RCL

RESOURCES *for* COLLEGE LIBRARIES

2007

This Edition of *Resources for College Libraries* was prepared by:

ACRL & Choice:
Project Editor: Marcus Elmore
Editorial Director, Choice: Francine Graf
Editor & Publisher, Choice: Irving Rockwood

Special Thanks to Our Proofreaders:
Monika Maslowski, Jinna Anderson, Chris Sullivan, Jennifer Donahue, Judith Douville,
Rebecca Bartlett, and Carolyn Wilcox

Record Entry Completed By:
Monika Maslowski, Laurie Trulock, and Sheila Laverty

R. R. Bowker LLC:
John Krafty: Product Manager, RCL
Ashley Ludwig: Managing Editor, RCL
Frank Morris: IT Director
Minh Huynh: Senior Programmer Analyst
Robert Zeisler: Senior Programmer Analyst

Editorial Staff:
Ian Singer: Vice President, Data Services
Roy Crego: Senior Managing Director, Editorial
Eleanor Schubauer: Managing Editor
Michael Olenick: Managing Editor
Beverly Palacio: Associate Editor

Production Department:
Doreen Gravesande: Senior Director, Production
Ralph Coviello, Manager, Manufacturing Services
Myriam Nunez: Project Manager, Product Development & Content Integrity
Kennard McGill: Production Consultant

Research Completed By:
Pat Diaz, Bobbie Ferraro, Kathy Griner, Becky Housel, and Diane Johnson.

Record Entry Completed By:
Jenny Marie DeJesus, Dorothy Perry-Gilchrist, Anthony Giuffra, and Steven Zaffuto

RESOURCES *for* COLLEGE LIBRARIES

2007

Volume 7:
Taxonomy Listing
Cumulative Author Index
Cumulative Title Index

Mary Ellen Davis, Executive Director, ACRL

Published by
R. R. Bowker LLC
630 Central Avenue, New Providence
New Jersey 07974

Annie Callanan, President and CEO

URL: http://www.rclweb.net
E-mail address: rclfeedback@bowker.com

Readers may send any corrections and/or updates to the information in this work to:
rclfeedback@bowker.com

International Standard Book Number:

7 Volume Set:	ISBN: 0-8352-4855-0
	ISBN13: 978-0-8352-4855-6
Vol. 1: Humanities:	ISBN: 0-8352-4856-9
	ISBN13: 978-0-8352-4856-3
Vol. 2: Language & Literature:	ISBN: 0-8352-4857-7
	ISBN13: 978-0-8352-4857-0
Vol. 3: History:	ISBN: 0-8352-4858-5
	ISBN13: 978-0-8352-4858-7
Vol. 4: Social Sciences:	ISBN: 0-8352-4859-3
	ISBN13: 978-0-8352-4859-4
Vol. 5: Science and Technology:	ISBN: 0-8352-4860-7
	ISBN13: 978-0-8352-4860-0
Vol. 6: Interdisciplinary & Area Studies:	ISBN: 0-8352-4861-5
	ISBN13: 978-0-8352-4861-7
Vol. 7: Indexes:	ISBN: 0-8352-4862-3
	ISBN13: 978-0-8352-4862-4

Printed and bound in the United States of America

Table of Contents

Taxonomy Listings *p.1*

Author Index *p.27*

Title Index *p.471*

Resources for College Libraries: General Introduction

Like its predecessors, the three editions of *Books for College Libraries* (BCL) that appeared in 1988, 1975, and 1964, *Resources for College Libraries* (RCL) is a bibliography of carefully selected works spanning the college curriculum and comprising a recommended core collection for all academic libraries. In the tradition of its predecessors, which drew on the such sources as the published catalog of Harvard's Lamont Library (1954), the shelflist of the undergraduate library of the University of Michigan, and, crucially, Charles Shaw's *List of Books for College Libraries* (1931), RCL attempts to balance multiple, often contradictory demands. It seeks to provide a balanced set of recommendations that take note of the weight of the various academic disciplines within the undergraduate curriculum, the degree to which those various disciplines depend on book materials for their essential teaching and research resources, and the extensive pattern of changes that have reshaped the academic curriculum since 1988, the year in which BCL3, the most recent edition of *Books for College Libraries,* appeared.

Of necessity, RCL also embodies a paradox identified by the late Virginia Clark, editor of BCL3: it "can fully succeed only by failing. It would be disastrous should the collection it suggests serve perfectly to ratify the finished work of book selection in any library."[1] Not only will individual institutions create collections significantly larger than the roughly 65,000 titles recommended by RCL, but they will tailor those collections to reflect the size and strength of their own individual departments, majors, and programs. RCL attempts to make general recommendations, within individual subject areas, of those titles most necessary for teaching the subject to undergraduates. In many cases, this means a foundation to which the smallest institutions should aspire but which larger collections will far surpass.

We describe RCL as a successor to, rather than a new edition of, BCL for two reasons. The first is formal, and lies behind the change in nomenclature: RCL includes in its recommendations a variety of electronic resources, including Web sites, subscription databases, e-books, and other electronic materials. The second, procedural reason follows from this: unlike its predecessors, RCL will appear as both a multivolume print edition and a searchable, continuously updated electronic database. In addition, there is a third, tacit distinction which may be made

between RCL and the various editions of BCL: although bibliographers compiling subject lists for RCL often took the titles listed in BCL3 as a starting point, our bibliographic work emphasized building a comprehensive, retrospective list of titles by reference to the current undergraduate curriculum, and thus much of the work on RCL was from scratch. In contrast, the relationship between the various editions of BCL was demonstrably that of revision; from one edition to the next, there was an expectation that a title would be retained unless it was actively removed (if, for instance, it had been superseded by a more recent work). Because so much more time had passed between the appearance of BCL3 and the development of RCL than between any successive editions of BCL, bibliographers faced the simultaneously daunting and liberating prospect of creating a subject list *de novo.* That this same period (1988-2006) has seen momentous sea changes in many of the academic disciplines in the humanities and the sciences, as well as the growth of interdisciplinary study across all the academic disciplines, made this an opportunity to take measure of the way subjects are taught to undergraduates, as well as the sorts of subjects which are taught, when developing our core list.

One result of this reassessment was the decision to recognize and include as separate subject divisions in RCL a number of interdisciplinary fields, e.g., Environmental Studies and Gender Studies. The decision about which fields to include was based primarily on the degree to which those subjects function as areas of formal study at undergraduate institutions in the U.S., whether as major programs, academic minors, or areas of concentration housed within another department (film studies, for instance, is often offered as a program or concentration within the departments of English, Comparative Literature, or Theater). We recognized that the lists of titles recommended for teaching interdisciplinary subjects, e.g., Asian American Studies, might overlap significantly with the corresponding title lists for related traditional fields, e.g., American Literature. At the same time, we were confident that many of the recommended interdisciplinary titles would be unique, and so it has proved. The degree of overlap between the various sections of RCL is, throughout, fortuitous and reflects actual overlap between various undergraduate curricula. Effort was made to regularize the editions selected, but the work of compiling the various subject lists proceeded on an independent basis.

---

1. Virginia Clark, "Introduction," *Books for College Libraries: A Core Collection of 50,000 Titles,* (3rd ed., Chicago: American Library Association, 1988), vii.

The other dramatic difference between RCL and BCL is the decision to move away from Library of Congress classification as the primary framework for the selection and classification of titles. Though this is bound to be regarded by many librarians as a controversial decision, we are confident that it will prove in retrospect to be a sound one. The rationale for doing so is the desire to have titles classified in a fashion which closely follows the contours of the undergraduate curriculum. While LC accomplishes this for some subjects (for instance, British or American Literature, which are taught by chronological periods, and within periods by major authors and by forms such as poetry or drama), other curricula fail to mesh well with LC classification: Business Administration, for example, is responsible for the largest portion of baccalaureate degrees conferred by U.S. colleges and universities,[2] yet the classification of materials in the business curriculum in LC class HB-HJ, while sufficient for cataloging purposes, offers no insight on the relationship between materials so classified and the curriculum in which they are used. It is, furthermore, an arrangement which makes perfect sense to, but only to, librarians. Not all copies of BCL resided in technical services departments, but it seems unlikely that they were much consulted by students or faculty. Our hope is that the new classification scheme will work to the advantage of all the academic library's constituencies: librarians, especially those lacking strong background in a given subject, will be able to see not only the recommended titles but also, in the subject taxonomy, a map of the undergraduate curriculum; faculty will find recommendations of essential works in a form more accessible than LC, and bearing a closer correspondence to the way their courses and departments are organized; students, searching for a place to begin research on a particular topic, will also be able to recognize in the classification scheme something corresponding to their own encounter with the subject matter in the classroom and laboratory. Finally, since each entry in RCL retains its LC classification, those who prefer to search for materials in this fashion will still be able to.

RCL is the result of the collaborative efforts of 332 contributors, almost exclusively teaching faculty or librarians at U.S. colleges and universities. There were three kinds of contributors: subject editors, bibliographers, and referees. Subject editors were selected on the basis of their subject expertise and teaching or collection development experience: eighteen hold doctorates, four are members of the teaching faculty at research universities, two are independent scholars, and the remainder are academic librarians. Many have previously contributed to or authored major bibliographies in their subject areas. They were responsible for developing the subject classification taxonomy for their respective subject areas, for recruiting bibliographers and coordinating their efforts, and for reviewing the results. The subject editors represented a change from the various editions of BCL, where the bibliographers (mainly Choice reviewers) dealt directly with the project editor. By inserting a layer of subject experts we sought to ensure that the titles selected and the taxonomies in which they were classified reflected as much as possible the realities of the contemporary undergraduate curriculum. The second class of RCL contributors, bibliographers, was responsible for the bulk of the actual selection of titles. Like the subject editors, they were faculty and librarians selected for their subject knowledge, often with particular expertise in one specific aspect of a field. Finally, a pool of sixty-four referees, senior faculty or subject-specialist librarians, provided independent assessment of the initial lists developed by the bibliographers; the subject editors used this feedback to further refine their lists prior to publication.

The development of RCL had presumed from the beginning that bibliographers would be manipulating electronic bibliographic records in some sort of online environment, but the decision of the Association of College and Research Libraries (ACRL) Board of Directors to partner with publisher R. R. Bowker to produce RCL allowed us access to Bowker's massive database of bibliographic records, as well as the extensive technical support and expertise Bowker deployed on behalf of the project. Bibliographers selected titles in Bowker's *booksinprint.com* database, in a particular edition, and then imported them to the online RCL Authoring System, where they assigned subject headings and recommended audience levels. In those instances where no bibliographic record existed for a desired title, one was created from a reliable source (preferably with book in hand, though this was not always possible). At the same time, bibliographers submitted corrections to Bowker records when they identified errors or inconsistencies. While this system allowed us to avoid much of the brute effort which was expended on the creation of bibliographic records for the various editions of BCL, it also meant that bibliographers spent thousands of person-hours in the *booksinprint.com* database, identifying the most recent and reliable edition of particular works; in some cases, editors elected to include multiple editions, especially where the differences between them are significant for undergraduate teaching (see, for instance, the decision to include multiple, equally worthwhile translations of Dante's *Divine Comedy* in the Italian literature section).

The use of an online system for the manipulation of electronic bibliographic records was in part a matter of

---

2. http://nces.ed.gov/fastfacts/display.asp?id=37: U.S. Department of Education, National Center for Education Statistics. (2006). *Digest of Education Statistics, 2005* (NCES 2006-030), chapter 3.

efficiency, but more importantly, it finally addresses one longstanding issue faced by BCL, that of obsolescence.

When *Choice* magazine was founded in 1964, it was envisioned as, among other things, an ongoing supplement to BCL1. This approach did not prove practical, and the second and third editions of BCL were required. In contrast, RCL will be updated on an ongoing basis beginning almost immediately after its initial publication; bibliographic records will reflect changes in print status, and new titles will be introduced at regular intervals, to supplement or replace extant titles.

In addition to the tireless efforts of the contributors, on whom I cannot lavish sufficient praise, special thanks to the ACRL Board of Directors and Mary Ellen Davis, ACRL Executive Director, without whose approval and generous support this project would not have been possible. Oversight and advice were provided throughout the project by the RCL Editorial Board: Carolyn Sheehy, North Central College, Chair; and other members Joan Ellen Broome, Georgia Southern University; Barbara Burd, College Misericordia; Brian E. Coutts, Western Kentucky University; Bradford Lee Eden, University of California, Santa Barbara; Stacey Marien, American University; and Richard Shaw, Technical College of the Lowcountry.

Thanks are also due the editorial staff of *Choice*, all of whom contributed effort and advice to the production of this work in varying degrees (and all of whom exhibited tremendous kindness in their efforts, especially in the final days): Becky Bartlett, Judith Douville, Fran Graf, Lisa Mitten, and Carolyn Wilcox. Fran Graf and Irv Rockwood, the Publisher of *Choice*, deserve another

helping of praise for their advice, encouragement, and oversight of the project, as well as for handling negotiations of our partnership with R. R. Bowker. Judith Douville made superhuman contributions to a number of subject areas in addition to her own responsibilities in Chemistry. Although almost every member of the *Choice* office staff contributed to this work, Sheila Laverty deserves special praise for her work on the Dance section. Finally, the work would not have been completed if it had not been for the tireless effort of a small cadre of freelance staff, namely Jennifer Donahue, Monika Maslowski, Teri Staab, and Laurie Trulock, who proofread and edited subject headings and section notes, entered titles, cataloged records, and helped maintain communication with subject editors, with extraordinary care, intelligence, and persistence.

With our partners at R. R. Bowker, we enjoyed the highest degree of collegiality and cooperation. Special thanks are due to Angela D'Agostino, Vice-President of Marketing; John Krafty, Product Manager of *Books In Print*; Ashley Ludwig, Managing Editor; Todd Rudloff, Project Manager of *Books In Print*; Frank Morris, Senior Programmer; Minh Huynh, Senior Programmer Analyst, all of whom made significant contributions to bringing this work to the light of day.

Finally, my deep thanks to my family, Colleen and Graham, for their patience and support throughout this project.

Marcus Elmore,

Editor

A Note on the RCL Subject Taxonomy

One of the distinctive features of *Resources for College Libraries* is the subject taxonomy used to organize the titles included in RCL. Developed specifically for RCL by the RCL editorial team, and in particular by the subject editors, the RCL taxonomy reflects the contours of today's undergraduate curriculum. The RCL taxonomy's major headings, therefore, generally correspond to academic majors, departments, or courses of study, e.g., anthropology, business administration, or physics. (In some cases an academic discipline has been further subdivided in order to create sections of manageable size, e.g., the subdivision of History by geographical region.) The goal is a classification scheme, which organizes materials as they would be taught by faculty and encountered in the classroom and the laboratory by undergraduate students.

In some subject areas, e.g. British and American literature, the RCL subject taxonomy closely resembles the Library of Congress classification scheme used in *Books for College Libraries,* 3rd edition. In most cases, however, the differences between LC and today's undergraduate curriculum, have been so substantial as to require the development of a new taxonomy from scratch. This has been especially true for the interdisciplinary subjects such as African American Studies, Criminal Justice, and Native American Studies, which draw upon materials from a dizzying range of LC classes. Gender Studies, for example, draws from a large array of academic disciplines, including (but not limited to) psychology, sociology, literature, philosophy, political science, medicine, and history.

The coverage of interdisciplinary subjects in RCL is another of its distinguishing features, and one deemed essential from the very inception of the project. Although there is some overlap between the interdisciplinary title lists and those of related traditional subjects, e.g., American literature and Chicano/a literature (a subsection of Latino Studies), the interdisciplinary sections inevitably include many unique titles. In addition, the inclusion of the interdisciplinary subjects makes it possible to distinguish those titles which have been selected as essential resources for a traditional subject such as American literature (e.g., Carson McCullers' *Collected Novels*), from those selected for an interdisciplinary area (e.g., Pat Mora's *Communion,* selected for Latino Studies > Humanities > Literature > Chicano/a Literature), and also from those selected for both (e.g., Mora's *Borders*).

By making the ways in which titles are actually used in the classroom the focus for our classification of titles in RCL, we hope to both dramatically increase its usefulness to students and faculty members and also to underscore the extent to which titles were selected on the basis of their importance to undergraduate study and teaching.

RCL Contributors

John Abbott, Graduate Student, GSLIS, University of Illinois, Urbana-Champaign.
Subject Editor: European History.

Randy Abbott, Head Reference Librarian, University of Evansville.
Referee.

Anthony Adam, Assistant Director, John B. Coleman Library, Prairie View A&M University.
Bibliographer: GLBT Studies.

Jan Adamczyk, Slavic Reference Service, University of Illinois.
Bibliographer: Russian Languages and Literatures.

Michael Adams, Librarian, CUNY Graduate Center.
Bibliographer: American Literature.

Paulita Aguilar, Curator, Indigenous Nations Library Program, University of New Mexico.
Bibliographer: Native American Studies.

Flavia Alaya, Professor of English, Ramapo College of New Jersey.
Referee.

Jean Alexander, Head of Reference, Hunt Library, Carnegie Mellon University.
Referee.

Duncan Alford, Head of Reference, Law Library, Georgetown University.
Bibliographer: Law.

Karen Antell, Head, Reference Department, University of Oklahoma.
Bibliographer: Technology and Engineering.

Ralph Arcari, Director Emeritus, Health Center Library, University of Connecticut.
Subject Editor: Medicine.

Susan Ariew, University Librarian, University of South Florida.
Bibliographer: Education.

Jan Armstrong, Professor of Education, University of New Mexico.
Referee.

Teresa Arrington, Associate Professor of Modern Languages, Blue Mountain College.
Bibliographer: Spanish Language and Literature.

Susan Awe, Director of Parish Memorial Library, University of New Mexico.
Referee.

David Azzolina, Reference librarian, University of Pennsylvania.
Bibliographer: General Language and Literature.

Pete Banholzer, Technical Information Specialist, NASA.
Bibliographer: Geology.

Ron Banks, Human Subjects Coordinator, Institutional Review Board, University of Illinois.
Bibliographer: Education.

David Bantz, Chief Information Architect, University of Alaska.
Referee.

Adele Barsh, Business and Economics Librarian, Carnegie Mellon University.
Bibliographer: Business Administration.

Jennifer Bartlett, Head of Research & Instructional Services, Murray State University.
Bibliographer: American Literature.

Edwin Battistella, Dean of Arts and Letters and Professor of English, University of Southern Oregon.
Bibliographer: General Language and Literature.

Frederic Baumgartner, Professor of History, Virginia Tech University.
Bibliographer: European History.

Robert Beauregard, Professor, Urban Policy Analysis and Management, New School University.
Referee.

Linda Behrend, Cataloging Librarian, University of Tennessee, Knoxville.
Bibliographer: American Literature.

Penny Beile, Head, Curriculum Materials Center, University of Central Florida.
Bibliographer: Education.

Dean Bell, Dean and Chief Academic Officer, Spertus Institute of Jewish Studies.
Bibliographer: European History.

Dennis Benamati, Director, Ryan-Matura Library, Sacred Heart University.
Referee.

Riva Berleant-Schiller, Professor emerita of Anthropology, University of Connecticut, emerita.
Subject Editor: Anthropology.

Jay Bernstein, Reader Services Librarian, Kingsborough Community College.
Referee.

John Berry, Native American Studies Librarian, University of California, Berkeley.
Subject Editor: Native American Studies.

Sharon Black, Librarian, Annenberg School for Communication, University of Pennsylvania.
Bibliographer: Journalism and Communication.

Steve Blackburn, Library Director, Hartford Seminary.
Referee.

Robert Bland, Associate University Librarian
Automation and Technical Services, University of North
Carolina, Asheville.
Bibliographer: Philosophy.

Richard Bleiler, Humanities Bibliographer, University of
Connecticut.
Bibliographer: General Language and Literature.

Laurel Blewett, Manager of Library Services,
Edward Hospital.
Referee.

Christopher Bloss, Instructional Services Librarian,
University of South Dakota.
Bibliographer: American Literature.

Ellen Bosman, Head of Technical Services, New Mexico
State University.
Subject Editor: GLBT Studies.

Jesús Bottaro, Instructor, CUNY / Medgar Evers
College.
Bibliographer: Spanish Language and Literature.

Steven Botterill, Professor of Italian, University of
California, Berkeley.
Referee.

Sally Bowdoin, Head of Serials, Brooklyn College.
Subject Editor: British Literature.

Linda Bowles-Adarkwa, Subject Specialist, Black
Studies and Women Studies, San Francisco State
University.
Bibliographer: African American Studies.

James Boxall, Director, GIS Centre, Dalhousie University.
Subject Editor: Geography.

James Bracken, Assistant Director for Main Library
Research and Reference Services, Ohio State University.
Subject Editor: Other Literatures in English.

Laura Braunstein, Research and Reference Services,
Dartmouth University.
Bibliographer: General Language and Literature.

Tony Bremholm, Life Sciences Librarian, Texas
A&M University.
Referee.

Karl Bridges, Coordinator of Electronic Instruction
Resources, University of Vermont.
Bibliographer: U.S. and Canadian History.

JoEllen Broome, Reference Specialist, Georgia Southern
University.
Subject Editor: Environmental Studies.

Mitchell Brown, Research Librarian for Chemistry and
Earth System Sciences, University of California,
Irvine.
Referee.

Mary Jane Brustman, Bibliographer for Social Welfare
and Criminal Justice, SUNY Albany.
Subject Editor: Criminal Justice.

Mark Bullock, Graduate Student, History Department,
University of Illinois at Chicago.
Bibliographer: European History.

Merry Burlingham, Chief Bibliographer and Collections
Officer, University of Texas.
**Bibliographer: Asian History, Languages, and
Literatures.**

Angela Cannon, Reference Librarian, Library of
Congress.
**Bibliographer: Russian Languages and
Literatures.**

Karen Cary, Head, Collection Management, Virginia
Commonwealth University.
Bibliographer: Sociology.

Melissa Cast, Reference Librarian and Subject Specialist
for Education, University of Nebraska Omaha.
Bibliographer: Education.

Rafaela Castro, Bibliographer, University of California,
Davis.
Subject Editor: Latino Studies.

Tina Ching, Reference Librarian, Arizona State
University.
Referee.

Diana Chlebek, English and Modern Languages and
Literature Bibliographer, University of Akron.
Bibliographer: French Language and Literature.

Michael Chromey, Humanities Librarian, Atlanta
University Center.
Bibliographer: African American Studies.

Hui Hua Chua, US Documents Librarian, Michigan
State University.
Bibliographer: Journalism and Communication.

Alan Church, Professor of English, University of
Texas at Brownsville.
Referee.

Janet Clarke, Asian American Studies Selector, Stony
Brook University.
Bibliographer: Asian American Studies.

Kim Clarke, Assistant Librarian, Selector for Women's
Studies, University of Minnesota, Twin Cities.
Subject Editor: Gender Studies.

Rudolph Clay, Subject Librarian, African and
African-American Studies, Washington University.
Bibliographer: African American Studies.

Ana Maria Cobos, Library Department Chair, Saddleback
College.
Subject Editor: Latino Studies.

Francesca Colecchia, Professor of Spanish, Duquesne
University.
Referee.

Gerardo Colmenar, Associate Librarian, Asian American Studies, University of California, Santa Barbara.
Subject Editor: Asian American Studies.

Mark Connell, Director, Center for Advancement of Technology in Education, SUNY College at Cortland.
Referee.

Paul Connors, Research Analyst, Michigan Legislative Service Bureau.
Bibliographer: U.S. and Canadian History.

Miriam Conteh-Morgan, Collection Manager for African Studies, Ohio State University.
Bibliographer: African American Studies.

Kate Corby, Education and Psychology Bibliographer, Michigan State University.
Subject Editor: Education.

Ronald Cormier, Professor of French, Longwood College.
Referee.

Alice Crosetto, Acquisitions Librarian, University of Toledo.
Bibliographer: British Literature.

Cynthia Crosser, Social Sciences and Humanities Librarian, University of Maine.
Bibliographer: Education.

Gwyneth Crowley, Coordinator of Collection Development, Social Science Libraries, Yale University.
Subject Editor: Economics.

Alice Daugherty, Reference Librarian, Louisiana State University.
Bibliographer: American Literature.

Stephanie Davis, Librarian, Spring Arbor University.
Bibliographer: Education.

Judith de Luce, Professor of Classics, Miami University of Ohio.
Referee.

Kathy Dean, Humanities Bibliographer, Ohio State University.
Bibliographer: Other Literatures in English.

Louise Deis, Science & Technology Reference Librarian, Princeton University.
Subject Editor: Environmental Sciences; General Science.

JoAnn DeVries, Associate Librarian, Reference/Bibliographer, University of Minnesota.
Bibliographer: Agriculture.

Jan Dixon, Reference Librarian, University of Arkansas.
Bibliographer: Geology.

Deborah Dolan, Social Science Librarian, Hofstra University.
Bibliographer: Psychology.

Travis Dolence, Instruction Librarian, Minnesota State University Moorhead.
Referee.

Michael Doorley, Associate Lecturer in Humanities, American College, Dublin.
Bibliographer: European History.

Judith Douville, Visual Arts, Science and Technology Editor, CHOICE.
Subject Editor: Chemistry.

Bill Drew, Associate Librarian, Systems and Reference, SUNY – Morrisville.
Referee.

Heather Dubnick, Field Bibliographer, Modern Language Assoc.
Subject Editor: Spanish Language and Literature.

Dana Dunn, Professor of Psychology, Moravian College.
Referee.

Lisa Dunn, Head of Reference, Colorado School of Mines.
Bibliographer: Geology.

Karin Durán, Teacher Curriculum Center Librarian, California State University Northridge.
Bibliographer: Latino Studies.

David Eastman, Doctoral Candidate, Department of Religious Studies, Yale University.
Bibliographer: Religion.

Mary Edsall, Professor of Library and Information Science, Catholic University of America.
Subject Editor: Dance.

Marcus Elmore, CHOICE.
Subject Editor: General Language and Literature.

Robert Elsie, Independent scholar.
Bibliographer: European History.

Kimberly Embelton, Literature and Languages Librarian, California State University Northridge.
Bibliographer: British Literature.

Michael Emery, Professor of English, Cottey College.
Bibliographer: GLBT Studies.

Mark Emmons, Head, Instruction Services, University of New Mexico.
Subject Editor: Film.

Carlene Engstrom, Director, D'Arcy McNickle Library, Salish Kootenai College.
Bibliographer: Native American Studies.

Pam Enrici, Associate Librarian, University of Maryland.
Bibliographer: Technology and Engineering.

Robert Entenmann, Professor of History, St. Olaf College.
Referee.

Isabel Espinal, Librarian for Afro American Studies, Anthropology, Native American Indian Studies, University of Massachussetts.
Bibliographer: African American Studies.

James Allan Evans, Professor Emeritus of Classical
Near Eastern and Religious Studies, University of British
Columbia.
Bibliographer: European History.

Angel Falcon, Harvard University, formerly.
Bibliographer: African American Studies.

David Feldman, Professor of Mathematics, University of
New Hampshire.
Referee.

Robert Fernekes, Information Services Librarian,
Business Specialist, Georgia Southern University.
Bibliographer: Business Administration.

Anne Fields, OSU Libraries Coordinator for Research
and Reference, Ohio State University.
Bibliographer: Education.

Jenifer Flaxbart, Head Librarian, Reference and
Information Services, University of Texas, Austin.
Bibliographer: Journalism and Communication.

Adonna Fleming, GIS / Maps Librarian,
University of Nebraska – Lincoln.
Bibliographer: Geology.

Nicole Fluhr, Professor of English, Southern Connecticut
State University.
Referee.

Michael Fosmire, Science Librarian, Purdue University.
Subject Editor: Physics.

Stephen Foster, University Librarian, Wright State
University.
Referee.

Gerri Foudy, Government and Politics, Public Affairs,
and Law Librarian, University of Maryland.
Bibliographer: Political Science.

Kathleen Fountain, Political Science and Social Work
Librarian, California State University, Chico.
Bibliographer: Political Science.

Kristine Fowler, Mathematics Librarian, University of
Minnesota, Twin Cities.
Subject Editor: Mathematics.

Stephen Fowlkes, Bibliographer for Sociology, Social
Work and Reference, Tulane University.
Bibliographer: Sociology.

Ann Fox, Professor of English, Davidson College.
Referee.

Joe Fugate, Professor of German, Kalamazoo College.
Referee.

Steve Fullwood, Manuscripts Librarian, Schomburg
Center for Research in Black Culture, New York Public
Library.
Bibliographer: African American Studies.

Ronald Ganze, Professor of English, Valparaiso
University.
Bibliographer: Medieval Studies.

Bill Gargan, Reference Librarian and Bibliographer,
Brooklyn College.
Bibliographer: British Literature.

Meryle Gaston, Islamic and Middle Eastern Studies
Librarian, University of California, Santa Barbara.
**Subject Editor: Middle Eastern History, Languages,
and Literatures.**

Cameron Gearen, Lecturer in English, Yale University.
**Bibliographer: General Language and
Literature.**

Caroline Geck, Librarian, Kean University.
Referee.

Jennifer Geddes, Research Associate Professor of
Religious Studies, University of Virginia.
Bibliographer: General Language and Literature.

Mary Gilles, Business Reference Librarian,
Washington State University.
Subject Editor: Law.

David Giovacchini, Arabic Librarian, Middle East
Collection, Stanford University.
Referee.

Ed Goedeken, Humanities Bibliographer, Iowa State
University.
Subject Editor: U.S. and Canadian History.

Melissa Goldsmith, Lecturer, Louisiana State University.
Referee.

Millie Gonzalez, Reference Librarian, Framingham
State College.
Bibliographer: Business Administration.

Olympia Gonzalez, Professor of Spanish, Loyola
University of Chicago.
Referee.

David Goodman, Professor of Library and Information
Science, Long Island University.
Subject Editor: Biology.

Candice Goucher, Professor of History, Washington State
University, Vancouver.
Referee.

Malaika Grant, Reference/Instruction Librarian,
University of Minnesota, Twin Cities.
Bibliographer: Gender Studies.

Laura Graves, Professor of History, South Plains
College.
Bibliographer: Native American Studies.

Chip Green, Professor of Geology, University of South
Carolina Upstate.
Referee.

Susan Green, Professor of History, California State
University, Chico.
Referee.

Cheryl Grossman, Electronic Services Supervisor, LearningWork Connection, Ohio State University.
Bibliographer: Education.

Anna Marie Guengerich, Librarian, College of Education, University of Iowa.
Bibliographer: Psychology.

Richard Hacken, European Studies Bibliographer, Brigham Young University.
Referee.

Michael Handis, Associate Librarian for Collection Management, CUNY Graduate Center.
Bibliographer: European History.

Shaun Hardy, Librarian, Carnegie Institution of Washington.
Bibliographer: Geology.

Sara Harrington, Art Librarian, Rutgers University.
Referee.

Jon Harrison, Social Sciences Collections Coordinator, Missouri State University.
Bibliographer: Criminal Justice.

Elizabeth Hartung, Professor of Sociology, California Sate University Channel Islands.
Bibliographer: Sociology.

Laurence Hauptman, Professor of History, SUNY New Paltz.
Bibliographer: Native American Studies.

Peter Hayes, Professor of History, Northwestern University.
Bibliographer: European History.

Charles Hayford, Research Fellow, Department of History, Northwestern University.
Subject Editor: Asian History, Languages, and Literatures.

Jeremy Hein, Professor of Sociology, University of Wisconsin – Eau Claire.
Referee.

Eileen Herring, Agriculture Librarian, University of Hawaii.
Bibliographer: Agriculture.

Martin Hewitt, Head of History Department, Trinity and All Saints College, University of Leeds.
Referee.

Terry Hill, Customer Representative for North America, OTTO HARRASSOWITZ GmbH & Co. KG.
Bibliographer: Political Science.

Baraba Hillson, Public and International Affairs and Psychology Liaison Librarian, George Mason University.
Referee.

Lee Hilyer, Mathematics Subject Librarian, University of Houston.
Bibliographer: Education.

Keith Hitchins, Professor of History, University of Illinois.
Bibliographer: European History.

Adrian Ho, Assistant Librarian, University of Houston.
Bibliographer: Journalism and Communication.

David Hogg, Astronomer, National Radio Astronomy Observatory.
Referee.

Jane Holmquist, Astrophysics Librarian, Princeton University.
Subject Editor: Astronomy.

Emily Horning, Librarian for Philosophy, Religious Studies and Anthropology, Yale University.
Subject Editor: Religion.

John Hunter, Science/Engineering Librarian, Rice University.
Bibliographer: Geology.

Carol Hutchins, Head Librarian, Courant Institute of Mathematical Sciences, New York University.
Subject Editor: Computing.

Robin Imhof, Reference Librarian, University of the Pacific.
Bibliographer: GLBT Studies.

Richard Irving, Associate Librarian, SUNY Albany.
Bibliographer: Criminal Justice.

Kristin Jacobi, Head, Catologing Department, Eastern Connecticut State University.
Bibliographer: Native American Studies.

James Jaffe, Professor of History, University of Wisconsin – Whitewater.
Bibliographer: European History.

Arif Jamal, Social Sciences Bibliographer, University of Pittsburgh.
Bibliographer: African American Studies.

Sylvia James, Sylvia James Consultancy.
Bibliographer: Business Administration.

Fred Jenkins, Head of Collection Management, University of Dayton.
Subject Editor: Ancient History; Classics.

Donald Clay Johnson, Curator, Ames Library of South Asia, University of Minnesota.
Bibliographer: Asian History, Languages, and Literatures.

Melissa Johnson, Reference and Instruction Librarian, Lynn University.
Bibliographer: European History.

Sarah Johnson, Librarian, Eastern Illinois University.
Bibliographer: General Language and Literature.

Lisa Johnston, Head of Public Services, Sweet Briar College.
Bibliographer: British Literature.

Scott Johnston, Librarian, CUNY Graduate Center.
Subject Editor: Urban Studies.

David P. Jordan, Professor of History, University of Illinois at Chicago.
Bibliographer: European History.

Jonathan Judaken, Professor of History, University of Memphis.
Bibliographer: European History.

Jeannie Kamerman, Director, Curriculum Materials Library, University of West Florida.
Bibliographer: Education.

James Kelly, Humanities Bibliographer, University of Massachussetts.
Subject Editor: American Literature.

Marcia Keyser, Instruction and Reference Librarian, Drake University.
Bibliographer: Education.

Shayee Khanaka, Librarian, Middle Eastern Collection, University of California Berkeley.
Bibliographer: Middle Eastern History, Languages, and Literatures.

Sherise Kimura, Reference Librarian, University of San Francisco.
Bibliographer: Asian American Studies.

Douglas King, Librarian, University of South Carolina.
Bibliographer: American Literature.

Laura Kinner, Coordinator, Cataloging Services, University of Toledo.
Bibliographer: British Literature.

Harold Kirkwood, Librarian, Purdue University.
Bibliographer: Business Administration.

Patricia Kirkwood, Science Librarian, University of Arkansas.
Bibliographer: Technology and Engineering.

Sheila Kirven, Education Services Librarian, New Jersey City University.
Bibliographer: Education.

Linda Klein, Reference Librarian, Eastern Kentucky University.
Bibliographer: British Literature.

Michael Knee, Science Bibliographer and Reference Librarian, University of Albany.
Bibliographer: Computing.

Norma Kobzina, Head of Information Services, Marian Koshland Bioscience and Natural Resources Library, University of California, Berkeley.
Subject Editor: Agriculture.

David Koenigstein, Librarian, Brooklyn College.
Bibliographer: British Literature.

Gayla Koerting, Special Collections Librarian, University of South Dakota.
Bibliographer: U.S. and Canadian History.

Laura Koltutsky, Information Services Librarian, University of Houston.
Bibliographer: Education.

Kwasi Konadu, Professor of History, Winston Salem State University.
Bibliographer: African History, Languages, and Literatures.

Svetlana Korolev, Science Librarian, University of Wisconsin, Madison.
Referee.

Wade Kotter, Social Sciences Librarian, Weber State University.
Bibliographer: Criminal Justice.

Joe Kraus, Science Librarian, University of Denver.
Referee.

Eiko Kuwana, Professor of History, University of the Sacred Heart, Tokyo.
Bibliographer: European History.

Sharon Ladenson, Gender Studies and Communications Bibliographer, Michigan State University.
Bibliographer: Journalism and Communication.

Carolyn Laffoon, Earth and Atmospheric Sciences Librarian, Purdue University.
Bibliographer: Geology.

Blake Landor, Bibliographer for Philosophy, Classics, and Religion, University of Florida.
Subject Editor: Philosophy.

Jeffry Larson, Librarian for Romance Languages and Literatures, Linguistics, and Classics, Yale University.
Subject Editor: French Language and Literature; Italian Language and Literature.

Jason E. Lavery, Professor of History, Oklahoma State University.
Bibliographer: European History.

Bernadette Lear, Behavioral Sciences and Education Librarian, Pennsylvania State University.
Bibliographer: Psychology.

Patrick Leary, Research Fellow, Department of History, Northwestern University.
Subject Editor: Victorian Studies.

Richard S. Levy, Professor of History, University of Illinois at Chicago.
Bibliographer: European History.

Kevin Lindstrom, Behavioral Sciences and Education Librarian, University of British Columbia.
Bibliographer: Geology.

Ken Liss, Communication Librarian, Boston College.
Bibliographer: Journalism and Communication.

Carol Loranger, Professor of English, Wright
State University.
Referee.

Jack Lynch, Professor of English, Rutgers University.
Bibliographer: British Literature.

Karen MacDonald, Business Subject Specialist
Librarian, Texas A&M University.
Bibliographer: Business Administration.

Peter Magierski, Librarian for the Middle East Studies,
New York University.
**Bibliographer: Middle Eastern History, Languages,
and Literatures.**

Diane Maher, University Archivist, University of San
Diego.
**Bibliographer: American Literature; British
Literature.**

Janice Mathews, Librarian for Urban Studies and Social
Work, University of Connecticut.
Referee.

Rhonda McGinnis, Business and Economics Librarian,
Wayne State University.
Bibliographer: Business Administration.

Glenn McGuigan, Business Reference Librarian, Penn
State University.
Subject Editor: Business Administration.

Peter McKay, Business Librarian, University of Florida.
Bibliographer: Business Administration.

Paula McMillen, Social Sciences Librarian, Oregon State
University.
Bibliographer: Education.

Lori Mestre, Digital Learning Librarian, University of
Illinois.
Bibliographer: Education.

Sue Metcalf, Social Sciences Librarian, New Mexico
State University.
Referee.

Marion Miller, Professor of History, University of Illinois
at Chicago, emerita.
Bibliographer: European History.

Lisa Mitten, CHOICE.
Subject Editor: Native American Studies.

Sandy Mooney, Design Librarian, Louisiana State
University.
Referee.

Fred Muratori, Bibliographer for Anglo-American and
Comparative Literature and Film, Cornell
University.
Bibliographer: Drama and Theater.

Paula Murphy, Library Consultant.
Referee.

Linda Musser, Head, Fletcher L. Byrom Earth and
Mineral Sciences Library, Pennsylvania State University.
Bibliographer: Geology.

Theodore Natsoulas, Professor of History, University of
Toledo.
Bibliographer: European History.

Sharon Naylor, Education, Psychology and TMC
Division Head, Illinois State University.
Bibliographer: Education.

Antoinette Nelson, Branch Manager, Science and
Engineering Library, University of Texas Arlington.
Subject Editor: Technology and Engineering.

Jan Newberry, Professor of Anthropology, University of
Lethbridge.
Referee.

Shawn Nicholson, Bibliographer for Sociology, Social
Work, Urban Planning, Michigan State University.
Referee.

Jim Niessen, World History Librarian, Rutgers
University.
Bibliographer: European History.

Byron Nordstrom, Professor of History, Gustavus
Adolphus University.
Bibliographer: European History.

Akilah Nosakhere, Manager, Reference and Research
Division, Auburn Avenue Research Library of
African American Culture and History.
Subject Editor: African American Studies.

Nancy O'Brien, Head, Education and Social Science
Library, University of Illinois.
Subject Editor: Education.

Darby Orcutt, Collection Manager for the Humanities
and Data Analysis, North Carolina State
University.
Bibliographer: Journalism and Communication.

Harriet Ottenheimer, Professor of Anthropology,
Kansas State University.
Bibliographer: Anthropology.

Mark Padnos, Coordinator of Public Services, Bronx
Community College.
**Subject Editor: Germanic Languages and
Literatures.**

John Page, Associate Dean, Learning Resources
Division, University of the District of Columbia.
Bibliographer: African American Studies.

Tim Parrish, Professor of English, Southern Connecticut
State University.
Bibliographer: General Language and Literature.

Lucy Patrick, Head of Special Collections, Florida
State University.
Referee.

Christopher Peebles, Associate Vice President for
Information Technology and Professor of Anthropology,
Indiana University.
Bibliographer: Anthropology.

Ed Peters, Professor of History, University of
Pennsylvania.
Bibliographer: European History.

Carmelita Pickett, African American Studies Librarian,
Emory University.
Bibliographer: African American Studies.

Lisa Pillow, Collection Development Librarian, University
of Wisconsin – River Falls.
Bibliographer: African American Studies.

Chestalene Pintozzi, Science-Engineering Librarian,
University of Arizona.
Bibliographer: Geology.

Don Polzella, Professor of Psychology and Associate
Dean for Faculty Development and Graduate Programs,
University of Dayton.
Subject Editor: Psychology.

Diethelm Prowe, Professor of History, Carleton College.
Bibliographer: European History.

Eleanor Randall, Reference Librarian, Edinboro
University of Pennsylvania.
Bibliographer: Biology.

Brenda Reed, Public Services Librarian, Education
Library, Queen's University.
Bibliographer: Education.

Ira Revels, Instruction Librarian, Cornell University.
Bibliographer: African American Studies.

Leslie Reynolds, Director of Policy Sciences and
Economics Library, Texas A&M University.
Bibliographer: Business Administration.

Amy Robb, Field Librarian for Women's Studies and
Communication, University of Michigan.
Bibliographer: Journalism and Communication.

Gloria Roberson, Reference Librarian, Adelphi
University.
Bibliographer: African American Studies.

Beth Roberts, Earth and Mineral Sciences Librarian,
Pennsylvania State University.
Bibliographer: Geology.

Elizabeth Robertson, Professor of English, University of
Colorado.
Bibliographer: British Literature.

Martin Roden, Professor emeritus of Engineering,
UCLA.
Bibliographer: Technology and Engineering.

Raquel Rodriguez, Librarian for the African American
Collection, University of Pittsburgh.
Bibliographer: African American Studies.

Lisa Romero, Communications Librarian, University of
Illinois.
Subject Editor: Journalism and Communication.

Lana Kay Rosenberg, Director, Dance Theatre,
Miami University of Ohio.
Referee.

Tony Rosso, Professor of English, Southern Connecticut
State University.
Bibliographer: British Literature.

Dana Roth, Chemistry Librarian, Caltech.
Bibliographer: Chemistry.

Linda Salem, Education Librarian, San Diego State
University.
Bibliographer: British Literature.

Mark Sanders, Student Outreach Reference Librarian,
East Carolina University.
Bibliographer: Environmental Studies.

Rachel Sandoval, Historical Records Project Archivist,
University of California, Irvine.
Bibliographer: Latino Studies.

Victoria Santana, Electronic Services Librarian,
Oklahoma City University.
Bibliographer: Native American Studies.

Román Santillán, Reference/Instruction Librarian,
CUNY / College of Staten Island.
Bibliographer: Spanish Language and Literature.

Vernon Schlotzhauer, Social Science Librarian,
Pennsylvania State University.
Bibliographer: Psychology.

Geoff Schmidt, Professor of English, Illinois State
University – Edwardsville.
Bibliographer: General Language and Literature.

Alan Schroeder, Business Librarian, California
State University Northridge.
Bibliographer: Business Administration.

Kate Schroeder, Doctoral Candidate, History Department,
Indiana University.
**Subject Editor: African History, Languages, and
Literatures.**

Friedrich Schuler, Professor of History, Portland State
University.
Subject Editor: Latin American History.

Katrin Schultheiss, Professor of History, University of
Illinois at Chicago.
Bibliographer: European History.

Jason Schultz, Communications Librarian, Georgia
State University.
Bibliographer: African American Studies.

Catherine Shreve, Librarian for Public Policy and Political
Science, Duke University.
Subject Editor: Political Science.

Jack Shreve, Professor of English, Allegany College.
Bibliographer: GLBT Studies.

Adam Siegel, Reference Librarian, University of California, Davis.
Bibliographer: Native American Studies.

Dorothy Siles, Librarian, Taylorville Public Library.
Bibliographer: Native American Studies.

Jane Sloan, Media Librarian, Rutgers University.
Subject Editor: Film.

Becky Smith, Head, Business and Economics Library, University of Illinois.
Bibliographer: Business Administration.

Helen Smith, Life Sciences Librarian, Penn State University.
Bibliographer: Agriculture.

Michael Smith, Business Librarian, Texas A&M University.
Bibliographer: Business Administration.

Jacqueline Snider, Librarian, ACT.
Bibliographer: Education.

Doug Southard, DRA International.
Bibliographer: Business Administration.

Roland Spickermann, Professor of History, University of Texas, Permian Basin.
Bibliographer: European History.

Jill Spreitzer, Assistant Librarian, Public Services, University of Detroit Mercy.
Bibliographer: Technology and Engineering.

Jennifer Stevens, Humanities Liaison Librarian, George Mason University.
Bibliographer: Other Literatures in English.

David Stoloff, Professor of Education, Eastern Connecticut State University.
Referee.

Fred Stoss, Biological Science Librarian, SUNY Buffalo.
Subject Editor: Biology.

Stephen Stratton, Head of Collection Development, California State University, Channel Islands.
Subject Editor: Sociology.

Cindy Stretch, Professor of English, Southern Connecticut State University.
Referee.

Leanne Strum, Library Liaison to the School of Business, Regent University.
Bibliographer: Business Administration.

Mila Su, Coordinator of Reference Services, Pennsylvania State University.
Subject Editor: Sport and Recreation.

Helen Sullivan, Head, Slavic Reference Service, University of Illinois.
Subject Editor: Russian Languages and Literatures.

Sarah Sussman, Curator, French and Italian Collections, Stanford University.
Bibliographer: European History.

Marek Suszko, Professor of History, Purdue University North Central.
Bibliographer: European History.

Laura Taddeo, Reference Librarian, SUNY Buffalo.
Bibliographer: British Literature.

Kornelia Tancheva, Director of Instructional Services, Cornell University.
Subject Editor: Drama and Theater.

Wendy Tann, Librarian, Federal Reserve Bank.
Bibliographer: Business Administration.

Cornelia Akins Taylor, Special Collections Librarian, Florida A & M University.
Bibliographer: African American Studies.

Betty Taylor-Thompson, Professor of English, Texas Southern University.
Referee.

Edward Teague, Head, Architecture & Allied Arts Library, University of Oregon.
Subject Editor: Visual Arts.

Samantha Teplitzky, Earth Sciences Librarian and Bibliographer, Stanford University.
Bibliographer: Geology.

Stephen Thompson, Co-Leader, Technical Services Department, Brown University.
Bibliographer: American Literature.

Erik Thomson, Collegiate Assistant Professor, Social Sciences, University of Chicago.
Bibliographer: European History.

Charles Thurston, Reference Librarian and Bibliographer, University of Texas at San Antonio.
Bibliographer: Education.

Judie Triplehorn, Librarian, Geophysical Institute, University of Alaska.
Bibliographer: Geology.

Markel Tumlin, English and American Literature Librarian, San Diego State University.
Bibliographer: American Literature.

Andrea Twiss-Brooks, Bibliographer for Chemical and Geophysical Sciences, University of Chicago.
Subject Editor: Geology.

Kent Underwood, Music Librarian, New York University.
Subject Editor: Music.

Alan Unsworth, Reference Librarian, University of Rochester.
Referee.

David Vaccari, Professor of Engineering, Stevens Institute of Technology.
Bibliographer: Technology and Engineering.

Susan Vega Garcia, Reference & Instruction Librarian, Bibliographer, Iowa State University.
Bibliographer: Latino Studies.

Tom Volkening, Engineering Librarian, Michigan State University.
Bibliographer: Technology and Engineering.

Heather Ward, University of Oregon, formerly.
Subject Editor: Medieval Studies.

Diane Warner, Monographs and Special Formats Cataloger, Texas Tech University.
Bibliographer: American Literature.

Gary Wasdin, Library Director, New School University.
Referee.

Matthew Wayman, Instruction Coordinator, Penn State University.
Bibliographer: U.S. and Canadian History.

Jeneen Willemssen, Librarian, Conserve School.
Bibliographer: Education.

Wendy Williamson, Economics Librarian, University of Minnesota.
Referee.

Suzanne Wise, Collection Development Librarian, Appalachia State University.
Referee.

Ada Woods, Reference Librarian, Towson University.
Bibliographer.

Peng Xu, Reference Librarian, Michigan State University.
Bibliographer: Business Administration.

Lisa Yuro, Reference Librarian/Humanities and Social Sciences Coordinator, University of Alabama.
Bibliographer: Journalism and Communication.

Ann Zawistoski, Reference and Instruction Librarian, Carleton College.
Bibliographer: Geology.

Linda Zellmer, Head, Geology Library, Indiana University.
Subject Editor: Geology.

HOW TO USE
RESOURCES FOR COLLEGE LIBRARIES

Resources for College Libraries (RCL) was designed to be easily searchable by author, title, and the RCL subject taxonomy. The set consists of seven volumes, Volumes 1-6 arranged by RCL Subject, and sorted alphabetically by author. Volume 7 is a comprehensive author, title and subject index. The volumes are arranged by *Resources for College Library* Subject Headings, a full listing of which is present in the Subject Headings Index in volume 7.

Each title in *Resources for College Libraries* has been classified with a specific RCL Subject and/or subjects. Titles can and often do appear within more than one RCL Subject area. Titles have been given a specific readership level through audience code: g=general, l=lower-division undergraduate, u=upper-division undergraduate graduate, and/or f=faculty level resources. Titles previously mentioned in *Books for College Libraries, 3rd Edition*, have been noted with a specific BCL3 icon *B*. Non-book entries can be easily identified with the icons for Web ▢, Ebook 🄴, or CD/DVD-ROM 💿.

Classification Number, Dewey Decimal Number, Library of Congress Control Number, Audience Code, and whether it has been reviewed in Choice Magazine.

Entries in the Author Index can include the following bibliographic information when available: author, co-author, editor, co-editor, translator, co-translator, along with page number(s) and volume number(s) of the selected works within the 6-volume set. Entries are not cross-referenced by other than primary author and/or first contributor. Entries in the Title Index include the title, page number(s) and volume number(s) of the selected works within the 6-volume set.

Titles in *Resources for College Libraries* have been alphabetized using the following rules:

- Initial articles of titles in English, French, German, Italian, and Spanish are not included for sorting purposes.

- Titles beginning with acronyms appear before those

SAMPLE RCL ENTRY

1 DRAMA AND THEATER ❯ Western Drama ❯ United States

2 Wilmeth, Don B. & Bigsby, Christopher (Editors)   PN2221

3 The Cambridge History of American Theater: **4** 1870-1945. **5** Ed. 2
6 Don B. Wilmeth & Christopher Bigsby (Contribution by). **7** Trade Paper.
8 Cambridge University Press. **9** New York, NY. **10** 2006. **11** 608p.
12 Cambridge History of American Theater Ser. **13** ISBN: 0-521-67984-2, ISBN13: 978-0-521-67984-8. **14** Dewey:792/.0973.
15 LCCN: 00-000000

16 Audience: l,u,f. **17** *Choice, 2005* *B*

1.	RCL Subject Heading
2.	Author/First Contributor
3.	Title
4.	Subtitle
5.	Ed. Info
6.	Additional Contributors
7.	Binding Type
8.	Publisher
9.	Publisher Location
10.	Publication Date
11.	Number of Pages
12.	Series Title
13.	ISBN, ISBN-13
14.	Dewey
15.	LCCN
16.	Audience Code
17.	Choice Review and Date

Title entries can include the following bibliographic information, when available: author, co-author, editor, co-editor, translator, co-translator, title, number of volumes, edition, series information, binding type, publisher, publisher location, date of publication, number of pages, ISBN, ISBN-13, Library of Congress

beginning with words. For example, B E A M A Directory would precede Baal, Babylon.

- As a general rule, U.S. and UN are filed in strict alphabetical order.

● Numeric Titles may be found near the end of the Title Index

Authors in *Resources for College Libraries* have been alphabetized using the following rules:

● Proper names beginning with "Mc" and "Mac" are filed in strict alphabetical order. For example, entries for contributors' names such as MacAdam, MacAvory, and MacCarthy are located prior to the pages with entries for names such as McAdam, McCoy, and McDermott.

● When author names are represented with initials, they are alphabetized before author first names. For example, Smith, H. C. appears before Smith, Harold A.

Any errors in bibliographic data should be E-mailed directly to: rclwebfeedback@bowker.com

ABBREVIATIONS AND CODE LIST:

BCL3	*Books for College Libraries, 3rd Edition*
Bk.(s.)	Book(s)
Ed.	Edition
F	Faculty
G	General
Inc.	Incorporated
Jr.	Junior
ISBN	International Standard Book Number
L	Lower-Division Undergraduate
LCCN	Library of Congress Control Number
p.	Pages
RCL	Resources for College Libraries
Ser.	Series
Sr.	Senior
U	Upper-Division Undergraduate

Geographical Abbreviations

AL	Alabama	NJ	New Jersey
AK	Alaska	NM	New Mexico
AB	Alberta	NSW	New South Wales
AE	American Europe	NY	New York
AS	American Samoa	NF	Newfoundland
AZ	Arizona	NC	North Carolina
AR	Arkansas	ND	North Dakota
ACT	Australian Capital Territory	NP	Northern Marianas
BC	British Columbia	N.T.	Northern Territory (Australia)
CA	California	NT	Northwest Territory
CM	Central Marianas	NS	Nova Scotia
CO	Colorado	NU	Nunavut
CT	Connecticut	OH	Ohio
DE	Delaware	OK	Oklahoma
DC	District Of Columbia	ON	Ontario
FM	Federated States Of Micronesia	OR	Oregon
FL	Florida	TT	Pacific Territories
GA	Georgia	PW	Pacific West
GU	Guam	PA	Pennsylvania
HI	Hawaii	PE	Prince Edward Island
ID	Idaho	PR	Puerto Rico
IL	Illinois	PQ	Quebec
IN	Indiana	QLD	Queensland
IA	Iowa	RI	Rhode Island
KS	Kansas	SK	Saskatchewan
KY	Kentucky	SA	South Australia
LA	Louisiana	SC	South Carolina
ME	Maine	SD	South Dakota
MB	Manitoba	TAS	Tasmania
MH	Marshall Islands	TN	Tennessee
MD	Maryland	TX	Texas
MA	Massachusetts	UT	Utah
MI	Michigan	VT	Vermont
MP	Middle Pacific	VIC	Victoria
MN	Minnesota	VI	Virgin Islands
MS	Mississippi	VA	Virginia
MO	Missouri	WA	Washington
MT	Montana	WV	West Virginia
NE	Nebraska	W.A.	Western Australia
NV	Nevada	WI	Wisconsin
NB	New Brunswick	WY	Wyoming
NH	New Hampshire	YT	Yukon Territory

Taxonomy Listings

AFRICAN AMERICAN STUDIES *v.6 p.1*

  History. *v.6 p.3*
    Africa *v.6 p.9*
    Diaspora. *v.6 p.11*
    Civil Rights Movement *v.6 p.12*
    Black Nationalism *v.6 p.12*
    Pan-Africanism. *v.6 p.13*
  Africana Studies *v.6 p.13*
    Diaspora. *v.6 p.14*
    Africa *v.6 p.14*
  Art *v.6 p.15*
    Performing Arts/Cinema/Television. . . *v.6 p.15*
    Visual arts *v.6 p.16*
  Anthropology and Archeology *v.6 p.16*
  Biography. *v.6 p.16*
  Civilization *v.6 p.19*
  Communication *v.6 p.20*
  Economics *v.6 p.20*
  Education *v.6 p.21*
  Health *v.6 p.21*
  Law *v.6 p.22*
  Literature *v.6 p.22*
    Africa *v.6 p.28*
    Diaspora. *v.6 p.29*
  Music. *v.6 p.29*
  Performing Arts *v.6 p.30*
  Politics *v.6 p.30*
  Psychology *v.6 p.32*
  Reference *v.6 p.33*
    General *v.6 p.33*
    Bibliography. *v.6 p.35*
  Religion and Philosophy *v.6 p.35*
  Reparations *v.6 p.36*
  Slavery and Slave Trade *v.6 p.37*
  Sociology *v.6 p.38*
  Sports. *v.6 p.41*
  Women *v.6 p.41*
  Science *v.6 p.48*

**AFRICAN HISTORY, LANGUAGES, AND
LITERATURES** *v.6 p.49*

  History of Africa. *v.6 p.51*
    General Works *v.6 p.51*
    Description and Travel *v.6 p.51*
    History *v.6 p.52*
    Egypt *v.6 p.56*
    Sudan *v.6 p.59*
    North Africa *v.6 p.59*
    Central Africa *v.6 p.61*

    East Africa. *v.6 p.63*
    West Africa *v.6 p.67*
    Southern Africa *v.6 p.74*
  African Languages and Literatures. *v.6 p.80*

AGRICULTURE *v.5 p.1*

  Agriculture *v.5 p.3*
    Agricultural Biotechnology *v.5 p.6*
    Agricultural Chemicals. *v.5 p.9*
    Agricultural Ecology *v.5 p.10*
    Agricultural Education *v.5 p.11*
    Agricultural Geography *v.5 p.12*
    Sustainable Agriculture *v.5 p.12*
    Urban Agriculture *v.5 p.13*
    Women in Agriculture *v.5 p.13*
    Agricultural Economics *v.5 p.13*
  Agronomy. *v.5 p.15*
  Botany, Agricultural *v.5 p.15*
  Botany, Economic *v.5 p.16*
  Conservation *v.5 p.16*
    Conservation of Natural Resources. *v.5 p.17*
    National Parks and Reserves *v.5 p.18*
    Water Conservation. *v.5 p.19*
    Wildlife Conservation. *v.5 p.19*
  Crops. *v.5 p.19*
    Field Crops *v.5 p.24*
    Horticultural Crops *v.5 p.25*
    Subtropical Crops *v.5 p.25*
    Tropical Crops *v.5 p.25*
    Vegetables *v.5 p.26*
  Entomology *v.5 p.26*
    Insect Pests *v.5 p.27*
    Insects. *v.5 p.27*
  Environment. *v.5 p.28*
    Environmental Management *v.5 p.28*
    Environmental Policy. *v.5 p.29*
  Farms. *v.5 p.29*
    Family Farms *v.5 p.30*
    Organic Farming *v.5 p.30*
  Fire. *v.5 p.31*
    Fire Management. *v.5 p.31*
    Forest Fires *v.5 p.31*
  Fisheries *v.5 p.32*
  Food *v.5 p.32*
    Food Composition *v.5 p.33*
    Food Policy *v.5 p.33*
    Food Science *v.5 p.33*
  Forestry. *v.5 p.36*
    Agroforestry *v.5 p.40*
    Deforestation. *v.5 p.40*
    Forest Ecology *v.5 p.40*
    Forest Policy *v.5 p.41*

Logging *v.5 p.41*
Rain Forests *v.5 p.41*
Silviculture *v.5 p.41*
Trees *v.5 p.41*
Wood *v.5 p.41*
Grasslands *v.5 p.41*
Rangelands *v.5 p.42*

Gardening *v.5 p.43*
Horticulture *v.5 p.44*
Organic Gardening *v.5 p.45*

Plants *v.5 p.45*
Plant Biotechnology *v.5 p.45*
Plant Diseases *v.5 p.45*

Seeds *v.5 p.47*

Soils *v.5 p.48*
Soil Chemistry *v.5 p.52*
Soil Classification *v.5 p.52*

Viticulture *v.5 p.52*

Wetlands *v.5 p.53*

Animal Science *v.5 p.53*

Veterinary Medicine *v.5 p.56*

AMERICAN LITERATURE *v.2 p.1*
History, Criticism *v.2 p.3*
Criticism *v.2 p.3*
History of American Literature *v.2 p.5*
Collected Essays. Collective Biography *v.2 p.6*
Women Authors *v.2 p.7*
Literary history, by period *v.2 p.9*
Literary history, by Region *v.2 p.12*
Literary history, by Form *v.2 p.15*

Collections of American Literature *v.2 p.17*
By Period *v.2 p.20*
By Region *v.2 p.21*
By Form *v.2 p.22*

Colonial Period (17th-18th Centuries) *v.2 p.28*

19th Century *v.2 p.30*
A *v.2 p.30*
Alcott, Louisa May *v.2 p.30*
B *v.2 p.31*
Bierce, Ambrose *v.2 p.31*
C *v.2 p.32*
Chesnutt, Charles *v.2 p.32*
Chopin, Kate *v.2 p.32*
Clemens, Samuel (Mark Twain) *v.2 p.33*
Cooper, James Fenimore *v.2 p.35*
Crane, Stephen *v.2 p.35*
D *v.2 p.36*
Dickinson, Emily *v.2 p.36*
E-F *v.2 p.37*
Emerson, Ralph Waldo *v.2 p.37*
Fuller, Margaret *v.2 p.38*
Garland, Hamlin *v.2 p.39*
G-H *v.2 p.39*
Harris, Joel Chandler *v.2 p.40*
Harte, Bret *v.2 p.40*
Hawthorne, Nathaniel *v.2 p.40*
Howells, William Dean *v.2 p.41*

Irving, Washington *v.2 p.42*
J-K *v.2 p.43*
James, Henry *v.2 p.43*
Jewett, Sarah Orne *v.2 p.46*
L-M *v.2 p.46*
Lanier, Sidney *v.2 p.47*
Longfellow, Henry Wadsworth *v.2 p.47*
Lowell, James Russell *v.2 p.47*
Melville, Herman *v.2 p.47*
N-R *v.2 p.49*
Norris, Frank *v.2 p.49*
Poe, Edgar Allen *v.2 p.50*
Porter, Sydney (O. Henry) *v.2 p.50*
S-T *v.2 p.51*
Stowe, Harriet Beecher *v.2 p.51*
Thoreau, Henry David *v.2 p.52*
V-W *v.2 p.53*
Whitman, Walt *v.2 p.53*
Whittier, James Greenleaf *v.2 p.55*

20th Century (1901-1960) *v.2 p.55*
A *v.2 p.55*
B *v.2 p.58*
C *v.2 p.64*
D *v.2 p.69*
E *v.2 p.70*
F *v.2 p.72*
G *v.2 p.78*
H *v.2 p.80*
I *v.2 p.89*
J *v.2 p.89*
K *v.2 p.91*
L *v.2 p.94*
M *v.2 p.97*
N *v.2 p.103*
O *v.2 p.105*
P *v.2 p.108*
R *v.2 p.113*
S *v.2 p.115*
T *v.2 p.124*
V *v.2 p.126*
W *v.2 p.128*
Z *v.2 p.138*

20th Century (1961-2000) *v.2 p.139*
A *v.2 p.139*
B *v.2 p.140*
Barth, John *v.2 p.142*
C *v.2 p.142*
D *v.2 p.143*
E *v.2 p.144*
F *v.2 p.145*
G *v.2 p.145*
H *v.2 p.146*
I *v.2 p.147*
J *v.2 p.147*
K *v.2 p.147*
L *v.2 p.148*
M *v.2 p.149*
N *v.2 p.151*
O *v.2 p.151*
Oates, Joyce Carol *v.2 p.152*
P *v.2 p.152*

R v.2 p.153
S v.2 p.154
T v.2 p.156
U v.2 p.157
V v.2 p.157
Vonnegut, Kurt v.2 p.157
W v.2 p.158
Y v.2 p.159
Z v.2 p.159
21st Century v.2 p.160

ANCIENT HISTORY v.3 p.1
General and Reference Works v.3 p.3
Ancient Near East v.3 p.4
General v.3 p.4
Mesopotamia v.3 p.5
Hittites v.3 p.6
Israel, Phoenicia, and Syria v.3 p.6
Egypt (PreDynastic to Arab Conquest) . . .v.3 p.8
Pharaonic Egypt v.3 p.8
Greco-Roman Egypt v.3 p.10
Egyptology v.3 p.11
Persia v.3 p.11
Greece v.3 p.12
General v.3 p.12
Sources v.3 p.13
Social History v.3 p.13
By Period v.3 p.15
Rome v.3 p.22
General v.3 p.22
Sources v.3 p.22
Social History v.3 p.22
By Period v.3 p.24

ANTHROPOLOGY v.4 p.1
Reference Works, Dictionaries, Encyclopedias,
Collections v.4 p.3
History and Biography v.4 p.3
Archaeology v.4 p.5
General and Introductory Works v.4 p.5
Theory and History of Archaeology . . .v.4 p.6
Analytic Methods v.4 p.6
Field Methods v.4 p.7
Archaeology by Continent v.4 p.7
Historical Archaeology v.4 p.13
Biological Anthropology v.4 p.14
General and Introductory Works v.4 p.14
Human Evolution v.4 p.15
Paleoanthropology v.4 p.16
Human Groups, Discussions of Race . . .v.4 p.17
Linguistic Anthropology v.4 p.17
General, Introductory, and Historical Works . . .v.4 p.17
Theory and Methods v.4 p.18
Origin and Evolution of Language and Language
Change v.4 p.19
Language and Culture v.4 p.20
Language in Relation to Gender, Ethnicity, and

Power v.4 p.20
Anthropology of Oral and Written Language . .v.4 p.21
Social and Cultural Anthropology v.4 p.22
General and Introductory Works v.4 p.22
Theory and Methodology v.4 p.23
Field Methods v.4 p.25
Anthropology of Art: Visual, Performing, Music,
Dance v.4 p.25
Cognitive Anthropology v.4 p.26
Critical and Engaged Anthropology . . .v.4 p.27
Economic Anthropology v.4 p.27
Educational Anthropology v.4 p.29
Anthropology and Environment v.4 p.29
Gender v.4 p.30
Kinship, Marriage, Family, Household Systems .v.4 p.31
Legal Anthropology v.4 p.33
Political Anthropology v.4 p.34
Psychological Anthropology v.4 p.35
Religion v.4 p.36
Urban Anthropology v.4 p.37
World Ethnography by Continent v.4 p.38
Applied Anthropology v.4 p.44
Electronic Resources v.4 p.45
Athropology of Food Habits, Cuisine, Drink, and
Nutrition v.4 p.45
Medical Anthropology v.4 p.46
Museum Anthropology v.4 p.47

ASIAN AMERICAN STUDIES v.6 p.83
General Works v.6 p.85
Databases v.6 p.85
Reference Works v.6 p.86
Arts and Humanities v.6 p.87
Arts and Culture v.6 p.87
Literature v.6 p.90
Philosophy v.6 p.105
Religion v.6 p.105
Social Sciences v.6 p.106
Business v.6 p.106
Civil Rights, Activism v.6 p.107
Education v.6 p.108
Family v.6 p.110
Gender and Sexuality v.6 p.111
History v.6 p.113
Labor v.6 p.116
Law v.6 p.117
Migration v.6 p.117
Politics v.6 p.120
Psychology v.6 p.121
Race v.6 p.122
Sociology v.6 p.125
Ethnic Groups v.6 p.125
Science, Health, and Technology v.6 p.141
Science v.6 p.141
Health v.6 p.141
Technology v.6 p.141

ASIAN HISTORY, LANGUAGES, AND
LITERATURES *v.6 p.143*
  South Asia, General *v.6 p.145*
    Languages and Literatures, General *v.6 p.147*
  Bangladesh *v.6 p.148*
  India *v.6 p.149*
    Social Life. Customs. Caste *v.6 p.149*
    Civilization *v.6 p.150*
    Languages and Literatures *v.6 p.150*
    Ethnography *v.6 p.153*
    History *v.6 p.155*
  Pakistan *v.6 p.162*
  Sri Lanka (Ceylon) *v.6 p.163*
  Nepal *v.6 p.163*
  Southeast Asia, General *v.6 p.164*
  Myanmar (Burma) *v.6 p.165*
    History *v.6 p.165*
  Vietnam *v.6 p.166*
    History *v.6 p.167*
    Language and Literature *v.6 p.169*
  Kampuchea (Cambodia) *v.6 p.169*
  Laos *v.6 p.171*
  Thailand (Siam) *v.6 p.171*
  Malaysia *v.6 p.172*
  Singapore *v.6 p.173*
  Indonesia *v.6 p.173*
    History *v.6 p.175*
    Language and Literature *v.6 p.178*
  Philippines *v.6 p.178*
  East Asia, General *v.6 p.180*
  China *v.6 p.181*
    History *v.6 p.183*
    Science and Technology *v.6 p.198*
    Biography, Memoirs *v.6 p.198*
    Foreign Relations *v.6 p.203*
    Regional History *v.6 p.205*
    Language *v.6 p.207*
    Literature *v.6 p.207*
    Taiwan *v.6 p.213*
    Foreign Views of China *v.6 p.214*
    Women in China *v.6 p.217*
    Foreign Presence in China (Missions, Business,
      Education) *v.6 p.217*
  Japan *v.6 p.218*
    Civilization *v.6 p.221*
    History *v.6 p.223*
    Biography, Memoirs *v.6 p.226*
    Japanese Literature *v.6 p.229*
    Okinawa *v.6 p.235*
  Korea *v.6 p.235*
    History *v.6 p.235*
    Language and Literature *v.6 p.237*
  Central Asia — General *v.6 p.238*
  Mongolia *v.6 p.239*
  Tibet *v.6 p.240*

ASTRONOMY *v.5 p.59*
  General Astronomy *v.5 p.61*
    Histories *v.5 p.61*
    Biographies *v.5 p.62*
    Dictionaries and Encyclopedias *v.5 p.62*
    Handbooks, Tables and Formulas *v.5 p.63*
    Atlases and Catalogs *v.5 p.63*
    Abstracts and Indexes *v.5 p.64*
    Yearbooks *v.5 p.64*
  Astronomy Texts and Textbooks *v.5 p.64*
    Mathematical Methods (QA) *v.5 p.64*
    General and Introductory *v.5 p.64*
    Astronomical Instrumentation *v.5 p.65*
    Practical and Spherical Astronomy *v.5 p.66*
    Theoretical Astronomy and Celestial Mechanics . *v.5 p.66*
    Astrophysics *v.5 p.66*
    Non-optical Methods of Astronomy *v.5 p.67*
    Descriptive Astronomy *v.5 p.68*
  Cosmology *v.5 p.71*
  Physics -- General Relativity *v.5 p.72*
  Light and Optics *v.5 p.73*
  Radiation Physics -- Cosmic Rays *v.5 p.73*
  Geophysics -- Cosmic Physics (QC) *v.5 p.73*
  Astrobiology *v.5 p.73*

BIOLOGY *v.5 p.75*
  History of Biology *v.5 p.77*
  Biological Techniques *v.5 p.82*
    Zoos and Botanical Gardens *v.5 p.82*
    Herbaria, Museums, and Culture Collections . . *v.5 p.85*
    Microscopy *v.5 p.86*
    General Field Methods *v.5 p.87*
    General Laboratory Methods *v.5 p.87*
    Statistical Analysis and Mathematics *v.5 p.90*
    Associations and Organizations *v.5 p.94*
    Library and Reference Works *v.5 p.94*
  Bioinformatics *v.5 p.96*
    Analytic Methods *v.5 p.99*
    Gene Sequencing *v.5 p.101*
    methods of gene sequencing *v.5 p.102*
    Protein Sequences *v.5 p.102*
    DNA and RNA Sequences *v.5 p.103*
    Proteomics *v.5 p.104*
    Computational Molecular Biology *v.5 p.105*
    Computer Applications *v.5 p.107*
    Microarray Data Analysis and Sequence
      Analysis *v.5 p.109*
  Biochemistry and Biophysics *v.5 p.110*
    General Biochemistry *v.5 p.111*
    Specific Substances *v.5 p.115*
    Plant Biochemistry *v.5 p.124*
    Biophysics *v.5 p.125*
  Cellular and Molecular Biology, Genetics *v.5 p.125*
    Molecular Biology, General *v.5 p.125*
    Genetics (General) *v.5 p.130*
    Medical Genetics *v.5 p.148*
    Genetic Engineering *v.5 p.152*
    Cell Biology, Eucaryotes *v.5 p.152*

Developmental Biology *v.5 p.153*
Organismic Biology (Anatomy, Physiology). . . . *v.5 p.155*
  Anatomy and Morphology *v.5 p.155*
  Histology. *v.5 p.158*
  Embryology *v.5 p.159*
  Physiology *v.5 p.163*
  Neurobiology *v.5 p.164*
  Immunology *v.5 p.165*
Behavioral Biology *v.5 p.165*
  Behavior of Microorganisms *v.5 p.166*
  Plant Behavior *v.5 p.166*
  Animal behavior *v.5 p.166*
  Social Behavior *v.5 p.167*
Integrative Biology *v.5 p.167*
  Biogeography. *v.5 p.167*
  General Ecology *v.5 p.169*
  Evolution. *v.5 p.189*
Descriptive Biology: General *v.5 p.204*
Descriptive Biology: Microorganisms. *v.5 p.205*
  Virology *v.5 p.206*
  Bacteriology *v.5 p.206*
Descriptive Biology: Plants *v.5 p.206*
  General. *v.5 p.206*
  Nomenclature. *v.5 p.207*
  Lower Plants (Cryptograms) *v.5 p.207*
  Higher Plants *v.5 p.211*
Descriptive Biology: Animals *v.5 p.211*
  Invertebrates *v.5 p.212*
  Vertebrates *v.5 p.213*
Biotechnology *v.5 p.217*
Natural History. *v.5 p.220*
  Reference. *v.5 p.224*
  Education. *v.5 p.227*
  Biographies. *v.5 p.229*
  Nature Writing *v.5 p.232*
  Bioregions and Bioregionalism *v.5 p.233*
Astrobiology and Exobiology *v.5 p.242*
Biology Education *v.5 p.244*
Bioethics. *v.5 p.246*
Biology Careers *v.5 p.250*

BRITISH LITERATURE. *v.2 p.161*
Criticism. *v.2 p.163*
Literary History, by Period *v.2 p.166*
  Anglo-Saxon. *v.2 p.167*
  Medieval. Middle English *v.2 p.168*
  Modern. *v.2 p.169*
Literary History, by Form *v.2 p.179*
  Poetry *v.2 p.179*
  Drama *v.2 p.185*
  Prose Fiction. The Novel. *v.2 p.189*
  Humor. Satire. *v.2 p.195*
Collections of British Literature *v.2 p.195*
  By Period *v.2 p.196*
  By Form *v.2 p.197*
Individual Authors and Works *v.2 p.203*
  Anglo-Saxon. Old and Middle English . . . *v.2 p.203*

English Renaissance (1500-1640) Prose. Poetry. *v.2 p.212*
English Renaissance (1500-1640) Drama . . . *v.2 p.217*
17th-18th C. *v.2 p.236*
19th C. *v.2 p.264*
20th C. *v.2 p.328*

BUSINESS ADMINISTRATION *v.4 p.49*
Business Environment *v.4 p.51*
  Social Policy. *v.4 p.51*
  International Trade and Foreign Investment . *v.4 p.57*
  Energy / Environment. *v.4 p.61*
Management Function *v.4 p.64*
  General Management *v.4 p.64*
  Finance *v.4 p.88*
  Accounting, Taxation, and Law. *v.4 p.103*
  Operations *v.4 p.112*
  Human Resource Management *v.4 p.119*
  Marketing *v.4 p.134*
Company and Industry Information. *v.4 p.146*
  Business History *v.4 p.146*
  Company Information *v.4 p.148*
  Industries and Markets (Selected). . . . *v.4 p.148*
Careers, Personal Skills Development,
and Vocational Guidance *v.4 p.166*
  Job-seeking. *v.4 p.168*
  Business Writing and Communications . . . *v.4 p.171*
  Business Mathematics *v.4 p.174*
  Management Education *v.4 p.176*
Business Information Sources *v.4 p.179*

CHEMISTRY *v.5 p.253*
Basic Chemistry *v.5 p.255*
  Guides to the Literature *v.5 p.255*
  Abstracting and Indexing Services *v.5 p.256*
  Encyclopedias. *v.5 p.256*
  Dictionaries. *v.5 p.257*
  Foreign Language Dictionaries *v.5 p.258*
  Handbooks and Tables of Data *v.5 p.258*
  Directories *v.5 p.259*
  Style Guide. *v.5 p.260*
  Biographies. *v.5 p.260*
  History of Chemistry *v.5 p.262*
  Chemistry Today *v.5 p.264*
  The Future of Chemistry. *v.5 p.265*
  Safety Literature *v.5 p.265*
  Problem Manuals, Educational Materials, and Computer
    Materials *v.5 p.266*
Analytical Chemistry *v.5 p.267*
  Encyclopedias. *v.5 p.267*
  General Handbooks and Data Compilations . *v.5 p.267*
  Analytical Methods *v.5 p.268*
  Special Topics *v.5 p.269*
  Treatises *v.5 p.273*
  Sampling and Statistical Methodology. . . *v.5 p.273*
  History and Bibliography *v.5 p.274*
  Problem Manuals and Software. *v.5 p.274*
  Guides to the Literature *v.5 p.274*
  Nomenclature. *v.5 p.274*

Physical Chemistry *v.5 p.274*
    Literature Retrieval *v.5 p.274*
    Encyclopedias. *v.5 p.275*
    Dictionary *v.5 p.275*
    General Handbooks *v.5 p.275*
    Databases and Literature Reviews. *v.5 p.275*
    Treatises, Monographs, and Advanced
      Textbooks. *v.5 p.275*
    Physicochemical Calculations *v.5 p.280*
    Physicochemical Properties and Data
      Compilations *v.5 p.280*
    Laboratory Texts and Manuals *v.5 p.287*
    Problem Manuals and Physical Chemistry
      Software *v.5 p.288*
Organic Chemistry *v.5 p.288*
    Guides to the Literature *v.5 p.288*
    Bibliographies, Indexes, and Reviews *v.5 p.288*
    Nomenclature. *v.5 p.288*
    Encyclopedias. *v.5 p.289*
    Dictionaries. *v.5 p.289*
    Handbooks and Tables of Data *v.5 p.289*
    History. *v.5 p.291*
    Compilations and Treatises. *v.5 p.291*
    Structure and Properties: Electronic/Physical. . *v.5 p.293*
    Synthetic Methods: *v.5 p.293*
    Reactions. *v.5 p.295*
    Organic Chemistry of Special Elements *v.5 p.296*
    Special Topics in Organic Chemistry *v.5 p.296*
    Organic Analytical Procedures *v.5 p.300*
    Laboratory Procedure Manuals *v.5 p.301*
    Problem Manuals *v.5 p.301*
Inorganic Chemistry. *v.5 p.301*
    General Surveys. *v.5 p.301*
    Nomenclature *v.5 p.301*
    Encyclopedia *v.5 p.302*
    Handbooks and Tables of Data *v.5 p.302*
    Compilations and Treatises. *v.5 p.302*
    Structure and Properties *v.5 p.303*
    Synthetic Methods. *v.5 p.304*
    Reactions. *v.5 p.304*
    Special Topics *v.5 p.305*
    Guides to the Literature *v.5 p.309*
Environmental Chemistry *v.5 p.309*
    Guides to the Literature *v.5 p.309*
    Abstracting and Indexing Services *v.5 p.309*
    General Environmental Chemistry *v.5 p.310*
    Dictionaries and Encyclopedia *v.5 p.310*
    Handbooks and Desk References *v.5 p.311*
    Chemical Analysis of Environmental Samples . *v.5 p.312*
    Special Topics in Environmental Chemistry . . *v.5 p.312*
    Educational Materials *v.5 p.315*
Industrial Chemistry *v.5 p.315*
    Handbooks and Encyclopedias *v.5 p.315*
    Dictionaries and Thesauri *v.5 p.316*
    History and Development of Chemical Industry. *v.5 p.316*
    Product Sources. *v.5 p.317*
    Economic and Financial Information *v.5 p.317*
    Standards and Specifications *v.5 p.318*
    Treatises and Comprehensive Works *v.5 p.318*
    Special Topics in Industrial Chemistry *v.5 p.318*
    Guides to the Internet *v.5 p.320*

Polymer Chemistry *v.5 p.321*
    Guides to the Literature *v.5 p.321*
    General Resources. *v.5 p.321*
    Nomenclature. *v.5 p.321*
    Encyclopedias. *v.5 p.321*
    Handbooks *v.5 p.322*
    Dictionary *v.5 p.322*
    History. *v.5 p.322*
    Treatises and Comprehensive Works *v.5 p.322*
    Techniques in Polymer Chemistry. *v.5 p.322*
    Characterization of Polymers. *v.5 p.323*
    Mechanical and Chemical Behavior of
      Polymers *v.5 p.324*
    Physical and Chemical Properties of Polymers . *v.5 p.324*
    Multicomponent Systems *v.5 p.324*
Biological Chemistry *v.5 p.324*
    Guides to the Literature *v.5 p.324*
    Abstracting and Indexing Services *v.5 p.325*
    Encyclopedias. *v.5 p.325*
    Nomenclature. *v.5 p.325*
    Dictionaries. *v.5 p.325*
    Glossaries *v.5 p.325*
    Review Literature *v.5 p.326*
    History. *v.5 p.326*
    Laboratory Methods *v.5 p.326*
    Tables of Data *v.5 p.326*
    Treatises *v.5 p.326*
    Special Topics *v.5 p.328*
    Laboratory Safety *v.5 p.330*
    Problem Manuals and Educational Materials . *v.5 p.331*

CLASSICAL LANGUAGES AND LITERATURES

CLASSICAL LANGUAGES AND
LITERATURES *v.2 p.397*
  General and Reference Works *v.2 p.399*
  Greek *v.2 p.399*
    Greek Language. *v.2 p.399*
    Greek Literature. *v.2 p.400*
    Genres *v.2 p.401*
    Individual Authors. *v.2 p.406*
  Latin *v.2 p.423*
    Latin Language *v.2 p.423*
    General Works *v.2 p.424*
    Genres *v.2 p.425*
    Individual Authors. *v.2 p.428*
    Medieval Latin *v.2 p.448*

COMPUTING

COMPUTING. *v.5 p.333*
  Data Structures *v.5 p.335*
  Data Encryption *v.5 p.335*
  Coding and Information Theory *v.5 p.335*
  Theory of Computation *v.5 p.335*
    General. *v.5 p.335*
    Analysis of Algorithms and Complexity. . . . *v.5 p.336*
    Logic and Semantics of Programs *v.5 p.336*
    Mathematical Logic and Formal Languages . *v.5 p.336*
  Math of Computing. *v.5 p.337*
    Numerical Analysis and Scientific Computing . *v.5 p.337*

Discrete Mathematics *v.5 p.337*
Information Systems *v.5 p.337*
   Database Management *v.5 p.337*
   Information Storage and Retrieval *v.5 p.338*
   World Wide Web *v.5 p.338*
   Information Systems Applications. *v.5 p.338*
Artificial Intelligence *v.5 p.339*
Computer Graphics *v.5 p.339*
Image Processing and Computer Vision. *v.5 p.340*
Pattern Recognition *v.5 p.340*
Simulation *v.5 p.340*
Document and Text Processing. *v.5 p.341*
Applications *v.5 p.341*
Millieux *v.5 p.342*
   Computer Industry *v.5 p.342*
   History of Computing *v.5 p.342*
   Computers and Society *v.5 p.342*
   Legal Aspects. *v.5 p.343*
General *v.5 p.343*
Reference *v.5 p.344*
Hardware *v.5 p.344*
System Organization *v.5 p.345*
   Processor Architecture *v.5 p.345*
   Computer and Communication Networks . . . *v.5 p.345*
   Performance *v.5 p.345*
Software *v.5 p.345*
   Software Engineering *v.5 p.345*
   Programming Languages *v.5 p.346*
   Operating Systems *v.5 p.348*
   Miscellany *v.5 p.348*
   General. *v.5 p.348*
   Programming Techniques *v.5 p.349*

CRIMINAL JUSTICE *v.6 p.243*
Criminal Justice, Generally *v.6 p.245*
   History of Criminal Justice. *v.6 p.245*
   Education, Teaching, and Careers *v.6 p.245*
   Comprehensive Reference Sources *v.6 p.245*
   Research *v.6 p.246*
Criminal Justice Systems and Processes. *v.6 p.246*
   Legal and Policy Issues *v.6 p.246*
   Criminal Justice Administration. *v.6 p.248*
   Ethical and Moral Issues *v.6 p.249*
Criminology *v.6 p.249*
   Criminology, Generally *v.6 p.249*
   Crime *v.6 p.250*
   Criminals and Criminal Behavior *v.6 p.254*
   Sociology of Crime *v.6 p.255*
   Victimology *v.6 p.258*
Law Enforcement. *v.6 p.259*
   Police and Law Enforcement Officers *v.6 p.259*
   Police Behavior *v.6 p.260*
   Law Enforcement, generally *v.6 p.261*
   Policing *v.6 p.263*
   Firearms *v.6 p.266*
   Investigation *v.6 p.266*
   Police and Terrorism. *v.6 p.267*

Law and Courts *v.6 p.267*
   Criminal Courts. *v.6 p.267*
   Law and Practice of Criminal Procedure. . . *v.6 p.269*
   Sentencing *v.6 p.271*
   Clemency/pardons. *v.6 p.272*
Corrections. *v.6 p.272*
   Corrections, Generally *v.6 p.272*
   Punishment *v.6 p.274*
   Prisons and Jails *v.6 p.275*
   Prisoners *v.6 p.276*
   Probation, Parole, and Community Corrections. *v.6 p.278*
   Restorative Justice. *v.6 p.278*
   Post-incarceration *v.6 p.279*

DANCE *v.1 p.1*
General Reference Works *v.1 p.3*
Historical Overviews *v.1 p.5*
Dance Biographies and Autobiographies *v.1 p.5*
Dance Styles, Forms, and Traditions. *v.1 p.14*
   Geographical Traditions. *v.1 p.14*
   African American Dance *v.1 p.17*
   African Caribbean Dance *v.1 p.19*
   Latin American Dance *v.1 p.20*
   Spanish Dance *v.1 p.20*
   Sacred and Liturgical Dance. *v.1 p.21*
   Western European Renaissance and Baroque
     Dance *v.1 p.21*
   Ballet *v.1 p.22*
   Contemporary Dance Traditions *v.1 p.25*
   Jazz Dance *v.1 p.31*
   Tap Dance *v.1 p.32*
   European and American Social Dance Traditions. *v.1 p.33*
   Variety Dance *v.1 p.34*
   Dance in Commercial Theater and Movies . . . *v.1 p.36*
   Television, Video, and New Media Dance . . . *v.1 p.36*
Choreography *v.1 p.37*
Dance Production and Administration *v.1 p.37*
Dance Notation *v.1 p.38*
Dance Criticism *v.1 p.38*
Dance Theory *v.1 p.40*
Dance and Related Arts *v.1 p.44*
Dance Education. *v.1 p.46*
Dance Ethnology and Anthropology *v.1 p.48*
Dance Science and Medicine *v.1 p.49*
Dance Therapy *v.1 p.50*
Somatic Studies *v.1 p.51*
Dance Documentation and Preservation *v.1 p.52*

DRAMA AND THEATER. *v.1 p.53*
General *v.1 p.55*
   History *v.1 p.55*
   Theory *v.1 p.55*
Reference *v.1 p.57*
Western Drama and Theater. *v.1 p.61*
   Individual Works *v.1 p.62*

Collections of Plays *v.1 p.62*
Periods *v.1 p.69*
Genres, Styles, and Types *v.1 p.87*
Europe *v.1 p.94*
United States *v.1 p.111*
Canada *v.1 p.126*
Latin America *v.1 p.127*
Australia *v.1 p.128*
Non-Western Drama and Theater *v.1 p.128*
Individual Works *v.1 p.128*
Collections of Plays *v.1 p.129*
Countries *v.1 p.129*
Periods, Genres, Styles, Types *v.1 p.133*
Theater Production *v.1 p.134*
Performance Studies *v.1 p.134*
General *v.1 p.136*
Reference *v.1 p.139*
Performance *v.1 p.142*

ECONOMICS *v.4 p.183*
General Economics *v.4 p.185*
Dictionaries. Handbooks *v.4 p.186*
Encyclopedias *v.4 p.192*
Biographical *v.4 p.193*
General Methodology *v.4 p.194*
Econometrics. Mathematical Economics *v.4 p.197*
General Equilibrium *v.4 p.205*
Simultaneous Equation Models. Multiple
Variables *v.4 p.206*
Panel Data *v.4 p.206*
Time-Series *v.4 p.206*
Modeling/Forecasting *v.4 p.206*
Game Theory *v.4 p.207*
Systems *v.4 p.207*
History *v.4 p.208*
Capitalist *v.4 p.214*
Socialist *v.4 p.235*
Comparative *v.4 p.237*
Macroeconomics and Monetary Economics . . . *v.4 p.237*
Models *v.4 p.239*
Marxian/Sraffian/Institutional/Evolutionary . . *v.4 p.241*
Business Cycles/Economic Growth/Prices . . . *v.4 p.242*
Consumption/Investment/Savings *v.4 p.245*
Central Banking and Monetary Policy/Interest
Rates *v.4 p.246*
Public *v.4 p.247*
Government Taxation and Expenditure *v.4 p.248*
Microeconomics *v.4 p.248*
Concepts *v.4 p.248*
Consumption/Consumer Behavior *v.4 p.249*
Market Structure and Pricing *v.4 p.251*
Competition *v.4 p.251*
Monopoly/Oligopoly *v.4 p.252*
Employment/Unemployment *v.4 p.252*
Labor and Demographic *v.4 p.253*
International *v.4 p.255*
Trade *v.4 p.256*
Economic Development *v.4 p.258*

Globalization *v.4 p.260*
Relations *v.4 p.262*
Financial Economics *v.4 p.262*
Health/Education/Welfare/Poverty *v.4 p.264*
Agricultural/Land/Environmental/Energy
Economics *v.4 p.267*
Urban and Rural Economics *v.4 p.268*
Cultural Economics. Social Economics *v.4 p.268*
Experimental Economics *v.4 p.271*
Cognitive Economics *v.4 p.272*
Feminist Economics *v.4 p.272*

EDUCATION *v.4 p.275*
Education and Training of Teachers and
Administrators *v.4 p.277*
Certification of Teachers *v.4 p.278*
Professional Aspects of Teaching and School
Administration *v.4 p.278*
Teacher Training in Universities and Colleges . *v.4 p.279*
School Administration and Organization *v.4 p.280*
Administrative Personnel *v.4 p.281*
Teaching Personnel, Work Conditions *v.4 p.282*
Classroom Management and Discipline *v.4 p.283*
School Facilities *v.4 p.288*
Student Life (Including Organizations and
Activities) *v.4 p.288*
Higher Education *v.4 p.289*
Institutions of Higher Education *v.4 p.289*
Teaching Personnel, Academic Freedom, Work
Conditions *v.4 p.292*
Scholarships, Grants, Student Financial Aid . . *v.4 p.293*
Administration and Finance *v.4 p.293*
Entrance Requirements. College Choice *v.4 p.294*
Curriculum *v.4 p.294*
Graduate and Professional Education *v.4 p.295*
Academic Degrees *v.4 p.295*
State and Federal policy *v.4 p.295*
Special Forms of Education *v.4 p.296*
Home Schooling *v.4 p.296*
Private schools. Boarding Schools *v.4 p.296*
Social Aspects of Education *v.4 p.297*
Economic Aspects of Education *v.4 p.297*
Education and the State *v.4 p.297*
Compulsory Education. Attendance. Dropouts . *v.4 p.299*
Literacy *v.4 p.299*
Educational Sociology *v.4 p.300*
Community and the School *v.4 p.303*
Types of Education *v.4 p.303*
Humanistic and Liberal Education *v.4 p.303*
Competency Based Education *v.4 p.303*
Basic Education (Including Basic Skills
Education) *v.4 p.304*
Career and Vocational Education *v.4 p.304*
Moral, Religious, and Character Education . . *v.4 p.306*
Multicultural Education (General) *v.4 p.308*
Comparative and International Education . . . *v.4 p.312*
Education in Developing Countries *v.4 p.314*

Rural Education. Urban Education *v.4 p.314*
Special Education. Exceptional Children and
    Youth. *v.4 p.315*
Adult and Continuing Education *v.4 p.319*
Distance Education *v.4 p.321*
Education (General). *v.4 p.322*
Philosophy of Education. *v.4 p.323*
History of Education *v.4 p.324*
General Education by Period, Level, and Type (Public
    or private). *v.4 p.324*
History of Higher Education *v.4 p.330*
By Place (Non-U.S. Regions or Countries) . . *v.4 p.333*
Biography *v.4 p.337*
Theory and Practice of Education *v.4 p.338*
Systems of Individual Educators *v.4 p.340*
Teaching (Principles and Practice) *v.4 p.346*
Educational Research *v.4 p.354*
Educational Psychology. Child Study. *v.4 p.355*
Education by Level (Includes Teaching of Individual
    Subjects) *v.4 p.359*
Primary Education. *v.4 p.360*
Elementary *v.4 p.361*
Secondary Education *v.4 p.366*
Kindergarten *v.4 p.368*
Early Childhood Education. *v.4 p.368*
Preschool Education. Nursery Schools. . . . *v.4 p.370*

ENVIRONMENTAL SCIENCES *v.5 p.351*
Agricultural Pollution *v.5 p.353*
Deforestation *v.5 p.353*
Groundwater Pollution. *v.5 p.354*
Pesticides. *v.5 p.354*
Air Pollution *v.5 p.354*
Biodegradation *v.5 p.355*
Bioremediation *v.5 p.355*
Brownfields *v.5 p.355*
Carbon. *v.5 p.355*
Dams *v.5 p.356*
Ecosystem Decline *v.5 p.356*
Anthropogenic Impact *v.5 p.357*
Biodiversity. *v.5 p.358*
Coral Reefs. *v.5 p.359*
Desertification *v.5 p.359*
Erosion. *v.5 p.359*
Energy Use. *v.5 p.359*
Energy Conservation. *v.5 p.361*
Renewable Energy Sources. *v.5 p.361*
Environmental Chemistry *v.5 p.363*
Environmental Disasters. *v.5 p.363*
Environmental Diseases and Health *v.5 p.364*
Infectious Diseases *v.5 p.365*
Toxicology *v.5 p.366*
Environmental Geology (A T-B) *v.5 p.366*
Environmental Impact Analysis *v.5 p.367*
Environmental Engineering. Environmental
    Audits *v.5 p.367*

Environmental Movement *v.5 p.369*
Environmentalists. *v.5 p.370*
Genetically Modified Foods *v.5 p.370*
Global Warming *v.5 p.370*
Climate Change. *v.5 p.371*
Heavy Metals: Environmental Aspects *v.5 p.371*
Cadmium. *v.5 p.372*
Lead *v.5 p.372*
Mercury *v.5 p.372*
Uranium *v.5 p.372*
Indoor Air Pollution. *v.5 p.372*
Industrialization: Environmental Aspects . . . *v.5 p.373*
Land Use *v.5 p.373*
Legislation *v.5 p.374*
Noise Pollution. *v.5 p.374*
Nuclear Power plants *v.5 p.374*
Radioactive Waste. *v.5 p.374*
Ozone Depletion *v.5 p.375*
Pollutants *v.5 p.375*
Carcinogens *v.5 p.375*
Hazardous Wastes *v.5 p.375*
Pollution Control Industry *v.5 p.376*
Radioactivity. *v.5 p.376*
Resource Recovery *v.5 p.376*
Recycling. *v.5 p.376*
Soil Pollution. *v.5 p.377*
Sustainability *v.5 p.377*
Toxic Waste *v.5 p.378*
Waste Disposal *v.5 p.378*
Water Pollution *v.5 p.378*
Marine Pollution *v.5 p.380*
Water resources *v.5 p.380*
Wildlife Management *v.5 p.380*

ENVIRONMENTAL STUDIES *v.6 p.281*
Reference Works *v.6 p.284*
Literature *v.6 p.287*
Philosophy and Religion. *v.6 p.288*
Science and Technology. *v.6 p.289*
Biological Sciences and Ecology *v.6 p.290*
General Science. *v.6 p.293*
Chemistry and Related Subjects *v.6 p.294*
Environmental History *v.6 p.294*
Social & Behavioral Sciences *v.6 p.297*
Economics and Development *v.6 p.297*
Political Science and Policy *v.6 p.299*

EUROPEAN HISTORY. *v.3 p.33*
General History *v.3 p.35*
European History, General Works *v.3 p.35*
Historiography *v.3 p.35*
Military and Naval history *v.3 p.35*
Communications and Media. *v.3 p.36*

Economic History *v.3 p.38*
History of Science *v.3 p.44*
Social and Cultural History *v.3 p.50*
Religious History. *v.3 p.55*
Nationalism *v.3 p.61*
By period *v.3 p.62*
Britain *v.3 p.88*
Historiography *v.3 p.88*
British Empire. Commonwealth of Nations . . . *v.3 p.88*
England *v.3 p.90*
English History *v.3 p.95*
Wales *v.3 p.132*
Scotland *v.3 p.132*
Ireland. Northern Ireland. *v.3 p.133*
Ireland *v.3 p.135*
Northern Ireland *v.3 p.139*
France *v.3 p.140*
History, General Works *v.3 p.140*
Military and Diplomatic History *v.3 p.141*
Social Life and Customs. Ethnography *v.3 p.141*
History *v.3 p.141*
Special topics *v.3 p.157*
Local History *v.3 p.158*
Germany *v.3 p.159*
General Works and Histories *v.3 p.159*
Military and Diplomatic History *v.3 p.160*
History *v.3 p.161*
Special Topics *v.3 p.178*
Regional, Provincial, and Local History . . . *v.3 p.181*
Austria. Austro-Hungarian Empire *v.3 p.181*
General Histories *v.3 p.181*
Military and Diplomatic History *v.3 p.182*
By Period *v.3 p.182*
Hungary *v.3 p.185*
General History *v.3 p.185*
Social Life. Ethnography *v.3 p.185*
By Period *v.3 p.185*
Czechoslovakia. Czech Republic. Slovakia. Bohemia.
Moravia *v.3 p.187*
General History *v.3 p.187*
By Period *v.3 p.188*
Ethnicity and Region *v.3 p.190*
Greece *v.3 p.191*
General History *v.3 p.191*
Civilization and Legacies *v.3 p.191*
By Period *v.3 p.191*
Local History and Description *v.3 p.196*
Cyprus *v.3 p.197*
Italy *v.3 p.197*
Regional History. Mezzogiorno, Sicily *v.3 p.197*
Urban History *v.3 p.197*
General History *v.3 p.197*
Foreign policy, Diplomacy *v.3 p.198*
By Period *v.3 p.198*
Netherlands (Low Countries) *v.3 p.204*
General Histories *v.3 p.204*
By Period *v.3 p.204*
Belgium, 1830 to present *v.3 p.205*
Central and Eastern Europe *v.3 p.206*

General Histories and Geographies *v.3 p.206*
By Period *v.3 p.207*
Russia *v.3 p.208*
General History *v.3 p.209*
Primary Source Collections *v.3 p.209*
Cultural and Intellectual History *v.3 p.210*
Social History *v.3 p.211*
Military and Diplomatic History *v.3 p.211*
Colonization and Empire *v.3 p.212*
Local and Regional History *v.3 p.214*
By period *v.3 p.214*
Commonwealth of Independent States (CIS) . *v.3 p.229*
Independent Successor States *v.3 p.231*
Scandinavia *v.3 p.231*
General Histories *v.3 p.231*
History *v.3 p.233*
Denmark *v.3 p.233*
Iceland *v.3 p.234*
Norway *v.3 p.234*
Sweden *v.3 p.234*
Foreign Relations, Diplomacy *v.3 p.235*
Vikings *v.3 p.235*
Finland *v.3 p.236*
Spain. Portugal *v.3 p.236*
Spain *v.3 p.236*
Portugal *v.3 p.243*
Switzerland *v.3 p.244*
Balkan Peninsula *v.3 p.245*
General Works *v.3 p.245*
By Period *v.3 p.246*
Yugoslavia *v.3 p.246*
Yugoslavian Successor State *v.3 p.247*
Romania *v.3 p.250*
Bulgaria *v.3 p.251*
Albania *v.3 p.251*
Poland *v.3 p.252*
General History *v.3 p.252*
By Period *v.3 p.252*
Special Topics *v.3 p.255*
Baltic States *v.3 p.255*
General Histories *v.3 p.255*
Latvia *v.3 p.256*
Estonia *v.3 p.256*
Lithuania *v.3 p.256*

FILM STUDIES *v.6 p.303*
General Reference *v.6 p.305*
Guides to Resources *v.6 p.305*
Indexes and Abstracts *v.6 p.305*
Bibliographies *v.6 p.305*
Filmographies *v.6 p.305*
Dictionaries and Encyclopedias *v.6 p.306*
Film Analysis and Criticism *v.6 p.307*
Animation *v.6 p.307*
Documentary Film *v.6 p.308*
Narrative Film and Genres *v.6 p.311*
Film Theory *v.6 p.327*
Society, Politics, and Culture *v.6 p.328*

Film and the State: Censorship, Propaganda . . *v.6 p.328*
Class. *v.6 p.328*
Gender and Sexuality *v.6 p.328*
Race and Ethnicity *v.6 p.329*
History *v.6 p.331*
By Period *v.6 p.332*
By Region and Country *v.6 p.333*
Individual Films: Analysis, Screenplays, Shooting
Scripts *v.6 p.344*
Film Industry. *v.6 p.344*
Production *v.6 p.345*
Distribution, Marketing, Exhibition *v.6 p.345*
Film Organizations *v.6 p.346*
Film Festivals. *v.6 p.346*
Film Awards *v.6 p.346*
Filmmaking *v.6 p.346*
General Filmmaking Guides *v.6 p.346*
Specialized Filmmaking Guides *v.6 p.347*

FRENCH LANGUAGE AND LITERATURE. *v.2 p.451*
French Language *v.2 p.453*
French Literature: History and Critcism. *v.2 p.454*
General. *v.2 p.454*
Special Periods *v.2 p.457*
Special Forms. *v.2 p.460*
Collections of French Literature *v.2 p.463*
Poetry *v.2 p.463*
Drama. Fiction *v.2 p.464*
Old French Literature *v.2 p.465*
Collections *v.2 p.465*
Individual Authors and Works to 1400 . . . *v.2 p.466*
Individual Authors and Works, 1400 to 1500. *v.2 p.468*
Modern French Literature *v.2 p.469*
16th C.. . . . . *v.2 p.469*
17th C.. . . . . *v.2 p.472*
18th C.. . . . . *v.2 p.478*
19th C.. . . . . *v.2 p.485*
Individual Authors, 20th C., to 1960 . . . . *v.2 p.506*
Individual Authors, 1960- *v.2 p.528*
French Literature Outside France. *v.2 p.535*
Belgium *v.2 p.535*
West Indies. *v.2 p.535*
Canada. *v.2 p.538*
Africa *v.2 p.541*

GAY, LESBIAN, BISEXUAL, AND TRANSGENDERED STUDIES *v.6 p.355*
General and Reference Works *v.6 p.357*
Encyclopedias. *v.6 p.358*
Dictionaries. *v.6 p.358*
Bibliographies *v.6 p.359*
Quotations *v.6 p.360*
Directories/Handbooks/Almanacs *v.6 p.360*
Indexes/Abstracts *v.6 p.361*
Databases. *v.6 p.361*
Periodicals *v.6 p.361*
History *v.6 p.362*

General and Reference Works *v.6 p.363*
Pre-20th Century *v.6 p.363*
Modern. *v.6 p.364*
Personal Identity *v.6 p.366*
Sexual *v.6 p.368*
Coming Out *v.6 p.368*
Gender Identity *v.6 p.369*
Sexual Orientation. *v.6 p.371*
Religion *v.6 p.372*
Christianity. *v.6 p.373*
Judaism *v.6 p.373*
Other religions *v.6 p.374*
Relationships. *v.6 p.374*
Dating *v.6 p.375*
Sex *v.6 p.375*
Family Relationships *v.6 p.376*
Parenting *v.6 p.376*
Abuse *v.6 p.377*
Health *v.6 p.377*
General Health *v.6 p.377*
AIDS *v.6 p.378*
Aging *v.6 p.380*
Mental Health and Psychology *v.6 p.380*
Economics and Business *v.6 p.382*
Advertising and Marketing. *v.6 p.382*
Careers. *v.6 p.383*
Sports *v.6 p.383*
Education *v.6 p.384*
Politics *v.6 p.386*
History *v.6 p.387*
Law/Civil Rights *v.6 p.387*
Marriage *v.6 p.388*
Military *v.6 p.389*
Biography *v.6 p.390*
Creative Production *v.6 p.390*
Literature. *v.6 p.391*
Art. *v.6 p.407*
Music *v.6 p.408*
Drama *v.6 p.410*
Dance *v.6 p.414*
Film *v.6 p.415*
Television *v.6 p.419*
Science *v.6 p.419*
Outside North America *v.6 p.420*

GENDER STUDIES *v.6 p.423*
Reference Works *v.6 p.425*
Feminist and Gender Theory. *v.6 p.426*
Gender Roles. Femininity. Masculinity *v.6 p.428*
Activism and Social Movements. Suffrage *v.6 p.430*
Feminism *v.6 p.432*
Body and Representation. Performativity *v.6 p.436*
Sports. Recreation *v.6 p.437*
Science and Technology. *v.6 p.438*
Politics. International Relations. War. Peace *v.6 p.439*
Health *v.6 p.443*

General Health *v.6 p.443*
Aging *v.6 p.444*
Psychology *v.6 p.445*
Sexuality *v.6 p.447*
Communications. Media. Popular Culture. Cultural
Studies *v.6 p.447*
History *v.6 p.449*
General History *v.6 p.449*
Pre-Historic to Classical *v.6 p.450*
Medieval *v.6 p.451*
Pre-Modern *v.6 p.451*
Modern *v.6 p.453*
Business and Economics. Employment.
Development *v.6 p.455*
Religion and Spirituality *v.6 p.458*
Philosophy and Ethics *v.6 p.460*
Education and Epistemologies *v.6 p.462*
Society *v.6 p.464*
Marriage. Relationships. Life Cycle *v.6 p.466*
Legal Issues. Social Issues *v.6 p.468*
Arts and Literature *v.6 p.472*
Fine Arts *v.6 p.472*
Performing Arts *v.6 p.473*
Language and Literature *v.6 p.475*

GENERAL LANGUAGE AND
LITERATURE *v.2 p.547*
Dictionaries, Encyclopedias *v.2 p.549*
Language *v.2 p.549*
English *v.2 p.550*
Linguistics *v.2 p.558*
Composition and Rhetoric *v.2 p.564*
Study, Teaching, Literary Research *v.2 p.566*
Theory, Philosophy, Aesthetics *v.2 p.566*
Criticism *v.2 p.567*
Special Approaches, Methods *v.2 p.570*
Special Topics *v.2 p.571*
History of Criticism *v.2 p.573*
Reading *v.2 p.573*
Authorship *v.2 p.573*
Translating *v.2 p.574*
Literary History, Biography *v.2 p.574*
Book History *v.2 p.576*
Special Forms of Literature *v.2 p.577*
Poetry *v.2 p.577*
Fiction *v.2 p.578*
Special Topics and Types of Fiction *v.2 p.579*
Comic Books. Graphic Novels *v.2 p.581*
Children's Literature *v.2 p.582*
Collections of Literature *v.2 p.582*
Poetry *v.2 p.582*
Fiction *v.2 p.583*
Essays *v.2 p.584*
Folklore *v.2 p.584*
Humor. Satire *v.2 p.585*

GENERAL SCIENCE *v.5 p.383*
Societies. Collected Works *v.5 p.385*
Dictionaries. Encyclopedias *v.5 p.386*
History *v.5 p.388*
Modern *v.5 p.390*
Special Periods. Special Topics *v.5 p.391*
By Country *v.5 p.392*
United States *v.5 p.393*
Biography *v.5 p.394*
Individual Biography *v.5 p.396*
Directories *v.5 p.397*
Science as a Profession *v.5 p.398*
Science: Early Works To 1800 . . . . *v.5 p.399*
Science: General Works, 1801- *v.5 p.399*
Addresses. Essays. Lectures *v.5 p.399*
Philosophy. Methodology *v.5 p.400*
General *v.5 p.405*
Addresses, Essays, Lectures *v.5 p.405*
Terminology *v.5 p.406*
Research. Study and Teaching. Tables *v.5 p.406*
General Works. History *v.5 p.406*
Special Topics. Methodology *v.5 p.406*
Study and Teaching. Tables *v.5 p.406*
System Theory *v.5 p.407*
Cybernetics *v.5 p.407*
Information Theory *v.5 p.408*
Scientific method *v.5 p.408*
Science and culture *v.5 p.409*
Science and art *v.5 p.411*
Science and Politics. Science and Technology
Policy *v.5 p.411*
Science and ethics *v.5 p.413*
Science and humor *v.5 p.413*
Scientific notation *v.5 p.413*
War and Science *v.5 p.413*

GEOGRAPHY *v.4 p.371*
General *v.4 p.373*
Reference *v.4 p.373*
Dictionaries *v.4 p.373*
Gazetteers *v.4 p.374*
General Works *v.4 p.374*
Philosophy *v.4 p.375*
Methodology *v.4 p.375*
Geographical Education *v.4 p.376*
Geography History *v.4 p.377*
Ancient *v.4 p.377*
Modern *v.4 p.377*
Exploration *v.4 p.378*
Atlases *v.4 p.379*
General *v.4 p.379*
Historic *v.4 p.380*

Subject *v.4 p.381*
Regions *v.4 p.381*
  United States *v.4 p.381*
  Mexico and Latin America *v.4 p.382*
  Europe *v.4 p.383*
  Africa *v.4 p.384*
  Asia *v.4 p.384*
  Oceania and Antarctica *v.4 p.384*
Cartography *v.4 p.385*
Geographic Information Systems *v.4 p.386*
Remote Sensing *v.4 p.388*
Surveying *v.4 p.389*
Global Positioning Systems *v.4 p.389*
Physical Geography *v.4 p.390*
  Geology *v.4 p.390*
  Topography *v.4 p.390*
  Geomorphology *v.4 p.390*
  Hydrology *v.4 p.391*
  Climatology *v.4 p.393*
  Biogeography *v.4 p.394*
Hazards and Disasters *v.4 p.394*
Urban Geography *v.4 p.395*
Rural Geography *v.4 p.395*
Human Geography *v.4 p.396*
  General *v.4 p.396*
  Regional *v.4 p.396*
  Development Studies *v.4 p.397*
  Economic Geography *v.4 p.398*
  Cultural Geography *v.4 p.399*
  Historical *v.4 p.399*
  Geopolitics *v.4 p.400*

GEOLOGY *v.5 p.415*
General Geology/Physical Geography *v.5 p.417*
  Reference Works *v.5 p.417*
  History, Biography, Directories *v.5 p.417*
  General Works *v.5 p.418*
  Geology Study and Teaching *v.5 p.419*
Geology: Special Topics *v.5 p.419*
  Computer Applications *v.5 p.419*
  Statistics *v.5 p.419*
  Mathematical Geology *v.5 p.420*
  Urban Geology *v.5 p.420*
  Field Geology *v.5 p.420*
  Remote Sensing (Satellite Applications) . . . *v.5 p.420*
  Engineering Geology *v.5 p.421*
  Natural Hazards *v.5 p.423*
Geologic Maps and Mapping *v.5 p.423*
Environmental Geology *v.5 p.423*
Surficial Geology (GB) *v.5 p.423*
  Geomorphology *v.5 p.423*
  Caves *v.5 p.424*
  Glaciers and Glacial Geology *v.5 p.424*
Meteorology and Climatology *v.5 p.425*
Hydrology and Hydrogeology *v.5 p.427*
  Surficial Hydrogeology (Rivers, Lakes,
   Streams, etc.) *v.5 p.427*

Groundwater/aquifer *v.5 p.428*
Marine Geology/Oceanography *v.5 p.428*
  Chemical Oceanography *v.5 p.429*
  Physical Oceanography *v.5 p.430*
  Waves, Tides, and Currents *v.5 p.430*
  Environmental Oceanography and Marine
   Resources *v.5 p.430*
  Biological Oceanography *v.5 p.431*
Regional Geology *v.5 p.431*
  North America *v.5 p.431*
  South America *v.5 p.432*
  Europe *v.5 p.432*
  Asia *v.5 p.432*
  Africa *v.5 p.433*
  Australasia *v.5 p.433*
  Oceans *v.5 p.433*
  Polar regions *v.5 p.434*
  Planets and Extraterrestrial Geology *v.5 p.434*
Mineralogy *v.5 p.435*
  Reference. General Works *v.5 p.435*
  Descriptive and Determinative Mineralogy
   (Methods of Mineral Analysis) *v.5 p.436*
  Crystallography (of Minerals) *v.5 p.436*
Igneous Rocks (Including Process of Formation) . . *v.5 p.437*
  Volcanoes/Volcanism *v.5 p.437*
Sedimentary Rocks, Sedimentation, Sedimentology,
Sedimentary Processes *v.5 p.438*
  Weathering *v.5 p.439*
  Erosion *v.5 p.439*
  Deposition *v.5 p.439*
  Sedimentary Structures *v.5 p.439*
  Carbonate Rocks *v.5 p.439*
Metamorphic Rocks and Processes
(Metamorphism) *v.5 p.440*
Geochemistry *v.5 p.440*
  Environmental Geochemistry *v.5 p.441*
Structural Geology *v.5 p.441*
  General Works *v.5 p.441*
  Earth Structure *v.5 p.442*
  Plate Tectonics *v.5 p.442*
  Earthquakes *v.5 p.442*
  Seismology *v.5 p.442*
Geophysics *v.5 p.443*
  General *v.5 p.443*
  Geodesy and Gravity *v.5 p.443*
  Geodynamics *v.5 p.443*
  Geomagnetism and Paleomagnetism *v.5 p.443*
  Heat Flow *v.5 p.444*
  Isotopes and Geochronology *v.5 p.444*
  Seismology *v.5 p.444*
  Space Physics (Solar Terrestrial Physics) . . *v.5 p.444*
  Applied and Exploration Geophysics *v.5 p.445*
Historical Geology *v.5 p.445*
  History of the earth *v.5 p.445*
  Paleoclimatology *v.5 p.445*
  Paleogeography *v.5 p.445*
Stratigraphy *v.5 p.446*
  General Works *v.5 p.446*
  Geologic Time *v.5 p.446*

Stratigraphic Units and Sequences *v.5 p.446*
Paleontology *v.5 p.446*
   Reference, General Works *v.5 p.446*
   Invertebrate Paleontology *v.5 p.447*
   Vertebrate Paleontology *v.5 p.447*
   Micropaleontology *v.5 p.448*
   Paleobotany. *v.5 p.449*
   Paleoecology *v.5 p.449*
   Extinction Theories *v.5 p.449*
   Trace fossils *v.5 p.450*
Economic Geology and Mineral Resources *v.5 p.450*
   Ore (Metallic Mineral) Deposits *v.5 p.450*
   Non-Metallic Resource Deposits *v.5 p.450*
   Gemology *v.5 p.452*
   Energy *v.5 p.452*

GERMANIC LANGUAGES AND LITERATURES *v.2 p.587*
German Literature *v.2 p.589*
   History. Criticism *v.2 p.589*
   Collections of German Literature *v.2 p.593*
   Middle High German Literature *v.2 p.594*
   German Literature: Individual Authors . . . *v.2 p.595*
   Swiss Literature in German *v.2 p.620*
German and Scandanavian Languages *v.2 p.620*
Dutch Literature *v.2 p.622*
   Collections *v.2 p.622*
   Individual Authors, by Period *v.2 p.622*
   Dutch Literature in Indonesia. *v.2 p.623*
   Flemish Literature. *v.2 p.623*
   Afrikaans Literature *v.2 p.623*
Scandanavia Literatures: General *v.2 p.624*
   Old Icelandic. Old Norwegian *v.2 p.624*
   Modern Icelandic *v.2 p.625*
   Danish *v.2 p.625*
   Norwegian *v.2 p.627*
   Swedish *v.2 p.629*

HISPANIC AND LUSO-BRAZILIAN LANGUAGES AND LITERATURES *v.2 p.633*
Spanish Language *v.2 p.635*
Portuguese Language *v.2 p.637*
Hispanic Literature *v.2 p.638*
   History, Criticism *v.2 p.638*
   Collections of Spanish Literature *v.2 p.642*
   Spanish Literature: Individual Authors and
     Works *v.2 p.645*
   Hispanic-American Literature. *v.2 p.663*
Luso-Brazilian Literature *v.2 p.687*
   History, Criticism *v.2 p.687*
   Individual Authors. *v.2 p.688*
   Lusophone Literature *v.2 p.689*

ITALIAN LANGUAGE AND LITERATURE. *v.2 p.695*
Italian Literature: History and Criticism. *v.2 p.697*
Italian Language *v.2 p.698*
Collections of Italian Literature *v.2 p.699*

Individual Authors and Works *v.2 p.700*
   To 1400 . . . . *v.2 p.700*
   1400-1700 . . . . *v.2 p.706*
   1701-1900 . . . . *v.2 p.710*
   1901-1960 . . . . *v.2 p.713*
   1961- *v.2 p.724*

JOURNALISM AND COMMUNICATION. . *v.4 p.401*
Journalism *v.4 p.403*
   History and Criticism *v.4 p.403*
   Law and Ethics *v.4 p.405*
   Special Topics *v.4 p.406*
   Print Journalism. *v.4 p.409*
   Broadcast Journalism *v.4 p.412*
Communication. *v.4 p.415*
   Mass Media *v.4 p.415*
   Telecommunications *v.4 p.419*
   Theory *v.4 p.422*
   Advertising *v.4 p.426*
   Public Relations *v.4 p.428*

LATIN AMERICAN HISTORY *v.3 p.257*
Latin America: General *v.3 p.259*
   Cultural History. *v.3 p.260*
   Environmental History. *v.3 p.268*
   History of Popular Culture *v.3 p.270*
   History of Civil Military Relations *v.3 p.273*
   Afro- Latin America. *v.3 p.278*
   Drugs *v.3 p.281*
   Women and Gender *v.3 p.282*
Mexico *v.3 p.284*
   Colonial Mexico *v.3 p.284*
   19th Century Mexico *v.3 p.288*
   20th Century Mexico *v.3 p.290*
Central America: General *v.3 p.296*
   Belize *v.3 p.296*
   Guatemala *v.3 p.298*
   El Salvador. *v.3 p.298*
   Honduras. *v.3 p.300*
   Nicaragua *v.3 p.300*
   Costa Rica *v.3 p.303*
   Panama. *v.3 p.304*
Caribbean: General *v.3 p.306*
   Cuba *v.3 p.306*
   Jamaica. Haiti. *v.3 p.314*
   Dominican Republic. *v.3 p.316*
   Other Islands *v.3 p.318*
South America: Individual Countries *v.3 p.322*
   Guayanas. *v.3 p.322*
   Bolivia. *v.3 p.323*
   Peru *v.3 p.325*
   Ecuador *v.3 p.332*
   Brazil *v.3 p.334*
   Paraguay *v.3 p.343*
   Uruguay *v.3 p.345*
   Argentina *v.3 p.346*
   Chile. *v.3 p.349*
   Colombia. *v.3 p.356*

Venezuela *v.3 p.359*

LATINO STUDIES *v.6 p.483*
  General Works *v.6 p.485*
    Reference Works *v.6 p.485*
    Discipline and Borderland Studies *v.6 p.485*
    Biography *v.6 p.488*
  Humanities *v.6 p.491*
    Art *v.6 p.491*
    Cinema *v.6 p.493*
    Communication and Mass Media *v.6 p.493*
    Language *v.6 p.494*
    Literature *v.6 p.495*
    Music and Dance *v.6 p.518*
    Religion *v.6 p.519*
  Social and Behavioral Sciences *v.6 p.520*
    Folklore *v.6 p.522*
    Economics and Business *v.6 p.524*
    Education *v.6 p.526*
    Migration *v.6 p.528*
    History *v.6 p.530*
    Politics, Government, and Law *v.6 p.536*
    Civil Rights Movement, Affirmative Action,
      Citizenship *v.6 p.539*
    Psychology *v.6 p.541*
    Sociology *v.6 p.542*
    Urban Studies *v.6 p.547*
  Science and Technology *v.6 p.551*
    Environmental Studies *v.6 p.551*
    Botany and Ethnobotany *v.6 p.551*
    Medicine and Public Health *v.6 p.551*
    Sports *v.6 p.552*

LAW *v.4 p.431*
  Law (General) *v.4 p.433*
    Law in General *v.4 p.433*
    History of Law. Biography. Anthropology . . *v.4 p.433*
    Jurisprudence. Philosophy and Theory *v.4 p.433*
    Comparative Law. International Uniform Law . *v.4 p.434*
  United Kingdom and Ireland *v.4 p.435*
  Canada *v.4 p.436*
  United States *v.4 p.436*
    Bibliography. Reference Works *v.4 p.436*
    Collections *v.4 p.437*
    Criminal Trials *v.4 p.437*
    Civil Trials *v.4 p.438*
    Legal Research. Legal Composition *v.4 p.439*
    Legal Education *v.4 p.439*
    Legal Profession *v.4 p.440*
    History of United States Law *v.4 p.440*
    Philosophy. General and Comprehensive Works. *v.4 p.441*
    Special Branches of United States Civil Law . *v.4 p.442*
    Intellectual Property. Copyright. Trademarks . *v.4 p.445*
    Labor Law *v.4 p.446*
    Social Insurance *v.4 p.447*
    Human Reproduction *v.4 p.447*
    Public Health. Medical Legislation *v.4 p.448*
    Veterinary Laws. Animals *v.4 p.448*

    Food, Drugs, Tobacco, Cosmetics, Alcohol . . *v.4 p.448*
    Public Safety. Firearms, Hazardous Materials,
      Explosives *v.4 p.449*
    Control of Social Activities. Amusements,
      Sports, Gaming *v.4 p.449*
    Education *v.4 p.449*
    Science and the Arts *v.4 p.451*
    Constitutional Law *v.4 p.451*
    Local Government *v.4 p.462*
    Administrative Organization and Procedure . . *v.4 p.463*
    Public Property: General Works. Water
      Resources. Public Land *v.4 p.463*
    Regional and City Planning. Zoning. Building . *v.4 p.463*
    Government Property. Public Records *v.4 p.464*
    Government Measures in Time of War, National
      Emergency, or Economic Crisis *v.4 p.464*
    Public Finance. Taxation *v.4 p.464*
    National Defense. Military Law *v.4 p.464*
    Indians *v.4 p.464*
    Courts. Procedure *v.4 p.465*
    Criminal Law. Criminal Procedure *v.4 p.471*
    States, A-W *v.4 p.474*
    Confederate States of America *v.4 p.474*
  Latin America *v.4 p.474*
  South America *v.4 p.474*
  Europe *v.4 p.474*
  Eurasia *v.4 p.475*
  Middle-East. Southwest Asia *v.4 p.475*
  South Asia. Southeast Asia. East Asia *v.4 p.475*
  Africa *v.4 p.475*
  Australia. New Zealand *v.4 p.476*
  Pacific Island Jurisdictions *v.4 p.476*
  Law of Nations *v.4 p.476*
    War Crimes Trials *v.4 p.477*
    20th Century *v.4 p.477*
    21st Century *v.4 p.477*
    United Nations *v.4 p.477*
    Law of the Sea *v.4 p.478*
    Law of War and Neutrality *v.4 p.478*

MATHEMATICS *v.5 p.455*
  General *v.5 p.457*
  Reference *v.5 p.460*
  Mathematics Education *v.5 p.462*
  Mathematics History *v.5 p.464*
  Recreational Mathematics *v.5 p.468*
  Logic, Foundations, and Philosophy *v.5 p.470*
    Set theory *v.5 p.471*
    Theory of Computing *v.5 p.471*
  Algebra and Number Theory *v.5 p.471*
    College Algebra *v.5 p.472*
    Linear Algebra *v.5 p.472*
    Abstract Algebra *v.5 p.473*
    Number Theory *v.5 p.475*
  Discrete Mathematics *v.5 p.477*
    Combinatorics *v.5 p.478*
    Graph Theory *v.5 p.479*

Statistics and Probability *v.5 p.480*
   Experimental Methodology/Design *v.5 p.481*
   Statistical Inference and Techniques. *v.5 p.482*
   Probability and Stochastic Processes *v.5 p.483*
Calculus *v.5 p.485*
   Precalculus *v.5 p.485*
   Advanced Calculus *v.5 p.486*
   Vector and Tensor Calculus *v.5 p.486*
Differential and Integral Equations *v.5 p.486*
   Ordinary Differential Equations. *v.5 p.487*
   Partial Differential Equations *v.5 p.487*
   Integral Equations *v.5 p.488*
   Dynamical Systems and Chaos *v.5 p.488*
Analysis *v.5 p.489*
   Real Analysis *v.5 p.490*
   Complex Analysis *v.5 p.490*
   Numerical Analysis *v.5 p.491*
   Calculus of Variations, Optimization and
     Control *v.5 p.492*
   Functional and Harmonic Analysis *v.5 p.493*
Geometry and Topology *v.5 p.494*
   Differential Geometry *v.5 p.496*
   Algebraic Geometry *v.5 p.497*
   Discrete and Computational Geometry . . . *v.5 p.497*
   Topology *v.5 p.498*
Applied Mathematics *v.5 p.500*
   Applications in the Physical Sciences or
     Engineering *v.5 p.500*
   Applications in the Biological Sciences *v.5 p.501*
   Applications in Business and the Social
     Sciences *v.5 p.503*

MEDICINE *v.5 p.507*
Medicine: General *v.5 p.509*
   Dictionaries. Terminology *v.5 p.509*
   History. Biography *v.5 p.509*
   Medical Ethics *v.5 p.511*
Public Aspects of Medicine *v.5 p.511*
   Medical Economics *v.5 p.511*
   Medicine and Society. Medical Sociology . . . *v.5 p.511*
   Public Health *v.5 p.512*
   Nutrition *v.5 p.512*
   Mental Health. *v.5 p.513*
   Hospitals. Nursing Homes *v.5 p.513*
   Toxicology *v.5 p.514*
Pathology *v.5 p.514*
Internal Medicine. Practice of Medicine. *v.5 p.514*
   Diseases *v.5 p.515*
   Neurology and Psychiatry. Neuropsychiatry . *v.5 p.516*
   Psychiatry. Mental retardation *v.5 p.516*
   Immunological Diseases. Allergy *v.5 p.517*
   Blood Diseases, Endocrinology *v.5 p.518*
   Respiratory Diseases. *v.5 p.518*
   Geriatrics. *v.5 p.518*
   Sports Medicine. Physiology of Sports *v.5 p.519*
   Gastrointestinal Diseases. *v.5 p.519*
   Musculoskeletal Diseases *v.5 p.519*
   Oncology. *v.5 p.520*
   Cardiology *v.5 p.520*

Medical Diagnosis. *v.5 p.520*
   Hematology. *v.5 p.521*
   Substance Abuse and Alcoholism *v.5 p.521*
Surgery. Orthopedia *v.5 p.522*
Audiology *v.5 p.523*
Gynecology. Obstetrics *v.5 p.523*
   Obstetrics. *v.5 p.524*
Pediatrics *v.5 p.524*
Dentistry. *v.5 p.525*
Therapeudics. Pharmacology. *v.5 p.526*
Pharmacy. Materia Medica. *v.5 p.526*
Nursing *v.5 p.526*
   History. Biography *v.5 p.528*
   General Works *v.5 p.529*
   Study. Teaching *v.5 p.529*
   Philosophy. Ethics. Psychological Aspects . . . *v.5 p.529*
   Special Topics *v.5 p.530*
   Community Health Nursing *v.5 p.530*
   Emergency Nursing *v.5 p.531*
Other Systems of Medicine *v.5 p.531*
End of Life Care *v.5 p.531*
Communicable Diseases. *v.5 p.532*
Medical Genetics *v.5 p.533*
Allied Health *v.5 p.533*
   Emergency Medical Technician *v.5 p.534*
   Medical Assistant *v.5 p.534*
   Physician Assistant *v.5 p.534*
   Radiology Technician *v.5 p.534*
   Occupational Therapy *v.5 p.535*
   Physical Therapy *v.5 p.535*
   Respiratory Therapy *v.5 p.536*
Medical Anthropology. *v.5 p.536*

MEDIEVAL STUDIES *v.6 p.553*
Archaeology *v.6 p.555*
Architecture *v.6 p.555*
Art History. *v.6 p.556*
Chivalry *v.6 p.556*
Crusades *v.6 p.556*
Daily Life *v.6 p.557*
Economics *v.6 p.557*
Education *v.6 p.558*
Gender. *v.6 p.559*
History. Historiography *v.6 p.561*
Literature *v.6 p.564*
Military history. *v.6 p.566*
Music *v.6 p.567*
Philosophy *v.6 p.567*
Politics and Law *v.6 p.568*
Reading and Literacy *v.6 p.568*
Religion *v.6 p.569*
   Paganism, Magic and Witchcraft *v.6 p.569*
   Christianity *v.6 p.569*
   Judaism *v.6 p.573*

Islam. *v.6 p.574*

Rural World *v.6 p.575*

Science and Medicine. *v.6 p.575*

Social History *v.6 p.576*

Urban World *v.6 p.577*

MIDDLE EASTERN HISTORY, LANGUAGES, AND LITERATURES *v.6 p.579*

Byzantine Empire 330-1453 . . . . *v.6 p.581*

Islamic Middle East. *v.6 p.581*

   Arab Countries in General *v.6 p.582*

   By Period *v.6 p.583*

Ethnography (Including Ethno-Religious Groups) *v.6 p.596*

   Bedouins *v.6 p.596*

   Jews (of the Middle East) *v.6 p.596*

   Kurds *v.6 p.598*

   All Others *v.6 p.600*

History of Specific Countries *v.6 p.601*

   Cyprus *v.6 p.601*

   Iraq *v.6 p.601*

   Lebanon *v.6 p.604*

   Syria. *v.6 p.606*

   Israel/Palestine *v.6 p.608*

   Jordan *v.6 p.620*

   Turkey *v.6 p.621*

   Saudi Arabia *v.6 p.625*

   Bahrain. *v.6 p.626*

   Kuwait *v.6 p.627*

   Oman *v.6 p.627*

   Yemen *v.6 p.628*

   United Arab Emirates *v.6 p.628*

   Iran *v.6 p.629*

   Armenia *v.6 p.633*

   Afghanistan. *v.6 p.633*

   Egypt *v.6 p.634*

   Sudan *v.6 p.640*

   Libya *v.6 p.640*

   Tunisia *v.6 p.641*

   Algeria. *v.6 p.642*

   Morocco *v.6 p.643*

   Muslims in India *v.6 p.644*

Middle Eastern Languages and Literatures *v.6 p.644*

   Hamitic Languages and Literatures *v.6 p.644*

   Semitic Languages and Literatures *v.6 p.645*

   Armenian Language and Literature *v.6 p.665*

   Caucasian Languages and Literatures *v.6 p.665*

   Turkic Languages and Literatures. *v.6 p.665*

   Iranian languages and literatures *v.6 p.668*

MUSIC *v.1 p.157*

Reference Resources *v.1 p.159*

   Dictionaries and Encyclopedias. *v.1 p.159*

   Indexes and Abstracts *v.1 p.163*

   Bibliographies and Catalogs *v.1 p.163*

   Discographies. *v.1 p.169*

   Directories and Information Sites *v.1 p.172*

Disciplines and Methodologies of Music

Scholarship *v.1 p.173*

Studies in Music History, Criticism, Analysis, and Appreciation *v.1 p.174*

   Western Classical Literature by Period *v.1 p.174*

   Western Classical Literature by Genre. *v.1 p.227*

   Western Classical Literature by European Nationality *v.1 p.245*

   Western Classical Literature: Miscellaneous Studies and Essays. *v.1 p.247*

   Musical Theatre. *v.1 p.248*

   Film, Television, and Video Music *v.1 p.254*

   Jazz and Blues *v.1 p.256*

   Rock, Pop, Rhythm and Blues, Soul, Hip Hop, and Country *v.1 p.265*

   Music In the United States and Canada *v.1 p.276*

   African American and African Diaspora *v.1 p.280*

   Folk and Traditional Music. *v.1 p.283*

Biographies and Studies of Composers and Performers *v.1 p.301*

   A *v.1 p.301*

   B *v.1 p.302*

   C *v.1 p.315*

   D *v.1 p.319*

   E *v.1 p.323*

   F *v.1 p.324*

   G *v.1 p.325*

   H *v.1 p.328*

   I *v.1 p.333*

   J *v.1 p.333*

   K *v.1 p.334*

   L *v.1 p.335*

   M *v.1 p.338*

   N *v.1 p.345*

   O *v.1 p.346*

   P *v.1 p.346*

   R *v.1 p.350*

   S *v.1 p.352*

   T *v.1 p.362*

   U *v.1 p.363*

   V *v.1 p.363*

   W *v.1 p.365*

   XYZ *v.1 p.368*

Music Theory and Composition *v.1 p.369*

Physics of Music, Acoustics, and Tuning *v.1 p.374*

Psychology and Physiology of Music. *v.1 p.375*

Sociology of Music. *v.1 p.376*

Gender and Sexuality Studies *v.1 p.377*

Philosophy and Aesthetics of Music *v.1 p.380*

Business and Industry of Music *v.1 p.383*

Music Technology *v.1 p.386*

Musical Instruments. *v.1 p.388*

Orchestration, Orchestras, and Notation. *v.1 p.392*

Performance Techniques and Interpretation *v.1 p.394*

   Vocal. *v.1 p.394*

   Instrumental *v.1 p.396*

   Historical Performance Practices *v.1 p.399*

   Conducting *v.1 p.402*

   Jazz and Improvisation *v.1 p.403*

   Stage Production *v.1 p.404*

Ear Training and Musicianship *v.1 p.404*

Music Education *v.1 p.404*

Music Therapy *v.1 p.406*

Librettos to Operas and Musicals. *v.1 p.407*

Lyrics and Texts to Songs and Choral Works . . . *v.1 p.411*

NATIVE AMERICAN STUDIES *v.6 p.675*

Art *v.6 p.678*

Education *v.6 p.680*

Environmental Issues *v.6 p.680*

History *v.6 p.681*

Contact and Exploration *v.6 p.684*

Colonial Period *v.6 p.685*

Early American *v.6 p.686*

Removal Period *v.6 p.687*

Manifest Destiny *v.6 p.687*

20th Century *v.6 p.688*

Languages and Linguistics. *v.6 p.690*

Language Preservation and Revitalization . . . *v.6 p.690*

Politics and Government *v.6 p.691*

Activism *v.6 p.693*

The Federal Relationship. Sovereignty and Treaty
Rights *v.6 p.695*

Literature, Music, Dance, and Film. *v.6 p.697*

Literature. *v.6 p.697*

Music *v.6 p.699*

Dance *v.6 p.699*

Film *v.6 p.700*

Religion and Philosophy. *v.6 p.700*

Health and Medicine *v.6 p.701*

Anthropology and Archeology *v.6 p.702*

Repatriation. *v.6 p.704*

Women and Gender. *v.6 p.704*

OTHER LITERATURES IN ENGLISH. . . . *v.2 p.725*

General and Reference Sources *v.2 p.727*

Canada *v.2 p.728*

Literary History and Criticism *v.2 p.728*

Collections *v.2 p.731*

Individual Authors. *v.2 p.732*

Australia/New Zealand *v.2 p.740*

Literary History and Criticism *v.2 p.740*

Collections *v.2 p.742*

Individual Authors. *v.2 p.743*

Africa *v.2 p.750*

Literary History and Criticism *v.2 p.750*

Collections *v.2 p.752*

Individual Authors. *v.2 p.752*

Asia *v.2 p.759*

India *v.2 p.761*

West Indies. *v.2 p.767*

Naipaul, V. S. *v.2 p.768*

Rhys, Jean *v.2 p.769*

Walcott, Derek *v.2 p.770*

PHILOSOPHY *v.1 p.413*

General Philosophy *v.1 p.415*

Reference Works *v.1 p.415*

Nature, Methods, Scope of Philosophy *v.1 p.416*

History of Philosophy. *v.1 p.417*

Ancient Oriental Philosophy *v.1 p.417*

Ancient Western Philosophy *v.1 p.419*

Medieval Philosophy *v.1 p.431*

Renaissance Philosophy *v.1 p.435*

Modern Philosophy *v.1 p.435*

Philosophy by Country *v.1 p.439*

American Philosophy *v.1 p.439*

Latin American Philosophy. *v.1 p.444*

British Philosophy. *v.1 p.444*

French Philosophy. *v.1 p.452*

German, Austrian Philosophy. *v.1 p.459*

Italian Philosophy *v.1 p.473*

Russian Philosophy *v.1 p.473*

Spanish Philosophy *v.1 p.474*

Asian Philosophy *v.1 p.474*

African Philosophy *v.1 p.476*

Dutch Philosophy *v.1 p.477*

Danish Philosophy *v.1 p.478*

Divisions of Philosophy *v.1 p.479*

Aesthetics *v.1 p.479*

Epistemology *v.1 p.481*

Ethics *v.1 p.483*

Metaphysics *v.1 p.488*

Philosophy of Language *v.1 p.489*

Philosophy of Law *v.1 p.490*

Logic *v.1 p.491*

Philosophy of Man *v.1 p.495*

Philosophy of Mind *v.1 p.496*

Philosophy of Nature *v.1 p.498*

Philosophy of Religion *v.1 p.498*

Philosophy of Science *v.1 p.499*

Political and Social Philosophy *v.1 p.500*

Philosophical Schools and Doctrines *v.1 p.501*

Altruism *v.1 p.501*

Analytic philosophy *v.1 p.501*

Critical Theory *v.1 p.502*

Determinism and Free Will. *v.1 p.503*

Dualism *v.1 p.504*

Egoism. *v.1 p.504*

Empiricism *v.1 p.504*

Essentialism *v.1 p.505*

Existentialism. *v.1 p.505*

Feminist Philosophy *v.1 p.506*

Frankfurt School *v.1 p.506*

Hedonism *v.1 p.507*

Hermeneutics *v.1 p.507*

Humanism *v.1 p.507*

Idealism *v.1 p.508*

Marxism *v.1 p.508*

Materialism. *v.1 p.509*

Nihilism *v.1 p.509*

Nominalism. *v.1 p.509*

Objectivism *v.1 p.510*

Ordinary Language Philosophy *v.1 p.510*

Phenomenology *v.1 p.510*

Positivism v.1 p.511
Postmodernism v.1 p.512
Poststucturalism. v.1 p.512
Pragmatism. v.1 p.512
Process Philosophy v.1 p.513
Rationalism. v.1 p.513
Realism v.1 p.514
Relativism v.1 p.514
Structuralism. v.1 p.515
Subjectivism v.1 p.515
Transcendentalism. v.1 p.515
Utilitarianism v.1 p.515
Darwinianism. v.1 p.516
Naturalism v.1 p.516
Skepticism v.1 p.516

PHYSICS v.5 p.537
General Physics v.5 p.539
Histories v.5 p.540
Popular Works v.5 p.540
Philosophy v.5 p.541
Biographies. v.5 p.542
Reference Works v.5 p.544
Dictionaries and Encyclopedias. v.5 p.545
Handbooks, Tables, and Formulas. v.5 p.545
Mechanics v.5 p.546
Fluid Mechanics v.5 p.547
Modern Physics v.5 p.547
Mathematical Physics v.5 p.548
Group Theory and Symmetry. v.5 p.548
Mathematical Methods. v.5 p.548
Quantum Mechanics/Quantum Theory v.5 p.548
Quantum Field Theories. v.5 p.550
Computational Physics v.5 p.551
Computer Simulations v.5 p.551
Quantum Computation. v.5 p.552
Particle Physics. v.5 p.552
Nuclear Physics v.5 p.553
Atomic and Molecular Physics. v.5 p.554
Condensed Matter Physics. v.5 p.554
Semiconductor Physics v.5 p.555
Gravitation. v.5 p.555
Relativity. v.5 p.556
Fifth Forces (Intermediate Range Forces) . . . v.5 p.558
Statistical Mechanics v.5 p.558
Phase Transitions v.5 p.559
Heat and Thermodynamics. v.5 p.559
Heat Transfer v.5 p.560
Optics v.5 p.560
Holography. v.5 p.561
Spectroscopy v.5 p.561
Color. v.5 p.562
Quantum Optics. v.5 p.562
Experimental Methods v.5 p.562
Data Handling v.5 p.562
Laboratory Techniques. v.5 p.563

Physics Education v.5 p.563
Biophysics v.5 p.564
Electricity and Magnetism. v.5 p.564
Superconductivity v.5 p.565
Quantum Hall Effect. v.5 p.565
Magnetism v.5 p.566
Quantum Electrodynamics (QED). v.5 p.566
Plasma Physics v.5 p.566
Acoustics v.5 p.566
Weights and Measures. v.5 p.567

POLITICAL SCIENCE. v.4 p.479
Political Science: General v.4 p.481
Government Documents v.4 p.481
Reference Works v.4 p.482
Research Methods. v.4 p.483
Relations to Other Subjects v.4 p.483
Political Theory. v.4 p.488
History of Political Thought v.4 p.488
Ancient. v.4 p.488
Medieval v.4 p.490
Modern. v.4 p.490
Theories of State v.4 p.493
Forms of the State. v.4 p.500
Purpose, Functions and Relations of the State . v.4 p.510
American Government and Politics. v.4 p.516
History of American Government. v.4 p.516
Federal Government v.4 p.522
State Government v.4 p.541
Local Government. v.4 p.542
Public Administration v.4 p.545
Citizenship v.4 p.547
Campaigns and Elections v.4 p.547
Mass Media and Politics. v.4 p.558
Public Policy v.4 p.559
Foreign Policy v.4 p.560
Environmental Policy v.4 p.566
Economic Policy v.4 p.566
Social Policy v.4 p.567
Political Issues v.4 p.567
Comparative Government v.4 p.574
Constitutional History. General v.4 p.574
Organs and Functions of Government v.4 p.574
Political Rights and Representation v.4 p.576
Political Participation v.4 p.577
Political Parties v.4 p.578
Public Administration v.4 p.580
Local Government. v.4 p.581
Colonies and Colonization v.4 p.582
Democratization. v.4 p.584
North America v.4 p.586
Latin America. v.4 p.591
Europe v.4 p.594
Africa v.4 p.610
Middle East. v.4 p.614
Asia v.4 p.616
Australia. New Zealand. Pacific Ocean Islands. v.4 p.624
International Relations. Transnational Relations . v.4 p.624

Theory. Study and Teaching *v.4 p.625*
History *v.4 p.627*
International Organization *v.4 p.628*
By Country, Territory, or Region *v.4 p.640*
Diplomacy *v.4 p.644*
War and Peace *v.4 p.646*
International Security *v.4 p.654*
Globalization *v.4 p.662*
Migration *v.4 p.667*
Global Health *v.4 p.668*
Human Rights *v.4 p.669*
Humanitarian Assistance *v.4 p.670*

PSYCHOLOGY *v.5 p.569*
Educational Psychology *v.5 p.571*
    Educational Administration and Personnel . . *v.5 p.573*
    Curriculum, Programs, and Teaching Methods . *v.5 p.573*
    Academic Learning and Achievement *v.5 p.574*
    Special and Remedial Education *v.5 p.574*
    Gifted and Talented *v.5 p.575*
    Educational/Vocational Counseling and Student
      Services *v.5 p.576*
Industrial and Organizational Psychology *v.5 p.577*
    Occupational Interests and Guidance *v.5 p.577*
    Personnel Attitudes. Job Satisfaction *v.5 p.578*
    Working Conditions and Industrial Safety . . . *v.5 p.580*
Sport Psychology and Leisure *v.5 p.581*
    Recreation and Leisure *v.5 p.583*
Military Psychology *v.5 p.583*
Consumer Psychology *v.5 p.585*
    Consumer Attitudes & Behavior *v.5 p.585*
    Marketing and Advertising *v.5 p.587*
Engineering and Environmental Psychology *v.5 p.587*
Intelligent Systems *v.5 p.589*
    Artificial Intelligence. Expert Systems *v.5 p.590*
    Neural Networks *v.5 p.591*
Forensic Psychology and Legal Issues *v.5 p.591*
General Psychology *v.5 p.593*
    History and Systems *v.5 p.595*
Psychometrics, Statistics, and Methodology . . . *v.5 p.599*
    Tests and Testing *v.5 p.600*
    Developmental Scales and Schedules *v.5 p.602*
    Personality Scales and Inventories *v.5 p.603*
    Educational Measurement *v.5 p.604*
    Consumer Opinion and Attitude Testing . . . *v.5 p.604*
Human Experimental Psychology *v.5 p.604*
    Sensory Perception *v.5 p.605*
    Visual Perception *v.5 p.606*
    Auditory and Speech Perception *v.5 p.607*
    Motor Processes *v.5 p.608*
    Cognitive Processes *v.5 p.608*
    Learning and Memory *v.5 p.609*
    Attention *v.5 p.611*
    Motivation and Emotion *v.5 p.611*
    Consciousness States *v.5 p.612*
    Parapsychology *v.5 p.613*
Animal Experimental and Comparative Psychology. *v.5 p.614*
    Learning and Motivation *v.5 p.616*

Physiological Psychology and Neuroscience *v.5 p.616*
Psychology and the Humanities *v.5 p.618*
    Literature and Fine Arts *v.5 p.618*
    Philosophy *v.5 p.619*
Communication Systems *v.5 p.620*
    Linguistics and Language & Speech *v.5 p.622*
    Mass Media Communications *v.5 p.624*
Developmental Psychology *v.5 p.625*
    Cognitive and Perceptual Development *v.5 p.629*
    Psychosocial and Personality Development . . *v.5 p.631*
    Gerontology *v.5 p.632*
Social Processes and Social Issues *v.5 p.632*
    Religion *v.5 p.632*
    Culture and Ethnology *v.5 p.636*
    Marriage and Family *v.5 p.638*
    Divorce and Remarriage *v.5 p.639*
    Childrearing and Child Care *v.5 p.640*
    Political Processes and Political Issues *v.5 p.642*
Social Psychology *v.5 p.645*
    Group and Interpersonal Processes *v.5 p.646*
    Social Perception and Cognition *v.5 p.649*
Personality Psychology *v.5 p.651*
    Personality Traits and Processes *v.5 p.651*
    Personality Theory *v.5 p.657*
    Psychoanalytic Theory *v.5 p.658*
Psychological and Physical Disorders *v.5 p.659*
    Affective Disorders *v.5 p.659*
    Schizophrenia and Psychotic States *v.5 p.660*
    Personality Disorders *v.5 p.661*
    Behavior Disorders and Antisocial Behavior . . *v.5 p.662*
    Substance Abuse and Addiction *v.5 p.663*
    Speech and Language Disorders *v.5 p.664*
Mental Health Treatment and Prevention *v.5 p.665*
    Cognitive Therapy *v.5 p.665*
    Behavior Therapy and Behavior Modification . *v.5 p.666*
    Group and Family Therapy *v.5 p.667*
    Self Help Groups *v.5 p.669*
    Promotion and Maintenance of Health and
      Wellness *v.5 p.670*
    Community and Social Services *v.5 p.670*
    Rehabilitation *v.5 p.672*
    Drug and Alcohol Rehabilitation *v.5 p.672*
    Speech and Language Therapy *v.5 p.673*
Professional Psychological and Health Personnel
Issues *v.5 p.674*
    Professional Ethics, Standards, and Liability . *v.5 p.674*
    Professional Education and Training *v.5 p.675*

RELIGION *v.1 p.519*
Religions. Mythology. Rationalism *v.1 p.521*
    General Works *v.1 p.521*
    Philosophy of Religion *v.1 p.522*
    Psychology of Religion *v.1 p.524*
    Religion: Relation to Other Subjects *v.1 p.524*
    Biography *v.1 p.525*
    Religions of the World *v.1 p.525*
    Natural Theology *v.1 p.525*
    Religion and the Sciences *v.1 p.526*

Myth. Comparative Mythology *v.1 p.526*
Religious Doctrines. Worship. *v.1 p.527*
Religious Life and Experience. Mysticism.
    Asceticism *v.1 p.530*
History and Principles of Religion *v.1 p.531*
Rationalism. Atheism. Secularism. *v.1 p.545*
Judaism *v.1 p.545*
    Pre-Talmudic Jewish literature *v.1 p.546*
    History. *v.1 p.546*
    Judaism and Christianity. *v.1 p.549*
    Principles of Judaism *v.1 p.551*
    Dogmatic Judaism. Apologetics. *v.1 p.551*
    Practical Judaism *v.1 p.552*
Islam *v.1 p.553*
    Biography. Muhammad *v.1 p.555*
    Islamic Civilization *v.1 p.555*
    Sacred Books. Koran *v.1 p.556*
    Islamic law. *v.1 p.556*
    Islam: General Works *v.1 p.556*
    Theology. *v.1 p.557*
    Islam and Other Religions *v.1 p.558*
    The Practice of Islam *v.1 p.559*
    Branches. Sects *v.1 p.560*
Bahaism *v.1 p.560*
Buddhism *v.1 p.561*
    Collected Works. History. Biography *v.1 p.561*
    Buddhist Literature: Sacred Texts *v.1 p.563*
    Buddhism: General Works *v.1 p.564*
    Doctrinal and Systematic Buddhism. *v.1 p.565*
    Deities. Rituals. Folklore. Shrines. *v.1 p.565*
    Modifications of Buddhism. *v.1 p.566*
Christianity. *v.1 p.568*
    Denominations *v.1 p.568*
    Early Christian Literature *v.1 p.590*
    Literature of Later Periods *v.1 p.593*
    Dictionaries. Encyclopedias *v.1 p.593*
    Philosophy and Psychology *v.1 p.594*
    Christianity: Relation to Other Topics *v.1 p.595*
    Christianity: General Works *v.1 p.596*
    Christianity and Other Religions *v.1 p.597*
    Church History *v.1 p.597*
    Persecution. Toleration. Liberalism *v.1 p.612*
    Biography *v.1 p.612*
    Bible. *v.1 p.613*
    Doctrinal theology. *v.1 p.632*
    Practical Theology. *v.1 p.647*
New Religious Movements *v.1 p.658*

**RUSSIAN AND EASTERN EUROPEAN
LANGUAGES AND LITERATURES.** *v.2 p.771*
    Slavic Languages. *v.2 p.773*
        General. *v.2 p.773*
        Baltic Languages *v.2 p.773*
        Bulgarian. *v.2 p.774*
        Croatian *v.2 p.774*
        Czech *v.2 p.774*
        Hungarian *v.2 p.774*
        Macedonian. *v.2 p.775*
        Polish *v.2 p.775*

        Russian. *v.2 p.775*
        Serbian. *v.2 p.776*
        Slovak *v.2 p.777*
        Slovenian. *v.2 p.777*
        Ukranian *v.2 p.777*
        Albanian *v.2 p.778*
        Romanian *v.2 p.778*
        Yugoslav *v.2 p.778*
    Slavic Literatures *v.2 p.778*
        General. *v.2 p.778*
        Bulgarian. *v.2 p.779*
        Baltic *v.2 p.780*
        Czech *v.2 p.781*
        Hungarian *v.2 p.784*
        Macedonian. *v.2 p.787*
        Polish *v.2 p.787*
        Russian. *v.2 p.792*
        Serbian. *v.2 p.810*
        Slovak *v.2 p.812*
        Slovenian. *v.2 p.812*
        Ukranian *v.2 p.813*
        Albanian *v.2 p.815*
        Romanian *v.2 p.815*
        Croatian *v.2 p.818*
        Yugoslav *v.2 p.818*

SOCIOLOGY *v.4 p.673*
    Principles *v.4 p.675*
        Teaching/Communicating *v.4 p.675*
        Dictionaries and Encyclopedias. *v.4 p.676*
        Theories *v.4 p.679*
        History of Sociology *v.4 p.682*
    Research Methods *v.4 p.686*
        Models. *v.4 p.687*
        Statistical Methods *v.4 p.689*
        Frameworks/Methodology *v.4 p.690*
    Social Psychology *v.4 p.691*
        History. *v.4 p.692*
        Theory. *v.4 p.692*
        Perception *v.4 p.692*
        Influence *v.4 p.695*
        Interaction *v.4 p.697*
    Social History *v.4 p.699*
        Culture. *v.4 p.699*
        Things *v.4 p.709*
        Mass Phenomena *v.4 p.710*
    Organizations. *v.4 p.716*
        Work. *v.4 p.717*
        Military *v.4 p.717*
        Bureaucracy *v.4 p.718*
        Sociology of Business *v.4 p.718*
        Voluntary Organizations *v.4 p.719*
        Secret Societies *v.4 p.719*
    Sociology of Religion *v.4 p.719*
        Christianity *v.4 p.720*
        Islam. *v.4 p.721*
        Other Religions *v.4 p.721*
    Stratification/Differentiation *v.4 p.722*
        Social Stratification *v.4 p.722*

Race *v.4 p.728*
Family Life *v.4 p.731*
   By Country or Region *v.4 p.732*
   Socialization *v.4 p.734*
   Childhood *v.4 p.735*
   Youth/Adolescence *v.4 p.735*
   Adulthood *v.4 p.736*
   Aging *v.4 p.740*
   Death/Dying *v.4 p.742*
   Family Violence *v.4 p.742*
Gender/Sexuality *v.4 p.743*
   Gender Role *v.4 p.743*
   Sexuality *v.4 p.746*
Social Problems *v.4 p.750*
   Gerontology *v.4 p.751*
   Criminology *v.4 p.751*
   Social Welfare Programs *v.4 p.754*
   Social Work Practice *v.4 p.757*
Social Change *v.4 p.759*
   Economics *v.4 p.759*
   Development *v.4 p.759*
   Revolution *v.4 p.760*
   Environmental Interactions *v.4 p.760*
   Technology *v.4 p.760*
Sociology of Education *v.4 p.761*
   Public Schools *v.4 p.762*
   Lifetime Learning *v.4 p.762*
   Colleges and Universities *v.4 p.762*
Demography *v.4 p.763*
   Assimilation *v.4 p.763*
   Immigration *v.4 p.763*
Political Sociology *v.4 p.765*
   War and Conflict *v.4 p.766*
   Political Systems *v.4 p.767*
   Policy Studies *v.4 p.768*
Community/Regional Studies *v.4 p.770*
   Urban *v.4 p.770*
   Rural *v.4 p.771*
   Electronic Communities *v.4 p.772*
Social Control *v.4 p.773*
   Power *v.4 p.773*
   Law *v.4 p.773*
   Police *v.4 p.774*
Health *v.4 p.774*
   Mental Health *v.4 p.774*
   Body *v.4 p.775*
   Compulsive Behaviors *v.4 p.775*
   Health Care *v.4 p.778*

SPORTS AND RECREATION *v.4 p.781*
Recreation and Leisure *v.4 p.783*
   General *v.4 p.783*
   Administration *v.4 p.785*
Outdoor Recreation *v.4 p.787*
   Hiking *v.4 p.788*
   Orienteering. Outward Bound *v.4 p.788*
   Canoeing *v.4 p.789*
   Mountaineering. Rock Climbing *v.4 p.789*

Fitness and Health *v.4 p.789*
   Weight Lifting *v.4 p.792*
   Aquatics *v.4 p.792*
   Health Clubs *v.4 p.792*
   Yoga *v.4 p.792*
   Pilates *v.4 p.793*
   Exercises *v.4 p.793*
Physical Education and Training *v.4 p.794*
   General *v.4 p.794*
   Elementary and Middle School *v.4 p.797*
   High School *v.4 p.799*
   College *v.4 p.800*
   Adaptive *v.4 p.800*
   Nutrition. Health and Hygiene *v.4 p.801*
Sport Studies *v.4 p.801*
   Philosophy *v.4 p.802*
   History *v.4 p.803*
   Literature (Including Sports Writing) *v.4 p.811*
   Research. Theory *v.4 p.812*
   Sociology *v.4 p.813*
   Education *v.4 p.820*
   General *v.4 p.823*
   Religion *v.4 p.824*
Sport Medicine *v.4 p.824*
   Doping. Drugs in Sport *v.4 p.826*
   Injuries and Rehabilitation *v.4 p.827*
   Athletic Training *v.4 p.828*
   Physical Therapy *v.4 p.829*
   Therapeutic Recreation *v.4 p.829*
Minorities and Specific Groups in Sport *v.4 p.830*
   African Americans *v.4 p.830*
   Latinos *v.4 p.833*
   Asians *v.4 p.834*
   Women *v.4 p.834*
   Gays and Lesbians *v.4 p.839*
   Youth *v.4 p.839*
   Seniors *v.4 p.840*
   Native Americans *v.4 p.841*
   Disabled *v.4 p.842*
   Jewish *v.4 p.842*
International Contests and Sporting Events . . . *v.4 p.842*
   General *v.4 p.842*
   Olympics *v.4 p.845*
   World Games *v.4 p.847*
   World Cups *v.4 p.847*
   Senior and Master Contests *v.4 p.847*
Sports A-L *v.4 p.847*
   General. Miscellaneous Sports, A-Z *v.4 p.847*
   Auto Racing *v.4 p.848*
   Baseball *v.4 p.849*
   Basketball *v.4 p.853*
   Billiards *v.4 p.855*
   Bodybuilding *v.4 p.855*
   Boxing *v.4 p.855*
   Bullfighting *v.4 p.856*
   Cricket *v.4 p.856*
   Cycling *v.4 p.856*
   Extreme *v.4 p.857*
   Fencing *v.4 p.857*
   Field Hockey *v.4 p.857*

Football (American) *v.4 p.858*
Diving *v.4 p.860*
Golf *v.4 p.860*
Gymnastics *v.4 p.861*
Ice Hockey *v.4 p.862*
Lacrosse *v.4 p.862*

Sports M-Z. *v.4 p.863*
Martial arts *v.4 p.863*
Marathon *v.4 p.863*
Polo *v.4 p.863*
Professional Wrestling *v.4 p.863*
Racquet Sports *v.4 p.863*
Rodeo *v.4 p.865*
Rowing. *v.4 p.865*
Rugby *v.4 p.865*
Running *v.4 p.866*
Sailing *v.4 p.866*
Shooting *v.4 p.866*
Skating (Roller, Ice) *v.4 p.866*
Skiing *v.4 p.866*
Soccer *v.4 p.867*
Softball. *v.4 p.868*
Surfing *v.4 p.868*
Swimming *v.4 p.868*
Track and Field *v.4 p.869*
Volleyball. *v.4 p.869*
Weight Lifting *v.4 p.869*
Wrestling *v.4 p.870*

Science of Sport *v.4 p.870*
Manufacture of Sporting Goods *v.4 p.870*
Physics and Mathematics of Sport *v.4 p.871*
Other Scientific Factors in Sport *v.4 p.871*

Exercise Science *v.4 p.872*
General. *v.4 p.872*
Exercise Physiology *v.4 p.874*
Sport Nutrition *v.4 p.876*
Sport Psychology *v.4 p.876*
Exercise Training *v.4 p.878*

Facilities and Structures *v.4 p.880*

Business of Sport *v.4 p.881*
Administration and Management *v.4 p.881*
Economics *v.4 p.886*
Politics and Government *v.4 p.890*
College. *v.4 p.893*
Professional. *v.4 p.895*
International *v.4 p.898*
Gambling. Entertainment. *v.4 p.899*
Law. Legal Issues *v.4 p.900*
Media *v.4 p.901*

Careers in Sport *v.4 p.903*
Coaching *v.4 p.904*
Officiating *v.4 p.905*
Law. Agents *v.4 p.905*
Management and Administration *v.4 p.905*
Media and Journalism *v.4 p.906*

Biomechanics *v.4 p.907*

Motor Learning. *v.4 p.909*

TECHNOLOGY AND ENGINEERING . . . *v.5 p.677*
General and Reference Works *v.5 p.679*
Technology: General *v.5 p.680*
Technical Writing *v.5 p.680*
Industrial Safety. *v.5 p.681*
Applied Mathematics *v.5 p.683*
Engineering Mathematics *v.5 p.683*
Computer Applications. *v.5 p.683*
Industrial Engineering. *v.5 p.683*
Invention and Patents *v.5 p.683*
Manufacturing *v.5 p.684*
Civil Engineering. *v.5 p.684*
Standards. *v.5 p.684*
Materials Science *v.5 p.686*
Structural Engineering. *v.5 p.692*
Construction: Concrete and Metal. *v.5 p.697*
Construction: Highways, Bridges, Roads, and
Buildings *v.5 p.697*
Soil Mechanics *v.5 p.698*
Transportation Engineering *v.5 p.699*
Applied Optics *v.5 p.701*
Water Resource Engineering *v.5 p.702*
Environmental Engineering *v.5 p.704*
Pollution *v.5 p.705*
Radioactive Waste. *v.5 p.706*
Reference Works *v.5 p.706*
Mechanical Engineering *v.5 p.707*
Power. Energy *v.5 p.708*
Control Engineering *v.5 p.710*
Heat. Thermodynamics *v.5 p.712*
Fluid Mechanics and Heat Transfer *v.5 p.712*
Machinery *v.5 p.714*
Motor Vehicles *v.5 p.715*
Aeronautical Engineering *v.5 p.717*
Aircraft. *v.5 p.717*
Rockets. Astronautics. Space Flight *v.5 p.718*
Electrical and Electronic Engineering. *v.5 p.720*
Circuits Analysis *v.5 p.720*
Analog and Digital Electronics *v.5 p.721*
Electric Power Transmission and Distribution . *v.5 p.723*
Telecommunications *v.5 p.725*
Computer Networks *v.5 p.727*
Antenna Theory *v.5 p.728*
Microwaves. *v.5 p.729*
Computer Engineering *v.5 p.729*
Lasers. Optoelectronics *v.5 p.730*
Metallurgy *v.5 p.730*
Metallography *v.5 p.734*
Corrosion. *v.5 p.734*
Iron and Steel. *v.5 p.736*
Other Ferrous Metals *v.5 p.736*
Nonferrous Metals. *v.5 p.736*
Alloys *v.5 p.736*
Joining *v.5 p.736*
Electroplating *v.5 p.737*
Mining. *v.5 p.737*
Nuclear Engineering *v.5 p.739*
Chemical Engineering *v.5 p.740*

Photography *v.1 p.761*
    Reference Works *v.1 p.761*
    Histories and Handbooks. *v.1 p.762*
    Individual Photographers. *v.1 p.765*
    Materials and Techniques *v.1 p.769*
Digital Art *v.1 p.770*
    Reference Works *v.1 p.770*
    Histories and Handbooks. *v.1 p.770*
    Individual Artists *v.1 p.772*
Sculpture. *v.1 p.774*
    Reference Works *v.1 p.774*
    Histories and Handbooks. *v.1 p.774*
    Individual Sculptors *v.1 p.778*
    Materials and Techniques *v.1 p.782*
Architecture *v.1 p.782*
    Reference Works *v.1 p.782*
    Histories and Handbooks. *v.1 p.785*
    Individual Architects. *v.1 p.791*
    Materials and Techniques *v.1 p.796*
    City Planning *v.1 p.796*
Interior Design and Decoration. *v.1 p.798*
    Reference Works *v.1 p.798*

Histories and Handbooks. *v.1 p.799*
Individual Designers. *v.1 p.801*
Materials, Techniques, and Practices *v.1 p.802*
Furniture *v.1 p.803*
Interior Objects and Decoration. *v.1 p.805*
Other Topics *v.1 p.811*
Landscape Architecture *v.1 p.811*
    Reference Works *v.1 p.811*
    Histories and Handbooks. *v.1 p.812*
    Individual Landscape Architects *v.1 p.815*
    Materials, Techniques, Practices *v.1 p.817*
    Gardens, Parks *v.1 p.818*
Cultural Heritage *v.1 p.820*
    Reference Works *v.1 p.820*
    Histories and Handbooks. *v.1 p.821*
    Materials, Techniques, Practices *v.1 p.824*
Arts Management. *v.1 p.825*
    Reference Works *v.1 p.825*
    Histories and Handbooks. *v.1 p.825*
    Business and Art *v.1 p.825*
    Art Law *v.1 p.826*
    Museum Studies *v.1 p.827*

Author Index

A

A. A. Services Staff, A. A. Services *v.5 p.672*

Aaker, David A. *v.4 p.141*

Aaron, Daniel *v.2 p.5*

Aaron, Hank & Wheeler, Lonnie *v.4 p.830, p.849*

Aaron, Jane *v.2 p.298*

Aaron, Melissa D. *v.1 p.149*

Aaron, Michele *v.6 p.415*

Aarons, Leroy *v.6 p.383*

Aaronson, Susan Ariel *v.4 p.663*

Aasved, Mikal J. *v.4 p.777*

Aav, Marianne & Stritzler-Levine,
Nina (Editors) *v.1 p.712, p.800*

Aav, Marianne (Editor) *v.1 p.809*

ABA Coordinating Committee on Nonprofit
Governance Staff (Contribution by) *v.4 p.85*

Abadie, Ann J. & Dollarhide, Louis D. (Editors) . . . *v.2 p.129*

Abalos, David T. *v.6 p.545*

Abate, Tom *v.5 p.217*

Abazov, Rafis *v.3 p.230, p.231*

Abbate, Carolyn & Parker,
Roger (Editors) *v.1 p.193, p.227, p.364, p.365*

Abbate, Carolyn *v.1 p.193, p.227*

Abbey, Edward *v.2 p.139*

Abbott, A. J. & Atkin, R. K. (Editors) *v.5 p.19*

Abbott, Allan V. & Wilson, David G. (Editors) . . . *v.5 p.715*

Abbott, Anthony S. *v.2 p.187*

Abbott, Carl, et al. *v.3 p.526*

Abbott, Carl *v.3 p.519, v.6 p.710*

Abbott, Chris *v.4 p.350*

Abbott, Edith *v.4 p.253*

Abbott, Edwin A. *v.5 p.494*

Abbott, Ira H. & Von Doenhoff, Albert E. *v.5 p.717*

Abbott, Jack Henry *v.6 p.276*

Abbott, Margery Post, et al. *v.1 p.585*

Abbott, Nabia *v.1 p.555*

Abbott, Philip *v.3 p.377*

Abbott, Richard H. *v.3 p.422, p.423, p.427*

Abbott, Stephen *v.5 p.489*

Abbott, Susan & Webb, Barbara *v.1 p.825*

Abbott, Walter M. (Editor) *v.1 p.570*

Abboud, Peret *v.6 p.653*

Abboud, Peter F. & McCarus, Ernest N. *v.6 p.653*

Abboud, Peter *v.6 p.653*

Abdel Kader, Soha *v.6 p.636*

Abdi, Herve, et al. *v.5 p.591*

Abduh, Muhammad *v.1 p.557*

Abdulla, Jamal & McCarus, Ernest N. (Editors) . . . *v.6 p.668*

Abdullah, King of Jordan *v.6 p.620*

Abdullah, Yahya Taher *v.6 p.655*

Abdullahi, Ahmed-An-Na'im *v.1 p.553*

Abel, Christopher *v.3 p.357*

Abel, Eddie & Dann, Sandra E. *v.5 p.305*

Abel, Elizabeth *v.2 p.392*

Abel, Richard (Editor) *v.6 p.332*

Abel, Richard L. *v.4 p.440*

Abel, Richard *v.6 p.340*

Abel, Theodore *v.3 p.171*

Abelard, Peter & Heloise *v.2 p.448*

Abelard, Peter *v.1 p.431, v.3 p.55*

Abeles, Harold F., et al. *v.1 p.404*

Abell, Martha L. & Braselton, James P. *v.5 p.460*

Abell, Martha L., et al. *v.5 p.482*

Abell, Peter (Editor) *v.4 p.194*

Abell, Robin A., et al. *v.5 p.174, p.233, p.241, v.6 p.290*

Abella, Irving M. & Troper, Harold *v.3 p.542*

Abelove, Henry (Editor), et al. *v.6 p.357*

Abelson, Harold, et al. *v.5 p.346, p.349*

Abelson, John N. & Simon,
Melvin I. (Editor-In-Chiefs) *v.5 p.115*

Abelson, John N. & Stone, Melvin I. (Editor-In-Chiefs) . *v.5 p.120*

Aberbach, Joel D., et al. *v.4 p.601*

Abercrombie, Michael, et al. *v.5 p.224*

Abercrombie, Stanley *v.1 p.720*

Abercrombie, Thomas A. *v.3 p.323*

Aberjhani, et al. *v.6 p.22, p.33*

Abernathy, Jeff *v.2 p.12*

Abernethy, Bruce, et al. *v.4 p.874, p.907, p.909*

Abernethy, David B. *v.3 p.73*

Abernethy, Thomas P. *v.3 p.504, p.510*

Abernethy, Thomas Perkins *v.3 p.407, p.494*

Abé, Ryûichi *v.1 p.567*

Abiodun, Rowland, et al. *v.1 p.689*

Abkariyus, Iskandar *v.6 p.604*

Ablemann, Nancy & Lie, John . . . *v.4 p.713, v.6 p.113, p.135*

Abler, Ronald F. (Editor), et al. *v.4 p.377*

Abler, Ronald (Introduction by) *v.4 p.373*

Abler, Thomas S. (Editor, Introduction by, Notes by) . *v.6 p.685*

Abler, Tom (Editor) *v.6 p.688*

Aboff, Marcie *v.1 p.62, p.107*

Abou-El-Haj, Rifa'at 'Ali *v.6 p.589*

Aboul-Magd, Osama S. *v.5 p.726*

Abouzeid, Leila (Author, Translator) *v.6 p.655*

Abouzeid, Leila *v.6 p.655*

Abragam, Anatole *v.5 p.553*

Abraham, Arthur *v.6 p.72*

Abraham, Gerald E. (Editor) *v.1 p.193*

Abraham, Gerald E. *v.1 p.193, p.350*

Abraham, Henry J. *v.4 p.434, p.466, p.535*

Abraham, Henry Julian & Perry, Barbara A. *v.4 p.455*

Abraham, Margaret *v.6 p.111, p.137*

Abraham, Richard *v.3 p.221*

Abraham, William J. *v.1 p.655*

Abrahamian, Ervand *v.6 p.630*

Abrahams, Peter H., et al. *v.5 p.158*

Abrahams, Roger D. (Editor) *v.6 p.80*

Abrahams, Roger D. *v.2 p.16*

Abram, John & Hawkes, Paul *v.4 p.143*

Abramovic´, Marina (Text by) *v.1 p.772*

Abramovitz, Moses *v.4 p.242*

Abramowicz, Janet & Morandi, Giorgio *v.1 p.734*

Abramowitz, Milton & Stegun, Irene A.
(Editors) *v.5 p.460, p.493*

Abrams, Bradley F. *v.3 p.189, v.4 p.506, p.507*

Abrams, Lynn *v.3 p.55, p.169, v.4 p.803*

Abrams, M. H. & Greenblatt *v.2 p.196*

Abrams, M. H. & Harpham, Geoffrey G. *v.2 p.549*

Abrams, M. H. (Editor) *v.2 p.322*

Abrams, M. H. *v.2 p.171, p.173, p.183, p.567*

Abrams, Sabrina Fuchs *v.2 p.99*

Abramson, Charles I. *v.5 p.614*

Abramson, Daniel *v.4 p.90*

Abramson, Jeffrey *v.4 p.470, v.6 p.270*

Abramson, Mark A. & Morin, Therese L. *v.4 p.546*

Abramson, Norman *v.5 p.391, p.408*

Abramson, Rudy & Haskell, Jean (Editors) *v.3 p.497*

Abramson, Rudy *v.3 p.455*

Abrikosov, A. A., et al. *v.5 p.558*

Abse, Dannie *v.2 p.328*

Abu Khaldun Sati Al Husri *v.6 p.591*

Abu Nowar, Maan *v.6 p.620*

Abu-Amr, Ziad *v.6 p.616*

Abueva, Jose V. *v.6 p.178*

Abu-Hakima, Ahmad M. *v.6 p.626, p.627*

Abu-Izzedin, Nejla M. *v.6 p.600*

AbuKhalil, Asad *v.4 p.643*

Abukhalil, Asad *v.6 p.604*

AbuKhalil, Asad *v.6 p.626*

Abulafia, David (Editor) *v.3 p.198*

Abulafia, David *v.3 p.65, p.163, p.198*

Abu-Lughod, Ibrahim *v.6 p.616*

Abu-Lughod, Janet L. *v.6 p.56, p.145, p.634, p.722*

Abu-Lughod, Lila (Editor) *v.6 p.591*

Abu-Lughod, Lila *v.4 p.30, v.6 p.596, p.639*

Abun-Nasr, Jamil M. (Editor) *v.6 p.59*

Abun-Nasr, Jamil M. *v.6 p.640, p.641, p.642, p.643*

Abuza, Zachary *v.4 p.622, p.657*

Aby, Stephen H. & Kuhn, James C. (Compiled by) . *v.4 p.298*

Abzug, Malcolm J. & Larrabee, E. Eugene *v.5 p.717*

Abzug, Robert H. *v.3 p.82, p.419*

Accad, Evelyne *v.6 p.605*

Accampo, Elinor A. *v.3 p.148*

Accardo, Pasquale J. (Editor), et al. *v.4 p.318*

Accessible Archives, Inc. *v.6 p.33*

Acemoglu, Daron (Editor) *v.4 p.242*

Acharya, Sabita *v.1 p.534*

Achebe, Chinua *v.2 p.753*

Achenbaum, W. Andrew *v.4 p.741*

Acheson, Alan *v.1 p.608*

Acheson, D. J. *v.5 p.547*

Acheson, Dean *v.3 p.450*

Aching, Gerard *v.3 p.266*

Achinstein, Peter *v.1 p.499, v.5 p.400*

Achinstein, Sharon *v.2 p.170*

Achtemeier, Paul J. *v.1 p.614*

ACIA - Arctic Climate Impact Assessment *v.4 p.393*

Ackelson, Richard W. *v.1 p.169, p.265, p.357*

Acker, Caroline J. & Tracy,
Sarah W. (Editors) *v.4 p.775, v.5 p.663*

Acker, James R. & Brody, David C. *v.6 p.269*

Acker, James R. (Editor), et al. *v.4 p.567*

Acker, James R. *v.6 p.247*

Ackerly, C. J. *v.2 p.332*

Ackerman, Bruce A. *v.4 p.451, p.452*

Ackerman, Bruce *v.4 p.522, p.535*

Ackerman, Evelyn Bernette *v.3 p.148*

Ackerman, Frank & Nadal, Alejandro *v.4 p.205*

Ackerman, Hal *v.6 p.352*

Ackerman, Jennifer G. *v.5 p.130*

Ackerman, John *v.2 p.385*

Ackerman, Kenneth D. *v.3 p.490*

Ackerman, Marc J. *v.5 p.591*

Ackerman, Robert *v.4 p.3*

Ackerman, Susan *v.6 p.391, p.646, p.664*

Ackermann, Robert J. *v.5 p.406*

Ackland, Michael *v.2 p.742, p.743*

Ackmann, Martha *v.5 p.718*

Ackoff, Russell L. *v.5 p.408*

Ackrill, J. L. (Editor) *v.1 p.425*

Ackrill, Margaret & Hannah, Leslie *v.4 p.90*

Ackroyd, Peter R. & Evans, C. F. (Editors) *v.1 p.614*

Ackroyd, Peter *v.2 p.207, p.238, p.282*

Acland, Charles R. *v.6 p.345*

Acocella, Joan R. *v.1 p.5*

Acocella, Joan *v.6 p.414*

Acock, Alan C. & Demo, David H. *v.4 p.731*

Acokamittiran *v.6 p.150*

Acorn, Annalise E. *v.4 p.754*

Acorn, Milton (Contribution by), et al. *v.2 p.731*

Acorn, Milton *v.2 p.733*

Acosta, Hernandez *v.4 p.882*

Acosta, Ivan *v.6 p.516*

Acosta, Oscar Z. *v.6 p.488, p.497*

Acosta, Teresa Palomo & Winegarten, Ruthe *v.3 p.508*

Acosta-Belén, Edna & Santiago, Carlos E. *v.6 p.520*

Acosta-Belén, Edna, et al. *v.6 p.520*

ACS Task Force on Laboratory Waste Management . . *v.5 p.265*

Acs, Zoltan & Armington, Catherine *v.4 p.381*

ACSM Staff & Berryman, Jack W. *v.4 p.803, p.824*

Acton, Edward (Editor), et al. *v.3 p.221*

Acton, Forman S. *v.5 p.491*

Acton, Harold *v.3 p.201*

Acuna, Rodolfo F. *v.6 p.521, p.535, p.548*

Acuna, Rodolfo *v.6 p.530, p.539*

Aczel, Amir D. *v.5 p.542*

Aczon, Michael *v.1 p.383*

Adair, John Eric *v.3 p.484*

Adair, Robert K. *v.5 p.540*

Adair, W. Steven (Editor) *v.5 p.206*

Adalian, Rouben Paul *v.6 p.633*

Adam, Antoine & Tint, Herbert *v.2 p.458*

Adam, Antoine *v.2 p.458, p.462, p.503*

Adam, Jan *v.3 p.208*

Adam, Karl *v.1 p.575*

Adam of Bremen *v.3 p.162*

Adamczyk, Alice J. *v.1 p.17*

Adamec, Ludwig W. *v.6 p.633*

Adamolekun, 'Ladipo *v.6 p.73*

Adams, A. E., et al. *v.5 p.438*

Adams, Bob & Morin, Laura *v.4 p.168*

Adams, Carol J. *v.6 p.447*

Adams, Carolyn *v.6 p.716*

Adams, Charles Francis *v.3 p.433*

Adams, Colin C., et al. *v.5 p.485*

Adams, Colin Conrad *v.5 p.498*

Adams, Colin, et al. *v.5 p.485*

Adams, David W. *v.4 p.311, p.763,v.6 p.680, p.681*

Adams, David *v.1 p.394, v.2 p.190*

Adams, Denise Wiles *v.1 p.811, p.821*

Adams, Don *v.2 p.100*

Adams, Doug & Apostolos-Cappadona, Diane (Editors) . *v.1 p.21*

Adams, Elsie B. *v.2 p.308*

Adams, Ephraim D. *v.3 p.432*

Adams, Ephraim Douglass *v.3 p.393*

Adams, Francis *v.4 p.584, p.640*

Adams, Frank D. *v.5 p.418*

Adams, Fred *v.5 p.190, p.242*

Adams, Gerald R. & Berzonsky,
  Michael D. (Editors) *v.5 p.625, p.640*

Adams, Gerald R. & Gullotta, Thomas P. (Editors) . *v.5 p.625*

Adams, Hazard & Searle, Leroy (Editors) . . . *v.2 p.566, p.573*

Adams, Hazard & Searle, Leroy *v.2 p.566, p.573*

Adams, Hazard *v.2 p.288, p.337*

Adams, Henry *v.1 p.734, v.2 p.30, v.3 p.373*

Adams, James E., et al. *v.6 p.735*

Adams, James E. *v.2 p.173, p.190, v.6 p.477*

Adams, James R. *v.4 p.90*

Adams, James T. *v.3 p.405, v.4 p.517*

Adams, James Truslow *v.3 p.405*

Adams, Jane *v.3 p.514*

Adams, John A. *v.4 p.382*

Adams, John Q. Jr. *v.3 p.416*

Adams, John Q. *v.3 p.416*

Adams, John R. *v.2 p.51*

Adams, Joseph Quincy *v.1 p.75, p.98, p.154*

Adams, Laurie Schneider *v.1 p.667*

Adams, Marilyn J. *v.4 p.361*

Adams, Michael Henry *v.1 p.788*

Adams, Michael *v.2 p.551*

Adams, Natalie Guice & Bettis, Pamela J. *v.4 p.847*

Adams, R L; Knowler, J T; Leader, D P *v.5 p.328*

Adams, R. L. *v.5 p.87*

Adams, Rachel & Savran,
  David (Editors) *v.4 p.745, v.6 p.369, p.428*

Adams, Randolph Greenfield *v.3 p.407*

Adams, R. *v.4 p.428*

Adams, Richard E. W. *v.4 p.9*

Adams, Richard *v.2 p.328*

Adams, Robert Martin *v.2 p.356*

Adams, Roger (Editor) *v.5 p.295*

Adams, S. M. *v.5 p.214*

Adams, Shelby L. *v.3 p.497*

Adams, Simon *v.4 p.383*

Adams, Stephen & Ross, Donald Jr. *v.2 p.52*

Adams, Vincanne *v.4 p.46, v.6 p.163*

Adams, Walter & Brock, James W. . *v.4 p.52, p.53, p.120, p.148*

Adams, William Yewdale *v.6 p.59*

Adams *v.4 p.168*

Adamson, Arthur W. & Gast, Alice P. *v.5 p.283*

Adamson, David *v.4 p.605*

Adamson, Glenn *v.1 p.717*

Adamson, Hugh C. & Hainsworth, Philip *v.1 p.560*

Adamson, Jeremy Elwell *v.1 p.720, p.803*

Adamson, Joni (Editor), et al. *v.6 p.287*

Adamson, Joni *v.6 p.287, p.697*

Adamson, Lynda G. *v.6 p.425*

Adamson, Melitta Weiss *v.5 p.32, v.6 p.557*

Adcock, Fleur E. (Editor) *v.2 p.448*

Adda, Jerome & Cooper, Russell W. *v.4 p.197*

Addams, Jane *v.4 p.757, p.769*

Addington, Larry H. *v.4 p.627, p.646*

Addis, Cameron *v.4 p.340*

Addis, William *v.5 p.692*

Addison, John T. & Schnabel, Claus *v.4 p.123*

Addison, Joseph, et al. *v.2 p.202, p.236*

Addison, Joseph *v.2 p.236*

Ade, George *v.2 p.30*

Adeli, Hojjat & Karim, Asim *v.5 p.699*

Adell, Sandra *v.6 p.22*

Adelman, Charlotte & Schwartz, Bernard L. . . *v.5 p.233, p.240*

Adelman, Howard & Suhrke, Astri (Editors) . . . *v.4 p.651*

Adelman, Irma & Morris, Cynthia T. *v.4 p.253, p.258*

Adelman, Irma & Thorbecke, Erik (Editors) . . . *v.4 p.258*

Adelman, Irma *v.4 p.242, p.252, p.264*

Adelman, Marcy R. (Editor) *v.6 p.374*

Adelson, Bruce *v.4 p.813, p.830, p.849*

Adelson, Warren, et al. *v.1 p.734*

Ades, Dawn (Editor) *v.1 p.676, p.683*

Ades, Dawn, et al. *v.1 p.695*

Ades, Dawn *v.1 p.695, p.762*
Adhya, Sankar & Garges, Susan (Editors) *v.5 p.130*
Adivar, Halide E. *v.6 p.623*
Adivar, Halide Edib *v.6 p.623*
Adjaye, Joseph K. *v.6 p.69*
Adkins, Lesley & Adkins, Roy A. *v.3 p.11*
Adkins, Lesley & Adkins, Roy *v.3 p.12, p.22*
Adkins, R. T. (Editor) *v.5 p.321*
Adlam, Carol *v.2 p.797*
Adler, Arlene M. & Carlton, Richard R. *v.5 p.534*
Adler, Bill Jr. & Adler, Bill *v.4 p.74*
Adler, Jacob *v.6 p.274*
Adler, Joanna (Editor) *v.5 p.591*
Adler, Kathleen & Garb, Tamar *v.1 p.734*
Adler, Kraig & Halliday, Tim (Editors) *v.5 p.95, p.214*
Adler, Mortimer J. & Van Doren, Charles *v.2 p.573*
Adler, Mortimer J. *v.1 p.495, v.4 p.324*
Adler, Nancy J., et al. *v.4 p.58, p.69*
Adler, Nancy J. *v.4 p.58, p.75*
Adler, Samuel *v.1 p.392*
Adler, Selig *v.3 p.451*
Adler, Susan M. *v.6 p.108, p.110, p.111, p.131*
Adler, William M. *v.4 p.759*
Adlington, Robert *v.1 p.207, p.208, p.301, p.311*
Adloff, J. P.; Guillaumont, Robert *v.5 p.307*
Adoff, Arnold *v.2 p.22*
Adomeit, Hannes *v.3 p.211*
Adonis, A. *v.6 p.655*
Adonis, et al. *v.6 p.655*
Adonis *v.6 p.655*
Adorno, Rolena *v.3 p.262*
Adorno, Theodor W. & Eisler, Hanns . . . *v.1 p.254, v.6 p.351*
Adorno, Theodor W., et al. *v.1 p.506, v.4 p.767*
Adorno, Theodor W. . *v.1 p.208, p.376, p.380, p.460, p.479, p.502*
Adriani, Gotz *v.1 p.734*
Adriano, D. C. *v.5 p.364, p.377*
Adrich, Robert & Wotherspoon, Garry (Editors) . . . *v.6 p.357*
Adshead, S. A. M. *v.6 p.238*
Adshead, Samuel Adrian M. *v.6 p.183*
Adshead-Lansdale, Janet (Editor) *v.1 p.5, p.46*
Advertising Red Books.com *v.4 p.141*
Advocates for Youth *v.5 p.670*
Aeschylus, et al. *v.1 p.63, p.70, p.88*
Aeschylus *v.1 p.70, p.87, p.88,v.2 p.352, p.406, p.407*
af Malmborg, Mikael *v.3 p.87*
Afanas'ev, Aleksandr Nikolaevich *v.2 p.793*
Afary, Janet *v.4 p.616, v.6 p.630*
Affe, Robert B. *v.4 p.417*
Affron, Charles & Affron, Mirella *v.6 p.348*
Afkhami, Mahnaz & Friedl, Erika (Editors) *v.6 p.631*
Afkhami, Mahnaz (Editor, Introduction by) *v.6 p.591*
Afnan, Soheil M. *v.1 p.431*
African Development Bank
  Staff (Contribution by) *v.4 p.384, p.397*
Afshari, Reza *v.4 p.512*

Afzal-Khan, Fawzia *v.2 p.761*
Agar, Herbert *v.3 p.451*
Agar, Michael H. *v.4 p.18, p.25*
Agarwal, Anant & Lang, Jeffrey *v.5 p.721*
Agarwal, Bina, et al. *v.4 p.272*
Agarwal, Dharam P. & Seitz,
  Helmut K. (Editors) *v.5 p.512, p.521*
Agawu, Kofi *v.1 p.284*
Agawu, V. K. *v.1 p.369*
Agay, Denes (Editor) *v.1 p.396*
Agbasiere, Joseph Therese & Ardener, Shirley . . . *v.4 p.700*
Agcaoili, T. D. (Editor) *v.6 p.179*
Agee, James *v.2 p.55*
Agehananda Bharati *v.1 p.567*
Agüeros, Jack *v.6 p.495, p.504*
Aggarwal, Vinod K., et al. *v.4 p.256*
Aghion, Philippe & Durlauf, Steven N. (Editors) . *v.4 p.186, p.194*
Aglesham, Allan E. (Editor), et al. *v.5 p.13*
Agnew, Hugh L. *v.3 p.188*
Agnew, John *v.4 p.487, p.495*
Agnon, Shmuel Yosef & Harshav, Barbara *v.6 p.647*
Agnon, Shmuel Yosef *v.6 p.646, p.647*
Agoncillo, Teodoro A. *v.6 p.179*
Agosín, Marjorie & Levison, Julie H. (Editors) . . *v.3 p.350*
Agosín, Marjorie (Editor) *v.3 p.351, v.6 p.430, p.432*
Agosín, Marjorie *v.2 p.679*
Agosta, Lucien L. *v.2 p.133*
Agranoff, Robert & McGuire, Michael . . . *v.4 p.542, p.543*
Agrawal, Arun *v.6 p.153*
Agrawal, Jai P. *v.5 p.723*
Agrawal, Shashi B. & Agrawal, Madhoolika . . . *v.6 p.290*
Agre, Philip E. *v.5 p.590*
Agren, Gvran I. & Bosatta, Ernesto *v.5 p.182, p.189*
Agresti, Alan & Finlay, Barbara *v.4 p.483*
Agresto, John *v.4 p.462*
Agricola, Georgius *v.5 p.731*
Agricola, Johann Friedrich & Tosi,
  Pier Francesco *v.1 p.182, p.394, p.399*
Agrios, George N. *v.5 p.45*
Aguero, Felipe & Stark, Jeffrey (Editors) . *v.3 p.273, v.4 p.591*
Aguilar Camín, Héctor & Meyer, Lorenzo *v.3 p.290*
Aguilar-San Juan, Karin (Editor) *v.6 p.107, p.108*
Aguilera, Pilar & Fredes, Ricardo (Editors) . . . *v.3 p.351*
Aguino, Benigno S. Jr. *v.6 p.179*
Aguirre, Adalberto Jr. & Baker, David V. *v.4 p.17*
Aguirre, Carlos *v.3 p.327*
Aguirre-Molina, Marilyn & Molina,
  Carlos W. (Editors) *v.5 p.523*
Agulhon, Maurice *v.3 p.140, p.148, p.153*
Agur, Anne M. (Author, Author) *v.5 p.158*
Agus, Irving A. *v.6 p.577*
Agustí, Jordi & Antón, Mauricio *v.5 p.448*
Agustin, Jose *v.2 p.666*
Aharoni, Yohanan, et al. *v.4 p.379*
Ahearn, Barry *v.2 p.135, p.138*

Ahearn, Laura M. *v.6 p.163*
Ahern, Emily M. *v.1 p.527*
Ahl, Diane C. *v.1 p.734*
Ahl, Diane Cole (Editor) *v.1 p.734*
Ahl, Frederick *v.2 p.436*
Ahlfors, Lars V. *v.5 p.490*
Ahlstrom, Gosta W. *v.3 p.6*
Ahlstrom, Sydney E. *v.1 p.604*
Ahlstrom, Sydney *v.1 p.633*
Ahmad, Abdel Ghaffar Muhammad *v.4 p.578, p.610*
Ahmad, Aijaz *v.2 p.759*
Ahmad, Aziz *v.1 p.553*
Ahmad, Feroz *v.6 p.623*
Ahmad, Imtiaz (Editor) *v.1 p.553*
Ahmadjian, Vernon *v.5 p.210*
Ahmadzadeh, Hashem *v.6 p.668, p.669*
Ahmed, Akbar & Shore, Chris (Editors) *v.4 p.27*
Ahmed, Akbar S. *v.1 p.553*
Ahmed, Leila *v.1 p.557, v.6 p.449, p.458*
Ahmed, Nafeez Mosaddeq *v.4 p.562*
Ahmed, Tarek *v.5 p.451*
Ahmida, Ali Abdullatif *v.4 p.582, v.6 p.60, p.640*
Aho, Alfred V., et al. *v.5 p.346, p.348*
Aho, James *v.4 p.766*
Ahrens, C. Donald *v.4 p.393*
Ahrens, T. J. (Editor) *v.5 p.443*
Ahroni, Reuben *v.6 p.596*
Ahuja, Ravindra K., et al. *v.5 p.478*
Ahuja, Sunil & Dewhirst, Robert E. *v.4 p.529*
Aichinger, Ilse *v.2 p.602*
Aidoo, Ama Ata *v.2 p.752*
Aiello, Rit & Sloboda, John A. (Editors) . . . *v.5 p.618*
Aigner, Martin & Ziegler, Günter M. *v.5 p.457*
Aigner, Martin *v.5 p.478*
Aiken, Conrad *v.2 p.56*
Aiken, Lewis R. & Groth-Marnat, Gary *v.5 p.600*
Aiken, Lewis R. *v.5 p.593, p.603*
Ailey, Alvin Jr. & Bailey, A. Peter *v.1 p.5, v.6 p.414*
Aimer, Peter & Mulgan, Richard *v.4 p.624*
Ainger, Michael *v.1 p.248, p.361*
Ainsworth, Patricia *v.5 p.659*
Ainsworth, Peter *v.6 p.251*
AISC Manual Committee *v.5 p.692*
AISE Staff *v.5 p.687, p.736*
Aitchison, Jean (Author, Contribution by) . . *v.2 p.553, p.559*
Aitchison, Jean *v.5 p.620, p.622*
Aitken, George *v.2 p.261*
Aitken, Ian (Editor) *v.4 p.413, v.6 p.308*
Aitken, Ian *v.6 p.308*
Aitken, R. Alan (Editor) *v.5 p.294*
Aitken, Richard & Looker, Michael (Editors) . *v.1 p.811, p.818*
Ajami, Fouad *v.6 p.582*
Ajayi, Jacob Festus Ade & Crowder, M. *v.6 p.67*
Ajayi, Jacob Festus Ade & Crowder, Michael (Editors) . *v.6 p.51*
Ajayi, Omofolabo S. *v.1 p.14*

Aji, Aron *v.2 p.782*
Ajzen, Icek *v.5 p.585, p.604*
Ajzenberg-Selove, Fay *v.5 p.542*
Ajzenstat, Janet (Editor), et al. *v.3 p.538*
Ak'abal, Humberto *v.2 p.673*
Akan, A. Osman & Houghtalen, Robert J. *v.5 p.702*
Akanazarova, S. L. & Kafarov, V. V. *v.5 p.743*
Akarli, Engin D. *v.6 p.604*
Akbar, M. J. *v.1 p.560*
Akcakaya, H. Resit, et al. *v.5 p.182, p.187, p.189*
Akcam, Taner *v.4 p.651*
Akehurst, F. R. & Davis, Judith M. (Editors) . *v.2 p.453*
Akelah, A; Moet, Abdelsamie *v.5 p.322*
Akenside, Mark *v.2 p.237*
Akenson, Donald Harman *v.3 p.133, v.4 p.333*
Akenson, James E. *v.1 p.265, p.377*
Akerlof, George A. *v.4 p.194*
Akerman, Susanna *v.3 p.234*
Akers, Ronald L. & Jensen, Gary F. (Editors) . *v.6 p.250*
Akers, Ronald L. *v.6 p.249*
Akhmadulina, Bella *v.2 p.800*
Akhmatova, Anna Andreevena *v.2 p.800*
Aki, Keiiti & Richards, Paul G. *v.5 p.442, p.444*
Akiba, Kin-ya (Editor) *v.5 p.308*
Akin, J. E. *v.5 p.692*
Akin, Wallace E. *v.5 p.48*
Akinjogbin *v.6 p.73*
Akira, Suehiro *v.6 p.171*
Akkermans, Peter M. & Schwartz, Glenn *v.4 p.8*
Akrigg, G. P. V. *v.3 p.101*
Akroyd, H. David *v.4 p.397*
Aksakov, Sergei *v.2 p.801, v.3 p.215*
Aksyonov, Vassily *v.2 p.801*
Akutagawa, Ryunosuke *v.6 p.229*
Akwesasne Notes (Editor) *v.6 p.691, p.700*
Al Ahmad, Jalal *v.6 p.669*
Al Munif, Abd Al-Rahman *v.6 p.655*
Al Qadiri, Muhammad *v.6 p.643*
Alagappa, Muthiah (Editor) *v.4 p.616, p.618*
Alagappa, Muthiah *v.4 p.616*
Alain-Fournier, Henri *v.2 p.515*
Alain-Fournier *v.2 p.506*
Al-Ali, Nadje *v.6 p.636*
Al-Amir, Daisy *v.6 p.655*
Alan, John (Editor) *v.6 p.693*
Aland, Kurt & Aland, Barbara *v.1 p.624*
Aland, Kurt (Editor) *v.1 p.628*
Alanen, Arnold R. & Melnick, Robert *v.1 p.812, p.821*
Alarcón, Norma (Editor), et al. *v.6 p.497, p.511, p.545*
Alarcón, Pedro Antonio de *v.2 p.653*
Alarcon, Alicia *v.4 p.763*
Alas Leopoldo Clarín, Leopoldo (Clarin) . . . *v.2 p.653*
Al-Ashour, Radwa *v.6 p.655*
Alavi, Bozorg, et al. *v.6 p.669*
Alavi, Bozorg *v.6 p.669*

Alba, Richard D. & Nee, Victor *v.6 p.117, p.122, p.125*

Albala, Joanna S. & Humphery-Smith, Ian *v.5 p.102, p.104, p.109, p.138*

Al-Baladuri, Ahmad Ibn Yahya. *v.6 p.584*

Alban, Juan Pedro Viqueira *v.3 p.262*

Albanese, Catherine L. *v.1 p.527, v.3 p.407, v.6 p.700*

Albanese, Denise *v.4 p.378*

Albarracin, Dolores (Editor), et al. *v.5 p.651*

Albee, Edward (Author, Author) *v.2 p.139*

Albee, Edward. *v.1 p.86, p.91, p.111, v.2 p.139*

Albee, George W. & Joffe, Justin M. (Editors). . . .*v.5 p.670*

Albelda, Randy P. & Tilly, Chris *v.4 p.272, v.6 p.455*

Albelda, Randy Pearl & Withorn, Ann (Editors) . . .*v.4 p.754*

Alberro, Alexander *v.1 p.825*

Albers, Donald J. & Alexanderson, G. L. (Editors). .*v.5 p.464*

Albers, Donald J. (Editor), et al. *v.5 p.464*

Albert, Adrien & Serjeant, E. P. *v.5 p.309*

Albert Ellis Institute. *v.5 p.666*

Albert, Jim, et al. *v.4 p.871*

Albert, Jim *v.5 p.482*

Albert R. Mann Library, Cornell University
Library. *v.4 p.151, p.163*

Albert, Walter. *v.2 p.579*

Alberti, Rafael *v.2 p.655*

Alberto, Eliseo *v.2 p.670*

Alberts, Bruce, et al. *v.5 p.154*

Alberts, Bruce *v.5 p.111, p.153*

Albertson, Chris *v.1 p.257, p.357, v.6 p.408*

Alberty, Robert A. & Silbey, Robert J. *v.5 p.275*

Alberty, Robert A.. . . . .*v.5 p.111*

Albó, Xavier *v.3 p.323*

Al-Bisatie, Mohamed *v.6 p.655, p.656*

Albom, Mitch. *v.2 p.160*

Alborg, J. L. *v.2 p.638*

Albrecht, Karl *v.4 p.78, p.119, p.166*

Albright, Ann Cooper & Gere, David (Editors) .*v.1 p.27, p.29*

Albright, Daniel (Editor, Commentaries by) *v.1 p.208*

Albright, Matthew *v.5 p.130, p.217*

Albus, Anita *v.1 p.750*

Alcalay, Ammiel (Editor, Introduction by). *v.6 p.647*

Alcalay, Ammiel *v.6 p.596*

Alcalay, Reuben *v.6 p.645*

Alcalá, Kathleen *v.6 p.497*

Alcamo, I. Edward *v.5 p.130*

Alciatore, David G. & Histand, Michael B. . . .*v.5 p.707*

Alcock, James E. *v.5 p.613*

Alcock, Leslie *v.3 p.96*

Alcock, Peter (Editor), et al. *v.4 p.676*

Alcock, Rutherford *v.6 p.223*

Alcock, Susan E. *v.3 p.191*

Alcoff, Linda & Potter, Elizabeth (Editors).*v.6 p.426, p.460, p.462*

Alcoff, Linda M. (Editor) *v.1 p.481*

Alcoholics Anonymous World
Services, Inc., Staff *v.5 p.669, p.672*

Alcott, Louisa May. *v.2 p.31*

Al-Daif, Rashid *v.6 p.656*

Aldama, Frederick Luis *v.6 p.497, p.511*

Aldama. *v.6 p.488, p.497, p.511*

Aldana, Francisco. *v.2 p.645*

Alden, Dauril *v.3 p.334*

Alden, John Richard *v.3 p.411, p.494*

Alden, Raymond MacDonald (Editor). *v.2 p.202*

Alder, Ken *v.3 p.146*

Alderman, Ellen & Kennedy, Caroline *v.4 p.455*

Alderman, John *v.1 p.383*

Alderman, Robert L. *v.1 p.802*

Aldersey-Williams, Hugh *v.5 p.305*

Alderson, Anthony D. & Iz, Fahir *v.6 p.665*

Aldous, Joan (Editor) *v.6 p.466*

Aldred, Cyril. *v.1 p.669, p.689, v.3 p.8, v.6 p.57*

Aldrich Chemical Company *v.5 p.259*

Aldrich, Elizabeth *v.1 p.34*

Aldrich, John H. *v.4 p.552, p.578*

Aldrich, Richard J. *v.4 p.583*

Aldrich, Robert & Connell, John *v.3 p.157*

Aldrich, Robert & Wotherspoon, Garry (Editors). . .*v.6 p.357*

Aldrich, Robert *v.3 p.157, v.4 p.583, v.6 p.391*

Aldrich, Tim E. & Griffith, Jack *v.5 p.364, p.365*

Aldridge, Alan *v.1 p.524*

Aldwell, Edward & Schachter, Carl. *v.1 p.369*

Alecto Historical Editions Board Staff, et al. . .*v.3 p.96, p.97*

Alegría, Claribel & Flakoll, Darwin J. *v.2 p.674*

Alegría, Claribel *v.2 p.674*

Aleiss, Angela *v.6 p.700*

Aleixandre, V. *v.2 p.655*

Aleixandre, Vicente *v.2 p.656*

Alejandro, Reynaldo G.. . . . .*v.1 p.17*

Alem, Raja *v.6 p.657*

Alencar, Jose de *v.2 p.689*

Aleramo, Sibilla *v.2 p.713*

Alesina, Alberto & Rosenthal, Howard *v.4 p.247*

Alesina, Alberto & Spolaore, Enrico *v.4 p.247*

Alesina, Alberto, et al.. . . . .*v.4 p.242*

Alexander, Barbara T.. . . . .*v.4 p.158*

Alexander, Brian *v.5 p.182, p.238*

Alexander, Catherine (Editor) *v.1 p.57, p.75, p.98*

Alexander, Charles & Sadiku, Matthew *v.5 p.720*

Alexander, Charles C. *v.3 p.464, v.4 p.849*

Alexander, Christopher *v.1 p.796*

Alexander, David *v.4 p.394*

Alexander, Doris. *v.1 p.79, p.81, p.111, v.2 p.107*

Alexander, Edward *v.2 p.120*

Alexander, James Heywood *v.1 p.276*

Alexander, Jeffrey C. *v.4 p.679*

Alexander, John T. *v.3 p.217*

Alexander, Keith (Editor) *v.4 p.112*

Alexander, Kern & Alexander, M. David *v.4 p.449*

Alexander, Kern & Hunter, Richard C. (Editors). . . .*v.4 p.315*

Alexander, Kern, et al. *v.4 p.90*

Alexander, M. Jacqui & Mohanty, Chandra T.
(Editors) *v.6 p.439*

Alexander, M. Jacqui *v.6 p.432*

Alexander, Meena *v.2 p.310, p.322,v.6 p.92,*
p.102,p.104,p.111,p.117,p.138

Alexander, Michael *v.2 p.111, p.166*

Alexander, Paul J. *v.3 p.56*

Alexander, R. McNeil *v.5 p.190*

Alexander, R. McNeill *v.5 p.111*

Alexander, R. S. & Alexander, Robert *v.3 p.153*

Alexander, R. S. *v.3 p.152*

Alexander, Robert J. (Contribution by) *v.4 p.588*

Alexander, Robert J. (Editor). *v.3 p.328*

Alexander, Robert J. *v.3 p.318, p.333,p.338,p.347*
,p.352,p.360, v.4 p.508

Alexander, Robin J. *v.4 p.312, p.338*

Alexander, Ruth M. *v.4 p.753, v.6 p.468*

Alexander, S. L. *v.4 p.406*

Alexander, Stella *v.3 p.246, p.247*

Alexander Street Press *v.1 p.57, p.122,p.139,v.6 p.14,*
p.22,p.28,p.29,p.30

Alexander, Thomas G. *v.3 p.529*

Alexander, Victoria D. *v.1 p.707*

Alexander, Yonah *v.4 p.614, v.6 p.616*

Alexanderson, Gerald (Editor), et al. *v.5 p.457*

Alexandra, Tsaritsa *v.3 p.219*

Alexandrov, Vladimir E. (Editor) *v.2 p.103*

Alexandrov, Vladimir E. *v.2 p.801*

Alexandrowicz, Harry J. *v.4 p.283*

Alexej Von Jawlensky Archive Staff *v.1 p.722, p.734*

Alexie, Sherman *v.2 p.139, v.6 p.697*

Alexievich, Svetlana. *v.3 p.228*

Alexis, Jacques S. *v.2 p.535*

Alexopoulos, Constantine J., et al. *v.5 p.209*

Alfieri, Vittorio *v.2 p.710*

Alfoldi, Jeanette *v.4 p.179*

Alford, C. Fred *v.4 p.483, v.5 p.642*

Alford, John A. *v.2 p.211*

Alford, William P. *v.4 p.475*

Algar, Hamid (Translator) *v.6 p.632*

Algar, Hamid. *v.6 p.630*

Algarin, Miguel & Holman, Bob (Editors) . .*v.6 p.505, p.509*

Algarin, Miguel & Pinero, Miguel *v.6 p.495, p.509*

Algarin, Miguel *v.6 p.505, p.509*

Algaze, Guillermo. *v.4 p.8*

Algeo, John & Pyles, Thomas *v.2 p.553*

Algeo, John (Editor). *v.2 p.553*

Alger, Chadwick F. (Editor) *v.4 p.632*

Alger, Mark *v.5 p.322*

Al-Ghazali *v.1 p.431*

Al-Ghitani, Gamal *v.6 p.656*

Algra, Keimpe (Editor), et al. *v.1 p.427*

Algren, Nelson *v.2 p.56, v.3 p.515*

Al-Hakim, Tawfiq & Eban, A. S. *v.6 p.656*

Al-Hakim, Tawfiq. *v.6 p.591, p.656*

Al-Hujwiri *v.1 p.559*

Ali, Abbas J. *v.4 p.718*

Ali, Daud (Editor). *v.6 p.145*

Ali, Daud *v.6 p.150*

Ali (Editor). *v.5 p.158*

Ali Khalidi, Muhammad (Editor) *v.1 p.431*

Ali, M. & El, Ali Bassam *v.5 p.315, p.740*

Ali, Paul & Gregoriou, Greg N. *v.4 p.85*

Ali, Saleem H. *v.6 p.680*

Aliber, Robert Z. *v.4 p.57, p.93,p.98,p.99,p.162*

Alice McGillivray, Richard Scammon,
and Rhodes Cook *v.4 p.547, p.555*

Alinder, Mary Street. *v.1 p.765*

Alisanka, Eugenijus *v.2 p.781*

Alison, Laurence John (Editor) *v.5 p.591*

Alitto, Guy S. *v.6 p.199*

Al-Jabarti, Abd Al-Rahman *v.6 p.636*

Al-Jahiz, Amir ibn Bahir. *v.6 p.656*

Al-Jami, 'Abd al-Rahman *v.1 p.557*

Alkalimat, Abdul (Editor). *v.6 p.13*

Alkalimat, Abdul. *v.6 p.12, p.13,p.16,p.33*

Alkemade, C. Theodorus J.; Herrmann, R. *v.5 p.273*

Al-Khalesi, Yasin M. *v.6 p.653*

Al-Kharrat, Edwar *v.6 p.656*

Allaby, Michael (Editor) *v.5 p.211*

Allaby, Michael *v.5 p.36, p.174,p.240*

Allain, Marie-Francoise *v.2 p.348*

Allan, Barbara & Livesey, Brian *v.5 p.255*

Allan, J. (Editor), et al. *v.5 p.699*

Allan, Walter (Editor) *v.4 p.226*

Allanbrook, Wye J. *v.1 p.188, p.227,p.338*

Alland, Alexander *v.4 p.17*

Allard, Kenneth *v.4 p.70*

Allardt, Erik, et. al. (editor) *v.3 p.231*

Allardyce, Gilbert *v.5 p.229*

Allaway, Roger, et al. *v.4 p.867*

Allchin, Bridget & Allchin, F. Raymond. *v.4 p.8*

Allchin, Bridget (Editor) *v.4 p.8*

Allchin, Raymond *v.4 p.8, v.6 p.145*

Alldritt, Keith *v.2 p.71*

Allen, Ann T. *v.3 p.52, p.159*

Allen, Beverly *v.4 p.651*

Allen, Brooke. *v.2 p.177*

Allen, Bud & Bosta, Diana *v.6 p.276*

Allen, Carol *v.1 p.120, p.122*

Allen, Catherine J. *v.4 p.36, p.700*

Allen, Charles W. *v.3 p.521*

Allen, Christopher; Radu, Michael; Baxter, Joan & Somerville,
Keith *v.6 p.73*

Allen, Christopher *v.1 p.694, p.730*

Allen, Connie *v.5 p.87*

Allen, David Elliston (Editor) *v.5 p.236*

Allen, Donald *v.2 p.22*

Allen, Ed. *v.2 p.160*

Allen, Edward & Iano, Joseph *v.1 p.796*

Allen, Edward & Zalewski, Waclaw *v.5 p.692*

Allen, Ethan *v.1 p.545*

Allen, Francis A. . . . . *.v.6 p.268*

Allen, Franklin & Gale, Douglas . . . . *.v.4 p.88*

Allen, Frederick L. . . . . *.v.3 p.365, p.445*

Allen, Frederick Lewis . . . . *.v.3 p.371, p.445*

Allen, G. C. & Donnithorne, Audrey G.. . . . . . *.v.4 p.258*

Allen, Gardner W.. . . . . *.v.3 p.413*

Allen, Geoffrey & Bevington, J. C. . . . . *.v.5 p.322*

Allen, Gerald R. . . . . *.v.5 p.172*

Allen, J. H. & Greenough, J. B. . . . . *.v.2 p.423*

Allen, J. J. *.v.6 p.369*

Allen, J. R. *.v.5 p.439*

Allen, James L. . . . . *.v.2 p.30*

Allen, James T. . . . . *.v.1 p.70, p.154*

Allen, Jessie & Pifer, Alan (Editors) . . . . *.v.6 p.444*

Allen, Jo Beth (Editor) . . . . *.v.4 p.361*

Allen, John B. . . . . *.v.4 p.866*

Allen, John R. . . . . *.v.5 p.438*

Allen, Judy . . . . *.v.4 p.161*

Allen, Linda J. S. . . . . *.v.5 p.501*

Allen, Lindsay . . . . *.v.3 p.11*

Allen, Louis . . . . *.v.6 p.173*

Allen, M. P. & Tildesley, D. J. (Editors). . . . . *.v.5 p.551*

Allen, Mark & Fisher, John H. . . . . *.v.3 p.68*

Allen, Mary . . . . *.v.4 p.823*

Allen, Michael Patrick. . . . . *.v.5 p.483*

Allen, Michael Thad. . . . . *.v.3 p.171*

Allen, Michael . . . . *.v.4 p.865*

Allen, Myron B. III & Isaacson, Eli L. . . . . . . *.v.5 p.491*

Allen, P. A. & Allen, John R. . . . . *.v.5 p.438*

Allen, P. A.. *.v.5 p.423*

Allen, Patricia (editor) . . . . *.v.5 p.12*

Allen, Patricia . . . . *.v.5 p.12*

Allen, Paula Gunn (Editor) . . . . . *.v.2 p.18, v.6 p.697*

Allen, Paula Gunn. . . . . *.v.2 p.3, v.6 p.477*

Allen, Peter Lewis . . . . *.v.4 p.746*

Allen, Philip M. . . . . *.v.6 p.67*

Allen, Phillip E. & Holberg, Douglas R. . . . . . . *.v.5 p.721*

Allen, Prudence . . . . *.v.6 p.433, p.460*

Allen, Richard & Trivedi, Harish (Editors) . . . . *.v.2 p.761*

Allen, Richard F. . . . . *.v.2 p.624*

Allen, Richard Hinck . . . . *.v.5 p.70*

Allen, Robert C.. . . . . *.v.4 p.267, v.5 p.3*

Allen, Robert (Editor) . . . . *.v.2 p.551*

Allen, Robert L. & Allen, Pamela P. . . . . *.v.4 p.700*

Allen, Roger (Editor) . . . . *.v.6 p.657*

Allen, Roger . . . . *.v.6 p.657*

Allen, Roy E.. . . . . *.v.4 p.242, p.246,p.260*

Allen, Roy F. *.v.2 p.591*

Allen, Susan Heuck . . . . *.v.3 p.15*

Allen, Theodore W.. . . . . *.v.4 p.729, p.731*

Allen, Thomas . . . . *.v.1 p.17*

Allen, Vernon L. . . . . *.v.4 p.264*

Allen, W. D. *.v.1 p.173*

Allen, William S. . . . . *.v.3 p.169*

Allende, Isabel . . . . *.v.2 p.679, v.3 p.352*

Allender, Judith Ann (Author, Author) . . . . *.v.5 p.530*

Alley, Michael . . . . *.v.5 p.267*

Alligood, Martha Raile & Marriner Tomey, Ann . . . *.v.5 p.530*

Allington, Richard L. & Johnston, Peter H. . . . . *.v.4 p.361*

Allione, Tsultrim . . . . *.v.1 p.566*

Allison, Anne. . . . . *.v.6 p.218*

Allison, Christine & Kreyenbroek, Philip (Editors). . *.v.6 p.598*

Allison, David B., et al. . . . . *.v.5 p.109, p.120*

Allison, Dorothy . . . . *.v.6 p.394*

Allison, Graham . . . . *.v.3 p.386, p.464*

Allison, Juliann Emmons (Editor) . . . . *.v.4 p.425*

Allison, Linda (Author, Illustrator) . . . . *.v.5 p.225*

Allison, Robert J. (Editor) . . . . *.v.5 p.423*

Allister, Mark Christopher . . . . *.v.6 p.287*

Allitt, Patrick . . . . *.v.1 p.543, v.4 p.337*

Allman, T. D.. . . . . *.v.3 p.482*

Allmand, Christopher . . . . *.v.3 p.68, v.6 p.566*

Allmendinger, Blake . . . . *.v.2 p.14*

Allmon, Warren & Bottjer, David J. (Editors) . . . *.v.5 p.449*

Allofs, Theo . . . . *.v.5 p.167, p.235,p.241*

Allott, Miriam (Editor) . . . . *.v.2 p.269*

Allport, Floyd Henry . . . . *.v.5 p.605*

Allport, Gordon W. . . . . *.v.5 p.646*

Allsen, Thomas T.. . . . . *.v.4 p.623, v.6 p.238*

Allsop, Peter . . . . *.v.1 p.182, p.319*

Allsopp, Michael E. & O'Keefe, John J. . . . . . . *.v.1 p.575*

Allsopp, Michael E. & Sundermeier,
  Michael W. (Editors). . . . . *.v.2 p.293*

Allstetter, William & Schuyler, Tami . . . . *.v.5 p.679*

Alluin, Bernard . . . . *.v.2 p.522*

Allworth, Edward A. . . . . *.v.3 p.230*

Allworth, Edward (Editor) . . . . *.v.3 p.212*

Allyn, David . . . . *.v.4 p.746*

Al-Maghut, Muhammad . . . . *.v.6 p.656*

Al-Maqrizi . . . . *.v.6 p.584*

Almekinder, Connie & De Boef, Walter . . . . *.v.5 p.182*

Almirol, Edwin B. . . . . *.v.6 p.129*

Almodóvar, Pedro. . . . . *.v.6 p.417*

Almog, Joseph . . . . *.v.1 p.453*

Almond, Gabriel Abraham & Verba, Sidney (Editors) *.v.5 p.642*

Almond, Gabriel Abraham . . . . *.v.3 p.451*

Almqvist, Ebbe . . . . *.v.5 p.391*

Al-Mughni, Haya . . . . *.v.6 p.627*

Al-Munif, Abd al-Rahman . . . . *.v.6 p.656*

Al-Muqaddasi. *.v.6 p.584*

Aloff, Mindy (Editor). . . . . *.v.1 p.44*

Alon, Uri . . . . *.v.5 p.125, p.138,p.144,p.148*

Alonso, Ana Maria . . . . *.v.3 p.290*

Alonso, Harriet H. . . . . *.v.6 p.439*

Aloysius, G. . . . . *.v.4 p.617, v.6 p.156*

Alpaydin, Ethem . . . . *.v.5 p.407*

Alper, Joseph S. & Geller, Lisa N. . . . . *.v.5 p.130*

Alperovitz, Gar . . . . . . *.v.3 p.464, v.4 p.493, p.502*

Alpers, David H., et al. . . . . *.v.5 p.512*

Alpert, Geoffrey P. & Dunham, Roger G. . . . . . . *.v.6 p.260*

Alpert, Hollis *v.1 p.228, p.248, p.325*
Alpert, Rebecca T. *v.6 p.373*
Al-Rahman Munif, Abd *v.6 p.620*
Al-Ramly, Lenin *v.6 p.656*
Al-Rasheed, Madawi *v.6 p.625*
Alreck, Pamela L. & Settle, Robert B. *v.4 p.137*
Alred, Gerald J., et al. *v.4 p.171, v.5 p.680*
Al-Saadawi, Nawal *v.6 p.656, p.657*
Al-Saud, Faisal Bin Salman *v.4 p.640*
Al-Sayyid-Marsot, Afaf L. *v.6 p.57, p.636*
Alsen, Eberhard *v.2 p.117*
Al-Sharqawi, Abdel Rahman *v.6 p.657*
Al-Shaykh, Hanan *v.6 p.657*
Als-Nielsen, Jens & McMorrow, Des *v.5 p.560*
Alsop, Ronald & Wall Street Journal Staff (Editors) . *v.4 p.176*
Alston, Margaret & Bowles, Wendy *v.4 p.757*
Alston, William P. (Editor) *v.1 p.514*
Alston, William P. *v.1 p.481, p.514, p.522*
Alt, A. Tilo *v.2 p.598*
Altamirano, Ignacio Manuel *v.2 p.666*
Altbach, Philip G. (Author, Editor), et al. *v.4 p.330*
Altbach, Philip G., et al. *v.4 p.330*
Altbach, Philip G. *v.4 p.330*
Altbach, Phillip G. *v.4 p.313*
Altcappenberg, Hein-Thomas Schulze, et al. *v.1 p.722*
Altemeyer, Bob *v.4 p.509, p.767*
Alter, Joseph S. . . . *v.4 p.790, p.792, p.802, p.803, v.6 p.156*
Alter, Max *v.4 p.233*
Alter, Michael J. *v.4 p.827, p.828, p.872*
Alter, Nora M. *v.6 p.338*
Alter, Robert & Cosman, Carol *v.2 p.501*
Alter, Robert *v.1 p.616, p.618, p.621,v.6 p.645, p.730*
Alteras, Isaac *v.3 p.386*
Alterman, Eric *v.4 p.416*
Alters, Brian J. & Alters, Sandra M. *v.5 p.202, p.244*
Alters, Brian J. *v.5 p.202, p.244*
Alters, Sandra M. *v.5 p.359*
Althaus, Horst *v.1 p.463*
Althoff, Gerd *v.3 p.162, v.4 p.501*
Altholz, Josef L. *v.6 p.758, p.763*
Althusser, Louis *v.1 p.455, p.473*
Altick, Richard D. & Fenstermaker, John J. *v.2 p.163*
Altick, Richard D. . . *v.2 p.163, p.173, p.576,v.3 p.36, p.110,v.6*
p.735, p.737, p.738, p.744, p.749, p.752, p.754, p.755, p.760,
p.762, p.763
Altieri, Miguel A. & Nicholls, Clara I. . . . *v.5 p.9, p.10, p.26*
Altieri, Miguel A. *v.5 p.10*
Altinay, Ayse Gul *v.6 p.623*
Altizer, Thomas J. (Editor) *v.1 p.637*
Altizer, Thomas J. J. *v.1 p.637*
Altman, A & Colwell, Rita R. *v.5 p.7*
Altman, Dennis (Author, Afterword by) *v.6 p.386*
Altman, Dennis, et al. *v.4 p.140*
Altman, Dennis *v.4 p.746, v.6 p.362, p.378*
Altman, Ida *v.3 p.284*

Altman, Micah, et al. *v.4 p.689*
Altman, Rick *v.6 p.311, p.315, p.351*
Altman, Stuart H. (Editor), et al. *v.4 p.778*
Altmann, Alexander *v.1 p.460*
Altmann, Barbara K. & McGrady, Deborah L. (Editors) . *v.2 p.468*
Altschiller, Donald *v.4 p.568*
Altschuld, James W. & Witkin, Belle Ruth *v.4 p.81*
Altschuler, Glenn C. *v.1 p.265*
Altschull, J. Herbert *v.4 p.403*
Altshuler, Alan A. & Luberoff, David E. *v.6 p.722*
Altstadt, Audrey L. *v.3 p.231*
al-Umari, Ibn Fadl Allah *v.6 p.609*
Alumit, Noel *v.6 p.394*
Alurista & Rojas-Urista, Xeliina (Editors) *v.2 p.21*
Alurista *v.2 p.139, v.6 p.497*
Alvarez, A. *v.2 p.785*
Alvarez, Al *v.2 p.574*
Alvarez, Alex *v.4 p.651*
Alvarez de Toledo, Cayetana *v.3 p.284*
Alvarez, Jose & Castellanos, Lazaro Pena *v.3 p.306*
Alvarez, Julia *v.3 p.316, v.6 p.505*
Alvarez, R. Michael & Brehm, John *v.4 p.425, p.559*
Alvarez, Robert R. Jr. *v.6 p.528, p.545*
Alvarez, Sonia E. *v.3 p.282, p.338, v.6 p.439*
Alvarez, Walter *v.5 p.449*
Alverson, Keith D. (Editor), et al. *v.5 p.425*
Alves, Maria H. *v.3 p.273, v.4 p.591*
Alves, Miriam *v.2 p.689*
Alvord, Clarence Walworth *v.3 p.505*
Alvord, Lori Arviso & Van Pelt, Elizabeth Cohen . *v.6 p.701*
Alwood, Edward *v.6 p.390*
Aly, Gotz *v.3 p.82*
Al-Zayer, Penni *v.1 p.16*
Al-Zayyat, Latifah *v.6 p.657*
AMA Staff (Editor) *v.5 p.511*
Amado, Jorge *v.2 p.689*
Amanda Quick *v.4 p.150*
Amar, Akhil R. *v.4 p.455, p.473, v.6 p.268*
Amar, Akhil Reed *v.4 p.452*
Amaratunga, Dhammika & Cabrera, Javier *v.5 p.120*
Ambedkar, B. R. *v.6 p.158*
Ambert, Alba N. & Alvarez, Maria D. *v.6 p.526*
Ambert, Alba N. *v.6 p.505*
Ambler, Eric *v.2 p.328, v.6 p.173*
Ambrose, Alice & Lazerowitz, Morris (Editors) . . *v.1 p.471*
Ambrose, Alice *v.1 p.445*
Ambrose, Stephen E. & Barber, James A. Jr. (Editors) . *v.4 p.717*
Ambrose, Stephen E. & Brinkley, Douglas *v.3 p.451*
Ambrose, Stephen E. *v.3 p.382, p.464, p.519*
Ambrose, Susan A., et al. *v.5 p.394, p.398, v.6 p.438*
Ambrosi, Gerhard Michael *v.4 p.226*
Ambrosius, Lloyd E. *v.3 p.464, p.465*
Ambrosoli, Mauro *v.3 p.42*
American Academy of Orthopaedic Surgeons Staff . *v.5 p.534*
American Academy of Religion Staff, 1972 & 1973 . *v.1 p.522*

American Assembly Staff *v.4 p.272*

American Association for Career Education *v.5 p.576*

American Association for the Advancement of Science . *v.4 p.284*

American Association of Cereal Chemists, Approved Methods
Committee Staff (Contribution by) *v.5 p.33*

American Association of Museums
Staff (Contribution by) *v.1 p.827*

American Bar Association Staff *v.4 p.87, p.444*

American Board of Professional Psychology *v.5 p.675*

American Chemical Society; Chemical
Abstracts Service *v.5 p.256, p.257*

American Chemical Society, Committee on Professional
Training *v.5 p.260*

American Chemical Society Staff (Contribution by) . . *v.5 p.267*

American Chemical Society, Task Force on Laboratory Waste
Management Staff *v.5 p.265*

American College of Emergency Physicians Staff . . *v.5 p.534*

American College of Sports Medicine Staff
(Contribution by) *v.4 p.783, p.829, p.842*

American College of Sports Medicine Staff . *v.4 p.790, p.873*

American College of Sports Medicine . *v.4 p.792, p.872, p.880 ,
p.882, v.5 p.519*

American Council for International Education *v.2 p.775*

American Council of Learned Societies Staff (Editor) . *v.5 p.464*

American Council on Education Staff *v.4 p.330*

American Council on the Teaching of Foreign
Languages *v.4 p.359*

American Counseling Association *v.5 p.674*

American Education Research Association . . *v.4 p.338, p.354,
p.355, p.361, v.5 p.571*

American Educational Research Association; American
Psychological Association; National Council on Measurement
in Education; Joint Committee on Standards for
Educational and Psychological Testing (U.S.) *v.5 p.604*

American Educational Research Association, et al. . . *v.4 p.285*

American Educational Research Association *v.5 p.571*

American Federation of Teachers *v.4 p.282*

American Football Coaches Association Staff *v.4 p.858*

American Geological Institute Staff
(Compiled by) *v.5 p.737, v.6 p.283*

American Geological Institute Staff *v.6 p.285, p.293*

American Geological Institute *v.5 p.417*

American Heritage Dictionary Editors (Editor) *v.5 p.386*

American Institute of Architects Staff &
Demkin, Joseph A. *v.1 p.796*

American Institute of Biological Sciences;
Meeting ; (1993 : Ames, Iowa) *v.5 p.155, p.190*

American Institute of Chemical Engineers, Center for Chemical
Process Safety Staff (Contribution by) *v.5 p.743*

American Institute of Chemical Engineers Staff & Center For
Chemical Process Safety CCPS Staff *v.5 p.743*

American Institute of Chemical Engineers Staff & Center for
Chemical Process Safety Staff *v.5 p.743*

American Institute of Chemical Engineers Staff . . . *v.5 p.743*

American Institute of Physics *v.5 p.280, p.544*

American Institute of Timber Construction Staff . *v.5 p.684, p.687*

American Kennel Club Staff (Contribution by) *v.5 p.53*

American Medical Association Staff *v.5 p.509*

American Mercury Staff *v.2 p.27*

American Museum of Natural History Staff, et al. . . *v.5 p.130*

American Musicological Society *v.1 p.172*

American National Election Studies *v.4 p.547*

American Physical Society *v.5 p.545*

American Psychiatric Association Staff *v.5 p.516*

American Psychiatric Association *v.5 p.662*

American Psychological Association, Committee on Animal
Research and Ethics *v.5 p.674*

American Psychological Association (Created by) . . *v.5 p.675*

American Psychological Association Education
Directorate *v.5 p.675*

American Psychological Association of
Graduate Students *v.5 p.675*

American Psychological Association Staff *v.5 p.600*

American Psychological Association *v.5 p.674*

American School Counselor Association *v.5 p.576*

American School Health Association *v.5 p.571*

American Sheep Industry Association *v.5 p.53*

American Social History Project *v.4 p.366*

American Society for Testing and Materials Committee D-18 on
Soil and Rock & American Society for Testing and
Materials Staff (Contribution by) *v.5 p.685*

American Society for Testing and Materials *v.5 p.318*

American Society for Training and Development Staff
(Contribution by) *v.4 p.304*

American Society of Agricultural Engineers *v.5 p.3*

American Society of Civil Engineers Staff . *v.4 p.390, v.5 p.685*

American Society of Composers,
Authors and Publishers *v.1 p.172, p.383*

American Society of Ichthyologists and Herpetologists; Food
and Agriculture Organization; European Commission . *v.5 p.172,
p.241*

American Society of Landscape Architects Staff . . . *v.1 p.815*

American Society of Lubrication Engineers Staff . . . *v.5 p.714*

American Sport Education Program
(Contribution by) *v.4 p.869, p.905*

American Sport Education Program Staff (Contribution by) . *v.4
p.794, p.839, p.862, p.869, p.904*

American Sport Education Program Staff . *v.4 p.794, p.795, p.839,
p.849, p.863, p.867, p.868, p.870, p.904, p.905*

American Welding Society Staff *v.5 p.736*

Americas Watch *v.3 p.328*

Ameriks, Karl (Editor) *v.1 p.508*

Ameriks, Karl *v.1 p.460*

Amerine, M. A., et al. *v.5 p.52*

Amerine, Maynard A. & Roessler, Edward B. *v.5 p.52*

Amerine, Maynard A. & Singleton, Vernon L. *v.5 p.52*

Ameringer, Charles D. (Editor) *v.4 p.588*

Ameringer, Charles D. *v.3 p.306*

Amerlinck, Mari-Jose (Editor) *v.4 p.25*

Ames, Kenneth M. & Maschner, Herbert D. . *v.4 p.10, v.6 p.702*

Ames, Michael M. *v.4 p.47*

Ames, Roger T. *v.6 p.183*

AMG: All Media Guide *v.6 p.305*

Amichai, Yehuda & Harshav, Benjamin *v.6 p.647*

Amichai, Yehuda *v.6 p.647*

Amico, Eleanor (Editor) *v.6 p.425*

Amidon, Jane *v.1 p.812, p.815*

Amihud, Yakov (Editor) *v.4 p.251*

Amin, Mohamed; Smyth, Annie & Seftel, Adam . . . *v.6 p.66*

Amin, Qasim *v.6 p.636*

Amin, Shahid *v.6 p.160*

Aminian, Ali & Kazimierczuk, Marian *v.5 p.721*

Aminzade, Ronald *v.3 p.148*

Amirahmadi, Hooshang & Entessar, Nader *v.6 p.591*

Amis, Kingsley (Editor) *v.2 p.198*

Amis, Kingsley *v.2 p.328, p.329*

Amis, Martin *v.2 p.329*

Amiss, John M., et al. *v.5 p.714*

Amit-Talai, Vered (Editor) *v.4 p.3*

Amjad, Ali *v.4 p.120*

Amman, Hans M. (Editor), et al. *v.4 p.186, p.197*

Ammer, Christine . . . *v.1 p.159, p.378, v.5 p.523, v.6 p.473*

Ammerman, R. T. (Editor) *v.1 p.501*

Ammerman, Robert T. & Hersen, Michel (Editors) . . *v.5 p.666*

Ammianus Marcellinus *v.2 p.428*

Ammon, Harry *v.3 p.416*

Ammon, Rob, et al. *v.4 p.880, p.882*

Ammons, A. R. *v.2 p.55*

Ammons, Elizabeth & Belasco, Susan (Editors) . . . *v.2 p.51*

Ammons, Elizabeth & White-Parks, Annette (Editors) . *v.2 p.5*

Ammons, Elizabeth *v.2 p.8*

Amnesty International *v.4 p.669, v.6 p.387*

Amodio, Mark C. *v.6 p.568*

Amos, Martyn (Editor) *v.5 p.105*

Amram, Martha (Author, Editor) *v.4 p.90, p.101*

Amrhein, James E. *v.5 p.692*

Amsel, Abram *v.5 p.614*

Amster, Randall *v.6 p.716*

Amstock, Joseph S. *v.5 p.687*

Amstrong, M. & Porter, R. H. (Editors) *v.4 p.186*

Amstutz, Mark R. *v.4 p.483, p.624*

Amt, Emilie (Editor) *v.6 p.559*

Amundson, Ronald *v.5 p.159, p.162, p.190*

Amussen, Susan D. *v.3 p.130*

Amuzegar, Hooshang & Amuzegar, Farideh *v.6 p.669*

Amy, Douglas J. *v.4 p.576*

Analoui *v.4 p.75*

Anand, Mulk Raj *v.2 p.764*

Anand, Nitya, et al. *v.5 p.293*

Anandalingam, G. & Lucas, Henry C. *v.4 p.84*

Anandalingam, G. & Raghavan, S. (Editors) *v.5 p.725*

Anastaplo, George *v.4 p.458, p.518*

Anastas, Paul T. & Warner, John *v.5 p.310*

Anastas, Paul T. *v.5 p.310*

Anastasi, Anne & Urbina, Susana *v.5 p.599*

Anastopoulos, Arthur D. & Shelton, Terri L. *v.4 p.318*

Anatolios, Khaled *v.1 p.612*

Anawalt, Patricia R. *v.3 p.260, v.6 p.684*

Anawalt, Sasha *v.1 p.5, p.22, v.6 p.414*

Anaya, Pilar Ortuno *v.3 p.242*

Anaya, Rudolfo A. & Lomelí, Francisco A. . . . *v.6 p.497, p.511*

Anaya, Rudolfo A. *v.6 p.497*

Anaya, Rudolfo *v.6 p.497*

Anbar, Ada *v.4 p.370*

Anbinder, Tyler G. *v.3 p.394*

Ancheta, Angelo N. *v.4 p.456, v.6 p.107, p.117, p.120*

Andaya, Barbara Watson & Andaya, Leonard Y. . . . *v.6 p.172*

Ander, Gregg D. *v.1 p.803*

Anderegg, Michael (Editor) *v.6 p.321*

Andermahr, Sonya, et al. *v.4 p.676, v.6 p.426, p.427*

Anders, Elizabeth *v.4 p.795, p.857*

Andersen, Alan N. (Editor), et al. *v.5 p.182, p.240*

Andersen, Esben S. *v.4 p.233*

Andersen, Francis I. & Freedman, David Noel . . . *v.1 p.622*

Andersen, Francis I. *v.1 p.622*

Andersen, Lykke E., et al. *v.4 p.267*

Andersen, Margaret *v.4 p.743, v.6 p.433*

Andersen, Mark B. (Editor) *v.4 p.876, v.5 p.581*

Andersen, Martin E. *v.3 p.347*

Andersen, Peter A. & Guerrero, Laura K. (Editors) . *v.5 p.646*

Andersen, Robert A. (Editor) *v.5 p.207*

Andersen, Stephen O. & Sarma, K. Madhava . . . *v.4 p.666*

Andersen, Svein S. & Eliassen, Kjell A. (Editors) . *v.4 p.636*

Andersen, Tom *v.5 p.173, v.6 p.294*

Andersen *v.2 p.626*

Anderson, Benedict R. O'G. . . . *v.4 p.493, v.6 p.173, p.175*

Anderson, Benedict *v.3 p.61*

Anderson, Bonnie S. &
Zinsser, Judith P. *v.3 p.50, v.6 p.449, p.559*

Anderson, Bonnie S. *v.3 p.52, v.4 p.710, v.6 p.430*

Anderson, Bryon D. *v.4 p.866, p.871*

Anderson, Charles L. *v.3 p.304*

Anderson, Charles R. *v.2 p.36*

Anderson, Christopher, et al. *v.1 p.694*

Anderson, D. T. (Editor) *v.5 p.212*

Anderson, D. T. *v.5 p.95, p.156*

Anderson, D. *v.2 p.702*

Anderson, David D. *v.2 p.56*

Anderson, David *v.6 p.64*

Anderson, Dennis *v.5 p.227*

Anderson, Donald K. Jr. (Editor) *v.2 p.218*

Anderson, Donna K. *v.1 p.208, p.327, p.328*

Anderson, E. N. *v.6 p.181*

Anderson, Elijah *v.4 p.692, p.723*

Anderson, Elizabeth T. & McFarlane, Judith M. . . . *v.5 p.531*

Anderson, Emily (Editor) *v.1 p.193, p.306*

Anderson, Eric *v.4 p.839, v.6 p.383*

Anderson, Eugene N. *v.4 p.609, p.610*

Anderson, Ewan (Editor) *v.4 p.487, p.495*

Anderson, Frank J. *v.5 p.82*

Anderson, Fred & Cayton, Andrew *v.3 p.382*

Anderson, Fred *v.3 p.405*

Anderson, Frederick *v.2 p.33*

Anderson, George K. (Translator) *v.2 p.624*

Anderson, George Kumler *v.2 p.167*

Anderson, Gerald H. (Editor) *v.1 p.633*

Anderson, Greg M. & Crerar, David A. *v.5 p.440*

Anderson, Greg *v.5 p.277*

Anderson, Harry R. *v.5 p.726*

Anderson, Ian *v.5 p.477*

Anderson, J. K. *v.2 p.422*

Anderson, J. L. *v.3 p.38*

Anderson, J. M. & Ingram, J. S. (Editors) *v.5 p.48*

Anderson, Jack *v.1 p.5, p.25, p.38*

Anderson, James F. & Dyson, Laronistine *v.6 p.249*

Anderson, James F., et al. *v.4 p.676, v.6 p.245*

Anderson, James Maxwell *v.3 p.243*

Anderson, Janet *v.1 p.27, p.29*

Anderson, Janice C. & Moore, Stephen D. (Editors) . *v.1 p.628*

Anderson, Jervis *v.4 p.123*

Anderson, John B. *v.5 p.434*

Anderson, John D. Jr. *v.5 p.717*

Anderson, John Q. (Editor) *v.3 p.427*

Anderson, John W. & Beardall, John *v.5 p.124, p.125*

Anderson, Joseph L. & Richie, Donald *v.6 p.335*

Anderson, Judith H. (Editor), et al. *v.2 p.212*

Anderson, Kay J. *v.6 p.710*

Anderson, Lars *v.4 p.813, p.853*

Anderson, Laura & Malaski, Christine *v.5 p.535*

Anderson, Laurie *v.1 p.208, p.301*

Anderson, Leslie E. & Dodd, Lawrence C. *v.3 p.300*

Anderson, Lisa M. *v.6 p.15, p.41*

Anderson, Lorin W., et al. *v.4 p.338, v.5 p.573*

Anderson, Lynn & Kress, Carla *v.4 p.787, p.842*

Anderson, M. S. *v.3 p.216*

Anderson, Malcolm *v.4 p.487, p.495*

Anderson, Marcia *v.4 p.827, v.5 p.519*

Anderson, Margaret L. *v.3 p.169*

Anderson, Margaret Lavinia *v.3 p.163*

Anderson, Margo J. (Editor) *v.4 p.676*

Anderson, Marian *v.1 p.280, p.301*

Anderson, Marlow & Feil, Todd *v.5 p.473*

Anderson, Marlow, et al. *v.5 p.464*

Anderson, Maxwell & Stallings, Laurence *v.2 p.55*

Anderson, Misty G. *v.2 p.187*

Anderson, Nancy K. *v.1 p.735*

Anderson, Noma B. & Shames, George H. . . *v.5 p.664, p.673*

Anderson, Olive *v.3 p.110, p.123*

Anderson, Patricia *v.6 p.737, p.738, p.743, p.763*

Anderson, Patrick *v.3 p.465*

Anderson, Paul M. *v.5 p.723*

Anderson, Paul S. & Lapp, Diane K. *v.4 p.361*

Anderson, R. D. Jr. *v.4 p.333*

Anderson, Richard, et al. *v.4 p.597*

Anderson, Rob (Editor), et al. *v.4 p.422, v.5 p.620*

Anderson, Robert D. *v.4 p.333*

Anderson, Roberta & Bellenger,
Dominic Aidan (Editors) *v.3 p.62*

Anderson, Robin L. *v.3 p.334*

Anderson, Roger B. & Debreczeny, Paul (Editors) . . *v.2 p.797*

Anderson, Roy M. & May, Robert M. *v.5 p.501*

Anderson, S. E. *v.6 p.11*

Anderson, Sean K. & Sloan, Stephen *v.4 p.657*

Anderson, Sherwood *v.2 p.56, p.57*

Anderson, Stanford *v.1 p.791*

Anderson, T. L. *v.5 p.687*

Anderson, Terry H. *v.4 p.57, p.108, p.133*

Anderson, Timothy *v.4 p.396*

Anderson, Tom *v.5 p.227*

Anderson, Virginia DeJohn *v.5 p.54, v.6 p.684*

Anderson, Warren D. *v.1 p.175*

Anderson, William S. (Editor) *v.2 p.434*

Anderson, William Scovil &
Quartarone, Lorina N. (Editors) *v.2 p.445*

Anderson, William Scovil *v.2 p.445*

Anderson, William *v.3 p.502*

Anderson-Levitt, Kathryn M. (Editor) *v.4 p.313*

Andersson, Ake E. & Andersson, David E. . . *v.4 p.256, p.260*

Andersson, Eve Astrid, et al. *v.5 p.338, p.349*

Andersson, Theodore Murdock *v.2 p.624*

Ando, Clifford *v.3 p.27*

Ando, Wataru (Editor) *v.5 p.291*

Andonian, Cathleen C. (Editor) *v.2 p.332*

Andors, Phyllis *v.6 p.433, p.453*

Andrade, M. A. (Editor) *v.5 p.105, p.107*

Andrade Muricy, Jose Candido de *v.2 p.689*

Andrae, Tor *v.1 p.555*

Andre, Judith *v.4 p.802, p.821*

Andre, Maria Claudia (Editor) *v.2 p.663*

Andre, Rae *v.4 p.736, v.6 p.466*

Andreadis, Harriette *v.6 p.391*

Andreas, Peter *v.6 p.486, p.537*

Andreasen, Alan R. *v.4 p.51, p.134*

Andreev, Leonid Nikolaevich *v.2 p.801*

Andreev-Khomiakov, Gennady *v.3 p.224*

Andreff, Wladimir *v.4 p.186*

Andres, Ramon *v.2 p.642*

Andres, Sophia *v.2 p.173, p.192*

Andresen, Jensine (Editor) *v.5 p.632*

Andresen, Julie T. *v.2 p.559*

Andrew, Christopher & Gordievsky, Oleg *v.3 p.211*

Andrew, Dudley *v.6 p.337*

Andrew, John *v.4 p.516*

Andrew, Neil (Editor) *v.5 p.173*

Andrew, Susan *v.4 p.870*

Andrewes, Anthony *v.3 p.16*

Andrews, Alexander *v.4 p.403*

Andrews, Carol (Editor) *v.3 p.8*

Andrews, Carol *v.3 p.8*

Andrews, Charles McLean *v.3 p.405, p.407, v.4 p.517*

Andrews, David G. *v.5 p.425*

Andrews, David L. (Editor), et al. *v.4 p.812*

Andrews, David L. (Editor) . . . *v.4 p.853, p.882, p.895, p.901*

Andrews, Deborah C. & Andrews, William D. *v.4 p.171*

Andrews, Elmer *v.2 p.352*
Andrews, George & Solomon, David (Editors) . . . *v.3 p.281*
Andrews, George E., et al. *v.5 p.493*
Andrews, George R. *v.3 p.338*
Andrews, George Reid *v.3 p.278*
Andrews, Gerald D. & Subramanian,
  Pallatheri M. (Editors) *v.5 p.376*
Andrews, Gregg *v.3 p.290*
Andrews, Henry N. *v.5 p.449*
Andrews, J. Cutler *v.3 p.424*
Andrews, J. E., et al. *v.5 p.423*
Andrews, Jac J. W. (Volume Editor), et al. . *v.4 p.285, v.5 p.602*
Andrews, Julian *v.1 p.778*
Andrews, Kenneth R. *v.3 p.88, p.93, p.101*
Andrews, Malcolm *v.1 p.702, v.2 p.282*
Andrews, Moya L. *v.5 p.518*
Andrews, Phil *v.4 p.408, p.906*
Andrews, Richard *v.1 p.91, p.106*
Andrews, Tamra *v.1 p.527*
Andrews, Tom (Editor) *v.2 p.115*
Andrews, Walter G. (Editor, Translator), et al. *v.6 p.666*
Andrews, Walter G. *v.6 p.666*
Andrews, William L. (Editor), et al. *v.6 p.22, p.33*
Andrews, William L. (Editor) *v.2 p.18, v.6 p.41*
Andrews, William L. *v.2 p.25*
Andric, Ivo *v.2 p.819*
Andrien, Kenneth J. & Adorno, Rolena (Editors) . . . *v.3 p.325*
Andrien, Kenneth J. & Johnson, Lyman L. *v.3 p.284*
Andrien, Kenneth J. *v.3 p.323, p.325*
Andriessen, Daniel *v.4 p.72*
Andriessen, Louis & Schonberger, Elmer . . . *v.1 p.208, p.359*
Andriote, John-Manuel *v.6 p.378*
Andrist, Linda C., et al. *v.5 p.527, p.529*
Andrukhovych, Yuri *v.2 p.814*
Andrzejewski, Jerzy *v.2 p.787, p.789*
Anfam, David *v.1 p.676, p.726, p.735*
Ang, Ien *v.4 p.418*
Ang, Tom *v.1 p.761, p.770*
Angel, Ronald J. *v.4 p.751*
Angelides, Steven *v.6 p.362, p.371*
Angelo, Joseph A. *v.3 p.49, v.5 p.359, p.739*
Angelo, Thomas A. & Cross, K. Patricia *v.4 p.285*
Angelou, Maya *v.2 p.139*
Angle, Paul M. (Editor) *v.3 p.424*
Anglim, Christopher Thomas *v.4 p.460*
Angold, Michael (Editor) *v.1 p.569*
Angold, Michael *v.1 p.568, v.3 p.192*
Angrist, Stanley W. *v.5 p.359*
Anguizola, Gustave *v.3 p.304*
Angus, David & Mirel, Jeffery *v.4 p.324*
Angus, Ian *v.3 p.534*
Anheier, Helmut K. (Editor) *v.4 p.85*
Ani, Marimba *v.6 p.3, p.19*
Anisimov, Evgenii V. *v.3 p.215*
Anitpa, Sebastian *v.5 p.167*

Anker, Philippe & Stroun, Maurice (Editors) *v.5 p.119*
Ankerberg, John & Weldon, John *v.5 p.77, p.202*
Anna, Timothy E. *v.3 p.273, p.288*
An-Na'im, Abdullahi A. (Editor) *v.4 p.33*
Annan, Kofi A. (Foreword by) *v.4 p.632*
Annan, Noel Gilroy, et al. *v.3 p.118, p.127*
Annan, Noel *v.6 p.739, p.749, p.758*
Annas, George J. *v.4 p.448*
Annas, Julia (Editor) *v.1 p.419*
Annas, Julia *v.1 p.419, p.423, p.426,
                          p.427, p.483, p.496, v.4 p.488*
Annesley, Claire (Editor) *v.4 p.186*
Annunzio, Susan & McGowan, Sharon *v.4 p.79*
Anonymous *v.1 p.534*
Anonymus, Gallus *v.3 p.252*
Anouilh, Jean *v.2 p.506*
Ansari, Sarah F. D. *v.6 p.148*
Anschutz, R. P. *v.1 p.444*
Anscombe, G. E. M. & von Wright, G. H. (Editors) . *v.1 p.471*
Anscombe, G. E. M. *v.1 p.491*
Ansel, Yves, et al. Berthier, Philippe, Nerlich, Michael . *v.2 p.501*
Ansell-Pearson, Keith *v.4 p.490*
Anselm, Saint & Anselm of Canterbury *v.1 p.431*
Anshaw, Carol *v.6 p.394*
Ansoff, H. Igor *v.4 p.81*
Antelman, Gordon *v.4 p.197*
Antheil, George *v.1 p.208, p.301*
Anthony, Carl Sferrazza *v.3 p.377*
Anthony, Douglas A. *v.6 p.71*
Anthony, James R. *v.1 p.182*
Anthony, John W., et al. *v.5 p.435*
Anthony, John W. *v.5 p.435*
Anthony, M. H. & Biggs, Norman L. *v.5 p.339, p.340*
Anthony, Rebecca J. & Roe, Gerald *v.4 p.168*
Antiphon & Andocides *v.2 p.405*
Antliff, Mark & Leighten, Patricia *v.1 p.676*
Antokoletz, Elliott (Editor), et al. *v.1 p.208, p.304*
Antokoletz, Elliott *v.1 p.163, p.208, p.304*
Anton, Thomas J. *v.4 p.523*
Antonio, Sheril D. *v.6 p.329, p.340*
Antonius, George *v.6 p.582*
Antonius, Rachad *v.4 p.689*
Antony, Arthur *v.5 p.255*
Anttalainen, Tarmo *v.4 p.115*
Antunes, Antonio Lobo *v.2 p.688*
Antush, John (Editor) *v.6 p.495, p.516*
Antush, John V. (Editor) *v.6 p.495, p.505, p.516*
Anyon, Jean *v.4 p.314*
Anzaldúa, Gloria (Editor) *v.6 p.477*
Anzaldúa, Gloria . . . *v.2 p.14, v.6 p.400, p.477, p.543, p.545*
Anzovin, Steve & Anzovin, Raf *v.6 p.348*
Aoki, Keith, et al. *v.4 p.445*
Aoki, Masahiko & Saxonhouse, Gary R. (Editors) . . *v.6 p.218*
Aparicio, Frances R. *v.1 p.291, v.3 p.266*
Apel, Willi *v.1 p.176, p.179*

Apollinaire, Guillaume & Revell, Donald *v.2 p.506*
Apollinaire, Guillaume *v.1 p.726, v.2 p.506, p.507*
Apollodorus *v.2 p.407*
Apollonius, Rhodius *v.2 p.406*
Apostol, Tom (Editor), et al. *v.5 p.494*
Apostol, Tom M. (Editor) *v.5 p.485*
Apostol, Tom M. *v.5 p.465, p.475, p.486*
Apostolic *v.1 p.590*
Appel, Andrew W. *v.5 p.348*
Appel, Toby A. *v.5 p.244*
Appelbaum, Nancy P. (Editor), et al. *v.3 p.278, p.296*
Appelbaum, Nancy P. *v.3 p.357*
Appelbaum, Peter *v.4 p.308*
Appelbaum, Stanley (Editor, Translator) *v.2 p.642, p.650, p.665*
Appelbaum, Stanley (Editor) *v.2 p.198, p.642, p.645*
Appelfeld, Aharon *v.6 p.647*
Appelo, C. A. & Postma, D. *v.5 p.440*
Appenzeller, Herb & Lewis, Guy *v.4 p.882, p.900, p.905*
Appenzeller, Herb *v.4 p.882, p.886, p.900*
Appenzeller, Thomas *v.4 p.785, p.882, p.900*
Appia, Adolphe *v.1 p.138*
Appiah, Anthony & Gates, Henry Louis Jr. . . *v.3 p.278*
Appiah, Anthony *v.1 p.416, v.4 p.693*
Appiah, Kwame Anthony; Gates, Henry Louis *v.6 p.33*
Appignanesi, Lisa & Forrester, John *v.5 p.595*
Apple, James M. *v.4 p.116*
Apple, Michael, et al. *v.4 p.361*
Apple, Michael W. *v.4 p.300*
Applebaum, Wilbur *v.5 p.386, p.391*
Applebee, Arthur N. *v.4 p.294, p.361*
Applebome, Peter *v.3 p.496*
Appleby, David P. *v.1 p.208, p.291, p.364*
Appleby, Joyce Oldham *v.3 p.373*
Applegate, Celia & Potter, Pamela Maxine . *v.1 p.245, v.3 p.178*
Applegate, Celia *v.3 p.178*
Applegate, E. C. *v.2 p.7*
Appleton, Thomas H. Jr. (Editor), et al. . . . *v.3 p.511*
Appleyard, Bryan *v.5 p.400*
Apps, Jerold W. *v.4 p.319*
ApRoberts, Ruth *v.2 p.265, p.316*
Apsimon, John W. (Editor) *v.5 p.299*
Aptekar, Lewis *v.4 p.760*
Apter, David E. & Rosberg, Carl G. *v.4 p.610*
Apter, David E. *v.4 p.494, p.610*
Apuleius *v.2 p.428*
Aquila, Richard (Editor) *v.6 p.323*
Aquin, Hubert *v.2 p.540, p.733*
Aquinas, Thomas & King, Peter *v.1 p.434*
Aquinas, Thomas, et al. *v.1 p.434*
Aquinas, Thomas *v.1 p.433, p.434, p.490, p.571*
                          , v.3 p.56, v.4 p.490
Arad, Yitzhak (Editor), et al. *v.3 p.82*
Aragon *v.2 p.507*
Arango, Luis Alfredo *v.2 p.674*
Arasse, Daniel *v.1 p.735*

Arato, Andrew & Gebhardt, Eike (Editors) *v.4 p.699*
Arbeau, Thoinot *v.1 p.21*
Arbena, Joseph & LaFrance, David G. (Editors) . . . *v.3 p.266*
Arbena, Joseph L. (Compiled by) . . . *v.4 p.812, p.813, p.833*
Arberry, Arthur John (Compiled by) *v.6 p.657*
Arberry, Arthur John (Editor) *v.6 p.670*
Arberry, Arthur John *v.1 p.556, p.559, v.6 p.657, p.670*
Arbib, Michael A. *v.5 p.407*
Archdeacon, William (Editor) *v.5 p.685*
Archdiocese of São Paulo Staff *v.3 p.338*
Archer, Christon I. (Editor) *v.3 p.284*
Archer, Christon I. *v.3 p.273*
Archer, Dane & Gartner, Rosemary *v.4 p.751*
Archer, Jack H., et al. *v.4 p.463*
Archer, John & Lloyd, Barbara B. (Editors) *v.4 p.746*
Archer, John *v.5 p.651*
Archer, Margaret S. & Tritter, Jonathon Q. (Editors) . *v.4 p.688*
Archer, Mary D. & Hill, Robert (Editors) . . . *v.5 p.362*
Archer, Michael *v.1 p.676*
Archer, Stanley *v.2 p.370*
Archer, Wesley L. *v.5 p.318*
Archetti, Eduardo P. *v.3 p.347*
Archibald, Douglas N. *v.2 p.326*
Archibald, E. H. *v.1 p.725*
Archibald, Elizabeth & Edwards, A. S. G. (Editors) . *v.2 p.212*
Archibald, Zosia (Editor), et al. *v.3 p.13*
Arciniegas, German *v.3 p.403*
Arco Staff *v.5 p.244*
Ardell, Jean Hastings *v.4 p.813, p.834, p.849*
Arden, Roy, et al. *v.1 p.772*
Ardis, Ann *v.2 p.173, v.6 p.746, p.755*
Ardissino, Erminia *v.2 p.697*
Arditti, Fred D. *v.4 p.92, p.93, p.101, p.103*
Ardizzone, Maria Luisa *v.2 p.702*
Ardon, Patricia *v.3 p.301*
Ardren, Traci *v.3 p.296*
Arellano, Manuel *v.4 p.198*
Arenas, Reinaldo *v.2 p.670, v.6 p.400, p.505*
Arendell, Terry (Editor) *v.5 p.638*
Arendt, Hannah *v.1 p.651, v.2 p.598, v.3 p.82,*
                          v.4 p.491, p.497, p.509, p.718
Arens, Moshe *v.6 p.609*
Arens, Richard (Editor) *v.3 p.344*
Arensberg, Conrad Maynadier *v.4 p.41*
Arestis, Philip & Chick, Victoria (Editors) *v.4 p.241*
Arestis, Philip & Sawyer, Malcolm C. (Editors) . . *v.4 p.193*
Aretino, Pietro *v.2 p.706, p.707*
Arfken, George B. & Weber, Hans J. *v.5 p.548*
Argan, Carlo Giulio & Contardi, Bruno *v.1 p.791*
Argersinger, Peter H. *v.3 p.519*
Arghezi, Tudor *v.2 p.816*
Arguedas, Jose Maria *v.3 p.328*
Arguedas, Jose M. *v.2 p.685*
Arguedas, José Maria (Editor) *v.3 p.328*
Argueta, Manlio *v.2 p.674*

Argyle, Michael *v.5 p.581, p.611, p.632*
Argyris, Chris (Contribution by), et al. *v.4 p.176*
Argyris, Chris *v.4 p.78*
Arian, Asher & Shamir, Michal (Editors) *v.4 p.615*
Arias, Arturo *v.2 p.674*
Arias, Joan *v.2 p.650*
Arias, Ron *v.6 p.497*
Arico, Santo L. (Editor) *v.2 p.697*
Aridjis, Homero *v.2 p.666, p.667*
Ariel, Avraham & Berger, Nora Ariel *v.4 p.389*
Aries, Philippe (Editor), et al. *v.4 p.732, v.6 p.557*
Aries, Philippe *v.4 p.735*
Arieti, Silvano *v.5 p.651*
Ariew, Roger & Grene, Marjorie (Editors) *v.1 p.453*
Ariew, Roger *v.1 p.436*
Ariès, Philippe *v.4 p.742*
Arima, E. Y. *v.4 p.789*
Ariosto, Lodovico *v.2 p.707*
Ariosto, Ludovico, et al. *v.2 p.707*
Ariosto, Ludovico *v.2 p.707*
Aris, Philippe A. *v.4 p.732*
Arishima, Takeo *v.6 p.229*
Aristophanes *v.1 p.70, p.89, v.2 p.423*
Aristotle *v.1 p.56, p.70, p.88, p.89, p.426, p.494,*
                ,v.2 p.408, p.566, p.577, v.4 p.488, v.5 p.399
Ariyoshi, Sawako *v.6 p.229*
Arjomand, Said A. *v.6 p.629*
Arkes, Hadley *v.4 p.453*
Arkin, Ronald C. *v.5 p.710*
Arksey, Hilary & Knight, Peter *v.4 p.691*
Arkush, Allan *v.1 p.460*
Arkush, R. David *v.6 p.189, p.199*
Arlen, Michael J. *v.4 p.414*
Arlington, Lewis C. & Lewisohn, William *v.6 p.205*
Armah, Ayi Kwei *v.2 p.752, p.753*
Armarego, W. L. & Perrin, D. D. *v.5 p.301*
Armes, Roy *v.6 p.333*
Armitage, Allan M. & Laushman, Judy M. *v.5 p.43*
Armitt, Lucie *v.2 p.286*
Armor, David J. *v.4 p.300, p.449, v.5 p.651*
Armour, Kathleen R. *v.4 p.795, p.903*
Armour, M. A. *v.5 p.266*
Armstead, H. C. *v.5 p.362*
Armstrong, Charles K. (Editor), et al. *v.6 p.236*
Armstrong, Charles *v.6 p.236*
Armstrong, D. M. (Editor) *v.1 p.430*
Armstrong, D. M. *v.1 p.498, p.509, p.510*
Armstrong, David M. *v.1 p.496*
Armstrong, David *v.2 p.434, v.5 p.511*
Armstrong, Gary *v.4 p.813, p.867*
Armstrong, Gaylene Styve *v.6 p.276*
Armstrong, Gordon M. *v.4 p.676*
Armstrong, Howard & Brasier, Martin *v.5 p.448*
Armstrong, Isobel & Blain, Virginia (Editors) . *v.2 p.173, p.184*
Armstrong, Isobel (Editor), et al. *v.2 p.196, p.198*

Armstrong, Isobel *v.2 p.173, p.183, v.6 p.755*
Armstrong, J. Scott (Editor) *v.4 p.118*
Armstrong, Jeannette (Editor) *v.2 p.728*
Armstrong, Jeannette *v.2 p.733*
Armstrong, Jerome & Moulitsas Zúniga, Markos . . . *v.4 p.554*
Armstrong, John A. *v.4 p.494*
Armstrong, Karen *v.1 p.527*
Armstrong, Lawrence E. *v.4 p.874, p.878*
Armstrong, Louis *v.1 p.257, p.302*
Armstrong, M. A. *v.5 p.474, p.494, p.498*
Armstrong, Nancy & Tennenhouse, Leonard *v.2 p.3*
Armstrong, Nancy *v.2 p.174, p.190, p.192, p.578*
                        ,v.6 p.746, p.755, p.764
Armstrong, Regis J. & Brady, Ignatius C. (Editors) . *v.1 p.571*
Armstrong, Richard B. & Armstrong, Mary Willems . *v.6 p.311*
Armstrong, Stephen *v.4 p.118*
Armstrong, William H. *v.6 p.681*
Arnaldi, Girolamo *v.4 p.643*
Arnason, H. Horvard *v.1 p.676*
Arnaud, Claude *v.2 p.514*
Arndt, Jörg & Haenel, Christoph *v.5 p.475*
Arnesen, Peter J. & Arnesen, Eric *v.6 p.3*
Arnett, David *v.5 p.70*
Arnett, Earl, et al. *v.3 p.493*
Arnett, Ross H. *v.5 p.27*
Arnett, William, et al. *v.1 p.704, p.809*
Arnheim, Daniel D. *v.1 p.49*
Arnheim, Rudolf *v.5 p.618*
Arnim, Ludwig Achim, Freiherr von *v.2 p.596*
Arno, Stephen F. & Fiedler, Carl E. *v.5 p.31, p.36*
Arnold, A. James (Editor), et al. *v.2 p.535*
Arnold, Ben *v.1 p.165*
Arnold, Benjamin *v.3 p.161*
Arnold, Brent, et al. *v.4 p.828*
Arnold, Bruce *v.1 p.685*
Arnold, Corliss Richard *v.1 p.238*
Arnold, David & Blackburn, Stuart (Editors) *v.6 p.155*
Arnold, Denis, et. al *v.1 p.193, p.306*
Arnold, Denis *v.1 p.179, p.325*
Arnold, Dieter *v.1 p.783*
Arnold E. Davidson, Cathy Davidson (Editor) *v.2 p.734*
Arnold, Edwin T. (Editor) *v.2 p.65*
Arnold, F. T. *v.1 p.182, p.399*
Arnold, George T. *v.4 p.413*
Arnold, Jeanne E. *v.4 p.10, v.6 p.684*
Arnold, June *v.6 p.394*
Arnold, Linda *v.3 p.284*
Arnold, M. Katz *v.5 p.520*
Arnold, Matthew *v.2 p.265*
Arnold, R. Douglas *v.4 p.406*
Arnold, Robert H. *v.4 p.388*
Arnold, Roslyn *v.4 p.361*
Arnold, Stephen H. (Editor) *v.2 p.543*
Arnold, Thomas K. *v.2 p.423*
Arnold, V. I. *v.5 p.487, p.494, p.546, p.548*

Arnold, Vladimir I. *v.5 p.487*

Arnoldo Mondadori editore Staff *v.2 p.647*

Arnott, Peter D. *v.1 p.70, p.88, p.89, p.137, v.2 p.401*

Arnove, Robert F. & Torres,
Carlos Alberto (Editors) *v.4 p.313, p.338*

Arnove, Robert F. (Editor), et al. *v.4 p.313*

Arnow, Harriette Louisa Simpson *v.3 p.510*

Arnstein, H. R. & Cox, R. H. *v.5 p.115*

Arnstein, Walter L. *v.3 p.110, p.120*

Arntzen, Etta *v.1 p.661*

Arny, Linda Ray *v.5 p.274*

Aron, Raymond *v.3 p.451, v.4 p.682, p.684*

Aron, Stephen *v.3 p.512*

Aronoff, Mark & Rees-Miller, Janie (Editors) *v.2 p.559*

Aronofsky, Darren & Selby, Hubert Jr. *v.2 p.139*

Aronowitz, Stanley *v.4 p.693, p.710, p.726*

Arons, Arnold B. *v.5 p.563*

Arons, Stephen *v.4 p.297*

Aronson, Arnold *v.1 p.84, p.111, p.146*

Aronson, Elliot & Meyers, David G. *v.4 p.692*

Aronson, Elliot & Pines, Ayala M. *v.5 p.580*

Aronson, I. Michael *v.3 p.59, p.219*

Aronson, Jerrold L., et al. *v.5 p.400*

Arrabal, Fernando *v.2 p.507*

Arredondo, Gabriela F. (Editor) *v.6 p.546*

Arreola, Daniel D. (Editor) *v.4 p.381*

Arreola, Daniel D. *v.6 p.530, p.543*

Arreola, Juan José *v.2 p.667*

Arriaga, Ximena B. & Oskamp, Stuart (Editors) . . . *v.5 p.670*

Arriagada, Genaro *v.3 p.273, p.352, v.4 p.591*

Arrigo, Bruce A. & Shipley, Stacey L. *v.5 p.591*

Arrigo, Bruce A. & Williams, Christopher R. (Editors) . *v.6 p.249*

Arrington, Leonard J. *v.1 p.587*

Arrington, Robert L. (Editor) *v.1 p.415*

Arrizon, Alicia *v.6 p.516*

Arrom, Silvia M. *v.3 p.282, p.284, p.288, v.6 p.453*

Arron, Deborah L. *v.4 p.440*

Arrow, Kenneth J. (Editor), et al. *v.4 p.186*

Arrow, Kenneth Joseph & Hahn, F. H. *v.4 p.198*

Arrow, Kenneth Joseph & Intriligator, Michael D. (Volume
Editors) *v.4 p.186, p.198*

Arrow, Kenneth Joseph *v.4 p.186, p.198, p.206, p.272*

Arseneau, Mary *v.2 p.303*

Arsuaga, Juan Luis & Martínez, Ignacio *v.4 p.15*

Arsuaga, Juan Luis de *v.4 p.16*

Art, Robert J. & Cronin, Patrick M. (Editors) . . . *v.4 p.644*

Art, Robert J. & Jervis, Robert *v.4 p.625*

Art, Robert J. & Waltz, Kenneth N. *v.4 p.654*

Artaud, Antonin *v.1 p.55, p.138, v.2 p.507*

Arter, David *v.3 p.232, p.233, v.4 p.578, p.584, p.597*

Arter, Judith, et al. *v.4 p.285*

Arthur, C. J. *v.4 p.235*

Arthur, Diane *v.4 p.75*

Arthur, John *v.4 p.454*

Arthur, Michael B. (Editor), et al. *v.5 p.577*

Arthur W. Diamond Law Library, Columia University . *v.4 p.476*

Arthur, Wallace *v.5 p.159, p.161, p.190*

Artibise, A. F. *v.4 p.700, v.6 p.710*

ArtsEdge—The National Arts and
Education Network *v.4 p.359*

Artz, Frederick B. *v.3 p.67, v.6 p.576*

Arundell, Dennis *v.1 p.98, p.143, p.149, p.154*

Aruri, Naseer Hasan *v.4 p.560, p.565, p.641*

Aruz, Joan (Editor) *v.1 p.669, v.3 p.4*

Arya, Atam Parkash *v.5 p.546*

Aryanpur-Kashani, Abbas &
Aryanpur-Kashani, Manoochehr *v.6 p.669*

Asacker, Tom *v.4 p.138*

Asad, Talal (Editor) *v.4 p.4*

Asante, Molefi K. & Mazama, Ama *v.6 p.13*

Asante, Molefi Kete & Mattson, Mark T. *v.6 p.3, p.33*

Asante, Molefi Kete & Vandi, Abdulai S. *v.6 p.38*

Asante, Molefi Kete *v.6 p.13, p.634*

Asbee, Sue *v.2 p.373*

Asbury, Herbert *v.4 p.714*

Asch, Ronald G. *v.3 p.165*

Ascham, R. *v.2 p.212*

Ascheid, Antje *v.6 p.328, p.338*

Aschenbrenner, Joyce *v.1 p.5, p.14, p.17, p.19*

Ascher, Abraham *v.3 p.219, p.220*

Ascher, Marcia *v.5 p.457, p.465*

Ascher, Steven & Pincus, Edward *v.6 p.346*

Ascher, William & Hirschfelder-Ascher, Barbara . . . *v.5 p.642*

Aschheim, Steven E. *v.3 p.59*

Ascoli, Albert Russell & von Henneberg,
Krystyna (Editors) *v.3 p.201*

Ascoli, Albert Russell (ed),
Von Henneberg, Krystyna (ed) *v.3 p.201*

Ash, Irene (Editor) *v.5 p.316*

Ash, Michael & Ash, Irene (Compiled by) *v.5 p.317*

Ash, Michael & Ash, Irene *v.5 p.318*

Ash, Mitchell G. *v.5 p.595*

Ash, Rhiannon *v.2 p.444*

Ash, Robert B. & Doleans-Dade, Catherine A. . . . *v.5 p.480*

Ash, Stephen V. *v.4 p.519*

Ash, Timothy Garton *v.3 p.208, p.255*

Ashare, Alan B. (Editor) *v.4 p.862, p.870, p.871*

Ash'ari, Abu al-Hasan 'Ali ibn Isma'il &
McCarthy, Richard Joseph *v.1 p.556*

Ashbee, Andrew (Editor) *v.1 p.182, p.335*

Ashbery, John *v.2 p.57*

Ashbrook, James B. *v.5 p.632*

Ashbrook, William *v.1 p.193, p.228, p.321, p.349*

Ashby, Arved (Editor) *v.1 p.208*

Ashby, Leroy *v.3 p.455*

Ashby, LeRoy *v.4 p.712*

Ashby, Michael F. & Jones, David. R. H. *v.5 p.687*

Ashcroft, Bill (Editor), et al. *v.2 p.571*

Ashcroft, Bill, et al. *v.2 p.571, p.727*

Ashcroft *v.5 p.554*

Ashe, A.R. *v.4 p.830, p.831*

Ashenfelter, Orley C. & Card, David (Editors) . *v.4 p.186, p.187*

Asher, Catherine B. & Talbot, Cynthia *v.6 p.155*

Asher, Catherine B. *v.1 p.788*

Asher, Kenneth *v.2 p.71*

Asher, Sandra Fenichel, et al. *v.1 p.143*

Ashfar, Haleh (Editor) *v.6 p.439*

Ashfield, Andrew & de Bolla, Peter (Editors) . . . *v.1 p.479*

Ashford, Robert D. *v.5 p.316*

Ashkenas, Ronald N., et al. *v.4 p.85*

Ashley, Benedict *v.1 p.577*

Ashley, Leonard R. *v.2 p.242*

Ashley, Merrill & Kaplan, Larry *v.1 p.6*

Ashley, Michael & Contento, William G. *v.2 p.580*

Ashley, Mike (Editor) *v.2 p.579*

Ashley, Mike *v.2 p.580*

Ashley, Perry J. *v.4 p.410*

Ashley, Richard *v.3 p.281*

Ashliman, D. L. *v.2 p.584*

Ashman, Keith M. & Zepf, Stephen E. *v.5 p.70*

Ashrawi, Hanan *v.6 p.616*

Ashtiany, Julia (Editor) *v.6 p.657*

Ashton, Dore & Hare, Denise B. *v.6 p.407*

Ashton, Dore *v.1 p.778*

Ashton, Jennifer *v.2 p.3*

Ashton, John *v.1 p.628*

Ashton, Rosemary *v.2 p.275, v.6 p.749, p.760*

Ashton, T. S. *v.3 p.122*

Ashton-Warner, Sylvia (Author, Author) *v.4 p.337*

Ashton-Warner, Sylvia *v.2 p.743*

Ashtor, Eliyahu *v.6 p.584, p.596*

Ashworth, William *v.6 p.288*

Asian Women United of California Staff (Editor) . . . *v.6 p.91*

Asimakopulos, Athanasios *v.4 p.226*

Asimov, Isaac *v.5 p.391, p.394*

Asinof, Eliot *v.4 p.849*

Askeland, Donald R. & Phule, Pradeep P. *v.5 p.687*

Askew, Kelly Michelle *v.1 p.284*

ASM International Staff *v.5 p.736*

Asma, Stephen T. *v.3 p.44*

Asmis, Elizabeth *v.1 p.429*

Asmus, Ronald D. *v.4 p.639*

Aspatore Books Staff *v.4 p.75*

Aspatore Books *v.4 p.905*

Aspinwall, Lisa G. & Staudinger,
Ursula M. (Editors) *v.5 p.593, p.670*

Aspromourgos, Tony *v.4 p.218*

Assayag, Jackie & Binio, Vironique (Editors) . . . *v.6 p.145*

Assmann, Jan *v.3 p.8*

Association for Behavioral and Cognitive Therapies . *v.5 p.666*

Association for Consumer Research *v.5 p.604*

Association of College & Research Libraries:
Women's Studies Section *v.6 p.433*

Association of Official Analytical Chemists *v.5 p.267*

Association of Psychology Postdoctoral
and Internship Centers *v.5 p.675*

Association of State and Interstate Water Pollution Control
Administrators *v.6 p.294*

Assouline, Pierre *v.1 p.765*

Astaire, Fred *v.1 p.6*

Astarita, Tommaso *v.3 p.197*

Astell, Ann W. & Wheeler, Bonnie (Editors) *v.3 p.143*

Astell, Mary, et al. *v.2 p.237*

Astell, Mary *v.2 p.237*

Astill, Grenville & Langdon, John (Editors) *v.3 p.42*

Astin, A. E. *v.3 p.24*

Astin, Alan E. *v.3 p.24*

Astin, Alexander W. *v.4 p.289, p.330*

Astley, Thea *v.2 p.743, p.744*

ASTM Subcommittee E06.81 on Building
Economics Staff (Contribution by) *v.5 p.685*

Aston, Elaine & Reinelt, Janelle (Editors) *v.1 p.57, p.98*

Aston, Elaine *v.1 p.98*

Aston, T. H. & Philpin, C. H. E. (Editors) *v.3 p.42*

Aston, Trevor (Editor) *v.3 p.38*

Aston, William G. (Translator) *v.6 p.223*

Astor, Bart *v.5 p.244*

Astorga Almanza, Luis Alejandro *v.3 p.281*

Astrom, Karl J. & Wittenmark, Bjorn *v.5 p.710*

Asturias, Miguel Ángel *v.2 p.674, p.675*

Astuto, Terry A., et al. *v.4 p.324*

Aswany, Ala Al *v.6 p.657*

Atchison, Ben *v.5 p.535*

Atchity, Kenneth J. (Editor) *v.2 p.424*

Atchley, Virginia G. *v.1 p.715*

Athanasius Nikitin O Staff, et al. *v.1 p.612*

Athanassoglou-Kallmyer, Nina Maria *v.1 p.735*

Athearn, James L. *v.4 p.163*

Athearn, Robert G. *v.6 p.323*

Atherton, James S. *v.2 p.357*

Atherton, Lewis E. *v.3 p.422, p.505, p.510, p.524*

Atherton, Margaret *v.1 p.436, p.449*

Atiya, Nayra *v.6 p.634*

Atkin, Brian & Brooks, Adrian *v.4 p.112*

Atkin, Nicholas & Tallatt, Frank (Editors) *v.3 p.140*

Atkins, Cholly & Malone, Jacqui *v.1 p.6, p.31, p.32*

Atkins, Dawn (Editor) *v.6 p.366*

Atkins, E. Taylor *v.6 p.218*

Atkins, G. Pope *v.3 p.273*

Atkins, P. W. & Friedman, R. S. *v.5 p.278*

Atkins, P. W. *v.5 p.264*

Atkins, Robert *v.1 p.662*

Atkinson, A. B. & Bourguignon, F. (Editors) *v.4 p.187*

Atkinson, Brooks *v.1 p.111*

Atkinson, Charles M. *v.1 p.444*

Atkinson, Clarissa W. (Editor), et al. *v.1 p.528*

Atkinson, Clarissa W. *v.6 p.559*

Atkinson, Cliff *v.4 p.171*

Atkinson, D. & Thorndyke, M. *v.5 p.161*

Atkinson, David N. *v.4 p.535*

Atkinson, David *v.1 p.297*

Atkinson, Donald R. & Hackett, Gail *v.5 p.636*

Atkinson, Giles, et al. *v.4 p.267, v.5 p.12, p.28*

Atkinson, John H. *v.5 p.698*
Atkinson, Kendall E. & Han, Weimin *v.5 p.491*
Atkinson, Kendall E. *v.5 p.488, p.491*
Atkinson, Michael M. & Chandler, Marsha A. (Editors) . *v.4 p.586*
Atkinson, R. *v.6 p.716*
Atkinson, Rick *v.6 p.604*
Atkinson, William Illsey *v.5 p.265*
Atlas, Allan W. *v.1 p.179*
Atlas, James *v.2 p.59, p.119*
Atleson, James B. *v.4 p.120*
Atran, Scott *v.4 p.26, p.36, v.5 p.632*
Attali, Jacques *v.1 p.376*
Attar, Farid Al-Din *v.6 p.670*
Atterbury, Paul & Batkin, Maureen *v.1 p.798, p.807*
Atterbury, Paul & Wainwright, Clive (Editors) . . . *v.6 p.736*
Attia, John Okyere *v.5 p.720*
Attig, Thomas A. *v.5 p.651*
Attridge, Derek & Jolly, Rosemary (Editors) . . . *v.2 p.750*
Attridge, Derek (Editor, Translator) *v.2 p.357*
Attridge, Derek (Editor) *v.2 p.357*
Attridge, Harold W. *v.1 p.630*
Attwell, David *v.2 p.753*
Attwood, Bain & Markus, Andrew (Editors) . . . *v.4 p.624*
Atwell, John E. *v.1 p.465*
Atwood, Christopher Pratt *v.6 p.239*
Atwood, Craig D. *v.1 p.590*
Atwood, Margaret Eleanor; Weaver, Robert . . . *v.2 p.731*
Atwood, Margaret Eleanor *v.2 p.728, p.731*
Atwood, Margaret *v.2 p.728, p.734*
Atwood, Roger *v.1 p.826*
Atwood, William G. *v.2 p.499*
Au, Susan *v.1 p.5*
Aubert, Charles & Sears, Edith *v.1 p.93, p.143*
Aubert de Gaspé, Philippe *v.2 p.538*
Aubigné, Agrippa d' *v.2 p.469*
Aubin, Jean Pierre *v.5 p.493*
Aubrey, Elizabeth *v.1 p.176*
Auburn, David *v.2 p.139*
Auchincloss, Louis *v.2 p.55, v.3 p.465*
Aucoin, James L. *v.4 p.408*
Auden, W. H. & Holmes, Norman (Editors) . . . *v.2 p.198*
Auden, W. H. & Isherwood, Christopher *v.2 p.329*
Auden, W. H. & Kallman, Chester *v.2 p.329*
Auden, W. H. *v.2 p.329, p.574*
Audi, Robert & Wainwright, William J. (Editors) . . *v.1 p.522*
Audi, Robert (Editor) *v.1 p.415*
Audi, Robert *v.1 p.513*
Audoin-Rouzeau, Stephane & Becker, Annette . . . *v.3 p.78*
Audoin-Rouzeau, Stephane *v.3 p.154*
Auerbach, Alan J. & Feldstein, Martin (Editors) . . *v.4 p.187*
Auerbach, Alan J. & Feldstein, Martin *v.4 p.187*
Auerbach, Alan J. *v.4 p.187*
Auerbach, E. *v.2 p.424*
Auerbach, Emily *v.2 p.266*
Auerbach, Erich *v.2 p.448, p.572, p.703*

Auerbach, Jeffrey *v.6 p.763*
Auerbach, Jonathan *v.2 p.95*
Auerbach, Nina *v.2 p.174, p.190*
Auge, Marc *v.4 p.22*
Augen, Jeff *v.5 p.101, p.102, p.104, p.144*
Augenbraum, Harold & Olmos,
   Margarite Fernández (Editors) *v.2 p.18, v.6 p.495*
Augenbraum, Harold Fernandez & Olmos,
   Margarite Fernandez (Editors) *v.6 p.511*
Augerot, James E. *v.2 p.778*
Augspurger, Michael *v.4 p.409*
Auguet, Roland *v.3 p.22*
August, Eugene R. *v.1 p.444, v.6 p.428*
Augustae *v.3 p.29*
Augustine, Dolores L. *v.3 p.180*
Augustine (Editor) *v.1 p.592, v.2 p.429*
Augustine, Saint, Bishop of Hippo. *v.1 p.592*
Augustine *v.1 p.430, p.431, p.503, p.592
                                     , v.2 p.429, p.430, v.3 p.56*
Auhagen, Ann Elisabeth & Von Salisch,
   Maria (Editors) *v.5 p.646*
Aulen, Gustaf E. *v.1 p.634, p.641*
Auletta, Ken *v.4 p.726*
Aulich, James & Sylvestrova, Marta *v.1 p.718*
Aullón de Haro, Pedro *v.2 p.650*
Aumann, R. J. & Hart, S. R. (Editors) . . . *v.4 p.187, v.5 p.504*
Aumann, Robert J. & Hart, Sergiu (Editors) . *v.4 p.187, v.5 p.504*
Aumente, Jerome, et al. *v.4 p.403*
Aune, David E. *v.1 p.624*
Auner, Joseph & Lochhead, Judy (Editors) *v.1 p.208*
Auner, Joseph Henry *v.1 p.208, p.353*
Aunesluoma, Juhana *v.3 p.236*
Auping, Michael (Editor) *v.1 p.735*
Auping, Michael *v.1 p.730*
Aurelius, Marcus *v.1 p.428*
Aurobindo, Sri *v.1 p.534*
Auron, Yair *v.4 p.651*
Ausland, John C. *v.3 p.386*
Auslander, Philip *v.1 p.86, p.112, p.265, p.378*
Aust, Anthony *v.4 p.477*
Austen, Jane *v.2 p.266*
Austen, Roger *v.6 p.391*
Austenfeld, Thomas C. *v.2 p.62, p.83, p.120*
Austen-Leigh, James E. *v.2 p.267*
Auster, Albert & Quart, Leonard *v.6 p.321, p.340*
Auster, Paul (Editor) *v.2 p.139, p.463*
Auster, Paul *v.2 p.139, p.140*
Austerlitz, Paul *v.1 p.291, v.3 p.266, p.316*
Austin, Allan W. *v.6 p.133*
Austin, David & Alcock, Leslie (Editors) *v.6 p.555*
Austin, David R. (Editor), et al. . . . *v.4 p.783, p.829, p.842*
Austin, G. T. *v.5 p.315*
Austin, J. L. *v.1 p.445, p.489, p.510*
Austin, James & Irwin, John *v.6 p.274*
Austin, James H. *v.5 p.632*
Austin, John & Carr, James E. *v.5 p.666*

Austin, John Langshaw *v.1 p.481*
Austin, M. M. *v.3 p.20*
Austin, Mary H. *v.2 p.28*
Austin, William W. *v.1 p.276, p.324*
AustLit *v.2 p.740*
Ausubel, David P. *v.5 p.574*
Ausubel, Frederick M. (Editor), et al. *v.5 p.87, p.125*
Autenreith, Georg *v.2 p.413 v.2 p.622, p.813, v.3 p.50*
Auxter, David, et al. *v.4 p.800*
Avallone, Eugene A. & Baumeister, Theodore . . . *v.5 p.731*
Avalon, Arthur *v.1 p.534*
Avalos, Hector *v.1 p.607, v.6 p.519*
Avedon, Richard (Editor) *v.1 p.765*
Avedon, Richard *v.1 p.765*
Avena, Thomas (Editor) *v.1 p.707*
Averill, Gage *v.1 p.265, p.291, p.295*
Averill, James H. *v.2 p.322*
Avers, Charlotte J. *v.5 p.190*
Avery, Emmett Langdon *v.2 p.244*
Avery, John *v.5 p.190*
Avery, Kevin J., et al. *v.1 p.721, p.730*
Avery, Kevin *v.1 p.730*
Avery, Peter (Editor), et al. *v.6 p.629*
Avery, Thomas Eugene & Burkhart, Harold E. . . . *v.5 p.36*
Avila, Eric *v.6 p.535, p.548*
Avi-Ran, Reuven *v.6 p.605*
Avis, Paul D. L. *v.1 p.655*
Avise, John C. *v.5 p.204*
Avison, Margaret *v.2 p.733*
Avi-Yonah, Michael *v.3 p.6, v.6 p.608*
Avrich, Paul *v.3 p.215, v.4 p.324*
Awde, Nicholas *v.6 p.668*
Awiakta, Marilou *v.6 p.680, p.704*
Awolowo, Obafemi *v.6 p.71*
Awwad, Tawfiq Y. *v.6 p.658*
Axel, Brian Keith *v.6 p.153*
Axelrod, Alan *v.3 p.455, v.4 p.719*
Axelrod, Joseph *v.4 p.292*
Axelrod, Paul & Reid, John G. (Editors) *v.4 p.333*
Axelrod, Paul *v.4 p.333*
Axelrod, Robert *v.4 p.625*
Axelrod, Stephen Gould (Editor) *v.2 p.96*
Axelrod, Steven G. & Deese, Helen (Editors) . . . *v.2 p.123*
Axelrod, Steven G. *v.2 p.96*
Axford, Elizabeth C. *v.1 p.172, p.386*
Axler, Sheldon J. *v.5 p.472*
Axline, Virginia M. *v.4 p.355*
Axsom, Richard H. & Platzker, David *v.1 p.755*
Axsom, Richard *v.1 p.755*
Axson, David A. J. & Hackett Group *v.4 p.81*
Axtell, James *v.6 p.685*
Axtell, Roger E., et al. *v.4 p.57*
Axtell, Roger E. *v.4 p.56, p.58*
Ayala, Cesar J. *v.3 p.316, p.318*
Ayala, Francisco J. (Editor) *v.5 p.198*

Ayala, Francisco *v.2 p.656*
Ayalon, Ami *v.4 p.403*
Ayandele, Emmanuel Ayankanmi *v.6 p.72*
Ayckbourn, Alan *v.2 p.328*
Aycock, Wendell M. & Schoenecke, Michael (Editors) . *v.6 p.325*
Aydin, Mustafa *v.6 p.623*
Ayer, A. J. *v.1 p.416*
Ayer, Alfred Jules . . . *v.1 p.438, p.445, p.447, p.451, p.511*
Ayers, David *v.2 p.177*
Ayers, Edward L. & Mittendorf, Bradley C. (Editors) . *v.2 p.21*
Ayers, Edward L. & Willis, John C. (Editors) . . . *v.3 p.498*
Ayers, Edward L. *v.3 p.394, p.496*
Ayers, Michael *v.1 p.447*
Aylett, B. J. *v.5 p.299*
Aylmer, G. E. *v.3 p.101, p.102*
Aymé, Marcel *v.2 p.506*
Aynsley, Jeremy *v.1 p.713*
Ayorinde, Christine *v.3 p.306*
Ayotte, Benjamin *v.1 p.163, p.369*
Ayoub, Mahmoud M. *v.1 p.556*
Ayoub, Raymond *v.5 p.470*
Ayral-Clause, Odile *v.1 p.778*
Ayres, David C. & Hellier, Desmond (Editors) . . . *v.5 p.706*
Ayres, Dianne & Hansen, Timothy *v.1 p.715, p.809*
Ayres, Frank & Mendelson, Elliott *v.5 p.485*
Ayres, Frank *v.5 p.473*
Ayres, James *v.1 p.800*
Ayres, Julia *v.1 p.759*
Ayres, Robert U., et al. *v.5 p.736*
Ayres, ... *v.5 p.310*
Ayubi, Nazih *v.4 p.500*
Azbel, David *v.5 p.742*
Azeiteiro, Ulisses *v.5 p.353*
Azevedo, Celia M. *v.3 p.335*
Azevedo, Milton M. *v.2 p.635*
Azicri, Max & Deal, Elsie (Editors) *v.3 p.306, v.4 p.506*
Azicri, Max *v.3 p.306*
Azikiwe, Nnamdi *v.6 p.71*
Azodo, Ada U. & Wilentz, Gay (Editors) *v.2 p.753*
Azodo, Ada Uzoamaka (Editor) *v.2 p.543*
Azorín Catena, Elena (Translator) *v.2 p.656*
Azorin *v.2 p.656*
Azuela, Mariano *v.2 p.667*
Azuma, Eiichiro *v.4 p.570, p.572, v.6 p.131*
Azzara, Alan J. *v.5 p.534*
Azzaro, Marian, et al. *v.4 p.427*
Azzi, Maria Susana & Collier, Simon *v.1 p.291, p.347*
Azzi, Stephen *v.3 p.540*

B

Ba, Mariama *v.2 p.543*
Baal-Teshuva, Jacob *v.1 p.735*
Baark, Erik *v.4 p.421*
Baars, Bernard J. (Editor), et al. *v.5 p.612*

Baase, Sara & Van Gelder, Allen *v.5 p.336*

Baase, Sara *v.5 p.342, p.343*

Babayan, Kathryn *v.6 p.630*

Babb, Florence E. *v.3 p.328*

Babb, Howard S. *v.2 p.267*

Babb, Lawrence A. *v.1 p.534, p.539*

Babb, Lawrence *v.2 p.213*

Babbitt, Milton *v.1 p.209, p.302*

Babcock, Arthur E. *v.2 p.463*

Babel, Isaac *v.2 p.801, v.3 p.224*

Baber, Zaheer *v.3 p.73*

Babinger, Franz *v.6 p.589, p.622*

Baboian, B. & Dean, S. (Editors) *v.5 p.734*

Baboian, Robert (Editor) *v.5 p.734*

Babor, Thomas F. & Del Boca, Frances K. (Editors) . *v.5 p.516*

Babor, Thomas *v.5 p.512, p.521*

Babson, Steve *v.4 p.124*

Babu, Gutti Jogesh, 1949- *v.5 p.64*

Babur, Emperor of Hindustan *v.6 p.644*

Babuscio, Jack & Dunn, Richard M. *v.4 p.601*

Bacchelli, Gabriella (Contribution by) *v.2 p.698*

Bacchelli, Riccardo *v.2 p.713*

Bacchylides *v.2 p.408, p.409*

Bacevich, Andrew J. *v.3 p.385, p.482*

Bach, Carl Philipp Emanuel *v.1 p.188, p.399*

Bach, Gerhard (Editor) *v.2 p.60*

Bach, Johann Sebastian *v.1 p.411*

Bach, Stanley J. & Smith, Steven S. *v.4 p.532*

Bacharach, Michael *v.4 p.83*

Bachchan, Harivansh Rai *v.6 p.150*

Bachelard, Gaston *v.1 p.40, p.455*

Bachelder, Daniel F. & Hunt, Norman J. *v.1 p.396*

Bacher, John C. *v.6 p.299*

Bachman, David *v.4 p.619*

Bachman, Gregg (Editor) *v.6 p.332*

Bachman, Ronet & Schutt, Russell K. *v.6 p.246*

Bachmann, Alberto *v.1 p.159, p.388, p.396*

Bachmann, Hugo *v.2 p.602*

Bachmann, Ingeborg *v.2 p.603*

Bachmann, Marie-Laure *v.1 p.404*

Bacho, Peter *v.6 p.99*

Bachor, Hans A. & Ralph, Timothy C. *v.5 p.562*

Backer, Bill *v.4 p.428*

Backett-Milburn, Kathryn & McKie, Linda (Editors) . *v.6 p.369*

Backhaus, Jurgen G. *v.4 p.187*

Backhouse, Roger & Bateman, Bradley (Editors) . . *v.4 p.226*

Backhouse, Roger E. & Salanti, Andrea (Editors) . *v.4 p.198, p.225*

Backhouse, Roger *v.4 p.194, p.226, p.239*

Backhurst, J. R. & Harker, J. H. *v.5 p.318*

Backscheider, Paula R. & Ingrassia, Catherine . *v.2 p.171, p.189*

Backscheider, Paula R. *v.2 p.245*

Backstrom, Charles H. & Hursh-Cesar, Gerald D. . *v.4 p.697*

Baclawski, Kenneth & Niu, Tianhua *v.5 p.105*

Bacon, David *v.4 p.726*

Bacon, Edwin & Sandle, Mark (Editors) *v.3 p.228*

Bacon, Francis *v.1 p.447, v.2 p.213*

Bacon, Jean *v.6 p.110, p.138*

Bacon, Lisa *v.3 p.499*

Bacon, Mike, et al. *v.5 p.444*

Bacquart, Jean-Baptiste *v.1 p.689*

Baczynski, Krzysztof Kamil *v.2 p.789*

Bad Object-Choices Staff (Editor) *v.6 p.415*

Badaracco, Claire Hoertz (Editor) *v.4 p.719*

Badaracco, Joseph L. Jr. *v.4 p.145*

Badaracco, Joseph L. *v.4 p.53*

Badasch, Shirley A. & Chesebro, Doreen S. . . . *v.5 p.533*

Badawi, M. M. (Editor) *v.6 p.658*

Badawi, M. M. *v.6 p.658*

Badcock, Blair *v.4 p.395, v.6 p.720*

Baddeley, Alan D. (Editor), et al. *v.5 p.609*

Baddeley, Alan D. *v.5 p.609*

Baddeley, Oriana & Fraser, Valerie *v.3 p.266*

Bader, Gloria E. & Rossi, Catherine A *v.4 p.136*

Bader, Robert S. *v.3 p.524*

Bader, Sara *v.4 p.141*

Badger, Anthony J. *v.3 p.439*

Badger, R. Reid *v.1 p.280, p.323*

Badgett, M. V. Lee *v.6 p.382*

Badian, E. (Editor) *v.3 p.25*

Badian, E. *v.3 p.25, p.26*

Badiou, Alain, et al. *v.1 p.455*

Badiou, Alain *v.1 p.455, p.483*

Bado-Fralick, Nikki *v.1 p.529*

Badr, Liyana *v.6 p.658*

Badran, Margot *v.6 p.634*

Baechle, Thomas & Earle, Roger W. *v.4 p.792*

Baechle, Thomas R. & Earle, Roger W. *v.4 p.792, p.878*

Baeck, Leo *v.1 p.551*

Baehr, Peter R. & Gordenker, Leon *v.4 p.632*

Baer, Ellen D. *v.5 p.527*

Baer, Gabriel *v.4 p.700*

Baer, Hans A., et al. *v.5 p.536*

Baer, Judith A. (Editor) *v.4 p.676*

Baer, Martha, et al. *v.4 p.561*

Baer, William (Editor) *v.2 p.770*

Baer, Yitzhak *v.3 p.65*

Baetzold, Roger C. & Rossiter, Bryant W. (Editors) . *v.5 p.275*

Baez, Antonio Carmona *v.3 p.306*

Baeza-Yates, Ricardo & Ribeiro-Neto, Berthier . . *v.5 p.338*

Bagby, Lewis (Editor) *v.2 p.801*

Bagehot, Walter . . . *v.2 p.166, v.4 p.99, p.146, p.154, p.604*

Bagemihl, Bruce *v.6 p.419*

Bagenal, Fran (Editor), et al. *v.5 p.68*

Bagger, Matthew C. *v.1 p.524*

Baggett, James Alex *v.4 p.519*

Baggott, Jim *v.5 p.279, p.305*

Baghramian, Maria *v.1 p.514*

Bagley, Constance E. & Dauchy, Craig E. . . . *v.4 p.67, p.108*

Bagley, Constance E. & Savage, Diane *v.4 p.51*

Bagley, Robert (Editor) *v.1 p.669, p.692, v.4 p.8*

Bagley, Will *v.1 p.587, v.3 p.529*

Bagnall, Roger & Cribiore, Raffaella *v.3 p.10*

Bagnall, Roger S. & Derow, Peter (Editors) *v.3 p.20*

Bagnall, Roger S. & Rathbone, Dominic W. (Editors) . *v.3 p.10*

Bagnall, Roger S. *v.3 p.10, v.6 p.58, p.635*

Baha'u'llah; 'Abdu'l-Baha *v.1 p.560*

Bahn, Paul G. *v.1 p.668*

Bahri, Deepika & Vasudeva, Mary (Editors) . *v.2 p.759, v.6 p.137*

Bahrke, Michael S. & Yesalis, Charles E. . . . *v.4 p.826, p.874*

Bai, Su, et al. *v.1 p.776*

Baier, Annette C. *v.1 p.451*

Baier, Stephen *v.6 p.70*

Baierlein, Ralph *v.5 p.559*

Baigell, Matthew *v.1 p.681*

Bailar, J. C. (Editor) *v.5 p.302*

Bailey, Alfred Goldsworthy *v.3 p.534, v.6 p.684*

Bailey, Anne C. *v.6 p.3, p.37*

Bailey, Benjamin H. *v.6 p.494, p.543*

Bailey, Britt & Lappe, Marc (Editors) *v.5 p.7*

Bailey, Clinton *v.6 p.596, p.658*

Bailey, Colin B. (Author, Contribution by) *v.1 p.735*

Bailey, Colin, et al. *v.1 p.730*

Bailey, D. Sherwin *v.6 p.362, p.373*

Bailey, Dennis *v.4 p.773*

Bailey, Edward P. Jr. *v.4 p.171*

Bailey, Eric J. *v.4 p.46*

Bailey, Frankie Y. & Green, Alice P. *v.6 p.257*

Bailey, Gauvin Alexander *v.1 p.676, p.683*

Bailey, Harold (Editor) *v.6 p.629*

Bailey, J. Michael *v.6 p.380*

Bailey, Jill *v.5 p.130*

Bailey, John J. & Godson, Roy S. *v.3 p.290*

Bailey, John J. *v.3 p.290*

Bailey, Jon S. & Burch, Mary R. *v.5 p.674*

Bailey, Kathryn *v.1 p.209, p.367*

Bailey, Liberty Hyde *v.5 p.3*

Bailey, Martha J. *v.5 p.394*

Bailey, Peter *v.3 p.91, p.110, p.130,v.6 p.743, p.763*

Bailey, Richard W. *v.2 p.553*

Bailey, Robert G. *v.5 p.356, v.6 p.293*

Bailey, Ronald (Editor) *v.6 p.285*

Bailey, Ronald *v.5 p.77*

Bailey, Stephen K. *v.4 p.446*

Bailey, Sydney D. *v.4 p.632*

Bailey, Thomas A. *v.3 p.377*

Bailey, Thomas Andrew, et al. *v.3 p.379*

Bailey, Thomas Andrew *v.3 p.385*

Bailey, Wilford S., et al. *v.4 p.821*

Bailey, William G. (Editor) *v.4 p.676*

Baily, John *v.1 p.286*

Baily, Samuel L. *v.4 p.763, v.6 p.716*

Bailyn, Bernard *v.3 p.407, p.487, v.4 p.324*

Bain, Kenneth R. *v.3 p.386*

Bain, Robert (Editor) *v.2 p.22*

Bainbridge, Beryl *v.2 p.330*

Bainbridge, Timothy *v.4 p.636*

Bainbridge-Cohen, Bonnie; Mills, Margaret *v.1 p.51*

Baine, Celeste *v.4 p.870, p.903, v.5 p.740*

Baines, Anthony *v.1 p.388*

Baines, Barbara J. *v.2 p.219*

Baines, Jocelyn *v.2 p.339*

Baines, John & Malek, Jaromir *v.6 p.56*

Baines, Paul & Burns, Edward (Editors) . *v.1 p.63, p.78, p.98*

Bains, William *v.5 p.7, p.325*

Bains, Yashdip S. *v.1 p.126*

Bainton, Roland H. *v.1 p.602*

Bair, Barbara & Cayleff, Susan E. (Editors) *v.6 p.443*

Bair, Deirdre *v.2 p.105, p.332, v.5 p.595*

Baird, Forrest E. & Heimbeck, Raeburne S. *v.1 p.474*

Baird, James *v.2 p.123*

Baird, Jay W. *v.3 p.171*

Baird, Robert M. & Rosenbaum, Stuart E. *v.6 p.388*

Baird, William *v.1 p.624, p.625*

Bajac, Quentin & Caujolle, Christian *v.1 p.761*

Bajaj, Y. P. S. (Editor) *v.5 p.19, p.24*

Bajic, Vladimir B. & Wee, Tan Tin (Editors) *v.5 p.96*

Bajohr, Frank *v.3 p.82, p.171*

Bak, Joseph & Newman, D. J. *v.5 p.490*

Bakal, Yitzhak & Polsky, Howard W. *v.6 p.274*

Bakeless, John E. *v.2 p.220*

Bakeless, John Edwin *v.3 p.403*

Baken, Ronald J. & Orlikoff, Robert F. *v.5 p.518*

Baker, A. A., et al. *v.5 p.717*

Baker, A. C. *v.5 p.362, p.363*

Baker, Aaron & Boyd, Todd *v.4 p.813, p.901*

Baker, Alan R. H. (Author, Contribution by) . *v.4 p.375, p.377*

Baker, Alison *v.6 p.61, p.643*

Baker, Arthur Ernest *v.2 p.313*

Baker, Barbara A. *v.2 p.3*

Baker, C. J., et al. *v.5 p.47*

Baker, C. L. *v.2 p.555*

Baker, Carlos *v.2 p.83, p.311*

Baker, Chris & Phongpaichit, Pasuk *v.6 p.171*

Baker, David & LeTendre, Gerald K. *v.4 p.313, p.333*

Baker, David *v.1 p.403*

Baker, G. P. *v.3 p.191*

Baker, Geoffrey H. *v.1 p.791*

Baker, George P. & Smith, George D. *v.4 p.90, p.99*

Baker, George P. *v.1 p.55, v.2 p.228, v.3 p.191*

Baker, Gordon & Morris, Katherine *v.1 p.504*

Baker, Hendrik *v.1 p.146, p.149*

Baker, Herschel C. *v.1 p.98, p.143*

Baker, Ian & Laird, Thomas *v.1 p.730*

Baker, James A. III & DeFrank, Thomas M. *v.3 p.465*

Baker, James M. *v.1 p.209, p.355*

Baker, Jean H. (Editor) *v.4 p.518, v.6 p.430, p.440*

Baker, Jean-Claude & Chase, Chris *v.1 p.6*

Baker, Jonathan & Aina, Tade Akin (Editors) *v.4 p.764*

Baker, Keith Michael *v.3 p.149*

Baker, Kenneth *v.1 p.677*
Baker, Lee D. *v.4 p.4*
Baker, Leonard *v.4 p.467*
Baker, Mark & Kusel, Jonathan *v.5 p.36*
Baker, Mark C. *v.2 p.559*
Baker, Mona (Editor) *v.2 p.574*
Baker, P. Randall *v.6 p.626*
Baker, Paul *v.6 p.358*
Baker, Peter & Glasser, Susan *v.3 p.229*
Baker, Randall (Editor) *v.4 p.545*
Baker, Ray Palmer *v.2 p.728*
Baker, Ross K. *v.4 p.529, p.533*
Baker, Sheridan Warner *v.2 p.83*
Baker, Stuart E. *v.2 p.309*
Baker, Susan & Gibson, Curtis S. *v.2 p.126*
Baker, Susan S. *v.6 p.524*
Baker, Tania A., et al. *v.5 p.138*
Baker, William & Ross, J. C. *v.2 p.286*
Baker, William & Womack, Kenneth (Editors) . . *v.2 p.192, v.6 p.755*
Baker, William J. *v.4 p.813, p.831, p.869*
Baker, William *v.2 p.778, p.779*
Baker-Cristales, Beth *v.6 p.528, p.543*
Bakewell, Peter (Editor) *v.3 p.325*
Bakewell, Peter *v.3 p.323*
Bakhash, Shaul *v.6 p.632*
Bakhtin, Mikhail M. *v.2 p.472, p.570, p.797, p.801*
Bakken, Børge *v.6 p.261*
Bakken, Gordon Morris & Kindell, Alexandra (Editors) . *v.4 p.570*
Bakker, Henk *v.5 p.20, p.25*
Bakker-Arkema, F. W. (Editor), et al. . . . *v.5 p.3*
Bakr, Salwa *v.6 p.658*
Baktiari, Bahman *v.4 p.616*
Bakvis, Herman & Chandler, William M. (Editors) . *v.4 p.586*
Balachandran, M. *v.4 p.88*
Balak, Benjamin *v.4 p.268*
Balakian, Anna Elizabeth *v.2 p.460*
Balakian, Anna *v.2 p.460*
Balakian, Peter *v.2 p.113, v.4 p.651*
Balakrishnan, Gopal (Editor) *v.3 p.61*
Balakrishnan, V. K. *v.5 p.477, p.478, p.479*
Balanchine, George & Mason, Francis *v.1 p.3*
Balanchine, George, et al. *v.1 p.3, p.228*
Balanis, Constantine A. *v.5 p.728*
Balasubramanyam, V. N. *v.4 p.255*
Balawyder, A. *v.3 p.537*
Balay, Robert (Editor), et al. *v.5 p.405*
Balay, Robert (Editor) *v.5 p.405*
Balazs, Eva H. *v.3 p.185*
Balcells, Albert *v.4 p.608*
Balda, Russell P., et al. *v.5 p.165*
Baldanza, Frank *v.2 p.339*
Baldassare, Mark (Editor) *v.4 p.713*
Baldassari, Anne, et al. *v.1 p.695*

Baldassaro, Lawrence & Johnson, Dick (Editors) . . *v.4 p.823, p.830, p.849*
Baldasty, Gerald J. *v.4 p.148*
Baldauf-Berdes, Jane J. *v.1 p.378*
Balderrama, Francisco E. & Rodriguez, Raymond . . *v.6 p.528, p.535*
Balderston, Daniel & Gonzalez, Mike (Editors) . . *v.2 p.663*
Balderston, Theo (Editor) *v.4 p.237*
Balderston, Theo *v.3 p.169*
Baldez, Lisa *v.3 p.352, v.4 p.710*
Baldi, Philip *v.2 p.423*
Baldi, Pierre & Brunak, Søren *v.5 p.107*
Baldi, Pierre & Hatfield, G. Wesley . . *v.5 p.109, p.120, p.130*
Baldick, Chris *v.2 p.177, p.549*
Baldick, Christopher *v.2 p.166*
Baldick, Robert *v.2 p.494*
Baldwin, Alice Mary *v.3 p.407*
Baldwin, Anna & Hutton, Sarah (Editors) . . *v.2 p.163*
Baldwin, Charles *v.3 p.455*
Baldwin, Deborah *v.3 p.290*
Baldwin, Gordon *v.1 p.761*
Baldwin, James *v.2 p.59, v.6 p.22, p.394*
Baldwin, John W. *v.3 p.142*
Baldwin, Kate A. *v.6 p.30*
Baldwin, Michelle *v.1 p.36*
Baldwin, Nicholas & Shell, Donald (Editors) . . *v.4 p.574*
Baldwin, Peter (Editor) *v.3 p.82*
Baldwin, Stanley P. *v.2 p.681*
Baldwin, Thomas *v.1 p.445*
Bale, John & Vertinsky, Patricia A. (Editors) . . *v.4 p.813*
Bale, John *v.4 p.813, p.821, p.893, p.898*
Bales, Kevin *v.4 p.27*
Bales, Richard (Editor) *v.2 p.523*
Bales, Richard F. *v.3 p.515*
Bales, Robert F. *v.4 p.695*
Bales, Robert Freed *v.4 p.692*
Balescu, Radu *v.5 p.558*
Balfour-Paul, Jenny *v.5 p.320*
Balick, Michael J. & Cox, Paul Alan *v.5 p.15, p.16*
Balick, Michael J. (Editor), et al. . . . *v.5 p.16, p.36, p.353*
Balido, Giselle *v.6 p.491, p.521*
Baliger, V. C. & Duncan, R. R. (Editors) . . *v.5 p.20*
Balim, Cigdem (Editor) *v.4 p.616*
Balina, Marina (Editor), et al. *v.2 p.794*
Balinski, M. L. & Young, Peyton H. *v.5 p.503*
Balio, Tino *v.6 p.345*
Balka, Christie & Rose, Andy (Editors) . . . *v.6 p.373*
Ball, Alan M. *v.3 p.224*
Ball, Catherine N. *v.2 p.203*
Ball, Howard & Cooper, Phillip J. *v.4 p.467*
Ball, Howard, et al. *v.4 p.461*
Ball, Howard *v.4 p.150, p.447, p.460, p.467*
Ball, Michael S. & Smith, Gregory W. *v.4 p.690*
Ball, Philip . . . *v.1 p.710, v.4 p.691, v.5 p.264, p.291, p.313*
Ball, Robert W. D. *v.1 p.806*

Ball, Stephen J. (Editor) *v.4 p.340*
Ball, W. W. Rouse *v.5 p.468*
Ballantyne, R. M. *v.2 p.264*
Ballard, Allen *v.4 p.309*
Ballard, F. J. *v.5 p.115, p.123, p.130*
Ballard, J. G. *v.2 p.330, v.6 p.214*
Ballard, Michael B. *v.4 p.519*
Ballard, Robert D. *v.6 p.293*
Ballaster, Ros (Editor) *v.2 p.196*
Ball *v.4 p.69*
Ballenger, Cynthia (Editor) *v.4 p.361*
Ballew, Vincent *v.4 p.87*
Ballhausen, Carl Johan; Gray, Harry B. *v.5 p.303*
Ballot, Michael *v.4 p.120*
Balls-Organista, Pamela & Chun, Kevin M. (Editors) *v.6 p.121*
Ballstadt, Carl (Editor) *v.2 p.728, p.731*
Ballweg, Ruth, et al. *v.5 p.534*
Bally, A. W. & Palmer, A. R. (Editors) *v.5 p.431*
Balmaceda, Margarita Mercedes *v.4 p.597*
Balmas, Enea Henri & Giraud, Yves *v.2 p.457*
Balmer, Paul *v.1 p.257, p.327*
Balmer, Randall H. *v.4 p.720*
Balmuth, Miriam *v.2 p.555*
Balsamo, Anne *v.6 p.438*
Balsdon, J. P. V. D. *v.3 p.22*
Baltagi, Badi H. (Editor) *v.4 p.198*
Baltagi, Badi H. *v.4 p.198, p.206*
Balter, Lawrence & McCall, Robert B. *v.4 p.676*
Balter, Michael *v.4 p.12*
Balthasar, Hans Urs Von *v.1 p.571*
Balthazar, Louis *v.3 p.535*
Balthazar, Scott L. (Editor) . . . *v.1 p.193, p.228, p.364*
Baltrusaityte, Jurgita *v.2 p.773*
Baltzell, Edward Digby *v.4 p.725, p.726*
Balutansky, Kathleen M. & Sourieau, Marie-Agnes (Editors) *v.3 p.314*
Balzac, Honore de *v.2 p.485*
Balzac, Honore De *v.2 p.485*
Balzac, Honoré de & Brooks, Peter *v.2 p.486*
Balzac, Honoré de *v.2 p.485, p.486*
Balzer, Harley D. (Editor) *v.3 p.211*
Bambara, Toni Cade *v.6 p.22, p.41*
Bamber, Greg (Editor) *v.4 p.120*
Bamberger, Jeanne *v.1 p.375*
Ban, A. W. van den, et al. *v.5 p.3*
Banac, Ivo *v.3 p.246, p.247*
Banani, Amin *v.6 p.631*
Banarsidass, Motilal *v.1 p.534*
Banaszak, Ronald Sr. (Editor) *v.6 p.271*
Banchoff, Thomas F. *v.5 p.494*
Bancroft, George *v.3 p.379*
Bancroft, John (Editor) *v.4 p.746*
Bandem, I. Made & DeBoer, Frederick E. *v.1 p.21*
Bandopadhyay, Bibhutibhushan *v.6 p.150*
Bandura, Albert *v.4 p.355, p.766,v.5 p.662, p.666*

Bandyopadhyay, Sekhar *v.6 p.149*
Bandyopadhyaya, Bibhutibhushana *v.6 p.150*
Bane, Mary J. & Ellwood, David T. *v.4 p.754*
Bane, Mary Jo (Editor), et al. *v.4 p.720*
Bane, Mary Jo *v.4 p.732*
Banerjee, Subhankar *v.5 p.82*
Banerji, Christiane & Donald, 6Diana (Edited and Translated by) *v.1 p.701, p.722*
Banerji, Sures Chandra *v.1 p.15*
Banes, Sally (Editor) *v.1 p.27, p.29*
Banes, Sally (Introduction by), et al. *v.6 p.414*
Banes, Sally *v.1 p.25, p.27, p.29, p.38, p.40, v.6 p.473*
Banfield, Edward C. & Wilson, James Q. *v.6 p.722*
Bang, Herman *v.2 p.626*
Bangash, M. Y. H. & Bangash, T. *v.5 p.692*
Bangerter, Lowell A. *v.2 p.609*
Bango, Isidro G. *v.6 p.573*
Bango Torviso, Isidro Gonzalo *v.3 p.236*
Bangs, Carl *v.1 p.583*
Bangs, Lester *v.1 p.265*
Bangura, Abdul Karim, et al. *v.4 p.483, v.5 p.642*
Banham, Martin (Editor), et al. . . . *v.1 p.57, p.128, p.130*
Banham, Martin (Editor) . *v.1 p.57, p.61, p.128, p.130, p.134*
Banham, Martin, et al. *v.2 p.750*
Banham, Reyner *v.1 p.702*
Banister, Manly *v.1 p.759*
Bank, Stephen & Kahn, Michael *v.5 p.625, p.631*
Bank, Stephen A. *v.4 p.106, p.109, p.112*
Bankier, David (Editor) *v.3 p.82*
Bankier, David *v.3 p.82*
Banks, Arthur S. (Editor), et al. *v.4 p.574*
Banks, Cameron *v.5 p.77*
Banks, Christopher P. & Green, John C. (Editors) . *v.4 p.535*
Banks, Dennis & Erdoes, Richard *v.6 p.688, p.693*
Banks, J.A. *v.6 p.764*
Banks, James A. & Banks, Cherry A. McGee . *v.4 p.300, p.308*
Banks, James A. (Editor) *v.4 p.313*
Banks, John C., et al. *v.5 p.95, p.158, p.214*
Banks, R. E. (Editor) *v.5 p.308*
Banks, Russell *v.2 p.140*
Bann, Stephen *v.1 p.677, p.685, p.778*
Bannantine, Julie A., et al. *v.5 p.687*
Banner, James M. Jr. & Cannon, Harold C. . *v.4 p.346, p.356*
Banner, Stuart *v.6 p.247, p.681, p.691*
Bannon, Ann *v.6 p.394*
Bannon, Joseph J. & Busser, James A. *v.4 p.785*
Banowetz, Joseph *v.1 p.397*
Banta, Trudy W. (Editor) *v.4 p.285*
Banti, Anna *v.2 p.707*
Banti, Luisa *v.3 p.24, v.6 p.710*
Banton, Michael P. *v.3 p.48*
Banville, John *v.2 p.330*
Bao, Quang & Yanagihara, Hanya (Editors) *v.6 p.91, p.111, p.405*
Bao, Xiaolan *v.6 p.111, p.116, p.126*
Baquero, Gastón *v.2 p.670*

Author Index

Baraadah, Muohammad *v.6 p.658*

Barab, Sasha A. (Editor), et al. *v.4 p.761*

Barac, Antun *v.2 p.818*

Baraheni, Reza *v.6 p.631*

Barak, Gregg (Editor) *v.6 p.262*

Barak, Gregg *v.4 p.750*

Baraka, Amiri & Jones, LeRoi *v.1 p.280, v.6 p.3, p.29*

Baraka, Amiri Imamu & Jones, LeRoi *v.2 p.140*

Baraka, Amiri Imamu *v.1 p.280, v.2 p.140*

Barakat, Halim I. *v.6 p.591, p.606, p.658*

Barakat, Hoda *v.6 p.658*

Baral, Robert *v.1 p.26*

Baralt, Guillermo A. *v.3 p.318*

Baram, Amatzia & Rubin, Barry (Editors) *v.6 p.604*

Baram, Amatzia *v.6 p.602*

Baram, Uzi & Carroll, Lynda (Editors) *v.4 p.13*

Baran, Stanley J. & Wallis, Roger *v.4 p.412*

Baranczak, Stanislaw & Cavanagh, Clare (Editors) . *v.2 p.787*

Baranczak, Stanislaw *v.2 p.788*

Baranovitch, Nimrod *v.1 p.288*

Baranowski, Shelley O. *v.3 p.169*

Baranski, Zymunt G. (Editor) *v.2 p.721*

Barany, George *v.3 p.186*

Barany, Zoltan & Volgyes, Ivan (Editors) *v.4 p.508*

Barany, Zoltan D. *v.3 p.187*

Barany, Zoltan *v.4 p.639*

Barash, David P. & Lipton, Judith Eve . . *v.4 p.731, v.5 p.614*

Barash, David P. *v.4 p.83, v.5 p.138*

Baratay, Eric & Hardouin-Fugier, Elisabeth . *v.1 p.818, v.5 p.82*

Baratta, Joseph P. (Compiled by) *v.4 p.632*

Barauh, Sanjib *v.6 p.160*

Barb, Alwyn *v.3 p.508*

Barba, Eugenio & Savarese, Nicola (Editors) . . . *v.1 p.151*

Barbash, Ilisa & Taylor, Lucien *v.6 p.310*

Barbazette, Jean *v.4 p.177*

Barber, Benjamin R. *v.4 p.502, p.554*

Barber, Bernard & Barber, Elinor G. *v.4 p.700, p.723*

Barber, Cesar L. *v.2 p.233*

Barber, Charles *v.2 p.553*

Barber, Elinor G. *v.4 p.723*

Barber, Karin (Editor) *v.2 p.750*

Barber, Karin, et al. *v.2 p.751*

Barber, Malcolm C. *v.3 p.63, p.142*

Barber, Malcolm *v.3 p.67*

Barber, Nigel & Donnelly, K. *v.5 p.640*

Barber, Nigel *v.5 p.651*

Barber, Noel *v.6 p.173*

Barber, Stanley A. *v.5 p.52, p.356*

Barber, Stephen *v.2 p.507, v.6 p.730*

Barber, William J. *v.3 p.439, v.4 p.522*

Barberie, Peter *v.1 p.765*

Barberis, Peter *v.4 p.605*

Barbero, Alessandro *v.3 p.142, p.162*

Barbero, Ever J. *v.5 p.687*

Barbieri, Marcello *v.5 p.97, p.199*

Barbour, Hugh (Editor) *v.1 p.585*

Barbour, James Murray *v.1 p.374*

Barbour, Michael G. & Billings,
William Dwight (Editors) *v.6 p.290*

Barbour, Philippe *v.4 p.602, p.636*

Barbour, Sarah & Herndon, Gerise (Editors) *v.2 p.535*

Barbuto, Domenica M. *v.4 p.178, p.179*

Barcham, William L. *v.1 p.735*

Barchiesi, Alessandro *v.2 p.438*

Barclay, David E. & Glaser-Schmidt,
Elisabeth (Editors) *v.3 p.386*

Barclay, David E. & Weitz, Eric D. (Editors) *v.3 p.159*

Bard, Allen J. & Faulkner, Larry R. *v.5 p.284*

Bard, Jonathan B. L. (Editor) *v.5 p.159*

Bard, Jonathan B. L. *v.5 p.159*

Bard, Mitchell G. *v.3 p.387*

Bardach, John E. (Editor) *v.5 p.32*

Bardakjian, Kevork B. *v.6 p.665*

Bardal, Einar *v.5 p.687, p.734*

Bardana, Emil J. *v.5 p.354*

Bard *v.5 p.284*

Bardhan, Kalpana (Editor) *v.6 p.151*

Bardis, Panos D. *v.4 p.676*

Bardon, Jonathan *v.3 p.139*

Bareham, Tony *v.2 p.367*

Barell, John *v.4 p.346*

Barends, F. B. J. (Editor), et al. *v.5 p.698*

Barfield, Thomas (Editor) *v.4 p.3*

Barfield, Thomas J. *v.4 p.623, v.6 p.238*

Barham, Peter *v.5 p.329*

Barickman, B. J. *v.3 p.334*

Barillas, William *v.2 p.14*

Barin, Ihsan, et al. *v.5 p.285*

Baring, Anne & Cashford, Jules *v.1 p.528*

Baritz, Loren (Editor) *v.4 p.709*

Baritz, Loren *v.3 p.365*

Bar-Joseph, Uri *v.6 p.613*

Bark, Dennis L. & Gress, David R. *v.3 p.176*

Barkai, Avraham *v.3 p.179*

Barkan, Diana Kormos *v.5 p.260*

Barker, Adele Marie & Gheith,
Jehanne M. (Editors) *v.2 p.797, v.6 p.477*

Barker, Andrew (Editor) *v.1 p.175*

Barker, Barbara *v.1 p.6*

Barker, Chris *v.4 p.676*

Barker, Christine R. & Last, Rex W. *v.2 p.613*

Barker, David *v.1 p.759*

Barker, Drucilla K. & Feiner, Susan F. . . . *v.4 p.273, v.6 p.455*

Barker, Ernest *v.4 p.488*

Barker, Francis (Editor), et al. *v.2 p.727*

Barker, Harley Granville *v.2 p.228*

Barker, James *v.5 p.271*

Barker, Juliet *v.2 p.269, p.322*

Barker, Lucius Jefferson & Walters,
Ronald W. (Editors) *v.3 p.445*

Barker, Lucius Jefferson, et al. *v.6 p.31*

Barker, Nancy N. *v.3 p.141*
Barker, Pat *v.2 p.330*
Barker, Paul *v.1 p.369*
Barker, Richard H. *v.2 p.242*
Barker, Robert L. *v.5 p.670*
Barker, Rocky *v.6 p.283*
Barker, Simon & Hinds,
   Hilary (Editors) *v.1 p.63, p.74, p.94, v.2 p.201*
Barker-Benfield, G. J. *v.4 p.743, v.6 p.428*
Barkin, Kenneth D. *v.3 p.163*
Barkley, Russell A. *v.5 p.662*
Barksdale, Richard & Kinnamon, Keneth *v.2 p.18*
Barkun, Michael *v.1 p.645*
Barlach, Ernst *v.2 p.603*
Barlet, Olivier *v.6 p.333*
Barlett, Peggy F. *v.5 p.29, p.30*
Barley, Stephen R. & Kunda, Gideon *v.4 p.268*
Barling, Julian (Editor), et al. *v.5 p.580*
Barlow, David E. & Barlow, Melissa Hickman . . . *v.6 p.265*
Barlow, Frank *v.1 p.608, v.3 p.96*
Barlow, Harold & Morgenstern, Sam *v.1 p.159*
Barlow, Harold *v.1 p.159, p.228, p.235*
Barlow, Judith E. (Editor) *v.1 p.120*
Barlow, Maude & Clarke, Tony *v.6 p.299*
Barlow, Philip L. *v.1 p.587*
Barlow, Shirley A. *v.2 p.409*
Barman, Jean *v.3 p.546*
Barman, Roderick J. *v.3 p.335*
Barme, Geremie & Minford, John (Editors) . *v.6 p.196, p.212*
Barme, Geremie R. *v.1 p.735, v.6 p.199, p.201*
Barme, Geremie *v.6 p.196*
Barmé, Geremie R. *v.6 p.196*
Barnaby, Frank & Huisken, Ronald (Editors) . . . *v.4 p.655*
Barnard, Alan & Spencer, Jonathan (Editors) . . . *v.4 p.3*
Barnard, Alan *v.4 p.38, v.6 p.74*
Barnard, Chester I. *v.4 p.64*
Barnard, Harry *v.3 p.435*
Barnard, John *v.4 p.124*
Barnard, Leslie W. *v.1 p.590*
Barnard, Rita *v.2 p.131*
Barnard, Robert (Author, Author) *v.2 p.166*
Barnard, T. C. *v.3 p.133, p.137*
Barnard-King, Caroline H. *v.2 p.115*
Barner, Robert W. *v.4 p.79*
Barner-Barry, Carol & Rosenwein, Robert . *v.4 p.483, v.5 p.642*
Barnes, Djuna *v.2 p.58, p.330, v.6 p.394*
Barnes, Gina L. *v.4 p.8, v.6 p.183*
Barnes, Harry E. *v.4 p.752*
Barnes, Hubert Lloyd (Editor) *v.5 p.450*
Barnes, Ian *v.3 p.413*
Barnes, James F. *v.6 p.63*
Barnes, James G. *v.4 p.143*
Barnes, John W. & Lisle, Richard J. *v.5 p.420, p.423*
Barnes, John *v.3 p.347*
Barnes, Jonathan (Editor) *v.1 p.426, v.2 p.408*

Barnes, Jonathan *v.1 p.421, p.516*
Barnes, Julian *v.2 p.332*
Barnes, Kenneth C. *v.4 p.764*
Barnes, Linda L. & Sered, Susan Starr (Editors) . . . *v.1 p.524*
Barnes, Michael R. & Gray, Ian C. (Editors) . *v.5 p.105, p.131*
Barnes, Noreen C. & Deutsch, Nicholas (Editors) . . *v.6 p.410*
Barnes, Pamela M. & Barnes, Ian G. . *v.4 p.602, v.6 p.297, p.299*
Barnes, R. F. W. & Beard, J. B. (Editors) *v.5 p.20*
Barnes, Richard S. K. (Editor) *v.5 p.204*
Barnes, Robert F., et al. *v.5 p.20, p.24*
Barnes, Susan J., et al. *v.1 p.735*
Barnes, Timothy D. *v.2 p.428, v.3 p.29, p.30*
Barnes, Virgil & Barnes, Mildred (Editors) *v.5 p.436*
Barnet, Miguel *v.2 p.670*
Barnet, Sylvan *v.1 p.57, p.662*
Barnett, Arthur Doak *v.6 p.189*
Barnett, Correlli (Editor) *v.3 p.80, p.174*
Barnett, Correlli *v.3 p.88, p.90, p.117, p.118*
Barnett, Dave *v.5 p.723*
Barnett, George L. *v.2 p.298*
Barnett, Louise K. *v.2 p.262*
Barnett, Michael N. *v.4 p.632, p.651*
Barnett, Ola W., et al. *v.6 p.259*
Barnett, Paul, et al. *v.1 p.770*
Barnett, Raymond A., et al. *v.5 p.503*
Barnett, Robert & Akiner, Shirin (Editors) *v.6 p.240*
Barnett, Robert W. & Blumner, Jacob S. *v.2 p.564*
Barnett, S. & Cameron, R. G. *v.5 p.492*
Barnett, Steven *v.4 p.803, p.813, p.886, p.901*
Barnett, Victoria *v.1 p.581, v.3 p.82, p.171*
Barnett, Vincent *v.4 p.211, p.235, p.255*
Barnett, Vivian E. (Editor) *v.1 p.735*
Barnett, Vivian E. *v.1 p.735*
Barnett, William A. (Editor), et al. *v.4 p.198, p.206*
Barnett-Friel, Patricia *v.5 p.632*
Barney, Darin *v.4 p.503, p.590*
Barney, Robert Knight, et al. . . *v.4 p.845, p.886, p.890, p.901*
Barney, Stephen A. *v.2 p.205, p.550*
Barney, William L. (Author, Introduction by) *v.3 p.504*
Barney, William L. *v.3 p.429*
Barnhart, John D. & Riker, Dorothy L. *v.3 p.514*
Barnhart, Richard M., et al. *v.1 p.692, p.730*
Barnhill, David Landis & Gottlieb, Roger S. (Editors) . *v.6 p.288*
Barnhisel, Gregory *v.2 p.111*
Barnhurst, Kevin G. *v.4 p.409*
Barnitz, Jacqueline *v.1 p.683*
Barnouw, Adriaan Jacob (Translator) *v.2 p.622*
Barnouw, Dagmar *v.2 p.768*
Barnouw, Erik *v.6 p.308*
Barnstone, Willis (Editor, Translator) *v.2 p.642*
Barnstone, Willis *v.2 p.663*
Barnum, Barbara Stevens *v.5 p.529*
Barnum, Susan R. *v.4 p.156*
Barnwell, Janet *v.6 p.348*
Baroja, Pío *v.2 p.656*

Baroja, Pio *v.2 p.656*
Baroja y Nessi, Pío *v.2 p.656*
Barolini, Teodolinda *v.2 p.703*
Baron, Beth *v.6 p.634, p.636*
Baron, Cynthia & Carson, Diane (Editors) *v.6 p.347*
Baron, David P. *v.4 p.51*
Baron, Dennis E. *v.2 p.553*
Baron, Devorah *v.6 p.647*
Baron, Jill S. (Editor) *v.6 p.299*
Baron, John H. *v.1 p.165, p.238*
Baron, Jonathan *v.4 p.82*
Bar-On, Mordechai *v.6 p.613*
Baron, Naomi S. *v.2 p.554*
Baron, Salo W. *v.6 p.645*
Baron, Samual H. & Kollmann, Nancy S. (Editors) . *v.3 p.210*
Barondes, Samuel H. *v.5 p.659*
Barone, Diane M. & Morrow, Lesley Mandel (Editors) . *v.4 p.368*
Barone, Diane M., et al. *v.4 p.360*
Bar-Or, Oded (Editor), et al. *v.4 p.828, p.874, p.878*
Barquist, David L. *v.1 p.806*
Barr, Alan (Editor) *v.1 p.63, p.94*
Barr, Andrew *v.4 p.699*
Barr, Carol, et al. *v.4 p.882*
Barr, James *v.1 p.616, p.618, v.6 p.394*
Barr, Michael D. *v.6 p.173*
Barr, Tery Lynn *v.5 p.273*
Barr, Thomas H. *v.5 p.486*
Barr, Tony *v.6 p.347*
Barra, Allen *v.3 p.526*
Barraclough, Geoffrey . *v.1 p.572, v.3 p.56, p.67, p.161, v.6 p.568*
Barraclough, Solon L. & Ghimire, Krishna B. *v.5 p.36*
Barrand, Anthony G. *v.1 p.33*
Barranger, Milly S. *v.6 p.413*
Barrass, Robert *v.5 p.680*
Barratt, Carrie Rebora & Miles, Ellen G. *v.1 p.735*
Barrault, Jean-Louis *v.1 p.105, p.143, p.151*
Barraza, Santa C. & Herrera-Sobek, María . *v.6 p.486, p.491*
Barreca, Regina *v.2 p.195, p.585*
Barrell, Barrie R. C. *v.4 p.366*
Barrell, John *v.2 p.281*
Barreno, Maria Isabel *v.2 p.688*
Barrera, Mario *v.4 p.729*
Barrett, Andrea *v.2 p.140*
Barrett, Anthony A. *v.3 p.27*
Barrett, G. C. & Elmore, D. T. *v.5 p.328*
Barrett, Gregory *v.6 p.335*
Barrett, Jack & Abel, Eddie *v.5 p.303*
Barrett, John W. (Editor) *v.5 p.36*
Barrett, John *v.4 p.847, p.864*
Barrett, Lisa Feldman (Editor), et al. *v.5 p.611*
Barrett, Marilyn *v.5 p.211*
Barrett, P. S. & Baldry, David *v.4 p.112*
Barrett, Stanley R. *v.4 p.701*
Barrett, Thomas M. *v.3 p.212*
Barrett, William E. *v.1 p.505*

Barrès, Maurice *v.2 p.508*
Barricelli, Gian P. *v.2 p.711, p.712*
Barrie, J. M. & Phelps, William Lyon *v.2 p.269*
Barrie, J. M. *v.2 p.269*
Barringer, Janice & Schlesinger, Sarah *v.1 p.22*
Barringer, Mark Daniel *v.6 p.297*
Barrio, Raymond *v.6 p.497*
Barrios, Richard *v.6 p.315, p.415*
Barr-Melej, Patrick *v.3 p.352*
Barro, Robert J. *v.4 p.242*
Barroll, J. Leeds *v.2 p.234*
Barron, David W. *v.5 p.346*
Barron, Jerome A. *v.4 p.458*
Barron, Neil *v.2 p.580*
Barron, Stephanie *v.1 p.677*
Barros, Carlos Pestana (Editor), et al. . . *v.4 p.843, p.882, p.887*
Barrow, Christine (Editor) *v.4 p.755*
Barrow, Clyde W. *v.4 p.491*
Barrow, Colin *v.4 p.87*
Barrow, Mark V. *v.5 p.77, p.214*
Barrow, Robin *v.4 p.340*
Barrow, Steve & Dalton, Peter *v.1 p.169, p.291*
Barrutia, Richard & Schwegler, Armin *v.2 p.635*
Barry, Deborah (Editor), et al. *v.3 p.268*
Barry, John & Frankland,
     E. Gene (Editors) *v.4 p.666, v.5 p.29, v.6 p.285*
Barry, John M. *v.3 p.505*
Barry, John Michael; Barry, E. M. *v.5 p.326*
Barry, John R., et al. *v.5 p.725*
Barry, Jonathan (Editor) *v.3 p.99, p.101, p.102*
Barry Jones, R. *v.4 p.260*
Barry, Joseph (Editor) *v.2 p.499*
Barry, Kathleen L. *v.6 p.468*
Barry, Kristen Lawton, et al. *v.4 p.775*
Barry, Patrick *v.1 p.577*
Barry, Philip *v.2 p.58*
Barsalou, Lawrence W. *v.5 p.608*
Barsam, Richard M. *v.6 p.308*
Barsby, John *v.2 p.438*
Barsom, John M. & Rolfe, Stanley T. (Editors) . . . *v.5 p.687*
Barston, R. *v.4 p.645*
Bart, Benjamin F. *v.2 p.490*
Bart, Pauline B. & O'Brien, Patricia H. *v.4 p.757*
Barta, Tony (Editor) *v.6 p.314*
Bar-Tal, Daniel (Editor), et al. *v.4 p.694*
Bartali, El Houssine (Editor), et al. *v.5 p.3*
Bartecki, Adam & Burgess, John *v.5 p.303*
Bartee, Wayne C. *v.3 p.176*
Bartels, Emily C. *v.2 p.220*
Bartels, Larry M. *v.4 p.556*
Bartels, Robert *v.4 p.134*
Bartelson, Jens *v.4 p.496*
Bartenieff, Irmgard & Davis, Martha Ann *v.1 p.50*
Bartenieff, Irmgard & Lewis, D. *v.1 p.50, p.51*
Bartenieff, Irmgard, et al. *v.1 p.50*

Barter, Judith A. *v.1 p.735*
Barth, Fredrik *v.4 p.34*
Barth, Gunther *v.3 p.365*
Barth, James R., et al. *v.4 p.90*
Barth, John *v.2 p.142*
Barth, Karl *v.1 p.588, p.596, p.630, p.633, p.634, p.655*
Barth, Markus *v.1 p.630*
Barth, Roland & Barth, Markus *v.1 p.630*
Barth, Roland S. *v.4 p.324*
Barthelme, Donald *v.2 p.140*
Barthes, Roland . *v.2 p.454, p.476, p.486, p.532, p.559, p.575*
Barthold, W. *v.6 p.629*
Bartholet, Elizabeth *v.4 p.737*
Bartholomew, D. (Editor), et al. *v.5 p.20, p.25*
Bartholomew, Robert E. *v.4 p.714*
Bartkowski, John P. & Regis, Helen A. *v.5 p.670*
Bartle, Keith D. & Myers, Peter (Editors) *v.5 p.269*
Bartlett, Beatrice S. *v.4 p.617, p.619*
Bartlett, C. J. *v.3 p.119*
Bartlett, Christopher A. & Ghoshal, Sumantra . . *v.4 p.58, p.64*
Bartlett, Eugene R. *v.4 p.421*
Bartlett, Frederic Charles *v.5 p.608*
Bartlett, Irving H. *v.3 p.415, p.419*
Bartlett, John R. (Editor) *v.1 p.617*
Bartlett, John *v.2 p.226*
Bartlett, Lee *v.2 p.70*
Bartlett, Neil *v.2 p.320*
Bartlett, Norman *v.3 p.387*
Bartlett, Richard *v.5 p.229*
Bartlett, Robert Merrill *v.3 p.67, p.97*
Bartlett, Roger *v.4 p.907*
Bartlett, Thomas & Hayton, David *v.3 p.134, p.137*
Bartlett, Thomas *v.3 p.134, p.137*
Bartlett, William *v.3 p.248*
Bartley, Numan V. *v.3 p.503*
Bartley, Paula *v.4 p.604*
Bartnikas, Ray & Srivastava, K. D. *v.5 p.723*
Bartok, Bela *v.1 p.297*
Bartol, Anne M. & Bartol, Curt R. (Editors) *v.5 p.591*
Bartol, Anne M. & Bartol, Curt *v.5 p.591*
Bartol, Curt R. & Bartol, Anne M. *v.5 p.591*
Bartolini, Stefano *v.4 p.601*
Bartollas, Clemens & Wood, Frank W. *v.6 p.275*
Bartolome, Lilia I. *v.4 p.349*
Bartolozzi, Bruno *v.1 p.393, p.397*
Barton, Angela C. *v.6 p.462*
Barton, Anne *v.2 p.219, p.228*
Barton, H. Arnold *v.3 p.232, p.233, p.234*
Barton, John (Editor) *v.1 p.615, p.618*
Barton, John H., et al. *v.4 p.61*
Barton, John *v.1 p.618*
Barton, Jonathan *v.4 p.267, v.5 p.28*
Barton, Lucy *v.1 p.150*
Barton, Margaret *v.1 p.98, p.151*
Barton, Miles *v.5 p.82*

Barton, Roy *v.4 p.367*
Barton, Simon & Fletcher, R. A. (Editors) *v.3 p.237*
Barton, Simon & Fletcher, Richard (Editors) *v.3 p.65*
Bartos, F. M. *v.3 p.188*
Bartov, Omer *v.3 p.174, v.4 p.651*
Bartra, Eli (Editor, Translator) *v.1 p.705*
Bartsch, Joel A. *v.1 p.715*
Bartusiak, Marcia *v.5 p.61*
Barua, Pradeep P. *v.6 p.145*
Baruch, Bernard *v.3 p.455*
Baruess, Imants *v.5 p.612*
Barvinok, Alexander *v.5 p.497*
Barwise, J. (Editor) *v.5 p.470*
Barwise, Jon & Etchemendy, John *v.1 p.493*
Barz, Gregory F. *v.1 p.284, v.4 p.701*
Barzelay, Michael & Amajani, Babak J. *v.4 p.529*
Barzilai, Gad *v.6 p.613*
Barzun, Jacques & Taylor, Wendell H. *v.2 p.579*
Barzun, Jacques *v.1 p.193, p.310, v.2 p.460*
 . . . . *, p.575, v.4 p.289, p.292, p.330*
Bascia, Nina (Editor), et al. *v.4 p.297*
Basdevant, Jean-Louis & Dalibard, J. *v.5 p.548*
Basevski, Dimitar & Brownjohn, Alan *v.2 p.787*
Basham, Kathryn Karusaitis & Miehls, Dennis *v.5 p.667*
Basham, Richard Dalton *v.3 p.543*
Bashmakova, Isabella & Smirnova, Galina . . *v.5 p.465, p.472*
Basho, Matsuo *v.6 p.229, p.234*
Basie, Count & Murray, Albert *v.1 p.257, p.305*
Basinger, Jeanine *v.6 p.322*
Basir, Vaikkam Muhammad *v.6 p.151*
Baskerville, David *v.1 p.383*
Baskerville, Peter A. *v.3 p.544*
Baskett, Mary W. *v.1 p.755*
Baskin, Judith *v.1 p.553*
Baskin, Yvonne *v.5 p.182, p.186, p.187*
Basler, Roy P. & Sandburg, Carl *v.3 p.424*
Basolo, Fred and Ralph G. Pearson *v.5 p.304*
Basolo, Fred *v.5 p.260*
Bass, Jack & Thompson, Marilyn W. *v.3 p.455*
Bass, Jack *v.4 p.470*
Bass, Michael *v.5 p.73, p.545, p.561*
Bass, Mike *v.4 p.849*
Bass, Rick *v.2 p.140, v.5 p.169, p.220*
Bass, Thomas A. *v.6 p.140*
Bassan, M. (Editor) *v.2 p.35*
Bassanese, Fiora A. *v.2 p.722*
Bassani, Ezio (Editor) *v.1 p.689*
Bassani, Giorgio *v.2 p.713*
Bassett, John Earl *v.2 p.57*
Bassett, Mark T. (Editor) *v.2 p.128*
Bassett, Patrick F. & Thorn, Craig (Illustrators) . . *v.4 p.296*
Bassett, Thomas J. *v.6 p.69*
Bassey, Magnus O. *v.6 p.16, p.32*
Bassnett, Susan *v.2 p.574*
Basso, Keith H. *v.4 p.20, v.6 p.690*

Basso, Matthew (Editor), et al. *v.4 p.745*

Bastéa, Eleni *v.3 p.194*

Bastiat, Frederic *v.4 p.187, p.208*

Bastide, Roger *v.1 p.543, v.3 p.338*

Bastien, Joseph W. *v.3 p.323*

Basu, Amrita *v.6 p.430*

Basye, Anne *v.4 p.171*

Baszkin, Adam & Norde, Willem (Contribution by) . *v.5 p.326*

Bataille, Georges *v.1 p.455, p.466*

Bataille, Gretchen M. & Lisa, Laurie (Editors) *v.6 p.425, p.705*

Bataille, Gretchen M. & Sands, Kathleen M. . *v.6 p.476, p.705*

Bataille, Gretchen M. & Silet, Charles L. (Editors) . *v.6 p.700*

Batalden, Stephen K. & Batalden, Sandra L. *v.3 p.229*

Batatu, Hanna *v.6 p.602, p.607, p.639*

Batatu, John *v.6 p.602*

Batchelor, G. K. *v.5 p.396, p.547*

Batchelor, John Calvin *v.2 p.339*

Batchelor, John *v.2 p.305*

Batchelor, R. E. & Offord, M. H. *v.2 p.453*

Batchelor, R. E. & Pountain, Christopher J. *v.2 p.635*

Bate, Jonathan *v.2 p.278, p.322*

Bate, Keith (Editor) *v.2 p.448*

Bate, Walter Jackson *v.2 p.250, p.294*

Bateman, Bradley W. & Davis, John B. (Editors) . . . *v.4 p.226*

Bates, Craig D. & Lee, Martha J. *v.1 p.805, v.6 p.678*

Bates, Crispin *v.6 p.118, p.137*

Bates, D. R. (Editor) *v.5 p.279*

Bates, Darrel *v.3 p.76*

Bates, David R. *v.5 p.279*

Bates, Evan (Editor) *v.2 p.594*

Bates, H. E. *v.5 p.174, p.228*

Bates, Jeffrey W. & Farmer, Andrew M. (Editors) . . *v.5 p.210*

Bates, Marston *v.5 p.227, v.6 p.293*

Bates, Milton J. *v.6 p.322*

Bates, Regis & Bates, Marcus *v.5 p.723*

Bates, Regis Bud J. *v.4 p.115, v.5 p.726*

Bates, Robert & Jackson, Julia A. *v.5 p.417*

Bates, Scott *v.2 p.507*

Bates Staff *v.3 p.97*

Bates, Suzanne *v.4 p.171*

Bateson, Gregory *v.4 p.23, p.42*

Bateson, Mary Catherine *v.6 p.653*

Bateson, William *v.5 p.198*

Bathurst, R. G. *v.5 p.439*

Batibo, Herman *v.6 p.80*

Batiza, Ann *v.5 p.97, p.104, p.144, p.148*

Batra, Ravi *v.4 p.256, p.260, p.264*

Batschmann, Oskar & Groys, Boris *v.1 p.772*

Batson, Benjamin A. *v.6 p.171*

Batson, C. Daniel, et al. . . . *v.1 p.524, v.5 p.632, p.633*

Battaglia, Bruno (Editor), et al. *v.5 p.204*

Battcock, Gregory (Editor) *v.1 p.677*

Battelle, John *v.4 p.157*

Battilossi, Stefano & Cassis, Youssef (Editors) . . . *v.4 p.88*

Battiscombe, Georgina *v.2 p.303*

Battistella, Edwin L. *v.2 p.551*

Battistini, Andrea (Editor) *v.2 p.697*

Battistini, Matilde *v.1 p.709*

Battle, Michael *v.1 p.607*

Battock, Gregory *v.1 p.40*

Battye, Adrian & Hintze, Marie-Anne *v.2 p.453*

Bauccio, Michael L. (Editor) *v.5 p.687, p.731*

Bauckham, Richard J. *v.1 p.630, p.632*

Bauckham, Richard *v.1 p.628*

Baud, Michiel *v.3 p.316*

Baudelaire, Charles *v.2 p.487*

Baudez, Claude-François *v.1 p.774*

Baudrillard, Jean *v.1 p.455, p.509*

Bauer, Arnold J. *v.3 p.271*

Bauer, Brian S. *v.3 p.260*

Bauer, Carl J. *v.3 p.352*

Bauer, Caroline Feller *v.4 p.362*

Bauer, Gretchen & Taylor, Scott D. . *v.4 p.610, p.613, v.6 p.74*

Bauer, K. Jack *v.3 p.418*

Bauer, Marion Dane *v.6 p.368*

Bauer, P. T. *v.4 p.242*

Bauer, Peter T. *v.4 p.242*

Bauer, Walter *v.1 p.646*

Bauer, Wolfgang *v.6 p.181*

Bauer, Yehuda & Keren, Nili *v.3 p.82*

Bauer, Yehuda *v.3 p.82*

Baugh, Albert C. (Editor) *v.2 p.166*

Baugh, Christopher *v.1 p.146*

Baugh, Edward *v.2 p.770*

Baugh, John *v.2 p.551*

Baughman, James L. *v.4 p.409, p.417*

Baulch, D. L., et al. *v.5 p.285*

Baulch, D. L. *v.5 p.285*

Baule, Steven *v.4 p.350*

Baum, Edward J. *v.5 p.280*

Baum, Joan *v.2 p.183*

Baum, Matthew A. *v.4 p.414, p.559*

Baum, Richard *v.6 p.196*

Baum, Wilhelm & Winkler, Dietmar W. *v.1 p.569*

Bauman, Richard & Sherzer, Joel (Editors) *v.4 p.18*

Bauman, Richard (Author, Editor) *v.6 p.522*

Bauman, Richard W. *v.4 p.340*

Bauman, Thomas *v.1 p.188, p.228, p.343*

Bauman, Zygmunt *v.4 p.699*

Baumbach, Jonathan & Spielberg, Peter (Editors) . . . *v.2 p.26*

Baumeister, R. F. *v.5 p.651*

Baumeister, Roy F. *v.5 p.645*

Baumgart, Winfried *v.3 p.76*

Baumgartner, Frederic J. *v.3 p.144*

Baumol, William J. & Blinder, Alan S. *v.4 p.187*

Baurmeister, Carl Leopold *v.3 p.413*

Bausano, William (Compiled by) *v.1 p.411*

Bautista, Gloria (Editor) *v.2 p.665*

Baver, Sherrie L. *v.3 p.318*

Baviskar, Amita *v.6 p.153*

Bawden, C. R. *v.6 p.239*

Baxandall, Rosalyn Fraad & Gordon, Linda . . *v.6 p.433, p.440*

Baxevanis, Andreas D. & Ouellette,
  B. F. Francis (Editors) . . *v.5 p.99, p.101, p.102, p.103, p.104,*
                              p.115, p.138, p.145

Baxevanis, Andreas D. (Editor) *v.5 p.87, p.99, p.101,*
                                         p.102, p.110

Baxter, James K. *v.2 p.744*

Baxter, James Phinney *v.5 p.393*

Baxter, Martin W. & Rennie, Andrew J. O. *v.5 p.503*

Baxter, Marty *v.1 p.695*

Baxter, Maurice G. *v.3 p.415*

Baxter, Richard *v.1 p.649*

Bay, Christian & Walker, Charles C. *v.4 p.497*

Bay, Christian *v.4 p.515*

Bay, Edna G. *v.4 p.610, v.6 p.453*

Bayard de Volo, Lorraine *v.3 p.301*

Bayart, Jean-Francois, et al. *v.4 p.611*

Bayart, Jean-Francois *v.4 p.611, p.699*

Bayati, Abd al-Wahhab *v.6 p.658*

Bay-Cheng, Sarah *v.2 p.121*

Bayer, Ronald *v.6 p.380*

Bayerle, Gustav *v.3 p.186*

Bayertz, Kurt (Editor) *v.5 p.77*

Bayley, Amanda (Editor) *v.1 p.209, p.305*

Bayley, David H. (Editor) *v.6 p.263*

Bayley, David H. *v.6 p.262, p.263*

Bayley, Edwin R. *v.3 p.455*

Bayley, John *v.2 p.371*

Baylor, Michael G. (Editor) *v.1 p.601*

Bayly, C. A. (Author, Contribution by) *v.6 p.156*

Bayly, C. A. *v.3 p.35, p.124, v.6 p.146*

Bayly, Christopher & Harper, Tim *v.6 p.164*

Bayly, M. Brian *v.5 p.441*

Bayly, Susan *v.4 p.722, v.6 p.149, p.160*

Baym, Nina (Editor) *v.2 p.18*

Baym, Nina *v.2 p.8, v.6 p.477*

Baynes, Cary F. & Wilhelm,
  Richard (Translators) *v.6 p.183, p.207*

Baynton, Barbara *v.2 p.744*

Bay'on, Dami'an *v.1 p.683*

Bayor, Ronald H. *v.3 p.503, v.6 p.118, p.122, p.710*

Bays, Daniel H. (Editor) *v.6 p.187, p.189*

Bazalgette, Cary *v.6 p.311*

Bazant, Jan *v.3 p.288*

Bazdulj, Muharem *v.2 p.811*

Bazelon, Irwin *v.1 p.254*

Bazerman, Max H. & Neale, Margaret A. *v.4 p.74*

Bazin, Andre & Cardullo, Bert (Contribution by) . . . *v.6 p.337*

Bazin, Germain *v.1 p.674*

Bazykin, Alexander *v.5 p.187, p.189*

Bazyler, Michael J. *v.4 p.464*

Bazzana, Kevin *v.1 p.209, p.327*

Büchner, Georg *v.2 p.596*

Beach, Christopher *v.2 p.15, p.111, v.6 p.312*

Beach, David *v.6 p.77*

Beach, Milo Cleveland *v.1 p.730*

Beach, Raymond W. & O'Leary, James S. *v.6 p.265*

Beacham, Richard C. *v.1 p.72, v.2 p.425*

Beacham, Walton (Editor) *v.5 p.224*

Beachey, Will *v.5 p.536*

Beadie, Nancy & Tolley, Kimberly (Editors) *v.4 p.296*

Beadle, Richard (Editor) *v.1 p.58, p.73, p.98, v.6 p.564*

Beagon, Mary *v.2 p.440*

Beal, Merrill D. *v.3 p.525*

Beale, Howard K. *v.3 p.394, p.435*

Beale, Philip O. *v.3 p.119*

Beales, Derek *v.3 p.71, p.182*

Beals, Katherine A. *v.4 p.801, p.824, p.876*

Beals, Kevin, et al. *v.5 p.190, p.244*

Beam, Joseph (Editor) *v.6 p.406*

Beamer, Glenn *v.4 p.523*

Bean, Annemarie (Editor), et al. *v.1 p.119*

Bean, Annemarie *v.6 p.15, p.30*

Bean, Billy & Bull, Chris *v.6 p.383*

Bean, Dawn Pawson *v.4 p.868*

Bean, Jennifer M. & Negra, Diane (Editors) . . *v.6 p.328, p.332*

Bean, J.M.W. *v.3 p.68*

Bean, Michael J. & Rowland, Melanie J. *v.4 p.463*

Bean, Michael J., et al. *v.5 p.178*

Bean, Ron *v.4 p.120*

Beard, Charles A. *v.4 p.454*

Beard, Charles Austin *v.3 p.379, p.465, v.4 p.518*

Beard, David & Gloag, Kenneth *v.1 p.173*

Beard, Mary & Henderson, John *v.1 p.669, p.685*

Beard, Mary, et al. *v.1 p.531, v.3 p.22, p.23*

Beard, Roger *v.4 p.354*

Bearden, Romare & Harry Henderson *v.6 p.15, p.16*

Beardon, Alan *v.5 p.490*

Beards, P. H. *v.5 p.722*

Beardsley, Aubrey & Wilde, Oscar *v.2 p.320*

Beardsley, Edward H. *v.4 p.774*

Beardsley, Monroe C. *v.1 p.435, p.479, p.480*

Beardsmore, G. R. & Cull, J. P. *v.5 p.444*

Beare, William *v.2 p.425*

Bearman, P. (Editor) *v.1 p.553*

Bearne, Eve & Watson, Victor (Editors) *v.2 p.582*

Bearor, Bob *v.3 p.537*

Beasley, Edward *v.3 p.88, p.124*

Beasley, Faith E. & Jensen, Katharine A. (Editors) . . *v.2 p.474*

Beasley, Jeffrey S. & Miller, Gary M. *v.5 p.725*

Beasley, Maurine H. & Gibbons, Sheila J. *v.6 p.447*

Beasley-Murray, George Raymond *v.1 p.657*

Beatles, The (Performed by) *v.1 p.265, p.305, p.411*

Beaton, Cecil *v.1 p.765*

Beattie, Andrew & Ehrlich, Paul R. *v.6 p.298*

Beattie, Ann *v.2 p.140*

Beattie, Donald A. (Editor) *v.5 p.712*

Beattie, J. M. *v.3 p.123*

Beattie, Keith *v.4 p.413, v.6 p.308*

Beattie, Peter M. *v.3 p.273, p.338*

Beatty, Barbara *v.4 p.370*

Beatty, Carol A. & Barker Scott, Brenda A. *v.4 p.79*

Beatty, J. Kelly (Editor), et al. *v.5 p.68*

Beaty, Frederick L. *v.2 p.387*

Beaucage, Serge L. *v.5 p.120*

Beauchamp, K. G. *v.4 p.421*

Beauchamp, Robin *v.6 p.348*

Beauchamp, Thomas L. & Bowie, Norman E. (Editors) . *v.1 p.485*

Beauchamp, Thomas L. & Childress, James F. . . *v.1 p.485, v.5*
                                            p.511, p.674

Beauchamp, Thomas L. & Rosenberg, Alexander . . . *v.1 p.451*

Beauchamp, Tom L. *v.1 p.485*

Beauchemin, Yves *v.2 p.540*

Beaud, Michel & Dostaler, Gilles . . . *v.4 p.187, p.188, p.208*

Beaudry, Mary C. (Editor) *v.4 p.6*

Beauman, Nicola *v.2 p.345, v.6 p.401*

Beaumarchais, Jean-Pierre de et al. *v.2 p.454*

Beaumarchais, Jean-Pierre de et at. *v.2 p.454*

Beaumarchais, Jean-Pierre de, et.al. *v.2 p.454*

Beaumarchais, Pierre De *v.2 p.478*

Beaumarchais, Pierre-Augustin Caron de *v.2 p.478*

Beaumarchais *v.2 p.478*

Beaumont, Cyril W. & Idzikowski, Stanislas *v.1 p.23*

Beaumont, Cyril W. *v.1 p.3, p.22*

Beaumont, Francis & Fletcher, John *v.2 p.217*

Beaumont, Keith *v.2 p.521*

Beauregard, Robert A. *v.6 p.710*

Beaurline, Lester A. *v.2 p.219*

Beaussant, Phillippe *v.1 p.182, p.319*

Beauvoir, Simone de . *v.2 p.508, p.509,v.4 p.743, v.6 p.366, p.427*

Beaver, Frank Eugene *v.6 p.306*

Beazley, Charles Raymond *v.4 p.377*

Beazley, John D. *v.5 p.220*

Bebbington, David *v.1 p.595*

Bebey, Francis *v.1 p.284*

Beccaria, Cesare *v.6 p.249*

Beccaria, Marcella *v.1 p.695*

Becher, Anne *v.6 p.285*

Becher, Bernd & Becher, Hilla *v.1 p.765*

Becher, Matthias *v.3 p.142, p.162*

Bechert, Heinz & Gombrich, Richard F. (Editors) . . *v.1 p.564*

Bechet, Sidney *v.1 p.257, p.306*

Bechhofer, Frank & Paterson, Lindsay *v.4 p.686*

Bechtel, Robert B. & Churchman, Arza (Editors) . . . *v.5 p.587*

Beck, Aaron T., et al. *v.5 p.665*

Beck, Béatrix *v.2 p.508*

Beck, Charlotte H. *v.2 p.12*

Beck, Haig & Cooper, Jackie (Editors) *v.1 p.791*

Beck, Hermann *v.3 p.168*

Beck, J. Murray *v.3 p.542, v.4 p.589*

Beck, Jill & Reiser, Joseph C. *v.1 p.38*

Beck, John *v.2 p.135*

Beck, Lewis W. *v.1 p.460, p.461*

Beck, Lois & Keddie, Nikki R. (Editors) . . *v.6 p.458, p.468*

Beck, Lois & Nashat, Guity (Editors) *v.6 p.629*

Beck, Lynn G. & Murphy, Joseph *v.4 p.281*

Beck, Peggy V.; Walters, Anna L. ; Fransisco, Nia . *v.6 p.700*

Beck, Richard (Editor) *v.2 p.625*

Beck, Robert J. *v.3 p.318*

Beck, Ulrich & Willms, Johannes *v.4 p.261, p.267*

Becker, Carl L. *v.3 p.71, v.4 p.518*

Becker, Edwin *v.1 p.695*

Becker, Elizabeth *v.6 p.168*

Becker, Gary S. *v.4 p.253*

Becker, Gary Stanley *v.4 p.133*

Becker, Gerhold K. (Editor) *v.5 p.246*

Becker, Howard S. *v.4 p.687, p.695, p.776*

Becker, Jared *v.2 p.718*

Becker, Jasper *v.6 p.181, p.196*

Becker, Lawrence C. & Becker, Charlotte B. (Editors) . *v.1 p.483*

Becker, Lawrence C. *v.1 p.428*

Becker, Marjorie *v.3 p.290*

Becker, Robert A. *v.5 p.546*

Becker, William E. & Watts, Michael (Editors) *v.4 p.185*

Becker, William H. & McClenahan, William M. *v.4 p.88*

Beckerman, Howard S. *v.6 p.348*

Beckerman, Michael B. *v.1 p.193, p.322*

Beckerman, Michael Brim (Editor) . . . *v.1 p.194, p.209, p.333*

Beckerman, Michael (Editor) *v.1 p.193, p.322*

Becket, Fiona *v.2 p.362*

Beckett, Andy *v.3 p.352*

Beckett, John V. *v.3 p.90*

Beckett, Lucy *v.1 p.194, p.228, p.365*

Beckett, Samuel, et al. *v.1 p.91, p.94, v.2 p.333*

Beckett, Samuel *v.1 p.81, p.91, p.94,v.2 p.332,*
                                    p.333, p.509, p.510

Beckett, Sheilah *v.5 p.329*

Beckford, Ruth *v.1 p.6*

Beckford, William *v.2 p.264*

Beckman, Linda J. & Harvey, S. Marie (Editors) . . . *v.4 p.775*

Beckson, Karl E. *v.2 p.320*

Beckson, Karl (Editor) *v.2 p.320*

Becksvoort, Christian *v.1 p.803*

Beckwith, John *v.1 p.671*

Beckwith, Martha W. *v.4 p.40*

Becquer, Gustavo Adolfo *v.2 p.653*

Bedau, Hugo Adam & Cassell, Paul G. (Editors) . . . *v.4 p.567*

Bedau, Hugo Adam *v.4 p.471, v.6 p.247*

Bede *v.1 p.608, v.2 p.448, v.3 p.66*

Beder, Sharon *v.6 p.298*

Bedeski, Robert E. *v.4 p.621*

Bedier, Joseph *v.2 p.466*

Bedingfield, Brad *v.2 p.203*

Bedini, Silvio A. *v.3 p.403, p.405*

Bednar, Michael J *v.6 p.727*

Bedworth, David D. & Bailey, James E. *v.4 p.117*

Beebe, Kenneth R., et al. *v.5 p.273*

Beebe, William (Editor) *v.5 p.77, p.225*

Beecher, Donald, et al. *v.2 p.707*

Beeman, Randal S. & Pritchard, James A. *v.5 p.10*

Beeman, Richard R. *v.3 p.499*

Beemsterboer, Phyllis L., et al. *v.5 p.525*

Beemyn, Brett & Eliason, Mickey (Editors) *v.6 p.366*

Beer, David F. & McMurrey, David *v.5 p.680*

Beer, David F. (Editor) *v.5 p.680*

Beer, Ferdinand Pierre, et al. *v.5 p.687*

Beer, Gillian *v.2 p.286, p.299, v.6 p.759*

Beer, John B. (Editor) *v.2 p.278*

Beer, John B. *v.2 p.278*

Beer, John *v.2 p.238*

Beer, Lawrence Ward & Maki, John M. *v.6 p.223*

Beer, Samuel Hutchison *v.4 p.523*

Beer, William R. *v.5 p.639*

Beerbohm, Max *v.2 p.331*

Beer-Hofmann, Richard *v.2 p.603*

Beerling, D. J. & Woodward, F. I. *v.5 p.167, p.190*

Beeson, Charles H. *v.2 p.448*

Beeston, A. F. L. (Editor), et al. *v.6 p.658*

Beeston, A. F. L. *v.6 p.653*

Beetham, David *v.4 p.503*

Beethoven, Ludwig van *v.1 p.194, p.228, p.306, p.407*

Beeton, Isabella *v.6 p.746, p.761*

Beevor, Antony & Cooper, Artemis *v.4 p.581*

Beevor, Antony *v.3 p.174, p.226*

Beezley, William H. & Curcio-Nagy, Linda (Editors) . *v.3 p.266*

Beezley, William H. & Lorey, David E. (Editors) . . . *v.3 p.290*

Beezley, William H. (Editor), et al. *v.3 p.264, p.290*

Beezley, William H. *v.3 p.264*

Begel, Daniel *v.5 p.581*

Begelman, Mitchell & Rees, Martin *v.5 p.72*

Begg, David K. *v.4 p.237*

Beggs, Clive *v.5 p.361*

Begin, Menachem *v.6 p.609*

Begleiter, Henri & Kissin, Benjamin (Editors) . *v.5 p.512, p.521*

Bego, Mark *v.1 p.265, p.324, p.325*

Begon, Michael, et al. *v.5 p.183, p.187, v.6 p.290*

Behague, Gerard H. (Editor) *v.1 p.280*

Behague, Gerard *v.1 p.291*

Behan, Brendan *v.2 p.333*

Behan, Tom *v.2 p.724*

Behar, Ruth (Editor) *v.3 p.306, v.6 p.495, p.505*

Behavior Analysis (APA Division 25) *v.5 p.662*

Behavior Analyst Certification Board *v.5 p.666*

Behe, Michael J. *v.5 p.111, p.199, p.202*

Behling, Laura L. *v.6 p.366*

Behn, Aphra *v.1 p.77, p.98, v.2 p.238*

Behn, Robin *v.2 p.577*

Behr, Edward *v.3 p.250*

Behrangi, Samad *v.6 p.670*

Behrendt, Stephen C. *v.2 p.238, p.253*

Behrens-Abouseif, Doris & Vernoit, Stephen . . . *v.1 p.673*

Behrensmeyer, Anna K., et al. *v.5 p.449*

Behringer, Wolfgang *v.3 p.165*

Behrman, Greg *v.4 p.769*

Behrman, Richard E. *v.5 p.524*

Behuniak, Susan M. *v.4 p.535*

Beichelt, Frank E. *v.5 p.483*

Beichman, Arnold *v.3 p.387*

Beiderwell, Bruce *v.2 p.306*

Beidler, Peter G. *v.2 p.43*

Beidler, W. *v.1 p.418*

Beier, Anne *v.4 p.534*

Beierlein, James G., et al. *v.4 p.151*

Beik, William *v.3 p.144*

Beilin, Yossi *v.4 p.629*

Beilstein, Friedrich Konrad *v.5 p.290*

Beim, Gloria & Winter, Ruth *v.4 p.827, p.874, p.878*

Beinart, Haim & Green, Jeffrey M. *v.3 p.58, p.238*

Beinart, Haim *v.6 p.573*

Beineke, John A. *v.4 p.340*

Beinin, Joel & Lockman, Zachary *v.6 p.636*

Beinin, Joel *v.6 p.596, p.616, p.634, p.639*

Beirne, Piers *v.6 p.249*

Beirne-Smith, Mary, et al. *v.5 p.517*

Beirne-Smith, Mary R., et al. *v.5 p.517*

Beiser, Arthur & Berg, Isabel *v.5 p.547*

Beiser, Frederick C. (Editor) *v.1 p.463, v.3 p.167*

Beiser, Frederick C. *v.3 p.166, p.167*

Beisner, Robert L. *v.3 p.394, p.435*

Beit-Hallahmi, Benjamin *v.5 p.633*

Beito, David T. (Editor), et al. *v.4 p.545, v.6 p.722*

Beja, Morris & Norris, David (Editors) *v.2 p.357*

Bejan, Adrian & Jones, J. S. *v.5 p.560, p.713*

Bejan, Adrian & Kraus, Allan D. (Editors) *v.5 p.740*

Bejan, Adrian *v.5 p.692*

Bek, Anna Nikolaevna & Rassweiler, Anne Dickason . *v.3 p.224*

Beker, Avi *v.4 p.655*

Bekes, Csaba & Byrne, Malcom (Editors) *v.4 p.641*

Bekh, Olena & Dingley, James *v.2 p.777*

Bekoff, Marc & Byers, John A. (Editors) *v.5 p.614*

Bekoff, Marc (Editor) *v.5 p.54, v.6 p.285, p.290*

Belchem, John *v.3 p.110, p.130*

Belden, Jack *v.6 p.192, p.214*

Belenko, Steven R. *v.4 p.568*

Belenky, Gregory (Editor) *v.5 p.583*

Belfield, Clive R. *v.4 p.297*

Belford, Barbara *v.2 p.320*

Belgrave, Faye Z. & Allison, Kevin W. *v.6 p.32*

Belkin, Aaron & Bateman,
  Geoffrey (Editors) *v.4 p.569, v.6 p.389*

Belknap, Joanne *v.6 p.260*

Bell, Adrienne Baxter *v.1 p.735*

Bell, Alan P. & Weinberg, Martin S. *v.6 p.371*

Bell, Alan P., et al. *v.6 p.371*

Bell, Albert A. Jr. & Allis, James B. *v.1 p.419*

Bell, Catharine (Editor) *v.5 p.82, p.95, p.224*

Bell, Catherine *v.1 p.530*

Bell, Colin & Newby, Howard *v.4 p.770*

Bell, Coral *v.3 p.465*

Bell, Daniel (Editor, Afterword by) *v.3 p.445, p.465*

Bell, Daniel *v.3 p.370, v.4 p.679, p.701, p.769, p.843*
Bell, David Andrew *v.1 p.469*
Bell, Derrick *v.4 p.449*
Bell, Elizabeth (Editor), et al. *v.6 p.311*
Bell, F. G., et al. *v.5 p.421*
Bell, F. G. *v.5 p.421, p.423*
Bell, Frederic G. *v.5 p.421*
Bell, Graham *v.5 p.190*
Bell, Harold I. *v.6 p.635*
Bell, Ian A. F. *v.2 p.312*
Bell, J. Bowyer (Introduction by) *v.6 p.609*
Bell, J. Bowyer *v.4 p.657*
Bell, Janis & Willette, Thomas (Editors) . . . *v.1 p.674, p.685*
Bell, J.Bowyer *v.3 p.134, p.139*
Bell, John D. (Editor) *v.3 p.251*
Bell, Julian *v.1 p.726*
Bell, Michael Davitt *v.2 p.40*
Bell, Millicent (Editor) *v.2 p.131*
Bell, Millicent *v.2 p.228*
Bell, Morag (Editor), et al. *v.4 p.502*
Bell, P. M. *v.3 p.141, v.4 p.643*
Bell, Paul A. *v.5 p.587*
Bell, Peter D. *v.4 p.701*
Bell, Peter *v.3 p.78*
Bell, Quentin *v.2 p.392*
Bell, Roger J. *v.3 p.533*
Bell, Steve *v.4 p.117*
Bell, Susan G. & Offen, Karen M. (Editors) *v.3 p.52*
Bell, Walter F. (Compiled by) *v.6 p.179*
Bellack, Alan S. (Editor) *v.5 p.666*
Bellah, Robert N., et al. *v.3 p.366, p.370, v.4 p.720*
Bellah, Robert N. *v.1 p.541, v.3 p.365, v.4 p.719*
Bellah, Robert Neelly *v.3 p.366*
Bellamy, Alex J. & Williams, Paul *v.4 p.648*
Bellamy, Edward *v.2 p.31*
Bellamy, L J *v.5 p.270*
Bellamy, Richard & Warleigh, Alex (Editors) . *v.4 p.602, p.636*
Bellas, Ralph A. *v.2 p.303*
Bellatín, Mario *v.2 p.667*
Bellatin, Mario *v.2 p.667*
Belleau, Remy *v.2 p.471*
Beller, Steven *v.3 p.58, p.59, p.183*
Bellesiles, Michael A. *v.3 p.411*
Bellet, Michel, et al. *v.4 p.233, p.246*
Belleville, Linda L., et al. *v.1 p.657*
Belli, G. G. *v.2 p.710*
Belli, Gioconda *v.3 p.301*
Belli, Giuseppe G. *v.2 p.710*
Bellitto, Christopher M. *v.1 p.570*
Bellman, Jonathan (Editor) *v.1 p.247*
Bellman, Jonathan *v.1 p.173, p.245*
Bell-Metereau, Rebecca Louise *v.6 p.415*
Bello, Andres *v.2 p.687*
Bellofiore, Riccardo (Editor) *v.4 p.261, p.262*
Bellos, David *v.2 p.532*

Bellosi, Luciano *v.1 p.695*
Bellow, Saul *v.2 p.60*
Bellringer, Alan W. *v.2 p.43*
Bell-Villada, Gene H. (Editor) *v.2 p.681*
Bell-Villada, Gene H. *v.2 p.677, p.682*
Bellwood, Peter S. *v.4 p.13*
Bellwood, Peter *v.4 p.5*
Belmonte, Dominic *v.4 p.346*
Belo, Jane (Selected by) *v.6 p.173, p.176*
Belongia, Michael T. & Garfinkel,
  Michelle R. (Editors) *v.4 p.242*
Belsey, Catherine *v.1 p.512*
Belting, Hans *v.1 p.700, p.735*
Belton, John *v.6 p.320*
Belton, Robert *v.1 p.667*
Bely, Andrei *v.2 p.801*
Belz, Herman *v.3 p.394, p.427, v.4 p.518*
Belzoni, Giovanni Battista *v.3 p.11*
Bembo, Pietro *v.2 p.708*
Bemis, Samuel F. *v.3 p.416*
Bemis, Samuel Flagg *v.3 p.413*
Bemis, William, et al. *v.5 p.157, p.190*
Ben Jelloun, Tahar *v.2 p.543, p.544*
Benade, Arthur H. *v.1 p.374*
Ben-Ami, Shlomo *v.4 p.646, p.648*
Benari, Naomi *v.1 p.46*
Ben-Arieh, Yehoshua & Davis, Moshe (Editors) . . . *v.6 p.609*
Ben-Arieh, Yehoshua *v.6 p.609*
Benatar, Raquel; Torrecilla, Pablo; Petersen, Patricia; Benatar,
  Raquel; Torrecilla, Pablo; Petersen, Patricia *v.2 p.682*
Benavente, Jacinto *v.2 p.656*
Benbi, D. K. & Nieder, R. (Editors) *v.5 p.48*
Benbow-Pfalzgraf, Taryn *v.2 p.8*
Benchley, Robert C. *v.2 p.58*
Benda, Harry J. *v.6 p.173*
Ben-David, Joseph *v.5 p.398*
Bendavid-Val, Leah (Editor) *v.1 p.763*
Bendazzi, Giannalberto *v.6 p.307*
Bender, Carl M. & Orszag, Steven A. *v.5 p.500*
Bender, David A. *v.5 p.33, p.329*
Bender, Gary & Johnson, Michael L. *v.4 p.408, p.906*
Bender, Gerald J. *v.6 p.75*
Bender, Margaret Clelland *v.4 p.20*
Bender, Robert M. & Squier, Charles L. (Editors) . *v.2 p.198*
Bender, Steven W. *v.4 p.456*
Bender, Thomas (Editor) *v.4 p.762*
Bender, Thomas *v.3 p.379, v.4 p.770*
Bender, William N. *v.4 p.283*
Bender, Wolfgang *v.1 p.285*
Bendix, Reinhard & Lipset, Seymour Martin (Editors) . *v.4 p.723*
Bendix, Reinhard *v.4 p.682, p.684*
Bendixen, Alfred & Zilverfsmit, Annette (Editors) . *v.2 p.131*
Bendsoe, Martin P. & Siegmund, Ole *v.5 p.693*
Benech-Arnold, Roberto L. & Sanchez, Rodolfo A. . *v.5 p.20, p.47*
Benecke, Gerhard *v.3 p.163, p.182*

Benedek, Wolfgang (Editor), et al. *v.6 p.440*

Benedetti, Jean (Editor) *v.1 p.137, p.143, v.6 p.347*

Benedetti, Mario *v.2 p.675, p.686*

Benedetti, Robert L. *v.1 p.138, p.143*

Benedict, Jeff *v.4 p.813, p.853*

Benedict, Kimberley M. *v.6 p.569*

Benedict, Michael L. *v.3 p.394, p.435*

Benedict of Nursia *v.2 p.448, v.3 p.56*

Benedict, Philip *v.1 p.588, p.601, v.3 p.144*

Benedict, Robert P. *v.5 p.713*

Benedict, Ruth *v.4 p.22, v.6 p.221*

Benedict, Stephen *v.4 p.523*

Benedict, William H. *v.3 p.542*

Benedictow, Ole J. *v.3 p.42*

Benedikt, Wel *v.2 p.461*

Benesh, Rudolf; Benesh, Joan *v.1 p.38*

Benestad, Finn & Schjelderup-Ebbe, Dag . . . *v.1 p.194, p.327*

Benet, Stephen Vincent *v.2 p.60, p.61*

Benezra, Neal *v.1 p.778*

Benítez Rojo, Antonio & Maraniss, James E. *v.2 p.670*

Benítez Rojo, Antonio *v.2 p.670*

Benfey, Christopher E. G., et al. *v.2 p.37*

Benfey, Otto Theodor (Editor) *v.5 p.262*

Benfey, Otto Theodor *v.5 p.291*

Benfey, Philip *v.5 p.138*

Ben-Ghiat, Ruth *v.3 p.202*

Ben-Gurion, David *v.6 p.613*

Benhabib, Seyla *v.4 p.576, p.669*

Benichou, Paul *v.2 p.458*

Beniscelli, Alberto *v.2 p.697*

Benitez Claros, Rafael *v.2 p.642*

Benjamin, Andrew (Editor) *v.1 p.456, p.702, p.770*

Benjamin, Arthur & Quinn, Jennifer *v.5 p.478*

Benjamin, Daniel & Simon, Steven *v.4 p.562*

Benjamin, Gerald & Nathan, Richard P. . . *v.4 p.542, v.6 p.722*

Benjamin, Jules R. *v.3 p.306*

Benjamin Kissin (Editor) *v.5 p.521*

Benjamin, Lois (Editor) *v.6 p.21, p.41*

Benjamin, Ludy Jr. *v.5 p.595*

Benjamin, Ludy T. & Baker, David *v.5 p.595*

Benjamin, Ludy T. Jr. & Lowman,
   Kathleen D. (Editors) *v.5 p.675*

Benjamin, Ludy T. Jr. (Editor), et al. *v.5 p.675*

Benjamin, Patricia & Lamp, Scott P. *v.4 p.790, p.828*

Benjamin, Patricia J. & Lamp, Scott P. *v.4 p.825, p.873*

Benjamin, Roger *v.1 p.750*

Benjamin, Thomas & Wasserman,
   Mark (Editors) *v.3 p.290*

Benjamin, Thomas *v.3 p.266, p.290*

Benjamin, Walter . . . *v.2 p.488, p.575, v.3 p.158, v.6 p.709*

Ben-Jochannan, Yosef *v.6 p.9*

Benke, Arthur C. & Cushing,
   Colbert E. (Editors) *v.5 p.173, p.233, p.241*

Benko, Georges & Strohmayer, Ulf *v.4 p.377*

Benman, B. E. & Persson, L. (Editors) . *v.5 p.183, p.187, p.198*

Benmayor, Rina, et al. *v.6 p.488*

Ben-Menahem, Yemina (Editor) *v.1 p.441*

Benn, Douglas I. & Evans, David J. A. *v.5 p.424*

Benn, Gottfried *v.2 p.603*

Benn, Maurice B. *v.2 p.596*

Benn, Stanley I. *v.4 p.515*

Bennahum, Judith *v.1 p.23, p.44, p.46*

Bennahum, Ninotchka D. *v.1 p.6*

Benne, Robert *v.4 p.307*

Benner, Dietrich & Lenzen, Dieter (Editors) *v.4 p.333*

Bennet, Alex & Bennet, David *v.4 p.78*

Bennet, Clinton *v.1 p.555*

Bennett, A. LeRoy *v.4 p.632*

Bennett, Alan, et al. *v.2 p.331*

Bennett, Andrew *v.2 p.574*

Bennett, Andy *v.1 p.265*

Bennett, Arnold *v.2 p.334*

Bennett, Benjamin *v.2 p.591, p.594*

Bennett, Betty T. *v.2 p.310*

Bennett, Bruce & Strauss, Jennifer (Editors) *v.2 p.740*

Bennett, Bruce *v.2 p.740*

Bennett, Deborah J. *v.1 p.491, v.5 p.480*

Bennett, Edward M. *v.3 p.387*

Bennett, Edwin K. *v.2 p.592*

Bennett, George W. (Introduction by) *v.5 p.32*

Bennett, Gordon A. & Montaperto, Ronald N. . *v.6 p.195, p.199*

Bennett, H. S. *v.3 p.99*

Bennett, H. *v.5 p.257*

Bennett, Herman L. *v.3 p.262, p.284*

Bennett, Jeffrey O., et al. *v.5 p.64, p.73, p.190, p.242*

Bennett, Joan *v.2 p.241*

Bennett, John W. *v.4 p.29*

Bennett, Jonathan *v.1 p.435, p.449, p.477*

Bennett, Judith M. & Hollister, C. Warren *v.3 p.68*

Bennett, Lerone Jr. *v.6 p.3*

Bennett, M. K. *v.5 p.494*

Bennett, Matthew R. & Glasser, Neil F. *v.5 p.425*

Bennett, Norman R. *v.6 p.66*

Bennett, Paula Bernat *v.2 p.9, p.15*

Bennett, Peter *v.4 p.134*

Bennett, Ralph Francis *v.3 p.80*

Bennett, Robert & Estall, Robert (Editors) *v.4 p.377*

Bennett, Robert J. (Editor) *v.4 p.581*

Bennett, Roger *v.4 p.134*

Bennett, Sean J. & Simon, Andrew *v.4 p.391*

Bennett, Susan *v.1 p.138*

Bennett, Warwick & Hudson, Patrick L. (Editors) . . *v.2 p.742*

Bennett, William J. *v.3 p.465*

Bennett *v.2 p.241*

Benningsen, Alexandre A. & Wimbush, Enders S. . . *v.3 p.212*

Bennis, Warren & Biederman, Patricia W. *v.4 p.65*

Bennis, Warren (Editor), et al. *v.4 p.70*

Bennis, Warren G. & Thomas, Robert J. *v.4 p.262*

Bennis, Warren *v.4 p.70*

Bennison, George M. & Moseley, Keith . *v.4 p.375, v.5 p.441*

Benowitz, June Melby *v.6 p.458*

Bensch, Stephen P. *v.6 p.577*
Bense, Judith A. *v.4 p.10*
Bensen, Robert (Editor) *v.4 p.755, v.6 p.680*
Benshoff, Harry M. & Griffin, Sean *v.6 p.415*
Benshoff, Harry M. *v.6 p.317, p.415*
Benson, Bruce L. *v.6 p.246*
Benson, C. David (Editor) *v.2 p.207*
Benson, C. David *v.2 p.207, p.211, v.6 p.564*
Benson, Carl *v.1 p.265, p.322*
Benson, Donald C. *v.5 p.457, p.465*
Benson, Elizabeth P. *v.3 p.268*
Benson, Eugene & Conolly,
   L. W. (Editors) *v.1 p.58, p.126, v.2 p.727, p.759*
Benson, Eugene ; Conolly, L. W. *v.2 p.728*
Benson, Eugene & Toye, William (Editors) *v.2 p.729*
Benson, Harry *v.1 p.765*
Benson, Jackson J. (Editor) *v.2 p.83, p.122*
Benson, Jackson J. *v.2 p.121*
Benson, Larry D. (Editor) *v.2 p.206*
Benson, Larry D., et al. *v.2 p.207*
Benson, Larry D. *v.2 p.212*
Benson, Lee *v.3 p.490*
Benson, Michael L. & Cullen, Francis T. *v.4 p.472*
Benson, Michael T. *v.3 p.465*
Benson, Michael *v.3 p.465*
Benson, Morton *v.2 p.774*
Benson, Robert L. & Constable, Giles (Editors) . . . *v.6 p.561*
Benstock, Bernard (Editor) *v.2 p.357*
Benstock, Bernard *v.2 p.357*
Benstock, Shari & Benstock, Bernard . . . *v.2 p.357*
Benstock, Shari (Author, Editor), et al. *v.6 p.477*
Benstock, Shari (Editor) *v.2 p.8*
Benstock, Shari, et al. *v.2 p.567*
Benstock, Shari *v.2 p.131*
Benston, George J., et al. *v.4 p.88*
Benston, George J. *v.4 p.90*
Benston, Kimberly W. *v.2 p.3*
Bent, Margaret *v.1 p.179, p.322*
Bentall, Richard P. *v.5 p.660*
Bent-Goodley, Tricia B. (Editor) *v.4 p.757, v.6 p.38*
Bentham, Jeremy & Hart, H. L. A. . . . *v.1 p.444, p.491*
Bentham, Jeremy & Mill, John Stuart *v.1 p.515*
Bentham, Jeremy *v.4 p.194, p.217, p.230, p.231, p.574*
Bentley, Arthur F. *v.4 p.482*
Bentley, E. C. *v.2 p.331*
Bentley, Eric (Editor) *v.3 p.445*
Bentley, Eric *v.1 p.55, p.63, p.94, v.2 p.699*
Bentley, Gerald E. Jr. *v.2 p.226*
Bentley, Gerald Eades *v.1 p.695, v.2 p.238*
Bentley, Toni *v.1 p.27, p.29*
Benton, Charlotte *v.1 p.776*
Benton, Gregor & Hunter, Alan *v.6 p.192*
Benton, Janetta Rebold *v.1 p.671*
Benton, M. J. *v.5 p.447*
Ben-Tor, Amnon (Editor) *v.3 p.7*

Bentsur, Eytan *v.4 p.648*
Bentur, A., et al. *v.5 p.693*
Bentwich, Norman D. *v.6 p.612*
Benveniste, Luis, et al. *v.4 p.296*
Benvenisti, Meron *v.6 p.609, p.613, p.616*
Benvenuto, E. *v.5 p.693*
Benvenuto, Edoardo *v.5 p.693*
Benvie, Sam *v.5 p.36*
Benward, Bruce & Kolosick, J. Timothy *v.1 p.404*
Ben-Yehuda, Eliezer (Editor) *v.6 p.645*
Benyo, Richard *v.4 p.840, p.847, p.866*
Ben-Yosef, Eldad *v.4 p.151, p.152*
Benyuch, Oleg *v.2 p.777*
Benyukh, Ksenia *v.2 p.773*
Benyus, Janine M. *v.5 p.83, p.166*
Benz, Christine *v.4 p.93*
Benzon, William *v.5 p.618*
Ben-Zvi, Linda *v.2 p.78*
Beran, Max A. *v.5 p.183, p.186*
Berardi, Gigi *v.1 p.50*
Bercaw, Nancy *v.6 p.453*
Berceo, Gonzalo *v.2 p.645*
Bercovitch, Sacvan *v.2 p.5, v.3 p.366*
Berdahl, Robert M. *v.3 p.167*
Berdanier, Carolyn D. *v.5 p.329*
Berdiaev, Nikolai A. & Berdyaev, Nicolas *v.3 p.210*
Berdichevsky, Norman *v.2 p.559*
Bereday, George Z. & Volpicelli, Luigi (Editors) . . . *v.4 p.324*
Bereiter, Carl *v.4 p.356*
Berenbaum, May R. *v.5 p.413*
Berenbaum, Michael *v.6 p.364*
Berend-Corinth, Charlotte & Hernad, Beatrice *v.1 p.736*
Berends, Mark, et al. *v.4 p.280*
Berendzen, Richard, et al. *v.5 p.71*
Berenson, Alex . . . *v.4 p.53, p.93, p.101, p.104, p.105, p.111*
Berenstein, Rhona J. *v.6 p.317*
Berentsen, William H. (Editor) *v.4 p.383*
Beresford, John (Editor) *v.3 p.106, p.108*
Beresford, Larry & Kubler-Ross *v.5 p.531*
Beresford, M. W. *v.3 p.126*
Berestetskii, V. B., et al. *v.5 p.566*
Berezin, Mabel & Schain, Martin (Editors) *v.4 p.383*
Berezin, Mabel *v.3 p.202*
Berg, Alban *v.1 p.209, p.228, p.309, p.407*
Berg, David R. & Ferrier, Grant *v.4 p.159*
Berg, Howard C. *v.5 p.564*
Berg, Ivar *v.4 p.297*
Berg, James J. & Freeman, Chris (Editors) *v.2 p.355*
Berg, Kris & Latin, Richard *v.4 p.795*
Berg, Mary (Editor) *v.3 p.306*
Berg, Maxine *v.3 p.90, p.122, v.6 p.749*
Berg, Stephen & Mezey, Robert (Editors) *v.2 p.22*
Berg, W. & Martin, L. *v.2 p.504*
Berg, William J. & Martin, Laurey K. *v.2 p.490*
Bergad, Laird W., et al. *v.3 p.306*

Bergad, Laird W. *v.3 p.306, p.318, p.335*

Bergant, Dianne & Karris, Robert J. (Editors) *v.1 p.615*

Bergdoll, Barry *v.1 p.788*

Berge, Zane L. & Clark, Thomas A. *v.4 p.321*

Bergen, Doris L. *v.3 p.82, v.4 p.651*

Bergen, Raquel K. *v.6 p.468*

Berger, Anna Maria Busse *v.1 p.176*

Berger, Arnold S. *v.4 p.114, v.5 p.345*

Berger, Arthur A. *v.3 p.370, v.4 p.416, v.5 p.620*

Berger, Arthur Asa *v.4 p.422, p.426*

Berger, Arthur V. *v.1 p.209, p.318*

Berger, Bennett M. *v.4 p.740*

Berger, Bonnie G., et al. *v.5 p.581*

Berger, Carl *v.3 p.535*

Berger, Dina *v.3 p.290*

Berger, Iris, et al. *v.6 p.52*

Berger, John *v.6 p.287*

Berger, Karen *v.4 p.788*

Berger, Mark T. & Borer, Douglas A. *v.6 p.180*

Berger, Maurice (Editor), et al. *v.6 p.428*

Berger, Maurice *v.1 p.772*

Berger, Melvin *v.1 p.238*

Berger, Morroe, et al. *v.1 p.257, p.316*

Berger, Morroe *v.4 p.456, v.6 p.636*

Berger, Peter L. *v.4 p.679, p.719*

Berger, Raoul *v.4 p.454, p.461, p.462, p.471*

Berger, Raymond M. *v.6 p.380*

Berger, Robert W. *v.3 p.144*

Berger, Stefan *v.3 p.159*

Berger, Warren *v.1 p.714*

Bergere, Marie-Claire *v.6 p.189, p.202*

Bergeron, Bryan & Chan, Paul *v.5 p.217*

Bergeron, Bryan *v.5 p.107*

Bergeron, Paul H. *v.3 p.416*

Bergethon, P. R. *v.5 p.111*

Bergfelder, Tim (Editor), et al. *v.6 p.338*

Bergh, Albert Ellery *v.1 p.63, p.95*

Berghahn, Daniela *v.6 p.338*

Berghahn, Volker R. *v.4 p.497*

Berghahn, Volker *v.3 p.169*

Berghaus, Günter *v.1 p.84, p.95, p.106*

Bergin, Joseph *v.3 p.144*

Bergin, Thomas G., et al. *v.2 p.463*

Bergin, Thomas G. *v.2 p.701, p.705, p.712, v.6 p.564*

Bergin, Thomas Goddard *v.2 p.703*

Bergman, David *v.6 p.392*

Bergman, Ingmar *v.2 p.629*

Bergman, Paul & Berman-Barrett, Sara J. *v.4 p.473*

Bergman, Paul *v.4 p.470*

Bergmann, Barbara R. *v.4 p.273*

Bergmann, Gustav *v.1 p.511*

Bergquist, Charles (Editor), et al. *v.3 p.273*

Bergquist, Charles W. *v.3 p.357*

Bergquist, Charles *v.3 p.346, p.349, p.356, p.359*

Bergreen, Laurence *v.1 p.248, p.310, v.2 p.55, v.3 p.72*

Berg-Schlosser, Dirk & Kersting, Norbert (Editors) . . *v.6 p.716*

Bergson, Henri *v.1 p.456, p.488, v.2 p.585*

Bergstein, Mary *v.1 p.778*

Bergstrom, Abram R. (Editor) *v.4 p.239*

Bergstrom, John C., et al. *v.4 p.267, v.5 p.17*

Bergum, Vangie *v.5 p.640*

Beringer, Richard E., et al. *v.4 p.519*

Berinsky, Adam J. *v.4 p.559*

Berinstein, Paula *v.5 p.452*

Beriss, David *v.4 p.40*

Berk, Fred *v.1 p.16*

Berk, Ronald A. *v.4 p.346*

Berkeley, George *v.1 p.449, p.481*

Berkeley, Kathleen *v.6 p.430*

Berkenstadt, Jim & Cross, Charles R. *v.1 p.266, p.345*

Berkes, Niyazi *v.6 p.623*

Berkes, Ross N. *v.4 p.632*

Berkey, Jonathan P. *v.4 p.721, v.6 p.581*

Berkhofer, Robert F. Jr. *v.6 p.681, p.686, p.697, p.700*

Berkhoff, Karel C. *v.3 p.229*

Berkin, Carol & Horowitz, Leslie (Editors) *v.6 p.451*

Berkin, Carol *v.3 p.407, v.6 p.451, p.453*

Berkman, Robert I. *v.4 p.180*

Berkouwer, G. C. *v.1 p.657*

Berkowitz, Edward D. *v.4 p.754*

Berkowitz, Freda P. *v.1 p.159*

Berkowitz, Gerald M. *v.1 p.112*

Berkowitz, Joel (Editor, Translator) *v.1 p.63, p.126*

Berkowitz, Joel (Editor) *v.1 p.126*

Berkowitz, Leonard *v.5 p.611*

Berkowitz, Norbert *v.5 p.320*

Berkshire Reference Works Staff *v.4 p.834, p.843*

Berlage, Gai I. & Gerard, Charley . . . *v.4 p.803, p.834, p.849*

Berle, Adolf A. Jr. & Means, Gardiner C. . . . *v.4 p.85, p.146*

Berlekamp, Elwyn R., et al. *v.5 p.457, p.468*

Berlin, Adele *v.1 p.616, p.622*

Berlin, Brent *v.4 p.26*

Berlin, Edward A. *v.1 p.257, p.334*

Berlin, Howard M. *v.4 p.188*

Berlin, Ira (Editor), et al. *v.3 p.429*

Berlin, Ira *v.6 p.3, p.37*

Berlin, Isaiah (Editor) *v.1 p.437*

Berlin, Isaiah *v.1 p.473, v.3 p.210, v.4 p.515*

Berliner, David C. & Biddle, Bruce J. *v.4 p.324*

Berliner, David C. & Calfee,
  Robert C. (Editors) *v.4 p.356, v.5 p.571*

Berliner, Nancy *v.1 p.788*

Berliner, Paul F. *v.1 p.257, p.285*

Berlinerblau, Jacques *v.6 p.3, p.21*

Berlinghoff, William & Gouvea, Fernando *v.5 p.465*

Berlinski, David *v.5 p.485*

Berlioz, Hector *v.1 p.194, p.306, p.310, p.393*

Berlo, Janet Catherine & Phillips, Ruth . . *v.1 p.681, v.6 p.678*

Berlow, Lawrence H. *v.5 p.679*

Berlyne, D. E. (Editor) *v.5 p.618*

Berman, Emanuel (Editor) *v.2 p.570*
Berman, Evan M., et al. *v.4 p.76*
Berman, Greg & Feinblatt, John *v.6 p.269*
Berman, Harold J. *v.4 p.433*
Berman, Jeffrey *v.2 p.564*
Berman, Karen, et al. *v.4 p.91*
Berman, Larry (Editor) *v.3 p.465*
Berman, Marshall *v.6 p.709*
Berman, Paul *v.4 p.562, p.657*
Berman, Ronald *v.2 p.75, p.83*
Berman, Russell A. *v.2 p.592*
Berman, William C. *v.3 p.465*
Bermann, Karl *v.3 p.387*
Bermel, Albert (Editor, Translator) *v.2 p.464*
Bermel, Albert *v.1 p.89*
Bermeo, Nancy Gina *v.4 p.503*
Bermingham, Ann *v.1 p.724*
Bermingham, Eldredge (Editor), et al. *v.5 p.174, p.238*
Bernal, Guillermo (Editor), et al. *v.5 p.636, v.6 p.121*
Bernal, Martin *v.3 p.12, v.6 p.10, p.19*
Bernanke, Ben S. & Woodford, Michael (Editors) . *v.4 p.246*
Bernanke, Ben S., et al. *v.4 p.246*
Bernanke, Ben S. *v.4 p.213*
Bernanos, Georges *v.2 p.508*
Bernard, H. Russell *v.4 p.25*
Bernard, Ian *v.6 p.348*
Bernard, Jessie Shirley *v.4 p.738*
Bernard, Jessie *v.4 p.738*
Bernard, Jonathan W. *v.1 p.209, p.363*
Bernard of Clairvaux *v.1 p.572*
Bernard, Paul P. *v.3 p.182*
Bernard, Sheila Curran *v.6 p.309*
Bernard, Thomas J., et al. *v.6 p.249*
Bernard *v.1 p.578*
Bernardin, Susan, et al. *v.1 p.705, p.763*
Bernardoni, James *v.6 p.340*
Bernasek, S. *v.5 p.275*
Bernath, Magdalena, et al. *v.3 p.244*
Bernath, Peter F. *v.5 p.561*
Bernauer, Thomas *v.5 p.7*
Bernault, Florence *v.6 p.273*
Bernbaum, Ernest *v.2 p.187, p.198*
Bernd, Clifford A. *v.2 p.590, p.598*
Berner, Elizabeth K. & Berner, Robert A. . . . *v.5 p.312, p.441*
Berners-Lee, Tim & Fischetti, Mark *v.5 p.338, p.342*
Berney, Kate & Templeton, N. G. (Editors) . . *v.2 p.188*
Bernfeld, Betsy *v.6 p.277*
Bernhard, Michael H. *v.3 p.255*
Bernhard, Thomas *v.2 p.616*
Bernhardsen, Tor *v.4 p.386*
Bernhardt, Sarah *v.1 p.105, p.143*
Bernier, Julie N. *v.4 p.828*
Bernier, Ronald M. *v.1 p.788*
Bernot, Alain *v.5 p.101, p.103, p.138*
Berns, Nancy *v.6 p.447, p.468*

Bernstein, Barton J. *v.3 p.373*
Bernstein, Carl & Woodward, Bob . . . *v.3 p.465, v.4 p.404*
Bernstein, Deborah S. (Editor) *v.6 p.612*
Bernstein, Deborah S. *v.6 p.612*
Bernstein, Eckhard *v.2 p.589*
Bernstein, Gail L. *v.6 p.226*
Bernstein, George L. *v.3 p.117*
Bernstein, J. M. (Editor) *v.1 p.480*
Bernstein, J. M. *v.1 p.506*
Bernstein, Jane A. (Editor) *v.1 p.378, v.6 p.473*
Bernstein, Jeremy *v.5 p.542*
Bernstein, Judith R. *v.5 p.651*
Bernstein, Leonard *v.1 p.247, p.311*
Bernstein, Mark F. *v.4 p.803, p.858*
Bernstein, Matthew & Studlar, Gaylyn (Editors) . . *v.6 p.329*
Bernstein, Nina *v.4 p.757*
Bernstein, Peter L. &
   Damodaran, Aswath (Editors) *v.4 p.94, p.162*
Bernstein, Peter L. . . . *v.4 p.91, p.92, p.93, p.94, p.99, p.162*
Bernstein, Richard J. *v.1 p.443*
Bernstein, Richard *v.6 p.196, p.202*
Bernstein, Ruth *v.5 p.93, p.183, p.187*
Bernthal, John E. & Bankson, Nicholas W. . . *v.5 p.665, p.673*
Bernus, P. (Editor), et al. *v.4 p.114*
Beroul *v.2 p.466*
Berra, Tim M. *v.5 p.190*
Berrar, Daniel P. (Editor), et al. *v.5 p.103, p.110*
Berrett, Joshua *v.1 p.257, p.302, p.368*
Berrick, A. J. & Keating, M. E. *v.5 p.473*
Berridge, G. R. (Editor), et al. *v.4 p.645*
Berridge, G. R. *v.4 p.645*
Berrill, Kevin T. (Author, Editor) . . *v.4 p.568, p.751, v.6 p.386*
Berring *v.4 p.439*
Berrizbeitia, Anita *v.1 p.815*
Berry, A. & Radford, S. (Editors) *v.5 p.115*
Berry, Anthony J., et al. *v.4 p.72*
Berry, Brian J.L. & Wheeler, James (Editors) . *v.4 p.381, v.6 p.720*
Berry, Chris *v.6 p.207, p.328, p.334*
Berry, Christopher J. & Farquhar, Mary Ann . . . *v.6 p.207*
Berry, Chuck *v.1 p.266, p.311*
Berry, Edward I. *v.2 p.233*
Berry, John D. *v.1 p.801*
Berry, L. G. *v.5 p.435*
Berry, Laura *v.2 p.174, p.190*
Berry, Lloyd E. & Crummey, Robert O. (Editors) . . *v.3 p.214*
Berry, Mary E. *v.6 p.226*
Berry, Mary F. & Blassingame, John W. *v.6 p.3*
Berry, Mary Frances *v.6 p.3*
Berry, Michael W. & Browne, Murray *v.5 p.338*
Berry, Michael W. (Editor) . . . *v.5 p.337, p.338, p.341*
Berry, Neil *v.4 p.403*
Berry, Nicholas O. *v.4 p.670*
Berry, R. J. *v.5 p.175, p.236*
Berry, R. Stephen, et al. *v.5 p.275*
Berry, R. Stephen *v.5 p.559*

Berry, Ralph	*v.2 p.235*
Berry, Richard & Burnell, James	***v.5 p.65***
Berry, Sara	***v.6 p.69, p.71***
Berry, Wallace	***v.1 p.369***
Berry, Wendell	*v.2 p.141, v.5 p.3, p.29*
Berry, William E.	***v.4 p.405***
Berryman, Alan A.	*v.5 p.183, p.187*
Berryman, Jack W. & Park, Roberta J. (Editors)	*v.4 p.803, p.825, p.873*
Berryman, John	*v.2 p.36, p.61*
Bersoff, Donald N. (Editor)	*v.5 p.674*
Berson, Jerome A.	*v.5 p.262*
Bertaud, Jean-Paul	*v.3 p.149*
Bertensson, Sergei & Leyda, Jay	*v.1 p.209, p.350*
Berthelot, Yves (Editor)	*v.4 p.633, p.663*
Berthold, Peter, et al.	*v.5 p.214*
Berto, Frank J.	*v.4 p.856*
Bertola, Giuseppe, et al.	*v.4 p.252, p.253*
Berton, Pierre	*v.3 p.416, p.533, p.534, p.537*
Bertonasco, Marc	*v.2 p.242*
Bertram, Christopher (Translator)	*v.1 p.454*
Bertram, Eva, et al.	*v.4 p.568*
Bertrand, Ina (Editor)	*v.6 p.337*
Bertrand, Jean-Pierre; Vrydaghs, David	*v.2 p.535*
Bertrand, Michael T.	*v.1 p.266, p.348*
Bertsch, Gary K. (Editor)	*v.4 p.623*
Bertsekas, Dimitri P.	*v.5 p.492*
Berube, Allan	*v.6 p.364, p.389*
Berube, Michael & Nelson, Cary (Editors)	*v.4 p.330*
Berwanger, Eugene H.	*v.4 p.565*
Bery, Ashok & Murray, Patricia (Editors)	*v.2 p.727*
Berys, Gaut & Dominic, Mover Lopes	*v.1 p.479*
Berzon, Betty	*v.6 p.374*
Beschloss, Michael R. & American Heritage Magazine Staff (Editors)	*v.3 p.377*
Beschloss, Michael R. & Talbott, Strobe	*v.4 p.643, p.645*
Beschloss, Michael R.	*v.3 p.439, p.455*
Beschloss, Michael	*v.3 p.455, p.465*
Besen, Wayne R. (Author, Editor)	*v.6 p.372*
Besner, Hilda F. & Spungin, Charlotte I.	*v.4 p.309, v.6 p.384*
Besnier, Niko	*v.4 p.21*
Bess, Michael D.	*v.3 p.156*
Besse, Susan K.	*v.3 p.338*
Bessel, Richard & Emsley, Clive	*v.6 p.262*
Bessel, Richard	*v.3 p.169*
Besser, Gretchen R.	*v.2 p.500*
Bessette, Alan E.	*v.5 p.209*
Bessette, Gerard	*v.2 p.540*
Bessinger, J. B. (Editor)	*v.2 p.203*
Besson, Jean-Louis	*v.4 p.40*
Best, Alan D. & Wolfshutz, Hans (Editors)	*v.2 p.590*
Best, Alan D.	*v.2 p.615*
Best, Gary D.	*v.3 p.465, p.466*
Best, Geoffrey	*v.4 p.478*
Best, Joel	*v.4 p.689, p.754, v.6 p.256, p.258*
Best, Myron G.	*v.5 p.437*
Best, Rick (Editor), et al.	*v.4 p.113*
Best, Victoria	*v.2 p.459*
Bestor, Arthur E.	*v.4 p.340*
Bestor, Theodore C.	*v.6 p.218*
Bestor, Theodore	*v.6 p.221*
Beswick, Stephanie	*v.6 p.59*
Beteille, Andre	*v.6 p.149*
Beth, Loren P.	*v.4 p.467*
Bethe, Hans A. & Jackiw, Roman V.	*v.5 p.549*
Bethe, Hans A. & Salpeter, E. E.	*v.5 p.549*
Bethe, Hans Albrecht	*v.5 p.553*
Bethell, Leslie (Editor, Contribution by)	*v.3 p.345*
Bethell, Leslie (Editor)	*v.3 p.307, p.334, p.335, p.350*
Bethell, Ursula & O'Sullivan, Vincent	*v.2 p.744*
Beti, Mongo	*v.2 p.544*
Betjeman, John	*v.2 p.331*
Bettelheim, Bruno & Zelan, Karen	*v.4 p.362*
Bettelheim, Bruno	*v.2 p.582, v.4 p.735*
Bettenson, Henry & Maunder, Chris (Editors)	*v.1 p.597, v.3 p.56*
Betti, Ugo	*v.2 p.713*
Bettie, Julie	*v.4 p.723*
Bettinger, Pete & Wing, Michael G.	*v.4 p.386, v.5 p.36*
Betts, John R.	*v.4 p.803*
Betts, Julian & Loveless, Tom (Editors)	*v.4 p.302*
Betts, Raymond F.	*v.3 p.76, v.4 p.584*
Betz, Albrecht	*v.1 p.209, p.323*
Betz, Cecily Lynn & Sowden, Linda A.	*v.5 p.524, p.527*
Betz, David	*v.4 p.597*
Betz, Hans D.	*v.1 p.630*
Betz, Hans-Georg	*v.4 p.601*
Betz, Nancy E., et al.	*v.5 p.577*
Beuka, Robert	*v.6 p.340, p.730*
Beukelman, David R. & Mirenda, Pat	*v.4 p.318*
Beus, Stanley S. (Editor)	*v.5 p.431*
Beuter, John H.	*v.5 p.36, v.6 p.297, p.298*
Beutler, Larry E. & Groth-Marnat, Gary	*v.5 p.603*
Bevacqua, Maria	*v.6 p.468*
Bevan, Alex & de Laeter, J. R.	*v.5 p.69, p.434*
Bevan, Clifford	*v.1 p.389*
Beveridge, Albert J.	*v.3 p.424*
Beveridge, Charles E. & Olmsted, Frederick Law	*v.1 p.815*
Beveridge, William I.	*v.5 p.408*
Beverley, John	*v.2 p.663*
Beverly, William	*v.6 p.340*
Bevington, David & Hunter, George K. (Editors)	*v.2 p.213*
Bevington, David M.	*v.2 p.228*
Bevington, David	*v.1 p.63, p.74, p.98, v.2 p.202*
Bevington, Merle M.	*v.6 p.739, p.750*
Bevington, Philip R. & Robinson, D. Keith	*v.5 p.64, p.562*
Bevis, Charlie	*v.4 p.803, p.824, p.849, p.890*
Bevis, Richard W.	*v.2 p.187*
Bewell, Alan J.	*v.2 p.323*
Bewley, J. D. & Black, M.	*v.5 p.20, p.47*
Bewley, Marius	*v.2 p.7*

Bex, Tony & Watts, Richard J. *v.2 p.551*
Beyala, Calixthe *v.2 p.544*
Beyaz'i, Bahram, et al. *v.6 p.670*
Beye, Charles R. *v.2 p.402*
Beye, Charles Rowan *v.2 p.400*
Beyer, Carl *v.1 p.755*
Beyer, Edward *v.2 p.627*
Beyer, Hans & Walter, Wolfgang *v.5 p.290*
Beyer, Harald *v.2 p.627*
Beyer, Robert T. *v.5 p.566*
Beyer, Stephan V. (Editor) *v.1 p.565*
Beyer, William H. (Editor) *v.5 p.460, p.480*
Beyer, William H. *v.5 p.460*
Beyerlein, Michael M., et al. *v.4 p.80*
Beyle, Thad L. (Editor) *v.4 p.548, p.557*
Beynon, R. J. *v.5 p.244*
Beytes, Chris & Hamrick, Debbie (Editors) *v.5 p.43*
Bezanson, Randall P. *v.4 p.458*
Bécquer, Gustavo Adolfo *v.2 p.653*
Bécquer, Gustavo Adolpho *v.2 p.653, p.654*
Béhar, Henri *v.2 p.511*
Bénichou, Paul *v.2 p.458*
Böhm, Florian, ... *v.1 p.720*
Böhm-Vitense, Erika *v.5 p.70*
Böll, Heinrich & Vennewitz, Leila *v.2 p.604*
Böll, Heinrich *v.2 p.604*
Bhabha, Homi K. *v.2 p.759*
Bhadra, Gautam (Editor), et al. *v.2 p.759*
Bhagat, Sanjai & Jefferis, Richard H. Jr. *v.4 p.198*
Bhagavan, Nadhipuram V. *v.5 p.329*
Bhagwati, Jagdish N. & Grossman, Gene M. (Editors) *v.4 p.243*
Bhagwati, Jagdish N. (Editor), et al. *v.4 p.256*
Bhagwati, Jagdish N. (Editor) *v.4 p.255, p.256*
Bhagwati, Jagdish N., et al. *v.4 p.256*
Bhagwati, Jagdish N. . . . *v.4 p.55, p.243, p.255, p.256, p.663*
Bhana, Surendra & Pachai, Bridglal *v.6 p.78*
Bhardwaj, Surinder M. *v.1 p.535*
Bhatia, Michael V. *v.4 p.670*
Bhattacharya, Nandini *v.2 p.171*
Bhatti, M. Asghar *v.5 p.693*
Bhide, Amar V. *v.4 p.67*
Bhushan, Bharat & Gupta, B. K. *v.5 p.707*
Bhushan, Bharat (Editor) *v.5 p.707*
Bhushan, Nalini & Rosenfeld, Stuart (Editors) *v.5 p.264*
Biagini, Eugenio F. *v.3 p.74*
Biagioli, Mario *v.3 p.46, v.5 p.62, p.396*
Bial, Henry (Compiled by) *v.1 p.134*
Bial, Raymond *v.3 p.380*
Biale, David (Editor) *v.1 p.546*
Bialec, Dana *v.2 p.775*
Bialik, C. N. *v.6 p.648*
Bialik, Hayyim Nahman *v.6 p.648*
Bianchi, Robert S. *v.4 p.701, v.6 p.59*
Bianchi, Suzanne M. (Editor), et al. *v.5 p.638*
Bianco, Lucien *v.6 p.192*

Bianquis, Th. (Editor), et al. *v.6 p.581*
Biasin, Gian-Paolo & Gieri, Manuela (Editors) . . . *v.2 p.722*
Biberaj, Elez *v.4 p.600*
Biblograf Editorial Staff (Compiled by) *v.2 p.635*
Bicat, Tina *v.1 p.150*
Bickel, Alexander M. *v.4 p.437*
Bickerman, Elias J. *v.3 p.3*
Bickers, Robert A. *v.6 p.203, p.214, p.217*
Bickerstaffe, George *v.4 p.176*
Bickert, William G., et al. *v.5 p.54*
Bickerton, Ian J. & Klausner, Carla L. *v.6 p.616*
Bickerton, James & Gagnon, Alain-G *v.4 p.586*
Bickley, Lynn S. & Szilagyi, Peter G. *v.5 p.520*
Bickley, R. Bruce Jr. *v.2 p.40*
Bickman, Martin *v.2 p.47, v.4 p.346*
Bidart, Frank *v.2 p.141*
Biddle, J. E. (Editor), et al. *v.4 p.194, p.208*
Biddle, Stuart J. H. & Mutrie, Nanette *v.4 p.876*
Biddle, Stuart J. H. (Editor) *v.4 p.812, p.876*
Bidney, David *v.4 p.23*
Bidwai, Praful & Vanaik, Achin *v.4 p.655*
Bieber, Judy *v.3 p.335*
Bieber, Margarete *v.1 p.69, p.70, p.72*
Biehle, James T., et al. *v.4 p.288*
Bielec, Dana *v.2 p.775*
Bielecki, Stanislaw, et al. *v.5 p.33*
Bien, Gloria, et al. *v.2 p.759*
Bienen, Henry S. & de Walle, Nicolas van *v.4 p.511*
Bienkowski, Piotr *v.3 p.4*
Bienvenut, Willy Vincent (Editor) *v.5 p.87, p.111*
Bierce, Ambrose & Joshi, S. T. *v.2 p.31*
Bierce, Ambrose, et al. *v.2 p.31*
Bierce, Ambrose *v.2 p.31, p.32*
Bieri, James *v.2 p.311*
Bierley, Paul E. *v.1 p.276, p.358*
Bierman, Irene A. (Editor) *v.6 p.637*
Biernson, George A. *v.5 p.710*
Bierregaard, Richard O. (Editor), et al. *v.5 p.175, p.235, p.239*
Biesold, Horst *v.3 p.171*
Biewener, Andrew A. *v.5 p.212*
Bigalike, Terence *v.4 p.701*
Biggs, Barton *v.4 p.94, p.99, p.162*
Biggs, D. L. (Editor) *v.5 p.431*
Biggs, Norman L. *v.5 p.337, p.480*
Bigham, Darrel E. (Editor) *v.3 p.514*
Biglaiser, Glen *v.3 p.273*
Bigler, Peter *v.5 p.272*
Bigsby, Christopher (Editor) *v.1 p.58, p.112, v.2 p.101*
Bigsby, Christopher *v.1 p.79, p.112, v.2 p.101*
Biguenet, John & Schulte, Rainer (Editors) *v.2 p.574*
Biko, Steve *v.6 p.78*
Bilaniuk, Laada *v.4 p.20*
Biles, Roger *v.3 p.496, p.514, p.515*
Bill, James A. *v.6 p.631*
Biller, Henry B. *v.5 p.581*

Billeskov-Jansen, F. J. & Mitchell, P. M. (Editors) . . *v.2 p.625*

Billet, Bret L. & Formwalt,
    Lance J. *v.4 p.804, p.830, p.849, p.890*

Billias, George A. (Editor) *v.3 p.411*

Billigmeier, Robert H. *v.3 p.244*

Billings, Warren M. (Editor) *v.3 p.499*

Billingsley, Andrew & Giovannoni, Jeanne M. *v.4 p.755*

Billingsley, Andrew *v.4 p.720*

Billingsley, Edward Baxter *v.3 p.327, p.350*

Billingsley, John *v.5 p.714*

Billingsley, Randall . . *v.4 p.91, p.92, p.94, p.98, p.101, p.103*

Billington, David P. & Jackson, Donald C. *v.5 p.702*

Billington, James H. *v.1 p.609, v.3 p.210*

Billington, Michael *v.2 p.376*

Billington, Ray A. & Ridge, Martin *v.3 p.380*

Billington, Ray A. (Editor) *v.3 p.380*

Billington, Ray A. *v.3 p.394, p.521*

Billington, Ray Allen *v.3 p.380, p.518*

Billman, Larry *v.1 p.3, p.37*

Billmeyer, Fred W. Jr. *v.5 p.322*

Billo, E. Joseph *v.5 p.267*

Bills, David B. *v.4 p.304, p.761*

Bills, Tim & Genasi, Chris *v.4 p.65*

Bilski, Emily *v.1 p.778*

Bilstein, Roger E. *v.5 p.717*

Bin Laden, Osama *v.4 p.658*

Bin Wahad, Dhoruba, et al. *v.6 p.3, p.31*

Binder, Kurt & Heermann, Dieter W. *v.5 p.551, p.558*

Binder, Kurt & Landau, David P. *v.5 p.551*

Binder, Sarah A. & Smith, Steven S. *v.4 p.533*

Binder, Wolfgang (Editor) *v.3 p.507*

Bindman, David *v.2 p.238*

Binford, Lewis Roberts *v.4 p.6*

Bingham, Clara & Gansler, Laura Leedy *v.4 p.130*

Bingham, Eula, et al. *v.5 p.364, p.367, p.374*

Bingying, Xie *v.6 p.202, p.217*

Binion, Rudolph *v.5 p.646*

Binmore, Ken *v.4 p.83*

Binneveld, Hans *v.5 p.583*

Binney, James & Merrifield, Michael *v.5 p.71*

Binney, James J. & Tremaine, Scot *v.5 p.71*

Binney, Marcus *v.1 p.785*

Binning, William C., et al. *v.4 p.547*

Binns, J. W. (Editor) *v.2 p.424*

Binns, John *v.1 p.569*

Binns, Tony (Author, Editor) *v.4 p.384*

Binns, Tony (Editor) *v.6 p.51*

Binstock, Robert H. & George, Linda K. (Editors) . *v.4 p.741*

Biocca, Frank & Levy, Mark R. (Editors) . . . *v.5 p.620, p.624*

Biolsi, Thomas & Zimmerman, Larry J. (Editors) . *v.4 p.27, v.6 p.702*

Biolsi, Thomas (Editor) *v.4 p.3*

Biolsi, Thomas *v.4 p.33*

Birch, Cyril (Editor, Translator) *v.6 p.207, p.211*

Birch, Sarah *v.4 p.577, p.584, p.597*

Birchall, Diana *v.6 p.92*

Birchard, William Jr. & Proudman, Robert D. . . . *v.5 p.229*

Birchfield, D. L. *v.6 p.697*

Birchwood, Max J. & Jackson, Chris *v.5 p.660*

Bird, Alan F. *v.1 p.730*

Bird, David M. *v.5 p.157, p.214*

Bird, Doni L. & Robinson, Debbie S. *v.5 p.525*

Bird, Dorothy & Greenberg, Joyce *v.1 p.28, p.29, p.36*

Bird, Eric C. *v.5 p.423*

Bird, Frederick Bruce *v.4 p.145*

Bird, Graham (Editor) *v.4 p.258*

Bird, Graham *v.1 p.439*

Bird, John *v.1 p.209, p.327*

Bird, Junius B. *v.4 p.11*

Bird, Richard J. *v.5 p.190*

Bird, Wendell R. *v.5 p.202*

Bird, William L. & Rubenstein, Harry R. *v.1 p.718*

Bird, William Larry Jr. *v.1 p.750*

Bird *v.6 p.214*

Birden, Susan *v.6 p.384*

Birdi, K. S. (Editor) *v.5 p.283*

Birdi, K.S. *v.5 p.283*

Birdsall, Stephen S., et al. *v.3 p.365*

Birdsell, Sandra *v.2 p.733*

Birgus, Vladimir *v.1 p.763*

Birkeland, Peter M. *v.4 p.164*

Birkeland, Peter W. *v.5 p.48*

Birkett, Jennifer & Kearns, James *v.2 p.457*

Birkhoff, Garrett D. & Mac Lane, Saunders . . . *v.5 p.473*

Birkhoff, Garrett D. & Rota, Gian-Carlo *v.5 p.487*

Birkin, Andrew *v.2 p.269*

Birla, Madan *v.4 p.165*

Birley, Anthony R. *v.3 p.27*

Birley, Anthony *v.3 p.27*

Birley, Derek *v.4 p.804*

Birmingham, David & Martin, Phyllis M. (Editors) . *v.6 p.61*

Birmingham, David & Martin, Phyllis *v.6 p.61*

Birmingham, David *v.3 p.243, p.244, v.4 p.582, v.6 p.55, p.74, p.75*

Birn, Randi *v.2 p.628*

Birn, Robin *v.4 p.135*

Birnbaum, Barry W. *v.4 p.321, p.350*

Birnbaum, Charles A. & Hughes, Mary V. . . . *v.1 p.817, p.822*

Birnbaum, Daniel, et al. *v.1 p.772*

Birnbaum, Philip *v.6 p.645*

Birnbaum, Pierre *v.3 p.140*

Birnbaum, Robert *v.4 p.289*

Birner, Jack (Editor), et al. *v.4 p.243*

Birney, Earle *v.2 p.729, p.733*

Birney, James G. *v.3 p.419*

Birns, Nicholas *v.2 p.377*

Birrell, Anne M. *v.6 p.209*

Birrell, Susan & Cole,
    Cheryl L. (Editors) *v.4 p.814, p.834, v.6 p.437*

Birrell, Susan & McDonald, Mary G. (Editors) . . . *v.4 p.814*

Birringer, Johannes H. *v.1 p.40*

Birringer, Johannes *v.1 p.40, p.55, p.86*

Birtchnell, John *v.5 p.646*

Birx, H. James (Editor) *v.4 p.3*

Bischoff, Bernhard & Cóinín, Dáibhí Ó *v.6 p.555*

Bisgrove, Richard *v.1 p.815*

Bisheff, Steve *v.4 p.853*

Bishop, Alan J. & Clements, M. A. (Ken) *v.5 p.462*

Bishop, Anne & Scudder, Jack *v.5 p.511, p.529*

Bishop, Claire *v.1 p.770*

Bishop, Elizabeth & Brasil, Emanuel (Editors) *v.2 p.689*

Bishop, Elizabeth *v.2 p.61*

Bishop, Jerry E. *v.5 p.131*

Bishop, John Christopher *v.1 p.503*

Bishop, Lloyd *v.2 p.454, p.457*

Bishop, Maurice *v.3 p.318*

Bishop, Michael *v.2 p.460*

Bishop, Morris *v.2 p.705, v.3 p.537*

Bishop, Peter *v.6 p.240*

Bishop, Robert & Atkins, Jacqueline M. *v.1 p.681*

Bishop Robert H Staff *v.5 p.714*

Bishop, Robert H. *v.5 p.714*

Bisio, Attilio & Boots, Sharon (Editors) *v.5 p.359*

Biskupski, Mieczysaw B. *v.3 p.252*

Bissell, R. Ward *v.1 p.736*

Bissell, Richard E. *v.3 p.387*

Bissinger, H. G. *v.4 p.814, p.840, p.858*

Bisson, Lillian M. *v.6 p.564*

Bissoondath, Neil *v.2 p.733*

Bitel, Lisa M. *v.1 p.577, v.3 p.51, v.6 p.559*

Bithell, Jethro *v.2 p.620*

Bitov, Andrei *v.2 p.801*

Bittencourt, J. A. *v.5 p.566*

Bix, Herbert P. *v.6 p.226*

Bizet, Georges *v.1 p.194, p.228, p.312, p.407*

Bizup, Joseph *v.6 p.765*

Bizzarini, Marco & Chater,
James (Translators) *v.1 p.179, p.339, p.340*

Bizzell, Patricia *v.2 p.564*

Bjarkman, Peter C. *v.4 p.804, p.833, p.849, p.853, p.890*

Bjarkman, Peter *v.3 p.316*

Bjelajac, David & Laurence, King *v.1 p.681*

Bjerkholt, Olav (Editor) *v.4 p.198*

Bjerre-Poulsen, Niels *v.4 p.516*

Björk, Christopher *v.4 p.333*

Björner and RP Stanley *v.5 p.478*

Bjomson, Richard *v.2 p.541, v.6 p.62*

Bjork, Daniel W. *v.5 p.595*

Bjorkegren, Dag *v.1 p.825*

Bjorken, James D. *v.5 p.549*

Black, Antony *v.1 p.556, v.4 p.490*

Black, Charles L. Jr. *v.4 p.461*

Black, Charles Lund *v.4 p.454*

Black, Cheryl *v.1 p.79, p.81, p.120*

Black, Christopher F. *v.3 p.200*

Black, David Alan & Beck, David R. (Editors) *v.1 p.628*

Black, David R. (Editor) *v.5 p.581*

Black, Don & Hampton, Christopher . *v.1 p.248, p.337, p.407*

Black, Earl & Black, Merle *v.4 p.550, p.556*

Black, Edwin R. *v.4 p.586*

Black, Edwin *v.4 p.775*

Black, Errol & Silver, Jim *v.4 p.124*

Black, J. *v.3 p.90, p.106*

Black, Jeremy (Editor), et al. *v.3 p.5, v.6 p.664*

Black, Jeremy *v.3 p.382, v.4 p.645*

Black, John R. *v.6 p.223*

Black, Kenneth Jr. & Skipper, Harold D. Jr. *v.4 p.163*

Black, Lydia T. *v.3 p.533*

Black, Max *v.1 p.471, p.489, p.502*

Black, Michael *v.2 p.362*

Black, Peter & Moorhead, Desiree *v.1 p.755*

Black, Peter E. *v.5 p.367*

Black, Richard & White, Howard (Editors) *v.4 p.258*

Black, Stephen A. *v.2 p.107*

Blackall, Eric A. *v.2 p.592, p.597, p.620*

Blackbourn, David & Eley, Geoffrey *v.3 p.159*

Blackbourn, David (Editor) *v.3 p.180*

Blackbourn, David *v.3 p.159, p.163*

Blackburn, Bonnie J. (Editor), et al. *v.1 p.179*

Blackburn, G. Meredith & Gait, Michael J. . . *v.5 p.131, p.328*

Blackburn, Joseph *v.4 p.119*

Blackburn, Julia *v.1 p.695*

Blackburn, Patrick, et al. *v.1 p.491*

Blackburn, Paul *v.2 p.58*

Blackburn, Philip & Partch, Harry *v.6 p.408*

Blackburn, Robert *v.4 p.606*

Blackburn, Simon *v.1 p.415, p.416*

Blackburn, Stanley (Editor) *v.5 p.300*

Blackburn, Stanley *v.5 p.300*

Blackburn, T. Henry & Sorensen, Jan (Editors) . . . *v.5 p.173*

Blacker, David J. *v.4 p.346*

Blackett, R. J. M. *v.4 p.519*

Blackford, Mansel G. *v.4 p.87, p.146*

Blackford, Russell, et al. *v.2 p.740*

Blacking, John & Nettl, Bruno *v.1 p.376*

Blacking, John *v.1 p.285*

Blackleeds, Alistair *v.6 p.738*

Blackman, Lisa & Walkerdine, Valerie *v.4 p.714*

Blackman, Philip (Translator) *v.1 p.550*

Blackman, William C. Jr. *v.5 p.313*

Blackmore, A. M. & Blackmore, E. H. (Editors) . . . *v.2 p.463*

Blackmore, Susan J. *v.5 p.613*

Blackmur, Richard P. *v.2 p.7*

Blackstone, Erwin A., et al. *v.4 p.546*

Blackstone, William (Translator) *v.4 p.435*

Blackwelder, Julia Kirk *v.6 p.455*

Blackwell, Roger *v.4 p.249*

Blackwell, Ron (Editor), et al. *v.4 p.208, p.240*

Blackwell Science Inc., Publishing Staff, et al. . . . *v.5 p.125*

Blackwood, Algernon *v.2 p.331*

Blackwood, Evelyn & Wieringa, Saskia . . *v.4 p.750, v.6 p.371, p.375, p.420*

Blades, James & Dean, Johnny *v.1 p.397*

Blades, James *v.1 p.389*

Blades, John *v.2 p.323*

Blaga, Lucian *v.2 p.816*

Blain, Virginia; Clements, Patricia; Grundy, Isobel . . *v.6 p.476*

Blain, Virginia (Editor) *v.2 p.198*

Blainey, Ann *v.2 p.290*

Blair, Clay & Blair, Joan *v.3 p.466*

Blair, Cornelia B. (Editor) *v.5 p.204*

Blair, Fredrika *v.1 p.6*

Blair, Hugh *v.2 p.564*

Blair, Margaret M. (Editor) *v.4 p.76, p.84*

Blair, Peter Hunter *v.2 p.203*

Blair, Sheila S. & Bloom, Jonathan *v.1 p.673*

Blair-Loy, Mary *v.5 p.578*

Blais, Marie-Claire *v.2 p.538*

Blake, Ann *v.2 p.748*

Blake, Nigel (Editor) *v.4 p.323, p.338*

Blake, Nigel, et al. *v.4 p.338*

Blake, R. D. *v.5 p.138*

Blake, R. M. *v.5 p.399, p.400*

Blake, Robert *v.3 p.90, p.93, p.110, v.4 p.606, v.6 p.757*

Blake, W. John *v.6 p.68*

Blake, William *v.1 p.716, v.2 p.239*

Blakelock, John H. *v.5 p.717*

Blakely, Edward J. & Snyder, Mary G. *v.6 p.716*

Blakemore, J. S. *v.5 p.554*

Blakemore, Robbie G. *v.1 p.799*

Blakemore, Steven (ed.) *v.3 p.301*

Blakey, Ellen Sue & Geiger, Rita *v.3 p.523*

Blakey, George T. *v.3 p.511*

Blalock, Eric M. (Editor) *v.5 p.103, p.110*

Blalock, H. M. Jr. (Editor) *v.4 p.687*

Blalock, Hubert M. *v.4 p.689*

Blaman, Anna *v.2 p.622*

Blamires, Alcuin (Editor) *v.2 p.196, v.6 p.559*

Blamires, Harry *v.2 p.357*

Blanchard, Dallas A. & Prewitt, Terry J. *v.4 p.569*

Blanchard, Ken, et al. *v.4 p.143*

Blanchard, Margaret A. (Editor) *v.4 p.415*

Blanchard, Paula *v.2 p.46*

Blanchard, Peter *v.3 p.327, p.328*

Blanchette, Arthur E. *v.3 p.540*

Blanchot, Maurice *v.2 p.483, p.510*

Blanck, Peter David (Editor) *v.4 p.446*

Blanco, Hugo & Camejo, Peter *v.3 p.328*

Blanco, Richard L. (Editor) *v.3 p.407, p.413*

Bland, Alexander *v.1 p.6, p.23*

Bland, Randall W. *v.4 p.467*

Bland, Will & Rolls, David *v.5 p.439*

Blandford, Percy W. *v.5 p.3*

Blandford, Steve (Editor), et al. *v.6 p.306*

Blaney, Joseph L. & Benoit, William L. *v.3 p.466*

Blank, Martin (Editor) *v.2 p.133*

Blank, Rebecca M. *v.4 p.264, p.754*

Blankart, Charles Beat & Mueller, Dennis C. (Editors) . *v.4 p.636*

Blann, Robinson *v.2 p.273*

Blanning, T. C. W. *v.3 p.149*

Blanning, Timothy C. W. *v.3 p.167, p.182*

Blansfield, Karen C. *v.2 p.50*

Blanton, Carlos Kevin *v.6 p.526*

Blasco Ibáñez, Vicente *v.2 p.656*

Blasi, Vincent *v.4 p.470*

Blasius, Mark & Phelan, Shane (Editors) . *v.6 p.358, p.363, p.386*

Blass, F. & Debrunner, A. *v.2 p.399*

Blass, Thomas *v.5 p.645*

Blassingame, John W. *v.3 p.394, v.6 p.3, p.37*

Blatnik, Andrej *v.2 p.812*

Blatt, Sidney J. *v.5 p.659*

Blattel, Harry *v.1 p.725*

Blatz, Perry K. *v.4 p.124*

Blau, Francine D., et al. *v.4 p.273*

Blau, Francine D. *v.4 p.253*

Blau, J. L. *v.3 p.414*

Blau, Joel *v.4 p.750*

Blau, Joshua *v.6 p.645, p.653*

Blau, Joyce *v.6 p.668*

Blau, Judith R. & Moncada, Alberto *v.4 p.768*

Blau, Judith R. *v.4 p.712*

Blau, Peter J. *v.5 p.707*

Blau, Peter M. & Duncan, Otis Dudley *v.4 p.726*

Blau, Peter M. (Editor) *v.4 p.718*

Blau, Peter Michael & Scott, W. Richard *v.4 p.717*

Blau, Peter *v.4 p.292*

Blau, Theodore H. *v.5 p.591*

Blaug, Mark & Vane, Howard R. (Editors) *v.4 p.193*

Blaug, Mark (Editor) *v.4 p.194, p.215, p.226*

Blaug, Mark, et al. *v.4 p.237*

Blaug, Mark *v.4 p.188, p.194, p.208, p.211, p.226*

Blauner, Bob *v.4 p.728*

Blaustein, Noah (Editor) *v.4 p.811*

Blay, Michel *v.5 p.400*

Blazer, Dan G. *v.5 p.659*

Blazewicz, Jacek (Editor), et al. *v.4 p.114*

Blea, Irene I. *v.6 p.542, p.546, p.548*

Blecker, Thorsten *v.4 p.117*

Bleecker, David & Csordas, George (Editors) *v.5 p.487*

Blegen, Theodore Christian *v.3 p.522*

Bleiler, Ellen H. (Editor, Translator) *v.1 p.394, p.411*

Bleiler, Everett F. & Bleiler, Richard J. *v.2 p.581*

Bleiler, Everett F. *v.2 p.581*

Bleiler, Richard J. *v.2 p.580*

Bleiler, Richard *v.2 p.581*

Blenkhorn, David L. & Fleisher, Craig S. (Editors) . *v.4 p.69, p.82*

Blenkinsopp, Joseph *v.1 p.622*

Blewett, Stephen E. *v.5 p.312*

Bleznick, Donald W. *v.2 p.638*

Blickle, Peter *v.3 p.165*

Blicq, Ron S. & Moretto, Lisa A. *v.4 p.172*

Blier, Suzanne Preston *v.1 p.689*

Blieszner, Rosemary H. & Bedford, Victoria H. (Editors) . . *v.5 p.638*

Blight, David W. *v.3 p.394*

Blight, James G. & Brenner, Philip *v.3 p.307*

Blight, James G. & Kornbluh, Peter *v.3 p.307*

Blij, H. J. de, et al. *v.4 p.396*

Blinder, Alan S. *v.4 p.88, p.154*

Blinkenberg, Lars *v.6 p.158*

Bliss, Michael *v.5 p.509*

Blix, Hans *v.4 p.655*

Bloch, Chana *v.2 p.249*

Bloch, E. Maurice *v.1 p.736*

Bloch, Marc *v.3 p.67, p.140, p.156, v.6 p.561*

Bloch, Maurice E. *v.4 p.27*

Bloch, Maurice *v.4 p.23, p.26*

Bloch, R. Howard *v.3 p.51*

Block, Adrienne F. *v.1 p.194, p.305, p.378*

Block, Alan A. & Weaver, Constance A. *v.6 p.251*

Block, Alan A. *v.4 p.751*

Block, Cathy Collins, et al. *v.4 p.360*

Block, Francesca Lia *v.6 p.394*

Block, Geoffrey Holden *v.1 p.209, p.248, p.333, p.351*

Block, Geoffrey *v.1 p.248, p.351*

Block, Jay A. *v.4 p.168*

Block, Martin E. *v.4 p.800*

Block, R. A. (Editor) *v.5 p.604*

Block, Richard N. & Beck, John P. *v.4 p.120*

Block, Richard N., et al. *v.4 p.109, p.111, p.112, p.120*

Blocker, Jack S. Jr., et al. *v.5 p.663*

Blocker, Jack S. Jr. *v.5 p.663*

Bloemink, Barbara & Cunningham, Joseph *v.1 p.712*

Blofeld, John Eaton Calthorpe *v.6 p.205*

Blofeld, John E. *v.1 p.561*

Blok, Aleksandr Aleksandrovich *v.2 p.801*

Blok, Aleksandr *v.2 p.801*

Blok, Anton *v.4 p.751*

Blom, J. C. & Lamberts, E. (Editors) *v.3 p.204*

Blomberg, Thomas G. & Lucken, Karol *v.6 p.273*

Blom-Cooper, Louis & Morris, Terence *v.6 p.252*

Blommaert, Jan *v.4 p.21*

Blomquist, Thomas W. & Mazzaoui, Maureen F. (Editors) *v.6 p.561*

Blomstermo, Anders (Editor), et al. *v.4 p.143*

Blondel, Jean & Thiebault, J. L. (Editors) *v.4 p.601*

Blondell, Ruby *v.1 p.423*

Blonsky, Marshall (Editor) *v.2 p.570*

Blood, Robert O. & Wolfe, Donald M. . *v.4 p.732, v.6 p.464, p.466*

Bloodstein, Oliver *v.5 p.665*

Bloom, Allan *v.3 p.366, v.4 p.289*

Bloom, Amy *v.4 p.746, v.6 p.369*

Bloom, Arthur L. *v.5 p.424*

Bloom, Benjamin S. (Editor) *v.5 p.575*

Bloom, Benjamin S. *v.5 p.625*

Bloom, Charles P. & Loftin, R. Bowen (Editors) . . . *v.5 p.589*

Bloom, Clive & Docherty, Brian (Editors) *v.2 p.15*

Bloom, Clive (Editor) *v.2 p.190*

Bloom, Clive *v.2 p.190*

Bloom, Edward A. & Bloom, Lillian D. *v.2 p.236*

Bloom, Harold (Editor, Introduction by) . *v.2 p.247, p.248, p.353, p.460, p.492, p.498, p.501, p.704*

Bloom, Harold (Editor, Translator, Introduction by) *v.2 p.677, v.6 p.22*

Bloom, Harold (Editor) *v.2 p.183, p.362, p.677, p.682*

Bloom, Harold, et al. *v.2 p.566, p.570*

Bloom, Harold (Introduction by) . *v.2 p.182, p.240, p.252, p.256, p.257, p.349, p.371, p.457, p.462, p.476, p.490, p.496, p.501, p.677, p.679, p.682, p.704, p.705, v.6 p.22*

Bloom, Harold . *v.2 p.66, p.183, p.239, p.311, p.326, p.566, p.573, p.582, p.682, p.767, p.782*

Bloom, John & Willard, Michael Nevin (Editors) . *v.4 p.814, p.830*

Bloom, John *v.4 p.841, v.6 p.680*

Bloom, Kenneth *v.1 p.165, p.248, p.254, v.6 p.315*

Bloom, Lois *v.4 p.368*

Bloom, Mia *v.4 p.658, v.6 p.251*

Bloom, Paul N. & Gundlach, Gregory T. *v.4 p.145*

Bloom, Paul *v.5 p.574*

Bloom, Peter (Editor) *v.1 p.194, p.310*

Bloom, Robert *v.2 p.337*

Bloom, Samuel William *v.4 p.774, v.5 p.511*

Bloomfield, B. C. *v.2 p.361*

Bloomfield, Leonard *v.2 p.559*

Bloomfield, Louis A. *v.5 p.539*

Bloomfield, Maxwell *v.4 p.440*

Bloomfield, Morton W. *v.2 p.211*

Bloomfield, Victor A., et al. *v.5 p.120*

Bloor, Michael *v.4 p.779*

Bloss, F. Donald *v.5 p.436*

Blot, Michel (Editor) *v.5 p.145*

Blotner, Joseph *v.2 p.73*

Blough, Glenn O. & Schwartz, Julius *v.4 p.362*

Blount, Ben G. (Editor) *v.4 p.17*

Blount, Jackie M. *v.4 p.309, v.6 p.384*

Blount *v.6 p.290*

Bloxham, Donald *v.4 p.651*

Bluestone, Barry & Harrison, Bennett *v.4 p.722*

Bluestone, Barry *v.4 p.722*

Blum, Cinzia S. *v.2 p.718*

Blum, Jerome *v.3 p.211, v.4 p.701, p.723*

Blum, John M. *v.3 p.439, p.456, p.466*

Blum, John Morton *v.3 p.373, p.439, p.445, p.466*

Blum, Louise A. *v.6 p.401*

Blum, Mark L. *v.1 p.567*

Blum, Richard H. *v.5 p.663*

Blum, Susan D. & Jensen, Lionel M. (Editors) . *v.6 p.181, p.196*

Bluman, Allan G. *v.4 p.174*

Blumberg, Arnold B. *v.6 p.609*

Blumberg, Paul *v.4 p.718*

Blume, Friedrich *v.1 p.235*

Blumenfeld, Erwin *v.1 p.765*

Blumenson, Martin *v.3 p.456*

Blumenthal, Eileen *v.1 p.93, p.133*

Blumenthal, Henry *v.3 p.387*

Blumenthal, Mark *v.5 p.531*

Blumenthal, Sidney *v.3 p.466*

Blumenthal, Uta-Renate *v.1 p.572*

Blumer, Herbert *v.4 p.682, p.692, p.695*

Blumer, Thomas John *v.1 p.807, v.6 p.678*

Blumhofer, Edith Waldvogel (Editor) *v.4 p.307*

Blumstein, Alfred (Editor, Contribution by) *v.6 p.251*

Blumstein, Philip & Schwartz, Pepper *v.4 p.731*

Blumstein, Philip *v.4 p.739, v.6 p.466*

Blundell, D. J. (Editor), et al. *v.5 p.432*

Blundell, Sue *v.3 p.13*

Blundell, Valda *v.4 p.25*

Blunden, Caroline & Elvin, Mark *v.6 p.181*

Blunden, Edmund *v.2 p.263, p.311*

Blunk, Tim & Levasseur, Raymond L. *v.6 p.23*

Blunt, Alison (Editor) *v.4 p.399*

Blunt, Anthony *v.1 p.685, p.730*

Blunt, Wilfrid; Stearn, William T. (William Thomas) *v.5 p.231*

Blunt, Wilfrid *v.5 p.231*

Blustein, Paul *v.4 p.94, p.98, p.99*

Bly, Robert W. *v.4 p.172*

Bly, Robert *v.2 p.629, v.4 p.745*

Blyden, Edward Wilmot *v.6 p.35, p.70*

Blyth, Mark *v.4 p.487, p.664*

Blyth, Myrna *v.6 p.447*

Blyth, R. H. *v.6 p.234*

Blyth, T. S. & Robertson, E. F. *v.5 p.472*

Blythe, James M. *v.4 p.490, p.501, v.6 p.568*

Blythe, Ronald *v.4 p.701*

Bmsa *v.5 p.90*

Bo, Shi *v.1 p.719*

Boahen, A. Adu *v.6 p.55*

Board on Agriculture Staff & National
  Research Council Staff *v.5 p.42*

Boardman, Anthony, et al. *v.4 p.82*

Boardman, Eunice (Editor, Compiled by) *v.1 p.404*

Boardman, John (Editor), et al. *v.3 p.3*

Boardman, John . *v.1 p.669, p.685, p.726, p.775, p.807, v.3 p.16*

Boardman, Kay & Jones, Shirley (Editors) *v.2 p.174*

Boardman, R., et al. *v.5 p.447*

Boas, Adrian *v.6 p.555, p.556, p.566*

Boas, Franz *v.4 p.3*

Boas, Franziska *v.1 p.46, p.48*

Boas, Frederick Samuel *v.2 p.220*

Boas, Frederick S. *v.2 p.187*

Boas, Mary L. *v.5 p.548*

Boas, Nancy *v.1 p.750*

Boas, Ralph P. Jr. *v.5 p.490*

Boase, Frederic *v.6 p.735*

Boase, Roger *v.2 p.457*

Boateng, Charles Adom *v.6 p.69*

Boatner, Mark M. III *v.3 p.429*

Boatright, Robert G. *v.4 p.548*

Boatwright, Mary T., et al. *v.3 p.22*

Boatwright, Mary Taliaferro *v.3 p.27, v.6 p.710*

Boatwright, Mary T. *v.3 p.27*

Boaz, Noel T. & Ciochon, Russell L. *v.4 p.16*

Bob, Clifford *v.4 p.497*

Bobbitt, Philip *v.4 p.454*

Bober, Phyllis Pray; Rubenstein, Ruth;
  Woodford, Susan *v.1 p.750*

Bobick, James, et al. *v.5 p.95*

Bobik, Joseph (Translator) *v.1 p.638*

Bobo, Jacqueline (Editor), et al. *v.6 p.13*

Bobo, Jacqueline *v.6 p.329, p.340*

Bobo, Mike & Dykes, Spike *v.4 p.858, p.904*

Bobrowsky, P. T. *v.4 p.376, v.5 p.423*

Boccaccio, Giovanni & Traversa, Vincenzo *v.2 p.701*

Boccaccio, Giovanni *v.2 p.701, p.704*

Boccagna, David (Composed by) *v.1 p.159*

Bochenek, Michael & Brown, A. Widney *v.6 p.384*

Bocher, E. & Mahérault, J. Armelhault *v.1 p.755*

Bochert, Till Holger *v.1 p.730*

Bock, Audie *v.6 p.335*

Bock, Darrell L. *v.1 p.598*

Bock, Gisela *v.3 p.50*

Bock, Philip K. (Editor) *v.4 p.35*

Bock, Philip K. *v.4 p.35*

Bocking, Richard C. *v.3 p.546*

Bockmuehl, Markus *v.1 p.630*

Bockris, John O'M. & Reddy, A. K. *v.5 p.285*

Bockris, John O'M. & Reddy, Amulya K. N. *v.5 p.285*

Bockris, John O'M., et al. *v.5 p.285*

Bockris, John O'M.; K. N. Amulya, Reddy *v.5 p.284*

Bockris, John O'M. *v.5 p.285*

Boczek, Boleslaw Adam *v.4 p.476*

Bodanis, David *v.5 p.390, p.391, p.409*

Bodansky, David *v.5 p.739*

Boddy, Janice *v.4 p.30*

Boddy, William *v.4 p.418*

Bode, Boyd H. *v.4 p.340*

Bode, Carl *v.3 p.366*

Bodel, John P. (Editor) *v.3 p.13*

Boden, Edward *v.5 p.54, p.56*

Boden, Margaret A. (Editor) *v.5 p.589, p.590*

Bodenhamer, David J. *v.6 p.271*

Bodenheimer, Rosemarie . . . *v.2 p.174, p.286, v.6 p.752, p.755*

Bodley, John H. *v.4 p.27*

Bodman, Sarah *v.1 p.759*

Bodmer, Walter *v.5 p.131*

Bodnar, John E. *v.6 p.710*

Bodnar, John (Editor) *v.3 p.366*

Bodnar, John, et al. *v.3 p.492*

Bodo, Peter *v.4 p.814, p.864, p.887*

Body-Gendrot, Sophie *v.6 p.716*

Boedeker, Deborah & Raaflaub, Kurt A. (Editors) . . . *v.3 p.17*

Boegehold, Alan L. & Scafuro, Adele C. *v.3 p.17*

Boehm, Barbara Drake & Fajt, Jiri (Editors) . *v.1 p.685, v.3 p.190*

Boehmer, Elleke *v.2 p.727*

Boeker, Egbert & Van Grondelle, Rienk *v.5 p.564*

Boeker, Paul H. *v.3 p.352*

Boerma, H. R. & Specht, J. E. (Editors) *v.5 p.20*

Boerner, Peter *v.2 p.597*

Boersma, L. L. (Editor) *v.5 p.48*

Boesch, Bruno & Taylor, Ronald *v.2 p.589*

Boesky, Lisa Melanie *v.6 p.278*

Boethius, Ancius *v.3 p.66*

Boethius *v.1 p.176, p.430, v.2 p.448*

Boettcher, Jennifer C. & Gaines,
Leonard M. *v.4 p.148, p.178, p.180*

Boettger, Suzaan *v.1 p.775*

Boff, Clodovis & Boff, Leonardo *v.1 p.637*

Boff, Leonardo *v.1 p.640*

Boga, Steven *v.4 p.795, p.864*

Bogadek, F. A. *v.2 p.774*

Bogadek, F. Y. *v.2 p.774*

Bogan, Louise *v.2 p.58, p.567*

Bogard, Travis *v.2 p.107, p.235*

Bogart, Anne *v.1 p.152*

Bogart, Kenneth P. *v.5 p.478*

Bogart, Theodore F. Jr., et al. *v.5 p.722*

Bogdanor, Vernon & Butler, David (Editors) *v.4 p.577*

Bogdanov, Vladimir (Editor), et al. . *v.1 p.169, p.170, p.257, p.266*

Bogdanov, Vladimir, et al. *v.1 p.170, p.257*

Bogert, Ralph *v.2 p.818*

Boggs, Grace L. *v.6 p.107, p.126*

Boggs, Jean S. & Maheux, Anne F. *v.1 p.722*

Boggs, Jean Sutherland *v.1 p.695*

Boggs, Sam Jr. *v.5 p.438, p.446*

Bogle, Donald . *v.1 p.18, p.32, p.36, v.6 p.3, p.15, p.329, p.340*

Bogle, John C. *v.4 p.88, p.94*

Bognanno, Mario F. & Coleman, Charles J. (Editors) . *v.4 p.120*

Bognar, Botond *v.1 p.791*

Bognar, Desi K. *v.6 p.306*

Bogoliubov, M. N. & Shirkov, D. V. *v.5 p.550*

Bogucki, Peter I. & Crabtree,
Pam J. (Editor, Translators) *v.4 p.12*

Bogue, Allan G. *v.3 p.427*

Bogue, E. Grady & Aper, Jeffery *v.4 p.330*

Bogue, E. Grady *v.4 p.289*

Bogue, Margaret B. *v.3 p.514*

Bogue, Margaret Beattie *v.5 p.77, v.6 p.294*

Bogus, Carl T. (Editor) *v.4 p.449*

Bohannan, Paul (Editor) *v.4 p.433*

Bohlen, Charles E. *v.3 p.456*

Bohlen, Janet Trowbridge *v.5 p.17, p.178, v.6 p.293*

Bohlman, Philip V. (Editor), et al. *v.1 p.276*

Bohlman, Philip V. *v.1 p.173, p.283, p.297, p.299*

Bohls, Elizabeth A. *v.6 p.477*

Bohm, David *v.5 p.541, p.549, p.556*

Bohm, Robert M. *v.6 p.247*

Bohm-Bawerk, Eugen von & Hilferding, Rudolph . *v.4 p.234*

Bohm-Bawerk, Eugen von *v.4 p.233, p.234*

Bohme, R. (Compiled by) *v.4 p.390*

Bohn, Babette *v.1 p.722*

Bohn, Hinrich L., et al. *v.5 p.48*

Bohn, Willard *v.2 p.699*

Bohner, Charles H. *v.2 p.129*

Bohner, Philotheus *v.6 p.567*

Bohnet, Matthias, et. al. (Editors) . . . *v.5 p.315, p.740*

Bohr, Niels Hendrik David *v.5 p.554*

Bohren, Craig F. & Huffman, Donald R. . . . *v.5 p.73, p.561*

Bohrer, Frederick N. *v.1 p.673, p.677*

Boia, Lucian *v.3 p.250*

Boianova, Snezhana, et al. *v.2 p.774*

Boianova, Snezhana *v.2 p.774*

Boiardo, Matteo Maria *v.2 p.708*

Boiardo, Matteo M. *v.2 p.708*

Boileau Despréaux, Nicolas *v.2 p.472*

Boime, Albert *v.1 p.707*

Boinski, Sue & Garber, Paul Alan (Editors) *v.5 p.614*

Boissevain *v.4 p.693*

Boissonnade, P. *v.3 p.67*

Boisvert, Raymond D. *v.1 p.443*

Boitani, Piero & Mann, Jill (Editors) . . *v.2 p.207, v.6 p.564*

Boix, Carles *v.4 p.503, p.550, p.578*

Bojer, Johan *v.2 p.628*

Bok, Derek C. *v.4 p.289, p.295, p.330*

Bok, Hilary *v.1 p.503*

Boklund, Gunnar *v.2 p.235*

Bol, Marsha C. & Carnegie Museum of
Natural History Staff (Editors) *v.6 p.680*

Bol, Peter K. *v.6 p.185*

Bolaño, Roberto *v.2 p.679*

Boland, Lawrence A. *v.4 p.194*

Boland, Mary L. *v.4 p.130*

Boland, Robert & Argentini, Paul *v.1 p.404*

Bold, Alan (Editor) *v.2 p.261*

Bold, Alan N. *v.2 p.272, p.383*

Bold, Harold C. & Wynne, Michael J. *v.5 p.208*

Bold, Harold C., et al. *v.5 p.207*

Boldy, Adrian P. & Radha Krishna, Hari C. (Editors) . *v.5 p.714*

Bolen, Eric G. & Robinson, William Laughlin . *v.5 p.19, p.356*

Boles, Janet K. & Hoeveler, Diane Long *v.6 p.433*

Boles, John B. & Johnson, Bethany L. (Editors) . . *v.3 p.496*

Boles, John B. *v.3 p.493*

Boleslavsky, Richard *v.1 p.143*

Bolgiano, Chris *v.5 p.36, v.6 p.297*

Bolin, Anne & Granskog, Jane (Editors) . . . *v.4 p.814, p.834*

Bolin, Inge *v.3 p.328*

Boling, Robert G. & Wright, Ernest *v.1 p.620*

Boling, Robert G. *v.1 p.620*

Boll, Heinrich *v.2 p.604*

Bolland, O. Nigel *v.3 p.296*

Bollen, Math H. J. *v.5 p.723*

Boller, Paul F. Jr. *v.3 p.377*

Bolles, A. Lynn *v.4 p.40*

Bolles, Mark Emery & Bolles, Richard Nelson *v.4 p.168*
Bolles, Richard Nelson & Brown, Dale S. *v.4 p.168*
Bolles, Richard Nelson *v.4 p.166*
Bolles, Robert C. (Editor) *v.5 p.606*
Bolles, Robert C. *v.5 p.595*
Bollier, David *v.4 p.773*
Bolling, G. Fredric & Withington, Valerie A. *v.1 p.755*
Bollinger, John G. & Duffie, Neil A. *v.5 p.710*
Bolloten, Burnett *v.3 p.241*
Bolongaro, Eugenio *v.2 p.714*
Bolozky, Shmuel *v.6 p.645*
Bolstad, William M. *v.5 p.480*
Bolt, Bruce *v.5 p.442*
Bolt, Robert *v.2 p.331*
Bolter, Jay David & Gromala, Diane *v.1 p.770*
Bolter, Jay David & Grusin, Richard *v.4 p.419*
Bolton, Brenda & Stuard, Susan Mosher *v.6 p.451*
Bolton, Herbert E. *v.3 p.528*
Bolton, Kenneth & Feagin, Joe R. *v.6 p.259*
Bolton, M. Kent *v.3 p.482*
Bolton, Ruthie *v.6 p.23, p.42*
Bolton, S. Charles *v.3 p.510*
Bolton, W. F. & Wrenn, C. L. (Editors) *v.2 p.203*
Bolz, Peter & Sanner, Hans-Ulrich *v.6 p.678*
Bomford, David (Editor) *v.1 p.721, p.750*
Bompa, Tudor & Carrera, Michael *v.4 p.792, p.878*
Bompa, Tudor O. & Cornacchia, Lorenzo J. . . *v.4 p.792, p.878*
Bonacich, Edna (Editor), et al. *v.6 p.116, p.118*
Bonanno, Alessandro (Editor), et al. *v.4 p.151*
Bonavita, Riccardo *v.2 p.697*
Bond, Beverley W. Jr. *v.3 p.512*
Bond, Bradley G. *v.3 p.504*
Bond, Brian (Editor) *v.3 p.78*
Bond, George C. (Editor), et al. *v.3 p.316, p.318*
Bondanella, Peter & Ciccarelli, Andrea (Editors) . . *v.2 p.697*
Bondanella, Peter C. & Shiffman, Jody R. (Editors) . *v.2 p.697*
Bonder, Bette R. & Wagner, Marilyn B. *v.5 p.535*
Bondy, Adrian J. & Murty, U. S. R. *v.5 p.480*
Bondy, Elizabeth & Ross, Dorene D. (Editors) . . . *v.4 p.279*
Bone, Jesse F. *v.5 p.156*
Bone, Q.; Marshall, N. B.; Blaxter, J. S. H. *v.5 p.214*
Bone, Robert M. *v.3 p.535*
Bonewit-West, Kathy *v.5 p.534*
Bonfante, Larissa & Bonfante-Warren,
    Alexandra (Translators) *v.2 p.448*
Bonhoeffer, Dietrich . . . *v.1 p.483, p.580, p.635, p.642, p.649*
Bonifacino, Juan S. (Editor), et al. *v.5 p.87*
Bonilla, Frank (Editor), et al. *v.6 p.521*
Bonilla-Silva, Eduardo *v.4 p.729*
Bonine, Michael E. (Editor) *v.6 p.716*
Bonino, Jose M. *v.1 p.637*
Bonino, Jose Miguez *v.1 p.641*
BonJour, Laurence & Sosa, Ernest *v.1 p.481*
Bonn, Keith E. (Editor) *v.3 p.80*
Bonnefoy, Yves & Schmidt, Paul *v.2 p.498*

Bonnefoy, Yves *v.2 p.460, p.498, p.510*
Bonnell, Victoria E. (Editor) *v.3 p.220*
Bonnell, Victoria E. *v.3 p.220, p.221*
Bonner, Arthur, et al. *v.6 p.158*
Bonner, Jeffrey P. *v.5 p.83*
Bonner, John T. *v.5 p.190*
Bonner, John Tyler *v.5 p.159*
Bonner, Philip *v.6 p.78*
Bonner, Stanley F. *v.3 p.23*
Bonnette, Dennis *v.5 p.201*
Bonney, Jo *v.2 p.24*
Bonney, Richard (Editor) *v.3 p.38*
Bonney, Richard *v.1 p.560*
Bonnichsen, Robson & Turnmire, Karen L. (Editors) . *v.4 p.10*
Bonnicksen, Thomas M. *v.5 p.175, p.239*
Bono, James J. *v.5 p.388*
Bonomi, Patricia U. *v.1 p.543, v.3 p.405*
Bonta, Marcia M. *v.5 p.229*
Bontekoe, Ron *v.1 p.474*
Bontemps, Arna (Editor) *v.2 p.22, p.58, v.6 p.23*
Bontemps, Arna Wendell *v.6 p.16, p.23*
Bontemps, Arna *v.6 p.16, p.23*
Bonus, Rick *v.6 p.89, p.129*
Bonwick, Colin *v.3 p.413*
Bony, Anne *v.1 p.799*
Bony, Jean *v.6 p.555*
Booch, Grady, et al. *v.5 p.345*
Booch, Grady et al. *v.5 p.349*
Booch, Grady, et al. *v.5 p.349*
Booher, Harold R. *v.5 p.77*
Booker, Christopher & North, Richard *v.4 p.602, p.636*
Booker, Christopher B. *v.6 p.449*
Booker, M. Keith (Editor) *v.2 p.753*
Booker, M. Keith *v.2 p.194, p.751, p.767*
Booker, P. J. *v.5 p.719*
Bookman, Ann & Morgen, Sandra (Editors) *v.6 p.440*
Bookstein, Fred L. *v.5 p.90, p.93*
Boole, George *v.1 p.491*
Boolos, George S. *v.1 p.495*
Boomgaard, Jeroen & Rutten, Bart (Editors) *v.1 p.770*
Boon, James A. *v.6 p.174, p.176*
Boon, Richard & Plastow, Jane (Editors) . . . *v.1 p.127, p.128*
Boone, Catherine *v.6 p.72*
Boone, Elizabeth Hill *v.1 p.683, v.3 p.260*
Boone, M., et al. *v.3 p.43*
Boone, Mary E. *v.4 p.172*
Boonin, David *v.1 p.485, v.4 p.775*
Boorman, Howard L. *v.6 p.189, p.198*
Boorse, Henry, et al. *v.3 p.49*
Boorstin, Daniel J. *v.3 p.366, p.405*
Boos, Florence S. & Silver, Carole G. (Editors) . . *v.2 p.301*
Booth, Alan & Dunn, Judith (Editors) *v.5 p.639*
Booth, Alison L. *v.4 p.124*
Booth, Anne & Weidemann, Anna (Editors) . *v.6 p.174, p.176*
Booth, Harold Simmons *v.5 p.304*

Booth, John *v.1 p.759*

Booth, Ken & Dunne, Timothy (Editors) *v.4 p.658*

Booth, Marilyn (Translator, Introduction by) *v.6 p.658*

Booth, Michael R. & Kaplan, Joel H. (Editors) *v.2 p.188*

Booth, Michael Richard *v.2 p.188, v.6 p.754*

Booth, Wayne, et al. *v.2 p.564, p.566*

Booth, Wayne *v.2 p.566, p.568, p.578, p.579*

Boothby, F., et al. *v.2 p.242*

Boots, B. N. (Editor), et al. *v.4 p.386*

Booty, Frank (Editor) *v.4 p.113*

Bootzin, Richard R. & McKnight, Patrick E. *v.5 p.599*

Booy, David *v.1 p.585*

Bopp, Mary S. *v.1 p.3*

Boras, Tom *v.1 p.393, p.403*

Borchardt-Ott, W. *v.5 p.284*

Borchert, Donald M. *v.1 p.416*

Borchert, Wolfgang & Meyer-Marwitz, Bernhard . . . *v.2 p.603*

Borchert, Wolfgang *v.2 p.603*

Bordley, James III & Harvey, A. McGehee *v.5 p.509*

Bordman, Gerald Martin & Hischak, Thomas S. . . *v.1 p.58, p.112*

Bordman, Gerald *v.1 p.31, p.112, p.248, p.334, p.335*

Bordo, Michael D. & Schwartz, Anna J. (Editors) . . *v.4 p.237*

Bordo, Michael D. (Editor), et al. *v.4 p.213*

Bordo, Michael D. (Editor) *v.4 p.255*

Bordo, Susan *v.6 p.369, p.428, p.436, p.447*

Bordonada, Angela Ena (Translator) *v.2 p.642*

Bordowitz, Hank *v.1 p.266, p.291, p.340*

Bordwell, David, et al. *v.6 p.345*

Bordwell, David *v.6 p.350*

Boreen, Jean, et al. *v.4 p.277*

Borevich, Z. I. & Shafarevich, I. R. *v.5 p.475*

Borg, Dorothy & Heinrichs, Waldo H. *v.3 p.387*

Borgatta, Edgar F. & Montgomery,
   Rhonda J. V. (Editors) *v.4 p.676*

Borge, Dan *v.4 p.92*

Borgerhoff, Elbert B. *v.2 p.455*

Borgerhoff, Joseph L. (Editor) *v.2 p.461*

Borges, Dain *v.3 p.338*

Borges, Jorge Luis *v.2 p.677, p.678*

Borgese, Elisabeth M. (Editor) *v.4 p.478*

Borghi, R. P. & Destriau, M. *v.5 p.279*

Borglin, Anders & Tvede, M. V. *v.4 p.206*

Borhek, Mary V. *v.6 p.368*

Borhi, Laszlo *v.3 p.187*

Boring, Edwin G. *v.5 p.595*

Boritt, Gabor S. *v.4 p.519*

Bork, Robert H. *v.4 p.444, p.462*

Borkman, Thomasina J. *v.5 p.669*

Borkowska, Grazyna *v.2 p.788*

Borkowski, John G., et al. *v.4 p.735*

Borlak, Jürgen (Editor) *v.5 p.125, p.138, p.145, p.183*

Borland, Hal, et al. *v.5 p.77*

Borland, Isabel A. *v.6 p.505, p.511*

Borland, James H. (Editor) *v.4 p.317*

Borlaug, N. E. *v.5 p.12*

Borlaug, Norman, et al. *v.5 p.29*

Born, Georgina & Hesmondhalgh, David (Editors) . . *v.1 p.378*

Born, Georgina *v.1 p.209*

Born, Max & Wolf, Emil *v.5 p.73*

Born, Max; Wolf, Emil *v.5 p.561*

Born, Max *v.5 p.554*

Born, Nicolas *v.2 p.616*

Borneman, John *v.3 p.177*

Borneman, Walter R. *v.3 p.533*

Bornet, Vaughn D. *v.3 p.466*

Bornholdt, Jenny (Editor), et al. *v.2 p.742*

Bornkamm, Gunther *v.1 p.627*

Bornstein, Kate *v.6 p.369*

Bornstein, Marc H. (Editor) *v.5 p.640, p.641, p.651*

Borodziej, Wlodzimierz *v.3 p.254*

Boron, Walter F. & Boulpaep, Emile L. *v.5 p.164*

Borowitz, Eugene B. *v.1 p.551*

Borowski, Tadeusz *v.2 p.789*

Borrelli, Mary Anne & Martin, Janet M. *v.4 p.526*

Borrelli, Mary Anne (Editor) *v.4 p.526*

Borroff, Marie *v.2 p.203, p.206*

Borror, Donald J. *v.5 p.225*

Borrowman, Merle L. *v.4 p.277*

Borsch, Stuart J. *v.3 p.42*

Borsellino, Nino & Pedullà, Walter *v.2 p.697*

Borsi, Franco & Portoghesi, Paolo *v.1 p.791*

Borsi, Franco *v.1 p.685*

Bortz, Jeff & Haber, Stephen H. (Editors) *v.3 p.290*

Borus, Daniel H. *v.2 p.41, p.46, p.49*

Borwein, Jonathan, et al. *v.5 p.457*

Borwein, Jonathan M. & Borwein, Peter B. *v.5 p.475*

Borzello, Frances *v.1 p.705, v.6 p.472*

Borzutzky, Silvia *v.3 p.352*

Bosch, David J. *v.1 p.647*

Bosch, Frans (Author, Illustrator) *v.4 p.878, p.907*

Bosch, Lynette M. F. *v.6 p.491*

Bosch, Robert & Robert Bosch GmbH Staff *v.5 p.715*

Bosco, Joseph (Editor), et al. *v.4 p.39*

Bosco, Ronald A. *v.2 p.28*

Bose, Bimal K. *v.5 p.723*

Bose, Purnima *v.6 p.156*

Bose, Sisir K. & Bose, Sugata (Editors) *v.6 p.158*

Boserup, Ester *v.3 p.42*

Bosha, Francis J. (Editor) *v.2 p.67*

Bosko, Mark Steven *v.6 p.345*

Boskovits, Miklos & Brown, David Alan . . . *v.1 p.726, p.730*

Bosma, Harke A. (Author, Editor) *v.5 p.651*

Bosque-Perez, Ramon & Morera,
   Jose Javier Colon (Editors) *v.3 p.318*

Boss, P. (Editor), et al. *v.5 p.638*

Boss, Pauline *v.5 p.651*

Bossan, Marie-Josephe *v.1 p.715*

Bosso, Christopher J. *v.4 p.449*

Bossy, John *v.1 p.572, v.3 p.120*

Bostock, David *v.1 p.422*

Bostock, Stephen S. *v.5 p.83*

Boston Lesbian Psychologies
  Collective Staff (Editor) *v.4 p.750, v.6 p.380*

Boston Women's Health Book Collective Staff & Boston
  Women's Health Book Collective *v.5 p.523*

Boston Women's Health Book Collective Staff *v.6 p.443*

Bostrvm, Antonia et al. *v.1 p.774*

Boswell, James & Johnson, Samuel *v.3 p.133*

Boswell, James, et al. *v.2 p.240, p.241*

Boswell, James *v.2 p.240*

Boswell, John *v.4 p.739, p.755, v.6 p.363, p.373, p.420*

Boswell, Thomas D. & Curtis, James R. *v.6 p.543*

Bosworth, A. B. *v.3 p.19, p.20*

Bosworth, Barry & Burtless, Gary (Editors) *v.4 p.741*

Bosworth, C. E. *v.1 p.556*

Bosworth, Clifford Edmund . . *v.6 p.581, p.630, p.634, p.644*

Bosworth, Edmund (Editor) *v.6 p.622*

Bosworth, Mary (Editor) *v.6 p.272*

Bosworth, Patricia *v.6 p.417*

Bosworth, R. J. B. *v.3 p.203*

Bosworth, Richard *v.3 p.202*

Bothwell, Robert *v.3 p.535, p.538, p.540*

Botkin, B. A. *v.3 p.424*

Botkin, Benjamin A. *v.3 p.394*

Botkin, Daniel B. *v.5 p.409, v.6 p.288*

Botkin, Jim *v.4 p.77*

Botstein, Leon (Editor) *v.1 p.194, p.313*

Bottero, Jean, et al. *v.3 p.5*

Bottero, Jean *v.1 p.538, v.3 p.5*

Bottéro, Jean *v.3 p.5*

Bottigheimer, Karl S. *v.3 p.137*

Botting, Douglas *v.5 p.237*

Bottjer, David J., et al. *v.5 p.446*

Botto, Francis *v.4 p.419*

Bottomore, Tom *v.4 p.675*

Bouchard, Claude (Editor), et al. *v.4 p.790*

Bouchard, Claude (Editor) *v.4 p.790, p.876*

Bouchard, Constance B. *v.3 p.142*

Boucher, Bruce *v.1 p.775*

Boucicault, Dion, et al. *v.2 p.202*

Boucicault, Dion *v.2 p.264*

Boucquey, Thierry & Diamond, Marie Josephine . . . *v.2 p.575*

Boudart, Marina (Editor), et al. *v.3 p.205*

Boudett, Kathryn Parker (Editor), et al. *v.5 p.600*

Boudon, Raymond & Bourricaud, Francois *v.4 p.676*

Boudreau, H. L. *v.2 p.641*

Boudreau, Thomas E. *v.4 p.633, p.648*

Boudreau, Vincent *v.6 p.179*

Boue, Juan Carlos *v.3 p.360*

Bouhdiba, Abdulwahab *v.1 p.559*

Boukreev, Anatoli & DeWalt, G. Weston *v.4 p.789*

Boulanger, Norman C. *v.1 p.148*

Boulby, Marion *v.6 p.621*

Boulby, Mark *v.2 p.617*

Boulden, Jane & Weiss, Thomas George . . . *v.4 p.633, p.658*

Boulden, Jane *v.4 p.648*

Boulding, Kenneth E. & Mukerjee, Tapan (Editors) . . *v.4 p.208*

Bouldrey, Brian (Editor) *v.6 p.406*

Boulez, Pierre *v.1 p.209, p.210, p.312*

Boullata, Issa J. & DeYoung, Terri (Editors) *v.6 p.658*

Boullata, Kamal (Editor, Translator) *v.6 p.658*

Boulton, Chris & Turner, Patrick *v.4 p.67*

Boumans, Marcel *v.4 p.198, p.240*

Bouquet, Mary & Porto, Nuno *v.4 p.47*

Bouquet, Mary (Editor) *v.4 p.47*

Bourantonis, Dimitris & Wiener, Jarrod (Editors) . . *v.4 p.633*

Bourantonis, Dimitris *v.4 p.655*

Bourdieu, Pierre & Johnson, Randal *v.1 p.825*

Bourdieu, Pierre *v.2 p.455, p.566,*
                                v.4 p.21, p.23, p.208, p.726, p.743

Bourgaize, David B., et al. *v.5 p.217*

Bourgault, Louise M. *v.4 p.415*

Bourgeacq, Jacques *v.2 p.541*

Bourgine, Paul & Nadal, Jean-Pierre (Editors) . . . *v.4 p.272*

Bourgois, Philippe I. *v.4 p.776*

Bourke, Joanna *v.3 p.78*

Bourliere, F. *v.5 p.357*

Bourne, Gilbert C. *v.4 p.865*

Bourne, Kenneth *v.3 p.91, p.93, p.108, p.110*

Bourne, Philip E. & Weissig, Helge (Editors) . *v.5 p.103, p.104,*
                                                          p.105

Bourne, Russell *v.6 p.685*

Bourne, Stephen *v.6 p.415*

Bournonville, August *v.1 p.6*

Bournoutian, George A. *v.3 p.231, v.6 p.633*

Bourque, Bruce J. *v.4 p.10, v.6 p.702*

Bourricaud, Francois *v.3 p.328*

Bouson, J. Brooks *v.2 p.767*

Boutelle, Sara H. *v.1 p.791*

Boutros-Ghali, Boutros (Introduction by) . *v.4 p.633, p.646, p.648*

Bouvard, Marguerite G. *v.6 p.430*

Bouvier, Virginia *v.3 p.530*

Bouwsma, William J. *v.1 p.580, p.600, p.602, v.3 p.70*

Bouyer, Louis *v.1 p.576*

Bouza, Anthony V. *v.6 p.260*

Bouzereau, Laurent *v.6 p.320*

Bove, Jose & Dufour, Francois *v.6 p.297*

Bovey, Frank A. & Mirau, Peter A. *v.5 p.323*

Bovey, Frank A. *v.5 p.290*

Bovon, Francois *v.1 p.628*

Bow, Leslie *v.6 p.95, p.111*

Bowden, Charles *v.4 p.764*

Bowden, Henry W. *v.1 p.525*

Bowden, John, John (Editor) *v.1 p.593*

Bowden, Mary E. *v.5 p.260*

Bowden, Mary Ellen, et al. *v.5 p.326*

Bowden, Muriel *v.2 p.207*

Bowden, Valmai *v.5 p.77, p.244*

Bowe, Patrick (Translator) *v.1 p.818*

Bowen, Catherine D. *v.4 p.467*

Bowen, Desmond *v.1 p.581*

Bowen, E. *v.2 p.334*

Bowen, Elizabeth & Greene, Graham . . *v.2 p.335, p.349, p.378*

Bowen, Elizabeth *v.2 p.334, p.335*

Bowen, Howard R; Schuster, Jack H *v.4 p.292*

Bowen, Howard R. *v.4 p.289, p.330*

Bowen, James & Bowen, Margarita *v.5 p.172*

Bowen, James *v.4 p.324*

Bowen, John *v.2 p.282*

Bowen, José Antonio (Editor) *v.1 p.402*

Bowen, Kevin (Editor, Translator) *v.6 p.169*

Bowen, Mark *v.6 p.293*

Bowen, Norman L. *v.5 p.437*

Bowen, Roger W. *v.4 p.621, v.6 p.223*

Bowen, William G. & Bok, Derek *v.4 p.294*

Bowen, William G. & Levin, Sarah A. *v.4 p.821, p.893*

Bowen, Zack R. *v.2 p.357*

Bower, D. I. & Maddams, W. F. *v.5 p.323*

Bower, Frank A. & Ward, Richard B. (Editors) . . . *v.5 p.375*

Bower, Gordon H. & Hilgard, Ernest J. *v.4 p.356*

Bower, James M. & Bolouri, Hamid (Editors) . *v.5 p.111, p.145*

Bowers, Fredson (Editor) *v.2 p.53*

Bowers, Fredson *v.2 p.228*

Bowers, James R. & Rich, Wilbur C. (Editors) . . . *v.4 p.543*

Bowers, Jane & Tick, Judith (Editors) . . . *v.1 p.378, v.6 p.474*

Bowers, Jeffrey S. & Marsolek, Chad J. (Editors) . *v.5 p.609*

Bowers, Michael W. *v.3 p.529*

Bowers, Newton L. Jr., et al. *v.5 p.504*

Bowers, Toni *v.6 p.477*

Bowersock, G. W. (Editor), et al. *v.3 p.30, p.191*

Bowersock, G. W. *v.3 p.30*

Bowersock, Glen W. *v.3 p.27, p.30*

Bowersox, Donald J. *v.4 p.143*

Bowes, D. R. *v.5 p.437*

Bowien, Botho & Durre, Peter (Editors) *v.5 p.120*

Bowker, Gordon *v.2 p.367*

Bowker, John (Editor) *v.1 p.522*

Bowker, John *v.1 p.526*

Bowker, Lee H. (Editor) *v.6 p.257*

Bowker, Robert *v.6 p.617*

Bowker Staff (Editor) *v.2 p.549*

Bowlby, John, et al. *v.4 p.735*

Bowlby, John *v.3 p.48, v.4 p.735*

Bowler, Ian R. (Editor), et al. *v.5 p.12*

Bowler, Peter J. *v.5 p.77, p.190, p.202*

Bowles, D. J. (Editor), et al. *v.5 p.124*

Bowles, Gloria *v.6 p.462*

Bowles, Jane *v.2 p.58, v.6 p.394*

Bowles, Joseph E. *v.5 p.421*

Bowles, Newton *v.4 p.633*

Bowles, Paul *v.2 p.62*

Bowles, Samuel (Editor), et al. *v.4 p.264*

Bowles, Samuel, et al. *v.4 p.214, p.251*

Bowles, Samuel *v.4 p.249, p.251, p.762*

Bowles, Stephen E. *v.6 p.305*

Bowley, Marian *v.4 p.217*

Bowley, Roger & Sanchez, Mariana *v.5 p.558*

Bowmaker, Simon W. (Editor) *v.4 p.185*

Bowman, Alan K. & Woolf, Greg (Editors) *v.3 p.3*

Bowman, Alan K. (Editor), et al. *v.3 p.22*

Bowman, Alan K. *v.3 p.10*

Bowman, Barbara A. & Russell, Robert M. (Editors) . *v.5 p.33*

Bowman, Kirk S. *v.3 p.273*

Bowman, Mary A. *v.6 p.570*

Bowman, Walter Parker *v.1 p.58*

Bowman, Wayne D. *v.1 p.380*

Bowness, Alan *v.1 p.677, p.685, p.778*

Bowra, C. M. *v.2 p.416*

Bowra, Maurice *v.2 p.403*

Bowring, Finn *v.5 p.217*

Bowring, Richard J. *v.6 p.226*

Bowring, Richard *v.1 p.541*

Bowron, Edgar Peters *v.1 p.674, p.685*

Bowser, Kathryn *v.6 p.346*

Bowser, Pearl & Spence, Louise *v.6 p.329, p.340*

Bowser, Pearl (Editor), et al. *v.6 p.329, p.340*

Bowtell, David & Sambrook, Joseph (Editors) . . . *v.5 p.110*

Bowyer, Justin (Editor) *v.6 p.334*

Box, George E. P., et al. *v.5 p.481*

Box, Harry C. *v.6 p.349*

Box, Richard C. *v.4 p.545, p.580*

Boxer, Barbara & Women of the Senate Members . . *v.3 p.455*

Boxer, C. R. *v.3 p.334*

Boxer, Marilyn J. & Quataert, Jean H. (Editors) . . . *v.3 p.52*

Boxer, Marilyn J. & Quataert, Jean H. . *v.3 p.50, v.6 p.451, p.453*

Boxer *v.3 p.73*

Boxill, Jan (Editor) *v.4 p.802*

Boyarin, Daniel, et al. *v.6 p.373*

Boyarin, Jonathan (Editor) *v.4 p.22*

Boyce, Charles *v.1 p.805, v.2 p.222*

Boyce, D. George *v.4 p.583*

Boyce, David George *v.3 p.134, p.138*

Boyce, Joseph M. *v.5 p.434*

Boyce, Mark S. & Haney, Alan W. (Editors) . *v.5 p.11, p.28, p.40, p.356*

Boyce, Mary (Editor, Translator) *v.1 p.538*

Boyce, Mary *v.1 p.538*

Boyce, William E. & DiPrima, Richard C. . *v.4 p.206, v.5 p.486*

Boyd, Andrew *v.4 p.381, p.413*

Boyd, Blanche M. *v.6 p.394*

Boyd, Brian *v.2 p.104*

Boyd, Carolyn P. *v.3 p.243*

Boyd, Douglas R. *v.4 p.412*

Boyd, E. *v.6 p.491, p.522*

Boyd, Helen *v.6 p.369*

Boyd, Herb *v.3 p.490, v.6 p.3, p.710*

Boyd, J. Patrick & Samuels, Richard J. *v.4 p.621*

Boyd, Kelly *v.6 p.746*

Boyd, Malcolm *v.1 p.182, p.302, p.352*

Boyd, Martin *v.2 p.744*

Boyd, Richard H. & Phillips, Paul J. *v.5 p.322*

Boyd, Susan C. *v.6 p.258*

Boyd, Valerie *v.2 p.80, v.6 p.16, p.23*

Boyd, William *v.2 p.335, v.4 p.324, p.341*

Boyde, Patrick *v.2 p.704*

Boyden, David D. *v.1 p.389, p.397, p.399*

Boyd-Franklin, Nancy *v.5 p.667*

Boydston, Jo Ann (Editor) *v.4 p.341*

Boyer, Carl B. *v.5 p.465*

Boyer, Christopher R. *v.3 p.290*

Boyer, Ernest L. & Carnegie Foundation for the Advancement
   of Teaching Staff *v.4 p.289, p.330*

Boyer, Ernest L. & Glassick, Charles E. *v.4 p.292, p.330*

Boyer, John W. *v.3 p.183*

Boyer, Kenneth K., et al. *v.4 p.117*

Boyer, Pascal *v.4 p.27, p.36, v.5 p.633*

Boyer, Patricia E. *v.1 p.84, p.95*

Boyer, Paul & Nissenbaum, Stephen *v.3 p.405*

Boyer, Paul (Editor) *v.3 p.466*

Boyer, Paul S. (Editor) *v.3 p.372*

Boyer, Paul S. *v.4 p.458*

Boyer, Richard G. & Spurling, Geoffrey (Editors) . *v.3 p.284*

Boyer, Richard O. *v.3 p.430*

Boyer, Richard *v.3 p.262, p.284*

Boyes, Walt *v.5 p.563*

Boykin, Anne & O'Bryan-Schoenhofer, Savina . . . *v.5 p.527*

Boykin, Keith *v.6 p.366, p.368, p.375, p.378*

Boyle, A. J. *v.2 p.425*

Boyle, Anne M. *v.2 p.78*

Boyle, Anthony James & Dominik, William J. *v.3 p.27*

Boyle, Anthony James *v.2 p.425*

Boyle, Catherine M. *v.3 p.352*

Boyle, Deirdre *v.4 p.413*

Boyle, Eloise M. & Gerhart, Genevra (Editors) . *v.2 p.775, p.776*

Boyle, Francis A. *v.4 p.627*

Boyle, Godfrey (Editor) *v.5 p.708*

Boyle, J. A. & Grossman, Stanley I. (Editors) . . . *v.6 p.629*

Boyle, John A. (Translator) *v.6 p.238*

Boyle, Kay *v.2 p.62, p.63*

Boyle, Kevin *v.4 p.124, p.438, v.5 p.728*

Boyle, Michael *v.4 p.790, p.878*

Boyle, Peter G. *v.4 p.560*

Boyle, Raymond & Haynes, Richard . *v.4 p.814, p.898, p.901*

Boyle, Raymond (Editor), et al. *v.4 p.882, p.887, p.901*

Boyle, Richard & Lemaire, Donald (Editors) *v.4 p.580*

Boyle, T. C. *v.2 p.141*

Boyle, Walden P. *v.1 p.154*

Boylestad, Robert L. & Nashelsky, Louis *v.5 p.722*

Boylestad, Robert L. *v.5 p.720*

Boyne, Daniel J. *v.4 p.835, p.865*

Boynton, Victoria & Malin, Jo *v.6 p.476*

Boyte, Harry Chatten *v.4 p.547*

Bozeman, Adda B. *v.4 p.477*

Bozo, Frederic *v.4 p.643*

Bozoki, Andras (Editor), et al. *v.4 p.595*

Bozzoli, Belinda & Nkotsoe, Mmantho *v.6 p.78*

Braad Thomsen, Christian *v.6 p.418*

Brabenec, Robert *v.5 p.490*

Brabner, J. H. F. (Editor) *v.4 p.374*

Bracamonte, Jose A. & Spencer, David E. *v.3 p.298*

Brace, Ian *v.4 p.137*

Bracewell, Ronald Newbold *v.5 p.64*

Bracey, Gerald W. *v.4 p.285, p.325*

Bracey, John H. & Sinha, Manisha *v.6 p.3*

Brach, Anthony R. *v.5 p.169*

Brachin, Pierre *v.2 p.620*

Bracken, Bruce A. (Editor) *v.4 p.356, v.5 p.602*

Bracken, James K. & Sterling, Christopher H. . . . *v.4 p.419*

Brackenridge, Celia *v.4 p.814, p.840*

Brackett, David *v.1 p.266*

Brackett, Nathan & Hoard, Christian (Editors) . *v.1 p.170, p.266*

Brackman, Arnold C. *v.3 p.5*

Brackman, Roman *v.3 p.223*

Bradbrook, M. C. *v.2 p.226*

Bradbrook, Muriel C. *v.2 p.185*

Bradburn, Norman M., et al. *v.4 p.137*

Bradbury, John M. *v.2 p.13*

Bradbury, Malcolm *v.2 p.60, p.189, p.194, p.331, p.345*

Bradbury, Ray *v.2 p.63*

Bradby, David *v.2 p.461*

Braddon, Mary Elizabeth *v.2 p.265*

Braden, Twain *v.4 p.866*

Brader, Ted *v.4 p.424*

Bradford, Peter *v.1 p.801*

Bradford, William *v.3 p.405, p.487*

Brading, D. A. *v.3 p.262, p.284*

Bradl, Heike *v.5 p.354, p.355, p.371, p.372, p.373*

Bradley, A. C. *v.2 p.234*

Bradley, Andrew C. *v.2 p.166*

Bradley, Bill *v.4 p.853*

Bradley, Carol June *v.1 p.165*

Bradley, Craig (Editor) *v.4 p.467*

Bradley, Diarmuid & Butterfield, Jeremy *v.2 p.635*

Bradley, Edwin M. *v.6 p.315*

Bradley, F. H. *v.1 p.445, p.488*

Bradley, Ian (Editor) *v.1 p.248, p.361, p.407*

Bradley, Ian *v.1 p.608*

Bradley, James E. & Muller, Richard A. *v.1 p.597*

Bradley, John R. (Editor) *v.2 p.43*

Bradley, John R., et al. *v.5 p.125*

Bradley, Keith R. *v.3 p.23, p.26*

Bradley, Keith *v.3 p.23*

Bradley, Lloyd *v.1 p.291*

Bradley, Marion Zimmer *v.2 p.141*

Bradley, Mark Philip *v.6 p.168*

Bradley, Patricia L. *v.2 p.129*

Bradley, Patricia *v.3 p.407*

Bradley, Raymond S. *v.5 p.445*

Bradley, Renee (Editor), et al. *v.4 p.318*

Bradley, Richard *v.4 p.12*

Bradley, Sculley (Editor, Compiled by) *v.2 p.18*

Bradner, Leicester *v.2 p.213*

Bradshaw, Brendan (Editor), et al. *v.3 p.136*

Bradshaw, David (Editor) *v.2 p.178, p.184*

Bradshaw, G. A. (Editor), et al. . . . *v.5 p.167, p.178, p.186*

Bradshaw, Michael J. *v.3 p.380, v.4 p.396*

Bradshaw, Paul F. & Hoffman, Lawrence A. *v.1 p.653*

Bradshaw, Terry *v.4 p.858*

Bradshaw, Timothy (Editor) *v.1 p.595*

Bradsher, Keith *v.4 p.153, v.5 p.715*

Bradstock, Ross A. (Editor), et al. . . *v.5 p.31, p.167, v.6 p.293*

Bradstreet, Anne D. *v.2 p.28*

Bradt, Hale *v.5 p.65*

Brady, Anne-Marie *v.6 p.203*

Brady, Bernard V. *v.1 p.651*

Brady, Ciaran & Gillespie, Raymond (Editors) *v.3 p.134, p.136*

Brady, Ciaran (Editor) *v.3 p.134*

Brady, Ciaran *v.3 p.136*

Brady, David W., et al. *v.4 p.548*

Brady, James *v.3 p.296*

Brady, Mary Pat *v.6 p.497, p.511*

Brady, Nyle C. & Weil, Ray R. *v.5 p.48*

Brady, Thomas A. Jr. (Editor), et al. *v.3 p.38*

Brady, Thomas A. Jr. (Editor) *v.1 p.600*

Brady, Thomas A. *v.3 p.165*

Braeman, John *v.3 p.456*

Braess, Dietrich *v.5 p.491, p.500*

Braga, Anthony A. *v.6 p.264*

Bragdon, Kathleen J. *v.6 p.702*

Bragg, Lois (Editor) *v.4 p.699*

Bragg, Steven M. & Roehl-Anderson, Janice M. . . . *v.4 p.106*

Bragg, Steven M. *v.4 p.104, p.174*

Braham, Randolph L. *v.3 p.82*

Brahms, Johannes *v.1 p.194, p.313*

Braidwood, Robert John & Willey, Gordon R. *v.4 p.37*

Brailsford, Dennis *v.4 p.804, p.855*

Brailsford, Henry Noel *v.3 p.102*

Braisted, William R. *v.3 p.382*

Braithwaite, John *v.6 p.278*

Braithwaite, Kamau *v.2 p.767*

Braithwaite, Rodric *v.3 p.228*

Brake, Laurel (Editor), et al. *v.6 p.740*

Brake, Laurel *v.6 p.740*

Brakeman, Lynne *v.6 p.425*

Brako, Lois (Editor), et al. *v.5 p.207*

Bram, Christopher *v.6 p.394*

Braman, Donald *v.6 p.276*

Brambilla Barcilon, Pinin & Marani, Pietro C. . . . *v.1 p.736*

Bramble, J. C. *v.2 p.439*

Brameld, Theodore Burghard Hurt *v.4 p.341*

Brammer, Robert *v.5 p.636*

Brams, Steven J. *v.4 p.83*

Bramstedt, Ernest K. *v.4 p.768*

Bramwell, Martyn *v.5 p.77, p.225*

Branan, Carl R. *v.5 p.740*

Brana-Shute, Gary *v.3 p.322*

Branca, Vittore *v.2 p.701*

Branch, Michael P. (Editor) *v.5 p.77*

Branch, Taylor *v.3 p.439, v.6 p.12*

Branch, Watson G. (Editor) *v.2 p.47*

Branch, William B. (Editor) *v.1 p.63, p.95, p.122, p.127, p.130*

Brand, C. P. *v.2 p.709*

Brand, Johanna *v.6 p.688, p.693*

Brand, Laurie A. *v.6 p.591, p.617*

Brand, Peter & Pertile, Lino (Editors) *v.2 p.697*

Brandabur, Edward *v.2 p.357*

Brandell, Gunnar *v.2 p.629*

Branden, Carl-Ivar & Tooze, John *v.5 p.115*

Brandenberger, David *v.3 p.225*

Brandes, Stanley *v.3 p.266, v.4 p.773*

Brandi, Karl *v.3 p.182*

Brandl, Steven G. & Barlow, David E. *v.6 p.261*

Brandon, Henry *v.3 p.466*

Brandon, James R. & Leiter, Samuel L. (Editors) . . *v.1 p.129,*
p.132, p.133, v.6 p.234

Brandon, James R. (Editor) *v.1 p.58, p.129, p.130, p.133*

Brandon, James R. *v.6 p.234*

Brandon, Robert N. *v.5 p.191*

Brandrup, J. *v.5 p.322*

Brands, H. W. & Schlesinger, Arthur M. Jr. *v.3 p.466*

Brands, H. W. Jr. (Editor) *v.3 p.466*

Brands, H. W. Jr. *v.3 p.385, p.446, p.466*

Brands, H. W. *v.3 p.415, p.508, p.530, v.4 p.517*

Brandt, Allan M. *v.5 p.516*

Brandt, Anthony *v.2 p.27*

Brandt, E. N. *v.5 p.316*

Brandt, Eric (Editor) *v.6 p.386*

Brandt, George W. *v.1 p.55*

Brandt, Nat *v.4 p.804, p.858, p.893, v.6 p.188, p.203*

Brandt, Richard B. *v.1 p.483, p.486*

Brandt, Richard M. *v.4 p.282*

Brandt, Siegmund *v.5 p.562*

Brandt, Steven A. *v.5 p.702*

Brandwood, Leonard *v.1 p.423*

Branford, Sue & Rocha, Jan *v.3 p.338*

Branham, R. Bracht *v.1 p.428, v.2 p.416*

Brann, Eva T. H. *v.1 p.481*

Brann, Eva *v.2 p.413*

Brannan, David A., et al. *v.5 p.494*

Branner, Hans Christian *v.2 p.626*

Brannigan, Augustine *v.5 p.409, p.411*

Brannigan, John *v.2 p.178, p.333, p.570*

Branscomb, Anne W. *v.4 p.445*

Branscombe, Peter *v.1 p.188, p.228, p.343*

Bransden, A. *v.5 p.554*

Bransden, B. H. & Joachain, C. J. *v.5 p.549*

Brant, Sebastian *v.2 p.594*

Brantingham, Jeffrey P. (Editor), et al. *v.4 p.15, p.16*

Brantlinger, Patrick . . *v.2 p.174, p.190, v.6 p.738, p.745, p.752,*
p.755, p.757, p.766

Brasch, Charles *v.2 p.744*
Brasch, Walter M. . *v.2 p.40, v.4 p.561, p.562, p.572, v.6 p.307*
Braschi, Giannina *v.6 p.491*
Brashear, Ronald & Lewis, Daniel *v.5 p.61*
Brasil, Emanuel & Smith, William J. (Editors) . . . *v.2 p.689*
Brasillach, Robert *v.2 p.508*
Brass, Paul R. *v.6 p.149*
Brasseaux, Carl A. *v.3 p.507*
Braswell, Geoffrey E. (Editor) *v.3 p.260*
Brater, Enoch (Editor) *v.2 p.101*
Brater, Enoch *v.2 p.333*
Brathwaite, Kamau *v.2 p.767*
Bratt, James D. *v.1 p.588*
Bratton, Michael & Walle,
  Nicholas van de *v.4 p.503, p.584, p.611*
Bratton, William W. & Knobler, Peter *v.6 p.259*
Braude, Benjamin & Lewis,
  Bernard (Editors) *v.6 p.589, p.596, p.600*
Braude, William G. (Editor) *v.1 p.550*
Braude, William G. (Translator) *v.1 p.550*
Braudel, Fernand *v.3 p.3, p.38*
Braudy, Leo *v.6 p.440*
Brauer, Fred & Castillo-Chavez,
  Carlos *v.5 p.91, p.93, p.188, p.189*
Brauer, Jurgen & Dunne, Paul J. *v.4 p.217, p.256, p.258*
Brauer *v.5 p.306*
Brault, Gerard J. (Editor) *v.2 p.466*
Brault, Gerard J. *v.2 p.466*
Brault, Jacques *v.2 p.540*
Brauman, J. I. & Streitwieser, Andrew Jr. *v.5 p.287*
Braun, Barbara & Roe, Peter *v.1 p.683*
Braun, E. *v.1 p.137, p.152*
Braun, Emily *v.1 p.736*
Braun, Eric *v.6 p.415*
Braun, Hans-Joachim *v.1 p.210, p.244, p.386*
Braun, Herbert *v.3 p.357*
Braun, Sidney D. (Editor) *v.2 p.455*
Braun, Volker *v.2 p.616*
Braunbehrens, Volkmar *v.1 p.188, p.352*
Braund, David *v.3 p.230*
Braund, Susan H. *v.2 p.427*
Braund, Susanna Morton *v.2 p.424*
Braunmuller, A. R. & Hattaway,
  Michael (Editors) *v.1 p.58, p.74, p.98, v.2 p.185*
Braunmuller, A. R. *v.2 p.221*
Braunstein, Peter & Doyle, Michael William (Editors) *v.4 p.712*
Braunstein, Susan L. *v.1 p.806*
Brautigan, Ianthe *v.2 p.58*
Brautigan, Richard *v.2 p.58, p.141*
Braveboy-Wagner, Jacqueline A. *v.3 p.359*
Bravman, Bill *v.6 p.64*
Brawley, Mark R. *v.4 p.662*
Braxton, Joanne M. *v.6 p.476*
Bray, Alan *v.6 p.364, p.421*
Bray, Donald E. & Stanley, Roderick K. *v.5 p.684*
Brazaitis, Peter *v.5 p.250*

Brazell, Karen (Translator) *v.6 p.229*
Brazell, Karen *v.1 p.129, p.132, p.133*
Brazelton, T. Berry & Greenspan, Stanley I. *v.5 p.641*
Braziel, Jana Evans & LeBesco, Kathleen (Editors) . *v.6 p.445*
Breakey, Kate *v.1 p.765*
Breasted, James H. (Editor) *v.3 p.8*
Breasted, James Henr *v.6 p.58*
Breasted, James Henry *v.6 p.57*
Breault, Donna Adair & Breault, Rick (Editors) . . . *v.4 p.341*
Brebner, John B. *v.3 p.403, p.405*
Brecht, Bertolt . *v.1 p.55, p.81, p.108, p.138, p.149, p.152, p.248,*
                    p.367, p.407, v.2 p.605
Brecht, Martin *v.1 p.602*
Brechtefeld, Jorg *v.3 p.160*
Breckenridge, Carol A. (Editor) *v.2 p.759, v.6 p.150*
Bredbenner, Candice Lewis *v.6 p.468*
Bredero, Adriaan H. *v.1 p.578*
Bredin, Jean-Denis *v.3 p.59, p.154*
Bredsdorff, Elias & Andersen *v.2 p.626*
Bree, Germaine *v.2 p.455, p.459, p.511, p.519*
Bree, Linda *v.2 p.248*
Breen, T. H. & Innes, Stephen *v.3 p.499*
Breen, T. H. *v.3 p.499*
Bregel, Yuri *v.4 p.384*
Breger, Louis *v.5 p.595*
Bregman, Albert S. *v.5 p.607*
Brehm, Barbara *v.4 p.790, p.878*
Breidbach, Olaf (Contribution by), et al. *v.5 p.230*
Breisach, Ernst A. *v.3 p.373*
Breitmaier, Eberhard and Gerhard Bauer *v.5 p.272*
Breitman, Richard, et al. *v.3 p.83*
Breitman, Richard *v.3 p.83*
Bremen, Brian *v.2 p.136*
Bremer, Francis J. *v.1 p.580, p.588, v.3 p.484, p.487*
Bremer, Michael *v.5 p.680*
Bremser, Martha (Editor) *v.1 p.3*
Bremser, Martha *v.1 p.3, p.6*
Brenan, Gerald *v.3 p.241*
Brenan *v.1 p.578*
Brenchley, ; Harper, ... *v.5 p.449*
Brend, Barbara *v.1 p.673*
Brendel, Otto J. *v.1 p.669, p.685*
Breneman, David W. *v.4 p.291*
Brennan, Elizabeth A. & Clarage, Elizabeth C. . . . *v.4 p.403*
Brennan, James P. (Editor), et al. *v.3 p.347*
Brennan, James P. *v.3 p.347*
Brennan, Marcia *v.1 p.705*
Brennan, Niamh *v.4 p.91, p.94, p.99*
Brennan, Richard P. *v.5 p.542*
Brenneis, Donald & Macaulay, Ronald K. S. (Editors) *v.4 p.18*
Brenner, Benjamin, et al. *v.5 p.521*
Brenner, Charles & Duggan, David J. (Editors) . . . *v.5 p.148*
Brenner, Louis *v.6 p.73*
Brenner, Michael *v.3 p.83, p.169, p.179*
Brenner, Neil & Keil, Roger (Editors) *v.6 p.716, p.720*

Brenner, Philip *v.3 p.307*

Brenner, Rachel Feldhay *v.6 p.648*

Brenner, Saul & Spaeth, Harold J. *v.4 p.535*

Brent, Joseph *v.1 p.440*

Brentano, Clemens *v.2 p.596*

Brentano, Robert *v.3 p.198, v.6 p.577*

Brenzinger, Matthias *v.6 p.80*

Brereton, Geoffrey *v.2 p.455, p.460, p.461*

Bresciani-Turroni, Constantino *v.4 p.237*

Breslin, Paul *v.2 p.770*

Breslow, Ronald *v.5 p.264*

Bresser Pereira, Luiz C. *v.3 p.338*

Bresser-Pereira, Luiz Carlos *v.4 p.545*

Bressoud, D. M. *v.5 p.475*

Bressoud, David M. & Wagon, Stan *v.5 p.475*

Bressoud, David M. *v.5 p.478*

Bressoud, David *v.5 p.490*

Bretall, Robert (Editor) *v.1 p.580*

Brethauer, Dale M. *v.4 p.118*

Breton, Andre *v.1 p.480, v.2 p.510*

Breton, André *v.2 p.511*

Breton, Nicholas *v.2 p.213*

Breton, Raymond *v.3 p.542*

Bretonne, Restif de la *v.2 p.478*

Brett, David *v.6 p.409*

Brett, George Sidney *v.5 p.595*

Brett, Jeanne M. *v.4 p.74*

Brett, Philip (Editor), et al. *v.1 p.378, v.6 p.408*

Brettell, Richard R. & Fonsmark, Anne-Birgitte . . . *v.1 p.736*

Brettell, Richard *v.1 p.677*

Brettler, Marc Zvi *v.6 p.645*

Breward, Christopher *v.1 p.715*

Brewer, Cynthia A. *v.4 p.386*

Brewer, Derek S. & Gibson, Jonathan (Editors) . . . *v.2 p.206*

Brewer, Derek S. (Editor) *v.2 p.207*

Brewer, Derek S. *v.2 p.207*

Brewer, Gay *v.2 p.141*

Brewer, John & Hunter, Albert *v.4 p.686*

Brewer, John & Styles,
John (Editors) *v.3 p.103, p.106, p.108, p.123*

Brewer, John D. *v.4 p.690, p.766, p.774*

Brewer, John *v.3 p.93, p.106, p.108, p.122*

Brewer, Neil & Wilson, Carlene (Editors) *v.5 p.591*

Brewer, Richard *v.6 p.298*

Brewster, Bill & Broughton, Frank *v.1 p.266*

Brewster, Dorothy P. *v.2 p.392, v.6 p.730*

Brexel, Bernadette *v.4 p.124*

Breyer, Donald E., et al. *v.5 p.685*

Breytenbach, Breyten *v.2 p.623*

Brezhneva, Luba *v.3 p.228*

Brezonik, Patrick L. *v.5 p.378*

Bréchon, Robert *v.2 p.522*

Brée, Germaine & Morot-Sir, Edouard *v.2 p.459*

Brian, Denis *v.5 p.394*

Brians, Paul *v.2 p.759*

Briant, Pierre *v.3 p.11*

Brick, Howard *v.3 p.366, p.370*

Bricke, John *v.1 p.451*

Bricker, David C. *v.4 p.362*

Bricker, Kathryn *v.4 p.793*

Brickhouse, Thomas C. & Smith,
Nicholas D. *v.1 p.422, v.2 p.417*

Brickman, Louis *v.5 p.683*

Brickman, William W. *v.4 p.333*

Bridenbaugh, Carl & Bridenbaugh, Jessica *v.3 p.492*

Bridenbaugh, Carl *v.3 p.101, p.499*

Bridenthal, Renate, et al. *v.3 p.50, v.6 p.449*

Bridge, F. R. *v.3 p.182*

Bridge, Gary & Watson, Sophie (Editors) *v.6 p.709*

Bridge, J. S. *v.5 p.427*

Bridges, E. M. *v.5 p.48*

Bridges, Robert S. *v.2 p.253*

Bridges, Roy; Hair, P E *v.4 p.378*

Bridges-Adams, William *v.1 p.98*

Bridgman, Richard *v.2 p.121*

Bridson, Gavin *v.5 p.224*

Brief, Arthur P. *v.5 p.578*

Brierly, James L. *v.4 p.477*

Briggs, Asa & Burke, Peter *v.3 p.37, v.4 p.415*

Briggs, Asa . *v.3 p.91, p.110, v.4 p.413, v.5 p.391, v.6 p.710, p.735,
p.757, p.761, p.762*

Briggs, Charles L. & Mantini-Briggs, Clara *v.3 p.360*

Briggs, Charles L. & Van Ness, John R. (Editors) . . *v.6 p.533*

Briggs, Charles L. *v.2 p.16, v.4 p.691*

Briggs, Clarence E. *v.3 p.304*

Briggs, Dennie *v.4 p.349*

Briggs, Jean L. *v.6 p.702*

Briggs, John C. *v.5 p.167*

Briggs, John (Editor), et al. *v.1 p.568*

Briggs, Julia *v.2 p.392*

Briggs, Laura *v.3 p.318*

Briggs, Leslie J. (Editor), et al. *v.4 p.346*

Briggs, Philip J. *v.3 p.451*

Briggs, Shirley A.; Rachel Carson Council Staff . . . *v.5 p.312*

Brigham, John *v.4 p.535*

Brighouse, Harry *v.4 p.346*

Bright, Chris *v.5 p.178*

Bright, Michael *v.5 p.224*

Brigstocke, Hugh *v.1 p.662*

Brill E *v.1 p.553*

Brillouin, Leon *v.5 p.408*

Brimblecombe, Peter & Lein, Alla Yu (Editors) . . . *v.5 p.111*

Brimelow, Peter *v.4 p.282*

Brinch Hansen, Per *v.5 p.348*

Brindle, Steven *v.1 p.720*

Bringa, Tone *v.3 p.249*

Bringmann, Wolfgang G. (Editor), et al. *v.5 p.595*

Brink, André *v.2 p.623*

Brink, David Owen *v.1 p.487, p.514*

Brink, Judy & Mencher, Joan (Editors) *v.6 p.458*

Brink, T. L. & Carmody, Denise L. *v.1 p.525*

Brinkerhoff, Derick W. & Brinkerhoff, Jennifer M. . . *v.4 p.166*

Brinkley, Alan & Dyer, Davis (Editors) *v.3 p.377*

Brinkley, Alan *v.3 p.439, p.446, p.466*

Brinkley, Douglas & Ambrose, Stephen E. . . . *v.3 p.365, p.371*

Brinkley, Douglas G. *v.4 p.153*

Brinkley, Douglas (Introduction by) *v.3 p.466*

Brinkley, Douglas *v.3 p.365, p.372, p.382, p.456*

Brinkmann, Reinhold & Wolff, Christoph . . . *v.1 p.245, p.299*

Brinkworth, Brian *v.4 p.391*

Brinnin, John M. *v.2 p.121*

Brinson, Peter *v.1 p.46, p.47*

Brint, Steven & Karabel, Jerome *v.4 p.291, p.330*

Brinton, Clarence C. *v.4 p.628*

Brinton, Laurel & Arnovick, Leslie *v.2 p.554*

Brinton, Mary C. (Editor) *v.6 p.218*

Brinton, Mary C. *v.6 p.218*

Briones, Claudia Luis & Lanata, Jose L. (Editors) . . *v.3 p.352*

Brisbin, Richard A. Jr. *v.4 p.467, p.535*

Brisco, Thomas V. *v.1 p.617*

Briscoe, James R. *v.1 p.163, p.210, p.320*

Brisk, Maria E. & Harrington, Margaret M. . . *v.4 p.299, p.312*

Brison, Karen J. *v.4 p.42*

Brissenden, Alan *v.1 p.44*

Brissenden, Rosemary *v.6 p.164*

Brisson, Luc *v.2 p.417*

Bristol, Evelyn *v.2 p.797*

Bristol, Michael D. & McLuskie,
Kathleen (Editors) *v.1 p.75, p.81, p.86, p.99*

Bristow, Joe *v.6 p.477*

Bristow, John A. *v.3 p.251*

Bristow, Joseph (Editor) . . . *v.2 p.174, p.184, p.320, v.6 p.755*

Bristow, Joseph *v.2 p.174, p.178, p.184, p.271*

British Library of Political and Economic Science Staff
(Contribution by) *v.4 p.3*

British Tunnelling Society *v.5 p.698*

Britt, Thomas W. (Editor), et al. *v.5 p.583*

Brittain, Victoria *v.6 p.75*

Brittan, Simon *v.2 p.181*

Brittin, Norman A. *v.2 p.97*

Britton, G. *v.5 p.330*

Britton, John A. (Editor) *v.4 p.333*

Britton, John A. *v.3 p.284*

Britton, N. F. *v.5 p.91*

Britvec, S. J. *v.5 p.693*

Briys, Eric C. & de Varenne, François *v.4 p.163*

Brizan, George I. *v.3 p.318*

Brkic, Svetozar *v.2 p.776*

Broad, C. D. *v.1 p.495*

Broadbent, Donald (Editor) *v.5 p.590*

Broadbent, Ed (Editor) *v.4 p.514*

Broadbent, R. J. *v.1 p.93*

Broadcast Music Inc. *v.1 p.172, p.383*

Broaddus, Dorothy C. *v.2 p.6, p.9, p.12*

Broadie, Alexander (Editor) *v.3 p.71*

Broadie, Alexander *v.1 p.494*

Broadie, Sarah *v.1 p.426*

Broadwater, Jeff *v.3 p.456*

Brobeck, Stephen (Editor) *v.5 p.585*

Broch, Hermann *v.2 p.603*

Brochu, Andre *v.2 p.538*

Brochu, Serge (Editor), et al. *v.6 p.255*

Brock, B. Peter (Editor), et al. *v.5 p.301*

Brock, Colin & Clarkson, Donald (Editors) *v.4 p.333*

Brock, Fred V. & Richardson, Scott J. *v.5 p.425*

Brock, Gerald W. *v.4 p.420*

Brock, James & Adams, Walter *v.4 p.148*

Brock, Lisa & Fuertes, Digna Castraneda (Editors) . . *v.3 p.307*

Brock, Peter & Young, Nigel *v.4 p.648*

Brock, Sebastian P. *v.1 p.569*

Brock, Timothy C. & Green, Melanie C. (Editors) . . *v.5 p.646*

Brock, William H. *v.5 p.262*

Brockelmann, Carl *v.6 p.581*

Brocken, Michael *v.1 p.298*

Brockett, Oscar Gross & Hildy, Franklin J. . . . *v.1 p.55, p.137*

Brockington, Lolita G. *v.3 p.284*

Brocklehurst, J. C. & Fillit, Howard M. *v.5 p.518*

Brockliss, Laurence *v.3 p.146, v.4 p.333*

Brod, Harry (Editor) *v.6 p.369, p.428*

Brod, Harry *v.4 p.491*

Broder, Henryk *v.3 p.179*

Broderick, Mick (Editor) *v.6 p.335*

Brodeur, Arthur Gilchrist *v.2 p.204*

Brodhead, Richard H. *v.2 p.9, p.40, p.47*

Brodie, Bernard *v.3 p.35*

Brodie, Fawn M. *v.3 p.411*

Brodie, Laura Fairchild *v.6 p.462*

Brodlie, K. W. (Editor), et al. *v.5 p.337, p.339, p.340*

Brodo, Irwin M., et al. *v.5 p.210*

Brodsgaard, Kjeld Erik & Heurlin, Bertel (Editors) . . *v.4 p.400*

Brodsky, Alyn *v.3 p.394, p.456, v.6 p.710*

Brodwin, Stanley (Editor) *v.2 p.42*

Brody, David C., et al. *v.6 p.268*

Brody, David *v.4 p.124*

Brody, Howard, et al. *v.4 p.864, p.871*

Brody, J. J. *v.1 p.730, v.6 p.678*

Brody, James & Campbell, Michael *v.1 p.266*

Brody, Jennifer D. *v.6 p.477*

Brody, Leslie . . *v.4 p.694, v.5 p.651, p.657,v.6 p.445, p.466*

Brody, Robert *v.6 p.573*

Brody, Tom *v.5 p.329*

Brodzinsky, David M. & Palacios, Jesus (Editors) . . *v.5 p.641*

Broe, Mary L. (Editor) *v.2 p.58*

Broeckelmann, Russ *v.4 p.116*

Broecker, Wallace S. *v.5 p.429*

Broek, David *v.5 p.687*

Broer, Lawrence R. & Holland, Gloria (Editors) . . . *v.2 p.83*

Broers, Michael *v.3 p.201*

Broesamle, John J. *v.3 p.446, p.456*

Brogan, D. W. *v.3 p.366*

Brogan, Denis W. *v.3 p.366, p.370*

Brogan, Jacqueline Vaught *v.2 p.123*

Brogyanyi, Eugene *v.1 p.63, p.108*

Broman, Sven *v.1 p.131, v.6 p.209*

Bromberg, J. Philip *v.5 p.275*

Bromberg, Ruth *v.1 p.755*

Brombert, Beth A. *v.1 p.736*

Brombert, Victor H. *v.2 p.462, p.501*

Brombert, Victor *v.2 p.492*

Brome, Alexander *v.2 p.237*

Brome, Richard *v.2 p.217*

Bromiley, Geoffrey N. *v.2 p.466*

Bromley, J. S., et al. *v.6 p.589*

Bromley, Richard *v.5 p.450*

Bromley, Roger *v.6 p.320*

Brondsted, Johannes *v.3 p.235*

Bronfenbrenner, Kate (Editor), et al. *v.4 p.124*

Bronfenbrenner, Urie *v.5 p.625*

Bronfman, Alejandra *v.3 p.307*

Bronmark, Christer & Hansson, Lars-Anders . *v.4 p.391, v.5 p.174*

Bronner, Simon J. *v.2 p.16*

Bronner, Stephen Eric & Thompson,
    Michael J. (Editors) *v.4 p.510*

Bronner, Stephen Eric . . *v.1 p.502, v.3 p.446, v.4 p.506, p.624,
                                                    p.658, p.669*

Bronowski, Jacob *v.5 p.400*

Bronson, Bertrand Harris, et al. *v.1 p.298*

Bronson, Fred *v.1 p.170, p.266*

Bronson, Richard & Costa, Gabriel *v.5 p.486*

Bronte, Charlotte *v.2 p.269, p.270*

Bronte, Patrick Branwell *v.2 p.270*

Brontë, Anne, et al. *v.2 p.270*

Brontë, Anne *v.2 p.270*

Brontë, Emily *v.2 p.270*

Brook, Andrew & Ross, Don (Editors) *v.1 p.441*

Brook, Barry S. & Viano, Richard J. *v.1 p.165*

Brook, Michael A. *v.5 p.296*

Brook, Peter *v.1 p.138, p.152*

Brook, Timothy & Wakabayashi, Bob Tadashi . . . *v.6 p.180*

Brook, Timothy (Editor) *v.6 p.193*

Brook, Timothy *v.6 p.185, p.186, p.193, p.196*

Brooke, Christopher N. L. *v.6 p.561*

Brooke, Frances *v.2 p.237*

Brooke, Henry *v.2 p.238*

Brooke, Iris & Landes, William-Alan *v.1 p.150*

Brooke, John Hedley (Editor) *v.6 p.288*

Brooke, Michael & Birkhead, Tim R. *v.5 p.95, p.214*

Brooke, Michael Z. & Mills, William R. *v.4 p.144*

Brooke, Rosalind B. & Brooke, Christopher N. L. . . *v.6 p.570*

Brooke, Rosalind B. *v.6 p.570*

Brooke, Rupert & Strachey, James *v.2 p.335*

Brooke, Rupert & Woodberry, George Edward . . . *v.2 p.335*

Brooke, Rupert *v.2 p.335*

Brooker, Jewel S. *v.2 p.71*

Brooker, Peter *v.4 p.676, v.6 p.730*

Brooker, Will *v.2 p.277*

Brookes, Andrew *v.5 p.704*

Brookes, Murray; Zietman, Anthony *v.5 p.162*

Brookes, Rod . *v.4 p.814, p.823, p.831, p.858, p.882, p.887, p.901*

Brookfield, H. C. (Editor), et al. *v.5 p.11*

Brookfield, Stephen D. & Preskill, Stephen . . *v.4 p.292, p.347*

Brookfield, Stephen D. *v.4 p.319*

Brookhart, Susan M. & AEHE Staff *v.4 p.285*

Brookhaven National Laboratory *v.5 p.545*

Brookman, Fiona *v.6 p.252*

Brookner, Anita *v.2 p.331*

Brooks, Brian S., et al. *v.4 p.411, p.416*

Brooks, Charles R. *v.5 p.687*

Brooks, Charlie R. *v.5 p.736*

Brooks, Chris *v.4 p.198*

Brooks, Cleanth & Faulkner, William *v.2 p.73*

Brooks, Cleanth & Tate, Allen *v.2 p.125*

Brooks, Cleanth *v.2 p.3, p.73, p.179, p.568*

Brooks, Dana D. & Althouse,
    Ronald C. (Editors) *v.4 p.814, p.831*

Brooks, Daniel R. & Wiley, Edward O. *v.5 p.191*

Brooks, David & Walker, Brenda (Editors) *v.2 p.740*

Brooks, David *v.3 p.467*

Brooks, Felicity *v.5 p.225*

Brooks, Frederick P. Jr. *v.5 p.345*

Brooks, Geo. F., et al. *v.5 p.515*

Brooks, George E. *v.6 p.68*

Brooks, Gwendolyn & Malcolm X *v.2 p.18, v.6 p.23*

Brooks, Gwendolyn *v.2 p.63*

Brooks, Jeffrey *v.3 p.217, p.225*

Brooks, Joanna & Saillant, John (Editor,
    Introduction by) *v.6 p.23*

Brooks, Joanna *v.6 p.23, p.35*

Brooks, Lynn Matluck & de Esquivel
    Navarro, Juan *v.1 p.16, p.20*

Brooks, Lynn Matluck *v.1 p.20*

Brooks, Michael *v.1 p.791*

Brooks, Nicholas *v.1 p.582*

Brooks, Peter *v.2 p.455, p.462, p.570*

Brooks, Roy L. *v.6 p.22, p.36*

Brooks, Tim & Marsh, Earle *v.4 p.418*

Brooks, Tim & Spottswood, Richard K. *v.1 p.280*

Brooks, Van Wyck *v.2 p.6, p.7, p.12, p.33*

Brooks, Virginia *v.5 p.374*

Brooks-Davies, Douglas (Editor, Introduction by) . . . *v.2 p.198*

Brookshaw, David *v.2 p.689*

Brook-Shepherd, Gordon *v.3 p.181, p.184*

Broome, Peter & Chesters, Graham (Editors) *v.2 p.463*

Broome, Richard *v.4 p.42*

Broomfield, Andrea & Mitchell, Sally . *v.2 p.196, p.202, v.6 p.739,
                                                    p.746, p.754*

Brooten, Bernadette J. *v.6 p.364, p.373*

Brophy, Alfred L. *v.3 p.523, v.6 p.3, p.20, p.36*

Brophy, James M. *v.3 p.168*

Brophy, Jere E. & Good, Thomas L. *v.4 p.349*

Brophy, Robert J. (Editor, Introduction by) *v.2 p.91*

Brose, Eric D. *v.3 p.167*
Brose, Eric Dorn *v.3 p.78, p.160*
Brosius, Maria *v.3 p.11, v.6 p.450*
Brosnan, Leila *v.2 p.392*
Brossard, Chandler *v.2 p.58*
Brossard, Nicole *v.2 p.540*
Broszat, Martin & Bestard-Camps, Joan *v.3 p.169*
Broszat, Martin *v.3 p.171*
Brotherton, David & Barrios, Luis *v.6 p.547*
Broto, Carles & Mostaedi, Arian (Editors) . . . *v.4 p.880, p.882*
Brottman, Mikita *v.6 p.313*
Brotton, Jerry *v.3 p.70*
Broude, Norma & Garrard,
   Mary D. (Editors) *v.1 p.706, v.6 p.472*
Broude, Norma & Garrard, Mary D. *v.6 p.472*
Broudy, Harry S. *v.4 p.341*
Brougher, Kerry *v.1 p.677*
Broughton, Panthea Reid *v.2 p.73*
Broughton, Simon et al. *v.1 p.170*
Broughton, Simon, et al. *v.1 p.170*
Broughton, Simon et al. *v.1 p.285, p.286*
Broughton, Simon, et al. *v.1 p.288, p.291, p.295*
Broughton, Simon et al. *v.1 p.298*
Broumas, Olga *v.2 p.141, v.6 p.404*
Broussard, Jinx Coleman *v.6 p.3, p.42*
Brouwer, Maria *v.4 p.230, p.234*
Brouwer, Roy & Pearce, David *v.5 p.702*
Broverman, Samuel A. *v.5 p.504*
Browder, Andrew *v.5 p.489*
Browder, Laura *v.2 p.69*
Brower, Daniel R. & Lazzerini, Edward J. (Editors) . *v.3 p.213*
Brower, Daniel R. *v.3 p.213*
Brower, Keith H., et al. *v.2 p.690*
Brower, Reuben A. *v.2 p.77, p.257*
Brower, Robert H. & Miner, Earl *v.6 p.234*
Browler, Kenneth & National
   Geographic Society Staff *v.5 p.18, p.41*
Brown, A. (Editor), et al. *v.5 p.15*
Brown, A. Peter . *v.1 p.188, p.194, p.238, p.306, p.329, p.343,
                                                   p.353*
Brown, Alice, et al. *v.4 p.607*
Brown, Andrew . *v.1 p.608, v.3 p.96, v.5 p.78, p.202, v.6 p.570*
Brown, Antony & Quine, Timothy *v.4 p.391*
Brown, Archie (Editor), et al. *v.3 p.209*
Brown, Archie (Editor) *v.4 p.597*
Brown, Brendan *v.4 p.636*
Brown, Brian E. *v.6 p.691, p.700*
Brown, Bruce Alan *v.1 p.188, p.228, p.343*
Brown, Candy Gunther *v.4 p.720*
Brown, Carolan & Reader's Digest Editors . . . *v.4 p.793*
Brown, Carolyn A. *v.6 p.71*
Brown, Charles Brockden *v.2 p.31*
Brown, Cheryl Render & Cookson, Catherine (Editors) *v.4 p.356*
Brown, Clarence (Contribution by, Notes by) . . *v.2 p.794*
Brown, Clive *v.1 p.188, p.194, p.195, p.340, p.399*

Brown, Colin D. *v.5 p.731*
Brown, Coreen *v.2 p.756*
Brown, Craig (Editor) *v.3 p.535*
Brown, Cynthia (Editor) *v.4 p.515*
Brown, D. S. *v.5 p.433*
Brown, David A. *v.1 p.736*
Brown, David H. *v.1 p.543, v.3 p.278*
Brown, David L. & Swanson, Louis E. (Editors) . . *v.4 p.771*
Brown, David S. *v.3 p.373*
Brown, David Wayne *v.4 p.444*
Brown, David *v.1 p.195, p.345, p.362, v.4 p.295*
Brown, Dee Alexander *v.3 p.518*
Brown, Dee . . . *v.3 p.394, p.518, v.4 p.572, p.646, v.6 p.682*
Brown, Dick & Henderson, Joe *v.4 p.866*
Brown, Donald E. *v.4 p.23*
Brown, Duane (Editor) *v.5 p.577*
Brown, E. Carey & Solow, Robert (Editors) . . . *v.4 p.213*
Brown, E. K. *v.2 p.66*
Brown, Elspeth (Editor), et al. *v.4 p.141*
Brown, Eugene *v.3 p.456*
Brown, Eurnestine & Burgess, Norma J. (Editors) . *v.6 p.42*
Brown, F., et al. *v.6 p.645*
Brown, Forman *v.6 p.395*
Brown, Fredda & Snell, Martha *v.4 p.318*
Brown, Frederick *v.2 p.490, p.504*
Brown, Gene (Editor) *v.6 p.305*
Brown, George H. *v.6 p.570*
Brown, Gillian *v.2 p.9*
Brown, Gordon S. *v.3 p.314*
Brown, Harriet *v.4 p.735*
Brown, Harry J. & Williams, Frederick D. (Editors) . *v.3 p.435*
Brown, Harry *v.2 p.58*
Brown, Herbert C. *v.5 p.296*
Brown, Herbert Ross *v.2 p.9*
Brown, Homer O. *v.2 p.189, p.357*
Brown, Howard Mayer & Sadie, Stanley (Editors) . *v.1 p.176,
                                        p.179, p.182, p.188, p.400*
Brown, Howard Mayer *v.1 p.179*
Brown, Howard *v.6 p.365*
Brown, Isabel Zakrzewski *v.3 p.316*
Brown, James & Tucker, Bruce *v.1 p.266, p.314*
Brown, James S. Jr. (Editor) *v.3 p.504*
Brown, James Ward & Churchill, Ruel V. . . . *v.5 p.487, p.490*
Brown, James *v.5 p.684*
Brown, Jane *v.1 p.818*
Brown, Jean E. (Editor, Introduction by) *v.4 p.298*
Brown, Jean (Editor), et al. *v.1 p.26, p.40*
Brown, Jeanne *v.1 p.783*
Brown, Jennifer M. & Heidensohn, Frances M. . . *v.6 p.260*
Brown, John M. & Lamb, Charles *v.2 p.298*
Brown, Jonathan C. (Editor) *v.4 p.124*
Brown, Jonathan C. *v.3 p.290, p.346*
Brown, Jonathan *v.1 p.726, p.731*
Brown, Joshua *v.4 p.409*

Brown, Judith M. & Louis, Roger
(Editors) *v.3 p.88, p.124, v.4 p.605*
Brown, Judith M. *v.6 p.156, p.158*
Brown, Judith *v.6 p.158*
Brown, Julian *v.5 p.552*
Brown, Karen McCarthy *v.1 p.542*
Brown, Keith *v.3 p.250*
Brown, Kendall W. *v.3 p.325*
Brown, L. Carl (Editor) *v.3 p.245, v.6 p.589*
Brown, L. Carl *v.6 p.641*
Brown, Laurie M., et al. *v.5 p.545*
Brown, Les *v.4 p.300*
Brown, Lester B., et al. *v.6 p.380*
Brown, Lester Russell *v.4 p.267*
Brown, Lois *v.6 p.23*
Brown, Lorene Byron *v.6 p.13, p.33*
Brown, Lucy M. *v.3 p.127, v.6 p.738, p.741*
Brown, M. Kathryn & Stanton, Travis W. (Editors) . . *v.3 p.296*
Brown, Malcolm Hamrick (Editor) *v.1 p.210, p.356*
Brown, Malcolm *v.3 p.78*
Brown, Marvin T. *v.4 p.697*
Brown, Matthew *v.1 p.210, p.320*
Brown, Maurice *v.4 p.218*
Brown, Melissa J. *v.6 p.213*
Brown, Mervyn *v.6 p.67*
Brown, Meta & Mulholland, Joyce L. . . . *v.5 p.526*
Brown, Michael F. & Fernández, Eduardo . . *v.3 p.329*
Brown, Michael F. *v.4 p.33*
Brown, Michael G. *v.3 p.542*
Brown, Mildred L. & Rounsley, Chloe Ann . *v.6 p.369, p.374*
Brown, Monica *v.6 p.495, p.511, p.547*
Brown, N. *v.2 p.776*
Brown, Nina W. *v.4 p.349*
Brown, Norman O. *v.5 p.658*
Brown, Patricia Fortini *v.1 p.674, p.685*
Brown, Peter (Editor) *v.2 p.207*
Brown, Peter . *v.1 p.430, p.577, p.598, p.612, p.652, v.2 p.430, v.3 p.30, p.56, v.5 p.536, v.6 p.570*
Brown, Rachel *v.1 p.389, p.400*
Brown, Ralph A. *v.3 p.416*
Brown, Raymond E. & Meier, John P. . . . *v.1 p.625*
Brown, Raymond E. (Editor), et al. . . . *v.1 p.626, p.642*
Brown, Raymond E., et al. *v.1 p.615*
Brown, Raymond E. *v.1 p.624, p.628*
Brown, Rebecca A. *v.4 p.789, p.835*
Brown, Rebecca *v.6 p.378, p.395*
Brown Reference Group *v.3 p.44, v.5 p.388*
Brown, Reginald A. *v.3 p.97*
Brown, Rex V. *v.4 p.83*
Brown, Richard D. & Tager, Jack *v.3 p.487*
Brown, Richard D. *v.3 p.488*
Brown, Rita Mae *v.6 p.368, p.395*
Brown, Robert Eldon *v.3 p.487*
Brown, Robert McAfee *v.1 p.568*
Brown, Roger H. *v.3 p.416*

Brown, Royal S. *v.1 p.255*
Brown, Rupert *v.4 p.692, v.5 p.649*
Brown, Sanborn C. *v.5 p.396*
Brown, Scott & Hilbert, Robert *v.1 p.257, p.334*
Brown, Seyom *v.3 p.446, p.451*
Brown, Sheila *v.6 p.256*
Brown, Sheldon S. *v.5 p.250*
Brown, Shona L. & Eisenhardt, Kathleen M. . . . *v.4 p.81*
Brown, Stanley *v.5 p.519*
Brown, Stephanie & Lewis, Virginia M. . . . *v.5 p.672*
Brown, Sterling A. *v.2 p.58*
Brown, Steve *v.4 p.119*
Brown, Steven D. & Lent, Robert W. (Editors) . *v.5 p.576, p.577*
Brown, Stewart (Author, Editor) *v.2 p.767*
Brown, Stewart J. & Tackett, Timothy (Editors) . . *v.1 p.611*
Brown, Stuart (Editor) *v.1 p.449*
Brown, Stuart Gerry *v.3 p.515*
Brown, Stuart M. *v.5 p.97, p.105, p.148*
Brown, T. A. *v.5 p.131*
Brown, Terence A. & BIOS Scientific
Publishers Staff (Editors) *v.5 p.131, p.148*
Brown, Thomas E. *v.5 p.662*
Brown, Warren S. (Editor), et al. *v.1 p.526*
Brown, Wendy *v.6 p.440*
Brown, William Wells *v.6 p.4, p.23*
Browne, Arthur, et al. *v.3 p.490*
Browne, Collette V. *v.6 p.444*
Browne, David *v.4 p.857, p.899*
Browne, Donald R. *v.4 p.413*
Browne, E. G. *v.6 p.670*
Browne, Eric C. & Dreijmanis, John (Editors) . . *v.4 p.574*
Browne, Irene (Editor) *v.4 p.133, v.6 p.455*
Browne, Janet *v.3 p.48*
Browne, Nick (Editor) *v.6 p.311*
Browne, Ray B. & Ambrosetti, Ronald J. (Editors) . *v.4 p.701*
Browne, Ray B. & Browne, Pat (Editors) . . *v.3 p.366*
Browne, Steven E. *v.6 p.350*
Browne, Thomas *v.2 p.241*
Browne, William H. *v.3 p.493*
Browne, William P. *v.4 p.559, v.5 p.13*
Brownell, Susan *v.6 p.451, p.453*
Browner, Tara *v.1 p.14*
Brown-Guillory, Elizabeth (Editor) . . . *v.6 p.15, p.23*
Browning, Barbara *v.1 p.19, p.20*
Browning, Christopher R. *v.3 p.83*
Browning, D. S. *v.2 p.163*
Browning, Don S. *v.5 p.633*
Browning, Douglas & Myers, William T. (Editors) . *v.1 p.513*
Browning, Elizabeth Barrett *v.2 p.271*
Browning, Harley L. *v.6 p.528, p.542*
Browning, Reed *v.4 p.849*
Browning, Robert & Barrett, Elizabeth Barrett . . *v.2 p.271*
Browning, Robert M. & Kerth, Thomas A. (Editors) . *v.2 p.590*
Browning, Robert M. *v.2 p.591*
Browning, Robert *v.2 p.271*

Browning, Rufus P., et al. *v.6 p.716*
Browning, Rufus P. *v.6 p.716*
Browning, W. R. F. *v.1 p.614*
Brown-John, C. Lloyd (Editor) *v.4 p.523*
Brownlee, W. Elliot & Graham, Hugh Davis (Editors) . *v.3 p.439*
Brownlee, W. Elliot *v.4 p.107*
Brownley, Martine Watson *v.2 p.343*
Brownlie, Ian & Goodwin-Gill, Guy S. (Editors) . . *v.4 p.434*
Brownlie, Ian *v.4 p.477*
Brownlow, Kevin *v.6 p.320*
Brownmiller, Susan *v.4 p.751, v.6 p.252, p.468*
Brownsey, Keith & Howlett, Michael (Editors) . . . *v.4 p.589*
Brownstein, Michael J. & Khodursky, Arkady (Editors) *v.5 p.138*
Brownworth, Victoria A. *v.6 p.401*
Brownworth, Victoria *v.6 p.377*
Broyles, Michael *v.1 p.277*
Broyles-González, Yolanda *v.1 p.124, v.6 p.517*
Brualdi, Richard A. *v.5 p.478*
Brubach, Holly *v.6 p.370*
Brubacher, John S. & Rudy, Willis *v.4 p.331*
Brubacher, John S. *v.4 p.289*
Brubaker, David C. & Ostroff, Joel H. (Editors) . *v.5 p.78, p.82*
Brubaker, George R. & Phipps, P. Beverley (Editors) *v.5 p.734*
Brubaker, Leslie & Smith, Julia M. H. (Editors) . . . *v.3 p.51*
Brubaker, Rogers *v.3 p.61, v.4 p.608, p.609*
Bruccoli, Matthew J. & Baughman, Judith S. *v.2 p.76*
Bruccoli, Matthew J. (Editor), et al. *v.2 p.796*
Bruccoli, Matthew J. (Editor) *v.2 p.75, p.106*
Bruccoli, Matthew J. *v.2 p.106*
Bruccoli, Matthew Joseph (Editor, Translator) *v.2 p.94*
Bruccoli, Matthew Joseph *v.2 p.76*
Bruce, F. F. *v.1 p.614, p.626, p.629*
Bruce, Frederick Fyvie *v.1 p.614*
Bruce, Robert V. *v.3 p.430*
Bruce, Steve *v.4 p.607, p.719*
Bruce, Tina *v.4 p.368*
Bruce, William, et al. *v.4 p.607*
Bruce-Novoa, Juan *v.6 p.497, p.509, p.511*
Bruchac, Joseph (Introduction by) *v.2 p.22, v.6 p.697*
Bruck, Connie *v.4 p.99*
Brucker, Gene Adam *v.4 p.738*
Brucker, Gene *v.3 p.197, p.199, p.203*
Bruckner, Matilda Tomaryn (Editor), et al. *v.2 p.463*
Bruder, Helen P. *v.2 p.239*
Brue, Stanley L. & McConnell, Campbell R. *v.4 p.194*
Brue, Stanley L., et al. *v.4 p.253*
Brueggemann, Brenda Jo *v.4 p.708*
Brueggemann, Walter *v.1 p.618*
Bruegmann, Robert (Editor) *v.1 p.792*
Bruegmann, Robert . . . *v.1 p.792, p.796, v.4 p.771, v.6 p.727*
Bruer, John T. *v.5 p.608*
Bruffee, Kenneth A. *v.4 p.349*
Bruford, Walter H. *v.3 p.167*
Bruhn, Erik *v.1 p.23*
Bruhn, Kathleen *v.3 p.290, v.4 p.593*

Bruhns, Karen Olsen *v.4 p.11*
Bruinessen, Martin van *v.6 p.598*
Bruinsma, Jelle (Editor) *v.5 p.12*
Brumberg, Joan Jacobs *v.6 p.466*
Brumble, H. David III (Translator) *v.2 p.622*
Brumfield, William Craft *v.1 p.788*
Brundage, James A. *v.3 p.51, v.6 p.568, p.570*
Brundell, Harry *v.1 p.452*
Brune, Lester H. & Burns, Richard Dean . . . *v.4 p.560, p.627*
Bruneau, Thomas C. *v.1 p.572*
Brunel, Pierre *v.1 p.526, v.2 p.549*
Bruner, Charlotte (Editor) *v.2 p.752*
Bruner, Charlotte *v.2 p.752*
Bruner, Edward M. *v.4 p.44*
Bruner, Jerome S. . . *v.4 p.341, p.347, p.356, v.5 p.571, p.573, p.604, p.622*
Bruner, Robert F. *v.4 p.177*
Bruni, Frank *v.4 p.485*
Brunicardi, F. Charles, et al. *v.5 p.522*
Brunier, Serge & Lagrange, Anne-Marie *v.5 p.65*
Brunner, C. Cryss (Editor) *v.4 p.281*
Brunner, Emil *v.1 p.642, p.645*
Brunner, K. & Meltzer, A. H. (Editors) . . . *v.4 p.240, p.255*
Brunner, K. F. & Meltzer, A. (Editors) . . . *v.4 p.253*
Brunner, Karl & Meltzer, Allan H. *v.4 p.231*
Brunner, Karl *v.2 p.550*
Bruno, Thomas J.; Svoronos, Paris D. N. *v.5 p.267*
Bruns, Roger A. *v.1 p.648*
Bruns, Roger *v.4 p.124*
Brunsdale, Mitzi M. *v.2 p.357*
Brunsdon, Charlotte *v.6 p.447*
Brunvand, Jan Harold (Editor) *v.2 p.16*
Brunvand, Jan Harold *v.2 p.16, p.17*
Bruscagli, Riccardo *v.2 p.697*
Bruscia, Kenneth E. (Editor) *v.1 p.406*
Bruscia, Kenneth E. *v.1 p.406*
Brush, Daniel, et al. *v.1 p.801*
Brush, Lisa D. *v.4 p.512*
Brush, Stephen B. *v.5 p.20*
Brush, Stephen G. *v.5 p.446*
Brussaard, L. & Ferrara-Cerrato, Ronald *v.5 p.11*
Brustad, Kristen, et al. *v.6 p.653*
Brustad, Kristen *v.6 p.653*
Brustein, Robert *v.1 p.81, p.95*
Bruyn, J., et al. *v.1 p.685*
Bruzzi, Stella *v.6 p.309, p.349*
Bry, Charlene *v.5 p.83*
Bryan, Violet H. *v.2 p.13*
Bryant, Clifton D. (Editor) *v.4 p.676, v.6 p.249*
Bryant, D. C., et al. *v.2 p.197*
Bryant, Dirk, et al. *v.5 p.359*
Bryant, Edward *v.5 p.423, p.425*
Bryant, Edwin & Ekstrand, Maria *v.1 p.535*
Bryant, Howard . *v.4 p.804, p.831, p.849, p.882, p.890, p.895*
Bryant, J. A. *v.2 p.219*

Bryant, James S. *v.5 p.720*
Bryant, John A. (Editor), et al. *v.5 p.246*
Bryant, John, et al. *v.5 p.246*
Bryant, Julius *v.1 p.778*
Bryant, Mark & Heneage, Simon *v.1 p.701, p.721*
Bryant, Mark *v.1 p.701, p.721*
Bryant, Wayne M. *v.6 p.415*
Bryce, Betty K. *v.1 p.711, p.751*
Bryce, Trevor (Revised by) *v.3 p.4*
Bryce, Trevor *v.3 p.6, p.15*
Bryce-Echenique, Alfredo *v.2 p.685*
Brydon, Diana *v.2 p.748*
Brydson, J. A. *v.5 p.319*
Bryer, Jackson R. (Editor), et al. *v.2 p.76*
Bryer, Jackson R. (Editor) *v.2 p.76*
Bryher, H. D. & H. D. *v.5 p.595*
Bryk, Anthony S., et al. *v.4 p.307*
Bryner, Gary C. & Thompson, Dennis L. (Editors) . . *v.4 p.463*
Bryon, Mike *v.5 p.600*
Bryson, Bill *v.5 p.399*
Bryson, Michael A. *v.6 p.287*
Bryson, Norman (Editor), et al. *v.1 p.700*
Buarque, Chico *v.2 p.690*
Bubenick, David V. *v.5 p.354, p.378*
Buber, Martin (Editor), et al. *v.6 p.610*
Buber, Martin . *v.1 p.467, p.468, p.522, p.546, p.638, v.4 p.499*
Bucaille, Laetitia *v.6 p.617*
Bucco, Martin *v.2 p.95*
Buch, A. *v.5 p.687*
Buchan, John *v.2 p.331*
Buchanan, Allen, et al. *v.5 p.131*
Buchanan, Bob B. (Editor), et al. *v.5 p.78, p.111, p.124*
Buchanan, Christy M., et al. *v.4 p.735*
Buchanan, J. M., et al. *v.4 p.226*
Buchanan, James M. *v.4 p.194, p.208, p.247*
Buchanan, Milton Alexander *v.2 p.642*
Buchanan, Scott (Editor) *v.1 p.266, p.411*
Buchanan, William (Editor) *v.1 p.765*
Buchanan, William J. *v.4 p.115*
Buchenau, Jürgen *v.3 p.291*
Bucher, Kurt & Frey, Martin *v.5 p.440*
Bucher, Ward (Editor) *v.1 p.821*
Buchler, Alexandra *v.2 p.781*
Buchner, Georg *v.2 p.596*
Bucholz, Arden *v.3 p.160, p.168*
Buchta, Wilfried *v.6 p.632*
Buchwald, Emilie (Editor) *v.6 p.727*
Buck, Elizabeth *v.3 p.533, v.6 p.130*
Buck, Louise E. & Lassoie, James P. *v.5 p.40*
Buck, Marilyn, et al. *v.4 p.797*
Buck, Marilyn M., et al. *v.4 p.794, p.903*
Buck, Pearl S. *v.2 p.58, v.6 p.200, p.214*
Buck, Philip W. *v.4 p.255*
Buck, Rebecca A. & Gilmore, Jean Allman . . . *v.1 p.828*
Buck, Robert N. *v.5 p.717*

Buck, Solon J. & Buck, Elizabeth H. *v.3 p.491*
Buck, Stephanie & Sander, Jochen *v.1 p.736*
Buckel, Werner & Kleiner, Reinhold *v.5 p.565*
Buckingham, J.; Hill, R. A. *v.5 p.297*
Buckingham, Marcus & Coffman, Curt *v.4 p.70, p.72*
Buckingham, William & Ross, George William . *v.3 p.539*
Buckland, S. T., et al. *v.5 p.92, p.188*
Buckland, S.T. (Editor), et al. . . *v.5 p.92, p.99, p.188, p.189*
Buckland, Theresa J. (Editor) *v.1 p.48*
Buckle, Richard & Taras, John *v.1 p.6*
Buckle, Richard *v.1 p.6, p.38*
Buckler, Ernest *v.2 p.733*
Buckler, John *v.3 p.19*
Buckley, Ann I (Editor) *v.1 p.175*
Buckley, Gail Lumet *v.4 p.717*
Buckley, Jerome H. . *v.2 p.174, v.3 p.110, p.127, v.6 p.750, p.752, p.763*
Buckley, Kerry W. *v.5 p.595*
Buckley, Laurene *v.1 p.736*
Buckley, Martin *v.5 p.175*
Buckley, Mary (Editor) *v.3 p.229*
Buckley, R. Michael & Gluckman, Stephen John . . . *v.5 p.515*
Buckley, William F. Jr. *v.3 p.446, v.4 p.292*
Buckley, William F. *v.3 p.446*
Buckley, William Joseph (Editor) *v.3 p.249*
Buckley, William K. (Editor) *v.2 p.515*
Buckman, Peter *v.1 p.33*
Buckman, Robert H. *v.4 p.77*
Buck-Morss, Susan *v.6 p.709*
Buckner, Phillip A. & Reid, John C. (Editors) . . . *v.3 p.542*
Buckser, Andrew & Glazier, Stephen D. (Editors) . . *v.4 p.36*
Buckworth, Janet & Dishman, Rodney . . *v.4 p.876, v.5 p.581*
Bucur, Maria & Wingfield, Nancy Merriwether . *v.3 p.181, p.183*
Bud, Robert F. *v.5 p.78, p.217*
Budd, John W. *v.4 p.120*
Budd, Leslie & Harris, Lisa *v.4 p.263*
Budd, Louis J. *v.2 p.33*
Budd, Malcolm *v.1 p.380*
Budden, Julian (Editor) *v.1 p.195, p.228, p.364*
Budden, Julian *v.1 p.195, p.228, p.349, p.364*
Buddenbaum, Judith *v.4 p.406*
Buddhaghosa, Acaeiya *v.1 p.563*
Buderi, Robert & Huang, Gregory T. *v.4 p.157*
Budevsky, O. *v.5 p.268*
Budge, E. A. Wallis . *v.1 p.542, v.6 p.644, p.645, p.659, p.664*
Budhu, Muniram *v.5 p.698*
Budinski, Ken & Budinski, Michael K. *v.5 p.687*
Budinski, Kenneth G. *v.5 p.680*
Budker, Dmitry, et al. *v.5 p.554*
Buechel, Eugene *v.6 p.690*
Buechler, Hans C. *v.3 p.323*
Buechner, Frederick *v.2 p.141*
Buehler, Lukas K. (Editor) *v.5 p.97*
Buehler *v.5 p.293*
Buehrer, Beverly B. *v.6 p.305, p.335*

Buehrig, Edward H. *v.3 p.467*
Buell, Lawrence *v.2 p.12, p.52, v.6 p.287*
Buell, Paul D. *v.6 p.238*
Buelow, George J. (Editor) *v.1 p.182*
Buelow, George J. *v.1 p.182*
Bueno de Mesquita, Bruce & Lalman, David *v.4 p.646*
Bueno de Mesquita, Bruce *v.4 p.625*
Bueno, Maria de Los Reyes Castillo . *v.3 p.278, p.307, v.4 p.40*
Bueno, Patricia *v.1 p.803*
Bueno, Salvador *v.2 p.671*
Buettner, Elizabeth *v.6 p.156*
Buffett, Warren *v.4 p.94*
Buffon, Georges-Louis Leclerc *v.5 p.220*
Buffum, Imbrie *v.2 p.469*
Bufwack, Mary A. & Oermann, Robert K. . . . *v.1 p.267, p.378*
Bugajski, Janusz *v.4 p.595, p.596, p.597, p.600*
Bugge, Anna, et al. *v.4 p.240*
Bugh, Glenn R. (Editor) *v.3 p.20*
Buglear, John *v.4 p.178*
Buhite, Russell D. *v.3 p.456, v.4 p.565*
Buhle, Paul & Rice-Maximin, Edward *v.3 p.373*
Buhler, Richard O. *v.3 p.297*
Buhler-Lynes, Barbara *v.1 p.695*
Bui, Hoan N. *v.6 p.111, p.117, p.259*
Buisseret, David (Editor) *v.6 p.720*
Buitrago Jimenez, A. *v.2 p.635*
Bukey, Evan B. *v.3 p.184*
Bukey, Evan Burr *v.3 p.83, p.185*
Bukhari, Zahid Hussain *v.4 p.721*
Bukharin, Nikolai *v.3 p.222*
Bukovansky, Mlada *v.4 p.496, p.591, p.608*
Bukowski, Charles *v.2 p.141*
Bulag, Uradyn E. *v.6 p.240*
Buley, R. Carlyle *v.3 p.512*
Bulgakov, Mikhail Afanasevich *v.2 p.801, p.802*
Bulger, Ruth E. (Editor), et al. *v.5 p.247*
Bulger, Ruth Ellen (Editor), et al. *v.5 p.246*
Bull, C. Neil *v.4 p.751*
Bull, Hedley (Editor), et al. *v.4 p.625*
Bull, Hedley *v.4 p.625, p.628, p.655*
Bull, John *v.2 p.264*
Bull, Malcolm *v.3 p.70*
Bull, Marcus *v.3 p.62*
Bull, Stephen J., et al. *v.5 p.581*
Bullen, J. B. *v.1 p.671, p.686*
Bulliet, Richard W. (Editor) *v.6 p.591*
Bulliet, Richard W. *v.6 p.294*
Bullinger, Hans-Jorg & Ziegler, Jurgen *v.5 p.589*
Bullock, Alan & Trombley, Stephen (Editors) . . . *v.2 p.549*
Bullock, Charles & Mahon, Michael . *v.4 p.785, p.829, p.842*
Bullock, Henry A. *v.4 p.309*
Bullock, Margaret E. *v.1 p.736*
Bullock, Steve *v.4 p.804, p.849, p.890*
Bullough, Geoffrey *v.2 p.228*
Bullough, Vern L. & Brundage,

James A. (Editors) *v.4 p.746, v.6 p.559*
Bullough, Vern L. & Bullough, Bonnie *v.6 p.370*
Bullough, Vern L. (Editor), et al. *v.5 p.528*
Bullough, Vern L. (Editor) *v.6 p.387*
Bullough, Vern L., et al. *v.6 p.359*
Bullough, Vern L. *v.4 p.746, p.749, v.6 p.362*
Bulman-May, James *v.2 p.740*
Bulosan, Carlos *v.6 p.93, p.99, p.129*
Bultmann, Rudolf *v.1 p.625, p.627, p.628, p.632*
Bumgarner, Jeffrey B. *v.6 p.264*
Bumsted, J. M. *v.3 p.542*
Bumsted, Jack & Bumsted, J. M. *v.3 p.535*
Bunce, Fredrick W. *v.1 p.709*
Bunce, R. G. & Howard, D. C. (Editors) . . *v.5 p.167, p.198*
Bunch, Lonnie G. III, et al. *v.3 p.377*
Bunch, Meribeth & Vaughn, Cynthia *v.1 p.394*
Bunck, Julie M. *v.3 p.307*
Bundles, A'Lelia *v.6 p.16, p.42*
Bundy, William P. *v.3 p.439, p.467*
Bunge, Mario *v.5 p.400*
Bunge, Nancy L. *v.2 p.574*
Bunin, Ivan A. *v.2 p.797, p.802*
Bunin, Ivan *v.2 p.802*
Bunnell, Fred L. & Johnson, Jacklyn F. (Editors) . . . *v.5 p.37*
Bunnell, Gene *v.6 p.726*
Bunnell, Peter C. *v.1 p.766*
Bunnin, Nicholas & Tsui-James, E. P. (Editors) . . . *v.1 p.415*
Bunnin, Nicholas & Yu, Jiyuan *v.1 p.415*
Bunting, Basil *v.2 p.331*
Bunton, Robin & Peterson, Alan *v.5 p.148*
Bunyan, John *v.1 p.593, v.2 p.241*
Buol, S. W. *v.5 p.48*
Buonarroti, Michelangelo & Nims, John F. *v.2 p.708*
Buonaventura, Wendy *v.1 p.28, p.29, p.40*
Buono, Anthony F. *v.4 p.64*
Burack, Jacob A., et al. *v.5 p.517*
Burbank, Douglas W. & Anderson, Robert S. . . . *v.5 p.424*
Burbank, Garin *v.4 p.548*
Burbank, Rex J. *v.2 p.133*
Burbidge, Peter & Sutton, Richard (Editors) . . *v.1 p.195, p.365*
Burch, Noel *v.6 p.335*
Burch, Susan *v.4 p.699*
Burchett, Kenneth E. *v.1 p.662, p.710*
Burchfield, R. W. *v.2 p.550, p.551, p.556*
Burchfield, Robert W. (Editor) *v.2 p.554*
Burciaga, José Antonio *v.6 p.497*
Burckhardt, Jacob *v.3 p.12, p.70, p.191, p.200*
Burckhardt, Sigurd *v.2 p.228*
Burczynski, Michael E. (Editor) *v.5 p.104, p.126, p.145*
Burden, Barry C. & Kimball, David C. *v.4 p.550*
Burden, Ernest E. *v.1 p.783, v.4 p.158*
Burden, Ernest *v.1 p.821*
Burden, Michael (Editor) *v.1 p.182, p.349*
Burden, Paul R. *v.4 p.283*

Author Index

Burden, Richard L. & Faires, J. Douglas *v.5 p.491*

Burdette, Marcia M. *v.6 p.77*

Burdette, Walter J. *v.5 p.148*

Burdick, Alan *v.5 p.186*

Burdick, Eugene & Wheeler, Harvey *v.2 p.59*

Burdick, John and Hewitt, W.E. (eds.) *v.3 p.301*

Burdick, John (ed.), Hewitt, W.E. (ed.) *v.3 p.298*

Burdick, John *v.3 p.338*

Bureau of Economic Analysis,
  U.S. Department of Commerce *v.4 p.59*

Burfoot, Amby (Editor) *v.4 p.790, p.863, p.866*

Burg, B. R. *v.6 p.389*

Burg, David F. *v.4 p.325*

Burg, Steven L. & Shoup, Paul S. . . . *v.3 p.246, p.248, p.249*

Burgat, Francois & Dowell, William *v.6 p.59*

Burge, David *v.1 p.210*

Burger, Edward B. & Starbird, Michael . . . *v.5 p.457, p.465*

Burger, Edward B. & Tubbs, Robert *v.5 p.475*

Burger, Edward B. *v.5 p.475*

Burger, Heinz Otto *v.2 p.589*

Burger, Joanna (Editor) *v.5 p.363*

Burger, Joanna *v.5 p.363, p.375*

Burger, Richard L. *v.3 p.260, v.4 p.11*

Burgess, Anthony *v.2 p.335, p.336, p.357, v.6 p.172*

Burgess, Ernest W. & Bogue,
  Donald J. (Editors) *v.4 p.770, v.6 p.716, p.717*

Burgess, Geoffrey & Haynes, Bruce *v.1 p.389*

Burgess, John *v.5 p.281*

Burgess, Jonathan S. *v.2 p.402*

Burgess, Michael & Bartle, Lisa R. *v.2 p.581*

Burgess, Stephen *v.4 p.633*

Burgess, Susan R. *v.4 p.531, p.535*

Burgess, William A. *v.5 p.313*

Burggraaff, Winfield J. *v.3 p.273*

Burgh, Hugo de *v.4 p.403*

Burghardt, Walter J. & Lawler, T. C. (Editors) . . . *v.1 p.590*

Burghardt, Walter J. (Editor), et al. *v.1 p.590, p.591*

Burgmann, Verity *v.4 p.710*

Burgos, William, et al. *v.6 p.528*

Burgoyne, Robert *v.6 p.314, p.340*

Burgwyn, H. James *v.3 p.78, p.202*

Burian, Edward R. (Editor) *v.3 p.266*

Burk, Robert F. *v.4 p.804, p.850, p.882, p.887, p.895*

Burke, Bernard F. & Graham-Smith, Francis *v.5 p.67*

Burke, Edmund R. (Editor) . . . *v.4 p.856, p.870, p.871*

Burke, Edmund R. *v.4 p.856*

Burke, Edmund *v.1 p.450, p.480, v.6 p.643*

Burke, Gwendolyn, et al. *v.5 p.706*

Burke, John Francis *v.6 p.537*

Burke, John P. *v.3 p.482*

Burke, Kenneth *v.1 p.489, v.2 p.59, p.568, p.575*

Burke, Peter (Editor) *v.3 p.70*

Burke, Peter *v.1 p.481, v.3 p.38, v.4 p.682, p.699*

Burke, Robert *v.5 p.313*

Burke, Roger Hopkins *v.6 p.249*

Burke, S. M. & Quraishi, Salim A. *v.6 p.162*

Burke, Sally *v.1 p.120*

Burkert, Walter . *v.1 p.421, p.530, p.531, p.532, v.3 p.12, p.13, p.16*

Burkett, Elinor *v.6 p.378*

Burkhard, Marianne *v.2 p.598*

Burkhardt, Barbara A. *v.2 p.97*

Burkhardt, Margaret A. & Nathaniel, Alvita K. . . *v.5 p.511, p.530*

Burkhart, Louise M. *v.3 p.262*

Burkholder, J. Peter (Editor) *v.1 p.210, p.333*

Burkholder, J. Peter *v.1 p.210, p.333*

Burkholder, Mark A. (Editor) *v.3 p.350*

Burkholder, Robert E. & Myerson, Joel *v.2 p.37*

Burki, Shahid Javed *v.6 p.162*

Burks, Barbara S., et al. *v.5 p.575*

Burleigh, Michael & Wippermann, Wolfgang *v.3 p.171*

Burleigh, Michael *v.3 p.171*

Burling, Robbins *v.2 p.559, v.4 p.18, p.19*

Burlingame, A. L. (Volume Editor) *v.5 p.87*

Burn, R. P. *v.5 p.475*

Burn, W. L. (William Laurence) *v.3 p.91, p.110*

Burn, W. L. *v.6 p.749*

Burner, David *v.3 p.439, p.467*

Burness, Donald *v.2 p.693*

Burnet, John *v.1 p.419, p.421*

Burnett, Anne P. *v.2 p.401, p.409*

Burnett, Cathleen *v.6 p.272*

Burnett, Christina Duffy & Marshall, Burke (Editors) . *v.3 p.319*

Burnett, John *v.5 p.209*

Burnett, Rebecca *v.4 p.167*

Burnett, Robert *v.1 p.383*

Burnett *v.5 p.680*

Burney, Charles *v.1 p.174, p.188*

Burney, Fanny *v.2 p.241, p.242*

Burney, Frances *v.2 p.242*

Burnham, John C. *v.4 p.709*

Burnham, Kenneth P. & Anderson, D. R. *v.5 p.92, p.93*

Burnham, Philip *v.6 p.299, p.680, p.691*

Burnham, W. Dean *v.4 p.556*

Burnham, Walter Dean *v.4 p.548*

Burnim, Kalman A. *v.1 p.99, p.152*

Burnley, David & Burnley, J. D. *v.2 p.554*

Burns, E. Bradford *v.3 p.339*

Burns, Eric *v.4 p.709*

Burns, Hobert Warren *v.4 p.323, p.339*

Burns, J. H. (Editor) . *v.3 p.106, p.108, p.123, p.127, v.4 p.490, p.501*

Burns, J. H. *v.4 p.502*

Burns, James M. *v.3 p.379, p.456*

Burns, John A. (Editor) *v.1 p.824*

Burns, John Horne *v.6 p.395*

Burns, Kate *v.6 p.265*

Burns, Kathryn *v.3 p.282, p.325*

Burns, Kristine H. (Editor) *v.6 p.474*

Burns, Lori & Lafrance, Melisse *v.1 p.378*

Burns, Marilyn *v.4 p.362*

86

Burns, Michael *v.3 p.59*
Burns, Nancy, et al. *v.4 p.503, p.550, v.6 p.440*
Burns, Paul *v.4 p.87*
Burns, Richard D. (Introduction by) *v.4 p.655*
Burns, Robert Ignatius *v.3 p.65*
Burns, Robert *v.2 p.272, p.273*
Burns, Ronald M. *v.3 p.536*
Burns, Sarah *v.1 p.682, p.731*
Burns, Stewart (Editor) *v.3 p.504*
Burns, Thomas S. & Eadie, John W. *v.3 p.30, v.6 p.711*
Burns, Thomas S. *v.3 p.22, p.30*
Burns, William E. *v.3 p.71*
Burnshaw, Stanley (Editor) *v.6 p.648*
Burnside, John *v.2 p.331*
Buros, Institute *v.5 p.600*
Burr, Chandler *v.6 p.420*
Burr, John R. & Burr, Charlotte A. *v.1 p.416, v.5 p.405*
Burr, John R. *v.1 p.438*
Burr, Ramiro *v.6 p.518*
Burr, Robert N. *v.3 p.350*
Burr, Zofia *v.2 p.8*
Burrell, David B. *v.1 p.638*
Burrin, Philippe *v.3 p.83*
Burrough, Bryan & Helyar, John *v.4 p.84*
Burroughs, Edgar Rice *v.2 p.59*
Burroughs, William S. *v.2 p.64, v.6 p.395*
Burrow, J. A. & Turville-Petre, Thorlac *v.2 p.550*
Burrow, J. A. *v.6 p.564*
Burroway, Janet & Weinberg, Susan *v.2 p.579*
Burrowes, Robert D. *v.6 p.628*
Burrows, David *v.1 p.380*
Burrows, Donald (Editor) *v.1 p.183, p.328*
Burrows, Donald *v.1 p.182, p.183, p.235, p.328*
Burrows, Edwin G. & Wallace, Mike . . . *v.3 p.490, v.6 p.711*
Burrows, Peter *v.4 p.84*
Burrows, Victoria *v.2 p.769*
Burrup, Percy E., et al. *v.4 p.280*
Burstyn, Varda (Editor) *v.4 p.747, v.6 p.456, p.468*
Burt, Brian A. & Eklund, Steven *v.5 p.525*
Burt, George D. *v.1 p.255, v.6 p.351*
Burt, John *v.2 p.129*
Burt, Jo-Marie & Mauceri, Philip (Editors) *v.3 p.332*
Burt, Peter *v.1 p.210, p.362*
Burt, Ramsey *v.1 p.40*
Burt, Richard & Boose, Lynda E. (Editors) *v.6 p.325*
Burt, Robert A. *v.4 p.462*
Burt, Stephen *v.2 p.90*
Burt, T. *v.4 p.390*
Burton, Allen W. & Miller, Daryl E. . *v.4 p.873, p.907, p.909*
Burton, Anthony (Editor) *v.1 p.188, p.195, p.400*
Burton, Antoinette (Editor) *v.6 p.745*
Burton, Antoinette M. & Burton, Antoinette *v.2 p.761*
Burton, David H. *v.3 p.439*
Burton, David Henry *v.3 p.439, p.467, v.4 p.631*
Burton, Gwendolyn R. & Englekirk, Paul *v.5 p.514*

Burton, Humphrey *v.1 p.210, p.311*
Burton, Ian, et al. *v.4 p.395*
Burton, Jeffrey F., et al. *v.6 p.133*
Burton, Richard D. *v.3 p.314*
Burton, Robert *v.2 p.213*
Burton, William W. (Editor) *v.1 p.210, p.311*
Burton, William *v.3 p.439*
Burton-Roberts, Noel *v.2 p.556*
Burum, Stephen H. (Editor) *v.6 p.349*
Buruma, Ian *v.6 p.219*
Burwell, Rose M. *v.2 p.83*
Bury, John B. *v.3 p.30, p.192*
Bury, R. G. (Editor) *v.4 p.215*
Busbee, Westley F. *v.3 p.504*
Busby, C. *v.5 p.438*
Busby, Cecilia *v.4 p.30*
Busby, Mark & Heaberlin, Dick (Editors) *v.2 p.108*
Busby, Mark *v.3 p.526*
Busby, Robert *v.3 p.467*
Busby, Sharon *v.1 p.806*
Busch, Andrew E. *v.3 p.446*
Busch, Frederick *v.2 p.141*
Busch, Wilhelm *v.2 p.603*
Buscombe, Edward & Pearson, Roberta E. (Editors) . *v.6 p.323*
Buscombe, Edward *v.6 p.700*
Buse, Peter *v.2 p.188*
Bush, Barbara *v.4 p.727*
Bush, David M., et al. *v.5 p.373*
Bush, Douglas *v.2 p.267*
Bush, George Herbert Walker & Scowcroft, Brent . . *v.3 p.467*
Bush, Peter R. (Editor) *v.2 p.671*
Bush, Robert *v.2 p.43*
Bush-Brown, James & Bush-Brown, Louise *v.5 p.43*
Bushkovitch, Paul *v.3 p.216*
Bushman, Richard L. *v.3 p.489*
Bushman, Richard Lyman *v.1 p.580*
Bushnell, David *v.3 p.357*
Bushnell, O. A. *v.6 p.130*
Bushnell, Rebecca W. (Editor) *v.1 p.58, p.88*
Bushong, Stewart C. *v.5 p.534*
Busia, K. A. *v.6 p.69*
Business Department, Carnegie
  Library of Pittsburgh Staff *v.4 p.172*
Business Information Agency, Inc. Staff *v.4 p.153*
Business Information Agency Staff *v.4 p.153*
Bussler, Christoph *v.4 p.113*
Butalia, Urashi (Editor) *v.2 p.763*
Butalia, Urvashi (Contribution by) *v.6 p.160*
Butcher, Judith, et al. *v.2 p.574*
Butcher, Kevin *v.3 p.27*
Butcher, Philip (Editor) *v.2 p.18*
Butcher, Russell D. *v.5 p.83*
Butcher, Samuel S. (Editor), et al. *v.5 p.167, p.183*
Butler, Alban *v.1 p.578*
Butler, Alfred J. *v.6 p.635*

Butler, Anne M. *v.4 p.747*

Butler, David & Ranney, Austin (Editors) *v.4 p.575*

Butler, David & Stokes, Donald E. *v.4 p.606*

Butler, David E. & Low, D. A. (Editors) *v.4 p.605*

Butler, David E. *v.1 p.375*

Butler, David (Editor) *v.4 p.606*

Butler, Diana H. *v.1 p.582*

Butler, Dom Cuthbert *v.1 p.652*

Butler, Edgar W. & Bustamante, Jorge A. (Editors) . *v.3 p.291*

Butler, Edward Cuthbert *v.1 p.577, v.3 p.56*

Butler, J. D. *v.5 p.313*

Butler, J. Douglas & Walbert, David F. (Editors) . . . *v.4 p.471*

Butler, James N. & Cogley, David R. *v.5 p.281*

Butler, John Sibley *v.6 p.20*

Butler, Johnnella E. *v.6 p.108*

Butler, Jon & Stout, Harry S. (Editors) *v.1 p.543, p.604*

Butler, Jon *v.1 p.543, p.606*

Butler, Joseph *v.1 p.645*

Butler, Judith *v.2 p.572, v.6 p.370*

Butler, Kim D. *v.3 p.278, p.339*

Butler, Lawrence F. *v.4 p.790, p.795*

Butler, Lee *v.4 p.726*

Butler, Marilyn . *v.2 p.171, p.174, p.183, p.184, p.267, p.286, v.3 p.127*

Butler, Mark J. *v.1 p.267*

Butler, Michael (Editor), et al. *v.3 p.244*

Butler, Michael *v.2 p.607*

Butler, Octavia *v.6 p.23, p.42*

Butler, Richard (Editor) *v.4 p.877, v.5 p.581*

Butler, Richard *v.4 p.655*

Butler, Robert Olen *v.2 p.141*

Butler, Ronnie *v.2 p.486*

Butler, Ruth *v.1 p.778*

Butler, Samuel & Mumford, Lewis *v.2 p.273*

Butler, Samuel *v.2 p.242, p.273*

Butler, Sandra & Rosenblum, Barbara *v.6 p.377*

Butler, Thomas *v.2 p.779*

Butlin, Martin *v.2 p.239*

Butor, Michel *v.2 p.511*

Butow, R. J. C. *v.6 p.223*

Butsch, Richard (Editor) *v.4 p.783, p.887*

Butt, Archibald W. *v.3 p.456*

Butt, Graham *v.4 p.376*

Butt, John & Benjamin, Carmen *v.2 p.635*

Butt, John (Editor) *v.1 p.183, p.303*

Butt, John *v.1 p.183, p.235, p.303, p.400*

Buttel, Frederick H. & McMichael,
  Philip David (Editors) *v.4 p.375*

Butterfield, Herbert, Sir *v.3 p.108, p.158*

Butterfield, Herbert *v.3 p.46, v.5 p.390*

Butters, Ronald R. (Editor), et al. *v.6 p.392*

Butterwick, Richard (Editor) *v.3 p.252*

Butterwick, Richard *v.3 p.253*

Buttino, Frank & Buttino, Lou *v.6 p.383*

Button, James W., et al. *v.6 p.387*

Butts, Barbara & Hendrix, Lee *v.1 p.721*

Butts, Jeffrey A. & Roman, John *v.6 p.267*

Butts, William (Editor) *v.2 p.128*

Buxton, Amity Pierce *v.6 p.368*

Buxton, Dwayne (Editor), et al. *v.5 p.20*

Buzura, Augustin *v.2 p.816*

Byatt, A. S. (Editor) *v.2 p.202*

Byatt, A. S. *v.2 p.331, p.332*

Byatt, Andrew et. al *v.5 p.172, p.241*

Bybee, Rodger W. (Editor) *v.5 p.191, p.244*

Byerman, Keith E. *v.2 p.36*

Byers, Michael *v.4 p.646*

Byers, Walter & Hammer, Charles *v.4 p.821, p.893*

Byford, Jim *v.5 p.173*

Byl, John *v.4 p.800*

Byland, Bruce E. & Pohl, John M. *v.3 p.260*

Byman, Daniel *v.4 p.658*

Bynagle, Hans E. *v.1 p.416, v.5 p.405*

Bynon, Theodora *v.2 p.559*

Bynum, Caroline Walker *v.3 p.56, v.6 p.570*

Bynum, Caroline W. *v.1 p.600, p.650, v.3 p.51*

Bynum, Victoria E. *v.6 p.451*

Bynum, William F. (Editor), et al. *v.5 p.390*

Byock, Ira *v.5 p.531*

Byock, Jesse *v.3 p.234*

Byrd, Ayana D. & Tharps, Lori *v.6 p.38, p.42*

Byrd, William *v.3 p.499*

Byrge, Duane & Milton, Robert G. *v.6 p.312*

Byrne, Alexander & Hilbert, David R. (Editors) . . . *v.1 p.710*

Byrne, Alexander *v.1 p.710, v.5 p.606*

Byrne, Dawson *v.1 p.108*

Byrne, Jane *v.3 p.515*

Byrne, Joseph Patrick *v.3 p.68*

Byrne, Julie *v.4 p.835, p.853*

Byrne, Malcom & Ostermann, Christian F. (Editors) . *v.4 p.641*

Byrne, Muriel S. & Boland, Bridget (Editors) . *v.3 p.92, p.99*

Byrnes, James Francis *v.3 p.456*

Byrnes, Rita M. *v.6 p.78*

Byrnes, William J. *v.1 p.825*

Byron, George Gordon *v.2 p.273, p.274*

Byron, John & Pack, Robert *v.6 p.199*

Byron, William *v.2 p.647*

Bytwerk, Randall *v.3 p.171, p.176*

Bywaters, David *v.2 p.246*

C

C. Q. Press Staff *v.4 p.547, p.548, p.556*

CA Plant Health Association Staff *v.5 p.48*

Cabalero, Cesar *v.6 p.677*

Caballero, Carlo *v.1 p.195, p.210, p.324*

Caban, Geoffrey (Editor) *v.1 p.712*

Cabanillas de Rodríguez, Berta *v.3 p.271*

Cabell, David W. E. & English, Deborah L. (Editors) . *v.4 p.148, p.149*

Cabell, James Branch *v.2 p.64*

Cabibbo, A. & Citterich, M. Helmer *v.5 p.97, p.126*

Cable, George W. *v.2 p.32*

Cabral, Amilcar *v.6 p.73*

Cabral de Melo Neto, Joao *v.2 p.690*

Cabrera, Lydia *v.2 p.671*

Cabri, Walter & Fabio, Romano Di *v.5 p.740*

Caccamo, Rita *v.4 p.679*

Cachel, Susan *v.4 p.15*

Cachey, Theodore J. (Editor) *v.2 p.704*

Caciola, Nancy *v.6 p.570*

Cacioppo, John T. (Editor), et al. *v.5 p.616*

Cadalso, Jose *v.2 p.654*

Cade, Jared *v.2 p.338*

Cadena, Marisol de (Contribution by) *v.3 p.329*

Cadge, Wendy *v.6 p.105*

Cadick, John *v.5 p.681*

Cadle, James & Yeates, Donald *v.4 p.114*

Cadogan, Gerald *v.3 p.15*

Cadwalader, Sandra L. & Deloria, Vine Jr. (Editors) *v.6 p.695*

Cadwallader, Allen & Gagne, David *v.1 p.369*

Cady, Edwin H. & Cady, Norma W. *v.2 p.41*

Cady, Edwin Harrison *v.2 p.28*

Cady, Edwin H. *v.2 p.36*

Cady, John F. *v.6 p.165*

Caesar, Judith *v.6 p.592*

Caesar, Julius *v.2 p.428*

Caesar, Michael *v.2 p.704*

Caffaro, John V. & Conn-Caffaro, Allison *v.5 p.667*

Caforio, Giuseppe (Editor) *v.4 p.717*

Cage, John M. *v.1 p.44, p.210, p.315*

Cahan, Abraham *v.2 p.32*

Cahen, Claude & Holt, P. M. *v.6 p.622*

Cahen, Claude *v.6 p.622*

Cahen, L., et al. *v.5 p.433*

Cahill, David *v.3 p.325*

Cahill, James *v.1 p.725, p.731*

Cahill, Lisa Sowle *v.5 p.247*

Cahill, Sean & Jason Cianciotto *v.6 p.384*

Cahill, Sean, Ken South, & Jane Spade *v.6 p.380*

Cahill, Sean *v.6 p.388*

Cahir, Linda Costanzo *v.6 p.325*

Cahn, Robert W. (Editor), et al. *v.5 p.318*

Cahn, Robert W. *v.5 p.318*

Cahn, Susan K. *v.4 p.804, p.835, v.6 p.437*

Cahuc, Pierre & Zylberberg, André *v.4 p.253*

Cai, Yong & Braids, Olin C. *v.5 p.112*

Cain, Gordon *v.5 p.316*

Cain, James M. *v.2 p.64*

Cain, Joe *v.5 p.131, p.191*

Cain, Peter & Hopkins, Tony *v.4 p.583*

Cain, William E. *v.2 p.52*

Caine, Dennis J. (Editor), et al. *v.4 p.827*

Caird, George B. *v.1 p.616*

Cairnes, John Elliott *v.4 p.217*

Cairns, Christopher (Editor) . *v.1 p.74, p.91, p.95, p.106, p.146*

Cairns, David *v.1 p.195, p.310*

Cairns, Douglas L. (Editor) *v.2 p.413*

Cairns, Robert B. & Stoff, David M. (Editors) . . . *v.5 p.662*

Caisse, Arthur J. Jr. *v.5 p.725*

Cajete, Gregory *v.4 p.311, v.6 p.680*

Calabrese, Edward J. *v.5 p.364*

Calabria, Frank M. *v.1 p.40*

Calafate Boyle, Susan *v.6 p.524, p.533*

Calais-Germain, Blandine *v.1 p.51*

Calasanti, Toni M. & Slevin, Kathleen F. *v.6 p.444*

Calavita, Kitty *v.4 p.570, v.6 p.525, p.528*

Caldeira, Teresa Pires Do Rio *v.4 p.773*

Calder, Andrew *v.1 p.89, p.105, p.143*

Calder, Bruce J. (Author, Introduction by) *v.3 p.316*

Calder, Daniel G. *v.2 p.203*

Calder, James D. *v.4 p.523*

Calder, John *v.2 p.333*

Calderón de la Barca, Pedro &
    Porqueras Mayo, Alberto *v.2 p.647*

Calderón de la Barca, Pedro . *v.1 p.74, p.107,v.2 p.646, p.647*

Calderón, Héctor *v.6 p.498, p.511*

Calderon, Hector & Saldivar, Jose D. (Editors) . *v.6 p.497, p.511*

Caldwell, Bruce J. (Editor) *v.4 p.194*

Caldwell, Bruce *v.4 p.194, p.198*

Caldwell, Dan *v.3 p.387*

Caldwell, Erskine *v.2 p.66*

Caldwell, Helen *v.1 p.6, v.2 p.690*

Caldwell, John *v.1 p.245*

Caldwell, Lynton K. *v.4 p.566*

Cale, John & Bockris, Victor *v.1 p.210, p.267, p.315*

Calhoon, Robert M. *v.3 p.407*

Calhoun, Arthur W. *v.4 p.732*

Calhoun, Charles C. *v.2 p.47*

Calhoun, Cheshire (Editor) *v.1 p.506*

Calhoun, Craig (Editor) *v.4 p.373, p.677*

Califano, Joseph A. Jr. *v.3 p.467*

Califia, Pat *v.6 p.368*

Califia, Patrick *v.4 p.746, v.6 p.370*

California University at Los Angeles African Studio Staff &
    Kuper, Hilda (Editors) *v.6 p.68*

Calin, William *v.2 p.455, v.6 p.564*

Calinescu, George *v.2 p.816*

Calkins, Robert G. *v.1 p.785*

Calladine, Chris R., et al. *v.5 p.120*

Callaghan, Dympna (Editor) . . . *v.1 p.75, p.86, p.99, v.2 p.228*

Callaham, Ludmilla Ignatiev, et al. *v.5 p.258, p.386*

Callahan, Christopher *v.4 p.413*

Callahan, Daniel & Singer, Peter (Editors) *v.1 p.485*

Callahan, Michael D. *v.4 p.631*

Callahan, Raymond E. *v.4 p.325*

Callahan, Sidney & Callahan, Daniel (Editors) . *v.6 p.464, p.468*

Callan, Patrick M. & Finney, Joni E. (Editors) . . . *v.4 p.295*

Callanan, Maggie & Kelley, Patricia *v.5 p.531*

Callanan, Valerie J. *v.6 p.258*

Callcott, Maria *v.3 p.350*

Callejo-Perez, David M. *v.4 p.300*

Callen, Anthea *v.1 p.750*

Callen, Herbert B. *v.5 p.559*

Callenbach, Ernest *v.6 p.293*

Callicott, J. Baird *v.5 p.357, p.369*

Callier, Pierre *v.1 p.755*

Callihan, Laurie Ann (Author, Editor) *v.5 p.244*

Callister, William D. Jr. *v.5 p.688*

Callow, Philip *v.2 p.53, p.312*

Callow, Simon *v.6 p.418*

Calloway, Colin G. *v.6 p.685, p.686, p.691*

Calomiris, Charles W. *v.4 p.111, p.154*

Calotychos, Vangelis (Editor) *v.3 p.197, v.6 p.601*

Calow, Peter (Editor) *v.5 p.28*

Calver, Giles *v.1 p.717*

Calvert, Jack G.; Pitts, James N. *v.5 p.278*

Calvert, Peter (Editor) *v.4 p.591*

Calvin, John *v.1 p.589*

Calvino, Italo (Editor) *v.2 p.714*

Calvino, Italo *v.2 p.697, p.714, p.715, v.6 p.730*

Calvocoressi, Peter, et al. *v.3 p.80*

Calvocoressi, Richard *v.1 p.766*

Calza, Gian Carlo & Carpenter, John T. (Editors) . *v.1 p.692, p.695*

Calza, Gian Carlo *v.1 p.692*

Camaj, Martin *v.2 p.815*

Camarillo, Albert *v.6 p.530, p.548*

Camayd-Freixas, Erik & Gonzalez,
  Jose Eduardo (Editors) *v.3 p.316*

Camazine, Scott *v.5 p.155, p.226*

Cambon, Glauco *v.2 p.710, p.718*

Camboni, Marina (Editor) *v.2 p.88*

Cambridge Center for Behavioral Studies *v.5 p.666*

Cambridge Educational (Produced by) *v.4 p.534*

Cambridge Scientific Abstracts, Inc. *v.5 p.731*

Cambridge Scientific Abstracts *v.5 p.670*

Cambridge University Press Staff *v.3 p.3*

Camejo, Peter, et al. *v.4 p.553*

Camenson, Blythe *v.4 p.168, v.5 p.250*

Camerer, Colin (Editor), et al. *v.4 p.249*

Cameron, A. & Ettles, C. M. *v.5 p.708*

Cameron, A. & Herrin, J. (Editors) *v.6 p.622*

Cameron, Alan & Long, Jacqueline *v.3 p.30*

Cameron, Averil & Conrad,
  Lawrence I. (Editors) *v.6 p.581, p.584*

Cameron, Averil *v.1 p.598, v.3 p.30, p.192*

Cameron, Deborah & Kulick, Don *v.4 p.21*

Cameron, Deborah *v.5 p.622*

Cameron, Don *v.4 p.124*

Cameron, Euan *v.1 p.601*

Cameron, H. D. *v.2 p.421*

Cameron, Keith *v.2 p.469*

Cameron, Kenneth M. *v.6 p.314*

Cameron, Kenneth N. (Editor) *v.2 p.311*

Cameron, Kenneth Neill *v.2 p.311*

Cameron, Kirk & White, Graham *v.4 p.589*

Cameron, Loren *v.6 p.370, p.407*

Cameron, Mary M. *v.6 p.163*

Cameron, Maxwell A. & Mauceri, Philip (Editors) . *v.3 p.329*

Cameron, Maxwell A. *v.3 p.329, v.4 p.591*

Cameron, Nigel M. de S. (Editor), et al. *v.5 p.247*

Cameron, Nigel *v.6 p.205*

Cameron, P. J. & Van Lint, J. H. *v.5 p.478*

Cameron, Rondo & Neal, Larry *v.3 p.38*

Cameron, Rondo *v.3 p.38*

Cameron, Sheila *v.4 p.176*

Camões, Luís de *v.2 p.688*

Camões, Luiz de *v.2 p.688*

Camille, Michael *v.1 p.654, p.671*

Caminero-Santangelo, Marta *v.6 p.477*

Cammarosano, Joseph R. *v.4 p.226*

Cammermeyer, Margarethe & Fisher, Chris *v.6 p.389*

Cammisa, Anne M. *v.4 p.523*

Camnitzer, Luis *v.1 p.684*

Camoes, Luis de *v.2 p.688*

Camoes, Luiz de *v.2 p.688*

Camp, John & Fisher, Elizabeth *v.3 p.12*

Camp, John M. *v.3 p.17*

Camp, Roderic A. *v.3 p.291*

Camp, Roderic Ai *v.3 p.291*

Campa, Arthur L. *v.6 p.530*

Campana, Dino *v.2 p.713, p.714*

Campbell, A. Malcolm & Heyer,
  Laurie J. *v.5 p.97, p.103, p.104, p.145*

Campbell, Alec *v.1 p.668, p.689*

Campbell, Angus, et al. *v.4 p.548*

Campbell, Anne *v.5 p.651*

Campbell, Barbara *v.2 p.160*

Campbell, Bruce M. S. *v.3 p.96*

Campbell, Bruce *v.3 p.266*

Campbell, C. Lee (Editor), et al. *v.5 p.45*

Campbell, Charles S. *v.3 p.432*

Campbell, Christy *v.5 p.46, p.52*

Campbell, Colin B. & Rockman,
  Bert A. (Editors) *v.3 p.467, p.482*

Campbell, Colin B. & Rockman, Bert A. *v.3 p.467*

Campbell, Colm *v.3 p.138*

Campbell, Colton C. & Rae, Nicol C. (Editors) . . *v.4 p.533*

Campbell, D. A. *v.2 p.403*

Campbell, D. M., Higgins, C. (Editors) *v.5 p.457*

Campbell, David A. (Editor, Translator) *v.2 p.403*

Campbell, David A. (Translator) *v.2 p.403*

Campbell, David A. *v.2 p.403*

Campbell, David G. *v.5 p.175, p.238, p.240*

Campbell, Douglas G. *v.6 p.269*

Campbell, Douglas S. *v.4 p.444*

Campbell, Elizabeth A. *v.2 p.282*

Campbell, Frederick L. (Editor), et al. *v.4 p.675*

Campbell, Gaylon S. & Norman, John M. *v.5 p.49*

Campbell, Gordon *v.1 p.674*

Campbell, Gwyn *v.6 p.67*
Campbell, J. B. *v.3 p.27*
Campbell, James B. *v.4 p.388*
Campbell, James (Editor), et al. *v.6 p.561*
Campbell, James (Editor) *v.3 p.96*
Campbell, James W. P. *v.1 p.796*
Campbell, James *v.2 p.10, v.6 p.730*
Campbell, Jeremy *v.5 p.408*
Campbell, John H. & DeNevi, Don (Editors) *v.6 p.254*
Campbell, John L. *v.4 p.261*
Campbell, John Y., et al. *v.4 p.198*
Campbell, Joseph & Abadie, M. J. *v.1 p.527*
Campbell, Joseph Keim (Editor), et al. . . *v.1 p.503*
Campbell, Joseph *v.1 p.527*
Campbell, Judith L. & Modrich, Paul (Volume Editors) *v.5 p.131*
Campbell, Kenneth J. *v.4 p.651*
Campbell, Kurt M. (Editor), et al. *v.4 p.655*
Campbell, Leon G. *v.3 p.273*
Campbell, Lily B. *v.2 p.233*
Campbell, Lily G. *v.2 p.234*
Campbell, Lyle *v.2 p.559*
Campbell, Marjorie Wilkins *v.3 p.545*
Campbell, Matthew *v.2 p.174, p.184, p.313*
Campbell, Mavis C. *v.6 p.70*
Campbell, Michael *v.1 p.267*
Campbell, Patricia S. & Scott-Kassner, Carol . . . *v.4 p.362*
Campbell, Patricia Shehan & Wade, Bonnie C. . *v.1 p.283, p.405*
Campbell, Patricia Shehan, et al. *v.1 p.405*
Campbell, R. H. & Skinner, Andrew S. . . . *v.4 p.211, p.218*
Campbell, Randolph B. *v.3 p.508*
Campbell, Russell *v.6 p.321*
Campbell, Sandra (Editor) *v.2 p.731*
Campbell, Scott & Fainstein, Susan S. (Editors) . . *v.6 p.727*
Campbell, Shirley Faye *v.4 p.25*
Campbell, Stephen & Milner, Stephen (Editors) *v.1 p.674, p.686*
Campbell, Stephen R. & Zazkis, Rina (Editors) . . *v.5 p.462*
Campbell, Stuart (Editor) *v.1 p.195, p.245*
Campbell, Sue *v.5 p.609*
Campbell, SueEllen *v.5 p.175, p.186*
Campbell, Ted A. *v.1 p.590*
Campbell, Thomas *v.2 p.243*
Campbell, Tom *v.4 p.514*
Campbell, W. A. *v.5 p.316, p.741*
Campbell, W. Joseph *v.4 p.403*
Campbell, Wallace H. *v.5 p.443*
Campbell-Allen, Denison & Roper, Harold *v.5 p.697*
Campbell *v.1 p.620*
Campbell-Kelly, Martin & Aspray,
    William *v.3 p.366, v.4 p.114, v.5 p.342, p.343*
Campion, Thomas *v.2 p.213*
Campo, Rafael *v.6 p.404, p.505, p.510*
Campoamor, Ramón de *v.2 p.654*
Campobello, Nellie *v.2 p.667*
Campos, David *v.6 p.385*
Campos, Frank Gabriel *v.1 p.397*

Camps, W. A. *v.2 p.446*
Camus, Albert *v.2 p.511, p.512*
Canada in World Affairs Staff *v.3 p.537*
Canada *v.4 p.586, p.587*
Canarache, A., et al. *v.5 p.49, v.6 p.285*
Canavaggio, Jean *v.2 p.645*
Canby, Sheila R. *v.1 p.691*
Canby, William C. *v.6 p.691*
Candland, Douglas K *v.5 p.595*
Candland, Douglas K. *v.5 p.614*
Canetti, Elias *v.2 p.605, p.606*
Canfield, Arthur G. *v.2 p.486*
Canfield, John V. (Editor) *v.1 p.438*
Canikova, Andrea *v.2 p.777*
Canizares-Esguerra, Jorge *v.3 p.71, p.262*
Cannadine, David . *v.3 p.110, p.130,v.6 p.736, p.742, p.744, p.745*
Cannan, Edwin *v.4 p.211*
Cannato, Vincent J. *v.3 p.490, v.6 p.711*
Canniff, Julie G. *v.6 p.138*
Canning, Kathleen *v.3 p.52, p.163*
Canning, Richard *v.6 p.392*
Cannon, Christopher *v.2 p.207*
Cannon, John *v.3 p.127*
Cannon, Joseph *v.5 p.329*
Cannon, Lou *v.3 p.467*
Canny, Nicholas (Editor) *v.3 p.88, p.124, v.4 p.605*
Canny, Nicholas P. *v.3 p.134, p.136, p.137*
Canny, Nicholas *v.3 p.136, p.137*
Canon, Bradley C. & Johnson, Charles A. *v.4 p.465*
Canovan, Margaret *v.4 p.494*
Cantalupo, Charles (Editor) *v.2 p.758*
Cantarella, Eva *v.6 p.364*
Cantarow, Ellen *v.6 p.433*
Canter, Larry W. *v.5 p.367*
Canterbery, E. Ray *v.4 p.185*
Cantú, Norma Elia &
    Nájera-Ramírez, Olga (Editors) *v.6 p.433, p.546*
Cantillon, Richard *v.4 p.215*
Cantner, Uwe (Editor), et al. *v.4 p.230, p.234*
Cantor, Charles R. & Smith, Cassandra L. *v.5 p.145*
Cantor, Harold *v.2 p.108*
Cantor, Norman F. *v.3 p.66, v.4 p.742, v.6 p.561*
Cantrell, Gregg *v.3 p.508*
Cantril, Hadley *v.4 p.710*
Cantwell, Robert S. *v.1 p.295*
Cao Xue Qin *v.6 p.211*
Capaldi, Nicholas *v.1 p.445*
Capek, Karel, et al. *v.2 p.783*
Capek, Karel *v.2 p.782, p.783, v.3 p.189*
Capel, W. & Piotrowski, Susan *v.4 p.795*
Capellanus, Andreas *v.2 p.457*
Capello, Roberta & Nijkamp, Peter (Editors) *v.6 p.722*
Capers, Gerald M. Jr. *v.3 p.510*
Capers, Gerald Mortimer . . . *v.3 p.415, p.422, p.423, p.427*
Capinera, John L. (Editor) *v.5 p.9, p.212*

Capinera, John *v.5 p.3, p.20, p.26*

Capinski, Marek & Zastawniak, Tomasz *v.5 p.503*

Capistrano de Abreu, Joao *v.3 p.334*

Caplan, David *v.2 p.178, p.179*

Caplan, Gerald *v.5 p.670*

Caplan, H. H. *v.1 p.662, p.663*

Caplan, Nathan, et al. *v.4 p.763, p.764, v.6 p.140*

Caplan, Pat & Topan, Farouk (Editors) . . . *v.4 p.38*

Caplan, Paula *v.4 p.292*

Caplan, Richard *v.4 p.628*

Caplan, Russell L. *v.4 p.454*

Caple, Chris *v.1 p.822*

Caplow, Theodore, et al. *v.4 p.732*

Caplow, Theodore *v.4 p.717*

Caponi, Gena D. (Editor) *v.2 p.62*

Caponi, Gena Dagel *v.2 p.62*

Caporale, Lynn H. (Editor) *v.5 p.199*

Caporale, Lynn Helena (Editor) *v.5 p.145, p.200*

Caporale, Lynn Helena *v.5 p.145, p.202*

Caporaso, James A. *v.4 p.602*

Capote, Truman *v.2 p.66, v.6 p.395*

Capp, B. S. *v.3 p.103*

Cappellato, Gabriele (Editor) *v.1 p.792*

Cappelli, Peter *v.4 p.85*

Capper, Charles *v.2 p.38*

Cappo, Joe *v.4 p.140, p.426*

Cappon, Lester (Editor) *v.3 p.407*

Cappuccino, Naomi & Price,
Peter W. (Editors) *v.5 p.143, p.183, p.188*

Capra, Fritjof *v.5 p.410, p.540, v.6 p.288*

Caprioli, Richard M. & Gross, Michael L. (Editors) . *v.5 p.271*

Caputi, Anthony *v.2 p.221*

Caputi, Jane *v.6 p.447, p.458*

Caputo, John D. (Editor) *v.1 p.512*

Caputo, Michael R. *v.4 p.198*

Carabelli, Anna M. *v.4 p.226*

Carabott, Philip (Editor) *v.3 p.194*

Caraley, Demetrios (Editor) *v.3 p.483*

Caramagno, Thomas C. *v.5 p.659*

Caraman, Philip *v.1 p.578*

Caranfa, Angelo *v.1 p.779*

Carapico, Sheila *v.4 p.614, v.6 p.628*

Caras, Roger A. (Editor) *v.5 p.78, p.226*

Carbert, Louise I. *v.4 p.590, v.6 p.440*

Carbo, Nick & Tabios, Eileen (Editors) *v.6 p.91*

Carbone, Greg *v.4 p.393*

Carbone, Peter F. *v.4 p.341*

Carbone, Teresa A. *v.1 p.736*

Carbonell, Nestor *v.3 p.307*

Carboni, Stefano, et al. *v.1 p.673, p.810*

Carby, Hazel V. *v.2 p.8*

Carcopino, Jerome *v.3 p.23*

Card, Claudia (Editor) *v.6 p.460*

Cardarelli, Francois *v.5 p.386, p.413, p.688*

Cardena, Etzel, et al. *v.5 p.613*

Cardenal, Ernesto *v.2 p.675*

Cardenas, Gilberto (Editor) *v.6 p.539*

Cardinal, Agnes (Editor), et al. *v.6 p.478*

Cardinal, Marie *v.2 p.528*

Cardona, Luis A. *v.6 p.535*

Cardoso, Eliana & Helwege, Ann *v.3 p.307*

Cardoso, Fernando E. & Faletto, Enzo *v.3 p.339*

Cardoso, Fernando Henrique *v.3 p.339*

Cardoza y Aragon, Luis *v.2 p.675*

Cardozo, Benjamin N. *v.4 p.433*

Carducci, Giosuè *v.2 p.710*

Cardullo, Bert & Knopf, Robert (Editors) . *v.1 p.63, p.84, p.95*

Cardullo, Bert (Editor), et al. *v.6 p.348*

Cardwell, Michael (Editor), et al. . . *v.4 p.256, p.267, v.5 p.14*

Cardy, Michael & Connon, Derek F. (Editors) . *v.1 p.105, p.127*

Career Planning and Adult Development Network . . *v.5 p.577*

Careless, James M. (Editor) *v.3 p.544*

Carens, James F. & Brady, Philip (Editors) *v.2 p.357*

Careri, Giovanni *v.1 p.674*

Carey, Anthony G. *v.3 p.503*

Carey, Charles W. *v.3 p.467*

Carey, Dennis & von Weichs, Marie-Caroline *v.4 p.85*

Carey, Francis A. & Sundberg, Richard J. *v.5 p.292*

Carey, Gary *v.2 p.94*

Carey, Gregory *v.5 p.131*

Carey, Henry F. (Editor) *v.4 p.600*

Carey, Henry *v.2 p.243*

Carey, James R. & Judge, Debra S. (Debra Suzan) . . *v.5 p.212*

Carey, James R. *v.5 p.167, p.212*

Carey, John *v.1 p.702, v.2 p.213*

Carey, Peter *v.2 p.744*

Carin, Arthur A. *v.4 p.362*

Carkoglu, Ali & Rubin, Barry (Editors) . . . *v.4 p.602, p.636*

Carle, David & Kaufmann, Je *v.5 p.31, v.6 p.290*

Carles, Emilie & Destanque, Robert *v.3 p.154*

Carleton, William *v.2 p.274*

Carley, Lionel *v.1 p.210, p.321*

Carlile, Lonny E. & Tilton, Mark (Editors) *v.6 p.219*

Carlin, Claire L. *v.2 p.473*

Carlin, Daniel *v.2 p.272*

Carlin, John *v.1 p.701*

Carliner, David, et al. *v.4 p.460*

Carlisle, Rodney P. *v.3 p.304, v.5 p.739*

Carlito, M. Delores *v.6 p.505, p.511*

Carlowicz, Michael J. & Lopez, Ramon E. . . . *v.5 p.73, p.444*

Carlson, A. Bruce, et al. *v.4 p.422, v.5 p.725*

Carlson, Allan *v.3 p.366*

Carlson, Alvar W. *v.6 p.530*

Carlson, Bruce M. *v.5 p.162*

Carlson, Daniel P. *v.6 p.265*

Carlson, David (Editor), et al. *v.5 p.472*

Carlson, Elof Axel *v.5 p.131*

Carlson, Gerald A. (Editor), et al. *v.5 p.14*

Carlson, Jon & Sperry, Len (Editors) *v.5 p.661, p.667*

Carlson, Karen J., et al. *v.5 p.523*

Carlson, Laurie Winn *v.5 p.14*

Carlson, Lori Marie & Hijuelos, Óscar (Editors) . . . *v.2 p.671*

Carlson, Marvin *v.1 p.56, p.86, p.89, p.138, p.154*

Carlson, Maura O'Brien, et al. *v.4 p.362*

Carlson, Paul H. *v.3 p.521*

Carlson, Rick J. & Stimeling, Gary *v.5 p.148*

Carlson, Sylvia E. & Carlson, Verne *v.6 p.349*

Carlson, Tony *v.4 p.172*

Carlton, David *v.4 p.658*

Carlton, Patrick W. *v.4 p.281*

Carlyle, Jane W. *v.2 p.275*

Carlyle, Thomas, et al. *v.2 p.276*

Carlyle, Thomas *v.2 p.275, p.276*

Carman, Taylor & Hansen, Mark (Editors) *v.1 p.456*

Carment, David (Editor), et al. *v.3 p.543*

Carmi, T. (Editor, Translator) *v.6 p.648*

Carmichael, Douglas R. & Rosenfield, Paul H. . *v.4 p.104, p.105*

Carmichael, Gordon (Editor) *v.5 p.131*

Carmichael, James V. Jr. (Editor) *v.6 p.383*

Carmody, Denise L. & Carmody, John T. *v.1 p.530*

Carmony, Donald F. *v.3 p.514*

Carnap, Rudolf *v.1 p.468, p.489, p.491, p.494, p.495*

Carnegie Commission on Higher Education, et al. . . *v.4 p.292*

Carnegie Forum on Education and the Economy Staff . *v.4 p.278*

Carnegie Foundation for the
Advancement of Teaching Staff *v.4 p.294*

Carnegie, M. Elizabeth *v.5 p.528*

Carneiro, Robert L. *v.4 p.23*

Carner, Gary (Compiled by) *v.1 p.165, p.257*

Carner, Mosco *v.1 p.195, p.228, p.349*

Carne-Ross, D. S. *v.2 p.416*

Carnes, Mark C. & Garraty, John A. *v.3 p.379*

Carnes, Mark C. *v.6 p.314*

Carnes, Tony & Yang, Fenggang (Editors) *v.6 p.105*

Carnevale, Anthony P. & Stone, Susan C. *v.4 p.131*

Carnibucci, Patricia *v.5 p.228*

Carnochan, W. B. *v.4 p.294*

Carnoy, Martin *v.4 p.325*

Caro, Robert A. *v.3 p.467, v.6 p.711*

Caro, Tim (Editor) *v.5 p.165, p.178*

Caroe, G. *v.5 p.385*

Caron, Timothy P. *v.2 p.73, p.138*

Caron, Vicki *v.3 p.154*

Carossa, Hans *v.2 p.606*

Carothers, Thomas *v.4 p.503, p.584, p.600*

Carp, E. Wayne *v.4 p.737*

Carp, Robert A. & Stidham, Ronald *v.4 p.465, p.534*

Carp, Robert A., et al. *v.4 p.534*

Carpenter, Allan *v.3 p.506*

Carpenter, D. A. *v.3 p.97*

Carpenter, Elizabeth *v.1 p.755*

Carpenter, Frederick Ives *v.2 p.91*

Carpenter, Humphrey . . . *v.1 p.211, p.314, v.2 p.366, v.6 p.409*

Carpenter, Joel A. *v.1 p.606*

Carpenter, Linda J. & Acosta, Vivian R. . *v.4 p.449, p.835, p.882,
p.893, p.900*

Carpenter, Linda J. *v.4 p.785, p.882, p.900*

Carpenter, Nan Cooke *v.1 p.179*

Carpenter, Rhys *v.2 p.413*

Carpenter, Ted Galen (Editor) *v.4 p.639*

Carpenter, Ted Galen *v.6 p.246, p.262*

Carpenter, Ted G. *v.4 p.633*

Carpenter, Thomas P., et al. *v.5 p.462*

Carpentier, Alejo *v.1 p.291, v.2 p.671*

Carr, Barry & Ellner, Steve (Editors) *v.3 p.352*

Carr, Brian & Mahalingam, Indira *v.1 p.474*

Carr, C *v.1 p.28, p.29, p.38*

Carr, David *v.3 p.370*

Carr, Emily *v.2 p.733*

Carr, Gerald L. *v.1 p.695, p.736*

Carr, Gerry *v.4 p.794, p.869, p.873, p.907*

Carr, Ian *v.1 p.257, p.320, p.334*

Carr, Janine C. *v.4 p.360*

Carr, Karen L. *v.1 p.509*

Carr, Kathleen T. *v.1 p.759*

Carr, Raymond (Editor) *v.3 p.243*

Carr, Virginia Spencer *v.2 p.100*

Carr, Virginia *v.2 p.62, v.6 p.409*

Carr, Wilfred (editor) *v.4 p.323*

Carraher, Jr., Charles *v.5 p.321*

Carrasco, David (Editor) *v.4 p.9*

Carrasco, David *v.3 p.261*

Carreiro, Assis *v.1 p.5*

Carrera, Margarita *v.2 p.675*

Carrere D'Encausse, Helene *v.3 p.220*

Carrese, Paul O. *v.4 p.541*

Carrier, David *v.2 p.581*

Carrier, Jeffrey C. (Editor) *v.5 p.214*

Carrier, Joseph *v.6 p.421*

Carrier, Roch *v.2 p.540*

Carrillo, Francisco Javier (Editor) *v.6 p.711*

Carrillo, Justo *v.3 p.307*

Carrington, Christopher *v.6 p.376*

Carroll, Anne Elizabeth *v.2 p.10*

Carroll, Bob (Editor), et al. *v.4 p.858*

Carroll, Bradley W. & Ostlie, Dale A. *v.5 p.66*

Carroll, David *v.2 p.286*

Carroll, John M. . *v.4 p.804, p.814, p.831, p.858, p.893, v.6 p.205*

Carroll, Lee Ann *v.2 p.564*

Carroll, Leo *v.6 p.274*

Carroll, Lewis & Clark *v.2 p.277*

Carroll, Lewis *v.2 p.277, v.5 p.468*

Carroll, Marilyn E. & Overmier, J. Bruce (Editors) . *v.5 p.614*

Carroll, Mark *v.1 p.211, p.376*

Carroll, Noel *v.6 p.317*

Carroll, Richard J. *v.4 p.566*

Carroll, Robert L. *v.5 p.447*

Carroll, Robert Lynn *v.5 p.447*

Carroll, Sean B., et al. *v.5 p.131, p.200*

Carroll, Sean B. *v.5 p.131, p.159*
Carroll, Susan J. (Editor) *v.6 p.440*
Carron, Albert V., et al. *v.5 p.581*
Carruth, Gorton (Editor) *v.3 p.372*
Carruth, Hayden & Podell, Susan Kagen *v.2 p.22*
Carruthers, Susan L. *v.3 p.87, v.4 p.406*
Carruthers, W. *v.5 p.293*
Carse, Adam Von Ahn *v.1 p.393*
Carse, Adam *v.1 p.393*
Carslaw, Horatio S. & Jaeger, J. C. *v.5 p.560*
Carson, Ben & Murphey, Cecil B. *v.6 p.17, p.48*
Carson, Clayborne (Editor) *v.6 p.12*
Carson, Clayborne *v.6 p.12*
Carson, David & Bull, Ray (Editors) *v.5 p.591*
Carson, Diane (Editor), et al. *v.6 p.474*
Carson, Rachel Louise *v.5 p.78*
Carson, Rachel . *v.5 p.17, p.27, p.354, p.369, p.514, v.6 p.290*
Carstairs, Andrew M. *v.4 p.601*
Carsten, F. L. *v.3 p.184*
Carsten, Janet (Editor) *v.4 p.31*
Carsten, Janet *v.4 p.31*
Carstensen, Frederick V. (Editor), et al. *v.5 p.3*
Carstensen, Vernon (Editor) *v.6 p.294*
Cartarescu, Mircea *v.2 p.816*
Carter, Angela & Uglow, Jennifer S. *v.2 p.336*
Carter, Angela *v.2 p.336*
Carter, Barbara L. *v.6 p.600, p.637*
Carter, Bernadette (Editor) *v.5 p.530*
Carter, Cynthia, et al. *v.4 p.414*
Carter, D. N. *v.2 p.348*
Carter, Dan T. *v.3 p.435, p.504, v.4 p.438*
Carter, David A. & Walker, Annette K. *v.5 p.221*
Carter, David E. *v.1 p.717*
Carter, David *v.4 p.710*
Carter, Elliott *v.1 p.211, p.316, p.369*
Carter, F. W. & Turnock, David (Editors) *v.5 p.705*
Carter, Giles F. *v.5 p.731*
Carter, Gregg Lee (Editor) *v.6 p.266*
Carter, Gregg Lee *v.4 p.485*
Carter, Gwendolen M. & O'Meara, Patrick (Editors) . . *v.6 p.54*
Carter, Gwendolen Margaret *v.6 p.78*
Carter, Howard & Mace, A. C. *v.3 p.8*
Carter, Howard *v.3 p.8*
Carter, Huntly . . . *v.1 p.81, p.84, p.108, p.146, p.148, p.152*
Carter, Jimmy *v.3 p.456, p.467*
Carter, John M. *v.4 p.783, p.804*
Carter, M. R. (Editor) *v.5 p.312*
Carter, Marcia Jean & LeConey,
  Stephen P. *v.4 p.783, p.785, p.829*
Carter, Mia *v.6 p.592*
Carter, Miranda *v.1 p.700*
Carter, Neil *v.5 p.29, v.6 p.299*
Carter, Paul A. *v.1 p.606, v.3 p.366*
Carter, R. W. & Woodroffe, C. D. (Editors) *v.5 p.366*
Carter, Robert A. *v.3 p.519*

Carter, Robert L. *v.6 p.17, p.22*
Carter, Ronald & McRae, John *v.2 p.166*
Carter, Sarah *v.5 p.14*
Carter, Steven R. *v.2 p.80*
Carter, Stewart *v.1 p.183, p.400*
Carter, Thomas & Cromley, Elizabeth C. *v.1 p.822*
Carter, Tim . . . *v.1 p.183, p.188, p.229, p.342, p.343*
Carter, William C. *v.2 p.523*
Carterette, Edward C. (Editor), et al. *v.5 p.606, p.609*
Cartianu, Ana & Johnston, R. C. (Editors) *v.2 p.815*
Cartledge, Paul & Spawforth, Antony *v.3 p.21*
Cartledge, Paul (Editor), et al. *v.3 p.13*
Cartledge, Paul (Editor) *v.3 p.12*
Cartledge, Paul, et al. *v.3 p.20*
Cartledge, Paul *v.3 p.17, p.19*
Cartlidge, Neil (Editor) *v.2 p.203*
Cartmell, Deborah *v.6 p.325*
Cartron, Jean-Luc E., et al. *v.5 p.178, p.183, p.233*
Cartwright, Justin *v.2 p.336*
Cartwright, Lorin A. & Pitney, William A. *v.4 p.828*
Cartwright, Roger *v.4 p.65*
Cartwright, Susan (Editor) *v.4 p.119, p.180*
Carty, Ken (Editor) *v.3 p.546, v.4 p.589*
Carty, R. Kenneth (Editor) *v.4 p.588*
Carty, Winthrop P. *v.5 p.230*
Cartz, Louis *v.5 p.688*
Caruana, Louis *v.5 p.401*
Caruana, Wally *v.1 p.668*
Carus-Wilson, Eleanora Mary *v.3 p.38*
Carver, Craig M. *v.2 p.551*
Carver, Martin *v.6 p.555*
Carver, Raymond *v.2 p.142*
Carver, Terrell (Editor) *v.1 p.464*
Cary, Joseph *v.2 p.697*
Cary, Joyce *v.2 p.337, p.338*
Cary, Noel D. *v.4 p.609*
Cary, Tristram *v.1 p.159, p.386*
Casadei, Alberto *v.2 p.697*
Casarett, Louis J., et al. *v.5 p.514*
Casazza, Jack & Delea, Frank *v.5 p.723*
Cascardi, Anthony J. (Editor) *v.2 p.647*
Cascardi, Anthony J. *v.2 p.647*
Cascudo, Luis da Camara *v.3 p.271*
Case, Arthur E. *v.2 p.262*
Case, Christopher *v.6 p.311*
Case, LeAnne *v.4 p.792*
Case, Linda P. *v.5 p.54, p.56*
Case, Sue-Ellen (Editor) *v.1 p.120, p.125, p.135*
Case, Ted J., et al. *v.5 p.167, p.172*
Casella, E. C. & Symonds, J. (Editors) *v.4 p.13*
Cases, Miguel Valcarcel *v.5 p.273*
Casey, Betty *v.1 p.33*
Casey, Calvert & Stavans, Ilan *v.2 p.671*
Casey, Eoghan *v.5 p.341, p.343, v.6 p.270*
Cash, Johnny & Carr, Patrick *v.1 p.267, p.316*

Cash, W. J. *v.3 p.493*

Cashen, Trish, et al. *v.1 p.770*

Cashman, Richard & Hughes, Anthony (Editors) . . *v.4 p.845, p.887, p.890, p.898*

Cashman, Sean D. *v.3 p.394, p.435, p.446*

Cashmore, Ellis *v.4 p.823, p.855, p.877*

Cashorali, Peter *v.6 p.406*

Casillo, Charles *v.6 p.407*

Casper, Scott E. & Long, Lucinda (Editors) *v.3 p.521*

Cassady, Carolyn *v.2 p.79, p.92*

Cassady, Neal *v.2 p.64*

Cassanelli, Lee V. *v.6 p.65*

Cassar, George H. *v.3 p.78*

Cassedy, Patrice *v.5 p.741*

Cassel, Christine K. (Editor), et al. *v.5 p.518*

Cassell, Justine & Jenkins, Henry (Editors) *v.6 p.438*

Cassell Staff *v.2 p.620*

Cassella, J. P., et al. *v.5 p.87*

Cassella-Blackburn, Michael *v.3 p.456*

Cassells Editors *v.2 p.620*

Casserly, Catherine M. *v.6 p.20, p.42*

Cassese, Antonio *v.6 p.268*

Cassidy, F. J. & Ringler, R. *v.2 p.205, p.550*

Cassidy, Frederic G. (Editor) *v.2 p.554*

Cassidy, Jude & Shaver,
  Phillip R. (Editors) *v.5 p.625, p.631, p.651*

Cassidy, Richard J. *v.1 p.630*

Cassidy, Tony *v.5 p.587*

Cassill, R. V. & Oates, Joyce Carol *v.2 p.26*

Cassimatis, Louis P. *v.3 p.195*

Cassin-Scott, Jack *v.1 p.146, p.150*

Cassirer, Ernst *v.1 p.435, p.437, p.461, p.468, p.481, p.495, v.3 p.71*

Cassirer, H W *v.1 p.461*

Cassis, Youssef & Bussiere, Eric *v.6 p.711*

Cassis, Yves & Cassis, Youssef (Editors) *v.4 p.91*

Casson, Lionel *v.3 p.3, p.8*

Cassuto, David N. *v.6 p.287*

Cassuto, Leonard & Eby, Clare Virginia (Editors) . . *v.2 p.70*

Castagno, John *v.1 p.663*

Castagno, Paul C. *v.1 p.91*

Castans, Raymond; Pagnol, Marcel *v.2 p.523*

Castel, Albert *v.3 p.394, p.435*

Castel-Bloom, Orly, et al. *v.6 p.648*

Castellan, Georges *v.3 p.250*

Castells, Manuel *v.4 p.761, v.6 p.717, p.729*

Casten, Thomas R. *v.5 p.713*

Casteras, Susan P. & Gordon, Susan *v.2 p.305*

Casteras, Susan P. *v.6 p.737, p.746*

Castex, Pierre Georges *v.2 p.458, p.465*

Casti, John L. *v.5 p.457*

Castiglione, Baldassarre, conte *v.2 p.708*

Castile, George P. & Bee, Robert L. (Editors) . . . *v.6 p.695*

Castile, George P. *v.6 p.695*

Castile *v.6 p.695*

Castilgione, Baldesar *v.2 p.708*

Castillo, Ana *v.6 p.498, p.510*

Castillo, Otto Rene *v.2 p.675*

Castle, Barbara *v.3 p.93, p.119*

Castle, Irene *v.1 p.6*

Castle, Terry *v.2 p.258, v.6 p.392*

Castle, Vernon & Castle, Irene *v.1 p.34*

Castleden, Rodney *v.3 p.15*

Castleman, Riva *v.1 p.752, p.754, p.755*

Castor, Belmiro V. J. *v.3 p.339*

Castorina, Jan & Stais, Dimitra *v.6 p.166*

Castree, Noel, et al. *v.4 p.375*

Castro, Americo *v.2 p.647*

Castro, Barry *v.4 p.52*

Castro, Donald S. *v.3 p.266*

Castro, Peter & Huber, Michael E. *v.5 p.171*

Castro, Rafaela G. *v.6 p.523*

Castro, Rosalía de *v.2 p.654*

Castro, Rosalia de, et al. *v.2 p.654*

Castro, Rosalia de *v.2 p.654*

Castro-Klaren, Sara *v.2 p.685*

Castronovo, David *v.2 p.137*

Casualty Actuarial Society Staff (Contribution by) . . *v.5 p.504*

Casway, Jerrold I. *v.4 p.804, p.850*

Catalyst Staff *v.4 p.57*

Catalyst *v.4 p.57*

Cate, Curtis *v.2 p.499*

Cate, Fred H. *v.4 p.449*

Cate, George A. *v.2 p.305*

Cate, Phillip D. *v.1 p.84, p.95*

Cate, Thomas (Editor), et al. *v.4 p.192*

Caterette, Edward C. (Editor), et al. *v.5 p.605*

Cath, Stanley H. (Editor), et al. *v.5 p.639*

Cather, Willa *v.2 p.67*

Catherine II *v.3 p.217*

Catholic Church Staff *v.1 p.571*

Catholic University of America Staff (Contribution by) . *v.1 p.571*

Cato Research *v.5 p.217*

Catteau, Jacques *v.2 p.797, p.802*

Cattermole, Peter *v.5 p.434*

Catto, Susan & Penrith, Deborah *v.4 p.169*

Catton, Bruce *v.3 p.430, p.435, p.516*

Catton, William & Catton, Bruce *v.3 p.427*

Catullus, Gaius Valerius *v.2 p.430*

Cauchon, Janet Wirth *v.5 p.661*

Caudill, Edward *v.5 p.78, p.202*

Caufield, Catherine *v.4 p.630*

Caufield, Sue Ann *v.3 p.282, p.339*

Caulfield, Sueann, et al. *v.3 p.283*

Causey, Andrew *v.1 p.775*

Causton, Helen, et al. *v.5 p.110*

Caute, David *v.3 p.87, p.446*

Cautela, Joseph R. & Ishaq, Waris (Editors) *v.5 p.666*

Cava, Roberta *v.4 p.130*

Cavalcanti, Guido *v.2 p.702*

Cavalcanti, Lauro *v.1 p.788*
Cavalier, Robert J. (Editor) *v.4 p.761*
Cavallaro, Claire C. & Haney, Michele *v.4 p.315*
Cavalli, Harriet *v.1 p.44, p.47, p.397*
Cavallo, Adolfo *v.1 p.709*
Cavallo, Guglielmo & Chartier, Roger (Editors) . . . *v.2 p.573*
Cavallo, Jo Ann *v.2 p.707, p.709*
Cavanagh, Clare *v.2 p.802*
Cavanagh, Peter R. (Editor) . . . *v.4 p.874, p.879, p.907, p.909*
Cavazos, Edward A. & Morin, Gavino *v.4 p.444*
Cave, Alfred A. *v.3 p.405, v.6 p.685*
Cave, Terence *v.2 p.471*
Cavell, Stanley *v.2 p.228, v.6 p.312*
Caveney, Graham *v.6 p.401*
Caves, Richard E. *v.1 p.826*
Caves, Roger W. (Editor) *v.6 p.709*
Cavicchi, Daniel & Keil, Charles (Editors) *v.1 p.376*
Cawelti, John G. & Rosenberg, Bruce A. *v.2 p.190*
Cawelti, John G. *v.2 p.577, v.6 p.323*
Caws, Mary A. (Editor) *v.2 p.460*
Caws, Mary A. *v.2 p.511, p.512*
Caws, Mary Ann (Editor) *v.1 p.677, v.2 p.464*
Caws, Mary Ann *v.2 p.460*
Caws, Peter *v.1 p.458, p.515*
Cayleff, Susan E. *v.4 p.835, p.860*
Cayou, Dolores K. *v.1 p.31*
Cayrol, Jean *v.2 p.512*
Cayton, Andrew R. & Onuf, Peter S. *v.3 p.512*
Cayton, Andrew R. L. *v.3 p.513*
Cayton, Andrew R. *v.3 p.513, p.514*
Cayton, Mary K. (Editor), et al. *v.4 p.677*
Cazdyn, Eric *v.6 p.328, p.335*
Cazeaux, Clive *v.1 p.479*
Cazes, Jack (Editor) *v.5 p.269*
Cazort, Mimi *v.1 p.721*
CBS News Staff *v.4 p.288*
CCH Editorial Staff *v.4 p.115*
CCPS *v.5 p.742*
Ceaser, James W. *v.3 p.370*
Cecchetti, Giovanni *v.2 p.713*
Cecelski, David S. & Tyson, Timothy B. (Editors) . . *v.3 p.501*
Cech, Donna J. & Martin, Suzanne *v.4 p.907, p.909*
Cech, Thomas R. & Pines, Maya *v.5 p.126*
Cecil, David *v.3 p.93, p.111*
Cedaro, Rod (Compiled by) *v.4 p.863, p.866*
Cedrins, Inara (Editor) *v.2 p.780*
Cejka, Jaroslav & Cernik, Michal *v.2 p.781*
Cela, Camilo Jose *v.2 p.657*
Cela, Camilo José *v.2 p.657*
Celan, Paul *v.2 p.606*
Celant, Germano *v.1 p.712*
Celentano, Suzanne C. & Marshall, Kevin *v.1 p.149*
Celenza, Christopher S. *v.3 p.199*
Celestin, Roger, et al. *v.6 p.433, p.453, p.456*
Celik, Zeynep (Editor), et al. *v.6 p.711*

Celine, Louis-Ferdinand *v.2 p.515*
Celis, Julio E. (Editor), et al. *v.5 p.154*
Cell, John Whitson *v.3 p.124*
Cellarius, Barbara A. *v.3 p.251*
Celletti, Rodolfo *v.1 p.229*
Cellini, Benvenuto *v.3 p.200*
Cellura, A. Raymond *v.5 p.138*
Cendrars, Blaise *v.2 p.512, p.513*
Cendrars, Miriam *v.2 p.513*
Censer, Jane T. *v.4 p.732*
Centeno, Miguel A. & Font, Mauricio (Editors) . . . *v.3 p.307*
Centeno, Miguel Angel *v.3 p.274, v.4 p.591*
Center for Biological Informatics of the
U.S. Geological Survey *v.5 p.204*
Center for Chemical Process Safety
Staff & Crowl, Daniel A. *v.5 p.743*
Center for Customer Driven Quality,
Purdue University *v.5 p.585, p.604*
Center for Education Staff & National
Research Council Staff *v.4 p.285*
Center for Gifted Education, College of
William and Mary *v.5 p.575*
Center for Gifted Education Staff *v.4 p.526*
Center for HIV Information *v.4 p.668*
Center for International Business Education and Research at
Michigan State University *v.4 p.59*
Center for Psychology in Schools *v.5 p.571*
Center for Responsive Politics *v.4 p.557, p.559*
Center for Russian, East European and Asian Studies, University
of Texas at Austin *v.4 p.595, p.596, p.597, p.600*
Center for Talented Youth, Johns Hopkins University . *v.5 p.575*
Center for World Indigenous Studies *v.4 p.482*
Center on Reinventing Public Education. Daniel J. Evans School
of Public Affairs. University of Washington *v.4 p.280*
Center on Urban Poverty and Social Change, Case Western
Reserve University *v.5 p.671, v.6 p.717*
Centlivre, Susanna & O'Brien, John *v.2 p.243*
Centlivre, Susanna *v.2 p.243*
Centner, Terence J. *v.6 p.290*
Central Intelligence Agency *v.4 p.481*
Centro De Estudios Sobre America Staff (Editor) . . . *v.3 p.307*
Cepeda, Raquel (Editor) *v.1 p.267*
Cepede, M. & Abensour, E. S. *v.4 p.701*
Ceram, C. W. *v.3 p.6*
Cerasano, Susan P. & Wynne-Davies, Marion . . *v.1 p.74, p.99*
Cerchiai, Luca, et al. *v.3 p.16, v.6 p.711*
Cercignani, Carlo *v.5 p.542*
Cernuda, Luis *v.2 p.657*
Cerquiglini-Toulet, Jacqueline *v.6 p.564, p.568*
Cerutti, Steven M. *v.2 p.431*
Ceruzzi, Paul E. *v.5 p.342*
Cervantes, Fernando *v.3 p.262, p.284*
Cervantes, Lorna Dee *v.2 p.142, v.6 p.498, p.510*
Cervantes Saavedra, Miguel de *v.2 p.647, p.648*
Cervero, Ron M. & Wilson, Arthur L. *v.4 p.319*
Cesaire, Aime *v.2 p.535, p.536*

Cesareni, Giovanni (Editor), et al. *v.5 p.115*
Cessac, Catherine *v.1 p.183, p.317*
Cestaro, Gary P. (Editor) *v.6 p.415*
Cániková, Andrea *v.2 p.777*
Céline, Louis-Ferdinand *v.2 p.515*
Césaire, Aimé *v.2 p.536*
Cha, Theresa Hak Kyung *v.6 p.95, p.102, p.104, p.122*
Chabal, Patrick & Daloz, Jean-Pascal *v.4 p.611*
Chabal, Patrick (Editor) *v.2 p.693*
Chabal, Patrick *v.4 p.498, p.611*
Chabay, Ruth W. & Sherwood, Bruce A. *v.5 p.539*
Chabon, Michael (Editor) *v.2 p.583*
Chabon, Michael *v.2 p.142, v.6 p.395*
Chabram-Dernersesian, Angie (Editor) . . . *v.6 p.486, p.491*
Chabrán, Richard & Chabrán, Rafael (Editors) . . . *v.6 p.485*
Chace, James *v.3 p.456, p.457, p.468*
Chace, William M. (Editor) *v.2 p.357*
Chadabe, Joel *v.1 p.211, p.244*
Chadarevian, Soraya de *v.5 p.126*
Chadda, Maya *v.4 p.617, v.6 p.158*
Chadwick, Bruce *v.4 p.804, p.831, p.850, p.890, p.896*
Chadwick, Henry *v.1 p.430, p.599,v.6 p.567, p.570*
Chadwick, John *v.3 p.15*
Chadwick, Owen . *v.1 p.545, p.572, p.582, p.598, p.601,v.3 p.111, p.120, v.6 p.758*
Chadwick, Whitney *v.1 p.706, v.6 p.472*
Chafe, Eric *v.1 p.183, p.235, p.303*
Chafe, Wallace L. *v.2 p.559*
Chafe, William Henry *v.3 p.439, p.468, v.4 p.522*
Chafer, Tony *v.4 p.584, v.6 p.68*
Chafetz, Janet S. & Dworkin, Anthony G. *v.6 p.430*
Chafetz, Janet S. *v.4 p.723, p.747*
Chaffee, Wilbur R. Jr. & Prevost, Gary (Editors) . . . *v.3 p.307*
Chaffin, Tom *v.3 p.307*
Chagall, Marc *v.1 p.695*
Chagall, Mark *v.1 p.755*
Chaikin, P. M. & Lubensky, T. C. *v.5 p.554*
Chainey, Spencer & Ratcliffe, Jerry *v.4 p.386, v.6 p.251*
Chairman of the Council of Economic Advisors . . . *v.4 p.481*
Chaison, Gary N. *v.4 p.124*
Chait, Richard P., et al. *v.4 p.293*
Chakalov, G. *v.5 p.386*
Chakrabarti, Dilip K. *v.4 p.8*
Chakrabarty, Dipesh *v.3 p.35, v.6 p.146*
Chakrabarty, Jagabanduhu *v.5 p.688*
Chakraborty, Tapash & Pietil-Ainen, Pekka *v.5 p.565*
Chalabi, Tamara *v.6 p.604*
Chalcraft, Edwin L. & Collins, Cary C. . . *v.4 p.755, v.6 p.680*
Chalet, Francois *v.1 p.772*
Chalfant, Henry & Prigoff, James *v.1 p.750*
Chaliand, Gerard *v.6 p.598*
Chalip, Laurence (Editor), et al. . *v.4 p.843, p.887, p.891, p.898*
Chalk, Frank & Jonassohn, Kurt *v.4 p.651, p.767*
Chalk, Peter & Rosenau, William *v.4 p.658*
Chalkley, John F. *v.3 p.291*

Chall, Jeanne S. *v.4 p.362, v.5 p.574*
Challener, Richard D. *v.3 p.451*
Chalmers, Alan F. *v.5 p.401*
Chalmers, David J. *v.1 p.496*
Chalmers, David John *v.1 p.496*
Chalmers, David M. *v.3 p.439, p.446*
Chalmers, David *v.1 p.496, v.3 p.468*
Chamberlain, Basil Hall *v.6 p.219*
Chamberlain, Bobby J. *v.2 p.690*
Chamberlain, Lesley & Marinetti, Filippo Tommaso . *v.2 p.718*
Chamberlain, Mariam K. *v.4 p.289*
Chamberlain, Michael *v.6 p.607*
Chamberlain, Neil W. & Schilling, Jane M. *v.4 p.124*
Chamberlin, William H. *v.3 p.221*
Chambers, Ann *v.5 p.708*
Chambers, Colin . . *v.1 p.58, p.76, p.99, p.136, p.140, p.149*
Chambers, Deborah, et al. *v.4 p.699*
Chambers, Donald A. (Editor) *v.5 p.131*
Chambers, E. K. *v.1 p.73, p.154*
Chambers, Edmund K. *v.2 p.226, p.227*
Chambers, Frank & Ogle, Michael (Editors) *v.4 p.393*
Chambers, John W. 2nd & Culbert, David *v.6 p.322*
Chambers, John Whiteclay (Editor) *v.3 p.382*
Chambers, R. W. *v.2 p.204*
Chambers, Robert W. *v.2 p.32*
Chambers, S. Allen, et al. *v.1 p.788*
Chambers, S. Allen *v.1 p.788*
Chambers, Sarah *v.3 p.283, p.325, p.327*
Chambers, Whittaker & Fox, John *v.3 p.446*
Chambers, William Nisbet *v.3 p.415*
Chambers-Schiller, Lee V. *v.4 p.735*
Chambliss, J. J. (Editor) *v.4 p.323, p.339*
Chameides, William L. & Perdue, E. M. *v.5 p.112*
Chametzky, Jules (Editor), et al. *v.2 p.18*
Chamisso, Adelbert von *v.2 p.596*
Chamley, Herve (Editor) *v.5 p.423*
Chamoiseau, Patrick *v.2 p.536*
Chamorro-Premuzic, Tomas & Furnham, Adrian . . . *v.5 p.651*
Champe, Pamela C. & Harvey, Richard A. *v.5 p.112*
Champion, Dean J. *v.6 p.260, p.278*
Champion, Dean John *v.4 p.677, v.6 p.246, p.278*
Champion, Larry S. *v.2 p.228*
Champion, Walter T. *v.4 p.883, p.900*
Champlin, Edward *v.3 p.27*
Chan, Anita, et al. *v.4 p.701, v.6 p.193*
Chan, Jeffery P *v.6 p.91*
Chan, Jeffrey P., et al. *v.6 p.91*
Chan, Mimi & Harris, Roy (Editors) *v.2 p.759*
Chan, Ming K. & Lo, Shiu Hing *v.6 p.205*
Chan, Ming K. & So, Alvin Y. (Editors) *v.6 p.205*
Chan, Ming K. (Editor) *v.6 p.205*
Chan, Patrick & Bentley, Jon *v.5 p.346, p.349*
Chan, Stephen *v.6 p.77*
Chan, Sucheng (Editor, Introduction by) *v.6 p.138*
Chan, Sucheng (Editor) . *v.6 p.85, p.93, p.113, p.115, p.139, p.140*

Chan, Sucheng . . . *v.6 p.85, p.113, p.116, p.118, p.126, p.138*

Chan, Wing-Tsit (Translator) *v.1 p.474*

Chancellor, Edward *v.4 p.88, p.99, p.101*

Chances, Ellen *v.2 p.797, p.802*

Chancy, Myriam J. *v.6 p.478*

Chanda, Nayan *v.6 p.167*

Chandler, Alfred D. Jr. *v.4 p.146, p.157*

Chandler, Alfred D. *v.3 p.38*

Chandler, Alice *v.6 p.750, p.752, p.763*

Chandler, Billy J. *v.3 p.339*

Chandler, D. S. *v.3 p.285*

Chandler, David G. *v.3 p.152, v.5 p.558*

Chandler, David L. *v.3 p.356*

Chandler, David P. *v.6 p.169, p.170*

Chandler, David *v.6 p.169*

Chandler, Harry *v.5 p.731*

Chandler, James K. *v.2 p.323*

Chandler, Raymond *v.2 p.64, p.65*

Chandler, Richard E. & Schwartz, Kessel *v.2 p.638*

Chandler, S. B. *v.2 p.712*

Chandler, Timothy J. L. &
  Nauright, John (Editors) *v.4 p.814, p.865*

Chandos, John *v.6 p.745*

Chandra, A. M. *v.4 p.386, p.388*

Chandra, Vikram *v.2 p.764*

Chandran, Satish (Editor) *v.5 p.728*

Chandrasekhar, B. S. *v.5 p.540*

Chandrasekhar, Indira (ed.) *v.6 p.147*

Chandrasekhar, S. *v.5 p.61, p.546, p.555, p.556*

Chandrasekhar, Sripati *v.4 p.736*

Chang, C. C. & Keisler, H. Jerome *v.5 p.470*

Chang, Chung-Li *v.4 p.701*

Chang, Diana *v.6 p.99*

Chang, Edward C. & Sanna, Lawrence J. (Editors) . . *v.5 p.651*

Chang, Edward C. *v.5 p.651*

Chang, Gengzhe & Sederberg, Thomas *v.5 p.457*

Chang, Gordon H. (Editor) *v.6 p.120*

Chang, Gordon H. *v.3 p.387*

Chang, Grace *v.6 p.456*

Chang, Hao *v.6 p.189, p.199*

Chang, Juliana (Editor) *v.6 p.102*

Chang, Jung & Halliday, Jon *v.6 p.201*

Chang, Jung *v.6 p.193, p.199, p.217*

Chang, K. C. (Editor) *v.6 p.181*

Chang, Kang-i Sun (Editor), et al. . . . *v.6 p.207, p.478*

Chang, Kevin O. & Chen, Wayne *v.1 p.291*

Chang, L. L. (Editor), et al. *v.5 p.436*

Chang, Lan Samantha *v.6 p.99*

Chang, Laurence & Kornbluh, Peter (Editors) . . . *v.3 p.468*

Chang, Mitchell (Editor), et al. *v.4 p.295, p.308, p.355*

Chang, Raymond *v.5 p.82, p.112, p.327*

Chang, Robert S. *v.4 p.456, v.6 p.107, p.117*

Chang, S. J. *v.5 p.550*

Chang, Tony H. (Compiled by) *v.6 p.195*

Chang, Victoria M. (Editor) *v.6 p.103*

Chang-Rodriguez, Raquel *v.3 p.262*

Channing, Edward *v.3 p.379*

Chanson, Hubert *v.5 p.378*

Chant, Christopher *v.5 p.700*

Chant, Sylvia & Craske, Nikki *v.6 p.429*

Chao, Buwei Y. *v.6 p.181*

Chapin, Bradley *v.6 p.245*

Chapin, F. Stuart III & Orner,
  Christian K. (Editors) *v.5 p.167, p.175, p.238*

Chapin Hall Center for Children, University of Chicago . *v.5 p.671*

Chapin, Suzanne H. & Johnson, Art *v.5 p.462*

Chaplin, David (Editor) *v.3 p.329*

Chaplin, Martin F. & Bucke, Christopher *v.5 p.119*

Chapman, Alan J. *v.5 p.560*

Chapman, Alison (Editor), et al. *v.2 p.174, p.184*

Chapman and Hall Staff *v.5 p.214*

Chapman, Carolyn & King, Rita S. *v.4 p.285*

Chapman, Chris S. *v.4 p.81*

Chapman, Forestine *v.4 p.151, p.164*

Chapman, George *v.2 p.217*

Chapman, Giles *v.1 p.717*

Chapman, Graham P. & Baker, Kathleen M. (Editors) . *v.4 p.384*

Chapman, Hugo *v.1 p.723*

Chapman, James *v.6 p.331*

Chapman, John (Editor) *v.1 p.63, p.112*

Chapman, John *v.1 p.578*

Chapman, K. E. & Higgins, S. J. (Editors) . . *v.5 p.101, p.112*

Chapman, Karen J. *v.4 p.178*

Chapman, R. W. *v.2 p.267*

Chapman, Raymond *v.6 p.751, p.755*

Chapman, Robert *v.4 p.12*

Chapman, Woodrow W. (Editor) *v.5 p.731*

Chapman, Woodrow W. *v.5 p.731*

Chapnick, Howard *v.4 p.409*

Chappell, Fred *v.2 p.142, p.143*

Chappell, James *v.1 p.807*

Chappell, Louise *v.6 p.440*

Chappell, Sally Anderson Kitt *v.1 p.792, v.4 p.10*

Chappell, Vere (Editor) *v.1 p.448*

Chappell, Warren & Bringhurst, Robert *v.3 p.37*

Chappell, Warren *v.2 p.576*

Chapple, J. A. V. *v.2 p.288*

Chapple, John A. & Sharps, J. G. *v.2 p.288*

Chapple, Richard *v.2 p.796*

Chapra, Steven C. *v.5 p.702, p.704*

Chapuis, Julien *v.1 p.779*

Chaput, Marcel *v.3 p.536*

Char, René *v.2 p.513*

Charan, Ram, et al. *v.4 p.70*

Charbeneau, Randall J. *v.5 p.379, v.6 p.289*

Chari, Srinivasa M. *v.1 p.535*

Charlebois, Lucile C. *v.2 p.657*

Charles, d'Orleans *v.2 p.468*

Charles, d'Orléans *v.2 p.468*

Charles, Maria & Grusky, David B. *v.4 p.723*

Charles, Ray & Ritz, David *v.1 p.267, p.316*
Charles Scribners Sons Staff (Contribution by) *v.5 p.394*
Charlesworth, James H. *v.1 p.623*
Charley, Helen G. & Weaver, Connie M. *v.5 p.33*
Charlier, Roger H. *v.5 p.361*
Charlton, David (Editor) *v.1 p.229*
Charlton, H. B. *v.2 p.233*
Charlton, Samuel G. & O'Brien, Thomas G. (Editors) . *v.5 p.587*
Charlton, Sue *v.4 p.616*
Charney, Israel W. (Editor) *v.4 p.652*
Charney, Leo & Schwartz, Vanessa R. (Editors) . . . *v.6 p.321*
Charney, Maurice (Editor) *v.1 p.58, p.89*
Charnon-Deutsch, Lou *v.2 p.641*
Charrad, Mounira M. *v.6 p.440, p.453, p.641*
Charriere, Isabelle De *v.2 p.478*
Charry, Eric S. *v.1 p.285*
Charters, Ann (Editor) *v.2 p.20*
Charters, Ann *v.2 p.20, p.92*
Charters, Samuel B. *v.1 p.258*
Chartier, Alain *v.2 p.468*
Chartier, Roger (Editor), et al. *v.3 p.70, v.4 p.732*
Chartier, Roger *v.3 p.149*
Chartrand, Gary & Zhang, Ping *v.5 p.480*
Chartrand, Gary and Lesniak, Linda *v.5 p.480*
Chartrand, Mark R. *v.4 p.421*
Chartrand, Rene *v.3 p.537*
Charvat, William & Kraus, Michael *v.2 p.49*
Charvet, Patrick Edward *v.2 p.455*
Chasdi, Richard J. *v.4 p.658*
Chase, Allan *v.4 p.728*
Chase, Cynthia *v.2 p.171*
Chase, Gilbert *v.1 p.245, p.277*
Chase, Karen & Levenson, Michael H. *v.6 p.764*
Chase, Kerry A. *v.4 p.60*
Chase, M. W. & National Institute of Standards and
   Technology Staff *v.5 p.286*
Chase, Malcolm W. *v.5 p.286*
Chase, Robert *v.1 p.235*
Chase, Salmon P. *v.3 p.394*
Chase, Salmon Portland *v.3 p.422, p.423, p.427*
Chase-Dunn, Christopher *v.4 p.723*
Chasek, Pamela S. *v.4 p.666, v.5 p.29, v.6 p.299*
Chase-Riboud, Barbara *v.6 p.23, p.42*
Chassen-Lopez, Francie R. *v.3 p.291*
Chasteen, John Charles & Castro-Klarén, Sara (Editors) . *v.3 p.264*
Chasteen, John Charles *v.3 p.266, p.278*
Chatani, N. *v.5 p.290*
Chateaubriand, Francois-Rene de *v.2 p.488*
Chatenay, Didier (Volume Editor), et al. . . . *v.5 p.121, p.123*
Chatfield, Michael & Vangermeersch, Richard (Editors) . *v.4 p.104*
Chatterjea, Ananya *v.1 p.28, p.30, p.40*
Chatterjee, Partha & Jeganathan, Pradeep (Editors) . *v.6 p.146*
Chatterjee, Partha *v.6 p.156, p.158, p.160*
Chatterjee, Samprit, et al. *v.5 p.483*
Chatterjee, Upamanyu *v.2 p.764*

Chatterji, Bankimcandra *v.6 p.151*
Chatterji, Joya *v.6 p.160*
Chatterji, Manas (Editor), et al. *v.4 p.262*
Chatterton, Thomas, et al. *v.2 p.243*
Chattopadhyay, Siddheswar *v.1 p.131, p.133*
Chatty, Dawn & Rabo, Annika (Editors) *v.6 p.592*
Chaturachinda, Gwyneth, et al. *v.1 p.663, p.691*
Chaturvedi, Ravi (Editor), et al. *v.1 p.58, p.131*
Chatzkel, Jay L. *v.4 p.77*
Chaucer, Geoffrey & De Lorris, Guillaume *v.2 p.208*
Chaucer, Geoffrey *v.2 p.207, p.208*
Chaudhuri, Amit *v.2 p.763, p.764*
Chauncey, George *v.6 p.362, p.717*
Chauveau, Jean-Pierre (Editor) *v.2 p.464*
Chauveau, Michel (Contribution by) *v.3 p.10*
Chauveau, Michel *v.6 p.58*
Chavalas, Mark & Mark Chavalas, Professor (Editors) . *v.3 p.4*
Chavalas, Mark W. & Younger, K. Lawson Jr. (Editors) . *v.3 p.4*
Chavan, Sunanda P *v.2 p.761*
Chavana, Herminia B. *v.3 p.526*
Chavarria, Jesus *v.3 p.329*
Chavarria, Joaquim *v.1 p.807*
Chaves, Jonathan (Editor, Translator) *v.6 p.209*
Chaves, Mark *v.1 p.658*
Chavez, Cesar, et al. *v.4 p.124*
Chavez, Denise & Feyder, Linda (Editors) . *v.1 p.120, p.124, v.6
                                                        p.517*
Chavez, Denise *v.6 p.498*
Chavez, Ernesto *v.6 p.540*
Chavez, John R. & Platts-Mills, John . . . *v.3 p.526, v.6 p.531*
Chavez, Linda *v.6 p.540*
Chavez, Thomas E. *v.3 p.528*
Chavkin, Samuel *v.3 p.352*
Chawaf, Chantal *v.2 p.528, p.529*
Chawla, Sohan L. & Gupta, R. K. *v.5 p.688, p.734*
Chayefsky, Paddy *v.2 p.65*
Chayes, Abram *v.3 p.468*
Chayko, Mary *v.4 p.772*
Chazin-Bennahum, Judith *v.1 p.5, p.6, p.23*
Checchi, Daniele *v.4 p.297*
Check, Joseph W. *v.4 p.314*
Chedid, Andree *v.2 p.464*
Chedid, Andrée *v.2 p.529*
Cheek, Timothy (Editor) *v.6 p.192, p.201*
Cheek, Timothy *v.1 p.211, p.229, p.333, p.407*
Cheeke, Peter R. *v.5 p.54*
Cheetham, A. K. & Day, Peter (Editors) *v.5 p.305*
Cheetham, A. K. & Day, Peter *v.5 p.305*
Cheever, John *v.2 p.67, v.6 p.395*
Cheever, Susan *v.2 p.65*
Cheikh, Nadia Maria El *v.6 p.581, p.584*
Chejne, Anwar G. *v.3 p.65*
Chekhov, Anton *v.1 p.108, v.2 p.802*
Chekhov, Michael *v.1 p.143, p.152*
Chela Flores, Julian *v.5 p.183, p.242*

Chelkowski, Peter J. & Dabashi, Hamid *v.6 p.632*

Chelladurai, P. *v.4 p.883, p.900*

Chemers, Martin M. & Ayman, Roya (Editors) . . . *v.5 p.647*

Chen, An *v.4 p.619*

Chen, C. H *v.5 p.710*

Chen, F. F. *v.5 p.566*

Chen, Fu Hua *v.5 p.421*

Chen, Gang *v.5 p.318*

Chen, Goong & Zhou, Jingmin *v.5 p.491*

Chen, H. -H. & Guizani, Mohsen *v.5 p.726*

Chen, Jie *v.4 p.619*

Chen, Jie-Qi & Horsch, Patricia (Translators) *v.4 p.368*

Ch'en, Kenneth *v.1 p.561*

Chen, Lin-Feng, et al. *v.5 p.729*

Chen, Ruoxi, et al. *v.6 p.212*

Chen, Shing-Ling & Hall, G. Jon *v.4 p.691*

Chen, Stephen *v.4 p.113*

Chen, Tina *v.6 p.95, p.123*

Chen, W. F. *v.5 p.685*

Chen, Xiaomei (Editor,
  Introduction by) *v.1 p.129, p.131, p.133, v.6 p.209*

Chen, Ying *v.2 p.540*

Chen, Yi-Ping Phoebe (Editor) *v.5 p.107*

Chen, Yong *v.6 p.126*

Chenery, Hollis B. (Editor), et al. *v.4 p.188*

Cheney, E. W. *v.5 p.491*

Cheney, George & Barnett, George A. *v.4 p.132*

Cheney, Margaret *v.6 p.409*

Cheney, Sheldon *v.1 p.81, p.95*

Cheng, H. H. (Editor) *v.5 p.49*

Cheng, K. S. & Romero, G. E. (Editors) *v.5 p.68*

Cheng, Lilly, et al. *v.6 p.108*

Cheng, Nien *v.6 p.195, p.199*

Cheng, Pang Guek *v.3 p.319*

Cheng, R Holland & Hammar, Lena (Editors) . *v.5 p.104, p.115*

Cheng, Sinkwan *v.1 p.491*

Cheng, Ta-Pei *v.5 p.72*

Cheng *v.5 p.693*

Chenier, Andre *v.2 p.478*

Chennels, David W. *v.3 p.536*

Chenok, P. B. (Editor) *v.4 p.104*

Chenu, M. D. *v.1 p.633*

Chenu, Marie-Dominique *v.6 p.570*

Cheremisinoff, Nicholas P. &
  Cheremisinoff, Paul N. (Editors) *v.5 p.688*

Cheremisinoff, Nicholas P. & Graffia, Madelyn *v.5 p.681*

Cheremisinoff, Nicholas P. (Editor) *v.5 p.367, p.713*

Cheremisinoff, Nicholas P. *v.5 p.321, p.688, p.713*

Cheremisinoff, Paul N., Nicholas P. Cheremisinoff, and
  Su Ling Cheng (Editors) *v.5 p.705*

Cherfas, Jeremy *v.5 p.138*

Cherkovski, Neeli *v.2 p.53*

Cherlin, Andrew J. & Furstenberg, Frank F. Jr. *v.4 p.740*

Cherlin, Andrew J. *v.4 p.739*

Chermayeff, Ivan, et al. *v.1 p.717*

Chernaik, Warren & Dzelzainis, Martin (Editors) . . . *v.2 p.252*

Cherniavsky, Felix *v.1 p.7*

Chernicoff, Stanley & Whitney, Donna *v.4 p.390*

Cherniss, Michael D. *v.2 p.167*

Chernoff, Barry (Editor), et al. *v.5 p.175, p.235*

Chernoff, Fred (Editor) *v.4 p.654*

Chernow, Ron *v.4 p.91, p.146, p.148, p.154, p.517*

Cherny, Robert W., et al. *v.4 p.120*

Cherny, Robert W. *v.3 p.433, p.524*

Cherrington, John *v.3 p.546*

Cherry, Deborah *v.6 p.746*

Cherry, Paul *v.4 p.142*

Cherry, Robert D. *v.4 p.133*

Cheryl Grossman *v.4 p.304, p.319*

Cheshire, Jenny (Editor, Introduction by) *v.2 p.551*

Cheshire, Jim *v.1 p.810*

Cheshire, P. C. & Mills, E. S. (Editors) *v.4 p.188*

Chesler, Phyllis *v.5 p.659*

Chesney-Lind, Meda & Hagedorn,
  John M. (Editors) *v.6 p.256, p.468*

Chesney-Lind, Meda & Pasko, Lisa . *v.6 p.255, p.258, p.468*

Chesney-Lind, Meda & Shelden, Randall G. . . *v.6 p.255, p.258*

Chesnut, Mary Boykin Miller *v.3 p.394, p.428*

Chesnutt, Charles Waddell *v.2 p.32, v.6 p.23*

Chesser, Ronald K. & Smith, Michael H. *v.5 p.188*

Chessex, Jacques *v.2 p.529*

Chester, Eric Thomas *v.3 p.316*

Chester, Eric *v.4 p.72*

Chester, Jonathan *v.5 p.434*

Chester, Roy *v.5 p.429*

Chesterfield, Philip Dormer Stanhope, Earl of . *v.3 p.106, p.127*

Chesterman, Sandra *v.1 p.750*

Chesterman, Simon *v.4 p.585*

Chesterton, G. K. *v.2 p.277, p.575*

Chesterton, Gilbert K. *v.1 p.596*

Cheung, Dominic *v.6 p.211, p.213*

Cheung, King-Kok & Yogi, Stan (Editors) *v.6 p.86, p.90*

Cheung, King-Kok (Editor) *v.6 p.95*

Cheung, King-Kok *v.6 p.95*

Chevlowe, Susan *v.1 p.736*

Chew, Donald H. Jr. *v.4 p.88*

Chew, Donald H. *v.4 p.91*

Chew, Samuel C. *v.2 p.274*

Cheyfitz, Eric *v.2 p.727, v.6 p.697*

Chénier, André *v.2 p.488*

Chhibber, Pradeep K. & Kollman, Ken *v.4 p.578*

Chhibber, Pradeep K. *v.4 p.617*

Ch'i, Hsi-sheng *v.4 p.619*

Chiarelli, Luigi, et al. *v.2 p.697*

Chiarmonte, Paula *v.6 p.472*

Chiasson, Robert B. *v.5 p.87*

Chibnall, Marjorie . . . *v.3 p.97, p.235, v.6 p.559, p.561, p.568*

Chicago Board of Education *v.4 p.285*

Chicago Board of Trade Staff *v.4 p.94, p.101, p.162*

Chichester, Page *v.5 p.228*

Chick, Victoria *v.4 p.226*

Chickering, Howell D. *v.2 p.203*

Chickering, Roger *v.3 p.163*

Chidester, David *v.1 p.543*

Ch'ien, Evelyn Nien-Ming *v.2 p.190*

Chierichetti, David *v.6 p.418*

Chiflet, Jean-Loup & Jacobs, Edgar-P . . *v.2 p.453*

Chiflet, Jean-Loup *v.2 p.453*

Chihuly, Dale, et al. *v.1 p.810*

Chikulo, Bornwell C. & Hope,
    Kempe Ronald (Editors) *v.4 p.611, p.664*

Chiland, Colette *v.6 p.370*

Chilcote, Ronald H. *v.4 p.502*

Child, Brenda J., et al. *v.4 p.312*

Child Development Institute,
    University of North Carolina *v.5 p.571*

Child, Francis James *v.2 p.198*

Child, Greg (Compiled by) *v.4 p.789*

Child, Lydia Maria *v.2 p.32*

Childers, Erskine *v.2 p.336*

Childers, Thomas *v.3 p.170, v.4 p.609*

Childress, James F. (Editor), et al. *v.5 p.674*

Childs, Brevard S. *v.1 p.618*

Childs, Donald J. *v.2 p.71*

Childs, Elizabeth C. (Editor) *v.1 p.827*

Childs, G. Tucker *v.6 p.80*

Childs, John Lawrence *v.4 p.341*

Childs, Marquis William *v.3 p.234*

Childs, Peter (Editor, Introduction by) *v.2 p.727*

Childs *v.1 p.620*

Chill, Emanuel *v.4 p.629*

Chilton, Bruce & Evans, Craig A. (Editors) *v.1 p.626*

Chilton, Bruce D. & Evans, Craig A. (Editors) *v.1 p.626*

Chilton, Bruce D. & Neusner, Jacob *v.1 p.549*

Chilton, John *v.1 p.258, p.329*

Chin, David *v.5 p.702*

Chin, Frank *v.6 p.98, p.99, p.104, p.131, p.133*

Chin, H. E. *v.3 p.322*

Chin, Jean L., et al. *v.6 p.121*

Chin, Jean Lau (Editor) *v.4 p.698, v.5 p.632*

Chin, Ko-lin *v.6 p.118, p.126*

Chin, Margaret *v.6 p.106, p.111, p.113*

Chin, Marilyn *v.6 p.103*

Chin, Pa *v.6 p.212*

Chin, Soo-Young (Editor), et al. *v.6 p.85, p.108*

Chin, Tung Pok & Chin, Winifred C. *v.6 p.93, p.126*

Chinea, Jorge Luis *v.3 p.319*

Ching, Francis D. K. *v.1 p.783*

Ching, Julia *v.1 p.539*

Ching-tzu, Wu *v.6 p.211*

Chinitz, David E. *v.2 p.71*

Chinn, Peggy L. & Watson, Jean *v.5 p.530*

Chinoy, Helen Krich & Jenkins, Linda Walsh (Editors) . *v.1 p.120*

Chipman, Donald E. *v.3 p.285, p.508*

Chipp, Herschel B. *v.1 p.736*

Chippindale, Christopher *v.4 p.12*

Chiriboga, David A. & Catron, Linda S. *v.4 p.739*

Chisholm, Dianne *v.2 p.88*

Chisholm, Roderick M. (Editor) *v.1 p.514*

Chisholm, Roderick M. *v.1 p.464*

Chisman, Forrest & Pifer, Alan *v.4 p.523*

Chiss, Jean-Louis, et al. *v.2 p.453*

Chitnis, Rajendra A. *v.2 p.778, p.797*

Chittick, Kathryn *v.2 p.282, v.6 p.739*

Chitty, Mary (Compiled and Edited by) *v.5 p.126, p.139*

Chiu, Monica *v.6 p.96*

Cho, Margaret *v.6 p.90, p.93*

Chodakiewicz, M. *v.3 p.254*

Chodorow, Joan *v.1 p.50*

Chodorow, Nancy Julia *v.4 p.736, v.6 p.427, p.445*

Chodorow, Nancy *v.6 p.445*

Chodorow, Stanley *v.1 p.572*

Ch'oe, Yongho (Editor), et al. *v.6 p.235*

Choi, Frederick D. S. (Editor) . . . *v.4 p.88, p.104, p.155, p.162*

Choi, Namkee G. (Editor) *v.6 p.121*

Choi, Susan *v.2 p.143*

Choi, Ying-Kit *v.5 p.685*

Chojnacki, Stanley *v.3 p.199*

Choksy, Lois *v.1 p.405*

Chomsky, Aviva (Editor), et al. *v.3 p.307*

Chomsky, Noam & Halle, Morris *v.2 p.556*

Chomsky, Noam . *v.2 p.559, v.3 p.387, p.440, p.451, p.468, v.4 p.658, v.5 p.620, p.622, p.623, p.624, v.6 p.617*

Chomsky, William & Kimhi, David *v.6 p.645*

Chong, Derrick *v.1 p.825*

Chong, Nilda & Baez, Francia *v.6 p.524*

Chong, Ping, et al. *v.6 p.98*

Chopin, Kate & Fearing, Kenneth *v.2 p.72*

Chopin, Kate *v.2 p.32*

Choppin, Gregory R., et al. *v.5 p.307*

Chopra, Anil K. *v.5 p.693*

Chopra, V. L. (Editor) *v.5 p.20, p.24*

Choquette, Leslie *v.3 p.537*

Choquette, Robert *v.1 p.543*

Chotner, Deborah (Editor) *v.1 p.731*

Choueiri, Youssef M. *v.6 p.582*

Choukri, Mohamed *v.6 p.659*

Chow, Tai L. *v.5 p.548*

Chow Tse-Tsung *v.6 p.189*

Chowning, Margaret *v.3 p.285*

Choy, Catherine Ceniza . *v.6 p.111, p.116, p.118, p.129, p.141*

Cho-yun Hsu *v.6 p.183*

Chretien de Troyes *v.2 p.466*

Chrétien de Troyes & Louis, Rene *v.2 p.466*

Chrétien de Troyes *v.2 p.466*

Chrétien, de Troyes *v.2 p.466*

Chrétien, Jean-Pierre *v.6 p.63*

Chris Beytes; Debbie Hamrick *v.5 p.43*

Chris Beytes (Editor) *v.5 p.43*

Chrislock, Carl H. *v.3 p.522*

Chrisman, Nicholas *v.4 p.386*

Chrispeels, Martin J. & Sadava, David E. *v.5 p.7*

Christ, Carol P. *v.1 p.528*

Christen, Barbara S. *v.1 p.792*

Christensen, C. Roland *v.4 p.177*

Christensen, Clayton M. & Raynor, Michael E. . . . *v.4 p.65*

Christensen, Clayton M., et al. *v.4 p.65, p.81*

Christensen, Clayton M. *v.4 p.51*

Christensen, Karen (Editor), et al. *v.6 p.437*

Christensen, Law & Kremer, Gary *v.3 p.512*

Christensen, Thomas (Editor) *v.1 p.369*

Christian, Barbara *v.6 p.478*

Christian, Charles M. *v.6 p.4*

Christian, Wolfgang & Belloni, Mario *v.5 p.563*

Christians, Clifford G. & Traber, Michael (Editors) . *v.4 p.405*

Christians, Clifford G., et al. *v.4 p.405*

Christiansen, Eric *v.3 p.56, p.63*

Christiansen, Keith & Arnsworth, Maryan W. (Editors) . *v.1 p.731*

Christiansen, Keith, et al. *v.1 p.736*

Christiansen, Rupert *v.2 p.278*

Christianson, John Robert *v.3 p.46*

Christianson, Scott *v.4 p.752, v.6 p.273*

Christie, Agatha *v.2 p.338, p.339*

Christie, John S. & Gonzalez, Jose B. *v.6 p.495*

Christie, John S. *v.6 p.512*

Christie, Neil *v.3 p.62*

Christie, R. M. *v.5 p.320*

Christine, de Pisan *v.2 p.469*

Christine de Pizan & Willard, Charity C. *v.2 p.469*

Christine de Pizan *v.2 p.468, p.469*

Christine, de Pizan *v.2 p.469*

Christofides, Koren (Editor) *v.2 p.473*

Christophe, Christophe Wiart (Author, Editor) . . . *v.5 p.211*

Christopher, A. J. *v.4 p.381*

Christopher, Renny *v.6 p.96, p.115, p.140*

Christopher, Robert *v.6 p.219*

Christou, Paul & Klee, Harry (Editor-In-Chiefs) . . . *v.5 p.7*

Christov-Bakargiev, Carolyn, et al. *v.1 p.737*

Chryssavgis, John *v.1 p.569*

Chu, Donald A. *v.4 p.289, p.793, p.864*

Chu, Donald *v.4 p.821, p.893*

Chu, Louis *v.6 p.99*

Chu, Patricia P. *v.6 p.96*

Chu, Petra ten-Doesschate *v.1 p.677, p.686*

Chu, Samuel C. *v.6 p.189, p.202, p.217*

Ch'u Tung-Tsu *v.4 p.475*

Ch'u, T'ung-tsu *v.4 p.701, v.6 p.185*

Chua, Amy *v.4 p.256, p.261, p.262*

Chuang Tzu *v.1 p.417, p.475*

Chubak, Sadeq *v.6 p.670*

Chubb, Basil *v.4 p.607*

Chujoy, Anatole & Manchester, P. W. *v.1 p.3*

Chumachenko, Tatiana A. *v.3 p.222*

Chun, Gloria H. *v.6 p.113, p.126*

Chung, Kai Lai & AitSahlia, Farid *v.5 p.483, p.503*

Chung, T. J. *v.5 p.547*

Chung, Young Yang *v.1 p.715, p.809*

Church, Forrest (Editor) *v.1 p.656*

Church, S. D. (Editor) *v.3 p.98*

Churchill, Caryl *v.1 p.99, v.2 p.337*

Churchill, Charles *v.2 p.243*

Churchill, Stuart W. (Introduction by) *v.5 p.743*

Churchill, Winston S. *v.3 p.93, p.111*

Churchland, Patricia S. & Sejnowski, Terrence J. . . . *v.5 p.591*

Churchland, Paul M. *v.1 p.496, v.5 p.616*

Chute, Marchette *v.2 p.208*

Chuter, David *v.6 p.257*

Chvany, Pete *v.6 p.368*

Chvatal, Vasek *v.5 p.492*

Chwin, Stefan *v.2 p.789*

Chyet, Michael L. *v.6 p.668*

Cialdini, Robert B. *v.4 p.139*

Ciardha, Eamonn O. *v.3 p.137*

Ciardi, John *v.2 p.65*

Ciarlet, P. G. (Editor), et al. *v.5 p.693*

Cibber, Colley *v.2 p.243*

Cicarelli, James & Cicarelli, Julianne *v.4 p.193*

Cicero, Marcus Tullius . *v.1 p.428, v.2 p.427, p.431, p.432, p.433*

Cichy, Ronald F. & Hickey, Philip J. *v.4 p.165*

Cicourel, Aaron V. *v.4 p.692*

Cigar, Norman *v.4 p.652*

Cikovsky, Nicolai Jr. *v.1 p.737*

Cimbala, Paul A. *v.3 p.503*

Ciment, James (Editor) *v.4 p.485*

Cimino, Richard (Editor) *v.1 p.585*

Cimoli, Mario (Editor) *v.4 p.383*

Cincura, Andrew *v.2 p.812*

Cinel, Dino *v.3 p.202*

Cingria, Charles Albert *v.2 p.513*

Cingria, Charles-Albert *v.2 p.513*

Ciobanu, Gabriel (Editor) *v.5 p.126*

Cioc, Mark & Cronon, William *v.3 p.159*

Cioc, Mark *v.3 p.159*

Cioffi, Kathleen *v.2 p.788*

Ciompi, Luc *v.5 p.660*

Cioranescu, Alexandre *v.2 p.816*

Cipolla, Carlo M. (Editor) *v.3 p.39, p.42*

Cipolla, Carlo M. *v.3 p.39*

Cipra, Barry *v.5 p.457*

Cipriani, Roberto *v.1 p.524*

Circa Reference Staff *v.4 p.188*

Cirillo, R. *v.4 p.195*

Cirincione, Joseph, et al. *v.4 p.655*

Cirque Du Soleil, et al. *v.4 p.65*

Cirules, Enrique *v.3 p.307*

Cisneros, Sandra *v.6 p.498*

Citino, Robert Michael *v.3 p.160*

Citron, Stephen . *v.1 p.248, p.249, p.328, p.331, p.335, p.337, p.357, p.404, v.6 p.413*

City College of New York Library *v.4 p.642*

City of Ann Arbor Natural Area Preservation
   Division Satff *v.5 p.233*
Ciulla, Joanne B. (Editor) *v.4 p.697*
Civardi, Giovanni *v.1 p.724*
Civello, Catherine A. *v.2 p.382*
Cixous, Helene, et al. *v.2 p.690*
Cixous, Helene *v.2 p.529*
Cixous, Hélène *v.2 p.529*
C.-J. Winter, R.L. Sizmann, and
   L.L. Vant-Hull (Editors) *v.5 p.708*
Claeys, Gregory *v.4 p.491*
Clagett, Marshall (Editor) *v.5 p.388*
Clagett, Marshall *v.5 p.390*
Clair, Jean *v.1 p.737*
Clamen, Stewart M. *v.6 p.307*
Clanchy, M. T. *v.6 p.569*
Clancy, Kevin J. & Krieg, Peter C. *v.4 p.134*
Clancy, Laurie *v.2 p.740*
Clancy, Paul, et al. *v.5 p.183, p.242*
Clancy-Smith, Julia A. *v.6 p.641, p.642*
Clanton, Reita E. & Dwight, Mary P. *v.4 p.847*
Clapp, Jennifer & Dauvergne, Peter *v.4 p.666*
Clapp, William Warland *v.1 p.112, p.140*
Clar, D. *v.6 p.12*
Clare, John *v.2 p.275, p.278*
Clare, Judith & Hamilton, Helen *v.4 p.689*
Clarence-Smith, W. G. & Topik,
   Steven (Editors) *v.3 p.271, p.303*
Claridge, Henry (Editor) *v.2 p.76*
Claridge, Laura *v.1 p.737*
Claridge, M. F. (Editor), et al. *v.5 p.198*
Clark, Alan *v.1 p.701*
Clark, Alvin L. Jr. (Editor), et al. *v.1 p.721*
Clark, Andrew H. *v.3 p.543*
Clark, Andrew J., et al. *v.1 p.663, p.669, p.807*
Clark, Andrew *v.5 p.435*
Clark, Anna *v.3 p.52, v.6 p.456, p.743, p.746, p.765*
Clark, Audrey N. *v.4 p.373*
Clark, Beverly Lyon & Higonnet, Margaret R. *v.2 p.582*
Clark, Blue *v.6 p.687, p.695*
Clark, C. A. & Moyer, J. W. *v.5 p.46*
Clark, Carol, et al. *v.1 p.695*
Clark, Caryl (Editor) *v.1 p.188, p.330*
Clark, Champ *v.3 p.433*
Clark, Charles E. (Editor), et al. *v.3 p.486*
Clark, Christopher *v.3 p.169*
Clark, Colin W. & Mangel, Marc *v.5 p.501*
Clark, Colin W. *v.5 p.503*
Clark, David P. *v.5 p.126*
Clark, Dennis *v.3 p.492, v.6 p.711*
Clark, Dick *v.4 p.804, p.831, p.850, p.896*
Clark, Donald N. (Editor) *v.6 p.236*
Clark, Donald N. *v.6 p.236*
Clark, Elizabeth Ann *v.1 p.599, p.642*
Clark, Ella E. & Edmonds, Margot *v.3 p.519*

Clark, Etta *v.4 p.841*
Clark, Eve V. *v.5 p.620, p.623*
Clark, G. Kitson *v.3 p.111, p.127, v.6 p.735*
Clark, Garth, et al. *v.1 p.807*
Clark, Garth *v.1 p.807*
Clark, George B. *v.3 p.301*
Clark, George (Editor) *v.2 p.204*
Clark, Gordon L. *v.4 p.543*
Clark, J. C. *v.3 p.93, p.106, p.108, p.127*
Clark, J. Desmond (Editor) *v.6 p.52*
Clark, J. E. *v.3 p.261*
Clark, J. Marshall & Ohkawa, Hideo *v.5 p.9*
Clark, James Midgley *v.6 p.570*
Clark, James *v.5 p.311*
Clark, Jim *v.4 p.157*
Clark, John Bates *v.4 p.208, p.223, p.252*
Clark, John (Editor) *v.4 p.163*
Clark, John Elwood Jr. *v.4 p.519*
Clark, John, et al. *v.2 p.559*
Clark, John O. E. & Stiegeler, Stella E. . . . *v.6 p.285*
Clark, John *v.4 p.208*
Clark, Katerina *v.2 p.797, v.3 p.214*
Clark, Keith (Editor) *v.6 p.24*
Clark, Keith *v.6 p.23*
Clark, Kenneth B. *v.5 p.625, p.631*
Clark, Kim B. & Fujimoto, Takahiro *v.4 p.144*
Clark, Leon E. *v.6 p.51*
Clark, Martin P. *v.4 p.422*
Clark, Mary E. *v.4 p.682*
Clark, Melody (Editor) *v.5 p.139*
Clark, Michael D. *v.3 p.366*
Clark, Nancy *v.4 p.801, p.876*
Clark, Paul *v.6 p.207*
Clark, Pete A. *v.3 p.92, p.123*
Clark, Peter & Hawley, Katherine (Editors) . *v.1 p.499, v.5 p.401*
Clark, Peter (Editor, Contribution by) *v.3 p.43*
Clark, Peter *v.1 p.538, v.3 p.126*
Clark, Ramsey *v.4 p.652*
Clark, Reginald M. *v.4 p.309*
Clark, Robert (Editor) *v.2 p.35*
Clark, Robert T. *v.2 p.598*
Clark, Roy Peter & Scanlan, Christopher . . . *v.4 p.410*
Clark, Samuel D. *v.3 p.536*
Clark, Sandra (Editor) *v.2 p.226*
Clark, Stuart *v.5 p.71*
Clark, T. J. *v.3 p.75, p.153*
Clark, Thomas Dionysius *v.3 p.496*
Clark, Tim & Koch, Rainer *v.5 p.279*
Clark, Timothy A. R., et al. *v.1 p.752, p.754*
Clark, Timothy J. *v.1 p.702*
Clark, Timothy W. (Editor) *v.6 p.290*
Clark, Tom *v.2 p.92*
Clark, Victoria *v.3 p.245*
Clark, Virginia L. & Bavoil, Patrik M. (Volume Editors) *v.5 p.166*
Clark, Walter Aaron (Editor) *v.1 p.291*

Clark, Walter Aaron *v.1 p.195, p.301*
Clark, Walter *v.2 p.65*
Clark, Wesley K. *v.4 p.561, p.563*
Clark, William A. V. *v.4 p.764*
Clark, William S. *v.1 p.108*
Clark *v.4 p.121*
Clarke, Anthony J. *v.5 p.361, p.362*
Clarke, Arthur C. & Kubrick, Stanley *v.2 p.337*
Clarke, Arthur C. *v.2 p.337*
Clarke, Austin *v.2 p.337*
Clarke, Cheryl *v.2 p.15, v.6 p.24, p.42*
Clarke, Colin, et al. *v.6 p.146*
Clarke, Colin *v.4 p.771*
Clarke, David B. *v.6 p.730*
Clarke, Desmond M. *v.5 p.401*
Clarke, Edith *v.4 p.40*
Clarke, Eric & Cook, Nicholas (Editors) *v.1 p.173*
Clarke, George Elliott (Editor) *v.2 p.729*
Clarke, George Elliott *v.2 p.733*
Clarke, Georgia *v.1 p.786*
Clarke, Gerald *v.6 p.401*
Clarke, Graham & Stillwell, John (Editors) *v.4 p.386*
Clarke, Graham *v.1 p.762, v.2 p.53*
Clarke, H. T. *v.5 p.300*
Clarke, Harold D.; Jenson, Jane; LeDuc, Lawrence; Pammett,
Jon H. *v.4 p.590*
Clarke, Helen *v.6 p.555*
Clarke, J. J. *v.1 p.475*
Clarke, Jeanne Nienaber *v.3 p.457*
Clarke, John Henrik (Editor) *v.6 p.24*
Clarke, John Henrik *v.6 p.10, p.24, p.37*
Clarke, Kamari Maxine *v.4 p.44*
Clarke, Katherine A. *v.4 p.377*
Clarke, M. L. *v.2 p.427*
Clarke, Mark A. *v.4 p.341*
Clarke, Mary & Crisp, Clement *v.1 p.5, p.23, p.37*
Clarke, Mary & Vaughn, David (Editors) *v.1 p.3*
Clarke, Micael M. *v.2 p.315, v.6 p.746, p.755*
Clarke, Michael *v.1 p.663*
Clarke, Paul Barry & Foweraker, Joe . . . *v.4 p.482, p.503*
Clarke, Peter *v.4 p.226*
Clarke, Richard A. *v.4 p.563*
Clarke, Ronald V. & Felson, Marcus (Editors) . . . *v.6 p.249*
Clarke, Sally H. *v.5 p.29*
Clarke, Simon & Ashwin, Sarah *v.4 p.124*
Clarke, Steve & Coakes, Elayne *v.4 p.321*
Clarke, Susan *v.6 p.722*
Clarke, Susanna *v.2 p.337*
Clarke, Thurston *v.6 p.61*
Clarke-Stewart, Alison & Brentano, Cornelia *v.5 p.639*
Clarkin, John F. & Lenzenweger, Mark F. (Editors) . . *v.5 p.661*
Clarkson, C. M. & Morgan, Rod (Editors) *v.6 p.269*
Clarkson, Euan N. K. *v.5 p.447*
Clarkson, L. A. *v.3 p.90, p.122*
Clarkson, Priscilla M. & Skrinar, Margaret (Editors) . . *v.1 p.49*

Clason, W. E. *v.5 p.739*
Clasper, James W. *v.5 p.739*
Classen, Constance *v.3 p.261, v.5 p.612*
Claude, Inis L. Jr. *v.4 p.628*
Claudel, Paul *v.2 p.513, p.514*
Claudi, Renata & Leach, Joseph H. (Editors) . *v.5 p.174, p.204*
Claugher, D. (Editor) *v.5 p.87, p.204*
Claus, Peter (Editor), et al. *v.6 p.146, p.147*
Clausen, Christopher *v.4 p.764*
Clausen, Meredith L. *v.1 p.786, p.792*
Clausen, Wendell (Editor, Commentaries by,
Introduction by) *v.2 p.446*
Clauss, James J. & Johnston, Sarah Iles (Editors) . . . *v.2 p.410*
Claverie, Jean-Michel & Notredame, Cedric *v.5 p.97*
Clavin, Tom *v.4 p.860*
Clawson, Calvin C. *v.5 p.465*
Clawson, David L., et al. *v.4 p.396*
Clawson, Marion *v.5 p.37*
Clay, Diskin *v.2 p.437*
Clay, Grady *v.6 p.717*
Clay, Jason & World Wildlife Fund Staff *v.5 p.14*
Clay, Jenny Strauss *v.2 p.413*
Clay, Marie M. *v.4 p.368*
Clayson, Hollis *v.1 p.677, p.686*
Clayton, Anthony *v.4 p.584, v.6 p.66*
Clayton, Cornell W. (Editor) *v.4 p.523*
Clayton, George D. & Clayton, Florence E. (Editors) . *v.5 p.314*
Clayton, J. Douglas *v.2 p.802*
Clayton, Jay *v.2 p.282, v.6 p.752*
Clayton, Julie & Dennis, Carina (Editors) *v.5 p.121*
Clayton, Lawrence A. *v.3 p.329*
Clayton, Lawrence, et al. *v.3 p.521*
Clayton, Lawrene A. *v.3 p.329*
Clayton, Philip *v.1 p.526*
Clear, Todd R. & Dammer, Harry R. *v.6 p.278*
Clear, Todd R. & Karp, David R. (Editors) *v.6 p.278*
Clear, Todd R., et al. *v.6 p.272*
Cleary, Edward L. & Steigenga, Timothy J. *v.4 p.591*
Cleary, Edward L. & Stewart-Gambino,
Hannah (Editors) *v.3 p.259*
Cleary, Edward L. (Editor) *v.1 p.572*
Cleary, Edward L. *v.1 p.572*
Cleary, Richard L. *v.1 p.796*
Cleary, Thomas *v.1 p.567*
Cleaveland, Timothy *v.6 p.70*
Cleaver, Tony *v.4 p.185*
Cleaves, Cheryl S. & Hobbs, Margie J. *v.4 p.175*
Clegern, Wayne M. *v.3 p.297*
Clegg, Elizabeth *v.1 p.677, p.686*
Cleland, Jane K. *v.4 p.172*
Cleland, John *v.2 p.243*
Cleland, Robert Glass (Editor) *v.3 p.531*
Clemence, Richard Vernon & Doody, Francis S. . *v.4 p.230, p.235*
Clemens, Clay (Editor) *v.4 p.639*
Clement, Catherine *v.1 p.378*

Clement, Clara E. *v.6 p.472*
Clement, Russell T., et al. *v.1 p.725*
Clement, Russell T. *v.1 p.662, p.696*
Clemente, Carmine D. *v.5 p.95, p.158*
Clemente, Linda & Clemente, Bill *v.2 p.538*
Clementi, Muzio *v.1 p.397, p.400*
Clements, Barbara Evans . . . *v.3 p.53, p.222,v.6 p.440, p.453*
Clements, Claire B. *v.4 p.785, p.790, p.841*
Clements, Douglas H. (Editor), et al. *v.4 p.360*
Clements, Frank A. *v.6 p.634*
Clements, Kendrick A. *v.3 p.440, p.468, v.6 p.298*
Clements, Rhonda L. & Kinzler, Suzanne K. . *v.4 p.797, p.799*
Clemmons, Janine R. & Buchholz, Richard (Editors) . *v.5 p.178*
Clendinen, Dudley & Nagourney, Adam *v.6 p.365, p.386*
Clendinnen, Inga *v.3 p.285*
Clendinning, Jane Piper *v.1 p.369*
Clepper, Henry *v.5 p.37*
Clerc, Jeanne-Marie *v.2 p.544*
Clerk of the U.S. House of Representatives *v.4 p.557*
Clery, E. J. *v.2 p.171*
Cleveland, Cutler J. & Morris, Christopher (Editors) . *v.5 p.708*
Cleveland, Cutler J. (Editor-In-Chief) *v.5 p.359, p.708*
Cleveland, Grover *v.3 p.435*
Cleveland, William L. *v.6 p.582, p.592*
Cleveland, William S. *v.5 p.480*
Cleverdon, Catherine Lyle *v.4 p.590*
Cleyre, Voltairine de *v.4 p.500*
Clément, Catherine & Kristeva, Julia *v.1 p.528*
Click, Patricia C. *v.3 p.501*
Cliff, Norman & Keats, John A. *v.5 p.599*
Clifford, Collette & Rutter, Michael *v.5 p.530*
Clifford, Craig E. & Pilkington, Tom (Editors) . . . *v.2 p.13*
Clifford, Deborah *v.2 p.39*
Clifford, Denis *v.4 p.443*
Clifford, James & Marcus, George E. (Editors) . . . *v.4 p.23*
Clifford, James Lowry *v.2 p.250*
Clifford, James *v.2 p.256*
Clifford, Nicholas R. *v.6 p.203*
Clifford, Richard J. *v.1 p.621*
Clift, Dominique *v.3 p.543*
Clift, Eleanor & Brazaitis, Tom *v.4 p.526*
Clifton, Lucille *v.2 p.143*
Clifton, Thomas *v.1 p.380*
Clifton-Taylor, Alec *v.1 p.608, p.789*
Clinard, Marshall B. & Meier, Robert F. *v.4 p.695*
Clinchy, Evans (Editor) *v.4 p.280*
Clinchy, Evans *v.4 p.325*
Cline, Sally *v.6 p.401*
Cline-Cole, Reginald & Robson, Elsbeth *v.4 p.384*
Cling, B. J. (Editor) *v.6 p.252*
Clingham, Greg (Editor) *v.2 p.250*
Clingham, Greg *v.2 p.250*
Clinton, Bill *v.3 p.468*
Clinton, Catherine *v.4 p.519, v.6 p.453*
Clinton, Hillary Rodham *v.3 p.457*

Clissold, Stephen *v.3 p.351*
Clive A. Edwards (Editor) *v.5 p.49*
Clive, John *v.3 p.88*
Clivio, Gianrenzo P. & Danesi, Marcel *v.2 p.698*
Clocksin, W. F. & Mellish, C. S. *v.5 p.346*
Cloetta, Yvonne *v.2 p.349*
Clogg, Richard (Editor) *v.3 p.194*
Clogg, Richard *v.3 p.194, p.195, v.4 p.597*
Cloke, Paul J. (Editor), et al. *v.4 p.396*
Clor, Harry M. *v.4 p.472*
Clore, Gerald L. & Martin, Leonard L. *v.5 p.657*
Close, Anthony *v.2 p.648*
Close, David *v.3 p.195*
Closs, August *v.2 p.591*
Closter, Susan V. *v.2 p.338, p.344*
Clot, Andre *v.6 p.589*
Clote, Peter & Backofen, Rolf . . . *v.5 p.105, p.341, p.501*
Clottes, Jean *v.1 p.668, v.4 p.16*
Cloudsley-Thompson, John L. *v.5 p.214*
Clough, Arthur Hugh *v.2 p.278*
Clough, Michael *v.6 p.56*
Clover, Carol J. & Lindow, John (Editors) *v.2 p.624*
Clover, Carol J. *v.6 p.317*
Clover, Frank M. *v.3 p.62*
Clowes, Edith W. (Editor), et al. *v.3 p.220*
Cloyd, Raymond A., et al. *v.5 p.43*
Clugston, M. J. *v.5 p.386*
Clum, John C. *v.6 p.410*
Clum, John M. (Editor) *v.2 p.24, v.6 p.411*
Clum, John M. *v.6 p.411*
Clumpner, Roy A. *v.4 p.797*
Clunas, Craig & Wen, Zhengming *v.1 p.693*
Clunas, Craig *v.1 p.693, v.6 p.186*
Clurman, Harold *v.1 p.112, p.143, p.152*
Clute, John & Grant, John (Editors) *v.2 p.581*
Clute, John & Nicholls, Peter *v.2 p.581*
Clutterbuck, Richard *v.6 p.172*
Clyman, Toby W. & Greene, Diana (Editors) *v.6 p.478*
Clymer, Kenton J. (Editor) *v.6 p.168*
Clymer, Kenton J. *v.6 p.170*
Coad, Oral *v.1 p.112, p.143*
Coakley, Jay J. & Donnelly, Peter *v.4 p.814*
Coakley, John & Gallagher, Michael (Editors) . . . *v.4 p.608*
Coakley, Sarah (Editor) *v.1 p.530*
Coaldrake, William H. *v.6 p.221*
Coates, Jennifer (Editor) *v.6 p.476*
Coates, Ken S. & Morrison, William *v.3 p.546*
Coates, Ken S. & Powell, Judith *v.3 p.546*
Coates, Kenneth S. *v.3 p.546*
Coates, Peter *v.5 p.78, p.221*
Coates, Robert M. & Denmark, Scott E. (Editors) . *v.5 p.290*
Coats, A. W. *v.4 p.211, p.268*
Coats, Joel R. & Yamamoto, Hiroki (Editors) *v.5 p.9*
Coatsworth, John H. *v.3 p.288*
Cobb, Cathy & Goldwhite, Harold *v.3 p.44, v.5 p.262*

Cobb, James C. *v.3 p.493*
Cobb, John B. Jr. & Griffin, David R. *v.1 p.637*
Cobb, John B. Jr. *v.1 p.641*
Cobb, Richard C. *v.3 p.149*
Cobb, Richard *v.3 p.149*
Cobb, Roger W. & Elder, Charles D. *v.4 p.554*
Cobban, Alfred (Editor) *v.3 p.91*
Cobban, Alfred *v.3 p.140*
Cobban, Helena *v.6 p.605*
Cobbett, William *v.3 p.108, p.126*
Coben, Diana (Editor), et al. *v.4 p.319*
Coben, Diana *v.4 p.762*
Coble, Parks M. *v.6 p.189, p.193*
Coburn, Kathleen & Harding, Anthony John (Editors) . *v.2 p.279*
Cocchiarale, Michael & Emmert, Scott (Editors) . . . *v.4 p.811*
Cocco de Filippis, Daisy & Gutierrez,
Franklin (Editors) *v.6 p.495, p.505*
Cochran, Pamela *v.1 p.590*
Cochran, Sherman (Editor), et al. *v.6 p.189*
Cochran, Sherman *v.6 p.189, p.218*
Cochrane, Allan *v.6 p.722*
Cochran-Smith, Marilyn & Zeichner,
Ken (Editors) *v.4 p.279, p.355*
Cockerham, William C. & Ritchey, Ferris J. *v.4 p.677*
Cockfield, Jamie H. *v.3 p.220*
Cockrell, Dale *v.1 p.119, p.281*
Cocks, Geoffrey & Jarausch, Konrad H. (Editors) . . *v.3 p.159*
Cocks, Joan *v.4 p.494*
Cockshut, A. O. J. *v.2 p.316*
Cockshutt, Nicholas R. (Editor) *v.1 p.812*
Cocteau, Jean *v.2 p.514, v.6 p.395*
Coddington, Alan *v.4 p.226*
Coddington, Earl A. & Levinson, Norman *v.5 p.487*
Coddington, Walter & Florian, Peter *v.4 p.63*
Code, Lorraine (Editor) *v.6 p.427*
Code, Lorraine *v.6 p.460, p.462*
CODEHUCA *v.3 p.304*
Codell, Julie F. *v.1 p.677, p.686*
Codina, Norberto *v.2 p.671*
Coduto, Donald P. *v.5 p.421*
Coe, Lewis *v.4 p.421*
Coe, Michael D. & Koontz, Rex *v.4 p.9*
Coe, Michael D. *v.4 p.9, p.22*
Coe, Michael, et al. *v.4 p.10*
Coe, Sophie D. *v.3 p.261, p.271*
Coedes, G. *v.6 p.164*
Coelho, Paulo *v.2 p.690*
Coelho, Victor Anand (Editor) . . . *v.1 p.389, p.400*
Coenen, Frans *v.2 p.622*
Coerver, Don, et al. *v.4 p.383*
Coerver, Don M. & Hall, Linda B. *v.3 p.291*
Coetzee, J. M. *v.2 p.753, p.754*
Coetzee, P. H. & Roux, A. P. J. (Editors) *v.1 p.476*
Coetzer, J. A. W. & Tustin, R. C. *v.6 p.283*
Cofer, Judith Ortiz *v.6 p.488, p.505, p.510*

Coffey, M. *v.2 p.427*
Coffey, S. (Editor) *v.5 p.292*
Coffey, Samuel (Editor) *v.5 p.292*
Coffey, Wayne *v.4 p.835, p.842, p.853*
Coffin, Berton & Singer, Werner *v.1 p.165, p.394*
Coffin, Berton *v.1 p.165, p.394, p.411*
Coffin, Edna A. & Bolozky, Shmuel *v.6 p.645*
Coffin, Edna A. *v.6 p.645*
Coffin, William Sloane *v.1 p.650*
Coffman, Curt & Gonzalez-Molina, Gabriel *v.4 p.76*
Coffman, Edward M. *v.3 p.468*
Coffman, Tom *v.3 p.533, v.6 p.130*
Cogan, Charles *v.4 p.643, p.645*
Cogan, Frances B. *v.2 p.9*
Cogan, Marc *v.2 p.704, v.6 p.564*
Cogan, Mordechai *v.1 p.620*
Cogan, Robert & Escot, Pozzi *v.1 p.370*
Cogeval, Guy *v.1 p.696*
Cogger, Harold C. & Zweifel,
Richard G. (Editors) *v.5 p.95, p.214*
Coggle, J. E. *v.5 p.376*
Coghlan, Brian *v.2 p.609*
Cogoli, Augusto (Editor) *v.5 p.153, p.217*
Cogswell, Fred & Elder, Jo-Ann *v.2 p.538*
Cogwell, Mathew T. *v.5 p.83*
Cohan, Steven (Editor) *v.1 p.249, p.255, v.6 p.315*
Cohen, Allan R. & Bradford, David L. *v.4 p.70, p.172*
Cohen, Andrew S. *v.5 p.427, p.449*
Cohen, Andrew *v.3 p.541*
Cohen, Arthur Allen *v.1 p.549*
Cohen, Arthur M. & Brawer, Florence B. *v.4 p.291*
Cohen, Arthur M. *v.4 p.331*
Cohen, Barbara Janson *v.5 p.164*
Cohen, Benjamin J. *v.4 p.246, p.261*
Cohen, Bonnie B. *v.1 p.51*
Cohen, Carl & Regan, Tom *v.6 p.288*
Cohen, Claudine *v.3 p.44*
Cohen, Dalia & Katz, Ruth *v.1 p.286*
Cohen, David B. & Wells, John W. (Editors) . *v.4 p.563, p.572*
Cohen, David S. *v.2 p.17*
Cohen, Deborah & O'Connor, Maura (Editors) . . . *v.3 p.35*
Cohen, E. Richard (Editor), et al. *v.5 p.545*
Cohen, Edward E. *v.3 p.13, p.17*
Cohen, Eliot A. *v.4 p.575*
Cohen, Elizabeth G. (Editor), et al. *v.4 p.349*
Cohen, Felix S., et al. *v.6 p.691*
Cohen, Felix S. *v.4 p.433, v.6 p.695*
Cohen, Gary B. *v.3 p.188*
Cohen, Gillian *v.5 p.610*
Cohen, Greta L. (Editor) *v.4 p.814, p.835*
Cohen, H. Floris *v.3 p.46, v.5 p.390*
Cohen, Hayyim J. *v.6 p.596*
Cohen, Hennig & Dillingham, William B. *v.2 p.21*
Cohen, Herb *v.4 p.74*
Cohen, Hermann *v.1 p.551*

Cohen, I. Bernard & Smith, George E. (Editors) . . . *v.5 p.542*
Cohen, I. Bernard *v.5 p.390, p.546, p.555, p.556*
Cohen, Ira M. & Kundu, Pijush K. *v.5 p.547*
Cohen, Irwin J. *v.3 p.516*
Cohen, Jean L. *v.4 p.471*
Cohen, Jeffrey E. *v.4 p.529*
Cohen, Jeffrey J. & Fish, Marian C. *v.4 p.352*
Cohen, Jerome A. (Editor) *v.4 p.475*
Cohen, Joel I. *v.5 p.7*
Cohen, Jonathan (Editor) *v.4 p.303, p.356, p.362*
Cohen, Joseph (Editor) *v.2 p.328*
Cohen, Karl F. *v.6 p.307*
Cohen, Lawrence *v.6 p.153*
Cohen, Leonard *v.2 p.734*
Cohen, Lester H. *v.3 p.407*
Cohen, Lizabeth *v.6 p.711*
Cohen, M. L. & Chelikowsky, J. R. *v.5 p.555*
Cohen, Mark A. *v.6 p.247*
Cohen, Mark R. . . *v.1 p.548, v.3 p.67, v.6 p.573, p.596, p.635*
Cohen, Mark *v.2 p.729*
Cohen, Matt *v.2 p.734*
Cohen, Michael *v.5 p.78*
Cohen, Morris R. & Nagel, Ernest *v.1 p.492*
Cohen, Morton N. *v.2 p.277*
Cohen, Norm *v.1 p.295*
Cohen, Paul A. & Townsend, Paul A. . . *v.6 p.183, p.188, p.203*
Cohen, Paul A. *v.6 p.188, p.203, p.218*
Cohen, Philip K. *v.2 p.320*
Cohen, R. *v.3 p.322*
Cohen, Rich *v.1 p.267, p.383*
Cohen, Robert *v.3 p.322, v.4 p.331*
Cohen, S. G. *v.5 p.292*
Cohen, Sarah B. (Editor, Introduction by) *v.2 p.24*
Cohen, Saul B. *v.3 p.372, v.4 p.374*
Cohen, Saul Bernard *v.4 p.487, p.495*
Cohen, Selma J. (Editor, Introduction by) . . . *v.1 p.26, p.40*
Cohen, Selma J. (Editor) *v.1 p.23, p.40, p.41*
Cohen, Selma Jeanne & Dorris, George (Editors) *v.1 p.3*
Cohen, Shaye J. D. *v.1 p.547, v.3 p.7*
Cohen, Sherrill & Taub, Nadine (Editors) *v.4 p.447*
Cohen, Stanley & Taylor, Laurie *v.4 p.774*
Cohen, Stanley *v.4 p.751*
Cohen, Stephen F. *v.3 p.222, p.387*
Cohen, Stephen Philip *v.4 p.643, p.645*
Cohen, Steve (Editor), et al. *v.4 p.178*
Cohen, Ted *v.2 p.585*
Cohen, Thomas V. & Cohen, Elizabeth S. *v.3 p.200*
Cohen, Walter *v.1 p.74, p.95*
Cohen, Warren I. & Tucker, Nancy B. (Editors) . . . *v.3 p.468*
Cohen, Warren I. . *v.3 p.385, p.387, p.440, p.446, p.468, v.6 p.180, p.182, p.203, p.218*
Cohen, William A. *v.4 p.70*
Cohen, William B. *v.6 p.56*
Cohen-Solal, Annie *v.2 p.527*

Cohen-Stratyner, Barbara (Introduction by) . . *v.1 p.112, p.137, p.140, p.143*
Cohen-Stratyner, Barbara *v.1 p.3*
Cohen-Tannoudji, Claude, et al. *v.5 p.549, p.566*
Cohen-Tanugi, Laurent *v.4 p.563*
Cohn, Arthur *v.1 p.238*
Cohn, Bernard S. *v.6 p.146*
Cohn, Bernard S *v.6 p.153*
Cohn, Norman *v.1 p.600*
Cohn, Robert G. & Gillespie, Gerald E. (Editors) . . . *v.2 p.496*
Cohn, Robert G. *v.2 p.496, p.498*
Cohn, Sam *v.3 p.42, p.70*
Cohn, Samuel K. Jr. *v.3 p.199*
Cohn-Sherbok, Daniel *v.4 p.381*
Cohodas, Nadine *v.1 p.383, v.3 p.457*
Cohoon, J. McGrath *v.5 p.342*
Coiro, Ann B. *v.2 p.249*
Coit, Margaret L. *v.3 p.457*
Coker, Paddy & Ganderton, Paul *v.4 p.394*
Cokinos, Christopher *v.6 p.290*
Colacurcio, Michael J. *v.2 p.40*
Colander, David C. & Holt, Richard P. F. *v.4 p.185*
Colander, David C. *v.4 p.195*
Colangelo, Nicholas & Davis, Gary A. *v.5 p.575*
Colbert, David (Editor) *v.3 p.371*
Coldewey, John C. (Editor) *v.1 p.63, p.73, p.99*
Coldiron, Margaret *v.1 p.132, p.144*
Colditz, Graham A. (Editor), et al. *v.5 p.523*
Coldstream, J. N. *v.3 p.16*
Coldstream, Nicola *v.1 p.786, p.796*
Cole, Arthur C. *v.3 p.394*
Cole Christensen, Darryl *v.3 p.268*
Cole, David *v.4 p.460, p.563, p.572*
Cole, Donald B. *v.3 p.416*
Cole, Donald Powell *v.6 p.596*
Cole, Douglas *v.2 p.220, v.4 p.4, v.6 p.678, p.702*
Cole, G. H. A. & Woolfson, M. M. *v.5 p.69, p.434*
Cole, Henri *v.2 p.143*
Cole, Herbert & Turner, Jane (Editors) *v.1 p.663, p.689*
Cole, Jeffrey A. *v.3 p.323*
Cole, John R. *v.2 p.476*
Cole, Johnnetta B. & Guy-Sheftall, Beverly . *v.4 p.743, v.6 p.4, p.42*
Cole, Jonathan R. & Cole, Stephen *v.5 p.410, p.411*
Cole, Joshua *v.3 p.53, p.148*
Cole, Juan R. & Keddie, Nikki R. *v.1 p.560*
Cole, Juan R.I. *v.6 p.637*
Cole, K. C. *v.5 p.457, p.470*
Cole, Kathleen M. & Sheath, Robert G. (Editors) . . . *v.5 p.208*
Cole, Leonard A. *v.4 p.655, v.5 p.410, p.411*
Cole, Margaret Isabel Postgate *v.4 p.273*
Cole, Michael Wayne *v.1 p.775*
Cole, Michael *v.1 p.389*
Cole, Stephanie & Parker, Alison M. (Editor, Translator, Introduction by) *v.3 p.498*

Cole, Stewart T. *v.5 p.153, p.158*

Cole, Susan *v.1 p.152*

Cole, Thomas R. *v.4 p.741*

Cole, Toby & Chinoy, Helen Krich *v.1 p.152*

Cole, Toby (Editor) *v.1 p.144*

Cole, Wayne S. *v.3 p.457, p.468*

Colebrook, Claire *v.1 p.512*

Coleman, Alexander *v.2 p.688*

Coleman, C. B. (Editor) *v.2 p.465*

Coleman, David C. & Hendrix, Paul F. *v.5 p.212*

Coleman, Debra (Editor), et al. *v.6 p.472*

Coleman, Graham & Jinpa, Thupten (Editors) . . . *v.1 p.565*

Coleman, James S. *v.4 p.716, v.6 p.55*

Coleman, Kathleen *v.2 p.460*

Coleman, Kenneth (Editor) *v.3 p.503*

Coleman, Kenneth *v.3 p.503*

Coleman, Penny *v.6 p.380*

Coleman, Ronny J. *v.5 p.311*

Coleman, Simon & Eade, John (Editors) *v.1 p.530*

Coleman, Walter *v.4 p.124*

Coleridge, Samuel Taylor & Jackson, J. R. *v.2 p.279*

Coleridge, Samuel Taylor *v.2 p.228, p.279, p.280*

Coles, Catherine & Mack, Beverly (Editors) *v.6 p.71*

Coles, Harry L. *v.3 p.416*

Coles, Robert . . . *v.4 p.719, p.736, p.755, v.5 p.633, v.6 p.29*

Coletta, Paolo E. *v.3 p.433, p.468*

Colette & McLeod, Enid *v.2 p.514*

Colette & Senhouse, Roger *v.2 p.515*

Colette, et al. *v.2 p.514*

Colette, Sidonie-Gabrielle *v.6 p.395*

Colette *v.2 p.514, p.515*

Cole-Turner, Ronald (Editor) *v.1 p.595*

Colón, Jesús *v.6 p.535, p.543*

Colón, Jesus *v.6 p.535, p.543*

Colón, Matilde *v.2 p.642*

Coligan, John E. *v.5 p.87, p.165*

Colin, Amery & Curran, Brian A. *v.1 p.821*

Colin, Jean-Paul, et al. *v.2 p.453*

Colish, Marcia *v.1 p.600*

Colker, Ruth *v.4 p.447, v.6 p.464, p.468*

Collado-Vides, Julio & Hofestädt,
Ralf (Editors) *v.5 p.101, p.139, p.148*

Collazos, Sharon P. *v.3 p.304*

Collecott, Diana *v.2 p.88, v.6 p.392*

Colledge, Edmund & McGinn, Bernard (Translators) . *v.1 p.652*

Colledge, Edmund (Editor and Translator) *v.2 p.622*

College Entrance Examination Board . . *v.4 p.293, p.294, p.295*

College Music Society *v.1 p.172, p.405*

Colleran, Jeanne & Spencer, Jenny S. (Editors) . . . *v.6 p.147*

Collett, Jonathan & Karakashian, Stephen (Editors) . *v.5 p.369*

Colletta, Lisa *v.2 p.195*

Collette, Alfred T. *v.5 p.406*

Colley, Ann C. *v.2 p.312*

Colley, Barbara C. *v.5 p.685*

Colley, John L., et al. *v.4 p.85*

Colley, John Scott *v.2 p.221*

Colley, Linda *v.3 p.93, p.106, v.6 p.757, p.763*

Collier, Christopher *v.4 p.542, p.543*

Collier Cochran, Alice *v.4 p.80*

Collier, David *v.3 p.329*

Collier, Gary *v.5 p.651*

Collier, Mark & Manley, Bill *v.3 p.8*

Collier, Maxie D. *v.6 p.346*

Collier, Nathan S., et al. *v.4 p.158*

Collier, Peter & Horowitz, David *v.3 p.455*

Collier, Peter *v.3 p.455*

Collier, Simon & Sater, William F. *v.3 p.350*

Collier, Simon, et al. *v.1 p.20*

Collier-Thomas, Betty & Franklin,
V. P. (Editors) *v.6 p.12, p.42, p.430*

Collier-Thomas, Bettye *v.6 p.35, p.42*

Collin, Finn & Guldmann, Finn *v.1 p.489*

Collin, Finn *v.1 p.500*

Collin, Robert E. *v.5 p.729*

Collin, Simon (Editor) *v.1 p.663*

Collingham, H. A. *v.3 p.153*

Collingwood, R. G. *v.1 p.416*

Collingwood, Robin George *v.1 p.481, p.488*

Collingwood, Tom *v.4 p.795*

Collini, Stefan, et al. *v.3 p.111, p.127*

Collini, Stefan . . . *v.2 p.265, v.3 p.111, p.127, v.6 p.750, p.757*

Collins, Adela Yarbro *v.1 p.632*

Collins, Alan F. (Editor), et al. *v.5 p.610*

Collins, Alan *v.4 p.643*

Collins, Allyson *v.6 p.260*

Collins, Bud (Editor) *v.4 p.843, p.864*

Collins, Catherine Fisher *v.6 p.38, p.42, p.277, p.469*

Collins, Dan S. *v.2 p.252*

Collins, E. J. T. (Editor) *v.4 p.701*

Collins, Edward A., et al. *v.5 p.322*

Collins, Harry M. & Pinch, Trevor *v.5 p.401*

Collins, Heidi *v.4 p.77*

Collins, Irene *v.2 p.267*

Collins, Jane L. *v.3 p.329*

Collins, Jim & Porras, Jerry I. *v.4 p.67*

Collins, Jim *v.4 p.70*

Collins, John J. (Editor) *v.1 p.529*

Collins, John J. *v.1 p.547, p.617, p.618,
p.619, v.5 p.633, v.6 p.700*

Collins, John W. & O'Brien, Nancy Patricia (Editors) . *v.4 p.322*

Collins, Lisa Gail *v.6 p.472*

Collins, Marva & Tamarkin, Civia *v.4 p.337*

Collins, Pamela A. & Scarborough, Kathryn E. . . . *v.6 p.260*

Collins, Patricia Hill *v.4 p.743, v.6 p.31, p.42, p.427*

Collins, Philip *v.2 p.282, v.6 p.744*

Collins, Randall *v.4 p.681, p.694*

Collins, Ray & Green, Pauline *v.4 p.637*

Collins, Robert 0. (Editor, Contribution by) *v.6 p.52*

Collins, Robert O. (Editor, Introduction by) *v.6 p.52*

Collins, Robert O. *v.6 p.59*

Collins, Robert *v.3 p.545*

Collins, Roger *v.3 p.65, p.237, p.243, v.6 p.562*

Collins, Scott *v.4 p.414*

Collins, Tony & Vamplew, Wray *v.4 p.814*

Collins, Tony *v.4 p.804, p.814, p.865*

Collins UK Staff *v.4 p.380*

Collins, Wilkie *v.2 p.280, p.281*

Collins, William C. *v.6 p.273*

Collins, William *v.2 p.243*

Collinson, Diane (Editor) *v.1 p.415*

Collinson, Diane *v.1 p.475*

Collinson, Helen *v.3 p.268*

Collinson, M. P. *v.5 p.4, p.29*

Collinson, Patrick *v.1 p.588, p.601, v.3 p.99, p.120*

Collis, David J., et al. *v.4 p.81*

Collis, John *v.4 p.12*

Collman, James P. *v.6 p.289*

Collodi, Carlo & Castellani Pollidori, Ornella . . . *v.2 p.710*

Collodi, Carlo *v.2 p.710*

Collop, John *v.2 p.243*

Colman, Andrew *v.5 p.593*

Colman, E. A. M. *v.2 p.228*

Colman, George *v.2 p.243*

Colomer, Josep (Editor) *v.4 p.577*

Colonna, M. & Hagemann, Harald (Editors) *v.4 p.234*

Colquhoun, Alan *v.1 p.786*

Colson, Charles W. & Cameron,
   Nigel M. de S. (Editors) *v.1 p.595*

Colton, Kent W. *v.4 p.158, v.6 p.722*

Coltrane, Scott *v.4 p.745*

Colum, Padraic *v.2 p.337*

Columbia University Libraries *v.4 p.611*

Colvim, E. W. *v.5 p.296*

Colvin, Howard *v.1 p.783*

Colvin, Leslie *v.5 p.225*

Colvin, Lucie G. *v.6 p.72*

Colvin, Mark *v.6 p.254*

Colvin, Vonnie, et al. *v.4 p.797*

Colwell, Richard & Richardson, Carol P. (Editors) . *v.1 p.405*

Colwell, Richard J. & Goolsby, Thomas W. . . *v.1 p.397, p.405*

Colwin, Cecil M. *v.4 p.868, p.879*

Coman, Katharine *v.4 p.248*

Comaroff, Jean & Comaroff, John L. *v.1 p.610*

Comaroff, Jean *v.1 p.610*

Comaroff, John L. & Comaroff, Jean *v.1 p.611*

Comas-Diaz, Lillian & Greene,
   Beverly (Editors) *v.6 p.111, p.122, p.141, p.445*

Comba, Peter & Hambley, Trevor W. *v.5 p.303*

Combs, Arthur W. *v.4 p.341, p.347*

Combs, James *v.3 p.370*

Combs, Jerald A. *v.3 p.385*

Comden, Betty & Green, Adolph . . . *v.1 p.249, p.311, p.407*

Comeau, Pauline & Santin, Aldo *v.6 p.688, p.691*

Comenetz, Michael *v.5 p.485*

Comenius, Johann Amos *v.4 p.341*

Comer, David J. & Comer, Donald T. *v.5 p.722*

Comer, Douglas E. & Droms, Ralph E. *v.5 p.345*

Comer, Douglas E. *v.5 p.729*

Comer, James P., et al. *v.4 p.280*

Comerchero, Victor *v.2 p.131*

Comey, Jeremiah *v.6 p.348*

Comfort, Nathaniel C. *v.5 p.131*

Comiskey, Michael *v.4 p.535*

Comito, Terry *v.2 p.128*

Comley, Nancy R. & Scholes, Robert *v.2 p.83*

Commager, Henry Steele & Morris,
   Richard B. (Editors) *v.3 p.407*

Commager, Henry Steele (Editor) *v.3 p.428*

Commager, Henry Steele *v.3 p.365, p.416*

Commager, Steele *v.2 p.434*

Commins, David Dean *v.6 p.606*

Commins, David *v.6 p.626*

Commins, Eugene D. & Bucksbaum, Philip H. . . . *v.5 p.553*

Commire, Anne & Klezmer, Deborah (Editors) . . . *v.6 p.425*

Committee on Animal Nutrition & National
   Research Council Staff *v.5 p.54*

Committee on Challenges for the Chemical
   Sciences in the 21st Century *v.5 p.741*

Committee on Environmental Epidemiolgy, National R . *v.5 p.364*

Committee on Integrating the Science of Early Childhood
   Development, et al. *v.5 p.513*

Committee on Scientific Issues in the Endangered-A . *v.5 p.178*

Committee on the Elimination of Tuberculosis in the United
   States, et al. *v.5 p.532*

Committee on the Role of Alternative
   Farming Methods Staff *v.5 p.4, p.30*

Committee Staff on Fuel Economy of Automobiles
   and L (Editor) *v.5 p.715*

Common Cause *v.4 p.516*

Commons, John R. *v.4 p.249*

Commons, John Rogers *v.4 p.208*

Commons, Michael L., et al. *v.5 p.606*

Commonwealth Secretariat *v.4 p.605*

Communion, The Anglican *v.1 p.582*

Comnena, Anna *v.3 p.63, p.192*

Comparetti, Domenico *v.2 p.446*

Compayre, Gabriel *v.4 p.325*

Compton, Ann *v.1 p.779*

Compton, Robert R. *v.5 p.419, p.420*

Compton-Burnett, Ivy *v.2 p.339*

Comrie, Bernard (Editor) *v.2 p.773*

Comrie, Bernard *v.4 p.18*

Comstock, Gary David *v.6 p.386*

Comstock, Gary (Editor) *v.5 p.78, p.247*

Comte, Auguste *v.1 p.455, p.511, v.4 p.679, p.684*

Conacher, D. J. *v.2 p.407, p.410*

Conan, Michel (Editor) *v.1 p.818*

Conant, James B. *v.4 p.325, v.5 p.408*

Conant, James Bryant *v.4 p.290, p.331, p.341, p.367*

Conant, Jennet *v.5 p.542*

Conant, Kenneth J. *v.1 p.786*

Conant, Roger & Collins, Joseph T. *v.5 p.214*
Conard, Robert C. *v.2 p.604, p.605*
Conaway, Charles F. *v.5 p.737*
Conboy, Katie, et al. *v.6 p.436, p.478*
Conboy, Kenneth J. & Morrison, James *v.6 p.240*
Concina, Ennio *v.1 p.789*
Conde, H. Victor *v.4 p.669*
Conde, Mary & Lonsdale, Thorunn (Editors) . . *v.2 p.767*
Condee, William F. *v.1 p.142, p.146, p.152, p.154*
Condé, Maryse *v.2 p.536*
Condie, Kent C. *v.5 p.442*
Condillac, Etienne Bonnot de *v.1 p.454*
Condominas, Georges & Foulke, Adrienne *v.6 p.166*
Condon, E. U. & Shortley, George H. *v.5 p.562*
Condon, E. W. & Odishaw, Hugh (Editors) *v.5 p.275*
Condon, Margaret E., et al. *v.5 p.600*
Cone, Edward T. *v.1 p.211, p.370*
Cone, James H. & Wilmore, Gayraud S. . *v.1 p.635, v.6 p.31, p.35*
Cone, James H. *v.1 p.635, p.642, v.6 p.29, p.31, p.35*
Cone, Joseph *v.5 p.428*
Cones, John W. *v.6 p.345*
Conforti, Joseph A. *v.1 p.584, v.3 p.484*
Confucius & Slingerland, Edward *v.1 p.418*
Confucius *v.6 p.184, p.207*
Congar, Yves *v.1 p.576*
Congdon, Kristin G. & Hallmark, Kara Kelley . *v.1 p.663, p.684*
Congressional Quarterly, Inc. Staff . *v.3 p.468, v.4 p.526, p.557*
Congressional Quarterly, Inc. *v.4 p.463*
Congreve, William *v.2 p.244*
Conisbee, Philip & Coutagne, Denis *v.1 p.737*
Conkelton, Sheryl (Editor) *v.1 p.766*
Conkey, Margaret W. *v.6 p.450*
Conkin, Paul K. *v.1 p.648*
Conkin, Paul Keith *v.3 p.468*
Conklin, Alfred R. *v.5 p.49*
Conklin, David W. (Editor) *v.4 p.69*
Conklin, Wm. Arthur, et al. *v.4 p.113*
Conlan, Timothy J., et al. *v.4 p.464*
Conlan, Timothy J. *v.4 p.523*
Conley, Patrick T. & Kaminski, John P. (Editors) . . *v.4 p.523*
Conlin, Diane A. *v.1 p.775*
Conlogue, William *v.6 p.287*
Conlon, Raymond (Editor) *v.1 p.63, p.74, p.95*
Conn, P. Michael (Volume Editor) *v.5 p.86*
Conn, P. Michael *v.5 p.115*
Conn, Peter *v.2 p.59, v.6 p.200, p.214*
Connah, Graham *v.4 p.7, v.6 p.52, p.71*
Connally, Nellie & Herskowitz, Mickey *v.4 p.485*
Connell, Des W. & Miller, Gregory J. *v.5 p.705*
Connell, Des. W. et al. (Editors) *v.5 p.310*
Connell, G. *v.2 p.642*
Connell, R. W. *v.4 p.743, p.745, v.6 p.429*
Connell, W. F. *v.4 p.341*
Connelly, John *v.3 p.207*
Connelly, Marc *v.2 p.65*

Connelly, Mark & Welch, David (Editors) *v.4 p.406*
Connelly, Mathew *v.6 p.60*
Connelly, N. G. (Editor), et al. *v.5 p.301*
Connelly, Owen *v.3 p.75*
Connelly, Thomas L. & Jones, Archer *v.3 p.428*
Connelly, Thomas Lawrence & Bellows, Barbara L. . *v.3 p.395*
Connelly, Thomas Lawrence & Jones, Archer *v.3 p.395*
Connelly, Thomas Lawrence *v.3 p.395*
Conner, Daryl R. *v.4 p.72*
Conner, Donna Berry (Editor) *v.5 p.563*
Conner, Janis & Rosenkrantz, Joel *v.1 p.776*
Conner, Jeffrey K. & Hartl, Daniel L. *v.5 p.131*
Conner, Randy P. & Sparks, David Hatfield *v.6 p.374*
Conner, Randy P., et al. *v.6 p.358, p.372*
Connery, Brian A. & Combe, Kirk (Editors) *v.2 p.195*
Conniff, Michael L. & Davis, Thomas J. *v.6 p.11*
Conniff, Michael L. *v.3 p.304*
Conniff, Richard *v.5 p.156*
Connolly, James J. *v.3 p.488, v.6 p.711*
Connolly, Joseph *v.2 p.389*
Connolly, Julian W. (Editor) *v.2 p.104*
Connolly, Peter (Editor) *v.1 p.521*
Connolly, Sean *v.3 p.137*
Connolly, Terry *v.5 p.398*
Connolly, Thomas E. (Editor) *v.2 p.357*
Connor, Marlene K. *v.4 p.745*
Connor, Rachel *v.2 p.88*
Connor, Seymour V. *v.3 p.418, v.6 p.533*
Connor, Steven (Editor) *v.1 p.512*
Connor, Walker *v.3 p.61, v.4 p.494*
Conolly, James & Lake, Mark *v.4 p.6, p.386*
Conolly, L. W. (Editor) *v.2 p.729*
Conolly-Smith, Peter *v.4 p.410*
Conot, Robert E. *v.4 p.477*
Conover, Ted *v.6 p.275*
Conquest, Robert *v.3 p.225*
Conquest, Wendy (Produced by), et al. *v.5 p.458*
Conrad, Alfred H.; Meyer, John Robert *v.4 p.208*
Conrad, Christine *v.1 p.7*
Conrad, David R. *v.4 p.341*
Conrad, James M. *v.5 p.714*
Conrad, Jessie *v.2 p.339*
Conrad, Joseph & Najder, Zdzislaw *v.2 p.340*
Conrad, Joseph *v.2 p.339, p.340, p.341*
Conrad, Margaret R. & Hiller, James K. *v.3 p.543*
Conrad, Peter *v.2 p.166*
Conrad, Robert E. (Editor) *v.3 p.278, p.335*
Conrad, Robert E. *v.3 p.336*
Conradi, Peter J. *v.2 p.372*
Conrads, Margaret C. *v.1 p.737*
Conroy, Hilary *v.6 p.236*
Conroy, Peter V. Jr. *v.2 p.480, p.481*
Considine, Douglas M. (Editor) *v.5 p.33, p.257*
Considine, Glenn D. *v.5 p.386*
Consoli, Joseph P. & Wilhelm, James J. (Editors) . . *v.2 p.700*

Constable, Edwin C. *v.5 p.299*
Constable, Giles *v.1 p.650, v.6 p.570*
Constable, Olivia R. (Editor) *v.3 p.237*
Constable, Olivia R. *v.3 p.237*
Constable, Olivia Remie *v.3 p.65*
Constanda, Christian *v.5 p.487*
Constant, Benjamin *v.2 p.478*
Constant, Caroline *v.1 p.792*
Constantelos, Demetrios J. *v.1 p.569*
Constantinides, G. M. (Editor), et al. *v.4 p.188*
Constantino, Steven M. *v.4 p.303*
Consumer Dummies Staff & Robinson , Tara Rodden . *v.5 p.131*
Contamine, Philippe *v.3 p.35, v.6 p.566*
Conte, Gian Biagio *v.2 p.424*
Conte, John E. Jr. *v.5 p.526*
Conteh-Morgan, Earl *v.4 p.503, p.585, p.611*
Conteh-Morgan, John & Olaniyan, Tejumola *v.2 p.751*
Conteh-Morgan, John *v.1 p.130*
Contento, William G. & Greenberg, Martin H. . . *v.2 p.580*
Contini, Gianfranco (Editor) *v.2 p.699*
Contini, Gianfranco *v.2 p.697*
Conway, Anne *v.1 p.448*
Conway, Brian E. *v.5 p.285*
Conway Greene Publishing Co. Editorial Staff . . *v.4 p.795*
Conway, J. B. *v.5 p.490, p.493*
Conway, Jill Ker, et al. *v.6 p.453*
Conway, John & Smith, Derek *v.5 p.473*
Conway, John B. *v.5 p.490*
Conway, John H. & Guy, Richard K. *v.5 p.475*
Conway, John *v.3 p.545*
Conway, Martin *v.3 p.206*
Conway Morris, Simon *v.5 p.183, p.242*
Conybeare, John A. C. *v.4 p.153, p.664*
Conyer, James L. Jr. & Thompson, Julius Eric . . *v.6 p.4, p.17*
Conyers, James L. (Editor) *v.6 p.14, p.21*
Conze, Edward (Editor, Translator) *v.1 p.563*
Conze, Edward, et al. *v.1 p.563*
Conze, Edward (Translator) *v.1 p.563*
Conze, Edward *v.1 p.561, p.564*
Conzelmann, Hans. *v.1 p.641*
Conzen, M. R. G. & Conzen, Michael P. . . *v.4 p.395, v.6 p.720*
Coogan, Michael D. (Editor), et al. *v.1 p.613*
Coogan, Michael D. *v.1 p.617, v.3 p.7*
Coogan, Tim Pat *v.3 p.138*
Coogan *v.3 p.134, p.138*
Cook, Albert Stanburrough & Tinker, Chauncey B. . *v.2 p.196*
Cook, Alexandra P. & Cook, Noble D. *v.3 p.285*
Cook, Bernard A. *v.3 p.206*
Cook, Blanche Wiesen *v.6 p.390*
Cook, Chris & Paxton, John (Editors) *v.4 p.601*
Cook, Constance E. *v.4 p.295*
Cook, Cornelia *v.2 p.338*
Cook, Curtis (Editor) *v.4 p.586*
Cook, David & Okenimkpe, Michael *v.2 p.758*
Cook, David A. *v.6 p.331*

Cook, David *v.1 p.560*
Cook, Edward Tyas Sr. *v.2 p.305*
Cook, G. Ramsay (Editor) *v.3 p.534*
Cook, G. Ramsay *v.3 p.534*
Cook, Gary D. *v.1 p.397*
Cook, Guy *v.5 p.20*
Cook, Haruko Taya & Cook, Theodore F. *v.6 p.223*
Cook, Ian *v.4 p.491*
Cook, James W. (Translator) *v.2 p.705*
Cook, Laurence Martin *v.5 p.169*
Cook, M. V. *v.5 p.717*
Cook, Maria Lorena *v.3 p.291*
Cook, Michael L. *v.2 p.580*
Cook, N.D. & Lovell, W.George (Editors) *v.3 p.350*
Cook, Nicholas & Pople, Anthony (Editors) . . . *v.1 p.211*
Cook, Nicholas . *v.1 p.195, p.235, p.238, p.306, p.370, p.380, v.5 p.618*
Cook, Nigel P. *v.5 p.722*
Cook, Noble D. *v.3 p.323*
Cook, Perry R. *v.1 p.374*
Cook, R. Dennis & Weisberg, Sanford *v.5 p.483*
Cook, R. James & Baker, Kenneth F. *v.5 p.7*
Cook, Ramsay *v.3 p.536*
Cook, Rebecca J. (Editor) *v.6 p.440*
Cook, Richard I. *v.2 p.251*
Cook, Robert M. *v.1 p.807*
Cook, Scott *v.4 p.28*
Cook, Sharon Anne (Editor), et al. *v.6 p.453*
Cook, Susan C. & Tsou, Judy S. (Editors) . *v.1 p.378, v.6 p.474*
Cook, Sylvia Jenkins *v.2 p.13*
Cook, Terrence E. *v.4 p.764*
Cook, Timothy *v.4 p.533*
Cook, Vivian J. & Newson, Mark *v.2 p.559*
Cook, Warren L. *v.3 p.530*
Cook-Deegan, Robert M. *v.5 p.132*
Cooke, Alan *v.3 p.546*
Cooke, David J., et al. *v.5 p.592*
Cooke, Donald *v.4 p.389*
Cooke, Edward S. Jr., et al. *v.1 p.803*
Cooke, James Francis *v.1 p.397*
Cooke, Mervyn & Horn, David (Editors) *v.1 p.258*
Cooke, Mervyn (Editor) *v.1 p.211, p.229, p.314*
Cooke, Mervyn *v.1 p.211, p.235, p.314*
Cooke, Miriam *v.6 p.478, p.659*
Cooke, Philip (Editor) *v.3 p.203*
Cooke, R. C. & Whipps, J. M. *v.5 p.209*
Cooke Ronald U. et al *v.5 p.424*
Cookson, Catharine (Editor) *v.1 p.656*
Cookson, Peter W. Jr. (Editor), et al. *v.4 p.325*
Cooley, Charles Horton *v.4 p.692, p.693*
Cooley, Dennis *v.6 p.262*
Cooley, John K. *v.4 p.641*
Cooley, Thomas M. *v.4 p.455*
Cooling, Benjamin Franklin III *v.3 p.433*
Coombs, Clyde Hamilton *v.5 p.599*

Coombs, Jan	*v.4 p.163*
Coombs, Philip H.	*v.4 p.325*
Cooney, Robert P. J. Jr.	*v.4 p.554, p.568*
Cooney, Terry A.	*v.3 p.367*
Coons, John E. & Sugarman, Stephen D.	*v.4 p.280*
Coontz, Stephanie	*v.4 p.732, v.5 p.638*
Cooper, Alan (Editor)	*v.4 p.427*
Cooper, Andrew F.	*v.3 p.537*
Cooper, Andrew	*v.4 p.824*
Cooper, Barbara M.	*v.6 p.70*
Cooper, Barry (Editor)	*v.1 p.196, p.306*
Cooper, Barry	*v.1 p.196, p.306*
Cooper, Bruce S. (Editor)	*v.4 p.121*
Cooper, Bruce S.	*v.4 p.296*
Cooper, C. & Darley-Usmar, V. (Editors)	*v.5 p.112*
Cooper, C. David & Alley, F. C.	*v.5 p.705*
Cooper, C. David, et al.	*v.5 p.704*
Cooper, Cary L. & Dewe, Philip	*v.4 p.698, v.5 p.580, p.652*
Cooper, David E.	*v.1 p.505*
Cooper, David (Editor)	*v.5 p.139*
Cooper, David	*v.1 p.211, p.238, p.255, p.305, p.332*
Cooper, Dennis	*v.6 p.395*
Cooper, Dona	*v.6 p.352*
Cooper, Douglas	*v.1 p.737*
Cooper, Edward S.	*v.1 p.779*
Cooper, Emmanuel	*v.1 p.807, v.6 p.407*
Cooper, Frederick	*v.6 p.54*
Cooper, Geoffrey M.	*v.5 p.154*
Cooper, Grosvenor & Meyer, Leonard B.	*v.1 p.370*
Cooper, Guy, et al.	*v.1 p.815*
Cooper, Helen	*v.2 p.168, p.208, p.209*
Cooper, Henry R. (Editor)	*v.2 p.812*
Cooper, James Fenimore	*v.1 p.584, v.2 p.35*
Cooper, James W.	*v.5 p.297*
Cooper, John C.	*v.1 p.633*
Cooper, John M. Jr.	*v.3 p.468*
Cooper, John M.	*v.1 p.163, p.196, p.340, p.426, v.3 p.440*
Cooper, John Michael & Prandi, Julie D. (Editors)	*v.1 p.196, p.331, p.340*
Cooper, John Michael	*v.1 p.196, p.238, p.340*
Cooper, John Milton Jr.	*v.3 p.440, p.468, v.4 p.631*
Cooper, Jonathan	*v.5 p.342, p.343*
Cooper, Martin	*v.1 p.196, p.306*
Cooper, Michael (Editor)	*v.6 p.223*
Cooper, Necia (Editor)	*v.5 p.132*
Cooper, Phillip J.	*v.4 p.461, p.466, p.535*
Cooper, Richard P., et al.	*v.5 p.590*
Cooper, Stephen	*v.2 p.361*
Cooper, Susan Fenimore	*v.5 p.78, p.221*
Cooper, Susan	*v.1 p.37*
Cooper, Wendy A.	*v.1 p.682*
Cooper, Wendy	*v.1 p.800*
Cooper, William C. & Terrill, Thomas E.	*v.3 p.493*
Cooper, William J. Jr.	*v.3 p.494, p.495, v.4 p.520*
Cooper, William S.	*v.5 p.78*
Cooper	*v.1 p.557*
Coopersmith, Stanley	*v.5 p.625, p.631*
Cooperson, Michael	*v.6 p.584*
Coote, Stephen (Editor)	*v.6 p.404*
Cope, Christopher	*v.3 p.158*
Cope, David	*v.1 p.211, p.370, p.386*
Cope, Edward A.	*v.5 p.43*
Cope, Jack	*v.2 p.623*
Cope, Jackson I.	*v.2 p.698*
Cope, Peter	*v.1 p.761, p.762, p.770*
Cope, R. Douglas	*v.3 p.285*
Cope, Richard	*v.6 p.78*
Cope, Wendy	*v.2 p.337*
Copeland, David A. (Editor-In-Chief)	*v.4 p.406*
Copeland, Edward & McMaster, Juliet (Editors)	*v.2 p.267*
Copeland, Robert A.	*v.5 p.119*
Copeland, Roger & Cohen, Marshall	*v.1 p.41*
Copeland, Roger	*v.1 p.28, p.30*
Copenhaver, Brian P.	*v.1 p.435*
Coperman, Harold	*v.1 p.395*
Copi, Irving M. & Cohen, Carl	*v.1 p.492*
Copland, Aaron & Perlis, Vivian	*v.1 p.211, p.318*
Copland, Aaron	*v.1 p.211, p.247, p.318*
Copleston, Frederick Charles	*v.1 p.428, p.431, p.437, p.438, p.455, p.508*
Copleston, Frederick J.	*v.1 p.431, p.432*
Copleston, Frederick	*v.1 p.417, p.450, p.473, p.511*
Copley, Antony	*v.1 p.539*
Copley, Paul	*v.5 p.620, p.623*
Copley, Stephen & Sutherland, Kathryn (Editors)	*v.4 p.218*
Copley, Terence	*v.4 p.333*
Copp, David (Editor)	*v.1 p.483*
Coppel, Stephan	*v.1 p.755*
Copper, John F.	*v.6 p.213*
Coppola, Eileen M.	*v.4 p.347, p.351*
Coquery-Vidrovitch, Catherine	*v.6 p.52, p.449*
Corbett, Edward P. J.	*v.2 p.163*
Corbett, H. Dickson, et al.	*v.4 p.314*
Corbett, Lionel	*v.5 p.633*
Corbin, Charles B. & Pangrazi, Robert B.	*v.4 p.790*
Corbitt, Duvon Clough	*v.3 p.308*
Corbitt, Robert A.	*v.5 p.367, p.706*
Corbridge, Stuart & Harriss, John	*v.6 p.159*
Corcoran, Michael	*v.4 p.860*
Corcos, Alain F.	*v.4 p.17*
Cordasco, Francesco & Bucchioni, Eugene	*v.4 p.311, v.6 p.526*
Cordell, Dennis D. & Gregory, Joel W.	*v.6 p.73*
Cordell, Karl & Antoszewski, Andrzej (Editors)	*v.4 p.596, p.602*
Cordell, Linda	*v.4 p.10*
Cordesman, Anthony H. & Hashim, Ahmed S.	*v.6 p.604*
Cordesman, Anthony H. & Obaid, Nawaf	*v.6 p.626*
Cordesman, Anthony H.	*v.6 p.613, p.626, p.627*
Cordesman, Anthony	*v.4 p.562, p.646, p.648*
Cordilia, Ann	*v.6 p.276*
Cordle, Thomas	*v.2 p.519*

Cordova, Carlos B. *v.6 p.529, p.542*

Cordova, Teresa (Editor), et al. *v.6 p.546*

Core, Harold *v.5 p.41*

Coren, Michael *v.2 p.319*

Corey, Elias James & Cheng, Xue-Min *v.5 p.294*

Corfield, Justin J. & Summers, Laura *v.6 p.170*

Corfield, Justin *v.6 p.173*

Corke, Thomas *v.5 p.717*

Corkin, Stanley *v.6 p.323*

Corlett, J. Angelo *v.6 p.20, p.36*

Corlett, William *v.4 p.501*

Corlew, Robert E. *v.3 p.510*

Corley, R. H. V. & Tinker, P. B. H. . . . *v.5 p.20, p.26*

Cormac, O'Grada *v.3 p.138*

Cormack, Malcolm *v.1 p.737*

Cormack, Robin *v.1 p.671*

Cormen, Thomas H., et al. *v.5 p.335, p.336*

Cormier, Jeffrey *v.3 p.535*

Cornblit, Oscar *v.3 p.325*

Corne, David W. & Fogel, Gary B. (Editors) . *v.5 p.107, p.108*

Corneille, Pierre & Couton, Georges (Editors) . . . *v.2 p.473*

Corneille, Pierre, et al. *v.1 p.63, p.78, p.105, v.2 p.465*

Corneille, Pierre *v.1 p.63, p.78, p.105, v.2 p.473*

Cornej, Petr & Pokorny, Jiri *v.3 p.187*

Cornelius, Steven *v.1 p.277*

Cornelius, Wayne A. *v.3 p.291, v.6 p.717*

Cornell, Joseph *v.5 p.227*

Cornell Legal Information Institute . . . *v.4 p.474, p.475, p.476*

Cornell, Saul *v.4 p.523*

Cornell, Tim *v.3 p.24, v.4 p.12*

Cornell University *v.4 p.367*

Corner, John *v.6 p.309*

Cornford, F. M. *v.1 p.421*

Cornford, Francis Macdonald . *v.1 p.419, p.423, p.500, v.2 p.421*

Cornforth, Derek *v.5 p.421, p.698*

Cornforth, John *v.1 p.799*

Corning, Peter *v.5 p.191, p.201*

Cornish, Alison *v.6 p.564, p.575*

Cornish, Dudley T. *v.3 p.395, p.430*

Cornish-Bowden, A. *v.5 p.119*

Cornish-Bowden, Athel *v.5 p.112*

Cornog, Evan & Whelan, Richard *v.3 p.377*

Corns, Thomas N. (Editor) *v.2 p.181, p.182*

Cornwall, Andrea (Editor) *v.6 p.51*

Cornwall, John & Cornwall, Wendy A. *v.4 p.214*

Cornwall, John & Cornwall, Wendy *v.4 p.241*

Cornwall, Mark *v.3 p.78, p.184*

Cornwell, John F. *v.5 p.548*

Cornwell, Neil (Editor) *v.2 p.793, p.795, p.796*

Cornwell, Neil *v.2 p.802*

Coronil, Fernando *v.3 p.360*

Corpi, Lucha *v.6 p.498*

Corr, Edwin G. & Sloan, Stephen (Editors) *v.3 p.298*

Corradi, Juan E. (Editor), et al. *v.4 p.515*

Corrales, Javier *v.3 p.347, p.360*

Correale, Robert M. & Hamel, Mary (Editors) *v.2 p.209*

Correard, Marie-Helene (Editor), et al. *v.2 p.453*

Corrigan, John (Author, Editor) *v.5 p.633*

Corrigan, John, et al. *v.1 p.525, v.5 p.633*

Corrigan, John S. & Hudson, Winthrop S. *v.1 p.604*

Corrigan, Oonagh & Tutton, Richard *v.5 p.121*

Corrigan, Robert W. (Editor) . *v.1 p.64, p.69, p.71, p.72, p.88*

Corrigan, Robert W. *v.1 p.64, p.69, p.70, p.72, p.90*

Corrigan, Timothy *v.6 p.305*

Corrin, Chris (Editor) *v.6 p.469*

Corrington, Robert S. *v.1 p.440*

Corrsin, Stephen D. *v.1 p.33*

Corsane, Gerard (Editor) *v.1 p.827*

Corsi, Pietro & Weindling, Paul *v.5 p.401*

Corsi, Pietro *v.5 p.230*

Corso, Gregory *v.2 p.65*

Corson, Richard & Glavan, James *v.1 p.150*

Corson, Richard *v.1 p.150*

Cort, John E. (Editor) *v.1 p.538*

Cortada, James W. . . *v.3 p.387, v.4 p.146, p.149, p.155, p.157, p.158, p.165*

Cortazar, Julio *v.2 p.678*

Cortes, Carlos E. (Editor) *v.6 p.519, p.521*

Cortes, Eladio & Barrea-Marlys, Mirta (Editors) . *v.1 p.58, p.127, v.2 p.663*

Cortese, Anthony J. *v.4 p.426, v.6 p.448*

Cortese, Anthony *v.4 p.422*

Cortina, Rodolfo *v.6 p.495, p.505, p.517*

Cortner, Richard C. *v.4 p.535*

Cortot, Alfred *v.1 p.397*

Corum, James S. *v.3 p.160*

Corvi, Roberta *v.1 p.445*

Corvino, John *v.6 p.420*

Corwin, E. S. *v.3 p.413*

Corwin, Edward S. *v.4 p.452, p.453, p.461*

Cory, Donald W. *v.6 p.362, p.381*

Corzo, Miguel A. (Editor) *v.1 p.822*

Cose, Ellis *v.4 p.723*

Cosentino, Marc *v.4 p.169*

Coser, Lewis A. & Rosenberg, B. (Editors) *v.4 p.679*

Coser, Lewis A. *v.4 p.682, p.766*

Cosío Villegas, Daniel *v.3 p.289*

Cosgrave, James F. (Editor) *v.4 p.715*

Cosgrove, Art (Editor) *v.3 p.136, v.6 p.562*

Cosgrove, Art *v.3 p.134, p.136*

Cosic, Bora *v.2 p.811*

Cosmas, Graham A. *v.3 p.435*

Costa, D. Margaret & Guthrie, Sharon R. (Editors) . *v.4 p.823, p.835, v.6 p.437*

Costa, Dora L. *v.4 p.741*

Costa Gomes, Rita *v.3 p.243*

Costa Pinto, Antonio *v.3 p.243*

Costain, Meredith *v.5 p.221*

Costas, Orlando E. *v.1 p.647*

Costello, Peter *v.2 p.503*

Coster, Will *v.4 p.708*
Costigan, Arthur T., et al. *v.4 p.277*
Costigliola, Frank *v.3 p.387*
Costill, David L., et al. *v.4 p.825, p.868, p.879*
Costin, Lela B. *v.4 p.273*
Coston, Charisse Tia Maria (Editor) . . . *v.6 p.258*
Cota-Cardenas, Margarita *v.6 p.498*
Cote, Isabelle & Reynolds, John (Editors) *v.4 p.391*
Cote, Jane M. *v.3 p.138*
Cotera, Martha P. *v.6 p.546*
Cothran, Helen (Editor) *v.6 p.261*
Cothran, James R. *v.1 p.818*
Cothren, Joe Tom & Smith, C. Wayne (Editors) . *v.5 p.20, p.24*
Cotler, Julio *v.3 p.281*
Coton, A.V. *v.1 p.7*
Cott, Nancy F. (Editor), et al. *v.6 p.449, p.453*
Cott, Nancy F. *v.4 p.723, p.739, v.6 p.433, p.466*
Cottam, Martha L., et al. *v.4 p.483, v.5 p.642*
Cotten, Doyice J. & Wolohan, John . *v.4 p.783, p.883, p.900*
Cotter, Anne-Marie Mooney *v.4 p.133*
Cotter, Joseph S. *v.3 p.291*
Cottingham, John G. (Editor) *v.1 p.453*
Cottingham, John G. *v.1 p.453, p.513*
Cottingham, W. N. & Greenwood, D. A. . . . *v.5 p.564*
Cottingham, W. Noel & Greenwood, Derek A. . . . *v.5 p.553*
Cottle, S., et al. *v.4 p.94*
Cottle, Simon *v.6 p.256*
Cotton, C. M. *v.5 p.15, p.16*
Cotton, Christine E., et al. *v.2 p.635*
Cotton, F. Albert, et al. *v.5 p.302*
Cotton, F. Albert *v.5 p.548*
Cotton, James *v.6 p.174, p.176*
Cotton, John L. *v.5 p.578*
Cotton, Simon *v.5 p.307*
Cottrell, Leonard S. & Eberhart, Sylvia *v.3 p.451*
Cottrell, Robert Charles *v.4 p.831, p.850*
Cottret, Bernard *v.1 p.602*
Cottrol, Robert J. (Editor, Translator), et al. *v.4 p.449*
Cottrol, Robert J. (Editor) *v.4 p.449*
Couch, Chris, et al. *v.6 p.727*
Couch, Leon W. II *v.5 p.725*
Coughlin, Lin (Editor), et al. *v.4 p.70*
Coulborn, Rushton (Editor) *v.4 p.490, p.501*
Coulby, David & Jones, Crispin *v.4 p.333*
Coulet, Henri (Editor) *v.2 p.465*
Coulet, Henri *v.2 p.462*
Coulmas, Florian (Editor) *v.4 p.18*
Coulmas, Florian *v.2 p.560, v.4 p.18, p.22*
Coulomb, Fanny *v.4 p.268*
Coulon, Jocelyn *v.4 p.633, p.648*
Coulson, J. & Richardson, J *v.5 p.318, p.741*
Coulson, J. M. & Richardson, J. F. . . . *v.5 p.741*
Coulson, J. M., et al. *v.5 p.318*
Coulson, John Metcalfe *v.5 p.741*
Coultate, T. P. *v.5 p.329*

Coulter, H. David *v.4 p.793*
Council for Agricultural Science and Technology Staff
    (Contribution by) *v.5 p.13*
Council for Exceptional Children
    Staff (Contribution by) *v.4 p.278, p.315*
Council for Exceptional Children *v.5 p.574*
Council of Europe *v.4 p.474*
Counihan, Carole & Van Esterik, Penny . . . *v.4 p.45*
Counihan, Carole (Editor) *v.4 p.45*
Counihan, Carole M. & Kaplan, Steven L. . . . *v.4 p.45*
Countryman, Edward *v.3 p.407*
Countryman, Vern (Editor) *v.4 p.437*
Coupe, Laurence *v.1 p.527*
Couper, Pen *v.5 p.742*
Couperus, Louis *v.2 p.622*
Coupland, A. (Editor) *v.6 p.727*
Coupland, Reginald *v.3 p.539*
Courant, Richard & Hilbert, D. *v.5 p.500*
Courant, Richard, et al. *v.5 p.458*
Courant, Richard *v.5 p.486, p.500*
Courlander, Harold (Editor) *v.2 p.752*
Courlander, Harold . . . *v.1 p.34, p.281, p.291, p.295*
Cournot, Augustin *v.4 p.198*
Courthion, Pierre *v.1 p.737*
Courthope, William J. *v.2 p.236*
Courthope, William John *v.2 p.179*
Courtillot, Vincent *v.5 p.449*
Courtney, Edward *v.2 p.424, p.440*
Courtney, James F., et al. *v.4 p.77*
Courtney, John C. *v.4 p.586, p.588*
Courtney, Susan *v.6 p.321*
Courtney, Thomas H. *v.5 p.324, p.731*
Courtney, Winifred F. *v.2 p.298*
Courtois, Stéphane, et al. *v.4 p.658*
Courtwright, David T. . . . *v.3 p.281, v.4 p.776, v.5 p.663*
Cousins, Ewert (Editor) *v.1 p.571*
Cousteau, Jacques & Dumas, Frederic . . . *v.6 p.293*
Coustillas, Pierre (Editor) *v.2 p.289*
Coutts, Howard *v.1 p.807*
Couturier, Edith Boorstein *v.3 p.285*
Couvillon, Arthur *v.4 p.869*
Covach, John & Boone, Graeme (Editors) . . . *v.1 p.267*
Covach, John *v.1 p.267*
CoVan, James *v.5 p.681*
Covel, Paul F. *v.5 p.233*
Covell, Maureen *v.6 p.67*
Covey, Herbert C. *v.4 p.714*
Cowan, Alexander *v.3 p.43*
Cowan, Brian *v.5 p.272*
Cowan, David *v.6 p.653*
Cowan, Henry J. & Smith, Peter R. *v.1 p.783*
Cowan, Ian B. *v.1 p.603, p.609*
Cowan, J. A. *v.5 p.112, p.327*
Cowan, James A. *v.5 p.327*
Cowan, James P. *v.5 p.367, p.374*

Cowan, Jane K. (Editor) *v.1 p.48*

Cowan, Jane K. *v.1 p.16*

Cowan, Louise *v.2 p.13*

Cowan, Ruth Schwartz *v.3 p.367*

Cowan, Thomas *v.6 p.357*

Cowans, Jon *v.3 p.243*

Coward, Barry *v.3 p.101*

Coward, David & Marivaux, Pierre
Carlet de Chamblain de *v.2 p.480*

Coward, Harold (Editor), et al. *v.6 p.105, p.137*

Coward, Harold (Editor) *v.1 p.529*

Coward, Harold *v.5 p.633*

Coward, Noel *v.1 p.249, p.407, p.411, v.2 p.342*

Coward, Richard (Translator) *v.2 p.465*

Cowasjee, Saros (Editor) *v.2 p.763*

Cowell, Adrian (Produced by, Directed By) . . *v.5 p.353, p.357,
p.370*

Cowell, Adrian *v.5 p.40, p.353, p.356, p.363*

Cowell, Henry *v.1 p.212, p.319, p.370*

Cowell, Mark W. *v.6 p.653*

Cowen, Perle Slavik, et al. *v.5 p.527*

Cowen, Roy C. *v.2 p.596*

Cowen, Tyler *v.1 p.826*

Cowley, John & Oliver, Paul *v.1 p.170, p.258*

Cowper, William *v.2 p.244*

Cox, A. *v.5 p.63*

Cox, Andrew & Kirby, Stephen *v.4 p.531*

Cox, C. Barry & Moore, Peter D. . . . *v.4 p.394, v.5 p.168*

Cox, Cheryl A. *v.3 p.14*

Cox, David R. *v.5 p.409*

Cox, Dianne L. (Editor) *v.2 p.73*

Cox, Donald D. *v.5 p.53, v.6 p.290*

Cox, E. J. *v.5 p.208*

Cox, Edward L. *v.3 p.319*

Cox, Gary P. *v.3 p.141*

Cox, Gary W. *v.4 p.577, p.578, p.604*

Cox, George W. *v.5 p.186, p.191*

Cox, James C., et al. *v.5 p.258*

Cox, Jeffrey N. & Gamer, Michael (Editors) *v.1 p.64, p.78, p.99*

Cox, Jim *v.1 p.267*

Cox, John D. & Kastan, David S. . . . *v.1 p.73, p.99, v.2 p.185*

Cox, Julian & Ford, Colin *v.1 p.766*

Cox, Karen Castellucci *v.2 p.679*

Cox, LaWanda *v.3 p.395, p.424*

Cox, Mary *v.1 p.667, p.712*

Cox, Michael & Drabble, Margaret (Editors) *v.2 p.163*

Cox, P. A. *v.5 p.303*

Cox, R. Merritt *v.2 p.654*

Cox, Richard H. *v.4 p.877*

Cox, Richard J. *v.4 p.115*

Cox, Richard William (Editor), et al. *v.4 p.867*

Cox, Thomas R. *v.5 p.37*

Cox, William Edwin *v.4 p.135*

Coxeter, Harold S. M. & Greitzer, S. L. *v.5 p.495*

Coxeter, Harold S. M. *v.5 p.495, p.497*

Cox-Rearick, Janet, et al. *v.1 p.723*

Coye, Dale F. *v.2 p.222, p.226, p.556*

Coyle, Adrian & Kitzinger, Celia (Editors) *v.6 p.381*

Coyle, Andrew (Editor), et al. *v.6 p.276*

Coyne, Gary S. *v.5 p.259*

Coyne, James C. (Editor) *v.5 p.659*

Coyne, Jerry A. & Orr, H. Allen *v.5 p.198*

Coyne, Michael *v.6 p.324*

Coysh, A. W. & Henrywood, R. K. *v.1 p.798, p.807*

Cozens, Frederick W. & Stumpf, Florence S. *v.4 p.814*

Cozzens, James Gould *v.2 p.65*

CQ Editors *v.4 p.557*

CQ Press Editors *v.4 p.559*

CQ Press Staff (Contribution by) *v.4 p.662*

CQ Press Staff (Editor) *v.4 p.559*

CQ Staff (Editor) *v.4 p.529*

Crabb, Cecil V. Jr. & Mulcahy, Kevin V. *v.3 p.451*

Crabb, Cecil V. Jr. *v.3 p.385*

Crabbe, George *v.2 p.281*

Crabbe, Katharyn W. *v.2 p.387*

Crabbe, M. James C. (Contribution by) *v.1 p.526*

Crabbs, Jack A. Jr. *v.6 p.58, p.637*

Crabtree, John *v.3 p.329*

Crabtree, Pamela (Editor) *v.6 p.555*

Crabtree, Phillip D., et al. *v.1 p.173*

Crace, Jim *v.2 p.337*

Craciun, Adriana & Lokke, Kari E. (Editors) *v.2 p.171*

Crack, Timothy Falcon *v.4 p.169*

Cracraft, James E. *v.3 p.216*

Cracraft, James *v.3 p.209, p.216*

Cracraft, Joel & Donoghue,
Michael J. (Editors) *v.5 p.191, p.198, p.201*

Craddock, Charles Egbert *v.2 p.32*

Craft, Anna *v.4 p.360*

Craft, Donna & Peck, Terrance W. (Contribution by) . *v.4 p.125*

Craft, Robert (Editor) *v.1 p.212, p.360*

Craft, Robert *v.1 p.212, p.359, p.360*

Crafton, Donald *v.6 p.307*

Crafts, N.F.R. *v.3 p.122*

Cragg, Kenneth & Speight, R. Marston (Editors) . . . *v.1 p.557*

Cragg, Kenneth *v.1 p.556, p.558*

Craggs, Stewart R. *v.1 p.159, v.6 p.316*

Craib, Raymond B. *v.4 p.383*

Craig, Albert M. & Shively, Donald H. (Editors) . . *v.6 p.226*

Craig, Albert M. *v.6 p.223*

Craig, Barbara H. & O'Brien,
David M. *v.4 p.569, v.6 p.464, p.469*

Craig, Carolyn Casey *v.1 p.58, p.121*

Craig, Colleen *v.4 p.793*

Craig, Edward (Editor) *v.1 p.416*

Craig, Edward Gordon *v.1 p.56, p.81, p.138*

Craig, Emily A. *v.6 p.266*

Craig, Gordon A. *v.3 p.159, p.160, p.163*

Craig, James R. & Vaughan, David J. *v.5 p.436*

Craig, John J. *v.5 p.710*

Craig, Patricia (Editor) *v.2 p.202*
Craig, Robert J. *v.5 p.603*
Craig, Robert L. *v.4 p.304*
Craig, William Lane & Flew, Antony *v.1 p.498*
Craig, Yvonne *v.4 p.757*
Craik, Derek J. *v.5 p.566*
Craik, T. W. *v.1 p.99, p.144, p.150, p.154*
Craine, Debra & Mackrell, Judith *v.1 p.3*
Crainer, Stuart & Dearlove, Des *v.4 p.176*
Crais, Clifton C. *v.6 p.78*
Cramer, Jan Salomon *v.4 p.199*
Cramer, Richard Ben *v.4 p.850*
Crampton, R. J. *v.3 p.207, p.246, p.251*
Crandall, Richard C. & Crandall, Susan M. *v.1 p.662*
Crandall, Robert W. *v.4 p.419*
Crandall, Russell (Editor), et al. *v.3 p.291*
Crandell, George W. (Editor) *v.2 p.134*
Crane, Eva *v.5 p.26, p.27, p.54*
Crane, Gregory *v.2 p.421*
Crane, Hart *v.2 p.68*
Crane, John O. & Crane, Sylvia *v.3 p.187*
Crane, Jonathan L. *v.6 p.317*
Crane, Stephen *v.2 p.36*
Crane, Susan *v.2 p.209*
Crane, Verner W. *v.3 p.501*
Crang, Mike *v.4 p.399*
Crank, John P. *v.6 p.263*
Crankshaw, Edward *v.3 p.184*
Cranmer, Jeff & Martin, Steven *v.6 p.171*
Crannell, Annalisa (Author, Author, Author) *v.5 p.462*
Cranor, Lorrie Faith & Wildman, Steven S. (Editors) *v.4 p.761*
Cranston, Maurice W. *v.3 p.147*
Cranston, Maurice *v.2 p.458, p.481, p.482, v.3 p.147*
Crapo, James D. (Editor), et al. *v.5 p.518*
Crapol, Edward P. (Editor) *v.4 p.566, p.568*
Crary, Catherine S. (Compiled by) *v.3 p.408*
Crashaw, Richard *v.2 p.243*
Craske, Matthew *v.1 p.686*
Crasnaru, Daniela *v.2 p.816*
Craven, Avery O. *v.3 p.395, p.414, p.424, p.495*
Craven, David *v.1 p.684, v.3 p.266*
Craven, Roy C. *v.1 p.691*
Craven, Toni & Kraemer, Ross S. (Editors) *v.1 p.616*
Craven, Wayne *v.1 p.682*
Craven, Wesley F. *v.3 p.499*
Craven, Wesley Frank *v.3 p.495*
Cravens, R. H. *v.1 p.762*
Craveri, Benedetta *v.3 p.71*
Craw, Robin C., et al. *v.5 p.168*
Crawford, Alan *v.1 p.792*
Crawford, Alistair *v.1 p.762*
Crawford, Bill *v.4 p.841, p.869*
Crawford, Fred & Mathews, Ryan *v.4 p.135*
Crawford, Isabella Valancy *v.2 p.732*
Crawford, James (Editor) *v.2 p.554*

Crawford, Karen & Heaton, Alan *v.5 p.274*
Crawford, Katherine *v.3 p.144*
Crawford, Mark *v.5 p.178, p.356*
Crawford, Michael & Whitehead, David (Editors) . . . *v.3 p.13*
Crawford, Michael *v.3 p.13, p.24, v.5 p.191*
Crawford, Paul *v.2 p.347*
Crawford, R. M. *v.5 p.175, p.183, p.238*
Crawford, Rachel *v.6 p.287*
Crawford, Richard *v.1 p.277*
Crawford, S. Cromwell *v.5 p.247*
Crawford, T. Hugh *v.2 p.136*
Crawford, T. *v.2 p.306*
Crawford, Walter B. *v.2 p.280*
Crawley, Eduardo *v.3 p.347*
Crawley, Jacqueline N. (Editor), et al. *v.5 p.88*
Crawshaw, Steve *v.3 p.159*
Cray, Ed (Editor), et al. *v.4 p.404*
Cray, Ed *v.1 p.295, p.328, v.3 p.457*
Creager, Angela N. H. (Editor), et al. *v.6 p.438*
Creamer, Robert W. *v.4 p.850*
Creasy, Edward Shepherd *v.6 p.589*
Creasy, Robert K., et al. *v.5 p.524*
Creath, Richard & Maienschein, Jane (Editors) *v.5 p.247*
Creed, Robert P. *v.2 p.204*
Creedon, Pamela J. (Editor) *v.4 p.835, p.901*
Creedy, John *v.4 p.195, p.208*
Creef, Elena Tajima *v.6 p.87, p.88, p.89, p.131*
Creel, George *v.3 p.457*
Creel, H. G. *v.6 p.184, p.199*
Creel, Herrlee G. *v.1 p.475*
Creeley, Robert *v.2 p.65*
Creese, Mary R. S. & Creese,
  Thomas M. (Contribution by) *v.5 p.395, v.6 p.438*
Creese, Mary R. *v.5 p.395, v.6 p.438*
Crehan, Kate A. F. *v.4 p.23*
Creighton, Colin & Shaw, Martin (Editors) *v.4 p.766*
Creighton, Donald G. *v.3 p.539*
Creighton, Donald *v.3 p.536*
Creighton, Thomas E. (Editor) *v.5 p.115*
Crellin, John K. *v.4 p.778*
Cremin, Lawrence *v.4 p.325*
Crenshaw, Ben & Hauser, Melanie *v.4 p.860*
Crenshaw, James L. *v.1 p.622*
Cressey, Paul G. *v.6 p.717*
Cresswell, Tim *v.4 p.373*
Cressy, David *v.3 p.99, p.102, p.105, p.127*
Crewe, Emma *v.4 p.606*
Crewe, Ivor & King, Anthony *v.4 p.606*
Crewe, Ivor, et al. *v.4 p.606*
Crews, Frederick C. *v.2 p.40, p.345*
Crews, Phillip, et al. *v.5 p.300*
Cribb, Robert & Brown, Colin *v.6 p.176*
Cribb, Robert & Hoadley, Mason C. *v.6 p.164*
Cribb, Robert *v.6 p.174, p.176*
Crickmer, D. F. & Zegeer, DAvid A. (Editors) *v.5 p.737*

Crim, Keith R. (Editor), et al. *v.1 p.522*

Crimp, Douglas *v.6 p.378*

Criscenti, Joseph T. (Editor) *v.3 p.347*

Crisci, Jorge Victor, et al. *v.5 p.168*

Crisfield, Deborah *v.4 p.840, p.869*

Crisman, Thomas L. *v.5 p.178, p.236, p.241*

Crisp, Colin *v.6 p.337*

Crisp, James E. *v.3 p.508*

Crisp, Quentin *v.6 p.401*

Crisp, Roger *v.1 p.445, p.516*

Cristianini, Nello & Shawe-Taylor, John . . . *v.5 p.340, p.407*

Critchfield, Richard *v.4 p.39*

Critchley, Simon & Schroeder, William (Editors) . . . *v.1 p.510*

Critchlow, Donald T. *v.4 p.523*

Crittenden, Camille *v.1 p.196, p.359*

Croce, Arlene *v.1 p.31, p.39*

Croce, Benedetto . . . *v.1 p.473, p.480, v.2 p.566, p.698, p.704*

Crochet, Treena M. *v.1 p.805*

Crocker, Chester A., et al. *v.4 p.645*

Crocker, Richard & Hiley, David (Editors) *v.1 p.177*

Crocker, Richard L. *v.1 p.176*

Crockett, David *v.3 p.510*

Croft, Janet Brennan *v.2 p.386*

Croft, Robert W. *v.2 p.80, v.6 p.24*

Crofton, Ian & Fraser, Don *v.1 p.159*

Croll, Elisabeth (Editor), et al. *v.4 p.731*

Croly, Herbert D. *v.3 p.436*

Crombie, A. C. *v.5 p.390, v.6 p.575*

Crombie, Alistair Cameron *v.5 p.390*

Cromer, Evelyn Baring *v.6 p.637*

Crompton, Louis *v.4 p.747, v.6 p.364*

Crompton, Paul H. *v.4 p.793*

Crompton, Rosemary & Mann, Michael *v.4 p.722*

Cromwell, Jason *v.6 p.370*

Cromwell, Peter R. *v.5 p.498*

Cronbach, Lee J. *v.5 p.571*

Crone, G. R. *v.4 p.377*

Crone, Gerald Roe *v.3 p.403*

Crone, Patricia & Hinds, Martin *v.1 p.557*

Crone, Patricia *v.6 p.583, p.584*

Crone, Rainer & Salzmann, Siegfried (Editors) *v.1 p.779*

Cronin, A. J. *v.2 p.337*

Cronin, Anthony *v.2 p.333*

Cronin, Gloria L. & Siegel, Ben (Editors) . . . *v.2 p.60, p.129*

Cronin, Gloria L. (Editor) *v.2 p.80*

Cronin, Gloria L. *v.2 p.60*

Cronin, James E. *v.4 p.606*

Cronk, Julie K. & Fennessy, M. Siobhan . *v.5 p.53, v.6 p.290*

Cronk, Quentin C. B. & Fuller, Janice L. *v.6 p.290*

Cronon, William *v.6 p.294, p.295, p.711*

Cronquist, Arthur *v.5 p.207*

Crook, D. P. *v.3 p.395, p.433*

Crook, Larry *v.1 p.291*

Crook, Malcolm *v.4 p.608*

Crook, Tim *v.1 p.94, v.4 p.413*

Crooker, Constance Emerson *v.6 p.266*

Crooks, James B. *v.4 p.543*

Crookshank, Anne & Knight of Glin *v.1 p.731*

Cropley, Arthur *v.4 p.356*

Cropper, William H. *v.5 p.288*

Crosbie, Michael J. & Watson, Donald *v.1 p.785*

Crosby, Alfred W. (Author, Contribution by) . *v.3 p.73, v.6 p.295*

Crosby, Alfred W. *v.3 p.70, p.268, p.271, v.6 p.291*

Crosby, Donald G. *v.5 p.314*

Crosby, Everett U. *v.6 p.555*

Crosby, Faye J. *v.4 p.133*

Crosby, John V. *v.4 p.137*

Crosier, Louis M. (Editor) *v.4 p.296*

Crosland, Margaret *v.2 p.457*

Crosman, Robert *v.2 p.253*

Cross, A. G. ; Smith, G. S. *v.2 p.795*

Cross, Anthony *v.3 p.215*

Cross, F. L. & Livingstone, E. A. (Editors) *v.1 p.594*

Cross, Frank Moore Jr. *v.3 p.7*

Cross, Gary S. *v.4 p.783, p.823*

Cross, Gary *v.4 p.716*

Cross, Ian *v.2 p.744*

Cross, Jonathan (Editor) *v.1 p.212, p.360*

Cross, Jonathan *v.1 p.212, p.312, p.360*

Cross, K. Patricia *v.4 p.319, p.331*

Cross, Nigel *v.3 p.119, v.6 p.739*

Cross, Richard *v.1 p.579*

Cross, Rob & Parker, Andrew *v.4 p.120*

Cross, Rod (Editor) *v.4 p.252*

Cross, Wilbur L. & Richey, Alice M. *v.4 p.172*

Cross, Wilbur L. *v.4 p.172*

Cross, William P. *v.4 p.588*

Crossan, John Dominic & Craig, William L. *v.1 p.642*

Crossan, John Dominic *v.1 p.627*

Crosset, Todd W. *v.4 p.815, p.835, p.860*

Crosskey, William W. & Jeffrey, William Jr. *v.4 p.452*

Crossley, John, et al. *v.4 p.786, p.883*

Crossley, Pamela K. *v.6 p.188, p.239*

Crossley, Paul & Frankl, Paul *v.1 p.786*

Crossley-Holland, Kevin *v.2 p.196*

Crossman, R. H. S. (Richard Howard Stafford) . *v.3 p.93, p.119*

Crossman, Richard (Editor) *v.4 p.508*

Croswell, Ken (Contribution by) *v.5 p.69, p.74*

Croswell, Ken *v.5 p.68, p.71*

Croteau, David *v.4 p.547*

Crotty, Shane *v.5 p.126*

Crotty, William (Editor) *v.4 p.503, p.658*

Crotty, William J. (Editor) *v.3 p.483, v.4 p.563*

Crouch, Colin *v.4 p.67, p.121*

Crouch, David *v.3 p.62*

Crouch, Harold *v.4 p.622*

Crouch, T. *v.4 p.847, p.867*

Croucher, Sheila L. *v.3 p.504, v.6 p.537, p.548*

Crouzet, Francois *v.3 p.111*

Crouzet-Pavan, Elisabeth *v.3 p.197, p.204*

Crow, Carl *v.6 p.214*
Crow, D. R. (Editor) *v.5 p.285*
Crow, John A. (Editor) *v.2 p.643*
Crowder, Ralph L. *v.6 p.4, p.17*
Crowder, Robert G. *v.5 p.574*
Crowdus, Gary (Editor) *v.6 p.328, p.340*
Crowl, Daniel A. & Louvar, Joseph F. *v.5 p.681*
Crowley & North *v.5 p.425, p.445*
Crowley, David & Heyer, Paul *v.3 p.37, v.4 p.415*
Crowley, David *v.1 p.719*
Crowley, Jocelyn Elise *v.4 p.739*
Crowley, John W. *v.2 p.3, v.5 p.663, p.673*
Crowley, Joseph Donald (Editor) *v.2 p.41*
Crowley, Leonard V. *v.5 p.514*
Crowley, Mart *v.6 p.411*
Crowley, Martin *v.2 p.515*
Crowley, Terry *v.2 p.560*
Crowley, Tony *v.2 p.551*
Crowne, John *v.2 p.243*
Crowson, Robert L. & Driscoll, Mary Erina *v.4 p.303*
Crowther, Christy & Campling, Jo *v.6 p.255*
Crowther, Jim & Sutherland, Peter (Editors) *v.4 p.319*
Crozier, Andrew J. *v.3 p.74*
Crozier, W. Ray *v.5 p.652*
Cruickshank, John (Editor) *v.2 p.455, p.463*
Cruickshank, John *v.2 p.512*
Cruikshank, Margaret *v.5 p.625, p.632, v.6 p.386, p.445*
Cruise O'Brien, Donal (Editor, Editor) *v.6 p.68*
Crum, Howard A. & Anderson, Lewis E. *v.5 p.209*
Crumley, Carole E. (Editor) *v.4 p.29*
Crumley, Carole E. *v.4 p.29*
Crumlish, Christina *v.4 p.425*
Crump, Andy *v.5 p.353*
Crump, David & Jacobs, George *v.6 p.269*
Crump, Donald J. (Editor) *v.5 p.179, p.233*
Crump, Galbraith M. *v.2 p.253*
Crunden, Robert M. (Editor, Introduction by) . . . *v.3 p.367*
Crunden, Robert M. *v.3 p.436*
Crunden, Robert Morse *v.3 p.367*
Cruse, Amy *v.6 p.738*
Cruse, Harold *v.6 p.24*
Cruse, Howard *v.6 p.395*
Crush, Jonathan *v.6 p.78*
Crutchfield, James A. *v.3 p.519*
Cruz, Angie *v.6 p.505*
Cruz, Arturo J. *v.3 p.301*
Cruz, Consuelo *v.3 p.301, p.303*
Cruz, J. Michael *v.6 p.380, p.381*
Cruz, Jon *v.1 p.281*
Cruz, Nilo *v.2 p.160*
Cruz-Torres, Maria Luz *v.4 p.28*
Crvenkovski *v.2 p.775*
Crystal, David . *v.2 p.226, p.549, p.551, p.552, p.554, p.560, v.4 p.19, v.5 p.620, p.623*
Crystal, Jill *v.6 p.627*

Cseke, Leland J.; Kaufman, Peter B. *v.5 p.126*
Csikszentmihalyi, Mark (Translator, Introduction by) . *v.1 p.418*
Csikszentmihalyi, Mihaly *v.5 p.583*
CSTB Staff *v.5 p.108*
Cua, Antonio S. (Editor) *v.1 p.475*
Cuban, Larry & Shipps, Dorothy (Editors) *v.4 p.325*
Cuban, Larry & Tyack, David B. *v.4 p.297, p.325*
Cuban, Larry & Usdan, Michael D. (Editors) . . . *v.4 p.314*
Cuban, Larry *v.4 p.325, p.351*
Cubberley, Ellwood P. (Editor) *v.4 p.325*
Cubberley, Ellwood Patterson *v.4 p.325*
Cubitt, Geoffrey *v.3 p.148*
Cubitt, Sean *v.4 p.690*
Cuca, Roberto & Pierce, Catherine S. *v.4 p.736*
Cucchi, Maurizio *v.2 p.699*
Cuddon, J. A. *v.2 p.549*
Cuddy-Keane, Melba *v.2 p.392*
Cuevas, Tomasa *v.3 p.242*
Cuff, David J. & Young, William J. *v.5 p.360, p.361*
Cuff, Robert D. *v.3 p.387*
Culbertson, Margaret (Compiled by) *v.1 p.711, p.783*
Cull, Nicholas J., et al. *v.4 p.425*
Cull, Nicholas J. *v.4 p.643, p.646*
Cullather, Nick *v.6 p.179*
Cullen, Christopher M. *v.1 p.432, p.579*
Cullen, Countee *v.2 p.65, v.6 p.24*
Cullen, Francis T. & Applegate, Brandon K. (Editors) . *v.6 p.277*
Cullen, Frank *v.1 p.58, p.90*
Cullen, L. M. (Louis M.) *v.3 p.135*
Cullen, L. M. *v.3 p.135*
Culler, A. Dwight *v.4 p.341, v.6 p.736, p.750*
Culler, Jonathan *v.2 p.566, p.570*
Culley, John H. *v.3 p.527*
Culley, Margo (Editor, Introduction by) *v.6 p.476*
Cullingworth, J. Barry *v.6 p.727*
Cullis, Christopher A. *v.5 p.124, p.139*
Cullwick, Hannah *v.6 p.743, p.747*
Culture Clash *v.6 p.517*
Culyer, A. J. & Newhouse, J. P. (Editors) . *v.4 p.188, p.199, p.264, v.5 p.511*
Cumberbatch, Ellis & Fitt, Alistair (Editors) *v.5 p.683*
Cumbers, Pauline (Translator) *v.1 p.696*
Cumings, Bruce *v.6 p.180, p.236*
Cumming, Elizabeth & Kaplan, Wendy *v.1 p.677, p.799*
cummings, e e *v.2 p.68*
Cummings, Michael R. *v.5 p.132*
Cummings, Robert (Editor) *v.2 p.198*
Cummins, Eric *v.6 p.273*
Cummins, J. G. *v.2 p.643*
Cummins, Light Townsend, et al. *v.3 p.507*
Cumpsty, Nicholas A. *v.5 p.717*
Cundari, Thomas R. (Editor) *v.5 p.299*
Cundy, Catherine *v.2 p.766*
Cuneen, Jacquelyn; Sidwell, M Joy *v.4 p.905*
Cuneo, Terence & van Woudenberg, Rene *v.1 p.450*

Cunha, Euclides Da *v.3 p.339*
Cunico, Robert L., et al. *v.5 p.326*
Cunliffe, Barry W. (Editor) *v.4 p.12*
Cunliffe, Barry W. *v.4 p.12*
Cunliffe-Jones, Hubert & Drewery, Benjamin (Editors) . *v.1 p.633*
Cunningham, Anne S. *v.1 p.818, v.5 p.83*
Cunningham, Anthony *v.5 p.16, p.17*
Cunningham, Conor *v.1 p.509*
Cunningham, Gary, et al. *v.5 p.524*
Cunningham, Helen & Greene, Brenda *v.4 p.172*
Cunningham, Hilary *v.6 p.519, p.540*
Cunningham, Imogen (Photographer) *v.1 p.766*
Cunningham, James P. *v.1 p.21*
Cunningham, John R. *v.4 p.169*
Cunningham, John *v.6 p.337*
Cunningham, Mary *v.1 p.569*
Cunningham, Megan *v.6 p.309*
Cunningham, Merce & Lesschaeve, Jacqueline . . . *v.1 p.7*
Cunningham, Merce *v.1 p.26*
Cunningham, Michael *v.2 p.143, v.6 p.395*
Cunningham, Noble E. Jr. *v.3 p.416*
Cunningham, Patricia M. & Allington, Richard L. . *v.4 p.362*
Cunningham, Stanley B. *v.4 p.425*
Cunningham, Suzanne *v.1 p.516*
Cunningham, Valentine & Wu, Duncan (Editors) . . . *v.2 p.198*
Cunningham, Valentine *v.2 p.178*
Cunningham, William P. (Editor) *v.5 p.353*
Cuno, Kenneth M. *v.6 p.637*
Cupchik, Gerald C. & László, Janos (Editors) . . . *v.5 p.618*
Curb, Rosemary & Manahan, Nancy (Editors) . . . *v.6 p.373*
Curchin, Leonard A. *v.3 p.237*
Curcio, Vincent *v.4 p.153*
Curcio-Nagy, Linda A. *v.3 p.262*
Curd, Patricia (Editor) *v.1 p.421*
Curl, James Stevens *v.1 p.783, p.811*
Curley, E. M. *v.1 p.453*
Curley, Edwin M. *v.1 p.477*
Curnow, Allen *v.2 p.744*
Curnutt, Kirk (Author, Editor) *v.2 p.76*
Curran, Charles E. *v.1 p.575*
Curran, Eileen *v.6 p.739*
Curran, James & Gurevitch, Michael (Editors) . . . *v.4 p.416*
Curran, Noel *v.1 p.500*
Curran, Stuart *v.2 p.311*
Currell, David *v.1 p.93*
Currell, Susan *v.4 p.783, p.823*
Curren, Randall R. *v.4 p.341*
Current, Richard Nelson & Current, Marcia E. *v.1 p.7*
Current, Richard Nelson & Escott, Paul D. (Editors) . *v.3 p.424, v.4 p.520*
Current, Richard Nelson & Lincoln, Abraham . . . *v.3 p.424*
Current, Richard Nelson . *v.3 p.395, p.422, p.423, p.428, p.517*
Current-Garcia, Eugene (Editor) *v.2 p.50*
Currie, David P. *v.4 p.453, p.536*
Currie, Dawn H. *v.6 p.448*

Currie, Elliott *v.4 p.723*
Currie, Philip J. & Padian, Kevin (Editors) . . . *v.5 p.448*
Curry, Anne *v.3 p.143, v.4 p.641, p.643, p.647*
Curry, E. R. *v.3 p.316*
Curry, Lynn & Wergin, Jon F. *v.4 p.295*
Curry, Richard O. (Editor) *v.4 p.458*
Curry, Walter C. *v.2 p.228*
Curta, Florin *v.3 p.62, p.192, p.214*
Curtain, Gregory G. (Editor), et al. *v.4 p.546*
Curti, Merle E. *v.3 p.367, v.4 p.647, p.648*
Curti, Merle Eugene *v.3 p.367*
Curtin, Leah L. *v.5 p.527*
Curtin, Michael *v.4 p.413*
Curtin, Philip D. (Editor) *v.6 p.68*
Curtin, Philip D., et al. *v.5 p.169, p.233*
Curtis, Anthony & Whitehead, John (Editors) . . . *v.2 p.370*
Curtis, C. Michael (Editor) *v.2 p.583*
Curtis, George William *v.2 p.32*
Curtis, Gerald L. (Editor) *v.4 p.621*
Curtis, Gerald L. *v.4 p.621, v.6 p.223*
Curtis, James *v.6 p.418*
Curtis, L. Perry Jr. *v.6 p.737, p.746, p.750*
Curtis, L. Perry *v.6 p.744*
Curtis, Lynn A. & Moyers, Bill (Editors) . . . *v.6 p.254*
Curtis, Michael *v.3 p.83*
Curtis P. Haugtvedt, Karen A. Machleit & Richard Yalch . . *v.4 p.139, p.140*
Curtis, Patricia A. *v.4 p.151, p.165*
Curtis, Penelope *v.1 p.775*
Curtis, Vanessa *v.2 p.392*
Curtis, Verna P. (Editor), et al. *v.1 p.766*
Curtis, Vesta Sarkhosh *v.6 p.670*
Curtis, Will *v.5 p.221*
Curtius, Ernst Robert *v.2 p.448*
Curzan, Anne *v.2 p.554*
Cushing, J. M. *v.5 p.183, p.188*
Cushing, Lincoln *v.1 p.761, v.3 p.308*
Cushman, Claire (Editor) *v.4 p.467*
Cushman, Clare *v.4 p.458*
Cushman, Keith & Ingersoll, Earl G. (Editors) . . . *v.2 p.362*
Cushman, Thomas & Mestrovic, Stjepan G. (Editors) . *v.4 p.652*
Cushner, Kenneth H. (Editor) *v.4 p.313*
Cushner, Nicholas P. *v.3 p.347*
Cusic, Don *v.1 p.267*
Cusimano-Love, Maryann K. *v.4 p.496*
Custen, George F. *v.6 p.314, p.327*
Custer, George Armstrong *v.3 p.519*
Custer, Robert L. & Milt, Harry *v.4 p.777*
Cutcher-Gershenfeld, Joel & Ford, Kevin *v.4 p.78*
Cutileiro, José *v.4 p.701*
Cutler, Brian L. & Penrod, Steven D. . . . *v.4 p.473, v.5 p.592*
Cutler, Irving *v.3 p.515*
Cutlip, Scott M., et al. *v.4 p.172*
Cutlip, Scott M. *v.4 p.428*
Cutnell, John D. & Johnson, Kenneth W. *v.5 p.539*

Cutrufelli, Maria Rosa (Editor) *v.2 p.699*

Cutter, Charles R. *v.3 p.285*

Cutter, Susan (Editor), et al. *v.4 p.374*

Cutter, Susan L. (Editor) *v.5 p.423*

Cutts, John P. (Editor) *v.2 p.198*

Cvancara, Alan M. *v.5 p.227*

Cvetkovich, Ann *v.2 p.190, v.6 p.747, p.755*

Cyert, Richard M. & March, James G. *v.4 p.72, p.83*

Cylkowski, Greg J. *v.4 p.883, p.905*

Cypher, James M. & Dietz, James L. *v.4 p.258*

Cyr, Arthur I. *v.4 p.485*

Cyr, Myriam *v.2 p.458*

Cyrano de Bergerac, Savinien *v.2 p.472*

Cyril of Alexandria *v.1 p.593*

Cytowic, Richard E. *v.5 p.616*

Cyzevs'kyj, Dmytro & Luckyj, George S. *v.2 p.814*

Czaja, Ronald & Blair, Johnny *v.4 p.137*

Czech, Brian, et al. *v.4 p.463*

Czekanowska, Anna *v.1 p.298*

Czepulkowski, B. H. (Editor) *v.5 p.132*

Czerniakow, Adam *v.3 p.83*

Czerniawski, Adam (Editor) *v.2 p.788*

Czerniawski, Adam (Translator) *v.2 p.789*

Czerniawski, Richard D. & Maloney, Michael W. . *v.4 p.427*

Czerwinski, E. J. (Editor) *v.2 p.788*

Czigany, Lorant *v.2 p.785*

Cziko, Gary *v.5 p.202*

D

Da Costa, Emilia Viotti *v.3 p.336*

Da Ponte, Lorenzo *v.1 p.188, p.319, p.320*

da Rosa, Aldo V. *v.5 p.361*

da Sousa Correa, Delia (Editor) *v.2 p.193*

da Vinci, Leonardo, et al. *v.1 p.723*

Daaku, Kwame Yeboah *v.6 p.70*

Daalder, Hans & Mair, Peter (Editors) *v.4 p.601*

Dabakis, Melissa *v.1 p.776*

Dabashi, Hamid *v.6 p.333, p.632*

Dabney, Lewis *v.2 p.137*

Dabney, Virginius *v.3 p.494, p.499*

Dack, M. R. *v.5 p.276*

Dackerman, Susan & Primeau, Thomas *v.1 p.752*

Daddario, Gina *v.4 p.835, p.845, p.902*

Daddow, Oliver J. *v.3 p.87*

Dadge, David *v.4 p.563*

Dadie, Bernard B. *v.2 p.541*

Dadie, Bernard Binlin *v.2 p.542*

Dadié, Bernard Binlin *v.2 p.542*

Dadlez, Anna R. *v.2 p.789*

Dadrian, Vahakn N. *v.4 p.652*

Daemmrich, Horst S. *v.2 p.598, p.599*

Daepp, Ulrich & Gorkin, Pamela *v.5 p.458*

Daftary, Farhad *v.1 p.560*

Dag Hammarskjold Library, United Nations *v.4 p.476*

Dagg, Anne Innis (Editor) *v.2 p.731*

Daglish, Neil D. *v.4 p.333*

Dahl, Carolyn A. *v.1 p.759*

Dahl, Gerhard Melvin *v.5 p.700*

Dahl, Linda *v.6 p.474*

Dahl, Per F. *v.5 p.540, p.542, p.565, p.739*

Dahl, Robert A. (Editor) *v.4 p.575*

Dahl, Robert A. *v.4 p.453, p.503*

Dahl, Robert Alan *v.4 p.503, p.575*

Dahl, Robert *v.6 p.722*

Dahlberg, Edward *v.2 p.69*

Dahlhaus, Carl *v.1 p.173, p.196, p.229, p.365, p.380*

Dahood, Mitchell *v.1 p.621*

Dahrendorf, Ralf *v.4 p.679, p.701, p.724*

Dai, David Yun & Sternberg, Robert J. (Editors) . . . *v.5 p.652*

Daiches, David & Woolf, Virginia *v.2 p.392*

Daiches, David *v.2 p.178, v.3 p.133*

Daiches *v.2 p.166*

Dailey, Denton J. *v.5 p.722*

Dailey, Jane Elizabeth (Editor), et al. *v.3 p.496*

Dailey, Nancy *v.6 p.456*

Dainian, Zhang *v.1 p.475*

Daintith, John (Editor) *v.5 p.112, p.257, p.545*

Daintith, John *v.6 p.285*

Daishonin, Nichiren & Yampolsky, Philip B. . *v.1 p.567, v.6 p.221*

Dake, L. P. *v.5 p.451*

Dakin, Douglas *v.3 p.194*

Dal Co, Francesco & Mazzariol, Giuseppe *v.1 p.792*

Dalai Lama XIV *v.1 p.566, v.6 p.240*

Dale, Alan S. *v.6 p.312*

Dale, Jeremy & Schantz, Malcolm von *v.5 p.132*

Dale, Jeremy W. & Park, Simon F. *v.5 p.132*

Dale, Peter A. *v.6 p.737, p.759*

Dale, Ronald J. *v.3 p.537*

D'Aleo, Joseph S. *v.6 p.285*

Dales, Richard C. *v.6 p.562*

Daley, Allen & Daley, Stella *v.5 p.229*

Daley, Kenneth *v.2 p.305*

Dalgleish, Tim & Power, Mick (Editors) *v.5 p.605*

Dalkir, Kimiz *v.4 p.77*

Dalla Costa, John *v.4 p.70*

Dallaire, Romeo & Beardsley, Brent *v.4 p.715*

Dallek, Robert *v.3 p.377, p.469*

Dalley, Stephanie (Author, Editor, Introduction by,
Notes by) *v.3 p.5*

Dalley, Stephanie (Author, Editor) *v.3 p.5*

Dalley, Stephanie (Editor) *v.1 p.538*

Dallin, Alexander & Firsov, Fridrikh I. (Editors) . . . *v.3 p.225*

Dallin, Alexander *v.3 p.174, p.226*

Dally, James W. & Riley, William F. *v.5 p.688*

Dally, William James & Towles, Brian Patrick *v.5 p.727*

D'Almeida, Irene A. *v.2 p.542*

Dalpe, Jean Marc *v.2 p.540*

Dalrymple, G. Brent *v.5 p.444, p.446*

Dalton, Jack P. (Author, Editor) *v.2 p.357*

Dalton, Kathleen *v.3 p.469*
Dalton, LeRoy C. & Snyder, Henry D. *v.5 p.462*
Dalton, Roque *v.2 p.675*
Dalton, Russell J. *v.4 p.578*
Dalton, Stephen (Author, Photographer) *v.5 p.221*
Dalton, Thomas C. *v.3 p.308*
D'Altroy, Terence N. *v.4 p.11*
Daly, Ann *v.1 p.7, p.26, p.39*
Daly, Augustine *v.2 p.36*
Daly, Brenda *v.2 p.152*
Daly, Herman E. & Farley, Joshua *v.5 p.14*
Daly, Howell V., et al. *v.5 p.26*
Daly, Jim *v.4 p.786, p.880, p.883*
Daly, John A. & Wiemann, John M. (Editors) . . . *v.5 p.647*
Daly, Kathleen *v.6 p.257*
Daly, Mary *v.1 p.655, v.6 p.459, p.461*
Daly, Okasha El *v.6 p.58*
Damas, Léon-Gontran *v.2 p.536*
DaMatta, Roberto *v.3 p.266*
D'Ambra, Eve *v.1 p.669, p.686*
D'Ambrosio, Anna Tobin (Editor) *v.1 p.803*
Dameron, George W. *v.3 p.198, p.199*
Damian, Carol *v.3 p.263*
Damiani, Bruno M. (Introduction by) *v.2 p.651*
D'Amico, Diane *v.2 p.303*
D'Amico, Robert *v.1 p.438*
Damjanov, Ivan *v.5 p.514*
Damon, Gene *v.6 p.361*
Damon, S. Foster *v.2 p.239*
Damon, William *v.5 p.625*
Dampier, William C. *v.5 p.390*
Damrosch, David *v.2 p.568*
Damrosch, Leo *v.3 p.147*
Damrosch, Leopold Jr. (Editor) *v.2 p.171*
Damrosch, Leopold Jr. *v.2 p.239*
Damschroder, David & Williams, David R. . . *v.1 p.165, p.370*
Dana, J. D. *v.5 p.436*
Dana, Nissim *v.6 p.600*
Dana, Richard (Editor) *v.5 p.603*
Dana, Richard Henry Jr. *v.3 p.422, p.423, p.428*
Dana, Samuel T. & Fairfax, Sally K. *v.5 p.37*
Danby, J. M. A. *v.5 p.66*
Dance, Stanley *v.1 p.258, p.332*
Danchin, Antoine *v.5 p.139*
Dancy, Jonathan & Sosa, Ernest (Editors) *v.1 p.482*
Dancyger, Ken & Rush, Jeff *v.6 p.352*
Dancyger, Ken *v.6 p.350*
Dandavati, Annie G. *v.3 p.352*
Dando, Malcolm R. *v.4 p.563*
D'Andrade, Roy G. & Strauss, Claudia J. (Editors) . . *v.4 p.27*
D'Andrade, Roy G. *v.4 p.27*
Dandridge, Rita B. *v.2 p.18, v.6 p.4, p.42*
Daneman, Meredith *v.1 p.23*
Danese, Tracy E. *v.3 p.504*
Daneshvar, Simin *v.6 p.670*

Danesi, Marcel (Editor) *v.4 p.423*
Danesi, Marcel *v.4 p.141*
Danesi, Marcello *v.4 p.424*
Danforth, Loring M. *v.3 p.250*
Dangarembga, Tsitsi *v.2 p.754*
Dangel, Julie Rainer *v.4 p.277*
D'Angelo, John P. *v.5 p.490*
Dangelo, Mark *v.4 p.66*
Dangerfield, George *v.3 p.117, p.118, p.414, p.416*
Dani, A. H. *v.4 p.8*
Danico, Mary Yu & Ng, Franklin *v.6 p.85*
Danico, Mary Yu *v.6 p.135*
Daniel, Carter A. *v.4 p.176*
Daniel, Clete *v.4 p.125, v.6 p.525*
Daniel, Cletus E. *v.6 p.525*
Daniel, E. Valentine *v.6 p.153*
Daniel, Isaac M. & Ishai, Ori *v.5 p.688*
Daniel, John (Editor), et al. *v.4 p.314*
Daniel, John *v.5 p.226*
Daniel, Lisa & Jackson, Claire (Editors) *v.6 p.416*
Daniel, M. *v.5 p.211*
Daniel, Norman *v.1 p.558*
Daniel, Pete *v.4 p.771, v.6 p.283*
Daniel, Samuel *v.2 p.213, p.217*
Daniel, Theodore W. & Helms, John *v.5 p.41*
Daniel, Yvonne *v.1 p.19, v.3 p.308*
Daniell, David *v.3 p.37*
Daniell, Henry & Chase, Christine D. (Editors) . *v.5 p.126, p.163*
Daniell, Jere R. *v.3 p.486*
Daniells, Lorna M. *v.4 p.180*
Danielou, Jean (Editor) *v.1 p.653*
Daniels, Bill, et al. *v.6 p.344*
Daniels, David *v.1 p.165, p.238*
Daniels, Farrington *v.5 p.287*
Daniels, George H. *v.5 p.393*
Daniels, Harvey & Zemelman, Steven *v.4 p.284*
Daniels, Jonathan (Introduction by) *v.3 p.496*
Daniels, Pamela & Weingarten, Kathy *v.4 p.736*
Daniels, Peter T. & Bright, William (Editors) . *v.2 p.560, v.4 p.18*
Daniels, Robert V. (Editor, Translator, Introduction by) . *v.3 p.222*
Daniels, Roger . *v.3 p.531, v.4 p.570, v.6 p.118, p.120, p.126, p.131, p.133*
Daniels, Sarah *v.1 p.99*
Daniels, Stephen *v.1 p.815*
Danielsen, Rolf, et al. *v.3 p.234*
Danielson, Dennis (Editor) *v.2 p.253*
Danielson, Dennis *v.2 p.253*
Danielson, Michael N. *v.4 p.883, p.887, p.896*
Danielson, Virginia *v.1 p.286, p.363, v.6 p.637*
D'Anieri, Paul, et al. *v.4 p.597*
Danilov, Nichita *v.2 p.816*
Danilova, Alexandra *v.1 p.7*
Danly, Robert Lyons *v.6 p.229*
Danly, Susan & Leibold, Cheryl *v.1 p.766*
Dann, Uriel *v.6 p.621*

Dannen, Fredric *v.1 p.383*

D'Annunzio, Gabriele *v.2 p.710, p.716*

D'Annunzio, Gabrielle *v.2 p.716*

Danow, David K. *v.2 p.802*

Danson, M. J. (Editor), et al. *v.5 p.112, p.205*

Dante Alighieri (Editor) *v.2 p.703*

Dante Alighieri . . . *v.2 p.448, p.702, p.703, p.704, v.3 p.69*

Danto, Arthur C. *v.1 p.441, p.466, p.479*

Dantzig, George B. & Thapa, Mukund N. . . . *v.5 p.492, p.493*

Dantzker, David R., et al. *v.5 p.536*

Danzger, M. Herbert *v.1 p.551*

Danziger, Pamela N. *v.4 p.138*

Danziger, Sheldon H. & Weinberg, Daniel H. (Editors) . *v.4 p.253, p.264*

D'Aponte, Mimi G. (Editor) *v.1 p.124, v.6 p.697*

D'Aragona, Tullia *v.1 p.435*

Darbishire, Helen *v.2 p.253*

Darby, H. C. & Versey, G. R. *v.3 p.126*

Darby, H. C. (Henry Clifford) *v.3 p.126*

Darby, Jaye T. & Fitzgerald, Stephanie (Editors) . *v.1 p.121, p.124, v.6 p.697*

Darby, John *v.4 p.648*

Darby, Paul *v.4 p.815, p.847, p.883, p.898*

Darby, Phillip *v.3 p.76*

Darby, William & Du Bois, Jack *v.1 p.255*

Darbyshire, Paul *v.4 p.351*

D'Arcy, Paul *v.4 p.384*

Darcy, Warren *v.1 p.196, p.229, p.365*

D'Arcy, William G. & Keating, Richard C. (Editors) . *v.5 p.155*

Darder, Antonia & Torres, Rodolfo D. (Editors) . . . *v.6 p.486*

Darder, Antonia (Editor) *v.6 p.526*

Dardis, Tom *v.2 p.56, p.73, p.76*

Darío, Rubén *v.2 p.675*

Darga, Amy (Editor) *v.4 p.169*

Darger, Henry *v.1 p.696*

Darian, Steven G. *v.5 p.401, p.406*

Darian-Smith, Kate *v.4 p.384*

Darion, Joe & Wasserman, Dale *v.1 p.249, p.407*

Darity, William A. Jr. & Myers, Samuel L. Jr. . *v.4 p.265, v.6 p.20*

Dark, Eleanor *v.2 p.744*

Darley, Andrew *v.1 p.771*

Darley, Gillian *v.1 p.792*

Darling, David *v.5 p.62, p.183, p.242*

Darlow, Michael *v.2 p.379*

Darmon, Adrian M. *v.1 p.663*

Darnay, Arsen J. (Editor) *v.4 p.166*

Darnell, Adrian C. *v.4 p.188, p.199*

Darnell, J. E. & Lodish, Harvey *v.5 p.154*

Darnell, Regna *v.4 p.4*

Darnton, Robert *v.3 p.147, p.177*

Darrah, Charles N. *v.4 p.39, p.44*

Darrieussecq, Marie *v.2 p.529*

Darst, Robert G. *v.6 p.299*

Dart, Mary M. *v.1 p.33*

Darvas, Ferenc, et al. *v.5 p.139*

Darwall, Stephen *v.1 p.450*

Darwin, Charles & Darwin, Charles *v.3 p.49*

Darwin, Charles . . *v.3 p.48, v.5 p.231, p.236, p.611, v.6 p.291*

Darwish, Mahmoud *v.6 p.606, p.659*

Darwish, Mahmud & Johnson-Davies, Denys . . . *v.6 p.659*

Darwish, Mahmud *v.6 p.659*

Dary, David *v.3 p.521, p.527*

Das, A. *v.5 p.550*

Das, Annapurna & Das, Sisir K. *v.5 p.729*

Das, Braja M. *v.5 p.421*

Das, Dilip K. *v.4 p.664*

Das Gupta, Ashin & Pearson, M. N. *v.6 p.155*

Das, P. K. *v.5 p.701, p.730*

Das, Suranjan *v.6 p.153*

Das, Veena & Poole, Deborah *v.4 p.34*

Das *v.5 p.698*

Dasch, E. Julius (Editor) *v.5 p.417*

Dasgupta, Romit & McLelland, Mark *v.6 p.421*

DasGupta, Shamita D. (Editor) *v.6 p.93, p.137*

Dash, Julie *v.6 p.24, p.42*

Dash, Samuel *v.4 p.473*

Dashefsky, H. Steven *v.5 p.228, p.229, p.244*

Daskalov, Roumen *v.3 p.251*

Daskalov, Rumen *v.3 p.251*

Dasmann, Raymond F. *v.5 p.17, p.29*

Daston, Lorraine & Park, Katharine (Editors) *v.3 p.44*

Date, C. J. *v.5 p.337*

Dates, Jannette L. & Barlow, William (Editors) *v.4 p.416, v.5 p.620, p.624*

Dathorne, O. R. *v.6 p.80*

Datnow, Amanda & Hubbard, Lea (Editors) *v.4 p.301*

Datta, Asim Kumar & Anantheswaran, R. C. (Editors) . *v.5 p.729*

Datta, Prabhat K. *v.4 p.617*

Daube, David *v.1 p.625*

Daubechies, Ingrid *v.5 p.493*

Daubert, T. E. & Danner, R. P. (Editors) *v.5 p.280*

Daubert, T. E. & Foster, Diane (Editors) . . . *v.5 p.281, p.741*

Daubney, Kate *v.1 p.255*

Daudet, Alphonse *v.2 p.488*

D'Augelli, Anthony R. & Patterson, Charlotte J. (Editors) *v.6 p.366, p.381*

Daulaire, Nils (Editor), et al. *v.4 p.668*

Daun, Holger *v.4 p.308*

Dauncey, Hugh & Cannon, Steve (Editors) *v.1 p.267*

Dauncey, Hugh & Hare, Geoff (Editors) . *v.4 p.804, p.843, p.856*

Dauster, Frank (Editor) *v.1 p.127*

D'Avenant, William *v.2 p.217*

D'Avennes, E. Prisse *v.1 p.669, p.690*

Davenport, Francis Garvin *v.3 p.511*

Davenport, John *v.3 p.527*

Davenport, Robert Ralsey *v.6 p.322*

Davenport, T. H. R. & Saunders, Christopher *v.6 p.79*

Davenport, Thomas H. & Prusak, Laurence . *v.4 p.66, p.72, p.78*

Davenport-Hines, Richard *v.2 p.329*

Daverio, John J. *v.1 p.196, p.245*

Daverio, John *v.1 p.196, p.313, p.353, p.354*

Davey, B. A. & Priestley, H. A. *v.5 p.478*

David, Abraham *v.6 p.610*

David, Alfred *v.2 p.209*

David, Charles-Philippe & Levesque, Jacques (Editors) *v.4 p.639*

David, Deirdre (Editor) *v.2 p.194, v.6 p.755*

David, Deirdre *v.2 p.286, v.6 p.478, p.747, p.750*

David, Gilbert et al. *v.2 p.540*

David, Hans T. *v.1 p.183, p.238, p.303*

David, Paul A. *v.3 p.419*

David, Rosalie *v.3 p.8, p.11*

David, Serge *v.5 p.330*

David-Fox, Michael (Editor), et al. *v.3 p.210*

Davidman, Lynn *v.5 p.626, p.652, v.6 p.445*

David-Neel, Alexandra *v.6 p.240*

Davidoff, Lenore *v.6 p.744, p.747, p.761*

Davidoff, Leonore & Hall, Catherine . *v.3 p.111, p.130,v.6 p.743, p.765*

Davidoff, Leonore *v.3 p.92, p.111, p.123*

Davidson, Amanda *v.1 p.779*

Davidson, Arnold E. (Editor) *v.2 p.729*

Davidson, Basil Risbridger *v.6 p.52, p.54*

Davidson, Bruce *v.6 p.12, p.16*

Davidson, Cathy N. *v.2 p.6*

Davidson, Chandler *v.4 p.554, p.573*

Davidson, Clifford *v.1 p.73, p.99*

Davidson, D. & Hintikka, K. J. (Editors) . . *v.1 p.441*

Davidson, D. Kirk *v.4 p.146*

Davidson, Donald *v.1 p.441, p.495, p.514*

Davidson, Douglas V. *v.4 p.724*

Davidson, Eric H. *v.5 p.132*

Davidson, Hilda Ellis *v.3 p.233*

Davidson, Hugh M. *v.1 p.452, v.2 p.476*

Davidson, J. N. *v.5 p.121*

Davidson, J. S. *v.3 p.319*

Davidson, James West *v.3 p.374, v.6 p.213*

Davidson, James *v.3 p.14*

Davidson, Jan, et al. *v.5 p.575*

Davidson, John *v.2 p.275*

Davidson, Marilyn J. & Burke, Ronald J. (Editors) . *v.6 p.456*

Davidson, Michael . *v.1 p.189, p.238, p.343, p.397, v.6 p.478*

Davidson, Miriam & Scott, Jeffry *v.6 p.486, p.521*

Davidson, P. A. *v.5 p.547, p.566*

Davidson, Pamela *v.2 p.797*

Davidson, Richard J. (Editor), et al. *v.5 p.611*

Davidson, Roderic H *v.6 p.621*

Davidson, Ronald M. *v.1 p.567*

Davidson, Russell & MacKinnon, James G. *v.4 p.199*

Davie, Donald *v.2 p.111, p.198, p.342*

Davie, Michael (Editor) *v.2 p.387*

Davies & Austin *v.5 p.329*

Davies, Alan & Elder, Catherine (Editors) . *v.2 p.560, v.5 p.620, p.623*

Davies, Alwyn G. *v.5 p.299*

Davies, Anthony & Wells, Stanley (Editors) *v.6 p.325*

Davies, Anthony *v.6 p.325*

Davies, Brian & Leftow, Brian (Editors) *v.1 p.432*

Davies, Catherine *v.2 p.638*

Davies, Charlotte A. *v.4 p.607*

Davies, David & Elliott, John H. *v.1 p.737*

Davies, David & Elliott, John *v.1 p.737*

Davies, David & Parke-Taylor, Michael *v.1 p.737*

Davies, David T. *v.5 p.298*

Davies, Douglas James *v.1 p.587*

Davies, E. R. *v.5 p.340*

Davies, Eden *v.1 p.41*

Davies, Geoffrey F. *v.5 p.442, p.443*

Davies, Gerald *v.4 p.847, p.865*

Davies, J. Clarence III & Mazurek, Jan *v.4 p.63*

Davies, J. G. (Editor) *v.1 p.654*

Davies, James C. *v.4 p.483, v.5 p.642*

Davies, James *v.4 p.760*

Davies, J.G. *v.1 p.21*

Davies, John Booth *v.1 p.375*

Davies, John H. *v.5 p.555*

Davies, John W. *v.5 p.680*

Davies, John *v.1 p.22, v.2 p.213*

Davies, K. G. (Editor) *v.3 p.408, p.409*

Davies, Kevin *v.5 p.121, p.132*

Davies, Llewelyn *v.3 p.53*

Davies, Mark *v.5 p.717*

Davies, Matt *v.3 p.352*

Davies, Norman *v.3 p.252, p.253, p.254*

Davies, Oliver *v.1 p.609*

Davies, Paul S. *v.5 p.191*

Davies, Paul *v.5 p.112, p.242*

Davies, Peter J. (Editor) *v.5 p.124*

Davies, Peter J. *v.1 p.196, p.306*

Davies, R. G. *v.5 p.212*

Davies, R. R. *v.3 p.132, v.6 p.562*

Davies, R. W. & Wheatcroft, Stephen G. *v.3 p.225*

Davies, R. W. *v.3 p.229*

Davies, Richard O. & Abram, Richard G. . *v.4 p.715, p.899, p.900*

Davies, Richard O. *v.4 p.805*

Davies, Richard W. (Editor), et al. *v.3 p.222*

Davies, Robertson *v.2 p.735*

Davies, Stephen *v.1 p.380*

Davies, Stevie *v.2 p.253*

Davies, Thomas M. Jr. *v.3 p.329*

Davies, W. D. & Finkelstein, Louis (Editors) *v.1 p.547*

Davies, W. D. *v.1 p.626, p.642*

Davies, Wayne K. *v.4 p.378*

Davila, Arlene M. . *v.3 p.319, v.4 p.132, p.138,v.6 p.526, p.548, p.717*

Davila, Thierry, et al. *v.1 p.772*

Davis, A. H. (Translator) *v.2 p.469*

Davis, Allison, et al. *v.4 p.701*

Davis, Angela Y. *v.6 p.29, p.42, p.474*

Davis, Angela *v.4 p.751, v.6 p.277*

Davis, B. *v.1 p.721, p.753*

Davis, Belinda J. *v.3 p.164*

Davis, Brent *v.4 p.339*

Davis, Burke *v.4 p.520*

Davis, Calvin D. *v.4 p.645, p.648*

Davis, Charles T. & Gates, Henry Louis Jr. (Editors) . . *v.2 p.3*

Davis, Charles T. *v.3 p.199*

Davis, Clive *v.1 p.383*

Davis, Cyprian *v.1 p.572*

Davis, Darrell William *v.6 p.335*

Davis, David B *v.4 p.727*

Davis, David Brion *v.3 p.395*

Davis, David E. *v.4 p.386*

Davis, Deta S. *v.1 p.165, p.166, p.386*

Davis, Dick *v.6 p.670*

Davis, Donald Edward *v.4 p.381*

Davis, E. Philip & Steil, Benn *v.4 p.99, p.155, p.162*

Davis, Elizabeth A. & Music Library Association Staff . *v.1 p.166*

Davis, Ellen F. & Hays, Richard B. (Editors) *v.1 p.615*

Davis, Francis *v.1 p.258*

Davis, G. H. *v.5 p.441*

Davis, Gerald (Editor), et al. *v.4 p.718*

Davis, Graham *v.3 p.291*

Davis, Gregson *v.2 p.536*

Davis, Harold Eugene *v.4 p.684*

Davis, Harold T. *v.5 p.486, p.488*

Davis, Herbert J. *v.2 p.262*

Davis, J. R. (Editor) *v.5 p.731, p.734*

Davis, James H. Jr. *v.2 p.473*

Davis, James W. *v.4 p.625*

Davis, Jane *v.4 p.416*

Davis, Jefferson *v.3 p.424, p.428*

Davis, Jennifer S. *v.2 p.160*

Davis, Jessica Milner *v.1 p.90*

Davis, Joel L. *v.5 p.132*

Davis, John B. *v.4 p.226*

Davis, John Bryan *v.5 p.511*

Davis, John C. *v.5 p.419*

Davis, Joseph R. (Editor) *v.5 p.688, p.736*

Davis, Kathy (Editor), et al. *v.6 p.425*

Davis, Kathy *v.6 p.443*

Davis, Kenneth S. *v.3 p.440, p.457, p.524*

Davis, Kenneth Sydney *v.3 p.457*

Davis, Lance E. & Huttenback, Robert A. . . . *v.6 p.745, p.746*

Davis, Madeleine (Editor) *v.3 p.352*

Davis, Martha *v.5 p.680*

Davis, Martin D., et al. *v.5 p.336, p.471*

Davis, Martin *v.5 p.335, p.336, p.342, p.471*

Davis, Meredith, et al. *v.4 p.356*

Davis, Michael D. *v.6 p.41, p.42*

Davis, Michael *v.4 p.489*

Davis, Mike *v.5 p.365, v.6 p.548, p.717*

Davis, Miles & Troupe, Quincy *v.1 p.258, p.320*

Davis, Moshe & Ben-Arieh, Yehoshua (Editors) . . *v.6 p.610*

Davis, Moshe (Editor) *v.6 p.610*

Davis, Moshe *v.6 p.610*

Davis, Natalie Zemon . *v.1 p.601, v.3 p.51, p.144, p.145, p.322, v.6 p.30, p.37*

Davis, Norman, et al. *v.2 p.209*

Davis, Paul *v.2 p.282*

Davis, Philip J. & Rabinowitz, Philip *v.5 p.492*

Davis, Philip J. *v.5 p.491*

Davis, Philip *v.2 p.174, v.6 p.752*

Davis, R. O. & Selvadurai, A. P. S. *v.5 p.698*

Davis, Ralph *v.3 p.39*

Davis, Rebecca Harding *v.2 p.36*

Davis, Richard A. & FitzGerald, Duncan *v.4 p.391*

Davis, Richard B. *v.3 p.495*

Davis, Richard *v.4 p.536, v.6 p.351*

Davis, Robert C. & Marvin, Garry R. *v.3 p.197, p.204*

Davis, Robert C. *v.4 p.727*

Davis, Robert M. *v.2 p.387, v.6 p.324*

Davis, Ronald L. *v.6 p.340*

Davis, Ronald W. *v.4 p.800*

Davis, Rowland H. *v.5 p.132*

Davis, Ruth Frances *v.1 p.286*

Davis, S. H. *v.3 p.339*

Davis, Sara D. & Beidler, Philip D. (Editors) . . *v.2 p.33*

Davis, Stephen F. *v.5 p.675*

Davis, Stephen J. *v.1 p.569, p.599*

Davis, T. Neil *v.5 p.73*

Davis, Thomas W. *v.1 p.617*

Davis, Tracy C. *v.6 p.745, p.747, p.754, p.762*

Davis, Uri *v.6 p.592*

Davis, Wayne A. *v.1 p.490*

Davis, William B., et al. *v.1 p.406*

Davis, William C. *v.3 p.395, p.430, p.508, v.4 p.520*

Davis, William Stearns *v.3 p.67*

Davis, Winston *v.6 p.219*

Davison, Andrew *v.6 p.623*

Davison, Annette *v.1 p.255*

Davison, Judith A. *v.5 p.525*

Davison, Kenneth E. *v.3 p.436*

Davison, Peter *v.2 p.374*

Davison, Richard A. (Editor) *v.1 p.249*

Davison, Roderic H. *v.6 p.589, p.623*

Davis-Russell, Elizabeth (Editor) *v.5 p.636*

Davydov, A. S. *v.5 p.549*

Dawes, Gregory W. (Editor) *v.1 p.627*

Dawesar, Abha *v.6 p.395*

Dawidoff, Nicholas (Editor) . . . *v.2 p.18, v.4 p.811, p.850*

Dawidoff, Robert *v.3 p.376*

Dawidowicz, Lucy S. *v.1 p.548*

Dawisha, A. I. *v.6 p.582*

Dawisha, Karen & Parrott, Bruce (Editor, Contribution by) *v.4 p.585, p.597*

Dawisha, Karen & Parrott, Bruce (Editors) . . *v.4 p.508, p.623*

Dawkins, Heather *v.1 p.677, p.686*

Dawkins, Marvin P. & Kinloch, Graham C. . . *v.4 p.805, p.831, p.860*

Dawkins, Richard & Dennett, Daniel Clement . *v.5 p.143, p.145*

Dawkins, Richard *v.5 p.191*

Dawn, Marva J. *v.1 p.654*

Dawson, Alma & Van Fleet, Connie (Editors) *v.6 p.24*

Dawson, Beth & Trapp, Robert G. *v.5 p.515*

Dawson, Buck *v.4 p.823, p.835, p.845, p.868*

Dawson, Carl (Editor) *v.2 p.265*

Dawson, Christopher *v.3 p.66*

Dawson, John P. *v.4 p.435*

Dawson, Joseph G. III (Editor) *v.3 p.507*

Dawson, Lorne L. *v.4 p.721*

Dawson, Michael C. *v.6 p.4, p.31*

Dawson, Robert MacGregor *v.3 p.539*

Dawson, Robert M. *v.4 p.587*

Day, A. Grove *v.2 p.22, v.6 p.697*

Day, Aiden *v.2 p.171*

Day, Alice T. *v.6 p.445*

Day, Barbara (Editor) *v.1 p.64, p.108*

Day, Clarence *v.2 p.69*

Day, Douglas *v.2 p.367*

Day, Frances Ann *v.6 p.359, p.391*

Day, Graham & Thompson, Andrew *v.4 p.494*

Day, I. N. M. & Ye, S. (Editors) *v.5 p.110, p.121, p.148*

Day, John *v.3 p.39*

Day Lewis, Cecil *v.2 p.342*

Day, Louis A. *v.4 p.417*

Day, Peter *v.1 p.598*

Day, Richard *v.3 p.542*

Day, Robert A. & Gastel, Barbara *v.5 p.680*

Day, Robert *v.5 p.421*

Day, Roger *v.5 p.462*

Day, Timothy *v.1 p.383, p.386*

Day, Trevor *v.4 p.391*

Day, William H. E. & McMorris, F. R. *v.5 p.91*

Dayan, Joan *v.3 p.314*

Dayan, Moshe *v.6 p.613*

Daynes, Kathryn M. *v.4 p.747*

Dazai, Osamu *v.6 p.229*

D'Costa, Gavin *v.1 p.597*

De Almeida, Manuel Antonio *v.2 p.690*

De Armas, Frederick A. (Editor), et al. *v.2 p.647*

De Armas, Frederick A. *v.2 p.640*

de Armas Wilson, Diana *v.2 p.648*

De Bary, W. Theodore & Lufrano, Richard J. . . . *v.6 p.182*

De Bary, William Theodore *v.4 p.616, p.617*

de Bary, Wm. Theodore (Translator) *v.4 p.619, v.6 p.186*

De Beaumarchais, Jean-Pierre *v.2 p.455*

De Bellis, Jack (Editor) *v.2 p.47*

De Berceo, Gonzalo *v.2 p.645*

de Berg, Henk *v.2 p.570*

De Bevoise, Ken *v.6 p.179*

de Blij, H. J. *v.4 p.374, p.376, p.379*

De Blij, Harm J. *v.4 p.373*

de Boer, Jelle Zeilinga & Sanders, Donald Theodore . *v.5 p.437*

De Borja, Riquer i Permanier *v.1 p.789*

de Boulay, Juliet *v.4 p.702*

de Brakelond, Jocelin *v.3 p.66*

De Bruyn, Günter *v.2 p.616*

De Burgh, Hugo (Editor) *v.4 p.408*

De Burgos, Julia *v.6 p.505, p.510*

De Capoa, Chiara *v.1 p.709*

De Carvalho, Fernando J. *v.4 p.226, p.242*

De Caso, Jacques *v.1 p.779*

De Catanzaro, C. J. *v.1 p.653*

de Caulaincourt, Armand *v.3 p.152*

De Certeau, Michel *v.1 p.530*

De Champlain, Samuel *v.3 p.538*

De Chiara, Joseph *v.1 p.785*

De Choisy, Abbe *v.6 p.171*

De Cieza De Le On, Pedro, et al. *v.3 p.325*

De Coulanges, Numa D. & Fustel de
Coulanges, Numa Denis *v.4 p.489*

De Cunzo, Lu Ann & Jameson, John H. *v.4 p.13*

De Datta, Surajit K. *v.5 p.20, p.25*

De Dos, Dirk *v.1 p.737*

de Duve, Christian *v.5 p.78, p.126*

De Duve, Christian *v.5 p.200*

De Felice, Renzo *v.6 p.597, p.640*

De Ferranti, Hugh *v.1 p.288*

De Filippo, Eduardo *v.2 p.715*

De Forest, John W. *v.2 p.36*

De Francis, John *v.6 p.207*

de Garine, I. & de Garine, Valerie *v.4 p.45*

De Gennaro, Angelo A. *v.1 p.473*

de Genova, Nicholas & Zayas, Ana Ramos *v.6 p.542*

De George, Richard T. & De George,
Fernande M. (Editors) *v.1 p.515*

De Geus, Arie *v.4 p.78*

De Gois, Damiao *v.3 p.243*

De Gonzalez, Nelly S. (Compiled by) *v.2 p.682*

de Gournay, Marie Le Jars *v.2 p.469*

De Grand, Alexander *v.3 p.202, p.203*

De Grazia, Edward & Newman, Roger K. *v.4 p.451*

De Grazia, Margreta & Wells, Stanley (Editors) . . . *v.2 p.228*

De Grazia, Victoria *v.3 p.53, p.203*

De Groot, Silvia W. *v.3 p.322*

De Guibert, Joseph *v.1 p.577*

De Gutiérrez, Edith *v.3 p.319*

de Hamel, Christopher *v.3 p.37*

De Hartog, Leo *v.3 p.214*

De Haven, Tom *v.2 p.143*

de Hoffmann, Edmond & Stroobant, Vincent *v.5 p.271*

De Hoveden, Roger *v.3 p.98*

De Hoyos, Angela & Milligan, Mary G. *v.6 p.495, p.510*

De Jesús Hernández-Gutiérrez, Manuel & Foster, David
(Editors) *v.6 p.495, p.498*

De Jesus, Carolina M. *v.3 p.278, p.283, p.336, v.6 p.29*

De Jesus, Joy L. (Editor) *v.6 p.495, p.505*

De Jesus, Melinda L. *v.6 p.111, p.129*

de Jongh, Edward *v.1 p.818*

De Jongh, Nicholas *v.6 p.411*

De Kadt, Emanuel & Williams, Gavin (Editors) . . . *v.4 p.258*

De Kerchove, Rene *v.6 p.285*

De Koster, Katie (Editor) *v.2 p.133*

De Krey, Gary S. *v.3 p.93, p.105, p.106*

de la Barca, Frances Calderon *v.3 p.289*

De La Bruyere, Jean *v.2 p.473, p.474*

De La Campa, Roman *v.3 p.308, v.6 p.488, p.543*

De la Campa, Romban *v.2 p.663*

De la Cruz, Sor Juana Ines *v.2 p.667*

De La Fuente, Alejandro *v.3 p.278, p.308*

De la Garza, Rodolfo O. & DeSipio, Louis (Editors) . *v.6 p.537*

De La Garza, Rodolfo O. & Pachon, Harry (Editors) . *v.6 p.537*

De la Garza, Rodolfo O. *v.6 p.537*

de La Grange, Henry L. *v.1 p.212, p.339*

De la Isla, José *v.6 p.537*

De La Roche, Elisa *v.6 p.517*

De la Taille, Jean *v.2 p.470*

De La Torre, Adela & Estrada, Antonio L. *v.6 p.551*

De La Torre, Adela & Pesquera, Beatriz M.
   (Editors) *v.6 p.486, p.546*

de la Torre, Carlos *v.3 p.333*

De La Torre, Miguel A. & Aponte, Edwin D. *v.6 p.520*

De La Torre, Miguel A. . . . *v.4 p.543, v.6 p.519, p.520, p.537*

De Lafayette, Madame *v.2 p.474*

De Laguna, Asela R. (Editor) *v.2 p.687, v.6 p.506, p.512*

De Lamartine, Alphonse *v.2 p.495*

De Lange, Nicholas R. M. (Editor) *v.6 p.645*

De Larra, Mariano J. *v.2 p.654*

De Lauretis, Teresa *v.6 p.474*

De León, Arnoldo *v.3 p.508*

De Leon, Arnoldo *v.3 p.508, v.6 p.531, p.534, p.548*

De Leon, Fray Luis *v.2 p.650*

De Lorris, Guillaume & De Meun, Jean *v.2 p.466*

De los Reyes, Paulina *v.3 p.352*

de Lucas Vallejo, Carmen *v.2 p.635*

De Madariaga, Isabel *v.3 p.214, p.217*

De Magalhaes De Gandavo, P. *v.3 p.339*

De Man, Paul *v.2 p.570*

De Manrique, Jorge *v.2 p.650*

de Marneffe, Peter & Husak, Douglas N. *v.6 p.253*

De Mauro, Tullio *v.2 p.698*

De Mel, Neloufer *v.2 p.760*

De Mendelssohn, Peter *v.2 p.613*

de Mesquita, Bruce Bueno, et al. *v.4 p.575*

De Mestre, Neville *v.4 p.871*

De Mille, Agnes *v.1 p.5, p.7*

De Mille, James *v.2 p.732*

De Molina, Tirso *v.2 p.650*

De Montclos, Jean-Marie Pérouse *v.1 p.686*

De Montemayor, Jorge *v.2 p.650*

De Montesquieu, Charles-Louis *v.2 p.480*

De Mourgues, Odette *v.2 p.477*

De Oliveira Martins, J. P. *v.3 p.243*

De Oliveira, Nicolas, et al. *v.1 p.771*

De Oliveira, Nicolas *v.1 p.771*

De Paor, Liam *v.1 p.609*

De Pater, Imke & Lissauer, Jack Jonathan . . . *v.5 p.69, p.434*

De Pillis, John *v.5 p.458, p.460*

De Pomerai, David *v.5 p.161*

De Pouplana, Lluis Ribbas (Editor) *v.5 p.200*

De Queiros Mattoso, Katia M. *v.3 p.334*

De Quevedo, Francisco *v.2 p.643, p.650*

De Quincey, Thomas *v.2 p.281, p.282*

De Renzo, D. J. (Editor) *v.5 p.311*

De Ridder-Symoens, Hilde (Editor) . *v.4 p.325, p.326, v.6 p.558*

De Rios, Marlene D. (Editor) *v.6 p.541, p.551*

De Risio, Sergio & Orsucci, Franco F. (Editors) . . . *v.5 p.247*

de Rivas Cherif, Cipriano *v.3 p.241*

de Rojas, Fernando *v.2 p.643*

De Romilly, Jacqueline *v.1 p.427, v.4 p.500*

De Roover, Raymond A. *v.6 p.557*

de Sade, Marquis *v.2 p.483*

De Sales, Francis *v.1 p.576*

De Sanctis, Francesco *v.2 p.698*

De Santis, Christpher C. (Editor) *v.2 p.87*

De Sauvigny, Guillaume *v.3 p.183*

De Sena, Jorge *v.2 p.688*

De Silva, K. M. & Wriggins, W. Howard *v.6 p.163*

De Silva, K. M. *v.6 p.159*

De Silva, Padmasiri *v.5 p.633*

de Soto, Hernando *v.3 p.329*

de Sousa, Geraldo U. *v.2 p.229*

de Souza Briggs, Xavier (Editor) *v.4 p.381, v.6 p.720*

de Souza, Eunice (Editor) *v.2 p.763*

De Sponde, Jean *v.2 p.472*

De Terra, Helmut *v.5 p.396*

de Tocqueville, Alexis . . . *v.3 p.153, p.157, v.4 p.491, p.517*

De Torres Villarroel, Diego *v.2 p.654*

De Valdes, Maria E. & Valdes, Mario J. (Editors) . *v.2 p.682*

De Vallejo, Catharina V. *v.2 p.665*

De Valois, Ninette *v.1 p.7*

De Vany, Arthur S. *v.6 p.344*

De Veaux, Scott *v.1 p.258*

De Vecchi, Pierluigi & Arasse, Daniel *v.1 p.737*

de Villagra, Gaspar Perez *v.6 p.510, p.533*

De Villehardouin, Geoffroi & De Joinville, Jean . . . *v.3 p.63*

De Villiers, Marq & Hirtle, Sheila . . *v.5 p.175, p.240, v.6 p.61*

De Visser, John *v.1 p.789*

De Voragine, Jacobus *v.1 p.579*

De Vos, George A. *v.4 p.702*

De Voto, Bernard A. *v.3 p.519*

De Voto, Bernard Augustine *v.3 p.519*

De Vries, Jan & Van der Woude, Ad *v.3 p.204*

De Vries, Jan *v.3 p.43*

De Vries, Louis & Theo M. Herrmann *v.5 p.387*

De Vries, Louis *v.5 p.387*

De Vroey, Michel *v.4 p.214*

de Waal, Cornelis *v.1 p.440*

de Waal, Edmund *v.1 p.775, p.807*

De Waal, Frans B. M. & Tyack, Peter L. (Editors) . *v.5 p.614*

De Waal, Frans *v.5 p.614*
De Waal, Thomas *v.3 p.231*
De Wagenheim, Olga Jimenez *v.3 p.319*
de Winter, W. P. & Aroroso, V. B. (Editors) *v.5 p.210*
De Witt, Norman W. *v.1 p.429*
De Young, David *v.5 p.68*
Deagan, Kathleen A. & Cruxent, Jose Maria . *v.3 p.316, v.4 p.13*
Deagan, Kathleen A. & MacMahon, Darcie A. *v.4 p.13*
Deak, Istvan (Editor), et al. *v.3 p.207*
Deak, Istvan *v.3 p.182, p.186*
Dean, Andrea Oppenheimer & Hursley, Timothy . . . *v.1 p.792*
Dean, Carolyn (Contribution by) *v.3 p.263, p.325*
Dean, Dennis R. *v.3 p.44, v.5 p.418*
Dean, John A. & Gokel, George W. *v.5 p.290*
Dean, John A. (Editor) *v.5 p.259*
Dean, John Aurie *v.5 p.267*
Dean, John *v.3 p.469*
Dean, Kathryn *v.5 p.642*
Dean, Peter *v.1 p.149*
Dean, Tacita & Millar, Jeremy *v.1 p.677*
Dean, Thomas L. *v.5 p.343*
Dean, Warren *v.3 p.268, p.336, p.339*
Dean, Winton & Knapp, John M. . . . *v.1 p.183, p.229, p.329*
Dean, Winton *v.1 p.183, p.196, p.235, p.312, p.328*
Deanesly, Margaret *v.1 p.609*
DeAngelis, D. L. (Donald Lee) (Editor) *v.5 p.183*
DeAngelis, D. L. (Donald Lee) *v.5 p.163*
DeAngelis, Michael *v.6 p.327, p.328, p.340, p.416*
Deans-Smith, Susan *v.3 p.285*
Dear, I. C. *v.3 p.80*
Dear, Michael J. (Editor) *v.6 p.709*
Dear, Michael *v.6 p.709*
Dear, Peter *v.3 p.46*
Dearborn, Mary V. *v.2 p.3, p.99*
Deardorff, Donald L. II *v.4 p.812*
Dearing, Ronda L. & Tangney, June Price *v.5 p.649*
DeArmond, Stephen J., et al. *v.5 p.616*
Deater-Deckard, Kirby D. *v.5 p.639, p.641*
Deatherage, Scott *v.3 p.387*
Deaver, Michael V. *v.4 p.656*
DeBary, William T. & Bloom, Irene (Editors) . . . *v.6 p.182*
Debary, William T. (Editor) *v.1 p.563*
DeBauche, Leslie Midkiff *v.6 p.322*
DeBenedetti, Charles *v.4 p.649*
DeBerri, Edward P., et al. *v.1 p.575*
Debicki, Andrew P. *v.2 p.639*
DeBonis, Steven *v.6 p.93, p.140*
Debost, Michel *v.1 p.397*
Debré, Patrice *v.5 p.396*
Debroise, Olivier *v.1 p.763*
Debus, Allen G. *v.3 p.46*
Debus, Allen George *v.5 p.391*
DeBusk, Ruth M. *v.5 p.148*
Debussy, Claude, et al. *v.1 p.212, p.320, p.333, p.381*
Debussy, Claude *v.1 p.212, p.229, p.407*

Decalo, Samuel *v.6 p.55*
Decarlo, Raymond A., et al. *v.5 p.720*
DeCew, Judith W. *v.4 p.443*
Decher, Reiner *v.5 p.360*
DeChiara, Joseph, et al. *v.1 p.803*
Decker, Diane C., et al. *v.4 p.167*
Decker, Julie & Chiei, Chris (Editors) *v.1 p.789*
Decker, June Irene & Mize, Monica . *v.4 p.797, p.799, p.800*
Decker, Robert & Decker, Barbara *v.5 p.437*
Decker, Scott *v.6 p.264*
Decker, Steve, et al. *v.6 p.256*
Decker, Wolfgang *v.4 p.805*
Deckker, Zilah Quezado *v.1 p.789*
DeConde, Alexander *v.3 p.387, p.411*
DeCosta-Willis, Miriam (Editor) *v.6 p.17, p.43*
DeCoster, Cyrus *v.2 p.654*
DeCoursey, Patricia J. *v.5 p.616*
Decredico, Mary A. *v.3 p.501*
DeCurtis, Anthony & Rolling Stone Magazine Staff . *v.1 p.267*
Dedijer, Vladimir *v.3 p.248*
Deeb, Lara *v.6 p.605*
Deeb, Marius K. *v.6 p.606, p.607*
Deeming, D. Charles & Ferguson, Mark W. J. (Editors) . *v.5 p.161*
Deepwell, Katy (Editor) *v.1 p.706*
Deer, W. A. (Editor), et al. *v.5 p.436*
Deere, Carmen D. *v.3 p.327*
Deere, Carolyn L. & Esty, Daniel C. (Editors) . *v.6 p.283, p.298*
Dees, Morris *v.4 p.441*
Deese, Helen & Axelrod, Steven G. *v.2 p.136*
Deetz, James *v.3 p.484*
Deffeyes, Kenneth S. . . . *v.4 p.160, v.5 p.451, p.452, p.737*
Deflem, Mathieu (Editor) *v.6 p.251*
DeFleur, Margaret H. *v.4 p.408*
Defoe, Daniel & Rivero, Albert J. *v.2 p.245*
Defoe, Daniel *v.2 p.245, v.3 p.105, p.126*
DeFrancis, John *v.2 p.560, v.6 p.207*
DeFrantz, Thomas (Editor) *v.1 p.18, p.41*
DeFrantz, Thomas F. *v.1 p.18, p.41*
DeFreitas, Gregory *v.6 p.524*
DeGeneres, Betty *v.6 p.419*
DeGeorge, Richard *v.1 p.485, v.4 p.298*
Degler, Carl N. . . *v.3 p.278, p.336, p.379, p.428, p.440, p.446*
DeGowin, Richard L., et al. *v.5 p.520*
DeGraaf, Kathy H., et al. *v.4 p.783, p.787*
DeGraff, Jeff & Lawrence, Katherine A. *v.4 p.66*
DeGregori, Thomas *v.5 p.7*
DeGregorio, Christine A. *v.4 p.533*
Deguy, Michel *v.2 p.529*
Dehejia, Vidya *v.1 p.691, p.777, v.6 p.151*
Dehmel, Richard *v.2 p.606*
Deissmann, Adolf *v.1 p.626*
Deist, Wilhelm & Messerschmidt, Manfred *v.3 p.174*
Dejnozka, Edward L., et al. *v.4 p.339*
Dekan, Jan *v.3 p.191*
Dekker, George *v.2 p.306*

Dekker, Sidney W. A. *v.5 p.587*

Dekker, Thomas, et al. *v.2 p.218*

Dekker, Thomas *v.2 p.217, p.218*

DeKnop, Paul (Editor), et al. *v.4 p.840*

DeKoven, Marianne *v.2 p.190*

Del Aguila, Juan M. *v.3 p.308*

Del Casal, Julian *v.2 p.671*

Del Castillo, Richard G. *v.3 p.527, v.6 p.531, p.545*

del Castillo, Richard Griswold *v.6 p.533*

del Mar, David Peterson *v.4 p.698*

Del Re, Giuseppe *v.5 p.401*

Del Rio, Angel *v.2 p.638*

del Valle-Inclán, Ramón *v.2 p.662*

Del Vecchio, John M *v.2 p.143*

DeLaat, Jacqueline *v.4 p.253, p.273*

Delacoste, Frederique & Alexander, Priscilla
(Editors) *v.6 p.456, p.469*

Delacroix, Eugene & Wellington, Hubert *v.1 p.696*

Delaforce, Angela *v.1 p.674, p.686*

Delahunt, Michael *v.1 p.661*

Delahunty, R. J. *v.1 p.477*

Delamar, Gloria T. *v.2 p.31*

Delamar, Penny *v.6 p.351*

Delamater, Jerome *v.1 p.37*

DeLamater, John & MacCorquodale, Patricia *v.4 p.737*

DeLamater, John D. (Editor) *v.5 p.645*

Delamont, Sara *v.4 p.41, p.743*

DeLamotte, Eugenia *v.4 p.493*

Deland, Margaret *v.2 p.36*

Delaney, C. F. (Editor) *v.1 p.522*

Delaney, Carol L. *v.6 p.621*

Delaney, Kevin J. & Eckstein, Rick . . *v.4 p.880, p.883, p.887*

Delany, Samuel R. *v.2 p.574, v.6 p.395*

Delaporte, Gillemette *v.1 p.802*

Delaporte-Idrissi, Guillemette *v.1 p.802*

Delbo, Charlotte *v.3 p.83*

Delbruck, Hans *v.3 p.35*

DelCarmen-Wiggins, Rebecca & Carter, Alice (Editors) . *v.5 p.602*

Deledda, Grazia & Kozma, Janice M. *v.2 p.717*

Deledda, Grazia *v.2 p.717*

Delehaye, Hippolyte *v.1 p.579*

Deletant, A. & Walker, B. (Translators) *v.2 p.816*

Deletant, Dennis & Alexandrescu, Yvonne *v.2 p.778*

Deletant, Dennis *v.3 p.250*

Deleuze, Gilles & Guattari, Félix *v.1 p.416*

Deleuze, Gilles & Parnet, Claire *v.1 p.456*

Deleuze, Gilles *v.1 p.415, p.456, p.466*

Delgado, Celeste F. & Munoz, Jose E.
(Editors) *v.1 p.19, p.20, v.3 p.266*

Delgado, Maria (Editor) *v.1 p.107*

Delgado, Maria M. *v.1 p.108*

Delgado, Ramon (Editor) *v.1 p.64, p.112, p.113*

Delgado, Ramon *v.1 p.64, p.112, p.113*

Delgado, Richard & Stefancic, Jean
(Editors) *v.4 p.456, v.6 p.521, p.540*

Delgado, Richard *v.4 p.729*

Deliege, Irene & Sloboda, John A. (Editors) . . . *v.1 p.375*

Deliege, Robert *v.4 p.702, v.6 p.153*

DeLillo, Don *v.2 p.143*

DeLio, Thomas *v.1 p.212, p.324*

Delisle, Richard G. *v.4 p.14*

Deliyannis, Deborah Mauskopf (Editor) *v.3 p.62*

Dell, Cecily *v.1 p.38*

Dell, Floyd *v.2 p.119*

Dell, Michael & Fredman, Catherine *v.4 p.157, p.158*

Dell, R. M. & Rand, D. A. J. *v.5 p.285*

Della Paolera, Gerardo & Taylor, Alan M. (Editors) . *v.3 p.346*

Delleur, Jacques W. (Editor) *v.5 p.702*

Delmarcel, Guy *v.1 p.809*

Delmas, Philippe *v.4 p.498*

Delmas, Robert J. (Editor) *v.5 p.112*

Delmendo, Sharon *v.3 p.388*

Delon, Michel (Editor) *v.3 p.71*

Delon, Michel et al. *v.2 p.458*

Deloney, Thomas *v.2 p.213*

DeLong, David W. *v.4 p.78*

DeLong-Bas, Natana J. *v.6 p.625, p.626*

Deloria, Vine & Wilkins, David E. *v.6 p.696*

Deloria, Vine Jr. & DeMallie, Raymond J. . *v.4 p.464, v.6 p.695*

Deloria, Vine Jr. & Lytle, Clifford M. *v.6 p.691, p.695*

Deloria, Vine Jr. & Wilkins, David E. *v.6 p.695*

Deloria, Vine Jr. (Editor) *v.3 p.440, p.446, v.6 p.689, p.691, p.695*

Deloria, Vine Jr. *v.4 p.721, v.6 p.693, p.695, p.700*

Deloria, Vine Jr *v.6 p.701*

Deloria, Vine Jr. *v.6 p.701*

Deloria, Vine *v.6 p.695*

Delpar, Helen *v.3 p.264, p.357*

Delpit, Lisa *v.4 p.309*

Delroy, Constantine-Simms *v.6 p.38*

Delteil, Loys *v.1 p.756*

DeLue, Rachael Ziady & Inness, George Jr. *v.1 p.737*

Delumeau, Jean *v.1 p.600*

DelVecchio, V.G. & Krcmery, V. (Editors) . *v.5 p.115, p.139, p.217*

Delworth, Ursula & Hanson, Gary R. *v.4 p.293*

Delzell, Charles F. *v.3 p.203*

Demana, Franklin D., et al. *v.5 p.485*

Demand, Nancy H. *v.3 p.17, v.6 p.711*

Demarest, Arthur A. & Conrad, Geoffrey W. (Editors) . *v.4 p.11*

DeMaria, Robert Jr. (Editor) *v.2 p.196*

Demastes, William W. (Editor) *v.1 p.58, p.79, p.113*

Demastes, William W. *v.1 p.79, p.113, p.138*

Dembski, William A. & Ruse, Michael (Editors) . . *v.5 p.202*

Dembski, William A. *v.5 p.191*

DeMers, Michael N. *v.4 p.386*

Demers, Patricia A. *v.5 p.247*

Demetrion, George *v.4 p.298, p.304*

Demetrion, James T. (Editor) *v.1 p.737*

Demetz, Peter (Editor) *v.2 p.605*

Demetz, Peter *v.2 p.590*

Demeunynck, Martine (Editor), et al. *v.5 p.121, p.124*

Demick, Jack & Andreoletti, Carrie (Editors) *v.5 p.626*
D'Emilio, John & Freedman, Estelle B. *v.6 p.362*
D'Emilio, John (Editor), et al. *v.4 p.569, v.6 p.388*
D'Emilio,
  John . *v.4 p.569, p.749, v.6 p.365, p.376, p.386, p.387, p.388, p.390*
D'Emillo, John *v.6 p.386*
Deming, Alison H. *v.5 p.78*
Demmel, James W. *v.5 p.472*
Demo, David H. (Editor), et al. *v.5 p.638*
Democratic National Committee *v.4 p.553*
Demorest, Amy *v.5 p.595*
Demos, John Putnam *v.4 p.731, p.733*
Demos, John *v.4 p.702*
Demosthenes *v.2 p.409*
Dempsey, Amy *v.1 p.663, p.677, p.678*
Dempster, Stuart *v.1 p.393, p.397*
Demtröder, W. *v.5 p.562*
Den Hartog, J. P. *v.5 p.688*
Denby, Edwin *v.1 p.39*
d'Encausse, Helene Carrere *v.3 p.223*
Denenberg, Thomas Andrew *v.1 p.802*
Denevan, William M. (Editor) *v.3 p.301, v.6 p.684*
Denham, John *v.2 p.244*
Denhardt, Janet Vinzant & Denhardt, Robert
  B. *v.4 p.545, p.546, p.580*
Denhardt, Robert B. *v.4 p.545, p.580*
Denieul-Cormier, Anne *v.3 p.143*
Denitch, Bogdan Denis *v.4 p.506, p.508*
Denizeau, Gerard *v.1 p.737*
Denligher, Ken *v.4 p.858, p.893*
Denmark, Florence L. & Paludi, Michele A. (Editors) *v.6 p.445*
Dennett, Daniel C. *v.1 p.503, p.545, v.5 p.202*
Dennett, Daniel Clement . . . *v.1 p.496, p.503, p.516, v.5 p.612*
Denney, Ronald C. *v.5 p.270*
Denning, Michael *v.2 p.577*
Dennis, Carina & Gallagher, Richard B. (Editors) . *v.5 p.139*
Dennis, David T. *v.5 p.124*
Dennis, David *v.3 p.178, v.5 p.124*
Dennis, E. S. & Llewellyn, D. J. (Editors) *v.5 p.7, p.20*
Dennis, Everette E. & Snyder, Robert W. *v.4 p.406*
Dennis, Everette E. (Editor), et al. *v.4 p.405*
Dennis, J. M. & Dennis, Mike *v.4 p.609*
Dennis, Lawrence J. & Eaton, William E. (Editors) . *v.4 p.341*
Dennis, Lawrence J. (Editor) *v.4 p.341*
Dennis, Mike *v.3 p.176*
Dennison, Stephanie & Shaw, Lisa *v.3 p.266*
Denniston, Dorothy H. *v.2 p.767*
Denniston, Lyle W. *v.4 p.444*
Denny, Fred I. & Dismukes, David E. *v.5 p.723*
Denny, Fred I. *v.5 p.360*
Denny, Mark W. & Gaines, Steven *v.5 p.92*
Denny, Mark W. *v.5 p.356, p.368, p.564*
Denny, Walter B. *v.1 p.673*
Denoon, Donald & Meleisea, Malama . . *v.4 p.42, v.6 p.130*
DeNora, Tia *v.1 p.377, p.381*

Densmore, Frances *v.1 p.295*
Dent, Borden D. *v.4 p.385*
Dent, D. R. & Walton, M. P. *v.5 p.11*
Dent, D. *v.5 p.9, p.26*
Dent, David W. *v.4 p.641*
Dent, Edward J. . . *v.1 p.99, p.144, p.149, p.154, p.183, p.352*
Dent, H. C. *v.4 p.334*
Dent, N. J. *v.2 p.482*
Dent, Nicholas *v.1 p.454*
Denton, Robert E. Jr. (Editor) *v.4 p.417, p.558*
Denton, Sally & Morris, Roger *v.3 p.529, v.6 p.711*
Denton, Sally *v.3 p.529*
Denvir, Bernard *v.1 p.726*
Department for Economic and Social Affairs Statistics Division
  Staff (Editor) *v.4 p.763*
Department of Animal Science Oklahoma State
  University *v.5 p.53, p.54*
Department of Economic and Social Affairs, Population Division
  Staff *v.4 p.668*
Department of Economic and Social Affairs Staff
  (Editor) *v.4 p.667*
Department of Economic and Social Affairs Staff . . *v.4 p.662*
Department of the Treasury Internal Revenue Service . *v.4 p.464*
DePastino, Todd *v.4 p.757*
Depauw, Karen P. & Gavron, Susan J. *v.4 p.800, p.842*
Depestre, Rene *v.2 p.536*
Depestre, René *v.2 p.535, p.536, p.537*
Depew, David J. & Weber, Bruce H. *v.5 p.202*
Deprez, Kas & Vos, Louis (Editors) *v.3 p.206*
Deputy, Janice (Editor) *v.1 p.52*
D'Erasmo, Stacey *v.6 p.395*
Derbes, Anne *v.1 p.727*
Derby, G. *v.3 p.376*
Derby, Stephen *v.5 p.714*
Derbyshire, John *v.5 p.475*
Derbyshire, William W. *v.2 p.777*
Derderian, Tom *v.4 p.843, p.866*
Deren, Maya *v.1 p.44*
Derks, Scott & Smith, Tony *v.4 p.188*
Derks, Scott *v.4 p.188*
Derleth, August (Editor) *v.2 p.18*
Derman, M. Ugur *v.1 p.673, p.719*
Derman, William *v.6 p.73*
DeRoche, Edward F. & Williams, Mary M. *v.4 p.370*
DeRose, Keith & Warfield, Ted A. (Editors) *v.1 p.517*
Derounian-Stodola, Kathryn Zabelle (Editor, Introduction by,
  Notes by) *v.6 p.478*
Derrida, Jacques & Vattimo, Gianni (Editors) . . . *v.1 p.521*
Derrida, Jacques . *v.1 p.479, v.2 p.567, p.570, v.4 p.496, p.509*
Derry, Gregory Neil *v.5 p.399*
Derry, T. K. *v.3 p.232, p.233, p.234*
Derry, Thomas K. *v.3 p.234*
Dershowitz, Alan M. *v.4 p.658*
Derus, Richard M. (Editor) *v.6 p.360*
Dery, Tibor *v.2 p.785*
Desai, Anita *v.2 p.764*

Author Index

Desai, Babasaheb B. *v.5 p.21, p.47*

DeSalle, Rob (Editor), et al. *v.5 p.126, p.200*

Desalle, Rob *v.5 p.132*

DeSalvo, Louise & Leaska, Mitchell A. (Editors) . . . *v.2 p.392*

Desan, Suzanne *v.3 p.150*

DesAutels, Peggy & Waugh, Joanne *v.1 p.483, v.6 p.461*

Descartes, Rene *v.5 p.399*

Descartes, René *v.1 p.453, p.482*

Deschaumes, Ghislaine Glasson & Ivekovic, Rada . . *v.6 p.159*

Deschodt, Anne-Marie & Davanzo Poli, Doretta . . . *v.1 p.720*

Descombes, Vincent *v.1 p.456*

DeSensi, Joy Theresa & Rosenberg, Danny *v.4 p.786, p.883, p.900*

De-Shalit, Avner *v.5 p.28, v.6 p.299*

Desharnais, Robert, et al *v.5 p.88*

DeShazer, Mary K. *v.3 p.298*

DeShazo, Peter *v.3 p.353*

Deshen, Shlomo & Zenner, Walter P. (Editors) *v.6 p.597*

Designers and Art Directors Association Staff . . . *v.4 p.427*

deSilva, David A. *v.1 p.623*

Desjardins, Chris *v.6 p.335*

Deskis, Susan E. *v.2 p.205*

Deslippe, Dennis A. *v.4 p.121*

Desmond, Adrian *v.5 p.396, v.6 p.750, p.759, p.762*

Desmond, Jane C. (Editor) *v.1 p.41, v.6 p.414*

Desmond, Jane C. *v.1 p.41*

Desnos, Robert, et al. *v.2 p.515*

Desnos, Robert *v.2 p.515*

DeSombre, Elizabeth R. *v.5 p.29, v.6 p.299*

Dess, Gregory G. & Picken, Joseph C. *v.4 p.72, p.78*

Dessaix, Robert (Editor) *v.2 p.742*

Dessen, Alan C. & Thomson, Leslie *v.1 p.140*

Dessen, Alan C. *v.2 p.219*

Dessen, Cynthia S. *v.2 p.439*

Desser, David & Jowett, Garth *v.6 p.344*

Desser, David (Editor) *v.6 p.335, p.344*

Desser, David *v.6 p.335*

Dessler, Andrew E. & Parson, Edward A. *v.6 p.283*

D'Este, Carlo *v.3 p.457, p.469*

Destexhe, Alain *v.4 p.652*

Desti, Mary *v.6 p.414*

Desti-Demanti, Zoe *v.1 p.121*

Destler, I. M. *v.4 p.57, p.567*

Dethloff, Henry C. & Schorn, Ronald A. *v.5 p.719*

DeTinguy, Anne *v.3 p.388*

Dettmar, Kevin J. & Richey, William (Editors) . . . *v.1 p.267*

Dettmar, Kevin J. H. *v.2 p.178, p.572*

Dettwyler, Katherine *v.4 p.45*

Detweiler, Robert & Jasper, David (Editors) *v.2 p.572*

Detwiler, Bruce *v.4 p.491*

Deuchler, Martina *v.6 p.236*

Deustua, Jose R. *v.3 p.327*

Deutsch, Charles *v.4 p.776, v.5 p.663*

Deutsch, Diana (Editor) *v.1 p.375, v.5 p.607, p.618*

Deutsch, Eliot, et al. *v.4 p.677*

Deutsch, Eliot *v.1 p.419*

Deutsch, Karl Wolfgang *v.3 p.61*

Deutsch, Morton & Coleman, Peter T. (Editors) . . . *v.5 p.647*

Deutsch, Otto Erich . *v.1 p.183, p.189, p.196, p.329, p.343, p.354*

Deutsch, Sandra M. *v.3 p.347*

Deutsch, Sandra McGee *v.3 p.334, p.346, p.350*

Deutsch, Sarah Jane *v.6 p.711*

Deutsches Nationalkomitee MAB; Unesco *v.5 p.233*

DeValeria, Dennis & Burke-DeValeria, Jeanne *v.4 p.850*

Devaney, Dennis, et al. *v.4 p.446*

Devaney, Robert L. *v.5 p.488*

Devault, Ileen A. *v.4 p.125*

DeVeaux, Alexis *v.6 p.24, p.43, p.401*

DeVenney, David P. (Annotations by, Compiled by) . . *v.1 p.277*

Dever, William G. *v.1 p.617, p.619*

Deverell, William *v.3 p.531*

Devereux, George (Author, Translator) *v.4 p.35*

Devi, Prathibha *v.5 p.124*

Devine, Jeremy M. *v.6 p.322*

Devine, Robert S. *v.5 p.166, p.182*

Devins, Neal & Whittington, Keith E. *v.4 p.531*

Devins, Neal *v.4 p.447*

DeVita, Vincent T., et al. *v.5 p.520*

DeVitis, A. A. *v.2 p.349*

DeVito, Stephen C. *v.5 p.310*

Devitt, Michael & Hanley, Richard (Editors) *v.1 p.490*

Devji, Faisal *v.4 p.658*

Devlin, Albert J. (Editor) *v.2 p.129*

Devlin, Ann Sloan *v.5 p.608*

Devlin, Bernie *v.5 p.652*

Devlin, James E. *v.2 p.66*

Devlin, Keith J. *v.5 p.458, p.465*

Devol, Kenneth S. *v.4 p.445*

Devon, Marjorie & Walch, Peter (Introduction by) . *v.1 p.759*

Devonyar, Jill, et al. *v.1 p.23, p.45*

Devore, Jay L. *v.5 p.480, p.500, p.683*

DeVorkin, David H. *v.5 p.62*

Devoto, Bernard (Editor) *v.3 p.520*

DeVoto, Bernard *v.2 p.33*

Devoto, Giacomo *v.2 p.699*

DeVotta, Neil *v.6 p.163*

Devries, Kelly *v.6 p.566*

DeVries, Mary A. *v.4 p.58, p.172*

DeVries, Raymond G. *v.4 p.445*

DeVries, Rheta *v.4 p.368*

Dew, Edward M. *v.3 p.322*

Dewar, James A. *v.5 p.719*

Dewar, Michael James Steuart *v.5 p.293*

Dewberry, Sidney O., et al. *v.4 p.158*

Dewey, John . *v.1 p.443, p.482, p.521, v.4 p.342, p.356, p.491, p.503, v.5 p.571*

Dewey, Scott Hamilton *v.4 p.566, v.6 p.299*

Dewey, Thomas E. *v.3 p.457*

DeWitt, Henry (Editor) *v.2 p.26*

Dews, Carlos L. & Law, Carolyn Leste (Editors) . . *v.6 p.368*

Dewsbury, Donald A. (Editor) *v.5 p.614*

Dewsbury, Donald A. *v.5 p.614*

Dexter, Emma *v.1 p.722*

Dey, P. M. & Harborne, J. B. *v.5 p.124*

DeYoung, Sandra *v.5 p.529*

Díaz-Cotto, Juanita *v.6 p.469*

Díaz-Plaja, Guillermo *v.2 p.638*

Décaudin, Michel & Leuwers, Daniel *v.2 p.457*

Dhada, Mustafah *v.6 p.73*

Dharmadasa, K. N. *v.6 p.163*

Dharwadker, Aparna Bhargava *v.1 p.131, p.134*

Dharwadker, Vinay *v.6 p.151*

Dhingra, Onkar D. & Sinclair, James B. *v.5 p.46*

Di Benedetto, Maria-Gabriella & Giancola, Guerino . *v.5 p.726*

Di Donato, Pietro *v.2 p.69*

Di Giovanni, Norman Thomas *v.2 p.678*

Di Leonardo, Micaela (Introduction by) *v.4 p.30*

Di Leonardo, Micaela *v.4 p.34*

di Lodovico Buonarroti Simoni, Michelangelo . . . *v.2 p.708*

Di Maria, Salvatore *v.1 p.74, p.106*

Di Prima, Diana *v.2 p.143*

Di Prima, Diane *v.2 p.143*

Di Renzo, Anthony *v.2 p.106*

Di Scala, Spencer M. *v.3 p.50*

Di Scala, Spencer *v.3 p.197*

Di Ventra, Massimiliano (Editor), et al. *v.5 p.742*

Diacon, Todd A. *v.3 p.339*

Diacu, Florin & Holmes, Philip *v.5 p.66, p.488*

Diagram Group *v.5 p.95, p.227*

Diamant, Louis & Lee, Jo Ann (Editors) *v.4 p.133*

Diamant, Louis *v.5 p.581*

Diamond, Beverley, et al. *v.1 p.295, p.389, v.6 p.699*

Diamond, Dan (Editor), et al. *v.4 p.862*

Diamond, Dermot & Hanratty, Venita C. A. *v.5 p.267*

Diamond, Harold J. *v.1 p.166*

Diamond, Jared M. *v.4 p.627, p.760*

Diamond, Jonathan *v.5 p.673*

Diamond, Larry & Diamond, Larry Jay *v.4 p.647*

Diamond, Larry & Plattner, Marc F. (Editors) . *v.4 p.214, p.235*

Diamond, Michael *v.6 p.759*

Diamond, Robert E. *v.2 p.205, p.550*

Dias, Maria O. *v.3 p.336*

Diaspro, Alberto (Editor) *v.5 p.88*

Diawara, Manthia (Editor) *v.6 p.329, p.341*

Diawara, Manthia *v.6 p.333*

Diaz, Arlene J. *v.3 p.360*

Diaz Diaz, Fernando *v.3 p.289*

Diaz, Junot *v.6 p.506*

Diaz, Maria Elena *v.3 p.308*

Diaz, Rafael M. *v.6 p.378*

Diaz-Briquets, Sergio & Perez-Lopez, Jorge *v.3 p.268*

Diaz-Stevens, Ana Maria & Stevens-Arroyo, Anthony M. *v.6 p.520*

Dib, Mohammed *v.2 p.542*

DiBattista, Maria *v.6 p.312, p.328, p.341*

Dibelius, Martin & Conzelmann, Hans *v.1 p.630*

Dibelius, Martin & Greeven, Heinrich *v.1 p.630*

Dibelius, Martin *v.1 p.628*

Dibrova, Volodymyr & Melnyczuk, Askold . . . *v.2 p.814*

DiCaprio, Lisa & Wiesner, Merry E. *v.3 p.50*

Dick, Auguste *v.5 p.465*

Dick, Bernard F. *v.2 p.127, v.6 p.322*

Dick, Everett *v.3 p.510, p.518*

Dick, Robert C. *v.3 p.419*

Dick, Steven J. & Strick, James E. *v.5 p.183, p.242*

Dick, Warren A. & Hatfield, Jerry L. (Editors) . *v.5 p.49, v.6 p.289*

Dickens, A.G. *v.1 p.604, p.609, v.3 p.99, p.120*

Dickens, Charles & Slater, Michael *v.6 p.754, p.756*

Dickens, Charles *v.2 p.282, p.283, p.284*

Dickerson, Donna L. *v.4 p.458*

Dickerson, Richard Earl *v.5 p.126*

Dickey, James *v.2 p.143*

Dickey, Stephanie *v.1 p.756*

Dickie, George, et al. *v.1 p.479*

Dickie, John *v.4 p.643, p.645*

Dickin, Alan P. *v.5 p.440, p.444*

Dickinson, Bob & Vladimir, Andy *v.4 p.161*

Dickinson, David K. & Neuman, Susan B. (Editors) *v.4 p.300, p.368*

Dickinson, Emily *v.2 p.37*

Dickinson, G. Lowes *v.4 p.647, p.649*

Dickinson, J. C. *v.6 p.570*

Dickinson, John Alexander & Young, Brian . *v.3 p.543, v.4 p.589*

Dickinson, Matthew J. *v.3 p.440, v.5 p.46*

Dickinson, Oliver *v.3 p.15*

Dickinson, Thomas H. (Editor) . *v.1 p.64, p.79, p.82, p.96, p.113*

Dickinson, Thomas H. . . *v.1 p.64, p.79, p.81, p.82, p.95, p.113*

Dickson, Bruce J. *v.4 p.619*

Dickson, David *v.3 p.137, v.5 p.393, p.411*

Dickson, Katherine M. *v.2 p.369*

Dickson, Mary H. & Fanelli, Mario (Editors) . . . *v.5 p.362*

Dickson, P. G. M. (Peter George Muir); Maria Theresa, Empress of Austria *v.3 p.183*

Dickson, Paul *v.4 p.850, p.868*

Dickson-Carr, Darryl *v.6 p.24*

Dickstein, Morris *v.2 p.265*

DiClemente, Carlo C. *v.5 p.663, p.673*

Dicum, Gregory, et al. *v.3 p.291*

Diderot, Denis & Alembert, Jean L. *v.1 p.154*

Diderot, Denis & d'Alembert, Jean le Rond *v.2 p.479*

Diderot, Denis *v.2 p.479, p.480, v.3 p.147*

Didion, Joan *v.2 p.143, p.144*

Diebolt, Claude, et al. *v.4 p.199, p.240*

Diefendorf, Barbara B. & Hesse, Carla (Editors) . . . *v.1 p.601*

Diefendorf, Barbara *v.3 p.145*

Diefendorf, Jeffry M. *v.3 p.176*

Diehl, J. F. *v.5 p.33*

Diehl, James M. *v.3 p.176*

Diehl, Joanne F. *v.2 p.61, p.102*

Diehl, Richard A. *v.4 p.9*

Diemert, Brian *v.2 p.349*

Diener, Ed & Suh, Eunkook M. (Editors) *v.5 p.670*

Dienhart, John W. & Curnutt, Jordan . . . *v.4 p.53, p.55, p.180*

Dierkes, Meinolf (Editor), et al. *v.4 p.78*

Dieter, George *v.5 p.688*

Dietrich, Richard *v.2 p.188*

Dietrich, William *v.3 p.530*

Dietz, Henry A. *v.3 p.329*

Dietz, James L. *v.3 p.319*

Diez, Thomas (Editor) *v.4 p.602, p.637*

Diffie, Whitfield & Landau, Susan *v.4 p.473*

DiGangi, Mario *v.6 p.411*

Digby, Anne *v.4 p.334*

DiGeorgio-Lutz, JoAnn (Editor) *v.6 p.462*

Diggins, John P. *v.3 p.203, p.367, p.374*

Dignan, James *v.6 p.258*

Digre, Brian *v.6 p.56*

DiIulio, John J. Jr. (Editor) *v.6 p.273*

Diiulio, John J. *v.6 p.275*

Dijksterhuis, E. J. *v.5 p.390, p.465*

Dijkstra, Bram *v.2 p.175, p.190*

Dika, Vera *v.6 p.317*

Dike, K. Onwuka *v.6 p.71*

Dikel, Margaret Riley & Roehm, Frances E. *v.4 p.169*

Dikotter, Frank *v.6 p.189, p.190*

Dikshit, R. D. *v.4 p.377*

Dileo, Cheryl (Editor) *v.1 p.406*

Dilg, Mary *v.4 p.309*

Dill, David D. *v.4 p.347*

Dill, Ken A. & Bromberg, Sarina *v.5 p.558*

Dillard, Annie *v.2 p.144, v.5 p.224, p.227*

Dillard, Joey L. *v.2 p.554*

Dillehay, Thomas D. *v.4 p.11*

Dillehay, Tom D. *v.4 p.11*

Diller, Daniel C. & Robertson, Stephen L. *v.3 p.378*

Dillery, John *v.2 p.422*

Dilley, Patrick *v.4 p.749, v.6 p.385*

Dillon, Janette *v.2 p.185*

Dillon, Jim & Naylor, David *v.1 p.113, p.154*

Dillon, John *v.1 p.430*

Dillon, Matthew & Garland, Lynda *v.3 p.13*

Dillon, Merton L. & Lovejoy, Elijah Parish *v.3 p.419*

Dils, Ann & Albright, Ann Cooper (Editors) *v.1 p.41*

Dilthey, Wilhelm & Makkreel, Rudolf A. *v.1 p.464*

Dilthey, Wilhelm *v.1 p.464*

Dilts, David A., et al. *v.4 p.130*

Dilworth, David A. & Viglielmo, Valdo H. (Editors) . *v.1 p.476*

Dilworth, Richardson *v.4 p.542, v.6 p.722*

Dimand, Mary Ann (Editor), et al. *v.4 p.273*

Dimand, Robert (Editor, Introduction
   by) *v.4 p.206, p.255, p.256, p.257, p.261, p.263*

Dimand, Robert W. (Editor), et al. *v.4 p.193*

Dimand, Robert W., et al. *v.4 p.193*

Dimand, Robert W. *v.4 p.255*

Dimand, Robert *v.4 p.227*

Dimbleby, Jonathan *v.6 p.201, p.205*

DiMeglio, John E. *v.1 p.35*

Dimijian, Greg & Dimijian, Mary B. (Photographers) *v.5 p.166*

Dimitri, Nicola (Editor, Translator), et al. . . . *v.4 p.249, p.272*

Dimitrova, Blaga, et al. *v.2 p.780*

Dimitrova, Blaga *v.2 p.780*

Dimock, Joseph J. *v.3 p.308*

Dinan, Desmond (Editor) *v.4 p.602, p.637*

Dinan, Desmond *v.4 p.602, p.637*

Dinan, Susan E. & Meyers, Debra (Editors) *v.1 p.655*

Dindal, Daniel L. (Editor) *v.5 p.87*

Dindia, Kathryn & Canary, Daniel J. (Editors) . . . *v.5 p.620*

Dindia, Kathryn & Duck, Steve (Editors) *v.5 p.647*

Dine, B. Joseph II & Gilmore, James H. *v.4 p.144*

Dinega, Alyssa W. (Editor) *v.2 p.796*

Diner, Judith B. (Editor, Translator) *v.2 p.469*

Dines, Nicholas T. & Harris, Charles W. . . . *v.1 p.785, p.817*

Dinesen, Isak *v.2 p.626*

Dinges, John *v.3 p.353*

Dinh, Linh *v.6 p.103*

Dinitiman, George & Ward, Bob *v.4 p.874, p.879*

Dinshaw, Carolyn & Wallace, David
   (Editors) *v.2 p.168, v.6 p.564*

Dinshaw, Carolyn *v.2 p.209*

D'Inverno, Ray A. *v.5 p.556*

Dinwiddie, Robert, et al. *v.5 p.65*

Dionysius of Halicarnassus *v.2 p.405*

Diop, Birago *v.2 p.544*

Diop, Cheikh Anta *v.4 p.702, v.6 p.10, p.52*

Diop, David *v.2 p.544*

Dipboye, Robert & Colella, Adrienne (Editors) *v.4 p.133*

DIPPR (AIChE Design Institute for Physical Property
   Data) *v.5 p.275*

DiPrima, Diane *v.2 p.144*

Dirac, Paul Adrien Maurice *v.5 p.549*

Dirda, Michael *v.2 p.573*

Diringer, David *v.3 p.37*

Dirix, A. (Editor), et al. *v.4 p.825*

Dirks, Nicholas B. *v.6 p.149, p.160*

Dirksen, Everett M. *v.3 p.457*

Dirlik, Arif & Yeung, Malcolm (Editors) . . . *v.6 p.113, p.126*

Dirlik, Arif *v.6 p.190, p.192*

Discenza, Richard (Editor), et al. *v.4 p.321*

Disher, Maurice Willson *v.1 p.88*

DiSilvestro, Roger L. *v.5 p.179*

Disraeli, Benjamin *v.2 p.275*

Dissanayake, Wimal (Editor) *v.6 p.334*

DiStefano, Anna (Editor), et al. *v.4 p.321*

DiStefano, Joseph J., et al. *v.5 p.710*

DiTomaso, Nancy & Post, Corinne (Editors) *v.4 p.132*

Dittmar, Linda & Michaud, Gene (Editors) *v.6 p.322*

Dittmer, Lowell (Editor), et al. *v.4 p.618*

Dittmer, Lowell *v.6 p.195, p.199*

Ditzen, Rudolf & Fallada, Hans *v.2 p.606*

Diubaldo, Richard J. *v.3 p.546*

Divakaruni, Chitra Banerjee *v.2 p.764, v.6 p.99, p.103*
Divine, Robert A. (Editor, Preface by) *v.3 p.469*
Divine, Robert A. (Editor) *v.3 p.440, p.469*
Divine, Robert A., et al. *v.3 p.379*
Divine, Robert A. *v.3 p.469*
Division for Ocean Affairs and the Law of the Sea, United
   Nations *v.4 p.478*
Division of Child, Youth, and Family Services (APA Division
   37) *v.5 p.671*
Division of School Psychology (APA Division 16) . . *v.5 p.576*
Dix, Edwin Asa *v.3 p.538*
Dix, Gregory *v.1 p.654*
Dix, Neville J; Webster, John *v.5 p.209*
Dix, Robin & Akenside, Mark *v.2 p.237*
Dix, Robin (Editor) *v.2 p.237*
Dixit, Avinash K. *v.4 p.248, p.252*
Dixit, Avinash *v.4 p.243*
Dixon, C. Scott (Editor) *v.3 p.165*
Dixon, C. Scott *v.3 p.165*
Dixon Gottschild, Brenda *v.1 p.18*
Dixon, Graham *v.1 p.183, p.316*
Dixon, Hepworth *v.3 p.491*
Dixon, J. B. & Weed, S. B. (Editors) *v.5 p.49*
Dixon, Joe B. & Schulze, Darrell G. (Editors) *v.5 p.49*
Dixon, Laurinda S. & Weisberg, Gabriel P. *v.1 p.709*
Dixon, Laurinda *v.1 p.738*
Dixon, Lloyd, et al. *v.5 p.716*
Dixon, Melvin *v.6 p.395*
Dixon, Mim & Roubideaux, Yvette (Editors) *v.6 p.701*
Dixon, Nancy M. *v.4 p.78*
Dixon, Peter *v.2 p.248*
Dixon, R. M. W. *v.2 p.556*
Dixon, Robert & Lee, Christopher *v.2 p.740*
Dixon, Simon *v.3 p.215*
Dixon, Suzanne *v.3 p.23*
Dixon, Wallace E. *v.5 p.641*
Dixon, Wheeler Winston (Editor) *v.6 p.311*
Dixon-Kennedy, Mike *v.1 p.534*
Dixon-Mueller, Ruth *v.4 p.569, v.6 p.469*
Dizikes, John *v.1 p.229, p.277*
Djebar, Assia *v.2 p.544, p.545, v.6 p.642*
Djerassi, Carl *v.5 p.260*
Djian, Jean-Michel *v.2 p.542*
Djilas, Milovan *v.3 p.247, p.248*
D'Ltri, Patricia W. *v.6 p.430*
Do, Hien Duc *v.6 p.140*
do Nascimento, Abdias & do Nascimento, Elisa L. . . *v.3 p.336*
Doan, Laura *v.6 p.368, p.392*
Doane, Alger N. *v.2 p.203*
Dobb, Maurice H. *v.4 p.217*
Dobb, Maurice Herbert *v.4 p.208, p.243*
Dobb, Maurice *v.4 p.208*
Dobbin, Frank (Editor) *v.4 p.195, p.268*
Dobbins, James C. *v.6 p.219*
Dobbins, James, et al. *v.4 p.633*

Dobbs, Brian & Dobbs, Judy *v.2 p.303*
Dobbs, Lou *v.4 p.252, p.261*
Dobbs, Michael *v.3 p.228*
Dobke, Dirk & Kellein, Thomas *v.1 p.696*
Dobkins, Rebecca J., et al. *v.1 p.738, v.6 p.678*
Dobkowski, Michael N. & Wallimann, Isidor
   (Editors) *v.4 p.652, p.662*
Doblin, Alfred *v.2 p.606*
Dobree, Bonamy *v.2 p.186*
Dobroszycki, Lucjan *v.3 p.83*
Dobrowolsky, Alexandra Z. & Hart, Vivien (Editors) *v.6 p.440*
Dobson, Alan P. *v.3 p.388*
Dobson, John F. *v.4 p.326*
Dobson, John M. *v.3 p.433*
Dobson, Michael & Wells, Stanley (Editors) . . . *v.2 p.222*
Dobson, Michael *v.2 p.229*
Dobson, R. B. & Taylor, J. *v.2 p.196*
Dobson, Sean *v.3 p.170*
Dobszay, Laszlo *v.1 p.245*
Dobychin, Leonid *v.2 p.802*
DoCarmo, Manfredo P. *v.5 p.496*
DoCarmo, Manfredo *v.5 p.496*
Docherty, David (Editor) *v.4 p.874*
Docherty, David *v.4 p.588*
Docherty, J. C. *v.4 p.125*
Doctorow, E. L. *v.2 p.144*
Dodd, C. H. *v.1 p.629, p.642*
Dodd, Christopher *v.4 p.843, p.865*
Dodd, David & Spaulding, Diana (Editors) . . *v.1 p.268, p.327*
Dodd, Janet S. (Editor) *v.5 p.260*
Dodd, Lawrence C. (Editor) *v.4 p.529*
Dodd, Thomas J. *v.3 p.301*
Dodd, William E. *v.3 p.395, p.424, p.495*
Doddannavar, Ravi, et al. *v.5 p.702*
Dodds, Eric R. *v.2 p.400*
Dodds, Gordon *v.3 p.532*
Dodds, Jerrilynn D. (Editor) *v.1 p.673, p.686*
Dodds, Jerrilynn *v.3 p.236*
Dodds, John W. *v.6 p.735*
Dodds, Klaus J. & Atkinson, David *v.4 p.488, p.495*
Dodds, Klaus *v.4 p.400*
Dodds, Sherril *v.1 p.36, p.37*
Dodelson, Scott *v.5 p.71*
Doder, Dusko *v.3 p.247, p.248*
Dodge, Charles & Jerse, Thomas A. *v.1 p.386*
Dodge, Pryor (Editor) *v.1 p.31*
Dodge, Pryor *v.4 p.857, p.870*
Dodge, Toby *v.4 p.643, v.6 p.602*
Dodgeon, Michael L. *v.3 p.11*
Dodgson, Elyse (Editor) *v.1 p.64, p.108*
Dodgson, Elyse *v.1 p.64, p.82, p.108*
Dodiya, Jaydipsinh & Surendran, K. V. (Editors) . . *v.2 p.762*
Dodson, James *v.4 p.860*
Dodson, Lisa *v.6 p.469*
Dodson, Michael & O'Shaughnessy, Laura N. . . . *v.3 p.301*

Dodson, Ronald G. *v.4 p.880, p.883, p.887*
Dodson, Stanley I. *v.4 p.391*
Dodwell, C. R. *v.1 p.671, p.727*
Dodwell, Henry H. *v.6 p.639*
Dodziuk, Helena *v.5 p.299*
Doe, Paula *v.6 p.229*
Doeg, Colin *v.4 p.160*
D'Oench, Ellen G. *v.1 p.755*
Doenecke, Justus D. *v.3 p.395, p.436*
Doeringer, Peter B. & Piore, Michael J. *v.4 p.717*
Doern, G. Bruce *v.5 p.392*
Doezema, Marianne & Milroy, Elizabeth (Editors) . . *v.1 p.682*
Doezema, Marianne *v.1 p.738*
Doggett, Hugh *v.5 p.21*
Doggett, Peter *v.1 p.268, p.305*
Dohan, Daniel *v.6 p.524, p.548*
Doherty, Gillian & Claybourne, Anna *v.4 p.399*
Doherty, Kieran *v.3 p.510*
Doherty, Thomas Patrick *v.4 p.418*
Dohrn-van Rossum, Gerhard *v.3 p.44*
Doi, Takeo *v.6 p.221, p.229*
Doisneau, Robert *v.1 p.766*
Dolan, Brian *v.1 p.802*
Dolan, Chris J. & Glad, Betty (Editors) *v.3 p.483*
Dolan, Jay P. *v.1 p.572, p.573, p.604*
Dolan, Jill *v.1 p.56, p.121, p.125, p.135*
Dolan, Kathleen A. *v.6 p.377*
Dolbow, Sandra W. *v.2 p.458*
Dolgin, Janet L. *v.4 p.448*
Dolin, Eric Jay *v.5 p.83*
Dolin, Raphael, et al. *v.5 p.515*
Dolkhart, Ronald H. (Editor) *v.3 p.348*
Doll, Ronald C. *v.4 p.362*
Dollard, John *v.3 p.496*
Dollimore, Jonathan & Sinfield, Alan (Editors) . . *v.2 p.229*
Dollish, Francis R. *v.5 p.297*
Dolman, Everett Carl *v.5 p.719*
Dolmetsch, Mabel *v.1 p.20*
Dols, Michael W. *v.6 p.584*
Domalski, Eugene S., William H. Evans, and Elizabeth D. Hearing *v.5 p.286*
Dombrowski, Daniel A. *v.4 p.510*
Domencich, T. *v.4 p.268*
Domenici, Pete V. *v.5 p.739*
Domenico, et al. *v.5 p.428*
Domhoff, G. William *v.4 p.702, p.719, p.726*
Domholdt, Elizabeth *v.5 p.535*
Dominguez, Jorge I. & Hernandez, Rafael (Editors) . *v.3 p.308*
Dominguez, Jorge I. & Poire, Alejandro (Editors) . *v.3 p.292*
Dominguez, Jorge I. (Editor), et al. *v.3 p.308*
Dominguez, Jorge I. (Introduction by) *v.1 p.573*
Dominguez, Jorge I. *v.3 p.308*
Dominick, William J. & Wehrle, William T. *v.2 p.427*
Dominik, William J. (Editor) *v.2 p.427*
Donagan, Alan *v.1 p.487*

Donaghy, Henry J. (Editor) *v.2 p.349*
Donahue, Brian *v.4 p.771, v.5 p.37*
Donahue, Debra L. *v.4 p.463*
Donahue, John *v.1 p.629*
Donald, David (Editor) *v.3 p.430*
Donald, David Herbert (Editor) *v.3 p.395*
Donald, David Herbert . . . *v.2 p.137, v.3 p.395, p.414, p.424*
Donald, David *v.3 p.422, p.423, p.428*
Donald, Merlin *v.5 p.608, p.612*
Donald, Stephanie Hemelryk & Benewick, Robert . . *v.6 p.182*
Donaldson, Greg *v.4 p.753*
Donaldson, Margaret *v.4 p.356*
Donaldson, Scott (Editor) *v.2 p.67, p.76*
Donaldson, Scott *v.2 p.68, p.76, p.84, v.6 p.401*
Donalson, Melvin *v.6 p.329, p.341*
Donchev, Anton *v.2 p.780*
Donchin, Anne & Purdy, Laura M. (Editors) *v.5 p.247*
Dongarra, Jack (Editor), et al. *v.5 p.349*
Donia, Robert J. & Fine, John V. A. Jr. *v.3 p.249*
Donia, Robert J. *v.3 p.249*
Doniach, N. & Kahane, A. *v.6 p.645*
Doniach, N. S. (Editor) *v.6 p.653*
Doniger, Wendy (Translator) *v.1 p.535*
Donin, Hayim H. *v.1 p.552*
Donington, Robert *v.1 p.196, p.229, p.365*
Donleavy, J. P. *v.2 p.69*
Donloe, Darlene *v.1 p.7*
Donne, John *v.1 p.582, p.652, v.2 p.213*
Donnell, Alison & Welsh, Sarah L. (Compiled by) . . *v.2 p.767*
Donnell, Alison *v.2 p.767*
Donnelly, James S. *v.3 p.138*
Donnelly, M. S. *v.4 p.589*
Donnelly, Marian C. *v.1 p.789*
Donnelly, Nancy D *v.6 p.111, p.139*
Donnelly, William J. *v.4 p.427*
Donner, Frank *v.6 p.260*
Donner, Fred *v.6 p.584*
Donner, Wendy *v.1 p.445*
Donoghue, Daniel *v.2 p.167*
Donoghue, Denis *v.2 p.71, p.163, p.302*
Donoghue, Eddie *v.4 p.727*
Donoghue, Emma *v.6 p.395, p.404*
Donohoe, Tom & Johnson, Neil *v.4 p.802, p.826*
Donohue, John J. *v.4 p.863*
Donohue, Joseph (Editor) . . . *v.2 p.186, p.187, p.188*
Donoso, José *v.2 p.679, p.680*
Donovan, Arthur *v.5 p.262*
Donovan, John *v.6 p.396*
Donovan, Josephine *v.2 p.51*
Donovan, Robert J. & Scherer, Raymond L. *v.4 p.414*
Donovan, Robert J. *v.3 p.469*
Donovan, Stephen K. & Paul, Christopher R. *v.5 p.446*
Donovan, Stephen K. (Editor) *v.5 p.450*
Donovan, Stephen K. *v.5 p.446*
Doob, Joseph L. *v.5 p.483*

Doody, Margaret Anne *v.2 p.242*

Dooley, Allan C. *v.3 p.119, v.6 p.739, p.741*

Dooley, Peter *v.4 p.195, p.253*

Doonan, S. *v.5 p.120*

Doordan, Dennis P. (Editor) *v.1 p.712*

Doorley, Michael *v.3 p.134*

Dopazo, Joaquin & Azuaje, Francisco (Editors) *v.5 p.93, p.104, p.105, p.108, p.115, p.126*

Doppelt, Bob, et al. *v.5 p.174, p.234, p.241*

Doran *v.1 p.99, p.140, p.144*

Dordick, Gwendolyn A. *v.4 p.737, p.750*

Dore, Elizabeth & Molyneux, Maxine (Editors) . *v.3 p.283, p.303*

Dore, Ronald P. *v.6 p.219, p.221*

Doreski, C. K. *v.2 p.61*

Doreski, William *v.2 p.96*

Doress-Worters, Paula B. & Siegal, Diana L. *v.6 p.445*

Dorf, Richard C. & Bishop, Robert H. *v.5 p.710*

Dorf, Richard C. & Kusiak, Andrew (Editors) *v.5 p.684*

Dorf, Richard C. & Svoboda, James A. *v.5 p.720*

Dorfman, Ariel & de la Parra, Marco Antonio *v.3 p.353*

Dorfman, Ariel *v.2 p.680*

Dorfman, Lisa *v.4 p.801, p.876*

Dorfman, Mark, et al. *v.5 p.363, p.373, p.378, p.705*

Dorfman, Mark S. *v.4 p.163*

Dorfman, Robert, et al. *v.4 p.199, p.243*

Dorian, A. F. (Editor) *v.5 p.387*

Dorian, A. F. *v.5 p.387*

Dorian, Angelo Francis *v.5 p.387*

Dorinson, Joseph & Warmund, Joram (Editors) . *v.4 p.805, p.831, p.850, p.887, p.896*

Doris, Ellen *v.5 p.212*

Dorland, Newman W. *v.5 p.325, p.509*

Dorling, Danny *v.4 p.373*

Dorling Kindersley Publishing Staff *v.4 p.380*

Dorman, Robert L. *v.6 p.287*

Dormer, Peter *v.1 p.702, p.712*

Dorn, Edward *v.2 p.69, p.144*

Dorn, Walter Louis *v.3 p.73*

Dorow, Sara K. *v.6 p.110, p.125*

Dorr, Ann & Paty, Alma Hale *v.5 p.737*

Dorrell, Nick (Volume Editor), et al. *v.5 p.132, p.153*

Dorris, Jonathon T. *v.3 p.395, p.436*

Dorsett, Lyle W. *v.3 p.512*

Dorsey, Jason *v.4 p.169*

Dorsey, Joseph C. *v.3 p.319*

Dorson, Richard M. (Editor) *v.2 p.17, p.28*

Dorson, Richard M. *v.2 p.584*

Dos Passos, John *v.2 p.69*

Dosi, Giovanni & Mazzucato, Mariana (Editors) . . *v.4 p.156*

Doss, Erika Lee (Editor) *v.4 p.409*

Doss, Erika *v.1 p.268, p.348, p.678, p.682*

Dosse, Francois *v.1 p.515*

Dossey, Barbara Montgomery *v.5 p.527, p.528*

Dostal, Robert J. (Editor) *v.1 p.468*

Dostoevsky, Fyodor M. *v.2 p.803*

Dostoevsky, Fyodor *v.2 p.803*

Dostoyevsky, Fyodor *v.2 p.803*

Dothan, Trude K. *v.3 p.7*

Dothan, Trude *v.3 p.7*

Doty, Alexander *v.6 p.390, p.416*

Doty, Mark *v.6 p.378, p.401, p.404*

Doty, William G. *v.1 p.527*

Double, Richard *v.1 p.503*

Dougherty, Kevin James *v.4 p.291*

Dougherty, Neil J. *v.4 p.795, p.883, p.900*

Doughty, Oswald *v.2 p.280, p.303*

Doughty, Robert A. *v.3 p.156*

Doughty, Robert, et al. *v.3 p.382*

Douglas, Alfred Bruce *v.6 p.401*

Douglas, Ann *v.2 p.8*

Douglas, David C. & Greenaway, G. W. (Editors) . . . *v.3 p.97*

Douglas, David C. *v.3 p.97, p.98*

Douglas, Edna *v.4 p.134*

Douglas, Gavin *v.2 p.213*

Douglas, George H. *v.2 p.137*

Douglas, Iain T. *v.1 p.582*

Douglas, Ian (Editor), et al. *v.4 p.373*

Douglas, Ian (Editor) *v.4 p.677*

Douglas, Jack D. *v.4 p.693*

Douglas, Keith *v.2 p.343*

Douglas, Mary Tew *v.4 p.36*

Douglas, Mary *v.1 p.521, v.4 p.28*

Douglas, Roy *v.3 p.88, p.124, p.126*

Douglas, Scott L. *v.6 p.289*

Douglas, Stephen Arnold *v.3 p.422, p.423, p.428*

Douglas, Susan J. *v.4 p.416, v.5 p.620, p.624, v.6 p.448*

Douglas, William O. *v.4 p.455, p.467*

Douglass, Frederick & Foner, Philip S. *v.3 p.419*

Douglass, Frederick . *v.2 p.36, v.3 p.395, p.419,v.6 p.4, p.17, p.24*

Douglass-Chin, Richard J. *v.1 p.648*

Doumani, Beshara (Editor) *v.6 p.592*

Doumani, Beshara *v.6 p.610*

Doumas, Christos G. *v.3 p.15*

Doumato, Eleanor Abdella & Posusney, Marsha Pripstein (Editors) *v.6 p.582*

Doumato, Eleanor Abdella *v.6 p.625*

Douville, Judith A. *v.5 p.255*

Dover, Gabriel *v.5 p.202*

Dover, Kenneth J. . *v.1 p.483, v.2 p.400, p.407, p.423,v.3 p.14, v.6 p.364, p.421*

Dovre, Paul J. (Editor) *v.4 p.307*

Dow, Bonnie J. *v.6 p.448*

Dow Chemical Company Staff *v.5 p.281*

Dow, Mark *v.4 p.764, v.6 p.275*

Dow, Sheila & Hillard, John (Editors) *v.4 p.227*

Dow, Sheila C. & Earl, Peter E. *v.4 p.227, p.237*

Dow, Sheila C. & Hillard, John (Editors) *v.4 p.199, p.227, p.232*

Dowd, Gregory Evans *v.6 p.685*

Dowd, Irene *v.1 p.49*

Dowden, Ken *v.1 p.531, v.6 p.569*

Dowden, Stephen D. (Editor) *v.2 p.612*

Dowden *v.1 p.532*

Dowdy, Thomas E. & McNamara, Patrick H. *v.1 p.524*

Dowe, Dieter *v.3 p.75*

Dower, Catherine *v.1 p.247*

Dower, J. W. *v.6 p.223, p.226*

Dower, John W. *v.6 p.223*

Dower, John *v.6 p.223*

Dowlah, Caf *v.4 p.664*

Dowley, Tim (Editor) *v.1 p.598*

Dowling, Ann & Williams, John E. *v.5 p.566*

Dowling, Carolyn & Kwok-Wing Lai (Editors) *v.4 p.351*

Dowling, Edward T. *v.4 p.175*

Dowling, Elizabeth M. & Scarlett, W. George (Editors) *v.1 p.650*

Dowling, Linda *v.6 p.760*

Downes, C. P. *v.5 p.153*

Downes, David A. *v.2 p.293*

Downes, John & Goodman, Jordan Elliot *v.4 p.94, p.101, p.103, p.162 p.162 p.162 p.162 p.162*

Downes, Larry & Mui, Chunka *v.4 p.51*

Downey, Dennis B. & Bremer, Francis J. (Editors) . .*v.3 p.491*

Downey, Greg *v.1 p.14*

Downey, Gregory J. *v.4 p.421*

Downey, Marlan W. (Editor), et al. *v.5 p.737*

Downey, Tom *v.4 p.94*

Downie, J. A. *v.2 p.262*

Downing, Brian M. *v.4 p.501*

Downing, John, et al. *v.4 p.416*

Downing, June E., et al. *v.4 p.318*

Downing, June E. *v.4 p.318*

Downing, Steven & Haladyna, Thomas M. (Editors) *v.5 p.600*

Downs, Alan *v.4 p.749, v.6 p.371, p.376*

Downs, Anthony *v.4 p.503, p.545, p.580*

Downs, Donald A. *v.4 p.458, v.6 p.469*

Downs, Laura Lee *v.4 p.711*

Downs, Philip G *v.1 p.189*

Downs, Robert B. *v.4 p.342*

Downward, Paul & Dawson, Alistair .*v.4 p.883, p.896, p.899*

Downward, Paul *v.4 p.232*

Dowson, Ernest *v.2 p.275*

Doxiadis, Euphrosyne *v.1 p.727*

Doxon, Lynn Ellen *v.5 p.742*

Doyal, Lesley *v.6 p.443, p.456*

Doyle, Arthur Conan *v.2 p.285*

Doyle, Don H. *v.3 p.494*

Doyle, Jack *v.5 p.7*

Doyle, Laura & Winkiel, Laura A. *v.3 p.314*

Doyle, Michael P. (Editor), et al. *v.5 p.33*

Doyle, Peter, et al. *v.5 p.446*

Doyle, Peter *v.5 p.447*

Doyle, Roddy *v.2 p.343*

Doyle, William (Editor) *v.3 p.147*

Doyle, William *v.3 p.150*

Doz, Yves L., et al. *v.4 p.69*

Dr. Dobbs Magazine *v.5 p.344*

Draaisma, Douwe *v.5 p.610*

Drabble, John H. *v.6 p.172*

Drabble, Margaret (Editor) *v.2 p.163*

Drabble, Margaret *v.2 p.343, p.344, p.389*

Drabek, Zdenek (Editor) *v.4 p.60*

Drabkin, William *v.1 p.197, p.235, p.306*

Drabowitch, Serge, et al. *v.5 p.728*

Drachman, Virginia G. *v.6 p.456*

Dracopoli, Nicolas C. (Editor), et al. *v.5 p.88*

Draghici, Soren *v.5 p.121*

Dragnich, Alex N. *v.3 p.248*

Drago, Russell S. *v.5 p.276*

Dragon, Gilbert *v.1 p.569*

Dragon, Osvaldo *v.2 p.678*

Drago-Severson, Eleanor *v.4 p.319*

Draguet, Michel *v.1 p.678*

Drakakis, John (Editor) *v.1 p.94, p.99*

Drake, Alexander *v.1 p.50*

Drake, Ellen T. & Jordan, William M. (Editors) *v.5 p.418, p.431*

Drake, Frances *v.5 p.425, v.6 p.294*

Drake, Frederick C. *v.3 p.382*

Drake, Frederick D. & Nelson, Lynn R. (Editors) . . .*v.4 p.523*

Drake, J. A. & Mooney, Harold A. *v.5 p.186*

Drake, Nathan *v.2 p.202*

Drake, Paul W. & Jaksic, Ivan (Editors) *v.3 p.353*

Drake, Paul W. (Editor) *v.3 p.259*

Drake, Paul W. *v.3 p.345, p.346, p.353*

Drake, Paul *v.3 p.353*

Drake, Peter G. *v.4 p.788*

Drake, Richard B. *v.3 p.497*

Drake, Richard L., et al. *v.5 p.158*

Drake, Richard *v.3 p.202*

Drake, St. Clair & Cayton, Horace R. *v.6 p.711*

Drake, Stillman *v.3 p.46*

Drakulic, Slavenka *v.2 p.818*

Draper, James D. *v.1 p.779*

Draper, James P. *v.6 p.24, p.33*

Draper, R. P. *v.2 p.184*

Drate, Spencer *v.1 p.717*

Draycott, Philip (Editor) *v.5 p.21*

Drayton, Michael *v.2 p.214*

Drayton, Richard *v.6 p.295*

Drazen, Patrick *v.6 p.307*

Drazin, P. G. *v.5 p.488*

Dreeben, Robert *v.4 p.300*

Drees, Clayton J. (Editor) *v.6 p.562*

Dreeszen, Craig, et al. *v.1 p.825*

Dreger, Alice Domurat *v.4 p.746*

Dregni, Michael *v.1 p.258, p.350*

Dreier, Peter, et al. *v.6 p.722*

Dreifelds, Juris *v.3 p.256*

Dreisbach, Robert Rickert, compiler *v.5 p.286*

Dreisbach, Robert Rickert *v.5 p.281*

Dreiser, Theodore & Riggio, Thomas P. *v.2 p.70*

Dreiser, Theodore *v.2 p.70*

Dreman, David N. *v.4 p.94*

Drenth, Pieter J. D. *v.5 p.579*

Dresch, Paul, et al. *v.4 p.25*

Dresch, Paul *v.6 p.628*

Drescher, John *v.3 p.501*

Dresser, Christopher *v.6 p.221*

Dresser, Peter D. *v.5 p.739*

Dressler, David *v.5 p.119*

Dressler, Joshua (Editor) *v.4 p.677, p.752, v.6 p.245*

Dretske, Fred I. *v.1 p.496*

Drever, James I. *v.5 p.441*

Drew, Clifford J. *v.5 p.409*

Drew, Elizabeth *v.3 p.469*

Drew, Horace R. & Pellegrino, Sergio . . . *v.5 p.693*

Drew, Katherine F. (Translator, Introduction by) . *v.3 p.142, p.162*

Drewal, Henry J., et al. *v.1 p.690*

Drewe, Sheryle Bergmann *v.4 p.794*

Drewett, Peter *v.4 p.7*

Drewnowski, Jan *v.4 p.265*

Drewry, Henry N. & Doermann, Humphrey . . . *v.4 p.291*

Drews, Robert *v.3 p.15*

Drexler, K. Eric *v.5 p.265, p.684*

Dreyer, Elizabeth A. & Burrows, Mark S. . . . *v.1 p.650*

Dreyer, June Teufel *v.4 p.619*

Dreyfus, Hubert L. & Rabinow, Paul . . . *v.1 p.458*

Dreyfus, Hubert L. *v.5 p.339, p.343*

Dreyfus, Laurence *v.1 p.183, p.303*

Dreyfuss, Hubert L. & Wrathall, Mark A. . . . *v.1 p.510*

Dreze, Jean & Sen, Amartya *v.4 p.265*

Drezon-Tepler, Marcia *v.4 p.615*

Driankov, D., et al. *v.5 p.710*

Drickamer, Karen D. & Dell, A. (Editors) . . . *v.5 p.112, p.139*

Driedger, Leo *v.3 p.542*

Drieu La Rochelle, Pierre *v.2 p.515, p.516*

Drijvers, Jan Willem & MacDonald, A. A. (Editors) . *v.4 p.334*

Drinan, Robert F. *v.1 p.656*

Drinkwater, Barbara L. *v.4 p.825, p.873*

Drinkwater, J. F. *v.3 p.142*

Drinkwater, John & Elton, Hugh (Editors) . . . *v.3 p.142*

Drinnon, Richard *v.6 p.682*

Dripps, Donald A. *v.6 p.267, p.268*

Driscoll, Margaret & Carliner, Saul . . . *v.4 p.321*

Driscoll, Mark J. *v.5 p.462*

Driskell, David C. *v.6 p.15*

Driskell, Judy A. & Wolinsky, I. R. A. (Editors) . *v.4 p.825, p.876*

Driver, Godfrey *v.6 p.664*

Driver, Harold E. *v.6 p.702*

Driver, Martha W. & Ray, Sid (Editors) . . . *v.6 p.562*

Driver, Rebecca & Thoenissen, C. . . . *v.4 p.257, p.263*

Driver, Tom F. *v.1 p.530*

Drlica, Karl *v.5 p.121*

Droeber, Julia *v.6 p.621*

Drogus, Carol A. *v.3 p.339*

Drogus, Carol Ann & Stewart-Gambino, Hannah . *v.3 p.339, p.353*

Drohojowska-Philip, Hunter *v.1 p.738*

Dronke, Peter (Editor) *v.1 p.432*

Dronke, Peter *v.6 p.559*

Drosdowski, Gunther & Duden, Konrad . . . *v.2 p.620*

Droste-Hülshoff, Annette von *v.2 p.596*

Drouet, Juliette *v.2 p.492*

Drower, Margaret (Editor) *v.3 p.11*

Drower, Margaret S. *v.3 p.11*

Dürrenmatt, Friedrich *v.2 p.606*

Dru, Jean-Marie *v.4 p.428*

Drucker Foundation Staff, et al. *v.4 p.66*

Drucker, Jane *v.6 p.376*

Drucker, Johanna *v.1 p.761*

Drucker, Peter F., et al. *v.4 p.767*

Drucker, Peter F. . . . *v.4 p.64, p.67, p.72, p.112, p.149*

Drucker, Philip *v.6 p.702*

Druckman, Daniel & Bjork, Robert A. . . . *v.5 p.605*

Druehl, Louis *v.5 p.208*

Druick, Douglas W. & Zegers, Peter . . . *v.1 p.738*

Druick, Douglas W. (Editor) *v.1 p.696*

Druick, Douglas W. *v.1 p.738*

Drukman, Mason *v.3 p.457*

Drummond, Carlos *v.2 p.690*

Drummond, John *v.1 p.7*

Drury, Allen *v.2 p.69*

Drury, John *v.1 p.709*

Drury, S. A. *v.5 p.420*

Drury, Shadia B. *v.4 p.658*

Dryden, John *v.2 p.246*

Dryden, Ken *v.4 p.862*

Dryer, Matthew S. & Comrie, Bernard (Editors) . . . *v.4 p.18*

D'Souza, Dinesh *v.3 p.470, v.4 p.331*

D'Souza, Gerard E. & Gebremedhin, Tesfa G. (Editors) . *v.5 p.12*

Du Bellay, Joachim *v.2 p.471*

Du Bois, W. E. B., et al. *v.6 p.31*

Du Bois, W. E. B. . . . *v.2 p.36, v.3 p.436, v.4 p.729, v.6 p.4, p.38*

Du Bois, William & Wright, R. Dean *v.4 p.675*

Du Boulay, F. R. H. *v.3 p.163*

Du Creux, Francois *v.3 p.538*

Du Maurier, Daphne *v.2 p.343*

du Maurier, George *v.2 p.275*

Du Plessix Gray, Francine *v.2 p.484*

Duany, Andres (Editor) *v.1 p.796*

Duany, Andres, et al. *v.4 p.770, v.6 p.726*

Duany, Jorge *v.3 p.319, v.6 p.543, p.548*

Duara, Prasenjit *v.4 p.496, v.6 p.190, p.205*

Dubasak, Marilyn *v.5 p.175, p.179*

DuBay, William H. *v.6 p.366*

Dubber, Markus Dirk *v.6 p.258*

Dubcek, Alexander *v.3 p.189*

Dube, Leela *v.6 p.153*

Dube, Marcel *v.2 p.540*

Dube, Saurabh *v.6 p.146, p.155*

Dube, Wolf-Dieter *v.1 p.678*

Duberman, Martin B. (Editor), et al. . . . *v.6 p.362*

Duberman, Martin B. . . . *v.6 p.364, p.365, p.381, p.401*

Duberman, Martin (Editor) *v.3 p.419, v.6 p.357, p.392*
Duberman, Martin .*v.3 p.424, v.6 p.4, p.17, p.365, p.387, p.388, p.390, p.401*
Dubin, Lois C. *v.3 p.58, p.183*
Dubin, Michael J. *v.4 p.557*
Dubisch, Jill & Winkelman, Michael *v.1 p.530*
Dubnow, Simon *v.1 p.548*
DuBoff, Leonard D. *v.1 p.827*
Duboff, Robert S. & Spaeth, Jim *v.4 p.135*
Dubofsky, Melvyn *v.4 p.125*
Dubois, David D. *v.4 p.76*
DuBois, Ellen Carol *v.3 p.396*
Dubois, Laurent & Garrigus, John *v.3 p.314, v.6 p.11*
Dubois, Lindsay *v.3 p.348*
Dubos, Rene Jules *v.4 p.760, v.5 p.396*
Dubrow, Gail Lee *v.1 p.822*
Dubus, Andre III *v.2 p.144*
Duby, Georges & Aries, Philippe (Editors) .*v.4 p.733, v.6 p.557*
Duby, Georges & Pantel, Pauline S. (Editors) *v.3 p.51*
Duby, Georges (Editor), et al. *v.3 p.52, v.6 p.559*
Duby, Georges .*v.3 p.67, v.4 p.682, p.733,v.6 p.556, p.557, p.559, p.562, p.575*
Ducey, Kevin *v.2 p.160*
Duchacek, Ivo D. *v.4 p.491*
Ducharme, Réjean *v.2 p.540*
DuChateau, Paul *v.5 p.487*
Duchen, Claire *v.6 p.433, p.453*
Duckers, Alexander *v.1 p.756*
Duckett, Eleanor S. *v.3 p.56, v.6 p.557*
Duckles, Vincent H., et al. *v.1 p.166*
Duckstein, Lucien & Plate, Erich J. (Editors) *v.5 p.702*
Duckworth, Douglas C. & Smith, D. H. *v.5 p.305*
Duckworth, George Eckel *v.1 p.72, p.90, v.2 p.425*
Duckworth, Jeannie *v.6 p.744*
Duckworth, William & Fleming, Richard (Editors) .*v.1 p.212, p.368, p.369*
Duckworth, William & Jansen, David A. . . .*v.1 p.212, p.213*
Duckworth, William *v.1 p.212, p.370, p.386*
Duda, Richard O., et al. *v.5 p.340, p.407*
Dudden, Arthur P. (Editor) *v.3 p.304*
Dudek, Louis; Michael Gnarowski *v.2 p.729*
Dudek, Louis *v.2 p.735*
DUDEN Editors *v.2 p.621*
Duden *v.2 p.620, p.621*
Dudeney, Henry E. *v.5 p.469*
Duderstadt, James J. *v.4 p.821, p.893*
Dudik, Evan Matthew *v.4 p.66*
Dudley, D. W. *v.5 p.714*
Dudley, Donald R. *v.1 p.428*
Dudley, Richard M. *v.5 p.483*
Dudley, Robert L. & Gitelson, Alan R. *v.4 p.548*
Dudley, Shannon & Wade, Bonnie C. *v.1 p.291*
Dudley, William S. *v.3 p.416*
Dudziak, Mary L. (Editor) *v.4 p.563*
Dueck, Robert K. *v.5 p.729*

Duellman, William E. & Trueb, Linda *v.5 p.214*
Duensing, Edward *v.5 p.228, p.245*
Duerksen, Christopher J. & Snyder, Cara *v.1 p.817*
Duerr, William A. *v.5 p.41*
Duetsch, Larry L. (Editor) *v.4 p.149*
Dufallo, Richard *v.1 p.213*
Duff, Alan *v.2 p.744*
Duff, J. Wight *v.2 p.424*
Duff, John W. *v.2 p.424*
Duff, P. M. (Editor) *v.5 p.418*
Duff, Tim *v.2 p.418*
Duffey, Bernard I. *v.2 p.14*
Duffield, John S. *v.4 p.639, p.654*
Duffin, Ross W. *v.1 p.177, p.179, p.400*
Duffin, W. J. *v.5 p.564*
Duffy, Eamon *v.1 p.604, p.609*
Duffy, John & Feeney, Vincent *v.3 p.486*
Duffy, John J. (Editor), et al. *v.3 p.486*
Duffy, Mary Lou & Forgan, James W. *v.4 p.277*
Duffy, Michael & Goodgame, Dan *v.3 p.470*
Duffy, Neill & Hooper, Jo *v.4 p.141*
Duffy, Patrick (Editor), et al. *v.3 p.134, p.136*
Duffy, Robert J. *v.5 p.360, p.374*
Duffy, Sean (Editor) *v.3 p.134, p.135, p.136, p.140*
Dufournet, Jean *v.2 p.466*
Dufrenne, Mikel *v.1 p.479*
Dufresne, John *v.2 p.574*
Dugan, Patrick (Editor) *v.5 p.53, v.6 p.293*
Dugas, H. *v.5 p.119, p.327*
Dugas, Hermann *v.5 p.119, p.327*
Dugdale, J.S *v.5 p.277*
Duggan, Joseph J. *v.2 p.467*
Dugger, Ronnie *v.3 p.470*
Duhem, Pierre M. *v.1 p.432, p.500*
Duignan, Peter J. & Gann, Lewis H. *v.6 p.531*
Duiker, William J. *v.6 p.167, p.168*
Duis, Perry R. *v.4 p.699, v.5 p.663*
Dujmovic, N. *v.3 p.319*
Duke, Benjamin C. O. *v.4 p.334*
Duke University Talent Indentification Program . . .*v.5 p.575*
Dukes, Gerry *v.2 p.333*
Dukes, H. H. & Reece, William O. *v.5 p.54*
Dukes, Paul *v.3 p.209, p.215,v.4 p.641, p.656*
Dukkipati, Rao V *v.5 p.716*
Duknovych, Aleksandr *v.2 p.814*
Dukore, B. F. *v.1 p.56*
Dukore, Bernard F. & Gerould, Daniel C. *v.1 p.84, p.96*
Dukore, Bernard Frank *v.2 p.309*
Dulaney, W. Marvin *v.6 p.259*
Dull, Jonathan R. *v.3 p.413*
Dulles, Foster R. *v.3 p.388, p.451*
Dulles, Foster Rhea *v.3 p.388*
Dulles, John W. F. *v.3 p.292*
Dulles, John W. *v.3 p.340*
Dumas, Alexandre *v.2 p.488, p.489*

Dumbrell, John . . . . *.v.3 p.388, p.470*

Dumenil, Lynn . . . . *.v.4 p.719*

Dumézil, Georges & Eliade, Mircea . . . . *.v.1 p.532*

Dummett, Michael . . . . . . *.v.1 p.488, p.494, p.502*

Dummit, David S. & Foote, Richard M. . . . . . . *.v.5 p.473*

Dumond, Don E. . . . . *.v.4 p.10*

Dumond, Dwight L. (Editor) . . . . *.v.3 p.365, p.419*

Dumont, Louis . . . . *.v.4 p.723*

Dumoulin, Heinrich . . . . *.v.1 p.567*

Dun and Bradstreet Information Services Staff . . . *.v.5 p.317*

Dun and Bradstreet Staff & Thomson Gale Staff . . . *.v.5 p.317*

Dunand, Francoise & Zivie-Coche, Christiane . . . . *.v.6 p.57*

Dunar, Andrew J. . . . . *.v.3 p.470*

Dunaway, David K. . . . . *.v.1 p.296, p.355*

Dunaway, Wilma A. . . . *.v.3 p.497, v.4 p.727, v.6 p.37, p.38*

Dunbabin, Jean . . . . *.v.3 p.142, p.198*

Dunbar, Paul Laurence . . . . *.v.2 p.36*

Dunbar, William . . . . *.v.2 p.214*

Dunbar, Willis F. & May, George S. . . . . . . *.v.3 p.516*

Dunbar-Nelson, Alice M. (Editor) . . . . . *.v.2 p.18, p.19*

Duncan, Acheson J. . . . . *.v.4 p.116*

Duncan, Alastair . . . . *.v.1 p.678*

Duncan, Alistair M. . . . . *.v.5 p.262*

Duncan, Charles . . . . *.v.2 p.32*

Duncan, Craig & Machan, Tibor R. . . . . *.v.4 p.510*

Duncan, David Ewing . . . . *.v.5 p.121*

Duncan, Doree (Editor), et al. . . . . *.v.1 p.26*

Duncan, Greg J. & Chase-Lansdale, P. Lindsay
　(Editors) . . . . *.v.4 p.755*

Duncan, Greg J. . . . . *.v.4 p.722, p.737*

Duncan, Isadora . . . . *.v.1 p.7*

Duncan, John B. . . . . *.v.4 p.621, v.6 p.236*

Duncan, Patti . . . . *.v.6 p.96, p.111*

Duncan, R. & Weston-Smith, Miranda (Editors) . . *.v.5 p.399*

Duncan, Robert Edward . . . . *.v.2 p.144*

Duncan, Robert . . . . *.v.2 p.69*

Duncan, Roger . . . . *.v.3 p.486*

Duncan, Thomas G. (Editor) . . . . . . *.v.2 p.168, v.6 p.564*

Duncan-Jones, Richard . . . . *.v.3 p.23*

Dundas, Paul . . . . *.v.1 p.538*

Dundes, Alan (Editor) . . . . *.v.2 p.17, p.584*

Dundes, Alan . . . . *.v.2 p.584*

Dundon, Tony & Rollinson, Derek . . . . *.v.4 p.121*

Dune, Eduard M. . . . . *.v.3 p.224*

Dungan, David Laird . . . . *.v.1 p.629*

Dunham, Katherine . . . . *.v.1 p.18, p.19*

Dunham, Vera Sandomirsky . . . . *.v.2 p.798*

Dunham, William . . . . *.v.5 p.465*

Dunitz, Robin J. & Prigoff, James . . . . *.v.1 p.704*

Dunkerley, James . . . . *.v.3 p.299*

Dunkerton, Jill, et al. . . . . *.v.1 p.727*

Dunkley, John . . . . *.v.2 p.478*

Dunlap, Knight . . . . *.v.5 p.666*

Dunlap, R. A. . . . . *.v.5 p.563*

Dunlap, Riley E. & Mertig, Angela G. (Editors) . . *.v.6 p.295*

Dunlap, Riley E. & Michelson, William (Editors) . . *.v.4 p.760*

Dunlap, Thomas R. . . . . *.v.5 p.9, p.354*

Dunlap, Thomas . . . . *.v.5 p.221*

Dunlap, William . . . . *.v.1 p.113*

Dunlop, John B. . . . . *.v.3 p.229*

Dunlop, Robert H. & Williams, David J. . . . . *.v.5 p.54, p.56*

Dunn, Ben M., et al. . . . . *.v.5 p.88*

Dunn, Charles W. & Woodard, J. David . . . . . *.v.4 p.516*

Dunn, Chris . . . . *.v.4 p.589*

Dunn, Christopher . . . . *.v.1 p.292, v.3 p.266*

Dunn, Dana, et al. . . . . *.v.4 p.285, v.5 p.593*

Dunn, Dana S. & Chew, Stephen L. (Editors) . . . *.v.5 p.675*

Dunn, Douglas . . . . *.v.2 p.343*

Dunn, Geoffrey D. . . . . *.v.1 p.593*

Dunn, James D. G. & McKnight, Scot . . . . . . *.v.1 p.627*

Dunn, James D. G. & Rogerson, John (Editors) . . *.v.1 p.615*

Dunn, James D. G. (Editor) . . . . *.v.1 p.630*

Dunn, James D. G. . . . . *.v.1 p.630, p.631*

Dunn, John . . . . *.v.1 p.448, v.3 p.106*

Dunn, Judy . . . . *.v.5 p.626, p.631*

Dunn, Kevin C. & Shaw, Timothy M. (Editors) *.v.4 p.641, p.643*

Dunn, Mark R. & Dunn, Mary W. . . . . *.v.4 p.542*

Dunn, Michael J. (Editor), et al. . . . . . . *.v.5 p.115, p.139*

Dunn, Michael J. (Editor) . . . . . . *.v.5 p.104, p.115, p.145*

Dunn, Peter N. . . . . *.v.2 p.641, p.651*

Dunn, Richard S. & Yeandle, Laetitia (Editors) . . . *.v.2 p.28*

Dunn, Richard S. . . . . *.v.3 p.487*

Dunn, Stephen . . . . *.v.2 p.144*

Dunn, Thomas Alexander . . . . *.v.2 p.221*

Dunn, Timothy J. . . . . *.v.6 p.486, p.529, p.537*

Dunnavant, Keith . . . . *.v.4 p.858, p.893*

Dunne, Gillian A. . . . . *.v.6 p.382*

Dunne, Michael . . . . *.v.6 p.316*

Dunne, Pete . . . . *.v.5 p.226*

Dunning, Eric (Editor), et al. . *.v.4 p.715, p.815, p.843, p.867*

Dunning, Eric G. (Editor), et al. . . . . *.v.4 p.815*

Dunning, Eric . . . . *.v.4 p.815*

Dunning, Jennifer . *.v.1 p.7, p.18, p.23, p.45, p.47, v.6 p.414*

Dunning, William A. . . . . *.v.3 p.396, p.436*

Dunning, William V. . . . . *.v.1 p.727*

Dunnington, Waldo . . . . *.v.5 p.465*

Dunsby, Jonathan . . . . *.v.1 p.213, p.235, p.353*

Dunstan, G. R. & Maruice, F. D. . . . . . . *.v.5 p.395, p.401*

Dunthorne, Gordon . . . . *.v.1 p.753*

Dunton, Chris . . . . *.v.1 p.58, p.130*

Dupeux, Georges . . . . *.v.4 p.702*

Duplessis, Rachel Blau . . . . *.v.2 p.15*

Duprbe, Louis K. & Wiseman, James A. . . . . . . *.v.1 p.653*

Dupre, Catherine . . . . *.v.2 p.347*

Dupree, Louis . . . . *.v.6 p.633*

Dupreez, Peter . . . . *.v.5 p.633*

Dupuis, Jacques . . . . *.v.1 p.597*

Dupuy, Alex . . . . *.v.3 p.314*

Duraiappah, Anantha Kumar . . . . *.v.4 p.207, p.267, v.5 p.14*

Duran, Jane . . . . *.v.6 p.462*

Duran, Manuel & Rogg, Fay *v.2 p.648*

Durand, Jorge & Massey, Douglas
S. *v.1 p.684, v.6 p.492, p.523, p.529*

Duranti, Alessandro (Editor) *v.2 p.560, v.4 p.18*

Duras, Marguerite *v.2 p.516*

Durback, Robert *v.1 p.577*

Durbin, Paul T. (Editor) *v.5 p.410, p.411*

Durbin, R., et al. *v.5 p.121*

Durch, William J. (Editor) *v.4 p.649*

Durch, William J. *v.4 p.633*

Durden, Robert F. *v.3 p.422, p.423, p.428*

Durell, Clement V. *v.5 p.556*

Durán, Manuel *v.2 p.648*

Durham, Jack L. & Teasley, John I. (Editors) *v.5 p.363*

Durham, John George Lambton *v.3 p.539*

Durham, Roger S. (Editor) *v.4 p.520*

Durham, Thomas *v.6 p.562*

Duric, Mira *v.3 p.388*

During, Jean, et al. *v.1 p.286*

During, Simon (Editor) *v.2 p.570*

Durkheim, Emile & Coser, Lewis A. *v.4 p.722*

Durkheim, Emile & Giddens, Anthony *v.4 p.684*

Durkheim,
Emile . *v.1 p.521, v.4 p.306, p.682, p.684, p.685, p.686, p.693*

Durney, Lawrence J. *v.5 p.737*

Duro, Richard J. (Editor), et al. *v.5 p.710*

Duroselle, Jean Baptiste *v.3 p.154*

Durozoi, Gerard *v.1 p.678*

Durr, Alfred *v.1 p.183, p.235, p.303*

Durrell, Gerald *v.5 p.227*

Durrell, Lawrence *v.2 p.344*

Durrenberger, E. Paul *v.4 p.28*

Durrenmatt, Friedrich *v.2 p.606*

Durrett, Richard *v.5 p.481*

Durrett, Rick *v.5 p.483*

Durrill, Wayne K. *v.4 p.520*

Durst, F. *v.5 p.708*

Dusinberre, Juliet *v.2 p.229*

Dussel, Enrique *v.1 p.608*

Duster, Troy *v.5 p.152*

Duthuit, Claude & Bois, Yve-Alain *v.1 p.779*

Dutka, Alan F. *v.4 p.136*

Dutro, J. T. Jr. (Editor), et al. *v.5 p.420*

Dutt, K. C. (Kartik Chandra) (Editor) *v.6 p.147*

Dutt, K.C. (ed.) *v.6 p.147*

Dutt, Nalinaksha *v.1 p.566*

Dutta, Hiran M. & Datta Munshi, J. S. *v.5 p.157*

Dutton, George *v.6 p.167*

Dutton, Michael (Editor) *v.6 p.196*

Dutton, Richard (Editor), et al. *v.2 p.229*

Dutton, Richard (Editor) *v.2 p.229*

Dutton, Richard *v.2 p.219*

Dutton, Robert R. *v.2 p.60*

Duus, Masayo *v.1 p.779, v.6 p.87, p.93*

Duus, Peter *v.6 p.236*

Duveau, Georges *v.3 p.75*

Duverger, Maurice *v.4 p.579*

Dvornik, Francis *v.3 p.214*

Dwivedi, A. N. *v.2 p.762*

Dwork, Deborah & Jan van Pelt, Robert *v.3 p.83*

Dworkin, Andrea *v.4 p.747, v.6 p.447, p.469*

Dworkin, Roger B. *v.4 p.448*

Dworkin, Ronald (Editor) *v.4 p.536*

Dworkin, Ronald M. (Editor) *v.4 p.434*

Dworkin, Ronald M. . . .*v.4 p.434, p.441, p.453, p.472, p.514*

Dwyer, James G. *v.4 p.450*

Dwyer, Judith A. (Editor) *v.1 p.571*

Dwyer, T. Ryle *v.3 p.138*

Dwyre, Diana & Farrar-Myers, Victoria *v.4 p.548*

Dybvig, R. Kent *v.5 p.346*

Dyck, Andrew R. *v.2 p.433*

Dyck, Perry Rand *v.4 p.589*

Dydo, Ulla E. *v.2 p.121*

Dye, David R. *v.3 p.301*

Dye, Frank J. *v.5 p.95, p.160*

Dye, Thomas R. *v.4 p.523, p.724*

Dyer, Alan *v.3 p.99*

Dyer, Betsey D. & Obar, Robert A. *v.5 p.153, p.191*

Dyer, Christopher *v.4 p.702, v.6 p.557*

Dyer, Donald *v.5 p.596*

Dyer, Gloria, et al. *v.5 p.245*

Dyer, Gwynne *v.3 p.483*

Dyer, Keith R. *v.4 p.391*

Dyer, Richard *v.6 p.416*

Dyhouse, Carol *v.3 p.111, v.6 p.745, p.747, p.765*

Dyke, Philip Peter George *v.5 p.458*

Dykeman, Wilma *v.2 p.144, v.3 p.510*

Dykstra, Clifford E. *v.5 p.279*

Dykstra, Robert R. *v.3 p.521*

Dylan, Bob *v.1 p.268, p.322, p.411*

Dym, Clive L. *v.5 p.693*

Dynes, Wayne R. & Donaldson, Stephen (Editors) . .*v.6 p.392*

Dynes, Wayne R. *v.6 p.360*

Dyos, H. J. & Wolff, Michael (Editors) .*v.3 p.111, v.6 p.711, p.762*

Dyrbye, Claës & Hansen, Svend Ole *v.5 p.693*

Dyreson, Mark *v.4 p.815, p.845, p.891, p.898*

Dysart, Dinah & Fink, Hannah *v.6 p.472*

Dyson, Anne Haas *v.4 p.360*

Dyson, Freeman J. *v.5 p.132, p.542*

Dyson, George Malcolm *v.5 p.292*

Dyson, H. V. & Dyson, B. *v.2 p.166*

Dyson, Kenneth & Featherstone, Kevin *v.4 p.629, p.637*

Dyson, Ketaki Kushari *v.6 p.151*

Dyson, Michael Eric *v.4 p.729, v.6 p.29, p.38*

Dyson, Stephen L. *v.3 p.198*

Dyson *v.4 p.656*

Dytham, Calvin *v.5 p.92*

Dziech, Billie W. & Hawkins, Michael W. *v.4 p.301*

Dzielska, Maria *v.1 p.430*

E

Eade, John & Mele, Christopher (Editors) *v.6 p.717*

Eadie, Jo *v.4 p.677*

Eadmer *v.1 p.579*

Eagle, Adam Fortunate & Findley, Tim *v.6 p.689, p.694*

Eagles, Charles W. (Editor) *v.3 p.494*

Eagles, Munroe (Editor), et al. *v.4 p.586*

Eagleton Institute of Politics, Rutgers University .*v.4 p.547, p.568*

Eagleton, Terry (Introduction by) *v.1 p.501*

Eagleton,
  Terry .*v.1 p.479, p.512, p.524, v.2 p.166, p.189, p.258, p.270, p.567*

Eagly, Alice & Chaiken, Shelly *v.5 p.652*

Eakin, Marshall C. *v.3 p.340*

Eakin, Nathan *v.1 p.159*

Eakin, Paul J. *v.4 p.693*

Eakins, Thomas *v.1 p.724*

Earl, Donald C. *v.2 p.442*

Earl, James W. *v.2 p.205*

Earl, P. E. & Kemp, S. (Editors) *v.5 p.604*

Earl, William L. *v.1 p.50*

Earle, Carville *v.3 p.380, v.4 p.381*

Earle, Jason & Kruse, Sharon D. *v.4 p.280*

Earle, Joe *v.1 p.693*

Earle, Peter (Editor) *v.3 p.39*

Earle, Peter *v.3 p.105, p.106, p.130, p.304*

Earle, Rebecca A. *v.3 p.357*

Earle, Sylvia A. & Wolcott, Henry *v.5 p.83*

Earle, Sylvia *v.5 p.428*

Earley Lawrenc *v.5 p.37*

Earley, P. Christopher & Erez, Miriam *v.4 p.56*

Earley, P. Christopher *v.4 p.58, p.172*

Earley, Pete & Shur, Gerald *v.6 p.271*

Earls, Irene *v.1 p.663, p.664, p.674*

Early, Evelyn A. *v.6 p.637*

Early, Gerald (Editor) *v.4 p.811, p.831, p.855*

Early, Gerald L. *v.6 p.4, p.15*

Early, Gerald *v.1 p.383*

Early, John D. & Headland, Thomas N. *v.4 p.39*

Earnshaw, Rae A. (Editor), et al. *v.4 p.772*

Earp, Lawrence *v.1 p.163, p.177, p.338*

Earth Pledge *v.1 p.817*

Easlea *v.5 p.410, p.411*

Easterby-Smith, Mark, et al. *v.4 p.119*

Easterday, Kenneth (Editor), et al. *v.5 p.462*

Easterday, Kenneth et al *v.5 p.462*

Easterlin, Richard A. *v.4 p.243*

Easterling, K E *v.4 p.871*

Easterling, P. E. (Editor) .*v.1 p.59, p.71, p.88, v.2 p.400, p.401*

Easterly, William *v.4 p.243*

Eastlake, Charles L. *v.1 p.750, p.751*

Eastlake, William *v.2 p.70*

Eastland, Terry (Editor) *v.4 p.536*

Eastland, Terry *v.4 p.536*

Eastman, Lloyd E., et al. *v.6 p.190*

Eastman, Lloyd E. *v.6 p.190*

Eastmond, Nick *v.4 p.351*

Easton, Carol *v.1 p.7*

Easton, Stewart C. & Wieruszowski, Helene *v.3 p.66*

Easttom II, William & Easttom, Chuck *v.4 p.113*

Eaton, Adrienne E. & Keefe, Jeffrey H. (Editors) . . .*v.4 p.121*

Eaton, Clement *v.3 p.396, p.415, p.425, p.428, p.495*

Eaton, Richard M. (Editor) *v.6 p.150*

Eaton, Richard M. *v.6 p.160*

Eaton, Walter P. *v.1 p.113, p.144, p.149, p.152*

Eatwell, John (Editor), et al. *v.4 p.192*

Eaves, Morris (Editor) *v.2 p.239*

Eaves, Morris *v.2 p.239*

Eaves, Thomas Cary Duncan & Kimpel, Ben *v.2 p.258*

Eayrs, James George *v.3 p.541*

Ebadi, Shirin *v.6 p.629*

Eban, Abba Solomon *v.6 p.613*

Eban, Abba *v.4 p.645, v.6 p.613*

Ebel, Robert D. (Editor), et al. *v.4 p.107*

Ebeling, Gerhard *v.1 p.602*

Ebeling, Walter *v.5 p.4, p.26*

Eber, Paula Holmes & Holmes-Eber, Paula *v.4 p.38*

Eberhardt, Piotr *v.3 p.207*

Eberhart, Richard *v.2 p.71*

Eberle, Suzanne *v.4 p.825, p.876*

Eberle-Sinatra, Michael (Editor) *v.2 p.568*

Eberly, Phillip K. *v.1 p.268*

Ebershoff, David *v.6 p.396*

Ebert, Thomas A. *v.5 p.188*

Ebert-Schifferer, Sybille *v.1 p.727*

Eberwein, Jane Donahue *v.2 p.37*

Eberwein, Robert T. (Introduction by) *v.6 p.322*

Eberwein, Wilhelm, et al. *v.4 p.121*

Ebihara, May M. (Editor), et al. *v.6 p.170*

Eble, Kenneth E. & McKeachie, Wilbert J. *v.4 p.292*

Eble, Kenneth E. *v.2 p.76*

Ebrey, Patricia B. *v.6 p.186, p.217, p.452*

Ebrey, Patricia Buckley, et al. *v.6 p.181, p.223*

Ebrey, Patricia Buckley *v.6 p.183*

Ebron, Paulla A. *v.1 p.285*

Ebsworth, E.A.V., et al. *v.5 p.303*

Eby, Frederick (Editor) *v.4 p.339*

Eby, G. Nelson *v.5 p.423, p.441*

Eca de Queiros, Jose Maria *v.2 p.688*

Eccles, William J. & Cooke, Jacob E.
  (Editors) *v.3 p.405, v.4 p.517*

Eccles, William J. *v.3 p.538*

Echaore-McDavid, Susan *v.4 p.151*

Echard, Siân (Editor) *v.2 p.211*

Echenberg, Myron *v.6 p.72*

Echenoz, Jean & Waldman, Guido *v.2 p.530*

Echenoz, Jean *v.2 p.529, p.530*

Echeruo, Michael J. *v.2 p.338*

Echevarría, Roberto González (Editor) *v.2 p.666*

Echevarría, Roberto González *v.2 p.664*

Echevarria, Antulio Joseph *v.3 p.160*

Echevarria, Roberto Gonzalez . . . *v.2 p.671, v.3 p.267, p.308*

Echols, Alice *v.6 p.427, p.433, p.453*

Echols, Harrison & Grossman, Carol *v.5 p.126*

Eck, Caroline van & Winters, Edward *v.1 p.702*

Eck, Diana L. *v.1 p.535, p.539*

Eck, Werner & Takacs, Sarolta A. *v.3 p.27*

Eckermann, Johann Peter, et al. *v.2 p.597*

Eckert, Kathryn Bishop *v.1 p.789*

Eckert, Penelope & McConnell-Ginet, Sally *v.4 p.21*

Eckstein, Rick *v.4 p.773*

Eckstein, Susan Eva *v.3 p.308, v.4 p.508*

Eco, Umberto . *v.1 p.702, v.2 p.560, p.568, p.570, p.724, v.4 p.424*

Economakis, Evel G. *v.3 p.220*

Economic Commission for Africa *v.4 p.664*

Economist Books Staff *v.4 p.172*

Economy, Elizabeth C. *v.6 p.196*

Edbury, Peter W. *v.3 p.64, v.6 p.601*

Eddington, Arthur S. (Author, Preface by) . . . *v.5 p.556, p.558*

Eddington, Arthur S. *v.5 p.556*

Eddington, Arthur Stanley *v.5 p.541*

Eddins, Dwight *v.2 p.326*

Eddison, John (John C.) *v.5 p.88*

Eddy, Beth *v.2 p.3*

Eddy, Mary Baker *v.1 p.583*

Edelman, Carole Lium & Mandle, Carol Lynn . . . *v.5 p.527*

Edelman, Gerald M. *v.5 p.160*

Edelman, Murray J. *v.5 p.642*

Edelman, Murray *v.5 p.642*

Edelman, Robert *v.4 p.805*

Edelson, Edward *v.5 p.132*

Edelson, Paula *v.6 p.437*

Edelstein-Keshet, Leah *v.5 p.91*

Eden, Lorraine & Dobson, Wendy . . . *v.4 p.243, p.261, p.263*

Edersheim, Elizabeth Haas *v.4 p.64, p.147*

Edey, Maitland A. *v.5 p.191*

Edgar, Adrienne Lynn *v.3 p.231*

Edgar, Gerald A. *v.5 p.498*

Edgar, Walter B. *v.3 p.501*

Edgecombe, Rodney S. *v.2 p.128*

Edgell, Penny *v.1 p.650*

Edgerton, Robert *v.6 p.62*

Edgerton, Samuel Y. & Perez de Lara, Jorge *v.3 p.263*

Edgerton, Samuel Y. Jr. *v.3 p.70*

Edgeworth, Francis Y. *v.4 p.223*

Edgeworth, Maria *v.2 p.286*

Edin, Kathryn & Kefalas, Maria *v.4 p.724*

Edin, Kathryn & Lein, Laura *v.6 p.466*

edited by Technische Universität Dresden, Zentrum für
Angewandte Sprachwissenschaft (Editor) *v.5 p.734*

Editions Grund (Editor) *v.1 p.664*

Edley, Christopher Jr. *v.4 p.456*

Edling, Max M. *v.4 p.523*

Edmonds, Ennis Barrington *v.4 p.711*

Edmonds, Martin *v.1 p.738*

Edmonds, Walter D. *v.2 p.71*

Edmundson, William A. *v.4 p.512, p.669*

Edsall, Nicholas C. *v.6 p.362*

Edsforth, Ronald W. & Bennett, Larry (Editors) . . . *v.3 p.367*

Edson, Margaret *v.2 p.144*

Edson, Sakre K. *v.4 p.281*

Education Atlas *v.4 p.326*

Educational Psychology (APA Division 15) *v.5 p.571*

Educational Testing Service . *v.4 p.176, p.286, v.5 p.576, p.577*

Edwards, Amelia *v.3 p.11*

Edwards, Anthony W. F. *v.5 p.143*

Edwards, C. H. Jr. *v.5 p.465, p.485*

Edwards, Catharine & Woolf, Greg (Editors) *v.3 p.22*

Edwards, Clive D. *v.1 p.803*

Edwards, Clive *v.1 p.805*

Edwards, David J. *v.1 p.712*

Edwards, David N. *v.6 p.59*

Edwards, Grace Toney (Editor), et al. *v.3 p.497*

Edwards, Gwynne *v.2 p.640*

Edwards, H. L. *v.2 p.214*

Edwards, Harold M. *v.5 p.470*

Edwards, Holly (Editor) *v.1 p.678, p.682*

Edwards, I. E. S. *v.3 p.8*

Edwards, Jeanette *v.4 p.31*

Edwards, Jess *v.4 p.399*

Edwards, John D. *v.5 p.700*

Edwards, John *v.3 p.238, v.4 p.115*

Edwards, Jonathan *v.1 p.483, p.584*

Edwards, Jorge *v.2 p.680*

Edwards, June *v.6 p.462*

Edwards, Laura F. *v.6 p.452*

Edwards, Lyman (Editor), et al. *v.5 p.360, p.362*

Edwards, Mark U. Jr. *v.1 p.603*

Edwards, Mike *v.2 p.270, p.345*

Edwards, Newton *v.4 p.450*

Edwards, P. D. *v.2 p.316*

Edwards, Paul M. *v.6 p.322*

Edwards, Paul *v.2 p.366*

Edwards, Penny *v.6 p.170*

Edwards, Ralph *v.1 p.805*

Edwards, Richard (Editor), et al. *v.4 p.320*

Edwards, Richard L. (Editor) *v.4 p.677*

Edwards, Robert R. *v.2 p.209, p.702*

Edwards, Stewart (Editor) *v.3 p.154*

Edwards, Victoria H. *v.5 p.179*

Eeckhoudt, Louis, et al. *v.4 p.207, p.263*

Efimov, Nina, et al. *v.2 p.778, p.779*

Efrati, Carol *v.2 p.290*

Efron, Bradley; Tibshirani, Robert *v.5 p.482*

Egan, David *v.2 p.803*

Egan, Eric *v.6 p.333*

Egan, Ferol *v.3 p.422, p.423, p.428*

Egan, Kieran *v.4 p.339, p.347*

Egan, Leona Rust *v.1 p.79, p.82, p.113, p.144, p.149*

Egan, Martha *v.1 p.709*

Egan, Ronald C. . . . . *.v.6 p.211*
Egan, Susan C. . . . . *.v.6 p.199*
Egar, Emmanuel Edame . . . . *.v.6 p.24, p.43*
Egendorf, Laura K. (Editor) . . . . *.v.6 p.265*
Egerton, Douglas . . . . *.v.3 p.501*
Egerton, Ray . . . . *.v.5 p.88*
Eggebrecht, Hans H. . . . . *.v.1 p.184, p.239, p.303*
Eggener, Keith L. . . . . *.v.1 p.815*
Eggert, Max . . . . *.v.4 p.169*
Eggleston, Edward . . . . *.v.2 p.37*
Egidi, Massimo & Rizzello, Salvatore (Editors) . . *.v.4 p.272*
Egloff, Gustav . . . . *.v.5 p.290*
Egret, Jean . . . . *.v.3 p.150*
Ehler, Sidney Z. & Morrall, John B. . . . . . . *.v.3 p.56*
Ehlers, J. & Gibbard, P. L. . . . . . . *.v.5 p.425, p.431, p.432*
Ehlers, Manfred & Michel, Ulrich . . . . *.v.4 p.388, v.5 p.366*
Ehlers, Manfred . . . . *.v.5 p.366, p.368*
Ehrenberg, John . . . . *.v.3 p.148*
Ehrenberg, Ronald G. . . . . *.v.4 p.293*
Ehrenberg, Victor L. . . . . *.v.3 p.17*
Ehrenfeld, David W. . . . . *.v.1 p.507*
Ehrenfreund, Pascale (Editor), et al. . . . . *.v.5 p.242*
Ehrenhalt, Alan . . . . *.v.4 p.516, p.554*
Ehrenkreutz, Andrew S. . . . . *.v.6 p.609*
Ehrenpreis, Irvin . . . . *.v.2 p.262*
Ehrenreich, Barbara & Hochschild, Arlie Russell
  (Editors) . . . . *.v.6 p.456*
Ehrenreich, Barbara . . . . *.v.4 p.265, v.6 p.464*
Ehrenreich, John H. . . . . *.v.4 p.757*
Ehrenstein, David . . . . *.v.6 p.416*
Ehret, Christopher . . . . *.v.6 p.52*
Ehrick, Christine . . . . *.v.3 p.345*
Ehrismann, Gustav . . . . *.v.2 p.589*
Ehrle, Elwood B. & Bennett, John B. . . . . *.v.4 p.293*
Ehrlich, Cyril . . . . . . *.v.1 p.389, v.3 p.111, p.127, v.6 p.757*
Ehrlich, Eugene H. & Carruth, Gorton . . . . *.v.2 p.7*
Ehrlich, Gretel . . . . *.v.6 p.293*
Ehrlich, Linda C. & Desser, David (Editors) . *.v.6 p.327, p.334*
Ehrlich, Paul R. & Ehrlich, Anne H. . . . . *.v.5 p.411*
Ehrlich, Paul R. *.v.5 p.652*
Ehrlichman, John D. . . . . *.v.3 p.470*
Ehrman, Bart D. & Apostolic . . . . *.v.1 p.591*
Ehrman, Bart D. . . . . *.v.1 p.599, p.624*
Ehrman, John . . . . *.v.3 p.451, p.470*
Ehrmann, Henry Walter & Schain, Martin A. . . . . *.v.4 p.608*
Ehsani, Mehrdad . . . . *.v.5 p.716*
Eibl-Eibesfeldt, Irenaus . . . . *.v.5 p.616*
Eichelberger, Martin R., et al. . . . . *.v.5 p.534*
Eichenbaum, Rose . . . . *.v.1 p.45*
Eichenberg, Fritz . . . . *.v.1 p.759*
Eichendorff, Joseph, Freiherr von . . . . *.v.2 p.596*
Eichendorff, Joseph . . . . *.v.2 p.596*
Eichengreen, Barry J. . . . . . . *.v.3 p.39, v.4 p.213, p.255*
Eichenwald, Kurt . . . . *.v.4 p.103, p.104*
Eichler, Magrit . . . . *.v.4 p.687*

Eichner, Alfred S. (Editor) . . . . *.v.4 p.232*
Eichstaedt, Peter H. . . . . *.v.6 p.681*
Eichstedt, Jennifer & Small, Stephen . . . . *.v.1 p.828*
Eickelman, Christine . . . . *.v.6 p.627*
Eickelman, Dale F. . . . . *.v.6 p.581*
Eid, Michael & Diener, Ed . . . . *.v.5 p.599, p.600*
Eide, Espen Barth . . . . *.v.6 p.262*
Eide, Yvind . . . . *.v.1 p.611*
Eidelberg, Paul . . . . *.v.4 p.518*
Eidelberg, Shlomo (Editor, Translator) . . . . *.v.6 p.597, p.609*
Eidintas, Alfonsas (Editor), et al. . . . . *.v.3 p.256*
Eig, Jonathan . . . . *.v.4 p.850*
Eigen, Manfred & Winkler, Ruthild . . . . *.v.5 p.401*
Eile, Stanislaw . . . . *.v.2 p.789*
Eils, Roland & Kriete, Andres (Editors) *.v.5 p.97, p.105, p.108*
Einarsson, Stefán . . . . *.v.2 p.625*
Einhard, et al. . . . . *.v.3 p.142, p.162*
Einhard . . . . *.v.3 p.66, v.6 p.562*
Einhorn, Eric S. *.v.3 p.232*
Einsele, G. (Editor), et al. . . . . *.v.5 p.446*
Einsele, Gerhard . . . . *.v.5 p.438*
Einsohn, Amy . . . . *.v.4 p.149*
Einstein, Albert & Infeld, Leopold . . . . *.v.5 p.541*
Einstein, Albert . . . . *.v.5 p.539, p.542, p.556*
Einstein, Alfred . . . . *.v.1 p.179, p.197*
Eire, Carlos M. N. . . . . *.v.1 p.601, v.3 p.238*
Eisaguirre, Lynne . . . . *.v.4 p.458*
Eisberg, Robert M. & Resnick, Robert E. . . . . . *.v.5 p.549*
Eisberg, Robert Martin . . . . *.v.5 p.547*
Eiseley, Loren C. *.v.5 p.221*
Eiseman, Elisa, et al. . . . . *.v.5 p.112, p.148*
Eiseman, Elisa . . . . *.v.5 p.247*
Eisen, Cliff . . . . *.v.1 p.189, p.343*
Eisen, George & Wiggins, David K. (Editors) *.v.4 p.805, p.830*
Eisenberg, Carolyn . . . . *.v.3 p.388*
Eisenberg, Evan . . . . *.v.1 p.377, p.386*
Eisenberg, Peter L. . . . . *.v.3 p.336*
Eisenbud, Merrill & Gesell, Thomas F. . . . . . . *.v.5 p.706*
Eisenhower, Dwight D. . . . . *.v.3 p.470*
Eisenhower, John S. D. . . . . *.v.3 p.470, v.6 p.534*
Eisenman, Stephen F. . . . . *.v.1 p.678*
Eisenmann, Linda (Editor) . . . . *.v.6 p.462*
Eisenstadt, Michael (Editor) . . . . *.v.4 p.561, p.643*
Eisenstadt, Samuel N. . . . . *.v.4 p.681, p.760*
Eisenstadt, Todd A. . . . . *.v.3 p.292*
Eisenstein, Elizabeth L. . . . . *.v.2 p.576, v.3 p.37*
Eisenstein, James & Jacob, Herbert . . . . *.v.6 p.267*
Eisenstein, Zillah R. . . . . *.v.4 p.458*
Eisenstock, Alan . . . . *.v.4 p.406*
Eiser, J. Richard . . . . *.v.5 p.585*
Eisinger, Robert M. . . . . *.v.4 p.526*
Eisner, Elliot W. . . . . *.v.4 p.342, p.362*
Eisner, Will (Author, Illustrator) . . . . *.v.2 p.581*
Eiss, Harry E. . . . . *.v.5 p.469*
Eitner, Lorenz . . . . *.v.1 p.727*

Eitzen, D. Stanley *v.4 p.815*

Ekblom, Bjorn (Editor) *v.4 p.867*

Ekeh, Peter P. *v.4 p.679*

Ekelund, Robert B. Jr. & Hebert, Robert F. *v.4 p.195*

Ekelund, Robert B. Jr. & Tollison, Robert D. *v.4 p.215*

Ekirch, Arthur A. Jr. *v.3 p.382, p.384*

Ekman, Paul & Davidson, Richard J. *v.5 p.611*

Ekserdjian, David *v.1 p.696*

Ekvall, Robert B. *v.4 p.39*

Ekwall, Eilert *v.3 p.126*

El Bushra, Judy & Gardner, Judith (Editors) *v.4 p.652*

El Kikhia, Mansour O. *v.6 p.640*

El Saadawi, Nawal *v.6 p.583*

El Saffar, Ruth A. & Wilson, Diana D. (Editors) . . . *v.2 p.649*

El Saffar, Ruth *v.2 p.649*

Elam, Harry J. Jr. & Alexander, Robert (Editors) . *v.1 p.65, p.122*

Elam, Harry J. Jr. *v.6 p.512, p.517*

Elaydi, Saber *v.5 p.477*

Elazar, Daniel J., et al. *v.4 p.543*

Elbow, Peter (Editor) *v.2 p.566*

Elbow, Peter *v.2 p.565*

Elcock, W. D. *v.2 p.635*

El-Deiry, Safik S. (Editor) *v.5 p.165*

Elder, Alan C. & Thom, Ian M. *v.1 p.678, p.682*

Elderfield, John *v.1 p.696*

Elderidge, Sarah (Editor) *v.5 p.34*

Eldredge, Charles C. *v.1 p.738*

Eldredge, Niles & Alcosser, Murray *v.5 p.447*

Eldredge, Niles & Grene, Marjorie *v.5 p.167*

Eldredge, Niles *v.5 p.191, p.203*

Eldridge, C. C. *v.3 p.88, p.124*

Eldridge, Elizabeth A. *v.6 p.75*

Eldridge, Larry D. *v.4 p.459*

Eldridge, Niles *v.5 p.198*

Eldridge, Philip J. *v.4 p.512*

Eldridge, Richard *v.1 p.479*

Elewa, Ashraf M. T. (Editor) *v.5 p.204*

Eley, Geoffrey & Suny, Ronald G. (Editors) *v.3 p.61*

Elfenbein, Andrew *v.6 p.739, p.755, p.763*

Elford, George W. *v.4 p.286*

Eliade, Mircea *v.1 p.530, p.542,v.2 p.816, p.817*

Eliaeson, Sven *v.4 p.681*

Elias, John L. & Merriam, Sharan B. *v.4 p.320*

Elias, Maurice J., et al. *v.5 p.671*

Elias, Norbert & Dunning, Eric *v.4 p.783, p.815*

Elias, Norbert *v.4 p.726*

Elias, Robert (Editor) *v.4 p.815, p.830, p.850*

Elias, Robert Henry *v.2 p.70*

Elias, Robert *v.4 p.752*

Elias, Stephen & Levinkind, Susan . . . *v.4 p.109, p.180, p.439*

Elias, Stephen & Stim, Richard *v.4 p.109, p.110, p.180*

Elias, Stephen *v.4 p.446*

Eliason, Michele *v.6 p.377*

Eliasson, Gunnar K. (Editor), et al. . . *v.4 p.230, p.235, p.243*

Eliel, Ernest L. & Wilen, Samuel H. *v.5 p.298*

Eliel, Ernest L. (Editor) *v.5 p.297*

Eliel, Ernest Ludwig, et al. *v.5 p.297*

Eliopoulos, Charlotte K. *v.5 p.518, p.531*

Eliot, Charles W. *v.1 p.816*

Eliot, Charles *v.1 p.561*

Eliot, George *v.2 p.286, p.287*

Eliot, Simon *v.6 p.741*

Eliot, T. S. *v.1 p.249, p.337, p.407,v.2 p.3, p.71, p.180*

Elizabeth, Lynne & Adams, Cassandra (Editors) . . . *v.1 p.796*

El-Khawas, Mohamed A. & Ndumbe, J. Anyu *v.4 p.398*

Elkin, A. P. *v.4 p.36*

Elkin *v.4 p.735*

Elkind, David *v.4 p.342, v.5 p.626, p.641*

Elkind, Sarah S. *v.4 p.543, v.6 p.722*

Elkins, James (Editor) *v.1 p.702*

Elkins, James *v.1 p.701*

Elkins, Marilyn *v.2 p.63*

Elkins, Stanley M. & McKitrick, Eric L. *v.4 p.517*

Elkins, T. H. & Hofmeister, B. *v.3 p.181*

Ellacuria, Ignacio, et al. *v.3 p.299*

Elledge, Scott *v.2 p.133*

Ellen, Roy *v.4 p.29*

Ellens, J. Harold & Rollins, Wayne G. (Editors) . . . *v.5 p.633*

Eller, Cynthia *v.3 p.51*

Ellerman, A. Denny, et al. *v.6 p.299*

Ellert, H. *v.6 p.77*

Ellin, Nan (Editor) *v.6 p.727*

Ellington, Duke *v.1 p.258, p.323*

Ellington, Lucien *v.6 p.166*

Ellingwood, Bruce Jr. & Kanda, Jun (Editors) *v.5 p.685*

Ellinwood, Leonard *v.1 p.277*

Elliot, Alison J. *v.4 p.356*

Elliott, Anthony & Ray, Larry (Editors) *v.4 p.677*

Elliott, Charles B. *v.6 p.179*

Elliott, Clark A. *v.5 p.395*

Elliott, David J. *v.1 p.405*

Elliott, Doug *v.5 p.221*

Elliott, Emory (Editor) *v.2 p.6*

Elliott, J. H. *v.3 p.73, p.238*

Elliott, J. K. (Editor) *v.1 p.632*

Elliott, Jean Leonard *v.3 p.542*

Elliott, John Hall *v.1 p.631*

Elliott, John H. *v.3 p.145*

Elliott, John Huxtable *v.3 p.238*

Elliott, Kamilla *v.6 p.325*

Elliott, Lawrence *v.3 p.457*

Elliott, Marianne *v.3 p.137*

Elliott, Martha *v.1 p.395, p.400*

Elliott, Robert S. *v.5 p.728*

Elliott, Russell R. & Rowley, William D. *v.3 p.529*

Elliott, Russell R. (Foreword by) *v.3 p.529*

Elliott, Stephen, et al. *v.4 p.356*

Elliott, Stephen *v.5 p.305*

Elliott, Ward E. *v.4 p.461*

Ellis, Alan, et al. *v.6 p.360*

Ellis, Alan L. & Riggle, Ellen D. (Editors) *v.4 p.133*
Ellis, Albert *v.5 p.665*
Ellis, Alexander J. *v.2 p.556*
Ellis, B. D. *v.1 p.505*
Ellis, Bruce J. & Bjorklund, David F. (Editors) *v.5 p.626*
Ellis, Charles D. & Vertin, James R. (Editors) *v.4 p.94*
Ellis, Charles D. & Vertin, James
   R. *v.4 p.88, p.89, p.94, p.146, p.147, p.155, p.162*
Ellis, Charles D. (Editor) *v.4 p.94*
Ellis, Charles D. *v.4 p.94*
Ellis, David M. *v.3 p.490*
Ellis, David *v.2 p.362*
Ellis, Edward Robb *v.3 p.490*
Ellis, Elisabeth *v.4 p.491*
Ellis, George *v.5 p.710*
Ellis, Havelock & Symonds, John Addington *v.6 p.381*
Ellis, Havelock *v.4 p.747, v.6 p.254*
Ellis, Jack C. & McLane, Betsy *v.6 p.309*
Ellis, Jack C. *v.6 p.309*
Ellis, Jack *v.6 p.305*
Ellis, Joseph H. *v.4 p.81*
Ellis, Joseph J. *v.4 p.485*
Ellis, Lewis Ethan *v.3 p.372, p.446*
Ellis, Lynn W. *v.4 p.118*
Ellis, R. J. *v.2 p.53*
Ellis, Richard E. *v.4 p.462*
Ellis, Richard J. *v.4 p.547*
Ellis, Richard *v.5 p.428*
Ellis, Roger & Zapel, Theodore O. (Editors) *v.1 p.120*
Ellis, Stephen & Mabandla, Oyama *v.4 p.613*
Ellis, Stephen & ter Haar, Gerrie *v.1 p.542*
Ellis, Steve (Editor) *v.2 p.209*
Ellis, Steve *v.2 p.209*
Ellis, Steven G. *v.3 p.136*
Ellis, Virginia R. *v.2 p.293*
Ellis, Willis D. *v.5 p.606*
Ellis-Fermor, Una *v.2 p.227, p.229*
Ellison, Michael & Pina, Leslie A. *v.1 p.804*
Ellison, Ralph *v.2 p.144, v.6 p.24*
Ellman, Richard *v.2 p.320, p.582*
Ellman, Steven J. & Antrobus, John S. (Editors) . . .*v.5 p.612*
Ellmann, Maud *v.2 p.335*
Ellmann, Richard & O'Clair, Robert (Editors) *v.2 p.22*
Ellmann, Richard (Editor) *v.2 p.22*
Ellmann, Richard *v.2 p.326, p.358, v.6 p.401*
Ellner, Steve & Hellinger, Daniel (Editors) *v.3 p.360*
Ellner, Steve *v.3 p.360*
Ellrodt, Robert *v.2 p.182*
Ellul, Jacques & Kings, Cecelia Gaul *v.1 p.643*
Ellul, Jacques *v.4 p.425, p.696*
Ellwood, Robert S. *v.1 p.530*
Elm, Susanna *v.1 p.653*
El-Mallah, Issam *v.1 p.287*
Elman, Benjamin A. *v.5 p.392, p.410*
Elmer, Laurel *v.6 p.69*

Elmessiri, Abdelwahab M. (Editor, Translator) . . .*v.6 p.659*
Elofson, W. M. *v.3 p.545*
Elon, Amos *v.6 p.610, p.613*
Elphick, Jonathan *v.5 p.78, p.214*
El-Rabbany, Ahmed *v.4 p.389*
El-Rewini, Hesham & Abd-El-Barr, Mostafa *v.5 p.729*
El-Rouayheb, Khaled *v.6 p.392*
El-Sadat, Anwar *v.6 p.639*
Elshtain, Jean Bethke *v.6 p.440, p.464*
Elsie, Robert (Editor, Translator) *v.2 p.815*
Elsie, Robert *v.2 p.815, v.3 p.251*
Elsner, J. R. *v.1 p.669, p.686*
Elson, Diane & Keklik, Hanse *v.6 p.456*
Elson, R. E. *v.6 p.174, p.176*
Elson Roessler, Shirley & Miklos, Reinhold *v.3 p.74*
Elson-Roessler, Shirley *v.6 p.453*
Elsschot, Willem *v.2 p.623*
Elster, Jon *v.5 p.643*
Elstun, Esther N. *v.2 p.603*
Elton, Arthur *v.6 p.737, p.763, p.765*
Elton, Charles S. *v.5 p.54, v.6 p.291*
Elton, Geoffrey R. *v.3 p.93, p.99, p.100*
Eluard, Paul *v.2 p.516, p.517*
Elvin, Mark & Liu, Ts'ui-jung *v.6 p.184, p.198*
Elvin, Mark *v.6 p.184*
Elwall, Robert (Editor) *v.1 p.762*
Elwell, Frank W. *v.4 p.221*
Elwell, Sue Levi (Editor), et al. *v.6 p.374*
Elwell-Sutton, L. P. *v.6 p.669*
Elwert, W. Theodor *v.2 p.453*
Elwes, Catherine *v.1 p.771*
Ely, James W. *v.4 p.467*
Elzea, Betty *v.1 p.696*
Elzea, Rowland *v.1 p.738*
Elzinga, Richard J. *v.5 p.212*
Emadi, Ali *v.5 p.716*
Emanoil, Mary (Editor) in association with IUCN-The World
   Conservation Union *v.5 p.221, p.225*
Emanuel, James A. (Editor) *v.2 p.19*
Ember, Carol R. & Ember, Melvin (Editors) *v.4 p.46*
Ember, Melvin & Ember, Carol R. (Editors) *v.6 p.717*
Embree, Ainslie T. & de Bary, Wm. Theodore *v.6 p.208*
Embree, Ainslie T. *v.1 p.535*
Embree, Lester (General Editor) *v.1 p.510*
Embretson, Susan E. & Hershberger, Scott L. (Editors) *v.5 p.600*
Embretson, Susan E. & Reise, Steven P. *v.5 p.600*
Embrey, Peter G. & Fuller, John P. *v.5 p.435*
Embry, Jessie L. *v.4 p.740*
Emden, Helmut F. van & Peakall, David P. *v.5 p.9*
Emecheta, Buchi *v.2 p.754*
Emenyonu, Ernest N. & Uko, Iniobong (Editors) . . .*v.2 p.753*
Emergency Nurses Association Staff & Newberry,
   Lorene *v.5 p.531*
Emerling, Jae *v.1 p.702*
Emerson, Caryl *v.1 p.197, p.345*

Emerson, D. *v.5 p.65*

Emerson, Edward Waldo *v.2 p.37*

Emerson, Everett H. *v.3 p.499*

Emerson, Ken *v.1 p.277, p.324*

Emerson, Ralph Waldo & Carlyle, Thomas . . *v.2 p.38, p.276*

Emerson, Ralph Waldo, et al. *v.2 p.38*

Emerson, Ralph Waldo *v.1 p.439, p.515, v.2 p.37, p.38*

Emerson, Robert W. *v.4 p.109*

Emerson, Thomas E. *v.4 p.10*

Emery, Lynne Fauley *v.1 p.14, p.18, p.19, p.31, p.34*

Emery, Michael, et al. *v.4 p.409*

Emery, Michael *v.4 p.406*

Emery, Robert E. *v.4 p.735, v.5 p.639*

Emery, William J. *v.5 p.430*

Eminescu, Mihai *v.2 p.817*

Emmanuel, Le Roy Ladurie *v.3 p.244*

Emmanuel, Steven M. (Editor) *v.1 p.436*

Emmel, Hildegard *v.2 p.592*

Emmelman, Debra S. *v.6 p.267*

Emmer, Michele (Editor) *v.1 p.702*

Emmerij, Louis, et al. *v.4 p.633*

Emmerson, Donald K. (Editor) *v.4 p.622*

Emmerson, Simon (Editor) *v.1 p.213, p.244, p.386*

Emmett, Ayala H. *v.6 p.617*

Emmons, Mark *v.6 p.305*

Emmons, Robert A. & McCullough, Michael E.
(Editors) *v.5 p.652*

Emmons, Robert A. *v.5 p.652*

Emmons, Shirlee & Sonntag, Stanley *v.1 p.395*

Emmons, Terence *v.4 p.726*

Emory, Jerry *v.5 p.83*

Empiricus, Sextus *v.1 p.517*

Empson, William *v.2 p.253, p.568*

Emrich, Duncan *v.2 p.22*

Emsley, Clive *v.3 p.74*

Emsley, John *v.5 p.264, p.308*

Enchi, Fumiko *v.6 p.229*

Enderle, Georges *v.4 p.53*

Enderlin, Charles *v.4 p.649*

Enders, Walter *v.4 p.206*

Endicott-West, E., et al. *v.4 p.623, v.6 p.239*

Endo, I. (Editor), et al. *v.5 p.126*

Endo, Shusaku *v.6 p.229*

Endres, Anthony M. & Fleming, Grant A. *v.4 p.630*

Ener, Mine *v.6 p.637*

Energy Information Administration, National Energy Information
Center, U.S. Dept. of Energy *v.5 p.452*

Energy Information Administration, U.S. Department of
Energy *v.5 p.452*

Enfield, N. J. (Editor) *v.4 p.20*

Eng, David L. & Hom, Alice Y. (Editors) *v.6 p.111*

Eng, David L. *v.6 p.96, p.111*

Eng, Lai A. *v.6 p.173*

Engberg, Siri & Banach, Joan *v.1 p.756*

Engel, Andreas & Van den Broeck, Christian P. L. . *v.5 p.558*

Engel, Barbara A. & Posadskaia-Vanderbeck, Anastasia
(Editors) *v.3 p.222*

Engel, Barbara A. (Editor), et al. *v.3 p.219*

Engel, Barbara Alpern . . . *v.3 p.53, p.211, p.217, v.6 p.454*

Engel, Barbara T. (Editor) *v.4 p.829, p.879*

Engel, Bernard F. *v.2 p.102*

Engel, James F. *v.4 p.134*

Engel, June *v.6 p.443*

Engel, Lehman *v.1 p.404*

Engel, M. & Macko, S. *v.5 p.440*

Engel, Michael *v.4 p.326*

Engel, Pal *v.3 p.186, v.6 p.562*

Engel, Pascal *v.1 p.492*

Engel, Susan L. *v.5 p.626*

Engelhardt, Elizabeth S. D. *v.2 p.8, p.12*

Engelhardt, H. Tristram *v.5 p.247*

Engelmann, Bernt *v.3 p.171*

Engels, Donald W. *v.3 p.21*

Engels, Friedrich *v.4 p.34, p.207, p.737*

Engels, John *v.2 p.144*

Engen, Rodney K. *v.1 p.751, p.752*

England, Crystal *v.4 p.302*

England, Paula & Farkas, George . *v.4 p.724, p.733, v.6 p.456*

England, Paula (Editor) *v.6 p.427*

England, Paula *v.4 p.133*

Engle, Margarita M. *v.6 p.506*

Engle, Paul *v.2 p.71*

Engle, R. F. & McFadden, D. L. (Editors) . . . *v.4 p.199*

Engle, R. F. (Editor) *v.4 p.199*

Engle, R. F. *v.4 p.199*

Engle, Ron & Miller, Tice L. (Editors) *v.1 p.113*

Engler, Mira *v.1 p.813*

English, Daylanne K. *v.2 p.10*

English, James (Editor) *v.2 p.178, p.194*

English, James F. *v.2 p.195*

English, John & McLaughlin, Kenneth *v.3 p.544*

English, John *v.3 p.539, p.541, v.4 p.588*

English, Leona M. (Editor) *v.4 p.320*

English, Richard A. (Editor) *v.4 p.677*

Englund, Harri (Editor) *v.4 p.611*

Engman, Max & Kirby, David (Editors) *v.4 p.594*

Engster, Daniel *v.4 p.491, p.496, p.498*

Enloe, Cynthia H. *v.6 p.440*

Enloe, Cynthia *v.6 p.440, p.464*

Ennis, Philip H. *v.1 p.268*

Ennius, Quintus *v.2 p.434*

Enoka, Roger *v.4 p.908, p.909*

Enoksen, Eystein, et al. *v.4 p.788, p.793*

Enright, Anne *v.3 p.343*

Enriquez, Juan *v.5 p.132*

Enser, A. G. S. *v.6 p.325*

Ensminger, Audrey H. et al. (Editors) *v.5 p.329*

Ensrud, Barbara *v.5 p.52*

Entelis, John P. (Editor) *v.1 p.553*

Entine, Jon, et al. *v.4 p.815, p.831*

Entman, Robert M. *v.4 p.558*

Entwhistle, Noel & Ramsden, Paul *v.5 p.574*

Entwistle, W. J. *v.2 p.635*

Environmental Action Coalition Staff, et al. *v.5 p.320*

Enz, Charles P. *v.5 p.542*

Enzensberger, Hans Magnus *v.2 p.606, p.607*

Epicurus *v.1 p.429, v.2 p.409*

Eppard, Philip B. (Editor) *v.2 p.106*

Eppel, Michael *v.6 p.602*

Epstein, Adam *v.4 p.883, p.900*

Epstein, Daniel Mark *v.2 p.97*

Epstein, Debbie (Editor) *v.6 p.385*

Epstein, Dena J. *v.1 p.281*

Epstein, Edward C. *v.4 p.121*

Epstein, Edward Jay *v.6 p.344*

Epstein, Emanuel & Bloom, Arnold J. *v.5 p.45*

Epstein, Irving (Editor) *v.4 p.334*

Epstein, Isidore *v.1 p.546*

Epstein, James A. *v.6 p.751, p.758*

Epstein, Jason *v.4 p.149*

Epstein, Joseph *v.4 p.739*

Epstein, Klaus W. *v.3 p.167*

Epstein, Lee *v.4 p.536*

Epstein, Lewis Carroll *v.5 p.556, p.563*

Epstein, Marc J. & Birchard, Bill *v.4 p.85*

Epstein, Marc J. *v.4 p.113*

Epstein, Richard A. *v.4 p.133*

Epstein, Richard J. *v.5 p.126*

Epstein, Rob & Friedman, Jeffrey (Directed
Bys) *v.6 p.365, p.388, p.421*

Epstein, Rob, and Jeffrey Friedman, producers . . .*v.6 p.378*

Epstein, Scarlett, et al. *v.4 p.771*

Epstein, Steven A. *v.3 p.199, v.6 p.562*

Epstein, Steven *v.6 p.378*

Equiano, Olaudah *v.2 p.28*

Equipo *v.2 p.635*

Erasmus, Desiderius & Luther, Martin *v.1 p.644*

Erasmus, Desiderius *v.1 p.593, v.2 p.623*

Erb, Uwe & Keller, Harald *v.5 p.387, p.679*

Erbisch, Frederic H. (Editor), et al. *v.5 p.7*

Erck, Dan, et al. *v.4 p.176*

Erdener, Yldray *v.6 p.665*

Erdey, Charles K. *v.5 p.693*

Erdman, David V. & Blake, William *v.2 p.239*

Erdman, David V. & Grant, John E. (Editors) . . .*v.2 p.239*

Erdman, David V. (ed.) *v.2 p.239*

Erdman, David V. *v.2 p.239*

Erdrich, Louise *v.2 p.144, p.145, v.6 p.697*

Ereaut, Gill (Editor), et al. *v.4 p.135*

Erenberg, Lewis A. *v.3 p.490*

Ereshefsky, Marc (Editor) *v.5 p.198, p.226*

Ereshefsky, Marc *v.5 p.204*

Ergas, Zaki (Editor) *v.4 p.611*

Ericksen, Robert P. & Heschel, Susannah (Editors) . .*v.1 p.609*

Erickson, Carolly *v.6 p.562*

Erickson, H. Lynn *v.4 p.362*

Erickson, Janet D. & Sproul, Adelaide *v.1 p.759*

Erickson, John A. *v.1 p.569*

Erickson, John *v.3 p.227*

Erickson, Jonathon S. *v.5 p.191*

Erickson, Jon *v.5 p.428*

Erickson, Lee *v.3 p.119, v.6 p.741*

Erickson, Millard J. *v.1 p.645*

Erickson, Paul A. & Murphy, Liam Donat (Editors) . *v.4 p.23*

Erickson, Paul A. & Murphy, Liam Donat *v.4 p.23*

Erickson, Raymond (Editor) *v.1 p.197, p.354*

Ericson, Margaret *v.6 p.474*

Eriksen, Thomas Hylland *v.4 p.34*

Erikson, Erik H. *v.4 p.735, v.5 p.513, p.658*

Erikson, Kai T. *v.4 p.760*

Eriksson, K., et al. *v.5 p.500*

Eriksson, Torsten *v.6 p.274*

Erisman, H. Michael *v.3 p.308*

Erlen, Jonathon & Spillane, Joseph F. *v.4 p.448*

Erler, Mary Carpenter & Kowaleski, Maryanne
(Editors) *v.6 p.559*

Erlich, Gloria C. *v.2 p.131*

Erlich, Haggai *v.6 p.67, p.637*

Erlich, H. *v.5 p.121*

Erlich, Victor *v.2 p.798*

Erlmann, Veit *v.1 p.285*

Erman, Adolf *v.6 p.57*

Ermatinger, Emil *v.2 p.591*

Ernaux, Annie *v.2 p.530*

Ernest, Paul A. *v.5 p.462*

Ernst & Young LLP, et al. *v.4 p.94*

Ernst & Young LLP Staff, et al. *v.4 p.85*

Ernst, Earle *v.1 p.132, p.134*

Ernst, Erika J. & Rogers, P. David *v.5 p.112*

Erofeev, Venedikt *v.2 p.803*

Erofeyev, Victor *v.2 p.803*

Erricker, Clive & Erricker, Jane *v.4 p.307*

Errington, J. Joseph *v.4 p.21*

Errington, Malcolm *v.3 p.19*

Erskine, James A., et al. *v.4 p.177*

Erskine, John *v.2 p.182*

Erskine, Robb *v.1 p.91, p.96*

Erskine, Robertson (Editor) *v.2 p.680*

Ertegun, Ahmet *v.1 p.268, p.383*

Ervin, David E. *v.5 p.7, p.21*

Ervin, Hazel Arnett & Holladay, Hilary (Editors) . . .*v.2 p.109*

Ervin, Hazel Arnett (Editor) *v.6 p.24, p.35*

Ervin, Hazel Arnett *v.6 p.24, p.35*

Ervin, Sam J. Jr. *v.3 p.470*

Erwin, D. C. & Stuteville, Donald L. (Editors) *v.5 p.46*

Erwin, Donald C. & Ribeiro, Olaf K. *v.5 p.46*

Erwin, Wallace M. *v.6 p.653*

Esack, Farid *v.1 p.558, p.559*

Esbensen, Finn-Aage (Editor), et al. *v.4 p.714*

Escobar, Anna María, et al. *v.2 p.635*

Escobar, Dario (Editor) . . . . *.v.6 p.90*

Escobar, Edward J. . . . . . *.v.4 p.774, v.6 p.265, p.537, p.548*

Escobar, Jesus . . . . *.v.1 p.796*

Escobar, Samuel E. . . . . *.v.1 p.647*

Escoffier, Jeffrey & Lore, Matthew (Editors) . . . *.v.1 p.28, p.30*

Escott, Colin, et al. . . . . *.v.1 p.268, p.368*

Esdaile, Charles J. . . . . *.v.3 p.75, p.152, p.240*

Esfandiari, Haleh . . . . *.v.6 p.632*

Eshelby, Martin E. *.v.5 p.717*

Esherick, Joseph & Rankin, Mary Backus . . . . . *.v.6 p.187*

Esherick, Joseph W. . . . . *.v.6 p.188*

eSipka, Danko . . . . *.v.2 p.774, p.776, p.778*

Eskridge, William N. Jr. (Editor) . . . . *.v.4 p.457*

Eskridge, William N. Jr. . . . . *.v.6 p.388*

Eslinger, Ellen . . . . *.v.1 p.648*

Esmonde, Jody & Murty, Maruti Ram . . . . *.v.5 p.475*

Espada, Martin . . . . *.v.6 p.506, p.512*

Espasa Staff (Editor) . . . . *.v.2 p.635*

Espejo, Roman (Editor) . . . . *.v.5 p.162, p.247*

Espenak, Liljan . . . . *.v.1 p.50*

Espie, Susan (Editor) . . . . *.v.2 p.643*

Espinosa, Aurelio M. . . . . *.v.6 p.523*

Espiritu, Yen Le . . *.v.6 p.85, p.93, p.111, p.120, p.123, p.129*

Esposito, David M. *.v.3 p.470*

Esposito, John L. & Voll, John O. . . . . *.v.4 p.500*

Esposito, John L. (Author, Editor) . . . . *.v.1 p.555*

Esposito, John L. (Editor) . . . . . . *.v.1 p.554, v.6 p.632*

Esposito, John L. . . . . *.v.1 p.557, v.4 p.658*

Esquibel, Catrióna Rueda . . . . . *.v.6 p.392, p.498, p.512*

Esquivel, Laura . . . . *.v.2 p.667*

Essed, Philomena & Goldberg, David Theo
(Editors) . . . . *.v.6 p.360, p.370, p.425, p.429*

Esser, K. (Editor), et al. . . . . *.v.5 p.209*

Esslin, Martin . . . . *.v.1 p.92, p.96, v.2 p.507*

Esslinger, Dean R. . . . . *.v.3 p.514, v.6 p.711*

Esteller, Manel (Editor) . . . . *.v.5 p.132*

Esterberg, Kristin G. . . . . *.v.6 p.366, p.374*

Estes, Jack C. . . . . *.v.4 p.163*

Esteves, Sandra M. . . . . *.v.6 p.506, p.510*

Estlund, David M. (Editor) . . . . *.v.4 p.503*

Estrin, Mark W. (Editor) . . . . *.v.2 p.107*

Etchemendy, John . . . . *.v.1 p.494*

Etcheson, Craig . . . . *.v.4 p.652*

Etherington, Norman (Contribution by) . . . . . *.v.3 p.88, p.124*

Etherington, Norman . . . . . . *.v.1 p.611, v.2 p.290, v.6 p.79*

Etiemble . . . . *.v.2 p.453*

Etkin, Bernard & Reid, Lloyd Duff . . . . *.v.5 p.717*

Ettedgui, Peter . . . . *.v.6 p.348*

Ettinger, Stephen J. & Feldman, Edward C.
(Editors) . . . . *.v.5 p.54, p.57*

Ettinghausen, Richard, et al. . . . . *.v.1 p.673, p.691*

Etue, Elizabeth & Williams, Megan K. . . . *.v.4 p.835, p.862*

Etulain, Richard W. (Editor) . . . . *.v.3 p.518, p.528*

Etzioni, Amitai & Lawrence, Paul R. (Editors) . . *.v.4 p.269*

Etzioni, Amitai & Marsh, Jason H. . . . . . *.v.4 p.563, p.572*

Etzioni, Amitai . . . . *.v.4 p.185, p.213, p.262, p.269, p.515,
p.626, p.628, p.629, p.716, p.750, p.768, p.770*

Euchner, Charles C. & McGovern, Stephen J. . . . *.v.6 p.723*

Euchner, Charles C. . . . . *.v.4 p.883, p.891, p.896*

Eucken, W. . . . . *.v.4 p.209*

Euclid . . . . *.v.5 p.465, p.495*

Eudes, Dominique . . . . *.v.3 p.195*

Eugenides, Jeffrey . . . . *.v.2 p.145, v.6 p.396*

Euraque, Darío A. *.v.3 p.300*

Euripides & Denniston, John D. . . . . *.v.2 p.410*

Euripides . . . . *.v.1 p.71, p.88, v.2 p.410, p.411*

European Commission Delegation to the United States *.v.4 p.474*

European Commission . . . . *.v.4 p.637*

European Parliament . . . . *.v.4 p.474*

European Society for the History of Economic Thoug *.v.4 p.227*

European Union - Delegation of the European Commission to
the United States . . . . *.v.4 p.603, p.637*

European Union . . . . . . *.v.4 p.474, p.482, p.603, p.637*

Eusebius . . . . *.v.3 p.30*

Evangelista, Matthew . . . . *.v.4 p.656*

Evangelista, Nick . . . . *.v.4 p.857, p.877*

Evangelou, V. P. . . . . *.v.5 p.313*

Evans, Alun . . . . *.v.6 p.322*

Evans, B. Ifor . . . . *.v.2 p.229*

Evans, Benjamin I. . . . . *.v.2 p.185*

Evans, C. Lawrence . . . . *.v.4 p.533*

Evans, C. Stephen . . . . *.v.1 p.478*

Evans, Craig A. & Porter, Stanley E. (Editors) . . . *.v.1 p.625*

Evans, Craig A. (Editor) . . . . *.v.1 p.615*

Evans, Craig A. . . . . *.v.1 p.617, p.625*

Evans, D. Fennell & Wennerström, Håkan . . . . . *.v.5 p.283*

Evans, David H. (Editor) . . . . *.v.5 p.214*

Evans, David J. A. (Editor) . . . . *.v.4 p.390*

Evans, David J. A. . . . . *.v.4 p.391*

Evans, David S. & Schmalensee,
Richard . . . . *.v.4 p.95, p.155, p.245, p.263*

Evans, Eli . . . . *.v.3 p.498*

Evans, Elizabeth . . . . *.v.2 p.94, p.118*

Evans, G. R. (Translator, Foreword by) . . . . . . *.v.3 p.56*

Evans, G. R. . . . . . . *.v.1 p.638, p.646, p.655, v.3 p.56*

Evans, Gail . . . . *.v.4 p.167*

Evans, Gerard . . . . *.v.2 p.594*

Evans, Gillian (Editor) . . . . *.v.1 p.649*

Evans, Gillian R. *.v.1 p.579*

Evans, Glen & Farberow, Norman L. . . . *.v.4 p.677, v.5 p.662*

Evans, Graham & Newnham, Richard . . . . . . *.v.4 p.626*

Evans, Grant . . . . *.v.6 p.171*

Evans, Gwynne A. . . . . *.v.5 p.492*

Evans, Harriet & Donald, Stephanie (Editors) . . . *.v.6 p.195*

Evans, Helen C. & Wixom, William D. (Editors) . . *.v.1 p.672*

Evans, Helen C. (Editor) . . . . *.v.1 p.671, p.686*

Evans, Howard E. & DeLahunta, Alexander . . . . *.v.5 p.88*

Evans, Howard E. *.v.5 p.230*

Evans, James A. . . . . *.v.3 p.192*

Evans, James Allan . . . . *.v.3 p.192*

Evans, James *v.5 p.61*

Evans, Janet M. *v.4 p.153*

Evans, John *v.1 p.696*

Evans, Julian & Turnball, John W. *v.5 p.37*

Evans, Karen (Editor), et al. *v.4 p.304*

Evans, L. T. *v.5 p.21*

Evans, Lawrence C. *v.5 p.487*

Evans, Leonard *v.5 p.682*

Evans, Mari *v.6 p.24, p.43*

Evans, Mari-Lynn (Editor), et al. *v.3 p.489*

Evans, Merran, et al. *v.5 p.481*

Evans, Michael & Ryan, Alan (Editors) *v.5 p.583*

Evans, Oliver *v.2 p.105*

Evans, Patricia R. *v.4 p.436*

Evans, Patrick *v.2 p.740*

Evans, Peter *v.1 p.213, p.314*

Evans, Philip & Wurster, Thomas S. *v.4 p.77*

Evans, R. J. *v.3 p.181*

Evans, Richard J. *v.3 p.35, p.83, p.178*

Evans, Robert & Pogge von Strandmann, Hartmut
(Editors) *v.3 p.76*

Evans, Rod L. & Berent, Irwin M. (Editors) *v.4 p.448*

Evans, Ronald W. *v.4 p.362*

Evans, Rowland & Novak, Robert *v.3 p.470*

Evans, Rowland *v.3 p.470*

Evans, Sara *v.6 p.449*

Evans, Sterling *v.3 p.268*

Evans, Walker & Hambourg, Maria Morris *v.1 p.766*

Evans, Warren J., et al. *v.5 p.54*

Evans-Pritchard, Edward E. *v.4 p.36, p.38, v.6 p.59*

Evans-Wentz, W. T. (Editor, Compiled by) *v.1 p.563*

Evans-Wentz, W. Y. & Lopez, Donald S. *v.1 p.561*

Eveleth, William T. (Editor) *v.5 p.318*

Evelyn, John *v.3 p.105*

Evensen, Bruce J. (Author, Editor) *v.1 p.648*

Even-Shoshan, Abraham (Editor) *v.6 p.646*

Evenson, Debra *v.3 p.308*

Evenson, R. E. & Gollin, D. (Editors) *v.5 p.21*

Everett, Anna *v.6 p.329, p.341*

Everett, Paul *v.1 p.184, p.239, p.364*

Everett, T. H. (Editor) *v.5 p.44*

Everett, T.H. (Editor) *v.5 p.44*

Everett, Walter *v.1 p.268, p.305*

Everett, William & Laird, Paul R. (Editors) . . *v.1 p.59, p.92*

Everett, William A. & Laird, Paul R. (Editors) . . . *v.1 p.249*

Everett, William *v.1 p.166, p.249*

Everhart, William C. *v.5 p.18*

Everist, Mark *v.1 p.177*

Evers, Frederick & Rush, James *v.4 p.303*

Everson, Stephen (Editor) *v.1 p.483*

Everson, William K. *v.6 p.312*

Everson, William *v.2 p.71, p.91*

Evert, Ray F. & Eichhorn, Susan E. *v.5 p.156*

Evertson, Carolyn & Weinstein, Carol S. (Editors) . . *v.4 p.283*

Eves, Charles K. *v.2 p.256*

Eves, Howard W. *v.5 p.465, p.495*

Evin, Ahmet O. *v.6 p.666*

Evliya Celebi *v.6 p.589*

Evliya, Efendi *v.6 p.622*

Evron, Boas *v.6 p.613*

Ewald, William Bragg Jr. *v.4 p.148, p.166*

Ewan, Elizabeth *v.6 p.577*

Ewans, Martin *v.6 p.633*

Ewbank, Alison J. & Papageorgiou, Fouli T. (Editors) *v.1 p.268*

Ewell, Judith *v.3 p.360, p.388*

Ewen, Stuart *v.4 p.52, p.428*

Ewens, W. J. & Grant, Gregory *v.5 p.107*

Ewens, Warren J. & Grant, Gregory . *v.5 p.107, p.482, p.502*

Ewing, Alfred C. *v.1 p.417*

Ewing, Galen Wood (Editor) *v.5 p.267*

Ewing, Kenneth D. *v.4 p.581*

Ewing, Tom *v.1 p.268, p.342*

Ewing, William A. *v.1 p.45*

Exbrayat, Jean-Marie *v.5 p.139*

Exiner, Johanna & Kelynak, Denis *v.1 p.50*

Eyck, Frank *v.3 p.168*

Eyerman, Ron & Jamison, Andrew *v.1 p.377*

Eyk, Jennifer E.Van & Dunn, Michael J.
(Editors) *v.5 p.116, p.148*

Eymann, Marcia & Wollenberg, Charles . *v.4 p.711, v.6 p.113*

Eymard, Pierre & Lafon, J. P. *v.5 p.475*

Eyre, Banning *v.1 p.285*

Eyring, Henry *v.5 p.276*

Eysenck, Hans J. & Martin, I. *v.5 p.666*

Eysenck, Hans Jürgen *v.5 p.612, p.652*

Ezekiel, Nissim, et al. *v.2 p.762*

Ezell, Margaret J. M. *v.2 p.169*

Ezergailis, Andrew *v.3 p.83, p.256*

Ezergailis, Inta M. *v.2 p.780*

F

Faass, Nancy *v.5 p.531*

Fabb, Nigel *v.2 p.552*

Fabbrizzi, Luigi & Poggi, Antonio (Editors) *v.5 p.265*

Faber, Daniel *v.3 p.268*

Faber, M. D. *v.5 p.633*

Faber, Melvin D. (Editor) *v.2 p.229*

Faber, Sebastiaan *v.3 p.292*

Faber, T. E. *v.5 p.547*

Fabian, Andrew (Editor), et al. *v.5 p.67*

Fabozzi, Frank J. *v.4 p.103*

Fabre, Genevieve & Feith, Michel (Editors) *v.2 p.126*

Fabre, Michel J. & Skinner, Robert E. (Editors) . . . *v.2 p.86*

Fabre, Michel J. *v.2 p.138*

Fabricant, Carole *v.2 p.263*

Fackenheim, Emil L. *v.1 p.551*

Fackre, Gabriel *v.1 p.633*

Facos, Michelle & Hirsh, Sharon (Editors) . . . *v.1 p.678, p.686*

Facts on File, Inc. Staff *v.5 p.387*

Fadala, Sam *v.4 p.795, p.847*

Faderman, Lillian & Eriksson, Brigitte . . . *v.6 p.362, p.421*

Faderman, Lillian & Xiong, Ghia *v.6 p.93, p.139*

Faderman, Lillian (Editor) *v.6 p.364, p.406*

Faderman, Lillian *v.4 p.750, v.6 p.364, p.401*

Fadiman, Anne *v.4 p.778, v.6 p.139, p.141*

Faery, Rebecca B. *v.2 p.3*

Faeth, Paul, et al. *v.5 p.29*

Fagan, Brian M. *v.4 p.10, v.5 p.425*

Fagan, Garrett G. *v.3 p.23*

Fagan, Jeffrey & Zimring, Franklin E. (Editors) . . . *v.6 p.269*

Fagan, Patrick *v.4 p.482*

Fagan, Thomas J. & Ax, Robert K. (Editors) *v.6 p.277*

Fage, J. D. & Tordoff, William *v.6 p.52*

Fage, J. D. *v.6 p.68*

Fagen, Herb *v.6 p.324*

Fagen, Richard R. & Tuohy, William S. *v.3 p.292*

Fagerberg, Jan (Editor), et al. *v.4 p.66*

Fageria, N. A., et al. *v.5 p.21, p.25*

Faggen, Robert (Editor) *v.2 p.77*

Fahey, Victora A. *v.5 p.527*

Fahim, Hussein M. *v.6 p.58, p.635*

Fahl, Ronald J. *v.4 p.164, v.5 p.37*

Fahlbusch, Erwin (Editor), et al. *v.1 p.594*

Fahlbusch, Erwin (Editor) *v.1 p.594*

Fahmy, Khaled *v.6 p.639*

Fahn, A. *v.5 p.155*

Fahy, Thomas; King, Kimball *v.1 p.86, p.94*

Fahy, Thomas Richard *v.2 p.682*

Faigman, David L. *v.4 p.536*

Faik, Sait *v.6 p.666*

Faille, Christopher C. *v.4 p.470*

Fain, Gerald S. (Editor) *v.4 p.783, p.802*

Fainaru, Steve & Sanchez, Ray *v.6 p.552*

Fainstein, Susan S. *v.6 p.723*

Fair, John D. *v.4 p.715*

Fair, Laura *v.6 p.66*

Fairbank, John K. & Teng, S. Y. *v.6 p.183*

Fairbank, John K. & Twitchett, Denis C. (Editor, Contribution by) *v.6 p.190*

Fairbank, John K. (Editor, Contribution by) . . *v.6 p.188, p.190*

Fairbank, John K. (Editor) *v.6 p.218*

Fairbank, John K. *v.3 p.388, v.6 p.201, p.214*

Fairbank, John King & Goldman, Merle *v.6 p.183*

Fairbank, Wilma *v.6 p.199*

Fairbrother, Trevor *v.1 p.738*

Fairer, David (Editor) *v.2 p.179*

Fairer, David *v.2 p.183*

Fairfax, Edmund *v.1 p.23*

Fairley, Barker *v.2 p.597, p.599*

Fairmont Press Staff & Kehlhofer, Rolf H. *v.5 p.708*

Fairris, David *v.4 p.121*

Fairservice, Don *v.6 p.350*

Faiz, Faiz Ahmad; Majeed, Sheema *v.6 p.162*

Faiz, Faiz Ahmad *v.6 p.151*

Faiz, Faiz Ahmed *v.6 p.151, p.162*

Fakhouri, Hani *v.4 p.702*

Fakhry, Majid *v.1 p.432*

Falah, Ghazi-Walid & Nagel, Caroline (Editors) . . . *v.6 p.581*

Falcón, Lidia *v.2 p.663*

Falcoff, Mark & Pike, Fredrick B. (Editors) . . *v.3 p.241, p.260*

Falcoff, Mark, et al. *v.3 p.353*

Falconer, John *v.1 p.763*

Falk, Doris V. *v.2 p.107*

Falk, Gerhard *v.4 p.805, p.858*

Falk, John H. & Dierking, Lynn D. *v.1 p.828*

Falk, Nancy Auer & Gross, Rita M. *v.1 p.528, v.6 p.459*

Falk, Peter H. (Editor) *v.1 p.664*

Falk, Quentin *v.2 p.349*

Falk, Richard A. *v.4 p.477, p.512, p.563, p.626*

Falk, Signi L. *v.2 p.134*

Falkner, David *v.4 p.805, p.831, p.850*

Fall, Aminata Sow *v.2 p.545*

Fallada, Hans *v.2 p.607*

Fallaize, Elizabeth (Editor) *v.2 p.465*

Fallon, Richard H. Jr. *v.4 p.536*

Fallon, Richard H. *v.4 p.453*

Fallon, Robert T. *v.2 p.253*

Fallows, David *v.1 p.179, p.322*

Falola, Toyin & Childs, Matt D. (Editors) . . . *v.3 p.303*

Falola, Toyin & Jennings, Christian (Editors) . . . *v.6 p.53*

Falola, Toyin (Editor) *v.6 p.52, p.53, p.71*

Falola, Toyin Omoyeni *v.4 p.702*

Falola, Toyin *v.6 p.51, p.55*

Faludi, Susan *v.6 p.429, p.433, p.469*

Families and Work Institute *v.5 p.580*

Fan, Gordon L. *v.5 p.154*

Fan, Hong Y. *v.4 p.835*

Fan, Jie, et al. *v.4 p.771*

Fanaroff, Avroy A., et al. *v.5 p.525*

Fancher, Gordon & Myers, Gerald (Editors) *v.1 p.41*

Fancher, Raymond E. *v.5 p.596*

Fane, Diana *v.3 p.263*

Fang, Hsai-Yang *v.5 p.421*

Fanning, Odom *v.5 p.250*

Fano, Ugo *v.5 p.554*

Fanon, Frantz *v.6 p.10, p.32, p.56, p.642*

Fanshel, David & Shinn, Eugene B. *v.4 p.756*

Fanshel, David, et al. *v.4 p.757*

Fante, John & Cooper, Stephen *v.2 p.72*

Fante, John *v.2 p.72*

Fantham, Elaine *v.2 p.424, p.438*

Fantina, Richard *v.2 p.84*

Fantoli, Annibale *v.3 p.46*

Fara, Patricia *v.5 p.231*

Farabee, David *v.6 p.277*

Faraday, Michael *v.5 p.564*

Farag, Ihab H. & Melsheimer, Stephen S. (Editors) . . *v.5 p.742*

Farah, Nuruddin *v.2 p.754*

Faraj, Maysaloun (Editor) *v.1 p.691*

Faranda, F. M., et al. *v.5 p.173, p.237*

Farazmand, Ali (Editor) *v.4 p.546*

Farazmand, Ali *v.4 p.616*

Farb, Peter *v.5 p.623*

Farber, David R. & Bailey, Beth L. *v.3 p.470*

Farber, David *v.3 p.515, v.4 p.153*

Farber, Eduard *v.5 p.260*

Farber, Paul Lawrence *v.3 p.44*

Farber, Vreneli *v.2 p.803*

Farcau, Bruce W. *v.3 p.274, v.4 p.591*

Farenga, Patrick & Holt, John *v.4 p.296*

Fares, Gustavo C., et al. *v.2 p.678*

Fargnoli, A. Nicholas & Gillespie, Michael P. *v.2 p.358*

Fargnoli, A. Nicholas *v.2 p.73*

Farhat, Hormoz *v.1 p.287*

Farkas, Miklós *v.5 p.90*

Farley, Edward *v.1 p.635*

Farley, Paul *v.2 p.344*

Farley, Reynolds & Haaga, John (Editors) *v.4 p.138*

Farley, Reynolds (Editor) *v.4 p.763*

Farley-Hills, David *v.2 p.259*

Farmaian, Sattareh F. *v.6 p.631*

Farmer, David Hugh *v.1 p.579, p.612*

Farmer, Henry G. *v.1 p.287*

Farmer, Paul *v.4 p.27, p.46, p.778*

Farmer, Peter J., et al. *v.4 p.880, p.883*

Farmer, Sharon A. *v.3 p.142*

Farneth, David *v.1 p.213, p.249, p.368*

Farnham, Christie Anne (Editor) *v.6 p.452*

Farnham, Willard *v.2 p.234*

Farnsworth, Jean M. (Editor), et al. *v.1 p.810*

Farnsworth, Paul (Editor) *v.4 p.13*

Farnsworth, Paul R. *v.1 p.375*

Farnsworth, Stephen J. & Lichter, S. Robert *v.4 p.558*

Farnsworth-Alvear, Ann *v.3 p.357*

Farnworth, Edward R. (Editor) *v.5 p.34*

Faro, Sebastian *v.5 p.516*

Faroqhi, Suraiya *v.4 p.641, v.6 p.589*

Farouk-Sluglett, Marion & Sluglett, Peter *v.6 p.602*

Farquhar, George *v.2 p.244*

Farquhar, Judith *v.6 p.193*

Farr, Dorothy Mary *v.2 p.218*

Farr, Marcia (Editor) *v.6 p.494, p.548*

Farr, Michael & Kursmark, Louise *v.4 p.169*

Farr, Michael J. (Based on a book by) *v.4 p.169*

Farr, Michael *v.4 p.167, p.169*

Farrand, Max *v.4 p.452*

Farrell, Brace *v.2 p.120*

Farrell, Edwin *v.4 p.299*

Farrell, Gerry *v.1 p.288*

Farrell, James T. *v.2 p.72*

Farrell, John A. *v.3 p.457*

Farrell, Joseph & Scuderi, Antonio *v.2 p.724*

Farrell, Joseph *v.1 p.107, v.2 p.423*

Farrell Lee, Grace *v.2 p.120*

Farrell, Michael P. & Rosenberg, Stanley . . *v.4 p.741, v.6 p.445*

Farrell, Michele L. *v.2 p.477*

Farrell, R. B. *v.2 p.621*

Farrell, Suzanne & Bentley, Toni *v.1 p.7*

Farrer, Austin & Conti, Charles Carl *v.1 p.634*

Farrier, Jasmine *v.4 p.531*

Farrington, Benjamin *v.5 p.392*

Farrington, David P. (Editor) *v.6 p.254*

Farrington, Karen *v.4 p.380*

Farrington, Lisa E. *v.1 p.704, p.706, v.6 p.16, p.43, p.472*

Farris, Phoebe M. (Editor) *v.1 p.706, v.6 p.472*

Farrokhzad, Forough *v.6 p.670*

Farrokhzad, Forugh *v.6 p.670*

Farsoun, Samih K. & Zacharia, Christina E. *v.6 p.617*

Farstrup, Alan E. & Samuels, S. Jay (Editors) . . . *v.4 p.363*

Fascione, Nina (Editor), et al. *v.6 p.283*

Fasham, M. J. R. (Editor) *v.5 p.112, p.172*

Fashola, Olatokunbo S. (Editor) *v.6 p.21, p.32*

Fashola, Olatokunbo S. *v.4 p.288*

Fasi, Allal *v.6 p.60, p.592*

Fass, Paula S. *v.4 p.326*

Fassett, Agatha *v.1 p.213, p.305*

Fast, Howard *v.2 p.73*

Fast, Susan *v.1 p.268, p.335*

Fast, Timothy H. & Fast, Cathy C. *v.6 p.425*

Fastovsky, David E. & Weishampel, David B. *v.5 p.448*

Fasulo, Michael, et al. *v.5 p.250*

Fath, Creekmore *v.1 p.756*

Fath, Manfred & Selz, Peter H. *v.1 p.779*

Faucheux, Sylvie (Editor), et al. *v.5 p.14*

Fauconnier, Gilles & Sweetser, Eve (Editors) . . . *v.2 p.560*

Fauconnier, Gilles, et al. *v.5 p.608*

Faul, Henry & Faul, Carol *v.5 p.418*

Faulkner, Harold U. *v.3 p.436*

Faulkner, L. L. & Logan, Earl *v.5 p.714*

Faulkner, Peter & Preston, Peter (Editors) *v.2 p.301*

Faulkner, Peter (Editor) *v.2 p.301*

Faulkner, Peter *v.2 p.301*

Faulkner, Virginia & Luebke, Frederick C. (Editors) . . *v.2 p.7*

Faulkner, William *v.2 p.73, p.74*

Faull, Katherine M. (Editor, Translator) *v.1 p.590*

Faunce, Roland Cleo *v.4 p.363*

Faundez, Julio *v.3 p.353*

Faura, Juan *v.4 p.138, v.6 p.526*

Faure, David & Pui-tak, Lee (Editors) *v.6 p.205*

Faure, David (Editor) *v.6 p.205*

Faure, Gunter & Mensing, Teresa M. *v.5 p.444*

Faurot, Jeannette L. *v.6 p.209*

Fausold, Martin L. *v.3 p.446, p.470*

Faust, David *v.5 p.401*

Faust, Drew G. *v.3 p.502, v.4 p.520*

Faust, Drew Gilpin *v.4 p.520*

Faust, Patricia L. (Editor) *v.3 p.430*

Faust, Rüdiger, et al. *v.5 p.259*

Faustman, Jean *v.2 p.537*

Fausto, Boris *v.3 p.340*

Fausto-Sterling, Anne *v.4 p.747, v.6 p.447*

Fauvel, John and Gray, Jeremy (Editors) *v.5 p.466*

Fauvel, John (Editor), et al. *v.1 p.374, v.3 p.46*

Favier, Jean *v.6 p.558*

Fawaz, Leila T. *v.6 p.605, p.607*

Fawcett, Millicent Garrett & Fawcett, Henry . *v.4 p.209, p.269*

Fawcett, Millicent Garrett *v.4 p.209, p.269, p.273*

Fawcett, Millicent *v.4 p.193, p.273*

Fawkes, Richard *v.6 p.316*

Fawn, Rick (Editor) *v.4 p.494*

Fawtier, Robert *v.3 p.142*

Fay, Elizabeth A. *v.2 p.323*

Fay, Elizabeth *v.2 p.171*

Fay, Laurel E. (Editor) *v.1 p.213, p.356*

Fay, Laurel *v.1 p.213, p.356*

Fay, Peter W. *v.6 p.187, p.204*

Çakmak, Ahmet S. & Freely, John *v.1 p.788*

Feagin, Joe R. & McKinney, Karyn D. *v.6 p.38*

Feagin, Joe R. & O'Brien, Eileen *v.4 p.729*

Feagin, Joe R. *v.4 p.680*

Fearing, James *v.4 p.130*

Fearing, Kenneth *v.2 p.73*

Fearn, Raymond *v.1 p.213, p.319*

Fearn-Banks, Kathleen *v.4 p.429, p.431, p.433*

Fearon, Peter *v.3 p.440, p.447*

Feather, John P. *v.2 p.576, v.3 p.119*

Feather, John *v.6 p.741*

Feather, Leonard & Gitler, Ira (Editors) . . .*v.1 p.159, p.258*

Feather, Leonard & Gitler, Ira *v.1 p.159, p.258*

Feather, Leonard *v.1 p.159, p.258*

Featherstone, Steve *v.4 p.390*

Feaver, Peter & Gelpi, Christopher *v.4 p.561*

Feaver, Peter & Kohn, Richard (Editors) *v.4 p.561*

Feaver, William *v.1 p.738*

Febvre, Lucien & Bataillon, Lionel *v.4 p.375*

Febvre, Lucien *v.2 p.472, p.576, v.3 p.37*

Feder, Martin E. & Burggren, Warren W.
(Editors) *v.5 p.163, p.184, p.214*

Feder, Stuart *v.1 p.213, p.333*

Federal Deposit Insurance Corporation *v.4 p.158*

Federal Election Commission *v.4 p.548, p.557*

Federal Register Office *v.4 p.481*

Federal Writers' Project Staff & Writers Program
Staff *v.3 p.485, p.486, p.489, p.491, p.493, p.502,
p.504, p.513, p.514, p.517, p.522, p.523, p.525, p.526, p.528,
p.529, p.531, p.533*

Federal Writers' Project
Staff *v.3 p.489, p.490, p.503, p.504, p.510, p.512
, p.515, p.516, p.522, p.523, p.524, p.525, p.526, p.532*

Federico, Giovanni *v.5 p.4*

Fedler, Fred *v.4 p.404*

Fedoroff, Nina & Botstein, David (Editors) *v.5 p.132*

Fee, Gordon D. *v.1 p.616, p.631*

Feeley, Malcolm M. & Rubin, Edward L. . . .*v.6 p.268, p.273*

Feelings, Tom *v.6 p.16, p.37*

Feeman, Timothy G. *v.5 p.500*

Feeney, Denis (Author, Contribution by) *v.1 p.532*

Feeney, Judith & Noller, Patricia *v.5 p.652, p.657*

Feenstra, Robert C. (Editor), et al. *v.4 p.257*

Feenstra, Robert C. *v.4 p.257*

Feenstra, Ronald & Plantinga, Cornelius Jr. *v.1 p.594*

Feest, Christian F. *v.1 p.682, v.6 p.678*

Feezell, Randolph *v.4 p.715*

Feher, Michel *v.2 p.465*

Fehervari, Geza *v.1 p.800*

Fehr, Beverley *v.5 p.647, p.652*

Fehr, W. R. & Hadley, H. H. (Editors) *v.5 p.21*

Fehrenbach, Heide *v.3 p.176*

Fehrenbach, T. R. *v.3 p.508, v.6 p.236*

Fehrenbacher, Don E. & Fehrenbacher, Virginia
(Editors) *v.3 p.396*

Fehrenbacher, Don E. *v.3 p.396, p.425, v.4 p.453*

Fei, Faye Chunfang (Editor) . . .*v.1 p.56, p.131, v.6 p.209*

Fei, Hsiao-tung *v.6 p.190*

Feierman, Steven *v.6 p.66*

Feifer, George *v.6 p.235*

Feigenbaum, Edward A. & Feldman, Julian (Editors) .*v.5 p.590*

Feigert, Frank *v.4 p.590*

Feigin, A., et al. *v.5 p.353, p.379*

Feigl, F. & Anger, V. *v.5 p.309*

Feigl, Fritz; Anger, Vinzenz *v.5 p.300*

Feigl, Herbert (Editor) *v.5 p.401*

Feigon, Lee *v.6 p.192, p.200, p.201*

Fein, David A. *v.2 p.469*

Feinberg, David B. *v.6 p.378, p.396, p.401*

Feinberg, Joel *v.1 p.491*

Feinberg, Leslie *v.6 p.362, p.366, p.370, p.396*

Feinberg, Richard & Ottenheimer, Martin (Editors) . .*v.4 p.32*

Feinendegen, Ludwig E. *v.5 p.148*

Feiner, Shmuel *v.3 p.179*

Feingold, Mordechai & Navarro-Brotons, Victor
(Editors) *v.4 p.334*

Feingold, Mordechai *v.3 p.47, v.4 p.334*

Feinstein, Elaine *v.2 p.352*

Feinstein, John & Auerbach, Red *v.4 p.823, p.853*

Feinstein, John (Author, Afterword by) *v.4 p.860*

Feinstein, John *v.4 p.853, p.893, p.902*

Feinstein, Karen *v.5 p.300*

Feinstein, Michael *v.6 p.409*

Feinstein, Sascha & Komunyakaa, Yusef (Editors) . .*v.2 p.583*

Feintuch, Burt (Editor) *v.2 p.584*

Feis, Herbert *v.3 p.76*

Feistritzer, C. Emily & Chester, David T. *v.4 p.278*

Feitell, Merrill *v.2 p.160*

Feith, Herbert & Castles, Lance (Editors) *v.6 p.174*

Feith, Herbert *v.6 p.174*

Feiwel, George R. (Editor) *v.4 p.213*

Feiwel, George R. *v.4 p.211*

Felbeck, David K. & Atkins, Anthony G. *v.5 p.688*

Feld, Barry C. *v.6 p.269, p.271*

Feld, Steven *v.1 p.298*

Feldenkrais, Moshe *v.1 p.50, p.51, p.52*
Felder, Raoul *v.4 p.74*
Feldhaus, Anne (Editor) *v.1 p.535*
Feldhaus, Anne *v.1 p.535, p.540*
Feldman, Anita *v.1 p.32*
Feldman, Daniel C. (Editor) *v.5 p.577*
Feldman, Elliot J. & Nevitte, Neil (Editors) *v.4 p.589*
Feldman, Frayda & Schellmann, Jorg (Editors) . . . *v.1 p.756*
Feldman, Fred *v.1 p.507*
Feldman, Gerald D. & Seibel, Wolfgang *v.3 p.171*
Feldman, Gerald D. *v.3 p.164, p.170*
Feldman, Jonathan *v.4 p.334*
Feldman, Marcus W. (Editor) *v.5 p.91, p.192*
Feldman, Martha S., et al. *v.4 p.690*
Feldman, Maurice (Editor) *v.4 p.316*
Feldman, Morton *v.1 p.213, p.324*
Feldman, Ofer & Valenty, Linda O. (Editors) *v.4 p.483, v.5 p.643*
Feldman, Paula R. & Kelley, Theresa M. (Editors) . . *v.2 p.171*
Feldman, Paula R. & Robinson, Daniel (Editors) . . . *v.2 p.199*
Feldman, Paula R. *v.2 p.199*
Feldman, Yael S. *v.6 p.648*
Feldstein, Martin *v.4 p.247*
Felig, Philip & Frohman, Lawrence A. *v.5 p.518*
Fell, Christine *v.6 p.559*
Feller, William *v.5 p.484*
Fellman, David (Editor) *v.4 p.450*
Fellman, Michael, et al. *v.3 p.396*
Fellowes, Edmund Horace *v.2 p.199*
Fellows, Otise E. *v.2 p.480*
Felluga, Dino *v.2 p.163, p.567*
Felner, Robert D. *v.5 p.671*
Felsenstein, Joseph *v.5 p.204*
Feltes, N. N. *v.2 p.193, v.6 p.756*
Felton, Lewis P. & Nelson, Richard B. *v.5 p.693*
Fenchel, T. M. & Fenchel, Tom *v.5 p.192*
Fendelman, Helaine & Taylor, Jonathan *v.1 p.809*
Fender, John *v.4 p.227*
Fendrich, James Max *v.4 p.710*
Fenelon, Francois de Salignac de La Mothe- *v.2 p.473*
Feng, Peter X. (Editor), et al. *v.6 p.88, p.89*
Feng, Peter X. *v.6 p.88, p.89, p.329, p.341*
Feng, Youlan *v.6 p.200*
Feng Yu-Lan *v.1 p.475*
Fenich, George G. *v.4 p.161*
Fenichell, Stephen *v.5 p.319*
Fenkl, Heinz Insu & Lew, Walter K. (Editors) . *v.6 p.91, p.100*
Fenlon, Iain *v.1 p.179*
Fenn, Elizabeth Anne *v.5 p.510, p.532*
Fenn, John *v.3 p.99*
Fenn, Richard K. & Capps, Donald (Editors) *v.5 p.633*
Fenn, Richard K. *v.1 p.545*
Fenna, Donald *v.5 p.567*
Fennell, John *v.1 p.569, v.3 p.215*
Fenno, Richard F. Jr. *v.4 p.533, p.550, p.557*
Fenoglio, Beppe *v.2 p.715*

Fenoglio-Preiser, Cecilia M., et al. *v.5 p.519*
Fenollosa, Ernest Francisco *v.1 p.132, p.134*
Fensch, Thomas (Editor) *v.2 p.122, p.125*
Fensham, Rachel & Eckersall, Peter (Editors) . *v.1 p.128, p.133*
Fenster, Julie *v.4 p.805, p.848*
Fenton, Charles A. *v.2 p.61*
Fenton, James *v.2 p.179, p.180, p.344*
Fenton, Jill R., et al. *v.6 p.305, p.325, p.327*
Fenton, John Joseph *v.5 p.314*
Fenton, John Y. *v.6 p.86, p.105, p.137*
Fenton, Steve & May, Stephen *v.4 p.767*
Fenton, Steve *v.4 p.731*
Fenton, William N. *v.6 p.682, p.691*
Feracho, Lesley *v.6 p.476, p.478*
Feraoun, Mouloud *v.6 p.60*
Ferber, Edna *v.2 p.73*
Ferber, Marianne A. & Nelson, Julie A. (Editors) . . . *v.4 p.273*
Ferber, Michael (Editor) *v.2 p.171, p.572*
Ferber, Michael *v.2 p.239*
Ferdowsi *v.6 p.670*
Fergus, Jan *v.2 p.267*
Ferguson, Arthur B. *v.3 p.100*
Ferguson, Carroy U. *v.6 p.32, p.38*
Ferguson, Charlene *v.4 p.392*
Ferguson, Charles D., et al. *v.4 p.658*
Ferguson, Charles E. *v.4 p.223, p.225*
Ferguson, Everett (Editor), et al. *v.1 p.599*
Ferguson, Everett (Editor) *v.1 p.597, p.646*
Ferguson, Everett *v.1 p.599, p.628*
Ferguson, Frances *v.2 p.323*
Ferguson, Gary *v.3 p.525*
Ferguson, Iain, et al. *v.4 p.768*
Ferguson, John *v.2 p.430*
Ferguson, Kitty *v.5 p.61, p.62, p.72*
Ferguson, Margaret *v.2 p.199*
Ferguson, Niall . *v.3 p.78, p.169, v.4 p.146, p.147, p.155, p.560*
Ferguson, Oliver Watkins *v.2 p.263*
Ferguson, Russell (Editor) *v.1 p.772*
Ferguson, Susan J. & Kasper, Anne S. *v.6 p.443*
Ferguson, Suzanne *v.2 p.90*
Fergusson, Erna *v.1 p.14*
Fergusson, J. E. *v.5 p.310*
Ferlinghetti, Lawrence *v.2 p.75*
Fermi, Enrico *v.5 p.560*
Fermi, Laura *v.5 p.542*
Fermon, An Jo *v.1 p.779*
Fermoselle, Rafael *v.3 p.308*
Fern, Edward F. *v.4 p.136*
Fern, Fanny *v.2 p.37*
Fernald, Theodore B. *v.6 p.690*
Fernandez, Alfredo L. *v.3 p.308*
Fernandez, Alina *v.3 p.308*
Fernandez, Damian J. & Camara, Madeline *v.3 p.309*
Fernandez, Damian J. (Editor) *v.3 p.301*
Fernandez De Calderon, Candida *v.1 p.684*

Author Index

Fernandez, Dominique *v.1 p.706*
Fernandez, John *v.4 p.133*
Fernandez, Raul A. *v.1 p.258, p.292*
Fernandez, Roberto G. *v.6 p.506*
Fernandez, Susan J. *v.3 p.309*
Fernandez-Kelly, Maria P. *v.4 p.729*
Fernea, Elizabeth W. (Editor) *v.6 p.592*
Fernea, Elizabeth Warnock (Editor, Introduction by) *v.6 p.592*
Fernea, Elizabeth W. *v.6 p.602*
Fernea, Robert A. & Fernea, Elizabeth Warnock . . *v.6 p.583*
Fernea, Robert A. & Gerster, Georg *v.6 p.58, p.635*
Fernea, Robert A. & Louis, William Roger (Editors) *v.6 p.602*
Fernett, Gene *v.6 p.306, p.341*
Fernández, Damián J. *v.3 p.309*
Fernández de Avellaneda, Alonso *v.2 p.646*
Fernández, Roberto (Editor) *v.2 p.19, v.6 p.495*
Fernie, Ewan, et al. *v.2 p.169*
Fernie, Sue & Metcalf, David (Editors) *v.4 p.253*
Fernihough, Anne (Editor) *v.2 p.362*
Feros, Antonio *v.3 p.238*
Ferrand, Alain & Torrigiani, Luiggino . *v.4 p.845, p.887, p.891*
Ferrante, Joan M. *v.6 p.559*
Ferrar, Marcus & Corsellis, John *v.3 p.249*
Ferrara, Lawrence *v.1 p.381*
Ferraresi, Franco *v.4 p.594*
Ferrater Mora, Jose *v.1 p.474*
Ferree, D. C. & Warrington, I. (Editors) *v.5 p.21*
Ferree, Myra Marx; Lorber, Judith; Hess, Beth B . *v.4 p.743*
Ferreira-Pinto, Cristina *v.2 p.690*
Ferreiro, Emilia *v.4 p.368*
Ferrell, Robert
  H. *v.3 p.378, p.385, p.440, p.447, p.451, p.470, p.512*
Ferren, John M. & Rutledge, Wiley *v.4 p.536*
Ferrer, Ada *v.3 p.278, p.309*
Ferrere, E. L. *v.2 p.519*
Ferrier, Carole (Editor) *v.2 p.740*
Ferrier, R. W. (Editor) *v.1 p.673, p.691*
Ferris, Timothy *v.5 p.61, p.71*
Ferriss, Susan & Sandoval, Ricardo *v.6 p.488, p.540*
Ferriter, Diarmaid *v.3 p.138*
Ferron, Jacques *v.2 p.540*
Ferruolo, Stephen C. *v.6 p.558*
Ferry, Anne *v.2 p.253*
Ferry, Georgina *v.5 p.262*
Ferry, Robert J. *v.3 p.359*
Fersh, Don & Thomas, Peter *v.4 p.131*
Fersht, Alan *v.5 p.119*
Fessner, Wolf-Dieter (Editor) *v.5 p.327*
Festinger, Leon *v.4 p.718, p.720, v.5 p.645*
Festle, Mary Jo *v.4 p.821, p.835*
Festou, Michel (Editor) *v.5 p.69*
Fetner, Gerald L. *v.3 p.374*
Fetrow, Alan G. *v.6 p.341*
Fetter, Alexander L. & Walecka, John Dirk *v.5 p.549*
Fetterley, Judith & Pryse, Marjorie (Editors) . . *v.2 p.21*

Fetterley, Judith (Editor) *v.2 p.20*
Fetzer, John F. *v.2 p.596*
Feuchtwang, Stephan *v.1 p.539*
Feuchtwanger, Edgar *v.2 p.275*
Feuchtwanger, Lion *v.2 p.607*
Feuer, Alan R. *v.5 p.346*
Feuer, Jane *v.6 p.316*
Feuerbach, Ludwig *v.1 p.464, p.498*
Feuerstein, Georg *v.1 p.475*
Few, Martha *v.3 p.263, p.298*
Few, Stephen *v.4 p.172, p.175*
Fewsmith, Joseph *v.4 p.619*
Fey, Harold E. (Editor) *v.1 p.568*
Feydeau, George & McLeish, Kenneth *v.2 p.517*
Feydeau, Georges *v.2 p.517*
Feyerabend, Paul K. *v.1 p.499, v.5 p.401*
Feynman, Richard Phillips, et al. *v.5 p.539*
Feynman, Richard
  Phillips . *v.5 p.539, p.540, p.541, p.542, p.556, p.558, p.566*
Fforde, Cressida (Editor), et al. *v.4 p.47*
Ficacci, Luigi *v.1 p.756*
Fichte, Johann G. *v.1 p.460*
Fichte, Johann Gottlieb *v.1 p.460*
Fichtenau, Heinrich *v.6 p.570, p.576*
Fichtner, Paula S. *v.3 p.181, p.183*
Ficken, Robert E. & LeWarne, Charles P. *v.3 p.532*
Ficken, Robert E. *v.3 p.547*
Ficowski, Jerzy *v.2 p.789*
Fiddian, Robin (Editor, Introduction by) *v.2 p.682*
Fiedler, Hermann Georg (Editor) *v.2 p.594*
Fiedler, Peggy Lee (Editor) *v.5 p.179*
Field, Edward *v.2 p.10*
Field, John *v.4 p.334*
Field, L. D., et al. *v.5 p.297*
Field, Martin J. *v.5 p.288*
Field, Syd *v.6 p.352*
Field, Thomas G. & Taylor, Robert W. *v.5 p.54*
Fielding, Henry & Fielding, Sarah *v.2 p.247, p.248*
Fielding, Henry *v.2 p.247*
Fielding, John P. *v.5 p.717*
Fielding, K. J. & Sorensen, David (Editors) . . . *v.2 p.276*
Fielding, Sarah *v.2 p.248*
Fields, K. *v.1 p.611*
Fields, Sarah K. . . *v.4 p.835, p.893, p.896, p.900, v.6 p.437*
Fields, Virginia & Zamudio-Taylor, Victor *v.6 p.492*
Fields, Virginia M. & Reents-Budet, Dorie . *v.1 p.669, p.684*
Fiell, Charlotte & Fiell, Peter *v.1 p.717, p.799, p.804*
Fiennes, Ranulph *v.4 p.378*
Fierro, Maribel *v.6 p.584*
Fierstein, Harvey *v.6 p.411*
Fieser, James *v.1 p.416*
Fieser, Louis F.; Fieser, Mary *v.5 p.292*
Fieser, Louis Frederick *v.5 p.292*
Fieser, Mary (Editor) *v.5 p.290*
Fife, Brian L. *v.4 p.300*

Fifer, J. Valerie *v.3 p.323*

Figart, Deborah M., et al. *v.4 p.273*

Figart, Deborah M. *v.4 p.250, p.252, p.265*

Figes, Orlando *v.3 p.210*

Figeys, Daniel (Editor) *v.4 p.156, v.5 p.217*

Figgis, Brian N. & Hitchman, Michael A. *v.5 p.303*

Figueredo, D. H. *v.2 p.767*

Figueroa, Luis A. *v.3 p.319*

Figueroa, Rafael (Compiled by) *v.1 p.166, p.292*

Fijnaut, Cyrille & Marx, Gary T. (Editors) *v.6 p.267*

Fikentscher, Kai *v.1 p.268*

Filisky, Michael *v.5 p.214*

Filk, G. (Editor), et al. *v.5 p.167*

Filler, Louis *v.3 p.396, p.419*

Filreis, Alan *v.2 p.10, p.123*

Filskov, Per, et al. *v.5 p.682*

Filson, Glen C. (Editor) *v.5 p.12*

Fimbel, Robert A. (Editor), et al. *v.5 p.37, p.41, p.353, v.6 p.291*

Finan, Christopher M. *v.3 p.458*

Financial Accounting Standards Board Staff . . *v.4 p.104, p.105*

Finch, Christopher *v.1 p.734*

Finch, Robert & Elder, John E. (Editors) *v.5 p.226*

Finch, Robert *v.5 p.226*

Fincham, Frank D. & Bradbury, Thomas N. (Editors) *v.5 p.638*

Findlay, Eileen Suarez *v.3 p.283, p.319*

Findlay, J. N. & Husserl, Edmund *v.1 p.469*

Findlay, J. N. *v.1 p.463*

Findlay, John M. & Gilchrist, Iain D. *v.5 p.606*

Findlen, Barbara (Editor) *v.6 p.433*

Findley, Carter V. *v.4 p.614, v.6 p.589*

Findley, Timothy *v.2 p.735*

Findling, John E. & Pelle, Kimberly D. (Editors) *v.4 p.805, p.845*

Findsen, Brian *v.4 p.320*

Fine, Aubrey H. & Fine, Nya M. . . . *v.4 p.783, p.800, p.829*

Fine, Ben & Saad-Filho, Alfredo *v.4 p.235*

Fine, Elizabeth C. *v.1 p.18, v.2 p.585*

Fine, Gail (Editor) *v.1 p.423*

Fine, Gary Alan & Turner, Patricia A. *v.2 p.17*

Fine, Gary Alan (Editor) *v.4 p.682*

Fine, Gary Alan *v.1 p.826, v.4 p.745*

Fine, John V. Jr. *v.3 p.246*

Fine, Lawrence *v.1 p.550*

Fine, Michelle *v.6 p.526, p.548*

Fine, Sidney *v.4 p.125*

Fineberg, Jonathan David *v.1 p.678, p.772*

Fine-Dare, Kathleen S. *v.4 p.464, v.6 p.694, p.704*

Finegan, Edward & Rickford, John R. (Editors) . . *v.2 p.552*

Finegan, Jack *v.1 p.617*

Finegold, David L., et al. *v.5 p.217, p.247*

Fineman, Daniel M. *v.6 p.171*

Finer, Herman *v.4 p.574*

Finer, S. E. *v.4 p.575*

Finger, Charles J. *v.2 p.236*

Finger, Seymour M. & Saltzman, Arnold A. *v.4 p.633*

Finger, Stanley *v.5 p.616*

Fingeroth, Danny *v.2 p.581*

Fini, Carlo *v.5 p.326*

Fink, Arthur E. (Editor), et al. *v.4 p.757*

Fink, Carole *v.3 p.154*

Fink, Conrad C. *v.4 p.406, p.407*

Fink, Gary M. & Graham, Hugh Davis (Editors) . . *v.3 p.471*

Fink, Gerald *v.5 p.139*

Fink, Leon *v.3 p.367*

Finke, Roger & Stark, Rodney *v.4 p.720*

Finkel, Alicia . . . *v.1 p.78, p.99, p.100, p.146, p.148, p.151*

Finkel, Alvin *v.3 p.536, p.541*

Finkel, Donald L. & Arney, William Ray *v.4 p.339*

Finkelhor, David (Editor), et al. *v.6 p.464, p.469*

Finkelman, Paul & Field van Tassel, Emily *v.4 p.462*

Finkelman, Paul & Urofsky, Melvin I. *v.4 p.453*

Finkelman, Paul & Wallenstein, Peter
(Editors) *v.3 p.384, v.4 p.485*

Finkelman, Paul (Editor) *v.1 p.656, v.4 p.453, p.459*

Finkelman, Paul *v.4 p.453*

Finkelstein, David & McCleery, Alistair (Editors) . . *v.2 p.576*

Finkelstein, David & McCleery, Alistair *v.2 p.576*

Finkelstein, David M. & Kivlehan, Maryanne (Editors) *v.4 p.619*

Finkelstein, David *v.6 p.741*

Finkelstein, Haim *v.1 p.696*

Finkelstein, Israel & Silberman, Neil Asher . . . *v.1 p.619*

Finkelstein, Leo *v.5 p.680*

Finkelstein, Martin J. *v.4 p.292*

Finkelstein, Norman G. *v.6 p.617*

Finkenbine, Roy E. *v.6 p.4*

Finkielman, Jorge *v.6 p.344*

Finkl, Charles W. (Editor) *v.5 p.417*

Finklestein, Norman G. *v.6 p.617*

Finlay, George *v.3 p.191*

Finlayson, Clive *v.4 p.15*

Finley, M. I. *v.2 p.413, v.3 p.3, p.15*

Finley, Moses I., et al. *v.3 p.197*

Finley, Moses I. *v.3 p.14*

Finley, Moses *v.4 p.489*

Finn, Margot C. (Author, Contribution by) . . *v.6 p.745, p.761*

Finn, Margot C. *v.6 p.758*

Finn, Patrick J. *v.4 p.302*

Finn, William & Lapine, James *v.1 p.249, p.407*

Finnerty, John D. & Emery, Douglas R. (Author, Editors) *v.4 p.91*

Finney, Joni E., et al. *v.4 p.295*

Finnie, David H. *v.6 p.627*

Finnigan, Dan, et al. *v.4 p.169*

Finnis, John (Editor) *v.4 p.490*

Finnis, John, et al. *v.4 p.656*

Finnish Metla Forest Research Institute *v.5 p.145*

Finocchiaro, Maurice A. *v.4 p.491, p.501*

Finson, Jon W. *v.1 p.197*

Finucane, Ronald C. *v.6 p.570*

Finucci, Valeria *v.2 p.707, p.709*

Fioerenza, Elisabeth S. *v.1 p.599*

Fiol-Matta, Licia *v.3 p.353*

Fiorani, Francesca . . . . *.v.3 p.200*

Fiore, Peter A. . . . . *.v.2 p.253*

Fiore, Robert L. . . . . *.v.2 p.650*

Fiorentino, Jon Paul (Editor) . . . . *.v.2 p.731*

Fiorenza, Francis S. . . . . *.v.1 p.635*

Fiorina, Morris P., et al. . . . . *.v.4 p.503*

Firbank, Ronald . . . . *.v.6 p.396*

Firchow, Peter E. & Firchow, Evelyn S. (Translators) *.v.2 p.594*

Firchow, Peter E. & Huxley, Aldous . . . . *.v.2 p.353*

Firchow, Peter E. . . . . *.v.2 p.341, p.353*

Firdawsi . . . . *.v.6 p.671*

Fireside, Harvey . . . . *.v.4 p.536*

Firestein, Beth A. (Editor) . . . . *.v.6 p.371*

Firestone, David (Editor) . . . . *.v.5 p.34*

Firestone, Reuven . . . . *.v.1 p.560*

Firestone, Richard B. & Chu, S. Y. Frank . . . . . . *.v.5 p.281*

Firestone, Richard B. . . . . *.v.5 p.545*

Firestone, Robert & Catlett, Joyce . . . . *.v.5 p.652*

Firestone, Ross . . . . *.v.1 p.258, p.326, p.327*

Firestone, Shulamith . . . . *.v.4 p.724, p.744, p.747*

Firestone, William A. (Editor), et al. . . . . *.v.4 p.286*

Firmat, Gustavo Perez . . . . *.v.2 p.671*

Firmin, Joseph-Antenor . . . . *.v.4 p.17*

Firth, Alan . . . . *.v.4 p.423*

Firth, Raymond William . . . . *.v.4 p.22, p.28, p.42*

Firth, Raymond . . . . *.v.1 p.530, v.4 p.36, p.39*

Fischbach, Ephraim & Talmadge, Carrick L. . . *.v.5 p.557, p.558*

Fischer, Agneta H. (Editor) . . . . *.v.4 p.694*

Fischer, Bernd . . . . *.v.3 p.251*

Fischer, Claude S. . . . . *.v.4 p.770, v.6 p.717*

Fischer, David Hackett . . . . *.v.3 p.409*

Fischer, David H. . . . . *.v.3 p.409, p.411*

Fischer, Dennis . . . . *.v.6 p.318*

Fischer, Irene . . . . *.v.4 p.389*

Fischer, John M. . . . . *.v.1 p.503*

Fischer, Joseph . . . . *.v.1 p.800*

Fischer, Kathleen B. . . . . *.v.3 p.353*

Fischer, Louis, et al. . . . . *.v.4 p.450*

Fischer, Louis . . . . *.v.1 p.540*

Fischer, Michael M. J. *.v.6 p.631*

Fischer, Phyllis E. . . . . *.v.2 p.556*

Fischer, Sibylle . . . . *.v.3 p.314, p.316*

Fischer, Wolfdietrich . . . . *.v.6 p.653*

Fischer-Dieskau, Dietrich . . . . *.v.2 p.593*

Fischer-Lichte, Erika . . . . *.v.1 p.55, p.96*

Fischerova, Daniela . . . . *.v.2 p.783*

Fischkin, Barbara . . . . *.v.6 p.488, p.543*

Fischman, Wendy, et al. *.v.4 p.55*

Fish, Jefferson M. (Editor) . . . . *.v.5 p.608, p.652*

Fish, John H. . . . . *.v.4 p.702*

Fish, L. . . . . *.v.5 p.85*

Fish, M. Steven . . . . *.v.4 p.597*

Fish, Stanley Eugene . . . . . *.v.2 p.214, p.249, p.253, p.568*

Fishbane, Michael A. . . . . *.v.1 p.551*

Fishbein, M. & Ajzen, Icek . . . . *.v.5 p.585, p.604*

Fishburn, Katherine . . . . *.v.2 p.138, p.754*

Fishel, Catherine . . . . *.v.1 p.717*

Fisher, Adrian T. (Editor), et al. . . . . *.v.5 p.649*

Fisher, Alan W. . . . . *.v.3 p.213*

Fisher, Alec . . . . *.v.1 p.492*

Fisher, Andy . . . . *.v.6 p.297*

Fisher, Celia B. . . . . *.v.5 p.674*

Fisher, Chris & Binns, Tony (Editors) . . . . *.v.4 p.376*

Fisher, Clive . . . . *.v.2 p.68*

Fisher, Donald M. . . . . *.v.4 p.805, p.841, p.862*

Fisher, Erik A. & Sharp, Steven W. . . . . *.v.5 p.647*

Fisher, Franklin M., et al. . . . . *.v.4 p.438*

Fisher, George . . . . *.v.4 p.473, v.6 p.270*

Fisher, Godfrey . . . . *.v.6 p.60*

Fisher, Irving . . . . . *.v.4 p.195, p.199, p.200, p.224, p.225,
p.243, p.246, p.247, p.251*

Fisher, James F. . . . . *.v.6 p.163*

Fisher, James T. . . . . *.v.1 p.573*

Fisher, James . . . . *.v.1 p.91, p.107*

Fisher, Jay M., et al. . . . . *.v.1 p.722*

Fisher, Jennifer . . . . *.v.1 p.23*

Fisher, John H. . . . . *.v.6 p.564*

Fisher, John . . . . *.v.3 p.325*

Fisher, Kathleen M., et al. . . . . *.v.5 p.245*

Fisher, Lawrence . . . . *.v.4 p.144*

Fisher, Lester E. . . . . *.v.5 p.83*

Fisher, Louis *.v.4 p.453, p.454, p.459, p.462, p.464, p.528, p.531*

Fisher, Nigel . . . . *.v.3 p.93, p.119*

Fisher, Peter . . . . *.v.6 p.366*

Fisher, Philip A. . . . . *.v.4 p.95*

Fisher, R. A. . . . . *.v.5 p.482*

Fisher, R. J. . . . . *.v.4 p.698*

Fisher, Robert & Kling, Joe (Editors) . . . . *.v.6 p.723*

Fisher, Robert E. . . . . *.v.1 p.691, p.693*

Fisher, Roger & Ury, William L. . . . . *.v.4 p.74*

Fisher, Sydney Nettleton & Ochsenwald, William . . *.v.6 p.581*

Fisher, W. B. & Grossman, Stanley I. (Editors) . . . *.v.6 p.629*

Fisher, William F. . . . . *.v.6 p.163*

Fisher, William H. . . . . *.v.5 p.41, v.6 p.297*

Fishkin, James S. . . . . *.v.4 p.503*

Fishman, Ethan . . . . *.v.5 p.652*

Fishman, Joshua A. & Keller, Gary D. (Editors) . . *.v.6 p.526*

Fishman, Katharine Davis . . . . *.v.1 p.18, p.28, p.30*

Fishman, Nina . . . . *.v.4 p.604, p.606*

Fishman, Stephen M. & McCarthy, Lucille P. . . . . *.v.4 p.342*

Fishman, Stephen . . . . *.v.4 p.441, p.446*

Fishman, Sylvia Barack . . . . *.v.4 p.721*

Fishman, Ted C. . . . . *.v.6 p.196*

Fishta, Gjergj . . . . *.v.2 p.815, v.3 p.252*

Fishwick, Marshall William . . . . *.v.3 p.371*

Fisk, Arthur D. . . . . *.v.5 p.587*

Fisk, Deborah Payne
(Editor) . . . . . . *.v.1 p.65, p.77, p.90, p.100, v.2 p.186*

Fisk, Robert . . . . *.v.6 p.606*

Fiske, Deborah Payne (Editor) . . . . . . *.v.1 p.59, p.77, p.100*

Fiss, Owen M. *v.4 p.515*

Fitch, J. Samuel *v.3 p.274*

Fitch, John S. 3rd *v.3 p.274*

Fitch, Kristine L. & Sanders, Robert E. (Editors) . . . *v.5 p.647*

Fitchen, Janet M. *v.4 p.702*

Fite, Gilbert C. *v.3 p.396, p.458*

Fitt, Sally S. *v.1 p.49*

Fitton, J. Lesley *v.3 p.15, p.191*

Fitts, Donald D. *v.5 p.279*

Fitz, Earl E. *v.2 p.690*

Fitzduff, Mari & Stout, Chris E. (Editors) *v.5 p.584*

Fitzgerald, Allan D. (Editor) *v.1 p.592*

Fitzgerald, Arthur E., et al. *v.5 p.725*

Fitzgerald, C. P. *v.6 p.183*

Fitzgerald, Deborah Kay *v.5 p.4, p.14, p.29*

Fitzgerald, E. V. K. *v.3 p.329*

Fitzgerald, Edward *v.6 p.671*

Fitzgerald, F. Scott *v.2 p.76*

FitzGerald, Frances *v.3 p.471*

Fitzgerald, Frank T. *v.3 p.309*

Fitzgerald, John *v.6 p.190*

Fitzgerald, Penelope *v.2 p.344*

Fitzgerald, Robert D. *v.2 p.744*

Fitzgerald, William *v.2 p.430*

Fitzgibbon, Marian *v.1 p.826*

Fitzgibbons, Athol *v.4 p.218*

Fitzharris, Tim *v.5 p.175, p.234, p.239*

Fitzhugh, George *v.3 p.396, p.419*

Fitzhugh, William W. & Chaussonnet, Valerie (Editors) *v.6 p.703*

Fitzmaurice, John *v.4 p.600*

Fitzmaurice, Tony & Shiel, Mark (Editors) *v.6 p.730*

Fitzmaurice, Tony *v.6 p.730*

Fitzmaurice-Kelly, James *v.2 p.649*

Fitzmier, John R. *v.1 p.584*

Fitzmyer, Joseph A. *v.6 p.664*

Fitzpatrick, Frank *v.4 p.831, p.853, p.893*

Fitzpatrick, Joseph P. *v.6 p.529*

Fitzpatrick, Sheila *v.3 p.225, v.4 p.334*

Fitzsimmons, Allan K. *v.5 p.179*

Fitzsimons, Cecilia *v.5 p.229*

Fitzwater, Terry *v.4 p.169*

Fivush, Robyn & Haden, Catherine A. (Editors) . . . *v.5 p.657*

Fixico, Donald Lee *v.6 p.295*

FIZ Chemie, Berlin (Editor) *v.5 p.258*

Fizel, John & Fort, Rodney D. (Editors) . . . *v.4 p.887, p.893*

Fizel, John L. (Editor), et al. *v.4 p.887*

Flaherty, M. Therese *v.4 p.119*

Flake, Kathleen *v.1 p.587*

Flamhaft, Ziva *v.6 p.613*

Flanagan, David *v.5 p.346*

Flanagan, Dawn P. & Harrison, Patti L. (Editors) . . . *v.5 p.602*

Flanagan, John T. (Editor) *v.2 p.21*

Flanagan, Lawrence B. (Editor), et al. *v.5 p.113*

Flanagan, Mary & Booth, Austin (Editors) *v.6 p.438*

Flanagan, Maureen A. *v.6 p.454*

Flanagan, Owen *v.1 p.496, v.5 p.619, p.652*

Flanagan, Richard *v.2 p.745*

Flanagan, Sabina *v.1 p.177, p.332, v.6 p.570*

Flanagan, Timothy J. (Editor) *v.6 p.273*

Flanagan, Tom *v.3 p.545*

Flanders, Judith *v.3 p.53, v.6 p.747, p.761, p.765*

Flanders, Ned A. *v.4 p.347*

Flannery, Austin P. *v.1 p.570*

Flannery, Austin *v.1 p.570*

Flannery, Kent V. & Marcus, Joyce (Editors) *v.4 p.9*

Flannery, Sarah & Flannery, David *v.5 p.476*

Flannery, Tim *v.5 p.168, p.371, v.6 p.295*

Flanz, Gisbert H. *v.4 p.601*

Flapan, Erica *v.5 p.298, p.498, p.501*

Flathman, Richard E. *v.4 p.515*

Flatley, Michael *v.1 p.7*

Flaubert, Gustave & Turgenev, Ivan *v.2 p.491*

Flaubert, Gustave *v.2 p.490, p.491, p.499*

Flavell, John H., et al. *v.5 p.626, p.629*

Fleche, Anne *v.1 p.79, p.82, p.113*

Fleck, Steven J. & Kraemer, William J. *v.4 p.790, p.879*

Fleet, Michael & Smith, Brian H. *v.3 p.329, p.353*

Flegg, Jim *v.5 p.175, p.240*

Fleischacker, Samuel *v.4 p.219*

Fleischer, Nat, et al. *v.4 p.855*

Fleischhauer, Carl & Brannan, Beverly W. (Editors) . *v.1 p.763*

Fleischman, Ellen *v.6 p.612*

Fleisher, Arthur A. III, et al. *v.4 p.883, p.887*

Fleisher, Mark S. *v.4 p.714, v.6 p.464, p.466*

Fleishman, Avrom *v.2 p.392, v.6 p.331*

Fleissner, Erwin *v.5 p.126*

Fleming, Denna F. *v.4 p.631*

Fleming, Fergus & Merullo, Annabel (Editors) *v.4 p.378*

Fleming, Fergus (As told by) *v.4 p.378*

Fleming, G. *v.1 p.738*

Fleming, Ian *v.2 p.344*

Fleming, John *v.2 p.384*

Fleming, Michael F. *v.5 p.245*

Fleming, Peter *v.6 p.240*

Fleming, Richard *v.1 p.510*

Fleming, Robert E. (Editor, Introduction by) *v.2 p.84*

Fleming, Robin *v.3 p.97*

Fleming, Thomas J. *v.3 p.458, p.471, p.491*

Fleming, Walter Lynwood *v.3 p.436*

Fleming-Williams, Ian *v.1 p.723*

Flemming, Roy B., et al. *v.6 p.267*

Fletcher, Alice C. *v.1 p.14*

Fletcher, Angus *v.2 p.572*

Fletcher, Anthony *v.4 p.582*

Fletcher, Banister *v.1 p.785*

Fletcher, Colin & Rawlins, C. L. *v.4 p.787*

Fletcher, Garth *v.5 p.596, p.647*

Fletcher, George P. *v.6 p.268, p.270*

Fletcher, Giles *v.2 p.214*

Fletcher, Harris F. *v.2 p.253*

Fletcher, Ifan K., et al. *v.1 p.22*

Fletcher, John G. *v.3 p.510*

Fletcher, Peri L. *v.6 p.529*

Fletcher, Richard *v.3 p.237, v.6 p.565*

Fletcher, Tom *v.1 p.34*

Flett, T. M. & Flett, J. P. *v.1 p.33*

Fleurant, Gerdes *v.1 p.21, p.292, v.3 p.314*

Fleury-Steiner, Benjamin D. *v.6 p.270*

Flew, Antony G. *v.1 p.415, p.451*

Flew, Terry *v.4 p.419*

Flexner, Abraham *v.4 p.326*

Flexner, Eleanor & Fitzpatrick, Ellen *v.6 p.430*

Flügge, Siegfried *v.5 p.549*

Flick, Alexander C. & Lobrano, Gustav . *v.3 p.422, p.423, p.428*

Flick, E. W. *v.5 p.318*

Flickinger, Michael C. & Drew, Stephen W. *v.5 p.325*

Flink, James J. *v.4 p.154*

Flinn, Caryl *v.6 p.338*

Flinn, Michael W. & Smout, T. C. (Editors) *v.3 p.40*

Flint, Colin (Author, Editor) *v.4 p.495*

Flint, Colin *v.4 p.400*

Flint, Kate *v.6 p.738*

Flint, Mary Louise & Dreistadt, Steve H. . . . *v.5 p.9, p.26*

Flint, Mary Louise *v.5 p.9, p.26*

Flint, Richard & Flint, Shirley Cushing *v.3 p.403*

Flint, Richard F. *v.5 p.425*

Flint, S. J., et al. *v.5 p.206, p.212*

Flint, Valerie I. *v.6 p.569*

Flippen, J. Brooks *v.4 p.566, v.6 p.299*

Flippo, Hyde *v.3 p.159*

Fliter, John A. *v.6 p.273*

Flngel, Erik *v.5 p.439*

Floistad, Guttorm (Editor) *v.1 p.438*

Flom, Eric L. *v.6 p.332*

Flood, Gavin *v.1 p.535, p.567*

Flood, James & Anders, Patricia (Editors) *v.4 p.360*

Flood, James (Editor), et al. *v.4 p.300, p.363*

Flood, Josephine *v.4 p.13*

Flood, Lawrence G. (Editor) *v.4 p.121*

Flood, Michael *v.6 p.425, p.429*

Flood, Robert L. & Daellenbach, Hans *v.4 p.119*

Flora, Joseph M. (Editor), et al. *v.2 p.7, p.13*

Flora, Stephen Ray *v.5 p.610*

Florence, Namulundah *v.4 p.310, p.342*

Flores, Angel (Editor) *v.2 p.643*

Flores, Angel *v.2 p.464, p.593, p.643*

Flores, Henry *v.6 p.537, p.548*

Flores, John *v.2 p.591*

Flores, Juan (Editor, Introduction by) . . *v.3 p.319, v.6 p.529*

Flores, Juan (Editor, Translator, Introduction by) . . *v.6 p.529*

Flores, Juan *v.6 p.543*

Flores, Lauro (Editor) *v.2 p.19*

Flores, Richard R. *v.6 p.517, p.523*

Flores, William & Benmayor, Rina (Editors) . *v.6 p.540, p.543*

Flores, Yolanda *v.1 p.121, p.127*

Florescano, Enrique *v.3 p.271*

Flores-Gonzalez, Nilda *v.6 p.526, p.543*

Florini, Ann *v.4 p.498*

Florit, Eugenio (Editor) *v.2 p.643*

Florka, Roger *v.1 p.453*

Florkin, Marcel *v.5 p.327*

Floud, Roderick & McCloskey, Donald N. (Editors) *v.3 p.111, p.122*

Floud, Roderick (Editor), et al. *v.3 p.122*

Floud, Roderick (Editor, Introduction by) *v.3 p.40*

Flower, E. & Murphey, M. G. *v.1 p.439*

Flower, Harriet I. *v.3 p.23*

Flowers, R. Barri *v.4 p.747, v.6 p.255*

Flowers, Sandra H. *v.6 p.12, p.25*

Floyd, James Michael & Sharp, Avery T. *v.1 p.166*

Floyd, Patricia A. *v.4 p.794, p.903*

Floyd, R. B., et al. *v.5 p.184, p.188*

Floyd, Samuel A. Jr. (Editor) *v.1 p.159, p.281*

Floyd, Thomas L. *v.5 p.722*

Fluharty, Vernon L. *v.3 p.357*

Flusche, Della M. & Korth, Eugene H. *v.3 p.350*

Flusche, Della M. *v.3 p.350*

Flynn, Charles L. Jr. *v.3 p.503*

Flynn, Leontia *v.2 p.344*

Flynn, Nancy *v.4 p.172*

Flynt, Wayne *v.3 p.504, v.4 p.541*

Fo, Dario *v.1 p.107, v.2 p.724, p.725, p.727*

Ó Máille, Pádraig *v.6 p.76*

Foakes, R. A. *v.1 p.76, p.100, p.154*

Foden, Giles *v.2 p.345*

Fodor, Jerry A. *v.1 p.482*

Foerstel, Herbert N. *v.4 p.451*

Foerster, Norman *v.2 p.3*

Fogarty, Gerald P. *v.1 p.573*

Fogel, Alan *v.5 p.626*

Fogel, Robert W. & Engerman, Stanley L. *v.3 p.419*

Fogel, Robert William *v.4 p.514*

Fogelin, Robert J. & Sinnott-Armstrong, Walter . . *v.1 p.492*

Fogelin, Robert J. *v.1 p.450, p.471*

Fogelquist, Donald F. *v.2 p.660*

Fogelson, Robert M. *v.3 p.531, v.6 p.712*

Fogg, G. E. *v.4 p.378, v.5 p.434*

Fogg, Neeta P., et al. *v.4 p.167*

Fogg, P. G. & Gerrard, W. *v.5 p.281*

Fog-Olwig, Karen (Editor) *v.4 p.40*

Fogu, Claudio *v.3 p.203*

Foister, Susan & Holbein, Hans *v.1 p.686, p.738*

Fokine, Michel *v.1 p.8*

Folbre, Nancy (Editor), et al. *v.4 p.273*

Folbre, Nancy *v.4 p.273*

Folda, Jaroslav *v.1 p.672*

Foley, Barbara H. *v.2 p.10*

Foley, Helene P. *v.6 p.450*

Foley, James D. *v.5 p.340*

Foley, John Miles *v.2 p.413*

Foley, Michael A. *v.4 p.471, v.6 p.268*

Foley, Michael *v.4 p.605*

Foley, Robert T. *v.3 p.160*

Foley, William A. *v.4 p.18*

Folkenflik, Robert *v.2 p.250*

Folkers, George F. (Translator), et al. *v.2 p.599*

Folks, Jeffrey J. & Folks, Nancy Summers (Editors) . . *v.2 p.13*

Folland, Gerald B. *v.5 p.486, p.490*

Folland, Sherman, et al. *v.4 p.163, v.5 p.511*

Follows, Mick & Oguz, Temel (Editors) . . . *v.4 p.392, v.5 p.429*

Folmer, Henk (Editor), et al. *v.4 p.62*

Folsing, Albrecht *v.3 p.46, v.5 p.542*

Folsom, Ed & Price, Kenneth M. *v.2 p.53*

Folsom, Ed (Editor) *v.2 p.53*

Folsom, Ed *v.2 p.53*

Folts, James A., et al. *v.1 p.769*

Folzenlogen, Darcy & Folzenlogen, Robert *v.5 p.83*

Fomby, Thomas & Terrell, Dek *v.4 p.200*

Fone, Byrne R. S. *v.2 p.10, v.6 p.392, p.406*

Fone, Byrne *v.6 p.362*

Foner, Eric & American Historical Association Staff,
    Commission on the social studies in the schools
    (Editors) *v.3 p.374*

Foner, Eric & Brown, Joshua *v.3 p.436, v.4 p.485*

Foner, Eric *v.3 p.374, p.376, p.379, p.396, v.4 p.727*

Foner, Nancy (Editor) *v.4 p.764*

Foner, Philip S. *v.3 p.396, p.420, p.433, v.4 p.125*

Foner, R. Eric *v.3 p.420*

Fong, I. W. & Drlica, Karl (Editors) *v.5 p.526*

Fong, Timothy P. *v.6 p.85, p.126, p.712*

Fong, Wen C. & Watt, James C. *v.1 p.693*

Font, Mauricio A. *v.3 p.340*

Fontana, Andrea *v.4 p.741*

Fontana, David *v.1 p.524, v.5 p.634*

Fontana, Josep *v.3 p.35*

Fontana, Mars G. *v.5 p.734*

Fontane, Theodor *v.2 p.596*

Fontein, Jan *v.1 p.777*

Fontenay, Charles L. *v.3 p.458*

Fonteyn, Margot *v.1 p.8*

Fonvizin, I *v.2 p.803*

Food and Agricultural Organization of the United
    Nations *v.5 p.7, p.32*

Food and Agriculture Organization (FAO) Staff *v.4 p.151, p.164*

Food and Agriculture Organization of the United Nations. ;
    Global Terrestrial Observing System (Organization) ;
    Integrated Global Observing Strategy Partnership. ; Food and
    Agriculture Organization of the United Nations.;
    Sustainable Development Dept. *v.5 p.113*

Food and Agriculture Organization of the United Nations Staff
    (Contribution by) *v.4 p.151*

Food and Agriculture Organization Staff, et
    al. *v.5 p.172, p.212, p.215*

Food Standards Agency Staff (Editor) *v.5 p.33*

Foot, C. *v.5 p.554*

Foot, Philippa R. (Editor) *v.1 p.487*

Foot, Philippa *v.1 p.484*

Foot, Rosemary (Editor), et al. *v.4 p.626, p.630*

Foot, Rosemary *v.4 p.669, v.6 p.236*

Foote, David *v.3 p.198, v.6 p.577*

Foote, Shelby *v.2 p.73, v.3 p.396*

Footitt, Hilary & Simmonds, John *v.3 p.156*

Forbath, William *v.4 p.125*

Forbes, Bruce David & Mahan, Jeffrey H. (Editors) . *v.4 p.720*

Forbes, David W. *v.1 p.682, p.694*

Forbes, E. R. & Muise, D. A. (Editors) *v.3 p.543*

Forbes, Ernest R. *v.3 p.543*

Forbes, Graeme *v.1 p.492*

Forbus, Kenneth & Feltovich, Paul (Editors) *v.5 p.590*

Force, Peter *v.3 p.405*

Forche, Carolyn *v.2 p.145*

Forcione, Alban K. *v.2 p.649*

Ford, Andrew *v.2 p.400*

Ford, Arthur L. *v.2 p.29*

Ford, Boris (Editor) *v.3 p.128*

Ford, Caroline *v.3 p.154*

Ford, Charles & Hammond, Robert *v.6 p.337*

Ford, Charles Henri & Tyler, Parker *v.6 p.396*

Ford, David & Muers, Rachel (Editors) . . . *v.1 p.633, p.635*

Ford, David F. & Soskice, Janet M. *v.1 p.521*

Ford, David F. *v.1 p.652*

Ford, Derek C. & Williams, Paul . . . *v.4 p.391, v.5 p.424*

Ford, Donna Y. & Harris, J. John *v.4 p.317*

Ford, Donna Y. *v.4 p.317*

Ford, Edward *v.2 p.119*

Ford, Ford Madox *v.2 p.345*

Ford, Gerald, et al. *v.4 p.548*

Ford, John *v.2 p.218*

Ford, Karen Jackson *v.2 p.126*

Ford, Kenneth W. & Hewitt, Paul *v.5 p.539*

Ford, Larry *v.6 p.727*

Ford, Lewis S. *v.1 p.637*

Ford, Marsha, et al. *v.5 p.514*

Ford, Richard *v.2 p.145*

Ford, Sara J. *v.2 p.121, p.124*

Forde, Daryll & Kaberry, P. M. (Editors) *v.6 p.68*

Forde, Daryll *v.4 p.29*

Fordham, Graham (Editor) *v.4 p.668*

Fordyce, C. J. *v.2 p.430*

Forell, Caroline *v.4 p.472*

Foreman, Dave *v.5 p.168, p.234*

Foreman, Grant *v.3 p.510*

Foreman, Lewis *v.1 p.166*

Forer, Lois G. *v.6 p.271*

Forer, Pip (Editor), et al. *v.4 p.387*

Forest Products Laboratory Staff *v.5 p.688*

Foresta, Merry A. *v.1 p.763, p.766*

Foresta, Ronald A. *v.3 p.269, v.5 p.18*

Forester, C. S. *v.2 p.345*

Forey, Alan *v.6 p.566, p.571*

Forey, Peter L., et al. *v.5 p.205*

Forgas, Joseph P. (Editor), et al. *v.5 p.649*

Forgas, Joseph P. (Editor) . *v.4 p.694, v.5 p.649, p.652, p.653*

Forge, Andrew *v.1 p.738*

Forget, Evelyn & Peart, Sandra (Editors) *v.4 p.217*

Forkner, Benjamin (Editor) *v.2 p.202*

Forlag, Albert B. & Magoc, Christopher J. . *v.5 p.18, v.6 p.295*

Forman, Michael H. *v.4 p.494*

Forman, Murray *v.1 p.268*

Forman, Robert K. (Editor) *v.5 p.634*

Forman, Shepard *v.4 p.28*

Formanek, Ruth & Gurian, Anita (Editors) *v.5 p.659*

Formisano, Roger *v.4 p.81*

Formisano, Ronald P. *v.3 p.488, v.6 p.712*

Fornara, Charles W. *v.2 p.402*

Forni, Pier M. *v.6 p.565*

Fornieri, Joseph R. *v.3 p.397*

Fornieri, Joseph *v.3 p.397*

Foroohar, Manzar *v.3 p.301*

Forouzan, Behrouz A. *v.5 p.726, p.727*

Forrer, Matthi *v.1 p.723, p.756*

Forrest, Alan *v.3 p.150, p.152*

Forrest, Katherine V. *v.6 p.396*

Forrest, Suzanne *v.6 p.535*

Forrester, Jay W. *v.4 p.119*

Forsdyke, Donald *v.5 p.78, p.203*

Forsdyke, Sara *v.3 p.17*

Forst, Brian & Manning, Peter K. *v.6 p.262*

Forster, E. M., et al. *v.2 p.346*

Forster, E. M. *v.2 p.345, p.346, p.579, v.6 p.396*

Forster, Marc R., et al. *v.1 p.601*

Forster, Marc R. *v.3 p.166*

Forsyth, James *v.3 p.214*

Forsyth, Tim (Editor) *v.4 p.192, p.373*

Forsythe, Charles E. *v.4 p.883*

Forsythe, David, et al. *v.4 p.633*

Forsythe, David P. & McMahon, Patrice C. (Editors) *v.4 p.669*

Forsythe, Diana *v.4 p.44*

Forsythe, Gary *v.2 p.426, v.3 p.24*

Forsythe, William E. *v.5 p.281, p.741*

Fort, Rodney D. & Fizel, John
(Editors) *v.4 p.843, p.884, p.891, p.898*

Forte, Allan & Gilbert, Steve *v.1 p.370*

Forte, Allen, et al. *v.1 p.268*

Forte, Allen *v.1 p.213, p.239, p.360, p.367, p.370*

Fortes, Meyer *v.4 p.32*

Fortescue, Peter W. (Editor), et al. *v.5 p.719*

Fortescue, William *v.2 p.495*

Fortey, Richard A. *v.5 p.447*

Fortey, Richard *v.5 p.192, p.445*

Fortier, Mark *v.1 p.56*

Fortney, Lloyd R. *v.5 p.722*

Fortunato, John A. *v.4 p.853, p.896, p.902*

Fortunato, Ray T. & Waddell, D. Geneva *v.4 p.292*

Fortuner, Renaud *v.5 p.105, p.108, p.109*

Forty, Adrian *v.1 p.713*

Foscolo, Ugo *v.2 p.710*

Foshay, Arthur W. *v.4 p.363*

Foskett, Daphne *v.1 p.725*

Foskett, Ken *v.4 p.536*

Fossedal, Gregory A. *v.3 p.244*

Fossett, Judith J. & Tucker, Jeffrey A. (Editors) . . . *v.6 p.14*

Fossier, Robert (Editor) *v.6 p.562*

Fossier, Robert *v.6 p.575*

Fossum, John A. *v.4 p.121*

Foster, Benjamin R. *v.1 p.539, v.6 p.664*

Foster, Carter E., et al. *v.1 p.722*

Foster, David R. & Aber, John D. (Editors) *v.5 p.357*

Foster, David R. & Overholt, James L. . . . *v.4 p.787, p.795*

Foster, David W. & Altamiranda, Daniel (Editors) . *v.2 p.664*

Foster, David W. (Editor) *v.6 p.392*

Foster, David W. *v.2 p.643, p.678, v.6 p.498, p.506, p.512*

Foster, David William, et al. *v.2 p.635, v.3 p.346*

Foster, David William *v.6 p.498, p.506, p.512*

Foster, Douglas A. (Editor), et al. *v.1 p.584*

Foster, Edward H. *v.2 p.10, p.13, p.118*

Foster, Gaines M. *v.4 p.520*

Foster, George McClelland *v.4 p.702*

Foster, Gwendolyn Audrey *v.6 p.333, p.474*

Foster, H. S. *v.3 p.451*

Foster, Hannah Webster *v.2 p.29*

Foster, Jeannette H. *v.6 p.392*

Foster, Jenny Ryun (Editor), et al. *v.6 p.87, p.135*

Foster, John L. (Translator) *v.6 p.644*

Foster, John L. *v.1 p.445, p.504*

Foster, John W. & Chesney, Helena C. *v.5 p.237*

Foster, Kenelm *v.2 p.705*

Foster, Lawrence *v.4 p.721*

Foster, Michael Beresford *v.4 p.489*

Foster, Nelson & Cordell, Linda S. (Editors) *v.3 p.271*

Foster, Philip J.; Zolberg, Aristide R. *v.6 p.69*

Foster, R. F. *v.2 p.326, v.3 p.134, p.138, v.6 p.746, p.763*

Foster, Richard & Kaplan, Sarah *v.4 p.67*

Foster, Stephen *v.3 p.485*

Foster, Susan L. (Editor) *v.1 p.41*

Foster, Susan L. *v.1 p.39*

Foster, Susan Leigh *v.1 p.41*

Foster, Thomas G. *v.2 p.346*

Foth, H. D. & Ellis, Boyd G. *v.5 p.49*

Foth, Henry D. & Schafer, John *v.5 p.366, p.373*

Foth, Henry D. *v.5 p.49*

Fothergill, Alastair *v.5 p.175, p.238*

Fotheringham, A. Stewart, et al. *v.4 p.376*

Fotion, Nick *v.1 p.441*

Fotitch, Tatiana Zurunitch *v.2 p.643*

FotoFest *v.1 p.763*

Fotsch, Paul Mason *v.5 p.700*

Foucault, Michel *v.1 p.458, p.495, v.3 p.55, v.4 p.747, p.752, v.6 p.275, p.364, p.370, p.429, p.447*

Fought, Carmen *v.6 p.494*

Foulkes, Julia L. *v.1 p.28, p.30, p.41*

Fountain, Charles *v.4 p.811, p.906*
Fountain, Gary & Brazeau, Peter *v.2 p.61*
Fouracre, Paul (Editor) *v.3 p.66, v.6 p.562*
Fouracre, Paul *v.3 p.142*
Fouz-Hernandez, Santiago & Jarman-Ivens,
  Freya *v.1 p.269, p.338*
Fowden, Garth *v.3 p.192*
Foweraker, Joe & Craig, Ann L. (Editors) *v.3 p.292, v.4 p.711*
Foweraker, Joe *v.3 p.340*
Fowler, Alastair *v.2 p.166, p.199*
Fowler, Alistair (Editor) *v.2 p.196, p.199*
Fowler, C. M. R. *v.5 p.443*
Fowler, Carolyn *v.2 p.537*
Fowler, Don *v.2 p.424*
Fowler, Edward *v.6 p.219*
Fowler, Floyd J. Jr. & Mangione, Thomas W. . . . *v.4 p.691*
Fowler, Gene Jr. *v.1 p.144*
Fowler, Kristine K. *v.5 p.458, p.461*
Fowler, Robert Booth, et al. *v.1 p.604*
Fowler, Robert (Editor) *v.2 p.413*
Fowler, T. Kenneth *v.5 p.362*
Fowler, Will (ed.) *v.3 p.260*
Fowler, Will *v.3 p.343*
Fowler, William M. Jr. *v.4 p.520*
Fowler, William M. *v.3 p.413*
Fowler-Salamini, Heather & Vaughan, Mary K.
  (Editors) *v.3 p.292, v.6 p.454*
Fowles, Grant R. & Cassiday, George L. *v.5 p.546*
Fowles, Grant R. *v.5 p.561*
Fowles, John *v.2 p.346, p.347*
Fowlie, Wallace *v.1 p.105, v.2 p.460, p.461, p.496*
Fox, Alistair *v.3 p.100, p.120, v.4 p.499*
Fox, Annette B. *v.3 p.541*
Fox, Anthony *v.2 p.621*
Fox, Denton & Palsson, Hermann (Translators) . . . *v.2 p.624*
Fox, Dixon Ryan *v.3 p.376*
Fox, Elizabeth & Waisbord, Silvio R. (Editors) . . . *v.4 p.415*
Fox, Geoffrey E. *v.6 p.537, p.543*
Fox, James A. & Tracy, Paul E. *v.4 p.691*
Fox, James Alan, et al. *v.6 p.252*
Fox, James R. *v.4 p.434*
Fox, John *v.2 p.455*
Fox, Karl A. *v.4 p.769*
Fox, Michael V. *v.1 p.621*
Fox, Michael W. *v.5 p.247*
Fox, Renee C. *v.4 p.778*
Fox, Richard G. *v.6 p.160*
Fox, Richard *v.5 p.571*
Fox, Robert B. & Powell, Warren H. *v.5 p.289*
Fox, Robin Lane *v.3 p.19*
Fox, Roddy & Rowntree, Kate (Editors) *v.4 p.384*
Fox, Ronald F. *v.5 p.192*
Fox, Ruth *v.2 p.214*
Fox, Stephen R. *v.4 p.426*
Fox, Susan (Editor) *v.2 p.26*

Fox, Thomas C. *v.1 p.573*
Fox Weber, Nicholas & Filler, Martin *v.1 p.720*
Foxall, Gordon R. *v.4 p.139*
Foxe, John *v.1 p.612*
Fox-Genovese, Elizabeth *v.6 p.452*
Fox-Lockert, Lucia *v.2 p.638*
Foye, Raymond & Percy, Ann *v.1 p.723*
Fraassen, Bas C. van *v.1 p.504*
Fracis, Sohrab Homi *v.2 p.160*
Frader, Laura L. & Rose, Sonya O. (Editors) . . . *v.3 p.53*
Fradkin, Philip L. *v.6 p.712*
Fradkin, Robert A. *v.1 p.159*
Frady, Marshall *v.1 p.648*
Fraenkel, Eduard *v.2 p.434*
Fraioli, Deborah A. *v.3 p.143*
Fraleigh, Sondra Horton *v.1 p.15, p.26, p.41*
Fraleigh, Sondra *v.1 p.41*
Frame, Donald M. *v.2 p.470*
Frame, Douglas *v.2 p.402*
Frame, Janet *v.2 p.745*
Frampton, Kenneth & Drew, Philip *v.1 p.792*
Frampton, Kenneth *v.1 p.786, p.792*
France, Anatole *v.2 p.489, p.490*
France, John *v.1 p.573, v.6 p.556, p.567*
France, Marie de *v.2 p.467*
France, Peter (Editor) *v.2 p.455, p.574*
Frances, Richard J. (Editor), et al. *v.5 p.512, p.521*
Franceschet, Susan *v.3 p.353*
Franceschina, John C. *v.6 p.411*
Francia, Luis H. & Gamalinda, Eric (Editors) . . . *v.6 p.91*
Francia, Luis H. (Editor, Introduction by) . . . *v.2 p.760*
Francia, Luis H. (Introduction by) *v.6 p.179*
Francione, Gary L. *v.4 p.448*
Franciosi, Robert J. *v.4 p.326*
Francis, A. J. *v.5 p.697*
Francis, Becky & Skelton, Christine *v.4 p.301*
Francis, Charles A. (Editor) *v.5 p.21*
Francis, David & Hester, Stephen *v.4 p.688*
Francis de Sales *v.1 p.576*
Francis, Elizabeth *v.2 p.11, v.4 p.772*
Francis, J. Michael & Kaufman, Will (Editors) . . . *v.4 p.591*
Francis, Mark & Foster, Hal *v.1 p.678*
Francis, Michael J. *v.3 p.348, p.353*
Francis, Peter & Oppenheimer, Clive *v.5 p.437*
Francis, R. A. *v.2 p.525*
Francis, Richard C. *v.5 p.653, p.657*
Franck, Thomas M. *v.4 p.633*
Francl, Michelle *v.5 p.288*
Franco, Jean *v.2 p.664*
Franco, Paul *v.4 p.491*
Francoeur, Robert T. (Editor), et al. *v.4 p.677, p.747*
Francome, Colin *v.4 p.778*
Franda, Marcus *v.4 p.624*
Frangieh, Bassam K. *v.6 p.659*
Frangsmyr, Tore (Introduction by) *v.5 p.231*

Franits, Wayne E. (Editor) *v.1 p.738*
Frank, Anna Marie *v.4 p.821, p.823*
Frank, Frederick S. & Magistrale, Anthony S. *v.2 p.50*
Frank, Grace *v.2 p.461*
Frank, Jerome & Frank, Barbara *v.4 p.438*
Frank, Jerome D. *v.4 p.437, p.647, p.649*
Frank, Juhan, et al. *v.5 p.66*
Frank, Lawrence *v.2 p.284, p.285, p.286*
Frank, Norman & Ramus, Erica *v.5 p.95, p.215*
Frank, Patrick (Editor) *v.1 p.684*
Frank, Philipp *v.5 p.401*
Frank, Robert G. & Elliott, Timothy R. *v.5 p.672*
Frank, Robert H. *v.4 p.53*
Frank, Ross *v.6 p.524, p.531*
Frank, Rusty E. *v.1 p.32*
Frank, Steven A. *v.5 p.192*
Frank, Waldo D. *v.3 p.367*
Frank, Zephyr L. *v.3 p.340*
Frankel, Aaron *v.1 p.404*
Frankel, Charles *v.5 p.434*
Frankel, Francine R. & Harding, Harry *v.6 p.155*
Frankel, Glenn *v.6 p.610*
Frankel, Jonathan & Zipperstein, Steven J. (Editors) . *v.3 p.59*
Frankel, Jonathan *v.3 p.59*
Frankel, Lois P. *v.4 p.167*
Frankel, Max *v.3 p.440, p.471*
Frankel, Michael E. S. *v.4 p.84*
Frankel, Richard M. (Editor), et al. *v.5 p.532*
Frankel, Theodore *v.5 p.496, p.501*
Frankenberry, Nancy K. (Editor) *v.1 p.521*
Frankfort, Henri A., et al. *v.3 p.4*
Frankfort, Henri A. *v.1 p.670, p.693, v.3 p.4*
Frankfurter, David *v.1 p.542*
Frankfurter, Felix & Landis, James M. *v.4 p.470*
Frankfurter, Felix *v.4 p.437, p.467*
Frankham, Richard, et al. *v.5 p.132*
Frank-Kamenetskii, D. A. *v.5 p.566*
Frankl, Razelle *v.1 p.655*
Frankl, Viktor E. *v.5 p.619*
Frankland, E. Gene *v.4 p.383*
Franklin, Benjamin *v.2 p.29, v.4 p.342*
Franklin, David *v.1 p.738*
Franklin, Donna L. *v.4 p.729*
Franklin, Eric N. *v.1 p.51*
Franklin, Gene F., et al. *v.5 p.710*
Franklin, J. L. *v.5 p.279*
Franklin, John H. & Moss, Alfred A. *v.6 p.4*
Franklin, John H. *v.3 p.430, p.436, p.495*
Franklin, John Hope *v.3 p.374*
Franklin, Mark N. *v.4 p.577*
Franklin, Miles *v.2 p.745*
Franklin, Peter *v.1 p.213, p.339*
Franklin, S. & Shepard, J. *v.3 p.215*
Franklin, Sarah & McKinnon, Susan (Editors) *v.4 p.32*
Franklin, Sarah & Ragone, Helena (Editors) *v.4 p.32*

Franklin, Simon (Translator) *v.2 p.813*
Franklin, Stan *v.5 p.589*
Franklin, V. P. (Editor) *v.6 p.21, p.38*
Franko, Ivan *v.2 p.814*
Franko, Mark & Richards, Annette (Editors) *v.1 p.42*
Franko, Mark *v.1 p.28, p.30, p.41, p.42*
Franks, Angela *v.4 p.775*
Franks, Don *v.6 p.346*
Franks, F. *v.5 p.313*
Franks, Jeffrey, et al. *v.3 p.344*
Franks, Joel S. *v.4 p.834, v.6 p.125*
Frank-Stromborg, Marilyn & Olsen, Sharon J. (Editors) . *v.5 p.529*
Franses, Philip Hans *v.4 p.200*
Frantz, Joe B. *v.3 p.508*
Frantz, Joe Bertram *v.3 p.521, v.6 p.324*
Frantzen, Allen J. *v.2 p.167, v.6 p.392*
Frantzich, Stephen E. & Schier, Steven E. *v.4 p.529*
Franzen, Jonathan *v.2 p.160*
Franzmann, Majella *v.1 p.528*
Frappier, Jean *v.2 p.467*
Frascina, Francis, et al. *v.1 p.727*
Fraser, Alan *v.1 p.397*
Fraser, Claire M. (Editor), et al. *v.5 p.139*
Fraser, Elisabeth A. *v.1 p.738*
Fraser, Gordon *v.5 p.540*
Fraser, James W. *v.4 p.307*
Fraser, Lauchlan H. & Keddy, Paul A. (Editors) . . . *v.4 p.392*
Fraser, Lyn M. & Ormiston, Aileen *v.4 p.91, p.95, p.105*
Fraser, Michael (editor) *v.2 p.549*
Fraser, Nancy & Bartky, Sandra L. (Editors) *v.6 p.427*
Fraser, Nancy *v.6 p.427*
Fraser, Neil *v.1 p.148*
Fraser, P M *v.3 p.10, v.6 p.57*
Fraser, Robert *v.2 p.756*
Fraser, Ronald, et al. *v.4 p.326*
Fraser, Russell A. *v.2 p.227*
Fraser, Sarah Elizabeth *v.1 p.727*
Fraser, Stephen D. *v.4 p.869*
Fraser, Steve & Gerstle, Gary (Editors) *v.3 p.471*
Fraser, Steven *v.4 p.126*
Fraser, Stewart *v.4 p.342*
Fraser, Valerie *v.3 p.263*
Fraser, W. Hamish *v.4 p.126*
Fraser *v.2 p.497*
Frausto da Silva, J. J. R. & Williams, R. J. *v.5 p.327*
Frawley, Maria H. *v.6 p.478*
Frawley, William J. (Editor) *v.2 p.560, v.5 p.620, p.623*
Frayling, Christopher *v.6 p.324*
Frayn, Michael *v.2 p.345*
Frazee, C. A. *v.6 p.589*
Frazer, William *v.4 p.227*
Frazier, Adrian *v.2 p.300*
Frazier, E. Franklin & Lincoln, C. Eric *v.6 p.35*
Frazier, Ian *v.3 p.518*
Frazier, Jane *v.2 p.101*

Frazier, John W. & Margai, Florence M. *v.4 p.382*
Frazier, Robert *v.3 p.195*
Frazier, W. J. & Schwimmer, D. R. *v.5 p.431*
Frears, John R. *v.4 p.609*
Freccero, Carla *v.3 p.367*
Freccero, John *v.2 p.704*
Frechet, Alec *v.2 p.347*
Frederic, Harold *v.2 p.37*
Frederick, William C. *v.4 p.53*
Frederick, William H. (Editor) *v.6 p.174*
Frederick, William H. *v.6 p.176*
Fredericks, Marcel, et al. *v.4 p.702*
Frederickson, Burton B. (Editor), et al. *v.1 p.708*
Frederickson, Greg N. *v.5 p.469*
Frederickson, H. George & Smith, Kevin B. . . *v.4 p.545, p.580*
Frederiksen, R. A. & Odvody, G. N. (Editors) *v.5 p.46*
Fredman, Stephen *v.2 p.108*
Fredrick, Edna C. *v.1 p.90, p.105*
Fredrickson, George M. *v.3 p.397, p.430*
Freeborn, Richard (Editor), et al. *v.2 p.794*
Freeborn, Richard *v.2 p.798*
Freed, Melvyn N., et al. *v.4 p.355*
Freedberg, David *v.1 p.702, v.5 p.396*
Freedberg, Sydney J. *v.1 p.727*
Freeden, Michael *v.1 p.501*
Freedheim, Donald K. (Editor) *v.5 p.596*
Freedman, David, et al. *v.5 p.481*
Freedman, David Noel *v.1 p.614*
Freedman, Eric M. *v.4 p.524*
Freedman, Estelle B. *v.6 p.433*
Freedman, Jonathan (Editor) *v.2 p.43*
Freedman, Jonathan *v.2 p.321*
Freedman, Lawrence (Editor) *v.3 p.35*
Freedman, Maurice *v.4 p.39*
Freedman, Paul *v.6 p.575*
Freedman, Robert O. *v.6 p.592*
Freedman, Robert Owen (Editor) *v.6 p.592, p.613*
Freedman, Robert Owen *v.6 p.613, p.617*
Freedman, Roger A. *v.5 p.65*
Freedom House Staff *v.4 p.409*
Freeh, Louis J. *v.6 p.259*
Freehling, William W. *v.3 p.397, p.416, v.4 p.520*
Freehof, Solomon B. *v.1 p.550*
Freeland, Cynthia A. *v.6 p.318*
Freeland, Richard M. *v.3 p.471*
Freeman, A. J. & Keller, C. (Editors) *v.5 p.307*
Freeman, A. J. & Lander, G. H. (Editors) *v.5 p.308*
Freeman, A. J. & Lander, G. H. *v.5 p.308*
Freeman, A. Myrick III *v.4 p.61*
Freeman, Carla C. *v.4 p.28*
Freeman, Charles *v.3 p.3*
Freeman, Douglas S. *v.3 p.425*
Freeman, Douglas Southall *v.3 p.397, p.430*
Freeman, Edith M. & Logan, Sadye Louise *v.6 p.38*
Freeman, Harry M. *v.5 p.368, p.373, p.376*

Freeman, James M. *v.6 p.140*
Freeman, Joan *v.5 p.543*
Freeman, Joanne B. *v.4 p.485*
Freeman, Jo *v.6 p.427*
Freeman, Joshua Benjamin *v.4 p.126*
Freeman, Kathleen *v.1 p.421*
Freeman, Lyn W. *v.5 p.531*
Freeman, Mark P. *v.1 p.702*
Freeman, Mary E. Wilkins *v.2 p.37*
Freeman, Michael & Jacques, Claude *v.6 p.170*
Freeman, Michael J. *v.6 p.765*
Freeman, Michael . *v.1 p.769, v.4 p.659, p.805, p.902, v.6 p.170*
Freeman, Nick & Bartels, Frank (Editors) *v.4 p.60*
Freeman, R. Edward, et al. *v.4 p.61, p.63*
Freeman, Ray *v.5 p.272*
Freeman, Richard B. & Rogers, Joel *v.5 p.579*
Freeman, Roger L. *v.5 p.725*
Freeman, Rosemary *v.2 p.214*
Freeman, Sandra *v.6 p.411*
Freeman, Walter J. *v.5 p.616*
Freeman-Grenville, G. S. (Editor) *v.6 p.63*
Freeman-Grenville, G. S. P. *v.6 p.581*
Freese, Barbara *v.4 p.146, p.160, v.5 p.450, p.737*
Freestone, Robert (Editor) *v.6 p.727*
Freeze, Alan R. & Cherry, John A. *v.5 p.428*
Frege, Gottlob *v.1 p.493*
Fregoso, Rosa Linda (Editor) *v.6 p.493*
Fregoso, Rosa Linda . . . *v.3 p.527, v.6 p.340, p.486, p.546*
Frei, Hans W. *v.1 p.635*
Frei, Norbert *v.3 p.176*
Freibert, Lucy M. & White, Barbara A. (Editors) . . . *v.2 p.29*
Freidberg, Errol, et al. *v.5 p.121*
Freidel, David, et al. *v.3 p.261, v.4 p.9*
Freidel, Frank & Pencak, William (Editors) *v.3 p.493*
Freidel, Frank *v.3 p.440, p.447, p.458*
Freidenberg, Judith *v.4 p.741, v.6 p.542, p.543, p.548*
Freifeld, Alice *v.3 p.186*
Freire, Paolo *v.4 p.300*
Freire, Paulo *v.3 p.340, v.4 p.342, p.761*
Freitag, Sandria B. (Editor) *v.6 p.160*
Freitag, Sandria B. *v.6 p.160*
Freitas, Gary A. *v.6 p.322*
Frelinghuysen, Alice Cooney, et al. *v.1 p.810*
Fremling, Calvin R. *v.3 p.506*
Fremont, John C. *v.3 p.520*
French, A. P. & Taylor, E. F. *v.5 p.549*
French, A. *v.2 p.782*
French, Alfred *v.2 p.781, p.782*
French, Anthony P. *v.5 p.546, p.557, p.558*
French, Hilary *v.6 p.300*
French, J. Milton (Editor) *v.2 p.253*
French, John D. & James, Daniel *v.3 p.283, v.6 p.456*
French, Peter A. (Editor), et al. *v.1 p.516*
French, Peter A. *v.4 p.715, p.802, p.821, p.893*
French, R. A. *v.6 p.720*

French, Roger *v.5 p.221*

French, Samuel E. *v.5 p.693*

French, Warren (Editor) *v.2 p.123*

French, Warren *v.2 p.49, p.92, p.117*

French, William E. *v.3 p.264, p.289, p.292*

Frend, W. H. C. *v.1 p.646*

Frend, W. H. *v.1 p.599, p.612, p.646*

Freneau, Philip M *v.2 p.29*

Frenkel, Daan & Smit, B. *v.5 p.551*

Fresenius, Philipp *v.5 p.289*

Fresonke, Kris & Spence, Mark David (Editors) . . .*v.3 p.520*

Freud, Anna & Burlingham, Dorothy T. *v.4 p.735*

Freud, Sigmund & Jung, C. G. *v.5 p.596, p.658*

Freud, Sigmund *v.1 p.524, v.2 p.585, v.4 p.748, v.5 p.634, p.658*

Freudenburg, Kirk (Editor) *v.2 p.427*

Freudenburg, Kirk *v.2 p.427*

Frevert, Ute *v.3 p.159, p.160*

Frey, Bruno S. *v.4 p.659*

Frey, Lawrence R. (Editor) *v.5 p.647*

Frey, R. G., et al. *v.1 p.485*

Freyre, Gilberto & Horton, Rod W. *v.3 p.336*

Freyre, Gilberto *v.3 p.271, p.340*

freysinger Valeria J *v.4 p.783*

Frick Art Reference Library Staff *v.1 p.664*

Frick, J. (Editor) *v.5 p.736*

Fricke, Aaron *v.6 p.401*

Fricke, Tom *v.6 p.164*

Fricker, Jon D. & Whitford, Robert K. *v.5 p.700*

Fricker, Lloyd D. (Editor) *v.5 p.328*

Fricker, Miranda & Hornsby, Jennifer (Editors) . . .*v.6 p.461*

Friday, Chris *v.6 p.116*

Friday, William C. & Hesburgh, Theodore M.
(Editors) *v.4 p.821, p.894*

Fridegard, Jan *v.2 p.629*

Fridson, Martin S. & Alvarez,
Fernando *v.4 p.91, p.95, p.105, p.106, p.175*

Friebolin, Horst *v.5 p.272*

Fried, Albert *v.3 p.447*

Fried, Gil, et al. *v.4 p.884, p.888, p.891*

Fried, Richard M. *v.3 p.447, p.458*

Friedan, Betty *v.6 p.433, p.445*

Friedberg, Aaron L. *v.4 p.498*

Friedberg, Errol C. *v.5 p.133*

Friedberg, Errol *v.5 p.78, p.127*

Friedel, Robert A. and Milton Orchin *v.5 p.297*

Friedelbaum, Stanley H. *v.4 p.536*

Frieden, Jeffry A. *v.4 p.664*

Friedenberg, Edgar Z. *v.4 p.736*

Friedenberg, Robert V. *v.4 p.550*

Friederici, Peter *v.5 p.233*

Friedl, Alfred E. & Koontz, Trish Yourst *v.4 p.363*

Friedl, Erika *v.6 p.629*

Friedl, Friedrich, et al. *v.1 p.719*

Friedlaender, Johnny *v.1 p.756*

Friedlaender, Walter *v.1 p.727*

Friedland, Bea *v.1 p.197, p.324*

Friedland, Roger & Mohr, John W. (Editors) *v.4 p.699*

Friedlander, G., et al. *v.5 p.308*

Friedlander, Henry *v.3 p.83, v.4 p.652*

Friedlander, Michael W. *v.5 p.73, p.388*

Friedlander, Saul *v.3 p.59, p.83, p.171*

Friedler, Sharon E. & Glazer, Susan B. (Editors) . . .*v.1 p.42*

Friedlob, G. Thomas & Welton, Ralph E. *v.4 p.175*

Friedman, A. & Littman, W. *v.5 p.500*

Friedman, Benjamin M. & Hahn, F. H. (Editors) *v.4 p.188, p.189*

Friedman, Clara H. *v.4 p.121*

Friedman, Edward (Editor, Contribution by) *v.4 p.619*

Friedman, Edward, et al. *v.6 p.193, p.194*

Friedman, Elisabeth J. *v.3 p.360*

Friedman, George *v.3 p.483*

Friedman, Herman (Editor), et al. *v.5 p.148, p.166*

Friedman, Howard S. (Editor), et al. *v.5 p.666*

Friedman, Isaiah *v.6 p.612, p.617*

Friedman, J. H., et al. *v.5 p.408*

Friedman, Jack P., et al. *v.4 p.95, p.166*

Friedman, Jonathan *v.3 p.84*

Friedman, Lawrence J. *v.3 p.420*

Friedman, Lawrence M. *v.4 p.440, p.442, p.471*

Friedman, Lawrence Meir *v.4 p.109, p.441*

Friedman, Lawrence S. (Editor), et al. *v.5 p.519*

Friedman, Leon & Israel, Fred L. (Editors) *v.4 p.467*

Friedman, Leon (Editor) *v.4 p.454, p.457*

Friedman, Lester D. (Editor) *v.6 p.329, p.339, p.341*

Friedman, Lester D. *v.4 p.774*

Friedman, Marilyn M., et al. *v.5 p.525, p.529*

Friedman, Maurice S. *v.1 p.468*

Friedman, Maurice *v.5 p.634*

Friedman, Melvin J. *v.2 p.100*

Friedman, Mildred & Giovannini, Joseph (Editors) . .*v.1 p.713*

Friedman, Milton & Friedman, Rose D. *v.4 p.232*

Friedman, Milton & Schwartz, A. J. *v.4 p.238*

Friedman, Milton & Schwartz, Anna J. *v.4 p.238*

Friedman, Milton (Editor) *v.4 p.231, p.237*

Friedman, Milton *v.4 p.214, p.231, p.237, p.250, p.269*

Friedman, Monroe *v.4 p.759*

Friedman, Norman *v.2 p.68*

Friedman, Raymond A. *v.4 p.121*

Friedman, Stanley *v.2 p.284*

Friedman, Susan S. *v.6 p.433, p.462*

Friedman, Susan W. *v.4 p.682*

Friedman, Thomas L. *v.3 p.483, v.4 p.55, p.89, v.6 p.592*

Friedman, Walter A. *v.4 p.146, p.165*

Friedmann, John *v.6 p.723*

Friedrich, Carl J. *v.4 p.574*

Friedrich, Hugo *v.2 p.470*

Friedrich, Otto *v.3 p.181*

Friedrich, Pia *v.2 p.721*

Friedrichs, Christopher R. *v.3 p.44*

Friedrichs, Jorg *v.4 p.626*

Friedrichsmeyer, Sara (Editor), et al. *v.4 p.584*

Friedwald, Will *v.1 p.258, p.269, p.357*

Friel, Joe *v.4 p.787, p.841, p.857*

Friel, Susan N. & House, Peggy A. (Editors) *v.5 p.462*

Frieling, Rudolf & Daniels, Dieter (Editors) *v.1 p.771*

Friend, Theodore *v.6 p.174, p.176, p.179*

Friendly, Fred *v.4 p.439*

Frierson, Cathy A. (Editor, Translator) *v.3 p.217*

Friesen, Abraham. *v.1 p.603*

Friesen, Gerald *v.3 p.546, v.6 p.682*

Friesen, Steven J.. . . . . *v.1 p.632*

Frigon, Normand L. & Mathews, David *v.5 p.683*

Frigstad, David B. *v.4 p.135*

Frijda, Nico H. (Editor), et al. *v.5 p.611*

Friman, H. Richard *v.3 p.281*

Frisch, Helmut. *v.4 p.230, p.235*

Frisch, Max & Ackermann, Paul Kurt *v.2 p.607*

Frisch, Max *v.2 p.607*

Frisch, Michael H.. . . . . *v.3 p.488*

Frisch, Otto R.. . . . . *v.5 p.554*

Frisch, Ragnar *v.4 p.195*

Frisch, Uriel *v.5 p.547*

Frisch, Walter (Editor) *v.1 p.213, p.353*

Frisch, Walter. *v.1 p.197, p.239, p.313, p.370*

Frison, George C. (Editor) *v.4 p.10*

Frison-Roche, Roger & Jouty, Sylvan *v.4 p.789*

Friswell, M. I. & Mottershead, J. E. *v.5 p.693*

Frith, Simon & Horne, Howard *v.1 p.269*

Frith, Simon & Marshall, Lee (Editors) *v.1 p.383, p.384*

Frith, Simon (Editor), et al. *v.1 p.269*

Frith, Simon (Editor, Translator, Introduction by) . . . *v.1 p.269*

Frith, Simon *v.1 p.269*

Fritsch-Bournazel, Renata *v.3 p.179*

Fritz, Harry W.. . . . . *v.3 p.525*

Fritz, Henry E.. . . . . *v.6 p.688*

Fritz, James S. *v.5 p.268*

Fritz, Robert *v.4 p.86*

Fritz, Stephen G.. . . . . *v.3 p.174*

Fritze, Ronald H.. . . . . *v.4 p.377*

Fritzer, Penelope J. & Bland, Bartholomew *v.2 p.195*

Fritzsche, Peter. *v.3 p.170*

Froelich, Paul *v.4 p.193*

Frohock, Wilbur M. *v.2 p.463*

Froissart, Jean. *v.3 p.69*

Frolic, B. Michael *v.4 p.702*

Frome, Michael. *v.4 p.407, v.5 p.18, p.233, p.234*

Frome, Shelly *v.1 p.137, p.144*

Fromentin, Eugene *v.2 p.490*

Fromentin, Eugène *v.2 p.490*

Fromkin, David *v.3 p.451, v.6 p.592*

Fromm,
  Erich. *v.1 p.484, v.4 p.235, p.768, p.775, v.5 p.585, p.611, p.645*

Frommer, Benjamin *v.3 p.189*

Frommer, Herbert H. & Stabulas-Savage, Jeanine J.. . *v.5 p.525*

Fromonot, Francoise *v.1 p.792*

Fronek, Josef *v.2 p.774*

Fronske, Hilda A. *v.4 p.798*

Frontera, Walter R. (Editor). *v.4 p.827, p.828, p.829*

Frost, Alan. *v.4 p.385*

Frost, Chris *v.4 p.409*

Frost, Ginger S. *v.6 p.747, p.765*

Frost, Helen. *v.1 p.33*

Frost, Lynda E. & Bonnie, Richard J. (Editors). *v.4 p.448, v.5 p.592*

Frost, Mark *v.4 p.823, p.860*

Frost, Nick (Editor). *v.4 p.757*

Frost, Robert *v.2 p.77*

Frost, T *v.5 p.272*

Frost, William *v.2 p.246*

Frost-Knappman, Elizabeth & Cullen-DuPont, Kathryn. *v.6 p.430*

Froude, James A.. . . . . *v.2 p.276*

Frouin, Robert J., et al. *v.4 p.388*

Frow, John. *v.2 p.577*

Frucht, Richard (Editor). *v.3 p.206*

Fruchtman, Jack Jr. (Editor). *v.2 p.264*

Frueh, Jamie *v.6 p.78*

Frueh, Joanna (Editor), et al. *v.6 p.472*

Fruehan, R. J. *v.5 p.736*

Frug, Gerald E. *v.6 p.723*

Frugoni, Chiara *v.6 p.577, p.712*

Fruhwirth, R., et al.. . . . . *v.5 p.562*

Frum, David. *v.3 p.440, p.483*

Frumkin, Howard, et al.. . . . . *v.6 p.727*

Frumkin, Norman *v.4 p.178*

Fruton, Joseph S. *v.5 p.116, p.119, p.326*

Fry, Brian R. *v.4 p.545, p.580*

Fry, Carrol L. *v.2 p.260*

Fry, Donald K.. . . . . *v.2 p.205*

Fry, Douglas P.. . . . . *v.4 p.766*

Fry, Iris *v.5 p.192*

Fry, Katherine *v.4 p.414*

Fry, Michael (Editor) *v.4 p.219*

Fry, Norman. *v.5 p.420, p.440*

Fry, Paul H. *v.2 p.180*

Fry, Ron. *v.4 p.169*

Frye, Keith (Editor) *v.5 p.435*

Frye, Northrop (Author, Introduction by) *v.2 p.180*

Frye, Northrop . *v.2 p.71, p.229, p.233, p.239, p.568, p.729, v.3 p.535*

Frye, R. N. & Grossman, Stanley I. (Editors) *v.6 p.629*

Frye, Richard N. *v.6 p.629*

Frye, Roland M.. . . . . *v.2 p.229, p.254*

Fryer, Peter *v.1 p.292, v.3 p.279*

Frykenberg, Robert E. (Editor) *v.6 p.160, p.712*

Frymer-Kensky, Tikva *v.1 p.529*

Fu G Staff *v.5 p.693*

Fu, Xinian, et al. *v.1 p.789*

Fubini, Enrico *v.1 p.189*

Fuccaro, Nelida *v.6 p.598, p.602*

Fuchs, B. *v.2 p.579*

Fuchs, Jurgen & Podda, Maurizio (Editors). . . *v.5 p.116, p.139*

Fuchs, Lawrence H. *v.4 p.702*

Fuchs, R. H. *v.1 p.731*

Fuchs, Rachel & Thompson, Victoria *v.3 p.53*

Fuchs, Rudi, et al. *v.1 p.773*

Fudge, Thomas A. *v.3 p.188*

Fuegi, John *v.2 p.605*

Fuentes, Agustin *v.4 p.14*

Fuentes, Carlos & Ortega, Julio (Editors) *v.2 p.666*

Fuentes, Carlos *v.2 p.668, v.3 p.73*

Fuerst, Oren & Geiger, Uri *v.4 p.89, p.91, p.95*

Fuerstenau, Maurice C. (Editor) *v.5 p.737*

Fuess, Claude M. *v.3 p.415*

Fugard, Athol, et al. *v.1 p.62, p.128, p.130, v.2 p.755*

Fugard, Athol *v.2 p.754, p.755*

Fugita, Stephen & Fernandez, Marilyn *v.6 p.133*

Fugita, Stephen S. & O'Brien, David J. . . *v.4 p.764, v.6 p.131*

Fuglestad, Finn *v.6 p.70*

Fuhrer, Ronald *v.1 p.731*

Fuhrmann, Horst *v.3 p.161, v.6 p.563*

Fuhrmann, Joseph T. (Editor) *v.3 p.220*

Fuhs, Allen E. & Schetz, Joseph A. (Editors) *v.5 p.713*

Fujii, I. *v.5 p.708*

Fujimoto, Takahiro *v.5 p.716*

Fujino, Diane Carol *v.6 p.93, p.107, p.131*

Fujioka, Yasuhiro *v.1 p.170, p.259, p.318*

Fujisawa, Chikao *v.1 p.476*

Fujitani, Takashi *v.6 p.226*

Fujita-Rony, Dorothy B. *v.6 p.116, p.129*

Fukurai, Hiroshi & Krooth, Richard *v.6 p.270*

Fukuyama, Francis *v.5 p.217, p.247*

Fulbright, J. William *v.3 p.451*

Fulbrook, Mary *v.3 p.176*

Fulcher, Jane F. (Editor) *v.1 p.213, p.320*

Fuld, James J. *v.1 p.160*

Fulford, Timothy, et al. *v.2 p.175*

Fulk, Mark *v.2 p.118*

Fulk, R. D., et al. *v.2 p.167, v.6 p.565*

Fuller, Bruce *v.4 p.298*

Fuller, C. J. (Editor) *v.6 p.149*

Fuller, C. J. *v.1 p.535*

Fuller, Charles *v.2 p.145*

Fuller, Dudley D. *v.5 p.708*

Fuller, George W. *v.3 p.530*

Fuller, Graham E. & Francke, Rend Rahim *v.1 p.560*

Fuller, Graham E. & Lesser, Ian O. *v.4 p.488, p.495*

Fuller, J. F. C. *v.3 p.397, p.430*

Fuller, James L. *v.5 p.710*

Fuller, John (Editor) *v.2 p.199*

Fuller, John *v.2 p.329*

Fuller, Lon L. *v.4 p.433, p.434*

Fuller, Margaret C. *v.5 p.32, p.358, p.373*

Fuller, Margaret *v.2 p.39*

Fuller, R. & Santos, Jorge A. (Editors) *v.5 p.716*

Fuller, R. *v.1 p.624*

Fuller, Reginald Horace *v.1 p.640*

Fuller, Sophie & Whitesell, Lloyd (Editors) . *v.1 p.378, v.6 p.408*

Fuller, Steve *v.1 p.499, v.5 p.401*

Fullerton, Carol S. & Ursano, Robert J. (Editors) . . . *v.4 p.699*

Fullerton, Mark D. *v.1 p.670, p.687*

Fullilove, Mindy Thompson *v.5 p.608*

Fullinwider, Robert K. (Editor) *v.4 p.547*

Fulmer, William E. *v.4 p.78*

Fultz, Julia H. & Sturt, Patty Ann *v.5 p.531*

Fulvi, Philip A. (Translator) *v.2 p.502*

Fumaroli, Marc *v.1 p.723*

Fumento, Michael *v.5 p.217*

Fung, Archon *v.4 p.504*

Fung, Edmund S. K. *v.4 p.619*

Fung, Karen *v.2 p.751, v.6 p.51*

Fung, Yuan-Cheng *v.4 p.908*

Fung, Yu-Lan *v.1 p.418, v.6 p.182*

Funge, John David *v.5 p.339, p.340*

Funk, Gary *v.4 p.821, p.894*

Funk, V. A., et al. *v.5 p.205*

Funke, Lewis *v.1 p.144*

Funkenstein, Amos *v.3 p.47*

Funston, Judith *v.2 p.43*

Fuquay, John W. & Fox, Patrick F. (Editors) . . . *v.5 p.34, p.54*

Furet, Francois & Marx, Karl *v.3 p.158*

Furet, Francois *v.3 p.150, p.158*

Furger, Roberta *v.6 p.438*

Furgurson, Ernest B. *v.3 p.499*

Furia, Philip *v.1 p.249, p.325, v.2 p.111*

Furley, David (Author, Contribution by) *v.1 p.419, p.500*

Furley, David (Editor) *v.1 p.419*

Furman, N. Howell (Editor) *v.5 p.268*

Furnham, Adrian & Taylor, John *v.4 p.130*

Furnish, Victor P. (Introduction by) *v.1 p.631*

Furniss, W. Todd & Graham, Patricia A. (Editors) . . *v.4 p.292*

Furnivall, J. S. *v.6 p.165, p.174, p.176*

Furnivall, John S. *v.6 p.176*

Furphy, Joseph *v.2 p.745*

Furr, A. Keith(Editory) *v.5 p.266*

Fursenko, Aleksandr & Naftali, Timothy . . . *v.3 p.228, p.309*

Furst, Peter T. *v.4 p.776, v.5 p.663*

Furst, Peter *v.3 p.317*

Furstenberg, Frank F. Jr. & Cherlin, Andrew J. . . *v.4 p.739, v.5 p.640*

Furstenberg, Frank F. Jr. *v.4 p.736*

Furtado, Ken & Hellner, Nancy *v.6 p.359, p.411*

Furth, George *v.1 p.249, p.357, p.407*

Furukawa, T. (Editor) *v.5 p.86*

Furukawa, Yasu *v.5 p.322*

Furuzan *v.6 p.666*

Fusco, Coco *v.6 p.492*

Fussell, Paul Jr. *v.2 p.578*

Fussell, Paul *v.2 p.178*

Fussell, Susan R. & Kreuz, Roger J. (Editors) . . . *v.5 p.620*

Fusso, Susanne *v.2 p.803*

Futuyma, Douglas J. *v.5 p.192*

Fux, Johann J. *v.1 p.370*
Fyfe, Aileen. *v.6 p.741, p.758, p.759*
Fyfe, Christopher *v.6 p.72*
Fyffe, Allen & Peter, Iain *v.4 p.789*
Fyle, C. Magbaily *v.6 p.53*

G

Gaar, Gillian G. *v.1 p.269, p.378, v.6 p.474*
Gaard, Greta (Editor) *v.6 p.433*
Gabasov, R. F., et al. *v.5 p.710*
Gabba, Emilio *v.3 p.24, p.26*
Gabbard, Krin *v.6 p.316, p.329, p.341*
Gabbert, Wolfgang *v.3 p.292*
Gabel, John B., et al. *v.1 p.616*
Gabin, Jane S.. . . . . *v.2 p.47*
Gabler, Robert E. (Author, Editor) *v.4 p.376*
Gabler, Ulrich *v.1 p.603*
Gaboriau, Emile *v.2 p.492*
Gabre-Sellassie, Zewde *v.6 p.64*
Gabriel, Jurg Martin & Fischer, Thomas (Editors) . . *v.3 p.244*
Gabriel, Mike *v.4 p.860*
Gabriel, Ralph Henry *v.3 p.367*
Gabriel, Richard A.. . . . . *v.5 p.584*
Gabrieli, Francesco *v.3 p.63, v.6 p.609*
Gackenbach, Jayne (Editor) *v.5 p.653*
Gacs, Ute D. (Editor), et al. *v.4 p.3, p.4*
Gad, Shayne Cox (Editor). . *v.5 p.95, p.104, p.113, p.145, p.217*
Gadamer, Hans Georg *v.1 p.420, p.468, p.507*
Gadd, David. *v.3 p.117, p.128*
Gadda, Carlo Emilio *v.2 p.715*
Gaddie, Ronald Keith. *v.4 p.550*
Gaddis, John Lewis (Editor), et al. *v.4 p.645, p.647*
Gaddis, John Lewis *v.3 p.388, p.452, v.4 p.628*
Gade, Daniel W.. . . . . *v.3 p.269*
Gadotti, Moacir *v.4 p.342*
Gaff, Jerry G. *v.4 p.294*
Gaffin, Harris *v.6 p.317*
Gage, Carolyn *v.6 p.411*
Gage, Nathaniel L.. . . . . *v.4 p.347, v.5 p.573*
Gager, John G.. . . . . *v.1 p.549*
Gagliano, Joseph A. *v.3 p.281, p.329*
Gagliardo, John G.. . . . . *v.3 p.164*
Gagne, Cole & Caras, Tracy. *v.1 p.213*
Gagne, Cole *v.1 p.213*
Gagne, Robert M., et al.. . . . . *v.4 p.342, v.5 p.573*
Gagnier, Regenia. *v.2 p.321, v.6 p.740, p.754*
Gagnon, V. P. *v.3 p.247*
Gahan, Peter. *v.2 p.309*
Gaile, Gary L. & Willmott, Cort J.. . . . . . *v.4 p.382*
Gaillard, Gerald *v.4 p.3*
Gaillardetz, Richard R. *v.1 p.575*
Gaines, Donna *v.4 p.736*
Gaines, Ernest J.. . . . . *v.2 p.145, v.6 p.25*
Gaines, James F. (Editor) *v.2 p.475*

Gaines, Jane & Renov, Michael (Editors) . . *v.4 p.413, v.6 p.309*
Gaines, Richard V., et al.. . . . . *v.5 p.435*
Gaines, William *v.4 p.408*
Gainey, Donald D. & Brucato, John M. *v.4 p.287*
Gainor, J. Ellen (Editor) *v.1 p.86, p.128, p.135*
Gainor, J. Ellen *v.2 p.78, p.309*
Gaisford, James D., et al. *v.5 p.218*
Gaite, Carmen M. *v.2 p.657*
Gaither, Carl C. & Cavazos-Gaither, Alma
    E. *v.5 p.225, p.458, p.461, p.545*
Gaither, Gerald H. *v.4 p.292*
Gaither, Milton. *v.4 p.326*
Gal, Reuven & Mangelsdorff, David (Editors) . . *v.5 p.584*
Galamian, Ivan *v.1 p.397*
Galan, Mark *v.5 p.179*
Galang, M. Evelina (Editor). *v.6 p.89, p.96*
Galang, M. Evelina *v.6 p.100*
Galanter, Marc & Kleber, Herbert D. *v.5 p.512, p.521*
Galarza, Ernesto *v.6 p.488, p.531, p.535, p.540*
Galas, David & McCormack, Stephen (Editors) . . *v.5 p.139*
Galassi, Peter *v.1 p.766*
Galbraith, John Kenneth . *v.3 p.440, p.447,v.4 p.95, p.99, p.193, p.209, p.211, p.213, p.214, p.243, p.265, p.773*
Galbraith, Michael W. (Editor) *v.4 p.315, p.320*
Galbraith, Stuart IV *v.6 p.226, p.335*
Galdós, Benito Pérez *v.2 p.654*
Galdman, Imogen *v.4 p.396*
Gale Editors (Editor) *v.1 p.76, p.100*
Gale Research Staff & McGrath, Kimberley A. . *v.5 p.95, p.156*
Gale Research Staff *v.5 p.395, v.6 p.285, p.291*
Gale, Richard M. (Editor). *v.1 p.488*
Gale, Robert L. . . . *v.2 p.43, p.46, p.47, p.77, p.113, v.6 p.358*
Gale, Steven H. (Editor) *v.2 p.111, p.195*
Gale, William F. & Totemeier, Terry C. (Editors) . . *v.5 p.732*
Gale, William G. & Orszag, Peter R.. . . . . . *v.4 p.107*
Gale, Zona *v.2 p.78*
Galen *v.2 p.404*
Galenson, Walter *v.4 p.126*
Galilei, Galileo & Drake, Stillman *v.5 p.62*
Galilei, Galileo *v.5 p.61, p.546*
Galilei, Vincenzo *v.1 p.179*
Galinsky, Karl (Editor). *v.3 p.27*
Galinsky, Philip *v.3 p.267*
Galkin, Elliott W.. . . . . *v.1 p.402*
Gall, C. (Editor). *v.5 p.54*
Gall, Gerald L.. . . . . *v.4 p.436*
Gall, Lothar & Underwood, J. A. *v.3 p.164*
Gall, Lothar *v.3 p.164*
Gallafent, Edward *v.6 p.316*
Gallagher, Catherine & Greenblatt, Stephen. . . *v.2 p.570*
Gallagher, Catherine & Laqueur, Thomas (Editors) . . *v.6 p.760*
Gallagher, Catherine . *v.2 p.170, p.193,v.6 p.756, p.761, p.765*
Gallagher, Gary W.. . . . . *v.4 p.520*
Gallagher, James J. & Gallagher, Shelagh A. . . . *v.4 p.317*
Gallagher, James J., et al.. . . . . *v.4 p.316*

Gallagher, Jean. *v.6 p.476*
Gallagher, Kelly *v.4 p.363*
Gallagher, Mary *v.2 p.537*
Gallagher, Michael & Mitchell, Paul (Editors) . . . *v.4 p.576*
Gallagher, Michael. *v.4 p.382*
Gallagher, Michela & Nelson, Randy J. (Editors) . . . *v.5 p.617*
Gallagher, Nancy E. *v.6 p.641*
Gallagher, Nora (Editor) *v.5 p.175, p.236*
Gallagher, Shaun. *v.4 p.323, p.339*
Gallant, Mavis *v.2 p.735*
Gallant, Thomas W. *v.3 p.194*
Gallas, Karen *v.4 p.360*
Galle, Jillian E. & Young, Amy L. (Editors) . . . *v.6 p.4, p.16*
Gallegos, Eloy J.. . . . . *v.3 p.498*
Gallegos, Rómulo *v.2 p.687*
Galli, Rosemary & Jones, Jocelyn. *v.6 p.73*
Galliano, Luciana *v.1 p.288*
Gallie, W. B.. . . . . *v.1 p.512*
Galliher, John F., et al. *v.6 p.247*
Gallin, Alice *v.4 p.307*
Galliou, Patrick & Jones, Michael *v.3 p.158*
Gallo, Gina *v.6 p.259*
Gallop, David *v.1 p.421*
Gallop, Jane. *v.2 p.568, p.571*
Galloway, David & Sabisch, Christian (Editors). . . . *v.6 p.406*
Galloway, J. H. *v.4 p.399*
Galluccio, Jon, et al. *v.6 p.376*
Gallup, Donald C. *v.2 p.107*
Gallup, George H. *v.4 p.697*
Gallup, George Jr. (Editor) *v.5 p.585*
Gallup, Joan Whaley *v.4 p.786, p.790, p.881, p.884*
Gallup, John Luke, et al. *v.4 p.397*
Galnoor, Itzhak. *v.6 p.617*
Galperin, Michael Y. & Koonin, Eugene V. (Editors) *v.5 p.139*
Galperin, William H.. . . . . *v.2 p.267, p.323*
Galpin, Francis W. *v.1 p.175*
Galston, Arthur W. & Peppard, Christiana Z. (Editors). *v.5 p.247*
Galston, William A. *v.4 p.510, p.511*
Galsworthy, John & Baker, George P. *v.2 p.348*
Galsworthy, John *v.2 p.347, p.348*
Galub, Arthur *v.4 p.536*
Galun, Esra *v.5 p.133*
Galun, Margalith (Editor) *v.5 p.210*
Galvin, Mary E. *v.6 p.392*
Galvin, Miles *v.3 p.319*
Gambaro, Griselda *v.2 p.678*
Gamber, Wendy (Editor), et al. *v.3 p.384*
Gambhir, M. L. *v.5 p.694*
Gamble, Clive. *v.4 p.16*
Gamble, David P.; Salmon, Linda K. & Njie, Alhaji
  Hassan *v.6 p.69*
Gamble, Harry Y.. . . . . *v.1 p.599*
Gamble, Vanessa N. *v.5 p.513*
Gamboa, Erasmo & Buan, Carolyn M. (Editors). *v.6 p.521, p.548*
Gamboa, Erasmo *v.6 p.525*

Gambogi, Joseph (Editor) *v.5 p.737*
Gambone, Michael D. *v.3 p.301*
Gamburd, Michele Ruth *v.6 p.154*
Game, Ann *v.4 p.679*
Gamelin, Theodore W. & Greene, Robert E. *v.5 p.499*
Gamma, Erich, et al.. . . . . *v.5 p.346, p.348, p.349*
Gammon, Bruce E.. *v.5 p.286*
Gammond, Peter. *v.1 p.197, p.249, p.346*
Gamow, George *v.5 p.399, p.539, p.540, p.543, p.554*
Gamson, Joshua *v.6 p.409*
Gamson, William A. *v.4 p.710*
Gamwell, Franklin I. *v.1 p.595*
Gander, Eric M. *v.5 p.653*
Gandhi, Leela *v.2 p.727*
Gandhi, Mahatma *v.4 p.766*
Gandhi, Mohandas K.. . . . . *v.1 p.540*
Gandhi, Mohandas *v.1 p.475*
Gandini, Lella & Edwards, Carolyn Pope (Editors) . *v.4 p.368*
Gandolfo, Christina *v.4 p.836, p.863, p.866*
Gandossy, Robert P. & Sonnenfeld, Jeffrey A.
  (Editors) *v.4 p.71, p.86*
Gandy, Matthew *v.6 p.727*
Gane, Mike J. *v.4 p.679*
Gane, Mike *v.4 p.681*
Ganeri, Jonardon *v.1 p.419*
Gangi, Jane M.. . . . . *v.4 p.360*
Gangolli, S. (Editor) *v.5 p.311*
Ganguly, Sumit & Hagerty, Devin T.. . . . . *v.6 p.159*
Ganguly, Sumit *v.6 p.159, p.160*
Ganjavi, Nizami *v.6 p.671*
Gann, Kyle *v.1 p.214, p.345, p.374*
Gannon, Michael V. (Editor) *v.3 p.504*
Gannon, Michael *v.3 p.504*
Ganong, Lawrence H. & Coleman,
  Marilyn *v.4 p.740, v.5 p.640, p.668*
Ganong, William F.. *v.5 p.164*
Gans, Herbert J. *v.3 p.371, v.4 p.702, p.754, v.6 p.717*
Ganshof, F. L.. . . . . *v.3 p.67*
Ganson, Barbara Anne *v.3 p.343, p.344*
Ganssle, Gregory E. & Woodruff, David M. (Editors) *v.1 p.594*
Ganti, Tibor *v.5 p.95, p.248*
Gantmakher, F. R. (Feliks Ruvimovich) *v.5 p.472*
Gantz, Timothy. *v.1 p.532, v.2 p.400*
Ganz, Cheryl & Strobel, Margaret (Editors). *v.1 p.808*
Ganzl, Kurt *v.1 p.160, p.249, p.250, p.337, p.407*
Gao, Bai. *v.6 p.219*
Gao, Mobo C. F. *v.6 p.195*
Gao Yuan *v.6 p.195, p.200*
Gaos, Vicente *v.2 p.643*
Gara, Larry *v.3 p.397, p.416, p.430*
Garafola, Lynn (Editor) *v.1 p.23*
Garafola, Lynn *v.1 p.23*
Garagi, Balawanta *v.1 p.131*
Garber, Daniel & Ayers, Michael (Editors) . . . *v.1 p.436, p.437*
Garber, Daniel & Nadler, Steven (Editors) *v.1 p.436*

Garber, Daniel & Nadler, Steven M. *v.1 p.436*

Garber, Frederick. *v.2 p.323*

Garber, James (Editor) *v.3 p.297*

Garber, Linda *v.6 p.359*

Garber, Marjorie B. *v.6 p.367, p.368, p.370*

Garber, Marjorie *v.2 p.229*

Garber, Steven D. *v.5 p.245*

Garber. *v.5 p.700*

Garbus, Martin. *v.4 p.536*

Garces, Maria Antonia *v.2 p.649*

García Acosta, Virginia *v.3 p.271*

García Bedolla, Lisa *v.6 p.538, p.549*

García Canclini, Néstor *v.3 p.267*

García, Cristina (Editor, Introduction
   by) *v.2 p.671, v.6 p.495, p.506*

García, Cristina. *v.2 p.145, v.6 p.506*

García, Ignacio M. *v.6 p.538*

García Lorca, Federico & Jiménez, Juan Ramón. *v.2 p.659, p.660*

García Lorca, Federico & Svich, Caridad. *v.2 p.660*

García Lorca,
   Federico. . . *v.1 p.84, p.107, v.2 p.658, p.659, p.660, v.6 p.396*

García, Mario T. (Editor) *v.6 p.486*

García, Mario
   T.. *v.3 p.508, v.6 p.488, p.512, p.531, p.535, p.538, p.544, p.549*

García Márquez, Gabriel *v.2 p.682, p.683*

Garcia, Alma (Editor) *v.6 p.486, p.546*

Garcia, Alma M. *v.6 p.521*

Garcia, Bernardo C. *v.6 p.367*

Garcia, Claire Watson. *v.1 p.724*

Garcia, Cristina *v.2 p.19*

Garcia, Eugene E. *v.4 p.311, p.312, v.6 p.527*

Garcia, F. Chris (Editor) *v.6 p.537*

Garcia, Jesus & Michaelis, John U. *v.4 p.363*

Garcia, John A. *v.6 p.538*

Garcia, Juan (Editor), et al. *v.6 p.521*

Garcia, Juan R. (Editor). *v.6 p.521*

Garcia, Juan R. *v.6 p.486, p.531, p.535, p.538, p.546*

Garcia, Lionel G.. . . . . *v.6 p.498*

Garcia, Manuel *v.1 p.395, p.400*

Garcia, Maria C. *v.6 p.543*

Garcia, Mario & Garcia, Alma (Editors) *v.6 p.427*

Garcia Marquez, Gabriel *v.2 p.682*

Garcia, Matthew *v.3 p.531, v.6 p.535, p.549, p.712*

Garcia, Nasario *v.6 p.488, p.498, p.512, p.523*

Garcia, Ricardo L. *v.2 p.160*

Garcia, Richard A.. . . . . *v.6 p.535, p.549*

Garcia, Rigoberto *v.3 p.351*

Garcia-Bryce, Inigo. *v.3 p.327*

Garcia-Marquez, Vicente *v.1 p.8*

Garcia-Mira, Ricardo (Editor), et al. *v.6 p.727*

Garcia-Perez, Gladys M. *v.3 p.309*

Garcma, Alfonso J.. . . . . *v.6 p.339, p.340*

Garden, Nancy. *v.6 p.396*

Gardenfors, Peter. *v.5 p.649*

Gardiner, Alan Henderson *v.3 p.8*

Gardiner, C. Harvey *v.3 p.329*

Gardiner, Harold (Photographer) *v.1 p.593*

Gardiner, John *v.6 p.735*

Gardiner, Judith Kegan *v.4 p.745, v.6 p.429*

Gardiner, Patrick (Editor) *v.1 p.438*

Gardiner, Samuel Rawson. *v.3 p.103*

Gardiner, Simon *v.4 p.884, p.900*

Gardner, Alexander *v.3 p.431*

Gardner, B. L. & Rausser, G. C.. . . . . *v.4 p.189*

Gardner, Bonnie Milne *v.1 p.113, p.137, p.152*

Gardner, Bruce L. & Rausser, Gordon C. (Editors) . . *v.4 p.189*

Gardner, Bruce L. *v.5 p.4*

Gardner, David G. & Shoback, Dolores M.. . . . . . *v.5 p.518*

Gardner, Erle Stanley *v.2 p.78*

Gardner, Hall *v.4 p.563*

Gardner, Helen (Editor, Introduction by) *v.2 p.199*

Gardner, Helen, et al.. . . . . *v.1 p.667*

Gardner, Howard & Laskin, Emma *v.5 p.647*

Gardner, Howard & Perkins, D. N. (Editors) . . . *v.5 p.618*

Gardner, Howard, et al.. . . . . *v.4 p.53, p.55*

Gardner, Howard. *v.4 p.303, p.343, p.356, v.5 p.571, p.608, p.653*

Gardner, James N. *v.5 p.192, p.243*

Gardner, James. *v.3 p.371*

Gardner, Jane F. & Wiedemann, Thomas *v.3 p.23*

Gardner, Jason (Editor) *v.5 p.232*

Gardner, John W.. . . . . *v.4 p.697*

Gardner, John *v.2 p.145, p.167*

Gardner, LeRoy *v.4 p.737*

Gardner, Lloyd C. *v.3 p.440, p.452*

Gardner, Martin *v.5 p.469, p.540*

Gardner, Paul D. (Editor) *v.1 p.616*

Gardner, Philip (Editor). *v.2 p.346*

Gardner, Robert L., et al. *v.4 p.107*

Gardner, Robert *v.4 p.347*

Gardner, Sebastian *v.1 p.461*

Garebian, Keith *v.1 p.250, p.311, p.337*

Garey, Michael R. & Johnson, David S. *v.5 p.336, p.471*

Garff, Joakim *v.1 p.478*

Garfield, Bob *v.4 p.427*

Garfield, Jay L. *v.5 p.593*

Garfield, Seth *v.3 p.340*

Garfield, Simon *v.5 p.262*

Garfinkel, Harold. *v.4 p.688*

Garfinkel, Simson, et al. *v.5 p.335, p.345, p.348*

Garfinkel, Simson *v.4 p.515*

Garfinkel, Yosef *v.4 p.26*

Garg, Ganga R. (Editor) *v.6 p.147*

Garg, Ganga R. *v.6 p.147, p.148*

Garganigo, John F., et al. *v.2 p.664*

Gargiulo, Terrence L. *v.4 p.78*

Garis, Robert *v.1 p.23*

Garlake, Peter *v.1 p.690*

Garland, David. *v.4 p.752, p.773, v.6 p.248*

Garland, Hamlin. *v.2 p.39*

Garland, Henry & Garland, Mary *v.2 p.589*

Garland, Henry B. (Henry Burnand) *v.2 p.599*

Garland, Henry B. *v.2 p.599*

Garland, Henry. *v.2 p.597*

Garland, Mary *v.2 p.599*

Garlick, Raymond & Mathias, Roland (Editors) *v.2 p.199*

Garlock, David (Editor) *v.4 p.412*

Garman, E. Thomas *v.4 p.250*

Garmezy, Norman *v.5 p.671*

Garnaut, Ross, et al. *v.4 p.86*

Garneau, Saint-Denys. *v.2 p.538*

Garner, Abigail *v.4 p.740, v.6 p.376*

Garner, Bryan A. *v.4 p.436*

Garner, Bryan *v.2 p.552, p.556*

Garner, Gretchen *v.1 p.764*

Garner, Wendell R. *v.5 p.594*

Garnets, Linda & Kimmel, Douglas C. *v.6 p.381*

Garon, Sheldon *v.6 p.224*

Garoogian, David *v.6 p.86*

Garrard, Greg *v.2 p.572, v.6 p.287*

Garraty, John A. & Carnes, Mark C. (Editors) *v.3 p.376*

Garraty, John A. *v.3 p.436, v.4 p.466*

Garreau, Joel *v.4 p.770, v.6 p.717*

Garret, Maxwell R., et al. *v.4 p.857*

Garretsen, Harry *v.4 p.227*

Garretson, Robert L. *v.1 p.402*

Garrett, David & Konkle, Lincoln (Editors) *v.2 p.61*

Garrett, David T. *v.3 p.265*

Garrett, Don & Barbanel, Edward (Editors) *v.1 p.504*

Garrett, Don (Editor) *v.1 p.477*

Garrett, Ian (Editor) *v.4 p.104*

Garrett, Laurie *v.4 p.668, v.6 p.283*

Garrett, Mark & Wachs, Martin *v.5 p.700*

Garrett, Paul *v.5 p.476*

Garrett, Stephen A. *v.3 p.80*

Garrett, William E. Jr., et al. *v.5 p.519*

Garrigan, Kristine O. *v.6 p.737, p.750*

Garrioch, David *v.3 p.147, p.158, v.6 p.712*

Garrison, Jean A. *v.3 p.388*

Garrison, Jim *v.3 p.471*

Garrison, Roger W. *v.4 p.245*

Garrison, Tom S. *v.5 p.428*

Garrison, W. L. *v.3 p.397*

Garrisson, Janine *v.3 p.145*

Garrity, George (Editor) *v.5 p.206*

Garrity, George M. (Editor) *v.5 p.206*

Garrity, Peter *v.4 p.175*

Garrod, H. W. *v.2 p.294*

Garros, Veronique (Editor), et al. *v.3 p.225*

Garrould, Ann (Editor) *v.1 p.723*

Garrow, David J. *v.1 p.581, v.4 p.447*

Garry, Ann & Pearsall, Marilyn (Editors) *v.6 p.461*

Garry, Jane, et al. *v.2 p.549, p.560*

Garsoian, Nina (Editor), et al. *v.1 p.569*

Garson, G. David. *v.5 p.591*

Garson, Helen S. *v.2 p.66*

Garten, Jeffrey E. *v.4 p.54*

Gartner, Barbara L. (Editor) *v.5 p.155*

Gartner, Leslie P. & Hiatt, James L. *v.5 p.159*

Gartner, Lloyd P. (Editor) *v.4 p.308*

Garton, Alison *v.5 p.626, p.630*

Garton Ash, Timothy *v.4 p.628*

Garton, Robin (Editor) *v.1 p.754*

Garvey, Marcus *v.6 p.12*

Garvin, Alexander *v.6 p.727*

Garvin, David A. *v.4 p.78*

Garvin, Tom *v.3 p.134, p.138*

Garvin *v.3 p.134*

Garwin, Richard L. & Charpak, Georges *v.5 p.553*

Garza, Hedda (Compiled by) *v.3 p.441, v.4 p.436*

Garza, Roberto J. *v.2 p.25*

Gascoigne, Bamber *v.1 p.752, p.759*

Gascoigne, David *v.2 p.532*

Gascoigne, George *v.2 p.214*

Gascuel, Olivier & Sagot, Marie-Frances *v.5 p.97*

Gash, Norman *v.3 p.94, p.108, p.111, p.130*

Gasiorowicz, Stephen. *v.5 p.549*

Gasiorowski, Mark J. & Byrne, Malcolm *v.6 p.631*

Gaskell, Elizabeth *v.2 p.270, p.288, p.289*

Gaskell, Philip *v.2 p.574, p.576*

Gaspar de Alba, Alicia, et al. *v.6 p.495, p.498, p.510*

Gaspar de Alba, Alicia *v.6 p.492*

Gass, Saul I. & Harris, Carl M. (Editors) *v.4 p.119*

Gassner, John & Quinn, Edward (Editors) *v.1 p.55*

Gassner, John (Editor, Introduction by) *v.2 p.25*

Gassner, John (Editor) *v.1 p.65, p.114, v.2 p.25*

Gassner, John (Introduction by) *v.1 p.65, p.114*

Gassner, John *v.1 p.65, p.69, p.73, p.100*

Gaster, Theodor Herzl *v.1 p.552*

Gaston, Anne-Marie *v.1 p.15*

Gaston, George M. A. *v.2 p.349*

Gaston, Kevin J. *v.5 p.168, p.205*

Gaston, Paul *v.3 p.494*

Gater, John & Gaffney, C. F. *v.4 p.7*

Gates, Barbara T. *v.2 p.270*

Gates, Bruce C. *v.5 p.278*

Gates, David *v.2 p.145*

Gates, Henry Louis Jr. & Appiah, Anthony
(Editors) *v.2 p.109, v.6 p.25, p.43*

Gates, Henry Louis Jr. & Appiah, Anthony . . *v.2 p.87, v.6 p.25*

Gates, Henry Louis Jr. & Burton, Jennifer (Editors) . . *v.6 p.14*

Gates, Henry Louis Jr. (Editor) *v.2 p.757, v.6 p.28*

Gates, Henry Louis Jr. *v.2 p.3, v.6 p.25, p.43*

Gates, Henry Louis. *v.2 p.29, v.6 p.4, p.19, p.25, p.43*

Gates, John M. *v.6 p.179*

Gates, Robert A. (Editor) *v.2 p.25*

Gates, Susan M., & Ringel, Jeanne S. *v.4 p.281*

Gates-Coon, Rebecca *v.3 p.186*

Gati, Charles *v.3 p.187*

Gatrell, Peter *v.3 p.220*

Gatti, Paolo L. & Ferrari, Vittorio *v.5 p.694*

Gattorna, John (Editor) *v.4 p.117*

Gatz, Margaret (Editor), et al.. . . . . *v.4 p.815, p.840*

Gaubatz, Kurt Taylor *v.4 p.504*

Gauderman, Kimberly *v.3 p.332*

Gaugler, William M.. . . . . *v.4 p.857*

Gaukroger, Stephen (Editor). *v.1 p.453*

Gaukroger, Stephen, et al. *v.1 p.454, p.498*

Gaukroger, Stephen *v.1 p.448, p.453*

Gauld, Alan *v.5 p.612*

Gauldin, Robert *v.1 p.370*

Gaunt, Simon & Kay, Sarah (Editors) *v.2 p.457*

Gaunt, Simon *v.2 p.457*

Gaunt, William. *v.1 p.731*

Gauntlett, David *v.4 p.743, p.744*

Gaus, Gerald F.. . . . . *v.1 p.501, v.4 p.511*

Gause, Jo Allen *v.1 p.797*

Gausman, Harold W. *v.5 p.124*

Gaustad, Edwin S. & Noll, Mark A. (Editors). . . . *v.1 p.543*

Gaustad, Edwin S. & Schmidt, Leigh Eric *v.1 p.604*

Gaustad, Edwin S. *v.1 p.604*

Gauthier, Anne H. *v.4 p.731*

Gauthier, Michelle M. *v.5 p.688*

Gautier, Théophile *v.2 p.492*

Gautschi, Walter *v.5 p.492*

Gauvain, Mary. *v.5 p.626, p.630*

Gauze, Rene *v.6 p.62*

Gavin, Christy *v.6 p.15, p.25, p.43*

Gavin, James & Gavin, Nettie. *v.4 p.790, p.905*

Gavora, Jessica . . . *v.4 p.821, p.836, p.894, p.900, v.6 p.437*

Gavosto, Estela A. (Editor), et al. *v.5 p.462*

Gavrilova, Raina *v.3 p.251*

Gavroglou, Stavros P.. . . . . *v.4 p.121*

Gavron, Daniel. *v.4 p.703*

Gavronsky, Serge (Translator) *v.2 p.464*

Gavronsky, Serge *v.2 p.459, p.464*

Gay, John *v.1 p.250, p.407*

Gay, Peter *v.2 p.284, v.3 p.72, p.170,v.6 p.760, p.761*

Gay, Timothy *v.4 p.858, p.871*

Gayle, Addison. *v.2 p.138*

Gaylin, Willard. *v.5 p.653*

Gayon, Jean *v.5 p.203*

Gazale, Midhat J. *v.5 p.466, p.476*

Gaze, Delia (Editor) *v.1 p.664, p.706, v.6 p.472*

Gazzaniga, Michael S. (Editor) *v.5 p.617*

Gazzaniga, Michael S. *v.5 p.617*

Gbadamosi, T. G. O.. . . . . *v.6 p.71*

Geach, Peter T. *v.1 p.496, p.651*

Gealt, Adelheid M., et al. *v.1 p.723*

Gealt, Adelheid M.. . . . . *v.1 p.725*

Geanakoplos, Deno John *v.3 p.192*

Geanakoplos, John *v.4 p.200, p.225*

Geary, David C. *v.5 p.653*

Geary, Laurence M. & Kelleher, Margaret *v.3 p.138*

Geary, Patrick J. *v.3 p.143, p.162, v.6 p.563*

Gebhard, David & Mansheim, Gerald *v.1 p.789*

Ged, Martin *v.3 p.539*

Gedalge, Andre *v.1 p.370*

Gedicks, Al *v.6 p.298, p.681*

Gedicks, Frederick M. *v.4 p.460*

Gee, Emma (Editor) *v.6 p.85, p.96*

Gee, Henry *v.5 p.133, p.201, p.205*

Gee, Maurice *v.2 p.746*

Geer, John G. *v.4 p.425*

Geertz,

 Clifford . *v.1 p.540, p.554,v.4 p.22, p.29, p.703,v.6 p.174, p.176*

Geffner, Andrea B. *v.4 p.58, p.172*

Geffner, Robert (Editor), et al.. . . . . *v.4 p.130*

Geggus, David P. (Editor) *v.3 p.314*

Geggus, David P.. . . . . *v.3 p.314*

Gehlbach, Frederick R. *v.3 p.269*

Gehring, Wes D. (Editor) *v.6 p.311*

Gehring, Wes D. *v.6 p.312*

Gehry, Frank O. *v.1 p.792*

Geiger, George Raymond *v.1 p.443*

Geiger, Louis G. *v.4 p.331*

Geiger, Roger L. (Editor) *v.4 p.331*

Geiger, Roger L. *v.5 p.393*

Geiger, Susan (Editor), et al. *v.6 p.53*

Geiger, Susan *v.6 p.66*

Geikie, Archibald Sir *v.5 p.418*

Geiogamah, Hanay & Darby, Jaye T. (Editors). *v.1 p.124, v.6 p.697*

Geiogamah, Hanay (Editor) *v.1 p.65, p.124, v.6 p.698*

Geiringer, Karl *v.1 p.184, p.302, p.303*

Geis, Deborah R. & Kruger, Steven F. (Editors) *v.6 p.411*

Geisler, Gisela *v.6 p.441*

Geisler, Norman L.. . . . . *v.1 p.645*

Geison, Gerald L. *v.5 p.396*

Geiss, Imanuel *v.6 p.55*

Geisst, Charles R. *v.4 p.84, p.89, p.155*

Geisst, Charles. *v.4 p.89, p.100, p.146, p.155, p.162*

Geist, Helmut (Editor) *v.1 p.812, v.4 p.267, v.5 p.17*

Geist, Helmut *v.6 p.285*

Geiter, Mary K. *v.1 p.585, v.3 p.492*

Gelb, Arthur *v.4 p.412*

Gelb, Leslie H. & Betts, Richard K. *v.3 p.388*

Gelbart, Larry, et al. *v.1 p.250, p.408*

Gelbaum, Bernard R. & Olmsted, J. M. *v.5 p.489*

Gelber, Katharine. *v.4 p.423*

Gelber, Michael Werth *v.2 p.246*

Gelbspan, Ross. *v.6 p.293*

Geld, Ellen Bromfield *v.3 p.334*

Geldard, Richard *v.1 p.515*

Geldenhuys, Deon *v.4 p.626*

Gelder, Ken *v.6 p.318*

Gelderen, D. M. van *v.5 p.37*

Gelderen, Elly van *v.2 p.552*

Gelderman, Carol (Editor) *v.2 p.99*

Geldern, James von & McReynolds, Louise (Editors) . *v.2 p.793*

Geldof, Lynn. *v.3 p.309*

Gelfand, David H. (Editor), et al. *v.5 p.133*
Gel'fand, I. M. & Fomin, S. V. *v.5 p.493*
Gelfand, Lawrence E. (Editor). *v.3 p.471*
Gelfand, Michele J. & Brett, Jeanne M. *v.4 p.74, p.698*
Gell, Alfred *v.4 p.26*
Gellately, Robert & Kiernan, Ben (Editors) *v.4 p.652*
Gellately, Robert & Stoltzfus, Nathan (Editors). . . *v.3 p.84*
Gellately, Robert *v.3 p.84, p.171*
Geller, Elizabeth & McGraw-Hill Staff *v.5 p.387*
Geller, Jay Howard *v.3 p.179*
Geller, Peter L.. . . . . *v.1 p.764*
Geller, William A. & Toch, Hans (Editors) *v.6 p.261*
Gellermann, William *v.3 p.458*
Gellert, Michael *v.3 p.367*
Gelles, Richard J. (Editor). *v.4 p.742*
Gelley, Alexander (Editor) *v.2 p.612*
Gellman, Irwin F. *v.4 p.485*
Gell-Mann, Murray. *v.5 p.543*
Gellner, David N. & Quigley, Declan (Editors) . . . *v.6 p.164*
Gellner, David N. *v.4 p.721*
Gellner, Ernest & Micaud, Charles Antoine . . . *v.6 p.61, p.600*
Gellner, Ernest. *v.1 p.558, v.3 p.61, v.4 p.494, p.515, p.679, p.700*
Gellrich, Jesse M. *v.6 p.565, p.569*
Gelpi, Albert (Editor) *v.2 p.71*
Gelpi, Albert. *v.2 p.343*
Gelpi, Christopher *v.4 p.649*
Gelsinon, Thomas (Editor) *v.6 p.527, p.544*
Gelven, Michael *v.1 p.470*
Gelvin, James L. & Gelvin, James *v.6 p.592*
Gelvin, James L.. . . . . *v.6 p.607, p.617*
Gelzer, Matthias *v.2 p.428*
Gemin, Massimo *v.1 p.739*
Gems, Gerald R. . . . *v.3 p.319, v.4 p.783, p.805, p.858, p.881*
Gendel, Steven M. (Editor), et al. *v.5 p.7*
Gendron, Bernard *v.1 p.269*
Genet, Jean *v.2 p.518, p.519, v.6 p.396*
Genette, Gerard *v.2 p.524*
Genevieve Lloyd (Editor) *v.1 p.506*
Geng, Hwaiyu *v.5 p.684*
Genicot, Léopold *v.6 p.575*
Gennaro, Rocco J. *v.1 p.504*
Genovese, Eugene D. *v.3 p.397, p.494, v.4 p.520, p.729*
Genovese, Michael A. *v.4 p.526*
Genovese, Michael *v.3 p.378*
Genoways, Hugh H. & Ireland, Lynne M. *v.1 p.828*
Gentile, Emilio. *v.3 p.203*
Gentleman, Judith A. (Editor) *v.3 p.292*
Gentleman, Robert (Editor), et al. *v.5 p.99, p.341*
Gentles, Ian *v.3 p.103*
Gentry, Francis G. (Editor) *v.2 p.594*
Gentz, William H. (Editor) *v.1 p.614*
Geoffrey of Monmouth. *v.3 p.95*
Geoffroy-Schneiter, Berenice *v.1 p.690, p.692, p.694*
Geok-lin Lim, Shirley & Chua, Cheng Lok (Editors) . . *v.6 p.91*
Geok-Lin Lim, Shirley & Ling, Amy (Editors) *v.6 p.96*

Geok-lin Lim, Shirley & Tsutakawa, Mayumi
  (Editors) *v.6 p.91, p.111*
Geological Survey (USGS) Staff. *v.6 p.285*
Georgalis, Nicholas. *v.1 p.515*
George, Alan. *v.4 p.616*
George, Alexander & Velleman, Daniel J. *v.5 p.470*
George, Alexander L. & Smoke, Richard *v.3 p.452*
George, Andrew *v.6 p.665*
George, Arthur L. & George, Elena *v.3 p.214*
George, David *v.1 p.127*
George, Gerald S. *v.4 p.861, p.908*
George, Henry *v.4 p.209*
George Lucas Educational Foundation Staff. . . . *v.4 p.351*
George, M. Dorothy *v.3 p.106, p.108*
George, Nelson *v.1 p.269, v.6 p.5, p.38*
George, Paul S. & Alexander, William M. *v.4 p.367*
George, Paul S. (Editor) *v.3 p.504*
George, Peter Bryan *v.2 p.347*
George, Sheba Mariam. *v.4 p.44*
George, Stefan Anton *v.2 p.609*
George, Stefan *v.2 p.609*
George, Stephen K. (Editor) *v.2 p.123*
George, Terry (Editor, Compiled by) *v.6 p.333*
George, Timothy & Dockery, David S. (Editors) . . *v.1 p.583*
George, Timothy (Editor) *v.1 p.648*
Georges, Robert A. & Jones, Michael O. *v.2 p.585*
Georgi, Howard *v.5 p.561*
Georgieva, Ana Ivanova. *v.2 p.774*
Geospatial & Statistical Data Center, University of Virginia
  Library. *v.4 p.556*
Gerard, Charley & Sheller, Marty *v.6 p.518*
Gerard, Charley *v.6 p.518*
Gerard, Kent & Hekma, Gert *v.6 p.364, p.375, p.421*
Gerard-Varet, L.A. (Editor), et al. *v.4 p.189*
Gerber, David A. & Kraut, Alan M. (Editors) . . . *v.4 p.764*
Gerber, Douglas E. (Editor) *v.2 p.403*
Gerber, Douglas E. *v.2 p.403*
Gerber, Ellen W., et al. *v.4 p.805, p.836*
Gerber, Gwendolyn L. *v.6 p.260*
Gerber, Haim *v.4 p.703*
Gerber, Jane S. *v.1 p.548, v.3 p.243*
Gerber, John C. (Editor) *v.2 p.41*
Gerber, Michael E. *v.4 p.67*
Gerber, Michele S.. . . . . *v.5 p.364, p.374*
Gerber, Rodney & Williams, Michael (Editors) . . . *v.4 p.377*
Gerber, Rodney (Editor) *v.4 p.377*
Gerber, Rudolph J. *v.4 p.568, v.6 p.253*
Gerber, Scott D. *v.4 p.467*
Gerdes, Dick. *v.2 p.685*
Gerdes, Louise (Editor) *v.4 p.485*
Gerdes, Louise I. (Editor) *v.5 p.430*
Gerdes, Louise I. *v.5 p.133*
Gerdts, William H.. . . . . . . *v.1 p.727, p.731, p.739*
Gerdy, John R. *v.4 p.805, p.815, p.821, p.894*

Gere, Charlotte *v.1 p.799*

Gere, David (Editor), et al. *v.1 p.39, p.42*

Gere, David *v.1 p.28, p.30, p.37, p.42, v.6 p.414*

Gere, James M. *v.5 p.688*

Güereña, Salvador *v.6 p.492*

Gergel, Thomas *v.3 p.490*

Gerhard, Peter *v.3 p.285*

Gerhardt, Juliette Cartwright *v.3 p.297*

Gerhardt, Michael J. *v.4 p.461*

Gerhardt, Uta *v.4 p.778*

Gerhart, Genevra *v.2 p.776*

Gerhart, John & Kirschner, Marc *v.5 p.160, p.192*

Gerin, Winifred *v.2 p.289*

Gerin-Lajoie, Paul *v.4 p.586*

Gerking, Shelby D. *v.5 p.215*

Gerlach, Allen *v.3 p.333*

Gerlach, Michael L. *v.6 p.219*

Gerlach, Wolfgang *v.3 p.84*

Gerli, E. Michael *v.2 p.649*

Gerli, Michael (Editor) *v.6 p.563*

Germain, Sylvie *v.2 p.530*

German, Randall M. *v.5 p.736*

Germic, Stephen A. *v.6 p.727*

Germond, Jack W. & Witcover, Jules *v.3 p.447*

Gerner, Deborah J. *v.6 p.617*

Gernet, Jacques *v.1 p.561, v.6 p.183, p.186*

Gero, Andras *v.3 p.186*

Gerolymatos, Andre *v.3 p.245*

Gerould, Gordon H. *v.2 p.196*

Gerould, Winifred *v.2 p.316*

Gerrard, Bill & Hillard, John (Editors) *v.4 p.227*

Gerrard, Christine (Editor) *v.2 p.171, p.183*

Gerrard, Christine *v.2 p.199*

Gerrard, Christopher *v.6 p.555*

Gerrard, John *v.5 p.424*

Gerrish, B. A. *v.1 p.581*

Gerrish, Brian A. *v.1 p.589*

Gerschenkron, Alexander *v.3 p.40*

Gershenfeld, Neil *v.5 p.500*

Gershevitch, Ilya & Grossman, Stanley I. (Editors) . *v.6 p.629*

Gershick, Zsa Zsa *v.6 p.389*

Gershoni, Israel & Jankowski, James P. *v.6 p.637*

Gershoy, Leo *v.3 p.150*

Gershuny, Jonathan *v.4 p.761*

Gershwin, Ira & Kimball, Robert . *v.1 p.250, p.325, p.408, p.411*

Gerson, Carole *v.2 p.729, p.731*

Gerson, Lloyd P. *v.1 p.430*

Gerstein, Alan S. *v.5 p.127*

Gerstenblith, Patty *v.1 p.827*

Gerster, Carole & Zlogar, Laura W. (Editors) *v.6 p.321*

Gerstle, C. Andrew *v.6 p.234*

Gerstmann, Evan *v.4 p.457, v.6 p.469*

Gerth, H. H. & Mills, C. Wright (Editor, Translator, Introduction
   by) *v.4 p.681*

Gerthold, Peter *v.5 p.215*

Gertler, Mark *v.4 p.189, p.200*

Gertsch, Richard E. & Bullock, Richard L. (Editors) . *v.5 p.737*

Gertz, SunHee Kim *v.2 p.169*

Gescheider, George A. *v.5 p.605*

Gesell, Arnold L. *v.5 p.626*

Gesensway, Deborah & Roseman, Mindy *v.6 p.88, p.133*

Gessner, David *v.5 p.221*

Gest, Ted *v.6 p.247*

Gesteland, Raymond F. (Editor), et al. *v.5 p.121*

Gesteland, Richard R. *v.4 p.56*

Gethin, Rupert *v.1 p.565*

Getscher, Robert H. *v.1 p.723*

Gettleman, Marvin E. (Editor), et al. *v.3 p.299*

Gettmann, R. A. *v.6 p.741, p.756*

Getty, J. Paul, Museum Staff *v.1 p.722, p.766*

Getty, Robert *v.5 p.54*

Getz, Wayne M. & Haight, Robert G. . . *v.5 p.184, p.188, p.215*

Getz, Wayne Marcus & Haight, Robert G. *v.5 p.212*

Getzels, Jacob W. *v.5 p.626, p.630*

Geuens, Jean-Pierre *v.6 p.346*

Geus, Theodor *v.3 p.506*

Geuter, Ulfried *v.5 p.596*

Geva, Tamara *v.1 p.8*

Gewald, Jan-Bart *v.6 p.76*

Gewirth, Alan *v.1 p.487, v.4 p.512*

Gewirtz, Arthur & Kolb, James J. (Editors) . *v.1 p.82, p.84, p.114*

Geyer, Alan F. *v.3 p.388*

Geyer, Georgie Anne *v.3 p.309*

Geyer, Robert (Editor), et al. *v.3 p.232, p.233*

Geyh, Charles Gardner *v.4 p.541*

Geyl, Pieter *v.3 p.158, p.204*

Gänzl, Kurt *v.1 p.59, p.92, p.160*

Gärtner, Heinz *v.1 p.189, p.302*

Gérin, Winifred *v.2 p.270*

Gómez de la Serna, Ramón, et al. *v.2 p.658*

Gómez-Quiñones, Juan *v.3 p.527, v.6 p.538*

Görlach, Manfred *v.2 p.552, p.554*

Gfroerer, Joseph, et al. *v.4 p.776*

Ghali, A. *v.5 p.694*

Ghanem, As'ad *v.4 p.614*

Ghanem, Fathy *v.6 p.659*

Ghani, Cyrus *v.6 p.631*

Ghannam, Farha *v.6 p.637*

Ghanoonparvar, Mohammad R. *v.6 p.671*

Ghareeb, Edmund *v.6 p.598, p.601*

Ghassemlou, A. R. *v.6 p.598*

Ghatak, Subrata *v.4 p.258*

Ghebre-Ab, Habtu (Compiled by, Introduction by) . . . *v.6 p.64*

Ghelderode, Michel de *v.2 p.517*

Ghemawat, Pankaj *v.4 p.177*

Ghent, Gretchen (Editor) *v.4 p.812*

Gheorghe, Marian *v.5 p.93, p.105, p.127*

Ghezzo, Marta Arkossy *v.1 p.404*

Ghidetti, Enrico; Luti, Giorgio *v.2 p.698*

Ghilani, Chuck, et al. *v.4 p.389*

Ghilani, Mary E. *v.4 p.167*

Ghirardo, Diane *v.1 p.786*

Ghiron, Chiara & Thomas, Russell *v.5 p.301*

Ghiselin, Michael T. *v.5 p.192*

Ghodse, Hamid *v.4 p.130*

Gholson, Barry (Editor), et al. *v.5 p.594*

Ghorayshi, Parvin (Compiled by) *v.6 p.456*

Ghosh, Amitav *v.2 p.764*

Ghosh, Bijoy K., et al. *v.5 p.710*

Ghosh, Partha S. *v.6 p.163*

Ghosh, S. N. & Desai, V. R. *v.5 p.702*

Ghysels, Eric & Osborn, Denise R. *v.4 p.200*

Giacalone, Robert A. & Greenberg, Jerald (Editors) . *v.4 p.130*

Giacomello, Giampiero *v.4 p.773*

Giacovazzo, Carmelo *v.5 p.284*

Giambattista, Alan, et al. *v.5 p.539*

Giamo, Ben *v.2 p.92*

Giampietro, Mario, et al. *v.5 p.11*

Giancoli, Douglas C. *v.5 p.539*

Gianguzza, Antonio (Editor), et al. *v.5 p.429*

Giannetti, Laura & Ruggiero, Guido *v.2 p.699*

Giannone, Richard *v.2 p.106*

Giannowe, Richard *v.2 p.106*

Gianturco, Carolyn *v.1 p.184, p.358*

Giard, Robert *v.6 p.391*

Giatzidis, Emile *v.3 p.251*

Giauque, Jeffrey Glen *v.4 p.637, p.654*

Gibaldi, Joseph *v.2 p.565, p.566*

Gibas, Cynthia & Jambeck, Per *v.5 p.108*

Gibb, H. A. R. & Bowen, Harold *v.6 p.589*

Gibbard, Philip L. *v.5 p.425*

Gibbon, Edward *v.3 p.31*

Gibboney, Richard A. *v.4 p.326*

Gibbons, Bob & Walters, Martin *v.5 p.237*

Gibbons, Bob *v.5 p.237*

Gibbs, A. M. (Editor) *v.2 p.309*

Gibbs, A. M. *v.2 p.309*

Gibbs, Christopher H. (Editor) *v.1 p.197, p.354*

Gibbs, Christopher H. *v.1 p.197, p.354*

Gibbs, J. Willard *v.5 p.558*

Gibbs, Jack P. *v.4 p.773*

Gibbs, James *v.2 p.757*

Gibbs, Jenny *v.1 p.809*

Gibbs, Josiah W. *v.5 p.385*

Gibellini, Rosino *v.1 p.638*

Giberson, Richard T. & Demaree, Richard S. Jr. (Editors) . *v.5 p.88*

Gibert, Stephen P. *v.3 p.452*

Giblett, Rod *v.5 p.53*

Gibney, Frank (Editor) *v.6 p.219*

Gibson, Aliona L. *v.6 p.5, p.17, p.43*

Gibson, Arrell M. *v.3 p.523*

Gibson, Arthur C. *v.5 p.155, p.240*

Gibson, Eleanor B. & Tapia, Elizabeth W. (Editors) . *v.5 p.732*

Gibson, Gail M. *v.2 p.185*

Gibson, Greg & Muse, Spencer V. . *v.5 p.133, p.139, p.140, p.502*

Gibson, H. N. *v.1 p.76, p.100*

Gibson, Ian *v.1 p.696, v.2 p.660*

Gibson, James J. *v.5 p.606*

Gibson, John S. *v.4 p.434*

Gibson, Mark *v.4 p.156*

Gibson, Mary *v.6 p.254*

Gibson, Michael *v.1 p.678, p.709*

Gibson, Ralph *v.3 p.148*

Gibson, Ray, et al. *v.5 p.172, p.237*

Gibson, Robert (Compiled by) *v.2 p.464*

Gibson, Robert *v.2 p.460*

Gibson, Roger F. Jr. (Editor) *v.1 p.443*

Gibson, Roger F. *v.1 p.443*

Gibson, Terry-Ann Spitzer & Hoeger, Wener W. K. . *v.4 p.792*

Gibson, William *v.1 p.609*

Gibson-Graham, J. K. *v.4 p.273*

Gicovate, Bernard *v.2 p.652*

Giddens, Anthony . *v.4 p.493, p.679, p.685, p.686, p.724, p.768*

Giddens-White, Bryon *v.4 p.534*

Giddings, Paula J. *v.4 p.729, v.6 p.25, p.38, p.43*

Giddings, Robert & Sheen, Erica (Editors) *v.6 p.325*

Giddins, Gary *v.1 p.259, p.269, p.302, p.319*

Gide, Andre *v.2 p.519, p.520, v.6 p.362, p.396*

Gide, André; Valéry, Paul *v.2 p.520, p.528*

Gide, André *v.2 p.520*

Gidengil, Elisabeth *v.4 p.586*

Gidron, Benjamin (Editor), et al. *v.4 p.640, p.649*

Giegerich, Heinz J. *v.2 p.556*

Gielen, Uwe P. & Roopnarine, Jaipaul L. (Editors) . *v.5 p.626*

Gielgud, John *v.1 p.144, v.6 p.418*

Gienapp, William E. *v.3 p.397*

Gier, Paul, et al. *v.5 p.245*

Giere, Ronald N. & Westfall, Richard S. (Editors) . *v.5 p.401*

Gierlowski-Kordesch, E. & Kelts, Kerry *v.5 p.438*

Gies, David T. (Editor) *v.2 p.638*

Gies, Frances & Gies, Joseph *v.4 p.703*

Gies, Frances *v.3 p.144*

Gies, Joseph *v.6 p.560*

Giese, Bernd *v.5 p.294*

Giese, F. *v.5 p.289*

Giesen, Rolf *v.6 p.338*

Gifford, Barry & Lee, Lawrence *v.2 p.92*

Gifford, Don *v.2 p.358*

Gifford, Paul *v.1 p.611, v.6 p.70*

Gifford, Prosser & Louis, Roger W. (Editors) . *v.3 p.76, v.6 p.56*

Gifford, Prosser & Louis, William Roger . *v.4 p.582, p.583, v.6 p.54*

Gifford, Prosser (Editor) *v.3 p.76, v.6 p.56*

Gigerenzer, Gerd, et al. *v.5 p.590*

Gigerenzer, Gerd *v.5 p.481*

Giglio, James N. *v.3 p.441, p.471*

Gijsen, Marnix *v.2 p.623*

Gikandi, Simon (Editor) *v.2 p.750, v.6 p.80*

Gikandi, Simon *v.2 p.751, p.753, p.758*

Gil, Moshe *v.6 p.573, p.574, p.608*

Gil, Patricio Robles, et al. *v.5 p.179, p.234*

Gil, Victor. *v.5 p.276*

Gilb, Dagoberto *v.6 p.499*

Gilberg, Trond. *v.4 p.508, p.600*

Gilbert, Charlene *v.6 p.20*

Gilbert, Christopher *v.1 p.804*

Gilbert, Creighton & Signorelli, Luca *v.1 p.739*

Gilbert, Creighton E. *v.1 p.739*

Gilbert, Daniel T. (Editor), et al. . . *v.4 p.691, v.5 p.645*

Gilbert, Dennis. *v.3 p.301, v.4 p.724*

Gilbert, Dorie J. & Wright, Ednita M. (Editors) *v.5 p.523*

Gilbert, Douglas. *v.1 p.35*

Gilbert, Helen (Editor) *v.2 p.727*

Gilbert, Jack G. *v.2 p.264*

Gilbert, Jack *v.2 p.145*

Gilbert, Jimmie & Gilbert, Linda *v.5 p.472*

Gilbert, Jorge *v.3 p.301*

Gilbert, Kevin (Editor) *v.2 p.742*

Gilbert, Marc Jason (Editor). *v.4 p.331*

Gilbert, Margaret. *v.4 p.713*

Gilbert, Martin (Author, Author) *v.4 p.380, v.6 p.617*

Gilbert,
    Martin. *v.3 p.118, p.381,v.4 p.380, p.485, p.644,v.6 p.608, p.610*

Gilbert, Pamela & Hamilton, Chris J. *v.5 p.213*

Gilbert, Pamela K. *v.6 p.750, p.759*

Gilbert, Paula R. *v.2 p.539*

Gilbert, Paul *v.5 p.659*

Gilbert, Roger. *v.2 p.55*

Gilbert, Sandra M. & Gubar, Susan (Editors) *v.2 p.195*

Gilbert, Sandra M. & Gubar,
    Susan *v.2 p.175, p.178,v.6 p.478, p.747, p.752*

Gilbert, Sandra M. (Editor). *v.2 p.19*

Gilbert, Scott F. & Raunio, Anne M. (Editors) *v.5 p.161*

Gilbert, Scott F. & Singer, Susan R. *v.5 p.161*

Gilbert, Scott F. *v.5 p.154, p.160*

Gilbert, Shirli *v.1 p.299*

Gilbert, Stephen G. *v.5 p.162*

Gilbert, Steven E. *v.1 p.214, p.250, p.325*

Gilbert, Stuart *v.2 p.358*

Gilbert, W. S. (William Schwenck). *v.2 p.288*

Gilboa, Eytan (Editor) *v.4 p.407*

Gilby, Thomas *v.4 p.490*

Gilchrist, Ellen *v.2 p.145, p.146*

Gilchrist, J. T. *v.6 p.558, p.571*

Gildea, Robert *v.3 p.156*

Gildersleeve, Basil L. & Lodge, Gonzalez *v.2 p.423*

Gildersleeve, Rich *v.4 p.178*

Giles, Mary E. *v.3 p.239*

Giles, Robert & Snyder, Robert W. (Editors) *v.6 p.270*

Giles, Wenona Mary & Hyndman, Jennifer (Editors) . *v.6 p.257*

Gill, Austin *v.2 p.496*

Gill, Diane L. *v.4 p.877, p.879, v.5 p.582*

Gill, Graeme J. & Pitty, Roderic . *v.4 p.508, p.579, p.597, p.599*

Gill, John *v.1 p.378, v.6 p.408*

Gill, LaVerne M. *v.4 p.485, p.530,v.6 p.31, p.43, p.441*

Gill, Lesley *v.3 p.323*

Gill, Richard & Gregory, Susan *v.2 p.267*

Gill, Stephen (Editor). *v.2 p.323*

Gill, Stephen J. *v.4 p.78*

Gill, Stephen. *v.2 p.323, v.6 p.738, p.755*

Gillan, Maria *v.2 p.26*

Gillan, Stuart L. & Chew, Donald H. *v.4 p.54*

Gille, Bertrand *v.3 p.70*

Gilleman, Luc *v.2 p.376*

Gillespie, Alexander *v.4 p.434*

Gillespie, Angus K. *v.1 p.797, v.6 p.728*

Gillespie, Charles C. *v.5 p.390*

Gillespie, Charles Guy *v.3 p.274, v.4 p.591*

Gillespie, Dizzy & Fraser, Al *v.1 p.259, p.326*

Gillespie, Gerald (Editor) *v.1 p.78, p.96*

Gillespie, Michael A. & Lienesch, Michael (Editors) . *v.4 p.452*

Gillespie, Michael Patrick & Gillespie, Paula *v.2 p.358*

Gillespie, Michael P. *v.2 p.321*

Gillett, Carl & Loewer, Barry (Editors). *v.1 p.509*

Gillett, Paula. *v.3 p.111, p.128*

Gillette, David D. & Lockley, Martin (Editors) . *v.5 p.448, p.450*

Gillette, J. Michael. *v.1 p.134, p.142*

Gillette, William *v.3 p.436, v.4 p.461*

Gilley, Jerry W. & Maycunich, Ann *v.4 p.76*

Gilley, Jerry W., et al. *v.4 p.78*

Gilley, Sheridan & Stanley, Brian (Editors) *v.1 p.611*

Gilliam, Bryan (Editor). *v.1 p.214, p.359*

Gilliam, Bryan Randolph (Editor) *v.1 p.245*

Gilliam, Bryan *v.1 p.214, p.229, p.359*

Gillies, Malcolm & Pear, David (Editors) . . . *v.1 p.214, p.327*

Gillies, Malcolm (Editor) *v.1 p.214, p.305*

Gillies, Malcolm *v.1 p.214, p.305*

Gillieson, David *v.5 p.424*

Gilligan, Carol, et al. *v.4 p.737*

Gilligan, Carol *v.4 p.692, v.6 p.445*

Gillingham, John. *v.3 p.98, p.99, p.100, v.6 p.568*

Gillis, Chester *v.1 p.573, p.604*

Gillis, John R. *v.4 p.736*

Gillispie, Charles C. (Editor) *v.5 p.395*

Gillispie, Charles C. *v.5 p.392, p.717*

Gillispie, Charles Coulston *v.5 p.392*

Gillman, Howard. *v.4 p.462*

Gillman, Ian & Klimkeit, Hans-Joachim *v.1 p.610*

Gillman, L. & Jerison, M.. . . . . *v.5 p.493*

Gillman, Neil *v.1 p.551*

Gillmeister, Heiner *v.4 p.815, p.864*

Gillmor, Alan M. *v.1 p.214, p.352*

Gillmor, C. Stewart. *v.5 p.396*

Gillon, Adam & Krzyzanowski, Ludwik (Editors) . . . *v.2 p.787*

Gillott, Cedric. *v.5 p.26*

Gilly, Adolfo. *v.3 p.292*

Gilman, Charlotte Perkins & Golden, Catherine *v.2 p.39*

Gilman, Charlotte Perkins . *v.2 p.39, v.4 p.681, p.737, v.6 p.466*

Gilman, Ernest B. *v.2 p.171*

Gilman, Henry(Editor-in-Chief) *v.5 p.293*

Gilman, Nils. *v.3 p.371*

Gilman, Richard. *v.1 p.82*

Gilman, Stephen. *v.2 p.649, p.651, p.654*

Gilmartin, Christina K. *v.6 p.192, p.217*

Gilmartin, David *v.6 p.160*

Gilmore, Bob *v.1 p.214, p.347*

Gilmore, David D. *v.3 p.242, v.4 p.703*

Gilmore, Grant. *v.4 p.440*

Gilmore, M. (Editor). *v.2 p.48*

Gilmore, Myron P.. . . . . *v.3 p.70*

Gilmore, Robert & Lefranc, Marc *v.5 p.499*

Gilmore, Robert K.. . . . . *v.3 p.512*

Gilmour, David *v.2 p.296, v.3 p.89*

Gilmour, Iain & Sephton, Mark A. (Editors) *v.5 p.74*

Gilmour, Pat. *v.1 p.754*

Gilmour, Robert S. & Halley, Alexis A. *v.4 p.526*

Gilmour, Robin *v.2 p.190, v.6 p.747, p.750, p.756, p.761*

Gilot, Francoise (Text by). *v.1 p.696*

Gilpin, George H. Jr. *v.2 p.323*

Gilpin, Michael E. & Hanski, Ilkka A.
(Editors) *v.5 p.91, p.184, p.188*

Gilpin, Robert. *v.4 p.55*

Gilsenan, Michael *v.6 p.605*

Gilson, Etienne. *v.1 p.430, p.432, p.434, p.479, p.489,
p.638, v.2 p.704, v.3 p.56, v.6 p.567, p.571*

Gilson, Stuart C.. . . . . *v.4 p.76, p.84*

Gilyard, Keith & Schuster, Charles (Editors) *v.2 p.565*

Gilyard, Keith & Wardi, Anissa Janine *v.6 p.25*

Gilyard, Keith *v.5 p.620*

Gimbel, John *v.3 p.175*

Gimbel, Wendy *v.3 p.309*

Gimble, Jeffrey. *v.5 p.250*

Gimbutas, Marija *v.1 p.527, p.529, p.531*

Gimferrer, Pere. *v.1 p.696*

Gimlin, Debra L.. . . . . *v.6 p.436*

Gimpel, James & Schuknecht, Jason *v.4 p.551*

Gimpel, James G. *v.4 p.530*

Ginat, Joseph & Winckler, Onn (Editors) *v.6 p.617*

Ginat, Joseph *v.6 p.596*

Ginger, Ray *v.3 p.515*

Gingerich, Owen *v.3 p.47, v.5 p.61*

Gingrich, Andre & Fox, Richard Gabriel (Editors) . . . *v.4 p.22*

Gini, Al *v.5 p.579*

Ginn, Victoria & Rizzoli *v.1 p.15*

Ginsberg, Allen & Ginsberg, Louis *v.2 p.79*

Ginsberg, Allen *v.2 p.79, v.6 p.404*

Ginsberg, Benjamin. *v.4 p.516*

Ginsborg, Paul *v.3 p.204, v.4 p.577, p.594*

Ginsburg, Mark *v.4 p.313*

Ginzberg, Eli (Editor). *v.4 p.735*

Ginzberg, Eli. *v.4 p.219, v.5 p.577*

Ginzberg, Louis *v.1 p.550*

Ginzburg, Carlo *v.1 p.610, p.739, v.3 p.200, p.201*

Ginzburg, Eugenia S. *v.2 p.803, v.3 p.224*

Ginzburg, Lev R. & Colyvan, Mark *v.5 p.184, p.188*

Ginzburg, Natalia *v.2 p.717, p.718*

Gioia, Dana & Gwynn, R. S. *v.2 p.583*

Gioia, Ted *v.1 p.259*

Gioncu, Victor & Mazzolani, Federico M. *v.5 p.694*

Giono, Jean *v.2 p.517*

Giordano, Gerard. *v.4 p.285*

Giordano, Gus *v.1 p.31*

Giordano, Nicholas J. & Nakanishi, Hisao *v.5 p.551*

Giordano, Ralph G.. . . . . *v.4 p.784*

Giovacchini, Saverio *v.6 p.321*

Giovannetti, J. *v.5 p.95, p.105, p.108, p.127*

Giovanni, Boccaccio. *v.3 p.69*

Giovanni, Nikki *v.2 p.146, v.6 p.25, p.43*

Gipe, Paul. *v.5 p.363, p.708*

Gipson, Lawrence Henry *v.3 p.409*

Güiraldes, Ricardo *v.2 p.678*

Giraldo, Javier *v.3 p.274*

Girard, Jolyon P. *v.3 p.384*

Girard, Philippe *v.3 p.314*

Girard, Rene *v.2 p.524*

Girard, René. *v.2 p.462, p.578*

Giraud, Marcel. *v.3 p.507*

Giraudoux, Jean *v.2 p.517, p.518*

Giraudoux, Jean, ... *v.2 p.518*

Girdlestone, Cuthbert M. *v.1 p.184, p.350*

Girgus, Sam B. *v.6 p.309, p.341*

Girling, Cynthia L. & Helphand, Kenneth I. *v.1 p.797*

Girouard, Mark . . . *v.3 p.111, p.130, v.4 p.726, v.6 p.737, p.744*

Giroud, Francoise *v.1 p.214, p.338, p.339, p.378*

Giroux, Henry A. & Epstein, Seymour *v.4 p.343*

Gissing, George R. *v.2 p.284, p.289, p.290*

Gitelman, Claudia (Editor, Compiled by) . . *v.1 p.16, p.28, p.30*

Gitenstein, Mark *v.4 p.536*

Gittings, Robert & Manton, Jo. *v.2 p.322*

Gittings, Robert *v.2 p.294*

Giuliano, Geoffrey *v.1 p.269, p.340*

Giulianotti, Richard (Editor) *v.4 p.715, p.815*

Giulianotti, Richard *v.4 p.815, p.843, p.867*

Givens, John. *v.2 p.803*

Givens, Terri E. *v.4 p.601*

Given-Wilson, Chris *v.6 p.576*

Givner, Joan *v.2 p.109*

Givnish, Thomas J. & Sytsma, Kenneth J. (Editors) . *v.5 p.200*

Gjecovi, Shtjefen & Logoreci, Anton (Editors) *v.2 p.815*

Gjerde, Jon *v.3 p.506*

Glaap, Albert-Reiner & Grace, Sherrill E. (Editors) . *v.1 p.127*

Glaathar, Joseph T.. . . . . *v.4 p.520*

Glad, Betty (Editor) *v.5 p.584*

Glad, Betty *v.3 p.458, p.471*

Glad, Paul W.. . . . . *v.3 p.397, p.433, p.517*

Gladdish, Ken *v.4 p.601*

Glade, T. *v.4 p.395*

Glade, William P. & Anderson, Charles W.. . . . . . *v.3 p.292*

Gladkov, Fyodor Vasilievich *v.2 p.803, v.3 p.224*

Gladman, T.. . . . . *v.5 p.736*

Gladstein, Mimi Reisel *v.2 p.113*

Gladwell, Malcolm *v.4 p.51, p.83, p.139, v.5 p.586*

Glancy, Diane H. *v.6 p.698*

Glancy, Diane *v.1 p.121, p.124, v.6 p.698*

Glandon, Shan *v.4 p.351*

Glannon, Walter (Editor) *v.1 p.486*

Glantz, David M. & House, Jonathan M. *v.3 p.175*

Glantz, David M. *v.3 p.174, p.227*

Glantz, Stanton A. *v.5 p.515*

Glanz, James & Lipton, Eric *v.1 p.792*

Glare, P. G. (Editor) *v.2 p.423*

Glaser, Hermann *v.3 p.176*

Glaser, Milton *v.1 p.720*

Glaser, Robert (Editor) *v.5 p.573*

Glasgow, Ellen *v.2 p.79*

Glasgow, Jackie (Editor) *v.4 p.286*

Glasgow, Neal A. & Hicks, Cathy *v.4 p.347*

Glashan, Roy (Compiled by) *v.4 p.557*

Glasheen, Adaline *v.2 p.358*

Glashow, Sheldon L. & Bova, Ben *v.5 p.543*

Glashow, Sheldon L. *v.5 p.552*

Glaspell, Susan *v.2 p.78*

Glasrud, Bruce A. & De Leon, Arnoldo . . . *v.6 p.485*

Glass, D. V. (Editor) *v.3 p.40, v.4 p.703*

Glass, Gene V. & Hopkins, Kenneth D. . . . *v.5 p.599*

Glass, Hiram B. *v.5 p.401*

Glass, I. S. *v.5 p.67*

Glass, Ian *v.5 p.62*

Glass, Leon & Kaplan, Daniel *v.5 p.488, p.501*

Glass, Philip *v.1 p.214, p.326*

Glassberg, David *v.3 p.374, p.376*

Glassco, John *v.2 p.735*

Glasser, Ruth *v.6 p.488, p.518*

Glasser, William *v.5 p.647*

Glassheim, Eagle *v.3 p.188*

Glassie, Henry H. *v.2 p.17*

Glassman, Irvin *v.5 p.279*

Glassman, Jonathon *v.6 p.63*

Glassmeier Amy *v.4 p.398*

Glassner, Andrew S. *v.5 p.340, p.341*

Glassner, Barry & Hertz, Rosanna (Editors) . . . *v.4 p.675*

Glassner, Jean-Jacques *v.3 p.5*

Glasstone, Samuel & Jordan, Walter H. . *v.5 p.360, p.374, p.376*

Glasstone, Samuel S. *v.5 p.276*

Glasstone, Samuel *v.5 p.360, p.374*

Glatzer, Nahum N. *v.1 p.547*

Glauser, Michel P. & Pizzo, Philip A. . . . *v.5 p.517*

Glavin, John (Editor) *v.6 p.326*

Glazebrook, G.P.De T. *v.3 p.544*

Glazebrook, Trish (Contribution by) *v.1 p.470*

Glazer, Deborah F. & Drescher, Jack (Editors) . . . *v.6 p.376*

Glazer-Raymo, Judith *v.4 p.293*

Glazier, Michael *v.1 p.571*

Glück, Louise *v.2 p.146*

Gleason, A. M. (Editor), et al. *v.5 p.458*

Gleason, Philip *v.4 p.291*

Gleason, Sandra E. *v.4 p.121*

Gleckner, Robert F. *v.2 p.274*

Gledhill, Christine (Editor) *v.6 p.331*

Gledhill, David *v.5 p.207*

Gledhill, John *v.4 p.34*

Gleditsch, Nils P. (Compiled by), et al. . . . *v.4 p.656*

Gleeson, David T. *v.3 p.498*

Gleeson, Michael & Maughan, Ronald J. . . . *v.4 p.874*

Gleeson-White, Sarah *v.2 p.100*

Gleick, James *v.5 p.488, p.543*

Gleick, Peter H. *v.5 p.19, v.6 p.293*

Gleijeses, Piero *v.3 p.309*

Glen, Duncan *v.2 p.368*

Glen, Heather (Editor) *v.2 p.270*

Glenday, Michael K. *v.2 p.99*

Glendinning, Victoria *v.2 p.316, p.335, p.380*

Glendon, Mary Ann *v.4 p.440, p.455*

Glenn, Darryl *v.6 p.29*

Glenn, Evelyn N. *v.6 p.112, p.131*

Glenn, H. Patrick *v.4 p.434*

Glenn, John *v.3 p.230*

Glenn, Kathleen M. *v.2 p.656*

Glenn, Phillip J. *v.4 p.423*

Gless, Darryl J. *v.2 p.229*

Glete, Jan *v.3 p.35*

Glick, Barry & Sturgeon, William *v.6 p.278*

Glick, Bernard & Pasternak, Jack (Editors) . . . *v.5 p.133*

Glick, Bernard R. (Editor) *v.5 p.133*

Glick, David *v.5 p.325, p.326*

Glick, Henry R. *v.4 p.448*

Glick, Leslie Alan *v.4 p.436*

Glick, Peter & Rudman, Laurie A. *v.5 p.653*

Glick, Thomas F. (Editor), et al. *v.5 p.79, p.203*

Glick, Thomas F. (Editor) *v.5 p.79, p.203*

Glick, Thomas F. *v.3 p.65, p.237*

Glickman, Todd S. *v.5 p.425*

Gliessman, Stephen R. (Editor) *v.5 p.11*

Glimcher, Paul W. *v.4 p.272*

Glinert, Lewis *v.6 p.646*

Glinsky, Albert *v.1 p.214, p.244, p.363*

Glissant, Edouard *v.2 p.537*

Glixon, Beth Lise, et al. *v.1 p.184, p.229, p.384*

Gloag, John *v.1 p.805*

Global IDP Survey Staff (Contribution by) . *v.4 p.667, p.765*

Global Investment Center Staff *v.4 p.151*

Glock, Hans Johann *v.1 p.471*

Glotfelty, Cheryll & Fromm, Harold (Editors) . . . *v.2 p.4*

Glover, David M. & Hames, B. David (Editors) . . . *v.5 p.160*

Glover, Denis *v.2 p.746*

Glover, Ian & Bellwood, Peter *v.4 p.13*

Glover, Jane . . . *v.1 p.184, p.189, p.316, p.343, p.379*

Glover, Jonathan *v.4 p.652*

Glover, Sarma, et al. *v.5 p.723*

Glover, Savion & Weber, Bruce *v.1 p.8, p.32*

Glover, Thomas & Mitchell, Kevin *v.5 p.99*

Glowka, Arthur W. *v.2 p.209*

Glowka, Wayne & Lance, Donald M. (Editors) . *v.2 p.552, p.556*

Gluck, Carol *v.6 p.224*

Gluck, Mary *v.3 p.158*

Gluck, Sherna B. & Patai, Daphne (Editors) . . *v.6 p.449, p.476*

Gluckel of Hameln Staff *v.3 p.180*

Gluckman, Amy & Reed, Betsy (Editors). *v.6 p.382*

Gluckman, Max *v.4 p.34, p.38, p.433*

Glushkova, Irina *v.6 p.154*

Glusker, Jenny P., et al. *v.5 p.284*

Gluyas, Jon & Swarbrick, Richard. *v.5 p.451, p.738*

Gmehling, J. & Onken, U. *v.5 p.281*

Gmehling, J. (Editor). *v.5 p.290, p.741*

Gmehling, J. *v.5 p.281*

Gmelch, George & Zenner, Walter P. (Editors). *v.4 p.37, v.6 p.722*

Gnedenko, Boris V. & Kovalenko, I. N. *v.5 p.683*

Günzler, Helmut & Williams, Alex (Editors) . . . *v.5 p.267*

Gobat, Jean-Michel (Editor), et al. *v.5 p.49*

Gobe, Marc *v.4 p.142*

Goble, Dale D. (Editor), et al. *v.6 p.291, p.295*

Goble, Danney *v.3 p.523*

Goble, Lou (Editor) *v.1 p.492*

Gocek, Fatma M. *v.6 p.589*

Gocek, Fatma Muge & Shiva, Balaghi *v.6 p.592*

Gockenbach, Mark S. *v.5 p.487, p.492*

Godbey, Geoffrey. *v.4 p.784*

Godbout, Jacques. *v.2 p.540*

Goddard, Harold C. *v.2 p.229*

Goddard, Victoria A. (Editor), et al. *v.4 p.41*

Godden, Malcolm R. & Lapidge, Michael
(Editors) *v.2 p.167, v.6 p.565*

Godden, Malcolm R. *v.2 p.211*

Godden, Rumer *v.2 p.347*

Godfrey, John *v.6 p.571*

Godfrey, Richard T. *v.1 p.754*

Godish, Thad *v.5 p.705*

Godly, Edward W. *v.5 p.289*

Godman, Peter & Murray, Oswyn (Editors). *v.2 p.449*

Godman, Peter (Editor) *v.2 p.449*

Godman, Peter *v.2 p.698*

Godoy, Ricardo A. *v.3 p.323*

Godsil, C. D. *v.5 p.478*

Godson, Susan H. *v.6 p.454*

Godwin, E. W., et al. *v.1 p.786*

Godwin, E. W. *v.1 p.793*

Godwin, Joscelyn *v.1 p.381*

Godwin, R. Kenneth & Kemerer, Frank R. *v.4 p.298*

Godwin, William *v.2 p.288*

Goedhart, Marc, et al. *v.4 p.89, p.91, p.95*

Goehlert, Robert U. & Martin, Fenton S. *v.4 p.439*

Goehr, Lydia. *v.1 p.381*

Goeliner, Ellen W. & Murphy, Jacqueline S. (Editors) . *v.1 p.45*

Goemans, Hein. *v.4 p.649*

Goen, C. C. *v.1 p.606*

Goering, John M. *v.4 p.524*

Goerke, Natasza *v.2 p.790*

Goertz, Hans-Jurgen *v.1 p.586, p.603*

Goertzel, Ted & Goertzel, Ben *v.5 p.260*

Goertzen, Chris *v.1 p.298*

Goethe, Johann Wolfgang von & Mueller, Carl
Richard *v.1 p.62, p.78, p.108*

Goethe, Johann Wolfgang von . *v.1 p.79, p.108, v.2 p.597, p.598*

Goetschel, Willi *v.1 p.477*

Goetzfridt, Nicholas J. *v.2 p.740*

Goetzmann, William H. & Williams, Glyndwr . . . *v.4 p.381*

Goetzmann, William H. *v.3 p.381, p.385*

Goetzmann, William N. & Rouwenhorst, K. Geert. *v.4 p.89, p.146*

Goetz-Stankiewicz, Marketa (Editor) *v.1 p.65, p.109*

Goetz-Stankiewicz, Marketa, et al. *v.2 p.783*

Goetz-Stankiewicz, Marketa *v.2 p.781, p.782*

Goff, Patricia M. & Dunn, Kevin C. (Editor, Translators). *v.4 p.483*

Goff, Patricia M. & Dunn, Kevin C. (Editors). . . . *v.5 p.643*

Goff, Robert & Abrams, Harry N., Staff *v.1 p.739*

Goff, Stanley. *v.3 p.315*

Goffart, Walter A. *v.3 p.31*

Goffen, Rona *v.1 p.739*

Goffin, Alvin M. *v.3 p.333*

Goffman, Daniel *v.6 p.589*

Goffman, Erving *v.4 p.423, p.694, p.697, v.5 p.623*

Gofman, John W. *v.5 p.364, p.374, p.376*

Gogarten, Friedrich *v.1 p.644*

Gogatz, Arthur & Mondejar, Reuben *v.4 p.66*

Goggans, Jan & Di Franco, Aaron *v.3 p.530*

Gogol, Miriam (Editor) *v.2 p.70*

Gogol, Nikolai. *v.2 p.803, p.804*

GoGwilt, Christopher Lloyd. *v.2 p.341*

Goheen, Miriam. *v.4 p.30*

Goitein, S. D. & Lassner, Jacob *v.6 p.597*

Goitein, S. D. (Editor) *v.6 p.597, p.628*

Goitein, S. D. *v.6 p.597*

Gokalp, Ziya. *v.6 p.623*

Gokay, Bulent & Walker, R. B. J. (Editors). *v.3 p.483*

Golant, Stephen M. *v.4 p.742*

Golash, Deirdre *v.6 p.275*

Golay, Michael. *v.3 p.532*

Gold, Alice Ross *v.4 p.326*

Gold, Carol *v.3 p.233*

Gold, Hazel *v.2 p.654*

Gold, Lisa. *v.1 p.288, v.6 p.174, p.176*

Gold, Penny S. *v.6 p.451, p.560*

Gold, Thomas B. *v.6 p.214*

Goldberg, David J. *v.3 p.372, p.441, p.447*

Goldberg, David T. *v.4 p.730*

Goldberg, Deborah T. *v.5 p.245*

Goldberg, Harvey E. (Editor) *v.6 p.597*

Goldberg, Harvey E. *v.6 p.597, p.640*

Goldberg, Jan *v.4 p.169*

Goldberg, Jonathan *v.2 p.67*

Goldberg, Lea *v.6 p.648*
Goldberg, Leah. *v.6 p.648*
Goldberg, Lewis R.. . . . . *v.5 p.603*
Goldberg, Rita *v.2 p.258*
Goldberg, Robert A. *v.3 p.458, v.4 p.486*
Goldberg, Ronald Allen. *v.3 p.447*
Goldberg, Rosalee *v.1 p.42*
Goldberg, Roselee & Anderson, Laurie *v.1 p.214, p.301*
Goldberg, Roselee & Verzotti, Giorgio (Contribution by). *v.1 p.773*
Goldberg, Roselee. *v.1 p.28, p.30, p.42*
Goldberg, Samuel *v.5 p.486, p.503*
Goldberg, Sander M. *v.2 p.416, p.445*
Goldberg, Steven. *v.4 p.451*
Goldberg, Vicki *v.1 p.762*
Goldberger, Arthur S.. . . . . *v.4 p.200*
Goldberger, Marvin L. & Watson, Kenneth M. . . . *v.5 p.553*
Goldberger, Paul *v.1 p.789, p.797, v.6 p.712*
Goldberg-Hiller, Jonathan *v.4 p.569*
Goldblat, Jozef. *v.4 p.656*
Goldblatt, Howard (Editor) *v.6 p.212*
Goldblatt, Patricia F. & Smith, Deirdre (Editors) . . . *v.4 p.277*
Goldemberg, Josbe, et al. *v.5 p.452*
Golden, Mark *v.3 p.14*
Golden, Miriam A.. . . . . *v.4 p.121*
Golden, Nancy. *v.4 p.382*
Goldensohn, Lorrie *v.2 p.61*
Goldfarb, Brian *v.4 p.347*
Goldfarb, Hilliard T. *v.1 p.722*
Goldfarb, Jeffrey C. *v.3 p.367, p.371*
Goldfarb, Ronald L. *v.4 p.472*
Goldfarb, Ronald *v.4 p.465, v.6 p.270*
Goldfarb, Theodore D. (Editor) *v.6 p.285*
Goldfarb, William *v.4 p.463*
Goldfinger, Eliot *v.1 p.722*
Goldfrank, Lewis R., et al. *v.5 p.514, p.534*
Goldgeier, James M. & McFaul, Michael. *v.3 p.388*
Goldhagen, Sarah Williams *v.1 p.793*
Goldhill, Simon *v.2 p.401, p.407*
Goldie, Matthew Boyd (Editor) *v.2 p.168*
Goldie, Peter. *v.1 p.496*
Goldie, Terry *v.2 p.729, p.740*
Goldin, Claudia D. *v.4 p.133*
Goldin, Frederick (Editor, Translator) *v.1 p.177, p.411*
Goldin, Frederick. *v.2 p.594*
Golding, Brian *v.3 p.97*
Golding, John *v.1 p.727, p.739*
Golding, Martin & Edmundson, William (Editors). . *v.1 p.491*
Golding, William. *v.2 p.347*
Goldleaf, Steven *v.2 p.106*
Goldman, Alan H. *v.1 p.479*
Goldman, Alvin I. *v.1 p.496*
Goldman, Emma. *v.4 p.506, p.553*
Goldman, Eric F. *v.3 p.436, p.447, p.471*
Goldman, Harvey *v.4 p.502*
Goldman, Judith *v.1 p.753*

Goldman, Karla *v.1 p.553*
Goldman, Martin *v.5 p.543*
Goldman, Merle & Perry, Elizabeth J. (Editors) . . . *v.4 p.619*
Goldman, Merle R.. . . . . *v.6 p.194, p.197*
Goldman, Merle *v.4 p.619*
Goldman, Michael. *v.1 p.56*
Goldman, Paul *v.1 p.664, p.721, p.752*
Goldman, R. P. & Goldman, S. S. (Translators) . . . *v.1 p.535*
Goldman, Ralph M. *v.4 p.551*
Goldman, Robert P. (Editor) *v.1 p.535, p.536*
Goldman, Robert P. (Translator) *v.1 p.536*
Goldman, Wendy
Z. *v.3 p.53, p.208, p.222, p.225, v.6 p.454, p.464, p.466*
Goldman *v.5 p.515*
Goldoni, Carlo *v.1 p.107, v.2 p.711*
Goldreich, Oded *v.5 p.335*
Goldrick-Jones, Amanda *v.6 p.434*
Goldring, Roland. *v.5 p.447*
Goldsby, John *v.1 p.403*
Goldsby, Thomas J. & Martichenko, Robert. *v.4 p.117*
Goldscheider, Calvin & Neusner, Jacob *v.4 p.721*
Goldschmidt, Arthur & Johnston, Robert *v.6 p.635*
Goldschmidt, Arthur (Editor), et al. *v.6 p.637*
Goldschmidt, Arthur Jr.. . . . . *v.6 p.581, p.637*
Goldschmidt, Henry (Author, Editor). *v.3 p.315*
Goldsmith, Donald (Author, Author) *v.5 p.74*
Goldsmith, Donald *v.5 p.71*
Goldsmith, Elizabeth C. & Goodman, Dena *v.2 p.457*
Goldsmith, F. B. (Editor) *v.5 p.175, p.239*
Goldsmith, Jack L. & Wu, Tim *v.4 p.115*
Goldsmith, John A. (Editor) *v.2 p.560*
Goldsmith, John A.. . . . . *v.2 p.560*
Goldsmith, Oliver *v.2 p.248*
Goldsmith, Sara K. (Editor) *v.5 p.662*
Goldsmith, Thomas (Editor). *v.1 p.269*
Goldsmith, Timothy H.. . . . . *v.5 p.166, p.167, p.192*
Goldsmith, Victor (Editor), et al.. . . . . *v.6 p.251*
Goldstein, Ann & Diederichsen, Diedrich. *v.1 p.678*
Goldstein, Avery N. *v.4 p.619*
Goldstein, Claire *v.1 p.813*
Goldstein, Daniel M. *v.3 p.323*
Goldstein, Donna M. *v.3 p.279*
Goldstein, Elyse (Editor) *v.1 p.553*
Goldstein, Fred. *v.4 p.111, p.165*
Goldstein, Herbert, et al.. . . . . *v.5 p.64, p.546*
Goldstein, Herman & McGraw-Hill Staff *v.6 p.264*
Goldstein, Inge F. & Goldstein, Martin. *v.6 p.285*
Goldstein, Jan Ellen *v.3 p.148*
Goldstein, Jeffrey H. *v.5 p.582*
Goldstein, Jonathan A. (Translator, Introduction by, Notes
by) *v.1 p.623*
Goldstein, Jonathan. *v.1 p.623*
Goldstein, Joseph, et al. *v.4 p.442, p.757*
Goldstein, Joshua S. *v.4 p.563, v.6 p.441*

Goldstein, Larry Joel, et al. *v.5 p.477*
Goldstein, Lisa. *v.4 p.368*
Goldstein, Malcom L.. . . . . *v.2 p.133*
Goldstein, Mel & Tanner, Dave *v.4 p.792, p.841, p.868*
Goldstein, Melvyn C. & Beall, Cynthia M.. . *v.4 p.28, v.6 p.240*
Goldstein, Melvyn C. & Kapstein, Matthew T. *v.6 p.240*
Goldstein, Melvyn C. & Robillard, Pierre *v.6 p.241*
Goldstein, Melvyn C.. . . . . *v.6 p.240*
Goldstein, Michael S. *v.4 p.790, p.805*
Goldstein, Norm (Editor) *v.4 p.412*
Goldstein, Paul *v.4 p.109, p.110, p.446*
Goldstein, Robert J. *v.4 p.438*
Goldstein, Robert Justin *v.3 p.74*
Goldstein, Sam & Brooks, Robert B. (Editors) . . . *v.5 p.626*
Goldstein, Sidney M.. . . . . *v.1 p.810*
Goldstein, Thomas *v.5 p.390*
Goldstein, Tom. *v.4 p.405*
Goldstone, Jack A. (Editor) *v.4 p.579, p.711*
Goldstone, Jack *v.4 p.486*
Goldstone, Robert L. (Editor), et al. *v.5 p.605*
Goldsworthy, Adrian K. *v.3 p.26*
Goldsworthy, Adrian *v.3 p.22, p.25*
Goldsworthy, Andy & Thompson, Jerry L.
   (Photographers). *v.1 p.779*
Goldsworthy, Andy. *v.1 p.697, p.779*
Goldsworthy, David *v.6 p.64*
Goldthorpe, J. E. *v.4 p.759*
Goldwater, Barry M. *v.3 p.452, p.458*
Goldwater, Robert *v.1 p.739*
Goldwhite, Harold *v.5 p.296*
Goldwin, Robert A.. . . . . *v.4 p.452*
Goldziher, Ignac *v.1 p.554*
Goldziher, Ignaz *v.1 p.557*
Gole, Nilufer. *v.6 p.623*
Golin, Steve *v.4 p.282*
Golley, Frank B. & Werger, Marinus J.
   (Editors) *v.5 p.41, p.353, p.357*
Gollnick, Donna M. & Chinn, Philip C. *v.4 p.363*
Golob, Richard & Brus, Eric *v.5 p.361*
Golomb, Jacob J.. . . . . *v.1 p.505*
Golomb, Solomon W.. . . . . *v.5 p.469*
Golub, Andrew Lang *v.4 p.83*
Golub, Gene H. & Van Loan, Charles F. *v.5 p.472*
Golub, Leon & Pasachoff, Jay M.. . . . . *v.5 p.68*
Goma, Paul *v.2 p.817*
Gombosi, Tamas I. *v.5 p.73, p.444*
Gombrich, E. H.. . . . . *v.1 p.668, p.702, p.703*
Gombrich, Richard F. & Obeyeskere, Gananth . . . *v.1 p.540*
Gombrowicz, Witold *v.2 p.787, p.790*
Gomex Torrego, L. *v.2 p.636*
Gomez, Alma (Editor), et al. *v.6 p.495*
Gomez, Jewelle *v.6 p.396*
Gomez, Michael A. *v.6 p.11*
Gomez, Ninoska. *v.1 p.52*
Gomez Torrego, Leonardo. *v.2 p.636*

Gomez-Lobo, Alfonso *v.1 p.422*
Gomez-Moriana, Antonio & Duran-Cogan, Mercedes
   (Editors) *v.4 p.703*
Gomez-Pena, Guillermo *v.6 p.492, p.499*
Gomori, George & Szirtes, George (Editors) . . . *v.2 p.785*
Gomulka, Stanislaw & Polonsky, Anthony *v.3 p.255*
Goncharov, Ivan A.. . . . . *v.2 p.804*
Goncourt, Edmond L. & Goncourt, Jules A. *v.2 p.492*
Gonda, Jan *v.1 p.536, p.540*
Gondicas, Dimitri & Issawi, Charles P. (Editors) . . . *v.3 p.195*
Gondola, Ch. Didier *v.6 p.62*
Gong, Gang & Semmler, Willi. *v.4 p.200*
Gongora y Argote, Luis de *v.2 p.650*
Gonick, Larry & Huffman, Art *v.5 p.540*
Gonon, Philipp (Editor). *v.4 p.305*
Gonzales, Manuel G. *v.6 p.531*
Gonzales, Michael J.. . . . . *v.3 p.292, p.329*
Gonzales, Patrisia & Rodriguez, Roberto *v.6 p.521*
Gonzales, Rodolfo *v.6 p.499, p.540*
Gonzales-Berry, Erlinda & Maciel, David (Editors) . *v.6 p.531*
Gonzales-Berry, Erlinda (Editor). *v.6 p.499, p.512*
Gonzalez Echevarria, Roberto (Editor) *v.2 p.649*
Gonzalez Echevarria, Roberto *v.2 p.649*
Gonzalez, Evelyn Diaz *v.3 p.491*
Gonzalez, Gilbert G. & Fernandez, Raul E.. . . . *v.6 p.531*
Gonzalez, Gilbert G. *v.6 p.525, p.527*
Gonzalez, Jovita *v.6 p.499*
Gonzalez, Juan *v.6 p.531*
Gonzalez, Lisa Sanchez *v.6 p.506, p.512*
Gonzalez, Maria Luisa (Editor), et al. *v.4 p.311*
Gonzalez, Maria Luisa, et al. *v.6 p.527*
Gonzalez, N. V. M. *v.6 p.179*
Gonzalez, Nancie L. *v.3 p.271, v.6 p.531*
Gonzalez, Otto-Raul *v.2 p.676*
Gonzalez, Rigoberto *v.6 p.499*
Gonzalez-Cruz, Luis F. & Colecchia, Francesca M. (Editor,
   Translators) *v.6 p.496, p.512, p.517*
Gonzalez-Pando, Miguel *v.3 p.309, v.6 p.521*
Gonzalez-Wippler, Migene *v.4 p.722*
González Casanova, Pablo, ed. *v.3 p.271*
González de la Vara, Martín. *v.3 p.271*
González, Deena J.. . . . . *v.6 p.531, p.546*
González, Gilbert G. *v.6 p.525*
González, Jovita & Raleigh, Eve. *v.6 p.499*
González, Justo L. *v.1 p.598*
González Navarro, Luis. *v.3 p.289*
Gooch, Anthony & Pareded, Angela Garcia de . . . *v.2 p.636*
Gooch, Brad *v.6 p.401*
Gooch, Bryan N. & Thatcher, David
   (Editors). *v.1 p.166, p.179, p.180*
Gooch, Paul W. *v.1 p.498*
Good, Anthony. *v.6 p.154*
Good, David F.. . . . . *v.3 p.181*
Good, Edwin M. *v.1 p.389*
Good, Gerry A. *v.5 p.70*

Good, Ralph E. (Editor), et al. *v.5 p.53, p.379*
Goodacre, Mark S. *v.1 p.629*
Goodale, Jane C. *v.4 p.43*
Goodale, Melvyn & Milner, David. *v.5 p.606*
Goodall, Brian *v.4 p.396*
Goodchild, Michael F. & Janelle, Donald G. (Editors) *v.4 p.375*
Goodchild, Peter *v.5 p.543*
Goode, William J. *v.4 p.739, p.740*
Goodell, Gregory. *v.6 p.346*
Goodenough, Ursula *v.5 p.221*
Goodich, Michael *v.6 p.362*
Goodin, Robert E., et al. *v.4 p.500*
Gooding-Williams, Robert (Editor) *v.6 p.123, p.135*
Goodis, David. *v.2 p.80*
Goodlad, John I. (Editor), et al. *v.4 p.282*
Goodlad, John I., et al. *v.4 p.326*
Goodlad, John I. *v.4 p.279, p.326, p.337, p.339*
Goodlad, Lauren M. E.. . . . *v.2 p.175, v.6 p.752, p.758, p.763*
Goodman, Alan H., et al.. . . . . *v.4 p.45*
Goodman, David S. *v.3 p.239, v.6 p.197, p.200*
Goodman, David *v.3 p.239*
Goodman, Dena *v.3 p.147*
Goodman, Jacob E. & O'Rourke, Joseph. . . . *v.5 p.337, p.340*
Goodman, James *v.3 p.441*
Goodman, Jane E. *v.6 p.600*
Goodman, J.. . . . . *v.1 p.434*
Goodman, Jennifer R.. . . . . *v.2 p.185*
Goodman, John C., et al. *v.4 p.768*
Goodman, Jordan (Editor), et al.. . . . . *v.3 p.281*
Goodman, Jordan. *v.5 p.241*
Goodman, Joyce & Martin, Jane. *v.6 p.462*
Goodman, Kenneth S. *v.5 p.574*
Goodman, Lenn E. *v.1 p.432*
Goodman, Louis W., et al. *v.3 p.274*
Goodman, Nelson *v.1 p.479, p.490, p.493*
Goodman, Paul. *v.3 p.397, v.4 p.347*
Goodman, Richard E.. . . . . *v.5 p.421*
Goodman, Susan & Dawson, Carl. *v.2 p.42*
Goodman, Susan E. *v.2 p.80*
Goodman/RobertM. *v.5 p.21*
Goodnough, David *v.2 p.680*
Goodpasture, H. McKennie *v.1 p.608*
Goodrich, Chauncey Allen *v.2 p.197*
Goodrich, L. Carrington & Fang, Chaoying
  (Editors). *v.6 p.186, p.198*
Goodrich, Thomas *v.3 p.397*
Goodrick-Clarke, Nicholas *v.4 p.768*
Goodsell, Don *v.5 p.716*
Goodspeed, Edgar Johnson & Owen, William B. . . . *v.2 p.413*
Goodstein, David. *v.4 p.160*
Goodwin, Albert *v.3 p.94, p.108, p.128*
Goodwin, Andrew *v.1 p.255*
Goodwin, Barbara & Taylor, Keith W. *v.4 p.499*
Goodwin, Barbara (Editor) *v.4 p.499*
Goodwin, Barbara *v.4 p.514*

Goodwin, Bill *v.4 p.385*
Goodwin, Brian *v.5 p.192*
Goodwin, Doris Kearns. *v.3 p.458, p.471*
Goodwin, Elaine M. *v.1 p.803*
Goodwin, Frederick K. & Jamison, Kay R. *v.5 p.517*
Goodwin, James *v.6 p.339*
Goodwin, Jeff *v.4 p.497*
Goodwin, John (Editor). *v.1 p.100, p.154*
Goodwin, Kenneth *v.2 p.740*
Goodwin, William Lawrence *v.4 p.356*
Goodwin, William W.. . . . . *v.2 p.400*
Goodwyn, Lawrence *v.3 p.397, p.436*
Goody, Esther N. *v.4 p.32*
Goody, Jack (Author, Contribution by) *v.4 p.32*
Goody, Jack. *v.4 p.32, v.6 p.557*
Goold, Benjamin J.. . . . . *v.6 p.265*
Goonatilake, Susantha *v.6 p.154*
Goonetilleke, D. C. R. A. (Editor) *v.2 p.727*
Goonetilleke, D. C. R. A. *v.2 p.760*
Goossen, Rachel W. *v.3 p.441*
Gootenberg, Paul *v.3 p.281, p.327, p.330*
Gootman, Elliot C. *v.5 p.485*
Gopaul-McNicol, Sharon-Ann & Armour-Thomas,
  Eleanor *v.5 p.600*
Gopnik, Adam *v.2 p.19*
Gorayska, Barbara & Mey, Jacob L. (Editors). *v.5 p.589*
Gorbachev, Mikhail. *v.3 p.388*
Gorbman, Claudia *v.1 p.255*
Gordenker, Leon *v.4 p.633*
Gordillo, Gaston R.. . . . . *v.3 p.267*
Gordimer, Nadine *v.2 p.583, p.755*
Gordin, Michael D. *v.3 p.44*
Gordis, Robert *v.4 p.722*
Gordo-Lopez, Angel J. & Parker, Ian (Editors) *v.5 p.589*
Gordon, Andrew M. & Newman, Steven M. (Editors) . *v.5 p.37*
Gordon, Andrew *v.6 p.224*
Gordon, Ann D., et al. *v.6 p.431*
Gordon, Arnold J. & Ford, Richard A. *v.5 p.259*
Gordon, Beate S.. . . . . *v.6 p.226*
Gordon, Bruce *v.1 p.604*
Gordon, Bryan. *v.4 p.11, v.6 p.703*
Gordon, Caroline *v.2 p.78*
Gordon, David J. *v.2 p.309*
Gordon, David T. (Editor). *v.4 p.326*
Gordon, Diana R. *v.6 p.263*
Gordon, Dillian & Syson, Luke *v.1 p.739*
Gordon, E. V. (Editor) *v.2 p.206*
Gordon, Edward E. & Gordon, Elaine H.. . . . . . *v.4 p.762*
Gordon, Edwin. *v.1 p.405*
Gordon, Eleanor & Nair, Gwyneth. *v.6 p.743, p.747*
Gordon, Eric A. *v.1 p.214, p.312, v.6 p.409*
Gordon, Gary *v.1 p.803*
Gordon, Haim (Editor) *v.1 p.505*
Gordon, Haim *v.6 p.617*
Gordon, Howard R. D. *v.4 p.305*

Gordon, I. *v.2 p.257*
Gordon, J. E. *v.5 p.697*
Gordon, Joel *v.6 p.639*
Gordon, John S.. . . . . . . *v.4 p.100, p.147, p.155, p.162*
Gordon, Jon *v.5 p.163*
Gordon, Lincoln *v.3 p.340*
Gordon, Linda (Editor) *v.4 p.754*
Gordon, Linda . *v.4 p.569, p.742, p.754, p.775, v.6 p.464, p.469*
Gordon, Lyndall *v.2 p.71, p.392*
Gordon, Malcolm S., et al. *v.5 p.198*
Gordon, Pamela *v.1 p.429*
Gordon, Raymond G., Jr. (Editor) *v.2 p.560*
Gordon, Richard *v.4 p.777*
Gordon, Robert J. & Friedman, Milton. . . . *v.4 p.232, p.238*
Gordon, Robert J. & Sholto-Douglas, Stuart *v.6 p.76*
Gordon, Robert S. *v.2 p.721*
Gordon, Sarah Barringer *v.1 p.587*
Gordon, Sarah. *v.3 p.59*
Gordon, Stacy B.. . . . . *v.4 p.530*
Gordon, Stewart *v.1 p.239, p.395, p.397, p.400, v.6 p.160*
Gordon, Suzanne *v.4 p.694*
Gordy, Berry Jr. *v.1 p.269, p.384*
Gore, Albert *v.6 p.291*
Gore, Chris *v.6 p.346*
Gore, Joan Elias *v.6 p.462*
Goreau, Angeline. *v.2 p.238*
Goreham, Gary A., et al. *v.5 p.12*
Gorer, Geoffrey *v.1 p.14*
Gorfein, David S. & Hoffman, Robert R. (Editors) . . *v.5 p.610*
Goring-Morris, A. Nigel & Belfer-Cohen, Anna (Editors). *v.4 p.16*
Goriunova, Olga & Shulgin, Alexei (Editors) *v.1 p.771*
Gorke, Martin *v.5 p.358, p.369*
Gorkin, Michael, et al. *v.3 p.299*
Gorky, Maxim *v.2 p.804*
Gorlizki, Yoram, et al. *v.3 p.225*
Gorman, Herbert *v.2 p.358*
Gorman, Hugh S.. . . . . *v.6 p.300*
Gorman, Joseph B. *v.3 p.458*
Gorman, Robert F. & Mihalkanin, Edward S.. . . . . *v.4 p.670*
Gorman, Robert F.. . . . . *v.4 p.633, p.667*
Gormley, Paul *v.6 p.321*
Gorn, Elliot J. (Editor) *v.4 p.831, p.855*
Gorn, Elliott J. *v.4 p.126, p.805, p.855*
Gorna, Robin *v.6 p.443*
Gorodetsky, Gabriel *v.3 p.227*
Gorostiza, Carlos, et al.. . . . . *v.2 p.678*
Gorr, Wilpen & Kurland, Kristen S. *v.4 p.387*
Gorra, Michael *v.2 p.762, p.768*
Gorriti, Gustavo *v.3 p.330*
Gorsuch, Anne E. *v.3 p.222*
Gorsuch, Richard L. *v.5 p.634*
Gorup, Radmila J. & Rakic, Bogdan (Editors) *v.2 p.778*
Gorup, Radmilla & Obradovic, Nadezda (Editors). . . *v.2 p.810*
Goryshkina, T. *v.6 p.285*
Goscilo, Helena (Editor, Translator) *v.2 p.787*

Goscilo, Helena (Editor) *v.2 p.794, p.798*
Goscilo, Helena (Introduction by) *v.2 p.794, v.6 p.478*
Goscilo, Helena *v.2 p.804*
Gosden, Chris & Knowles, Chantal *v.4 p.47*
Gosling, J. C. B. *v.1 p.423*
Gosling, James, et al.. . . . . *v.5 p.346*
Gosling, L. Morris & Sutherland, William J.
   (Editors) *v.5 p.17, v.6 p.291*
Goslinga, Cornelis C.. . . . . *v.3 p.322*
Goslinga, Cornelis Cornelis Christiaan . . *v.3 p.322*
Gosnell, Harold F. *v.4 p.577*
Gosner, Kevin *v.3 p.285*
Goss Lucas, Sandra & Bernstein, Douglas A.. . . . . *v.5 p.675*
Gosse, Edmund William *v.2 p.214*
Gosse, Edmund *v.6 p.758, p.765*
Gosse, Siegfried, et al. *v.2 p.594*
Gosse, Van. *v.3 p.309*
Gossen, Gary H., South and Leon Portilla, Miguel (eds.). *v.3 p.296*
Gossett, Thomas F. *v.2 p.51*
Gossfeld, Lynn M., et al.. . . . . . . *v.5 p.520, p.523, p.530*
Gostin, Larry (Editor). *v.4 p.442*
Goswami, Amit & Goswami, Maggie *v.5 p.399*
Goswami, B. N. & Fischer, Eberhard. *v.1 p.731*
Goswami, Manu *v.6 p.157*
Goswami, Usha (Editor) *v.5 p.626, p.630*
Gotanda, Philip Kan *v.6 p.98*
Gotelli, Nicholas J.. . . . . *v.5 p.169*
Gotlib, Ian H. & Hammen, Constance L. (Editors) . . *v.5 p.659*
Gotoff, Harold C.. . . . . *v.2 p.433*
Gott, J. Richard *v.5 p.72*
Gott, Richard *v.3 p.309*
Gottdiener, Mark & Budd, Leslie *v.6 p.717*
Gottdiener, Mark & Pickvance, Chris G. (Editors). . *v.6 p.717*
Gottdiener, Mark. *v.6 p.712, p.723*
Gottdiener, M.. . . . . *v.6 p.709, p.723*
Gottesman, Evan R. *v.6 p.170*
Gottfredson, Gary D. & Holland, John L.. . . . . . *v.5 p.577*
Gottfried, Heidi (Editor) *v.6 p.427*
Gottfried, Kurt & Weisskopf, Victor F.. . . . . . *v.5 p.552*
Gottfried, Kurt & Yan, Tung-Mow *v.5 p.549*
Gottfried, Martin *v.1 p.8, p.31, v.2 p.101*
Gottfried, von Strassburg, 13th cent.. . . . . . *v.2 p.594*
Gottlieb, Daniel W.. . . . . *v.5 p.706*
Gottlieb, Jack *v.1 p.299*
Gottlieb, Richard (Editor). *v.4 p.160*
Gottlieb, Robert & Kimball, Robert *v.1 p.411*
Gottlieb, Robert (Editor) *v.1 p.259*
Gottlieb, Robert. *v.1 p.8, p.23*
Gottlieb, Roger S. (Editor) *v.1 p.508*
Gottlieb, Vera & Allain, Paul (Editors) *v.2 p.804*
Gottlob, Michael *v.6 p.150*
Gottmann, Jean *v.4 p.495*
Gottry, Steve *v.4 p.87*
Gottschalk, Louis M.. . . . . *v.1 p.197, p.327*

Gottschalk, Peter *v.6 p.154*

Gottschild, Brenda D. *v.1 p.18*

Gottschild, Brenda Dixon *v.1 p.18*

Gottstein, Günter *v.5 p.732*

Goubert, Pierre *v.3 p.145*

Goudie, Andrew (Editor) *v.4 p.391, v.5 p.417*

Goudie, Andrew S. *v.4 p.373, v.5 p.417*

Goudriaan, Teun *v.1 p.536*

Gougeon, Gilles (Editor) *v.3 p.543*

Gough, Barry M. *v.3 p.534*

Gough, Barry *v.3 p.545*

Gough, Cal & Greenblatt, Ellen (Editors) *v.6 p.383*

Gough, Leo *v.5 p.218*

Goulbourne, Harry (Editor) *v.4 p.3*

Gould, Allan *v.6 p.360*

Gould, Carol C. & Wartofsky, Marx W. *v.6 p.461*

Gould, Carol (Editor) *v.6 p.461*

Gould, Cecil *v.1 p.739*

Gould, Edwin S. *v.5 p.304*

Gould, Eric *v.4 p.297*

Gould, Evlyn *v.2 p.497*

Gould, Frederick E.. . . . . *v.4 p.158*

Gould, Glenn & Page, Tim *v.1 p.214, p.247*

Gould, Grant F. & Gould, James L. *v.5 p.92*

Gould, H. & Gould, J. Whiteley *v.2 p.435*

Gould, Harold A.. . . . . *v.4 p.703*

Gould, Jay E. *v.5 p.88*

Gould, Jeffrey L.. . . . . *v.3 p.301*

Gould, Lewis L. . . *v.3 p.378, p.397, p.436, p.441, p.471, p.526*

Gould, Roger V. (Editor) *v.4 p.688*

Gould, Stephen
Jay . . *v.5 p.79, p.192, p.221, p.226, p.410, p.446, p.608, p.653*

Gould Todd *v.4 p.806, p.854*

Gould, William B. IV. *v.4 p.109, p.111, p.112, p.121, p.126, p.446*

Gouldner, Alvin Ward. *v.4 p.682*

Gouldner, Alvin W.. . . . . *v.4 p.695*

Gouma-Peterson, Thalia. *v.1 p.697*

Gourevitch, Peter Alexis & Shinn, James *v.4 p.86*

Gourevitch, Philip *v.4 p.715, v.6 p.65*

Gourgouris, Stathis *v.3 p.194*

Gouri, Haim *v.6 p.648*

Gourieroux, Christian & Jasiak, Joann *v.4 p.200*

Gourieroux, Christian. *v.4 p.200*

Gourse, Leslie. *v.1 p.259, p.281, p.312, p.317, p.324, p.332, p.342*

Gouvea, Fernando Q. *v.5 p.476*

Gouveia, Georgette *v.1 p.739*

Gouyon, Pierre-Henri, et al. *v.5 p.200*

Gove, H. E. *v.5 p.540*

Gover, Daniel (Editor), et al. *v.2 p.751*

Government Printing Office Staff *v.4 p.51*

Govindarajan, Vijay & Gupta, Anil K.. . . . . . . *v.4 p.69*

Govindarajan, Vijay & Trimble, Chris *v.4 p.68*

Govindarajulu, Z. *v.5 p.92*

Govoni, Norman *v.4 p.134*

Gow, James & Carmichael, Cathie *v.3 p.250*

Gowans, Alan *v.1 p.789*

Gower, John & Othman, Ossama *v.2 p.211*

Gower, John, et al. *v.2 p.212*

Gower, John *v.2 p.211*

Gowers, Ernest. *v.2 p.550*

Gowers, Timothy *v.5 p.458*

Gowing, Laura *v.3 p.52*

Gowing, Lawrence (Editor) *v.1 p.664*

Gowing, Lawrence *v.1 p.739*

Gowland, D. A., et al. *v.4 p.383*

Goyen, William *v.2 p.78*

Goytisolo, Jose Agustin *v.2 p.668*

Goytisolo, Juan *v.2 p.657, p.658*

Gozzano, Guido *v.2 p.715*

Gozzi, Carlo *v.2 p.710*

Grabar, Oleg . . . *v.1 p.673, p.691, p.731, v.6 p.574*

Grabbe, Christian D. *v.2 p.597*

Grabbe, Christian Dietrich *v.2 p.597*

Grabbe, Lester L.. . . . . *v.1 p.547*

Graber, Julia A. (Editor), et al.. . . . . *v.5 p.626*

Grace, Eric S. *v.4 p.156*

Grace, Patricia *v.2 p.746*

Grace, Sherrill E.. . . . . *v.3 p.547*

Gracia, Jorge J. & De Greiff, Pablo *v.6 p.540, p.544*

Gracia, Jorge J. E. (Editor) *v.1 p.444*

Gracia, Jorge J. *v.6 p.544*

Gracian, Baltasar & Maurer, Christopher *v.2 p.650*

Gracian, Baltasar *v.2 p.650*

Gracitua-Mario, Estanislao & Wodon, Quentin
(Editors) *v.4 p.687, p.731*

Gracq, Julien. *v.2 p.518*

Gracyk, Theodore *v.1 p.270*

Gradenwitz, Peter E. *v.1 p.299*

Gradshteyn, I. S. *v.5 p.63, p.461, p.486*

Gradstein, Felix M. (Editor), et al.. . . . . . . *v.5 p.444, p.446*

Gradstein, Mark, et al. *v.4 p.297*

Graebner, Norman A. (Editor) *v.3 p.452*

Graebner, Norman A. *v.3 p.381*

Graebner, Norman Arthur *v.3 p.452*

Graebner, William *v.3 p.441*

Graedel, Thomas & Howard-Grenville,
Jennifer *v.5 p.373, p.376, p.377*

Graetz, Michael J. & Mashaw, Jerry L.. . . . . . *v.4 p.722*

Graetz, Michael J. & Shapiro, Ian *v.4 p.107*

Graetz, Michael J. *v.4 p.107*

Graeub, Ralph *v.6 p.291*

Graf, W. L. (Editor) *v.5 p.431*

Graf, William L.. . . . . *v.5 p.739*

Grafakos, Loukas. *v.5 p.493*

Graff, David *v.6 p.185*

Graff, Ellen *v.1 p.26*

Graff, Henry F. (Editor). *v.3 p.378*

Graff, Violette (Editor) *v.6 p.161*

Graffagnino, J. Kevin *v.3 p.486*

Graffy, Julian & Hosking, Geoffrey Alan (Editors) . . *v.3 p.228*

Grafton, Anthony (Editor) *v.5 p.79, p.237*
Grafton, Anthony *v.3 p.47*
Graham, Benjamin *v.4 p.89, p.95*
Graham, Billy *v.1 p.581, p.648*
Graham, Brian *v.3 p.87*
Graham, Bruce *v.4 p.617*
Graham, Carol *v.3 p.330*
Graham, Charles & Morgenstern, Dan *v.1 p.259*
Graham, Dan *v.1 p.779*
Graham, Dee L., et al. *v.4 p.742*
Graham, Don *v.2 p.49*
Graham, Elspeth (Editor), et al. *v.2 p.196*
Graham, Frank Jr. *v.6 p.293, p.295*
Graham, George *v.4 p.798*
Graham, Gerald S. *v.3 p.76*
Graham, Gordon *v.1 p.479, v.5 p.133*
Graham, Helen *v.3 p.241*
Graham, Hugh Davis & Diamond, Nancy *v.4 p.331*
Graham, Hugh Davis *v.4 p.486, p.570*
Graham, Hugh *v.3 p.302*
Graham, James W. *v.3 p.16*
Graham, Jeffrey B. (Editor) *v.5 p.215*
Graham, Joe S. (Compiled by) *v.6 p.485*
Graham, Joe S. (Editor) *v.6 p.492, p.523*
Graham, John R. & Naglieri, Jack A. (Editors) . . . *v.5 p.599*
Graham, John W. & Havlick, Wendy *v.4 p.172*
Graham, Judith S. *v.3 p.487*
Graham, Katharine *v.4 p.410*
Graham, Laura R. *v.3 p.340*
Graham, Linda E. & Wilcox, Lee W. *v.5 p.208*
Graham, Loren R. . *v.3 p.44, p.210, p.222,v.5 p.392, p.410, p.411*
Graham, Martha *v.1 p.8*
Graham, Maryemma *v.6 p.25, p.43*
Graham, Otis L. *v.3 p.441, p.447*
Graham, Patricia Albjerg *v.4 p.326*
Graham, Peg & Hudson-Ross, Sally (Editors) . . . *v.4 p.279*
Graham, Philip *v.1 p.114*
Graham, R. *v.3 p.336*
Graham, Richard (Editor) *v.2 p.690*
Graham, Richard *v.3 p.336*
Graham, Ronald L., et al. *v.5 p.337*
Graham, Sara H. *v.4 p.519*
Graham, Stedman, et al. *v.4 p.884*
Graham, Stephen & Marvin, Simon *v.6 p.718, p.720*
Graham, Stephen (Editor) . . . *v.4 p.659, v.6 p.723, p.729*
Grahame, Kenneth *v.2 p.347*
Graham-Jones, Jean *v.1 p.127*
Grahn, Judy Rae *v.6 p.360, p.393*
Grainger, John D. (Editor) *v.3 p.345*
Grainger, John D. *v.3 p.27*
Grainger, Percy *v.1 p.215, p.247*
Gramick, Jeannine (Editor), et al. *v.6 p.373*
Grammer, Leslie C. *v.5 p.517*
Grams, Martin Jr. *v.1 p.94, p.114*
Gramsci, Antonio *v.2 p.568*

Granatstein, J. L. *v.3 p.539*
Granatstein, Jack L. & Hillmer, Norman *v.3 p.541*
Granatstein, Jack L. *v.3 p.537, p.541, v.4 p.588*
Grand, Steve *v.5 p.218*
Grandazzi, Alexandre *v.3 p.24*
Grandbois, Alain *v.2 p.539*
Grandi, Guido (Editor) *v.5 p.116, p.140, p.149*
Grandison, A.S. & Lewis, M.J. (Editors) . . . *v.5 p.741*
Granger Book Company, Editorial Board Staff (Editor) . *v.2 p.23*
Granger Book Company, Editorial Board Staff . . *v.2 p.22, p.23*
Granger, Bruce I. *v.2 p.29*
Granger, C. W. & Hatanaka, Michio *v.4 p.206*
Granger, C. W. (Editor) *v.4 p.206*
Granger, Clive & Terasvirta, Timo *v.4 p.207*
Granger, Clive W. J. *v.4 p.200*
Granger, Clive *v.4 p.200, p.201, p.207*
Granovetter, Mark S. & Swedberg, Richard *v.4 p.185*
Grant, Barry K. & Sloniowski, Jeannette (Editors) . . *v.6 p.309*
Grant, Barry K. (Editor) *v.6 p.318*
Grant, Barry Keith (Editor) *v.6 p.311*
Grant, Carl A. & Sleeter, Christine E. *v.4 p.300*
Grant, E. *v.5 p.399*
Grant, Edward *v.1 p.526, v.5 p.61*
Grant, Elliott M. *v.2 p.504*
Grant, H. Roger *v.4 p.499*
Grant, Heath, et al. *v.6 p.261*
Grant, J. Andrew & Soderbaum, Fredrik (Editors) . . *v.4 p.611*
Grant, James L. *v.4 p.89*
Grant, John *v.6 p.307*
Grant, Kim *v.1 p.678*
Grant, Mark N. *v.1 p.277*
Grant, Michael *v.1 p.532, v.3 p.10, p.27, p.28*
Grant, Nathan *v.2 p.126*
Grant, R. M. *v.4 p.51*
Grant, Rebecca & Newland, Kathleen (Editors) . . . *v.6 p.441*
Grant, Richard B. *v.2 p.492*
Grant, Richard P. (Editor) *v.5 p.106, p.108, p.140*
Grant, Robert M. *v.1 p.612*
Grant, Robert McQueen, 1917- *v.1 p.639*
Grant, S. G. *v.4 p.367*
Grant, William R. *v.6 p.15, p.38*
Grantham, Dewey W. *v.3 p.496*
Grantham, William C., et al. *v.4 p.792, p.906*
Grants Program Staff *v.4 p.293*
Grantz, A. (Editor), et al. *v.5 p.434*
Granville, Wilfred *v.1 p.59*
Granville-Barker, Harley *v.2 p.227*
Graslund, Bo *v.4 p.16*
Grasmuck, Sherri & Pessar, Patricia R. . *v.4 p.570, v.6 p.529*
Grass, Günter *v.2 p.607, p.608*
Grasselli, Jeanette G., Ritchey, William M. (eds.) . . . *v.5 p.297*
Grasselli, Margaret Morgan, et al. *v.1 p.753*
Grattan-Guinness, Ivor (Editor) *v.5 p.466*
Grattan-Guinness, Ivor *v.5 p.466*
Gratton, Bartlett & Rolf *v.4 p.812*

Gratton, Chris & Jones, Ian *v.4 p.812*

Gratton, Chris & Taylor, Peter *v.4 p.884, p.888*

Gratton, Johnnie & Le Juez, Brigitte (Editors) . . . *v.2 p.465*

Gratzer, George A. *v.5 p.461*

Gratzer, Walter Bruno. *v.5 p.230*

Grau, Gunter & Shoppmann, Claudia (Editors). *v.3 p.84*

Grau, Gunter; Schoppmann, Claudia *v.6 p.365*

Grau, Oliver *v.1 p.771*

Graubard, Stephen *v.3 p.441*

Graulich, Melody & Tatum, Stephen (Editors) . . . *v.2 p.128*

Graupner, Helmut & Tahmindjis, Phillip (Editors) . . . *v.6 p.421*

Graur, Dan & Li, Wen-Hsiung. *v.5 p.113*

Grave, Floyd K. & Grave, Margaret
  G. *v.1 p.163, p.189, p.239, p.330*

Graver, David (Editor) *v.2 p.752*

Graver, David *v.1 p.82, p.84, p.96*

Graver, Dennis. *v.4 p.787, p.847*

Graver, Jack. *v.5 p.501, p.683*

Graves, Donald E., et al. *v.3 p.537*

Graves, Frank P. *v.4 p.326*

Graves, Joseph L. Jr.. . . . . *v.4 p.17*

Graves, Lee *v.3 p.525*

Graves, Nadine George *v.1 p.18, p.35*

Graves, Richard P. *v.2 p.348*

Graves, Richard *v.2 p.245*

Graves, Robert (Author, Editor) *v.2 p.348*

Graves, Robert. *v.2 p.181, p.348, v.3 p.118*

Gravil, Robert *v.3 p.348*

Gray, Alasdair *v.2 p.347*

Gray, Christopher J. *v.6 p.63*

Gray, Douglas (Editor) *v.2 p.199*

Gray, Dulce Maria *v.6 p.527*

Gray, Elaine *v.5 p.242*

Gray, Frances Clayton & Lamb, Yanick
  Rice *v.4 p.832, p.836, p.864*

Gray, Fred D. *v.6 p.5*

Gray, James Henry *v.3 p.545*

Gray, Janet *v.2 p.15*

Gray, Jeremy *v.5 p.466, p.495*

Gray, Jim & Reuter, Andreas *v.5 p.337, p.338*

Gray, John Chipman *v.4 p.441*

Gray, John, et al. *v.1 p.739*

Gray, John Milner *v.6 p.66*

Gray, John S. (Editor), et al.. . . . . *v.5 p.171*

Gray, John. *v.1 p.166, p.281, p.285, v.4 p.211*

Gray, Marion W. *v.3 p.167*

Gray, Mary Lackritz *v.1 p.731*

Gray, N. F. *v.5 p.368, p.379*

Gray, Paul R., et al. *v.5 p.722*

Gray, Peter *v.3 p.138*

Gray, Piers *v.2 p.72*

Gray, Richard J. & Robinson, Owen *v.2 p.13*

Gray, Richard *v.2 p.13*

Gray, Robert F. & Gulliver, P. *v.4 p.32*

Gray, Ronald D. *v.2 p.591*

Gray, Susan Kimberly *v.1 p.799*

Gray, Terry *v.2 p.222*

Gray, Thomas *v.2 p.249*

Gray, William Glenn *v.3 p.177*

Gray, William *v.2 p.312*

Grayling, A. C. *v.1 p.447, p.492*

Graymont, Barbara *v.6 p.685*

Grayson, David *v.1 p.239, p.343*

Grayson, Edward & Bond, Catherine . *v.4 p.825, p.884, p.901*

Grayson, Jane (Editor), et al. *v.2 p.104*

Grayson, Michael A. (Editor) *v.5 p.271*

Grayzel, Solomon *v.6 p.571, p.573*

Grayzel, Susan R. *v.3 p.53, p.78, p.208*

Grazulis, Thomas P. *v.5 p.426*

Greasley, Philip A.. . . . . *v.2 p.15*

Great Books Foundation Staff (Contribution by). . . . *v.5 p.232*

Greatrex, Geoffrey & Lieu, Samuel N. C. (Editors). . *v.3 p.12*

Greaves, Harold R.. . . . . *v.4 p.631*

Greaves, Richard L. *v.2 p.241*

Greco, Albert N. *v.4 p.149*

Greeley, Andrew M. *v.4 p.720*

Greeley, Ronald & Batson, Raymond *v.5 p.63, p.68, p.69*

Green, Brent *v.4 p.138*

Green, Charles *v.4 p.142*

Green, Christopher D. & Groff, Philip R.. . . . . . *v.5 p.596*

Green, Christopher D., et al.. . . . . *v.5 p.596*

Green, Christopher D. *v.5 p.596*

Green, Christopher. *v.1 p.678, p.687, p.739*

Green, Constance McLaughlin. *v.3 p.493*

Green, Dan *v.5 p.552*

Green, David M. & Swets, John A. *v.5 p.606*

Green, Douglas B. *v.1 p.270*

Green, Dudley *v.4 p.789*

Green, Elna C. *v.4 p.519, p.568, v.6 p.431, p.454*

Green, Garrett *v.1 p.635*

Green, Gill & Sobo, E. J. *v.4 p.779, v.6 p.378*

Green, Harvey *v.4 p.126*

Green, J. Ronald. *v.6 p.329, p.341*

Green, James H., et al. *v.4 p.115*

Green, Jeff *v.1 p.160, p.170*

Green, Jesse *v.6 p.376*

Green, Joel B. (Editor), et al. *v.1 p.629*

Green, John C. & Herrnson, Paul S. (Editors) . *v.4 p.551, p.552*

Green, John C. (Editor), et al. *v.4 p.511*

Green, Julien. *v.2 p.518*

Green, Laura Morgan. *v.2 p.175, p.190*

Green, Lucy *v.1 p.379, p.405*

Green, Marianne E.. . . . . *v.4 p.169*

Green, Martin *v.2 p.245, v.5 p.723*

Green, Michael D.. . . . . *v.6 p.687, p.691*

Green, Michael. *v.6 p.224*

Green, Paul M. (Editor, Afterword by) *v.3 p.515*

Green, Penny & Ward, Tony *v.6 p.253*

Green, Peter (Editor). *v.3 p.21*

Green, Peter *v.3 p.17, p.19, p.21*

Green, Phil *v.1 p.759*

Green, Robert P. (Editor) *v.6 p.5*

Green, Roger Lancelyn & Hooper, Walter *v.2 p.366*

Green, Roger Lancelyn (Editor) *v.2 p.296*

Green, Rosario; Smith, Peter H. *v.3 p.292*

Green, Sarah F. *v.4 p.42*

Green, Scott *v.4 p.86*

Green, Stanley *v.6 p.316*

Green, Stephen W. & Ernest, Douglas J. (Editors) . . . *v.4 p.482*

Green, Thomas A. & Svinth, Joseph R. (Editors) . . . *v.4 p.863*

Green, Timothy D. & Brown, Abbie *v.4 p.351*

Green, W. John. *v.3 p.357*

Greenan, David E. & Tunnell, Gil *v.6 p.381*

Greenawalt, Kent *v.4 p.298, p.307, p.459*

Greenaway, Theresa & Dorling Kindersley Publishing
Staff. *v.5 p.168, p.175*

Greenbaum, Sidney & Nelson, Gerald *v.2 p.556*

Greenbaum, Sidney. *v.2 p.556*

Greenbaum, Susan D. *v.6 p.544, p.549*

Greenberg, Amy S. *v.3 p.381*

Greenberg, Arthur *v.5 p.262*

Greenberg, Blu. *v.1 p.553*

Greenberg, David. *v.3 p.471*

Greenberg, Ellen *v.4 p.533*

Greenberg, James B. *v.4 p.772*

Greenberg, Joseph H. *v.6 p.80, p.690*

Greenberg, Karen J. (Editor) *v.4 p.562, p.659*

Greenberg, Michael D. *v.5 p.501*

Greenberg, Moshe *v.1 p.622, v.6 p.646*

Greenberg, Richard *v.6 p.411*

Greenberg, Steven *v.6 p.374*

Greenblatt, David *v.4 p.422*

Greenblatt, Stephen (Editor). *v.2 p.196*

Greenblatt, Stephen. *v.2 p.227, p.229, v.3 p.128*

Greene, Alexis (Editor) *v.1 p.121*

Greene, Brian *v.5 p.552, p.557*

Greene, David L. & Santini, Danilo J. *v.5 p.700*

Greene, Donald *v.2 p.250*

Greene, Ellen (Editor) *v.2 p.419*

Greene, Gayle *v.2 p.364, v.6 p.478*

Greene, Graham. *v.2 p.166, p.349, p.350, p.351*

Greene, Hank *v.1 p.33*

Greene, Jack P. & Pole, J. R. (Editors) *v.3 p.409*

Greene, James H.. . . . . *v.4 p.116*

Greene, Jeffrey P.. . . . . *v.1 p.804*

Greene, John C. *v.5 p.79, p.192, p.388, p.393*

Greene, John R. *v.3 p.471, p.472*

Greene, John Robert *v.3 p.471*

Greene, Julie. *v.4 p.126*

Greene, Kathanne W.. . . . . *v.4 p.446*

Greene, Lord, et al.. . . . . *v.5 p.600*

Greene, Maxine *v.4 p.302, p.343*

Greene, Molly *v.3 p.192*

Greene, Mott T. *v.5 p.418*

Greene, Naomi. *v.6 p.338*

Greene, Paul D. & Porcello, Thomas *v.1 p.283, p.386*

Greene, Rachel. *v.1 p.771*

Greene, Richard L. (Editor) *v.2 p.199*

Greene, Richard Leighton (Author, Editor) *v.2 p.199*

Greene, Richard P. & Pick, James B.. . . . . . . *v.6 p.723*

Greene, Richard *v.1 p.215, p.239, p.332*

Greene, Robert W.. . . . . *v.2 p.460*

Greene, Robert. *v.2 p.218*

Greene, Ross W. *v.4 p.283*

Greene, Stanley A.. . . . . *v.5 p.707*

Greene, Theodora *v.5 p.294*

Greene, William H.. . . . . *v.4 p.201*

Greenfeld, Howard *v.1 p.739*

Greenfeld, Liah *v.1 p.708, v.3 p.61*

Greenfield, Gerald M.. . . . . *v.3 p.260*

Greenfield, Lesley Ripley *v.6 p.425*

Greenfield, Lois *v.1 p.26*

Greenfield, Stanley B. (Translator). *v.2 p.204*

Greenfield, Stanley B.. . . . . . *v.2 p.167, v.6 p.565*

Greenfield, Sumner M. *v.2 p.643*

Greengrass, Mark. *v.1 p.604, v.3 p.145*

Greenhalgh, Paul *v.1 p.799*

Greenhill, Pauline *v.3 p.544*

Greenhouse, Carol J., et al.. . . . . *v.4 p.33*

Greenhouse, Linda *v.4 p.467, p.536*

Greenidge, A. H. J. *v.4 p.489*

Greenleaf, Richard E.. . . . . *v.1 p.573*

Greenleaf, W. H.. . . . . *v.4 p.607*

Greenlee, Sam *v.6 p.25*

Green-Lewis, Jennifer *v.6 p.737, p.750*

Greenough, J. B.. . . . . *v.2 p.423*

Greenough, Sarah *v.1 p.766*

Greenslade, S. L. (Editor) *v.1 p.615*

Greenslade, S. L.. . . . . *v.1 p.591*

Greenslade, William *v.2 p.291*

Greenspan, Amy L.. . . . . *v.4 p.131*

Greenspan, Ralph *v.5 p.133*

Greenspan, Stanley I. & Shanker, Stuart *v.5 p.620, p.623*

Greenstein, Fred I. (Editor) *v.3 p.378*

Greenstein, Fred I. *v.3 p.472, p.483*

Greenwald, Douglas (Editor) *v.4 p.189*

Greenwald, Marilyn & Bernt, Joseph (Editors) *v.4 p.408*

Greenway, John L.. . . . . *v.2 p.624*

Greenwood, Addison & National Academy of Sciences
Staff. *v.5 p.399*

Greenwood Electronic Media *v.6 p.33, p.37*

Greenwood, Justin *v.4 p.603*

Greenwood, Norman & Earnshaw, A. *v.5 p.303*

Greenwood, Peter W. *v.6 p.255*

Greenya, John *v.4 p.536*

Greer, Allan *v.3 p.538*

Greer, Jim *v.6 p.409*

Greer, Margaret R. *v.2 p.647*

Greer, Rowan A. (Editor) *v.1 p.593*

Greer, Scott L. (Editor) *v.4 p.400*

Greever, William S. *v.3 p.518*
Greg, Walter W. *v.2 p.229*
Gregersen, Hans (Editor), et al. *v.5 p.37*
Gregersen, Niels Henrik (Editor), et al. *v.1 p.526*
Gregg, Edward *v.3 p.106, p.108*
Gregg, Gary L. & Rozell, Mark J. (Editors) *v.3 p.483*
Gregg, Robert C. (Editor) *v.1 p.591*
Gregg, Susan A. *v.4 p.12*
Gregor, A. James *v.3 p.203, v.4 p.510*
Gregor-Dellin, Martin *v.1 p.197, p.365*
Gregorich, E. G. et al. (Editors) *v.5 p.311*
Gregory, Anne *v.4 p.429*
Gregory, Brad S. *v.1 p.601*
Gregory, Cedric E. *v.5 p.738*
Gregory, Dennis E. *v.4 p.288*
Gregory, Derek & Pratt, Geraldine *v.4 p.373*
Gregory, Derek (Editor) *v.4 p.396*
Gregory, Derek, et al. *v.6 p.709*
Gregory, Derek *v.6 p.603, p.610, p.634*
Gregory, Desmond *v.3 p.265*
Gregory, Gayle H. & Chapman, Carolyn *v.4 p.349*
Gregory, Gayle H. & Kuzmich, Lin *v.4 p.349*
Gregory I, Pope *v.1 p.579*
Gregory, Ian N. *v.4 p.387*
Gregory, Isabella Augusta *v.2 p.288*
Gregory, John *v.1 p.430*
Gregory, Justina (Editor) *v.1 p.71, v.2 p.401*
Gregory, Justina *v.2 p.411*
Gregory of Tours *v.3 p.66*
Gregory, Peter N. & Getz, Daniel A. (Editors) *v.1 p.561*
Gregory, R. L. & Zangwill, O. L. *v.1 p.496*
Gregory, Raymond F. *v.4 p.446*
Gregory, Richard *v.5 p.606*
Gregory, Robert J. *v.5 p.600*
Gregory, Robin *v.1 p.389*
Gregory, Saint Bishop of Tours *v.3 p.162*
Gregory, T. Ryan (Editor) *v.5 p.140*
Gregory, Timothy *v.3 p.193*
Gregory, William A. *v.4 p.75*
Greider, William *v.4 p.246, p.561, p.664*
Greilsamer, Laurent *v.2 p.513*
Greimas, Algirdas Julien & Maupassant, Guy de . . *v.2 p.497*
Greimas, Algirdas Julien *v.2 p.453*
Greimas, Algirdas-Julien; Keane, Teresa Mary . . . *v.2 p.453*
Greiner, Alfred, et al. *v.4 p.243*
Greiner, Walter, et al. *v.5 p.560*
Greiner, Walter *v.5 p.549*
Grekova, I. *v.2 p.804*
Grellmann, Wolfgang & Seidler, Sabine *v.5 p.688*
Gremillion, Kristen J. (Editor) *v.4 p.7*
Grenberg, Bruce L. *v.2 p.48*
Grendler, Paul F. *v.3 p.199, v.4 p.334*
Grene, Marjorie & Depew, David *v.5 p.79*
Grene, Marjorie *v.1 p.454*
Grenfell, Michael *v.4 p.682*

Grenier, Guillermo & Stepick, Alex III (Editors) . *v.6 p.544, p.549*
Grenier, Guillermo J., et al. *v.6 p.538, p.544*
Grenier, Yvon *v.3 p.299*
Grente, Georges (Editor) *v.2 p.455, p.456*
Grenthe, Ingmar (Editor) *v.5 p.261*
Grenville, J. A. S. *v.4 p.629*
Grenville, Kate *v.2 p.746*
Greskovic, Robert *v.1 p.3, p.24*
Gressley, Gene M. (Editor) *v.3 p.518*
Greuter, W. (Editor), et al. *v.5 p.207*
Greve, Henrich R. *v.4 p.78*
Greven, Philip J. Jr. *v.3 p.488*
Greville, Charles *v.3 p.94, p.112*
Greville, Fulke *v.2 p.214*
Grevisse, Maurice; Goosse, André *v.2 p.453*
Grew, Joseph C. *v.3 p.458, v.6 p.226*
Grewal, J. S. *v.1 p.540, v.6 p.161*
Grey, Christopher *v.1 p.759*
Grey, Gene W. *v.5 p.37*
Grey, J. David (Editor) *v.2 p.267*
Grey, Thomas S. (Editor) *v.1 p.197, p.229, p.365*
Grey, Zane *v.2 p.78*
Gribbin, John *v.5 p.540, p.552*
Gribbin, Mary & Gribbin, John *v.5 p.539*
Grice, Paul *v.1 p.490*
Gridley, Mark C. *v.1 p.259*
Grieco, Joseph M. & Ikenberry, G. John *v.4 p.626*
Grieder, Jerome B. *v.6 p.190*
Grier, Barbara *v.6 p.359, p.391*
Grier, James W. & Burk, Ted *v.5 p.166*
Grierson, Donald E. (Editor), et al. *v.5 p.694*
Grierson, H. J. (Editor) *v.2 p.199*
Grierson, Herbert J. *v.2 p.166*
Gries, Peter Hays *v.6 p.197, p.204*
Griess, Thomas E. *v.3 p.382*
Griest, Guinevere L. *v.3 p.119*
Grieve, Alastair *v.1 p.779*
Grieves, Keith *v.3 p.78*
Grieveson, Lee *v.6 p.341*
Griffin, Alice & Thorsten, Geraldine *v.2 p.83*
Griffin, Alice *v.2 p.101, p.134*
Griffin, Dale (Editor), et al. *v.4 p.195*
Griffin, David Ray *v.1 p.639*
Griffin, Donald R. *v.6 p.291*
Griffin, Dustin H. *v.2 p.195, p.259*
Griffin, Farah J. *v.6 p.25*
Griffin, Gary A. (Editor) *v.4 p.279*
Griffin, Jack *v.4 p.173*
Griffin, Jasper *v.2 p.413*
Griffin, Joe L. & DeNevi, Don *v.6 p.259*
Griffin, John Howard *v.4 p.730*
Griffin, Miriam D. (Editor) *v.4 p.489*
Griffin, Miriam T. *v.3 p.28*
Griffin, Nicholas (Editor) *v.1 p.447*
Griffin, Patricia J. *v.4 p.815, p.839, v.6 p.384*

Griffin, Robert S.. . . . . *v.4 p.840*

Griffin, Susan M. (Editor) *v.2 p.43, v.6 p.326*

Griffin, Susan *v.5 p.584*

Griffin-Nolan, Ed. *v.3 p.302*

Griffin-Pierce, Trudy *v.6 p.703*

Griffis, William Elliot *v.6 p.227, p.236*

Griffith, Gareth. *v.2 p.309*

Griffith, H. Winter *v.4 p.827, p.828, p.829*

Griffith, James S. *v.6 p.486, p.523*

Griffith, James *v.6 p.492, p.523*

Griffith, John F. (Editor) *v.5 p.49*

Griffith, John W.. *v.2 p.341*

Griffith, Lois. *v.6 p.506, p.517*

Griffith, Niall & Todd, Peter M. (Editors). *v.1 p.375*

Griffith, Nicola & Pagel, Stephen (Editors) *v.6 p.406*

Griffith, Nicola & Pagel, Stephen *v.6 p.406*

Griffith, Nicola. *v.6 p.406*

Griffith, Robert. *v.3 p.458*

Griffith, Sally Fore *v.4 p.410*

Griffith, Susan *v.4 p.169*

Griffith, W. Thomas *v.5 p.539*

Griffiths, A., et al.. . . . . *v.5 p.133*

Griffiths, Alison *v.6 p.310*

Griffiths, Anne M. *v.4 p.32*

Griffiths, Anthony J. F., et al.. . . . . . . *v.5 p.99, p.133*

Griffiths, Antony *v.1 p.753, p.759*

Griffiths, David F. *v.5 p.552, p.564*

Griffiths, David J. *v.5 p.549*

Griffiths, Gareth, et al. *v.2 p.727*

Griffiths, Gareth *v.2 p.751*

Griffiths, Martin & O'Callaghan, Terry *v.4 p.626*

Griffiths, Martin (Editor) *v.4 p.626*

Griffiths, Martin *v.4 p.628*

Griffiths, N. E. S.. *v.3 p.543*

Griffiths, Naomi E. *v.3 p.543*

Griffiths, Nicholas *v.3 p.263, p.326*

Griffiths, Paul E. *v.5 p.653*

Griffiths, Paul *v.1 p.215, p.336*

Griffiths, Phillip & Harris, Joseph *v.5 p.497*

Griffiths, Trevor (Editor) *v.1 p.65, p.77, p.90, p.100*

Griffiths, Trevor R. *v.1 p.59*

Grigg, Carolyn D. (Compiled by) *v.1 p.160*

Grigg, David B.. . . . . *v.3 p.43, v.4 p.395, v.5 p.4, p.12*

Grigg, John. *v.3 p.94, p.117, p.118*

Grigg, Neil S. & Criswell, Marvin E. *v.5 p.685*

Grigg, Neil S. *v.5 p.19, p.368, p.380*

Griggs, William E. *v.6 p.5, p.16*

Grigorenko, E.V. *v.5 p.121*

Grijzenhout, Frans (Editor), et al. *v.1 p.731*

Griliches, Zvi & Intriligator, Michael D. (Editors). *v.4 p.189, p.201*

Grillmeier, Aloys & Hainthaler, Theresia *v.1 p.640*

Grillmeier, Aloys. *v.1 p.640*

Grillmeier, S. J., et al. *v.1 p.640*

Grillo, Evelio *v.6 p.489, p.542*

Grillparzer, Franz. *v.2 p.597*

Grima, Benedicte. *v.6 p.634*

Grimes, Kimberly M. & Milgram, B. Lynne (Editors) . *v.4 p.44*

Grimes, Michael D. & Morris, Joan M. *v.4 p.682*

Grimes, Ronald L.. *v.1 p.530*

Grimley, Daniel M. & Rushton, Julian (Editors). *v.1 p.197, p.323*

Grimley, Daniel M. (Editor). *v.1 p.215, p.356*

Grimm, Jacob & Grimm, Wilhelm K. *v.2 p.593*

Grimm, Jacob & Grimm, Wilhelm *v.2 p.592*

Grimm, Jacob W. & Grimm, Wilhelm K.. . . . . . *v.2 p.621*

Grimm, Jacob W., et al.. . . . . *v.2 p.593*

Grimmelshausen, Hans Jakob Christoph von *v.2 p.595*

Grimmelshausen, Johann J. *v.2 p.595*

Grimsley, Jim *v.6 p.396*

Grimsley, Mark & Simpson, Brooks D. (Editors) . . . *v.3 p.397*

Grimsley, Mark *v.3 p.397*

Grimsley, Ronald (Editor). *v.2 p.458*

Grimsley, Ronald. *v.2 p.482*

Grimsley, Wayne *v.3 p.502*

Grinde, Donald & Johansen, Bruce *v.6 p.681*

Grindle, Merilee S. & Domingo, Pilar *v.3 p.324*

Grindle, Merilee S.. . . . . *v.4 p.772*

Grindon, Leger. *v.6 p.314*

Gringauz, Alex. *v.5 p.329*

Grinker, Roy R. & Steiner, Christopher B.. . . . . . *v.4 p.38*

Grinker, Roy R. *v.4 p.772*

Grinker, Roy Richard *v.4 p.4*

Grinspoon, Lester & Bakalar, James B.. . . . . . . *v.3 p.281*

Grinstein, Louise S. (Editor), et al. *v.5 p.221, p.261*

Grippo, Charles *v.1 p.150*

Griset, Pamala L. & Mahan, Sue *v.6 p.251*

Griskey, Richard A.. . . . . *v.5 p.741*

Griswold del Castillo, Richard & De Leon, Arnoldo. *v.6 p.531*

Griswold del Castillo, Richard & Garcia, Richard
A. *v.4 p.126, v.6 p.489, p.526*

Griswold del Castillo, Richard (Editor), et al.. . . . . *v.6 p.492*

Griswold del Castillo, Richard *v.6 p.534, p.549*

Gritsch, Eric W. *v.1 p.585*

Grünfeld, Mihai G.. . . . . *v.2 p.666*

Grob, Alan. *v.2 p.323*

Grob, Robert L. & Barry, Eugene F. (Editors). *v.5 p.269*

Groddeck, Georg Walther *v.5 p.619*

Groden, Michael *v.2 p.358*

Grodzins, Dean *v.1 p.589*

Grodzki, Lynn & Allen, Wendy. *v.4 p.64*

Groeneveld, Richard F. *v.6 p.263*

Groenewegen, P. D. *v.4 p.215*

Groenewegen, Peter & Marshall, Alfred *v.4 p.224*

Groetsch, Charles W. *v.5 p.488*

Grofman, Bernard N. & Davidson, Chandler (Editors) . *v.4 p.461*

Grofman, Bernard N. & Lijphart, Arend (Editors) . . . *v.4 p.576*

Grofman, Bernard N. (Editor) *v.4 p.530*

Grogan, Denis Joseph. *v.5 p.405*

Grogan, Paul & Proscio, Tony *v.6 p.728*

Grogin, Robert C. *v.3 p.389*

Gronbech, Bo *v.2 p.626*
Grondin, Jean *v.1 p.507*
Gronke, Paul. *v.4 p.533*
Gronow, Pekka & Saunio, Ilpo *v.1 p.384*
Groom, A. J. R. *v.4 p.633*
Groos, Arthur & Parker, Roger
  (Editors) *v.1 p.197, p.229, p.230, p.349*
Groover, Mikell P. Jr. *v.4 p.116*
Groover, Mikell P. *v.4 p.116*
Groppa, Carlos G. *v.1 p.15, p.34*
Grose, Peter L. *v.3 p.458*
Grose, Philip Jr. *v.4 p.541*
Grosfoguel, Ramon. *v.3 p.320, v.6 p.529, p.536*
Groslier, B. P. *v.6 p.170*
Gross, David, et al. *v.5 p.481*
Gross, David. *v.5 p.610*
Gross, Ernie *v.3 p.372*
Gross, Hanns *v.3 p.201*
Gross, Harvey *v.2 p.578*
Gross, James A. (Editor) *v.4 p.131*
Gross, James A. *v.4 p.121, p.446*
Gross, Jan T. *v.3 p.84, p.229, p.254, p.255*
Gross, John (Editor) *v.2 p.199, p.202*
Gross, John . *v.2 p.175, p.202, v.3 p.112, p.120, p.128, v.6 p.740*
Gross, Jonathan L. & Tucker, Thomas W. . . . *v.5 p.480, p.499*
Gross, Larry (Editor), et al. *v.4 p.412*
Gross, Larry P. *v.4 p.416, v.6 p.390*
Gross, Larry. *v.6 p.368, p.386*
Gross, M. L. & Caprioli, R. *v.5 p.271*
Gross, Maurice. *v.5 p.503*
Gross, Michael L. & Caprioli, Richard M. (Editors) . *v.5 p.271*
Gross, Rita M. *v.1 p.528, v.6 p.459*
Gross, Robert A. *v.3 p.409, p.488*
Gross, Robert E. & West, Mona (Editors) *v.6 p.373*
Grossberg, Lawrence (Editor), et al. *v.1 p.255*
Grossel, Stanley S., et al. *v.5 p.743*
Grosseteste, Robert. *v.2 p.449*
Grossfeld, Stan. *v.1 p.766*
Grossinger, Richard. *v.5 p.243*
Grossman, Andrew David (Editor) *v.6 p.416*
Grossman,
  Avraham . *v.3 p.51, p.58, v.6 p.434, p.459, p.465, p.560, p.571*
Grossman, Dave *v.5 p.584*
Grossman, David *v.6 p.614, p.648*
Grossman, G. M. & Rogoff, K. (Editors) *v.4 p.189*
Grossman, Gene M. & Rogoff, Kenneth S. (Editors). *v.4 p.189*
Grossman, James R. (Editor), et al. *v.3 p.515*
Grossman, James R. *v.6 p.712*
Grossman, Mark & ABC-CLIO Inc. Staff,
  Inc *v.4 p.464, v.6 p.689, p.694*
Grossman, Mark (Editor) *v.4 p.516, p.557*
Grossman, Nathaniel. *v.5 p.66*
Grossman, Pamela *v.4 p.279*
Grossman, Robert B. *v.5 p.295*
Grossman, Vasily Semenovich *v.2 p.804, v.3 p.227*

Grossman, Vasily *v.2 p.804, v.3 p.227*
Grossmann, Klaus E. (Editor), et al. *v.5 p.627, p.631*
Grossmann, Reinhardt *v.1 p.464*
Grossvogel, David I. *v.1 p.82, p.85, p.92, p.96, v.2 p.461*
Grosz, Elizabeth *v.6 p.436*
Grotberg, Edith Henderson (Editor) *v.5 p.653*
Grotewold, Erich (Editor) *v.5 p.133*
Groth, Chuck *v.1 p.718*
Groth, Janet *v.2 p.137*
Groth, Paul *v.4 p.771*
Grotowski, Jerzy *v.1 p.85, p.109, p.138*
Groulx, Lionel *v.2 p.539*
Grousset, Rene *v.3 p.230*
Grout, A. J. *v.5 p.209*
Grout, Donald Jay & Williams, Hermine Weigel . . *v.1 p.230*
Grove, A. T. & Rackham, Oliver. *v.5 p.79, p.168, p.176, p.237*
Grove, A. T. *v.6 p.51*
Grove, Andrew S. *v.4 p.81*
Grove, Carol. *v.1 p.813*
Grove, Frederick Philip *v.2 p.732*
Grove, Jean M. *v.4 p.393, v.5 p.426*
Grove, Noel *v.5 p.82, p.179, p.221*
Grover, Kathryn (Editor). *v.4 p.716, p.784, p.791, p.806*
Grover, Velma I. *v.5 p.702*
Groves, Alan & Shipton, Alyn *v.1 p.259, p.348*
Groves, R. H. & Di Castri, F. (Editors) *v.5 p.168, p.237*
Groves, Robert M. (Editor), et al. *v.4 p.691*
Grow, Michael *v.3 p.344*
Grubb & Ellis *v.4 p.158*
Grubb, Kevin B. *v.1 p.8*
Grubb, W. Norton & Lazerson, Marvin. *v.4 p.305*
Grubb, W. Norton & Ryan, Paul *v.4 p.305*
Grubbs, Bruce *v.4 p.390*
Grubbs, Judith E. *v.3 p.23*
Grube, Ernst J; Sims, Eleanor G; Bayani, Manijeh; Nassar,
  Nahla *v.1 p.673, p.691*
Grube, G. M. *v.1 p.424*
Gruber, Helmut *v.3 p.184*
Gruber, Howard E. & Voneche, J. Jacques
  (Editors) *v.5 p.627, p.630*
Gruber, Ira D. *v.3 p.411*
Gruchy, Allan G. *v.4 p.247*
Gruden, Dusan (Volume Editor) *v.5 p.354, p.368*
Gruen, Erich S. *v.3 p.21, p.25, p.26*
Gruen, John *v.1 p.8, v.6 p.407*
Gruenwald, Geza. *v.5 p.320*
Gruesser, John Cullen *v.6 p.25*
Gruesser, John *v.6 p.25*
Grumet, Madeleine R. *v.4 p.282*
Grunbaum, Branko & Shephard, Geoffrey C. . . . *v.5 p.498*
Grundman, Adolph H. *v.4 p.854*
Grundy, Kenneth W. & Weinstein, Michael A. . . *v.4 p.497*
Grundy, Pamela *v.4 p.815, p.821, p.894*
Gruneau, Richard. *v.4 p.816*
Gruner, Elliott *v.6 p.322*

Grunfeld, A. Tom *v.6 p.241*
Grunfeld, Frederic V. *v.5 p.237*
Gruntman, Mike *v.5 p.719*
Grunwald, Ernest. *v.5 p.279*
Grunwald, Geza *v.5 p.320*
Grunwald, Michael *v.4 p.541*
Grupp, Hariolf *v.4 p.241*
Grusa, Jiri *v.2 p.783*
Grusin, Richard *v.1 p.818, v.5 p.18, v.6 p.297*
Gruskin, Elisabeth Paige *v.6 p.377*
Grusky, David B. (Editor). *v.4 p.722*
Grut, Marina *v.1 p.20*
Gruzinksi, Serge *v.3 p.263*
Grynberg, Michal (Editor) *v.3 p.84*
Gryphius, Andreas *v.2 p.595*
Gryskiewicz, Stan & Taylor, Sylvester. *v.4 p.66*
Grzymala-Busse, Anna *v.4 p.601*
Gschneidner, K. A. Jr. & Eyring, Leroy (Editors) . . *v.5 p.308*
Gschneidner, K. A. Jr. & Eyring, LeRoy *v.5 p.308*
Guajardo, Paul. *v.6 p.499, p.512*
Guardia, Ricardo F. *v.3 p.303*
Guardino, Peter F. *v.3 p.289*
Guardino, Peter *v.3 p.285*
Guarini, Battista *v.2 p.708*
Guarino-Ghezzi, Susan & Loughran, Edward J. . . . *v.6 p.248*
Guarracino, F. & Walker, A.. . . . . *v.5 p.694*
Guastalla, Giorgio & Guastalla, Guido *v.1 p.756*
Gubar, Susan & Hoff, Joan (Editors) *v.4 p.748*
Gubbins, David *v.5 p.442, p.443, p.444*
Gudykunst, William B. *v.5 p.647*
Guede, Alain *v.1 p.189, p.281, p.352*
Guelzo, Allen C. *v.1 p.582*
Guenther, Herbert V. *v.1 p.565*
Gueraseva, Stacy *v.1 p.384*
Guerin, Philip J. Jr. (Editor) *v.5 p.668*
Guerin-Gonzales, Camille. *v.6 p.525, p.529*
Guernsey, Otis L. Jr. & Sweet, Jeffrey
   (Editors). *v.1 p.65, p.66, p.114, p.115*
Guernsey, Otis L. Jr. (Editor). *v.1 p.65, p.114*
Guernsey, Otis L. Jr.. . . . . *v.1 p.65, p.114*
Guerra, Lillian *v.3 p.309*
Guesnerie, Roger *v.4 p.201, p.250*
Guest, Ann H., et al.. . . . . *v.1 p.45*
Guest, Ann Hutchinson *v.1 p.38*
Guest, Ivor F. (Editor, Translator) *v.1 p.39*
Guest, Ivor F.. . . . . *v.1 p.8, p.24*
Guest, Ivor. *v.1 p.8*
Guest, Kenneth J. *v.6 p.105, p.126*
Guevremont, Germaine *v.2 p.539*
Guggenheim, E. A.. . . . . *v.5 p.275*
Gugler, Josef *v.6 p.15, p.30, p.333, p.718*
Guha, Ranajit (Editor) *v.6 p.146*
Guha, Ranajit *v.6 p.157*
Guha, Sumit *v.6 p.161*
Guiat, Cyrille *v.4 p.594, p.609*

Guibernau, Montserrat *v.4 p.494*
Guibet, Jean-Claude & Faure-Birchem, Emmanuelle. *v.5 p.742*
Guicciardini, Niccoló *v.5 p.466*
Guicharnaud, Jacques & Guicharnaud, June. *v.2 p.461*
Guidolotti, Pino *v.1 p.793*
Guidot, Raymond (Editor). *v.1 p.717*
Guidry, John A. (Editor), et al. *v.3 p.302*
Guignon, Charles & Hiley, David (Editors) *v.1 p.441*
Guignon, Charles B. *v.1 p.505*
Guignon, Charles (Editor) *v.1 p.470*
Guilbault, Jocelyne, et al. *v.1 p.292*
Guilbert, John M. & Park, Charles F. Jr. *v.5 p.436, p.450*
Guilford, J. P. *v.5 p.599*
Guillaume, Alfred *v.1 p.556*
Guillaume, de Lorris & Jean, de Meun. *v.2 p.467*
Guillaume, de Lorris *v.2 p.467*
Guillaumin, Emile *v.3 p.155*
Guillen, Mauro F. *v.3 p.348*
Guilleragues, Gabriel Joseph de Lavergne *v.2 p.473*
Guillermo, Artemio R. *v.6 p.179*
Guillermoprieto, Alma *v.1 p.20, p.28, p.30, v.3 p.309*
Guillet, David *v.3 p.330*
Guillet de Monthoux, Pierre. *v.4 p.215*
Guillet, Edwin Clarence *v.3 p.539, p.544*
Guillevic, Eugène *v.2 p.518*
Guillén, Jorge *v.2 p.654, p.658*
Guillén, Nicolas *v.2 p.672*
Guillén, Nicolás *v.2 p.672*
Guillory, John *v.2 p.163*
Guindon, Hubert *v.3 p.543*
Guiney, Louise I. *v.2 p.39*
Guinn, David E. & Orenstein, Harold *v.1 p.150*
Guirdham, Maureen *v.4 p.132*
Guisso, Richard W., et al.. . . . . *v.6 p.184, p.202*
Gujarati, Damodar N.. . . . . *v.4 p.201*
Gujarati *v.4 p.201*
Gulanick, Meg & Myers, Judith L. (Editors) *v.5 p.527*
Gullace, Nicoletta F. *v.3 p.53, p.79, v.4 p.604*
Gullan, P. J. & Cranston, P. S.. . . . . *v.5 p.213*
Gullan, P. J.; Cranston, P. S.. . . . . *v.5 p.213*
Gullette, David. *v.3 p.302*
Gulley, Norman *v.1 p.424*
Gullón, Germán *v.2 p.641*
Gullón, Ricardo *v.2 p.639*
Gullick, J. M. (Compiled by) *v.6 p.164*
Gullickson, Arlen R. *v.5 p.604*
Gulliford, Andrew *v.1 p.822, v.6 p.701*
Gulliver, P. H.. . . . . *v.4 p.38*
Gulliver, Philip H. & Silverman, Marilyn *v.4 p.42*
Gump, Margaret *v.2 p.599*
Gumpert, Gary & Drucker, Susan J. (Editors) *v.4 p.408, p.906*
Gumperz, John J. & Levinson, Stephen C. (Editors) . *v.4 p.20*
Gumperz, John J. (Editor, Contribution by) *v.5 p.623*
Gumport, Patricia J. *v.6 p.462*
Gunaratne, Shelton A. (Editor). *v.4 p.415*

Gundel, Marc *v.1 p.718, p.720*

Gundersen, Joan R.. . . . . *v.6 p.452*

Gunderson, Robert Gray *v.3 p.365, p.420*

Gundle, Stephen & Parker, Simon (Editors). *v.4 p.594*

Gundolf, Friedrich *v.2 p.599*

Gunesekera, Romesh *v.2 p.760*

Gunn, Elizabeth *v.2 p.322*

Gunn, Giles. *v.2 p.48*

Gunn, Ian & Hart, Clive *v.2 p.358*

Gunn, John (Editor) *v.5 p.424*

Gunn, Simon. *v.6 p.743*

Gunn, Thom *v.6 p.404*

Gunning, Thomas G. *v.4 p.363*

Gunston, Bill (Editor). *v.5 p.717*

Gunston, Bill *v.4 p.151*

Gunstone, Frank D., Harwood, John L.. . . . . *v.5 p.329*

Gunter, Barrie, et al. *v.4 p.140, p.427*

Gunter, Michael M.. . . . . *v.4 p.640, p.666, v.6 p.598*

Gunther, Gerald *v.4 p.441*

Gunther, Richard, et al. *v.4 p.608*

Gunther, Werner *v.2 p.620*

Gunton, Colin E. (Editor) *v.1 p.635*

Gunton, Colin E.. . . . . *v.1 p.635*

Guo, Yugui *v.4 p.334*

Guohua, Xu & Peel, L. J. (Editors). *v.5 p.4*

Guppy, Shusha. *v.6 p.631*

Gupta, Akhil & Ferguson, James (Editors) *v.4 p.23*

Gupta, Akhil *v.4 p.34*

Gupta, Avijit (Editor) *v.4 p.384*

Gupta, Chiranjib Kumar *v.5 p.732*

Gupta, Dipankar *v.6 p.154*

Gupta, G. S.. . . . . *v.5 p.116, p.153*

Gupta, R. P. *v.4 p.388*

Gupta, Ram S. *v.5 p.704*

Gupta, Ravi P. *v.5 p.420*

Gupta, Sunil & Lehmann, Donald *v.4 p.143*

Gupta, U. S. *v.5 p.21*

Gura, Philip F. & Bollman, James F.. . . . . . *v.1 p.277, p.389*

Gura, Philip F.. . . . . *v.3 p.485*

Gurak, Laura J. & Lannon, John M. *v.5 p.680*

Guralnick, Peter. *v.1 p.259, p.270, p.334, p.348*

Guran, Ardeshir (Editor), et al. *v.5 p.694*

Gurevich, A. J.. . . . . *v.6 p.563*

Gurevich, Aron I.. . . . . *v.6 p.571*

Gurganus, Allan *v.6 p.378, p.396*

Gurnett, Donald A. & Bhattacharjee, Amitava. *v.5 p.566*

Gurney, O. R. *v.3 p.6*

Gurr, Andrew *v.1 p.76, p.100, p.144, v.2 p.227, p.229*

Gurr, M. I. *v.5 p.34*

Guru, Bhag & Warrier, Ravi K. *v.5 p.721*

Guru, Bhag S. & Hiziroglu, Huseyin R. *v.5 p.723*

Guruswamy, Rosemary Fithian *v.2 p.29*

Gurvich, L. V.; Veyts, I. V.; Alcock, C. B. *v.5 p.286*

Gusfield, Joseph R.. . . . . *v.4 p.776, v.5 p.663*

Guss, David M. *v.3 p.267, p.360*

Gustafson, Alrik (Introduction by) *v.2 p.624*

Gustafson, Alrik *v.2 p.629*

Gustav, Bergmann *v.5 p.401*

Gustavson, Carl G. *v.3 p.234*

Gustavsson, Nora S. & Segal, Elizabeth A.. . . . . . *v.4 p.756*

Gustav-Wrathall, John Donald. . . . *v.4 p.719, v.6 p.365, p.384*

Gut, Allan *v.5 p.484*

Gutek, Barbara A.. . . . . *v.4 p.253*

Gutek, Gerald L.. . . . . *v.4 p.326, p.343*

Guth, Alan H.. . . . . *v.5 p.71*

Guthman, Julie *v.5 p.31*

Guthrie, A. B. Jr. *v.2 p.78*

Guthrie, Christine & Fink, Gerald R. (Volume Editors). *v.5 p.153*

Guthrie, Edwin R. *v.5 p.571*

Guthrie, James W. (Editor) *v.4 p.322*

Guthrie, Janet *v.4 p.836, p.848*

Guthrie, John T. & Givermann, Donna E. (Editors) . . *v.4 p.354*

Guthrie, John T. (Editor), et al. *v.4 p.363*

Guthrie, R. Dale. *v.1 p.668, v.4 p.17*

Guthrie, Ramon *v.2 p.79*

Guthrie, Robert V. *v.5 p.596*

Guthrie, Tyrone *v.1 p.140, p.152*

Guthrie, W. K. C. *v.1 p.420, p.427*

Guthrie, William K *v.1 p.532*

Guthrie, William Keith Chambers *v.1 p.532*

Guthrie, Woody *v.1 p.296, p.328*

Gutierrez, Andrew Paul. *v.5 p.184, p.188*

Gutierrez, Donald. *v.2 p.114*

Gutierrez Elorza, M. *v.4 p.391*

Gutierrez, Felix F. & Schement, Jorge Reina *v.6 p.493*

Gutierrez, Gustavo *v.1 p.643*

Gutierrez, Jose Angel *v.6 p.489, p.538, p.540*

Gutierrez, Margo (Author, Contribution by). *v.6 p.540*

Gutierrez, Ramon A.. . . . . *v.6 p.534*

Gutiérrez, David G. . . *v.4 p.764, v.6 p.521, p.529, p.536, p.538*

Gutjahr, Paul C. (Editor). *v.2 p.20*

Gutman, Arthur *v.4 p.131*

Gutman, Bill & Frederick, Shawn *v.4 p.857*

Gutman, Israel *v.3 p.84*

Gutman, Roy & Rieff, David (Editors) *v.4 p.652*

Gutmann, Amy & Thompson, Dennis *v.4 p.504*

Gutmann, Amy (Editor). *v.4 p.524*

Gutmann, Viktor *v.5 p.309*

Guttenplan, Samuel (Editor). *v.1 p.496*

Guttentag, Roger M.. . . . . *v.4 p.159*

Gutting, Gary (Editor) *v.1 p.459, v.5 p.399, p.402*

Gutting, Gary *v.1 p.456*

Guttman, Joseph *v.5 p.640*

Guttmann, Allen & Thompson, Lee B.. . . . . . *v.4 p.806, p.834*

Guttmann,
  Allen . *v.4 p.715, p.806, p.816, p.836, p.845, p.846, v.6 p.437*

Guttsman, Willi *v.3 p.170*

Gutwirth, Madelyn *v.2 p.500*

Gutzwiller, Kathryn J. *v.2 p.421*

Gutzwiller, M. C.. . . . . *v.5 p.546*

Guy, John S. *v.3 p.100*
Guy, Josephine (Editor) *v.2 p.175*
Guy, Nancy *v.1 p.288*
Guyer, Paul (Editor) *v.1 p.461*
Guyotat, Pierre *v.2 p.530*
Guy-Sheftall, Beverly (Editor) *v.6 p.427*
Guyton, Arthur C. & Hall, John E. *v.5 p.164*
Guzman, Kristin *v.6 p.492*
Guzmán, Martín Luis *v.2 p.668*
Gvosdev, Nikolas K. *v.3 p.213*
Gwartney, James D. *v.4 p.189*
Gwin, Minrose C. *v.6 p.478*
Gwynne, Margaret Anderson *v.4 p.44*
Gyani, Gabor *v.3 p.186, p.187*
Gyatso, Janet & Havnevik, Hanna *v.6 p.241*
Gyatso, Janet *v.6 p.241*
Gyekye, Kwame. *v.6 p.36*
Gygax, Franziska. *v.2 p.121*
Gyory, Andrew *v.6 p.118, p.123, p.126*

H

H. Bennett, (Editor) *v.5 p.407*
H. D. *v.2 p.88, p.89, p.111*
H. W. Wilson Company. *v.5 p.571*
Haac, Oscar A. *v.2 p.480, p.498*
Haack, Susan & Lane, Robert (Editors) *v.1 p.513*
Haack, Susan *v.1 p.493*
Haak, Bob. *v.1 p.731*
Haakonssen, Knud *v.1 p.437, p.491*
Haar, Ingo & Fahlbusch, Michael (Editors) . . . *v.3 p.84, p.171*
Haas, Christopher *v.3 p.10*
Haas, Ernst B., et al. *v.5 p.410, p.412*
Haas, Ernst B. *v.4 p.626, p.629, p.637*
Haas, Ken (Photographer) *v.1 p.20*
Haas, Kenneth C. & Alpert, Geoffrey P. (Editors) . . . *v.6 p.274*
Haas, Linda (Editor), et al. *v.6 p.465, p.466*
Haas, Lisbeth *v.6 p.531*
Haas, Michael E. *v.4 p.634*
Haas, Michael *v.3 p.389*
Haas, Robert, et al. *v.1 p.174*
Haas, Violet B. & Perrucci, Carolyn C. (Editors) . . . *v.5 p.398*
Haass, Richard N. & O'Sullivan, Meghan L. (Editors). *v.4 p.642*
Haass, Richard N. *v.3 p.483*
Habashi, Fathi (Editor) *v.5 p.732*
Habeck, Mary *v.4 p.659*
Habeeb, William M. & Zartman, I. William. *v.3 p.304*
Habegger, Alfred *v.2 p.4, p.43*
Habegger, Jerryll *v.1 p.805*
Habel, Dorothy. *v.1 p.797*
Habel, Janette *v.3 p.309*
Habell-Pall'an, Michelle & Romero, Mary (Editors) . *v.6 p.493*
Habell-Pallan, Michelle. *v.6 p.491, p.512*
Haber, Jeffry R. *v.4 p.105*
Haber, Stephen, ed. *v.3 p.285*

Haber, Stephen H. *v.3 p.289*
Haberfeld, M. R. *v.6 p.263*
Haberly, David T. *v.2 p.691*
Haberman, David L. *v.1 p.536*
Haberman, Donald *v.2 p.133*
Habermas,
    Jürgen . *v.1 p.468, p.482, p.490, p.522, v.4 p.484, p.494, p.511,*
                              p.765, p.767, v.5 p.620
Habermas, Jurgen *v.1 p.495, v.4 p.696, p.770*
Habermas *v.1 p.482*
Habib, Irfan (Editor) *v.6 p.155, p.156*
Habib, M. A. R. *v.2 p.573*
Habiby, Emile *v.6 p.659*
Habicht, Christian *v.2 p.433, v.3 p.12, p.21*
Habinek, Thomas N. *v.2 p.424*
Habing, H. J. & Olofsson, Hans (Editors) *v.5 p.70*
Haboush, JaHyun Kim (Editor, Translator, Annotations by,
    Introduction by) *v.6 p.237*
Haboush, JaHyun Kim (Editor) *v.6 p.236*
Haboush, JaHyun Kim *v.6 p.236*
Haccou, Patsy, et al. *v.5 p.184, p.188*
Haché, Alain *v.4 p.862, p.871*
Hachten, William A. *v.4 p.403*
Hack, Robert (Editor), et al. *v.5 p.698*
Hacker, Andrew *v.4 p.730*
Hacker, Jacob & Pierson, Paul. *v.4 p.553*
Hacker, Kenneth L. *v.4 p.696*
Hacker, Marilyn (Compiled by) *v.2 p.146*
Hacker, Marilyn *v.2 p.146, v.6 p.404, p.405*
Hacker, P. M. *v.1 p.468, p.502*
Hackett, Robin *v.2 p.190*
Hackett, Rosalind I. (Editor) *v.6 p.71*
Hackh, Ingo Waldemar Dagobert *v.5 p.258*
Hacking, Ian *v.5 p.402, p.470, p.484*
Hackley, Chris *v.4 p.140*
Hadas, Moses *v.2 p.400*
Hadda, Janet. *v.2 p.120*
Haddad, Michael *v.6 p.352*
Haddad, Robert M *v.6 p.600, p.606*
Haddad, William W. & Ochsenwald, William L.
    (Editors) *v.6 p.590*
Haddad, Yvonne Yazbeck & Esposito, John L. (Editors). *v.6 p.592*
Haddad, Yvonne Yazbeck & Esposito, John L. *v.1 p.558*
Haddad, Yvonne Yazbeck & Smith, Jane I. (Editors). *v.1 p.554*
Haddad, Yvonne Yazbeck & Stowasser, Barbara Freyer. *v.1 p.556*
Hadden, Peggy. *v.1 p.664*
Haddon, Mark *v.2 p.351*
Hadenius, Stig *v.3 p.235*
Hadfield, Andrew. *v.2 p.169*
Hadjian, Asadour *v.5 p.694*
Hadjimatheou, George *v.4 p.232, p.245, p.250*
Hadjor, Kofi B. *v.4 p.573*
Hadleigh, Boze *v.6 p.408, p.416*
Hadley, Elaine *v.6 p.754, p.758*
Hadlock, Charles. *v.5 p.473, p.502*
Hadow, G. E., et al. *v.2 p.249*

Haeberle, Erwin J. & Gindorf, Rolf
  (Editors) *v.4 p.750, v.6 p.370, p.372*

Haeckel, Ernst *v.5 p.230*

Haefner, James W. *v.5 p.91, p.93, p.502*

Haeri, Niloofar *v.6 p.637*

Haetta, Odd Mathis *v.3 p.232*

Haeussler, Ernest F., et al. *v.4 p.175, v.5 p.503*

Hafen, Leroy R. (Editor) *v.3 p.520*

Hafen, Leroy R. *v.3 p.522, p.526*

Hafer, R. W. *v.4 p.155*

Hafez, Kai & Paletz, David L. (Editors) . . . *v.4 p.415*

Hafez, Mohammed Zakirul *v.4 p.61*

Haffenden, John (Editor) *v.2 p.329*

Haffenden, John *v.2 p.61*

Haffenden, Philip Spencer *v.3 p.485*

Hafiz, Shamsedin *v.6 p.671*

Hafiz *v.6 p.671*

Haft, Lloyd (Editor) *v.6 p.211*

Hagan, John & McCarthy, Bill *v.6 p.255*

Hagan, Kenneth J. & Roberts, William R. (Editors) . *v.3 p.382*

Hagan, Philip (Editor), et al. *v.5 p.682*

Hagan, Philip, et al. *v.5 p.682*

Hagberg, Karen A. *v.1 p.395, p.398*

Hage, Jerald & Powers, Charles *v.4 p.733*

Hagedorn, Jessica (Editor) *v.6 p.91*

Hagedorn, Jessica *v.6 p.100, p.103*

Hagedorn, John M. *v.4 p.753*

Hagedorn, Katherine J. *v.1 p.292*

Hagel, John & Brown, John Seely *v.4 p.73*

Hagen, Uta & Frankel, Haskel *v.1 p.144*

Hagen, William W. *v.3 p.181*

Hagener, Malte; Töteberg, Michael *v.6 p.305*

Hagg, Tomas & Rousseau, Philip (Editors) . . . *v.2 p.401*

Hagg, Tomas *v.2 p.405*

Haggard, H. Rider *v.2 p.290*

Haggard, Stephan & Kaufman, Robert R. . . . *v.4 p.487, p.504*

Haggard, William *v.4 p.558*

Hagger, Martin & Chatzisarantis, Nikos *v.5 p.582*

Haggerty, George (Editor) *v.4 p.748, v.6 p.358, p.363*

Hagopian, Frances *v.3 p.340*

Hagstrom, Robert G. Jr. *v.4 p.848, p.888, p.896, p.902*

Hague, Paul N. & Hague, Nick *v.4 p.135*

Hahl-Koch, Jelena *v.1 p.739*

Hahm, Sung D. & Plein, L. Christopher *v.4 p.621*

Hahn, Kimiko *v.6 p.100, p.103*

Hahn, Lewis E. & Schilpp, Paul Arthur (Editors) . *v.1 p.443*

Hahn, Lewis E. (Editor) *v.1 p.441, p.468*

Hahn, Otto *v.5 p.261*

Hahn, Robert A. (Editor) *v.4 p.44*

Hahn, Roger *v.5 p.385, p.396*

Hahner, June E. (Editor) *v.3 p.283*

Hahner, June E. *v.3 p.336*

Haidt, Jonathan *v.5 p.670*

Haig, Alan *v.3 p.112, p.120*

Haig, Alexander M. *v.3 p.472*

Haig, Matt *v.4 p.142*

Haig, Stirling *v.2 p.474, p.501*

Haigh, Christopher (Editor) *v.3 p.100, p.120*

Haigh, Christopher *v.1 p.604, p.609*

Haigh, John *v.5 p.481*

Haigh, R. H., et al. *v.4 p.631, p.645*

Haigh, Sam *v.2 p.537*

Haigh *v.3 p.100*

Haight, G. Timothy & Singer, Daniel D. . . . *v.4 p.95, p.166*

Haight, Gordon S. *v.2 p.287*

Haight, Roger *v.1 p.635, p.655*

Haiken, Elizabeth *v.4 p.774, v.6 p.443*

Haile, Harry G. *v.2 p.593*

Haile, J. M. *v.5 p.287, p.551*

Haim, Soleyman *v.6 p.669*

Haiman, Franklyn S. & Haiman, Franklyn Saul . . *v.4 p.459*

Haiman, Franklyn S. *v.4 p.459*

Haimo, Ethan *v.1 p.189, p.215, p.239, p.330, p.353*

Haimson, Leopold H. *v.3 p.220*

Haines, Alan H. *v.5 p.295*

Haines, Aubrey L. *v.3 p.525*

Haines, Charles Grove *v.4 p.454*

Haines, David W. (Editor) *v.4 p.570, v.6 p.139, p.140*

Haines, John *v.1 p.177*

Hainstock, Elizabeth G. *v.4 p.343*

Hainsworth, Peter, et al. *v.2 p.698*

Hainsworth, Peter *v.2 p.706*

Hair, Donald S. *v.2 p.313*

Hais, Karel, et al. *v.2 p.774*

Haisston, Ann J. *v.5 p.179*

Hajdu, David *v.1 p.259, p.361, v.6 p.409*

Hajian, Harry G. *v.5 p.266*

Hajnal, Peter I. (Editor) *v.4 p.630, p.640*

Hajnal, Peter I. *v.4 p.630*

Hake, Kathryn *v.4 p.305*

Hake, Sabine *v.6 p.338*

Hakeda, Yoshita S. (Translator) *v.6 p.221*

Hakeda, Yoshito S. *v.1 p.563*

Haken, H. *v.5 p.561*

Hakim, Catherine *v.4 p.733*

Hakim, Ida, et al. *v.6 p.36, p.38*

Hakon, Sven & Stockenstrom, Goran (Editors) . . *v.2 p.629*

Hakuseki, Arai *v.6 p.227*

Halberstam, David & Stout, Glenn (Editors) . . . *v.2 p.19*

Halberstam,
  David *v.3 p.472, v.4 p.408, p.410, p.806, p.823, p.854,
                      p.858, p.896, p.902, p.906*

Halberstam, Judith *v.6 p.318, p.368, p.370, p.429*

Halbertal, Moshe & Margalit, Avishai *v.1 p.527*

Halbrook, Stephen P. *v.3 p.244*

Halden-Brown, Susan *v.5 p.582*

Haldon, John F. *v.3 p.193*

Hale, Bruce (Editor) *v.4 p.865*

Hale, Charles A. *v.3 p.289, p.292*

Hale, Charles R. *v.3 p.302*

Hale, Francis J. *v.5 p.719*

Hale, Grace E. *v.3 p.496*
Hale, Horatio *v.6 p.682, p.690, p.701, p.703*
Hale, J. R. *v.3 p.35, p.70*
Hale, Janice E. *v.4 p.310*
Hale, John Rigby. *v.4 p.766*
Hale, John *v.3 p.70*
Hale, Mason E., et al. *v.5 p.210*
Hale, Mason E. *v.5 p.210*
Hale, William *v.6 p.621*
Halebsky, Sandor & Kirk, John M. (Editors) *v.3 p.309*
Halebsky, Sandor (Editor), et al. *v.3 p.310*
Halecki, Oscar *v.3 p.206*
Halecki, Oskar *v.3 p.206*
Hales, Robert E. (Editor), et al. *v.5 p.517*
Haley, Alex *v.6 p.5*
Haley, Bruce *v.6 p.763*
Haley, James L. *v.3 p.508*
Haley, Jay & Hoffman, Lynn *v.5 p.668*
Haley, John O. *v.4 p.475, v.6 p.219*
Haley, Michael C. & Lunsford, Ronald F. *v.2 p.560*
Halévy, Elie *v.3 p.112*
Halfon, Neal (Editor), et al. *v.5 p.641*
Halford, Nigel G. (Editor). *v.5 p.218*
Halford, Nigel G. *v.5 p.7, p.21*
Halfpenny, Peter *v.4 p.680*
Halfyard, Janet K. *v.1 p.255*
Haliburton, Thomas Chandler *v.2 p.732*
Haliczer, Stephen *v.3 p.55, p.59, p.239*
Halio, Jay (Editor) *v.2 p.389*
Halkin, A. S. *v.6 p.646*
Hall, A. Rupert *v.3 p.47, v.5 p.391*
Hall, Allan, et al. *v.4 p.902, p.906*
Hall, Brian K. & Hallgrímsson, Benedikt (Editors) . . *v.5 p.192*
Hall, Brian K. *v.5 p.160*
Hall, Brian Keith & Olson, Wendy (Editors) *v.5 p.160*
Hall, Calvin S. *v.5 p.659*
Hall, Carl W. *v.5 p.407*
Hall, Carolyn & Brignoli, Hector Perez. . . *v.3 p.298, v.4 p.399*
Hall, Catherine, et al. *v.6 p.758*
Hall, Catherine *v.6 p.434, p.746*
Hall, Charles J. (Compiled by) *v.1 p.189, p.197, p.215*
Hall, Charles J. *v.1 p.277*
Hall, Charles John *v.1 p.174*
Hall, Cheryl Ann *v.5 p.643*
Hall, Christopher A. *v.1 p.616*
Hall, Christopher D. *v.5 p.322*
Hall, Clifton D. & Coleman, Samuel S. *v.2 p.595*
Hall, Colin M. *v.5 p.371*
Hall, Colin Michael & Boyd, Stephen W. *v.5 p.357*
Hall, D. J. *v.3 p.539*
Hall, Daniel G. *v.6 p.164*
Hall, David D. *v.1 p.584, v.3 p.405*
Hall, Derek R. *v.4 p.259*
Hall, Donald E. *v.1 p.374*
Hall, Donald (Editor) *v.2 p.23*

Hall, Donald *v.2 p.4, p.82*
Hall, Doug & Fifer, Sally Jo (Editors) *v.1 p.771*
Hall, Edward T. *v.4 p.696*
Hall, Edwin *v.1 p.740*
Hall, Fred M. *v.1 p.260, p.314*
Hall, G. D. (Editor) *v.3 p.98*
Hall, G. Emlen *v.6 p.300*
Hall, Gordon C. Nagayama & Okazaki, Sumie (Editors). *v.6 p.122*
Hall, Granville Davisson *v.3 p.499*
Hall, Gwendolyn M. *v.4 p.728*
Hall, J. R. *v.2 p.206, p.550*
Hall, James & Steinmann, Martin *v.2 p.326*
Hall, Jeffrey C. (Editor), et al. *v.5 p.133*
Hall, Jerome *v.4 p.434*
Hall, Joan Houston (Editor) *v.2 p.552*
Hall, Joan W. *v.2 p.90*
Hall, John A. & Trentmann, Frank (Editors) *v.4 p.498*
Hall, John A. (Editor). *v.4 p.494*
Hall, Jonathan M. *v.3 p.14*
Hall, Joseph *v.2 p.214*
Hall, Kenneth B. & Porterfield, Gerald A. . *v.1 p.797, v.6 p.728*
Hall, Kermit, et al. *v.4 p.466, p.537*
Hall, Kermit L. & McGuire, Kevin T. (Editors) . . . *v.4 p.534*
Hall, Kermit L. (Editor) *v.4 p.454, p.534*
Hall, Kermit L. *v.4 p.440*
Hall, Kim F. *v.6 p.478*
Hall, Lesley & Porter, Roy *v.3 p.55*
Hall, Linda B. & Coerver, Don M. *v.3 p.292*
Hall, M. Ann *v.4 p.806, p.813, p.836, v.6 p.437*
Hall, Marcia B. (Editor, Contribution by) . . . *v.1 p.675, p.687*
Hall, Marcia (Editor) *v.1 p.697, p.740*
Hall, Marie B. *v.5 p.385, p.391*
Hall, Marshall *v.5 p.474*
Hall, Martin. *v.6 p.74*
Hall, Michael (Editor) *v.1 p.198, p.235, p.354*
Hall, Michael R. *v.3 p.317*
Hall, N. John *v.2 p.316*
Hall, Nigel (Editor), et al. *v.4 p.368*
Hall, Nina (Editor) *v.5 p.265*
Hall, Patricia Wong & Hwang, Victor M. (Editors) . *v.6 p.123*
Hall, Perry A. *v.6 p.5, p.14*
Hall, Peter. *v.1 p.139, p.152,v.6 p.712, p.726, p.728*
Hall, R. & Blundell, D. J. (Editors) *v.5 p.432*
Hall, Radclyffe *v.2 p.351, v.6 p.397*
Hall, Rex & Shayler, David *v.5 p.719*
Hall, Richard C. *v.3 p.251*
Hall, Richard Seymour. *v.6 p.51*
Hall, Richard *v.4 p.378*
Hall, Robert T. *v.4 p.681*
Hall, Robert *v.4 p.489*
Hall, Rodney Bruce & Biersteker, Thomas J. (Editors). *v.4 p.663*
Hall, Spencer & Ramsey, Jonathan (Editors) *v.2 p.323*
Hall, Steven K. *v.5 p.266*
Hall, Stuart & du Gay, Paul (Editors) *v.2 p.571*

Hall, Susan J. *v.4 p.908*
Hall, Susan T. *v.4 p.360*
Hall, Thomas E. & Ferguson, J. David *v.4 p.213*
Hall, Tim *v.4 p.395, v.6 p.721*
Hall, Timothy L. & Moose, Christian J. (Editors) . . . *v.4 p.629*
Halladay, Eric *v.4 p.816, p.865*
Hallam, Arne *v.5 p.4*
Hallam, Arthur Henry *v.2 p.290*
Hallam, Elizabeth M. & Everard, Judith . . *v.3 p.143, v.6 p.568*
Hallam, Tony *v.5 p.450*
Hallaq, Wael B. *v.1 p.556*
Hallas, James H. (Editor) *v.3 p.472*
Hallberg, M. C. (Editor) *v.5 p.12*
Hallberg, Milton C. *v.5 p.14*
Hallberg, Peter *v.2 p.624, p.625*
Halldór Hermannsson *v.2 p.624*
Halldór Laxness *v.2 p.625*
Halle, Louis J. *v.3 p.389*
Hallen, B. *v.1 p.476*
Hallenbeck, Cleve *v.3 p.403*
Haller, John S. Jr. & Haller, Robin M. *v.4 p.774*
Haller, William & Davies, Godfrey *v.3 p.103*
Hallett, Christopher H. *v.1 p.775*
Hallett, Michael A. *v.6 p.276*
Halley, Janet E. *v.6 p.389*
Halliday, David, et al. *v.5 p.539, p.546*
Halliday, F. E. *v.2 p.291*
Halliday, Fred *v.6 p.592, p.593, p.628*
Halliday, M. A. K. *v.2 p.561*
Hallin, Daniel C. *v.4 p.407, p.414*
Halline, Allan G. *v.2 p.25*
Halliwell, Ruth *v.1 p.189, p.343*
Hallmundsson, Hallberg *v.2 p.624*
Hallowell, A. Irving *v.4 p.35*
Hallowell, Gerald (Editor) *v.3 p.536*
Halls, Peter, et al. *v.4 p.387, v.5 p.28*
Hall-Wallace, Michelle K., et al. *v.4 p.387*
Halm, Heinz *v.6 p.636*
Halman, Talat S. (Editor, Introduction by) *v.6 p.666*
Halman, Talat S., et al. *v.6 p.666*
Halman, Talat S. *v.6 p.665, p.666*
Halmos, P. R. *v.5 p.466, p.471, p.472*
Halpenny, Francess (Editor) *v.3 p.534*
Halper, Jeff *v.6 p.610*
Halper, Stefan & Clarke, Jonathan *v.4 p.516*
Halperin, Charles J. *v.3 p.215*
Halperin, David M. *v.6 p.364*
Halperin, John *v.2 p.267*
Halperin, Maurice *v.3 p.310*
Halperin-Kaddari, Ruth *v.6 p.614*
Halpern, Daniel *v.5 p.232*
Halpern, Diane F. *v.5 p.608*
Halpern, Joseph *v.2 p.527*
Halpern, Martin *v.4 p.122, p.126*
Halpern, Paul *v.5 p.557*

Halpern, Sue *v.2 p.160*
Halpin, Anne M. (Editor) *v.5 p.43*
Halsaa, Beatrice (Editor), et al. *v.6 p.434*
Halsall, Albert W. *v.2 p.492*
Halsband, Robert *v.2 p.257*
Halsby, Julian, et al. *v.1 p.725*
Halton, Thomas P. & O'Leary, Stella *v.2 p.399*
Halttunen, Karen *v.4 p.724*
Halualani, Rona Tamiko *v.6 p.130*
Halzen, Francis & Martin, Alan D. *v.5 p.552*
Ham, Roswell G. *v.2 p.251*
Hamadeh, Hisham K. & Afshari, Cynthia A. (Editors) . *v.5 p.149*
Hamakawa, Yoshihiro (Volume Editor) *v.5 p.362*
Hamalian, Leo & Hatch, James V. (Editors) . . . *v.1 p.66, p.122*
Hamalian, Linda *v.2 p.114*
Hamamoto, Darrell Y. *v.6 p.89*
Hamann, Brigitte *v.3 p.183*
Hambleton, Ronald K. (Editor), et al. *v.5 p.600*
Hambley, Allan R. *v.5 p.722*
Hamblin, W. Kenneth & Christiansen, Eric H. . *v.4 p.390, v.5 p.418*
Hambourg, Maria Morris *v.1 p.762*
Hambrey, Michael & Alean, Jürg *v.5 p.425*
Hambrey, Michael J. & Harland, W. B. *v.5 p.425*
Hambrey, Michael J. *v.5 p.425*
Hambrick-Stowe, Charles E. *v.1 p.584*
Hamburger, Joseph *v.3 p.88*
Hamburger, Michael *v.2 p.593*
Hamburger, Viktor *v.5 p.160*
Hamby, Alonzo L. (Editor) *v.3 p.472*
Hamby, Alonzo L. *v.3 p.447, p.472, v.4 p.522*
Hamdan, Mahmoud H. & Righetti, Pier G. . *v.5 p.88, p.110, p.116*
Hamdi, Mohamed E. *v.6 p.641*
Hamel, Gary & Prahalad, C. *v.4 p.81*
Hamel, Gary *v.4 p.66, p.71, p.73*
Hamer, David *v.4 p.624*
Hamer, Dean & Copeland, Peter *v.6 p.420*
Hamer, Dean H. *v.5 p.634*
Hamermesh, Daniel S. & Bean, Frank D. (Editors) . . . *v.4 p.570*
Hamermesh, Daniel S. *v.4 p.247*
Hamermesh, Morton *v.5 p.548*
Hameroff, Stuart R. (Editor), et al. *v.5 p.613*
Hamerow, Theodore S. *v.3 p.168, p.171*
Hames, B. D. & Hooper, N. M. *v.5 p.331*
Hames, Peter *v.6 p.337*
Hamid, Mohsin *v.2 p.760*
Hamid, S. Halim; Amin, Mohamed B. &
    Maadhah, Ali G. *v.5 p.324*
Hamilton, A. C., et al. *v.2 p.214*
Hamilton, A. C. *v.2 p.729*
Hamilton, Alexander, James Madison and John Jay . . . *v.4 p.518*
Hamilton, Alexander *v.4 p.213*
Hamilton, Bernard *v.3 p.64, p.69*
Hamilton, Charles V. *v.4 p.461*
Hamilton, Daniel & Quinlan, Joseph *v.4 p.60*

Hamilton, Gary *v.4 p.214, p.257, p.259*
Hamilton, George H. **v.1** *p.678, p.687*
Hamilton, Holman *v.3 p.420, p.436*
Hamilton, Ian (Editor) *v.2 p.178, p.184*
Hamilton, Ian *v.2 p.96, p.118, p.265*
Hamilton, James T. *v.4 p.414*
Hamilton, James *v.1 p.779*
Hamilton, John D. *v.3 p.547*
Hamilton, Kenneth & Liszt, Franz . . . *v.1 p.198, p.239, p.336*
Hamilton, Kenneth (Editor) *v.1 p.198, p.336*
Hamilton, Nigel *v.2 p.612, v.3 p.472*
Hamilton, Nora & Chinchilla, Norma Stoltz . . *v.6 p.542, p.549*
Hamilton, Nora *v.3 p.292*
Hamilton, Paul *v.2 p.323*
Hamilton, Richard F. & Herwig, Holger H. (Editors) . . *v.3 p.79*
Hamilton, Rita *v.2 p.646*
Hamilton, Roy W. *v.1 p.692*
Hamilton, Russell G. *v.2 p.693, p.695, p.697*
Hamilton, Sue *v.1 p.475*
Hamilton, Virginia Van der Veer *v.3 p.504*
Hamilton, Walter *v.2 p.180*
Hamlet, Desmond M *v.2 p.254*
Hamlin, William M. *v.2 p.169, p.186*
Hamlisch, Marvin *v.1 p.250, p.328*
Hamlyn, D. W. *v.1 p.465*
Hamm, Charles *v.1 p.277*
Hamm, Mark S. *v.4 p.524*
Hamm, Richard F. *v.4 p.449*
Hamm, Thomas D. *v.1 p.585*
Hammacher, A. M. *v.1 p.780*
Hammacher, Abraham Marie *v.1 p.740*
Hammack, David C. *v.3 p.490, v.6 p.712*
Hammack, Floyd M. *v.4 p.327*
Hammarberg, Gitta *v.2 p.793, p.804*
Hammer, Louis & Schyfter, Sara (Translators) . . . *v.2 p.643*
Hammer, Michael & Champy, James *v.4 p.86*
Hammerback, John C. & Jensen, Richard J. . . *v.6 p.489, p.526*
Hammermeister, Kai *v.1 p.480*
Hammersley, J. M. & Handscomb, D. C. *v.5 p.551*
Hammerstein, Oscar II (Lyrics by) *v.1 p.250, p.328, p.408, p.411*
Hammerton, James *v.6 p.765*
Hammes, Gordon G. *v.5 p.327*
Hammett, Dashiell *v.2 p.80*
Hammill, Donald D. & Bartel, Nettie R. *v.4 p.318*
Hammond, Allen L. (Editor) *v.5 p.395*
Hammond, Anne (Editor) *v.1 p.767*
Hammond, Anne *v.1 p.766*
Hammond, Brean *v.2 p.257*
Hammond, Christopher *v.5 p.284, p.436*
Hammond, D. (Editor) *v.5 p.168, p.176, p.236, p.239*
Hammond, Frederick *v.1 p.184, p.325*
Hammond, George P. (Editor, Translator) *v.3 p.403*
Hammond, George Peter *v.3 p.528*
Hammond, J. Daniel (Editor) *v.4 p.232*
Hammond, J. Daniel *v.4 p.232*

Hammond, J. R. *v.2 p.319*
Hammond, John L. *v.3 p.299*
Hammond, John *v.2 p.319*
Hammond, Lila *v.2 p.777*
Hammond, Mason *v.2 p.423*
Hammond, N. G. L. *v.3 p.19*
Hammond, Nicholas (Editor) *v.1 p.452, v.2 p.476*
Hammond, Nicholas G. *v.3 p.12, p.17, p.19*
Hammond, Nicholas *v.1 p.751, v.2 p.459*
Hammond, Phillip E., et al. *v.4 p.537*
Hammond World Atlas Corporation Staff *v.6 p.593*
Hamner, Robert D. *v.2 p.770*
Hamnett, Andrew, et al. *v.5 p.285*
Hamnett, Brian R. *v.3 p.285*
Hamon, Raeann & Ingoldsby, Bron (Editors) . *v.4 p.738, p.742*
Hamouda, O. G. & Smithin, J. (Editors) *v.4 p.227*
Hamouda, Omar F. & Rowley, J. C. (Editors) . . . *v.4 p.201*
Hamouda, Omar F. & Smithin, John N. (Editors) . . . *v.4 p.227*
Hampe, Karl & Baethgen, Friedrich *v.3 p.161*
Hampel, Clifford A. & Hawley, Gessner G. *v.5 p.258*
Hampel, Clifford A. (Editor) *v.5 p.285*
Hampel, Clifford A. *v.5 p.257*
Hampshire, Stuart *v.1 p.437, p.477*
Hampton, David *v.4 p.385*
Hampton, Lionel & Haskins, James *v.1 p.260, p.328*
Hamrock, Bernard J., et al. *v.5 p.708*
Hamrock, Bernard J. *v.5 p.708*
Hamsun, Knut *v.2 p.628*
Hamzeh, A.Nizar *v.4 p.616*
Han, Arar & Hsu, John Y. (Editors) . . . *v.6 p.93, p.122, p.123*
Han, Beatrice *v.1 p.459*
Han, Hyun Sook & Ruth, Kari *v.6 p.93, p.110*
Han, Jiawei & Kamber, Micheline *v.5 p.337*
Han, Jie (Editor), et al. *v.5 p.698*
Hanak, Peter *v.3 p.186*
Hanan, Mack *v.4 p.142*
Hanaway, William, et al. *v.6 p.632*
Hanchar, John M. (Editor), et al. *v.5 p.375*
Hanchard, Michael George *v.3 p.279*
Hancock, Harold B. *v.3 p.409*
Hancock, James F. & Hancock, J. F. *v.5 p.21, p.45*
Hancock, John M. & Zvelebil, Marketa J. (Editors) . *v.5 p.97*
Hancock, Paul L. (Editor) *v.5 p.441*
Hancock, Peter A. (Editor) *v.5 p.587*
Hancocks, David *v.5 p.83*
Hand, John Oliver & Wolff, Martha *v.1 p.727*
Hand, John Oliver *v.1 p.726, p.740*
Hand, Learned *v.4 p.437, p.455*
Hand, Louis N. & Finch, Janet D. *v.5 p.546*
Hand, Richard J. *v.2 p.341*
Handal, Nathalie (Editor) *v.6 p.659*
Handel, Henry *v.2 p.746*
Handelman, Howard *v.3 p.330*
Handke, Peter *v.1 p.109, v.2 p.617*
Handler, Jerome & Lange, Frederick *v.4 p.14*

Handler, Jerome S. & Lange, Fredrick W. *v.4 p.728*

Handler, Richard *v.3 p.543, v.4 p.581*

Handler, Sarah *v.1 p.804*

Handley, John *v.4 p.111, p.166*

Handlin, David P. *v.1 p.789*

Handlin, Lilian *v.3 p.415*

Handlin, Oscar . . . *v.3 p.367, p.376, p.441, p.447, p.458, p.487, p.488, v.4 p.571, v.6 p.712*

Handy, Robert T. *v.1 p.605*

Handy, W. C. *v.1 p.260, p.329, v.6 p.17, p.25, p.29*

Handy-Marchello, Barbara *v.3 p.523*

Hane, Mikiso *v.4 p.703, v.6 p.224, p.227*

Hanelt, Peter *v.5 p.21, p.25*

Hanes, Jeffrey E. & Seki, Hajime *v.6 p.224*

Haney, Jack V. (Editor) *v.2 p.793*

Haney, Lynne, and Pollard Lisa (eds.) *v.3 p.260*

Haney, Robert W. *v.4 p.472*

Haney-López, Ian *v.6 p.540*

Hanf, Theodor *v.4 p.614, p.616*

Hanfling, Oswald *v.1 p.510*

Hanford Cultural and Historic Resources Program Staff (Contribution by) *v.5 p.375, p.391, p.413, p.415, p.417*

Hangen, Eva C. *v.2 p.214*

Hanin, Yuri L. *v.4 p.877*

Hanke, Ken *v.6 p.330*

Hankins, John E. *v.2 p.214*

Hankins, Thomas L. *v.5 p.390*

Hankinson, R. J. *v.1 p.517*

Hanks, David & Hoy, Anne *v.1 p.713*

Hanley, Lynne *v.2 p.191*

Hanlon, Joseph F., et al. *v.4 p.116*

Hanlon, Joseph *v.6 p.74, p.76*

Hanna, Judith L. *v.1 p.48, v.6 p.474*

Hanna, Judith Lynn *v.1 p.48*

Hanna, Judith Lynne *v.1 p.47*

Hanna, Martha *v.3 p.79, p.155*

Hanna, Nelly *v.4 p.726, v.6 p.637*

Hanna, Thomas P. *v.5 p.155*

Hanna, Thomas *v.1 p.52*

Hanna, William S. *v.3 p.492*

Hannam, June *v.6 p.431*

Hannay, Alastair & Marino, Gordon Daniel (Editors) . *v.1 p.581*

Hannay, Alastair *v.1 p.478*

Hannay, Lord *v.3 p.197*

Hannay, Margaret P. (Editor) *v.2 p.381*

Hannay, Margaret Patterson *v.2 p.366*

Hannay, Norman B. *v.5 p.305*

Hannerz, Ulf *v.4 p.407*

Hannesson, Jóhann S. *v.2 p.624*

Hannigan, John A. *v.6 p.712*

Hannigan, Robert E. *v.3 p.452*

Hanning, Robert W. *v.2 p.467*

Hannon, Charles *v.2 p.74*

Hannula, Dick & Thornton, Nort (Editors) . *v.4 p.794, p.868, p.904*

Hans, Nicholas *v.4 p.334*

Hans, Valerie P. *v.4 p.109, p.112*

Hansberry, Lorraine *v.2 p.80*

Hansch, Corwin (Editor) *v.5 p.330*

Hansel, C. E. M. *v.5 p.613*

Hansell, Michael H. *v.5 p.212*

Hanselman, Duane & Littlefield, Bruce R. *v.5 p.461*

Hansen, Alvin H. *v.4 p.243, p.246*

Hansen, Birthe & Heurlin, Bertel (Editors) . . *v.4 p.641, p.644*

Hansen, Brad *v.1 p.770*

Hansen, Charles M. *v.5 p.282*

Hansen, Ejvind Damsgaard *v.4 p.211, p.215*

Hansen, Elaine T. *v.2 p.209*

Hansen, Henny H. *v.6 p.598*

Hansen, Jorn & Nielsen, Niels Kayser (Editors) . *v.4 p.876, p.879*

Hansen, Karen T. *v.4 p.37, p.703*

Hansen, Katharine *v.4 p.169*

Hansen, Katherine *v.4 p.170*

Hansen, Marcus L. *v.4 p.667*

Hansen, Martin A. *v.2 p.626*

Hansen, P. E. & Jorgensen, Sven E. (Editors) *v.5 p.704*

Hansen, Randall et al. *v.4 p.167, p.170*

Hansen, Roger D. *v.3 p.292*

Hansen, Ruth Ann (Editor) *v.5 p.535*

Hansen, Thomas B. *v.1 p.540*

Hansen, Thomas Blom & Stepputat, Finn (Editors) . . . *v.4 p.34*

Hansen, William F. *v.2 p.229*

Hansen, William P. *v.3 p.384*

Hanski, Ilkka A. & Gaggiotti, Oscar E. (Editors) *v.5 p.133, p.184, p.188*

Hanski, Ilkka A. & Gilpin, Michael E. (Editors) . *v.5 p.184, p.188*

Hanski, Ilkka A. *v.5 p.184, p.188*

Hanslick, Eduard *v.1 p.198, p.381*

Hanson, A. A. (Editor), et al. *v.5 p.21, p.25*

Hanson, Bryan *v.5 p.211*

Hanson, Carol R., et al. *v.4 p.436, p.669*

Hanson, Clare *v.2 p.191*

Hanson, Duane, et al. *v.1 p.780*

Hanson, Elizabeth *v.5 p.83*

Hanson, Ellis *v.6 p.416*

Hanson, Holly Elisabeth *v.6 p.66*

Hanson, J. Arthur (Translator) *v.2 p.429*

Hanson, Joyce Ann *v.6 p.5, p.17, p.43*

Hanson, Norwood R. *v.5 p.402*

Hanson, Peter *v.6 p.332*

Hanson, Stephanie L., et al. *v.5 p.674*

Hanson, Victor Davis & Keegan, John *v.3 p.12*

Hanson, Victor Davis (Editor) *v.3 p.17*

Hanson, Victor Davis *v.3 p.17, p.18*

Hanssen, Beatrice *v.6 p.710*

Hansson, Lennart *v.5 p.179*

Hantke, Steffen (Editor) *v.6 p.318*

Hao-Heyi-Suichu *v.6 p.184*

Hapke, Laura *v.2 p.4, p.8*

Happle, Stephen K. *v.4 p.219*

Haqqani, Husain *v.4 p.617*
Haqqi, Yahya *v.6 p.659*
Haralson (Editor) *v.2 p.96*
Haraway, Donna Jeanne *v.4 p.30, v.6 p.439*
Harbage, Alfred *v.2 p.218*
Harbaugh, William H. *v.3 p.472*
Harbeck, Karen M. *v.4 p.309, v.6 p.383, p.385*
Harbison, Craig *v.1 p.675, p.687*
Harbison, Peter. *v.3 p.136*
Harbord, Heather *v.3 p.547*
Harbour, Frances V. *v.4 p.641, p.644*
Harclerode, Peter *v.4 p.561, p.659*
Harcourt, Bernard E. (Editor) *v.6 p.266*
Harcourt, Bernard E. *v.6 p.263*
Harcourt, G. C. & Riach, P. A. (Editors) *v.4 p.227*
Harcourt, G. C. *v.4 p.225*
Harcourt, Geoffrey C. (Editor). *v.4 p.227*
Hardach, Karl *v.3 p.172*
Hardacre, Helen *v.1 p.541, p.567, v.6 p.221*
Hardeman, D. B. & Bacon, Donald C. *v.3 p.458*
Harden, Edgar F. *v.2 p.43, p.315*
Hardesty, Donald L. & Little, Barbara J. *v.4 p.7*
Hardgrave, Robert L. Jr. & Kochanek, Stanley A. . . . *v.4 p.617*
Hardie, D. Grahame *v.5 p.330*
Hardie, Martin & Carter, Charles *v.1 p.756*
Hardie, Philip (Editor) *v.2 p.438*
Hardie, Philip R. *v.2 p.446*
Hardie, Philip *v.2 p.425, p.438, p.446*
Hardiman, David (Editor) *v.6 p.157*
Hardiman, David. *v.6 p.157, p.159*
Hardiman, Gary *v.5 p.127*
Hardin, Garrett, et al. *v.5 p.41*
Hardin, Garrett. *v.4 p.763*
Hardin, Kimeron & Hall, Marny. *v.6 p.381*
Hardin, Russell. *v.4 p.766*
Hardin, Terri. *v.1 p.154*
Harding, A. F. *v.4 p.12*
Harding, C. J. (Editor), et al. *v.5 p.303*
Harding, James H.. . . . . *v.5 p.174, p.215, p.234*
Harding, James M. (Editor) *v.1 p.85, p.96*
Harding, Lee E. & McCullum, Emily (Editors) . *v.5 p.179, p.234*
Harding, Rachel E. *v.3 p.340*
Harding, Robert C. *v.3 p.304*
Harding, Robert R. *v.3 p.145*
Harding, Sandra & Hintikka, Merrill B. (Editors). *v.6 p.461, p.462*
Harding, Sandra (Editor) *v.4 p.690, v.5 p.388*
Harding, Sandra *v.6 p.439, p.462*
Harding, T. Swann *v.5 p.4*
Harding, Vincent *v.6 p.5*
Harding, Walter *v.2 p.52*
Hardison, O. B. Jr. *v.1 p.577*
Hardman, John. *v.3 p.147*
Hardouin-Fugier, Elisabeth, et al. *v.1 p.725*
Hardt, Michael & Negri, Antonio *v.4 p.504*
Hardwick, Elizabeth *v.2 p.80, p.575*

Hardy, Barbara. *v.2 p.267*
Hardy, Dennis *v.4 p.733*
Hardy, Edward R. (Editor) *v.1 p.640*
Hardy, Emma & Hardy, Florence E. *v.2 p.291*
Hardy, Florence E. *v.2 p.291*
Hardy, Friedhelm. *v.1 p.540*
Hardy, G. H. *v.5 p.458, p.489, p.490*
Hardy, Gayle J. *v.6 p.431*
Hardy, Godfrey H. & Wright, E. M. *v.5 p.476*
Hardy, Godfrey H., et al. *v.5 p.489*
Hardy, Henry R. *v.3 p.539*
Hardy, James Earl *v.6 p.397*
Hardy, Jim & Andrisani, John *v.4 p.860*
Hardy, John T. *v.5 p.426*
Hardy, Lew, et al. *v.5 p.582*
Hardy, Melissa A. & Bryman, Alan E. (Editors). . . *v.4 p.178*
Hardy, Phil (Editor) *v.6 p.318, p.324*
Hardy, Stephen *v.4 p.806, p.816*
Hardy, Thomas *v.2 p.291, p.292*
Hardy-Fanta, Carol & Gerson, Jeffrey *v.6 p.538*
Hare, A. Paul (Editor), et al.. . . . . *v.5 p.647*
Hare, A. Paul, et al. *v.5 p.647*
Hare, Bruce R. (Editor) *v.4 p.730*
Hare, David *v.1 p.100*
Hare, Richard M. *v.1 p.484, p.487*
Hare, William *v.4 p.339*
Harel, David & Feldman, Yishai A. *v.5 p.335, p.343*
Harel, David *v.5 p.343*
Haren, Michael. *v.1 p.432, v.6 p.567*
Harer, John B. *v.4 p.459*
Hareven, Shulamith. *v.6 p.648*
Hargittai, I. & Hargittai, M.. . . . . *v.5 p.276*
Hargittai, Istvan *v.5 p.261, p.326*
Hargreaves, Andy *v.4 p.347*
Hargreaves, David & North, Adrian C.
(Editors) *v.1 p.375, v.5 p.618*
Hargreaves Heap, Shaun & Varoufakis, Yanis *v.4 p.688*
Hargreaves, Jennifer *v.4 p.806, p.816, p.836, v.6 p.437*
Hargreaves, John D.. . . . . *v.4 p.583, p.584, v.6 p.53, p.68*
Hargreaves, John *v.4 p.816*
Hargreaves, Mary W. *v.3 p.417*
Harich, Walther *v.2 p.599*
Harik, Iliya F. *v.6 p.605, p.639*
Haring, Keith *v.1 p.45*
Hariot, Thomas. *v.5 p.396*
Harjo, Joy (Editor) *v.6 p.705*
Harjo, Joy *v.2 p.19, p.146*
Harkins, Anthony. *v.4 p.709*
Harkins, William Edward *v.2 p.781*
Harkness, E. M. *v.5 p.52*
Harlan, Elizabeth *v.2 p.499*
Harlan, Jack Rodney *v.5 p.4*
Harlan, Lindsey *v.6 p.154, p.161*
Harland, David M. (Editor). *v.5 p.71*
Harland, David M. *v.5 p.69, p.719*

Harland, Richard *v.1 p.512*

Harle, J. C. *v.1 p.692*

Harle, Vilho *v.4 p.773*

Harley, Debra A. & Dillard, John M. *v.6 p.21*

Harley, James *v.1 p.215, p.368*

Harley, John *v.1 p.180, p.315*

Harley, Sharon & Terborg-Penn, Rosalyn (Editors) . *v.6 p.5, p.43*

Harley, Sharon (Editor) *v.6 p.39, p.43*

Harley, Sharon *v.6 p.5, p.17*

Harlow, Francis Harvey & Lanmon, Dwight P. . . . *v.1 p.808*

Harlow, Neal *v.3 p.531*

Harman, Gilbert & Thomson, Judith J. *v.1 p.514*

Harman, Gilbert *v.1 p.487*

Harmless, William *v.1 p.577*

Harmon, Daniel E. *v.4 p.378*

Harmon, Deborah A. & Jones, Toni Stokes *v.4 p.363*

Harmon, Jay, et al. *v.5 p.55*

Harmon, John E. & Anderson, Steven J. *v.4 p.387*

Harmon, William *v.2 p.549*

Harmon *v.2 p.68*

Harnack, Adolf *v.1 p.633, v.3 p.56*

Harnad, Stevan R. (Editor) *v.5 p.605*

Harner, James L. *v.2 p.549, p.566*

Harnett, Richard M. & Ferguson, Billy G. *v.4 p.404*

Harold, Elliotte Rusty *v.5 p.346*

Harold, Frank M. *v.5 p.154*

Harootunian, H. D. *v.6 p.224*

Harootunian, Harry D. *v.6 p.224*

Haroutunian, Joseph *v.1 p.633*

Harper, Charles A. (Editor) *v.5 p.319*

Harper, Doug & Lawson, Helene (Editors) *v.4 p.717*

Harper, Frances Ellen Watkins *v.2 p.39*

Harper, George M. *v.2 p.326*

Harper, Janice *v.4 p.46*

Harper, Judith E. *v.6 p.452*

Harper, Katherine Anne & Brown, Robert L. (Editors) . *v.1 p.536*

Harper, William Rainey *v.6 p.646*

HarperCollins Spiritual Classics Staff *v.1 p.585*

HarperCollins Staff (Contribution by) *v.2 p.637*

HarperCollins Staff *v.2 p.636*

HarperCollins UK Staff *v.4 p.379*

Harper's Magazine Staff *v.2 p.19*

Harpole, Charles (Editor) *v.6 p.344*

Harpsfield, Nicholas *v.2 p.214*

Harpur, James & Braybrooke, Marcus *v.1 p.617*

Harr, J. Scott & Hess, Kären M. *v.6 p.245*

Harr, Jonathan *v.1 p.740*

Harran, Don *v.1 p.180, p.184, p.299, p.351*

Harrap's Staff *v.2 p.453*

Harre, Rom *v.5 p.402, p.409*

Harrell, David Edwin Jr. *v.1 p.648*

Harrell, Richard S., et al. *v.6 p.654*

Harrell, Richard S. *v.6 p.653*

Harrell, Stevan *v.4 p.708*

Harrer, Heinrich *v.6 p.241*

Harré, Rom *v.1 p.497, v.5 p.594*

Harries, Jill & Wood, Ian (Editors) *v.3 p.192*

Harrigan, George G. & Goodacre, Royston (Editors) . *v.5 p.127*

Harriger, Katy J. *v.4 p.524*

Harring, Sidney L. *v.4 p.464, v.6 p.688, p.696*

Harrington, Austin *v.1 p.708*

Harrington, Christina *v.1 p.609*

Harrington, Daniel J. *v.1 p.629*

Harrington, J. W. *v.4 p.387*

Harrington, Joel F. *v.3 p.166*

Harrington, John P. (Editor) *v.2 p.202*

Harrington, Karl P. & Pucci, Joseph M. *v.2 p.449*

Harrington, Michael *v.4 p.506, p.703*

Harrington, Walt (Editor) *v.4 p.408*

Harris, Albert J. & Sipay, Edward R. *v.4 p.363*

Harris, Andrew J. *v.6 p.247*

Harris, Bertha *v.6 p.397*

Harris, Charles H. & Sadler, Louis R. . . . *v.3 p.293, v.6 p.536*

Harris, Charles H. III & Sadler, Louis R. *v.3 p.293*

Harris, Charles W. *v.4 p.524*

Harris, Cyril M. *v.1 p.783*

Harris, Daniel *v.4 p.712, v.6 p.365, p.387*

Harris, David A. *v.6 p.263, p.264*

Harris, David E. *v.4 p.716, p.784*

Harris, David V. & Kiver, Eugene P. *v.5 p.419*

Harris, Derek (Editor) *v.2 p.639*

Harris, Donald (Editor), et al. *v.1 p.215, p.309, p.353*

Harris, E. Lynn *v.6 p.397, p.401, p.406*

Harris, Eddy L. *v.3 p.506*

Harris, Edward D. Jr., et al. *v.5 p.519, p.520*

Harris, Ellen T. *v.6 p.408*

Harris, Fran *v.4 p.836, p.854, p.896*

Harris, Frank *v.2 p.321*

Harris, Fred R. *v.4 p.530*

Harris, George W. *v.2 p.39*

Harris, Gordon (Compiled by) *v.4 p.630*

Harris, H. A. *v.4 p.806*

Harris, Harold Arthur *v.4 p.806*

Harris, Henry *v.5 p.79, p.113*

Harris, Ian *v.4 p.491, v.6 p.170*

Harris, James E. & Weeks, Kent R. *v.6 p.57*

Harris, James G. & Harris, Melinda Woolf *v.5 p.207*

Harris, Jennifer *v.1 p.809*

Harris, Jesse W. *v.2 p.214*

Harris, Joanne *v.2 p.351*

Harris, Joe *v.5 p.497*

Harris, Joel Chandler *v.2 p.40*

Harris, John F. *v.3 p.472*

Harris, John M., et al. *v.5 p.480*

Harris, John W. (Editor), et al. *v.5 p.545*

Harris, Jonathan *v.1 p.703, v.3 p.193*

Harris, Judith Rich *v.5 p.513*

Harris, Julia F. *v.2 p.40*

Harris, Kathleen M. *v.4 p.756*

Harris, Larry D., et al. *v.5 p.179*

Harris, Larry D. *v.5 p.37, p.40, p.358, p.373*
Harris, Leslie M. (Editor) *v.4 p.138*
Harris, Leslie M. *v.6 p.712*
Harris, Mark W. *v.1 p.589*
Harris, Mark *v.2 p.80, p.81*
Harris, Marvin & Ross, Eric B. *v.4 p.736*
Harris, Marvin *v.4 p.22, p.23*
Harris, Mary B. (Editor) *v.4 p.309*
Harris, Mary E. *v.1 p.682*
Harris, Max *v.3 p.263*
Harris, Michael *v.4 p.542*
Harris, Oliver & Lieb, Frederick G. *v.2 p.64*
Harris, Paul; Halsby, Julian *v.1 p.725*
Harris, Paul *v.1 p.93*
Harris, R. Cole & Warkentin, John *v.3 p.536*
Harris, R. W. *v.3 p.103, p.105*
Harris, Randy A. *v.2 p.561, v.4 p.18, v.5 p.621, p.623*
Harris, Richard A. & Milkis, Sidney M. *v.4 p.463*
Harris, Richard C. *v.2 p.51*
Harris, Richard W. *v.5 p.41*
Harris, Richard Wilson, et al. *v.5 p.43*
Harris, Richard *v.6 p.713*
Harris, Robert L. (Editor) *v.5 p.314, p.682*
Harris, Seymour E. (Editor) *v.4 p.211, p.230, p.235*
Harris, Stephen L. *v.6 p.5*
Harris, Stephen *v.2 p.127*
Harris, Thomas L. *v.4 p.144*
Harris, Tim *v.3 p.94, p.105*
Harris, Trudier *v.6 p.26, p.44*
Harris, Wendy Beech & Beech, Wendy *v.4 p.68*
Harris, William C. *v.3 p.504*
Harris, William J. *v.2 p.142*
Harris, William V. *v.2 p.576, v.3 p.25*
Harris, William *v.6 p.583, p.604*
Harrison, A. F. (Editor) *v.5 p.184*
Harrison, Antony H. *v.2 p.175, p.184*
Harrison, Bernard *v.1 p.189, p.239, p.330*
Harrison, Beverly Wildung *v.6 p.465, p.469*
Harrison, Brian H. *v.3 p.112, p.123, v.6 p.761*
Harrison, Brian *v.3 p.112*
Harrison, Charles & Wood, Paul (Editors) *v.1 p.703*
Harrison, Charles *v.2 p.735*
Harrison, Daniel *v.1 p.370*
Harrison, Edward R. *v.5 p.72*
Harrison, Elizabeth J. (Editor) *v.1 p.82, p.85, p.96, p.115*
Harrison, Faye V. (Editor) *v.4 p.27*
Harrison, G. B. *v.2 p.196, p.227, p.234*
Harrison, George B. *v.2 p.227*
Harrison, Gordon *v.5 p.356, p.364*
Harrison, Henrietta *v.6 p.190, p.200*
Harrison, Ian T. & Harrison, Shuyen *v.5 p.294*
Harrison, J. F. *v.3 p.90, v.4 p.703*
Harrison, Jackie *v.4 p.412*
Harrison, Jane E. *v.1 p.532*
Harrison, Lowell H. & Klotter, James C. *v.3 p.511*

Harrison, Lowell H. (Editor) *v.3 p.511*
Harrison, Mark (Editor) *v.3 p.81*
Harrison, Mark *v.6 p.157*
Harrison, Martin *v.1 p.59, p.140*
Harrison, Paul Mansfield *v.1 p.583*
Harrison, Pegram *v.1 p.756*
Harrison, R. M. (Editor), et al. *v.5 p.310*
Harrison, R. M. (Editor) *v.5 p.310, p.375*
Harrison, Richard W. *v.3 p.211*
Harrison, Robert (Translator) *v.2 p.467*
Harrison, Robert *v.3 p.441, v.4 p.531*
Harrison, Roger (Editor) *v.4 p.320*
Harrison, Ross *v.1 p.445*
Harrison, Russell *v.2 p.86*
Harrison, S. J. (Editor) *v.2 p.446*
Harrison, S. J. *v.2 p.425*
Harrison, S L *v.4 p.404*
Harrison, Selig S. (Editor), et al. *v.6 p.159*
Harrison, Selig S. *v.6 p.236*
Harrison, Stephen (Editor) *v.2 p.424*
Harris-Shapiro, Carol *v.1 p.597*
Harrist, Robert E. & Fong, Wen C. *v.1 p.732*
Harrod, Howard L. *v.6 p.288*
Harrod, Roy F. *v.4 p.211, p.227*
Harrod, Tanya *v.1 p.800*
Harrold, Charles Frederick *v.2 p.276*
Harrop, Jeffrey *v.4 p.211, p.240, p.255*
Harrop, Martin & Miller, William L. (Editors) *v.4 p.577*
Harry Fox Agency *v.1 p.172, p.384*
Harry, Joseph & Devall, William B. *v.4 p.749, v.6 p.375*
Hart, Armando *v.3 p.310*
Hart, Betty & Risley, Todd R. *v.4 p.356, p.368*
Hart, Clive & Hayman, David (Editors) *v.2 p.358*
Hart, Clive *v.2 p.358*
Hart, D. G. *v.1 p.587*
Hart, Dianne W. *v.3 p.302, v.6 p.489, p.529*
Hart, Francis R. *v.2 p.189*
Hart, H. L. *v.4 p.434*
Hart, Henry *v.2 p.96*
Hart, Hillary *v.5 p.680*
Hart, Ivor B. *v.5 p.396*
Hart, James David, 1911- *v.2 p.3*
Hart, John Fraser *v.4 p.395*
Hart, John M. *v.3 p.293*
Hart, John *v.4 p.524, v.6 p.350*
Hart, Jonathan *v.2 p.729, v.3 p.76*
Hart, Lorenz *v.1 p.250, p.329, p.408, p.411*
Hart, Parker T. *v.3 p.389*
Hart, Paul & Reynolds, John (Editors) *v.5 p.215*
Hart, Stephen M. *v.2 p.639, p.664*
Hart, Thomas R. *v.2 p.649*
Hart, Vivien *v.6 p.456, p.469*
Harte, Bret *v.2 p.40*
Harteis, Richard; Meredith, William *v.2 p.779*
Hartemann, Frederic & Hauptman, Robert *v.6 p.283*

Harter, Eugene C. *v.3 p.340*

Harth, Erica (Editor) *v.6 p.133*

Harthan, John *v.1 p.716*

Hart-Hewins, Linda & Wells, Jan *v.4 p.360*

Hartigan, Lynda Roscoe, et al. *v.1 p.697*

Hartl, Daniel L. & Jones, Elizabeth W. . . *v.5 p.99, p.133, p.134*

Hartl, Daniel L. & Jones, Elizabeth *v.5 p.99, p.133*

Hartley, F. R., et al. *v.5 p.282*

Hartley, John *v.4 p.416*

Hartley, Keith & Sandler, Todd (Editors) *v.4 p.189*

Hartley, Peter *v.5 p.647*

Hartlyn, Jonathan *v.3 p.317*

Hartman, G. L. (Editor), et al. *v.5 p.46*

Hartman, Geoffrey H. & O'Hara, Daniel T. *v.2 p.568*

Hartman, Geoffrey H. (editor) *v.2 p.293*

Hartman, Geoffrey H. *v.2 p.323, p.567, p.571*

Hartman, Howard L. & Mutmansky, Jan M. *v.5 p.738*

Hartman, Howard L. (Editor) *v.5 p.738*

Hartman, Joan E. & Messer-Davidow, Ellen (Editors) *v.6 p.463*

Hartman, Laura P. (Editor), et al. *v.4 p.69, p.664*

Hartman, Louis F. *v.1 p.622*

Hartman, Monte *v.4 p.382*

Hartmann, Betsy *v.6 p.447*

Hartmann, Dennis L. *v.5 p.426*

Hartmann, Ernest *v.5 p.613*

Hartmann, Friedel & Katz, Casimir *v.5 p.694*

Hartmann, Heidi I. *v.4 p.254*

Hartmann, Hudson T., et al. *v.5 p.15, p.43*

Hartmann Von Aue *v.2 p.595*

Hartmann, William K. & Miller, Ron *v.5 p.68*

Hartmann, William K. *v.5 p.69, p.434*

Hartmann, William M. *v.5 p.606*

Hartmann-Tews, Ilse *v.4 p.716, p.816, p.836, v.6 p.437*

Hartnack, Justus *v.1 p.463*

Hartnoll, Phyllis (Editor) *v.1 p.55, p.59, p.61, p.128*

Hartog, Francois *v.2 p.412*

Hartog, Hendrik *v.4 p.442, p.739*

Hartquist, T. W., et al. *v.5 p.66*

Hartsfield, Nora & Ringel, Gerhard (Editors) *v.5 p.480*

Hartshorne, Charles *v.1 p.432, p.525, p.639*

Hartshorne, Richard *v.4 p.375*

Hartshorne, Robin *v.5 p.466, p.495, p.497*

Hartsock, Nancy C. *v.4 p.273*

Hartt, Frederick *v.1 p.675, p.687, p.740*

Hartung, Jan-Peter & Reifeld, Helmut (Editors) *v.4 p.308, p.334*

Hartwell, Leland, et al. *v.5 p.134*

Harty, Kevin J. (Editor) *v.2 p.185*

Harty, Kevin J. *v.6 p.314*

Hartz, Louis *v.3 p.376*

Harvard Business Reference Staff *v.4 p.180*

Harvard Business Review Staff *v.4 p.177*

Harvard Business School Press Staff *v.4 p.80*

Harvard Business School Staff (Contribution by) *v.4 p.130, p.167*

Harvard Business School Staff (Editor) *v.4 p.71, p.73*

Harvard University. Committee on the Objectives of General

Education in a Free Society. *v.4 p.290, p.294*

Harvey, Andrew *v.6 p.374*

Harvey, Archer St. Clair & O'Keefe, Patrick J. (Editors) . *v.1 p.827*

Harvey, B. Peter *v.1 p.565*

Harvey, Brian *v.5 p.719*

Harvey, Daniel Cobb *v.3 p.543*

Harvey, David *v.3 p.158, p.447, v.6 p.713, p.721*

Harvey, John *v.1 p.784*

Harvey, L. P. *v.3 p.237, p.239, v.6 p.584*

Harvey, Mark *v.4 p.788, p.884*

Harvey, Neil *v.4 p.711*

Harvey, Paul H. & Heseltine, Janet E. (Editors) . . . *v.2 p.456*

Harvey, Paul H. & Pagel, Mark D. *v.5 p.192*

Harvey, Paul *v.1 p.583*

Harvey, Philip (Editor) *v.5 p.689*

Harvey, R. (Editor) *v.1 p.577*

Harvey, Robert C. *v.2 p.581*

Harvey, Ronald G. *v.5 p.292*

Harvey, Susan (Translator) *v.1 p.612*

Harvie, Charles & Lee, Boon-Chye (Editors) . *v.4 p.243, p.259*

Harvie, Christopher T. *v.3 p.133, v.6 p.756, p.758*

Harvie, Christopher *v.3 p.133*

Harwell, George C. *v.5 p.680*

Harwell, Joan M. *v.4 p.318*

Harwin, Lorna *v.2 p.399*

Harwit, Martin D. *v.5 p.66*

Harwood, Britton J. *v.2 p.211*

Harwood, Gregory W. *v.1 p.164, p.198, p.364*

Harwood, John T. *v.2 p.186*

Harwood, L. M. *v.5 p.292*

Hasan, Ira *v.2 p.333*

Hasan, Mushirul & Asaduddin, M. (Editors) . . *v.6 p.146, p.148*

Hasan, Mushirul (Editor) *v.6 p.157, p.159*

Hasan, Sana *v.6 p.637*

Haschak, Paul G. *v.4 p.173*

Hasegawa, Tsuyoshi *v.3 p.81, p.87, p.227, v.4 p.647*

Hasek, Jaroslav *v.2 p.783*

Hasenfratz, Robert J. (Editor) *v.2 p.204*

Hasenfratz, Robert J. *v.2 p.205*

Hashmi, Sohail H. (Editor) *v.4 p.500*

Haskell, Charles M. *v.5 p.520*

Haskell, Molly *v.6 p.474*

Haskett, Robert *v.3 p.285*

Haskins, Charles H. *v.3 p.67, v.6 p.563*

Haskins, Charles Homer *v.6 p.558*

Haskins, James S. *v.1 p.8*

Haskins, James *v.1 p.18, v.3 p.458*

Haslam, Malcolm *v.1 p.664*

Haslam, Nick (Editor) *v.5 p.647*

Haslam, S. M. *v.4 p.392*

Haslett, Adam *v.2 p.160*

Haslett, Beth & Samter, Wendy *v.5 p.627*

Haslett, Simon K. *v.5 p.366, p.371, p.448*

Haslip-Viera (Editor), et al. *v.6 p.542, p.549*

Haslip-Viera, Gabriel & Falcon, Angelo (Author, Editors) *v.6 p.544, p.549*

Haslip-Viera, Gabriel *v.3 p.285*

Hass, Robert *v.2 p.146*

Hassall, Christopher *v.2 p.335*

Hassan, Fekri A. (Editor) *v.4 p.7*

Hassanpour, Amir *v.6 p.668*

Hassel, Bryan C. *v.4 p.280*

Hassenbruch, Arne (Editor) *v.3 p.45, v.5 p.388*

Hassenstein, B. *v.5 p.408*

Hassid, Aviv *v.5 p.113*

Hassig, Ross *v.3 p.261, p.285, p.286*

Hassine, Victor *v.6 p.276*

Hassler, Warren W. Jr. *v.3 p.425*

Hassner, Alfred & Stumer, C. *v.5 p.294*

Hassrick, Peter H. & Webster, Melissa J. *v.1 p.697*

Hassrick, Royal B. *v.6 p.687, p.703*

Hassumani, Sabrina *v.2 p.766*

Hastie, Amelie (Editor), et al. *v.6 p.418*

Hastie, Peter A. *v.4 p.799, p.800*

Hastie, Reid, et al. *v.4 p.471*

Hastings, A. *v.5 p.91, p.93, p.188*

Hastings, Adrian (Editor), et al. *v.1 p.594, p.632*

Hastings, Adrian (Editor) *v.1 p.598*

Hastings, Adrian *v.1 p.573*

Hastings, Alan *v.5 p.94, p.189, p.502*

Hastings, Baird *v.1 p.164, p.189, p.343*

Hastings, Max *v.3 p.175, v.4 p.647*

Hastings, Selina *v.2 p.387*

Hastorf, Christine A. & Popper, Virginia S. (Editors) . . *v.4 p.7*

Hastrup, Kirsten & Hervik, Peter *v.4 p.25*

Hastrup, Kirsten *v.4 p.42*

Hasty, Christopher *v.1 p.370*

Haswell, Janis Tedesco *v.2 p.382*

Hatakeyama, T & Quinn, F. X. *v.5 p.323*

Hatamiya, Leslie T. *v.4 p.571, v.6 p.133*

Hatano, Giyoo & Inagaki, Kayoko *v.5 p.245*

Hatch, J. Amos (Editor) *v.4 p.356*

Hatch, James V. & Shine, Ted (Editors) *v.2 p.25*

Hatch, James V., et al. *v.1 p.123*

Hatch, Nathan O. *v.1 p.605*

Hatch, Thom *v.3 p.508*

Hatcher, Allen *v.5 p.499*

Hatcher, John & Bailey, Mark *v.3 p.40, p.96*

Hatcher, William S. & Martin, Douglas J. *v.1 p.561*

Hatchuel, Sarah *v.6 p.326*

Hatfield, Gary *v.1 p.454*

Hatfield, Henry Caraway *v.2 p.590*

Hatfield, Henry C. *v.2 p.598*

Hatfield, J. L. & Baker, J. M. (Editors) *v.5 p.29*

Hatfield, J. L. & Stewart, B. A. (Editors) . . . *v.5 p.87, p.176*

Hathaway, Heather *v.2 p.767*

Hathaway, Jane *v.6 p.628, p.638*

Hathway, D. C. *v.5 p.387*

Hatoum, Milton *v.2 p.691*

Hatt, Michael & Klonk, Charlotte *v.1 p.701*

Hattaway, Herman & Beringer, Richard E. . *v.3 p.398, v.4 p.520*

Hattaway, Herman & Jones, Archer *v.3 p.398*

Hattaway, Herman *v.3 p.397*

Hattaway, Michael (Editor) *v.2 p.233*

Hattenhauer, Darryl *v.2 p.90*

Hatto, A. T. (Translator) *v.2 p.595*

Hatton, Ragnhild H. *v.3 p.106*

Hatzfeld, Jean *v.6 p.65*

Hauff, Wilhelm *v.2 p.599*

Haug, Marc & Whalen, Richard E. (Editors) . . . *v.5 p.614*

Hauge, Kjetil Ra *v.2 p.774*

Haugeland, John *v.5 p.590*

Haugerud, Angelique (Editor), et al. *v.4 p.28*

Haughton, Hugh (Editor), et al. *v.2 p.278*

Haule, James M. & Smith, Philip H. Jr. *v.2 p.392*

Haule, James M. & Stape, J. H. (Editors) *v.2 p.392*

Hauptman, Judith *v.1 p.553*

Hauptman, Laurence M. *v.6 p.687, p.689*

Hauptman, William *v.1 p.740*

Hauptmann, Gerhart *v.2 p.609*

Haury, Emil W. *v.4 p.11*

Hausam, Wiley (Editor) *v.1 p.250, p.408*

Hausberg, Margaret D. *v.1 p.759*

Hauser, Arnold *v.1 p.708*

Hauser, Barbara R. (Editor) *v.4 p.442, v.6 p.469*

Hauser, Marc D. *v.5 p.621, p.623*

Hauser, Marc *v.5 p.614*

Hauser, Robert Mason *v.4 p.724*

Hauser, Ronald *v.2 p.597*

Hauser, Stuart T. & Kasendorf, E. *v.5 p.627*

Hauser, Thomas *v.4 p.855, p.896*

Hauser-Cram, Penny, et al. *v.4 p.368*

Hausmann, Rudolf *v.5 p.127*

Hausner, H. H. & Mal, M. K. *v.5 p.732*

Haussman, Melissa *v.4 p.768*

Haut, Woody *v.6 p.326*

Havard, Gilles *v.4 p.630, v.6 p.685*

Havard, Robert G. *v.2 p.643*

Havel, Vaclav *v.2 p.782, p.783*

Havel, Václav *v.3 p.189*

Havelock, Eric A. *v.1 p.424*

Havens, Thomas R. *v.6 p.168, p.224*

Haverkamp, Alfred *v.3 p.161*

Havighurst, Walter *v.3 p.513*

Havlice, Patricia Pate *v.1 p.662, p.711*

Havlice, Patricia P. *v.1 p.711*

Hawass, Zahi *v.1 p.706*

Hawes, Chris & Satiat-Jeunemaitre, Beatrice (Editors) . *v.5 p.154*

Hawes, Joseph M. & Shores, Elizabeth F. (Editors) . . *v.5 p.638*

Hawke, Constance S. *v.4 p.441*

Hawkes, David C. (Editor) *v.4 p.588*

Hawkes, David *v.6 p.209*

Hawkes, John *v.2 p.82, p.83*

Hawkes, Nena Rey & Seggar, John F. *v.4 p.836*

Hawkes, Terence *v.2 p.561*

Hawkesworth, Celia. *v.2 p.818, v.3 p.248, v.6 p.478*

Hawking, Stephen W. . . . *v.5 p.72, p.540, p.555, p.556, p.557*

Hawkins, Alma M. *v.1 p.47*

Hawkins, Angus *v.3 p.112*

Hawkins, Darnell Felix & Kempf-Leonard, Kimberly
  (Editors) *v.6 p.248*

Hawkins, Darnell Felix (Editor), et al. *v.6 p.248, p.263*

Hawkins, Darren G. *v.3 p.353, v.4 p.512*

Hawkins, David B. *v.4 p.339*

Hawkins, Dawn *v.5 p.90*

Hawkins, Freda *v.4 p.667*

Hawkins, Frederick William. . . . *v.1 p.59, p.105, p.106, p.140*

Hawkins, Joan *v.6 p.318*

Hawkins, John *v.1 p.174*

Hawkins, Mike. *v.3 p.49, p.77*

Hawkins, Peter & Jacoff, Rachel (Editors) *v.2 p.704*

Hawkins, Roger & Towell, Richard *v.2 p.453*

Hawksworth, D. L. (Editor) *v.5 p.237*

Hawksworth, D. L. *v.5 p.179*

Hawksworth, David L. (Editor) *v.5 p.205*

Hawley, Ellis W. *v.3 p.441*

Hawley, John C. (Editor) *v.2 p.727*

Hawley, John S. & Wulff, Donna M. *v.1 p.540*

Hawley, John Stratton & Wulff, Donna Marie (Editors). *v.1 p.536*

Hawley, R. Scott, et al. *v.5 p.140*

Hawley, Scott & Mori, Catherine A. *v.5 p.134*

Hawlin, Stefan *v.2 p.272*

Haworth, J. T. & Veal, Anthony James (Editors) . . . *v.4 p.250*

Hawthorne, Gerald F. (Editor), et al. *v.1 p.631*

Hawthorne, Julian *v.2 p.41*

Hawthorne, Nathaniel *v.2 p.41*

Hawting, Gerald R. *v.6 p.584*

Hay, Ashley & Stacey, Robyn *v.5 p.85*

Hay, Deborah *v.1 p.28, p.30*

Hay, George E. *v.5 p.486*

Hay, Harry *v.6 p.365, p.390*

Hay, Iain (Editor) *v.4 p.376, p.396*

Hay, Iain *v.4 p.376*

Hay, James G. *v.4 p.873, p.908*

Hay, John M. & Burlingame, Michael *v.3 p.434*

Hay, John M. *v.3 p.434*

Hay, John *v.5 p.221*

Hay, Margaret Jean (Editor) *v.2 p.751, v.6 p.80*

Hay, Samuel A. *v.1 p.123*

Hay, William W., et al. *v.5 p.525*

Hayashi, Brian Masaru *v.6 p.133*

Hayashi, Fumio *v.4 p.201*

Haycox, Stephen W. *v.3 p.533, v.6 p.300*

Hayden, Corinne P. *v.6 p.283*

Hayden, Dolores. *v.6 p.713, p.718, p.726*

Hayden, Jacqueline *v.3 p.255*

Hayden, John O. (Editor) *v.2 p.307*

Hayden, Joseph R. *v.6 p.179*

Hayden, Mary & Thompson, Jeff (Editors) *v.4 p.313*

Hayden, Mary (Editor), et al. *v.4 p.313*

Hayden, Robert *v.2 p.81*

Haydn, Joseph *v.1 p.189, p.330*

Hayek, Friedrich A. *v.4 p.211, p.227, p.234, p.238, p.243, p.248*

Hayek, Lee-Ann C. & Buzas, Martin A. *v.5 p.189*

Hayes, Cassandra. *v.4 p.167*

Hayes, Dade & Bing, Jonathan *v.6 p.344*

Hayes, David & Shubin, Tatiana (Editors) *v.5 p.458*

Hayes, David K. & Ninemeier, Jack D. *v.4 p.165*

Hayes, Dawn Marie *v.6 p.571*

Hayes, Derek *v.4 p.379, p.382*

Hayes, James *v.6 p.205*

Hayes, John (Editor) *v.1 p.616*

Hayes, John H. & Miller, J. Maxwell *v.1 p.619, v.3 p.7*

Hayes, Joy Elizabeth *v.3 p.267*

Hayes, Kevin J. (Editor) *v.2 p.43, p.50, p.92*

Hayes, Michael T. *v.4 p.575*

Hayes, Peter *v.3 p.84, p.172*

Hayes, Robert A. *v.3 p.274*

Hayes, Wayland J. *v.5 p.9, p.354, p.366*

Hayes, William. *v.4 p.322*

Hayes-Bautista, David E. *v.6 p.521, p.544, p.551*

Hayford, Charles W. *v.6 p.190, p.202*

Hayford, Charles Wishart *v.6 p.182*

Haygood, Wil *v.1 p.8, p.36*

Hayhoe, Ruth *v.4 p.334*

Haykal, M. H. *v.1 p.555*

Haykal, Muhammad Hasanayan *v.6 p.58, p.639*

Haykin, Simon & Moher, Michael *v.5 p.725*

Haykin, Simon *v.4 p.422, v.5 p.725*

Hayman, David *v.2 p.358*

Hayman, Ronald *v.2 p.605*

Haynes, Bruce. *v.1 p.375, p.389*

Haynes, Charles C., et al. *v.4 p.450*

Haynes, Felicity & McKenna, Tarquam (Editors) . . . *v.6 p.370*

Haynes, Roslynn D. *v.2 p.740*

Hays, Mary & Opie, Amelia. *v.2 p.290*

Hays, Mary *v.2 p.290*

Hays, Michael & Nikolopoulou, Anastasia
  (Editors) *v.1 p.88, p.96, p.115, v.2 p.188*

Hays, R. Allen *v.4 p.524*

Hays, Richard B. *v.1 p.625*

Hays, Samuel P. *v.3 p.436, v.4 p.566, v.5 p.4, p.17, v.6 p.283, p.300*

Hays, Sharon *v.6 p.466, p.469*

Hays, Terence E. (Editor) *v.4 p.4*

Hayslip, Le Ly & Wurts, Jay. *v.6 p.93, p.140*

Hayslip, Le Ly *v.6 p.93, p.140*

Hayt, William H., et al. *v.5 p.721*

Haythornthwaite, Philip J. *v.3 p.74*

Hayward, Jack Ernest Shalom (Editor), et al. . . *v.4 p.603, p.637*

Hayward, Jennifer P. *v.2 p.284*

Hayward, O. T. (Editor). *v.5 p.431*

Hayward, Susan & Vincendeau, Ginette (Editors) . . *v.6 p.338*

HAYWARD *v.6 p.306*

Haywood, Ian *v.6 p.738, p.758, p.763*
Haywood, J. A. & Nahmad, H. M. *v.6 p.654*
Haywood, John *v.3 p.3, v.4 p.380*
Haywood, Kathleen M. & Getchell, Nancy *v.4 p.909*
Haywood, Richard *v.3 p.218*
Hayworth, Gene *v.4 p.146*
Hazard, Nicolas Auguste & Delteil, Loys *v.1 p.756*
Hazard, Paul *v.3 p.72*
Hazareesingh, Sudhir *v.3 p.140, p.149*
Hazaz, Haim *v.6 p.649*
Hazen, Margaret H. & Hazen, Robert M. *v.1 p.277*
Hazen, Robert M. (Editor) *v.5 p.431*
Hazewinkel, Michiel *v.5 p.458, p.461*
Hazlitt, William & Wu, Duncan . . . *v.2 p.292, p.293*
Hazlitt, William *v.2 p.166, p.181, p.229, p.292*
Hazon, N. & Flik, G. (Editors) *v.5 p.163*
Hazzard, William R., et al. *v.5 p.519*
Hazzard-Gordon, Katrina *v.1 p.31*
H'Doubler, Margaret N. *v.1 p.47*
Heaberlin, S. W. *v.5 p.709, p.739*
Heacox, Kim *v.5 p.234*
Head, Bessie *v.2 p.756*
Head, Dominic *v.2 p.194, p.754*
Head, Lesley *v.6 p.297*
Head, Simon *v.4 p.69*
Head, Thomas *v.1 p.613, v.6 p.571*
Headlam, Dave *v.1 p.215, p.309*
Headland, Thomas N. (Editor), et al. *v.4 p.18*
Headrick, Daniel R. *v.3 p.76*
Headrick, David *v.5 p.96, p.213*
Heady, Harold F. & Child, R. Dennis *v.5 p.42*
Heale, Elizabeth *v.2 p.182*
Healey, George H. (Editor) *v.2 p.358*
Healey, Patsy (Editor), et al. *v.4 p.543, v.6 p.723*
Healy, Alice F. & Bourne, Lyle E. Jr. (Editors) *v.5 p.610*
Healy, Alice F. *v.5 p.608*
Healy, David *v.5 p.659*
Healy, J. J. *v.2 p.740*
Healy, Kevin *v.3 p.324*
Healy, Nicholas M. *v.1 p.655*
Healy, Thomas *v.2 p.252*
Heaney, Duska Radosavljevic & Awde, Nicholas . . . *v.2 p.776*
Heaney, Seamus (Translator) *v.2 p.352*
Heaney, Seamus *v.2 p.204, p.326, p.352*
Heaphy, Leslie A. *v.4 p.806, p.832, p.850, v.6 p.41*
Heard-Bey, Frauke *v.6 p.628*
Hearder, Harry *v.3 p.198, p.201*
Hearn, Charles R. *v.3 p.367*
Hearn, E. J. *v.5 p.689*
Hearn, Fil *v.1 p.703, p.786*
Hearn, Lafcadio *v.2 p.39, p.40*
Hearn, Maxwell K. *v.1 p.732*
Hearne, Samuel *v.3 p.545*
Hearnshaw, J. B. *v.5 p.65*
Heartney, Eleanor & Gopnik, Adam *v.1 p.825*

Heartz, Daniel *v.1 p.189, p.190, p.230, p.330, p.343*
Heasley Cox, Martha & Chatterton, Wayne *v.2 p.56*
Heater, Derek *v.4 p.577*
Heath, Anthony *v.4 p.606*
Heath, Duncan, et al. *v.2 p.171, p.183, p.568*
Heath, Jeffrey M. *v.2 p.387*
Heath John Staff *v.4 p.177*
Heath, Julian *v.5 p.86*
Heath, Kingston William *v.1 p.822*
Heath, Maurice E. *v.5 p.42*
Heath, Michael T. *v.5 p.337*
Heath, Robert L. (Editor) *v.4 p.428*
Heath, Shirley Brice *v.4 p.357*
Heath, Stephen C. *v.2 p.491*
Heath, Thomas L. *v.5 p.466*
Heather, Peter J. *v.3 p.31*
Heather, Peter *v.3 p.31, p.62*
Heat-Moon, William Least *v.2 p.146*
Heaton, Donald D. *v.5 p.21, p.26*
Heaviside, Oliver *v.5 p.564*
Heavysege, Charles *v.2 p.732*
Hebb, D. O. *v.5 p.617*
Hebbel, Friedrich *v.2 p.599*
Hebblethwaite, Peter *v.1 p.573*
Hebel, Johann Peter *v.2 p.599*
Hebert, Elizabeth A. *v.4 p.286, p.347, p.363*
Heble, Ajay (Editor), et al. *v.2 p.729*
Hechemy, Karim E. *v.5 p.206*
Hecht, Anthony *v.2 p.146, p.329*
Hecht, Ben *v.2 p.81*
Hecht, Bennett L. *v.4 p.158*
Hecht, Eugene *v.5 p.73, p.561*
Hecht, Hans *v.2 p.273*
Hecht, Heiko (Editor), et al. *v.5 p.606*
Hecht, Jeff *v.5 p.701*
Hecht, Sidney M. (Editor) *v.5 p.121*
Hecht, Susanna B. & Cockburn, Alexander *v.3 p.269*
Hecht, Tobias (Editor) *v.3 p.286*
Hecht, Tobias *v.3 p.279*
Heck, Shirley F. & Williams, C. Ray *v.4 p.278*
Heckel, Robert V. & Shumaker, David M. *v.5 p.592*
Heckel, Waldemar & Yardley, John (Editors) *v.3 p.20*
Heckel, Waldemar *v.3 p.19*
Heckenberger, Michael J. *v.4 p.11*
Heckethorn, Charles W. *v.4 p.719*
Heckman, J. J. & Leamer, E. E. (Editors) . . . *v.4 p.189, p.201*
Heckman, James J. & Singer, Burton S. (Editors) . . *v.4 p.254*
Heckscher, Charles C. *v.4 p.122*
Heckscher, Eli F. *v.4 p.215*
Heckscher, Eli Filip *v.3 p.152*
Hedayat, Sadeq *v.6 p.671*
Hedgecoe, John *v.1 p.769, p.780*
Hedges, William L. & Irving, Washington *v.2 p.42*
Hedgpeth, Kevin & Missal, Stephen *v.6 p.348*
Hedin, Benjamin *v.1 p.270, p.322, p.323*

Hedman, Eva-Lotta E. *v.6 p.179*

Hedrick, Brad, et al. *v.4 p.842, p.854*

Hedrick, Joan D. *v.2 p.51*

Hedrick, Philip W. *v.5 p.134*

Hedrick, Tace *v.3 p.267*

Hedrick, Tom & McKenzie, Mike *v.4 p.906*

Heenk, Liesbeth *v.1 p.756*

Heer, C. V. *v.5 p.558*

Heer, David M. *v.6 p.529*

Heermann, Dieter W. *v.5 p.551*

Heertje, Arnold & Perlman, Mark (Editors) . . *v.4 p.230, p.235*

Heertje, Arnold (Editor) *v.4 p.193, p.215, p.223*

Heertje, Arnold *v.4 p.193, p.215, p.217, p.223*

Heffer, Simon *v.2 p.276*

Heffley, Mike *v.1 p.215, p.260, p.313*

Hefley, James & Hefley, Marti *v.1 p.612*

Hefling, Charles & Shattuck, Cynthia (Editors) . . . *v.1 p.582*

Hefling, Stephen E. *v.1 p.215, p.235, p.339*

Hefling, Stephen *v.1 p.198, p.239*

Hefner, Robert W. *v.6 p.174, p.176*

Heftmann, E. (Editor) *v.5 p.269*

Hegedus, Louis *v.5 p.299*

Hegel, G. W. F. *v.1 p.463, p.491*

Hegel, Georg Wilhelm Fredrich *v.4 p.491, p.502*

Hegel, Georg Wilhelm Friedrich *v.1 p.463, p.522*

Heger, Heinz *v.3 p.84, v.6 p.365*

Heggen, Thomas *v.2 p.81*

Hehir, Bryan, et al. *v.4 p.515, p.641, p.642*

Hehn, Anton H. *v.5 p.709*

Heiber, Helmut & Glantz, David M. (Editors) . . . *v.3 p.175*

Heiber, Helmut *v.3 p.81*

Heiberger, Mary Morris & Vick, Julia Miller *v.4 p.170*

Heidar, Knut *v.4 p.594*

Heidbreder, Edna *v.5 p.596*

Heidegger, Martin . *v.1 p.417, p.421, p.461, p.463, p.466, p.468, p.470, p.471, p.489, p.511*

Heidel, Alexander *v.6 p.665*

Heidenheimer, Arnold J. & Johnston, Michael (Editors) . *v.4 p.580*

Heidenrich, John G. *v.4 p.652*

Heider, Fritz *v.5 p.646*

Heidler, David S. & Heidler, Jeanne T. *v.3 p.424*

Heij, Christiaan, et al. *v.4 p.201*

Heijke, Hans & Muysken, Joan (Editors) *v.4 p.297*

Heikal, Mohamed H. *v.6 p.639*

Heil, John & Mele, Alfred R. (Editors) *v.1 p.497*

Heilbron, J. L. *v.3 p.47, v.5 p.466, p.495, p.543*

Heilbron, John L. & Seidel, Robert W. *v.5 p.543*

Heilbron, John L. (Editor) *v.3 p.45*

Heilbroner, Robert L. & Milberg, William *v.4 p.209*

Heilbroner, Robert L. . *v.3 p.40, v.4 p.195, p.209, p.214, p.235, p.243, p.244*

Heilbrun, Kirk, et al. *v.5 p.592, v.6 p.248*

Heilbrun, Kirk *v.5 p.592*

Heilbrunn, Jeffrey *v.4 p.134*

Heilbut, Anthony *v.6 p.402*

Heilemann, John *v.4 p.158*

Heiler, Friedrich *v.1 p.654*

Heilman, Anna *v.2 p.191*

Heilman, Arthur W., et al. *v.4 p.363*

Heilman, Arthur W. *v.4 p.363*

Heilman, Robert B. *v.2 p.230*

Heilman, Samuel C. *v.4 p.764*

Heim, Scott *v.6 p.397*

Heiman, Gary W. *v.5 p.600*

Heimann, Jim (Editor) *v.4 p.141*

Heimer, Karen & Kruttschnitt, Candace *v.6 p.258*

Hein, Jeremy . . *v.4 p.571, p.763, p.764, v.6 p.118, p.138, p.139*

Hein, Jotun, et al. *v.5 p.140*

Hein, Laura Elizabeth & Selden, Mark (Editors) . . . *v.6 p.235*

Heinberg, Richar *v.4 p.62*

Heine, Bernd & Nurse, Derek (Editors) *v.6 p.80*

Heine, Heinrich *v.2 p.599, v.3 p.168*

Heine, Jorge *v.3 p.320*

Heine, Steven & Prebish, Charles S. (Editors) . . . *v.1 p.561*

Heineke, Walt & Willis, Jerry (Editors) *v.4 p.351*

Heineman, Elizabeth D. *v.3 p.53, p.172*

Heineman, Kenneth J. *v.4 p.331*

Heinemann, Bruce W. *v.5 p.222*

Heinemann, Margot *v.2 p.221*

Heininger, Janet *v.4 p.649*

Heinl, Robert *v.3 p.315*

Heinsohn, Robert Jennings & Cimbala, John M. . *v.5 p.354, p.368, p.372, p.376*

Heintz, James, et al. *v.4 p.269*

Heintze, James R. *v.1 p.166, p.277*

Heintzelman, Greta & Smith Howard, Alycia . . . *v.2 p.134*

Heintzman, James *v.5 p.232*

Heinze, Richard *v.2 p.446*

Heiple, Daniel L. *v.2 p.652*

Heisenberg, Werner *v.5 p.402, p.541, p.553*

Heiser, Charles B. Jr. *v.5 p.4*

Heiserman, Arthur Ray *v.2 p.214*

Heisig, James W. *v.1 p.476, p.509*

Heisler, Sanford I. *v.5 p.679*

Heisner, Beverly *v.6 p.348*

Heissig, Walther *v.6 p.240*

Heitner, Robert R. (Editor) *v.2 p.592*

Heitschmidt, Rodney K. & Stuth, Jerry W. (Editors) . *v.5 p.42*

Heitzenrater, Richard P. *v.1 p.586*

Heitzmann, William Ray *v.4 p.903*

Hejlsberg, Anders; Wiltamuth, Scott; Golde, Peter . *v.5 p.346*

Helbing, Terry (Selected by) *v.6 p.411*

Helbling, Robert E. *v.2 p.599*

Held, David & McGrew, Anthony G. (Editors) . . . *v.4 p.663*

Held, David *v.4 p.504, p.659*

Heldman, Dennis R. (Editor) *v.5 p.4*

Helfand, Jessica *v.1 p.717*

Helfrich, Kurt Gerard Frederick *v.1 p.816*

Helg, Aline *v.3 p.279, p.310, p.356, p.357*
Helitzer, Melvin *v.4 p.906*
Helle, Knut (Editor, Contribution by) *v.3 p.232, p.233*
Hellegouarch, Yves *v.5 p.476*
Helleiner, Jane *v.4 p.731*
Heller, Charles E. & Stofft, William A. (Editors) . . . *v.3 p.383*
Heller, Henry *v.3 p.49, p.145*
Heller, Joseph *v.2 p.146*
Heller, Jules & Heller, Nancy G.
(Editors) *v.1 p.664, p.706, v.6 p.472*
Heller, K. A. (Editor), et al. *v.4 p.317*
Heller, Kurt A. (Editor), et al. *v.5 p.575*
Heller, Morton & Schiff, William (Editors) . . . *v.5 p.606*
Heller, Nancy G. *v.6 p.472*
Heller, Peter B. *v.4 p.634*
Heller, Stephen R. (Editor) *v.5 p.288*
Heller, Steven & Anderson, Gail *v.1 p.701*
Heller, Steven & Ballance, Georgette (Editors) . . . *v.1 p.713*
Heller, Steven & Chwast, Seymour *v.1 p.719*
Heller, Steven & Pomeroy, Karen *v.1 p.716*
Heller, Steven (Editor) *v.1 p.714*
Heller, Terry *v.2 p.43*
Hellie, Richard *v.4 p.728*
Hellinger, Stephen H. & Hellinger, Douglas A. . *v.4 p.253, p.263*
Hellman, Lillian & Bates, Kathy *v.2 p.83*
Hellman, Lillian *v.1 p.121, v.2 p.83, v.6 p.411*
Hellmann, Paul T. *v.4 p.374*
Hellwig, David J. (Editor) *v.3 p.279*
Hellwinkel, D. *v.5 p.289*
Helm, Dieter R. (Editor) *v.4 p.227*
Helm, Paul *v.1 p.645*
Helmholtz, Hermann *v.1 p.375, v.5 p.607*
Helmick, Raymond G. *v.4 p.649*
Helminiak, Daniel A. *v.5 p.634, v.6 p.373*
Helmke, Gretchen *v.3 p.274, p.348*
Helmreich, Anne *v.1 p.818*
Helmreich, Ernst *v.1 p.610*
Helmreich, Jonathan E. *v.3 p.389*
Helmreich, William B. *v.4 p.694*
Helms, Christine M. *v.6 p.626*
Helms, Jesse *v.4 p.486*
Helms, Mary W. *v.3 p.304*
Helms, Ronald N. & Belcher, M. Clay *v.5 p.723*
Helmstadter, Richard (Editor) *v.1 p.656*
Helper, Hinton Rowan *v.3 p.398, p.420*
Helpern, Alice *v.1 p.26*
Helphand, Kenneth I. *v.1 p.813*
Helsinger, Elizabeth K., et al. *v.6 p.747, p.761*
Helton, Arthur C. *v.4 p.667, p.670*
Helton, Lonnie R. & Smith, Mieko Kotake . . . *v.5 p.513*
Helvarg, David *v.5 p.430*
Helyer, Neil & Brown, Kevin *v.5 p.27*
Hema Maps Staff (Author, Illustrator) *v.4 p.385*
Hemelrijk, Charlotte (Editor) *v.5 p.193*
Hemelrijk, Emily Ann *v.6 p.451, p.463*

Hemenway, David *v.6 p.266*
Hemenway, Robert E. *v.6 p.17*
Hemingway, Ernest, et al. *v.2 p.13, p.84*
Hemingway, Ernest *v.2 p.84, p.85*
Hemlow, Joyce *v.2 p.242*
Hemmasi, Harriette & Rowley, Fred (Compiled by) . . *v.1 p.167*
Hemmings, Annette B. *v.4 p.29*
Hemmings, F. W. J. (Editor) *v.2 p.459*
Hemmings, F. W. J. *v.2 p.489*
Hemmings, Frederic William John *v.2 p.488, p.504*
Hemmons, Willa Mae *v.6 p.259*
Hempel, Carl G. *v.1 p.499, v.5 p.402*
Hemphill, Essex (Editor) *v.6 p.406*
Hemphill, Essex *v.6 p.397, p.405*
Hemphill, Hellen & Haines, Ray *v.4 p.132*
Hempstead, Colin & Worthington, William E. . . . *v.5 p.679*
Hempstead, Colin A. *v.5 p.387*
Hempton, David *v.1 p.586*
Hendel, Yehudit *v.6 p.649*
Hendershot, Cyndy *v.4 p.712*
Hendershot, Heather *v.1 p.655*
Hendershott, Anne B. *v.4 p.696*
Henderson, C. J. *v.6 p.318*
Henderson, David W. *v.5 p.496*
Henderson, Errol A. *v.6 p.14, p.31*
Henderson, George *v.1 p.672, p.687, v.4 p.132*
Henderson, Harold P. & Roberts, Gary L. (Editors) . . *v.3 p.503*
Henderson, Harry *v.4 p.471, p.563, v.5 p.709, p.740*
Henderson, James D. *v.3 p.357*
Henderson, Jeffrey *v.2 p.401*
Henderson, John Cleaves *v.4 p.298*
Henderson, Karla A., et al. *v.4 p.784, p.836*
Henderson, Mary C. *v.1 p.115, p.154*
Henderson, Paula *v.1 p.786*
Henderson, Peter V. N. *v.3 p.293*
Henderson, Robert W. *v.4 p.806, p.850*
Henderson, V. & Thisse, J. F. (Editors) *v.4 p.189*
Henderson, Virginia A. *v.5 p.527*
Henderson, William & Abel, Eddie *v.5 p.303*
Hendin, Josephine *v.3 p.441*
Hendon, Julia A. & Joyce, Rosemary A. (Editors) . . . *v.4 p.9*
Hendrick, Burton J. *v.3 p.425*
Hendrick, Clyde & Hendrick, Susan S. (Editors) . . *v.5 p.647*
Hendricks, Glenn *v.6 p.529, p.549*
Hendrickson, Carol *v.3 p.267*
Hendrickson Publishers, Inc. Staff *v.1 p.613*
Hendrix, Scott & Gassmann, Gunther *v.1 p.585*
Hendry, David F. & Morgan, Mary S. (Editors) . . . *v.4 p.201*
Hendry, David F. & Morgan, Mary S. *v.4 p.201*
Hendry, David F. *v.4 p.201*
Hendry, Joy *v.6 p.221*
Heng, Liang & Shapiro, Judith *v.6 p.195, p.200*
Hengel, Martin & Bowden, John *v.1 p.640*
Hengel, Martin *v.1 p.629, p.630, p.640, p.643*
Hengeveld, R. *v.5 p.168, p.184*

Henig, Jeffrey R. & Rich, Wilbur C. (Editors) . . . *v.4 p.543*
Henig, Jeffrey R. *v.4 p.315*
Henig, Jeffrey *v.4 p.347*
Henig, Robin Marantz *v.5 p.230*
Henig, Ruth *v.4 p.631*
Henige, David P. *v.6 p.53*
Henisch, Heinz K. & Henisch, Bridget A. . *v.1 p.701, p.762, p.763*
Henke, Holger & Reno, Fred (Editors) . . . *v.3 p.315*
Henke, Robert *v.1 p.91, p.135, p.144*
Henkin, Louis *v.4 p.455*
Henkle, Roger B. *v.6 p.752*
Henle, Michael *v.5 p.478, p.499*
Henley, Beth *v.2 p.146*
Henley, William Ernest *v.2 p.290*
Henman, Anthony *v.3 p.281*
Henneman, John B. *v.3 p.144*
Hennen, John *v.3 p.501*
Hennessey, Maureen Hart & Larson, Judy L. *v.1 p.740*
Hennessey, Thomas *v.3 p.139*
Hennessy, Brendan *v.4 p.407*
Hennessy, John L. & Patterson, David A. . *v.5 p.344, p.345, p.730*
Hennig, W. (Editor) *v.5 p.161*
Henning, Daniel H. & Mangun, William R. *v.4 p.62*
Henricksson, John (Editor) *v.5 p.230*
Henrion, Claudia *v.5 p.458, p.466, v.6 p.439*
Henry, J. David *v.5 p.176, p.211, p.234, p.239*
Henry, J. Glynn & Heinke, Gary W. *v.5 p.704*
Henry, Jules *v.4 p.22, p.343*
Henry M. Leicester, ed.-in-chief. *v.5 p.263*
Henry, Mark & Armstrong, Leslie (Editors) *v.4 p.382*
Henry, Mary E. *v.6 p.463*
Henry, Nancy *v.2 p.287*
Henry, O. & Porter, Sydney *v.2 p.51*
Henry Yuhuai He *v.4 p.620*
Henshall Momsen, Janet *v.4 p.259, p.273*
Hensler, Kate *v.4 p.792, p.881*
Henson, Matthew A. *v.6 p.5, p.17*
Hentoff, Nat *v.4 p.563, p.572*
Henty, G. A. *v.2 p.290*
Henze, Hans W. & Spencer, Stewart *v.1 p.215, p.331*
Henze, Paul B. *v.6 p.64*
Henzold, G. *v.5 p.684*
Heon, Laura S., et al. *v.1 p.714*
Hepburn, Allan *v.2 p.191*
Heper, Metin & Evin, Ahmet O. *v.6 p.623*
Heper, Metin & Sayari, Sabri (Editors) . . . *v.6 p.623*
Heper, Metin (Editor), et al. *v.6 p.623*
Heper, Metin *v.6 p.621*
Hepokoski, James A. . *v.1 p.198, p.215, p.230, p.239, p.356, p.364*
Hepper, Peter G. (Editor) *v.5 p.614*
Heppner, Christopher *v.2 p.239*
Hepworth, James R. (Editor) *v.2 p.121*
Heraclitus *v.1 p.421*
herausgegeben von der Dudenredaktion . . . *v.2 p.621*
Herberg, Will *v.1 p.543*

Herbert, Christopher *v.2 p.316, v.6 p.756, p.763*
Herbert, Edward Herbert *v.2 p.214*
Herbert, Frank *v.2 p.146*
Herbert, George *v.2 p.249*
Herbert, Melissa S. *v.4 p.717*
Herbert, Nick *v.5 p.541*
Herbert, Robert L. *v.1 p.740*
Herbert, Robert *v.1 p.728*
Herbert, Rosemary (Editor) *v.2 p.580*
Herbert, Steven Kelly *v.4 p.774, v.6 p.264*
Herbert, Trevor (Editor) *v.1 p.389*
Herbert, Trevor *v.1 p.389*
Herbert, Ulrich *v.3 p.172*
Herbert, Zbigniew *v.2 p.790*
Herbich, John B. (Editor) *v.5 p.702*
Herbst, Anri (Editor) *v.1 p.285*
Herbst, Edward *v.6 p.174, p.176*
Herbst, Jeffrey Ira *v.4 p.611*
Herbst, Josephine *v.2 p.81*
Herbst, Jurgen *v.4 p.327*
Herbst, Peter (Editor) *v.1 p.270*
Herbst, Philip *v.4 p.659*
Herd, David *v.2 p.57*
Herda, D J *v.3 p.510*
Herder, Johann Gottfried *v.2 p.599*
Herder, Ronald (Editor) *v.1 p.411*
Herdt, Gilbert H. & de Vries, Brian (Editors) . . . *v.6 p.380*
Herdt, Gilbert H. & Leavitt, Stephen C. (Editors) . . . *v.4 p.43*
Herf, Jeffrey *v.3 p.159, p.178*
Hergenhan, Laurie (Author, Editor) *v.2 p.743*
Hergenhan, Laurie (Editor) *v.2 p.741*
Hergenhan, Laurie *v.2 p.741*
Herholdt, Elizabeth M. *v.5 p.227*
Heriot, Angus *v.1 p.230*
Heritage, John *v.4 p.688*
Herken, Gregg *v.5 p.543*
Herlihy, Barbara & Corey, Gerald *v.5 p.674*
Herlihy, David (Editor) *v.6 p.576*
Herlihy, David V. (Contribution by) *v.4 p.857*
Herlihy, David *v.3 p.43, p.51, v.6 p.557*
Herling, Gustaw *v.2 p.790*
Herling-Grudzinski, Gustaw *v.2 p.790*
Herman, Andrew & Swiss, Thomas (Editors) *v.4 p.761*
Herman, Barry & United Nations Staff *v.4 p.664*
Herman, Bohuslav & Tinbergen, Jan *v.4 p.254*
Herman, Didi *v.6 p.373*
Herman, Ellen *v.5 p.596*
Herman Hansen, Mogens *v.4 p.500*
Herman, Jerry & Stasio, Marilyn *v.1 p.250, p.331, p.332*
Herman, Jerry (Composed by) *v.6 p.411*
Herman, Judith L. *v.4 p.737*
Herman, Lee & Mandell, Alan *v.4 p.320*
Herman Mark, John J. McKetta, Jr., Donald F. Othmer, ed.
board *v.5 p.257*
Herman, Michael *v.4 p.546, p.580*

Hermand, Jost *v.2 p.617*
Hermann, Bernd & Hummel, Susanne (Editors) *v.5 p.121*
Hermann, W. A. *v.5 p.306*
Hermans, T. J. (Editor) *v.3 p.206*
Hermes, Matthew E. (Editor) *v.5 p.316*
Hernandez, Felisberto. *v.2 p.686*
Hernandez, Francisco. *v.5 p.234*
Hernandez, Guillermo E. *v.6 p.499, p.512*
Hernandez, Rafael *v.3 p.310*
Hernandez, Ramona *v.6 p.524, p.529*
Hernández, Carmen D. *v.6 p.506, p.512*
Hernández Catá, Ernesto *v.3 p.310*
Hernández Cruz, Victor. *v.6 p.506, p.510*
Hernández, Eugenio and Guido L. Weiss *v.5 p.494*
Hernández, José M.. . . . . *v.3 p.310*
Hernández, José *v.2 p.678*
Hernández, Rafael & Rojas, Rafael *v.2 p.672*
Hero, Alfred O. Jr. & Balthazar, Louis *v.4 p.581*
Hero, Rodney E. *v.6 p.538*
Herodotus *v.2 p.412*
Herold, J. Christopher *v.3 p.152*
Heron, Ann (Editor) *v.6 p.406*
Herr, Christopher J.. . . . . *v.2 p.108*
Herr, Richard *v.3 p.240*
Herrara-Sobek, Maria (Editor). *v.6 p.499, p.512*
Herrera, Andrea O'Reilly *v.6 p.489, p.542*
Herrera, Hayden *v.1 p.697, p.740*
Herrera Serna, Laura *v.3 p.289*
Herrera-Sobek, María & Viramontes, Helena Maria
    (Editors). *v.6 p.499, p.513*
Herrera-Sobek, María (Editor) *v.6 p.499, p.512, p.513*
Herrera-Sobek, María *v.6 p.513, p.523*
Herrick, John & Stuart, Paul H. (Editors). *v.4 p.754*
Herrick, Rebekah. *v.4 p.533*
Herrick, Robert *v.2 p.250*
Herrigel, Eugene. *v.4 p.802, p.847*
Herrin, Judith *v.6 p.563*
Herring, George C.. . . . . *v.6 p.168*
Herring, Peter *v.5 p.173*
Herring, Phillip F. *v.6 p.402*
Herrity, Peter *v.2 p.777*
Herrmann, Claudine *v.6 p.434*
Herrmann, Keith R.. . . . . *v.4 p.173*
Herrmann, W. A. & Brauer, G. *v.5 p.306*
Herrmann, W. A. & Brauer *v.5 p.306*
Herrmann, W. A. (Editor) *v.5 p.306*
Herrmann, Wolfgang A. (Editor). *v.5 p.306, p.307*
Herrnson, Paul (Editor), et al. *v.4 p.548*
Herrnson, Paul S.. . . . . *v.4 p.549*
Herrnstein, Richard J. & Boring, Edwin G. (Editors) *v.5 p.596*
Herrnstein, Richard J. *v.5 p.608, p.632, p.653*
Herron, R. E. & Sutton-Smith, Brian. *v.5 p.627*
Herrup, Cynthia B.. . . . . *v.3 p.123*
Herschy, R. W. & Fairbridge, R. W. (Editors) . . . *v.6 p.283*
Hersen, Michel & Bellack, Alan S. (Editors) *v.5 p.667*

Hersen, Michel (Editor) *v.5 p.665, p.666*
Hersen, Michel (Editor-In-Chief), et al.. . . . . . *v.5 p.603*
Hersen, Michel, et al.. . . . . *v.5 p.667*
Hersen, Michel. *v.5 p.666*
Hersey, John *v.2 p.81, v.6 p.218*
Hersh, Richard H. & Merrow, John (Editors) *v.4 p.331*
Hersh, Seymour M.. . . . . *v.3 p.483, v.4 p.659*
Hershatter, Gail *v.6 p.217*
Hershberg, Eric *v.4 p.512*
Hershenson, Herbert M. *v.5 p.270, p.272*
Hershenson, Maurice *v.5 p.606*
Hershman, D. Jablow & Lieb, Julian. *v.5 p.659*
Herskovic, Marika Jr. (Editor) *v.1 p.728*
Herskovits, Melville Jean *v.6 p.10*
Hersman, Rebecca K. C. *v.4 p.528, p.531*
Herspring, Dale R.. . . . . *v.3 p.447*
Herstein, I. N. (Text by) *v.5 p.473*
Herstein, Israel N. *v.5 p.473*
Hertsgaard, Mark *v.5 p.358, p.370*
Hertz, Joseph H., trans.. . . . . *v.1 p.552*
Hertz, Robert *v.4 p.24*
Hertzberg, Arthur (Editor, Introduction by) *v.1 p.549*
Hertzberg, Richard W. *v.5 p.689*
Hertzke, Allen D.. . . . . *v.3 p.447*
Herwig, Holger & Sater, William F. *v.3 p.274, p.351*
Herwig, Holger H. & Bercuson, David J.. . . . . . *v.4 p.628*
Herwig, Holger H. *v.3 p.79, p.160, p.184*
Heryanto, Ariel *v.6 p.174, p.176*
Herz, Judith S.. . . . . *v.2 p.346*
Herz, Monica & Nogueira, Joao Pontes *v.4 p.649*
Herzberg, Frederick. *v.5 p.579*
Herzberg, Gerhard *v.5 p.270, p.562*
Herzberger, David K.. . . . . *v.2 p.641*
Herzen, Alexander *v.3 p.217*
Herzfeld, Michael *v.3 p.196, v.4 p.24, p.718*
Herzog, Chaim *v.6 p.593, p.614*
Herzog, Dagmar *v.3 p.168*
Herzog, Hanna. *v.6 p.614*
Herzog, Tamar *v.3 p.239*
Heschel, Abraham Joshua *v.1 p.522, p.551, p.552*
Heschel, Susannah *v.1 p.553*
Hesiod, ; West, M L *v.2 p.413*
Hesiod. *v.1 p.532, v.2 p.413*
Heskes, Irene (Compiled by) *v.1 p.167, p.300*
Heskes, Irene *v.1 p.300*
Heskett, John *v.1 p.717*
Heskins, Jeffrey *v.1 p.650*
Heslep, Robert D. *v.4 p.343*
Hess, Andrew C. *v.6 p.60*
Hess, Carol A. (Contribution by) *v.1 p.215, p.324*
Hess, Frederick M. & Finn, Chester E. Jr. (Editors) . *v.4 p.347*
Hess, Frederick M.. . . . . *v.4 p.280, p.315*
Hess, Jonathan M. *v.3 p.180*
Hess, Peter N.. . . . . *v.4 p.201*

Hess, Rob & Stewart, Bob (Editors). *v.4 p.806, p.816, p.843, p.847*

Hess, Stephen & Kalb, Marvin (Editors) *v.4 p.563*

Hess, Stephen *v.4 p.414*

Hesse, Hermann & Roloff, Michael *v.2 p.610*

Hesse, Hermann & Vennewitz, Leila *v.2 p.610*

Hesse, Hermann *v.2 p.609, p.610*

Hesse, Manfred *v.5 p.299*

Hesse, Mary *v.5 p.402*

Hesse-Biber, Sharlene *v.4 p.778, v.5 p.653, v.6 p.445*

Hessel, Dieter T. (Editor) *v.6 p.288*

Hessel, Volker, et al. *v.5 p.743*

Hesselbein, Frances (Editor), et al. *v.4 p.71, p.73*

Hesselbein, Frances *v.4 p.71*

Hesselink, Nathan (Editor) *v.1 p.288*

Hesselink, Nathan *v.1 p.15*

Hesseltine, William B. (Editor) *v.3 p.398, p.428*

Hesseltine, William B. *v.3 p.425*

Hesseltine, William Best *v.3 p.398*

Hessler, Julie. *v.4 p.257*

Hessler, Peter *v.6 p.214*

Heth, Charlotte (Editor) *v.1 p.15, v.6 p.699*

Hetherington, E. Mavis & Kelly, John *v.5 p.640*

Hetherington, Stephen Cade. *v.1 p.482*

Hetzel, Bill *v.5 p.346*

Hetzron, Robert *v.6 p.665*

Heumann, Milton & Cassak, Lance *v.4 p.573, v.6 p.264*

Heurgon, Jacques *v.3 p.25*

Heuring, Vincent P., et al. *v.5 p.730*

Heuser, Beatrice *v.4 p.639, p.654*

Heussenstamm, George *v.1 p.393*

Heuvel, Jon Vanden *v.3 p.168*

Heuving, Jeanne *v.2 p.102*

Hevia, James L. *v.6 p.204*

Hevia, James Louis. *v.6 p.204*

Hewes, Dean E. (Editor) *v.5 p.621*

Hewett, Ed A. & Winston, Victor H. (Editors) *v.3 p.228*

Hewett-Thayer, Harvey W. *v.2 p.592*

Hewison, Kevin *v.6 p.171*

Hewitson, Gillian J. *v.4 p.273*

Hewitt, Andrew *v.1 p.37, p.42*

Hewitt, Barnard *v.1 p.115*

Hewitt, Christopher & Cheetham, Tom *v.4 p.628*

Hewitt, Christopher. *v.4 p.563*

Hewitt, Mark Allen. *v.1 p.793*

Hewitt, Nicholas *v.2 p.515*

Hewitt, Paul G. (Illustrator) *v.5 p.539*

Hewstone, Miles *v.4 p.693, v.5 p.611, p.646, p.653*

Hexter, Jack H. *v.3 p.102, p.103*

Hey, Jody *v.5 p.134, p.198*

Heyck, Denis Lynn Daly *v.3 p.269*

Heyck, T. W.. . . . . *v.3 p.112, p.128, v.6 p.750*

Heyde, C. C. & Seneta, E. (Editors) *v.5 p.466, p.481*

Heyde, K. *v.5 p.553*

Heydemann, Steven (Editor). *v.4 p.614*

Heydenreich, Ludwig H. *v.1 p.786*

Heyen, William (Editor) *v.2 p.23*

Heyer, Anna H. *v.1 p.167*

Heyer, John Hajdu (Editor) *v.1 p.184, p.338*

Heylin, Clinton *v.1 p.270, p.356, p.384*

Heyman, Barbara B. *v.1 p.215, p.304, v.6 p.409*

Heyman, Jacques. *v.1 p.796, v.5 p.694, p.697*

Heyman, Theresa Thau *v.1 p.718*

Heymann, C. David. *v.2 p.111*

Heymann, David *v.5 p.532*

Heymann, Jody *v.4 p.759*

Heymann, Philip B. *v.4 p.563, p.659*

Heyne, E. G. (Editor). *v.5 p.22, p.25*

Heyneman, Stephen P. (Editor) *v.4 p.721*

Heyns, Michiel. *v.2 p.191*

Heyrman, Christine L. *v.1 p.583, p.607*

Heyward, DuBose *v.2 p.81*

Heyward, Vivian H. *v.4 p.879*

Heywood, Christopher *v.6 p.80*

Heywood, John *v.2 p.219*

Heywood, Leslie & Dworkin, Shari L.. . . . . *v.4 p.816, p.836*

Heywood, Linda M.. . . . . *v.6 p.75*

Heywood, Paul. *v.4 p.608*

Heywood, Thomas *v.2 p.219*

Hébert, Anne & Gallant, Mavis *v.2 p.539*

Hébert, Anne. *v.2 p.539*

Hölderlin, Friedrich. *v.2 p.600*

Hholbl, Ghunther *v.6 p.58*

Hibbard, Allen (Editor) *v.2 p.64*

Hibbard, Caroline M.. . . . . *v.3 p.102, p.120*

Hibbeler, R. C. & Tan, Kiang Hwee *v.5 p.694*

Hibbeler, Russell C. *v.5 p.689*

Hibbett, Howard *v.6 p.229*

Hibbing, John R. & Theiss-Morse, Elizabeth *v.4 p.554*

Hibbing, John R.. . . . . *v.4 p.533*

Hibbs, Alan R. *v.5 p.86*

Hick, John Harwood *v.1 p.639*

Hick, John *v.1 p.523, p.597*

Hickenlooper Sowell, Debra. *v.1 p.9*

Hickey, Dave, et al. *v.1 p.697, p.728*

Hickey, Gerald C. *v.6 p.168*

Hickey, Thomas J.. . . . . *v.1 p.499*

Hickman, Cleveland P., et al. *v.5 p.189, p.215*

Hickman, Larry A. & Alexander, Thomas M. (Editors). *v.1 p.443*

Hickman, Money L. (Editor) *v.1 p.693*

Hicks, Dan & Beaudry, Mary C. (Editors) *v.4 p.14*

Hicks, J. R. *v.4 p.238*

Hicks, John Richard, Sir *v.4 p.254*

Hicks, John Richard *v.4 p.209, p.214*

Hicks, Malcolm (Editor) *v.2 p.238*

Hicks, Michael *v.1 p.215, p.277, p.319, v.6 p.409*

Hicks, Tyler G.. . . . . *v.5 p.685*

Hidayat, Sadiq *v.6 p.671*

Hiden, John & Lane, Thomas (Editors). *v.3 p.255*

Hiemenez, Paul C. & Rajagopalan, Raj. *v.5 p.283*

Hiesinger, Kathryn B. & Fischer, Felice *v.1 p.713, p.714*

Hiesinger, Kathryn B. & Marcus, George H. *v.1 p.798*

Hiesinger, Ulrich W. *v.1 p.728*

Hietala, Thomas R. *v.3 p.381, v.4 p.816, p.832, p.855*

Higdon, Hal *v.4 p.791, p.841, p.866*

Higdon *v.5 p.689*

Higginbotham, A. Leon Jr. *v.4 p.457*

Higginbotham, Donald (Editor) *v.3 p.409*

Higginbotham, Donald *v.3 p.413*

Higginbotham, Peter *v.6 p.743, p.761, p.766*

Higgins, C. G. & Coates, D. R. (Editors) *v.5 p.428*

Higgins, D. & Taylor, Willie (Editors) *v.5 p.101*

Higgins, Des & Taylor, Willie (Editors) *v.5 p.97*

Higgins, E. Tory & Kruglanski, Arie W. (Editors) . . *v.5 p.646*

Higgins, E. Tory & Sorrentino, Richard M. (Editors) *v.5 p.649*

Higgins, J. (Editor) *v.2 p.685*

Higgins, Kathleen J. *v.3 p.334*

Higgins, Kathleen M. & Solomon, Robert C. (Editors) *v.1 p.508*

Higgins, Loretta P. (Editor), et al. *v.5 p.527, p.529*

Higgins, Monica C. *v.4 p.71*

Higgins, Patricia J. & Paredes, J. Anthony (Editors) . *v.4 p.44*

Higgins, Patrick (Editor) *v.6 p.406*

Higgins, Paula (Editor) *v.1 p.180, p.314, p.315*

Higgins, Reynold *v.1 p.670, p.687, v.3 p.16*

Higgins, S. J. & Banting, G. (Editors) *v.5 p.113*

Higginson, John, et al. *v.5 p.364, p.375*

Higginson, Thomas W. *v.3 p.431*

Higgs, Eric S. *v.6 p.283*

Higgs, Robert J. & Braswell, Michael C. *v.4 p.824*

Higgs, Robert J. *v.4 p.823*

High, Peter B. *v.6 p.336*

Higham, Charles *v.4 p.8, v.6 p.170*

Higham, John (Editor) *v.3 p.374*

Higham, John *v.3 p.374*

Higham, Nicholas J. *v.5 p.458, p.461*

Higham, Robin & Kagan, Frederick W. (Editors) . . *v.3 p.211*

Higham, Robin & Mrozek, Donald J. (Editors) . . . *v.3 p.383*

Higham, Robin (Editor) *v.3 p.383*

Highet, Gilbert *v.2 p.427, p.435, v.4 p.348*

Highfill, Philip H., et al. *v.1 p.100, p.140, p.142*

Highsmith, Carol M. & Landphair, Ted *v.1 p.822*

Highsmith, Patricia *v.2 p.86, v.6 p.397*

Highwater, Jamake *v.1 p.42*

Highway Innovative Technology Evaluation Center Staff
(Contribution by) *v.5 p.698*

Higonnet, Margaret R. (Editor) *v.3 p.208*

Higonnet, Margaret R. *v.6 p.454*

Higson, Andrew (Editor) *v.6 p.339*

Higson, Andrew *v.6 p.339*

Hijuelos, Óscar *v.2 p.147, v.6 p.506*

Hikmet, Nazim *v.6 p.666*

Hilberg, Raul *v.1 p.548*

Hilbert, David & Cohn-Vossen, S. *v.5 p.495*

Hilbert, David *v.5 p.466, p.495*

Hilbert, Richard A. *v.4 p.688*

Hildebrand, Joel, et al. *v.5 p.282*

Hildebrand, Milton & Goslow, George Jr. *v.5 p.157*

Hildebrand, Sharon (Editor) *v.6 p.285*

Hildebrandt, Stefan & Tromba, Anthony J. *v.5 p.495*

Hildenbrand, W. & Sonnenschein, H. (Editors) . . . *v.4 p.189*

Hildenbrand, Werner *v.4 p.201*

Hilderbrand, Robert C. *v.4 p.654*

Hiley, David *v.1 p.177*

Hilger, Michael *v.6 p.700*

Hill, Andrew E. (Editor) *v.1 p.622*

Hill, Anita *v.4 p.441*

Hill, Anne *v.4 p.348*

Hill, Anthony F. *v.5 p.307*

Hill, Charles & Jones, Gareth *v.4 p.81*

Hill, Christopher . *v.2 p.254, v.3 p.102, p.103, p.120, p.121, p.128, p.130, p.131, v.4 p.628*

Hill, Claude *v.2 p.605*

Hill, Constance Valis *v.1 p.32*

Hill, Daniel D. *v.4 p.426*

Hill, Donald R. *v.1 p.292, v.3 p.320*

Hill, Elizabeth, et al. *v.1 p.826*

Hill, Errol G. & Hatch, James V. *v.6 p.15, p.30*

Hill, George R. & Stephens, Norris L. *v.1 p.167*

Hill, John Walter *v.1 p.184*

Hill, Jonathan & Maughan, Barbara (Editors) . . . *v.5 p.662*

Hill, Jonathan *v.1 p.595*

Hill, Karen Lee *v.4 p.877*

Hill, Kathleen Thompson & Hill, Gerald N. *v.4 p.516*

Hill, Leslie *v.2 p.517*

Hill, Lynn & Child, Greg *v.4 p.789, p.836*

Hill, M. L. (Editor) *v.5 p.432*

Hill, Marquita K. *v.5 p.705*

Hill, Michael R. & Hoecker-Drysdale, Susan (Editors) . *v.4 p.690*

Hill, Patricia Liggins, et al. *v.6 p.5, p.26*

Hill, Peter & Simeone, Nigel *v.1 p.216, p.341*

Hill, Peter (Editor) *v.1 p.216, p.341*

Hill, Peter *v.1 p.216, p.239, p.360*

Hill, Philip G. & Peterson, Carl R. *v.5 p.719*

Hill, Philip G. (Editor) . *v.1 p.66, p.69, p.70, p.71, p.72, p.73, p.74, p.78, p.79, p.82, p.108*

Hill, R. Carter, et al. *v.4 p.201*

Hill, Richard & McWilliams, Jim (Editors) *v.2 p.33*

Hill, Robert M. 3rd *v.3 p.298*

Hill, Robert M. II *v.3 p.298*

Hill, Ronald *v.4 p.384*

Hill, Samuel S. & Owen, Dennis E. *v.3 p.472*

Hill, Sarah H. *v.1 p.806, v.6 p.472, p.678, p.705*

Hill, Selima *v.2 p.351*

Hill, Stephen M. & Malik, Shahin P. (Editors) . . . *v.4 p.649*

Hill, Tom & Hill, Richard W. Sr. (Editors) *v.6 p.678*

Hill, William E. *v.3 p.520*

Hill, William H., et al. . . . *v.1 p.184, p.358, p.359, p.389*

Hill, Winfred F. *v.4 p.357*

Hillard, James M. *v.5 p.83*

Hillard, John (Editor) *v.4 p.227*

Hillebrand, Harold N. *v.1 p.100, p.144*

Hillel, Daniel & Elrick, David E. *v.5 p.49*

Hillel, Daniel J. (Editor-In-Chief) *v.5 p.49*

Hillel, Daniel *v.5 p.49*

Hillenbrand, Carole *v.3 p.63*

Hillenbrand, Robert *v.1 p.674, p.691*

Hiller, James & Neary, Peter (Editors) *v.3 p.547*

Hillerbrand, Hans J. (Editor) *v.1 p.580*

Hillers, Delbert R. *v.1 p.622*

Hillert, Mats *v.5 p.282*

Hillgarth, J. N. *v.3 p.237, p.239*

Hillier, Frederick S. & Lieberman, Gerald J. *v.5 p.493*

Hillier, Paul *v.1 p.216, p.347*

Hillis, David M. (Editor), et al. *v.5 p.127*

Hillman, Brenda *v.2 p.147*

Hillman, James *v.5 p.584*

Hillman, Michael *v.6 p.671*

Hillman, Susan Kay *v.4 p.828*

Hillman, Tim & Thorn, Craig IV (Editors) *v.4 p.296*

Hillmann, Michael C. *v.6 p.671*

Hillmer, Norman (Editor) *v.3 p.541*

Hills, Alice *v.6 p.262*

Hills, L. Rust (Introduction by) *v.2 p.26*

Hills, Paul *v.1 p.710*

Hills, Richard Leslie *v.5 p.709*

Hillstrom, Kevin & Hillstrom, Laurie Collier *v.4 p.385*

Hillstrom, Laurie Collier & Hillstrom,
Kevin *v.1 p.664, p.706, v.6 p.473*

Hillyard, Paddy (Editor), et al. *v.6 p.249*

Hillyer, Barbara *v.6 p.443*

Hilmes, Michele *v.4 p.412, p.417*

Hilpert, Ulrich (Editor) *v.4 p.397*

Hiltebeitel, Alf & Erndl, Kathleen M. (Editors) . . . *v.1 p.540*

Hiltermann, Joost R. *v.6 p.454, p.617*

Hilton, Boyd *v.3 p.112, p.121, v.6 p.758*

Hilton, James *v.2 p.351, v.6 p.215*

Hilton, Peter J., et al. *v.5 p.458*

Hilton, Stanley E. *v.3 p.340*

Hilton, Tim *v.1 p.780, v.2 p.305*

Hilton, Wendy *v.1 p.22*

Himanen, Pekka *v.4 p.761*

Himes, Chester B. *v.2 p.86*

Himes, Chester *v.6 p.26*

Himmelblau, David M. & Riggs, James B. *v.5 p.741*

Himmelfarb, Gertrude . . . *v.1 p.437, v.3 p.112, p.128, v.4 p.754,
v.6 p.743, p.745, p.758, p.766

Himmelstein, Jerome L. *v.5 p.663*

Himmerich Y Valencia, Robert *v.3 p.286*

Himmich, Bensalem *v.6 p.659*

Himonas, Alex *v.5 p.314*

Hinchliffe, Alan *v.5 p.277*

Hinchman, Hannah *v.5 p.232*

Hincks, Francis *v.3 p.539*

Hind, Arthur M. *v.1 p.753*

Hinde, John R. *v.3 p.244*

Hinde, Robert A. & Watson, Helen E. (Editors) . . . *v.5 p.584*

Hindelang, Michael J., et al. *v.6 p.255*

Hindemith, Paul *v.1 p.371, p.404*

Hindery, Leo & Cauley, Leslie *v.4 p.84*

Hindley, Alan, et al. *v.2 p.453*

Hindman, Elizabeth B. *v.4 p.405*

Hinds, Pamela & Kiesler, Sara (Editors) *v.4 p.69*

Hindus, Milton *v.2 p.524*

Hine, Darlene Clark & McLeod, Jacqueline A. (Editors). *v.3 p.320*

Hine, Darlene Clark & Thompsom, Kathleen . . . *v.6 p.6, p.44*

Hine, Darlene Clark (Editor), et al. *v.6 p.5, p.44*

Hine, Darlene Clark, et al. *v.6 p.5*

Hine, Darlene Clark . . . *v.5 p.529, v.6 p.6, p.39, p.434, p.449*

Hine, Daryl & Parisi, Joseph (Editors) *v.2 p.23*

Hine, David *v.4 p.594*

Hine, Jack Sylvester *v.5 p.292*

Hine, Jack *v.5 p.292*

Hine, John *v.4 p.793*

Hine, Robert (Editor) *v.5 p.154*

Hine, Robert V. & Faragher, John *v.3 p.518*

Hines, Maxwell S. (Contribution by) *v.4 p.367*

Hines, Terence *v.5 p.613*

Hines, William E. *v.6 p.347*

Hiney, Tom *v.2 p.65*

Hing, Bill Ong & Lee, Ronald (Editors) *v.6 p.118*

Hing, Bill Ong *v.4 p.571, p.763, v.6 p.118, p.121*

Hinman, Lawrence M. *v.1 p.484*

Hinnebusch, Raymond A. *v.6 p.638*

Hinnebusch, Raymond *v.6 p.593, p.607*

Hinnells, John R. *v.1 p.522*

Hinojosa, Rolando *v.6 p.499, p.500, p.513*

Hinrichsen, Don *v.5 p.241*

Hinsch, Bret *v.6 p.185, p.421*

Hinshaw, John *v.4 p.126*

Hinsley, Curtis M. *v.4 p.47*

Hinsley, Francis H. *v.4 p.649*

Hinson, Maurice *v.1 p.160, p.167, p.239, p.389, p.398*

Hinterding, Erik (Editor), et al. *v.1 p.756*

Hintikka, Jaakko *v.1 p.472*

Hintjens, Helen M. *v.4 p.583, p.584*

Hinton, Alexander Laban *v.6 p.170*

Hinton, Carma & Gordon, Richard (Directed Bys) . . *v.6 p.197*

Hinton, David *v.1 p.418*

Hinton, Harold C. (Editor) *v.6 p.194, p.197*

Hinton, Leanne & Hale, Kenneth (Editors) *v.4 p.19*

Hinton, Leanne *v.6 p.690, p.691*

Hinton, Stephen (Editor) *v.1 p.250, p.368*

Hinton, William *v.6 p.192*

Hippius, Zinaida *v.2 p.804*

Hippler, Mike *v.6 p.389*

Hippocrates *v.2 p.404, v.5 p.510*

Hirabayashi, Lane R. (Editor) *v.6 p.108*

Hirabayashi, Lane Ryo (Editor), et al. *v.6 p.118, p.131*

Hirakawa, Akira *v.1 p.561*

Hirano, Kyoko *v.6 p.336*
Hirata, Keiko *v.4 p.640, p.663*
Hirning, Harvey J. *v.5 p.55*
Hiro, Dilip *v.6 p.603, p.631, p.632*
Hironaka, Ann *v.4 p.647*
Hirsal, Josef *v.2 p.783*
Hirsch, A. *v.5 p.306*
Hirsch, Abraham & De Marchi, Neil *v.4 p.232*
Hirsch, Andrew Von (Editor), et al. *v.6 p.278*
Hirsch, E. D. Jr. *v.4 p.327*
Hirsch, Foster *v.1 p.251, p.348*
Hirsch, Francine *v.3 p.213*
Hirsch, H. N. *v.4 p.467*
Hirsch, Jerrold *v.3 p.374*
Hirsch, Joshua Francis *v.6 p.322*
Hirsch, Marianne & Keller, Evelyn F. (Editors) *v.6 p.427*
Hirsch, Morris W., et al. *v.5 p.488*
Hirsch, S. R. *v.1 p.545*
Hirsch, Susan Eleanor *v.4 p.122*
Hirschfeld, Al *v.1 p.701*
Hirschfeld, Christian C. *v.1 p.818*
Hirschfeld, Magnus . . *v.4 p.743, p.748,v.6 p.370, p.381, p.420*
Hirschhorn, Clive *v.1 p.9*
Hirschi, Travis *v.6 p.255*
Hirsh, John C. (Editor) *v.2 p.199*
Hirsh, John *v.2 p.209*
Hirsh, Sharon *v.1 p.709*
Hirshberg, Jehoash *v.1 p.300*
Hirshson, Stanley P. *v.3 p.436*
Hirst, David *v.6 p.617*
Hirst, Derek *v.3 p.94, p.102, p.103, p.121*
Hirst, Michael, et al. *v.1 p.740*
Hirst, Michael *v.1 p.723*
Hirst, Monica *v.3 p.389*
Hirst, Paul H. & White, Patricia . . . *v.4 p.323, p.339*
Hirst, Paul Q. (Editor) *v.4 p.497*
Hirszowicz, Maria *v.4 p.708*
Hirt, Paul W. *v.5 p.37*
Hischak, Thomas S. . . . *v.1 p.59, p.92, p.115,v.6 p.316, p.326*
Hischak, Thomas *v.6 p.316*
Hiscox, Gardner Dexter *v.5 p.407*
Hise, Greg *v.6 p.728*
Hiskett, Mervyn *v.1 p.554, v.6 p.68*
Hiss, Alger *v.3 p.459*
Histand, Michael B. & Alciatore, David G. *v.5 p.714*
History of Education Society *v.4 p.327*
History Project Staff *v.6 p.362*
Hitchcock, H. Wiley & Sadie, Stanley (Editors) . *v.1 p.160, p.278*
Hitchcock, H. Wiley *v.1 p.277*
Hitchcock, Henry Russell *v.1 p.786*
Hitchcock, James *v.4 p.460*
Hitchcock, Susan Tyler *v.2 p.298*
Hitchcock, William I. *v.3 p.79, p.157*
Hitchens, Christopher *v.2 p.374*
Hitchins, Keith *v.3 p.250*

Hitchman, James H. *v.3 p.530*
Hitler, Adolf *v.3 p.172*
Hitti, Philip K. *v.6 p.583, p.600*
Hitti, Philip Khuri *v.6 p.604*
Hitti, Phillip K. *v.6 p.604, p.606, p.608*
Hix, H. L. *v.2 p.101*
Hix, Simon & Lord, Christopher *v.4 p.603*
Hix, Simon *v.4 p.603, p.637*
Hixon, Don L. & Hennessee, Don A. . . *v.1 p.160, p.379, v.6 p.474*
Hixon, Donald L. *v.1 p.160*
Hixson, Richard F. *v.4 p.405, p.445*
Hixson, Walter L. *v.3 p.459*
Hjort, Mette & MacKenzie, Scott (Editors) . . . *v.6 p.331*
Hladczuk, Sharon (Compiled by), et al. *v.4 p.300*
Hlasko, Marek *v.2 p.790*
Hlihor, Constantin & Scurtu, Ioan *v.3 p.250*
Hlophe, Stephen S. *v.4 p.703, v.6 p.70*
Ho, Allan & Feofanov, Dmitry *v.1 p.216, p.356*
Ho, C. Y. *v.5 p.286*
Ho, Chimei & Bronson, Bennet (Editors) *v.1 p.693*
Ho, Fred W. (Editor) *v.6 p.107, p.120*
Ho, Rodney J. Y. & Gibaldi, Milo *v.5 p.218*
Hoage, Robert J. & Deiss, William A. *v.5 p.83*
Hoagland, Alison K. *v.1 p.789*
Hoaglin, David C. (Editor), et al. *v.5 p.482*
Hoagwood, Terence A. *v.2 p.290*
Hoare, Anthony *v.4 p.373*
Hoare, Jim & Pares, Susan (Editors) *v.4 p.189*
Hoare, Marko Attila *v.3 p.249*
Hoare, Michael Rand *v.4 p.389*
Hobart, Alice Tisdale *v.6 p.215*
Hobart, Michael E. & Schiffman, Zachary S. . . . *v.5 p.406*
Hobbes, Thomas & Gaskin, J. C. A. *v.1 p.448*
Hobbes, Thomas *v.1 p.448, v.4 p.491*
Hobbs, Colleen A. *v.5 p.527, p.529*
Hobbs, Joseph J. *v.4 p.397*
Hobbs, Robert Carleton *v.1 p.740*
Hobbs, Robert *v.1 p.740*
Hobby, Elaine & White, Chris (Editors) *v.6 p.393*
Hoberg, Annegret & Friedel, Helmut (Editors) . . . *v.1 p.740*
Hoberman, J. *v.4 p.508, v.6 p.321*
Hoberman, John M. *v.4 p.802, p.806, p.832, p.873*
Hoberman, John *v.4 p.802, p.816, p.832*
Hoberman, Loise Schell & Migden Socolow, Susan (Editors) . *v.3 p.286*
Hoberman, Louisa S. *v.3 p.286*
Hobhouse, Janet *v.2 p.121*
Hobsbaum, Philip *v.2 p.181*
Hobsbawm, E. J. (Eric John), et al. *v.3 p.112, p.131*
Hobsbawm, E. J. *v.3 p.61, v.4 p.494, p.703*
Hobsbawm, Eric J. & Ranger, Terence (Editors) . . . *v.3 p.61*
Hobsbawm, Eric J. . *v.3 p.76, p.77, p.89, p.123, p.125, p.158*
Hobson, Archie *v.4 p.374*
Hobson, Charles F. *v.4 p.467*
Hobson, Christopher Z. *v.2 p.240*

Hobson, Fred *v.2 p.13*
Hobson, Geary (Editor). *v.2 p.19, v.6 p.698*
Hobson, John M. *v.3 p.74*
Hobson, Mary (Author, Translator). *v.2 p.804*
Hoch, Stephen L.. . . . . *v.3 p.217*
Hochberg, Julian E. (Editor), et al.. . . . . *v.5 p.605*
Hochedlinger, Michael *v.3 p.182*
Hochhuth, Rolf. *v.2 p.617*
Hochman, Barbara. *v.2 p.49*
Hochman, Elaine S. *v.1 p.679*
Hochschild, Adam. *v.3 p.77, p.206*
Hochschild, Arlie Russell & Machung, Anne *v.6 p.467*
Hochschild, Arlie Russell . . . *v.4 p.731, v.5 p.580, v.6 p.467*
Hochschild, Jennifer & Scovronick, Nathan. *v.4 p.300*
Hochsmann, Hyun *v.1 p.475*
Hockenberry, Marilyn J. *v.5 p.525, p.527*
Hockett, Charles Francis *v.2 p.561*
Hockin, Thomas A.. . . . . *v.4 p.588*
Hockings, Paul. *v.6 p.310*
Hockney, David *v.1 p.751*
Hocks, Mary E. & Kendrick, Michelle R.
   (Editors). *v.1 p.703, p.771*
Hocks, Richard A.. . . . . *v.2 p.43*
Hodder, Alan D.. . . . . *v.2 p.52*
Hodder, Ian *v.4 p.6*
Hoddeson, Lillian & Daitch, Vicki *v.5 p.543*
Hodge, Bob & Mishra, Vijay *v.2 p.741*
Hodge, Francis *v.1 p.115*
Hodge, Michael J.. . . . . *v.5 p.79, p.203*
Hodge, R. I. *v.2 p.252*
Hodge, Sheida *v.4 p.56*
Hodgen, Margaret Trabue *v.4 p.4*
Hodges, Ben *v.1 p.100, p.126, v.6 p.411*
Hodges, Donald C. & Gandy, Ross *v.4 p.593*
Hodges, Donald C.. . . . . *v.3 p.293, p.348*
Hodges, H. A. *v.1 p.464*
Hodges, Tony *v.6 p.61*
Hodgetts, J. E., et al. *v.4 p.588*
Hodgetts, John Edwin *v.4 p.588*
Hodgetts, Richard M., et al. *v.4 p.69*
Hodgins, Paul *v.1 p.42*
Hodgson, Barbara *v.5 p.232*
Hodgson, David A. & Thomas, Christopher M.
   (Editors). *v.5 p.153, p.206*
Hodgson, Ernest, et al. *v.5 p.311*
Hodgson, Godfrey *v.3 p.459*
Hodgson, J. & Illius, A. W. (Editors) *v.5 p.42*
Hodgson, James F. & Orban, Catherine (Editors). *v.6 p.262, p.267*
Hodgson, J.. *v.5 p.42*
Hodgson, Marshall G. *v.1 p.555, p.556, v.6 p.581*
Hodgson, Peter C. & King, Robert H. (Editors) . . *v.1 p.636*
Hoebel, E. Adamson *v.4 p.433*
Hoefs, Jochen *v.5 p.440*
Hoehler-Fatton, Cynthia *v.4 p.36*
Hoehling, A. A. *v.3 p.431*

Hoekema, Anthony A. *v.1 p.645*
Hoel, Paul G., et al. *v.5 p.484*
Hoel, Paul G. *v.5 p.482, p.484*
Hoenig, Steven L. *v.5 p.264*
Hoenigswald, Henry M.. . . . . *v.2 p.561*
Hoensch, J. *v.3 p.185*
Hoenselaars, Ton (Editor) *v.1 p.76, p.100, p.135*
Hoeppner, Edward H. *v.2 p.57*
Hoermann, Roland *v.2 p.597*
Hoess, Rudolf. *v.3 p.84*
Hofacker, Erich *v.2 p.613*
Hoff, Joan *v.3 p.472*
Hoffe, Otfried *v.1 p.461*
Hoffecker, Carol E. (Editor) *v.3 p.493*
Hoffecker, Carol E.. . . . . *v.3 p.493*
Hoffer, Eric *v.4 p.710*
Hoffer, Peter C. & Hull, N. E.. . . . . *v.4 p.461*
Hoffer, Peter C. *v.4 p.440, p.474*
Hoffleit, Dorrit & Jaschek, Carlos. *v.5 p.64*
Hoffleit, Dorrit, et al. *v.5 p.64*
Hoffman, Andrew J. *v.4 p.61, p.63, v.6 p.298*
Hoffman, Barbara T. (Editor) *v.1 p.827*
Hoffman, Barry *v.1 p.714, v.4 p.140, p.141*
Hoffman, Bruce *v.4 p.659*
Hoffman, Darleane C., et al.. . . . . *v.5 p.308*
Hoffman, David & Hoffman, Donald D. *v.5 p.607*
Hoffman, David J. *v.5 p.311, v.6 p.283*
Hoffman, Ethan (Photographer). *v.1 p.15*
Hoffman, Eva *v.3 p.84, p.254, p.255*
Hoffman, Frederick J. *v.2 p.74*
Hoffman, Joel *v.6 p.646*
Hoffman, Joshua & Rosenkrantz, Gary S.. . . . . . *v.1 p.488*
Hoffman, Katherine. *v.1 p.767*
Hoffman, Kenneth & Kunze, Ray *v.5 p.472*
Hoffman, Michael A. *v.3 p.8*
Hoffman, Michael J. *v.2 p.578*
Hoffman, Nancy (Editor) *v.4 p.282*
Hoffman, Paul *v.3 p.341, v.5 p.466*
Hoffman, Ronald & Albert, Peter J. (Editors) . . . *v.4 p.630*
Hoffman, Shirl J. (Editor). *v.4 p.873, p.903*
Hoffman, William M., et al. *v.6 p.412*
Hoffman, William M.. . . . . *v.6 p.378, p.412*
Hoffmann, David L. *v.3 p.225*
Hoffmann, E. T. A. (Ernst Theodor Amadeus). *v.1 p.198, v.2 p.599*
Hoffmann, E. T. A. *v.2 p.599*
Hoffmann, Frank & Cooper, B. Lee *v.1 p.167, p.270*
Hoffmann, Frank W. (Editor) *v.1 p.160, p.387*
Hoffmann, Frank. *v.1 p.167, p.270*
Hoffmann, Gretchen McCord *v.4 p.446*
Hoffmann, Jens *v.1 p.679*
Hoffmann, John (Editor) *v.3 p.515*
Hoffmann, Laurence D., et al.. . . . . *v.5 p.503*
Hoffmann, Peter *v.3 p.172, v.5 p.742*
Hoffmann, Roald. *v.5 p.264*
Hoffmann, Steven A. *v.6 p.159*

Hoffmann, Yoel *v.6 p.649*

Hoffmeier, James K. . . . . *. v.3 p.7*

Hoffpauir, Richard *v.2 p.77*

Hofmann, Werner *v.1 p.740*

Hofmannsthal, Hugo von *v.2 p.609*

Hofmann-Wellenhof, Bernhard, et al. . . . *v.4 p.389, v.5 p.719*

Hofrichter, Robert (Editor) *v.5 p.215*

Hofstadter, Douglas R. (Author, Preface by) *v.5 p.470*

Hofstadter, Richard (Editor) *v.3 p.448*

Hofstadter, Richard . *v.3 p.368, p.380, p.441, p.447, p.448, v.4 p.298, p.331, p.683, p.685*

Hofstede, Geert & Hofstede, Gert Jan *v.4 p.58, p.75*

Hofstede, Geert *v.4 p.718*

Hofstetter, Eleanore O. *v.4 p.667, v.6 p.470*

Hogan, Ben & Wind, Herbert W. *v.4 p.861*

Hogan, Charles Beecher *v.1 p.100, p.101, p.140*

Hogan, David J. *v.6 p.318*

Hogan, James C. *v.2 p.407, p.419*

Hogan, John C. *v.4 p.450*

Hogan, Linda *v.2 p.147, v.6 p.698*

Hogan, Michael J. & Paterson, Thomas G. (Editors) . *v.3 p.385*

Hogan, Michael J. (Editor) . *v.3 p.385, p.448, p.452, v.4 p.486*

Hogan, Michael J. *v.3 p.472, v.4 p.486*

Hogan, Patrick Colm *v.4 p.695*

Hogan, Robert (Editor), et al. *v.5 p.657*

Hogan, Robert T. (Editor) *v.2 p.163*

Hogan, Sean (Editor) *v.5 p.43*

Hogan, Sean O. *v.4 p.541*

Hogan, Sean *v.5 p.43*

Hogan, Steve *v.6 p.358*

Hogan, Thomas P. *v.5 p.601*

Hogarth, David *v.6 p.309*

Hoge, James F. Jr. & Rose, Gideon (Editors) . . . *v.4 p.564*

Hogg, Margaret (Editor) *v.5 p.586*

Hogg, Margaret K. (Editor) *v.5 p.586, p.604*

Hogg, Michael & Abrams, Dominic *v.4 p.713*

Hogg, Michael A. & Cooper, Joel (Editors) . . . *v.5 p.646*

Hogg, Michael A. *v.5 p.649*

Hogg, Richard M. (Contribution by) *v.2 p.554*

Hogg, Russell & Carrington, Kerry (Editors) . . . *v.4 p.752*

Hogg, Thomas J. *v.2 p.311*

Hoggart, Keith, et al. *v.4 p.396*

Hoggart, Richard . *v.3 p.112, p.128, v.4 p.696, v.5 p.621, p.624*

Hoghughi, Masud S. & Long, Nicholas (Editors) . . . *v.5 p.641*

Hogler, Raymond L. *v.4 p.109, p.122, p.126*

Hogue, W. Lawrence *v.6 p.26, p.39*

Hogwood, Christopher *v.1 p.184, p.329*

Hohberg, Jorg-Martin *v.5 p.694*

Hohenberg, John *v.4 p.405, p.556*

Hohenberg, Paul M. & Lees, Lynn H. . . . *v.3 p.44, v.6 p.713*

Hohendahl, Peter U. (Editor) *v.2 p.589*

Hohn, Michael Edward *v.5 p.420*

Hoidal, Oddvar K. *v.3 p.234*

Hoig, Stanley *v.6 p.684, p.685, p.686, p.687, p.688*

Hoisington, Sona S. *v.2 p.798*

Hoisington, Thomas H. (Editor, Translator) *v.2 p.794*

Hokenson, Jan *v.1 p.56, p.90*

Hokkanen, Heikki M. T. & Lynch, James M. (Editors) . *v.5 p.8*

Holahan, Carole K., et al. *v.5 p.575*

Holberg, Ludvig *v.2 p.627*

Holbert, Steve & Rose, Lisa *v.6 p.264*

Holborn, Hajo *v.3 p.178*

Holcombe, Charles *v.6 p.185*

Holcombe, Lee *v.6 p.747*

Holcroft, Thomas *v.2 p.245*

Holden, Anthony *v.2 p.290, v.6 p.409*

Holden, John H., et al. *v.5 p.8, p.22, p.45*

Holden, Matthew Jr. *v.4 p.545, p.580*

Holden, Palmer J., et al. *v.5 p.55*

Holden, Robert H. *v.4 p.659*

Holder, Arthur G. *v.1 p.650*

Holder, John J. (Editor, Translator) *v.1 p.418*

Holderlin, Friedrich *v.2 p.600*

Holderness, Graham *v.2 p.234*

Holding, Dennis H. (Author, Editor) *v.5 p.605*

Holditch, Kenneth & Leavitt, Richard Freeman *v.2 p.134*

Holifield, E. Brooks *v.1 p.605, p.607, p.657*

Holihan, Mary *v.4 p.87*

Hollahan, Eugene (Editor) *v.2 p.293*

Holland, Barbara *v.4 p.772*

Holland, Bart K. *v.4 p.178*

Holland, D. K. (Editor) *v.4 p.140*

Holland, Dorothy & Quinn, Naomi (Editors) *v.4 p.27*

Holland, H. D. & Turekian, K. K. *v.5 p.363, p.367*

Holland, Heidi *v.4 p.613*

Holland, James *v.1 p.390*

Holland, John L. *v.5 p.577*

Holland, Julie (Editor) *v.4 p.776*

Holland, Kathleen E., et al. *v.4 p.363*

Holland, Martin *v.4 p.603*

Holland, Norman N. *v.2 p.571*

Holland, Norman Norwood Jr. *v.2 p.244*

Holland, Vyvyan Beresford *v.2 p.321*

Holland, Vyvyan *v.2 p.321*

Hollander, Gayle D. *v.4 p.703*

Hollander, John (Editor) *v.2 p.23, v.6 p.698*

Hollander, John *v.1 p.247, v.2 p.87*

Hollander, Myles & Wolfe, Douglas A. *v.5 p.482*

Hollander, Robert (Editor) *v.2 p.703*

Hollander, Robert *v.2 p.704*

Hollander, Samuel (Editor) *v.4 p.221*

Hollander, Samuel . *v.4 p.211, p.212, p.217, p.219, p.220, p.222*

Hollander, S *v.4 p.223*

Hollander, Stacy C. & Anderson, Brook Davis *v.1 p.800*

Hollandsworth, J. G. Jr. *v.5 p.659, p.660*

Hollas, J. Michael *v.5 p.273, p.562*

Hollenbach, David *v.1 p.575*

Hollenberg, Donna Krolik *v.2 p.89*

Hollender, Jeffrey & Fenichell, Stephen *v.4 p.54*

Hollender, Jeffrey *v.4 p.52*

Holleran, Andrew *v.6 p.397, p.406*

Holleran, Michael *v.1 p.822, v.6 p.726*

Holli, Melvin G. & Jones, Peter d' A. (Editors) *v.3 p.515*

Holliday, J. S. & Swain, William *v.3 p.531*

Holliday, Paul. *v.5 p.46*

Hollier, Denis (Editor) *v.2 p.456*

Hollier, Denis *v.2 p.456*

Hollifield, James F. & Jillson, Calvin C. *v.4 p.504*

Hollin, Clive R. (Editor) *v.6 p.277*

Hollingdale, R. J.. . . . . *v.1 p.466*

Hollinger, David A. & Capper, Charles. *v.3 p.368*

Hollinghurst, Alan *v.2 p.352, v.6 p.397*

Hollingsworth, Joseph Rogers *v.3 p.437*

Hollington, Michael *v.2 p.608*

Hollingworth, Leta S.. . . . . *v.5 p.575*

Hollis, Martin *v.1 p.492*

Hollis, Susan T. *v.6 p.644*

Hollister, C. Warren, et al. *v.3 p.97, p.98*

Hollister, C. Warren *v.3 p.97, p.98*

Hollnagel, Erik (Editor). *v.5 p.587*

Hollos, Marida C. *v.3 p.185*

Holloway, Brian R.. . . . . *v.5 p.680*

Holloway, D. G. & Tawney, D. A. *v.5 p.689*

Holloway, David *v.3 p.49, p.208, p.225*

Holloway, John. *v.1 p.147, v.2 p.234, v.6 p.750, p.752*

Holloway, Joseph E. (Editor) *v.6 p.6, p.11, p.39*

Holloway, Julian (Editor), et al. *v.4 p.395*

Holloway, Karla F. *v.6 p.479*

Holloway, R. Ross. *v.1 p.670, p.687, v.3 p.24*

Holloway, Sarah (Editor), et al. *v.4 p.376*

Holloway, Thomas H.. . . . . *v.3 p.341*

Hollyn, Norman *v.6 p.350*

Holman, C. Hugh *v.2 p.13*

Holman, David (Editor), et al.. . . . . *v.5 p.580*

Holman, J. K.. . . . . *v.1 p.198, p.230, p.365*

Holman, J. P. *v.5 p.560*

Holman, Peter *v.1 p.180, p.184, p.239, p.322, p.349*

Holman, Tomlinson. *v.6 p.351*

Holman Weisbard, Phyllis. *v.6 p.459*

Holmberg, Arthur *v.1 p.45*

Holmes, Anne *v.2 p.495*

Holmes, Brian, et al. *v.4 p.335*

Holmes, Charles S. (Editor), et al. *v.2 p.163*

Holmes, Charles S.. . . . . *v.2 p.125*

Holmes, Colin *v.3 p.112*

Holmes, David, et al.. . . . . *v.5 p.127*

Holmes, Frederic L. & Levere, Trevor Harvey (Editors). *v.5 p.263*

Holmes, Frederic Lawrence *v.5 p.122*

Holmes, Geoffrey S.. . . . . *v.3 p.94, p.106*

Holmes, George *v.3 p.69*

Holmes, James R. *v.3 p.304*

Holmes, John Clellon *v.2 p.81*

Holmes, Justice *v.4 p.468*

Holmes, King K. (Editor), et al. *v.5 p.516*

Holmes, Megan *v.1 p.740*

Holmes, Michael William (Editor) *v.1 p.591*

Holmes, Oliver Wendell. *v.4 p.434*

Holmes, Richard *v.4 p.703*

Holmes, Thom. *v.1 p.216, p.244*

Holmes, Urban T. Jr. & Neckam,
  Alexander *v.6 p.557, p.577, p.713*

Holmes-Eber, Paula. *v.6 p.641*

Holmgren, Beth (Editor) *v.2 p.798*

Holmgren, Beth *v.2 p.798, p.804*

Holmgren, Richard A. *v.5 p.477, p.488*

Holmlund, Chris & Fuchs, Cynthia *v.6 p.416*

Holmstrom, Lakshmi *v.2 p.763*

Holoman, D. Kern *v.1 p.198, p.240, p.310*

Holroyd, Michael (Introduction by) *v.2 p.343*

Holroyd, Michael. *v.2 p.309*

Holst, B., et al. *v.5 p.176, p.236*

Holst, Gail. *v.1 p.298*

Holst, Johan Jorgen (editor) *v.3 p.235*

Holstein, James A. & Gubrium, Jaber F. (Editors). . *v.5 p.646*

Holstein, James A. & Gubrium, Jaber F. *v.5 p.653*

Holsti, Kalevi J. *v.4 p.624*

Holt, Bradley P. *v.1 p.650*

Holt, Claire (Editor) *v.6 p.174*

Holt, Elizabeth G. (Editor) *v.1 p.679, p.687*

Holt, Elizabeth G. *v.1 p.672, p.675*

Holt, Frank Lee *v.3 p.20*

Holt, J. C. *v.3 p.68, p.98*

Holt, James C. *v.6 p.565*

Holt, John *v.4 p.327, p.343, p.357, p.364*

Holt, Mack P. *v.1 p.610, v.3 p.145*

Holt, Marilyn Irvin *v.3 p.521*

Holt, Marion P. (Editor) *v.1 p.66, p.108, v.2 p.643*

Holt, Marion P.. . . . . *v.2 p.640*

Holt, Michael F. *v.3 p.398*

Holt, P. M. (Editor). *v.6 p.581*

Holt, P. M. *v.3 p.64, v.6 p.584, p.609, p.640*

Holt, Peter M. *v.6 p.583*

Holt, Richard & Rosser, Gervase (Editors) *v.6 p.577*

Holt, Richard *v.4 p.806*

Holthe, Tess Uriza *v.6 p.179*

Holtman, Robert B.. . . . . *v.3 p.152*

Holton, Elwood F. III, et al.. . . . . *v.4 p.320*

Holton, Gerald. *v.3 p.46, p.49, v.5 p.390, p.391, p.395, p.400, p.402*

Holton, Jim *v.6 p.690*

Holton, Milne & Kuhner, Herbert (Editors). *v.2 p.591*

Holton, Milne & Mihailovich, Vasa D. (Editors). . . *v.2 p.811*

Holton, Milne & Mihailovich, Vasa D. *v.2 p.810*

Holton, Robert *v.2 p.92*

Holtz, Robert D. & Kovacs, William D. *v.5 p.421*

Holtz, Shel *v.4 p.144*

Holub, Miroslav, et al. *v.2 p.783*

Holub, Miroslav *v.2 p.783*

Holub, Robert C.. . . . . *v.2 p.589*

Holubova, Miloslava *v.2 p.783*

Holum, Kenneth G. *v.3 p.31*

Holway, John *v.6 p.41*

Holy, Ladislav *v.4 p.36*

Holz, Arno. *v.2 p.609*

Holzgrefe, J. L. (Author, Editor). *v.4 p.669, p.671*

Holzhey, Helmut & Mudroch, Vilem. *v.1 p.460, p.461*

Holzman, Jac & Daws, Gavan. *v.1 p.384*

Holzman, Richard S. *v.3 p.425*

Hom, Marion K. *v.6 p.211*

Homan, Lynn M. & Reilly, Thomas. *v.6 p.6, p.17*

Homan, Sidney. *v.1 p.139*

Homans, George C., et al.. . . . . *v.4 p.692*

Homans, Margaret *v.2 p.175, p.270, p.322, v.6 p.763*

Home School Legal Defense Association *v.4 p.296*

Homer, Bruce D. & Tamis-LeMonda, Catherine S.
(Editors) *v.5 p.621*

Homer, Sidney & Leibowitz, Martin L.. . . . . *v.4 p.103*

Homer, Sidney & Sylla, Richard. *v.4 p.155*

Homer, William I. & Goodrich, Lloyd *v.1 p.741*

Homer, William I. *v.1 p.740*

Homer. *v.2 p.414*

Homza, Lu Ann. *v.3 p.59, p.239*

Honan, Park *v.2 p.227, p.265, p.267, p.272*

Honda, Hiromu, et al.. . . . . *v.1 p.808*

Hondagneu-Sotelo, Pierrette. *v.6 p.524, p.546*

Honderich, Ted (Editor). *v.1 p.415*

Honderich, Ted. *v.1 p.503*

Hondermarck, Hubert (Editor) *v.5 p.116*

Hondros, John L.. . . . . *v.3 p.195*

Hone, Ralph E.. . . . . *v.2 p.381*

Honen. *v.6 p.221*

Honey, J. R. *v.3 p.112, p.128, v.6 p.745, p.747*

Honey, Martha *v.6 p.283*

Honeycombe, Robert *v.5 p.689*

Hong, Fan & Mangan, J. A.
(Editors). *v.4 p.836, p.844, p.867, v.6 p.437*

Hong, Howard V. & Hong, Edna H. (Editors). *v.1 p.478*

Hong, Maria *v.6 p.91*

Hong, Young-Sun *v.3 p.170*

Hong Yung Lee *v.4 p.620*

Hongo, Garrett K.. . . . . *v.6 p.91, p.103*

Hongo, Garrett *v.2 p.147, v.6 p.103*

Honig, Bruce & Rostain, Alain *v.4 p.66*

Honig, Emily *v.6 p.194*

Honig, J. M. (Editor) *v.5 p.277*

Honigmann, E. A. J. *v.2 p.234*

Honigsheim, Paul *v.4 p.681*

Honna, Jun *v.4 p.622*

Honolka, Kurt *v.1 p.190, p.353*

Honour, Hugh & Fleming, John *v.1 p.668*

Honour, Hugh *v.1 p.704*

Honsberger, Ross *v.5 p.476, p.478, p.495*

Honthaner, Eve Light *v.6 p.347*

Hoobler, Dorothy & Hoobler, Thomas *v.3 p.499*

Hood, Clifton *v.6 p.713*

Hood, James W. *v.2 p.313*

Hood, Mantle *v.1 p.173*

Hood, Ralph W. Jr., et al.. . . . . *v.5 p.634*

Hood, Robert E. *v.1 p.608, v.4 p.720*

Hood, Sinclair *v.1 p.668, p.687*

Hood, Steven J. *v.6 p.168*

Hood, Stuart *v.2 p.484*

Hood, Thomas. *v.2 p.290, p.291*

Hood, William *v.1 p.741*

Hoodfar, Homa *v.6 p.456, p.638*

Hooft, Stan Van *v.5 p.248*

Hoogenboom, Ari *v.3 p.398*

Hoogers, Gregor *v.5 p.362*

Hook, Andrew *v.2 p.69*

Hook, Brian & Twitchett, Denis C. (Editors) *v.6 p.183*

Hook, Diana H., et al. *v.4 p.420*

Hook, Glenn D. & McCormack, Gavan (Editors) . . . *v.6 p.224*

Hook, J. R. & Hall, H. E. *v.5 p.554*

Hook, Sidney *v.1 p.441, p.468*

Hook, Steven W. & Spanier, John *v.3 p.452*

Hooker, John. *v.4 p.762*

Hooker, Mark T. *v.3 p.204*

Hooker, Richard *v.1 p.582*

hooks, bell *v.4 p.730, v.6 p.26, p.44, p.330, p.427*

Hooley, D. M. *v.2 p.439, p.440*

Hooper, Charlotte *v.6 p.441*

Hooper, John. *v.3 p.243*

Hooper, Judith *v.5 p.193*

Hoopes, John W. *v.4 p.9*

Hoopes, Roy *v.2 p.65*

Hoopes, Townsend & Brinkley, Douglas *v.3 p.459*

Hooton, Cornell G. *v.4 p.527*

Hoover, Evalyn & Mercier, Sheryl *v.5 p.229*

Hoover, Herbert T. *v.3 p.523*

Hoover, Herbert *v.3 p.459, p.472, v.4 p.213*

Hoover, Kenneth R., et al.. . . . . *v.5 p.643*

Hoover, Kevin D. (Editor) *v.4 p.202, p.217, p.233*

Hoover, Kevin D. *v.4 p.195, p.240*

Hoover, W. G. *v.5 p.551*

Hopcroft, Rosemary L.. . . . . *v.3 p.43*

Hope, Debra A. (Editor) *v.5 p.612*

Hope, Marjorie & Young, James. *v.5 p.740*

Hopes, David B. *v.5 p.222*

Hopf, Henning *v.5 p.291*

Hopkins, A. G. *v.6 p.68*

Hopkins, Adam *v.3 p.196*

Hopkins, Alan (Editor). *v.5 p.42*

Hopkins, Andrew. *v.1 p.786*

Hopkins, Anthony *v.1 p.198, p.240, p.306*

Hopkins, David S. P. & Massy, William F. *v.4 p.293*

Hopkins, David. *v.1 p.679, v.2 p.181*

Hopkins, Dwight N.. . . . . *v.6 p.6, p.36*

Hopkins, E. Washburn *v.1 p.536*

Hopkins, Gerard Manley . . . *v.2 p.293, p.294, p.578, v.3 p.534*

Hopkins, Keith. *v.4 p.501*

Hopkins, Lisa *v.2 p.186, v.6 p.326*

Hopkins, MaryCarol *v.6 p.118, p.139*

Hopkins, Nicholas & Westergaard, Kirsten *v.6 p.639*

Hopkins, Nicholas S. & Ibrahim,
Saad Eddin (Contribution by) *v.4 p.703*

Hopkins, Willie E. *v.4 p.132*

Hopkinson, Michael *v.3 p.134, p.138*

Hopkirk, Peter *v.6 p.204, p.239*

Hopler, Robert B. (Editor) *v.5 p.738*

Hopp, Wallace & Spearman, Mark *v.4 p.119*

Hoppen, K. Theodore *v.6 p.735*

Hoppensteadt, Frank C. & Peskin, Charles S. *v.5 p.94*

Hopper, Paul J. & Traugott, Elizabeth Closs *v.2 p.561*

Hoppin, Richard H. *v.1 p.177*

Hoppit, Julian *v.3 p.106, p.108*

Hopps, Walter & Bois, Yve-Alain *v.1 p.741*

Hopps, Walter, et al. *v.1 p.767*

Hopwood, Derek *v.6 p.58, p.607*

Horace *v.2 p.434*

Horak, Ray *v.4 p.115*

Horan, Nigel J. & Lowe, Paul *v.5 p.376, p.378, p.379*

Horbury, William (Editor), et al. *v.1 p.547*

Horden, Peregrine (Editor) *v.1 p.406*

Hordern, Edward *v.5 p.469*

Hordeski, Michael F. *v.5 p.361*

Horgan, Paul *v.2 p.81, v.3 p.509*

Hori, Ichiro *v.1 p.541*

Hori, Muneo *v.5 p.694*

Horio, Teruhisa *v.6 p.224*

Horkheimer, Max & Adorno, Theodor W. *v.1 p.468*

Horkheimer, Max *v.1 p.468*

Horle, Craig W. (Editor) *v.3 p.492*

Horn, Berthold K. *v.5 p.710*

Horn, David & Jackson, Richard *v.1 p.167, p.278*

Horn, David *v.1 p.167, p.278*

Horn, James *v.3 p.499*

Horn, Jane *v.4 p.836, p.861*

Horn, Laurence R. & Ward, Gregory L. (Editors) . . . *v.4 p.424*

Horn, Pamela *v.3 p.53*

Horn, Thelma *v.5 p.582*

Hornblow, Arthur *v.1 p.115*

Hornblower, Simon & Spawforth, Antony (Editors) . . *v.2 p.399*

Hornblower, Simon (Editor) *v.2 p.402*

Horne, Alan *v.1 p.712*

Horne, Alistair *v.3 p.152, p.157, v.4 p.584, v.6 p.643*

Horne, Gerald . . *v.3 p.293, p.389, p.531, v.6 p.328, p.341, p.713*

Horne, John N. & Kramer, Alan *v.3 p.79, p.161*

Horneck, G. & Baumstark-Khan, C. *v.5 p.243*

Horner, Shari *v.2 p.167*

Horner, Tom *v.6 p.359, p.373*

Horney, Karen *v.6 p.445*

Hornick (Editor) *v.5 p.165*

Horno Delgado, Asunción (Editor), et al. . *v.6 p.500, p.506, p.513*

Hornsby, Alton (Editor) *v.6 p.6, p.14*

Hornsby, Alton Jr. *v.6 p.6*

Hornung, E. W. *v.2 p.352*

Hornung, Erik & Bryan, Betsy *v.3 p.9*

Hornung, Erik *v.3 p.9*

Horobin, R. W. & Kiernan, J. A. (Editors) *v.5 p.88*

Horosko, Marian *v.1 p.9, p.28, p.30, p.42*

Horovitz, David *v.6 p.614*

Horowitz, Dan & Lissak, Moshe *v.4 p.615, v.6 p.612*

Horowitz, David A. *v.3 p.441*

Horowitz, Donald L. *v.4 p.713*

Horowitz, Helen L. *v.4 p.290, p.331*

Horowitz, Irving L. (Editor) *v.4 p.703*

Horowitz, Irving L. *v.4 p.685*

Horowitz, Irwin A. *v.5 p.592*

Horowitz, Maryanne Cline *v.1 p.416*

Horowitz, Shale Asher & Schnabel, Albrecht *v.4 p.670*

Horowitz, Steven *v.4 p.234*

Horrox, Rosemary (Translator) *v.3 p.69*

Horsfield, Kate & Hilderbrand, Lucas (Editors) . . . *v.1 p.770*

Horsley, Imogene *v.1 p.371*

Horsley, L. H.; Tamplin, William S. *v.5 p.282*

Horsley, Richard A. (Editor) *v.1 p.599*

Horsman, Reginald *v.3 p.417, v.6 p.686*

Horst, Louis & Russell, Carroll *v.1 p.26*

Horstmann, Cay & Cornell, Gary *v.5 p.346, p.347*

Horton, Andrew S. (Editor) *v.6 p.312*

Horton, Andrew *v.6 p.352*

Horton, James O. & Horton, Lois E. *v.3 p.488*

Horton, Mark & Middleton, John *v.4 p.724, v.6 p.63*

Horton, William K. *v.4 p.321*

Hortorium, L. H. Bailey & Hortorium, Bailey *v.5 p.44*

Horvat, Michael A., et al. *v.4 p.800*

Horvath, Ari L. *v.5 p.282, p.407*

Horvath, Brooke *v.2 p.56*

Horvath, Istvan T. (Editor-In-Chief) *v.5 p.278*

Horwath, Alexander (Editor), et al. *v.6 p.341*

Horwich, George & Samuelson, Paul Anthony (Editors) . *v.4 p.257*

Horwich, Paul *v.1 p.490, v.5 p.402*

Horwitz, A. V. *v.5 p.649*

Horwitz, Dawn L. *v.1 p.9*

Horwitz, Marshall *v.5 p.149*

Horwitz, Morton J. *v.4 p.440, p.441*

Horwitz, Richard P. *v.3 p.486*

Horwitz, Tony *v.4 p.521*

Horwitz, Williams (Editor) *v.5 p.34*

Hosford, William F. *v.5 p.732*

Hoshi, Takeo & Kashyap, Anil *v.6 p.224*

Hoskin, Michael *v.5 p.61*

Hosking, Eric & Hosking, David (Photographers) . *v.5 p.176, p.238*

Hosking, Geoffrey Alan *v.3 p.213*

Hosking, Geoffrey *v.3 p.209*

Hoskins, Colin, et al. *v.6 p.344*

Hoskins, Jim *v.1 p.45*

Hoskins, P. W. O. (Editor) *v.5 p.367, p.376, p.378*

Hoskins, Tina *v.4 p.864*

Hoskins, W. G.. . . . . *v.6 p.575*

Hoskins, W.G.. . . . . *v.3 p.126*

Hoskote, Ranjit (Editor). *v.2 p.763*

Hosler, Mary M.. *v.2 p.556*

Hosoume, Kimi & Barber, Jacqueline *v.5 p.229*

Hospital, Carolina & Cantera, Jorge (Editors). *v.6 p.496, p.507*

Hospital, Carolina *v.6 p.506, p.510*

Hossain, Rokeya S.. . . . . *v.2 p.764*

Hosseini, Khaled *v.2 p.160*

Hossler, Don, et al.. . . . . *v.4 p.294*

Hostetler, John A.. . . . . *v.1 p.586*

Hostetter, Anthony *v.1 p.82, p.85, p.109, p.152, p.154*

Hostettmann, K., et al.. . . . . *v.5 p.299*

Hotaling, Edward *v.4 p.832, p.847*

Hothersall, David. *v.5 p.596*

Hotson, J. Leslie *v.2 p.221*

Hotson, Leslie *v.1 p.77, p.101, p.144, v.2 p.227*

Hottenstein, David S.. . . . . *v.4 p.287*

Houchin, John H. (Editor). *v.2 p.107*

Houck, Lynne D. & Drickamer, Lee C.
(Editors). *v.5 p.166, p.167, p.614*

Houellebecq, Michel *v.2 p.530*

Houfe, Simon *v.1 p.712, v.6 p.737*

Hough, Derek *v.5 p.193*

Hough, Graham Goulden *v.2 p.214*

Hough, Jerry F.. . . . . *v.4 p.598*

Hough, Michael *v.1 p.813*

Hough, Richard & Richards, Denis *v.3 p.81*

Hough, Richard *v.3 p.91*

Hough, Susan Elizabeth. *v.5 p.442*

Houghton, Buck *v.6 p.351*

Houghton, David *v.3 p.389, p.441, p.442*

Houghton, E. L. & Carpenter, P. W. *v.5 p.718*

Houghton, John T. (Editor), et al. *v.5 p.371*

Houghton, John T. *v.5 p.426*

Houghton, Norris *v.1 p.251, p.311, p.408*

Houghton, R. P. *v.5 p.299*

Houghton, Walter E. (Editor) *v.6 p.735, p.752*

Houghton, Walter E. *v.6 p.750*

Houghton, Walter Edwards *v.3 p.112, p.128*

Houglum, Peggy A., et al. *v.4 p.827, p.828, p.829*

Houk, Walter *v.5 p.83*

Houle, Cyril O. *v.4 p.320*

Houlihan, Barrie (Editor) *v.4 p.816*

Hounshell, David A.. . . . . *v.3 p.368*

Houpt, Katherine A.. . . . . *v.5 p.55, p.57*

Hourani, Albert H. & Ruthven, Malise *v.6 p.583*

Hourani, Albert H. & Shehadi, Nadim (Editors). . . *v.6 p.605*

Hourani, Albert H. (Editor), et al. *v.6 p.593*

Hourani, Albert H.. . . . . *v.6 p.593*

Hourigan, Maureen M.. . . . . *v.4 p.29*

Hourihane, Colum (Editor) *v.1 p.672, p.687*

Housby, J. Nicholas (Editor) *v.5 p.88*

House Committee on Ways and Means. *v.4 p.481*

House, Herbert O.. . . . . *v.5 p.294*

House, Humphry *v.2 p.284*

House, Jane & Attisani, Antonio
(Editors) *v.1 p.67, p.107, v.2 p.699*

House, Robert J. (Editor), et al. *v.4 p.69, p.71*

Houser, Nathan & Kloesel, Christian J.. . . . . . . *v.1 p.440*

Housh, Terry J. & Housh, Dona J. (Editors) *v.4 p.873*

Housley, Kathleen L.. . . . . *v.1 p.741*

Housley, Norman. *v.6 p.556*

Housman, A. E.. . . . . *v.2 p.291*

Houston, Brant. *v.4 p.414*

Houston, Cecil J. & Smyth, William J.. . . . . *v.3 p.542*

Houston, Christopher. *v.6 p.598, p.621*

Houston, David Franklin *v.3 p.472*

Houston, James G.. . . . . *v.6 p.248*

Houston, Jeanne Wakatsuki & Houston, James D.. *v.6 p.93, p.134*

Houston, Michael E.. . . . . *v.4 p.874*

Houston, Penelope *v.6 p.346*

Houston, R. A.. . . . . *v.4 p.335*

Houston, Rab A. *v.3 p.43, p.99, p.128, p.132, p.134*

Houston, Velina H. (Editor,
Introduction by). *v.1 p.67, p.125, v.6 p.98*

Houston, Velina H. (Editor). . . *v.1 p.67, p.125, v.6 p.91, p.98*

Houtkoop-Steenstra, Hanneke *v.4 p.691*

Hovannisian, Richard C. & Sabagh, Georges (Editors). *v.6 p.659*

Hovannisian, Richard G. (Editor) *v.6 p.623, p.633*

Hovannisian, Richard G.. . . . *v.3 p.231, v.6 p.624, p.633*

Hovenkamp, Herbert *v.4 p.444*

Hovland, Carl I.. *v.5 p.586*

Hovland, Carl Iver *v.4 p.423, v.5 p.624*

Howard, Allen M. & Shain, Richard M. *v.4 p.384*

Howard, Angela & Kavenik, Frances M. (Editors). . *v.6 p.450*

Howard, Angela Falco, et al.. . . . . *v.1 p.777*

Howard, Caroline (Editor). *v.4 p.321*

Howard, Christopher. *v.4 p.66*

Howard, Daniel J. & Berlocher, Stewart H. (Editors) . *v.5 p.199*

Howard, David & Angus, James. *v.1 p.375*

Howard, David. *v.6 p.352*

Howard, Dennis R. & Crompton, John L. . . . *v.4 p.888, p.891*

Howard, Dennis Ramsay & Crompton, John L.. *v.4 p.884, p.888*

Howard, Donald R.. . . . . *v.2 p.209*

Howard, Gary C. (Editor) *v.5 p.116*

Howard, Harold P.. . . . . *v.3 p.520*

Howard, Henry & Surrey, Henry Howard Earl of . . . *v.2 p.214*

Howard, J. Woodford Jr.. . . . . *v.4 p.468*

Howard, Jean *v.2 p.225, p.233, p.234*

Howard, Joseph Kinsey.. . . . . *v.3 p.525, p.545*

Howard, Judith A. & Allen, Carolyn (Editors) *v.6 p.434*

Howard, June (Editor). *v.2 p.46*

Howard, Keith *v.1 p.288*

Howard, Kim & Stevens, Annie (Editors). *v.6 p.385*

Howard, Leon.. . . . . *v.2 p.47*

Howard, Marc Morje *v.4 p.640*

Howard, Maureen (Editor) *v.2 p.27*

Howard, Michael C. (Editor) *v.4 p.478*

Howard, Michael Eliot *v.4 p.647, p.649*

Howard, Michael *v.3 p.36, p.79*
Howard, Patricia *v.1 p.190, p.230, p.326*
Howard, Philip & Jones, Steve (Editors) *v.4 p.425*
Howard, Philip A. *v.3 p.310*
Howard, Philip H. & Neal, Michael W. *v.5 p.258*
Howard, Philip H. *v.5 p.311, p.318*
Howard, Philip K. *v.4 p.441*
Howard, Rhoda E. *v.4 p.512, v.6 p.55*
Howard, Ronnalie R. *v.2 p.303*
Howard, Russell & Sawyer, Reid *v.4 p.564*
Howard-Snyder, Daniel (Editor) *v.1 p.594*
Howarth, R. W., et al. *v.5 p.173*
Howarth, W. D. *v.2 p.478*
Howarth, William D. (Editor) *v.1 p.78, p.106*
Howarth, William L. *v.3 p.535*
Howat, Roy *v.1 p.216, p.320*
Howatson, Margaret *v.2 p.399*
Howe, A. Elizabeth *v.1 p.756*
Howe, Daniel W. *v.1 p.589, v.4 p.694*
Howe, Dennis *v.5 p.344*
Howe, Florence (Editor) *v.2 p.23, v.6 p.463*
Howe, Irving *v.2 p.74*
Howe, Jeffrey *v.1 p.784*
Howe, Leland W. *v.4 p.306*
Howe, Leo *v.4 p.39*
Howe, Linda S. *v.3 p.310*
Howe, Mark Antony de Wolfe (Editor) . . . *v.3 p.425*
Howe, Mark D. (Editor) *v.4 p.468*
Howe, Mark D. *v.4 p.468*
Howe, Marvine *v.6 p.643*
Howe, Nicholas *v.2 p.167*
Howe, Stephen *v.3 p.125*
Howell, Benita J. (Editor) *v.1 p.822*
Howell, Colin D. *v.4 p.807*
Howell, Colin *v.4 p.806, p.816, p.850*
Howell, Joseph H. & Dunnivant, Stephen W. *v.4 p.351*
Howell, Jude *v.4 p.620*
Howell, M. G., et al. *v.5 p.287*
Howell, M. G. *v.5 p.287*
Howell, Mark D. *v.4 p.848, p.888*
Howell, P. *v.2 p.437*
Howell, Scott L. & Hricko, Mary *v.5 p.601*
Howell, William G. & Peterson, Paul E. *v.4 p.298*
Howells, Christina (Editor) *v.1 p.458, p.506*
Howells, Coral Ann (Editor) *v.2 p.734*
Howells, Coral Ann *v.2 p.729, p.734, p.737*
Howells, William Dean *v.2 p.33, p.42, p.578*
Howes, Carollee & Ritchie, Sharon *v.4 p.369*
Howes, Elaine V. *v.4 p.367*
Howes, John F. *v.6 p.227*
Howey, Noelle & Samuels, Ellen *v.6 p.367, p.375*
Howie, John Mackintosh *v.5 p.491*
Howitt, Arnold M. & Pangi, Robyn L. (Editors) . . . *v.4 p.564*
Howitt, Dennis *v.5 p.592*
Howkins, Alun *v.6 p.759*

Howland Kenney, William *v.4 p.712*
Howlett, Kathy M. *v.6 p.326*
Howley, Edward T. & Franks, B. Don *v.4 p.791, p.906*
Howsam, Leslie *v.3 p.37, v.5 p.395, v.6 p.741, p.759*
Howse, Justin, et al. *v.1 p.49*
Hoxie, Frederick E. (Editor) *v.6 p.682*
Hoxie, Frederick E. *v.6 p.688, p.689*
Hoy, David (Editor) *v.1 p.459*
Hoy, Jim & Isern, Tom *v.3 p.520*
Hoyle, David (Editor) *v.4 p.117*
Hoyle, David *v.4 p.117*
Hoyle, Fred *v.3 p.47*
Hoyle *v.5 p.358, p.360*
Hoyles, Celia *v.5 p.463*
Hoyos, Dexter *v.3 p.25*
Hoyt, Edwin P. *v.3 p.509, v.6 p.227*
Hrabal, Bohumil, et al. *v.2 p.783*
Hrabal, Bohumil *v.2 p.783*
Hranicky, W. Jack *v.4 p.390*
Hrdy, Sarah Blaffer *v.4 p.744*
Hroch, Miroslav *v.3 p.61*
Hrotsvitha *v.1 p.62, p.73, p.109*
Hruby, Peter *v.2 p.782*
Hryhorenko, Hrytsko & Ukrainka, Lesya *v.2 p.813*
Hsia, C. T. *v.6 p.208*
Hsia, R. Po-chia (Editor) *v.1 p.604*
Hsia, R. Po-chia *v.1 p.612, v.3 p.166*
Hsiao, Cheng *v.4 p.202, p.206*
Hsiao, Kung-Chuan *v.6 p.187*
Hsiung, James C. & Levine, Steven I. (Editors) . . . *v.6 p.193*
Hsu, Elisabeth *v.4 p.46*
Hsu, Francis L. *v.6 p.182*
Hsu, Hui-Hwang *v.5 p.106, p.109*
Hsu, Immanuel C. *v.6 p.183*
Hsu, Madeline Y. *v.6 p.118, p.127*
Hsu, Tao-Ching *v.1 p.56, p.131, v.6 p.209*
Hsu, Teng H. *v.5 p.694*
Hüttermann, Aloys & Godbold, Douglas (Editors) . . . *v.5 p.38*
Hu, Hua-ling *v.6 p.193, p.202*
Hu, Shi Ming & Seifman, Eli (Editors) *v.4 p.335*
Hu, Shizhang *v.3 p.459*
Hua, Cai & Hustvedt, Asti *v.4 p.32*
Huang, Chungliang A. *v.4 p.793*
Huang, Guiyou (Editor) *v.6 p.86, p.93, p.100*
Huang, Guiyou *v.6 p.86, p.90*
Huang, Kerson *v.5 p.552, p.558*
Huang, Ray *v.6 p.183, p.186*
Hubbard, Arthur T. *v.5 p.283*
Hubbard, Bryn & Glasser, Neil F. *v.4 p.391*
Hubbard, John L. (Featuring) *v.5 p.498*
Hubbard, Margaret *v.2 p.441*
Hubbard, Michael W., et al. *v.5 p.513*
Hubbard, R. Glenn *v.4 p.247, p.263*
Hubbard, Thomas K. (Editor) *v.3 p.14*
Hubbartt, William S. *v.4 p.446*

Hubbell, Sue. *v.5 p.156*

Hubbs, Carl L. & Lagler, Karl F. *v.5 p.215*

Hubbs, G. Ward *v.4 p.521*

Hubbs, Nadine *v.1 p.379, v.6 p.408*

Hubel, David H. & Wiesel, Torsten N. *v.5 p.617*

Huber, Bernhard A. (Editor), et al.. . . . . . *v.5 p.184, p.236*

Huber, Brian T. (Editor), et al.. . . . . *v.5 p.445*

Huber, Charles F.. . . . . *v.5 p.255*

Huber, Evelyne & Stephens, John D.. . . . . . *v.4 p.594*

Huber, Peter W. *v.4 p.445*

Huber, Thomas M. *v.6 p.224*

Huber, Thomas P. & Huber, Carole J. *v.3 p.545*

Hubert, Judd David. *v.2 p.475*

Hubin, Allen J.. . . . . *v.2 p.580*

Hubka, Thomas C. *v.1 p.789*

Hubler, Edward *v.2 p.225*

Hubner, Kurt. *v.5 p.402*

Huc, Evariste Regis & Gabet, Joseph *v.6 p.215*

Hucho, Wolf *v.5 p.716*

Huchthausen, Peter *v.3 p.304*

Huck, Charlotte S., et al. *v.4 p.364*

Huddleston, Rodney & Pullum, Geoffrey K. *v.2 p.556*

Hu-DeHart, Evelyn (Editor) *v.6 p.85, p.118*

Hudík, Pavol, et al. *v.2 p.812*

Hudgins, Sharon *v.3 p.214*

Hudler, George W. *v.5 p.209*

Hudlicky, Milos *v.5 p.296*

Hudson, Frederic *v.4 p.405*

Hudson, Frederick, et al. *v.4 p.405*

Hudson, John B. *v.5 p.554*

Hudson, John C. *v.3 p.506, v.5 p.4*

Hudson, John *v.3 p.97, p.98, v.5 p.263*

Hudson, Marc *v.2 p.205*

Hudson, Mark J. *v.6 p.221*

Hudson, Michael C. *v.6 p.605*

Hudson, Michael *v.6 p.583*

Hudson, Richard *v.1 p.400*

Hudson-Weems, Clenora *v.6 p.26, p.44*

Hudspeth, Robert N. (Editor). *v.2 p.39*

Huebener, Theodore *v.2 p.590*

Huelle, Pawel *v.2 p.790*

Huerta, Jorge A. (Editor). *v.6 p.496, p.517*

Huerta, Jorge *v.6 p.513, p.517*

Huerta-Macias, Ana *v.4 p.304, p.305, v.6 p.527*

Huether, Sue E. & McCance, Kathryn L.. . . . . *v.5 p.514*

Huettenmueller, Rhonda. *v.4 p.175*

Huettich, H. G.. . . . . *v.2 p.591*

Hufbauer, Gary Clyde & Grieco, Paul L. E. *v.4 p.107*

Huff, Archie Vernon *v.3 p.417*

Huff, C. Ronald, et al. *v.4 p.567*

Huffaker, Carl B. & Gutierrez, Andrew Paul (Editors). *v.5 p.170, p.213*

Huffaker, Carl B. *v.5 p.9, p.368, p.380*

Huffman, James L. *v.6 p.227*

Huffman, Joseph P. *v.3 p.161*

Huffman, Wallace & Evenson, Robert *v.5 p.30*

Hufton, Olwen H.. . . . . *v.3 p.53, p.150*

Hufton, Olwen *v.3 p.52*

Hug, Simon *v.4 p.579*

Hugenberger, Charles E. *v.6 p.493*

Huggett, Richard J.. . . . . *v.5 p.168, p.358*

Huggett, Stephen & Jordan, David *v.5 p.499*

Huggins, Martha K.. . . . . . . *v.3 p.336, v.6 p.262*

Huggins, Nathan I. (Editor). *v.2 p.19*

Huggins, Nathan Irvin *v.3 p.420*

Hugh of Saint Victor *v.1 p.577*

Hughes, Aaron W. & Ibn Ezra, Abraham ben Meir. *v.6 p.573, p.574*

Hughes, Alan *v.5 p.643*

Hughes, Alex & Williams, James S. (Editors) . *v.6 p.327, p.338*

Hughes, Alex (Editor), et al.. . . . . *v.2 p.459*

Hughes, Andrew S. *v.6 p.567*

Hughes, Anne *v.3 p.103*

Hughes, Austin L.. . . . . . *v.5 p.144, p.145, p.200*

Hughes, Bob *v.4 p.784, p.795*

Hughes, Charles E.. . . . . *v.3 p.434*

Hughes, Christopher *v.3 p.244*

Hughes, Derek & Todd, Janet (Editors) *v.1 p.59, p.77, p.101, v.2 p.238*

Hughes, Derek. *v.2 p.186, p.246*

Hughes, G. E. & Cresswell, Maxwell J. *v.1 p.492*

Hughes, Geoffrey. *v.2 p.554*

Hughes, Gerard J. *v.1 p.426*

Hughes, Glenn *v.1 p.115*

Hughes, Holly & Roman, David (Editors) *v.6 p.412*

Hughes, Howard C.. . . . . *v.5 p.614*

Hughes, John, et al. *v.4 p.683*

Hughes, Kathleen *v.6 p.563*

Hughes, Langston & Meltzer, Milton *v.1 p.34*

Hughes, Langston, et al. *v.2 p.87*

Hughes, Langston *v.2 p.87, p.88*

Hughes, Linda K. & Lund, Michael *v.6 p.741, p.756*

Hughes, Linda K. *v.2 p.313*

Hughes, Lindsey A.. . . . . *v.3 p.216*

Hughes, Lindsey *v.3 p.217*

Hughes, Louis *v.6 p.6, p.17*

Hughes, M. Vivian *v.6 p.765*

Hughes, Merritt Y. *v.2 p.254*

Hughes, Michael & Kroehler, Carolyn J. *v.4 p.675*

Hughes, Peter C. *v.5 p.719*

Hughes, Richard L. & Beatty, Katherine M. *v.4 p.71*

Hughes, Richard T. & Adrian, William B. (Editors) . *v.4 p.308*

Hughes, Robert *v.1 p.682, p.697, p.741*

Hughes, Russell Meriwether *v.1 p.20*

Hughes, Stephen H. *v.6 p.643*

Hughes, T., et al.. . . . . *v.4 p.864, p.870*

Hughes, Ted *v.2 p.353*

Hughes, Thomas P. *v.3 p.49, v.4 p.159*

Hughes, Thomas *v.2 p.291*

Hughes-Wilson, John & Corns, Cathryn M. *v.3 p.79*

Hugo, Richard *v.2 p.81, p.578*

Hugo, Victor & Janc, John J. *v.2 p.494*

Hugo, Victor. *v.2 p.493, p.494*

Huhn, Tom (Editor) *v.1 p.506, p.507*

Hui, Wei. *v.6 p.212*

Hui, Yiu H. & Khachatourians, George G. (Editors) . . *v.5 p.34*

Huidobro, Matias M. *v.2 p.672*

Huidobro, Vicente *v.2 p.680*

Huijsing, J. H. (Editor), et al. *v.5 p.721*

Huitt, W. *v.4 p.306*

Huizinga, Johan H.. . . . . *v.3 p.204*

Huizinga, Johan *v.1 p.600, v.6 p.563*

Huk, Romana *v.2 p.382*

Hulbert, Ann. *v.2 p.120*

Hulek, Klaus. *v.5 p.497*

Hulet, Claude L. *v.2 p.691*

Hull, Brent *v.1 p.824*

Hull, Caroline & Jotischky, Andrew *v.4 p.380*

Hull, Clark L. *v.4 p.357, v.5 p.613*

Hull, Clark Leonard *v.5 p.615*

Hull, Cordell. *v.3 p.459*

Hull, D. & Clyne, T. W. *v.5 p.689*

Hull, David L. (Editor) *v.5 p.193*

Hull, David L.. . . . . *v.5 p.193, p.226*

Hull, Geoffrey P.. . . . . *v.1 p.384*

Hull, Gloria T. (Editor), et al. *v.6 p.463*

Hull, Isabel V. *v.3 p.55, p.161, p.167*

Hull, John C. *v.5 p.503*

Hull, N. E. H. & Hoffer, Peter Charles *v.4 p.439*

Hull, N. E. H., et al. *v.4 p.447*

Hullfish, Henry G. & Smith, Phillip G.. . . . . . *v.4 p.357*

Hulme, Derick L.. . . . . *v.3 p.389*

Hulme, Keri (Author, Preface by) *v.2 p.746*

Hulme, Keri *v.2 p.746*

Huls, Mary E. *v.6 p.425*

Hulse, James. *v.3 p.529*

Hulsey, Byron C.. . . . . *v.3 p.459*

Hult, Joan S. & Trekell, Marianna
(Editors). *v.4 p.807, p.836, p.854*

Hulteng, John L.. . . . . *v.4 p.405*

Hultgren, Arland J. *v.1 p.646*

Hultgren, Ralph; Desai, Pramod D. *v.5 p.286*

Hultgren, Ralph R. et al. *v.5 p.286*

Hults, Linda C.. . . . . *v.1 p.753*

Human Kinetics Staff. *v.4 p.798, p.799*

Human Relations Media Staff (Produced by) *v.6 p.385*

Human Rights Watch, Helsinki Staff *v.6 p.603*

Human Rights Watch, Middle East Staff (Editor). *v.6 p.598, p.603*

Human Rights Watch Staff *v.4 p.512, p.613*

Human Rights Watch. *v.4 p.670*

Human Services Policy Center, University of
Washington. *v.5 p.671*

HumanGenome Project (ed.) . . . *v.5 p.140, p.145, p.149, p.245*

Humble, Nicola *v.2 p.191*

Humboldt, Alexander von & Fernandez, Luis Martinez. *v.3 p.310*

Hume, Cameron R.. . . . . *v.4 p.649*

Hume, David & Sayre-McCord, Geoffrey. *v.1 p.451*

Hume, David *v.1 p.451, p.523, v.4 p.217*

Hume, Robert D.. . . . . *v.2 p.187*

Humez, Jean McMahon *v.6 p.6, p.17*

Humfrey, Peter (Editor). *v.1 p.741*

Humm, Maggie *v.6 p.427*

Hummel, Arthur W. *v.6 p.187, p.199*

Hummel, Monte *v.5 p.179, p.234*

Hummel, Rolf E.. . . . . *v.5 p.732*

Hummer, Hans J.. . . . . *v.3 p.143*

Humpherys, Anne *v.2 p.298*

Humphrey, Carol Sue. *v.3 p.315*

Humphrey, Doris *v.1 p.9*

Humphrey, Hubert H.. . . . . *v.3 p.459*

Humphrey, James H. & Yow, Deborah A.. . . . . *v.4 p.840*

Humphrey, James Harry *v.5 p.627*

Humphrey, James H. *v.4 p.799*

Humphreys, Arthur Raleigh *v.2 p.260*

Humphreys, James E.. . . . . *v.5 p.473*

Humphreys, Keith *v.5 p.669*

Humphreys, R. Stephen. *v.6 p.584, p.593*

Humphreys, Robert A. *v.3 p.297*

Humphreys, Sheila M. *v.5 p.398*

Humphries, Christopher J. & Parenti, Lynne R.. *v.5 p.170, p.201*

Humphries, John. *v.1 p.390, p.400*

Humphries, Reynold *v.6 p.318*

Humphries, Rolfe *v.2 p.81*

Humpston, Giles & Jacobson, David M. *v.5 p.737*

Hums, Mary A. & MacLean, Joanne . *v.4 p.844, p.891, p.898*

Hune, Shirley & Nomura, Gail M. (Editors) . *v.6 p.112, p.114*

Hune, Shirley (Editor), et al. *v.6 p.85*

Hunefeldt, Christine *v.3 p.327*

Hung, Chang-tai *v.1 p.693, v.6 p.193*

Hung, George K. & Pallis, Jani Macari (Editors) . . . *v.4 p.872*

Hung, William *v.6 p.185, p.200, p.209*

Hungarian National Library *v.2 p.785*

Hungerford, Constance Cain. *v.1 p.741*

Hunn, Bruce D. (Editor) *v.5 p.360, p.361, p.362, p.368*

Hunnisett, Basil *v.1 p.752*

Hunnisett, Jean. *v.1 p.151*

Hunt, Anthony *v.2 p.154*

Hunt, B J; James, M I *v.5 p.323*

Hunt, Constance E., et al.. . . . . *v.5 p.179*

Hunt, Edward D.. . . . . *v.6 p.608*

Hunt, Edwin S. & Murray, James M. *v.3 p.40, p.62*

Hunt, Herbert James *v.2 p.486*

Hunt, James W. & Strongin, Patricia K. *v.4 p.131*

Hunt, John D. (Editor) *v.1 p.818*

Hunt, John D. *v.1 p.818*

Hunt, John M. *v.5 p.451*

Hunt, Leigh *v.2 p.291*

Hunt, Lord. *v.1 p.819*

Hunt, Lynn A. *v.3 p.150*

Hunt, Marsha *v.6 p.332*

Hunt, Michael H.. . . . . *v.3 p.385, p.452, v.6 p.168*

Hunt, Nancy & Marshall, Kathleen *v.4 p.316*

Hunt, Peter *v.2 p.582*

Hunt, Ronald J. *v.6 p.358, p.363*

Hunt, Roy E.. . . . . *v.5 p.421*

Hunt, Stephen (Editor) *v.1 p.524*

Hunt, William R.. . . . . *v.3 p.533*

Hunt, William *v.3 p.103, p.121*

Hunter, C. G. *v.3 p.217*

Hunter, D.. . . . . *v.6 p.367, p.406*

Hunter, G. K. *v.2 p.235, p.254*

Hunter, Geoffrey *v.1 p.494*

Hunter, Graeme K. *v.5 p.79, p.127, p.154*

Hunter, Ian & Saunders, David (Editors) *v.4 p.496*

Hunter, Ian *v.1 p.459*

Hunter, J. Paul. *v.2 p.192, p.247*

Hunter, Jack (Editor) *v.6 p.416*

Hunter, James Davison *v.4 p.306*

Hunter, Jane *v.6 p.201, p.218*

Hunter, Janet E. *v.6 p.224*

Hunter, Jefferson *v.1 p.763, v.2 p.194*

Hunter, John E. & Schmidt, Frank L. *v.4 p.689*

Hunter, Louis C.. . . . . *v.5 p.406*

Hunter, Michael & Wootton, David (Editors) *v.1 p.545*

Hunter, Michael *v.5 p.385, p.392*

Hunter, Nan D., et al.. . . . . *v.4 p.457*

Hunter, R. L.. . . . . *v.2 p.406*

Hunter, Richard (Editor) *v.2 p.413*

Hunter, Robin *v.4 p.343*

Hunter, Rodney J. & Ramsay, Nancy J. *v.1 p.649*

Hunter, Sam, et al. *v.1 p.679*

Hunter, Sam *v.1 p.741*

Hunter, Susan *v.4 p.704*

Hunter, Tab *v.6 p.418*

Hunter, Tera W. *v.6 p.6, p.44*

Hunter, Wendy. *v.3 p.274, p.341, v.4 p.592*

Hunter, William *v.5 p.134*

Huntington, Samuel P. & Harrison, Lawrence E. (Editors). *v.4 p.269, p.700*

Huntington, Samuel P. *v.3 p.36, v.4 p.482*

Hunwick, John O. *v.6 p.640*

Hupchick, Dennis P. *v.3 p.246*

Huppe, Bernard F. *v.2 p.205*

Huppert, George *v.1 p.601*

Hurd, Charles *v.2 p.27*

Hurd, Richard *v.2 p.245*

Hurdzan, Michael *v.4 p.881*

Hurewicz, Witold. *v.5 p.487*

Hurewitz, J. C. (Editor, Translator). *v.6 p.582*

Hurewitz, J. C.. . . . . *v.6 p.593*

Hurewitz, Jacob C. *v.6 p.617*

Hurford, Peter *v.1 p.398*

Hurlburt, Laurence P.. . . . . *v.1 p.732, p.741*

Hurley, Donna W. *v.2 p.443*

Hurley, S. L.. . . . . *v.1 p.497, v.5 p.613*

Hurst, Beth *v.4 p.364*

Hurst, G. Cameron 3rd & Hurst I, G. *v.4 p.863*

Hurst, James W.. . . . . *v.5 p.37, v.6 p.295*

Hurst, Ronald L., et al.. . . . . *v.1 p.804*

Hurston, Lucy. *v.2 p.81*

Hurston, Zora
Neale. . . . *v.2 p.17, p.81, v.6 p.6, p.16, p.17, p.26, p.39, p.44*

Hurt, C. D. *v.5 p.405*

Hurt, R. Douglas & Hurt, Mary E.. . . . . . . *v.5 p.5*

Hurt, R. Douglas (Editor, Introduction by). . . . *v.6 p.6, p.39*

Hurt, R. Douglas. *v.3 p.513, v.5 p.4, p.30, v.6 p.681*

Hurtado, Aida *v.6 p.434*

Hurtado, Larry W. *v.1 p.626*

Hurvitz, Leon (Translator). *v.1 p.563*

Hurwit, Jeffrey M. *v.3 p.16, p.18*

Husain, Initzar & Memon, Mohammad U. *v.6 p.151*

Husayn, Taha *v.6 p.659, p.660*

Husband, William *v.3 p.222*

Husch, Bertram, et al. *v.5 p.38*

Huse, Norbert & Wolters, Wolfgang *v.1 p.675, p.687*

Huselid, Mark & Becker, Brian *v.4 p.120*

Huselid, Mark, et al.. . . . . *v.4 p.76*

Husen, Torsten *v.4 p.327*

Husén, Torsten & Postlethwaite, T. Neville (Editors). *v.4 p.313, p.322*

Husmeier, Dirk (Editor), et al. *v.5 p.97*

Hussain, Intizar (Editor) *v.6 p.151*

Huss-Ashmore, Rebecca (Editor) *v.4 p.45*

Hussein, King of Jordan *v.6 p.621*

Hussein, M. Kamel *v.6 p.660*

Husserl, Edmund *v.1 p.468, p.469, p.511*

Hussey, Joan M.. . . . . *v.1 p.569, v.3 p.56*

Hussey, Mark *v.2 p.392*

Hussey, Roger, et al. *v.4 p.91, p.106*

Hussey, Roland D. *v.3 p.359*

Hussey, S. S.. . . . . *v.2 p.209*

Hussey, Stanley *v.2 p.556*

Huston, Nancy *v.2 p.540*

Hutchby, Ian. *v.4 p.418*

Hutcheon, Linda & Hutcheon, Michael. *v.1 p.230*

Hutcheon, Linda *v.2 p.729*

Hutcheson, Ernest & Ganz, Rudolph. *v.1 p.240, p.398*

Hutcheson, Francis. *v.1 p.450, p.484*

Hutcheson, John D. Jr. (Editor), et al. *v.4 p.787*

Hutchings, Arthur *v.1 p.190, p.240, p.344*

Hutchings, Stephen C. *v.2 p.798*

Hutchings, Vincent L.. . . . . *v.4 p.559*

Hutchins, Loraine & Kaahumanu, Lani (Editors) . . . *v.6 p.372*

Hutchins, Michael (Editor), et al.. . . . . *v.5 p.83, p.179, p.248*

Hutchins, Robert M. *v.4 p.290, p.343*

Hutchins, Robert Maynard *v.4 p.327*

Hutchinson, Amelia P. & Lloyd, Janet *v.2 p.637*

Hutchinson, Amélia P. & Lloyd, Janet *v.2 p.637*

Hutchinson, Barbara S. & Greider, Antoinette Paris (Editors). *v.5 p.309*

Hutchinson, Dennis J. *v.4 p.468*
Hutchinson, Earl O. *v.4 p.568*
Hutchinson, F. E. *v.2 p.264*
Hutchinson, G. O. *v.2 p.403, p.433*
Hutchinson, John & Smith, Anthony D. *v.3 p.61*
Hutchinson, John F. *v.3 p.36*
Hutchinson, Seth, et al. *v.5 p.711*
Hutchinson, Thomas *v.3 p.487*
Hutchinson, William T. *v.3 p.459*
Hutchison, Bruce *v.3 p.535*
Hutchison, Elizabeth Q. *v.3 p.353*
Hutchison, Terence Wilmot *v.4 p.215*
Hutchison, William R. *v.1 p.580, p.636*
Hutchisson, James M. (Editor) *v.2 p.95*
Huth, Hans *v.5 p.79, p.234*
Hutson, James H. *v.3 p.413*
Hutt, Michael J. *v.6 p.151, p.164*
Hutten, Ernest H. *v.5 p.402*
Huttenback, Robert A. *v.6 p.161*
Hutton, Ronald *v.3 p.94, p.105, p.121*
Hutton Turner, Elizabeth *v.1 p.741*
Huurdeman, Anton A. *v.4 p.420*
Huxley, Aldous *v.2 p.353, p.354, v.4 p.696, p.750*
Huxley, Anthony (Editor), et al. *v.5 p.43*
Huxley, Michael & Witts, Noel (Compiled by) *v.1 p.42*
Huxley, Thomas Henry & Huxley, Julian S. *v.1 p.484*
Huxtable, Ada Louise *v.1 p.793*
Huxtable, Marion & Blyth, Eric (Editors) *v.4 p.757*
Huynh Sanh Thong (Translator) *v.6 p.169*
Huynh Sanh Thong *v.6 p.169*
Huysmans, J. K. & Baldick, Robert *v.2 p.494*
Huysmans, J. K., et al. *v.2 p.494*
Huysmans, J. K. *v.2 p.494*
Huysmans, Joris Karl *v.2 p.494*
Huysmans, Joris K. *v.2 p.494, p.495*
Huysmans, Joris-Karl *v.2 p.495*
Hwang, David Henry (Foreword by) *v.6 p.88*
Hwang, David Henry *v.2 p.147, v.6 p.98, p.99*
Hyam, Ronald *v.3 p.125*
Hyatt, Richard *v.3 p.503*
Hyatt, Robert E., et al. *v.5 p.518*
Hybels, Saundra & Weaver, Richard L. *v.4 p.423*
Hyde, Bruce & Andersson, Sten *v.5 p.304*
Hyde, Charles K. *v.4 p.154*
Hyde, Edward *v.3 p.103*
Hyde, Elizabeth *v.1 p.813*
Hyde, George E. *v.6 p.703*
Hyde, J. K. *v.3 p.198*
Hyde, Lewis (Editor) *v.2 p.79*
Hyde, Mary *v.2 p.263*
Hyde, Robin *v.2 p.746*
Hyland, Peter *v.2 p.230*
Hyland, Sabine *v.3 p.326*
Hyland, William G. *v.1 p.216, p.325, v.3 p.473*
Hylton, John *v.1 p.395*

Hylton, P *v.1 p.443*
Hylton, Peter *v.1 p.502*
Hyman, Arthur & Walsh, James J. (Editors) *v.1 p.432*
Hyman, Harold Melvin *v.3 p.428*
Hyman, Irwin A. & Snook, Pamela A. *v.4 p.284*
Hyman, Irwin A. *v.4 p.284*
Hyman, Isabelle *v.1 p.793*
Hyman, Paula E. & Moore, Deborah Dash
(Editors) *v.1 p.553, v.6 p.459*
Hyman, Paula E. *v.6 p.454, p.459*
Hyman, Paula *v.3 p.155*
Hyman, Richard *v.4 p.126*
Hyman, Stanley E. *v.2 p.575*
Hyman, Timothy *v.1 p.741*
Hymes, Dell H. *v.4 p.18*
Hymes, Dell *v.4 p.19, p.24*
Hymes, James L. *v.4 p.284*
Hyne, Norman J. *v.5 p.451, p.738*
Hyneman, Charles S. & Lutz, Donald S. (Editors) . . *v.4 p.517*
Hynes, J. Dennis, and Loewenstein, Mark J. *v.4 p.75*
Hynes, Joseph (Editor) *v.2 p.383*
Hynes, Samuel *v.3 p.79, p.117*
Hyppolite, Jean *v.1 p.463*
Hysa, Ramazan John *v.2 p.778*
Hyser, Raymond M. & Arndt, J. Chris (Compiled by) . *v.3 p.372*
Hyslop, Marjorie R. *v.5 p.732*
Hyslop, Stephen G. *v.3 p.528*
Hyson, Marilou *v.4 p.369*
Hyun, Theresa *v.6 p.237*

I

Iaccino, James F. *v.6 p.318*
Iacopone da Todi *v.2 p.701*
Iacovetta, Franca *v.3 p.542*
Iannone, A. Pablo *v.1 p.415*
Iannucci, Amilcare (Editor) *v.2 p.704*
Iatrides, John O. (Editor) *v.3 p.195*
Ibach, Harald & Lüth, Hans *v.5 p.554*
Ibarbourou, Juana *v.2 p.687*
Ibarra, F. & Da Rosa, A. M. *v.2 p.643*
Ibarra, Jorge *v.3 p.310*
Iber, Jorge & De León, Arnoldo *v.3 p.521*
Iber, Jorge & De Leon, Arnoldo *v.3 p.518*
Iber, Jorge *v.6 p.536*
Iberall, A. S. *v.5 p.407*
Ibn Al-Firkah & Ibrahim ibn Abd Al-Rahman *v.6 p.609*
ibn 'Ali Ibn Babawayh al-Qummi, Muhammad & Asaf Ali
Asghar Fayzee *v.1 p.560*
Ibn Al-Qalanisi *v.6 p.609*
Ibn Battuta *v.6 p.584*
Ibn Batuta, et al. *v.6 p.63*
Ibn Munqidh, Usamah *v.6 p.609*
Ibn Taghribirdi, Abu *v.6 p.636*
Ibn 'Abd, Al-Hakam *v.6 p.584*

Ibrahim, Ferhad & Gurbey, Gulistan (Editors) . *v.6 p.599, p.622*
Ibrahim, Huma (Editor) *v.2 p.756*
Ibrahim, Saad Eddin *v.6 p.639*
Ibrahim, Sonallah *v.6 p.660*
Ibrahim, Sun'Allah *v.6 p.660*
Ibsen, Henrick *v.2 p.628*
Ibsen, Henrik *v.1 p.80, p.82, p.109, v.2 p.628*
Ibsen, Olga A. *v.5 p.525*
Ibson, John *v.1 p.708*
Ibuse, Masuji *v.6 p.229*
Icaza, Jorge *v.2 p.685*
Ichioka, Yuji *v.6 p.131, p.134*
Ickes, Harold L. & Sternsher, Bernard . . . *v.3 p.459*
Icon Group International, Inc. Staff (Compiled by) . . *v.4 p.153*
IDC: Internal Displacement Monitoring Centre . . . *v.4 p.667*
Idelsohn, A. Z. *v.1 p.300*
Idilbi, Ulfat *v.6 p.660*
Idowu, E. Bolaji *v.1 p.542*
Idowu, E. Bolasi *v.1 p.542*
Idris, Yusuf *v.6 p.660*
Ife, B. W. *v.2 p.641*
Ifekwunigwe, Jayne O. *v.4 p.31, p.709*
Iggers, Wilma A. *v.3 p.190*
Iggers, Wilma (Editor, Translator) *v.3 p.190*
Ignacimuthu, S. *v.5 p.97*
Ignacio, Emily *v.6 p.89, p.129, p.141*
Ignashev, Diane M. & Krive, Sarah (Editors) . . . *v.2 p.796*
Ignatieff, Michael & Appiah, Anthony *v.4 p.512*
Ignatieff, Michael (Editor) *v.4 p.512*
Ignatieff, Michael *v.4 p.494, p.659, p.753*
Ignatow, David *v.2 p.89*
Ignjatic, Zdravko *v.2 p.776, p.777*
Igoe, Lynn M. & Igoe, James *v.1 p.662, p.704*
Ihara, Saikaku *v.6 p.229*
Ihde, Aaron J. *v.5 p.263*
Ihimaera, Witi *v.2 p.746*
Ihonvbere, Julius Omozuanvbo & Mbaku, John Mukum
(Editors) *v.4 p.585, p.611*
Ikard, Robert W. *v.4 p.837, p.854, p.884*
Ikas, Karin Rosa *v.6 p.500, p.513*
Ikegami, Eiko *v.6 p.224*
Ikenberry, G. John (Editor) *v.3 p.448*
Ikenberry, G. John *v.4 p.560, p.626*
Ikram, Salima *v.6 p.57*
Ilahiane, Hsain *v.6 p.600*
Ilarione *v.3 p.286*
Ilbery, Brian W. (Editor), et al. *v.5 p.14*
Iles, Chrissie & Zummer, Thomas *v.1 p.771*
Iliffe, John *v.6 p.77*
Illes, Lajos (ed.) *v.2 p.785*
Illich, Ivan *v.4 p.327*
Illick, Joseph E. *v.3 p.492*
Illingworth, Valerie (Editor) *v.5 p.545*
Illingworth, Valerie *v.5 p.62*
Illyes, Gyula *v.2 p.786*

Ilnytzkyj, O. S. *v.2 p.814*
Imanishi, Kinji *v.5 p.237*
Imberger, Jorg (Editor) *v.4 p.392*
Imbert, Dorothee *v.1 p.819*
Imbo, Samuel O. *v.1 p.476*
Imbriale, W. A. *v.5 p.728*
Imbroscio, David L. *v.4 p.544*
Immelmann, Klaus & Beer, Colin *v.5 p.96, p.166*
Immerman, Richard H. *v.3 p.459*
Immerso, Michael *v.3 p.491*
Immerwahr, Sara A. *v.1 p.728*
Impelluso, Lucia *v.1 p.664, p.709*
Inabinett, Mark *v.4 p.811, p.907*
Inada, Lawson Fusao (Editor) *v.6 p.134*
Inada, Lawson Fusao *v.6 p.103, p.134*
Inalcik, Halil *v.6 p.590, p.622*
Inbar, Efraim *v.4 p.615, v.6 p.614*
Inbau, Fred Edward, et al. *v.6 p.267*
Incledon, Lori *v.4 p.791, p.879*
Incropera, Frank P., et al. *v.5 p.560*
Indergaard, Michael *v.6 p.723*
Infante, Guillermo Cabrena . . . *v.2 p.672, v.3 p.310*
Infante, Guillermo Cabrera *v.2 p.672*
Infeld, Leopold *v.5 p.543*
Infochem Gmbh Staff *v.5 p.288*
Information Today, Inc. Staff (Editor) . . . *v.4 p.149*
Ingber, Judith B. *v.1 p.9*
Inge, M. T. (Editor) *v.2 p.66*
Inge, M. Thomas & Hall, Dennis (Editors) . . . *v.3 p.368*
Inge, Tonette B. (Editor) *v.2 p.13*
Inge, William *v.2 p.89*
Ingebritsen, Christine *v.3 p.232, p.233*
Ingebritsen, Steven E. & Sanford, Ward E. . . . *v.5 p.428*
Ingegnoli, V. *v.6 p.291*
Ingersoll, Earl G. (Editor) *v.2 p.119*
Ingersoll, Richard M. *v.4 p.283*
Ingham, Alan G. & Loy, John W. Jr. (Editors) . . . *v.4 p.816*
Ingham, John M. *v.4 p.35*
Ingham, Patricia *v.2 p.271*
Ingham, Richard (Editor) *v.1 p.390*
Ingham, Rosemary & Covey, Liz *v.6 p.349*
Ingham, Rosemary *v.1 p.147*
Ingle, H. Larry *v.1 p.585*
Inglefield, Ruth K, et al. *v.1 p.393, p.398*
Inglehart, Ronald & Norris, Pippa *v.6 p.441*
Inglehart, Ronald F., et al. *v.3 p.293*
Inglis, Andrew F. & Luther, Arch *v.4 p.421*
Inglis, Fred *v.4 p.403*
Inglis, John (Editor), et al. *v.5 p.134*
Inglis, John (Editor) *v.1 p.432, v.6 p.567, p.571*
Inglis, Kenneth Stanley *v.3 p.112, p.121*
Ingold, Tim (Editor), et al. *v.4 p.29*
Ingold, Tim (Editor) *v.4 p.24*
Ingold, Tim *v.4 p.29*
Ingpen, Roger *v.2 p.311*

Ingraham, Patricia W. & Lynn, Laurence E. (Editors) . *v.4 p.580*
Ingram, David & Simon-Ingram, Julia *v.1 p.502*
Ingram, David *v.4 p.576, v.6 p.300*
Ingram, Edward *v.3 p.77*
Ingram, James C.. . . . . *v.6 p.171*
Ingram, Richard T. *v.4 p.291*
Ingram, R.Winnington *v.2 p.411*
Ingrao, Charles W. (Editor) *v.3 p.181*
Ingrao, Charles W. *v.3 p.181*
Ingrassia, Paul J. *v.4 p.154*
Ingstad, Anne S; Ingstad, Helge *v.3 p.403, p.405*
Ingstad, Helge *v.3 p.547*
Ingwersen, Faith & Ingwersen, Niels. *v.2 p.627*
Ingwersen, Niels (Editor) *v.2 p.626*
Inhaber, Herbert *v.5 p.360, p.368*
Inhorn, Marcia C. *v.6 p.639*
Inhorn, Marcia Claire & van Balen, Frank (Editors) . *v.6 p.443*
Inkpen, Robert (Editor) *v.4 p.375*
Inman, James A. *v.2 p.565*
Inman, Keith; Rudin, Norah. *v.5 p.326*
Innes, Abby *v.3 p.190*
Innes, Brian *v.6 p.266*
Innes, Christopher (Editor) *v.2 p.309*
Innes, Christopher *v.1 p.83, p.85, p.96, p.101,*
                                              p.147,v.2 p.188, p.591
Innis, Harold Adams *v.3 p.545, v.6 p.684*
Innocent & Lewis, Robert E. *v.1 p.643*
Inorganic Chemistry Staff, et al. *v.5 p.286*
Inscoe, John C. & McKinney, Gordon B.. . . . . . *v.4 p.521*
Inscoe, John C. (Editor). *v.3 p.497*
Insingel, Mark *v.2 p.623*
Insoll, Timothy (Editor). *v.1 p.524*
Institute for Career Research *v.5 p.250, p.251*
Institute for Research (Chicago, Ill.) *v.5 p.218, p.251*
Institute for Sex Research Staff, et al. . . *v.4 p.748, v.6 p.420*
Institute for the Study of Educational Policy Staf . . . *v.4 p.310*
Institute of Medicine Staff. *v.6 p.377*
Institute of Medicine (U.S.) Staff (Contribution by) . . *v.5 p.530*
Institute of National Science Staff & Chinese Academy of
   Science Staff *v.5 p.392*
Institute on Money in State Politics *v.4 p.558*
Institution of Mechanical Engineers (Great Britain), Pressure
   Systems Group Staff (Contribution by) *v.5 p.702*
Interdata Staff (Compiled by) *v.4 p.156*
Intergovernmental Panel on Climate Change (Editor) . *v.4 p.394*
International Alliance for Women in Music. . . *v.1 p.172, p.379*
International Code Council *v.1 p.785, v.5 p.685*
International Federation of Film Archives . . . *v.6 p.305, p.346*
International Federation of Library Associations. Section of Art
   Libraries. *v.1 p.667*
International Food Information Service Staff *v.5 p.34*
International Information Centre and Archives for the Women's
   Movement *v.6 p.432*
International Labour Office *v.4 p.254*
International Labour Organisation Library *v.5 p.580*
International Organization for Migration (IOM) *v.4 p.764*

International Organization for Migration
   Staff (Contribution by) *v.4 p.667*
International Phonetic Association Staff
   (Contribution by) *v.2 p.561*
International Society for Technology in Education Staff. *v.4 p.351*
International Symposium on Circulating Nucleic Acids in
   Plasma/Serum 2003 : Santa Monica, Calif.) . . *v.5 p.116, p.120*
International Theatre Institute Staff *v.1 p.55, p.61, p.128*
International Tribunal for the Law of the Sea *v.4 p.476*
International Union of Pure and Applied Chemistry . . *v.5 p.289*
Internet Archive *v.6 p.344*
Internet Center for Corruption Research *v.4 p.55*
Interrante, Leonard V. & Hampden-Smith, Mark J.
   (Editors) *v.5 p.318*
Intriligator, Michael D. *v.4 p.175*
Investigative Reporters and Editors, Missouri School of
   Journalism *v.4 p.558*
Inwood, Brad & Gerson, Lloyd P. (Editors). *v.1 p.428*
Inwood, Brad (Editor) *v.1 p.421, p.428*
Inwood, Brad *v.1 p.429*
Inwood, M. J. *v.1 p.464*
Inwood, Michael J. (Editor) *v.1 p.471*
Inwood, Michael J. *v.1 p.464*
Inwood, Michael *v.1 p.471*
Ioanid, Radu *v.3 p.84, p.250*
IOMA Staff *v.4 p.118*
Ionesco, Eugène *v.2 p.520*
Ippolito, Dennis S. *v.4 p.524*
Ipsen, Carl. *v.3 p.203*
Iqbal, Mohammed & Yunus, Mohammed (Editors) . . *v.5 p.354*
Irby-Massie, Georgia L. & Keyser, Paul T. *v.2 p.404*
Ireland, Alleyne *v.4 p.410*
Ireland, Kenneth & Rosen, Michael *v.5 p.476*
Ireland, Patrick. *v.4 p.601*
Ireland, Robert E. *v.5 p.294*
Irele, Abiola *v.6 p.80*
Irele, F. Abiola & Gikandi, Simon *v.2 p.751*
Ireson, Carol J. *v.6 p.454, p.456*
Irigaray, Luce *v.1 p.456, v.6 p.434, p.445, p.461*
Irish, Sharon. *v.1 p.793*
Iriye, Akira *v.3 p.385, p.389, v.4 p.640, v.6 p.181*
Irokawa, Daikichi *v.6 p.227*
Irons, Peter H. (Editor) *v.6 p.134*
Irons, Peter H.. . *v.4 p.450, p.455, p.464, p.537,v.6 p.115, p.134*
Irons, Peter *v.4 p.470, p.537*
Irschick, Eugene F. *v.6 p.161*
Irvin, Dale T. & Sunquist, Scott W. *v.1 p.598*
Irvine, Demar *v.1 p.173, p.198, p.340*
Irvine, Janice M. *v.4 p.569*
Irvine, Sidney H. & Kyllonen, Patrick C. (Editors) . . *v.5 p.601*
Irving, Edward B. Jr. *v.2 p.205*
Irving, J.D., Shae (Editor). *v.4 p.441*
Irving, John *v.1 p.190, p.240, p.344, v.2 p.147*
Irving, Pierre M. *v.2 p.42*
Irving, Washington *v.2 p.42*
Irwin, Douglas A. *v.4 p.55, p.257, p.261, p.664*

Irwin, Geoffrey. *v.4 p.379*
Irwin, J. David & Nelms, R. Mark *v.5 p.721*
Irwin, John *v.6 p.275*
Irwin, Judith W. *v.4 p.283*
Irwin, Paul B. *v.6 p.73*
Irwin, Richard L., et al. *v.4 p.906*
Irwin, Robert *v.6 p.660*
Irwin, Terence H. (Editor). *v.1 p.424*
Irwin, Terence H. *v.1 p.420, p.426*
Irwin, Terence *v.1 p.424*
Isaac, Benjamin H. *v.3 p.3*
Isaac, R. Mark & Smith, Vernon L. (Editors) *v.4 p.271*
Isaac, Rhys *v.3 p.499*
Isaacman, Allen & Roberts, Richard (Editors) *v.6 p.53*
Isaacman, Allen F. & Isaacman, Barbara. *v.6 p.76*
Isaacs, Alan (Author,
    Editor) *v.4 p.91, p.95, p.102, p.103, p.155, p.162*
Isaacs, Anita. *v.3 p.274, p.333*
Isaacs, Arnold R. *v.6 p.168*
Isaacs, Harold R. *v.6 p.215*
Isaacs, Harold Robert *v.6 p.192, p.215*
Isaacs, Jorge *v.2 p.683*
Isaacs, Nathan & Isaacs, Susan S. *v.4 p.357*
Isaacson, Walter & Thomas, Evan *v.3 p.455*
Isaev, Alexander *v.5 p.107*
Isaksson, Hans *v.2 p.629*
Isard, Peter *v.4 p.261, p.263*
Isard, Walter *v.4 p.397*
Isay, Richard A. *v.6 p.368*
Ise, John. *v.3 p.524*
Isenberg, Alison *v.6 p.713*
Isenberg, Joan P. & Jalongo, Mary Renck (Editors) . . *v.4 p.369*
Isenberg, Michael T. *v.4 p.807, p.816, p.855*
Iser, Wolfgang. *v.2 p.567, p.572, p.573*
Iserles, Arieh (Editor) *v.5 p.486, p.492*
Isfort, Robert J. & Lederberg, Joshua (Editors) . . . *v.5 p.163*
Ishaaya, Isaac *v.5 p.22, p.27*
Ishaq, I. *v.1 p.555*
Ishay, Micheline *v.4 p.512*
Isherwood, Christopher *v.2 p.355, p.356, v.6 p.397, p.402*
Ishida, Takeshi & Krauss, Ellis S. (Editors). *v.4 p.621*
Ishiguro, Hide *v.1 p.459*
Ishiguro, Kazuo *v.2 p.355*
Ishii, Yoneo *v.6 p.171*
Ishikawa, Chiyo (Editor, Introduction by) *v.3 p.73, p.239*
Ishikawa, Takuboku *v.6 p.230*
Isichei, Elizabeth. *v.1 p.542, p.611*
Isin, Engin F.. . . . . *v.4 p.544, v.6 p.723*
Island, David & Letellier, Patrick *v.6 p.377*
Islas, Arturo *v.6 p.500*
Ismael, J. S. *v.6 p.627*
Ismael, Jacqueline S. *v.6 p.627*
Ismael, Tareq Y. & El-Sa'id, Rifa'at *v.6 p.638*
Ismael, Tareq Y. (Editor) *v.6 p.593*
Ismael, Tareq Y. *v.4 p.614, v.6 p.593*

Isozaki, Arata, et al. *v.1 p.789*
Isozaki, Arata *v.1 p.793*
Israel, G. & Gasca, A. M.. . . . . *v.5 p.79, p.91*
Israel, Jonathan I. *v.3 p.72, p.204*
Israel, Jonathan Irvine *v.3 p.205, p.239*
Israel, Milton *v.6 p.157*
Israeli, Raphael *v.6 p.604*
Issaq, Haleem J. *v.5 p.274*
Issawi, Charles. *v.6 p.582*
Isserman, Maurice & Kazin, Michael. *v.3 p.473*
Istas, Jacques *v.5 p.99*
Istrail, Sorin, et al. *v.5 p.106, p.127*
Italia, Iona. *v.4 p.405*
Itaya, Kikuo *v.6 p.230*
I'tisami, Parvin. *v.6 p.671*
Ito, Takatoshi & Krueger, Anne O. (Editors) *v.4 p.60*
Itoh, Teiji *v.6 p.221*
Itti, Laurent (Editor), et al. *v.5 p.611*
Itzkoff, Seymour W. *v.5 p.193*
Itzkowitz, Norman *v.3 p.69, v.6 p.590*
IUPAC. Commission on Thermodynamics and
    Thermochemistry.. . . . . *v.5 p.286*
IUPAC, Physical Chemistry Division. *v.5 p.286*
Ivan Franko National University of Lviv *v.2 p.814*
Ivanits, Linda J. *v.2 p.793*
Ivanov, Viacheslav *v.2 p.804*
Ivanova, Anna. *v.1 p.20*
Ivers, Karen S.. . . . . *v.4 p.351*
Iverson, Peter J. *v.3 p.459*
Iverson, Peter *v.3 p.459*
Ives, Edward D. *v.2 p.585*
Ivie, Robert L. *v.4 p.564*
Ivy, Robert A. Jr.. . . . . *v.1 p.793*
Iwamura, Jane & Spickard, Paul (Editors) *v.6 p.105*
Iwanska, Lucja M. & Shapiro, Stuart C. (Editors). *v.5 p.339, p.341*
Iyanaga, Shokichi & Kawada, Yukiyosi (Editors) . . . *v.5 p.461*
Iyas, Ibn *v.6 p.635*
Iyengar, K Srinivasa *v.2 p.763*
Iyengar, Shanto & McGuire, William J. (Editors) . . . *v.5 p.643*
Iz, Fahir (Editor), et al. *v.6 p.665*
Iz, Fahir *v.6 p.666*
Izady, Mehrdad *v.6 p.599*
Izard, Carroll E. *v.5 p.612*
Izawa, Chizuko (Editor). *v.5 p.610*
Izenour, George C.. . . . . *v.1 p.71, p.72, p.155*
Izod, John (Editor), et al. *v.6 p.309*
Izutsu, Toshihiko. *v.1 p.556*
Izzo, David Garrett *v.2 p.356*

J

J Kirton, John & I Hajnal, Peter *v.4 p.663*
J., Naughton *v.2 p.774*
J., Stangroom *v.5 p.96*
Jabès, Edmond *v.2 p.521*

Jablonka, Eva & Lamb, Marion J. *v.5 p.193*

Jablonski, Edward & Stewart, Lawrence D. . . *v.1 p.251, p.325*

Jablonski, Edward . *v.1 p.216, p.251, p.301, p.302, p.310, p.325, p.336, v.6 p.409*

Jablonski, Stanley *v.5 p.509*

Jabra, Jabra I. *v.6 p.660*

Jabra, Jabra Ibrahim & Boullata, Issa J. *v.6 p.660*

Jaccottet, Philippe *v.2 p.530, p.531*

Jack, Belinda *v.2 p.535*

Jack, Ian *v.2 p.175, p.272, p.274, p.295, p.307*

Jackendoff, Ray *v.2 p.550, p.561*

Jackman, Robert W. *v.4 p.498*

Jacko, Julie A. & Stephanidis, Constantine (Editors) . *v.5 p.589*

Jackson Allen, Patricia & Vessey, Judith A. *v.5 p.525*

Jackson, Allen W., et al. *v.4 p.791*

Jackson, Anna & Jaffer, Amin *v.1 p.693*

Jackson, Betty P. et al. *v.5 p.96, p.155*

Jackson, Bruce *v.4 p.690*

Jackson, Christine E. *v.1 p.664*

Jackson, Cynthia L. *v.4 p.310*

Jackson, Daphne F. *v.5 p.553*

Jackson, Dennis & Jackson, Fleda B. *v.2 p.362*

Jackson, Donald (Editor) *v.3 p.520*

Jackson, Donald W. *v.4 p.458*

Jackson, Donald *v.3 p.411*

Jackson, Faith R. *v.1 p.816*

Jackson, Frank & Smith, Michael (Editors) . . . *v.1 p.417*

Jackson, Gordon S. *v.4 p.410*

Jackson, Jerma A. *v.1 p.270*

Jackson, Jerome A. *v.6 p.291*

Jackson, John David *v.5 p.564*

Jackson, John G. *v.6 p.10*

Jackson, John H. *v.4 p.435*

Jackson, Jonathan Jr. (Foreword by) *v.6 p.6, p.26*

Jackson, Joy J. *v.3 p.507, v.6 p.713*

Jackson, Julian *v.3 p.156*

Jackson, K. David *v.2 p.691*

Jackson, Kenneth T. (Editor) *v.3 p.491, v.6 p.713*

Jackson, Kenneth T. *v.6 p.718*

Jackson, Kevin *v.6 p.307*

Jackson, Laura Riding & Jacobs, Mark *v.2 p.89*

Jackson, Laura Riding *v.2 p.89*

Jackson, Lawrence *v.3 p.547*

Jackson, Lee *v.6 p.763*

Jackson, Lesley *v.1 p.720, p.802*

Jackson, M., et al. *v.5 p.140, p.145, p.149, p.201*

Jackson, Naomi M. *v.1 p.26*

Jackson, Peter (Editor), et al. *v.6 p.629*

Jackson, Peter *v.6 p.156*

Jackson, Phil & Rosen, Charley *v.4 p.832, p.854*

Jackson, Phil *v.4 p.802, p.854*

Jackson, Philip L. & Kimerling, A. Jon (Editors) . . . *v.5 p.38*

Jackson, R. G. *v.5 p.742*

Jackson, Radway *v.1 p.664*

Jackson, Richard (Editor) *v.2 p.812*

Jackson, Richard *v.2 p.664*

Jackson, Robert H. (Editor) *v.3 p.527*

Jackson, Robert H. Jr. & Rosberg, Carl G. *v.6 p.54*

Jackson, Robert H. *v.3 p.176, p.324*

Jackson, Robert L. & Nelson, Lowry Jr. (Editors) . . *v.2 p.805*

Jackson, Roland *v.1 p.160, p.400*

Jackson, Ron S. *v.5 p.52*

Jackson, Ronald L. & Richardson, Elaine B. (Editors) . *v.6 p.20*

Jackson, Ronald L. II (Editor) *v.6 p.6, p.32, p.39*

Jackson, Rosie & Lawrence, Frieda *v.2 p.362*

Jackson, Russell (Editor) *v.6 p.326*

Jackson, S. P. (Editor), et al. *v.5 p.127*

Jackson, Shirley *v.2 p.90*

Jackson, Stanley W. *v.5 p.659*

Jackson, Susan A. & Csikszentmihalyi, Mihaly . *v.4 p.802, p.877*

Jackson, Susan E. (Editor), et al. *v.4 p.76*

Jackson, Timothy L. *v.1 p.198, p.240, p.362*

Jackson, Timothy P. *v.1 p.651*

Jackson, Wallace & Yoder, R. Paul (Editors) *v.2 p.257*

Jackson, Wes (Editor), et al. *v.5 p.12*

Jackson, William T. *v.2 p.595*

Jacob, Christian *v.4 p.385*

Jacob, E. & Cathie Jordan (Editors) *v.4 p.302, p.312*

Jacob, Ernest F. *v.6 p.563*

Jacob, James E. *v.3 p.158*

Jacob, Max *v.2 p.521*

Jacob, Pierre & Jeannerod, Marc *v.5 p.607*

Jacob, Susan & Hartshorne, Timothy S. *v.5 p.576*

Jacob, Walter (Editor) *v.1 p.552*

Jacobs, Andrew S. *v.1 p.549*

Jacobs, Bonita C. *v.4 p.294*

Jacobs, Bruce A. *v.6 p.253*

Jacobs, Clyde E. *v.4 p.443*

Jacobs, Dick & Jacobs, Harriet *v.1 p.167, p.251, p.270*

Jacobs, George M., et al. *v.4 p.349*

Jacobs, Harriet A. *v.2 p.43*

Jacobs, Heidi Hayes (Editor) *v.4 p.364*

Jacobs, James B. & Potter, Kimberly . *v.4 p.472, p.568, v.6 p.252*

Jacobs, James B., et al. *v.4 p.438*

Jacobs, James B. *v.6 p.266, p.273*

Jacobs, Jane *v.6 p.718*

Jacobs, Janet Liebman & Capps, Donald (Editors) . . *v.5 p.634*

Jacobs, Karen (Editor) *v.5 p.535*

Jacobs, Louis *v.1 p.551, p.552*

Jacobs, Meg (Editor), et al. *v.3 p.384*

Jacobs, Philip Walker *v.1 p.767*

Jacobs, Roderick A. *v.2 p.557*

Jacobs, Seth *v.3 p.389*

Jacobsen, Douglas G. & Jacobsen, Rhonda Hustedt . *v.4 p.307*

Jacobsen, Douglas G. & Trollinger, William Vance Jr. (Editors) . *v.1 p.606*

Jacobsen, Douglas G. *v.1 p.587*

Jacobsen, J. P. *v.2 p.627*

Jacobsen, Jens Peter *v.2 p.627*

Jacobsen, Knut A. & Pratap, Kumar P. *v.4 p.764*

Jacobsen, Nils & Aljovín de Losada, Cristóbal *v.3 p.327*
Jacobsen, Nils *v.3 p.326, p.327*
Jacobsohn, Gary J. *v.6 p.614*
Jacobson, Carl Alfred (ed.) *v.5 p.304*
Jacobson, Gary C. *v.4 p.530, p.549, p.557, p.558*
Jacobson, Howard *v.2 p.438*
Jacobson, Matthew F. *v.4 p.571*
Jacobson, Matthew Frye *v.4 p.571*
Jacobson, Michael, et al. *v.5 p.168, p.426*
Jacobson, Michael *v.6 p.274*
Jacobson, Nathan *v.5 p.473*
Jacobson-Hardy, Michael (Photographer, Text by) . . *v.6 p.275*
Jacobus, Lee A. (Editor) *v.2 p.25*
Jacobus, Lee A. *v.1 p.67*
Jacobus, Mary *v.2 p.323*
Jacoby, Karl *v.6 p.297*
Jacoby, Sanford M. *v.4 p.86*
Jacoby, Tamar *v.4 p.571*
Jacoby, Wade *v.4 p.585, p.603, p.609, p.637*
Jacoff, Michael (Editor) *v.1 p.775*
Jacoff, Rachel (Editor) *v.2 p.704, v.6 p.565*
Jacquard, Roland *v.4 p.659*
Jacquart, Danielle & Thomasset, Claude *v.3 p.50*
Jacques, Edwin E. *v.3 p.252*
Jacques, Peter & Smith, Zachary A. *v.5 p.430*
Jacquette, Dale (Editor) *v.1 p.465, p.492*
Jacquot, Raymond G. *v.5 p.711*
Jacyna, L. S. *v.5 p.621, p.623, p.665, p.673*
Jadhav, Narendra *v.4 p.733*
Jaeckel, Ralph & Erciyes, Gulna Doganata *v.6 p.665*
Jaeger, C. Stephen *v.6 p.556, p.565*
Jaeger, Paul T.; Bowman, Cynthia Ann *v.4 p.450*
Jaeger, Richard C. & Blalock, Travis *v.5 p.722*
Jaeger, Richard M. (Editor) *v.4 p.355*
Jaeger, Werner W. *v.1 p.426, v.2 p.408*
Jafari, Jafar (Editor) *v.4 p.161*
Jaffa, Harry V. *v.3 p.425*
Jaffard, Stephane, et al. *v.5 p.494, p.501*
Jaffary, Nora E. *v.3 p.286*
Jaffe, A. J. & Sperber, C. *v.4 p.764*
Jaffe, Abram J., et al. *v.4 p.178*
Jaffe, Alexandra *v.4 p.21*
Jaffe, Bernard *v.5 p.261, p.388, p.393*
Jaffe, Daniel *v.1 p.216, p.348*
Jaffe, W. *v.4 p.215*
Jaffrelot, Christophe *v.1 p.540, v.6 p.149, p.157, p.159*
Jagchid, Sechin & Symons, Van J. *v.6 p.204*
Jager, Ronald & Jager, Grace *v.3 p.486*
Jaggar, Alison M. & Bordo, Susan R. (Editors) . . . *v.6 p.463*
Jaggar, Alison M. & Rothenberg, Paula S. *v.6 p.470*
Jaggar, Alison M. (Editor) *v.6 p.461*
Jaggar, Alison M. *v.4 p.744, v.6 p.441*
Jagota, Arun K. *v.5 p.106, p.108, p.110*
Jahan, Rounaq *v.6 p.457*
Jahn, Hubertus F. *v.3 p.220*

Jahoda, Gloria Love *v.3 p.505*
Jahoda, Gustav *v.4 p.35*
Jain, Devaki *v.4 p.634*
Jain, Jasbir & Amin, Amina (Editors) *v.2 p.762*
Jain, Jasbir & Singh, Veena (Editors) *v.2 p.760*
Jain, Manju *v.2 p.72*
Jain, R. P. *v.5 p.722*
Jain, Subodh K. & Botsford, L. W. (Editors) . . . *v.5 p.189*
Jain, Subodh K. & Wohrmann, K. (Editors) *v.5 p.189*
Jakle, John A. & Sculle, Keith A. *v.1 p.715, p.797*
Jakle, John A. *v.3 p.513*
Jakobson, Max *v.3 p.236*
Jakobson, Roman & Halle, Morris *v.2 p.550, p.561*
Jakobson, Roman & Waugh, Linda R. *v.2 p.561*
Jakobson, Roman *v.2 p.561*
Jaksic, Ivan *v.3 p.265, p.354*
Jalal Al-e, Ahmad *v.6 p.632*
Jalal, Ayesha *v.6 p.157, p.162*
Jalland, Pat *v.3 p.112, v.6 p.765*
Jamalzada, Mohammad A. *v.6 p.671*
James, C. L. R. *v.6 p.6, p.18*
James, Christopher *v.1 p.769*
James, Cynthia *v.2 p.767*
James, David E. & Berg, Rick (Editors) *v.6 p.321*
James, David E *v.5 p.443*
James, Edward *v.3 p.237*
James, Edwin O. *v.6 p.576*
James, George *v.6 p.10*
James, Glenn & James, Robert C. *v.5 p.458, p.461*
James, Harold *v.4 p.664*
James, Henry & Hollander, John *v.2 p.44*
James, Henry (Editor), et al. *v.2 p.45*
James, Henry . . . *v.1 p.56, p.136, v.2 p.4, p.7, p.44, p.45, p.456,*
p.575, p.578, v.6 p.397
James, I. M. *v.5 p.499*
James I of Aragon *v.3 p.65*
James, Ioan *v.5 p.466*
James, James Alton *v.3 p.533*
James, Joy (Author, Editor) *v.6 p.26, p.44*
James, Joy *v.6 p.434, p.441*
James, Lawrence *v.3 p.89, p.125, p.126*
James, Laylin K. (Editor) *v.5 p.261*
James, Louis *v.2 p.175, p.193, v.6 p.743, p.754, p.756*
James, P. D. *v.2 p.355*
James, P. (Editor) *v.5 p.116*
James, Patricia *v.4 p.221*
James, Patrick, et al. *v.3 p.537*
James, Robert Rhodes *v.3 p.94, p.113*
James, Scott C. *v.4 p.551, p.552, p.579*
James, Sharon L. *v.2 p.426*
James, Stanlie M. & Busia, Abena P. (Editors) . *v.6 p.6, p.44, p.428*
James, Sydney V. *v.3 p.489*
James, T. G. H. *v.3 p.9, p.11, v.6 p.57*
James, Thomas L. (Volume Editor) *v.5 p.88, p.134*
James, Thomas *v.6 p.108, p.134*

James, Thurston *v.1 p.147*
James, W. Martin *v.6 p.75*
James, Wendy *v.4 p.22*
James, William (Editor), et al. *v.1 p.439*
James, William (Editor) *v.1 p.521*
James, William *v.1 p.439, p.513, p.524,*
                v.4 p.357, v.5 p.594, p.613, p.634
Jameson, Fredric *v.2 p.367, p.561, p.568*
Jameson, John F. *v.3 p.409*
Jameux, Dominique *v.1 p.216, p.312, p.313*
Jamieson, Kathleen Hall & Waldman, Paul *v.4 p.404*
Jamieson, Ross W. *v.4 p.14*
Jamison, Andrew *v.6 p.300*
Jamison, D. Curtis *v.5 p.109*
Jamison, Judith & Kaplan, Howard *v.1 p.9*
Jamison, Kay Redfield *v.5 p.653, p.659, p.660*
Janabi, Hatif *v.6 p.660*
Janacek, Leos & Cheek, Timothy . *v.1 p.216, p.230, p.333, p.408*
Janaway, Christopher (Editor) *v.1 p.465*
Jancar, Drago *v.2 p.813*
Jancovich, Mark (Editor), et al. *v.6 p.313*
Janda, Laura A.; Townsend, Charles Edward *v.2 p.774*
Janda, Louis *v.5 p.601*
Janda, Richard D. *v.2 p.561, v.5 p.621, p.623*
Janelle, Donald G. *v.4 p.374*
Janes, Regina *v.2 p.683*
Janicak, Philip G., et al. *v.5 p.517*
Janicaud, Dominique *v.1 p.507*
Janick, Jules *v.5 p.44*
Janko, Richard *v.1 p.90*
Jankowiak, William (Editor) *v.5 p.653*
Jankowiak, William R. & Bradburd, Daniel (Editors) . *v.3 p.281*
Jankowski, Dorothy A. & Selover, Theodore B. Jr.
   (Editors) *v.5 p.741*
Jankowski, James *v.6 p.58*
Jankowski, Jerry *v.1 p.718*
Jankowski, Martin S. *v.4 p.714*
Jann, Rosemary *v.6 p.750, p.754*
Jannot, Jean-Rene *v.1 p.532*
Janos, A. C. *v.3 p.186*
Janoschka, Anja *v.4 p.428*
Janosik, Robert J. (Editor) *v.4 p.437*
Janovy, John Jr. *v.5 p.245*
Janowitz, Morris *v.4 p.704, p.759*
Jansen, Eilev S., et al. *v.4 p.202, p.240*
Jansen, F. J. *v.2 p.627*
Jansen, Katherine Ludwig *v.6 p.571*
Jansen, Marije *v.1 p.757*
Jansen, Marius B. *v.6 p.224, p.227*
Jansiti, Carlo *v.2 p.521*
Janson, Anthony *v.1 p.668*
Janson, Jan-Christer & Rydén, Lars (Editors) . . . *v.5 p.328*
Janson, Tore *v.2 p.423*
Janssen, Peter *v.5 p.430*
Jantz, Harold *v.2 p.598*

Jantzen, Grace M. *v.6 p.459, p.560, p.571*
Januszewski, Alan *v.4 p.351*
Janzen, John *v.5 p.536*
Janzen, Rod A. *v.4 p.720*
Japp, Phyllis M., et al. *v.4 p.417*
Jaques-Dalcroze, Emile *v.1 p.47*
Jaquette, Jane S. & Wolchik, Sharon L. (Editors) . . *v.6 p.441*
Jarausch, Konrad H. & Gransow, Volker *v.3 p.177*
Jarausch, Konrad H. *v.3 p.180, v.4 p.609*
Jarausch, Konrad Hugo & Geyer, Michael *v.3 p.178*
Jardine, Lisa *v.3 p.47, p.70*
Jardine, N. (Editor), et al. *v.5 p.222*
Jargowsky, Paul A. *v.4 p.771*
Jarman, Beatriz Galimberti & Carvajal, Carol Styles . *v.2 p.636*
Jarman, Douglas (Editor) *v.1 p.216, p.230, p.309*
Jarman, Douglas *v.1 p.216, p.230, p.309*
Jarnow, Jesse *v.3 p.381*
Jarrell, Hampton M. *v.3 p.425*
Jarrell, Randall, et al. *v.2 p.296*
Jarrell, Randall *v.2 p.90, p.91*
Jarrett, Bede *v.6 p.563*
Jarrett, Derek *v.3 p.108, p.128*
Jarry, Alfred *v.2 p.520, p.521*
Jarvie, Ian *v.6 p.341*
Jarvinen, Alfred W. & Ankley, Gerald T. . *v.5 p.366, p.368, p.380*
Jarvis, Matt *v.4 p.877*
Jarvis, Peter *v.4 p.320*
Jarvis, Robin *v.2 p.172*
Jasanoff, Sheila (Editor) *v.5 p.364, p.373*
Jasen, David A. & Jones, Gene *v.1 p.260*
Jasen, David A. *v.1 p.160, p.270*
Jashemski, Wilhelmina Feemster & Meyer, Frederick G.
   (Editors) *v.5 p.236*
Jaskoski, Helen (Editor) *v.2 p.4*
Jasmin, Claude *v.2 p.540*
Jason, Neville *v.1 p.780*
Jason, Philip K. (Editor) *v.2 p.105*
Jasper, David *v.2 p.572*
Jaspers, Karl & Bultmann, Rudolf *v.1 p.523*
Jaspers, Karl *v.1 p.468, p.505, v.3 p.178*
Jastrjembskaia, Nadejda & Titov, Yuri *v.4 p.795, p.861*
Jastrzebski, Zbigniew D. *v.5 p.689*
Jaszi, Oazkar *v.3 p.183*
Jawlensky, Angelica, et al. *v.1 p.741*
Jawlensky, Maria, et al. *v.1 p.741*
Jaworski, Leon *v.4 p.439*
Jay, Antony (Editor) *v.4 p.482*
Jay, Joelle Kristin *v.4 p.348*
Jay, Karla *v.6 p.365, p.390, p.402*
Jay, Kathryn *v.4 p.716, p.816*
Jay, Richard *v.3 p.94, p.113*
Jay, Timothy *v.2 p.552*
Jaynes, Julian *v.5 p.596*
Jayyusi, Salma K. (Editor) *v.3 p.236, v.6 p.660*
Jazbec, Milan *v.4 p.641, p.644*

Jean Paul *v.2 p.600*

Jean, Yves & Volatron, Francois *v.5 p.304*

Jeannet, Angela M. & Sanguinetti Katz, Giuliana
(Editors) *v.2 p.718*

Jeannet, Angela M. *v.2 p.715*

Jeanteur, Ph *v.5 p.124, p.152*

Jebb, Richard C. (Editor) *v.2 p.405*

Jebens, Holger (Editor) *v.4 p.711*

Jedicke, Peter & Scientific American Editors . . *v.5 p.215, p.222*

Jeep, John M. (Editor) *v.3 p.161*

Jeeves, Malcolm (Editor) *v.1 p.526*

Jeffares, A. Norman (Editor). *v.2 p.326*

Jeffares, A. Norman *v.2 p.163, p.326*

Jefferies, Matthew *v.3 p.169*

Jeffers, H. Paul. *v.6 p.418*

Jeffers, Robinson & Gelpi, Albert *v.2 p.91*

Jeffers, Robinson *v.2 p.91*

Jefferson, Alan *v.1 p.216, p.230, p.359*

Jefferson, Ann (Contribution by). *v.2 p.527*

Jefferson, Ian, et al.. . . . . *v.5 p.698*

Jefferson, Thomas *v.3 p.499*

Jeffery, Brian. *v.2 p.457*

Jeffery, Keith. *v.3 p.138*

Jeffery, Peter *v.1 p.177*

Jefferys, Steve *v.4 p.122*

Jefford, Clayton N. *v.1 p.591*

Jeffords, Susan *v.6 p.328, p.341, p.474*

Jeffrey, Charles; Systematics Association *v.5 p.96*

Jeffrey, G. A.. *v.5 p.277*

Jeffrey, Ian. *v.1 p.762*

Jeffrey, Julie R. *v.6 p.454*

Jeffrey M. Heath (Editor) *v.2 p.729*

Jeffrey, Richard *v.1 p.492, p.495*

Jeffreys, Harold *v.5 p.402*

Jeffries, John C. Jr. *v.4 p.468*

Jeffries, John W. *v.3 p.489*

Jeffries, Judson L. *v.3 p.499*

Jefremovas, Villia *v.4 p.652*

Jehlen, Myra & Warner, Michael (Editors). *v.2 p.20*

Jejeebhoy, Shireen J. *v.6 p.447*

Jelavich, Barbara. *v.3 p.211, p.246*

Jelavich, Charles & Jelavich, Barbara *v.3 p.246*

Jelavich, Peter *v.3 p.178*

Jellison, Charles A.. . . . . *v.3 p.411*

Jember, Gregory K. *v.2 p.206, p.550*

Jemi, Onwuchekwa & Madubuike, Ihechukwu. *v.2 p.751, v.6 p.80*

Jen, Gish *v.6 p.100*

Jencks, Charles. *v.1 p.786*

Jencks, Christopher & Riesman, David *v.4 p.290*

Jencks, Christopher *v.4 p.722, p.750*

Jenkins, Alan *v.4 p.122*

Jenkins, Alice & John, Juliet (Editors) *v.2 p.175, p.193*

Jenkins, Annibel *v.2 p.258*

Jenkins, Anthony *v.2 p.188*

Jenkins, Brian *v.3 p.433*

Jenkins, David (Editor). *v.1 p.809, v.3 p.40*

Jenkins, Dennis R. *v.5 p.719*

Jenkins, Elizabeth *v.2 p.267*

Jenkins, Everett Jr. *v.1 p.559*

Jenkins, Everett, Jr.. . . . . *v.1 p.559*

Jenkins, Everett Jr. *v.6 p.10, p.11*

Jenkins, Francis A. & White, Harvey E.. . . . . *v.5 p.73, p.561*

Jenkins, Fred W. *v.2 p.399*

Jenkins, Henry *v.4 p.422, v.6 p.312*

Jenkins, Hugh M. *v.4 p.290*

Jenkins, J. J. *v.1 p.448*

Jenkins, Jean F. *v.5 p.533*

Jenkins, Jeffrey Eric *v.1 p.67, p.115*

Jenkins, John & Pigram, John (Editors) . *v.4 p.784, p.787, p.823*

Jenkins, John J. *v.1 p.451*

Jenkins, John R. *v.3 p.245*

Jenkins, Morton *v.5 p.134*

Jenkins, Philip *v.1 p.543, p.576, p.596, p.647, v.4 p.659*

Jenkins, Rhys Owen (Editor), et al. *v.4 p.131*

Jenkins, Richard *v.4 p.736*

Jenkins, Rob. *v.4 p.617*

Jenkins, Ron *v.5 p.273*

Jenkins, Sharron *v.6 p.21, p.39*

Jenkins, Simon P.R. *v.4 p.873*

Jenkins, Todd S. *v.1 p.160, p.260*

Jenkins, Virginia S.. . . . . *v.1 p.813*

Jenks, William Furness *v.5 p.432*

Jenkyns, Richard *v.3 p.113, p.128,v.6 p.750, p.764*

Jenness, David & Velsey, Donald *v.1 p.270*

Jenness, Diamond *v.6 p.703*

Jennings, Alan *v.5 p.694*

Jennings, Francis & Fenton, William N.
(Editors). *v.6 p.684, p.685, p.696*

Jennings, Francis *v.3 p.485, v.4 p.517, v.6 p.684, p.686*

Jennings, J. N. *v.5 p.424*

Jennings, Kenneth M.. . . . . *v.4 p.122*

Jennings, Kevin (Editor) *v.6 p.383, p.385*

Jennings, Lawrence C. *v.3 p.149*

Jennings, Lawrence Charles *v.3 p.76, p.153*

Jennings, Ronald C. *v.6 p.601*

Jennings, Sue *v.1 p.94*

Jennings, Walter, et al. *v.5 p.269*

Jenny, Hans *v.5 p.49, p.52, v.6 p.293*

Jenrette, Richard Hampton *v.1 p.824*

Jens, Walter *v.2 p.590*

Jensen, Clayne R. & Guthrie, Steven P. *v.4 p.787, p.823*

Jensen, Eric Frederick *v.1 p.198, p.354*

Jensen, Frede (Editor, Translator) *v.2 p.699*

Jensen, Frede (Editor) *v.2 p.698*

Jensen, Gordon E. & Netzer, David W. (Editors) . . . *v.5 p.719*

Jensen, Karol L. *v.6 p.368*

Jensen, Klaus *v.4 p.414*

Jensen, Larry R. *v.3 p.310*

Jensen, Line (Editor), et al. *v.2 p.626*

Jensen, Merrill *v.3 p.405, v.4 p.517*

Jensen, N. M. *v.4 p.59*

Jensen, Niels L. . . . . *.v.2 p.627*

Jensen, Ole B. & Richardson, Tim . . . . *.v.4 p.397*

Jensen, Peter R. . . . . *.v.4 p.420*

Jensen, Richard J. . . . . *.v.3 p.515*

Jensen, Richard . . . . *.v.3 p.506*

Jensen, Ronald J.. . . . . *.v.3 p.437*

Jensen, Vickie . . . . *.v.1 p.782*

Jenson, Deborah, et al. . . . . *.v.3 p.315*

Jenson, Jane & Mahon, Rianne (Editors) . . . . . . *.v.4 p.122*

Jenson, Robert W. . . . . *.v.1 p.639*

Jentleson, Bruce W. & Paterson, Thomas G. (Editors) . *v.4 p.628*

Jeppesen, Knud *v.1 p.180, p.346, p.371*

Jeremias, Joachim *v.1 p.641, p.642, p.657*

Jergovic, Miljenko . . . . *.v.2 p.811*

Jermy, A. Clive . . . . *.v.5 p.210*

Jernegan, Marcus W. . . . . *.v.4 p.724*

Jerrard, H G; McNeill, D B *v.5 p.63, p.567, p.569, p.571*

Jerris, Rand . . . . *.v.4 p.861*

Jerrold, Walter C.. . . . . *.v.2 p.291*

Jersch-Wenzel, Stefi . . . . *.v.3 p.180*

Jersild, Arthur Thomas . . . . *.v.4 p.357*

Jersild, Austin . . . . *.v.3 p.213*

Jervis, Robert *v.3 p.483, v.4 p.656*

Jespersen, Otto *v.2 p.554, p.557, p.561*

Jespersen, T. Christopher . . . . *.v.6 p.215*

Jessop, Ralph . . . . *.v.2 p.276*

Jessup, Helen Ibbitson . . . . *.v.1 p.692*

Jessup, Philip C.. . . . . *v.3 p.398, p.434*

Jeukendrup, Asker & Gleeson, Michael. . . . . . . *.v.4 p.876*

Jeung, Russell . . . . *.v.6 p.105*

Jevons, Frederick Raphael *v.5 p.327, p.410, p.412*

Jevons, W. Stanley (William Stanley) . . . . . . *.v.4 p.212*

Jevons, W. Stanley *v.4 p.231, v.5 p.402*

Jevons, William Stanley. . . . . *.v.4 p.231*

Jevons, Willian Stanley . . . . *.v.4 p.231*

Jewell, K. Sue *v.6 p.39, p.44*

Jewett, Sarah Orne . . . . *.v.2 p.46*

Jewish Publication Society Staff . . . . *.v.1 p.618*

Jewkes, Yvonne . . . . *.v.6 p.256*

Jeyifo, Biodun (Editor) . . . . *.v.2 p.757*

Jeyifo, Biodun *v.1 p.130, v.2 p.752, p.757*

Jeynes, William . . . . *.v.4 p.307*

Jezic, Diane P. . . . . *.v.1 p.379*

Jezierski, John Vincent *v.1 p.704, p.767*

Jördening, Hans-Joachim & Winter, Josef (Editors) . *v.5 p.704*

Jha, Prem Shankar . . . . *.v.6 p.161*

Jhabvala, Ruth Prawer . . . . *.v.2 p.355*

Jiang, Tao (Editor), et al. . . . . *.v.5 p.127*

Jiji, Latif M.. . . . . *.v.5 p.713*

Jiles, David C . . . . *.v.5 p.566*

Jillson, Calvin . . . . *.v.3 p.385*

Jimenez, Juan Ramon & Harter, Hugh A.. . . . . . . *.v.2 p.660*

Jimenez, Juan Ramon. . . . . *.v.2 p.660*

Jimerson, Lorna . . . . *.v.4 p.278*

Jiménez, Francisco (Editor) *v.6 p.500, p.513*

Jiménez, José Olivio . . . . *.v.2 p.664*

Jiménez, Juan Ramón. . . . . *.v.2 p.660*

Jiminez, Jill (Editor) . . . . *.v.1 p.664*

Jin, Ha *v.2 p.147, v.6 p.103*

Jing, Jun. . . . . *.v.6 p.197*

Jinkins, Michael . . . . *.v.1 p.655*

Jippensha, Ikku . . . . *.v.6 p.230*

Jirasek, Alois . . . . *.v.2 p.783*

Jirásek, Jan E. (Jan Evangelista) . . . . *.v.5 p.162*

Jünger, Ernst. . . . . *.v.2 p.610*

Joachim, Harold H. & Harris, Errol E.. . . . . . . *.v.1 p.454*

Joannou, Maroula . . . . *.v.6 p.479*

Jobe, Jared B. (Editor), et al. . . . . *.v.6 p.389*

Jobert, Barthelemy . . . . *.v.1 p.741*

Jobling, Malcom . . . . *.v.5 p.215*

Jobling, Mark, et al. . . . . *.v.5 p.134*

Jochens, Jenny *v.3 p.51, v.6 p.560*

Jochum, Markus & Murtugudde, Raghu
(Editors) *v.4 p.392, v.5 p.430*

Joel, Lucille A. & Kelly, Lucie Young . . . . . . *.v.5 p.527*

Johannesson, Eric O. . . . . *.v.2 p.629*

Johannis, Theodore B. & Bull, Neil (Editors) . . . *.v.4 p.716*

Johannsen, Robert W. *v.3 p.398, p.418, p.422,
p.423, p.428, v.6 p.534*

Johansen, Anja. . . . . *.v.3 p.155, p.169*

Johansen, Bruce E.
(Editor) *v.4 p.192, p.464, v.6 p.682, p.691, p.703*

Johansen, Bruce E. . . . . *.v.4 p.30*

Johanssen, Terje (Editor) . . . . *.v.2 p.627*

Johansson, Sven A. E. (Editor), et al. . . . . . . *.v.5 p.273*

Johansson, Warren & Percy, William. . . . . *.v.6 p.368*

John, Elizabeth A. *v.6 p.684, p.685*

John Gorman, Michael . . . . *.v.1 p.793*

John H. Heinz III Center for Science, Economics and the
Environment *v.5 p.17, p.170, p.356, v.6 p.291*

John, J. A. & Quenouille, M. H.. . . . . *.v.5 p.409*

John, Juliet . . . . *.v.2 p.284*

John of Salisbury. *v.1 p.432, v.4 p.490*

John of the Cross & Teresa of Avila . . . . *.v.2 p.646*

John of the Cross. . . . . *.v.2 p.646*

John S. and James L. Knight Foundation. *v.4 p.821, p.884, p.894*

John Scagliotti, director. . . . . *.v.6 p.365*

John W. Hartman Center for Sales, Advertising & Marketing
History. . . . . *.v.4 p.141*

Johns, Alger F.. . . . . *.v.6 p.652*

Johns, Christina J. & Johnson, P. Ward. . . . . . *.v.3 p.304*

Johns, Michael . . . . *.v.3 p.289*

Johnsgard, Paul A. . . . . *.v.3 p.524*

Johnson, Addie & Proctor, Robert W. . . . . *.v.5 p.611*

Johnson, Allan G.. . . . . *.v.4 p.677, v.6 p.429*

Johnson, AnnMae . . . . *.v.3 p.506*

Johnson, Ben F. III . . . . *.v.3 p.510*

Johnson, Benjamin Heber . . . . *.v.6 p.534*

Johnson, Carroll B.. . . . . *v.2 p.649, p.651*

Johnson, Catherine J. & Snyder, Allegra F. . . . . *.v.1 p.52*

Author Index

Johnson, Cathy *v.5 p.227*
Johnson, Cecil *v.4 p.832, p.865*
Johnson, Chalmers A. *v.4 p.760, v.6 p.192, p.224*
Johnson, Chalmers *v.6 p.145, p.235*
Johnson, Charles A. & Brickman, Danette *v.4 p.462*
Johnson Charles W.; Ney, Robert *v.4 p.461*
Johnson, Christopher H. *v.3 p.158*
Johnson, Christopher *v.4 p.24*
Johnson, Claudia Durst *v.3 p.485*
Johnson, Claudia L. *v.2 p.267*
Johnson, D. W. & Van Hook, R. I. (Editors) *v.5 p.176*
Johnson, David E., et al. *v.5 p.721*
Johnson, David E. *v.3 p.374*
Johnson, David K. *v.6 p.365, p.383, p.388*
Johnson, David W. & Johnson, Roger T. *v.4 p.286*
Johnson, David W., et al. *v.5 p.184*
Johnson, David *v.5 p.433, p.463, p.694*
Johnson, Denis *v.2 p.355*
Johnson, Diane *v.2 p.147*
Johnson, Donald J., et al. *v.6 p.51*
Johnson, Donald *v.3 p.538*
Johnson, Don *v.4 p.811*
Johnson, Douglas, et al. *v.1 p.198, p.307*
Johnson, Douglas Hamilton *v.6 p.59*
Johnson, Edgar A. *v.4 p.212*
Johnson, Edgar *v.2 p.284*
Johnson, Edward A. *v.5 p.38*
Johnson, Edward D. *v.2 p.184, v.6 p.755*
Johnson, Elaine B. *v.4 p.348*
Johnson, Elizabeth A. *v.1 p.639*
Johnson, Elizabeth S. & Johnson, Harry G. *v.4 p.228*
Johnson, Eric & Reuband, Karl-Heinz *v.3 p.172*
Johnson, Eric L. & Jones, Stanton L. (Editors) . . . *v.5 p.634*
Johnson, Eyvind *v.2 p.629*
Johnson, Fenton *v.6 p.379, p.402*
Johnson, George *v.5 p.62, p.543*
Johnson, Graham & Stokes, Richard *v.1 p.395, p.411*
Johnson, Graham E. & Peterson, Glen D. *v.6 p.205*
Johnson, H. Thomas & Kaplan, Robert S. *v.4 p.106*
Johnson, Harry G. & Swoboda, Alexander K. *v.4 p.238*
Johnson, Haynes B. *v.3 p.473*
Johnson, Haynes *v.3 p.442, p.473, v.4 p.486*
Johnson, Herbert Alan & Wolfe, Nancy Travis . . . *v.6 p.245*
Johnson, Howard & Watson, Karl (Editors) *v.3 p.297*
Johnson, Hugh *v.5 p.32*
Johnson, Ian *v.4 p.620*
Johnson, Ida M. & Sigler, Robert T. *v.4 p.742*
Johnson, J. K. *v.3 p.544*
Johnson, James H. *v.1 p.245*
Johnson, James Weldon *v.2 p.89, v.6 p.6, p.18*
Johnson, Jane & Greutzner, A. (Compiled by) . . . *v.1 p.664*
Johnson, Janet Buttolph & Reynolds, H. T. *v.4 p.483*
Johnson, Jeff *v.1 p.585, v.5 p.338*
Johnson, Jeffrey S. & VGM Career Books Staff . . . *v.4 p.170*
Johnson, John J. *v.3 p.274, v.4 p.717*

Johnson, John W. (Editor) *v.4 p.441*
Johnson, Joyce *v.2 p.90*
Johnson, Judith L. *v.4 p.321*
Johnson, Julie G. *v.3 p.263*
Johnson, Kelli Lyon *v.6 p.507, p.513*
Johnson, Kenneth F. & Bezdek, Robert R. *v.3 p.293*
Johnson, Kevin R. *v.4 p.460, v.6 p.489, p.544*
Johnson, Kurt & Coates, Steven L. *v.2 p.104*
Johnson, Leanor Boulin & Staples, Robert *v.4 p.734*
Johnson, Lee *v.1 p.741*
Johnson, Leonard R. (Editor) *v.5 p.164*
Johnson, Linda C. *v.6 p.205*
Johnson, Lionel P. *v.2 p.292*
Johnson, Loch & Inderfurth, Karl F. (Editors) . . . *v.4 p.562*
Johnson, Lonnie R. *v.3 p.206*
Johnson, Luke Timothy *v.1 p.624, p.629, p.630, p.631*
Johnson, Lyman L. & Lipsett-Rivera, Sonya . . *v.3 p.263, p.283*
Johnson, Lyman L. (Editor) *v.3 p.345*
Johnson, Lymon L. & Tandeter, Enrique (Editors) . . *v.3 p.286*
Johnson, Lyndon B. *v.3 p.473*
Johnson, Marilynn S. *v.6 p.261*
Johnson, Marshall D. *v.1 p.617*
Johnson, Mary Elizabeth & Kiracofe, Roderick . . . *v.1 p.809*
Johnson, Matthew V. *v.4 p.6*
Johnson, Maxwell E. *v.1 p.657*
Johnson, Michael D. & Gustaffson, Anders *v.4 p.139*
Johnson, Michael G. & Henley, Tracy B. (Editors) . . *v.5 p.596*
Johnson, Michael L. *v.4 p.303*
Johnson, Michael P. *v.3 p.503*
Johnson, Norman F. & Triplehorn, Charles A. *v.5 p.27*
Johnson, Ollie Andrew III *v.3 p.341*
Johnson, Paula C. *v.6 p.277*
Johnson, Penelope D. *v.3 p.51, p.143*
Johnson, Philip, et al. *v.1 p.793*
Johnson, Phillip E. *v.5 p.203*
Johnson, Phylis & Keith, Michael C. *v.6 p.419*
Johnson, R. W. *v.4 p.613*
Johnson, Rebecca L. *v.5 p.134*
Johnson, Robert B. & DeGraff, Jerome V. *v.5 p.421*
Johnson, Robert D. *v.3 p.452*
Johnson, Robert F. & Bertazzoni, Giovanna *v.1 p.757*
Johnson, Roberta *v.2 p.641*
Johnson, Robert *v.6 p.274*
Johnson, Ronald W. & Schene, Michael G. *v.1 p.822*
Johnson, Samuel *v.2 p.230, p.250, v.6 p.71*
Johnson, Sherry *v.3 p.310*
Johnson, Spencer *v.4 p.79*
Johnson, Steven (Editor) *v.1 p.207*
Johnson, Steven *v.5 p.617*
Johnson, Susan Lee *v.3 p.531*
Johnson, Susan M. *v.5 p.668*
Johnson, Susan Moore *v.4 p.278, p.281*
Johnson, Theodore O. *v.1 p.184, p.240, p.303*
Johnson, Tim (Editor) *v.1 p.764, v.6 p.678*
Johnson, Timothy Russell *v.4 p.537*

Johnson, Troy R. (Editor) *v.6 p.689, p.694*
Johnson, Troy R., et al. *v.6 p.694*
Johnson, Troy R. *v.6 p.689, p.694*
Johnson, Troy *v.6 p.689, p.694*
Johnson, Uwe *v.2 p.618*
Johnson, W. R. *v.2 p.437*
Johnson, Wallace R. *v.3 p.297*
Johnson, Walter Ralph *v.2 p.433*
Johnson, Winslow *v.4 p.134*
Johnson-Davies, Denys (Editor, Translator) *v.6 p.660*
Johnson-Davies, Denys (Translator) *v.6 p.660*
Johnson-Davies, Denys *v.2 p.583*
Johnson-Laird, Philip *v.5 p.590*
Johnson-Odim, Cheryl *v.6 p.28, p.44*
Johnston, Carol A. *v.2 p.129*
Johnston, David Cay *v.4 p.107*
Johnston, David *v.4 p.493, p.511*
Johnston, Donald H. (Editor) *v.4 p.415*
Johnston, E. H. *v.1 p.563*
Johnston, James Scott *v.4 p.337*
Johnston, Janet R. & Campbell, Linda E. G. *v.5 p.668*
Johnston, Jennifer *v.2 p.355*
Johnston, Jill *v.1 p.39*
Johnston, Kenneth R. & Ruoff, Gene W. (Editors) . *v.2 p.324*
Johnston, Kenneth R. *v.2 p.323*
Johnston, Patricia A. *v.1 p.708*
Johnston, R. J. (Editor), et al. *v.4 p.373, p.374, p.378*
Johnston, R. J. *v.4 p.378*
Johnston, Richard, et al. *v.4 p.590*
Johnston, Ron *v.4 p.374, p.378*
Johnston, William M. (Editor) *v.1 p.531*
Johnston, William M. *v.3 p.181*
Johnstone, D. Bruce *v.4 p.295*
Johnstone, G. *v.6 p.279*
Johoda, Gustav & Lewis, Ioan M. (Editors) . *v.5 p.627, p.631*
Joint Center for Housing Studies, Harvard University . *v.4 p.158*
Joint Commission on Mental Illness and Health . . *v.5 p.671*
Joint Committee on Printing *v.4 p.481*
Joint United Nations Programme on HIV/AIDS . . *v.4 p.668*
Jokilehto, Jukka *v.1 p.822*
Joll, Evelyn (Author, Editor) *v.1 p.741*
Joll, James *v.3 p.79*
Jolles, P. & Jornvall, H. (Editors) . . *v.5 p.116*
Jolley, Nicholas (Editor) *v.1 p.459*
Jolliffe, Genevieve *v.6 p.347*
Jolly, Margaret *v.4 p.31*
Jolly, Richard *v.4 p.634, p.664*
Jonakait, Randolph N. *v.6 p.270*
Jonas, Joan *v.1 p.773*
Jonas, Manfred *v.3 p.389, p.452*
Jonas, Wayne B. & Levin, Jeffrey S. *v.5 p.531*
Jonassaint, Jean *v.2 p.537*
Jonassen, David H. (Editor) *v.4 p.351*
Jones, A. H. M. & Monroe, Elizabeth *v.6 p.64*
Jones, A. H. M. *v.3 p.28, p.31, p.192, v.4 p.500*

Jones, Adam (Editor) *v.4 p.652, v.6 p.257*
Jones, Adam *v.3 p.302*
Jones, Alan *v.6 p.654*
Jones, Aled *v.6 p.738*
Jones, Alexander (Editor) *v.1 p.613*
Jones, Alice Hanson *v.3 p.409*
Jones, Alice H. *v.3 p.405*
Jones, Andrew *v.3 p.113, v.4 p.6*
Jones, Ann *v.4 p.752*
Jones, Anny Brooksbank *v.3 p.242*
Jones, Archer *v.3 p.398*
Jones, B. J. *v.6 p.691*
Jones, Bill T. & Zane, Arnie *v.1 p.9*
Jones, Bill T. *v.1 p.9*
Jones, Billie J., et al. *v.4 p.904*
Jones, Brian W. & Milns, R. D. *v.2 p.444*
Jones, Bruce Anthony (Editor) *v.4 p.281*
Jones, C. Jessie & Rose, Debra J. (Editors) . *v.4 p.795, p.841*
Jones, Caroline *v.1 p.732*
Jones, Charisse & Shorter-Gooden, Kumea *v.6 p.434*
Jones, Charles E. (Editor) *v.6 p.12*
Jones, Charles O. *v.4 p.532*
Jones, Charles *v.2 p.551, p.557*
Jones, Cheslyn, et al. *v.1 p.650*
Jones, Cheslyn *v.1 p.654*
Jones, Chris & Jolliffe, Genevieve *v.6 p.347*
Jones, Chris J. & Abel, Eddie *v.5 p.303*
Jones, Chris *v.4 p.789*
Jones, Claude E. *v.2 p.261*
Jones, Cleve & Dawson, Jeff *v.6 p.379, p.402*
Jones, Clive & Murphy, Emma C. *v.6 p.614*
Jones, Colin *v.3 p.147, p.159*
Jones, D. Mervyn *v.2 p.785*
Jones, D. S. (Douglas Samuel); Sleeman, B. D. . . . *v.5 p.91*
Jones, Dan Burne *v.1 p.757*
Jones, Daniel *v.2 p.557*
Jones, Darryl *v.6 p.318*
Jones, David A. *v.6 p.245, p.250*
Jones, David Wyn (Editor) *v.1 p.199, p.240, p.307*
Jones, Derek C. (Editor) *v.4 p.190*
Jones, Donald G. & Daley, Elaine L. *v.4 p.802, p.813*
Jones, Douglas G. *v.2 p.729*
Jones, Edmund D. (Editor) *v.2 p.175*
Jones, Edmund D. *v.2 p.169, p.170, p.172*
Jones, Edward P. *v.2 p.147*
Jones, Emrys (Editor) *v.2 p.197, p.199*
Jones, Eric L. *v.4 p.209*
Jones, Eric *v.3 p.40*
Jones, Evan John *v.1 p.21*
Jones, F. Stanley (Editor) *v.1 p.642*
Jones, Franklin D. *v.5 p.714*
Jones, Gareth E. *v.3 p.132*
Jones, Gareth Stedman *v.3 p.113, p.131*
Jones, Gavin W. *v.4 p.733*
Jones, Grant D. *v.3 p.286, p.297*

Jones, Gwyn *v.3 p.62, p.235*
Jones, Hamlyn G. (Editor), et al.. . . . . *v.5 p.124*
Jones, Harry V.. . . . . *v.2 p.215*
Jones, Howard M. *v.2 p.7, v.4 p.343*
Jones, Howard *v.1 p.429, v.3 p.385, p.417, v.4 p.521*
Jones, J. Benton Jr. *v.5 p.49*
Jones, J. R. *v.3 p.105, p.107*
Jones, Jacqueline *v.4 p.708, v.6 p.7, p.44, p.457*
Jones, James R. *v.3 p.107*
Jones, James T. *v.2 p.92*
Jones, James W. *v.3 p.485, v.5 p.634*
Jones, James *v.2 p.90*
Jones, Janna *v.1 p.822*
Jones, John Bush. *v.1 p.251*
Jones, John Paul *v.3 p.411*
Jones, John Philip (Editor) *v.4 p.426*
Jones, John *v.2 p.402, v.5 p.328*
Jones, Joseph L., et al.. . . . . *v.5 p.339, p.341*
Jones, K. R. *v.2 p.470, p.471*
Jones, Kenneth W. *v.1 p.536*
Jones, Kent Albert & Jones, Kent *v.4 p.55, p.61, p.664*
Jones, Kirkland C.. . . . . *v.6 p.18*
Jones, Lawrence *v.2 p.741*
Jones, Lindsay *v.1 p.522*
Jones, Loyal *v.3 p.497*
Jones Luong, Pauline *v.3 p.230, v.4 p.623*
Jones, Lyle V. & Olkin, Ingram *v.4 p.355*
Jones, M. Gail, et al. *v.4 p.286*
Jones, Malcolm V. & Miller, Robin Feuer
  (Editors). *v.2 p.793, p.798*
Jones, Malcolm *v.6 p.555*
Jones, Mari R. & Holleran, Susan (Editors). *v.1 p.375*
Jones, Martin *v.5 p.122*
Jones, Mary *v.4 p.126*
Jones, Michael E. *v.3 p.63*
Jones, Neil C. & Pevzner, Pavel . . . *v.5 p.107, p.336, p.341*
Jones, Nicholas F. *v.3 p.18*
Jones, Nigel *v.2 p.335*
Jones, Norman *v.5 p.697*
Jones, Oakah L. Jr.. . . . . *v.3 p.298, p.528*
Jones, Paul C.. . . . . *v.2 p.13*
Jones, Phil. *v.5 p.695*
Jones, Phyllis M. (Editor) *v.2 p.178*
Jones, Quincy *v.1 p.270, p.334*
Jones, R. J. Barry *v.4 p.192*
Jones, Reginald L. (Editor). *v.6 p.33*
Jones, Richard A.. . . . . *v.5 p.554*
Jones, Richard M. *v.4 p.357*
Jones, Robert Edmond *v.1 p.139, p.147*
Jones, Robert O. (Compiled by) *v.1 p.810*
Jones, Robert; Oyung, Robert; Pace, Lise *v.4 p.80*
Jones, Robert T. *v.5 p.718*
Jones, Robyn & Cassidy, Tania *v.4 p.904*
Jones, Rodney *v.2 p.147*
Jones, Ronald W. & Kenen, Peter B. (Editors) . . . *v.4 p.190*

Jones, Russell H. (Editor) *v.5 p.734*
Jones, Samantha & Carswell, Grace (Editors). *v.4 p.268, v.5 p.28*
Jones, Serene *v.1 p.636*
Jones, Sharon L.. . . . . *v.2 p.81*
Jones, Stanley *v.2 p.293*
Jones, Stephen R. & Cushman, Ruth Carol . . . *v.5 p.176, p.240*
Jones, Stephen *v.1 p.288, v.6 p.318*
Jones, Steve (Editor) *v.4 p.419, v.5 p.621, p.625*
Jones, Steve *v.5 p.134, p.203*
Jones, Susan, et al. *v.4 p.423*
Jones, Suzanne W. (Editor) *v.2 p.26*
Jones, Terry *v.2 p.209*
Jones, Timothy *v.1 p.199, p.240, p.307*
Jones, Tom *v.1 p.404*
Jones, W. H. (Translator) *v.2 p.404, v.5 p.510*
Jones, William David *v.4 p.510*
Jones, William, ed. *v.5 p.292*
Jones, William K. *v.4 p.443*
Jones, Wilmer L. *v.4 p.521*
Jones-Correa, Michael (Editor) *v.4 p.544*
Jones-Correa, Michael *v.6 p.538, p.549, p.718*
Jong, Steven M. de & Meer, Freek D. van der (Editors). *v.4 p.388*
Jonin, Pierre (Editor) *v.2 p.465*
Jonson, Ben & Jonnes, Jill *v.2 p.220*
Jonson, Ben *v.2 p.219, p.220*
Joosten, Joop M. & Welsh, Robert P.. . . . . *v.1 p.697*
Jopek, Norbert *v.1 p.777*
Joralemon, Donald *v.5 p.536*
Joravsky, David *v.5 p.402*
Jordan, Bella Bychkova & Jordan, Terry G.. . . . . *v.3 p.214*
Jordan, Bertrand *v.5 p.102, p.122*
Jordan, David C. *v.3 p.310*
Jordan, David M.. . . . . *v.3 p.434*
Jordan, David P.. . . . . *v.3 p.150, p.154, p.159*
Jordan, Ellen R.. . . . . . *v.3 p.53, v.6 p.431, p.457*
Jordan, Frank (Editor) *v.2 p.183*
Jordan, John C. *v.2 p.218*
Jordan, John E.. . . . . *v.2 p.324*
Jordan, John O. & Patten, Robert L.
  (Editors). *v.6 p.738, p.741, p.752*
Jordan, John O. (Editor) *v.2 p.285*
Jordan, Nicole *v.3 p.155*
Jordan, Pascual. *v.5 p.402*
Jordan, Peter C. *v.5 p.279*
Jordan, Robert B.. . . . . *v.5 p.304*
Jordan, Robert S., et al. *v.4 p.629*
Jordan, Stephanie & Allen, Dave (Editors) . *v.1 p.37, p.42, p.45*
Jordan, Stephanie *v.1 p.42*
Jordan, Thomas Earl *v.5 p.281*
Jordan, William C. *v.3 p.43, p.69, v.6 p.555*
Jordan, William R. *v.6 p.283*
Jordan, Winthrop D.. . . . . *v.3 p.398, v.6 p.7*
Jordan-Bychkov, Terry *v.4 p.382*
Jordanes *v.3 p.63*
Jordans *v.1 p.536*

Jorde, Lynn B., et al. *v.5 p.149*

Jorde, Lynn B. *v.5 p.149*

Jordy, William H. *v.1 p.789*

Jorgensen, Christine T. *v.6 p.370, p.402*

Jorgensen, Danny L. *v.4 p.690*

Jorgensen, Owen *v.1 p.375, p.401*

Jorgensen, Paul A. *v.2 p.230*

Jorgensen, Theodore P. *v.4 p.861, p.871*

Jorgensen, William L. & Salem, Lionel *v.5 p.293*

Jorgenson, Dale W. *v.4 p.202, p.207*

Jose, F. Sionil *v.6 p.179*

Josefsson, Lars & Persson, Patrik *v.5 p.728*

Joselit, David *v.1 p.679, p.682*

Joseph, Bertram Leon *v.1 p.101, p.145*

Joseph, Charles M. *v.1 p.24, p.217, p.360*

Joseph, George G. *v.3 p.47, v.5 p.466*

Joseph, George *v.2 p.470*

Joseph, Gilbert M. *v.3 p.293*

Joseph, Herbert S. (Editor) *v.6 p.649*

Joseph, Jay *v.5 p.658*

Joseph, Joel D. *v.4 p.537*

Joseph, John E. *v.4 p.694*

Joseph, John *v.6 p.600, p.606, p.607*

Joseph, Rhawn *v.5 p.203, p.243*

Joseph, Richard A. *v.6 p.62*

Joseph, Richard (Editor) *v.4 p.611*

Joseph, Richard *v.4 p.611*

Joseph, Suad (Editor) *v.6 p.459, p.582, p.593*

Joseph, Suad *v.6 p.593*

Joseph, William A. (Editor), et al. *v.6 p.195*

Josephson, John R. & Josephson, Susan G. (Editors) *v.1 p.495*

Josephson, Matthew *v.3 p.437, p.442*

Josephson, Peter *v.4 p.491, p.497*

Josephus, Flavius *v.1 p.546*

Josephy, Alvin M. Jr. *v.6 p.682, p.685, p.687, p.703*

José, Jorge V. & Saletan, Eugene J. *v.5 p.546*

Joshi, Priya *v.2 p.191, p.762*

Joshi, S. T. & Dziemianowicz, Stefan (Editors) . . . *v.2 p.581*

Joslyn, M. A. & Amerine, M. A. *v.5 p.52*

Josselin, Daphne & Wallace, William (Editors) . . *v.4 p.640*

Jossey-Bass Inc. Staff *v.4 p.327*

Jost, Ekkehard *v.1 p.260*

Jost, John T. & Sidanius, James (Editors) . *v.4 p.483, v.5 p.643*

Jost, Jurgen *v.5 p.496*

Jost, Kenneth & CQ Editors *v.4 p.537*

Joughin, Louis; Morgan, Edmund Morris *v.4 p.471*

Jourda, Pierre *v.2 p.465*

Joussan, John & Chadwick, Matthew *v.5 p.703*

Jouvet, Michel *v.5 p.613*

Jovanovski, Meto *v.2 p.787*

Jowers, Sidney Jackson *v.1 p.140, p.151*

Jowitt, Deborah (Editor) *v.1 p.9, p.26, p.217, p.342*

Jowitt, Deborah *v.1 p.9, p.36, p.39, v.6 p.414*

Jowitt, Glenn & Shaw, Peter *v.1 p.790*

Jowitt, Kenneth *v.4 p.491*

Joyce, Alice *v.1 p.812*

Joyce, Davis D. *v.3 p.374*

Joyce, Elisabeth W. (Editor) *v.2 p.102*

Joyce, James Avery *v.4 p.631*

Joyce, James *v.2 p.358, p.359*

Joyce, Patrick D. . . *v.6 p.114, p.123, p.135, p.742, p.743, p.758*

Joyce, Patrick W. *v.6 p.742*

Joyce, Patrick *v.3 p.113, v.6 p.743*

Joyce, Stanislaus, et al. *v.2 p.359*

Joyner, Christopher C. (Editor) *v.4 p.477, p.478, p.634*

Joyner, Christopher C. *v.4 p.477*

Joyner, David *v.5 p.469, p.474*

Joynson, R. B. *v.5 p.596*

Jozsa, Frank P. Jr. *v.4 p.884, p.888, p.896*

Jozsef, Attila *v.2 p.786*

Jozwiak, Don *v.4 p.848*

Jrade, Cathy L. *v.2 p.664*

Juan, E. San Jr. *v.6 p.104, p.129*

Jubayr, ibn *v.6 p.585*

Jubien, Michael *v.1 p.488*

Juckes, Tim J. *v.6 p.79*

Judah, Tim *v.3 p.249*

Judd, Denis & Surridge, Keith *v.6 p.79*

Judd, Denis *v.3 p.77, p.89, p.125*

Judd, Dennis R. & Kantor, Paul *v.6 p.728*

Judd, Dennis R. & Swanstrom, Todd *v.6 p.723*

Judd, Kenneth L. & Tesfatsion, Leigh (Editors) . . . *v.4 p.190*

Judd, Kenneth L. *v.4 p.202*

Judge, Anne & Healey, Frederick G. *v.2 p.453*

Judges, Donald P. *v.4 p.448*

Judson, William V. *v.3 p.221*

Judt, Tony *v.4 p.564*

Jue, Joyce & Williams, Chuck *v.6 p.164*

Juergensmeyer, Mark *v.1 p.524*

Juárez, José Luis *v.3 p.271*

Juhn, Tricia *v.3 p.299*

Jukofsky, Diane *v.5 p.176, p.211, p.225, p.239*

Jules-Rosette, Bennetta *v.2 p.542*

Julesz, Bela, et al. *v.5 p.605*

Julian Dierkes *v.4 p.675*

Julian of Norwich *v.1 p.652, p.653*

July, Robert W. *v.6 p.54*

July, Robert *v.6 p.54*

Juma, Calestous *v.5 p.218*

Jumars, Peter A. *v.4 p.392, v.5 p.431*

Jumonville, Neil *v.3 p.374*

Jung, C. G. *v.1 p.524, p.594,v.5 p.634, p.659*

Jung, Courtney Elizabeth *v.4 p.614*

Jung Ha Kim *v.6 p.105, p.112, p.135*

Jung, Sandro *v.2 p.237, p.260*

Jungmann *v.1 p.654*

Junker, Detlef (Editor) *v.3 p.389*

Junker, Patricia *v.1 p.742*

Juola, Patrick *v.5 p.730*

Juran, Joseph M. & Godfrey, A. Blanton *v.5 p.685*

Juravich, Tom & Bronfenbrenner, Kate *v.4 p.126*
Jurca, Catherine *v.6 p.731*
Jurd, Richard D. *v.5 p.212*
Jurgen, Ronald K. *v.5 p.716*
Jurinski, James John *v.4 p.464*
Jurisica, Igor & Wigle, Dennis. *v.5 p.116*
Jurkanin, Thomas J., et al. *v.6 p.265*
Jurkowski, Henryk *v.1 p.93, p.96*
Jurs, Peter C. *v.5 p.267*
Jury, David *v.1 p.719*
Jury, William A. & Horton, Robert *v.5 p.49*
Juslin, Patrik N. & Sloboda, John A.
   (Editors) *v.1 p.375, v.5 p.612, p.619*
Jusserand, Jean A. *v.2 p.166*
Just, Roger *v.4 p.42*
Just, Ward *v.2 p.147*
Juster, Susan *v.1 p.583*
Justice, Donald Rodney *v.2 p.90*
Justice, Donald *v.2 p.90*
Jutikkala, Eino *v.3 p.236*
Juvenal & Persius *v.2 p.435*
Juvenal *v.2 p.435*
Juviler, Peter H. *v.4 p.512*
Juvinall, Robert C. & Marshek, Kurt M. *v.5 p.714*
Jwaideh, Wadie *v.6 p.599*

K

K., Voltmer *v.4 p.424*
Kabasele, Francois L. *v.1 p.573*
Kabbani, Nizar *v.6 p.661*
Kabir *v.6 p.151*
Kabisama, Henslay W. *v.5 p.724*
Kacmarek, Robert M. *v.5 p.518*
Kaczor, Christopher *v.5 p.248*
Kaczor, W. J. & Nowak, M. T. *v.5 p.489*
Kadac, Sadik *v.5 p.713*
Kadare, Ismail *v.2 p.815*
Kadarkay, Arpad *v.3 p.187*
Kadera, Kelly M. *v.4 p.626, p.647*
Kadish, Karl M. & Ruoff, Rodney S. (Editors) *v.5 p.306*
Kadohata, Cynthia *v.6 p.100*
Kadushin, Alfred & Harkness, Daniel *v.4 p.757*
Kadushin, Alfred & Kadushin, Goldie *v.4 p.757*
Kadushin, Max *v.1 p.552*
Kaegi, Walter E. *v.6 p.581, p.585*
Kaemmer, John E. *v.4 p.26*
Kaempfer, Engelbert & Beatrice, M. Bodart-Bailey . . *v.6 p.225*
Kaempfer, Engelbert *v.6 p.224*
Kaen, Fred R. *v.4 p.86*
Kaeppler, Adrienne L., et al. *v.1 p.694*
Kaeppler, Adrienne L. *v.1 p.17*
Kaeppler, Adrienne Lois *v.1 p.48*
Kaes, Anton, et al. *v.3 p.170*
Kaesche, Helmut *v.5 p.689, p.734*

Kaeser, Gigi (Photographer) *v.6 p.368, p.372, p.376*
Kaestle, Carl *v.4 p.327*
Kaeuper, Richard W. *v.3 p.69, p.96, p.143, p.144*
Kafadar, Cemal *v.6 p.590*
Kafka, Franz, et al. *v.2 p.610*
Kafka, Franz *v.2 p.610, p.611*
Kafka, Phillipa *v.6 p.500, p.507, p.513*
Kagan, Donald *v.3 p.18*
Kagan, Frederick W. *v.3 p.219*
Kagan, Henri *v.5 p.298*
Kagan, Jerome & Gall, Susan (Editors) *v.5 p.627*
Kagan, Jerome *v.5 p.627, p.649*
Kagan, Richard L. *v.3 p.237*
Kagan, Robert *v.4 p.637, p.641*
Kagan, Sharon L. & Neville, Peter *v.4 p.754*
Kagan, Sharon Lynn *v.4 p.369*
Kagan, Shelly *v.1 p.484*
Kagehiro, D. & Laufer, William S. (Editors) *v.5 p.592*
Kager, Reni *v.2 p.561*
Kahan, Yitzhak, et al. *v.6 p.606*
Kahane, Ahuvia (Editor), et al. *v.2 p.414*
Kahin, George M. *v.6 p.168*
Kahin, George McTurnan *v.6 p.177*
Kahk, Juhan; Tarvel, Enn *v.3 p.255*
Kahl, Günter *v.5 p.116, p.140*
Kahlenberg, Richard D. (Editor) *v.4 p.294*
Kahlo, Frida & Lozano, Luis-Martin *v.1 p.742*
Kahn, Albert E. *v.1 p.9*
Kahn, Ashley *v.1 p.260, p.318, p.320*
Kahn, Charles H. *v.1 p.421, p.424*
Kahn, Cynthia M. (Editor) *v.5 p.55, p.57*
Kahn, Harold L. *v.6 p.187, p.200*
Kahn, Jetty *v.5 p.222*
Kahn, Kenneth B. (Editor) *v.4 p.144*
Kahn, Kenneth B. *v.4 p.144*
Kahn, Kim Fridkin & Kenney, Patrick J. . *v.4 p.530, p.551, p.557*
Kahn, Paul *v.6 p.239*
Kahn, Roger *v.4 p.811, p.851*
Kahn, Ronald *v.4 p.470*
Kahn, Sharon E. & Pavlich, Dennis J. (Editors) . . . *v.4 p.298*
Kahn, Susan Martha *v.4 p.32*
Kahneman, Daniel & Tversky, Amos (Editors) . . . *v.4 p.272*
Kahneman, Daniel (Editor), et al. . . *v.4 p.195, v.5 p.608, p.670*
Kahnweiler, William & Kahnweiler, Jennifer *v.4 p.76*
Kain, Geoffrey R. (Editor) *v.2 p.765*
Kain, Richard Morgan *v.2 p.359*
Kairys, David & Cramer, Rene (Editors) *v.4 p.465*
Kaiser, David E. *v.3 p.442, v.4 p.486*
Kaiser, Georg *v.2 p.611*
Kaish, Stanley (Editor), et al. *v.4 p.190*
Kakar, Mohammad Hassan *v.6 p.634*
Kakar, Sudhir *v.6 p.149*
Kaku, Michio *v.5 p.391, p.392, p.403, p.550, p.557*
Kalaidjian, Walter (Editor) *v.2 p.11*
Kalbagh, Chetana (Editor) *v.5 p.13*

Kalberg, Stephen *v.4 p.681*

Kalbfeld, Brad *v.4 p.414*

Kaldor, Mary *v.4 p.498*

Kaldor, Nicholas *v.4 p.209, p.244, p.248*

Kalecki, Michal *v.4 p.202, p.244, p.259, p.269*

Kaler, James B. *v.5 p.70*

Kalff, Jacob *v.5 p.173, p.174, p.427*

Kalichman, Seth C. *v.4 p.756*

Kalicki, Jan H. & Goldwyn, David L. *v.4 p.62*

Kalidasa *v.6 p.151*

Kalinak, Kathryn *v.1 p.255, v.6 p.341*

Kalinowska, Izabela *v.2 p.778, p.789, p.798*

Kalisch, Philip Arthur, et al. *v.5 p.527, p.529*

Kallberg, Jeffrey *v.1 p.199, p.317, p.379*

Kallen, Stuart A. *v.6 p.431*

Kallir, Jane *v.1 p.217, p.353, p.742*

Kalman, Dan *v.5 p.500*

Kalman, Harold D. *v.1 p.790*

Kalman, Laura *v.4 p.468*

Kalstone, David *v.2 p.62, p.102*

Kaluarachchi, Jagath J. *v.5 p.368, p.375, p.379*

Kalunta-Crumpton, Anita & Agozino, Biko (Editors) . *v.6 p.250*

Kalupahana, David J. *v.1 p.565*

Kalven, Harry Jr. & Zeisel, Hans *v.4 p.473*

Kalven, Harry Jr. *v.4 p.459*

Kalyanpur, Maya & Harry, Beth *v.4 p.316*

Kalyvas, Stathis N. *v.4 p.601*

Kamber, Richard *v.1 p.456*

Kambhampati, Uma S. *v.4 p.259*

Kamboureli, Smaro *v.2 p.729*

Kamen, Henry A. *v.3 p.239*

Kamen, Henry Arthur Francis *v.3 p.40, p.70, p.239*

Kamen, Henry *v.3 p.65, p.74, p.239*

Kamenetsky, Christa *v.3 p.172*

Kamens, Edward *v.6 p.230*

Kamerman, Sheila B. & Kahn, Alfred J. *v.6 p.465, p.467*

Kamerman, Sheila B. *v.4 p.732*

Kamien, Morton I. & Schwartz, Nancy Lou *v.4 p.269*

Kamil, Michael L. (Editor), et al. *v.4 p.354*

Kaminer, Wendy *v.4 p.458*

Kaminski, Bartlomiej *v.4 p.506, p.508, p.596*

Kaminski, John P. (Editor) *v.4 p.451*

Kaminsky, Amy K. (Editor) *v.2 p.644*

Kaminsky, Amy K. *v.6 p.479*

Kaminsky, Stuart M. *v.6 p.311*

Kamke, E. *v.5 p.471*

Kamm, Antony *v.3 p.7*

Kammen, Daniel M; Hassenzahl, David M *v.5 p.504*

Kammen, Michael G. . *v.1 p.742, v.3 p.365, p.368, p.406, p.490, v.4 p.518*

Kamp, R. M. & Choli-Papadopoulou, Theodora . . . *v.5 p.116*

Kampen-O'Riley, Michael *v.1 p.668*

Kamshad, Hassan *v.6 p.671*

Kamsteeg, Frans H. *v.3 p.354*

Kamtekar, Rachana *v.1 p.422*

Kamuf, Peggy *v.2 p.456*

Kanaaneh, Rhoda Ann *v.6 p.618*

Kanafani, Ghassan *v.6 p.661*

Kanaganayakam, Chelva *v.2 p.760, p.762*

Kanahele, George S. (Editor) *v.1 p.288, p.296*

Kanani, N. (Editor) *v.5 p.737*

Kanbur, S. M. Ravi, et al. *v.4 p.397*

Kandeh, Jimmy D. *v.4 p.498, p.611*

Kandel, Eric R. *v.5 p.617*

Kander, John, et al. *v.6 p.412*

Kandinsky, Wassily, et al. *v.1 p.697*

Kandinsky, Wassily *v.1 p.703*

Kandiyoti, Deniz & Saktanber, Ayse (Editors) . . . *v.6 p.624*

Kane, Cheikh H. *v.2 p.545*

Kane, George (Editor) *v.2 p.211*

Kane, George *v.2 p.168*

Kane, Gordon *v.5 p.552*

Kane, Hamidou *v.2 p.545*

Kane, Joseph Nathan & Aiken, Charles Curry *v.3 p.381*

Kane, Joseph N. *v.3 p.378*

Kane, Patricia E. *v.1 p.798*

Kane, Pearl R. *v.4 p.296*

Kane, Penny *v.6 p.443, p.756, p.765*

Kane, Robert (Editor) *v.1 p.503*

Kane, Thomas S. *v.2 p.565*

Kanehisa, Minoru *v.5 p.145*

Kanellos, Nicolas *v.6 p.500, p.507, p.513*

Kanellos, Nicolás & Fabregat, Claudio E. (Editors) . *v.6 p.485*

Kanellos, Nicolás & Martell, Helvetia *v.6 p.485*

Kanellos, Nicolás (Editor) . *v.2 p.19, v.6 p.485, p.496, p.500, p.507, p.513*

Kanellos, Nicolás *v.1 p.124, v.6 p.485, p.513, p.517*

Kanes, Martin *v.2 p.487*

Kang, David C. *v.4 p.621*

Kang, L. H. & Kim, Elaine H. *v.6 p.96, p.112*

Kang, Laura Hyun Yi *v.6 p.96, p.112*

Kang, Sung-Mo Steve & Leblebici, Yusuf *v.5 p.722*

Kang, Younghill *v.6 p.94*

Kanigel, Robert *v.5 p.466*

Kanin, Garson *v.2 p.91*

Kanipe, Jeff *v.5 p.71*

Kaniuk, Yoram *v.6 p.649*

Kankyusha *v.6 p.230*

Kann, Robert A. *v.3 p.181*

Kanner, Barbara *v.6 p.476*

Kanner, Bernice *v.4 p.139*

Kannicht, Christoph (Editor) *v.5 p.116*

Kano, Jigoro *v.4 p.863*

Kant, Immanuel . *v.1 p.461, p.462, p.480, p.481, p.484, p.498, p.523, v.3 p.167, v.4 p.343, p.649*

Kanter, Laurence & Palladino, Pia *v.1 p.742*

Kanter, Rosabeth Moss *v.4 p.76, p.733, v.6 p.457*

Kantor, Harvey & Tyack, David B. (Editors) . *v.4 p.305, p.353*

Kantor, MacKinlay *v.2 p.91*

Kantor, Martin *v.5 p.660*

Kantor, Shawn Everett *v.5 p.42, v.6 p.298*

Kantor, Sybil Gordon *v.1 p.679*

Kantor, Tadeusz *v.1 p.109, p.152*

Kantorowicz, Ernst Hartwig *v.3 p.163*

Kantorowicz, Ernst H. *v.3 p.69*

Kantowicz, Edward *v.3 p.515*

Kanwar, Pamela *v.6 p.161*

Kanze, Edward *v.5 p.233*

Kao, Deborah Martin, et al. *v.1 p.767*

Kao, Patricia & Tien, Susan *v.4 p.167*

Kapardis, Andreas *v.5 p.592*

Kapchan, Deborah A. *v.4 p.31*

Kapcia, Antoni *v.3 p.310*

Kapiszewski, Diana & Kazan, Alexander (Editors) . . *v.4 p.592*

Kaplan, Alice *v.3 p.156*

Kaplan, Ann E. *v.6 p.474*

Kaplan, Bert *v.4 p.35*

Kaplan, Carla (Editor) *v.6 p.16, p.18, p.44*

Kaplan, Carola (Editor), et al. *v.2 p.341*

Kaplan, Charles & Anderson, William (Editors) . . . *v.2 p.568*

Kaplan, David E. & Dubro, Alec *v.6 p.251*

Kaplan, E. Ann *v.4 p.558*

Kaplan, Elliott D. (Author, Editor) *v.4 p.390*

Kaplan, Fred, et al. *v.5 p.289*

Kaplan, Fred *v.2 p.33, p.127, p.277, p.285, v.6 p.402*

Kaplan, Gilbert E. (Editor) *v.1 p.753*

Kaplan, Herbert H. *v.3 p.217*

Kaplan, Jack M. *v.4 p.68*

Kaplan, Jeffrey P. *v.2 p.557*

Kaplan, Jonathan Michael *v.5 p.140*

Kaplan, Justin E. *v.2 p.33*

Kaplan, Lawrence S. *v.3 p.452*

Kaplan, Leonard V. & Moran, Beverly I. (Editors) . . *v.3 p.442, p.473, v.4 p.528*

Kaplan, Marion A. *v.3 p.164, p.180*

Kaplan, Norman M. & Flynn, Joseph T. *v.5 p.520*

Kaplan, Rachel & Marani, Pietro C. . . . *v.1 p.742*

Kaplan, Robert S. & Norton, David P. . . *v.4 p.73, p.81, p.82*

Kaplan, Robert *v.5 p.476*

Kaplan, Sandra N., et al. *v.5 p.573*

Kaplan Staff, et al. *v.4 p.395*

Kaplan, Steven L. *v.3 p.150*

Kaplan, Steven M. *v.5 p.258*

Kaplan, Sydney J. *v.2 p.369*

Kaplan, Wendy *v.1 p.798*

Kaplan *v.5 p.245*

Kapleau, Roshi P. *v.1 p.567*

Kaplin, William A. & Lee, Barbara A. . . . *v.4 p.450*

Kaplow, Louis & Shavell, Steven *v.4 p.83*

Kappeler, Victor E., et al. *v.6 p.261*

Kappen, Sebastian *v.1 p.641*

Kappler, Charles J. (Editor) *v.4 p.465, v.6 p.696*

Kapteyn & Koojmans *v.4 p.634*

Kar, Law & Bren, Frank *v.6 p.335*

Karaagac, John *v.3 p.442*

Karakasidou, Anastasia N. *v.3 p.195*

Karamanski, Theodore *v.3 p.515*

Karas, Joza *v.1 p.246, p.300*

Karasch, Mary C. *v.3 p.279, p.336*

Karasek, Krzysztof, et al. *v.2 p.787*

Karasek, Robert A. & Theorell, Torres *v.5 p.580*

Karassik, Igor J., et al. *v.5 p.713*

Karasu, Bilge *v.6 p.667*

Karatani, Rieko *v.4 p.605, p.667*

Karato, Shun'ichirao *v.5 p.442, p.443*

Karch, Steven *v.3 p.281*

Karcz, Andrzej *v.2 p.779, p.789, p.798*

Kardong, Kenneth V. *v.5 p.157, p.193*

Karenga, Maulana & Carruthers, Jacob *v.6 p.14, p.15*

Karenga, Maulana *v.6 p.14*

Karetnikova, Inga *v.6 p.352*

Kargel, J. S. *v.5 p.69*

Karger, Gunther (Author, Editor) *v.4 p.86*

Karier, Clarence J. *v.4 p.327*

Karim, Kahn Fazle *v.4 p.398*

Karimi-Hakkak, Ahmad (Editor, Translator) . . . *v.6 p.671*

Karl, Barry D. *v.3 p.448*

Karl, Frederick R. *v.2 p.287*

Karl, Frederick Robert *v.2 p.194*

Karl, Rebecca E. *v.4 p.494*

Karl, Terry L. *v.3 p.360*

Karlekar, Malavika *v.6 p.154*

Karlen, Delmar *v.4 p.465*

Karlin, Daniel (Editor) *v.2 p.200*

Karlin, Fred & Wright, Doris *v.6 p.351*

Karlin, Fred & Wright, Rayburn *v.1 p.255*

Karlin, Fred *v.1 p.255*

Karlin, Len *v.4 p.903*

Karlin, Samuel (Editor), et al. *v.4 p.206*

Karloff, Howard *v.5 p.683*

Karlqvist, Anders, et al. *v.4 p.202*

Karlson, P. *v.5 p.327*

Karlsson, Gunnar *v.3 p.234*

Karman, James *v.2 p.91*

Karmel, Pepe *v.1 p.742*

Karmis, Michael (Editor) *v.5 p.738*

Karnad, Girish *v.6 p.151*

Karnes, Frances A. & Bean, Suzanne M. (Editors) . . *v.4 p.317*

Karnick, Kristine B. & Jenkins, Henry (Editors) . . *v.6 p.312*

Karnouk, Liliane *v.1 p.679, p.690*

Karnow, Stanley *v.6 p.168*

Karp, Abraham J. *v.1 p.549*

Karp, Rashelle S. (Editor) *v.4 p.180*

Karp, Theodore *v.1 p.177*

Karpat, Kemal H. (Editor) *v.6 p.590*

Karpat, Kemal H. *v.6 p.590*

Karras R M Staff *v.3 p.55*

Karsavina, Tamara *v.1 p.9, p.24*

Karsh, Efraim & Karsh, Inari *v.6 p.593*

Karsh, Efraim (Editor) *v.6 p.614*

Karsh, Efraim *v.6 p.614*
Karson, Robin *v.1 p.816*
Karst, Kenneth L. *v.4 p.455*
Karsten, Peter (Editor) *v.5 p.584*
Karsten, Peter *v.4 p.717*
Kartomi, Margaret J. *v.1 p.390*
Karttunen, Hannu (Editor), et al. *v.5 p.65*
Karukstis, Kerry K. & Van Hecke, Gerald R. *v.5 p.264*
Karush, Matthew B. *v.3 p.348*
Karvonen, Lauri (Editor), et al. *v.4 p.554, p.579*
Karwowski, Waldemar (Editor) *v.5 p.679*
Kasaba, Resat *v.6 p.590*
Kasack, Wolfgang *v.2 p.796*
Kasahara, Kazuo *v.1 p.541*
Kaschak, Ellyn *v.6 p.446*
Kasekamp, Andres *v.3 p.256*
Kasemann, Ernst *v.1 p.625*
Kasfir, Sidney Littlefield *v.1 p.679, p.690*
Kashatus, William C. *v.3 p.375*
Kashima, Tetsuden (Editor) *v.6 p.134*
Kashima, Tetsuden *v.6 p.115, p.134*
Kashiwahara, Yusen *v.6 p.221*
Kashua, Sayed *v.6 p.649*
Kaske, R. E., et al. *v.6 p.565, p.571*
Kaslow, Florence W. & Schwartz, Lita L. *v.5 p.640*
Kasper, Dennis L., et al. *v.5 p.515*
Kasper, Sherryl *v.4 p.240*
Kasper, Walter *v.1 p.641*
Kass, Leon R. *v.5 p.248*
Kass, Leon *v.5 p.158*
Kassanoff, Jennie A. *v.2 p.131*
Kassarjian, Harold H. & Robertson, Thomas S. *v.5 p.586*
Kassay, John *v.1 p.804*
Kassem, Maye *v.4 p.500, p.611*
Kasser, Susan A. & Lytle, Rebecca K. *v.4 p.801*
Kasser, Tim & Kanner, Allen (Editors) *v.5 p.586*
Kasser, Tim *v.5 p.586*
Kassimeris, George *v.4 p.659*
Kassis, Hanna E. *v.1 p.556*
Kasson, John F. *v.3 p.409*
Kassow, Samuel D. *v.3 p.220*
Kastenbaum, Robert J. *v.5 p.627*
Kastner, Jeffrey *v.1 p.679*
Kastner, Victoria *v.1 p.793*
Kasza, Gregory J. *v.4 p.510*
Kataev, Valentin *v.2 p.805*
Katchmer, George A. *v.6 p.324*
Kateb, Yacine *v.2 p.545*
Kater, Michael H. *v.1 p.246, v.3 p.172, v.4 p.609*
Katerberg, William H. *v.1 p.582*
Kates, Robert William *v.4 p.395*
Kates, Steven M. *v.6 p.382*
Kathryl Wolff, Susan M. O'Connell, and Valerie J. Montenegro,
    comp. and ed. *v.5 p.405*
Kato, Shuichi *v.6 p.221*

Katouzian, Homa *v.6 p.629, p.631*
Katritzky, Alan R. & Rees, C. W. (Editors) *v.5 p.298*
Katritzky, Alan R. (Editor), et al. *v.5 p.294*
Katritzky, Alan R. *v.5 p.298*
Katsaros, John & Christy, Peter *v.4 p.82*
Katsh, M. Ethan *v.4 p.445*
Katsu Kokichi *v.6 p.227*
Kattan, Naim *v.2 p.540*
Kattenburg, Paul M. *v.3 p.389*
Katz, Alfred H. (Editor) *v.5 p.669*
Katz, Alfred H. *v.5 p.669*
Katz, Cathie *v.5 p.222*
Katz, Daniel & Kahn, Robert L. *v.4 p.716*
Katz, David & Spillman, Rob *v.1 p.292*
Katz, Donald *v.4 p.884, p.888*
Katz, Elihu & Wedell, George *v.4 p.412*
Katz, Ephraim *v.6 p.307*
Katz, Friedrich *v.3 p.293*
Katz, Harry C. (Editor) *v.4 p.419*
Katz, Helen E. *v.4 p.427*
Katz, J. J. (Editor), et al. *v.5 p.308*
Katz, J J; Seaborg, Glenn Theodore; Morss, L R . . . *v.5 p.308*
Katz, Jacob *v.1 p.199, p.300, p.365, v.3 p.59, p.178*
Katz, James E. *v.5 p.388, p.393, p.412*
Katz, Jonathan I. *v.5 p.68*
Katz, Jonathan N. (Editor) *v.6 p.359, p.363*
Katz, Jonathan N. *v.6 p.357, p.360, p.372*
Katz, Jonathan Ned *v.6 p.363*
Katz, Jonathan *v.3 p.431*
Katz, Mark N. *v.4 p.497*
Katz, Mark *v.1 p.167, p.387, p.390*
Katz, Michael & Thornton, Dorothy *v.5 p.707*
Katz, Michael B. *v.4 p.758*
Katz, Richard S. *v.4 p.579*
Katz, Sali B. *v.1 p.804*
Katz, Samuel L., et al. *v.5 p.532*
Katz, Sheila H. *v.6 p.610*
Katz, Sidney A. & Salem, Harry *v.5 p.313*
Katz, Solomon H. & Weaver, William Woys (Editors) . . *v.5 p.34*
Katz, Steven T. (Editor) *v.1 p.531*
Katz, Steven T. *v.1 p.531*
Katz, Steven *v.6 p.347*
Katz, Tamar *v.2 p.191*
Katz, Victor & Michalowica, Karen Dee (Editors) . *v.5 p.463, p.467*
Katz, Victor J. *v.5 p.466*
Katz, Vincent *v.1 p.757*
Katz, William Loren *v.6 p.7*
Katzenbach, Jon R. & Smith, Douglas K. *v.4 p.80*
Katzenbach, Rolf & Turek, Jens (Editors) *v.5 p.698*
Katzenberg, M. Anne & Saunders, Shelley R. (Editors) . *v.4 p.14*
Katzenstein, Mary F. & Reppy, Judith
    (Editors) *v.4 p.717, v.6 p.390*
Katzenstein, Mary F. *v.4 p.745, v.6 p.431*
Katzenstein, Peter J. (Editor), et al. *v.4 p.624, p.629*

Katzenstein, Peter J. *v.4 p.609*

Ka-Tzetnik *v.6 p.649*

Katzew, Ilona *v.3 p.263*

Katzmann, Gary S. (Editor) *v.6 p.248*

Katzmann, Robert A. *v.4 p.537*

Katznelson, Ira *v.4 p.511, v.6 p.723*

Kauders, Anthony D. *v.3 p.59*

Kauders, Anthony *v.3 p.180*

Kauffman, Bill *v.4 p.486*

Kauffman, Kyle Dean (Editor) *v.5 p.14*

Kauffman, Stuart A. *v.5 p.127*

Kauffmann, Jean-Paul *v.3 p.152*

Kauffmann, Norman L., et al. *v.4 p.313*

Kaufman, Alan & Griffin, S. A. (Editors) *v.2 p.23*

Kaufman, Andrew L. *v.4 p.468*

Kaufman, Bob *v.2 p.91, p.147*

Kaufman, Bruce E. & Taras, Daphne Gottlieb (Editors) . *v.4 p.122*

Kaufman, Burton I. *v.3 p.473*

Kaufman, David *v.6 p.413*

Kaufman, Edy *v.3 p.354*

Kaufman, Gordon D. *v.1 p.639*

Kaufman, Heidi & Fauske, Christopher J. *v.2 p.286*

Kaufman, Herbert *v.5 p.38*

Kaufman, Ilana (Editor) *v.6 p.614*

Kaufman, James A. (Editor) *v.5 p.266*

Kaufman, Leonard & Rousseeuw, Peter J. *v.4 p.689*

Kaufman, Roy S. *v.1 p.827*

Kaufman, Sharon R. *v.5 p.532*

Kaufmann, Jerome E. & Schwitters, Karen L. *v.5 p.472*

Kaufmann, Karen M. *v.4 p.544*

Kaufmann, Thomas DaCosta *v.1 p.687*

Kaufmann, Walter A. *v.1 p.466*

Kaufmann, Walter *v.1 p.505*

Kaufmann, Yehezkel *v.1 p.547*

Kaul, Asha *v.4 p.423*

Kaul, H. K. (Editor) *v.6 p.161*

Kaup, Monika *v.6 p.486, p.500, p.513*

Kaur, Amarjit *v.6 p.172*

Kaushik, Asha *v.2 p.762*

Kausler, Donald H. & Kausler, Barry C. *v.4 p.677*

Kauss, David *v.5 p.582*

Kautmann, Walter (Translator) *v.1 p.466*

Kautsky, Karl *v.4 p.214*

Kavanagh, Barry F. *v.4 p.389*

Kavanagh, Julie *v.6 p.414*

Kavanaugh, Kieran & Rodriguez, Otilio (Translators) . *v.1 p.571*

Kavanaugh, Kieran *v.1 p.571*

Kaveh, A. *v.5 p.695*

Kaveney, Roz *v.6 p.318*

Kavenik, Frances M. *v.2 p.187*

Kawabata, Yasunari *v.6 p.230*

Kawakami, Barbara F. *v.6 p.87, p.132*

Kawanishi, Hirosuke *v.4 p.126*

Kay, B. H. *v.5 p.703*

Kay, George R. *v.2 p.700*

Kay, Lily E. *v.5 p.122*

Kay, Paul *v.4 p.27*

Kay, Robert & Alder, Jackie *v.6 p.283*

Kay, Sarah *v.2 p.467*

Kayal, Philip M. *v.4 p.779, v.6 p.379*

Kayali, Hasan *v.6 p.593*

Kayden, Jerold S., et al. *v.6 p.726*

Kaye, G. W. C. & Laby, T. H. *v.5 p.281*

Kaye, Nick *v.1 p.86, p.135*

Kayne, Richard S. & Zanuttini, Raffaella (Editors) . *v.2 p.561*

Kays, W. M., et al. *v.5 p.560*

Kazarinoff, Nicholas D. *v.5 p.498*

Kazdin, Alan E. *v.5 p.594*

Kazepov, Yuri (Editor) *v.6 p.723*

Kazin, Alfred & Solotaroff, Ted *v.2 p.91*

Kazin, Alfred *v.2 p.4, p.575*

Kazuko, Ono *v.6 p.454*

Kean, Thomas H. & Hamilton, Lee *v.4 p.564, p.659*

Keane, Christopher *v.6 p.352*

Keane, John *v.4 p.498*

Keane, Molly *v.2 p.360*

Keane, Robert N. (Editor) *v.2 p.321*

Kearey, P., et al. *v.5 p.445*

Kearney, Colbert *v.2 p.373*

Kearney, Leslie (Editor) *v.1 p.199, p.362*

Kearney, Milo & Medrano, Manuel *v.6 p.486, p.534*

Kearney, Nolan Charles *v.4 p.364*

Kearney, Richard (Editor) *v.1 p.438*

Kearns, George *v.2 p.111*

Kearon, John *v.2 p.636*

Kearsley,Greg *v.4 p.357*

Keasey, Kevin (Editor), et al. *v.4 p.86*

Keates, Jonathan *v.2 p.501*

Keating, AnaLouise & Anzaldúa, Gloria (Editors) . . *v.6 p.479*

Keating, AnaLouise *v.6 p.479*

Keating, Elizabeth A. *v.4 p.21*

Keating, Michael *v.4 p.607*

Keating, Peter (Editor) *v.6 p.742, p.761*

Keating, Peter *v.6 p.740, p.741*

Keating, Sarah B. *v.5 p.529*

Keating, Tom *v.3 p.541*

Keats, John *v.2 p.295*

Keaveney, Arthur *v.3 p.26*

Keay, S. J. *v.3 p.237*

Kechichian, Joseph A. *v.6 p.626, p.627*

Keck, Leander E. (Editor), et al. *v.1 p.615*

Keck, Margaret E. & Sikkink, Kathryn *v.4 p.640*

Keck, Margaret E. *v.3 p.341*

Keck, Robert & Patterson, Richard R. *v.5 p.91*

Keck, Thomas M. *v.4 p.470, p.537*

Kedar, Benjamin Z. *v.6 p.556*

Keddie, Nikki R. & Baron, Beth (Editors) . . *v.6 p.454, p.593*

Keddie, Nikki R. & Richard, Yann *v.6 p.631*

Keddie, Nikki R. *v.1 p.555*

Kedlaya, Kiran S., et al. *v.5 p.458*

Kedourie, Elie & Haim, Sylvia G. (Editors) *v.6 p.610*
Kedourie, Elie *v.4 p.614*
Kedourie, Sylvia (Editor) *v.6 p.624*
Kedward, H. R. (Harry Roderick) *v.3 p.140*
Kedward, Harry R. *v.3 p.156*
Kee, Howard C. *v.1 p.655*
Kee, Howard Clark *v.1 p.615*
Kee, Joyce LeFever *v.5 p.527*
Keech, William R. *v.4 p.214*
Keefe, James W. & Jenkins, John M. *v.4 p.349*
Keefe, Simon P. (Editor) *v.1 p.190, p.240, p.344*
Keefe, Susan E. & Padilla, Amado M. *v.6 p.544*
Keegan, John *v.3 p.36, v.6 p.567*
Keegan, Lynn & Dossey, Barbara Montgomery *v.5 p.529*
Keegan, Timothy J. *v.6 p.79*
Keeling, Richard *v.1 p.167, p.296*
Keen, Ernest *v.5 p.596*
Keen, Maurice H. *v.6 p.568*
Keen, Maurice *v.6 p.556*
Keen, Mike Forrest & Mucha, Janusz L. (Editors) . . *v.4 p.683*
Keen, Mike Forrest *v.4 p.683*
Keenan, Alan *v.4 p.504*
Keenan, Andrea & Georges, Danielle . *v.4 p.63, p.158, v.5 p.685*
Keenan, Jeremy *v.6 p.60*
Keenan, Philip E. (Photographer,
    Text by) *v.5 p.84, p.87, p.215, p.229*
Keene, Donald (Translator) *v.6 p.230*
Keene, Donald *v.1 p.132, p.134, v.6 p.227, p.230, p.234*
Keene, Manuel & Kaoukji, Salam *v.1 p.715*
Keener, James, et al. *v.5 p.502*
Keeney, Gavin *v.1 p.813*
Keenoy, Ray & Brown, Saskia (Editors) *v.2 p.698*
Kees, Weldon *v.2 p.91*
Keesing, Roger M. *v.1 p.544*
Keeves, John P. (Editor) *v.4 p.286, p.355*
Kefauver, Alan P. *v.1 p.387*
Kegan, Robert *v.5 p.627*
Kegley, Charles W. Jr. *v.1 p.581*
Kehoe, Alice B. *v.4 p.22*
Kehoe, Alice Beck *v.1 p.542, v.4 p.36*
Kehoe, Vincent J. *v.6 p.351*
Keiger, John *v.3 p.141*
Keightley, David N. *v.6 p.184*
Keil, Charles & Feld, Steven *v.1 p.377, p.381*
Keil, Charles, et al. *v.1 p.296, p.381*
Keil, Charles *v.1 p.260*
Keillor, Garrison (Selected by, Introduction by) . . . *v.2 p.23*
Keillor, Garrison *v.2 p.23, p.147*
Keiser, Richard A. *v.4 p.555, p.573*
Keister, Lisa A. *v.4 p.245, p.265*
Keith, A. B. (Editor) *v.1 p.536*
Keith, A. M. *v.2 p.425, p.426*
Keith, Jennie *v.4 p.742*
Keith, Lawrence H. & Walters, Douglas B. *v.5 p.744*
Keith, Lawrence H. (Editor) *v.5 p.268*

Keith-Smith, Brian *v.2 p.603*
Kekes, John *v.4 p.511*
Kelemen, R. Daniel *v.4 p.637*
Kelen, Leslie G. & Stone, Eileen Hallet *v.3 p.529*
Kelertas, Violeta (Editor) *v.2 p.781*
Kelidar, Abbas R. (Editor) *v.6 p.603*
Keljik, Jeff *v.5 p.725*
Kelleghan, Fiona (Editor) *v.2 p.580*
Kelleher, Margaret & O'Leary, Philip (Editors) . . . *v.2 p.163*
Kellenbenz, Hermann *v.3 p.40*
Keller, Edward A. *v.5 p.423*
Keller, Edward B. & Berry, Jonathan L. *v.4 p.145*
Keller, Evelyn F. & Longino, Helen E. (Editors) . . *v.6 p.439*
Keller, Evelyn F. *v.5 p.403*
Keller, Evelyn Fox & Winship, L. L. *v.5 p.134*
Keller, Gary D. & Candelaria, Cordelia (Editors) . . *v.6 p.534*
Keller, Gary D. (Editor) *v.6 p.500, p.513*
Keller, Gary D., et al. *v.6 p.492*
Keller, Gary D. *v.6 p.489, p.493*
Keller, Gary, et al. *v.6 p.492*
Keller, George *v.4 p.293*
Keller, Gerald *v.4 p.178*
Keller, Gottfried *v.2 p.600*
Keller, Helen *v.4 p.337*
Keller, Hermann *v.1 p.184, p.401*
Keller, James R. & Stratyner, Leslie (Editors) . *v.6 p.326, p.419*
Keller, James R. *v.6 p.419*
Keller, Judith *v.1 p.767*
Keller, Laurent (Editor) *v.5 p.193*
Keller, Mary *v.1 p.527*
Keller, Morton *v.3 p.437*
Keller, Nora (Editor) *v.6 p.91, p.135*
Keller, Nora O. *v.6 p.100*
Keller, Rosemary Skinner (Editor), et al. . . . *v.1 p.528*
Keller, Rosemary Skinner, et al. *v.1 p.543, p.605*
Keller, Rosemary Skinner *v.1 p.605*
Keller, Shoshana *v.3 p.230*
Keller, Suzanne *v.4 p.724*
Kellerman, Barbara & Barilleaux, Ryan J. *v.4 p.527*
Kellerman, Barbara *v.4 p.697*
Kellerman, Henry (Editor) *v.5 p.613*
Kelley, Alice V. *v.2 p.392*
Kelley, Amy *v.3 p.98*
Kelley, Beverly Merrill *v.6 p.342*
Kelley, Christopher S. (Editor) *v.4 p.527*
Kelley, David & Khalfa, Jean (Translators) . . . *v.2 p.464*
Kelley, David H. & Milone, E. F. *v.5 p.63*
Kelley, Donald R. *v.4 p.598*
Kelley, Edith S. *v.2 p.91*
Kelley, Harold H., et al. *v.5 p.648*
Kelley, Larry D. & Jugenheimer, Donald W. . . . *v.4 p.428*
Kelley, Mark R. (Editor), et al. *v.2 p.254*
Kelley, Ninette & Trebilcock, Michael J. *v.4 p.764*
Kelley, Robin D. *v.4 p.508, p.553*
Kelling, George H. *v.3 p.197*

Kellison, Stephen G. *v.5 p.504*

Kellman, Steven G. *v.2 p.113*

Kellner, George & Lemons, J. Stanley *v.3 p.489*

Kellner, Menachem M *v.1 p.552*

Kellner, R. (Editor) *v.5 p.273*

Kellogg, Frederick *v.3 p.250*

Kellogg, Louise Phelps *v.3 p.512*

Kellogg, Louise T. *v.3 p.517*

Kellogg, Michael *v.4 p.711*

Kellogg, Susan *v.3 p.286*

Kellogg, William W. & Schware, Robert . . . *v.5 p.355, p.371*

Kelloway, E. Kevin (Editor), et al. *v.4 p.130*

Kelly, A.F. *v.5 p.47*

Kelly, Aileen *v.2 p.798*

Kelly, Alfred H. *v.3 p.49, p.164*

Kelly, Andrew *v.6 p.322*

Kelly, Anita E. *v.5 p.646*

Kelly, Ann Cline *v.2 p.263*

Kelly, Anthony *v.4 p.83*

Kelly, Barbara L. *v.1 p.217, p.341*

Kelly, Brigit Pegeen *v.2 p.148*

Kelly, Caroline & Breinlinger, Sara *v.5 p.648*

Kelly, Catriona & Lovell, Stephen (Editors) *v.2 p.798*

Kelly, Catriona (Editor) *v.2 p.794*

Kelly, Catriona *v.2 p.798, v.3 p.210*

Kelly, Christine *v.4 p.711*

Kelly, Christopher *v.3 p.31*

Kelly, David H. & Kelly, Gail P. *v.4 p.314*

Kelly, Deirdre A. (Editor) *v.5 p.519*

Kelly, Deirdre *v.4 p.299*

Kelly, Douglas *v.2 p.457*

Kelly, Gail, et al. *v.6 p.425*

Kelly, Gail P. (Editor) *v.4 p.301, p.313, p.314*

Kelly, Henry Ansgar . . . *v.1 p.56, p.70, p.71, p.72, p.73, p.88*

Kelly, J. N. D. *v.1 p.633*

Kelly, J. N. *v.1 p.613, p.646, v.6 p.571*

Kelly, James G. *v.5 p.671*

Kelly, John M. *v.4 p.434*

Kelly, John *v.5 p.532*

Kelly, Katherine E. (Editor) *v.2 p.384*

Kelly, Kevin *v.6 p.414*

Kelly, Luke E. & Melograno, Vincent J. *v.4 p.795*

Kelly, Luke E. (Editor) *v.4 p.801*

Kelly, Marjorie (Editor) *v.1 p.557*

Kelly, Mary J. (Editor), et al. *v.4 p.415*

Kelly, Michael (Editor) *v.1 p.479*

Kelly, Rosemary *v.2 p.351*

Kelly, Thomas Forrest *v.1 p.174, p.230*

Kelly, Thomas *v.3 p.16*

Kelman, James *v.2 p.360*

Kelsen, Hans *v.4 p.477*

Kelsey, David H. *v.1 p.638*

Kelsey, W. Michael *v.6 p.230*

Kelsky, Karen *v.6 p.448, p.454, p.479*

Kelso, J. R. & Hartig, J. H. (Editors) *v.5 p.174, p.234*

Kemal, Salim & Gaskell, Ivan (Editors) *v.1 p.703*

Kemal, Salim *v.1 p.481*

Kemal, Yashar (Author, Introduction by) *v.6 p.667*

Kemal, Yashar *v.6 p.667*

Kembhavi, Ajit K. & Narlikar, Jayant V. *v.5 p.71*

Kemble, John H. *v.3 p.304*

Kemeny, John G., et al. *v.5 p.478*

Kemeny, John G. *v.5 p.403*

Kemerling, Garth *v.1 p.415*

Kemmis, Daniel *v.6 p.300*

Kemp, Anthony E. *v.1 p.376, v.5 p.619*

Kemp, Barry J. *v.4 p.8*

Kemp, Charles & Rasbridge, Lance *v.4 p.668*

Kemp, Ian (Editor) *v.1 p.199, p.230, p.310*

Kemp, Martin *v.1 p.742, v.5 p.397*

Kemp, Peter *v.2 p.319*

Kemp, Roger L. (Editor) *v.1 p.826*

Kemp, Sandra (Editor), et al. *v.2 p.194*

Kemp, Sandra *v.2 p.296*

Kemp, Sid *v.4 p.73*

Kemp, Steven M. & Kemp, Sid *v.4 p.179*

Kemp, Tom *v.5 p.448*

Kempadoo, Kamala & Doezema, Jo *v.6 p.457, p.470*

Kempe, Margery B. *v.1 p.653, v.2 p.206, p.207, v.3 p.57*

Kempe, Margery *v.2 p.206*

Kemper, Robert V. & Royce, Anya Peterson (Editors) . *v.4 p.25*

Kemper, Steve *v.5 p.716*

Kempfert, Hans-Georg & Gebreselassie, Berhane . . . *v.5 p.699*

Kempf-Leonard, Kimberly (Editor-In-Chief) *v.4 p.677*

Kempton, Willett M., et al. *v.4 p.30*

Kenaz, Yehoshua *v.6 p.649*

Kendall, Elisabeth *v.6 p.654*

Kendall, Elizabeth *v.1 p.9, p.26, v.6 p.313*

Kendall, John S. and Marzano, Robert J. *v.4 p.359*

Kendall, Maurice *v.5 p.64, p.482*

Kendall, Richard *v.1 p.45, p.742*

Kendall-Tackett, Kathleen A. *v.5 p.660*

Kendon, Adam *v.4 p.22*

Kendrew, John & Lawrence, Elleanor (Editors) . . . *v.5 p.325*

Kendrick, David, et al. *v.4 p.202*

Kendrick, John *v.3 p.73, p.240*

Kendrick, Laura *v.1 p.719*

Kendrick, Robert L. *v.1 p.184, p.379*

Keneally, Thomas *v.2 p.746, v.4 p.517*

Kenez, Peter *v.3 p.222*

Kengor, Paul & Schweizer, Peter *v.3 p.473*

Kenkel, John V., et al. *v.5 p.267*

Kenkel, John V. *v.5 p.274*

Kennan, George F. *v.3 p.211, p.389, p.452, p.459, p.473*

Kennan, George Frost *v.3 p.459, p.473*

Kennan, Kent *v.1 p.371*

Kenneally, James J. *v.1 p.573, p.605*

Kennedy, Adrienne *v.1 p.121*

Kennedy, B. A. (Editor) *v.5 p.738*

Kennedy, Charles H. (Editor), et al. *v.6 p.162*

Kennedy, Charles W. *v.2 p.197*
Kennedy, Dane. *v.6 p.157*
Kennedy, David M. *v.3 p.442, p.448, p.473*
Kennedy, Dennis (Editor) . . *v.1 p.59, p.76, p.101, p.135, p.140*
Kennedy, Donald. *v.4 p.293*
Kennedy, Duncan F. *v.2 p.426*
Kennedy, Elizabeth L. & Davis, Madeline D. *v.6 p.365*
Kennedy, Ellen C. (Editor) *v.2 p.535*
Kennedy, George A. *v.1 p.625, v.2 p.405, p.427*
Kennedy, George Alexander. *v.2 p.427*
Kennedy, George E. & Montgomery, Tracy T. . . . *v.5 p.680*
Kennedy, Hubert *v.6 p.402*
Kennedy, Hugh & Barbir, Karl *v.6 p.585*
Kennedy, Hugh N. *v.6 p.585*
Kennedy, Hugh *v.3 p.65, p.237, v.6 p.585*
Kennedy, J. Gerald & Bryer, Jackson R. (Editors). *v.2 p.77, p.85*
Kennedy, J. Gerald & Weissberg, Liliane (Editors) . . . *v.2 p.50*
Kennedy, John F. *v.3 p.376*
Kennedy, John H. *v.6 p.41*
Kennedy, John Pendleton. *v.2 p.43*
Kennedy, Joseph *v.3 p.281*
Kennedy, Kenneth A. R. *v.4 p.15*
Kennedy, Liam. *v.6 p.718*
Kennedy, Mary L. (Editor) *v.2 p.565*
Kennedy, Mary M. (Editor) *v.4 p.348*
Kennedy, Michael *v.1 p.199, p.217, p.323, p.359, p.363, v.4 p.387*
Kennedy, Paul M. (Editor) *v.3 p.36*
Kennedy, Paul M. *v.3 p.36, p.91*
Kennedy, Peter. *v.4 p.202*
Kennedy, Randall *v.4 p.442, p.471*
Kennedy, Richard *v.2 p.68*
Kennedy, Rick & McNutt, Randy *v.1 p.384*
Kennedy, Robert F.. . . . . *v.3 p.389, p.473*
Kennedy, Roger G. *v.5 p.5*
Kennedy, Scott *v.3 p.390, v.4 p.145*
Kennedy, Susan E. *v.6 p.454*
Kennedy, William *v.2 p.147*
Kennedy-Glans, Donna & Schulz, Robert *v.4 p.86*
Kennelly, Brendan (Editor) *v.2 p.200*
Kenner, Hugh (Editor) *v.2 p.72*
Kenner, Hugh *v.2 p.111, p.178, p.359*
Kenneth Thompson. *v.4 p.685*
Kennett, Jiyu. *v.1 p.568*
Kenney, Dennis Jay & Finckenauer, James O. . . . *v.6 p.251*
Kenney, Edwin J. & Clausen, W. V. (Editors). . . . *v.2 p.425*
Kenney, George C. *v.1 p.757*
Kenney, Padraic *v.3 p.208*
Kenney, Patrick J. & Kahn, Kim Fridkin *v.4 p.530*
Kennington, Richard, et al. *v.1 p.437*
Kennon, Donald R.. . . . . *v.4 p.533*
Kenny, Anthony (Editor) *v.1 p.417*
Kenny, Anthony John Patrick *v.1 p.420*
Kenny, Anthony *v.1 p.432, p.472, p.579, p.639, v.2 p.278, v.3 p.100*

Kenny, Judith T. & Fyfe, Nicholas (Editors). *v.4 p.395, v.6 p.721*
Kenny, Kevin *v.3 p.134, v.4 p.126*
Kenny, Peter M., et al. *v.1 p.802, p.804*
Kenoyer, Jonathan M.. . . . . . . *v.4 p.9, v.6 p.150, p.713*
Kenrick, Paul & Crane, Peter R.. . . . . *v.5 p.449*
Kenrick, Paul & Davis, Paul *v.5 p.449*
Kenstowicz, Michael J. *v.2 p.562*
Kent, Allegra. *v.1 p.9*
Kent, Ann. *v.4 p.513, p.620*
Kent, David A. (Editor). *v.2 p.303*
Kent, Eliza F. *v.6 p.459*
Kent, George C. & Carr, Robert K. *v.5 p.157*
Kent, George E.. . . . . *v.2 p.64*
Kent, James *v.4 p.441*
Kent, Kathryn R. *v.2 p.6, p.11*
Kent, Michael *v.4 p.825, p.873*
Kent, Neil *v.1 p.687*
Kent, Raymond D. (Editor). *v.5 p.621, p.665, p.673*
Kent, Robert B. *v.4 p.397*
Kent, Stephen *v.4 p.710*
Kent, Susan K.. . . . . *v.3 p.53, p.92*
Kentgens-Craig, Margret *v.1 p.786*
Kentula, Mary E., et al. *v.5 p.173, p.179, p.242*
Kenyatta, Jomo *v.6 p.65*
Kenyon, Amy Maria *v.6 p.713*
Kenyon, Cecelia M. (Editor) *v.4 p.518*
Kenyon, Daphne A. & Kincaid, John (Editors) . . . *v.4 p.524*
Kenyon, J. P. (John Philipps) *v.3 p.105, p.121*
Kenyon, John S. *v.2 p.557*
Kenyon, Nicholas (Editor) *v.1 p.401*
Keogh, Dermot F. (Editor) *v.3 p.300, p.344*
Keogh, Dermot. *v.3 p.138*
Keohane, Alan *v.6 p.600*
Keohane, Robert O. & Levy, Marc A. (Editors) . . . *v.4 p.666*
Keohane, Robert O. & Nye, Joseph S. *v.4 p.626*
Keohane, Robert O. *v.4 p.626, p.663, p.664*
Kepel, Gilles *v.6 p.593, p.638*
Kepler, Johannes *v.5 p.61*
Keppie, Lawrence J.. . . . . *v.3 p.22*
Keppie, Lawrence *v.3 p.28*
Ker, Ian (Editor) *v.1 p.572*
Kerans, David *v.3 p.217*
Kerbel, Matthew Robert *v.4 p.527*
Kerber, Linda K. & Kessler-Harris, Alice (Editors) . . *v.6 p.450*
Kerber, Linda K. (Author, Editor) *v.6 p.450*
Kerber, Linda K.. . . . . *v.6 p.441, p.450*
Kerchache, Jacques, et al.. . . . . *v.1 p.777*
Kerensky, Oleg. *v.2 p.188*
Kerenyi, Carl *v.1 p.532*
Kerényi, Karl & Holme, Christopher. *v.1 p.532*
Kerferd, George B. *v.1 p.427*
Kerkering, John D. *v.2 p.9*
Kerkhoff, Blair. *v.4 p.905*
Kerkvliet, Benedict J.. . . . . *v.6 p.179*
Kerman, Cynthia E. & Eldridge, Richard. *v.2 p.126*

Kerman, Joseph . . *v.1 p.173, p.185, p.230, p.240, p.247, p.303*

Kermode, Anita *v.2 p.203*

Kermode, Frank (Editor) *v.2 p.200*

Kermode, Frank *v.1 p.67, p.74, p.76, p.101,
p.632, v.2 p.230, p.568*

Kern, Edith *v.2 p.527*

Kern, Kathi *v.6 p.431, p.459*

Kernan, Alvin *v.2 p.250, v.3 p.120*

Kernfeld, Barry D. & Kernfeld, Barry (Editors). *v.1 p.160, p.260*

Kernfeld, Barry D. *v.1 p.170, p.260*

Kernighan, Brian W. & Ritchie, Dennis M. *v.5 p.347*

Kernodle, Tammy L. *v.1 p.260, p.368*

Kerns, Virginia *v.4 p.4*

Kerolgue, Fiona *v.1 p.692*

Kerouac, Jack *v.2 p.93*

Kerr, Anne *v.5 p.140*

Kerr, Clark & Gade, Marian L. *v.4 p.293*

Kerr, Clark *v.4 p.290*

Kerr, David (Editor) *v.1 p.130*

Kerr, Elizabeth M. *v.2 p.74*

Kerr, George H. *v.6 p.235*

Kerr, James L. *v.2 p.307*

Kerr, John *v.4 p.802, p.817*

Kerr, M. E. *v.6 p.379, p.397*

Kerr, Mary Margaret & Nelson, C. Michael *v.4 p.284*

Kerrane, Kevin & Yagoda, Ben (Editors) *v.4 p.403*

Kerrigan, Anthony (Editor) *v.2 p.678*

Kerrigan, William *v.2 p.230*

Kerry, K. R. & Hempel, G. (Editors) *v.5 p.180, p.238*

Kershaw, Baz & Milling, Jane (Editors) . *v.2 p.185, p.186, p.187*

Kershaw, Baz (Editor) *v.2 p.188*

Kershaw, Ian *v.3 p.84, p.172*

Kershner, Bruce & Leverett, Robert T. *v.5 p.38*

Kersnowski, Frank L. (Editor) *v.2 p.348*

Kersnowski, Frank L. *v.2 p.348*

Kertesz, Louise *v.2 p.113*

Kertész, Imre *v.2 p.786*

Kerth, Thomas & Schoolfield, George (Editors) . . . *v.2 p.594*

Kertzer, David I. *v.3 p.59, p.201, v.4 p.594, p.765*

Kerwin, Cornelius M. *v.4 p.463*

Kesey, Ken *v.2 p.148*

Kesler, Stephen E. *v.5 p.738*

Kessel, Joseph *v.2 p.521*

Kesselring, Joseph *v.2 p.92*

Kessen, William (Editor), et al. *v.5 p.605*

Kessler, David P. & Greenkorn, Robert A. *v.5 p.743*

Kessler, David *v.4 p.449, v.5 p.532*

Kessler, Francis P. *v.4 p.527*

Kessler, Lauren *v.6 p.134*

Kessler, Rachael *v.4 p.357, p.364*

Kesteloot, Lilyan *v.2 p.535, p.537*

Kesten, Seymour R. *v.4 p.499*

Kestenbaum, Justin L. (Editor) *v.3 p.516*

Kester, Gerard & Sidibe, Ousmane O. *v.4 p.122*

Kester, Norman G. (Editor) *v.6 p.383*

Kester-Shelton, Pamela *v.6 p.479*

Ketcham, Katherine, et al. *v.5 p.673*

Ketcham, Michael G. *v.2 p.258, p.261*

Ketcham, Ralph Louis *v.3 p.368, v.4 p.504*

Ketcham, Ralph *v.3 p.417*

Ketner, Joseph D. *v.1 p.705*

Keto, C. Tsehloane *v.6 p.14*

Ketterer, David *v.2 p.729*

Ketterson, John B. (Editor) *v.5 p.565*

Kettle, S. F. *v.5 p.303*

Kettle, Sidney F. *v.5 p.276*

Keuls, Eva C. *v.3 p.14*

Keuth, Herbert *v.1 p.445*

Keuzenkamp, Hugo A. *v.4 p.202*

Keve, Paul W. *v.6 p.273, p.275*

Key, V. O. Jr. *v.3 p.496*

Keyes, Cheryl L. *v.1 p.270*

Keyes, Corey L. M. & Haidt, Jonathan (Editors) . . . *v.5 p.670*

Keyes, Daniel C. (Editor), et al. *v.5 p.532*

Keyes, Daniel *v.2 p.148*

Keyes, George S. (Editor) *v.1 p.675, p.687*

Keyes, Roger *v.3 p.206*

Keyfitz, Nathan *v.5 p.502*

Keyishian, Harry (Editor) *v.2 p.118*

Keylor, William R. *v.4 p.628*

Keymer, Thomas & Mee, Jon (Editors) *v.2 p.172*

Keymer, Thomas (Editor) *v.2 p.262*

Keynes, John Maynard . . . *v.1 p.495, v.3 p.79, v.4 p.193, p.228*

Keynes, R. D. & Darwin, Charles *v.5 p.231*

Keynes, R. D. *v.5 p.233*

Keynes, Randal *v.5 p.222*

Keyser, Daniel J. & Sweetland, Richard C. (Editors) . *v.5 p.601*

Keyssar, Alexander *v.4 p.519*

Köchel, Ludwig *v.1 p.164, p.190, p.344*

Körner, Christian & Schulze, Ernst-Detlef
(Editors) *v.5 p.176, p.180*

Körner, T. W. *v.5 p.459*

Khadduri, Majid *v.6 p.603, p.641*

Khaitov, Nikolai *v.2 p.780*

Khakhina, Liya N. *v.5 p.193*

Khalaf, Samir *v.6 p.605*

Khaldun, Ibn *v.6 p.585*

Khalidi, Rashid (Editor), et al. *v.6 p.583*

Khalidi, Rashid *v.4 p.641, v.6 p.618*

Khalidi, Tarif *v.6 p.585*

Khalidi, Walid & Khalidi, Muhammad A. (Editors) . *v.6 p.618*

Khalidi, Walid *v.6 p.618*

Khalifeh, Sahar *v.6 p.661*

Khalil, Elias L. (Editor) *v.4 p.195*

Khan, Badruddin *v.6 p.367*

Khan, Badrul Huda *v.4 p.322*

Khan, Muhammad Akram *v.4 p.190*

Kharasch, Morris Selig and Otto Reinmuth *v.5 p.295*

Kharms, Daniil & Vvedensky, Alexander *v.2 p.794*

Khater, Akram Fouad *v.6 p.605*

Khayyam, Omar *v.6 p.671*

Khazanov, Anatoly M. *v.4 p.708*

Khilnani, Sunil *v.3 p.157, p.158*

Khlebnikov, Velimir *v.2 p.805*

Khlevniuk, Oleg V. *v.3 p.226*

Khodarkovsky, Michael *v.3 p.213*

Khomeini, Iman *v.6 p.632*

Khorrami, Mohammad Mehdi & Vatanabadi, Shouleh
(Editors) *v.6 p.671*

Khouri, Mounah A. & Algar, Hamid (Editor,
Translators) *v.6 p.661*

Khoury, Elias *v.6 p.661*

Khoury, Philip S. & Kostiner, Joseph (Editors) *v.6 p.593*

Khoury, Philip S. *v.6 p.607*

Khrushchev, Nikita Sergeevich & Khrushchev, Sergeaei
(Editors) *v.3 p.224*

Khusraw, Nasir-I *v.6 p.671*

Khwaja, Waqas A. (Editor) *v.2 p.760*

Kianush, Mahmud (Author, Translator) *v.6 p.672*

Kibert, Charles *v.1 p.796, v.4 p.158*

Kibler, William W. (Editor), et al. *v.3 p.141*

Kibler, William W. *v.2 p.453*

Kibria, Nazli *v.6 p.110, p.127, p.135, p.140*

Kicza, John E. (Editor) *v.3 p.298*

Kidd, Bruce *v.4 p.807, p.817*

Kidd, Sue Monk *v.2 p.160*

Kidder, Chris *v.3 p.502*

Kidder, Stanley Q. & Vonder Haar, Thomas H. . *v.5 p.367, p.371*

Kidder, Tracy *v.4 p.704*

Kidman, Fiona *v.2 p.747*

Kids First Staff *v.6 p.311*

Kidwell, Roland E. Jr. & Martin, Christopher L (Editors) . *v.4 p.131*

Kieckhefer, Richard & Bond, George D. (Editors) . . . *v.1 p.527*

Kieckhefer, Richard *v.6 p.569*

Kieff, F. Scott (Editor) *v.5 p.140*

Kieft, David Owen *v.3 p.206*

Kiel, Dyke & Adams, K. Gary *v.1 p.164, p.185, p.342*

Kielan-Jaworowska, Zofia, et al. *v.5 p.448*

Kiely, David M. *v.2 p.306*

Kienast, Dieter *v.1 p.813*

Kieniewicz, Stefan *v.3 p.253*

Kier, Elizabeth *v.3 p.74*

Kier, Kathleen E. (Compiled by) *v.2 p.48*

Kierkegaard, Soren *v.1 p.478, p.523, p.593, p.594, p.595,
p.643, p.650, p.652, v.2 p.627*

Kiernan, Ben (Introduction by) *v.4 p.653*

Kiernan, Ben *v.4 p.652, v.6 p.170*

Kiernan, Brian (Editor) *v.2 p.747*

Kiernan, Frances *v.2 p.99*

Kiernan, J. A. & Mason, I. (Editors) *v.5 p.86, p.159*

Kiernan, Kathy & Powers, Retha (Editors) *v.2 p.19*

Kiernan, Kevin S. *v.2 p.205*

Kiernan, Kevin. *v.2 p.204*

Kiernan, Robert F. *v.2 p.127*

Kiernan, V.G. *v.6 p.151*

Kiernan, Victor *v.3 p.78*

Kiers, Judikje & Tissink, Fieke *v.1 p.732*

Kiersch, George A. *v.5 p.421*

Kierszenbaum, Abraham L. *v.5 p.153, p.159*

Kiesling, Eugenia C. *v.3 p.155*

Kiesling, Stephen. *v.4 p.865*

Kiessling, Ann & Anderson, Scott C. *v.5 p.162*

Kiessling, Wolfgang; Flügel, Erik; Golonka, Jan . . . *v.5 p.438*

Kiev, Ari *v.6 p.523, p.551*

Kieval, Hillel J. *v.3 p.188, p.190*

Kievlenko Evgenii IAkovlevich *v.5 p.452*

Kiggundu, Moses N. *v.4 p.665*

Kikoski, Catherine Kano & Kikoski, John F. *v.4 p.79*

Kilbourn, William *v.3 p.539*

Kilcup, Karen *v.2 p.19, v.6 p.698*

Killam, Douglas & Rowe, Ruth (Editors) *v.2 p.750*

Killenbeck, Mark R. *v.4 p.524*

Killian, James R. Jr. *v.5 p.397*

Killingray, David (Editor), et al. *v.3 p.297*

Killingsworth, M. Jimmie *v.2 p.53*

Killingsworth, Mark R. *v.4 p.253*

Killoran, Helen. *v.2 p.131*

Kilminster, Richard *v.4 p.685*

Kilpatrick, Hilary. *v.6 p.661*

Kilpatrick, J Swafford. Findell, B. (eds.) *v.5 p.463*

Kilpatrick, Jacquelyn *v.6 p.700*

Kilpatrick, Jeremy (Editor), et al. *v.5 p.463*

Kilpatrick, Joel. *v.3 p.483*

Kilpatrick, Sarah *v.2 p.242*

Kilson, Marion *v.6 p.73*

Kim, Claire Jean. *v.6 p.123, p.135*

Kim, Elaine H. & Choi, Chungmoo (Editors) . . *v.6 p.112, p.135*

Kim, Elaine H. & Kang, Laura Hyun Yi (Editors) . *v.6 p.91, p.135*

Kim, Elaine H. & Lowe, Lisa (Editors) *v.6 p.108*

Kim, Elaine H. (Editor), et al. *v.6 p.91*

Kim, Elaine H., et al. *v.6 p.88*

Kim, Elaine M. & Yu, Eui-Young *v.6 p.94, p.135*

Kim, Elaine. *v.6 p.96*

Kim, Hunggyu *v.6 p.238*

Kim, Hyung-chan (Editor) *v.6 p.86*

Kim, Ilpyong J. *v.6 p.236*

Kim, Jaegwon & Sosa, Ernest (Editors) *v.1 p.488*

Kim, Jaegwon *v.1 p.497, p.509*

Kim, Kichung *v.6 p.238*

Kim, Kwang Chung & Warner, R. Stephen. . . *v.6 p.105, p.136*

Kim, Kwang Chung (Editor) *v.6 p.123, p.135*

Kim, Kyung Hyun *v.6 p.334*

Kim, Myung Mi *v.6 p.103*

Kim, Richard E. *v.2 p.760*

Kim, Ronyoung *v.6 p.100*

Kim, Suji Kwock. *v.2 p.160*

Kim, Sunhyuk *v.4 p.621*

Kimball, Arthur G. *v.6 p.230*

Kimball, Michelle & Von Schlegell, Barbara R. *v.6 p.459*

Kimball, Richard Ian *v.4 p.807, p.824*

Kimball, Robert & Berlin, Irving . *v.1 p.251, p.310, p.408, p.412*

Kimball, Robert & Nelson, Steve *v.1 p.251, p.408, p.412*

Kimball, Roger. *v.3 p.371*

Kimbell, David R. B. *v.1 p.199, p.230, p.231, p.246, p.308*

Kimble, Gregory A. *v.5 p.597*

Kimeldorf, Howard. *v.4 p.127*

Kimmel, Marek *v.5 p.154*

Kimmel, Michael (Editor). *v.4 p.677*

Kimmel, Michael S. & Aronson, Amy *v.6 p.425*

Kimmel, Michael S. & Ferber, Abby L. *v.4 p.724*

Kimmel, Michael S. *v.4 p.744, p.745, v.6 p.429*

Kimmerling, Baruch & Migdal, Joel S.. . . . . *v.6 p.618*

Kimmerling, Baruch *v.6 p.618*

Kimmins, J. P. *v.5 p.38*

Kimura, Doreen *v.5 p.608*

Kimura, Toshio, et al.. . . . . *v.5 p.432*

Kincaid, David & Cheney, E. W. *v.5 p.492*

Kincaid, Jamaica. *v.2 p.767, p.768*

Kincaid, James R. *v.2 p.316*

Kinch, John A.. . . . . *v.5 p.222*

Kincheloe, Joe L.. . . . . *v.4 p.355*

Kinchen, Oscar Arvle. *v.3 p.539*

Kindall, Jerry & Winkin, John (Editors) . . . *v.4 p.795, p.851*

Kindem, Gorham A. (Editor) *v.6 p.345*

Kinder, Marsha. *v.6 p.311*

Kinderman, William & Krebs, Harald (Editors) . *v.1 p.199, p.371*

Kinderman, William (Editor) *v.1 p.199, p.307*

Kinderman, William *v.1 p.199, p.240, p.307*

Kindi *v.6 p.635*

Kindleberger, Charles P. & Aliber,
Robert. *v.4 p.95, p.100, p.147, p.244, p.263*

Kindleberger, Charles P.. . . . . *v.4 p.244*

Kindlon, Daniel J., et al. *v.5 p.641*

Kindsvatter, Peter S. *v.3 p.383*

Kinealy, Christine *v.3 p.138*

King, Anthony *v.3 p.142, p.161, v.4 p.817, p.844, p.867*

King, B. B. & Ritz, David *v.1 p.260, p.335*

King, Barbara J. (Editor). *v.4 p.19*

King, Bruce *v.1 p.47, v.2 p.178, p.727, p.763*

King, C. Richard & Springwood, Charles F.
(Editors). *v.4 p.817, p.841*

King, C. Richard & Springwood, Charles
Fruehling *v.4 p.817, p.822, p.830, p.894*

King, C. Richard (Editor) *v.4 p.841*

King, Charles *v.3 p.230*

King, D. Brett & Wertheimer, Michael *v.5 p.597*

King, David C.. . . . . *v.4 p.524*

King, David *v.1 p.793*

King, Debra & Flam, Helena *v.4 p.694*

King, Desmond *v.4 p.524*

King, Emily *v.1 p.718*

King, F. H. *v.5 p.5, v.6 p.181, p.198, p.295*

King, Gary, et al.. . . . . *v.4 p.483*

King, Geoff & Krzywinska, Tanya *v.6 p.318*

King, Gillian A. (Editor), et al. *v.5 p.653*

King, Grace Eilzabeth *v.2 p.43*

King, Henry *v.2 p.245*

King, J. E. (Editor) *v.4 p.232*

King, J. E.. . . . . *v.4 p.269*

King, J. L. & Hunter, Karen. *v.4 p.750, v.6 p.369, p.375*

King, James R.. . . . . *v.4 p.278*

King, Jeremy *v.3 p.190*

King, Jerry P. *v.5 p.459*

King, John R. *v.2 p.644*

King, Joyce E. (Editor). *v.4 p.301, p.310, p.355*

King, Julia & Miletic-Vejzovic, Laila (Editors) . . . *v.2 p.392*

King, Karen L. (Editor) *v.1 p.528*

King, Karen L.. . . . . *v.1 p.646*

King, Kathleen P. *v.4 p.320*

King, Kenneth *v.1 p.28, p.30, p.42*

King, Kimball *v.1 p.101, p.115, v.2 p.188*

King, Lester J. & Opelka, James H. (Editors). . . . *v.5 p.744*

King, Margaret L. *v.3 p.52*

King, Martha *v.2 p.717*

King, Max *v.5 p.199*

King, Phillip B. *v.5 p.432*

King, R. Bruce (Editor), et al. *v.5 p.302*

King, R. Bruce (Editor). *v.5 p.302*

King, Richard A. (Editor), et al. *v.5 p.149*

King, Richard H. *v.2 p.14*

King, Richard *v.1 p.419, p.540*

King, Rita M. *v.5 p.245*

King, Robert C., et al. *v.5 p.134*

King, Ross *v.1 p.732, p.742, p.787, v.3 p.200*

King, Stephen A.. . . . . *v.1 p.292*

King, Stephen J. *v.4 p.585, p.611, v.6 p.641*

King, Stephen *v.2 p.148*

King, Terry A. & Smith, F. Graham. *v.5 p.73, p.561*

King, Thomas (Editor) *v.2 p.732, v.6 p.698*

King, Thomas R.. . . . . *v.6 p.418*

King, Victor T. & Wilder, William D. *v.4 p.39*

King, Woodie & Milner, Ron (Editors) *v.2 p.25*

King, Woodie (Editor) *v.2 p.26*

King, Woodie Jr. (Editor) *v.1 p.67, p.123*

Kingdon, David G. & Turkington, Douglas. . . *v.5 p.660, p.665*

Kingdon, Jonathan. *v.4 p.15*

Kingdon, Robert McCune. *v.3 p.145*

King-Hele, D. G.. . . . . *v.5 p.719*

King-Hele, Desmond G.. . . . . *v.2 p.311*

Kingman, Daniel *v.1 p.278*

King-Meadows, Tyson & Schaller, Thomas F.. . . . . *v.4 p.530*

Kingsbury, Damien *v.4 p.622, v.6 p.175, p.177*

Kingsbury, Jack D. *v.1 p.629*

Kingsbury, Paul (Editor) *v.1 p.160, p.270*

Kingsland, Sharon E. *v.5 p.184*

Kingsley, Charles & Hughes, Thomas *v.2 p.296*

Kingsley, Charles. *v.2 p.296*

Kingsley, Karen *v.1 p.790*

Kingsley, Peter. *v.1 p.421*

Kingsley, Z. *v.3 p.315*

Kingsolver, Barbara *v.2 p.148, v.5 p.234*

Kingston, Helen M. *v.5 p.149*

Kingston, Maxine Hong *v.6 p.94, p.100*

Kingston, Paul W. & Lewis, Lionel S. (Editors) . . . *v.4 p.296*

Kinkead-Weekes, Mark *v.2 p.258, p.362*

Kinnaird, John *v.2 p.293*

Kinnamon, Keneth *v.2 p.138*

Kinnard, Roy *v.6 p.318, p.322*

Kinne, Wisner P. *v.1 p.116*

Kinnell, Galway *v.2 p.92*

Kinney, Arthur F. (Editor) *v.1 p.67, p.75, v.2 p.169*

Kinney, Harrison (Editor) *v.2 p.125*

Kinney, Harrison *v.2 p.125*

Kinoshita Junji *v.6 p.230*

Kinross, Lord *v.6 p.624*

Kinsbruner, Jay *v.3 p.286, p.347*

Kinsella, James *v.6 p.379*

Kinsella, John & Wark, McKenzie . . . *v.4 p.817, p.844, p.902*

Kinsella, John *v.2 p.747*

Kinsey, Alfred C., et al. *v.4 p.748, v.6 p.420*

Kinsler, Lawrence E., et al. *v.5 p.567*

Kinsley, David R. *v.1 p.536*

Kinsley, David *v.1 p.536*

Kintsch, Walter *v.5 p.605*

Kinzbrunner, Barry M., et al. *v.5 p.532*

Kinzer, Stephen *v.4 p.654*

Kionka, Edward J. *v.4 p.443*

Kiple, Kenneth F. & Ornelas, Kriemhild Coneè (Editors) . *v.5 p.34*

Kiple, Kenneth F. *v.3 p.271*

Kipling, Rudyard *v.2 p.296, p.297*

Kippenhahn, Rudolf *v.5 p.408*

Kippenhahn, Rudolph & Weigert, A. *v.5 p.70*

Kipphan, Helmut (Editor) *v.4 p.417*

Kipping, Matthias & Engwall, Lars (Editors) *v.4 p.64*

Kiraly, Bela K. & Jonas, Paul *v.3 p.187*

Kirby, David *v.2 p.48, v.3 p.256*

Kirby, F. E. *v.1 p.240*

Kirby, Lorne T. *v.5 p.122*

Kirby, Sandra, et al. *v.4 p.817, p.840*

Kirby, William C. (Editor), et al. *v.3 p.390*

Kirby, William C. (Editor) *v.4 p.515*

Kirch, Patrick V. *v.4 p.13*

Kirchhoff, Frederick *v.2 p.301*

Kirchner, Bill (Editor) *v.1 p.260, p.320*

Kirchner, Bill *v.6 p.30*

Kirdar, Uner & Silk, Leonard *v.4 p.504*

Kirihara, Donald *v.6 p.336*

Kirilov, Nikolai; Kirk, Frank *v.2 p.779*

Kirk, Connie Ann *v.2 p.37*

Kirk, G. S. *v.2 p.414*

Kirk, John A. *v.3 p.510*

Kirk, John M. *v.3 p.310*

Kirk, John T. *v.1 p.804*

Kirk, P. M. (Editor), et al. *v.5 p.45*

Kirk, Randy W. *v.4 p.87*

Kirk, Russell *v.3 p.368*

Kirkendall, Andrew J. *v.3 p.337*

Kirkendall, Rich *v.3 p.512*

Kirkham, Michael *v.2 p.348*

Kirkham, Pat (Editor) *v.1 p.706, p.714*

Kirkham, Richard L. *v.1 p.482, p.493*

Kirkland, Caroline M. *v.2 p.43*

Kirkland, Gelsey & Lawrence, D. H. *v.1 p.9*

Kirkman, Andrew & Slavin, Dennis (Editors) . *v.1 p.180, p.311*

Kirk-Othmer *v.5 p.257, p.741*

Kirkpatrick, Donald L. & Kirkpatrick, James D. . . . *v.4 p.79*

Kirkpatrick, John & Ives, Charles *v.1 p.217, p.333*

Kirkpatrick, Lee A. *v.5 p.634*

Kirkpatrick, Ralph *v.1 p.185, p.352*

Kirkpatrick, Robin *v.2 p.168, p.169, p.230, p.704*

Kirkwood, G. M. *v.2 p.419*

Kirkwood, James, et al. *v.1 p.251, p.408*

Kirpal, Viney *v.2 p.760, p.762*

Kirsch, George B. *v.4 p.807, p.851*

Kirsch, Uri *v.5 p.695*

Kirschbaum, Leo *v.2 p.230*

Kirschbaum, Stanislav J. *v.3 p.190*

Kirschner, Marc W. & Gerhart, John C. *v.5 p.203*

Kirschten, Robert *v.2 p.55*

Kirsch-Volders, Micheline (Editor) . . . *v.5 p.364, p.373, p.375*

Kirsh, Andrea & Levenson, Rustin S. *v.1 p.751*

Kirshenblatt-Gimblett, Barbara *v.4 p.47*

Kirstein, Lincoln . . . *v.1 p.5, p.9, p.24, p.42, p.45, v.6 p.414*

Kirtzman, Andrew *v.3 p.491*

Kirwan, Albert D. *v.3 p.415, p.505*

Kirwan, Frances *v.5 p.491, p.497*

Kis, Danilo *v.2 p.811*

Kis, Janos *v.4 p.504*

Kisiel, Theodore J. *v.1 p.471*

Kislan, Richard *v.1 p.31, p.32*

Kisling, Vernon N. *v.5 p.84*

Kissane, Bill *v.3 p.139*

Kissane, Noel (Editor) *v.3 p.139*

Kissen, Rita M. *v.4 p.283, p.309, v.6 p.383, p.385*

Kissin, Benjamin & Begleiter, Henri (Editors) . *v.5 p.512, p.522*

Kissin, Benjamin (Editor) *v.5 p.521, p.522*

Kissinger, Henry A. & Summers, Lawrence H. . *v.4 p.560, p.562*

Kissinger, Henry A. . *v.3 p.76, p.452, p.453, p.459, p.460, v.4 p.645*

Kiste, Robert C. & Marshall, Mac (Editors) *v.4 p.4*

Kistler, Mark O. *v.2 p.591*

Kitani, Osamu (Editor), et al. *v.5 p.5*

Kitano, Harry H. *v.6 p.132*

Kitano, Hiroaki (Editor) *v.5 p.106, p.127, p.146, p.149*

Kitch, Carolyn . . . *v.4 p.141, p.416, p.697, v.5 p.621, p.625*

Kitchen, Helen A. *v.6 p.74*

Kitchen, Philip J. (Editor) *v.4 p.137*

Kitcher, Philip & Schacht, Richard . . . *v.1 p.199, p.231, p.365*

Kitchin, C. R. *v.5 p.65*

Kitching, Ian, et al. *v.5 p.199, p.201*
Kite-Powell, Jeffery T. (Editor) *v.1 p.180, p.401*
Kitfield, James. *v.4 p.560, p.564*
Kitromilides, Paschalis M. *v.3 p.194*
Kitses, Jim. *v.6 p.324*
Kitson Clark, G. S. R. (George Sidney Roberts). . . . *v.3 p.113*
Kittay, Eva Feder & Alcoff, Linda (Editors) *v.1 p.506*
Kittel, Bonnie Pedrotti, et al. *v.6 p.646*
Kittel, Charles & Kroemer, Herbert *v.5 p.560*
Kittel, Charles *v.5 p.554*
Kittler, Pamela Goyan & Sucher, Kathryn P. *v.5 p.34*
Kittleson, James M. *v.3 p.166*
Kitto, Humphrey D. *v.2 p.402, p.419*
Kittredge, George Lyman *v.2 p.206*
Kitzinger, Celia *v.4 p.750, v.6 p.372, p.381*
Kitzinger, Rachel & Grant, Michael (Editors) *v.3 p.3*
Kivelson, Valerie A. & Greene, Robert H. (Editors) . *v.1 p.569*
Kiver, Eugene P. & Harris, David V. *v.5 p.419*
Kivy, Peter (Editor). *v.1 p.479*
Kivy, Peter *v.1 p.381, p.401*
Kiy, Richard & Wirth, John D. (Editors) *v.3 p.269*
Kiyooka, Roy *v.6 p.94*
Kiyota, Minoru. *v.1 p.566*
Kjellberg, Pierre *v.1 p.774*
Kjellgren, Eric & Ivory, Carol. *v.1 p.694*
Klaeber *v.2 p.204*
Klahr, David & Kotovsky, K. (Editors). *v.5 p.590*
Klaiber, Jeffrey L. *v.3 p.330*
Klaiber, Jeffrey. *v.3 p.260*
Klamer, Arjo. *v.4 p.233*
Klamkin, Murray S. (Editor) *v.5 p.500*
Klammer, Martin *v.2 p.54*
Klammer, Thomas P. *v.2 p.557*
Klaniczay, Tibor *v.2 p.785*
Klapisch-Zuber, Christiane (Editor), et al. *v.6 p.560*
Klaren, Peter F. *v.3 p.330*
Klaren, Peter Flindell *v.3 p.330*
Klarer, Mario *v.2 p.163*
Klarman, Michael J. *v.4 p.457, p.537*
Klarner, David A. (Editor). *v.5 p.469*
Klass, Donald L.. . . . . *v.5 p.362, p.377*
Klass, Morton *v.4 p.704*
Klauenberg, B. Jon & Miklavicic, Damijan. *v.5 p.376*
Klawans, Harold L.. . . . . *v.5 p.516*
Klawitter, George (Editor). *v.6 p.405*
Kleberg, Lars *v.1 p.85, p.109*
Klee, Carol A. & Ramos-Garcia, Luis A. (Editors) . *v.2 p.636*
Klee, Ernst, et al. *v.3 p.85*
Klee, Robert *v.5 p.403*
Kleene, S. C. *v.5 p.470*
Kleidman, Robert *v.4 p.559*
Kleimann, Julian & Rohlmann, Michael . . . *v.1 p.728, p.732*
Klein, A. M. *v.2 p.735*
Klein, Alan M.. . . . . *v.4 p.817, p.855*
Klein, Alec *v.4 p.157*

Klein, Ann G. *v.4 p.337, v.5 p.575, p.597*
Klein, Carole *v.2 p.364*
Klein, Dan. *v.1 p.810*
Klein, David A. *v.4 p.79*
Klein, Dennis A.. . . . . *v.2 p.660*
Klein, Donald & Clark, Anne B. *v.6 p.194, p.199*
Klein, Felix *v.5 p.495*
Klein, Herbert & Luna, Francisco Vidal *v.3 p.341*
Klein, Herbert S. *v.3 p.279, p.324, v.4 p.728*
Klein, Ingo & Mittnik, Stefan (Editors). *v.4 p.202*
Klein, Isaac *v.1 p.552*
Klein, Joe *v.3 p.473*
Klein, Malcolm W. (Editor), et al. *v.6 p.256*
Klein, Malcolm W. *v.6 p.256*
Klein, Martin A. *v.6 p.68, p.72*
Klein, Mason & Berger, Maurice *v.1 p.742*
Klein, Maury *v.4 p.66*
Klein, Menachem *v.6 p.713*
Klein, Milton M. (Editor) *v.3 p.490*
Klein, Norman M. *v.6 p.307*
Klein, Philip S. & Hoogenboom, Ari *v.3 p.492, v.4 p.713*
Klein, Philip S. *v.3 p.420, p.437*
Klein, Richard G. *v.4 p.15*
Klein, Ulrike. *v.1 p.826*
Klein, William J.. . . . . *v.5 p.222*
Kleinberg, Aviad M. *v.6 p.571*
Kleiner, Diana E. E. *v.3 p.10*
Kleiner, Diana E.. . . . . *v.1 p.775*
Kleinert, Hagen *v.5 p.549*
Kleinert, Sylvia & Neale, Margo
   (Editors) *v.1 p.668, p.694, v.4 p.26*
Kleinhenz, Christopher (Editor) *v.6 p.563*
Kleinig, John & Smith, Margaret L. *v.6 p.245*
Kleinknecht, Alfred. *v.4 p.235*
Kleinman, Daniel Lee *v.5 p.218*
Kleinman, Isobel R. *v.4 p.798, p.799*
Kleist, Heinrich von *v.2 p.600*
Kleit, Andrew N. (Editor) *v.4 p.252*
Kleitz, William. *v.5 p.722*
Klekh, Igor *v.2 p.814*
Klement, Alice *v.3 p.543*
Klement, Frank L. *v.3 p.398, p.428*
Kleniewski, Nancy (Editor) *v.6 p.718*
Klepper, Robert K. *v.6 p.332*
Kleppner, Paul *v.3 p.515*
Klesse, Edward J. *v.4 p.288*
Klessinger, Martin & Michl, Josef *v.5 p.297*
Klevar, Harvey L. *v.2 p.66*
Klibbe, Lawrence H. *v.2 p.654*
Klicka, Christopher J. *v.4 p.296, p.450*
Kliebard, Herbert M. *v.4 p.305*
Klieman, Aaron (Editor, Introduction by) *v.6 p.612*
Klieman, Aaron (Editor) *v.6 p.618*
Klier, John D. *v.3 p.219*
Klier, John Doyle & Lambroza, Shlomo (Editors) . . . *v.3 p.60*

Klier, John. *v.3 p.216*

Klima, Ivan, et al. *v.2 p.783*

Klima, Ivan *v.2 p.783, v.3 p.189*

Klinck, Carl F. & Bailey, Alfred G. (Editors) *v.2 p.730*

Klinck, Carl Frederick *v.2 p.730*

Kline, David *v.5 p.79*

Kline, Morris *v.5 p.467*

Kline, Theresa J. B. *v.5 p.601*

Kling, Rob (Editor), et al. *v.6 p.713*

Klingemann, Hans-Dieter, et al. *v.4 p.579*

Klinghoffer, Arthur J. *v.4 p.385*

Klingman, Peter D. *v.3 p.434*

Klinkenborg, Verlyn *v.5 p.233*

Klinkowitz, Jerome & Knowlton, James *v.2 p.617*

Klitzman, Robert & Bayer, Ronald. *v.6 p.379*

Klock, Geoff. *v.2 p.581*

Klonsky, Milton *v.2 p.240*

Klopp, Charles. *v.2 p.716*

Kloppenberg, Lisa A. *v.4 p.537*

Kloppenborg, John S. *v.1 p.629*

Kloppenburg, Jack Ralph. *v.5 p.8, p.47*

Klopstock, Freidrich G. *v.2 p.600*

Klopstock, Friedrich Gottlieb *v.2 p.600*

Klosko, George *v.4 p.498*

Klossner, Michael *v.6 p.314*

Klostermaier, Klaus K. *v.1 p.536, p.537*

Klosty, James (Editor) *v.1 p.9*

Klotman, Phyllis R. & Gibson, Gloria J. *v.6 p.330, p.342*

Klotman, Phyllis R. (Editor) *v.6 p.330, p.342*

Klotman, Phyllis Rauch & Cutler, Janet K. . . . *v.6 p.330, p.342*

Klotter, James C. *v.3 p.511*

Klotz, Irwing M. *v.5 p.327*

Klubock, Thomas M. *v.3 p.354*

Kluckhohn, Clyde & Leighton, Dorothea C. *v.6 p.703*

Klug, William S. & Cummings, Michael R. *v.5 p.134*

Kluge, Friedrich *v.2 p.621*

Kluger, Richard *v.4 p.450*

Kluger, Ruth *v.3 p.85*

Kluka, Darlene & Schilling, Guido
(Editors). *v.4 p.884, p.891, p.896*

Kluka, Darlene A., et al. *v.4 p.884, p.891*

Klute, Ed A. (Editor) *v.5 p.50*

Kluwin, Thomas N. (Editor), et al. *v.4 p.312*

Klyne, W. & Buckingham, John B. *v.5 p.298*

Klyza, Christopher M. & Trombulak, Stephen C. . . . *v.3 p.486*

Kmenta, Jan *v.4 p.202*

Kümmel, Werner Georg, et al. *v.1 p.625*

Knacke, O. (Editor), et al. *v.5 p.302*

Knacke, O., et al. *v.5 p.302*

Knacke, O., Kubaschewski, O., Hesselmann, K. . . . *v.5 p.302*

Knackstedt, Mary V. *v.1 p.803*

Knapp, Alan K. (Editor), et al. *v.5 p.170, p.240*

Knapp, Andrew *v.4 p.609*

Knapp, Bettina L. *v.2 p.462, p.484, p.504, p.514, p.519*

Knapp, Bettina. *v.1 p.106, p.152*

Knapp, Jeffrey *v.2 p.163, p.186*

Knapp, Mark & Daly, John (Editors) *v.5 p.648*

Knapp, Mark L. & Hall, Judith A. *v.4 p.424*

Knapp, Raymond. *v.1 p.251*

Knappman, Edward W. (Editor), et al. *v.4 p.438*

Knauft, Bruce M. *v.4 p.43*

Knaus, Christopher *v.4 p.301*

Knauss, John A. *v.4 p.392, v.5 p.430*

Kneale, Matthew *v.2 p.360*

Kneale, Pauline E. *v.4 p.377*

Kneale, William & Kneale, Martha *v.1 p.494*

Knecht, R. J. *v.3 p.145*

Knee, Michael *v.5 p.344*

Kneese, Allen V. & Sweeney, J. L. (Editors) *v.4 p.190*

Knepper, George W. *v.3 p.513*

Knäblein, Jörg & Muller, Rainer H. (Editors) *v.4 p.156*

Knickman, James R. (Editor) *v.5 p.513*

Knight, Alan E. *v.2 p.462*

Knight, Alan *v.3 p.293*

Knight, Arthur. *v.6 p.316, p.330, p.342*

Knight, Brenda *v.2 p.11*

Knight, Charles A. *v.2 p.195, p.236, p.261*

Knight, David (Author, Contribution by) *v.5 p.261*

Knight, David (Editor) *v.5 p.263*

Knight, David *v.5 p.263*

Knight, Denise D. (Editor) *v.2 p.29, v.6 p.479*

Knight, Franklin W. & Martínez Vergne, Teresita. . . . *v.4 p.40*

Knight, G. Wilson *v.2 p.230, p.235*

Knight, George Wilson *v.2 p.225*

Knight, John R. *v.4 p.165*

Knight, Peter (Editor). *v.3 p.371*

Knight, R. C. *v.2 p.473*

Knight, Randall D. *v.5 p.563*

Knight, Rolf. *v.6 p.688, p.689*

Knight, Sarah Kemble & Winship, George Parker . . . *v.2 p.29*

Knight, Stephen, et al. *v.2 p.197*

Knight, Stephen *v.2 p.741*

Knight, Vernon J. Jr. & Steponaitis, Vin (Editors). . . *v.4 p.11*

Knight, W. Andy (Editor) *v.4 p.634*

Knight, W. Andy *v.4 p.634*

Knightley, Phillip. *v.4 p.403*

Knighton, David *v.5 p.427*

Knighton, Tess & Fallows, David (Editors) *v.1 p.177*

Knights, L. C. *v.2 p.230*

Knights, Michael Andrew *v.4 p.647*

Knisely, Karen *v.5 p.245*

Knobel, Roger *v.5 p.501*

Knoche, Ulrich. *v.2 p.427*

Knock, Thomas J. *v.3 p.473, v.4 p.631*

Knoepflmacher, U. C. & Tennyson, G. B.
(Editors). *v.6 p.737, p.764*

Knoll, Andrew H. *v.5 p.193, p.445, p.447*

Knoll, Arthur J. *v.6 p.73*

Knoll, Glenn F. *v.5 p.563*

Knopp, Lisa *v.5 p.222*

Knoppers, Bartha Maria. *v.5 p.149*
Knoppers, Gary N. *v.1 p.620*
Knoppers, Gary *v.1 p.620*
Knoppers, Laura L. *v.2 p.254*
Knott, Kim *v.1 p.537*
Knowles, Anne Kelly (Editor) *v.4 p.387*
Knowles, David & Hadcock, R. Neville *v.1 p.578*
Knowles, David, et al. *v.1 p.578*
Knowles, David *v.1 p.577, p.578, p.609, v.6 p.571*
Knowles, Dom David *v.3 p.57, v.6 p.572*
Knowles, Elizabeth (Contribution by) *v.2 p.549*
Knowles, Gerald *v.2 p.554*
Knowles, John *v.2 p.92*
Knowles, Karen (Editor) *v.5 p.79*
Knowles, Malcolm S. *v.4 p.320*
Knowles, Mark *v.1 p.3, p.32*
Knowles, Owen & Moore, Gene M. *v.2 p.341*
Knowles, Ronald. *v.2 p.234, p.376*
Knowlson, James R. *v.2 p.333*
Knowlton, James & Cates, Truett (Translators) . . . *v.3 p.178*
Knowlton, Steven R. & Parsons, Patrick R. (Editors) . *v.4 p.405*
Knox, Alan B. *v.4 p.320*
Knox, Bernard M. *v.2 p.419*
Knox, Brian *v.3 p.190*
Knox, Edward C. *v.2 p.473*
Knox, George A. *v.5 p.431*
Knox, MacGregor. *v.3 p.81, p.203*
Knox, Melissa *v.2 p.321*
Knox, Paul L. & Marston, Sallie A. *v.4 p.396*
Knox-Shaw, Peter *v.2 p.267*
Knudsen, Steen *v.5 p.100, p.103, p.110, p.122*
Knudson, Duane V. & Morrison, Craig S. . . . *v.4 p.873, p.909*
Knudson, Jerry W. *v.3 p.354, v.4 p.412*
Knuth, Donald E. *v.5 p.336, p.461*
Knutson, Anne Classen *v.1 p.742*
Knutsson, Johannes (Editor) *v.6 p.264*
Ko, Dorothy (Editor), et al. *v.6 p.181, p.217*
Ko, Dorothy *v.6 p.452*
Kobach, Kris W. *v.4 p.595*
Kobayashi, Hideo *v.6 p.231*
Koblitz, Neal *v.5 p.476, p.497*
Kobylianska, Olha & Yaroshynska, Yevheniya . . . *v.2 p.813*
Kocanda, S. *v.5 p.689*
Kocay, William, and Donald L. Kreher. *v.5 p.480*
Kocbek, Edvard *v.2 p.813*
Koch, C. J. *v.2 p.747, v.6 p.178*
Koch, Dave *v.6 p.307*
Koch, Kenneth *v.2 p.92*
Koch, Lawrence O. *v.1 p.170, p.261, p.346*
Koch, Sigmund & Leary, David E. (Editors) *v.5 p.597*
Koch, Stephen *v.2 p.574*
Koch, Vivienne. *v.2 p.326*
Kocher, Paul Harold *v.2 p.221*
Kochin, Michael S. *v.4 p.489*
Kocka, Jurgen & Mitchell, Allan (Editors) *v.3 p.74*

Kocks, Dorothee E. *v.6 p.287*
Koda, Harold *v.1 p.715*
Kodansha International Staff. *v.6 p.219*
Kodansha Ltd. Staff *v.6 p.219*
Kodrich, Kris *v.3 p.302*
Koebner, Linda *v.5 p.84*
Koegel, Robert L. *v.4 p.318*
Koehler, G. Stanley. *v.2 p.136*
Koehler, Michael D. *v.4 p.858, p.904*
Koelb, Clayton & Downing, Eric (Editors) *v.2 p.590*
Koelewijn, Cees *v.3 p.322*
Koenig, Daniel J. *v.6 p.262*
Koenig, Harold George (Editor) *v.5 p.634*
Koenig, Jack L. *v.5 p.323*
Koenig, William J. *v.6 p.166*
Koenigsberger, Dorothy. *v.1 p.435*
Koepplin, Leslie *v.3 p.530*
Koerner, Joseph L. *v.1 p.675, p.688*
Koerner, Lisbet. *v.5 p.231*
Koestenbaum, Wayne *v.1 p.379, v.6 p.408*
Koester, Helmut (Editor) *v.1 p.625*
Koester, Helmut *v.1 p.626, p.627*
Koestler, Arthur *v.3 p.47, p.226, v.5 p.654*
Kofas, Jon V. *v.3 p.195, p.354*
Koff, Clea *v.4 p.33*
Koff, Raymond S. (Editor) *v.5 p.515*
Kofman, Jan *v.3 p.207*
Kofsky, Frank *v.1 p.261, p.318*
Kogan, Deborah Copaken *v.1 p.767*
Kogan, Maurice & Hawksworth, Mary (Editors) . . . *v.4 p.482*
Kogawa, Joy. *v.2 p.735, v.6 p.100*
Kogel, Jessica Elzea *v.5 p.450*
Koger, Larry (Compiled by). *v.4 p.727*
Kogevinas, Manolis; Pearce, Neil; Susser,
  Mervyn; Boffetta, P *v.4 p.778*
Kogler, Peter. *v.1 p.773*
Koh, Frances M. *v.6 p.110*
Koh, Masuda *v.6 p.231*
Kohak, Erazim V. *v.6 p.288*
Kohane, Isaac S., et al. *v.5 p.100, p.110, p.127, p.135*
Kohfeldt, Mary L. *v.2 p.288*
Kohl, Herbert R. *v.4 p.310, p.337, p.348, v.5 p.573*
Kohl, Lawrence F. *v.4 p.551, p.552*
Kohlenberger, John R. III & Strong, James *v.1 p.614*
Kohlenberger, John R. III (Editor) *v.1 p.613*
Kohler, Joachim *v.1 p.199, p.365*
Kohler, Peter A. & Zacher, Hans F. *v.4 p.247*
Kohler, Robert E. *v.5 p.326*
Kohler, Wolfgang *v.5 p.606, p.615*
Kohli, Atul (Editor). *v.4 p.617*
Kohli, Atul, et al.. . . . . *v.4 p.665*
Kohlmeier, Albert L. *v.3 p.512*
Kohlstedt, Sally G. & Rossiter, Margaret
  (Editors). *v.5 p.388, p.393, p.394*
Kohn, Alfie *v.4 p.284, p.286, p.327*

Kohn, Livia & LaFargue, Michael (Editors) *v.1 p.418*

Kohn, Livia *v.1 p.539*

Kohn, Margaret *v.6 p.723*

Kohn, Melvin L. *v.4 p.695, p.724*

Kohn, Richard H. *v.3 p.383*

Kohn, Stephen M., et al. *v.4 p.109, p.131*

Kohno, Masaru. *v.4 p.621*

Kohonen, Teuvo *v.5 p.340*

Kohout, Pavel *v.2 p.783*

Koht, Halvdan *v.2 p.628*

Kohut, David R. *v.3 p.348, p.354*

Koine, J.. . . . . *v.6 p.231*

Kojeve, Alexandre *v.1 p.464*

Kojiro, Yoshikawa *v.6 p.209, p.210*

Kola, Paulin *v.3 p.249*

Kolakowski, Leszek *v.1 p.469, p.508*

Kolata, Alan L.. . . . . *v.3 p.261*

Kolata, Gina *v.4 p.791, v.5 p.510, p.532*

Kolb, Charles *v.3 p.473*

Kolb, Eberhard. *v.3 p.170*

Kolb, Edward W. & Turner, Michael S. *v.5 p.72*

Kolb, Robert & Wengert, Timothy J. (Editors) *v.1 p.585*

Kolb, Robert W. &
   Overdahl, James A. *v.4 p.89, p.95, p.100, p.102*

Kolb, Rocky *v.5 p.62*

Kolbert, Elizabeth *v.5 p.371*

Kolchanov, Nikolay & Hofestaedt, Ralf
   (Editors). *v.5 p.102, p.127, p.140*

Kolen, Michael J. & Brennan, Robert L. *v.5 p.601*

Kolin, Philip C. (Editor) *v.1 p.116, v.2 p.134, p.230*

Kolinski, Charles J.. . . . . *v.3 p.344*

Koliopoulos, Giannaes & Veremaes, Thanos *v.3 p.194*

Koliopoulos, John S. *v.3 p.195*

Kolko, Gabriel. *v.3 p.448, p.453*

Kolko, Joyce. *v.3 p.453*

Kollin, Susan *v.6 p.286*

Kollmann, Nancy S. *v.3 p.215*

Kollmann, Nancy Shields *v.3 p.215*

Kolm, Serge-Christophe & Mercier Ythier, Jean
   (Editors) *v.4 p.190*

Kolmerten, Carol A. *v.4 p.499*

Kolodny, Annette *v.2 p.6, v.4 p.331*

Kolodziej, Edward A.. . . . . *v.4 p.608*

Kolokotrones, Theodoros ; Tertsetes, Georgios *v.3 p.195*

Kolp, John G. *v.3 p.500*

Kolsto, Pal. *v.4 p.598*

Kolthoff, I. M.; Stenger, V. A.. . . . . *v.5 p.268*

Kolthoff, Izaak M. *v.5 p.273*

Koltun, Elizabeth (Editor). *v.1 p.553*

Koltyk, Jo A. & Foner, Nancy *v.6 p.139*

Kolve, V. A. *v.2 p.209*

Komar, Vitaly, et al. *v.1 p.703*

Komara, Edward (Editor). *v.1 p.160, p.261*

Komaroff, Linda & Carboni, Stefano (Editors) *v.1 p.674, p.691*

Komarovsky, Mirra *v.4 p.739*

Komen, G. J., et al.. . . . . *v.5 p.430*

Komi, Paavo V. (Editor) *v.4 p.825, p.874, p.879*

Kondepudi, Dilip K. & Prigogine, Ilya. *v.5 p.277, p.560*

Kondo, Dorinne K. *v.4 p.39, v.6 p.90, p.99, p.123, p.221*

Kondolf, G. Mathias & Piégay, Hervé (Editors). . . . *v.4 p.391*

Koneman, Elmer W., et al. *v.5 p.515*

Koner, Pauline *v.1 p.10*

Kong, F. K., et al. *v.5 p.689*

Kongstvedt, Peter R. *v.5 p.509*

Kongstvedt, Peter *v.5 p.509*

Konhauser, Joseph D., et al.. . . . . *v.5 p.469*

Konig, David T. *v.4 p.474*

Konigsberg, Ira. *v.6 p.307*

Kono, Juliet S. & Song, Cathy (Editors). *v.6 p.92*

Konopka, Andrzej & Crabbe, M. James C. . . . *v.5 p.90, p.107*

Konrad, George *v.2 p.784, p.785, v.3 p.187*

Konrad, Victor *v.3 p.535*

Konstam, Angus *v.4 p.380, p.383*

Konter, S. *v.3 p.503*

Kontje, Todd. *v.2 p.592*

Kontler, Laszlo. *v.3 p.185*

Kontos, Louis (Editor), et al. *v.4 p.714*

Konvitz, Milton R. (Editor) *v.4 p.455*

Konwicki, Tadeusz *v.2 p.790*

Konzal, Jean L. & Dodd, Anne Wescott *v.4 p.303*

Kooden, Harold & Flowers, Charles *v.6 p.380*

Koohi-Kamali, Farideh *v.6 p.599, p.631*

Kooijman, S. A. L. M. *v.5 p.113*

Kooistra, Lorraine Janzen *v.2 p.303*

Kook, Abraham Isaac. *v.1 p.545*

Koolhaas, Rem & Mau, Bruce. *v.1 p.797*

Koolhaas, Rem *v.1 p.797, p.813*

Koonin, Eugene V. & Galperin, Michael Y.. . *v.5 p.102, p.140*

Koonin, Eugene V. (Volume Editor), et al. *v.5 p.127*

Koonin, Steven E. *v.5 p.551*

Koonz, Claudia *v.3 p.53, p.172*

Kooser, Ted *v.2 p.148*

Koot, Gerard M. *v.4 p.212, p.215*

Kopay, David & Young, Perry D. *v.6 p.384*

Kopecký, Jan *v.5 p.278*

Kopecky, Petr *v.4 p.575, p.596*

Kopelev, Lev Z. *v.3 p.224*

Kopka, Helmut & Daly, Patrick W. *v.5 p.461*

Koplos, Janet *v.1 p.777*

Koponen, Wilfrid R. *v.6 p.393*

Kopp, David *v.1 p.371*

Kopper, Edward A. Jr. (Editor) *v.2 p.306*

Kopper, Philip *v.3 p.500*

Koppett, Leonard *v.4 p.854, p.902, p.907*

Koprulu, Mehmed Fuad. *v.6 p.590*

Korbel, Josef. *v.3 p.189*

Korbonski, Stefan (Introduction by) *v.3 p.254*

Korbonski, Stefan *v.3 p.254*

Kordal, Richard Joseph, et al.. . . . . *v.5 p.100, p.122*

Koren, Herman & Bisesi, Michael S. *v.5 p.358, p.364*

Koren, Herman *v.5 p.682*

Koren, Yoram *v.5 p.711*

Korenman, Joan *v.6 p.463*

Korf, Bruce R. *v.5 p.135, p.533*

Korf, Ian F., et al. *v.5 p.103*

Korff, H. A. *v.2 p.590*

Korg, Jacob *v.2 p.89, p.111, p.326*

Kornberg, Allan & Clarke, Harold D. *v.4 p.586*

Kornberg, Allan *v.4 p.589*

Kornberg, Arthur & Baker, Tania *v.5 p.122*

Kornberg, Arthur *v.5 p.119*

Kornblatt, Judith D. *v.2 p.798*

Kornbluh, Mark Lawrence *v.4 p.549*

Kornbluh, Peter *v.3 p.354*

Kornhauser, Elizabeth & McDonnell, Patricia *v.1 p.742*

Kornicki, Peter F. *v.6 p.225*

Kornprobst, Jacques *v.5 p.440*

Kornwolf, James D. *v.6 p.713*

Korosenyi, Andras *v.4 p.595*

Korr, Charles P. *v.4 p.851, p.888, p.891*

Kors, Alan C. *v.3 p.70, v.6 p.569*

Kors, Alan Charles (Editor) *v.1 p.437, p.438*

Kors, Alan Charles *v.3 p.72*

Korsgaard, Christine M. *v.1 p.484*

Korstvedt, Benjamin M. *v.1 p.199, p.240, p.314*

Kort, Carol *v.2 p.7*

Kort, Michael G. *v.3 p.442*

Kort, Wesley A. *v.2 p.191*

Kort, Wolfgang *v.2 p.617*

Korth, Eugene H. *v.3 p.350*

Korthals, Michiel & Bogers, Robert J. (Editors) . . . *v.5 p.248*

Kortum, G.; Vogel, Gustav W.; Andrussow, K. *v.5 p.300*

Korve, Hans W. *v.5 p.700*

Koshal, D. (Editor) *v.5 p.684*

Koshar, Rudy (Editor) *v.4 p.716, p.784*

Koshar, Rudy *v.1 p.822, v.3 p.159*

Koshy, Susan *v.6 p.96, p.123*

Kosinski, Dorothy (Editor) *v.1 p.780*

Kosinski, Dorothy M. (Editor) *v.1 p.742*

Kosinski, Jerzy N. *v.2 p.148*

Koskoff, Ellen (Editor) *v.6 p.474*

Koskoff, Ellen *v.1 p.278, p.296*

Koslow, Diane R. & Salett, Elizabeth P. (Editors) . . *v.5 p.637*

Koslow, Stephen H. & Huerta, Michael F. (Editors) . . *v.5 p.589*

Koss, Mary P., et al. *v.6 p.446, p.470*

Kossak, Steven & Singer, Jane Casey *v.1 p.732*

Kosseff, Alex *v.4 p.786, p.787*

Kossek, Ellen Ernst & Lambert, Susan J. (Editors) . . *v.5 p.580*

Kossew, Sue *v.2 p.754*

Kossman, E. H. *v.3 p.205*

Kostelanetz, Richard (Editor) . . *v.1 p.217, p.261, p.315, p.335, p.363, v.6 p.408*

Kostelanetz, Richard . *v.1 p.86, p.217, p.271, p.315, p.326, p.369*

Kostelnick, Charles & Hassett, Michael *v.4 p.423*

Kostelnick, Marjorie, et al. *v.4 p.316*

Kostenevich, Albert Grigor'evich *v.1 p.728*

Koster, Eduard A. (Editor) *v.4 p.383*

Koster, Robert *v.6 p.345*

Kostiner, Joseph (Editor) *v.4 p.614, v.6 p.593*

Kostiner, Joseph *v.6 p.626*

Kostka, Stefan *v.1 p.371*

Kosto, Adam J. *v.3 p.238*

Kostof, Spiro *v.1 p.785, p.797, v.6 p.713, p.728*

Kostrovitskaya, Vera S. & Pisarev, Alexei *v.1 p.24*

Kostyrchenko, Gennadi V. *v.3 p.60, p.226*

Kosuge, K. *v.5 p.304*

Kosztolanyi, D. *v.2 p.786*

Kot, Mark *v.5 p.91, p.170*

Kota, Sastri L., et al. *v.5 p.726*

Kotabe, Masaaki & Mol, Michael J. (Editors) . . . *v.4 p.118*

Koth, Karl B. *v.3 p.284*

Kothari, D.P. & Nagrath, I. J. *v.5 p.724*

Kotis, Greg & Hollmann, Mark *v.1 p.251, p.408*

Kotkin, Joel *v.4 p.772, v.6 p.713*

Kotkin, Stephen & Wolff, David (Editors) *v.3 p.214*

Kotkin, Stephen (Editor) *v.6 p.240*

Kotkin, Stephen *v.3 p.226*

Kotler, Philip & Lee, Nancy *v.4 p.54*

Kotler, Philip, et al. *v.4 p.51, p.134*

Kotler, Philip *v.4 p.134*

Kotler, Phillip R., et al. *v.4 p.161*

Kott, Jan (Editor) *v.2 p.787*

Kotter, John P. & Cohen, Dan S. *v.4 p.73*

Kotter, John P. *v.4 p.71*

Kottick, Edward L. *v.1 p.390*

Kotz, Mary Lynn *v.1 p.697*

Kotz, Samuel (Editor) *v.5 p.481*

Kou, Sindo *v.5 p.737*

Koul, Opender & Dhaliwal, G. S. (Editors) . . . *v.5 p.8, p.22*

Koul, Opender (Editor), et al. *v.5 p.9*

Kourouma, Ahmadou *v.2 p.545*

Kousha, Mahnaz *v.6 p.632*

Kousoulas, D. G. *v.3 p.192*

Kousser, J. Morgan *v.4 p.555, p.573, p.579*

Kousser, Thad *v.4 p.530*

Kouwenberg, Silvia & Singler, John Victor (Editors) . *v.2 p.562*

Kouzes, James M. & Posner, Barry Z. *v.4 p.71*

Kovacich, Gerald *v.4 p.113*

Kovacs, David & Euripides *v.2 p.411*

Kovaly, Heda *v.3 p.190*

Kovecses, Zoltan *v.5 p.654*

Koven, Seth *v.3 p.53*

Kovic, Ron *v.6 p.168*

Kovner, Abba *v.6 p.649, p.650*

Kowalchik, Claire *v.4 p.837, p.866*

Kowaleski, Maryanne *v.6 p.558, p.577*

Kowalski, Jeff K. (Editor) *v.3 p.261*

Kowalski, Theodore J. *v.4 p.288*

Kowalsky, Arnold A. & Kowalsky, Dorothy E. . . . *v.1 p.798*

Koyre, Alexandre *v.1 p.488, v.3 p.47*

Kozaczuk, Wladyslaw & Straszak, Jerzy *v.3 p.254*

Kozinn, Allan, et al. *v.1 p.390*

Kozinn, Allan *v.1 p.271, p.306*

Kozloff, Max *v.1 p.764*

Kozlov, Vladimir A. *v.3 p.228*

Kozlowski, T. T. *v.5 p.38*

Kozlowski, Theodore T. & Pallardy, Stephen G. *v.5 p.38*

Kozol, Jonathan *v.4 p.302, p.315, p.327, p.335*

Kozulin, Alex (Editor), et al. *v.4 p.357, v.5 p.571*

Kozulin, Alex *v.5 p.597*

Küpper, Heinz *v.2 p.621*

Kraay, Hendrik & Whigham, Thomas L. . *v.3 p.274, p.344, p.345*

Kraay, Hendrik *v.3 p.274, p.337*

Krabbenhoft, Ken (Translator) *v.2 p.646*

Kraditor, Aileen S. *v.3 p.398, p.420*

Kraeft, Norman & Kraeft, June K. *v.1 p.757*

Kraehe, Enno E. *v.3 p.183, p.184*

Kraemer, H. (Hendrik *v.1 p.597*

Kraemer, Ross S. & D'Angelo, Mary R. (Editors) . . *v.1 p.599*

Kraemer, Ross Shepard *v.1 p.531*

Kraemer, William J. *v.4 p.875, p.879*

Kraenzel, Carl Frederick *v.3 p.518*

Krafft, Manfred & Mantrala, Murali K. (Editors) . . . *v.4 p.164*

Kraft, Elizabeth *v.2 p.262*

Kraft, James P. *v.1 p.384*

Kraft, John M. & Pfleger, Frank L. (Editors) *v.5 p.46*

Kraft, Leo *v.1 p.371*

Kragh, Helge *v.5 p.540*

Krailsheimer, A. J. & Coupe, W. A. *v.2 p.458*

Krailsheimer, A. J. *v.2 p.459, p.476*

Kraitchik, Maurice *v.5 p.469*

Krajka, W. *v.2 p.341*

Krakauer, Jon *v.4 p.789*

Krall, Hanna *v.2 p.790*

Kramarae, Cheris & Spender, Dale (Editors) *v.6 p.425*

Kramer, Christina E. *v.2 p.775*

Kramer, Gudrun *v.6 p.597, p.638*

Kramer, Jonathan D. *v.1 p.240, p.371*

Kramer, Larry *v.6 p.379, p.397, p.402, p.412*

Kramer, Lawrence *v.1 p.199, p.377, p.381, v.2 p.54*

Kramer, Leonie & Mitchell, Adrian (Editors) *v.2 p.743*

Kramer, Paul A. *v.6 p.180*

Kramer, Rita *v.4 p.343*

Kramer, Samuel N. *v.3 p.5*

Kramer, Victor A. *v.2 p.56*

Kramer, Wendy *v.3 p.298*

Krames, Jeffrey A. *v.4 p.71*

Kramnick, Isaac & Moore, R. Laurence *v.1 p.656*

Kramnick, Isaac (Editor) *v.3 p.72*

Kramnick, Isaac *v.3 p.107*

Krane, Dan E. & Raymer, Michael L. *v.5 p.97*

Krane, Kenneth S. *v.5 p.547*

Krantz, S. G. *v.5 p.491*

Krantz, Steven G. *v.5 p.461, p.494*

Krantz, Steven George *v.5 p.459, p.461*

Krantz, Steven *v.5 p.459, p.491, p.495*

Kranz, Rachel & Cusick, Tim *v.6 p.360, p.388*

Kranz, Rachel *v.4 p.446*

Krapohl, Robert H. & Lippy, Charles H. *v.1 p.648*

Krapp, Kristine (Editor) *v.5 p.395*

Krase, Andreas *v.1 p.767*

Krasemann, Stephen J. *v.5 p.238*

Krasicki, Ignacy *v.2 p.790*

Krasilovsky, M. William & Schemel, Sidney *v.1 p.384*

Krasinski, Zygmunt *v.2 p.790*

Kraska, Peter B. (Editor) *v.6 p.261*

Krasner, David (Editor) *v.1 p.116, p.139, p.145*

Krasner, David *v.1 p.123, v.2 p.16*

Krasno, Jean E. & Sutterlin, James S. . . . *v.4 p.656, v.6 p.603*

Krasnow, Erwin G., et al. *v.4 p.445*

Krasny, Marianne E. *v.5 p.186*

Kraszewski, Charles S. *v.2 p.789*

Krasznahorkai, Laszlo *v.2 p.786*

Kraus, Christina S. & Woodman, Anthony J. *v.2 p.426*

Kraus International Publications Staff, ; Freidus, Helen . *v.4 p.369*

Kraus, John D. & Marhefka, Ronald J. *v.5 p.728*

Kraus, John Daniel & Marhefka, Ronald J. *v.5 p.728*

Kraus, Karl *v.2 p.611*

Kraus, Michael *v.3 p.368*

Kraus, Richard & Charman, Sarah *v.1 p.5, p.47*

Kraus, Richard C. *v.1 p.719*

Kraus, Richard, et al. *v.4 p.784, p.903*

Krause, Jerry V., et al. *v.4 p.796, p.854, p.904*

Krause, Jerry *v.4 p.854, p.904*

Krause, Linda & Petro, Patrice (Editors) *v.6 p.730*

Krause, Micki *v.4 p.114*

Krauskopf, Konrad B. & Bird, Dennis K. *v.5 p.440*

Krauss, Ellis S. *v.3 p.390*

Krauss, Lawrence M. *v.5 p.541*

Krauss, Melvyn B. & Lazear, Edward P. (Editors) . . *v.5 p.664*

Krauss, Rosalind E. *v.1 p.706*

Krausz, Michael (Editor) *v.1 p.381*

Kraut, Alan M. (Editor) *v.3 p.420*

Kraut, Alan M. *v.3 p.442, v.4 p.667*

Kraut, Richard (Editor) . *v.1 p.424, p.426, v.2 p.417, v.4 p.489*

Kraut, Richard *v.4 p.489*

Krautheimer, Richard . *v.1 p.599, v.3 p.197, p.204, v.6 p.577*

Krauze, Enrique *v.3 p.293*

Kravchenko, Viktor Andreevich *v.3 p.224*

Kravetz, Stacy *v.4 p.95*

Krawetz, Stephen A. & Womble, David D. (Editors) . . *v.5 p.97*

Kraybill, Donald B. & Bowman, Carl Desportes . . . *v.1 p.586*

Kraybill, Donald B. & Nolt, Steven M. *v.1 p.586*

Kraye, Jill (Editor) *v.1 p.435*

Krebs, Charles J. *v.5 p.170*

Krebs, Harald *v.1 p.200, p.354*

Krebs, Robert E. & Krebs, Carolyn A. . . . *v.3 p.45, v.5 p.389*

Krebs, Robert E. *v.3 p.45, v.5 p.263, p.388, v.6 p.575*

Krech, Shepard *v.6 p.295, p.681*

Kreeft, Peter & Tacelli, Ronald K. *v.1 p.646*

Kreider, Richard B. (Editor), et al.. *v.4 p.827, p.828, p.875, p.879*

Kreighbaum, Ellen F. & Smith, Mark A. (Editors). *v.4 p.870, p.872*

Kreimeier, Klaus *v.3 p.178*

Kreisel, Martha *v.1 p.761, p.806*

Krejci, Oskar *v.4 p.574, p.577, p.596*

Krell, Alan. *v.1 p.742*

Kremenyuk, Victor A. (Editor). *v.4 p.645*

Kremer, John M. & Scully, Deirdre M.. . . . *v.4 p.877, v.5 p.582*

Kren, Emil; Marx, Daniel *v.1 p.711*

Kren, Thomas & Barstow, Kurt *v.1 p.672, p.716*

Kren, Thomas & McKendrick, Scot *v.1 p.732, p.734*

Krenk, S.. . . . . *v.5 p.695*

Krenn, Michael L. & Finkelman, Paul (Editors). . . . *v.3 p.315*

Krensky, Stephen. *v.5 p.230*

Krentz, Edgar *v.1 p.616*

Krepon, Michael & Caldwell, Dan (Editors) . . *v.4 p.562, p.630*

Kreps, Christina F.. . . . . *v.4 p.47*

Kreps, David M. (Editor), et al. *v.4 p.202*

Kreps, Juanita & Clark, Robert *v.4 p.254, p.269*

Kreps, Juanita M. *v.4 p.265*

Kreps, Juanita *v.4 p.273*

Kresin, V. Z. & Wolf, S. A.. . . . . *v.5 p.565*

Kresina, Thomas F. (Editor). *v.5 p.149, p.152*

Kress, George J. & Snyder, John *v.4 p.137*

Kress, Gunther & Leeuwen, Theo Van *v.1 p.703*

Kress, Rainer *v.5 p.488*

Kressel, Gideon *v.6 p.596*

Kressel, Neil J. & Kressel, Dorit F. *v.6 p.270*

Kretchmar, Scott R.. . . . . *v.4 p.796*

Kretzmann, Norman & Stump, Eleonore (Editors). . . *v.1 p.434*

Kretzmann, Norman (Editor), et al. *v.1 p.432*

Kreutz, Barbara M.. . . . . *v.6 p.563*

Krevolin, Richard W.. . . . . *v.6 p.326*

Kreyenbroek, Philip G. & Sperl, Stefan (Editors) . . . *v.6 p.599*

Kreyling, Michael *v.2 p.130*

Kreyszig, Erwin *v.5 p.501, p.683*

Kröller, Eva-Marie (Editor) *v.2 p.730*

Kribbs, Jayne K. *v.2 p.55*

Kricher, John C.. . . . . *v.5 p.38*

Krieg, Joann P. *v.2 p.54*

Kriegel, Lorraine, et al. *v.1 p.32*

Kriegel, Lorraine P. & Chandler-Vaccaro, Kimberly . . *v.1 p.32*

Krieger, Alex D., et al. *v.6 p.534*

Krieger, Gary R. & Balge, Marci Z.. . . . . . . *v.5 p.682*

Krieger, Gary R. *v.5 p.682*

Krieger, Robert (Editor) *v.5 p.9, p.312, p.354*

Kriegsman, Sali A. *v.1 p.26*

Krier, Dan *v.4 p.86*

Krige, John *v.5 p.403*

Krikos, Linda & Ingold, Cindy *v.6 p.426*

Krill, Rosemary Troy & Eversmann, Pauline K.. . . . *v.1 p.800*

Krimsky, Sheldon *v.5 p.355, p.366, p.375*

Kripke, Saul A. *v.1 p.472, p.490*

Kris, Ernst. *v.5 p.619*

Krishna, Valerie S. *v.2 p.206*

Krishnamoorti, Ramanan & Vaia, Richard A. (Editors). *v.5 p.689*

Krishnaswamy, Revathi *v.6 p.157*

Krismann, Carol H. *v.4 p.57*

Krispyn, Egbert (Editor) *v.2 p.622*

Kristal, Efraín (Editor) *v.2 p.664*

Kristal, Efrain *v.2 p.685, v.3 p.327*

Kristeller, Paul O. *v.1 p.435*

Kristeller, Paul Oskar *v.3 p.71*

Kristensen, Tom *v.2 p.627*

Kristeva, Julia, et al. *v.2 p.571*

Kristeva, Julia *v.2 p.531, p.571*

Kristof, Nicholas D. & WuDunn, Sheryl *v.6 p.145*

Kristol, Irving *v.4 p.511, p.516*

Kritzeck, James *v.1 p.558*

Kritzer, Amelia H. (Editor, Compiled by) . . *v.1 p.121, v.2 p.25*

Kritzer, Herbert M. (Editor) *v.4 p.433*

Kritzman, Lawrence D. & Nora, Pierre. *v.3 p.140*

Krivchenko, G. I.. . . . . *v.5 p.714*

Krleza, Miroslav *v.2 p.818*

Kroeber, A. L. *v.4 p.24, v.6 p.703*

Kroeber, Karl & Ruoff, Gene W. (Editors) *v.2 p.324*

Kroeger, Otto, et al. *v.4 p.173*

Kroen, Sheryl *v.3 p.153*

Kroetsch, Robert *v.2 p.730, p.735, p.736*

Krogh, David *v.5 p.222*

Krolik, Julian H. *v.5 p.71*

Kroll, Barry M. *v.6 p.169*

Kroll, Mark *v.1 p.401*

Kronenberger, Louis. *v.3 p.94, p.109*

Kronenfeld, Jennie J. & Whicker, Marcia L. *v.4 p.170*

Kronenfeld, Jennie J.. . . . . *v.4 p.160, p.161*

Kronenwetter, Michael *v.4 p.659*

Kronish, Amy & Safirman, Costel *v.6 p.333*

Krooss, Herman E. (Editor) *v.4 p.246*

Kropotkin, Peter *v.4 p.493*

Kropotkin, Petr Alekseevich *v.2 p.799, p.805*

Kroschwitz, Jacqueline I. & Menges, George *v.5 p.321*

Kroschwitz, Jacqueline I. (Executive Editor) *v.5 p.257*

Kroschwitz, Jacqueline I. *v.5 p.257*

Krudy, Gyula & Szirtes, George *v.2 p.786*

Krudy, Gyula *v.2 p.786*

Krueger, Brian D. *v.4 p.170*

Krueger, Richard A. & Casey, Mary Anne *v.4 p.686*

Krueger, Richard A. & King, Jean A. *v.4 p.136*

Krueger, Richard A. *v.4 p.136*

Krueger, Roberta L. (Editor). *v.2 p.168, v.6 p.565*

Krug, Edward A.. . . . . *v.4 p.327*

Krug, Gary J. *v.4 p.760*

Krug, Steve *v.5 p.338, p.339*

Kruger, Arnd & Murray, William (Editors). *v.4 p.807, p.846, p.891*

Kruger, Arnd & Riordan, James (Editors) . . . *v.4 p.807, p.888*

Kruger, Lawrence (Editor) *v.5 p.606*

Krugman, Paul *v.4 p.244*

Kruijt, Dirk *v.3 p.275*
Kruk, Herman. *v.3 p.85*
Krukowski, Lucian *v.1 p.481*
Krumboltz, John D. & Hamel, Daniel A. *v.5 p.577*
Krumhansl, Carol L. *v.1 p.376*
Krummel, Donald W. & Sadie, Stanley (Editors). *v.1 p.168, p.384*
Krummel, Donald W. (Editor), et al. *v.1 p.167, p.278*
Krupnick, Charles *v.4 p.639, p.654*
Kruschke, Earl R. & Jackson, Byron M. *v.5 p.740*
Krutch, Joseph Wood *v.5 p.79, p.230*
Krutilla, John V. & Fisher, Anthony C. *v.4 p.62*
Krutnik, Frank *v.6 p.314, p.328, p.342*
Kryt, Dobromila (Editor) *v.5 p.258*
Kryter, Karl D. *v.5 p.364, p.374*
Kryzanek, Michael J. & Wiarda, Howard J.. . . . . *v.4 p.592*
Kubasek, Nancy K., et al. *v.4 p.51*
Kubiak, Greg D. *v.4 p.534*
Kubicek, Paul J. *v.4 p.127*
Kubik, Gerhard *v.1 p.261*
Kubler-Ross, Elisabeth *v.4 p.742*
Kucer, Stephen B. *v.4 p.354, p.364*
Kucera, Antonin *v.5 p.387*
Kuchel, Philip W. *v.5 p.331, p.333, p.335*
Kucich, John & Sadoff, Dianne F. (Editors). *v.2 p.175*
Kucich, John, et al. *v.2 p.297, p.312, p.341*
Kuczma, Marcin *v.5 p.459*
Kuczynski, Leon (Editor) *v.5 p.641*
Kuczynski, P. *v.3 p.330*
Kudaka, Geraldine & Leong, Russell. *v.6 p.100*
Kudryavtsev, A. B., et al. *v.5 p.278*
Kuehl, Karl, et al. *v.5 p.582*
Kuehn, Manfred *v.3 p.167*
Kuehn, Robert E. (Editor). *v.2 p.354*
Kuehni, Rolf G. *v.1 p.710*
Kuethe, Allan J.. . . . . *v.3 p.275, p.310, p.356*
Kugler, Eileen Gale. *v.4 p.309*
Kuhlmann, Hilke *v.4 p.499*
Kuhn, Annette *v.6 p.318, p.474*
Kuhn, Bowie *v.4 p.807, p.851, p.884*
Kuhn, Cynthia, et al. *v.4 p.826*
Kuhn, Philip A. & Brook, Timothy (Editors) *v.4 p.620*
Kuhn, Philip A. *v.6 p.187*
Kuhn, Robert Lawrence *v.6 p.197, p.200*
Kuhn, Thomas S. *v.1 p.499, v.3 p.47, v.5 p.61, p.403*
Kuhrt, Amelie & Sherwin-White, Susan (Editors) . . . *v.3 p.21*
Kuhrt, Amelie *v.3 p.4*
Kuiper, Edith & Barker, Drucilla K. *v.4 p.274*
Kuiper, Edith & Sap, Jolande *v.4 p.274*
Kuitert, Wybe *v.1 p.819*
Kuklick, Bruce. *v.1 p.439*
Kuklick, Henrika *v.4 p.4*
Kuklinski, James H. (Editor, Contribution by). . . . *v.5 p.643*
Kuklinski, Jim (Editor) *v.4 p.483, v.5 p.643*
Kukreja, Veena *v.4 p.617, p.618*
Kularatna, Nihal & Dias, Dileeka *v.4 p.115*

Kulavig, Erik *v.3 p.228*
Kulczycki, John J. *v.3 p.253*
Kulick, Don (Author, Contribution by) *v.4 p.19*
Kulick, Don *v.4 p.746*
Kulikoff, Allan *v.5 p.5*
Kull, Andrew *v.4 p.457*
Kullman, Colby H. & Young, William C.
  (Editors). *v.1 p.96, p.127, p.128, p.130, p.136*
Kulp, Karel & Ponterotto, Joseph G.. . . . . . *v.5 p.22, p.32*
Kumar, A. & Srivastava, A. K. *v.5 p.128*
Kumar, Amitava *v.6 p.118, p.138*
Kumar, Nita *v.6 p.154*
Kumar, Radha *v.6 p.431*
Kumar, Shiv K. *v.6 p.151*
Kumar, Vinay, et al. *v.5 p.514*
Kumashiro, Kevin K. (Editor) *v.6 p.94, p.107, p.112*
Kumin, Maxine *v.2 p.92*
Kummel, Werner G. *v.1 p.624*
Kump, Lee R., et al. *v.5 p.248*
Kuna, Franz *v.2 p.611*
Kunda, Ziva *v.5 p.649*
Kundera, Milan, et al. *v.2 p.784*
Kundera, Milan *v.2 p.784*
Kundur, Prabha *v.5 p.724*
Kunert, Gunter *v.2 p.611*
Kung, Hans *v.1 p.529, p.573, p.639, p.644, p.646, p.655*
Kunin, W. & Gaston, Kevin J. (Editors) *v.5 p.155*
Kunitz, Stanley *v.2 p.92*
Kunstler, Barton Lee. *v.4 p.66*
Kunstler, James Howard *v.4 p.771*
Kunz, Diane B. (Editor). *v.3 p.473*
Kunz, George Frederick & Stevenson, Charles Hugh . *v.1 p.715*
Kunzig, Robert. *v.5 p.428*
Kunzle, David *v.3 p.302*
Kuo, Benjamin C. & Golnaraghi, Farid. *v.5 p.711*
Kuo, Benjamin C. *v.5 p.711*
Kuo, Michael *v.5 p.209*
Kupchan, Charles *v.4 p.642*
Kuper, Leo *v.4 p.435*
Kupfer, David J. & Bloom, Floyd E. (Editors) . . . *v.5 p.517*
Kupiec, Mary (Editor), et al. *v.3 p.368*
Kupperman, Joel J. *v.1 p.475*
Kupperman, Karen O. *v.3 p.500*
Kupperman, Karen Ordahl *v.6 p.685*
Kuppers, Petra *v.1 p.86, p.135*
Kuprin, Aleksandr I. *v.2 p.805*
Kurain, George T. (Editor), et al. *v.4 p.517*
Kuran, Timur *v.4 p.207, p.237*
Kurasaki, Karen S. (Editor), et al. *v.6 p.122*
Kurashige, Lon. *v.6 p.132*
Kurath, Gertrude P. & Lewis, Robert E. (Editors) . . *v.2 p.551*
Kurath, Gertrude P. *v.1 p.15*
Kurath, Gertrude Prokosch; Garcia, Antonio *v.1 p.49*
Kureishi, Hanif *v.2 p.360, p.361*
Kureishi, M. *v.1 p.271*

Kurian, George Thomas, et al. *v.4 p.575*

Kurihara, Kenneth K. (Editor) *v.4 p.232*

Kurin, Richard *v.1 p.826*

Kuriyama, Constance Brown *v.2 p.221*

Kurke, Leslie *v.2 p.417*

Kurland, Philip B. *v.4 p.470*

Kurlansky, Mark *v.5 p.319, v.6 p.291*

Kuroda, Yasumasa *v.4 p.622*

Kurosawa, Akira *v.6 p.344*

Kurose, James F. & Ross, Keith W. *v.5 p.727*

Kuroyanagi, Tetsuko *v.6 p.227*

Kursmark, Louise M. *v.4 p.170*

Kurtén, Bjö & Anderson, Elaine *v.5 p.448*

Kurth, Peter *v.1 p.10, v.6 p.414*

Kurtz, Barbara E. *v.2 p.647*

Kurtz, Donald V. *v.4 p.34*

Kurtz, Ernest *v.4 p.776, v.5 p.673*

Kurtz, Michael *v.1 p.217, p.358*

Kurtz, Stephen G. & Hutson, James H. (Editors) . . . *v.3 p.409*

Kurtzman, Jeffrey *v.1 p.185, p.342*

Kuruvilla, M I *v.2 p.760*

Kurz, Heinz D. & Salvadori, Neri (Editors) *v.4 p.218*

Kurz, Heinz-Dieter & Salvadori, Neri *v.4 p.218*

Kurzman, Charles *v.1 p.557, v.6 p.632*

Kurzweil, Hans & Stellmacher, Bernd *v.5 p.474*

Kurzweil, Jack *v.5 p.726*

Kus, Sally *v.4 p.794, p.869, p.904*

Kushell, Jennifer *v.4 p.167*

Kushner, Harvey W. *v.4 p.678*

Kushner, Tony & Knox, Katharine *v.4 p.668*

Kushner, Tony . . . *v.1 p.62, p.126, p.723, v.2 p.148, v.6 p.412*

Kuska, Bob *v.4 p.807, p.832, p.854*

Kusky, Timothy M. *v.5 p.417, p.423*

Kusnitz, Leonard A. *v.3 p.390*

Kuspit, Donald B. *v.1 p.802, p.810*

Kuspit, Donald *v.1 p.679*

Kuss, Malena (Editor) *v.1 p.292*

Kusserow, Adrie *v.4 p.733*

Kuster, Konrad *v.1 p.190, p.344*

Kuther, Tara L. *v.5 p.675*

Kutler, Stanley I. *v.3 p.373, p.442, p.448, p.473*

Kutliroff, David *v.5 p.563*

Kutnjak Ivkovic, Sanja *v.6 p.260*

Kutska, Kenneth S., et al. *v.4 p.787, p.796*

Kuttner, Robert *v.4 p.665*

Kutz, Myer (Editor) *v.5 p.689*

Kutz, Myer *v.5 p.700*

Kutzinski, Vera M. *v.2 p.672*

Kuwana, Theodore (Editor) *v.5 p.268*

Kux, Dennis *v.4 p.644*

Kuyk, Betty M. *v.6 p.26*

Kuykendall, Ralph S. *v.3 p.534*

Kuzenski, John C., et al. *v.3 p.507*

Kuzio, Taras & D'Anieri, Paul J. (Editors) . . *v.4 p.585, p.598*

Kuzio, Taras *v.4 p.598*

Kuznar, Lawrence A. *v.4 p.24*

Kuzniar, Alice A. *v.6 p.416*

Kvistad, Gregg *v.4 p.609*

Kwak, Jenny & Fried, Liz *v.6 p.235*

Kwasny, Mark V. *v.3 p.409*

Kweit, Robert W. & Kweit, Mary G. *v.6 p.723*

Kwok, Sun *v.5 p.69*

Kwoka, John E. & White, Lawrence J. (Editors) . *v.4 p.84, p.109*

Kwolek-Folland, Angel *v.4 p.57*

Kwon, Youngmin (Editor) *v.6 p.238*

Kwong, Peter *v.6 p.106, p.114, p.116, p.120, p.127*

Kyambalesa, Henry & Houngnikpo, Mathurin C. . . . *v.4 p.384*

Kyd, Thomas *v.2 p.218*

Kydd, Andrew *v.4 p.624*

Kydland, Finn E. (Editor) *v.4 p.244*

Kyle, Keith *v.6 p.65*

Kymlicka, Will *v.4 p.547, p.551, p.573, p.579*

Kyriacou, Demetrios K. *v.5 p.294*

Kyrk, Hazel *v.4 p.265*

Kyte, Jack *v.5 p.116*

Kythe, Prem K. & Wei, Dongming *v.5 p.695*

Kyvig, David E. *v.4 p.454*

L

La Bruyère, Jean de *v.2 p.474*

La Fayette, Madame de *v.2 p.474*

La Follette, Robert M. *v.3 p.434*

La Fontaine, Jean De *v.2 p.474*

La Fontaine, Jean de *v.2 p.474*

La Fontaine, Jean De *v.2 p.474*

La Grange, Henry-Louis de *v.1 p.217, p.339*

La Laurencie, Lionel D. *v.6 p.408, p.412*

La Mothe, Jacques *v.2 p.511*

La Rocca, Cristina (Editor) *v.3 p.198*

La Rochefoucauld, Francois de *v.2 p.474, p.477*

La Rosa Corzo, Gabino *v.3 p.311*

La Rosa, Michael & Mejia, German R. (eds.) . . . *v.3 p.305*

La Vere, David *v.6 p.687*

Laban, Rudolf *v.1 p.10, p.47*

Laband, John *v.6 p.79*

Labanyi, Jo *v.2 p.641*

Labaree, Benjamin W. *v.3 p.487*

Labaree, Leonard W. *v.3 p.406, v.4 p.553*

LaBarre, Weston *v.4 p.36*

L'Abate, Luciano *v.5 p.658, p.661, p.668*

Labe, Louise *v.2 p.470*

LaBelle, Maurice M. *v.2 p.521*

Laberge, Marie *v.2 p.540*

Labé, Louise *v.2 p.470*

Labiche, Eugene, et al. *v.2 p.465*

Labiche, Eugene *v.2 p.495*

Labiche, Eugène *v.2 p.495*

Labon, Joanna (Editor) *v.2 p.818*

Labov, William *v.2 p.562*

Labovitz, John R. *v.4 p.462*

Labuta, Joseph A. & Smith, Deborah *v.1 p.405*

Labuta, Joseph A. *v.1 p.402*

Lacey, A. R. *v.1 p.456*

Lacey, Alan *v.1 p.415*

Lacey, Michael J. *v.5 p.369, p.371, p.374*

Lacey, Stephen *v.1 p.80, p.101*

Lach, Donald F. & Van Kley, Edwin J. *v.6 p.145, p.215*

Lach, Donald F. *v.6 p.145, p.215*

Lach, Donald *v.3 p.74*

Lachapelle, Guy, et al. *v.4 p.589*

Lachs, John *v.1 p.439*

Lackey, Scott A. *v.3 p.182*

Lackie, J. M. *v.5 p.153*

Laclos, Choderlos de *v.2 p.480*

Lacouture, Jean *v.3 p.155, p.157*

LaCroix, Isobyl (Consultant Editor) *v.5 p.43*

Lacroix, Zoé & Critchlow, Terence (Editors) *v.5 p.97*

LaCugna, Charles S. *v.4 p.122*

Lacy, Norris J. & Asher, Martha *v.2 p.467*

Lacy, Norris J. & Grimbert, Joan Tasker (Editors) . *v.2 p.467*

Lacy, Norris J. (Editor) *v.2 p.467*

Laczkovich, Miklos *v.5 p.470*

Ladd, Brian *v.3 p.169, p.181, v.4 p.582, v.6 p.726*

Ladd, Gary W. *v.5 p.627, p.631*

Ladd, George Eldon *v.1 p.625*

Ladd, Helen F. & Yinger, John M. *v.4 p.544, v.6 p.724*

Ladd, M. F. *v.5 p.306*

Ladd, Mark *v.5 p.284*

Ladefoged, Peter & Maddieson, Ian *v.2 p.562*

Ladefoged, Peter *v.2 p.562*

Lader, Lawrence *v.6 p.470*

Laderman, Carol & Roseman, Marina (Editors) . . . *v.4 p.46*

Laderman, Carol *v.4 p.46*

Ladha, J. K. (Editor), et al. *v.5 p.12*

Ladies Professional Golf Association Staff . . . *v.4 p.837, p.861*

Ladner, Joyce A. (Editor) *v.4 p.683, v.6 p.39*

Ladson-Billings, Gloria *v.4 p.310*

LaDuke, Winona *v.6 p.681*

Ladurie, Emmanuel Le Roy *v.3 p.143, p.145*

Ladurie, LeRoy *v.3 p.145*

Ladygina-Kohts, N. N. *v.5 p.615*

Ladyman, James *v.5 p.403*

Lafayette, Le Marquis de *v.3 p.411*

Lafayette, Madame de *v.2 p.474*

Lafayette, Marie-Madeleine *v.2 p.474*

LaFeber, Walter *v.3 p.305, p.385, p.398*

Lafeber, Walter *v.3 p.433*

LaFeber, Walter *v.3 p.453, p.474*

LaFerla, Jane & Gunter, Veronika A. (Editors) . . . *v.1 p.761*

Laferriere, Dany *v.2 p.540*

Laffan, Michael *v.3 p.139*

Laffan, R. G. *v.3 p.248*

Laffaye, Horace A. *v.4 p.844, p.863*

Lafferty, James M. (Editor) *v.5 p.563*

LaFollette, Hugh (Editor) *v.1 p.486*

Lafond, Paul *v.1 p.757*

Laforest, Guy *v.3 p.541*

Laforet, Carmen *v.2 p.661*

Laforgue, Jules *v.2 p.495*

LaForgue, Jules *v.2 p.495*

LaFrance, David G. *v.3 p.293*

LaGamma, Alisa *v.1 p.777*

Lagarde, André (Editor) *v.2 p.463*

Lagemann, Ellen Condliffe *v.4 p.355*

Lagendijk, Arnoud & Oinas, Päivi *v.4 p.397*

Lager, Fred C. *v.4 p.52*

Lagercrantz, Olof *v.2 p.630*

Lagergren, Jens (Editor) *v.5 p.140*

Lagerkvist, Par *v.2 p.630*

Lagerkvist, Pär *v.2 p.630*

Lagerkvist, Ulf *v.5 p.122*

Lagerlöf, Selma *v.2 p.630*

Lagerquist, L. DeAne *v.1 p.585*

Lagerwey, John (Editor) *v.1 p.539*

Lagnese, John E. & Schmidt, E. J. *v.5 p.695*

Lago, Mary *v.2 p.346*

Lagos, Maria L. *v.3 p.324*

Lagowski, Joseph J. (Editor) *v.5 p.257*

LaGrega, Michael D., et al. *v.5 p.705*

Lahav, Gallya *v.4 p.637, p.668*

Lahey, Benjamin B. (Editor), et al. *v.5 p.662*

Lahiri, Jhumpa *v.2 p.148, v.6 p.100*

Lahita, Robert G., et al. *v.5 p.517*

Lahr, John *v.2 p.374, v.6 p.413*

Lai, Eric Yo Ping (Editor) *v.6 p.86*

Lai, Him M., et al. *v.6 p.103, p.118, p.127*

Lai, Him Mark *v.6 p.86, p.127*

Lai, James & Nakanishi, Don T. (Editors) *v.6 p.120*

Lai, Whalen & Lancaster, Lewis R. (Editors) *v.1 p.568*

Laidler, David *v.4 p.225, p.238*

Laidler, Keith J. *v.5 p.391*

Laine, James W. *v.6 p.156*

Laing, Dave *v.1 p.271*

Laing, Ellen J. *v.1 p.711*

Laing, Lloyd Robert & Laing, Jennifer *v.1 p.670, p.688*

Laing, Lloyd Robert *v.3 p.96*

Laiou, Angeliki E. (Editor) *v.3 p.193*

Laird, Mark *v.1 p.819*

Laird, Pamela Walker *v.4 p.53, p.132, p.147*

Laird, Sally (Editor) *v.2 p.799*

Laistner, Max L. *v.2 p.426, p.449, v.6 p.567*

Laitin, David D. *v.6 p.71*

Laitinen, Herbert A. *v.5 p.274*

Laity, Cassandra *v.2 p.89*

Lajoie, Susanne (Editor) *v.5 p.590*

Lajoie, Susanne P. (Editor) *v.5 p.463*

Lajolo, Davide *v.2 p.720*

Lajoux, Alexandra Reed & Nesvold, H. Peter *v.4 p.84*

Lakatos, Imre & Musgrave, Alan E. (Editors) *v.5 p.403*

Lakatos, Imre (Editor), et al. *v.5 p.470*

Lake, David A. & Powell, Robert (Editors) *v.4 p.625*

Lake, David A.. . . . . *v.3 p.453*

Lake, Peter *v.1 p.588*

Lakeman, Enid. *v.4 p.577*

Laker, Anthony (Editor) *v.4 p.796, p.817*

Laker, Anthony *v.4 p.796, p.798, p.799*

Laki, Peter *v.1 p.217, p.305*

Lakoff, George & Johnson, Mark . . . *v.2 p.562, v.4 p.20, p.27*

Lakoff, George *v.4 p.20, v.5 p.619*

Lakoff, Robin Tolmach *v.2 p.557, p.562, v.4 p.21*

Lakoff, Sanford *v.4 p.504*

Lakshminarayana, Budugur *v.5 p.713*

Lal, Ananda (Editor) *v.1 p.59, p.131*

Lal, Rattan *v.5 p.187, p.359, p.367*

Lal, R *v.5 p.50*

Lal, Vinay (Editor) *v.6 p.150*

Lal, Vinay *v.6 p.146*

Lalic, Ivan V. & Jones, Francis R. *v.2 p.811*

Lalli, Carol M. & Parsons, Timothy *v.4 p.392, v.5 p.431*

Lam, Andrew *v.6 p.94, p.140*

Lam, Truong B. *v.6 p.167*

Lamadrid, Enrique R. & Gandert, Miguel A. *v.6 p.523*

Lamanna, Mary Ann *v.4 p.681*

Lamantia, Philip. *v.2 p.94*

Lamar, Howard R. (Editor) *v.3 p.518*

Lamar, Howard Roberts *v.3 p.523, p.527*

Lamarsh, John R. & Baratta, Anthony J. *v.5 p.740*

Lamb, Andrew *v.1 p.92*

Lamb, B. C. *v.5 p.135*

Lamb, Charles & Lamb, Mary. *v.2 p.298*

Lamb, Charles *v.2 p.298*

Lamb, Chris *v.4 p.409, p.417, p.807, p.832, p.851*

Lamb, Hubert *v.6 p.293*

Lamb, Margaret & Tarling, Nicholas. *v.6 p.164*

Lamb, Margaret (Editor), et al. *v.4 p.107*

Lamb, Michael E. (Editor) *v.5 p.641*

Lamb, Sharon *v.5 p.641*

Lamb, Simon & Sington, David. *v.5 p.419, p.445*

Lamb, Simon *v.5 p.432*

Lamb, Trevor & Bourriau, Janine (Editors) *v.5 p.607*

Lambdin, Laura Cooner & Lambdin, Robert Thomas
(Editors). *v.2 p.167, p.168*

Lambdin, Robert T. & Lambdin, Laura C. (Editors) . . *v.6 p.565*

Lambek, Michael *v.4 p.36*

Lambert Colomeda, Lorelei A.. . . . . *v.6 p.681*

Lambert, David & Diagram Group. *v.5 p.419*

Lambert, David M. & Spencer, Hamish G. *v.5 p.199*

Lambert, Eddie & Norsworthy, Elaine *v.1 p.261, p.323*

Lambert, Francis J. D. *v.3 p.311*

Lambert, Joseph B., et al. *v.5 p.297*

Lambert, Joseph B.. . . . . *v.5 p.263*

Lambert, Josiah Bartlett. *v.4 p.127*

Lambert, Malcolm *v.1 p.646, v.3 p.57, p.69, v.6 p.572*

Lambert, Nadine M. & McCombs, Barbara L. (Editors). *v.5 p.574*

Lambert, Peter *v.3 p.344*

Lambert, Philip *v.1 p.217, p.333*

Lambert, Phyllis & Van der Rohe, Ludwig Mies . . . *v.1 p.793*

Lambert, Robert A. *v.5 p.79, p.237*

Lambert, Robert Stansbury *v.3 p.409*

Lambert, Stephen E. & Decotis, Ruth *v.5 p.459*

Lambert, Stephen E. *v.4 p.170*

Lambert, Susan *v.1 p.759*

Lamberti, Jean-Claude *v.4 p.492*

Lamberton, Robert. *v.2 p.413, p.418*

Lamberts, Koen & Goldstone, Rob (Editors) *v.5 p.649*

Lambeth, Edmund B.. . . . . *v.4 p.405*

Lambourne, Lionel *v.1 p.728*

Lamboy, Edwin M.. . . . . *v.6 p.494*

Lambrechts, James R. (Editor), et al.. . . . . . . *v.5 p.422*

Lambright, W. Henry (Editor) *v.5 p.719*

Lambright, W. Henry. *v.5 p.394, p.412*

Lambsdorff, Johann Graf, et al. *v.4 p.252, p.263*

Lambton, Ann K. S. *v.6 p.630, p.669*

Lambton, Ann Katharine Swynford. [from old catalog]. *v.6 p.669*

Lamiell, James T. *v.5 p.597*

Laming, D. R. J. *v.5 p.658*

Lamis, Alexander P. (Editor) *v.3 p.496*

Lamm, Martin *v.2 p.630*

Lamming, George *v.2 p.768*

Lamont, Corliss *v.1 p.507*

Lamont, Michele (Editor) *v.4 p.728*

Lamont, Rosette C. (Editor). *v.1 p.67, p.87, p.121*

LaMonte, J. L. *v.3 p.64*

Lamotte, E. *v.1 p.561*

Lampard, Marie Turbow (Editor), et al. *v.1 p.780*

Lampe, G. W. (Editor) *v.1 p.615*

Lampe, John R. *v.3 p.247, p.248*

Lampe Kingston, Armando *v.3 p.315*

Lampert, Ada *v.5 p.654*

Lampert, Laurence *v.1 p.466*

Lampert, Magdalene & Ball, Deborah *v.5 p.463*

Lampert, Magdalene *v.5 p.463*

Lampkin, N. H. & Padel, S. (Editors) *v.5 p.30, p.31*

Lampkin, Nicolas *v.5 p.30, p.31*

Lampman, Archibald *v.2 p.732*

Lampman, Steve *v.5 p.732*

Lamport, Leslie *v.5 p.461*

Lan, Feng *v.2 p.111*

Lan, Yi-Chen & Unhelkar, Bhuvan *v.4 p.69*

Lancaster, Jane F. *v.6 p.687*

Lancaster, Jordan *v.3 p.197, p.204*

Lancaster, Lynne C. & Stillman, David. *v.4 p.132*

Lancaster, M. *v.5 p.310*

Lancaster, Roger & Di Leonardo, Micaela
(Editors). *v.6 p.428, p.436*

Lancaster, William *v.6 p.596*

Lanchester, John *v.2 p.361*

Lanchner, Carolyn *v.1 p.697*

Lanctot, Neil *v.4 p.807, p.832, p.851, p.884, p.888, p.896*

Lanczos, Cornelius *v.5 p.548*

Land, Aubrey C. *v.3 p.493*

Land, Myrick & Land, Barbara *v.3 p.529, v.6 p.713*

Land, Myrick E. & Land, Barbara N. *v.3 p.529*

Landau, David & Parshall, Peter W. *v.1 p.753*

Landau, Ellen G. *v.1 p.742*

Landau, Jacob M., et al. *v.3 p.230*

Landau, Jacob M. *v.6 p.597, p.638*

Landau, L. D. & Lifshitz, E. M. . . . *v.5 p.546, p.547, p.549*

Landau, L. D., et al. *v.5 p.546, p.550, p.559, p.565*

Landau, L. D. *v.5 p.546, p.548, p.564*

Landau, Ralph (Editor), et al. *v.4 p.244*

Landau, Rubin H., et al. *v.5 p.551*

Landau, Sarah B. *v.1 p.793*

Landau, Saul *v.3 p.299, p.302*

Landauer, Susan *v.1 p.743*

Lande, Russell, et al. *v.5 p.180, p.189*

Landels, John G. *v.1 p.175*

Lander, Guy *v.4 p.109, p.111, p.112*

Landers, Robert K. *v.2 p.73*

Landes, David S. *v.3 p.40, p.77, v.4 p.237, p.265*

Landes, Ruth *v.6 p.703, p.705*

Landgrebe, John A. *v.5 p.301*

Landis, Deborah Nadoolman & Makovsky, Judianna . *v.6 p.349*

Landis, Deborah Nadoolman *v.6 p.349*

Landis, Jacquelyn *v.6 p.489, p.531*

Landis, Mark *v.3 p.460*

Landis, Wayne G. & Yu, Ming-Ho *v.5 p.330, p.704*

Landman, Bruce M. & Robertson, Aaron *v.5 p.476*

Landon, H. C. & Wyn Jones, David *v.1 p.191, p.330*

Landon, H. C. Robbins *v.1 p.190, p.241, p.330, p.344*

Landon, H. C. *v.1 p.200, p.307*

Landon, J. R. *v.5 p.50*

Landow, George P. *v.2 p.305, v.6 p.750, p.752*

Landow, George *v.2 p.751, v.6 p.749, p.750, p.752*

Landry, Paul & McNair, Matty *v.4 p.788, p.789*

Landsberg, Brian K. *v.4 p.532*

Landsmann, Liliana Tolchinsky *v.4 p.369*

Landweber, Laura F. & Dobson, Andrew P. (Editors) . *v.5 p.122*

Landy, Joanne M. & Burridge, Keith R. *v.4 p.798*

Landy, Marcia (Editor) *v.6 p.315*

Landy, Marcia *v.6 p.331*

Lane, Barbara Miller *v.1 p.787*

Lane, Christina *v.6 p.328, p.342*

Lane, Edward William *v.6 p.638*

Lane, Eric & Shengold, Nina *v.6 p.412*

Lane, Frederic C. *v.3 p.198*

Lane, Frederick C. (Editor) *v.3 p.40*

Lane, Harold E. & Dupré, Denise *v.4 p.161*

Lane, James B. & Escobar, Edward J. (Editors) . . . *v.6 p.536*

Lane, Jan-Erik *v.4 p.75*

Lane, John *v.5 p.79, p.234*

Lane, Kris E. *v.3 p.332*

Lane, Richard D. & Nadel, Lynn (Editors) *v.5 p.612*

Lane, Robert E. *v.5 p.643*

Lane, Saunders Mac & Birkhoff, Garrett D. *v.5 p.473*

Lane, Terrance & Serk, Jessie *v.1 p.800*

Lane, Thomas *v.3 p.256*

Lanes, Selma G. *v.2 p.582*

Lang, Bernhard *v.1 p.654*

Lang, Frieder R. & Fingerman, Karen L. . . . *v.4 p.741, v.5 p.648*

Lang, G. A. (Editor) *v.5 p.124*

Lang, Gladys E. & Lang, Kurt *v.3 p.474*

Lang, Helen S. *v.5 p.399*

Lang, Jack *v.5 p.727*

Lang, Kenneth R. & Gingerich, Owen (Editors) . . . *v.5 p.61*

Lang, Kenneth R. *v.5 p.63, p.68*

Lang, Paul Henry *v.1 p.174*

Lang, Robert J. *v.5 p.469*

Lang, Sabine *v.6 p.370*

Lang, Serge A. *v.5 p.459*

Langan, Thomas *v.1 p.471*

Langbaum, Robert *v.2 p.181*

Langbein, John H. *v.6 p.270*

Langdell, Cheri Colby *v.2 p.115*

Langdon, George D. *v.3 p.487*

Langdon, John W. *v.3 p.79*

Langdon, Philip *v.6 p.718*

Lange, Victor *v.2 p.590*

Langen, Timothy & Weir, Justin
(Editors) *v.1 p.67, p.109, v.2 p.794*

Langenheim, Jean H. *v.5 p.16*

Langenkamp, Robert D. *v.5 p.738*

Langer, Adam & Barsanti, Chris *v.6 p.346*

Langer, Arthur M. *v.4 p.79*

Langer, Ellen J. *v.5 p.611*

Langer, Erick D. *v.3 p.324*

Langer, Georgea M., et al. *v.4 p.286*

Langer, John *v.4 p.414*

Langer, Judith *v.4 p.136*

Langer, Lawrence L. *v.2 p.572, v.3 p.85*

Langer, Susanne K. *v.1 p.441, p.442*

Langer, Ullrich (Editor) *v.2 p.470*

Langer, William H. & Glanzman, V. M. *v.5 p.452*

Langer, William H. *v.5 p.452*

Langer, William L. & Gleason, S. Everett *v.3 p.453*

Langevin, Andre *v.2 p.541*

Langfeld, Herbert Sidney *v.5 p.618*

Langford, Cooper Harold; Gray, Harry B. *v.5 p.304*

Langford, Paul *v.3 p.107, p.109, p.128*

Langford, Wendy *v.5 p.654, v.6 p.465, p.467*

Langford-Wood, Naomi & Salter, Brian *v.4 p.173*

Langhans, Edward A. (Editor), et al. *v.1 p.59*

Langland, Elizabeth *v.6 p.744, p.747, p.756, p.765*

Langland, Tuck *v.1 p.782*

Langland, William *v.2 p.211*

Langley, J. Ayodele (Editor) *v.6 p.10, p.31, p.36*

Langley, Jabez Ayodele *v.6 p.68*

Langley, Lester D. *v.3 p.315*

Langley, Stephen *v.1 p.116, p.137*

Langley, Winston E. *v.4 p.513*
Langman, Larry *v.6 p.324*
Langmead, Donald *v.1 p.662, p.697, p.783, p.793*
Langmuir, Erika & Lynton, Norbert *v.1 p.665*
Langsdon, Phillip R. *v.3 p.510*
Langston, Craig & Lauge-Kristensen, Rima *v.4 p.113*
Langston, Nancy & Cronon, William *v.6 p.295*
Langstroth, Lovell & Langstroth, Libby *v.5 p.84*
Langton, Phyllis & Kammerer, Dianne *v.4 p.675*
Langton, Robert *v.2 p.285*
Langton, Stephen *v.2 p.449*
Langum, David J. *v.4 p.473*
Langwill, Lyndesay G. *v.1 p.390*
Lanham, Richard A. *v.4 p.173*
LANIC: Latin American Network Information Center . *v.6 p.463*
Lanier, Doris *v.4 p.776*
Lanier, Drew Noble *v.4 p.537*
Lanier, Parks Jr. (Editor) *v.2 p.12*
Lanier, Sidney *v.2 p.47*
Lankevich, George *v.3 p.491, v.6 p.714*
Lankford, John & Rothenberg, Marc (Editors) *v.5 p.61*
Lankford, Ronald D. Jr. & Lankford, Ronald D. . . . *v.1 p.296*
Lannering, J. *v.2 p.237*
Lanning, Michael L. *v.6 p.7*
Lannon, John M. *v.5 p.680*
Lannoo, Michael J. (Editor) *v.5 p.215*
Lansbury, Coral *v.6 p.748*
Lansdown, Richard (Editor) *v.4 p.385*
Lansford, Tom *v.3 p.390, v.4 p.564, p.631, p.660*
Lansing, Carol *v.3 p.199*
Lansing, Richard (Editor) *v.2 p.705*
Lansing, Richard H. (Editor) *v.2 p.705*
Lansing, Robert Jr. *v.4 p.631*
Lanson, Jerry & Fought, Barbara Croll *v.4 p.414*
Lantz, Kenneth *v.2 p.805*
Lanyon, Richard I. & Goodstein, Leonard D. *v.5 p.603*
Lanza, Joseph *v.1 p.376*
Lanzmann, Claude *v.3 p.85*
Lao She *v.6 p.212*
Lao-Montes, Agustin & Davila, Arlene M.
(Editors) *v.6 p.542, p.549*
LaPalombara, Joseph *v.4 p.594*
Lapan, Maureen & Houghton, Raymond *v.4 p.357*
Lapchick, Richard E. (Editor) *v.4 p.822, p.894*
Lape, Noreen Groover *v.2 p.15*
Lapesa, Rafael *v.2 p.639*
Lapham, Lewis H. & Rosenbush, Ellen (Editors) . *v.2 p.19, p.584*
Lapidus, Ira M. *v.1 p.554*
Lapine, James & Sondheim, Stephen . *v.1 p.251, p.357, p.408*
Laplante, Phillip A. *v.5 p.106, p.108*
Lapointe, Paul-Marie *v.2 p.541*
Laporte, Joseph *v.5 p.155*
Lappin, A. G. *v.5 p.304*
Lappin, Elena *v.2 p.781*
Laqueur, Thomas W. *v.3 p.113, p.121*

Laqueur, Walter & Rubin, Barry (Editors) *v.6 p.618*
Laqueur, Walter (Editor) *v.3 p.85*
Laqueur, Walter *v.1 p.549, v.4 p.510, p.660*
Larana, Enrique (Editor), et al. *v.4 p.710*
Larbaud, Valéry *v.2 p.521*
Lardas, John *v.2 p.64, p.79, p.93*
Lardner, James & Reppetto, Thomas A. *v.6 p.261*
Lardner, Ring W. *v.2 p.94*
Lareau, Annette *v.4 p.728*
Large, David Clay *v.3 p.181*
Large, E. C. (Ernest Charles) *v.5 p.46*
Largey, Michael *v.4 p.26*
Larkin, Colin (Editor) *v.1 p.160, p.271*
Larkin, Colin *v.1 p.292, v.6 p.30*
Larkin, David *v.5 p.233*
Larkin, Emma *v.2 p.374*
Larkin, Emmet *v.3 p.139*
Larkin, John A. *v.6 p.180*
Larkin, Philip, et al. *v.2 p.361*
Larkin, Philip *v.2 p.361, p.362*
Larkum, Anthony W. D., et al. *v.5 p.208*
Larminie, James & Dicks, Andrew *v.5 p.742*
Larminie, James & Lowry, John *v.5 p.716*
Larmour, David H. J. *v.2 p.104*
Larner, John *v.3 p.199, v.6 p.215, p.563*
Laroche-Claire, Yves *v.2 p.454*
Larock, Richard C. *v.5 p.294*
Larossa, Ralph *v.4 p.739, v.6 p.467*
Laroui, Abdallah *v.6 p.641, p.642, p.643*
Larousse Editors (Editor) *v.2 p.636*
Larousse Mexico Staff *v.2 p.664*
Larrabee, Aimée & Altman, John *v.5 p.240*
Larres, Klaus *v.4 p.645*
Larrissy, Edward *v.2 p.240*
Lars, Claudia *v.2 p.676*
Larsen, Clark Spencer *v.4 p.14*
Larsen, Jakob Aall Ottesen *v.3 p.12, p.21*
Larsen, Jeffrey Arthur & Smith, James M. *v.4 p.656*
Larsen, Jens P. *v.1 p.185, p.235, p.329*
Larsen, Karen *v.3 p.234*
Larsen, Lawrence H. & Hulston, Nancy J. *v.3 p.512*
Larsen, Nella *v.2 p.94*
Larsen, Stein U; Hagtvet, Bernt; Myklebust, Jan P . *v.4 p.768*
Larsen, Timothy (Editor), et al. *v.1 p.590*
Larsen, William J. *v.5 p.162*
Larson, Brooke (Editor), et al. *v.3 p.324*
Larson, Brooke *v.3 p.324, p.327*
Larson, Catherine *v.2 p.640*
Larson, Charles R. (Editor, Introduction by) . *v.2 p.752, v.6 p.80*
Larson, Charles R. *v.6 p.80*
Larson, Donald R. *v.2 p.652*
Larson, Edward J. . *v.3 p.442, v.4 p.438, v.5 p.79, p.193, p.236*
Larson, Eric V. & Levin, Norman D. *v.3 p.390*
Larson, Jennifer *v.1 p.532*
Larson, Jill *v.2 p.189*

Larson, Kate Clifford *v.6 p.7, p.18, p.44*
Larson, Kelli A. *v.2 p.136*
Larson, Orville K. *v.1 p.147*
Larson, Peggy *v.5 p.234, p.240*
Larson, Pier Martin *v.6 p.67*
Larson, Reed & Eccles, Jacquelynne S. (Editors) . . . *v.4 p.288*
Larson, Ron, et al. *v.5 p.472*
Larson, T. A. *v.3 p.526*
LaRue, Jan *v.1 p.371*
LaSalle, Mick *v.6 p.328, p.332*
Lascelles, Mary *v.2 p.267*
Lasch, Christopher *v.4 p.704, p.768*
Lash, Joseph P. *v.3 p.460*
Lashley, Felissa R. *v.5 p.149*
Lashley, Karl S. *v.5 p.617*
Lasker, Bruno *v.6 p.119, p.129*
Laski, Harold J. *v.3 p.368, v.4 p.767*
Laskier, Michael M. *v.6 p.597, p.638, p.643*
Lasko, Peter *v.1 p.672*
Laslett, John M. (Editor) *v.4 p.127*
Laslett, Peter (Editor), et al. *v.4 p.740*
Laslett, Peter *v.3 p.92, v.4 p.704, p.737*
Lass, Roger (Editor) *v.2 p.554*
Lass, William E. *v.3 p.522*
Lasser, William *v.4 p.537*
Lassus, Bernard *v.1 p.813*
Lasswell, Harold D. (Editor), et al. . . . *v.4 p.696, p.697*
Lasswell, Harold D. (Editor) *v.4 p.696*
Lasswell, Harold Dwight *v.4 p.483*
Laszlo, Ervin *v.5 p.403*
Laszlo, Pierre & Mader, Mary Beth *v.5 p.451*
Laszlo, Pierre *v.5 p.319*
Latacz, Joachim *v.2 p.414*
Latash, Mark L. & Zatsiorsky, Vladimir M.
   (Editors). *v.4 p.873, p.908, p.909*
Latash, Mark L. *v.4 p.908, p.909*
Lateiner, Donald *v.2 p.412*
Latham, Alison (Editor) *v.1 p.161*
Latham, Earl *v.3 p.448*
Latham, Ronald E. (Editor) *v.2 p.423*
Latham, Sean *v.2 p.191*
Lather, Patricia A. & Smithies, Chris. . . . *v.6 p.443*
Lathi, Bhagwandas P. *v.5 p.726*
Latimer, Elizabeth Wormeley (Translator). . . *v.3 p.152*
Latimer, Wendell Mitchell. *v.5 p.285*
Latin American Network Information Center (LANIC). *v.4 p.704*
Latombe, Jean-Claude. *v.5 p.711*
Latsis, Spiro J. (Editor) *v.4 p.269*
Lattimore, Owen *v.3 p.460, v.6 p.239*
Lattimore, Richmond A. *v.2 p.402*
Lattin, Vernon E. (Editor), et al. *v.6 p.500, p.513*
Lattin, Vernon E. (Editor, Introduction by) . . . *v.6 p.500, p.514*
Latzer, Barry *v.6 p.268, p.269*
Latzko, William J. & Saunders, David M. . . . *v.4 p.73*
Lau, Evelyn *v.2 p.736*

Lau, Jenny Kwok Wah (Editor) *v.6 p.334*
Lau, Joseph S. (Editor), et al. *v.6 p.213*
Lau, Joseph S. M. & Goldblatt, Howard (Editors). *v.6 p.208, p.212*
Laub, John H. & Sampson, Robert J. *v.4 p.753, v.6 p.255*
Lauber, Daniel & Atkin, Jennifer *v.4 p.170*
Lauber, Daniel & Rice, Kraig *v.4 p.170*
Lauber, Daniel *v.4 p.170*
Lauber, Volkmar (Editor) *v.5 p.709*
Laubin, Reginald & Laubin, Gladys *v.6 p.700*
Lauck, Jon *v.5 p.14*
Laudan, Larry *v.5 p.389, p.394, p.400, p.403, p.409*
Laudan, Rachel *v.5 p.418*
Laude, Jean, et al. *v.1 p.21*
Lauder, Everlyn H. *v.5 p.222*
Lauderdale Graham, Sandra *v.3 p.279, p.337, p.341*
Laudicina, Paul A. *v.4 p.69*
Laue, Thomas M. & Plagens, Andreas *v.5 p.295*
Lauer, Quentin *v.1 p.464*
Laufer, Gabriel *v.5 p.701, p.730, p.731*
Lauffer, Robert Butch & Kater, April *v.4 p.837, p.867*
Laughton, Bruce *v.1 p.697*
Lauglo, Jon & Maclean, Rupert (Contribution by). . . *v.4 p.305*
Laugwitz, Detlef *v.5 p.467*
Laumann, Edward O. (Editor), et al. *v.4 p.748*
Laumann, Edward O., et al. *v.4 p.748*
Launay, Robert *v.6 p.69*
Launius, Roger D. & Jenkins, Dennis R. (Editors). . . *v.5 p.719*
Laurance, William F. & Bierregaard, Richard O. Jr.
   (Editors) *v.5 p.41, p.353, p.373*
Laurance, William F. *v.5 p.239*
Laurel, Brenda *v.4 p.55, p.57, p.63*
Lauren, Paul G. *v.4 p.513*
Lauren, Paul Gordon. *v.3 p.78*
Laurence, Frank M. *v.2 p.85*
Laurence, Margaret. *v.2 p.736*
Laurentis, Giacomo De (Editor) *v.4 p.155*
Laurents, Arthur *v.6 p.418*
Lauria-Santiago, Aldo & Binford, Leigh *v.3 p.299*
Laurie, Joe *v.1 p.35*
Laurie, Simon S. *v.4 p.327*
Lauring, Palle *v.3 p.234*
Lauritzen, Paul (Editor) *v.5 p.162*
Lautens, M. *v.5 p.290*
Lautreamont, Isidore de. *v.2 p.495*
Laux, James M. *v.4 p.154*
Lavalle, David, et al. *v.5 p.582*
Lavallee, Daniele *v.4 p.12*
Lavallee, David & Wylleman, Paul (Editors) *v.4 p.903*
Lavallee, David, et al. *v.4 p.877*
LaValley, Albert J. *v.2 p.277*
Lave, Jean *v.4 p.27*
Lavender, David *v.3 p.525, p.531*
Lavender, Larry *v.1 p.47*
Laver, James *v.1 p.151, p.715*

Lavidrine, Bertrand, et al. *v.1 p.824*

Laviera, Tato *v.6 p.507, p.510*

Lavin, David E. & Hyllegard, David *v.4 p.294*

Lavin, Marilyn A. *v.1 p.728, p.732*

Lavin, Michael R. *v.4 p.180*

Lavin, Michael *v.4 p.180*

Lavinia, Stan (Editor) *v.4 p.600*

Lavoie, Marc (Editor) *v.4 p.232*

Lavrin, Asuncion *v.3 p.283, p.346, p.348, p.354*

Law Commission of Canada (Editor) *v.6 p.250*

Law, Graham *v.6 p.741, p.756*

Law, Jonathan; Wright, John *v.6 p.307*

Law, Jonathan *v.1 p.59*

Law, Kam-Yee (Editor) *v.6 p.195*

Law Library of Congress . *v.4 p.437, p.440, p.474, p.475, p.476*

Law, Robin *v.6 p.68, p.73*

Lawal, H. Bayo *v.4 p.690*

Lawhorne, Clifton O. & Long, Howard R. *v.4 p.443*

Lawler, E. L., et al. *v.4 p.119*

Lawler, Edward E. III. *v.5 p.579*

Lawler, Edward E. *v.5 p.579*

Lawler, Jennifer *v.6 p.451*

Lawler, Justus George *v.1 p.573*

Lawler, Lillian B. *v.1 p.16*

Lawler, Thomas C. & Burghart, Johannes (Editors) . . *v.1 p.591*

Lawless, Richard (Editor) *v.4 p.765*

Lawoti, Mahendra *v.4 p.617*

Lawrence, A. W. *v.1 p.787*

Lawrence Berkeley National Laboratory *v.5 p.552*

Lawrence, Bruce B. *v.6 p.106*

Lawrence, C. H. *v.1 p.578, v.3 p.66, v.6 p.572*

Lawrence, D. H. *v.2 p.7, p.362, p.363*

Lawrence, David, et al. *v.5 p.173*

Lawrence, David M. *v.5 p.428*

Lawrence, Eleanor *v.5 p.225*

Lawrence, Frederick M.. . . . . *v.4 p.568*

Lawrence, John T. *v.3 p.209*

Lawrence, Keith & Cheung, Floyd (Editors) *v.6 p.96*

Lawrence, T. J. *v.4 p.631*

Lawrence, Tim *v.1 p.271*

Lawrence, Vera B. *v.1 p.278*

Lawrence, Vera Brodsky *v.1 p.278*

Lawrence-Lightfoot, Sara *v.4 p.353*

Lawrie, Stephen *v.5 p.34*

Laws, Gordon D. & Laws, Lauren M. *v.3 p.543, p.546*

Laws, Kenneth & Laws, Kenneth L. *v.1 p.42*

Laws, Kenneth *v.1 p.49*

Laws, Richard *v.5 p.176, p.238*

Lawson, Alan, et al. *v.2 p.727*

Lawson, Bruce (Editor), et al. *v.2 p.565*

Lawson, Colin (Editor) *v.1 p.393*

Lawson, Colin J. & Stowell, Robin *v.1 p.401*

Lawson, Colin J. (Editor) *v.1 p.390*

Lawson, Colin J. *v.1 p.191, p.241, p.344*

Lawson, E. Thomas & McCauley, Robert N. *v.5 p.634*

Lawson, Ellen N.. . . . . *v.6 p.21, p.45*

Lawson, Henry. *v.2 p.747*

Lawson, Jack *v.1 p.218, p.345*

Lawson, Joan *v.1 p.37*

Lawson, Joseph Chappell H. *v.4 p.409*

Lawson, M. K. *v.3 p.97, p.98*

Lawson Mack, Raneta & Kelly, Michael J. *v.4 p.564*

Lawson, Philip *v.3 p.539*

Lawson, Russell. *v.4 p.87*

Lawson, Stephanie *v.4 p.624*

Lawson, Tim & Persons, Alisa. *v.6 p.307*

Lawson-Borders, Gracie *v.4 p.418*

Lawson-Peebles, Robert (Editor). *v.6 p.316*

Lawton, Denis & Gordon, Peter *v.4 p.339*

Lawton, John H. & May, Robert M. (Editors). . . . *v.5 p.170*

Lawvere, F. William & Rosebrugh, Robert *v.5 p.471*

Lawvere, F. William & Schanuel, Stephen Hoel. . . . *v.5 p.473*

Lax, Roger & Smith, Frederick *v.1 p.168, p.251, p.271*

Laxalt, Robert *v.3 p.529*

Laxness, Halldor Kiljan. *v.2 p.625*

Lay, David C. *v.5 p.472*

Lay, Steven R. *v.5 p.498*

Layard, Austen *v.3 p.5*

Layard, Henry Austin *v.3 p.5*

Laybourn, Keith *v.4 p.127*

Laye, Camara *v.2 p.542, v.6 p.28*

Layman, Dale P. *v.5 p.245*

Layman, Nancy S. *v.4 p.450*

Layne, Linda L. *v.6 p.620*

Layton, Bentley *v.1 p.646*

Layton, Irving *v.2 p.736*

Layton, Peter *v.1 p.810*

Layton, Robert (Editor) *v.1 p.241*

Layton, Susan *v.2 p.799*

Lazard, Naomi *v.6 p.162*

Lazare, Aaron *v.5 p.648*

Lazare, Bernard *v.3 p.60*

Lazare, Lucien *v.3 p.85*

Lazaroff, David W. & Arizona-Sonora Desert Museum
Staff. *v.5 p.234, p.240*

Lazarsfeld, Patricia K. (Editor) *v.4 p.685*

Lazarus, Edward *v.4 p.537*

Lazarus, Neil (Editor). *v.4 p.485*

Lazarus, Richard J. *v.4 p.448*

Lazarus, Richard S. *v.5 p.612, p.654*

Lazenby, J. F. *v.3 p.25*

Lazenby, John. *v.3 p.25*

Lazenby, Walter *v.2 p.302*

Lazer, David (Editor). *v.6 p.266, p.270*

Lazerson, Marvin & Grubb, W. Norton (Editors) . . *v.4 p.353*

Lazic, Radmila *v.2 p.811*

Lazic, Zivorad R.. . . . . *v.5 p.743*

Le Billon, Philippe (Editor) *v.4 p.400*

Le Bon, Gustave *v.4 p.713*

Le Breton, Binka *v.4 p.728*

Le Carré, John *v.2 p.361*
Le, Chap T. *v.5 p.100*
Le Clezio, J. M. G. *v.2 p.531*
Le Clézio, J.-M. G. *v.2 p.531*
Le Fanu, J. Sheridan *v.2 p.361*
Le Fort, Gertrud, Freiin von *v.2 p.612*
Le Fort, Gertrud von *v.2 p.612*
Le Goff, Jacques . . . *v.1 p.645, v.6 p.558, p.563, p.572, p.576*
Le Guin, Ursula K. *v.2 p.148*
Le Maitre, R. W. (Editor), et al. *v.5 p.437*
Le Naour, Jean-Yves *v.3 p.79*
Le Patourel, John *v.6 p.568*
Le Play, Frederic *v.4 p.685*
Le Poidevin, Robin *v.1 p.500*
Le Quesne, A. L. *v.2 p.277*
Le Rider, Jacques *v.3 p.184*
Le Strange, Guy *v.6 p.585*
Le Van, Marthe *v.1 p.715, p.720*
Le Vine, Victor T. *v.4 p.612, v.6 p.54*
Lea, Peter J. & Leegood, R. C. (Editors) . . . *v.5 p.124, p.128*
Lea, Sydney *v.2 p.148*
Lea, Tom *v.2 p.94*
Leab, Daniel J. *v.4 p.524*
Leach, E. R. *v.4 p.34*
Leach, Eleanor W. *v.1 p.728*
Leach, John *v.4 p.247*
Leach, Maria *v.2 p.585*
Leach, Melissa (Editor), et al. *v.5 p.167, p.218, p.248*
Leach, Neil (Editor) *v.6 p.728*
Leach, Neil *v.1 p.703*
Leach, Richard H., et al. *v.4 p.582*
Leach, Robert & Borovsky, Victor *v.1 p.109*
Leach, Robert *v.1 p.109, p.139, p.153*
Leach, Rodney *v.4 p.603, p.637*
Leacock, Eleanor Burke & Safa, Helen I. *v.6 p.457*
Leacock, Ruth *v.3 p.341*
Leacock, Stephen *v.2 p.736, v.4 p.379, v.6 p.685*
Leacroft, Richard *v.1 p.101, p.155*
Leahey, Thomas H. *v.5 p.597*
Leahy, James E. *v.4 p.537*
Leahy, Robert L. *v.4 p.272*
Leake, Elizabeth *v.2 p.723*
Leakey, F. W. *v.2 p.488*
Leaman, Oliver (Editor) *v.1 p.475, v.6 p.333*
Leaman, Oliver *v.1 p.432, p.475*
Leamer, Edward E. *v.4 p.202*
Leamon, James S. *v.3 p.486*
Leaptrott and Company Staff & Leaptrott, Nan *v.4 p.56*
Lear, John *v.3 p.293*
Lear, Jonathan *v.1 p.426*
Lear, Roma *v.4 p.784, p.801, p.830*
Learned, Andrea & Johnson, Lisa *v.5 p.587*
Lears, T. J. Jackson *v.3 p.368*
Leary, Lewis & Auchard, John (Compiled by) *v.2 p.4*
Leary, Lewis (Editor) *v.2 p.4*

Leary, Lewis *v.2 p.4*
Leary, Mark R. & Kowalski, Robin Mark *v.5 p.654*
Leary, Patrick *v.6 p.735, p.749*
Leary, William M. (Editor) *v.3 p.460*
Lease, Ronald C., et al. *v.4 p.91, p.95*
Leaska, Mitchell A. & Phillips, John (Editors) *v.2 p.380*
Least Heat-Moon, William *v.6 p.698*
Leatherbarrow, David *v.1 p.813*
Leatherbarrow, William J. (Editor) *v.2 p.805*
Leatherbarrow, William J. *v.2 p.805*
Leathers, Howard D. & Foster, Phillips *v.5 p.34*
Leavis, F. R. *v.2 p.164*
Leavis, Frank R. (Editor) *v.2 p.164, p.568*
Leavis, Frank R. *v.2 p.164, p.181*
Leavitt, David *v.5 p.590, v.6 p.397*
Leavitt, Howard B. (Editor) *v.4 p.277, p.313*
Leavitt, Judith W. *v.5 p.523*
Leavitt, Lewis A. & Fox, Nathan A. (Editors) *v.5 p.584*
Leavitt, Richard F. *v.2 p.134*
Lebacqz, Karen & Driskill, Joseph D. *v.1 p.649*
LeBaron, Dean & Vaitilingam, Romesh *v.4 p.95*
Lebenson, Richard & Creighton, Kathleen (Editors) . *v.1 p.712*
Lebergott, Stanley *v.5 p.586*
Leblanc, Hugues *v.1 p.495*
LeBlanc, Robin M. *v.6 p.219, p.441*
Lebovics, Herman . *v.2 p.522, v.3 p.140, p.180, p.181, v.4 p.608*
Lebow, Irwin *v.4 p.420*
LeBow, Richard Ned *v.4 p.484, p.626*
Lebra, Takie S. *v.6 p.221*
Lebrecht, Norman *v.2 p.361*
Lebreton, Jules & Zeiller, Jacques *v.3 p.57*
Lecarme, Jacques *v.2 p.517*
Leccese, Michael & McCormick, Kathleen (Editors) . *v.1 p.797*
Lechner, Frank & Boli, John (Editors) *v.4 p.55*
Lechte, John & Zournazi, Mary (Editors) *v.2 p.456*
Lechte, John *v.1 p.512*
Lecker, Robert (Editor), et al. *v.2 p.730*
Lecker, Robert (Editor) *v.2 p.730*
Leckie, Robert *v.3 p.383*
Leckie, William H. *v.4 p.718*
Leclerc, Ivor *v.1 p.446*
Leclercq, Jean & Misrahi, Catharine *v.6 p.572*
Leclercq, Jean *v.1 p.578, v.3 p.57*
LeCompte, Mary Lou *v.4 p.837, p.865*
Lecomte, Paul *v.5 p.50, v.6 p.289*
Lecomte-Tilouine, Marie & Dollfus, Pascale (Editors) . *v.6 p.161*
Leconte de Lisle *v.2 p.495*
Ledbetter, David *v.1 p.185, p.241, p.303*
Leddick, David *v.6 p.414*
Lederer, Herbert (Editor) *v.2 p.621*
Lederer, Ivo *v.3 p.247*
Lederer, Laura (Editor) *v.4 p.748*
Lederer, Michael *v.5 p.309*
Lederer, William J. & Burdick, Eugene *v.2 p.94*
Lederman, Daniel *v.3 p.350*

Lederman, Leon & Teresi, Dick *v.5 p.541*

Lederman, Muriel & Bartsch,
 Ingrid (Editors) *v.5 p.398, v.6 p.439*

Ledkovsky, Marina (Editor), et al. *v.2 p.793, p.796*

LeDonne, John P. *v.3 p.212, p.216*

Leduc, Joanne (Editor) *v.3 p.545*

Leduc, Violette *v.2 p.521, v.6 p.397*

Lee, A. Collingwood *v.2 p.702*

Lee, Alfred McClung *v.4 p.410*

Lee, Alvin *v.2 p.205*

Lee, Anthony W. & Pultz, John *v.1 p.767*

Lee, Anthony W. *v.6 p.88, p.90, p.127*

Lee, Antoinette J. *v.1 p.822*

Lee, Briant H. *v.1 p.96, p.155*

Lee, Byeong Gi & Kim, Woo-June. *v.5 p.727*

Lee, C. C. *v.5 p.707*

Lee, Cecilia Hae-Jin *v.6 p.235*

Lee, Chang-Rae *v.6 p.100, p.101*

Lee, Charles R. Jr. *v.4 p.474*

Lee, Courtland C. (Editor) *v.4 p.353*

Lee, David L. & Axelrod, Saul *v.5 p.667*

Lee, Don *v.6 p.101*

Lee, Douglas *v.1 p.218, p.241*

Lee, Erika *v.6 p.119, p.127*

Lee, Esther Kim *v.1 p.125*

Lee, Francis Graham *v.1 p.656, v.4 p.486*

Lee, Frederic S. *v.4 p.233, p.242*

Lee, Gypsy Rose *v.1 p.36*

Lee, Harper *v.2 p.94*

Lee, Henry C. & O'Neill, Thomas W. *v.6 p.266*

Lee, Hermione *v.2 p.67, p.335, p.392*

Lee, Jay & Wong, David W. S. *v.4 p.387*

Lee, Jennifer & Zhou, Min (Editors) . . . *v.6 p.85, p.110, p.123*

Lee, Jennifer *v.6 p.106, p.123, p.136*

Lee, John A. *v.6 p.380*

Lee, Joseph J. *v.3 p.139*

Lee, Joseph *v.3 p.139*

Lee, Josephine D. *v.6 p.90, p.96, p.99*

Lee, Josephine (Editor), et al. *v.6 p.114*

Lee, Joyce G. *v.6 p.500, p.514*

Lee, Leo O. (Editor) *v.6 p.200, p.213*

Lee, Leo Ou-fan. *v.6 p.190, p.205, p.213*

Lee, Li-Young *v.6 p.103*

Lee, Martin A. & Shlain, Bruce *v.4 p.704*

Lee, Mary P. *v.6 p.94, p.114, p.136*

Lee, Maurice A. (Editor) *v.2 p.574*

Lee, Mei-Ling Ting. *v.5 p.102*

Lee, Mike S. *v.5 p.88, p.218*

Lee, Nathaniel *v.2 p.251*

Lee, Ou-Fan Leo *v.6 p.208*

Lee, P. K. (Editor) *v.5 p.695*

Lee, Peter H. (Editor) *v.6 p.238*

Lee, Peter H. (Translator) *v.6 p.238*

Lee, Peter H. *v.6 p.238*

Lee, Priscilla. *v.6 p.104*

Lee, Rachel C. & Wong, Sau-Ling Cynthia
 (Editors) *v.6 p.89, p.90, p.123, p.141, p.143*

Lee, Rachel C. *v.6 p.96, p.112*

Lee, Richard B. & Daly, Richard (Editors) *v.4 p.3*

Lee, Richard B. & DeVore, Irven *v.4 p.38*

Lee, Robert E. *v.5 p.208*

Lee, Robert G. *v.6 p.88, p.90*

Lee, Sang Hyun (Editor) *v.1 p.584*

Lee, Sherman E *v.1 p.693*

Lee, Simon *v.1 p.743*

Lee, Spike & Aftab, Kaleem *v.6 p.330, p.342*

Lee, Stacey J. *v.6 p.108, p.122*

Lee, Steven H. *v.6 p.169, p.236*

Lee, Stuart M. (Editor) *v.5 p.689*

Lee, Tanith & Caws, Mary Ann *v.2 p.524*

Lee, Thomas F. *v.5 p.135*

Lee, Thomas W. *v.4 p.689*

Lee, Wanda M. L. *v.5 p.637*

Lee, Wen Ho & Zia, Helen *v.6 p.94, p.117, p.141*

Lee, Wendy Lynne *v.1 p.508*

Lee, William H. K. (Editor), et al. *v.5 p.442*

Lee, Y. C. *v.6 p.101*

Lee, Yeonwoo *v.4 p.230, p.235*

Lee, Yuan-Yuan & Shen, Sinyan *v.1 p.288*

Lee, Yueh-Ting (Editor), et al. *v.5 p.637*

Lee, Yur-Bok & Patterson, Wayne (Editors). *v.3 p.390*

Leebaert, Derek *v.3 p.453*

Leech, Clifford (Editor), et al. *v.2 p.185*

Leech, Clifford. *v.2 p.235*

Leech, Geoffrey N. & Svartvik, Jan *v.2 p.557*

Leech, Margaret *v.3 p.398, p.431, p.437*

Leech-Wilkinson, Daniel *v.1 p.177, p.235, p.338*

Leeder, M. R. *v.5 p.438*

Leeder, S. H. *v.6 p.638*

Leeds, Anthony *v.4 p.37, v.6 p.722*

Leedy, Paul D. & Ormrod, Jeanne Ellis *v.5 p.409*

Leeman, Richard W. *v.4 p.660*

Leeman, Richard *v.1 p.697*

Leeming, David A. *v.2 p.384*

Leeming, David *v.1 p.527, v.6 p.26, p.402*

Leenders, Michiel R., James A. Erskine and Louise A.
 Mauffette-Leenders *v.4 p.177*

Leeper, Alexander W. *v.6 p.563*

Leepson, Marc *v.1 p.822*

Lees, Andrew *v.3 p.164*

Lees, D. R. & Edwards, D. (Editors). *v.5 p.193*

Lees, Gene *v.1 p.251, p.336, p.337, p.338*

Lees, Nigel *v.5 p.255*

Lees, Stan *v.4 p.84*

Lees, Stella *v.2 p.741*

Leese, Elizabeth *v.6 p.349*

Leeson, Robert (Editor) *v.4 p.225, p.228, p.232*

Lee-Treweek, Geraldine & Linkogle, Stephanie *v.4 p.690*

Lefcourt, Herbert M. *v.5 p.654*

Lefebvre, Georges *v.3 p.150, p.152*

Lefebvre, Henri & Le Bas, Elizabeth. *v.6 p.710*

Lefebvre, Henri. *v.1 p.508, v.4 p.680, v.6 p.710*

Lefebvre, Jeffrey *v.3 p.390*

Lefevre, Marc J. *v.5 p.266*

Leff, Carol. *v.3 p.190*

Leff, Laurel *v.4 p.411*

Leff, Leonard J. *v.2 p.85*

Lefèvre, Edwin & Marketplace Books *v.4 p.95, p.102*

Leffler, Melvyn P. *v.3 p.453*

Leffler, William L. & Raymond, Martin S. *v.5 p.738*

Leffman, David, et al. *v.6 p.182, p.197*

Lefkovitch, L. P. *v.5 p.100*

Lefkowitz, M. M. *v.5 p.627*

Lefkowitz, Mary R. & Fant, Maureen Brown. *v.3 p.13, v.6 p.451*

Lefkowitz, Mary R. & Rogers, Guy (Editors) *v.3 p.12*

Lefkowitz, Mary. *v.3 p.12, v.6 p.10, p.20*

Lefler, Hugh Talmage. *v.3 p.502*

León, Luis D. *v.6 p.487, p.520*

Leftow, Brian & Davies, Brian (Editors). *v.1 p.434, p.575, p.595*

LeGates, Richard T. & Stout, Frederic (Editors). . . *v.1 p.797*

LeGates, Richard. *v.4 p.387*

Legault, Albert & Fortmann, Michel. *v.4 p.644, p.656*

Leggatt, Alexander (Editor) *v.2 p.233*

Leggatt, Alexander *v.2 p.235*

Legge, James (Translator). *v.6 p.184, p.208*

Leggett, Anthony J.. . . . . *v.5 p.541*

Leggett, Jeremy *v.6 p.300*

Leggett, John. *v.2 p.118*

Leggott, Michele and Brian Flaherty *v.2 p.743*

LeGrand, Catherine. *v.3 p.357*

Lehane, Brendan *v.5 p.237*

Lehaney, Brian (Editor) *v.4 p.77*

Lehar, Steven *v.5 p.613*

Leheny, David Richard. *v.4 p.784, p.834, p.898*

Lehman, David (Editor) *v.2 p.58, p.578*

Lehman, David *v.2 p.23*

Lehman, Jeffrey & Phelps, Shirelle *v.4 p.437*

Lehman, Tim *v.5 p.30*

Lehmann, E. L. & Romano, Joseph P. *v.5 p.482*

Lehmann, Michael B. *v.4 p.96*

Lehmann, Ruth P. M. (Translator) *v.2 p.204*

Lehmann, Winfred P. *v.2 p.562*

Lehmann-Haupt, Hellmut *v.3 p.172*

Lehman-Wilzig, Sam N. *v.4 p.615*

Lehner, Marcus *v.1 p.22*

Lehner, Philip N.. . . . . *v.5 p.615*

Lehninger, Albert L., et al. *v.5 p.111, p.327*

Lehninger, Albert L. *v.5 p.327*

Lehr, Valerie. *v.6 p.376*

Lehrer, Keith *v.1 p.450, p.482*

Lehring, Gary L. *v.6 p.390*

Leiber, Michael J. *v.6 p.271*

Leibniz, Gottfried Wilhelm & Clarke, Samuel. . . . *v.1 p.459*

Leibniz, Gottfried Wilhelm *v.1 p.459*

Leibold, Mathew A. (Editor), et al.. . . . . *v.4 p.394*

Leibovitz, Annie & Sontag, Susan *v.1 p.767*

Leicester, Henry Marshall. *v.2 p.209*

Leick, Alfred. *v.4 p.390*

Leick, Gwendolyn *v.1 p.784, v.3 p.5*

Leider, Emily Wortis *v.6 p.418*

Leifer, Eric M. *v.4 p.851, p.888, p.891, p.896*

Leigh, G. J. (Editor) *v.5 p.50*

Leigh, G. J. *v.5 p.5*

Leigh, J. R. *v.5 p.711*

Leigh, John *v.2 p.459*

Leighton, Angela & Reynolds, Margaret (Editors). *v.2 p.197, p.200*

Leighton, George R. (Photographer) *v.3 p.293*

Leighton, Isabel *v.3 p.368*

Leighton, Lauren G. *v.2 p.805*

Leighton, Walter L.. . . . . *v.1 p.515*

Leijonhufvud, Axel. *v.4 p.225, p.240*

Leinberger, Charles *v.1 p.255*

Leinen, Stephen *v.6 p.383*

Leininger, Madeleine & McFarland, Marilyn R.. . . *v.5 p.530*

Leininger, Madeleine M. & McFarland, Marilyn . . . *v.5 p.530*

Leiris, Michel *v.2 p.521*

Leishman, J. B. *v.2 p.225*

Leishman, Rory *v.4 p.541*

Leisner, Tony *v.1 p.34*

Leiss, William, et al. *v.4 p.140*

Leitch, Vincent B. *v.2 p.567, p.568*

Leiter, Brian *v.1 p.466*

Leiter, Richard A. *v.4 p.441*

Leiter, Samuel L. & Hill, Holly (Contribution by). *v.1 p.60, p.116*

Leiter, Samuel L. *v.1 p.59, p.60, p.97, p.116, p.129, p.132, p.134, p.153, v.6 p.235*

Leith, Dick *v.2 p.554*

Lejeune, Jean-Francois *v.1 p.790, v.6 p.728*

Lekai, Louis J. *v.6 p.572*

Lekic, Anita *v.2 p.818*

Lekis, Lisa *v.1 p.19, p.20, p.33*

Leksukhum, Santi *v.1 p.732*

Leland, John *v.5 p.187*

Leland, Suzanne M. & Thurmaier, Kurt M.. . . *v.4 p.542, p.544*

Lele, Milind *v.4 p.82*

Lele, Subhash; Richtsmeier, Joan T. *v.5 p.100*

Lellinger, David B.. . . . . *v.5 p.210*

Lem, Stanislaw. *v.2 p.790*

Lemaitre, Georges Edouard *v.2 p.459*

Lemaitre, Jean P. (Editor) *v.5 p.689*

Lemann, Nicholas *v.4 p.286*

Lemarchand, Reni *v.4 p.653, v.6 p.63*

LeMaster, J. R. & Kummings, Donald D. (Editors). . *v.2 p.54*

Lemay, J. Leo. *v.2 p.29*

Lembke, Janet *v.5 p.222*

Lemcke, Dawn P., et al.. . . . . *v.5 p.523*

Lemco, Jonathan *v.4 p.524, p.581, p.590*

Lemelin, Roger *v.2 p.539*

Lemert, Charles C.. . . . . *v.4 p.683, p.685*

Lemert, Charles *v.4 p.675, p.683*

Lemire, Maurice *v.2 p.538*

Lemoine, Bertrand *v.1 p.790*

Lemoine, Serge *v.1 p.728*

Lemon, Ralph *v.1 p.28, p.30*

Lemonick, Michael D. *v.5 p.74*

Lems-Dworkin, Carol *v.1 p.168, p.285, p.287*

Lena, Pierre & Lebrun, Francoise *v.5 p.65*

Lenau, Nicolaus *v.2 p.600*

Lenburg, Jeff. *v.6 p.307*

Lencioni, Patrick M. & Lencioni, Patrick *v.4 p.80*

Lender, Mark Edward & Martin, James K. . *v.4 p.700, v.5 p.664*

Lendvai, Paul *v.3 p.185*

Lenehan, Pat. *v.4 p.826*

L'Enfant, Julie *v.1 p.720*

Lengauer, Thomas (Editor) *v.5 p.97, p.146, p.149, p.152*

Lengermann, Patricia Madoo &
  Niebrugge-Brantley, Jill *v.4 p.680*

L'Engle, Madeleine *v.2 p.148, p.149*

Lengnick-Hall, Mark L. & Lengnick-Hall, Cynthia A. . *v.4 p.76*

Lengwiler, Yvan *v.4 p.263*

Lenihan, John H. *v.6 p.324*

Lenin, V. I. *v.4 p.237, p.506, p.508*

Lenman, Bruce. *v.3 p.133*

Lenman, Robin (Editor). *v.1 p.762*

Lennard, John *v.2 p.577*

Lenneberg, Eric H. (Editor) *v.4 p.357*

Lennon, Alexander T. J. (Editor). *v.3 p.483*

Lennon, Colm *v.3 p.135, p.136*

Lennon, Thomas M. *v.1 p.436*

Lennox, Charlotte *v.2 p.251*

Lennox, Gina & Mitterand, Danielle *v.6 p.668*

Lennox, James G. *v.5 p.80*

Lens, Sidney. *v.3 p.386*

Lenski, Gerhard E. *v.4 p.722*

Lenski, Noel (Editor) *v.3 p.31, p.192*

Lenski, Noel Emmanuel *v.3 p.31*

Lenskyj, Helen Jefferson *v.4 p.846, p.884, p.888, p.891*

Lent, Adam *v.4 p.711*

Lent, John A. (Compiled by) *v.6 p.448*

Lent, John A. (Editor) *v.6 p.308*

Lentner, Cornelus (Editor). *v.5 p.326*

Lentricchia, Frank & Dubois, Andrew (Editors) . . . *v.2 p.164*

Lentricchia, Frank *v.2 p.72, p.77, p.111, p.124*

Lentz, Harris M. III *v.6 p.319, p.324*

Lentz, Robert J. *v.6 p.322*

Lenz, Carolyn R. (Editor), et al. *v.2 p.230*

Lenz, Siegfried. *v.2 p.612*

Leo, Richard A. & Thomas, George C. III (Editors) . *v.4 p.473*

Leon, Joseph J. Sr., et al. *v.4 p.691*

Leon, Victor *v.2 p.636*

Leonard, Barry (Editor). *v.6 p.295, p.300*

Leonard, Bill J. *v.1 p.583*

Leonard, Carol S. *v.3 p.216*

Leonard, David C. *v.5 p.571*

Leonard, David K. & Straus, Scott *v.6 p.55*

Leonard, Dorothy & Swap, Walter. *v.4 p.66, p.80*

Leonard, George J. (Editor) *v.6 p.86, p.96*

Leonard, George *v.4 p.327*

Leonard, H. Jeffrey *v.4 p.63*

Leonard, Irving A. *v.3 p.403*

Leonard, J *v.5 p.292*

Leonard, Karen I. *v.6 p.110, p.123, p.137*

Leonard, Kathy S. *v.6 p.500, p.507, p.514*

Leonard, Kenneth E. & Blane, Howard Thomas
  (Editors) *v.5 p.664*

Leonard, Laurence B. *v.5 p.665, p.673*

Leonard, R.L. (Richard Lawrence) *v.4 p.638*

Leonard, Thomas C. *v.4 p.404*

Leonard, Thomas M. *v.3 p.311, p.390*

Leonard, Wilbert Marcellus *v.4 p.817*

Leonardsen, Dag *v.6 p.250*

Leon-Dermota, Ken *v.3 p.354*

Leone, Richard C. & Anrig, Gregory . *v.4 p.564, p.572, p.660*

Leong, Frederick (Editor) *v.5 p.577*

Leong, Karen J. *v.6 p.88, p.90, p.94, p.96, p.112, p.215*

Leong, Roger *v.1 p.45*

Leong, Russell Charles *v.6 p.101*

Leong, Russell (Editor) *v.6 p.92, p.112*

Leong, Russell (Introduction by) *v.6 p.88*

Leon-Portilla, Miguel (Editor, Introduction by) *v.3 p.286*

Leon-Portilla, Miguel. *v.3 p.261, p.286*

Leontief, Wassily *v.4 p.213, p.259*

Leopardi, Giacomo. *v.2 p.711, p.712*

Leopold, Aldo *v.5 p.17, p.224, p.226, p.370, v.6 p.288*

Leopold, Luna B., et al. *v.5 p.427*

Leopold, Richard W. *v.3 p.434*

Leopold, Rudolf (Editor) *v.1 p.743*

Leopoldseder, Hannes (Editor), et al.. . . . . . . *v.1 p.771*

Lepecki, Andre *v.1 p.43*

Lepenies, Wolf *v.3 p.178*

Lepore, Ernest & Ludwig, Kirk *v.1 p.442*

Lepore, Ernest *v.1 p.493*

Lepore, Jill. *v.3 p.406, v.6 p.686*

Lepore, Monica, et al. *v.4 p.792, p.801*

Leppert, Richard D. & McClary, Susan (Editors) . . . *v.1 p.377*

Leppert, Richard D. *v.1 p.377*

Leppmann, Wolfgang *v.2 p.614*

Lepschy, Anna Laura & Lepschy, Giulio C.. . . . . *v.2 p.699*

Lerdahl, Fred & Jackendoff, Ray S. *v.1 p.371*

Lerer, Seth. *v.2 p.209*

Lerman, A. (Editor). *v.5 p.427*

Lerman, Abraham (Editor), et al. *v.5 p.427*

Lerman, Liz. *v.1 p.47*

Lerman, Zvi, et al.. . . . . *v.5 p.14*

Lermontov, Mikhail *v.2 p.805*

Lerner, A. W. *v.5 p.643*

Lerner, Alan J. & Green, Benny . . . *v.1 p.252, p.336, p.408*

Lerner, Alan J.. . . . . *v.1 p.252, p.336*

Lerner, Gerda (Compiled by) *v.6 p.450*

Lerner, Gerda *v.3 p.51, p.374, p.398,*
                                    p.420, v.6 p.434, p.450, p.467
Lerner, Janet W. *v.4 p.318*
Lerner, Loren R. *v.1 p.662*
Lerner, Max *v.3 p.368, v.4 p.343*
Lerner, Michael (Editor) *v.2 p.19*
Lerner, Richard M. & Steinberg, Laurence (Editors) . . *v.5 p.642*
Lerner, Richard M. *v.5 p.627, p.641*
Lerner, Rita G. & Trigg, George L. (Editors) *v.5 p.545*
Leroy, Francis (Editor) *v.5 p.389*
Lesbian History Group Staff. *v.6 p.363*
Lesch, Ann Mosely & Tessler, Mark *v.6 p.618, p.639*
LeShan, Lawrence *v.5 p.584*
Lesinka, Zofia P. *v.2 p.63, p.121, p.388*
Lesk, Arthur M. (Editor) *v.5 p.128*
Lesk, Arthur M. *v.5 p.98, p.502*
Leskov, N. S. *v.2 p.805*
Lesky, Albin *v.2 p.401*
Leslie, Clare Walker & Roth, Charles E. *v.5 p.232*
Leslie, G. B. & Lunau, F. W. (Editors) *v.5 p.372*
Leslie, Marina *v.4 p.499*
Lesmian, Boreslaw *v.2 p.790*
Lessard, Michel *v.1 p.804*
Lesser, Charles H. *v.3 p.502*
Lesser, Jeff *v.3 p.341*
Lesser, Jeffrey *v.3 p.341*
Lessig, Lawrence *v.4 p.435, p.446*
Lessing, Doris *v.2 p.364, p.365*
Lessing, Gotthold Ephraim *v.1 p.460, p.481, v.2 p.600*
Lester, Alan *v.6 p.78*
Lester, James P., et al. *v.4 p.566*
Lester, James *v.1 p.261, p.362*
Lester, Joel *v.1 p.185, p.191, p.241, p.303, p.371*
Lester, Patrick D. (Editor) *v.1 p.725, v.6 p.679*
Lester, Paul Martin & Ross, Susan Dente (Editors) . *v.4 p.416*
Lester, Robert (Editor) *v.1 p.827*
Lester, Robin *v.4 p.807, p.858, p.894*
Lester, Toni P. (Editor) *v.6 p.371*
Lestrel, Pete E. (Editor). *v.5 p.91, p.94*
Lestrel, Pete E. *v.5 p.155*
LeTendre, Gerald K. (Editor) *v.4 p.335, v.6 p.221*
LeTendre, Gerald K. *v.6 p.219*
Lethbridge, Henry J. *v.6 p.206*
Letts, Malcolm (Editor) *v.3 p.334*
Letts, William J. IV & Sears, James T.
   (Editors) *v.4 p.309, v.6 p.385*
Letwin, William *v.4 p.444*
Leuba, S. H. & Zlatanova, J. (Editors) *v.5 p.128*
Leuchars, Chris *v.3 p.344*
Leuchtenburg, William E. . *v.3 p.378, p.442, p.448, p.474, v.4 p.466*
Leuchtenburg, William Edward *v.3 p.474*
Leung, Edwin Pak-Wah (Editor) *v.6 p.199*
Leuschner, William A. *v.5 p.38, p.41, p.354*
Lev, Arlene Istar *v.6 p.377, p.381*
Lev, Daniel S. *v.6 p.175*

Lev, Peter *v.6 p.342*
Levack, Brian P. (Editor) *v.6 p.569*
Levant, Howard *v.2 p.123*
Levathes, Louise *v.6 p.204*
LeVay, Simon *v.6 p.420*
Levens, R. G. (Editor) *v.2 p.426*
Levenson, Alan T. *v.3 p.180*
Levenson, Jay (Editor). *v.3 p.73, p.243*
Levenson, Jon D. *v.1 p.619*
Levenson, Joseph Richmond *v.6 p.190*
Levenson, Michael (Editor) *v.2 p.175, p.179, p.572*
Levenstein, Harvey A. *v.4 p.127, v.5 p.34*
Levenstein, Harvey *v.5 p.34*
Levenston, Edward A. & Sivan, Reuban (Editors) . . . *v.6 p.646*
LeVeque, William J. (Editor) *v.5 p.476*
Lever, Evelyne *v.3 p.147*
Lever, Maurice & Goldhammer, Arthur. *v.2 p.484*
Lever, Richard, et al. *v.2 p.741*
Lever, Susan *v.2 p.743*
Levere, Trevor Harvey *v.5 p.263*
Leverett, Flynt (Editor) *v.4 p.564*
Leverich, Lyle *v.2 p.134, v.6 p.402*
Levering, Robert *v.5 p.579*
Levertov, Denise *v.2 p.149*
Levesque, Jacques *v.3 p.208, p.222*
Levey, Michael *v.1 p.679, p.688, p.726, p.728*
Levi, Carlo *v.3 p.197*
Levi, Edward H. *v.4 p.441*
Levi, Erik *v.3 p.172*
Levi, Isaac *v.5 p.400, p.409*
Levi, Jan H. *v.2 p.113*
Levi, Jean *v.6 p.215*
Levi, Peter *v.2 p.313*
Levi, Primo *v.2 p.715, v.3 p.85*
Levi, Vicki Gold & Heller, Steven *v.1 p.714*
Levick, Barbara *v.3 p.28*
Levin, Amy K. *v.6 p.26, p.45*
Levin, Barbara B. *v.4 p.277*
Levin, Bruce Lubotsky (Editor), et al. *v.5 p.671*
Levin, Dov *v.3 p.85, p.226*
Levin, Eve *v.3 p.211*
Levin, Gail *v.1 p.697, p.743*
Levin, Hanoch *v.6 p.650*
Levin, Harold L. *v.5 p.447*
Levin, Harry *v.2 p.230, p.359, p.462*
Levin, Henry M. *v.4 p.299*
Levin, Jack & Rabrenovic, Gordana *v.6 p.252*
Levin, James & Nolan, James F. *v.4 p.284*
Levin, James *v.6 p.393*
Levin, Louis *v.4 p.777*
Levin, N. Gordon Jr. *v.3 p.474*
Levin, Nora *v.3 p.222*
Levin, Phillis (Editor) *v.2 p.200*
Levin, Susan *v.2 p.322*

Levin, Ted *v.5 p.222*

Levin, Theodore *v.1 p.300*

Levinas, Emmanuel *v.1 p.456, p.469, p.508*

Levine, Alan J. *v.3 p.81, p.175*

Levine, Andrew *v.4 p.504, p.506, p.507*

Levine, Arthur & Weingart, John R. *v.4 p.294*

Levine, Arthur (Editor) *v.4 p.331*

Levine, Arthur *v.4 p.294*

Levine, Baruch A. *v.1 p.620*

Levine, Baruch. *v.1 p.620*

Levine, Carol *v.5 p.135, p.248*

Levine, Daniel H.. . . . . *v.1 p.573, v.3 p.360*

Levine, Daniel S.. . . . . *v.5 p.591*

Levine, David A. & Wrightson, Keith *v.3 p.100, p.123*

Levine, George & Madden, William *v.2 p.176, v.6 p.754*

Levine, George (Editor). *v.2 p.287*

Levine, George L. *v.2 p.175, p.191*

Levine, Gustav & Parkinson, Stanley. *v.5 p.605*

Levine, Ira N. *v.5 p.279*

Levine, Joseph & Suzuki, David. *v.5 p.154*

Levine, Linda Gould *v.2 p.680*

Levine, Mark *v.1 p.403*

LeVine, Mark *v.6 p.610*

Levine, Martin L. (Editor). *v.5 p.592*

Levine, Murray & Perkins, David V.. . . . . *v.5 p.650, p.671*

Levine, Murray & Wallach, Leah *v.5 p.592*

Levine, Myron A. & Ross, Bernard H. *v.6 p.724*

Levine, Nancy E.. . . . . *v.6 p.164*

Levine, P. J. A. *v.6 p.750, p.754*

Levine, Philip *v.2 p.149*

Levine, Philippa (Editor). *v.3 p.89, p.125*

Levine, Robert A. (Editor) *v.4 p.35*

Levine, Robert M. & Sebebom Meihy, Jose Carlos . . *v.3 p.279*

Levine, Robert M. *v.3 p.311, p.337, p.341*

Levine, Robert V. *v.5 p.587, p.648*

Levine, Robert. *v.1 p.315, p.316*

Levine, Steven I.. . . . . *v.6 p.192, p.206*

Levine, Steven Z. *v.1 p.743*

Levine, Victor T. *v.6 p.62*

Levinger, Matthew *v.3 p.168*

Levins, Lynn Gartrell *v.2 p.74*

Levinson, Andre. *v.1 p.10*

Levinson, Bradley A. U. (Editor), et al. *v.4 p.302*

Levinson, Daniel J. & Levinson, Judy D.. . . . . . *v.4 p.741*

Levinson, Daniel J.. . . . . *v.4 p.741*

Levinson, David & Christensen, Karen . . . *v.4 p.848, v.6 p.145*

Levinson, David & Ponzetti, James J. Jr. *v.5 p.654*

Levinson, David (Editor, Compiled by) . . . *v.6 p.245, p.246*

Levinson, David (Editor) *v.4 p.678*

Levinson, Marc. *v.4 p.96, p.102, p.103*

Levinson, Marjorie *v.2 p.324*

Levinson, Orde (Compiled by) *v.1 p.757*

Levinson, Ralph & Reiss, Michael (Editors) *v.5 p.248*

Levinson, R. *v.5 p.268*

Levinton, Jeffrey S.. . . . . *v.5 p.193*

Levi-Strauss, Claude. *v.4 p.24*

Levi-Strauss, David. *v.1 p.767*

Levit, Alexandra *v.4 p.167*

Levit, Nancy *v.4 p.442, v.6 p.470*

Levitan, Sar A., et al. *v.4 p.253, p.254, p.265*

Levitas, Ruth *v.4 p.499*

Levitchi, Leon; Bantas, Andrei *v.2 p.778*

Levitchi, Leon *v.2 p.778*

Levitin, Daniel J. (Editor). *v.5 p.608*

Levitt, Arthur & Dwyer, Paula *v.4 p.96*

Levitt, Geoffrey M.. . . . . *v.4 p.564*

Levitt, I. M. *v.4 p.135*

Levitt, Joseph *v.4 p.644, p.656*

Levitt, Marcus C. (Editor). *v.2 p.796*

Levitt, Matthew *v.4 p.564*

Levitt, Peggy *v.4 p.44*

Levitt, Steven D. & Dubner, Stephen J. *v.4 p.185, p.271*

Levtzion, Nehemia *v.6 p.53*

Levtzion, Nehemiah *v.6 p.68*

Levy, Alan H.. . . . . *v.1 p.200, p.338,*
v.4 p.524, p.817, p.832, p.859, p.896

Levy, Alan *v.2 p.112*

Levy, Andre & Weingrod, Alex *v.6 p.614*

Levy, Avigdor (Editor) *v.6 p.590, p.597*

Levy, Azriel *v.5 p.471*

Levy, Babette M. *v.2 p.29*

Levy, Barry S. *v.5 p.535*

Levy, Charles K. *v.5 p.193*

Levy, Daniel C. & Bruhn, Kathleen *v.3 p.293*

Levy, David Benjamin. *v.1 p.200, p.235, p.241, p.307*

Levy, Fran J. (Editor) *v.1 p.51*

Levy, Fran J. *v.1 p.51*

Levy, Frank & Murnane, Richard J. *v.4 p.253, p.254*

Levy, Frank. *v.4 p.244, p.245, p.254, p.265*

Levy, John M. *v.1 p.797, v.6 p.728*

Levy, Leon & Linden, Eugene *v.4 p.96, p.100*

Levy, Leonard W. & Karst, Kenneth L. (Editors) . . . *v.4 p.454*

Levy, Leonard W. (Author, Editor). *v.4 p.452*

Levy, Leonard W.. *v.4 p.435, p.452, p.456, p.459, p.473, v.6 p.271*

Levy, Matthys & Salvadori, Mario G. *v.5 p.697*

Levy, Peter B. (Editor) *v.3 p.372*

Levy, Reuben *v.6 p.672*

Levy, Richard S.. . . . . *v.3 p.60, v.4 p.609*

Levy, Robert I. *v.4 p.43*

Levy, Robert M. & Rubenstein, Leonard S.. . . . . . *v.4 p.442*

Levy, Sidney J. & Rook, Dennis W. (Editors). *v.4 p.135, v.5 p.587*

Levy-Livermore, Amnon (Editor) *v.4 p.261*

Lew, Jamie *v.6 p.109, p.136*

Lew, Walter K. (Editor) *v.6 p.92, p.104*

Lew, Walter K.. . . . . *v.6 p.104*

Lewalski, Barbara *v.2 p.254*

Lewand, Robert Edward *v.5 p.476*

Lewens, Tim. *v.5 p.222*

Lewin, Abraham. *v.3 p.85*

Lewin, Ariel *v.4 p.9*

Lewin, Benjamin *v.5 p.122, p.135*

Lewin, David *v.1 p.371*

Lewin, Ellen & Leap, William L. (Editors) . . . *v.4 p.24, p.25*

Lewin, Ellen *v.6 p.375*

Lewin, Kurt *v.4 p.695*

Lewin, Linda *v.3 p.334, p.337*

Lewin, Moshe *v.3 p.222, p.228*

Lewine, Richard, et al. *v.1 p.168, p.252*

Lewis, Adam *v.1 p.802*

Lewis, Anthony *v.4 p.405, p.443, p.473, v.6 p.269*

Lewis, Archibald Ross *v.6 p.567*

Lewis, Bernard . . *v.1 p.558, v.4 p.614, v.6 p.573, p.574, p.582, p.583, p.594, p.597, p.622, p.624*

Lewis, C. S. (Editor, Compiled by) *v.1 p.597*

Lewis, C. S. . . *v.1 p.484, p.597, p.651, p.652, v.2 p.164, p.168, p.169, p.254, p.366, v.6 p.565*

Lewis, Catherine C. *v.4 p.364, p.370*

Lewis, Charles L. *v.3 p.425*

Lewis, Charlton T. & Short, Charles *v.2 p.424*

Lewis, Colin D. *v.4 p.117*

Lewis, Daniel (Editor) *v.1 p.20*

Lewis, David H. *v.4 p.844, p.866*

Lewis, David Levering *v.3 p.493, v.6 p.26*

Lewis, David M. & Pickard-Cambridge, Arthur W. . . *v.2 p.402*

Lewis, David *v.1 p.493, p.502*

Lewis, Don *v.5 p.599*

Lewis, E. D. (Editor) *v.6 p.310*

Lewis, Edward S. *v.5 p.261*

Lewis, Geoffrey *v.6 p.665*

Lewis, Gordon K. *v.3 p.320*

Lewis, Grace Ross *v.5 p.264*

Lewis, Griselda *v.1 p.808*

Lewis, H. D. *v.1 p.446*

Lewis, H. W. *v.5 p.711*

Lewis, Herschell Gordon & Nelson, Carol *v.4 p.140*

Lewis, Herschell Gordon *v.4 p.173*

Lewis, I. M. *v.4 p.36*

Lewis, Ioan M. *v.6 p.65*

Lewis, J. Lowell *v.1 p.20*

Lewis, James G. (James Graham) *v.5 p.38*

Lewis, James R. (Editor) *v.1 p.658*

Lewis, Jane *v.3 p.113*

Lewis, John S. *v.5 p.68*

Lewis, Jon *v.6 p.345*

Lewis, Justin *v.4 p.425*

Lewis, Lancelot S. *v.3 p.305*

Lewis, Laura A. *v.3 p.263, p.286*

Lewis, Leslie W. & Ardis, Ann L. *v.2 p.6*

Lewis, Lloyd *v.3 p.425, p.437*

Lewis, Lynette & Ross, Michael *v.6 p.414*

Lewis, Meriwether & Clark, William *v.3 p.520*

Lewis, Michael J. *v.1 p.682, p.787*

Lewis, Michael M. *v.4 p.89, p.92, p.96, p.100, p.103*

Lewis, Naphtali & Reinhold, Meyer *v.3 p.22*

Lewis, Naphtali *v.3 p.10, v.6 p.58*

Lewis, Norman N. *v.6 p.607, p.621*

Lewis, Oscar *v.4 p.704, p.733*

Lewis, P. S. *v.4 p.704*

Lewis, Paul (Editor) *v.4 p.259*

Lewis, Paul G. *v.6 p.724*

Lewis, Paul H. *v.3 p.275, p.344, p.345, p.348, v.4 p.592*

Lewis, Penny & Johnson, David Read (Editors) *v.1 p.94*

Lewis, Peter & Booth, Jerry (Editors) *v.4 p.413*

Lewis, R. W. B. *v.2 p.131*

Lewis, Randolph *v.6 p.342*

Lewis, Raphaela *v.6 p.590*

Lewis, Reina & Mills, Sara (Editors) *v.6 p.428, p.434*

Lewis, Richard D. *v.4 p.56*

Lewis, Richard J., Sr. *v.5 p.312*

Lewis, Richard J. *v.5 p.258, p.311, p.313, p.682*

Lewis, Ricki *v.5 p.80, p.135*

Lewis, Robert A. (Editor) *v.5 p.311*

Lewis, Robert *v.6 p.714*

Lewis, Roger *v.2 p.336*

Lewis, Ronald L. *v.5 p.40, p.354, p.356, p.373*

Lewis, Roy *v.2 p.460*

Lewis, Samella S. *v.1 p.705*

Lewis, Sinclair *v.2 p.95*

Lewis, Stephen E. *v.3 p.294*

Lewis, Thomas, et al. *v.4 p.738, v.5 p.650, p.654*

Lewis, Victoria *v.1 p.67*

Lewis, W. Arthur *v.4 p.259, p.268*

Lewis, W. H. *v.3 p.145*

Lewis, Wyndham *v.2 p.367, p.575*

Lewis-Beck, Michael S. (Editor), et al. *v.4 p.686*

Lewis-Beck, Michael S. (Editor) *v.4 p.609*

Lewisohn, Mark *v.1 p.170, p.306*

Lewis-Williams, David *v.1 p.668*

Lewontin, Richard C. . . . *v.5 p.80, p.122, p.128, p.135, p.200*

Lewy, Guenter *v.1 p.573, v.3 p.85, v.6 p.624*

Lexer, Matthias *v.2 p.621*

Lexis Nexis Staff, et al. *v.4 p.105, p.106, p.107*

LexisNexis *v.4 p.140, p.150*

Ley, David *v.6 p.724*

Leyens, Jacques-Philippe, et al. *v.4 p.694*

Leyland, Winston (Editor) *v.6 p.374, p.406*

Leymarie, Isabelle *v.1 p.292, v.6 p.518*

Leyser, Henrietta *v.6 p.560*

Lezama Lima, Jose *v.2 p.672*

Lezama Lima, José (Editor) *v.2 p.672*

Lönnroth, Lars *v.2 p.624*

López, Juan J. *v.3 p.311*

López Luján, Leonardo & Levin, Judy *v.4 p.10*

López, Miguel R. *v.6 p.501, p.514*

López-Santamaría, Maya *v.6 p.518*

López-Stafford, Gloria *v.6 p.489, p.501*

Lâm, Maivân Clech *v.4 p.33*

Lörinczy, Dénes *v.5 p.88, p.113*

Li, Chao-Jun & Chan, Tak-Hang *v.5 p.296*

Li, David Leiwei *v.6 p.97*

Li, J. J. *v.5 p.296*

Li Ju-chen *v.6 p.211*

Li, Ming, et al. *v.4 p.888*

Li, Peter S. *v.3 p.542*

Li, Yuan-Hui *v.5 p.440*

Li, Yu-ning (Editor) *v.6 p.199, p.217*

Li, Zhisui *v.6 p.201*

Liang, David Mingyue *v.1 p.288*

Liang, G. H. & Skinner, D. Z. . . *v.5 p.8, p.16, p.22*

Liang, Zhang, et al. *v.6 p.197*

Liano, Dante *v.2 p.676*

Lias, Sharon G. *v.5 p.282*

Libaridian, Gerard J. *v.6 p.633*

Libeskind, Daniel & Terragni, Attilio . . *v.1 p.793*

Liboff, Richard L. *v.5 p.550, p.560*

Library of America Staff (Editor) *v.2 p.23*

Library of Congress, Federal Research
  Division Staff (Editor), et al. *v.6 p.62*

Library of Congress Staff, et al. *v.4 p.767*

Library of Congress *v.4 p.367, p.437, p.476, p.481,*
  p.517, p.574, p.612, v.6 p.148, p.582

Lich, Glen E. (Editor) *v.3 p.509*

Lichtenberg, Joseph D. *v.5 p.627*

Lichtenstein, Grace & Dankner, Laura . . *v.1 p.278*

Lichtenstein, Nelson *v.4 p.127*

Lichtenthal, J. David (Editor) *v.4 p.176*

Lichtheim, Miriam *v.3 p.9, v.6 p.644*

Lichtman, Marshall Al , et al. *v.5 p.521*

Lickorish, W. B. *v.5 p.499*

Lida De Malkiel, Maria Rosa *v.2 p.651, p.652*

Liddell, Henry G. & Scott, Robert (Compiled by) . *v.2 p.400*

Liddell, Janice *v.6 p.26, p.45*

Liddell, Robert *v.2 p.267*

Liddell-Hart, Basil H. *v.3 p.36, p.81, p.175*

Liddick, Donald R. *v.6 p.251*

Liddle, Andrew *v.5 p.72*

Liddle, Peter & Cecil, Hugh *v.3 p.79*

Lide, David, Milne, G. W. A. (eds.) . . . *v.5 p.290*

Lide, David R. and Henry V. Kehiaian . . *v.5 p.275*

Lide, David R. (Editor-in-Chief) *v.5 p.259*

Lide, David R.; Kehiaian, Henry V. . . . *v.5 p.275*

Lide, David R., Milne, G.W.A. . . . *v.5 p.289, p.290*

Lide, David R. *v.5 p.290, p.316*

Lidl, Rudolf & Pilz, Günter *v.5 p.473*

Lidor, Ronnie & Henschen, Keith P. (Editors). *v.4 p.877, v.5 p.582*

Lidor, Ronnie, et al. *v.4 p.877*

Lidz, Carol S. *v.5 p.602*

Lieb, Elliott H. & Loss, Michael *v.5 p.489*

Lieb, Michael & Shawcross, John T. (Editors) . *v.2 p.254*

Lieb, Michael *v.2 p.254*

Liebau, F. *v.5 p.307*

Liebeck, M. W. *v.5 p.459*

Liebenow, J. Gus *v.6 p.70*

Lieber, Robert J. *v.4 p.625, p.641, p.642*

Lieber, Sherman *v.6 p.610*

Lieberman, Alicia F. *v.5 p.642*

Lieberman, Jethro K. *v.4 p.441, p.454*

Lieberman, Phil & Anderson, John A. . . *v.5 p.517*

Lieberman, Phil L. & Blaiss, Michael S. . *v.5 p.517*

Lieberman, Philip & Blumstein, Sheila E. . *v.2 p.562*

Lieberman, Philip *v.4 p.19*

Lieberman, Victor B. *v.6 p.164*

Liebert, Georges *v.1 p.200, p.381*

Lieberthal, Kenneth & Dickson, Bruce . . *v.4 p.620*

Lieberthal, Kenneth (Editor), et al. . . *v.6 p.183*

Liebler, Daniel C. (Editor), et al. . . *v.5 p.117*

Liebler, Daniel C. (Editor) *v.5 p.117*

Liebman, Matt, et al. *v.5 p.5, p.11, p.12*

Liebovich, Louis W. *v.3 p.474*

Liebow, Elliot *v.4 p.704*

Liebson, Milt *v.1 p.782*

Liedtke, Walter, et al. *v.1 p.697*

Lien, Pei-Te, et al. *v.6 p.120*

Lien, Pei-Te *v.6 p.120*

Lienhard, John H. *v.5 p.406, p.410*

Lier, Rudolf *v.3 p.322*

Lieser, Karl Heinrich *v.5 p.308*

Lieu, Samuel & Montserrat, Dominic (Editors) . *v.3 p.31*

Lieu, Samuel N. & Montserrat, Dominic . . *v.3 p.31*

Lieu, Samuel N. *v.1 p.646*

Lieuwen, Edwin *v.3 p.275, p.294*

Lieven, Anatol & Trenin, Dmitri (Editors) . *v.4 p.638*

Lieven, Anatol *v.3 p.256, p.368*

Lieven, Dominic C. *v.3 p.220*

Lifar, Serge *v.6 p.414*

Lifshitz, E. M. & Pitaevskii, L. P. . . *v.5 p.566*

Lifson, David S. (Translator) . . . *v.1 p.67, p.126*

Lifton, Betty J. *v.4 p.343*

Lifton, Paul *v.2 p.133*

Lifton, Robert J. *v.3 p.172, v.4 p.653*

Lifton, Robert Jay *v.5 p.654*

Light, Andrew & Rolston, Holmes (Editors) . *v.1 p.486*

Light, Ivan H. & Bonacich, Edna . . *v.6 p.106, p.136*

Light, Leah L. & Burke, Deborah M.
  (Editors) *v.5 p.627, p.630, p.632*

Light, Michael *v.1 p.767*

Light, Paul Charles *v.4 p.546*

Lightbown, Ronald *v.1 p.698*

Lightfoot, David *v.2 p.562*

Lightfoot, Sara Lawrence *v.4 p.303*

Lijphart, Arend & Grofman, Bernard N. (Editors) . *v.4 p.576*

Lijphart, Arend & Waisman, Carlos H. (Editors) . *v.4 p.504*

Lijphart, Arend *v.4 p.502, p.504*

Likhovski, Assaf *v.6 p.612*

Likoff, Laurie *v.5 p.576, p.578*

Lilar, Suzanne; Ronse, Henri *v.2 p.521, p.522*

Lilar, Suzanne *v.2 p.521*

Lillard, Angeline Stoll *v.4 p.337*

Lillard, Paula P. *v.4 p.343*

Lillehoj, Elizabeth (Editor) *v.1 p.732*

Lilleker, Darren G. & Lees-Marshment, Jennifer (Editors) *v.4 p.545, p.577*
Lilleker, Darren G. *v.4 p.425*
Lillesand, Thomas M., et al. *v.4 p.388*
Lillie, Amanda *v.1 p.790*
Lillo, George. *v.2 p.251*
Lilly, Carol S. *v.3 p.247*
Lim, Catherine *v.2 p.760*
Lim, Kyung S. (Editor) *v.5 p.684*
Lim, Shirley (Editor), et al. *v.6 p.97, p.119*
Lim, Shirley *v.6 p.92*
Lima, Elon Lages *v.5 p.474, p.499*
Lima, Jose Lezama *v.2 p.672*
LIM *v.4 p.400*
Limbacher, James L. & Wright, H. Stephen . . *v.1 p.168, p.256*
Limbacher, James L. *v.1 p.168, p.256, v.6 p.317*
Limerick, Patricia N. (Editor), et al. . . *v.3 p.518*
Limerick, Patricia Nelson *v.3 p.518*
Lim-Hing, Sharon (Editor) *v.6 p.92, p.112*
Limon, Graciela *v.6 p.500, p.501*
Limon, Jose E. *v.6 p.523*
Limon, Jose *v.1 p.10*
Lim-Wilson, Fatima *v.6 p.104*
Lin, C. C. & Segel, Lee A. *v.5 p.501*
Lin, Nan *v.4 p.269*
Lin, Simon M. & Johnson, Kimberly F. (Editors). *v.5 p.100, p.110*
Lin, Yutang & Chua, Cheng Lok *v.6 p.94*
Lin, Yutang *v.6 p.208*
Lincoln, Abraham & Basler, Roy Prentice . . *v.3 p.425*
Lincoln, Abraham & Shaw, Archer H. . . . *v.3 p.426*
Lincoln, Abraham *v.3 p.425*
Lincoln, Bruce *v.4 p.564, p.660*
Lincoln, C. Eric & Mamiya, Lawrence . *v.1 p.608, v.6 p.7, p.36*
Lincoln, C. Eric *v.1 p.560, v.6 p.7, p.36*
Lincoln, Chris *v.4 p.885, p.888, p.894*
Lincoln, Edward J. *v.6 p.219*
Lincoln, Evelyn *v.1 p.753*
Lincoln, R. J. & Boxshall, G. A. *v.5 p.225*
Lincoln, W. Bruce *v.3 p.214, p.219, p.225*
Lind, Amy, et al. *v.6 p.426*
Lind, David & Sanders, Scott Patrick . . *v.4 p.867, p.871*
Lind, Levi Robert *v.2 p.700*
Lind, Michael *v.3 p.509*
Lindahl, Carl (Editor), et al. *v.2 p.585*
Lindbeck, George A. *v.1 p.568, p.570, p.636*
Lindberg, Carter (Editor) *v.1 p.602*
Lindberg, Carter *v.1 p.601*
Lindberg, David C. (Editor) *v.5 p.389, v.6 p.576*
Lindberg, Jill A., et al. *v.4 p.284*
Lindeburg, Michael R. *v.5 p.685*
Lindee, M. Susan *v.5 p.149*
Lindemann, Erika C. *v.2 p.565*
Lindemann, Mary *v.3 p.47, p.50, p.167, v.5 p.510*
Linden, Eugene *v.4 p.394, v.5 p.426*
Linden, Walther *v.2 p.589*

Lindenbaum, Shirley *v.4 p.46*
Linder, Douglas O. *v.4 p.438*
Linder, Greg (Editor), et al. *v.6 p.291*
Linder, M. C. (Editor) *v.5 p.124*
Linderman, Gerald F. *v.3 p.398*
Lindesmith, Alfred R. *v.4 p.449*
Lindfors, Bernth & Sander, Reinhard W. (Editors) . . *v.2 p.751*
Lindfors, Bernth (Editor), et al. *v.2 p.758*
Lindfors, Bernth (Editor) *v.2 p.753, p.757*
Lindfors, Bernth *v.2 p.751*
Lindfors, Judith Wells *v.4 p.423*
Lindgren, Mats & Bandhold, Hans *v.4 p.82*
Lindgren *v.5 p.482*
Lindheim, Ralph & Luckyj, George S. (Editors) . . *v.2 p.814*
Lindner, Rudi Paul *v.6 p.623*
Lindo, Hugo *v.2 p.676*
Lindow, John *v.1 p.533*
Lindqvist, Sven *v.4 p.817, p.869, p.870*
Lindsay, David *v.2 p.215, p.219*
Lindsay, James & Daalder, Ivo *v.3 p.483, v.4 p.560*
Lindsay, James F. & Katz, Silas *v.5 p.711*
Lindsay, James M. & Daalder, Ivo H. . . . *v.3 p.483*
Lindsay, James M. *v.2 p.600*
Lindsay, Maurice & Duncan, Lesley . . . *v.2 p.200*
Lindsay, Maurice *v.2 p.164*
Lindsay, Vachel *v.2 p.94*
Lindsay, W. M. *v.2 p.440*
Lindsay-Poland, John *v.3 p.269, p.305*
Lindsey, Almont *v.4 p.127*
Lindsey, Charles *v.3 p.539*
Lindsey, Duncan *v.4 p.756*
Lindsey, J. K. *v.5 p.481, p.503*
Lindstrom, Matthew J. & Smith, Zachary A. . . *v.5 p.29, v.6 p.300*
Lindstrom, Naomi *v.2 p.664, p.678*
Lindzey, Gardner (Editor) *v.5 p.597*
Lindzey, Gardner *v.5 p.597*
Linehan, Peter & Nelson, Janet L. (Editors) . . *v.6 p.555*
Linehan, Peter *v.3 p.243*
Linehan, Thomas P. *v.4 p.582*
Linfert, Carl *v.1 p.743*
Ling, Amy & White-Parks, Annette (Editors) . . *v.6 p.101*
Ling, Amy (Editor) *v.6 p.88*
Ling, Amy *v.6 p.97*
Ling, Dwight L. *v.6 p.61*
Ling, Jan *v.1 p.298*
Ling, Jinqi *v.6 p.97*
Ling, Roger *v.1 p.728, p.811*
Lingard, Bob & Douglas, Peter *v.6 p.463*
Lingard, C. Cecil *v.4 p.590*
Lingeman, Richard R. *v.2 p.70*
Lingeman, Richard *v.3 p.474*
Linger, Daniel Touro *v.4 p.39*
Lingle, Walter L. & Kuykendall, John W. . . *v.1 p.588*
Lings, Martin *v.1 p.555*
Linhard, Tabea Alexa *v.3 p.294*

Link, Andrew J. *v.5 p.117*

Link, Arthur S. & McCormick, Richard L. *v.3 p.448*

Link, Arthur S. (Editor) *v.3 p.474*

Link, Arthur S. *v.3 p.442, p.474*

Link, Perry (Editor) *v.6 p.213*

Link, Perry *v.6 p.208*

Link, Stuart B *v.5 p.635*

Link, William A. *v.3 p.443, p.448, p.497*

Linke, William F. *v.5 p.282*

Linkogle, Stephanie *v.3 p.302*

Linkon, Sherry L. (Editor) *v.4 p.302*

Linkon, Sherry Lee & Russo, John. *v.3 p.513*

Links, J. G. *v.1 p.743*

Linley, David *v.1 p.804*

Linmark, R. Zamora *v.6 p.101, p.112*

Linn, Brian McAllister *v.6 p.180*

Linn, Karen *v.1 p.278, p.390*

Linn, Robert L. & Miller, M. David *v.5 p.604*

Linn, Robert L. (Editor) *v.5 p.604*

Linné, Carl von & Freer, Stephen *v.5 p.207*

Lins, Osman *v.2 p.691*

Linsky, Arnold, et al. *v.4 p.699*

Linsley, Ray K., et al. *v.5 p.368, p.380*

Linteau, Paul-Ande, et al. *v.3 p.544*

Lintner, Bertil *v.6 p.166*

Linton, C. M. *v.5 p.62*

Linton, Joan P. *v.2 p.170*

Linton, Ralph *v.4 p.695*

Lintott, Andrew *v.3 p.25, p.26, v.4 p.501*

Lints, Richard S. (Editor), et al. *v.1 p.643*

Linz, Juan J. & Stepan, Alfred. *v.4 p.505*

Lion, Jean Pierre. *v.1 p.261, p.308*

Lionnet, Francoise *v.6 p.477*

Liotta, Dennis C. & Volmer, Mark *v.5 p.293*

Lipham, James M., et al. *v.4 p.282*

Lipka, Richard P. & Brinthaupt, Thomas M. (Editors) . *v.4 p.279*

Lipkin, Arthur *v.6 p.385*

Lipking, Lawrence I. *v.2 p.250*

Liponski, Wojciech *v.4 p.848*

Lipoveetiskiaei, M. N. *v.2 p.796*

Lipp, Solomon *v.3 p.350*

Lipper, Joanna *v.4 p.759*

Lippi-Green, Rosina L. *v.2 p.552, v.4 p.21*

Lippincott Williams and Wilkins Staff (Contribution by). *v.5 p.531*

Lippit, Victor *v.4 p.214*

Lippitt, John. *v.1 p.478, p.479*

Lippman, Edward A. (Contribution by). *v.1 p.382*

Lippman, Edward A. (Editor) *v.1 p.382*

Lippman, Edward A. *v.1 p.175, p.382*

Lippman, Stanley B. & Lajoie, Jose *v.5 p.347*

Lippman, Thomas W. *v.3 p.390*

Lippman, Walter *v.1 p.484*

Lippmann, Morton *v.5 p.365, p.366*

Lippmann, Walter . . . *v.3 p.455, p.474, v.4 p.425, p.697, p.768*

Lippold, John C. & Kotecki, Damian J. *v.5 p.737*

Lipschultz, Jeremy Harris & Hilt, Michael L. *v.4 p.407*

Lipschutz, Martin *v.5 p.496*

Lipschutz, Ronnie D. *v.6 p.322*

Lipschutz, Seymour & Lipson, Marc Lars *v.5 p.478*

Lipschutz, Seymour and Lipson, Marc *v.5 p.472*

Lipset, Seymour Martin & Bendix, Reinhard . *v.4 p.722, p.726*

Lipset, Seymour Martin & Lakin, Jason M.. . . . . *v.4 p.505*

Lipset, Seymour Martin & Marks, Gary *v.4 p.507, p.554*

Lipset, Seymour Martin & Meltz, Noah M. *v.4 p.122*

Lipset, Seymour Martin . . . *v.3 p.368, v.4 p.586, p.589, p.591*

Lipsey, Mark W. & Wilson, David B. *v.4 p.687*

Lipsey, Mark W. *v.4 p.686*

Lipsitz, George, et al.. . . . . *v.6 p.492*

Lipsitz, Joan. *v.4 p.367, p.736*

Lipska, Ewa *v.2 p.790*

Lipski, John M. *v.2 p.636*

Lipsman, Ron *v.4 p.175*

Lipson, Carol S. & Day, Michael J. (Editors) *v.5 p.589*

Lipson, Juliene G. & Dibble, Suzanne L. (Editors) . . *v.5 p.530*

Lipton, Michael *v.4 p.265*

Lipton, Ronnie *v.1 p.721*

Lisanti, Thomas *v.6 p.342*

Lisanti, Tom *v.6 p.332*

Lischer, Richard *v.1 p.649*

Liscombe, Rhodri W. *v.1 p.790*

Lisle, Laurie *v.1 p.780*

Lisle, Richard J. *v.5 p.441*

Lispector, Clarice. *v.2 p.691*

List, George *v.1 p.292*

Lister, Raymond *v.1 p.752*

Lister, T. *v.5 p.140, p.328*

Lister, Ted (Editor) *v.5 p.265*

Litalien, Raymonde & Vaugeois, Denis (Editors) . . . *v.3 p.538*

Litan, Robert E. & Nordhaus, William D. *v.4 p.444*

Litan, Robert E. (Editor) *v.4 p.471*

Little & Mirlees *v.4 p.259*

Little, Barbara J. (Editor) *v.1 p.823, v.4 p.7*

Little, Charles E. & Ashworth, William. . . *v.5 p.707, v.6 p.286*

Little, Colin *v.5 p.182, p.193*

Little, Jeffrey B. *v.4 p.96, p.100*

Little, John, et al. *v.5 p.473, p.497*

Little, Judy *v.2 p.393*

Little, Kenneth E. *v.4 p.87*

Little, Lester K. *v.1 p.651, v.6 p.572*

Little, Meredith & Jenne, Natalie (Editors). *v.1 p.45, p.185, p.303*

Little, Michael R. *v.3 p.390*

Little, Peter (Editor) *v.5 p.135*

Little, Stephen, et al. *v.1 p.693*

Littleboy, Bruce *v.4 p.228*

Littlefield, Daniel F., Jr. *v.2 p.49*

Littlewood, Antony R., et al. *v.1 p.819*

Littlewood, Ian. *v.6 p.219*

Littré, Emile, et. al.. . . . . *v.2 p.454*

Litwak, Robert S. *v.3 p.474*

Litweiler, John *v.1 p.261*
Litz, A. Walton *v.2 p.268, p.359*
Litz, R. E. *v.5 p.8, p.22*
Litz, Walton *v.2 p.268*
Litzinger, Boyd *v.2 p.272*
Liu, Alan *v.2 p.324, p.549, p.727*
Liu, David H. and Bela G. Liptak, eds.. . . . . *v.5 p.707*
Liu, David H.F., ed. *v.5 p.707*
Liu, David H.F. *v.5 p.368*
Liu, Eric *v.6 p.94, p.127*
Liu, Henry. *v.5 p.697*
Liu, James J. *v.6 p.208, p.210*
Liu, Jun S.. . . . . *v.5 p.551*
Liu, Lin & Madej *v.4 p.385, p.387*
Liu, Lydia H. *v.6 p.204*
Liu, Lydia He *v.6 p.204*
Liu, Miles Xian (Editor) *v.1 p.60, p.125,v.6 p.86, p.99*
Liu, Sandra & Hamamoto, Darrell Y. (Editors) . . *v.6 p.89, p.97*
Liu, Tessie P. *v.3 p.149*
Liu, Wu-Chi & Lo, Irving Y. (Editors) *v.6 p.210, p.211*
Liu, Xiaoyuan *v.4 p.620*
Liu, Xiusheng & Ivanhoe, P. J. (Editors) *v.1 p.418*
Liu, Ying (Editor) *v.4 p.167*
Liulevicius, Vejas Gabriel *v.3 p.161*
Liuzza, R. M. (Editor) *v.2 p.167*
Lively, Donald E. *v.4 p.457, p.537*
Liverani, Mario. *v.3 p.4*
Livermore, Harold U.. . . . . *v.3 p.243*
Livermore, Shaw *v.3 p.414*
Livesay, Dorothy *v.2 p.736*
Livesay, Harold C. *v.4 p.127*
Livesley, W. John (Editor). *v.5 p.661*
Livezeanu, Irina *v.3 p.250*
Livezey, Lowell W. (Editor). *v.6 p.718*
Livezey, William Edmund. *v.3 p.383*
Livia, Anna & Hall, Kira (Editors) *v.4 p.21*
Livingston, Alan & Livingston, Isabella *v.1 p.712*
Livingston, Charles. *v.5 p.499*
Livingston, Donald W. *v.1 p.451*
Livingston, Ivor L. (Editor) *v.6 p.22, p.39*
Livingston, James D. *v.5 p.732*
Livingston, Jane, et al. *v.1 p.743*
Livingston, Lili Cockerille *v.1 p.10*
Livingston, Robert J. *v.5 p.173*
Livingstone, David N. & Withers, Charles W. J.
    (Editors) *v.4 p.375*
Livingstone, David N. *v.4 p.374*
Livingstone, Marco *v.1 p.679, p.698*
Livingstone, Margaret S. *v.1 p.703*
Livingston-Isenhour, Tamara Elena & Garcia,
    Thomas George Caracas. *v.1 p.292*
Livio, Mario. *v.5 p.467, p.476*
Livolsi, Virginia A. & Asa, Sylvia *v.5 p.518*
Livy, Titus Livius *v.2 p.436*
Livy *v.2 p.435, p.436*

Lleshanaku, Luljeta. *v.2 p.815*
Llewellyn, Karl N. & Hoebel, E. Adamson. . . *v.6 p.691, p.703*
Llewellyn, Karl N. *v.4 p.439*
Llewellyn, Richard *v.2 p.361*
Llobera, Josep R. *v.3 p.61*
Lloyd, Christopher *v.2 p.495*
Lloyd, David G. (Editor) *v.5 p.206*
Lloyd Evans, Gareth & Lloyd Evans,
    Barbara (Revised by) *v.2 p.230*
Lloyd, G. E. R.. . . . . *v.2 p.404, v.5 p.392*
Lloyd, Genevieve *v.1 p.477*
Lloyd, Margaret *v.1 p.26*
Lloyd, Paul *v.2 p.636*
Lloyd, Peter *v.3 p.330*
Lloyd, Richard D. *v.6 p.718*
Lloyd, Rosemary (Editor) *v.2 p.488*
Lloyd, Rosemary *v.2 p.488, p.491, p.496*
Lloyd, Sandra Mackenzie, et al.. . . . . . . *v.1 p.823, p.828*
Lloyd, Seton *v.3 p.4*
Lloyd, T. H. *v.3 p.96, p.161*
Lloyd, T. O. *v.3 p.89, p.119, p.125*
Lloyd, Trevor Owen. *v.3 p.89, p.125*
Lloyd Webber, Andrew & Rice, Tim . . *v.1 p.252, p.337, p.408*
Lloyd-Jones, Antonia (Translator) *v.2 p.791*
Lo, Andrew W. (Editor). *v.4 p.263*
Lo, Irving Y. & Schultz, William (Editors) *v.6 p.210*
Lo, Kai-yin *v.1 p.804*
Lo Kuan-Chung & Roberts, Moss *v.6 p.211*
Lo, Vai Io (Contribution by). *v.4 p.122*
Loades, David M. *v.3 p.100, p.121*
Loasby, Brian J. *v.4 p.195, p.215*
Lobban, Christopher S. & Harrison, Paul J.. . . . . *v.5 p.208*
Lobdell, Jared *v.5 p.664*
Lobeck, Anne *v.2 p.557*
Lobenthal, Joel. *v.6 p.418*
Lobo Antunes, Antonio *v.2 p.688*
Lobo Montalvo, Maria Luisa *v.1 p.790*
Lobo, Susan *v.3 p.330*
Lobo, Tatiana *v.2 p.676*
LoBrutto, Vincent *v.6 p.348, p.350*
Lochrie, Karma *v.6 p.567*
Lock, F. P. *v.2 p.243*
Lock, G. S. *v.5 p.713*
Lock, Gary. *v.4 p.7*
Lock, Margaret (Editor, Contribution by) *v.4 p.47*
Lock, Margaret M. *v.6 p.222*
Lock, Peter *v.3 p.193*
Locke, Alain L.. . . . . *v.6 p.7, p.39*
Locke, Edwin A. & Latham, Gary P.. . . . . . . *v.5 p.579*
Locke, John & Fraser, Alexander Campbell. *v.4 p.195*
Locke, John *v.1 p.448, p.482, p.597,
                          v.4 p.215, p.216, p.343, p.492*
Locke, Nancy *v.1 p.743*
Locke, Robert & Schöne, Katja *v.4 p.176*
Locker, J. L. *v.1 p.757*

Lockeretz, William (Editor) *v.5 p.13*

Lockhart, Bruce McFarland & Duiker, William J. . . . *v.6 p.167*

Lockhart, James *v.3 p.286, p.326*

Lockhart, Paul *v.3 p.235*

Lockheed, Marlaine E. & Verspoor, Adriaan M. . . . *v.4 p.314*

Lockman Foundation Staff (Editor, Translator) *v.1 p.613*

Lockridge, Kenneth A. *v.3 p.500*

Lockshin, Richard A. & Zakeri, Zahra (Editors) . . . *v.5 p.159*

Lockwood, David (Editor) *v.6 p.759, p.761*

Lockwood, Lewis & Kroll, Mark (Editors) *v.1 p.200, p.241, p.307*

Lockwood, Lewis *v.1 p.200, p.307*

Lockwood, Thomas (Editor) *v.2 p.247*

Lockwood, Victoria S. *v.4 p.385*

Lodders, Katharina & Fegley, Bruce Jr. *v.5 p.69*

Lodge, David & Wood, Nigel *v.2 p.567, p.568*

Lodge, David *v.2 p.169, p.189, p.361*

Lodge, Henry Cabot *v.3 p.474*

Lodge, Milton & McGraw, Kathleen M. (Editors) . . . *v.5 p.643*

Lodge, Thomas *v.2 p.215*

Lodwick, Marcus *v.1 p.665*

Loeb, Lori A. *v.6 p.739, p.748*

Loeffelholz, Mary *v.2 p.8*

Loening, K. L. (Editor) *v.5 p.321*

Loescher, Gil *v.4 p.634, p.670*

Loesser, Arthur *v.1 p.377, p.390*

Loesser, Susan *v.1 p.252, p.337*

Loevy, Robert D. (Editor) *v.4 p.457*

Loewe, Michael & Shaughnessy, Edward L. *v.4 p.9*

Loewenberg, Alfred *v.1 p.161, p.231*

Loewenstein, David & Mueller, Janel (Editors) . . . *v.2 p.170*

Loewenstein, Werner R. *v.5 p.154*

Loewenthal, Erich & Schneider, Lambert (Editors) . *v.2 p.590*

Loewenthal, Lillian *v.1 p.10*

Loewer, Peter H. *v.5 p.156*

Lofaro, Michael A. & Davis, Hugh (Editors) *v.2 p.56*

Lofaro, Michael A. *v.3 p.511*

Loffreda, Beth *v.6 p.387*

Lofland, John Jr. *v.4 p.692*

Lofland, John *v.4 p.696*

Lofland, Lyn H. *v.4 p.771, v.6 p.718*

Lofquist, Lloyd H. & Dawis, Rene V. *v.5 p.578*

Loftis, John C. *v.2 p.260*

Loftis, John *v.2 p.187*

Loftus, Elizabeth F. *v.4 p.473, v.5 p.592, v.6 p.271*

Loftus, Ronald P. (Editor, Translator) *v.6 p.477*

Logan, Bruce E. *v.5 p.704*

Logan, Charles H. *v.6 p.276*

Logan, Deborah Anna & Sanders, Valerie (Editors) . *v.4 p.195*

Logan, Deborah Anna *v.2 p.299*

Logan, Fern *v.6 p.16*

Logan, John R. & Molotch, Harvey L. (Editors) . . . *v.6 p.724*

Logan, Michael F. *v.4 p.544*

Logan, Rayford W. & Winston, Michael R. (Editors) *v.6 p.14, p.33*

Logan, Rayford W. *v.6 p.7*

Logan, Rayford Whittingham *v.3 p.317*

Logan, Sadye Louise & Freeman, Edith M. (Editors) . . *v.6 p.22*

Logan, Thad *v.6 p.761*

Logan, William & Gioia, Dana (Editors) *v.2 p.90*

Logevall, Fredrik *v.6 p.169*

Logsdon, Bette J. *v.4 p.798*

Logsdon, Joseph *v.3 p.422, p.423, p.428*

Logsdon, Tom *v.5 p.720*

Logue, John *v.3 p.234*

Lohner, Edgar & Hannum, H. G. *v.2 p.594*

Lohr, Eric & Poe, Marshall T. (Editors) *v.3 p.212*

Lohr, Eric *v.4 p.653*

Lohrli, Anne *v.6 p.741, p.754*

Lohse, Bernhard *v.1 p.633*

Lohse, Edward *v.1 p.627, p.631*

Lohse, Jon C. & Valdez, Fred (Editors) *v.3 p.297*

Loidl, Hans-Wolfgang & Bernard, Stefan *v.1 p.813*

Loizos, Peter & Papataxiarchis, Evthmios (Editors) . *v.3 p.195*

Loizos, Peter *v.6 p.310*

Lomax, Alan *v.1 p.261, p.296, p.343*

Lomax, Derek W. *v.3 p.65*

Lomax, John *v.2 p.20*

Lomax, Michael E. . *v.4 p.807, p.832, p.851, p.885, p.888, p.897*

Lomax, Paul, et al. *v.5 p.347*

Lomax, Richard G. *v.4 p.355, v.5 p.482, p.503*

Lombardi, John V. *v.3 p.359, p.360*

Lombardi, Marilyn M. (Editor) *v.2 p.62*

Lombardi, Vince *v.4 p.697*

Lombardo, John *v.4 p.859, p.894*

Lomborg, Bjorn *v.6 p.291*

Lombroso-Ferrero, Gina &
Savitz, Leonard D. *v.4 p.752, v.6 p.254*

Lomelí, Francisco A. & Shirley, Carl R. *v.6 p.501, p.514*

Lommel, Cookie *v.6 p.330, p.342*

Lomnicki, Adam *v.5 p.184, p.189*

Lomnitz, Larissa Adler de *v.4 p.704*

Lomolino, Mark V. & Heaney, Lawrence R. . *v.4 p.394, v.5 p.168*

Lomolino, Mark V. (Editor), et al. . *v.4 p.394, v.5 p.168, p.226*

Lomperis, Timothy J. *v.6 p.169*

London, Bette Lynn *v.6 p.479*

London, Jack *v.2 p.95*

London, Richard L. and Nicholas Mocciolo *v.5 p.504*

London Times Staff, London Times *v.4 p.379*

Londono-Vega, Patricia *v.3 p.357*

Lone, Stewart *v.3 p.341*

Lonergan, Bernard *v.1 p.639*

Loney, Glenn Meredith *v.1 p.32*

Loney, Glenn *v.1 p.10, p.32, v.6 p.415*

Long, A. A. & Sedley, D. N. *v.1 p.428*

Long, A. A. (Editor) *v.1 p.421*

Long, A. A. *v.1 p.428, p.429*

Long, Carolyn N. *v.4 p.439, v.6 p.696, p.701*

Long, David & Schmidt, Brian C. (Editors) *v.4 p.625*

Long, David E. & Reich, Bernard *v.6 p.594*

Long, David E.. . . . . *v.6 p.626*
Long, David F.. . . . . *v.3 p.417*
Long, Douglas *v.4 p.118*
Long, E. B. *v.3 p.437*
Long, Edward L. Jr. *v.4 p.290*
Long, Frank (Editor) *v.4 p.202*
Long, Huey P. *v.3 p.460*
Long, J. Scott *v.4 p.689*
Long, Janet, ed. *v.3 p.271*
Long, John A. *v.5 p.215*
Long, John L. *v.6 p.283*
Long, John *v.4 p.789*
Long, Lynellen D. *v.6 p.443*
Long, Michael *v.2 p.235*
Long, Ngo Vinh *v.4 p.704, v.6 p.167*
Long, Patrick D. & Ricard, Laura *v.6 p.140*
Long, Richard A. & Collier, Eugenia W. (Editors) . . . *v.2 p.20*
Long, Richard A. *v.1 p.32*
Long, Richard *v.1 p.780*
Long, Robert Emmet. *v.1 p.36, v.6 p.416*
Long, Roger D. (Editor) *v.3 p.89, p.125*
Long, Thomas G.. . . . . *v.1 p.649*
Longair, Malcolm S. *v.5 p.62, p.66, p.548*
Longenecker, Stephen L. *v.1 p.607*
Longfellow, Henry Wadsworth *v.2 p.47*
Longfield, Bradley J.. . . . . *v.1 p.588*
Longford, Elizabeth *v.3 p.91, p.113, p.119*
Longinus *v.2 p.416*
Longley, Paul A. (Editor), et al. *v.4 p.387*
Longley, Paul A., et al. *v.4 p.387*
Longman, Stanley Vincent *v.1 p.139*
Longoria, Arturo *v.3 p.269, v.5 p.222*
Longrigg, James (Editor) *v.2 p.404*
Longrigg, James *v.2 p.405*
Longrigg, Stephen H.. . . . . *v.6 p.605, p.607*
Longrigg, Stephen Hemsley *v.6 p.603*
Long-Solis, Jane *v.3 p.271*
Longstreet, Stephen. *v.4 p.777*
Longva, Anh Nga *v.6 p.627*
Lonsdale, Roger (Editor) *v.2 p.180, p.200*
Loo, Chalsa M. *v.6 p.127*
Looijen, Rick C. *v.5 p.184*
Loomba, Ania *v.2 p.572*
Loomis, Burdett A. (Editor) *v.4 p.534*
Loomis, Jeffrey B. *v.2 p.294*
Loomis, John B.. . . . . *v.5 p.38*
Loomis, R. S. & Connor, D. J. *v.5 p.22*
Loomis, Roger S. & Wells, Henry W.
  (Editors) *v.1 p.67, p.70, p.73, p.101*
Loomis, William F.. . . . . *v.5 p.193*
Looney, Stephen W. *v.5 p.100*
Loos, Anita (Editor), et al. *v.2 p.94*
Loos, Anita *v.2 p.94*
Looser, Devoney *v.2 p.268*
Lopata, Helena Z. (Editor) *v.4 p.741*

Lopata, Helena Z. *v.4 p.741*
Lopata, Helena Znaniecka *v.6 p.465, p.467*
Lopate, Phillip *v.2 p.21, p.584*
Lopes, Rosaly M. C. & Gregg, Tracy K. P.. . . *v.5 p.434, p.437*
Lopez, Adalberto (Editor). *v.6 p.531*
Lopez, Barry *v.2 p.149, v.5 p.238*
Lopez, Daniel *v.6 p.311*
Lopez, Donald S. (Editor). *v.1 p.534*
Lopez, Donald S. Jr. (Editor). . . *v.1 p.539, p.540, p.561, p.565*
Lopez, Donald S. Jr. *v.6 p.241*
Lopez, Donald S.. . . . . *v.1 p.563, p.566, v.6 p.241*
Lopez, Ian F.. . . . . *v.4 p.457*
Lopez Jr., Donald S. *v.6 p.241*
Lopez, Nancy *v.4 p.315*
Lopez, Robert S. & Raymond, Irving W.
  (Translators). *v.3 p.69, p.198, v.6 p.558*
Lopez Tijerina, Reies. *v.6 p.536, p.540*
Lopukhov, Fedor Vasil'evich *v.1 p.24, p.45*
Lorange, Peter (Editor) *v.4 p.176*
Lorant, Stefan, et al. *v.3 p.492, v.6 p.714*
Loraux, Nicole. *v.3 p.14, p.20*
Lorber, Judith & Moore, Lisa Jean. *v.6 p.443*
Lorber, Judith *v.4 p.746, v.6 p.429*
Lorca, Federico García *v.2 p.660*
Lorch, Jennifer. *v.2 p.722*
Lord, Albert B. *v.2 p.415, p.819*
Lord, Barry & Dexter, Gail (Editors). *v.1 p.828*
Lord, Barry & Lord, Gail Dexter *v.1 p.828*
Lord, Bette Bao *v.6 p.201, p.217*
Lord, Charles R. *v.5 p.679*
Lord, George D. (Editor) *v.2 p.200*
Lord, James *v.1 p.780*
Lord, John. *v.4 p.338*
Lord Shaftesbury. *v.1 p.437*
Lorde, Audre Geraldine. *v.2 p.149, v.4 p.744,*
                                       v.6 p.372, p.402, p.405, p.434
Lorentz, John H.. . . . . *v.6 p.629*
Lorentzen, Lois A. & Turpin, Jennifer (Editors) . . . *v.6 p.465*
Lorenz, Richard *v.1 p.767*
Lorenzen, David N.. . . . . *v.1 p.537, v.6 p.151*
Lorey, David E. *v.4 p.335*
Lorimer, D. L. R. (Editor). *v.6 p.672*
Lorimer, Douglas A.. . . . . *v.3 p.92*
Lorin, Philippe & Alonso, Cristina. *v.4 p.141*
Loring, John. *v.1 p.802, p.806*
Lorion, Raymond P. (Editor), et al.. . . . . *v.5 p.643*
Lornell, Kip & Rasmussen, Anne K.. . . . . *v.1 p.296*
Lornell, Kip *v.1 p.296*
Lorquin, Bertrand *v.1 p.780*
Lorr, Maurice *v.4 p.689*
Lorrick, Peter *v.1 p.15*
Lorsch, Jay W. (Editor), et al.. . . . . *v.4 p.54, p.86, p.109*
Losambe, Lokangaka & Sarinjeive, Devi (Editors) . . *v.1 p.130*
Losee, John. *v.3 p.45*
Losey, Mike (Editor), et al.. . . . . *v.4 p.76*

Loshitzky, Yosefa. *v.6 p.333*

Losito, Linda, et al.. . . . . *v.5 p.156*

Loti, Pierre & Cambon, M. Jules *v.2 p.496*

Lott, Bernice & Maluso, Diane (Editors) *v.4 p.698*

Lott, Dale F. *v.6 p.284*

Lott, Eric *v.1 p.281*

Lott, John R.. *v.4 p.541*

Lottman, Herbert R. *v.1 p.767, v.2 p.503*

Lotz, Wolfgang. *v.1 p.787*

Lotze, Dieter P. *v.2 p.603*

Loud, G. A. & Metcalfe, A. (Editors) *v.3 p.198*

Loud, G. A. *v.3 p.198*

Louden, Robert B. & Kuehn, Manfred (Editors). . . . *v.1 p.462*

Loudon, Rodney *v.5 p.562*

Lough, John *v.2 p.456, v.3 p.147*

Loughery, John *v.6 p.367, p.375, p.376*

Loughman, Michael *v.4 p.789*

Louie, David W. *v.6 p.101*

Louie, David Wong. *v.6 p.101*

Louie, Miriam Ching Yoon *v.6 p.457*

Louie, Steven G. & Omatsu, Glenn K. (Editors). *v.6 p.107, p.120*

Louie, Vivian S.. . . . . *v.6 p.109, p.127*

Louis, Murray *v.1 p.10, p.43*

Louis, William Roger & Stookey, Robert W. (Editors) . *v.6 p.610*

Louis, William Roger, et al. *v.3 p.77*

Louis, William Roger. *v.6 p.63, p.64*

Louise, Chandra B. *v.5 p.251*

Lounsbury, Carl R. *v.1 p.784*

Lounsbury, Thomas RaynesFord. *v.2 p.555, p.557*

Lounsbury, Warren C. & Boulanger, Norman C.. . . . *v.1 p.140*

Loup Pivin, Jean (Editor) *v.1 p.690*

Lourandos, Harry *v.4 p.13*

Lourie, Richard *v.3 p.223*

Loux, Michael J. & Zimmerman, Dean W. (Editors). . *v.1 p.488*

Loux, Michael J.. . . . . *v.1 p.510*

Lovato, Andrew *v.6 p.534*

Love, Harold. *v.2 p.244*

Love, Jean O. *v.2 p.393*

Love, Paul *v.1 p.4*

Love, Ronald S. *v.3 p.145*

Love, Rosaleen *v.5 p.173, p.241, v.6 p.293*

Lovecraft, H. P. *v.2 p.94*

Lovejoy, Arthur Oncken *v.1 p.442, p.488, p.504*

Lovejoy, David S. *v.3 p.406*

Lovejoy, Margot *v.1 p.771*

Lovejoy, Paul E. & Hogendorn, Jan S. *v.6 p.71*

Lovejoy, Paul E. *v.4 p.728, v.6 p.11, p.39, p.53, p.68*

Lovejoy, Thomas E. & Hannah, Lee (Editors). *v.4 p.394*

Lovelace, Richard *v.2 p.251*

Loveland, Walter D.; Morrissey, David J.;
Seaborg, Glenn T.. . . . . *v.5 p.308*

Lovell, Charles M. *v.1 p.732*

Lovell, John Jr.. . . . . *v.1 p.281*

Lovell, John P. (Editor) *v.6 p.321*

Lovell, Margaretta M. *v.1 p.682*

Lovell, Mary S. *v.2 p.371*

Lovell, Stephen *v.3 p.210*

Lovell, Terry *v.2 p.193, v.6 p.756*

Lovell, W. George *v.3 p.298*

Lovelock, James *v.5 p.248*

Loveman, Brian (Editor), et al. *v.3 p.275*

Loveman, Brian *v.3 p.275, p.350, v.4 p.592*

Lovera, José Rafael. *v.3 p.271*

Lovesey, Oliver *v.2 p.758*

Lovett, Charlie. *v.4 p.846, p.863*

Lovett, Patricia. *v.1 p.719*

Lovász, Laszio. *v.5 p.479*

Lovász, Laszlo, et al.. . . . . *v.5 p.478*

Loving, Jerome *v.2 p.70*

Lovinger, King F. (Compiled by) *v.4 p.529*

Lovrick, Peter *v.1 p.288*

Low, Alfred D.. . . . . *v.3 p.185*

Low, Anthony *v.2 p.182, v.6 p.576*

Low, D. A. *v.3 p.87, v.6 p.157*

Low, Gail C.. *v.2 p.176*

Low, Linda (Editor) *v.4 p.398*

Low, Nicholas & Gleeson, Brendan (Editors) *v.6 p.728*

Low, Pak Sum (Editor) *v.4 p.394*

Low, Setha & Smith, Neil (Editors) *v.6 p.724*

Low, Setha, et al.. . . . . *v.6 p.297*

Low, Setha M. & Lawrence-Zuaniga, Denise (Editors). *v.6 p.721*

Low, Setha M.. . . . . *v.6 p.710, p.718*

Low, Tim *v.5 p.185*

Lowance, Mason I. (Editor), et al. *v.2 p.51*

Lowance, Mason I. Jr.. . . . . *v.2 p.12*

Lowdermilk, Deitra Leonard & Perry, Shannon E.. . . *v.5 p.524*

Lowe, Benjamin *v.4 p.811*

Lowe Besteman, Catherine *v.6 p.65, p.66*

Lowe, David A. (Editor) *v.2 p.805*

Lowe, Denise *v.6 p.332*

Lowe, Donald M. *v.4 p.775*

Lowe, E. J. *v.1 p.448, p.488, p.497*

Lowe, Ian *v.1 p.757*

Lowe, Lisa *v.6 p.97*

Lowe, Margaret A.. . . . . *v.6 p.446, p.463*

Lowe, Peter *v.6 p.237*

Lowe, Stephen R. *v.4 p.861, p.885, p.891, p.897*

Lowe, Truman (Editor) *v.6 p.679*

Lowell, Amy *v.2 p.95, p.461*

Lowell, James Russell *v.2 p.47, p.95*

Lowell, Mary Gardner *v.3 p.311*

Lowell, Robert *v.2 p.96*

Lowenstein, Roger. *v.4 p.96, p.98, p.100, p.147*

Lowenstein, Steven M. *v.3 p.180*

Lowenthal, Abraham F. & Fitch, J. Samuel (Editors) . *v.3 p.275*

Lowenthal, Abraham F.. . . . . *v.3 p.330*

Lowenthal, Cynthia. *v.2 p.187*

Lowenthal, David ; Comitos, Lambros *v.4 p.704*

Lowenthal, Gerhart & Airey, Peter. *v.5 p.740*

Lower, Arthur R.. . . . . *v.3 p.535*

Lower, Richard Coke *v.3 p.460*
Lowes, John L.. *v.2 p.280*
Lowes, Mark D. *v.4 p.407*
Lowi, Theodore J. *v.6 p.724*
Lowie, Robert H.. . . . . *v.4 p.3*
Lowinson, Joyce H., et al. *v.5 p.512, p.522*
Lowitt, Richard & Norris, George W. *v.3 p.460*
Lowitt, Richard *v.3 p.460*
Lowman, Rodney L. *v.5 p.578*
Lowney, Christopher *v.3 p.238*
Lowney, John *v.2 p.136*
Lowrance, William W. *v.5 p.410, p.412, p.413*
Lowry, Beverly *v.6 p.7, p.18, p.45*
Lowry, Donal (Editor) *v.6 p.79*
Lowry, Malcolm *v.2 p.367*
Lox, Curt, et al. *v.4 p.875, p.877, v.5 p.582*
Loyd, Sam. *v.5 p.469*
Loyn, Henry *v.3 p.63*
Loyrette, Henry & Pantazzi, Michael. *v.3 p.153*
Loza, Steven J.. . . . . *v.1 p.293, p.349, v.6 p.489, p.518*
Loza, Steven *v.6 p.518, p.549*
Lu, David John *v.6 p.225*
Lu, Li & Lai, Man O. *v.5 p.736*
Lu, Xiaobo & Perry, Elizabeth J. (Editors) *v.6 p.194*
Lu, Xiaobo *v.4 p.620*
Lu Xun *v.6 p.213*
Lubac, Henri De *v.1 p.575*
Lubbock, Jules *v.1 p.800*
Lubenow, W. C. *v.6 p.745, p.751*
Lublin, David *v.4 p.551, p.553*
Lubman, Stanley B. *v.4 p.475*
Lubrano, Annteresa. *v.4 p.421*
Lucan *v.2 p.436, p.437*
Lucas, Christopher J. *v.4 p.331*
Lucas, Colin R. *v.3 p.150*
Lucas, Gavin *v.4 p.6*
Lucas, George L., et al. *v.4 p.908*
Lucas, Henry S. *v.3 p.69*
Lucas, J. R. *v.5 p.470*
Lucas, John A. *v.4 p.846*
Lucas, K. A. *v.5 p.734*
Lucas, Kintto *v.3 p.333*
Lucas, Robert E. B. *v.4 p.259, p.265*
Lucas, Robert E. Jr. & Sargent, Thomas J.
  (Editors). *v.4 p.203, p.233, p.238*
Lucas, Robert E. Jr. *v.4 p.233, p.238, p.244*
Lucas, Rosemary & McCredden, Lyn *v.2 p.741*
Lucas, St. John & Jones, P. M. (Editors) *v.2 p.464*
Luce, Mary Frances, et al. *v.4 p.203*
Luce, R. Duncan & Raiffa, Howard *v.5 p.504*
Luce, T. James (Editor) *v.2 p.399*
Luce, T. James *v.2 p.402*
Luce, T. J. *v.2 p.436*
Lucero, Helen R. & Baizerman, Suzanne. *v.6 p.489, p.492, p.523*
Luchetti, Cathy. *v.3 p.521*

Lucian. *v.2 p.416*
Luciani, Vincent *v.1 p.107*
Luciano, Lynne *v.6 p.446*
Lucie-Smith, Edward & Chicago, Judy *v.1 p.698*
Lucie-Smith, Edward . . . *v.1 p.665, p.679, p.680, p.682, p.684,
                                   p.706, p.728, p.743, p.780*
Luck, Georg *v.2 p.426*
Luck, J. Murray (Editor), et al. *v.3 p.245*
Luck, J. Murray *v.3 p.245*
Luckasson, Ruth A.. . . . . *v.5 p.517*
Luckingham, Bradford *v.3 p.528*
Luckyj, George S. (Editor) *v.2 p.813*
Luckyj, George S. *v.2 p.813, p.814*
Lucow, Ben *v.2 p.221*
Lucretius Carus, ; Bailey, Cyril *v.2 p.437*
Lucretius Carus, Titus *v.2 p.437*
Lucy, John Arthur *v.4 p.20*
Ludden, David (Editor) *v.6 p.149*
Luderer, Bernd, et al.. . . . . *v.4 p.175*
Ludewig, Burkhard & Hoffmann, Matthias W. *v.5 p.165*
Ludman, Joan, et al. *v.1 p.743*
Ludwig, Arnold M.. . . . . *v.4 p.483, v.5 p.643, p.654*
Ludwig, Coy. *v.1 p.720*
Ludwig, Jens & Cook, Philip J. (Editors). *v.6 p.266*
Ludwig, Kirk (Editor) *v.1 p.442*
Luebke, David M. (Editor) *v.3 p.57*
Luebke, Frederick C. (Editor) *v.3 p.521*
Lueders, Edward, et al. *v.5 p.232*
Luft, David S. *v.2 p.614*
Luftig, Stacy *v.1 p.271, p.342, p.357*
Lugard, Frederick J. *v.6 p.56*
Luger, Dan & Pook, Paul. *v.4 p.865, p.879*
Luger, Stan *v.4 p.154*
Lugones, Leopoldo *v.2 p.678*
Luhr, James F. (Editor) *v.5 p.419*
Luhrmann, Tanya M. *v.4 p.36*
Luis, William *v.3 p.311, v.6 p.507, p.514*
Lukacs, John *v.3 p.186, p.369*
Lukas, J. Anthony *v.3 p.474, p.488*
Lukas, Richard C. *v.3 p.254*
Lukenbill, Grant *v.6 p.382*
Lukens, Rebecca J. *v.2 p.582*
Luker, Kristin *v.4 p.768, p.775, v.6 p.465, p.470*
Luker, Nicholas (Editor) *v.2 p.794*
Lukes, Igor *v.3 p.189*
Lukács, Georg *v.2 p.572*
Lukács, György & Bostock, Anna *v.2 p.462*
Lukács, György *v.2 p.487, p.501, p.504*
Lukin, Alexander *v.3 p.212*
Lukk, Tiiu *v.6 p.345*
Lukowski, Jerzy & Zawadzki, Hubert *v.3 p.252*
Lukowski, Jerzy *v.3 p.253*
Lulat, Y. G-M. *v.4 p.335*
Lull, Timothy F. & Russell, William R.
  (Editors) *v.1 p.603, v.3 p.166*

Lum, Darrell H. Y. *v.6 p.101*
Lum, Grande *v.4 p.74*
Lum, Wing T. *v.6 p.104*
Lumet, Sidney *v.6 p.347*
Lumpkin, Angela, et al. *v.4 p.802*
Lumpkin, Grace *v.2 p.95*
Lumsden, Ian *v.6 p.421*
Lumsden, Linda J. *v.4 p.519, v.6 p.431*
Lumsden, Peter (Editor) *v.5 p.354, p.356, p.375*
Lumumba, Patrice *v.6 p.18, p.29, p.62*
Luna, Francisco Vidal & Klein, Herbert S. *v.3 p.334*
Lund, Henning & Hammerich, Ole *v.5 p.293*
Lund, Herbert F. *v.5 p.376, p.377*
Lund, Jacalyn Lea & Kirk, Mary Fortman . . . *v.4 p.798, p.799*
Lund, Roger D. *v.2 p.246*
Lundblad, Roger L. *v.5 p.117*
Lundbom, Jack R. *v.1 p.623*
Lundestad, Geir *v.4 p.638, p.642*
Lundin, Anne H. *v.2 p.582*
Lunenfeld, Peter *v.1 p.771*
Lunine, Jonathan I. *v.5 p.74, p.243*
Lunn, Eugene *v.1 p.508*
Lunn, George & Sansone, Eric B. *v.5 p.313*
Lunt, J. *v.6 p.621*
Luo, Yiqi & Zhou, Xuhui *v.5 p.699*
Lupack, Barbara T. (Editor) *v.6 p.326*
Lupack, Barbara Tepa (Editor) *v.6 p.326*
Lupack, Barbara Tepa *v.6 p.326, p.330, p.342*
Lupton, Ellen *v.1 p.714*
Lupton, Robert *v.5 p.64*
Luraghi, Raimondo *v.4 p.521*
Luria, Aleksandr R. *v.5 p.610*
Luria, Maxwell *v.2 p.467*
Lurie, Alison *v.2 p.149, v.6 p.402*
Lurie, Rosanne *v.4 p.170*
Lurquin, Paul F. *v.5 p.8, p.194, p.243, p.370*
Lury, Celia *v.4 p.261*
Luscombe, David *v.1 p.433*
Lust, Herbert C. *v.1 p.757*
Lustick, Ian (Editor) *v.6 p.618*
Lustick, Ian S. (Editor) *v.6 p.594, p.618, p.661*
Lustig, Arnost *v.2 p.784*
Lust-Okar, Ellen *v.4 p.615*
Luther, Martin *v.3 p.57*
Luthuli, Albert *v.6 p.79*
Luton, Larry S. *v.4 p.542*
Luttwak, Edward N. *v.3 p.28*
Lutz, Christopher H. *v.3 p.298*
Lutz, Donald S. *v.4 p.452*
Lutz, James M. & Lutz, Brenda J. *v.4 p.660*
Lutz, Mark A. *v.4 p.207, p.209*
Lutz, Tom *v.5 p.654*
Lutzker, John R. *v.6 p.259*
Lux, David S. *v.3 p.145*
Lux, Maureen *v.6 p.702*

Luxemburg, Rosa & Bukharin, Nikolai I. *v.4 p.236*
Luxemburg, Rosa & Graf, William David *v.4 p.236*
Luxemburg, Rosa, et al. *v.4 p.236*
Luxemburg, Rosa *v.4 p.236, p.245*
Luxon, S. G. (Editor) *v.5 p.266*
Luykx, Aurolyn *v.3 p.324*
Luz Montes, Amelia María de la & Goldman, Anne Elizabeth
   (Editors) *v.6 p.501, p.514*
Luz, Ulrich *v.1 p.629*
Luza, Radomir & Vella, Christina *v.3 p.189*
Luza, Radomir V. *v.3 p.185*
Luza, Radomir *v.3 p.190*
Luzi, Mario *v.2 p.715, p.716*
Lyall, Charles J. *v.6 p.661*
Lybbert, Blair *v.4 p.287*
Lybyer, Albert Howe *v.6 p.590*
Lycett, Andrew *v.2 p.385*
Lydon, James F. *v.3 p.135*
Lydon, Michael *v.1 p.271, p.317*
Lye, Colleen *v.4 p.485*
Lyles, Marjorie A. & Crossan, Mary *v.4 p.79*
Lyly, John *v.2 p.215*
Lyman, Edward L. *v.3 p.529*
Lyman, R. Lee *v.5 p.448*
Lyman, Stanley David, et al. *v.6 p.694*
Lynch, Allen C. *v.3 p.212*
Lynch, David K. & Livingston, William *v.5 p.73*
Lynch, Deidre (Editor) *v.2 p.268*
Lynch, Eleanor W. & Hanson, Marci J. (Editors) . . . *v.4 p.316*
Lynch, Gordon *v.1 p.595*
Lynch, Hollis R. *v.6 p.70*
Lynch, James (Editor), et al. *v.4 p.309*
Lynch, John & Kilmartin, Christopher T. *v.5 p.660*
Lynch, John *v.3 p.347, v.4 p.592*
Lynch, Joseph H. *v.1 p.600, v.3 p.57, p.68*
Lynch, Katherine A. (Editor) *v.6 p.7, p.39*
Lynch, Kevin *v.6 p.726*
Lynch, L. *v.2 p.503*
Lynch, Marc *v.4 p.415, v.6 p.594*
Lynch, Nancy A. *v.5 p.345*
Lynch, Owen M. (Editor) *v.6 p.154*
Lynch, Sharon J. *v.4 p.367*
Lynch, Wayne *v.5 p.241*
Lynd, Helen M. *v.4 p.704*
Lynd, Robert S. & Lynd, Helen M. *v.4 p.704*
Lynd, Staughton & Lynd, Alice (Editors) . . . *v.4 p.127, p.766*
Lyndon, R. F. *v.5 p.161*
Lyne, R. O. *v.2 p.446*
Lynes, Barbara Buhler, et al. *v.1 p.743*
Lynes, Russell *v.3 p.369*
Lynham, Deryck *v.1 p.10*
Lynn, Barry C. *v.4 p.665*
Lynn, Joanne & Schuster, Janice Lynch (Editors) . . . *v.5 p.532*
Lynn, John A. *v.3 p.145*
Lynn, Kenneth S. *v.2 p.42*

Lynn, Laurence E. Jr. *v.4 p.178, p.545, p.580*

Lynn, Martha Drexler *v.1 p.775, p.810*

Lynn, Steven Jay & McConkey, Kevin M. (Editors) *v.5 p.610*

Lynton, Norbert *v.1 p.680*

Lyon, David *v.4 p.562, p.572*

Lyon, Eugene *v.3 p.505*

Lyon, James K. *v.2 p.605*

Lyon, Thomas J. (Introduction by) *v.5 p.232*

Lyon, Thomas P. & Maxwell, John W. *v.4 p.61, p.63*

Lyons, Albert S. & Petrucelli, Joseph A. *v.5 p.510*

Lyons, David *v.1 p.487, p.516*

Lyons, F. S. L. (Francis Stewart Leland) *v.3 p.135*

Lyons, F. S. *v.3 p.135*

Lyons, Greg *v.2 p.21*

Lyons, James *v.3 p.443*

Lyons, Joan (Editor) *v.1 p.761*

Lyons, John *v.2 p.562*

Lyons, Malcolm C. & Jackson, D. E. P. . . . *v.6 p.585*

Lyons, Oren, et al. *v.6 p.692*

Lyons, Paddy & Morgan, Fideles (Editors) . *v.1 p.67, p.78, p.90,*
p.101

Lyons, Phyllis I. *v.6 p.227, p.231*

Lyons, Tanya & Pye, Geralyn *v.4 p.384*

Lyons, W. E., et al. *v.4 p.542, v.6 p.724*

Lyons, William C. & Plisga, Gary J. . . . *v.5 p.451, p.738*

Lyotard, Jean François *v.2 p.522*

Lyotard, Jean-Francois *v.1 p.457, p.511*

Lyra, Carmen *v.2 p.676*

Lysengen, Janet D. & Rathke, Ann M. (Editors) . . *v.3 p.523*

Lyshevski, Sergey Edward *v.5 p.711*

Lysias *v.2 p.407, p.408*

Lysloff, Rene T. A. & Gay, Leslie C. (Editors) . *v.1 p.218, p.387*

Lyson, Thomas A. *v.5 p.14*

Lytle, Andrew *v.2 p.95*

Lytle, Donald E. (Editor) *v.4 p.357*

Lyttelton, Adrian (Editor) *v.3 p.202*

Lyttelton, Adrian (editor) *v.3 p.202*

Lyttelton, Adrian *v.3 p.202*

Lytton, Timothy (Editor) *v.6 p.266*

M

M, Clauss *v.1 p.538*

Ma, John *v.3 p.21, v.6 p.714*

Ma, Laurence J. C. & Cartier, Carolyn L. . *v.4 p.765, v.6 p.119,*
p.127

Ma, Liping *v.4 p.364*

Ma, Shang-Keng *v.5 p.559*

Ma, Sheng-mei *v.6 p.97*

Maaba, Brown, et al. *v.4 p.335*

Maag, Karin & Witvliet, John D. *v.1 p.654*

Maalouf, Amin *v.2 p.545, v.6 p.556*

Maantay, Juliana & Ziegler, John *v.4 p.387, v.6 p.721*

Maas, Martha & Snyder, Jane M. *v.1 p.175*

Maas, Michael (Editor) *v.3 p.31, p.192*

Mabberley, David *v.5 p.155, p.232*

Mabert, Vincent A. & Jacobs, F. Robert (Editors) . . . *v.4 p.116*

Mabey, Richard (Editor) *v.5 p.232*

Mabry, Donald J. *v.3 p.294*

Mabry, Sharon *v.1 p.395*

Mac Donald, Heather *v.6 p.264*

Macalady, Donald L. (Editor) *v.5 p.310*

MacAndrew, Craig & Edgerton, Robert B. *v.4 p.776*

MacArthur, Douglas *v.3 p.460*

MacArthur, Robert H. & Wilson, Edward O. . . . *v.5 p.168*

Macartney, C. A. *v.3 p.183*

Macartney, Carlile A. *v.3 p.63*

Macaulay, Neill *v.3 p.302*

Macaulay, Ronald K. *v.2 p.562*

Macaulay, Thomas Babington, el al. *v.3 p.105*

Macaulay, Thomas Babington Macaulay, Baron . . . *v.2 p.299*

MacAvoy, Paul & Millstein, Ira M. *v.4 p.86*

MacAvoy, Paul W. & Millstein, Ira M. . *v.4 p.52, p.54, p.111*

MacBeath, Murray *v.1 p.500*

MacCaffrey, Isabel G. *v.2 p.215, p.254*

MacCaffrey, Wallace T. *v.3 p.100*

MacCambridge, Michael . *v.4 p.807, p.859, p.897, p.902, p.907*

MacCarthy, Fiona *v.2 p.301*

Macchi, Vladimiro *v.2 p.699*

MacCleery, Douglas W. *v.5 p.38*

MacCoby, Eleanor E. *v.4 p.737*

MacCormack, Sabine *v.2 p.430, v.3 p.31, p.263*

MacCoun, Robert J. & Reuter, Peter *v.4 p.777*

Maccoy, Peter *v.1 p.150*

MacCulloch, Diarmaid *v.3 p.57*

MacCurdy, Raymond R. *v.2 p.644*

MacDermot, Galt, et al. *v.1 p.252, p.408*

MacDermott, Felim & McGrath, Declan *v.6 p.353*

MacDiarmid, Hugh, et al. *v.2 p.368*

MacDiarmid, Hugh *v.2 p.368*

MacDonagh, Oliver *v.3 p.113, p.136*

Macdonald, Barbara & Rich, Cynthia *v.6 p.380*

MacDonald, Callum *v.3 p.189*

MacDonald, George *v.2 p.299*

MacDonald, Glen M. *v.5 p.168*

Macdonald, Glynn *v.1 p.52*

MacDonald, Hugh (Editor) *v.1 p.200, p.310*

MacDonald, Ian *v.1 p.218, p.356*

MacDonald, Jeffery L. *v.6 p.140*

MacDonald, Laurence E. *v.1 p.256*

Macdonald, Lyn *v.3 p.79*

Macdonald, Lynda A. C. *v.4 p.131*

MacDonald, Malcolm *v.1 p.200, p.218, p.313, p.363*

MacDonald, Margaret F. *v.1 p.723*

MacDonald, Margaret Read (Editor) *v.2 p.585*

MacDonald, Raymond R. (Editor), et al. *v.1 p.376*

MacDonald, Ronald *v.4 p.414*

MacDonald, Ross *v.2 p.97*

MacDonald, Scott B. (Editor), et al. *v.3 p.320*

MacDonnell, Lawrence J. & Bates, Sarah F. (Editors) . *v.4 p.463*

MacDougall, David. *v.6 p.310*

MacDougall, Elizabeth B. & Jashemski, Wilhelmina Feemster (Editors) *v.1 p.819*

MacDougall, J. D. *v.5 p.445*

MacDowell, Douglas M. *v.4 p.433*

MacEachern, Alan *v.5 p.18, v.6 p.295*

Macedo, Donaldo P. & Koike, Dale A. *v.2 p.638*

Macedo, Helder & De Melo e Castro, E. M. (Editors). *v.2 p.687, p.688*

Macedo, Stephen. *v.4 p.328, p.547*

Macey, David *v.6 p.402*

MacFadyen, David *v.1 p.298*

MacFarquhar, Roderick (Editor) *v.6 p.194*

MacFarquhar, Roderick. *v.6 p.195, p.196*

Macfie, A. L. *v.3 p.246*

MacGaffey, Janet & Bazenguissa-Ganga, Remy . . . *v.4 p.44*

MacGaffey, Wyatt *v.1 p.611*

Macgillivray, Ian K. *v.6 p.385*

MacGillivray, Joseph Alexander *v.3 p.16*

MacGowan, Kenneth *v.1 p.80, p.83, p.97*

MacGregor, Brent *v.4 p.415*

MacGregor, James G.. . . . . *v.3 p.546*

MacHado, Ana Maria & Delicado, Federico *v.2 p.692*

Machado, Antonio *v.2 p.661*

Machado de Assis, Joaquim Maria. *v.2 p.691, p.692*

Machado de Assis *v.2 p.691*

Machado de Assis *v.2 p.692*

Machado, Manuel *v.2 p.661*

Machado y Ruiz, Antonio. *v.2 p.661*

Machan, Tibor R.; Cheser, James E. *v.1 p.486*

MacHann, Clinton & Burt, Forrest D. (Editors) . . . *v.2 p.266*

MacHann, Clinton *v.2 p.266*

Machen, Arthur *v.2 p.367*

Machiavelli, Niccolò *v.2 p.709*

Machiavelli, Niccolo & Ariosto, Ludovico . *v.1 p.67, p.75, p.107*

Machiavelli, Niccolo *v.2 p.709, v.4 p.492, p.502*

Machin, G. I. *v.3 p.113, p.121*

Machin, Stephen & Vignoles, Anna *v.4 p.297*

Machlis, Joseph & Forney, Kristine *v.1 p.174*

Machobane, L. B. *v.6 p.75, p.76*

Machovec, Milan. *v.1 p.641*

Machover, Carl. *v.4 p.116*

Macieira-Coelho, Alvaro (Editor) *v.5 p.152, p.164*

Maciel, David & Ortiz, Isidro D. (Editors) *v.6 p.521*

Maciel, David R. & Herrera-Sobek, María . . *v.6 p.493, p.529*

Maciel, David R. (Editor), et al. *v.6 p.491*

MacInnes, Colin *v.2 p.367*

Macintosh, Donald & Hawes, Michael *v.4 p.891, p.898*

Macintosh, Donald & Whitson, David *v.4 p.891, p.898*

Macintosh, Donald, et al. *v.4 p.588*

MacIntyre, Alasdair. *v.1 p.484, p.514, v.6 p.288*

MacIntyre, Bruce *v.1 p.191, p.236, p.330*

Macintyre, J. E. (Executive Editor) *v.5 p.302*

Macintyre, Jane E. & Hodgson, A.J. *v.5 p.302*

Maciuszko, Jerzy J.. . . . . *v.2 p.788*

Mack, Arien & Rock, Irvin *v.5 p.611*

Mack, Arien (Editor) *v.4 p.778*

Mack, Maynard *v.2 p.257*

Mack, Robert L. *v.2 p.249*

Mack, Sara *v.2 p.438*

MacKay, Angus *v.3 p.238, v.6 p.563*

MacKay, Charles. *v.4 p.244*

Mackay, Donald *v.5 p.286, p.293*

MacKay, Don *v.5 p.293*

MacKay, Fiona. *v.6 p.441*

Mackay, James. *v.1 p.774*

Mackay, K. M., et al. *v.5 p.301*

MacKay, William M. & Conte, Mario *v.5 p.552*

Mackendrick, Alexander *v.6 p.350*

MacKendrick, Paul L. *v.2 p.433*

MacKenna, Stephen *v.1 p.430*

MacKenzie, Craig *v.2 p.756*

MacKenzie, D. N. *v.6 p.668*

MacKenzie, Doris L. & Armstrong, Gaylene S. (Editors). *v.6 p.274*

MacKenzie, Doris L. *v.6 p.272*

MacKenzie, Henry *v.2 p.251*

Mackenzie, Hettie Millicent Hughes *v.4 p.343*

Mackenzie, Ian. *v.1 p.752*

Mackenzie, John M. (Editor) *v.3 p.89, p.125*

MacKenzie, Norman & MacKenzie, Jeanne. *v.2 p.319*

MacKenzie, Norman H. (Editor). *v.2 p.294*

MacKenzie, Norman H.. . . . . *v.2 p.294*

Mackenzie, W. J.. . . . . *v.5 p.643*

MacKenzie, W. S. & Guilford, C. *v.5 p.435*

MacKenzie, W. S., et al. *v.5 p.437*

Mackerras, Colin. *v.1 p.288*

Mackesy, Piers. *v.3 p.409*

Mackethan, Lucinda Hardwick *v.2 p.14*

Mackey, Frank *v.3 p.544*

Mackey, Robert Russell. *v.4 p.521*

Mackie, Gerry *v.4 p.505*

Mackie, J. L. *v.1 p.451, p.523*

Mackie, John L. *v.1 p.494*

Mackie, Richard *v.3 p.545*

Mackie, Thomas T. & Rohds, Richard *v.4 p.577*

Mackie, Vera. *v.6 p.434*

MacKillop, Ian & Sinyard, Neil (Editors). *v.6 p.339*

MacKillop, Ian (Editor). *v.2 p.164*

MacKinnon, Catharine A.. . . *v.4 p.442, p.446, p.459, v.6 p.441*

MacKinnon, Frank *v.4 p.590*

MacKinnon, Janice R. & MacKinnon, Stephen R.. . . *v.6 p.201*

MacKinnon, Kenneth *v.4 p.416*

MacKinnon, Stephen R. & Friesen, Oris *v.6 p.190, p.215*

Mack-Kirschner, Adrienne *v.4 p.278, p.338, p.348*

Macksey, Richard & Moorer, Frank E. (Editors) . . . *v.2 p.138*

Mack-Smith, Denis M. *v.3 p.202*

MacLachlan, Colin M. *v.6 p.536*

MacLaran, Andrew (Author, Editor) *v.6 p.728*

MacLean, Elizabeth K. *v.3 p.460*

Maclean, Norman F. *v.5 p.31*
Maclear, J. F. *v.1 p.611*
MacLeish, A. Bruce *v.1 p.824*
MacLeish, Archibald *v.2 p.98*
Macleish, Archibald *v.2 p.98*
MacLeish, Archibald *v.2 p.98, p.99*
MacLennan, Hugh *v.3 p.535*
MacLeod, Bruce A. *v.1 p.384*
Macleod, David I. *v.4 p.719*
MacLeod, Dianne Sachko. *v.6 p.737, p.744*
MacLeod, Iain A. *v.5 p.698*
MacLeod, Murdo J., et al. *v.3 p.345*
MacLeod, Norman (Editor) *v.5 p.155, p.199*
MacLeod, Roy *v.3 p.21*
MacManus, Susan A *v.4 p.524*
MacMaster, Neil (Editor) *v.3 p.157*
Macmillan Library Reference
  Staff *v.4 p.678, p.777, v.5 p.638, p.664*
Macmillan, Malcolm *v.5 p.658*
MacMillan, Margaret *v.4 p.630*
Macmillan Publishing Company Staff *v.5 p.222*
MacMullen, Ramsay & Lane, Eugene N. (Editors) . . *v.1 p.599*
MacMullen, Ramsay *v.3 p.23, p.28, p.31*
MacNabb, Elizabeth L. (Editor), et al. *v.6 p.463*
MacNamara, John *v.5 p.597*
Macnaughton, William R. *v.2 p.45*
MacNeice, Louis *v.2 p.326, p.368, p.369*
MacNeil, Robert *v.2 p.130*
MacNiven, Ian S. *v.2 p.344*
Macomber, Roger S. *v.5 p.272*
Maconie, Robin *v.1 p.218, p.358, p.375*
MacPherson, Allen *v.5 p.235*
Macpherson, C. B. *v.4 p.590*
Macquarrie, John. *v.1 p.636*
MacQuarrie, John *v.1 p.657*
Macqueen, J. G. *v.3 p.6, v.4 p.9*
MacQueen, John & Scott, Tom (Editors) *v.2 p.200*
MacQueen, Norrie. *v.4 p.584, p.649, v.6 p.56*
MacQuoid, Percy & Edwards, Ralph *v.1 p.805*
MacRae, Duncan Jr. *v.4 p.769*
MacRae, Greg *v.5 p.695*
Macrae, Norman *v.5 p.397*
MacRaild, Donald M. & Hepburn, A. C. (Editors). . *v.3 p.135*
Macrakis, Kristie. *v.5 p.392, p.412*
Macre, Norman *v.5 p.397*
MacShane, Denis. *v.4 p.127*
Macwan, Joseph *v.6 p.152*
Madame de Stael. *v.2 p.501*
Madan, T. N. & Barnes, J. A. *v.6 p.154*
Madan, T. N., et al. *v.1 p.537*
Madan, Vandana *v.4 p.772*
Madariaga, Isabel de *v.3 p.217*
Maddala, G. S. *v.4 p.203*
Madden & Wydeven, Joseph F. *v.2 p.103*
Madden, David *v.2 p.14, p.65*

Madden, Frederick & Darwin, John (Editors) . . . *v.4 p.435*
Madden, Frederick & Fieldhouse, David (Editors). . *v.4 p.436*
Madden, Frederick (Editor) *v.4 p.435*
Madden, Kirsten & Seitz, Janet *v.4 p.214, p.274*
Madden, Thomas (Editor). *v.6 p.556*
Madden, Thomas F. & Rees, Ronald *v.3 p.199*
Maddex, Jack P. *v.3 p.500*
Maddex, Robert L. *v.4 p.435, p.574*
Maddicott, J. R. *v.3 p.143*
Maddox, Brenda *v.5 p.122*
Maddox, Donald *v.2 p.467*
Maddox, Graham. *v.1 p.596*
Maddox, Robert J. *v.3 p.460*
Madelung, Otfried *v.5 p.554*
Madge, Tim *v.4 p.777*
Madigan, Mary Jean *v.1 p.810*
Madinger, John. *v.6 p.267*
Madison, G. B. *v.1 p.457*
Madison, James H. (Editor) *v.3 p.506*
Madison, James H. *v.3 p.514*
Madoff, Steven Henry *v.1 p.780*
Madrigal, Luis Íñigo & Ainsa, Fernando *v.2 p.664*
Madrigal, Luis Íñigo & Alvar, Manuel *v.2 p.665*
Madsen, Axel *v.6 p.416, p.418*
Madsen, Deborah L. *v.6 p.479, p.501, p.514*
Madson, John *v.5 p.241*
Maeroff, Gene I. *v.4 p.322*
Maestripieri, Dario (Editor) *v.5 p.615*
Maeterlinck, Maurice, et al. *v.1 p.85, p.109*
Maeterlinck, Maurice *v.2 p.522*
Maffetone, Phillip *v.4 p.827, p.829*
Maffly-Kipp, Laurie R. *v.1 p.607*
Maga, Timothy P. *v.3 p.474*
Magai, Carol & Haviland-Jones, Jeannette M. . . *v.5 p.654*
Magalaner, Marvin & Kain, Richard M. *v.2 p.360*
Magalaner, Marvin. *v.2 p.359, p.360*
Magaldi, Cristina. *v.3 p.265*
Magalini, Sabina I. & Magalini, Sergio C. . . . *v.5 p.509*
Magay, Tamas & Orszagh, Laszlo *v.2 p.774*
Magdalino, Paul *v.3 p.193*
Magee, Bryan. *v.1 p.200, p.365, p.446, p.465*
Magee, David *v.4 p.69*
Magee, Jeffrey. *v.1 p.261, p.331*
Magennis, Hugh *v.2 p.168*
Mager Stellman, Jeanne & International Labor Office Staff
  (Editors) *v.5 p.365*
Maggin, Donald L. *v.1 p.261, p.326*
Maggiore, Dolores J. *v.6 p.359*
Magill, Frank N. & Irons-Georges, Tracy (Editors) . *v.2 p.575*
Magill, Frank N. (Editor) . . *v.2 p.180, p.549, p.580, v.6 p.306*
Magill, Frank N *v.6 p.306*
Magill, Frank Northen *v.6 p.26, p.33*
Magill, Richard A. *v.4 p.909*
Magleby, David *v.4 p.460*
Maglischo, Ernest W. *v.4 p.868, p.879*

Magnavita, Jeffrey J. (Editor) *v.5 p.661*

Magnello, Eileen & Hardy, Anne (Editors) *v.5 p.100*

Magner, Lois N. *v.5 p.80*

Magness, Jodi *v.1 p.546*

Magnus, Philip Sir (Philip Montefiore) *v.3 p.89, p.125*

Magnus, Wilhelm, et al. *v.5 p.475, p.479*

Magnuson, Paul *v.2 p.280, p.324*

Magnusson, Lars (Editor) *v.4 p.216, p.233*

Magnusson, Lars *v.3 p.235*

Magocsi, Paul R. (Editor) *v.3 p.534*

Magocsi, Paul Robert *v.3 p.206*

Magone, Jose M. *v.4 p.603, p.638*

Magriel, Paul *v.6 p.414*

Maguire, Henry *v.3 p.193*

Maguire, Mike (Editor), et al. *v.6 p.249*

Mah, Harold *v.3 p.72*

Mahadeva, Lavan & Sinclair, Peter *v.4 p.246*

Mahan, A. T. (Alfred Thayer) *v.3 p.383*

Mahan, Alfred Thayer *v.3 p.36, p.383, p.417*

Mahan, Gerald D. *v.5 p.546*

Mahaney, Ian F. *v.4 p.390*

Mahar, William J. *v.1 p.281*

Maharidge, Dale *v.4 p.767*

Mahdi, Mushin & Haddawy, Husain *v.6 p.661*

Maher, Frances A. & Thompson Tetreault, Mary Kay . *v.6 p.463*

Maher, Paul A. Jr. *v.2 p.93*

Maher, Paul *v.2 p.93*

Maheshwari, Ramesh *v.5 p.209*

Mahfouz, Naguib *v.6 p.661, p.662*

Mahler, Gregory S. *v.4 p.615, v.6 p.614*

Mahler, Henry R. & Cordes, Eugene H. *v.5 p.327*

Mahler, Jonathan *v.6 p.714*

Mahler, Margaret S., et al. *v.5 p.627*

Mahmutcehajic, Rusmir *v.3 p.249*

Mahon, Alyce *v.1 p.706*

Mahon, Michael *v.1 p.459*

Mahoney, James *v.3 p.300, p.302*

Mahoney, John *v.1 p.574*

Mahoney, Rosemary *v.6 p.197, p.202, p.216*

Mahood, Molly M. *v.2 p.180*

Mahota, William J. *v.2 p.776*

Mahowald, Mary B., et al. *v.5 p.149, p.533*

Mahowald, Mary Briody *v.5 p.80, p.135, v.6 p.444*

Mahta, Tarla *v.1 p.131, p.134*

Mai, Larry L., et al. *v.4 p.15*

Maiden, Martin, et al. *v.2 p.699*

Maiden, Martin *v.2 p.699*

Maidment, Brian *v.1 p.753, v.6 p.737*

Maidment, David R. *v.5 p.703*

Maier, Charles S. *v.3 p.170, p.177, p.178*

Maier, Ernest (Editor), et al. *v.4 p.180*

Maier, Henry W. *v.5 p.628*

Maier, Karl *v.6 p.75*

Maier, Klaus A., et al. *v.3 p.175*

Maier, Mark H. *v.4 p.690*

Maier, Pauline *v.3 p.409*

Maier, Raina M., et al. *v.5 p.355, p.356, p.377, p.379*

Maier, Thomas *v.3 p.455*

Mailer, Norman *v.2 p.99*

Mailhot, Laurent; Nepveu, Pierre *v.2 p.538*

Maillet, Antonine *v.2 p.541*

Maimonides & Twersky, Isadore *v.1 p.550*

Maimonides, Moses & Kellner, Menachem Marc . . . *v.1 p.550*

Maimonides, Moses *v.1 p.433*

Maimonides *v.1 p.550*

Main, Jackson Turner *v.3 p.409, v.4 p.518*

Main, Mary *v.2 p.680*

Maine, Barry *v.2 p.69*

Maine, Henry Sumner *v.4 p.433*

Maine, Sir, Henry Sumner *v.4 p.33*

Mainga, Mutumba *v.6 p.77*

Maiorino, Giancarlo (Editor) *v.2 p.641*

Mair, Charles *v.2 p.732*

Mair, Douglas & Miller, Anne *v.4 p.195*

Mair, Peter (Editor) *v.4 p.602*

Mair, Victor H. (Editor) *v.6 p.208*

Mair, Victor H. *v.4 p.9, v.6 p.208, p.211*

Maira, Sunaina & Srikanth, Rajini (Editors) . *v.6 p.92, p.137*

Maira, Sunaina *v.4 p.704, v.6 p.110, p.137*

Mairowitz, David Zane *v.2 p.512*

Maisel, Edward *v.6 p.409*

Maisel, L. Sandy (Editor) *v.4 p.551*

Maisel, Louis S. (Editor) *v.4 p.548, p.551*

Maistre, Xavier de *v.2 p.498*

Maisy, John *v.5 p.215*

Maitland, Sara & Appignanesi, Lisa (Editors) . . *v.2 p.766*

Maiwald, Eric *v.4 p.114*

Maizell, Robert E. *v.5 p.255*

Maizlish, Stephen E. *v.3 p.513*

Majer, Vladimir; Vaclav Svoboda; H. V. Kehiaian . *v.5 p.300*

Majmudar, Uma *v.6 p.159*

Major, J. Russell *v.3 p.145*

Major, John *v.3 p.390*

Major, Mabel *v.2 p.15*

Major, Patrick & Mitter, Rana (Editor, Translators) . *v.4 p.486*

Majors, William R. *v.3 p.511*

Majumadara, Ramendu (Editor) *v.1 p.55, p.61, p.128*

Majumdar, Shyamal K. (Editor), et al. *v.4 p.392*

Majumdar, Sumit (Editor), et al. *v.4 p.190*

Mak, King K. & Sickling, Dean L. *v.5 p.695*

Mak Lau Fong *v.4 p.719*

Mak, Thomas C. W. & Zhou, Gong-Du *v.5 p.284*

Makar, Ragai N. & Bloyer, Christen T. *v.6 p.662*

Makarim, Sami N. *v.1 p.539*

Makarov, B. M., et al. *v.5 p.490*

Makarov, Sergey N. *v.5 p.728*

Makarova, Natalia *v.1 p.10*

Makdisi, Ussama S. *v.6 p.605*

Maker, C. June & Nielson, Aleene B. *v.4 p.317*

Maker, C. June & Shiever, Shirley W. *v.5 p.575*

Maki, Mitchell T., et al. *v.6 p.134*

Makiko, Nakano (Translator) *v.6 p.227*

Makin, Peter *v.2 p.112*

Makinson, Randell & Heinz, Thomas *v.1 p.802*

Makosky, Vivian P. (Editor), et al. *v.5 p.675*

Makoto, Kumazawa, et al. *v.4 p.122*

Makower, Joel. *v.1 p.271, v.4 p.63*

Makward, Christiane P. & Miller, Judith G. (Editors) . *v.2 p.465*

Malachowski, Alan *v.1 p.442*

Malacinski, George M. (Editor) *v.5 p.160*

Malacinski, George M. *v.5 p.128*

Malamud, Bernard *v.2 p.149*

Malamud, Martha A. *v.2 p.442*

Malamud, Randy *v.5 p.84*

Malamuth, Neil M. & Donnerstein, Edward *v.4 p.748*

Malaparte, Curzio *v.2 p.716*

Malaspina, Margaret A. *v.4 p.96, p.109*

Malavet, Pedro A. *v.6 p.538*

Malbert, Roger & White, Jessica (Editors) *v.1 p.757*

Malbon, Ben *v.1 p.34*

Malcolm, Bill & Malcolm, Nancy *v.5 p.209*

Malcolm E. Sumner (editor) *v.5 p.50*

Malcolm, Noel *v.3 p.249*

Malcolm, Norman *v.1 p.472*

Malcolmson, Cristina *v.2 p.249*

Malcolmson, Malcolm *v.3 p.92, p.107, p.109*

Maldonado, Alex W. *v.3 p.320*

Maldonado, Carlos & Garcia, Gilbert *v.6 p.521*

Maldonado, Carlos S. *v.6 p.527*

Male, Emile *v.1 p.688*

Malebranche, Nicolas *v.1 p.452*

Maleh, Ghassan (Editor), et al. *v.1 p.60, p.129, p.130*

Malesevic, Sinisa *v.3 p.247, v.4 p.600*

Maley, Terry S. *v.5 p.420*

Maley, William *v.6 p.634*

Malherbe, Abraham J. *v.1 p.631*

Malherbe *v.2 p.474*

Malhotra, V. M. & Carino, Nicholas J. *v.5 p.689*

Malia, Martin E. *v.4 p.508, p.598*

Malia, Martin *v.3 p.209, p.218*

Malik, Aditya *v.6 p.152*

Malik, Yogendra K. & Singh, V. B. *v.4 p.618*

Malik, Yogendra K. *v.3 p.390, v.4 p.642, p.644*

Malin, Irving. *v.2 p.131*

Malin, J. C. *v.3 p.420*

Malin, James. *v.3 p.524*

Malin, Jo & Boynton, Victoria (Editors) *v.6 p.477*

Malina, Bruce J. *v.1 p.625*

Malinowski, Bronislaw . *v.1 p.17, v.4 p.3, p.4, p.28, p.700, p.737*

Malinowski, Edmund R. *v.5 p.280*

Malinowski, Sharon (Editor) *v.6 p.391*

Malinowsky, H. Robert *v.6 p.361*

Malins, Edward Greenway *v.2 p.326*

Malinvaud, Edmond *v.4 p.256*

Malitz, Jürgen. *v.3 p.28*

Malka, Eli S. *v.6 p.597, p.640*

Malkiel, Burton Gordon *v.4 p.96*

Malkiewicz, Kris & Mullen, M. David *v.6 p.349*

Malkin, Mary Ann O'Brian *v.1 p.4*

Mallaby, Sebastian *v.4 p.244, p.265*

Mallach, Alan *v.1 p.218, p.231, p.340*

Mallalieu, H. L. *v.1 p.725*

Mallarmé, Stéphane *v.2 p.496*

Malle, Bertram F. (Editor), et al. *v.5 p.650*

Mallett, Margaret. *v.4 p.364*

Mallett, Phillip *v.2 p.297*

Mallgrave, Harry F. *v.1 p.794*

Mallgrave, Harry. *v.1 p.703, p.787*

Mallick, P. K. *v.5 p.690*

Mallie & McKittrick *v.3 p.135, p.140*

Mallinson, William *v.6 p.601*

Mallios, William S. *v.4 p.203, p.207*

Mallon, Bill & Buchanan, Ian *v.4 p.807, p.846*

Mallon, Florencia E. *v.3 p.327, p.354*

Mallon, Florenica E. *v.3 p.330*

Mallon, Gerald *v.4 p.756, v.6 p.377*

Mallory, Sean. *v.1 p.695*

Mallory, Bruce & New, Rebecca. *v.4 p.369*

Malloy, Robin P. & Evensky, Jerry (Editors) *v.4 p.219*

Malm, William P. *v.1 p.283, p.287, p.288, p.289*

Malmfors, Birgitta *v.5 p.681*

Malmkjaer, Kirsten (Editor). *v.2 p.562*

Malnig, Julie *v.1 p.34*

Malo, Jean-Jacques & Williams, Tony (Editors) . . . *v.6 p.323*

Malone, Bill C. & Stricklin, David. *v.1 p.271*

Malone, Bill C. *v.1 p.271*

Malone, David M. & Khong, Yuen Koong (Editors) . *v.4 p.642*

Malone, David M. (Editor) *v.4 p.634*

Malone, Dumas *v.3 p.412*

Malone, Jacqui *v.1 p.32*

Malone, John W. *v.4 p.866*

Malone, Linda A. *v.6 p.300*

Malone, Lyn, et al. *v.4 p.387*

Malone, Michael P. *v.3 p.525*

Malone, Thomas W. (Editor), et al. *v.4 p.77*

Malone *v.3 p.525*

Malonis, Jane A. (Editor) *v.4 p.113*

Maloon, Terence & Art Gallery of New South Wales
Staff. *v.1 p.743*

Malory, Thomas *v.2 p.212*

Malouf, David *v.2 p.747*

Maloy, Otis C. & Murray, Timothy D. *v.5 p.46*

Malpezzi, Stephen & Green, Richard (Editors) . . . *v.4 p.166*

Malraux, Andre. *v.2 p.522, v.6 p.216*

Malraux, André. *v.2 p.480, p.522, v.6 p.192, p.216*

Malsberger, John W. *v.4 p.534*

Maltby, Marc S. *v.4 p.807, p.859*

Maltese, John A. *v.4 p.537*

Malthus, T. J. *v.4 p.389*

Malthus, Thomas. R. *v.4 p.763*

Malthus, Thomas Robert *v.4 p.218, p.221, p.222*
Malti-Douglas, Fedwa *v.6 p.662*
Maltin, Leonard *v.6 p.308*
Maltz, Earl M. *v.4 p.468, p.537*
Maluccio, Anthony N. (Editor), et al. *v.4 p.758*
Malveaux, Julianne & Green, Reginna A. (Editors) . . *v.4 p.564*
Malyavskaya, Greta R. & Shveyeva, Natalia K. . . . *v.5 p.387*
Mamdani, Mahmood, et al. *v.4 p.711*
Mamdani, Mahmood *v.6 p.55*
Mamet, David . *v.1 p.62, p.80, p.87, p.116, v.2 p.149, v.6 p.350*
Mamlouk, Michael S. & Zaniewski, John P. *v.5 p.690*
Manafy, A. *v.6 p.599*
Manahan, Stanley E. *v.5 p.310, p.314, p.704, p.706*
Manalansan, Martin F. IV (Editor) *v.6 p.105, p.123*
Manalansan, Martin F. *v.6 p.112, p.129*
Manatu, Norma *v.6 p.15, p.39, p.45, p.474*
Manchel, Frank *v.6 p.305*
Manchester, Richard N. & Taylor, Joseph H. *v.5 p.70*
Manchester, William *v.3 p.118, p.475*
Manchuelle, Francois *v.6 p.73*
Mancing, Howard *v.2 p.640, p.649*
Mancini, Henry *v.1 p.256, p.339*
Mancini, Marc *v.4 p.161*
Mancoff, Debra N. (Editor) *v.1 p.743*
Mandala, Elias C. *v.6 p.297*
Mandel, Eli *v.2 p.736*
Mandel, Maud *v.4 p.653*
Mandela, Nelson *v.6 p.78*
Mandela, Winnie *v.6 p.29, p.45*
Mandelbaum, Allen & Richardson, Robert D. (Editors) *v.2 p.24*
Mandelbaum, Michael *v.4 p.817*
Mandelbrot, Benoit B. *v.5 p.498, p.502*
Mandell, Gerald L., et al. *v.5 p.533*
Mandell, Howard *v.1 p.261*
Mandell, Richard D. *v.3 p.172, v.4 p.807, p.846*
Mandelshtam, Osip *v.2 p.805, p.806*
Mandelstam, Nadezhda *v.2 p.806*
Mander, Jane *v.2 p.747*
Mander, Raymond & Mitchenson, Joe *v.1 p.101, p.155*
Mandeville, Bernard *v.1 p.484, v.2 p.251*
Mandl, Franz *v.5 p.559*
Mandler, Peter *v.3 p.113, p.131, v.6 p.744*
Manea, Norman *v.2 p.817*
Manent, Pierre *v.4 p.492*
Manes, Stephen & Andrews, Paul *v.4 p.158*
Maney, Patrick J. *v.3 p.460*
Mangan, J. A. & Da Costa, Lamartine P. (Editors) . . *v.4 p.716*
Mangan, James A. & Walvin, James (Editors) *v.4 p.817*
Mango, Andrew *v.6 p.624*
Mangone, Gerard J. *v.4 p.629*
Manguel, Alberto *v.2 p.573, v.3 p.37, v.5 p.232*
Mangun, William R. & Henning, Daniel H. . . . *v.4 p.62*
Manheim, Jarol B. *v.4 p.52, p.54, p.145*
Manheim, Michael (Editor) *v.1 p.60, p.116, v.2 p.107*
Manheim, Michael *v.1 p.80, p.83, p.109*

Mani, Vettam *v.1 p.537*
Manion, Melanie *v.4 p.620*
Manion, Paul D. & Lachance, Denis (Editors) *v.5 p.38*
Manjhan Shattari Rajgiri, Mir Sayyid *v.6 p.152*
Manke, Mary Phillips *v.4 p.349*
Mankekar, Purnima *v.6 p.448*
Mankiller, Wilma (Editor), et al. *v.6 p.450*
Mankiw, N. Gregory & Romer, David (Editors) . . . *v.4 p.225*
Mankiw, N. Gregory (Editor) *v.4 p.246*
Manley, Bill (Editor) *v.3 p.9*
Manley, Bill *v.3 p.9*
Manly, Bryan F. *v.5 p.100*
Mann, Alfred K. *v.4 p.525*
Mann, Alfred *v.1 p.185, p.241, p.329, p.371*
Mann, Barbara E. *v.6 p.714*
Mann, Bruce J. (Editor) *v.1 p.87, p.92, p.116*
Mann, Carlos G. *v.3 p.275, p.305*
Mann, Carol *v.1 p.743*
Mann, Charles C. & Plummer, Mark L. *v.5 p.180*
Mann, Gurinder S. *v.1 p.540*
Mann, Gurinder Singh, et al. *v.6 p.106*
Mann, Gurinder Singh *v.1 p.540*
Mann, Heinrich *v.2 p.614*
Mann, Horace *v.4 p.344*
Mann, Jacob *v.6 p.597, p.609, p.636*
Mann, James (Editor) *v.1 p.718*
Mann, James H. *v.3 p.390*
Mann, James *v.3 p.483*
Mann, Jill *v.2 p.210*
Mann, Klaus *v.2 p.618*
Mann, Michael *v.4 p.660, p.715*
Mann, Nicholas *v.2 p.706*
Mann, Sally *v.1 p.767*
Mann, Thomas E. & Ornstein, Norman J. *v.4 p.530*
Mann, Thomas E. *v.4 p.549*
Mann, Thomas *v.2 p.590, p.612, p.613, v.6 p.397*
Mann, Vivian B. (Editor) *v.1 p.703*
Mann, William Edward *v.1 p.498*
Mann, William J. *v.6 p.418*
Mann, William *v.6 p.417*
Mannell, Roger C. & Kleiber, Douglas A. *v.5 p.582*
Mannes, Aaron *v.4 p.660*
Mannheim, Hermann *v.6 p.245, p.250*
Mannheim, Karl *v.4 p.685*
Manniche, Lise *v.1 p.175, v.3 p.9*
Mannikka, Eleanor *v.1 p.692, p.777*
Manning, Brian *v.3 p.92, p.104*
Manning, Frederic *v.2 p.747*
Manning, Kenneth R. *v.6 p.18, p.48*
Manning, Matt *v.4 p.149*
Manning, Patrick *v.6 p.56, p.74*
Manning, Peter D. *v.1 p.218, p.244*
Manning, Robert E. *v.4 p.786, p.787*
Manning, Susan A. *v.1 p.26*
Manning, Susan *v.1 p.10, p.18, p.29, p.30*

Mannings, David *v.1 p.743*
Mannion, A. M. *v.5 p.29*
Manns, James *v.1 p.480*
Mano, M. Morris *v.5 p.730*
Manogaran, Chelvadurai *v.6 p.163*
Manor, James *v.6 p.163*
Manovich, Lev *v.4 p.419*
Manring, M. M. *v.6 p.39*
Manrique, Jaime *v.6 p.402, p.496, p.507*
Mansbach, S. A. *v.1 p.680, p.688*
Mansbridge, Jane J. *v.6 p.470*
Mansbridge, Michael *v.1 p.794*
Mansel, Philip *v.3 p.149, v.6 p.622*
Mansergh, Nicholas *v.3 p.89*
Mansfield, Harvey C. Jr. *v.4 p.492*
Mansfield, Howard *v.1 p.823*
Mansfield, Katherine *v.2 p.369*
Mansfield, Peter & Pelham, Nicolas *v.6 p.582*
Mansfield, Sue *v.5 p.584*
Manson, Neil A. (Editor) *v.1 p.596*
Manson, William C. *v.4 p.35*
Mansour, Joyce *v.2 p.532*
Manstead, Antony S. R. (Editor), et al. *v.5 p.612*
Mantel, Hilary *v.2 p.367*
Mantell, Martin E. *v.3 p.437*
Mantello, F. A. & Rigg, A. G. (Editors) . . . *v.2 p.449*
Mantle, Burns (Editor) *v.1 p.68, p.116, p.117*
Manto, Sa'adat Hasan *v.6 p.152*
Manton, Catherine *v.4 p.778, v.6 p.446*
Manuel, Juan, et al. *v.2 p.651*
Manuel, Juan *v.2 p.651, p.661*
Manuel, Peter, et al. *v.1 p.293*
Manuel, Peter *v.1 p.271, p.283*
Manusov, Valerie & Patterson, Miles L. (Editors) . . . *v.4 p.424*
Manusov, Valerie Lynn (Editor) *v.4 p.424*
Manwaring, Max G. & Prisk, Court (Editors) *v.3 p.299*
Manzano, Juan F. *v.3 p.279*
Manzetti, Luigi *v.3 p.348*
Manzoni, Alessandro *v.2 p.712*
Manzoni, Jean-Francois & Barsoux, Jean-Louis . . *v.4 p.131*
Mao Zedong *v.6 p.202*
Maogoto, Jackson Nyamuya . . . *v.4 p.653, v.6 p.257*
Maor, Eli *v.5 p.485*
Maoz, Zeev *v.4 p.650*
Mapel, David & Nardin, Terry *v.4 p.766*
Mapp, Edward *v.1 p.4*
Mappes, Thomas A. & DeGrazia, David . *v.1 p.486, v.5 p.511*
Mappes, Thomas A. & Zembaty, Jane S. . . . *v.4 p.484, p.770*
Maqrizi *v.6 p.635*
Marable, Manning, et al. *v.6 p.7, p.33*
Marable, Manning . . . *v.3 p.320, v.4 p.573, v.6 p.7, p.14, p.21*
Maraini, Dacia *v.2 p.491*
Maran, Rita *v.3 p.157*
Marangoni, Alejandro G. *v.5 p.119*
Maraniss, David *v.3 p.475, v.4 p.859*

Maraniss, James E. *v.2 p.647*
Maranon, Jon *v.3 p.269*
Marar, Ziyad *v.5 p.654*
Marashi, Mehdi *v.6 p.669*
Marc, David *v.4 p.418*
Marcel, Gabriel *v.1 p.439, p.457, p.505, p.523*
Marcel Pagnol *v.2 p.523*
Marcel, Valerie & Mitchell, John V. *v.4 p.398*
Marcet, Jane H. *v.4 p.195*
Marcet, Jane *v.4 p.218*
March, James G; Olsen, Johan P *v.4 p.280*
March, Kathleen N. (Editor) *v.2 p.692*
March, Kathryn S. *v.6 p.164*
March, Peyton C. *v.3 p.475*
March, Robert H. *v.5 p.540*
March, William *v.2 p.97*
Marchak, M. Patricia & Marchak, William . . . *v.4 p.660*
Marchak, M. Patricia *v.4 p.164*
Marchak, Patricia *v.3 p.348*
Marchand, Leslie A. *v.6 p.741, p.751, p.752*
Marchand, Peter J. *v.5 p.222*
Marchand, Roland *v.4 p.144, p.145, p.426, p.429*
Marchand, Suzanne L. *v.3 p.178, p.191*
Marchant, Alexander N. *v.3 p.335*
Marchant, Mary A. & Williamson, Handy Jr. (Editors) . *v.4 p.268*
Marchello-Nizia, Christiane & Boyer, Régis . . . *v.2 p.467*
Marchessault, Jovette *v.2 p.541*
Marchetti, Gina *v.6 p.89, p.112, p.328, p.330, p.342*
Marchildon Greg *v.5 p.700*
Marciniak, Arkadiusz *v.4 p.12*
Marclay, Christian *v.1 p.773*
Marco, Guy A. et al. *v.1 p.168, p.278*
Marco, Guy A. *v.1 p.168, p.231, p.278*
Marconi, Joe *v.4 p.145*
Marcosson, Samuel A. *v.4 p.538*
Marcus, Abraham *v.6 p.607*
Marcus, Clare Cooper & Francis, Carolyn (Editors) . *v.6 p.728*
Marcus, Daniel M. *v.5 p.479*
Marcus, Eric *v.6 p.365, p.387*
Marcus, George E., et al. *v.5 p.643*
Marcus, Greil *v.1 p.271*
Marcus, Harold G. *v.6 p.64*
Marcus, Jacob R. (Editor) . *v.3 p.322, v.6 p.434, p.452, p.454,
                                                   p.459, p.465*
Marcus, Jacob R. . . . *v.1 p.548, p.549, v.6 p.434, p.459, p.465*
Marcus, Jane (Editor) *v.2 p.393*
Marcus, Jane *v.2 p.164, p.191*
Marcus, Joel *v.1 p.629*
Marcus, Joyce *v.3 p.261*
Marcus, Laura & Nicholls, Peter (Editors) . . . *v.2 p.179*
Marcus, Leslie F. (Editor), et al. *v.5 p.100*
Marcus, Steven *v.6 p.759, p.760*
Marcus, Yizhak *v.5 p.282*
Marcuse, Herbert & Kellner, Douglas *v.1 p.502*
Marcuse, Herbert . . . *v.4 p.508, p.685, p.700, p.761, v.5 p.644*

Marcuse, Peter & van Kempen, Ronald (Editors). *v.6 p.721, p.728*

Marder, Herbert *v.2 p.393*

Marder, Louis *v.2 p.231*

Marder, Michael P. *v.5 p.555*

Marder, T. A. *v.1 p.794*

Mardin, Yusuf *v.6 p.665*

Maredia, Karim M. (Editor), et al. *v.5 p.10*

Marenbon, John (Editor) *v.1 p.433*

Marenbon, John *v.1 p.433, p.579, v.3 p.57*

Mares, David R. (Editor) *v.3 p.275*

Mares, Michael A. *v.5 p.424*

Marías, Javier *v.2 p.661*

Marfleet, Philip *v.4 p.400*

Margadant, Ted W. *v.3 p.153*

Margesin, Rosa & Schinner, Franz (Contribution by) . . *v.5 p.50*

Margolick, David *v.4 p.808, p.855*

Margolin, Leslie *v.4 p.737, p.758*

Margolin, Victor (Editor) *v.1 p.703, p.713*

Margolis, Simeon. *v.5 p.526*

Margolis, Wendy (Editor), et al. *v.4 p.439*

Marguerite, de Navarre *v.2 p.470*

Marguerite, Queen consort of Henry II King of Navarre. *v.2 p.470*

Marguiles, Donald *v.2 p.149*

Margulies, Herbert F. *v.3 p.517*

Margulies, Phillip (Editor) *v.3 p.372, p.448*

Margulis, Alexander & Kholodnaya, Asya (Editors) . *v.2 p.776*

Margulis, Lynn & Dolan, Michael *v.5 p.194*

Margulis, Lynn & Olendzenski, Lorraine
  (Editors). *v.5 p.185, p.187, p.194*

Margulis, Lynn & Sagan, Dorion *v.5 p.199*

Margulis, Lynn, et al.. . . . . *v.5 p.205*

Mariampolski, Hy *v.4 p.139*

Mariani, Paul L. *v.2 p.61, p.294*

Mariani, Paul *v.2 p.96*

Marich, Robert. *v.6 p.346*

Marie De France *v.2 p.467*

Marie, de France *v.2 p.467*

Marieb, Elaine N. *v.5 p.164*

Marien, Mary Warner *v.1 p.764, p.767*

Maril, Robert Lee *v.6 p.487, p.538*

Marill, Alvin H. *v.1 p.168, p.256*

Marilley, Suzanne M. *v.6 p.431*

Marin, Cheech (Editor) *v.6 p.492*

Marin, Diego *v.2 p.644*

Marincola, John & Dewald, Carolyn (Editors) . . . *v.2 p.412*

Marincola, John *v.2 p.402*

Marinel, Alan Le *v.4 p.87*

Marinetti, Filippo Tommaso *v.2 p.718*

Marini, Stephen A. *v.1 p.278*

Marinjnissen, R. H. *v.1 p.751*

Marino, Giambattista *v.2 p.708*

Marino, Gordon (Editor, Introduction by). *v.1 p.505*

Marino, John A. (Editor) *v.3 p.201*

Marion, Jerry B. & Heald, Mark A. *v.5 p.565*

Marion, Nancy E. *v.4 p.567*

Mariqa, Jacqueline (Editor) *v.1 p.581*

Maritain, Jacques. *v.1 p.457, v.4 p.344, p.513*

Marius, Richard *v.3 p.100*

Marivaux, A.. . . . . *v.2 p.481*

Marivaux, Pierre Carlet de Chamblain de. *v.2 p.481*

Marivaux *v.2 p.481*

Mark, Herman F. (Editorial Board Member), et al. . . *v.5 p.321*

Mark, Herman F. *v.5 p.321*

Mark, James E. (Editor) *v.5 p.324, p.690*

Mark, James E., et al.. . . . . *v.5 p.301*

Mark, Margaret & Pearson, Carol S. *v.4 p.144*

Mark, Mary Ellen *v.1 p.767*

Mark, Michael L. & Gary, Charles L. *v.1 p.405*

Mark, Michael L. (Editor). *v.1 p.405*

Mark, Rebecca & Vaughan, Robert *v.3 p.494*

Mark, Stephen R.. . . . . *v.5 p.370*

Markel, Mike *v.5 p.681*

Markel, Scott & León, Darryl *v.5 p.102*

Markell, Patchen. *v.4 p.513, p.514*

Marker, David *v.5 p.470*

Marker, F. J. & Innes, Christopher (Editors) . . . *v.1 p.83, p.97*

Marker, Frederick & Marker, Lise-Lone *v.2 p.624*

Marker, Gary (Editor). *v.3 p.209*

Markham, Felix M.. . . . . *v.3 p.152*

Markham, Jerry W.. . . . . . *v.4 p.89, p.104, p.109, p.147*

Markley, A. A.. . . . . *v.2 p.313*

Markoe, Glenn, et al. *v.1 p.670, p.690, p.706*

Markoe, Glenn *v.3 p.7*

Markoff, Arseni (Editor) *v.5 p.120, p.122, p.135*

Markoff, John *v.4 p.772, p.773*

Markos, Anton *v.5 p.194*

Markov, Georgi *v.2 p.780*

Markovits, Claude *v.3 p.305*

Markovitz, Irving L. (Editor) *v.6 p.55*

Markovitz, Irving Leonard *v.6 p.72*

Markowe, Laura *v.6 p.369*

Markowitz, Judith A. *v.6 p.391*

Markowitz, Linda *v.4 p.127*

Marks, Frederick W. III *v.3 p.475*

Marks, Jonathan *v.4 p.14, p.15, p.17*

Marks, Joseph E. (Editor) *v.1 p.22*

Marks, Robert B. *v.6 p.186, p.206*

Marks, Stephen P. *v.4 p.668, p.670*

Markstein, Donald D.. . . . . *v.6 p.308*

Markus, R. A. *v.1 p.579*

Markvart, Tomas (Editor) *v.5 p.362*

Markwick, Margaret *v.2 p.316*

Marlatt, G. Alan (Editor) *v.4 p.779, p.781, p.783*

Marley, David F. *v.6 p.709*

Marley, James A.. . . . . *v.5 p.661*

Marling, Karal Ann. *v.1 p.714*

Marling, William. *v.2 p.65, p.82*

Marlowe, Christopher. *v.2 p.221*

Marmol, Jose *v.2 p.678*

Mar-Molinero, Clare *v.2 p.636*

Marmor, Max & Ross, Alex *v.1 p.662*

Marmorstein, Gary *v.6 p.342*

Marnham, Patrick *v.1 p.744*

Maroni, Gustavo (Editor) *v.5 p.135*

Marot, Clément *v.2 p.470*

Marotta, Toby *v.6 p.366, p.388*

Marotti, Giorgio *v.2 p.692*

Marples, David R. *v.3 p.229*

Marquand, C. & Croft, D. *v.5 p.712*

Marquand, John P. *v.2 p.97*

Marquardt, Elizabeth *v.5 p.640*

Marquardt, Michael, et al. *v.4 p.79*

Marquart, James W., et al. *v.4 p.567*

Marques, A. H. de Oliveira *v.3 p.244, v.6 p.557*

Marquis, Alice G. *v.1 p.698*

Marquis, Donald M. *v.1 p.261, p.312*

Marquis, Don *v.2 p.97*

Marquis Who's Who, Inc. *v.5 p.397, p.398*

Marr, David G. *v.6 p.167*

Marr, David *v.2 p.749*

Marr, Phebe *v.6 p.603*

Marr, W. Allen (Editor) *v.5 p.422*

Marrese, Michelle Lamarche *v.3 p.216, v.6 p.452*

Marrett, Allan *v.1 p.289*

Marrs, Suzanne *v.2 p.130*

Marrus, Michael R. & Paxton, Robert O. *v.3 p.60, p.156*

Marrus, Michael R. *v.3 p.60, p.85, p.176*

Marryat, Frederick *v.2 p.299*

Marschark, Marc & Spencer, Patricia Elizabeth (Editors). *v.4 p.318*

Marschark, Marc, et al. *v.4 p.318*

Marsden, George M. (Editor) *v.1 p.605*

Marsden, George M. *v.1 p.581, p.584, p.606, p.636*

Marsden, George M *v.4 p.331*

Marsden, Gordon *v.6 p.735, p.764*

Marsden, Richard C. & Orchard, Andrew P. . . . *v.2 p.206, p.550*

Marsh, Charles, et al. *v.4 p.173*

Marsh, Dave *v.1 p.272, p.348, p.358*

Marsh, David C. *v.4 p.704*

Marsh, Derick R. C. *v.2 p.235*

Marsh, George Perkins *v.5 p.354, p.355, p.370*

Marsh, Ian *v.4 p.618, p.622*

Marsh, Jan *v.2 p.303, p.304*

Marsh, Joss *v.6 p.744*

Marsh, Margaret & Ronner, Wanda *v.6 p.470*

Marsh, Nicholas *v.2 p.364*

Marsh, Peter (Editor) *v.4 p.295*

Marsh, Rosalind & Korosteleva, Elena *v.3 p.230*

Marsh, Rosalind J. (Editor) *v.2 p.799*

Marsh, Rosalind J. *v.2 p.799*

Marshak, David *v.4 p.287*

Marshall, Adre *v.2 p.45*

Marshall, Alex *v.4 p.771, v.6 p.728*

Marshall, Alfred & Marshall, Mary P. *v.4 p.224*

Marshall, Alfred *v.4 p.224, p.238*

Marshall, Anthony D. *v.5 p.84*

Marshall, Barbara *v.6 p.441*

Marshall, Catherine & Rossman, Gretchen B. *v.4 p.687*

Marshall Cavendish Corporation Staff (Contribution
by) *v.5 p.176, p.239*

Marshall, Clare P. & Fairbridge, Rhodes W. (Editors) . *v.5 p.440*

Marshall, Dorothy *v.3 p.107, p.109*

Marshall, Douglas W. & Peckham, Howard Henry . *v.3 p.413*

Marshall, Elizabeth L. *v.5 p.135*

Marshall, George Catlett *v.3 p.460*

Marshall, Herbert *v.1 p.123, p.145*

Marshall, I. Howard (Editor) *v.1 p.625*

Marshall, I. *v.1 p.631*

Marshall, Lee *v.1 p.384*

Marshall, Louise H. & Magoun, Horace W. (Editors) . *v.5 p.617*

Marshall, Mac (Editor) *v.4 p.776*

Marshall, Mac *v.4 p.43, p.45*

Marshall, P. J. & Low, Alaine (Editors). *v.3 p.89, p.125, v.4 p.605*

Marshall, P. J. (Editor) *v.3 p.89, p.125, v.6 p.156*

Marshall, P. J. *v.3 p.74, v.6 p.161*

Marshall, Paul *v.1 p.605*

Marshall, Paule *v.2 p.768*

Marshall, Richard D. *v.1 p.698*

Marshall, Robert L. (Editor) *v.1 p.191, p.241*

Marshall, Robert L. *v.1 p.185, p.303*

Marshall, Rosalind K. *v.3 p.92, p.124, p.132*

Marshall, Rosalind *v.1 p.588*

Marshall, Samuel L. *v.6 p.237*

Marshall, Wayne E. *v.5 p.34*

Marshall, William Harvey *v.2 p.274*

Marsh-Lockett, Carol P. (Editor) *v.6 p.15, p.45*

Marsilius of Padua *v.4 p.490*

Marsoobian, Armen & Ryder, John *v.1 p.439*

Marsot, Afaf Lutfi al-Sayyid *v.6 p.58, p.639*

Marstine, Janet *v.1 p.828*

Marston, Gwen *v.1 p.802, p.809*

Marston, John *v.2 p.222*

Marston, Nicholas *v.1 p.200, p.241, p.355*

Marston, R.M. *v.5 p.709*

Martel, Gordon (Editor) *v.3 p.164*

Martell, Arthur Earl; Smith, Robert M. *v.5 p.302*

Martell, Christopher R., et al. *v.5 p.665, v.6 p.381*

Martens, Rainer *v.4 p.904*

Marter, Joan M. *v.1 p.780*

Martí, José *v.2 p.672*

Martín Gaite, Carmen *v.2 p.661*

Martínez, Demetria *v.6 p.501*

Martínez, Julio A. & Lomelí, Francisco A.
(Editors) *v.6 p.501, p.514*

Martínez, Julio A. (Editor) *v.2 p.672, v.6 p.507, p.514*

Martínez, Manuel Luis *v.6 p.501, p.514*

Martínez, Oscar J. (Editor) *v.3 p.527*

Martínez, Oscar J. *v.3 p.527, v.6 p.487, p.522, p.532*

Martínez, Richard Edward *v.6 p.520*

Martínez, Rubén *v.4 p.765*

Martínez, Tomás Eloy *v.3 p.348*

Martínez Vergne, Teresita *v.3 p.317*

Martín-Rodríguez, Manuel M. *v.6 p.501, p.514*

Martial *v.2 p.437, p.438*

Martijn, Jan K. *v.4 p.257*

Marti-Lopez, Elisa *v.2 p.641*

Martin, A. Lynn *v.3 p.146*

Martin, Andrew & Ross, George (Editors) *v.4 p.212*

Martin, Benjamin *v.3 p.241*

Martin, Bill & Avakian, Bob *v.4 p.507, p.508*

Martin, Bruce, et al. *v.4 p.787*

Martin, Burns *v.2 p.258*

Martin, Calvin (Editor) *v.6 p.682*

Martin, Catherine *v.2 p.747*

Martin, Charles *v.2 p.430*

Martin, Cheryl English *v.3 p.286*

Martin, Chester *v.4 p.587, p.605*

Martin, Christopher *v.4 p.127*

Martin, David *v.1 p.580*

Martin, Del *v.6 p.367*

Martin, Diana & Haller, Lynn *v.1 p.721*

Martin Du Gard, Roger *v.2 p.522*

Martin, Emily *v.4 p.47, v.6 p.444*

Martin, Fenton S. & Goehlert, Robert *v.4 p.466, p.530*

Martin, Frederick N. & Clark, John Greer *v.5 p.523*

Martin, Gary J. *v.5 p.16*

Martin, Geoffrey J. *v.3 p.45, v.4 p.378*

Martin, George *v.1 p.218, p.231*

Martin Grayson and David Eckroth, executive eds. . . . *v.5 p.257*

Martin, Guy *v.6 p.13, p.31, p.55*

Martin, Henri-Jean *v.3 p.37, p.144*

Martin, Henry *v.1 p.261, p.346*

Martin, James A. Jr. *v.1 p.524*

Martin, Janet L. B. *v.3 p.215*

Martin, Janet M. *v.4 p.527*

Martin, Jay *v.2 p.131*

Martin, Jeanette S. & Chaney, Lillian H. *v.4 p.56*

Martin, Joel W. *v.1 p.544, v.6 p.701*

Martin, John D. (Author, Editor) *v.4 p.64, p.91*

Martin, John. *v.1 p.5, p.10, p.27, p.39, v.3 p.197, p.204, v.5 p.732*

Martin, Joyce *v.4 p.66*

Martin, Judy *v.1 p.752, p.759*

Martin, Julian *v.3 p.129*

Martin, Lawrence *v.3 p.541*

Martin, Lenore & Keridis, Dimitris (Editors) *v.6 p.624*

Martin, Mary L. *v.2 p.467*

Martin, Michael *v.1 p.545, v.5 p.176, p.240*

Martin, Patricia P. *v.3 p.271*

Martin, Patricia Preciado (Editor, Translator) . *v.6 p.489, p.523*

Martin, Peter *v.4 p.117*

Martin, Phyllis M. & O'Meara, Patrick (Editors) *v.6 p.51*

Martin, Phyllis *v.6 p.62*

Martin, Priscilla *v.2 p.210*

Martin, Ralph P. *v.1 p.624*

Martin, Randy & Miller, Toby *v.4 p.817*

Martin, Randy *v.1 p.43, v.3 p.302*

Martin, R. *v.5 p.326*

Martin, Richard C. (Editor) *v.1 p.554*

Martin, Robert A. *v.2 p.134, v.5 p.447, v.6 p.393*

Martin, Robert B. *v.2 p.294*

Martin, Robert K. (Editor) *v.6 p.393*

Martin, Robert M. *v.1 p.492*

Martin, Ronald E. *v.5 p.447*

Martin, Seelye *v.4 p.389, v.5 p.428*

Martin, Shannon E. & Copeland, David A.
(Editors) *v.4 p.411, p.417*

Martin, Simon *v.4 p.808, p.817, p.867, p.891*

Martin, Terence *v.2 p.41*

Martin, Terry J. *v.2 p.41, p.48, p.50*

Martin, Terry *v.3 p.213*

Martin, Thomas R. *v.3 p.12*

Martin, Vance & Tyler, Nicholas (Editors) . . . *v.5 p.176, p.238*

Martin, W. & Tops, Guy A. *v.2 p.621*

Martin, Waldo E. Jr. *v.3 p.420*

Martin, Waldo E. *v.4 p.439*

Martin, Walter R. & Ober, Warren *v.2 p.45*

Martin, Wendy *v.2 p.26, p.583*

Martin, William, et al. *v.3 p.245*

Martindale, Andrew *v.1 p.672*

Martindale, Charles (Editor) *v.2 p.446*

Martindale, Colin (Editor), et al. *v.5 p.619*

Martindale, Don *v.4 p.680*

Martine, James J. *v.2 p.107*

Martineau, Harriet *v.2 p.299, v.4 p.193, p.209, p.218,
p.269, v.6 p.740, p.748, p.764*

Martineau, Jane & Robison, Andrew (Editors) . *v.1 p.675, p.688*

Martineau, Robert J. & Novello, David P. *v.6 p.300*

Martineau, Robert J. & Novello, David. *v.6 p.300*

Martines, Lauro *v.3 p.200*

Martinez Arias, Alfonso & Stewart, Alison *v.5 p.164*

Martinez, J. Michael (Editor), et al. *v.4 p.567*

Martinez, Joe L. Jr. & Mendoza, Richard H. (Editors) . *v.6 p.541*

Martinez, Nancy C. & Martinez, Joseph G. *v.6 p.565*

Martinez, Ruben *v.6 p.521*

Martinez, Samuel *v.4 p.41*

Martinez-Duenas Espejo, Jose Luis & Perez Fernandez, Jose
Maria *v.2 p.770*

Martinez-Fernandez, Luis. *v.3 p.311, p.317, p.320*

Martinez-Vergne, Teresita & Knight, Franklin W.
(Editors) *v.4 p.41*

Martinez-Vergne, Teresita *v.3 p.320*

Marting, Diane E. (Editor) *v.2 p.692*

Martini, Fritz *v.2 p.589, p.590*

Martinich, A. P. & Sosa, David (Editors) *v.1 p.502*

Martinich, A. P. *v.1 p.448, p.490, v.2 p.550, p.562*

Martino, Joseph P. *v.5 p.412*

Martins, Peter & Cornfield, Robert *v.1 p.10*

Martins, Peter *v.1 p.24*

Martins, Wilson *v.2 p.692*

Martinsen, Deborah A. *v.2 p.806*

Martinson, Deborah *v.2 p.83*

Martinson, Harry. *v.2 p.630*

Martland, Peter. *v.1 p.384*

Martorella, Rosanne *v.1 p.826*

Marty, Martin E. & Appleby, R. Scott (Editors) . . . *v.4 p.722*

Marty, Martin E. & Moore, Jonathan *v.4 p.307, p.486*

Marty, Martin E.. . . . . *v.1 p.545, p.605*

Martyn, J. Louis *v.1 p.631*

Martz, Louis L. *v.2 p.182, p.254, p.261*

Marullo, Sam *v.4 p.561*

Maruna, Shadd & Immarigeon, Russ (Editors) . . . *v.6 p.279*

Maruna, Shadd. *v.6 p.279*

Maruyama, Hiroshi, et al.. . . . . . *v.5 p.338, p.349*

Maruyama, Masao *v.6 p.225*

Marvell, Andrew & Smith, Nigel *v.2 p.252*

Marvell, Andrew *v.2 p.252*

Marvin, Carolyn & Ingle, David W. *v.4 p.767*

Marvin, Carolyn *v.4 p.416*

Marvin, Clara *v.1 p.164, p.180, p.346*

Marvin, Thomas F. *v.2 p.157*

Marwick, Arthur *v.3 p.118, v.4 p.705, p.724*

Marx, Anthony W. *v.4 p.494*

Marx, Elisabeth *v.4 p.56*

Marx, Emanuel (Editor). *v.6 p.596*

Marx, Emanuel. *v.6 p.596*

Marx, Karl & Engels,
  Friedrich . *v.1 p.545, v.2 p.569, v.4 p.222, p.236, p.507, p.509*

Marx, Karl & Tucker, Robert C.. . . . . *v.4 p.507*

Marx, Karl, et al. *v.4 p.507, p.508*

Marx, Karl *v.1 p.465, v.4 p.215, p.218,*
                              p.236, p.238, p.492, p.681

Marx, Leo. *v.3 p.369*

Maryland Institute for Technology in the
  Humanities *v.3 p.404, p.406, p.409, p.414*

Marzano, Robert J. & Kendall, John S.. . . . . . *v.4 p.286*

Marzano, Robert J., et al. *v.4 p.284*

Marzano, Robert J.. . . . . *v.4 p.364*

Marzec, Robert P. *v.3 p.490*

Marzola, Alessandra & Silva, Francesco (Editors) . . . *v.4 p.228*

Masalha, Nur (Editor) *v.6 p.618*

Masalha, Nur *v.6 p.618*

Masaryk, Tomas G.. . . . . *v.3 p.210*

Mascelli, Joseph V.. . . . . *v.6 p.349*

Masciandaro, Donato *v.6 p.253*

Mascie-Taylor, C. G. Nicholas (Editor, Contribution by). *v.4 p.14*

Masel, Richard I.. . . . . *v.5 p.279*

Maser, Chris & Silberstein, Jane. *v.5 p.373, p.377*

Maser, Chris *v.5 p.38*

Maser, Jack D. (Editor), et al. *v.5 p.661*

Mashek, Debra J. & Aron, Arthur (Editors). . . *v.5 p.648, p.654*

Masiello, Francine *v.3 p.267*

Masing-Delic, Irene *v.2 p.799*

Masini, Eleonora and Susan Stratigos *v.3 p.354*

Maslach, Christina & Leiter, Michael P. *v.5 p.580*

Maslow, Abraham H. *v.5 p.635*

Maslow, Jonathan Evan. *v.5 p.236, p.239*

Maslowska, Dorota *v.2 p.791*

Mason, Alpheus T. *v.4 p.468, p.470*

Mason, Christopher. *v.1 p.827*

Mason, David *v.4 p.147, p.155*

Mason, Diana J., et al. *v.5 p.530*

Mason, Francis *v.1 p.10*

Mason, Haydn Trevos *v.2 p.484*

Mason, Haydn *v.2 p.459*

Mason, I. L. *v.5 p.55*

Mason, John Edwin *v.4 p.727*

Mason, Laura & Rizzo, Tracey *v.3 p.151*

Mason, Laura *v.1 p.246*

Mason, Lauris & Ludman, Joan *v.1 p.757*

Mason, Mary A. *v.4 p.442, p.740, v.6 p.467*

Mason, Mary Ann (Editor), et al. *v.4 p.733*

Mason, Michael *v.6 p.760*

Mason, Penelope *v.1 p.693, v.6 p.219*

Mason, Robert J. & Mattson, Mark T. *v.4 p.159*

Mason, Ronald, J. *v.4 p.11*

Mason, Stephen Finney *v.5 p.263*

Mason, Tony *v.4 p.817, p.844, p.867*

Mason, W. Dale *v.4 p.465, v.6 p.696*

Masonry Standards Joint Committee (MSJC), Masonry
  society. *v.5 p.686*

Mass, Lawrence D. (Editor). *v.6 p.402, p.412*

Massa, Mark S. . . *v.1 p.574, v.4 p.817, p.859, p.894*

Massa, Werner *v.5 p.284*

Massai, Sonia (Editor) *v.1 p.76, p.101, p.135*

Massaquoi, Hans J. *v.6 p.29*

Masschaele, James *v.6 p.558*

Masselink, Gerd & Hughes, Michael. *v.5 p.424*

Massengale, John & Swanson, Richard A.
  (Editors). *v.4 p.808, p.873*

Massey, Anne *v.1 p.800*

Massey, Douglas S. & Denton, Nancy A.. . . . . *v.4 p.730*

Massey, Douglas S., et al. . *v.4 p.571, v.6 p.525, p.529, p.530*

Massey, Reginald & Massey, Jamila. *v.1 p.15*

Massie, Robert K. *v.3 p.217*

Massignon, Louis *v.1 p.555*

Massine, Leonide *v.1 p.10*

Massing, Paul W. *v.3 p.60*

Massinger, Philip. *v.2 p.221*

Massironi, Manfredo *v.5 p.594, p.607*

Masson, Jeffrey Moussaieff *v.5 p.615*

Masson, Marilyn A. *v.4 p.10*

Masson, Paul R. & Pattillo, Catherine *v.4 p.398*

Masson, Raphael, et al. *v.1 p.780*

Massood, Paula J. *v.6 p.330, p.342*

Mast, Gerald & Kawin, Bruce F.. . . . . *v.6 p.331*

Mast, Gerald. *v.6 p.313*

Masteroff, Joe, et al. *v.1 p.252, p.408*

Masters, Bruce Alan *v.6 p.590, p.597, p.601*

Masters, Edgar Lee *v.2 p.97*

Masters, Gilbert M. *v.5 p.361, p.377, p.724*

Masters, Jamie *v.2 p.437*

Masters, William H., et al. *v.4 p.748*

Masterson, Daniel M.. . . . . *v.3 p.275*
Masterson, James W., et al. *v.5 p.714*
Masterson, William H. *v.4 p.644, p.645*
Mastny, Vojtech *v.3 p.87, p.189, p.226*
Mastoon, Adam *v.6 p.369*
Mas'Ud Ibn Umar Al-Taftazani *v.1 p.557*
Masuda, Sayo *v.6 p.227*
Masudi *v.6 p.585*
Masud-Piloto, Felix *v.3 p.311*
Masur, Gerhard *v.3 p.260*
Masuzawa, Tomoko *v.1 p.521*
Masyny, Vojtech & Byrne, Malcolm (Editors). . . . *v.4 p.630*
Mata de Lopez, Sara *v.3 p.347*
Matar, Muhammad A. *v.6 p.662*
Mate, Mavis E.. . . . . *v.6 p.560*
Mateas, Michael & Sengers, Phoebe (Editors). . . . *v.5 p.589*
Matejic, Mateja, et al. *v.2 p.780*
Matejko, Alexander J.. . . . . *v.4 p.705*
Matelski, Marilyn J. & Nancy, Lynch Street (Editor, Translators) *v.6 p.323*
Mates, Benson. *v.1 p.492, p.494*
Mates, Julian *v.1 p.32, p.252*
Mathabane, Mark. *v.4 p.731*
Mather, Betty B. & Karns, Dean M. . . . *v.1 p.22, p.185, p.401*
Mather, Cotton (Editor) *v.3 p.485*
Mather, Cotton. *v.1 p.584*
Mather, Kirtley F. & Mason, Shirley L. *v.5 p.418*
Mather, Kirtley F. *v.5 p.418*
Mather, Paul M. *v.4 p.389*
Matheson Hooker, Virginia *v.6 p.172*
Matheson, Peter (Editor, Translator) *v.3 p.166*
Mathew, Gervase. *v.6 p.556*
Mathews, Christopher K., et al. *v.5 p.327*
Mathews, Donald G. *v.1 p.607*
Mathews, Thomas F. *v.1 p.599*
Mathews. *v.5 p.327*
Mathewson, Rufus W. Jr. *v.2 p.799*
Mathez, Edmond A. & Webster, James D. *v.5 p.419*
Mathias, Elizabeth & Raspa, Richard *v.2 p.17*
Mathias, P. & Pollard, Sidney (Editors) *v.3 p.41*
Mathias, Peter & Postan, M. M. (Editors) *v.3 p.40*
Mathias, Peter *v.3 p.113*
Mathiassen, Terje. *v.2 p.773*
Mathiesen, Thomas J.. . . . . *v.1 p.175*
Mathijs, Ernest & Mendik, Xavier (Editors) *v.6 p.314*
Mathis, Robert L. & Jackson, John H.. . . . . . . *v.4 p.76*
Mathre, D. E. (Editor) *v.5 p.46*
Matibag, Eugenio *v.3 p.315, p.317*
Matida, Kasyo *v.1 p.16*
Matis, James H. & Kiffe, Thomas R.. . . . . *v.5 p.100*
Matisse, Henri & Castleman, Riva *v.1 p.806*
Matlack, Albert S. *v.5 p.310*
Matlak, Richard *v.2 p.280*
Matless, David *v.4 p.399*
Matloff, Maurice *v.3 p.383*

Mator, Carlos A.. . . . . *v.2 p.651*
Matory, J. Lorand *v.6 p.71, p.459*
Matos-Rodriquez, Felix V. & Delgado, Linda C. (Editors) *v.3 p.320*
Matossian, Mary K. *v.4 p.778*
Matovina, Timothy M. *v.6 p.520, p.532, p.549*
Matsumoto, Brian *v.5 p.86*
Matsumoto, Valerie J.. . . . . *v.6 p.132*
Matsumoto, Y. *v.5 p.499*
Matsuyama, Akira *v.6 p.164*
Matt, Daniel Chanan (Introduction by) *v.1 p.550*
Matt, Daniel Chanan *v.1 p.500*
Mattar, Philip *v.6 p.608*
Matter, E. Ann & Coakley, John (Editors) . *v.3 p.201, v.6 p.560*
Mattern, Susan P. *v.3 p.28*
Mattfeld, Julius *v.1 p.168, p.278*
Matthaei, Julie A. *v.6 p.457*
Matthew, Donald *v.3 p.97*
Matthew, H. C. G. & Harrison, Brian (Editors) . . . *v.6 p.735*
Matthew, H. C. G. (Henry Colin Gray) . . . *v.3 p.113, v.6 p.758*
Matthews, Brander (Editor) *v.1 p.56, p.136*
Matthews, Brander *v.1 p.68, p.97*
Matthews, Christopher *v.3 p.475*
Matthews, Fred H. *v.4 p.685*
Matthews, G. M. (Editor) *v.2 p.295*
Matthews, Gareth B. *v.1 p.498*
Matthews, Gerald, et al.. . . . . *v.5 p.654*
Matthews, J. F. *v.3 p.31*
Matthews, Jana B., et al.. . . . . *v.4 p.68*
Matthews, Janet R. & Walker, C. Eugene. *v.5 p.675*
Matthews, John A. (Editor) *v.6 p.284, p.286*
Matthews, John F. *v.2 p.428, v.3 p.32*
Matthews, Joseph L. & Matthews Berman, Dorothy. *v.4 p.96, p.98*
Matthews, Mervyn *v.4 p.705*
Matthews, Nicole. *v.6 p.313*
Matthews, Peter H. *v.2 p.562, v.4 p.18*
Matthews, Roger *v.3 p.6*
Matthews, Stephen & Yip, Virginia *v.6 p.207*
Matthews, Steven *v.2 p.179*
Matthews, W. K. *v.2 p.781*
Matthews, William J. *v.5 p.216*
Matthews, William *v.2 p.149, p.206*
Matthewson, Tim. *v.3 p.315*
Matthias, John & Printz-Pahlson, Goran (Translators) . *v.2 p.629*
Matthias, John *v.3 p.248*
Matthiessen, Francis O. *v.2 p.24*
Matthiessen, Peter . . *v.2 p.149, v.6 p.489, p.526, p.689, p.694*
Mattimore, Bryan W. *v.4 p.66*
Mattingly, Carol *v.6 p.431, p.448*
Mattingly, Garrett *v.3 p.71, p.91, p.100*
Mattingly, Jack D., et al. *v.5 p.718*
Mattingly, Paul H. *v.6 p.718*
Matto de Turner, Clorinda. *v.2 p.685, v.3 p.283, p.327*
Mattock, John. *v.4 p.59*

Mattox, Gale A. & Rachwald, Arthur R. (Editors) . . *v.4 p.630, p.639*

Mattsson, Einar *v.5 p.735*

Mattusch, Carol C. *v.1 p.775*

Maturin, Charles R. *v.2 p.299*

Matusky, Patricia & Tan, Sooi Beng (Editors) *v.1 p.289*

Matusow, Allen J. *v.3 p.475*

Matute, Ana M. *v.2 p.661*

Matuz, Roger (Editor) *v.1 p.665, v.6 p.679*

Matz, Jesse *v.2 p.194*

Matz, Samuel A. *v.5 p.34*

Matzke, Gary R., et al. *v.5 p.526*

Matzner, Egbert (Volume Editor) *v.5 p.176*

Matzner, Richard A., ed. *v.5 p.63, p.443*

Maud, Peter J. & Foster, Carl (Editors) . . . *v.4 p.791, p.875*

Maud, Ralph *v.2 p.108*

Mauer, Marc & Chesney-Lind, Meda (Editors) . . . *v.6 p.249*

Mauer, Marc *v.4 p.753, p.773*

Maufort, Marc (Editor) *v.1 p.87, p.120*

Maugham, W. Somerset *v.2 p.370, p.371, p.578*

Maughan, Ronald J. *v.4 p.825, p.876*

Maughan, Ron *v.4 p.825, p.876*

Mauleon, Rebeca *v.1 p.403*

Maullin, Richard *v.3 p.275*

Maultsby, Portia & Burnim, Mellonee V. *v.6 p.30*

Maume, Patrick *v.3 p.139*

Maunder, W. J. *v.5 p.371*

Mauner, George *v.1 p.744*

Maung Maung, U. *v.6 p.166*

Maung, Mya *v.4 p.617*

Maupassant, Guy de *v.2 p.497*

Maupin, Armistead *v.6 p.397*

Maupin, Molly A. & Barber, Nancy L. *v.6 p.294*

Maurel, Sylvie *v.2 p.769*

Maurer, Armand A. *v.1 p.433*

Maurer, Bill *v.4 p.41*

Maurer, Brian A. *v.5 p.100*

Maurer, Stephen B. & Ralston, Anthony *v.5 p.478*

Maurer, Warren *v.2 p.609*

Mauriac, François *v.2 p.522*

Maurice, Donald G. *v.1 p.218, p.241, p.305*

Maurois, Andre *v.2 p.311, p.487, p.489*

Maury, Matthew Fontaine *v.4 p.394*

Mauser, Gary A. *v.4 p.558*

Mauskopf, Seymour H. (Editor) *v.5 p.263*

Mauss, Marcel *v.4 p.28*

Mauthner, Melanie L. *v.5 p.628, p.631*

Maveety, Nancy *v.4 p.468*

Mawdsley, Evan & White, Stephen . . . *v.3 p.222, v.4 p.598*

Mawdsley, Evan *v.3 p.225*

Mawer, Deborah (Editor) *v.1 p.218, p.350*

Mawer, Noel *v.2 p.86*

Max-Muller, F. (Editor) *v.1 p.538*

Maxton, Graeme P. & Wormald, John *v.4 p.154*

Maxwell, Bruce *v.4 p.660*

Maxwell, Daniel G. & Barrett, Christopher B. . *v.4 p.259, p.265*

Maxwell, David *v.6 p.77*

Maxwell, Gavin *v.6 p.61*

Maxwell, James Clerk (Editor) *v.5 p.543*

Maxwell, James Clerk *v.5 p.565*

Maxwell, Jane & Gretton, Monica (Editors) *v.5 p.690*

Maxwell, John C. *v.4 p.71*

Maxwell, Kenneth R. *v.3 p.341*

Maxwell, Kenneth *v.3 p.244, p.335, v.4 p.608*

Maxwell, Moreau *v.4 p.11*

Maxwell, Richard (Editor) *v.6 p.737, p.740*

Maxwell, Robert & Muirhead, Thomas *v.1 p.794*

Maxwell, Robert S. *v.3 p.434*

Maxwell, William *v.2 p.97*

May, Charles E. *v.2 p.50*

May, David C. *v.6 p.255*

May, Dean L. *v.3 p.532*

May, Dean *v.3 p.529*

May, Elizabeth *v.5 p.182*

May, Ernest R. & Zelikow, Philip D. (Editors) . *v.3 p.443, p.475*

May, Ernest R. *v.3 p.417, p.433, p.453*

May, Gary *v.3 p.460*

May, Glenn A. *v.6 p.180*

May, Henry F. *v.3 p.369, p.406*

May, Jacques M. & McLellan, Donna L. (Editors) . . *v.3 p.271*

May, James M. (Editor) *v.2 p.433*

May, Jerry R. & Asken, Michael J. (Editors) *v.5 p.582*

May, Keith M. *v.2 p.354*

May, Larry *v.4 p.713*

May, Lary (Editor) *v.3 p.371, p.443*

May, Rollo *v.5 p.654*

May, Steve (Editor) *v.4 p.53, p.173*

May, Steven W. *v.2 p.182*

May, William V. & Tolin, Craig *v.1 p.395*

Mayakovsky, Vladimir *v.2 p.806*

Mayaram, Shail *v.6 p.154*

Mayberry, Katherine J. *v.2 p.304*

Maydeu-Olivares, Albert & McArdle, John J. (Editors) . *v.5 p.601*

Mayell, Mark *v.3 p.547*

Mayer, A. M. & Poljakoff-Mayber, A. *v.5 p.47*

Mayer, Ann Elizabeth *v.1 p.559*

Mayer, Anton *v.1 p.200, p.359*

Mayer, Bernard S. *v.4 p.74*

Mayer, Enrique *v.3 p.326*

Mayer, Frank & Hoppert, Michael *v.5 p.86, p.218*

Mayer, George H. *v.3 p.522*

Mayer, Hans E. *v.6 p.556*

Mayer, Harold M. & Wade, Richard C. *v.3 p.516*

Mayer, Kenneth R. *v.4 p.462*

Mayer, Lauryn S. *v.6 p.569*

Mayer, Margit & Ely, John *v.4 p.610*

Mayer, Robert (Editor) *v.6 p.326*

Mayer, Roland H. & Horace *v.2 p.434*

Mayer, Susan & Peterson, Paul E. (Editors) *v.4 p.265*

Mayer, Tamar *v.6 p.618*

Mayer, Thomas *v.4 p.195, p.238, p.246*
Mayer, Wendy & Allen, Pauline *v.1 p.593*
Mayer, William G. & Busch, Andrew E. *v.4 p.549*
Mayer, William G. *v.4 p.551, p.553*
Mayers, David *v.3 p.390*
Mayes, Frances *v.2 p.578*
Mayes, Stanley *v.3 p.11*
Mayewski, Pawel. *v.2 p.787*
Mayhall, C. Glen. *v.5 p.533*
Mayhew, David R. *v.3 p.443, v.4 p.551*
Mayhew, David *v.4 p.551, p.552*
Mayhew, Henry *v.2 p.299, v.6 p.743, p.744, p.761*
Mayhew, Robert J. *v.2 p.251, v.4 p.375*
Mayhew, Susan *v.4 p.373*
Maynard, Donald N. & Hochmuth, George J.. . . *v.5 p.22, p.26*
Maynard, Kimberly A. *v.4 p.671*
Maynard, Kyle. *v.4 p.842, p.870*
Maynard Smith, John & Szathmary, Eors. *v.5 p.194*
Maynard Smith, John *v.5 p.160, p.194, p.200*
Maynard, W. Barksdale *v.1 p.790*
Mayne, Judith *v.6 p.418*
Mayne, Thom *v.1 p.794*
Maynes, Mary Jo, et al. *v.3 p.54*
Mayo, Elton *v.5 p.579*
Mayo, John *v.3 p.351*
Mayo, Katherine *v.6 p.150*
Mayo, Mike (Editor) *v.6 p.323*
Mayo, Robert S. *v.2 p.600*
Mayor, A. Hyatt *v.1 p.760*
Mayr, Ernst & Ashlock, Peter D. *v.5 p.212*
Mayr, Ernst W. *v.3 p.49, v.5 p.203*
Mayr, Ernst. *v.5 p.80, p.194*
Mayr-Harting, Henry *v.6 p.572*
Mays, Annabelle *v.4 p.335*
Mays, James L. & Gaventa, Beverly R. *v.1 p.615*
Mays, James L., et al. *v.1 p.619*
Mays, Larry W. *v.5 p.703*
Mays, Terry M. *v.4 p.650*
Maza, Sarah C.. . . . . *v.3 p.149*
Mazama, Ama (Editor). *v.6 p.14*
Mazar, Amihai *v.1 p.617*
Mazón, Mauricio. *v.6 p.536, p.540*
Mazierska, Ewa & Rascaroli, Laura *v.6 p.337*
Mazour, Anatole G. *v.3 p.210, p.218*
Mazower, Mark *v.3 p.194, p.195, p.196*
Mazrui, Alamin M. & Mazuri, Ail A. *v.6 p.20, p.36*
Mazrui, Ali A. & Tidy, Michael. *v.6 p.54*
Mazrui, Ali A. *v.2 p.756*
Mazrui, Ali Al'Amin *v.6 p.7, p.10*
Mazrui, Ali (Hosted by) *v.6 p.53*
Mazumdar, Sanjay K.. . . . . *v.5 p.690*
Mazur, Barry. *v.5 p.476*
Mazur, Bolesaw W.. . . . . *v.2 p.775*
Mazur, Eric Michael & McCarthy, Kate *v.4 p.712*
Mazur, Eric *v.5 p.563*

Mazur, Nicole. *v.5 p.84*
Mazurana, Dyan E., et al.. . . . . *v.4 p.650*
Mazurek, Kas & Winzer, M. A. *v.4 p.316*
Mazza, Enrico *v.1 p.657*
Mazzaro, Jerome *v.2 p.705*
Mazzeo, Karen S. *v.4 p.793*
Mazzotta, Giuseppe *v.2 p.705, p.706*
Mba, Nina E. *v.6 p.71*
Mbaku, John M. & Ihonvbere, Julius O.
(Editors). *v.4 p.505, p.585, p.612*
Mbaku, John M.. . . . . *v.4 p.612*
Mbaku, John Mukum & Ihonvbere, Julius Omozuanvbo
(Editors) *v.4 p.585, p.612*
Mbaku, John Mukum *v.4 p.612*
Mbiti, John Samuel. *v.1 p.525*
Mbiti, John S. *v.1 p.542, v.6 p.36*
Mboya, Tom *v.6 p.65*
McAdams, A. James *v.4 p.610*
McAdams, Dan P. (Editor), et al. *v.5 p.655*
McAdams, Dan P., et al. *v.5 p.655*
McAdams, Dan P. *v.5 p.655*
McAdams, Frank J.. . . . . *v.6 p.323*
McAdams, Janet *v.6 p.698*
McAdoo, William G. *v.3 p.460*
McAfee, R. Preston *v.4 p.83*
McAleer, Kevin *v.3 p.169*
McAlister, Elizabeth A. *v.1 p.293*
McAlister, Lyle N. *v.3 p.275, p.404*
McAllister, James A. *v.3 p.546*
McAllister, James W. *v.3 p.45*
McAllister, Mary Louise *v.4 p.581, p.587*
McAllister, Matthew P. *v.4 p.697*
McAllister, William B. *v.3 p.282*
McAlmon, Robert & Boyle, Kay *v.2 p.63*
McArdle, William D., et al.. . . . . . . *v.4 p.801, p.876*
McArdle. *v.4 p.875, v.5 p.519*
McArthur, Benjamin *v.1 p.117, p.145*
McArthur, Hugh & Spalding, Duncan *v.5 p.732*
McArthur, Thomas *v.2 p.552*
McAuley, James (Editor) *v.2 p.741*
McBain, Ed. *v.2 p.97*
McBeth, B. S. *v.3 p.360*
McBeth, Brian S.. . . . . *v.3 p.361*
McBeth, Leon *v.1 p.583*
McBirney, Alexander R. *v.5 p.437*
McBride, Dwight A. (Editor) *v.2 p.59, v.6 p.26*
McBrien, Richard P. *v.1 p.575, p.579*
McBrien, Richard *v.1 p.574*
McBrien, William *v.1 p.252, p.347, v.6 p.409*
McCabe, J. Terrence *v.4 p.30*
McCabe, Marsha & Thomas, Joseph D. *v.1 p.823*
McCabe, Susan *v.2 p.62*
McCabe, Warren L., et al.. . . . . *v.5 p.744*
McCaffery, Peter. *v.4 p.551, p.552, p.553*
McCaffrey, Donald W. & Jacobs, Christopher P.. . . *v.6 p.332*

McCaffrey, Donald W. *v.6 p.313*
McCaffrey, Katherine T. *v.3 p.320*
McCall, Dan *v.2 p.48*
McCall, G. J. & De Mulder, E. F. *v.5 p.420*
McCall, Morgan W. & Hollenbeck, George P. . . *v.4 p.59, p.120*
McCalla, James *v.1 p.218, p.241*
McCallum, Hamish *v.5 p.100*
McCallum, Lawrence *v.6 p.338*
McCalman, Iain *v.3 p.113, p.131, v.6 p.739, p.760, p.766*
McCalpin, James P. & Nelson, Alan R. (Editors) . . . *v.5 p.422*
McCamant, James D. *v.5 p.218*
McCandless, Stanley *v.1 p.148*
McCann, Bryan *v.1 p.293, v.3 p.267*
McCann, Carole R. & Kim, Seung-Kyung (Editors) . *v.6 p.428*
McCann, Charles R. (Editor) *v.4 p.191*
McCann, Charles R. Jr. (Editor) *v.4 p.203*
McCann, Charles R. *v.4 p.228*
McCann, Colum *v.1 p.46*
McCann, David R. *v.6 p.238*
McCann, Frank D. *v.3 p.275, p.337*
McCann, Franklin Thresher *v.3 p.404*
McCann, James C. *v.5 p.22*
McCannon, John *v.3 p.223*
McCardle, Peggy & Chhabra, Vinita (Editors) . . . *v.4 p.364*
McCarren, Felicia M. *v.1 p.49*
McCarry, John & O'Leary, Brendan (Editors) *v.4 p.607*
McCarter, P. Kyle Jr. *v.1 p.620*
McCarter, Robert *v.1 p.794*
McCarthy, Cormac *v.2 p.149*
McCarthy, David F. *v.5 p.699*
McCarthy, George E. *v.4 p.683*
McCarthy, Jack *v.2 p.360*
McCarthy, Jane & Epstein, Laurily K. *v.1 p.774, p.812*
McCarthy, John A. *v.2 p.615*
McCarthy, Justin *v.6 p.590, p.610*
McCarthy, Martha M., et al. *v.4 p.450*
McCarthy, Mary *v.2 p.99*
McCarthy, Patrick *v.2 p.512*
McCarthy, P. *v.2 p.360*
McCarthy, Ronald & Sharp, Gene *v.4 p.650*
McCarthy, Terence *v.2 p.212*
McCarthy-Arnolds, Eileen (Editor), et al. *v.6 p.55*
McCartney, Bruce L. *v.5 p.703*
McCarus, Ernest N. (Editor), et al. *v.6 p.654*
McCash, Elaine M. *v.5 p.283*
McCash, William B. *v.3 p.503*
McCaskie, T. C. *v.6 p.70*
McCaughey, Martha & King, Neal (Editors) *v.6 p.321*
McCauley, Deborah V. *v.3 p.498*
McCauley, Joseph L. *v.5 p.547*
McCauley, Michael J. *v.2 p.124*
McCauley, Robert N. & Lawson, E. Thomas *v.5 p.635*
McCawley, James D. *v.2 p.557*
McChesney, Robert Waterman & Scott, Ben *v.4 p.558*
McChesney, Robert W. *v.4 p.416, p.425*

McClain, Carol S. (Editor) *v.4 p.47*
McClain, Charles J. *v.4 p.457*
McClary, Susan *v.1 p.180, p.200, p.231, p.247, p.312, p.379, v.6 p.475*
McClatchy, J. D. (Editor) *v.6 p.405*
McClatchy, J. D. *v.2 p.24, p.149, v.6 p.405*
McClaurin, Irma (Editor) *v.4 p.31, v.6 p.435*
McClay, Kenneth R. *v.5 p.420*
McCleary, Richard *v.6 p.278*
McClellan, A. L. *v.5 p.287*
McClellan, B. Edward *v.4 p.306*
McClellan, Edwin *v.6 p.227, p.231*
McClellan, James E. *v.5 p.385*
McClellan, James *v.4 p.468*
McClellan, Keith *v.4 p.859, p.897, p.902*
McClellan, Michael *v.4 p.118*
McClelland, Charles E. *v.3 p.160, p.179*
McClelland, Linda F. *v.1 p.819, v.6 p.295*
McCleverty, J. A. & Meyer, Thomas J. (Editors) . . . *v.5 p.299*
McClintock, Cynthia & Lowenthal, Abraham F. (Editors) *v.3 p.330*
McCloskey, Barbara *v.1 p.680*
McCloskey, Deirdre N. *v.3 p.41, v.4 p.185, v.6 p.402*
McCloskey, Robert G. *v.4 p.466*
McCloud, Scott *v.2 p.582*
McClung, William A. *v.2 p.182*
McClure, George W. *v.3 p.200*
McClure, Michael *v.2 p.4, p.150*
McClurg, Andrew J. (Editor), et al. *v.6 p.266*
McClusky, Pamela & Thompson, Robert Farris . *v.1 p.690, v.4 p.26*
McClymond, Michael James *v.1 p.648*
McColley, Diane K. *v.2 p.254*
McCollum, James K. *v.4 p.509*
McComb, William David *v.5 p.559*
McCombs, Maxwell *v.4 p.697*
McConkey, Edwin H. *v.5 p.135, p.141*
McConnell, Andy *v.1 p.810*
McConnell, David L. *v.6 p.220*
McConnell, Frank D. *v.2 p.319*
McConnell, Steve *v.5 p.346, p.348*
McConnell, Winder (Editor) *v.2 p.595*
McCook, Stuart George *v.3 p.269*
McCool, Daniel *v.6 p.681, p.689, p.696*
McCord, Edward Allen *v.6 p.190*
McCord, Joan (Editor) *v.6 p.250*
McCord, Norman *v.3 p.113*
McCormac, Jack C. *v.4 p.389, v.5 p.695*
McCormack, Allen E. *v.1 p.4*
McCormick, James M. *v.3 p.386*
McCormick, John & Pratasik, Bennie *v.1 p.93, p.97*
McCormick, John *v.1 p.93, p.101, v.3 p.87*
McCormick, Michael *v.3 p.66*
McCormick, Peter & Elliston, Frederick A. (Editors) . *v.1 p.470*
McCormick, Richard W. *v.6 p.338*

McCormmach, Russell K.. . . . . *v.5 p.543*
McCourt, Frank *v.4 p.338*
McCoy, Alfred W. & De Jesus, Ed. C. (Editors). . . . *v.4 p.705*
McCoy, Alfred W. *v.6 p.164*
McCoy, Alfred *v.4 p.562*
McCoy, Donald R.. . . . . *v.3 p.448, p.461, p.475*
McCoy, Drew R.. . . . . *v.6 p.295*
McCoy, Horace, et al.. . . . . *v.2 p.20*
McCoy, Horace *v.2 p.97*
McCoy, Judy *v.1 p.168, p.272, p.281*
McCoy, Neal H. *v.5 p.474*
McCoy, Roger M. *v.4 p.389*
McCracken, Ellen (Editor) *v.6 p.491, p.514*
McCracken-Flesher, Caroline *v.2 p.307*
McCrady, Barbara S. & Epstein, Elizabeth E.
(Editors). *v.5 p.512, p.517, p.522*
McCrae, Robert R. & Costa, Paul T. Jr. *v.5 p.658*
McCrary, Peyton *v.3 p.507*
McCraw, Thomas K. (Introduction by). . . . *v.4 p.147, p.148*
McCray, W. Patrick *v.5 p.65*
McCrea, Scott *v.2 p.231*
McCrisken, Trevor B. & Pepper, Andrew . . *v.6 p.315, p.342*
McCrone, Kathleen E. *v.4 p.808, p.837*
McCrum, Robert, et al.. . . . . *v.2 p.555*
McCrum, Robert *v.2 p.390*
McCullers, Carson & Dews, C. L. Barney *v.2 p.100*
McCullers, Carson *v.2 p.100*
McCulloch, Alan *v.1 p.665*
McCulloch, Jock *v.6 p.74*
McCulloch, John R. *v.4 p.216, p.240*
McCullough, Colleen *v.2 p.747*
McCullough, David *v.3 p.415, p.475*
McCullough, Helen Craig (Translator) *v.6 p.231*
McCullough, Helen Craig *v.6 p.225*
McCullough, James P. Jr.. . . . . . . *v.5 p.660, p.665*
McCullough, Laura L. & Tanner, Brenda M. . . . *v.4 p.288*
McCumber, John *v.1 p.471*
McCunn, Ruthanne Lum *v.6 p.94*
McCunney, Robert J., et al. *v.5 p.535*
McCusker, John J. *v.4 p.57, p.147, p.175, p.180*
McCutcheon, Chuck *v.6 p.300*
McCutcheon, Russell T. (Editor). *v.1 p.521*
McCutcheon, Scott & McCutcheon, Bobbi *v.5 p.428*
McDaniel, Anita K. & McDaniel, Clyde O. *v.6 p.40*
McDaniel, Carl N. & Gowdy, John M.. . . . . . *v.6 p.298*
McDannell, Colleen *v.1 p.764*
McDarrah, Timothy S., et al. *v.1 p.762*
McDavid, Raven I. Jr. *v.2 p.552*
McDermott, Alice *v.2 p.150*
McDermott, Henry J.. . . . . *v.5 p.355, p.378*
McDermott, Kevin & Agnew, Jeremy *v.4 p.509*
McDermott, Rachel Fell *v.6 p.152*
McDermott, Rose *v.4 p.484, p.642, v.5 p.644*
McDonagh, Don *v.1 p.4, p.10, p.27*
McDonagh, Eileen *v.4 p.472*

McDonagh, Maitland *v.6 p.314*
McDonald, Archie P. (Editor) *v.6 p.324*
McDonald, David A. (Editor) *v.6 p.300*
McDonald, Forrest. *v.3 p.378, p.412, p.414, p.415, p.417, v.4 p.517*
McDonald, Gail. *v.2 p.72, p.112*
McDonald, Hamish. *v.6 p.177*
McDonald, Ian & Brown, Stewart *v.2 p.768*
McDonald, James H.. . . . . *v.4 p.45*
McDonald, Keiko (Editor) *v.6 p.344*
McDonald, Keiko I. *v.6 p.327, p.336*
McDonald, Lee Martin & Porter, Stanley E. *v.1 p.624*
McDonald, Lynn *v.4 p.683*
McDonald, Malcolm & Keegan, Warren J. *v.4 p.144*
McDonald, Malcolm & Morris, Peter *v.4 p.135*
McDonald, Miller B. & Copeland, Lawrence O.. . . *v.5 p.48*
McDonald, Nan & Fisher, Douglas. *v.4 p.364*
McDonald, Nicola (Editor) *v.6 p.565*
McDonald, Patrick H.. . . . . *v.5 p.686*
McDonald, Peter & Lassoie, James P. (Editors). *v.4 p.164, v.5 p.38*
McDonald, Peter (Editor) *v.5 p.50*
McDonald, Robert A. *v.6 p.714*
McDonald, Robert L. (Editor) *v.2 p.66*
McDonald, Roderick P. *v.4 p.689*
McDonald, Russ (Editor) *v.1 p.76, p.101, v.2 p.222, p.231*
McDonogh, Gary (Editor), et al.. . . . . *v.3 p.443*
McDonough, John (Editor) *v.4 p.140, p.426*
McDonough, Kevin & Feinberg, Walter (Editors) . . . *v.4 p.323*
McDonough, Peter, et al. *v.4 p.608*
McDonough, William & Braungart, Michael *v.5 p.319*
McDonough, William. *v.6 p.298*
McDougal, Myres Smith *v.4 p.478*
McDougall, Len *v.4 p.788*
McDougall, Richard *v.2 p.119*
McDowall, David *v.6 p.599*
McDowell, Deborah E.. . . . . . . *v.6 p.27, p.45, p.479*
McDowell, Gary L.. . . . . *v.4 p.538*
McDowell, George R.. . . . . *v.5 p.5*
McDowell, John (Translator) *v.1 p.424*
McDowell, Margaret B.. . . . . *v.2 p.100*
McEachern, Claire (Editor) *v.1 p.76, v.2 p.235*
McElheny, Victor K. *v.5 p.122*
McElheran, Brock *v.1 p.402*
McElhinny, Michael W. & McFadden, Phillip L. . . . *v.5 p.443*
McEliece, Robert J.. . . . . *v.5 p.408*
McEllhennery, John G. (Editor), et al. *v.1 p.586*
McElrath, J.. . . . . *v.2 p.49*
McElrath, Joseph R. (Editor) *v.2 p.32*
McElrath, Joseph R. Jr. & Crisler, Jesse S.. . . . . *v.2 p.49*
McElroy, Ann & Townsend, Patricia K. *v.5 p.536, p.537, p.539*
McElroy, Michael B. *v.5 p.426*
McElvaine, Robert S. (Editor) *v.3 p.443*
McElvaine, Robert S.. . . . . *v.3 p.475*
McErlain, Alex. *v.1 p.808*

McEuen, Melissa A. *v.1 p.706, p.764*
McEvedy, Colin *v.3 p.3*
McEvoy, James E. (Editor) *v.5 p.264*
McEvoy, James *v.1 p.433*
McEvoy, John & McEvoy, Julia *v.4 p.837, p.848*
McEvoy, Thom J. *v.5 p.39*
McEwan, Bonnie G. (Editor) *v.4 p.11, v.6 p.703*
McEwan, Colin (Editor), et al. *v.4 p.12*
McEwan, Elaine K. *v.4 p.360*
McEwan, Ian *v.2 p.367, p.368*
McEwan, Peter J. *v.1 p.665*
McEwen, John *v.1 p.780*
McEwen, William J. *v.4 p.142*
McFadden, D. & Fuss, M. *v.4 p.248*
McFadden, George *v.2 p.246*
McFadden, Johnjoe. *v.5 p.194*
McFadyen, Alistair Iain *v.1 p.643*
McFadyen, Alistair I. *v.1 p.643*
McFall, Liz *v.4 p.141*
McFarland, David J. *v.5 p.166, p.170*
McFarland, Linda *v.3 p.461*
McFarlane, Anthony *v.3 p.356*
McFarlane, Brian (Editor), et al. *v.6 p.337*
McFarlane, I. D. *v.2 p.456*
McFarlane, James (Editor) *v.2 p.627*
McFarlane, James W. *v.2 p.627*
McFarlane, K. B. *v.6 p.572*
McFarlane, Kenneth Bruce *v.6 p.576*
McFarlane, Robert C. & Smardz, Zofia. *v.3 p.475*
McFee, Graham *v.1 p.43, p.47*
McFeely, William S. *v.3 p.399, p.437*
McGahan, Anita M. *v.4 p.81, p.149*
McGann, Jerome J. (Editor) *v.2 p.197, p.200*
McGann, Jerome J. *v.2 p.164, p.172, p.183, p.191,
                                    p.274, p.306, p.567, p.569*
McGann, Jerome J.,(ed) *v.2 p.304*
McGann, Jerome. *v.6 p.737, p.755*
McGaugh, James L. *v.5 p.610*
McGavin, George C. *v.5 p.213*
McGavran, Donald A. *v.1 p.647*
McGeary, M. Nelson *v.3 p.434*
McGee, Glenn *v.5 p.122, p.135*
McGee, Harold *v.5 p.34, p.35*
McGee, Lea M. & Richgels, Donald J. *v.4 p.368*
McGee, Marty *v.6 p.351*
McGee, Micki *v.5 p.669*
McGee, Owen *v.3 p.139*
McGee, Timothy J. & Rosenfield, Randall A. . . . *v.1 p.177*
McGee, Timothy J. (Editor) *v.1 p.177*
McGee, Timothy J. *v.1 p.278*
McGerr, Michael E. *v.4 p.552*
McGhee, George R. Jr. *v.5 p.155*
McGhee, Robert. *v.4 p.11, p.379*
McGill, Dan, et al. *v.4 p.98*
McGill, Ralph *v.3 p.497*

McGilligan, Patrick. *v.6 p.419*
McGillivray, Alice V., et al. *v.4 p.556*
McGimpsey, David. *v.4 p.818, p.851*
McGinn, Bernard A. (Editor) *v.1 p.529*
McGinn, Bernard (Translator) *v.1 p.645*
McGinn, Bernard *v.1 p.600, p.645, p.653*
McGinn, Colin. *v.1 p.497*
McGinn, Marie & Wittgenstein, Ludwig Josef Johann . *v.1 p.472*
McGinniss, Joe. *v.3 p.449*
McGlew, James F. *v.4 p.500*
McGoldrick, Dominic, et al. *v.6 p.268*
McGoldrick, Dominic *v.4 p.655, p.660*
McGoldrick, Monica (Editor), et al. *v.5 p.668*
McGough, Lucy S. *v.4 p.473*
McGovern, George *v.4 p.247*
McGovern, James R. *v.3 p.475*
McGovern, Patrick E. *v.5 p.52*
McGovern, Thomas V. (Editor) *v.5 p.676*
McGovern, William Montgomery *v.6 p.241*
McGowan, Christopher *v.3 p.49, p.50, v.5 p.157*
McGowan, Danny & Alexander, F. M. (Editors) . . . *v.1 p.52*
McGowan, Margaret M. *v.3 p.146*
McGowan, Maryrose *v.1 p.803*
McGown, Carl, et al. *v.4 p.869, p.904*
McGrade, A. S. (Editor) *v.1 p.433*
McGrade, Arthur Stephen *v.4 p.490*
McGrath, Alister E. & Marks, Darren C. (Editors). . *v.1 p.580*
McGrath, Alister E. (Editor, Introduction by) . . . *v.1 p.594*
McGrath, Alister E. *v.1 p.526, p.545, p.597, p.602,
                                    p.632, p.644, p.645, p.650*
McGrath, Declan. *v.6 p.350*
McGrath, Patrick J. *v.5 p.394, p.412*
McGrath, Rita Gunther & MacMillan, Ian C. *v.4 p.68*
McGrath, Tom. *v.1 p.256, p.272*
McGraw-Hill Staff. *v.1 p.60, v.5 p.28, p.245, p.387,
                                    p.395, p.545, p.679, v.6 p.286*
McGraw-Hill *v.5 p.387, p.417, v.6 p.284*
McGrayne, Sharon Bertsch *v.5 p.261*
McGreal, Wilfred. *v.1 p.579*
McGreevey, Tom & Yeck, Joanne L. *v.6 p.331*
McGreevey, W. P. *v.3 p.357*
McGreevy, John T. *v.4 p.486*
McGregor, Douglas. *v.4 p.120*
McGregor, J. F. *v.3 p.104, p.121*
McGregor, James H. S. *v.6 p.194, p.197*
McGregor, Richard (Editor). *v.1 p.218, p.320*
Mcgregor, Robert K. *v.2 p.52*
McGregor, Robert Kuhn & Lewis, Ethan *v.2 p.381*
McGrew, Roderick E. *v.3 p.216*
McGrew, William C. *v.5 p.615*
McGuane, Thomas *v.2 p.150*
McGuckin, John Anthony *v.1 p.633*
McGuigan, Patrick B. & Weyrich, Dawn M. *v.4 p.538*
McGuinness, Kevin. *v.4 p.298*
McGuire, C. B. & Radner, Roy (Editors) *v.4 p.269*

McGuirk, Bernard & Cardwell, Richard (Editors) . . . *v.2 p.683*

McGuirk, Carol (Editor) *v.2 p.273*

McHale, James P. & Grolnick, Wendy S. (Editors) . *v.5 p.639*

McHam, Sarah Blake (Editor,
   Contribution by) *v.1 p.774, p.775, p.777*

McHaney, Pearl A. *v.2 p.130*

McHenry, Elizabeth *v.6 p.27*

McHugh, Heather *v.2 p.150*

McHugh, Roland & Joyce, James *v.2 p.360*

McIllwain, Jeffrey Scott *v.6 p.119, p.124, p.127*

McIlvaine, Eileen, et al. *v.2 p.390*

McInerny, D. Q. *v.1 p.492*

McInnis, Thomas N. *v.6 p.269*

McIntire, Sandra A. & Miller, Leslie A. *v.5 p.601*

McIntosh, Roderick J. *v.6 p.68*

McIntyre, Angus *v.6 p.175, p.177*

McIntyre, Ian *v.2 p.273*

McIntyre, Rosemary *v.5 p.530*

McIver, Stuart B. *v.6 p.295*

McJimsey, George *v.3 p.443, p.461, p.475*

McKay, Ailsa *v.4 p.274*

McKay, Alexander G. & Shepherd, D. M. (Editors) . *v.2 p.427*

McKay, Claude *v.2 p.97, v.3 p.491, v.6 p.714*

McKay, David P. & Crawford, Richard. . . . *v.1 p.279, p.311*

McKay, George *v.4 p.709*

McKay, Jim, et al. *v.4 p.818, p.837*

McKay, Jim *v.4 p.837*

McKay, Nellie Y. *v.2 p.126*

McKay, Susan *v.3 p.135, p.140*

McKeague, Charles P. & Turner, Mark *v.5 p.485*

McKee, Christopher *v.3 p.412*

McKee, Robert. *v.6 p.353*

McKeen, William (Editor). *v.1 p.272*

McKeever, Daniel (Editor) *v.4 p.297*

McKeever, Robert J. *v.4 p.538*

McKeever-Furst, Jill L. *v.3 p.261*

McKelvey, Blake. *v.6 p.273*

McKelvey, Maureen & Orsenigo, Luigi *v.4 p.156*

McKendrick, Jamie. *v.2 p.700*

McKendrick, Melveena *v.2 p.640*

McKendrick, Neil, et al. *v.3 p.123, p.129*

McKenna, Neil. *v.6 p.402*

McKenna, Peter & Oh, Tomasina *v.5 p.661*

McKenna, Richard *v.6 p.190, p.216*

McKenna, Teresa *v.6 p.501, p.514*

McKenna, Wayne *v.2 p.298*

McKenry, Leda M., et al. *v.5 p.526*

McKenzie, Brian Angus. *v.3 p.390*

McKenzie, D. F. *v.2 p.577*

McKenzie, Norman & McKenzie, Jeanne (Editors) . *v.4 p.193*

McKenzie, Phyllis *v.6 p.532*

McKenzie, Richard B. *v.4 p.82*

McKenzie, Walter *v.4 p.351*

McKeon, Michael (Author, Introduction by) . . *v.2 p.192, p.578*

McKeon, Michael *v.2 p.578*

McKeon, Richard & Aristotle *v.1 p.426*

McKercher, B J; Aronsen, Lawrence *v.3 p.537*

McKercher, B. J. *v.3 p.390*

McKerrow, Raymie E. & Gronbeck, Bruce *v.4 p.423*

McKerrow, Ronald B. *v.2 p.231*

McKerrow, Ronald Brunlees *v.2 p.231*

McKetta, Frank *v.6 p.260*

McKibben, Bill (Editor) *v.5 p.80, p.226*

McKie, Linda *v.6 p.259*

McKiernan, Kevin *v.6 p.599*

McKillop, A. B. *v.3 p.535*

McKim, Donald K. (Editor) *v.1 p.589, v.3 p.166*

McKim, Donald K. *v.1 p.589*

McKim, Robert & McMahan, Jeff (Editors). *v.4 p.494*

McKinion, Steven A. (Editor) *v.1 p.655*

McKinley, Catherine E. *v.6 p.407*

McKinley, Edward H. *v.1 p.589, v.6 p.56*

McKinney, Francis F. *v.3 p.426*

McKinney, Gordon B. *v.4 p.542*

McKinney, James C. *v.1 p.395, p.405*

McKinney, John *v.4 p.788*

McKinney, Louise *v.3 p.507*

McKinney, M. L. & McNamara, K. J. *v.5 p.194*

McKinney, M. L. *v.5 p.194*

McKinnon, James W. (Editor) *v.1 p.175*

McKinnon, James *v.1 p.178*

McKinnon, Sharon M. & Bruns, William J. Jr. . . . *v.4 p.106*

McKinnon, Susan & Silverman, Sydel (Editors) . . . *v.4 p.24*

McKitrick, Eric L. (Editor) *v.3 p.420*

McKitrick, Eric L. *v.3 p.437*

McKitterick, David *v.3 p.37*

McKitterick, Rosamond (Editor) *v.4 p.381, v.6 p.569*

McKitterick, Rosamond *v.3 p.143, p.162*

McKivigan, John R. *v.3 p.420*

McKnight, Edgar V. & Via, Dan O. Jr. *v.1 p.616*

McKnight, Kathryn Joy *v.3 p.263*

McKnight, Lee W. (Editor), et al. *v.4 p.421*

McKnight, Scot & Osborne, Grant R. (Editors) . . . *v.1 p.625*

McKnight, Thomas K. *v.4 p.68*

McKnight, Thomas *v.1 p.760*

McKnight, Tom L. *v.4 p.382, p.397*

McKusick, James C. *v.3 p.45, v.6 p.287*

McLachlan, Geoffrey J., et al. *v.5 p.102, p.141*

McLafferty, Fred W. & Stauffer, Douglas B. *v.5 p.271*

McLafferty, Fred W. & Turecek, Frantisek *v.5 p.271*

McLafferty, Fred W. *v.5 p.271*

McLanahan, Sara & Sandefur, Gary D. *v.4 p.739*

McLanahan, Sara S. (Editor), et al. *v.4 p.756*

McLane, Joan B. & McNamee, Gillian D. *v.4 p.360*

McLaren, John & Coward, Harold (Editors) *v.1 p.656*

McLaren, Peter. *v.4 p.297*

McLaughlin, Andrew Cunningham. *v.4 p.518*

McLaughlin, Eugene & Muncie, John (Editors) . . . *v.6 p.246*

McLaughlin, Martin L. *v.2 p.715*

McLaughlin, Mary Martin *v.3 p.68*

McLaughlin, Peter *v.5 p.170, p.194*

McLaughlin, R. E. *v.1 p.603*

McLean, Bethany & Elkind, Peter *v.4 p.91, p.105, p.106, p.109, p.148*

McLean, David *v.3 p.345*

McLean, Iain & McMillan, Alistair *v.4 p.482*

McLean, Mervyn. *v.1 p.289*

McLeary, Joseph Webb, et al. *v.4 p.173, p.175*

McLeavey, Dennis W. & Solnik, Bruno *v.4 p.96*

McLeish, Kenneth & Griffiths, Trevor *v.1 p.71*

McLellan, David *v.4 p.236*

McLellan, John *v.1 p.596*

McLendon, Jacquelyn Y. *v.2 p.4*

McLennan, A.G., et al. *v.5 p.128*

McLeod, Hugh (Editor) *v.1 p.611, p.612*

McLeod, Hugh *v.1 p.531, p.609*

McLeod, Mary & Aujame, Roger *v.1 p.802*

McLeod, Peter, et al. *v.5 p.591*

McLeod, Robin J. Y. & Baart, M. Louisa. *v.5 p.497*

McLeod, W. H. *v.1 p.540, p.541*

M'Closkey, Kathy *v.1 p.716, p.809, v.6 p.679*

McLoughlin, Leslie. *v.6 p.654*

McLoughlin, Thomas *v.3 p.137*

McLoughlin, William G. . *v.1 p.583, v.3 p.489, v.6 p.687, p.688*

McLuhan, Marshall & Fiore, Quentin *v.5 p.625*

McLuhan, Marshall *v.2 p.577, v.4 p.416, v.5 p.625*

McLure, Roger. *v.1 p.500*

McLynn, Neil *v.3 p.32*

McMahan, Jeff *v.1 p.486, v.3 p.475*

McMahon, Anthony. *v.4 p.745, v.6 p.446*

McMahon, April M. S. *v.2 p.563*

McMahon, Darrin M. *v.3 p.72*

McMahon, Kevin J. (Editor), et al. *v.3 p.484*

McMahon, Robert J. *v.3 p.391*

McMahon, Robert *v.6 p.300*

McMahon, Thomas A. *v.4 p.909*

McMann, Evelyn D. (Compiled by) *v.1 p.665*

McManners, John (Editor) *v.1 p.598*

McManners, John *v.3 p.151*

McManus, Barbara F. *v.2 p.399, v.6 p.463*

McManus, Chris *v.5 p.594*

McMaster, Carolyn *v.6 p.76*

McMaster, Graham (comp./editor) *v.2 p.324*

McMaster, Marvin & McMaster, Christopher *v.5 p.271*

McMaster, Marvin C. *v.5 p.269*

McMaster, Susan E. *v.4 p.166*

McMeekin, Robert *v.4 p.280*

McMenamin, Donna *v.1 p.684*

McMenamin, Mark A. & McMenamin, Dianna L. . . . *v.5 p.176*

McMillan, Gregory K. & Considine, Douglas M. . . . *v.4 p.116*

McMillan, James B. & Montgomery, Michael. . . . *v.2 p.552*

McMillan, Victoria E.. . . . . *v.5 p.245*

McMillin, Arnold (Editor). *v.2 p.799*

McMinn, Winston G.. . . . . *v.4 p.624*

McMullen, Emerson Thomas (Editor, Translator) . . . *v.5 p.510*

McMullin, Ernan (Editor) *v.5 p.410*

McMullin, Neil *v.1 p.562*

McMullin, Thomas A. & Walker, David *v.3 p.376*

McMurray, Emily J. & Olendorf, Donna (Editors). . . *v.5 p.395*

McMurray, George R. (Editor). *v.2 p.683*

McMurray, George R. *v.2 p.680, p.684*

McMurray Robert G *v.4 p.791, p.903*

McMurrer, Daniel P. & Sawhill, Isabel V. *v.4 p.266*

McMurry, Sally Ann. *v.5 p.30*

McMurtrey, Martin. *v.6 p.489, p.520*

McMurtry, Larry *v.2 p.150*

McNair, Harold M. & Miller, James M. *v.5 p.269*

Mcnair, Jeffrey L. *v.3 p.544*

McNally, Dennis *v.2 p.93*

McNally, Michael J. *v.6 p.520, p.532*

McNally, Terrence *v.6 p.412*

McNamara, Kenneth J. *v.5 p.194*

McNamara, Robert P. *v.6 p.256*

McNamara, Robert S. & Blight, James G. *v.4 p.562*

McNamee, Mike (Editor) *v.4 p.802, p.873*

McNaron, Toni A. *v.6 p.385*

McNaught, Brian. *v.6 p.369*

McNeely, Jeffrey A. & Miller, Kenton R. (Editors). *v.5 p.17, p.18*

McNeese, Tim *v.3 p.522*

McNeil, Genna Rae *v.6 p.12, p.21, p.22*

McNeil, John D. *v.4 p.364*

McNeil, Legs & McCain, Gillian *v.1 p.272*

McNeil, Legs & Osborne, Jennifer. *v.6 p.317*

McNeil, W. K. *v.1 p.161, p.296*

McNeill, F. Martin & Thro, Ellen *v.5 p.711*

McNeill, J. R. *v.5 p.28, p.356, p.358, v.6 p.296*

McNeill, John J. *v.6 p.373*

McNeill, John Thomas *v.1 p.589*

McNeill, William H. *v.3 p.36, v.5 p.370, v.6 p.296*

McNeillie, Andrew (Editor) *v.2 p.393*

McNeillie, Andrew (Introduction by). *v.2 p.393*

McNerney, Kathleen *v.2 p.684*

McNett, Jeanne *v.4 p.57, p.64, p.180*

McNickle, D'Arcy. *v.2 p.97, v.6 p.692*

McPeck, John E., et al. *v.4 p.344*

McPhail, Helen & Guest, Philip *v.2 p.348*

McPhee, Colin. *v.1 p.289, v.6 p.175, p.177*

McPhee, John *v.5 p.432*

McPherran, Mark L. *v.1 p.422*

McPherson, Alan L. *v.3 p.305*

McPherson, James Alan. *v.2 p.150*

McPherson, James M. . . . *v.3 p.399, p.420, p.431, v.4 p.521*

McPherson, Maggie & Nunes, Miguel Baptista . . . *v.4 p.322*

McPherson, Michael S. & Schapiro, Morton Owen . *v.4 p.293*

McQuarrie, Donald & Simon, John *v.5 p.278*

McQuarrie, Donald A. & Simon, John D.. . . . . *v.5 p.278*

McQuarrie, Donald A. *v.5 p.559*

McQuarrie, Edward F. *v.4 p.136*

McQueen, E. I. *v.2 p.412*

McQuiston, Liz *v.1 p.713*

McRae, Andrew. *v.1 p.75, p.101, v.2 p.195*
McRae, John R. *v.1 p.568*
McRay, John. *v.1 p.626*
McRoberts, Kenneth (Editor) *v.3 p.541*
McRoy, Jay (Editor) *v.6 p.319, p.336*
McRue, Robert. *v.6 p.393*
McShea, William J. & Healy, William M. . . . *v.5 p.185, p.240*
McSherry, Corynne. *v.4 p.446*
McSherry, J. Patrice *v.3 p.275, v.4 p.660*
McSween, Harry Y. Jr., et al. *v.5 p.440*
McSweeney's Editors (Created by). *v.2 p.583*
McTyre, Ruthann B. (Compiled by) *v.1 p.168, p.395*
McVeigh, Simon & Hirshberg, Jehoash. *v.1 p.185*
McVey, Ruth (Editor) *v.6 p.171*
McWhinney, Edward *v.4 p.590*
McWhorter, John. *v.2 p.552*
McWilliams, Carey & Meier, Matt S.. . . . *v.3 p.527, v.6 p.532*
McWilliams, Carey *v.5 p.5, p.30*
McWilliams, Dean. *v.2 p.32*
McWilliams, Margaret *v.5 p.35*
Mda, Zakes *v.2 p.756*
Meacham, Standish. *v.3 p.113, p.131*
Mead, Andrew. *v.1 p.218, p.302*
Mead, Chris *v.4 p.832, p.855*
Mead, Frank S. *v.1 p.544, p.605*
Mead, George Herbert *v.1 p.438, p.442, v.4 p.693*
Mead, Margaret & Lutkehaus, Nancy *v.4 p.23*
Mead, Margaret & Wolfenstein, Martha (Editors) . . . *v.4 p.735*
Mead, Margaret *v.3 p.369, v.4 p.23, p.43, p.748*
Mead, Robert Douglas (Author, Illustrator) *v.4 p.700*
Mead, W. R. & Hall, Wendy *v.3 p.232, p.233*
Mead, W. R.. . . . . *v.3 p.232, p.233*
Mead, Walter Russell *v.4 p.560, p.564, p.642*
Meade, Guthrie Jr.. . . . . *v.1 p.168, p.170, p.272*
Meade, Marion *v.2 p.11, p.110*
Meade, Teresa A.. . . . . *v.3 p.341*
Meadow, Charles T. *v.4 p.418, p.422*
Meadows, Dennis, et al. *v.4 p.763*
Meadows, Eddie S. *v.1 p.168, p.261, p.262, p.405*
Meadows, James D. *v.5 p.535*
Meale, Carol M. (Editor) *v.6 p.560, p.565*
Mealing, Stuart (Editor). *v.1 p.771*
Means, Barbara, et al. *v.4 p.351*
Means, Russell & Wolf, Marvin J.. . . . . *v.6 p.694*
Meckier, Jerome (Editor) *v.2 p.354*
Meckier, Jerome *v.2 p.354*
Meconi, Honey *v.1 p.180, p.335*
Medalie, David. *v.2 p.346*
Medawar, Peter Brian *v.5 p.400, p.403*
Medding, Peter Y. *v.4 p.615*
Medema, Steven G. & Samuels, Warren J. *v.4 p.209*
Mediamark Research Inc. *v.4 p.137, p.138, p.139*
Medical Economics Staff, et al. *v.5 p.526*
Medical Economics Staff *v.5 p.526*
Medin, Douglas L. (Editor) *v.5 p.574*

Medin, Tzvi *v.3 p.311*
Medina, Lara. *v.6 p.435, p.459, p.465, p.520, p.546*
Medina, Pablo *v.3 p.311, v.6 p.489, p.507*
Medley, H. Anthony *v.4 p.170*
Medlik, S.. *v.4 p.161*
Medved, Michael. *v.6 p.321*
Mee, Erin (Editor) *v.1 p.129, p.131, v.6 p.148*
Mee, Jon *v.2 p.240*
Meek, Christine & Lawless, Catherine (Editors). . . *v.6 p.560*
Meek, Margaret *v.4 p.361*
Meeks, Brian ; Lindahl, Folke. *v.4 p.685*
Meeks, Brian *v.3 p.302, p.320*
Meeks, Wayne A.. . . . . *v.1 p.627*
Meese, Edwin III. *v.3 p.475*
Meester, Ronald *v.5 p.484*
Meeus, Jean H. *v.5 p.64*
Megarry, Tim *v.4 p.17*
Megged, Aharon *v.6 p.650*
Meggitt, Mervyn J. *v.4 p.43*
Meglitsch, Paul A. & Schram, Frederick R.. . . . . *v.5 p.213*
Mehlinger, Howard D. & Powers, Susan M. *v.4 p.352*
Mehlman, Maxwell J. & Botkin, Jeffrey R.. . . . . *v.5 p.135*
Mehmed, Pasha *v.6 p.590*
Meho, Lokman I. & Maglaughlin,
    Kelly L. (Compiled by) *v.6 p.599, p.668*
Meho, Lokman I. *v.6 p.599*
Mehra, Jagdish & Milton, Kimball. *v.5 p.543*
Mehrens, William A. & Lehmann, Irvin J. *v.5 p.604*
Mehring, Margaret *v.6 p.353*
Mehrotra, Arvind Krishna. *v.2 p.762*
Mehta, Dinesh P. & Sahni, Sartaj (Editors). . . *v.5 p.335, p.344*
Mehta, Kishor C. & Delahay, James M. *v.5 p.686*
Mehta, Kishor *v.5 p.686*
Mehta, Uday Singh. *v.4 p.511, p.583*
Mehta, Ved *v.1 p.446*
Meid, Volker. *v.2 p.591*
Meier, Andrew. *v.3 p.229*
Meier, Christian *v.2 p.428, v.3 p.18*
Meier, Daniel *v.4 p.315, p.361*
Meier, David *v.4 p.68*
Meier, Deborah *v.4 p.328*
Meier, Heinz K. *v.3 p.245*
Meier, John & Rishel, Thomas *v.5 p.463*
Meier, John P. *v.1 p.627*
Meier, Kenneth J. & Stewart, Joseph Jr. *v.6 p.527*
Meier, Matt S. & Gutierrez, Margo *v.6 p.485*
Meier, Matt S. & Rivera, Feliciano *v.6 p.532*
Meier, Matt S., et al. *v.6 p.485, p.489*
Meier, Richard & Allen, Stan *v.1 p.794*
Meiggs, Russell & Lewis, David M. (Editors) *v.3 p.18*
Meiggs, Russell *v.3 p.18*
Meij, Bram (Contribution by), et al. *v.1 p.722*
Meijer, Fik J. & Van Nifj, Onno *v.3 p.23*
Meijer, Fik *v.3 p.23*
Meijer, Reinder P. *v.2 p.622*

Meikle, Jeffrey L.. . . . . *v.1 p.714, v.5 p.319*

Meiklejohn, Alexander *v.4 p.290, p.344*

Meillassoux, Claude *v.4 p.28*

Meilman, Patricia (Editor). *v.1 p.744*

Meinardus, Otto F.. . . . . *v.1 p.569*

Meine, Franklin J.. . . . . *v.2 p.21*

Meinecke, Friedrich *v.3 p.178*

Meiners, Harry F. (Editor). *v.5 p.563*

Meiners, R. K.. . . . . *v.2 p.125*

Meinesz, Alexandre. *v.5 p.208*

Meinig, D. W. *v.3 p.509*

Meinig, Donald W. *v.3 p.380, p.527, p.530*

Meintjes, Louise *v.1 p.285*

Meir, Avinoam *v.6 p.596*

Meisami, Julie S. (Editor, Translator). *v.6 p.630*

Meisel, John. *v.4 p.587*

Meisel, Joseph S.. . . . . *v.6 p.758*

Meisel, Martin *v.6 p.737*

Meisler, Stanley *v.4 p.634*

Meislich, Herbert, et al.. . . . . *v.5 p.301*

Meisner, Maurice J. *v.6 p.192, p.200*

Meisner, Maurice. *v.6 p.194*

Meissner, Rolf *v.5 p.419*

Meister, David & Enderwick, Thomas P.. . . . . . *v.5 p.587*

Meister, David *v.5 p.587*

Meister, Maureen (Editor). *v.1 p.794*

Meital, Yoram *v.6 p.618*

Mekenkamp, Monique (Editor), et al. *v.4 p.623, p.650*

Melady, Thomas & Melady, Margaret *v.6 p.66*

Melakopides, Costas *v.3 p.541*

Melamed, Daniel R. & Marissen, Michael. *v.1 p.164, p.185, p.304*

Melamed, Daniel R.. . . . . . . *v.1 p.185, p.236, p.303*

Melamed, Leo & Tamarkin, Bob *v.4 p.89, p.148*

Melaragno, Michele G. *v.5 p.698*

Melby, Pete & Cathcart, Tom *v.1 p.817*

Melendez, Edgardo. *v.6 p.538*

Melendez, Edwin & Melendez, Edgardo (Editors). . . *v.6 p.522*

Melendez, Miguel *v.6 p.540*

Melendez Valdes, Juan *v.2 p.655*

Melendy, H. Brett *v.3 p.534*

Melfi, Rudy C., et al.. . . . . *v.5 p.525*

Melhado, Evan M. & Frängsmyr, Tore (Editors). . . *v.5 p.263*

Melhus, Bjorn (Editor), et al. *v.1 p.773*

Meli, Francis *v.4 p.614, v.6 p.79*

Melia, Fulvio *v.5 p.71*

Melissa Cast *v.4 p.280*

Melissinos, Adrian C. & Napolitano, Jim *v.5 p.563*

Mellars, Paul *v.4 p.17*

Mellen, Joan. *v.2 p.684, v.6 p.336, p.344*

Meller, Susan & Elffers, Joost *v.1 p.809*

Mellerio, Andre *v.1 p.757*

Mellers, Wilfrid *v.1 p.185, p.218, p.319, p.348, v.6 p.409*

Melley, Timothy (Contribution by) *v.4 p.709*

Melling, David J. & Griffith, Sidney H. *v.1 p.569*

Mello, Renato Gonzalez & Ades, Dawn *v.1 p.744*

Mellon, M. G.. . . . . *v.5 p.255*

Mellor, Anne K.. . . . . *v.2 p.172, p.310*

Mellor, Joseph William *v.5 p.303*

Mellor, Ronald (Editor) *v.3 p.22*

Mellor, Ronald. *v.2 p.426, p.444*

Mellor, Roy *v.4 p.495*

Mellow, James R. (Author, Illustrator). *v.2 p.77*

Mellow, James R. *v.2 p.85*

Melnyk, Andrew *v.1 p.509*

Melnyk, Bernadette (Author, Author). *v.5 p.528*

Melnyk, Steven A. & Christensen,
 R. T. (Contribution by) *v.4 p.119*

Meloan, Clifton E.. . . . . *v.5 p.274*

Melone, Albert P. *v.4 p.585, p.600*

Melosh, H. J. *v.5 p.434*

Melosi, Martin V.. . . . . *v.5 p.706, v.6 p.728*

Melot, Michel *v.1 p.753*

Melson, Robert *v.3 p.85, v.4 p.653*

Melton, J. Gordon (Editor) . . . *v.1 p.527, p.528, p.544, p.605*

Melton, J. Gordon *v.1 p.544*

Melton, James Van Horn *v.3 p.72, p.167, p.183*

Melton, Reginald F. *v.4 p.322*

Meltsner, Michael *v.4 p.471*

Meltz, Robert, et al. *v.4 p.463*

Meltzer, Allan H.. . . . . *v.4 p.228*

Meltzer, Richard *v.1 p.272*

Melvern, Linda. *v.4 p.653, v.6 p.257*

Melville, Charles. *v.6 p.630*

Melville, Elinor G. K. *v.3 p.269, p.286*

Melville, Herman *v.2 p.48*

Melville, Joy *v.1 p.102, p.145*

Melville, Pauline *v.2 p.368*

Melville, Sara E. *v.5 p.141*

Melville, Tom *v.4 p.808, p.856*

Memon, Amina, et al.. . . . . *v.5 p.592*

Mena, Maria C.. . . . . *v.6 p.501*

Menair, Peter, et al.. . . . . *v.1 p.777, v.6 p.679*

Menand, Louis *v.1 p.439, p.513, v.2 p.72, v.4 p.298*

Menander *v.1 p.71, p.90, v.2 p.416*

Menard, Henry W. *v.5 p.391*

Menard, Scott *v.4 p.686*

MENC, the National Association for Music Education Staff
 (Contribution by) *v.1 p.405*

Menchaca, Martha. *v.6 p.532, p.540, p.544*

Menchu, Rigoberta *v.2 p.676*

Mencius *v.1 p.418*

Mencken, H. L. (Author, Editor). *v.3 p.443*

Mencken, H. L. *v.2 p.4, p.97, p.552, v.3 p.449*

Mendelsohn, Berk, et al. *v.5 p.520*

Mendelsohn, Oliver & Vicziany, Marika *v.6 p.149*

Mendelson, Edward *v.2 p.329*

Mendelson, Sara & Crawford, Patricia. . . . *v.3 p.52, v.6 p.452*

Mendelson, Wallace *v.4 p.470*

Mendelssohn, Moses *v.1 p.460*

Mendenhall, William, et al. *v.4 p.179, v.5 p.482*

Mendez, Miguel *v.6 p.501*

Mendez Rodenas, Adriana. *v.3 p.311*

Mendieta, Eduardo & Lange-Churion, Pedro (Editors) *v.1 p.444*

Mendieta, Eduardo (Editor) *v.1 p.444*

Mendoza, Louis Gerard. *v.6 p.514, p.532*

Mendoza, Susanah L. *v.6 p.129*

Mendoza, Tony. *v.3 p.311*

Mendras, Henri & Cole, Alistair *v.3 p.141, v.4 p.42*

Mendras, Henri *v.4 p.705*

Menendez, Albert J. *v.4 p.382*

Meney, Lionel *v.2 p.454*

Menéndez Pidal, Ramón *v.2 p.636, p.640, v.3 p.65*

Mengaldo, Pier von. *v.2 p.700*

Mengel, Konrad, et al. *v.5 p.22, p.45*

Menger, Carl. *v.4 p.234*

Menger, F. M. & Mandell, L. *v.5 p.301*

Menglin, Zhao & Jiqing, Yan *v.1 p.131, p.140, p.151*

Menifield, Charles E. & Shaffer, Stephen D. (Editors) *v.4 p.530*

Menikoff, Barry *v.2 p.312*

Menjivar, Cecilia. *v.6 p.530*

Menke, William *v.5 p.443*

Menkes, John H. *v.5 p.516*

Menkes, Justin *v.4 p.71*

Mennel, Robert M. *v.6 p.255*

Mennell, Stephen; Murcott, Anne Otterloo,
    Anneke H van *v.4 p.778*

Menning, Bruce W.. . . . . *v.3 p.212*

Menocal, Maria Rosa (Editor), et al. *v.6 p.662*

Menocal, Maria Rosa. *v.3 p.238*

Menon, Dilip M. *v.6 p.161*

Menon, Patricia *v.2 p.193*

Menon, Ritu & Bhasin, Kamla *v.6 p.159, p.454*

Menotti, Francesco *v.4 p.12*

Mensah, Joseph *v.3 p.542*

Mentasti, Rosa Barovier *v.1 p.810*

Mentzer, John T. & Moon, Mark A. *v.4 p.137*

Mentzer, John T. *v.4 p.118*

Menz, Christopher *v.1 p.802*

Menzel, Peter & D'Aluisio, Faith *v.5 p.711*

Menzies, John *v.5 p.425*

Mepham, Ben *v.5 p.248*

Mercatante, Anthony S. *v.1 p.527*

Mercer, Gina. *v.2 p.745*

Mercer, Michelle. *v.1 p.262, p.356*

Mercer-Taylor, Peter (Editor) *v.1 p.200, p.340*

Merchant, Carolyn *v.5 p.398, v.6 p.284, p.286*

Merck Staff, et al. *v.5 p.515*

Mercurio, Gianni & Morera, Danila (Editors) . . . *v.1 p.698*

Mercuro, Nicholas, et al.. . . . . *v.4 p.62*

Meredith, Anthony & Gregory. *v.1 p.593*

Meredith, George. *v.2 p.300*

Meredith, Martin *v.6 p.78*

Meredith, William. *v.2 p.97, p.780*

Meri, Josef W. (Editor) *v.6 p.574*

Meriwether, Margaret Lee & Tucker, Judith (Editors) *v.6 p.594*

Meriwether, Margaret Lee. *v.6 p.607*

Merk, Frederick & Merk, Lois B. *v.3 p.417*

Merk, Frederick *v.3 p.381, p.420, p.532*

Merkel, Jayne *v.1 p.794*

Merker, Paul & Stammler, Wolfgang *v.2 p.589*

Merkl, Peter H. (Editor). *v.4 p.602*

Merkl, Peter H. *v.3 p.170*

Merleau-Ponty, Maurice *v.1 p.457, p.508, p.511*

Merli, Frank J. *v.3 p.386*

Merlo, Alida V. & Benekos, Peter J. *v.6 p.248*

Mermin, Dorothy. *v.2 p.272, v.6 p.740, p.748*

Mernissi, Fatema *v.6 p.594*

Mernissi, Fatima *v.1 p.557, v.6 p.450, p.643*

Merot, Alain *v.1 p.744*

Merrell, Kenneth W. *v.5 p.602*

Merrens, H. Roy (Editor) *v.3 p.502*

Merriam, Alan P. *v.1 p.285*

Merriam, Sharan B. & Caffarella, Rosemary S. . . . *v.4 p.320*

Merriam-Webster, Inc. Staff *v.2 p.549, p.557, v.4 p.373*

Merrick, Gordon *v.6 p.397*

Merrick, Jeffrey W. & Sebalis, Michael (Editors) . . *v.6 p.421*

Merridale, Catherine *v.3 p.226, p.227*

Merrifield, Andrew *v.6 p.718*

Merrifield, Ralph *v.3 p.96, p.126*

Merrill, Christopher *v.3 p.247*

Merrill, George P. *v.5 p.418*

Merrill, Harwood F.. . . . . *v.4 p.116*

Merrill, Horace S. *v.3 p.506*

Merrill, James *v.2 p.100, p.101, v.6 p.398, p.405, p.412*

Merrill, John C. *v.4 p.405*

Merrill, Lisa. *v.6 p.413, p.414*

Merrill, Richard T., et al. *v.5 p.444*

Merrill, Robert *v.2 p.99, p.157*

Merrills, A. H. *v.6 p.60*

Merriman, A. *v.5 p.732*

Merriman, John (Editor). *v.3 p.149, v.4 p.705*

Merriman, John M.. . . . . *v.3 p.149*

Merriman, Nick & Schadla-Hall, Tim (Editors) *v.4 p.5*

Merriman, Roger B. *v.6 p.590*

Merriner, James L. *v.3 p.516*

Merritt, Frederick S., et al. *v.5 p.686*

Merritt, Helen & Yamada, Nanako *v.1 p.753*

Merritt, Jane T.. . . . . *v.6 p.686*

Merritt, Jennifer *v.4 p.176*

Merritt, Russell *v.6 p.308*

Merry, Henry J. *v.4 p.532*

Merry, Sally E. *v.4 p.33*

Merry, Sally Engle & Brenneis, Donald Lawrence . . . *v.4 p.43*

Merry, Sally Engle. *v.4 p.33, v.6 p.130*

Mersereau, Russell, et al. *v.5 p.721*

Mersmann, A. (Editor) *v.5 p.284*

Mertins, Detlef. *v.1 p.794*

Merton, Robert C. *v.4 p.238*

Merton, Robert K. *v.4 p.680, p.699*

Merton, Thomas. *v.1 p.578, p.643, v.2 p.98*

Mertus, Julie. *v.4 p.513*

Mertz, Annelise (Editor) *v.1 p.47*

Mertz, Barbara. *v.3 p.9, v.6 p.57*

Mervin, David *v.3 p.475*

Merwin, W. S.. . . . . *v.2 p.101, p.206, p.467, v.6 p.565*

Merzbacher, Eugen. *v.5 p.550*

Mes, Tom & Sharp, Jasper *v.6 p.306, p.336*

Mesa-Lago, Carmelo (Editor) *v.3 p.311*

Meserole, Harrison T. (Editor) *v.2 p.24*

Mesibov, Gary B., et al.. . . . . *v.5 p.658*

Meskell, Lynn. *v.6 p.57*

Mesquita, Ivo, et al. *v.1 p.816*

Messaris, Paul *v.1 p.715*

Messenger, Christian K.. . . . . *v.4 p.812*

Messenger, Troy *v.4 p.720*

Messent, Peter B. *v.2 p.33*

Messer, Robert & Straffin, Philip *v.5 p.499*

Messer, Thomas M.. . . . . *v.1 p.744*

Messerli, Jonathan *v.4 p.344*

Messerly, John G. *v.5 p.597*

Messerschmidt, James W.. . . . . *v.6 p.257*

Messiaen, Oliver *v.1 p.218, p.341, p.372*

Messiaen, Olivier, et al. *v.1 p.218, p.341*

Messiah, Albert *v.5 p.550*

Messick, David M. & Kramer, Roderick Moreland
(Editors) *v.5 p.648*

Messick, Samuel *v.5 p.601*

Messina, Anthony M.. . . . . *v.4 p.606*

Messina, Lynn *v.5 p.122, p.218*

Messing, Karen *v.6 p.444, p.457*

Messinger, Lisa Mintz *v.1 p.744*

Messner, Michael A. & Sabo, Donald F. *v.4 p.818*

Messner, Michael A.. . . . . . . *v.4 p.745, p.818, v.6 p.437*

Mester, Terri A.. . . . . *v.1 p.46*

Metastasio, Pietro *v.2 p.712*

Metcalf, Alida C.. . . . . *v.3 p.335*

Metcalf, Bill *v.4 p.740*

Metcalf, Michael, et al.. . . . . *v.5 p.347, p.349*

Metcalf, Peter *v.4 p.23*

Metcalf, Robert L. & Luckmann, William H.
(Editors) *v.5 p.10, p.27*

Metcalf, Thomas R. *v.6 p.157*

Metress, Christopher (Editor) *v.3 p.505*

Metropolitan Museum of Art Staff (Contribution by) . *v.1 p.668*

Metsger, Deborah A. & Byers, Sheila C.. . . . . *v.5 p.85, p.86*

Mettes, L. & Zuman, Petr. *v.5 p.290*

Mettler, Barbara *v.1 p.47*

Metz, A. & Benson, C.. . . . . *v.1 p.272, p.338*

Metz, Clyde R.. . . . . *v.5 p.288*

Metz, Helen C. (Editor) *v.6 p.67*

Metzer, David Joel *v.1 p.218*

Metzger, Bruce M. & Coogan, Michael D. (Editors). *v.1 p.614*

Metzger, Bruce M. & Ehrman, Bart D.. . . . . . . *v.1 p.626*

Metzger, Bruce M. *v.1 p.624*

Metzger, Linda & Ryan, Alan. *v.6 p.501, p.507, p.514*

Metzger, Linda (Editor) *v.6 p.501, p.507, p.514*

Metzinger, Thomas. *v.5 p.613*

Metzler, David *v.5 p.113*

Metzler, Michael W. *v.4 p.796*

Mewes, H. W. (Editor), et al.. . . . . *v.5 p.106, p.141, p.146*

Mews, C. J. *v.1 p.579*

Mews, Siegfried & Knust, Herbert (Editors) *v.2 p.605*

Mews, Siegfried *v.2 p.615*

Meyendorff, John *v.1 p.570, p.640*

Meyer, Adolph E. *v.4 p.328*

Meyer, Alfred G. *v.3 p.54*

Meyer, Christopher *v.4 p.645*

Meyer, Conrad Ferdinand *v.2 p.600*

Meyer, David R. *v.6 p.714*

Meyer, George H. *v.1 p.716*

Meyer, Hans G. *v.2 p.628*

Meyer, James H. *v.5 p.5*

Meyer, James S. *v.1 p.680*

Meyer, John M. *v.6 p.288*

Meyer, John P. & Allen, Natalie J.. . . . . *v.5 p.579*

Meyer, Karl E. & Brysac, Shareen Blair . . *v.4 p.623, v.6 p.239*

Meyer, Karl E.. . . . . *v.4 p.642*

Meyer, Leisa D. *v.4 p.766, v.6 p.465*

Meyer, Leonard B. *v.1 p.382*

Meyer, Marshall W. *v.4 p.82*

Meyer, Michael A. (Editor), et al. *v.3 p.180*

Meyer, Michael A. *v.1 p.547, p.548*

Meyer, Michael C. & Beezley, William H. (Editors). . *v.3 p.284*

Meyer, Michael *v.2 p.628*

Meyer, Nicholas E.. . . . . *v.6 p.485, p.490*

Meyer, Philip *v.4 p.149, p.405, p.411*

Meyer, Rudolph X.. . . . . *v.5 p.720*

Meyer, Stefan G.. . . . . *v.6 p.662*

Meyer, Thomas *v.4 p.766*

Meyer, von R. J. *v.5 p.302*

Meyer-Arendt, Jurgen R. *v.5 p.561*

Meyerhoff, Miriam *v.2 p.563*

Meyering, Sheryl L.. . . . . *v.2 p.67*

Meyerowitz, Joanne (Editor) *v.6 p.455*

Meyerowitz, Joanne *v.4 p.744, v.6 p.363, p.371*

Meyers, Carol & Meyers, Eric. *v.1 p.623*

Meyers, Carol L. & Meyers, Eric M.. . . . . *v.1 p.623*

Meyers, Chet & Jones, Thomas B.. . . . . *v.4 p.348*

Meyers, Diana Tietjens (Editor) *v.6 p.461*

Meyers, Diana Tietjens *v.6 p.446, p.461*

Meyers, Eric M. (Editor) *v.1 p.617*

Meyers, Fred E. & Stephens, Matthew P.. . . . . . *v.4 p.116*

Meyers, Herbert M. & Gerstman, Richard *v.4 p.144*

Meyers, Jacob M. *v.1 p.620, p.623*

Meyers, Jeffrey (Editor). *v.2 p.85, p.96*

Meyers, Jeffrey. *v.2 p.85, p.137, p.341, p.367, p.369, p.371, p.375*

Meyers, Marc A. & Chawla, K. K.. . . . . *v.5 p.690*

Meyers, Marian & Paletz, David L. (Editors) *v.6 p.448*

Meyers, Marvin *v.3 p.414*

Meyers, Robert A. (Editor) *v.5 p.8, p.387*

Meyers, Robert A. (Editor-In-Chief) *v.5 p.267*

Meyers, Robert A. *v.5 p.96, p.141, p.142, p.149,*
p.150, p.153, p.311

Meyers, Steven J. *v.5 p.230*

Meyers, William K.. . . . . *v.3 p.294*

Meyerson, Julia *v.3 p.330*

Meyerson, Mark D. *v.3 p.58, p.59, p.239*

Mezey, Michael L. *v.4 p.527*

Mezey, Paul G.. . . . . *v.5 p.298*

Mezirow, Jack & Jack Meizirow and Associates Staff . *v.4 p.320*

Mezu, S. Okechukwu & Mezu,
Rose Ure (Editor, Contribution by) *v.6 p.13*

Mezu, S. Okechukwu. *v.2 p.543*

Mäler, Karl-Göran & Vincent, Jeffrey R. (Editors). . *v.4 p.191*

Márai, Sándor *v.2 p.786*

Ménard, Kim S. *v.6 p.251*

Méndez G, Cecilia *v.3 p.328*

Méndez-Méndez, Serafin, et al. *v.6 p.485, p.490*

Mérimée, Prosper *v.2 p.498*

Mörike, Eduard Friedrich *v.2 p.600*

Mújica, Bárbara & Florensa, Eva *v.2 p.644*

Mújica, Bárbara & Zahareas, Anthony N. (Editors) . *v.2 p.644*

Mújica, Bárbara *v.2 p.644*

M'Gonigle, Michael & Starke, Justine *v.4 p.398*

Miah, Andy (Editor), et al. *v.4 p.870*

Miah, Andy. *v.4 p.802, p.825, p.872, p.875*

Miall, Andrew D. *v.5 p.427, p.438*

Miaskowski, Christine & Buchsel, Patricia . . . *v.5 p.520, p.528*

Miceli, Melinda *v.6 p.385*

Michael, Eugene *v.6 p.332*

Michael, Franz & Chang, Chung-Li *v.6 p.188*

Michael, Ian *v.2 p.644*

Michael, Sami *v.6 p.650*

Michael, Thomas *v.1 p.418*

Michaelides, Solon *v.1 p.176*

Michaels, Albert L. *v.3 p.354*

Michaels, Anne *v.2 p.736*

Michaels, Lloyd *v.6 p.331*

Michaelsen, Larry K. (Editor), et al. *v.4 p.350*

Michal, Gerhard (Editor) *v.5 p.113, p.154*

Michalos, Alex *v.2 p.309*

Michalson, Edgar L.; Papendick, Robert I.;
Carlson, John E. *v.5 p.17, p.30*

Michaud, Guy *v.2 p.461*

Michaud, Nelson & Nossal, Kim Richard (Editors) . *v.3 p.541*

Michaux, Henri *v.2 p.522, p.523*

Michel, De Montaigne *v.2 p.470*

Michelet, Jules *v.3 p.158*

Micheli, Lyle J. & Jenkins, Mark . . . *v.4 p.825, p.866, p.879*

Micheline, Jack *v.2 p.98*

Michell, George & Zebrowski, Mark. *v.1 p.691*

Michell, George *v.1 p.692*

Michell, Joel. *v.5 p.599*

Michelucci, Stefania *v.2 p.364*

Michener, James A. *v.2 p.98*

Michener, James. *v.2 p.98*

Michie, Elsie B. (Editor) *v.2 p.271*

Michman, Ronald D. & Mazze, Edward M.. . . . . . *v.4 p.160*

Michod, Richard E.. . . . . *v.5 p.203*

Michon, Heather K. *v.1 p.416*

Michrina, Barry P. & Richards, CherylAnne *v.4 p.25*

Michta, Andrew A. *v.4 p.639*

Mickel, Elijah *v.6 p.22, p.33*

Mickel, Emanuel J.. . . . . *v.2 p.468*

Mickelson, Roslyn Arlin *v.4 p.335*

Mickey, Thomas J. *v.4 p.429*

Mickiewicz, Adam *v.2 p.791*

Micklem, Niel *v.4 p.714*

Micklos, David & Freyer, Greg *v.5 p.122*

Mico International (Produced by) *v.1 p.132, p.134*

Micone, Marco. *v.2 p.541*

Micozzi, Mark S (Editor) *v.5 p.531*

Micucci, Joseph A. *v.5 p.668*

Middlebrook, Diane W. & Yalom, Marilyn (Editors) . . . *v.2 p.8*

Middlebrook, Diane W. *v.2 p.115*

Middlebrook, Diane Wood *v.6 p.371, p.409*

Middlebrook, Diane *v.2 p.353*

Middlebrook, Kevin J. (Editor), et al. *v.3 p.294*

Middlebrook, Kevin J. (Editor) *v.3 p.294*

Middlebrook, Kevin J. *v.3 p.294*

Middlekauff, Robert *v.3 p.409, p.487*

Middleton, Frank *v.6 p.450*

Middleton, Gerard V. (Editor) *v.5 p.438*

Middleton, John & Beidelman, Thomas O.. . . . . . *v.4 p.36*

Middleton, John & Campbell, Jane *v.6 p.66*

Middleton, Nick *v.4 p.159*

Middleton, Richard (Editor) *v.1 p.272*

Middleton, Richard *v.1 p.272*

Middleton, Stephen (Editor) *v.6 p.7, p.31*

Middleton, Susan & Liittschwager, David . . . *v.5 p.358, p.359*

Middleton, Susan. *v.5 p.180*

Middleton, Thomas. *v.2 p.215, p.221*

Middleton, William D. *v.5 p.700*

Midgley, James (Contribution by), et al. *v.4 p.769*

Midgley, Mary *v.1 p.484, p.486, p.503*

Midwest Plan Service Engineers Staff *v.5 p.55*

Midwest Plan Service Personnel *v.5 p.55*

Mieczkowski, Yanek *v.3 p.475*

Miele, Chris *v.1 p.823*

Mielke, Howard *v.5 p.168*

Mielke, James H., et al. *v.4 p.17, v.5 p.164*

Miell, Dorothy (Editor), et al. *v.1 p.376*

Miers, Suzanne & Roberts, Richard L. (Editors) *v.6 p.53*

Mierzwik, Diane *v.4 p.353*

Mies, Maria *v.6 p.457*

Miesner, Thomas O. & Leffler, William L. *v.5 p.738*

Miettinen, Jukka O. *v.1 p.133, p.134*

Migdal, Joel S. (Editor). *v.4 p.495*

Migdal, Joel S. *v.4 p.773, v.6 p.614*

Miglani, Gurbachen S. *v.5 p.135*

Miglietta, John P.. . . . . *v.3 p.391*

Migliorini, Bruno. *v.2 p.699*

Mihailovich, Vasa D. (Editor, Translator) *v.2 p.811*

Mihesuah, Devon A. & Wilson, Angela
Cavender. *v.4 p.312, v.6 p.680*

Mikalson, Jon D. *v.1 p.533, v.3 p.14*

Mikell, Gwendolyn (Editor). *v.6 p.435, p.457*

Mikhail, Mona H. *v.6 p.479, p.662*

Mikhailov, M. D. & Ozisik, M. Necati *v.5 p.713*

Mikhelson, Ilya *v.5 p.695*

Mikkeli, Heikki *v.3 p.35*

Mikos, Michael J. (Translator) *v.2 p.787, p.788, p.791*

Mikos, Michael J. *v.2 p.788, p.789*

Mikotowicz, Tom (Editor) *v.1 p.140, p.147*

Milani, Farzaneh *v.6 p.672*

Milani, Mohsen M.. . . . . *v.6 p.631*

Milanovic, Branko *v.4 p.261, p.266*

Milbank Memorial Fund *v.5 p.671*

Milburn, Gerard J. *v.5 p.552*

Milburn, Michael A. & Conrad, Sheree D. *v.5 p.644*

Milder, Robert *v.2 p.48*

Mileck, Joseph *v.2 p.610*

Miles, Alan *v.1 p.38*

Miles, Ann *v.4 p.44*

Miles, Barry *v.1 p.219, p.272, p.369, v.2 p.79*

Miles, Dudley H.. . . . . *v.3 p.114, p.131*

Miles, Ellen G.. . . . . *v.1 p.732*

Miles, Emma B.. . . . . *v.2 p.46*

Miles, Gary B.. . . . . *v.2 p.436*

Miles, Hugh *v.4 p.415*

Miles, John C. & Priest, Simon (Editors) *v.4 p.796*

Miles, Josephine. *v.2 p.98*

Miles, Julia. *v.1 p.68, p.121*

Miles, Margaret R. *v.1 p.643*

Miles, Matthew B. & Huberman, A. Michael (Editors). *v.4 p.690*

Miles, Raymond E., et al. *v.4 p.68*

Miles, Rosalind *v.2 p.220*

Miles, Wyndham D. *v.5 p.261*

Mileti, Dennis *v.5 p.423*

Milford, Nancy *v.2 p.77, p.98*

Milgram, Stanley, et al. *v.5 p.646*

Milgram, Stanley. *v.4 p.695*

Milgrom, Jacob *v.1 p.620, p.621*

Milgrom, Lionel R.. . . . . *v.5 p.330*

Milhailovich, Vasa D. (Editor). *v.2 p.779*

Milhaud, Darius *v.1 p.219, p.341*

Milhaupt, Curtis J. (Editor), et al. *v.6 p.220*

Milhous, Judith & Hume, Robert D. (Editors). *v.1 p.102, v.2 p.187*

Milis, Ludo J. R.. . . . . *v.6 p.572*

Military Family Research Institute, Purdue University . *v.5 p.579*

Milkis, Sidney M. & Mileur, Jerome M.
(Editors) *v.3 p.443, v.4 p.522*

Milkis, Sidney M. & Nelson, Michael *v.4 p.527*

Milkis, Sidney M. (Editor), et al. *v.3 p.476*

Milkis, Sidney M. *v.4 p.527*

Milkman, Ruth & Voss, Kim *v.4 p.122*

Mill, James *v.1 p.445*

Mill, John Stuart & Mill, Harriet Taylor *v.6 p.452*

Mill, John Stuart (Editor) *v.4 p.222*

Mill, John Stuart *v.1 p.445, p.494, p.511, p.516, p.523,
                                    v.4 p.222, p.223, p.344, p.515*

Millar, Dan Pyle & Heath, Robert L. (Editors) *v.4 p.173*

Millar, Fergus & Segal, Erich (Editors) *v.3 p.28*

Millar, Fergus. *v.3 p.26, p.28, p.32, v.4 p.489*

Millar, James R. (Editor) *v.4 p.598, p.599*

Millard, Andre *v.1 p.387*

Millard, André (Editor) *v.1 p.390*

Millard, F.. . . . . *v.4 p.596*

Millay, Edna St. Vincent *v.2 p.98*

Miller, Alexei & Rieber, Alfred J. (Editors). *v.3 p.213*

Miller, Alice. *v.5 p.628, p.658*

Miller, Anita (Editor) *v.4 p.538*

Miller, Ann *v.4 p.532*

Miller, Arthur, et al. *v.2 p.102*

Miller, Arthur G. (Editor) *v.4 p.698, v.5 p.655*

Miller, Arthur I.. . . . . *v.5 p.62*

Miller, Arthur *v.1 p.117, v.2 p.101, p.102, v.6 p.216*

Miller, Audrey & Solomon, Philippa H. *v.5 p.296*

Miller, Barbara S. & Miller, Barbara Stoler (Translators). *v.6 p.152*

Miller, Blair. *v.6 p.307, p.313, p.332*

Miller, Brian Cole *v.4 p.80*

Miller, Bruce G. *v.5 p.361*

Miller, Carl *v.6 p.412*

Miller, Carol A. *v.5 p.519*

Miller, Carol P. & Wheeler, Robert *v.3 p.513*

Miller, Char (Editor) *v.5 p.5, p.28, p.39, p.353*

Miller, Char; Staebler, Rebecca *v.5 p.39*

Miller, Char. *v.5 p.39*

Miller, Charles B.. . . . . *v.4 p.392, v.5 p.431*

Miller, Christopher L.. . . . . *v.2 p.542, v.6 p.682, p.701*

Miller, Clark & Edwards, Paul N. (Editors). *v.4 p.666*

Miller, Cristanne *v.2 p.102*

Miller, D. A. *v.2 p.193, p.268, v.6 p.412, p.756*

Miller, D. Quentin (Editor). *v.2 p.59*

Miller, Danny L. (Editor), et al.. . . . . *v.2 p.12*

Miller, David H. *v.4 p.631*

Miller, David M. & Wertz, Dorothy C.. . . . . . . *v.1 p.537*

Miller, David M. *v.2 p.254*

Miller, David. *v.3 p.140, v.4 p.494*

Miller, Delbert C. & Salkind, Neil J.. . . . . *v.4 p.686*

Miller, Donald E. & Miller, Lorna Touryan *v.6 p.633*

Miller, E. Willard & Miller, Ruby M. *v.5 p.313, p.707*

Miller, Edwin H. *v.2 p.41*

Miller, Elmer S.. . . . . *v.4 p.37*

Miller, Ericka M. *v.6 p.7, p.18*

Miller, Errol *v.4 p.335*

Miller, Eugene & Pollack, Neuman F. *v.4 p.176*

Miller, Frederick A. & Katz, Judith H. *v.4 p.132*

Miller, G. Wayne *v.4 p.848*

Miller, Gabriel *v.2 p.108*
Miller, Gene H. *v.5 p.730*
Miller, George A., et al. *v.5 p.594*
Miller, George A. *v.4 p.357*
Miller, George H. *v.4 p.445*
Miller, Gerald A. (Editor), et al. *v.5 p.699*
Miller, Gloria E. *v.4 p.357, v.5 p.571*
Miller, Henry Knight *v.2 p.248*
Miller, Henry *v.2 p.102*
Miller, Ingrid W. (Editor) *v.2 p.666*
Miller, Isabel. *v.6 p.398*
Miller, J. Hillis Jr. & Wolfreys, Julian *v.2 p.164*
Miller, J. Hillis Jr. *v.2 p.164, p.176, p.179*
Miller, J. Mitchell & Wright, Richard A. Jr. (Editors) *v.4 p.678*
Miller, James Andrew *v.6 p.601, p.643*
Miller, James D. *v.4 p.83*
Miller, James E. & Miller, James E. Jr. *v.2 p.72*
Miller, James Edward. *v.3 p.204*
Miller, James *v.6 p.407*
Miller, Jane E. *v.4 p.173, p.179, v.5 p.681*
Miller, Janet L. *v.4 p.279*
Miller, Jason *v.2 p.150*
Miller, Jay (Compiled by), et al. *v.6 p.682*
Miller, Jerome G. *v.4 p.730*
Miller, John E. *v.3 p.517*
Miller, John *v.3 p.94, p.105, p.121*
Miller, Jon & Inwood, Brad (Editors) *v.1 p.436*
Miller, Joseph C. *v.6 p.75*
Miller, Judith G. *v.2 p.526*
Miller, Julia R., et al. *v.5 p.358*
Miller, Kenneth E. *v.4 p.594*
Miller, Leonard W. *v.4 p.832, p.848*
Miller, Leta E. & Lieberman, Fredric *v.1 p.219, p.329*
Miller, Margaret Christina *v.3 p.18*
Miller, Marilyn Grace. *v.3 p.267*
Miller, Marshall L. *v.3 p.251*
Miller, Mary E. *v.1 p.670, p.684, v.3 p.261*
Miller, Mary Ellen *v.1 p.670, p.684*
Miller, Melvin D. *v.4 p.305, p.353*
Miller, Melvin E. & Young-Eisendrath, Polly (Editors). *v.5 p.635*
Miller, Merle. *v.3 p.476*
Miller, Michael V. *v.5 p.655*
Miller, Nathan *v.3 p.372, p.449*
Miller, Neal E. & Dollard, John *v.4 p.357*
Miller, Neil *v.6 p.363, p.366, p.421*
Miller, Norma. *v.1 p.10*
Miller, O. J. & Therman, Eeva *v.5 p.142*
Miller, P. M. & Wilson, M. J. *v.4 p.687*
Miller, Patricia D. (Editor) *v.4 p.784, p.791, p.801*
Miller, Patrick B. & Wiggins, David K. (Editors). *v.4 p.818, p.832*
Miller, Patrick B. (Editor) *v.4 p.818*
Miller, Paul Allen (Editor) *v.2 p.427*
Miller, Paul Allen *v.2 p.426*
Miller, Pepper & Kemp, Herb *v.4 p.138*
Miller, Perry G. (Editor) *v.1 p.515*

Miller, Perry G. *v.1 p.588, v.2 p.4, p.20, p.29,*
 v.3 p.369, p.406, p.485
Miller, Perry. *v.1 p.584*
Miller, Peter M. & Nirenberg, Ted D. (Editors) . . . *v.5 p.673*
Miller, Philip L. (Introduction by) *v.1 p.236, p.412*
Miller, Phillip L. (Editor), et al. *v.1 p.236, p.246, p.412*
Miller, R. Robin & Browning, Sandra Lee *v.4 p.773*
Miller, Randall M. & Pencak, William A. (Editors) . . *v.3 p.492*
Miller, Ray & Donahue, Roy L. *v.5 p.50*
Miller, Raymond W. & Gardiner, Duane T. *v.6 p.294*
Miller, Rex & Miller, Mark Richard *v.5 p.714*
Miller, Richard B. *v.1 p.486*
Miller, Richard E. *v.4 p.332*
Miller, Richard *v.1 p.200, p.236, p.355, p.395, p.401*
Miller, Rowland S. *v.5 p.648, p.655*
Miller, Russell *v.4 p.486*
Miller, Seumas & Blackler, John. *v.6 p.263*
Miller, Shawn William *v.3 p.269*
Miller, Stephen G. *v.3 p.14*
Miller, Stephen T., et. al. *v.2 p.581*
Miller, Stephen *v.3 p.14*
Miller, Stuart C. *v.6 p.180*
Miller, Terry E. *v.1 p.168, p.289, p.296*
Miller, Tim *v.6 p.412*
Miller, Timothy (Editor) *v.1 p.544*
Miller, Timothy *v.4 p.499, p.740*
Miller, Toby. *v.6 p.384, p.437, p.448*
Miller, Tyrus *v.2 p.11*
Miller, Walter (Translator). *v.2 p.422*
Miller, Walter *v.2 p.98*
Miller, William & Zemke, Ron *v.4 p.143*
Miller, William L. (Editor), et al. *v.4 p.582*
Miller, William Lee. *v.1 p.657*
Miller, William R. & Carroll, Kathleen M.
 (Editors). *v.5 p.512, p.522*
Miller, William R. & Delaney, Harold D. *v.5 p.635*
Miller-McLemore, Bonnie J. *v.1 p.649*
Millet, Bella. *v.2 p.204*
Millett, Allan R. & Maslowski, Peter. *v.3 p.383*
Millett, Allan R. & Murray, Williamson R.
 (Editor, Contribution by) *v.3 p.79*
Millett, Allan R. *v.3 p.383*
Millett, Allan Reed *v.6 p.237*
Millett, Bella (Editor). *v.2 p.204*
Millett, Kate. *v.6 p.403, p.479*
Millett, Richard & Gold-Biss, Michael (Editors) . . *v.3 p.276*
Millett, Richard *v.3 p.275*
Millán-Zaibert, Elizabeth & Salles, Arleen (Editors). *v.1 p.444*
Millgram, Abraham E. *v.1 p.552*
Millhauser, Steven *v.2 p.150*
Millier, Brett C. *v.2 p.62*
Milligan, Barry *v.6 p.746, p.754, p.760*
Milligan, George (Editor), et al. *v.5 p.117*
Milligan, Jeffrey Ayala *v.4 p.335*
Milligan, Thomas A. *v.5 p.728*

Millington, Andrew C.
(Editor), et al. *v.5 p.87, p.88, p.94, p.169, p.185*
Millington, Barry (Editor) *v.1 p.200, p.365*
Millis, Walter *v.3 p.383, p.399, p.437, p.453*
Millon, Theodore (Editor), et al. *v.5 p.661*
Milloy, John *v.4 p.335, v.6 p.680*
Mills, C. Wright & Jacoby, Russell *v.4 p.724*
Mills, C. Wright *v.4 p.681, p.724, p.762, p.763, p.769*
Mills, Cynthia *v.5 p.194*
Mills, D. L. *v.5 p.561*
Mills, E. S. (Editor) *v.4 p.191*
Mills, Edwin S. *v.6 p.724*
Mills, Eric L. *v.4 p.392, v.5 p.431*
Mills, Ian (Compiled by) *v.5 p.280*
Mills, John A. *v.5 p.667*
Mills, Judson & Herman-Jones, Eddie (Editors) . . . *v.5 p.650*
Mills, Kenneth *v.3 p.326*
Mills, Sara. *v.1 p.459*
Mills, T. M. *v.5 p.484*
Millstone, Eric *v.4 p.152, p.165*
Millward, C. M. *v.2 p.555, p.557*
Milne, A. A. *v.2 p.368*
Milne, Antony *v.5 p.720*
Milne, G. W. A. (Editor) *v.5 p.312*
Milne, Geoffrey *v.2 p.741*
Milne, George W. (Editor) *v.5 p.259*
Milne, R. J. *v.5 p.695*
Milne, R. S. & Mauzy, Diane K. *v.6 p.173*
Milne, Tom, et al. *v.6 p.319*
Milner, Andrew *v.2 p.254*
Milner, Clyde A. II (Editor), et al. *v.3 p.518*
Milner, Henry *v.3 p.235*
Milner, John *v.1 p.665*
Milner, Max & Pichois, Claude *v.2 p.459*
Milner-Gulland, Robin R. *v.3 p.209*
Milnor, John *v.5 p.499*
Milojkovic-Djuric, Jelena *v.2 p.811, v.3 p.246*
Milosch, Jane C. (Editor) *v.1 p.744*
Milosz, Czeslaw *v.2 p.789, v.3 p.255*
Milroy, James *v.2 p.555*
Milson, Menahem *v.6 p.662*
Milton, Giles *v.6 p.60, p.177*
Milton, John & Fowler, Alastair *v.2 p.255*
Milton, John & Hughes, Merritt Y. (Editors) *v.2 p.255*
Milton, John & Potter, G. R. *v.3 p.245*
Milton, John R. *v.3 p.523*
Milton, John *v.2 p.254, p.255*
Milton, Kay *v.4 p.30*
Milton, Richard *v.5 p.203*
Milunsky, Aubrey *v.5 p.533*
Milward, Alan S. *v.3 p.81*
Mims, Edwin *v.2 p.47*
Min, Pyong G. & Kim, Jung H. (Editors) . . . *v.6 p.106, p.136*
Min, Pyong G. & Kim, Rose *v.6 p.106, p.116, p.136*
Min, Pyong Gap & Foner, Nancy *v.6 p.110, p.119, p.136*

Min, Pyong Gap (Editor) *v.6 p.86, p.124*
Min, Pyong Gap . . *v.6 p.106, p.114, p.116, p.122, p.124, p.136*
Min, Pyrong Gap *v.6 p.85*
Mina, Hanna. *v.6 p.662*
Minchin, Timothy J. *v.4 p.127*
Mindell, David P.. . . . . *v.5 p.194*
Mindell, Phyllis *v.4 p.173*
Mindich, David T. Z. *v.4 p.417*
Mindich, David T. *v.4 p.404*
Mindiola, Tatcho Jr., et al. *v.6 p.542*
Minear, Richard H. *v.4 p.477*
Minelli, A.. . . . . *v.5 p.199*
Miner, Craig *v.3 p.524*
Miner, Earl (Editor) *v.2 p.246*
Miner, Earl, et al. *v.6 p.231*
Miner, Earl. *v.2 p.246, v.6 p.231*
Miner, H. Craig *v.3 p.524*
Mines, Diane P. *v.6 p.154*
Minesuah, Devon Abbott *v.6 p.435, p.705*
Mingay, G. E. *v.4 p.705, p.726*
Mingione, Enzo *v.4 p.771*
Mingos, D. M. *v.5 p.301*
Mingst, Karen A. & Karns, Margaret P. *v.4 p.634*
Mingst, Karen A. & Snyder, Jack L. *v.4 p.625*
Mingus, Charles *v.1 p.262, p.341*
Minh-ha, Trinh T. *v.6 p.88, p.89, p.90, p.97, p.112, p.479*
Mini, Piero V. *v.4 p.228*
Minifie, Fred D. *v.5 p.665*
Mink, Gwendolyn *v.4 p.755, v.6 p.441, p.470*
Minkin, Mary & Wright, Carol *v.5 p.523*
Minkin, Mary Jane & Wright, Carol V. . . . *v.5 p.523, v.6 p.444*
Minkler, Meredith *v.4 p.778*
Minkoff, Eli C. & Baker, Pamela J. *v.5 p.245*
Minkoff, Eli C., et al.. . . . . *v.5 p.448*
Minor, Vernon H. *v.1 p.675*
Minority Rights Group Staff (Editor). *v.3 p.279*
Minoura, K. (Editor) . . . *v.5 p.174, p.187, p.237, p.238, p.242*
Minow, Mary & Lipinski, Tomas A. *v.4 p.451*
Minow, Newton & Lamay, Craig *v.4 p.445*
Minowitz, Peter *v.4 p.219*
Minsky, Marvin L. & Papert, Seymour A. *v.5 p.498*
Minsky, Morton & Machlin, Milt *v.1 p.35, p.36*
Minta, Stephen. *v.2 p.684*
Minteer, Ben A. *v.6 p.289*
Mintel Group *v.5 p.586*
Minter, David L.. . . . . *v.2 p.11*
Minter, David *v.2 p.74*
Minton, Henry L.. . . . . *v.5 p.597*
Minturn, Neil *v.1 p.219, p.348*
Mintz, Alan (Editor) *v.6 p.646, p.650*
Mintz, Alan L. *v.6 p.650*
Mintz, Alan *v.6 p.650*
Mintz, Jeanne S. *v.6 p.175*
Mintz, Jerome R. *v.4 p.42*
Mintz, Ruth F. *v.6 p.650*

Mintz, Sidney W. & Price, Richard *v.4 p.41*

Mintz, Sidney W. *v.3 p.272, p.282,v.4 p.41, p.46*

Mintzberg, Henry *v.4 p.64, p.176*

Mintzer, Irving M. *v.5 p.371*

Minuchin, Salvador & Fishman, H. Charles. *v.5 p.668*

Minus, Paul M. *v.1 p.576*

Minutaglio, Bill *v.3 p.509*

Mira, Alberto *v.6 p.339*

Mirabella, Francis M. (Editor). *v.5 p.273*

Miracle, Andrew W. Jr. & Rees, C. Roger. *v.4 p.822, p.840, p.885*

Miraldi, Robert. *v.4 p.406*

Miranda, Carlos R. *v.3 p.345*

Miranda, Malvin *v.6 p.532*

Mirandé, Alfredo & Enriquez, Evangelina *v.6 p.546*

Mirandé, Alfredo *v.6 p.522*

Mir-Hosseini, Ziba *v.6 p.632*

Mirikitani, Janice. *v.6 p.104*

Miroff, Bruce *v.3 p.476*

Miron, Douglas B. *v.5 p.728*

Miron, Gaston *v.2 p.541*

Mironov, Boris N. & Eklof, Ben *v.3 p.211*

Mirovitskaya, Natalia & Ascher, William L. (Editors) *v.6 p.286*

Mirowsky, John & Ross, Catherine E. *v.4 p.699*

Mirrlees, J. *v.4 p.244*

Mirsky, Dimitry S. *v.2 p.799*

Mirvis, Philip H., et al. *v.4 p.84*

Misak, C. J. *v.1 p.482, p.504*

Misak, Cheryl (Editor) *v.1 p.440*

Miscamble, Wilson D. *v.3 p.461*

Misener, Stephen & Krawetz, Stephen A. (Editors) . *v.5 p.100*

Mish, Charles C. (Editor) *v.2 p.203*

Mishal, Shaul & Sela, Avraham *v.6 p.618*

Mishal, Shaul *v.6 p.621*

Mishaqah, Mikhail *v.6 p.605*

Mishell, William W. *v.3 p.85, p.256*

Mishima, Yukio *v.6 p.231, p.235, p.398*

Mishkin, Julie Russo & Schill, Marta *v.1 p.16*

Mishler, Elliot G. *v.4 p.691*

Mishra, Pankaj *v.2 p.764*

Misiunas, Romuald J. & Taagepera, Rein. *v.3 p.256*

Miskimin, Harry A. *v.3 p.41*

Mislow, Kurt. *v.5 p.298*

Misnad, Sheikha *v.4 p.335*

Misner, Charles W., et al. *v.5 p.72, p.556, p.557*

Misra, Gauri S.. . . . . *v.5 p.322*

Misra, J. C. (Editor) *v.5 p.100*

Missouri Group Staff, et al. *v.4 p.414*

Mistral, Gabriela, et al.. . . . . *v.2 p.680*

Mistral, Gabriela *v.2 p.681*

Mistrík, Jozef *v.2 p.777*

Mistron, Deborah. *v.2 p.768*

Mistry, Rohinton *v.2 p.765*

Mitchell, Alanna *v.6 p.292*

Mitchell, Andrew W. *v.5 p.223*

Mitchell, Andy. *v.4 p.387, p.388*

Mitchell, Angelyn *v.6 p.37, p.40, p.45*

Mitchell, B. R. *v.4 p.385*

Mitchell, Basil (Editor) *v.1 p.498*

Mitchell, Brian S. *v.5 p.732*

Mitchell, Bruce & Robinson, Fred C. (Editors) . *v.2 p.206, p.550*

Mitchell, Charles P.. . . . . *v.6 p.321*

Mitchell, Debby, et al. *v.4 p.796, p.862*

Mitchell, Donald (Author, Editor) *v.1 p.219, p.339*

Mitchell, Donald. *v.1 p.219, p.339*

Mitchell, James K. & Soga, Kenichi *v.5 p.422*

Mitchell, John Cameron & Trask, Stephen. *v.1 p.252, p.379, p.409*

Mitchell, John D. & Watanabe, Miyoko . . . *v.1 p.132, p.135*

Mitchell, John G.. . . . . *v.5 p.230*

Mitchell, Joseph. *v.2 p.98*

Mitchell, Kenneth Edward *v.3 p.272*

Mitchell, Lee C. *v.6 p.324*

Mitchell, Leif (Editor) *v.6 p.385*

Mitchell, Margaret. *v.2 p.98*

Mitchell, Mitch *v.6 p.352*

Mitchell, Olivia S. (Editor) *v.4 p.98*

Mitchell, P. M. & Ober, Kenneth H. (Translators) . . *v.2 p.626*

Mitchell, Paul & Wilford, Rick (Editors) *v.4 p.607*

Mitchell, Peter (Editor) *v.4 p.384*

Mitchell, Peter J. *v.4 p.8*

Mitchell, Richard S. *v.5 p.435*

Mitchell, Robert W. (Editor), et al.. . . . . *v.5 p.615*

Mitchell, Sally *v.6 p.479, p.735, p.740, p.748, p.761*

Mitchell, Sandra D.. . . . . *v.5 p.170*

Mitchell, Silas Weir *v.2 p.46*

Mitchell, Stephen. *v.6 p.665*

Mitchell, Susan. *v.4 p.138, v.5 p.586*

Mitchell, T. F. *v.6 p.654*

Mitchell, Thomas M.. . . . . *v.5 p.339, p.408*

Mitchell, Thomas N. *v.2 p.433*

Mitchell, Timothy *v.4 p.808, p.856,v.6 p.638, p.639*

Mitchell, Tony (Editor) *v.1 p.272*

Mitchell, W. J. *v.2 p.240*

Mitchell, W. O. *v.2 p.736*

Mitchell, William J. *v.6 p.730*

Mitchell-Boyask, Robin (Editor) *v.2 p.411*

Mitchell-Tavener, Claire *v.4 p.796, p.857*

Mitchelson, Keith R. & Cheng, Jing (Editors). . . . *v.5 p.120*

Mitchelson, Keith R. (Editor) *v.5 p.120*

Mitchinson, David *v.1 p.780*

Mitchison, Rosalind *v.3 p.133*

Mitford, Jessica *v.2 p.371*

Mitford, Nancy. *v.2 p.371*

Mitgang, Herbert *v.3 p.426*

Mithun, Marianne *v.6 p.690*

Mitra, Shankar *v.5 p.441*

Mitra, Subrata (Editor) *v.4 p.191*

Mitrakos, Alexander S. *v.3 p.196*

Mitrani, Isi *v.5 p.484*

Mitrasca, Marcel *v.3 p.230*

Mitroff, Ian I. & Denton, Elizabeth A. *v.4 p.52, p.54*

Mitry, Jean *v.6 p.327*

Mitsui, Toru & Hosokawa, Shuhei . . . *v.1 p.272, p.283, p.387*

Mittal, Sushil & Thursby, G. R. *v.1 p.541*

Mittelhammer, Ron C., et al. *v.4 p.203*

Mittelman, Mary S., et al.. . . . . *v.5 p.519*

Mitten, Lisa *v.6 p.677*

Mitter, Partha *v.1 p.692*

Mitter, Shomit. *v.1 p.109, p.145*

Mittermeier, Russell A., et al. *v.5 p.356, v.6 p.286, p.292*

Mitton, Jeffry B.. . . . . *v.5 p.189, p.194*

Mitton, Simon. *v.5 p.62*

Mix, Paul E.. . . . . *v.5 p.690*

Miyagi, Masako *v.5 p.718*

Miyamoto, Michael M. & Cracraft, Joel (Editors). *v.5 p.122, p.194*

Miyan, J. A. (Editor), et al. *v.5 p.165*

Miyares, Ines M., et al. *v.4 p.383*

Miyares, Ines *v.6 p.139*

Miyashiro, A. *v.5 p.440*

Miyazaki, Koji *v.5 p.498*

Miyazaki, Toten *v.6 p.227*

Miyoshi, Masao *v.6 p.231*

Mizener, Arthur *v.2 p.77*

Mizrahi, Yemile *v.3 p.294*

Mjagkij, Nina (Editor) *v.6 p.7*

GLSEN Staff (Createdby) *v.6 p.385*

Mladen, Davidovic *v.2 p.777*

Müller, Franz (Editor) *v.5 p.10*

Müller, Gerd & Newman, Stuart (Editors) *v.5 p.160*

Müller, H. J. & Roeder, Thomas *v.5 p.110*

Müller, Werner E. G. *v.5 p.113*

Mnacko, Ladislav *v.2 p.812*

Moallem, Minoo *v.6 p.632*

Mobberley, Martin. *v.5 p.63*

Mobberly, Martin *v.5 p.65*

Moberg, G. & Mench, J. A. (Editors) *v.5 p.166*

Moberg, Mark *v.3 p.297*

Moberg, Vilhelm *v.2 p.630, v.3 p.235*

Mobily, Kenneth E. & MacNeil, Richard. *v.4 p.786, p.801, p.830*

Mobley, Jonnie P. *v.1 p.140*

Mobley, Marilyn Sanders *v.2 p.46, p.150*

Moch, Leslie Page *v.4 p.602*

Mockaitis, Thomas R. & Rich, Paul . . . *v.4 p.564, p.660*

Moctezuma, Eduardo M. *v.3 p.261*

Modarres-Sadeqi, Jafar *v.6 p.672*

Modell, Arnold H. *v.4 p.693, v.5 p.655*

Modell, Judith. *v.4 p.32*

Modiano, Patrick *v.2 p.532*

Modigliani, Franco & Friedman, Milton *v.4 p.232*

Modigliani, Franco *v.4 p.210*

Modleski, Tania *v.6 p.475*

Modoc Press Staff & American Association of Colleges for Teacher Education Staff (Contribution by). . . . *v.4 p.279*

Mody, Ashoka & Pattilo, Catherine (Editors) . *v.4 p.240, p.266*

Mody, Bella (Editor), et al. *v.4 p.420*

Moe, Nelson. *v.3 p.197*

Moeller, Bernard *v.1 p.602*

Moeller, Robert G. (Editor) *v.3 p.177*

Moeller, Robert G. *v.3 p.177*

Moeller, Susan D. *v.4 p.407*

Moeller, Therald B.. . . . . *v.5 p.301*

Moeller, Thomas G. *v.5 p.628, p.631, p.662*

Moelwyn Hughes, E. A. *v.5 p.276*

Moelwyn-Hughes, E. A. *v.5 p.276*

Moen, Phyllis (Editor), et al. *v.4 p.725*

Moens, Alexander *v.3 p.484*

Moeran, Brian. *v.4 p.39*

Moerk, Ernst L. *v.4 p.358*

Moerman, Daniel E.. . . . . *v.4 p.47*

Moerman, Michael *v.4 p.19*

Moffett, Charles S. *v.1 p.732*

Moffett, Samuel H. *v.1 p.610*

Moffitt, John F. *v.1 p.688, v.3 p.236*

Moffitt, Terrie E., et al. *v.5 p.662*

Mofty, Soraya (Author, Read by) *v.6 p.668*

Moger, Allen W. *v.3 p.500*

Moggridge, Donald E. (Editor) *v.4 p.228*

Moggridge, Donald E. *v.4 p.212, p.228*

Moghadam, Valentine M. (Editor) *v.6 p.429, p.435*

Moghaddam, Fathali M. & Marsella, Anthony J. (Editors). *v.4 p.660, p.767*

Moghissi, Hiadeh *v.6 p.435, p.460, p.465*

Moglen, Helene *v.2 p.571*

Mohanram, Radhika & Rajan, Gita (Editors) . . . *v.2 p.727*

Mohanty, Chandra T. (Editor), et al. *v.6 p.457*

Mohanty, Chandra Talpade *v.6 p.428, p.457*

Mohanty, J. N. *v.1 p.419*

Mohanty, Jitendra N. & Gupta, Bina *v.1 p.419*

Mohanty, Jitendra N. *v.1 p.419*

Mohl, Raymond A. & Betten, Neil. *v.3 p.514*

Mohl, Ruth *v.2 p.569, v.6 p.566*

Moholy-Nagy, László *v.1 p.768*

Mohr, James C. *v.4 p.472*

Mohr, Nicholasa *v.6 p.507*

Mohr, Richard D. *v.1 p.808*

Mohsen Manutchehr-Danai, Regensburg *v.5 p.435, p.452*

Moi, Toril *v.6 p.479*

Moir, Alfred *v.1 p.744*

Moisala, Pirkko & Diamond, Beverley *v.1 p.379*

Mokri, M. *v.6 p.668*

Mokyr, Joel (Editor) *v.3 p.41, p.123, v.4 p.192, p.212*

Mokyr, Joel *v.3 p.41*

Mol, Serge. *v.4 p.863*

Molasky, Michael & Rabson, Steve (Editors) . . *v.6 p.235*

Molasky, Michael S. *v.6 p.231, p.235*

Moldenhauer, Hans & Moldenhauer, Rosaleen . *v.1 p.219, p.367*

Moler, Kenneth L. *v.2 p.268*

Moley, Raymond *v.3 p.476*

Moliere, Jean-Baptiste & Couton (Editors) . . . *v.2 p.475*

Moliere, Jean-Baptiste & Wilbur, Richard . . . *v.2 p.475*

Moliere, Jean-Baptiste *v.2 p.475*

Molin, Donald H. *v.1 p.141*

Molina, Antonio Munoz. *v.2 p.661*

Moliner, Maria D. *v.2 p.636*

Mollat, Michel *v.6 p.576*

Molle, Elizabeth A. *v.5 p.534*

Mollenhoff, David V. *v.3 p.517*

Mollenkopf, John H. *v.6 p.714*

Mollenkopf, John Hull *v.6 p.724*

Mollin, Richard A. *v.5 p.476*

Molloy, Molly E *v.3 p.260*

Molnar, Ferenc. *v.2 p.786*

Molnar, Miklos. *v.3 p.185*

Molnar, Stephen. *v.4 p.17*

Moloney, Francis J.. . . . . *v.1 p.629*

Moltmann, Jurgen *v.1 p.639, p.641, p.645*

Moltz, Barry *v.4 p.68*

Molyneux, Maxine *v.6 p.431*

Momaday, N. Scott *v.2 p.150, v.6 p.698*

Momigliano, Arnaldo D. *v.2 p.401, v.3 p.21*

Mommsen, Hans. *v.3 p.170, p.173*

Mommsen, Wolfgang J.. . . . . *v.3 p.164*

Momsen, Janet H. (Editor) *v.4 p.31, v.6 p.457*

Monaghan, Jay *v.3 p.327, p.351, p.433*

Monaghan, Leila Frances (Editor). *v.4 p.22*

Monahan, Dave (Editor) *v.5 p.429*

Monahan, Patrick J. *v.4 p.587*

Moncrief, Gary F., et al. *v.4 p.530*

Mondale, Sarah & Patton, Sarah B. (Editors) . . . *v.4 p.328*

Mondimore, Francis M.. . . . . *v.6 p.372, p.420*

Monegal, Emir R. (Editor) *v.2 p.666*

Moneta, Howard (Editor) *v.1 p.708*

Monette, Paul *v.6 p.379, p.398, p.403*

Money, Keith *v.1 p.11*

Moneyhon, Carl H. *v.3 p.509, p.511, v.4 p.521*

Monga, Celestin *v.4 p.497, p.585, p.612*

Mongerson, Paul *v.4 p.404*

Mongia, Padmini *v.2 p.728*

Monier, Charles J. *v.5 p.721*

Monkkonen, Eric H. *v.6 p.245*

Monmonier, Mark S. *v.4 p.386*

Monmonier, Mark *v.4 p.375, p.385, p.386*

Monnett, John H. & McCarthy, Michael *v.3 p.526*

Monod, Paul K. *v.3 p.107, p.109*

Monroe, Jonathan (Editor) *v.2 p.565*

Monroe, Kristen Renwick (Editor) *v.5 p.644*

Monroy, Douglas *v.6 p.534, p.536, p.549*

Monshipouri, Mahmood. *v.4 p.513*

Monson, Ingrid *v.1 p.262, p.281*

Montagu, Ashley . *v.4 p.14, p.344, p.729, p.737, p.744, p.760, v.6 p.435, p.461*

Montagu, Jennifer *v.1 p.775*

Montagu, Jeremy *v.1 p.176, p.390*

Montagu, Lady Mary Wortley *v.2 p.256, v.3 p.107, p.129*

Montaigne, Michel de & Florio, John *v.2 p.471*

Montaigne, Michel de *v.2 p.471*

Montale, Eugenio & Reed, Jeremy. *v.2 p.719*

Montale, Eugenio *v.2 p.718, p.719*

Montalvo-Barbot, Alfredo *v.3 p.320*

Montana, John C., et al.. . . . . *v.4 p.115*

MONTANES *v.5 p.703*

Montano, Mary & Montaano, Mary Caroline . *v.6 p.492, p.523*

Montaudo, Giorgio *v.5 p.323*

Montauk, Richard *v.4 p.177*

Montefiore, Alan (Editor) *v.1 p.457*

Montefiore, C. G. & Loewe, H. (Editors). *v.1 p.550*

Montefiore, Sebag *v.3 p.216*

Montefiore, Simon Sebag *v.3 p.223*

Monteforte Toledo, Mario *v.2 p.676*

Monteith, Sharon, et al.. . . . . *v.2 p.194*

Montejano, David (Editor) *v.6 p.538*

Montejano, David *v.6 p.532*

Montejo, Esteban. *v.3 p.279*

Montell, William L. *v.2 p.17*

Montemayor, Jorge de *v.2 p.651*

Monteon, Michael *v.3 p.351*

Monter, E. William *v.1 p.612*

Montero, Marta Iris & Burle Marx, Roberto *v.1 p.816*

Monterroso, Augusto, et al. *v.2 p.668*

Montes Huidobro, Matías. *v.2 p.672, p.673*

Montesquieu, Charles de Secondat *v.2 p.481, v.3 p.147*

Montessori, Maria & Hunt, J. *v.4 p.344*

Montessori, Maria *v.4 p.344*

Montet, Christian & Serra, Daniel. *v.4 p.84*

Monteverdi, Claudio. *v.1 p.185, p.231, p.342, p.409*

Montgomery, Carla W. *v.5 p.423*

Montgomery, Charles H. *v.6 p.534*

Montgomery, John H. *v.5 p.312, p.313*

Montgomery, L. M.. . . . . *v.2 p.736*

Montgomery, Marion *v.2 p.14*

Montgomery, Maureen E. *v.2 p.131*

Montgomery, Robert L. *v.2 p.215*

Montgomery, Scott L.. . . . . *v.5 p.389*

Montgomery, Sy *v.5 p.223, p.227*

Montgomery, William. *v.1 p.558*

Montherlant, Henry de *v.2 p.523*

Montiel-Argüello, Alejandro. *v.3 p.302*

Montney, Charles. *v.2 p.580*

Montoya, Richard *v.6 p.517*

Mood, Dale P., et al.. . . . . *v.4 p.784, p.796*

Moodie, Susanna *v.2 p.732*

Moodie, T. Dunbar *v.6 p.79*

Moody, A. David (Editor) *v.2 p.72*

Moody, Christopher J. & Whitham, Gordon H. . . . *v.5 p.296*

Moody, Ernest A.. . . . . *v.1 p.494*

Moody, Glyn *v.5 p.98*

Moody, James L.. . . . . *v.1 p.147, p.150*

Moody, Peter R. Jr. *v.4 p.618*

Moody, Richard (Author, Editor) *v.2 p.25*

Moody, T. W. & Martin, F. X. (Editors) *v.3 p.135, p.136*

Moody, T. W. (Editor), et al. *v.3 p.137*

Moody, T. W. (Editor) *v.3 p.136, p.137*

Moody, William Vaughn *v.2 p.98*

Moogk, Peter M. *v.3 p.538*

Moogk, Peter *v.2 p.60*

Mooij, Marieke K. de. *v.4 p.427*

Mook, Douglas. *v.5 p.597*

Moon, Ailee & Song, Young I. (Editors) *v.6 p.112, p.136*

Moon, Jeremy; Sharman, Campbell *v.4 p.624*

Moon, Katherine H. *v.6 p.237*

Moon, Krystyn R. *v.1 p.296*

Mooney, Chris *v.4 p.566*

Mooney, Douglas D. & Swift, Randall *v.5 p.500*

Mooney, Harold A. & Hobbs, Richard J.
(Editors) *v.5 p.180, v.6 p.292*

Mooney, Harold A. (Editor), et al. *v.5 p.180*

Mooney, James *v.4 p.37, v.6 p.688, p.701, p.703*

Mooney, Patrick H. & Majka, Theo J.. . . . . *v.5 p.5, p.30*

Moor, Andrew *v.1 p.810*

Moorcock, Michael. *v.2 p.368*

Moorcroft, William H. & Belcher, Paula *v.5 p.613*

Moore, Allan (Editor). *v.1 p.262*

Moore, Allan F. *v.1 p.272*

Moore, Barrington Jr.. . . . . *v.4 p.767*

Moore, Brian C. (Editor) *v.5 p.607*

Moore, Carey A.. . . . . . . *v.1 p.621, p.623, p.624*

Moore, Carlos *v.3 p.311*

Moore, Charles W., et al. *v.1 p.819*

Moore, Chris (Author, Editor) *v.5 p.630*

Moore, Christopher *v.6 p.8*

Moore, D. R., et al.. . . . . *v.5 p.690*

Moore, David Cresap *v.3 p.114*

Moore, David S. & Notz, William I. *v.5 p.481*

Moore, David *v.5 p.161*

Moore, Denton R. *v.3 p.533*

Moore, Dorothy Perrin *v.4 p.68*

Moore, Edward C. *v.1 p.513*

Moore, Elaine *v.5 p.293*

Moore, F. Richard *v.1 p.387*

Moore, G. E. *v.1 p.446, p.487, p.507*

Moore, Gene M. (Editor) *v.6 p.326*

Moore, George Edward *v.1 p.446*

Moore, George Foot *v.1 p.548*

Moore, George W. & Sullivan, Nicholas *v.5 p.424*

Moore, George. *v.2 p.300, p.301*

Moore, Gerald *v.6 p.80*

Moore, Glover *v.3 p.417*

Moore, Harry Thornton *v.2 p.344*

Moore, Henrietta L., et al. *v.4 p.31*

Moore, Henrietta L. *v.4 p.24*

Moore, Henrietta *v.4 p.31*

Moore, J. M. & Brunt, P. A. (Editors) *v.3 p.28*

Moore, James *v.3 p.484*

Moore, Jim & Vermilyea, Natalie *v.2 p.51*

Moore, Joan & Pinderhughes, Raquel (Editors) . *v.6 p.522, p.525*

Moore, Joan W. & Pachon, Harry *v.6 p.522*

Moore, Joan W. *v.6 p.547, p.549*

Moore, John A. Jr. & Pubantz, Jerry *v.4 p.634*

Moore, John A. *v.5 p.135*

Moore, John Allphin & Pubantz, Jerry *v.4 p.634*

Moore, John N. *v.3 p.302*

Moore, Kathleen D. *v.5 p.242*

Moore, Kathleen Dean *v.5 p.226*

Moore, Keith L. & Dalley, Arthur F. II *v.5 p.158*

Moore, Keith L. & Persaud, T. V. N.. . . . . . *v.5 p.162*

Moore, Keith L., et al. *v.5 p.162, p.163*

Moore, Keith M. *v.4 p.268, v.5 p.13, p.17, v.6 p.297*

Moore, Leonard N. *v.3 p.513*

Moore, Lisa C. (Editor). *v.6 p.369, p.407*

Moore, Lois Merriweather *v.6 p.40*

Moore, Madeline *v.2 p.393*

Moore, Marianne *v.2 p.103*

Moore, Marijo *v.6 p.698*

Moore, Mark H. *v.4 p.545, p.546*

Moore, Michael G. & Anderson, William (Editors) . . *v.4 p.322*

Moore, Michael L. & Outslay, Edmund *v.4 p.92, p.108*

Moore, Mike. *v.4 p.665*

Moore, Pamela (Editor) *v.4 p.818, p.844, p.855*

Moore, Pete W. *v.6 p.594*

Moore, R. I. *v.3 p.68*

Moore, Robin D.. . . . . *v.3 p.267, p.279*

Moore, Roy L.. . . . . *v.4 p.406*

Moore, Schuyler M. *v.6 p.345*

Moore, Stephen D. *v.1 p.626*

Moore, Thomas (Editor) *v.5 p.482*

Moore, Thomas *v.2 p.260, p.274*

Moore, W. J.. . . . . *v.5 p.276*

Moore, Wilbert E. *v.4 p.725*

Moore, Will Grayburn. . . *v.2 p.456, p.458, p.459, p.475, p.477*

Moore *v.5 p.154, p.160*

Moorefield, Virgil *v.1 p.272, p.387*

Moore-Gilbert, Bart (Editor). *v.2 p.762*

Moore-Gilbert, Bart *v.2 p.728*

Moorehead, Alan *v.6 p.51*

Moorehead, Caroline *v.4 p.765*

Moores, Eldridge M. & Fairbridge, Rhodes W. (Editors). *v.5 p.432*

Moorhead, James H. *v.1 p.606*

Moorhead, John *v.1 p.593*

Moorhouse, Michael & Barry, Paul *v.5 p.109*

Moorman, Frederic William *v.2 p.250*

Moorman, John R. H.. . . . . *v.6 p.572*

Moorman, John R.. . . . . *v.1 p.582, p.609*

Moorman, Mary Trevelyan *v.2 p.324*

Moos, Rudolf H. *v.4 p.699*

Moosa, Matti *v.6 p.652*

Mor Barak, Michàlle *v.4 p.132*

Mora, Jose Ferrater *v.1 p.474*

Mora, Pat *v.2 p.150, v.6 p.501, p.510*

Moraga, Cherríe & Anzaldúa, Gloria
(Editors) *v.6 p.97, p.113, p.479*

Moraga, Cherríe & Castillo, Ana (Editors) . . . *v.6 p.515, p.546*
Moraga, Cherríe *v.6 p.501, p.510*
Morales, Alejandro *v.2 p.150, v.6 p.502*
Morales, Aurora L. & Morales, Rosario *v.6 p.496, p.507*
Morales, Ed *v.1 p.293, v.3 p.317*
Morales, Edmundo. *v.3 p.272, p.282, p.330*
Morales, Maria H. *v.4 p.223*
Morales, Rebecca & Bonilla, Frank (Editors) *v.6 p.525*
Moran, Aidan P. *v.4 p.877, v.5 p.582*
Moran, Albert & Vieth, Errol *v.6 p.337*
Moran, Albert (Editor) *v.6 p.345*
Moran, Dermot & Mooney, Tim (Editors) *v.1 p.511*
Moran, Dermot. *v.1 p.511*
Moran, Emilio F. (Editor) *v.4 p.30*
Moran, Emilio F. *v.4 p.30*
Moran, Jeffrey P. *v.4 p.438, p.736*
Moran, John P. *v.4 p.598*
Moran, Michael *v.4 p.385*
Moran, Rachel F. *v.4 p.457, p.737*
Moran, Robbin Craig *v.5 p.210*
Moran, Robert T. & Abbott, Jeffrey D. *v.4 p.61*
Moran, Theodore, et al. *v.4 p.60*
Moran, Theodore *v.4 p.60*
Morange, Michel *v.5 p.80, p.128, p.135*
Morante, Elsa *v.2 p.719*
Moran-Zenteno, Dante *v.5 p.432*
Morash, Christopher *v.1 p.109*
Morash, Merry & Ford, J. Kevin (Editors) *v.6 p.264*
Morath, Inge & Miller, Arthur. *v.6 p.197, p.216*
Moravec, Hans *v.5 p.339, p.343*
Moravia, Alberto. *v.2 p.719, p.720*
Morawska, Ewa *v.3 p.492, p.493*
Morcillo, Aurora G. *v.3 p.242*
Mordden, Ethan *v.1 p.252, v.6 p.398*
More, Ellen S. *v.6 p.439*
More, Thomas (Editor), et al. *v.2 p.215*
More, Thomas *v.2 p.215, v.4 p.499*
Moreau, Joseph *v.4 p.285*
Moreen, Vera Basch *v.6 p.597, p.629*
Morel, Gérard; Raccurt, Mireille *v.5 p.89*
Morel, Jacques. *v.2 p.458*
Moreland, Richard C. *v.2 p.74*
Moreno Fraginals, Manuel (Editor), et al.. . . . . *v.3 p.317*
Moreno Gomez, Francisco *v.2 p.639*
Moreno, Jonathan D. (Editor) *v.4 p.660, p.669*
Moreno, Jose A. *v.3 p.317*
Moreno, Paul D. *v.4 p.133, p.447*
Morín, José Luis *v.6 p.540*
Morford, Mark P. O. *v.1 p.428*
Morford, M. *v.2 p.437*
Morgagni, Giambattista *v.5 p.510*
Morgan, Ann L. (Editor) *v.1 p.784*
Morgan, Barbara & Patnaik, Deba P. *v.1 p.29, p.30, p.46*
Morgan, Barbara *v.1 p.27*
Morgan, Catherine. *v.3 p.16*

Morgan, Dale L. *v.3 p.529*
Morgan, David L. *v.4 p.137, p.687*
Morgan, David. *v.6 p.239, p.351*
Morgan, Edmund S. & Morgan, Helen M. *v.3 p.410*
Morgan, Edmund S. . . *v.1 p.588, v.3 p.410, p.485, p.487, p.500*
Morgan, Esther (Editor) *v.2 p.200, p.577, p.583*
Morgan, Frank *v.5 p.496*
Morgan, Gareth *v.4 p.66*
Morgan, H. Wayne & Morgan, Anne H. *v.3 p.524*
Morgan, H. Wayne *v.3 p.437*
Morgan, Harry *v.4 p.310*
Morgan, Hiram *v.3 p.135, p.137*
Morgan, Howard, et al. *v.4 p.65*
Morgan, Howard W. *v.3 p.437*
Morgan, Iwan *v.3 p.476*
Morgan, Jessica, et al. *v.1 p.771*
Morgan, Kenneth O. *v.3 p.94, p.95, p.118, p.119, p.132*
Morgan, Kenneth W. *v.1 p.565*
Morgan, Lewis H. *v.6 p.703*
Morgan, M. Gwyn. *v.3 p.29*
Morgan, Marcyliena *v.4 p.21*
Morgan, Margery. *v.2 p.630*
Morgan, Mary S. & Morrison, Margaret (Editors) . . . *v.4 p.687*
Morgan, Mary S.. . . . . *v.4 p.203*
Morgan, Richard G. (Editor). *v.2 p.110*
Morgan, Robert C. *v.1 p.773*
Morgan, Robert J. *v.3 p.417*
Morgan, Robert P. & Barton, John *v.1 p.616*
Morgan, Robert P. *v.1 p.219*
Morgan, Robert *v.2 p.151*
Morgan, Robin (Editor, Compiled by) *v.6 p.431*
Morgan, Robin (Editor). *v.6 p.431*
Morgan, Ronald J. *v.3 p.263, p.326*
Morgan, Sally & Lalor, Pauline *v.5 p.173*
Morgan, Ted *v.2 p.64, v.3 p.156, p.449, p.518*
Morgan, Teresa *v.3 p.23*
Morgan, Thais E. (Editor) *v.6 p.748, p.764*
Morgan, William J. & Meier, Klaus V. *v.4 p.803*
Morgan, William *v.1 p.784*
Morgen, Sandra *v.5 p.524*
Morgenstern, Christian *v.2 p.614*
Morgenstern, Richard D. *v.4 p.62*
Morgenstern, Sam (Editor) *v.1 p.174, p.247*
Morgenthau, Hans J., et al. *v.4 p.626*
Morgenthau, Hans J. *v.3 p.453, v.4 p.626*
Morgner, Irmtraud *v.2 p.618*
Mori, Ogai. *v.6 p.231*
Mori, Toshio & Inada, Lawson Fusao *v.6 p.101*
Moriarty, Catherine *v.1 p.780*
Moriarty, Laura J. (Editor) *v.6 p.248*
Moriarty, Laura J. *v.6 p.258*
Moricz, Zsigmond *v.2 p.786*
Morike, Eduard Friedrich *v.2 p.600*
Morin, Edward *v.6 p.211*
Morine, David E. *v.5 p.180, p.230*

Morisawa, Marie E. *v.5 p.427*

Morison, Samuel Eliot, et al. *v.3 p.380*

Morison, Samuel Eliot; Obregón, Mauricio *v.3 p.404*

Morison, Samuel Eliot. *v.3 p.383, p.404, p.485, p.487*

Morkot, Robert *v.3 p.12*

Morley, Christopher *v.2 p.98*

Morley, James W. & Nishihara, Masashi (Editors). . . *v.6 p.168*

Morley, John M. *v.3 p.95, p.114*

Morley, John. *v.1 p.800*

Morley, Morris H. & McGillion, Chris *v.3 p.311*

Morley, Morris H. (Editor) *v.3 p.476*

Morley, Morris H. *v.3 p.391*

Morley, Richard *v.4 p.238*

Morley, Thomas *v.1 p.180*

Morner, Magnus *v.3 p.328*

Morone, James A. *v.4 p.555, p.579*

Morony, Michael G. *v.6 p.602*

Morowitz, Laura & Emery, Elizabeth *v.3 p.155*

Morphy, Howard & Perkins, Morgan *v.1 p.708, v.4 p.26*

Morrall, John B. *v.4 p.489, p.490, v.6 p.568*

Morreale, Joanne *v.4 p.551, v.6 p.342*

Morrell, Jack & Thackray, Arnold W.. . . . *v.3 p.114, v.5 p.385*

Morrill, John (Editor). *v.3 p.104*

Morrill, John. *v.3 p.104*

Morris, Adalaide Kirby *v.2 p.89*

Morris, Alan *v.2 p.532*

Morris, Alistair. *v.1 p.819*

Morris, Andrew D. *v.4 p.808, v.6 p.194*

Morris, Benny. *v.6 p.611, p.614, p.619*

Morris, Colin (Editor) *v.3 p.57*

Morris, Craig & Thompson, Donald E.. . . . . *v.3 p.261*

Morris, Cynthia T. & Adelman, Irma *v.4 p.237, p.259*

Morris, Daniel *v.2 p.136, v.4 p.862*

Morris, David B. *v.2 p.257*

Morris, David G. & Abel, Eddie *v.5 p.298*

Morris, Desmond *v.5 p.201, p.617*

Morris, Dick. *v.3 p.476*

Morris, Donald R.. . . . . *v.6 p.79*

Morris, Edmund *v.3 p.443*

Morris, Evan. *v.4 p.142*

Morris, G. S. Don & Stiehl, Jim. *v.4 p.364*

Morris, Gay (Editor) *v.1 p.39, p.43*

Morris, Gay *v.1 p.29, p.30, p.43*

Morris, G.S. Don & Stiehl, Jim (Authors) *v.4 p.304*

Morris, Ivan. *v.6 p.228, p.232*

Morris, J. A. *v.3 p.311*

Morris, James A.. . . . . *v.3 p.276*

Morris, James M. & Kross, Andrea L. *v.4 p.678*

Morris, Jan *v.6 p.206, p.371, p.403*

Morris, Joseph M. & Gole, William J.. . . . . *v.4 p.84*

Morris, Kenneth E. *v.3 p.476*

Morris, Kenneth M. & Morris, Virginia B.. . . . . . *v.4 p.96*

Morris, Lynn A. (Editor) *v.4 p.784, p.813*

Morris, Marcia A. *v.2 p.799*

Morris, Norval & Tonry, Michael H.. . . . . . *v.6 p.271, p.275*

Morris, Norval *v.6 p.273*

Morris, Patrick, et al. *v.5 p.236*

Morris, Peter J. T. & Benfrey, Otto Theodor (Editors) . *v.5 p.261*

Morris, R. J. *v.3 p.114, p.131*

Morris, Reginald O. *v.1 p.372*

Morris, Richard B. *v.3 p.372, v.5 p.409*

Morris, Robert D. *v.1 p.372*

Morris, Rod & Balance, Alison *v.5 p.241*

Morris, Roger *v.3 p.476*

Morris, Sarah P. *v.1 p.670*

Morris, Stephen D. *v.3 p.294*

Morris, Stephen J. *v.6 p.168*

Morris, Thomas D.. . . . . *v.4 p.442, p.453*

Morris, Thomas V. (Editor) *v.1 p.499*

Morris, W. N. *v.5 p.660*

Morris, William & Shankland, Graeme *v.2 p.302*

Morris, William O'Connor *v.2 p.302*

Morris, William *v.2 p.301, p.302, v.4 p.499*

Morris, Wright *v.2 p.103*

Morrison, Alec (Editor). *v.4 p.812, p.861*

Morrison, Andrea M. & Mann, Barbara J. *v.4 p.60*

Morrison, Blake *v.2 p.200*

Morrison, Craig *v.1 p.155*

Morrison, Dane A. & Schultz, Nancy Lusignan (Editors). *v.3 p.488*

Morrison, David & Owen, Tobias C. *v.5 p.69*

Morrison, Jago. *v.2 p.194, p.578*

Morrison, James D. (Editor). *v.5 p.295*

Morrison, James *v.2 p.415*

Morrison, R. Bruce & Wilson, Rod . . . *v.6 p.682, p.692, p.703*

Morrison, Robert (Editor) *v.2 p.268*

Morrison, Terri & Conaway, Wayne A. *v.4 p.56*

Morrison, Terri, et al. *v.4 p.56*

Morrison, Terri. *v.4 p.173*

Morrison, Toni. *v.2 p.151, v.6 p.27, p.45, p.470*

Morrison, William F.. . . . . *v.4 p.74*

Morrison, William R.. . . . . *v.3 p.547*

Morrisroe, Patricia *v.1 p.768, v.6 p.407*

Morrissey, Charles T.. . . . . *v.3 p.486*

Morrissey, Katherine G.. . . . . *v.3 p.530*

Morrissey, Marietta. *v.4 p.728*

Morrissey, Robert John *v.3 p.140*

Morrow, Charlene & Perl, Teri (Editors) *v.5 p.467*

Morrow, Deana F. & Messinger, Lori *v.6 p.381*

Morrow, Don & Wamsley, Kevin *v.4 p.808*

Morrow, Mary S. *v.1 p.191, p.330*

Morrow, Raymond A. & Brown, David D. *v.4 p.680*

Morrow, Raymond Allen & Torres, Carlos Alberto . *v.4 p.762*

Morse, Carl & Larkin, Joan (Editors) *v.6 p.405*

Morse, David *v.2 p.170, p.172*

Morse, Donald E. *v.2 p.158*

Morse, Flo. *v.1 p.589*

Morse, Janice M. (Editor). *v.5 p.529*

Morse, Kathryn Taylor *v.3 p.533, p.547*

Morse, Peter *v.1 p.757*

Morse, Philip M. & Ingard, K. Uno *v.5 p.567*

Morse, Philip McCord *v.5 p.548*

Morse, Roger & Flottum, Kim (Editors) *v.5 p.27, p.55*

Morse, Stephen A., et al. *v.5 p.515, p.516*

Morsink, Johannes *v.4 p.435*

Morss, Lester R. *v.5 p.308*

Mort, Jo-Ann (Editor) *v.4 p.127*

Mortensen, Dale T. *v.4 p.203, p.244, p.254, p.266*

Mortensen, Vigo (Editor) *v.5 p.218, p.248*

Mortenson, Philip B. *v.5 p.80, p.246*

Mortier, Roland & Trousson, Raymond. *v.2 p.480*

Mortimer, Geoff *v.3 p.166*

Mortimer, Jeylan T. & Shanahan, Michael J.
(Editors). *v.5 p.628, p.632*

Mortimer, M. & Taylor, P. G. (Editors). *v.5 p.279*

Mortimer, Robert G. *v.5 p.278*

Mortimer, William Golden *v.3 p.282*

Morton, Andrew *v.3 p.476*

Morton, Brian (Editor) *v.5 p.171*

Morton, Carlos *v.6 p.502, p.517*

Morton, David. *v.1 p.289, p.387*

Morton, Desmond *v.3 p.535, p.536, p.537*

Morton, Donald (Editor) *v.6 p.357*

Morton, Fred & Ramsay, Jeff. *v.6 p.75*

Morton, Frederic *v.3 p.184*

Morton, Jacqueline (Author, Editor) *v.2 p.557*

Morton, Joann B.. . . . . *v.6 p.277*

Morton, Margaret. *v.4 p.751, v.6 p.718*

Morton, Richard Lee *v.3 p.500*

Morton, Timothy (Editor) *v.2 p.311*

Morton, William Lewis *v.3 p.537*

Mortvedt, J. J. (Editor), et al.. . . . . *v.5 p.50*

Morwood, James *v.2 p.400*

Mosby, David & Weissman, Michael *v.4 p.73*

Moschovitis, Christos J. P., et al. *v.5 p.679*

Mosco, Vincent *v.4 p.425*

Mosconi, Willie & Cohen, Stanley. *v.4 p.855*

Moseley, Alexander & Norman, Richard (Editors). . *v.4 p.513*

Moseley, Charles J. (Editor). *v.4 p.159, p.160*

Moseley, Christopher *v.2 p.781*

Moseley, Fred (Editor) *v.4 p.236*

Moser, Charles A. (Editor) *v.2 p.799*

Moser, Charles A. *v.2 p.780*

Moser, L. E., et al. *v.5 p.50*

Moser, Michael E. & Finlayson, Max
(Editors) *v.5 p.53, p.357, p.380*

Moser, Paul K. & Carson, Thomas L. (Editors) . . . *v.1 p.515*

Moser, Paul K. & Copan, Paul (Editors) *v.1 p.499, p.595*

Moser, Paul K. & Trout, J. D. (Editors) *v.1 p.509*

Moser, Paul K. (Editor). *v.1 p.482*

Moser, Paul K., et al. *v.1 p.482*

Moser, Rodney L. *v.5 p.534*

Moses, Catherine *v.3 p.311*

Moses, Daniel D. (Editor). *v.2 p.732*

Moses, Larry W. *v.6 p.240*

Moses, Montrose J. (Editor) *v.2 p.25*

Moses, Wilson J. (Editor) *v.6 p.13*

Moses, Wilson J.. . . . . *v.6 p.13, p.31*

Mosher, Clayton James, et al. *v.6 p.251*

Moskos, Charles C. Jr. *v.4 p.634, p.650*

Moskowitz, David V.. . . . . *v.1 p.161, p.293*

Moskowitz, Gordon B. *v.5 p.650*

Mosley, Leonard *v.3 p.461*

Mosley, Stephen R. *v.6 p.289, p.296*

Moss, David A.. . . . . *v.4 p.92*

Moss, Dorian & Roy, David. *v.5 p.180*

Moss, Henry S. *v.3 p.66*

Moss, Kary L. (Editor) *v.6 p.444*

Moss, Lenny. *v.5 p.135*

Moss, Leonard *v.2 p.102*

Moss, M. E. *v.1 p.473*

Moss, Norman *v.4 p.647*

Moss, Philip & Tilly, Chris *v.4 p.133*

Moss, Richard J. *v.4 p.716*

Moss, Rita W. *v.4 p.96, p.180*

Moss, Sanford *v.5 p.238*

Moss, Walter G. *v.3 p.209*

Moss, Walter. *v.3 p.209*

Moss, Wes *v.4 p.68*

Mosse, George L.. *v.3 p.60, p.61, p.78, p.179, v.4 p.510, v.5 p.584*

Mosse, W. E. *v.3 p.180, p.218, p.219*

Mossé, Fernand *v.2 p.551*

Mossman, Judith *v.2 p.411*

Mossner, E. C. *v.1 p.451*

Mosston, Muska & Ashworth, Sara *v.4 p.798, p.799*

Most, Andrea *v.1 p.253, p.300*

Most, Benjamin A.. . . . . *v.3 p.348*

Mosteghanemi, Ahlam *v.6 p.662*

Mostofsky, David I. & Zaichkowsky, Leonard (Editors). *v.5 p.582*

Mostow, Joshua (Editor) *v.6 p.181*

Mostow, Joshua S. (Editor), et al. *v.6 p.473*

Mostyn, Trevor & Hourani, Albert H. (Editors) . . . *v.6 p.60*

Moszynska, Anna *v.1 p.680*

Motala, Ziyad *v.4 p.614*

Mote, Frederick W. & Twitchett, Denis C. *v.6 p.186*

Mote, Frederick W. (Editor) *v.6 p.186*

Mote, Frederick W. *v.6 p.182, p.184, p.185*

Mote, Victor L. *v.3 p.214*

Motherwell, Robert; Terenzio, Stephania *v.1 p.744*

Motion, Andrew *v.2 p.295*

Motloch, John L.. . . . . *v.1 p.817*

Mott, Frank L.. . . . . *v.4 p.409*

Mott, Frank Luther *v.4 p.411*

Mott, Lawrence V. *v.6 p.567*

Mott, Wesley T. (Editor) *v.1 p.515*

Mottahedeh, Roy P. *v.6 p.585*

Mottahedeh, Roy *v.6 p.632*

Mottana, Annibale, et al. *v.5 p.435*

Mottola, Anthony & St. Ignatius of
Loyola Staff *v.1 p.577, p.612*

Mottram, D. R.. . . . . *v.4 p.826*

Motulsky, Harvey & Christopoulos, Arthur *v.5 p.101*

Motyl, Alexander (Editor), et al.. . . . . *v.4 p.644*

Motyl, Alexander J. (Editor-In-Chief) *v.4 p.494*

Moua, Mai Neng (Editor) *v.6 p.92, p.139, p.140*

Moubayed, Sami M.. . . . . *v.6 p.607*

Moul, Charles C. (Editor) *v.6 p.345*

Moulakis, Athanasios *v.4 p.303*

Mounce, Robert H.. . . . . *v.1 p.632*

Mounfield, Peter R.. . . . . *v.5 p.740*

Mount, David *v.5 p.102, p.142*

Mount, Ferdinand *v.4 p.733*

Mouritsen, Henrik *v.3 p.26*

Mouritzen, Hans & Wivel, Anders. *v.4 p.383, p.400*

Mousley, Andy. *v.2 p.186*

Moussa, Naima Moustaid &
  Berdanier, Carolyn *v.5 p.104, p.117, p.146*

Moussa, Sabri *v.6 p.662*

Moussalli, Carole. *v.5 p.251*

Mousseau, Timothy A., et al.. . . . . *v.5 p.195*

Moussinac, Leon (Compiled by). *v.1 p.142*

Moussis, Nicholas *v.4 p.603, p.638*

Mouzelis, Nicos *v.4 p.680*

Mowat, Charles Loch *v.3 p.118*

Mower, A. Glenn Jr. *v.4 p.435*

Mowle, Thomas *v.4 p.642*

Mowrer, O. Hobart. *v.5 p.571, p.572*

Mowrer, Orval Hobart *v.4 p.358*

Mowrey, Peter C.. . . . . *v.6 p.346*

Mowry, George E. & Brownell, Blaine A. . . . *v.3 p.443, p.449*

Mowshowitz, Abbe. *v.4 p.718*

Moxey, Keith *v.1 p.753*

Moy, Patricia & Pfau, Michael *v.4 p.558*

Moyer, David B.. . . . . *v.4 p.153*

Moyer, Imogene *v.6 p.250*

Moyle, Peter B. & Cech, Joseph J.. . . . . *v.5 p.216*

Moynihan, Daniel P. *v.4 p.266, p.769*

Mozaffari, Nahid *v.6 p.672*

Mozart, Leopold *v.1 p.398, p.401*

Mozart, Wolfgang Amadeus. *v.1 p.164, p.191, p.231, p.344, p.409*

Mozick, Martin (Editor). *v.2 p.662*

Mozzam, Sheikh (Editor) *v.6 p.162*

Mphahlele, Ezekiel *v.2 p.756*

Mr. Fresh and the Supreme Rockers Staff *v.1 p.18*

Mrazek, Jan (Editor) *v.1 p.133, p.134*

Mrozek, Donald J.. . . . . *v.4 p.808, p.818*

Mrozek, Slawomir *v.2 p.791*

Müsch, Irmgard, et al. *v.5 p.224*

Muchembled, Robert *v.1 p.709, v.3 p.146*

Mucke, Ulrich *v.3 p.328*

Mudd, John *v.4 p.544*

Mudrick, Marvin *v.2 p.268*

Mudrooroo. *v.2 p.747*

Muehlbauer, Gene *v.4 p.753*

Mueller, Dennis C.. . . . . *v.4 p.576*

Mueller, John *v.1 p.37, p.46*

Mueller, Laurence D.. . . . . *v.5 p.170*

Mueller-Harvey, I. & Baker, R. M.. . . . . *v.5 p.268*

Muendel, Renate *v.2 p.300*

Muftuler-Bac, Meltem *v.4 p.638*

Mugglestone, Lynda *v.6 p.751*

Muggleton, David &
  Weinzierl, Rupert *v.4 p.818, p.846, p.888, p.892*

Muggleton, David *v.4 p.709*

Muhamad, Ibn Sasra *v.6 p.607*

Muhanji, Cherry *v.6 p.398*

Muhlberger, Detlef (Editor) *v.4 p.768*

Muhle, Eduard (Editor) *v.3 p.161*

Muhlstein, Anka *v.3 p.538*

Muir, Edward *v.1 p.530*

Muir, John *v.3 p.533, v.6 p.287*

Muir, Kenneth *v.2 p.225, p.231*

Muir, Lynette R. *v.1 p.73, p.97*

Muir, William *v.6 p.585*

Muirhead, J. H. *v.1 p.446*

Muirhead, Kimberly Free *v.2 p.41*

Muirhead, Robb J. *v.5 p.482*

Muise, D. A. (Editor) *v.6 p.682*

Mujica, Barbara *v.2 p.644*

Mukherjee, Bharati *v.2 p.765, v.6 p.101*

Mukherjee, Dipika (Editor), et al. *v.2 p.760*

Mukherjee, Meenakshi *v.2 p.762*

Mukherjee, Tutun (Editor) *v.6 p.146, p.148*

Muksian, Robert *v.4 p.175*

Mulamoottil, George *v.5 p.357*

Mulcahy, D. G. *v.4 p.344*

Mulder, Philip N.. . . . . *v.1 p.607*

Muldoon, James P. Jr.. . . . . *v.4 p.629*

Muldoon, James. *v.3 p.74, v.4 p.501, p.583*

Mulford, Carla (Editor), et al. *v.2 p.21*

Mulford, Charles W. &
  Comiskey, Eugene E. . . . *v.4 p.96, p.102, p.105, p.106, p.111*

Mulgan, Aurelia George *v.6 p.220, p.225*

Mulgan, John *v.2 p.747*

Mulhall, Douglas *v.5 p.136, p.265*

Mulhall, Stephen *v.1 p.471*

Mulhauser, Ruth *v.2 p.472*

Mulisch, Harry. *v.2 p.623*

Mull, Richard F., et al. *v.4 p.786*

Mullaney, Marie M. (Compiled by) *v.4 p.557*

Mullaney, Marie M. *v.3 p.377*

Mullen, Bill. *v.6 p.11*

Mullen, Megan Gwynne *v.4 p.421*

Mullen, Michelle. *v.4 p.796, p.848*

Mullen, Richard *v.2 p.317*

Mullender, Sape *v.5 p.345*

Muller, Carol Ann *v.1 p.285*

Muller, Eric L.. . . . . *v.6 p.107, p.134*

Muller, F. Max (Editor). *v.1 p.537, p.564*

Muller, F. Max. *v.1 p.537, p.564*

Muller, Filip *v.3 p.85*

Muller, Gilbert H. *v.2 p.86*

Muller, Hans W. *v.1 p.806*

Muller, Heiner *v.2 p.618*

Muller, Keith E. & Fetterman, Bethel A. *v.5 p.483*

Muller, Nathan J. *v.4 p.420, p.422*

Muller, Richard & Corum, James S. (Translators) . . . *v.3 p.175*

Muller, Richard A. *v.1 p.603*

Muller, Robert & Roche, Douglas *v.4 p.634*

Muller, Robert J. *v.5 p.337*

Muller, Theodor *v.1 p.777*

Muller, Thomas *v.4 p.571, v.6 p.714*

Muller, Ulrich (Editor), et al. *v.1 p.200, p.366*

Muller-Brockmann, Josef & Muller-Brockmann,
Shizuko *v.1 p.718*

Mulligan, Catherine N. *v.5 p.706*

Mulligan, Joseph F. & Mulligan, Kevin T. *v.4 p.907*

Mulligan, Therese & Wooters, David (Editors) . . . *v.1 p.763*

Mullin, Bernard J., et al. *v.4 p.885*

Mullin, Robert Bruce *v.1 p.584*

Mullings, Leith *v.6 p.40, p.45, p.470*

Mullins, Mark R. (Editor) *v.1 p.610*

Mullins, Paul R. *v.6 p.20*

Mullins *v.4 p.675*

Mullis, Kary B. & Gibbs, Richard (Editors) *v.5 p.154*

Mullner, S. *v.5 p.117, p.205*

Mulroy, Elizabeth A. (Editor) *v.6 p.465, p.467*

Mulryan, Lenore Hoag *v.1 p.684, p.777*

Mulryne, Ronnie (Editor), et al. . . . *v.1 p.155, v.2 p.227*

Multatuli *v.2 p.623*

Multhauf, Robert P. *v.5 p.317*

Mulvenon, James C. (Editor) *v.6 p.197*

Mulvey, Laura *v.6 p.473*

Mulvihill, James *v.2 p.302*

Mulzer, Johann, et al. *v.5 p.294*

Mumford, Lewis *v.4 p.771, v.6 p.714*

Mun, Thomas *v.4 p.216, p.257*

Muncie, John (Editor), et al. *v.5 p.639*

Munck, Gerardo L. *v.3 p.276*

Munck, Ronaldo *v.4 p.236*

Munck, Thomas *v.3 p.72*

Muncy, Mitchell S. (Editor) *v.4 p.525*

Muncy, Raymond Lee *v.4 p.733*

Mundell, Robert A. *v.4 p.247*

Mundell, Robert *v.4 p.238*

Mundhenk, Rosemary J. *v.2 p.203*

Mundy, Barbara E. *v.3 p.287*

Mundy, Bradford P. & Ellerd, Michael G. *v.5 p.296*

Mundy, Jean *v.4 p.784*

Mundy, John H. *v.1 p.256, v.6 p.564*

Mundy, Martha *v.6 p.596, p.628*

Mungello, David E. *v.6 p.186, p.216, p.218*

Mungo, Ray *v.6 p.409*

Munhall, Edgar *v.1 p.723*

Munich, Adrienne & Bradshaw, Melissa (Editors) . . . *v.2 p.95*

Munich, Adrienne *v.6 p.764*

Munif, Abd al-Rahma. *v.6 p.621*

Munif, Abd al-Rahman *v.6 p.662*

Munitz, Milton K. *v.1 p.488*

Munk, Nina *v.4 p.84*

Munk, Petr & Aminabhavi, Tejraj M. *v.5 p.322*

Munkres, James R. *v.5 p.499*

Munn, Mark D. *v.3 p.18, p.20*

Munn, Ted (Editor) *v.6 p.286*

Munnell, Alicia H. & Sunden, Annika *v.4 p.97, p.99*

Munoz, Carlos *v.6 p.538, p.539, p.541*

Munoz, Elias M. *v.6 p.507, p.508*

Munro, Alice *v.2 p.737*

Munro, Donald J. *v.1 p.418*

Munro, J. Forbes *v.6 p.65*

Munroe, Alexandra, et al. *v.1 p.773*

Munroe, Alexandra *v.6 p.222*

Munroe, John A. *v.3 p.493, v.4 p.542*

Munson, Henry Jr. *v.6 p.61, p.643*

Munter, Mary & Haley, Thea *v.4 p.173*

Mura, David *v.6 p.94, p.113, p.132*

Murakami, Haruki *v.6 p.232*

Murasaki, Shikibu *v.6 p.232*

Murase, Miyeko & Tosa, Mitsuoki *v.1 p.733*

Muraskin, William A. *v.4 p.719*

Murat, Michel *v.2 p.518*

Muravchik, Joshua *v.4 p.507*

Murayama, Milton *v.6 p.101*

Murch, Walter (Author, Preface by) *v.6 p.350*

Murck, Alfreda & Fong, Wen C. *v.6 p.208*

Murdin, Paul & Penston, Margaret (Editors) *v.5 p.63*

Murdin, Paul (Editor) *v.5 p.63*

Murdoch, Brian O. *v.2 p.589*

Murdoch, H. Adlai *v.2 p.537*

Murdoch, Iris *v.1 p.424, p.487, p.488, v.2 p.372*

Murdoch, John E. *v.5 p.399*

Murdoch, Joyce & Price, Deb *v.6 p.388*

Murdock, Catherine Gilbert *v.5 p.664, v.6 p.470*

Murdock, Eugene C. *v.3 p.431*

Murdock, George P. & O'Leary, Timothy J. *v.6 p.703*

Murdock, John E. & Sylla, Edith D. (Editors) *v.6 p.576*

Murdock, Kenneth Ballard *v.3 p.487*

Murdy, Anne-Elizabeth *v.6 p.8, p.21, p.45*

Mure, Geoffrey R. *v.1 p.427*

Murfree, Mary N. *v.2 p.46, p.47*

Murguìa, Alejandro *v.6 p.490, p.536*

Murillo, Fernando *v.2 p.687*

Murillo, Maria Victoria *v.4 p.128*

Muriuki, Godfrey *v.6 p.65*

Muron, Louis *v.2 p.508*

Murphey, Rhoads *v.3 p.36*

Murphy, Alexandra R., et al. *v.1 p.723*

Murphy, Andrew *v.2 p.170*

Murphy, Brenda (Editor) *v.1 p.60, p.121, v.2 p.16*

Murphy, Brenda *v.1 p.80, p.83, p.117, v.2 p.134*
Murphy, Bruce A. *v.4 p.468*
Murphy, Bruce Allen *v.4 p.468*
Murphy, Bruce *v.2 p.549*
Murphy, C. F. & Peterson, D. M. (Editors) *v.5 p.8, p.22*
Murphy, David E. *v.3 p.227*
Murphy, Donald J. *v.3 p.476*
Murphy, Douglas B. *v.5 p.86*
Murphy, Emma C. *v.6 p.641*
Murphy, Frederick J. *v.1 p.632*
Murphy, Gardner *v.4 p.358*
Murphy, James B., et al. *v.5 p.84*
Murphy, James J. (Editor) *v.2 p.565*
Murphy, James J. *v.6 p.558, p.569*
Murphy, Jeffrie G. & Hampton, Jean *v.1 p.651*
Murphy, Jeffrie G. *v.1 p.462*
Murphy, John F. *v.4 p.477*
Murphy, John J. (Editor) *v.2 p.67*
Murphy, Kevin R. & Davidshofer, Charles O. . . . *v.5 p.601*
Murphy, Larry G. (Editor), et al. *v.1 p.544*
Murphy, Linda L. (Editor), et al. *v.5 p.601*
Murphy, Mark *v.1 p.491*
Murphy, Michael (Editor) *v.4 p.587*
Murphy, N. T. *v.2 p.390*
Murphy, Patrick D. (Editor) *v.2 p.154*
Murphy, Patrick D. *v.2 p.155*
Murphy, Patrick E. *v.4 p.173*
Murphy, Paul L. *v.4 p.452*
Murphy, Paul V. *v.4 p.516*
Murphy, Peter F. (Editor) *v.6 p.367, p.429*
Murphy, Raymond *v.4 p.680*
Murphy, Robert *v.6 p.339*
Murphy, Robin R. *v.5 p.711*
Murphy, Shane M. *v.4 p.818, p.840*
Murphy, Shane *v.4 p.877, v.5 p.582*
Murphy, Sharon, et al. *v.4 p.354*
Murphy, Timothy (Editor) *v.6 p.357*
Murphy, Timothy F. & Poirier, Suzanne *v.6 p.393*
Murphy, Timothy F. *v.6 p.420*
Murphy, Timothy S. *v.2 p.64*
Murphy, Trevor *v.2 p.440, v.5 p.225*
Murphy, Walter F., et al. *v.4 p.465, p.466*
Murphy, William M. *v.2 p.326*
Murra, John V. *v.3 p.324*
Murray, Alan S. *v.4 p.107*
Murray, Alan V. (Editor) *v.3 p.232*
Murray, Alice Yang *v.6 p.134*
Murray, Bill *v.4 p.844, p.867*
Murray, Carl D. & Dermott, Stanley F. *v.5 p.68*
Murray, Charles Shaar *v.1 p.272, p.331*
Murray, David *v.4 p.728*
Murray, Douglas L. *v.3 p.269*
Murray, G. T. (Editor) *v.5 p.690*
Murray, G. T. *v.5 p.319, p.732*
Murray, Graeme I. & Curran, Stephanie *v.5 p.89*

Murray, James D. & VanRyper, William *v.5 p.340*
Murray, James D. *v.5 p.91, p.94, p.502*
Murray, Janet Horowitz *v.5 p.341, p.342*
Murray, Jocelyn *v.6 p.51*
Murray, John A. *v.5 p.232*
Murray, Les A. *v.2 p.743*
Murray, Linda & Murray, Peter (Editors) *v.1 p.665*
Murray, Linda *v.1 p.675, p.688, p.698*
Murray, Mary *v.3 p.312*
Murray, Michael P. *v.4 p.203*
Murray, Nicholas *v.2 p.252*
Murray, Oswyn & Price, Simon (Editors) *v.3 p.13*
Murray, Oswyn *v.3 p.17*
Murray, Pamela S. *v.3 p.358*
Murray, Peter & Murray, Linda *v.1 p.665, p.675, p.688*
Murray, R. Emmett *v.4 p.122*
Murray, Raymond *v.6 p.358, p.417*
Murray, Robert K., et al. *v.5 p.111*
Murray, Robert K. *v.3 p.443, p.449, p.476, v.4 p.714*
Murray, Robert *v.1 p.656*
Murray, Ruth L. *v.1 p.48*
Murray, Stephen O. & Roscoe, Will (Editors) . *v.6 p.374, p.421*
Murray, Stephen O. *v.4 p.748, v.6 p.367, p.372, p.421*
Murray, Stuart (Contribution by) *v.2 p.741*
Murray, Stuart *v.3 p.383*
Murray, Tim (Editor) *v.4 p.5*
Murray, Williamson & Millett, Allan R. *v.3 p.81*
Murray-Brown, Jeremy *v.6 p.65*
Murrell, J. N. & Boucher, E. A. *v.5 p.282*
Murrell, Peter C. Jr. *v.4 p.310*
Murry, John M. *v.2 p.263, p.295*
Murshed, Syed Mansoob (Editor) *v.3 p.300*
Murtagh, William J. *v.1 p.823, v.6 p.728*
Murtha, Thomas P., et al. *v.4 p.69*
Murthy, A. S. Narasimha & Mohle, R. Henry *v.5 p.700*
Murthy, V. N. *v.5 p.422*
Murti, T. R. *v.1 p.566*
Murty, Komanduri, et al. *v.6 p.277*
Muscatine, Charles *v.2 p.210*
Muscatine, Doris (Editor), et al. *v.5 p.52*
Musciano, Chuck & Kennedy, Bill *v.5 p.338, p.347*
Muse, Erika A. *v.6 p.106, p.127*
Musgrave, Michael & Sherman, Bernard D.
  (Editors) *v.1 p.201, p.313, p.401*
Musgrave, Michael (Editor) *v.1 p.201, p.313*
Musgrave, Michael *v.1 p.201, p.236, p.313*
Musgrave, Peter *v.3 p.41, p.70*
Musgrave, Richard Abel *v.4 p.247*
Musgrove, Jan *v.6 p.351*
Music, David W. *v.1 p.390*
Music Library Association *v.1 p.384, p.406*
Music Publishers' Association of the United
  States *v.1 p.172, p.385*
Musico, Giuliana *v.6 p.343*
Musil, Robert *v.2 p.614*

Musser, Charles *v.6 p.332, p.343*

Musser, Donald W. & Price,
  Joseph L. (Editors) *v.1 p.633*

Musset, Alfred de & Meyer, Peter *v.2 p.498*

Musset, Alfred de *v.2 p.498*

Mussorgsky, Modest *v.1 p.201, p.231, p.345, p.409*

Musto, David F. & Korsmeyer, Pamela . . . *v.4 p.568, v.5 p.664*

Musto, David F. *v.3 p.282*

Mutawi, Samir A. *v.6 p.621*

Mutch, Robert E. *v.4 p.525*

Muthu, Sankar *v.3 p.72*

Mutibwa, Phares M. *v.6 p.67*

Mutibwa, Phares *v.6 p.66*

Mutis, Alvaro *v.2 p.684*

Mwanakatwe, J. M. *v.6 p.77*

MWH, Inc. Staff *v.5 p.704*

Mycio, Mary *v.5 p.364*

Myer, Valerie G. (Editor) *v.2 p.262*

Myers, A. R. *v.3 p.96, p.126, v.6 p.577*

Myers, Alan A. & Giller, Paul S. *v.5 p.169*

Myers, Arnold, et al. *v.1 p.390*

Myers, Brad. *v.5 p.343, p.344, p.348*

Myers, Brian. *v.6 p.238*

Myers, David B. *v.4 p.655*

Myers, David G. *v.5 p.608*

Myers, David J. *v.3 p.361*

Myers, Drew. *v.5 p.283*

Myers, Helen (Editor) *v.1 p.173*

Myers, Helen *v.1 p.293*

Myers, Jack & Weingarten,
  Roger (Editors) *v.2 p.24*

Myers, Jacob M. (Editor) *v.1 p.621*

Myers, Jeffrey *v.2 p.4*

Myers, JoAnne *v.6 p.358, p.363, p.387*

Myers, John E. B. *v.1 p.289*

Myers, John G. *v.4 p.136*

Myers, Keith. *v.5 p.446*

Myers, Margaret G. *v.4 p.247*

Myers, Mary L. *v.1 p.722*

Myers, Paul *v.1 p.219, p.311*

Myers, Peter C. *v.4 p.492, p.502*

Myers, William Starr *v.3 p.476*

Myerson, Joel (Editor) *v.2 p.52, p.54*

Myerson, Joel *v.2 p.52*

Myint-U, Thant *v.6 p.165, p.166*

Mylne, Vivienne *v.2 p.462*

Mylonas, George E. *v.3 p.16*

Myrdal, Gunnar *v.4 p.210, p.214, p.233,
                                   p.239, p.244, p.256,
                                   p.259, p.269, p.730*

Myrdal, Gunner *v.4 p.730*

Myres, Sandra L. *v.6 p.455*

Myrick, Kenneth *v.2 p.215*

Myrnyi, I. P. *v.2 p.815*

Mysnyk, Mark, et al. *v.4 p.870*

N

Naam, Ramez *v.5 p.152*

Nabhan, Gary Paul *v.5 p.136*

Nabokov, Peter *v.4 p.841, v.6 p.682*

Nabokov, Vladimir (Translator) *v.2 p.793, p.806*

Nabokov, Vladimir Vladimirovich *v.2 p.104*

Nabokov, Vladimir *v.2 p.104, p.799*

Nachmani, Amikam *v.4 p.647, p.650*

Nacos, Brigitte Lebens *v.4 p.558*

Nadal, Jean-Pierre *v.4 p.272*

Nadeau, Maurice *v.2 p.458, p.463, p.491*

Nadel, Alan *v.3 p.371, v.6 p.343*

Nadel, Ira B. (Editor) *v.2 p.112*

Nadel, Ira B. *v.2 p.112, p.385*

Nadel, Lynn (Editor) *v.5 p.609*

Nadelhaft, Jerome J. *v.3 p.410*

Nadell, Martha Jane *v.2 p.11*

Nadelmann, Ethan A. *v.3 p.282*

Nadelson, Theodore *v.5 p.584*

Nadenicek, Daniel J. *v.1 p.813*

Nader, Helen. *v.3 p.240*

Nader, Laura *v.4 p.33, p.433*

Nader, Ralph. *v.5 p.716*

Nadler, David, et al. *v.4 p.86*

Nadler, Steven (Editor). *v.1 p.436, p.437, p.452*

Nadler, Steven *v.1 p.477, p.698*

NAEMT. *v.5 p.534*

Naficy, Hamid *v.6 p.321*

Nafisi, Azar *v.6 p.632*

Naftali, Timothy *v.4 p.565*

Nagal, Robert F. *v.4 p.462*

Nagappan, Ramu *v.6 p.334*

Nagarjuna *v.1 p.564*

Nagel, Alexander & Buonarroti, Michelangelo *v.1 p.698*

Nagel, Ernest & Newman, James R. *v.5 p.470*

Nagel, Ernest *v.5 p.403*

Nagel, James *v.2 p.36*

Nagel, Joane *v.4 p.730, v.6 p.694*

Nagel, Paul C. *v.3 p.369, p.415, p.512*

Nagel, Robert F. *v.4 p.525*

Nagel, Thomas & Scanlon, Thomas *v.1 p.486*

Nagel, Thomas *v.1 p.486, p.501, p.514, v.4 p.514*

Nagengast, Carole &
  Velez-Ibanez, Carlos G. (Editors) *v.4 p.45*

Naginski, Isabelle H. *v.2 p.499*

Nagl-Docekal, Herta &
  Vester, Katharina *v.4 p.744*

Nagle, Joan G. *v.5 p.681*

Nagrin, Daniel *v.1 p.37, p.43*

Nagy, Gregory *v.2 p.415, p.417*

Nagy, L. (Editor), et al. *v.5 p.169*

Nagy, Thomas F. *v.5 p.674*

Nahaylo, Bohdan & Swoboda, Victor *v.3 p.213*

Nahin, Paul J. *v.5 p.469, p.476, p.484*
Nahm, Andrew C. & Hoare, James *v.6 p.237*
Nahshon, Edna. *v.1 p.126*
Nahuis, Richard *v.4 p.254, p.259*
Nahum, Peter *v.1 p.726*
Naidu, R. (Editor), et al. *v.5 p.379*
Naidu, Som *v.4 p.352*
Naifeh, Steven & Smith, Gregory W.. . . . . . . *v.1 p.744*
Naik, M. K. *v.2 p.762*
Naim, A. E. & Stehli, F. G. *v.5 p.433*
Naim, A. E., et al. *v.5 p.433*
Naima. *v.6 p.591*
Naimark, Norman & Gibianskii, Leonid (Editors) . . . *v.3 p.207*
Naimark, Norman M. & Case, Holly (Editors) *v.3 p.247*
Naimark, Norman M.. . . . . *v.3 p.176*
Naipaul, V. S. *v.2 p.768, p.769*
Nair, Mohan *v.4 p.82*
Nair, P. K. (Editor) *v.5 p.39*
Nair, Supriya. *v.2 p.768*
Nairn, Alan E. & Stehli, Francis G. (Editors) *v.5 p.433*
Nairn, Allan *v.6 p.175, p.177*
Nairn, Roderick & Helbert, Matthew. *v.5 p.518*
Naison, Mark *v.4 p.552, p.554*
Najder, Zdzislaw *v.2 p.341*
Najita, Joyce M. & Stern, James L. (Editors) *v.4 p.123*
Najjar, Orayb A. *v.6 p.619*
Najmabadi, Afsaneh *v.6 p.629, p.630*
Nakamoto, Kazuo *v.5 p.305*
Nakamura, Hajime *v.1 p.476*
Nakamura, Kyoko M. (Translator, Annotations
     by, Introduction by) *v.1 p.566*
Nakamura, Robert T. &
     Church, Thomas W. *v.4 p.109, p.111, v.6 p.301*
Nakane, Chie, et al. *v.6 p.225*
Nakane, Chie *v.4 p.705*
Nakanishi, Don T. & Lai, James S. *v.6 p.117, p.121*
Nakanishi, Don T. & Wu, Ellen D. *v.6 p.86, p.94, p.120*
Nakanishi, Donald T. & Nishida, Tina Y.
     (Editors) *v.4 p.311, v.6 p.109*
Nakanishi, Koji & Meth-Cohn, Otto (Editors). . . . *v.5 p.299*
Nakanishi, Koji *v.5 p.299*
Nakash, Yitzhak *v.6 p.602*
Nakashizuka, T. & Matsumoto, Y. (Editors). *v.5 p.176*
Nakasone, Henry Y. & Paull, Robert E. *v.5 p.22, p.26*
Nalbantian, Suzanne *v.2 p.105*
Nalivkin, D. V. *v.5 p.432*
Nalkowska, Zofia. *v.2 p.791*
Nalty, Bernard C.. . . . . *v.6 p.8*
Nalven, Gail (Editor) *v.5 p.706*
Nalven, Joseph & Jarvis, J. D.. . . . . *v.1 p.772*
Nalwa, Hari Singh, (Editor) *v.5 p.275*
Nalwa, Hari Singh (Editor) *v.5 p.690*
Nalwa, H.S. *v.5 p.679*
Nam, Vickie *v.6 p.94, p.113, p.122*
Namaste, Viviane K. *v.6 p.371*

Namier, Lewis B.. . . . . *v.3 p.76, p.107, p.109*
Namier, Lewis Bernstein, Sir *v.3 p.114*
Nanamoli, Bhikkhu. *v.1 p.562*
Nance, William L.. . . . . *v.2 p.66*
Nanda, B. R. *v.6 p.157, p.159*
Nanda, Serena *v.4 p.746, v.6 p.374, p.421*
Nandy, Ashis. *v.2 p.760, v.6 p.150, p.157*
Nanney, Donald C. *v.2 p.70*
Nansen, Ralph *v.5 p.709*
Naokes, Jeremy & Pridham, G. (Editors) *v.3 p.173*
Naphy, William G.. . . . . *v.1 p.604*
Napier, Susan Jolliffe *v.6 p.308*
Napier, Winston *v.6 p.27*
Napoleoni, Loretta *v.4 p.660*
Napoli, Donna Jo *v.2 p.550, p.563*
Naqshi, A. R. *v.5 p.207*
Naquin, Susan & Rawski, Evelyn S.. . . . . *v.6 p.187*
Naquin, Susan & Yü, Chün-fang (Editors) *v.1 p.566*
Naranjo, Carmen *v.2 p.676*
Narasimhaiah, C. D. *v.2 p.762*
Narayan, R. K. *v.2 p.765*
Narayan, Uma *v.6 p.435*
Narayanan, R. S. & Beeby, A. W. *v.5 p.686*
Narayanaravu, Velceru *v.6 p.152*
Nardi, Peter M. *v.6 p.375*
Nardin, Jane *v.2 p.317*
Naremore, James *v.2 p.393, v.6 p.348*
Narlikar, Amrita. *v.4 p.61*
Narlikar, Jayant Vishnu. *v.5 p.556, p.557*
Naro, Nancy Priscilla (Editor) *v.3 p.337*
Naro, Nancy *v.3 p.337*
Naroditskaya, Inna *v.1 p.287*
Nasar, Sylvia. *v.5 p.661*
Nasaw, David *v.4 p.149, p.328, p.411*
Nash, Elizabeth *v.3 p.237*
Nash, Gary B. (Editor) *v.3 p.373*
Nash, Gary B. *v.3 p.406, p.492, v.4 p.380, v.6 p.714*
Nash, George H.. . . . . *v.3 p.449, p.476, p.477*
Nash, Gerald D. *v.3 p.477, p.518*
Nash, Jay R. & Ross, Stanley R.. . . . . *v.6 p.306*
Nash, June C. & Fernandez-Kelly, Maria P. (Editors) . . *v.4 p.28*
Nash, June *v.3 p.324, v.4 p.34*
Nash, Manning. *v.6 p.166*
Nash, Margaret A. *v.6 p.463*
Nash, Ogden. *v.2 p.103*
Nash, Paul. *v.4 p.344*
Nash, Robert J. *v.4 p.306, p.307*
Nash, Roderick & Graves, Gregory *v.3 p.380*
Nash, Roderick *v.3 p.369, v.5 p.17, p.28, v.6 p.289*
Nash, Steven A. (Editor) *v.1 p.744*
Nash, Thomas *v.2 p.222*
Nashat, Guity & Beck, Lois (Editors) . . *v.6 p.435, p.452, p.630*
Nashat, Guity *v.6 p.632*
Naske, Claus M. & Slotnick, Herman E.. . . . . . . *v.3 p.533*

Nasr, Seyyed Hossein (Editor), et al.. . . . . *v.1 p.560*
Nasr, Seyyed Hossein. *v.1 p.557*
Nasr, Seyyed Vali Reza. *v.4 p.615, p.617*
Nasrallah, Emily *v.6 p.662*
Nassar, Jamal R.. . . . . *v.4 p.660, p.663*
Nassau, Kurt. *v.5 p.562*
Nasta, Dominique *v.1 p.256*
Nasta, Susheila. *v.2 p.760*
Nastasi, Bonnie K., et al. *v.5 p.576*
Natali, Denise *v.6 p.599*
Natanson, I. P.. . . . . *v.5 p.490*
Natarajan, Mangai *v.6 p.260*
Natarajan, Nalini (Editor) *v.2 p.762*
Naterer, Greg F.. . . . . *v.5 p.713*
Nathan, Andrew J. *v.6 p.194*
Nathan, David G., et al.. . . . . *v.5 p.521*
Nathan, Hans *v.1 p.35*
Nathans, Benjamin *v.3 p.60, p.218*
Nathanson, Tenney *v.2 p.54*
Nation, James L.. . . . . *v.5 p.213*
National Academic Advising Association *v.5 p.576*
National Academy of Engineering Staff *v.5 p.684*
National Academy of Sciences Staff &
Vedral, Joyce L. *v.5 p.195, p.246*
National Academy of Sciences Staff . *v.4 p.561, p.656, v.5 p.395*
National Academy of Sciences. *v.4 p.359*
National Academy Press (Created by) *v.5 p.195*
National Academy Press Staff (Contribution by). . . *v.5 p.674*
National Academy Press Staff *v.5 p.10*
National Advisory Commission Staff & Kerner, Otto . *v.6 p.254*
National Aeronautics & Space Administration. . . . *v.5 p.420*
National Aeronautics and Space Administration . . . *v.5 p.417*
National Agricultural Library *v.4 p.152, p.164*
National Archives and Records Administration
(NARA). *v.4 p.481, p.556, p.557*
National Archives and Records Administration's (NARA) Office
of the Federal Register (OFR) *v.4 p.481*
National Archives Staff *v.3 p.375*
National Association for Gifted Children *v.5 p.575*
National Association for Rural Mental Health. . . . *v.5 p.671*
National Association for the Advancement of Colored People
Staff, et al.. . . . . *v.6 p.261*
National Association of Elementary School Principals . *v.4 p.282*
National Association of Home Builders. *v.4 p.159*
National Association of School Psychologists. . . . *v.5 p.577*
National Association of Secretaries of State (NASS) . *v.4 p.549*
National Audubon Society Staff &
Thompson, Ida. *v.5 p.417, p.447*
National Audubon Society Staff, et al. *v.5 p.216*
National Career Development Association *v.5 p.578*
National Center for Biotechnology Information, U.S. National
Library of Medicine. *v.5 p.205*
National Center for Children in Poverty, Columbia
University *v.5 p.671*
National Center for Education Statistics *v.4 p.322*
National Center for Fair and Open Testing *v.4 p.286*

National Center for Health Statistics Staff
(Contribution by) *v.4 p.739*
National Center for History *v.4 p.359*
National Center for Manufacturing Sciences *v.4 p.159*
National Center for Post-Traumatic Stress Disorder, U.S.
Department of Veterans Affairs. *v.5 p.662*
National Center for Research and Data, Child Welfare League of
America *v.5 p.671*
National Child Welfare Resource Center, Muskie School of
Public Service, University of Southern Maine *v.5 p.671*
National Clearinghouse on Child Abuse and Neglect
Information. *v.4 p.756*
National Commission on Excellence in Education. . . *v.4 p.322*
National Commission on Terrorist Attacks Against the United
States *v.4 p.481*
National Council for Accreditation of Teacher Education
(NCATE). *v.4 p.359*
National Council for the Social Studies. *v.4 p.359*
National Council of Teachers of Mathematics Staff . . *v.5 p.463*
National Council of Teachers of Mathematics. . . . *v.4 p.360*
National Council on Measurement in Education. . . . *v.5 p.604*
National Dance Association Staff. *v.1 p.4*
National Education Association *v.4 p.283*
National Endowment for the Humanities. *v.4 p.303, p.348, p.350*
National Geographic Society Staff. . . . *v.4 p.380, p.382, p.392*
National Geographic Society. *v.4 p.360, v.6 p.594*
National Historical Society Staff & Davis, Jenny . . . *v.3 p.431*
National Historical Society Staff & Davis, William C.. *v.3 p.431*
National Historical Society Staff. *v.3 p.431*
National Home Education Research Institute *v.4 p.296*
National Institute for Occupational Safety and Health, Centers
for Disease Control *v.5 p.580*
National Institute for Research Advancement *v.4 p.560*
National Institute of Mental Health *v.5 p.671*
National Institute of Standards and Technology . . . *v.5 p.545*
National Intramural Recreational Sports Association (Nirsa)
(Created by) *v.4 p.800*
National Library of Medicine *v.6 p.702*
National Mental Health Association *v.5 p.671*
National Middle School Association Staff
(Contribution by) *v.4 p.367*
National Museum and Archive of Lesbian and Gay History &
Program of the Lesbian and Gay Community Services
Staff. *v.6 p.360*
National Music Publishers' Association *v.1 p.172, p.385*
National Oceanic & Atmospheric Administration
(NOAA). *v.5 p.426*
National Oceanic and Atmospheric
Administration *v.5 p.417, p.426*
National O*Net Consortium. *v.5 p.577, p.578*
National Research Center on the Gifted and Talented (University
of Connecticut). *v.5 p.575*
National Research Council, Committee on Undergraduate
Biology Education to Prepare Research Scientists for the 21st
Century (Contribution by) *v.5 p.246*
National Research Council, Office of Critical Tables. *v.5 p.281*
National Research Council Staff & Alberts, Betty . . *v.4 p.361*

National Research Council Staff & Committee on Early
    Childhood Pedagogy Staff *v.4 p.370*
National Research Council Staff & Institute of Medicine
    Staff *v.6 p.248*
National Research Council Staff (Editor) *v.5 p.574*
National Research Council
    Staff, et al. *v.5 p.173, p.353, p.357, p.379*
National Research Council
    Staff *v.4 p.110, p.111, p.254, p.295, p.542,*
    v.5 p.11, p.13, p.22, p.55, p.136, p.246, p.266, p.365, p.368,
    p.380, p.398, p.463, p.572, p.588, p.605, p.671, p.703, p.716,
    p.718, v.6 p.724
National Research Council (U.S.), Committee on California
    Agricultural Research Priorities: Pierce's Disease Staff
    (Contribution by) *v.5 p.46*
National Research Council (U.S.), Committee on NASA-NOAA
    Transition from Research to Operations Staff
    (Contribution by) *v.5 p.720*
National Restaurant Association *v.4 p.165*
National Safety Council *v.5 p.580*
National Science Teachers Association; United States;
    Environmental Protection Agency; Office of Research and
    Development *v.5 p.180*
National Security Agency *v.4 p.481*
National Soccer Coaches of America Staff . . . *v.4 p.867, p.905*
National Staff Development Council *v.4 p.283*
National Strength Training and Conditioning
    Association *v.4 p.791, p.903*
National Textbook Company Staff & Vox Staff *v.2 p.636*
National Wetlands Policy Forum Staff *v.5 p.176*
National Wildlife Federation Staff *v.5 p.18, v.6 p.286*
National Writing Project Staff & Nagin, Carl *v.4 p.364*
Natoli, Joseph P. *v.6 p.332*
Natoli, Joseph *v.6 p.332*
Natriello, Gary *v.4 p.299*
Natsume Soseki *v.6 p.232*
Nattiez, Jean-Jacques *v.1 p.372*
Natvig, Mary (Editor) *v.1 p.406*
Naughton, Leonie *v.6 p.338*
Naum, Gellu *v.2 p.779*
Naumann, Francis M. & Duchamp, Marcel *v.1 p.698*
Naumes, William & Naumes, Margaret J. *v.4 p.178*
Nava, Michael *v.6 p.502*
Nava'i, Alisher *v.6 p.667*
Navaretti, Giorgio Barba & Venables, Anthony J. . *v.4 p.257, p.261*
Navarra, Tova & Lipowitz, Myron A. *v.5 p.329*
Navarro, Armando *v.6 p.539, p.541*
Navarro, Joe *v.6 p.252*
Navarro, Jose-Manuel *v.3 p.320*
Navarro, Peter *v.4 p.177*
Navarro, Sharon Ann & Mejia, Armando Xavier . . . *v.6 p.539*
Navarro Tomas, Tomás *v.2 p.636*
Naveh, Hannah (Editor) *v.6 p.614*
Navia, Luis E. *v.1 p.422*
Navratilova, Martina & Vecsey, George *v.6 p.384*
Nawy, Edward G. *v.5 p.690, p.695*
Nayar, B. K. *v.5 p.210*

Nayar, Baldev Raj & Paul, T. V. *v.6 p.146*
Nayar, Baldev Raj *v.4 p.400*
Nayder, Lillian *v.2 p.281, p.285, v.6 p.740*
Naylor, Colin (Editor) *v.1 p.665, p.712, p.762*
Naylor, Gloria (Editor) *v.2 p.26*
Naylor, Gloria *v.2 p.151*
Naylor, Phillip C. & Heggoy, Alf A. *v.6 p.642*
Naylor, Phillip C. *v.4 p.584, v.6 p.642*
Naylor, Robert A. *v.3 p.297*
Nazareth, J. L. *v.5 p.683*
Nazareth, Peter *v.2 p.751, p.758*
Nazzal, Nafez & Nazzal, Laila A. *v.6 p.608*
Nazzari, Muriel *v.3 p.337*
NC-IUBMB & Webb, Edwin C. (Editors) . . . *v.5 p.119, p.325*
NCTM Commission on Teaching Standards
    for School M. *v.5 p.463*
Ndiaye, Christiane *v.2 p.535*
Ndubisi, Forster *v.1 p.813*
Neack, Laura *v.3 p.477*
Nead, Lynda *v.6 p.731, p.763*
Neal, Dick *v.5 p.170*
Neal, Mark Anthony *v.6 p.8, p.40*
Neal, Steve *v.3 p.461*
Neale, Caroline *v.6 p.53*
Neale, J. E. Sir (John Ernest) *v.3 p.95, p.100*
Neale, John E. *v.3 p.100*
Neale, M. J. *v.5 p.708*
Neale, Michael J. *v.5 p.708*
Neale, Steve & Krutnik, Frank *v.6 p.313*
Neale, Steve (Editor) *v.6 p.311*
Neale, Steve *v.6 p.327, p.343*
Neamen, Donald *v.5 p.722*
Near, Holly *v.6 p.409*
Neass, Harald *v.2 p.628*
Neate, Patrick *v.2 p.368*
Neathery, T. L. (Editor) *v.5 p.432*
Nebelsick, Harold P. *v.3 p.47*
Necipoglu, Gulru *v.1 p.787*
Nectoux, Jean-Michel *v.1 p.219, p.324*
Nedelkov, Dobrin & Nelson, Randall W. *v.5 p.117*
Nee, Victor & Swedberg, Richard (Editors) . . . *v.4 p.215, p.271*
Nee, Victor G. & De Bary Nee, Brett *v.6 p.127*
Needell, Jeffrey D. *v.3 p.337*
Needham, Joseph (Author, Contribution by) . . *v.6 p.182, p.198*
Needham, Joseph *v.5 p.392, p.403, v.6 p.198*
Needham, Tristan *v.5 p.491*
Needleman, A., et al. *v.5 p.690*
Needleman, Herbert L. *v.5 p.372*
Needler, Martin C. *v.4 p.593*
Neeley, Kathryn A. & Somerville, Mary *v.5 p.397*
Neely, Mark E. Jr. *v.3 p.399, v.4 p.521*
Neely, Mark E. *v.3 p.426*
Neely, W. Brock *v.5 p.365, p.375*
Nees, Lawrence *v.1 p.672*
Neff, Emily Ballew & Phelan, Wynne H. *v.1 p.744*

Negev, Avraham (Editor) *v.1 p.617*

Negishi, Ei-ichi & Meijere, Armin De (Editors) *v.5 p.299*

Negri, Paul (Editor) *v.2 p.200*

Negron-Muntaner, Frances & Grosfoguel, Ramon
(Editors) *v.3 p.320*

Negron-Muntaner, Frances. *v.4 p.712, v.6 p.493*

Negus, Keith *v.1 p.273, p.385*

Nehaniv, Chrystopher L. & Dautenhahn, Kerstin
(Editors) *v.5 p.589*

Neher, Andrew. *v.5 p.613*

Nehmzow, Ulrich. *v.5 p.711*

Nehru, Jawaharlal *v.6 p.159*

Nei, Masatoshi & Kumar, Sudhir *v.5 p.200*

Neider, Charles *v.2 p.33*

Neier, Aryeh. *v.4 p.653*

Neihardt, John G. *v.2 p.103*

Neihart, Maureen. *v.4 p.317*

Neill, Michael *v.2 p.186*

Neill, Stephen & Wright, N. T. *v.1 p.626*

Neill, Stephen *v.1 p.610, p.647*

Neill, William J. V. *v.4 p.395, v.6 p.728*

Neillands, Robin *v.3 p.81*

Neils, Jenifer. *v.1 p.775*

Neilson, Alasdair *v.5 p.10, p.379*

Neiman, Susan *v.1 p.484*

Neimark, Peninah Rhodes & Mott, Peter
(Editors) *v.4 p.566, v.6 p.301*

Neimeyer, Robert A. (Editor) *v.5 p.655*

Neipert, David *v.4 p.57, p.110*

Neises, Charles P. *v.1 p.273, p.306*

Neiwert, David A. *v.6 p.252, p.253*

Nekoogar, Faranak *v.5 p.727*

Nekrich, Aleksandr M. & Freeze, Gregory L.. . *v.3 p.161, p.212*

Nelkin, Dorothy. *v.5 p.392, p.407, p.410, p.412*

Nell, Edward J. *v.4 p.228*

Nelli, Humbert S. *v.3 p.516*

Nelligan, Emile, et al. *v.2 p.539*

Nelsen, Brent F. & Stubb, Alexander (Editors) *v.3 p.87*

Nelsen, Roger B. (Editor) *v.5 p.459*

Nelsen, Roger B.. . . . . *v.5 p.459*

Nelson, Adam R.. . . . . *v.4 p.344*

Nelson, Andrew N *v.6 p.232*

Nelson, Ardis L. *v.2 p.673*

Nelson, Barbara J. & Chowdhury, Najma (Editors) . . *v.6 p.441*

Nelson, Brian (Editor) *v.1 p.68, p.125, v.6 p.92, p.99*

Nelson, Bruce *v.4 p.128*

Nelson, Carl A. *v.4 p.56*

Nelson, Cary *v.2 p.15*

Nelson, Claudia *v.2 p.176, v.6 p.748, p.756, p.765*

Nelson, Daniel *v.4 p.128*

Nelson, David M. *v.4 p.808, p.859*

Nelson, Douglas R. & Vandenbussche, Hylke
(Editors). *v.4 p.257, p.262*

Nelson, E. Clifford (Editor) *v.1 p.585, p.586*

Nelson, Emmanuel S.
(Editor). . . *v.2 p.762, p.765, v.6 p.18, p.33, p.34, p.391, p.393*

Nelson, Gary M., et al. *v.4 p.758*

Nelson, Gaylord, et al. *v.6 p.296*

Nelson, Geoffrey & Prilleltensky, Isaac. *v.5 p.672*

Nelson, Gerald C. *v.5 p.8*

Nelson, Glenn C. & Burkett, Richard *v.1 p.808*

Nelson, Harold N. (Editor) *v.4 p.459*

Nelson, John D. & Miller, Debora J. *v.5 p.422*

Nelson, Julie A. *v.4 p.196, p.270*

Nelson, L. *v.2 p.649*

Nelson, Lyle Emerson *v.4 p.528*

Nelson, Lynn H. *v.6 p.461, p.463*

Nelson, Mariah B. *v.4 p.818, p.837, v.6 p.438*

Nelson, Paul David. *v.3 p.412*

Nelson, Paul V. *v.5 p.43*

Nelson, Philip *v.5 p.564*

Nelson, Richard D. *v.1 p.621*

Nelson, Richard R. & Winter, Sidney G. *v.4 p.233*

Nelson, Robert C. *v.5 p.718*

Nelson, Robert J.. . . . . *v.2 p.473*

Nelson, Robert L. & Bridges, William P.. . . . . . . *v.4 p.447*

Nelson, Robert S. & Shiff, Richard (Editors) *v.1 p.665*

Nelson, Roy P.. . . . . *v.1 p.719*

Nelson, Sarah Milledge *v.4 p.9*

Nelson, Theresa *v.6 p.379, p.398*

Nelson, William E. *v.4 p.455, p.457, p.474, p.538*

Nelson *v.1 p.541*

Nemcova, Bozena *v.2 p.784*

Nemerov, Howard *v.2 p.105*

Nemes, Robert *v.3 p.186*

Nemeth, Charles P. *v.6 p.270*

Nemeth, Neil. *v.4 p.411*

Nemhauser, George L. & Wolsey, Laurence A. . . *v.5 p.479, p.493*

Nemiro, Jill. *v.4 p.67*

Nemiroff, Robert *v.6 p.27, p.45*

Nemoy, Leon *v.6 p.566, p.573*

Nene, Y. L. (Editor), et al. *v.5 p.22*

Nerdinger, Winfried (Editor). *v.1 p.794*

Nering, Evar D. & Tucker, Albert W.. . . . . *v.5 p.683*

Nerlich, Graham *v.1 p.500*

Nerlove, Marc *v.4 p.203*

Neruda, Jan, et al. *v.2 p.784*

Neruda, Pablo & Walsh, Donald Devenish *v.2 p.681*

Neruda, Pablo *v.2 p.681*

Nerval, Gérard de *v.2 p.492*

Nesbett, Peter T. & DuBois, Michelle *v.1 p.744*

Nesbett, Peter T. *v.1 p.757*

Nesbit, Robert C.. . . . . *v.3 p.517*

Nesin, Aziz *v.6 p.667*

Nesper, Larry *v.6 p.689, p.694, p.696*

Ness, Bryan D. (Editor). *v.5 p.136*

Ness, Immanuel & Ciment, James *v.4 p.678*

Ness, Immanuel (Editor) *v.4 p.678*

Ness, Immanuel *v.4 p.128, v.6 p.709*

Ness, Sally Ann *v.1 p.17, p.49*

Nessen, Ron *v.3 p.477*

Nestle, Joan & Preston, John (Editors) *v.6 p.375*
Nestle, Joan (Editor) *v.6 p.367*
Nestle, Joan, et al. *v.6 p.371*
Nestle, Joan *v.6 p.403*
Nestle, Marion *v.5 p.35*
Nestler, Eric J. *v.5 p.617*
Netanyahu, Benjamin *v.3 p.57, p.240*
Netter, Frank H.. . . . . *v.5 p.96, p.158*
Nettina, Sandra M. *v.5 p.528*
Nettl, Bruno & Russell, Melinda (Editors) *v.1 p.283*
Nettl, Bruno (Editor), et al.. . . . . *v.1 p.161, p.283*
Nettl, Bruno (Editor) *v.1 p.283, p.287*
Nettl, Bruno, et al.. . . . . *v.1 p.287, p.293*
Nettl, Bruno *v.1 p.173, p.283, p.296, p.406, v.4 p.26*
Nettl, J. P. *v.4 p.193*
Nettle, Daniel & Romaine, Suzanne *v.2 p.563, v.4 p.19*
Nettleford, Rex *v.1 p.19*
Netzley, Patricia D.. . . . . *v.6 p.352*
Neubauer, John. *v.2 p.601*
Neuberger, A. & Van Deenen, L. L. (Editors) *v.5 p.326*
Neuburger, Mary *v.3 p.251*
Neufeldt, Leonard N. *v.2 p.52*
Neufeldt, Susan A. *v.5 p.676*
Neuhauser, Claudia *v.5 p.91, p.485, p.502*
Neuhold, Lisa A. (Volume Editor) *v.5 p.117*
Neuls-Bates, Carol (Editor) *v.1 p.379*
Neuman, Shirley & Nadel, Ira B. (Editors) *v.2 p.122*
Neuman, Susan B. & Dickinson, David K.
   (Editors). *v.4 p.358, p.369*
Neumann, Franz L.. . . . . *v.3 p.173*
Neumann, Roderick P. *v.5 p.18, p.19*
Neumann, William L.. . . . . *v.3 p.391*
Neumayer, Eric *v.4 p.63*
Neumeyer, David, et al.. . . . . *v.1 p.372*
Neumeyer, David *v.1 p.219, p.332*
Neundorf, Alyse *v.6 p.690*
Neupert, Richard John *v.6 p.338*
Neurath, Otto (Editor), et al. *v.5 p.388*
Neurath, Otto (Editor) *v.5 p.388*
Neusner, Jacob & Avery-Peck, Alan J. *v.1 p.550, p.551*
Neusner, Jacob (Editor) *v.1 p.548*
Neusner, Jacob *v.1 p.548, p.549, p.550*
Neustadt, Richard E. *v.3 p.378*
Nevaer, Louis E. V.. . . . . *v.6 p.526*
Neve, Brian *v.6 p.343*
Nevett, Lisa C. *v.3 p.14*
Nevin, Jeff. *v.1 p.293*
Nevins, Allan . . . *v.3 p.423, p.426, p.431, p.434, p.437, p.453*
Nevins, Joseph. *v.6 p.487, p.530*
New, Melvyn (Editor) *v.2 p.262*
New Mexico Architectural Foundation Staff & American
   Institute of Architects Staff (Editors) *v.1 p.823*
New Strategist Publications, Inc. Staff (Editor) . . . *v.4 p.138*
New Strategist Publications, Inc. Staff *v.4 p.138*
New, W. H. (Editor) *v.2 p.730*

New, W. H. *v.2 p.730*
New York Public Library, ProQuest Information and
   Learning *v.6 p.14, p.34*
New York Public Library Staff. *v.1 p.4*
New York Public Library *v.6 p.14, p.34*
New York (State). *v.5 p.700*
New York Times Staff (Contribution by) . *v.1 p.117, p.137, p.141*
New York Times Staff *v.2 p.566, p.584, v.5 p.80, p.230*
New York University School of Law Staff & Kaczorowski,
   Robert J. *v.4 p.525*
New Yorker Magazine Staff *v.2 p.26*
New Zealand, Ministry of Foreign Affairs *v.4 p.634*
Newberg, Andrew, et al. *v.5 p.635*
Newberger, Eli H. *v.5 p.642, v.6 p.446*
Newbigin, Lesslie *v.1 p.596*
Newbould, Brian. *v.1 p.201, p.354*
Newbould, Ian *v.3 p.114*
Newburn, Tim & Sparks, Richard (Editors). *v.6 p.247*
Newbury, Catharine *v.4 p.582, p.584, p.612*
Newby, Hayes A. & Popelka, Gerald R. *v.5 p.523*
Newby, Howard (Author, Editor) *v.4 p.772*
Newby, Rick. *v.3 p.525*
Newcomb, Horace (Editor) *v.4 p.415*
Newcomb, Horace *v.4 p.418*
Newell, Karl M. (Editor) *v.4 p.908, p.909*
Newell, Robert & Rubio, Luis.. . . . . *v.3 p.294*
Newey, Glen. *v.1 p.448*
Newey, Vincent (Editor) *v.2 p.241*
Newhouse, Victoria. *v.1 p.790*
Newitt, M. D. D. (Editor) *v.6 p.63*
Newitt, M. D. D. *v.6 p.56*
Newitt, Malyn. *v.6 p.76*
Newland, Amy Reigle *v.1 p.752, p.754*
Newlands, Anne *v.1 p.682*
Newlin, Keith (Editor) *v.2 p.70*
Newlyn, Lucy *v.2 p.324*
Newman, Amy. *v.1 p.703*
Newman, Barbara. *v.1 p.11, p.37, p.52, p.53, p.55*
Newman, Ernest *v.1 p.191, p.201, p.231, p.326, p.366*
Newman, Frank, et al. *v.4 p.332*
Newman, Graeme & Clarke, Ronald V.. . . . . *v.6 p.253*
Newman, Harold & Newman, Jon O. (Compiled by) . *v.1 p.533*
Newman, Jacqueline M. *v.5 p.35, v.6 p.182*
Newman, James R. (Editor) *v.5 p.459*
Newman, James. *v.6 p.51*
Newman, John Henry . . . *v.1 p.575, p.579, p.595, v.4 p.290*
Newman, John K. *v.2 p.402*
Newman, Karen *v.2 p.233*
Newman, Katherine S.. . . . . *v.4 p.33, p.725, p.771, v.6 p.265*
Newman, Lea & Frost, Robert *v.2 p.77*
Newman, Leslea *v.6 p.398*
Newman, Lex (Editor) *v.4 p.196*
Newman, Louise *v.6 p.435*
Newman, Mark & Barkema, G. T. *v.5 p.551, p.559*
Newman, Michael C. & Unger, Michael A.. . . . . . *v.5 p.704*

Newman, Michael *v.4 p.603*

Newman, Paul & Ratliff, Martha (Editors) *v.4 p.19*

Newman, Peter & Thornley, Andrew *v.6 p.729*

Newman, Peter (Editor) *v.4 p.191, p.434*

Newman, Richard (Editor), et al. *v.4 p.572*

Newman, Robert P.. . . . . *v.6 p.201, p.216*

Newman, Roger B. & Luke, Barbara. *v.5 p.524*

Newman, Roger K.. . . . . *v.4 p.468, p.538*

Newman, William S. *v.1 p.186, p.191, p.201, p.219,
p.241, p.307, p.401*

Newmarch, Rosa H. *v.1 p.246*

Newmark, Charles S.. . . . . *v.5 p.601*

Newmark, Leonard D. *v.2 p.778*

Newmark, Maxim *v.2 p.639*

Newmeyer, Frederick J. (Editor) *v.2 p.563*

Newmeyer, Frederick J.. . . . . *v.2 p.563*

Newmyer, R. Kent *v.4 p.468*

Newsinger, John *v.2 p.375*

Newsome, David *v.3 p.114, p.121,
v.6 p.745, p.749, p.759, p.764*

Newson, Linda A. *v.3 p.302, p.332*

Newth, Michael (Translator) *v.2 p.464, p.466*

Newton, Candelas *v.2 p.660*

Newton, Cathryn & Laporte, Leo F. *v.5 p.449*

Newton, Dale & Gaspard, John *v.6 p.347*

Newton, David E. *v.5 p.264, v.6 p.284*

Newton, Douglas P. *v.4 p.348, p.364*

Newton, Esther. *v.6 p.371*

Newton, Huey P.. . . . . *v.6 p.13, p.27*

Newton, Isaac. *v.5 p.467, p.556, p.557, p.561*

Newton, Judith L. & Rosenfelt, D. (Editors) *v.2 p.8*

Newton, Judith Lowder *v.4 p.711*

Newton, K., et al. *v.5 p.716*

Newton, Lisa H. *v.4 p.61, p.64*

Newton, Michael T. *v.4 p.582, p.608*

Newton, Ronald C. *v.3 p.348*

Newton, Roy & Davison, Sandra *v.1 p.824*

Newton, Stephen James. *v.1 p.708*

Newton, Velma. *v.3 p.305*

Nexo, Martin Anderson *v.2 p.627*

Nezval, Vitezslav. *v.2 p.784*

Nfah-Abbenyi, Juliana M.. . . . . *v.6 p.479*

Nölting, Bengt. *v.5 p.117, p.125*

NFPA Staff *v.5 p.682, p.686*

Ng, Fae M. *v.6 p.101*

Ng, Franklin (Editor), et al. *v.6 p.85, p.109*

Ng, Franklin (Editor) *v.6 p.86*

Ng, Sek H. & Warner, Malcolm *v.4 p.128*

Ng, Wendy L. *v.6 p.115, p.134*

Ngaboh-Smart, Francis *v.2 p.755*

Ngai, Mae M. *v.4 p.460, p.571, v.6 p.119, p.124, p.125*

Ngugi wa Thiong'o. *v.2 p.759*

Nguyen, B. Minh & Shreve, Porter *v.2 p.26*

Nguyen, Dac B. & Luong, Hy V. *v.6 p.169*

Nguyen, Dat & Burson, Rusty *v.4 p.834, p.859*

Nguyen, Kien. *v.6 p.94, p.141*

Nguyen, Viet Thanh *v.6 p.97*

Niamir-Fuller, Maryam *v.6 p.294*

Niane, D. T.. . . . . *v.6 p.69*

Niblock, Tim *v.6 p.594, p.640*

Niblock, Timothy. *v.6 p.626*

Nicassio, Susan VanDiver. *v.3 p.201*

Niccols, Richard *v.2 p.215*

Nice, David C.. . . . . *v.4 p.525*

Nice, David *v.1 p.219, p.348*

Nicholas Colangelo, Susan G. Assouline,
and Miraca U. M. Gross. *v.5 p.575*

Nicholas, David *v.3 p.41, p.44, v.6 p.560, p.564, p.577*

Nicholas, H. G. *v.4 p.635*

Nicholas, Lynn H. *v.1 p.823*

Nicholas, Sarah Anne, et al. *v.5 p.736*

Nicholas, Sian *v.4 p.413*

Nicholas. *v.1 p.433*

Nicholl, Charles *v.1 p.698, v.2 p.498*

Nicholl, Desmond S.. . . . . *v.5 p.136, p.218*

Nicholls, A. J. *v.3 p.177*

Nicholls, David (Editor) . . . *v.1 p.219, p.279, p.315, v.6 p.408*

Nicholls, David G. *v.2 p.5*

Nichols, Aidan *v.1 p.579*

Nichols, Beverly *v.4 p.796, p.798*

Nichols, Bill *v.6 p.309*

Nichols, Gary J. *v.5 p.446*

Nichols, Geraldine C.. . . . . *v.2 p.661*

Nichols, John A. & Shank, M. Thomas (Editors). *v.6 p.560, p.572*

Nichols, John *v.2 p.151*

Nichols, Michael P. & Schwartz, Richard C. *v.5 p.668*

Nichols, Mike (Photographer) *v.5 p.84*

Nichols, Roger & Smith, Richard
Langham *v.1 p.220, p.231, p.320*

Nichols, Roger. *v.1 p.220, p.320*

Nichols, Roy F. & Berwanger, Eugene H. *v.3 p.399*

Nichols, Roy F. *v.3 p.399, p.421*

Nichols, S. W. & Schuh, R. T. *v.5 p.10*

Nichols, William C. (Editor), et al.. . . . . . . *v.5 p.639*

Nicholsen, Shierry Weber *v.6 p.287*

Nicholson, D. H. & Lee, A. H. (Editors) *v.2 p.200*

Nicholson, Dwight R.. . . . . *v.5 p.566*

Nicholson, Helen *v.3 p.63*

Nicholson, Ian A. M. *v.5 p.597*

Nicholson, Linda J. (Editor, Introduction by) . . *v.6 p.428, p.461*

Nicholson, Norman. *v.2 p.244, v.3 p.536, p.537*

Nicholson, Peter *v.2 p.212*

Nicholson, Philip Yale *v.4 p.128*

Nicholson, Reynold A.. . . . . *v.6 p.662, p.663*

Nicholson, Stuart *v.1 p.262, p.323*

Nickel, Douglas R. & Carroll, Lewis. *v.1 p.764*

Nickell, Joe & Fischer, John F. *v.6 p.266*

Nickels, Cameron C.. . . . . *v.2 p.12*

Nicklaus, Jack *v.4 p.861*

Nicol, Donald M.. . . . . *v.3 p.193*

Nicolau, Dan (Editor) *v.5 p.110*

Nicolet, Claude *v.4 p.377*

Nicoletta, Julie *v.1 p.790*

Nicolin, Pierluigi & Repishti, Francesco *v.1 p.812*

Nicoll, Allardyce (Editor) *v.1 p.75, p.102, v.2 p.186*

Nicoll, Allardyce *v.1 p.56, p.76, p.87, p.91, p.93,*
p.97, p.102,v.2 p.185, p.188

Nicolle, David *v.4 p.380*

Nicolson, Harold G. *v.2 p.274*

Nicolson, Harold *v.3 p.152*

Nicolson, Nigel *v.2 p.380*

Nicolson, Vanessa & Panourgias, Klio K.. . . . . . *v.1 p.781*

Nicosia, Francis R. & Huener, Jonathan *v.3 p.173*

Nicosia, Gerald *v.2 p.93*

Nidel, Richard *v.1 p.283*

Nie, Norman H., et al. *v.4 p.505, p.547*

Nieboer, Evert & Nriagu, Jerome O. (Editors) *v.5 p.366*

Niebuhr, H. Richard *v.1 p.638*

Niebuhr, Helmut Richard *v.1 p.596, p.644*

Niebuhr, Reinhold & Heimert, Alan *v.3 p.376*

Niebuhr, Reinhold *v.1 p.485, p.643,*
v.3 p.369, p.453,v.4 p.484, p.496, p.770

Niebuhr, Richa H. *v.1 p.639*

Nieh, Hualing (Editor) *v.6 p.213*

Nieh, Hualing *v.6 p.101, p.213*

Niehardt, John G. & Elk, Nicholas Black . . *v.2 p.31, v.6 p.701*

Nielsen, Jakob. *v.5 p.338, p.339*

Nielsen, Kai. *v.1 p.487, p.504, p.516*

Nielsen, Nancy J.. . . . . *v.6 p.694*

Nielsen, Stevan Lars & Johnson, W. Brad *v.5 p.665*

Niemeyer, Paul J. *v.6 p.326*

Nienhauser, William H. Jr. (Editor, Compiled by) . . . *v.6 p.208*

Nienhauser, William H. Jr. (Editor), et al.. . . . . *v.6 p.208*

Nierenberg, William A. (Editor) *v.5 p.417*

Nierenberg, William A. (Editor-In-Chief) *v.5 p.357*

Nieto, Sonia (Editor) *v.4 p.311, v.6 p.527*

Nietz, John Alfred *v.4 p.285*

Nietzsche, Friedrich Wilhelm *v.1 p.466*

Nietzsche, Friedrich *v.1 p.56, p.88, p.467, v.4 p.344*

Nieuwenhuijsen, Mark (Editor) *v.5 p.365*

Nieuwenhuis, Paul; Wells, P. E. *v.5 p.716*

Nieuwenhuis, Tom *v.6 p.603*

Nieuwenhuys, Olga *v.4 p.40*

Nieuwenhuys, Rob *v.2 p.623*

Nievo, Ippolito. *v.2 p.712*

Niewyk, Donald L. (Editor) *v.3 p.85*

Niewyk, Donald L. *v.3 p.60, p.180*

Nigel of Canterbury *v.2 p.449*

Nigg, Erich A. (Editor) *v.5 p.152*

Nigro, Salvatore S.. . . . . *v.1 p.744*

Nijeholt, Geertje A. & Wieringa, Saskia . . *v.3 p.283, v.6 p.441*

Nijinska, Bronislava *v.1 p.11*

Nijinsky, Vaslav *v.1 p.11*

Nijkamp, Peter & Mills, E. S. *v.4 p.191*

Nijkamp, Peter (Editor) *v.4 p.191*

Nikitenko, Aleksandr *v.3 p.218*

Niklas, Karl J.. . . . . *v.5 p.449*

Niklaus, Robert *v.2 p.456, p.459, p.478*

Nikolajeva, Maria *v.2 p.582*

Niku, Saeed B.. . . . . *v.5 p.711*

Niles, John D. *v.2 p.205*

Niles, Susan A.. . . . . *v.3 p.261*

Nill KimballR. *v.4 p.156*

Nilsen, Don L. *v.2 p.195*

Nilson, Arthur H. & Darwin, David *v.5 p.695*

Nilsson, James W. & Riedel, Susan A. *v.5 p.721*

Nimmo, Dan D. *v.4 p.549*

Nimmons, David *v.6 p.381*

Nims, John Frederick *v.2 p.103*

Nin, Anais *v.2 p.105*

Ninkovich, Frank A. *v.3 p.477*

Nipperdey, Thomas *v.3 p.164*

Nisbet, Lee (Editor) *v.6 p.266*

Nisbet, R. G. M. & Rudd, Niall *v.2 p.435*

Nisbet, Robert A. & Himmelfard, Gertrude. . . *v.4 p.290, p.332*

Nisbet, Robert A. *v.4 p.680, p.683, p.685, p.700*

Nisbet, Robin G. & Hubbard, Margaret. *v.2 p.435*

Nisbett, Richard E. & Cohen, Dov *v.5 p.637*

Nisbett, Richard E. *v.5 p.637*

Nisenson, Eric. *v.1 p.262, p.320, p.351*

Nishida, Mieko *v.3 p.265, p.337*

Nishiguchi, Toshihiro (Editor) *v.4 p.118*

Nishitani, Keiji. *v.1 p.509*

Nishiyama, Matsunosuke *v.6 p.225*

Niskanen, William A. *v.4 p.86*

Nissen, Bruce (Editor) *v.4 p.128, p.572, p.665*

Nissen, Henrik S. (Editor) *v.3 p.232, p.233*

Nisula, Dasha Culic *v.2 p.779*

Nitecki, Matthew H. (Editor) *v.5 p.195*

Nitti, John J. & Ferreira, Michael J. *v.2 p.638*

Nitz, Genoveva & Berta Hummel Museum Staff . . . *v.1 p.698*

Niu, Xiaodong *v.4 p.344*

Niven, Ivan, et al. *v.5 p.476*

Niven, Ivan (Text by). *v.5 p.476*

Niven, Ivan *v.5 p.479, p.489*

Niven, John *v.3 p.417, p.426*

Niven, Paul R. *v.4 p.73, p.82*

Niven, Penelope *v.2 p.115*

Nivola, Pietro S. *v.6 p.724*

Nixon, C. E. & Rodgers, Barbara S. *v.3 p.32*

Nixon, Jude V.. . . . . *v.2 p.294*

Nixon, Judith M.. . . . . *v.4 p.161*

Nixon, Raymond B. *v.3 p.434*

Nixon, Richard M. *v.3 p.477*

Nizami, N.. . . . . *v.6 p.672*

Nkashama, Pius Ngandu *v.2 p.542*

Nketia, Joseph H. Kwabena *v.1 p.285*

Nkrumah, Kwame *v.2 p.760, v.6 p.54*

NOAA National Climatic Data Center *v.5 p.426*

Noakes, Jeremy & Pridham, G. (Editors) *v.3 p.173*
Noakes, Jeremy & Pridham, Geoffrey (Editors) . . . *v.3 p.173*
Noakes, Timothy D. *v.4 p.866, p.875, p.879*
Noam, Eli *v.4 p.420*
Nobel, Philip. *v.1 p.797, v.6 p.729*
Noble, David F. *v.4 p.170*
Noble, David W.. . . . . *v.3 p.369, p.376, p.443*
Noble, Elmer R. *v.5 p.213*
Noble, Jean Bobby *v.6 p.429, p.480*
Noble, Kate *v.5 p.635*
Noble, Keith A. (Editor, Compiled by) *v.4 p.339*
Noble, Peter S.. . . . . *v.2 p.468*
Noble, Thomas F. *v.3 p.199*
Nobles, Melissa *v.3 p.279*
Noblit, George W. & Hare, R. Dwight. *v.4 p.24*
Nocedal, Jorge & Wright, Stephen J.. . . . *v.5 p.492, p.493*
Nochlin, Linda. *v.1 p.706, v.6 p.473, p.475*
Noddings, Nel. *v.4 p.306, p.307, p.339*
Nodelman, Sheldon. *v.1 p.744*
Noel, Joseph P. & Robertson, Dan *v.5 p.117*
Noel, Roden B. *v.2 p.274*
Noel, S. J. *v.3 p.544*
Noel, Thomas J. *v.1 p.790*
Noel-Hume, Ivor *v.4 p.14*
Noer, Deliar *v.1 p.554*
Noether, D. & Noeter, Herman *v.5 p.316*
Noever, Peter (Editor) *v.1 p.720*
Nof, Shimon Y. (Editor). *v.4 p.116*
Noë, Alva & Thompson, Evan T. (Editors) *v.5 p.607*
Nofsinger, John & Kim, Kenneth *v.4 p.87*
Nofsinger, John R. & Kim, Kenneth *v.4 p.86*
Nofsinger, John R.. . . . . *v.4 p.97*
Noggle, Anne *v.3 p.227*
Nogradi, M. *v.5 p.295*
Noguera, Pedro *v.4 p.315*
Nohlen, Dieter (Editor), et al. *v.4 p.612*
Nolan, David *v.3 p.303*
Nolan, Deborah (Editor) *v.5 p.459, p.464*
Nolan, Dennis R.. . . . . *v.4 p.123*
Nolan, Fredrick. *v.1 p.329, v.6 p.409*
Nolan, James L. Jr. & Meister, Denise G. *v.4 p.283*
Nolan, James L. *v.4 p.449*
Nolan, Janet A.. . . . . *v.3 p.135*
Nolan, Mary *v.3 p.170*
Nolan, Riall. *v.4 p.45*
Nolen, John *v.1 p.814*
Nolen-Hoeksema, Susan & Larson, Judith *v.5 p.655*
Nolen-Hoeksema, Susan *v.5 p.660*
Noll, Mark A. & Blumhofer, Edith L. (Editors) . . . *v.1 p.606*
Noll, Mark A. (Editor) *v.1 p.606*
Noll, Mark A., et al. *v.1 p.606*
Noll, Mark A.. *v.1 p.590, p.598, p.605, p.606, p.648, v.3 p.410*
Noll, Mark *v.1 p.584, p.585*
Noll, Richard *v.5 p.597, p.661*
Noll, Roger G. & Zimbalist, Andrew (Editors) *v.4 p.888, p.897*

Nollen, Scott A. *v.6 p.331*
Noller, Patricia & Feeney, Judith A. (Editors) *v.5 p.639*
Nolletti, Arthur Jr. & Desser, David (Editors). . *v.6 p.327, p.336*
Nollman, Jim (Editor) *v.5 p.212*
Nolt, John *v.4 p.382*
Nolutshungu, Sam C. *v.6 p.62*
Nomura, Gail M. (Editor) *v.6 p.90, p.109*
Nonhebel, D. C., et al. *v.5 p.276*
Nonini, Donald M. *v.6 p.172*
Noonan, Bonnie *v.6 p.319*
Noonan, Harold W.. . . . . *v.1 p.451, p.468*
Noonan, John T. Jr. *v.1 p.657, v.4 p.443, p.444*
Noonan, John Thomas *v.4 p.538*
Noonan, John *v.1 p.574*
Nor Faridah Abdul Manaf & Quayum, Mohammad A.. *v.2 p.760*
Nora, Pierre & Kritzman, Lawrence D.. . . . . . . *v.3 p.141*
Nora, Pierre *v.3 p.141*
Norbeck, Joseph M. et al.. . . . . *v.5 p.700*
Norberg, Dag Ludvig *v.2 p.449*
Norcliffe, Glen. *v.4 p.808, p.857*
Norcross, John C., et al. *v.5 p.669*
Nord, David Paul. *v.4 p.149*
Nord, Deborah E. *v.6 p.748*
Nord, Philip G.. . . . . *v.3 p.149*
Nord, Warren A. *v.4 p.307*
Nordbruch, Claus. *v.2 p.612*
Norden, Deborah L. *v.3 p.276, p.348, v.4 p.592*
Nordhoff, Charles & Hall, James Norman *v.2 p.103*
Nordin, Margareta & Frankel, Victor H. *v.4 p.908*
Nordland, Gerald. *v.1 p.744*
Nordlund, Marcie *v.4 p.316, p.350*
Nordlund, Willis J. *v.4 p.128*
Nordmann, Alfred *v.1 p.472*
Nordquist, Joan (Editor, Compiled by) *v.6 p.359*
Nordquist, Joan (Editor) *v.6 p.359*
Nordstrom, Byron J. (Editor) *v.3 p.232, p.233*
Nordstrom, Byron J. *v.3 p.232, p.233, p.235*
Nordstrom, Karl F. (Author, Editor) *v.4 p.392*
Nordstrown, Kirk & Munoz, James L. *v.5 p.440*
Norgate, Kate. *v.3 p.98*
Norgren, Jill *v.4 p.465*
Noriega, Chon A. & Belcher, Wendy L. (Editors). *v.6 p.490, p.544*
Noriega, Chon A. & Lopez, Ana M. (Editors). . . . *v.6 p.493*
Noriega, Chon A. (Editor) *v.6 p.487, p.493*
Noriega, Chon A.. . . . . *v.6 p.493*
Noriega, Manuel & Eisner, Peter. *v.3 p.305*
Norman, Charles *v.2 p.112*
Norman, Diana. *v.6 p.556*
Norman, Donald A.. . . . . *v.5 p.588*
Norman, E. Herbert. *v.6 p.225*
Norman, E. R. *v.1 p.609*
Norman, Geoffrey A. (Editor) *v.5 p.22, p.25*
Norman, George & LaManna, Manfred (Editors). *v.4 p.207, p.252*
Norman, Jerry *v.6 p.207*
Norman L. Allinger, Norman L. *v.5 p.298*

Norman, Marsha *v.1 p.121, v.2 p.151*
Norman, Sylva *v.2 p.311*
Nornes, Markus *v.6 p.309*
Norris, Christopher *v.1 p.512*
Norris, David O. & Carr, James A. *v.5 p.366*
Norris, Frank *v.2 p.49*
Norris, Geoffrey *v.1 p.220, p.350*
Norris, H. T. *v.6 p.663*
Norris, James D. *v.4 p.426*
Norris, John *v.4 p.644*
Norris, Kathleen *v.1 p.650, v.3 p.523*
Norris, Lacy J. *v.2 p.468*
Norris, Margot (Editor) *v.2 p.360*
Norris, Pippa (Editor) *v.6 p.448*
Norris, Pippa. *v.4 p.577*
Norris, Richard A. Jr. & Rusch, William G. (Editors) *v.1 p.640*
Norris, Robert F., et al. *v.5 p.10, p.27*
North American Commission on Stratigraphic Nomenclature and
  American Association of Petroleum Geologists . . . *v.5 p.446*
North, Douglass C. & Thomas, Robert Paul *v.3 p.41*
North, Douglass Cecil *v.3 p.41, v.4 p.196, p.210, p.248*
North, J. D. *v.6 p.576*
North, John David *v.1 p.744*
North, John *v.5 p.62, v.6 p.735*
North, Michael *v.3 p.205*
Northam, John *v.2 p.628*
Northedge, F. S. *v.4 p.631*
Northern, Jerry *v.5 p.523*
Northern, Rebecca T. *v.5 p.43*
Northey, Margot & Knight, David B. *v.4 p.376*
Northrop, Douglas *v.3 p.213*
Northrup, Jim *v.6 p.698*
Northup, George T. *v.2 p.639*
Norton, Anne *v.5 p.644*
Norton, Bryan G. *v.5 p.357, p.378*
Norton, David Fate (Editor) *v.1 p.451*
Norton, Derek & Reading, Nigel *v.1 p.777, v.6 p.679*
Norton, Leslie *v.1 p.24*
Norton, O. Richard *v.5 p.69*
Norton, Philip (Editor) *v.4 p.575*
Norton, Richard C. (Editor) *v.1 p.253*
Norton, Robert L. *v.5 p.714*
Norton, Roger D. *v.5 p.14*
Norton, William *v.4 p.396*
Norton-Smith, Richard *v.3 p.461*
Norwich, John Julius *v.3 p.193*
Norwick, Kenneth P. & Chasen, Jerry S. *v.4 p.441*
Norwid, Cyprian Kamil & Czerniawski, Adam *v.2 p.791*
Norwood, Frederick A. *v.1 p.586*
Norwood, Vera *v.5 p.230*
Nosakhere, Akilah Shukura (Compiled by), et al. . *v.6 p.14, p.34*
Noss, Luther *v.1 p.220, p.332*
Noss, Reed F. & Cooperrider, Allen Y. *v.5 p.180*
Noss, Reed F., et al. *v.5 p.180*
Nossack, Hans Erich & Drenttel, William *v.3 p.175*

Nostrand, Richard L. *v.6 p.532*
Notehelfer, F. G. *v.6 p.225, p.228*
Notestein, Wallace *v.3 p.104, p.121*
Notley, Alice *v.2 p.151*
Nottingham, John *v.6 p.65*
Nottingham, Stephen *v.6 p.284*
Novacek, Michael J. (Editor) *v.5 p.84*
Novack, Cynthia J. *v.1 p.43*
Novak, Arne; Harkins, et al. *v.2 p.782*
Novak, Gregor, et al. *v.5 p.564*
Novak, John (Editor) *v.4 p.277*
Novak, Joseph D. *v.4 p.358, v.5 p.572*
Novak, Maximillian E. *v.2 p.246*
Novak, Melinda A. & Petto, Andrew J. (Editors) . . *v.5 p.615*
Novak, Michael *v.4 p.55, p.167, p.803*
Novak, Paul *v.5 p.703*
Novak, Steven J. *v.4 p.332*
Novak, William J. *v.4 p.440*
Novalis *v.2 p.601*
Novartis Foundation Symposium Staff *v.5 p.113*
Novartis Staff *v.5 p.218*
Novick, Peter *v.3 p.86, p.376*
Novick, Sheldon M. *v.4 p.469*
Novotny, Fritz *v.1 p.728*
Novshek, William *v.4 p.203*
Novy, Marianne (Editor) *v.1 p.76, p.102, p.135*
Nowell-Smith, Geoffrey *v.6 p.419*
Nowlan, Robert A. & Nowlan, Gwendolyn L. *v.6 p.332*
Nowlan, Robert A. & Nowlan, Gwendolyn W. . *v.6 p.333, p.346*
Noxon, James *v.1 p.451*
Noyelle, Thierry J. & Stanback, Thomas M. Jr. . . . *v.6 p.724*
Noyori, Ryoji *v.5 p.295*
Nozick, Robert . *v.1 p.417, p.493, p.501, p.512, p.514, v.4 p.511*
Nriagu, Jerome O. (Editor) *v.5 p.366*
Nsamenang, A. Bame *v.4 p.335*
Nuccetelli, Susana *v.1 p.444*
Nuckolls, Charles W. *v.4 p.35*
Nuclear Data Evaluation Lab *v.5 p.545*
Nudds, J. R. & Pettitt, C. W. (Editors) *v.5 p.227*
Nuechterlein, Jonathan E. &
  Weiser, Philip J. *v.4 p.52, p.111, p.166, p.420*
Nuernberg, Susan M. (Editor) *v.2 p.95*
Nuffield, Edward W. *v.3 p.545*
Nugent, David *v.3 p.328*
Nugent, Paul *v.6 p.54, p.74*
Nugent, Richard Bruce *v.6 p.27, p.403*
Nugent, Robert *v.2 p.517*
Nugent, Walter & Ridge, Martin (Editors) *v.3 p.518*
Nugent, Walter *v.4 p.571, p.765*
Nuhanovic, Gordan *v.2 p.818*
Nuland, Sherwin B. *v.5 p.509, p.510, p.532*
Nun, Jose *v.3 p.276*
Nunberg, Geoffrey *v.2 p.558*
Nunez, Sigrid *v.6 p.101*
Nunn, Frederick M. *v.3 p.276*

Nunnally, Brian K. *v.5 p.136*
Nunnally, Jum C. & Bernstein, Ira H. *v.5 p.599*
Nunokawa, Jeff *v.2 p.193, v.6 p.756, p.765*
Nurse, Paul *v.5 p.80*
Nurse, Peter H.. . . . . *v.2 p.458*
Nusinovich, Gregory S.. . . . . *v.5 p.729*
Nussbaum, Felicity (Editor) *v.2 p.172*
Nussbaum, Martha C. & Rorty, Amelie O. (Editors) . *v.1 p.427*
Nussbaum, Martha C. & Sen, Amartya (Editors) . . . *v.4 p.266*
Nussbaum, Martha C. *v.1 p.420, p.428, p.497, v.5 p.655*
Nussbaum, Martha Craven *v.1 p.491*
Nussbaum, Martha (Editor), et al. *v.2 p.375*
Nussbaum, Robert L., et al. *v.5 p.150*
Nutt, Paul C. *v.4 p.83*
Nuttall, Ena Vazquez, et al. *v.5 p.572*
Nuttall, Mark (Editor) *v.6 p.284*
Nuwer, Hank. *v.4 p.288*
Nwapa, Flora *v.2 p.756*
Nweke, Felix I., et al. *v.5 p.22*
Nwoga, Donatus I. (Editor) *v.2 p.756*
Nybakken, James W.. . . . . *v.5 p.171*
Nybakken, James Willard (Editor), et al. . . *v.5 p.429, v.6 p.284*
Nybakken, Oscar E. *v.5 p.406*
Nyberg, Tore *v.3 p.232, p.233*
Nydell, Margaret K. *v.6 p.654*
Nye, Andrea *v.1 p.506*
Nye, David *v.3 p.381*
Nye, Joseph S.. . . . . *v.4 p.626*
Nye, Mary J.. *v.5 p.263*
Nye, Robert A.. . . . . *v.4 p.705*
Nyerere, Julius K. *v.6 p.66*
Nyhart, Lynn K. & Broman, Thomas H. (Editors) . . . *v.3 p.45*
Nyhart, Lynn K.. . . . . *v.3 p.45*
Nyhuis, Allen W. *v.5 p.84*
Nylander, Jane C. & Nylander, Richard C. *v.1 p.824*
Nyman, Michael *v.1 p.220*
Nyquist, Richard A., et al.. . . . . *v.5 p.305*
Nyquist, Richard A. *v.5 p.270*
Nyren, Chuck *v.4 p.138*
Nyren, Ron & Stone, Sarah *v.2 p.579*

O

O. S. H. A. Staff *v.5 p.312*
OABITAR, (Objectivity, Accuracy, and Balance In Teaching
   About Religion) *v.4 p.299*
Oakes, Elizabeth H. *v.4 p.825*
Oakeshott, Michael. *v.1 p.485, v.4 p.492, p.493*
Oakley, Allen *v.4 p.230, p.236*
Oakley, Francis & Russett, Bruce M.. . . . . *v.1 p.576*
Oakley, Francis. *v.1 p.600, v.6 p.572*
Oakley, Stewart P. *v.3 p.234*
Oaks, Laury *v.5 p.524*
Oakshott, Les *v.4 p.179*
Oates, Joan & Oates, David *v.3 p.6*

Oates, Joyce Carol (Compiled by) *v.2 p.7*
Oates, Joyce Carol (Editor) *v.2 p.26, p.28*
Oates, Joyce Carol *v.2 p.152, v.4 p.812, p.856*
Oates, Stephen B. & Errico, Charles J.. . . . . . . *v.3 p.380*
Oates, Stephen B. *v.3 p.399, p.426, p.431*
Oatley, Keith (Author, Contribution by) *v.5 p.655*
Obaldia, René de. *v.2 p.523*
O'Ballance, Edgar *v.6 p.62*
Obata, Chiura. *v.6 p.88, p.134*
Obejas, Achy *v.6 p.398, p.508*
Ober, Josiah. *v.3 p.18*
Oberdorfer, Don *v.6 p.237*
Oberg, et al.. . . . . *v.5 p.715, p.732*
Oberhelman, Harvey D.. . . . . *v.2 p.684*
Oberman, Heiko A. . *v.1 p.549, p.581, p.603, p.632, p.633, p.634*
Oberman, Heiko *v.3 p.166*
Obeyesekere, Gananath *v.4 p.43*
Obiakor, Festus E. & Gordon, Jacob U. (Editors). . . *v.6 p.21*
Obolensky, Dimitri *v.3 p.193*
Oboler, Suzanne & González, Deena J. (Editors) . . . *v.6 p.485*
Oboler, Suzanne *v.6 p.539, p.544*
Obolonsky, Alexander V. *v.3 p.209*
O'Brien, Bob R.. . . . . *v.5 p.18*
O'Brien, Catherine (Editor) *v.2 p.700*
O'Brien, Catherine *v.2 p.700*
O'Brien, D. P. *v.4 p.218*
O'Brien, David & Shannon, Thomas A. (Editors) . . . *v.1 p.572*
O'Brien, David J. & Fugita, Stephen S. *v.6 p.132*
O'Brien, David J., et al. *v.5 p.14*
O'Brien, David M. *v.4 p.443, p.464, p.466, p.538*
O'Brien, Edna *v.2 p.372, p.373*
O'Brien, Edward J. *v.2 p.26*
O'Brien, Eugene *v.2 p.352*
O'Brien, Flann *v.2 p.373*
O'Brien, George Dennis *v.4 p.290*
O'Brien, Joan V. *v.1 p.533*
O'Brien, John. *v.1 p.94, p.102*
O'Brien, Kevin J. *v.4 p.620*
O'Brien, Mary Elizabeth *v.5 p.528, p.530*
O'Brien, Mary *v.6 p.301*
O'Brien, Michael J., et al.. . . . . *v.4 p.6*
O'Brien, Michael *v.3 p.477, p.495, p.497*
O'Brien, Nancy P. & Fabiano, Emily S. *v.4 p.339*
O'Brien, Patrick K. (Editor). *v.4 p.381*
O'Brien, Robert & Martin, Harold (Editors) *v.3 p.494*
O'Brien, Robert F. (Editor) *v.1 p.169*
O'Brien, Ron *v.4 p.860*
O'Brien, Teri S. *v.4 p.791, p.904*
O'Brien, Thomas F.. . . . . *v.3 p.351*
O'Brien, Thomas J. *v.4 p.256, p.263*
O'Brien, Tim *v.2 p.151, v.5 p.84*
O'Callaghan, Joseph F. *v.3 p.65, p.238*
O'Casey, Sean *v.2 p.373, p.374*
Occhiogrosso, Frank (Editor) *v.1 p.76, p.102, p.135*
Occhipinti, John D. *v.6 p.262*

Occupational Safety and Health Administration, U.S.
  Department of Labor *v.5 p.580*
OceanLaw *v.4 p.478*
Océano Staff *v.3 p.299*
Ochoa, Enrique & Ochoa, Gilda L. *v.6 p.544, p.550*
Ochoa, Enrique C. *v.3 p.272*
Ochoa, George & Corey, Melinda *v.6 p.305*
Ochoa, George *v.3 p.477*
Ochs, Carol *v.1 p.651*
Ochs, Robyn (Editor) *v.6 p.360*
Ochse, Orpha C. *v.1 p.279, p.390*
Ockerman, Herbert W. *v.5 p.259*
Ockey, James *v.4 p.622*
O'Connell, David *v.2 p.515*
O'Connell, Mark *v.5 p.639*
O'Connell, P. J. *v.6 p.309*
O'Connor, Alice (Editor), et al. *v.6 p.724*
O'Connor, David E. *v.4 p.192*
O'Connor, David *v.1 p.452*
O'Connor, Flannery *v.2 p.106*
O'Connor, Francis V. (Editor) *v.1 p.698*
O'Connor, Frank (Editor) *v.2 p.374*
O'Connor, Frank *v.2 p.374, p.579*
O'Connor, J. J., and Robertson, E. F. (Editors) . . . *v.5 p.467*
O'Connor, Kevin *v.3 p.256*
O'Connor, Margaret *v.5 p.528*
O'Connor, Patricia W. & Pasquariello, Anthony M.
  (Editors) *v.2 p.644*
O'Connor, Patricia W. *v.2 p.644*
O'Connor, Rob, et al. *v.4 p.827, p.828, p.829*
O'Connor, Sandra Day *v.4 p.466*
O'Connor, Sean *v.6 p.412*
O'Connor, Thomas A. *v.2 p.647*
O'Connor, Thomas H. *v.3 p.487, v.6 p.714*
O'Croinin, Daibhi (Editor) *v.3 p.137*
Oda, Hiroshi *v.6 p.220*
Odamtten, Vincent O. *v.2 p.753*
O'Day, Alan *v.3 p.135, p.139*
Oddo, Vincent *v.1 p.398, p.406*
Oded, Arye *v.6 p.65*
Odegaard, Nancy & Sadongei, Alyce *v.1 p.828*
O'Dell, C. Robert *v.5 p.70*
Odell, George C. *v.1 p.4, p.55, p.117, p.137*
Odem, Mary E. *v.4 p.736, v.6 p.467*
Odets, Clifford *v.2 p.108*
Odifreddi, Piergiorgio *v.5 p.459, p.467*
Odo, Franklin S. *v.6 p.116, p.132*
Odo, Franklin *v.6 p.87, p.119*
Odoevsky, Vladimir F. *v.2 p.806*
Odoevsky, Vladimir Fedorovich *v.2 p.806*
Odom, Thomas P. *v.4 p.653, p.715*
O'Donnell, James J. *v.1 p.430, v.2 p.430*
O'Donnell, Joe *v.1 p.768*
O'Donnell, R. M. *v.4 p.228*
O'Donnol, Shirley M. *v.1 p.151*

O'Donoghue, Michael (Editor) *v.5 p.452*
O'Donohue, William T. & Ferguson, Kyle E.
  (Editors) *v.5 p.594, p.674*
O'Donohue, William T. & Levensky, Eric R. (Editors) . *v.5 p.592*
O'Donohue, William T. (Editor) *v.5 p.667*
O'Donohue, William *v.5 p.667*
Odorico, J. S. (Editor), et al. *v.5 p.159*
O'Dougherty, Maureen *v.3 p.341*
O'Driscoll, Gerald P., et al. *v.4 p.270*
O'Driscoll, Gerald P. Jr. (Editor) *v.4 p.219*
O'Driscoll, Robert *v.2 p.327*
Odum, Howard T. *v.5 p.53, p.368, p.372, p.379*
Oe, Kenzaburo *v.6 p.232*
Oehlers, D. J. & Bradford, M. A. *v.5 p.695, p.697*
Oehlert, Gary W. *v.5 p.482*
Oehser, Paul H. & Ripley, S. Dillon *v.5 p.385*
Oehser, Paul H. *v.5 p.385*
Oergel, Maike *v.2 p.176*
Oesterle, Dale A. *v.4 p.85*
Oesterley, W. O. E. *v.1 p.21*
Offer, D., et al. *v.4 p.693*
Offerman-Zuckerberg, J. *v.5 p.644*
Office of Educational Research and Improvement, U.S.
  Department of Education *v.5 p.576*
Office of Management and Budget *v.4 p.481*
Office of Program Consultation and Accreditation . . . *v.5 p.676*
Office of the Federal Register, National Archives and Records
  Administration *v.4 p.481*
Office of the Law Revision Counsel of the U.S. House of
  Representatives *v.4 p.481*
Offner, Arnold A. & Wilson, Theodore A. (Editors) . . *v.3 p.391*
Offner, Arnold A. *v.3 p.453, p.477*
Offord, Malcolm *v.2 p.454*
Offutt, Leslie Scott *v.3 p.287*
Ofiara, Douglas D. & Seneca, Joseph J. *v.6 p.298*
O'Flaherty, Michael & Gisvold, Gregory *v.4 p.513*
O'Flaherty, Patrick *v.3 p.547*
O'Flaherty, Wendy Doniger *v.1 p.537*
Ofshe, Richard & Watters, Ethan *v.4 p.714*
O'Gara, Gordon C. *v.3 p.384*
Ogbaa, Kalu *v.2 p.753*
Ogborn, Jane & Buckroyd, Peter *v.2 p.195*
Ogden, August R. *v.3 p.449*
Ogden, J. Alexander & Kalb, Judith E. *v.2 p.793, p.796*
Ogden Nature Center Staff & Sterling Publishing Company
  Staff *v.1 p.760*
Ogden, Philip E. & White, Paul E. (Editors) *v.3 p.157*
Ogden, Schubert M. *v.1 p.636, p.641*
Ogershok, David & Pray, Richard (Editors) *v.4 p.159*
Ogg, Frederick Austin *v.3 p.513*
Ogilvie, Marilyn & Harvey, Joy (Editors) . *v.5 p.395, v.6 p.439*
Ogilvie, Marilyn B. *v.5 p.398*
Ogilvie, Robert M. *v.2 p.436*
Ogilvie, Sheilagh (Editor) *v.3 p.164*
Ogilvy, J. D. & Baker, Donald C. *v.2 p.205*

Oglesby, Carole A. (Editor), et al. *v.6 p.438*

Ogletree, Charles Jr.. . . . . *v.6 p.12, p.21, p.22*

Ogloff, James R. (Editor) *v.5 p.592*

O'Gorman, Francis (Editor). *v.2 p.176, p.193*

O'Gorman, Francis *v.2 p.176, p.193, p.200, p.305*

O'Gorman, Frank. *v.3 p.114, v.4 p.604, p.606*

O'Grada, Cormac *v.3 p.139*

O'Grady, Timothy *v.4 p.861*

O'Grady, William, et al.. . . . . *v.2 p.563*

Ogude, James *v.2 p.759*

Ogunjimi, Bayo & Na'allah, Abdul Rasheed *v.2 p.751*

Oh, Sadaharu & Falkner, David *v.6 p.228*

Ohaegbulam, Festus Ugboaja. *v.6 p.56*

O'Hagan, Howard *v.2 p.733*

O'Hagan, Timothy *v.1 p.454*

O'Hanlon, Rosalind *v.6 p.149*

O'Hara, Frank *v.2 p.105, p.106, v.6 p.405*

O'Hara, James *v.2 p.68*

O'Hara, John *v.2 p.106, p.107*

O'Hara, Phillip Anthony *v.4 p.192*

O'Hare, Greg, et al. *v.5 p.426*

O'Healy, Anne-Marie *v.2 p.720*

O'Hear, Anthony (Editor) *v.5 p.248*

O'Hear, Anthony *v.1 p.446*

Ohl, John K.. . . . . *v.3 p.461*

Ohles, Frederik M., et al. *v.4 p.338*

Ohles, John F. (Editor) *v.4 p.338*

Ohmae, Kenichi. *v.4 p.70*

Ohnuki-Tierney, Emiko *v.6 p.222*

Oja, Carol J. & Tick, Judith (Editors) . *v.1 p.220, p.318, p.319*

Oja, Carol J.. . . . . *v.1 p.220, p.279*

Ojaide, Tanure & Sallah, Tijan M. (Editors) . *v.2 p.752, v.6 p.80*

Ojinmah, Umelo *v.2 p.741*

Oka, Yoshitake. *v.6 p.228*

Okada, John *v.6 p.101*

Okafor, Dubem. *v.2 p.756*

Okamoto, Shiro *v.6 p.228*

Okamura, Jonathan Y. *v.6 p.119, p.129*

O'Kane, Rosemary H. *v.4 p.497*

Okano, Kaori & Tsuchiya, Motonori *v.4 p.335*

Okano, Kaori, et al. *v.6 p.222*

O'Keefe, John *v.2 p.252*

O'Keeffe, Michael & Navrotsky, Alexandra (Editors) . *v.5 p.284*

Okey, Robin. *v.3 p.181, v.4 p.509, p.596, p.600*

Okigbo, Charl *v.4 p.398*

Okigbo, Christopher *v.2 p.756*

Okihiro, Gary Y. (Editor) *v.6 p.109*

Okihiro, Gary Y; Ito, Leslie A. *v.6 p.114, p.132*

Okihiro, Gary Y. . *v.3 p.376, v.6 p.85, p.87, p.105, p.109, p.114, p.116, p.124, p.132, p.134*

Okin, Susan Moller . *v.4 p.488, p.490, p.493, p.517, v.6 p.441*

Okker, Patricia. *v.4 p.409*

Oklobdzija, Vojin. *v.5 p.730*

Okorocha, Cyril C. *v.6 p.72*

Okpewho, Isidore (Editor). *v.2 p.753*

Okpewho, Isidore *v.2 p.752*

Okrent, Daniel *v.1 p.790*

Okri, Ben *v.2 p.756*

Okubo, A.. . . . . *v.5 p.502*

Okuda, T. (Editor), et al. *v.5 p.177, p.185*

Okuda, Ted & Watz, Edward *v.6 p.313*

Okun, Arthur M. *v.4 p.239*

Okuno-Fujiwara, Masahiro & Okazaki, Tetsuji (Editors). *v.6 p.220*

Olah, George A. & Molnár, Árpád *v.5 p.292*

Olah, George A.. . . . . *v.5 p.261, p.296*

Olaniyan, Tejumola. *v.1 p.286, p.335, v.2 p.768*

Olasky, Marvin N. *v.4 p.404*

Olatunji, Babatunde & Atkinson, Robert *v.1 p.11, p.14*

Olbracht, Ivan *v.2 p.784*

Olby, Robert C. (Editor), et al. *v.3 p.45*

Olcott, Anthony *v.2 p.799*

Olcott, Jocelyn *v.3 p.294*

Olcott, Martha Brill *v.3 p.231*

Old, Hughes Oliphant. *v.1 p.654*

Oldenberg, H.. . . . . *v.1 p.538*

Oldfield, Ronald Jowett & Rost, Fred W. D. *v.5 p.86*

Oldfield, Sara *v.5 p.239, p.240*

Oldham, Gabriella *v.6 p.350*

Oldham, John *v.2 p.252*

Oldknow, Tina *v.1 p.811*

Oldroyd, David R. *v.5 p.418*

Olds, C., et al. *v.5 p.477*

O'Leary, De Lacy E. *v.6 p.625*

O'Leary, John (Editor) *v.4 p.826, p.901*

O'Leary, Virginia (Editor), et al. . *v.6 p.429, p.446, p.467, p.470*

Oleksak, Michael M. & Oleksak,
Mary A. *v.4 p.808, p.833, p.844, p.851, p.899*

Olesha, Yuri *v.2 p.806*

Oleszek, Walter J. *v.4 p.532*

Olevnik, Peter P., et al. *v.4 p.290*

Olfman, Sharna (Editor) *v.4 p.370*

Olin, John C. *v.1 p.612*

Olin, Laurie *v.1 p.816, p.819*

Olin, Spencer C. *v.3 p.531*

Olinick, Michael *v.5 p.503*

Olivares, Julian *v.2 p.651*

Olivares, Rafael A. *v.2 p.636*

Olivas, Michael A. (Editor) *v.6 p.527*

Olivas, Michael A. *v.4 p.312*

Olivas Weston, Rosario *v.3 p.272*

Olive, Jenny *v.5 p.459*

Oliveira, Carlos Sousa, et al. *v.5 p.695*

Oliveira, Carmen L. *v.6 p.403*

Oliveira, Marques A. *v.3 p.244*

Oliveira, Paulo S. & Marquis, Robert J. . . *v.5 p.236, v.6 p.292*

Olivelle, Patrick (Author, Translator). *v.6 p.152*

Olivelle, Patrick (Editor) *v.1 p.537, v.6 p.152*

Olivelle, Patrick (Translator) *v.1 p.537*

Olivelle, Patrick *v.1 p.537*

Oliver, Anne Marie & Steinberg, Paul *v.4 p.661*

Oliver, Charles M.. . . . . *v.2 p.85*
Oliver, Douglas L.. . . . . *v.4 p.43*
Oliver, Douglas *v.4 p.43*
Oliver, H. J. *v.2 p.218*
Oliver, James H. *v.3 p.21*
Oliver, John E. (Editor) *v.5 p.426, v.6 p.284*
Oliver, John E. Jr. & Hidore, John J.. . . . . . . *v.5 p.426*
Oliver, Melvin L. & Shapiro, Thomas M.. . . . . . *v.4 p.730*
Oliver, Paul. *v.1 p.262, p.281, p.784, p.821*
Oliver, Peter *v.3 p.545*
Oliver, R. E. *v.4 p.87*
Oliver, Richard L. *v.5 p.218*
Oliver, Richard W. *v.5 p.219*
Oliver, Roland & Atmore, Anthony *v.6 p.53*
Oliver, Roland Anthony & Crowder, Michael (Editors) . *v.6 p.51*
Oliver, Roland *v.6 p.53*
Oliveros, Pauline. *v.1 p.220, p.346*
Oliver-Smith, Anthony *v.3 p.330*
Oliverson, Ray & McKenna, Ted *v.5 p.679*
Olivo, Christiane *v.4 p.610*
Olkowski, William, et al.. . . . . *v.5 p.44*
Ollard, Richard. *v.2 p.256*
Oller, D. Kimbrough & Griebel, Ulrike (Editors). *v.5 p.166, p.195*
Ollier, Claude *v.2 p.532*
Ollinger-Zinqu, Gisèle *v.1 p.745*
Ollman, Bertell. *v.4 p.507*
Olmo, Lauro *v.2 p.663*
Olmstead, Arthur T. *v.3 p.12, v.6 p.630*
Olmstead, Neil (Composed by) *v.1 p.403*
Olmsted, Anthony *v.1 p.385*
Olmsted, Frederick Law, et al.. . . . . *v.1 p.816*
Olmsted, Frederick Law *v.1 p.816, v.3 p.495, p.509*
Olrik, Axel (Editor). *v.2 p.626*
Olsen, Alexandra Hennessey (Editor). *v.2 p.197*
Olsen, Dale A. & Sheehy, Daniel E. (Editors). . . . *v.1 p.293*
Olsen, Dale A. *v.1 p.293*
Olsen, Donald J. *v.3 p.114*
Olsen, Eric, et al. *v.1 p.161, p.273, p.387*
Olsen, Kirstin *v.2 p.222, p.268, v.6 p.426*
Olsen, Margaret M.. . . . . *v.3 p.356*
Olsen, Wallace C. (Editor) *v.5 p.22*
Olson, Carl (Editor) *v.1 p.529*
Olson, Charles *v.2 p.108*
Olson, David M. *v.4 p.575*
Olson, Eric T. *v.1 p.495*
Olson, James C. & Naugle, Ronald C.. . . . . *v.3 p.524*
Olson, James C. *v.3 p.461*
Olson, James S. (Editor) *v.3 p.477, v.4 p.465, p.583*
Olson, Kent *v.4 p.439*
Olson, Leonard T. *v.4 p.841, p.847, p.869*
Olson, Lynne *v.6 p.12, p.45*
Olson, Marc O. J. (Editor). *v.5 p.113*
Olson, Mary C. *v.6 p.556*
Olson, Paul R. *v.2 p.661*
Olson, Paulette I. & Emami, Zohren *v.4 p.185, p.274*

Olson, R. A. & Frey, K. J. *v.5 p.15, p.23*
Olson, Richard (Editor) *v.5 p.395*
Olson, Robert W. *v.6 p.599, p.624*
Olson, Roberta J. M. & Pasachoff, Jay M. *v.1 p.688*
Olson, Roberta J. M. *v.1 p.776*
Olson, Robert *v.6 p.349, p.599*
Olson, Roger E. *v.1 p.598*
Olson, Sigurd F. *v.5 p.80, p.224*
Olson, Steve *v.5 p.195, p.235, p.459*
Olssen, Mark *v.4 p.344*
Oltuski, Enrique *v.3 p.312*
Olufs, Dick W. 3rd *v.4 p.420*
Olwig, Karen F. *v.4 p.41*
O'Malley, Brendan & Craig, Ian. *v.3 p.197*
O'Malley, John W.. . . . . *v.1 p.570, p.578, p.612*
O'Malley, Robert E. Jr. *v.5 p.487*
O'Malley, Therese & Treib, Marc (Editors) *v.1 p.819*
Oman, Charles William Chadwick *v.3 p.69*
Omar, M. Ali *v.5 p.555*
O'Meara, Dominic J.. . . . . *v.1 p.430*
Omenka, Nicholas I. *v.1 p.574*
Omer-Cooper, John D.. . . . . *v.6 p.74*
Omi, Michael & Winant, Howard A.. . . . . *v.6 p.124*
Omnes, Roland. *v.5 p.542*
Omoto, Allen Martin & Kurtzman, Howard S. *v.6 p.382*
Omoto, Charlotte K. & Lurquin, Paul F. *v.5 p.123, p.136*
On, Bat-Ami Bar (Editor). *v.1 p.506*
Ondaatje, Michael *v.2 p.730, p.732, p.737*
One Club Staff. *v.1 p.715*
O'Neil, Dennis. *v.4 p.140*
O'Neil, Harold F.. . . . . *v.4 p.322*
O'Neil, Maryadele J. (Editor), et al. *v.5 p.259, v.6 p.286*
O'Neil, Patrick *v.4 p.509, p.595*
O'Neil, Peter V.. . . . . *v.5 p.501, p.683*
O'Neil, Tom *v.6 p.346*
O'Neill, Bard E. *v.4 p.661*
O'Neill, Barrett *v.5 p.496*
O'Neill, C. & Anderton, B.. . . . . *v.5 p.165*
O'Neill, Dan. *v.5 p.434*
O'Neill, Eugene *v.1 p.117, v.2 p.107*
O'Neill, Jamie *v.6 p.398*
O'Neill, Kathleen *v.4 p.582*
O'Neill, Mary *v.2 p.457*
O'Neill, Michael & Reeves, Gareth . . . *v.2 p.329, p.369, p.384*
O'Neill, Michael J. *v.5 p.84*
O'Neill, Michael *v.4 p.602*
O'Neill, Thomas P. Jr. & Novak, William *v.3 p.461*
O'Neill, William L.. . . . . . . *v.3 p.443, p.477, v.4 p.486*
Onetti, Juan Carlos *v.2 p.687*
Ong, Aihwa (Editor) *v.6 p.204*
Ong, Aihwa *v.6 p.107, p.119*
Ong, Paul & Hee, Suzanne *v.6 p.106, p.124, p.136*
Ong, Paul M. (Editor) *v.6 p.85, p.109*
Ong, Walter J.. . . . . *v.2 p.294, v.3 p.37*
Onians, John (Editor). *v.1 p.665*

Author Index

Onions, Charles T. *v.2 p.226*

Onkvisit, Sak & Shaw, John J. *v.4 p.144*

Onnepalu, Tonu *v.2 p.781*

Ono, Noboru. *v.5 p.295*

Onslow, Barbara *v.6 p.448, p.740, p.748, p.754*

Onuf, Peter S. & Sadosky, Leonard J. *v.4 p.525*

Onwubolu, Godfrey *v.5 p.715*

Ooka, Shohei *v.6 p.232*

Oostendorp, Herre Van (Editor), et al. *v.5 p.621, p.625*

Oosterhuis, Harry *v.4 p.748*

Opdycke, Sandra *v.6 p.426*

Open University Staff *v.5 p.429, p.430*

Ophir, Adi *v.4 p.489*

Opie, Iona & Opie, Peter *v.2 p.200*

Opie, Jennifer Hawkins *v.1 p.811*

Opie, John *v.5 p.11*

Opitz, Glenn B. (Editor) *v.1 p.774*

Opland, Jeff *v.2 p.168*

Opler, Morris E. *v.6 p.704*

Oppen, George *v.2 p.106*

Oppenheim, Felix E. *v.4 p.646*

Oppenheim, Janet *v.3 p.114, p.129, v.6 p.760*

Oppenheim, Lois (Editor) *v.2 p.511*

Oppenheimer, Andres *v.3 p.312*

Oppenheimer, Jerry *v.3 p.477*

Oppenheimer, Mark *v.4 p.720*

Oppenheimer, Paul (Translator) *v.2 p.593*

Oppenheimer, Robert *v.5 p.543*

Oppermann, Ian (Author, Editor) *v.5 p.727*

Oppliger, Patrice A. *v.4 p.818, p.863, p.870*

Opresko, Lee *v.5 p.128, p.142, p.151*

OptimumFinance.net *v.4 p.152*

O'Quinn, Garland Jr. & Hickman, E. Jessica *v.4 p.798*

Oquist, Paul *v.3 p.358*

Orbakh, Doron *v.5 p.285*

Orchard, Andy *v.2 p.205*

O'Reilley, Mary Rose *v.4 p.348*

O'Reilly, Gerald (Editor) *v.5 p.420*

O'Reilly, James T., et al. *v.5 p.682*

O'Reilly, James T. *v.6 p.264, p.265*

Orel, Harold (Editor) *v.2 p.297*

Orel, Vladimir E. *v.2 p.778*

Orellana, Sandra L. *v.3 p.298*

Orelove, Fred P. (Editor), et al. *v.4 p.318*

Orem, Dorthea E., et al. *v.5 p.530*

Oren, Aras *v.6 p.667*

Oren, Tasha G. & Petro, Patrice *v.4 p.419*

Orend, Brian *v.4 p.513*

Orengo, C.A. (Editor), et al. *v.5 p.98*

Orenstein, Arbie *v.1 p.220, p.350*

Oreskes, Naomi *v.5 p.418, p.443*

Orey, Michael, et al. *v.4 p.352*

Orfield, Gary (Editor) *v.4 p.299*

Orfield, Gary, et al. *v.4 p.301*

Orfield, Myron W. *v.6 p.724*

Organ, Dennis W., et al. *v.5 p.579*

Organisation for Economic Co-operation and Development.;
Working Group on Economic Aspects of Biodiversity. *v.5 p.223*

Organisation for Economic Co-operation and
Development *v.5 p.223*

Organization of American States *v.4 p.437, p.474, p.476*

Orgel, Stephen (Editor) *v.2 p.231*

Orgel, Stephen *v.1 p.76, p.78, p.102, v.2 p.231*

Oriard, Michael *v.4 p.808, p.812, p.818, p.823, p.859,
p.885, p.894, p.897, p.902*

Oriel, Charles *v.2 p.640*

Oring, Elliott. *v.2 p.585*

Orizio, Riccardo *v.3 p.315*

Orlans, Harold *v.4 p.705*

Orlean, Susan (Editor) *v.2 p.28, p.584*

Orleans, Leo A. (Editor) *v.5 p.393*

Orledge, Robert *v.1 p.220, p.352*

Orlich, Ileana Alexandra *v.2 p.816*

Orlick, Terry *v.4 p.877*

Orlova, Alexandra (Editor) *v.1 p.201, p.345*

Orlova, Alexandra *v.1 p.201, p.362*

Orlove, Benjamin S. & Custred, Glynn (Editors) *v.4 p.28*

Orlove, Benjamin S. (Editor) *v.3 p.272*

Orme, Nicholas *v.4 p.336, v.6 p.558*

Ormerod, Beverley *v.2 p.537*

Ormiston, Gayle L. & Schrift, Alan D. (Editors) . . . *v.1 p.507*

Ormond, Richard & Kilmurray, Elaine *v.1 p.745*

Ormond, Richard, et al. *v.1 p.745*

Ormrod, David *v.4 p.212*

Ormsby, Tim, et al. *v.4 p.388*

Orna, Mary V. (Editor) *v.5 p.263*

Orndorff, Kata (Editor) *v.6 p.372*

Ornstein, Martha *v.5 p.392*

Ornstein, Norman J. (Editor) *v.4 p.575*

Oropeza, Lorena *v.6 p.539, p.541*

O'Rourke, Joseph *v.5 p.337, p.340*

O'Rourke, Kevin (Translator) *v.6 p.238*

O'Rourke, P. J. *v.4 p.185, p.196, p.251*

Orpen, Valerie *v.6 p.350*

Orr, Bridget *v.2 p.187*

Orr, C. W. *v.6 p.601*

Orr, Gregory *v.2 p.92*

Orr, John *v.1 p.57, p.87, p.89, p.92*

Orrell, John *v.2 p.227*

Orr-Stav, Jonathan & Lotan, Jon *v.6 p.646*

Orser, Charles E. *v.4 p.14*

Orsi, Robert A. (Editor) *v.6 p.718*

Orsi, Robert A. *v.1 p.544, p.607*

Orszagh, Laszlo *v.2 p.775*

Ortega, Adolfo *v.6 p.494*

Ortega, Julio & Fuentes, Carlos *v.2 p.666*

Ortega, Julio (Editor) *v.2 p.684*

Ortega y Gasset, Jose *v.1 p.474, v.2 p.651*

Ortega y Gasset, José *v.1 p.474, p.481, v.2 p.661*

Ortigao, José A. & Sayao, Alberto (Editors) *v.5 p.699*

Ortiz, Alicia Dujovne *v.3 p.349*
Ortiz, Altagracia (Editor) *v.3 p.320*
Ortiz De Montellano, Bernard R. *v.3 p.261*
Ortiz Griffin, Julia & Griffin, William D. *v.3 p.242*
Ortiz, Simon J.. . . . . *v.2 p.20, p.26, p.151, v.6 p.698*
Ortner, Sherry B.. *v.1 p.541*
Ortolani, Benito *v.1 p.133*
Orton, Clive, et al. *v.4 p.7*
Orton, Clive *v.4 p.7*
Orton, Joe *v.2 p.374*
Orton, Keith *v.1 p.147*
Orton, Lawrence D. *v.3 p.188*
Orttung, Robert W. & Reddaway, Peter (Editors) . . . *v.4 p.598*
Orvell, Miles *v.1 p.764*
Orwell, George *v.2 p.375, p.376, p.584, v.3 p.241*
Orwin, Clifford & Tarcov, Nathan (Editors) . . *v.4 p.492*
Orwin, Donna T. (Editor) *v.2 p.797, p.806*
Osaragi, Jiro *v.6 p.232*
Osato, Sono *v.1 p.11*
Osawa, Syozo *v.5 p.200*
Osborn, Eric *v.1 p.613*
Osborn, M. Elizabeth (Editor). *v.6 p.496, p.517*
Osborn, Marilyn, et al. *v.4 p.336*
Osborne, Charles . . *v.1 p.201, p.231, p.309, p.321, p.351, p.366*
Osborne, Graham (Photographer) *v.5 p.177, p.235, p.239*
Osborne, John. *v.1 p.80, p.102, v.2 p.376*
Osborne, Martin J. & Rubinstein, Ariel . . *v.4 p.207, v.5 p.504*
Osborne, Milton E.. . . . . *v.6 p.167, p.170*
Osborne, Peter (Author, Editor) *v.1 p.680*
Osborne, Richard *v.1 p.201, p.351*
Osborne, Robert D.. . . . . *v.4 p.336*
Osborne, Robert *v.6 p.346*
Osborne, Robin & Cunliffe, Barry W. (Editors) *v.4 p.12*
Osborne, Robin *v.1 p.670, v.3 p.18*
Osborne, Roger (Editor), et al. *v.5 p.445, p.446*
Osborne, Thomas J. *v.3 p.534*
Osbourne, Lloyd & Stevenson, Robert Louis *v.2 p.312*
Osen, Lynn M.. . . . . *v.5 p.467*
Oser, Fritz K. *v.4 p.348*
Osers, Ewald (Editor, Translator) *v.2 p.787*
Osgood, Charles E., et al.. . . . . *v.5 p.604*
Osgood, Charles G.. . . . . *v.2 p.215*
Osgood, Herbert L.. . . . . *v.3 p.406, v.4 p.518*
Osgood, Herbert Levi *v.3 p.406, v.4 p.518*
O'Shaughnessy, Hugh *v.3 p.354*
O'Shaughnessy, John. *v.4 p.139, p.426*
O'Shea, James & Madigan, Charles *v.4 p.65*
O'Shea, Maria Theresa *v.6 p.599*
Oshinsky, David M.. . . . . *v.3 p.461, v.5 p.533*
Osif, Bonnie A.; Baratta, Anthony J. &
  Conkling, Thomas W.. . . . . *v.5 p.364, p.740*
Osler, William, Sir *v.5 p.510*
Oslin, George P. *v.4 p.420*
Osmanczyk, Edmund Jan & Mango, Anthony (Editors). *v.4 p.635*
Osmond-Smith, David *v.1 p.220, p.236, p.309, p.310*

Osofisan, Femi *v.2 p.757*
Osofsky, Gilbert *v.6 p.714*
Osorio, Jonathan K. K. *v.6 p.131*
Ostaijen, Paul Van *v.2 p.623*
Ostashevsky, Eugene (Editor) *v.2 p.794*
Osterbrock, Donald E. & Ferland, Gary J. *v.5 p.67*
Osterburg, Bertil O. *v.6 p.315*
Ostergren, Robert C. *v.4 p.571*
Ostergren, Robert Clifford & Rice, John G. *v.4 p.397*
Osterhammel, Jürgen *v.4 p.583*
Osterlind, Steven J.. . . . . *v.5 p.601*
Osterman, Paul. *v.4 p.555*
Osterweis, Rollin Gustav *v.3 p.495*
Ostler, Jeffrey *v.3 p.522, v.6 p.682*
Ostler, Nicholas *v.2 p.563*
Ostriker, Alicia S. *v.2 p.8*
Ostroff, Frank *v.4 p.80*
Ostrogorsky, George. *v.3 p.66, p.193*
Ostrom, Alan *v.2 p.136*
Ostrom, Hans & Macey, J. David (Editors) *v.2 p.6*
Ostrom, Hans A. & Macey, J. David *v.6 p.27, p.34*
Ostrom, Hans A. *v.2 p.88*
Ostrovsky, Aleksandr Nikolaevich *v.2 p.806*
Ostrovsky, Erika *v.2 p.532*
Ostrow, Eileen J. (Editor) *v.1 p.68, p.123*
Ostrow, James (Editor), et al. *v.4 p.675*
Ostrower, Francie *v.4 p.719*
Ostwald, Martin *v.4 p.501*
Ostwald, Peter F.. . . . . . . *v.1 p.201, p.355, v.6 p.415*
O'Sullivan, Donal *v.1 p.298, p.316*
O'Sullivan, Ellen L. & Spangler, Kathy J.. *v.4 p.786, p.787, p.885*
O'Sullivan, Meghan L.. . . . . *v.4 p.565*
O'Sullivan, Michael *v.2 p.333, p.334*
O'Sullivan, Vincent (Editor). *v.2 p.743*
O'Sullivan, Vincent (Selected by) *v.2 p.743*
O'Sullivan, Vincent *v.2 p.747, p.748*
Osuna, Alfonso J. Garcia (Editor) *v.2 p.651*
Otero, Gerardo (Editor) *v.4 p.383*
Otieno, Wambui Waiyaki *v.6 p.18, p.29, p.45*
Otis, Brooks *v.2 p.407, p.438, p.446*
Otis, Carol L. & Goldingay, Roger. *v.4 p.825*
Otis, Delos S. *v.6 p.696*
O'Toole, Fintan *v.2 p.235, p.260*
O'Toole, Laurence J. *v.6 p.317*
O'Toole, Thomas *v.6 p.62*
Otsuka, Julie. *v.6 p.101*
Ott, Peggy J., et al.. . . . . *v.5 p.512, p.522*
Ottati, Victor C. (Editor), et al. *v.5 p.644*
Ottaway, Marina & Carothers, Thomas (Editors) . . . *v.4 p.615*
Ottaway, Marina (Editor) *v.4 p.612*
Otte, Daniel & Endler, John A. (Editors) *v.5 p.199*
Otten, Anna (Editor) *v.2 p.610*
Otten, Robert M. *v.2 p.237*
Ottenberg, Hans-Gunter. *v.1 p.191, p.302*

Ottenberg, Simon & Falola, Toyin *v.4 p.38*

Ottenberg, Simon *v.4 p.38*

Ottenheimer, Harriet Joseph *v.4 p.18*

Otterstedt, Annette *v.1 p.391*

Otterstrom, Samuel *v.4 p.382, v.6 p.721*

Otteson, James R. *v.4 p.219*

Ottman, Robert & Rogers, Nancy *v.1 p.404*

Otto, et al. *v.3 p.163*

Otto, Matthias *v.5 p.274*

Otto, Rudolf *v.1 p.521*

Otto, Shirley E. *v.5 p.520, p.528*

Otto, Walter F *v.1 p.533*

Ottoboni, M. Alice *v.5 p.314*

Otuathail, Gearoid, et al. *v.4 p.488, p.496*

Otway, Thomas *v.2 p.252*

Ou, S. H. *v.5 p.46*

Ouaknin, Marc-Alain *v.2 p.563*

Oueijan, Naji B. *v.2 p.164*

Ough, Cornelius S. *v.5 p.52*

Ouimet, Matthew J. *v.3 p.212*

Oum, Tae Hoon, et al. *v.4 p.152*

Oura, K. *v.5 p.555*

Outka, Gene *v.1 p.651*

Outlaw, Lucius T. Jr. *v.6 p.40*

Outler, Albert Cook *v.1 p.568*

Outram, Dorinda *v.3 p.72*

Outten, Wayne N., et al. *v.4 p.447*

Ouzgane, Lahoucine & Morrell, Robert (Editors) . . *v.4 p.733*

Oved, Yaacov *v.4 p.740*

Ovendale, Ritchie *v.6 p.594, p.611*

Over, Kristen Lee *v.6 p.566*

Overbury, Thomas *v.2 p.215*

Overholt, Catherine (Editor) *v.6 p.457*

Overholt, Thomas W. *v.1 p.619*

Overmyer, Daniel L. (Editor) *v.1 p.539*

Overmyer, Daniel L. *v.1 p.562*

Oversby, Virginia M. & Werme, Lars O.
(Editors) *v.5 p.372, p.375, p.376*

Overy, R. J. *v.3 p.173*

Overy, Richard & Ogilvie, Sheilagh (Author, Editors) . *v.3 p.164*

Overy, Richard *v.3 p.81, p.176, p.227, v.4 p.380*

Ovid *v.2 p.438, p.439*

Owen, Bobbi *v.1 p.117, p.141, p.147, p.148*

Owen, Bruce M., et al. *v.6 p.298*

Owen, Bruce M. *v.4 p.422*

Owen, C. James & York, Willbern *v.4 p.543*

Owen, Charles A. (Editor) *v.2 p.210*

Owen, Eric Trevor *v.2 p.415*

Owen, Margaret *v.4 p.741*

Owen, Nancy E. *v.1 p.707, p.808, p.826*

Owen, Norman G. *v.6 p.165*

Owen, Roger (Editor) *v.6 p.611*

Owen, Roy (Editor, Translator) *v.2 p.468*

Owen, Stephen (Editor, Translator) *v.6 p.208*

Owen, Stephen *v.6 p.210, p.212*

Owen, Sue *v.2 p.187*

Owen, Tobias (Editor), et al. *v.5 p.243*

Owens, Jessie Ann *v.1 p.180*

Owens, Joseph *v.1 p.427, p.488*

Owens, Lori J. *v.4 p.541*

Owens, Philip N. & Slaymaker, Olav *v.4 p.391*

Owens, Rosemary Cullen *v.3 p.135, p.139*

Owings, Alison *v.3 p.54, p.86, p.173*

Owomoyela, Oyekan (Editor) *v.2 p.752, v.6 p.80*

Owomoyela, Oyekan *v.2 p.757, v.6 p.77*

Owram, Doug *v.3 p.545*

Owsley, Frank L. Jr. *v.3 p.417*

Owsley, Frank L. *v.3 p.399*

Owsley, Frank Lawrence *v.3 p.399, p.429, p.495*

Owtram, Francis *v.6 p.627*

Oxford University Press (Created by) *v.4 p.104, p.380*

Oxford University Press Staff (Compiled by) . . . *v.5 p.225*

Oxford University Press Staff (Editor) . . . *v.4 p.380*

Oxford University Press Staff *v.4 p.380*

Oxford University Press *v.6 p.34*

Oyama, Susan *v.5 p.160, p.170, p.195*

Oyewumi, Oyeronke (Editor) *v.4 p.744, v.6 p.429*

Oyono, Ferdinand *v.2 p.543*

Oz, Amos *v.6 p.606, p.611, p.615, p.650, p.651*

Ozbudun, Ergun *v.4 p.616, v.6 p.624*

Ozeki, Ruth L. *v.6 p.101*

Ozick, Cynthia *v.2 p.151, p.152*

Ozieblo Rajkowska, Barbara *v.2 p.79*

Ozinga, James R., et al. *v.4 p.598, p.600*

Ozkirimli, Umut *v.4 p.495*

Ozment, Steven *v.1 p.600, p.602, v.3 p.69, p.166*

Ozsvbath, Zsuzsanna & Radnboti, Miklbos . . . *v.2 p.785*

Ozyegin, Gul *v.6 p.624*

P

P., Taylor *v.4 p.419*

Paarlberg, Don & Paarlberg, Phillip *v.5 p.15*

Pabla, A. S. *v.5 p.724*

Pacelle, Richard L. Jr. *v.4 p.470*

Pach, Chester J. Jr. & Richardson, Elmo . . . *v.3 p.477*

Pach, János & Agarwal, Pankaj K. *v.5 p.479, p.498*

Pach, Walter *v.1 p.745*

Pachai, Bridglal *v.6 p.76*

Pacheco, Ferdie *v.6 p.490, p.536*

Pacht, Otto *v.1 p.672*

Pachter, L. & Sturmfels, B. (Editors) *v.5 p.92, p.107*

Pacifici, Sergio *v.2 p.698*

Pacini-Hernandez, Deborah *v.1 p.293, v.3 p.267, p.317*

Paciorek, Michael J. & Jones, Jeffrey A. . *v.4 p.784, p.801, p.842*

Pack, Phillip E. *v.5 p.246*

Pack, Robert & Parini, Jay (Editors) *v.2 p.26*

Pack, Robert *v.2 p.77*

Pack, Spencer J. *v.4 p.219*

Packard, Chris *v.2 p.9*
Packard, Randall M. *v.6 p.63*
Pack-Brown, Sherlon P. & Williams, Carmen Braun . *v.5 p.674*
Packel, Edward W. *v.5 p.484*
Packer, James E. *v.3 p.29*
Paczkowski, Andrzej *v.3 p.255, v.4 p.596*
Padden, Carol & Humphries, Tom *v.4 p.700*
Padden, Carol A. & Humphries, Tom L. *v.4 p.709*
Paddison, Max *v.1 p.382*
Paddle, Robert *v.6 p.292*
Paddock, Lisa Olson & Rollyson, Carl E. *v.2 p.271*
Padilla, Felix M. *v.6 p.532, p.544, p.550*
Padilla, Genaro M. *v.6 p.490, p.532*
Padilla, Herberto *v.3 p.312*
Padmanabhan, T. *v.5 p.72*
Padmanabhan, Thanu *v.5 p.72*
Padoch, Christine, et al. *v.5 p.39*
Padro, Fernando F. *v.4 p.758*
Paehlke, Robert *v.4 p.505, p.667*
Paetro, Maxine *v.4 p.428*
Pagan, Eduardo Obregon *v.6 p.536, p.541, p.550*
Pagano, Michael A. & Bowman, Ann O. *v.6 p.724*
Pagano, Michael A. & Moore, Richard . . *v.4 p.544, v.6 p.724*
Pagano, Robert R., et al. *v.5 p.93*
Pagden, Anthony *v.3 p.74*
Page, C. N. *v.5 p.210*
Page, Christopher *v.1 p.178*
Page, Denys L. (Editor) *v.2 p.403*
Page, Denys L. *v.2 p.415, p.419*
Page, Edward C. & Goldsmith, Michael J. (Editors) . *v.4 p.582*
Page, Eugene R. *v.2 p.243*
Page, G. William *v.5 p.706*
Page, Jake & Officer, Charles B. *v.6 p.294*
Page, Jake *v.5 p.84*
Page, Judith W. *v.2 p.324*
Page, Max & Mason, Randall (Editors) *v.1 p.823*
Page, Max *v.6 p.714*
Page, Melvin E. *v.6 p.76*
Page, Norman *v.2 p.313, p.330, p.356, v.6 p.403*
Page, P. K. *v.2 p.738*
Page, Roderic D. & Holmes, Edward C. *v.5 p.200*
Page, Sophie *v.6 p.569*
Page, Thomas Nelson *v.2 p.49*
Page, Tim *v.1 p.247, v.2 p.112*
Pagel, Mark D. (Editor) *v.5 p.195*
Pagell, Ruth A. & Halperin, Michael *v.4 p.180*
Pagiola, Stefano, et al. *v.5 p.13*
Pagis, Dan *v.6 p.651*
Paglia, Camille *v.5 p.618*
Pagliaro, Harold E. *v.2 p.309*
Pagliarulo, Michael A. *v.5 p.535*
Pagnol, Marcel *v.2 p.523*
Pahlavi, Mohammad R. *v.6 p.631*
Pai Hsien-yung (Author, Translator) *v.6 p.213, p.214*
Paidar, Parvin *v.6 p.631*

Paige, Jeffery M. *v.3 p.303*
Paik, Nam June *v.1 p.773*
Pain, Rachel, et al. *v.4 p.399*
Paine, Albert B. *v.2 p.33*
Paine, Lynn Sharp *v.4 p.54*
Paine, Thomas *v.1 p.545, v.3 p.410*
Painter, Borden *v.3 p.197, p.204*
Painter, George D. *v.2 p.488*
Painter, Karen (Editor) *v.1 p.220, p.339*
Painter, Michael & Durham, William H. (Editors) . . . *v.3 p.269*
Painter, Nell Irvin *v.6 p.8*
Painter, Paul C.; Coleman, Michael M. *v.5 p.322*
Painter, Sidney *v.3 p.66, p.98, v.6 p.576*
Pais, Abraham, et al. *v.5 p.543*
Pais, Abraham *v.3 p.46, v.5 p.540, p.544*
Pak, Gary *v.6 p.102*
Pakaluk, Michael *v.1 p.427*
Pakenhaam, Thomas *v.3 p.135, p.137*
Pakenham, Thomas *v.3 p.77, v.4 p.583*
Pakroo, Peri *v.4 p.87*
Pal, Pratapaditya *v.1 p.692*
Palacios, Marco *v.3 p.358*
Palagia, Olga (Editor) *v.1 p.776*
Palazzo, Lynda *v.2 p.304*
Palazzolo, Daniel J. *v.4 p.533*
Palda, Kristian S. *v.4 p.144*
Palermo, George B. & Kocsis, Richard N. . . . *v.6 p.254, p.267*
Paletz, David L. & Schmid, Alex P. (Editors) . . *v.4 p.559, p.661*
Paley, Grace *v.2 p.152*
Paley, Morton D. *v.2 p.240*
Paley, Vivian G. *v.4 p.310, p.365, p.370*
Paley, Vivian Gussin *v.4 p.310*
Palgrave Macmillan Staff (Editor) *v.4 p.293*
Palika, Liz *v.5 p.216*
Palisca, Claude V. (Editor) *v.1 p.178*
Palisca, Claude V., et al. *v.1 p.174*
Palisca, Claude V. *v.1 p.180, p.186*
Palisca, Claude *v.1 p.181*
Palka, B. P. *v.5 p.491, p.494*
Palladino, Michael A. *v.5 p.136*
Palladino, Pia *v.1 p.728*
Paller, Michael *v.2 p.134, v.6 p.412*
Pallister, Janis L. (Editor) *v.2 p.539*
Pallister, John, et al. *v.4 p.173*
Palloff, Rena M. *v.4 p.322*
Pallone, Dave & Steinberg, Alan *v.6 p.384*
Palmedo, Philip F. *v.1 p.781*
Palmer, Alan Warwick *v.3 p.218*
Palmer, Bryan D. *v.4 p.709*
Palmer, Colin A. *v.4 p.728, v.6 p.8*
Palmer, Daniel D. *v.5 p.210*
Palmer, David Scott (Editor) *v.3 p.330*
Palmer, Frederick *v.3 p.477*
Palmer, Gene V. *v.2 p.795*
Palmer, Heather *v.4 p.796, p.862*

Palmer, Howard *v.3 p.546*

Palmer, John W. & Palmer, Stephen E. *v.6 p.276*

Palmer, Joy A. (Editor) *v.4 p.340*

Palmer, L. R. *v.2 p.400*

Palmer, Leonard R. *v.2 p.424*

Palmer, Michael F. *v.5 p.635*

Palmer, Monte *v.6 p.594*

Palmer, Paulina *v.6 p.393*

Palmer, R. R., et al. *v.3 p.35*

Palmer, R. R. (Robert Roswell) *v.3 p.75*

Palmer, R. R. *v.3 p.151*

Palmer, Richard H. *v.1 p.57, p.89*

Palmer, Robert R. (Author, Preface by) *v.3 p.75*

Palmer, Robert R. (Editor, Translator) *v.3 p.149*

Palmer, Stephen & Laungani, Pittu D. (Editors) . . . *v.5 p.637*

Palmer, Stephen (Author, Editor) *v.5 p.637*

Palmer, Ted *v.6 p.274*

Palmer, Tim *v.5 p.174, p.180*

Palmer, William *v.3 p.374*

Palmie, Stephan *v.3 p.312*

Palmieri, Robert & Palmieri, Margaret W.
(Editors) *v.1 p.161, p.391*

Palmiotto, Michael J. *v.6 p.260*

Paloscia, Raffaele *v.6 p.729*

Paloutzian, Raymond F. & Park, Crystal L. (Editors) . *v.5 p.635*

Pals, Daniel L. *v.1 p.521*

Palsson, Bernhard O. *v.5 p.128, p.142, p.151*

Palsson, Herman & Edwards, Paul (Translators) . . . *v.2 p.625*

Palsson, Hermann *v.2 p.624*

Paltock, Robert *v.2 p.256*

Paludan, Phillip S. *v.3 p.399*

Paludan, Phillip Shaw *v.3 p.502*

Palumbi, Stephen R. *v.5 p.195*

Palumbo, Patrizia *v.3 p.198*

Palumbo-Liu, David *v.6 p.114, p.124*

Palzkill, Timothy *v.5 p.117*

Pam, Alvin & Pearson, Judith *v.5 p.640*

Pammer, William J. Jr. *v.4 p.544*

Pampel, Fred C. *v.4 p.153*

Pamphile, Leon D. *v.3 p.315*

Pamphili, Eusebius *v.3 p.67*

Pamphilus, Eusebius *v.1 p.591, v.3 p.57*

Pamuk, Ayse *v.4 p.388, v.6 p.721*

Pamuk, Orhan *v.6 p.624, p.667*

Pamuk, Sevket *v.6 p.624*

Panayotova, S. & Binski, Paul *v.1 p.672*

Panchen, Alec L. *v.5 p.201*

Panday, R. M. N. (Radjnarain Mohanpersad Nannan) . *v.3 p.322*

Pande, Govind Chandra *v.1 p.562*

Pandey, Gyanendra *v.6 p.159, p.161*

Pandya, Mukul, et al. *v.4 p.71*

Panel to Study Gender Differences in Career Outcom . *v.5 p.398*

Pang, Eul-Soo *v.3 p.341*

Pang, Valerie Ooka & Cheng, Li-Rong Lilly (Editors) . *v.6 p.109*

Pangallo, Karen L. (Editor) *v.2 p.287*

Pangle, Lorraine S. & Pangle, Thomas L. *v.4 p.328*

Pangrazi, Robert P., et al. *v.4 p.798, p.799*

Pangrazi, Robert P. *v.4 p.798*

Panichas, George A. *v.2 p.341*

Panicucci, Jane *v.4 p.787, p.798*

Panikkar, Kavalam N. *v.4 p.705*

Pankhurst, C. (Editor), et al. *v.5 p.89*

Pankhurst, E. Sylvia *v.4 p.604*

Pankhurst, Emmeline *v.4 p.604, p.606*

Pankhurst, Richard J. *v.5 p.170, p.207*

Pankow, James F. *v.5 p.313*

Pannell, David J. *v.5 p.683*

Pannenberg, Wolfhart (As told by) *v.1 p.636*

Pannenberg, Wolfhart . . . *v.1 p.636, p.638, p.641, p.643, p.646*

Panno, Joseph *v.5 p.154*

Panny, Judith Dell *v.2 p.745, p.746*

Panofsky, Wolfgang K. H. & Phillips, Melba *v.5 p.565*

Pansini, Anthony J. & Smalling, Kenneth D. *v.5 p.724*

Pansini, Anthony J. *v.5 p.724*

Pantazzi, Michael, et al. *v.1 p.745*

Panteli, Stavros *v.6 p.601*

Panter-Brick, Catherine (Editor, Contribution by) . . . *v.4 p.28*

Paoletti, John T. & Radke, Gary M. *v.1 p.675, p.688*

Paolino, Thomas J. & McCrady, Barbara S. (Editors) . *v.5 p.668*

Paolucci, Anne *v.2 p.722*

Papacosma, S. Victor & Heiss, Mary A. (Editors) . . . *v.4 p.639*

Papacosma, S. Victor *v.3 p.196*

Papadakis, Yiannis (Editor), et al. *v.6 p.601*

Papadakis, Yiannis *v.3 p.197*

Papadimitriou, Christos H. *v.5 p.336*

Papageorgiou, M. (Editor) *v.5 p.700*

Papandreou, Andreas George *v.3 p.196*

Papashvily, Helen Waite *v.2 p.8*

Papayanis, Marilyn A. *v.2 p.760*

Paper, Jordan D. *v.6 p.212*

Paper, Jordan *v.1 p.528*

Paper, Lewis J. *v.3 p.477*

Paperny, Vladimir *v.1 p.787*

Papineau, David *v.1 p.417, p.497*

Papp, Daniel S., et al. *v.3 p.386*

Papp, Peggy *v.5 p.668*

Pappano, Laura *v.4 p.694*

Pappas, Nickolas *v.1 p.424*

Pappe, H. O. *v.4 p.212*

Pappe, Ilan *v.6 p.611*

Pappe, Illan *v.6 p.619*

Paquette, L. A. *v.5 p.289*

Paquette, Leo A. *v.5 p.289*

Paquette, Robert L. *v.3 p.312*

Paquette, Robert Louis & Ferieger, Louis A. (Editors) . *v.4 p.521*

Parasecoli, Fabio *v.5 p.35*

Parasuraman, Raja *v.5 p.617*

Parati, Graziella *v.2 p.698*

Paravisini-Gebert, Lizabeth *v.2 p.768*

Pardo Bazán, Emilia *v.2 p.662*
Pardo, Mary. *v.6 p.431, p.546, p.550*
Pardo-Maurer, R.. . . . . *v.3 p.303*
Parducci, Allen. *v.5 p.655*
Paredes, Americo & Bauman, Dick (Editors) *v.2 p.585*
Paredes, Americo . . . *v.2 p.109, v.6 p.487, p.502, p.523, p.524*
Paredes, Américo *v.2 p.109, v.6 p.487, p.519, p.524*
Parekh, Bhikhu C.. . . . . *v.4 p.484, p.768*
Parekh, Bhikhu. *v.6 p.159*
Parent, D. P. *v.5 p.477*
Parente, Stephen L. & Prescott, Edward C.. . *v.4 p.196, p.259*
Parenti, Michael J. *v.3 p.477*
Parenti, Michael. *v.4 p.498, p.509, p.510*
Pares, Richard. *v.3 p.88, p.95, p.107, p.109*
Paret, Peter (Editor), et al. *v.3 p.36*
Pareto, Vilfredo *v.4 p.212, p.248, p.249, p.685*
Parezo, Nancy *v.4 p.4*
Parédes, Americo. *v.6 p.502*
Parfit, Derek *v.1 p.514*
Parfitt, Tudor. *v.6 p.611*
Pargament, Kenneth I. *v.5 p.635*
Parhami, Behrooz *v.5 p.344, p.345, p.730*
Paringer, William Andrew. *v.4 p.344*
Parini, Jay & Miller, Brett C. (Editors) *v.2 p.15*
Parini, Jay (Editor) *v.2 p.728*
Parini, Jay *v.2 p.75, p.77, p.123, p.127*
Parins, James W.. . . . . *v.2 p.49, v.6 p.698*
Parins, Marylyn *v.2 p.212*
Paris, Bernard J. *v.2 p.287*
Paris, Erna. *v.4 p.767*
Paris, Margaret L. *v.6 p.490, p.508*
Paris, Michael (Editor) *v.6 p.323*
Paris Review Staff *v.2 p.583, p.584*
Paris, Scott G. & Stahl, Steven A. (Editors). *v.4 p.365*
Parish, James R. & Pitts, Michael R.. . . . . *v.6 p.316*
Parish, James Robert & Pitts, Michael R.. . . . . . *v.6 p.316*
Parish, James Robert *v.6 p.419*
Parish, Peter J. *v.3 p.432*
Parish, R. V. *v.5 p.305*
Parish, William L. & Whyte, Martin K. *v.4 p.734*
Park, David A.. . . . . *v.5 p.540*
Park, Edward J. W. & Park, John S. W. . . . *v.6 p.117, p.121*
Park, John. *v.6 p.107, p.117*
Park, Ken *v.4 p.374*
Park, Kyeyoung *v.6 p.106, p.136*
Park, Lisa Sun-Hee *v.6 p.107, p.110, p.127, p.136*
Park, Michael Alan *v.4 p.14*
Park, Robert Ezra & Burgess, Ernest W. . . *v.4 p.680, v.6 p.718*
Park, Robert Ezra *v.4 p.713, p.729*
Park, Roberta J. & Mangan, James A.
  (Editors) *v.4 p.818, p.837, v.6 p.438*
Park, Thomas K.. . . . . *v.6 p.643*
Parker, Alexander A. *v.2 p.647*
Parker, Alexander Augustine. *v.2 p.647*
Parker, Arthur C.. . . . . *v.6 p.704*

Parker, D. S.. *v.3 p.331*
Parker, David, & Siegel, Esther. *v.1 p.36*
Parker, David A. & De Cecco, John P. (Editors). . . *v.6 p.420*
Parker, DeWitt H. *v.1 p.480*
Parker, Dorothy R. *v.2 p.110*
Parker, Dorothy *v.2 p.110*
Parker, Douglas M.. . . . . *v.2 p.103*
Parker, Eldon M. & Alexander, Robert Jackson *v.3 p.346*
Parker, Ellen M. *v.5 p.475*
Parker, Frank R.. . . . . *v.4 p.555, p.573, p.579*
Parker, Fred *v.2 p.251, p.257, p.262*
Parker, Geoffrey & Smith, Lesley M. *v.3 p.41, v.6 p.165*
Parker, Geoffrey *v.3 p.36, p.205, p.240*
Parker, Glenn M. *v.4 p.80*
Parker, Hershel *v.2 p.48*
Parker, Keith L., et al. *v.5 p.526*
Parker, L. Craig Jr. *v.6 p.262*
Parker, Mara E. *v.1 p.169, p.191, p.241*
Parker, Marla (Editor) *v.5 p.459*
Parker, Mary Ann *v.1 p.164, p.186, p.329*
Parker, Michael & Starkey, Roger (Editors). *v.2 p.752*
Parker, Peter & Kermode, Frank (Editors) *v.2 p.179*
Parker, Peter *v.2 p.356, v.6 p.403*
Parker, Phyllis R.. . . . . *v.3 p.342*
Parker, Richard B. *v.6 p.594*
Parker, Richard G.. . . . . *v.4 p.31*
Parker, Robert A.. . . . . *v.3 p.79*
Parker, Roger (Editor) *v.1 p.231*
Parker, Rozsika & Pollock, Griselda (Editors). *v.6 p.473*
Parker, S. *v.5 p.388*
Parker, Steve. *v.4 p.381*
Parker, Sue Taylor & McKinney, Michael L. *v.5 p.609*
Parker, Sue Taylor (Editor), et al. *v.5 p.615*
Parker, Sybil P. *v.5 p.274, p.275*
Parker, T. H. *v.1 p.589*
Parker, W. Oren, et al. *v.1 p.147, p.148, p.149*
Parker, Walter *v.4 p.365*
Parker, William N. & Jones, Eric L. (Editors) *v.3 p.41*
Parker, William R. *v.2 p.255*
Parker, William *v.6 p.359*
Parker, Woodrow M. (Editor) *v.5 p.637*
Parker-Jenkins, Marie, et al.. . . . . *v.4 p.308*
Parkes, Alan *v.5 p.471*
Parkes, Colin Murray. *v.5 p.655*
Parkes, Graham *v.5 p.597*
Parkes, M. B.. *v.3 p.37*
Parkhouse, Bonnie L.. . . . . *v.4 p.786, p.885*
Parkin, David *v.4 p.38*
Parkin, R. J. & Stone, Linda (Editors). *v.4 p.32*
Parkinson, Brian *v.5 p.612*
Parkinson, G. H. R. & Shanker, S. G. (Editors) *v.1 p.417*
Parkinson, G. H. R. (Editor). *v.1 p.435*
Parkinson, R. B. (Translator) *v.6 p.644*
Parkinson, R. B.. . . . . *v.6 p.644*

Author Index

Parkinson, Richard *v.3 p.9*
Parkman, Francis & Morison, Samuel Eliot *v.3 p.538*
Parkman, Francis *v.3 p.406, p.520, p.538*
Parkman, Patricia *v.3 p.299*
Parks, Craig D. & Sanna, Lawrence J. *v.5 p.648*
Parks, George *v.5 p.444*
Parks, Gordon Jr. *v.1 p.768*
Parks, Gordon *v.6 p.18, p.27*
Parks, Janet B. & Quarterman, Jerome (Editors) . *v.4 p.885, p.889*
Parks, John G. *v.2 p.26*
Parks, Joseph H. *v.3 p.434*
Parks, Richard S. *v.1 p.220, p.321*
Parks, Roger (Editor) *v.3 p.485*
Parks, Suzan-Lori *v.2 p.152*
Parks, Theodore E. (Editor) *v.5 p.607*
Parla, Taha & Davison, Andrew *v.6 p.624*
Parlar, Mahmut *v.5 p.683*
Parmet, Herbert S. *v.3 p.378, p.477, p.478*
Parmet, Robert D. *v.4 p.128*
Parmigiani, Giovanni (Editor), et al. *v.5 p.102*
Parmley, Robert O. *v.5 p.686*
Parncutt, Richard & McPherson, Gary (Editors) . *v.1 p.376, p.406*
Parodi, Jorge *v.3 p.331*
Parr, Robert G. & Weitao, Yang *v.5 p.551*
Parrenas, Rhacel
  Salazar . . *v.4 p.44, v.6 p.110, p.113, p.116, p.119, p.129, p.130*
Parrill, Sue *v.2 p.268, v.6 p.326*
Parrinder, Geoffrey *v.1 p.558*
Parrinder, Patrick & Parr, Adrian *v.2 p.164*
Parrinder, Patrick (Editor) *v.2 p.319*
Parrinder, Patrick *v.2 p.189, p.319*
Parrington, Vernon L. *v.2 p.6*
Parrini, Paolo (Editor), et al. *v.1 p.512*
Parrish, Michael E. *v.3 p.449*
Parrish, William E. *v.3 p.512*
Parrott, Andrew *v.1 p.186, p.304, p.401*
Parry, Benita *v.2 p.571*
Parry, David L. *v.6 p.248*
Parry, Ellwood C. III *v.1 p.698*
Parry, J. H. (John Horace) *v.3 p.404*
Parry, J. H. *v.3 p.73, p.74, v.4 p.592*
Parry, John Horace *v.3 p.404*
Parry, Linda *v.1 p.720, p.802*
Parry, Milman *v.2 p.415*
Parry-Jones, Jemima *v.5 p.157*
Parsa, Misagh *v.3 p.303, v.4 p.500*
Parsad, Basmat & Lewis, Laurie *v.4 p.277*
Parshall, Peter W. & Schoch, Rainer *v.1 p.753*
Parshall, Peter W., et al. *v.1 p.754*
Parsipur, Shahrnush *v.6 p.672*
Parsons, Craig *v.4 p.638*
Parsons, James (Editor) *v.1 p.236, p.246*
Parsons, James J. *v.3 p.358*
Parsons, John C. *v.6 p.560*
Parsons, Keith M. *v.5 p.448*
Parsons, Neil *v.6 p.75*
Parsons, Philip & Chance, Victoria (Editors) . . *v.2 p.741*
Parsons, Talcott & Shils, Edward A. *v.4 p.692*
Parsons, Talcott & Smelser, Neil J. *v.4 p.270*
Parsons, Talcott & Turner, Bryan S. *v.4 p.675*
Parsons, Talcott (Editor) *v.4 p.683*
Parsons, Talcott, et al. *v.4 p.738*
Parsons, Talcott *v.4 p.680, p.716*
Partch, Harry *v.1 p.220, p.221, p.347*
Parthe, Kathleen *v.2 p.799*
Parthé, Kathleen *v.2 p.799*
Particle Data Group *v.5 p.545*
Partin, Ronald L. *v.4 p.284*
Partington, James R. *v.5 p.263*
Partner, Peter *v.3 p.199, p.200*
Partnow, Elaine & Hyatt, Lesley *v.1 p.60*
Parton, Anthony *v.1 p.698*
Partridge, Christopher (Editor) *v.1 p.525*
Partridge, Christopher H. (Editor) . . *v.1 p.658, p.659, p.661*
Partridge, Edward B. *v.2 p.220*
Partridge, Eric *v.2 p.231, p.552*
Parvu, Sorin *v.2 p.816*
Pascal, Blaise & Ariew, Roger *v.1 p.452*
Pascal, Blaise *v.1 p.452, p.595, v.2 p.476*
Pascal, Elizabeth *v.4 p.598*
Pascal, Paul *v.2 p.449*
Pascal, Roy *v.2 p.590, p.592*
Pascarella, Ernest T. & Terenzini, Patrick T. . *v.4 p.290, p.332*
Pascoli, Giovanni *v.2 p.720*
Pasek, Jan Chryzostom *v.2 p.791*
Pashler, Harold E. *v.5 p.611*
Paskevska, Anna *v.1 p.49*
Pasolini, Pier Paolo *v.2 p.721*
Pasqualetti, Martin, et al. *v.5 p.709*
Pass, Susan *v.4 p.345*
Passage, Charles E. *v.2 p.601*
Passantino, Erika D. & Scott, David W. (Editors) . *v.1 p.709*
Passerini, Luisa *v.3 p.203*
Passfield, et al. *v.4 p.212, p.254*
Passman, Donald S. *v.1 p.385*
Passmore, John *v.3 p.129*
Passonneau, Joseph *v.3 p.493*
Passport Books Staff & Alcaraz, Daniel *v.2 p.637*
Pasternak, Boris Leonidovich *v.2 p.806*
Pasternak, Boris *v.2 p.806*
Pasternak, Burton *v.4 p.705*
Pasternak, Charles A. *v.5 p.80*
Pasternak, Jack J. *v.5 p.123, p.151*
Pastore, Jose & Haller, Archibald O. *v.4 p.705*
Pastor-Satorras, Romualdo & Vespignani,
  Alessandro *v.5 p.338, p.345*
Pasztor, Suzanne B. *v.3 p.294*
Pasztory, Esther *v.3 p.261*
Patai, Daphne *v.2 p.376, v.3 p.342*
Patai, Saul E. *v.5 p.296*

336

Patai, Saul. *v.5 p.289, p.290*
Patankar, Suhas V. *v.5 p.560*
Patch, Robert W.. . . . . *v.3 p.287, p.294*
Patchen, Kenneth *v.2 p.110*
Patel, Mukund R.. . . . . *v.5 p.709*
Pateman, Roy & Gros, Jean-Germain . . . *v.4 p.612*
Pateman, Roy *v.6 p.67*
Pater, Walter. *v.2 p.302, p.303*
Paterek, Josephine *v.1 p.716, v.6 p.679*
Paterson, Andrew Barton 'Banjo' *v.2 p.748*
Paterson, Chris & Sreberny, Annabelle (Editors) . . . *v.4 p.407*
Paterson, Don *v.2 p.373*
Paterson, Hugh E. & McEvey, Shane F. *v.5 p.199*
Paterson, Lindsay *v.4 p.336*
Paterson, Matthew *v.6 p.301*
Paterson, Thomas G., et al. *v.3 p.386*
Paterson, Thomas G. *v.3 p.312, p.453, p.454, p.478*
Paterson *v.1 p.504*
Patey, Douglas Lane *v.2 p.387*
Pathelin, Pierre. *v.2 p.469*
Pathelin *v.2 p.469*
Pathria, R. K. *v.5 p.559*
Patinkin, Don & Leith, J. Clark *v.4 p.223, p.225*
Patinkin, Don *v.4 p.225*
Patnaik, Pradyot *v.5 p.302, p.312*
Paton, Herbert J. *v.1 p.462*
Paton, John Glenn & Christy, Van A.. . . . . *v.1 p.396*
Patoski, Joe N.. . . . . *v.6 p.490, p.519*
Patriarca, Silvana. *v.3 p.201*
Patricia Schwarz *v.5 p.550*
Patrick, Christian C. *v.5 p.518*
Patrick, Dale R. & Fardo, Stephen *v.4 p.116*
Patrick, Dale R. *v.5 p.725*
Patrick, Donna *v.4 p.21*
Patrick, Graham L.. . . . . *v.5 p.301*
Patrick, Hugh T. & Aoki, M. (Editors) *v.6 p.220*
Patrick, Rembert W. *v.3 p.399, p.429*
Patrick, Robert *v.6 p.405*
Patrick, Ruth & Reimer, Charles W. *v.5 p.208*
Patrides, C. A. & Waddington, Raymond B. *v.2 p.170*
Patrides, G. A. (Editor) *v.2 p.249*
Patt, Beatrice P. & Nozick, Martin (Editors) *v.2 p.644*
Patten, Chris. *v.4 p.642*
Patten, M. N. (Editor) *v.5 p.733*
Patten, Robert & Bowen, John (Editors) *v.2 p.285*
Patten, Robert L. *v.1 p.758, v.3 p.120, v.6 p.737, p.741*
Patterson, Annabel *v.2 p.170, p.252*
Patterson, Austin McDowell *v.5 p.258, p.288, p.289*
Patterson, Colin *v.5 p.195*
Patterson, Cynthia B. *v.3 p.14*
Patterson, Daniel W. *v.1 p.297*
Patterson, David (Editor, Translator). *v.3 p.86*
Patterson, David *v.2 p.799*
Patterson, E. Palmer; Patterson, Nancy-Lou. *v.6 p.682*
Patterson, E. Palmer *v.6 p.682*

Patterson, Gerald R. *v.5 p.660, p.662*
Patterson, James T. *v.3 p.461, p.478,*
                               v.4 p.450, p.522, p.758, p.778, p.779
Patterson, Kelly D. & Shea, Daniel *v.4 p.530*
Patterson, Kerry & Mills, Terence C. (Editors) *v.4 p.203*
Patterson, Lee *v.2 p.210*
Patterson, Orlando *v.4 p.727, p.729*
Patterson, Thomas C. *v.4 p.4*
Patterson, Thomas E.. . . . . *v.4 p.549, p.555*
Patterson, Tiffany Ruby *v.2 p.82*
Patterson, Wayne *v.6 p.114, p.121, p.136*
Pattie, David *v.1 p.92, p.97, v.2 p.333*
Pattie, Frank A. *v.5 p.597*
Pattillo, Mary E., et al. *v.6 p.272*
Pattillo-McCoy, Mary *v.4 p.725, p.730*
Pattison, Eliot *v.6 p.241*
Pattison, George & Thompson, Diane Oenning (Editors). *v.2 p.806*
Pattison, George *v.1 p.471*
Pattison, Stephen *v.1 p.649*
Pattison, Walter T. & Bleznick, Donald W. (Editors). *v.2 p.644*
Pattison, Walter T. *v.2 p.655*
Patton, Cindy *v.6 p.379, p.387*
Patton, George S. & Blumenson, Martin *v.3 p.461*
Patton, George S.. . . . . *v.3 p.461*
Patton, John *v.1 p.649*
Patton, Sharon F. *v.1 p.705*
Patyra, M. J. & Mlynek, D. J. (Editors) *v.5 p.711*
Pauck, Wilhelm & Pauck, Marion *v.1 p.581*
Pauck, Wilhelm (Editor) *v.1 p.631*
Paul, Anne. *v.3 p.261*
Paul, Annie Murphy *v.5 p.603, p.655*
Paul, Catherine E. *v.2 p.103, p.112, p.122*
Paul, Christiane *v.1 p.772*
Paul Cloke, Professor, et al.. . . . . *v.4 p.396*
Paul, Diana M.. . . . . *v.1 p.566*
Paul, Eldor A. & Clark, Francis E. *v.5 p.50, p.113*
Paul, Ellen Frankel (Editor), et al. *v.4 p.507*
Paul, G. M. *v.2 p.442*
Paul, James C. & Schwartz, Murray L.. . . . . . . *v.4 p.445*
Paul, James L. & Smith, Terry Jo (Editors) *v.4 p.338*
Paul, Lissa (Editor), et al. *v.2 p.582*
Paul, Mariani *v.2 p.68*
Paul, Pamela. *v.4 p.739*
Paul, Rodman W.. . . . . *v.3 p.519*
Paul, William *v.6 p.313, p.319*
Pauley, Bruce F. *v.3 p.60, p.185*
Pauley, Garth E. *v.3 p.378*
Paulin, Tom *v.2 p.293*
Pauling, Linus & Wilson, E. Bright *v.5 p.550*
Pauling, Linus *v.5 p.282*
Paulson, Ed. *v.4 p.85*
Paulson, L. C. *v.5 p.347*
Paulson, Ronald *v.3 p.129*
Paulu, Burton *v.4 p.412*
Paulus, Paul B. (Editor), et al.. . . . . *v.5 p.648*

Pauly, Reinhard G. *v.1 p.191*

Pausewang, Siegfried (Editor), et al. *v.4 p.612, v.6 p.64*

Pavelka, Margit & Roth, Jurgen *v.5 p.159*

Pavese, Cesar *v.2 p.720*

Pavese, Cesare. *v.2 p.720, p.721*

Pavia, Audrey *v.5 p.251*

Pavic, Milorad *v.2 p.811*

Pavis, Patrice *v.1 p.43, p.46, p.60*

Pavlich, George *v.4 p.754*

Pavlik, John V. *v.4 p.419*

Pavlov, Konstantin; Popova-Wightman, Ludmilla G. . *v.2 p.780*

Pawel, Ernst *v.2 p.611*

Pawlikowski, John T. *v.1 p.642*

Paxton, John R. & Eschmeyer, William N. (Editors) . *v.5 p.216*

Paxton, Nancy L. *v.6 p.157*

Paxton, Robert O. *v.3 p.156, v.4 p.510*

Payen, Jean Charles *v.2 p.457*

Payn, Graham & Morley, Sheridan *v.2 p.342*

Payne, Brian K. *v.6 p.276*

Payne, Charles *v.1 p.24*

Payne, Christopher (Editor) *v.1 p.805*

Payne, Christopher *v.1 p.776*

Payne, Daniel A. *v.1 p.586*

Payne, David *v.2 p.285, p.287, p.315*

Payne, Helen (Editor) *v.1 p.51*

Payne, Helen *v.1 p.51*

Payne, James L., et al. *v.5 p.644*

Payne, Matthew J. *v.3 p.231*

Payne, Michael *v.4 p.142*

Payne, Richard J. *v.3 p.391*

Payne, Richard K. & Tanaka, Kenneth K. (Editors) . *v.1 p.567*

Payne, Richard K. (Editor) *v.1 p.562*

Payne, Stanley G. . . *v.1 p.574, v.3 p.241, p.242, v.4 p.510, p.608*

Payne, V. Gregory & Isaacs, Larry D. *v.4 p.910*

Payne-Palacio, June & Theis, Monica *v.4 p.165*

Paynter, Maria Nicolai *v.2 p.723*

Payson, Steven *v.4 p.196, p.263*

Payton, Rodney J. *v.2 p.705*

Paz, Octavio & Paz, Marie Jose *v.2 p.668*

Paz, Octavio (Introduction by) *v.1 p.684*

Paz, Octavio *v.2 p.484, p.577, p.668, p.669, v.3 p.294*

p'Bitek, Okot & Liyong, Taban lo *v.2 p.757*

P'Bitek, Okot *v.2 p.757*

Pchilka, Olena, et al. *v.2 p.813*

PDR Staff *v.5 p.526*

Peabody, Richard & Ebersole, Lucinda (Editors) . . *v.2 p.127*

Peabody, Sue *v.3 p.147*

Peacock, John A. *v.5 p.72*

Peacock, Thomas Love *v.2 p.302*

Peacocke, Arthur R. *v.5 p.114*

Peak, Lois *v.6 p.222*

Peakall, David *v.5 p.365*

Peake, Mervyn *v.2 p.373*

Pearce, Craig L. *v.4 p.80*

Pearce, David & Barbier, Edward B. *v.5 p.13, v.6 p.298*

Pearce, Fred *v.4 p.394*

Pearce, George F. *v.4 p.521*

Pearce, John E. *v.3 p.511*

Pearce, Lynne (Editor) *v.4 p.174*

Pearcy, Thomas L. *v.3 p.305*

Peard, Julyan G. *v.3 p.342*

Pearl, Judea *v.5 p.339*

Pearlstein, Richard M. *v.4 p.661*

Pears, Peter *v.6 p.410*

Pearsall, Deborah M. *v.4 p.7*

Pearsall, Derek Albert & Wu, Duncan
  (Editors) *v.2 p.181, p.182, p.210*

Pearsall, Derek Albert *v.2 p.181, p.205, p.210*

Pearson, Anthony J. & Roush, William R. (Editors) . *v.5 p.290*

Pearson, Barry Lee & McCulloch, Bill *v.1 p.262, p.334*

Pearson, C. J., et al. *v.5 p.11, p.23, p.26, p.28*

Pearson, Carl E. (Editor) *v.5 p.461, p.500*

Pearson, Daniel . *v.4 p.808, p.851, p.885, p.889, p.892, p.897*

Pearson, Hesketh *v.1 p.102, p.145, p.150, v.2 p.321*

Pearson, Karl *v.5 p.403*

Pearson, Lester B. *v.3 p.541*

Pearson, Lionel . *v.2 p.402, p.403, p.409, v.3 p.17, p.18, p.21*

Pearson, M. N. *v.6 p.147, p.155*

Pearson, Michael N. *v.6 p.156*

Pearson, Richard J. *v.4 p.9*

Pearson, Roberta E. (Editor), et al. *v.6 p.307*

Pearson, Roger *v.2 p.484, p.501, v.3 p.147*

Pease, Bob & Pringle, Keith (Editors) . . . *v.4 p.744, v.6 p.430*

Pease, Neal *v.3 p.391*

Peate, Iorwerth C. *v.3 p.132*

Peattie, Antony *v.1 p.232*

Peattie, Mark R. *v.6 p.228*

Peavy, Linda S. & Smith, Ursula *v.3 p.521*

Pech, Stanley Z. *v.3 p.188*

Pechenik, Jan A. *v.5 p.246*

Pechkova, Eugenia & Nicolini, Claudio A. . . . *v.5 p.114, p.117*

Peck, H. Daniel *v.2 p.52*

Peck, Helen *v.4 p.143*

Peck, Linda Levy *v.3 p.95, p.102*

Peck, Robert B. *v.4 p.451*

Peck, Robert S. *v.4 p.456*

Peckham, Howard H. *v.3 p.413, p.514*

Peckner, Donald & Bernstein, I. M. *v.5 p.736*

Pecktal, Lynn *v.1 p.37, p.147*

Pedelty, Mark *v.1 p.293*

Peden, G. C. *v.4 p.228*

Peden, George *v.4 p.228*

Pedersen, Olaf *v.4 p.336*

Pedersen, Paul B. (Editor) *v.5 p.637*

Pedersen, Paul, et al. *v.5 p.637*

Pedersen, Paul *v.5 p.637, p.676*

Pedersen, Susan *v.3 p.54*

Pederson, Judith (Editor) *v.5 p.180*

Pedley, J. B., et al. *v.5 p.300*

Pedraza-Bailey, Silvia *v.6 p.530*

Pedrero, Paloma *v.2 p.638*

Pedrotti, Frank L., et al.. . . . . *v.5 p.561*

Pedrycz, Witold & Gomide, Fernando *v.5 p.470*

Peebles, P. J. *v.5 p.72*

Peebles, Patrick *v.6 p.163*

Peebles, Phillip James Edwin. *v.5 p.72*

Peel, John David Yeadon. *v.6 p.72*

Peel, Robert *v.1 p.583*

Peel, Robin *v.2 p.131*

Peele, George *v.2 p.222*

Peele, Stanton *v.4 p.777*

Peeples, Scott *v.2 p.50*

Peers, Edgar A. (Editor). *v.2 p.644*

Peers, Laura L. & Brown, Alison K. (Editors) *v.4 p.48*

Peet, Richard *v.4 p.375*

Peña, Devon G.. . . . . *v.6 p.487, p.522, p.525, p.551*

Peña, Manuel H.. . . . . *v.1 p.293*

Peña, Manuel *v.6 p.519*

Pegg, Carole *v.1 p.43*

Pegis, Anton C.. . . . . *v.1 p.434*

Pegis, Anton Charles *v.1 p.572*

Peguero, Valentina *v.3 p.317*

Pei, Minxin *v.6 p.197*

Peierls, R. E.. . . . . *v.5 p.555*

Peikoff, Leonard *v.1 p.510*

Peimani, Hooman *v.4 p.661*

Peirce, Charles Sanders *v.1 p.440, p.441, p.513*

Peirce, Leslie P.. . . . . *v.6 p.591*

Peirce, Neal R. *v.3 p.525, p.530*

Peitgen, Heinz-Otto, et al.. . . . . *v.5 p.488*

Peixoto, Afranio *v.2 p.692*

Peixoto, J. P.. . . . . *v.5 p.426*

Pekic, Borislav *v.2 p.811*

Pelayo, Ruben *v.2 p.684*

Peleg, Ilan *v.6 p.619*

Peleggi, Maurizio *v.6 p.171*

Pelevin, Victor *v.2 p.807*

Pelikan, Jaroslav & Hotchkiss, Valerie R. (Editors) . *v.1 p.646*

Pelikan, Jaroslav & Lehmann, Helmut T. (Editors) . *v.1 p.603*

Pelikan, Jaroslav J. *v.1 p.634, p.645, v.3 p.57, v.4 p.303*

Pelikan, Jaroslav. *v.1 p.615, p.640*

Pelinka, Anton & Plasser, Fritz (Editors). . . . *v.4 p.579, p.595*

Pelinka, Anton *v.4 p.595*

Pelissero, John P. (Editor). *v.6 p.725*

Pellegrin, Pierre *v.1 p.420*

Pelletier, Paul A.. . . . . *v.5 p.395*

Pelletier, Ray *v.4 p.143*

Pelletier, Theo (Photographer) *v.1 p.279*

Pelley, Patricia M.. . . . . *v.6 p.166*

Pellicani, Luciano *v.4 p.661*

Pelling, Henry & Reid, Alastair J.. . . . . *v.4 p.606*

Pelling, Henry *v.3 p.95, p.119*

Pells, Richard H.. . . . . *v.3 p.369, p.371*

Peloso, Vincent C. & Tenenbaum, Barbara A. (Editors) *v.3 p.345*

Peloso, Vincent C.. . . . . *v.3 p.331*

Peltier, Leonard F. *v.6 p.694*

Peltier, W. Richard (Editor) *v.5 p.442*

Peltonen, Markku (Editor). *v.1 p.448*

Peltzman, Barbara R.. . . . . *v.4 p.338*

Peluso, Nancy L. *v.5 p.39*

Pelz, Dave & Frank, James A.. . . . . *v.4 p.861*

Pelzmann, Linda *v.4 p.263*

Pember, Don R. & Calvert, Clay. *v.4 p.445*

Pemberton, Cynthia Lee A.. . . . . . *v.4 p.822, p.837, p.901*

Pemberton, John *v.6 p.175, p.177*

Pempel, T. J. (Editor). *v.4 p.618*

Pempel, T. J.. . . . . *v.6 p.220*

Pencak, William *v.6 p.417*

Pence, Gregory E. *v.5 p.370, v.6 p.294*

Pendarvis, Edwina D., et al.. . . . . *v.4 p.317*

Pender, Nola J., et al.. . . . . *v.5 p.528*

Pendergast, Sara & Pendergast, Tom

(Editors) *v.1 p.665, p.680, v.3 p.443*

Pendergast, Sara *v.1 p.712*

Pendergrast, Mark *v.3 p.282*

Pendgracs, Doreen & Chafe, Dawn *v.3 p.547*

Pendle, Karin (Editor) *v.6 p.475*

Pendle, Karin *v.1 p.169, p.379*

Pendlebury, J.D.S.. . . . . *v.3 p.16*

Pendleton, Wade C. *v.6 p.76*

Penelhum, Terence. *v.1 p.450, p.452, p.517*

Pener, Degen *v.1 p.34*

Penguin Books Staff *v.2 p.292*

Penley, Constance *v.6 p.319, p.475*

Penlington, Norman *v.3 p.540*

Penman, Bruce (Editor). *v.2 p.700*

Penn, Helen *v.4 p.756*

Penn, Ira A., et al.. . . . . *v.4 p.115*

Pennell, Allison A. (Editor), et al.. . . . . *v.4 p.62*

Pennell, C. R. (Editor) *v.6 p.641*

Pennell, C. R.. . . . . *v.6 p.61, p.644*

Pennell, Richard *v.6 p.644*

Penney, Dawn (Editor) *v.4 p.796*

Penniman, Howard R. (Editor). *v.4 p.590*

Penningroth, Dylan C. *v.4 p.705*

Pennington, H. C. *v.5 p.63*

Pennington, Jean A.. . . . . *v.5 p.35, p.513*

Pennington, Renee & Harpending, Henry *v.6 p.75*

Pennington, S. & Dunn, M. J. (Editors). *v.5 p.117*

Pennington, Sandra (Editor) *v.5 p.136*

Penn-Nabrit, Paula *v.4 p.296*

Pennock, James Roland & Chapman, John W. (Editors). *v.4 p.458*

Pennock, Robert T.. . . . . *v.5 p.195*

PennWell Books *v.4 p.160*

Penny, Laura. *v.4 p.141*

Penny, Nicholas *v.1 p.729, p.733, p.782*

Penny, Ralph. *v.2 p.637*

Penrith, Deborah (Editor) *v.4 p.170*

Penrod, Lynn *v.2 p.531*

Penrose, Roger. *v.5 p.541*

Penson, John B., et al. *v.5 p.15*

Peper, George, et al. *v.4 p.861*

Pepper, David *v.5 p.370*

Pepper, John V., et al.. . . . . *v.6 p.246*

Pepper, Stephen C. *v.1 p.480*

Pepper, Suzanne (Editor) *v.6 p.190*

Pepper, Suzanne *v.4 p.336, v.6 p.191, p.194*

Pepper, William F. *v.4 p.486*

Peppers, Don & Rogers, Martha *v.4 p.143*

Pepys, Samuel *v.3 p.105*

Peraino, Judith Ann. *v.1 p.379, v.6 p.408*

Peralta-Ramos, Monica *v.3 p.349*

Perces, Marjorie, et al.. . . . . *v.1 p.27*

Percoco, James A. *v.3 p.375*

Percox, David. *v.6 p.65*

Percus, Jerome K. *v.5 p.136, p.142*

Percy, Larry & Elliott, Richard *v.4 p.427*

Percy, Walker *v.2 p.152*

Perdue, Leo G.. . . . . *v.1 p.619*

Perdue, Peter C. *v.6 p.239*

Pereboom, Derk (Editor) *v.1 p.503*

Pereboom, Maarten *v.3 p.75*

Perec, Georges. *v.2 p.532, p.533*

Pereira, Anthony W. *v.3 p.342*

Pereira, Kim *v.6 p.27*

Perelman, Michael *v.4 p.67, p.698*

Perelman, S. J. *v.2 p.111*

Peres, Shimon, et al. *v.6 p.615*

Peres, Shimon *v.6 p.594, p.615*

Peretti, Terri J. *v.4 p.538*

Peretz, Don & Doron, Gideon *v.6 p.615*

Peretz, Don *v.6 p.594, p.619*

Peretz, Isabelle (Editor). *v.1 p.376*

Perez, Bertha *v.6 p.494, p.527*

Perez de Cuellar, Javier. *v.4 p.635, p.650*

Perez, Emma. *v.6 p.546*

Perez Firmat, Gustavo *v.6 p.493*

Perez, Gina M. *v.6 p.530, p.550*

Perez, Janet & Horn, Paul W. *v.2 p.639*

Perez, Janet & Ihrie, Maureen (Editors) *v.2 p.639*

Perez, Janet *v.2 p.657*

Perez, Joseph *v.3 p.240*

Perez, Loida Maritza *v.6 p.508*

Perez, Louis A. Jr. (Editor) *v.3 p.312*

Perez, Louis A. Jr. *v.3 p.312*

Perez, Louis A.. . . . . *v.3 p.276*

Perez, Louis G. *v.6 p.228*

Perez, Nissan *v.1 p.768*

Perez, Ruperto M. (Editor), et al. *v.5 p.637*

Perez Sarduy, Pedro & Stubbs, Jean *v.3 p.279, p.312*

Perez-Lopez, Jorge & Travieso-Diaz, Matias F. . . . *v.3 p.312*

Perez-Lopez, Jorge F. *v.3 p.312*

Perez-Reverte, Arturo *v.2 p.662, p.663*

Perez-Stable, Marifeli. *v.3 p.312*

Perez-Torres, Rafael *v.6 p.544*

Perez-Venero, Alex *v.3 p.305*

Perinbam, B. Marie. *v.4 p.705*

Perisic, Zoran *v.6 p.352*

Peristiany, J. G. & Pitt-Rivers, Julian (Editors) *v.4 p.42*

Perkampus, Heinz-Helmut *v.5 p.270, p.297*

Perkell, Christine G. *v.2 p.446*

Perkin, Harold J. *v.3 p.114*

Perkin, Harold *v.3 p.114, v.6 p.735, p.742*

Perkins, Bradford *v.3 p.386, p.417*

Perkins, Dexter *v.3 p.386, p.461, p.478*

Perkins, Donald H. *v.5 p.552*

Perkins, Howard C. *v.3 p.365, p.421*

Perkins, Kathy A. & Uno, Roberta
(Editors) . . . *v.1 p.68, p.121, p.123, p.124, p.125, v.2 p.25*

Perkins, Kathy A.
(Editor) *v.1 p.68, p.121, p.123, v.6 p.15, p.18, p.34*

Perkins, Kenneth J. *v.6 p.60, p.641*

Perkins, Leeman L.. . . . . *v.1 p.181*

Perkinson, Henry J. *v.4 p.323, p.328*

Perl, Jed *v.1 p.680, p.682*

Perle, George & Berg, Alban *v.1 p.221, p.241, p.309*

Perle, George *v.1 p.221, p.232, p.309, p.372*

Perlin, George C.. . . . . *v.4 p.589*

Perlin, John *v.5 p.362*

Perlin, Michael L. *v.5 p.592*

Perlis, Vivian *v.1 p.221, p.333*

Perlman, Dan L. & Milder, Jeffrey C. *v.1 p.797*

Perlman, Jim *v.2 p.54*

Perlmann, Joel *v.4 p.765*

Perlmutter, Donna *v.1 p.11*

Perloff, Marjorie *v.2 p.106*

Perloff, Richard M. *v.5 p.646*

Perlow, Leslie A.. . . . . *v.5 p.579, p.580*

Perman, M. *v.3 p.437*

Perman, Michael *v.3 p.399, p.497, v.4 p.519, p.573*

Pernicone, Nunzio *v.3 p.202*

Perone, James E.. . . . . *v.1 p.273, p.279*

Perova, Natasha & Tait, Arch (Editors). *v.2 p.794*

Perova, Natasha (Editor) *v.2 p.794*

Perpener, John O. III. *v.1 p.18*

Perpetusa-Seva, Inmaculada & Torres, Lourdes (Editors). *v.6 p.393*

Perraton, H. D.. . . . . *v.4 p.314*

Perrault, Charles *v.2 p.476*

Perret, Geoffrey *v.3 p.461, p.478*

Perrett, Geoffrey *v.3 p.478*

Perrie, Maureen & Pavlov, Andrei *v.3 p.215*

Perrie, Maureen *v.3 p.226*

Perrin, D. D. (Editor) *v.5 p.302*

Perrin, D. D.. *v.5 p.300*

Perrin, Noel *v.6 p.225*

Perrin, Norman *v.1 p.616, p.627, p.638, p.640*

Perrin, Tom *v.4 p.808, p.859*

Perrine, C. M. (Editor), et al. *v.5 p.216*

Perrings, Charles (Editor), et al. *v.5 p.180*

Perris, Arnold *v.1 p.376*

Perritt, Henry H. *v.4 p.447*

Perron, Wendy (Editor). *v.1 p.11*

Perrone, Charles A. & Dunn, Christopher. *v.1 p.293*

Perrone, Charles A.. . . . . *v.2 p.692*

Perrot, Michelle (Editor), et al. *v.4 p.734*

Perrotta, Cosimo. *v.4 p.246, p.250*

Perrottet, Tony *v.4 p.808*

Perrow, Charles *v.4 p.717*

Perrow, Martin R. & Davy, Anthony J. (Editors) . . . *v.6 p.284*

Perrucci, Robert & Wysong, Earl *v.4 p.725*

Perry, Anne Griffin & Potter, Patricia Ann *v.5 p.528*

Perry, Barbara A.. . . . . . *v.3 p.443, p.461,v.4 p.466, p.538*

Perry, Ben Edwin *v.2 p.405*

Perry, Bliss *v.2 p.6*

Perry, Carolyn & Weaks, Mary Louise (Editors) *v.2 p.14*

Perry, Dale L. *v.5 p.302*

Perry, Duncan M. *v.3 p.251*

Perry, Elizabeth & Li, Xun *v.6 p.196, p.206*

Perry, George *v.1 p.253, p.337, p.409*

Perry, Glenn E.. . . . . *v.6 p.58, p.635*

Perry, H. W.. . . . . *v.4 p.466, p.538*

Perry, John *v.1 p.273, p.351, p.497*

Perry, Laurens B.. . . . . *v.3 p.289*

Perry, Lewis & Fellman, Michael (Editors) *v.3 p.421*

Perry, M. E. *v.3 p.240*

Perry, Marvin (Author, Compiled by), et al. *v.3 p.75*

Perry, Matt *v.1 p.508*

Perry, Michael J. *v.4 p.455, p.456, p.538*

Perry, Ralph B.. . . . . *v.1 p.439, v.3 p.369*

Perry, Robert H. & Green, Donald W. *v.5 p.316, p.741*

Perry, Ruth *v.2 p.192*

Perse, Saint-John. *v.2 p.523*

Persell, Stuart M.. . . . . *v.5 p.80, p.195*

Perseus Publishing Staff (Editor). *v.4 p.180*

Perseus Publishing Staff *v.4 p.71, p.174*

Pershing, John J. *v.3 p.478*

Persichetti, Vincent *v.1 p.372*

Persinger, Michael A.. . . . . *v.5 p.635*

Persky, Joseph & Wiewel, Wim *v.4 p.543*

Persley, G. J.. . . . . *v.5 p.8*

Personal Narratives Group Staff *v.6 p.477*

Persons, Jacqueline B., et al. *v.5 p.665*

Persoon, James. *v.2 p.184*

Pertschuk, Michael *v.4 p.52, p.53*

Perttula, Timothy K. *v.6 p.704*

Pesaran, M. Hashem & Schmidt, Peter (Editors). *v.4 p.191, p.203*

Pescador, Juan Javier *v.3 p.287*

Pesce, Dolores (Editor) *v.1 p.178*

Peschard-Sverdrup, Armand B. & Rioff, Sara *v.3 p.294*

Peshkin, Alan. *v.4 p.297, p.303, p.308, p.315, p.367*

Pesic, Peter *v.5 p.467, p.471, p.472*

Peskin, Allan & Davis, Jim *v.3 p.399, p.437*

Peskin, Allan. *v.3 p.399*

Pessar, Patricia R. & Foner, Nancy. *v.6 p.530*

Pessar, Patricia R. (Translator) *v.3 p.265, p.342*

Pessen, Edward *v.3 p.414*

Pessoa, Fernando *v.2 p.688, p.689*

Petchesky, Rosalind P. *v.4 p.669*

Pete, Geradino A. *v.5 p.724*

Peteet, Julie M. *v.6 p.455, p.619*

Peter, J. Paul & Jerry C. Olson *v.4 p.139*

Peter The Venerable *v.2 p.449*

Peter, Van Der Veer. *v.1 p.541*

Peterkin, Julia Mood *v.2 p.109*

Peterkin, Julia *v.2 p.109*

Peters, B. Guy & Pierre, Jon (Editors) *v.4 p.545, p.580*

Peters, Charles & Nelson, Michael. *v.4 p.527*

Peters, Edward (Editor) *v.1 p.646*

Peters, Edward M.. . . . . *v.3 p.57*

Peters, Emrys L.. . . . . *v.4 p.40*

Peters, Erskine. *v.1 p.281, p.412*

Peters, F. E. *v.1 p.547, v.3 p.21, v.6 p.625*

Peters, J. S. & Wolper, Andrea (Editors) *v.6 p.442*

Peters, Jacqueline S.. . . . . *v.1 p.406*

Peters, John Durham & Simonson, Peter *v.4 p.696*

Peters, John Durham *v.4 p.416, v.5 p.621*

Peters, John G.. . . . . *v.2 p.341*

Peters, Julie Anne *v.6 p.398*

Peters, Margot *v.2 p.271, v.6 p.403*

Peters, Max Stone *v.5 p.743*

Peters, Michael A. *v.4 p.345*

Peters, Pam *v.2 p.558*

Peters, Ronald W. Jr. *v.4 p.533*

Peters, Rudolph (Author, Translator). *v.1 p.559, p.560*

Peters, Sally *v.2 p.309*

Peters, Shawn Francis *v.4 p.308*

Peters, Thomas J. & Waterman, Robert H. Jr. . . . *v.4 p.81, p.148*

Peters, Tom *v.4 p.67, p.73*

Petersen, Andrew. *v.1 p.784*

Petersen, Carolyn Collins & Brandt, John C.. . . . . . *v.5 p.65*

Petersen, David. *v.1 p.623, v.5 p.232*

Petersen, Norman R. *v.1 p.626*

Petersen, Roger Dale *v.3 p.207*

Petersen, Shannon C.. . . . . *v.4 p.463*

Petersen, William & Petersen, Renee. *v.4 p.678*

Petersen, William L. *v.1 p.591*

Petersen, William. *v.4 p.222*

Petersilia, Joan *v.4 p.753, v.6 p.278*

Peterson, Anna L. (Editor), et al.. . . . . *v.3 p.299*

Peterson, Bernard L. Jr. . . *v.1 p.123, p.141, p.142,v.6 p.18, p.34*

Peterson, Bernard L. *v.1 p.60, p.93*

Peterson, Brooks *v.4 p.59*

Peterson, Carla L. *v.6 p.8, p.45*

Peterson, Charles S. *v.3 p.530*

Peterson, Christopher & Seligman, Martin E. P.. . . . *v.5 p.670*

Peterson, D. J. *v.3 p.223*

Peterson del Mar, David *v.3 p.532*

Peterson, Donald R. *v.5 p.676*

Peterson, E. Wesley F. *v.5 p.15*

Peterson, Edward N. *v.3 p.176*

Peterson, Eugene *v.1 p.613*
Peterson, Florence *v.4 p.128*
Peterson, Ivars *v.5 p.459, p.467, p.469*
Peterson, J. E. *v.6 p.625*
Peterson, Janice & Lewis, Margaret (Editors) *v.6 p.457*
Peterson, Jeanette F. *v.3 p.263*
Peterson, John E. & Peters, Ronald M. *v.6 p.628*
Peterson, Jon A. *v.1 p.797, v.6 p.729*
Peterson, Kate Dempsey & Burns, Vincent . . . *v.4 p.565, p.661*
Peterson, Larry L. & Davie, Bruce S. *v.5 p.345, p.727*
Peterson, Lars & Renstrom, Per *v.4 p.827*
Peterson, Linda H. *v.6 p.480, p.740, p.748, p.754*
Peterson, M. Jeanne . *v.3 p.114, v.6 p.744, p.748, p.762, p.765*
Peterson, M. P. (Editor) *v.4 p.386*
Peterson, Mark A., et al. *v.6 p.276*
Peterson, Mark A. *v.3 p.444, v.4 p.532*
Peterson, Merrill D. *v.3 p.412*
Peterson, Nancy L. *v.4 p.738*
Peterson, Norma L. *v.3 p.417*
Peterson, Oscar *v.1 p.262, p.347*
Peterson, Paul E. (Editor) *v.4 p.328, p.450, v.6 p.719*
Peterson, Paul E., et al. *v.4 p.525*
Peterson, Paul E. *v.4 p.328, p.525*
Peterson, Richard A. *v.1 p.273*
Peterson, Roger T. & Pough, Frederick H. *v.5 p.436*
Peterson, Susan *v.1 p.808, v.6 p.228, p.679*
Peterson, Theodore B. *v.4 p.410*
Peterson, Willard J. *v.6 p.188*
Peterson, William *v.6 p.173*
Peterson's Guides Staff *v.5 p.246*
Peterson's *v.4 p.170*
Petesch, Natalie L. *v.2 p.153*
Petipa, Marius *v.1 p.11*
Petitpas, Al, et al. *v.4 p.904*
Petkov, Steven & Mustazza, Leonard (Editors) *v.1 p.273, p.357*
Petocz, Agnes *v.5 p.598*
Petofi, Sandor *v.2 p.786*
Petraglia, Joseph *v.4 p.358*
Petraglia, M. D. & Korisettar, Ravi *v.4 p.17*
Petran, Tabitha *v.6 p.606*
Petrarca, Francesco *v.2 p.706*
Petrarch, Francesco *v.2 p.706*
Petras, James F. & Veltmeyer, Henry *v.3 p.333*
Petrie, Duncan *v.6 p.339*
Petrill, Stephen A. (Editor), et al. *v.5 p.658*
Petro, Nicolai N. *v.4 p.585, p.598*
Petro, Peter *v.2 p.812*
Petrone, Penny *v.2 p.731*
Petronius Arbiter *v.2 p.440*
Petropoulos, John Anthony *v.3 p.195*
Petropoulos, Jonathan *v.3 p.173*
Petroski, Henry *v.2 p.577*
Petrov, Evgeni I. & Ilf, Ilya *v.2 p.807*
Petrovich, Janice & Wells, Amy Stuart (Editors) *v.4 p.299, p.302*
Petrovich, Sandra Marie *v.3 p.305*

Petrovskii, Sergei V. & Li, Bai-Lian . . . *v.5 p.169, p.185, p.187*
Petrucci, Armando *v.6 p.569*
Petrushevskaya, Ludmilla *v.2 p.807*
Petry, Ann *v.2 p.109*
Petry, Carl F. (Editor) *v.6 p.635*
Petry, Carl F. *v.6 p.635, p.636*
Petry, Nancy M. *v.5 p.661*
Petsko, Gregory A. & Ringe, Dagmar *v.5 p.117*
Pettavino, Paula J. & Pye, Geralyn . . . *v.4 p.885, p.892, p.899*
Pettegree, Andrew (Editor) *v.1 p.602*
Pettegree, Andrew *v.1 p.602*
Pettengill, Ray W. (Translator) *v.3 p.410*
Petters, S. W. *v.5 p.433*
Petterson, Donald *v.6 p.640*
Pettet, E. C. *v.2 p.295*
Pettet, E. *v.2 p.233*
Pettigrew, Neil *v.6 p.308*
Pettijohn, F. J. & Potter, P. E. *v.5 p.439*
Pettijohn, F. J., et al. *v.5 p.438*
Pettinato, Giovanni *v.3 p.7*
Pettinger, Peter *v.1 p.262, p.323*
Pettis, Joyce *v.2 p.768*
Pettit, Arthur G. *v.2 p.33*
Pettit, Clare *v.6 p.756*
Pettit, Rhonda S. *v.2 p.110*
Pettiway, Leon E. *v.6 p.371*
Petty, William *v.4 p.216, p.254*
Petzinger, Thomas Jr. *v.4 p.717*
Peuckert, Detley J. & Peukert, Detlev J. K. . . . *v.3 p.173*
Peukert, Detlev J. *v.3 p.170*
Pevar, Stephen L. *v.4 p.465, v.6 p.696*
Pevsner, Jonathan *v.5 p.98, p.142, p.146*
Pevsner, Nikolaus, et al. *v.1 p.784, p.812*
Pevsner, Nikolaus *v.1 p.790*
Pevzner, Pavel A. *v.5 p.107, p.123, p.128*
Peyre, Henri & Seronde, Joseph (Editors) *v.2 p.465*
Peyre, Henri *v.2 p.456, p.461*
Pezeshkzad, Iraj *v.6 p.672*
Pèrez-Torres, Rafael *v.6 p.502, p.510, p.515*
Pfaff, Francoise (Editor) *v.6 p.334*
Pfaff, Francoise *v.6 p.334*
Pfaff-Czarnecka, Joanna, et al. *v.6 p.147*
Pfafflin, James R. & Edward N.
    Ziegler *v.5 p.355, p.368, p.377, p.379*
Pfafflin, James R. & Ziegler, Edward N. (Editors) . . *v.5 p.353*
Pfaller, Michael A., et al. *v.5 p.515*
Pfanz, Donald *v.4 p.521*
Pfeffer, Jeffrey *v.4 p.73*
Péguy, Charles *v.2 p.523*
Pfeifer, Michael J. *v.4 p.753*
Pfeiffer, Rudolph *v.2 p.399*
Pfeiffer, William S. *v.5 p.681*
Péret, Benjamin *v.2 p.523*
Pérez Arroyo, Rafael *v.1 p.176*
Pérez Firmat, Gustavo *v.6 p.490, p.542*

Pérez Galdós, Benito *v.2 p.655*

Pérez Sarduy, Pedro & Stubbs, Jean *v.2 p.673*

Pérez y González, María E. *v.6 p.532*

Pérez-Reverte, Arturo *v.2 p.662*

Pfiffner, James P. *v.4 p.527*

Pfitzer, Gregory M. *v.3 p.374*

Pflanze, Otto *v.3 p.164*

Pfungst, Oskar *v.5 p.615*

Phaidon Press Editors *v.1 p.784*

Phalen, Rick, et al. *v.3 p.369*

Pham, Andrew X. *v.6 p.94, p.141*

Phan, Aimee *v.6 p.102, p.141*

Phan, Peter C. *v.1 p.608*

Phares, Vicky *v.5 p.642*

Pharies, David A., et al. *v.2 p.637*

Pharr, Clyde & Wright, John *v.2 p.415*

Phayer, Michael *v.3 p.86*

Phelan, Craig *v.4 p.128*

Phelan, John L. *v.3 p.332, p.358*

Phelan, Richard M. *v.5 p.715*

Phelps, Charles E. *v.5 p.511*

Phelps, Edmund S. *v.4 p.240*

Phelps, Roger P., et al. *v.1 p.173, p.406*

Phifer, Paul *v.4 p.167*

Philander, S. George *v.5 p.430*

Philanthropic Research, Inc., ... *v.4 p.545*

Philbrick, Thomas *v.2 p.29*

Philip, George D. E. *v.3 p.276*

Philip, R. *v.6 p.324*

Philip, Robert *v.1 p.387, p.401*

Philipp, Thomas & Haarmann, Ulrich
(Editor, Contribution by) *v.6 p.636*

Philippi, Donald L. (Translator) *v.6 p.222, p.225*

Philippot, Pierre & Feldman, Robert S. (Editors) . . . *v.5 p.655*

Philips, Ambrose *v.2 p.256*

Philips, Beeman N. *v.4 p.353*

Philips, G. *v.3 p.331*

Philips, John Edward (Editor) *v.6 p.51*

Philleo, Joanne (Editor), et al. *v.4 p.758*

Phillipps, K. C. *v.6 p.742, p.751, p.752*

Phillippy, Patricia B. *v.2 p.182*

Phillips & Axelrod *v.3 p.519*

Phillips, Betty Lou *v.1 p.800*

Phillips, Cabell B. H. *v.3 p.369*

Phillips, Carla R. & Phillips, William D. Jr. *v.3 p.243*

Phillips, Carl *v.6 p.405*

Phillips, Catherine (Editor) *v.2 p.294*

Phillips, Charles & Axelrod, Alan *v.4 p.476*

Phillips, Charles L. & Nagle, H. Troy *v.5 p.711*

Phillips, Charles L. *v.5 p.711*

Phillips, Charles *v.4 p.10*

Phillips, Clare *v.1 p.716*

Phillips, Clifton J. *v.3 p.514*

Phillips, Dana *v.2 p.5*

Phillips, Derek L. *v.4 p.770*

Phillips, Edward J. *v.3 p.217*

Phillips, Elizabeth B. & Jackson,
John-Paul C. *v.1 p.178, p.181, p.402*

Phillips, G. M. *v.5 p.467*

Phillips, Gene D. *v.2 p.65*

Phillips, George Harwood *v.4 p.542, v.6 p.687*

Phillips, Helen *v.2 p.210*

Phillips, J. B. *v.1 p.613*

Phillips, J. R. *v.3 p.69, v.4 p.379*

Phillips, Jack *v.4 p.65*

Phillips, John L. Jr. *v.4 p.870*

Phillips, John *v.2 p.484, v.3 p.250*

Phillips, Johnthan P. *v.3 p.64*

Phillips, Jonathan *v.3 p.63, p.238, p.244*

Phillips, Kendall R. *v.6 p.319*

Phillips, Kevin *v.4 p.486, p.572, p.726*

Phillips, Larissa *v.6 p.602*

Phillips, Norman R. *v.4 p.345*

Phillips, Peggy A. *v.3 p.157*

Phillips, Peter *v.1 p.181*

Phillips, R. A. J. *v.3 p.545*

Phillips, R. Cody *v.3 p.305*

Phillips, R. *v.6 p.324*

Phillips, Richard & McConnell, Charles *v.6 p.275*

Phillips, Richard *v.2 p.246*

Phillips, Robert *v.4 p.87*

Phillips, Roderick *v.4 p.740*

Phillips, Roger & Rix, Martyn *v.5 p.84*

Phillips, Steven J. *v.1 p.821*

Phillips, Susan *v.4 p.714*

Phillips, Tom (Editor) *v.1 p.690*

Phillips, Tony *v.5 p.444*

Phillips, Ulrich Bon *v.3 p.494*

Phillips, W. Revell & Griffen, Dana T. *v.5 p.436*

Phillips, Warren F. *v.5 p.718*

Phillips, Wendel *v.6 p.627*

Phillips, William D. Jr. & Phillips, Carla
Rahn *v.3 p.73, p.404, p.406*

Phillips, William H. *v.6 p.353*

Phillips-Matz, Mary Jane *v.1 p.201, p.349*

Phillips-Matz, Mary J. *v.1 p.201, p.364*

Phillipson, David W. *v.4 p.8, v.6 p.53*

Phillipson, N. T. (Nicholas T.) *v.3 p.129*

Philo & Lewy, Yochanan *v.1 p.431*

Philoponus & Simplicius *v.1 p.500*

Philp, Kenneth R. (Editor) *v.6 p.689, p.692*

Philp, Kenneth R. *v.6 p.689, p.696*

Philpott, Simon *v.6 p.175, p.177*

Philpott *v.3 p.516*

Phinnemore, David & McGowan, Lee *v.4 p.603, p.638*

Phipps, William E. *v.1 p.649*

Phipps, Wilma J., et al. *v.5 p.522*

Phoggeler, Otto *v.1 p.471*

Physicians for Human Rights Staff *v.6 p.599, p.604*

Piaget, Jean & Inhelder, Barbel *v.5 p.628, p.630*

Piaget, Jean, et al. *v.4 p.358*
Piaget, Jean . *v.1 p.417, v.4 p.345, p.358,v.5 p.513, p.628, p.630*
Piaseckyj, Oksana *v.2 p.814*
Piattelli-Palmarini, Massimo (Editor). *v.2 p.563*
Picano, Felice *v.6 p.379, p.398*
Picard, Elizabeth *v.6 p.605*
Picard, Gilbert C. & Picard, Colette *v.6 p.60*
Picard, Raymond (Editor) et al. Lafond, Jean (Editor), Cuénin,
    Micheline (Editor), Chupeau, Jacques (Editor) *v.2 p.465*
Picard, Rosalind W.. . . . . *v.5 p.589*
Picart, Caroline Joan ("Kay") (Editor) *v.6 p.315*
Picart, Caroline Joan S. *v.6 p.331*
Picasso Project Staff (Author, Introduction by) *v.1 p.745*
Picchione, John & Smith, Lawrence R. (Editors) . . . *v.2 p.700*
Pick, Daniel *v.3 p.201*
Pick, James B. *v.4 p.388*
Pick, Lucy K. *v.6 p.572, p.574*
Pickard, George L. & Emery, W. J. *v.5 p.430*
Pickard, Robert *v.1 p.823*
Pickard-Cambridge, Arthur W.. . . . . *v.2 p.402*
Picker, John M. *v.6 p.754, p.762, p.764*
Pickerill, J. Mitchell *v.4 p.538*
Pickering, Andrew *v.5 p.403*
Pickering, Charles W. Sr. *v.4 p.541*
Pickering, David (Editor) . . . *v.1 p.141, p.145, p.147, p.153*
Pickett, K. H. Spencer & Pickett, Jennifer M.. . . . *v.6 p.267*
Pickett, Steward T. (Editor) *v.5 p.180, p.185*
Pickles, John. *v.4 p.375*
Pickover, Clifford A. *v.5 p.411, p.498*
Pickren, Wade E. & Dewsbury, Donald A. (Editors) . *v.5 p.598*
Pico, Fernando *v.3 p.320*
Picon, Gaetan *v.2 p.459*
Pielou, E. C.. . . . . *v.5 p.238, p.449*
Pienitz , Reinhar (Editor), et al. *v.5 p.174, p.187*
Pieper, Josef *v.4 p.784*
Pierangelo, Roger & Giuliani, George A.. . . . . . *v.4 p.316*
Pierangelo, Roger *v.4 p.316*
Pierce, Bessie Louise *v.3 p.516*
Pierce Colfer, Carol J. & Byron, Yvonne (Editors). . *v.4 p.164*
Pierce, Donna, et al. *v.3 p.287*
Pierce, G. Alvin & Hodges, Dewey H.. . . . . . . *v.5 p.718*
Pierce, Gregory R. (Editor), et al. *v.5 p.650*
Pierce, James Smith *v.1 p.665*
Pierce, John Robinson *v.1 p.375*
Pierce, T. Jones *v.4 p.705*
Pierce, Yolanda Nicole *v.6 p.36*
Piercy, Marge *v.2 p.153*
Pieroth, Doris Hinson . . . *v.4 p.808, p.837, p.846, p.860, p.868*
Pierre, D. B. C. *v.2 p.373*
Pierre, Jon & Peters, B. Guy *v.4 p.580*
Pierson, Michele *v.6 p.319, p.352*
Piesarskas, Bronius & Svecevicius, Bronius. *v.2 p.773*
Pietersen, Jacques & Pietersen, Willie *v.4 p.79*
Pietramala, David G. & Grauer, Neil A. *v.4 p.862*
Pietri, Pedro. *v.6 p.496, p.508, p.517*

Pietrusza, David *v.4 p.808, p.851, p.885, p.889,
                                        p.892, p.897, p.902*
Pieyre de Mandiargues, André. *v.2 p.523*
Pifer, Ellen (Editor). *v.2 p.105*
Pifer, Ellen *v.2 p.60*
Piñera, Virgilio. *v.2 p.673*
Pióro, Michal & Medhi, Deepankar *v.5 p.727*
Pigeat, Jean-Paul *v.1 p.819*
Pigford, Lois. *v.4 p.170*
Piggott, Derek. *v.4 p.787, p.788, p.848*
Piggott, Stuart *v.1 p.534*
Pigliucci, Massimo *v.5 p.195*
Pigman, Ward & Horton, Derek *v.5 p.330*
Pigou, Arthur C. *v.4 p.210, p.228, p.252, p.254*
Pike, Fredrick B.. . . . . *v.3 p.331*
Pike, Kenneth L. *v.2 p.563*
Pike, Lionel . *v.1 p.202, p.221, p.241, p.242, p.307, p.356, p.363*
Pike, Ruth L. *v.5 p.329*
Pike, Ruth *v.3 p.240*
Pike, Zebulon M.. . . . . *v.3 p.520*
Pikirayi, Innocent *v.6 p.77*
Pikkert, P. (Peter). *v.6 p.668*
Piland, Sherry *v.6 p.473*
Pilbrow, Richard *v.1 p.149*
Pilch, Jerzy *v.2 p.791*
Pilcher, Jane & Whelehan, Imelda *v.6 p.426*
Pilcher, Jeffrey M. *v.3 p.267, p.272*
Pile, John *v.1 p.799*
Pilkey, Walter D.; Wunderlich, Walter *v.5 p.696*
Pilkey, Walter D. *v.5 p.696*
Pilkington, Doris & Garimara, Nugi *v.2 p.748*
Pillar, Paul R. *v.4 p.565*
Pillay, T. V. R. & Kutty, M. N. *v.5 p.32*
Pilling, Claudia, et al.. . . . . *v.2 p.601*
Pilling, Michael J. & Seakins, Paul W. *v.5 p.276*
Pillsbury, Richard & Florin, John (Editors) *v.5 p.5*
Pilniak, Boris *v.2 p.807*
Pilsner, Brenda. *v.6 p.18, p.34*
Pimentel, David (Editor), et al. *v.6 p.289*
Pimentel, David (Editor) *v.5 p.10, p.27*
Pimm, Stuart L. *v.5 p.357, v.6 p.294*
Pinar, William F. (Editor) *v.4 p.365*
Pinar, William F. *v.4 p.365*
Pinault, David *v.6 p.663*
Pinchot, Gifford *v.3 p.434, v.5 p.17, p.39*
Pinchuk, Ben-Cion *v.3 p.86*
Pinciss, G. M. *v.2 p.186, p.231*
Pincus, Fred L. *v.4 p.516, v.6 p.470*
Pincus, Harold A. (Editor), et al.. . . . . *v.5 p.675*
Pindar *v.2 p.417*
Pinder, David *v.6 p.725*
Pindsdorf, Marion K. *v.4 p.174*
Pindyck, Robert S. & Rubinfeld, Daniel L.. . . *v.4 p.203, p.207*
Pine, Lisa *v.3 p.173*
Pinedo, Isabel Cristina *v.6 p.319*

Pinello, Daniel R. *v.4 p.457*

Pinero, Arthur Wing *v.2 p.302*

Pinero, Eugenio *v.3 p.359*

Pinero, Miguel *v.6 p.508, p.517, p.518*

Pinget, Robert *v.2 p.523*

Pingoud, Alfred, et al. *v.5 p.89, p.114*

Ping-Robbins, Nancy R. & Marco, Guy

(Editors). *v.1 p.164, p.281, p.334*

Pinion, Frank B. *v.2 p.313*

Pink, Sarah *v.4 p.818, p.837, p.856*

Pinkard, Terry *v.3 p.168*

Pinker, Steven . *v.2 p.563, v.5 p.621, p.623, p.628, p.650, p.658*

Pinkney, Robert *v.4 p.576, p.612*

Pinn, Anthony B. *v.6 p.36*

Pinney, Christopher *v.6 p.150, p.154*

Pino, David *v.1 p.391, p.398*

Pinochet Ugarte, Augusto *v.3 p.354*

Pinon, Nelida *v.2 p.692*

Pinsky, Robert *v.2 p.153*

Pinsky, Valerie & Wylie, Alison (Editors) *v.4 p.6*

Pinsof, William M. & Lebow, Jay *v.5 p.639*

Pinson, Koppel S. *v.3 p.164*

Pinson, Linda & Jinnett, Jerry *v.4 p.87*

Pinson, Linda *v.4 p.174*

Pinson, Mark (Editor). *v.3 p.249*

Pinstrup-Andersen, Per & Schiøler, Ebbe *v.5 p.8, p.33*

Pinteau, Pascal. *v.6 p.352*

Pinter, Harold (Editor), et al. *v.2 p.583*

Pinter, Harold, et al. *v.2 p.377*

Pinter, Harold *v.1 p.62, p.92, p.102, v.2 p.377*

Pion-Berlin, David (Editor) *v.3 p.276*

Pion-Berlin, David *v.3 p.276, v.4 p.592*

Piot, Charles *v.6 p.74*

Piotrowski, Christine M. *v.1 p.801*

Pipa, Arshi. *v.2 p.815*

Piper, Paul (Editor). *v.3 p.444*

Piper, Thomas R., et al. *v.4 p.53, p.177*

Piperno, Dolores R. & Pearsall, Deborah M. *v.5 p.16*

Pipes, Richard *v.4 p.509, p.661*

Pipher, Mary. *v.5 p.642*

Pippin, Robert (Editor) *v.1 p.467*

Pira, Edward S. *v.4 p.872, p.881, p.906*

Pirandello, Luigi & Reed, Henry. *v.2 p.722*

Pirandello, Luigi. *v.1 p.83, p.107, v.2 p.722, p.723*

Pirazzoli-t'Serstevens, Michele *v.6 p.185*

Pirenne, Henri *v.3 p.67, p.69, v.6 p.577*

Pirro, D. M., et al. *v.5 p.708*

Pirsig, Robert M.. . . . . *v.2 p.153*

Piscatori, James P. (Editor) *v.1 p.558*

Piscatori, James P. *v.4 p.500*

Pisciotta, Alexander W. *v.6 p.274*

Piston, Walter, et al. *v.1 p.372*

Piston, Walter *v.1 p.372*

Piszkiewicz, Dennis *v.4 p.565*

Pitard, Wayne T. *v.3 p.7*

Pitblado, Robin, et al.. . . . . *v.5 p.682*

Pitcher, Gayle D. & Poland, Scott *v.4 p.353*

Pitcher, George. *v.1 p.450*

Pite, Raloh (Editor), et al.. . . . . *v.2 p.281, p.315, v.6 p.752*

Pite, Ralph & Mullan, John (Editors). *v.6 p.753*

Pite, Ralph (Editor), et al. . . *v.2 p.277, p.289, p.305, v.6 p.753*

Pite, Ralph (Editor) *v.2 p.271, p.272, p.304, v.6 p.753*

Piterberg, Gabriel. *v.6 p.591*

Pitkin, Hanna F. *v.4 p.576*

Pitkin, Linda M. *v.5 p.216*

Pitruzzella, Salvo *v.1 p.94*

Pitt, David C. *v.5 p.223*

Pitt, Ivan L. & Norsworthy, J. R. *v.4 p.152*

Pitt, Leonard. *v.6 p.535*

Pittaway, Mark. *v.3 p.207*

Pittman, John P. *v.1 p.442*

Pitt-Rivers, Julian A.. . . . . *v.4 p.42*

Pitt-Rivers, Julian Alfred ; Abu Zayd, Ahmad. . . . *v.4 p.705*

Pitts, Brenda G. & Stotlar, David K.. . . . . *v.4 p.786, p.885*

Pitts, Michael R. *v.6 p.324*

Pitts, Victoria *v.4 p.26*

Pitz, Mary E. *v.4 p.546*

Pitzer, Donald E. (Editor) *v.4 p.499*

Pivar, Stuart *v.1 p.698*

Piven, Frances Fox & Cloward, Richard A.. . . . . *v.4 p.549*

Pix, Mary, et al. *v.2 p.202*

Pixley, Jocelyn. *v.4 p.250, p.261*

Pizam, Abraham (Editor-In-Chief) *v.4 p.161*

Pizarro, Marcos *v.4 p.301*

Pizer, Donald. *v.2 p.21, p.49, p.50*

Pizzi, William T. *v.6 p.269*

Pizzo, Philip A. & Wilfert, Catherine M. (Editors). . *v.5 p.515*

Pizzo, Philip A. *v.5 p.520, p.525*

Place, Edwin & Behm, Herbert (Translators) *v.2 p.646*

Place, Susan E. (Editor), et al.. . . . . *v.3 p.269*

Placher, William C. *v.1 p.634, p.636*

Plack, Christopher J. *v.5 p.607*

Plakans, Andrejs *v.3 p.256*

Planalp, Sally *v.5 p.648*

Planel, Hubert *v.5 p.243*

Plank, Steven Eric *v.1 p.396, p.402*

Plant, Richard *v.6 p.366*

Plante, Thomas G. & Sherman, Allen C. (Editors). . *v.5 p.635*

Plantinga, Alvin & Wolterstorff, Nicholas (Editors) . *v.1 p.523*

Plantinga, Alvin. *v.1 p.493, p.523, p.595, p.639*

Plantinga, Carl R. *v.6 p.309*

Plantinga, Cornelius Jr. *v.1 p.643*

Plantinga, Leon. *v.1 p.191, p.202, p.242, p.307, p.317*

Plaskow, Judith *v.1 p.528, p.643*

Plasmans, Joseph, et al.. . . . . *v.4 p.203, p.240*

Plasmans, Joseph. *v.4 p.203*

Plass, Paul *v.2 p.426, v.3 p.23*

Plastow, Jane & Banham, Martin (Editors) . . . *v.1 p.129, p.130*

Plath, Sylvia *v.2 p.153*

Plato & Bloom, Allan. *v.4 p.489*

Plato, et al. *v.2 p.417*

Plato *v.1 p.422, p.423, p.424, p.425, p.427, p.482, p.489, v.2 p.417, p.418, v.4 p.216, p.489*

Platonov, Andrei *v.2 p.807*

Platonov, Andrey *v.2 p.807*

Platonov, Sergei Fedorovich *v.3 p.215*

Platt, Anthony M. *v.4 p.683*

Platt, Brian *v.4 p.336*

Platt, Harold L. *v.6 p.714*

Platt, Heather (Editor) *v.1 p.164, p.202, p.313*

Platt, Jerome J. *v.5 p.664, p.673*

Platt, John *v.1 p.273, p.319*

Platt, Rutherford H. *v.4 p.382, p.464*

Platt, Tristan *v.3 p.324*

Platzker, David & Wyckoff, Elizabeth *v.1 p.760*

Platzman, Steven *v.1 p.745*

Plauger, P. J., et al. *v.5 p.347, p.349*

Plauger, P. J. *v.5 p.346, p.348*

Plaut, W. Gunther & Meyer, Michael. *v.1 p.552*

Plautus, Titus Maccius & Terence . . . *v.1 p.72, p.90, v.2 p.440*

Plautus, Titus Maccius *v.2 p.440*

Playfair, Susan R. *v.5 p.216*

Playford, John *v.1 p.22*

Pleasants, Henry *v.1 p.232*

Pleck, Elizabeth Hafkin *v.4 p.742*

Pleck, Elizabeth H. *v.4 p.705, p.734*

Pleck, Joseph H. *v.4 p.734, v.6 p.465, p.467*

Plekon, Michael *v.4 p.721*

Plenzdorf, Ulrich *v.2 p.618*

Plenzdorf *v.2 p.618*

Pleshakov, Constantine *v.3 p.227*

Pless, Vera *v.5 p.477*

Plessis, Alain *v.3 p.154*

Plesur, Milton *v.3 p.433*

Pletcher, David M. *v.3 p.381, p.400, p.433, p.437*

Plimpton, George *v.2 p.66*

Pliny the Elder *v.2 p.440, p.441, v.5 p.223*

Pliny the Younger *v.2 p.441*

Plokhy, Serhii *v.3 p.229*

Plomp, Reinier *v.5 p.607, p.608*

Plotkin, Henry C. (Editor) *v.5 p.195*

Plotkin, Mariano Ben *v.3 p.349*

Plotkin, Mark J. & Shnayerson, Michael *v.5 p.526*

Plotnick, Amy (Editor) *v.5 p.672*

Plous, Scott *v.5 p.609*

Plowden, Martha Ward *v.6 p.41, p.45*

Plucknett, Donald, et al. *v.5 p.370*

Plucknett, Theodore F. T. *v.4 p.436*

Pluim, Babette & Safran, Marc . *v.4 p.828, p.864, p.875, p.879*

Plum, Sydney L. (Editor, Introduction by) *v.5 p.80, p.232*

Plumb, J. H. (John Harold) *v.3 p.107*

Plumb, J. H. *v.3 p.107, p.109*

Plumly, Stanley *v.2 p.153*

Plummer, Charles C., et al. *v.4 p.390, v.5 p.419*

Plunkett, Jack W.
 (Editor) *v.4 p.115, p.150, p.151, p.152, p.153, v.5 p.361*

Plunkett, Jack W. *v.4 p.113, p.114, p.118, p.153, p.154, p.156, p.170*

Plunkett Research, Ltd *v.4 p.157*

Pluschke, Peter (Editor) *v.5 p.355, v.6 p.292*

Plutarch *v.2 p.418, p.419*

Poag, C. Wylie *v.5 p.441*

Pobell, F. *v.5 p.563*

Poch, Robert K. & AEHE Staff *v.4 p.298*

Pocock, J. G. *v.3 p.107*

Podair, Jerald E. *v.4 p.283*

Podalsky, Laura *v.3 p.349*

Podeh, Elie & Winckler, Onn *v.6 p.640*

Podlecki, Anthony J. *v.2 p.407*

Podnieks, Andrew, et al. *v.4 p.844, p.862*

Poe, Daryl Zizwe *v.6 p.13, p.18*

Poe, Edgar Allan *v.2 p.50*

Poe, Marshall T. *v.3 p.209*

Poe, Richard *v.6 p.10, p.20*

Poehlman, John M. & Sleper, David A. . . . *v.5 p.8, p.15, p.23*

Poeta Movima *v.2 p.692*

Poey, Delia *v.6 p.496, p.502, p.508, p.515*

Pogrebin, Mark (Editor) *v.6 p.254*

Pogue, Forrest C. *v.3 p.461*

Pohanish, Richard P. & Greene, Stanley A. *v.6 p.286*

Pohl, Frances K. *v.1 p.682, p.708*

Pohlmann, Egert & West, Martin L. *v.1 p.176*

Pohlmann, Marcus D. (Editor, Introduction by) *v.6 p.31*

Pohren, D. E. *v.1 p.21*

Poincare, Henri *v.5 p.66*

Poincare, Jules Henri *v.5 p.403*

Poincelot, Raymond P. *v.5 p.44*

Poirier, Dale J. *v.4 p.203*

Poirier, Jean-Pierre *v.5 p.261*

Poirier, Richard *v.2 p.6, p.77*

Poirion, Daniel (Editor) & Berthelot, Anne (Editor) . . *v.2 p.468*

Poitras, Geoffrey *v.4 p.204, p.264*

Pojman, Louis P. *v.1 p.523*

Pokrovskii, M. N. *v.3 p.209*

Polachek, James M. *v.6 p.188*

Polakoff, Keith I. *v.3 p.437*

Polakow, Valerie (Editor), et al. *v.6 p.463*

Poland, Jeffrey *v.1 p.509*

Polanyi, Karl *v.3 p.41, v.4 p.196, p.210, p.270*

Polanyi, Michael & Prosch, Harry *v.1 p.490*

Pole, J. R. *v.4 p.458*

Polenz, Peter Von *v.2 p.621*

Polhemus, Robert M. *v.2 p.176, p.191*

Poliakov, Leon *v.3 p.60*

Poling, Bruce E., et al. *v.5 p.282*

Polish, Mark, et al. *v.6 p.347*

Polit, Denise F. *v.5 p.529*

Polito, Robert *v.2 p.124*

Politzer, Heinz *v.2 p.611*

Poliziano, Angelo *v.2 p.708, p.709*

Polizzotti, Mark (Introduction by) *v.1 p.729*

Polk, James K.. . . . . *v.3 p.421*

Polk, William R. & Chambers, Richard L. (Editors) . *v.6 p.594*

Polk, William R.. . . . . *v.6 p.602*

POLKING, et al.. . . . . *v.5 p.486*

Polkinghorn, Bette & Thomson, Dorothy L. *v.4 p.194*

Polkinghorne, John C.. . . . . *v.1 p.526, p.596*

Polkinghorne, John.. . . . . *v.1 p.526, p.596*

Pollack, H.. . . . . *v.5 p.690*

Pollack, Howard *v.6 p.410*

Pollack, Jack.. . . . . *v.4 p.469*

Pollack, Jill S.. . . . . *v.6 p.377*

Pollack, Kenneth M.. . . . . *v.3 p.391*

Pollack, Marcelo *v.3 p.354*

Pollack, Rachel & Schwartz, Cheryl *v.6 p.369*

Pollack, Robert & Brenner, Margaret.. . . . . . *v.5 p.574*

Pollack, Robert.. . . . . *v.5 p.123*

Pollack, Sandra & Knight, Denise D. (Editors) . . *v.6 p.391*

Pollack, William *v.5 p.642*

Pollak, Otto *v.4 p.752*

Pollak, Vivian R. (Editor) *v.2 p.37*

Pollak, Vivian R. *v.2 p.54*

Pollan, Michael *v.5 p.16, p.45*

Pollard, Albert F.. . . . . *v.3 p.100, p.121*

Pollard, Andrew (Editor), et al.. . . . . *v.4 p.353*

Pollard, Arthur (Editor) *v.2 p.281*

Pollard, Charles W.. . . . . *v.2 p.768*

Pollard, John F.. . . . . *v.3 p.203*

Pollens, Stewart *v.1 p.391*

Polletta, Francesca *v.4 p.711*

Pollitt, Jerome Jordan.. . . . . *v.1 p.670*

Pollitt, Katha.. . . . . *v.6 p.442*

Pollock, David *v.3 p.391*

Pollock, Frederick & Maitland, Frederic
   William *v.3 p.98, v.4 p.436*

Pollock, Griselda (Editor). *v.6 p.473*

Pollock, Griselda *v.1 p.745, v.6 p.473*

Pollock, John *v.3 p.109*

Pollock, Joycelyn M. *v.6 p.278*

Pollock, Linda A. *v.3 p.92, v.4 p.735*

Pollock, Raphael E. & O'Sullivan, Brian *v.5 p.164*

Pollock, Sharon *v.2 p.738*

Pollock, Sheldon I. (Editor) *v.2 p.761*

Pollock, Susan *v.3 p.6*

Polo, Marco, et al.. . . . . . . *v.6 p.186, p.216, p.239*

Polo, Marco. *v.6 p.186, p.216*

Polonsky, Anthony (Editor) *v.3 p.255*

Polonsky, Antony & Adamczyk-Garbowska, Monika
   (Editors). *v.2 p.788*

Polonsky, Antony & Davies, Norman (Editors). . . . *v.3 p.86*

Polonsky, Antony & Michlic, Joanna B.
   (Editors) *v.3 p.86, p.254, p.255*

Polonsky, Rachel. *v.2 p.164*

Pols, Edward.. . . . . *v.1 p.497*

Polsby, Nelson W. *v.4 p.527*

Polsky, Ned *v.4 p.706*

Polt, John Herman Richard (Translator) *v.2 p.644*

Polukhina, Valentina & Weissbort, Daniel (Editors) . *v.2 p.794*

Polunov, Alexander. *v.3 p.218*

Polvinen, Tuomo. *v.3 p.213, p.236*

Poly, Jean-Pierre & Bournazel, Eric *v.3 p.143*

Polya, G. *v.5 p.460*

Polya, George, et al. *v.5 p.489*

Polya, George *v.5 p.464*

Polyakov, A. M. *v.5 p.550*

Polyanin, Andrei Dmitrievich *v.5 p.743*

Polybius *v.2 p.406*

Pomata, Gianna & Siraisi, Nancy G. (Editors) *v.5 p.80*

Pomerance, Murray (Editor). *v.6 p.314*

Pomeranz, Kenneth & Topik, Steven . *v.4 p.57, p.147, v.6 p.145*

Pomeranz, Kenneth *v.6 p.181*

Pomeroy, Earl S. *v.3 p.530*

Pomeroy, Sarah B. (Editor) *v.2 p.419, v.6 p.451*

Pomeroy, Sarah B., et al.. . . . . *v.3 p.13*

Pomeroy, Sarah B.. . . . . . . *v.3 p.14, v.6 p.451, p.635*

Pomeroy, William J. *v.3 p.391, v.6 p.180*

Pommersheim, Frank *v.6 p.692*

Pompa, Leon (Editor). *v.1 p.473*

Pomper, Gerald M. & Weiner, Marc D. (Editors) . . . *v.4 p.555*

Pomper, Gerald M. (Editor) *v.4 p.531*

Pomper, Philip *v.3 p.218*

Pond, S. & Pickard, George L. *v.5 p.430*

Pond, Steven F. *v.1 p.262, p.328*

Pond, Wilson & Bell, Alan *v.5 p.56*

Ponge, Francis *v.2 p.523*

Pons, Frank M.. . . . . *v.3 p.317*

Pont, Sally *v.4 p.809, p.859, p.894*

Pontiero, G.. . . . . *v.2 p.692*

Pontuso, James F.. . . . . *v.4 p.492*

Ponzanesi, Sandra *v.2 p.761*

Poo, Mu-chou *v.4 p.644*

Pook, Les *v.5 p.469*

Pool, David. *v.6 p.67*

Poole, Austin Lane (Editor) *v.3 p.96*

Poole, Charles K., et al.. . . . . *v.5 p.565*

Poole, Charles P.. . . . . *v.5 p.545, p.546*

Poole, Deborah & Renique, Gerardo *v.3 p.331*

Poole, Deborah.. . . . . *v.3 p.331*

Poole, Peter A.. . . . . *v.4 p.638*

Poole, Ross *v.4 p.495*

Poole, Stafford. *v.3 p.264, p.287*

Pooler, Jim *v.5 p.586*

Pooler, Marilyn, et al.. . . . . *v.5 p.534*

Poon, Irene *v.1 p.683, v.6 p.88*

Poon, Leonard W. (Editor), et al. *v.5 p.628, p.630*

Poorvu, William J. & Cruikshank, Jeffrey L.. . . *v.4 p.97, p.166*

Poovey, Mary *v.2 p.176, p.268, p.310, v.6 p.748, p.751*

Popa, Radu *v.5 p.243*

Pope, Alexander *v.2 p.257*
Pope, Carl E., et al.. . . . . *v.6 p.246*
Pope, Kenneth S. & Vasquez, Melba Jean Trinidad . *v.5 p.676*
Pope, Marvin H.. . . . . *v.1 p.621*
Pope, Peter E. *v.4 p.379*
Pope, Randolph D. *v.2 p.658*
Pope, Stephen Bailey *v.5 p.547*
Pope, Steven W. (Editor) *v.4 p.809, p.813*
Pope, Steven W. *v.4 p.809*
Pope-Davis, Donald, et al. *v.5 p.637*
Pope-Hennessy, John W. *v.1 p.781*
Pope-Levison, Priscilla *v.1 p.648*
Popesko, Peter, et al. *v.5 p.157*
Popham, James W. *v.4 p.286*
Popham, W. James *v.4 p.328*
Popkewitz, Thomas S. & Brennan, Marie. *v.4 p.345*
Popkewitz, Thomas S. *v.4 p.315*
Popkin, Jeremy D. (Editor). *v.3 p.37*
Popkin, Jeremy D.. . . . . *v.3 p.151, p.153*
Popkin, Richard H. & Stroll, Avrum *v.1 p.517*
Popkin, Richard H. *v.1 p.417, p.435, p.437, p.517*
Popkin, Richard Henry *v.1 p.517*
Poplack, Shana (Editor). *v.2 p.555*
Pople, Anthony (Editor) *v.1 p.221, p.309*
Pople, Anthony *v.1 p.221, p.242, p.309, p.341*
Popov, Evgeny *v.2 p.807*
Popovics, Sandor (Editor) *v.5 p.690*
Popper, Frank *v.1 p.772*
Popper, Karl R. & Eccles, John C.. . . . . *v.5 p.619*
Popper, Karl R.. . . . . *v.1 p.446, p.482, p.499, p.501,*
  v.4 p.488, p.490, p.493, p.517, v.5 p.403, p.409
Popper, William & Ibn Taghribirdi, Abu al-Mahasin
  Yusuf *v.6 p.607, p.636*
Popplestone, John A. & McPherson, Marion White . *v.5 p.598*
Population Research Center, RAND Corporation . . . *v.5 p.580*
Porath, Yehoshua. *v.6 p.612*
Porch, Douglas *v.3 p.81, v.6 p.61*
Porche, Demetrius James *v.5 p.531*
Pordzik, Ralph *v.4 p.485*
Porrata-Doria, Rafael *v.4 p.61*
Porshnev, B. F. & Dukes, Paul *v.3 p.216*
Port, Kenneth L. & McAlinn, Gerald Paul *v.6 p.220*
Porta, Carlo Antonio Melchiore Filippo *v.2 p.712*
Portal, Jane. *v.1 p.693, v.4 p.9*
Porte, Daniel, et al. *v.5 p.518*
Porte, Joel & Morris, Saundra (Editors) *v.2 p.38*
Porte, Joel *v.2 p.38, p.52*
Porteous, I. R. *v.5 p.496*
Porter, A. N. & Stockwell, A. J.. . . . . *v.3 p.125*
Porter, Andrew *v.3 p.89, p.125, v.4 p.605*
Porter, Bernard *v.3 p.89, p.125, v.6 p.746*
Porter, Beth *v.4 p.425*
Porter, Brian *v.3 p.253*
Porter, Carol *v.4 p.288*
Porter, Cole & Kimball,

Robert *v.1 p.253, p.347, p.348, p.409, p.412*
Porter, David Dixon *v.3 p.432*
Porter, David L. (Editor) *v.4 p.832, p.833*
Porter, David *v.2 p.37*
Porter, Douglas R. & Salveson, David A.
  (Editors). *v.5 p.177, p.181*
Porter, Eric *v.1 p.262*
Porter, Frank W. III (Editor). *v.1 p.806*
Porter, Glenn. *v.4 p.567*
Porter, Hal *v.2 p.748*
Porter, John *v.4 p.706*
Porter, Karra *v.4 p.809, p.837, p.854*
Porter, Katherine Anne *v.2 p.109*
Porter, Kay (As told to) *v.5 p.582*
Porter, Lewis (Editor) *v.1 p.263, p.369*
Porter, Lewis *v.1 p.262, p.318, p.369*
Porter, Michael E.. . *v.4 p.51, p.57, p.59, p.61, p.64, p.81, p.665*
Porter, Michael, et al. *v.4 p.73, v.6 p.220*
Porter, Micheal E. *v.4 p.73*
Porter, Robert A. (Editor) *v.1 p.825*
Porter, Robert O. *v.6 p.696*
Porter, Robert *v.2 p.782*
Porter, Roy & Ogilvie, Marilyn B. (Editors) *v.5 p.62*
Porter, Roy & Teich, Mikulas (Editors) *v.3 p.71*
Porter, Roy (Editor) *v.3 p.50*
Porter, Roy *v.1 p.450, v.3 p.50, p.72, p.90, p.92,*
  v.4 p.706, v.5 p.418, p.510
Porter Sargent Staff (Editor) *v.4 p.316, v.5 p.574*
Porter, Stanley & Evans, Craig *v.1 p.631*
Porter, Stanley E.. . . . . *v.2 p.405*
Porter, Steven *v.1 p.93, p.117*
Porter, Susan L. *v.1 p.253*
Porter, Theodore M. *v.5 p.467*
Porter, Yves & Thevenart, Arthur *v.1 p.819*
Portes, Alejandro & Bach, Robert L. *v.4 p.571, v.6 p.530*
Portes, Alejandro *v.3 p.505*
Portman, Janet & Stewart, Marcia *v.4 p.442*
Portner, Hal *v.4 p.277*
Portney, Paul & Haas, Ruth B. (Editors) *v.4 p.62*
Porto, Brian L. *v.4 p.822, p.837, p.894, p.901*
Porzecanski, Arturo C. *v.3 p.346*
Posa, Francesco & Ehlers, Manfred *v.5 p.367, p.368*
Posada-Carbo, Eduardo, ed. *v.3 p.345*
Posada-Carbo, Eduardo *v.3 p.358*
Posadas, Barbara M. *v.6 p.130*
Poschl, Viktor *v.2 p.446*
Posey, Alexander Lawrence. *v.2 p.49*
Posey, Alexander *v.2 p.49*
Posey, Amy J. & Wrightsman, Lawrence S.. . . . . . *v.6 p.271*
Posey, Carl A. *v.4 p.846*
Posner, Daniel N. *v.4 p.612*
Posner, Michael I. (Editor) *v.5 p.611*
Posner, Michael J. & Raichle, Marcus E.. . . . . . *v.5 p.617*
Posner, Richard A.. . . . . . . *v.4 p.442, p.462, p.528*
Posnick, Michael & Schiff, Ellen (Editors) . . . *v.1 p.68, p.126*

Pospísil, Leopold *v.4 p.33*

Pospielovsky, Dimitry V. *v.1 p.570*

Post, Gaines *v.6 p.568*

Post, James, et al. *v.4 p.52*

Post, Jennifer C. *v.1 p.169, p.283*

Post, Jerrold M. (Editor) *v.4 p.512, v.5 p.644*

Post, Jerrold M. *v.4 p.512, p.698, v.5 p.644*

Post, Jonathan F. S. (Editor). *v.2 p.182*

Post, Jonathan F. S. *v.2 p.182*

Post, Karen *v.4 p.142*

Post, Peggy & Post, Peter *v.4 p.57, p.174*

Post, Robert C. *v.4 p.848*

Post, Stephen G., et al. *v.1 p.501, v.5 p.655*

Postan, M. M. & Miller, E (Editors). . . . *v.3 p.41, v.6 p.558*

Postan, M. M. (Editor), et al. *v.3 p.41, v.6 p.558*

Postan, M. M. (Editor). *v.3 p.41, v.6 p.558, p.575*

Post *v.4 p.26*

Postel, Sandra & Richter, Brian D. *v.5 p.356, p.380*

Postel, Sandra *v.5 p.357, p.380, v.6 p.289*

Postgate, John Raymond *v.5 p.50*

Postlethwaite, Diana *v.6 p.751, p.756*

Postlethwaite, T. Neville (Editor) *v.4 p.313*

Postlewait, Thomas & Paradis, James G.
(Editors). *v.5 p.410, p.412*

Postlewait, Thomas *v.1 p.55, p.56, p.117, p.137*

Postma, G. & Oti, M. N. *v.4 p.392*

Postman, Neil *v.4 p.323, p.417*

Posusney, Marsha Pripstein & Angrist, Michele Penner
(Editors). *v.6 p.594*

Potash, Chris *v.1 p.273, p.294, p.331*

Potash, Robert A. *v.3 p.276, p.349, v.4 p.592*

Potkay, Adam & Burr, Sandra (Editors) *v.2 p.9, p.172*

Potocki, Jan *v.2 p.791*

Potter, Caroline *v.1 p.221, p.322*

Potter, Clare (Compiled by). *v.6 p.361, p.362*

Potter, D. S. & Mattingly, D. J. (Editors) *v.3 p.23*

Potter, David & Thomas, Gordon L. (Editors) *v.2 p.28*

Potter, David (Editor). *v.1 p.610*

Potter, David M. *v.3 p.365, p.369, p.400, p.421, p.429,
p.495, p.497, v.4 p.695*

Potter, David S. *v.2 p.426, v.3 p.29*

Potter, David *v.3 p.144, p.146*

Potter, Elizabeth *v.1 p.499, p.506*

Potter, G. R. (Editor) *v.3 p.71*

Potter, John (Editor) *v.1 p.236, p.396*

Potter, Karl H. & Bhattacharyya, Sibajiban (Editors) . *v.1 p.419*

Potter, Keith *v.1 p.221*

Potter, P. E., et al. *v.5 p.438*

Potter, Paul (Translator). *v.5 p.510*

Potter, Robert B., et al. *v.4 p.398*

Potter, Stephen R. *v.4 p.11*

Potter, Sulamith Heins & Potter, Jack M. *v.4 p.40*

Potter, Sulamith Heins *v.4 p.40*

Potter, Thomas D. & Colman, Bradley R. (Editors) . . *v.5 p.426*

Potter, Van R. *v.5 p.248*

Potterfield, Peter *v.4 p.789, p.790*

Pottinger, George *v.3 p.90, p.114*

Pottker, Janice & Fishel, Andrew (Editors) *v.4 p.301*

Potts, D. T. *v.3 p.6*

Potuchek, Jean L. *v.4 p.732, v.6 p.467*

Pouchert, Charles J. *v.5 p.270, p.272*

Pouchet, F.-A. (Félix-Archimède) *v.5 p.225*

Pough, Frederick H. *v.5 p.436*

Poulet, Georges *v.2 p.456, p.461*

Poulin, Jacques. *v.2 p.541*

Poultney, David *v.1 p.174*

Poulton, Diana. *v.1 p.181, p.322*

Pouncy, Carolyn J. (Editor, Translator) *v.3 p.215*

Pound, Ezra & Fenollosa, Ernest. *v.1 p.129, p.133, p.134, v.6 p.235*

Pound, Ezra & Kehew, Robert (Editors) *v.2 p.466*

Pound, Ezra & Williams, William Carlos. . . . *v.2 p.112, p.136*

Pound, Ezra *v.2 p.112, p.457, p.569, p.573, p.575*

Pound, Richard W. *v.4 p.846, p.885, p.889, p.892*

Pound, Roscoe (Editor) *v.4 p.440*

Pound, Roscoe. *v.4 p.433, p.434*

Pounds, Norman J. G. *v.3 p.35*

Poupeye, Veerle *v.1 p.684*

Poutsma, Hendrik *v.2 p.558*

Powdermaker, Hortense. *v.4 p.25, p.43*

Powe, Lucas A. Jr. *v.4 p.459*

Powell, Anthony *v.2 p.377, p.378*

Powell, Ardal *v.1 p.391*

Powell, Arthur B. & Frankenstein, Marilyn (Editors) . *v.5 p.464*

Powell, B. B. & Morris, I. *v.2 p.415*

Powell, Barry B. *v.2 p.415*

Powell, Charles C. & Lindquist, Richard K. *v.5 p.44*

Powell, Chris & Paton, George E. (Editors). *v.4 p.773*

Powell, Colin L. & Persico, Joseph E. *v.3 p.461*

Powell, David A. *v.2 p.499*

Powell, Dawn *v.2 p.113*

Powell, G. Bingham Jr. *v.4 p.577*

Powell, G. Bingham *v.4 p.577*

Powell, Gary N. & Graves, Laura M. *v.6 p.457*

Powell, J. Enoch *v.2 p.412*

Powell, James Lawrence *v.5 p.446*

Powell, James M. (Editor). *v.6 p.555*

Powell, John (Editor), et al. . . . *v.2 p.176, p.184, p.188, p.193*

Powell, John W. *v.3 p.527*

Powell, John Wesley *v.6 p.294*

Powell, Jonathan & Paterson, Jeremy (Editors) . . . *v.2 p.434*

Powell, Kerry (Editor). *v.1 p.60, p.79, p.80, p.103, v.2 p.176, p.188*

Powell, Mark Allan *v.1 p.161, p.273*

Powell, Neil (Editor, Introduction by) *v.6 p.405*

Powell, Richard J. & Reynolds, Jock. *v.1 p.705*

Powell, Richard J. *v.1 p.705*

Powell, Robert. *v.4 p.498, p.625*

Powell, Sumner C. *v.3 p.488*

Powell, Thomas J. (Editor) *v.5 p.669*

Powell, William S. *v.3 p.502*

Powelson, David R. & Powelson,
Melinda A. *v.5 p.377, p.378, p.704*
Power, Daniel *v.3 p.143*
Power, Edward J. *v.4 p.323, p.340*
Power, Eileen *v.6 p.451, p.560*
Power, F. Clark, et al. *v.5 p.572*
Power, J. F. (Editor, Introduction by) *v.5 p.50*
Power, James F. (Editor) *v.5 p.50*
Power, Marcus. *v.4 p.260, p.268*
Power, Margaret *v.3 p.354*
Power, Paul W. *v.4 p.305, p.353*
Power, Richard L. *v.3 p.513*
Power, Samantha. *v.4 p.715*
Power, Susan C. *v.1 p.683, v.6 p.679*
Powers, David S. *v.6 p.641, p.642, p.643*
Powers, Karen Vieira. *v.3 p.332, p.333*
Powers, Richard G. (Editor), et al.. . . . . . *v.6 p.222, p.232*
Powers, Richard G. *v.3 p.449, v.6 p.259*
Powers, Shelley, et al. *v.5 p.348, p.349*
Powers, Stephen & Rothman, Stanley *v.4 p.535, p.541*
Powers, Thomas. *v.3 p.49*
Powers-Beck, Jeff *v.4 p.809, p.818, p.841, p.851*
Powrie, Phil *v.6 p.338*
Powrie, William *v.5 p.422, p.699*
Powys, John Cowper *v.2 p.373*
Poyatos, Fernando *v.4 p.424*
Poynor, Rick (Editor). *v.1 p.714, p.715*
Poynor, Rick. *v.1 p.713*
Poyo, Gerald E. & Hinojosa, Gilberto M.
(Editors). *v.6 p.534, p.550*
Poyo, Gerald E. *v.3 p.312*
Pozar, David M. *v.5 p.729*
Poznanski, Renie *v.3 p.156*
Poznansky, Alexander & Langston,
Brett *v.1 p.164, p.202, p.362, p.363*
Poznansky, Alexander. *v.1 p.202, p.362, v.6 p.410*
Prache, Anne *v.6 p.555, p.572*
Prade, Rolf *v.5 p.125, p.136*
Prados-Torreira, Teresa *v.3 p.312*
Prager, Ellen & Earle, Sylvia *v.5 p.429*
Prahalad, C. K., et al.. . . . . *v.4 p.52, p.54*
Prahalad, C. K.. . . . . *v.4 p.665*
Prak, Maarten Roy *v.3 p.41*
Prakash, Aseem *v.4 p.63*
Prakash, Gyan *v.6 p.158*
Prance, Ghillean *v.5 p.177, p.239*
Prange, R. E. & Girvin, S. M. (Editors) . . . *v.5 p.565, p.566*
Prasad, M. N. V. (Editor) *v.5 p.170, p.219*
Prasad, Paras N.. . . . . *v.5 p.219, p.562*
Prasad, Pushkala (Editor), et al. *v.4 p.132*
Prasad, Pushkala, et al. *v.4 p.132*
Prashad, Vijay (Contribution by) *v.6 p.124, p.137*
Prashad, Vijay *v.4 p.723, v.6 p.149*
Prasolov, V. V.. . . . . *v.5 p.499*
Prasow, Paul & Peters, Edward *v.4 p.447*

Prater, Donald A.. . . . . *v.2 p.613*
Prater, Donald *v.2 p.615*
Prats, A. J. *v.6 p.324, p.700*
Pratt, Annis *v.6 p.460*
Pratt, E. J. (Author, Editor) *v.2 p.738*
Pratt, E. J. *v.2 p.738*
Pratt, Julius W.. . . . . *v.3 p.417*
Pratt, Julius *v.3 p.400, p.438*
Pratt, Keith *v.1 p.289, v.6 p.237*
Pratt, Minnie B. *v.6 p.405*
Pratt, Minnie Bruce *v.6 p.403, p.405*
Pratt, Ray *v.1 p.273*
Pratt, Richard H.. . . . . *v.3 p.400*
Pratt, Richard Henry *v.6 p.680, p.683*
Pratt, Walter F.. . . . . *v.4 p.469*
Prawer, Joshua (Editor) *v.6 p.609*
Prawer, Siegbert (Editor) *v.2 p.593*
Praz, Mario *v.2 p.165*
Prazmowska, Anita J. *v.3 p.81, p.254*
Prazmowska, Anita *v.3 p.254*
Prebish, Charles S. (Editor) *v.1 p.565*
Prebish, Charles S. *v.1 p.564, v.4 p.824*
Preble, Christopher A. *v.4 p.565*
Preece, Christopher N. (Editor), et al. *v.4 p.159*
Prejean, Helen *v.6 p.247*
Prelinger, Catherine M. (Editor) *v.1 p.582*
Prelinger, Elizabeth. *v.1 p.695*
Prem, Boris *v.2 p.613*
Premchand, Munshi *v.6 p.152*
Premchand. *v.6 p.152*
Premo, Bianca *v.3 p.326*
Prendergast, Christopher (Editor) *v.2 p.461*
Prendergast, Christopher *v.2 p.487*
Prendergast, Roy M. *v.1 p.256*
Prenshaw, Peggy W. (Editor) *v.2 p.130*
Prentice, Alison & Theobald, Marjorie R. (Editors) . . *v.4 p.283*
Prentice, Alison *v.4 p.336*
Prentice, Penelope *v.2 p.377*
Prentice, William E. & Arnheim, Daniel D.. *v.4 p.827, p.828, p.829*
Prentice, William E. *v.5 p.519, p.535*
Prentice *v.4 p.828*
Prentice-Hall Staff *v.4 p.399*
Prentis, Steve *v.5 p.219, p.742*
Prepared by the Committee on Patents and Related
Matters *v.5 p.264*
Presberg, Charles D. *v.2 p.649*
Presbyterian Church Staff *v.1 p.588*
Prescott, G. W. (Gerald Webber). *v.5 p.208*
Prescott, Laurence E.. . . . . *v.4 p.336*
Preskill, Stephen L. & Jacobvitz, Robin S. . . . *v.4 p.348*
Presniakov, Alexander E. *v.3 p.219*
Press, Frank, et al. *v.5 p.419*
Press, Ian & Pugh, Stefan *v.2 p.777*
Press, Ian & Ramoniene, Meilute *v.2 p.773, p.774*

Press, Stephen D. *v.1 p.24*
Press, William H., et al. *v.5 p.337, p.347, p.492*
Presser, Harriet B. *v.5 p.581*
Pressley, Michael *v.4 p.365, v.5 p.573*
Pressman, Steven *v.4 p.185, p.208, p.216*
Prest, John *v.3 p.95, p.114*
Prest, Wilfrid R. *v.3 p.124*
Presthus, R. *v.4 p.591*
Preston, Dennis Richard *v.2 p.553*
Preston, Dickson J. *v.3 p.421*
Preston, John & Lowenthal, Michael (Editors) *v.6 p.375*
Preston, John (Editor) *v.6 p.375*
Preston, Laurence W. *v.6 p.161*
Preston, Paul *v.3 p.241, p.242, p.243*
Preston, Richard Joseph & Braham, Richard R. *v.5 p.39*
Preston, Ward *v.6 p.349*
Preston, William Jr. *v.3 p.444, p.449*
Preston-Dunlop, Valerie (Compiled by) *v.1 p.4*
Preston-Dunlop, Valerie (Editor) *v.1 p.27*
Preston-Dunlop, Valerie M. *v.1 p.48*
Preston-Dunlop, Valerie Monthland &
   Sanchez-Colberg, Ana *v.1 p.43*
Preston-Dunlop, Valerie *v.1 p.48*
Prestowitz, Clyde & Prestowitz, Clyde V. *v.4 p.51*
Prestwich, Michael *v.3 p.68, p.98, v.6 p.567*
Pretsch, Ernho, et al. *v.5 p.291*
Prettejohn, Elizabeth *v.1 p.703, p.729*
Pretty, Jules N. *v.5 p.13*
Preucel, Robert *v.4 p.6*
Preuss, Holger *v.4 p.846, p.889*
Preuss, Peter *v.1 p.429*
Preuss, Ulrich K. *v.4 p.576*
Preves, Sharon E. *v.6 p.371*
Previts, Gary J. & Merino, Barbara Dubis *v.4 p.104*
Prevost, Abbe *v.2 p.481*
Prevost, Robert *v.1 p.499, v.3 p.544*
Prevots, Naima *v.1 p.11, p.29, p.31, p.37*
Preziosi, Donald & Hitchcock, Louise *v.1 p.670*
Preziosi, Donald (Editor) *v.1 p.701*
Preziosi, Donald *v.1 p.709*
Prévert, Jacques *v.2 p.523*
Prial, Dunstan *v.1 p.385*
Priami, Corrado (Contribution by) *v.5 p.128, p.142, p.151*
Pribichevich, Stoyan *v.3 p.250*
Pribram, E. Deidre *v.6 p.343*
Price, Alan *v.2 p.132*
Price, B. Byron *v.1 p.683*
Price, Curtis (Editor) *v.1 p.186*
Price, Curtis *v.1 p.186, p.232, p.349*
Price, Derek D. *v.5 p.389*
Price, George R. *v.2 p.218*
Price, Glanville *v.2 p.454*
Price, J. L. *v.3 p.205*
Price, Janet *v.6 p.436*
Price, Jennifer *v.5 p.235*

Price, Kenneth M. *v.2 p.54*
Price, Lorna *v.3 p.245*
Price, Miles O., et al. *v.4 p.439*
Price, Monroe E. & Clinton, Robert *v.6 p.696*
Price, Neville J. & Cosgrove, John W. *v.5 p.441*
Price, Renee (Editor) *v.1 p.699*
Price, Reynolds *v.2 p.153, v.6 p.379, p.398*
Price, Richard (Editor) *v.4 p.41*
Price, Richard *v.3 p.410, v.4 p.41*
Price, Roger (Editor) *v.3 p.153*
Price, Roger *v.3 p.154*
Price, Ron *v.5 p.727*
Price, Sally *v.4 p.41, p.48*
Price, Simon & Kearns, Emily (Editors) *v.1 p.533*
Price, Simon *v.1 p.533*
Price-Cohen, Cynthia (Editor) *v.4 p.34*
PricewaterhouseCoopers LLP Staff *v.4 p.92, p.107*
PricewaterhouseCoopers Staff, et al. *v.4 p.92, p.105, p.106, p.111*
Prichett, Gordon D. & Saber, John C. *v.5 p.503*
Pricken, Mario *v.4 p.427*
Prickett, Stephen *v.2 p.172, p.176, p.191*
Prida, Dolores *v.6 p.508, p.518*
Pride, Armistead S. & Wilson, Clint C. II *v.4 p.404*
Prideaux, Sue *v.1 p.699*
Pridemore, William Alex *v.6 p.250*
Pridham, Brian R. (Editor) *v.6 p.627*
Priebsch, Robert & Collinson, William Edward *v.2 p.621*
Priest, Simon & Gass, Michael A. *v.4 p.788, p.789*
Priest, Stephen *v.1 p.457*
Priestley, J. B. & Brett, R. L. *v.2 p.293*
Priestley, J. B. *v.2 p.285, p.300, p.378, v.3 p.126*
Priestley, J.B. *v.2 p.378*
Priestly, George *v.3 p.305*
Priestman, Martin (Editor) *v.2 p.191, p.580*
Prieto, Jose Manuel *v.2 p.673*
Prigann, Herman, et al. *v.1 p.814*
Prigogine, Ilya (Editor) *v.5 p.276*
Prigozy, Ruth (Editor) *v.2 p.77*
Prilleltensky, Isaac *v.5 p.675*
Primack, Richard & Corlett, Richard . *v.5 p.169, p.177, p.181*
Primack, Richard B. *v.5 p.17, p.18, p.357, p.358*
Primakov, Yevgeny M. *v.4 p.661*
Primakov, Yevgeny *v.4 p.598*
Primoratz, Igor (Editor) *v.4 p.661*
Primoratz, Igor *v.6 p.275*
Primrose, S. B. & Twyman, Richard M. *v.5 p.146*
Primrose, Sandy, et al. *v.5 p.142*
Prince, Stephen (Editor, Translator, Introduction by) . *v.6 p.319*
Prince, Stephen (Editor) *v.6 p.343*
Prince, Stephen *v.6 p.321, p.336*
Princeton Review Publishing Staff *v.4 p.170, p.171*
Princeton Review Staff & Wright, Judene *v.5 p.246*
Princeton Review Staff *v.4 p.171, v.5 p.246*
Princeton University Conference Staff *v.4 p.207*

Pringle, Keith *v.4 p.755, v.6 p.470*
Pringle, Peter *v.4 p.439*
Prins, Gwyn *v.6 p.77*
Prins, Yopie *v.2 p.176*
Prinstein, Mitchell J. & Patterson, Marcus D. (Editors). *v.5 p.676*
Prinz, Jesse J. *v.1 p.504, v.5 p.655*
Prior, Arthur N. *v.1 p.492*
Prior, Katherine & Adamson, John *v.1 p.716*
Prior, Lindsay *v.4 p.687, p.775*
Prior, Matthew *v.2 p.256*
Prior, Moody E. *v.2 p.234*
Priscu, John C. (Editor). *v.5 p.185, p.187*
Pritchard, D. J. & Korf, Bruce R. *v.5 p.151*
Pritchard, Hayden N. & Bradt, Patricia T. . . . *v.5 p.206, p.207*
Pritchard, James B. (Editor) *v.1 p.619, v.3 p.4*
Pritchard, John Paul *v.2 p.5*
Pritchard, Seth G. & Amthor, Jeffrey S. *v.5 p.23, p.28*
Pritchard, William H. *v.2 p.78*
Pritchett, C. Herman *v.4 p.456*
Pritchett, James A. *v.4 p.38, v.6 p.77*
Pritchett, James *v.1 p.221, p.315*
Pritchett, V. S. *v.2 p.378, p.487*
Pritchett, Wendell E. *v.6 p.725*
Pritsak, Omeljan *v.2 p.814*
Proakis, John G. & Manolakis, Dimitris G.. . . *v.5 p.336, p.341*
Proakis, John G. & Salehi, Masoud *v.5 p.726*
Prochazka, Theodore Sr. *v.3 p.189*
Procida, Mary A.. . . . . *v.6 p.150*
Procopiow, Norma. *v.2 p.96*
Procopius. *v.3 p.67*
Procter, Garry *v.5 p.295*
Proctor, Alexander Phimister & Hassrick, Peter H. (Translators) *v.1 p.781*
Proctor, James D. *v.4 p.375*
Proctor, Rob (Photographer). *v.1 p.812*
Proctor, Robert W. & Kim-Phuong, L.Vu (Editors) . *v.5 p.588*
Procyk, Anna M.. . . . . *v.3 p.229*
Proehl, Jean A.. . . . . *v.5 p.531*
Proffer, Carl & Proffer, Ellendea C. (Editors) . . . *v.2 p.794*
Proffer, Carl R. (Compiled by). *v.2 p.795*
Prokhorov, Vadim *v.1 p.298*
Prokhovnik, Raia *v.1 p.506, v.6 p.461*
Prokofiev, Sergei. *v.1 p.221, p.348*
Prokopetz, Andrew T. *v.5 p.330, p.331*
Prokop-Janiec, Eugenia *v.2 p.789*
Pronger, Brian *v.4 p.839, v.6 p.384*
Pronko, Leonard C. . . *v.1 p.85, p.106,v.2 p.462, p.506, p.517*
Pronzini, Bill & Adrian, Jack (Editors) *v.2 p.26*
Pronzini, Bill & Greenberg, Martin H. (Editors) . . . *v.2 p.27*
Propertius *v.2 p.441, p.442*
Propp, William H. *v.1 p.621*
ProQuest Company *v.6 p.14, p.18, p.34*
Pross, Addy *v.5 p.296*
Prost, Gary L. *v.5 p.421*
Prothero, Donald R. & Dott, Robert H.. . . . . . . *v.5 p.445*

Prothrow-Stith, Deborah *v.4 p.775*
Proto, Francesco (Editor) *v.1 p.704, p.787*
Protter, Philip *v.5 p.484, p.487*
Protzen, Jean-Pierre *v.3 p.262*
Proudfoot, Richard, et al. *v.1 p.76, p.103*
Proulx, Annie (Author, Adapted by) *v.2 p.153*
Proust, Marcel *v.2 p.524*
Prouty, Charles Tyler *v.1 p.75, p.103*
Prouty, Chris *v.6 p.64*
Provan, Iain W., et al.. . . . . *v.1 p.619*
Provenzo, Eugene F. Jr.. . . . . *v.4 p.307, p.345*
Provine, Robert R. *v.5 p.656*
Prucha, Francis Paul (Editor) *v.6 p.692*
Prucha, Francis Paul *v.3 p.384*
Prucha, Francis P.. . . . . *v.4 p.465, p.573, p.729, v.6 p.683, p.686, p.688, p.692, p.696, p.701*
Prudentius. *v.2 p.442*
Prud'homme van Reine, W. F. & Trono, G. C. Jr. (Editors) *v.5 p.208*
Prunier, Gerard *v.4 p.653, v.6 p.59*
Prunier, Gérard. *v.4 p.653*
Prunster, N. & Victoria University Staff *v.2 p.700*
Prus, Bolesiaw *v.2 p.791*
Prus, Boleslav *v.2 p.791*
Prus, Robert *v.4 p.687*
Pruter, Robert *v.1 p.171, p.273*
Pryke, Kenneth G. *v.3 p.543*
Pryor, Esther & Kraines, Minda Goodman *v.4 p.793*
Pryor, Frederic L. & Schaffer, David L. *v.4 p.305*
Pryor, Frederic L. *v.3 p.321*
Pryor, Jan & Rodgers, Bryan *v.4 p.740*
Przeworski, Adam (Author, Contribution by) . . . *v.4 p.505*
Przeworski, Adam *v.4 p.507, p.592*
Przeworski, Joanne F.. . . . . *v.3 p.351*
Psellus, Michael *v.3 p.193*
Psi Chi *v.5 p.676*
Ptolemy, Claudius *v.4 p.377*
Pu Yi, Aisin-Gioro. *v.6 p.188, p.191, p.200*
Pucci, Pietro *v.2 p.413*
Pucci, Suzanne R. & Thompson, James (Editors) . . . *v.2 p.268*
Puccini, Giacomo *v.1 p.202, p.232, p.349, p.409*
Pucel, David J.. . . . . *v.4 p.305*
Puchner, Martin *v.2 p.189*
Puddington, Arch.. . . . . *v.4 p.128*
Pudney, Stephen *v.4 p.204*
Pudup, Mary B. (Editor), et al. *v.3 p.498*
Puente, Antonio E. (Editor), et al. *v.5 p.676*
Puerto, Cecilia. *v.6 p.473, p.475*
Puette, William J. *v.6 p.232*
Puffett, Derrick (Editor) *v.1 p.221, p.222, p.232, p.359*
Puga, María Luisa *v.2 p.669*
Pugh, C. C. *v.5 p.490*
Pugh, David G. & Bacon, Terry R. *v.4 p.174*
Pugh, Martin *v.3 p.95, p.114, v.4 p.604*
Pugh, Stefan M. & Press, J. Ian *v.2 p.777*

Puhalla, Jim, et al.. . . . . *v.4 p.872, p.881, p.906*

Puig, Manuel. *v.2 p.678, v.6 p.398*

Pulci, Luigi *v.2 p.708*

Pulera, Dominic J.. . . . . *v.4 p.730*

Pulera, Dominic *v.6 p.470*

Pulido, Laura *v.6 p.108, p.116, p.124, p.525, p.551*

Pullman, Philip.. . . . . *v.2 p.373*

Pullum, Geoffrey K. & Ladusaw, William A.. . . . . *v.2 p.563*

Pulzer, Peter *v.3 p.60, p.160*

Punch, Maurice *v.4 p.690*

Puniello, Francoise S. & Rusak, Halina R.. . . . . *v.1 p.725*

Punja, Zamir K.. . . . . *v.5 p.46*

Puntila, L. A.. . . . . *v.3 p.236*

Purcell, Susan K.. . . . . *v.3 p.295*

Purcell-Gates, Victoria, et al. *v.4 p.304, p.354*

Purdie, Edna *v.2 p.601*

Purdy, Al *v.2 p.738*

Purdy, James *v.2 p.110, v.6 p.398*

Purdy, Laura M.. . . . . *v.6 p.444, p.461*

Puretz, Susan, et al. *v.4 p.801, p.802, p.880*

Purlevskii, Savva Dmitrievich *v.3 p.211*

Purpel, David E. & McLaurin, William M.. . . *v.4 p.306, p.307*

Purrington, Robert D.. . . . . *v.5 p.540*

Purseglove, J. W.. . . . . *v.5 p.23, p.33*

Pursell, Brennan C.. . . . . *v.3 p.188*

Purver, Margery *v.5 p.385*

Purves, Andrew *v.1 p.649*

Purvis, Alston W. & Le Coultre, Martijn F.. . . . . *v.1 p.718*

Purvis, Alston W.. . . . . *v.1 p.720*

Pusey, James R.. . . . . *v.6 p.191*

Pushkin, Alexander *v.2 p.807*

Pushkin, Alexandr & Brett, Simon *v.2 p.807*

Pushkin, Alexandr, et al.. . . . . *v.2 p.807*

Pushkin, Alexandr *v.2 p.807*

Putnam, Hilary (Editor), et al.. . . . . *v.5 p.471*

Putnam, Hilary *v.1 p.442, p.493, p.513, p.514*

Putnam, Lara *v.3 p.280*

Putnam, Linda L. & Jablin, Fredric M.. . . . . . *v.4 p.174*

Putnam, Michael C.. . . . . *v.2 p.426, p.445, p.446*

Putnam, Robert D., et al.. . . . . . . *v.3 p.204, v.4 p.719*

Putnam, Robert D.. . . . . *v.4 p.594, p.706*

Putnam, Samuel *v.2 p.692*

Puttaswamaiah, K.. . . . . *v.4 p.83*

Puttnam, David *v.6 p.345*

Pybus, Cassandra.. . . . . *v.6 p.11, p.37*

Pybus, D. & Sell, C.. . . . . *v.5 p.319*

Pye, K. & Allen, J. R. L. (Editors). *v.4 p.392*

Pye, Kenneth (Editor). *v.5 p.439*

Pykett, Lyn *v.2 p.281*

Pyle, Andrew *v.1 p.452*

Pyle, Christopher H.. . . . . *v.4 p.473*

Pym, Barbara *v.2 p.379*

Pynchon, Thomas *v.2 p.153*

Pyne, Hnin Hnin, et al.. . . . . *v.4 p.776*

Pyne, Stephen J., et al.. . . . . *v.5 p.31*

Pyne, Stephen J.. . . . . *v.5 p.31, v.6 p.284*

Pyron, Darden A. (Editor) *v.2 p.98*

Pyron, Darden Asbury *v.6 p.410*

Pyszczynski, Thomas A., et al. *v.5 p.632*

Pyysiainen, Ilkka & Anttonen, Veikko (Editors). . . . *v.5 p.635*

Q

Qaim, Matin, et al. *v.5 p.8*

Qian, Zhaoming (Editor) *v.2 p.112*

Qin, Duo *v.4 p.204*

Qing, Dai *v.4 p.620*

Qiu, Renzong *v.5 p.248*

Quade, Quentin *v.4 p.280*

Quaghebeur, Marc (Editor) *v.2 p.535*

Quah, Jon S.. . . . . *v.6 p.173*

Quain, Kevin *v.1 p.273, p.348*

Quam, Jean K. (Editor) *v.6 p.382*

Quammen, David *v.5 p.223, p.358, p.359, p.370*

Quandt, William B. *v.6 p.594, p.619, p.626, p.642*

Quantrill, Malcolm *v.1 p.794*

Quantz, Johann J. *v.1 p.398, p.402*

Quarles, Benjamin (Editor) *v.3 p.432*

Quarles, Benjamin . . . *v.3 p.400, p.410, p.421, p.426, p.432*

Quarles, Francis *v.2 p.256*

Quarles, Mike *v.6 p.314*

Quarteroni, Alfio & Valli, A. *v.5 p.488, p.492*

Quarteroni, Alfio, et al. *v.5 p.492*

Quaschning, Volker. *v.5 p.361*

Quasha, George (Text by). *v.1 p.773*

Quashie, Kevin Everod *v.6 p.45*

Quataert, Donald & Zurcher, Eric J. (Editors) . *v.6 p.591, p.622*

Quataert, Donald. *v.6 p.591*

Quatrano, Ralph (Editor) *v.5 p.136*

Quay, Herbert C. & Hogan, A. E. (Editors). *v.5 p.662*

Quayd, Muhammad Y.. . . . . *v.6 p.663*

Queen, Carol. *v.4 p.746, v.6 p.367*

Queen, J. Allen.. . . . . *v.4 p.288*

Queiros, Eca de *v.2 p.689*

Quelch, John A. & Deshpande, Rohit (Editors). . . . *v.4 p.73*

Queller, Donald E.. . . . . *v.3 p.63*

Queneau, Raymond. *v.2 p.525*

Quenot, Michael *v.1 p.570*

Quesada, Roberto *v.6 p.508*

Quesenberry, Peter J. (Editor), et al. *v.5 p.152*

Quesenberry, Peter J.. . . . . *v.5 p.151, p.152*

Quesnay, Francois *v.4 p.217*

Quevedo. *v.2 p.651*

Quick, James C. & Tetrick, Lois E. (Editors) *v.5 p.581*

Quick, James C., et al. *v.5 p.581*

Quicke, Donald L. J.. . . . . *v.5 p.170, p.195*

Quigley, Christine *v.4 p.15*

Quigley, Declan *v.4 p.723*

Quigley, Kevin F. F.. . . . . *v.4 p.585, p.640*

Quijano, Anibal *v.3 p.331*
Quillen, Rita *v.2 p.12*
Quiller-Couch, Arthur Thomas *v.2 p.569, p.575*
Quilligan, Edward J. & Zuspan, Frederick P. *v.5 p.524*
Quimby, George Irving *v.6 p.704*
Quin, Louis D. *v.5 p.296*
Quincy, John Jr. *v.1 p.823*
Quincy, Keith *v.6 p.171*
Quine, Willard V. . . *v.1 p.443, p.444, p.490, p.492, p.493, p.510*
Quinkert, Gerhard, et al. *v.5 p.293*
Quinn, D. B. & Ryan, A. N. *v.3 p.100, p.102*
Quinn, Daniel *v.6 p.287*
Quinn, David B. *v.3 p.404*
Quinn, Herbert F. *v.4 p.590*
Quinn, Jane Bryant *v.4 p.97*
Quinn, Jay (Editor) *v.2 p.27, v.6 p.407*
Quinn, John R. *v.1 p.576*
Quinn, Karen J. & Quinn, Kenneth P. *v.2 p.168*
Quinn, Kenneth *v.2 p.430, p.446*
Quinn, T. J. *v.5 p.560*
Quinonez, Naomi Helena *v.6 p.487, p.493*
Quint, David *v.2 p.649*
Quintana, Alvina E. *v.6 p.480, p.502, p.508, p.515*
Quintana, Leroy V. *v.6 p.502*
Quintilian *v.2 p.442*
Quirk, Charles E. (Editor) *v.4 p.786, p.885, p.901*
Quirk, James & Fort, Rodney D. *v.4 p.889, p.897*
Quirk, Randolph & Svartvik, Jan *v.2 p.553*
Quirk, Randolph, et al. *v.2 p.558*
Quirk, Randolph *v.2 p.558*
Quirk, Robert E. *v.3 p.295, p.312*
Quirk, William J. & Bridwell, R. Randall . . . *v.4 p.486, p.538*
Quiroga, Horacio *v.2 p.687*
Quiroz, Alfonso W. *v.3 p.331*
Quitslund, Jon A. *v.2 p.215*
Qureshi, Emran & Sells, Michael Anthony (Editors) . *v.4 p.661*
Qureshi, Mohsin (Editor) *v.5 p.309*
Qureshi, Regula B. *v.1 p.289*

R

R. S. Means Company Staff *v.1 p.784, v.5 p.686*
R Spitzer, Cary *v.5 p.718*
Raabe, Paul R. *v.1 p.623*
Raabe, W. *v.2 p.601*
Raabe, Wilhelm *v.2 p.601*
Raabe, William A., et al. *v.4 p.107*
Raad, Boele De & Perugini, Marco (Editors) *v.5 p.603*
Raaflaub, Kurt A. *v.3 p.18, p.25*
Raat, W. Dirk *v.3 p.391*
Rabaey, Jan M., et al. *v.5 p.722*
Rabasa, Jose *v.3 p.264*
Rabb, Theodore K. *v.3 p.71*
Rabban, David M. *v.4 p.459*
Rabe, David *v.2 p.153*

Rabe, Monica *v.4 p.168*
Rabearivelo, Jean-Joseph *v.2 p.543*
Rabelais, Francois *v.2 p.472*
Rabelais, François *v.2 p.472*
Rabiger, Michael *v.6 p.309, p.350*
Rabilloud, T. (Editor) *v.5 p.89, p.117*
Rabin, Albert I. *v.5 p.635*
Rabin, Yitzak *v.6 p.615*
Rabinbach, Anson *v.3 p.170, p.185*
Rabinovich, Itamar *v.4 p.650, v.6 p.606*
Rabinovich, Semyon *v.5 p.562*
Rabinovitz, Lauren *v.6 p.343*
Rabinow, Paul *v.5 p.219, v.6 p.643*
Rabinowicz, Tzvi M. (Editor) *v.1 p.547*
Rabinowitz, Alan *v.6 p.725*
Rabinowitz, Dan & Abu-Baker, Khawla *v.6 p.619*
Rabinowitz, Dan *v.6 p.615*
Rabinowitz, Nancy S. & Richlin, Amy (Editors) . . *v.2 p.399*
Rabinowitz, Nancy S. *v.2 p.412*
Rabinowitz, Paula *v.2 p.8*
Rabinyan, Dorit *v.6 p.651*
Rabkin, Rhoda P. *v.3 p.312*
Rable, George C. *v.3 p.400, v.4 p.521*
Raboteau, Albert J. *v.1 p.608*
Rabun, J. Stanley *v.1 p.824*
Raby, F. J. E. *v.2 p.449, v.6 p.566*
Raby, Frederick J. (Editor) *v.2 p.449*
Raby, Peter (Editor) . . . *v.1 p.60, p.92, p.103, v.2 p.321, p.377*
Rachels, James & Rachels, Stuart *v.1 p.485*
Rachlin, Howard *v.5 p.612*
Racine, Daniel L. *v.2 p.537*
Racine, Jean & Wilbur, Richard *v.2 p.477*
Racine, Jean *v.1 p.78, p.106, v.2 p.476, p.477*
Racine, Jean-Luc & Viramma, Josiane Racine *v.4 p.40*
Racine, Karen *v.3 p.359*
Racke, Kenneth D. *v.5 p.10*
Rackham, Oliver *v.6 p.575*
Rackin, Phyllis *v.2 p.234, p.235*
Racster, Olga *v.1 p.11*
Racy, A. J. *v.1 p.287*
Radak, Zsolt *v.4 p.875*
Radano, Ronald M. & Bohlman, Philip V.
(Editors) *v.1 p.282, p.377*
Radano, Ronald M. *v.1 p.222, p.263, p.282, p.314*
Radcliffe, Ann *v.2 p.303*
Radcliffe-Brown, A. R. & Forde, Daryll (Editors) . . *v.4 p.32*
Radcliffe-Brown, A. R. *v.4 p.24*
Radcliffe-Smith, A. *v.5 p.207*
Radden, Jennifer (Editor) *v.5 p.660*
Radding, Cynthia R. *v.3 p.269, p.287*
Rade, Lennart & Westergren, Bertil *v.5 p.461, p.500*
Radelet, Michael L., et al. *v.6 p.268*
Rademacher, Hans *v.5 p.477*
Raden, Adjeng K. & Geertz, Hildred *v.6 p.177*
Rader, Benjamin G. *v.4 p.809, p.818, p.851, p.902*

Rader, Debra & Sittig, Linda Harris *v.4 p.312, p.365*
Rader, Russell B. (Editor), et al.. . . . . *v.5 p.380*
Radford, Andrew. *v.2 p.558*
Radhakrishnan, S. *v.1 p.419*
Radice, Lisanne *v.4 p.606*
Radice, Mark A.. . . . . *v.1 p.232, p.404*
Radiguet, Raymond. *v.2 p.525*
Radin, Charles A. *v.5 p.498*
Radin, Paul A. *v.4 p.24*
Radin, Paul *v.6 p.704*
Radishchev, Alexander *v.2 p.807, v.3 p.216*
Radnoti, Miklos *v.2 p.786*
Rados, David L. *v.4 p.135*
Radosh, Ronald & Milton, Joyce *v.4 p.438*
Radosh, Ronald *v.3 p.454*
Radostits, O. M., et al. *v.5 p.56, p.57*
Radovich, Don *v.6 p.419*
Radwanski, George. *v.3 p.541*
Radway, Janice A.. . . . . *v.2 p.572, p.577*
Radzinowicz, Leon & Hood, Roger G.. . . . . . . *v.4 p.436*
Radzinowicz, Leon *v.4 p.752, v.6 p.250*
Radzinowicz, Mary A. *v.2 p.255*
Radzinsky, Edvard *v.3 p.219, p.220*
Rae, Catherine M. *v.2 p.132*
Rae, Charles B. *v.1 p.222, p.338*
Rae, Douglas W. *v.6 p.719*
Rae, Ian & Witzel, Morgen (Editors) *v.4 p.60*
Rae, John *v.4 p.219*
Rae, Kenneth *v.1 p.141*
Raeburn, Nicole C. *v.6 p.382*
Raeff, Marc *v.3 p.167, p.210, p.216*
Rafael, Vicente L. *v.6 p.180*
Rafalovich, Adam *v.4 p.319*
Raff, Rudolf A.. . . . . *v.5 p.200*
Raffaelli, Tiziano *v.4 p.228*
Raffan, James (Editor) *v.5 p.240*
Raffe, Walter George *v.1 p.4*
Raffles, Hugh *v.3 p.269*
Raffles, Stamford. *v.6 p.177*
Raffman, Diana *v.1 p.382*
Rafiee, Abdi *v.6 p.669*
Rafiquzzaman, M. *v.5 p.344, p.730*
Rafter, Nicole H. *v.6 p.254*
Raghavachari, Ramesh & Tan, Weihong . *v.5 p.104, p.117, p.146*
Raghavan, Valayamghat *v.5 p.161, p.210*
Raghavan, V.. . . . . *v.5 p.161*
Ragheb, J. Fiona *v.1 p.794*
Raghu Dorairaja Staff. *v.5 p.699*
Rago, Stephen A. & Stevens, W. Richard . . . *v.5 p.348, p.349*
Ragone, David V. *v.5 p.324, p.712*
Ragsdale, Cliff T.. . . . . *v.4 p.179*
Ragsdale, Hugh (Editor) *v.3 p.212*
Raheja, Gloria G.. . . . . *v.6 p.154*
Rahimieh, Nasrin. *v.6 p.672*
Rahm, Dianne *v.4 p.63, v.6 p.301*

Rahman, A. (Editor) *v.6 p.155*
Rahman, Anika & Toubia, Nahid *v.6 p.444*
Rahman, Fazlur *v.1 p.556, p.557, p.558*
Rahn, Jay *v.1 p.382*
Rahn, John *v.1 p.372*
Rahn, Perry H.. . . . . *v.5 p.422*
Rahnema, Ali (Editor) *v.1 p.557*
Rahner, Karl & O'Hara, William Joseph *v.1 p.572, p.642*
Rahner, Karl & Vorgrimler, Herbert *v.1 p.594*
Rahner, Karl, 1904-. *v.1 p.645*
Rahner, Karl *v.1 p.575, p.577, p.579, p.636*
Rahtz, Howard. *v.6 p.261, p.264*
Rahula, Walpola *v.1 p.565*
Rahv, Philip *v.2 p.569*
Raiffa, Howard, et al. *v.4 p.74*
Raiffa, Howard. *v.5 p.504*
Raimo, John W. (Editor) *v.3 p.377, p.406*
Raimond, Jean & Watson, Richard (Editors) . . . *v.2 p.172*
Rainbird, Sean *v.1 p.760*
Rainer, Yvonne *v.1 p.11*
Rainger, Ronald (Editor), et al. *v.5 p.80*
Rainsford, Peter & Bangs, David H. Jr.. . . . . *v.4 p.165*
Rainwater, Lee & Smeeding, Timothy M. *v.4 p.756*
Rainwater, Lee. *v.4 p.775, v.6 p.465, p.471*
Raitt, Jill, et al. *v.6 p.572*
Raizen, Esther *v.6 p.646*
Raizman, David *v.1 p.713*
Rajan, Balachandra. *v.2 p.165*
Rajan, Gita & Mohanram, Radhika (Editors) . . . *v.2 p.728*
Rajan, Gita & Sharma, Shailja. *v.6 p.137*
Rajan, S. D. *v.5 p.696*
Rakove, Jack N. *v.4 p.452*
Rakudzhiev, Rumen, et al. *v.2 p.774*
Raleigh, Walter & Rudick, Michael *v.2 p.215*
Ralls-Mcleod, Karen & Harvey, Graham (Editors). . . *v.1 p.284*
Ralph, Richard *v.1 p.22*
Ralston, Anthony (Editor), et al.. . . . . . *v.5 p.343, p.344*
Ramachandran, V. S. & Blakeslee, Sandra *v.5 p.617*
Ramachandran, V. S. *v.5 p.617*
Ramage, Janet *v.5 p.361*
Ramage, Nancy H. & Ramage, Andrew *v.1 p.670*
Ramakrishnan, S. Karthick *v.4 p.571*
Ramamurthy, Vaidhyanathan & Schanze, Kirk S.
(Editors) *v.5 p.278*
Ramamurti, K S *v.2 p.762*
Raman, M. & Sharma, S. *v.5 p.681*
Ramanathan, Ramu *v.4 p.204*
Ramanujan, A. K. (Editor, Translator) *v.6 p.152*
Ramazani, Jahan (Editor), et al. *v.2 p.200*
Ramazani, Nesta *v.1 p.11, p.17*
Ramazani, Rouhollah K. *v.6 p.632*
Rambert, Marie *v.1 p.11*
Rameau, Jean Philippe *v.1 p.372*
Ramen, Fred *v.4 p.380, v.6 p.685*
Ramet, Sabrina P. & Pavlakovic, Vjeran *v.3 p.248*

Ramet, Sabrina P. *v.3 p.247*

Ramirez, Arturo *v.6 p.515, p.524*

Ramirez, Bruno & Otis, Yves *v.4 p.571*

Ramirez de Arellano, Annette B. & Seipp, Conrad . *v.3 p.321*

Ramirez, Elizabeth C. *v.1 p.122, p.125, v.6 p.518*

Ramirez, J. David *v.6 p.21*

Ramirez, Susan E. *v.3 p.326*

Ramirez, Susan Elizabeth *v.3 p.326*

Ramljak, Suzanne *v.1 p.800*

Ramond, Pierre *v.1 p.809*

Ramos, Henry A. J. *v.6 p.541*

Ramos, Juanita (Compiled by). *v.6 p.496*

Ramos, Manuel *v.6 p.502*

Ramos-Garcia, Luis A. (Editor) *v.2 p.644*

Ramos-Garcia, Luis (Editor) *v.6 p.515, p.518*

Ramos-Zayas, Ana Y.. . . . . *v.6 p.539, p.550*

Rampal, Jang B. (Editor) *v.5 p.103*

Rampersad, Arnold *v.4 p.832, p.851, v.6 p.27*

Rampersand, Arnold *v.2 p.88, v.6 p.19, p.27*

Rampley, Matthew (Editor) *v.1 p.704*

Ramras-Rauch, Gila & Michman-Melkman, Joseph
(Editors) *v.6 p.651*

Ramsamy, Edward *v.4 p.260, p.268*

Ramsay, Allan *v.2 p.258*

Ramsay, Anne Fla (Editor) *v.4 p.603, p.638*

Ramsay, Burt *v.1 p.27*

Ramsay, John G. & Huber, Martin *v.5 p.441*

Ramsay, John G. & Lisle, Richard J.. . . . . . *v.5 p.441*

Ramsay, O. Bertrand *v.5 p.298*

Ramsay, William M. *v.1 p.615*

Ramsdell, Charles W.. . . . . *v.3 p.429*

Ramsden, Elsa *v.5 p.533*

Ramsden, Jeremy *v.5 p.98*

Ramsey, Boniface (Editor, Translator) *v.1 p.591, p.653*

Ramsey, Charles B. & Modarres, Mohammad . *v.5 p.709, p.740*

Ramsey, Charles George, et al. *v.1 p.785*

Ramsey, F. P. *v.1 p.446*

Ramsey, Guthrie P. *v.1 p.282*

Ramsey, Norman F.. . . . . *v.5 p.554*

Ramsey, Patricia G., et al.. . . . . *v.4 p.309*

Ramsey, S. Robert *v.6 p.207*

Ramusack, Barbara N. *v.6 p.161*

Rana, Fazale & Ross, Hugh *v.5 p.195*

Rand, Ayn *v.1 p.504, p.510, v.2 p.113*

Rand, Gary M. & Petrocelli, Sam R. (Editors) . . . *v.5 p.704*

Rand McNally Inc. Staff, et al. *v.4 p.380*

Randal, Jonathan C. *v.6 p.606*

Randal, Jonathan *v.4 p.661*

Randall, Ian & Hilborn, David. *v.1 p.568*

Randall, J. G. & Current, Richard Nelson . . . *v.3 p.400, p.426*

Randall, James G. & Donald, David Herbert . . . *v.3 p.432*

Randall, John H. 3rd.. . . . . *v.2 p.67*

Randall, Laura (Editor) *v.4 p.383, p.593*

Randall, Lisa. *v.5 p.541*

Randall, Richard S.. . . . . *v.4 p.451*

Randall, Ruth Painter *v.3 p.426*

Randall, Stephen J.. . . . . *v.3 p.391*

Randel, Don M. (Editor) *v.1 p.161*

Randel, Don Michael (Editor) *v.1 p.161*

Randolph, Theron G. & Moss, Ralph W.. . . . . . *v.5 p.365*

Randolph, Vance *v.2 p.21*

Random House Staff *v.1 p.117, p.137, p.141*

Ranft, Patricia *v.1 p.656*

Rangel-Ribeiro, Victor *v.2 p.765*

Ranger, T. O. & Kimambo, Isaria Ndelahiyosa *v.1 p.542, p.543*

Ranger, Terence *v.6 p.77*

Ranguy, Bismark & Staiano-Ross, Kathryn *v.3 p.297*

Rank, Otto. *v.5 p.635*

Ranki, Vera *v.3 p.60, p.86, p.186, p.187*

Rankin, Charles E. (Editor) *v.6 p.688*

Rankin, Sue *v.6 p.385*

Rankin, Susan R.. . . . . *v.6 p.386*

Ranney, Austin (Editor) *v.3 p.449*

Ranney, David *v.6 p.725*

Ranney, Victoria P. (Editor), et al. *v.1 p.816*

Ransford, Oliver. *v.6 p.74*

Ranshofen-Wertheimer, E. F. *v.4 p.632*

Ransom, John Crowe & Mazer, Ben *v.2 p.113*

Ranum, Orest A.. . . . . *v.3 p.146*

Rao, C. N. & Raveau, Bernard *v.5 p.309*

Rao, C. N. R.; Muller, A.; Cheetham, A. K. . . . *v.5 p.319*

Rao, M. A., et al. *v.5 p.5, p.35*

Rao, M. Govinda & Singh, Nirvikar *v.4 p.618*

Rao, Raja *v.2 p.765*

Rao, Velcheru Narayana & Shulman, David
(Editors) *v.6 p.147, p.148*

Rapaport, D. C. & Rapaport, Dennis. *v.5 p.551, p.552*

Raper, Julius R. (Editor), et al. *v.2 p.344*

Raphael, Chad *v.4 p.408*

Raphael, D. D., et al. *v.4 p.228*

Raphael, D. D.. . . . . *v.4 p.212, p.219*

Raphael, Lee. *v.6 p.374*

Rapley, Elizabeth. *v.3 p.147*

Rapley, Ralph & Harbron, Stuart (Editors) . . . *v.5 p.128*

Rapoport, Basil *v.5 p.106, p.200*

Rapoport, David C. & Weinberg, Leonard (Author,
Editors) *v.4 p.497*

Rapoport, Ron (Editor) *v.4 p.812, p.837*

Rapp, Rayna *v.4 p.47*

Rappaport, Joanne *v.3 p.358*

Rappaport, Julian & Seidman, Edward (Editors). *v.5 p.650, p.672*

Rappaport, Roy A. *v.1 p.530, v.4 p.30, p.37*

Rappaport, Theodore *v.5 p.726*

Rappe, Anthony K. & Casewit, Carla J. *v.5 p.276*

Rappoport, Zvi, (Comjpiler). *v.5 p.291*

Rapport, Nigel & Overing, Joanna *v.4 p.23*

Rasdall, Hastings. *v.1 p.507*

Rashdall, Hastings; Powicke, Frederick M;
Emden, A B *v.6 p.558, p.559*

Rashid, Ahmed. *v.6 p.634*

Rashid, Al M. *v.3 p.391*

Rashid, M. H. *v.5 p.724*

Rashid, Muhammad H. (Editor) *v.5 p.709*

Rashidi, Hooman H.; Buehler, Lukas K. *v.5 p.98*

Rashkin, Elissa J. *v.6 p.340*

Raskin, David (Editor) *v.5 p.593*

Raskin, Jamin B. *v.4 p.450*

Raskin, Jonah *v.2 p.79*

Rasmussen, David M. (Editor). *v.1 p.502*

Rasmussen, R. Kent *v.2 p.33*

Rasmussen, Randy *v.6 p.319*

Rasmussen, Tom & Spivey, Nigel J. (Editors) . *v.1 p.670, p.808*

Rasmussen, Wayne David *v.5 p.5*

Rasmusson, D. C. *v.5 p.23, p.25*

Rasnake, Roger N. *v.3 p.324, p.331*

Rasputin, Valentin *v.2 p.807, p.808, v.3 p.214*

Rassias, J. M. *v.5 p.487*

Rassool, Hussein. *v.5 p.512, p.522*

Rastall, Richard *v.1 p.372*

Ratay, Robert T. *v.5 p.686*

Ratcliff, Kathryn S.. . . . . *v.5 p.524*

Rath, Tom & Clifton, Donald O. *v.4 p.83*

Rathbone, Eliza E. & Shackelford, George M. . . . *v.1 p.729*

Rathbone, Richard. *v.6 p.70*

Rathburn, Elizabeth & Drummond, Siobhan
(Contribution by). *v.4 p.824, p.837, p.846*

Rathje, William & Murphy, Cullen *v.5 p.377, p.378*

Rathjen, Frederick *v.3 p.509*

Rathvon, Natalie *v.4 p.361*

Ratledge, Colin & Kristiansen, Bjorn (Editors) . . . *v.4 p.156*

Ratliff, William E. & Miranda, Roger *v.3 p.303*

Ratner, Julie (Editor), et al. *v.5 p.589*

Ratner, Julie (Editor) *v.5 p.588*

Ratner, Leonard G.. . . . . *v.1 p.191, p.202*

Ratner, Mark A. & Schatz, George C. *v.5 p.279*

Rattansi, Ali & Westwood, Sallie (Editors). *v.4 p.44*

Rattenbury, Ken *v.1 p.263, p.323*

Rattigan, Terence. *v.2 p.379*

Rauch, Alan *v.6 p.751*

Rauch, George V.. . . . . *v.3 p.276*

Rauch, Karen & Fessler, Jeff *v.6 p.358*

Rauchhaus, Robert W. (Editor) *v.4 p.639*

Raudzens, George *v.3 p.74*

Rauk, Arvi. *v.5 p.293*

Raun, Toivo U.. . . . . *v.3 p.256*

Raup, David M. *v.5 p.181*

Rausch, Jane M. *v.3 p.358*

Rauschenbusch, Walter *v.1 p.643*

Rauschkolb, Roy S. & Hornsby, Arthur G.. . . . . . *v.5 p.50*

Rauter, Amélia Pilar (Editor), et al. *v.5 p.219*

Ravel, Maurice *v.1 p.222, p.350*

Raven, John E.. . . . . *v.1 p.425*

Raven, Peter H. & Berg, Linda R.. . . . . *v.5 p.704*

Raven-Hansen, Peter (Editor) *v.4 p.532*

Raverat, Gwen. *v.6 p.762, p.765*

Ravetz, Joe, et al.. . . . . *v.4 p.395, v.6 p.721*

Ravikovitch, Dahlia *v.6 p.651*

Ravina, Mark *v.6 p.228*

Ravitch, Diane & Viteritti, Joseph P. (Editors) . . . *v.4 p.315*

Ravitch, Diane *v.4 p.328*

Ravitch, Frank S.. . . . . *v.4 p.450*

Ravve, A. *v.5 p.322*

Rawley, James A. & Behrend, Stephen D. *v.4 p.727*

Rawley, James A. *v.3 p.400, p.421, p.426*

Rawling, Eleanor M., et al. *v.4 p.378*

Rawlings, Hunter R. *v.2 p.421*

Rawlings, Marjorie Kinnan *v.2 p.113*

Rawlins, William K. *v.4 p.697, v.5 p.621*

Rawls, James J. & Bean, Walton. *v.3 p.531*

Rawls, John *v.1 p.501, v.4 p.511, p.514, p.625*

Rawls, Walton *v.1 p.718*

Rawski, Thomas G.. . . . . *v.6 p.191*

Rawson, Claude (Editor) *v.2 p.263*

Rawson, Claude *v.2 p.248*

Rawson, Elizabeth (Editor) *v.2 p.434*

Rawson, Elizabeth *v.3 p.191*

Rawson, Jessica (Editor) *v.4 p.9*

Rawson, Philip S. *v.1 p.692*

Ray, Arthur J. *v.6 p.685*

Ray, Benjamin C. *v.6 p.67*

Ray, Brian D. *v.4 p.296*

Ray, Larry (Editor) *v.4 p.196*

Ray, Nicholas *v.1 p.794*

Ray Ollie M.. *v.1 p.4*

Ray, Pradeep *v.4 p.60*

Ray, Richard. *v.4 p.829*

Ray, Robert H.. . . . . *v.2 p.252*

Ray, William B. *v.4 p.445*

Raychaudhuri, Soumya *v.5 p.106, p.142, p.146, p.341*

Raychaudhuri, Tapan *v.6 p.161*

Rayfield, Donald *v.2 p.808*

Raykov, Mariana *v.2 p.774*

Rayleigh, Strutt *v.5 p.567*

Raymo, Chet *v.5 p.405, p.406*

Raymond, Andre *v.6 p.57, p.635*

Raymond, Eric S. *v.5 p.342, p.343, p.348*

Raymond, Jack *v.1 p.171, p.253*

Raymond, James C. & Russell, I. Willis (Editors) . . . *v.2 p.553*

Raymond, Marcel *v.2 p.461*

Rayner, Jonathan.. . . . . *v.6 p.337*

Rayner-Canham, Marelene F. & Rayner-Canham, Geoffrey W.
(Author, Editors). *v.3 p.49*

Rayner-Canham, Marelene F. & Rayner-Canham,
Geoffrey W. *v.5 p.261, p.544*

Rayno, Don *v.1 p.263, p.368*

Rayor, Diane J. & Batstone, William W. (Editors). . . *v.2 p.426*

Rayor, Diane J. (Translator) *v.2 p.415*

Rayor, Diane. *v.2 p.419*

Razi, Najm A. *v.1 p.559*

Razin, Shmuel & Herrmann, Richard (Editors) *v.5 p.128*

Rea, Louis M. & Parker, Richard A. *v.4 p.691*

Read, Anthony & Fisher, David *v.3 p.226*

Read, Bendict (Editor) *v.1 p.781*

Read, Christopher (Editor) *v.3 p.226*

Read, Christopher *v.3 p.221*

Read, Colin *v.3 p.540*

Read, Donald *v.3 p.92, p.95, p.114, p.115, v.4 p.403*

Read, Gardner- *v.1 p.393, p.398*

Read, Herbert & Stangos, Nikos *v.1 p.665*

Read, Herbert E. *v.1 p.729, p.776, v.2 p.379*

Read, Herbert Edward (Introduction by) *v.2 p.379, p.575*

Read, Herbert Edward *v.4 p.345*

Read, Herbert *v.2 p.379*

Read, Jen'nan Ghazal. *v.4 p.763*

Read, Malcolm & Wade, Paul *v.4 p.825*

Read, Peter L. & Lewis, Stephen R.. . . . . *v.5 p.69*

Read, Stephen *v.1 p.493*

Reade, Charles *v.2 p.303*

Reader, Ian *v.1 p.541*

Reader, W. J. (William Joseph) . . . *v.3 p.115, p.131, v.6 p.744*

Reader's Digest Editors *v.5 p.212, p.239, p.526*

Reading, Harold G. (Editor) *v.5 p.438*

Ready, Milton *v.3 p.502*

Reagan, Leslie J.. . . . . *v.6 p.455, p.471*

Reagan, Nancy & Novak, William *v.3 p.478*

Reagan, Ronald *v.3 p.478*

Reagan, Timothy G. *v.4 p.313*

Reagin, Nancy Ruth. *v.3 p.54, p.160*

Reagon, Bernice Johnson (Editor). *v.6 p.30*

Reagon, Bernice Johnson. *v.6 p.30*

Real Academia Espanola Staff *v.2 p.637*

Reale, Giovanni *v.1 p.420*

Realuyo, Bino A. (Editor), et al. *v.6 p.92*

Ream, Walt & Field, Katharine G. *v.5 p.89, p.128*

Reamer, Frederic G. *v.4 p.758, v.6 p.252*

Reaney, Gilbert *v.1 p.178, p.338*

Reardon, B. P. (Editor) *v.2 p.405*

Reardon, Betty A. *v.6 p.442*

Reardon, Jenny *v.5 p.136, p.146*

Reason, James *v.5 p.588, p.609*

Reaves, Joseph A.. . . . . *v.4 p.819, p.834, p.844, p.851, p.899*

Reay, Barry (Editor). *v.3 p.102, p.104, p.105, p.129*

Reay, Barry *v.3 p.104, p.121*

Rebach, Howard M. & Bruhn, John G. (Editors) . . . *v.4 p.692*

Rebay, Luciano (Editor). *v.2 p.698*

Rebellato, Dan *v.2 p.189*

Rebenich, Stefan *v.1 p.613*

Reber, Arthur S. & Reber, Emily S. *v.5 p.594*

Rebert, Paula *v.6 p.487, p.535*

Rebolledo, Tey D. & Marquez, Maria T.
(Editors). *v.6 p.496, p.502, p.524*

Rebolledo, Tey D. & Rivero, Eliana S. (Editors). *v.6 p.496, p.502*

Rebolledo, Tey D. *v.6 p.480, p.502, p.515*

Rebolledo, Tey Diana *v.6 p.502, p.508, p.515*

Reboussin, Dan *v.2 p.752*

Rebreanu, Liviu *v.2 p.817*

Rechcigl, Jack E. & Rechcigl, Nancy A.. . . . . . . *v.5 p.10*

Rechtschaffen, Clifford & Gauna, Eileen P. *v.5 p.374*

Rechy, John *v.2 p.154, v.6 p.398, p.502*

Recinos, Adrian (Translator), et al.. . . . . *v.2 p.676*

Recinos, Adrian (Translator). *v.2 p.676*

Reck-Malleczewen, Freidrich *v.3 p.173*

Record, Jeffrey *v.4 p.561, v.6 p.604*

Recording Industry Association of
America *v.1 p.172, p.173, p.385*

Rector, John L.. . . . . *v.3 p.350*

Rector, Liam (Editor) *v.2 p.82*

Rector, Monica. *v.2 p.692*

Reddaway, Darlene & Pruul, Kajar (Editors) *v.2 p.781*

Reddaway, Peter *v.4 p.582, p.598*

Redden, John D. *v.4 p.345*

Reddick, John *v.2 p.608, p.609*

Reddington, Frances P. & Kreisel, Betsy W. . . *v.6 p.252, p.259*

Reddington, Martin, et al. *v.4 p.76*

Reddock, Rhoda E., ed *v.3 p.297*

Reddock, Rhoda *v.6 p.442, p.458*

Reddy, K. Ramesh *v.5 p.177*

Reddy, William M. *v.3 p.153*

Reder, Michael R. (Editor) *v.2 p.766*

Redfern, Ron *v.5 p.432, p.445*

Redfield, Robert. *v.4 p.24*

Redford, Bruce (Editor). *v.2 p.251*

Redford, Bruce. *v.2 p.256*

Redford, Donald B. (Editor) *v.1 p.543, v.3 p.9, p.10*

Redford, Donald B. *v.3 p.7, p.9, v.6 p.57*

Redgrave, Michael *v.1 p.145*

Redgrave, Richard & Redgrave, Samuel *v.1 p.733*

Redhouse, Sir James *v.6 p.666*

Redish, Edward F. *v.5 p.564*

Redish, Martin H. *v.4 p.525*

Redlich, Josef *v.3 p.184*

Redman, Eric *v.4 p.461*

Redmond, Sean (Editor) *v.6 p.319*

Redonnet, Marie *v.2 p.519, p.533*

Redwood, David *v.4 p.379, p.381*

Reece, Richard J.. . . . . *v.5 p.136*

Reed, Adolph Jr. *v.4 p.484*

Reed, Eli *v.1 p.768*

Reed, Francis *v.1 p.141, p.149*

Reed, Graham *v.5 p.605*

Reed, Ishmael *v.2 p.154, v.6 p.27*

Reed, Jeffrey H. *v.5 p.727*

Reed, John & Wake, Clive (Editors) *v.2 p.542*

Reed, John Calvin et. al. *v.5 p.432*

Reed, John R. *v.2 p.176, p.193, p.319, v.6 p.753, p.762*

Reed, John *v.1 p.202, p.236, p.354, v.3 p.221*

Reed, Maxine K. & Reed, Robert M. *v.6 p.347*

Reed, Nelson A. *v.3 p.289*

Reed, Peter *v.1 p.814*

Reed, Ronald F. *v.4 p.323, p.340*

Reed, Roy *v.3 p.511*

Reed, Sue W.; Wallace, Richard *v.1 p.754*

Reed, T. J. *v.2 p.613*

Reed, T.V. *v.4 p.710*

Reed, Walt. *v.1 p.716*

Reed-Danahay, Deborah *v.4 p.29*

Reeder, Linda *v.3 p.202*

Rees, Amanda *v.3 p.519*

Rees, Dai & Rose, Steven (Editors) *v.5 p.617*

Rees, David W. E. *v.4 p.421*

Rees, Ennis *v.2 p.217*

Rees, Helen *v.1 p.289*

Rees, James *v.1 p.141, p.145*

Rees, Joan *v.2 p.218*

Rees, Margaret A. *v.2 p.498*

Rees, Martin J.. . . . . *v.5 p.541*

Rees, Martin. *v.4 p.661, p.667*

Reese, Anne C. & Vallera-Rickerson, Irini . . . *v.4 p.809, p.838*

Reese, Charles D. *v.5 p.686*

Reese, Gustave. *v.1 p.174, p.181, v.6 p.567*

Reese, William J.. . . . . *v.4 p.328*

Reese, Willy Peter *v.3 p.175*

Reesman, Jeanne Campbell. *v.2 p.96*

Reeve, Andrew & Ware, Alan *v.4 p.577*

Reeve, C. D.. . . . . *v.1 p.423, p.427, v.4 p.489*

Reeve, Clara & Watt, James. *v.2 p.258*

Reeve, Clara. *v.2 p.258*

Reeve, Fiona (Editor), et al.. . . . . *v.4 p.320*

Reeves, Douglas B. *v.4 p.65*

Reeves, Marjorie *v.3 p.62*

Reeves, Miriam G. *v.3 p.507*

Reeves, Richard *v.3 p.478*

Reeves, Robert *v.5 p.65*

Reeves, Scott D. *v.1 p.403*

Reeves, Thomas C. (Editor) *v.3 p.478*

Reeves, Thomas C.. . . . . *v.3 p.438, p.462*

Reeves, William D.. . . . . *v.3 p.507*

Reeves-Ellington, Richard H. & Anderson, Adele . . . *v.4 p.145*

Referee Magazine Staff & National Association of Sports
Officials Staff. *v.4 p.905*

Regalado, Samuel O. *v.4 p.809, p.834, p.851, p.897*

Regan, Donald T.. . . . . *v.4 p.529*

Regan, John *v.3 p.139*

Regan, Stephan (Editor) *v.2 p.176, p.193*

Regev, Motti & Seroussi, Edwin *v.1 p.300*

Rüegg, Walter (Editor) *v.4 p.329*

Regier, C. C.. . . . . *v.3 p.444*

Regier, Cornelius C. *v.3 p.449*

Regier, Willis Goth (Introduction by). *v.6 p.698*

Reguer, Sara *v.6 p.598*

Rehabilitation Research and Training Center, University of
South Florida. *v.5 p.667*

Rehfeld, Andrew *v.4 p.576*

Rehfeldt, Phillip *v.1 p.393, p.398*

Rehg, James A. *v.5 p.712*

Rehm, Hubert *v.5 p.118*

Rehm, Rush *v.1 p.71, p.137*

Rehm, S. & Espig, G. *v.5 p.25, p.26*

Rehman, Javaid *v.4 p.661*

Rehnquist, William H. *v.4 p.456, p.466*

Rehrig, William H.. . . . . *v.1 p.161*

Reich, Bernard & Goldberg, David H. *v.6 p.615*

Reich, Bernard & Kieval, Gershon R. (Editors) *v.4 p.615*

Reich, Bernard & Kieval, Gershon R. *v.6 p.615*

Reich, Bernard. *v.4 p.615, v.6 p.594, p.608*

Reich, Hans J. & Rigby, James H. (Editors) *v.5 p.291*

Reich, Nancy B. *v.1 p.202, p.354*

Reich, Peter L.. . . . . *v.3 p.295*

Reich, Steve. *v.1 p.222, p.350*

Reich, Walter (Editor) *v.4 p.661*

Reichenbach, Hans . . . *v.1 p.417, p.482, p.500, v.5 p.400, p.403*

Reichert, Tom *v.4 p.426*

Reichheld, Frederick F. *v.4 p.143*

Reichl, Alexander J. *v.6 p.726*

Reichl, Linda E. *v.5 p.559*

Reichley, A. James *v.3 p.478*

Reichmann, Rebecca L.. . . . . *v.3 p.342*

Reid, Alastair J. *v.3 p.115, p.131, v.4 p.128*

Reid, Anthony *v.6 p.165, p.177*

Reid, Bill *v.6 p.679*

Reid, Constance *v.5 p.467*

Reid, Cornelius L. *v.1 p.161, p.396*

Reid, Daniel G. (Editor), et al.. . . . . *v.1 p.606*

Reid, Daniel *v.4 p.793*

Reid, David A. & Plank, Richard E. (Editors). . . . *v.4 p.136*

Reid, David *v.2 p.182*

Reid, Donna K. *v.1 p.701*

Reid, Francis *v.1 p.139, p.147*

Reid, J. K. (Editor) *v.1 p.589*

Reid, John & Tobias, Andrew *v.6 p.403*

Reid, John P. *v.4 p.452, p.456*

Reid, Joyce M. (Editor). *v.2 p.456*

Reid, Margaret *v.2 p.9*

Reid, Mark A.. . . . . *v.6 p.330, p.343*

Reid, Miles *v.5 p.474, p.497*

Reid, Randall *v.2 p.131*

Reid, Richard J.. . . . . *v.4 p.582, p.612, v.6 p.67*

Reid, Robin Anne *v.2 p.63*

Reid, Ronald F. & Klumpp, James F. (Editors) *v.2 p.28*

Reid, T. R.. . . . . *v.4 p.638*

Reid, Thomas *v.1 p.450*

Reid, William J. *v.4 p.758*

Reid-Pharr, Robert F.. . . . . *v.6 p.27, p.40, p.367*

Reif, Frederick *v.5 p.559*

Reigstad, Paul *v.2 p.629*

Reilly, Bernard F. (Author, Preface by). *v.3 p.238*

Reilly, Bernard F. *v.3 p.65, p.66, p.238*

Reilly, C. N. (Editor) *v.5 p.268*

Reilly, Charlie (Editor) *v.2 p.142*

Reilly, John M. (Editor). *v.2 p.138*
Reilly, Mary (Editor) *v.4 p.358*
Reilly, Philip R. *v.5 p.80, p.123, p.151*
Reilly, Tom & Williams, Mark (Editors) . *v.4 p.868, p.872, p.880*
Rein, Monica *v.3 p.349*
Rein, Raanan *v.3 p.242*
Reinarman, Craig & Levine, Harry G. *v.4 p.777*
Reindl, Sheila M.. . . . . *v.5 p.524*
Reineck, H. E. & Singh, I. B.. . . . . *v.5 p.438, p.439*
Reinelt, Janelle G. and Joseph R. Roach *v.1 p.56, p.139*
Reinerman, Alan J. *v.3 p.182*
Reinert, Kenneth A. *v.4 p.196*
Reingold, Nathan & Reingold, Ida H. (Editors) . . . *v.5 p.394*
Reingold, Nathan (Editor) . . . *v.5 p.385, p.386, p.389, p.394*
Reinhard, Thilo (Editor) *v.1 p.202, p.236, p.355, p.412*
Reinhardt, Karl. *v.2 p.419*
Reinhart, Robert C.. . . . . *v.6 p.412*
Reinharz, Jehuda & Mendes-Flohr, Paul R.
  (Editors). *v.1 p.548, v.3 p.60*
Reinharz, Shulamit & Davidman, Lynn . . *v.4 p.688, v.6 p.426*
Reinharz, Shulamit *v.4 p.688*
Reis, Harry T. & Judd, Charles M. (Editors) *v.5 p.646*
Reis, Joao Jose *v.3 p.265, p.342*
Reis, João José *v.3 p.280, p.337*
Reisberg, Daniel & Hertel, Paula (Editors) *v.5 p.610*
Reisch, Michael & Andrews, Janice *v.4 p.758*
Reischauer, August Karl *v.1 p.562*
Reischauer, Edwin O. (Translator) *v.6 p.185*
Reischauer, Edwin O. *v.6 p.185, p.216, p.218, p.220*
Reischauer, Haru M. *v.6 p.228*
Reisman, Sorel (Editor), et al.. . . . . *v.4 p.322*
Reiss, Alvin H. *v.1 p.825, p.826*
Reiss, Mitchell *v.4 p.656*
Reiss, Timothy J. (Editor). *v.2 p.768*
Reisz, Karl & Millar, Gavin. *v.6 p.350*
Reitz, Caroline *v.2 p.191*
Reitz, Elizabeth J. & Wing, Elizabeth S. *v.4 p.7*
Reitz, John R., et al. *v.5 p.565*
Rejda, George E.. . . . . *v.4 p.163*
Rejwan, Nissim *v.6 p.598, p.603, p.611, p.615*
Reksten, Linda E. *v.4 p.352*
Relethford, John H.. . . . . *v.5 p.201*
Relihan, Joel C. *v.2 p.427, p.428*
Remak, Joachim *v.3 p.245*
Remarque, Erich Maria *v.2 p.614, p.618*
Rembar, Charles, et al.. . . . . *v.4 p.472, p.473*
Remedi, Fernando J. *v.3 p.272*
Remedi, Gustavo *v.3 p.267*
Remington, Jack S., et al.. . . . . *v.5 p.533*
Remington, Thomas F. *v.4 p.598*
Remini, Robert V. *v.3 p.417, p.418*
Remmer, Karen L.. . . . . *v.3 p.276, p.349, p.354*
Remnick, David *v.2 p.584, v.3 p.228, v.4 p.833, p.856*
Remy, H. *v.5 p.303*
Renard, Jules *v.2 p.525*

Renaud, Michelle L. *v.6 p.471*
Renault, Mary *v.6 p.398*
Renaut, R. W. & Last, W. M. (Editors) *v.5 p.438*
Rencher, Alvin C. *v.5 p.483*
Renda, Mary A. *v.3 p.315*
Rendall, Jonathan *v.4 p.856*
Rendall, Steven (Editor, Translator) *v.2 p.474, p.475*
Rendell, Ruth *v.2 p.379*
Render, Barry, et al. *v.4 p.119*
Render, Sylvia L. (Editor) *v.2 p.32*
Renford, Raymond K. *v.6 p.150*
Renfrew, Colin & Bahn, Paul G. (Editors) *v.4 p.6*
Renfrew, Colin & Bahn, Paul *v.4 p.5*
Rengel, Zdenko (Editor) *v.5 p.23*
Renninger, K. Ann & Shumar, Wesley (Editors). . . . *v.4 p.762*
Renninger, K. Ann & Shumar, Wesley *v.4 p.762*
Reno, William *v.4 p.612, v.6 p.73*
Renold, Emma *v.4 p.748*
Renouard, Yves & Bethell, Denis *v.1 p.574*
Renov, Michael (Editor) *v.6 p.310*
Renov, Michael *v.6 p.310*
Rensch, Roslyn *v.1 p.391*
Renshaw, Eric *v.5 p.170*
Renshaw, Geoff & Ireland, Norman J. *v.4 p.204*
Renshaw, John *v.3 p.344*
Renshon, Stanley A. & Duckitt, John (Editors) *v.5 p.644*
Renshon, Stanley A. *v.3 p.478, v.5 p.644*
Renstrom, P. A. (Editor) *v.4 p.827*
Renstrom, Peter G. *v.4 p.437*
Renwick, W. L. *v.2 p.167*
Renzetti, Claire M. & Miley, Charles H. (Editors). . . *v.6 p.377*
Renzetti, Claire M. *v.6 p.377*
Renzulli, Joseph S., et al. *v.5 p.576*
Repa, Barbara Kate. *v.4 p.131*
Repetto, Robert C. & Gillis, Malcolm (Editors) . . . *v.5 p.39*
Repetto, Robert C.. . . . . *v.5 p.39*
Repic, Oljan *v.5 p.330*
Reporters Without Borders Staff (Editor) *v.6 p.619*
Repp, Kevin *v.3 p.169*
Reppetto, Thomas A.. . . . . *v.6 p.251*
Republican National Committee *v.4 p.553*
Rescher, Nicholas. *v.1 p.459, p.460, p.482, p.492,*
                          p.501, p.513, v.5 p.404
Research and Education Association Staff *v.4 p.440*
Reséndez, Andrés *v.6 p.534*
Resh, Vincent H. & Cardé, Ring T. (Editors) . . . *v.5 p.27, p.28*
Reskin, Barbara F. & Hartmann, Heidi I. *v.4 p.254*
Reskin, Barbara F. & Roos, Patricia A.. . . . . . . *v.4 p.725*
Resnick, Philip. *v.3 p.547*
Resnick, Robert E. *v.5 p.564*
Resnick, Seymour & Pasmantier, Jeanne *v.2 p.645*
Resnik, David B. *v.5 p.136*
Resource Discovery Network *v.5 p.343, p.344*
Restall, Matthew *v.3 p.287*
Restivo, Sal P. *v.4 p.678*

Reti, Rudolph *v.1 p.372*

Rettig, Michael D. & Canady, Robert Lynn *v.4 p.288*

Reuben, Julie A. *v.4 p.332*

Reuque Paillalef, Rosa Isolde *v.3 p.354*

Reuvid, Jonathan & Hinks, John *v.4 p.113*

Reuvid, Jonathan *v.4 p.171*

Revard, Carter C.. . . . . *v.6 p.699*

Revard, Carter *v.6 p.699*

Revard, Stella P. *v.2 p.255*

Revel, Jacques & Naddabb, Ramona (Editors) *v.3 p.157*

Revelle, William, Director *v.5 p.603*

Revenson, Tracey A., et al. *v.5 p.668*

Reverby, Susan M. (Editor) *v.6 p.8*

Reverdy, Pierre. *v.2 p.525*

Revie, R. Winston & Uhlig, Herbert Henry (Editors) . *v.5 p.690*

Rewald, John, et al. *v.1 p.745*

Rewald, John *v.1 p.745, p.781*

Rexer, Lyle *v.1 p.768*

Rexroat, Cynthia *v.6 p.20, p.40*

Rexroth, Kenneth & Ling Chung (Translators) *v.6 p.210*

Rexroth, Kenneth. *v.2 p.114, p.115*

Rey, H. A. *v.5 p.70*

Rey, Terry *v.3 p.315*

Reydon, Thomas A. C. & Hemerik, Lia (Editors) . . . *v.5 p.114*

Reyerson, Kathryn L. & Drendel, J. (Editors) *v.3 p.142*

Reyes, Adelaida *v.1 p.279, p.297, v.6 p.89, p.141*

Reyes, Alfonso (Editor, Prologue by). *v.2 p.669*

Reyes, Angelita Dianne *v.6 p.480*

Reyes, David & Waldman, Tom *v.6 p.519*

Reyes, Luis & Rubie, Peter (Editors) *v.6 p.490, p.493*

Reyes Mateo, C. (Editor), et al. *v.5 p.118*

Reyes, Rogelio. *v.2 p.645*

Reyhner, Jon Allan & Eder, Jeanne Oyawin . *v.4 p.312, v.6 p.680*

Reyhner, Jon Allan *v.6 p.691*

Reymundo, Ana Cristina & Cruz, Celia *v.1 p.294, p.319*

Reyna, Stephen P. *v.4 p.27*

Reynolds, Andrew *v.2 p.794*

Reynolds, Arthur J.. . . . . *v.4 p.316*

Reynolds, Barbara (Editor) *v.2 p.699*

Reynolds, Barbara *v.2 p.705*

Reynolds, C. S. & O'Sullivan, P. (Editors) *v.5 p.174*

Reynolds, Cecil R. & Fletcher-Janzen, Elaine (Editors). *v.4 p.316*

Reynolds, Cecil R. & Fletcher-Janzen, Elaine. *v.4 p.316, v.5 p.572*

Reynolds, Cecil R. & Gutkin, Terry B.
(Editors) *v.4 p.358, v.5 p.577*

Reynolds, Cecil R. & Kamphaus, Randy W. (Editors) . *v.5 p.602*

Reynolds, Craig J. (Author, Translator). *v.6 p.171*

Reynolds, David S. *v.2 p.9, p.54*

Reynolds, Douglas R.. . . . . *v.6 p.188*

Reynolds, E. Bruce *v.6 p.171, p.172, p.181*

Reynolds, Leighton D. & Wilson, N. G. *v.2 p.399*

Reynolds, Leighton D. (Editor) *v.2 p.425*

Reynolds, Michael S. *v.2 p.85*

Reynolds, Nancy & McCormick, Malcolm *v.1 p.5*

Reynolds, Nancy *v.1 p.24*

Reynolds, Nicholas E. *v.3 p.305*

Reynolds, Philip L.. . . . . *v.1 p.657*

Reynolds Roger *v.1 p.222*

Reynolds, Simon & Press, Joy. *v.6 p.475*

Reynolds, Simon *v.1 p.273*

Reynolds, Susan *v.3 p.68, v.6 p.577*

Reynolds, Suzanne *v.2 p.449*

Reynolds, Verne *v.1 p.391, p.398*

Reynolds, William & Trembley, Elizabeth (Editors) . . *v.6 p.326*

Rezulli, Joseph S. & Reis, Sally M. *v.5 p.573*

Rezun, Miron *v.3 p.45, p.208, p.209*

Réage, Pauline; Paulhan, Jean *v.2 p.533*

Réage, Pauline *v.2 p.533*

Rédei, George P. *v.5 p.96, p.104, p.106, p.146*

Röhl, John C. G.. . . . . *v.3 p.164*

Rheda, Regina *v.2 p.692*

Rheingold, Howard *v.4 p.712, v.5 p.408*

Rhine, Stanley *v.4 p.15*

Rhines, Jesse A. *v.6 p.330*

Rhoades, Everett R. *v.6 p.702*

Rhoads, Edward J. M. *v.4 p.623, v.6 p.191*

Rhoads, Edward J. *v.6 p.188*

Rhoads, Robert A. *v.4 p.398*

Rhoden, Nancy L. *v.1 p.582*

Rhodes, Frank Harold Trevor *v.4 p.332*

Rhodes, Gale *v.5 p.328*

Rhodes, James Ford *v.3 p.400*

Rhodes, Jane *v.6 p.431, p.435, p.448, p.455*

Rhodes, John A. & Allman, Elizabeth S. *v.5 p.91, p.94*

Rhodes, Lisa L. *v.1 p.379*

Rhodes, P. J. & Osborne, Robin (Editor, Translators) . . *v.3 p.20*

Rhodes, P. J. (Author, Editor). *v.3 p.19*

Rhodes, P. J. *v.3 p.19, v.4 p.489*

Rhodes, Richard *v.1 p.745, v.3 p.506*

Rhodes, Sybil *v.3 p.355*

Rhys, Jean & Bronte, Charlotte *v.2 p.769*

Rhys, Jean. *v.2 p.769*

Riall, Lucy *v.3 p.201*

Riasanovsky, Nicholas Valentine & Steinberg, Mark D.. *v.3 p.209*

Riasanovsky, Nicholas V. *v.3 p.218*

Ribeiro, Darcy & Rabassa, Gregory *v.3 p.342*

Ribeyro, Julio Ramon. *v.2 p.685*

Ribéreau-Gayon, Pascal (Editor), et al. *v.5 p.53*

Ribner, Neil G. (Editor). *v.5 p.593*

Ribowsky, Mark *v.1 p.273, v.4 p.809, p.833, p.852*

Ricard, Francois *v.2 p.539*

Ricard, Robert *v.1 p.574*

Ricardo, David & Dobb, M. H. *v.4 p.221*

Ricardo, David & McCulloch, J. R. *v.4 p.221*

Ricardo, David, et al.. . . . . *v.4 p.221*

Ricardo, David *v.4 p.220, p.221*

Ricci, Franco (Editor). *v.2 p.715*

Ricci, Nino *v.2 p.738*

Riccucci, Norma M. *v.4 p.525, p.546*

Rice, Anthony *v.3 p.322, v.5 p.223, p.230*
Rice, David G. & Stambaugh, John E. *v.1 p.533*
Rice, David Talbot *v.1 p.672*
Rice, Donald E. *v.3 p.312*
Rice, Eugene F. Jr. *v.1 p.602*
Rice, Frank A. & Said, Majed F.. . . . . . . *v.6 p.654*
Rice, Howard C. *v.3 p.413*
Rice, Marcelle Smith *v.2 p.113*
Rice, Mitchell F. *v.4 p.545, p.580*
Rice, Otis K. & Brown, Stephen W. *v.3 p.501*
Rice, Prudence M. *v.1 p.808*
Rice, Richard, et al. *v.3 p.531*
Rice, Tamara T. *v.3 p.193*
Rice, Tim *v.1 p.253, p.337, p.409*
Rice, Timothy & Wade, Bonnie C. *v.1 p.298*
Rice, Timothy *v.1 p.298*
Rice-Evans, Catherine A. & Halliwell, B.. . . . *v.5 p.163*
Rich, Adrienne Cecile. *v.2 p.115*
Rich, Adrienne . . . *v.2 p.115, v.4 p.737, v.6 p.405, p.465, p.467*
Rich, E. E. & Wilson, C. H. (Editors) *v.3 p.42*
Rich, E. E. (Editor), et al. *v.3 p.42*
Rich, Jason R.. . . . . *v.4 p.67*
Rich, Nathaniel *v.6 p.730*
Rich, Norman M.. . . . . *v.3 p.219*
Rich, Wilbur (Editor) *v.4 p.881, p.885, p.889, p.892*
Richani, Nazih *v.4 p.616*
Richard, Alfred C. Jr.. . . . . *v.6 p.330*
Richard, Alfred. *v.3 p.391*
Richard Bett (Editor) *v.1 p.517*
Richard, Carl J. *v.3 p.369*
Richard, David A. *v.3 p.212*
Richard III, Golden, et al.. . . . . *v.4 p.114*
Richard, Jean *v.3 p.143*
Richard, Jean-Pierre *v.2 p.459*
Richard, Mark (Editor) *v.1 p.490*
Richard, Nelly *v.3 p.355*
Richard, Suzanne (Editor) *v.3 p.4*
Richard-Allerdyce, Diane *v.2 p.105*
Richards, Andrew J. *v.4 p.128*
Richards, Annette *v.1 p.191*
Richards, Audrey I. *v.4 p.46*
Richards, David Adams *v.2 p.738*
Richards, David G. *v.2 p.597*
Richards, David *v.4 p.454*
Richards, Dick *v.1 p.808*
Richards, Gary *v.2 p.14*
Richards, Glyn *v.1 p.475*
Richards, I. A. *v.2 p.569*
Richards, Jack C., et al.. . . . . *v.4 p.423*
Richards, Jeffrey *v.1 p.574*
Richards, John A. & Jia, Xiuping *v.4 p.389*
Richards, John F. (Author, Contribution by) *v.6 p.156*
Richards, John H.; Hendrickson, James B. *v.5 p.330*
Richards, Keith *v.5 p.427*
Richards, Larry *v.6 p.330, p.343*

Richards, Leonard L. *v.3 p.488*
Richards, Michael *v.3 p.242*
Richards, P. Scott & Bergin, Allen E. (Editors) *v.5 p.635*
Richards, Pamela, et al.. . . . . *v.4 p.753*
Richards, Pamela S. *v.3 p.81*
Richards, Paul. *v.4 p.34*
Richards, Stanley *v.1 p.253, p.409*
Richards, Tazz (Editor). *v.1 p.17*
Richards, Thomas. *v.1 p.110, p.145, p.153, v.6 p.745, p.762, p.764*
Richardson, Alan & Bowden, John (Editors) *v.1 p.594*
Richardson, Bob *v.5 p.230*
Richardson, Bonham C.. . . . . *v.3 p.305*
Richardson, Brian W.. . . . . *v.4 p.379*
Richardson, Cyril C. *v.1 p.591*
Richardson, F. M. *v.5 p.584*
Richardson, Glenn W. Jr.. . . . . *v.4 p.548*
Richardson, Henry Handel *v.2 p.748*
Richardson, James. *v.2 p.304, p.313, p.327*
Richardson, Joanna *v.2 p.494*
Richardson, John E. *v.4 p.53*
Richardson, John. *v.2 p.733*
Richardson, Louise *v.3 p.391*
Richardson, Margaret & Stevens, Mary Anne (Editors). *v.1 p.794*
Richardson, Michael D., et al.. . . . . . *v.4 p.280, p.282*
Richardson, Michael *v.1 p.457*
Richardson, Nathan E. *v.2 p.641, v.6 p.339*
Richardson, R. C.. . . . . *v.3 p.88, p.104, p.121*
Richardson, Rupert Norval, et al. *v.3 p.509*
Richardson, Ruth. *v.3 p.115, p.124*
Richardson, Samuel & Fielding, Henry. *v.2 p.258*
Richardson, Samuel & Sherburn, George *v.2 p.259*
Richardson, Samuel *v.2 p.258, p.259*
Richardson, Tim (Editor) *v.1 p.816*
Richardson, Virginia (Editor) *v.4 p.355*
Richardson, W. J.. . . . . *v.1 p.471*
Richardson, Willis *v.2 p.25*
Riche, Martha Farnsworth (Editor) *v.4 p.179*
Riche, Pierre *v.3 p.143, p.162, v.6 p.557, p.559*
Richerson, Peter J. & Boyd, Robert *v.4 p.15*
Riches, John *v.1 p.615*
Richetti, John (Editor) *v.2 p.170, p.172, p.192*
Richetti, John J., et al. *v.2 p.189*
Richetti, John J. *v.2 p.246*
Richey, Russell E. (Editor), et al. *v.1 p.586*
Richie, Alexandra *v.3 p.181*
Richie, Donald. *v.6 p.228, p.336*
Richler, Mordecai *v.2 p.738*
Richman, David *v.2 p.231*
Richman, Karen E. *v.4 p.41*
Richman, Paula *v.6 p.152*
Richmond, Colin. *v.6 p.576, p.577*
Richmond, Hugh Macrae. *v.1 p.60, p.76, p.103, p.137*
Richmond, Mary E.. . . . . *v.4 p.758*
Richter, Conrad *v.2 p.113*

Richter, Daniel K. *v.6 p.686*

Richter, Gerhard *v.1 p.745*

Richter, Hans *v.1 p.680*

Richter, Judith *v.4 p.145*

Richter, Linda & Morrell, Robert (Editors) *v.4 p.734*

Richter, Michael *v.3 p.137*

Rickard, Peter *v.2 p.454*

Rickards, Guy *v.1 p.222, p.357*

Rickards, Maurice *v.1 p.798*

Ricke, Helmut & Schmitt, Eva *v.1 p.811*

Ricke, Helmut *v.1 p.811*

Rickerl, Diane & Francis, Charles (Editors) *v.5 p.11*

Ricketts, Harry *v.2 p.297*

Ricketts, Martin *v.4 p.224, p.248*

Ricketts, Taylor H., et al. *v.5 p.169, p.185, p.235*

Rickitt, Richard *v.6 p.352*

Ricklefs, M. C. *v.6 p.177*

Ricklefs, M.C. *v.6 p.177*

Ricklefs, Merle C. *v.6 p.177*

Rickman, Cheryl D. *v.4 p.88*

Rickman, Gregg *v.6 p.319*

Ricks, Christopher (Editor) *v.2 p.197, p.201, p.291*

Ricks, Christopher . . . *v.2 p.180, p.181, p.201, p.255, p.313*

Ricks, David & Bertola, Giuseppe *v.4 p.70*

Rickwood, David & Hames, B. D. (Editors) *v.5 p.123*

Rico, Francisco *v.2 p.641*

Ricoeur, Paul *v.1 p.457, p.491, p.507, p.644, v.2 p.572*

Ricourt, Milagros & Danta, Ruby *v.6 p.545, p.550*

Ricourt, Milagros *v.6 p.544, p.550*

Riddell, Peter *v.4 p.605, p.606*

Riddick, Carol & Russell, Ruth V. *v.4 p.786*

Riddick, John A., Bunger, William B.,
    Sakano,Theodore K. *v.5 p.291*

Riddle, Brett R., et al. *v.4 p.394, v.5 p.169*

Riddle, John M. *v.4 p.778*

Riddle, Ronald *v.1 p.297*

Ridener, Larry E. *v.4 p.675*

Rideout, Walter B. *v.2 p.11*

Ridge, John Rollins *v.2 p.49, v.6 p.699*

Ridge, Martin *v.3 p.434*

Ridgway, Brunilde Sismondo *v.1 p.776*

Ridinger, Robert B. & Zhuravlev, Andrey (Editors) . . *v.5 p.449*

Ridinger, Robert B. (Compiled by) *v.6 p.359*

Ridinger, Robert B. (Editor) *v.6 p.363, p.388*

Ridinger, Robert B. *v.6 p.363*

Ridings, Eugene *v.3 p.342*

Ridley, Aaron (Editor) *v.1 p.467*

Ridley, Damon D. *v.5 p.255, p.256*

Ridley, Jasper Godwin *v.3 p.101, p.122*

Ridley, Jasper *v.3 p.101*

Ridley, Mark (Editor) *v.5 p.195, p.226*

Ridley, Matt *v.5 p.123, p.136, p.195*

Ridley, Maurice R. *v.2 p.295*

Ridlon, Florence *v.6 p.19, p.48*

Ridolfi, Carlo *v.1 p.745*

Ridolfi, Roberto *v.2 p.709*

Ridpath, Ian (Editor) *v.5 p.64*

Riduttori, Bonfiglioli (Editor) *v.5 p.715*

Rieber, R. W. *v.5 p.584*

Rieber, Robert W. & Wollock, Jeffrey (Editors) *v.5 p.572*

Rieber, Robert W. (Editor) *v.5 p.572, p.621, p.623*

Riede, David G. *v.2 p.304*

Riede, David *v.2 p.304*

Rieder, Jonathan & Steinlight, Stephen (Editors) . . . *v.3 p.371*

Riedling, Marlow (Compiled by) *v.3 p.484*

Riedt, Heinz *v.2 p.711*

Rieff, David *v.4 p.671, v.6 p.542*

Riegel, Emil Raymond *v.5 p.316, p.741*

Riegel, R. E. & Athearn, R. G. *v.3 p.519*

Riegelman, Richard K. *v.5 p.515*

Rieke, George *v.5 p.65*

Rieman, Timothy D. & Burks, Jean M. *v.1 p.804, p.805*

Riera, Carmen *v.2 p.663*

Ries, Al & Ries, Laura *v.4 p.142*

Rieselbach, Leroy N. *v.4 p.531*

Riesenberg, Peter N. *v.4 p.578*

Rieser, Andrew Chamberlin *v.4 p.721*

Riesman, David *v.4 p.212, p.332*

Riesman, Paul *v.4 p.38*

Riess, Steven A. . . *v.4 p.809, p.819, p.842, p.843, p.852, p.897*

Riessman, Catherine K. *v.6 p.467*

Riessman, Frank & Carroll, David *v.5 p.669*

Rietbergen, Peter *v.3 p.50*

Rifaat, Alifa *v.6 p.663*

Riffaterre, Hermine *v.2 p.461*

Rifkin, Jeremy *v.5 p.709*

Rigau, Jorge *v.1 p.790*

Rigby, James H. *v.5 p.291*

Rigden, John S. *v.5 p.309*

Rigg, Jonathan *v.4 p.384*

Riggers, Shelley *v.6 p.214*

Riggio, Ronald E. & Feldman, Robert S. (Editors) . . . *v.4 p.424*

Riggle, Ellen D. & Tadlock, Barry L. (Editors) *v.4 p.569*

Riggs, Robert Edwon *v.4 p.635*

Riggs, Stephen Return *v.6 p.690*

Riggs, Thomas (Editor) *v.1 p.141, v.6 p.490, p.493*

Riggs, Thomas *v.1 p.665, p.705*

Righetti, P. G., et al. *v.5 p.89, p.118*

Righter, Robert W. *v.6 p.296*

Righter, Rosemary *v.4 p.635*

Rightmire, G. Philip *v.4 p.16*

Rignall, John (Editor) *v.2 p.288*

Rigoutsos, Isidore &
    Stephanopoulos, G. *v.5 p.106, p.114, p.142, p.151*

Rigoutsos, Isidore & Stephanopoulos, Gregory
    (Editors) *v.5 p.114, p.128, p.142, p.146*

Riha, Thomas (Editor) *v.3 p.209, p.210*

Rihll, Tracey-Elizabeth *v.2 p.405*

Riis, Jacob A. *v.4 p.755*

Riis, Thomas L. *v.1 p.120*

Riker, William H. *v.4 p.505*

Rikli, Roberta E. & Jones, C. Jessie *v.4 p.841, p.880*

Riley, Charles A. II *v.1 p.710*

Riley, Christopher *v.6 p.353*

Riley, Denise *v.6 p.435*

Riley, Dick & McAllister, Pam *v.2 p.339*

Riley, E. C. *v.2 p.649*

Riley, Glenda (Editor) *v.3 p.522*

Riley, Glenda. . *v.3 p.521, v.4 p.838, p.866, v.5 p.640, v.6 p.292*

Riley, Jo *v.1 p.132, p.145*

Riley, Laura & Riley, William *v.5 p.84, p.235*

Riley, Patrick *v.1 p.454*

Riley, Robert Q. *v.4 p.154, v.5 p.701*

Riley, Sam G. (Editor) *v.4 p.410*

Riley, Stephen P. *v.6 p.70*

Riley, Terence & Bergdoll, Barry (Editors) *v.1 p.794*

Riley-Smith, Jonathan Simon Christopher *v.3 p.63*

Riley-Smith, Jonathan *v.3 p.63, p.64*

Rilke, Rainer Maria *v.2 p.614, p.615*

Rima, Ingrid H. (Editor) *v.4 p.204, p.257, p.264, p.270*

Rima, Ingrid H. *v.4 p.196*

Rimbaud, Arthur *v.2 p.498, p.499*

Rimer, J. Thomas *v.6 p.228, p.232*

Rimmerman, Craig A. (Editor) *v.6 p.390*

Rimmerman, Craig A.. . . . . *v.4 p.570, v.6 p.387*

Rimoin, David L., et al.. . . . . *v.5 p.151*

Rimsky-Korsakov, Nikolay *v.1 p.372, p.393*

Rinder, Lawrence. *v.1 p.699*

Rindler, Wolfgang *v.5 p.558*

Rinehart, Mary Roberts *v.1 p.579*

Rinehart, Robert E. & Sydnor, Synthia (Editors) . . *v.4 p.857*

Ring, Johannes and Heidrun Behrendt *v.5 p.365*

Ring, Johannes, et al.. . . . . *v.5 p.365*

Ring, Malvin E. *v.5 p.525*

Ringe, Donald A. *v.2 p.35*

Ringer, Alexander *v.1 p.202*

Ringer, Fritz K. *v.3 p.179, v.4 p.336, p.681*

Ringius, Lasse. *v.5 p.376, p.379, p.706, v.6 p.301*

Ringo, John *v.5 p.136*

Ringrose, David R.. . . . . *v.3 p.241*

Ringuet *v.2 p.539*

Ringvald, Vardit, et al. *v.6 p.646*

Rinhart, Floyd, et al. *v.1 p.764*

Rink, John *v.1 p.202, p.242, p.317*

Rinsler, Norma. *v.2 p.492*

Riordan, Cornelius H.. . . . . *v.4 p.301*

Riordan, James & Jones, Robin *v.4 p.796, v.6 p.194*

Riordan, James (Translator) *v.2 p.794*

Riordan, James. *v.2 p.793*

Riordan, J. *v.4 p.844, p.892, p.899*

Riordan, Jim & Kruger, Arnd (Editors) . *v.4 p.844, p.892, p.899*

Rios, Alberto *v.6 p.502, p.511*

Rios, Francisco A. (Editor) *v.4 p.350*

Rios-Bustamante, Antonio. *v.6 p.525*

Ripley, C. Peter (Editor) *v.3 p.421*

Ripley, Earle A., et al. *v.5 p.706*

Ripley, Randall B. & Lindsay, James M. (Editors). . *v.4 p.531*

Rippin, Andrew *v.1 p.559*

Rippley, La Vern J.. . . . . *v.3 p.517*

Rischar Davis, Pat *v.4 p.375*

Rischin, Rebecca *v.1 p.222, p.242, p.341*

Riseng, Karen & Jensen, Montambault . *v.5 p.172, p.185, p.236*

Risjord, Mark W.. . . . . *v.4 p.688*

Risjord, Norman K.. . . . . *v.3 p.522*

Risman, Barbara J.. . . . . *v.6 p.467*

Rissler, Jane & Mellon, Margaret G. *v.5 p.8, p.11*

Rist, John M. *v.1 p.430, p.431, v.2 p.409*

Rist, Ray C. (Author, Introduction by) *v.4 p.301, p.310*

Riste, Olav *v.3 p.234*

Rister, Carl C. *v.3 p.524*

Ristock, Janice L. *v.6 p.377*

Ritchie, David & Gates, Alexander E. *v.5 p.437, p.442*

Ritchie, George H. & Stauffer, George B. . . . *v.1 p.398, p.402*

Ritchie, J. M *v.2 p.591, p.592*

Ritchie, J. T. & Hanks, R. J. *v.5 p.50*

Ritchie, James McPherson *v.2 p.603, p.604*

Ritchie, Jane & Lewis, Jane (Editors) *v.4 p.136, p.137*

Ritter, Archibald R. M. & Kirk, John M. (Editors) . . *v.3 p.313*

Ritter, Archibald R. M. *v.3 p.312*

Ritter, Dale F., et al. *v.5 p.424*

Ritter, Gerhard A. *v.3 p.167*

Ritter, Harry *v.3 p.532*

Ritter, R. M. & Hart, Horace *v.2 p.574*

Rittner, Carol Ann (Editor), et al. *v.4 p.653*

Rittner, Carol (Author, Editor), et al. *v.4 p.653*

Ritvo, Harriet *v.6 p.760, p.764*

Ritzer, George (Editor) *v.4 p.678, p.680*

Ritzer, George *v.4 p.683*

Riva, Maria E. *v.6 p.419*

Rival, Laura M. *v.3 p.269*

Rivas, Angel de Saavedra (Author, Editor) . . . *v.2 p.655*

Rivas, Darlene *v.3 p.361*

Rivas, Manuel *v.2 p.692*

Rivera, Beatriz *v.6 p.508*

Rivera, Carmen S.. . . . . *v.6 p.508, p.515*

Rivera Cusicanqui, Silvia *v.3 p.324*

Rivera, José A. *v.6 p.522, p.551*

Rivera, Raquel Z. *v.6 p.519*

Rivera, Tomás *v.6 p.503*

Rivero, Albert J. *v.2 p.248*

Rivero Marín, Rosanna *v.6 p.508, p.515*

Rivero, Yeidy M.. . . . . *v.3 p.321*

Rivers, Elias (Editor) *v.2 p.645*

Rivers, Isabel (Editor) *v.2 p.172*

Rivers, Isabel *v.2 p.182*

Rivkin, Steve & Sutherland, Fraser *v.4 p.142*

Rivlin, Alice M.. . . . . *v.4 p.266, p.525*

Rivoli, Pietra *v.4 p.55, p.58*

Rizal, Jose. *v.2 p.687*

Rizgar, Baran *v.6 p.668, p.669*

Rizzello, Salvatore (Editor) *v.4 p.272*
Rn, Lucy Hood *v.5 p.528*
Roach, Colleen (Editor). *v.4 p.766*
Roach, Kent *v.4 p.661*
Roads, Curtis *v.1 p.222, p.245, p.387*
Roark, James L. *v.3 p.400, p.438*
Roazen, Paul. *v.5 p.644*
Robarge, David Scott *v.4 p.538*
Robb, Christina *v.5 p.648*
Robb, Graham . . . *v.2 p.487, p.499, v.3 p.153, v.6 p.364, p.421*
Robb, John D. *v.6 p.519, p.524*
Robb, L. J. *v.5 p.450*
Robb, Peter *v.1 p.745*
Robbe-Grillet, Alain & Howard, Richard *v.2 p.525, p.579*
Robbe-Grillet, Alain *v.2 p.525, p.526*
Robbelen, G., et al. *v.5 p.23*
Robbins, Allan & Miller, Wilhelm *v.5 p.721*
Robbins, Edward & El-Khoury, Rodolphe (Editors) . *v.6 p.726*
Robbins, John *v.5 p.33, p.35*
Robbins, Keith *v.3 p.95, p.115, v.6 p.735*
Robbins, Lionel C. *v.4 p.210*
Robbins, Lionel *v.4 p.210*
Robbins, Pam, et al. *v.4 p.288*
Robbins, Paul R. *v.5 p.656*
Robbins, Peter T. *v.4 p.63*
Robbins, Warren M. & Nooter, Nancy Ingram . . . *v.1 p.777*
Robbins-Roth, Cynthia *v.5 p.219*
Roberge, Pierre R. *v.5 p.735*
Robergs, Robert A. & Keteyian, Steven J. *v.4 p.875*
Robert, Alain *v.5 p.489*
Robert, Andre *v.5 p.427*
Robert C. Byrd. *v.4 p.150*
Robert Cialdini Staff *v.5 p.586*
Robert, Dana L. *v.1 p.647*
Robert Gregory Staff *v.5 p.601*
Robert, Henry M. & Evans, William J. (Editors) . . *v.4 p.575*
Robert, Jason Scott. *v.5 p.160*
Robert, Paul & Rey, Alain *v.2 p.454*
Robert, Paul & Rey-Debove, Josette *v.2 p.454*
Roberts, Adam & Kingsbury, Benedict (Editors) . . *v.4 p.635*
Roberts, Adam & Robertson, Carol *v.1 p.760*
Roberts, Adam *v.2 p.176, p.272*
Roberts, Albert R. (Editor) *v.6 p.248*
Roberts, Alexander & Donaldson, James (Editors). . *v.1 p.591*
Roberts, Andrew D. *v.6 p.77*
Roberts, Andrew. *v.3 p.152, v.6 p.77*
Roberts, Anna (Editor) *v.6 p.560*
Roberts, Brian K. *v.4 p.395*
Roberts, Charles G. D. *v.2 p.738*
Roberts, Cokie *v.4 p.487, p.517, p.569*
Roberts, David *v.2 p.120, v.3 p.520*
Roberts, Diane *v.6 p.36, p.40, p.45*
Roberts, Dorothy *v.6 p.40, p.46, p.447, p.471*
Roberts, Elizabeth Madox. *v.2 p.113*
Roberts, Elizabeth. *v.3 p.92, p.115, p.131*

Roberts, Fred & Tesman, Barry *v.5 p.479*
Roberts, Graham *v.2 p.799*
Roberts, Helene E. (Editor) *v.1 p.666, p.709*
Roberts, Hugh *v.6 p.60, p.642*
Roberts, Ian W. *v.3 p.186, p.219*
Roberts, J. C. *v.5 p.320*
Roberts, J. Deotis *v.1 p.636*
Roberts, J. J. *v.1 p.623*
Roberts, J. Timmons & Thanos, Nikki Demetria . . *v.3 p.270*
Roberts, J. W. *v.1 p.110, p.153*
Roberts, Jerry *v.5 p.177, p.181, p.224, p.239, v.6 p.327*
Roberts, Jimmy Jack *v.1 p.539*
Roberts, John & Crossley, Nick (Editors) . . . *v.4 p.766, p.774*
Roberts, John D.; Stewart, Ross; Caserio, Marjorie . *v.5 p.292*
Roberts, John D.. . . . . *v.5 p.272, p.293, p.297*
Roberts, John S. *v.1 p.282, p.294, v.6 p.519*
Roberts, John Storm *v.1 p.294*
Roberts, John W. *v.2 p.17*
Roberts, Ken. *v.4 p.786*
Roberts, Kenneth *v.2 p.113*
Roberts, L. E., et al. *v.5 p.704, p.709*
Roberts, Leonard & Wildman, Stephen *v.1 p.745*
Roberts, Marcus *v.1 p.508*
Roberts, Mary L. *v.3 p.54, p.79, p.155*
Roberts, Mary Louise *v.3 p.54, p.155*
Roberts, Mervin F. *v.5 p.228*
Roberts, Michael C. (Editor) *v.5 p.642*
Roberts, Michael *v.2 p.442, v.3 p.235*
Roberts, Monty & Grealy, Lucy *v.4 p.848*
Roberts, Neil (Editor). *v.2 p.184*
Roberts, Nick *v.2 p.700*
Roberts, Nora Ruth. *v.4 p.485*
Roberts, Pam *v.1 p.768*
Roberts, Paul *v.1 p.222, p.242, p.321, v.6 p.298*
Roberts, Peter (Editor) *v.1 p.68, p.117*
Roberts, Peter *v.4 p.345*
Roberts, Randy *v.4 p.819, p.856*
Roberts, R. *v.4 p.706*
Roberts, Robert North & Hammond, Scott J. *v.4 p.556*
Roberts, Russell *v.4 p.185*
Roberts, S. M., et al. *v.5 p.119*
Roberts, Tim S. *v.4 p.350*
Roberts, Walter R. *v.3 p.247*
Roberts, Warren *v.1 p.745*
Roberts, Willard L *v.5 p.435*
Robertson, A. H. & Moon, Nick *v.4 p.435*
Robertson, Agnes J. *v.4 p.436*
Robertson, Anne W. *v.1 p.178, p.338*
Robertson, Claire C. *v.6 p.65*
Robertson, D. W. *v.2 p.210*
Robertson, David Brian *v.4 p.123*
Robertson, David (Editor). *v.4 p.482*
Robertson, David. *v.3 p.462*
Robertson, Douglas (Editor). *v.5 p.701*
Robertson, Fiona *v.2 p.307*

Robertson, G. Lindsay *v.6 p.692*

Robertson, George (Editor) *v.5 p.248*

Robertson, Jack S. *v.1 p.662*

Robertson, Jennifer E. *v.6 p.222, p.448*

Robertson, Jennifer (Editor) *v.6 p.357*

Robertson, John George. *v.2 p.589*

Robertson, Martin *v.1 p.729, p.808*

Robertson, Priscilla *v.3 p.76*

Robertson-Lorant, Laurie. *v.2 p.48*

Robeson, Paul. *v.6 p.19*

Robeson, Virginia R. (Author, Editor) *v.3 p.540*

Robichaux, Robert H. & Yetman, David A.. . . *v.5 p.177, p.185*

Robin, Arthur L. & Foster, Sharon L. *v.5 p.668*

Robin, Corey. *v.4 p.484, v.5 p.644*

Robin, Gerald D.. . . . . *v.6 p.264*

Robin, M. *v.4 p.589*

Robin, Regine *v.2 p.541*

Robin, Ron *v.3 p.454*

Robin, Stephane, et al.. . . . . . *v.5 p.107, p.123, p.146, p.219*

Robins, C. Richard *v.5 p.216*

Robins, Elizabeth. *v.2 p.113*

Robins, Nicholas A. *v.3 p.313, p.326*

Robins, Philip *v.6 p.621*

Robins, Robert S. & Post, Jerrold M. *v.5 p.644*

Robinson, Alice M.; Roberts, Vera Mowry;

  & Barranger, Milly S.. . . . . *v.6 p.475*

Robinson, Allan R. & Brink, Kenneth H.. . . . *v.4 p.392*

Robinson, Andrew *v.5 p.426*

Robinson, Archie. *v.4 p.128*

Robinson, Armstead L. *v.4 p.521*

Robinson, B. W. *v.6 p.672*

Robinson, Bryan E.. . . . . *v.4 p.737*

Robinson, Cecil *v.6 p.503, p.515*

Robinson, Chase F. *v.6 p.574, p.585, p.602*

Robinson, Christopher *v.2 p.416*

Robinson, D. A. & Williams, R. B. G. (Editors). . . *v.5 p.439*

Robinson, Daniel N. *v.5 p.598, p.619*

Robinson, David (Editor) *v.1 p.590*

Robinson, David J. (Editor). *v.3 p.287, p.303, p.304*

Robinson, David *v.6 p.54, p.72*

Robinson, Dean E. *v.4 p.573*

Robinson, Doane. *v.3 p.523*

Robinson, Edward Arlington. *v.2 p.114*

Robinson, Elwyn B. *v.3 p.523*

Robinson, Francis *v.6 p.582*

Robinson, Fred C. *v.2 p.205*

Robinson, G. M. *v.4 p.395*

Robinson, Geoffrey B. *v.6 p.175, p.177*

Robinson, Glen O. & Robinson, O. F. *v.5 p.18, p.39*

Robinson, Glen O. *v.4 p.463, v.5 p.39, v.6 p.296*

Robinson, Glenn E.. . . . . *v.6 p.619*

Robinson, Greg *v.6 p.134*

Robinson, Gregory H. (Editor). *v.5 p.300*

Robinson, Harlow (Author, Foreword by, Afterword

by) *v.1 p.222, p.349*

Robinson, I. S. *v.3 p.57, p.162, v.6 p.572*

Robinson, Ian S. *v.1 p.574*

Robinson, J. C. *v.5 p.23, p.25, p.26*

Robinson, J. W. (Editor) *v.5 p.270*

Robinson, J. W. *v.2 p.185*

Robinson, Jackie W. & Duckett, Alfred *v.4 p.833, p.852*

Robinson, Jeffrey C. *v.2 p.295*

Robinson, J.M. (Editor). *v.1 p.647*

Robinson, Jo Ann Ooiman (Editor) *v.4 p.487, p.573*

Robinson, Joan . *v.4 p.185, p.196, p.236, p.239, p.241, p.244,
               p.251, p.252, p.253, p.260, p.270*

Robinson, John A. T. *v.1 p.624*

Robinson, John P. (Editor), et al. *v.5 p.603, p.644*

Robinson, Joy M. *v.2 p.526*

Robinson, Judith *v.4 p.149, p.411*

Robinson, Katy *v.6 p.95, p.110, p.136*

Robinson, Marilynne *v.2 p.154*

Robinson, Matthew J., et al. *v.4 p.905, p.906*

Robinson, Orrin W. *v.2 p.206, p.550*

Robinson, Patricia A. & Etter, Ryn. *v.5 p.681*

Robinson, Paul (Editor) *v.1 p.202, p.232, p.307*

Robinson, Paul H. *v.4 p.471, v.6 p.268*

Robinson, Paul. *v.4 p.570, v.6 p.387, p.393*

Robinson, Peter M.. . . . . *v.4 p.204*

Robinson, Phillip T. *v.5 p.85, p.251*

Robinson, Piers *v.4 p.407, p.415*

Robinson, Rachael *v.3 p.244*

Robinson, R. *v.3 p.77*

Robinson, Ray *v.4 p.859*

Robinson, Richard B. *v.1 p.494*

Robinson, Richard H.. . . . . *v.1 p.565*

Robinson, Roger & Wattie, Nelson (Editors) *v.2 p.741*

Robinson, Ronald Edward *v.6 p.56*

Robinson, Solveig C. (Editor). *v.2 p.176, p.203*

Robinson, Stewart *v.5 p.341*

Robinson, Susan B. & Pirog, John *v.1 p.758*

Robinson, T. H. & Brockington, L. H. (Editors). . . *v.6 p.652*

Robinson, T. M. *v.1 p.422*

Robinson, W. H. *v.5 p.213*

Robinson, William A.. . . . . *v.3 p.434*

Robinson, William I. *v.3 p.303*

Robinson, William *v.1 p.497*

Robisheaux, Thomas *v.3 p.166*

Roblès, Emmanuel *v.2 p.526*

Roblyer, Margaret D. *v.4 p.352*

Robson, Catherine *v.2 p.277, v.6 p.748*

Robson, David W. *v.4 p.332*

Robson, J. (Translator) *v.1 p.556*

Robson, John M. *v.3 p.115, p.129, v.4 p.223*

Robyt, John F. *v.5 p.330*

Roca, Iggy M. & Johnson, Wyn *v.2 p.563*

Rocamora, Carol *v.2 p.784*

Rocard, Marcienne. *v.6 p.503, p.515*

Rocco, John *v.1 p.273, p.321, p.322, p.346*
Rochberg, George *v.1 p.222, p.350, p.351*
Roche, Daniel *v.3 p.148*
Roche, George *v.4 p.525*
Roche, Jerome *v.1 p.181*
Roche, Maurice *v.4 p.846, p.889, p.892*
Rochelle, A. (Editor) *v.5 p.153*
Rochester, John W. *v.2 p.259*
Rochin, Refugio & Valdés, Dennis (Editors) *v.6 p.532*
Rochlin, James F. *v.4 p.592, p.593*
Rock, David (Editor) *v.3 p.346*
Rock, David *v.3 p.346*
Rock, Irvin *v.5 p.607*
Rock, Peter A. *v.5 p.278*
Rock, Stephen R. *v.4 p.646*
Rockett, Will H. *v.6 p.319*
Rockhill, William W. *v.6 p.241*
Rockmore, Tom *v.1 p.465, v.4 p.236*
Rockson, Stanley G. (Editor) *v.5 p.163*
Roco, Mihail C. & Montemagno, Carlo D. *v.5 p.589*
Rodan *v.4 p.623*
Rodas, Ana Maria *v.2 p.676*
Rodd, E. H. (Editor) *v.5 p.292*
Rodden, John *v.2 p.376*
Roddy, Dennis *v.4 p.421, p.422*
Rode, Linda & Gerwel, G. J. (Compiled by) . . *v.2 p.623, p.624*
Rodel, Kevin P. & Binzen, Jonathan *v.1 p.804*
Roden, Frederick S. (Editor) *v.2 p.321*
Roden, Martin S., et al. *v.5 p.722*
Roden, Martin S. *v.5 p.726*
Rodenas, Adriana M. *v.3 p.313*
Roderick, Melissa *v.4 p.299*
Rodgens, Bruce *v.6 p.358*
Rodgers, Daniel T. *v.3 p.444, p.449*
Rodgers, Hilary, et al. *v.4 p.385*
Rodgers, Richard & Hammerstein,
   Oscar II. *v.1 p.253, p.328, p.351, p.409*
Rodgers, Richard *v.1 p.253, p.351*
Rodgers, Susan (Editor) *v.6 p.175, p.177*
Rodinson, Maxine *v.1 p.555*
Rodis-Lewis, Genevieve *v.1 p.454*
Rodley, Lyn *v.1 p.672*
Rodmell, Graham E. & Marivaux, Pierre Carlet de
   Chamblain de. *v.2 p.481*
Rodney, Walter. *v.6 p.55, p.69*
Rodo, Jose E. *v.2 p.687*
Rodríguez O, Jaime E. *v.4 p.583*
Rodríguez, Victoria E. *v.6 p.442*
Rodríguez-Salgado, Maria J. *v.3 p.240*
Rodrigue, Aron. *v.6 p.598*
Rodriguez, Abraham Jr. *v.6 p.508*
Rodriguez, America (Contribution by) *v.6 p.494*
Rodriguez, Camille & Perez, Ramon B. (Editors) . . *v.6 p.527*
Rodriguez, Clara E. (Editor), et al. *v.6 p.542*
Rodriguez, Clara E. (Editor) *v.6 p.493, p.494*

Rodriguez, Clara E. *v.6 p.545*
Rodriguez, Clara *v.6 p.545*
Rodriguez de Montalvo, Garci. *v.2 p.646*
Rodriguez del Pino, Salvador (Editor) *v.1 p.127*
Rodriguez, Felix V. Matos *v.3 p.321*
Rodriguez, Joseph A. *v.6 p.719*
Rodriguez, Juana Maria. *v.6 p.545*
Rodriguez, Linda A. (Editor) *v.3 p.277*
Rodriguez, Linda. *v.3 p.333*
Rodriguez, Luis J. *v.4 p.714, v.6 p.490, p.503, p.547*
Rodriguez, Suzanne *v.6 p.403*
Rodriguez, Victoria *v.3 p.295, v.6 p.442*
Rodriguez-Fraticelli, Carlos *v.6 p.527*
Rodriguez-Pereyra, Gonzalo. *v.1 p.510*
Rodrik, Dani (Editor, Introduction by) *v.4 p.240*
Rodriquez de Montalvo, Garci. *v.2 p.646*
Rodriquez, M. J. & Adams, Simon. *v.3 p.240*
Roe, Anne *v.5 p.395*
Roe, Jill & Bettison, Margaret. *v.2 p.745*
Roe, Nicholas . . . *v.2 p.172, p.183, p.291, p.295, p.324, p.569*
Roeder, Michael T. *v.1 p.242*
Roederer, Juan G. *v.5 p.224*
Roediger, David R. *v.4 p.571*
Roehrig, Alysia D., et al. *v.4 p.279*
Roehrig, Catharine H. (Editor), et al. . *v.1 p.670, p.690, v.3 p.10*
Roelker, Nancy L. *v.3 p.146*
Roell, Craig H. *v.1 p.279, p.391*
Roemer, Kenneth M. & Porter, Joy (Editors) *v.6 p.699*
Roemer, Nils H. *v.3 p.180*
Roerdink, F. H. & Kroon, A. M. (Editors) *v.5 p.219*
Roesdahl, Else *v.3 p.236*
Roesgaard, Marie H. *v.4 p.336*
Roess, Roger P., et al. *v.5 p.701*
Roessler, Shirley *v.3 p.54, p.151, p.158*
Roethke, Theodore *v.2 p.114*
Roett, Riordan & Sacks, Richard S. *v.3 p.344, p.345*
Roett, Riordan (Editor) *v.3 p.295*
Rofes, Eric E. & Stulberg, Lisa M. (Editors) . . . *v.4 p.281*
Roff, Derek A. *v.5 p.195*
Roff, Derek *v.5 p.101*
Roff, William R. *v.6 p.173*
Rogak, Lisa. *v.4 p.88*
Rogal, Samuel J. (Compiled by) *v.5 p.5*
Rogan, Eugene & Tell, Tariq (Editors) *v.6 p.620*
Rogan, Eugene (Editor) *v.6 p.611*
Rogan, Eugene L. *v.6 p.621*
Rogelberg, Steven G. (Editor) *v.5 p.579*
Rogers, Alan J. *v.5 p.701*
Rogers, Alan. *v.3 p.406*
Rogers, Arthur & Durand de Bousingen, Denis *v.5 p.248*
Rogers, Bonnie. *v.5 p.535*
Rogers, Carl Ransom & Freiberg, H. Jerome *v.4 p.358*
Rogers, Carl Ransom *v.4 p.739*
Rogers, Clifford J. *v.3 p.91, p.144*

Rogers, Colin D.. . . . . *v.4 p.247, p.270*
Rogers, Daniel E. . . . . *. v.4 p.610*
Rogers, Dwight L. & Babinski, Leslie M. *v.4 p.279*
Rogers, Elizabeth Barlow *v.5 p.44*
Rogers, Everett M. *v.4 p.761*
Rogers, Frederick R.. . . . . *v.1 p.48*
Rogers, Hartley Jr. *v.5 p.471*
Rogers, J. *v.1 p.588*
Rogers, John J. W. & Santosh, M.. . . . *v.5 p.442, p.443*
Rogers, John James William. *v.5 p.445*
Rogers, John . . . . *. v.3 p.48*
Rogers, Katharine M.. . . . . *v.2 p.264*
Rogers, Lesley J.. . . . . *v.6 p.420*
Rogers, Mary F. *v.4 p.688*
Rogers, Pat *v.2 p.251*
Rogers, Patricia L. (Editor) *v.4 p.352*
Rogers, Richard & Shuman, Daniel W. . . . *v.5 p.593, v.6 p.270*
Rogers, Richard G., et al. *v.4 p.742*
Rogers, Susan F. (Editor) *v.4 p.839*
Rogers, Will & Day, Donald *v.1 p.90, p.117*
Rogers, William W., et al.. . . . . *v.3 p.505*
Rogerson, John (Editor). *v.1 p.614*
Rogerson, Peter A. *v.4 p.376*
Rogerson, Peter *v.4 p.376*
Rogerson Staff *v.4 p.396*
Rogger, Hans *v.3 p.60, p.220*
Rogoff, Barbara, et al. *v.4 p.348*
Rogoff, Edward G. . . . . *. v.4 p.82*
Rogoff, Irit (Editor) *v.1 p.680, p.688*
Rogol, Alan D. *v.4 p.826, p.875*
Rogstad, David H., et al. *v.5 p.728*
Roguez, Richard *v.6 p.490, p.527*
Rohde, Fred C., et al.. . . . . *v.5 p.216*
Rohen, Johannes W., et al. *v.5 p.158*
Rohlen, Thomas P. & LeTendre, Gerald K.
    (Editors) *v.4 p.336, v.6 p.222*
Rohlfs, K. & Wilson, T. L. *v.5 p.67*
Rohlich, Thomas H. (Translator). *v.6 p.233*
Rohmer, Sax. *v.2 p.379*
Rohner, Ronald P. & Bettauer, Evelyn C.. . . . *v.6 p.704*
Rohou, Jean *v.2 p.477*
Rohr, John A. *v.4 p.546*
Rohrbough, Malcolm J.. . . . . *v.3 p.513*
Rohrschneider, Robert *v.4 p.610*
Rohsenow, Warren M., et al. *v.5 p.713*
Rohwer, Claude D. & Skroki, Anthony M. *v.4 p.443*
Rohwer, Jurgen & Monakov, Mikhail *v.3 p.212*
Rohy, Valerie *v.2 p.5, v.6 p.393*
Ro'i, Yaacov *v.3 p.231*
Roider, Karl A. Jr. *v.3 p.183*
Roitman, Janet L. *v.4 p.260*
Rojas, Fernando de. *v.2 p.651, p.652*
Rojavin, Marina & Reid, Allan *v.2 p.776*
Rojewski, Jay W. & Rojewski, Jacy L. . . *v.6 p.110, p.125, p.127*
Roland, Charles G. . . . . *. v.3 p.86*

Roland, Charles P. *v.3 p.429, p.497*
Roldan, Mary *v.3 p.358*
Roley, Brian Ascalon. *v.6 p.102, p.130*
Rolfe, J. C. (Translator). *v.2 p.442*
Rolland, Romain *v.2 p.526*
Rolle, Richard *v.2 p.449*
Roller, Lynn E.. . . . . *v.1 p.533*
Rolleston, Thomas W. *v.2 p.601*
Rollin, Roger B.. . . . . *v.2 p.250*
Rolling Stones *v.1 p.274, p.351*
Rollins, Peter C. & O'Connor, John E.
    (Editors). *v.6 p.315, p.323, p.700*
Rollins, Peter C. *v.6 p.315*
Rollyson, Carl & Magill, Frank N. (Editors) . . *v.2 p.165, p.569*
Rollyson, Carl & Paddock, Lisa *v.2 p.48*
Rollyson, Carl *v.2 p.75, p.389*
Rolvaag, Ole Edvart *v.2 p.629*
Romaine, Suzanne (Editor) *v.2 p.555*
Romains, Jules *v.2 p.526*
Roman, David *v.6 p.412*
Roman, Eric *v.3 p.187*
Roman, Steven A. *v.5 p.335, p.484*
Romanek, Broc & Krus, Cynthia M. *v.4 p.85*
Romanell, Patrick *v.3 p.295*
Romanes, George J. *v.5 p.158*
Romano, David *v.6 p.599*
Romano, Joseph P. and Siegel, Andrew F. *v.5 p.481*
Romano, Mary A. *v.4 p.270*
Romanowksi, Patricia (Editor), et al.. . . . . *v.1 p.161, p.274*
Romanucci-Ross, Lola E. & Moerman, Daniel R.
    (Editors) *v.4 p.47*
Roman-Velazquez, Patria *v.3 p.267*
Romasco, Albert U.. . . . . *v.3 p.444*
Romberger, John A., et al.. . . . . *v.5 p.156*
Rombough, Lon *v.5 p.53*
Rome, Dennis *v.6 p.256*
Romer, David *v.4 p.204*
Romer, Grant B. *v.1 p.764*
Romero, Jose L. *v.4 p.592*
Romero, Luis Alberto. *v.3 p.349*
Romero, Raul R. *v.1 p.294*
Romero Salvadbo, Francisco J. *v.3 p.241*
Román, Antonio *v.1 p.795*
Romm, James S. *v.2 p.412*
Romm, Norma R. A. *v.4 p.687*
Romney, Jonathan & Wootton, Adrian (Editors) . . *v.6 p.316*
Romo, David Dorado *v.3 p.295*
Romo, Ricardo *v.6 p.536, p.550*
Rompilla, Ethel *v.1 p.803*
Rompkey, Bill *v.3 p.547*
Rona, Jeff *v.1 p.256, v.6 p.351*
Ronan, Colin A. *v.5 p.389, v.6 p.198*
Ronda, James P. *v.6 p.686*
Rondinelli, Dennis A., et al.. . . . . . . *v.4 p.314*
Ronen, Dov. . . . . *. v.6 p.74*

Roney, C. W. *v.4 p.137*
Roney, R. Craig *v.4 p.365*
Ronfeldt, David F. (Editor) *v.3 p.277*
Ronfeldt, David F. *v.3 p.300*
Rong, Xue Lan & Preissle, Judith *v.6 p.109*
Roniger, Luis & Herzog, Tamar (Editors). *v.3 p.260*
Ronkin, Noa *v.1 p.418*
Ronning, C. Neale *v.3 p.313*
Ronot, Xavier; Usson, Yves *v.5 p.120*
Ronsard, Pierre de *v.2 p.471*
Ronsard, Pierre. *v.2 p.472*
Ronshin, Valery *v.2 p.808*
Ronstadt, Robert C.. . . . . *v.4 p.178*
Rony, Fatimah T.. . . . . *v.6 p.310*
Roodenburg, Herman *v.4 p.773*
Roojen, Pepin Van *v.1 p.718*
Rooks, Noliwe M.. . . . . *v.6 p.40, p.46, p.448*
Rooks, Noliwe *v.6 p.14*
Rooksby, Rikky & Shrimpton, Nicholas (Editors) . . . *v.2 p.313*
Room, Adrian & Ayto, John. *v.2 p.549*
Room, Adrian *v.1 p.666*
Rooney, John W. Jr. *v.3 p.206*
Rooney, Phyllis *v.1 p.506*
Roorda, Eric. *v.3 p.317, p.391*
Roose-Evans, James *v.1 p.80, p.83, p.85, p.87, p.137*
Roosens, Laurent P. & Salu, Luc *v.1 p.761*
Roosens, Laurent P.. . . . . *v.1 p.761*
Roosevelt, Eleanor & Black, Allida M.. *v.3 p.462, v.4 p.487, p.569*
Roosevelt, Eleanor *v.3 p.462*
Roosevelt, Elliott. *v.3 p.462*
Roosevelt, Franklin D. *v.3 p.478*
Roosevelt, Kermit III *v.4 p.541*
Roosevelt, Nicholas *v.6 p.180*
Roosevelt, Priscilla *v.3 p.211*
Roosevelt, Theodore *v.3 p.381, p.418, p.478*
Root, Hilton L. *v.4 p.260, p.261*
Root, Maria P. (Editor) *v.4 p.706, v.6 p.124, p.130*
Root, Robert K. *v.2 p.231*
Root, Robert Kilburn *v.2 p.210*
Root, Robert L. Jr. *v.2 p.133*
Root, Robert. *v.2 p.133*
Roper, John Herbert *v.3 p.374*
Roper, Lyndal. *v.3 p.52*
Ropka, Mary & Williams, Ann *v.5 p.515*
Ropp, Paul S. (Editor) *v.6 p.182*
Ropp, Theodore. *v.3 p.36*
Roque, Alfredo Vilchis *v.1 p.733*
Rorabaugh, W. J.. . . . . *v.3 p.531, v.5 p.664*
Rorem, Ned *v.1 p.247, p.351, v.6 p.410*
Rorlich, Azade-Ayse *v.3 p.213*
Rorty, Amelie O. (Editor) *v.2 p.408*
Rorty, Amelie *v.4 p.323, p.340*
Rorty, Amélie (Editor) *v.1 p.427*
Rorty, Richard McKay. *v.1 p.417, p.442, p.490,*

p.513, p.514, v.4 p.493
Rosaldo, Michelle Zimbalist *v.4 p.35*
Rosaldo, Renato *v.6 p.180*
Rosales, F. Arturo *v.6 p.541*
Rosales, Francisco A.. . . . . *v.6 p.536, p.541*
Rosales, Gaudencio & Arevalo, Catalino (Editors). . . *v.1 p.574*
Rosales, Vicente Perez *v.3 p.351*
Rosand, David *v.1 p.729, p.733*
Rosand, Ellen *v.1 p.186, p.232, p.246*
Rosario, Nelly *v.6 p.508*
Roschelle, Anne R.. . . . . *v.4 p.734*
Rosco, Jerry *v.6 p.403*
Roscoe, Will & Murray, Stephen O. (Editors). *v.6 p.372, p.421*
Roscoe, Will (Editor) *v.4 p.746, v.6 p.371, p.705, p.707, p.709*
Roscoe, Will *v.4 p.31, v.6 p.371*
Rosdolsky, Roman *v.4 p.236*
Rose, Anne C. *v.3 p.400*
Rose, Arnold M. (Editor) *v.4 p.718*
Rose, Carolyn L. (Editor), et al. *v.5 p.228*
Rose, Dan *v.4 p.25*
Rose, Debra J. & Christina, Robert W. *v.4 p.874, p.908, p.910*
Rose, Ernst *v.2 p.589*
Rose, H. J. & Hard, Robin *v.1 p.533, v.2 p.401*
Rose, H. J. *v.2 p.401, p.425*
Rose, Ingrid & Quiroz, Roderick S. (Editors) *v.1 p.746*
Rose, Jessica *v.4 p.791, p.910*
Rose, Jonathan & Anderson, Patricia. *v.6 p.742*
Rose, Jonathan *v.3 p.120, v.4 p.726, v.6 p.739*
Rose, Lisle A. *v.3 p.479*
Rose, Lisle Abbott *v.3 p.479, p.495*
Rose, Mark *v.2 p.215, v.3 p.37*
Rose, Michael R.. . . . . *v.5 p.203*
Rose, Michael *v.5 p.196*
Rose, Mike *v.2 p.565*
Rose, Phyllis *v.1 p.11*
Rose, R. B. *v.3 p.151*
Rose, Richard & Munro, Neil. *v.4 p.578, p.599*
Rose, Richard & Suleiman, Ezra N. (Editors) *v.4 p.575*
Rose, Sonya O. *v.3 p.81*
Rose, Susan D.. . . . . *v.4 p.308*
Rose, Tricia *v.1 p.274*
Rose, William (Editor) *v.2 p.593*
Rose, William *v.2 p.593*
Rose, Willie L.. . . . . *v.3 p.502, v.6 p.8*
Roseberry, Lord *v.3 p.152*
Roseberry, William. *v.3 p.361, v.4 p.24*
Roseboom, Eugene Holloway *v.3 p.513*
Rosecrance, Richard *v.4 p.498*
Rosemann, Philipp W. *v.1 p.580*
Rosemblatt, Karin Alejandra. *v.3 p.355*
Rosemont, Franklin & Radcliffe, Charles *v.4 p.554*
Rosemont, Penelope (Editor) *v.1 p.680*
Rosen, Allen D. *v.4 p.514*
Rosen, Andrew. *v.3 p.117*

Rosen, Bernard Carl *v.4 p.693*
Rosen, Charles. *v.1 p.191, p.203, p.242, p.247, p.307, p.330, p.344*
Rosen, David *v.1 p.203, p.236, p.364*
Rosen, Edward *v.3 p.48*
Rosen, Elizabeth *v.1 p.51*
Rosen, Ellen Doree. *v.4 p.128*
Rosen, Ellen Israel *v.4 p.665*
Rosen, Fred S. & Strom, Terry B. *v.5 p.518*
Rosen, Greg *v.2 p.197, p.198, v.4 p.606*
Rosen, Jeffrey *v.4 p.443*
Rosen, Robert N. *v.3 p.498, v.4 p.521*
Rosen, Ruth *v.6 p.455*
Rosen, Stanley *v.2 p.418*
Rosen, Stephen L. *v.5 p.690*
Rosen, Stephen Peter *v.5 p.584*
Rosen, Tova. *v.6 p.560, p.566, p.574*
Rosenau, Pauline Marie. *v.4 p.682*
Rosenbaum, David A.. . . . . *v.5 p.608*
Rosenbaum, James E. *v.4 p.305, p.353, v.5 p.577, p.578*
Rosenbaum, Robert J. (Author, Afterword by) *v.6 p.535*
Rosenberg, Beth C. & Dubino, Jeanne *v.2 p.393*
Rosenberg, Charles E. *v.5 p.389, p.394, p.410, p.513*
Rosenberg, Deena *v.1 p.253, p.325, p.326*
Rosenberg, Emily S. *v.3 p.454*
Rosenberg, Hans *v.3 p.167*
Rosenberg, Jakob & Slive, Seymour *v.1 p.729, p.733*
Rosenberg, Jakob, et al.. . . . . *v.1 p.688*
Rosenberg, John D. *v.2 p.184, p.305*
Rosenberg, Kenneth A. *v.5 p.181*
Rosenberg, Marvin *v.2 p.231*
Rosenberg, Neil V. *v.1 p.274*
Rosenberg, Pierre & Prat, Louis-Antoine *v.1 p.724*
Rosenberg, Pierre. *v.1 p.722*
Rosenberg, Shawn, et al. *v.5 p.645*
Rosenberg, Tina *v.3 p.208*
Rosenberger, Nancy R. (Editor) *v.4 p.693*
Rosenberger, Nancy R. *v.6 p.446*
Rosenblatt, Louise M. *v.2 p.571*
Rosenblatt, Paul C. & Wallace, Beverly R. . . . *v.6 p.22, p.33*
Rosenblum, Jonathan D. *v.4 p.128*
Rosenblum, Nancy L. & Post, Robert C. (Editors). . . *v.4 p.499*
Rosenblum, Naomi. *v.1 p.707, p.763, p.764, v.6 p.473*
Rosenblum, Robert & Janson, H. W.. . . . . . . *v.1 p.680*
Rosenblum, Robert *v.1 p.746*
Rosenblum, Sandra P. *v.1 p.398, p.402*
Rosendahl, Mona *v.4 p.41*
Rosener, Werner *v.6 p.575*
Rosenfeld, Dana. *v.6 p.367, p.380, p.387*
Rosenfeld, Jo Ann (Editor) *v.6 p.444*
Rosenfeld, Lawrence B.. . . . . *v.4 p.758*
Rosenfeld, Natania *v.2 p.393*
Rosenfeld, Sybil Marion *v.1 p.103*
Rosengrant, Martha. *v.5 p.724*
Rosengren, John. *v.4 p.819, p.840, p.862*
Rosenheim, Margaret K. (Editor) *v.4 p.473*

Rosenkranz, E. Joshua & Schwartz, Bernard (Editors) . *v.4 p.469*
Rosenmeier, Rosamond *v.2 p.29*
Rosenmeyer, Thomas G. *v.2 p.407*
Rosenof, Theodore *v.4 p.549*
Rosenstein, Nathan S. *v.3 p.26*
Rosenstein, Nathan Stewart. *v.3 p.26*
Rosenstiel, Leonie *v.1 p.222, p.312, v.6 p.410*
Rosenstock, Linda, et al.. . . . . *v.5 p.535*
Rosenstone, Robert A. (Editor) *v.6 p.331*
Rosenstone, Robert A. *v.6 p.315*
Rosenstone, Steven J. & Hansen, John Mark *v.4 p.547*
Rosenstreich, Peter *v.4 p.89, p.97, p.98, p.100*
Rosenthal, A. & Vakalopoulou, L.
 (Editors). *v.5 p.142, p.146, p.151*
Rosenthal, Alan & Corner, John (Editors). *v.6 p.310*
Rosenthal, Alan *v.4 p.413, p.531, p.541*
Rosenthal, David M. (Editor) *v.1 p.509*
Rosenthal, Debra J. (Editor) *v.2 p.51*
Rosenthal, Elizabeth J. *v.6 p.410*
Rosenthal, Franz *v.6 p.663*
Rosenthal, Joel Thomas (Editor) *v.6 p.561*
Rosenthal, Lisa *v.1 p.707, p.746*
Rosenthal, Mark, et al.. . . . . *v.5 p.85*
Rosenthal, Mark *v.1 p.772*
Rosenthal, Michael & Myrone, Martin *v.1 p.746*
Rosenthal, Michael *v.1 p.746*
Rosenthal, Robert & Jacobson, Lenore *v.4 p.358*
Rosenthal, T. G. *v.1 p.699*
Rosentraub, Mark S. (Editor) *v.4 p.525*
Rosentraub, Mark S.. . . . . *v.4 p.886, p.889, p.892, p.897*
Rosenwaike, Ira (Editor) *v.6 p.551*
Rosenwein, Barbara H. *v.1 p.600, v.3 p.62, v.6 p.564*
Rosenzweig, Cynthia & Hillel, Daniel. *v.5 p.28*
Rosenzweig, Franz *v.1 p.551*
Rosenzweig, M. R. & Stark, O. (Editors). *v.4 p.191*
Rosenzweig, Robert M. *v.4 p.295*
Rosenzweig, Roy & Blackmar, Elizabeth . . *v.1 p.819, v.6 p.715*
Roses, Lorraine E. & Randolph, Ruth E. (Editors) . . *v.2 p.20*
Roses, Lorraine E. *v.6 p.19, p.27, p.34*
Roshwald, Aviel & Stites, Richard (Editors) *v.3 p.80*
Rosin, Gary S. & Closen, Michael L.. . . . . . . *v.4 p.75*
Roskams, Steve *v.4 p.7*
Roskos, Kathleen & Christie, James F. (Editors) . . *v.4 p.369*
Roslavleva, Natalia *v.1 p.11*
Roslof, Edward E. *v.3 p.223*
Rosner, Bernard *v.5 p.93*
Rosovsky, Henry *v.4 p.290*
Ross, Alexander M.. . . . . *v.3 p.432*
Ross, Alison *v.2 p.195*
Ross, Andrew C.. . . . . *v.1 p.647*
Ross, Andrew *v.4 p.254, p.261*
Ross, C. R. *v.2 p.601*
Ross, Carl T. *v.5 p.696*
Ross, Charles K.. . . . . *v.4 p.833, p.852*
Ross, Corey *v.3 p.177*

Ross, D. O. *v.2 p.427*
Ross, D. W.. *v.5 p.151*
Ross, David (Editor) *v.1 p.427*
Ross, David F. (Editor) *v.4 p.118*
Ross, David Frank (Editor), et al. *v.6 p.271*
Ross, David Frederick *v.4 p.118*
Ross, David O.. . . . . *v.2 p.430*
Ross, David *v.1 p.487*
Ross, Dennis B. *v.4 p.650*
Ross, Don *v.4 p.272*
Ross, Doran H. & Marzio, Frances *v.1 p.746*
Ross, Doran H. (Editor). *v.1 p.690*
Ross, Earle D. *v.4 p.332*
Ross, Ellen *v.3 p.54, v.6 p.748*
Ross, Fred *v.4 p.128*
Ross, George M. (Editor), et al. *v.4 p.609*
Ross, Heather L. & Sawhill, Isabel V. . . . *v.4 p.266*
Ross, Ian Campbell. *v.2 p.262*
Ross, Ian S. *v.4 p.219*
Ross, Irwin *v.3 p.479*
Ross, Ivan A. (Editor). *v.5 p.211*
Ross, Ivan A. *v.5 p.211*
Ross, James B. & McLaughlin, Mary M. (Editors) . . *v.6 p.555*
Ross, Jan (Editor) *v.2 p.263*
Ross, Janice *v.1 p.11, p.29, p.31, p.48*
Ross, Jeffrey Ian & Richards, Stephen C.. . . . . . *v.6 p.276*
Ross, Jeffrey Ian (Editor) *v.6 p.250*
Ross, Jeffrey S. & Hortobagyi, Gabriel N.
(Editors). *v.5 p.159, p.163*
Ross, John, et al.. . . . . *v.1 p.760*
Ross, John *v.4 p.383*
Ross, Josephine *v.2 p.268*
Ross, Kristin. *v.3 p.157*
Ross, Lawrence C. Jr. & Kensington Publishing Corporation
Staff. *v.4 p.289*
Ross, Leslie. *v.1 p.666, p.672, p.709*
Ross, M. J. *v.4 p.379*
Ross, Michael A.. . . . . *v.4 p.469, p.538*
Ross, Michael H. *v.5 p.128, p.153, p.159*
Ross, Michael R.. . . . . *v.5 p.18, p.32*
Ross, Ralph (Introduction by) *v.4 p.345*
Ross, Raymon R.. . . . . *v.4 p.365*
Ross, Robert B. *v.5 p.691*
Ross, Robert (Editor) *v.2 p.728*
Ross, Robert J.. . . . . *v.6 p.169*
Ross, Robert M. & Allmon, Warren D. (Editors) . . *v.5 p.196*
Ross, Robert S. & Jiang, Changbin (Editors) *v.3 p.392*
Ross, Robert S. *v.3 p.391*
Ross, Ronald G. *v.4 p.114*
Ross, Sinclair *v.2 p.738, p.739*
Ross, Stephanie *v.1 p.819*
Ross, Stephen A. *v.4 p.89, p.264*
Ross, Stephen *v.2 p.341*
Ross, Ted *v.1 p.387*
Ross, W. David *v.1 p.487*

Ross, William David *v.2 p.408*
Rossabi, Morris (Editor) *v.6 p.204*
Rossabi, Morris *v.4 p.620, v.6 p.186, p.201, p.239, p.240*
Rosse, Joseph G. & Levin, Robert A. *v.4 p.76*
Rosseau, Jean-Jacques *v.2 p.482*
Rossel, Sven Hakon (Editor) *v.2 p.626*
Rossel, Sven Hakon *v.2 p.624*
Rossell, Deac *v.6 p.331*
Rosselli, John. *v.1 p.191, p.203, p.232, p.246, p.309, p.344, p.385*
Rossells, Beatriz *v.3 p.272*
Rosser, B. R.. *v.4 p.779*
Rosser, John Barkley & Rosser, Marina V. *v.4 p.237*
Rosser, M. J.. *v.4 p.175*
Rossett, Allison *v.4 p.305*
Rossetti, Christina Georgina. *v.2 p.304*
Rossetti, Dante Gabriel. *v.2 p.304, p.305, p.700*
Rossetti, William M. *v.2 p.305*
Rossi, Paolo *v.5 p.391*
Rossides, Eugene T. (Editor) *v.3 p.392*
Rossing, Thomas D. & Fletcher, Neville H.. . . . . *v.5 p.567*
Rossing, Thomas D., et al. *v.5 p.567*
Rossini, Frederick D. [and others] *v.5 p.286*
Rossini, Frederick D., et al *v.5 p.286*
Rossini, Gioacchino Antonio . . . *v.1 p.203, p.232, p.352, p.409*
Rossino, Alexander B. *v.3 p.254*
Rossiter, Andrew & Kawanabe, Hiroya (Volume
Editors) *v.5 p.174, p.196*
Rossiter, Bryant W. & Baetzold, Roger C. (Editors) . . *v.5 p.276*
Rossiter, Bryant W. & Hamilton, John F. (Editors). *v.5 p.276, p.277*
Rossiter, Bryant W. (Editor), et al.. . . . . . . *v.5 p.276, p.277*
Rossiter, Bryant W. *v.5 p.276, p.277*
Rossiter, Clinton Lawrence *v.4 p.575*
Rossiter, Clinton *v.3 p.385, v.4 p.464, p.518*
Rossiter, Margaret W.. . . . . *v.5 p.5, p.398*
Rossman, Wulf. *v.5 p.475*
Rossotti, Charles O. *v.4 p.107*
Rossow, Edwin C. *v.5 p.696*
Rossum, Ralph A. *v.4 p.525, p.534*
Rostand, Edmond *v.2 p.336, p.498*
Rostislavov, Dmitriaei Ivanovich. *v.3 p.216*
Roston, Murray *v.2 p.255*
Rostovtzeff, Mikhail I *v.3 p.14*
Rostovtzeff, Mikhail I. *v.3 p.24*
Rostow, Eugene V. *v.4 p.470*
Rostow, W. W. *v.4 p.559*
Rostworowski de Diez Canseco, Maria *v.3 p.326*
Roszak, Theodore *v.4 p.761*
Rota, Gian-Carlo (Editor) *v.5 p.479*
Rotberg, Robert I. & Rabb, Theodore K. (Editors). . *v.4 p.647*
Rotberg, Robert I. & Robb, Theodore K. (Editors) . . *v.3 p.43*
Rotberg, Robert I. *v.3 p.126*
Rotella, Carlo *v.6 p.731*
Rotella, Guy L. *v.2 p.101*
Rotella, Guy *v.2 p.62, p.78, p.103, p.124*

Rotenberg, K. J. (Editor) *v.5 p.628, p.631*

Rotenstreich, Nathan *v.4 p.499*

Rotgers, Frederick (Editor), et al. *v.5 p.673*

Roth, Cecil. *v.1 p.548, v.6 p.574*

Roth, David M. & Meyer, Freeman *v.3 p.489*

Roth, David M. *v.3 p.489*

Roth, Dennis M. *v.5 p.223, p.235*

Roth, Henry *v.2 p.114*

Roth, John K. & Rittner, Carol (Editors). *v.3 p.86*

Roth, John K. (Editor) *v.1 p.416, v.5 p.405*

Roth, Joseph *v.2 p.614, v.3 p.184*

Roth, Joshua Hotaka *v.6 p.119, p.132*

Roth, Lawrence O. & Field, Harry L. *v.5 p.5*

Roth, Leland M. *v.1 p.787*

Roth, Leland *v.1 p.790*

Roth, László & Wybenga, George L. *v.1 p.718*

Roth, Martin *v.2 p.42*

Roth, Mitchel *v.6 p.261*

Roth, Norman *v.3 p.66*

Roth, Philip *v.2 p.154*

Roth Publishing, Inc. Staff *v.2 p.24*

Roth, Rachel. *v.4 p.442, p.774, v.6 p.471*

Roth, Wolff-Michael & Tobin, Kenneth George *v.4 p.277*

Rothbart, Harold A. & Brown, Thomas H. *v.5 p.715*

Rothbart, Harold A.. . . . . *v.5 p.715*

Rothberg, Helen & Erickson, G. Scott *v.4 p.77, p.83*

Rothblatt, Sheldon *v.3 p.115, p.129, v.6 p.745*

Rothenberg, Marc (Editor) *v.5 p.386*

Rothenberg, Marc *v.5 p.386*

Rothenberg, Paula S. *v.6 p.471*

Rothera, Ellen *v.5 p.365*

Rothermund, Dietmar *v.5 p.15*

Rothfels, Nigel *v.5 p.85*

Rothko, Mark *v.1 p.746*

Rothman, David J. *v.6 p.273*

Rothman, Ellen K. *v.4 p.738*

Rothman, Hal K. *v.4 p.62*

Rothman, Philip (Editor) *v.4 p.204*

Rothman, S. S. *v.5 p.159, p.163*

Rothman, Stanley, et al.. . . . . *v.6 p.343*

Rothman, William (Author, Contribution by) *v.6 p.310*

Rothmüller, Aron Marko *v.1 p.300*

Rothschild, Bruce J. (Editor) *v.4 p.392*

Rothschild, Deborah, et al. *v.1 p.718*

Rothschild, Emma *v.3 p.72*

Rothschild, Joseph *v.3 p.207*

Rothschild, Lynn & Lister, Adrian (Editors). . . . *v.5 p.196*

Rothschild, V. & Logothetis, Nicholas *v.5 p.484*

Rothstein, Edward *v.5 p.460*

Rothstein, Frances A. & Blim, Michael L.. . . . *v.4 p.28*

Rothstein, Joseph. *v.1 p.387*

Rothstein, Larry & Belson, Matthew *v.4 p.830*

Rothstein, Stanley W. & Garubo, Raymond C. . . . *v.4 p.282*

Rothstein, Stanley W. (Editor) *v.4 p.315*

Rothstein, William *v.1 p.372*

Rothstein *v.4 p.450*

Rothwell, Evelyn. *v.1 p.398*

Rothwell, Kenneth S. *v.2 p.231, v.6 p.327*

Rothwell, Nancy *v.5 p.398*

Rothwell, William J., et al.. . . . . *v.4 p.79, p.352*

Rotimi, Ola *v.2 p.757*

Rotman, Joseph J. *v.5 p.474, p.475*

Rotskoff, Lori *v.5 p.664*

Rotundo, E. Anthony. *v.4 p.745, v.6 p.430, p.452, p.455*

Rotundo, L. *v.3 p.227*

Roubik, David W. (Editor), et al. *v.5 p.185, p.239*

Rouch, Alain & Clavreuil, Gérard *v.2 p.535*

Rouchdy, Aleya (Editor) *v.6 p.654*

Roucoux, Katherine *v.5 p.223*

Roudané, Matthew C. (Editor). *v.2 p.134*

Roudani, Matthew. *v.1 p.61, p.118*

Roudiez, S. Leon. *v.2 p.462*

Roudinesco, Elizabeth *v.5 p.598*

Roudometof, Victor. *v.3 p.250*

Rouessac, Annick & Rouessac, Francis. *v.5 p.268*

Rougemont, Denis de *v.2 p.526, v.3 p.88*

Rough Guides Staff & Brown, Jules *v.6 p.206*

Roughgarden, Joan *v.4 p.744, p.746, v.6 p.420*

Roughgarden, Jonathan *v.5 p.502*

Roumain, Jacques *v.2 p.537*

Rounds, Carol & Solyom, Erika *v.2 p.775*

Rounds, Carol *v.2 p.775*

Rouquie, Alain *v.3 p.277, v.4 p.592*

Rourke, Constance *v.2 p.586*

Rouse, Ruth & Neill, Stephen Charles (Editors). . . . *v.1 p.568*

Rousseau, Denise M. *v.4 p.74*

Rousseau, G. S. *v.2 p.249*

Rousseau, George S. *v.2 p.261*

Rousseau, Jean-Jacques & Kelly, Christopher *v.2 p.482*

Rousseau, Jean-Jacques & Wu, Michael *v.3 p.148*

Rousseau, Jean-Jacques, et al. *v.2 p.482*

Rousseau, Jean-Jacques *v.1 p.139, p.454, v.2 p.482, p.483, v.3 p.148, v.4 p.492*

Rousseau, Philip. *v.1 p.613, p.653, v.3 p.11*

Rousso, Henry *v.3 p.157*

Rout, Leslie B.. . . . . *v.3 p.280*

Routh, C. R. & Birley, R. (Foreword by) *v.3 p.90*

Rouyer, Philippe & Nagy, Peter (Editors). *v.1 p.61, p.97*

Roveda, Vittorio *v.1 p.692*

Rovere, Richard H.. . . . . *v.3 p.449, p.462*

Rovine, Victoria *v.4 p.26*

Rowan, Carl Thomas *v.4 p.538*

Rowe, David C. *v.5 p.656*

Rowe, David Charles. *v.4 p.819, p.902*

Rowe, George E. Jr. *v.2 p.221*

Rowe, James K. & Lipschutz, Ronnie D.. . . . *v.4 p.261, p.262*

Rowe, John C. *v.2 p.45*

Rowe, Margaret M.. . . . . *v.2 p.365*

Rowe, Michael *v.3 p.168, v.4 p.774, v.6 p.265*

Rowe, Nicholas *v.2 p.258*

Rowe, R. K. *v.5 p.367, p.422*
Rowe, R. Kerry, et al. *v.5 p.377*
Rowe, Robert *v.1 p.388*
Rowe, William (Editor) *v.2 p.685*
Rowe *v.2 p.372*
Rowell, Charles Henry *v.6 p.27, p.29*
Rowell, David L. *v.5 p.50*
Rowell, Galen (Photographer, Introduction by) *v.6 p.241*
Rowell, George & Jackson, Anthony *v.1 p.103*
Rowell, S. C. *v.3 p.256*
Rowen, Herbert H. *v.3 p.205*
Rowland, A. Westley *v.4 p.293*
Rowland, Christopher *v.1 p.617*
Rowland, David (Editor) *v.1 p.391*
Rowland, David *v.1 p.391, p.402*
Rowland, Don *v.4 p.376*
Rowland, Fytton & Rhodes, Peter (Editors) *v.5 p.256*
Rowland, Ingrid D. *v.3 p.71*
Rowland, Lewis P. *v.5 p.516*
Rowland, Steve, et al. *v.5 p.441*
Rowland, Susan (Editor) *v.6 p.435, p.446*
Rowland, Thomas W. *v.4 p.875*
Rowlandson, Jane (Editor) *v.3 p.11*
Rowlandson, Mary White *v.2 p.29*
Rowley, Charles Kershaw & Schneider, Friedrich
(Editors) *v.4 p.192*
Rowley, Hazel *v.2 p.748*
Rowse, A. L. *v.3 p.92, p.101, p.126*
Rowse, Alfred L. *v.3 p.406*
Rowson, Susanna *v.2 p.30*
Roxburgh, David J. *v.1 p.674, p.691*
Roy, Arundhati *v.2 p.765, p.766*
Roy, Ashok *v.1 p.751*
Roy, D. C. (Editor) *v.5 p.432*
Roy, David T. (Translator) *v.6 p.212*
Roy, David Tod (Edited and Translated by) *v.6 p.212*
Roy, David Tod (Translator) *v.6 p.212*
Roy, Denny *v.6 p.214*
Roy, G. D. *v.5 p.720*
Roy, Gabrielle *v.2 p.539, p.540*
Roy, Maya *v.1 p.294*
Roy, Olivier (Editor) *v.6 p.624*
Roy, Olivier *v.6 p.634*
Roy, Raja Rammohun *v.6 p.158*
Royal Society of Chemistry Staff *v.5 p.302*
Royce, Anya Peterson *v.1 p.49, v.4 p.26*
Royce, Anya *v.1 p.43*
Royce, James E. & Scratchley, David *v.4 p.776*
Royce, Josiah *v.1 p.436, p.439, p.639*
Roy-Fequiere, Magali *v.3 p.321*
Royka, Paul A. *v.1 p.804*
Royko, Mike (Author, Introduction by) *v.3 p.516*
Royle, Tony & Towers, Brian *v.4 p.123*
Roysircar, Gargi (Editor), et al. *v.5 p.637*
Royster, Charles *v.3 p.410, p.413*

Roza, Marguerite & Celio, Mary Beth *v.4 p.282*
Rozalski, Michael E. *v.4 p.284*
Rozell, Mark J. & Barilleaux, Ryan J. *v.3 p.479, p.484*
Rozell, Mark J. & Wilcox, Clyde (Editors) *v.3 p.479*
Rozewicz, Tadeusz *v.2 p.791*
Rozwadowski, Helen M. *v.5 p.429*
Ruan, Shigui (Editor), et al. *v.5 p.91*
Ruane, Joseph & Todd, Jennifer *v.3 p.140, v.4 p.607*
Ruane, Kevin *v.4 p.638, p.655*
Ruay, Deng D. Akol *v.6 p.59*
Rubal-Lopez, Alma & Anselmo, Angela *v.6 p.527*
Rubashow-Katznelson, Rachel (Editor) *v.6 p.612*
Ruben, Alan Miles (Editor) *v.4 p.447*
Ruben, Brent D. *v.4 p.332*
Rubenberg, Cheryl A. *v.6 p.619*
Rubenfeld, Jed *v.4 p.454*
Rubens, Philip *v.5 p.681*
Rubenstein, Anne *v.3 p.267*
Rubenstein, Bruce A. & Ziewacz, Lawrence E. *v.3 p.516*
Rubenstein, Rheta Norma Pollock, et al. *v.5 p.464*
Rubenstein, William B., et al. *v.4 p.448*
Rubenzer, Steven J. & Faschingbauer, Thomas R. . . . *v.4 p.698*
Ruber, Peter A. *v.2 p.27*
Rubiés, Joan-Pau *v.6 p.154*
Rubin, Anne S. *v.4 p.522*
Rubin, Barnett R. *v.6 p.634*
Rubin, Barry & Kirisci, Kemal (Editors) *v.6 p.624*
Rubin, Barry & Rubin, Judith Colp (Editors) *v.1 p.560*
Rubin, Barry (Editor) *v.6 p.595*
Rubin, Barry M. & Heper, Metin (Editors) . *v.4 p.616, v.6 p.624*
Rubin, Barry *v.4 p.615, v.6 p.594, p.595, p.619*
Rubin, David C. (Editor) *v.5 p.610*
Rubin, Don (Editor), et al. *v.1 p.61, p.130*
Rubin, Don (Editor) *v.1 p.61, p.127*
Rubin, Don *v.1 p.61*
Rubin, Eva R. (Editor) *v.4 p.448*
Rubin, Frances & Rowley, John *v.4 p.65*
Rubin, Harvey W. *v.4 p.163*
Rubin, Herbert J. & Rubin, Irene *v.4 p.691*
Rubin, Herbert J. *v.4 p.719*
Rubin, James Henry *v.1 p.729, p.746*
Rubin, Jay *v.6 p.233*
Rubin, Lillian B. *v.4 p.706*
Rubin, Louis Decimus Jr. (Editor), et al. *v.2 p.14*
Rubin, Louis Decimus Jr. (Editor) *v.3 p.494*
Rubin, Louis Decimus Jr. *v.2 p.14, v.3 p.500*
Rubin, Martin *v.6 p.316*
Rubin, Miri *v.1 p.657*
Rubin, Ruth *v.1 p.300*
Rubinfeld, Mark D. *v.6 p.313, p.317, p.328, p.343*
Rubinstein, Alvin Z. *v.6 p.619*
Rubinstein, Ariel *v.4 p.207*
Rubinstein, Charlotte S. *v.1 p.777*
Rubinstein, Michael & Colby, Ralph H. *v.5 p.564*

Rubinstein, Murray A. (Editor) *v.6 p.214*

Rubinstein, W. D. *v.3 p.115, p.123*

Rubulis, Aleksis *v.2 p.780*

Ruccio, David F. & Amariglio, Jack *v.4 p.196*

Ruck, Rob. *v.3 p.267, p.317*

Ruckert, George E. *v.1 p.289*

Rudacille, Deborah *v.4 p.744*

Rudalevige, Andrew *v.4 p.527*

Rudall, Paula *v.5 p.156*

Rudd, Niall *v.2 p.435*

Ruddiman, William F. . . . *v.5 p.355, p.358, p.360, p.371, p.373*

Rude, George *v.3 p.95, p.107, p.109, p.126,*
v.4 p.706, p.710, p.713, p.753

Rudebush, George *v.1 p.423*

Rudenstine, David *v.4 p.439*

Ruderman, David B. *v.3 p.48*

Rudgley, Richard *v.3 p.282, v.4 p.776*

Rudin, Harry R. *v.6 p.62*

Rudin, Walter *v.5 p.489, p.494*

Rudinsky, Norma, et al. *v.2 p.812*

Rudisill, Richard, et al. *v.1 p.761*

Rudland, S. (Editor), et al. *v.5 p.165*

Rudlin, John *v.1 p.91, p.135*

Rudner, David W. *v.6 p.154*

Rudney, Gwen L. *v.4 p.353*

Rudnick, Paul *v.6 p.414*

Rudnitsky, Konstantin *v.1 p.85, p.110*

Rudolf, Max *v.1 p.403*

Rudolph, Colin David (Editor). *v.5 p.525*

Rudolph, Frederick B. & McIntire, Larry V.
(Editors) *v.5 p.219, p.249*

Rudolph, Frederick *v.4 p.332*

Rudolph, James D. *v.4 p.593*

Rudolph, Kurt *v.1 p.647*

Rudolph, Susanne Hoeber, et al. *v.6 p.161*

Rudrum, Alan (Editor), et al. *v.2 p.197, p.201*

Rudwick, Martin J. *v.5 p.418*

Rudy, Gordon *v.6 p.569*

Rue, Loyal D. *v.5 p.635*

Ruedy, John *v.6 p.642*

Ruether, Rosemary Radford . . . *v.1 p.528, p.644, v.6 p.460*

Ruff, Shawn S. *v.6 p.407*

Ruffo-Fiore, Silvia *v.2 p.709*

Rugeley, Terry *v.3 p.265, p.289*

Ruggie, John G. *v.4 p.625*

Ruggiero, Kristin Hoffman *v.4 p.706*

Ruggiero, Vincent R. *v.4 p.676*

Ruggles, Eleanor *v.1 p.118, p.145*

Ruggles, Fairchild D. *v.1 p.674, p.814*

Rugh, William A. *v.6 p.583*

Rugman, Alan M. (Editor) *v.4 p.177*

Rugoff, Ralph & Storr, Robert. *v.1 p.773*

Ruh, Brian. *v.6 p.336*

Ruiz de Alarcón, Juan *v.2 p.652*

Ruiz de Alarcon, Juan *v.2 p.652*

Ruiz de Burton, Maria A. *v.6 p.503*

Ruiz de Burton, Maria Amparo *v.6 p.503*

Ruiz, Gregory M. & Carlton, James T. (Editors) . . . *v.5 p.181*

Ruiz, Juan *v.2 p.652*

Ruiz Ramón, Francisco *v.2 p.640*

Ruiz, Vicki L. & Korrol, Virginia Sanchez . . . *v.6 p.490, p.547*

Ruiz, Vicki L. (Editor) *v.6 p.547*

Ruiz, Vicki L. . *v.6 p.40, p.46, p.450, p.455, p.526, p.546, p.547*

Ruiz Zafon, Carlos *v.2 p.662*

Rukeyser, Muriel & Rich, Adrienne *v.2 p.114*

Rukeyser, Muriel *v.2 p.114*

Rukl, Antonin *v.5 p.64*

Rule, Amy & Lorenz, Richard (Editors) *v.1 p.768*

Rule, Gordon & Hitchens, T. Kevin *v.5 p.118*

Rule, Jane. *v.6 p.393, p.398*

Rulfo, Juan, et al. *v.2 p.669*

Rulfo, Juan *v.2 p.669*

Rumbaugh, Duane M. & Washburn, David A. *v.5 p.615*

Rumbaugh, James, et al. *v.5 p.347, p.348*

Rumble, Patrick & Testa, Bart (Editors) . . *v.2 p.721, v.6 p.417*

Rumble, Patrick A. *v.6 p.339*

Rumelin, Christian *v.1 p.760*

Rumer, Boris (Editor) *v.4 p.599, p.624*

Rumi, Jalaluddin *v.6 p.672*

Rumi, Jalalu'L-Dein & Nicholson, Reynold A. *v.6 p.672*

Rumi *v.6 p.672*

Rummel, Erika *v.1 p.603*

Rumney, Thomas A. *v.4 p.396*

Rumrich, John Peter *v.2 p.366*

Runciman, Steven *v.1 p.570, p.600, p.601,*
v.3 p.57, p.58, p.63, p.193, p.194, v.6 p.581

Rundell, Michael *v.4 p.856*

Rung, Margaret C. *v.4 p.546*

Runge, C. Ford, et al. *v.4 p.665*

Runte, Alfred *v.5 p.18, v.6 p.296*

Runyon, Damon *v.2 p.114*

Ruoff, Gene W. *v.2 p.268, p.324*

Ruoff, James E. *v.2 p.170*

Ruoff, Kenneth J. *v.4 p.622, v.6 p.225*

Ruowang, Wang *v.6 p.213*

Rupesinghe, Kumar *v.4 p.497, p.613*

Rupp, Gordon *v.1 p.603, p.609*

Rupp, Leila J. *v.6 p.432*

Ruppert, Edward E., et al. *v.5 p.156, p.196, p.213*

Rury, John L. *v.4 p.297, p.328, p.762*

Rusch, Frederik L. (Editor) *v.2 p.126*

Rusch, William G. (Editor, Translator) *v.1 p.639*

Ruscher, Janet B. *v.4 p.698, v.5 p.621*

Rusco, Elmer R. *v.6 p.692*

Ruse, Michael & Castle, David (Editors) *v.5 p.219*

Ruse, Michael (Editor) *v.5 p.81, p.196*

Ruse, Michael *v.1 p.516, v.3 p.49, v.5 p.81, p.196,*
p.203, p.204, p.226

Rush, Anne Kent. *v.4 p.791, p.874*

Rush, Fred (Editor). *v.1 p.502*

Rush, George E. *v.6 p.246*
Rush, James R.. . . . . *v.6 p.177*
Rush, Michael *v.1 p.772*
Rush, Norman *v.2 p.154*
Rushdie, Salman & West, Elizabeth (Editors) *v.2 p.763*
Rushdie, Salman. *v.2 p.165, p.569, p.766*
Rushing, W. Jackson (Editor) *v.1 p.683, v.6 p.679*
Rushing, W. Jackson III *v.1 p.781, v.6 p.679*
Rushton, Julian (Author, Contribution by). *v.1 p.203, p.242, p.323*
Rushton, Julian . . . *v.1 p.192, p.203, p.232, p.236, p.311, p.344*
Rusinko, Susan. *v.2 p.189*
Rusinow, Dennison *v.3 p.247*
Rusk, David *v.6 p.709, p.725*
Rusk, Dean & Rusk, Richard *v.3 p.462*
Rusk, Jerrold G.. . . . . *v.4 p.548, p.549, p.555*
Rusk, Ralph Leslie *v.2 p.15*
Rusk, Tom & Miller, D. Patrick. *v.4 p.74*
Ruskin, John *v.2 p.305, p.306, v.6 p.738, p.755*
Ruspoli, Mario *v.1 p.669*
Russ, Charles V. *v.2 p.621*
Russ, Michael *v.1 p.203, p.242, p.345*
Russ, William A. Jr. *v.3 p.534*
Russell, Alan & Lee, Kok Loong *v.5 p.697, p.733*
Russell, Bertrand & Marsh, Robert C. (Editors) *v.1 p.483*
Russell, Bertrand Arthur *v.4 p.656*
Russell, Bertrand *v.1 p.417, p.447, p.460, p.483, p.485,*
                           p.494, v.4 p.345, p.656, v.5 p.404, p.557
Russell, Catherine *v.6 p.311*
Russell, Colin A.. *v.5 p.261*
Russell, Conrad (Editor) *v.3 p.104*
Russell, Conrad *v.3 p.95, p.101, p.104, p.122*
Russell, D. A. *v.2 p.399*
Russell, D.. . . . . *v.2 p.419*
Russell, Delbert W.. . . . . *v.2 p.540*
Russell, Denise. *v.5 p.660, v.6 p.446*
Russell, Douglas A. (Editor, Introduction
   by) *v.1 p.68, p.110, v.2 p.594*
Russell, Edmund *v.6 p.296*
Russell, Francis *v.4 p.438*
Russell, Frederick H. *v.1 p.644*
Russell, George A. *v.1 p.403*
Russell, Gordon W.. . . . . *v.5 p.583*
Russell, Howard S.. . . . . *v.3 p.485*
Russell, James A. & Fernandez-Dols, Josi-Miguel
   (Editors) *v.5 p.648*
Russell, Jan Jarboe *v.3 p.462*
Russell, Jeffrey B. *v.1 p.529, p.645, v.6 p.569, p.573*
Russell, John M. *v.3 p.6*
Russell, John *v.1 p.746, p.812*
Russell, Letty M. & Clarkson, J. Shannon (Editors) . *v.6 p.460*
Russell, Letty M. (Editor). *v.1 p.617*
Russell, Letty M.. *v.1 p.644*
Russell, Michael S.. . . . . *v.5 p.320, p.321*
Russell, Mona L. *v.6 p.58*
Russell, P. E.. . . . . *v.2 p.650*

Russell, Paul *v.6 p.358, p.398*
Russell, Peter E. *v.3 p.73, p.244*
Russell, Peter J. *v.5 p.136*
Russell, Philip *v.4 p.594*
Russell, Ralph (Editor) *v.6 p.152*
Russell, Sharman Apt. *v.5 p.156*
Russell, Sharon A. *v.6 p.334*
Russell, Stuart J. & Norvig, Peter *v.5 p.339*
Russell, Thaddeus *v.4 p.129*
Russell, Tony *v.1 p.263*
Russell-Brown, Kathryn. *v.6 p.257*
Russell-Chapin, Lori Ann & Ivey, Allen E. *v.5 p.676*
Russell-Wood, A. J.. . . . . *v.3 p.335*
Russett, Bruce M. *v.4 p.629*
Russett, Cynthia *v.6 p.748*
Russmann, Edna R. & Finn, David *v.1 p.776*
Russmann, Edna R. (Editor) *v.1 p.670, p.690*
Russo, Charles J. (Editor) *v.4 p.451*
Russo, Richard *v.2 p.154*
Russo, Vito *v.6 p.417*
Russo, William *v.1 p.394, p.403*
Russolo, Luigi *v.1 p.222, p.372*
Rust, E. Gardner *v.1 p.21, p.169, p.284*
Rust, John & Golombok, Susan *v.5 p.601*
Rust, Paula C.. . . . . *v.4 p.750, v.6 p.372, p.375, p.376*
Rustaveli, Shota *v.6 p.665*
Ruth, Henry S. & Reitz, Kevin R. *v.6 p.250*
Rutherford, Donald *v.1 p.460, v.4 p.191*
Rutherford, R. B. *v.1 p.429*
Rutherford, Richard *v.2 p.415*
Ruthven, K. K.. . . . . *v.2 p.165*
Rutland, Robert A. *v.3 p.418, v.4 p.518*
Rutland, Robert Allen (Editor). *v.3 p.374*
Rutledge, A. J. & Molnar, Donald J.. . . . . *v.5 p.17, p.18*
Rutledge, Leigh & Hancock, Gregory R. (Editors) . . *v.6 p.360*
Rutman, Darrett Bruce *v.3 p.384, p.488*
Ruttan, Vernon W. (Editor) *v.5 p.13*
Rutter, Michael. *v.5 p.251*
Ruud, Charles A. & Stepanov, S. A. *v.3 p.218*
Ruud, Paul A. *v.4 p.204*
Ruud, Warren L. *v.5 p.485*
Ruyter, Nancy L. *v.1 p.27*
Ruyter, Nancy Lee Chalfa *v.1 p.48*
Ruz, Alberto & Cardoza y Aragón, Luis *v.2 p.676*
Ruzaik, Ibn *v.6 p.627*
Ruzek, Sheryl B., et al.. . . . . *v.6 p.444*
Ruzic, Neil P. *v.5 p.720*
Ryals, Clyde de L. *v.2 p.272*
Ryan, Allan J. & Stephens, Robert E. (Editors). *v.1 p.50*
Ryan, Allan J. & Stephens, Robert E. *v.1 p.50*
Ryan, Allan J. *v.1 p.701, v.6 p.679*
Ryan, Christopher *v.2 p.708*
Ryan, Frank *v.5 p.204*
Ryan, Halford R. *v.2 p.28*

Ryan, James *v.1 p.764*
Ryan, Joan *v.4 p.819, p.838*
Ryan, Judith (Editor) *v.3 p.160*
Ryan, Judith *v.2 p.592*
Ryan, Mark *v.6 p.301*
Ryan, Marleigh G. *v.6 p.233*
Ryan, Mary P. *v.4 p.734*
Ryan, Michael J. *v.5 p.171*
Ryan, Patrick J. *v.5 p.495*
Ryan, William E. & Conover, Theodore E. *v.1 p.713*
Ryan, William *v.4 p.706*
Ryan-Hayes, Karen (Editor) *v.2 p.808*
Ryan-Hayes, Karen L. *v.2 p.800*
Rybczynski, Witold *v.1 p.795, p.816, v.6 p.715, p.729*
Rybicki, George B. & Lightman, Alan P. *v.5 p.67*
Rychlak, Joseph F. *v.5 p.598*
Rydel, Christine (Editor, Translator) *v.2 p.795*
Rydel, Christine (Editor) *v.2 p.796*
Ryden, David K. *v.4 p.461*
Ryder, Frank G. (Translator) *v.2 p.595*
Ryder, John (Editor) *v.1 p.516*
Ryder, Lewis H. *v.5 p.550*
Ryding, Karin C. & Mehall, David *v.6 p.654*
Ryding, Karin C. *v.6 p.654*
Ryding, Sven-Olof *v.5 p.707*
Rydstrom, Helle *v.4 p.772*
Rykwert, Joseph *v.1 p.795*
Ryle, Gilbert *v.1 p.446, p.497*
Ryman, Rhonda *v.1 p.4*
Rymer, Thomas *v.2 p.258*
Rymes, Betsy *v.4 p.315*
Rynne, Xavier *v.1 p.570*
Rynning, Sten *v.3 p.141*
Rypka, J. *v.6 p.672*
Ryscavage, Paul *v.4 p.133*
Ryser, Herbert J. *v.5 p.479*
Ryskamp, Charles *v.2 p.244*
Rystad, Goran (editor) *v.3 p.235*
Rytkonen, Paulina *v.3 p.355*
Rywerant, Yochanan & Feldenkrais, Moshe *v.1 p.52*
Rzhevsky, Nicholas (Editor) *v.2 p.795, v.3 p.210*

S

Saadat, Hadi *v.5 p.724*
Saagpakk, Paul F. *v.2 p.773*
Saari, Carolyn *v.4 p.758*
Saari, D. *v.5 p.504*
Saba, Umberto *v.2 p.723*
Sabaliunas, Leonas *v.3 p.256, p.257, p.259*
Saban Center for Middle East Policy, Brookings
   Institute *v.4 p.616*
Sabato, Larry J. *v.4 p.549, p.558*
Sabbagh, Suha *v.6 p.619*
Sabbioni, Jennifer (Editor), et al. *v.2 p.743*

Sabia, Debra *v.3 p.303*
Sabin, Roger *v.2 p.582*
Sabin, William A. *v.4 p.174*
Sabina, Leslie M. *v.1 p.394, p.403*
Sabine, Maureen *v.6 p.97, p.128*
Sableman, Mark *v.4 p.406, p.445*
Sablosky, Irving *v.1 p.279*
Sabra, Adam Abdelhamid *v.6 p.636*
Saccio, Peter *v.2 p.234*
Saccomanno, Fabio *v.5 p.360, p.369, p.724*
Saccone, Cecilia & Pesole, Graziano *v.5 p.96, p.146*
Sachar, Howard M. *v.1 p.548, p.549*
Sachar, Howard Morley *v.1 p.549, v.6 p.598, p.611*
Sachedina, Abdulaziz A. *v.1 p.558*
Sacher, John M. *v.3 p.507*
Sachov, V. N. *v.5 p.479, p.484*
Sachs, Carolyn E. *v.4 p.772, v.5 p.13, v.6 p.458*
Sachs, Curt *v.1 p.5, p.49, p.176*
Sachs, Edwin O. & Woodrow, Ernest A. *v.1 p.155*
Sachs, Harvey *v.1 p.246*
Sachs, Jeffrey D. *v.4 p.266*
Sachs, Nelly *v.2 p.615*
Sachs, Paul D. & Luff, Richard T. . . *v.4 p.788, p.872, p.881, p.886*
Sack, Allen L. & Staurowsky, Ellen J. . . *v.4 p.822, p.889, p.894*
Sackett, Susan *v.6 p.316*
Sacknoff, Scott *v.4 p.151*
Sacks, David H. *v.3 p.91*
Sacks, Howard L. & Sacks, Judith Rose *v.1 p.282*
Sacks, Oliver *v.5 p.326, p.516*
Sacks, Peter M. *v.2 p.180*
Sackville-West, Vita *v.2 p.380, p.381*
Saddhatissa, H. *v.1 p.562*
Sadek, Paul C. *v.5 p.269*
Sa'di *v.6 p.672*
Sadie, Julie Anne & Samuel, Rhian (Editors) . . *v.1 p.161, p.380*
Sadie, Julie Anne (Contribution by) *v.1 p.186*
Sadie, Stanley & Tyrrell, John (Editors) *v.1 p.162*
Sadie, Stanley (Editor) . . *v.1 p.162, p.203, p.232, p.233, p.366*
Sadie, Stanley *v.1 p.161, p.391*
Sadik, Nafis *v.6 p.426*
Sadiki, Larbi *v.4 p.615*
Sadker, David M. & Sadker, Myra P. *v.4 p.302*
Sadleir, Michael *v.2 p.317*
Sadler, Graham & Wood, Caroline . . . *v.1 p.186, p.233, p.246*
Sadler, Thomas *v.5 p.160*
Sadlier, Darlene J. (Editor, Translator) *v.2 p.693*
Sadlier, Darlene J. *v.2 p.689*
Sadock, Benjamin J. (Author, Author) *v.5 p.517*
Sadoveanu, Mihail (Translator) *v.2 p.817*
Sadovnik, Alan R. & Semel, Susan F. (Editors) . . *v.6 p.463*
Sadovskii, L. E. & Sadovskii, A. L. *v.4 p.871*
Sadowski, Michael (Editor) *v.4 p.312*
Sadtler Research Labs, Inc., Staff . . . *v.5 p.270, p.272, p.273*
Sadzeck, Tom *v.4 p.864*
Saeger, James Schofield *v.3 p.343*

Saenger, Paul H. *v.6 p.569*

Saenz-Badillos, Angel *v.6 p.646*

Saettler, L. Paul *v.4 p.352*

Saff, Donald & Sacilotto, Deli. *v.1 p.760*

Saffar, Ruth E. *v.2 p.650*

Saffle, Michael *v.1 p.164, p.203, p.336, p.366*

Safford, Frank *v.3 p.358*

Safire, William *v.3 p.479*

Safranski, Rudiger *v.1 p.467*

Saftig, Paul (Volume Editor). *v.5 p.114*

Sagan, Francoise *v.2 p.526*

Sagar, Keith *v.2 p.353, p.364*

Sagarra, Eda *v.4 p.706*

Sag'as, Ernesto & Inoa, Orlando (Editors) *v.3 p.317*

Sag'as, Ernesto. *v.3 p.317*

Sage, Leland L. *v.3 p.522*

SAGE. *v.4 p.819*

Saggers, Sherry & Gray, Dennis *v.4 p.46, v.5 p.664*

Sagner-Duchting, Karin. *v.1 p.746*

Sagolla, Lisa Jo *v.1 p.12*

Saha, Lawrence J. *v.4 p.762*

Saheb-Ettaba, Mouncef, et al. *v.6 p.654*

Sahlins, Marshall David *v.4 p.24, p.28*

Sahlins, Peter *v.3 p.243*

Saich, Tony & Van de Ven, Hans (Editors) *v.6 p.192*

Saich, Tony (Editor) *v.6 p.192*

Said, Edward W.. . . . . *v.2 p.572, v.4 p.630, p.650,*
v.6 p.97, p.114, p.124, p.595, p.619,
p.620, p.746, p.757

Said, Edward *v.6 p.619*

Said, Suzanne & Trede, Monique *v.2 p.401*

Sa'idi, Ghulam Husayn. *v.6 p.672*

Saigyo. *v.6 p.233*

Saikaku, Ihara & De Bary, William T. *v.6 p.233*

Saikal, Amin *v.4 p.642, v.6 p.634*

Sailes, Gary A. (Editor). *v.4 p.819, p.833*

Sainsbury, Malcolm *v.5 p.298*

Sainsbury, M. *v.5 p.292*

Sainsbury, R. M.. . . . . *v.1 p.447, p.493*

Saint, Assoto (Editor). *v.6 p.405*

Saint Cyprian of Carthage. *v.1 p.592*

Saint Gregory of Nyssa *v.1 p.592*

Saint Sing, Susan *v.4 p.803, p.865*

Saint-Denis, Michel *v.1 p.153*

Saint-Exupéry, Antoine de. *v.2 p.526*

Saintsbury, George E. *v.2 p.165, p.189*

Sakakida-Rawski, Evelyn *v.6 p.187*

Sakano, Theodore K., et al. *v.5 p.291*

Sakata, Hiromi Lorraine *v.1 p.287*

Sakata, Yasuo. *v.6 p.87, p.132*

Saki & Baring, Maurice. *v.2 p.381*

Saki & Chesterton, G. K. *v.2 p.381*

Saki & Milne, A. A. *v.2 p.381*

Saki & Nevinson, H. W. *v.2 p.381*

Saki & Squire, J. C. *v.2 p.381*

Saki & Walpole, Hugh *v.2 p.381*

Saklatvala, J. (Editor), et al.. . . . . *v.5 p.114*

Saklofske, Donald H. & Zeidner, Moshe (Editors). . *v.5 p.656*

Sakmyster, Thomas L. *v.3 p.187*

Saks, Elyn R. & Behnke, Stephen H.. . . . . . . *v.5 p.593*

Sakurai, J. J. & Taun, San F. *v.5 p.550*

Salacuse, Jeswald W.. . . . . *v.4 p.59, p.74*

Salaff, Janet W. *v.6 p.206*

Salaman, Graeme (Editor), et al. *v.4 p.76*

Salamensky, S. I. *v.5 p.648*

Salamo, Lin, et al.. . . . . *v.2 p.33*

Salamon, George *v.2 p.615*

Salamone, Joseph C. (Editor) *v.5 p.321, p.322*

Salamun, Tomaz *v.2 p.813*

Salanié, Bernard *v.4 p.107*

Salas, Eduardo & Fiore, Stephen M. *v.4 p.80*

Salas, Eduardo & Stone, Dianna (Editors) *v.5 p.588*

Salas, Floyd *v.6 p.503*

Salas, Susan (Editor) *v.2 p.665*

Salazar, Max *v.1 p.294, v.6 p.519*

Salazar, Ruben *v.6 p.494*

Salazar-Carrillo, Jorge & West, Bernadette *v.3 p.361*

Saldaana, Johnny (Editor) *v.2 p.25*

Saldívar, Jose D.. . . . . *v.6 p.487, p.491, p.515*

Saldivar, Ramon *v.6 p.503, p.515*

Saldivar-Hull, Sonia *v.6 p.480, p.503, p.515*

Sale, Peter F. (Editor). *v.4 p.393*

Salem, Deborah J. & Rowan, Andrew N. (Editors) . . *v.5 p.85*

Salem, Dorothy C. (Editor) *v.6 p.19, p.34, p.46*

Salem, Dorothy *v.6 p.40, p.46*

Salem, Ibtihal *v.6 p.663*

Salem, Norma *v.6 p.642*

Salemi, Marco & Vandamme, Anne-Mieke (Editors). . *v.5 p.137*

Sales and marketing management *v.4 p.143*

Saletan, Eugene J. & Cromer, Alan H. *v.5 p.547*

Salgado, Gamini *v.2 p.364*

Salgado, Maria Antonia (Editor) *v.2 p.665*

Salgado, Sebastiao *v.1 p.768*

Salhi, Kamal (Editor) *v.2 p.535*

Saliba, Therese (Editor), et al.. . . . . *v.6 p.460*

Salibi, Kamal S.. . . . . *v.6 p.604, p.605, p.620*

Saliers, Don E.. . . . . *v.1 p.654*

Salih, Halil I. *v.6 p.601*

Salih, Khaled (Editor) *v.6 p.603*

Salih, Mohamed Abdel Rahim M. *v.4 p.505, p.613*

Salih, Tayeb & Johnson-Davies, Denys. *v.6 p.663*

Salih, Tayeb *v.6 p.663*

Salinas (Editor) *v.5 p.89, p.129, p.146, p.206*

Salinger, Herman (Editor). *v.2 p.593*

Salinger, J. D. *v.2 p.118*

Salinger, Pierre. *v.3 p.479*

Salisbury, Neal. *v.6 p.683*

Salisbury, Rollin D.. . . . . *v.4 p.390*

Salk, Jonas *v.5 p.404*

Salkever, Stephen G. *v.4 p.489*

Salkin, J. *v.1 p.51*

Salkovskis, Paul M. (Editor). *v.5 p.666*

Salles-Reese, Verónica *v.3 p.264*

Sallis, James *v.2 p.80, p.86, p.87, p.124*

Sallis, John *v.1 p.511*

Sallust *v.2 p.442, p.443*

Salman, Ton (Editor) *v.3 p.268*

Salmón, Josefa *v.3 p.324*

Salmon, E. T. *v.3 p.25*

Salmon, J. H. M. *v.3 p.146*

Salmon, Nathan U. *v.1 p.505*

Salmon, Patrick *v.3 p.235, p.236*

Salmon, Paul. *v.2 p.589*

Salmon, Trevor C. & Nicoll, William (Editors). . . . *v.3 p.88*

Salmon, Trevor C. & Shepherd, Alistair J. K. *v.4 p.638*

Salmon, Wesley Charles *v.5 p.400, p.404, p.409*

Salny, S. M. *v.1 p.802*

Salomon, David *v.5 p.335, p.348*

Salomon, Nanette *v.1 p.688, p.707*

Salovey, Peter (Editor) *v.5 p.656*

Salowe, Allen E. *v.4 p.303*

Salsburg, David *v.5 p.467, p.481*

Salthouse, T. A. (Editor) *v.5 p.628, p.632*

Saltykov-Shchedrin, Mikhail Evgrafovich. *v.2 p.808*

Salucci, Ilario *v.6 p.603*

Salusineszky, Imre (Editor) *v.2 p.743*

Salvador, Amos (Editor) *v.5 p.446*

Salvador, Amos *v.5 p.450, p.452*

Salvador, Mari L., et al.. . . . . *v.3 p.305*

Salvato, Joseph A. *v.5 p.704*

Salvatore, Ricardo D. & Aguirre, Carlos (Editors) . . . *v.3 p.351*

Salvendy, Gavriel (Editor) *v.4 p.119, v.5 p.588*

Salvesen, David *v.5 p.177*

Salvesen, Magda & Cousineau, Diane *v.1 p.827*

Salvucci, Richard J. *v.3 p.287*

Salwak, Dale. *v.2 p.379*

Salwen, Micheal B. & Garrison, Bruce *v.4 p.404*

Salyers, Abigail A. & Whitt, Dixie D. *v.6 p.284*

Salzberg, Charles *v.4 p.854, p.897*

Salzberg, Hugh, Jack I. Morrow, and Stephen R. Cohen. *v.5 p.287*

Salzberg, Hugh W. *v.5 p.263*

Salzer, Felix & Schachter, Carl *v.1 p.373*

Salzer, Felix *v.1 p.372*

Salzman, Eric *v.1 p.222*

Salzman, Mark *v.6 p.197, p.216*

Salzman, Michele R.. . . . . *v.3 p.32*

Salzman, Michele Renee *v.3 p.32*

Salzman, Paul *v.2 p.203*

Salzman, Philip Carl. *v.4 p.30*

Samarco, C. Vincent *v.4 p.302*

Sambereus *v.5 p.56*

Samet, Hanan *v.5 p.335, p.340*

Samet, James M., et al. *v.5 p.96*

Samii, Kuross A.. . . . . *v.3 p.392*

Samli, A. Coskun. *v.4 p.145*

Samman, Ghada *v.6 p.663*

Sammond, Nicholas (Editor) *v.4 p.819, p.863*

Sammons, Jeffrey L. (Editor) *v.2 p.601*

Sammons, Jeffrey L. *v.2 p.601*

Sammons, Jeffrey T. *v.4 p.819, p.856*

Sammons, Vivian O. *v.6 p.22, p.34, p.48*

Samora, Julian, et al. *v.6 p.532*

Sampson, Anthony. *v.6 p.78*

Sampson, Edward C. *v.2 p.133*

Sampson, Gary & Whalley, John
(Editors) *v.4 p.257, p.268, v.5 p.29*

Sampson, Gary P. & Woolcock, Stephen (Editor, Contribution
by) *v.4 p.630, p.665*

Sampson, Gary P., et al.. . . . . *v.6 p.298*

Sampson, Geoffrey *v.2 p.564*

Sampson, George. *v.2 p.167*

Sampson, Henry T.. . . . . . *v.1 p.35, p.282,v.6 p.308, p.330*

Sampson, Karen L. *v.4 p.115, p.116*

Sams, Eric *v.1 p.203, p.236, p.355*

Samson, Jane (Editor) *v.3 p.90*

Samson, Jim (Editor). . . . *v.1 p.203, p.204, p.317, v.6 p.757*

Samson, Jim *v.1 p.203, p.204, p.222, p.242, p.317, p.373*

Samuel, Lawrence R. *v.4 p.426*

Samuel, Pierre & Zariski, Oscar *v.5 p.474*

Samuel, Raphael (Editor) *v.3 p.115, p.124*

Samuels, Andrew. *v.5 p.645*

Samuels, Martin *v.3 p.80*

Samuels, Myra L. & Witmer, Jeffrey A. *v.5 p.93*

Samuels, Raymond II (Editor) *v.3 p.540*

Samuels, Richard J.. . . . . . . *v.4 p.622, v.6 p.225*

Samuels, Shirley (Editor). *v.2 p.10*

Samuels, Steven *v.2 p.679*

Samuels, Warren J. (Editor), et al. *v.4 p.210*

Samuels, Warren J. (Editor) *v.4 p.186*

Samuelson, Paul Anthony . . . *v.4 p.196, p.197, p.204, p.210*

San Juan, E. Jr. *v.6 p.97*

San Juan, E., Jr. *v.6 p.97*

San Juan, E. Jr. *v.6 p.130*

San Juan, E., Jr. *v.6 p.130*

San Juan, E. *v.2 p.321, v.6 p.97, p.119, p.124, p.130*

San Juan, Epifanio, Jr. . . . *v.6 p.114, p.119, p.121, p.124, p.130*

San Miguel, Guadalupe Jr. *v.6 p.528*

San Miguel, Guadalupe. *v.6 p.527, p.550*

San Miguel, Pedro Luis *v.3 p.315, p.318*

Sanabria, Harry *v.3 p.282*

Sanasarian, Eliz (Editor) *v.6 p.631*

Sanasarian, Eliz *v.6 p.630*

Sanchez, Alex *v.6 p.399*

Sanchez, David A. *v.5 p.487*

Sanchez, Gonzalo J. *v.3 p.358*

Sanchez, Jean-Charles (Editor), et al. *v.5 p.104, p.118*

Sanchez, Julio *v.3 p.321*

Sanchez Korrol, Virginia *v.6 p.532*

Sanchez, Rosaura & Cruz, Rosa M. (Editors) *v.6 p.547*

Sanchez, Rosaura. *v.6 p.494*

Sanchez-Casal, Susan & MacDonald, Amie A. (Editors). *v.6 p.464*

Sanchez-Romeralo, Antonio, et al. *v.2 p.645*

Sand, George & Miles, Siân. *v.2 p.500*

Sand, George *v.2 p.499, p.500*

Sandage, Allan & Bedke, John *v.5 p.64*

Sandage, Scott A. *v.4 p.706*

Sandall, Susan, et al. *v.4 p.316*

Sandars, N. K. *v.3 p.7*

Sandars, Nancy K. *v.1 p.669*

Sanday, Peggy Reeves *v.4 p.744, v.6 p.430*

Sandbach, F. H. *v.1 p.429*

Sandburg, Carl *v.2 p.115, v.3 p.426*

Sande, Merle A. & Volberding, Paul A. *v.5 p.515, p.516*

Sandeen, Ernest Robert *v.1 p.636*

Sandel, Michael J. *v.4 p.555*

Sandemose, Aksel *v.2 p.628*

Sander, Gordon *v.3 p.205*

Sanders, Alan J. K. *v.6 p.240*

Sanders, Andrew *v.2 p.167*

Sanders, E. P. & Davies, Margaret *v.1 p.629*

Sanders, E. P. *v.1 p.548, p.627, p.631*

Sanders, James E. *v.3 p.280, p.358*

Sanders, James *v.6 p.730*

Sanders, Paula. *v.6 p.568, p.575, p.636*

Sanders, Randy *v.4 p.549*

Sanders, Robert & Campling, Jo *v.5 p.628, p.631, p.668*

Sanderson, R. T. *v.5 p.304*

Sanderson, Robert Thomas *v.5 p.304*

Sanderson, Stephen *v.4 p.760*

Sanderson, Steven E. *v.3 p.272*

Sandfort, Theo (Editor), et al. *v.6 p.357*

Sandgren, David P. *v.1 p.611*

Sandhu, Daya Singh (Editor) *v.6 p.122*

Sandin, Lyn Di Iorio *v.6 p.508, p.515*

Sandler, Ben Zion *v.5 p.715*

Sandler, Irving. *v.1 p.680, p.781*

Sandler, Stanley R. & Karo, Wolf *v.5 p.323*

Sandler, Stanley R. *v.5 p.295*

Sandler, Stephanie *v.2 p.800*

Sandlund, O. T. (Odd Terje) (Editor). *v.5 p.181*

Sandmel, Ben. *v.1 p.15*

Sandmel, Samuel. *v.1 p.550*

Sandon, John *v.1 p.798, p.808*

Sandor, Bela I. *v.5 p.691*

Sandor, Bela Imre *v.5 p.691*

Sandos, James A.. . . . . *v.3 p.295*

Sandoval, Armbruster. *v.4 p.262*

Sandoval, Jonathan (Editor) *v.4 p.353*

Sandoval, Jonathan H. (Editor), et al. *v.4 p.286*

Sandoval-Sanchez, Alberto & Sternbach, Nancy S.
(Editors) *v.1 p.68, p.125, v.2 p.25*

Sandoval-Sanchez, Alberto *v.6 p.493, p.515, p.518*

Sandoz, Mari *v.3 p.521, p.525*

Sandrow, Nahma *v.1 p.97, p.126*

Sands, Donald B. (Editor) *v.2 p.197, p.206*

Sands, Robert R. (Editor) *v.4 p.819*

Sands, Robert R. *v.4 p.819, p.859, p.894*

Sandstrom, Alan R.. . . . . *v.3 p.272*

Sandulescu, C. George (Editor) *v.2 p.321*

Sandweiss, Lee Ann (Editor) *v.3 p.512*

Sandweiss, Martha A.. . . . . *v.1 p.764*

Sandys, John Edwin *v.2 p.399*

Sanford, David H. *v.1 p.494*

Sanford, George *v.3 p.254, v.4 p.505, p.596*

Sanford, Nevitt & Comstock, Craig *v.4 p.683*

Sanford, Nevitt *v.4 p.290, p.291, p.332*

Sanford, R. J. *v.5 p.691*

Sanford, William R. & Green, Carl R. *v.3 p.509*

Sangster, Charles & Johnston, Gordon *v.2 p.733*

Sanjek, Roger (Editor) *v.4 p.24*

Sanjek, Russell *v.1 p.279, p.385*

Sanjian, Avedis K. *v.6 p.608*

Sanjines C, Javier *v.3 p.324*

Sanjur, Diva. *v.3 p.272, v.5 p.35*

Sankoff, David & Kruskal, Joseph P.. . . . . *v.5 p.336, p.341*

Sanlo, Ronni L. (Editor) *v.6 p.386*

Sanlo, Ronni L. *v.6 p.383, p.386*

Sanneh, Lamin O. & Carpenter, Joel A. (Editors) . . *v.1 p.611*

Sanneh, Lamin *v.1 p.554, p.596, p.647, v.6 p.69*

Sansom, George Bailey. *v.6 p.225*

Sansone, Carol & Sansone, Livio *v.3 p.280*

Sansone, David *v.4 p.809*

Santa Ana, Otto *v.4 p.312, v.6 p.494, p.522*

Santaniello, V. & Evenson, R. E. (Editors) *v.5 p.8*

Santaniello, V.. . . . . *v.5 p.15*

Santas, Gerasimos X.. . . . . *v.1 p.423*

Santas, Gerasimos Xenophon (Editor) *v.1 p.425*

Santayana, George *v.1 p.440, v.2 p.576*

Santelli, Maurice and Jean-Marc Pons *v.5 p.295*

Santiago, Carlos E.. . . . . *v.3 p.321*

Santiago, Esmeralda *v.2 p.155, v.6 p.490, p.508*

Santiago, Michael *v.6 p.262*

Santiago, Roberto *v.2 p.20, v.6 p.496, p.509*

Santiago, Silviano *v.2 p.693*

Santoni, Pedro *v.3 p.289*

Santoro, Gene. *v.1 p.263, p.274, p.341, p.342*

Santos, Bienvenido N. *v.6 p.102*

Santos, Hector J. de los *v.5 p.729*

Sapia, Yvonne V. *v.6 p.509*

Sapienza, Alice M. & Stork, Diana *v.5 p.219*

Sapinkopf, Lisa *v.2 p.780*

Sapir, Edward *v.4 p.20, v.5 p.624*

Sapiro, Virginia (Editor) *v.6 p.442*

Sapiro, Virginia *v.4 p.492, p.502, v.6 p.442*

Sapora, Allen Victor Heimback *v.4 p.358*

Sapoval, Bernard & Hermann, Claudine *v.5 p.555*

Sapoznik, Henry *v.1 p.300*

Sapp, Jan *v.5 p.81*

Sappho *v.2 p.419*

Sarabianov, Dmitri V. *v.1 p.688*
Saracco, Roberto, et al. *v.4 p.420*
Saracho, Olivia N. & Spodek, Bernard (Editors) . . *v.4 p.369*
Sarang, Vilas. *v.2 p.763*
Sarantakes, Nicholas Evan *v.6 p.235*
Saraphes, Stephanos G. *v.3 p.195*
Sarasohn, Lisa T. & Gassendi, Pierre *v.1 p.452, p.453*
Sarason, Seymour B. *v.4 p.277, p.281, p.329, p.348*
Sarason, Seymour Bernard. *v.4 p.329, v.5 p.572*
Sarat, Austin (Editor) *v.4 p.471*
Sarat, Austin *v.4 p.451, v.6 p.272*
Sardar, Ziauddin & Cubitt, Sean (Editors) *v.6 p.319*
Sardar, Ziauddin *v.5 p.393*
Sarduy, Severo *v.2 p.673*
Sargent, Carolyn F. & Brettell, Caroline B. *v.4 p.47*
Sargent, Carolyn F. & Johnson, Thomas M. (Editors) . *v.4 p.47*
Sargent, Paul. *v.4 p.279*
Sargeson, Frank *v.2 p.748*
Sarkar, Husain *v.1 p.454*
Sarkar, Sahotra. *v.1 p.512, v.5 p.129*
Sarkar, Tapan, et al. *v.5 p.728*
Sarkisyanz, Manuel. *v.1 p.562*
Sarlos, Robert K. *v.1 p.80, p.83, p.118*
Sarma, G P *v.2 p.762*
Sarma, Ramacandra *v.6 p.152*
Sarmiento, Jorge Louis & Gruber,
  Nicolas *v.4 p.393, v.5 p.429, p.430*
Sarna, Jonathan D. *v.1 p.549*
Sarna *v.1 p.621*
Saroyan, William *v.2 p.118*
Sarraute, Nathalie *v.2 p.527, p.579*
Sarrazin, Albertine *v.2 p.533*
Sarti, Roland *v.3 p.201, p.202*
Sarton, George *v.5 p.393, p.400, p.410*
Sarton, May *v.2 p.119, v.6 p.399*
Sartori, Giovanni. *v.4 p.574, p.579*
Sartori, Leo *v.5 p.557*
Sartre, Jean-Paul, et al. *v.2 p.528*
Sartre, Jean-Paul *v.1 p.458, p.505, p.508,*
  v.2 p.488, p.519, p.527, p.528, p.576
Sasaki, R. A. *v.6 p.102*
Saslow, James M. . . . *v.1 p.707, v.2 p.709, v.6 p.405, p.407*
Sassen, Saskia (Editor) *v.6 p.725*
Sassen, Saskia *v.4 p.496, v.6 p.719, p.721*
Sasson, Jack (Editor) *v.1 p.619*
Sasson, Jack M. (Editor) *v.6 p.651, p.665*
Sasson, Jack M. *v.1 p.623*
Sassone, Adriana Boidi, et al. *v.1 p.805*
Sassoon, Anne Showstack. *v.4 p.492*
Sassoon, David S. *v.6 p.598, p.602*
Sassoon, Donald *v.4 p.507, p.594*
Sassoon, Siegfried *v.2 p.300, p.379, p.380*
Sataloff, Robert Thayer (Editor). *v.1 p.50*
Satchell, Geoffrey H. *v.5 p.216*
Satchell, William *v.2 p.748*

Satchidanandan, K. (Editor) *v.6 p.148*
Sater, William F. *v.3 p.277, p.355, p.392*
Satie, Erik. *v.1 p.222, p.352*
Satlow, Michael L. *v.1 p.545, p.552*
Sato, Hiroaki & Watson, Burton *v.6 p.235*
Sato, Hiroaki. *v.6 p.225*
Sato, Ikuya *v.4 p.753*
Sato, Shigeru *v.6 p.178*
Satoh, Noriyuki *v.5 p.162*
Satow, Ernest M. *v.6 p.228*
Satterfield, Terre *v.5 p.39, p.41, v.6 p.292*
Sattler, Jerome M. *v.5 p.602, p.603*
Satz, Ronald N. *v.6 p.686, p.687, p.692*
Satzewich, V. *v.3 p.542*
Saucier, Gene A. *v.1 p.398*
Sauer, Carl Ortwin *v.3 p.404*
Sauer, David B. (Editor) *v.5 p.23*
Saul, John Ralston *v.4 p.510*
Saul, John S. *v.6 p.74*
Saul, Mahir *v.6 p.74*
Saul, Norman E. *v.3 p.392*
Saunders, Corinne & Bradshaw, David (Editors) . . *v.2 p.210*
Saunders, Edward Manning *v.3 p.540*
Saunders, G. Thomas *v.5 p.266*
Saunders, Michael W. *v.6 p.417*
Saunders, Peter. *v.6 p.719*
Saunders, Richard H. *v.1 p.746*
Saunders, Simon R. *v.5 p.728*
Saunders, Thomas B. *v.2 p.252*
Saunders, Vivien. *v.4 p.838, p.861*
Saunders, William S. (Editor) *v.1 p.814*
Saura, Carlos *v.1 p.21, p.36*
Saussure, Ferdinand de *v.2 p.564*
Sauter, Marc Rodolphe *v.3 p.245*
Sauveur, Albert. *v.5 p.735*
Savage, Barbara D. *v.4 p.487, p.573*
Savage, Candace C. *v.5 p.427*
Savage, Candace *v.5 p.73, p.241, p.444, p.445*
Savage, David G. & Biskupic, Joan *v.4 p.466, p.539*
Savage, David *v.4 p.456*
Savage, Jon *v.1 p.274, p.356*
Savage, Richard *v.2 p.259*
Savage-Rumbaugh, E. Sue, et al. *v.5 p.615*
Savage-Rumbaugh, Sue *v.4 p.19*
Savedoff, Barbara E. *v.1 p.764*
Savelle, Max *v.3 p.369, p.538*
Savickas, Mark L. & Spokane, Arnold R. (Editors) . *v.5 p.578*
Savickas, Mark L. & Walsh, W. Bruce (Editors). . . *v.5 p.578*
Savigliano, Marta E. *v.1 p.15, p.19, p.20*
Savigliano, Marta *v.1 p.15, p.43*
Savigneau, Josyane *v.2 p.100, v.6 p.403*
Savile, Anthony & Leibniz, Gottfried Wilhelm . . . *v.1 p.460*
Saville, John *v.4 p.604*
Saville-Troike, Muriel *v.4 p.19*

Savin-Williams, Ritch C. (Author, Editor) *v.6 p.382*
Savitch, H. V. & Kantor, Paul *v.6 p.725*
Savitz, Andrew, et al.. . . . . *v.4 p.61, p.64*
Savoie, Donald J. *v.4 p.587, p.588*
Savona, Ernesto U. (Editor) *v.6 p.253*
Savory, Elaine *v.2 p.769*
Savran, David *v.2 p.102, p.134, v.6 p.413*
Sawicki, Jana *v.6 p.461*
Sawik, Tadeusz. *v.4 p.116*
Sawin, Philip (Compiled by), et al. *v.4 p.161*
Sawyer, Birgit & Sawyer, Peter *v.3 p.232, p.233*
Sawyer, Birgit (Editor), et al. *v.3 p.236*
Sawyer, Clair N., et al. *v.5 p.310*
Sawyer, Donald T., et al. *v.5 p.285*
Sawyer, Donald T. *v.5 p.309*
Sawyer, John F. *v.1 p.525*
Sawyer, P. H. *v.3 p.236*
Sawyer, R. Keith *v.4 p.423*
Sawyer, Ralph D. *v.6 p.184*
Sawyer, Richard C. *v.5 p.27*
Sawyer, Suzana *v.4 p.711*
Sawyer, Thomas H., et al. . *v.4 p.886, p.889, p.892, p.897, p.899*
Sawyer, W. W. *v.5 p.485*
Sawyer-Lauçanno, Christopher *v.2 p.62, p.68, p.69*
Sawyers, June Skinner (Author, Editor) *v.1 p.274, p.358*
Sawyers, June Skinner *v.1 p.298*
Sax, Dov F. (Editor), et al. *v.4 p.394, v.5 p.169, p.181*
Saxe, Karen *v.5 p.494*
Saxena, Jitendra & Fischer, Farley (Editors) . . *v.5 p.363, p.376*
Saxena, Jitendra (Editor) . *v.5 p.363, p.369, p.373, p.375, p.376*
Saxonberg, Steven *v.3 p.208, v.4 p.509, p.596, p.600*
Saxton, Alexander *v.6 p.117, p.121, p.128*
Saxton, Martha *v.2 p.31*
Saxton, Ruth & Tobin, Jean (Editors) *v.2 p.366*
Sayag, Alain, et al. *v.1 p.768*
Sayari, Sabri & Esmer, Yilmaz (Editors) *v.4 p.616*
Sayer, Bill. *v.4 p.788, p.865*
Sayer, Derek *v.3 p.191*
Sayer, George *v.2 p.366*
Sayer, John W.. . . . . *v.6 p.690, p.694*
Sayers, Andrew *v.1 p.695*
Sayers, Dorothy L.. . . . . *v.2 p.381, p.382*
Sayers, Jane *v.6 p.568, p.573*
Sayers, Janet *v.5 p.629, p.631*
Sayigh, Yezid *v.6 p.620*
Sayler, Oliver M. (Editor) *v.1 p.83, p.85, p.148, p.153*
Sayler, Oliver Martin *v.1 p.110*
Sayles, Leonard R. & Smith, Cynthia J. . . *v.4 p.54, p.72, p.110*
Sayre, Kenneth M. *v.1 p.425, p.483*
Sayre, Nathan F. *v.5 p.42*
Sayre, Shay *v.4 p.136*
Sayre, Wallace S.. . . . . *v.6 p.725*
Saywell, John T. *v.3 p.544, v.4 p.590*
Sayyab, Badr Shakir *v.6 p.663*
Scafella, Frank (Editor) *v.2 p.85*

Scagel, R. F., et al.. . . . . *v.5 p.206, p.207*
Scagell, Robin *v.5 p.66*
Scaglione, Aldo *v.3 p.162*
Scagliotti, John, and Greta Schiller, directors *v.6 p.366*
Scala, Dante J.. . . . . *v.4 p.549*
Scales, James R. & Goble, Danny *v.3 p.524*
Scales, L.E. *v.5 p.493*
Scambler, Graham & Higgs, Paul *v.5 p.511*
Scammell, Geoffrey V.. . . . . *v.3 p.74*
Scammon, Richard M. *v.4 p.549*
Scancarelli, Janine (Editor) *v.6 p.690*
Scanes, C. G. *v.5 p.56*
Scanes, Colin G. *v.5 p.13*
Scanlan, James P. & Zeldin, Mary-Barbara . . . *v.1 p.473, p.474*
Scanlan, James P. (Editor), et al.. . . . . *v.1 p.473*
Scanlan, Margaret *v.2 p.191*
Scanlon, Jennifer. *v.6 p.435, p.458*
Scanlon, Paul A. *v.2 p.752*
Scanlon, T. M. *v.1 p.485*
Scanlon, Valerie C. & Sanders, Tina *v.5 p.164*
Scannell, Paddy & Cardiff, David *v.4 p.413*
Scannell, Paddy (Editor) *v.4 p.412*
Scannell, Paddy *v.4 p.412*
Scanzoni, John H. *v.4 p.734*
Scanzoni, Letha D. & Mollenkott, Virginia R.. . . . *v.6 p.373*
Scarano, Francisco A.. . . . . *v.3 p.321*
Scarborough, Elizabeth Ann & Furumoto, Laurel . . . *v.5 p.598*
Scarborough, Vernon L. & Wilcox, David R. (Editors). *v.3 p.262*
Scarce, Michael *v.6 p.378*
Scarf, Maggie *v.5 p.639*
Scarisbrick, J. J. *v.3 p.101*
Scarpaci, Joseph L.. . . . . *v.1 p.823*
Scarre, Chris. *v.4 p.6*
Scarre, Christopher *v.3 p.3, p.22*
Scarrott, Martin *v.4 p.161, p.785, p.813*
Scarry, Elaine (Editor) *v.2 p.181*
Scatton, Ernest A. *v.2 p.774*
Sceve, Maurice & Sieburth, Richard *v.2 p.472*
Sceve, Maurice. *v.2 p.472*
Schaaf, Fred *v.5 p.70*
Schaaf, Larry J. *v.1 p.768*
Schaaf, Larry John *v.1 p.724, p.763*
Schaal, Benoist (Editor), et al.. . . . . *v.5 p.607*
Schaap, Jeremy *v.4 p.856*
Schabas, William A. *v.4 p.435, p.653, v.6 p.247, p.268*
Schacht, Joseph *v.1 p.556*
Schacht, Richard (Editor) *v.1 p.467*
Schacht, Richard. *v.1 p.438, p.467*
Schacter, Bernice *v.5 p.219, p.249*
Schacter, Daniel L.. . . . . *v.5 p.610*
Schade-Poulsen, Marc *v.6 p.644*
Schaechter, Elio *v.5 p.209*
Schaefer, Eric *v.6 p.314*
Schaeffer, Jean-Marie *v.1 p.480*
Schaeffer, Neil *v.2 p.484*

Schaeper, Thomas J. *v.3 p.151*

Schafer, Edward H. *v.6 p.185, p.204*

Schafer, R. Murray. *v.1 p.375, p.382*

Schafer, William J. *v.2 p.741*

Schaff, Philip *v.1 p.598, v.3 p.58*

Schaffer, Dylan. *v.2 p.734*

Schaffer, Frederic C. *v.4 p.505, p.585, p.613*

Schaffer, Kay & Smith, Sidonie (Editors) . . . *v.4 p.846, p.892*

Schaffer, Kristen *v.6 p.715*

Schaffer, Moselle *v.5 p.85*

Schaffner, Ingrid & Abrams, Harry N., Staff *v.1 p.746*

Schain, Martin A. (Editor), et al.. . . . . . . *v.4 p.129*

Schakel, Peter J. (Editor) *v.2 p.366*

Schaller, Mark & Crandall, Christian S. (Editors) . . . *v.5 p.637*

Schaller, Michael *v.3 p.392, p.479*

Schalock, Robert L. *v.5 p.672*

Schama, Simon. *v.1 p.814, v.3 p.205*

Schamschula, Walter (Editor) *v.2 p.781, p.782*

Schanberg, Sydney H. *v.6 p.170*

Schank, Roger C. (Editor). *v.5 p.590*

Schanke, Robert A. & Marra, Kimberely Bell
    (Editors). *v.1 p.126, p.135*

Schanke, Robert A. & Marra, Kimberley B.
    (Editors). *v.1 p.126, p.135, v.2 p.16, v.6 p.413*

Schanke, Robert A. & Marra, Kimberley Bell (Editors). *v.6 p.413*

Schanke, Robert A.
    (Editor), et al. *v.1 p.126, v.6 p.358, p.359, p.413*

Schanke, Robert A.. . . . . *v.6 p.403*

Schantz, Hans *v.5 p.728*

Schanz, Tom (Editor) *v.5 p.699*

Schanzer, Ernest *v.2 p.231*

Schaper, Michael *v.4 p.51, p.52, p.54*

Schapiro, Meyer *v.1 p.746*

Schapsmeier, Edward L. &
    Schapsmeier, Frederick H.. . . . . . *v.3 p.462, p.479*

Schapsmeier, Frederick H. & Schapsmeier, Edward L. . . *v.5 p.6*

Scharff, Robert C. *v.1 p.455*

Scharfstein, Ben-Ami. *v.1 p.417*

Scharlin, Craig & Villanueva, Lilia V.. *v.6 p.95, p.117, p.119, p.130*

Scharnhorst, Gary (Editor). *v.2 p.5*

Scharnhorst, Gary *v.2 p.40*

Schattschneider, Doris & Escher, M. C. *v.5 p.460*

Schatz, Edward *v.3 p.231*

Schatz, Thomas G. *v.6 p.311*

Schatzberg, Michael G.. . . . . . *v.4 p.513, p.613, v.6 p.442*

Schatzberg, Rufus & Kelly, Robert J. *v.6 p.251*

Schatzman, Michelle *v.5 p.492*

Schawlow, Arthur L. & Townes, C. H. *v.5 p.562*

Schebera, Jurgen. *v.1 p.223, p.253, p.368*

Schechner, Richard & Schuman, Mady (Editors) . . . *v.1 p.136*

Schechner, Richard. *v.1 p.135, p.136*

Schechter, Danny. *v.4 p.417*

Schechter, John Mendell *v.1 p.294, v.3 p.270, p.271*

Schechter, Patricia A.. . . . . . . *v.6 p.8, p.19, p.46*

Schechter, Solomon. *v.1 p.547*

Schechter, Susan *v.4 p.752*

Schecter, Barnet *v.4 p.713*

Schecter, Sandra R. & Bayley, Robert *v.6 p.494*

Scheer, Edward *v.2 p.507*

Scheese, Don *v.6 p.288*

Schefer, Jean Louis. *v.1 p.704*

Scheff, Thomas J. *v.4 p.775*

Scheffler, Israel (Editor), et al.. . . . . *v.4 p.308*

Scheffler, Israel *v.4 p.329, p.345, v.5 p.404*

Schefold, Karl *v.1 p.671*

Scheibe, Karl E. *v.5 p.594*

Scheick, William J. (Editor) *v.2 p.319*

Scheick, William *v.2 p.8*

Scheid, Francis J.. . . . . *v.5 p.492*

Scheid, John *v.1 p.533, v.3 p.24*

Scheid, Rickne C. & Woelfel, Julian B. *v.5 p.525, p.526*

Schein, Edgar H. *v.4 p.75*

Schein, Richard H. *v.4 p.382*

Scheina, Robert L. *v.3 p.277*

Scheindlin, Raymond P. *v.6 p.566, p.574, p.654*

Scheiner, Ethan *v.4 p.622*

Scheiner, Samuel M. & Gurevitch, Jessica *v.5 p.171*

Scheingold, Stuart A. *v.4 p.442*

Scheirs, John. *v.5 p.691*

Schelbert, Leo (Editor) *v.3 p.245*

Schelde, Per *v.6 p.319*

Schele, Linda & Freidel, David *v.3 p.262*

Schele, Linda & Miller, Mary Ellen *v.1 p.684*

Scheler, Max Ferdinand *v.1 p.523, p.768*

Schell, Herbert Samuel *v.3 p.523*

Schell, Jonathan *v.3 p.479, v.4 p.656, p.657*

Schell, Orville *v.6 p.241*

Schell, Patience A.. . . . . *v.4 p.336*

Schelle, Bernadette & Martin, Clemens. *v.6 p.253*

Schelling, Friedrich Wilhelm Joseph *v.1 p.465*

Schellmann, Jorg, et al. *v.1 p.758*

Schemann, Hans *v.2 p.621*

Schement, Jorge Reina (Editor) *v.4 p.423*

Schempp, Paul *v.4 p.797*

Schena, Mark (Editor) *v.5 p.110*

Schena, Mark *v.5 p.110, p.111, p.146*

Schenker, Alexander M.. . . . . *v.2 p.788*

Schenker, Heinrich. *v.1 p.204, p.307, p.373*

Schenkkan, Robert *v.2 p.155*

Scheper-Hughes, Nancy & Wacquant, Loic (Editors) . *v.5 p.249*

Scheper-Hughes, Nancy *v.3 p.280, v.4 p.46*

Schepers, Ute *v.5 p.137*

Scher, Paula *v.1 p.713*

Scher, Philip W.. . . . . *v.4 p.44*

Scher, Richard K. *v.3 p.497*

Scher, Steven Paul (Editor) *v.1 p.382*

Scherer, F. M. *v.1 p.385, v.4 p.230, p.235*

Scherer, Nancy *v.4 p.525*

Schermerhorn, John R.. . . . . *v.4 p.73*

Scheuerle, Angela *v.5 p.151*

Scheuerman, William E. *v.4 p.470*

Scheurer, Timothy E. *v.1 p.274*

Schey, H. M.. . . . . *v.5 p.486*

Schávelzon, Daniel *v.3 p.272*

Schérer, Jacques *v.2 p.462*

Schölkopf, Bernhard (Editor), et al.. *v.5 p.107, p.109, p.339, p.341*

Schönfelder, Volker *v.5 p.67*

Schick, Allen *v.4 p.543*

Schick, Kathy D. & Toth, Nicholas *v.4 p.17*

Schiebinger, Londa *v.3 p.48*

Schieffelin, Bambi B. & Ochs, Elinor (Editor, Contribution
by) *v.4 p.20*

Schieffelin, Bambi B. (Editor), et al. *v.4 p.21*

Schieffelin, Bambi B. *v.4 p.20*

Schieffelin, Edward L. & Crittenden, Robert *v.4 p.43*

Schiemer, Suzanne *v.4 p.798*

Schier, Steven E. (Editor). *v.3 p.479, p.484*

Schier, Steven E. *v.4 p.549*

Schiff, David *v.1 p.223, p.242, p.316, p.325*

Schiff, Leonard I.. . . . . *v.5 p.550*

Schiff, Maurice. *v.5 p.724*

Schiff, Stacy. *v.2 p.105, p.527*

Schiff, Ze'ev & Ya'ari, Ehud *v.6 p.606, p.615*

Schiff, Zeev *v.6 p.620*

Schiffer, Michael Brian *v.4 p.6*

Schiffman, Lawrence H. & VanderKam, James C.
(Editors) *v.1 p.546*

Schiffman, Lawrence H. *v.1 p.548*

Schiffman, Susan, et al.. . . . . *v.5 p.599*

Schiffrin, Andre *v.4 p.149*

Schilit, Howard M. *v.4 p.92, p.97, p.105, p.106, p.111*

Schillebeeckx, Edward & Smith, David *v.1 p.639*

Schillebeeckx, Edward *v.1 p.577, p.638, p.641*

Schiller, Friedrich & Passage, Charles E. *v.2 p.601*

Schiller, Friedrich *v.1 p.460, p.481, v.2 p.601*

Schiller, Wendy J. *v.4 p.534*

Schilling, Govert *v.5 p.67*

Schilling, Mark *v.6 p.306, p.317, p.336*

Schilling, Robert J.. . . . . *v.5 p.712*

Schillinger, Joseph *v.1 p.373*

Schilpp, Paul Arthur (Editor) *v.1 p.446, p.458, p.469*

Schilpp, Paul Arthur *v.1 p.443, p.469*

Schilthuizen, Menno *v.5 p.199*

Schimel, Lawrence (Editor). *v.6 p.369, p.374*

Schimmel, Annemarie. *v.1 p.559, p.560, v.6 p.663, p.673*

Schindeler, Fred F. *v.4 p.590*

Schindler, Anton F. & Macardle, Donald W. . . *v.1 p.204, p.308*

Schinka, John A. & Velicer, Wayne F. *v.5 p.594*

Schinner, Franz F. (Editor), et al. *v.5 p.89*

Schirazi, Asghar *v.6 p.633*

Schirmer, Daniel B. & Shalom, Stephen R. (Editors) *v.3 p.392*

Schirmer, Jennifer *v.3 p.277*

Schirmer, Sherry Lamb *v.3 p.512*

Schiro, Michael Stephen *v.4 p.365*

Schirokauer, Conrad, et al. *v.6 p.181*

Schissler, Hanna *v.3 p.177*

Schivelbusch,
Wolfgang *v.3 p.176, p.282, v.4 p.706, p.710, v.6 p.766*

Schlagel, Richard H. *v.3 p.45, v.5 p.389*

Schlager, Neil (Editor) *v.4 p.129*

Schlager, Nell Y. *v.5 p.684*

Schlaich, Joan & DuPont, Betty (Editors) *v.1 p.37*

Schlam, Carl C. *v.2 p.429*

Schlauch, Margaret (Translator) *v.2 p.625*

Schlegel, Eric M. *v.5 p.67, p.541*

Schlegel, Friedrich *v.2 p.601*

Schleien, Stuart J. *v.4 p.785, p.801*

Schleiermacher, Friedrich Daniel Ernst. . . . *v.1 p.521, p.642*

Schleiermacher, Friedrich *v.1 p.636*

Schlein, Alan M. *v.5 p.679*

Schlemmer, Oskar *v.1 p.148*

Schlesinger, Arthur M. Jr. *v.3 p.372, p.375, p.418,
p.444, p.450, p.479, v.4 p.522, p.642*

Schlesinger, Stephen *v.4 p.635*

Schlesinger, William H.. . . . . *v.5 p.440, p.441*

Schleunes, Karl A. *v.3 p.86, p.173*

Schleuter, June (Editor) *v.1 p.122*

Schleyer, Paul von Ragué *v.5 p.275*

Schlick, Mary D. *v.1 p.806*

Schliemann, Heinrich *v.3 p.16*

Schliwa, Manfred (Editor). *v.5 p.114*

Schloezer, Boris *v.1 p.223, p.355*

Schloss, Joseph G. *v.1 p.274, p.388*

Schlossberg, David *v.5 p.533*

Schlossberg, Herbert *v.6 p.759*

Schlosser, Eric *v.5 p.35*

Schlossman, Steven L. *v.4 p.473*

Schlüter, Thomas *v.5 p.433*

Schlueter, June *v.2 p.617*

Schlundt, Christina L. *v.1 p.4, p.37*

Schmalenbach, Werner *v.1 p.699*

Schmalensee, Richard & Willig, Robert D. (Editors). *v.4 p.191*

Schmandt, Jurgen (Editor), et al.. . . . . *v.4 p.420*

Schmid, Alex Peter & Jongman, A. J. *v.4 p.661*

Schmid, Andre *v.6 p.237*

Schmid, Carol L. *v.4 p.706*

Schmid, David *v.6 p.256*

Schmidbauer, Hubert *v.5 p.309*

Schmidgall, Gary *v.1 p.233, v.6 p.403*

Schmidt, Alvin J.. . . . . *v.4 p.719*

Schmidt, Dennis J. *v.1 p.57, p.71, p.89*

Schmidt, Diane, et al.. . . . . *v.5 p.324*

Schmidt, Elizabeth. *v.6 p.77*

Schmidt, Gustav (Editor) *v.4 p.639*

Schmidt, Harvey & Jones, Tom *v.1 p.253, p.409*

Schmidt, Hugo. *v.2 p.601*

Schmidt, James (Editor) *v.3 p.72*

Schmidt, Kerstin *v.1 p.87, p.118*

Schmidt, Kimberly D. (Author, Editor), et al.. . . . *v.3 p.344*

Schmidt, Michael. *v.2 p.180*

Schmidt, Nancy J. *v.6 p.334*

Schmidt, Peter *v.4 p.14*

Schmidt, Richard A. & Wrisberg, Craig A. *v.4 p.910*

Schmidt, Susanne K. & Werle, Raymund *v.4 p.420*

Schmidt-Kittler, N. & Vogel, K. (Editors) . . . *v.5 p.196, p.205*

Schmidt-Nowara, Christopher *v.3 p.241*

Schmidtz, David (Editor) *v.1 p.442*

Schmied, Wieland & Fuerst, Andrea *v.1 p.699*

Schmied, Wieland & Whitford, Frank *v.1 p.666*

Schmied, Wieland *v.1 p.746*

Schmieder, Wolfgang *v.1 p.164, p.186, p.304*

Schmincke, Hans-Ulrich *v.5 p.437*

Schmitt, Arno & Sofer, Jehoeda *v.6 p.374*

Schmitt, Bernadotte Everly *v.3 p.249*

Schmitt, Bernd H. *v.4 p.135*

Schmitt, C. B. (Editor), et al. *v.1 p.435, v.3 p.71*

Schmitt, Charles B. *v.3 p.71*

Schmitt, Fritz; Unter Mitarbeit von Gerhard Fricke . . *v.2 p.589*

Schmitt, Karl Michael *v.3 p.392*

Schmitt, Peter J. *v.3 p.369*

Schmitt, Richard *v.1 p.505*

Schmitz, David F. & Jespersen, T. Christopher (Editors). *v.3 p.454*

Schmitz, David F. (Editor) *v.3 p.444, p.462*

Schmottlach, Neil & McManama, Jerre . *v.4 p.798, p.799, p.800*

Schmuck, Richard A. & Schmuck, Patricia A. *v.4 p.350*

Schnabel, Julian *v.1 p.699*

Schnadelbach, R. Terry *v.1 p.816, p.817*

Schnapp, Jeffrey T. *v.1 p.718*

Schneemelcher, Wilhelm (Editor) *v.1 p.632*

Schneemelcher, Wilhelm *v.1 p.632*

Schneider, Arnd & Wright, Christopher (Editors) . . . *v.4 p.26*

Schneider, Ben R. Jr. (Compiled by) *v.1 p.103, p.141*

Schneider, Ben Ross *v.3 p.260*

Schneider, Benjamin & Smith, D. Brent (Editors) . . . *v.5 p.656*

Schneider, Carl E. (Editor) *v.4 p.448, p.539*

Schneider, Cathy L. *v.3 p.355*

Schneider, David J. *v.4 p.694, v.5 p.605, p.650*

Schneider, David M. *v.4 p.32, p.734*

Schneider, David Murray *v.4 p.32*

Schneider, Elizabeth M. *v.4 p.472*

Schneider, Jane & Schneider, Peter T. *v.3 p.204*

Schneider, Mark *v.4 p.543*

Schneider, Mary W. *v.2 p.266*

Schneider, Michael *v.4 p.266*

Schneider, P., et al. *v.5 p.67*

Schneider, Richard E. & Ford, Mary Jo *v.1 p.150*

Schneider, Richard J. (Editor) *v.2 p.52, v.6 p.288*

Schneider, Stephen H. (Editor), et al. *v.6 p.301*

Schneider, Stephen Henry (Editor), et al. *v.5 p.249*

Schneider, Steven Jay & Shaw, Daniel (Editors) . . . *v.6 p.319*

Schneider, Wayne (Editor) *v.1 p.223, p.325*

Schneider, Wolfgang & Pressley, Michael . . . *v.5 p.629, p.630*

Schneiderman, Leo *v.5 p.636*

Schneiders, Sandra M. *v.1 p.578*

Schneier, Bruce *v.5 p.335, p.342, p.343*

Schneier, Edward V. & Gross, Bertram M. *v.4 p.531*

Schneirov, Matthew *v.4 p.410*

Schnittke, Alfred *v.1 p.223, p.353*

Schnitzler, Arthur & Hutter, Catherine *v.2 p.615*

Schnitzler, Arthur *v.2 p.615*

Schobert, Harold H. *v.5 p.738*

Schoch, Richard W. *v.2 p.189*

Schock, Kurt *v.4 p.766, p.767*

Schodt, David W. *v.3 p.333*

Schodt, Frederik L. *v.6 p.228*

Schoeck, Richard J. *v.2 p.210*

Schoen, Johanna *v.4 p.756*

Schoenbaum, David *v.3 p.173*

Schoenbaum, Samuel *v.2 p.221, p.227, p.228*

Schoenberg, Arnold *v.1 p.223, p.353, p.373*

Schoenborn, Christoph *v.1 p.654*

Schoenbrod, David *v.4 p.532*

Schoenfeld, Alan H. *v.5 p.460, p.464*

Schoenfeld, Bruce *v.4 p.809, p.833, p.838, p.864*

Schoenhals, Kai P. *v.3 p.175*

Schoenhals, Michael (Editor) *v.6 p.196*

Schoenrich, Otto *v.3 p.404, p.406*

Schoep, Arthur & Harris, Daniel *v.1 p.396, p.412*

Schoffeleers, J. Matthew *v.6 p.76*

Schofield, Andrew *v.5 p.699*

Schofield, Malcolm (Editor), et al. *v.1 p.517*

Schofield, Malcolm, et al. *v.1 p.422*

Schofield, Malcolm *v.1 p.422*

Schofield, Norman *v.4 p.484, p.769*

Schofield, W. B. *v.5 p.209*

Scholarly Resources Staff & Gallup, George Jr. *v.5 p.586*

Scholastic, Inc. Staff (Contribution by) *v.4 p.535*

Scholberg, Kenneth R. *v.2 p.651*

Scholem, Gershom Gerhard *v.1 p.547*

Scholem, Gershom *v.1 p.551, p.552*

Scholes, Myron S., et al. *v.4 p.248*

Scholes, Robert E. *v.2 p.165*

Scholes, Robert *v.2 p.567, p.571*

Scholl, Tim *v.1 p.24, p.25*

Scholle, Peter A. & Ulmer-Scholle, Dana S. . . . *v.5 p.439, p.440*

Schollgen, Gregor (Editor) *v.3 p.80, p.161*

Scholz, Eugen *v.5 p.268*

Schomburg Center for Research in Black Culture . . . *v.6 p.476*

Schonberg, Harold C. *v.1 p.332, p.333, p.391, p.403*

Schonberger, Richard J. *v.4 p.119*

Schonfeld, Martin *v.1 p.462*

Schonle, Andreas *v.2 p.800*

School and Community Safety Society of America
Staff *v.4 p.786, p.788*

Schoolfield, George C. (Editor) *v.2 p.593*

Schoolfield, George C. *v.3 p.236*

Schoonhoven, Louis M., et al. *v.5 p.27*

Schoonmaker, Frances *v.4 p.277*

Schoonmaker, Trevor (Editor) *v.1 p.286, p.335*

Schoonover, Thomas D. *v.3 p.305*

Schoonover, Thomas *v.3 p.400*

Schoop, Trudi & Mitchell, Peggy *v.1 p.51*
Schopen, Gregory *v.1 p.566*
Schopenhauer, Arthur. *v.1 p.465, p.466*
Schopf, J. William (Editor). *v.5 p.81, p.196*
Schopf, J. William *v.5 p.447, p.449*
Schopp, Claude *v.2 p.489*
Schoppa, R. Keith *v.6 p.189, p.191, p.202, p.206*
Schor, Esther (Editor). *v.2 p.310*
Schor, Joel A. *v.3 p.421*
Schor, Juliet B. *v.5 p.581, p.587*
Schor, Mira *v.6 p.473*
Schorer, Suki *v.1 p.25*
Schork, M. Anthony & Remington, Richard D.. . . . *v.5 p.93*
Schorr, Thelma M. & Kennedy, Maureen Shawn . . . *v.5 p.529*
Schorske, Carl E.. . . . . *v.3 p.184, v.4 p.610*
Schott, Matthew & Conrad, Glenn R. (Editors) *v.3 p.507*
Schouls, Peter A.. . . . . *v.1 p.448*
Schouvaloff, Alexander & Wadsworth, Atheneum. . . . *v.1 p.46*
Schouvaloff, Alexander *v.1 p.46*
Schrader, Abby M.. . . . . *v.3 p.218*
Schrage, Michael *v.4 p.67*
Schram, Stuart R. (Editor). *v.6 p.202*
Schreck, C. B. & Moyle, Peter B. (Editors). *v.5 p.216*
Schrecker, Ellen *v.3 p.450*
Schrecker, John E. *v.6 p.183*
Schreiber, B. Charlotte (Editor) *v.5 p.451*
Schreiber, Gerhard, et al. *v.3 p.175*
Schreiner, Claus *v.1 p.21, p.294, p.299*
Schreiner, Olive *v.2 p.757*
Schreuder, Deryck M. *v.6 p.75*
Schröder, Monika J. A. *v.4 p.160*
Schröder, Thies (Volume Editor). *v.1 p.814*
Schriber, Mary S. *v.6 p.480*
Schrieffer, J. Robert *v.5 p.565*
Schrire, Robert A. (Editor) *v.4 p.614*
Schroedel, Jean
  Reith *v.4 p.527, p.528, p.531, p.532, p.569, v.6 p.471*
Schroeder, Alan *v.4 p.556*
Schroeder, Daniel J.. . . . . *v.5 p.66*
Schroeder, Daniel V. *v.5 p.560*
Schroeder, David P. *v.1 p.192, p.242, p.331*
Schroeder, H. J. (Translator). *v.1 p.570*
Schroeder, John Herman *v.3 p.401, p.418*
Schroeder, Manfred R. *v.5 p.498*
Schroeder, Patricia R. *v.1 p.263, p.282, p.334*
Schroeder, Paul W. *v.3 p.75*
Schroeder, Susan (Editor) *v.3 p.287*
Schroeder, Susan. *v.3 p.287*
Schroeder, W. L., et al. *v.5 p.422*
Schroeer, Dietrich *v.5 p.411*
Schroer, Craig *v.6 p.487, p.519*
Schroeter, Daniel J. *v.6 p.598, p.644*
Schubert, William H. *v.4 p.365*
Schuchard, Ronald. *v.2 p.72*
Schueller, Wolfgang *v.5 p.698*

Schuetz, Janice & Snedaker, Kathryn H. *v.4 p.438*
Schugerl, K. & Zeng, A. P. (Editors) *v.5 p.742*
Schugurensky, Daniel. *v.4 p.329*
Schuh, Randall T. *v.5 p.171*
Schulberg, Budd *v.2 p.115*
Schulenberg, David *v.1 p.186, p.242, p.304*
Schuler, Friedrich E. *v.3 p.295*
Schulhofer, Stephen J. *v.4 p.472*
Schulkin, Jay *v.5 p.617*
Schuller, Gunther A. *v.1 p.263*
Schuller, Gunther *v.1 p.223, p.263, p.403*
Schulman, Sarah *v.1 p.253, p.380, v.6 p.399, p.413*
Schulte, Theo. *v.3 p.86, p.175*
Schulten, Susan *v.4 p.378*
Schultes, Richard E., et al. *v.5 p.16*
Schultz, Bradley *v.4 p.408, p.409, p.902, p.907*
Schultz, David *v.4 p.539*
Schultz, Debra L.. . . . . *v.6 p.432*
Schultz, Don E. & Barnes, Beth *v.4 p.427*
Schultz, James A. *v.3 p.55, p.162*
Schultz, Jane E. *v.4 p.522*
Schultz, Jeffrey D. (Editor), et al. . . . *v.4 p.573, v.6 p.87, p.121*
Schultz, Jeffrey. *v.2 p.123, v.4 p.559*
Schultz, Jnrgen *v.5 p.185*
Schultz, Juergen *v.1 p.787, v.6 p.555, p.577, p.579, p.581*
Schultz, Kirsten *v.3 p.77, p.244, p.337*
Schultz, Nancy L. *v.3 p.370*
Schultz, Susan M. (Editor) *v.2 p.58*
Schultz, Theodore W. (Editor) *v.4 p.266*
Schultz *v.2 p.503*
Schultze, Quentin J. *v.1 p.656*
Schulz, Andrew *v.1 p.758*
Schulz, Bruno, et al. *v.2 p.791*
Schulz, Donald E. (Editor) *v.3 p.313*
Schulz, Dorothy Moses *v.6 p.260*
Schulz, Eckehard *v.6 p.654*
Schulz, Norbert *v.5 p.70*
Schulz, Richard *v.4 p.751*
Schulze, Ernst-Detlef (Editor) *v.5 p.185*
Schulze, Franz *v.1 p.795*
Schulze, Hagen & Schneider, Deborah L.. . . . . . *v.3 p.160*
Schulze, Hagen *v.3 p.179*
Schulze, Ralf *v.4 p.689*
Schulze-Makuch, Dirk & Irwin, Louis N.. . . . . . . *v.5 p.243*
Schulzinger, Robert D. (Editor) *v.3 p.386*
Schulzinger, Robert D. *v.3 p.454, p.479*
Schumacher, Michael *v.2 p.79, v.6 p.403*
Schumaker, Lyn *v.4 p.38*
Schumaker, Paul D. & Loomis, Burdett A. (Editors). . *v.4 p.527*
Schuman, Howard & Presser, Stanley *v.4 p.691*
Schumann, Robert *v.1 p.204, p.355*
Schumm, Stanley A. *v.5 p.427*
Schumpeter, Joseph
  Alois.*v.4 p.210, p.212, p.229, p.230, p.235, p.245, p.500, p.505, p.507*
Schuparra, Kurt *v.3 p.531*

Schur, Edwin M. *v.4 p.697, v.6 p.446*
Schur, Max *v.5 p.598*
Schurer, Ernst (Editor) *v.1 p.68, p.85, p.110*
Schurer, Ernst *v.2 p.612*
Schurmann-Zeggel, Heinz *v.2 p.741*
Schurz, Carl *v.3 p.434*
Schuster, Angela M. H. & Polk, Milbry *v.1 p.823*
Schutt, Hans-Werner *v.5 p.261*
Schutte, Ofelia *v.4 p.685*
Schutz, Alfred *v.4 p.685, p.686*
Schutz, Bernard F. *v.5 p.72, p.558*
Schuurman, Nadine *v.4 p.388*
Schwab, Donald P. *v.4 p.179*
Schwab, Glenn O., et al. *v.5 p.703*
Schwab, Peter *v.3 p.313*
Schwade, Arcadio *v.6 p.222*
Schwaller, John F. *v.3 p.287*
Schwanauer, Stephen & Levitt, David *v.1 p.388*
Schwandner-Sievers, Stephanie & Fischer, Bernd Jurgen
   (Editors) *v.3 p.252*
Schwandt, Thomas A. *v.4 p.689*
Schwantes, Carlos A. *v.3 p.530*
Schwarcz, Joseph & Schwarcz, Chava . . . *v.1 p.716*
Schwarcz, Lilia Moritz *v.3 p.337*
Schwarcz, Lilia *v.3 p.342*
Schwartz, Arthur & Schwartz, Ruth M. *v.5 p.660*
Schwartz, Arthur, et al. *v.4 p.758*
Schwartz, Barry *v.5 p.650*
Schwartz, Barth D. *v.2 p.722*
Schwartz, Benjamin I. *v.6 p.191, p.203*
Schwartz, Bernard (Editor) *v.4 p.456, p.539*
Schwartz, Bernard . . . *v.4 p.440, p.452, p.466, p.469, p.539*
Schwartz, David G. *v.6 p.253*
Schwartz, Delmore *v.2 p.119*
Schwartz, Elliott & Godfrey, Daniel *v.1 p.223*
Schwartz, Elliott, et al. *v.1 p.223*
Schwartz, Elliott *v.1 p.223, p.245*
Schwartz, Evan I. *v.4 p.67*
Schwartz, Frederic J. *v.1 p.713*
Schwartz, Herman (Author, Editor, Introduction by) . *v.4 p.539*
Schwartz, Herman (Editor) *v.4 p.539, p.541*
Schwartz, Howard F. (Editor), et al. *v.5 p.47*
Schwartz, Jeffrey H., et al. *v.4 p.16*
Schwartz, Jeffrey H. *v.5 p.199*
Schwartz, Jerry R. *v.4 p.414*
Schwartz, John A. *v.4 p.332*
Schwartz, Judith L. & Schlundt, Christina L. . . . *v.1 p.22*
Schwartz, Karlene V. & Margulis, Alexander R. . . . *v.5 p.205*
Schwartz, Lita Linzer & Kaslow, Florence W. . . . *v.5 p.640*
Schwartz, Lloyd & Estess, Sybil P. (Editors) . . . *v.2 p.62*
Schwartz, M. (Editor) *v.5 p.429, v.6 p.284*
Schwartz, Marie Jenkins *v.4 p.706*
Schwartz, Matthew *v.4 p.143*
Schwartz, Mel *v.5 p.679, p.691*
Schwartz, Melvin M. *v.5 p.691*

Schwartz, Mildred A. *v.4 p.587*
Schwartz, Mischa *v.4 p.422*
Schwartz, Murray M. & Kahn, Coppelia *v.2 p.231*
Schwartz, Pedro *v.4 p.223*
Schwartz, Peter & Gibb, Blair *v.4 p.145*
Schwartz, Richard A. *v.3 p.444*
Schwartz, Richard B. *v.3 p.109, p.129*
Schwartz, Ronald D. *v.6 p.241*
Schwartz, Rosalie *v.3 p.313*
Schwartz, Sheila (Editor), et al. *v.1 p.773*
Schwartz, Stuart B. (Editor) *v.3 p.287*
Schwartz, Stuart B. *v.3 p.280, p.335*
Schwartz, Susan L. *v.1 p.16*
Schwartz, Thomas A. *v.3 p.176*
Schwarz, A. B. Christa *v.6 p.393*
Schwarz, Boris *v.1 p.246*
Schwarz, Cindy *v.5 p.552*
Schwarz, Daniel R. *v.2 p.114, v.6 p.731*
Schwarz, Egon *v.2 p.597*
Schwarz, Hans P. *v.3 p.177*
Schwarz, Hans-Peter *v.3 p.177*
Schwarz, James A., et al. *v.5 p.679*
Schwarz, James A. *v.5 p.275*
Schwarz, Jordan A. *v.3 p.462*
Schwarz, Philip J. *v.4 p.474*
Schwarz, Roberto *v.2 p.693*
Schwarz, Roger *v.4 p.174*
Schwarz-Bart, Simone; Schwarz-Bart, André . . . *v.2 p.538*
Schwarz-Bart, Simone *v.2 p.538*
Schwarzenbach, René P., et al. *v.5 p.310*
Schwarzmantel, J. J. *v.4 p.487, p.554*
Schwarzschild, Martin *v.5 p.70, p.71*
Schwebel, Andrew I. & Fine, Mark A. . . . *v.5 p.666, p.668*
Schwebel, Sara L., et al. *v.4 p.277*
Schweber, Silvan S. *v.5 p.544, p.566*
Schwedler, Jillian (Editor) *v.6 p.595*
Schweidler, Max *v.1 p.824*
Schweikert, Harry C. (Editor) *v.2 p.795*
Schweitzer, Albert *v.1 p.627, p.638*
Schweitzer, Philip A. (Editor) *v.5 p.735*
Schweitzer, Philip A. *v.5 p.691, p.735*
Schweizer, Bernard *v.2 p.389*
Schweizer, Peter & Schweizer, Rochelle *v.3 p.484*
Schweizer, Peter *v.3 p.479*
Schwieder, Dorothy *v.3 p.522*
Schwinger, Julian Seymour, et al. *v.5 p.565*
Schwinger, Wolfram *v.1 p.223, p.347*
Schwitters, Kurt *v.1 p.699*
Schwoerer, Lois G. *v.3 p.107*
Scientific American Editors *v.5 p.388*
Scientific American Staff *v.5 p.146*
Scigliano, Eric *v.1 p.781*
Sclater, Neil & Chironis, Nicholas P. *v.5 p.715*
Scliar, Moacyr & Giacomelli, Eloah F. *v.2 p.693*

Scliar, Moacyr *v.2 p.693*
Scobbie, Irene *v.3 p.235*
Scobie, Ingrid W. *v.3 p.462*
Scobie, James R. *v.4 p.706*
Scodari, Paul F. *v.5 p.177, p.181*
Scollon, Ronald & Scollon, Suzanne Wong *v.4 p.20*
Sconce, Jeffrey *v.4 p.419*
Scoppettone, Sandra *v.6 p.399*
Scott, A. C. (Author, Illustrator) *v.1 p.132, p.134*
Scott, A. C. *v.1 p.133, p.134*
Scott, Allen J. (Editor) *v.6 p.725*
Scott, Allen J. *v.4 p.398*
Scott, Allen John *v.6 p.345*
Scott, Claudia D. *v.5 p.511*
Scott, Clive *v.2 p.461*
Scott, David (Editor) *v.4 p.286*
Scott, David L. *v.4 p.97*
Scott, Derek B. (Editor) *v.1 p.377*
Scott, Franklin Daniel *v.3 p.232, p.235*
Scott, H. M. *v.4 p.583*
Scott, Hilda *v.4 p.706*
Scott, Ivan *v.2 p.119*
Scott, J. Michael (Editor), et al. *v.6 p.292, p.296*
Scott, Jacqueline L. (Editor), et al. *v.4 p.732*
Scott, James M. *v.3 p.479, v.4 p.377*
Scott, Janelle T. *v.4 p.367*
Scott, Joan Wallach *v.3 p.54, v.6 p.450*
Scott, Joan W. *v.3 p.54*
Scott, Joanna *v.2 p.155*
Scott, John A. (Editor) *v.3 p.151*
Scott, John A. *v.2 p.705*
Scott, John F. *v.1 p.684*
Scott, John *v.3 p.224, v.4 p.682*
Scott, Joseph *v.4 p.161*
Scott, Katie & Warwick, Genevieve (Editors) *v.1 p.746*
Scott, Michael L. *v.5 p.347*
Scott, Michael *v.1 p.236, p.396, v.2 p.222*
Scott, Pamela & Lee, Antoinette J. *v.1 p.790*
Scott, Paul *v.2 p.382*
Scott, R. & Liddell, Henry G. *v.2 p.400*
Scott, Rebecca J., et al. *v.3 p.337*
Scott, Rebecca J. *v.3 p.280*
Scott, Robert A., 1935- *v.1 p.787*
Scott, Ron *v.5 p.535, p.536*
Scott, Sarah *v.2 p.259*
Scott, Stanley, et al. *v.1 p.299*
Scott, Thomas A. & Mercer, E. Ian (Translators) *v.5 p.114, p.325*
Scott, Tom (Editor) *v.3 p.43*
Scott, Tom *v.3 p.163, p.166*
Scott, Virginia *v.2 p.476*
Scott, W. Richard *v.4 p.716*
Scott, Walter Dill *v.5 p.581*
Scott, Walter Sr. & Garside, P. D. *v.2 p.307*
Scott, Walter Sr. & Hewitt, David *v.2 p.307*
Scott, Walter Sr., et al. *v.2 p.308*

Scott, Walter Sr. *v.2 p.247, p.307, p.308*
Scott, William C. *v.1 p.176*
Scott, Yolanda M. *v.6 p.258*
Scott-Ram, N. R. *v.5 p.171, p.201*
Scotus, John D. *v.1 p.433, p.503*
Scoullos, Michael J., et al. *v.5 p.372, p.374*
Scrambler, Graham *v.4 p.756*
Scrase, Timothy *v.4 p.314*
Scribner, Bob *v.3 p.164*
Scribner, R. W. & Dixon, C. Scott *v.1 p.604*
Scribner, R. W. *v.3 p.165*
Scribner Reference Staff *v.3 p.377*
Scribners Reference Staff *v.3 p.377*
Scriven, Katritzky R., et al. *v.5 p.298, p.299*
Scrivener, Laurie & Barnes, J. Suzanne *v.6 p.444*
Scriver, Charles R. (Editor) *v.5 p.533*
Scruggs, Afi-Odelia E. *v.6 p.11, p.40*
Scruggs, Lyle *v.4 p.63*
Scruton, Roger *v.1 p.382, p.436, p.477*
Scudery, Madeleine de *v.2 p.477*
Scullard, Howard H. *v.3 p.24, p.25, p.26, p.29, v.6 p.715*
Scullion, Hugh & Linehan, Margaret *v.4 p.77*
Scully, J. C. *v.5 p.691*
Scully, Marlan Orvil & Zubairy, Muhammad Suhail . *v.5 p.562*
Scully, Roger *v.4 p.603*
Scully, Timothy R. *v.3 p.351, p.355*
Scully, Vincent *v.1 p.787*
Scura, Dorothy M. (Editor) *v.2 p.80*
Seaborg, Glenn T. & Seaborg, Eric *v.5 p.262*
Seabury, Paul & McDougall, Walter A. (Editors) . . . *v.3 p.321*
Seager, Allan *v.2 p.114*
Seager, Joni *v.6 p.426*
Seager, Robin *v.3 p.26*
Seager, William *v.1 p.497*
Seal, Graham *v.2 p.585*
Seale, Bobby *v.6 p.13*
Seale, Patrick *v.6 p.608*
Sealey, Alison & Carter, Bob *v.2 p.564, v.5 p.622, p.624*
Sealey, Raphael *v.3 p.13, p.20*
Sealts, Merton Miller, et al. *v.2 p.38*
Sear, Frank *v.1 p.72, p.155*
Search Institute *v.5 p.672*
Searing, James F. *v.6 p.72*
Searle, Chris *v.3 p.321*
Searle, G. R. *v.4 p.604, p.605, p.607*
Searle, J. R. (Editor) *v.1 p.442, p.490*
Searle, John R. *v.1 p.442, p.490, p.497, p.501, v.5 p.619*
Searle, Shayle R. & Willett, Lois Schertz . . . *v.4 p.175, p.204*
Sears, David O. (Editor), et al. *v.4 p.484, v.5 p.645*
Sears, James T. & Williams, Walter L. *v.6 p.382*
Sears, James T. *v.6 p.366, p.386*
Sears, Laurie J. *v.6 p.178*
Sears, R. Bradley, Gary Gates, & William B.
Rubenstein *v.6 p.376, p.377*
Sears, Stephen W. *v.3 p.401*

Sears, Stephen *v.3 p.432*

Seashore, Carl E.. . . . . *v.1 p.376*

Seaton, Douglas *v.1 p.169, p.236, p.396*

Seaver, Kirsten A. *v.4 p.399*

Seaver, Paul S. *v.3 p.92, p.122*

Seaward, Paul *v.3 p.105*

Seay, Albert *v.6 p.567*

Sebald, W. G. *v.2 p.618*

Sebbar, Leïla. *v.2 p.545*

Sebbar, Leila. *v.2 p.545*

Sebeok, Thomas A.. . . . . *v.2 p.571, v.4 p.424*

Sebesky, Don *v.1 p.394*

Secada, Walter G. (Editor), et al.. . . . . *v.5 p.464*

Seccombe, Wally. *v.4 p.738*

Secher, Reynald *v.4 p.653*

Seckbach, Joseph & Rubin, Eitan (Editors) . . . *v.5 p.98, p.243*

Seckbach, Joseph (Editor). *v.5 p.196*

Seco, Manuel *v.2 p.637*

Secord, James A. *v.6 p.739, p.751, p.760*

Secrest, Meryle . *v.1 p.223, p.253, p.311, p.357, p.709, v.6 p.410*

Seddon, David & Zeilig, Leo (Editors) *v.4 p.191*

Seddon, George *v.1 p.814, v.6 p.294*

Seddon, John M. & Gale, Julian D. *v.5 p.277*

Seddon, Terri *v.4 p.336*

Sedelmeier, Ulrich & Schimmelfennig, Frank
(Editors). *v.4 p.400, p.603*

Sedgewick, Robert *v.5 p.336, p.347*

Sedgwick, Catharine Maria. *v.2 p.51*

Sedgwick, Eve K. *v.2 p.192, p.572, v.6 p.393, p.760*

Sedgwick, Fred *v.4 p.365*

Sedgwick, John & Pokorny, Michael (Editors) . . . *v.6 p.345*

Sedgwick, John *v.5 p.85*

Sedgwick, Peter H.. . . . . *v.1 p.596*

Sedgwick, Peter *v.1 p.436*

Sedley, Charles. *v.2 p.259*

Sedley, David (Editor) *v.1 p.428*

Sedley, David N.. . . . . *v.2 p.437*

Sedriks, A. John *v.5 p.735*

Seeberg, Vilma. *v.4 p.336*

Seed, David (Editor) *v.2 p.581*

Seed, David *v.6 p.319*

Seed, Patricia *v.3 p.264, p.287*

Seefeldt, Carol (Editor) *v.4 p.369*

Seeger, Anthony *v.1 p.294*

Seeger, Falk (Editor), et al. *v.5 p.464*

Seeger, Karlheinz. *v.5 p.555*

Seeger, Pete *v.1 p.297*

Seeger, Ruth Crawford *v.1 p.297*

Seekins, Donald M.. . . . . *v.6 p.166*

Seelye, John *v.3 p.488*

Seethala, Ramakrishna & Fernandes, P. B. (Editors) . . *v.5 p.219*

Seevers, Brenda S.. . . . . *v.5 p.12*

Sefton, James E. *v.3 p.438*

Segal, Charles. *v.2 p.403, p.412, p.420*

Segal, Erich (Editor) *v.2 p.423, p.425*

Segal, Erich *v.2 p.402, p.440*

Segal, Jeffrey A. & Spaeth, Harold J. *v.4 p.466*

Segal, Lynne & McIntosh, Mary (Editors). *v.6 p.435, p.447, p.471*

Segal, Lynne *v.6 p.430, p.446*

Segal, Robert A. (Editor, Introduction by) *v.5 p.636*

Segall, Marshall H.. . . . . *v.5 p.645*

Segel, Binjamin W. *v.3 p.60*

Segel, Harold B. (Author, Editor, Translator) *v.3 p.252*

Segel, Harold B. (Editor) *v.1 p.68, p.110, v.2 p.788, p.789*

Segel, Harold B. *v.1 p.85, p.93, v.2 p.779, p.795*

Segel, Lee A. *v.5 p.502*

Seger, Linda (Author, Preface by) *v.6 p.353*

Seger, Linda. *v.6 p.347, p.353*

Segev, Tom & Lewis, Anthony *v.6 p.615*

Segev, Tom & Watzman, Haim *v.6 p.615*

Segev, Tom *v.6 p.612, p.615*

Segil, Larraine (Editor), et al.. . . . . *v.4 p.72*

Segovia, Fernando F. (Editor) *v.1 p.617*

Segrave, Kerry . *v.4 p.131, p.134, p.140, p.141, p.774, v.6 p.343*

Segre, Cesare & Ossola, Carlo. *v.2 p.700*

Segre, Cesare (Editor) *v.2 p.468*

Segre, Emilio *v.5 p.544, p.553*

Segrè, Emilio *v.5 p.544*

Seguin, Juan N. *v.6 p.534*

Segundo, Juan L.. . . . . *v.1 p.575*

Segundo, Juan Luis. *v.1 p.638*

Segura, Julio. *v.4 p.192*

Sehoole, M.T. *v.4 p.336*

Seib, Philip *v.4 p.406*

Seiber, James N. *v.5 p.8*

Seiberling, Grace & Bloore, Carolyn *v.6 p.738*

Seibold, Eugen & Berger, W. H. *v.5 p.429*

Seidel, Henry M., et al.. . . . . *v.5 p.521*

Seidel, K. W., et al. *v.5 p.42*

Seidel, Michael. *v.2 p.246, v.4 p.852*

Seidell, Atherton *v.5 p.282*

Seidelmann, P. Kenneth (Editor) *v.5 p.66*

Seidensticker, Edward G. (Translator) *v.6 p.233*

Seidensticker, Edward G. *v.6 p.228*

Seidler, Victor J. *v.6 p.430*

Seidlin, Oskar *v.2 p.590*

Seidman, Gay W.. . . . . *v.3 p.342*

Seidman, Michael *v.3 p.242*

Seidman, Steven *v.4 p.686*

Seifert, Jaroslav *v.2 p.784*

Seiffert, Udo (Editor), et al. *v.5 p.106, p.109*

Seifrid, Thomas *v.2 p.776, p.793, p.808*

Seigel, Catharine F. *v.2 p.56*

Seigle, Cecilia S., et al. *v.1 p.754*

Seilhamer, George O.. . . . . *v.1 p.118*

Seinfeld, John H. & Pandis,
Spyros N.. . . . . . *v.5 p.313, p.363, p.371, p.427, p.705*

Seitz, A. & Loeschcke, V. (Editors) *v.5 p.171, p.181*

Seitz, Wesley D., et al.. . . . . *v.4 p.152, p.160, p.164*

Seitz, William C.. . . . . *v.1 p.729, p.747*

Seivert, Sharon & Cavaleri, Steven A. *v.4 p.77*

Seixas, Judith S. & Youcha, Geraldine *v.5 p.664*

Sekules, Veronica. *v.1 p.672*

Sela, Avraham (Editor) *v.6 p.595*

Selby, Hubert Jr. *v.2 p.155*

Selby, Martha Ann *v.6 p.148*

Selby, Nick *v.2 p.112*

Selcraig, James T. *v.3 p.506*

Selden, David *v.4 p.283*

Selden, Mark *v.6 p.192*

Seldes, Gilbert *v.1 p.35, p.118*

Seldon, Anthony & Ball, Stuart (Editors) *v.4 p.607*

Seldon, Anthony & Kavanagh, Dennis (Editors) . . . *v.4 p.605*

Seldon, Anthony (Editor) *v.4 p.605*

Self, Geoffrey *v.1 p.204, p.282, p.318*

Self, Robert O. *v.6 p.719*

Self, Will *v.2 p.380*

Selfridge-Field, Eleanor (Editor) *v.1 p.388*

Selig, J. M. *v.5 p.715*

Selig, Robert *v.2 p.290*

Seligman, Amanda I. *v.6 p.715*

Seligman, Joel *v.4 p.92, p.100, p.147, p.155, p.162*

Seligman, Milton & Darling, Rosalyn Benjamin . . . *v.5 p.668*

Seligman, Patricia *v.1 p.751*

Seligmann, Linda J. *v.3 p.331*

Selimovic, Mesa *v.2 p.812*

Selin, Helaine (Editor) *v.5 p.389*

Selin, Helaine *v.5 p.467*

Sell, Michael *v.1 p.61, p.103*

Sell, Mike *v.1 p.85, p.118*

Sellars, John *v.1 p.429*

Sellars, Richard W. *v.5 p.18, v.6 p.296*

Sellars, Wilfrid, et al. *v.1 p.497*

Sellars, Wilfrid *v.1 p.489, p.499*

Sellassie, Haile *v.6 p.64*

Sellekaerts, Willy (Editor) *v.4 p.204, p.258, p.260*

Seller, Maxine S. (Editor) *v.1 p.87, p.120*

Seller, Robert H. *v.5 p.521*

Sellers, Charles Grier *v.3 p.421, p.494*

Sellers, Jeffrey M. *v.4 p.543*

Sellers, Susan (Editor) *v.2 p.532*

Selley, Richard C. *v.5 p.451, p.738*

Sells, Michael Anthony *v.1 p.556*

Sells, Michael (Translator, Introduction by) *v.6 p.663*

Seltzer, Richard A., et al. *v.6 p.442*

Seltzer, Thomas (Editor) *v.2 p.795*

Selvadurai, Shyam (Editor) *v.2 p.584*

Selvadurai, Shyam *v.2 p.761, p.766, v.6 p.399*

Selz, Peter *v.1 p.680*

Sembene, Ousmane *v.2 p.545*

Sembène, Ousmane *v.2 p.545*

Semel, Susan F. & Sadovnik, Alan R. *v.4 p.348*

Semetko, Holli A., et al. *v.4 p.549, p.558, p.559*

Semmel, Bernard *v.3 p.77*

Semmes, Clovis E. *v.1 p.18, v.4 p.700*

Semonche, John E. *v.4 p.466, p.539*

Semple, Charles & Steel, Mike *v.5 p.205*

Semple, Janet *v.3 p.115, p.129*

Sen, Amartya *v.4 p.266, p.514, p.515*

Sen, Gita (Editor), et al. *v.6 p.444*

Sen, Krishna *v.6 p.175*

Sender, Katherine *v.6 p.383*

Seneca, Lucius Annaeus *v.1 p.73, p.89, p.429, v.2 p.443*

Seneca the Elder *v.2 p.443*

Seneci, Pierfausto *v.5 p.295*

Senelick, Laurence (Editor) *v.3 p.62, v.6 p.475*

Senelick, Laurence *v.6 p.413*

Sener, Bilge (Editor) *v.5 p.185, p.200*

Senese, Guy B. *v.4 p.312, v.6 p.680, p.692*

Senge, Peter M. *v.4 p.79, p.80*

Sengers, Gerda *v.6 p.635, p.638*

Senghor, Leopold S. *v.2 p.535*

Senghor, Leopold Sedar *v.2 p.543*

Senghor, Léopold Sédar *v.2 p.543, v.6 p.72*

Senici, Emanuele (Editor) *v.1 p.204, p.352*

Senker, Cath *v.5 p.81*

Senn, Alfred Erich *v.4 p.846, p.892*

Sennett, Herbert *v.2 p.258*

Sennett, Richard (Compiled by) *v.6 p.719*

Sennett, Richard *v.4 p.695, p.717, p.734*

Sennott, R. Stephen (Editor) *v.1 p.784*

Senor, Thomas D. (Editor) *v.1 p.523*

Sensbach, Jon F. *v.1 p.648*

Sensen, Christoph W. (Editor) *v.5 p.98, p.105, p.106, p.108, p.118, p.142, p.143, p.147, p.249*

Sentance, Bryan *v.1 p.806, p.810*

Seow, Choon-Leong *v.1 p.622*

Sepinuck, Stephen L. & Treuthart, Mary P. *v.4 p.539*

Sepulveda, Juan A. *v.6 p.490, p.541*

Serafin, Steven (Editor) *v.2 p.779, p.782, p.785, p.788*

Serafini, Anthony *v.5 p.81*

Serageldin, Ismail (Editor), et al. *v.1 p.823, v.6 p.729*

Serbin, Kenneth P. *v.3 p.277*

Serebrennikov, Nikolai Nikolaevich & Horosko, Marian *v.1 p.25, p.48*

Sered, Susan Starr *v.1 p.528*

Sereny, Gitta *v.3 p.86, p.178*

Sergeant, Elizabeth S. *v.2 p.67*

Sergiovanni, Thomas *v.4 p.281, p.282*

Serjeant, E. P. & Dempsey, B. (Editors) *v.5 p.300*

Serlio, Sebastiano *v.1 p.75, p.138, p.148, p.155*

Serpell, James (Editor) *v.5 p.166*

Serre, Jean Pierre *v.5 p.474, p.477*

Serrin, Judith & Serrin, William (Editors) *v.4 p.404*

Sertorio, L. (Editor) *v.5 p.564*

Serulnikov, Sergio *v.3 p.324*

Service, Alastair *v.1 p.787*

Service, Robert *v.3 p.209, p.223*

Servos, Norbert *v.1 p.12*

Sessions, Roger & Cone, Edward T. (Editors) *v.1 p.223*

Sessions, William Lad *v.1 p.452*
Setel, Philip (Editor), et al.. . . . . *v.6 p.55*
Seth, Vikram. *v.2 p.766*
Sethi, Ravi. *v.5 p.347*
Sethi, Suresh P., et al.. . . . . *v.4 p.118*
Seton-Watson, Hugh *v.3 p.62, p.207, p.218*
Settle, Frank A. (Editor) *v.5 p.268*
Settle, Mary Lee *v.2 p.115*
Setton, Kenneth M. & Baldwin, Marshall W. (Editors) . *v.3 p.64*
Setton, Kenneth M. & Hazard, Harry W. (Editors) . . . *v.3 p.64*
Setton, Kenneth M. (Editor), et al. *v.3 p.64, v.6 p.557*
Setton, Kenneth M.. . . . . *v.3 p.63, p.64*
Seuffert, Bernhard & Kurrelmeyer, W. *v.2 p.615*
Sever, Dave *v.4 p.287*
Severin, Dorothy S.. . . . . *v.2 p.652*
Sevigne, Mme De *v.2 p.477, p.478*
Sevilla Arroyo, Florencio (Editor) *v.2 p.662*
Sewall, Richard Benson *v.2 p.37*
Sewell, Darrel (Editor) *v.1 p.699*
Sewell, Darrel *v.1 p.699*
Sewell, James D. & Egger, Steven A. *v.6 p.262*
Sewell, Richard H. *v.3 p.401, p.421, p.422, p.423, p.429*
Sewell, William H. Jr.. . . . . *v.3 p.149, v.4 p.706*
Sexton, Anne. *v.2 p.115*
Sexton, Patricia Cayo *v.4 p.123, p.329*
Sexton, Virginia S. & Hogan, John D. (Editors) . . . *v.5 p.594*
Seybert, Thomas A.. . . . . *v.5 p.703*
Seyersted, Per *v.2 p.33*
Seyh Galip. *v.6 p.667*
Seymour, Bruce *v.1 p.12*
Seymour, M. J.. . . . . *v.4 p.379*
Seymour, Miranda *v.2 p.46, p.310, v.4 p.838, p.848*
Seymour, Nancy N.. . . . . *v.1 p.666*
Seymour, Raymond B. *v.5 p.323*
Seznec, Jean *v.1 p.533*
Sánchez, George Isidore *v.6 p.533*
Sánchez, Gonzalo & Meertens, Donny *v.3 p.359*
Sánchez Korrol, Virginia *v.6 p.533, p.550*
Sánchez, Magdalena S.. . . . . *v.3 p.240*
Sánchez, Marta Ester *v.6 p.480, p.503, p.511, p.516*
Shaaban, Bouthaina. *v.6 p.583*
Shaara, Michael *v.2 p.155*
Shaban, M. A.. . . . . *v.6 p.585, p.586*
Shabtai, Yaakov *v.6 p.651*
Shace, Joseph & Epstein, David G. *v.4 p.110*
Shachtman, Tom *v.4 p.423*
Shackelford, George T. M. & Wissman, Fronia E.. . . *v.1 p.733*
Shackelford, James F. & Alexander, W.. . . . . *v.5 p.691*
Shackelford, James F., ed.. . . . . *v.5 p.322*
Shackelford, James M. *v.5 p.316*
Shackelford, Laurel & Weinberg, Bill (Editors) . . . *v.3 p.498*
Shackford, James A. *v.3 p.511*
Shackleton Bailey, D. R. *v.2 p.435*
Shackleton, J. R. (Editor) *v.4 p.197*
Shacochis, Bob (Foreword by). *v.3 p.313*

Shadbolt, Doris. *v.1 p.699, v.6 p.679*
Shadbolt, Maurice *v.2 p.748*
Shade, William Gerald (Editor), et al. *v.4 p.550, p.556*
Shadish, William R., et al. *v.4 p.690*
Shadur, Joseph & Shadur, Yehudity *v.1 p.807*
Shadwell, Thomas *v.2 p.259*
Shaeffer, Ronald E.. . . . . *v.5 p.696*
Shafaeddin, Mehdi. *v.4 p.60*
Shafer, Byron E. (Editor) *v.4 p.548, p.552*
Shafer, Byron E.. . . . . *v.4 p.551*
Shafer, Yvonne. *v.1 p.122*
Shaffer, Arthur H. *v.3 p.410*
Shaffer, Brian W. (Editor). *v.2 p.179, p.194*
Shaffer, Brian *v.2 p.194*
Shaffer, Kirwin R. *v.3 p.313*
Shaffer, William R.. . . . . *v.4 p.594*
Shafir, Gershon & Peled, Yoav (Editors) . . . *v.6 p.615*
Shafir, Gershon & Peled, Yoav *v.6 p.615*
Shafritz, Jay M.. . . . . *v.4 p.482, p.483*
Shah, Anwar. *v.4 p.755*
Shah, Ghanshyam *v.4 p.711*
Shah, Nayan. *v.6 p.128, p.141*
Shah, Sonia (Editor) *v.6 p.108, p.113, p.435*
Shah, Sonia *v.5 p.738*
Shaham, Nathan *v.6 p.651*
Shaheen, Jack *v.6 p.330*
Shaheen, Mohammad *v.2 p.346*
Shahid, Irfan *v.6 p.581, p.583, p.586*
Shaikh, Farzana *v.6 p.158*
Shain, Yossi *v.4 p.571*
Shaked, Gershon *v.6 p.651*
Shakely, Ferhad *v.6 p.669*
Shakespeare, William & Bevington, David . . . *v.1 p.77, p.103*
Shakespeare, William (Editor) *v.2 p.223*
Shakespeare, William, et al. *v.2 p.226*
Shakespeare, William *v.2 p.223, p.224, p.225, p.226*
Shaktini, Namascar (Editor) *v.2 p.533*
Shakur, Assata *v.6 p.19, p.46*
Shakur, Sanyika *v.4 p.714*
Shakya, Tsering *v.6 p.241*
Shalamov, Varlam *v.2 p.808*
Shalev, Meir *v.6 p.651*
Shalit, Ben. *v.5 p.584*
Shamah, Shani Beverly *v.4 p.89, p.97, p.98, p.100*
Shami, Seteney, et al.. . . . . *v.6 p.583*
Shamir, Moshe *v.6 p.651*
Shamir, R. & Frasconi, P. (Editors) *v.5 p.109*
Shamir, Yitzhak *v.6 p.616*
Shammas, Anton *v.6 p.651*
Shamos, Michael Ian *v.4 p.855*
Shamos, Morris H. *v.5 p.407*
Shampine, Lawrence F.. . . . . *v.5 p.487, p.492*
Shamsie, Muneeza (Editor) *v.2 p.761*
Shanahan, Timothy *v.5 p.204*
Shane, Ed. *v.5 p.622, p.625*

Shangren, Kong *v.6 p.209*

Shank, David A.. . . . . *v.1 p.648, v.6 p.69*

Shank, Matthew D.. . . . . *v.4 p.886*

Shankar, Lavina Dhingra & Srikanth, Rajini
(Editors). *v.6 p.124, p.138*

Shankar, R. *v.5 p.550*

Shankar, Ravi *v.1 p.289, p.356*

Shanker, Stuart G. (Editor) *v.1 p.499, p.500*

Shanley, John Patrick *v.2 p.155*

Shanley, Mary L. & Pateman, Carole (Editors) . . . *v.6 p.442*

Shanley, Mary L.. . . . . *v.4 p.734, v.6 p.376, p.377*

Shanley, Mary Lyndon *v.6 p.748*

Shanmugam Ne Staff *v.5 p.696*

Shannon, Jonathan Holt *v.1 p.287*

Shannon, Joyce Brennfleck (Editor) *v.4 p.826*

Shannon, Magdaline W *v.3 p.316*

Shannon, Mike *v.4 p.812, p.852*

Shannon, Richard. *v.3 p.115*

Shannon, Sandra & Williams, Dana *v.6 p.27*

Shannon, Thomas A. & Walter, James J. *v.5 p.151*

Shanty, Frank G. (Editor), et al. *v.4 p.661*

Shapin, Steven & Schaffer, Simon *v.3 p.48*

Shapin, Steven *v.3 p.48*

Shapira, Anita *v.6 p.611*

Shapiro, Ann-Louise *v.3 p.54, p.155, v.6 p.471*

Shapiro, Arthur. *v.4 p.317*

Shapiro, Barbara J. *v.6 p.270*

Shapiro, Carol & Varian, Hal R. *v.4 p.51*

Shapiro, David & Shapiro, Cecile *v.1 p.729*

Shapiro, David L. *v.4 p.455*

Shapiro, David. *v.5 p.658, p.661*

Shapiro, Edward S. & Kratochwill, Thomas R. (Editors). *v.5 p.572*

Shapiro, Edward S.. . . . . *v.4 p.287*

Shapiro, Gerald (Editor) *v.2 p.27*

Shapiro, Henry D. *v.3 p.498*

Shapiro, James *v.2 p.231, v.3 p.61*

Shapiro, Jerome F. *v.6 p.320*

Shapiro, Judith *v.6 p.194*

Shapiro, Karl Jay *v.2 p.116*

Shapiro, Norman R., et al. *v.2 p.465*

Shapiro, Norman R. *v.2 p.464, p.472*

Shapiro, Norman *v.2 p.776*

Shapiro, Peter *v.6 p.408*

Shapiro, Sherry B. (Editor). *v.1 p.48*

Shapiro, Sherry *v.1 p.48*

Shapiro, Sidney A. & Glicksman, Robert L.. *v.4 p.92, p.110, p.111*

Shapiro, Thomas M. *v.6 p.20, p.40*

Shapouri, Hosein *v.5 p.742*

Sharan, Nagendra N. *v.2 p.765*

Sharan, Shlomo (Editor) *v.4 p.350*

Sharer, Robert J. *v.4 p.10*

Shariati, Ali *v.4 p.721*

Sharkansky, Ira. *v.4 p.615, p.616, v.6 p.616*

Sharma, A. K. & Sharma, A. (Editors) *v.5 p.125*

Sharma, Arun Kumar & Sharma, Archana (Editors) . . *v.5 p.125*

Sharma, Arvind & Young, Katherine K.
(Editors). *v.1 p.528, v.6 p.435, p.460, p.466*

Sharma, Arvind (Editor) *v.1 p.529*

Sharma, Arvind. *v.1 p.541, v.4 p.723*

Sharma, C. D. *v.1 p.475*

Sharma, Hari D. & Reddy, Krishna R.. . *v.5 p.369, p.377, p.422*

Sharma, Kanhayalal L. *v.4 p.706*

Sharma, Parnesh *v.6 p.696*

Sharma, Prem V.. . . . . *v.5 p.445*

Sharma, Sanjay P. (Editor), et al. *v.4 p.26*

Sharma, Soumitra (Editor) *v.4 p.229*

Sharma, Sunil *v.6 p.673*

Sharma, Suresh *v.6 p.154*

Sharman, Campbell & Moon, Jeremy (Editors) . . . *v.4 p.624*

Sharoni, Simona *v.6 p.620*

Sharot, Stephen. *v.1 p.525, v.4 p.722*

Sharouni, Yusuf *v.6 p.663*

Sharp, Alan *v.4 p.650*

Sharp, Avery T. & Floyd, James Michael. *v.1 p.169, p.236, p.396*

Sharp, Cecil J. & Karpeles, Maud. *v.1 p.33*

Sharp, Cecil J. *v.1 p.16*

Sharp, Charles Dee *v.1 p.714*

Sharp, David W. A.. . . . . *v.5 p.258*

Sharp, Elaine B. *v.4 p.567, v.6 p.725*

Sharp, Gene *v.4 p.650*

Sharp, James R. *v.3 p.418*

Sharp, Lewis I.. . . . . *v.1 p.781*

Sharp, Maurice L. *v.5 p.697, p.736*

Sharp, William F.. . . . . *v.3 p.358*

Sharpe, Errol. *v.3 p.543*

Sharpe, Grant William, et al. *v.4 p.164*

Sharpe, J. A.. . . . . *v.4 p.707*

Sharpe, Jenny *v.2 p.728, v.3 p.322*

Sharpe, Kenneth E.. . . . . *v.3 p.318*

Sharpe, Tony. *v.2 p.124*

Sharpes, Donald K.. . . . . *v.4 p.329*

Sharples, R. W. *v.1 p.428*

Sharpless, Richard E. *v.3 p.358*

Sharpley, Andrew N. (Editor) *v.5 p.11*

Sharrett, Christopher *v.6 p.320*

Sharrock, Roger *v.2 p.241*

Shasha, Dennis E. & Lazere, Cathy *v.5 p.342, p.344*

Shasha, Dennis. *v.5 p.469*

Shattock, Joanne & Wolff, Michael (Editors) *v.6 p.753*

Shattock, Joanne (Editor) *v.2 p.177, v.6 p.753*

Shattuck, George C. *v.6 p.683, p.696*

Shattuck, Roger *v.2 p.524*

Shatzer, Robert. *v.3 p.544*

Shatzmiller, Maya *v.6 p.586, p.601*

Shaughnessy, Edward L. *v.2 p.108*

Shaughnessy, Mary Angela. . . . *v.1 p.263, p.274, p.347, p.388*

Shaughnessy, Mina P.. . . . . *v.2 p.565*

Shaughnessy, Robert (Editor) *v.1 p.77, p.87, p.103, p.136*

Shaughnessy, Robert *v.1 p.69, p.75, p.103*

Shavit, Jacob & Naor, Chaya *v.6 p.611*

Shavitt, Sharon. *v.5 p.648*

Shaw, A. Jonathan & Goffinet, Bernard (Editors). *v.5 p.209, p.210*

Shaw, Bradley A. & Vera-Godwin, Nova (Editors) . *v.2 p.684*

Shaw, Colin & Ivens, John *v.4 p.143*

Shaw, D.L. *v.2 p.687*

Shaw, Donald L. *v.2 p.665, p.673*

Shaw, Eric *v.4 p.607*

Shaw, G. K. *v.4 p.226, p.229*

Shaw, George Bernard & Lerner, Alan Jay. *v.1 p.253, p.336, p.409*

Shaw, George Bernard. *v.1 p.56, p.80, p.103, p.248,*
v.2 p.232, p.309, p.310, p.628

Shaw, Harry E.. . . . . *v.2 p.308*

Shaw, Ian (Author, Editor) *v.6 p.58*

Shaw, Ian (Editor). *v.3 p.10*

Shaw, Lisa & Dennison, Stephanie. *v.4 p.712*

Shaw, Lisa *v.1 p.294, v.3 p.268*

Shaw, Marion *v.2 p.313*

Shaw, Martin *v.4 p.653*

Shaw, Mary *v.2 p.461*

Shaw, Michael J. (Editor) *v.4 p.113*

Shaw, Stanford J. *v.6 p.591, p.598, p.622, p.625*

Shaw, Stephen K. (Editor), et al. *v.3 p.444, v.4 p.539*

Shaw, Thurstan (Editor), et al. *v.4 p.8*

Shaw, Victor N. *v.4 p.777, v.5 p.664*

Shaw, W. David *v.2 p.180*

Shaw, William & Piozzi, Hester Lynch *v.2 p.251*

Shaw, William H. (Editor) *v.4 p.54, p.55*

Shawcross, John T. *v.2 p.255*

Shawcross, William. *v.4 p.647, v.6 p.170*

Shawker, Thomas H. *v.5 p.137*

Shawn, Ted. *v.1 p.12, p.27, p.43*

Shay, Anthony & Sellers-Young, Barbara (Editors). *v.1 p.16, p.17*

Shay, Anthony *v.1 p.17, p.43*

Shayne, Julie D. *v.3 p.283, p.299*

Shea, Daniel M. *v.4 p.531*

Shea, Edward J.. . . . . . *v.4 p.797, p.803, p.822, p.840*

Shea, William R.. . . . . *v.5 p.391, p.395*

Sheaffer, Louis *v.2 p.108*

Sheahan, John *v.3 p.331*

Shean, Glenn *v.5 p.661*

Shearer, Alistair *v.1 p.692, p.693, p.710*

Shearer, Benjamin F. & Shearer, Barbara S.
(Editors). *v.5 p.224, p.396*

Shearer, David R. *v.3 p.226*

Shearman, John *v.1 p.675*

Sheckels, Theodore F.. . . . . *v.6 p.337*

Shectman, Jonathan *v.3 p.45, v.5 p.389*

Shedd, Joseph B. & Bacharach, Samuel B. *v.4 p.283*

Sheehan, Bernard W. *v.6 p.686*

Sheehan, James J. *v.3 p.160, p.165*

Sheehan, Michael M. & Murray, Jacqueline (Editors) . *v.6 p.557*

Sheehan, Richard G. *v.4 p.889, p.897*

Sheehan, William *v.5 p.68*

Sheehy, Colleen J. *v.1 p.777*

Sheehy, Daniel *v.1 p.294, v.6 p.519*

Sheehy, Helen *v.1 p.141, p.145*

Sheehy, Noel (Editor), et al.. . . . . *v.5 p.598*

Sheehy, Noel. *v.5 p.598*

Sheets-Johnstone, Maxine *v.1 p.43*

Sheffer, Martin S. *v.4 p.539*

Shefrin, Hersh *v.4 p.97, p.102, p.103, v.5 p.586*

Shefter, Martin *v.6 p.725*

Shehadeh, Lamia R. *v.6 p.606*

Shehadeh, Raja. *v.6 p.620*

Sheikh, Moazzam (ed.) *v.6 p.152*

Shein, Louis J. *v.1 p.474*

Sheinin, David *v.4 p.631*

Shekhar, Shashi & Chawla, Sanjay *v.5 p.335, p.337*

Sheldon, Garrett Ward *v.4 p.492*

Sheldon, Henry D. *v.4 p.289*

Sheldon, Kathleen E. *v.6 p.76*

Sheldrake, Philip *v.1 p.651*

Shelemay, Kay Kaufman *v.1 p.284, p.300*

Shell, G. Richard *v.4 p.75*

Shell, Marc *v.1 p.826*

Shell, Robert C.. . . . . *v.6 p.79*

Shellabarger, Samuel *v.3 p.107, p.129*

Sheller, Mimi *v.3 p.316*

Shelley, Mary Wollstonecraft & Harper, Henry H.. . . *v.2 p.310*

Shelley, Mary Wollstonecraft *v.2 p.310, p.311*

Shelley, Percy Bysshe *v.2 p.311, p.312*

Shelton, Dinah *v.4 p.653*

Shelton, Jo-Ann *v.3 p.24*

Shelton, Lewis E. *v.1 p.118, p.153*

Shelton, Patrick J. *v.5 p.513*

Shelton, Suzanne *v.1 p.12*

Shen, Grant *v.1 p.132, p.134*

Shen, Sin-Yan *v.1 p.289, p.290*

Shen, Sinyan. *v.1 p.290*

Shen, Vivian *v.6 p.334*

Shen, Y. R. *v.5 p.561*

Shenefield, John H. & Stelzer,
Irwin M. *v.4 p.85, p.110, p.111, p.112, p.444*

Shenfield, Stephen D.. . . . . *v.4 p.510*

Shenk, Ellen *v.5 p.251*

Shennan, Stephen. *v.4 p.7*

Shenstone, William *v.2 p.260*

Shepard, Paul *v.5 p.226*

Shepard, Robert B. *v.3 p.392*

Shepard, Roy J. & Astrand, Per-Olof
(Editors). *v.4 p.826, p.875, p.880*

Shepard, Sam. *v.1 p.118, v.2 p.155*

Shephard, Ben *v.5 p.585*

Shephard, Roy J. *v.4 p.791, p.793, p.841*

Shepherd, Elizabeth *v.5 p.96, p.157*

Shepherd, John & Wicke, Peter *v.1 p.377*

Shepherd, John (Editor) *v.1 p.162, p.274, p.284*

Shepherd, John Robert *v.6 p.214*

Shepherd, John *v.1 p.162, p.274, p.284*

Shepherd, Naomi *v.6 p.611*

Shepherd, Robin E. H. *v.3 p.190*

Shepherd, Simon & Womack, Peter *v.2 p.185*

Shepherdson, David J. (Editor), et al. *v.5 p.85*

Sheppard, Anne *v.1 p.480*

Sheppard, Francis. *v.3 p.115, v.6 p.715*

Sheptycki, James *v.6 p.263*

Sherbell, Shepard. *v.1 p.768*

Sherbo, Arthur *v.2 p.251, p.259*

Sherbon, Elizabeth. *v.1 p.38*

Sherburn, George Wiley *v.2 p.257, p.258*

Sheridan, Alan *v.2 p.520*

Sheridan, Eugene R. *v.3 p.491*

Sheridan, Richard Brinsley *v.2 p.260*

Sheridan, Susan *v.2 p.741*

Sheridan, Thomas E. *v.3 p.527, p.528, v.6 p.533, p.550*

Sheridan, Thomas *v.2 p.709*

Sherif, Muzafer & Brannigan, Augustine *v.4 p.692*

Sherif, Muzafer *v.4 p.692, p.717*

Sheriff, Abdul *v.6 p.66*

Sheriff, Mary D. *v.1 p.747*

Sheriff, Robert E.. . . . . *v.5 p.445*

Sheriff, Robin E. *v.3 p.280, p.342, v.4 p.37*

Sherley-Price, Leo (Translator) *v.1 p.652*

Sherma, Joseph & Zweig, G. *v.5 p.330*

Sherman, A. J. *v.4 p.668, v.6 p.612*

Sherman, Alfred *v.4 p.607*

Sherman, Andrew J. & Hart, Milledge A. *v.4 p.85*

Sherman, Daniel J. *v.1 p.828*

Sherman, George *v.3 p.535*

Sherman, Irwin W. *v.5 p.206*

Sherman, Janann *v.3 p.462*

Sherman, Jane & Mumaw, Barton *v.1 p.12*

Sherman, Jane. *v.1 p.12*

Sherman, Joe *v.4 p.154*

Sherman, Lawrence W. (Editor) *v.4 p.680*

Sherman, Martin *v.6 p.413*

Sherman, Robert, et al. *v.5 p.669*

Sherman, Sarah W. *v.2 p.46*

Sherman, Sharon R. *v.6 p.310*

Sherman, W. F.. . . . . *v.5 p.563*

Sherman, William C. & Thorson, Playford V. (Editors) *v.3 p.523*

Shermer, Michael & Grobman, Alex *v.3 p.86*

Shermer, Michael. *v.5 p.636*

Shernoff, Michael (Editor) *v.6 p.376, p.382*

Sherr, Richard (Editor) *v.1 p.181, p.334*

Sherrill, Claudine. *v.4 p.801*

Sherrow, Victoria. *v.1 p.716*

Sherry, John W. *v.6 p.695*

Sherry, Norman *v.2 p.341, p.342, p.351*

Sherry, Vincent B. & Sherry, Vincent. *v.2 p.179*

Sherry, Vincent *v.2 p.11*

Sherwin, Susan & Parish, Barbara *v.5 p.524*

Sherwin, Susan *v.6 p.444, p.461*

Sherwin-White, Adrian Nicholas *v.4 p.501*

Sherwin-White, Susan & Kuhrt, Amelie *v.3 p.21*

Sherwood, Dolly *v.1 p.781*

Sherwood, Gayle *v.1 p.164, p.223, p.333*

Sherwood, Joan *v.3 p.241*

Sherwood, Marika & Adi, Hakim *v.6 p.13, p.55*

Sherwood, Robert E. *v.2 p.116, v.3 p.462*

Sherzer, Joel *v.4 p.19*

Shestov, Lev *v.1 p.474*

Shetler, Jan Bender *v.6 p.66*

Shevchenko, Taras *v.2 p.815*

Shevchenko, T.. . . . . *v.2 p.815*

Shevell, S. K. (Editor) *v.5 p.562*

Shewey, Don (Editor). *v.6 p.413*

Shewry, Peter R. (Editor) *v.5 p.9, p.23*

Shi, David E. & Mayer, Holly A. *v.3 p.372*

Shi, David E. *v.3 p.370*

Shi Nai'an & Guanzhong, Luo *v.6 p.212*

Shi, Tianjian *v.4 p.620*

Shiach, Morag *v.2 p.532*

Shiblak, Abbas. *v.6 p.598, p.603*

Shibutani, Tamotsu ; Kwan, Kian M.. . . . . . . *v.4 p.725*

Shichor, David & Gilbert, Michael J.. . . . . . *v.6 p.247*

Shichor, David & Sechrest, Dale K. (Editors) . . *v.6 p.271*

Shick, Allen & Lostracco, Felix *v.4 p.567*

Shidlo, Ariel (Editor), et al. *v.6 p.382*

Shields, Carol *v.2 p.739*

Shields, Christopher (Editor) *v.1 p.420*

Shields, James J. Jr. (Editor) *v.6 p.222*

Shields, Martin *v.5 p.89, p.246*

Shiell, Timothy C. *v.4 p.459*

Shiff, Richard, et al. *v.1 p.699*

Shiff, Richard *v.1 p.747*

Shifflett, Crandall. *v.3 p.406*

Shiffrin, Steven H. *v.4 p.459*

Shifman, Barry & Walton, Guy *v.1 p.801*

Shiga Naoya. *v.6 p.233*

Shigesada, Nanako & Kawasaki, Kohkichi *v.5 p.181*

Shigley, Joseph, et al. *v.5 p.708, p.715*

Shigo, Alex L.. . . . . *v.5 p.156*

Shikibu, Murasaki *v.6 p.233*

Shiklomanov, I. A. & Rodda, John C. (Editors). *v.5 p.359, p.371, p.380*

Shiller, Robert J.. *v.4 p.90, p.92, p.97, p.100, p.245, p.250, p.264*

Shillinglaw, Susan & Hearle, Kevin (Editors) . . . *v.2 p.123*

Shillingsburg, Peter L. *v.2 p.315, v.6 p.742*

Shillington, Kevin (Editor) *v.6 p.54*

Shillington, Kevin *v.6 p.54*

Shillony, Ben-Ami *v.6 p.225*

Shiloah, Amnon *v.1 p.287, p.300*

Shilts, Randy *v.6 p.379, p.390*

Shim, Jae K.. . . . . *v.4 p.137*

Shimabukuro, Robert Sadamu *v.6 p.134*

Shimakawa, Karen *v.6 p.90, p.99*

Shimazaki, Toson. *v.6 p.233*

Shimizu, Hidetada & Levine, Robert A. (Editors) . . . *v.5 p.598*

Shimkets, Richard A. (Editor), et al. *v.5 p.165*

Shimokawa, Koichi S. *v.4 p.154*
Shin, Doh C.. . . . . *v.4 p.621*
Shin, Gi-Wook & Robinson, Michael E. *v.6 p.237*
Shin, Gi-Wook *v.4 p.711*
Shin, Sarah J. *v.6 p.109, p.136*
Shiner, Larry E. *v.1 p.704*
Shinoda, Minoru *v.6 p.225*
Shipan, Charles R. *v.4 p.539*
Shipler, David K.. . . . . *v.4 p.726*
Shipley, Bill *v.5 p.90*
Shipley, Graham. *v.3 p.21*
Shipp, Steve. *v.1 p.666, p.684*
Shippey, Karla C. *v.4 p.58, p.110*
Shipton, Alyn *v.1 p.263, p.326, p.367*
Shipton, Clifford K. *v.3 p.485*
Shiraev, Eric & Zubok, Vladislav *v.3 p.212*
Shiraishi, Takashi (Editor) *v.6 p.175, p.178*
Shiraishi, Takashi. *v.6 p.178*
Shire, Helena Mennie. *v.2 p.215*
Shiri, Keith (Editor) *v.6 p.334*
Shirk, David A. *v.3 p.295*
Shirley, James *v.2 p.222*
Shirley, John W. *v.5 p.397*
Shirley, Peter & Morley, R. Keith *v.5 p.340*
Shirreff, David. . . . *v.4 p.90, p.93, p.97, p.100, p.102, p.103*
Shirwadkar, Meena *v.2 p.761*
Shivers, Alfred S. *v.2 p.130*
Shivers, Jay S. & DeLisle, Lee J. *v.4 p.785*
Shivers, Jay S. *v.4 p.786*
Shklar, Judith N. *v.2 p.481*
Shlaim, Avi *v.6 p.595, p.616, p.621*
Shlapentokh, Vladimir *v.3 p.223*
Shleifer, Andrei *v.4 p.97, p.100*
Shloss, Carol Loeb *v.1 p.12, p.46*
Shneer, David & Aviv, Caryn (Editors) *v.6 p.374*
Shneiderman, Ben & Plaisant, Catherine *v.5 p.339*
Shneiderman, Ben *v.5 p.343, p.344*
Shneidman, Edwin S. (Author, Editor) *v.5 p.663*
Shneidman, Edwin S.. . . . . *v.5 p.663*
Shneidman, N N *v.2 p.800*
Shneidman, N. N. *v.2 p.800, p.808*
Shockley, Ann A.. . . . . *v.6 p.399*
Shoemaker, Adam *v.2 p.742*
Shoemaker, Candace (Editor). *v.1 p.812, p.819, v.5 p.44*
Shoemaker, David P., et al. *v.5 p.287*
Shoemaker, J. S. & Lin, S. M. (Editors) . . . *v.5 p.101, p.137*
Shoemaker, Robert & Vincent, Mary (Editors) . . . *v.3 p.55*
Shoemaker, Stephen J. *v.1 p.642*
Shofner, Jerrell H. *v.3 p.505*
Shogan, Robert. *v.3 p.378, v.4 p.129*
Shohat, Ella *v.6 p.334*
Shoilevska, Sanya *v.1 p.256, p.346*
Sholokhov, Mikhail. *v.2 p.808*
Shondell, Don & Raynaud, Cecil (Editors) . . . *v.4 p.869, p.905*
Shoptaw, John. *v.2 p.58*

Shor, Ira. *v.4 p.300*
Shore, Bradd *v.4 p.24*
Shore, Harvey *v.1 p.825*
Shore, Kenneth. *v.4 p.284*
Shore, Stephen *v.1 p.768*
Shore, William H.. . . . . *v.5 p.81, p.226*
Shorris, Earl. *v.6 p.490, p.533*
Shorrocks, Brian & Swingland, Ian R. (Editors). . . *v.5 p.223*
Short, Bob. *v.3 p.503*
Short, Brian *v.4 p.399*
Short, John Rennie *v.4 p.395, v.6 p.710, p.721*
Short, Philip *v.6 p.170, p.171, p.202*
Short, Tom *v.5 p.360, p.724*
Shorter, Edward *v.4 p.739*
Shortland, Michael *v.5 p.407*
Shorto, Russell *v.3 p.491, v.6 p.715*
Shortridge, James R. *v.3 p.506*
Shorts, Don Allen *v.1 p.666, p.685*
Shoshan, Boaz. *v.6 p.635, p.636*
Shoshani, Jesheskel, et al. *v.4 p.707, p.710*
Shostak, Arthur B. (Editor) *v.4 p.500*
Shostak, Marjorie *v.4 p.38*
Shostakovich, Dmitrii Dmitrievich. . . . *v.1 p.223, p.356*
Shoumatoff, Nicholas & Shoumatoff, Nina *v.3 p.245*
Shouyi, Bai *v.6 p.183*
Shou-Yu Liang & Wen-Ching Wu *v.4 p.793*
Showalter, Elaine (Editor, Introduction by, Selected by) . *v.2 p.27*
Showalter,
   Elaine . . . *v.2 p.169, p.177, p.566, v.4 p.714, v.6 p.748, p.757*
Showalter, English *v.2 p.462*
Shrank, Cathy *v.2 p.170*
Shrayer, Maxim D. (Editor) *v.2 p.795*
Shreeve, James *v.5 p.81, p.129, p.137*
Shreir, L. L., et al. *v.5 p.735*
Shriner, Ralph L., et al.. . . . . *v.5 p.300*
Shropshire, Kenneth L. & Davis, Timothy *v.4 p.905*
Shropshire, Kenneth L. *v.4 p.819, p.833, p.905, v.6 p.41*
Shryock, Andrew *v.6 p.620*
Shteir, Rachel *v.1 p.36*
Shu, Frank H. *v.5 p.67, p.72*
Shubik, Martin. *v.4 p.252, p.689*
Shue, Vivienne *v.4 p.620*
Shuffleton, Frank (Editor) *v.2 p.9*
Shugar, Gershon J. & Ballinger, Jack T. *v.5 p.259, p.260*
Shugar, Gershon J.; Dean, John A.. . . . . . . *v.5 p.259*
Shugg, Roger W. *v.3 p.507*
Shuker, Roy *v.1 p.162, p.274*
Shukshin, Vasily *v.2 p.808*
Shula Marks, and Peter Richardson, eds. *v.3 p.322*
Shull, Michael S. & Wilt, David E. *v.6 p.308, p.323*
Shull, Michael S.. . . . . *v.6 p.333*
Shull, Steven A. & Shaw, Thomas C. *v.4 p.527*
Shull, Steven A.. . . . . *v.3 p.444*
Shulman, David D. *v.1 p.537*
Shulman, Frank Joseph *v.6 p.220*

Shulman, James Lawrence & Bowen, William G. *v.4 p.293, p.822, p.895*

Shulman, Judith, et al. *v.4 p.350*

Shulman, Lee S. *v.4 p.348*

Shulman, Max *v.2 p.116*

Shulman, Steven & Darity, William Jr. (Editors) . . . *v.4 p.134*

Shu-min, Huang *v.6 p.197*

Shumsky, Neil Larry *v.6 p.709*

Shumway-Cook, Anne & Wollacott, Marjorie H. . . . *v.4 p.910*

Shun, Kwong-Loi *v.1 p.418*

Shur, Michael *v.5 p.555*

Shurts, John *v.6 p.681, p.697*

Shusta, Robert M., et al. *v.6 p.265*

Shuttleworth, Sally *v.2 p.271*

Shvidkovsky, Dmitri *v.3 p.214*

Shweder, Richard A. *v.5 p.637*

Shy, John W. *v.3 p.414*

Shy, John *v.3 p.414*

Siavelis, Peter *v.3 p.355*

Sibelius Academy *v.1 p.173*

Sibley, William F. *v.6 p.233*

Sicher, Efraim *v.2 p.800*

Siciliano, Enzo *v.2 p.722*

Sick, Gary G. *v.3 p.480*

Sicker, Martin *v.6 p.584, p.595, p.612*

Sicking, Louis *v.3 p.205*

Sickman, Laurence & Soper, Alexander C. *v.1 p.693*

Sidanius, Jim & Pratto, Felicia *v.5 p.656*

Siddiqui, Ataullah *v.1 p.558*

Siddle Walker, Vanessa & Snarey, John R. *v.6 p.33*

Sidel, Mark *v.4 p.565, p.572*

Sidel, Ruth *v.6 p.458*

Sideman, S. & Landesberg, Amir (Editors) *v.5 p.86*

Sider, Theodore & Conee, Earl Brink *v.1 p.488*

Sides, Charles H. *v.5 p.681*

Sidey, Hugh *v.3 p.378*

Sidgwick, Henry *v.1 p.485*

Sidgwick, Nevil Vincent *v.5 p.301*

Sidhwa, Bapsi *v.2 p.766*

Sidlow, Edward I. *v.4 p.550*

Sidney, Mara S. *v.4 p.567, v.6 p.725*

Sidney, Philip *v.2 p.215, p.216*

Sidorkin, Alexander M. *v.4 p.345*

Sidwell, Keith C. *v.2 p.450*

Siebel-Achenbach, Sebastian *v.3 p.255*

Sieber, Harry *v.2 p.652*

Sieber, Roy & Herreman, Frank *v.1 p.716*

Siebers, Tobin Anthony *v.1 p.515*

Siebert, Charles *v.5 p.242*

Siebert, Fredrick S., et al. *v.4 p.406*

Siebs, Theodor *v.2 p.621*

Sieburth, Stephanie *v.2 p.642*

Siedel, George J. *v.4 p.82, p.110*

Siedentop, Daryl, et al. *v.4 p.797*

Siedentop, Larry *v.4 p.603, p.638*

Siegal, Mordecai *v.5 p.56*

Siegel, Ben *v.2 p.131*

Siegel, Carl L. *v.5 p.491, p.494*

Siegel, David, et al. *v.4 p.138*

Siegel, Elaine V. *v.1 p.51*

Siegel, George J. (Editor), et al. *v.5 p.516*

Siegel, Jacob S. & Swanson, David A. (Editors) . . . *v.4 p.376*

Siegel, James T. *v.6 p.175, p.178*

Siegel, Jay A. (Editor), et al. *v.4 p.678*

Siegel, Jeremy J. *v.4 p.97, p.100, p.102*

Siegel, Jerome H. *v.5 p.617*

Siegel, Jonah *v.1 p.680*

Siegel, Jules Paul (Editor) *v.2 p.277*

Siegel, Katherine A. *v.3 p.392*

Siegel, Katy & Mattick, Paul *v.1 p.826*

Siegel, Larry J. *v.6 p.249*

Siegel, Lawrence M. *v.4 p.451*

Siegel, M. B. *v.1 p.39*

Siegel, Marc *v.4 p.694*

Siegel, Marcia B. *v.1 p.12, p.27, p.39, p.44*

Siegel, Marcia *v.1 p.12, p.29, p.31*

Siegel, Peter E. (Editor) *v.3 p.321*

Siegel, Ronald K. *v.5 p.661*

Siegelbaum, Lewis H. & Sokolov, Andrei (Editors) . . *v.3 p.226*

Siegelbaum, Lewis H. & Suny, Ronald G. (Editors) . . *v.3 p.223*

Siegle, Joe, et al. *v.4 p.505*

Siegwart, Roland & Nourbakhsh, Illah Reza *v.5 p.339, p.342, p.712*

Sieh, Edward W. *v.6 p.278*

Sielke, Sabine *v.2 p.37*

Sienkiewicz, Henryka *v.2 p.791, p.792*

Sierakowiak, Dawid *v.3 p.86*

Sieverding, Katharina *v.1 p.769*

Sievers, Allen M. *v.6 p.175, p.178*

Sievers, Harry J. *v.3 p.438*

Sifakis, Carl *v.4 p.678*

Sigal, Leon V. *v.4 p.566, p.644, p.657*

Sigal, Pete *v.3 p.264*

Sigee, David C. *v.5 p.47*

Sigel, Lisa Z. *v.6 p.739, p.742, p.760, p.764*

Sigel, Roberta S. *v.4 p.746, v.6 p.430*

Sigmund, Paul E. (Edited and Translated by) *v.1 p.576*

Signorile, Michelangelo *v.6 p.369, p.372, p.382, p.390*

Sigoloff, Marc *v.6 p.333*

Sigurdson, Jon *v.5 p.393*

Sigurdsson, Haraldur, et al. *v.5 p.438, v.6 p.286*

Sigurdsson, Haraldur *v.5 p.437*

Sihler, Andrew L. *v.2 p.400*

Sikkink, Kathryn *v.4 p.513*

Siklos, Andras *v.3 p.187*

Sikorski, Zdzislaw E. (Editor) *v.5 p.329*

Sikov, Ed *v.6 p.313*

Silber, Irwin *v.4 p.507*

Silberger, Julius *v.1 p.583*

Silberman, Bernard S. *v.4 p.545, p.581*

Silbey, Joel H. (Editor) *v.4 p.575*

Silbey, Joel H. *v.3 p.415, p.509, v.4 p.542*

Silcox, David P. *v.1 p.747*

Silesky, Barry *v.2 p.145*

Silk, Joseph *v.5 p.72*

Silkin, Jon (Editor) *v.2 p.201*

Silko, Leslie Marmon *v.2 p.155, v.6 p.699*

Sill, Geoffrey M. & Tarbell, Roberta K. (Editors) . . . *v.2 p.54*

Silla, Eric *v.6 p.74*

Sillery, A. *v.6 p.75*

Sillén, Lars Gunnar *v.5 p.282*

Silliman, Elaine R. & Wilkinson, Louise Cherry
(Editors) *v.4 p.365*

Silliman, Stephen *v.4 p.14*

Sillitoe, Alan *v.2 p.380*

Sillitoe, Paul (Editor), et al. *v.4 p.45*

Sillitoe, Paul *v.4 p.43*

Sills, Chip & Jensen, George H. (Editors) *v.1 p.438*

Sills, Chip & Jensen, George H. *v.1 p.438*

Silone, Ignazio, et al. *v.2 p.700*

Silone, Ignazio *v.2 p.723*

Silva, Ajit *v.4 p.73*

Silva, John M. & Stevens, Diane E. *v.4 p.877, v.5 p.583*

Silva, José Asunción *v.2 p.684*

Silva, Noenoe K. *v.6 p.131*

Silva, Patricio (Editor) *v.3 p.277, v.4 p.593*

Silver, A. I. *v.3 p.536*

Silver, Alain & Ursini, James (Editors) *v.6 p.320*

Silver, Alain & Ursini, James *v.6 p.320, p.730*

Silver, Alain & Ward, Elizabeth (Editors) . *v.6 p.307, p.314, p.343*

Silver, Alain *v.6 p.311, p.336*

Silver, Archie A. & Hagin, Rosa A. *v.5 p.574*

Silver, Beverly J. *v.4 p.129*

Silver, Brenda R. *v.2 p.393*

Silver, Brian L. *v.5 p.391*

Silver, Carole *v.2 p.302*

Silver, Daniel J. & Martin, Bernard *v.1 p.547*

Silver, Harold & Silver, Pamela *v.4 p.337*

Silver, Harold *v.4 p.336*

Silver, J *v.5 p.309*

Silvera, Makeda (Editor) *v.6 p.405*

Silverblatt, Irene Marsha *v.3 p.264, p.283, p.326*

Silverfarb, Daniel *v.6 p.603*

Silverman, Eli B. *v.6 p.263*

Silverman, J. H. & Tate, John *v.5 p.497*

Silverman, Joseph *v.5 p.477*

Silverman, Kaja *v.2 p.567, p.571*

Silverman, Kenneth *v.1 p.581, v.3 p.488*

Silverman, Maxwell & Bowman, Ned A. *v.1 p.155*

Silverman, Stephen M. *v.6 p.313*

Silverman, Stephen *v.4 p.798, p.799*

Silverman, Sydel (Editor) *v.4 p.4*

Silverman, Sydel, et al. *v.4 p.4*

Silverman, Sydel *v.4 p.42*

Silverstein, Josef *v.6 p.165, p.166*

Silverstein, Robert M. & Webster, Francis X. *v.5 p.297*

Silverthorne, Elizabeth *v.2 p.46*

Silvester, Jeremy & Gewald, Jan-Bart *v.6 p.76*

Silvester, Peter J. *v.1 p.263*

Silvet, J. *v.2 p.773*

Silz, Walter *v.2 p.592*

Sim, Stuart *v.1 p.512*

Sime, Ruth L. *v.5 p.544*

Simecka, Martin M. *v.2 p.812*

Simeon, Richard *v.4 p.587*

Simerka, Barbara (Editor) *v.2 p.640*

Simic, Charles *v.2 p.155, p.811*

Simion, Eugen *v.2 p.817*

Simiu, Emil & Miyata, Toshio *v.5 p.686, p.696*

Simiu, Emil & Scanlan, Robert H. *v.5 p.696*

Simkins, Francis Butler *v.3 p.434*

Simmel, Georg & Wolff, Kurt H. *v.4 p.686*

Simmel, Georg *v.1 p.525, v.4 p.766, v.6 p.719*

Simmers, Louise *v.5 p.533*

Simmon, Scott *v.6 p.324*

Simmonds, J. G. *v.5 p.486*

Simmonds, N. W. & Smartt, Joseph (Editors) . . . *v.5 p.15, p.23*

Simmons, A. John *v.4 p.773*

Simmons, Annette *v.4 p.74*

Simmons, Charles A. *v.4 p.411*

Simmons, Cynthia & Perlina, Nina *v.3 p.227*

Simmons, Donald C. *v.3 p.297*

Simmons, George F. *v.5 p.489, p.499*

Simmons, Jack *v.3 p.115, v.6 p.766*

Simmons, Marc *v.3 p.528*

Simmons, Margaret R. (Editor, Music by) *v.6 p.30*

Simmons Market Research Bureau *v.4 p.139, p.142*

Simmons, Matthew R. *v.4 p.268*

Simmons, Tracy Lee *v.4 p.303*

Simms, Brendan *v.3 p.167*

Simms, Bryan R. *v.1 p.224, p.353*

Simms, J. G. *v.3 p.138*

Simms, Karl *v.1 p.457*

Simms, Rob *v.1 p.287*

Simms, William Gilmore *v.2 p.51*

Simo, Melanie Louise *v.1 p.814*

Simon, Anne *v.5 p.243*

Simon, Carl P. & Blume, Lawrence E. *v.4 p.204*

Simon, Carl P. & Witte, Ann D. *v.4 p.270*

Simon, David J. (Editor) *v.4 p.463*

Simon, David R. & Love, Tamar *v.6 p.256*

Simon, Denis F. & Goldman, Merle R. (Editors) . . *v.5 p.393*

Simon, Francoise & Kotler, Philip *v.5 p.219*

Simon, Herbert A. (Author, Preface by) *v.4 p.248*

Simon, Herbert A. *v.4 p.74, p.75, p.83, v.5 p.404*

Simon, Herbert, et al. *v.4 p.250, p.272*

Simon, James F. *v.4 p.452, p.469, p.539*

Simon, Joan *v.1 p.747*

Simon, Joel *v.3 p.270*

Simon, John Y. & Stevens, Michael E. *v.3 p.401*
Simon, Katherine G. *v.4 p.306*
Simon, Kevin (Editor) *v.3 p.511, p.512*
Simon, Laurence R. *v.5 p.645*
Simon, Louis *v.4 p.345*
Simon, Neil *v.2 p.116*
Simon, Paul *v.4 p.539*
Simon, Reeva S. & Tejirian, Eleanor Harvey *v.6 p.604*
Simon, Reeva Spector *v.6 p.603*
Simon, Richard M. *v.5 p.101, p.123*
Simon, Rita J. & Blaskovich, Dagny A. *v.6 p.247*
Simon, Rita J. (Editor). *v.4 p.809, p.822, p.838, p.901*
Simon, Rita James & Heitfield, Heather *v.6 p.258, p.471*
Simon, Robert I. & Gold, Liza H. *v.5 p.593*
Simon, Robert I. *v.5 p.661, p.662*
Simon, Robert L. *v.4 p.803*
Simon, Robin *v.1 p.666*
Simon, Sidney B., et al. *v.4 p.350*
Simonarson, Olafur H. *v.1 p.69, p.110, v.2 p.624*
Simonds, John Ormsbee & Starke, Barry W. *v.1 p.817*
Simonds, Nina *v.6 p.182*
Simonelli, Rocco & Frumkes, Roy. *v.6 p.347*
Simonett, Helena *v.1 p.294*
Simoni, Mary *v.1 p.224, p.245, p.373*
Simonian, Lane *v.3 p.270*
Simons, Eric N. *v.5 p.733*
Simons, Geoff *v.3 p.313, v.4 p.560*
Simons, Jack & Nichols, Jeff *v.5 p.279*
Simons, John D. *v.2 p.602*
Simons, Jon *v.1 p.503*
Simons, Judy (Editor). *v.2 p.268*
Simons, Minot II. *v.4 p.838, p.862*
Simons, W. W. & Zanger, M. *v.5 p.272, p.323*
Simons, Walter *v.6 p.561, p.573*
Simonson, Harold P. *v.2 p.15*
Simonson, Lee *v.1 p.139, p.148, p.149*
Simonton, Dean Keith *v.5 p.598*
Simonton *v.3 p.51*
Simosko, Vladimir & Tepperman, Barry *v.1 p.263, p.321*
Simpkins, Robert A. *v.4 p.143*
Simpson, Amelia S. *v.3 p.342*
Simpson, Anne B. *v.2 p.770*
Simpson, Caroline Chung *v.6 p.132*
Simpson, D. P. *v.2 p.424*
Simpson, David *v.2 p.324*
Simpson, Douglas J., et al. *v.4 p.345*
Simpson, George E. *v.1 p.544, v.4 p.37*
Simpson, Georgiana Kennedy . . . *v.1 p.683, p.806, v.6 p.679*
Simpson, James W. (Editor) *v.2 p.42*
Simpson, James *v.2 p.168, p.204, p.211*
Simpson, Jeffrey *v.3 p.541*
Simpson, Jeffry A. & Rholes, W. Steven (Editors). . . *v.5 p.656*
Simpson, Joe L. & Elias, Sherman *v.5 p.151*
Simpson, Lewis P. (Editor), et al. *v.2 p.27*
Simpson, Louis Aston Marantz *v.2 p.116*

Simpson, Louis. *v.2 p.116*
Simpson, Richard J. *v.5 p.89, p.118*
Simpson, Robert *v.1 p.204, p.314*
Simpson, Roger & Coté, William E. *v.4 p.407*
Simpson, Ronald D. & Frost, Susan H.. . . . . . *v.4 p.291*
Simpson, William Kelly (Editor). *v.6 p.645*
Simrock, K. H., et al. *v.5 p.281, p.741*
Sims, Brenda R. *v.5 p.681*
Sims, James L., et al. *v.6 p.10*
Sims, Martha C. & Stephens, Martine *v.2 p.585*
Sims, Patsy *v.1 p.649*
Sims, Ronald R. & Quatro, Scott A. (Editors). . . . *v.4 p.698*
Sinclair, A. (Editor), et al.. . . . . *v.5 p.624*
Sinclair, A. R. & Arcese, Peter (Editors) *v.5 p.358*
Sinclair, Barbara *v.4 p.533*
Sinclair, R. K. *v.4 p.501*
Sinclair, Upton . . . *v.1 p.545, v.2 p.119, p.120, v.4 p.404, p.751*
Sinclair, Wayne A. & Lyon, Howard H. *v.5 p.47*
Sindell, Kathleen *v.4 p.97*
Sinden, Richard R. *v.5 p.123*
Sindermann, C. J. *v.5 p.409*
Sindler, Allan P. & Long, Huey Pierce Jr.. . . . . . *v.3 p.507*
Sinfield, Alan *v.2 p.16*
Singer, Amy *v.6 p.611*
Singer, Bayla *v.5 p.718*
Singer, Ben *v.6 p.327, p.333, p.343*
Singer, Bennett L. (Editor) *v.6 p.407*
Singer, Beth J. *v.4 p.513*
Singer, Beverly R. *v.6 p.700*
Singer, Charles. *v.5 p.389*
Singer, Dorothy G. & Revenson, Tracey A.. . . . . . *v.5 p.629*
Singer, Dorothy G. & Singer, Jerome L. (Editors). . . *v.4 p.417*
Singer, Hans *v.1 p.758*
Singer, Harvey *v.4 p.279*
Singer, I. M. & Thorpe, J. A. *v.5 p.495*
Singer, Isaac Bashevis *v.2 p.120*
Singer, Jerome L. *v.5 p.656*
Singer, Marcus George *v.1 p.487*
Singer, Merrill & Baer, Hans *v.4 p.47*
Singer, Noel F. *v.1 p.16, p.133*
Singer, Peter Albert David (Editor), et al. . . . *v.5 p.160, p.249*
Singer, Peter Albert David (Editor) *v.1 p.485, p.486*
Singer, Peter (Editor) *v.1 p.486, v.6 p.289*
Singer, Peter. *v.1 p.464, p.486*
Singer, Robert N. (Editor), et al. *v.4 p.877, v.5 p.583*
Singer, Robert T. *v.1 p.693*
Singer, Ronald (Editor) *v.5 p.447*
Singer, S. Jonathan *v.5 p.249*
Singer, Stephanie F. *v.5 p.548*
Singer, T. E. (Editor) *v.5 p.256*
Singerman, Diane & Hoodfar, Homa (Editors) *v.6 p.638*
Singh, Balwant. *v.6 p.166*
Singh, G. *v.2 p.112*
Singh, Hanwant B. (Editor) *v.5 p.355*
Singh, Jane (Editor, Preface by) *v.6 p.87, p.138*

Singh, Jyotsna G. *v.2 p.165, p.762*
Singh, K. S. (Editor), et al. *v.6 p.155*
Singh, K. S. (Editor) *v.4 p.707, v.6 p.149, p.155*
Singh, K. S. *v.6 p.149*
Singh, Khushwant *v.2 p.766*
Singh, Kirpal (Editor). *v.2 p.761*
Singh, Nanua *v.5 p.684*
Singh, R. Paul & Heldman, Dennis R. *v.5 p.6, p.35*
Singh, Rama S. & Krimbas, Costas B. (Editors). . . . *v.5 p.200*
Singh, Shailendra. *v.5 p.219*
Singh, Simon *v.5 p.468, p.477*
Singh, Upinder. *v.6 p.162*
Singh, Vijay P. (Editor) *v.5 p.703*
Singh, Vijay P.. . . . . *v.5 p.369, p.379*
Singletary, Otis A. *v.3 p.418, p.438*
Singleton, Fred. *v.3 p.236*
Singleton, John (Editor). *v.6 p.222*
Singleton, Marvin K. *v.4 p.410*
Singley, Carol J. (Editor) *v.2 p.132*
Singley, Mark K. & Anderson, John R.. . . . . . *v.4 p.358*
Sinha, Anil Kumar *v.5 p.733*
Sinha, Manisha. *v.3 p.502*
Sinnott, Richard *v.4 p.608*
Sinnott-Armstrong, Walter & Howarth, Richard B.
  (Editors) *v.4 p.394*
Sinor, Denis (Editor) *v.6 p.239*
Sinyard, Neil. *v.2 p.351*
Siorvanes, Lucas *v.1 p.431*
Siouris, George M. *v.5 p.712*
Sipe, Thomas *v.1 p.204, p.243, p.308*
Sipes, I. G. (Editor), et al. *v.5 p.314, p.365*
Sipser, Michael. *v.5 p.337*
Siracusa, Joseph M. *v.3 p.454*
Siraisi, Nancy G. *v.3 p.50*
Sirat, Colette *v.6 p.568, p.574*
Sircar, D. C. *v.1 p.541*
Sirias, Silvio. *v.6 p.509, p.516*
Sirica, John J. *v.4 p.438*
Sirmans, Marion E.. . . . . *v.3 p.502*
Sirotnik, Kenneth A. & Soder, Roger (Editors) *v.4 p.340*
Sirotnik, Kenneth A. *v.4 p.281*
Sisk, Timothy D. & Reynolds, Andrew *v.4 p.578, p.613*
Sisk, Timothy D. *v.4 p.614*
Sisman, Elaine Rochelle *v.1 p.192, p.243, p.344*
Sisson, Charles Jasper (Editor) *v.2 p.216*
Sisson, Richard & Rose, Leo E. *v.6 p.148*
Sithole, Ndabaningi *v.6 p.55*
Sitsky, Larry (Editor) *v.1 p.224*
Sitter, John *v.2 p.195*
Sittig, Marshall *v.5 p.315, p.682, v.6 p.286*
Sittser, Jerry *v.1 p.652*
Sitwell, Edith *v.2 p.382*
Sitwell, Osbert *v.2 p.382*
Siu, Lok C. D. *v.3 p.306*
Siu, Paul C. *v.6 p.128*

Sivan, Emmanuel & Friedman, Menachem (Editors). . *v.6 p.595*
Sivin, Nathan (Editor) *v.6 p.182*
Sivulka, Juliann *v.4 p.426*
Siwiak, Kazimierz & McKeown, Debra *v.5 p.727*
Sizer, Nigel & Rice, Richard *v.3 p.322*
Sizer, Theodore R. *v.4 p.329, p.367*
Sjahrir, Soetan *v.6 p.175, p.178*
Skaggs, Peggy *v.2 p.33*
Skaine, Rosemarie *v.4 p.838, p.854*
Skal, David J. *v.6 p.320*
Skandera-Trombley, Laura E.. . . . . *v.6 p.97*
Skar, Sarah L *v.4 p.763*
Skau, Michael. *v.2 p.75*
Sked, Alan. *v.3 p.182*
Skeel, David A.. . . . . *v.4 p.97, p.110, p.444*
Skeen, C. Edward *v.4 p.487*
Skeet, Ian *v.6 p.627*
Skehan, Patrick W. *v.1 p.624*
Skelton, Geoffrey *v.1 p.224, p.332*
Skelton, John *v.2 p.216*
Skelton, Oscar D. *v.3 p.540*
Skelton, Peter, et al. *v.5 p.202*
Skemp, Richard R.. . . . . *v.5 p.464*
Skemp, Sheila L. *v.2 p.30*
Skerl, Jennie & Lydenberg, Robin (Editors) *v.2 p.64*
Skerl, Jennie (Editor) *v.2 p.59*
Skerl, Jennie *v.2 p.64*
Skidelsky, Robert (Editor). *v.4 p.229*
Skidelsky, Robert Jacob Alexander *v.3 p.119*
Skidelsky, Robert J. *v.4 p.507*
Skidelsky, Robert. *v.4 p.229*
Skidmore, David G. *v.3 p.480*
Skidmore, Monique (Editor) *v.6 p.165, p.166*
Skidmore, Thomas E. *v.3 p.280, p.342*
Skillen, James W. *v.3 p.450*
Skilling, H. Gordon (Editor). *v.3 p.188*
Skilling, H. Gordon. *v.3 p.188*
Skinner, Andrew S. & Wilson, Thomas. *v.4 p.219*
Skinner, Andrew S. *v.4 p.212*
Skinner, B. F. *v.5 p.615, p.622, p.624, p.646*
Skinner, Burrhus Frederic *v.4 p.500*
Skinner, James M. *v.3 p.306, v.6 p.328, p.343*
Skirton, H. & Patch, C. *v.5 p.151*
Sklair, Leslie *v.4 p.759, p.760*
Sklar, Bernard *v.5 p.726*
Sklar, Larry A. (Editor) *v.5 p.219*
Skocpol, Theda & Fiorina, Morris (Editors) . . *v.4 p.547, p.555*
Skocpol, Theda *v.4 p.547, p.555, p.760, p.769*
Skogan, Wesley G.. . . . . *v.6 p.264*
Skolnick, Jerome H., et al. *v.6 p.261*
Skolnick, Joan, et al. *v.5 p.407*
Skolnik, Herman *v.5 p.263*
Skolnikoff, Eugene B. *v.3 p.454*
Skorupski, John (Editor) *v.1 p.445*

Skorupski, John *v.1 p.445*
Skousen, Mark & Taylor, Kenna C. *v.4 p.186*
Skov, Lise & Moeran, Brian (Editors) *v.6 p.222*
Skowronski, JoAnn *v.1 p.169, p.282*
Skoyles, John & Sagan, Dorion *v.5 p.656*
Skramstad, Harold & Skramstad, Susan *v.1 p.828*
Skrentny, John D. *v.4 p.495, p.511, p.516*
Skutt, Alexander G. & Roberts, James B. *v.4 p.856*
Skvarenina, Tim L. *v.5 p.709*
Skvarenina, Timothy L. & DeWitt, William E. . . . *v.5 p.724*
Skvorecky, Josef, et al. *v.2 p.784*
Sky, Theodore *v.4 p.525*
Skyrms, Brian *v.1 p.495*
Slack, J. M. *v.5 p.160*
Slack, Laura *v.1 p.717*
Slack, Paul A. *v.3 p.120*
Slack, Trevor & Parent, Milena *v.4 p.886, p.889*
Slack, Trevor *v.4 p.819, p.886*
Slade, Joseph W. & Lee, Judith Yaross *v.3 p.513*
Slade, Ruth M. *v.6 p.63*
Slater, Adrian, et al. *v.5 p.219*
Slater, Candace *v.4 p.707, v.5 p.177*
Slater, David & Taylor, Peter (Editors) *v.3 p.370*
Slater, David *v.3 p.331, v.4 p.400*
Slater, John C. *v.5 p.550*
Slater, Michael *v.6 p.754, p.755*
Slater, Niall W. *v.1 p.73, p.90, v.2 p.440*
Slater, Peter J. B. *v.5 p.166*
Slater, Philip Elliot *v.3 p.371*
Slater, Rebecca *v.1 p.754, p.755*
Slater, Robert *v.4 p.157*
Slatkin, Wendy *v.1 p.707, v.6 p.473*
Slaughter, Jane *v.3 p.54, p.203, v.6 p.455*
Slaughter, Sheila A. & Rhoades, Gary *v.4 p.290*
Slaughter, Thomas P. *v.3 p.520*
Slavin, Arthur Joseph *v.3 p.101*
Slavin, Robert E. & Madden, Nancy A. (Editors). *v.4 p.281, p.365*
Slavin, Robert E. (Editor), et al. *v.4 p.361*
Slavitt, David R. *v.1 p.73, p.90*
Slavov, Atanas *v.2 p.780*
Slaybaugh, Douglas *v.5 p.6*
Slayton, Robert A. *v.3 p.462, v.4 p.707*
Sledd, James *v.2 p.558*
Sleinis, E. E. *v.1 p.467*
Slemrod, Joel & Bakija, Jon *v.4 p.108*
Slemrod, Joel (Editor) *v.4 p.108*
Slemrod, Joel *v.4 p.107*
Slessor, Kenneth *v.2 p.748*
Sletcher, Michael (Editor) *v.3 p.485*
Slide, Anthony (Editor) *v.6 p.306*
Slide, Anthony *v.6 p.313, p.391*
Slive, Seymour *v.1 p.699, p.729, p.747*
Sloan, Alfred P. Jr. *v.4 p.154*
Sloan, Bill *v.4 p.411*
Sloan, Douglas (Author, Editor) *v.4 p.329*

Sloan, Elinor C. *v.4 p.631, p.655*
Sloan, Ethel & Sloane-White, Patricia *v.5 p.524*
Sloan, Jeffrey & Sloan, Richard *v.4 p.68*
Sloan, W. David & Parcell, Lisa Mullikin (Editors) . *v.4 p.404*
Sloan, W. David (Compiled by) *v.4 p.404*
Sloane, Arthur A. *v.4 p.129*
Sloane, David E. *v.2 p.12*
Sloane, Eugene A. *v.4 p.857*
Slobin, Mark (Editor) *v.1 p.246, p.299*
Slobin, Mark *v.1 p.284, p.300, p.301*
Sloboda, John A. *v.1 p.376, v.5 p.619*
Sloboda, John (Editor) *v.1 p.376, v.5 p.619*
Sloboda, Zili & Bukoski, William J. (Editors) . *v.5 p.512, p.522*
Slocum, Terry A., et al. *v.4 p.376*
Slomp, Hans *v.4 p.123*
Slonim, Marc *v.1 p.110*
Slonimsky, Nicolas & Kassell, Richard (Editors) . *v.1 p.162*
Slonimsky, Nicolas (Editor) *v.1 p.162*
Slonimsky, Nicolas, et al. *v.1 p.224*
Slonimsky, Nicolas *v.1 p.162, p.248, p.373*
Slotkin, James S. *v.4 p.4*
Slotkin, Richard *v.2 p.9, v.3 p.381, v.6 p.324*
Slowacki, Juliusz *v.2 p.792*
Sluga, Hans D. & Stern, David G. (Editors) . . . *v.1 p.472*
Sluga, Hans D. *v.1 p.469*
Sluka, Jeffrey A. (Editor) *v.4 p.34*
Slyomovics, Susan *v.6 p.611*
Smaczny, Jan *v.1 p.204, p.243, p.322*
Smagorinsky, Peter & Taxel, Joel (Editors) *v.4 p.306*
Smakov, Gennady *v.1 p.12*
Smale, Melinda *v.5 p.9, p.16, p.23*
Smaling, E. M. A. (Editor), et al. *v.5 p.11*
Small, Christopher *v.1 p.377*
Small, Helen *v.6 p.749, p.757, p.760*
Small, Ian (Editor) *v.2 p.321*
Small, Ian *v.2 p.321*
Small, John, et al. *v.4 p.374*
Small, Melvin & Singer, J. David *v.3 p.36*
Small, Melvin *v.3 p.386, p.444, p.480*
Smalley, Donald (Editor) *v.2 p.317*
Smallman, Basil *v.1 p.186, p.243, p.355*
Smallman, Shawn C. *v.3 p.277, p.342*
Smallman-Raynor, Matthew *v.4 p.381*
Smalls, Charlie (Music by, Lyrics by) *v.1 p.254, p.409*
Smallwood, Philip *v.2 p.251*
Smallwood, Robert (Editor) *v.1 p.77, p.104, p.136*
Smart, Carol, et al. *v.4 p.735*
Smart, Carol *v.6 p.269*
Smart, Christopher *v.2 p.259*
Smart, L. E. & Gagan, J. M. F. (Editors) *v.5 p.293*
Smart, L. E. (Editor) *v.5 p.268*
Smart, Mary Ann *v.1 p.380*
Smart, Ninian *v.1 p.476, p.521, p.525*
Smart, William B. *v.3 p.530*
Smartt, J. *v.5 p.23, p.45*

Smartt, Joseph & Simmonds, Norman W. (Editors) . . . *v.5 p.23*
SME Staff *v.5 p.733*
Smedley, Agnes *v.6 p.192, p.203*
Smeenk, Wilma & Malsch, Marijke *v.6 p.259, p.265*
Smejkal, Gary B. (Editor) *v.5 p.118*
Smeliansky, Anatoly *v.2 p.800*
Smelik, Anneke M. *v.6 p.475*
Smeloff, Edward & Asmus, Peter *v.5 p.724*
Smelser, Marshall *v.3 p.415*
Smelser, Neil J. & Baltes, Paul B. *v.4 p.678*
Smelser, Neil J. & Swedberg, Richard (Editors) . . . *v.4 p.718*
Smelser, Neil J. *v.4 p.675, p.692*
Smelser, Ronald M. *v.3 p.189*
Smeltzer, Suzanne C. O'Connell, et al. *v.5 p.522*
Smernoff, Richard A. *v.2 p.479, p.481*
Smethurst, Colin (Editor) *v.2 p.504*
Smethurst, Colin *v.2 p.488*
Smethurst, James Edward *v.6 p.13, p.28*
Smialek, William *v.1 p.164, p.204, p.317*
Smienk, Gerrit & Steenbergen, Clemens *v.1 p.820*
Smil, Vaclav *v.4 p.667, v.6 p.195, p.197*
Smilevski, Goce *v.2 p.787*
Smiley, Jane *v.2 p.155, p.285, p.579*
Smiley, Robert A.; Jackson, Harold L. *v.5 p.317*
Smit, J. Henry *v.2 p.348*
Smit, W. A., et al. *v.5 p.294*
Smith, A. C. (Editor) *v.6 p.289*
Smith, A. D. (Editor), et al. *v.5 p.325*
Smith, A. D. (Editor) *v.5 p.114*
Smith, A. D. *v.1 p.483*
Smith, A. J. *v.2 p.182, p.216*
Smith, Adam . *v.1 p.450, p.485,v.2 p.565, v.4 p.218, p.219, p.220*
Smith, Alfred Emanuel *v.3 p.462*
Smith, Alison *v.6 p.338*
Smith, Andrew Brodie *v.6 p.325*
Smith, Andrew F. (Editor) *v.5 p.35*
Smith, Andrew *v.1 p.431, v.2 p.177, p.192, v.6 p.76*
Smith, Angela *v.2 p.369, p.393*
Smith, Anna Deavere *v.1 p.122*
Smith, Anne Marie *v.2 p.532*
Smith, Anthony & Hutchinson, John (Editors) *v.4 p.495*
Smith, Anthony D. *v.1 p.525, v.3 p.62, v.4 p.495*
Smith, Arthur H. *v.6 p.187, p.206, p.216*
Smith, B. Mark *v.4 p.97, p.102, p.162*
Smith, Barbara. *v.6 p.432, p.480*
Smith, Bardwell L. (Editor) *v.1 p.562*
Smith, Barry & Smith, David Woodruff (Editors) . . . *v.1 p.470*
Smith, Barry (Editor) *v.1 p.442*
Smith, Barry *v.1 p.465*
Smith, Bernard, et al. *v.1 p.733*
Smith, Betty *v.2 p.116*
Smith, Bill *v.1 p.35*
Smith, B.L. (Editor) *v.1 p.562*
Smith, Bonnie G. (Editor) *v.6 p.428, p.435*
Smith, Brent L. *v.4 p.565*

Smith, Brian C. *v.5 p.270*
Smith, Brian H. *v.3 p.355*
Smith, Bruce D. *v.4 p.6*
Smith, Bruce. *v.2 p.155*
Smith, Bryan John (Editor) *v.5 p.103*
Smith, C. S. *v.1 p.118, p.138, p.141*
Smith, C. Wayne & Dilday, Robert H. (Editors) . . *v.5 p.23, p.25*
Smith, C. Wayne & Frederiksen, Richard A. (Editors) . *v.5 p.24*
Smith, C. Wayne (Editor), et al. *v.5 p.23, p.25*
Smith, C. Wayne *v.5 p.23*
Smith, Carolyn J.. . . . . *v.6 p.410*
Smith, Catherine P. *v.1 p.224, p.282, p.358*
Smith, C. *v.2 p.645*
Smith, Cecil & Litton, Glenn. *v.1 p.93, p.118*
Smith, Charlotte, et al. *v.2 p.261*
Smith, Charlotte *v.2 p.260, p.261*
Smith, Christian & Prokopy, Joshua *v.1 p.544*
Smith, Christian *v.4 p.721*
Smith, Christopher E., et al.. . . . . . . *v.6 p.249, p.268*
Smith, Christopher E.. . . . . *v.4 p.539, p.540, v.6 p.274*
Smith, Colin J. *v.2 p.646*
Smith, Constance. *v.1 p.826*
Smith, Craig B. & Hawass, Zahi *v.6 p.57*
Smith, Craig *v.4 p.220*
Smith, Dan *v.4 p.381*
Smith, Daniel B. *v.4 p.734*
Smith, Daniel M.. . . . . *v.3 p.480*
Smith, Darren L. (Editor) *v.4 p.783, p.788, v.5 p.19*
Smith, Dave & Bottoms, David (Editors) *v.2 p.24*
Smith, David & Schenk, Michael *v.5 p.89*
Smith, David E. *v.4 p.588, p.590*
Smith, David G. *v.4 p.756, p.757*
Smith, David Marshall *v.4 p.398*
Smith, David M. *v.6 p.79*
Smith, David. *v.2 p.376*
Smith, Dennis *v.3 p.541*
Smith, Donald E.. . . . . *v.1 p.751*
Smith, Dorothy E. *v.4 p.744*
Smith, Douglas Alton. *v.1 p.391*
Smith, Duane A. *v.3 p.525, v.6 p.296*
Smith, Edward W. *v.5 p.583*
Smith, Elbert B. *v.3 p.418*
Smith, Elise L.. . . . . *v.1 p.747*
Smith, Elton E.. . . . . *v.2 p.313*
Smith, Emma (Editor) *v.2 p.233, p.234*
Smith, F. B.. . . . . *v.3 p.92, p.115*
Smith, F. Leslie, et al. *v.4 p.412*
Smith, Frederick Key *v.1 p.246*
Smith, G. E. Kidder *v.1 p.791*
Smith, G. Rex (Translator) *v.6 p.586*
Smith, Gaddis *v.3 p.480*
Smith, Gary A. *v.6 p.315, p.339*
Smith, Gavin. *v.3 p.331*
Smith, Gene. *v.3 p.462, p.480*
Smith, George Patrick *v.5 p.220, p.249*

Smith, George P. *v.4 p.738*

Smith, Graham. *v.3 p.229*

Smith, H. Shelton *v.1 p.644*

Smith, Harmon. *v.2 p.38, p.52*

Smith, Hazel. *v.4 p.603, p.638, v.6 p.393*

Smith, Helaine *v.1 p.71*

Smith, Helmut Walser *v.3 p.169*

Smith, Helmut W. *v.3 p.165*

Smith, Henrietta M. & Hirahara, Naomi. *v.6 p.87, p.107*

Smith, Henry N. *v.3 p.519*

Smith, Howard M. *v.5 p.561*

Smith, Huston *v.4 p.291*

Smith, Ian *v.5 p.699*

Smith, J. C. *v.5 p.697*

Smith, J. Clay Jr. (Editor) *v.6 p.442*

Smith, J. Douglas *v.3 p.500*

Smith, J. Maynard *v.5 p.196*

Smith, Jackie & Johnston, Hank. *v.4 p.640, p.663*

Smith, James R. *v.5 p.443*

Smith, Jane F. & Kvasnicka, Robert M. (Editors). *v.6 p.683, p.692*

Smith, Jean E. *v.4 p.469*

Smith, Jeff *v.1 p.256, p.385*

Smith, Jeffery A. *v.4 p.459*

Smith, Jeffrey Chipps. *v.1 p.675*

Smith, Jeffrey K., et al. *v.4 p.287*

Smith, Jennifer. *v.4 p.587*

Smith, Jeremy *v.2 p.555*

Smith, Jessie Carney (Editor) *v.6 p.19, p.34, p.46*

Smith, Jessie Carney *v.6 p.19, p.34*

Smith, Jessie C.. . . . . *v.6 p.19, p.34, p.46*

Smith, Jim & Beresford, Nicholas A.. . . . . . *v.5 p.364*

Smith, Jim *v.6 p.265, p.266*

Smith, Joel *v.1 p.702, p.769*

Smith, John E.. . . . . *v.5 p.220*

Smith, John K.. . . . . *v.4 p.355*

Smith, John M.. . . . . *v.5 p.204*

Smith, John *v.1 p.439, v.3 p.500*

Smith, Jonathan D. H. & Romanowska, Anna B. . . . *v.5 p.474*

Smith, Jonathan Z. *v.1 p.521*

Smith, Joseph P. *v.1 p.592*

Smith, Joseph (Translator). *v.1 p.587*

Smith, Joseph *v.1 p.587, v.3 p.342*

Smith, Justin H. *v.3 p.418, p.419*

Smith, K. T. *v.5 p.489*

Smith, Karen E., et al. *v.5 p.497*

Smith, Katharine Capshaw *v.6 p.28*

Smith, Keith. *v.4 p.395*

Smith, L. Glenn & Smith, Joan K.. . . . . . . *v.4 p.338*

Smith, Lacey Baldwin *v.3 p.101*

Smith, Larry *v.2 p.75, p.111*

Smith, Lawrence R. (Editor). *v.2 p.700*

Smith, Lee. *v.2 p.155*

Smith, Leonard V., et al. *v.3 p.155*

Smith, Leonora. *v.6 p.503*

Smith, Lillian *v.2 p.116*

Smith, Lissa (Editor) *v.4 p.809, p.838*

Smith, M. Cecil & Pourchot, Thomas (Editors) *v.4 p.321, v.5 p.572*

Smith, Margaret *v.1 p.555*

Smith, Marian. *v.1 p.25*

Smith, Mark M. (Editor) *v.3 p.495*

Smith, Mark *v.4 p.639*

Smith, Marquard (Editor) *v.1 p.773*

Smith, Melissa T. (Translator) *v.2 p.795*

Smith, Michael C. & Fossey, Richard W.. . . . . *v.4 p.451*

Smith, Michael E. *v.4 p.638*

Smith, Michael J.. . . . . *v.4 p.627*

Smith, Michael L. *v.3 p.196, p.197*

Smith, Michael Llewellyn *v.3 p.196, v.6 p.715*

Smith, Michael P. & Bender, Thomas *v.6 p.719*

Smith, Mickey C., et al.. . . . . *v.4 p.156*

Smith, Myron J. Jr.. . . . . *v.4 p.844, p.859*

Smith, N. Craig & Quelch, John. *v.4 p.146*

Smith, Neil & Williams, Peter (Editors) *v.6 p.721*

Smith, Neil *v.4 p.378, v.6 p.729*

Smith, Nicholas D. & Brickhouse, Thomas C. . . . *v.1 p.423*

Smith, Nigel *v.2 p.253*

Smith, Norman Kemp *v.1 p.462*

Smith, P. G. & Scott, J. S. *v.5 p.707*

Smith, Pamela H. *v.3 p.48, v.5 p.392, p.411*

Smith, Patricia Juliana (Editor) *v.6 p.360*

Smith, Patrick A. *v.2 p.75*

Smith, Patti *v.2 p.156*

Smith, Paul Chaat & Warrior, Robert Allen. . *v.6 p.690, p.695*

Smith, Paul (Editor, Contribution by) *v.2 p.85*

Smith, Paul G.. . . . . *v.5 p.379, p.380*

Smith, Paul J. (Editor) *v.4 p.662*

Smith, Paul J. *v.1 p.721*

Smith, Paul Julian *v.2 p.660*

Smith, Perry M. *v.4 p.407*

Smith, Peter & Jones, O. R. *v.1 p.497*

Smith, Peter H. *v.3 p.295, v.4 p.593*

Smith, Peter *v.1 p.561*

Smith, Philip L. *v.4 p.345*

Smith, R. Martin & Busch, Kenneth L.. . . . . . *v.5 p.271*

Smith, R. R. *v.1 p.776*

Smith, Raymond A. & Haider-Markel, Donald P. *v.4 p.570, v.6 p.360, p.387*

Smith, Raymond A. (Editor). *v.6 p.379*

Smith, Raymond J. *v.2 p.243*

Smith, Raymond T. *v.4 p.33*

Smith, Richard J. *v.6 p.182, p.187*

Smith, Richard N. *v.3 p.480, v.4 p.411*

Smith, Richard Norton *v.3 p.462*

Smith, Richard. *v.6 p.408*

Smith, Robert A.. . . . . *v.4 p.819, p.857*

Smith, Robert H., et al.. . . . . *v.5 p.171*

Smith, Robert J. & Wiswell, Ella L. *v.6 p.222*

Smith, Robert J. *v.4 p.707*

Smith, Robert Michael *v.4 p.129*

Smith, Robert S.. . . . . *v.6 p.69*
Smith, Robert W. *v.5 p.62*
Smith, Robin. *v.5 p.743*
Smith, Roger C.. . . . . *v.3 p.73*
Smith, Roger (Editor) *v.5 p.683, p.684*
Smith, Roger. *v.5 p.396*
Smith, Ron F. *v.4 p.406*
Smith, Ronald A. *v.4 p.810, p.822, p.895, p.902*
Smith, Roy C. & Walter,
   Ingo *v.4 p.92, p.98, p.102, p.103, p.156, p.163*
Smith, Sarah *v.6 p.312*
Smith, Scott T. (Photographer). *v.5 p.235*
Smith, Sidonie & Watson, Julia (Editors) *v.6 p.477*
Smith, Stan (Editor) *v.2 p.330*
Smith, Stephen L. *v.4 p.785*
Smith, Steven C.. . . . . *v.1 p.256, p.332*
Smith, Steven S., et al.
   . . . . *v.4 p.531*
Smith, Steven S. *v.4 p.534*
Smith, Stevie (Illustrator) *v.2 p.383*
Smith, Stevie *v.2 p.382, p.383*
Smith, Stuart S. & DeLio, Thomas (Editors) *v.1 p.224*
Smith, Susan L. *v.6 p.22, p.46, p.444*
Smith, Suzanne E. *v.1 p.385*
Smith, Tara *v.1 p.510*
Smith, Teresa H. *v.2 p.788*
Smith, Theodore Clarke. *v.3 p.438*
Smith, Thorne *v.2 p.116*
Smith, Timothy B. *v.5 p.638*
Smith, Toby. *v.4 p.63*
Smith, Tony *v.3 p.454*
Smith, V. L. (Editor) *v.4 p.268*
Smith, Valerie (Editor) *v.6 p.330*
Smith, Verity (Editor). *v.2 p.665*
Smith, Vernon L. *v.4 p.248, p.264, p.272*
Smith, Vivian & Hubber, Brian *v.2 p.749*
Smith, W. Stevenson *v.1 p.671*
Smith, Wayne S. & Dominguez, Esteban M. (Editors) . *v.3 p.313*
Smith, Whitney *v.4 p.499*
Smith, Wilfred C. *v.1 p.554*
Smith, William B. *v.5 p.293*
Smith, William F. *v.5 p.691*
Smith, William J. & Holmes, James S. *v.2 p.622*
Smith, William Jr. *v.4 p.329*
Smith, William Robertson. *v.3 p.385*
Smith, Woodruff D. *v.3 p.77, v.4 p.584*
Smith, Zadie *v.2 p.380*
Smith-Autard, Jacqueline M. *v.1 p.48*
Smithells, Colin J., et al. *v.5 p.319*
Smither, Howard E.. . . . *v.1 p.186, p.192, p.204, p.224, p.237*
Smitherman, Geneva & Villanueva, Victor (Editors) . *v.2 p.565*
Smitherman, Geneva (Editor) *v.6 p.40, p.46*
Smithers, Don L.. . . . . *v.1 p.186, p.391*
Smithers, Janice A.. . . . . *v.4 p.742*
Smithers, Peter *v.2 p.237*
Smith-Hefner, Nancy Joan *v.6 p.139*

Smithies, Michael (Compiled by) *v.6 p.172*
Smith-Shomade, Beretta E. *v.6 p.15, p.46, p.448*
Smithsonian American Art Museum Staff & Slowik,
   Theresa J. *v.1 p.683*
Smithsonian Institution Staff. *v.6 p.677*
Smocovitis, Vassiliki B. *v.5 p.81, p.196*
Smolin, Lee *v.5 p.556, p.557*
Smoll, Frank L. & Smith, Ronald E.. . . . *v.4 p.824, p.840*
Smollett, Tobias George. *v.2 p.261*
Smoodin, Eric (Editor) *v.6 p.308*
Smoodin, Eric *v.6 p.308*
Smorkaloff, Pamela Maria. . . . *v.2 p.673, v.6 p.509, p.516*
Smorodinskii, Iakov A. & Landau, L. D. *v.5 p.553*
Smout, T. C. (Thomas Christopher) *v.3 p.133*
Smout, T. C.. . . . . *v.3 p.132, p.133*
Smrekar, Claire & Goldring, Ellen *v.4 p.367*
Smulders, Sharon. *v.2 p.305*
Smutny, Joan F. (Editor) *v.4 p.317*
Smutny, Joan Franklin *v.4 p.317*
Smuul, Juhan *v.2 p.781*
Smyers, Virginia L. & Winship, Michael *v.2 p.6*
Smylie, James H.. . . . . *v.1 p.588*
Smylie, Mark A. & Miretzky, Debra (Editors). . . . *v.4 p.278*
Smyrl, Marc *v.4 p.528*
Smyrniw, Walter *v.2 p.778*
Smyser, W. R. *v.3 p.177*
Smyth, Herbert W. *v.2 p.400*
Smyth, Malcolm R. (Editor). *v.5 p.268*
Smyth, Sarah & Crosbie, Elena V. *v.2 p.776*
Smythe, Donald *v.3 p.463, p.480*
Smythe, Ted Curtis *v.4 p.411*
Snapp, J. Russell *v.3 p.495*
Snay, Mitchell *v.3 p.401*
Snedecor, George W. & Cochran, William G.. . . . . *v.5 p.483*
Sneed, M. Cannon *v.5 p.303*
Snell, Clete *v.6 p.258*
Snell, Daniel C. *v.3 p.4*
Snell, Daniel (Editor) *v.3 p.4*
Snell, K. D. M. & Ell, Paul S.. . . . . *v.6 p.759*
Snell, Richard S. *v.5 p.158*
Snellgrove, David L. *v.1 p.564*
Snelson, John *v.1 p.254, p.337*
Sneppen, Kim & Zocchi, Giovanni *v.5 p.125, p.129*
Snider, Bruce C. (Editor), et al. *v.4 p.709*
Sniderman, Paul M., et al.. . . . . *v.5 p.645*
Snoddy, Theo *v.1 p.666*
Snodgrass, Michael. *v.3 p.295*
Snodgrass, W. D. *v.2 p.116*
Snodin, Michael & Styles, John *v.1 p.801*
Snodin, Michael (Editor) *v.1 p.795*
Snoeyink, Vernon L. & Jenkins, David *v.5 p.705*
Snoj, Nina *v.2 p.777*
Snorri Sturluson *v.2 p.625*
Snow, C. P. *v.2 p.317, v.4 p.291*
Snow, David A. & Anderson, Leon *v.4 p.751*

Snow, David A. (Editor), et al. *v.4 p.710*

Snow, Dean R. *v.4 p.11*

Snow, Edgar R. *v.6 p.192*

Snow, Philip *v.6 p.56, p.206*

Snow, Richard E., et al. *v.5 p.572*

Snowden, Don & Dixon, Willie *v.1 p.263, p.321*

Snowden, Frank M. Jr. *v.3 p.3*

Snowden, Frank M. *v.3 p.202*

Snowdon, Brian & Vane, Howard R. (Editors) . *v.4 p.193, p.241*

Snowdon, Brian & Vane, Howard R. . . *v.4 p.192, p.240, p.241*

Snowdon, Brian, et al. *v.4 p.241*

Snowdon, Brian *v.4 p.245, p.258*

Snustad, D. Peter & Simmons, Michael J. *v.5 p.137*

Snyder, C. Arnold *v.1 p.603*

Snyder, C. R. & Lopez, S. J. (Editors) *v.5 p.670*

Snyder, C. R. (Editor) *v.5 p.656*

Snyder, Gary. *v.2 p.156*

Snyder, Gordon F. *v.5 p.726*

Snyder, Graydon F. *v.1 p.609*

Snyder, Jack L. *v.4 p.505*

Snyder, James C. *v.1 p.672*

Snyder, James, et al. *v.1 p.675*

Snyder, James *v.1 p.672, p.675, p.688*

Snyder, Jane M. *v.2 p.419, v.6 p.393*

Snyder, Kerala J. *v.1 p.186, p.315*

Snyder, Kirk *v.4 p.168, v.6 p.382*

Snyder, Lloyd R., et al. *v.5 p.269*

Snyder, Margaret C. & Tadesse, Mary *v.6 p.458*

Snyder, Margaret C. *v.6 p.458*

Snyder, Mariah & Lindquist, Ruth *v.5 p.531*

Snyder, Noel F. & Snyder, Helen *v.6 p.292*

Snyder, Pat (Directed By), et al. *v.6 p.380*

Snyder, Paula *v.6 p.426*

Snyder, R. Claire. *v.6 p.389*

Snyder, Robert W. *v.1 p.35*

Snyder, Scott *v.4 p.644, p.646*

Snyder, Timothy *v.3 p.207, p.252*

So, Alvin Y. *v.4 p.618*

So, Jenny F. *v.1 p.290*

Soames, Scott *v.1 p.438, p.439*

Soares, Andre *v.6 p.419*

Soares, Eric J. *v.4 p.136*

Soares, Janet M. *v.1 p.12*

Sobchack, Vivian C. *v.6 p.320*

Sobel, Bernard *v.1 p.35, p.36, p.90, p.91*

Sobel, Matthew J. & Heyman, Daniel P. *v.5 p.484, p.493*

Sobel, Richard *v.3 p.454*

Sobel, Robert & Sicilia, David B. (Editors). *v.4 p.529*

Sobel, Robert (Editor) *v.3 p.377*

Sobel, Robert *v.3 p.480, v.4 p.487, p.528*

Sobell, Mark G. *v.5 p.348, p.349*

Sober, Elliot & Wilson, David S. *v.5 p.650*

Sober, Elliott. *v.1 p.516, v.5 p.196, p.249*

Soble, Alan *v.6 p.436, p.462*

Sobol, Ilya M. *v.5 p.483*

Sobol, Julie Macfie & Sobol, Ken *v.3 p.516*

Soboul, Albert *v.3 p.151*

Sobrino, Jon & Barr, Robert R. *v.3 p.299*

Sobrino, Jon *v.1 p.641*

Social Psychology Network *v.5 p.676*

Social Science Research and Instructional Council, California
　State University. *v.4 p.676*

Society for Community Research and Action (APA
　Division 27) *v.5 p.672*

Society for Consumer Psychology (APA Division 23) . *v.5 p.585*

Society for Developmental Biology (SDB) *v.5 p.161*

Society for Historical Archaeology Staff. *v.4 p.14*

Society for the Psychological Study of Social Issues (APA
　Division 9). *v.5 p.672*

Society for the Teaching of Psychology (APA
　Division 2). *v.5 p.676*

Society of European Stage Authors and
　Composers. *v.1 p.173, p.385*

Society of Manufacturing Engineers Staff. *v.5 p.733*

Sociometrics *v.4 p.689*

Socolofsky, Homer E. & Spetter, Allan. *v.3 p.438*

Socolofsky, Homer E. *v.3 p.525*

Socolow, Susan M. *v.3 p.347*

Socolow, Susan Migden. *v.3 p.283*

Soderberg, Nancy *v.4 p.562*

Soesastro, Hadi & Findlay, Christopher C. *v.4 p.398*

Sofer, Andrew *v.1 p.148*

Soffer, O. & Praslov, N. D. *v.4 p.17*

Soffer, Reba N. *v.3 p.115, p.129*

Sofsky, Wolfgang *v.3 p.86*

Sohail, Muhammad (Editor). *v.5 p.137*

Sohn, Louis B. & Clark, Grenville. *v.4 p.635*

Sohn, Louis B. & Gustafson, Kristen. *v.4 p.478*

Soja, Edward W. *v.6 p.721*

Sokel, Walter H. (Editor) *v.1 p.69, p.83, p.85, p.110*

Sokel, Walter H. *v.2 p.611*

Sokol, Stanley S. *v.1 p.666*

Sokolow, Gary A. *v.6 p.692*

Sokolowski, Robert. *v.1 p.470, p.511*

Sola-Morales, Ignasi De *v.1 p.795*

Solan, Lawrence M. & Tiersma, Peter M. *v.6 p.245*

Solbach, Andreas. *v.2 p.596*

Solberg, Carl *v.3 p.463*

Solecki, Sam. *v.2 p.737*

Soley, Lawrence *v.4 p.515*

Solie, Ruth A. (Editor) *v.1 p.380, v.6 p.475*

Solinger, Rickie (Editor) *v.6 p.447, p.471*

Solinger, Rickie *v.4 p.769, v.6 p.471*

Solis, Jose *v.4 p.337*

Sollers, Philippe *v.2 p.533, p.534*

Solnit, Rebecca *v.1 p.707*

Sologub, Fedor. *v.2 p.808*

Solomon, Barbara M. *v.4 p.302*

Solomon, Deborah *v.1 p.46, p.747*

Solomon, Edward I. & Lever, A. B. P. (Editors). . . . *v.5 p.304*

Solomon, Edward I. & Lever, A. B. P. *v.5 p.304*

Solomon, Edward I. & Lever, A. Barry P. (Editors) . *v.5 p.304*

Solomon, Edward I., Lever, A.B.P. (eds.) *v.5 p.304*

Solomon, Eric *v.2 p.36*

Solomon, Jean W. & O'Brien, Jane Clifford (Editors) *v.5 p.535*

Solomon, John & Solomon, Ruth (Editors) *v.1 p.49*

Solomon, Jon *v.6 p.315*

Solomon, Judith Y. *v.5 p.669*

Solomon, Mark *v.4 p.509, p.554*

Solomon, Maynard *v.1 p.192, p.204, p.308, p.344*

Solomon, Robert C. & Higgins, Kathleen M. (Editors). *v.1 p.508*

Solomon, Robert C. & Higgins, Kathleen M. *v.1 p.467*

Solomon, Robert C. & Sherman, David L. (Editors) . . *v.1 p.511*

Solomon, Robert C. *v.1 p.497, p.506, v.5 p.656*

Solomon, Robert *v.4 p.239*

Solorzano, Carlos (Editor) *v.1 p.61, p.118, p.127*

Solorzano, Carlos *v.2 p.676*

Soloveitchik, Joseph B. *v.1 p.552*

Soloviev, Vladimir & Wozniuk, Vladimir (Editors) . *v.1 p.474*

Solow, Daniel *v.5 p.471*

Solow, R. *v.4 p.245*

Solow, Robert M. & Taylor, John B. *v.4 p.245*

Solow, Robert *v.4 p.245*

Solso, Robert L. *v.1 p.704, v.5 p.609, p.619*

Solt, Leo F. (Leo Frank) *v.3 p.104, p.122*

Soluri, John *v.3 p.270*

Solway, Diane *v.1 p.12, v.6 p.415*

Solzhenitsyn, Aleksandr *v.2 p.808, v.4 p.753*

Somakian, Manoug *v.3 p.231*

Somasundaram, Daya *v.6 p.163*

Someck, Ronny *v.6 p.651*

Somel, Selcuk Aksin *v.6 p.591*

Somer, Elizabeth & Health Media of America Staff . *v.5 p.329*

Somervell, D. C. (David Churchill) *v.3 p.115, p.129*

Somervill, Barbara A. *v.4 p.393, v.5 p.172*

Somme, Axel (Editor) *v.3 p.232, p.233*

Sommer, Deborah (Editor) *v.1 p.539*

Sommer, Doris *v.3 p.265*

Sommer, Sally & Harris, Margaret *v.1 p.12*

Sommerfeld, Arnold *v.5 p.547*

Sommers, Ira Brant & Baskin, Deborah R. . . . *v.6 p.253, p.254*

Sommers, Paul M. (Editor) . . . *v.4 p.852, p.886, p.889, p.897*

Sommerville, C. John *v.4 p.418*

Sommerville, Ian *v.5 p.346, p.348*

Sommerville, Johann P. (Introduction by) *v.3 p.95, p.102*

Sonbol, Amira El Azhary *v.6 p.620*

Sonbol, Amira El-Azhary (Editor) *v.6 p.582*

Sonbol, Amira El-Azhary *v.6 p.640*

Sondheim, Stephen & Goldman, James . *v.1 p.254, p.357, p.410*

Sondheim, Stephen & Horowitz, Mark Eden . *v.1 p.254, p.357*

Sondheim, Stephen & Laurents, Arthur . . . *v.1 p.254, p.410*

Sondheim, Stephen (Lyrics by, Music by). *v.1 p.254, p.357, p.410*

Sone, Monica Itoi *v.6 p.95*

Sonenshein, Raphael *v.3 p.444, v.4 p.544*

Sonesson, Birgit *v.3 p.321*

Song, Bang-song *v.1 p.290*

Song, Cathy *v.6 p.104*

Song, Min *v.6 p.97, p.105*

Song Ong Siang *v.6 p.173*

Song, Yongyi & Sun, Dajin *v.6 p.196*

Songer, Donald R., et al. *v.4 p.470*

Sonn, Tamara *v.6 p.595*

Sonneck, Oscar G. (Editor) *v.1 p.204, p.308*

Sonnenschein, David (Editor) *v.6 p.352*

Sonnert, Gerhard & Holton, Gerald . . . *v.5 p.398, v.6 p.439*

Sonnichsen, Charles L. *v.3 p.528, v.6 p.715*

Sonnino, Paul *v.3 p.146*

Sontag, Susan *v.1 p.704, v.2 p.567, p.569,*
v.4 p.778, v.6 p.378, p.379

Soper, Alexander C. & Paine, Robert T. *v.1 p.694*

Sophocles *v.1 p.72, p.89, v.2 p.420*

Sorabji, Richard (Editor) *v.1 p.427*

Sorabji, Richard *v.1 p.498, v.5 p.615*

Soranus *v.2 p.405*

Sorel, Georges *v.4 p.507, p.759*

Sorell, Tom (Editor) *v.1 p.448*

Sorell, Tom *v.1 p.449, p.454*

Sorell, Walter (Editor) *v.1 p.44*

Sorell, Walter *v.1 p.12, p.39*

Sorensen, Andre (Editor), et al. *v.6 p.729*

Sorensen, Bent *v.5 p.361*

Sorensen, Roy *v.1 p.495*

Sorensen, Theodore C. *v.3 p.480*

Sorenson, Helen & Thorson, James A. *v.5 p.536*

Sorenson, W. Conner *v.5 p.81, p.213*

Sorenson, Wayne R.; Campbell, Tod W. *v.5 p.323*

Sorescu, Marin *v.2 p.817*

Soria, Regina *v.1 p.666*

Sorin, Gerald *v.1 p.549, v.3 p.421*

Sorkin, Michael & Zukin, Sharon (Editors) *v.6 p.715*

Sorkin, Michael (Editor) *v.6 p.719, p.726*

Sornson, Robert (Editor) *v.4 p.361*

Soroka, Stuart Neil *v.4 p.587*

Sorokin, Pitirim A. & Lunden, Walter A. . . . *v.4 p.484, p.770*

Sorokin, Pitirim A. *v.4 p.680, p.683, p.700, p.760*

Sorokin, Pitirim Aleksandrovich *v.4 p.694*

Soros, George *v.4 p.665*

Soros, Susan W. *v.1 p.802, p.805*

Soros, Tivadar *v.3 p.86, p.187*

Sorrell, Martin (Translator) *v.2 p.464*

Sorrell, Neil *v.1 p.290*

Sorrentino, Richard M. & Higgins, E. Tory (Editors) . *v.5 p.650*

Sosa, David *v.1 p.502*

Sosa, Ernest (Author, Contribution by) *v.1 p.483*

Sosa, Ernest *v.1 p.488*

Sosa, Juan B. *v.3 p.306*

Sosare, M. & Birzvalka, I. *v.2 p.773*

Soseki, Natsume *v.6 p.233*

Sosin, Jack M. *v.3 p.513*

Sosna, Morton *v.3 p.497*

Sotelo, Susan Baker *v.6 p.503, p.516*
Soto, Gary. *v.2 p.673, v.6 p.503, p.511*
Soto, Pedro Juan *v.6 p.509*
Soto, Shirlene A.. . . . . *v.6 p.432, p.436*
Soucek, Svat *v.6 p.239*
Souckova, Milada *v.2 p.782*
Soufas, C. Christopher *v.2 p.640*
Soufas, Theresa Scott. *v.2 p.639*
Sougou, Omar *v.2 p.754*
Souhami, Diana *v.6 p.403*
Soule, David C. (Editor) *v.6 p.284*
Soule, George *v.2 p.379*
Souritz, Elizabeth *v.1 p.12*
Souster, Raymond *v.2 p.739*
Southall, Aidan. *v.6 p.719*
Southall, Humphrey *v.6 p.735*
Southam, B. C. *v.2 p.72, p.268*
Southam, Jem (Author, Photographer) *v.1 p.814*
Southern, Eileen & Wright, Josephine *v.1 p.282, v.6 p.30*
Southern, Eileen *v.1 p.162, p.282,v.6 p.30, p.34*
Southern, Pat *v.3 p.29, v.4 p.718*
Southern, R. W. *v.3 p.58, p.68*
Southern, Richard W.. . . . . *v.1 p.155, p.559, p.580, v.6 p.564*
Southern, Thomas *v.2 p.260*
Southgate, Minoo (Editor, Translator) *v.6 p.673*
Southgate, Paul & Lucas, John (Editors). *v.5 p.32*
Southgate. *v.3 p.95, p.115*
Southon, Ian *v.5 p.299*
Southwell, Robert *v.2 p.216*
Southwood, Richard & Southwood, R. *v.5 p.249*
Southworth, Franklin C. *v.6 p.147, p.148*
Soux, María Luisa *v.3 p.282*
Souza, Laura de Mello e *v.3 p.264, p.335*
Sova, Dawn B. *v.2 p.50*
Sowell, David *v.3 p.333, p.358*
Sowell, John. *v.5 p.177, p.240*
Sowell, Thomas *v.4 p.186, p.218, p.310*
Sowerwine, Charles *v.3 p.141*
Soyinka, Wole (Editor). *v.6 p.81*
Soyinka, Wole *v.1 p.128, p.130,v.2 p.758, v.6 p.19, p.29*
Spacks, Patricia Meyer *v.2 p.172*
Spaeth, Harold J. & Segal, Jeffrey A. *v.4 p.540*
Spaethling, Robert (Editor, Translator) *v.1 p.192, p.344*
Spain, Louise *v.1 p.4*
Spalding, Frances *v.1 p.680, p.689*
Spalding, Francis & Collins, Judith *v.1 p.666*
Spalding, Julian *v.1 p.668, p.828*
Spalding, Mark D., et al. *v.4 p.393*
Spalding, Mark. *v.4 p.393*
Spalding, Phinizy (Author, Editor). *v.3 p.503, p.504*
Spalding, Phinizy. *v.3 p.503*
Spalding, Susan E. & Woodside, Jane H. *v.1 p.33*
Spallholz, Julian E.. . . . . *v.5 p.329*
Spandorfer, Merle, et al. *v.1 p.751, p.760*
Spangler, Mary M. *v.4 p.345*

Spanier, John W. & Hook, Steven W. *v.4 p.560*
Spann, Girardeau A.. . . . . *v.4 p.457, p.540*
Spargo, John. *v.4 p.236*
Spark, Muriel *v.2 p.383, p.384*
Sparke, Linda S. & Gallagher, John S. *v.5 p.71*
Sparke, Penny (Editor) *v.5 p.319*
Sparkman, O. David *v.5 p.272*
Sparks, D. L., et al. *v.5 p.51*
Sparks, Donald L. *v.5 p.51*
Sparks, Sheila & Cynthia, Taylor *v.5 p.528*
Sparr, Pamela (Editor) *v.6 p.458*
Sparrow, Andrew. *v.3 p.120*
Sparshott, Francis *v.1 p.44*
Spary, E. C.. *v.5 p.81*
Spate, Virginia *v.1 p.747*
Spater, George. *v.3 p.109, p.131*
Speaight, Robert *v.2 p.227*
Speake, Graham (Editor). *v.3 p.3, p.13*
Speake, Jennifer *v.1 p.666, p.710*
Spear, Thomas G. *v.6 p.65*
Spear, Thomas *v.6 p.63*
Special Collections, Duke University. *v.6 p.432*
Speck, Frank G. *v.1 p.15, v.6 p.704*
Speck, W. A. *v.3 p.91, p.109*
Speck, William A. *v.3 p.133*
Speckmann, Johan Dirk. *v.3 p.323*
Spector, David L. & Goldman, Robert D. *v.5 p.86*
Spector, Irwin *v.1 p.12*
Spector, Jack J. *v.1 p.681*
Spector, Paul E. *v.5 p.579*
Spector, Robert D. *v.2 p.261*
Spector, Robert. *v.4 p.165*
Speed, Terry (ed.) *v.5 p.101, p.102*
Speel, Erika *v.1 p.798*
Speer, Kevin P. *v.4 p.826, p.875, p.880*
Speicher, David W. (Editor) *v.5 p.105, p.118*
Speiser, Ephraim A. *v.1 p.621*
Spektorowski, Alberto *v.3 p.349*
Spellerberg, Ian F. & Sawyer, John W. D. *v.5 p.169*
Spellerberg, Ian F. *v.5 p.359*
Spellman, Frank R. and Nancy E. Whiting *v.5 p.707*
Spellman, Frank R.. . . . . *v.5 p.706*
Spellman, Kathryn. *v.4 p.44*
Spellman, W. M. & Spellman, William *v.4 p.502*
Spence, A. Michael. *v.4 p.254*
Spence, Clark C.. . . . . *v.3 p.526*
Spence, Jonathan D.. *v.6 p.183, p.187, p.188, p.189, p.191, p.193, p.200, p.201, p.202, p.203, p.216, p.217, p.218*
Spence, Jonathan *v.6 p.216*
Spence, Kenneth Wartenbee *v.5 p.616*
Spence, Sarah (Editor) *v.2 p.446*
Spencer, Albert & Luy, Jack. *v.5 p.691*
Spencer, Elizabeth *v.2 p.116*
Spencer, Hanna *v.2 p.602*
Spencer,

Author Index

Herbert . *v.1 p.719, v.4 p.345, p.346, p.484, p.511, p.683, p.684*

Spencer, John, et al. *v.4 p.390*

Spencer, John H. *v.6 p.64*

Spencer, Jonathan *v.6 p.163*

Spencer, M. C. *v.2 p.511*

Spencer, Paul (Editor) *v.1 p.49*

Spencer, Richard & Ghausi, Mohammed *v.5 p.722*

Spencer, T. J. *v.2 p.165*

Spencer, Thomas S. & Russell, John J. *v.1 p.812*

Spencer, Warren *v.3 p.432*

Spencer, William. *v.6 p.595, p.642*

Spender, Dale (Editor) *v.6 p.464*

Spender, Dale *v.2 p.742*

Spender, Stephen & Hall, Donald *v.2 p.15, p.16, p.180*

Spender, Stephen. *v.2 p.384*

Spener, David & Staudt, Kathleen
(Editors) *v.3 p.527, v.6 p.487, p.522*

Spengemann, William C. & Roberts, Jessica F. (Editors). *v.2 p.24*

Spengler, John D., et al.. . . . . *v.5 p.372*

Spenser, Edmund. *v.2 p.216*

Spera, David A. (Editor) *v.5 p.363*

Sperber, Jonathan *v.3 p.76, p.168*

Sperling, Daniel (Editor) *v.5 p.742*

Sperling, Daniel *v.5 p.701*

Sperling, L. H. *v.5 p.324*

Sperling, Michael B. & Sack, Amy *v.4 p.399*

Spero, Joshua B.. . . . . *v.4 p.397*

Speroff, Leon *v.5 p.524*

Speth, James Gustave (Editor). *v.4 p.667*

Speth, James Gustave *v.5 p.358, p.378*

Spevack, Marvin (Editor) *v.2 p.226*

Speziale-Bagliacca, Roberto *v.2 p.232*

Spicehandler, Ezra & Arnson, Curtis (Editors) . . . *v.6 p.652*

Spicer, Edward Holland. *v.6 p.683*

Spicer, Jack *v.2 p.156*

Spicer, Joaneath (Editor) *v.1 p.747*

Spicer, Kevin P. *v.3 p.173*

Spickard, Paul (Editor), et al. *v.6 p.131*

Spickard, Paul R.. . . . . *v.6 p.132*

Spiegel, Alan *v.2 p.56*

Spiegel, Harriet *v.2 p.468*

Spiegel, Leonard & Limbrunner, George F.. . . . . *v.5 p.696*

Spiegel, Leonard F., et al.. . . . . *v.5 p.696*

Spiegel, Ross & Meadows, Dru *v.1 p.785*

Spiegelberg, Herbert *v.1 p.511*

Spiegelman, Art (Author, Illustrator) *v.2 p.156*

Spiegelman, Art. *v.2 p.156, v.3 p.87*

Spiegelman, Willard *v.2 p.578, p.583*

Spiegel-Rosing, Ina & Price, Derek De Solla
(Editors). *v.5 p.411, p.412*

Spielman, John P.. . . . . *v.3 p.183*

Spielvogel, Laura *v.4 p.792, p.819*

Spiers, Edward M. *v.3 p.116*

Spies, Robert A. (Editor), et al. *v.5 p.601*

Spies, Werner & Rewald, Sabine (Editors) *v.1 p.699*

Spies, Werner *v.1 p.781*

Spigel, Lynn *v.6 p.448*

Spike, John T. *v.1 p.747*

Spilka, Bernard, et al.. . . . . *v.5 p.636*

Spilken, Terry L. *v.1 p.50*

Spillane, Joseph E. & Kosofsky, Barry E. *v.3 p.282*

Spillane, Mickey *v.2 p.117*

Spiller, Robert E. *v.2 p.7*

Spillers, Hortense J. *v.6 p.28*

Spillman, Robert *v.1 p.399*

Spilner, Maggie *v.4 p.788, p.791*

Spindler, George D. & Hammond, Lorie (Editors) . . . *v.4 p.29*

Spindler, George D. (Editor) *v.4 p.29, p.35, p.303*

Spindler, Louise S. *v.4 p.29*

Spinelli, Emily. *v.2 p.558*

Spink, Nesta, et al. *v.1 p.758*

Spinoza, Baruch & Spinoza, Benedict de *v.1 p.477*

Spinoza, Baruch *v.1 p.454, p.477*

Spinoza, Benedict de *v.1 p.477*

Spinoza, Benedictus De *v.1 p.478*

Spinrad, Hyron *v.5 p.71*

Spira, S. F.. . . . . *v.1 p.763*

Spirduso, Waneen W., et al.. . . . . *v.4 p.875, p.880*

Spires, Robert C.. . . . . *v.2 p.642*

Spirn, Anne Whiston *v.1 p.814*

Spiro, Melford E. *v.1 p.562, v.4 p.36*

Spirou, Costas & Bennett, Larry. *v.6 p.729*

Spisak, James W. & Matthews, William (Editors) . . . *v.2 p.212*

Spitz, Peter H. *v.4 p.157*

Spitzer, Alan B. *v.3 p.153*

Spitzer, John & Zaslaw, Neal *v.1 p.186, p.192, p.394*

Spitzer, Leo *v.3 p.343, v.6 p.73*

Spitzer, Lyman *v.5 p.70*

Spitzer, Manfred *v.5 p.591*

Spitzer, Robert J.. . . . . *v.4 p.527*

Spitzer, Robert. *v.4 p.528, p.532*

Spivak, Burton *v.3 p.412*

Spivak, Gayatri Chakravorty *v.2 p.761, v.6 p.97*

Spivak, Michael. *v.5 p.486, p.496, p.497, p.499*

Spivey, Nigel *v.1 p.671, v.3 p.15, v.4 p.810*

Spleth, Janice (Editor) *v.2 p.543*

Spleth, Janice *v.2 p.543*

Splittstoesser, Walter E *v.5 p.24, p.26, p.31*

Spoerri, Elka, et al.. . . . . *v.1 p.724*

Spohn, Cassia *v.6 p.271*

Spolsky, Joel *v.5 p.339, p.346, p.349*

Spong, Mark W., et al. *v.5 p.712*

Sponsel, Leslie E. & Gregor, Thomas (Editors) *v.4 p.35*

Sponsel, Leslie E. (Editor), et al. *v.5 p.39*

Spooner, Mary H. *v.3 p.355*

Sposito, Garrison *v.5 p.51*

Spoto, Donald *v.2 p.135*

Spotts, Frederic *v.3 p.179*

Spotts, Merhyle Franklin, et al. *v.5 p.715*

Spottswood, Richard K. *v.1 p.171, p.279, p.280*
Sprackland, Robert G. *v.5 p.89*
Spragens, Thomas A. Jr. *v.4 p.505*
Sprague, Claire & Tiger, Virginia *v.2 p.366*
Sprague, George F. & Dudley, J. W. (Editors) *v.5 p.24*
Sprague, Marshall *v.3 p.526*
Sprague, Milton A. & Triplett, Golver B. (Editors) . . . *v.5 p.51*
Sprague, Rosamond Kent (Editor) *v.1 p.427*
Spray, Sharon L. *v.4 p.393*
Sprecher, Drexel A. *v.3 p.87, v.4 p.477*
Spreyer, Leon *v.4 p.348*
Sprigg, June *v.1 p.714*
Sprigge, Timothy L. S. *v.1 p.440*
Spriggs, Matthew *v.4 p.13*
Sprinchorn, Evert. *v.2 p.630*
Spring, Eileen *v.3 p.52*
Spring, Joel H. *v.4 p.313, p.314, p.329*
Spring, Justin & Abrams, Harry N., Staff *v.1 p.747*
Spring, Justin & Skolnick, Arnold *v.1 p.724*
Spring, Justin *v.1 p.747*
Springborg, Robert & Henry, Clement M. *v.6 p.595*
Springer, Kimberly (Editor) *v.6 p.31, p.46*
Springer, Otto (Editor) *v.2 p.621*
Springford, Michael (Editor) *v.5 p.541*
Springhall, John *v.4 p.583*
Springhouse Staff. *v.5 p.528*
Sprinkle, Robert H.. . . . . *v.5 p.249*
Sprinz, Detlef F. & Wolinsky-Nahmias, Yael (Editors) . *v.4 p.627*
Sproat, John G. *v.3 p.438*
Sproule, J. Michael *v.4 p.418*
Sproule, William J. (Editor), et al. *v.5 p.701*
Sproule-Jones, Mark *v.6 p.301*
Sprout, Harold H. & Sprout, Margaret *v.3 p.384*
Sprout, Harold H. *v.3 p.384*
Spruyt, Hendrik *v.4 p.496, p.497*
Spry, Irene M. *v.3 p.546*
Spufford, Margaret *v.3 p.129*
Spufford, Peter *v.6 p.558*
Spurling, Hilary *v.1 p.699, p.747, v.2 p.339, p.382*
Spurr, Russell *v.6 p.237*
Squier, Charles L. *v.2 p.260*
Squier, Susan M. *v.2 p.393, v.6 p.731*
Squire, Peverill & Hamm, Keith E. *v.4 p.550*
Squires, Gregory D., et al. *v.4 p.544*
Squires, James D. *v.4 p.411*
Squires, Michael & Talbot, Lynn K. *v.2 p.364*
Srikanth, Rajini & Iwanaga, Esther Y. (Editors). *v.2 p.20, v.6 p.92*
Srikanth, Rajini *v.6 p.97, p.138*
Srinivasan, T. N. (Editor), et al. *v.4 p.192*
Sriramesh, Krishnamurthy & Vereciec, Dejan (Editors). *v.4 p.428*
Srivastava, Sudhir (Editor) *v.5 p.103*
Sroufe, L. Alan, et al.. . . . . *v.5 p.629*
Ssb *v.5 p.243*
Ssu-ma Chien *v.6 p.184*
St. Anselm. *v.1 p.433*

St. Aubyn, F. C. *v.2 p.497, p.499*
St. Bonaventure *v.1 p.433*
St. Clair, William. *v.3 p.195, v.6 p.739*
St. Denis, Ruth *v.1 p.12*
St. James Press Staff *v.1 p.4, v.6 p.360, p.391*
St. John, Bob *v.4 p.859*
St. John de Crevecoeur, J. Hector *v.2 p.30*
St. John, Ronald Bruce *v.6 p.640*
St Martin, Hardie (Editor). *v.2 p.645*
St. Martin's Press Staff & Young, Allen M. . . *v.5 p.177, p.239*
Staar, Richard F. (Editor) *v.4 p.585, p.596*
Stabb, Martin S. *v.2 p.679*
Stableford, Brian M. *v.2 p.192*
Stabler, Arthur P. (Editor) *v.2 p.465*
Stabler, Jane *v.2 p.274*
Stacey, C. P.. . . . . *v.3 p.537, p.540*
Stacey, Charles P. *v.3 p.540*
Stacey, Judith *v.4 p.732, p.734*
Stacey, William A. & Shupe, Anson *v.4 p.743*
Stachowitsch, Michael *v.5 p.96, p.157*
Stachura, Peter D. *v.3 p.253*
Stack, Carol B. *v.4 p.37*
Stackelberg, Roderick. *v.3 p.174*
Stackhouse, Max L. *v.1 p.644*
Stade, George & Jackson, William T. (Editors) *v.2 p.576*
Stadler, Quandra P. (Editor) *v.2 p.27*
Stadter, Philip A. (Editor) *v.2 p.419*
Stael, Germaine de & Berger, Morroe . . . *v.2 p.501, v.3 p.152*
Stael, Germaine de & Folkenflik, Vivian *v.2 p.501*
Stael, Germaine de *v.2 p.501, v.3 p.153*
Staël, Madame de *v.2 p.501*
Stafford, Charles J., et al. *v.5 p.312*
Stafford, Charles *v.4 p.40*
Stafford, J.. . . . . *v.2 p.120*
Stafford, Jean *v.2 p.120*
Stafford, Marla R. & Faber, Ronald J. (Editors) . . . *v.4 p.428*
Stafford, Mary E. & Robinson-Kurpius, Sharon E. . . *v.5 p.602*
Stafford Poole, C. M.. . . . . *v.3 p.287*
Stafford, William *v.2 p.117*
Stagg, John C. *v.3 p.418*
Stagliano, Vito A. *v.4 p.62, p.63*
Stahl, Ann (Editor) *v.6 p.54*
Stahl, Ernest L. (Editor). *v.2 p.594*
Stahl, Franklin W. & Hershey, A. D. *v.5 p.81, p.129*
Stahl, Hans-Peter. *v.2 p.421*
Stahl, J. D., et al.. . . . . *v.2 p.582*
Stahl, Saul *v.5 p.468, p.474, p.505*
Staib, Richard *v.4 p.62, p.64*
Staiger, Emil *v.2 p.598*
Staiger, Janet (Editor). *v.6 p.343*
Staikos, K. (Editor), et al.. . . . . *v.3 p.196*
Staines, David *v.2 p.468*
Stainton, Leslie. *v.2 p.660, v.6 p.403*
Staiti, Paul J.. . . . . *v.1 p.699*
Stakman, E. C. *v.5 p.47*

Staley, Thomas F. (Author, Introduction by) *v.2 p.360*
Stalk, George *v.4 p.119*
Stallabrass, Julian *v.1 p.681*
Staller, Natasha E. *v.1 p.700*
Stalley, R. F. *v.4 p.489*
Stalley, Roger *v.1 p.787*
Stallings, William *v.4 p.422, v.5 p.335, p.345, p.727*
Stallworthy, Jon (Editor) *v.2 p.583*
Stallworthy, Jon *v.2 p.327, p.369*
Stam, Robert & Raengo, Alessandra (Editors). . . . *v.6 p.327*
Stam, Robert. *v.6 p.327*
Stamatoyannopoulos, George, et al. *v.5 p.521*
Stambach, Amy *v.4 p.29*
Stambler, Irwin & Stambler,
  Lyndon *v.1 p.162, p.263, p.264, p.297*
Stamos, David N. *v.5 p.249*
Stamp, Shelley. *v.6 p.329, p.475*
Stampino, Maria Galli *v.2 p.709*
Stampp, Kenneth M. *v.3 p.365, p.401, p.421, p.429,
                                     p.438, v.6 p.37*
Stampp, Kenneth Milton *v.3 p.514*
Stan, Adele M.. . . . . *v.6 p.471*
Stanberry, D. Elaine *v.2 p.602*
Stanbury, E. E. & Buchanan, R. A. *v.5 p.735*
Stanbury, Sarah (Editor) *v.2 p.204*
Stancey, Gary; Burris, Robert H; Evans, Harold J . *v.5 p.24, p.51*
Stanciu, Ion & Cernovodeanu, Paul *v.3 p.392*
Standaert, Nicolas (Editor) *v.1 p.610*
Standage, Tom *v.3 p.37, v.4 p.421, p.710*
Standish, Isolde *v.6 p.336*
Standish, Peter *v.2 p.679*
Standley, Fred L. *v.6 p.28*
Standring, Susan *v.5 p.158*
Stanescu, Nichita. *v.2 p.817*
Stanfield, John H. II & Dennis, Rutledge M. (Editors). *v.4 p.687*
Stanfield, Peggy S. & Hui, Y. H. *v.5 p.533, p.534*
Stanfield, Peter. *v.6 p.316*
Stanford, Ann *v.2 p.30*
Stanford Arms Control Group Staff *v.4 p.657*
Stanford University. *v.6 p.436*
Stanford, William Bedell *v.2 p.407*
Stang, H. & Li, Victor C. *v.5 p.696*
Stangos, Nikos (Editor) *v.1 p.681*
Stangroom, J. (Jeremy) *v.5 p.230*
Stanhope, Marcia & Lancaster, Jeanette *v.5 p.531*
Staniforth, Maxwell (Translator) *v.3 p.58*
Stanislavski, Constantin. *v.1 p.139, p.145, v.6 p.348*
Stanislavsky, Constantin *v.1 p.138, p.139, p.146*
Stanislawski, Jan. *v.2 p.775*
Stanislawski, Michael. *v.3 p.219*
Stanko, Elizabeth A. *v.4 p.752*
Stanko, Stephen, et al. *v.6 p.273*
Stankovic, Sinisa & Campbell, Neil *v.5 p.696*
Stanley, David *v.2 p.17*
Stanley, George Edward. *v.4 p.382*

Stanley, George F. G.. . . . . *v.3 p.546*
Stanley, Glenn (Editor) *v.1 p.204, p.308*
Stanley, H. Eugene *v.5 p.559*
Stanley, Henry M.. . . . . *v.6 p.52*
Stanley, Lawrence A. (Editor) *v.1 p.274, p.412*
Stanley, Peter W.. . . . . *v.6 p.180*
Stanley, Richard P. *v.5 p.479*
Stanley, William D. & Harrington, Richard F.. . . . *v.4 p.422*
Stanley, William D.. . . . . *v.5 p.721*
Stanley, William *v.3 p.299*
Stanley-Baker, Joan. *v.1 p.694*
Stannard, David E. *v.1 p.645, v.6 p.131*
Stannard, Martin (Editor) *v.2 p.388*
Stannard, Martin *v.2 p.388*
Stansfield, Gareth R. V. *v.6 p.604*
Stansfield, William D., et al.. . . . . *v.5 p.129*
Stansfield, William D. *v.5 p.249*
Stansfield, William *v.5 p.137*
Stansky, Peter *v.2 p.376*
Stanton, D. W. & White, D. E. *v.5 p.479*
Stanton, G. R.. *v.3 p.13*
Stanton-Salazar, Richard D. *v.6 p.528*
Stape, J. H. (Editor) *v.2 p.342*
Staples, George & Herbst, Derral R. *v.5 p.44*
Staples, Robert. *v.4 p.738, v.6 p.466, p.467*
Staples, William G.. . . . . *v.4 p.773*
Stapleton, Michael *v.2 p.167*
Starck, Jean-Luc *v.5 p.501*
Starfield, A. M. ; Bleloch, A. L. (Andrew L.) *v.5 p.223*
Stark, Joan S. & Lattuca, Lisa R. *v.4 p.295*
Stark, Rodney & Finke, Roger. *v.1 p.525*
Stark, Rodney *v.1 p.525*
Starkey, Brigid, et al.. . . . . *v.4 p.646*
Starkey, Chad *v.4 p.829*
Starkey, Paul & Meisami, Julie S. (Editors). *v.6 p.663*
Starkie, Enid *v.2 p.165, p.499*
Starkweather, C. Woodruff & Givens-Ackerman,
  Janet *v.5 p.665, p.673*
Starling, Christopher L. & Blocker, H. Gene *v.1 p.476*
Starn, Orin, et al.. . . . . *v.3 p.331*
Starn, Orin. *v.3 p.331*
Starobinski, Jean *v.2 p.456, p.459, p.471, p.483*
Starr, Amory. *v.4 p.712*
Starr, Chester G. Jr. (Editor) *v.3 p.4*
Starr, Chester G. *v.3 p.15, p.17*
Starr, June & Collier, Jane F. (Editors) *v.4 p.34*
Starr, June & Goodale, Mark (Editors) *v.4 p.25*
Starr, Kenneth W. *v.4 p.540*
Starr, Kenneth *v.3 p.480*
Starr, Kevin *v.3 p.531, p.532*
Starr, Larry, et al. *v.1 p.274*
Starr, Paul *v.5 p.510*
Starr, S. Frederick *v.1 p.204, p.327*
Starr, Stephen Z.. . . . . *v.3 p.432*

Stasiuk, Andrzej *v.2 p.792*

Stasz, Cathleen, et al.. . . . . *v.4 p.305*

Staten, Clifford L. *v.3 p.313*

Stathis, Stephen W.. . . . . *v.4 p.560, p.630*

Statius, Publius Papinius *v.2 p.443*

Staub, Ervin *v.4 p.715*

Staudinger, Jeff. *v.5 p.707, v.6 p.286*

Staudohar, Paul D.. . . . . . *v.4 p.886, p.889, p.897*

Staudt, Kathleen & Coronado, Irasema. *v.4 p.560, p.640*

Staudt, Kathleen A. & Coronado, Irasema . . . *v.6 p.487, p.541*

Staudt, Kathleen *v.6 p.487, p.525*

Stauffer, David M., et al. *v.1 p.754*

Stauffer, Dietrich *v.5 p.559*

Stauffer, George B. *v.1 p.187, p.237, p.304*

Staunton, Irene (Compiled by). *v.6 p.77, p.78*

Staunton, M. (Editor) *v.3 p.98*

Stavans, Ilan & Augenbraum, Harold *v.6 p.485, p.486*

Stavans, Ilan (Editor) . *v.2 p.665, p.666,v.6 p.491, p.503, p.516*

Stavans, Ilan *v.2 p.679, v.6 p.503, p.516, p.522, p.545*

Stavely, Keith W.. . . . . *v.2 p.255*

Staver, Ruth Johnston. *v.2 p.205*

Stavig, Ward. *v.3 p.326*

Stavrianos, Leften Stavros. *v.3 p.246*

Stead, C. K. *v.2 p.72, p.112, p.327, p.748*

Stead, Christina *v.2 p.749*

Stead, C.K. *v.2 p.749*

Steadman, Henry J., et al.. . . . . *v.6 p.277*

Steamer, Robert J. *v.4 p.540*

Steane, J. B. *v.1 p.233, p.237, p.396*

Steans, Jill. *v.6 p.442*

Stearn, William T. *v.5 p.207*

Stearns, Beverly P. & Stearns, Stephen C. *v.5 p.181*

Stearns, Jean & Stearns, Marshall W. *v.1 p.19, p.33*

Stearns, Maxwell L. *v.4 p.540*

Stearns, Monteagle. *v.4 p.560, p.566*

Stearns, Peter (Editor) *v.4 p.699, p.707*

Stearns, Peter N. *v.3 p.76, p.371, p.444, v.4 p.425*

Stearns, Stephen C.. . . . . *v.5 p.196*

Stebbins, Theodore E. *v.1 p.700, p.747*

Stebbins, William C. *v.5 p.618*

Steblin, Rita *v.1 p.192, p.374*

Stecher, Brian & Kirby, Sheila Nataraj (Editors) . . . *v.4 p.281*

Stechow, Wolfgang *v.1 p.747*

Stedman, John Gabriel *v.3 p.323*

Stedman, John G. *v.3 p.323*

Stedman, Thomas L. *v.5 p.325*

Stedman-Jones, Gareth *v.3 p.116, p.131, v.6 p.743*

Stedman's Staff *v.5 p.509*

Steed, Robert P. (Editor), et al. *v.4 p.551, p.554*

Steedman, Carolyn *v.4 p.346*

Steedman, Ian *v.4 p.246*

Steegmuller, Francis (Editor) *v.1 p.13*

Steegmuller, Francis . *v.1 p.13, v.2 p.491, p.497, p.507, v.6 p.419*

Steel, Ronald. *v.3 p.454, v.4 p.409*

Steele, Beverley A.. . . . . *v.3 p.321*

Steele, E. D.. . . . . *v.3 p.116*

Steele, Elizabeth *v.2 p.393*

Steele, Gerry. *v.4 p.229*

Steele, Guy Jr. *v.5 p.347*

Steele, Ian K. *v.3 p.106, p.107*

Steele, James *v.1 p.795*

Steele, John H. (Editor), et al. *v.5 p.429*

Steele, Linda. *v.2 p.42, p.43*

Steele, Philip *v.6 p.168, p.169*

Steele, Richard. *v.2 p.262*

Steele, Valerie *v.1 p.716*

Steele-Perkins, Crispian. *v.1 p.391*

Steelwater, Eliza *v.6 p.247*

Steen, Harold K. & Tucker, Richard P. (Editors) . . . *v.3 p.270*

Steen, Harold K. *v.4 p.152, p.164, v.5 p.39*

Steen, Lynn Arthur (Editor). *v.5 p.246, p.464*

Steen, R. Grant *v.5 p.612, p.658*

Steen, Wim J. van der *v.5 p.197, p.249*

Steenbergen, Clemens & Reh, Wouter *v.1 p.820*

Steenland, Kyle & Savitz, David A. (Editors). *v.5 p.365*

Steenstrup, Carl *v.6 p.226*

Steers, Richard M. & Nardon, Luciara *v.4 p.70*

Stefanakis, Emmanuel *v.4 p.388*

Stefancic, David R.. . . . . *v.4 p.129*

Stefanidis, Yiannis D.. . . . . *v.6 p.601*

Stefanllari, Ilo *v.2 p.773*

Stefansson, Vihjalmur. *v.3 p.547*

Steffe, Leslie P. *v.5 p.464*

Steffy, Gary R.. . . . . *v.1 p.803*

Stegelin, Dolores A. & Borman, Kathryn M. (Editors). *v.4 p.369*

Steger, Manfred B. & Carver, Terrell. *v.4 p.509*

Steger, Manfred B. *v.4 p.55, p.665*

Stegner, Wallace *v.2 p.121, v.5 p.397*

Stehney, Ann K., et al., eds.. . . . . *v.5 p.495*

Steichen, Joanna *v.1 p.769*

Steier, David M. & Mitchell, Tom (Editors). *v.5 p.590*

Steigman, Andrew L.. . . . . *v.4 p.529*

Steigmann-Gall, Richard *v.3 p.174*

Steimanis, Josifs *v.3 p.256*

Stein, Agnes (Editor, Translator). *v.2 p.594*

Stein, Alfred (Editor), et al. *v.4 p.389*

Stein, Arlene *v.4 p.570, v.6 p.387*

Stein, Arnold Sidney *v.2 p.216*

Stein, Arnold *v.2 p.249, p.255*

Stein, Bruce A. (Editor), et al.. . . . . . . *v.6 p.286, p.292*

Stein, Burton. *v.6 p.162*

Stein, Charles W. *v.1 p.35*

Stein, David, et al. *v.4 p.321*

Stein, Deborah & Spillman, Robert *v.1 p.396*

Stein, Elias M. & Shakarchi, Rami. *v.5 p.494*

Stein, Gertrude *v.2 p.122, v.6 p.404*

Stein, H. N. (Editor) *v.5 p.283*

Stein, Howard & Young, Glenn (Editors) *v.1 p.69*

Stein, Howard F. & Hill, Robert F. (Editors) *v.3 p.524*

Stein, Jay M. (Editor) *v.1 p.797, v.6 p.729*

Stein, Joseph, et al. *v.1 p.254, p.410*

Stein, Kenneth W. *v.4 p.566, p.642, p.646, p.650*

Stein, Louise K. *v.1 p.187*

Stein, Marc (Editor) *v.6 p.358, p.363*

Stein, Murray & Hollwitz, John (Editors). *v.5 p.583*

Stein, Perrin *v.1 p.722*

Stein, Richard L. *v.6 p.753, p.758, p.762*

Stein, Samuel (Editor) *v.5 p.636*

Stein, Seth & Wysession, Michael. . . . *v.5 p.442, p.443, p.444*

Stein, Sherman K. *v.5 p.468*

Stein, Stanley J. & Stein, Barbara H.. . . . . . *v.3 p.288*

Stein, Stanley J. *v.3 p.280, p.337*

Stein, Stephen J. (Editor) *v.1 p.529*

Stein, Stephen J. *v.1 p.589*

Steinbeck, John *v.2 p.123*

Steinberg, David I. *v.6 p.165, p.166*

Steinberg, David J. (Editor) *v.6 p.165*

Steinberg, Dominique Moyse *v.5 p.669*

Steinberg, Jonathan *v.3 p.245*

Steinberg, Leo *v.1 p.747*

Steinberg, Mark D. & Khrustalev, Vladimir M. *v.3 p.220*

Steinberg, Mark D. *v.3 p.221*

Steinberg, Mark L. & Cosloy, Sharon D. *v.5 p.96, p.220*

Steinberg, Michael *v.1 p.243*

Steinberg, Milton *v.1 p.551*

Steinberg, Peter L. *v.3 p.450*

Steinberg, Sigfrid H. *v.2 p.577*

Steinberg, Steven J. & Steinberg, Sheila L. . *v.4 p.388, v.6 p.721*

Steinberg, Ted *v.6 p.296*

Steiner, Bernard C. *v.3 p.493*

Steiner, Christopher B. *v.1 p.690*

Steiner, Erich *v.5 p.267*

Steiner, Franklin *v.3 p.378*

Steiner, George *v.1 p.89, v.2 p.421, p.569, p.576*

Steiner, Hans (Editor). *v.5 p.513*

Steiner, John F. & Steiner, George A. *v.4 p.52*

Steiner, Peter. *v.2 p.782, v.3 p.188*

Steinfels, Margaret O'Brien *v.4 p.721*

Steinfirst, Susan *v.1 p.4*

Steingass, F. *v.6 p.654, p.669*

Steingold, Fred S. *v.4 p.444*

Steingold, Fred *v.4 p.88*

Steinhart, Peter. *v.1 p.724*

Steinheimer, Thomas R. (Editor), et al. *v.5 p.10*

Steinitz, Richard *v.1 p.224, p.336*

Steinkraus, Keith H. (Editor) *v.5 p.35*

Steinman, Ralph M. *v.5 p.165*

Steinweis, Alan E. *v.3 p.174*

Stekel, Dov *v.5 p.101*

Stell, W. Joseph *v.1 p.148*

Stemberger, Gunter *v.1 p.551*

Sten, Christopher *v.2 p.48*

Stendhal & Knight, B. C. J. G. *v.2 p.502*

Stendhal. *v.2 p.501, p.502*

Steneck, Nicholas H. *v.6 p.568, p.576*

Stenesh, Jochanan *v.5 p.114*

Stengers, Isabelle. *v.5 p.404*

Stengers, Jean & Van Neck, Anne *v.4 p.748*

Stepan, Alfred C. *v.3 p.277, p.331*

Stepan, Alfred *v.3 p.277, v.4 p.593*

Stepan, Nancy L.. . . . . *v.3 p.280*

Stepan-Norris, Judith & Zeitlin, Maurice *v.4 p.123*

Stephan, Cookie & Stephan, Walter G.. . . . . . . *v.5 p.648*

Stephanson, Anders. *v.3 p.463*

Stephen, H., et al. *v.5 p.282*

Stephen, Leslie. *v.1 p.516*

Stephen, Lynn *v.3 p.283, v.6 p.432, p.458*

Stephens, Alan (Editor) *v.5 p.6*

Stephens, Chris *v.1 p.781*

Stephens, Elizabeth *v.3 p.392*

Stephens, Evelyne H. *v.3 p.332*

Stephens, G. Lynn & Graham, George *v.4 p.693*

Stephens, G. Ross & Wikstrom, Nelson *v.4 p.543*

Stephens, John Russell *v.6 p.740*

Stephens, Mitchell & Olson, Beth *v.4 p.414*

Stephens, Mitchell *v.4 p.403*

Stephens, Ralph I., et al. *v.5 p.691*

Stephens, Richard C. *v.5 p.664*

Stephens, Susan A. & Winkler, John J. (Editors) . . . *v.2 p.405*

Stephens, W. P. *v.1 p.581, p.603*

Stephens, Walter *v.6 p.569*

Stephenson, Bruce, et al.. . . . . *v.5 p.66*

Stephenson, Carl *v.3 p.68*

Stephenson, D. Grier *v.4 p.540*

Stephenson, Frank H.. . . . . . *v.5 p.90, p.107, p.108, p.129*

Stephenson, G. Ennis (Editor) *v.2 p.27*

Stephenson, Ken *v.1 p.275*

Stephenson, Marcia. *v.3 p.325*

Stephenson, Richard M. *v.1 p.34*

Stepick, Alex *v.6 p.539, p.550*

Steppe, Wolfhard & Gabler, Hans W. (Contribution by). *v.2 p.360*

Steptoe, Andrew (Editor) *v.5 p.656*

Sterba, Gunther & Mills, Dick (Editors) *v.5 p.56*

Sterba, James P. *v.4 p.514*

Sterelny, Kim *v.5 p.197*

Sterling, Christopher H. & Kittross, John M. *v.4 p.412*

Sterling, Christopher H. (Editor). *v.4 p.413, p.418*

Sterling, Christopher H., et al.. . . . . . . *v.4 p.166, p.421*

Sterling, Christopher H.. . . . . *v.4 p.421*

Sterling, Keir B. (Editor), et al. *v.5 p.231, p.232*

Stern, Claudio (Editor) *v.5 p.161*

Stern, Daniel N. *v.5 p.629, p.631*

Stern, David & Mirsky, Mark J. (Editors). *v.6 p.652*

Stern, David G. *v.1 p.472*

Stern, Ephraim *v.1 p.618*

Stern, Fritz R. *v.3 p.179*

Stern, Fritz Richard. *v.3 p.165*

Stern, Gary M. & Halperin, Morton H. (Editors). *v.4 p.462, p.532*

Stern, Gerald. *v.2 p.156*

Stern, Harold P. & Mahmoud, Samy *v.5 p.726*

Stern, Irwin (Contribution by) *v.2 p.693*

Stern, Jerome *v.2 p.579*

Stern, Jessica *v.4 p.662*

Stern, Jewel *v.1 p.713, p.806*

Stern, Joel M., et al. *v.4 p.92*

Stern, Kenneth S. *v.4 p.438, v.6 p.695*

Stern, Lawrence *v.1 p.150*

Stern, Madeleine B. *v.2 p.31*

Stern, Robert A. M., et al. *v.1 p.791*

Stern, Robert W. *v.6 p.158*

Stern, Robert. *v.1 p.464*

Stern, Steve J. (Editor) *v.3 p.325*

Stern, Steve J. *v.3 p.288, p.332, p.355, v.6 p.452*

Sternberg, Robert & Davidson, Janet (Editors) . . . *v.5 p.576*

Sternberg, Robert J. & Barnes, Michael L. *v.5 p.657*

Sternberg, Robert J. & Davidson, Janet (Editors) . . . *v.5 p.609*

Sternberg, Robert J. & Grigorenko, Elena (Editors) . *v.5 p.572*

Sternberg, Robert J. & Grigorenko, Elena . . . *v.4 p.287, p.319*

Sternberg, Robert J. & Preiss, David D. (Editors) . . . *v.5 p.588*

Sternberg, Robert J. (Editor), et al. *v.5 p.657*

Sternberg, Robert J. (Editor) . . . *v.5 p.598, p.609, p.656, p.676*

Sternberg, Robert J., et al. *v.5 p.657*

Sternberg, Robert J. *v.5 p.572, p.594, p.609, p.613, p.656*

Sterne, Jonathan *v.1 p.377, p.388*

Sterne, Laurence *v.2 p.262*

Sterne, Netta *v.3 p.547*

Sterner, Olov *v.5 p.315*

Sterner, Robert Warner & Elser, James J. . *v.5 p.114, p.185, p.200*

Sternfeld, F. W. *v.1 p.181, p.187, p.233*

Sternheimer, Karen *v.4 p.712, p.713*

Sternlicht, Sanford (Editor) *v.2 p.337*

Sternlicht, Sanford V. *v.2 p.189*

Sternlicht, Sanford *v.2 p.189, p.348*

Sternsher, Bernard *v.3 p.463*

Sterrett, Andrew (Editor) *v.5 p.460*

Sterrett, Frances (Editor) *v.5 p.705, v.6 p.289*

Sterritt, David *v.6 p.343*

Stessel, Richard I. *v.5 p.377, p.378*

Stetson, Erlene *v.2 p.24*

Steuart-Denham, James *v.4 p.217*

Steuerle, C. Eugene *v.4 p.108*

Steuerle, Eugene C. *v.4 p.108*

Stevanovic, Bosiljka & Wertsman, Vladimir . *v.2 p.795, p.796*

Stevens, Anthony *v.5 p.585*

Stevens, Brian L. & Lewis, Frank L. *v.5 p.718*

Stevens, David *v.2 p.172, p.183, p.569*

Stevens, Denis *v.1 p.187, p.237, p.342*

Stevens, Dennis J. *v.6 p.264*

Stevens, Donald F. *v.3 p.289*

Stevens, E. S. *v.5 p.320, v.6 p.294*

Stevens, Graham *v.1 p.502*

Stevens, Halsey *v.1 p.224, p.305*

Stevens, John E. *v.1 p.178*

Stevens, John *v.4 p.803, p.863*

Stevens, Laura M. *v.6 p.686*

Stevens, Malcolm P. *v.5 p.322*

Stevens, Mark & Swan, Annalyn *v.1 p.700*

Stevens, Mitchell L. *v.4 p.296*

Stevens, Peter F. *v.5 p.171, p.197*

Stevens, Richard G. & Franck, Matthew J. (Editors) . *v.4 p.540*

Stevens, Robert Bocking *v.4 p.447*

Stevens, Robert E., et al. *v.4 p.136*

Stevens, Rosemary *v.5 p.514*

Stevens, S. S. *v.5 p.605*

Stevens, Wallace & Kermode, Frank *v.2 p.124*

Stevens, Wallace *v.2 p.124*

Stevens, William S. *v.4 p.163*

Stevens-Arroyo, Anthony M. & Pantoja, Segundo (Editors) *v.6 p.520*

Stevens-Arroyo, Anthony M. & Sanchez, Maria E. . . *v.6 p.487*

Stevenson, Adlai E. *v.4 p.635*

Stevenson, Anne *v.2 p.380*

Stevenson, David *v.3 p.80*

Stevenson, Elizabeth *v.2 p.30*

Stevenson, F. J. & Cole, M. A. *v.5 p.51*

Stevenson, F. J. *v.5 p.51*

Stevenson, Garth *v.4 p.581, p.587*

Stevenson, Howard Jr. (Editor) *v.4 p.304*

Stevenson, L. Harold & Wyman, Bruce *v.5 p.707*

Stevenson, Ollie & Huebler, Dana *v.4 p.168*

Stevenson, Randall *v.2 p.179*

Stevenson, Richard C. *v.2 p.300*

Stevenson, Robert G. (Editor) *v.4 p.353*

Stevenson, Robert Louis & Dury, Richard . . . *v.2 p.312*

Stevenson, Robert Louis & Katz, Wendy R. . . . *v.2 p.312*

Stevenson, Robert Louis *v.2 p.312, p.313*

Stevenson, Robert Murrell *v.1 p.280*

Stevenson, Robert *v.1 p.181, p.294, v.3 p.262*

Stevenson, Thomas B. *v.4 p.707*

Stevenson, Tom *v.5 p.53*

Stevenson *v.1 p.599, p.600*

Steward, Julian H. *v.4 p.30*

Stewart, Abigail J., et al. *v.5 p.640*

Stewart, Andrew *v.1 p.776, v.3 p.20*

Stewart, B. A. & Lal, Rattan (Editors) *v.5 p.51*

Stewart, Brian *v.1 p.725*

Stewart, Charles Cameron & Stewart, E. K. . . *v.6 p.70*

Stewart, Chuck *v.4 p.457*

Stewart, David & Shamdasani, Prem N. *v.4 p.687*

Stewart, David A. *v.4 p.830*

Stewart, David *v.1 p.511*

Stewart, Earl L. *v.1 p.282*

Stewart, Frank Henderson *v.6 p.596*

Stewart, Garrett *v.2 p.177, p.193, v.6 p.739, p.757*

Stewart, Gary *v.1 p.286*

Stewart, George R. *v.2 p.40, p.117*

Stewart, Gordon T. *v.3 p.392, p.538*

Stewart, Hilary *v.1 p.778*

Stewart, Ian . *v.5 p.90, p.229, p.460, p.469, p.474, p.495, p.502*

Stewart, Jacqueline (Author, Illustrator) . . . *v.6 p.8, p.15, p.331*

Author Index

Stewart, James B. *v.4 p.100, p.110, p.147*
Stewart, James *v.4 p.206, v.5 p.485*
Stewart, John *v.4 p.284, v.6 p.51*
Stewart, Mary L. *v.3 p.54*
Stewart, Michael *v.4 p.42, p.229*
Stewart, Miranda *v.2 p.637*
Stewart, Steve *v.6 p.417*
Stewart-Gambino, Hannah W. *v.3 p.355*
Stewart-Howe, Kathleen (Editor) *v.1 p.760*
Steyaert, Michiel (Editor), et al. *v.5 p.721*
Stöckmann, H. -J. *v.5 p.550*
Sthapitanonda, N. *v.1 p.791*
Stich, Stephen P. & Warfield, Ted A. . . . *v.1 p.498*
Stichter, Sharon B. & Hay, Jean *v.6 p.52*
Stick, David *v.3 p.500, p.502*
Stick, Robert V. *v.5 p.330*
Stickney, Robert R. *v.5 p.32*
Stid, Daniel D. *v.4 p.528*
Stieglitz, Perry *v.3 p.392*
Stiff, Ruth L. *v.5 p.85*
Stifter, Adalbert *v.2 p.602*
Stigler, George J. & Kindahl, James K. . . . *v.4 p.239*
Stigler, George J. *v.4 p.210, p.223, p.249*
Stigler, James W. (Editor) *v.4 p.36*
Stigler, Stephen M. *v.5 p.468, p.481*
Stiglitz, Joseph E. & Charlton, Andrew . *v.4 p.53, p.56, p.665*
Stiglitz, Joseph E. & Walsh, Carl E. *v.4 p.186*
Stiglitz, Joseph E. *v.4 p.56, p.58, p.256, p.262, p.665*
Stigum, Bernt P. *v.4 p.204*
Stiles, Kristine & Selz, Peter H. *v.1 p.681*
Stiles, Kristine *v.1 p.681*
Stilgitz, Joseph E. (Author, Afterword by) *v.4 p.262*
Still, James *v.2 p.117, p.156*
Stille, Alexander *v.1 p.823*
Stiller, David M. *v.5 p.706*
Stillinger, Jack *v.2 p.324*
Stillinger, Thomas C. (Editor) *v.2 p.210*
Stillman, Amy K. *v.1 p.17*
Stillman, Bruce & Stewart, David
(Editors) *v.5 p.143, p.147, p.151, p.201*
Stillman, Bruce (Editor) *v.5 p.129*
Stillman, John Maxson *v.5 p.263*
Stillman, Norman A. *v.1 p.548, v.6 p.598*
Stillwell, John C. *v.5 p.472*
Stillwell, John *v.5 p.477, p.496*
Stilo, Donald, et al. *v.6 p.669*
Stilwell, Joseph W. *v.6 p.193, p.201, p.216*
Stimpson, Michael *v.1 p.391*
Stimson, Henry L. & Bundy, McGeorge *v.3 p.463*
Stinchcombe, Arthur L. *v.4 p.718*
Stinger, Charles L. *v.3 p.200*
Stinson, John J. *v.2 p.336*
Stinson, Russell *v.1 p.187, p.243, p.304*
Stipanuk, David M. & Roffman, Harold *v.4 p.161*
Stipanuk, Martha H. *v.5 p.513*

Stirati, Antonella *v.4 p.220*
Stites, Richard (Editor) *v.3 p.227*
Stites, Richard *v.3 p.210, p.223*
Stith, Anthony *v.4 p.134*
Stith, Kate & Cabranes, Jose A. *v.6 p.272*
Stitt, Megan P. *v.2 p.289, p.296, p.308*
Stivender, David *v.1 p.224, p.340*
Stivers, Richard *v.4 p.695*
Stock, Ann M. (Editor) *v.6 p.344*
Stock, Brian *v.2 p.564*
Stock, Catherine McNicol & Johnston, Robert D. (Editors). *v.5 p.6*
Stock, Gregory B. & Campbell, John *v.5 p.152*
Stock, James H. & Watson, Mark W. *v.4 p.204*
Stock, Leo Francis (Editor) *v.3 p.406*
Stock, M. *v.5 p.409*
Stock, R. D. *v.2 p.232*
Stock, Robert *v.4 p.397*
Stockdale, Margaret S. & Crosby, Faye J. (Editors) . . *v.4 p.132*
Stockenstrom, Goran (Editor) *v.2 p.630*
Stocker, Barry *v.1 p.457*
Stockford, Marjorie A. *v.4 p.134, p.445*
Stockhausen, Karlheinz. *v.1 p.224, p.358*
Stocking, George W. (Author, Editor) *v.4 p.5*
Stocking, George W. Jr. (Author, Editor) *v.4 p.5*
Stocking, George W. Jr. (Editor) . *v.4 p.3, p.5, p.48, p.49, p.51*
Stocking, George W. Jr. *v.4 p.5*
Stocking, George W. *v.6 p.751*
Stocklein, Marc C. *v.1 p.817*
Stockton, David *v.2 p.434, v.3 p.26, v.4 p.501*
Stockwin, J. A. A. *v.6 p.220*
Stoddard, Charles H. & Stoddard, Glenn M. . . *v.5 p.40, p.354*
Stoddard, Charles H. *v.5 p.40*
Stoddard, Elizabeth *v.2 p.51*
Stoddard, Ellwyn R. (Editor), et al. *v.6 p.677*
Stoddard, Whitney S. *v.1 p.781, v.6 p.556*
Stoddart, Judith *v.2 p.306*
Stoddart, L. A., et al. *v.5 p.42*
Stoecker, H. (Editor). *v.6 p.56*
Stoecker, Sally W. *v.3 p.212*
Stoehr, Taylor *v.2 p.41*
Stoessinger, John G. *v.3 p.454*
Stoessinger, John George *v.4 p.635*
Stoewer, Heinz & Feuerbacher, Berndt P. (Editors) . *v.5 p.720*
Stoherer Sharon *v.1 p.396*
Stohl, Michael (Editor) *v.4 p.662*
Stoica, Ion (Editor). *v.2 p.816*
Stojkovic, Stan & Farkas, Mary Ann *v.6 p.275*
Stokell, Ian *v.4 p.800, p.838, p.868, p.905*
Stoker, Bram. *v.2 p.306*
Stoker, Robert P. *v.4 p.525*
Stokes, Eric & Bayly, C. A. *v.6 p.158*
Stokes, Francis G. *v.2 p.226*
Stokes, Gale *v.3 p.208, p.248, v.4 p.579, p.600*
Stokes, John *v.2 p.321*

Stokes, Martin & Bohlman, Philip Vilas (Editors) . . . *v.1 p.299*
Stokes, Martin *v.1 p.287*
Stokes, Simon *v.1 p.827*
Stokes, Susan C. *v.3 p.332*
Stokey, Nancy L. & Lucas, Robert E. Jr. *v.4 p.205, p.239*
Stokstad, Marilyn *v.1 p.668, p.673, v.6 p.556*
Stolba, K. Marie *v.1 p.174*
Stolberg, Benjamin *v.4 p.129*
Stoldt, G. Clayton, et al. *v.4 p.886, p.903, p.907*
Stoler, Mark A. *v.3 p.463, v.4 p.561*
Stoll, Anita K. & Smith, Dawn L. (Editors) . . *v.2 p.640, p.641*
Stoll, Anita K. & Smith, Dawn L. *v.2 p.640*
Stoll, Clifford *v.5 p.408*
Stoll, David *v.3 p.283, p.298*
Stoll, Elmer E. *v.2 p.232*
Stolleis, Michael *v.3 p.174*
Stoller, Paul & Olkes, Cheryl. *v.4 p.37*
Stoller, Paul *v.4 p.25, p.759*
Stolley, Paul D. & Lasky, Tamar. *v.5 p.365*
Stolz, Barbara Ann *v.6 p.247*
Stolzfus, Nathan. *v.3 p.87*
Stolzoff, Norman C. (Contribution by) *v.1 p.294*
Stone, Albert E. *v.2 p.11*
Stone, Andrea J. *v.3 p.262*
Stone, Bailey *v.3 p.75*
Stone, Christopher D. *v.4 p.435, p.444*
Stone, Clarence N. & Sanders, Heywood T. (Editors) *v.6 p.725*
Stone, Dan (Editor) *v.3 p.87*
Stone, Daniel *v.3 p.252, p.253*
Stone, Donald (Editor) *v.2 p.465*
Stone, Geoffrey *v.4 p.505, p.565, p.567*
Stone, George W. Jr. & Kahrl, George M. *v.1 p.104, p.141, p.153*
Stone, Glenn D. *v.4 p.38*
Stone, I. F. *v.6 p.237*
Stone, Jacqueline I. *v.1 p.562*
Stone, Jon R. (Editor). *v.1 p.522*
Stone, Jonathan *v.1 p.781*
Stone, Julius *v.4 p.478*
Stone, Kurt *v.1 p.394*
Stone, Lawrence. *v.3 p.92, p.101, p.102, p.104,
                                  p.124, p.131, v.4 p.726, p.734*
Stone, Linda (Editor) *v.4 p.33*
Stone, Marla. *v.3 p.203*
Stone, Michael E. (Editor) *v.1 p.546*
Stone, Michael. *v.5 p.550*
Stone, Norman & Strouhal, Eduard (Editors) . . *v.3 p.188*
Stone, Norman *v.3 p.80*
Stone, Robert *v.2 p.156*
Stone, Ruth M. (Editor). *v.1 p.286*
Stone, Ruth M. *v.1 p.286*
Stone, Thomas Ryan *v.1 p.415*
Stone, William F. & Shaffner, P. E. *v.5 p.645*
Stoneall, Linda. *v.4 p.770*
Stonecash, Jeffrey M. & McGuire, Mary P. . . . *v.4 p.552, p.554*
Stonecash, Jeffrey M. *v.4 p.552, p.555*

Stonehouse, B. (Editor) *v.5 p.434*
Stonehouse, B. *v.5 p.186*
Stoneman, Patsy *v.2 p.289*
Stoneman, Richard *v.3 p.196*
Stone-Miller, Rebecca *v.1 p.671, p.685*
Stoner, K. Lynn & Perez, Luis Hipolito Serrano (Editor,
    Compiled by). *v.6 p.547*
Stoppard, Tom *v.1 p.87, p.104, v.2 p.385*
Stoppelman, Gabriela. *v.2 p.507, p.508*
Stopple, Jeffrey *v.5 p.468, p.477*
Stora, Benjamin *v.6 p.61*
Storer, Donald. *v.5 p.51*
Storey, Graham *v.2 p.294*
Storey, John & Salaman, Graeme *v.4 p.67*
Storey, Mark (Editor) *v.2 p.278*
Storey, Moorfield & Lichauco, Marcial P. *v.6 p.180*
Storm, Theodor *v.2 p.602*
Storr, Anthony *v.5 p.619*
Storr, Merl. *v.4 p.750, v.6 p.372*
Storr, Robert *v.1 p.700, p.747, p.748*
Storrer, William A. *v.1 p.795*
Story, Ronald *v.4 p.380, p.707*
Stott, Rebecca & Avery, Simon *v.2 p.272*
Stott, Rebecca *v.5 p.231*
Stouck, David (Editor) *v.2 p.731*
Stouck, David *v.2 p.731*
Stouffer, Samuel A., et al. *v.5 p.585*
Stout, B. A. & Cheze, B. (Editors) *v.5 p.6, p.45*
Stout, Chris E. *v.4 p.662*
Stout, Harry S. *v.1 p.586, p.587, p.588, p.607, p.649*
Stout, Janis P. *v.2 p.67, p.110*
Stout, Joseph A. Jr. *v.3 p.295*
Stout, Neil R. *v.3 p.414*
Stout, Rex *v.2 p.117*
Stout, Rowland. *v.1 p.514*
Stover, Eric *v.4 p.654*
Stow, John. *v.3 p.127*
Stow, Kenneth *v.6 p.574*
Stowasser, Barbara Freyer. *v.6 p.460*
Stowe, David W. *v.1 p.280*
Stowe, Harriet Beecher & Johnson, Charles *v.2 p.51*
Stowe, Harriet Beecher *v.2 p.51, p.52, v.3 p.421*
Stowe, Judith A. *v.6 p.172*
Stowe, Richard S. *v.2 p.489*
Stowe, William W. *v.2 p.487*
Stowell, John C. *v.5 p.295*
Stowell, Robin
    (Editor) *v.1 p.204, p.243, p.308, p.391, p.392, p.402*
Stowell, Robin *v.1 p.205, p.243, p.308, p.392, p.402*
Stowers, Stanley K. *v.1 p.631*
Straayer, Chris *v.6 p.417*
Strachan, Hew *v.3 p.80, v.4 p.627, p.647*
Strachan, Tom & Read, Andrew P. (Translators). . . *v.5 p.143*
Strachey, Lytton *v.2 p.380, v.3 p.116, p.129, v.6 p.735*
Straczynski, J. Michael *v.6 p.353*

Strahan, David B. *v.4 p.358*
Straight, Michael *v.1 p.825*
Strain, Phillip S. (Editor) *v.4 p.353*
Strakhovsky, Leonid I. *v.3 p.218*
Straley, Dona S. *v.6 p.664*
Strand, David *v.6 p.191, p.206*
Strand, Mark *v.2 p.156, p.583*
Strang, Gilbert *v.5 p.473, p.500*
Strang, Heather *v.4 p.754, v.6 p.258, p.279*
Strange, Patricia & Strange, Allen *v.1 p.394, p.399*
Strange, Richard N. *v.5 p.47*
Strange, Steven K. & Zupko, Jack (Editors) *v.1 p.429*
Stranges, Anthony N. *v.5 p.282*
Strasser, Hermann *v.4 p.680*
Strasser, Mark P. *v.4 p.442, p.570, v.6 p.389*
Strasser, Mark Philip *v.6 p.389*
Strasser, Susan *v.4 p.140, v.6 p.296*
Strathdee, Robert *v.4 p.305*
Strathern, Andrew (Editor), et al. *v.6 p.252*
Strathern, Marilyn *v.4 p.33*
Strathern, Paul *v.2 p.684*
Stratton, David H. (Editor) *v.3 p.533*
Stratton, David H. *v.3 p.463*
Stratton-Pruitt, Suzanne L. (Editor) *v.1 p.748*
Stratyner, Barbara *v.1 p.35, p.36*
Straub, Deborah Gillan (Editor) *v.2 p.28*
Straumanis, Alfreds *v.2 p.781*
Straus, Joseph Nathan *v.1 p.374*
Straus, Joseph N. *v.1 p.224, p.225, p.355, p.360*
Straus, Kenneth M. *v.3 p.226*
Straus, L. G. *v.4 p.17*
Straus, Murray A., et al. *v.4 p.743*
Strauss, Anselm L. & Corbin, Juliet M. *v.4 p.688*
Strauss, Anselm L. *v.4 p.682*
Strauss, Anselm *v.6 p.719*
Strauss, Barry S. *v.3 p.19, p.20*
Strauss, Botho *v.2 p.619*
Strauss, Gerald (Introduction by) *v.3 p.163*
Strauss, Herbert A. *v.3 p.180*
Strauss, Leo & Cropsey, Joseph (Editors) *v.4 p.488*
Strauss, Leo *v.4 p.502, p.511*
Strauss, Richard *v.1 p.225, p.233, p.359, p.410*
Strauss, Sarah *v.4 p.793*
Strauss, Steven *v.4 p.114, p.119*
Straussner, Shulamith Lala Ashenberg
  (Editor) *v.4 p.777, v.5 p.512, p.522, p.673*
Stravinsky, Igor & Craft, Robert *v.1 p.225, p.360*
Stravinsky, Igor, et al. *v.1 p.225, p.360*
Stravinsky, Igor *v.1 p.225, p.233, p.360, p.382, p.410*
Stravinsky, Vera & Craft, Robert *v.1 p.225, p.361*
Straw, Richard Alan & Blethen, Tyler *v.3 p.498*
Strawson, P. F. *v.1 p.446, p.490*
Strawson, Peter F. *v.1 p.462, p.489, p.502*
Strayer, J. K. *v.5 p.683*
Strayer, Joseph R. (Editor) *v.6 p.555*

Strayer, Joseph R. *v.3 p.68, p.69*
Strayer, Robert *v.3 p.229*
Strazny, Philipp *v.2 p.564*
Strecker, Georg *v.1 p.631*
Streeck, Wolfgang & Yamamura, Kozo *v.6 p.226*
Street, Harry *v.4 p.436*
Street, Jack D. & Umlas, Rod (Editors) *v.1 p.107*
Street, Paul *v.3 p.484*
Street, Sarah *v.6 p.350*
Streeter, Burnett Hillman, 1874-1937 . . . . . . *v.1 p.629*
Streetman, Ben & Banerjee, Sanjay *v.5 p.723*
Streets, Heather *v.3 p.126*
Strege, Mark A. & Lagu, Avinash L. *v.5 p.89*
Strehlke, Carl Brandon *v.1 p.733*
Streissguth, Michael *v.1 p.275, p.316*
Streissler, Erich W. *v.4 p.258, p.264*
Streitmatter, Janice L. *v.6 p.464*
Streitmatter, Rodger *v.4 p.404, v.6 p.404*
Streitwieser, Andrew, Jr.; Brauman, John I. *v.5 p.287*
Strick, James Edgar *v.5 p.81*
Strickland, Dorothy S. & Alvermann, Donna E. . . . *v.4 p.365*
Strickland, Edward *v.1 p.225*
Strickland, Rennard F. & Wilkinson, Charles F. (Editors). *v.4 p.465*
Strickland, Ruth Ann (Translator) *v.6 p.279*
Stricoff, R. Scott & Walters, Douglas B. *v.5 p.266*
Strier, Richard *v.2 p.249*
Strieter, Terry W. *v.1 p.666*
Striff, Erin (Editor) *v.1 p.136*
Striffler, Steve & Moberg, Mark *v.3 p.272*
Striffler, Steve *v.3 p.333, p.334*
Strikwerda, Carl *v.3 p.206*
Strindberg, August (Translator) *v.2 p.631*
Strindberg, August *v.1 p.83, p.110, v.2 p.630, p.631*
Stringer, Chris *v.4 p.16*
Stringer, Christopher & McKie, Robin *v.4 p.16*
Stringer, Julian (Editor) *v.6 p.331*
Stringer, Martin D. *v.1 p.654*
Strittmatter, Erwin *v.2 p.615*
Strober, Deborah H. & Strober, Gerald S. (Translators). *v.3 p.480*
Strobl, Gert R. *v.5 p.324*
Strock, Herbert L. *v.6 p.347*
Stroebel, Leslie & Zakia, Richard D. (Editors) *v.1 p.762*
Stroh, Linda K. & Johnson, Homer H. *v.4 p.65*
Stroh, Linda K., et al. *v.4 p.70*
Strohm, Paul *v.2 p.168, p.210*
Strohm, Reinhard *v.1 p.192, p.233, p.246*
Stroker, Elisabeth *v.1 p.470*
Stroll, Avrum *v.1 p.502*
Strom, Kaare (Editor), et al. *v.4 p.576*
Strom, Robert G. & Sprague, Anne L. *v.5 p.69, p.434*
Strom, Steven, et al. *v.1 p.817*
Stromquist, Annie *v.1 p.760*
Strong, George Templeton . *v.3 p.422, p.423, p.424, p.426, p.429*
Strong, George V. *v.4 p.510, p.595*

Strong, John S.. *v.1 p.562*
Strong, John *v.1 p.566*
Strong, Martin C.. . . . . *v.1 p.171, p.275*
Strong, Robert A.. . . . . *v.4 p.560*
Strong, Roy *v.1 p.671, p.820, v.6 p.738*
Strong, Simon *v.3 p.332*
Strong, William S. *v.4 p.446*
Stronge, James *v.4 p.349*
Stroock, Daniel W.. . . . . *v.5 p.489*
Strossen, Nadine *v.4 p.748, v.6 p.471*
Stroud, Barry *v.1 p.452, p.517*
Strout, Cushing *v.3 p.376*
Strozier, Charles B.. . . . . *v.3 p.426*
Structural Engineering Institute (Contribution by) . . . *v.5 p.686*
Struik, Dirk J.. . . . . *v.5 p.389, p.394, p.468*
Strum, Philippa *v.4 p.469*
Strum, Shirley C. & Lindburg, Donald G.. . . . . . . *v.4 p.15*
Struna, Nancy L.. . . . . *v.4 p.810, p.819*
Strunk, Oliver & Treitler, Leo (Editors) *v.1 p.174*
Strunk, William Jr. & White, E. B.. . . . . *v.2 p.565*
Struve, Lynn A. (Editor, Translator) *v.6 p.188*
Strychacz, Thomas F. (Translator). *v.2 p.85*
Stryer, Lubert, et al. *v.5 p.114*
Stryer, Lubert *v.5 p.327*
Stuard, Susan M. (Editor) *v.6 p.561*
Stuart, Barbara *v.5 p.271*
Stuart, David C. *v.1 p.820*
Stuart, Duane R. *v.2 p.401*
Stuart, Gary L.. . . . . *v.6 p.267, p.271*
Stuart, Jesse H. *v.2 p.117*
Stuart, Jesse (Introduction by) *v.2 p.117*
Stuart, John Leighton. *v.6 p.201, p.218*
Stuart, Robert C. *v.3 p.155*
Stuart-Fox, Martin *v.6 p.171*
Stub, Holger R. *v.4 p.741*
Stubben, Jerry D. & Sokolow, Gary A.. . . . . *v.6 p.692*
Stubbendieck, James, et al. *v.5 p.40, p.42*
Stubbs, Liz *v.6 p.310*
Stuckenschmidt, Hans Heinz *v.1 p.225, p.353*
Stuckey, Mary E.. . . . . *v.3 p.370*
Stucky, Nathan & Wimmer, Cynthia (Editors). *v.1 p.136*
Studd, Stephen *v.6 p.410*
Studenmund, A. H. *v.4 p.205*
Studwell, William E. *v.1 p.237*
Stueck, William (Editor) *v.6 p.237*
Stueck, William W.. . . . . *v.3 p.392*
Stueck, William Whitney *v.6 p.237*
Stuempfle, Stephen *v.1 p.294*
Stuhler, Barbara *v.4 p.519, p.569*
Stull, D. R.; Prophet, Harold *v.5 p.286*
Stumm, Werner & Morgan, James J.. . . . . *v.5 p.313*
Stumm, Werner *v.5 p.313*
Stump, Eleonore & Kretzmann, Norman
    (Editors). *v.1 p.431, p.592, p.593, v.2 p.430*
Stump, Eleonore *v.1 p.435*

Stump, Phillip H.. . . . . *v.1 p.571*
Sturgis, Matthew *v.1 p.720*
Sturluson, Snorri *v.1 p.534, v.2 p.625, v.3 p.234*
Sturluson, Storri & Tiruvalluvar *v.2 p.625*
Sturm, Terry (Editor) *v.2 p.742*
Sturman, Andrew & Tapper, Nigel *v.4 p.385*
Sturman, Janet Lynn *v.1 p.233, p.246*
Sturrock, John . *v.1 p.515, v.2 p.460, p.511, p.526, p.567, p.571*
Sturtevant, David R. *v.6 p.180*
Sturtevant, Edgar Howard *v.2 p.555, p.564*
Sturtevant, William C. & Damas, David *v.6 p.677*
Sturtevant, William C. & D'Azevedo, Warren L.
    (Editors) *v.6 p.677*
Sturtevant, William C. & Heizer, Robert *v.6 p.677*
Sturtevant, William C. & Helm, June *v.6 p.677*
Sturtevant, William C. & Ortiz, Alfonso *v.6 p.677*
Sturtevant, William C. & Suttles, Wayne *v.6 p.677*
Sturtevant, William C. & Trigger, Bruce G.. . . . . *v.6 p.677*
Sturtevant, William C. & Washburn, Wilcomb E.
    (Editors) *v.6 p.683*
Sturtevant, William C., et al. *v.6 p.677*
Sturtz, Linda. *v.6 p.452*
Stuster, Jack *v.5 p.392*
Stutely, Richard *v.4 p.175*
Stutts, Alan T. & Wortman, James *v.4 p.161*
Stwertka, Eve & Viscusi, Margo (Editors). . . . *v.2 p.99, p.100*
Styan, John L. (Editor) *v.1 p.83, p.97*
Styan, John L.. . *v.1 p.55, p.77, p.81, p.86, p.97, p.104, p.142*
Styron, William *v.2 p.156*
Suarez, Jose I. & Tomlins, Jack E.. . . . . *v.2 p.693*
Suarez, Juan A. *v.6 p.417*
Suarez, Virgil & Poey, Delia (Editors) *v.6 p.496, p.509*
Suarez, Virgil *v.6 p.509*
Subba Rao, D. V.. . . . . *v.5 p.208*
Subcommittee on Poultry Nutrition Staff, Committee . . *v.5 p.56*
Sublett, Michael D.. . . . . *v.4 p.542*
Sublette, Ned *v.1 p.295*
Subotnik, Rose R. *v.1 p.382*
Subrahmanyam, Sanjay (Contribution by) *v.6 p.156*
Subrahmanyam, Sanjay *v.3 p.73, v.6 p.156, p.162*
Subtelny, Orest. *v.3 p.230*
Suchlicki, Jaime; Morris, James A; Fernandez, Damian J; Del
    Aguila, Juan; Suarez, Andres. *v.3 p.277*
Suchodolski, Bogdan *v.3 p.252*
Suchoff, Benjamin *v.1 p.225, p.243, p.305*
Suckling, Colin J. & Suckling, Keith E. *v.5 p.328*
Suckling, John *v.2 p.260*
Suckow, Ruth *v.2 p.117*
Sudarkasa, Niara *v.4 p.39*
Sudhakar, A.. . . . . *v.5 p.721*
Sudnow, David *v.1 p.382, p.403, p.404*
Sudraka, et al.. . . . . *v.1 p.128, p.131*
Sue, David & Sue, Derald Wing *v.5 p.638*
Suetonius *v.2 p.444*
Suárez, Mario, et al. *v.6 p.503*

Suárez-Orozco, Carola & Suárez-Orozco, Marcelo M. . *v.6 p.530*

Suárez-Orozco, Marcelo M. & Paez, Mariela (Editors). *v.6 p.522*

Suárez-Orozco, Marcelo M. *v.6 p.528*

Sugar, Max (Editor) *v.5 p.629*

Sugar, Pete F. *v.3 p.246*

Sugar, Peter F. (Editor), et al. *v.3 p.185*

Sugar, Steve *v.4 p.84*

Sugarman, Jeremy & Sulmasy, Daniel P. (Editors). . . *v.5 p.511*

Sugasawa, Shigehiko; Nakai, Seijiro *v.5 p.293*

Sugata, Bose. *v.6 p.158*

Sugawara Takasue no Musume & Morris, Ivan *v.6 p.233*

Sugden, John P. *v.4 p.820, p.844, p.856*

Suggs, Welch *v.6 p.438*

Sugimoto, Yoshio (Author, Contribution by) . . . *v.6 p.220*

Sugrue, Thomas J. *v.3 p.517, v.4 p.771, v.6 p.725*

Suh, Sharon A. *v.6 p.106, p.136*

Suhai, Sándor *v.5 p.106, p.118, p.147*

Suhl, Benjamin. *v.2 p.528*

Suid, Lawrence H. *v.6 p.323*

Sukhanov, N. N. *v.3 p.221*

Sukhwal, B. L. & Sukhwal, Lilawati *v.4 p.496*

Sukthankar, Ashwini *v.2 p.763*

Suleiman, Ezra. *v.4 p.581*

Suleiman, Susan Rubin & Forgacs, Eva (Editors) . . *v.2 p.785*

Suleiman, Susan Rubin (Editor) *v.6 p.437, p.473*

Suleiman, Yasir *v.6 p.583, p.655*

Suleri, Sara *v.2 p.763*

Sull, Donald N. & Wang, Yong . . *v.4 p.59, p.68*

Sullerot, Evelyne *v.2 p.456*

Sullivan, Alvin (Editor) *v.6 p.736, p.742, p.753*

Sullivan, Andrew (Editor) *v.4 p.570, v.6 p.389*

Sullivan, Andrew *v.6 p.387, p.389*

Sullivan, Bruce M. *v.1 p.537*

Sullivan, Charles L. *v.5 p.53*

Sullivan, Edward J. & Tasset, Jean-Marie (Text by) . *v.1 p.748*

Sullivan, Garrett A., et al. *v.1 p.75, p.104, v.2 p.186*

Sullivan, J. L. *v.4 p.608*

Sullivan, J. P. *v.2 p.438, p.442*

Sullivan, John L., et al. *v.5 p.645*

Sullivan, Larry E. (Editor), et al.. . . . . . *v.6 p.261*

Sullivan, Lawrence (Editor) *v.6 p.701, p.704*

Sullivan, Lawrence *v.1 p.13*

Sullivan, Mark *v.3 p.450*

Sullivan, Martin E., et al. *v.1 p.828*

Sullivan, Michael & Mizrahi, Abe *v.5 p.500*

Sullivan, Michael P. *v.4 p.627*

Sullivan, Michael . . . *v.1 p.681, p.694,v.5 p.472, p.485, p.486*

Sullivan, Patricia *v.3 p.444*

Sullivan, Robert *v.6 p.695*

Sullivan, Roger J. *v.1 p.462, p.487*

Sullivan, Rosemary (Editor) *v.2 p.732*

Sullivan, Teresa A., et al. *v.4 p.250, p.271*

Sullivan, Walter *v.2 p.14, v.5 p.443*

Sullivan, Zohreh T. *v.2 p.298*

Sulloway, Alison G. *v.2 p.268, p.294*

Sully, Melanie A.. . . . . *v.4 p.595*

Sultan Bahu *v.6 p.153*

Sultan, Stanley. *v.2 p.327, p.360*

Sultan, Terrie, et al.. . . . . *v.1 p.748*

Sultan, Terrie *v.1 p.758*

Sultz, Harry A. & Young, Kristina M. *v.5 p.514*

Sumarsam *v.1 p.290*

Sumer, Faruk (Editor), et al.. . . . . *v.6 p.668*

Sumich, James L. *v.5 p.172*

Sumida, Stephen H. *v.6 p.98, p.131*

Summ, G. Harvey & Kelly, Tom (Editors) *v.3 p.306*

Summerfield, Maurice J. *v.1 p.264*

Summerhayes, C. P. & Thorpe, S. A.. . . . . . *v.5 p.429*

Summers, Claude J. & Pebworth, Ted L. *v.2 p.220*

Summers, Claude J. (Editor) *v.1 p.666, p.707*

Summers, Claude J., editor *v.6 p.358*

Summers, Claude J. (Editor) . . . *v.6 p.360, p.391, p.417, p.419*

Summers, Claude J. *v.6 p.393*

Summers, Joseph H. *v.2 p.249, p.255*

Summerson, John N. *v.1 p.787*

Sumner, Judith *v.5 p.16*

Sumner, William Graham.. . . . . *v.4 p.686*

Sumner, William Graham *v.4 p.770*

Sumner, William L.. . . . . *v.1 p.392*

Sumption, Jonathan *v.3 p.144, v.6 p.567*

Sun, Yan. *v.4 p.620*

Sun, Youli. *v.6 p.193, p.204*

Sunagawa, Ichiro *v.5 p.436, p.437*

Sundaram, Rangarajan K. *v.4 p.207*

Sundelius, Bengt (Editor) *v.3 p.235, p.236*

Sunderland, Willard *v.3 p.213*

Sunderrajan & Park. *v.2 p.269*

Sundkler, Bengt G. *v.1 p.611*

Sundman, Per Olof & Sandbach, Mary . *v.2 p.631, p.633, p.635*

Sundquist, Eric J.. . . . . *v.2 p.5*

Sundstrom, Michael, et al.. . . . . *v.5 p.118*

Sunquist, Mel & Sunquist, Fiona *v.6 p.292*

Sunquist, Scott W. (Editor), et al. *v.1 p.610*

Sunseri, Thaddeus *v.6 p.66*

Sunstein, Cass R. & Epstein, Richard A. (Editors). . *v.4 p.462*

Sunstein, Cass R. *v.4 p.110, p.111, p.434, p.447, p.497, p.540, p.695, v.6 p.442*

Sunstein, Cass. *v.4 p.425, p.426, p.761*

Suny, Ronald G.. . . . . . . *v.3 p.223, p.230, p.231*

Suny, Ronald Grigor & Martin, Terry (Editors) *v.3 p.213*

Super, Carol & Gold, Ronald *v.4 p.143*

Super, Charles M., et al. *v.5 p.578*

Super, Donald E.. . . . . *v.5 p.577, p.578*

Super, John C.. . . . . *v.3 p.270, p.272*

Super, R. H. *v.2 p.317*

Supervielle, Jules. *v.2 p.527*

Suplee, Curt *v.5 p.541*

Suppes, Galen J. & Storvick, Truman . *v.5 p.360, p.374, p.378*

Suppes, Patrick & Hill, Shirley A.. . . . . . . *v.5 p.471*

Suppes, Patrick. *v.1 p.493*

Suranna, Pingali *v.6 p.153*
Surdam, David G. *v.4 p.522*
Surgenor, Christopher. *v.4 p.151*
Suri, Manil *v.2 p.766*
Surmanek, Jim *v.4 p.428*
Surmelian, Leon (Translator) *v.6 p.665*
Surmelian, Leon *v.6 p.665*
Suro, Roberto *v.6 p.530*
Surowiecki, James *v.4 p.51, p.135, v.5 p.649*
Surtees, Robert J. *v.6 p.683, p.693*
Surtevant, William C. (Editor) *v.6 p.678*
Surtz, Ronald E. *v.2 p.639*
Suryadinata, Leo *v.4 p.623*
Surzycki, Stefan *v.5 p.129*
Susanka, Sarah & Obolensky, Kira. *v.1 p.801*
Susman, Warren *v.3 p.370*
Susser, Bernard *v.4 p.768*
Susskind, Lawrence E., et al. *v.4 p.566, v.6 p.301*
Sussman, Herbert L. *v.6 p.757, p.762*
Sussman, Herbert. *v.6 p.749*
Sussman, Hillary E. & Smit, Maria A. (Editors). . . *v.5 p.147*
Sussman, Robert W. (Author, Editor) *v.4 p.15*
Sutcliffe, W. Dean. *v.1 p.187, p.243, p.352, p.353*
Suter, Keith *v.4 p.262, p.640, p.663*
Sutherland, Charmain *v.4 p.800*
Sutherland, D. M. *v.3 p.151*
Sutherland, J. A.. . . . . *v.6 p.740, p.742, p.757*
Sutherland, John & Engel, Karl-Heinz *v.2 p.222*
Sutherland, John *v.2 p.177, p.192, p.193, p.308, p.384,*
                              v.6 p.736, p.738, p.740, p.753, p.757
Sutherland, Nicola M. *v.3 p.146*
Sutherland, William J. (Editor) *v.5 p.171*
Sutter, Herb *v.5 p.347, p.349, p.351*
Sutter, Paul S. *v.6 p.296*
Suttles, Gerald D. *v.4 p.707*
Sutton, Constance R. & Chaney, Elsa M.
  (Editors). *v.6 p.542, p.550*
Sutton, David E.. . . . . *v.4 p.46*
Sutton, David *v.3 p.196*
Sutton, George P. & Biblarz, Oscar *v.5 p.720*
Sutton, Imre & Clow, Richmond L. (Editors). *v.6 p.681, p.693*
Sutton, Mark Q. & Anderson, E. N.. . . . . . . *v.4 p.30*
Sutton, Peter & Wieseman, Marjorie *v.1 p.748*
Sutton, R. Anderson *v.1 p.290*
Sutton, Robert I. *v.4 p.67, p.74*
Sutton, Robert P. *v.4 p.500*
Suvin, Darko. *v.2 p.192*
Suzman, James. *v.6 p.76, p.77*
Suzman, Mark *v.4 p.495*
Suzman, Richard M. (Editor), et al. *v.4 p.742*
Suzuki, D. T. *v.1 p.476, p.562*
Suzuki, Daisetz Teitaro *v.1 p.531*
Suzuki, Diasetz Teitaro *v.1 p.564*
Sveinsson, Einar Ol *v.2 p.625*
Svensson, Birte. *v.5 p.114*

Sverdrup, Keith A., et al. *v.5 p.429*
Svetlietiskiaei, Valery A. *v.5 p.696*
Svevo, Italo *v.2 p.723, p.724*
Svich, Caridad & Marrero, Maria Teresa (Editors). *v.6 p.516, p.518*
Swaddle, Thomas W. *v.5 p.303*
Swaffield, Simon R. (Editor) *v.1 p.814*
Swafford, Jan *v.1 p.313*
Swagerty, W. R. (Editor) *v.6 p.678*
Swagman, Charles F. *v.6 p.628*
Swain, Geoffrey & Swain, Nigel. *v.3 p.208*
Swain, Joseph Peter *v.1 p.254*
Swain, Roger B. *v.5 p.228*
Swain, Simon *v.2 p.405, p.406*
Swain, Tony & Trompf, Garry. *v.1 p.544*
Swain, Tony *v.4 p.43*
Swales, Martin & Swales, Erika *v.2 p.602*
Swales, Martin *v.2 p.592*
Swan, A. R. H. & Sandilands, M. H. *v.5 p.419, p.420*
Swan, Karen (Editor), et al. *v.4 p.418*
Swan, Maureen *v.6 p.79*
Swan, Oscar E., et al.. . . . . *v.2 p.777*
Swan, Oscar E.. . . . . *v.2 p.775*
Swan, Wallace (Editor) *v.6 p.372*
Swanberg, W. A. *v.4 p.411*
Swann, Brian (Editor) *v.6 p.699*
Swann, Charles *v.2 p.41*
Swann, Julian *v.3 p.148*
Swann, Paul *v.6 p.310*
Swanson, Ellen & O'Sean, Arlene A. *v.5 p.461*
Swanson, H. Lee (Editor), et al. *v.5 p.575*
Swanson, Larry W.. . . . . *v.5 p.618*
Swanson, Mark & Langley, Jacqueline D. (Illustrators). *v.3 p.424*
Swanson, Meg (Editor) *v.1 p.120*
Swanson, Timothy M. (Editor). *v.6 p.298*
Swanton, John R. *v.6 p.683, p.704*
Swart, Juani, et al.. . . . . *v.4 p.77*
Swartz, Clifford E. *v.5 p.541*
Swartz, David *v.4 p.682*
Swartz, Mark H. *v.5 p.521*
Swatos, William H. *v.4 p.678, p.720*
Swayd, Samy S. *v.6 p.601*
Swayne, David & Fadly, Aly M.. . . . . . . *v.5 p.56, p.57*
Swearer, Donald K.. . . . . *v.1 p.565*
Swearingen, James E.. . . . . *v.2 p.262*
Swedberg, Richard *v.4 p.271, p.681*
Sweden.; Statens naturvårdsverk. *v.5 p.177, p.181*
Swedenburg, Ted *v.6 p.612*
Sweeney, Del *v.3 p.43*
Sweeney, Douglas A.. . . . . *v.1 p.590*
Sweeney, Kep *v.4 p.165*
Sweeney, Lauren J.. . . . . *v.5 p.161*
Sweet, Doris V. (Editor) *v.5 p.315*
Sweet, Frank W. *v.1 p.120*
Sweet, Henry *v.2 p.555, p.558*

Sweet, James H. *v.3 p.264, p.280, p.335*

Sweet, Matthew *v.6 p.749*

Sweet, Paul R. *v.3 p.184*

Sweet, Timothy *v.6 p.288*

Sweet, Waldo E. *v.4 p.810, p.813*

Sweet, William *v.5 p.356, p.361, p.371*

Sweetman, David. *v.6 p.404*

Sweetman, Jack *v.3 p.384*

Sweetman, John *v.6 p.743, p.760*

Sweetman, Sean *v.5 p.526*

Sweets, John F. *v.3 p.156*

Sweetser, Marie-Odile *v.2 p.474*

Sweezy, Paul M. *v.4 p.236*

Sweig, Julia E. *v.3 p.313*

Sweigard, Lulu E. *v.1 p.51, p.52*

Swenberg, Charles E. & Conklin, James J. (Editors) . . *v.5 p.86*

Swenson, May *v.2 p.117*

Swenson-Wright, John *v.3 p.392*

Swern, Daniel (Editor) *v.5 p.742*

Swetz, Frank J. (Editor), et al. *v.5 p.468*

Swidler, Ann. *v.4 p.738*

Swidler, Arlene (Editor). *v.6 p.373*

Swift, Charles I. *v.1 p.149*

Swift, David E. *v.1 p.607*

Swift, Graham *v.2 p.380*

Swift, Jonathan. *v.2 p.263*

Swift, K. G. & Booker, J. D. *v.4 p.117*

Swift, Mark Stanley *v.2 p.809*

Swift, Mary G. *v.1 p.13*

Swinburne, Algernon Charles & McGann, Jerome . . . *v.2 p.313*

Swinburne, Algernon Charles, et al. *v.2 p.700*

Swinburne, Algernon Charles *v.2 p.313*

Swinburne, Richard *v.1 p.499, p.523, p.595, p.639, p.640*

Swinfield, Rosemarie *v.1 p.151*

Swishchuk, Anatoly V. & Jianhong Wu, ... *v.5 p.92, p.171*

Swisher, Carl B. *v.4 p.469*

Swissler, Becky. *v.4 p.799, p.800, p.838, p.840,*
p.857, p.858, p.862

Switzer, Les (Editor). *v.6 p.79*

Switzer, Richard (Editor) *v.2 p.465*

Switzer, Richard *v.2 p.488*

Swonk, Diane *v.4 p.271*

Swystun, Jeff (Editor). *v.4 p.142*

Syal, Meera *v.2 p.766*

Sydenham, M. J. *v.3 p.151*

Sydenham, Michael J. *v.3 p.151*

Sydnor, Charles S. *v.3 p.495*

Sykes, Bryan. *v.4 p.745*

Sykes, Christopher *v.6 p.612*

Sykes, Egerton. *v.1 p.527*

Sykes, Percy & McLane, Charles B. *v.6 p.633*

Sykes, Percy. *v.6 p.630*

Sykes, Peter *v.5 p.292*

Sykes, S. W. & Clayton, J. P. (Editors) *v.1 p.641*

Sylvan, Robin *v.1 p.275*

Sylvester, Christine *v.6 p.442*

Sylvester, David *v.1 p.748*

Sylvester, Judith L. & Huffman, Suzanne *v.4 p.407*

Sylvie, George & Witherspoon, Patricia D. *v.4 p.149*

Syme, Ronald *v.2 p.439, p.443, p.444, v.3 p.26*

Symes, Colin *v.1 p.385*

Symonds, Craig L. *v.3 p.384*

Symons, Julian. *v.2 p.580*

Symposium on Science, Reason, and
Modern Democracy S *v.4 p.573*

Synan, Vinson *v.1 p.587*

Synge, John Millington *v.2 p.306*

Syrett, David *v.3 p.81*

Syrett, Michel & Lammiman, Jean *v.4 p.67*

Szabo, Albert & Barfield, Thomas J. *v.1 p.791*

Szabo, Magda *v.2 p.786*

Szakolczay, Lajos *v.2 p.785*

Szalay, Michael *v.2 p.11*

Szalay, Miklós *v.6 p.79*

Szarkowski, John. *v.1 p.769*

Szasz, Thomas. *v.4 p.471, p.770, p.775, v.6 p.269*

Szatmary, David P. *v.1 p.275*

Szczerbiak, Aleksander Andrzej *v.4 p.579, p.597*

Sze, Arthur *v.6 p.102*

Sze, Simon M. & Ng, Kwok K, ... *v.5 p.555*

Szebehely, Victor G. & Mark, Hans *v.5 p.66*

Szeemann, Harald (Editor) *v.1 p.700*

Szell, Gyorgy (Editor) *v.4 p.123*

Szenberg, Michael & Ramrattan, Lall (Editors) . . . *v.4 p.197*

Szenberg, Michael (Editor) *v.4 p.186*

Szenberg, Michael, et al. *v.4 p.186*

Szewc, Piotr *v.2 p.792*

Szmatka, Jacek (Editor), et al. *v.4 p.690*

Szpilman, Wladyslaw *v.3 p.87, p.255*

Szporluk, Roman *v.3 p.230*

Sztompka, Piotr *v.4 p.695*

Szuchman, Mark D. *v.3 p.349*

Szulanski, Gabriel *v.4 p.79*

Szwed, John F. *v.1 p.264, p.361, p.362*

Szymanski, Stefan & Zimbalist,
Andrew S. *v.4 p.820, p.844, p.852, p.899*

Szymborska, Wislawa. *v.2 p.792*

Szymusiak, Karen & Sibberson, Franki. *v.4 p.365*

t' Hooft, Gerard *v.5 p.544*

T

Taagepera, Rein & Shugart, Matthew *v.4 p.578*

Taatjes, Douglas J. & Mossman, Brooke T. (Editors) . . *v.5 p.86*

Tabacco, Giovanni *v.3 p.200*

Tabachnikov, Serge. *v.4 p.855, p.871*

Tabakoff, Boris (Editor) *v.5 p.512, p.522*

Tabari *v.6 p.586, p.587, p.588*

Tabatabai, M. Ali & Sparks, Donald L. (Editors) *v.5 p.51*

Tabataba'i, Muhammad Husayn *v.1 p.560*

Tabbi, Joseph & Wutz, Michael (Editors) *v.4 p.419*

Taber, K. *v.5 p.264*

Tablino, Paolo *v.1 p.574*

Tabor, David *v.5 p.277*

Taborsky, Edward *v.3 p.189*

Tabrah, Ruth M. *v.3 p.534*

Tacey, David J. *v.2 p.750*

Tacitus, Cornelius *v.2 p.444, p.445, v.3 p.67, p.161*

Tackett, Timothy *v.3 p.151*

Tadie, Jean-Yves *v.2 p.525*

Taeuber, Cynthia M. (Editor) *v.6 p.426*

Taft, Michael *v.1 p.264, p.412*

Taft, William Howard *v.4 p.632*

Tagami, Jeff *v.6 p.104*

Tager, Jack *v.4 p.713, v.6 p.715*

Taghizadegan, Salman *v.4 p.117*

Tagil, Sven *v.3 p.232, p.233*

Tagore, Rabindranath *v.2 p.766, v.6 p.153*

Taguchi, Genichi, et al. *v.5 p.686*

Tahara, Mildred (Translator) *v.6 p.233*

Taher, Bahaa *v.6 p.664*

Tai, Hue-Tam H. *v.6 p.167*

Tai, Hue-Tam Ho *v.6 p.168*

Taibo, Paco Ignacio II *v.2 p.669*

Taine, Hippolyte A. *v.2 p.167*

Tait, Katharine *v.1 p.447*

T'ai-t'ai, Ning L. *v.6 p.203, p.217*

Taithe, Bertrand *v.3 p.155*

Tajbakhsh, Kian *v.6 p.719*

Takagi, Dana Y. *v.6 p.109, p.121, p.124*

Takahashi, Jere *v.6 p.132*

Takahashi, Lois *v.4 p.722*

Takahashi, Takao (Editor) *v.5 p.249*

Takahata, Naoyuki & Clark, Andrew G. (Editors) . . . *v.5 p.201*

Takaki, Ronald
    T. . *v.2 p.10, v.4 p.707, v.6 p.85, p.86, p.114, p.117, p.119, p.137*

Takeda, Kiyoko *v.4 p.622*

Takemitsu, Toru *v.1 p.225, p.362*

Takeuchi, Hirotaka & Nonaka, Ikujiro *v.4 p.77*

Takeuchi, Y. *v.5 p.98, p.197*

Takezawa, Yasuko I. *v.6 p.135*

Takougang, Joseph & Krieger, Milton *v.4 p.613*

Talattof, Kamran *v.6 p.673*

Talbert, Richard J. *v.4 p.501*

Talbot, Cynthia *v.6 p.162*

Talbot, David (David E. J.) &Talbot, James (James D.
    R.) *v.5 p.735*

Talbot, Emile J. *v.2 p.502*

Talbot, Ian *v.6 p.159*

Talbot, Michael *v.1 p.187, p.301, p.365*

Talbot, William Henry Fox, et al. *v.1 p.765*

Talbott, Strobe & Chanda, Nayan (Editors) . . *v.4 p.487, p.662*

Talbott, Strobe *v.3 p.392, v.4 p.562, p.644, p.646, p.657*

Talbott, William *v.4 p.513, p.670*

Talboys, Graeme K. *v.1 p.828*

Talburt, Susan & Steinberg, Shirley R. (Editors) . . . *v.6 p.386*

Talen, Emily *v.6 p.715*

Talhami, Ghada H. *v.6 p.620, p.638*

Taliaferro, Charles *v.1 p.504, p.526*

Taliaferro, John *v.2 p.59*

Talisse, Robert & Hester, Micah *v.1 p.440*

Talisse, Robert B. *v.4 p.505, p.511*

Tallapaka Annamacharya & Narayanaravu, Velceru . . *v.6 p.153*

Tallchief, Maria & Kaplan, Larry *v.1 p.13*

Talley, P. Forrest *v.4 p.756*

Tallman, Irving (Editor), et al. *v.4 p.736*

Tallman, Susan *v.1 p.754*

Tallmer, Margot, et al. *v.5 p.532*

Talmagne, Florence *v.6 p.421*

Talwar, Jennifer Parker *v.6 p.107, p.117, p.126*

Tam, Kwok-kan & Dissanayake, Wimal *v.6 p.335*

Tamagne, Florence *v.3 p.55*

Tamarin, David *v.3 p.349*

Tamarkin, Robert A. *v.4 p.102, p.163*

Tambiah, Stanley J. *v.1 p.562, v.4 p.713, p.714, v.6 p.163*

Tambling, Jeremy *v.2 p.705*

Tamburri, Anthony J., et al. *v.2 p.20*

Tamir, Zakariya *v.6 p.664*

Tamm, C. O. *v.5 p.187*

Tamm, Eric *v.1 p.275, p.323, p.324*

Tamparo, Carol D. & Lewis, Marcia A. *v.5 p.514*

Tamrat, Taddesse *v.1 p.611*

Tam'si, Tchicaya U *v.2 p.545, p.546*

Tamulevich, Susan, et al. *v.1 p.820*

Tamura, Eileen H. *v.6 p.132*

Tamura, Linda *v.6 p.114, p.132*

Tan & REN *v.5 p.703*

Tan, Amy *v.2 p.156, v.6 p.102*

Tan, Kim H. *v.5 p.51*

Tanabe, George J. Jr. (Editor) *v.1 p.542*

Tanaka, Stefan *v.6 p.220*

Tanaka, Yuki *v.6 p.455*

Tancredi, Laurence R. *v.5 p.618*

Tandeter, Enrique *v.3 p.325*

Tandon, Bharat *v.2 p.269*

Tandori, Dezso *v.2 p.786*

Tanenbaum, Andrew S. *v.5 p.348, p.730*

Tanenbaum, Andrew *v.4 p.422, v.5 p.727, p.728*

Tanenhaus, David S. *v.6 p.249*

Tanenhaus, Sam *v.3 p.450, p.463*

Tang, Li *v.1 p.570*

Tang, Tong B. *v.5 p.393*

Tang, Xianzu *v.1 p.129, p.132, v.6 p.209*

Tangermann, Stefan & Banse, M. (Editors) *v.5 p.15*

Tangires, Helen *v.6 p.725*

Tangney, June Price & Dearing, Ronda L. *v.5 p.657*

Taniguchi, Yoshio *v.1 p.795*

Tanizaki, Jun'ichiro *v.6 p.233*

Tanizaki, Junichiro *v.6 p.233*
Tanizaki, Jun'ichiro. *v.6 p.233*
Tank, Patrick W.. . . . . *v.5 p.89*
Tank, Ronald W. *v.4 p.444*
Tankard, Judith B. *v.1 p.820*
Tannen, Deborah. *v.4 p.21, v.5 p.581*
Tannenbaum, Frank. *v.3 p.280*
Tannenbaum, Leslie *v.2 p.240*
Tannenbaum, Peter & Arnold, Robert *v.5 p.460*
Tanner, Daniel & Tanner, Laurel N. *v.4 p.365*
Tanner, Kathryn E.. . . . . *v.1 p.636, p.637*
Tanner, Kathryn *v.1 p.596, p.636*
Tanner, Marcus *v.3 p.248, p.249*
Tanner, Michael *v.1 p.205, p.366*
Tanner, Norman P. (Editor) *v.1 p.571, v.3 p.58*
Tanner, Ogden & Auchincloss, Adele *v.5 p.85*
Tanner, Roland. *v.6 p.566*
Tanpinar, Ahmet Hamdi. *v.6 p.668*
Tansey, Geoff & Worsley, Tony *v.4 p.152*
Tansi, Sony Lab'Ou *v.2 p.546*
Tansi, Sony Labou *v.2 p.546*
Tansi, Sony L.. . . . . *v.2 p.546*
Tansill, Charles C. *v.3 p.480*
Tanton, James *v.5 p.460, p.469*
Tanur, Judith M., et al. (Editors). *v.5 p.483, p.504*
Tanur, Judith M., et al. *v.5 p.483*
Tapia, John E. *v.4 p.321*
Tapié, Victor Lucien *v.3 p.182*
Taplin, D.T. (Editor) *v.1 p.44*
Taplin, Oliver (Editor) *v.2 p.401, p.425*
Taplin, Oliver *v.2 p.402, p.407, p.415*
Tapper, Richard (Editor) *v.6 p.334*
Taragano, Martin. *v.4 p.854*
Taraghi, Goli. *v.6 p.673*
Taranto, James & Leo, Leonardo (Editors) *v.3 p.378*
Taras H. Shevchenko Museum and Memorial Park
  Foundation. *v.2 p.814, p.815*
Taras, Ray & Castle, Marjorie. *v.4 p.506, p.597*
Tarbell, Dean S. & Tarbell, Ann T.. . . . . . . *v.5 p.291*
Tarbell, Ida *v.4 p.147, p.148*
Tarbox, Gwen. *v.2 p.10*
Tarkington, Booth *v.2 p.124*
Tarleton, Raymond J. *v.5 p.6*
Tarling, Nicholas *v.6 p.165*
Tarlo, Emma. *v.6 p.160*
Tarn, W. W.. . . . . *v.3 p.20*
Tarn, William W.. . . . . *v.3 p.20, p.21, p.22*
Tarr, Carrie & Rollet, Brigitte *v.6 p.329*
Tarr, Edward H. *v.1 p.392*
Tarr, G. Alan. *v.4 p.454*
Tarr, Joel A. *v.5 p.358, v.6 p.715*
Tarrant, Harold. *v.1 p.425*
Tarrow, Sidney (Author, Contribution by). *v.4 p.625*
Tarrow, Sidney. *v.4 p.594, p.713*
Tarski, Alfred *v.1 p.494*

Tarter, Ralph E. *v.5 p.709*
Taruskin, Richard
  F. *v.1 p.175, p.226, p.247, p.361, p.402, v.3 p.210*
Taruskin, Richard. *v.1 p.174*
Tarver, H. Micheal & Frederick, Julia C.. . . . . . *v.3 p.361*
Tashiro, C. S. *v.6 p.349*
Tasie, G. O.. *v.6 p.72*
Tasker, Fiona L. & Golombok, Susan *v.6 p.376*
Tasker, Yvonne. *v.6 p.475*
Tasman, Dan *v.1 p.783, p.798*
Taspinar, Omer *v.6 p.599, p.625*
Tasso, Torquato *v.2 p.709, p.710*
Tastsoglou, Evangelia & Dobrowolsky, Alexandra
  (Editors) *v.4 p.668*
Tate, Allen *v.2 p.125, p.576*
Tate, Gayle T. *v.6 p.8, p.32, p.46*
Tate, Mary J. & Bruccoli, Matthew J.. . . . . *v.2 p.77*
Tate, Merze *v.3 p.393*
Tate, Michael L. *v.3 p.521*
Tate, Robert L. *v.5 p.51*
Tatham, David *v.1 p.720*
Tatlow, Ruth. *v.1 p.187, p.304*
Taton, Rene (Editor) *v.5 p.389*
Tattersall, Ian, et al. *v.4 p.16*
Tattersall, Ian *v.4 p.16*
Tatum, Beverly Daniel *v.4 p.310*
Tatum, Charles M. (Editor). . . . *v.6 p.496, p.503, p.504, p.516*
Tatum, Charles M.. . . . . *v.6 p.491, p.494*
Tatum, George B. & MacDougall, Elisabeth B. (Editors). *v.1 p.817*
Tatum, Georgia L. *v.3 p.429*
Tatz, Colin. *v.4 p.830*
Taub, Eric *v.6 p.347*
Taub, Michael (Editor) *v.6 p.652*
Taub, Robert *v.1 p.205, p.243, p.308, p.399*
Tauber, Alfred I.. . . . . *v.2 p.52*
Taubes, Clifford Henry *v.5 p.92, p.94*
Taubman, William *v.3 p.228*
Taucar, Christopher Edward *v.4 p.581*
Taufer, Veno (Author, Translator) *v.2 p.813*
Tauney, R. H. *v.3 p.122*
Taussig, Frank W. *v.4 p.258*
Taussig, Michael *v.3 p.356*
Tavani, Herman T.. . . . . . *v.5 p.106, p.129, p.147, p.249*
Tavard, Georges H.. . . . . *v.1 p.638*
Tavener, John *v.1 p.226, p.362*
Taves, Ann *v.5 p.636*
Taw, Jennifer M. *v.3 p.306*
Tawa, Nicholas E. *v.1 p.275, p.280*
Tawfiq, Sahar *v.6 p.664*
Tawil, Raymonda H. *v.6 p.620*
Tawney, Richard H. *v.6 p.191*
Tayeb, Monir *v.4 p.77*
Taylor, A. E. *v.1 p.425, v.2 p.418*
Taylor, A. J. P.. . . . . *v.3 p.117, p.118, p.119, p.182*
Taylor, Alan *v.3 p.407, v.4 p.581, v.6 p.686*

Taylor, Andrew *v.2 p.742, v.4 p.129*
Taylor, Archer *v.2 p.589*
Taylor, Arnold H.. . . . . *v.3 p.282*
Taylor, Arthur J. (Editor). *v.3 p.88, p.116*
Taylor, Arthur *v.1 p.264*
Taylor, Barbara B. *v.1 p.650*
Taylor, Barbara (Editor), et al.. . . . . *v.4 p.366*
Taylor, Barbara *v.3 p.54, p.116,v.6 p.442, p.749*
Taylor, Billy *v.1 p.264*
Taylor, Bonnie B. *v.4 p.451*
Taylor, Brian D. *v.4 p.599*
Taylor, C. C. (Commentaries by) *v.1 p.422*
Taylor, C. C. W. (Editor) *v.1 p.421*
Taylor, Carole Anne (Editor). *v.2 p.5*
Taylor, Charles. *v.1 p.495, p.496, v.4 p.587, v.5 p.636*
Taylor, Christopher *v.1 p.423*
Taylor, Craig E. & Vanmarcke, Erik *v.5 p.686, p.687*
Taylor, D. J.. . . . . *v.2 p.315, p.376*
Taylor, D. Lansing & Wang, Yu-Li (Volume Editors) . *v.5 p.86*
Taylor, D. R. F. (Editor) *v.4 p.386*
Taylor, D. R.. *v.4 p.375*
Taylor, Denny & Dorsey-Gaines, Catherine *v.4 p.762*
Taylor, Diana & Villegas, Juan (Editors) *v.6 p.516, p.518*
Taylor, Donald M. *v.5 p.632*
Taylor, Dorothy L. *v.6 p.245*
Taylor, Edward *v.2 p.30*
Taylor, Edwin F. & Wheeler, John Archibald . . *v.5 p.73, p.557*
Taylor, Elizabeth & Cohen, Adam *v.3 p.516*
Taylor, Eugene *v.5 p.636*
Taylor, Frederick Winslow *v.4 p.64*
Taylor, Frederick *v.3 p.175*
Taylor, Gary & Jowett, John. *v.2 p.232*
Taylor, Gary *v.2 p.232*
Taylor, Greg *v.6 p.344*
Taylor, Helen (Introduction by) *v.2 p.385*
Taylor, Ina. *v.1 p.724*
Taylor, J. B. & Woodford, Michael (Editors) . . . *v.4 p.192*
Taylor, J. Edward & Adelman, Irma *v.4 p.241, p.271*
Taylor, James L. *v.2 p.638*
Taylor, James S. *v.4 p.340*
Taylor, Jane *v.3 p.7*
Taylor, Jay *v.6 p.200, p.214*
Taylor, Jeffrey H. (Editor) *v.4 p.792, p.881*
Taylor, Jeremy *v.2 p.263*
Taylor, Joe G. *v.3 p.507*
Taylor, Joe G *v.3 p.507*
Taylor, John B. (Author, Illustrator) *v.6 p.271*
Taylor, John R.. . . . . *v.5 p.64, p.563*
Taylor, John Russell *v.2 p.189*
Taylor, John *v.1 p.795, v.4 p.854*
Taylor, Judith M. *v.5 p.24*
Taylor, Julie *v.1 p.21, p.49*
Taylor, Kathleen, et al. *v.4 p.321*
Taylor, Keith W. *v.6 p.167*
Taylor, Larissa J.. . . . . *v.3 p.146*

Taylor, Larry R., et al. *v.5 p.269*
Taylor, Leighton R. *v.5 p.85*
Taylor, Lily R.. . . . . *v.3 p.25, p.26*
Taylor, Mark C. *v.1 p.436*
Taylor, Mark *v.2 p.232, v.6 p.169*
Taylor, Maxwell D.. . . . . *v.3 p.463*
Taylor, Michael John Haddrick *v.4 p.151*
Taylor, Miles & Wolff, Michael (Editors). . . . *v.6 p.736, p.751*
Taylor, P. G. (Editor) *v.5 p.328*
Taylor, Patrick & Dorling Kindersley Publishing Staff . *v.5 p.44*
Taylor, Paul. *v.1 p.13*
Taylor, Peter J., et al. *v.5 p.249*
Taylor, Peter *v.2 p.157*
Taylor, Philip A. M. *v.4 p.668*
Taylor, Philip Bates. *v.4 p.593*
Taylor, Philip L. & Heinonen, Olle G. *v.5 p.555*
Taylor, Quintard & Moore, Shirley Ann Wilson
    (Editors). *v.6 p.452, p.455*
Taylor, Quintard *v.6 p.715*
Taylor, Rabun M.. . . . . *v.1 p.796*
Taylor, Richard & Christie, Ian *v.6 p.339*
Taylor, Robert H. (Editor) *v.6 p.165, p.166*
Taylor, Robert H. *v.6 p.165, p.166*
Taylor, Robert J. *v.3 p.489*
Taylor, Robert W., et al.. . . . . *v.6 p.253*
Taylor, Rogan *v.4 p.820, p.868*
Taylor, Ronald *v.2 p.591*
Taylor, Samuel H. & Roberts, Robert E. *v.4 p.758*
Taylor, Sandra C.. . . . . *v.6 p.135*
Taylor, Stuart Ross *v.5 p.68*
Taylor, Therese *v.3 p.54, p.154*
Taylor, Verta, et al. *v.6 p.436*
Taylor, Victor E. & Lambert, Gregg *v.1 p.457*
Taylor, Welford Dunaway & Longest, George C. (Editors). *v.2 p.80*
Taylor, Welford Dunaway *v.1 p.758*
Taylor, William B. *v.3 p.264, p.288*
Taylor, William N. *v.4 p.826*
Taylor, William R. *v.3 p.494*
Taylour, William *v.3 p.16*
Taymiya, Ibn. *v.1 p.558*
Tchaikovsky, Peter Ilyitch *v.1 p.374*
Tchen, John Kuo Wei *v.6 p.114, p.124, p.128*
Tcherikover, Victor *v.3 p.22*
Tcherviakov, Alexander F.. . . . . *v.1 p.807*
Tchobanoglous, George, et al.. . . . . *v.5 p.369, p.379, p.706*
Teachers College Press *v.4 p.277*
Teachout, Terry *v.1 p.13, p.46*
Teaford, Jon C. *v.4 p.526, p.544, v.6 p.715*
Teague, Edward H. (Compiled by) *v.1 p.711*
Teasdale, Sara *v.2 p.124*
Tebbel, John W. & Zuckerman, Mary E. *v.4 p.410*
Tebbett, Ian (Editor) *v.5 p.269*
Tebbit, Mark. *v.1 p.491*
Tebbutt, Peter *v.5 p.267*
Tebeau, Charlton W. & Marina, William *v.3 p.505*

Technical University of Dresden Staff (Editor) *v.5 p.258*

Technische Universitat Dresden Staff (Editor). *v.5 p.258*

Technische Universitat Dresden, Zentrum für Angewandte
   Sprachwissenschaft *v.5 p.316*

Teck, Katherine *v.1 p.404*

Tedlock, Barbara *v.6 p.704*

Tedlock, Dennis *v.2 p.677*

Teich, Mikulas (Editor, Contribution by) *v.3 p.191*

Teicher, Hendel *v.1 p.29, p.31*

Teichgraeber, Richard F. 3rd *v.2 p.38, p.52*

Teichman, Judith A. *v.3 p.295, p.349, p.355*

Teicholz, Tom (Editor) *v.2 p.111*

Teitelbaum, Joshua *v.6 p.626*

Tejirian, Edward J. *v.4 p.750, v.6 p.372*

Telander, Rick *v.4 p.822, p.895*

Telford, W. M., et al. *v.5 p.445*

Tellenbach, Gerd *v.1 p.576*

Teller, Edward & Shoolery, Judith *v.5 p.544*

Teller, Edward *v.5 p.360*

Teller, Walter & Whitman, Walt. *v.2 p.54*

Telles, Edward Eric *v.3 p.280, p.343*

Tellis, Gerard J. & Golder, Peter N. *v.4 p.135*

Tellman, Barbara (Editor) *v.5 p.181*

Telmissany, May *v.6 p.664*

Telotte, J. P. *v.6 p.320*

Tembeck, Iro *v.1 p.15*

Temin, Peter. *v.4 p.214, p.421*

Temkin, Owsei *v.1 p.525, v.2 p.405, v.5 p.516*

Temperley, Howard (Editor) *v.3 p.316, v.4 p.728*

Temperley, Nicholas (Editor) *v.6 p.757*

Temperley, Nicholas *v.1 p.192, p.237, p.331*

Temple, Christel N.. . . . . *v.6 p.13, p.28*

Temple, Michael *v.4 p.582*

Temple, Norman J., et al. *v.5 p.513*

Temple, Robert. *v.6 p.198*

Templer, Robert *v.6 p.166, p.167*

Temple-Raston, Dina *v.6 p.257*

Templeton, Alice *v.2 p.115*

Templeton, Mary E. *v.4 p.171*

Temu, A. J. & Swai, B. *v.6 p.54*

Ten Broek, Jacobus. *v.3 p.421*

Ten, C. L. (Editor) *v.1 p.438*

Tendulkar, Vijay *v.1 p.129, p.131, v.6 p.153*

Tenenbaum, Barbara *v.3 p.289*

Tenenbaum, Frances (Editor) *v.1 p.812*

Tenenbaum, Gerald & Mendaes France, Michel *v.5 p.477*

Tenenbaum, Gershon (Editor) *v.4 p.878, v.5 p.583*

Teng Ssu-Yu. *v.6 p.187, p.191*

Tenhula, John *v.6 p.95, p.120, p.138*

Tennekes, Henk *v.5 p.718*

Tennent, John & Friend, Graham *v.4 p.179*

Tennent, Timothy C. *v.1 p.597*

Tennyson, Alfred Lord & Hill, Robert W.. . . . . . . *v.2 p.314*

Tennyson, Alfred Lord *v.2 p.313, p.314*

Tennyson, Alfred Tennyson, Baron. *v.2 p.314*

Tennyson, Hallam *v.2 p.315*

Tenorio-Trillo, Mauricio *v.3 p.265*

Tentler, Leslie W.. . . . . *v.3 p.444*

Tentler, T. *v.1 p.657*

Tenzer, Michael *v.1 p.290*

Teodoreanu, Ionel *v.2 p.817*

Teorey, Toby; Lightstone, Sam & Nadeau, Tom *v.5 p.337*

TePaske, John J. (Editor) *v.3 p.332*

Terborg-Penn, Rosalyn & Rushing, Andrea B.
   (Editors) *v.6 p.11, p.46*

Terborg-Penn, Rosalyn *v.4 p.519, v.6 p.32, p.46*

TERC Staff *v.5 p.223, p.228*

Terchek, Ronald & Conte, Thomas C. (Editors) *v.4 p.506*

Terence *v.2 p.445*

Terkel, Studs. *v.3 p.480, v.4 p.717, p.730*

Terman, Lewis M. & Oden, Melita H. *v.5 p.576*

Terman, Lewis M. *v.5 p.576*

Terraciano, Kevin *v.3 p.288*

Terraine, John. *v.3 p.91*

Terras, Victor *v.2 p.793, p.797, p.800, p.809*

Terrett, Nicholas K.. . . . . *v.5 p.328*

Terrill, Ross. *v.6 p.200, p.202, p.217*

Terrill, William. *v.6 p.261*

Terry, Arthur *v.2 p.640*

Terry, Patricia & Gavronsky, Serge. *v.2 p.464*

Terry, Patricia (Translator) *v.2 p.468*

Terry, R. C. (Editor) *v.2 p.317*

Terry, R. C. *v.6 p.739, p.757*

Terry, Walter *v.6 p.415*

Tersine, Richard J. *v.4 p.116*

Terzaghi, Karl, et al. *v.5 p.422*

Teski, Marea. *v.4 p.742*

Tesser, Abraham (Editor), et al. *v.5 p.646, p.657*

Tessler, Mark A. *v.6 p.620*

Tessler, Mark (Editor), et al.. . . . . *v.6 p.595*

Tester, Jefferson W., et al.. . . . . *v.5 p.452*

Tetel, Marcel *v.2 p.470, p.471*

Tetlock, Philip E.. . . . . *v.5 p.645*

Tetreault, Mary A. (Editor) *v.3 p.284, v.6 p.442*

Tettey, Wisdom (Editor), et al.. . . . . *v.4 p.613*

Teweles, Richard J. & Bradley, Edward S.. *v.4 p.97, p.102, p.163*

Teweles, Richard J., et al. *v.4 p.98, p.102*

Teynard, Felix *v.1 p.700*

Tétreault, Mary Ann *v.6 p.627*

Tökés, Rudolf L.. . . . . *v.4 p.595*

Tönnies, Ferdinand *v.6 p.719*

Thacker, Eugene *v.5 p.129, p.220*

Thacker, John *v.4 p.319*

Thacker, Strom C. *v.3 p.295*

Thackeray, William Makepeace *v.2 p.315, p.316*

Thackrah, J. R.. . . . . *v.4 p.662*

Thackray, Arnold W. & Myers, Minor Jr. *v.5 p.262*

Thackray, Arnold W. (Editor) *v.5 p.220*

Thackrcy, Susan *v.2 p.106*

Thackston, Wheeler M. (Editor) *v.6 p.156*

Thackston, Wheeler M. Jr. *v.6 p.652, p.673*

Thackston, Wheeler M. *v.6 p.655*

Thain, Michael & Hickman, Michael. *v.5 p.225*

Thakur, Ramesh (Editor) *v.4 p.635*

Thakurta, Paranjoy Guha & Raghuraman, Shankar . . *v.4 p.618*

Thal, Erwin R., et al. *v.5 p.522*

Thaler, Alwin *v.1 p.77, p.104*

Thaler, Richard H. (Editor). *v.4 p.98, p.101*

Thaler, Richard *v.4 p.98*

Thall, Bob *v.6 p.729*

Thalmann, William G. *v.2 p.402, p.407*

Thamm, Gerhardt B. *v.3 p.175*

Thapar, Romila. *v.6 p.155*

Thapar, Romilla *v.6 p.155*

Tharoor, Shashi *v.2 p.766, p.767*

Tharp, Roland G. & Gallimore, Ronald G. *v.4 p.349*

Tharp, Twyla *v.1 p.13, p.37, p.44*

Tharu, Susie J. & Lalita, K.
(Editors) *v.2 p.763, p.764, v.6 p.147, p.148*

Thatcher, Ian D. *v.3 p.221, p.224*

Thayer, Alexander Wheelock *v.1 p.205, p.308*

Thayer, Carlyle A. *v.4 p.622*

Thayer, Ernest Lawrence *v.2 p.51*

Thayer, H. Standish *v.1 p.513*

The Alliance for Technology Access Staff *v.4 p.317*

The Animal Welfare Information Center, U.S. Department of
Agriculture, Agricultural Research Service, National
Agricultural Library. *v.5 p.56, p.57*

The Center for Middle Eastern Studies at the University of
Texas at Austin *v.4 p.615, v.6 p.595*

The Department of Neurology and Neuroscience at Cornell
University Medical College *v.5 p.164*

The Department of Physiology and Biophysics, Weill Medical
College of Cornell University *v.5 p.163*

The European Commission *v.5 p.250*

The Forum for Scientific Excellence, Inc. (Editor). . . *v.5 p.266*

The Society of News Design Staff (Editor) *v.4 p.409*

The Society of Publication Designers Staff (Editor) . *v.1 p.719*

The Urban Institute and The Brookings Institution . . *v.4 p.108*

The World Bank (Created by) *v.4 p.58, p.110, p.112*

The World Bank. *v.4 p.59, p.60, p.665*

The World's Great Classics (Editor) *v.1 p.69, p.97*

Theado, Matt (Editor) *v.2 p.11*

Theado, Matt *v.2 p.93*

Theberge, Nancy. *v.4 p.820, p.838, p.862, v.6 p.438*

Thelen, David P. (Editor) *v.3 p.375*

Thelen, David P. *v.3 p.517*

Thelen, Lawrence *v.1 p.93, p.118, p.153*

Thelen Reid and Priest LLP *v.4 p.159*

Thelin, John R. & Wiseman, Lawrence L. . . . *v.4 p.822, p.895*

Thelin, John R. *v.4 p.291, p.332, p.822, p.895*

Then, Danny & McGregor, Wes *v.4 p.113*

Theobald, Mary Miley *v.1 p.828*

Theocritus. *v.2 p.421*

Theodore, Louis & Kunz, Robert G. *v.5 p.705*

Theodore, Louis; Kunz, Robert G. *v.5 p.318*

Theodores, Diana *v.1 p.40*

Theodorson, George A. (Editor) *v.6 p.719*

Theoharis, Athan G. *v.3 p.480, v.6 p.261*

Theophano, Teresa *v.6 p.360*

Theophrastus. *v.2 p.421*

Theriault, Yves. *v.2 p.540*

Thernstrom, Stephan A. *v.4 p.707*

Thesing, William B.. . . . . *v.2 p.98, p.177, p.193*

Thérèse & Foley, Marc *v.1 p.580*

Thibodeau, Gary A. & Patton, Kevin T. *v.5 p.164*

Thiel, Teresa, et al.. . . . . *v.5 p.129, p.220*

Thiele, Felix & R.E. Ashcroft, Imperial College of Science
(Editors) *v.5 p.250*

Thielemann, Selina *v.1 p.290*

Thieme, Horst R. *v.5 p.92, p.189*

Thier, Marlene & Daviss, Bennett *v.4 p.366*

Thies, Jochen *v.3 p.80*

Thiessen, Gesa Elsbeth (Editor) *v.1 p.596*

Thietmar. *v.3 p.162*

Thiher, Allen *v.5 p.406, p.411*

Thijssen, J. M. *v.5 p.551*

Thiongo, Ngugi Wa. *v.2 p.759*

Thirlwall, A. P. (Editor) *v.4 p.229*

Thirring, W. *v.5 p.548*

Thirsk, Joan *v.3 p.43, p.101, p.102, p.123, v.5 p.13*

Thistlethwaite, Nicholas & Webber, Geoffrey (Editors). *v.1 p.392*

Thistlethwaite, Susan Brooks *v.5 p.137*

Thody, Philip & Read, Howard *v.2 p.528*

Thody, Philip *v.2 p.528*

Thody, Phillip *v.2 p.481*

Thom, Ian & Hill, Charles (Editors) *v.1 p.748*

Thomas, A. M.. . . . . *v.3 p.393*

Thomas, Alan G. & LoVuolo, Ralph L. *v.4 p.80*

Thomas, Alfred *v.2 p.782*

Thomas, Alison *v.5 p.137*

Thomas, Andrew Peyton *v.4 p.540*

Thomas, Andrew *v.5 p.718*

Thomas B. Fordham Foundation *v.4 p.287*

Thomas, Baylis. *v.6 p.611*

Thomas, Benjamin P., et al. *v.3 p.426*

Thomas, Benjamin P. *v.3 p.426*

Thomas, Brook *v.2 p.5, v.4 p.438*

Thomas, Catherine (Editor) *v.1 p.829*

Thomas, Charles. *v.1 p.127, p.128*

Thomas, D. N. & Dieckmann, G. S. (Editors). . . . *v.5 p.430*

Thomas, David & Morgan, Prys *v.3 p.132*

Thomas, David C. & Inkson, Kerr *v.4 p.59*

Thomas, David C. *v.4 p.70*

Thomas, David (Editor). *v.4 p.587*

Thomas, David Hurst, et al. *v.6 p.683*

Thomas, David S. G. (Editor) *v.5 p.424*

Thomas, Deborah A. *v.2 p.316*

Thomas, Donald (Editor) *v.2 p.201*

Thomas, Donald. *v.3 p.91*

Thomas, Douglas. *v.4 p.709*

Thomas, Duncan C. *v.5 p.93, p.144, p.152*

Thomas, Dylan *v.2 p.385, p.386*

Thomas, Edward J. *v.1 p.562, p.565*

Thomas, Edward *v.2 p.385*

Thomas, Emory M. *v.3 p.401, p.429, v.4 p.522*

Thomas, Francis G. & Henze, Gunter *v.5 p.273*

Thomas, Frank & Johnston, Ollie A. *v.6 p.308*

Thomas, G. Scott *v.4 p.556*

Thomas, Gareth *v.2 p.642*

Thomas, Helen (Editor) *v.1 p.44*

Thomas, Helen *v.1 p.44*

Thomas, Henry W. *v.4 p.852, p.898*

Thomas, Hugh *v.3 p.242, p.313*

Thomas, Jill *v.6 p.276*

Thomas, Jim *v.4 p.75*

Thomas, Keith *v.3 p.122*

Thomas, Larry *v.5 p.450, p.738*

Thomas, Leslie C.; Chamberlin, Gordon J. . . . *v.5 p.269*

Thomas, Lewis H. *v.4 p.590*

Thomas, Lindon C. *v.5 p.713*

Thomas, Lorenzo *v.6 p.28*

Thomas, Lyn *v.2 p.532*

Thomas, Martin *v.3 p.157*

Thomas, Nicholas *v.4 p.385*

Thomas, Nick *v.3 p.177, v.4 p.610, p.712*

Thomas, Norman E. (Editor) *v.1 p.647*

Thomas of Celano *v.1 p.580*

Thomas, P. G. *v.2 p.169*

Thomas, Peter D. *v.3 p.109*

Thomas, Piri *v.6 p.491, p.509*

Thomas, R. Murray *v.5 p.629*

Thomas, Raju G. C. *v.4 p.618*

Thomas, Randall (Editor) *v.5 p.705*

Thomas, Richard & Martindale, Charles (Editors) . . . *v.2 p.399*

Thomas, Richard F. *v.2 p.446, p.447*

Thomas, Robert D. *v.1 p.583, p.584*

Thomas, Robert *v.3 p.248*

Thomas, Roland E. & Rosa, Albert J. *v.5 p.721*

Thomas, Ron *v.4 p.833, p.854, p.898*

Thomas, Rosalind *v.2 p.412, p.413, v.3 p.19*

Thomas, S. Bernard *v.6 p.201*

Thomas, Sue & Wilcox, Clyde *v.6 p.443*

Thomas, Susan E. *v.5 p.296, p.297*

Thomas, Veronica G. (Compiled by), et al. *v.6 p.35, p.47*

Thomas Vinod *v.4 p.398*

Thomas, Ward *v.4 p.484*

Thomas, William I. & Volkart, Edmund H. *v.4 p.688*

Thomas, William I. *v.4 p.684, p.749, p.752*

Thomas, William L. Jr. (Editor) *v.6 p.297*

Thomas *v.3 p.81, p.156, v.5 p.485*

Thomason, Jeffrey J. (Editor) *v.5 p.448*

Thomason, Sarah G. *v.4 p.20*

Thomison, Dennis *v.1 p.711*

Thommen, Jean-Paul & Richter, Ansgar *v.4 p.65*

Thompkins, Vincent (Editor) *v.3 p.370*

Thompson, A. M. *v.3 p.517*

Thompson, A. Richard, et al. *v.5 p.67*

Thompson, Andrew *v.3 p.90, p.126*

Thompson, Ann & McMullan, Gordon *v.2 p.232*

Thompson, Augustine *v.3 p.199*

Thompson, Bard *v.1 p.602*

Thompson, Bob *v.5 p.53*

Thompson, Bruce *v.2 p.597, v.5 p.602*

Thompson, C. Bradley *v.4 p.515, p.516*

Thompson, Charles P. (Editor), et al. *v.5 p.610*

Thompson, Colin P. *v.2 p.646*

Thompson, Donald (Editor, Translator) *v.1 p.295*

Thompson, Dorothy *v.3 p.116, p.123, v.6 p.749, p.758*

Thompson, Doug & Thompson, A. D. *v.2 p.721*

Thompson, E. A. *v.3 p.58, p.63*

Thompson, E. P. (Edward Palmer) *v.3 p.124*

Thompson, E. P. . . . *v.2 p.240, p.302, v.3 p.116, p.131, v.4 p.725*

Thompson, Edward H. Jr. (Compiled by) *v.6 p.445*

Thompson, Edward P. *v.3 p.107, p.109, p.124, p.131*

Thompson, F. M. L. (Editor) *v.6 p.736, p.762*

Thompson, F. M. L. (Francis Michael Longstreth). *v.3 p.116, p.132*

Thompson, F. M. *v.3 p.116, p.132, v.6 p.736, p.743*

Thompson, Flora *v.3 p.92, p.109, p.116, p.127, v.6 p.759, p.762*

Thompson, Gail L. *v.4 p.310*

Thompson, Heather Ann *v.3 p.517*

Thompson, I. A. A. & Casalilla, Bartolomi Yun (Editors). *v.3 p.240*

Thompson, J. M. *v.3 p.151*

Thompson, James *v.1 p.94*

Thompson, Jason *v.3 p.11*

Thompson, Jennifer L. (Editor), et al. *v.4 p.15*

Thompson, Jim, et al. *v.2 p.21*

Thompson, Jim *v.2 p.124, p.125*

Thompson, John N. *v.5 p.197*

Thompson, June M., et al. *v.5 p.522*

Thompson, Kathleen & Mac Austin, Hilary
(Editors) *v.6 p.11, p.47*

Thompson, Kenneth W. (Editor) *v.4 p.528*

Thompson, Kenneth W. *v.3 p.386*

Thompson, Kenneth *v.4 p.678*

Thompson, Kristin *v.2 p.390, v.6 p.353*

Thompson, Laura *v.2 p.371, v.6 p.704*

Thompson, Leonard Monteath *v.6 p.79*

Thompson, Linda *v.3 p.527*

Thompson, Mark R. *v.6 p.180*

Thompson, N. S. *v.2 p.210*

Thompson, Nicola D. (Editor) *v.2 p.177, p.193*

Thompson, Paul B. & Hilde, Thomas C. (Editors) . . . *v.6 p.289*

Thompson, Paul B. *v.5 p.35*

Thompson, Paul (Editor) *v.2 p.302*

Thompson, Paul *v.5 p.197*

Thompson, R. Alan *v.6 p.259, p.260*

Thompson, Richard F. & Madigan, Stephen A. . . . *v.5 p.610*

Thompson, Robert Bruce & Thompson, Barbara
Fritchman *v.4 p.114, v.5 p.344*

Thompson, Ross A. & Amato, Paul R. (Editors) *v.5 p.640*

Thompson, Roy *v.6 p.349, p.351*

Thompson, Russell D. & Perry, Allen H. *v.5 p.427*

Thompson, Stephen A. *v.5 p.703*

Thompson, Stephen J. *v.2 p.637*

Thompson, Stith *v.2 p.585*

Thompson, Susan J. *v.5 p.418*

Thompson, Thomas. *v.5 p.479*

Thompson, William J. (Editor). *v.2 p.488*

Thompson, William N. *v.4 p.777, p.899, p.900*

Thompson, William R. *v.4 p.628*

Thompson Wylder, Vicki D., et al. *v.1 p.700*

Thomsen, Moritz. *v.4 p.707*

Thomsett, Michael C. (Compiled by). *v.4 p.163*

Thomson Delmar Learning Staff. *v.5 p.701*

Thomson, Elizabeth & Gutman, David. *v.1 p.275, p.313*

Thomson, Elizabeth, et al. *v.1 p.275, p.335*

Thomson Gale Staff (Contribution
  by) *v.3 p.386, v.4 p.374, p.561, p.628*

Thomson Gale Staff (Editor) *v.4 p.142*

Thomson Gale Staff *v.3 p.484, v.4 p.88, v.5 p.396*

Thomson, Guy P.. . . . . *v.3 p.288*

Thomson, Guy *v.3 p.260*

Thomson, J. J. *v.5 p.544*

Thomson, J. K. J. *v.3 p.71*

Thomson, James A.. . . . . *v.2 p.165*

Thomson, James *v.2 p.263*

Thomson, John Mansfield & Rowland-Jones, Anthony
  (Editors) *v.1 p.392*

Thomson, Judith J. *v.1 p.496*

Thomson, Keith S. *v.5 p.226, p.231*

Thomson, Patricia (Editor) *v.2 p.216*

Thomson, Patricia *v.2 p.216*

Thomson, P. *v.3 p.297*

Thomson PDR Staff *v.5 p.526*

Thomson, Richard, et al. *v.1 p.700*

Thomson, Sinclair *v.3 p.325, p.326*

Thomson, Virgil *v.1 p.237, p.374*

Thong, Huynh Sanh (Editor, Translator) *v.6 p.169*

Thongchai, Winichakul *v.6 p.172*

Thorburn, Hugh G.. . . . . *v.4 p.589, p.590*

Thorburn, Hugh *v.4 p.589*

Thoreau, Henry
  David *v.1 p.501, v.2 p.53, v.3 p.489, p.544, v.5 p.227*

Thorlby, Anthony. *v.2 p.809*

Thorley, John *v.2 p.450*

Thormählen, Marianne *v.2 p.259*

Thorn, Craig (Editor). *v.4 p.297*

Thorn, Frank *v.3 p.97*

Thorn, John, et al. *v.4 p.852*

Thornberry, Terence P., et al. *v.6 p.256*

Thornbrough, Emma L.. . . . . *v.3 p.514*

Thornbury, William D. *v.4 p.391, v.5 p.424*

Thorndike, David *v.4 p.175, p.181*

Thorndike, Edward L. *v.4 p.359*

Thorndike, Edward Lee, et al. *v.4 p.359*

Thorndike, Edward Lee *v.4 p.359, v.5 p.599, p.615*

Thorndike, Joseph & Ventry, Dennis (Editors) . . . *v.4 p.108*

Thorndike, Robert M. *v.5 p.602, p.604*

Thorne, Barrie & Yalom, Marilyn (Editors). . *v.6 p.466, p.467*

Thorne, Barrie (Editor) *v.5 p.624*

Thorne, Barrie *v.6 p.464*

Thorne, Florence C. *v.4 p.129*

Thorne, Kip S. *v.5 p.73, p.557*

Thorne, Tanis C. *v.3 p.522*

Thornham, Sue. *v.6 p.475*

Thornley, Gail (Editor) *v.4 p.116*

Thornton, A. P.. . . . . *v.3 p.126*

Thornton, Arland (Editor) *v.5 p.639*

Thornton, Bruce S.. . . . . *v.6 p.364, p.422*

Thornton, Joe *v.5 p.315*

Thornton, John F. & Varenne, Susan B. (Editors) . . *v.1 p.564*

Thornton, John *v.6 p.63*

Thornton, R. Gordon *v.3 p.497*

Thornton, Richard C. *v.3 p.480*

Thornton, Sarah *v.1 p.34*

Thornton, Stephen J. *v.4 p.366*

Thornton, Stephen T. & Marion, Jerry B.. . . . . . *v.5 p.547*

Thornton, Weldon *v.2 p.360*

Thorp, Rosemary, et al.. . . . . *v.3 p.332*

Thorp, Rosemary *v.3 p.332*

Thorpe, Edward *v.1 p.13*

Thorpe, J. A.. . . . . *v.5 p.497*

Thorpe, James *v.2 p.165, p.255*

Thorpe, Michael (Editor) *v.2 p.278*

Thorpe, Richard S. & Brown, Geoffrey C. . . . *v.5 p.420, p.437*

Thorslev, Peter Larsen *v.2 p.274*

Thorton, Stephen J. & Flinders, David J. (Editors) . . *v.4 p.366*

Thrall, Miriam M. *v.6 p.742, p.753*

Thrapp, Dan L. *v.3 p.521, p.522*

Thrasher, Alan R. *v.1 p.290*

Thrasher, Frederic M.. . . . . *v.4 p.752, v.6 p.256*

Thucydides *v.2 p.422*

Thudium, Laura *v.1 p.151*

Thulborn, Tony *v.5 p.448, p.450*

Thurber, James A. & Nelson, Candice J. (Editors). . . *v.4 p.558*

Thurber, James *v.2 p.125, p.126*

Thurin, Erik I.. . . . . *v.2 p.54*

Thurman, E. M. & Mills, M. S. *v.5 p.268*

Thurman, Judith *v.2 p.627*

Thurman, Robert A. F. *v.6 p.241*

Thurman, Robert A. (Translator) *v.1 p.564, v.6 p.241*

Thurman, Wallace *v.2 p.124*

Thurner, Mark & Guerrero, Andrés (Editors) *v.3 p.328*

Thurner, Mark *v.3 p.265, p.328*

Thurow, Lester C. *v.4 p.78, p.248, p.266*

Thurston, Anne F. *v.6 p.203*

Thurston, H. David *v.5 p.47*

Thurston, John *v.2 p.733*

Thurston, Robert W. & Bonwetsch, Bernd *v.3 p.227*

Thurston, William P. *v.5 p.496*
Tian, Chenchan *v.1 p.476, p.508*
Tibawi, A. L. *v.6 p.605, p.608, p.611*
Tibawi, Abdul Latif. *v.4 p.337*
Tibbetts, John C. & Welsh, James M. *v.6 p.327*
Tibbetts, John C. & Welsh, James Michael *v.6 p.327*
Tibble, Steven *v.3 p.64, p.65*
Tibi, Bassam *v.6 p.583, p.595*
Tibor, Palankai *v.4 p.638*
Tibullus *v.2 p.445*
Tice, George A. *v.3 p.491*
Tice, Karen W. *v.4 p.755, p.758*
Tice, Terrence N. & Slavens, Thomas P. *v.1 p.417*
Tick, Judith *v.1 p.226, p.355, p.356*
Tickell, Adam (Editor), et al. *v.4 p.398*
Tickner, J. Ann. *v.6 p.443*
Ticknor, George *v.2 p.639*
Tideiksaar, Rein *v.5 p.519*
Tidwell, William D. *v.5 p.449*
Tieck, Ludwig *v.2 p.602*
Tiedemann, Joseph S. *v.3 p.491*
Tiedt, Pamela L. & Tiedt, Iris M. *v.4 p.309*
Tieghem, Philippe van *v.2 p.458*
Tienda, Marta & Wilson, William Julius (Editors) . . *v.4 p.753*
Tierney, B. *v.1 p.576*
Tierney, Brian *v.1 p.656, v.3 p.58, p.68*
Tierney, Helen (Editor) *v.4 p.678, v.6 p.426*
Tierney, Kathleen J., et al. *v.5 p.423*
Tierney, Lawrence M. Jr. (Editor) *v.5 p.515*
Tierney, William G. *v.4 p.332*
Tiersten, Lisa *v.3 p.54*
Tietenberg, T. H. *v.4 p.63*
Tifft, Susan E. & Jones, Alex S. *v.4 p.149, p.411*
Tiger, Lionel & Shepher, Joseph *v.6 p.616*
Tigerstedt, E. N. *v.4 p.490*
Tight, Malcolm. *v.4 p.321*
Tilden, Paul Q. *v.6 p.28*
Tiles, Jim E. *v.1 p.443*
Tiles, Mary *v.1 p.457*
Tileston, Donna E. Walker *v.4 p.287*
Till, Karen E. *v.3 p.181*
Tillard, Francoise *v.1 p.205, p.331*
Tiller, Veronica E. (Editor) *v.6 p.678*
Tilley, D. R. & Tilley, J. *v.5 p.565*
Tilley, Virginia Q. *v.3 p.299, v.4 p.650*
Tillich, Paul Johannes *v.1 p.632, p.633, p.651*
Tillich, Paul *v.1 p.581, p.634, p.637, p.644*
Tillinghast, Richard (Editor) *v.2 p.96*
Tillis, Steve. *v.1 p.93*
Tillman, Ray M. & Cummings, Michael S. (Editors) *v.4 p.129*
Till-Mobley, Mamie & Benson, Christopher *v.6 p.8, p.40*
Tillotson, Geoffrey (Editor) *v.2 p.316*
Tillotson, Kathleen *v.2 p.194, v.6 p.757*
Tillson, Albert H. Jr. *v.3 p.500*
Tilly, Charles & Blockmans, Wim P. (Editors) . . . *v.3 p.44*

Tilly, Charles (Editor). *v.4 p.602*
Tilly, Charles, et al.. . . . . *v.4 p.707*
Tilly, Charles . . . *v.3 p.62, p.151, v.4 p.501, p.602, p.684, p.712*
Tilly, Louise & Scott, Joan W.. . . . . *v.6 p.458*
Tillyard, Eustace M. *v.2 p.165, p.232*
Timberlake, Andrea (Editor), et al. *v.6 p.8, p.47*
Timberlake, Craig. *v.1 p.81, p.138, p.141*
Time-Life Books Editors *v.1 p.769*
Timerman, Jacobo *v.3 p.349, v.6 p.606, p.616*
Timmerman, John H. *v.2 p.78*
Timmerman, Peter (Editor) *v.4 p.375, p.678*
Timmermans, Jean. *v.5 p.282, p.300, p.301*
Timmons, Stuart *v.6 p.404*
Timmons, W. H. *v.3 p.509*
Timonen, Virpi *v.4 p.594, p.595*
Timoshenko, S. *v.5 p.691*
Timoshenko, Stephen & Young, Donovan H. *v.5 p.691*
Timpone, Anthony *v.6 p.351*
Tims, Frank M. (Editor), et al.. . . . . *v.5 p.673*
Tinbergen, Jan & Fischer, Dietrich. *v.4 p.262, p.267*
Tinbergen, Jan; Bos, Hendricus Cornelis *v.4 p.205*
Tinbergen, Jan (Editor) *v.4 p.245*
Tinbergen, Jan, et al. *v.4 p.262, p.266*
Tinbergen, Jan . . . *v.4 p.197, p.205, p.235, p.237, p.245, p.249,*
                              p.256, p.260, p.262, p.266
Tinbergen, Niko *v.5 p.615*
Tindale, R. S., et al. *v.4 p.688*
Tindall, George B.. . . . . . *v.3 p.444, p.450, p.497, p.498*
Tindall, William Y. *v.2 p.241*
Tindall, William York *v.2 p.360, p.386*
Tiner, Ralph W. *v.4 p.393*
Tinkham, Michael *v.5 p.565*
Tinniswood, Adrian. *v.1 p.795*
Tinoco, Ignacio, et al. *v.5 p.114, p.328*
Tinsley, Ian J. *v.5 p.363, p.375*
Tinsman, Heidi. *v.3 p.355*
Tinter, Adeline R. *v.2 p.132*
Tinterow, Gary & Conisbee, Philip (Editors) . . . *v.1 p.748*
Tinterow, Gary & Conisbee, Phillip (Editors) . . . *v.1 p.748*
Tinterow, Gary & Lacambre, Genevieve *v.1 p.733*
Tintner, Adeline R. *v.2 p.46*
Tipler, Paul A. & Llewellyn, Ralph A. *v.5 p.547*
Tipton, Charles M. (Editor) *v.4 p.810, p.874*
Tipton, Frank B. *v.3 p.165*
Tipton, Harold F. & Krause, Micki (Editors) . . . *v.4 p.114*
Tipton, Harold F. & Krause, Micki. *v.4 p.114*
Tiradritti, Francesco *v.1 p.671*
Tiruneh, Andargachew *v.6 p.64*
Tisdale, Samuel L., et al.. . . . . *v.5 p.51*
Tisdall, Caroline & Bozollo, Angelo *v.1 p.681*
Tisdell, Clement A. *v.4 p.62*
Tishkov, Valery *v.3 p.229*
Tishler, William H. (Editor) *v.1 p.814*
Tisma, Aleksandar *v.2 p.812*
Tismaneanu, Vladimir (Editor). *v.4 p.599*

Tismaneanu, Vladimir. *v.3 p.208, p.250,v.4 p.509, p.600*

Tissol, Garth. *v.2 p.439*

Titon, Jeff Todd & Carlin, Bob (Editors) *v.1 p.297*

Titon, Jeff Todd (General Editor) *v.1 p.284*

Titon, Jeff Todd *v.1 p.264, p.297*

Titone, Connie. *v.4 p.346*

Titterington, D. M. & Cox, D. R. (Editors) . . . *v.5 p.81, p.90*

Titus, Mary *v.2 p.110*

Tiusanen, Timo. *v.2 p.607*

Tivey, L. J. (Editor) *v.4 p.607*

Tlou, Thomas & Campbell, Alec C.. . . . . *v.6 p.75*

Tlumak, Jeffrey *v.1 p.436*

Tobar, Hector *v.6 p.509, p.545*

Tobias, Andrew *v.4 p.98*

Tobias, Sheila *v.5 p.464*

Tobin, Beth Fowkes *v.2 p.173*

Tobin, James. *v.4 p.239*

Tobin, J.. . . . . *v.4 p.205*

Tobin, Joseph J. (Editor) *v.4 p.369*

Tobin, Joseph J., et al. *v.4 p.370, p.371, p.373*

Tobin, Richard *v.5 p.181*

Tobin, Robert *v.4 p.535*

Tobin, Ronald W.. . . . . *v.2 p.477*

Tocci, Ronald J. & Ambrosio, Frank J.. . . . . *v.5 p.344, p.730*

Toch, Hans & Adams, Kenneth *v.6 p.277*

Toch, Hans, et al.. . . . . *v.6 p.277*

Toch, Hans *v.6 p.272, p.276, p.277*

Todd, Andrew & Lecat, Jean Guys *v.1 p.148, p.153*

Todd, David Keith & Mays, Larry W. *v.5 p.428*

Todd, Janet *v.2 p.318*

Todd, Kim *v.6 p.292*

Todd, Larry (Editor) *v.1 p.205, p.355*

Todd, Larry *v.1 p.205, p.243*

Todd, Mabel E. *v.1 p.52*

Todd, Malcolm. *v.3 p.161*

Todd, Margo. *v.1 p.581, p.582*

Todd, Olivier *v.2 p.512, p.522*

Todd, R. Larry *v.1 p.205, p.243, p.341*

Todd, Robert H., et al. *v.5 p.684*

Todorov, Tzvetan. *v.1 p.507, p.508,v.3 p.251,*
p.404, v.4 p.629, v.5 p.622

Todorova, Maria N.. . . . . *v.3 p.246*

Toelken, Barre *v.2 p.585*

Toer, Pramoedya Ananta *v.6 p.178*

Toesca, Maurice *v.2 p.526*

Toff, Nancy *v.1 p.392, p.399*

Toffler, Alvin. *v.4 p.769*

Toft, Monica Duffy *v.4 p.488, p.496, p.497*

Toibin, Colm *v.6 p.394, p.399*

Toker, Franklin. *v.1 p.795*

Tokheim, Roger L.. . . . . *v.5 p.723*

Toklas, Alice B. *v.2 p.124*

Tokunaga, Howard & Keppel, Geoffrey *v.5 p.602*

Tolan, John Victor *v.6 p.573, p.575*

Tolansky, S.. . . . . *v.5 p.561*

Toledo Maya Cultural Council Staff & Toledo Alcaldes
Association Staff *v.3 p.297*

Toliyat, Hamid A. *v.5 p.725*

Tolkien, J. R. R. *v.2 p.386*

Toll, Robert C.. . . . . *v.1 p.35, p.36*

Tolles, Thayer (Editor) *v.1 p.778*

Tolley, Kimberly *v.4 p.367*

Tollner, Ernest W. *v.5 p.6*

Tolman, Beth & Page, Ralph *v.1 p.33, p.34*

Tolman, Richard C.. . . . . *v.5 p.559*

Tolson, Melvin B. *v.2 p.124*

Tolstaya, Tatyana. *v.2 p.809*

Tolstoy, Alexei *v.2 p.809*

Tolstoy, Leo *v.1 p.481, v.2 p.809, v.4 p.346*

Toma, J. D.. . . . . *v.4 p.716, p.820, p.822, p.859, p.895*

Tomal, Daniel R.. . . . . *v.4 p.355*

Tomalin, Claire *v.2 p.369, p.370*

Tomalonis, Alexandra *v.1 p.13*

Toman, Walter *v.5 p.629, p.631*

Tomas, Carmelo R. (Editor) *v.5 p.208*

Tomasello, Michael *v.5 p.638, p.650*

Tomasi di Lampedusa, Giuseppe. *v.2 p.723*

Tomasi Di Lampedusa, Giuseppe *v.2 p.723*

Tomaszewski, Fiona K. *v.3 p.221*

Tomback, Diana F. (Editor), et al.. . . . . *v.5 p.40, v.6 p.292*

Tomczak, Matthias & Godfrey, J. Stuart . *v.5 p.429, p.433, p.434*

Tomei, Christine D. (Editor) *v.2 p.796, p.800*

Tomei, Lawrence A. (Editor) *v.4 p.352*

Tomei, Lawrence A. *v.4 p.352*

Tomelleri, Joseph R. & Eberle, Mark E. *v.5 p.216*

Tomes, Jason *v.3 p.252*

Tomey, Ann Marriner & Alligood, Martha Raile . . *v.5 p.530*

Tomita, Mary Kimoto *v.6 p.95, p.114, p.133*

Tomlin, Lily (Narrated by) *v.6 p.417*

Tomlins, Christopher L.. . . . . *v.4 p.447*

Tomlinson, Alan & Sugden, John *v.4 p.845, p.847, p.868*

Tomlinson, Carol A. & Allan, Susan D. *v.4 p.350*

Tomlinson, Carol Ann, et al.. . . . . *v.5 p.574*

Tomlinson, Carol Ann *v.4 p.350*

Tomlinson, Gary *v.1 p.187, p.342*

Tomlinson, Janis A.. . . . . *v.1 p.700*

Tomlinson, R. A. *v.3 p.19*

Tompar-Tiu, Aurora & Sustento-Severicher,
Juliana. *v.6 p.122, p.130*

Tompkins, Eugene *v.1 p.118*

Tompkins, Jane P.. . . . . *v.2 p.10, v.6 p.325*

Tonchev, Belin *v.2 p.780*

Tone, Andrea. *v.4 p.775*

Tone, John Lawrence *v.3 p.75, p.241*

Tonelli, Alan E. *v.5 p.321*

Tong, Benson (Editor) *v.6 p.87, p.110*

Tong, Benson *v.6 p.113, p.128*

Tong, Ho-Ming, et al.. . . . . *v.5 p.323*

Tong, Rosemarie, et al. *v.5 p.250*

Tong, Rosemarie Putnam *v.6 p.428*

Tong, Rosemarie *v.4 p.472*

Tonkiss, Fran *v.6 p.710*

Tonnies, Ferdinand *v.4 p.686*

Tonomura, Hitomi (Editor), et al. *v.6 p.226*

Tonry, Michael H. & Farrington, David P. (Editors) . *v.6 p.273*

Tonry, Michael H. & Petersilia, Joan (Editors) *v.6 p.275*

Tonry, Michael H. (Editor) *v.6 p.250*

Tonry, Michael H. *v.6 p.272, p.274, p.277*

Toobin, Jeffrey *v.3 p.480*

Toogood, Alan *v.5 p.45*

Took, J. F. *v.2 p.705*

Toole, John Kennedy *v.2 p.157*

Toole, K. Ross *v.3 p.526*

Toomer, Jean *v.2 p.126*

Toop, David *v.1 p.226, p.275*

Toop, Richard *v.1 p.226, p.336*

Tootill, Elizabeth (Editor) *v.5 p.225*

Topaz, Muriel *v.1 p.38*

Topik, Steven C. *v.3 p.338*

Topik, Steven *v.3 p.343*

Toplin, Robert B. *v.6 p.315*

Toplin, Robert Brent *v.6 p.315*

Topol, Jachym *v.2 p.784*

Topos - European Landscape Magazine Staff *v.1 p.814*

Toppin, Gilbert & Czerniawska, Fiona *v.4 p.65*

Topping, Donna Hooker & McManus, Roberta Ann . *v.4 p.366*

Topping, Keith & Ehly, Stewart (Editors) *v.4 p.350*

Topping, Keith J. *v.4 p.350*

Topsfield, L. T. *v.2 p.468*

Toranska, Teresa *v.3 p.255*

Torbiorn, Kjell M. *v.4 p.638*

Torchia, Robert Wilson, et al. *v.1 p.733*

Tordoff, William *v.4 p.613*

Torge, Wolfgang *v.5 p.443*

Torgerson, Warren S. *v.5 p.599*

Torgoff, Martin *v.4 p.777*

Tornqvist, Egil *v.1 p.81, p.83, p.118*

Toropov, Brandon *v.2 p.222, p.223*

Torp, Linda & Sage, Sara *v.4 p.349*

Torp, Lisbet *v.1 p.16*

Torr, James D. *v.6 p.266*

Torrans, Thomas *v.3 p.527, v.6 p.487, p.488, p.491, p.533*

Torre, Adela de la *v.6 p.539*

Torre, Josbe de la, et al. *v.5 p.703*

Torrence, Gaylord & Danoff, I. Michael *v.6 p.679*

Torres, Andrés & Velázquez, José E. (Editors) *v.6 p.539*

Torres, Arlene & Whitten, Norman E. Jr. (Editors) . *v.3 p.280*

Torres, Eliseo & Sawyer, Tim *v.6 p.524, p.551*

Torres, Eliseo *v.6 p.524, p.551*

Torres, Felipe, et al, ed. *v.3 p.272*

Torres, Maria de los Angeles *v.6 p.539*

Torres, Rodolfo D. *v.6 p.539*

Torres, Sergio & Eagleson, John (Editors) *v.1 p.578*

Torres-Cuevas, Eduardo *v.3 p.313*

Torres-Saillant, Silvio & Hernandez, Ramona *v.6 p.522*

Torricelli, Robert G. & Carroll, Andrew (Editors) . . . *v.2 p.28*

Torruella, Juan R. *v.3 p.321*

Torstrick, Rebecca L. *v.6 p.608*

Tosh, John *v.6 p.67, p.749*

Tost, Tony *v.2 p.160, p.161*

Toth, Istvan Gyorgy *v.4 p.337*

Toth, Jennifer *v.4 p.709*

Toth, Jozsef *v.5 p.283, p.284*

Totman, Conrad *v.6 p.226, p.228*

Totosy de Zepetnek, Steven *v.2 p.738*

Totten, George & MacKenzie, D. Scott *v.5 p.736*

Tottle, C. R. *v.5 p.733*

Totton, Robin *v.1 p.299*

Toulmin, Stephen E. & Goodfield, June *v.1 p.500*

Toulmin, Stephen E. *v.1 p.487, v.5 p.404*

Toulmin, Stephen Edelston *v.1 p.493*

Toulmin, Stephen *v.5 p.404*

Touma, Habib Hassan *v.1 p.287, p.288*

Tourneur, Cyril *v.2 p.222*

Tournier, Michel *v.2 p.534, v.6 p.288*

Tournikiotis, Panayotis (Editor) *v.3 p.191*

Tournikiotis, Panayotis *v.1 p.795*

Tourtillott, Suzanne J. E. *v.1 p.782, p.783*

Toussaint-Samson, Adele *v.3 p.338*

Touval, Saadia *v.4 p.650*

Towle, Charlotte *v.4 p.755, p.758*

Towle, Philip *v.4 p.657*

Townes, Charles H. *v.5 p.544*

Townley, Eric *v.1 p.163, p.171, p.264*

Townsend, Camilla *v.3 p.333*

Townsend, Charles Edward *v.2 p.774*

Townsend, Chris *v.5 p.147*

Townsend, Courtney M. Jr. *v.5 p.523*

Townsend, Dabney *v.1 p.480*

Townsend, James Benjamin *v.2 p.275*

Townsend, Janet G. *v.3 p.270*

Townsend, Joyce H. (Editor) *v.1 p.748*

Townsend, R. S. (Translator) *v.2 p.795*

Townshend, Alan (Editor) *v.5 p.267*

Townshend, Charles *v.3 p.135, p.139*

Townson, Nigel *v.3 p.242*

Toye, J. F. J. & Toye, Richard *v.4 p.665*

Toye, John *v.4 p.229*

Toye, William (Editor) *v.2 p.731*

Toynbee, Arnold J. *v.3 p.370*

Toynbee, Paget *v.2 p.705*

Tozeren, Aydin & Byers, Stephen W. *v.5 p.98*

Trabaud, Louis (Editor) *v.5 p.237*

Tracey, Grant *v.6 p.315*

Trachtenberg, Alan *v.3 p.401, p.438, p.445*

Trachtenberg, Joshua *v.6 p.574*

Trachtenberg, Marc *v.4 p.629, p.647*

Trachtenberg, Marvin *v.1 p.785*

Tracy, Brian S. *v.4 p.68*

Tracy, David *v.1 p.634, p.637*

Tracy, James D. (Editor), et al. *v.1 p.601*
Tracy, James D. (Editor) *v.4 p.771*
Tracy, James D. *v.1 p.602, p.603, v.3 p.205*
Tracy, John A.. . . . . *v.4 p.92, p.98, p.105, p.176*
Tracy, Karen *v.4 p.423*
Tracy, Kathleen *v.5 p.81, p.120*
Tracy, Robert (Editor) *v.1 p.27*
Tracy, Robert *v.1 p.19, p.29, p.31*
Tracy, Stephen V.. . . . . *v.2 p.415*
Tracy, Steven C. (Editor). *v.2 p.88*
Tracy, Steven C.. . . . . *v.2 p.88*
Trafzer, Clifford E. *v.6 p.702*
Trager, Philip *v.1 p.27*
Trahan, Elizabeth Welt *v.2 p.593*
Traherne, Thomas *v.1 p.652*
Traill, Catharine Parr *v.2 p.733*
Traill, David A. *v.3 p.16*
Traina, Cristina L. *v.1 p.576*
Training Management Corporation Staff *v.4 p.57*
Trainor, Lynn E. H.. . . . . *v.5 p.137*
Trakl, Georg *v.2 p.615*
Trambley, Estela P.. . . . . *v.6 p.504*
Tran, Barbara (Editor), et al.. . . . . . . *v.6 p.92, p.141*
Trani, Eugene P. & Wilson, David L. . . . *v.3 p.445, p.450, p.481*
Transparency International *v.4 p.54*
Tranter, George E. & Holmes, John L. (Editors). . . . *v.5 p.270*
Tranter, John & Mead, Philip (Editors) *v.2 p.743*
Tranter, John. *v.2 p.743*
Tranter, Neil L. *v.4 p.810, p.889, p.892*
Tranter, William, et al. *v.5 p.726*
Trapp, J. B. (Editor), et al. *v.2 p.197*
Trapp, Kenneth R. (Editor) *v.1 p.800*
Trapp, Michael (Editor). *v.2 p.426*
Trapp, Stefan & McFarlane, Craig (Editors) . . . *v.5 p.355*
Trappl, Robert (Editor), et al. *v.5 p.590*
Trask, David F. *v.3 p.401, p.438, p.481*
Trask, Michael *v.2 p.11*
Trask, R. L. (Editor) *v.2 p.564, v.5 p.622, p.624*
Trask, R. L. *v.2 p.564, v.5 p.622, p.624*
Trask, Samuel, et al.. . . . . *v.5 p.40*
Trattner, Walter I. (Editor). *v.4 p.758*
Traubner, Richard *v.1 p.233, p.254*
Traupman, John (Editor) *v.2 p.424*
Trautman, Neal E. *v.6 p.263*
Trautmann, Thomas R. *v.6 p.150*
Travers, Max. *v.4 p.179*
Traverse, A. *v.5 p.449*
Traversi, Derek *v.2 p.233, p.234*
Travis, David *v.1 p.769*
Travis, Dempsey J. *v.3 p.516*
Travis, Jeremy & Visher, Christy (Editors) *v.6 p.279*
Travis, Jeremy & Waul, Michelle (Editors). . . *v.6 p.279, p.281*
Travis, Peter W. *v.2 p.185*
Travisano, Thomas *v.2 p.61, p.62, p.91, p.96, p.97*
Traxel, David *v.3 p.450, p.481*

Traynham, James G. (Editor) *v.5 p.291*
Treacy, Michael & Wiersema, Fred *v.4 p.135*
Treadgold, Warren T.. . . . . *v.3 p.193*
Treasure, Geoffrey *v.3 p.146*
Treece, David *v.3 p.343*
Trefousse, Hans L.. . . . . . . *v.3 p.401, p.421, p.434*
Trefousse, Hans *v.3 p.401*
Tregear, Mary *v.1 p.694*
Treggiari, Susan M.. . . . . *v.3 p.24*
Tregle, Joseph G. Jr. *v.3 p.508*
Treglown, Jeremy & Bennett, Bridget (Editors) *v.4 p.403*
Treglown, Jeremy (Editor) *v.2 p.259*
Treglown, Jeremy *v.2 p.378, p.379*
Treharne, Elaine M. *v.2 p.197*
Treharne, Elaine *v.2 p.168*
Treib, Marc & Imbert, Dorothee *v.1 p.817*
Treib, Marc (Editor) *v.1 p.815*
Treib, Marc *v.1 p.226, p.363*
Treiman, Donald J. & Hartmann, Heidi I.. . . . . . *v.4 p.255*
Treitler, Leo. *v.1 p.178, p.383*
Trejo, Arnulfo D. (Editor). *v.6 p.545*
Trela, D. J. & Tarr, Rodger L. (Editors) *v.2 p.277*
Trelease, Allen W.. . . . . *v.3 p.402, p.438*
Trelease, Jim. *v.4 p.366*
Tremain, Rose *v.2 p.385*
Tremblay, Michel. *v.2 p.541*
Tremlin, Todd *v.1 p.524*
Trench, Charles C. *v.3 p.90, p.116*
Trench, Lucy (Editor) *v.1 p.798, p.799, p.803*
Trenka, Jane Jeong *v.6 p.95, p.137*
Trenn, Thaddeus J.. . . . . . *v.5 p.308, p.394, p.412*
Trensky, Paul I., et al. *v.2 p.784*
Trensky, Paul I. *v.2 p.782*
Trent, Judith S. & Friedenberg, Robert V. *v.4 p.578*
Trent, R. J. *v.5 p.129*
Treptow, Kurt W. (Editor, Translator). *v.2 p.816*
Tresidder, Jack *v.1 p.710*
Trethewey, Kenneth R. & Chamberlain, John *v.5 p.735*
Trevelyan, George Macaulay *v.3 p.90, p.92, p.108*
Trevelyan, George O.. . . . . *v.3 p.410*
Treviano, A. Javier (Editor) *v.4 p.687*
Trevino, Jesus Salvador *v.6 p.541*
Trevor, Harley *v.5 p.622, p.624*
Trevor, William *v.2 p.385*
Trevor-Roper, Hugh R.. . . . . *v.6 p.201, p.216*
Trexler, Richard C. *v.3 p.268*
Trezise, Simon (Editor). *v.1 p.226, p.321*
Trezise, Simon *v.1 p.226, p.243, p.321*
Tribe, Ivan M. *v.1 p.275*
Tribe, John *v.4 p.785, p.889*
Tribe, Laurence H. *v.4 p.454, p.472*
Trible, Phyllis *v.1 p.619*
Tricard, Louise Mead . . . *v.4 p.810, p.838, p.869, v.6 p.438*
Trice, Harrison M. *v.5 p.579*
Tricomi, F. G. *v.5 p.488*

Tricot, Xavier *v.1 p.748*
Triechler, Paula A. *v.4 p.779*
Trifonov, Yuri *v.2 p.809*
Trigg, George L. (Editor) *v.5 p.545*
Trigg, Heather B.. . . . . *v.4 p.383*
Trigg, Joseph W. *v.1 p.613*
Trigg, Roger *v.1 p.523*
Trigger, Bruce G. & Washburn, Wilcomb E. (Editors) . *v.6 p.683*
Trigger, Bruce G.. . . . . *v.4 p.6*
Trigiano, R. N. (Robert Nicholas) & Gray, Dennis J.
  (Editors) *v.5 p.156*
Trigo Boix, Nuri *v.5 p.177, p.223*
Trilling, James *v.1 p.713*
Trilling, Lionel *v.2 p.5, p.165, p.266, p.569*
Trimble, Stephen (Editor) *v.5 p.235*
Trimble, Virginia & Williams, Thomas *v.5 p.62*
Trimingham, J. Spencer *v.1 p.554, v.6 p.63, p.584, p.601*
Trimpi, Wesley. *v.2 p.220*
Trinkaus, Erik. *v.4 p.17*
Trinkunas, Harold A. *v.3 p.361*
Tripp, Aili Mari *v.6 p.443*
Tripp, C. A. *v.6 p.390*
Trippi, Peter *v.1 p.748*
Triptow, Robert (Editor) *v.6 p.407*
Tristan, Flora *v.3 p.328*
Trites, Roberta Seelinger *v.6 p.480*
Tritton, D. J. *v.5 p.547*
Troccoli, Joan C. & Hunt, Sarah Anschutz *v.1 p.733*
Trochimczyk, Maja (Editor). *v.1 p.226, p.301*
Trocki, Carl A. *v.6 p.145, p.173*
Troeger, Richard *v.1 p.187, p.243, p.304, p.402*
Troeh, Frederick R. & Donahue, Roy Luther. . . . *v.5 p.6, p.28*
Troeh, Frederick R; Thompson, Louis M. *v.5 p.51*
Trofimenkoff, Susan Mann *v.3 p.544*
Troll, Christian W. *v.1 p.555*
Trolldal, Bjorn *v.4 p.153*
Trollope, Anthony & Skilton *v.2 p.318*
Trollope, Anthony *v.2 p.317, p.318*
Trompenaars, Fons & Woolliams, Peter *v.4 p.59*
Trompenaars, Fons *v.4 p.59, p.132*
Trompf, G. W. *v.1 p.544*
Troost, Linda & Greenfield, Sayre (Editors) . *v.6 p.327, p.344*
Tropiano, Stephen *v.6 p.419*
Trost, B. M. & Fleming, I. (Editors) *v.5 p.294*
Trotman, Clive *v.5 p.243*
Trotsky, Len *v.6 p.193, p.216*
Trotsky, Leon *v.2 p.800*
Trotter, Hale F. & Williamson, Richard E. *v.5 p.486*
Trotter, Joe (Editor), et al.. . . . . *v.6 p.8*
Trotter, Robert T. 2nd & Chavira, Juan A.. *v.6 p.524, p.551, p.552*
Trotter, William R. *v.3 p.236, v.6 p.410*
Trottier, David *v.6 p.353, p.355*
Troubetzkoy, Alexis S. *v.3 p.218*
Trousson, Raymond & Eigeldinger, Frédéric *v.2 p.483*
Trousson, Raymond & Vercruysse, Jeroom *v.2 p.484*

Trowbridge, Leslie W., et al. *v.4 p.367*
Trowbridge, Peter J. & Bassuk, Nina L. *v.1 p.817*
Trowell, Margaret *v.1 p.714*
Troxel, Tiffany A.. . . . . *v.3 p.229, v.4 p.599*
Troxell, Kay *v.1 p.21*
Troy, Gil *v.3 p.371*
Troy, Leo *v.4 p.123*
Troy, Nancy J. *v.1 p.801*
Trubowitz, Sidney & Robins, Maureen Picard *v.4 p.278*
Trudeau, Lawrence J. (Editor) *v.6 p.87, p.98*
Trudeau, Pierre E. *v.3 p.542*
Trudgill, Peter & Bauer, Laurie (Editors). . . . *v.2 p.550, p.564*
True, Michael *v.2 p.5*
Trueba, Enrique T. *v.4 p.311, v.6 p.545*
Trueblood, Alan S. *v.2 p.662*
Trugo, Luiz & Finglas, Paul (Editors) *v.5 p.35*
Trujillo, Carla (Introduction by) *v.6 p.547*
Trujillo, Carla *v.6 p.428, p.547*
Truman, Harry S. & Koenig, Louis W. *v.3 p.481*
Truman, Harry S.. *v.3 p.481*
Trumbach, Randolph. *v.3 p.55*
Trumbull, Elise. *v.4 p.311, p.312, v.6 p.528*
Trump, Kenneth S. *v.4 p.281*
Trun, Nancy Jo & Trempy, J. E.. . . . . *v.5 p.137*
Trungpa, Chogyam *v.6 p.242*
Trunk, Isaiah *v.3 p.87*
Truong, Monique *v.6 p.102, p.399*
Trussler, Simon *v.2 p.185*
Trusted, Jennifer *v.1 p.500*
Truth and Reconciliation Commission of South Africa . *v.4 p.731*
Tryphonopoulos, Demetres P. & Adams, Stephen J.
  (Editors) *v.2 p.112*
Trzeciakowski, Lech *v.3 p.253*
Trzynadlowski, Andrzej M. *v.5 p.725*
Tsai, Eugenie *v.1 p.724*
Tsang, Pamela S. & Vidulich, Michael A. (Editors) . *v.5 p.588*
Tsang, Steve *v.6 p.206*
Tsay, Ruey S. *v.4 p.205, p.206, p.264*
Tschirhart, John & Shogren, Jason F. (Editors) . . . *v.6 p.301*
Tschirhart, Mary *v.1 p.825*
Tschizewskij, Dmitrij. *v.2 p.779, p.800*
Tsebelis, George *v.4 p.575*
Tsering, Tashi, et al. *v.6 p.242, p.243, p.245*
Tsesis, Alexander. *v.4 p.423*
Tsing, Anna Lowenhaupt. *v.4 p.27*
Tsomo, Karma Lekshe (Editor) *v.6 p.436, p.460*
Tsou, Tang. *v.6 p.204*
Tsoukalis, Loukas *v.4 p.383*
Tsuchimochi, Gary H. & Kawabe, Daito *v.6 p.222*
Tsuda, Takeyuki *v.6 p.115, p.133*
Tsui, Chia-Chi *v.5 p.712*
Tsuji, Jiro *v.5 p.295*
Tsujimoto, Karen *v.1 p.748*
Tsukamoto, Zenryv *v.1 p.562*
Tsukerblat, Boris S.. . . . . *v.5 p.280*

Tsuneyoshi, Ryoko *v.6 p.222*

Tsur, Samuel A. *v.5 p.246*

Tsurumi, Kazuko *v.4 p.707*

Tsvetaeva, Marina I. *v.2 p.810*

Tu, Weiming & De Bary, William Theodore (Editors) *v.4 p.513*

Tuan, Mia *v.6 p.124*

Tuan, Rocky S. & Lo, Cecilia W. (Editors) *v.5 p.161*

Tuan, Yi-Fu (Editor) *v.6 p.721*

Tuan, Yi-Fu *v.4 p.375*

Tuana, Nancy (Editor), et al.. . . . . . . *v.4 p.745, v.6 p.437*

Tuana, Nancy (Editor) *v.6 p.439*

Tuaolo, Esera & Rosengren, John *v.4 p.839, p.860*

Tuathail, Gearsid S., et al. *v.4 p.400, p.401, p.403*

Tubb, Jonathan N. *v.3 p.7*

Tubbs, Stephenie Ambrose & Jenkinson, Clay Straus *v.3 p.520*

Tucci, Giuseppe *v.1 p.566, p.567*

Tuchman, Barbara W.. . . . . . . *v.3 p.463, v.6 p.193, p.201*

Tucholsky, Kurt *v.2 p.615*

Tuck, Anthony *v.6 p.568*

Tuck, Richard *v.4 p.477*

Tucker, Alan *v.5 p.479*

Tucker, Allan (Editor). *v.4 p.294*

Tucker, Anne, et al.. . . . . *v.1 p.765*

Tucker, David M.. . . . . *v.3 p.511*

Tucker, David *v.4 p.540*

Tucker, Gene M. & Knight, Douglas A. *v.1 p.619*

Tucker, Herbert F. & Mermin, Dorothy (Editors) . . *v.2 p.197*

Tucker, Herbert F. (Editor) *v.2 p.177, v.6 p.736*

Tucker, Herbert F. *v.2 p.272, p.315*

Tucker, Judith E. *v.6 p.608, p.611, p.612, p.638*

Tucker, M. E. *v.5 p.439*

Tucker, Mark (Editor) *v.1 p.264, p.323*

Tucker, Maurice E.. . . . . *v.5 p.420*

Tucker, Nancy B. *v.3 p.393, v.4 p.561, p.566, p.644*

Tucker, Nancy Bernkopf *v.3 p.393, v.6 p.214*

Tucker, Patrick (Translator) *v.6 p.348*

Tucker, Paul H. *v.1 p.748*

Tucker, Paul *v.1 p.748*

Tucker, Priscilla M.. . . . . *v.5 p.228*

Tucker, Richard P. *v.6 p.299*

Tucker, Robert C. (Editor) *v.3 p.225*

Tucker, Robert C. *v.3 p.224*

Tucker, Susan (Editor), et al. *v.1 p.765*

Tucker, Wallace & Tucker, Karen *v.5 p.67, p.68*

Tucker, William P.. . . . . *v.3 p.295*

Tuckerman, Frederick Goddard *v.2 p.51*

Tuckerman, Nancy, et al.. . . . . *v.1 p.486*

Tuckwell, Barry *v.1 p.392*

Tuden, Arthur & Plotnicov, Leonard *v.4 p.707*

Tudge, Colin *v.5 p.223, p.533*

Tudor, Andrew *v.6 p.320*

Tufte, Edward R. *v.1 p.721, v.4 p.174, v.5 p.481, p.588*

Tulchin, Joseph S. & Brown, Amelia (Editors) . . . *v.4 p.506*

Tulchin, Joseph S. & Selee, Andrew D. *v.4 p.585, p.613*

Tulchin, Joseph S. & Varas, Augusto (Editors) . . . *v.3 p.355*

Tulchin, Joseph S. (Editor), et al. *v.3 p.313*

Tulchin, Joseph S. *v.3 p.277, p.393, v.4 p.593*

Tuljapurkar, Shripad & Caswell, Hal *v.5 p.172*

Tulli, Magdalena *v.2 p.792*

Tulli, Magdelena *v.2 p.792*

Tulliu, Steve & Schmalberger, Thomas *v.4 p.657*

Tully, James *v.4 p.526*

Tully, R. Brent & Fisher, J. Richard. *v.5 p.64*

Tulving, Endel & Craik, Fergus I. M. (Editors) . . . *v.5 p.611*

Tuma, Keith (Editor) *v.2 p.201*

Tumarkin, Nina *v.3 p.227*

Tumielewicz, P. J. & Lyons, Peg (Editors) *v.1 p.141*

Tumin, Melvin M. & Feldman, Arnold S. *v.4 p.707*

Tumulty, Joseph P. *v.3 p.481*

Tun, Mao *v.6 p.213*

Tune, Tommy *v.6 p.415*

Tung, Anthony Max *v.1 p.824*

Tung Chieh-Yuan. *v.6 p.209*

Tung, Fei *v.4 p.475*

Tung, May Paomay *v.6 p.110, p.128*

Tung, W. K. *v.5 p.548*

T'ung-tsu Ch'u. *v.6 p.187*

Tunick, Mark *v.6 p.275*

Tunick, Susan *v.1 p.778*

Tunkin, G. I. *v.4 p.627*

Tunnell, Kenneth D. *v.4 p.131*

Tuohy, Thomas. *v.3 p.200*

Turan, Kenneth & Zito, Stephen F.. . . . . *v.6 p.317*

Turan, Kenneth. *v.6 p.346*

Turbet, Richard *v.1 p.165, p.181, p.315*

Turbide, David A. *v.5 p.684*

Turcan, Robert *v.1 p.533*

Turchin, Peter *v.5 p.186*

Turcotte, Donald L. & Schubert, Gerald *v.5 p.443*

Turcotte, Donald L.. . . . . *v.5 p.420*

Turetzky, Bertram *v.1 p.394, p.399*

Turfan, Naim *v.6 p.622*

Turgenev, Ivan *v.2 p.810*

Turiel, Isaac. *v.5 p.366, p.372, p.373*

Turim, Maureen *v.6 p.337*

Turino, Thomas *v.1 p.286, p.295*

Turits, Richard Lee *v.3 p.318*

Turk, Daniel Gottlob *v.1 p.399, p.402*

Turk, Eleanor L. *v.3 p.160*

Turkington, Carol & Harris, Joseph *v.4 p.319*

Turnbaugh, Douglas *v.6 p.415*

Turnbull, Andrew *v.2 p.77*

Turnbull, C. Mary *v.6 p.173*

Turnbull, C. M. *v.6 p.173*

Turnbull, Colin M. *v.4 p.39, v.6 p.63*

Turnbull, Eleanor L. *v.2 p.645*

Turnbull, George (Editor) *v.4 p.346*

Turnbull, William *v.5 p.622, p.624*

Turncock, David *v.3 p.207*

Turnell, Martin *v.2 p.462, p.463*

Turner, A. Keith & Schuster, Robert L. (Editors) . . . *v.5 p.422*
Turner, Barry (Editor) *v.4 p.374, p.575, p.625*
Turner, Bryan (Introduction by) *v.4 p.692, p.762*
Turner, Bryan S. *v.1 p.559, v.4 p.686, v.5 p.511, p.512*
Turner, Cheryl *v.2 p.192*
Turner, Darwin T. (Editor) *v.2 p.126*
Turner, Darwin T. (Introduction by) *v.2 p.25*
Turner, Dwayne *v.6 p.379*
Turner, Ed & Clouse, Woody *v.4 p.864*
Turner, Eric G. *v.2 p.401*
Turner, Ernest S. *v.6 p.739, p.757*
Turner, Evan H. *v.1 p.769*
Turner, Faythe (Introduction by) *v.6 p.496, p.509*
Turner, Frank M. *v.3 p.116, p.129, v.6 p.751, p.753, p.764*
Turner, Frank *v.1 p.580*
Turner, Frederick Jackson *v.3 p.415, p.520*
Turner, Frederick J. *v.3 p.381, p.402*
Turner, Frederick *v.3 p.295*
Turner, Harriet S. & López de Martínez, Adelaida
(Editors) *v.2 p.639, p.642*
Turner, Harriet S. *v.2 p.655*
Turner, Henry A. Jr. *v.3 p.170*
Turner, Henry Ashby *v.3 p.174*
Turner, Jack *v.5 p.223, v.6 p.284*
Turner, Jacques *v.1 p.751*
Turner, James *v.1 p.545*
Turner, Jane (Editor) *v.1 p.666, p.667*
Turner, J. *v.1 p.87, p.107, p.153*
Turner, Jonathan H. *v.4 p.684, p.707, p.718*
Turner, Justin G. & Turner, Linda L. (Editors) . . . *v.3 p.427*
Turner, L. F. & Turner, Susan Lilliman *v.4 p.797, p.799*
Turner, Lowell (Editor), et al. *v.4 p.129*
Turner, Lynn W. *v.3 p.486*
Turner, Marjorie S. *v.4 p.271*
Turner, Mark *v.2 p.573, v.4 p.272*
Turner, Mary *v.4 p.728*
Turner, Michael R. *v.2 p.201*
Turner, Nancy J. & Szczawinski, Adam F. *v.5 p.209*
Turner, Patricia A. *v.2 p.17*
Turner, Paul *v.2 p.177, p.203, p.416*
Turner, Ralph V. & Heiser, Richard R. *v.3 p.99*
Turner, Ralph V. *v.3 p.98*
Turner, Richard Brent *v.6 p.36*
Turner, Silvie, et al. *v.1 p.758*
Turner, Stansfield *v.4 p.562*
Turner, Stephen & Sica, Alan (Editors) *v.4 p.684*
Turner, Stephen P. & Roth, Paul Andrew (Editors) . . *v.1 p.501*
Turner, Thomas R. *v.3 p.427*
Turner, Tom *v.5 p.81*
Turner, Tyya N. *v.4 p.156*
Turner, Victor W. *v.1 p.55, p.136, v.4 p.37, v.6 p.77*
Turner, W. Craig & Harding, Lee E. *v.2 p.130*
Turney, Jon *v.5 p.250*
Turnpenny, Peter D. & Ellard, Sian *v.5 p.152*
Turoff, Fred *v.4 p.797, p.862*

Turow, Joseph *v.4 p.696*
Turow, Scott *v.4 p.441*
Turpin, Jennifer (Editor) *v.4 p.679*
Turton, Richard John *v.5 p.555*
Turville-Petre, E. O. *v.2 p.625*
Turville-Petre, Gabriel *v.2 p.625*
Turville-Petre, Thorlac *v.2 p.551*
Tushnet, Mark (Editor) *v.4 p.462*
Tushnet, Mark V. *v.4 p.457, p.469*
Tushnet, Mark *v.4 p.540*
Tuska, Jon (Editor, Introduction by) *v.2 p.27*
Tuska, Jon *v.3 p.527*
Tuszynski, Jack A. *v.5 p.125*
Tuten, Nancy Lewis & Zubizarreta, John (Editors) . . *v.2 p.78*
Tutino, John *v.3 p.295*
Tuttle, Richard *v.1 p.700*
Tuttle, William M. Jr. *v.3 p.516*
Tuttleton, James W. (Editor), et al. *v.2 p.132*
Tutuola, Amos *v.2 p.757*
Tuwhare, Hone (Contribution by) *v.2 p.749*
Tuwhare, Hone *v.2 p.749*
Twaddle, Michael *v.6 p.67*
Twagilimana, Aimable *v.4 p.654*
Twain, Mark & Salamo, Lin *v.2 p.35*
Twain, Mark *v.2 p.34, p.35, v.3 p.506*
Twardowska, I., et al. *v.5 p.369, p.377, p.378*
Tweed, Thomas A. & Prothero, Stephen (Editors) . . . *v.6 p.106*
Tweeten, Luther G. & Thompson, Stanley R. (Editors) . *v.5 p.15*
Tweeten, Luther G. *v.5 p.15*
Tweit, Susan J. *v.5 p.178, p.233*
Twersky, Isadore (Editor, Introduction by, Notes by) . *v.1 p.551*
Twidell, John, et al. *v.5 p.361*
Twigg, Judyth L. *v.4 p.669*
Twinam, Ann *v.3 p.356, p.359*
Twine, Frances W. *v.3 p.280, p.343*
Twiss, Robert J. & Moores, Eldridge M. *v.5 p.442*
Twitchell, James B. *v.4 p.427*
Twitchett, Denis C. & Franke, Herbert (Editors) . *v.6 p.186, p.204*
Twitchett, Denis C. (Editor, Contribution by) . . *v.6 p.184, p.185*
Twohig, E. S. *v.1 p.669*
Twombly, Robert C. *v.1 p.795*
Twomey, David P. *v.4 p.134*
Tworzecki, Hubert *v.4 p.579, p.597*
Twyman, Richard M. *v.5 p.118, p.154, p.155*
Ty, Eleanor Rose & Goellnicht, Donald C.
(Editors) *v.6 p.98, p.125, p.126*
Tyack, David B. & Hansot, Elisabeth *v.4 p.282*
Tyack, David *v.4 p.298*
Tyacke, Nicholas *v.3 p.122*
Tydeman, William (Editor) *v.1 p.73, p.97, p.98, p.155*
Tydeman, William *v.1 p.73, p.97, p.155*
Tye, Barbara Benham & Tye, Kenneth A. *v.4 p.314*
Tye, Larry *v.4 p.429*
Tygiel, Jules *v.4 p.810, p.833, p.852, p.898*
Tyldesley, Joyce A. *v.6 p.57, p.58*

Tyler, Alice *v.3 p.402*
Tyler, Anne *v.2 p.157*
Tyler, Howard, et al.. . . . . *v.5 p.56*
Tyler, James & Sparks, Paul. *v.1 p.392*
Tyler, Lyon G. *v.3 p.500*
Tyler, Ralph W. *v.4 p.366*
Tyler, Ron (Editor) *v.1 p.760*
Tyler, Ron, et al. *v.1 p.733*
Tyler, Royall *v.2 p.30*
Tyler *v.6 p.417*
Tymn, Marshall B. & Ashley, Mike (Editors) *v.2 p.581*
Tyner, James A. *v.6 p.117, p.120, p.130*
Tyrrell, Ian R. *v.3 p.375*
Tyrrell, Ian. *v.4 p.776*
Tyrrell, John (Editor). *v.1 p.226, p.233, p.333*
Tyrrell, John *v.1 p.226, p.233, p.333*
Tyrrell, William B. & Brown, Frieda S. *v.3 p.15*
Tyrrell, William Blake *v.4 p.810*
Tyson, Timothy B.. . . . . *v.6 p.13*
Tyson-Ward, Sue *v.2 p.638*
Tytler, Harriet *v.6 p.158*
Tzu, Lao *v.1 p.418*

U

U Maung Maung *v.6 p.166*
U. S. Bureau of Mines Staff & American Geological Institute
 Staff. *v.5 p.450, p.739*
U S Bureau of Mines Staff *v.5 p.733, p.738*
U. S. Bureau of Mines Staff. *v.5 p.739*
U. S. Department of Labor, Employment and Training Staff
 (Contribution by) *v.5 p.578*
U. S. Department of Labor Staff. *v.5 p.577, p.578*
U. S. Food and Drug Administration Dept. of Health and
 Human Services *v.5 p.33*
U. S. Institute of Museum and Library
 Services. *v.3 p.404, p.407, p.410, p.414*
U. S. Laws and Statutes Staff, Statutes *v.6 p.693*
U. S. News and World Report Staff *v.4 p.278*
U. S. Office of Education Staff & Coleman, James S. . *v.4 p.301*
U. S. Tennis Association Staff & Ellenbecker, Todd S.. *v.4 p.864*
Uba, Laura *v.6 p.122*
Ubbelohde, Carl, et al. *v.3 p.526*
Ubicini, M. A.. *v.6 p.623*
Uchida, Hiroshi (Editor) *v.4 p.237*
Uchida, Yoshiko *v.6 p.95, p.115, p.135*
Ucko, Peter J. (Editor) *v.4 p.6*
Ucko *v.3 p.10*
Udall, Nicholas *v.2 p.222*
Ueda, Akinari *v.6 p.233*
Ueda, Makoto *v.6 p.234*
Uehling, Greta *v.3 p.213*
Ueno, Keihei, Toshiaki Imamura, and K.L. Cheng. . *v.5 p.291*
Ueno, Kenji, et al.. . . . . . *v.5 p.460, p.474, p.494, p.496*
Ueshiba, Kisshomaru *v.4 p.863*

Uffenbeck, John E. *v.5 p.344, p.345, p.730*
Ugalde, Luis Carlos. *v.3 p.296, v.4 p.594*
Uglow, Jenny *v.2 p.289*
Ugresic, Dubravka *v.2 p.818*
Ugur, Mehmet *v.4 p.239*
Uhland, Ludwig *v.2 p.602*
Uhlendorf, Bernard A. (Editor) *v.3 p.414*
Uhlig, Herbert H. & Revie, R. Winston *v.5 p.735, p.736*
Uhry, Alfred *v.2 p.157*
Uitti, Karl D. & Freeman, Michelle A.. . . . . *v.2 p.468*
Ukadike, N. Frank *v.6 p.334*
Ulam, Adam B. *v.3 p.219, p.223*
Ulam, Adam Bruno. *v.3 p.393*
Ulanov, Ann & Ulanov, Barry *v.5 p.657*
Ulanov, Ann Belford *v.6 p.460*
Ulanov, Barry & Ulanov, Ann Belford *v.5 p.636*
Uledi-Kamanga, Brighton J.. . . . . *v.2 p.755*
Ulfstrand, Staffan. *v.5 p.181*
Ulibarrí, Sabine R. *v.6 p.504*
Ulich, Robert (Editor) *v.4 p.323, p.329*
Ulicky, Ladislav & Kemp, T. J. *v.5 p.275*
Ulin, David L. (Editor) *v.2 p.584*
Ulin, David L. *v.2 p.21, p.22, v.6 p.730*
Ulitskaya, Ludmila *v.2 p.810*
Ullman, Jeffrey D. & Widom, Jennifer. *v.5 p.337, p.338*
Ullmann, Fritz *v.5 p.316*
Ullmann, Stephen *v.2 p.463*
Ullmann, Walter *v.1 p.574, v.3 p.58, p.69*
Ulmschneider, Peter *v.5 p.243*
Ulrich, Dave & Brockbank, Wayne *v.4 p.77*
Ulrich, Gael D.. . . . . *v.5 p.743*
Ulrich, Laurel Thatcher *v.3 p.487*
Ulrich, Paul S., et.al *v.1 p.4, p.5*
Ulrich, Susan Puderbaugh & Canale, Suzanne Weyland. *v.5 p.528*
Umar, Asad (Editor), et al. *v.5 p.98*
Umar, Badruddin *v.6 p.148*
Umberger, Emily and Tom Cummins, eds *v.3 p.264*
Umeh, Marie (Editor). *v.2 p.754*
Umphlett, Wiley L. (Editor) *v.4 p.812*
Umphlett, Wiley L. *v.4 p.810, p.860, p.895*
Umphlett, Wiley Lee *v.4 p.418*
Umstattd, William D. & Davis, Charles W.. . . . . . *v.1 p.805*
Umstead, Douglas R.. . . . . *v.2 p.711*
UN Office for the Coordination of Humanitarian Affairs
 (UNOCHA) *v.4 p.668, p.669, p.670, p.671*
UNAIDS/WHO *v.4 p.669*
Unamuno, Miguel de, et al. *v.2 p.645*
Unamuno, Miguel de *v.1 p.474, v.2 p.662, p.663*
UNC Institute for Transportation Research and Education Staff
 (Contribution by), et al. *v.5 p.701*
Underdown, David *v.3 p.95, p.104, p.122*
Underhill, Ruth M.. . . . . *v.6 p.701, p.704*
Underwood, Dale. *v.2 p.245*
Underwood, James R. & Guth, Peter L. *v.5 p.422*
Underwood, Jim. *v.4 p.79*

Underwood, Marion K. *v.5 p.629*
Underwood, Thomas A. *v.2 p.125*
Undset, Sigrid, et al. *v.2 p.628*
Undset, Sigrid *v.2 p.628, p.629*
UNESCO Staff. *v.5 p.250*
Ung, Loung *v.6 p.95, p.139*
Ungar, Michael (Editor). *v.5 p.629*
Ungar, Sanford J. *v.3 p.481, v.4 p.438*
Ungaretti, Giuseppe *v.2 p.723*
Unger, Craig *v.1 p.13, v.3 p.484*
Unger, Douglas *v.2 p.157*
Unger, Harlow G. *v.4 p.340*
Unger, Irwin & Unger, Debi. *v.3 p.481*
Unger, Irwin *v.4 p.332*
Unger, Jonathan (Editor) *v.4 p.620*
Unger, Jonathan *v.4 p.337*
Unger, Nancy C. *v.3 p.402*
Unger, Peter K. *v.1 p.489*
Unger, Rhoda K. (Editor) *v.6 p.446*
Unger, Richard. *v.2 p.602*
Ungvary, Krisztian *v.3 p.187*
UNICEF Staff *v.4 p.670*
UNICEF. *v.4 p.670*
United Kingdom. Central Office of Information.. . . *v.4 p.604*
United Kingdom. Office for National Statistics . . . *v.4 p.604*
United Kingdom. Prime Minister. . . . *v.4 p.604, p.605, p.606*
United Nations Association Staff. *v.4 p.669*
United Nations Conference on International Organization
    Staff. *v.4 p.635*
United Nations Conference on Trade and Development. *v.4 p.666*
United Nations. Crime and Justice Information Network. *v.6 p.246*
United Nations, Department of Economic and Social Affairs,
    Population Division Staff *v.4 p.663*
United Nations, Department of Economic and Social Affairs
    Staff *v.4 p.547*
United Nations, Dept. of Economic and Social Affairs Staff
    (Contribution by) *v.4 p.666*
United Nations Development Programme Staff & Arab Fund for
    Economic and Social Development Staff *v.4 p.615*
United Nations Development Programme
    Staff *v.4 p.258, p.262, p.586, p.666*
United Nations Environment Programme Staff *v.5 p.367*
United Nations Environment Programme *v.5 p.353*
United Nations High Commissioner for Refugees Staff. *v.4 p.765*
United Nations: Human Settlements
    Programme. *v.4 p.663, v.6 p.725*
United Nations. OHCHR *v.4 p.670*
United Nations
    Staff. . . . *v.4 p.586, p.635, p.636, p.651, p.655, p.657, p.667*
United Nations, Statistical Division Staff (Contribution
    by) *v.4 p.388*
United Nations Timber Committee. *v.4 p.152, p.164*
United Nations (UN) *v.4 p.666*
United Nations. *v.4 p.476, p.482, p.635, p.657, p.662,
                p.663, p.666, p.669, v.5 p.701, v.6 p.436*
United States.; Bureau of the Budget. *v.4 p.248*

United States Census Bureau, Systems Support Division. *v.4 p.179*
United States Census Bureau *v.4 p.159*
United States Central Intelligence Agency *v.4 p.60, p.61*
United States; Clean Air Act Advisory Committee; United
    States; Environmental Protection Agency *v.5 p.355*
United States. Congress. House. Committee on Natural
    Resources *v.5 p.181, p.186*
United States Department of Agriculture, Agricultural Marketing
    Service *v.4 p.152, p.164*
United States Department of Agriculture, Economic Research
    Service. *v.4 p.152*
United States Department of Agriculture Foreign Agricultural
    Service *v.4 p.152, p.164*
United States Department of Agriculture *v.4 p.152*
United States Department of Commerce, International Trade
    Administration *v.4 p.161*
United States Department of Commerce. *v.4 p.60*
United States, Department of Defense Staff. *v.3 p.393*
United States Department of Education. *v.5 p.573*
United States Department of Health and Human Services, Office
    of Applied Studies, Substance Abuse and Mental Health
    Services Administration (SAMHSA) *v.4 p.777*
United States Department of State. *v.4 p.437, p.476*
United States; Environmental Protection Agency; Office of
    Policy, Planning, and Evaluation *v.5 p.182, p.187*
United States, General Accounting Office. *v.3 p.300*
United States Geological Survey. *v.5 p.450*
United States Green Building Council *v.4 p.159*
United States. National Commission on Excellence in
    Education *v.4 p.323*
United States, Naval History Division *v.3 p.414*
United States. President's Commission on Campus
    Unrest *v.4 p.332*
United States Senate *v.4 p.532, p.534*
United States. Supreme Court.. . . . . *v.4 p.437*
United States Tennis Association. *v.4 p.864*
United States.Congress. Senate. Committee on Appropriations.
    Subcommittee on Departments of Labor, Health and
    Human Services, Education, and Related Agencies. *v.4 p.337*
United Way *v.5 p.672*
Universities Federation for Animal Welfare Staff . . . *v.5 p.56*
University of Auckland Library *v.4 p.179*
University of California at Berkeley Wellness Lett & White,
    Timothy P. *v.4 p.791*
University of California, Berkeley *v.6 p.436*
University of California Museum of Paleontology, The
    Paleontological Society, Society of Vertebrate Paleontology,
    and United States Geological Survey *v.5 p.447*
University of California, Santa Barbara. *v.6 p.390*
University of Colorado at Boulder *v.5 p.548*
University of Hawaii at Manoa, Industrial Relation Staff. *v.4 p.123*
University of Illinois Communications Library . . . *v.4 p.141*
University of Michigan Documents Center *v.4 p.482*
University of Minnesota Human Rights Center *v.4 p.670*
University of Minnesota Law Library *v.4 p.477*
University of Surrey *v.4 p.675*

University of Toronto Press (Created by) *v.3 p.534*

Uno, Roberta (Editor) *v.1 p.69, p.122, p.125*

Uno, Roberta *v.6 p.99*

Unrue, Darlene Harbour. *v.2 p.110*

Unrue, Darlene H. *v.2 p.110*

Unruh, David R. *v.4 p.742*

Unruh, John D. Jr. *v.3 p.520*

Unsöld, Albrecht & Baschek, Bodo *v.5 p.65*

Unterberger, Betty Miller *v.3 p.188, p.189*

Unterecker, John E. (Editor) *v.2 p.327*

Unterecker, John E. *v.2 p.327*

Untermeyer, Louis *v.2 p.201*

Unwin, Tim *v.4 p.373*

Unwin, Timothy (Editor) *v.2 p.463, p.491, p.492*

Updike, John & Kenison, Katrina (Editors) . . . *v.2 p.27*

Updike, John. *v.1 p.683, v.2 p.157*

Upfield, Arthur. *v.2 p.749*

Upham, Frank K. *v.6 p.220*

Upham, Paul (Editor) *v.5 p.718*

Uphoff, Norman T. & Ilchman, Warren F. (Editors) . . *v.4 p.574*

Upor, Laszlo (Editor) *v.1 p.69, p.110*

Upton, Clive, et al. *v.2 p.558*

Upton, Dell *v.1 p.791*

Uraizee, Joya F. (Contribution by) *v.2 p.755, p.756*

Urbach, Reinhard. *v.2 p.615*

Urban, Joan Barth & Solovei, Valerii D. *v.4 p.599, p.600*

Urban Land Institute Staff *v.4 p.159, p.166*

Urban, Martin *v.1 p.748*

Urban, Wayne J. & Wagoner, Jennings L. *v.4 p.329*

Urban, Wayne J. *v.4 p.283*

Urbawski, Marie (Editor). *v.2 p.39*

Urben, Peter (Revised by). *v.5 p.312*

Urben, Peter. *v.5 p.312, p.682*

Urbina, Susana. *v.5 p.602*

Urciuoli, Bonnie *v.6 p.494, p.542*

Urdang, Stephanie *v.6 p.74*

Ure, Peter *v.2 p.327*

Uribe-Uran, Victor M. (Editor) *v.3 p.359*

Uribe-Uran, Victor M. *v.3 p.356*

Urmson, J. O. & Ree, Jonathan (Editors) *v.1 p.416*

Urofsky, Melvin I. & Finkelman, Paul (Editors). *v.4 p.440, p.441*

Urofsky, Melvin I. & Finkelman, Paul *v.4 p.452*

Urofsky, Melvin I. & Levy, David W. (Editors) . . . *v.4 p.469*

Urofsky, Melvin I. . . . *v.3 p.379, p.435, v.4 p.440, p.448, p.469*

Urquhart, Jane *v.2 p.739*

Urquidi, Marjory (Translator) *v.3 p.332*

Urrea, Luis Alberto. *v.4 p.765, v.6 p.504, p.530*

Urrutia, Miguel *v.3 p.359*

Urton, Gary *v.3 p.262*

U.S. Census Bureau *v.4 p.482, p.679*

U.S. Commission on Civil Rights *v.6 p.702*

U.S. Department of Agriculture. *v.5 p.51*

U.S. Department of Education. *v.4 p.323*

U.S. Department of Health and Human
    Services *v.5 p.672, v.6 p.702*

U.S. Department of Labor Staff *v.4 p.168*

U.S. Department of State   *v.4 p.482, p.561, p.566, p.643, p.670*

U.S. Dept. of Energy, Office of Scientific and Technical
    Information. *v.5 p.394*

U.S. Geological Survey EROS Data Center. *v.5 p.421*

U.S. Geological Survey . . *v.5 p.417, p.428, p.435, p.451, p.452*

U.S. Government Accountability Office (GAO) *v.4 p.481*

U.S. Government Printing Office. *v.4 p.482*

U.S. House of Representatives, Committee on Ways and
    Means *v.5 p.672*

U.S. National Bureau of Standards. *v.5 p.287*

U.S. Naval Observatory *v.5 p.63*

U.S. Navy. Dudley Knox Library. Naval Postgraduate
    School *v.4 p.565*

Usborne, Richard. *v.2 p.390*

USDA Forest Products Staff. *v.5 p.691*

Useem, Michael *v.4 p.90*

USGS World Energy Assessment Team. *v.5 p.451*

Usigli, Rodolfo. *v.2 p.669*

Usmiani, Renate *v.2 p.541*

Usner, Daniel H. Jr. *v.3 p.506*

Ustin, Susan L. *v.4 p.389*

Usukawa, Saejo *v.6 p.360*

Utermark, Walther; Schicke, Walter *v.5 p.291*

Utley, Robert
    Marshall. *v.3 p.402, p.509, p.520, p.521, p.528, v.6 p.684, p.687, p.688*

Uttal, William R. *v.5 p.594, p.606, p.618*

Utter, Glenn H. *v.4 p.449*

Utterback, Paul J. & Nelson, David A. (Editors) . . . *v.5 p.315*

Utz, Peter *v.1 p.388*

Uviller, H. Richard *v.4 p.471*

Uyeda, Akinari. *v.6 p.234*

Uyemura, John P. *v.5 p.723*

V

Vacalopoulos, Apostolos E. *v.3 p.191*

Vacca, Richard T. & Vacca, Jo Anne L. *v.4 p.366*

Vacca, Richard T., et al. *v.4 p.361*

Vaccari, David A., et al. *v.5 p.705*

Vaccari, John A., et al. *v.5 p.691*

Vaccaro, Richard *v.5 p.712*

Vacek, Edward C. *v.1 p.651*

Vacha, Keith. *v.6 p.380*

Vaculik, Ludvik *v.2 p.784*

Vaderlind, Paul, et al. *v.5 p.460, p.469*

Vaggi, Gianni *v.4 p.217*

Vagi, David L. *v.3 p.22*

Vagts, Alfred *v.3 p.36*

Vaid, Urvashi *v.6 p.388*

Vaidhyanathan, Siva *v.4 p.761*

Vaidya, Ashish K. *v.4 p.56, p.58, p.181*

Vaidyanathan, Seetharaman (Editor), et
    al. *v.5 p.108, p.143, p.147, p.152*

Vaihinger, H. *v.1 p.469*

Author Index

Vail, Leroy (Editor) *v.6 p.75*

Vaillant, Janet G.. . . . . *v.2 p.543*

Vaitheeswaran, Vijay V. *v.5 p.362, p.369, p.709*

Valafar, Faramarz (Editor) *v.5 p.98*

Valantasis, Richard *v.1 p.531*

Valavanis, Panos *v.3 p.15*

Valbuena Prat, Angel *v.2 p.639, p.645*

Valder, Peter *v.5 p.44*

Valderrama Fernández, Ricardo *v.3 p.332*

Valdes, Dennis N. *v.6 p.525*

Valdes, Isabel & Seoane, Marta *v.4 p.136*

Valdes, Isabel *v.6 p.526*

Valdes, M. Isabel *v.4 p.139, v.6 p.526*

Valdes, Mario J. & Kadir, Djelal. *v.2 p.665*

Valdez, Luis *v.1 p.125, v.6 p.504, p.518*

Valdez, Stephen & Wood, Julian . *v.4 p.58, p.98, p.102, p.103*

Valdés, Dionicio Nodín. *v.6 p.536, p.550*

Valdés Domínguez, Fermín & Stebbins, Consuelo E. . *v.3 p.313*

Valdés, Guadalupe *v.4 p.311, p.312, v.6 p.528*

Valdés, Zoé *v.2 p.673*

Valdivia, Angharad N. (Editor) *v.6 p.448*

Valdivia, Angharad N. *v.6 p.449, p.494*

Vale, Brian *v.3 p.277*

Vale, Lawrence J. & Campanella, Thomas J.. *v.4 p.760, v.6 p.729*

Vale, Lawrence J.. . . . . *v.4 p.757, v.6 p.726*

Valelly, Richard M. *v.3 p.522, v.6 p.8, p.32*

Valencia, Reynaldo Anaya *v.4 p.458, v.6 p.541*

Valencia, Richard R. (Editor) *v.4 p.311, v.6 p.528*

Valensi, Lucette *v.6 p.623, p.642*

Valenta, Jiri & Ellison, Herbert J. *v.3 p.321*

Valentine, Penny & Wickham, Vicki *v.6 p.410*

Valentine, Richard *v.5 p.725*

Valentini, Riccardo (Editor) *v.5 p.178*

Valentino, Benjamin A. *v.4 p.654, p.715, v.6 p.257*

Valenty, Linda O. & Feldman, Ofer (Editors) *v.5 p.645*

Valenzuela, Arturo *v.3 p.350*

Valera, Juan *v.2 p.655*

Valesio, Paolo *v.2 p.716*

Valéry, Paul *v.2 p.528*

Vali, Abbas (Editor) *v.6 p.600*

Vali, Abbas *v.6 p.600, p.630*

Valiela, Ivan. *v.5 p.399, p.409*

Valier, Claire. *v.6 p.247*

Valis, Noel & Maier, Carol (Editors) *v.2 p.639*

Valis, Noel M. *v.2 p.655*

Valis, Noël Maureen *v.2 p.655*

Valk, Arnoud van der *v.4 p.393*

Valk, Barbara G. (Editor) *v.6 p.684, p.693*

Vallacher, Robin R. & Nowak, Andrzej . . . *v.5 p.586, p.622*

Vallega, Adalberto *v.5 p.430*

Valle-Inclán, Ramón del *v.2 p.663*

Vallejo, Antonio Buero *v.2 p.656, p.657*

Vallejo, César & Fogden, Barry *v.2 p.685*

Vallejo, César, et al. *v.2 p.685*

Vallejo, César *v.2 p.685*

Vallely, Fintan *v.1 p.163, p.299*

Vallentine, John F. *v.5 p.42, p.43*

Vallieres, Pierre *v.3 p.536*

Valls, Andrew (Editor) *v.4 p.484*

Valls, Andrew *v.4 p.484, p.627*

Valmiki, Omprakash & Mukherjee, Arun Prabha. *v.6 p.149, p.153*

Valocchi, Stephen & Corber, Robert J. (Editors). . . . *v.6 p.357*

Valsaraj, Kalliat T. *v.5 p.705, p.712*

Vamplew, Wray (Editor), et al.. . . . . *v.4 p.824*

Vamplew, Wray *v.4 p.810, p.898, p.899*

Van Aken, Mark J. *v.3 p.333*

Van Alphen, Ernst *v.1 p.749*

Van Alstyne, Richard Warner *v.3 p.382*

van Assendelft, Laura *v.4 p.569*

Van Belle, Gerald, et al. *v.5 p.90, p.93*

Van Beusekom, Monica M.. . . . . *v.6 p.71*

Van Bottenburg, Marten. *v.4 p.845*

Van Bremen, Riet *v.6 p.451*

Van Briessen, Fritz *v.1 p.751*

Van Bruinessen, Martin *v.6 p.600*

Van Brunt, Bruce. *v.5 p.493*

Van Buitenen, J. A. & Dimmet, Cornelia (Editors) . . *v.1 p.537*

Van Buren, Martin *v.3 p.418*

Van Buren *v.1 p.637*

Van Cleve, Libby *v.1 p.394, p.399*

Van Dale *v.2 p.622*

Van Dalen, Deobold B. *v.4 p.797*

Van Dam, Nikolaos. *v.6 p.608*

Van Dam, Raymond *v.3 p.32*

Van De Graaff, John H., et al.. . . . . . . *v.4 p.295, p.296*

van de Leur, Walter *v.1 p.264, p.361*

Van de Mieroop, Marc *v.3 p.5, p.6*

Van De Vijver, Gertrudis, et al. *v.5 p.197*

Van de Walle, John *v.5 p.464*

Van Deburg, William L. *v.3 p.402, v.6 p.40, p.256*

Van Den Berg, Leo, et al. *v.6 p.726*

van Den Berg, Richard *v.4 p.205*

Van den Bergh, Jeroen C. (Editor) *v.4 p.62*

Van den Berghe, Pierre L. *v.4 p.684, p.729*

Van den Bosch, R., et al.. . . . . *v.5 p.27*

van den Broek, Antonie Gerard & Baker, William (Editors) *v.2 p.288*

Van den Toorn, Pieter C. *v.1 p.226, p.233, p.361*

Van Der Bliek, Rob (Editor) *v.1 p.264, p.342*

Van der Leeden, Frits (Editor), et al. *v.5 p.313*

Van der Linden, R. Robert *v.4 p.152, p.153*

Van der Merwe, Peter *v.1 p.175, p.275*

Van der Pluijm, Ben A. & Marshak, Stephen *v.5 p.442*

Van der Put, P. J. *v.5 p.303*

Van der Toorn, Karel (Editor), et al. *v.1 p.618*

Van der Tuin, J. D. *v.5 p.703*

van der Velde, Christiaan D.. . . . . *v.5 p.650*

Van der Woude, Ad (Editor), et al. *v.3 p.44*

Van Deursen, A. *v.3 p.205*

Van Deusen, Kira *v.2 p.793*

van Dijk, Jan *v.4 p.419*
Van Dijk, Teun A.. . . . . *v.4 p.21, p.731*
Van Doren, Mark *v.2 p.232, p.247*
Van Dorsten, Brent (Editor) *v.5 p.593*
Van Dover, J. Kenneth *v.2 p.580*
Van Driesche, Jason & Van Driesche, Roy G.. . . . . *v.5 p.182*
Van Duyn, Mona. *v.2 p.126*
Van Dyne, George M.. . . . . *v.5 p.42, p.358*
Van (Editor) *v.5 p.593*
Van Eeden, Frederik *v.2 p.623*
Van Engen, John *v.1 p.601*
Van Fraassen, Bas C.. . . . . *v.1 p.498, p.504*
Van Galen, Jane (Editor), et al. *v.4 p.296*
Van Gennep, Arnold *v.4 p.37*
Van Gerven, Walter *v.4 p.604, p.638*
van Ginneken, Jaap. . . *v.4 p.408, p.713,v.5 p.586, p.622, p.625*
Van Gogh, Vincent *v.1 p.749*
Van Gulik, Robert H.. . . . . *v.6 p.212*
Van Hear, Nicholas *v.4 p.765*
Van Hecke, Gerald R. & Karukstis, Kerry K.. . . . . *v.5 p.278*
Van Herk, Aritha *v.2 p.739*
Van Hoorn, Judith L., et al. *v.4 p.707*
Van Horn, Carl E. & Schaffner, Herbert A. (Author,
   Editors) *v.4 p.123*
Van Houten, R. & Axelrod, Saul (Editors) *v.5 p.667*
Van Ingen, John F. *v.1 p.504*
Van Inwagen, Peter *v.1 p.489, p.503*
Van Kemenade, Willem. *v.6 p.206*
Van Kirk, Sylvia *v.3 p.546*
Van Kley, Dale K. *v.3 p.151*
Van Lier, H. N. (Editor), et al.. . . . . *v.5 p.6*
van Lint, Jacobus H. & Wilson, Richard M. *v.5 p.479*
Van Loon, Jon C.. . . . . *v.5 p.273*
Van Norman Baer, Nancy *v.1 p.25*
Van Onselen, Charles. *v.6 p.77, p.79*
Van Orden, Kate *v.1 p.22*
Van Orman Quine, Willard *v.1 p.444*
Van Oss, Adriaan C. *v.3 p.298*
Van Pelt, Robert. *v.5 p.40*
Van Praagh, David *v.6 p.160*
Van Raalte, Judy L. & Brewer, Britton W.
   (Editors). *v.4 p.878, p.904, v.5 p.583*
Van Riper, Charles & Erickson, Robert L. *v.5 p.674*
Van Sant, John E. *v.6 p.120, p.133*
Van Sertima, Ivan (Editor). *v.6 p.9, p.11, p.12, p.19*
Van Sertima, Ivan. *v.6 p.9, p.48, p.49, p.51*
Van Spanckeren, Kathryn & Castro, Jan G.
   (Editors). *v.2 p.734, p.735*
Van Tine, Warren R. & Pierce, Michael D. (Editors). . *v.3 p.513*
Van Vechten, Carl *v.1 p.40, v.2 p.126*
Van Vlack, Lawrence H. *v.5 p.692*
Van Vliet, Willem (Editor) *v.6 p.709*
Van Vynckt, Randall (Editor) *v.1 p.784*
Van Wagoner, Richard S. *v.4 p.740, p.749*
Van Wart, Montgomery. *v.4 p.546, p.698*

Van West, Carroll (Editor). *v.3 p.511*
Van Wienen, Mark W.. . . . . *v.2 p.11*
Van Witsen, Leo *v.1 p.234, p.404*
Van Woerkens, Martine *v.6 p.149*
Van Wolferen, Karel *v.4 p.622*
Van Wyk, Ben-Erik *v.5 p.24, p.44, p.45*
Van Young, Eric *v.3 p.288*
Van Zijp, Rudy *v.4 p.233, p.234*
Van Zile, Judy A.. . . . . *v.1 p.17*
Van Zile, Judy *v.1 p.16*
Vanaik, Achin *v.4 p.618*
VanAlstyne, Judith S.. . . . . *v.5 p.681*
Vanbrugh, John *v.2 p.263*
VanBurkleo, Sandra F. (Editor), et al. *v.4 p.453*
VanBurkleo, Sandra F. *v.4 p.458*
Vance, Carole S. *v.4 p.749, v.6 p.447*
Vance, Cyrus R. *v.3 p.481*
Vance, Dennis E. & Vance, Jean E. (Editors) *v.5 p.111*
Vance, Eugène *v.2 p.468*
Vance, John A.. . . . . *v.2 p.264*
Vandeloise, Claude & Anselmo, Frank A.. . . . . . *v.2 p.454*
Vanden Auweele, Yves (Editor), et al. *v.4 p.797*
Vanden, Harry E. & Prevost, Gary *v.3 p.260*
Vandeputte, Omer *v.2 p.622*
Vander, Judith *v.1 p.297, v.6 p.699*
Vander Voort, George F. *v.5 p.734*
Vander Weg, etval.. . . . . *v.1 p.169, p.374*
Vanderbilt, Arthur T. *v.4 p.440*
Vanderbilt, Tom *v.4 p.870, p.881*
Vanderhaeghe, Guy. *v.2 p.739*
VanderKam, James C. & Flint, Peter W.. . . . . . *v.1 p.546*
VanderKam, James C. *v.1 p.619*
VanderLippe, John M. *v.6 p.625*
Vanderlugt, Anthony *v.5 p.701*
Vandermeer, John H. & Goldberg, Deborah Esther . . *v.5 p.171*
Vandermeer, John *v.5 p.137*
Vanderwerken, David L. & Wertz, Spencer K.
   (Editors). *v.4 p.803, p.812*
Vanderwood, Paul J. *v.3 p.289*
VanderZwaag, Harold J.. . . . . *v.4 p.886*
Vandewalle, Dirk. *v.6 p.641*
Vandiver, Frank E. *v.3 p.384*
VanDiver, Frank E. *v.3 p.384*
Vandiver, Frank E. *v.3 p.402, p.427, p.429, p.432,
                                   p.445, p.463, p.481*
Vando, Gloria *v.6 p.509, p.511*
Vangelisti, Anita L. (Editor). *v.5 p.622, p.639*
Vanhoozer, Kevin J. (Editor), et al.. . . . . . . *v.1 p.616*
Vanita, Ruth (Editor) *v.2 p.763, v.6 p.422*
Vann, J. Don & Van Ardsel, Rosemary. *v.6 p.742, p.753*
Vann, J. Don & VanArsdel, Rosemary T. (Editors) . . *v.2 p.728*
Vannatta, Dennis *v.2 p.135*
Vansina, Jan *v.6 p.61, p.65*
Vanstrum, Glenn S.. . . . . *v.5 p.241*

VanTassel-Baska, Joyce & Reis, Sally M.
(Editors) *v.4 p.317, p.318*

Vantuono, William (Translator) *v.2 p.204*

Varano, Charles S. *v.4 p.727*

Varela, Lucia G; Smith, Rhonda J.;Phillips, Phil A.; Purcell,
Alexander *v.5 p.53*

Varese, Louise *v.1 p.226, p.363*

Varey, Simon *v.2 p.248*

Varg, Paul A. *v.3 p.393*

Vargas Llosa, Mario & Grossman, Edith *v.2 p.686*

Vargas Llosa, Mario, et al. *v.2 p.645*

Vargas Llosa, Mario *v.2 p.685, p.686, v.3 p.332*

Vargas, Luis A. & Koss-Chioino, Joan D. (Editors) . *v.6 p.122*

Vargas, Luis Alberto & Long-Solis, Janet . *v.3 p.272, v.5 p.35*

Vargas, Zaragosa *v.4 p.255*

Vargo, Marc E. *v.6 p.410*

Vargyas, Lajos *v.1 p.299*

Varia, Radu *v.1 p.781*

Varian, H. R. *v.4 p.249*

Varisco, Daniel Martin *v.4 p.37*

Varley, Paul H. *v.6 p.220*

Varnedoe, Kirk *v.1 p.681, p.749*

Varon Gabar, Rafael *v.3 p.326*

Varon, Jeremy *v.3 p.445*

Varshney, Ashutosh *v.6 p.149, p.150*

Vasari, Giorgio. *v.1 p.676, p.689*

Vasilenko, Svetlana *v.2 p.810*

Vasiliev, Alexander A. *v.3 p.67*

Vasiliev, Alexander Alexandrovich *v.3 p.194*

Vasquez, Manuel A. & Marquardt, Marie F. *v.4 p.720*

Vasquez, Richard *v.6 p.504*

Vassanji, M. G. *v.2 p.759*

Vassiliev, Alexei *v.6 p.625*

Vasudev, Aruna, et al. *v.6 p.334*

Vasudeva, Somadeva (Editor) *v.1 p.129, p.131*

Vatanabadi, Shouleh & Khorrami, Mohammad Mehdi
(Editors) *v.6 p.673*

Vatican Council Two *v.1 p.571*

Vatikiotis, Michael R. J. *v.6 p.175, p.178*

Vatikiotis, P. J. *v.6 p.595, p.638, p.639*

Vatikiotis, Panayiotis J.. . . . . *v.3 p.196, v.6 p.57*

Vatsyayana, Mallanaga *v.6 p.153*

Vauchez, Andre (Editor) *v.6 p.555*

Vauclair, Jacques *v.5 p.615*

Vaudeville, Charlotte *v.6 p.153*

Vaughan, Alden T. & Vaughan, Virginia M. *v.2 p.232*

Vaughan, Alden T. (Editor) *v.3 p.486*

Vaughan, Alden T. *v.3 p.486, p.500, v.6 p.686*

Vaughan, David & Chapman, John V. (Editors) . . . *v.1 p.25*

Vaughan, David & Harris, Melissa *v.1 p.13*

Vaughan, David *v.1 p.13, p.25, p.29, p.31*

Vaughan, J. G., et al. *v.5 p.24*

Vaughan, Mary Kay (Editor) *v.3 p.296*

Vaughan, Richard (Editor) *v.3 p.99*

Vaughan, Virginia M.. . . . . *v.2 p.232*

Vaughan, William *v.1 p.733*

Vaughan-Whitehead, Daniel *v.3 p.252*

Vaughn, Jack A. (Editor) *v.2 p.245*

Vaughn, Karen I. *v.4 p.234*

Vaughn, Robie *v.4 p.846*

Vaughn, William *v.1 p.749*

Vavrus, Michael J. *v.4 p.280*

Vaz, Kim M. (Editor) *v.6 p.450*

Vazov, Ivan Minchov *v.2 p.780*

Vazquez de Espinosa, Antonio *v.3 p.404*

Vazquez, Francisco H. & Torres, Rodolfo D. *v.6 p.522*

Veal, A. J. (Editor), et al. *v.4 p.785, p.899*

Veatch, Robert M. *v.5 p.511*

Veblen, Thorstein B. & Ardzrooni, Leon *v.4 p.197*

Veblen, Thorstein B. *v.4 p.214, p.250, p.251, p.725*

Veblen, Thorstein *v.4 p.210, p.212, p.214, p.250, p.651*

Veccia, Susan H. *v.3 p.375*

Vecsey, Christopher & Starna, William A.
(Editors) *v.6 p.684, p.697*

Veenstra, Timothy D. & Smith, Richard D. (Editors) . *v.5 p.118*

Veeser, Cyrus *v.3 p.318*

Veeser, Harold (Editor) *v.2 p.571*

Vega, Bernardo *v.6 p.491, p.536, p.537*

Vega, Ed *v.6 p.509*

Vega, Garcilaso de la *v.2 p.652, v.3 p.404, p.405*

Vega, Gina *v.4 p.143, p.144*

Vega, Lope de & Zorrilla, Rojas. *v.1 p.69, p.75, p.108, v.2 p.653*

Vega, Lope de *v.2 p.653*

Vega, Marta Moreno *v.1 p.19, p.20,v.6 p.491, p.545*

Veitch, Jonathan *v.2 p.131*

Velarde-Mayol, Victor *v.1 p.470*

Velasquez, Roberto (Editor), et al. . *v.5 p.638, v.6 p.541, p.542*

Velez-Ibanez, Carlos G. . . *v.3 p.528, v.4 p.770, v.6 p.488, p.533*

Veli, Orhan *v.6 p.668*

Vella, Jane Kathryn *v.4 p.321*

Vella, Jane. *v.4 p.321*

Vella, Walter F. & Vella, Dorothy *v.6 p.172*

Vella, Walter F.. . . . . *v.6 p.172*

Vellacott, Philip *v.2 p.407*

Veloso, Caetano *v.1 p.295*

Veltman, M. G. *v.5 p.553*

Veltman, Martinus *v.5 p.553*

Vemuri, V. Rao. *v.5 p.407*

Venclova, Thomas *v.2 p.781*

Vendelin, George D., et al. *v.5 p.729*

Vendler, Helen H. *v.2 p.181, p.295, p.327*

Venegas, Daniel & Brammer, Ethriam C. *v.6 p.504*

Venes, Donald *v.5 p.509*

Venezky, Richard L. *v.2 p.558*

Veni, George, et al. *v.5 p.424*

Venkatesa Iyengar, Masti *v.6 p.153*

Vennum, Thomas Jr.. . . . *v.4 p.810, p.841, p.842, p.863*

Ventelou, Bruno *v.4 p.229*

Ventura, Gabriela Baeza *v.6 p.497*

Venturi, Franco *v.3 p.75*
Venturo, David F. *v.2 p.251*
Venuti, Lawrence *v.2 p.574, v.4 p.709*
Vera, Eugenia Roldan. *v.3 p.265*
Vera, Yvonne *v.2 p.752, p.759*
Verba, Ericka Kim *v.3 p.355*
Verba, Sidney & Nie, Norman H. *v.4 p.506, p.555, p.580*
Verba, Sidney, et al. *v.4 p.578, p.580*
Verbeek, Marno *v.4 p.205*
Verbitskaya, Anastasya *v.2 p.810*
Verbrugghe, Gerald P. & Wickersham, John M. *v.3 p.11*
Verderame, Lori *v.1 p.781*
Verdery, Katherine *v.3 p.185, p.208, p.251, v.4 p.42*
Verdi, Giuseppe *v.1 p.205, p.234, p.364, p.410*
Verdi, Richard *v.1 p.700*
Verdoorn, Frans (Editor) *v.5 p.210, p.211*
Verene, Donald Phillip *v.1 p.473*
Vereshchagin, Nikolai Konstantinovich & Shen, A. . *v.5 p.471*
Verga, Giovanni & Lan, David *v.2 p.713*
Verga, Giovanni *v.2 p.713*
Vergara, Camilo J. (Author, Photographer) *v.6 p.719*
Vergara, Camilo Jose *v.1 p.656*
Vergara, Jose M. & Varas, Florencia *v.3 p.356*
Vergason, Glenn A. & Anderegg, M. L. *v.4 p.317*
Verger, Fernand, et al. *v.5 p.720*
Vergote, A. *v.5 p.636*
Verhoeven, Ludo T. & Snow, Catherine E. (Editors) . *v.4 p.354*
Verissimo, Erico *v.2 p.693*
Verkade, John G. *v.5 p.277*
Verlaine, Paul M.. . . . . *v.2 p.503*
Verlaine, Paul *v.2 p.503*
Verma, K. D. *v.2 p.763*
Verma, Som Prakash *v.1 p.733*
Vermes, Geza (Translator) *v.1 p.546, p.620*
Vermes, Geza *v.1 p.641*
Vermeule, Emily T. *v.3 p.16*
Vermeulen, Han & Roldan, Arturo A. (Editors) . . . *v.4 p.5*
Vernadsky, George (Editor), et al. *v.3 p.210*
Vernadsky, George *v.3 p.215*
Vernallis, Carol *v.1 p.256*
Vernant, Jean-Pierre *v.3 p.15*
Verne, Jules *v.2 p.503, p.504*
Verner, Andrew M. *v.3 p.221*
Verner, Miroslav. *v.6 p.57*
Verney, Jack *v.4 p.581*
Vernon, Irene S. *v.6 p.702*
Vernon, Paul *v.1 p.299*
Vernon, Raymond *v.3 p.296*
Verschueren, Karel *v.5 p.312, p.363*
Versényi, Adam (Editor) *v.2 p.665*
Versluis, Arthur *v.6 p.701*
Verswijver, Leo *v.6 p.344*
Vertes, Attila; Nagy, Sandor; Klencsar, Zoltan. . . *v.5 p.308*
Vertinsky, Patricia A.. . . . . *v.4 p.810, p.838*
Vertova, Giovanna *v.4 p.398, p.399*

Very, Jones *v.2 p.53*
Vesalius, Andreas et al *v.5 p.510, p.511*
Vesilind, P. Aarne & Gunn, Alastair S. *v.5 p.705*
Vestal, Theodore M. *v.4 p.314, p.540*
Vettel-Becker, Patricia *v.1 p.765*
Vettriano, Jack *v.1 p.749*
Veyne, Paul *v.1 p.533*
Veysey, Laurence R. *v.4 p.333*
Vázquez, Diego *v.6 p.504*
Vögtle, Fritz (Editor), et al. *v.5 p.265*
Võ, Linda Trinh *v.6 p.108, p.121*
VGM Career Books Staff (Editor) *v.4 p.171*
VGM Career Books Staff *v.5 p.251*
Via, Dan O. & Gagnon, Robert A. J.. . . . . *v.1 p.618*
Vianna, Hermano *v.1 p.20, p.295*
Vibert, Conor *v.4 p.83*
Vicardo y Guzman, Juan Pablo *v.3 p.288*
Vicarelli, Fausto *v.4 p.229*
Vicente, Gil *v.2 p.689*
Vicinus, Martha (Editor). *v.3 p.116, v.6 p.749*
Vicinus, Martha. *v.2 p.177, p.194, v.4 p.738, v.6 p.466, p.468, p.749*
Vick, Brian E. *v.3 p.168*
Vickers, Adrian (Editor) *v.6 p.175, p.178*
Vickers, Adrian *v.6 p.178*
Vickers, Amy *v.5 p.19, p.380, v.6 p.286*
Vickers, Brian *v.2 p.232*
Vickers, Miranda *v.3 p.252*
Vickery, James D. *v.5 p.231*
Vickery, Olga W. *v.2 p.75*
Vickrey, William S.. . . . . *v.4 p.248*
Vickrey, William *v.4 p.247, p.248*
Vico, Giambattista *v.1 p.473, v.2 p.709*
Vicsek, Tamas & Vicsek, Thomas (Editors) *v.5 p.92*
Victor, David G. *v.6 p.299, p.301*
Victor, Edward & Kellough, Richard D. *v.4 p.366*
Victor, R. F. *v.4 p.229*
Vicuana Mackenna, Benjamin *v.3 p.351*
Vidal, Gore *v.2 p.127, p.128, v.6 p.399, p.404*
Vidal, Mary *v.1 p.749*
Vidaling, Raphaelle; McLuhan, Marshall *v.1 p.719*
Vidhyasekaran, P. *v.5 p.47*
Vidyasagar, M. & Spong, Mark W.. . . . . *v.5 p.712*
Vieira, Mark A. *v.6 p.314*
Viereck, Peter R. *v.2 p.126*
Vierhaus, Rudolf *v.3 p.167*
Viessman, Warren Jr. & Hammer, Mark J. . . . *v.5 p.369, p.380*
Vieth, Errol *v.6 p.320*
Vigarello, Georges *v.3 p.141*
Vigeland, Carl & Marsalis, Wynton *v.1 p.264, p.340*
Vigil, Ernesto B. *v.6 p.541*
Vigil, Evangelina. *v.6 p.504, p.511*
Vigil, James Diego. *v.4 p.714, p.715, v.6 p.125, p.547, p.550, p.551*
Vigil, Maurilio E. *v.6 p.539*
Vigil, Ralph H. (Editor), et al.. . . . . *v.3 p.529*
Vigil, Ralph H.. . . . . *v.3 p.318*

Vigne, Georges. *v.1 p.749*

Vigny, Alfred de *v.2 p.502*

Vigod, Bernard L. *v.4 p.581*

Vikers, Brian (Editor) *v.2 p.232*

Vila, Bryan & Morris, Cynthia (Editors) *v.4 p.487, p.568*

Vila, Pablo (Editor) *v.3 p.528*

Vila, Pablo. *v.4 p.727, v.6 p.488, p.522*

Viladesau, Richard *v.1 p.654*

Vile, John R.. . . . . *v.4 p.454*

Vile, M. J. *v.4 p.576*

Vilikovsky, Pavel. *v.2 p.812*

Villa, Dana (Editor) *v.4 p.493*

Villa, Jose G. *v.6 p.104, p.130*

Villa, Raúl Homero *v.6 p.504, p.516*

Villalon, Leonardo A. (Contribution by), et al. *v.6 p.72*

Villanueva, Victor (Editor) *v.2 p.565*

Villard, Henry Serrano & Allen, Willis M. Jr. *v.1 p.718*

Villard, Oswald Garrison *v.3 p.432*

Villarino, Jose Pepe *v.6 p.519*

Villaronga, Gabriel *v.3 p.321*

Villarreal, Jose A. *v.6 p.504*

Villaseñor, Victor. *v.6 p.504*

Villaurrutia, Xavier & Paz, Octavio *v.2 p.669*

Villaverde, Cirilo. *v.2 p.673*

Villedieu, Madame De *v.2 p.478*

Villella, Edward & Kaplan, Larry *v.1 p.13*

Villiers de l'Isle-Adam, P.. . . . . *v.2 p.503*

Villiers de l'Isle-Adam, Philippe A. *v.2 p.502*

Villon, Francois *v.2 p.469*

Villon, François *v.2 p.469*

Vinat de la Mata, Raquel *v.3 p.314*

Vinay, Jean-Paul & Darbelnet, Jean *v.2 p.454*

Vince, Ronald W.. . . . . *v.1 p.78, p.106*

Vincent, David *v.2 p.577, v.3 p.37, p.38, p.116, p.120, p.129, p.132, v.6 p.738, p.739, p.743*

Vincent, Jeffrey R. & Mäler, Karl-Göran (Editors). . *v.4 p.192*

Vincent, Joan (Editor) *v.4 p.35*

Vincent, Terrace *v.6 p.333*

Vincent, Thomas L. & Grantham, Walter J.. . . . . . *v.5 p.712*

Vincentelli, Moira *v.1 p.707*

Vincenti, Walter G.. . . . . *v.5 p.718*

Vineberg, Steve *v.6 p.313*

Vines, Lois D. (Editor). *v.2 p.50*

Viney, Ethna *v.4 p.749, v.6 p.447*

Viney, Michael *v.5 p.237*

Vining, Elizabeth G. *v.6 p.228*

Vinogradoff, Paul *v.4 p.433, p.501*

Vinovskis, Maris A. (Editor). *v.3 p.402*

Vinovskis, Maris A. *v.4 p.329, p.330*

Vinson, Ben *v.3 p.288*

Vinson, Betsy Partin *v.5 p.665, p.674*

Vinther, Janus *v.6 p.351*

Viola, Bill, et al. *v.1 p.773*

Viola, Bill *v.1 p.773*

Viola, Herman J. & Margolis, Carolyn J. (Editors) . . *v.3 p.273*

Viollet-le-Duc, Eugène-Emmanuel . . . *v.1 p.704, p.787, p.788*

Viqueira Alban, Juan Pedro *v.3 p.288*

Viramontes, Helena M. *v.6 p.504*

Virchow, Detlef (Editor) *v.5 p.9, p.24*

Virchow, Rudolf Ludwig Karl *v.5 p.514*

Vircondelet, Alain *v.2 p.517*

Virgil *v.2 p.447, p.448*

Virilio, Paul *v.6 p.323*

Viroli, Maurizio *v.3 p.200*

Viscomi, Joseph S. *v.2 p.240*

Viscusi, W. Kip (Editor) *v.4 p.110, p.112*

Vise, David A. & Malseed, Mark *v.4 p.68*

Visher, Emily B. & Visher, John S. *v.4 p.732*

Visram, Rozina. *v.6 p.158*

Visser, F. Th *v.2 p.555*

Visser, Hubregt. *v.5 p.729*

Visvanathan, Nalini. *v.6 p.458*

Viswanathan, Gauri. *v.2 p.763*

Viswanathan, T., et al. *v.1 p.290*

Vitebsky, Piers *v.4 p.772*

Vittorini, Elio *v.2 p.723*

Vittucci, Matteo M. & Goya, Carola *v.1 p.21*

Vivien, Renee *v.6 p.399*

Vizcarra Bordi, Ivonne *v.3 p.273*

Vizenor, Gerald R.. . . . . *v.2 p.20*

Vizentini, Paulo Gilberto Fagundes & Wiesebron, Marianne (Editors) *v.4 p.61*

Vlacic, Ljubo, et al. *v.5 p.716*

Vlastos, Gregory (Editor) *v.1 p.425*

Vlastos, Gregory *v.1 p.421, p.423, p.425*

Vlavianos, Haris *v.3 p.196*

Vlieghe, Hans *v.1 p.676, p.689*

Vlock, Deborah *v.2 p.285*

Vloyantes, John P. *v.3 p.236*

Vo, Linda Trinh & Bonus, Rick (Editors). *v.6 p.120*

Vo-Dinh. *v.5 p.118, p.220*

Voegelin, Eric & Wizer, James L. *v.1 p.469*

Voekel, Pamela *v.3 p.264, p.288*

Voet, Donald & Voet, Judith G. *v.5 p.328*

Vogel, A. I., et al. *v.5 p.292*

Vogel, Arthur Israel. *v.5 p.309*

Vogel, David *v.4 p.52, p.54, p.112*

Vogel, Ezra F.. . *v.4 p.725, v.6 p.181, p.195, p.197, p.206, p.220*

Vogel, Joseph O. *v.4 p.8*

Vogel, Morris J. *v.5 p.514*

Vogel, Paula *v.1 p.62, p.122, v.2 p.157*

Vogel, Ronald K. (Editor) *v.4 p.544, v.6 p.709*

Vogel, Steven K.. . . . . *v.6 p.220, p.221*

Vogel, Steven *v.4 p.908, v.5 p.564*

Vogel, Todd (Editor) *v.4 p.411*

Vogel, Virgil J.. . . . . *v.6 p.702*

Vogelsang, Willem *v.6 p.633*

Vogelsong, Diana L. *v.1 p.811*

Vogelstein, Bert & Kinzler, Kenneth W. *v.5 p.520*

Vogler, Richard *v.6 p.269*

Vogt, Christian (Photographer). *v.1 p.815*
Vogt, Eric W. *v.2 p.646*
Vogt, W. Paul *v.4 p.679*
Vogtle, Fritz (Editor), et al. *v.5 p.300*
Vohra, Rakesh *v.4 p.205*
Voiculescu, Vasile *v.2 p.818*
Voit, Eberhard O. *v.5 p.92, p.94, p.114*
Voit, Johannes *v.5 p.559*
Volavka, Zdenka *v.4 p.708*
Volk, Terese M. *v.1 p.406*
Volk, Tyler. *v.5 p.250*
Volkema, Roger *v.4 p.75*
Volkman, Toby Alice (Editor) *.v.4 p.708, v.6 p.110, p.111, p.125*
Volkmar, Fred R. (Editor), et al. *v.5 p.663*
Volkogonov, Dmitri. *v.3 p.224*
Volkov, Solomon *v.1 p.46*
Voll, John O.. . . . . *v.1 p.554*
Vollmann, William T. *v.4 p.751*
Volo, James M. & Volo, Dorothy Denneen *v.3 p.496*
Volosinov, V. N. *v.1 p.509*
Volpe, Edmond Loris *v.2 p.75*
Volpi, Frederic. *v.4 p.586, p.613*
Voltaire, Francois. *v.2 p.484*
Voltaire *v.1 p.454, p.455, v.2 p.484, p.485, v.3 p.148*
Volti, Rudi. *v.4 p.154, v.5 p.388*
Von Abele, Rudolph R. *v.3 p.427*
von Ankum, Katharina (Editor) *v.3 p.170*
von Aue, Hartmann. *v.2 p.595*
Von Baeyer, Hans Christian . . . *v.5 p.405, p.407, p.408, p.560*
Von Campenhausen, Hans *v.1 p.615, p.638*
Von Clausewitz, Carl *v.3 p.36*
Von der Osten, Gert & Vey, Horst *v.1 p.676, p.689*
Von Dittersdorf, Karl D. *v.1 p.192, p.321*
Von Drehle, David *v.4 p.129*
Von Fritz, Kurt. *v.4 p.490*
von Furer-Haimendorf, Christoph *v.6 p.155*
Von Glahn, Richard *v.6 p.186, p.187, p.206*
Von Goethe, Johann Wolfgang. *v.2 p.598*
Von Grimmelshausen, Hans J. *v.2 p.596*
Von Gunden, Heidi. *v.1 p.226, p.346*
Von Hartmann, Aue. *v.2 p.595*
von Heyking, John *v.4 p.490*
Von Hirsch, Andrew & Ashworth, Andrew (Editors). *v.6 p.272*
Von Hoff, Daniel D. & Hruban, Ralph H. *v.5 p.165*
Von Hofmannsthal, Hugo *v.2 p.609*
Von Kalnein, Wend *v.1 p.676, p.689*
Von Kleist, Heinrich *v.1 p.79, p.89, p.110*
Von Klemperer, Klemens *v.3 p.174*
Von Krafft-Ebing, Richard. *v.4 p.749, v.6 p.420*
von Krogh, Georg, et al. *v.4 p.79*
Von Laue, Theodore H.. . . . . *v.3 p.221, p.223*
Von Mehren, Joan *v.2 p.39*
Von Meier, Alexandra. *v.5 p.724*
von Metternich, Prince Clemens *v.3 p.184*
von Mises, Ludwig. *v.4 p.197, p.212*

Von Mises, Richard. *v.5 p.481*
Von Molnár, Stephan *v.5 p.566*
von Neumann, John & Morgenstern, Oskar *v.5 p.505*
Von Rad, Gerhard *v.1 p.620*
Von Rauch, Georg *v.3 p.256*
Von Reis, Siri V. & Schultes, Richard E. (Editors) . . . *v.5 p.16*
Von Rohr, John *v.1 p.584*
Von Rosenstiel, Helene & Winkler, Gail Caskey. *v.1 p.824, p.825*
Von Sneidern, Maja-Lisa *v.2 p.202*
von Soden, Wolfram *v.3 p.5*
Von Treitschke, Heinrich G.. . . . . *v.3 p.165*
Von Westernhagen, Curt *v.1 p.205, p.234, p.366*
Von Zelewsky, Alexander *v.5 p.304*
Vonnegut, Kurt. *v.2 p.158*
Voorhees, Richard J. *v.2 p.376*
Vora, Rajendra & Palshikar, Suhas (Editors) *v.4 p.618*
Vorenberg, Michael. *v.4 p.453*
Vorgrimler, Herbert *v.1 p.580*
Vorlicky, Robert *v.2 p.5, v.6 p.480*
Vose, Clement E.. . . . . *v.4 p.443*
Voss, Ralph F. (Editor) *v.2 p.135*
Voss-Hubbard, Mark *v.4 p.552, p.553*
Votolato, Gregory *v.1 p.714*
Vox *v.2 p.637*
Vrasidas, Charalambos & Glass, Gene V. (Editors) . *v.4 p.352*
Vrato, Elizabeth & Running Press Staff. *v.6 p.426*
Vreeland, James (Editor), et al. *v.4 p.262*
Vries, Jan De *v.3 p.42*
Vrkljan, Irena *v.2 p.818*
Vroom, Victor H.. . . . . *v.5 p.579*
Vryhof, Steven C. *v.4 p.308*
Vryonis, Speros Jr. *v.6 p.622*
Vryonis, Speros. *v.3 p.194, v.6 p.588*
Vuchic, Vukan R. *v.6 p.729*
Vucinich, Alexander S.. . . . . *v.3 p.45, p.223, v.5 p.393*
Vygotsky, L. S. *v.4 p.695, v.5 p.573, p.622, p.624*
Vyverberg, Henry. *v.3 p.148*

W

Wace, A. J. B. *v.2 p.415*
Wachman, Alan M.. . . . . *v.6 p.214*
Wachman, Gay *v.2 p.179, p.192*
Wachsmann, Nikolaus *v.3 p.174*
Wachtel, Andrew B. *v.2 p.800*
Wachtel, Andrew *v.2 p.819*
Wachtel, Michael. *v.2 p.793*
Wachtel, Nathan *v.3 p.325*
Wachtel, Paul L.. . . . . *v.5 p.585, p.667*
Wachterhauser, Brice R.. . . . . *v.1 p.507*
Wacker, Grant *v.1 p.587*
Wacks, Raymond. *v.1 p.491*
Wada, Yoko (Editor) *v.2 p.204*
Waddell, Helen. *v.2 p.450*

Waddell, Tom & Schaap, Dick. *v.4 p.839, v.6 p.384*

Waddington, Ivan *v.4 p.820, p.826*

Waddington, Miriam *v.2 p.739*

Waddington, P. A. J. *v.6 p.263*

Waddington, Raymond B. *v.2 p.707*

Waddock, Sandra; Graves, Samuel *v.4 p.54*

Wade, Bonnie C.. . . . . *v.1 p.284, p.290*

Wade, Christine J., et al. *v.3 p.300, p.303*

Wade, Mason *v.3 p.536*

Wade, Nicholas (Editor). *v.5 p.216*

Wade, Nicholas *v.5 p.137, p.143, p.152, p.598*

Wade, Peter *v.1 p.295, v.3 p.281, p.359, v.4 p.731*

Wade, Rex A. *v.3 p.221*

Wade, Richard C. *v.3 p.514*

Wade, Terence R.. . . . . *v.2 p.776*

Wadhams, Wayne *v.1 p.163, p.388*

Wadley, Susan S.. . . . . *v.6 p.155*

Waerden, Bartel L. van der *v.5 p.474*

Wagar, Jeannine *v.1 p.403*

Wagar, W. Warren *v.2 p.319*

Wagener, Hans. *v.2 p.592, p.616*

Wagenheim, Kal & De Wagenheim, Olga Jimenez
(Editors) *v.6 p.533*

Wagenknecht, Edward C.. . . . . *v.2 p.47*

Wagenknecht, Edward *v.2 p.47, p.308*

Wagg, Stephen *v.6 p.313*

Waggoner, Hyatt Howe *v.2 p.38*

Waghorne, Joanne P., et al. *v.1 p.538*

Wagman, Donald D. et al.(Editors). *v.5 p.302*

Wagman, Donald D.; Rossini, Frederick D.. . . . *v.5 p.287*

Wagman, Morton *v.5 p.589, p.590, p.591*

Wagner, Andreas *v.5 p.201*

Wagner, Ann L. *v.1 p.5*

Wagner, Anne Middleton *v.1 p.778*

Wagner, Anton; Bryan, Bonita J. Orosz. *v.2 p.731*

Wagner, Erica *v.2 p.353*

Wagner, Fritz W. (Editor), et al. *v.6 p.726*

Wagner, Harvey M.. . . . . *v.5 p.504*

Wagner, Heather Lehr. *v.6 p.600*

Wagner, Helmut R. *v.4 p.686*

Wagner, Richard *v.1 p.205, p.206, p.234, p.366,
p.367, p.403, p.410*

Wagner, Steven J. & Warner, Richard (Editors) . . . *v.1 p.516*

Wagner, Tony *v.4 p.330*

Wagner-Martin, Linda (Editor) *v.2 p.85*

Wagner-Martin, Linda. *v.2 p.117, p.122, v.6 p.404*

Wagoner, David *v.2 p.128*

Wagoner, Robert H. & Chenot, Jean-Loup *v.5 p.692*

Wahl, Elizabeth S. *v.2 p.173*

Wahrig, Gerhard *v.2 p.622*

Wahrman, Dror. *v.6 p.744*

Waidson, H. M. *v.2 p.620*

Wain, John (Editor). *v.2 p.201*

Wainwright, Clive *v.1 p.801*

Wainwright, Geoffrey & Westerfield Tucker, Karen B.
(Editors) *v.1 p.654*

Wainwright, Geoffrey (Editor), et al. *v.1 p.568*

Wainwright, Geoffrey. *v.1 p.637*

Wainwright, Peter C. & Reilly, Stephen M. (Editors) *v.5 p.197*

Wainwright, Stephen A. *v.5 p.92, p.156*

Waisman, Carlos H. & Peralta-Ramos, Monica
(Editors) *v.3 p.277, v.4 p.593*

Waisman, Carlos H. & Rein, Raanan (Editors) . . . *v.3 p.345*

Waismann, Friedrich *v.1 p.472, v.5 p.464, p.468*

Waite, P. B. *v.3 p.540, v.4 p.587*

Waite, Peter B.. . . . . *v.3 p.540*

Waith, Eugene M. *v.2 p.187, p.217*

Wake, Marvalee H. (Editor) *v.5 p.157*

Wakefield, Suzy Mygatt (Editor) *v.4 p.306, p.353*

Wakefield, Wanda Ellen. *v.4 p.810*

Wakelyn, Jon L. & Vandiver, Frank E. *v.3 p.427*

Wakelyn, Jon L. *v.4 p.526*

Wakeman, Frederic Jr. *v.6 p.191*

Wakerly, John F. *v.5 p.730*

Waksman, Gabriel (Editor) *v.5 p.118, p.220*

Waksman, Steve. *v.1 p.275, p.377, p.392*

Walbank, F. W.. . . . . *v.2 p.406*

Walbank, Frank W. *v.3 p.25*

Walbank, F.W. *v.2 p.406*

Walcott, Derek *v.2 p.576, p.770, p.771, p.773*

Wald, Elijah *v.1 p.264, p.334*

Wald, Kenneth D. & Calhoun-Brown, Allison. *v.1 p.606*

Wald Lasowski, Patrick (Editor) *v.2 p.464*

Wald, Michael S., et al. *v.4 p.756*

Waldau, Roy S. *v.1 p.118, p.146, p.150, p.153*

Walder, Andrew G. *v.4 p.509, v.6 p.195*

Walder, Dennis (Editor) *v.2 p.177, p.194*

Waldhorn, Arthur *v.2 p.86*

Waldinger, Roger *v.4 p.730, v.6 p.719*

Waldman, Anne *v.2 p.20, p.21, p.158*

Waldman, Carl & Wexler, Alan *v.4 p.379*

Waldman, Diane (Author, Editor) *v.6 p.310*

Waldmann, Herbert (Editor) *v.5 p.294*

Waldmeir, Joseph J. & Waldmeir, John C. (Editors). . . *v.2 p.66*

Waldmeir, Patti *v.6 p.79*

Waldner, J. B. *v.5 p.684*

Waldrep, Christopher (Editor) *v.6 p.252*

Waldron, Ann *v.2 p.130*

Waldron, Kenneth J. & Kinzel, Gary L. *v.5 p.715*

Waldron, Mary. *v.2 p.269*

Walecka, John Dirk. *v.5 p.553*

Walesa, Lech. *v.4 p.129*

Waley, Arthur D. (Editor) *v.6 p.210*

Waley, Arthur (Translator). *v.6 p.210*

Waley, Arthur . *v.1 p.418, v.6 p.188, p.203, p.204, p.208, p.212*

Waley, Daniel Philip & Denley, Peter *v.3 p.70*

Waley *v.1 p.565*

Walicki, Andrzej *v.3 p.211, p.253, v.4 p.509*

Walker, Alan *v.1 p.206, p.336*
Walker, Alice *v.2 p.158, v.6 p.28, p.47, p.399*
Walker, Barbara K.. . . . . *v.6 p.668*
Walker, Brian *v.1 p.702*
Walker, C. H. & Livingstone, D. R. *v.5 p.363, p.380*
Walker, Charles *v.3 p.265, p.326, p.327, p.328*
Walker, Cheryl *v.2 p.8*
Walker, Dale L. (Editor) *v.2 p.96*
Walker, Danielle Medina & Walker, Thomas *v.4 p.59*
Walker, David M. (Editor) *v.4 p.433*
Walker, David. *v.6 p.9, p.37*
Walker, Donald A. (Editor) *v.4 p.213, p.217*
Walker, E. Paul *v.6 p.588*
Walker, Gabrielle. *v.5 p.450*
Walker, George A.. . . . . *v.1 p.760*
Walker, Hallam *v.2 p.476*
Walker, J. Samuel & Wallace, Henry A. *v.3 p.463*
Walker, J. Samuel *v.5 p.364, p.412*
Walker, Janet A.. . . . . *v.6 p.234*
Walker, Janet *v.6 p.325*
Walker, Jearl. *v.5 p.541*
Walker, Jim *v.5 p.120*
Walker, John M.. . . . . *v.5 p.118*
Walker, John R. & Lundberg, Donald E. *v.4 p.165*
Walker, Julia. *v.1 p.83, p.86, p.118*
Walker, Lenore E. & Shapiro, David L. *v.5 p.593*
Walker, Lenore E. *v.4 p.743, p.759*
Walker, Margaret *v.2 p.128, v.6 p.47*
Walker, Mark *v.6 p.323*
Walker, Peter (Editor) *v.5 p.360, p.740*
Walker, Peter *v.1 p.817*
Walker, Ralph Charles Sutherland *v.1 p.462*
Walker, Rebecca Edby *v.6 p.428, p.436*
Walker, Samuel, et al. *v.6 p.257*
Walker, Samuel. *v.4 p.472, p.568, v.6 p.245, p.247*
Walker, Scott *v.2 p.27*
Walker, Shirley. *v.2 p.749*
Walker, Warren F. & Homberger, Dominique G. *v.5 p.89*
Walker, Warren F. Jr. & Homberger, Dominique G.. *v.5 p.89, p.157*
Walker *v.3 p.282*
Walker-Hill, Helen *v.1 p.282, v.6 p.30, p.35, p.47*
Walker-Moffat, Wendy *v.4 p.311, v.6 p.109*
Walkowitz, Daniel J. (Editor) *v.3 p.300, p.303*
Walkowitz, Judith R.. . . . *v.3 p.54, v.4 p.749, v.6 p.471, p.749*
Wall, Cheryl A. *v.6 p.28, p.47*
Wall, Cynthia (Editor) *v.2 p.173*
Wall, James T.. . . . . *v.3 p.382*
Wall, Joseph Frazier *v.3 p.522*
Wall, Robert *v.5 p.162*
Wall, William Douglas *v.4 p.359*
Wallace, Alfred R. *v.5 p.197*
Wallace, Anthony F.. . . . . . *v.4 p.25, p.37, v.6 p.684, p.704*
Wallace, Aurora *v.4 p.411*
Wallace, David (Editor) *v.2 p.169, v.6 p.566*
Wallace, David J.. . . . . *v.2 p.702*

Wallace, David Rains *v.3 p.46, p.270, v.5 p.197*
Wallace, David. *v.2 p.210*
Wallace, Deborah. *v.5 p.320*
Wallace, Edgar *v.2 p.386*
Wallace, Ernest, et al.. . . . . *v.3 p.509*
Wallace, Ian *v.5 p.682*
Wallace, Joseph E. *v.5 p.238*
Wallace, Kendra R. *v.6 p.109, p.125*
Wallace, Lew *v.2 p.128*
Wallace, Maurice O.. . . . . *v.6 p.41*
Wallace, Michelle *v.6 p.41, p.47*
Wallace, Patricia M. *v.5 p.588*
Wallace, Patricia W. & McCormick, N.. . . . . . *v.3 p.463*
Wallace, Phyllis A., et al. *v.4 p.271*
Wallace, R. Jay *v.1 p.503*
Wallace, Richard (Editor) *v.4 p.171*
Wallace, Robert L. & Taylor, Walter K. *v.5 p.213*
Wallace, Robert *v.4 p.69*
Wallace, Robin *v.1 p.206, p.308*
Wallace, Ruth A. (Editor) *v.4 p.744*
Wallace, Willard Mosher *v.3 p.414*
Wallace-Hadrill, Andrew *v.2 p.444*
Wallace-Hadrill, J. M. *v.3 p.67*
Wallace-Sanders, Kimberly (Editor) *v.6 p.437, p.449*
Wallach, Bret *v.4 p.399*
Wallach, Michael A. & Kogan, Nathan . *v.5 p.629, p.630, p.631*
Wallach, Yona *v.6 p.652*
Wallenberg, Raoul *v.3 p.187*
Waller, Derek *v.4 p.118*
Waller, Edmund *v.2 p.264*
Waller, Gregory A. (Editor) *v.6 p.320*
Waller, J. Michael *v.3 p.300*
Waller, James *v.4 p.654, p.698, v.6 p.257, p.258*
Waller, Willard W. *v.4 p.732*
Wallerstein, Immanuel. *v.3 p.42, v.4 p.680, p.759, p.762*
Wallerstein, Judith S., et al. *v.5 p.640*
Wallert, Arie (Editor), et al. *v.1 p.751*
Wallimann, Isidor & Dobkowski, Michael N. (Editors). *v.4 p.654*
Wallin, Nils L. (Editor), et al. *v.1 p.284*
Walling, Gerald C. *v.2 p.351*
Walling, Karl-Friedrich *v.4 p.493*
Wallis, Geoff & Wilson, Sue *v.1 p.171, p.299*
Wallis, Lawrence B. *v.2 p.217*
Wallis, Michael & Mankiller, Wilma. *v.6 p.690, p.693*
Wallmann, Jeffrey M.. . . . . *v.6 p.325*
Walls, Andrew F.. . . . . *v.1 p.647, p.648*
Walmsley, Andrew S.. . . . . *v.3 p.488*
Walmsley, Sean A. (Editor) *v.5 p.229, p.246*
Walpole, Horace *v.2 p.264, v.3 p.108, p.109, p.110, p.130*
Walpole, Josephine *v.1 p.726*
Walpole, Ronald E., et al. *v.5 p.481, p.501, p.683*
Walras, Leon *v.4 p.197, p.213, p.217*
Walraven, Klaas van *v.4 p.631*
Walser, Hans. *v.5 p.496*
Walser, Martin *v.2 p.619*

Walser, M.. *v.2 p.619*

Walser, Robert (Editor) *v.1 p.264*

Walser, Robert *v.1 p.275*

Walsh, Anthony & Ellis, Lee (Editors) *v.6 p.250*

Walsh, Anthony *v.6 p.257*

Walsh, Catherine E. *v.6 p.494, p.495, p.528*

Walsh, Froma (Editor) *v.5 p.639*

Walsh, George, et al.. . . . . *v.4 p.65*

Walsh, James (Editor). *v.1 p.653*

Walsh, John Evangelist *v.2 p.50, p.296*

Walsh, Lawrence E. *v.3 p.445, p.481*

Walsh, Margaret *v.3 p.519*

Walsh, Mary R. (Editor) *v.6 p.430, p.446*

Walsh, Mary-Paula *v.6 p.460*

Walsh, Michael J. (Editor) *v.1 p.613*

Walsh, P. G. (Editor) *v.2 p.436*

Walsh, P. G.. . . . . *v.2 p.436, p.450*

Walsh, P. *v.2 p.425*

Walsh, Stephen *v.1 p.226, p.227, p.237, p.361*

Walsh, Vivian & Gram, Harvey N.. *v.4 p.206, p.218, p.224, p.271*

Walsh, W. Bruce & Heppner, Mary J. (Editors) . *v.4 p.306, p.354*

Walsh, W. Bruce & Savickas, Mark (Editors). *v.4 p.306, v.5 p.578*

Walsh, W. Bruce (Editor), et al. *v.5 p.588*

Walsh, William *v.2 p.763, p.765*

Walshe, Maurice O'C. (Maurice O'Connell) . . . *v.2 p.589*

Walter, Barbara F. *v.4 p.651*

Walter, Jennifer & Klein, Eran (Editors) *v.5 p.250*

Walter, John & Schofield, Roger S. (Editors). . . . *v.3 p.43*

Walter, Lynn & Desai, Manisha (Editors) *v.4 p.679*

Walter, Lynn (Editor) *v.6 p.432*

Walter, Mariko Namba. *v.4 p.37*

Walter, Richard J. *v.3 p.356*

Walters, D. Gareth *v.2 p.639, p.640*

Walters, F. P. *v.4 p.632*

Walters, Michael *v.5 p.81, p.216*

Walters, Reece. *v.6 p.246, p.247*

Walters, Ronald G.. . . . . *v.3 p.402, p.421*

Walters, Ronald W. & Johnson, Cedric. *v.6 p.32, p.35*

Walters, Ronald W. & Smith, Robert C. *v.6 p.41*

Walters, Ronald W. . *v.4 p.519, p.555, p.556, p.573, v.6 p.9, p.32*

Walters, Suzanna Danuta *v.6 p.366, p.369*

Walters, Suzanna D.. . *v.4 p.738, v.6 p.428, p.436, p.449, p.468*

Walthall, Anne *v.6 p.228*

Waltham, David *v.5 p.420*

Waltham, Tony *v.5 p.422*

Walton, Anthony *v.3 p.506*

Walton, Douglas N.. . . . . *v.1 p.493*

Walton, Douglas *v.1 p.493*

Walton, Hanes Jr & Smith, Robert C. *v.6 p.32*

Walton, Hanes Jr.. . . . . *v.4 p.529*

Walton, Hanes *v.4 p.574*

Walton, Harold F.; Rocklin, Roy D. *v.5 p.269*

Walton, Harold Frederic. *v.5 p.304*

Walton, Izaak *v.3 p.90*

Walton, J. Michael, et al. *v.1 p.72, p.89*

Walton, John *v.4 p.697, p.759*

Walton, Richard E., et al. *v.4 p.123*

Walton, Stuart *v.4 p.777*

Waltz, Kenneth N. *v.4 p.625, p.627*

Walvin, James. *v.3 p.93*

Walz, Garry Richard & Bleuer, Jeanne *v.5 p.602*

Walz, Wolfgang *v.5 p.118, p.163*

Walzel, Oskar F. *v.2 p.590*

Walzer, Lee *v.6 p.388*

Walzer, Michael *v.4 p.511, p.513, p.514*

Wandycz, Piotr S. *v.3 p.253, p.254, p.393*

Wandycz, Piotr Stefan *v.3 p.207*

Wandycz, Piotr Stephan, et al.. . . . . *v.3 p.253*

Wang, Chu-Kia & Salmon, Charles G. *v.5 p.696*

Wang, David & Tai, Jeanne (Editors). *v.6 p.213*

Wang, Jason T. L. (Editor), et al.. . . . . *v.5 p.98, p.143, p.147*

Wang, Jing & Barlow, Tani E. (Editors) *v.6 p.335*

Wang, Jing *v.6 p.198, p.208*

Wang, Joseph *v.5 p.273*

Wang, Ke-wen (Editor). *v.6 p.191, p.195*

Wang, L. G. (Editor) *v.6 p.259*

Wang, Lawrence K. *v.5 p.707*

Wang, Z. L. (Editor), et al. *v.5 p.692*

Wangermann, Ernst. *v.3 p.183*

Wangersky, Peter J. (Editor) *v.4 p.393*

Wangersky, Peter J. (Volume Editor) *v.4 p.393*

Wannenwetsch, Bernd *v.1 p.654*

Wansbeek, Tom J. & Meijer, Erik *v.4 p.205*

Waplington, Nick. *v.1 p.773*

Wapner, Paul & Falk, Richard A. *v.4 p.484, p.485, p.627*

Wappingers Central School District *v.4 p.287*

Warburg, Aby M.. . . . . *v.1 p.676*

Warburg, Gabriel *v.6 p.640*

Warburton, Christopher *v.4 p.384*

Warburton, Nigel (Editor) *v.1 p.769*

Ward, Aileen. *v.2 p.296*

Ward, Alan *v.5 p.223*

Ward, Allen M. *v.3 p.26, p.27*

Ward, Artemus *v.4 p.540*

Ward, Barbara (Editor), et al. *v.4 p.260, p.271*

Ward, Barbara *v.4 p.267, p.271*

Ward, Ben *v.2 p.553*

Ward, Benedicta *v.6 p.573*

Ward, C. *v.3 p.306*

Ward, Charles E.. . . . . *v.2 p.247*

Ward, Christopher *v.3 p.410*

Ward, Colleen A. (Editor) *v.5 p.638*

Ward, David *v.2 p.722*

Ward, Evan R. *v.3 p.270*

Ward, Geoffrey C. & Burns, Kenneth *v.4 p.810, p.852*

Ward, Geoffrey C. (Contribution by, Narrated by) . . . *v.3 p.519*

Ward, Geoffrey C. *v.3 p.463, v.6 p.41*

Ward, Harry M. *v.3 p.500*

Ward, J. V. & Uehlinger, U. *v.5 p.178*

Ward, James G. & Anthony, Patricia (Editors) *v.4 p.281*

Ward, Jennifer. *v.3 p.51*

Ward, John & Peppard, Joe *v.4 p.115*

Ward, John William *v.3 p.418*

Ward, Keith *v.1 p.597*

Ward, Kennan *v.5 p.235*

Ward, Lawrence *v.5 p.609*

Ward, Lester F. & Gerver, Israel (Introduction by). . . *v.4 p.686*

Ward, Lester F.. . . . . *v.4 p.684*

Ward, Maisie. *v.2 p.278*

Ward, Margaret *v.3 p.135, p.139*

Ward, Mary J. *v.2 p.128*

Ward, Michael *v.4 p.636*

Ward, Nathaniel *v.2 p.30*

Ward, Peter D. & Brownlee, Donald *v.5 p.74, p.75, p.77*

Ward, Peter D. *v.5 p.450, v.6 p.294*

Ward, Peter M.. . . . . *v.6 p.551*

Ward, R. Gerard & Kingdon, Elizabeth (Editors) . . . *v.4 p.43*

Ward, Robert David & Rogers, William Warren. . . . *v.4 p.542*

Ward, Simon. *v.1 p.106*

Ward, Stephen J. A. *v.4 p.406*

Ward, Stephen V.. . . . . *v.6 p.715*

Ward, W. R. *v.1 p.590*

Ward, W. Reginald *v.1 p.649*

Ward, William S. *v.2 p.14*

Wardale, Edith E. *v.2 p.551*

Warder, A. K. *v.1 p.563*

Wardhaugh, Robert A. *v.3 p.546*

Wardhaugh, Ronald *v.2 p.553, p.558*

Ward-Jackson, Peter *v.5 p.197*

Wardlaw, Alastair C.. . . . . *v.5 p.93*

Wardlaw, Grant *v.4 p.662*

Wardle, David A.. . . . . *v.6 p.292*

Wardle, Lynn D. (Editor), et al. *v.6 p.389*

Wardlow, Daniel L. (Editor). *v.6 p.383*

Ward-Perkins, Bryan. *v.3 p.32*

Ward-Perkins, J. B.. . . . . *v.1 p.671*

Wardwell, Allen *v.1 p.683, v.6 p.679, p.701*

Wardy, Robert *v.1 p.421*

Ware, Alan *v.4 p.550, p.553*

Ware, Clifton *v.1 p.396, p.406*

Ware, Leslie *v.4 p.144*

Ware, Susan & Braukman, Stacy (Editors) *v.6 p.426*

Ware, Timothy *v.1 p.570*

Warf, Barney (Editor). *v.4 p.396*

Warhol, Robyn R. & Herndl, Diane P.
(Editors) *v.2 p.569, v.6 p.480*

Warhol, Robyn R. *v.4 p.695*

Warhurst, John & MacKerras, Malcolm (Editors) . . . *v.4 p.624*

Wark, McKenzie *v.4 p.761*

Warlaumont, Hazel G. *v.4 p.141*

Warman, Arturo *v.3 p.273, v.5 p.24*

Warmbrunn, Erika *v.1 p.124*

Warmbrunn, Werner *v.3 p.205, p.206*

Warmington, E. H. (Editor) . . . *v.2 p.425, v.3 p.32, p.33, p.35*

Warmus, William, et al.. . . . . *v.1 p.782*

Warner, Elizabeth *v.1 p.534*

Warner, Ezra J.. . . . . *v.3 p.427*

Warner, Janet *v.2 p.240*

Warner, Keith Q. (Editor) *v.2 p.538*

Warner, Lloyd W. & Low, V. O.. . . . . *v.4 p.708*

Warner, Marina *v.6 p.189, p.203, p.217, p.573*

Warner, Michael (Editor) *v.1 p.650, v.2 p.28*

Warner, Michael *v.6 p.389*

Warner, Pamela *v.1 p.716, p.809*

Warner, Sam Bass Jr. *v.3 p.492, v.6 p.296*

Warner, Sylvia Townsend *v.2 p.387*

Warner, Timothy *v.1 p.275*

Warner, Tom *v.4 p.712*

Warner, W. Lloyd *v.4 p.725*

Warner, William B. *v.2 p.259*

Warner, William L. & Lunt, Paul S. *v.4 p.725*

Warner, William L. *v.4 p.708*

Warner, William W.. . . . . *v.5 p.231*

Warneryd, Karl Erik *v.4 p.246, p.251*

Warnlock, Geoffrey. *v.1 p.447*

Warnock, Geoffrey J. *v.1 p.447*

Warnock. *v.1 p.450*

Warr, Mark *v.6 p.256, p.257*

Warr, Wendy A. (Editor), et al. *v.5 p.260*

Warrack, John. *v.1 p.206, p.234, p.247, p.367*

Warren, Austin *v.2 p.569, v.3 p.486*

Warren, Carol A.. . . . . *v.6 p.367*

Warren, Charles (Editor) *v.6 p.310*

Warren, Charles *v.4 p.440*

Warren, Christian. *v.5 p.363, p.372, v.6 p.297*

Warren, David B. & Museum of Fine Arts Staff. . . . *v.1 p.801*

Warren, Donald R.. . . . . *v.4 p.281, p.324*

Warren, Earl *v.4 p.469*

Warren, Elizabeth & Tyagi, Amelia Warren *v.4 p.98*

Warren, Gordon H. *v.3 p.433*

Warren, Harris G. *v.3 p.344*

Warren, Henry Clarke. *v.1 p.564*

Warren, J. K.. . . . . *v.5 p.451*

Warren, James. *v.2 p.14*

Warren, Jonathan W. *v.3 p.343*

Warren, Karen S. & Cady, Duane L. (Editors) *v.6 p.471*

Warren, Larry *v.1 p.13*

Warren, Lynne (Editor) *v.1 p.762*

Warren, Michelle P. & Shangold, Mona M.. . . *v.4 p.826, p.878*

Warren, Patricia N. *v.6 p.399*

Warren, Raymond *v.1 p.234, p.404*

Warren, Richard A.. . . . . *v.3 p.288*

Warren, Robert Penn & Brooks, Cleanth *v.2 p.579*

Warren, Robert Penn *v.2 p.7, p.12, p.129*

Warren, W. L. *v.3 p.99*

Warren, Warren S. *v.5 p.277*

Warren, Wini. *v.5 p.396*

Warrior, Robert *v.6 p.699*

Warshaw, Matt.. . . . . *v.4 p.788, p.868*

Warshaw, Shirley Anne *v.4 p.528*

Warshawsky, David (Editor) *v.5 p.129, p.143*

Wartick, Steven L. & Wood, Donna J. *v.4 p.145*

Warton, Thomas *v.2 p.216*

Warung, Price *v.2 p.749*

Warwick, Ronald *v.2 p.728*

Wasburn, Philo C. *v.4 p.408*

Washburn, Dennis & Cavanaugh, Carole (Editors) . . *v.6 p.337*

Washburn, Dorothy K. & Crowe, Donald W. *v.1 p.721*

Washburn, Dorothy Koster & Crowe, Donald W.
(Editors) *v.1 p.704, p.714*

Washburn, Margaret F. *v.5 p.616*

Washburn, Michael *v.5 p.636*

Washburn, Wilcomb E. *v.3 p.500, v.4 p.465, v.6 p.693*

Washburne, Christopher J. & Derno, Maiken (Editors). *v.1 p.383*

Washington, Booker T. & Du Bois, W. E. B. *v.6 p.9*

Washington, Booker T. *v.2 p.53*

Washington, Booker T *v.6 p.19, p.32*

Washington, George *v.2 p.30*

Washington, Peter (Editor) *v.2 p.272*

Washofsky, Mark *v.1 p.552, p.553*

Waskow, Arthur I. & Waskow, Howard . . . *v.5 p.629, p.631*

Wasowski, Andy; Wasowski, Sally; Morrison, Darrel G. *v.1 p.824*

Wasserman, David & Wachbroit, Robert (Editors) . . *v.6 p.254*

Wasserman, Earl R. & Bennett, Betty T. *v.2 p.312*

Wasserman, George *v.2 p.242*

Wasserman, Gerhard (Editor) *v.5 p.250*

Wasserman, Jack *v.1 p.749*

Wasserman, Mark *v.3 p.265, p.289, p.290, p.296*

Wasserstein, Bernard *v.6 p.613*

Wasserstein, Bruce *v.4 p.85, p.92*

Wasserstein, Wendy *v.1 p.122, v.2 p.158*

Wasserstrom, Jeff *v.6 p.206*

Wasserstrom, Jeffrey N. *v.6 p.191, p.206*

Wasson, Haidee *v.6 p.331, p.332*

Waste, Robert J. *v.4 p.544*

Wat, Aleksander *v.2 p.792, v.3 p.254*

Wat, Eric C.. . . . . *v.6 p.113, p.115, p.366, p.367*

Watanabe, Sylvia & Bruchac, Carol (Editors) . . *v.6 p.92, p.102*

Watanna, Onoto *v.6 p.102*

Watelet, Claude-Henri *v.1 p.820*

Waterbury, John *v.6 p.640*

Waterfield, Robin *v.5 p.613*

Waterhouse, Ellis K. *v.1 p.729*

Waterhouse, Ellis *v.1 p.726*

Waterhouse, William *v.1 p.392*

Waterman, Christopher A.. . . . . *v.1 p.286*

Waterman, David *v.6 p.345*

Waterman, John T. *v.2 p.622*

Waterman, Laura & Waterman, Guy . . . *v.5 p.224, p.250*

Waterman, Michael *v.5 p.342, p.502*

Waterman, Richard W., et al. *v.4 p.546, v.6 p.301*

Waterman, Richard W. *v.4 p.528*

Waters, Brent & Cole-Turner, Ronald (Editors) . . . *v.1 p.526*

Waters, John *v.6 p.417*

Waters, M. Dane *v.4 p.460*

Waters, Neil L.. . . . . *v.4 p.627*

Waters, Sarah *v.6 p.399*

Waters, T. F. *v.5 p.684*

Waterston, Elizabeth *v.2 p.731, p.737*

Watkin, David (Editor) *v.1 p.795*

Watkin, David *v.1 p.788*

Watkins, Andrea & Clarkson, Priscilla. *v.1 p.50*

Watkins, Daniel P. *v.2 p.280*

Watkins, Evan *v.4 p.759*

Watkins, Glenn *v.1 p.181, p.326*

Watkins, John J. *v.5 p.470, p.480*

Watkins, John *v.2 p.216*

Watkins, Marie & Braun, Linda *v.4 p.168*

Watkins, Michael & Rosegrant, Susan *v.4 p.646*

Watkins, S. Craig. *v.6 p.331*

Watkins, Sharon B. *v.3 p.154*

Watkins, Susan. *v.2 p.569*

Watkins, T. H. & Byrnes, Patricia (Editors) *v.5 p.227*

Watkins, T. H. *v.3 p.463*

Watkinson, John *v.1 p.388*

Watrous, James. *v.1 p.754*

Watson, Alan. *v.4 p.433*

Watson, Alaric *v.3 p.29*

Watson, Burton
(Translator) *v.1 p.564, v.6 p.184, p.208, p.210, p.234*

Watson, Burton *v.6 p.184, p.208, p.209, p.210*

Watson, C. A. *v.5 p.268*

Watson, Cynthia A.. . . . . *v.4 p.562*

Watson, Dana Cairns *v.2 p.122*

Watson, David L. & Tharp, Roland G. *v.5 p.669*

Watson, David *v.5 p.657*

Watson, Derek. *v.1 p.206, p.314, p.367*

Watson, Donald, et al. *v.1 p.798*

Watson, Donald R. *v.3 p.155*

Watson, Donald *v.1 p.796*

Watson, Elwood & Martin, Darcy (Editors) *v.6 p.449*

Watson, Ernest Bradlee *v.1 p.104, p.142*

Watson, Fred *v.5 p.66*

Watson, George *v.2 p.165*

Watson, Ian (Editor) *v.1 p.136, p.142, p.143*

Watson, J. R.. . . . . *v.1 p.655*

Watson, J. Wreford *v.4 p.708*

Watson, James & Hill, Anne *v.4 p.424*

Watson, James D. & Berry, Andrew *v.5 p.123*

Watson, James D., et al. *v.5 p.123*

Watson, James D. *v.3 p.463, v.5 p.82, p.123, p.137*

Watson, James G. *v.2 p.75*

Watson, James L. & Caldwell, Melissa (Editors) . . . *v.4 p.46*

Watson, Jean & NLN Staff *v.5 p.528*

Watson, John B. *v.5 p.616*

Watson, Leslie & Dallwitz, M. J. *v.5 p.42*

Watson, Oliver *v.1 p.801*

Watson, P. *v.5 p.288*

Watson, Robert P. & Campbell, Colton C. (Editors) . . *v.4 p.552*

Watson, Robert P. & Gordon, Ann (Editors) *v.4 p.528*
Watson, Robert P. *v.4 p.550*
Watson, Ruth *v.6 p.72*
Watson, T. Steuart & Gresham, Frank M. (Editors) . . *v.5 p.667*
Watson, Tom *v.4 p.861*
Watson, Virginia D. *v.4 p.43*
Watson, W. Martin & Markman, Sherwin *v.4 p.528*
Watson, William *v.1 p.694*
Watson *v.5 p.585*
Watson-Jones, Virginia *v.1 p.774*
Watstein, Sarah & Stratton, Stephen E. *v.4 p.669*
Watt, Donald Cameron *v.4 p.628*
Watt, Dougal *v.4 p.113*
Watt, Ian (Editor) *v.2 p.194, p.269*
Watt, Ian P. *v.2 p.190, p.342, p.579, v.3 p.130*
Watt, Ian *v.2 p.342*
Watt, Stephen & Richardson, Gary A. *v.1 p.119*
Watt, Tessa *v.3 p.102, p.122, p.130*
Watt, W. Montgomery. *v.1 p.555, v.3 p.66, v.6 p.575, p.588, p.625*
Watt, William M. & Cachia, Pierre A. *v.6 p.564*
Watt, William M. *v.1 p.555, p.558, v.6 p.588*
Wattar, Tahir *v.6 p.664*
Wattenberg, Martin P. & Shugart, Matthew Soberg . . *v.4 p.576*
Wattenberg, Martin P. *v.4 p.550, p.556*
Watterson, John Sayle *v.4 p.810, p.860, p.895*
Watts, Alan *v.1 p.476*
Watts, Cedric T. *v.2 p.351*
Watts, Derek A. *v.2 p.473, p.478*
Watts, Duncan J., et al. *v.4 p.422*
Watts, Duncan J. *v.5 p.336, p.345*
Watts, Edward *v.3 p.506*
Watts, Jennifer A. *v.1 p.769*
Watts, Jerry G. *v.2 p.142*
Watts, Linda S. *v.2 p.122*
Watts, Meredith *v.4 p.752*
Watts, Michael (Editor, Commentaries by) *v.4 p.186*
Watts, Robert G. & Bahill, A. Terry *v.4 p.848, p.871*
Watts, Sheldon J. *v.4 p.708*
Watts, Steven *v.3 p.463, v.4 p.154*
Watts, Tim J. *v.6 p.359*
Waugh, Colin M. *v.4 p.654*
Waugh, Evelyn *v.2 p.388, v.6 p.399*
Waugh, Thomas *v.6 p.417*
Wawro, Geoffrey *v.3 p.154, p.168, p.182, v.4 p.628, p.648*
Wawro, Gregory *v.4 p.533*
Waxer, Lise (Editor) *v.3 p.268*
Waxer, Lise *v.3 p.268*
Waxman, Samuel M. *v.1 p.81, p.106, p.153*
Waxman, Stephen G. *v.5 p.516*
Waxman, Stephen *v.5 p.165*
Wayman, Alex & Wayman, Hideko (Translators) . . . *v.1 p.564*
Wayne, Kathryn M. *v.1 p.783*
Wcislo, Francis W. *v.3 p.219*
Weales, Gerald *v.2 p.108*
Wearing, Betsy *v.4 p.785, p.838*

Wearing, J. P. *v.1 p.104, p.142*
Weart, Spencer R. . . . *v.4 p.506, p.627, p.648, p.651, v.5 p.427*
Weast, Robert C. *v.5 p.291*
Weatherford, Doris (Editor) *v.6 p.426*
Weatherford, Jack *v.6 p.239*
Weatherson, Michael A. & Bochin, Hal W. *v.3 p.463*
Weaver, C. E. *v.5 p.439*
Weaver, David B. (Editor) *v.4 p.161*
Weaver, Jace (Editor) *v.6 p.681*
Weaver, Jace *v.4 p.541*
Weaver, John *v.1 p.14*
Weaver, Mary J. & Appleby, R. Scott (Editors) *v.1 p.574*
Weaver, Mike (Editor) *v.1 p.769*
Weaver, Peter L. *v.3 p.297, p.298*
Weaver, R. Kent (Editor) *v.4 p.587*
Weaver, R. W. (Editor) *v.5 p.51*
Weaver, Robert Franklin *v.5 p.129*
Weaver, Sally M. *v.6 p.690, p.693*
Weaver, Tom *v.6 p.320*
Weaver, Warren *v.5 p.484, p.485*
Weaver, William & Chusid, Martin (Editors) . . *v.1 p.207, p.364*
Weaver, William & Puccini, Simonetta *v.1 p.207, p.349*
Weaver, William D. Jr. & North, Mack O. *v.5 p.56*
Weaver-Zercher, David *v.1 p.586*
Webb, Beatrice *v.4 p.271*
Webb, Diana *v.1 p.601*
Webb, Duncan M. *v.1 p.150*
Webb, Geoffrey Fairbank *v.6 p.556*
Webb, Graham *v.6 p.308*
Webb, James L. Jr. *v.6 p.69*
Webb, Jennifer & Schirato, Tony *v.4 p.424*
Webb, Marilynn & Lonie, Bridie *v.1 p.758*
Webb, Mary *v.2 p.386, v.5 p.701*
Webb, Phyllis *v.2 p.739*
Webb, R. H. & Wilshire, H. G. (Editors) *v.6 p.290*
Webb, R. K. (Robert Kiefer) *v.3 p.116, p.132*
Webb, Ralph L. & Kim, Nae-Hyun *v.5 p.713, p.714*
Webb, Robert K. *v.3 p.116*
Webb, Samuel L. & Armbrester, Margaret E. (Editors) *v.3 p.505*
Webb, Stephen S. (Author, Preface by) *v.3 p.500*
Webb, Stephen *v.5 p.72*
Webb, Vic & Kembo-Sure (Editors) *v.6 p.81*
Webb, Walter Prescott *v.3 p.509, p.519*
Webber, David W. *v.4 p.448*
Webber, Joan *v.2 p.216, p.255*
Webber, Roger *v.5 p.365*
Webby, Elizabeth (Editor) *v.2 p.742*
Webel, Charles *v.4 p.662*
Weber, Adna F. *v.6 p.716*
Weber, Bruce A. (Editor), et al. *v.4 p.755*
Weber, Bruce H. (Editor), et al. *v.5 p.197*
Weber, Carl (Editor) *v.1 p.69, p.110*
Weber, Carl M. *v.1 p.207, p.367*
Weber, Cynthia *v.6 p.323*
Weber, David J. & Rausch, Jane M. (Editors) *v.3 p.260*

Weber, David J. *v.3 p.528, p.529, v.6 p.533, p.686*

Weber, Devra *v.6 p.525*

Weber, E. *v.5 p.6, v.6 p.287*

Weber, Elka *v.6 p.573, p.574, p.575*

Weber, Eugen *v.3 p.155*

Weber, Lillian & Alberty, Beth *v.4 p.346*

Weber, Max M. . . . *v.1 p.539, p.596, v.4 p.718, p.721, v.6 p.720*

Weber, Max . *v.4 p.211, p.213, p.435, p.681, p.720, p.722, p.725*

Weber, Nicholas Fox *v.1 p.681, p.683*

Weber, Ronald *v.2 p.15*

Weber, Timothy P. *v.1 p.607*

Weber, Walter J. Jr. & DiGiano, Francis A. . . *v.5 p.369, p.705*

Weber, William (Editor), et al. *v.5 p.186*

Websdale, Neil *v.4 p.743*

Webster, Brenda *v.2 p.240*

Webster, Charles *v.3 p.48, v.5 p.393, p.404*

Webster, Donald E. *v.6 p.625*

Webster, Donovan *v.5 p.585*

Webster, Fred & Webster, Marie S. *v.3 p.270*

Webster, Grady L. & Bahre, Conrad J. *v.6 p.488, p.551*

Webster, Graham *v.3 p.29*

Webster, James K. (Editor) *v.5 p.309, p.310*

Webster, John B. (Editor) *v.1 p.581*

Webster, John C. B. *v.1 p.541, v.6 p.155*

Webster, John *v.2 p.235, p.236*

Webster, Juliet *v.4 p.761, v.6 p.458*

Webster, L. F. (Editor) *v.5 p.707*

Webster, R. & Oliver, M. A. *v.5 p.52*

Webster, Robert K. & Gunnell, Pamela S. (Editors). . *v.5 p.47*

Webster-Stratton, Carolyn *v.4 p.354*

Wechsler, Jeffrey *v.6 p.88*

Wedde, Ian & McQueen, Harvey (Editors) *v.2 p.743*

Wedding, Danny & Stevens, Michael J. (Editors) . . . *v.5 p.594*

Weddle, Robert S. *v.3 p.506*

Wedeen, Lisa *v.6 p.608*

Wedeen, Richard P. *v.5 p.366, p.372*

Wedekind, Frank & Mueller, Carl Richard *v.2 p.616*

Wedekind, Frank *v.2 p.616*

Wedgwood, C. V. & Kennedy, Paul *v.3 p.166*

Wedgwood, C. V. *v.3 p.104*

Wedgwood, Cicely V. *v.3 p.104, p.205*

Weed, Frank J. *v.4 p.754*

Weedon, Alexis *v.6 p.742*

Weeks, Albert Loren *v.3 p.227*

Weeks, Gregory *v.3 p.277, p.356, v.4 p.593*

Weeks, J. M. *v.5 p.366*

Weeks, Jeffrey *v.4 p.570, p.749, v.6 p.363, p.388, p.422*

Weeks, Mary Elvira *v.5 p.264*

Weeks, Philip *v.3 p.402, v.6 p.687*

Weeks, William Earl *v.3 p.505*

Weeks, William E. *v.3 p.382*

Weevers, Theodor *v.2 p.622*

Wegman, Rob C. *v.1 p.181, p.346*

Wegner, Daniel M. *v.5 p.609, p.619, p.657*

Wegren, Stephen K. *v.5 p.6*

Wegs, J. Robert *v.3 p.185*

Wehle, Philippa (Editor) *v.1 p.69, p.106*

Wehler, Hans-Ulrich *v.3 p.165*

Wehmeyer, Michael L. & Patton, James R. *v.5 p.517*

Wehmeyer, Michael L., et al. *v.4 p.319*

Wehr, Hans *v.6 p.655*

Wehr, John D. & Sheath, Robert G. *v.5 p.208*

Wehr, Michael & Frank, Joseph H. (Editors) *v.5 p.35*

Wehrs, Donald R. *v.6 p.81, p.83, p.85*

Wei, William *v.6 p.108, p.115*

Weick, Karl E. *v.4 p.174*

Weidensaul, Scott. *v.5 p.182, v.6 p.292*

Weidman, John & Sondheim,
Stephen *v.1 p.254, p.357, p.358, p.410, p.411*

Weidner, Marsha (Editor) *v.6 p.473*

Weiers, Ronald M. *v.4 p.179*

Weigall, David *v.4 p.627*

Weigand, Hermann J. *v.2 p.595*

Weigel, George *v.1 p.580*

Weightman, Barbara A. *v.4 p.384, p.399*

Weigl, Bruce (Editor, Translator). *v.6 p.169*

Weigle, Marta & White, Peter *v.2 p.17*

Weigle, Marta *v.1 p.578*

Weigley, Russell F. (Editor) *v.3 p.492*

Weigley, Russell F. *v.3 p.384*

Weigley, Russell Frank *v.3 p.384*

Weiglin, Peter C. *v.4 p.176*

Weihmiller, Gordon R. *v.3 p.393*

Weikart, Richard *v.3 p.49, p.78, p.165*

Weil, Andre *v.5 p.468, p.477*

Weil, Danny & Kincheloe, Joe L. (Editors) *v.4 p.366*

Weil, Danny *v.4 p.299*

Weil, Jiri, et al. *v.2 p.784*

Weil, Simone *v.1 p.458, p.652*

Weil, Stephen E. *v.1 p.829*

Weilacher, Udo. *v.1 p.815*

Weiler, C. Susan & Penhale, Polly A. (Editors). . . . *v.5 p.90*

Weiler, Joseph H. & Wind, Marlene (Editors). . . . *v.4 p.639*

Weiler, Paul C. *v.4 p.445*

Weimann, Robert *v.2 p.232*

Weimer, Walter B. (Editor) *v.5 p.409*

Weinberg, Adam S., et al. *v.6 p.299, p.727*

Weinberg, Bill *v.3 p.270*

Weinberg, Elizabeth Ann *v.4 p.684*

Weinberg, Gerald M. *v.5 p.407*

Weinberg, Gerhard L. *v.3 p.81, p.175*

Weinberg, H. Barbara *v.1 p.749*

Weinberg, Jonathan *v.1 p.707, v.6 p.407*

Weinberg, Julius Rudolf *v.1 p.433, v.6 p.568*

Weinberg, Leonard *v.4 p.662*

Weinberg, Martin & Bell, Alan (Editors) *v.6 p.359*

Weinberg, Martin S., et al. *v.6 p.367*

Weinberg, Meyer *v.4 p.311, v.6 p.109*

Weinberg, Robert S. & Gould, Daniel *v.5 p.583*

Weinberg, Robert S. & Richardson, Peggy A. . . *v.4 p.878, p.905*

Weinberg, Robert. *v.3 p.221*

Weinberg, Steve, et al. *v.4 p.408*

Weinberg, Steven *v.5 p.73, p.541, p.544, p.553, p.557*

Weinberger, Eliot & Paz, Octavio *v.6 p.210*

Weinberger, Hans F. *v.5 p.488, p.491*

Weinberger, Naomi. *v.6 p.606, p.608*

Weinberger-Thomas, Catherine *v.6 p.460, p.471*

Weinbrot, Howard D.. . . . . *v.2 p.195*

Weiner, Annette B.. . . . . *v.4 p.43, p.44*

Weiner, Edward *v.4 p.166, v.6 p.716*

Weiner, Irving B. & Hess, Allen K. (Editors) *v.5 p.593*

Weiner, J. S. *v.4 p.16*

Weiner, Joel H. (Editor) *v.6 p.740, p.753*

Weiner, Marc A.. . . . . *v.1 p.207, p.301, p.367*

Weiner, Mark S. *v.4 p.723*

Weiner, Rex & Stillman, Deanne *v.4 p.736*

Weinfeld, Moshe. *v.1 p.621*

Weinfurter, Stefan *v.3 p.163*

Weingart, Richard E.. . . . . *v.1 p.644*

Weingart, Wolfgang *v.1 p.719, p.720*

Weingarten, Marc *v.4 p.403*

Weinreich, Gabriel *v.5 p.496*

Weinreich, Regina. *v.2 p.94*

Weinreich, Uriel *v.2 p.564*

Weinstein, Allen *v.3 p.450, p.464*

Weinstein, Barbara. *v.3 p.270, p.338, p.343*

Weinstein, Donald & Bell, Rudolph M.. . . . . . *v.6 p.573*

Weinstein, James. *v.3 p.445, p.450, v.4 p.493*

Weinstein, Martin E. *v.3 p.346*

Weinstein, Michael M. *v.4 p.663*

Weinstein, Philip M. (Editor) *v.2 p.75*

Weinstein, Philip. *v.2 p.573*

Weinstein, Rhona S. *v.5 p.573*

Weinstock, John M. & Rovinsky, Robert T. (Editors) . *v.2 p.624*

Weintraub, E. Roy *v.4 p.176*

Weintraub, Sidney (Editor) *v.4 p.61*

Weintraub, Sidney *v.3 p.296*

Weintraub, Stanley *v.2 p.310*

Weir, John. *v.6 p.380, p.400*

Weir, Margaret (Editor), et al.. . . . . . *v.4 p.526, p.571, p.572*

Weir, Robert E. & Hanlan, James P. (Editors). . . . *v.4 p.123*

Weir, Robert E.. . . . . *v.4 p.130*

Weir, Robert M. *v.3 p.502*

Weir, Walter *v.4 p.428*

Weis, Elisabeth & Belton, John (Editors) *v.6 p.352*

Weis, Lois & Fine, Michelle (Editors) *v.4 p.302*

Weis, Rene *v.6 p.573*

Weisberg, Arthur. *v.1 p.399, p.403*

Weisberg, Herbert F. *v.4 p.531*

Weisberg, Sanford *v.5 p.483*

Weisberger, Bernard A. *v.3 p.455*

Weisbrot, Robert *v.3 p.481*

Weisburd, A. Mark. *v.4 p.648, p.651*

Weisburd, David, et al. *v.4 p.774, v.6 p.253, p.255*

Weise, Elizabeth R. & Cherny, Lynn (Editors) *v.6 p.439*

Weisenburger, Steven C. *v.2 p.16*

Weishampel, David B., et al. *v.5 p.448*

Weiskel, Timothy C.. . . . . *v.6 p.69*

Weisman, Alan. *v.3 p.270*

Weisman, Leslie K.. . . . . . . *v.1 p.707, p.800, v.6 p.473*

Weisman, Steven R. *v.4 p.108, p.147*

Weismantel, Mary J. *v.3 p.273*

Weiss, Alan *v.4 p.65*

Weiss, Andrea *v.6 p.417*

Weiss, Anita M. & Gilani, S. Zulfiger (Editors) . . . *v.6 p.162*

Weiss, Beno. *v.2 p.715, p.724*

Weiss, Bernard G. *v.1 p.556*

Weiss, Bernhard *v.1 p.514*

Weiss, Donald H.. . . . . *v.4 p.447*

Weiss, Johannes *v.1 p.627*

Weiss, Kenneth M. & Buchanan, Anne V. *v.5 p.137*

Weiss, M. Lynn *v.2 p.122, p.138*

Weiss, Maureen R. *v.4 p.878, v.5 p.583*

Weiss, Paul *v.1 p.513, v.4 p.803*

Weiss, Penny A. *v.6 p.462*

Weiss, Peter *v.2 p.619*

Weiss, Piero (Author, Compiled by) *v.1 p.234*

Weiss, Piero *v.1 p.175*

Weiss, Sholom M. & Kulikowski, Casimir A.
(Editors) *v.5 p.339, p.408*

Weiss, Thomas G., et al. *v.4 p.636*

Weiss, Thomas George, et al. *v.4 p.565*

Weissberg, Robert *v.4 p.559*

Weissberg, Ted. *v.4 p.822, p.895*

Weissberger, Arnold (Editor) *v.5 p.277*

Weissberger, Arnold *v.5 p.277*

Weisse, Ralf & Storch, Hans v. *v.4 p.394*

Weisser, Thomas *v.6 p.325*

Weisskopf, Victor F. *v.5 p.399*

Weisskopf, Victor *v.5 p.544*

Weissman, Dick *v.1 p.264*

Weissman, Harold, et al. *v.4 p.759*

Weissman, James C. & DuPont, Robert L. (Editors). . *v.5 p.664*

Weissman, Jerry *v.4 p.174*

Weisstein, Eric W. *v.5 p.460, p.461*

Weisstein, Eric *v.5 p.63*

Weisstein *v.5 p.460, p.461*

Weitkamp, Jens & Puppe, Lothar (Editors) *v.5 p.278*

Weitz, Eric D. *v.4 p.715*

Weitz, Rose (Editor) *v.6 p.437*

Weitz, Rose *v.4 p.774*

Weizman, Ezer. *v.6 p.616*

Weizmann, Chaim *v.6 p.616*

Weizsacker, Carl F. Von. *v.5 p.404*

Wekerle, Christine *v.5 p.512, p.522*

Welaratna, Usha *v.6 p.139*

Welch, Claude E. *v.4 p.640, p.670*

Welch, Claude *v.1 p.634*

Welch, Cliff *v.3 p.343*

Welch, Evelyn. *v.1 p.676, p.689*

Welch, Holmes H. *v.1 p.563*
Welch, Holmes *v.1 p.563*
Welch, Jack & Byrne, John A. *v.4 p.72*
Welch, Jack *v.4 p.82*
Welch, James & Stekler, Paul *v.6 p.688*
Welch, Lew *v.2 p.158*
Welch, Michael *v.6 p.272*
Welch, Paula D. *v.4 p.797*
Welch, Richard E. Jr. *v.3 p.393, p.435, p.438*
Welch, Susan, et al. *v.3 p.517, v.6 p.720*
Welch, Walter L. & Stenzel Burt, Leah B. . . . *v.1 p.386, p.388*
Welden, Dan & Muir, Pauline *v.1 p.760*
Weldon, Fay *v.2 p.269*
Welish, Marjorie *v.1 p.681*
Wellek, Rene & Warren, Austin *v.2 p.567*
Wellek, Rene *v.2 p.573, p.782*
Weller, Richard *v.1 p.817*
Weller, Robert P. *v.4 p.618, p.620*
Weller, Sam *v.2 p.63*
Welles, Benjamin *v.3 p.445, p.464*
Wellesley, Kenneth *v.3 p.29*
Wellesz, Egon *v.1 p.178*
Wellhausen, Julius *v.6 p.589*
Wellington, Jerry *v.4 p.367, p.368*
Wellins, Mike *v.6 p.348*
Wellins, Richard S., et al. *v.4 p.80*
Wellman, Kathleen *v.3 p.50, p.148*
Wellner, Alison Stein *v.4 p.788, p.824*
Wells, Amy Stuart & Crain, Robert L. . . . *v.4 p.301*
Wells, Amy Stuart *v.4 p.299*
Wells, Colin *v.3 p.29*
Wells, David *v.5 p.496*
Wells, Donald R. *v.4 p.90*
Wells, H. G. & Sawyer, Andy *v.2 p.320*
Wells, H. G. *v.2 p.319, p.320*
Wells, Henry W. *v.2 p.186*
Wells, Jess (Editor) *v.6 p.377*
Wells, John C. *v.2 p.558*
Wells, Jonathan *v.5 p.197*
Wells, Paul *v.6 p.308*
Wells, Peter S. *v.3 p.29*
Wells, Sandra K. & Alt, Betty L. . . *v.6 p.260*
Wells, Stanley & Edmondson, Paul . . *v.2 p.226*
Wells, Stanley & Stanton, Sarah
  (Editors) *v.1 p.61, p.77, p.104, v.2 p.232*
Wells, Stanley W. & Wells, Stanley . . *v.2 p.227*
Wells, Stanley *v.2 p.226, p.232*
Wells-Barnett, Ida B., et al. *v.6 p.19*
Wells-Barnett, Ida B. *v.4 p.752, v.6 p.9*
Welsby, Derek A. *v.6 p.59*
Welsch, Gabe *v.2 p.684*
Welsh, Alexander *v.2 p.285, p.308*
Welsh, Frank *v.6 p.206*
Welsh, Jennifer M. (Editor) *v.4 p.671*
Welsh, Kate Shoup *v.4 p.168*

Welsh-Asante, Kariamu (Editor) *v.1 p.14*
Welter, Volker M. & Whyte, Iain Boyd . . . *v.6 p.716*
Weltman, Sharon A. *v.2 p.306*
Weltman-Aron, Brigitte *v.1 p.815*
Welty, Eudora *v.2 p.130*
Wempen, Faithe *v.4 p.174*
Wemple, Suzanne F. *v.6 p.561*
Wendel, C. H. *v.5 p.6, p.30*
Wendell, Barrett *v.2 p.6*
Wendell, Susan *v.6 p.444*
Wendorf, Fred, et al. *v.4 p.8*
Wendorf, Richard *v.2 p.243, p.244*
Wendt, Alexander *v.4 p.627*
Wenger, Karl F. (Editor) *v.5 p.40*
Wenglinsky, Harold *v.4 p.352*
Wenk, Arthur B. *v.1 p.169, p.207, p.227*
Wenke, John *v.2 p.49, p.118*
Wenner, Lawrence A. *v.4 p.820, p.892, p.903, p.907*
Wenner, Manfred W. *v.6 p.628*
Wensinck, Arent J. *v.1 p.557, p.558*
Wenske, Gerhard *v.5 p.258, p.259*
Wentz, Charles A. *v.5 p.314*
Wenz, Peter S. *v.1 p.486, v.6 p.289*
Weores, Sandor, et al. *v.2 p.786, p.787*
Weores, Sandor *v.2 p.786*
Werblowsky, Zvi & Wigoder, Geoffrey (Editors) . . . *v.1 p.546*
Werbner, Richard P. & Ranger, Terence (Editors) . *v.4 p.582, p.613*
Werfel, Franz *v.2 p.616*
Werhane, P. H. & Freeman, R. Edward . . *v.4 p.54, p.55, p.181*
Werner, Emmy E. & Smith, Ruth S. *v.5 p.672*
Werner, Eric *v.1 p.301*
Werner, Frank D. & Greig,
  Richard C. *v.4 p.861, p.870, p.871, p.872*
Werner, Heinz *v.5 p.594, p.595*
Werner, Peter H. *v.4 p.799, p.862*
Werner, Sarah *v.1 p.77, p.87, p.105*
Werness, Hope B. *v.1 p.667, v.6 p.680*
Wernham, R. B. *v.3 p.101*
Wernick, Andrew *v.1 p.455*
Wert, Jeffry D. *v.4 p.522*
Wertenbaker, Thomas J. *v.3 p.407*
Wertenbaker, Thomas Jefferson *v.3 p.500, p.501*
Werth, Alexander *v.3 p.228*
Werth, Barry *v.6 p.404*
Werth, James L. Jr. (Editor) *v.5 p.532*
Wertheim, Albert *v.2 p.755*
Wertkin, Gerard C. (Editor) *v.1 p.667*
Wertsman, Vladimir F. *v.4 p.168*
Wescoat, James L. Jr. *v.1 p.820*
Wescott, Glenway *v.2 p.128*
Wesemael, Sabine van *v.2 p.532*
Weslager, Clinton A. *v.6 p.704*
Wesley, Charles *v.2 p.264*
Wesley, John *v.1 p.644, p.645*
Wesley, Marilyn C. *v.2 p.152*

Wess, Julius & Bagger, Jonathan. *v.5 p.553*
Wessel, James K. (Editor-In-Chief). *v.5 p.692*
Wesseling, H. L. *v.3 p.77, v.4 p.583, v.6 p.11*
Wessels, Tom *v.5 p.235*
Wesson, John *v.4 p.868, p.871*
Wesson, Robert *v.5 p.197*
West, Alan (Editor) *v.6 p.504, p.509, p.516*
West, Alan. *v.3 p.314*
West, Bernadette M., et al. *v.4 p.407*
West, Cornel & Glaude, Eddie S. (Editors) *v.6 p.36*
West, Cornel (Editor) *v.4 p.730, v.6 p.41*
West, Cornel *v.1 p.513, v.6 p.20, p.32, p.41*
West, D. J.. . . . . *v.4 p.749*
West, David *v.2 p.437*
West, Douglas B.. . . . . *v.5 p.480*
West, Elliott *v.6 p.687*
West, Henry *v.1 p.516*
West, James L. W. III *v.2 p.77*
West, Jessamyn *v.2 p.130, p.131*
West, John B. *v.5 p.536*
West, John F. *v.3 p.234*
West, John G. Jr. & Maclean, Iain. *v.4 p.487, p.560*
West, M. L. (Editor, Translator) *v.2 p.415*
West, M. L. (Editor) *v.2 p.403*
West, M. L. (Translator, Introduction by). . . . *v.2 p.403, p.404*
West, M. L. *v.1 p.176*
West, Malcolm L. & Sheldon-Keller,
    Adrienne E. *v.5 p.649, p.657, p.658*
West, Margaret Genevieve *v.2 p.82*
West, Michael *v.4 p.80, p.81*
West, Nancy Martha *v.4 p.427*
West, Nathanael *v.2 p.131*
West, Philip & Ji-Moon, Suh (Editors) *v.6 p.237*
West, Rebecca J.. . . . . *v.2 p.719*
West, Rebecca *v.2 p.389, v.3 p.247, p.248*
West, Richard *v.3 p.247, p.248*
West, Robert C. (Author, Translator) *v.4 p.378*
West, Robert Cooper *v.3 p.357, p.359*
West, Shearer *v.1 p.708*
West, Thomas G.. . . . . *v.5 p.607*
West, W. Richard Jr. (Foreword by) *v.6 p.678*
Westad, Odd Arne (Editor) *v.3 p.212*
Westad *v.6 p.168*
Westbrook, Deeanne *v.4 p.812, p.852*
Westbrook, Paul & Westbrook, Alonzo T. . . . *v.1 p.163, p.276*
Westbrook, Perry D. *v.2 p.12*
Westbrook, Robert B.. . . . . *v.3 p.481, v.4 p.493*
Westcott, Cynthia & Horst, R. Kenneth *v.5 p.47*
Westcott, Edward Noyes *v.2 p.53*
Westehead, D. R. & Parish, J. H. *v.5 p.98*
Westerbeek, Hans & Smith, Aaron. *v.4 p.845, p.886, p.892, p.899*
Westerhoff, John H. *v.1 p.656*
Westerkamp, Marilyn J.. . . . . *v.1 p.607*
Westerman, R. L. (Editor) *v.5 p.52*
Westermann, W. L.. . . . . *v.4 p.727*

Westermeier, Reiner & Naven, Tom *v.5 p.119*
Westermeier, Reiner. *v.5 p.90, p.103, p.104*
Western Literature Association Staff. *v.2 p.15*
Westervelt, Saundra D. & Humphrey, John A. (Editors). *v.6 p.270*
Westervelt, Saundra D. *v.4 p.754*
Westfahl, Gary (Editor) *v.2 p.581*
Westfal, Richard E. (Editor) *v.5 p.534*
Westfall, Richard S. *v.3 p.48, p.130,v.5 p.468, p.544*
Westing, Arthur H. (Editor) *v.5 p.10, p.354, p.355*
Westlake, E. J.. . . . . *v.3 p.303*
Westland, Pamela. *v.5 p.229*
Westley, A. *v.1 p.760*
Westley, Frances R. & Miller, Philip S. (Editors) . . . *v.6 p.284*
Westlye, Mark C. *v.4 p.550, p.557*
Westmacott, Richard *v.1 p.820*
Westmeier, Karl-Wilhelm *v.1 p.587*
Weston, Andrea *v.5 p.269*
Weston, Judith *v.6 p.350*
Weston, Kath *v.4 p.33, p.740, v.6 p.375*
Weston, Paul. *v.5 p.109*
Weston, Richard *v.1 p.795*
Weston, Ruth D. *v.2 p.130*
Westphal, Merold *v.1 p.523, p.524, p.595*
WetFeet. *v.4 p.65, v.5 p.251*
WetFeet.com (Firm) Staff. *v.4 p.171, p.178*
Wethered, Audrey G. *v.1 p.51*
Wetmore, Kevin J. *v.1 p.72, p.123*
Wetta, Frank J. & Curley, Stephen J.. . . . . *v.6 p.323*
Wetteroth, Debbra *v.4 p.115*
Wetzel, David *v.3 p.168*
Wetzel, Robert G. *v.5 p.172, p.427, p.428*
Wever, Kirsten S.. . . . . *v.4 p.123*
Wexler, Alan. *v.4 p.381*
Wexler, Jerry & Ritz, David. *v.1 p.386*
Wexler, Laura *v.1 p.765*
Wexo, John Bonnett *v.5 p.85*
Weydt, Günther *v.2 p.596*
Weyenth, Robert *v.1 p.824*
Weyl, Hermann *v.5 p.496*
Weyl, Nathaniel *v.3 p.370*
Weyland, Kurt Gerhard *v.3 p.332, p.343, p.349, p.361*
Whalen, Carmen Teresa & Vazquez-Hernandez, Victor
    (Editors). *v.6 p.530, p.533*
Whalen, Carmen Teresa. *v.3 p.321*
Whalen, James W. *v.5 p.278*
Whalen, Mollie *v.4 p.751, v.6 p.446, p.471*
Whalen, Philip. *v.2 p.128, p.158*
Whalen, Thomas J. *v.4 p.534*
Whannel, Garry *v.4 p.820, p.903*
Wharton, Edith. *v.2 p.132*
Wharton, William *v.2 p.158*
Whatmore, Sarah. *v.4 p.399*
Whayne, Jeannie M. *v.3 p.511*
Whealey, Robert H. *v.3 p.174, p.242*
Wheatcroft, Geoffrey *v.4 p.845, p.857*

Wheatcroft, Stephen G. (Editor) *v.3 p.209*

Wheater, C. Philip & Cook, Penny A. *v.5 p.483, p.502*

Wheatley, Kim *v.2 p.312*

Wheatley, Margaret J. *v.4 p.72*

Wheatley, Phillis *v.2 p.30*

Wheeden, Richard & Zygmund, Antoni *v.5 p.490*

Wheeler, Alina *v.4 p.142*

Wheeler, Arthur L. *v.2 p.431*

Wheeler, Barbara L. (Editor) *v.1 p.406, p.407*

Wheeler, Burton K. & Healy, Paul F. *v.3 p.464*

Wheeler, Darrell *v.1 p.443*

Wheeler, Douglas L. & Pelissier, Rene *v.6 p.75*

Wheeler, Eileen *v.5 p.56*

Wheeler, Elizabeth A. *v.2 p.11*

Wheeler, Helen R. *v.6 p.445*

Wheeler, Hoyt N., et al. *v.4 p.131*

Wheeler, Hoyt N. *v.4 p.130*

Wheeler, J. Craig *v.5 p.67*

Wheeler, John A. *v.5 p.73, p.556, p.557, p.558*

Wheeler, John Archibald & Ford, Kenneth William . *v.5 p.544*

Wheeler, Lesley *v.2 p.9*

Wheeler, Marcus (Editor), et al. *v.2 p.776*

Wheeler, Michael *v.2 p.177, v.6 p.753, p.759, p.764*

Wheeler, Nicholas J. *v.4 p.671, p.673, p.675*

Wheeler, Paul *v.6 p.349*

Wheeler, Post (Editor, Translator) *v.1 p.542*

Wheeler, Quentin & Meier, Rudolf *v.5 p.199*

Wheeler, Rebecca S. (Editor) *v.2 p.553*

Wheeler, Stephen & Beatley, Timothy (Editors) . . . *v.4 p.268*

Wheeler, Thomas *v.2 p.253*

Wheeler, William B. & Becker, Susan D. . . . *v.3 p.375, p.376*

Wheeler, Willis B. *v.5 p.10, p.27*

Wheelock, Arthur K. Jr. & Broos, Ben *v.1 p.749*

Wheelock, Arthur K. Jr. *v.1 p.749*

Wheelock, Arthur K. *v.1 p.749*

Wheelock, Gretchen A. *v.1 p.192, p.331*

Wheelwright, Julie (Author, Introduction by) *v.6 p.367*

Wheelwright, Philip Ellis *v.1 p.422*

Wheen, Francis *v.4 p.237*

Whelchel, L. H. *v.6 p.36, p.37*

Whelpton, John *v.6 p.164*

Whenham, John *v.1 p.187, p.234, p.237, p.342, p.343*

Whetten, Nathan L. *v.4 p.772*

Whewell, William *v.5 p.404*

Whicker, Jules *v.2 p.646*

Whigham, Thomas & Cooney, Jerry W. *v.3 p.344*

Whigham, Thomas L. *v.3 p.278*

Whigham, Thomas *v.3 p.345*

Whillock, Rita K. *v.4 p.550, p.558, p.559*

Whinney, Margaret *v.1 p.778*

Whishaw, Ian Q. & Kolb, Bryan *v.5 p.616*

Whisnant, David E. *v.3 p.498*

Whitaker, Allan *v.5 p.96, p.220*

Whitaker, Arthur P. *v.3 p.506, p.507*

Whitaker, Arthur Preston *v.3 p.346, p.356*

Whitaker, Kent *v.5 p.536*

Whitaker, Reginald *v.4 p.589*

Whitaker, Rick *v.2 p.106*

Whitakker, G., et al. *v.5 p.288*

Whitburn, Joel *v.1 p.171, p.172, p.276*

White, Antonia *v.2 p.386*

White, Barbara A. *v.2 p.132*

White, Barbara J. & Madara, Edward J. (Editors) . . . *v.5 p.669*

White, Bruce A. (Editor) *v.5 p.90, p.101, p.102*

White, Bruce (Photographer) *v.1 p.801*

White, Bud & White, Charles B. *v.4 p.881, p.886, p.906*

White, Christine A. & Carver, Gavin *v.1 p.148*

White, D. *v.5 p.733*

White, David A. & Sofge, Donald A. *v.5 p.712*

White, David Gordon (Editor) *v.1 p.567*

White, David R. *v.1 p.38*

White, Deborah Gray *v.6 p.12, p.47, p.452*

White, Donald G. (Editor) *v.5 p.47*

White, E. B. *v.2 p.133*

White, E. Francis *v.6 p.9, p.47*

White, Edmund (Editor) *v.1 p.708, v.6 p.390, p.391*

White, Edmund *v.1 p.61, p.92, p.106,
                                   v.2 p.519, v.6 p.366, p.380, p.400, p.404*

White, Elizabeth *v.1 p.805*

White, Eric W. *v.1 p.227, p.234, p.247, p.361*

White, G. Edward *v.4 p.443, p.469, p.540, p.852*

White, Gary W. (Editor) *v.4 p.181*

White, George W. *v.3 p.246, v.4 p.383, p.384, p.399,
                                        p.400, p.488, p.496*

White, Glenn D. & Louie, Gary J. *v.1 p.163, p.388*

White, Graham & Maze, John *v.3 p.464*

White, Graham *v.4 p.588*

White, Guy & Meeson, Philip *v.5 p.563*

White, Halbert *v.4 p.205*

White House Office of Faith-Based and Community
Initiatives *v.5 p.672*

White, J. R. & Campbell, D. *v.5 p.323*

White, James B. *v.2 p.249, v.4 p.497*

White, James D. *v.3 p.224*

White, James F. *v.1 p.655, p.657*

White, James L. *v.5 p.320*

White, James M. *v.4 p.735, v.5 p.639*

White, John Kenneth & Shea, Daniel M. *v.4 p.552, p.553*

White, John Kenneth *v.3 p.481*

White, John M. *v.5 p.287, p.288*

White, John *v.1 p.673, p.689*

White, Joseph F. *v.5 p.729*

White, Judy (Editor) *v.3 p.356*

White, L. Michael & Yarbrough, O. Larry (Editors) . . *v.1 p.628*

White, Landeg *v.6 p.76*

White, Lucy Mueller *v.1 p.761*

White, Luise *v.6 p.455*

White, Lynn Jr. *v.3 p.68*

White, Maurice E. *v.5 p.56, p.57, p.59, p.61*

White, Mel *v.6 p.373*

White, Merry I. *v.6 p.222*
White, Michael & Gribbin, John. *v.5 p.544*
White, Michael. *v.5 p.397*
White, Nicholas P. *v.1 p.425, v.4 p.490*
White, Norman. *v.2 p.294*
White, Patricia. *v.6 p.417*
White, Patrick, et al. *v.2 p.454*
White, Patrick *v.2 p.750, v.6 p.400*
White, Philip & Young, Kevin (Editors) *v.4 p.820*
White, Randall. *v.1 p.669*
White, Richard A. *v.3 p.344*
White, Richard Alan *v.3 p.345*
White, Richard D. Jr. *v.3 p.464*
White, Richard D. *v.4 p.546*
White, Richard *v.6 p.684, p.686, p.687*
White, Ronald C. Jr. & Hopkins, C. Howard *v.1 p.644*
White, Sarah C. *v.4 p.31*
White, Shane & White, Graham J. *v.1 p.19, v.6 p.9, p.37*
White, Sol *v.4 p.810, p.833, p.852*
White, Stephen (Editor), et al. *v.3 p.207*
White, Stephen, et al. *v.4 p.599*
White, Stephen K. (Editor) *v.1 p.469*
White, Stephen. *v.3 p.229*
White, T. H. *v.2 p.387*
White, Theodore H. & Jacoby, Annalee . *v.6 p.191, p.216, p.217*
White, Theodore H. *v.3 p.450*
White, Timothy *v.1 p.276, p.340*
White, Welsh S. *v.4 p.474, v.6 p.267, p.270, p.271*
White, William Allen. *v.3 p.379, p.481*
Whiteford, Scott & Ferguson, Ann (Editors) *v.3 p.273*
Whitehead, Alfred North. *v.1 p.447, p.489, p.522,*
v.4 p.291, p.340, p.346, v.5 p.400, p.404
Whitehead, Bruce M., et al. *v.4 p.352*
Whitehead, Colson *v.2 p.159*
Whitehead, John S. *v.3 p.533*
Whitehead, John T. *v.6 p.272, p.276*
Whitehead, Neil L. *v.3 p.359*
Whitehead, Por. *v.3 p.234*
Whitehead, Randall. *v.1 p.803*
Whitehill, Walter Muir (Author, Illustrator) . *v.3 p.489, v.6 p.721*
Whitelaw, Nancy. *v.4 p.150*
Whitelegg, John *v.5 p.701*
Whiteley, Gillian *v.1 p.782*
Whiteley, Sheila *v.6 p.475*
Whitelock, Dorothy (Editor, Introduction by). *v.3 p.96*
Whitenack, Judith *v.2 p.646*
Whitener, Scott *v.1 p.392, p.399*
White-Parks, Annette *v.6 p.95*
Whiteside, Andrew G. *v.3 p.184*
Whitfield, Peter *v.4 p.379, v.5 p.62, v.6 p.716*
Whitfield, Philip *v.5 p.197*
Whitfield, Sarah, et al. *v.1 p.749*
Whitfield, Sarah *v.1 p.729*
Whitfield, Teresa *v.3 p.300*
Whitford, Frank *v.1 p.713, p.749, p.788*

Whiting, Robert . . *v.4 p.820, p.834, p.852, p.890, p.898, p.899*
Whitley, Bernard E. & Kite, Mary E. *v.5 p.650*
Whitley, James *v.3 p.19, v.4 p.13*
Whitley, M. Stanley *v.2 p.637*
Whitman, Marina V. *v.4 p.271*
Whitman, Marina von Neumann *v.4 p.264*
Whitman, Mark *v.4 p.451*
Whitman, Walt. *v.2 p.54, p.55*
Whitmarsh, Blair *v.5 p.583*
Whitmarsh, Tim *v.2 p.401*
Whitmore, Sarah *v.4 p.576, p.586, p.599*
Whitmore, T. C. (Timothy Charles) (Editor) *v.5 p.182*
Whitmore, Thomas M. *v.3 p.288*
Whitnah, Donald R. & Erickson, Edgar L. *v.3 p.185*
Whitney, Gordon G. *v.6 p.284*
Whitney, Robert *v.3 p.314*
Whitsett, Tim *v.1 p.163, p.386*
Whitson, Kathy J. *v.6 p.480*
Whittaker, C. R.. . . . . *v.3 p.29*
Whittaker, Cynthia H.. . . . . *v.3 p.218, v.4 p.599*
Whittaker, E. T. & Watson, G. N. *v.5 p.490*
Whittaker, Edmund T. *v.5 p.404*
Whittaker, Ruth *v.2 p.366, p.384*
Whittall, Arnold *v.1 p.227*
Whitten, Norman E. Jr. & Torres, Arlene (Editors) . . *v.3 p.281*
Whitten, Phillip *v.4 p.869*
Whittier, John Greenleaf & Wineapple, Brenda. *v.2 p.55*
Whittier, John Greenleaf *v.2 p.55*
Whittington, Michael & Williams, Glen (Editors) . . . *v.4 p.587*
Whittle, Alasdair W. R. *v.4 p.13*
Whittle, Peter *v.5 p.712*
Whitton, Brian A. (Editor), et al. *v.5 p.208, p.209*
Whittow, Mark. *v.3 p.194*
Whitworth, Ben *v.1 p.782*
Whorf, Benjamin Lee *v.4 p.20, v.5 p.624*
Whorton, James C. *v.5 p.10, p.354*
Whyte, John H. *v.1 p.575*
Whyte, William F. *v.4 p.752, v.6 p.720*
Whyte, William H. Jr. (Editor). *v.6 p.729*
Wiarda, Howard J. & Kline, Harvey F.. . . . . . . *v.4 p.593*
Wiarda, Howard J. *v.3 p.278, p.318,v.4 p.510, p.593*
Wiart *v.5 p.211*
Wiber, Melanie G.. . . . . *v.4 p.31*
Wiberg, Kenneth B. *v.5 p.293*
Wicharaya, Tamasak *v.6 p.269*
Wichterich, Christa *v.4 p.666*
Wick, Denis *v.1 p.399*
Wickelgren, Ingrid *v.5 p.82, p.220*
Wickens, Christopher D., et al. *v.5 p.588, p.718*
Wickens, G. E. *v.5 p.16*
Wickens, Gerald E. *v.5 p.44*
Wicker, Tom & Schlesinger, Arthur M. Jr. . . . *v.4 p.528, p.529*
Wicker, Tom. *v.3 p.481, p.482*
Wickert, Jonathan *v.5 p.422, p.699*

Wickett, Murray R. *v.3 p.524, v.6 p.688*

Wickham, Chris *v.3 p.199*

Wickham, Glynne W. *v.1 p.74, p.105, p.155*

Wickham-Crowley, Timothy P. *v.4 p.498*

Wickramasinghe, Chandra. *v.5 p.243*

Wicks, Robert *v.1 p.458*

Wicksell, Knut & Sandelin, Bo *v.4 p.241*

Wicksell, Knut. *v.4 p.239, p.241*

Widdifield, Stacie G. *v.3 p.265*

Widdis, Randy William *v.4 p.765*

Wideman, John Edgar . . *v.2 p.159, v.6 p.19, p.28, p.254, p.255*

Widenor, William C. *v.3 p.402, p.435*

Widick, B. J. *v.3 p.517*

Wiebe, Robert H. *v.3 p.402, p.438, p.445*

Wiebe, Rudy. *v.2 p.739*

Wiecek, William M. *v.4 p.455*

Wieck, Roger S. *v.1 p.729, p.749*

Wiedemann, Thomas E. J. *v.3 p.15, p.24*

Wiemken, Helmut & Schotus, Fridericus *v.2 p.593*

Wienand, Peter, et al. *v.1 p.827*

Wiener, Joel H. *v.3 p.110, v.6 p.742*

Wiener, Leo (Compiled by) *v.2 p.818*

Wiener, Martin J. *v.3 p.93, p.117, p.123, p.130, v.6 p.744*

Wiener, Martin Joel. *v.3 p.117, p.124,v.6 p.744, p.745, p.751, p.766*

Wiener, Norbert *v.5 p.408*

Wieners, John *v.2 p.159*

Wiens, John J. (Editor). *v.5 p.155, p.199, p.201*

Wierzbicki, James Eugene *v.1 p.245, p.256*

Wiese, Andrew. *v.6 p.716*

Wiese, Benno von *v.2 p.592*

Wiesen, David S. (Translator) *v.2 p.430*

Wiesen, S. Jonathan *v.3 p.177*

Wiesner, Jerome B. *v.5 p.394, p.404, p.412*

Wiesner, Merry E. *v.3 p.52, v.6 p.451, p.452, p.453*

Wiesner-Hanks, Merry E.. . . . . . . *v.3 p.51, v.6 p.450*

Wiet, Gaston. *v.6 p.602*

Wieting, Stephen G. (Editor) *v.4 p.811, p.820*

Wiggin, Addison & Bonner, William. *v.4 p.246, p.267*

Wiggin, Gladys Anna *v.4 p.298*

Wiggins, Arthur W. & Wynn, Charles M. *v.5 p.82*

Wiggins, David K. (Editor) *v.4 p.811*

Wiggins, David K.. . . . . . . *v.4 p.822, p.833, v.6 p.41*

Wiggins, David *v.1 p.505*

Wiggins, Gary D. *v.5 p.256*

Wiggins, Grant P. *v.4 p.287*

Wiggins, Jerry S. (Editor) *v.5 p.658*

Wiggins, Jerry S. *v.5 p.603, p.604*

Wiggins, Marianne *v.2 p.159*

Wiggins, Sarah W. *v.3 p.505*

Wigglesworth, Neil. *v.4 p.811, p.865*

Wightman, Alistair *v.1 p.227, p.362*

Wightman, William P.. . . . . *v.5 p.389*

Wigmore, John H. *v.4 p.435*

Wigmore, Richard

(Translator) *v.1 p.207, p.237, p.354, p.412, p.413*

Wigmosta, Mark S., et al.. . . . . *v.5 p.703, p.704*

Wignall, Jeff. *v.1 p.770, p.772*

Wigoder, Geoffrey & Seckbach, Fern (Editors) *v.1 p.546*

Wijesinha, Rajiva. *v.2 p.761*

Wikan, Unni & Wiggins, Peter *v.6 p.628*

Wikan, Unni *v.4 p.39, p.40*

Wiktorowicz, Quintan (Editor). *v.4 p.712*

Wilansky, Susan & Willerson, James T. *v.5 p.520*

Wilber, Ken *v.5 p.636*

Wilbur, Richard *v.2 p.128*

Wilchins, Riki A.. . . . . *v.6 p.367*

Wilcken, Ulrich *v.3 p.20*

Wilcox, Clifford *v.4 p.5*

Wilcox, Earl J. & Barron, Jonathan N. (Editors) . . . *v.2 p.78*

Wilcox, Helen (Editor) *v.6 p.480*

Wilcox, Jarrod W. *v.4 p.205*

Wilcox, John C. *v.6 p.480*

Wilcox, Ralph C. (Editor) *v.4 p.845, p.899*

Wilczek, Piotr *v.2 p.789*

Wild, Ray *v.4 p.119*

Wild, Tony. *v.4 p.117*

Wild, Trevor *v.4 p.772*

Wildavsky, Aaron B. & Caiden, Naomi. *v.6 p.301*

Wilde, Alan *v.2 p.346*

Wilde, Larry (Author, Interviewed By) *v.6 p.313*

Wilde, Oscar. *v.2 p.321, p.322, v.6 p.400*

Wilde, Sandra *v.4 p.287*

Wilde, William H. *v.2 p.742*

Wilde *v.2 p.356*

Wildenstein, Daniel *v.1 p.749, p.750*

Wilder, Alec *v.1 p.276*

Wilder, Amos N. *v.1 p.626*

Wilder, Claudyne & Rotondo, Jennifer *v.4 p.174*

Wilder, Frank Van (Editor) *v.1 p.726*

Wilder, Robert J. *v.5 p.430, p.431*

Wilder, Thornton. *v.2 p.133, p.134*

Wildhagen, Karl *v.2 p.622*

Wilding, Michael (Editor). *v.2 p.743*

Wilding, Michael. *v.2 p.742*

Wilentz, Gay *v.6 p.29*

Wilentz, Sean *v.3 p.415*

Wiles, David *v.1 p.72, p.138, v.2 p.402*

Wiley, Bell I. *v.3 p.402, p.427, p.432*

Wiley, Bell Irvin *v.3 p.496*

Wiley, Carol A. (Editor) *v.4 p.838, p.863*

Wiley, John P. Jr. *v.5 p.224*

Wiley, Roland J. *v.1 p.14, p.25*

Wiley, Ronald John *v.1 p.25*

Wiley, William L. *v.1 p.106*

Wilf, Herbert S. *v.5 p.478*

Wilhelm, Gernot *v.3 p.7, p.8*

Wilhelm, Hellmut & Wilhelm, Richard. *v.6 p.184*

Wilhelm, James J. *v.2 p.457*

Wilhelms, Don E. *v.5 p.418, p.435*

Wilhite, Barbara C. & Keller, M. Jean. . *v.4 p.786, p.787, p.830*

Wilhoit, R. C. and B. J. Zwolinski. *v.5 p.287*

Wilk, Kevin E. *v.5 p.519*

Wilke, Rebecca Lynn *v.4 p.279*

Wilken, Robert L. *v.1 p.600*

Wilkin, Karen *v.1 p.782*

Wilkins, David & Lomawaima, Tsianina *v.6 p.697*

Wilkins, David E. & Lomawaima, K. Tsianina *v.4 p.526*

Wilkins, David E. *v.4 p.465, v.6 p.693, p.697*

Wilkins, David G., et al. *v.1 p.668*

Wilkins, Ernest Hatch. *v.2 p.706*

Wilkins, Ernest H. *v.2 p.698*

Wilkins, Lee & Coleman, Renita. *v.4 p.417*

Wilkins, M. R. *v.5 p.105, p.147*

Wilkins, Robert L., et al. *v.5 p.536*

Wilkins, Robert P. & Wilkins, Wynona H. *v.3 p.523*

Wilkinson, A. J. & Moody, P. C.. . . . . *v.5 p.329*

Wilkinson, Charles F. *v.4 p.463, p.465, p.540, v.6 p.693*

Wilkinson, Charles. *v.6 p.690, p.693*

Wilkinson, Endymion Porter. *v.6 p.182*

Wilkinson, Geoffrey (Editor) *v.5 p.300*

Wilkinson, Geoffrey *v.5 p.307*

Wilkinson, J. Harvie *v.3 p.501, v.5 p.473, p.492*

Wilkinson, John C. *v.6 p.628*

Wilkinson, L. P. *v.2 p.439, p.448*

Wilkinson, Paul *v.4 p.498, p.662*

Wilkinson, Richard H. *v.1 p.543*

Wilkinson, Steven *v.4 p.618*

Wilkinson, Toby A. H.. . . . . *v.6 p.58*

Wilkinson, Toby A. *v.3 p.10*

Wilkinson, Toby. *v.3 p.10*

Wilkinson, Todd *v.4 p.566*

Wilks, Ivor *v.6 p.70*

Will, Barbara *v.2 p.122*

Willard, Helen S., et al.. . . . . *v.5 p.535*

Willard, Margaret W. (Editor) *v.3 p.410*

Willard, Stephen *v.5 p.500*

Willats, John. *v.5 p.629*

Willbern, David *v.2 p.233*

Willcock, Malcolm M. *v.2 p.416*

Willem, Van Vliet (Editor) *v.4 p.544, p.545*

Willerton, John P. *v.4 p.599*

Willet, Frank *v.1 p.690, p.691*

Willett, Edward *v.5 p.137*

Willett, John. *v.1 p.139, p.153*

Willett, Thomas D. (Editor) *v.4 p.245*

Willetts, R. F. *v.1 p.533, v.3 p.16*

Willey, Basil *v.6 p.751, p.753, p.754*

Willhoite, Michael *v.6 p.400*

William and Gayle Cook Music Library, Indiana University
School of Music *v.1 p.173*

William C Sturtevant (Editor) *v.6 p.690*

William M. McDonald and Associates Staff & McDonald,

William M. (Editors) *v.4 p.333*

William M. White Business Library, Leeds School of Business,
University of Colorado at Boulder. *v.4 p.53*

William of Ockham *v.1 p.433, p.510*

William Still Underground Railroad Foundation *v.6 p.37*

Williams, A. *v.2 p.763*

Williams, Adrian. *v.1 p.207, p.337*

Williams, Alan (Editor) *v.6 p.321*

Williams, Alan *v.5 p.696*

Williams, Angela & Nussbaum, Jon F. *v.5 p.622*

Williams, Arnold *v.1 p.74, p.105*

Williams, Aubrey L. *v.2 p.244*

Williams, Bernard. *v.1 p.454, p.485, p.487, p.488*

Williams, Brian Glyn. *v.3 p.213, p.214*

Williams, C. K. *v.2 p.159*

Williams, Caroline *v.1 p.458, p.515*

Williams, Cedric E.. . . . . *v.2 p.590*

Williams, Chancellor. *v.6 p.11*

Williams, Charles *v.2 p.387, p.705, v.3 p.155*

Williams, Christine L. (Editor). *v.6 p.458*

Williams, Clarence G. *v.6 p.21*

Williams, Clyde R. (Editor) *v.5 p.143, p.147*

Williams, Colin & Clearwater, S. *v.5 p.552*

Williams, Craig A. & James, David V. B.. . . . . . *v.4 p.874*

Williams, Dana A. *v.6 p.15, p.16, p.35, p.47*

Williams, Daryle *v.3 p.343*

Williams, David B. (Editor), et al. *v.5 p.692*

Williams, David Brian & Webster, Peter Richard . . . *v.1 p.388*

Williams, David M. & Forey, Peter (Editors) *v.5 p.171*

Williams, David *v.3 p.432, v.4 p.179*

Williams, Deborah Lindsay *v.2 p.67, p.132*

Williams, Drid *v.1 p.49*

Williams, Emily Allen *v.2 p.768*

Williams, Eric *v.6 p.20, p.37*

Williams, George C. *v.5 p.198*

Williams, George H. & Mergal, Angel M. (Editors) . . *v.1 p.602*

Williams, George H. *v.1 p.602*

Williams, Gordon *v.2 p.425*

Williams, Gwyn A.. . . . . *v.3 p.132*

Williams, Heather Andrea. *v.6 p.21, p.37*

Williams, J. D. *v.5 p.505, p.507, p.509*

Williams, J. G. *v.5 p.692*

Williams, Jack. *v.4 p.811, p.820, p.856*

Williams, Jean. *v.4 p.811, p.845, p.868*

Williams, Jen R. & Carcillo, Joseph V.. . . . . . . *v.4 p.105*

Williams, Jerome D. (Editor), et al. *v.4 p.426*

Williams, John A. (Editor) *v.1 p.554, p.555*

Williams, John Alexander. *v.3 p.498, p.501*

Williams, John B. *v.2 p.38, p.49*

Williams, John E. & Best, Deborah L.. . . . . *v.4 p.693*

Williams, John H. *v.3 p.344, p.509*

Williams, Johnathan M. (Editor) *v.5 p.294*

Williams, John. *v.2 p.598*

Williams, Joseph M. *v.2 p.555, p.565*

Williams, Joy *v.2 p.159*

Williams, Juan & Dixie, Quinton *v.6 p.36*

Williams, Juan *v.4 p.469, p.470, v.6 p.12*

Williams, Juanita H. *v.6 p.446, p.447*

Williams, Kathleen *v.2 p.216*

Williams, Kipling D. *v.5 p.649*

Williams, L. Pearce. *v.5 p.391*

Williams, Leslie R. & Fromberg, Doris P. (Editors) . *v.4 p.369*

Williams, Linda *v.4 p.749, v.6 p.317*

Williams, Lynn B. *v.1 p.711, p.712, p.751*

Williams, Mark & Leggott, Michele (Editors). . . . *v.2 p.742*

Williams, Mark (Editor), et al. *v.4 p.874, p.908, p.910*

Williams, Mark *v.2 p.742, p.750, p.761*

Williams, Melvin D. *v.1 p.587*

Williams, Melvin H. *v.4 p.791, p.876*

Williams, Michael . *v.1 p.517, p.519, p.521, v.5 p.40, v.6 p.296, p.301, p.419*

Williams, Nancy S. *v.4 p.366*

Williams, Norma *v.6 p.545*

Williams, Paul & Tribe, Anthony *v.1 p.565*

Williams, Paul L. *v.4 p.662*

Williams, Paul *v.1 p.566*

Williams, Peter F. *v.1 p.187, p.244, p.304*

Williams, Peter *v.1 p.38, p.178, p.392, v.4 p.716, p.853*

Williams, Philip J. & Walter, Knut *v.3 p.278, v.4 p.593*

Williams, R. Hal *v.3 p.438*

Williams, R. J. P.; da Silva, J. J. R. Frausto. *v.5 p.264*

Williams, Ralph Vaughan *v.1 p.227, p.363*

Williams, Raymond B. *v.6 p.106, p.138*

Williams, Raymond (Contribution by) *v.6 p.288*

Williams, Raymond L. *v.2 p.665, p.684, p.686*

Williams, Raymond Leslie *v.2 p.665*

Williams, Raymond. . . . *v.2 p.169, p.173, p.177, p.179, p.184, p.185, p.194, p.195, p.376, p.571, v.3 p.93, p.117, p.130, v.6 p.736, p.763*

Williams, Richard *v.4 p.730*

Williams, Robert A. Jr. *v.4 p.574, v.6 p.693*

Williams, Robert C. *v.5 p.6, p.30*

Williams, Robert Hardin, et al. *v.5 p.518*

Williams, Robin & Tollett, John *v.4 p.428*

Williams, Roger J. *v.5 p.115*

Williams, Rowan . *v.1 p.582, p.583, p.598, p.637, p.647, p.656*

Williams, Scott P. & Petersen, Randy *v.4 p.864*

Williams, T. David *v.6 p.76*

Williams, T. Harry . . . *v.3 p.384, p.403, p.427, p.432, p.464*

Williams, Tennessee. *v.1 p.119, v.2 p.135, v.6 p.400*

Williams, Thomas H. *v.3 p.427*

Williams, Tony & Hunter, Gordon. *v.4 p.865, p.866*

Williams, Tony *v.6 p.320, p.339*

Williams, W. S. *v.5 p.553*

Williams, Walter L. & Retter, Yolanda (Editors). . . *v.6 p.388*

Williams, Walter L. *v.6 p.367, p.368*

Williams, Walter. *v.4 p.526, p.567, p.770*

Williams, William Appleman (Editor), et al. . . *v.3 p.454, p.455*

Williams, William Appleman (Editor) *v.3 p.454*

Williams, William Appleman *v.3 p.393, p.454*

Williams, William Carlos *v.2 p.136, p.137*

Williams-Leon, Teresa & Nakashima, Cynthia L. (Editors) *v.6 p.125*

Williams-Nickelson, Carol & Prinstein, Mitchell J. (Editors). *v.5 p.676, p.677, p.679*

Williamson, Charles T. *v.3 p.316*

Williamson, Craig *v.2 p.204*

Williamson, D. I. (Donald Irving) *v.5 p.213*

Williamson, David (Editor), et al. *v.1 p.128, v.2 p.743*

Williamson, Donald S. *v.5 p.669*

Williamson, Edward C. *v.3 p.505*

Williamson, Edwin *v.2 p.679*

Williamson, George *v.2 p.72, p.183*

Williamson, Joel. *v.2 p.75*

Williamson, John (Editor). *v.1 p.207, p.314*

Williamson, John *v.1 p.207, p.244, p.359*

Williamson, Margaret. *v.6 p.480*

Williamson, Mark *v.5 p.182, p.720*

Williamson, Paul *v.1 p.776*

Williamson, Richard S. *v.4 p.526*

Williamson, Samuel R. Jr. *v.3 p.80, p.185*

Williamson *v.5 p.301*

Willinger, David *v.1 p.84, p.86, p.111*

Willingham, Warren W. & Cole, Nancy S. (Editors) . . *v.4 p.287*

Willink, Philip W. (Editor), et al. *v.5 p.172, p.186*

Willinsky, John. *v.2 p.553*

Willis, Carol *v.6 p.729*

Willis, Christopher *v.5 p.198*

Willis, Deborah *v.1 p.705, p.769, v.6 p.9, p.16*

Willis, Delta *v.5 p.99*

Willis, H. Lee & Scott, Walter G. (Contribution by) . *v.5 p.724*

Willis, J. H. Jr. *v.2 p.393*

Willis, James F. *v.4 p.477*

Willis, Jim *v.4 p.412, p.413*

Willis, John R. (Editor) *v.4 p.728*

Willis, Justin *v.6 p.65*

Willis, Kathy & McElwain, Jenny *v.5 p.449*

Willis, Roy *v.6 p.66*

Willis, Sherry (Editor), et al. *v.4 p.741*

Willis *v.4 p.42*

Willmer, Pat, et al. *v.5 p.357*

Wills, Christopher & Bada, Jeffrey. *v.5 p.204*

Wills, Christopher *v.5 p.365*

Wills, Garry *v.3 p.410, p.464, p.482, v.4 p.72*

Wills, John E. *v.6 p.199*

Willson, K. C. *v.5 p.24, p.35*

Willson, Perry R. *v.3 p.203*

Willumson, Glenn G. *v.1 p.769*

Wilmeth, Don B. & Bigsby, Christopher (Editors) . . . *v.1 p.119*

Wilmore, Jack H. & Costill, David L. *v.4 p.878*

Wilshire, Bruce *v.4 p.662*

Wilson, A. N. *v.1 p.526*

Wilson, Amos N. *v.6 p.9, p.20, p.32*

Wilson, Andrew *v.2 p.86, v.4 p.599, v.6 p.404*

Wilson, Angus *v.2 p.389, p.504, v.6 p.400*

Wilson, Arthur M. *v.2 p.480*

Wilson, Arthur *v.6 p.290*

Wilson, August (Preface by). *v.1 p.123*

Wilson, August. *v.1 p.123, v.2 p.159*

Wilson, Carol Shiner & Haefner, Joel (Editors) . . . *v.6 p.480*

Wilson, Carter A.. . . . . *v.4 p.727*

Wilson, Cecil L. *v.5 p.273*

Wilson, Charles Reagan, et al.. . . . . *v.3 p.494*

Wilson, Charles *v.6 p.742*

Wilson, Chris *v.6 p.533, p.551*

Wilson, Clyde N. (Editor), et al.. . . . . *v.3 p.412, p.413*

Wilson, Clyde N. (Editor). *v.3 p.375, p.412*

Wilson, Constance M. *v.6 p.172*

Wilson, Daniel G. *v.1 p.761*

Wilson, Daniel J.. . . . . *v.5 p.533*

Wilson, David F.. . . . . *v.1 p.178*

Wilson, David M.. . . . . *v.3 p.97*

Wilson, David Sloan *v.4 p.720*

Wilson, David *v.6 p.257, p.722*

Wilson, Dianne. *v.2 p.650*

Wilson, Don E. (Editor), et al.. . . . . *v.5 p.359*

Wilson, Douglas *v.4 p.308*

Wilson, Dreck Spurlock (Editor) *v.1 p.705, p.784*

Wilson, Dreck Spurlock *v.6 p.33*

Wilson, Duff *v.5 p.353, p.355, p.375, p.377*

Wilson, Edmund *v.2 p.137, p.570, p.576,v.6 p.684, p.704*

Wilson, Edward O. *v.1 p.483, v.5 p.359, p.397,*
                                p.619, p.620, v.6 p.292

Wilson, Emma *v.6 p.338*

Wilson, Ethel *v.2 p.739*

Wilson, F. P. *v.2 p.185*

Wilson, George Earl *v.3 p.540*

Wilson, George M.. . . . . *v.6 p.228*

Wilson, Golder N. *v.5 p.152*

Wilson, Gregory S. (Editor) *v.5 p.583*

Wilson, H. T. *v.4 p.546*

Wilson, Harold *v.3 p.95, p.119*

Wilson, Harriet E. & Gates,
  Henry Louis Jr. *v.2 p.53, v.6 p.28, p.47*

Wilson, Heather A. *v.4 p.478, p.479, p.481*

Wilson, J. S. G. *v.4 p.241*

Wilson, James Q. & Petersilia, Joan (Editors). . . . *v.6 p.263*

Wilson, James Q. *v.6 p.250, p.251, p.269*

Wilson, James *v.1 p.750*

Wilson, Janet *v.4 p.729*

Wilson, Jean M. *v.2 p.380*

Wilson, Jean. *v.2 p.228*

Wilson, Joan H. *v.3 p.482*

Wilson, John & Fotheringham, Stewart (Editors) . . . *v.4 p.388*

Wilson, John A. *v.3 p.10, p.11, v.6 p.57*

Wilson, John Albert *v.6 p.57*

Wilson, John D. *v.2 p.203, p.216*

Wilson, John Dover *v.2 p.233*

Wilson, John G. (John Grenell) *v.5 p.231, p.232*

Wilson, John H.. . . . . *v.2 p.217*

Wilson, John Q. *v.6 p.726*

Wilson, John T. *v.5 p.394, p.412*

Wilson, John *v.4 p.716, p.820, p.892*

Wilson, Joseph. *v.4 p.562, p.648*

Wilson, Josleen & National Audubon Society Staff . . *v.5 p.216*

Wilson, Katharina M. & Margolis, Nadia. *v.6 p.561*

Wilson, Katharina M. (Editor). *v.6 p.561, p.566*

Wilson, Lanford *v.2 p.159*

Wilson, Leslie (Editor), et al. *v.5 p.86, p.87*

Wilson, Logan *v.4 p.294*

Wilson, Lori Lee *v.3 p.489*

Wilson, Major L. *v.3 p.415, p.418*

Wilson, Margaret Dauler *v.1 p.454*

Wilson, Margaret. *v.2 p.641*

Wilson, Mary A. *v.2 p.120, p.121*

Wilson, Mary Christina *v.6 p.621*

Wilson, Matthew *v.2 p.32*

Wilson, Michael, et al. *v.5 p.265*

Wilson, Nick C. *v.6 p.491, p.552, p.553*

Wilson, Paul. *v.1 p.227, p.305*

Wilson, Peter H. *v.3 p.165*

Wilson, Peter J. *v.4 p.17, p.39*

Wilson, Peter N.. . . . . *v.1 p.264, p.317, p.318*

Wilson, Raymond Jackson *v.4 p.684*

Wilson, Raymond L.. . . . . *v.1 p.725, p.751*

Wilson, Richard A. *v.6 p.78*

Wilson, Richard (Editor) *v.4 p.34*

Wilson, Richard Guy *v.1 p.791*

Wilson, Richard L.. . . . . *v.1 p.808, p.809*

Wilson, Richard *v.2 p.233, v.6 p.223*

Wilson, Rob *v.6 p.115, p.131*

Wilson, Robert A. & Keil, Frank (Editors) *v.5 p.609*

Wilson, Robert A. (Editor) *v.5 p.205*

Wilson, Robert F. *v.4 p.785, p.904*

Wilson, Robert. *v.5 p.138*

Wilson, Robin J. *v.5 p.480*

Wilson, Robin *v.5 p.468, p.480*

Wilson, Rodney (Editor) *v.6 p.621*

Wilson, Rodney, et al. *v.6 p.626*

Wilson, Sam *v.5 p.242*

Wilson, Samuel M. *v.4 p.41*

Wilson, S *v.5 p.280*

Wilson, Sloan *v.2 p.128*

Wilson, Sondra Kathryn (Editor) *v.2 p.90*

Wilson, Stephen *v.3 p.61*

Wilson, Timothy D. *v.5 p.657*

Wilson, Wayne & Derse, Edward (Editors) . . . *v.4 p.826, p.846*

Wilson, Wendy S. & Herman, Gerald *v.3 p.375*

Wilson, William H.. . . . . *v.6 p.729*

Wilson, William Julius *v.4 p.730, p.759, p.771, v.6 p.720*

Wilson, William W. *v.4 p.630, p.644, p.666*

Wilson, Wilson & Dutton, Richard. *v.2 p.186*

Author Index

Wilson-Bareau, Juliet *v.1 p.724*
Wilson-Tagoe, Nana *v.2 p.753*
Wilstein, Steve *v.4 p.407, p.903, p.907*
Wilt, Alan F. *v.3 p.82*
Wilt, Judith *v.2 p.308*
Wilton, Andrew *v.1 p.734*
Wilton, Carol *v.3 p.544, p.545*
Wilton, Tamsin *v.4 p.750, v.6 p.371*
Wiltse, Charles M. *v.3 p.416*
Wiltshire, David *v.4 p.686*
Wiltshire, John *v.2 p.269*
Wimbush, Vincent L. & Rodman, Rosemary C. (Editors).*v.4 p.721*
Wimbush, Vincent L. & Valantasis, Richard (Editors) . *v.1 p.531*
Winant, Howard *v.4 p.731, p.767, p.768*
Winbush, Raymond (Editor). *v.6 p.20, p.37*
Winch, Christopher & Gingell, John *v.4 p.324, p.340*
Winch, Christopher *v.4 p.306*
Winch, D. *v.4 p.220*
Winch, Robert F. *v.4 p.739*
Winch, Robert G. *v.5 p.702*
Winchell, Mark R. *v.2 p.5*
Winchester, Simon *v.2 p.553, v.3 p.532*
Wind, Jerry, et al. *v.4 p.135*
Windeatt, Barry *v.2 p.211*
Windelspecht, Michael *v.3 p.46, v.5 p.389, p.390*
Winder, R. Bayly *v.6 p.626*
Windfuhr, Gernot L. & Tehranisa *v.6 p.669*
Windfuhr, Gernot L. *v.6 p.669*
Windlesham, Lord *v.4 p.567*
Windmeyer, Shane L. (Editor) *v.6 p.386*
Windsor, Alan *v.1 p.734, p.754, p.774*
Wine, Humphrey *v.1 p.730*
Winecoff, Charles *v.6 p.419*
Winegarten, Renee *v.2 p.500, p.501*
Wines, James *v.1 p.788*
Winfeld, Liz & Spielman, Susan . *v.4 p.132, p.168, v.6 p.382*
Winfield, Jerry P. (Editor) *v.2 p.640*
Winfield, Percy H. *v.4 p.433*
Wing, Adrien Katherine (Editor). *v.6 p.436, p.472*
Wing, Bret & Walker, Sharon *v.4 p.156*
Wing, G. Milton *v.5 p.488*
Wingell, Richard *v.1 p.174*
Wingerd, Bruce D. *v.5 p.90*
Wingerson, Lois *v.5 p.138*
Wingfield, Mary A. *v.1 p.667*
Wingfield, Nancy M. *v.3 p.189*
Wingfield, Paul *v.1 p.227, p.237, p.333*
Wingler, Hans *v.3 p.179*
Winick, Charles *v.4 p.3*
Wink, Andre *v.6 p.162*
Wink, Michael (Editor) *v.4 p.157, v.5 p.125*
Winkler, A. J., et al. *v.5 p.36*
Winkler, Allan M. *v.5 p.740*
Winkler, Carol K. *v.4 p.565*
Winkler, E. M. *v.5 p.452*

Winkler, John J. *v.2 p.429, v.6 p.364, p.422, p.423, p.425*
Winkler, Kenneth P. *v.1 p.450, p.451*
Winkler, Peter *v.5 p.470*
Winks, Robin & Louis, Roger (Editors) *v.3 p.35, p.90*
Winks, Robin W. (Editor) *v.2 p.580*
Winks, Robin W. *v.3 p.382, p.433, p.536, p.542*
Winn, James A. *v.2 p.247*
Winn, James Anderson *v.1 p.248*
Winn, Neil *v.3 p.322*
Winn, Peter *v.3 p.356*
Winnan, Audur H. *v.1 p.758*
Winner, Ellen *v.5 p.576*
Winnick, Joseph P. *v.4 p.801*
Winnifrith, Tom *v.2 p.271*
Winnington-Ingram, R. P. *v.2 p.421*
Winock, Michel *v.3 p.61*
Winquist, Charles E. & Taylor, Victor E. (Editors) . *v.1 p.512*
Winskel, Glynn *v.5 p.336, p.347, p.348, p.349*
Winslow, Calvin *v.4 p.130*
Winslow, Ola Elizabeth *v.2 p.241, v.3 p.489*
Winsor, Mary P. *v.5 p.85*
Winston, Brian *v.4 p.419*
Winston, David *v.1 p.624*
Winston, Diane H. *v.1 p.589*
Winston, Judith E. *v.5 p.199, p.205*
Winter, Alison *v.6 p.751*
Winter, Carl K. *v.5 p.310*
Winter, Charles A. *v.5 p.251, p.253, p.255*
Winter, David A. *v.4 p.875, p.876, p.908, p.910*
Winter, Henry J. *v.5 p.405*
Winter, J. M. *v.3 p.42, p.93, p.118*
Winter, James *v.6 p.296, p.759, p.766*
Winter, Jay *v.3 p.80*
Winter, John D. *v.5 p.437*
Winter, Marian Hannah *v.1 p.22*
Winter, Mark *v.5 p.407*
Winter, Michael *v.6 p.58, p.59*
Winter, Robert & Martin, Robert (Editors). *v.1 p.207, p.244, p.308*
Winter, William . . . *v.1 p.81, p.119, p.142, p.146, p.153, p.154*
Winterbone, D. E. *v.5 p.712*
Winterbottom, Daniel M. *v.1 p.818*
Winterbottom, Michael (Editor) *v.2 p.450, p.451, p.453*
Winternitz, Emanuel *v.1 p.175, p.392*
Winternitz, Maurice *v.1 p.541*
Winters, Yvor *v.2 p.7, p.128, p.180*
Winterson, Jeanette *v.2 p.387, v.6 p.400*
Winton, Andrew Lincoln & Winton, Kate Grace Barber. *v.5 p.33*
Winton, Tim *v.2 p.749*
Wintz, Cary D. & Finkelman, Paul (Editors) . . *v.6 p.28, p.35*
Wipperfurth, Alex *v.4 p.142*
Wiredu, Kwasi (Editor) *v.1 p.476, p.477*
Wirls, Daniel & Wirls, Stephen *v.4 p.534*
Wirt, Frederick M. & Kirst, Michael W. *v.4 p.298*
Wirth, Louis *v.6 p.720*
Wirth-Nesher, Hana *v.6 p.731, p.733, p.735*

Wischnitzer, Saul *v.5 p.90*

Wisconsin Cartographers Guild Staff & Wisc Cart Guild Staff. *v.3 p.517, p.518*

Wisdom, J. O.. *v.1 p.417*

Wise, David A. (Editor). *v.4 p.267*

Wise, Edwin *v.5 p.715*

Wise, Marian & Kenworthy, Lauren. . . *v.5 p.366, p.373, p.376*

Wise, Stephen R.. . . . . *v.4 p.522*

Wise, Suzanne *v.4 p.820*

Wiseman, Adele *v.2 p.739, p.740*

Wiseman, Carter *v.1 p.795*

Wiseman, Donald J. (Editor), et al.. . . . . . . *v.1 p.614*

Wiseman, T. P.. . . . . *v.2 p.426, p.431*

Wiseman, Timothy Peter (Editor) *v.3 p.24*

Wiseman, T.P.. *v.1 p.533*

Wiser, William & Wiser, Charlotte V. *v.4 p.40*

Wish, Harvey *v.3 p.375*

Wishart, David J.. . . . . *v.3 p.519*

Wiskemann, Elizabeth *v.3 p.190*

Wisker, Gina. *v.2 p.728*

Wister, Owen *v.2 p.128*

Wit, Ernst & McClure, John. *v.5 p.101*

Witalec, Janet ; Chapman, Jeffery ; Giroux, Christopher. *v.6 p.699*

Witalec, Janet (Editor) *v.2 p.11*

Witcover, Jules. *v.3 p.482*

Witham, Barry B. *v.1 p.119, p.146, p.150*

Witham, Larry A. *v.1 p.650*

Wither, George. *v.2 p.216*

Witherington, Ben III. *v.1 p.627, p.628*

Witherly, Jeffre L., et al. *v.5 p.123*

Witherspoon, Alexander M. & Warnke, Frank J. . . . *v.2 p.197*

Witherspoon, Gary *v.6 p.704*

Witke, Roxanne *v.6 p.196, p.200, p.217*

Witkiewicz, Stanislaw I. *v.2 p.792*

Witkin, Belle Ruth & Altschuld, James W.. . . . . . *v.4 p.82*

Witkin, Zara *v.3 p.226*

Witkowski, Jan *v.5 p.82*

Witt, Charlotte. *v.1 p.427, p.505*

Witt Library of the Courtauld Institute Staff *v.1 p.725*

Witt, Lynn (Editor), et al.. . . . . *v.6 p.361*

Wittcoff, Harold A. & Reuben, Bryan G. *v.5 p.318*

Witte, John Jr. *v.4 p.459*

Wittek, Paul *v.6 p.591, p.666*

Wittels, Fritz. *v.5 p.598*

Witten, Ian H., et al. *v.5 p.341, p.342*

Witten, Thomas A.. . . . . *v.5 p.555*

Wittfogel, Karl August *v.6 p.182*

Wittgenstein, Ludwig & Anscombe, Gertrude Elizabeth Margaret *v.1 p.472*

Wittgenstein, Ludwig & Docherty, Peter *v.1 p.473*

Wittgenstein, Ludwig Josef Johann. *v.1 p.472*

Wittgenstein, Ludwig. *v.1 p.472, p.483*

Witthoft, Brucia *v.1 p.758*

Wittig, Kurt *v.2 p.165*

Wittig, Monique *v.2 p.534, v.4 p.749, v.6 p.368, p.400*

Wittke, Carl F.. . . . . *v.1 p.35, p.120*

Wittkower, Rudolf, et al. *v.1 p.676*

Wittkower, Rudolf *v.1 p.788*

Wittlich, Gary E. & Martin, Deborah S. *v.1 p.374*

Wittman, Donald A. *v.4 p.506*

Wittner, Lawrence S.. . . . . *v.3 p.196, v.4 p.572, p.651, p.657*

Wittreich, Joseph *v.2 p.256*

Witvliet, Theo *v.1 p.638*

Witwer, David *v.4 p.130*

Witzel, Morgen *v.4 p.177*

Witzleben, J. Lawrence. *v.1 p.290, p.291*

Wizelius, Tore *v.5 p.709*

Wlaschin, Ken *v.6 p.316*

Wünschiers, Röbbe *v.5 p.106*

Wodak, Ruth & Pelinka, Anton (Editors). . . . *v.4 p.595, p.596*

Wodehouse, P. G., et al.. . . . . *v.2 p.391*

Wodehouse, P. G. *v.2 p.390, p.391, p.392*

Wodrich, David L.. . . . . *v.5 p.603*

Wogalter, Michael S. (Editor) *v.5 p.588*

Wohl, Anthony S. *v.3 p.117*

Wohl, Ellen E.. . . . . *v.5 p.172, p.242*

Wohl, Hellmut *v.1 p.676*

Wohlauer, Gabriele E. *v.5 p.258*

Woideck, Carl *v.1 p.264, p.265, p.318, p.346, p.347*

Wojcik, Pamela Robertson *v.6 p.348*

Wojcik-Andrews, Ian *v.6 p.312*

Wojnarowicz, David *v.6 p.408*

Wolanski, Eric (Editor). *v.5 p.173, p.213, p.241*

Wolcott, Harry F. *v.4 p.282, p.687*

Woledge, Brian (Editor), et al.. . . . . *v.2 p.464*

Wolf, Arthur P. & Durham, William H.. . . . . *v.4 p.738*

Wolf, Christa *v.2 p.619, p.620*

Wolf, Eric R. *v.3 p.35, v.4 p.25, p.29, p.35*

Wolf, Friedrich A. *v.2 p.416*

Wolf, John B. (Editor) *v.3 p.146*

Wolf, John Baptist. *v.6 p.61*

Wolf, John P. & Deeks, Andrew J.. . . . . *v.5 p.697*

Wolf, Margery *v.6 p.214*

Wolf, Martin *v.4 p.56, p.58, p.666*

Wolf, Naomi. *v.6 p.436*

Wolf, Robert S. *v.5 p.471*

Wolf, Stacy *v.1 p.380, v.6 p.413*

Wolf, Stephanie G.. . . . . *v.4 p.708*

Wolf, Sylvia *v.1 p.774*

Wolf, Theta H.. *v.5 p.574*

Wolf, Thomas P. (Editor), et al. *v.3 p.482*

Wolfe, Alan *v.4 p.299, p.697*

Wolfe, Charles & Lornell, Kip *v.1 p.297, p.335*

Wolfe, David A. & Mash, Eric J. (Editors) *v.5 p.663*

Wolfe, David *v.6 p.292, p.293*

Wolfe, J. N. (Editor) *v.4 p.260*

Wolfe, Joel D.. *v.3 p.343*

Wolfe, Joseph & Keys, J. Bernard (Editors). *v.4 p.177*

Wolfe, Michael. *v.3 p.146*

Wolfe, Thomas & Conroy, Pat. *v.2 p.138*
Wolfe, Thomas *v.2 p.137, p.138*
Wolfe, Tom *v.2 p.159, v.5 p.720*
Wolfer, Loreen. *v.4 p.376*
Wolff, Alexander. *v.4 p.845, p.855*
Wolff, Charlotte *v.6 p.404*
Wolff, Christoph *v.1 p.187, p.192, p.237, p.304, p.345*
Wolff, Geoffrey *v.2 p.107*
Wolff, George *v.5 p.220*
Wolff, Janice M. (Editor) *v.2 p.565, p.566*
Wolff, Konrad *v.1 p.244*
Wolff, Larry *v.3 p.72, p.207*
Wolff, Robert Lee *v.2 p.265, p.275*
Wolff, Robert P. *v.4 p.237, p.511*
Wolff, Ronald G.. . . . . *v.5 p.157, p.158*
Wolfflin, Heinrich *v.1 p.676*
Wolfgang, Charles H.. . . . . *v.4 p.284*
Wolfgang, Marvin E., et al. *v.4 p.753, p.754, v.6 p.255*
Wolfgang, Marvin E. *v.6 p.252*
Wolford, Lisa & Schechner, Richard (Editors) . *v.1 p.111, p.146*
Wolfram, Herwig *v.3 p.63*
Wolfram, Stephen *v.5 p.462, p.501*
Wolfram von Eschenbach *v.2 p.595*
Wolfram, von Eschenbach. *v.2 p.595*
Wolfram, Walt & Johnson, Robert *v.2 p.558*
Wolfram, Walt & Schilling-Estes, Natalie. . . . *v.2 p.553*
Wolfram, Walt & Thomas, Erik R.. . . . . . *v.2 p.555*
Wolfreys, Julian (Editor) *v.2 p.292*
Wolfson, Elliot R. *v.6 p.574*
Wolfson, Evan *v.6 p.389*
Wolfson, Harry A. *v.1 p.431, p.634*
Wolfson, Nicholas *v.4 p.460, p.749*
Wolfson, Richard *v.5 p.360, p.374*
Wolfson, Susan J. (Editor) *v.2 p.296*
Wolfson, Susan J. *v.2 p.324*
Wolgemuth, Ken *v.5 p.224*
Wolin, Richard. *v.4 p.510*
Wolin, Sheldon S. *v.4 p.493*
Wolkstein, Diane & Kramer, Samuel N. *v.1 p.539*
Woll, Allen L.. . . . . . *v.1 p.61, p.123, p.124, p.254, p.283*
Woll, Allen *v.3 p.351*
Woll, Gerd. *v.1 p.758*
Woll, Josephine *v.2 p.810*
Wollheim, Richard. *v.1 p.498, p.701*
Wollons, Roberta Lyn (Editor). *v.4 p.368*
Wollstonecraft, Mary . . *v.2 p.318, p.319, v.4 p.745, v.6 p.432*
Wolman, Yecheskel.. . . . . *v.5 p.256*
Woloch, Isser *v.3 p.153*
Woloch, Nancy. *v.4 p.439*
Wolpe, Joseph & Lazarus, A. *v.5 p.667*
Wolpe, Joseph *v.5 p.667*
Wolper, Lawrence F. *v.5 p.514*
Wolpert, Andrew *v.3 p.20*
Wolpert, Lewis. *v.2 p.405, v.5 p.162*
Wolpert, Stanley A. *v.6 p.162, p.163*

Wolpert, Stanley *v.6 p.155, p.160*
Wolpin, Miles D.. . . . . *v.4 p.574*
Wolpoff, Milford H. *v.4 p.16*
Wolschke-Bulmahn, Joachim (Editor) *v.1 p.820*
Wolt, Jeffrey D. *v.5 p.52*
Wolterstorff, Nicholas *v.1 p.596, p.652*
Wolverton, Lisa *v.3 p.188*
Wolverton, Mimi & Penley, Larry Edward (Editors) . *v.4 p.177*
Womack, Craig S. *v.6 p.699*
Womack, Mari *v.1 p.710*
Women of South Asian Descent Collective Staff
  (Editor). *v.6 p.92, p.138*
Womersley, David (Editor) *v.2 p.170, p.173*
Wong, Bernice Y. L. (Editor) *v.4 p.319*
Wong, C. -H & Whitesides, G. M.. . . . . *v.5 p.119, p.295*
Wong, Deborah A.. . . . . *v.1 p.16*
Wong, Deborah Anne *v.1 p.297*
Wong, Glenn M.. . . . . *v.4 p.449, p.901*
Wong, J. Y. *v.5 p.716, p.717*
Wong, Jade *v.6 p.95*
Wong, K. Scott & Chan, Sucheng (Editors). . *v.6 p.115, p.128*
Wong, K. Scott *v.6 p.116, p.128*
Wong, Kin-Lu *v.5 p.729*
Wong, Limsoon *v.5 p.99*
Wong, Ming H. *v.5 p.178*
Wong, Nellie, et al.. . . . . *v.6 p.105, p.113*
Wong, Paul T. P. & Wong, Lilian C. J. (Editors) . *v.4 p.699*
Wong, R. Bin *v.6 p.182, p.183, p.204*
Wong, Rita *v.1 p.750*
Wong, Roderick *v.5 p.658*
Wong, Rosemary T.. . . . . *v.4 p.278*
Wong, Samuel S. M. *v.5 p.554*
Wong, Sau-Ling Cynthia & Sumida, Stephen H.
  (Editors). *v.6 p.87, p.91*
Wong, Sau-Ling Cynthia. *v.6 p.98*
Wong, Shawn. *v.6 p.92, p.102*
Wong, Stanley. *v.4 p.197, p.251*
Wong, Young-Tsu *v.1 p.820*
Wong *v.4 p.904*
Wonnacott, Ronald J. & Wonnacott, Gordon P. . . *v.4 p.258*
Woo, Deborah *v.4 p.134, v.6 p.107*
Woo, P. (Editor). *v.5 p.32*
Wood, Allen W. *v.1 p.465*
Wood, Andrew G. *v.3 p.296*
Wood, Andrew Grant *v.4 p.765*
Wood, B. J. B. *v.5 p.36*
Wood, Charles H. & Porro, Roberto (Editors) . . *v.5 p.40*
Wood, Charles T. *v.3 p.96, p.144*
Wood, Christopher *v.1 p.667, p.724, p.725, p.726*
Wood, David (Editor). *v.1 p.458*
Wood, David. *v.5 p.699*
Wood, Dennis *v.2 p.479*
Wood, Douglas J. *v.4 p.427*
Wood, E. J., et al. *v.5 p.129*
Wood, Edward J. et al *v.5 p.129*

Wood, Elisabeth J. *v.3 p.300*
Wood, Elisabeth Jean *v.4 p.614*
Wood, Elizabeth A. *v.3 p.55, p.225, v.6 p.443*
Wood, Ellen *v.2 p.319*
Wood, Eric F. & Princeton Water Resources Group
   Staff. *v.5 p.369, p.380*
Wood, Floris W. *v.5 p.586, p.587*
Wood, Frances *v.6 p.239*
Wood, Gordon S. & Institute of Early American History and
   Culture Staff *v.3 p.410*
Wood, Gordon S. *v.4 p.517*
Wood, Houston. *v.6 p.131*
Wood, Ian *v.3 p.67*
Wood, James B. *v.3 p.146*
Wood, Jeryldene M. (Editor) *v.1 p.750*
Wood, John C. & Woods, Ronald N. (Editors) . . . *v.4 p.197*
Wood, John C. (Editor) *v.4 p.229*
Wood, John Cunningham & McLure, Michael *v.4 p.197*
Wood, John Cunningham & Wood, Michael C. *v.5 p.580*
Wood, John (Editor) *v.1 p.763*
Wood, John H. *v.4 p.156*
Wood, Marcus *v.1 p.705*
Wood, Marilynn J., et al. *v.5 p.529*
Wood, Martin *v.5 p.90*
Wood, M. *v.5 p.90*
Wood, Michael *v.2 p.684, p.685*
Wood, Paul & Gaiger, Jason. *v.1 p.704*
Wood, Paul (Editor) *v.5 p.227*
Wood, Peter *v.4 p.709*
Wood, Rega *v.1 p.651, p.652*
Wood, Robert E. *v.1 p.480*
Wood, Sharon *v.2 p.698*
Wood, Stanley. *v.5 p.11*
Wood, Stephanie Gail. *v.3 p.288*
Wood, Stephanie *v.3 p.264*
Wood, Stephen B. *v.4 p.447*
Wood, Terry Lee (Editor), et al. *v.4 p.366*
Wood, William A. *v.6 p.172*
Wood, William Burke *v.1 p.119, p.155, p.157, p.159*
Woodall, James *v.2 p.679*
Woodard, Helena. *v.2 p.173*
Woodbridge, Frederick J. *v.1 p.498*
Woodbridge, Linda *v.2 p.170*
Woodbridge, Sally B. *v.1 p.795, p.796*
Woodcock, E. C. *v.2 p.424*
Woodcock, George *v.2 p.355, p.376*
Woodcock, Sarah C. *v.1 p.25*
Wooden, Wayne S. & Ehringer, Gavin . *v.4 p.865, p.881, p.882*
Woodford, Arthur M. *v.3 p.517*
Woodford, Neil & Johnson, Alan
   (Editors) *v.5 p.105, p.119, p.143, p.147*
Woodford, Susan. *v.1 p.671, p.689*
Woodham, Jonathan M. *v.1 p.713*
Woodham, Jonathan *v.1 p.712*
Woodham Smith, Cecil Blanche Fitz Gerald . . . *v.3 p.91, p.117*

Woodham-Smith, Cecil *v.3 p.139*
Woodhead, A. G. *v.3 p.13*
Woodhead, James A. (Editor) *v.5 p.419*
Woodhouse, C. M. *v.3 p.194*
Woodhouse, John *v.2 p.716, p.717*
Woodhouse, Reed *v.6 p.394*
Woodhull, Victoria C. *v.4 p.708*
Woodhull, Winifred. *v.2 p.542*
Woodill, Gary (Editor), et al. . . *v.4 p.314, p.359, p.369, p.370*
Woodin, S. & British Ecological Society *v.5 p.178*
Woodman, A. J. *v.2 p.426, p.445*
Woodring, Carl R. & Shapiro, James (Editors) . . . *v.2 p.180*
Woodroffe, C. D. *v.5 p.424*
Woodroffe, Colin D. *v.4 p.393*
Woodroffe, John *v.1 p.538*
Woods, Charles A. and Sergile, Florence E. . *v.3 p.316, v.5 p.169*
Woods, Donald *v.6 p.80*
Woods, James D. & Lucas, Jay H. *v.6 p.382*
Woods, Lawrence T. *v.4 p.640*
Woods, Michael *v.4 p.396*
Woods, Randall B. *v.3 p.393*
Woods, Randall Bennett (Editor). *v.3 p.445*
Woods, Randall Bennett. *v.3 p.464*
Woods, Richard (Editor) *v.1 p.531*
Woods, Thomas A. *v.5 p.6, p.7*
Woodside, Alexander B. *v.6 p.167, p.168*
Woodside, Alexander. *v.6 p.167, p.237*
Woodside, Gayle & Kocurek, Dianna *v.5 p.682, p.683*
Woodson, Carter Godwin. *v.4 p.310, p.311, v.6 p.21*
Woodson, Jacqueline *v.6 p.376, p.400*
Woodstra, Chris, et al. . . *v.1 p.172, p.234, p.235, p.238, p.244*
Woodward, Arthur E. *v.5 p.323, p.324*
Woodward, Bob *v.3 p.482, p.484, v.4 p.90, p.156, p.565*
Woodward, C. Vann & Muhlenfeld, Elisabeth (Editors). *v.3 p.429*
Woodward, C. Vann. *v.3 p.403, p.435, p.439, p.494,*
                                        p.497, v.6 p.9, p.41
Woodward, David *v.3 p.80*
Woodward, G.W.O. *v.1 p.578*
Woodward, J. (Editor) *v.2 p.810*
Woodward, Peggy *v.5 p.534, p.535*
Woodward, Peter *v.3 p.393, v.6 p.59*
Woodward, Richard B. *v.1 p.769*
Woodworth, David & Hobbs, Guy (Editors) *v.4 p.171*
Woodworth, David *v.4 p.171*
Woodworth, Lynn (Editor) *v.5 p.434*
Woodworth, Steven E. & Winkle, Kenneth J. *v.4 p.381*
Woodworth, Steven E. (Editor) *v.4 p.522*
Woodworth, Steven E. *v.4 p.522*
Woody, Robert & Woody, Jane (Editors) *v.5 p.675*
Woof, Robert *v.2 p.324*
Woog, Dan *v.4 p.839, v.6 p.384, p.386*
Wooldridge, Jeffrey M. *v.4 p.205, p.206*
Woolf, D. R. *v.3 p.88, p.102, p.104*
Woolf, Greg (Editor). *v.3 p.22*

Woolf, Greg *v.3 p.29, p.142*

Woolf, Stuart J. *v.3 p.75*

Woolf, Vicki *v.1 p.14*

Woolf, Virginia & Prose, Francine *v.2 p.395*

Woolf, Virginia. *v.2 p.393, p.394, p.395, p.397, p.399,*
p.570, p.576, v.6 p.400, p.480

Woolfenden, Gregory W. *v.1 p.655*

Woolford, John & Karlin, Daniel *v.2 p.272*

Woolfson, Adrian. *v.5 p.138*

Woolfson, Michael & Hai-fu, Fan *v.5 p.284*

Woolhouse, Roger S. *v.1 p.504, p.505*

Woollcombe, Tamsyn. *v.1 p.782*

Woolley, Leonard. *v.3 p.6*

Woolrych, Austin. *v.3 p.104*

Woolum, Janet *v.4 p.838*

Wooster, Ralph A. *v.3 p.365, p.421*

Wooster, Robert *v.6 p.688, p.693*

Wootton, R. J. *v.5 p.216*

Wootton, Robert J. *v.5 p.217*

Worcester, Nancy & Whately, Marianne *v.5 p.524*

Worden, Blair *v.2 p.170, p.217*

Worden, J. William. *v.5 p.629*

Worden, Nigel. *v.6 p.80*

Wordsworth, Dorothy. *v.2 p.322*

Wordsworth, Jonathan *v.2 p.173, p.324*

Wordsworth, Jonathon & Wordsworth, Jessica (Contribution
by) *v.2 p.201, p.583*

Wordsworth, William & Coleridge, Samuel
Taylor. *v.2 p.280, p.325*

Wordsworth, William & Wordsworth, Mary. *v.2 p.325*

Wordsworth, William, et al. *v.2 p.325*

Wordsworth, William *v.2 p.324, p.325, v.3 p.110, p.127*

Worell, Judith (Editor) *v.4 p.679, v.6 p.426*

Worell, Judy (Editor). *v.5 p.642*

Worger, William H., et al. *v.6 p.56*

Workers of the WPA Writers Program Staff (Compiled
by) *v.3 p.501*

World Bank Group *v.4 p.56*

World Bank Institute Staff. *v.6 p.726*

World Bank Staff (Contribution by) *v.4 p.337*

World Bank Staff. *v.4 p.260, p.373, v.6 p.181*

World Conservation Monitoring Centre. *v.5 p.224*

World Health Organization Staff & International Union of Pure
and Applied Chemistry Staff. *v.5 p.314*

World Health Organization *v.4 p.669, v.5 p.672*

World Legal Information Institute. *v.4 p.436, p.475, p.476, p.477*

World Resources Institute (Created by) . . . *v.6 p.299, p.301*

World Resources Institute
Staff *v.4 p.177, v.5 p.357, p.367, p.370, p.378*

World Tourism Organization (WTO) Staff *v.4 p.162*

World Wildlife Fund Staff *v.5 p.178, p.182*

Worldwatch Institute. *v.5 p.357, p.360, p.367*

Wormald, Jennifer *v.3 p.122, p.133*

Wormeli, Rick *v.4 p.366*

Wormuth, Francis D. & Firmage, Edwin B.. . . . . *v.4 p.461*

Wormuth, Francis D., et al. *v.4 p.532*

Worobec, Christine D. *v.3 p.218*

Worrall, Anne & Hoy, Claire *v.6 p.278*

Worrall, Linda & Hickson, Louise M. *v.5 p.665*

Worrall, Nick *v.1 p.81, p.84, p.111, p.138*

Worsley, Peter. *v.1 p.544, p.545, v.4 p.37*

Worster, Donald *v.3 p.528, v.6 p.297*

Worth, George J.. . . . . *v.6 p.740, p.742*

Worth, Katharine. *v.2 p.249, p.260*

Worth, Richard. *v.3 p.508*

Worthen, James *v.2 p.364*

Worthen, John & Harrison, Andrew *v.2 p.364*

Worthen, John *v.2 p.280, p.325, p.326, p.364*

Worthen, W. B. *v.1 p.69, p.75, p.77, p.105, p.129, p.136*

Worthen, William B.. . . . . *v.1 p.57, p.70, p.105, p.119, p.138*

Worthington, Ian (Editor). *v.3 p.20*

Worthington, Ian *v.2 p.409*

Wortman, Richard *v.3 p.211*

Worton, Michael *v.2 p.535*

Wou, Odoric Y. K. *v.6 p.193, p.207*

Wouk, Herman *v.2 p.129*

Wouters, Cas. *v.4 p.738*

Woy, James (Editor) *v.4 p.181*

Wozniak, Danielle *v.4 p.759*

Wrangham, Richard W. (Editor), et al. *v.5 p.616*

Wrathall, Mark A. *v.1 p.471*

Wray, L. Randall *v.4 p.233*

Wren, J. Thomas *v.4 p.72*

Wriggins, Sally Hovey *v.6 p.185, p.203, p.239*

Wright, Alison *v.1 p.700*

Wright, Allen *v.2 p.269*

Wright, Andrew *v.2 p.269*

Wright, Angus & Wolford, Wendy. *v.3 p.270, p.343*

Wright, Angus *v.3 p.270*

Wright, Arthur F. & Twitchett, Denis Crispin (Editors). *v.6 p.185*

Wright, Arthur F. *v.1 p.563, v.6 p.185*

Wright, Barbara *v.2 p.490*

Wright, Charles *v.2 p.159*

Wright, Christopher. *v.1 p.726*

Wright, Conrad. *v.1 p.590*

Wright, Craig *v.1 p.178*

Wright, D. F. (Editor). *v.1 p.603*

Wright, Dawn J. & Bartlett, Darius J. *v.4 p.393*

Wright, Derek (Editor) *v.2 p.755*

Wright, Derek. *v.2 p.752, p.758*

Wright, Donald R.. . . . . *v.6 p.69*

Wright, Doug & Mahlsdorf, Charlotte von . *v.2 p.159, v.6 p.413*

Wright, Esmond *v.3 p.410*

Wright, Franz *v.2 p.159*

Wright, Georg H. *v.1 p.503, p.504*

Wright, James D., et al.. . . . . *v.4 p.751, p.769*

Wright, James *v.2 p.129*

Wright, Jim *v.4 p.820, p.848, p.849*

Wright, John & Wright, Richardson. *v.6 p.60, p.641*

Wright, Jonathan. *v.3 p.170, p.171*

Wright, Joseph & Wright, Elizabeth M. *v.2 p.551*

Wright, Judith *v.2 p.749*

Wright, Judy *v.1 p.34*

Wright, Kevin N.. . . . . *v.6 p.275*

Wright, Laura (Editor) *v.2 p.555*

Wright, Lorraine M. & Leahey, Maureen. . . . *v.5 p.525, p.528*

Wright, Louis B.. . . . . *v.3 p.407, p.501*

Wright, M. R. *v.1 p.500*

Wright, Mabel Osgood & Philippon, Daniel J. *v.5 p.235*

Wright, Marcia *v.6 p.62*

Wright, Mary C. *v.6 p.189*

Wright, N. T. *v.1 p.631, p.632, p.642*

Wright, Paul & Herivel, Tara (Editors) *v.6 p.274*

Wright, Paul H., et al. *v.5 p.701*

Wright, Quincy *v.3 p.36, v.4 p.628*

Wright, Richard A.. . . . . *v.6 p.274*

Wright, Richard T. & Decker, Scott H.. . . . . . *v.6 p.253*

Wright, Richard *v.2 p.138, v.6 p.9, p.41*

Wright, Robert A. *v.3 p.535*

Wright, Robert E. & Cowen, David J.. . . . . . *v.4 p.90, p.148*

Wright, Russell O. *v.4 p.424, p.811, p.853, p.886, p.890, p.892, p.893, p.898*

Wright, Sam *v.4 p.713*

Wright, Sarah B.. . . . . *v.2 p.132, p.133*

Wright, Sarah Bird *v.2 p.292*

Wright, Stephen C. (Editor) *v.2 p.64*

Wright, Stephen G. & Duncan, J. Michael *v.5 p.699*

Wright, Susan (Editor) *v.4 p.657*

Wright, Vincent *v.4 p.609*

Wright, Walter F.. . . . . *v.2 p.300*

Wright, Will *v.6 p.325*

Wright, William (Abridged by) *v.6 p.653*

Wright, William *v.6 p.655*

Wright, Winthrop R.. . . . . *v.3 p.281, p.360, p.361*

Wright-McLeod, Brian *v.6 p.699*

Wrightsman, Lawrence S., et al. *v.5 p.593*

Wrightsman, Lawrence S. *v.5 p.593, p.629, p.632*

Wrigley, Chris (Editor) *v.4 p.213*

Wrigley, E. Anthony & Schofield, Roger S.. . . . *v.3 p.43, p.90*

Wrigley, E. Anthony, et al. *v.3 p.43*

Writers' Program of the Work Projects Administration in th Staff *v.3 p.509, p.510*

Writers Program Staff *v.3 p.501, p.505*

Wrobel, David M. *v.3 p.382*

Wrolstad, Ronald E., et al. *v.5 p.36*

Wrong, Michela. *v.6 p.67*

Wronka, Joseph *v.4 p.670*

Wu, Carl & Allis, C. David *v.5 p.143*

Wu, Catherine H. & McLarty, Jerry W.. . *v.5 p.99, p.143, p.147*

Wu Ch'eng-en *v.6 p.212*

Wu, Chi-Yuen *v.4 p.251*

Wu, Diana T.. . . . . *v.6 p.117*

Wu, Duncan & DeMaria, Robert Jr. (Editors) *v.2 p.201*

Wu, Duncan & Treharne, Elaine (Editors). *v.2 p.168, p.169, p.201*

Wu, Duncan & Womersley, David (Editors). *v.2 p.202*

Wu, Duncan (Editor) *v.2 p.173, p.201*

Wu, Duncan *v.2 p.189*

Wu, Frank *v.4 p.729, p.731, v.6 p.108, p.125*

Wu, Harry & Wakeman, Carolyn *v.6 p.203*

Wu, Hung *v.1 p.694*

Wu Hung *v.1 p.778*

Wu, John C. H. *v.1 p.568*

Wu, Qingyun *v.6 p.481*

Wu, Tai Te (Editor). *v.5 p.129*

Wu, Wei & Yu, H. -S. (Editors) *v.5 p.699*

Wu, William F. *v.6 p.98, p.128*

Wuerth, Louis A.. . . . . *v.1 p.758*

Wuest, Deborah A. & Bucher, Charles A.. . . . . . *v.4 p.797*

Wulfemeyer, K. Tim & Buckalew, James K. *v.4 p.417*

Wulff, David H. *v.5 p.636*

Wullschlager, Jackie *v.2 p.177*

Wunder, Heide *v.3 p.52, p.165*

Wunder, John R. *v.4 p.465, v.6 p.693*

Wunderlin, Clarence E. *v.3 p.464*

Wuorinen, John Henry *v.3 p.236*

Wurgaft, Lewis D. *v.2 p.298*

Wurzel, Rudiger K. *v.4 p.604, v.6 p.301, p.303, p.305*

Wushanley, Ying *v.4 p.811, p.839, v.6 p.438*

Wuthnow, Robert. *v.4 p.720, p.755, v.5 p.670*

Wyandt, Herman Edwin & Tonk, Vijay S. (Editors) . *v.5 p.138*

Wyatt, David K. *v.6 p.172*

Wyatt, Donald *v.2 p.355*

Wyatt, H. V. (Editor) *v.5 p.325*

Wyatt, Robert & Johnson, John Andrew (Editors). *v.1 p.227, p.254, p.325*

Wyatt, Thomas *v.1 p.538, v.2 p.217*

Wyatt-Brown, Bertram *v.3 p.422, p.494, p.496*

Wybrew, Hugh *v.1 p.570*

Wycherley, R. E. *v.3 p.19*

Wycherley, William. *v.2 p.264*

Wyckoff, Lydia & Jones, Ruthe B.. . . . . *v.1 p.734*

Wyckoff, William & Dilsaver, Lary M. (Editors) . . . *v.3 p.525*

Wyer, Mary (Editor), et al. *v.5 p.398, v.6 p.439*

Wyer, Robert S. Jr. & Srull, Thomas K. (Editors). *v.4 p.692, p.693*

Wyeth, N. C. *v.1 p.716, p.717*

Wyke, Maria. *v.6 p.315*

Wykes, David *v.2 p.247*

Wykes, Maggie *v.4 p.407*

Wyld, Henry Cecil Kennedy. *v.2 p.555*

Wylie, Elinor H. *v.2 p.129*

Wylie, Laurence William *v.3 p.141*

Wylie, Philip. *v.3 p.370*

WYLIE *v.4 p.399*

Wyman, Matthew, et al. *v.4 p.578, p.599*

Wymer, Rowland. *v.6 p.419*

Wyn Jones, David, et al. *v.1 p.192, p.331*

Wyndham-Lewis, D. B. & Lee, Charles (Editors). *v.2 p.586, p.587, p.589*

Wynn, Graeme & Oke, Timothy *v.3 p.547*

Wynn, Neil A. *v.3 p.482*

Wynne, Clive D. L.. . . . . *v.5 p.616*

Wynne-Davies, Marion (Editor) *v.2 p.165, p.166*
Wypych, George *v.5 p.741*
Wyschogrod, Edith *v.1 p.501*
Wyse, Akintola J. *v.6 p.73*
Wyspianski, Stanislaw *v.2 p.792*

X

Xanthakos, Petros P. *v.5 p.697*
Xenakis, Christopher I. *v.3 p.223*
Xenakis, Iannis *v.1 p.227, p.368, p.374*
Xenophon *v.1 p.423, v.2 p.422, p.423, v.3 p.15*
Xianguo, L. *v.5 p.742*
Xiaolong, Qiu *v.6 p.207, p.213*
Xie, Yu & Shauman, Kimberlee A. *v.5 p.398, v.6 p.439*
Xing, Jun & Hirabayashi, Ryo (Editors) . . . *v.6 p.475, p.476*
Xing, Jun *v.6 p.89, p.90*
Xing, Wan-Li & Cheng, Jing (Editors) *v.5 p.130*
Xiong, Jin *v.5 p.99*
Xu, Xi & Ingham, Mike (Editors) *v.2 p.761*

Y

Yü, Chün-fang *v.1 p.566*
Yacine, Kateb *v.2 p.546, p.547*
Yaeger, Don *v.4 p.822, p.823, p.895, p.901*
Yaffee, Steven L., et al. *v.5 p.186, p.235*
Yager, Fred & Yager, Jan *v.4 p.150*
Yagoda, Ben *v.4 p.410*
Yakhlif, Yahya *v.6 p.664*
Yakovleva, Natalia *v.6 p.297*
Yale Law School *v.4 p.451*
Yalom, Irvin D. & Leszcz, Molyn *v.5 p.669*
Yalom, Marilyn (Author,
  Introduction by) *v.3 p.55, p.151, p.152, p.158*
Yamada, Haru *v.4 p.20*
Yamada, Koun *v.6 p.223, p.235*
Yamada, Mitsuye *v.6 p.104*
Yamaguchi, Kaoru *v.4 p.229, p.230*
Yamamoto, Akio *v.5 p.307*
Yamamoto, Eric K. *v.6 p.117, p.125*
Yamamoto, Hisaye *v.6 p.102*
Yamamoto, Mari *v.4 p.712*
Yamamoto, Traise *v.6 p.98, p.113, p.133, p.481*
Yamamuro, Jerry A. & Kaliakin, Victor N. (Editors) . *v.5 p.699*
Yamanaka, Lois-Ann *v.6 p.102, p.104*
Yamashita, Karen T. *v.6 p.102*
Yamauchi, Edwin M. *v.1 p.618, p.647*
Yamauchi, Wakako *v.6 p.95, p.99, p.105*
Yamayee, Zia A. & Bala, Juan L. Jr. *v.5 p.725*
Yamey, Basil S. *v.1 p.826*
Yan, Mo *v.6 p.213*
Yan, Peter V. (Editor) *v.5 p.99*
Yan, Yunxiang *v.4 p.734, p.772*
Yanagisako, Sylvia J. *v.6 p.133*

Yanak, Ted & Cornelison, Pamela *v.3 p.373*
Yancey, George *v.6 p.125*
Yancey, Kathleen Blake *v.2 p.566*
Yandell, Benjamin *v.5 p.468*
Yanez, Agustin *v.2 p.669, p.670*
Yanez, Mirta (Editor) *v.2 p.673*
Yang, Alice, et al. *v.6 p.87*
Yang, Bingen *v.5 p.697*
Yang, Ch'ing-k'un *v.4 p.708*
Yang, Fenggang *v.1 p.608, v.6 p.106, p.128*
Yang, Hsin, et al. *v.1 p.734*
Yang, Rae *v.6 p.196*
Yaniv, Avner (Editor) *v.6 p.616*
Yannella, Donald (Editor) *v.2 p.49*
Yannella, Donald *v.2 p.38*
Yanow, Scott *v.1 p.265, v.6 p.317*
Yans-McLaughlin, Virginia *v.3 p.491*
Yantis, Steven (Editor) *v.5 p.607*
Yao, Xinzhong *v.1 p.418*
Yapp, M. E. *v.3 p.77*
Yaqub, Salim (Instructed by) *v.6 p.595*
Yarbro-Bejarano, Yvonne *v.6 p.504, p.516*
Yarbrough, Tinsley E. *v.4 p.467, p.540*
Yardeni, Ada *v.6 p.646*
Yardley, Anne Bagnall *v.1 p.178, p.380*
Yardley, Bruce W. *v.5 p.440*
Yardley, John *v.2 p.445*
Yared, NazikSaba *v.6 p.664*
Yaremko, Jason M. *v.3 p.314*
Yarmolinsky, Adam, et al. *v.4 p.301*
Yarnell, Susan L. *v.3 p.498*
Yarnold, Edward S. *v.1 p.593*
Yarrington, Douglas *v.3 p.361, p.363*
Yarrow, Philip John *v.2 p.456, p.457*
Yarshater, E. (Editor) *v.6 p.630*
Yarshater, Ehsan (Editor) *v.6 p.630*
Yarshater, Ehsan *v.6 p.673, p.675, p.677*
Yasser, Joseph *v.1 p.374*
Yastrebtsev, V. V. & Jonas, Florence *v.1 p.207, p.350*
Yatchew, Adonis *v.4 p.205*
Yate, Martin *v.4 p.171*
Yates, Frances A. *v.1 p.473, v.3 p.48*
Yates, Jeff *v.4 p.540, p.541*
Yates, Richard *v.2 p.159*
Yates, W. E. *v.2 p.597*
Yau, John *v.6 p.104*
Yavuz, M. Hakan & Esposito, John L. (Editors) . . . *v.6 p.625*
Yaws, Carl L. *v.5 p.287*
Yaws, Carl *v.5 p.316*
Yazawa, Melvin (Editor) *v.3 p.488*
Ybarra, Raul E. & López, Nancy *v.4 p.301*
Ye, Weili & Xiadong, Ma *v.6 p.196, p.203, p.217*
Yeager, Gertrude M. *v.3 p.296*
Yeager, Rodger *v.6 p.66*
Yeang, Ken *v.5 p.367*

Yeang, Kenneth *v.5 p.361, p.374*
Yeaple, Franklin D.. . . . . *v.5 p.709*
Yeargers, E. K., et al.. . . . . *v.5 p.502*
Yeargers, Edward K.. . . . . *v.5 p.125*
Yeats, Robert S., et al.. . . . . *v.5 p.442*
Yeats, W. B.. . . . . *v.2 p.327, p.328*
Yee, Rodney & Zolotow, Nina. *v.4 p.793*
Yee, Shirley J.. . . . . *v.6 p.37, p.47*
Yefremov, Ivan, et al.. . . . . *v.2 p.810*
Yegenoglu, Meyda *v.6 p.595, p.596*
Yeh, Michelle *v.6 p.211*
Yeh, Wen-hsin *v.6 p.191*
Yehoshua, A. B.. . . . . *v.6 p.652*
Yeide, Nancy H., et al.. . . . . *v.1 p.827*
Yellin, Jean Fagan *v.6 p.19, p.38, p.47*
Yellin, Victor F.. . . . . *v.1 p.374*
Yellow Robe, William S.. . . *v.1 p.124, v.6 p.699*
Yelon, Stephen L.. . . . . *v.4 p.349*
Yelvington, Kevin A.. . . . . *v.4 p.41*
Yen Ho, Alice *v.6 p.165*
Yena, Donna J.. . . . . *v.4 p.168*
Yeo, Robert *v.2 p.761*
Yeoman, Ian (Editor), et al.. . . . . *v.1 p.825*
Yeomans, J. M.. . . . . *v.5 p.559*
Yepsen, Roger B.. . . . . . *v.5 p.370, p.381, p.383, p.385*
Yergin, Daniel & Stanislaw, Joseph *v.4 p.56, p.58*
Yergin, Daniel *v.4 p.160*
Yerkes, Robert M. & Stevenson, Fanny *v.5 p.616*
Yerkes, Robert M.. . . . . *v.5 p.616*
Yesalis, Charles E. & Cowart, Virginia S. . . *v.4 p.826, p.827*
Yesalis, Charles E.. . . . . *v.4 p.826*
Yeschke, Charles L.. . . . . *v.6 p.267*
Yeung, Yue-man & Li, Xiaojian *v.4 p.397*
Yevtushenko, Yevgeny *v.2 p.810*
Yew, Lee Kuan. *v.6 p.173*
Yglesias, José *v.6 p.509*
Yi, Nam-ho, et al. *v.6 p.238*
Yi, Xiong; Qingkui, Li. *v.5 p.52*
Yiannias, John L. (Editor). *v.3 p.191*
Yildiz, Kerim & Blass, Tom *v.6 p.600, p.602*
Yildiz, Kerim *v.6 p.600, p.622*
Yin, An & Harrison, Mark (Editors) *v.5 p.433*
Yin, Robert K.. . . . . *v.4 p.688*
Yin, Xiao-Huang *v.6 p.98, p.128*
Yinger, John (Editor) *v.4 p.302*
Ying-Hsing, Sung *v.6 p.198*
Yingling, Thomas E.. . . . . . . *v.2 p.68, v.6 p.394*
Yishai, Yael *v.6 p.616*
Ylinen, Jari & Cash, Mel *v.4 p.826*
YMCA of the USA Staff *v.4 p.792, p.797*
YMCA of the USA.. . . . . *v.4 p.792*
Yoast, Bill R.. . . . . *v.4 p.860*
Yockey, Hubert P.. . . . . *v.5 p.198*
Yoder, Edwin *v.3 p.376*
Yoder, H. S. Jr.. . . . . *v.5 p.437*

Yoder, Jennifer A.. . . . . *v.4 p.610*
Yodzis, Peter.. . . . . *v.5 p.503*
Yoffee, Norman (Editor, Contribution by). *v.4 p.6*
Yoke, Ho Peng. *v.6 p.198*
Yoke, Mary & Carol, Kennedy *v.4 p.793, p.794, p.880*
Yokoi, Yuho & Victoria, Daizen *v.1 p.568*
Yolton, John W. (Introduction by) *v.1 p.449*
Yolton, John W.. . . . . *v.1 p.436, p.449*
Yonemoto, Marcia *v.6 p.226*
Yonemura, Ann, et al.. . . . . *v.1 p.694*
Yoneyama, Shoko *v.6 p.223*
Yong, Raymond N.. . . . . *v.5 p.422, p.423*
Yonge, C. D. (Translator) *v.1 p.546*
Yoo, David K.. . . . . *v.6 p.115, p.133*
Yoon, In-Jin. *v.6 p.107, p.125, p.137*
Yorke, James A.. . . . . *v.5 p.489*
Yosef, Raz.. . . . . *v.6 p.417*
Yoshida, Shigeru *v.6 p.229*
Yoshida, Yoshishige *v.6 p.337*
Yoshihara, Mari *v.6 p.98, p.115*
Yoshimoto, Banana. *v.6 p.234*
Yosso, Tara *v.6 p.528*
Yost, David S.. . . . . . . *v.4 p.639, p.640, p.655*
Yost, Jeffrey R. *v.4 p.158, v.5 p.405, p.406*
Youens, Susan *v.1 p.207, p.238, p.354, p.368*
Young & Shane (Editors). *v.5 p.733, p.734*
Young, Alexandra Patricia & Morton, Tammy B. . . . *v.5 p.534*
Young, Alfred F. (Editor) *v.3 p.410, p.411*
Young, Alfred F.. . . . . *v.3 p.411*
Young, Anthony *v.5 p.370, p.371, p.374*
Young, Barbara, et al.. . . . . *v.5 p.159*
Young, Brigitte. *v.3 p.177, p.178, v.4 p.610*
Young, Christine A.. . . . . *v.3 p.489*
Young, Copeland H., et al. *v.4 p.689*
Young, Crawford *v.4 p.574, p.576, p.577*
Young, David A.. . . . . *v.5 p.282*
Young, David C.. . . . . *v.4 p.847*
Young, David G. *v.5 p.82, p.198*
Young, Davis A.. . . . . *v.5 p.437*
Young, Edward. *v.2 p.264*
Young, Elizabeth *v.2 p.10, v.6 p.481*
Young, Elliott *v.3 p.296, v.6 p.488, p.533*
Young, Ernest P.. . . . . *v.6 p.191, p.203*
Young, Frances & Mitchell, Margaret (Editors) . . . *v.1 p.600*
Young, Frances (Editor), et al.. . . . . *v.1 p.593*
Young, Frances. *v.1 p.646*
Young, G. M. (George Malcolm) *v.3 p.117, p.130*
Young, George F.. . . . . *v.3 p.351*
Young, George M.. . . . . *v.6 p.736, p.751*
Young, Ian *v.6 p.359, p.360, p.391*
Young, Iris Marion.. . . . . *v.4 p.506, p.514*
Young, J. Francis, et al.. . . . . *v.5 p.692*
Young, James F. & Shane (Editors) *v.5 p.733*
Young, James P.. . . . . *v.3 p.375*
Young, James S.. . . . . *v.3 p.415*

Young, James Webb *v.4 p.428*
Young, Jay A. (Editor) *v.5 p.266*
Young, Jay A.; Kinglsey, Warren K.;
  Wahl, George H., Jr. *v.5 p.266, p.267*
Young, Jeffrey T. *v.4 p.220*
Young, John W. *v.3 p.157*
Young, Julian *v.1 p.509*
Young, Kate *v.6 p.458*
Young, Katherine & Sharma, Arvind *v.1 p.529*
Young, Kevin (Editor) *v.6 p.28*
Young, Lisa & Everitt, Joanna. *v.4 p.591*
Young, M. J. L. (Editor), et al. *v.6 p.664*
Young, Margaret Labash (Editor) *v.5 p.386*
Young, Margaret Levine *v.5 p.679*
Young, Marilyn *v.6 p.169*
Young, Matt *v.5 p.561*
Young, Michael & Willmott, Peter *v.4 p.37, p.38*
Young, Michael W. *v.4 p.5*
Young, Paul H.. . . . . *v.5 p.726*
Young, Paul *v.5 p.99, p.143, p.147*
Young, Philip *v.2 p.86*
Young, R. G.. . . . . *v.6 p.320*
Young, Richard B. *v.2 p.217, v.4 p.291*
Young, Robert A.. . . . . *v.3 p.544*
Young, Robert (Editor) *v.4 p.581*
Young, Robert J. *v.3 p.82, p.141, p.156*
Young, Robert M. *v.3 p.117*
Young, Roland A. *v.3 p.482*
Young, Serinity (Editor). *v.1 p.529*
Young, Serinity *v.6 p.460*
Young, Simon S. *v.5 p.92, p.93, p.94, p.95, p.99*
Young, Steven B.. . . . . *v.5 p.238*
Young, Terence & Riley, Robert B. (Editors) . . *v.1 p.820, p.821*
Young, Terence. *v.1 p.820*
Young, Theodore Cuyler *v.6 p.582*
Young, Virginia Heyer *v.4 p.5*
Young, W. Arthur. *v.2 p.298*
Young, Walter D.. . . . . *v.4 p.589*
Young-Jin, Kim (Editor) *v.5 p.697*
Youngkin, Ellis Quinn & Davis, Marcia Szmania . . . *v.5 p.524*
Youngquist, Walter L.. . . . . *v.5 p.739*
Youngson, A. J. (Editor) *v.3 p.42*
Yount, Lisa *v.5 p.138, p.220, p.396, p.710*
Yount, Sylvia *v.1 p.750*
Yourcenar, Marguerite *v.6 p.400*
Yourdon, Edward *v.4 p.70*
Youssef, Saadi *v.6 p.664*
Ysursa, John M.. . . . . *v.1 p.33*
Yu, Anthony C. (Editor). *v.6 p.212*
Yu, Anthony C. (Translator). *v.6 p.212*
Yu, Eden S H & Kwan, Yum K *v.4 p.398*
Yu, Eui-Young (Editor). *v.6 p.115, p.125, p.137*
Yu, Francis T. S. & Yang, Xiangyang *v.5 p.702*
Yu, Guangyuan. *v.6 p.198*
Yu, Henry. *v.6 p.115, p.120, p.125*

Yu, Pauline *v.6 p.210*
Yu, Renqiu *v.6 p.107, p.128*
Yuan, Qu *v.6 p.210, p.211*
Yudkin, Jeremy *v.1 p.178, p.179*
Yudkin, Leon I. (Editor) *v.6 p.652*
Yudkoff, Alvin *v.1 p.14, p.32*
Yue, Gang. *v.6 p.209*
Yuh, Ji-Yeon Yuh. *v.6 p.237*
Yuh, Ji-Yeon. *v.6 p.116, p.137*
Yukichi, Fukuzawa *v.6 p.229*
Yu-ming, Shaw *v.6 p.201, p.204, p.218*
Yun, Grace (Introduction by) *v.6 p.108*
Yung, Judy, et al.. . . . . *v.6 p.115, p.128*
Yung, Judy *v.6 p.113, p.128*
Yungman, V. S. (Editor), et al.. . . . . *v.5 p.287*
Yunis, Harvey (Editor) *v.2 p.401*
Yurchak, Alexei *v.3 p.223*
Yuri, Tsivian *v.6 p.339*
Yusa, Michiko *v.1 p.476*

Z

Zabarko, Boris (Editor) *v.3 p.87, p.230*
Zablocki, Benjamin D. *v.4 p.740*
Zafar, Rafia. *v.2 p.9, p.10*
Zafirovski, Milan. *v.4 p.193*
Zafrani, Haim *v.6 p.598, p.643*
Zagare, Frank C.. . . . . *v.4 p.657*
Zagona, Karen *v.2 p.637*
Zagorin, Perez . . . *v.1 p.449, v.2 p.422, v.3 p.48, p.102, p.105*
Zagorski, Paul W. *v.4 p.593*
Zagorsky, Jay L.. . . . . *v.4 p.181, p.183, p.185*
Zahan, Dominique *v.1 p.543*
Zahava, Irene *v.2 p.27, v.6 p.407*
Zahlan, Rosemarie Said *v.6 p.626, p.627, p.628, p.629*
Zaidel, Dahlia W.. . . . . *v.5 p.619*
Zajas, Jay J. & Church, Olive D. *v.4 p.420*
Zak, Albin *v.1 p.276, p.363, p.364*
Zakin, Susan. *v.6 p.288*
Zakrajsek, Dorothy B., et al. *v.4 p.800*
Zalk, Sue R. & Gordon-Kelter, Janice
  (Editors) *v.4 p.255, p.267, p.274, p.275, p.277*
Zaller, Robert (Editor) *v.2 p.91*
Zalokar, Nadja. *v.6 p.20, p.21, p.47, p.48*
Zaltman, Gerald *v.5 p.587*
Zamagni, Stefano (Editor). *v.4 p.267*
Zaman, Niaz (Editor). *v.6 p.148, p.149*
Zaman, Niaz *v.2 p.761*
Zameret, Zvi *v.4 p.337*
Zamiatin, Eugene & Zamiatin, Yevgeny *v.2 p.810*
Zammattio, Carlo, et al.. . . . . *v.5 p.397*
Zamora, Daisy *v.2 p.677*
Zamosc, Leon *v.3 p.359*
Zamoyski, Adam *v.3 p.153, p.252, p.253, p.255*

Zanca, Kenneth J. *v.1 p.575*

Zanders (Editor) *v.5 p.147*

Zane, Arnie *v.1 p.46*

Zane, Nolan W. *v.6 p.87, p.122*

Zang, David W. *v.4 p.811, p.833, p.853*

Zang, David. *v.4 p.811, p.820, p.821*

Zanker, Paul *v.3 p.24, p.29*

Zapanta-Manlapaz, Edna *v.2 p.761*

Zappa, Frank *v.1 p.276, p.369*

Zaprudnik, Jan *v.3 p.230*

Zarate, Juan C. *v.3 p.303*

Zarb, Janet M. *v.5 p.666*

Zarembka, Paul & Soederberg, Susanne (Editors) . . . *v.4 p.239*

Zaretsky, Eli *v.4 p.692*

Zaretsky, Robert *v.3 p.156*

Zariski, Oscar & Samuel, Pierre *v.5 p.474*

Zarlino, Gioseffo. *v.1 p.181, p.182*

Zarnowska, Anna *v.3 p.253, p.254*

Zartman, I. William & Rubin, Jeffrey Z. (Editors) . . . *v.4 p.646*

Zartman, I. William (Editor) *v.4 p.613, v.6 p.72*

Zartman, I. William *v.6 p.60*

Zarur, Elizabeth Netto Calil & Lovell, Charles M. (Editors). *v.3 p.265, p.266*

Zaslaw, Neal & Cowdery, William. *v.1 p.193, p.345*

Zaslaw, Neal & Fiel, Fiona M. (Editors) *v.1 p.165, p.193, p.345*

Zaslaw, Neal (Editor) *v.1 p.193, p.244, p.345*

Zaslaw, Neal *v.1 p.192, p.193, p.244, p.345*

Zastoupil, Lynn *v.6 p.158*

Zatsiorsky, Vladimir M. (Editor). *v.4 p.827, p.828, p.829, p.880, p.908*

Zatsiorsky, Vladimir M. . . *v.4 p.880, p.908, p.909, p.910*

Zautra, Alex J. *v.4 p.699*

Zavos, John (Editor), et al. *v.6 p.158*

Zawacki, Andrew (Editor). *v.2 p.812*

Zawati, Hilmi M. & Mahmoud, Ibtisam M. *v.4 p.654*

Zayas, Maria De *v.2 p.653*

Zayas y Sotomayor, María de *v.2 p.653*

Zboray, Ronald J. *v.2 p.10*

Zea, Leopoldo *v.1 p.444*

Zebiri, Kate *v.1 p.559*

Zebovitz, Thomas C. *v.5 p.744*

Zedler, Joy B. *v.5 p.241, p.242*

Zedner, Lucia. *v.3 p.55, v.6 p.744, p.745, p.749*

Zee, A. *v.5 p.550*

Zeffirelli, Franco *v.6 p.419*

Zega, Michael E. & Gruber, John E. *v.1 p.719*

Zegura, Elizabeth & Tetel, Marcel *v.2 p.472*

Zegura, Elizabeth Chesney (Editor) *v.2 p.472*

Zehr, Howard & Toews, Barb (Editors). *v.6 p.279*

Zeidan, Joseph T. *v.6 p.481*

Zeidman, Irving *v.1 p.36*

Zeigler, Earle F. (Editor) *v.4 p.797*

Zeilinga de Boer, Jelle & Sanders, Donald Theodore . *v.5 p.442*

Zeine, Zeine N. *v.6 p.583*

Zein-Elabdin, Eiman O. & Charusheela, S. (Editors) *v.4 p.211, p.271*

Zeisel, Hans & Kaye, D. H. *v.4 p.179*

Zeitlin, Maurice *v.3 p.350*

Zeitz, Paul. *v.4 p.197*

Zelanski, Paul & Fisher, Mary Pat *v.1 p.710, p.711*

Zelazny, Gene *v.4 p.174*

Zeldin, Theodore *v.3 p.141*

Zelditch, Miriam, et al. *v.5 p.155*

Zelditch, Miriam Leah (Editor) *v.5 p.198*

Zelikow, Philip. *v.3 p.482*

Zelizer, Barbie *v.4 p.403*

Zelizer, Viviana A. Rotman *v.4 p.738*

Zelizer, Viviana A.. . . . . . . *v.4 p.718, p.719, p.735*

Zeller, Edward *v.1 p.428*

Zeman, Adam *v.5 p.618*

Zemanová, Mirka *v.1 p.227, p.333, p.334*

Zemans, Joyce *v.1 p.829*

Zemansky, Mark W. & Dittman, Richard *v.5 p.560*

Zemansky, Mark W. *v.5 p.560*

Zemelman, Steven *v.4 p.366*

Zemke, Ron, et al. *v.4 p.132*

Zenderland, Leila . . . *v.4 p.287, v.5 p.599, p.600, p.609, p.657*

Zenger, John Peter *v.4 p.438*

Zenios, S. A. & Ziemba, W. T. (Editors) *v.4 p.192*

Zenkovsky, Serge A. (Editor) *v.2 p.795*

Zenkovsky, V. V. *v.1 p.474*

Zentella, Ana C. *v.4 p.21*

Zenzen, Joan M. *v.1 p.824*

Zernov, Nicolas *v.1 p.610*

Zeromski, Stefan *v.2 p.792, v.3 p.253*

Zertal, Idith *v.6 p.616*

Zerubavel, Eviatar *v.5 p.650, p.651*

Zettl, Herbert *v.6 p.347*

Zewail, Ahmed H. (Editor) *v.5 p.282, p.283*

Zewail, Ahmed. *v.5 p.262*

Zewde, Bahru *v.6 p.64*

Zeyl, Donald (Editor). *v.1 p.421*

Zhai, Qiang *v.3 p.393, v.6 p.169*

Zhan, Lin & National League for Nursing Staff. *v.6 p.121, p.141*

Zhan, Lin *v.6 p.121, p.141*

Zhang, Wei & Shmulevich, Ilya (Editors) *v.5 p.93, p.130, p.147, p.148*

Zhang, Wei, et al. *v.5 p.101, p.102*

Zhang, Yumei *v.4 p.618, p.619, p.622*

Zhao, Quansheng. *v.4 p.622*

Zhao, Suisheng . . . *v.4 p.621, v.6 p.191, p.192, p.195*

Zhao, Xiaojian. *v.6 p.120, p.128*

Zhao, Xiao-Qiang *v.5 p.171*

Zhao, Yong (Editor) *v.4 p.352*

Zhen, Ni *v.6 p.209, p.335*

Zheng, Shiping. *v.4 p.621*

Zhi Ning, Chen & Michael Yan Wah, Chia *v.5 p.729*

Zhiti, Visar *v.2 p.815*

Zhong, Xueping (Editor), et al. *v.6 p.195, p.217*

Zhou, Jizhong, et al. *v.5 p.153*

Zhou, Min & Bankston, Carl L. III . . . *v.6 p.109, p.110, p.141*

Zhou, Xiaojing & Najmi, Samina *v.6 p.98*

Zhu, Liping *v.6 p.115, p.129*

Zi, Zhongyun *v.3 p.393, v.6 p.205*

Zia, Helen *v.6 p.105*

Ziad, Zeenut (Editor) *v.6 p.156*

Ziadeh, Nicola *v.6 p.607*

Ziblatt, Daniel. *v.3 p.168, p.169, p.202*

Zieger, Robert H.. . . . . *v.4 p.130*

Ziegler, P. A.. . . . . *v.5 p.432*

Ziegler, Philip *v.3 p.117, v.6 p.576*

Zielenbach, John W. *v.6 p.727*

Zielinski, T. J. & Swift, M. (Editors) *v.5 p.267*

Zielonka, Jan *v.4 p.599*

Zienkiewicz, O. C. & Taylor, R. L. *v.5 p.697*

Zierdt-Warshaw, Linda, et al.. . . . . . . *v.5 p.679, p.680*

Ziermann, Horst *v.1 p.750*

Zigerell, James. *v.2 p.252*

Zigler, Edward F. (Editor), et al. *v.4 p.304, p.354, p.359*

Zilboorg, Caroline *v.6 p.404*

Zilles, Klaus. *v.6 p.504, p.516*

Zim, Herbert S. *v.5 p.435*

Ziman, J. M.. . . . . *v.5 p.555*

Ziman, John M.. . . . . . . *v.5 p.405, p.411, p.412, p.413*

Zimbalist, Andrew & Brundenius, Claes *v.3 p.314*

Zimbalist, Andrew (Editor) *v.4 p.890*

Zimbalist, Andrew *v.4 p.853, p.890, p.895*

Zimdahl, Robert L.. . . . . *v.5 p.11, p.24*

Zimmer, Carl *v.5 p.198*

Zimmer, Elizabeth A. & Roalson, Eric (Volume
    Editors) *v.5 p.115, p.201*

Zimmer, Marc *v.5 p.96, p.220, p.227*

Zimmer, Oliver. *v.3 p.245*

Zimmerman, Barry J. & Schunk, Dale H.
    (Editors) *v.4 p.359, v.5 p.573*

Zimmerman, Bonnie (Editor) . . . *v.4 p.749, v.6 p.358, p.363*

Zimmerman, Bonnie *v.6 p.394*

Zimmerman, Cynthia *v.2 p.731*

Zimmerman, Franklin B. *v.1 p.165, p.187, p.188, p.349, p.350*

Zimmerman, Jonathan *v.4 p.762*

Zimmerman, Joseph F. & Rule, Wilma (Editors) . . . *v.4 p.533*

Zimmerman, Joseph F.. . . . . *v.4 p.462, p.463*

Zimmerman, Larry J. *v.1 p.829*

Zimmermann, Michael F. (Editor) *v.1 p.701*

Zimring, Franklin E. & Hawkins, Gordon J. . . *v.6 p.272, p.273*

Zimring, Franklin E. & Hawkins, Gordon. . *v.4 p.753, v.6 p.272*

Zimring, Franklin E. (Author, Foreword by) *v.6 p.255*

Zimring, Franklin E., et al. *v.6 p.275*

Zimring, Franklin E.. . . . . *v.6 p.248, p.249*

Zinberg, Israel & Martin, Bernard *v.6 p.566, p.574*

Zindel, Paul *v.2 p.159*

Zingg, Paul J. *v.4 p.853*

Zinn, Howard & Arnove, Anthony (Editors) . . *v.3 p.380, p.445*

Zinn, Howard (Editor) *v.3 p.482, v.4 p.522*

Zinovieff, Sofka *v.3 p.196*

Zinser, Charles I.. . . . . *v.4 p.788*

Zinsser, Hans *v.5 p.366*

Zinsser, Judith P.. . . . . *v.6 p.436, p.450*

Zinsser, William *v.2 p.574*

Ziolkowski, Theodore J. *v.2 p.448, p.610*

Ziomek, Henryk *v.2 p.641*

Zipes, Douglas P., et al.. . . . . *v.5 p.520*

Zipes, Jack D. (Editor) *v.2 p.585*

Zipes, Jack D. *v.2 p.582*

Zipkin, Paul Herbert *v.4 p.117*

Zipper, Ricardo Israel. *v.3 p.356*

Zips, Werner *v.6 p.9*

Ziring, Lawrence, et al.. . . . . *v.4 p.636*

Zitser, Ernest A. (Editor) *v.3 p.217*

Zivkovic, Zoran *v.2 p.812*

Zizek, Slavoj.. . . . . *v.1 p.501*

Zlatar, Zdenko *v.2 p.779*

Zlotnick, Susan *v.6 p.481, p.483, p.485*

Zmora, Hillay (Contribution by) *v.4 p.502*

Zmuda, Allison & Tomaino, Mary *v.4 p.304*

Zoch, Paul A. *v.4 p.340*

Zohary, Daniel & Hopf, Maria *v.5 p.24, p.45*

Zohn, Harry *v.2 p.612, p.616*

Zola, Emile *v.2 p.504, p.505,v.3 p.155, p.156*

Zola, Émile *v.2 p.506*

Zolberg, Aristide R., et al.. . . . . *v.4 p.765*

Zolberg, Vera L. *v.1 p.708*

Zoller, Gunter *v.1 p.462, p.463*

Zoller, Michael. *v.1 p.575*

Zoller, Paul; Walsh, David J. *v.5 p.324*

Zollo, Peter *v.4 p.139, p.140, v.5 p.587*

Zolov, Eric *v.3 p.268*

Zoltai, Tibor & Stout, James H.. . . . . . *v.5 p.435, p.436*

Zomaya, Albert Y. (Editor) . . . *v.5 p.106, p.107, p.108, p.109*

Zona, Kirstin H. *v.2 p.62, p.103*

Zonabend, Francoise *v.4 p.708*

Zonderman, Jon *v.6 p.267*

Zondervan *v.1 p.614*

Zonneveld, Sjaak. *v.2 p.294*

Zook, David H., ... *v.3 p.278*

Zook, David H. *v.3 p.278*

Zoomers, A. & Van Den Haar, G. (Editors) *v.3 p.300*

Zorach, Cecile & Melin, Charlotte *v.2 p.558*

Zorilla, José *v.2 p.655*

Zornow, William Frank *v.3 p.403, p.429*

Zoshchenko, Mikhail *v.2 p.810*

Zott, Lynn M. *v.2 p.11, p.12*

Zürcher, Erik. *v.1 p.563*

Zsambok, Caroline E. & Klein, Gary A. (Editors) . . . *v.5 p.589*

Zubay, Geoffrey L.. . . . . *v.5 p.243, p.244*

Zuber, Jean Bernard & Itzykson, Claude *v.5 p.550, p.551*

Zuber, Roger & Cuénin, Micheline. *v.2 p.459*

Zubkova, Elena *v.3 p.228*
Zubov, B. V. (Editor) *v.5 p.178*
Zubrick, James W. *v.5 p.301*
Zuccotti, Susan *v.3 p.156, v.4 p.654*
Zuck, Lowell H. (Editor) *v.1 p.602*
Zucker, Andrew A. & Kozma, Robert *v.4 p.322*
Zucker, Carole (Editor) *v.6 p.348*
Zucker, Ross *v.4 p.515*
Zuckerman, Edward L. *v.5 p.663*
Zuckerman, Frederic S. *v.3 p.221*
Zuckerman, Harriet *v.5 p.399*
Zuckerman, J J. *v.5 p.305*
Zuckerman, Larry *v.3 p.206*
Zuckerman, Mary E. *v.4 p.410*
Zuckerman, Solly *v.5 p.409*
Zuckert, Michael P. *v.4 p.513, p.514*
Zuckmayer, Carl *v.2 p.616*
Zuczek, Richard *v.3 p.502*
Zuffi, Stefano *v.1 p.710*
Zufofsky, Louis & Zukofsky, Louis *v.2 p.507*
Zug, George R., et al. *v.5 p.217*
Zug, James *v.4 p.864, p.865*
Zuhlsdorff, Volkmar *v.3 p.179*
Zuhur, Sherifa *v.6 p.640*
Zuidervaart, Lambert *v.1 p.480*
Zukav, Gary *v.5 p.541*
Zukin, Sharon *v.6 p.720*
Zukofsky, Louis & Scroggins, Mark *v.2 p.139*
Zukofsky, Louis *v.2 p.139*
Zukowsky, John & Thorne, Martha *v.1 p.791*
Zulawski, Ann *v.3 p.325*
Zulawski, David E. & Wicklander, Douglas E. *v.6 p.267*
Zumerchik, John *v.4 p.861, p.871,v.5 p.360,
                                          p.361, p.453, p.455, p.457
Zumthor, Paul *v.3 p.205*

Zumwalt, Rosemary L. *v.2 p.17, p.18*
Zunes, Stephen *v.4 p.565*
Zung, Cecilia S. L. *v.1 p.61, p.132*
Zunz, Olivier (Editor), et al. *v.4 p.725*
Zurcher, Erik J. *v.6 p.625*
Zureik, Elia & Nakhleh, Khalil *v.4 p.708*
Zurick, David & Karan, P. P. *v.6 p.162*
Zusne, Leonard & Jones, Warren H. (Editors) *v.5 p.614*
Zusne, Leonard *v.5 p.598, p.599*
Zussman, John (Editor) *v.5 p.436*
Zutshi, Chitralekha *v.6 p.162*
Zweibel, Ken *v.5 p.362, p.363*
Zweig, Arnold *v.2 p.616*
Zweig, Gunter and Joseph Sherma (eds.) *v.5 p.269, p.270*
Zweig, Michael *v.4 p.727*
Zweig, Paul *v.2 p.160*
Zweig, Stefan *v.2 p.616, v.3 p.184*
Zweigenhaft, Richard L. & Domhoff, G. William . . . *v.4 p.133*
Zweiger, Gary *v.5 p.130*
Zweiniger-Bargielowska, Ina *v.3 p.55, v.6 p.455*
Zwicker, Steven N. (Editor) . . . *v.2 p.170, p.171, p.173, p.247*
Zwicker, Steven N. *v.2 p.247*
Zwillinger, Daniel (Editor) *v.5 p.462*
Zwillinger, Daniel *v.5 p.462, p.487*
Zwinger, Ann Haymond *v.5 p.231*
Zwinger, Ann *v.5 p.231, p.235*
Zwirn, Jerrold (Compiled by) *v.4 p.529*
Zwonitzer, Mark & Hirshberg, Charles *v.1 p.276, p.316*
Zychowicz, James L. *v.1 p.227, p.244, p.339*
Zygmund, A. *v.5 p.494*
Zygulski, Zdzislaw Jr. *v.1 p.674, p.801*
Zykov, C. *v.5 p.225*
Zymberi, Isa *v.2 p.778,*

Title Index

A

A. E. Housman: A Collection of Critical Essays. . . . *.v.2 p.291*

A. E. Housman Revisited. . . . . *.v.2 p.290*

A. M. Klein - Complete Poems: Original Poems, 1926-1934; Original Poems, 1937-1955 and Poetry Translations, Vol. 2. . . . . *.v.2 p.735*

A. Philip Randolph: A Biographical Portrait. . . *.v.4 p.123, p.124*

A. R. Ammons: Collected Poems, 1951-1971. . . . . *.v.2 p.55*

An A to Z of DNA Science: What Scientists Mean When They Talk about Genes and Genomes. . . . . *.v.5 p.123*

The A to Z of Foreign Musical Terms: From Adagio to Zierlich - A Dictionary for Performers and Students. . . . *.v.1 p.159*

AAAS Science Book List, 1978-1986. . . . . *.v.5 p.405*

The AAM Guide to Collections Planning. . . . . . . *.v.1 p.828*

The AAM Guide to Provenance Research. . . . . . *.v.1 p.827*

Aaron Copland A Reader: Selected Writings 1923-1972. . . . . *.v.1 p.211, p.318*

Aaron Copland and His World. . . . . *.v.1 p.220, p.318, p.319*

Aaron Copland: The Life and Work of an Uncommon Man. *.v.6 p.410*

Aaron Copland. . . . . *.v.1 p.209, p.318*

Aaron's Rod. . . . . *.v.2 p.362*

☐ AATA Online ; Abstracts of International Conservation Literature. . . . . *.v.1 p.821*

☐ AAUP web site. . . . . *.v.4 p.292*

The Abacus and the Sword: The Japanese Penetration of Korea, 1895-1910. . . . . *.v.6 p.236*

ABA-LSAC Official Guide to ABA-Approved Law Schools 2006. . . . . *.v.4 p.439, p.440*

Abandoned in the Wasteland: Children, Television, and the First Amendment. . . . . *.v.4 p.445*

Abandoned: The Betrayal of the American Middle Class since World War II. . . . . *.v.4 p.486, p.487*

'Abbasid Belles Lettres. . . . . *.v.6 p.657*

The Abbasid Revolution. . . . . *.v.6 p.585, p.586*

L' Abbe Prevost. . . . . *.v.2 p.481*

The Abbess of Crewe. . . . . *.v.2 p.383*

Abbey Road - Let It Be: The Beatles. . . . . *.v.1 p.268, p.305*

The Abbot. . . . . *.v.2 p.308*

☐ Abbreviations of Chemical Compounds. . . . . . *.v.5 p.257*

The ABC and XYZ of Bee Culture: An Encyclopedia of Beekeeping. . . . . *.v.5 p.27, p.28, p.55*

ABC Chinese-English Comprehensive Dictionary. . . *.v.6 p.207*

ABC of Clinical Genetics. . . . . *.v.5 p.149*

ABC of Influence: Ezra Pound and the Remaking of American Poetic Tradition. . . . . *.v.2 p.111*

ABC of Reading. . . . . *.v.2 p.573*

ABC of Relativity. . . . . *.v.5 p.557*

The ABC of Stage Lighting. . . . . *.v.1 p.141, p.149*

The ABC Presidents: Conversations and Correspondence with the Presidents of Argentina, Brazil, and Chile. . . . . *.v.3 p.338, p.347, p.352*

'Abd Al Rahman III: The First Cordoban Caliph, Vol. 3. *.v.6 p.584*

'Abd Al-Malik. . . . . *.v.6 p.585*

Abductive Inference: Computation, Philosophy, Technology. . . . . *.v.1 p.495*

Abe Fortas: A Biography. . . . . *.v.4 p.468*

Abe Lincoln in Illinois. . . . . *.v.2 p.116*

Abel Sanchez and Other Stories. . . . . *.v.2 p.663*

Abel Sanchez. . . . . *.v.2 p.662*

Abelard and Heloise. . . . . *.v.1 p.579*

Abelard and the Origin and Early History of the Universities. . . . . *.v.4 p.325*

Abel's Proof: An Essay on the Sources and Meaning of Mathematical Unsolvability. . . . . *.v.5 p.467, p.471, p.472*

Abingdon Dictionary of Living Religions. . . . . . *.v.1 p.522*

Abinger Harvest. . . . . *.v.2 p.345*

☐ Abkurtzungen Chemischer Verbindungen/Abbreviations of Chemical Compounds. . . . . *.v.5 p.257*

Abnormal: Lectures at the College de France, 1974-1975. . . . . *.v.1 p.495*

Abolish the FCC: Common Law Telecosm. . . . . . *.v.4 p.445*

Abolishing Death: A Salvation Myth of Russian Twentieth-Century Literature. . . . . *.v.2 p.799*

The Abolition of Slavery and the Aftermath of Emancipation in Brazil. . . . . *.v.3 p.337*

The Abolition of the Death Penalty in International Law. . . . . *.v.4 p.435, v.6 p.247*

Abolitionism: A New Perspective. . . . . *.v.3 p.421*

Abolitionism in the United States and Brazil: A Comparative Perspective. . . . . *.v.3 p.335*

Aboriginal Art. . . . . *.v.1 p.668*

Aboriginal Australians. . . . . *.v.4 p.42*

Aboriginal Fishing Rights: Laws, Courts, Politics. . . *.v.6 p.696*

Aboriginal Men of High Degree: Initiation and Sorcery in the World's Oldest Tradition. . . . . *.v.4 p.36*

Aboriginal Peoples and Government Responsibility: Exploring Federal and Provincial Roles, No. 12. . . . . . *.v.4 p.588*

Abortion and American Politics. . . *.v.4 p.569, v.6 p.464, p.469*

Abortion and Common Sense. . . . . . *.v.4 p.569, v.6 p.469*

ⓔ Abortion and Dialogue: Pro-Choice, Pro-Life, and American Law. . . . . *.v.6 p.464, p.468*

Abortion and Dialogue: Pro-Choice, Pro-Life and American Law. . . . . *.v.4 p.447*

Abortion and the Politics of Motherhood. . . . . . . *.v.4 p.768, p.769, v.6 p.465, p.470*

The Abortion Controversy: A Documentary History. . *.v.4 p.448*

Abortion in America: The Origins and Evolution of National Policy, 1800-1900. . . . . *.v.4 p.472*

Abortion, Medicine and the Law. *v.4 p.471*

Abortion Politics in North America. *v.4 p.768*

Abortion Practice in Britain and the United States. . .*v.4 p.778*

The Abortion Rights Controversy in America: A Legal
  Reader. *v.4 p.447, p.448*

Abortion: The Clash of Absolutes. *v.4 p.472*

Abortion: Understanding Differences. *v.6 p.464, p.468*

Abortion Wars: A Half Century of Struggle,
  1950-2000. . . . .*v.6 p.447, p.471*

The Abortive Revolution: China under Nationalist Rule,
  1927-1937. . . . .*v.6 p.190*

About Arts Management. *v.1 p.825*

About Criminals: A View of the Offender's World. . .*v.6 p.254*

About Face: A History of America's Curious Relationship with
  China, from Nixon to Clinton. *v.3 p.390*

About Face: Performing Race in Fashion and
  Theater. *v.6 p.90, p.99, p.123*

About French Poetry from Dada to "Tel Quel": Text and
  Theory. *v.2 p.460*

About Guilt and Innocence: The Origins, Development, and
  Future of Constitutional Criminal Procedure. .*v.6 p.267, p.268*

About Landscape: Essays on Design, Style, Time and
  Space. *v.1 p.814*

About Teaching Mathematics: A K-8 Resource. . . .*v.4 p.362*

About Time: Exploring the Gay Past. *v.6 p.364, p.365*

About Town: The New Yorker and the World It Made. .*v.4 p.410*

About Writing: Seven Essays, Four Letters, and Five
  Interviews. *v.2 p.574*

Above the Law: Police and the Excessive Use of Force.*v.6 p.261*

Abracadabra, and Other Satires. *v.2 p.347*

Abraham Isaac Kook: The Lights of Penitence, the Moral
  Principles, Lights of Holiness, Essays Letters and
  Poems. *v.1 p.545*

Abraham Lincoln: A Biography. *v.3 p.426*

Abraham Lincoln and Civil War America: A Biography..*v.3 p.397*

Abraham Lincoln and His Times: A Constitutional
  Biography. *v.4 p.518*

Abraham Lincoln and Reconstruction: The Louisiana
  Experiment. *v.3 p.507*

Abraham Lincoln: Constitutionalism and Equal Rights in the
  Civil War Era. *v.3 p.394, v.4 p.518*

Abraham Lincoln: Eighteen Nine to Eighteen
  Fifty-Eight. *v.3 p.424*

The Abraham Lincoln Encyclopedia. *v.3 p.426*

Abraham Lincoln: His Speeches and Writings. . . .*v.3 p.424*

Abraham Lincoln: The Man Behind the Myths. . . .*v.3 p.426*

Abraham Lincoln: The Prairie Years and the War Years.*v.3 p.426*

Abraham Lincoln the Prairie Years, Vol. 2. . . . . .*v.3 p.426*

Abraham Lincoln: The War Years. *v.3 p.426*

Abraham Lincoln's DNA and Other Adventures in
  Genetics. *v.5 p.80, p.81, p.123, p.151*

Abraham Lincoln's Political Faith. *v.3 p.397*

The Abrams Encyclopedia of Photography. *v.1 p.761*

The Abrams Guide to American House Styles. . . .*v.1 p.784*

The Abruzzo Trilogy: Fontamara, Bread and Wine, The Seed
  Beneath the Snow. *v.2 p.723*

Abs on the Ball: A Pilates Approach to Building Superb
  Abdominals. *v.4 p.793*

The Absent Man: The Narrative Craft of Charles W.
  Chesnutt. *v.2 p.32*

Absent Mandate: Canadian Electoral Politics in an Era of
  Restructuring. *v.4 p.590*

An Absent Presence: Japanese-Americans in Postwar American
  Culture, 1945-1960. . . . .*v.6 p.132*

Absent Without Leave: French Literature under the Threat of
  War. *v.2 p.456*

Absentee Ownership and Business Enterprise in Recent Times:
  The Case of America. *v.4 p.214, p.250*

The Absentee. *v.2 p.286*

The Absent-Minded Imperialists: Empire, Society and Culture in
  Britain. *v.6 p.746*

Absinthe, the Cocaine of the Nineteenth Century: A History of
  the Hallucinogenic Drug and Its Effect on Artists and
  Writers in Europe and the United States. .*v.4 p.776, p.777*

The Absolute at Large. *v.2 p.783*

The Absolute Bourgeois: Artists and Politics in France
  1848-1851. . . . .*v.3 p.75*

The absolute bourgeois: artists and politics in France,
  1848-1851. . . . .*v.3 p.153*

Absolute Destruction. *v.3 p.161*

Absolutism and Ruling Class: The Formation of the Russian
  Political Order, 1700-1825. . . . .*v.3 p.216*

Absolutism and Society in Seventeenth-Century France: State
  Power and Provincial Aristocracy in Languedoc. .*v.3 p.144*

Absolutism and the Eighteenth-Century Origins of Compulsory
  Schooling in Prussia and Austria. *v.3 p.167, p.183*

Absorption and Scattering of Light by Small
  Particles. *v.5 p.73, p.561*

Abstract Algebra. *v.5 p.473*

Abstract Art. *v.1 p.680*

Abstract Expressionism: A Critical Record. *v.1 p.729*

Abstract Expressionism: The Critical Developments. . .*v.1 p.730*

Abstract Expressionism. *v.1 p.676, p.726*

Abstract Expressionist Painting in America. *v.1 p.729*

Abstract Expressionist Women Painters: An Annotated
  Bibliography: Elaine de Kooning, Helen Frankenthaler, Grace
  Hartigan, Lee Krasner, Joan Mitchell, Ethel
  Schwabacher. *v.1 p.725*

The Abstract Wild. *v.5 p.223*

⬜ Abstracting and Indexing Resources for Historical Chemistry
  Journals. *v.5 p.256*

An Absurd Vice: A Biography of Cesare Pavese. . . .*v.2 p.720*

The Abuse of Police Authority: A National Study of Police
  Officers' Attitude. *v.4 p.774*

Abuse of Power: The New Nixon Tapes. *v.3 p.473, p.474*

⬜ ABZU: A Guide to Information Related to the Study of the
  Ancient Near East on the Web. *v.3 p.4*

⬜ ACA Code of Ethics. *v.5 p.674*

ACA Ethical Standards Casebook. *v.5 p.674*

Academia to Biotechnology: Career Changes at any
  Stage. *v.5 p.250*

Academic Anthropology and the Museum: Back to the
  Future. *v.4 p.47*

Academic Capitalism and the New Economy: Markets, State, and Higher Education. . . . . *.v.4 p.290, p.291*

Academic Discourse and Critical Consciousness. . . *.v.2 p.564*

Academic Duty. . . . . *.v.4 p.293*

Academic Freedom: A Guide to the Literature. . . . *.v.4 p.298*

Academic Freedom and Tenure: Ethical Issues. . . . *.v.4 p.298*

Academic Freedom and the Inclusive University. . . *.v.4 p.298*

Academic Freedom: Education and Human Rights, Vol. 3. . . . . *.v.4 p.314*

Academic Freedom in American Higher Education: Rights, Responsibilities, and Limitations, Vol. 22. . . . . *.v.4 p.298*

Academic Freedom in the Age of the College. . . . *.v.4 p.298*

The Academic Job Search Handbook. . . . . . . *.v.4 p.170*

The Academic Man: A Study in the Sociology of a Profession. . . . . *.v.4 p.294*

Academic Pathfinders: Knowledge Creation and Feminist Scholarship. . . . . *.v.6 p.462*

Academic Power: Patterns of Authority in Seven National Systems of Higher Education. . . . . . . *.v.4 p.295, p.296*

[Academic Press] Encyclopedia of Physical Science and Technology. . . . . *.v.5 p.386*

Academic Rebels in Chile: The Role of Philosophy in Higher Education and Politics. . . . . *.v.3 p.354*

The Academic Revolution. . . . . *.v.4 p.290, p.332*

Academic Science, Higher Education, and the Federal Government, 1950-1983: Programs and Policies. . . . . *.v.5 p.394, p.412*

Academic Skills Problems: Direct Assessment and Intervention. . . . . *.v.4 p.287*

Academic Strategy: The Management Revolution in American Higher Education. . . . . *.v.4 p.293*

Academy of American Poets. . . . . *.v.2 p.577, p.582*

Acceleration and Improvement of Protein Identification by Mass Spectrometry. . . . . *.v.5 p.87, p.111*

An Accented Cinema: Exilic and Diasporic Filmmaking. . . . . *.v.6 p.321*

Accents of English: Beyond the British Isles. . . . . *.v.2 p.558*

Accents of English, Vol. 1. . . . . *.v.2 p.558*

Accents of English, Vol. 2. . . . . *.v.2 p.558*

Access to the Genome: The Challenge to Equality. . *.v.5 p.135*

Accessing U. S. Government Information: Subject Guide to Jurisdiction of the Executive and Legislative Branches. . . . . *.v.4 p.529*

Accident Prevention Manual for Business and Industry: Administration and Programs. . . . . *.v.5 p.682*

Accident Prevention Manual for Business and Industry: Engineering and Technology. . . . . *.v.5 p.682*

Accident Prevention Manual for Business and Industry: Environmental Management. . . . . *.v.5 p.682*

The Accidental Asian: Notes of a Native Speaker. *.v.6 p.94, p.127*

An Accidental Man. . . . . *.v.2 p.372*

The Accidental President of Brazil: A Memoir. . . . *.v.3 p.339*

The Accidental Tourist. . . . . *.v.2 p.157*

Accomplices of Silence: The Modern Japanese Novel. *.v.6 p.231*

According to Jake and the Kid. . . . . *.v.2 p.736*

According to Kotler. . . . . *.v.4 p.134*

According to the Rolling Stones. . . . . *.v.1 p.274, p.351*

The Account of Mary Rowlandson and Other Indian Captivity Narratives. . . . . *.v.2 p.29, p.30*

An Account of the Manners and Customs of the Modern Egyptians: The Definitve 1860 Edition. . . . . . *.v.6 p.638*

An Account of the Ottoman Conquest of Egypt in the Year A. H. 922 (A. D. 1516). . . . . *.v.6 p.635*

Accountability in Social Research: Issues and Debates. *.v.4 p.687*

Accountants' Handbook, Set. . . . . *.v.4 p.104, p.105*

Accounting Best Practices. . . . . *.v.4 p.104*

Accounting Demystified. . . . . *.v.4 p.105*

Accounting. . . . . *.v.4 p.91, p.94, p.99*

Accreditation. . . . . *.v.5 p.676*

Accretion Power in Astrophysics. . . . . *.v.5 p.66*

The Accumulation of Capital: An Anti-Critique Imperialism and the Accumulation of Capital. . . . . *.v.4 p.236*

The Accumulation of Capital. . . . . . . *.v.4 p.245, p.246*

The Accumulation of Capital. . . . . *.v.4 p.236*

Accumulation of Capital. . . . . *.v.4 p.236*

The Accumulation of Capital. . . . . . *.v.4 p.244, p.245, p.270*

Ace Your Case!: The WetFeet Insider Guide to Consulting Interviews. . . . . *.v.4 p.171, p.178*

Acequia Culture: Water, Land and Community in the Southwest. . . . . *.v.6 p.522, p.551*

Acheson: The Secretary of State Who Created the American World. . . . . *.v.3 p.456, p.457*

Acheson: The Secretary of State Who Created the American World. . . . . *.v.3 p.457*

The Achievement of American Liberalism: The New Deal and Its Legacies. . . . . *.v.3 p.439, p.468,v.4 p.522*

The Achievement of American Sport Literature: A Critical Appraisal. . . . . *.v.4 p.812*

The Achievement of Christina Rossetti. . . . . *.v.2 p.303*

The Achievement of Samuel Johnson. . . . . *.v.2 p.250*

Achievements of the Left Hand: Essays on the Prose of John Milton. . . . . *.v.2 p.254*

Achieving Diversity: The Status and Progress of Women and African Americans in the Agricultural Economics Profession. . . . . *.v.4 p.268*

Achieving Our Country: Leftist Thought in Twentieth-Century America. . . . . *.v.4 p.493*

Achieving the Impossible Dream: How Japanese Americans Obtained Redress. . . . . *.v.6 p.134*

Achim von Arnim. . . . . *.v.2 p.597*

Acid Dreams: The CIA, LSD and the Sixties Rebellion. *.v.4 p.704*

Acid Rain Information Book. . . . . *.v.5 p.354, p.378*

Acid-Base Interactions to Vinyl Chloride Polymers. . *.v.5 p.321*

ACM Computing Reviews. . . . *.v.5 p.341, p.343, p.344*

The Acoustic Sense of Animals. . . . . *.v.5 p.618*

Acoustics and Psychoacoustics. . . . . *.v.1 p.375*

ACP Medicine. . . . . *.v.5 p.514, p.515*

Acquainted with Grief. . . . . *.v.2 p.715*

Acquiring Culture: Cross-Cultural Studies in Child Development. . . . . *.v.5 p.627, p.631*

Acquiring Genomes: A Theory of the Origins of Species. . . . . *.v.5 p.199*

The Acquisition and Retention of Knowledge: A Cognitive View. *v.5 p.574*

Across the Acheron. *v.2 p.534*

Across the Blocs: Exploring Comparative Cold War Cultural and Social History. *v.4 p.486*

Across the Board: The Mathematics of Chessboard Problems. *v.5 p.470, p.480*

Across the Bridge. *v.2 p.735*

Across the Great Divide: Cultures of Manhood in the American West. *v.4 p.745*

Across the Moscow River: The World Turned Upside Down. *v.3 p.228*

Across the Open Field: Essays Drawn from English Landscapes. *v.1 p.819*

Across the Pacific: An Inner History of American-East Asian Relations. *v.3 p.389, v.6 p.181*

Across the Pacific: Asian Americans and Globalization. *v.6 p.85, p.118*

Across the River and into the Trees. *v.2 p.84*

Across the Wide Missouri. *v.3 p.519, 520*

☐ ACS Division of Chemical Health and Safety. . . .*v.5 p.265*

☐ ACS Journals. *v.5 p.256*

☐ ACS Publications. *v.5 p.255*

The ACS Style Guide: A Manual for Authors and Editors. *v.5 p.260*

ACSM Fitness Book: A Proven Step-by-Step Program from the Experts. *v.4 p.790, p.873*

ACSM's Exercise Management for Persons with Chronic Diseases and Disabilities. *v.4 p.783, p.829, p.842*

ACSM's Guidelines for Exercise Testing and Prescription. *v.4 p.872, p.873,v.5 p.519*

ACSM's Health/Fitness Facility Standards and Guidelines. *v.4 p.792, p.880, p.882*

Act and Being. *v.1 p.635*

The Act and the Place of Poetry: Selected Essays. . .*v.2 p.460*

Act Like a Man: Challenging Masculinities in American Drama. *v.2 p.5, v.6 p.480*

Act of Creation: The Founding of the United Nations. *v.4 p.635*

The Act of Creation. *v.5 p.654*

The Act of Reading: A Theory of Aesthetic Response. *v.2 p.567, p.572, p.573*

An Act of State: The Execution of Martin Luther King Jr. *v.4 p.486*

☐ ACTE online (Association for Career and Technical Education). *v.4 p.304*

Actex Study Manual. SOA Exam FM, CAS Exam 2. *v.5 p.504*

Actex Study Manual. SOA Exam P, CAS Exam 1. . *v.5 p.504*

Acting as a Way of Salvation: A Study of Raganuga Bhakti Sadhana. *v.1 p.536*

Acting for Endangered Species: The Statutory Ark. . *v.4 p.463*

Acting for the Camera. *v.6 p.347*

Acting Gay: Male Homosexuality in Modern Drama. *v.6 p.410, p.411*

Acting in the Cinema. *v.6 p.348*

Acting on the Past: Historical Performance Across the Disciplines. *v.1 p.42*

Acting Out: Maladaptive Behavior in Confinement. . *v.6 p.277*

Acting: The First Six Lessons. *v.1 p.143*

Action for Mental Health. *v.5 p.671*

Action Francaise: French Canadian Nationalism in the Twenties. *v.3 p.544*

Action Research for Educators. *v.4 p.355*

Actions and Reactions. *v.2 p.296*

Action. *v.6 p.506, p.517*

Activating Agents and Protecting Groups. . . .*v.5 p.290, p.291*

Active Galactic Nuclei: From the Central Black Hole to the Galactic Environment. *v.5 p.71*

Active Technical Communication: Concepts and Applications. *v.5 p.681*

Active Vision: The Psychology of Looking and Seeing. *v.5 p.606*

Activism Replaces Isolationism: U. S. Public Attitudes 1940-1975. . . . .*v.3 p.451*

Activist Faith: Grassroots Women in Democratic Brazil and Chile. *v.3 p.339, p.340, p.353*

Activists Beyond Borders: Advocacy Networks in International Politics. *v.4 p.640*

Activities for Junior High and Middle School Mathematics, Vol. 1. . . . .*v.5 p.462*

Activities for Junior High and Middle School Mathematics, Vol. 2. . . . .*v.5 p.462*

Activities Handbook for the Teaching of Psychology, Vol. 1. . . . .*v.5 p.675*

Activities Handbook for the Teaching of Psychology, Vol. 3. . . . .*v.5 p.675*

Activities Handbook for the Teaching of Psychology, Vol. 4. . . . .*v.5 p.675*

Actor at Work. *v.1 p.138, p.143*

An Actor Prepares. *v.1 p.139, p.145*

Actors and American Culture, 1880-1920. . . .*v.1 p.117, p.145*

Actors and Singers. *v.1 p.205, p.206, p.366*

The Actor's Book of Gay and Lesbian Plays. *v.6 p.412*

Actor's Encyclopedia of Dialects. *v.1 p.141*

An Actor's Handbook. *v.6 p.348*

The Actor's Image: Print Makers of the Katsukawa School. *v.1 p.752*

Actors on Acting: The Theories, Techniques, and Practices of the World's Great Actors, Told in Their Own Words. *v.1 p.144*

The Actors Studio: A History. *v.1 p.137, p.144*

Actors Talk about Acting: Fourteen Interviews with Stars of the Theatre. *v.1 p.144*

The Actor's Ways and Means. *v.1 p.145*

Actresses As Working Women: Their Social Identity in Victorian England. *v.6 p.747*

Acts and Other Events. *v.1 p.496*

Acts and the History of Earliest Christianity. *v.1 p.630*

Acts of Courage: Vaclav Havel's Life in the Theater. *v.2 p.784*

Acts of Faith: Explaining the Human Side of Religion. *v.1 p.525*

Acts of Faith. *v.2 p.761*

Acts of Hope: Creating Authority in Literature, Law, and Politics. *v.4 p.497*

Acts of Intervention, Performance, Gay Culture and AIDS, Unnatural Acts: Theorizing the Performative. *v.6 p.412, p.413*

Acts of Meaning: Four Lectures on Mind and
Culture. *v.5 p.604, p.605*

Acts of Resistance: Plays by Women, in
Translation. *v.6 p.146, p.148*

The Acts of the Apostles. *v.1 p.630*

Actuarial Mathematics. *v.5 p.504*

☐ Ad* Access. *v.4 p.141, p.426*

☐ Ad Council Campaigns. *v.4 p.427*

☐ ADA Home Page; Americans with Disabilities Act. *v.1 p.785*

Adalbert Stifter: A Critical Study. *v.2 p.602*

Adalbert Stifter. *v.2 p.599*

Adam and Eve. *v.2 p.817*

Adam Bede. *v.2 p.287*

Adam Clayton Powell: Portrait of a Marching
Black. *v.3 p.458, p.459*

Adam, Eve, and The Genome: The Human Genome Project and
Theology. *v.5 p.137*

🐟 A.D.A.M. Interactive Anatomy 4. . . . . . *v.5 p.157*

The Adam of Two Edens: Poems. *v.6 p.659*

Adam Resurrected. *v.6 p.649*

Adam Smith and Modern Political Economy: Bicentennial
Essays on The Wealth of Nations. *v.4 p.219*

Adam Smith and Modern Political Economy: Bicentennial
Essays on the Wealth of Nations. *v.4 p.219*

Adam Smith and the Founding of Market Economics. *v.4 p.219*

Adam Smith and the Philosophy of Law and
Economics. *v.4 p.219*

Adam Smith: The Theory of Moral Sentiments. *v.1 p.450, p.485*

Adam Smith's Daughters: Eight Prominent Women Economists
from the Eighteenth Century to the Present. . . . *v.4 p.194*

Adam Smith's Economics: Its Place in the Development of
Economic Thought. *v.4 p.218*

Adam Smith's Legacy: His Place in the Development of
Modern Economics. *v.4 p.219*

Adam Smith's Marketplace of Life. *v.4 p.219*

Adam Smiths Political Philosophy: The Invisible Hand and
Spontaneous Order. *v.4 p.220*

Adam Smith's Politics. *v.4 p.220*

Adam Smith's System of Liberty, Wealth, and Virtue: The
Moral and Political Foundations of the Wealth of
Nations. *v.4 p.218, p.219*

Adam Smith's Wealth of Nations: New Interdisciplinary
Essays. *v.4 p.218*

Adam Smith. *v.4 p.211, p.212, p.218, p.219*

Adams and Jefferson: A Revolutionary Dialogue. . . *v.3 p.412*

Adams Cover Letter Almanac. *v.4 p.171*

Adam's Curse: A Future Without Men. *v.4 p.745*

Adapted Aquatics Programming: A Professional
Guide. *v.4 p.792, p.801*

Adapted Physical Activity. *v.4 p.801*

Adapted Physical Education and Sport. *v.4 p.801*

Adapted Physical Education National Standards: National
Consortium for Physical Education and Recreation
for Individuals with Disabilities (U. S.). *v.4 p.801*

Adapting Educational and Psychological Tests for Cross-Cultural
Assessment. *v.5 p.600*

Adapting the United Nations to a Postmodern Era: Lessons
Learned. *v.4 p.634*

Adaptive Antenna Arrays. *v.5 p.728*

Adaptive Control. *v.5 p.710*

Adaptive Evolution of Genes and
Genomes. *v.5 p.144, p.145, p.200*

Adaptive Genetic Variation in the Wild. *v.5 p.195*

The Addict and the Law. *v.4 p.449*

Addiction and Change: How Addictions Develop and Addicted
People Recover. *v.5 p.663, p.673*

Addiction at Work: Tackling Drug Use and Misuse in the
Workplace. *v.4 p.130*

Addictions: A Comprehensive Guidebook. *v.5 p.512, p.517, p.522*

Adding It Up: Helping Children Learn Mathematics. *v.5 p.463*

☐ Adding It Up: Helping Children Learn Mathematics. *v.5 p.463*

The Adding Machine: Selected Essays. *v.2 p.64*

Addison. *v.2 p.236*

Addressing Community Problems: Psychological Research and
Interventions. *v.5 p.670*

Adenauer's Germany and the Nazi Past: The Politics of
Amnesty and Integration. *v.3 p.176*

The Adequacy of the Fossil Record. *v.5 p.446*

Ade's Fables. *v.2 p.30*

Adieu Babylone. *v.2 p.540*

Adieux: A Farewell to Sartre. *v.2 p.509*

Adlai Stevenson and American Politics: The Odyssey of a Cold
War Liberal. *v.3 p.456*

Administering Special Education: In Pursuit of Dignity and
Autonomy. *v.4 p.315*

The Administration of Fraternal Organizations on North
American Campuses: A Pattern for the New
Millennium. *v.4 p.288*

Administration of High School Athletics. . . . *v.4 p.883, p.884*

Administrative Behavior: A Study of Decision-Making Processes
in Administrative Organizations. *v.4 p.74, p.75, p.83*

The Administrative Medical Assistant. *v.5 p.534*

Administrators of Empire. *v.3 p.350*

Admiral of the Ocean Sea: A Life of Christopher
Columbus. *v.3 p.404*

Admirals, Generals, and American Foreign Policy,
1898-1914. . . . . *v.3 p.451*

Adolescence in Pacific Island Communities. *v.4 p.43*

Adolescent Development and Rapid Social Change: Perspectives
from Eastern Europe. *v.4 p.707, p.708*

Adolescent Fear of Crime and Defensive Behaviors: An
Alternative Explanation of Violent Delinquency. . *v.6 p.255*

The Adolescent in Family Therapy: Breaking the Cycle of
Conflict and Control. *v.5 p.668*

Adolescent Socialization in Cross-Cultural Perspective. *v.4 p.736*

Adolescents after Divorce. *v.4 p.735*

The Adolescent. *v.2 p.803*

Adolf Loos. *v.1 p.795*

Adolphe. *v.2 p.478*

Adoptive Immunotherapy: Methods and Protocols. . *v.5 p.165*

Adorning the World: Art of the Marquesas Islands. . *v.1 p.694*

Adorno: Disenchantment and Ethics. *v.1 p.506*

Adorno, Modernism and Mass Culture: Essays in Critical Theory and Music. *v.1 p.382*

Adrian Piper - A Retrospective, 1965-2000: Issues in Cultural Theory. *v.1 p.772*

Adrienne Rich: The Moment of Change. *v.2 p.115*

Adrienne Rich's Poetry. *v.2 p.115*

Adrienne Rich. *v.2 p.115*

Adrift on the Nile. *v.6 p.661*

Adrift: The Cuban Raft People. *v.3 p.308*

Ads, Fads, and Consumer Culture: Advertising's Impact on American Character and Society. *v.4 p.426*

Adsorption: Theory, Modeling, and Analysis, Vol. 107..*v.5 p.283*

Adult Attachment: Theory, Research, and Clinical Implications. *v.5 p.656*

Adult Attachment. *v.5 p.652, p.657*

Adult Education and Lifelong Learning: Theory and Practice. *v.4 p.320*

Adult Eyewitness Testimony: Current Trends and Developments. *v.6 p.271*

Adult Guide to Children's Team Sports. *v.4 p.840*

Adult Learner: The Definitive Classic in Adult Education and Human Resource Development. *v.4 p.320*

Adult Learning and Development: Perspectives from Educational Psychology. *v.4 p.321, v.5 p.572*

Adult Learning Methods: A Guide for Effective Instruction. *v.4 p.320*

Adult Personality Development: Applications. .*v.5 p.629, 632*

Adult Personality Development: Theories and Concepts. *v.5 p.629, 632*

Adults as Learners: Increasing Participation and Facilitating Learning. *v.4 p.319*

The Advance of the Fungi. *v.5 p.46*

Advanced Calculus. *v.5 p.486*

Advanced Computer Architecture and Parallel Processing. *v.5 p.729, p.730*

Advanced Data Mining Technologies in Bioinformatics. *v.5 p.106, p.109*

Advanced Distance Sampling: Estimating Abundance of Biological Populations. *v.5 p.92, p.99, p.188, p.189*

Advanced Educational Foundations for Teachers: The History, Philosophy and Culture of Schooling. *v.4 p.329*

Advanced Engineering Mathematics. *v.5 p.501, p.683*

Advanced Fitness Assessment and Exercise Prescription. *v.4 p.879*

Advanced Focus Group Research. *v.4 p.136*

Advanced Genetics. *v.5 p.135*

Advanced Inorganic Chemistry. *v.5 p.302, p.303*

Advanced International Trade: Theory and Evidence. .*v.4 p.257*

Advanced Macroeconomics. *v.4 p.204*

Advanced Materials in Sports Equipment. . . .*v.4 p.871, p.872*

Advanced Mathematical Economics. *v.4 p.205*

Advanced Mathematical Methods for Scientists and Engineers: Asymptotic Methods and Perturbation Theory. . . .*v.5 p.500*

Advanced Molecular Biology: A Concise Reference. *v.5 p.154, p.155*

Advanced Organic Chemistry: Reactions and Synthesis. .*v.5 p.292*

Advanced Organic Chemistry: Structure and Mechanisms, Pt. A. *v.5 p.292*

Advanced Organic Chemistry. *v.5 p.292*

Advanced Practical Organic Chemistry. *v.5 p.292*

Advanced Programming in the UNIX Environment. *v.5 p.348, p.349*

Advanced Strength of Materials. *v.5 p.688*

Advanced Structural Mechanics. *v.5 p.694, p.695*

Advanced Thermodynamics for Engineers. *v.5 p.712*

Advanced Topics in Finite Element Analysis of Structures: With Mathematica and MATLAB Computations. . . .*v.5 p.693*

Advanced Topics in Molecular Biology. *v.5 p.128*

Advanced Web-Based Training Strategies: Unlocking Instructionally Sound Online Learning. *v.4 p.321*

The Advancement of Learning. *v.1 p.447*

Advances in African American Psychology. *v.6 p.33*

Advances in Agricultural Economic History, Vol. 2. . .*v.5 p.14*

Advances in Analytical Chemistry and Instrumentation, 1960-1973, Vols. 1-11. . . . .*v.5 p.268*

Advances in Behavioral Economics. *v.4 p.249*

Advances in Behavioral Finance, Vol. 2. . . . . . .*v.4 p.98*

Advances in Behavioral Finance. *v.4 p.98, p.101*

Advances in Chemical Physics. *v.5 p.276*

Advances in Chemical Propulsion : Science to Technology. *v.5 p.720*

Advances in Computer Methods for Systematic Biology: Artificial Intelligence, Databases, Computer Vision. *v.5 p.105, p.108, p.109*

Advances in Earth Structures: Research to Practice: Proceedings of Sessions of GeoShanghai, June 6-8, 2006, Shanghai, China. *v.5 p.698*

Advances in Economics and Econometrics: Theory and Applications, Eighth World Congress. *v.4 p.202*

Advances in GIS Research. *v.4 p.387*

Advances in Human Performance and Cognitive Engineering Research. *v.5 p.588*

Advances in Morphometrics: Proceedings of the NATO ASI Held in IL Ciocco, Tuscany, Italy, July 18-30,1993.*v.5 p.100*

Advances in Safety and Structural Integrity. *v.5 p.697*

Advances in Sport Psychology. *v.5 p.582*

Advances in Systems Biology. *v.5 p.128, p.142, p.151*

Advancing Women in Business—The Catalyst Guide: Best Practices from the Corporate Leaders. *v.4 p.57*

Adventure Curriculum for Physical Education: Middle School. *v.4 p.787, p.798*

An Adventure in Multidimensional Space: The Art and Geometry of Polygons, Polyhedra and Polytopes. .*v.5 p.498*

Adventure Programming. *v.4 p.796*

Adventure with a Genius: Recollections of Joseph Pulitzer. *v.4 p.410*

Adventures and Encounters: Europeans in South-East Asia. *v.6 p.164*

Adventures in Celestial Mechanics. *v.5 p.66*

Adventures in Criticism. *v.2 p.569*

Adventures in Group Theory: Rubik's Cube, Merlin's Machine and Other Mathematical Toys. *v.5 p.469, p.474*

Adventures in Paradox: Don Quixote and the Western
  Tradition. . . . .*.v.2 p.649*

Adventures in Pataphysics: Collected Writings. . . . *.v.2 p.521*

Adventures in Speech: Rhetoric and Narration in Boccaccio's
  Decameron. . . . .*.v.6 p.565*

Adventures in the Atomic Age: From Watts to
  Washington. . . . .*.v.5 p.262*

Adventures in the Skin Trade, and Other Stories. *.v.2 p.385, p.386*

The Adventures of Antar: An Early Arab Epic Approaches to
  Arabic. . . . .*.v.6 p.663*

The Adventures of Captain Hatteras. . . . .*.v.2 p.504*

The Adventures of David Simple and Volume the Last. *.v.2 p.248*

The Adventures of David Simple: Containing an Account of His
  Travels Through the Cities of London and Westminster
  in the Search of a Real Friend. . . . .*.v.2 p.248*

The Adventures of Don Chipote: Or When Parrots
  Breast-Feed. . . . .*.v.6 p.504*

The Adventures of Don Quixote de la Mancha. . . . *.v.2 p.648*

The Adventures of Ferdinand Count Fathom. . . . . *.v.2 p.261*

Adventures of Huckleberry Finn: An Authoritative Text,
  Contexts and Sources, Criticism. . . . .*.v.2 p.34*

The Adventures of Lindamira, a Lady of Quality. . . *.v.2 p.236*

The Adventures of Oliver Twist. by Charles Dickens. *.v.2 p.282*

The Adventures of Peregrine Pickle. . . . . *.v.2 p.261*

The Adventures of Philip on His Way Through the World;
  Showing Who Robbed Him, Who Helped Him, and
  Who Passed Him By. by W. M. Thackeray. . . . *.v.2 p.315*

The Adventures of Pinocchio. . . . .*.v.2 p.710*

The Adventures of Roderick Random. . . . . *.v.2 p.261*

The Adventures of Sindbad. . . . .*.v.2 p.786*

Adventures of the Dialectic. . . . .*.v.1 p.508*

Adventures of the Rat Family. . . . . *.v.2 p.504*

Adventures with Old Houses. . . . .*.v.1 p.824*

Adversaries of Dance: From the Puritans to the Present. *.v.1 p.5*

The Adversary Within: Dissident Writers in Afrikaans. *.v.2 p.623*

Advertising: A Cultural Economy. . . . .*.v.4 p.141*

The Advertising Age Encyclopedia of Advertising,
  Set. . . . .*.v.4 p.140, p.426*

Advertising Age: Handbook of Advertising. . . . . .*.v.4 p.140*

Advertising Age. . . . .*.v.4 p.139, p.150*

Advertising and Promotion: Communicating Brands. . *.v.4 p.140*

Advertising and the Business of Brands. . . . . . .*.v.4 p.140*

Advertising and the Transformation of American Society,
  1865-1920, Vol. 110. . . . .*.v.4 p.426*

Advertising in the 60s: Turncoats, Traditionalists, and Waste
  Makers in America's Turbulent Decade. . . . . .*.v.4 p.141*

Advertising Media Planning: A Brand Management
  Approach. . . . .*.v.4 p.428*

☐ Advertising Principles. . . . .*.v.4 p.426*

Advertising, Promotion, and New Media. . . . . . .*.v.4 p.428*

The Advertising Red Books. Agencies. . . . . *.v.4 p.140, p.150*

Advertising the American Dream: Making Way for Modernity,
  1920-1940. . . . .*.v.4 p.426*

Advertising to Baby Boomers. . . . .*.v.4 p.138*

Advertising to Children on TV: Content, Impact, and
  Regulation. . . . .*.v.4 p.140, p.427*

Advertising to the American Woman, 1900-1999. . . .*.v.4 p.426*

Advertising Today. . . . .*.v.1 p.714*

Advertising's Best Print, Design, Radio, and TV. . . *.v.1 p.715*

Advice and Consent: Clarence Thomas, Robert Bork and the
  Intriguing History of the Supreme Court's Nomination
  Battles. . . . .*.v.4 p.539*

Advise and Consent. . . . .*.v.2 p.69*

Advocacy, Counselling and Mediation in Casework: Processes
  of Empowerment. . . . .*.v.4 p.757*

Advocacy Groups. . . . .*.v.4 p.591*

☐ Advocates for Youth. . . . .*.v.5 p.670*

The Advocate. . . . .*.v.6 p.361*

Adweek. . . . .*.v.4 p.139, p.150*

The AEF and Coalition Warmaking, 1917-1918. . . . *.v.3 p.481*

Aegean Art and Architecture. . . . .*.v.1 p.670*

The Aegean Bronze Age. . . . .*.v.3 p.15*

Aegean Painting in the Bronze Age. . . . .*.v.1 p.728*

The Aeneid of Virgil. . . . . *.v.2 p.447*

Aeneidos: Liber Primus. . . . . *.v.2 p.447*

Aeneidos: Liber Quartus. . . . .*.v.2 p.447*

Aeneidos: Liber Secundus. . . . . *.v.2 p.447*

Aeneidos: Liber Sextus. . . . . *.v.2 p.447*

The Aeneid. . . . .*.v.2 p.447*

Aeneid. . . . .*.v.2 p.447*

Aerobic Fitness and Health. . . . . *.v.4 p.793*

Aerodynamics for Engineering Students. . . . . . .*.v.5 p.718*

Aerodynamics of Road Vehicles: From Fluid Mechanics to
  Vehicle Engineering. . . . .*.v.5 p.716*

Aeschylus: Choephori. . . . . *.v.2 p.406*

Aeschylus: Eumenides. . . . . *.v.2 p.407*

Aeschylus in His Style, a Study in Language and
  Personality. . . . .*.v.2 p.407*

Aeschylus' "Prometheus Bound": A Literary
  Commentary. . . . .*.v.2 p.407*

Aeschylus: Plays One. . . . .*.v.1 p.70, p.88*

Aeschylus: Plays Two. . . . .*.v.1 p.70, p.87, p.88*

Aeschylus: Prometheus Bound. . . . .*.v.2 p.406, p.407*

Aeschylus: The Oresteia. . . . .*.v.2 p.407*

Aeschylus: The Persians. . . . .*.v.2 p.407*

Aeschylus, Vol. 1. . . . .*.v.2 p.406*

The Aesthetic and Critical Theories of John Ruskin. . *.v.2 p.305*

Aesthetic Approaches to Children's Literature: An
  Introduction. . . . .*.v.2 p.582*

The Aesthetic Attitude. . . . . *.v.5 p.618*

Aesthetic Legacies. . . . . *.v.1 p.481*

Aesthetic Movement Architect and Designer. . . . . *.v.1 p.786*

Aesthetic Paganism in German Literature, from Winckelmann to
  the Death of Goethe. . . . .*.v.2 p.590*

Aesthetic Quality: A Contextualistic Theory of Beauty. *.v.1 p.480*

Aesthetic Theory. . . . .*.v.1 p.479*

Aesthetic Value. . . . .*.v.1 p.479*

Aesthetics: A Critical Anthology. . . . .*.v.1 p.479*

Aesthetics: An Introduction to the Philosophy of Art. *.v.1 p.480*

Aesthetics from Classical Greece to the Present: A Short
  History. . . . .*.v.1 p.480*

The Aesthetics of Comics. *v.2 p.581*

The Aesthetics of Disturbance: Anti-Art in Avant-Garde
Drama. *v.1 p.82, p.84, p.85, p.96*

Aesthetics of Ecology. *v.1 p.814*

The Aesthetics of Italian Renaissance Art: A Reconsideration of
Style. *v.1 p.676*

The Aesthetics of Music. *v.1 p.382*

The Aesthetics of Rock. *v.1 p.272*

The Aesthetics of Survival: A Composer's View of
Twentieth-Century Music. *v.1 p.222, p.350, p.351*

Aesthetics: Problems in the Philosophy of Criticism. . *v.1 p.479*

Aesthetics. *v.1 p.480*

AFCA's Defensive Football Drills. *v.4 p.858*

An Affair of State: The Investigation, Impeachment, and Trial of
President Clinton. *v.4 p.462, p.528*

The Affair: The Case of Alfred Dreyfus. *v.3 p.59, p.154*

Affairs of Honor: National Politics in the New Republic. .*v.4 p.485*

Affairs of State: Public Life in Late Nineteenth Century
America, 1977. . . . .*v.3 p.437*

Affective Computing. *v.5 p.589*

Affine and Projective Geometry. *v.5 p.494*

Affinity. *v.6 p.399*

Affirmative Action: A Documentary History. . .*v.4 p.487, p.573*

Affirmative Action and Principles of Justice: Contributions in
Legal Studies. *v.4 p.446*

The Affirmative Action Empire: Nations and Nationalism in the
Soviet Union, 1923-1939. . . . .*v.3 p.213*

Affirmative Action Is Dead: Long Live Affirmative
Action. *v.4 p.133*

Affirmative Action. *v.4 p.446*

The Affluent Society. *v.4 p.213*

The Afghan Connection: The Extraordinary Adventures of Major
Eldred Pottinger. *v.3 p.90, p.114*

Afghanistan: A Short History of Its People and Politics. .*v.6 p.633*

Afghanistan: An Atlas of Indigenous Domestic
Architecture. *v.1 p.791*

The Afghanistan Wars. *v.6 p.634*

Afghanistan. *v.6 p.633*

The Afghans. *v.6 p.633*

Afican Film: Reimaging a Continent. *v.6 p.15, p.30*

Afrekete: An Anthology of Black Lesbian Writing. . *v.6 p.407*

Africa: African Cultures and Societies Before 1885. . *v.6 p.53*

Africa: African History Before 1885. . . . .*v.6 p.53*

Africa and Africans in the Making of the Atlantic World,
1400-1800. . . . .*v.6 p.63*

Africa and the Bible. *v.1 p.618*

Africa and the Blues. *v.1 p.261*

Africa and the Victorians: The Climax of Imperialism in the
Dark Continent,. *v.6 p.56*

Africa and the Victorians: The Official Mind of
Imperialism. *v.3 p.77*

Africa and the West: A Documentary History from the Slave
Trade to Independence. *v.6 p.56*

Africa and the West: Intellectual Responses to European
Culture. *v.6 p.68*

Africa: Colonial Africa 1885-1939, Vol. 3. . . . . .*v.6 p.53*

Africa: Contemporary Africa, Vol. 5. . . . .*v.6 p.53*

Africa Dances. *v.1 p.14*

Africa, Football and FIFA: Politics, Colonialism and
Resistance. *v.4 p.815, p.847, p.883, p.898*

Africa, Human Rights, and the Global System: The Political
Economy of Human Rights in a Changing World, 15. .*v.6 p.55*

Africa in History. *v.6 p.52*

Africa in World Politics: A Pan-African
Perspective. *v.6 p.13, p.31, p.55*

Africa Must Unite. *v.6 p.54*

Africa on a Global Stage. *v.4 p.384*

Africa Since 1800. . . . .*v.6 p.53*

Africa since 1940: The Past of the Present. *v.6 p.54*

Africa since Independence: A Comparative History. *v.6 p.54, p.55*

Africa South of the Sahara: A Geographical
Interpretation. *v.4 p.397*

☐ Africa South of the Sahara: African Literature and Writers on
the Internet. *v.2 p.751*

☐ Africa South of the Sahara: African Politics and
Government. *v.4 p.610*

☐ Africa South of the Sahara. *v.6 p.51*

Africa: The Art of a Continent. *v.1 p.690*

Africa Today: An Atlas of Reproducible Papers. . . .*v.6 p.51*

Africa, Vol. 4. . . . .*v.6 p.52, p.53*

Africa Works: The Political Instrumentalisation of
Disorder. *v.4 p.611*

Africa-Centered Reality Therapy and Choice
Theory. *v.6 p.22, p.33*

The African Aesthetic: Keeper of the Traditions. . . .*v.1 p.14*

African American and Latina Women at Work: Race, Gender
and Economic Inequality. *v.4 p.133, v.6 p.455, p.456*

African American Architects: A Biographical Dictionary,
1865-1945. . . . .*v.1 p.705, p.784,v.6 p.33*

African American Art and Artists. *v.1 p.705*

African American Authors, 1745-1945: A Bio-Bibliographical
Critical Sourcebook. *v.6 p.18, p.33, p.34*

☐ African American Biographical Database
(AADB). *v.6 p.18, p.19, p.34*

African American Communication and Identities: Essential
Readings. *v.6 p.6, p.32, p.33, p.39*

African American Concert Singers Before 1950. . . . .*v.6 p.29*

ⓔ African American Education: A Reference
Handbook. *v.4 p.310*

The African American Experience in Cyberspace: A Resource
Guide to the Best Web Sites on Black Culture and
History. *v.6 p.13, p.33*

African American Films Through 1959: A Comprehensive,
Illustrated Filmography. *v.6 p.330, p.343*

African American Fraternal Associations and the History of
Civil Society in the United States. *v.6 p.7, p.39*

African American Golfers During the Jim Crow
Era. *v.4 p.805, p.831, p.860*

African American Health Disparities. *v.6 p.21, p.22, p.39*

African American Leadership. *v.6 p.41*

African American Life in the Rural South,
1900-1950. . . . .*v.6 p.6, p.39*

African American Literary Criticism: 1773-2000. .*v.6 p.24, p.35*

African American Literary Theory: A Reader. *v.6 p.27*

African American Literature: A Guide to Reading
 Interests. *v.6 p.24*

African American Literature. *v.6 p.25*

The African American Male, Writing, and Difference: A
 Polycentric Approach to African American
 Literature, Criticism, and History. *v.6 p.26, p.39*

African American Mosaic: A Documentary History from the
 Slave Trade to the Twenty-First Century. *v.6 p.3*

African American Music; An Introduction. *v.6 p.30*

African American Music Reference. *v.6 p.29*

African American Nationalist Literature of the 1960s: Pens of
 Fire. *v.6 p.12, p.25*

African American Newsapers: the 19th century. . . .*v.6 p.33*

African American Political Thought, 1890-1930: Washington,
 Du Bois, Garvey, and Randolph. *v.6 p.31*

African American Political Thought. *v.6 p.31*

African American Power and Politics: The Political Context
 Variable. *v.4 p.574*

The African American Press: A History of News Coverage
 During National Crises, with Special Reference to
 Four Black Newspapers, 1827-1965. . . . .*v.4 p.411*

African American Psychology: From Africa to America. .*v.6 p.32*

African American Religious Thought: An Anthology. . .*v.6 p.36*

African American Song. *v.6 p.29*

African American Studies Reader. *v.6 p.14*

African American Theatre: An Historical and Critical
 Analysis. *v.1 p.123*

The African American Urban Experience: Perspectives from the
 Colonial Period to the Present. *v.6 p.8*

African American Women: A Biographical
 Dictionary. *v.6 p.19, p.34, p.46*

African American Women: An Annotated
 Bibliography. *v.6 p.35, p.47*

African American Women and HIV/AIDS: Critical
 Responses. *v.5 p.523*

African American Women and Sexuality in the
 Cinema. *v.6 p.15, p.39, p.45, p.474, p.475*

African American Women and the Vote, 1837-1965. . .*v.6 p.431*

African American Women Confront the West:
 1600-2000. . . . .*v.6 p.452, p.455*

African American Women in
 Congress. *v.4 p.485, p.486, p.530, v.6 p.31, p.43, p.441*

African American Women in the Struggle for the Vote,
 1850-1920. . . . .*v.4 p.519, v.6 p.32, p.46*

African American Women Playwrights: A Research
 Guide. *v.6 p.15, p.25, p.43*

African American Women Speak Out on Anita Hill - Clarence
 Thomas. *v.6 p.40, p.46*

African American Women Writers of the
 19thCentury. *v.6 p.476*

African Americans and the American Political System. .*v.6 p.31*

African Americans and the Bible: Sacred Texts and Social
 Textures. *v.4 p.721*

African Americans in Sport: Contemporary
 Themes. *v.4 p.819, p.833*

African Americans in Sports. *v.6 p.41*

African Americans Mosaic: A Documentary History from the
 Slave Trade to the Twenty-First Century. *v.6 p.3*

African and Caribbean Politics: From Kwame Nkrumah to the
 Grenada Revolution. *v.3 p.320*

African Archaeology: A Critical Introduction. *v.6 p.54*

African Archaeology. *v.4 p.8, v.6 p.53, p.54*

African Art in American Collections. *v.1 p.777*

African Art in Transit. *v.1 p.690*

African Art. *v.1 p.690, p.691*

African Biodiversity: Molecules, Organisms,
 Ecosystems. *v.5 p.184, p.236*

African Biographical Dictionary. *v.6 p.51*

African Catholicism: Essays in Discovery. *v.1 p.573*

African Cinema: Politics and Culture. *v.6 p.333*

African Cinemas: Decolonizing the Gaze. *v.6 p.333*

African Civilizations: An Archaeological
 Perspective. *v.4 p.7, v.6 p.52*

African Dance: An Artistic, Historical and Philosophical
 Inquiry. *v.1 p.14*

African Democracies and African Politics. . . .*v.4 p.505, p.613*

African Design: An Illustrated Survey of Traditional
 Craftwork. *v.1 p.714*

African Development Report 2005. . . . . .*v.4 p.384, p.397*

The African Diaspora: A Musical Perspective. *v.1 p.281*

African Drama and Performance. *v.2 p.751*

African Exodus: The Origins of Modern Humanity. . .*v.4 p.16*

African Experience: From Olduvai Gorge to the 21st
 Century. *v.6 p.53*

African Experience in Literature and Ideology. *v.6 p.80*

The African Experience in Spanish America. *v.3 p.280*

African Feminism: The Politics of Survival in Sub-Saharan
 Africa. *v.6 p.435, p.457*

African Feminist Fiction and Indigenous
 Values. *v.6 p.81, p.83, p.85*

African Film: Re-Imagining a Continent. *v.6 p.333*

African Folktales: Traditional Stories of the Black World. .*v.6 p.80*

African Gender Studies. *v.4 p.744, v.6 p.429, p.430*

An African in Paris. *v.2 p.542*

African Independence: The First Twenty-Five Years. . .*v.6 p.54*

African Languages: An Introduction. *v.6 p.80*

African Literatures in English: East and West. *v.2 p.751*

African Masculinities: Men in Africa from the Late Nineteenth
 Century to the Present. *v.4 p.733, p.734*

African Music: A Bibliographical Guide to the Traditional,
 Popular, Art, and Liturgical Musics of Sub-Saharan
 Africa. *v.1 p.166, p.281, p.285*

African Music: A Pan African Annotated
 Bibliography. *v.1 p.168, p.285, p.287*

African Music: A People's Art. *v.1 p.284, p.285*

African Music in Perspective. *v.1 p.285*

African Nationalism. *v.6 p.55*

The African Novel in English: An Introduction. *v.2 p.751*

African Novels in the Classroom. *v.2 p.751, v.6 p.80*

African Oral Literature: Backgrounds, Character and
 Continuity. *v.2 p.752*

The African Origin of Civilization: Myth or
Reality. *v.4 p.702, v.6 p.10, p.52*

African Passions: And Other Stories. *v.6 p.508*

African People in World History: A Lecture and Illustrated
History. *v.6 p.10*

African Perspectives in American Higher Education: Invisible
Voices. *v.6 p.21*

African Perspectives on Colonialism. *v.6 p.55*

The African Philosophy Reader. *v.1 p.476*

African Political Parties: Evolution, Institutionalisation and
Governance. *v.4 p.578, p.610*

☐ African Postcolonial Literature. *v.2 p.751*

The African Predicament and the American Experience: A Tale
of Two Edens. *v.6 p.7, p.10*

African Presence in Early Europe. *v.6 p.11, p.12*

The African Queen. *v.2 p.345*

🅔 The African Quest for Freedom and Identity: Cameroonian
Writing and the National Experience. *v.6 p.62*

The African Quest for Freedom and Identity: Cameroonian
Writing and the National Experience. *v.2 p.541*

African Rain Forest Ecology and Conservation: An
Interdisciplinary Perspective. *v.5 p.186*

African Religions and Philosophy. *v.1 p.542, v.6 p.36*

The African Religions of Brazil: Toward a Sociology of the
Interpenetration of Civilizations. . . .*v.1 p.543, v.3 p.338*

African Rhythm: A Northern Ewe Perspective. *v.1 p.284*

African Rock Art: Paintings and Engravings on
Stone. *v.1 p.668, p.689*

African Slave Trade. *v.6 p.52*

African Slavery in Latin America and the
Caribbean. *v.3 p.279, v.4 p.728*

African Stars: Studies in Black South African
Performance. *v.1 p.285*

African State and Society in the 1990s: Cameroon's Political
Crossroads. *v.4 p.613*

The African State in Transition. *v.4 p.611*

African States and Rulers. *v.6 p.51*

☐ African Studies: Human Rights and Governance in
Africa. *v.4 p.611*

African Studies in Social Movements and Democracy. .*v.4 p.711*

African Systems of Kinship and Marriage. *v.4 p.32*

African Theatre in Development. *v.2 p.750*

African Theatre: Southern Africa. *v.1 p.130*

African Traditional Religion: A Definition. *v.1 p.542*

African Urban Kinsmen: The Ga of Central Accra. . . .*v.6 p.73*

An African View of Literature. *v.2 p.751*

An African Voice: The Role of the Humanities in African
Independence. *v.6 p.54*

African Voices: An Introduction to the Languages and
Linguistics of Africa. *v.6 p.81*

African Voices in the African American Heritage. . . .*v.6 p.26*

African Voices of the Atlantic Slave Trade: Beyond the Silence
and the Shame. *v.6 p.3, p.37*

African Women: A Modern History. *v.6 p.52, p.449*

African Women and Development: A History. *v.6 p.458*

☐ African Women on the Internet. *v.6 p.436*

African Women South of the Sahara. *v.6 p.52*

☐ African Women's Bibliographical Database. *v.6 p.432*

☐ African Writers: Voices of Change. *v.2 p.752*

Africana: The Encyclopedia of the African and African
American Experience. *v.3 p.278*

Africana Womanism: Reclaiming Ourselves. . . .*v.6 p.26, p.44*

African-American Art. *v.1 p.705*

African-American Century: How Black Americans Shaped Our
Country. *v.6 p.4, p.5, p.19, p.20*

African-American Concert Dance: The Harlem Renaissance and
Beyond. *v.1 p.18*

African-American Exploration in West Africa: Four
Nineteenth-Century Diaries. *v.6 p.10, p.11*

The African-American Family in Slavery and
Emancipation. *v.6 p.37, p.38*

African-American Folktales: Stories from Black Traditions in
the New World. *v.2 p.16*

African-American Gardens and Yards in the Rural
South. *v.1 p.820*

African-American Grief. *v.6 p.22, p.33*

African-American Literature: Overview and
Bibliography. *v.6 p.28*

African-American Music: An Introduction. *v.1 p.282*

The African-American Odyssey, Vol. I (Chapters 1-13). .*v.6 p.5*

African-American Organized Crime: A Social History. .*v.6 p.251*

African-American Reflections on Brazil's Racial
Paradise. *v.3 p.279*

African-American Social Workers and Social
Policy. *v.4 p.757, v.6 p.38*

The African-American Soldier. *v.6 p.7*

African-American Studies Core List of Resources. .*v.6 p.14, p.34*

The African-American Woman: An Ecological
Perspective. *v.6 p.42*

African-American Women and Poverty: Can Education Alone
Change the Status Quo? *v.6 p.20, p.42*

African-American Writers: A Dictionary. *v.6 p.18, p.34*

African-British Writings in the Eighteenth Century: The Politics
of Race and Reason. *v.2 p.173*

African-Centered Pedagogy: Developing Schools of
Achievement for African American Children. . . .*v.4 p.310*

Africanism and Authenticity in African-American Women's
Novels. *v.6 p.26, p.45*

Africanisms in American Culture. *v.6 p.6, p.11, p.39*

Africanizing Anthropology: Fieldwork, Networks and the
Making of Cultural Knowledge in Central Africa. . .*v.4 p.38*

Africans in Brazil: A Pan-African Perspective. *v.3 p.336*

🅔 Africans in Colonial Mexico: Absolutism, Christianity, and
Afro-Creole Consciousness, 1570-1640. . . . . . .*v.3 p.284*

Africans in Colonial Mexico: Absolutism, Christianity, and
Afro-Creole Consciousness, 1570-1640. . . . . . .*v.3 p.262*

Africans in the Americas: A History of the Black
Diaspora. *v.6 p.11*

🕊 The Africans Series. *v.6 p.53*

Africa's Challenge to International Relations
Theory. *v.4 p.641, p.643*

Africa's Stalled Development: International Causes and
Cures. *v.6 p.55*

Africa. *v.1 p.61, p.130,v.6 p.51*

The Afro-American Woman: Struggles and
  Images. *v.6 p.5, p.43, p.44*

Afro-American Women Writers. *v.2 p.3, v.6 p.25, p.43*

Afro-American Writing: An Anthology of Prose and
  Poetry. *v.2 p.20*

The Afrocentric Idea. *v.6 p.13*

The Afrocentric Paradigm. *v.6 p.14*

Afrocentricity and the Academy: Essays on Theory and
  Practice. *v.6 p.14, p.21*

Afrocentrism and World Politics: Towards a New
  Paradigm. *v.6 p.14, p.31*

Afro-Creole: Power, Opposition and Play in the
  Caribbean. *v.3 p.314*

Afrocuba: Una Antología de Escritos Cubanos Sobre Raza,
  Política y Cultura. *v.2 p.673*

Afro-Cuban Religiosity, Revolution, and National
  Identity. *v.3 p.306*

Afro-Cuban Tales. *v.2 p.671*

Afro-Cuban Voices: On Race and Identity in Contemporary
  Cuba. *v.3 p.279, p.280, p.312*

Afro-Hispanic Literature: An Anthology of Hispanic Writers of
  Hispanic Ancestry. *v.2 p.666*

Afro-Latin America, 1800-2000. . . . .*v.3 p.278*

Afro-Orientalism. *v.6 p.11*

◻ AFT: A Union of Professionals. *v.4 p.282*

After Adorno: Rethinking Music Sociology. *v.1 p.381*

After and Before the Lightning. *v.2 p.20, v.6 p.698*

After Bipolarity: The Vanishing Threat, Theories of Cooperation
  and the Future of the Atlantic Alliance. *v.4 p.654*

After Chartism: Class and Nation in English Radical Politics
  1848-1874. . . . .*v.6 p.758*

After Clausewitz: German Military Thinkers Before the Great
  War. *v.3 p.160*

After Communism: Perspectives on Democracy. . . .*v.4 p.598*

After Crime and Punishment: Pathways to Offender
  Reintegration. *v.6 p.279*

After Dark My Sweet. *v.2 p.124, p.125*

After Delores. *v.6 p.399*

After Development: The Transformation of the Korean
  Presidency and Bureaucracy. *v.4 p.621*

After Empire: Scott, Naipaul, Rushdie. *v.2 p.762, p.768*

After Enron: Lessons for Public Policy. *v.4 p.86*

After Fifty: How the Baby Boom Will Redefine the Mature
  Market. *v.4 p.138*

After Habermas: New Perspectives on the Public
  Sphere. *v.4 p.766, p.774*

After Hegemony: Cooperation and Discord in the World
  Political Economy. *v.4 p.626, p.664, p.665*

After Jews and Arabs: Remaking Levantine Culture. .*v.6 p.596*

After Kinship. *v.4 p.31*

After Leaving Mr. MacKenzie. *v.2 p.769*

After Many a Summer Dies the Swan. *v.2 p.353, p.354*

After Many Years. *v.2 p.715*

After Modern Art, 1945-2000. . . . .*v.1 p.679*

After Nature's Revolt: Eco-Justice and Theology. . .*v.6 p.288*

After Nature. *v.2 p.618*

After Postcolonialism: Remapping Philippines - U. S.
  Confrontations. *v.6 p.114, p.119, p.121, p.124, p.130*

After Seven Years. *v.3 p.476*

After Slavery: Emancipation and Its
  Discontents. *v.3 p.316, v.4 p.728*

After Socialism, Vol. 20, Pt. 1. . . . .*v.4 p.507*

After Spanish Rule: Postcolonial Predicaments of the
  Americas. *v.3 p.328*

✦ After Stonewall: From the Riots to the Millennium. *v.6 p.365*

After Such Knowledge: Memory, History, and the Legacy of the
  Holocaust. *v.3 p.84*

After the Ark?: Environmental Policy-Making and the
  Zoo. *v.5 p.84*

After the Armada: Elizabethan England and the Struggle for
  Western Europe, 1588-1595. . . . .*v.3 p.101*

After the Black Death: A Social History of Early Modern
  Europe. *v.1 p.601*

After the Bombs: A Novel. *v.2 p.674*

After the Cold War: American Foreign Policy in Europe and
  Asia. *v.4 p.485*

After the Divorce. *v.2 p.717*

After the Eclipse: Poems. *v.2 p.731*

After the Fact: The Art of Historical Detection. . . .*v.3 p.374*

After the Fall: Essays in Russian and Soviet
  Historiography. *v.3 p.210*

After the Fall. *v.2 p.101*

After the First Death There Is No Other. *v.2 p.153*

After the First Three Minutes: The Story of Our
  Universe. *v.5 p.72*

After the Holocaust: Rebuilding Jewish Lives in Postwar
  Germany. *v.3 p.83, p.179*

After the Ice Age: The Return of Life to Glaciated North
  America. *v.5 p.449*

After the Killing Fields: Lessons from the Cambodian
  Genocide. *v.4 p.652*

After the Rights Revolution: Reconceiving the Regulatory
  State. *v.4 p.447*

After the School Bell Rings. *v.4 p.300*

After the Storm: The Eiteljorg Fellowship for Native American
  Fine Art, 2001. . . . .*v.6 p.679*

After the Strike: A Century of Labor Struggle at
  Pullman. *v.4 p.122*

After the Thunder: Fourteen Men Who Shaped Post-Civil War
  America. *v.4 p.521*

After the Trail of Tears: The Cherokees' Struggle for
  Sovereignty, 1839-1880. . . . .*v.6 p.687, p.688*

After the Wall: East Meets West in the New Berlin. .*v.3 p.177*

After the War Was Over: Reconstructing the Family, Nation, and
  State in Greece, 1943-1960. . . . .*v.3 p.195, p.196*

After the World Trade Center: Rethinking New York
  City. *v.6 p.715*

After Tylor. *v.4 p.5*

After Virtue: A Study in Moral Theory. *v.1 p.484*

After Yalta. *v.3 p.479*

After-Dinner Conversation: The Diary of a Decadent. *v.2 p.684*

Afterimage: Film, Trauma, and the Holocaust. . . .*v.6 p.322*

Afterimages. *v.1 p.39*

The Afterlife of Edgar Allan Poe. *v.2 p.50*

Afterlife of Gardens. *v.1 p.819*

The Afterlife of Property: Domestic Security and the Victorian Novel. *v.2 p.193, v.6 p.756, p.765*

Afterlife. *v.6 p.398*

Aftermath: The Clinton Impeachment and the Presidency in the Age of Political Spectacle. *v.3 p.442, p.473,v.4 p.528*

Aftermath: The Landscape of War. *v.5 p.585*

Afternoon of a Faun: Mallarme, Debussy, Nijinsky. . .*v.1 p.45*

Afterwards: Slovenian Writing, 1945-1995. . . . . . .*v.2 p.812*

Agaguk: Roman. *v.2 p.540*

Against All Enemies: Inside America's War on Terror. .*v.4 p.563*

Against All Enemies: Interpretations of American Military History from Colonial Times to the Present, 51. . . . .*v.3 p.382, p.383*

Against All Odds: Ten Entrepreneurs Who Followed Their Hearts and Found Success. *v.4 p.68*

Against Criminology. *v.4 p.751*

Against History, Against State: Counterperspectives from the Margins. *v.6 p.154*

Against Interpretation: And Other Essays. *v.2 p.569*

Against Judicial Activism: The Decline of Freedom and Democracy in Canada. *v.4 p.541*

Against Method: Outline of an Anarchistic Theory of Knowledge. *v.5 p.401*

Against Nature: A Rebours. *v.2 p.495*

Against Nature. *v.2 p.494*

Against Our Will: Men, Women and Rape. *v.4 p.751*

Against Our Will: Men, Women, and Rape. *v.6 p.252*

Against Our Will: Men, Women, and Rape. *v.6 p.468*

Against the Academicians and the Teacher. . . .*v.1 p.430, p.592*

Against the Age: An Introduction to William Morris. .*v.2 p.301*

Against the Current: Privatization, Water Markets and the State in Chile. *v.3 p.352*

Against the Evidence: Selected Poems, 1934-1994. . . .*v.2 p.89*

Against the Gods: The Remarkable Story of Risk. *v.4 p.92, p.99, p.162*

Against the Grain: Essays Nineteen Seventy-Five to Nineteen Eighty-Five. *v.2 p.166*

Against the Grain. *v.2 p.494, p.495*

Against the Tide: An Intellectual History of Free Trade. .*v.4 p.664*

Agamemnon. *v.2 p.406*

Agape: An Ethical Analysis. *v.1 p.651*

Agassiz: A Novel in Stories. *v.2 p.733*

Agatha Christie and the Eleven Missing Days. *v.2 p.338*

Age Discrimination by Employers. *v.4 p.134*

An Age in Motion: Popular Radicalism in Java, 1912-1926. . . . .*v.6 p.178*

The Age of Atonement: The Influence of Evangelicalism on Social and Economic Thought 1785-1865. . . . .*v.3 p.112, p.121,v.6 p.758, p.759*

The Age of Augustus. *v.3 p.27*

Age of Charles Martel. *v.3 p.142, p.143*

The Age of Conquest: Wales 1063-1415. . . . . . .*v.6 p.562*

Age of Contradiction: American Thought and Culture in the 1960's. *v.3 p.366, p.370*

The Age of Conversation. *v.3 p.71*

The Age of Doubt: American Thought and Culture in the 1940s. *v.3 p.441*

The Age of Empire. *v.3 p.76, p.77, p.89, p.125*

Age of Enlightenment, 1715-89. . . . .*v.2 p.458, p.459*

The Age of Enlightenment. *v.1 p.437*

The Age of Equipoise: A Study of the Mid-Victorian Generation. *v.3 p.91, p.92, p.110*

Age of Equipoise: A Study of the Mid-Victorian Generation. *v.6 p.749*

Age of Extremism: The End of Compromise in American Politics, Culture, and Race Relations. *v.3 p.371*

The Age of Federalism. *v.4 p.517*

The Age of German Idealism. *v.1 p.508*

The Age of Gold: The California Gold Rush and the New American Dream. *v.3 p.530, p.531*

The Age of Hirohito: In Search of Modern Japan. . . .*v.6 p.227*

The Age of Ideology: Political Ideologies from the American Revolution to Postmodern Times. *v.4 p.487, p.554*

The Age of Improvement. *v.3 p.110, v.6 p.735*

Age of Iron. *v.2 p.753*

The Age of Jackson. *v.3 p.418*

The Age of Justinian: The Circumstances of Imperial Power. *v.3 p.192*

The Age of Lamark. *v.5 p.230*

The Age of Liberty: Sweden 1719-1772. . . . .*v.3 p.235*

The Age of Manufactures, 1700-1820: Industry, Innovation, and Work in Britain. *v.3 p.122*

The Age of Manufactures: Industry, Innovation, and Work in Britain, 1700-1820. . . . .*v.3 p.90*

The Age of McCarthyism: A Brief History with Documents. *v.3 p.450*

The Age of Melancholy: Major Depression and Its Social Origins. *v.5 p.659*

The Age of Milton: Backgrounds to Seventeenth-Century Literature. *v.2 p.170*

The Age of Paradox: A Biography of England 1841. . .*v.6 p.735*

The Age of Realism. *v.2 p.459*

The Age of Reason: The Seventeenth Century Philosophers. *v.1 p.437*

The Age of Reason. *v.1 p.545, v.2 p.528*

The Age of Reconnaissance: Discovery, Exploration, and Settlement, 1450-1650. . . . .*v.3 p.73*

The Age of Reform, 1250-1550: An Intellectual and Religious History of Late Medieval and Reformation Europe. *v.1 p.600, v.3 p.69*

Age of Reform: From Bryan to F. D. R. *v.3 p.368, p.441, p.447, p.448*

The Age of Rights. *v.4 p.455*

The Age of Robert Guiscard: Southern Italy and the Norman Conquest. *v.3 p.198*

The Age of Shakespeare. *v.1 p.76, p.101,v.2 p.230*

Age of Sinan: Architectural Culture in the Ottoman Empire. *v.1 p.787*

The Age of Suspicion. *v.2 p.579*

The Age of Terror: America and the World after September
11. . . . . *v.4 p.487, p.662*

The Age of Terrorism. *v.4 p.660*

The Age of the Baroque in Portugal. *v.3 p.243*

The Age of the Crusades: The Near East from 11th
C-1517. . . . .*v.3 p.64, v.6 p.584*

The Age of the Democratic Revolution: A Political History of
Europe and America, 1760-1800. . . . .*v.3 p.75*

Age of the Democratic Revolution: The Challenge. . . .*v.3 p.75*

Age of the Democratic Revolution: The Struggle, Vol. 2. .*v.3 p.75*

Age of the Earth. *v.5 p.444*

The Age of Uncertainty. *v.4 p.209*

The Age of Van Eyck: The Mediterranean World and Early
Netherlandish Painting, 1430-1530. . . . .*v.1 p.730*

The Age of Virtue: British Culture from the Restoration to
Romanticism. *v.2 p.170, p.172*

The Age of Watteau, Chardin, and Fragonard: Masterpieces of
French Genre Painting. *v.1 p.730*

The Age of William Wordsworth: Critical Essays on the
Romantic Tradition. *v.2 p.324*

The Age of Wonders. *v.6 p.647*

☐ AgEcon Search: Research in Agricultural and Applied
Economics. *v.5 p.13*

Agency, Partnership, and the LLC in a Nutshell. . . .*v.4 p.75*

Agency, Partnerships, and Limited Liability Companies: Cases
and Materials. *v.4 p.75*

Agency-Based Social Work: Neglected Aspects of Clinical
Practice. *v.4 p.759*

Agenda for Progressive Taxation. *v.4 p.248*

The Agenda: Inside the Clinton White House. *v.3 p.482*

Agenda-Setting Dynamics in Canada. *v.4 p.587*

Agents of Apocalypse: Epidemic Disease in the Colonial
Philippines. *v.6 p.179*

Agents of Opportunity: Sports Agents and Corruption in
Collegiate Sports. *v.4 p.905*

Ages of American Law. *v.4 p.440*

Aggression: A Social Learning Analysis. . .*v.4 p.766, v.5 p.662*

Aggression and Violence: Genetic, Neurobiological, and
Biosocial Perspectives. *v.5 p.662*

Aggression in Organizations: Violence, Abuse, and Harassment
at Work and in Schools. *v.4 p.130*

The Aggressions of Civilization: Federal Indian Policy Since the
1880s. *v.6 p.695*

Agha, Shaikh and State: The Social and Political Structures of
Kurdistan. *v.6 p.600*

AGI Data Sheets: For Geology In The Field, Laboratory and
Office. *v.5 p.420*

Aging in Rural America. *v.4 p.751*

Aging, Physical Activity, and Health. *v.4 p.791, p.841*

Aging Societies: The Global Dimension. *v.4 p.741*

Aglaia: The Poetry of Alcman, Sappho, Pindar, Bacchylides and
Corinna. *v.2 p.403*

Agnes Grey. *v.2 p.270*

Agnes Smedley: The Life and Times of an American
Radical. *v.6 p.201*

☐ AgNIC: The Agriculture Network Information Center.*v.5 p.3*

The Agony of Christianity and Essays on Faith. .*v.2 p.662, p.663*

The Agony of Modernization: Labor and Industrialization in
Spain. *v.3 p.241*

Agrarian Dreams: The Paradox of Organic Farming in
California. *v.5 p.31*

Agrarian Feminism: The Politics of Ontario Farm
Women. *v.4 p.590, v.6 p.440*

The Agrarian History of England and Wales, 1850-1914,
Set. *v.4 p.701*

The Agrarian Question and the Peasant Movement in Colombia:
Struggles of the National Peasant Association,
1967-1981. . . . .*v.3 p.359*

Agrarian Reform and Peasant Economy in Southern
Peru. *v.3 p.330*

Agrarian Roots of Pragmatism. *v.6 p.289*

Agrarian Socialism: The Cooperative Commonwealth Federation
in Saskatchewan: A Study in Political Sociology. . .*v.4 p.589*

The Agrarian Sociology of Ancient Civilizations. . . .*v.4 p.211*

Agricola - Germania: Dialogue on Oratory, Vol. 1. . .*v.2 p.445*

Agricola and Germany. *v.2 p.444, v.3 p.161*

Agricultural and Environmental Resource Economics. . .*v.5 p.14*

Agricultural Biotechnology: Challenges and
Prospects. *v.5 p.8, p.9*

Agricultural Biotechnology: Finding Common International
Goals. *v.5 p.6*

Agricultural Biotechnology in Developing Countries: Towards
Optimizing the Benefits for the Poor. *v.5 p.8*

🖱 Agricultural Biotechnology. *v.5 p.7*

Agricultural Crop Issues and Policies. *v.5 p.22*

Agricultural Development Policy: Concepts and
Experiences. *v.5 p.14*

Agricultural Involution: The Processes of Ecological Change in
Indonesia. *v.4 p.29, v.6 p.174*

☐ Agricultural Marketing Service @ USDA
Portal. *v.4 p.152, p.164*

Agricultural Policy for the Twenty-First Century. . . .*v.5 p.15*

Agricultural Restructuring and Sustainability: A Geographical
Perspective. *v.5 p.14*

The Agricultural Revolution of the 20th Century. . . .*v.5 p.15*

The Agricultural Revolution. *v.3 p.90*

☐ Agricultural Statistics. *v.4 p.151, p.164*

Agricultural Trade under CUSTA. . . .*v.4 p.630, p.644, p.666*

Agriculture and Environmental Change: Temporal and Spatial
Dimensions. *v.5 p.29*

Agriculture and Intellectual Property Rights: Economic,
Institutional and Implementation Issues in
Biotechnology. *v.5 p.15*

Agriculture and International Trade: Law, Policy, and the
WTO. *v.4 p.256, p.267, v.5 p.14*

Agriculture and Modern Technology: A Defense. *v.5 p.7*

Agriculture and Rural Development Planning: A Process in
Transition. *v.4 p.397*

Agriculture and the State in Soviet and Post-Soviet Russia. *v.5 p.6*

Agriculture, Environment, and Health: Sustainable Development
in the 21st Century. *v.5 p.13*

☐ Agriculture Fact Book. *v.4 p.152*

Agriculture in Britain and America, 1660-1820: An Annotated Bibliography of the Eighteenth-Century Literature. . *.v.5 p.5*

Agriculture in Surinam, 1650-1950: An Panday, R. M. N. (Radjnarain Mohanpersad Nannan): An Inquiry into the Causes of its Decline. . . . . *.v.3 p.322*

Agriculture in the Middle Ages: Technology, Practice, and Representation. . . . . *.v.3 p.43*

Agriculture in Transition: Land Policies and Evolving Farm Structures in Post Soviet Countries. . . . . *.v.5 p.14*

The Agriculture of China. . . . . *.v.5 p.4*

Agrippa d'Aubigne's "Les Tragiques": A Study of the Baroque Style in Poetry. . . . . *.v.2 p.469*

Agrippa d'Aubigne. . . . . *.v.2 p.469*

Agrippina: Sex, Power, and Politics in the Early Empire. *.v.3 p.27*

☐ AGRIS/CARIS: International Information System for the Agricultural Sciences and Technology. . . . . *.v.5 p.3*

Agrochemical Fate and Movement: Perspectives and Scale of Study. *.v.5 p.10*

Agrochemicals: Composition, Production, Toxicology, Applications. . . . . *.v.5 p.10*

Agrochemicals Desk Reference. . . . . *.v.5 p.312*

Agrodiversity: Learning from Farmers Across the World. *.v.5 p.11*

Agroecology: Ecological Processes in Sustainable Agriculture. . . . . *.v.5 p.11*

Agroecology: The Science of Sustainable Agriculture. *.v.5 p.10*

Agroecosystems Analysis. . . . . *.v.5 p.11*

Agroforestry in Sustainable Agricultural Systems. . . *.v.5 p.40*

Agroforestry Systems in the Tropics. . . . . . . *.v.5 p.39*

Agronomic Handbook: Management of Crops, Soils and Their Fertility. . . . . *.v.5 p.49*

Agua Viva: Ficcao. . . . . *.v.2 p.691*

The Aguero Sisters. . . . . *.v.2 p.145, v.6 p.506*

AHA Guide to the Health Care Field. . . . . . . *.v.5 p.509*

Ahead of the Curve: A Commonsense Guide to Forecasting Business and Market Cycles. . . . . *.v.4 p.81*

Ahead of the Curve: David Baltimore's Life in Science. *.v.5 p.126*

🄴 Ahead of the Curve?: U. N. Ideas and Global Challenges. . . . . *.v.4 p.633*

AI for Games and Animation: A Cognitive Modeling Approach. . . . . *.v.5 p.339, p.340*

Aias. . . . . *.v.2 p.420*

☐ AICPA: American Institute of Certified Public Accountants. . . . . *.v.4 p.103*

Aiding and Abetting. . . . . *.v.2 p.384*

Aiding Democracy Abroad: The Learning Curve. . . *.v.4 p.503*

Aidios, Borinquen Querida: The Puerto Rican Diaspora, Its History and Contributions. . . . . *.v.6 p.520*

AIDS and Accusation: Haiti and Geography of Blame. *.v.4 p.46*

AIDS and the Law. . . . . *.v.4 p.448*

☐ AIDS Epidemic Update: December 2005. . . . . *.v.4 p.669*

AIDS in Africa and the Caribbean. . . . . *.v.3 p.316, p.318*

AIDS in Asia: A Continent in Peril. . . . . . . *.v.4 p.704*

AIDS in the Mind of America: The Social, Political and Psychological Impact of a New Epidemic. . . . . *.v.6 p.378*

AIDS Therapy. . . . . *.v.5 p.515*

☐ AIGA Design Archives. . . . . . . *.v.1 p.710, p.712*

Aiieeeee: An Anthology of Asian-American Writers. . *.v.6 p.91*

Ailey Spirit: The Journey of an American Dance Company. . . . . *.v.1 p.19, p.29, p.31*

Aime Cesaire. . . . . *.v.2 p.537*

☐ AIME: The American Institute of Mining, Metallurgical, and Petroleum Engineers. . . . . *.v.5 p.730*

Aimez-Vous Brahms?. . . . . *.v.2 p.526*

Aimé Césaire. . . . . *.v.2 p.536*

The Aims of Education. . . . . *.v.4 p.291, p.346*

Ainsworth and Bisby's Dictionary of the Fungi. . . . *.v.5 p.45*

Ain't I a Woman: Black Women and Feminism. *.v.6 p.44, p.427*

AIP Physics Desk Reference. . . . . *.v.5 p.545*

Air and Water: The Biology and Physics of Life's Media. . . . . *.v.5 p.564*

Air Monitoring for Toxic Exposures. . . . . . *.v.5 p.355, p.378*

Air Pollution Chemistry. . . . . *.v.5 p.313*

Air Pollution Control: A Design Approach. . . . . *.v.5 p.705*

Airborne: The New Dance Photography of Lois Greenfield. . . . . *.v.1 p.26*

Air-Breathing Fishes: Evolution, Diversity, and Adaptation. . . . . *.v.5 p.215*

Aircraft Control and Simulation. . . . . *.v.5 p.718*

Aircraft Engine Design. . . . . *.v.5 p.718*

Aircraft Maintenance & Engineering Directory 2005. *.v.4 p.151*

Aircraft Performance: Theory and Practice. . . . . *.v.5 p.717*

Aire de las Colinas: Cartas a Clara. . . . . . . *.v.2 p.669*

Aire Frio. . . . . *.v.2 p.673*

🄴 Airline Industry - Global Best Practices: 2005 Edition. . . . . *.v.4 p.152*

Airlines and Air Mail: The Post Office and the Birth of the Commercial Aviation Industry. . . . . . *.v.4 p.152, p.153*

The Airplane, a History of Its Technology. . . . . *.v.5 p.717*

Airplane Stability and Control: A History of the Technologies That Made Aviation Possible. . . . . *.v.5 p.717*

Aishah: The Beloved of Mohammed. . . . . . . *.v.1 p.555*

The AIVF Guide to International Film and Video Festivals. . . . . *.v.6 p.346*

Ajyuq', el Animalero. . . . . *.v.2 p.673, p.674*

Akbar and His India. . . . . *.v.6 p.156*

Akenfield: Portrait of an English Village. . . . . *.v.4 p.701*

Akhenaten and the Religion of Light. . . . . . . *.v.3 p.9*

Akhenaten: King of Egypt. . . . . *.v.6 p.57, p.58*

Akhenaten: The Heretic King. . . . . *.v.3 p.9*

Aksel Sandemose: Exile in Search of a Home, 2. . . *.v.2 p.628*

Al Filo Del Agua. . . . . *.v.2 p.669, p.670*

Al Jazeera: The Inside Story of the Arab News Channel That Is Challenging the West. . . . . *.v.4 p.415*

Al Norte: Agricultural Workers in the Great Lakes Region, 1917-1970. . . . . *.v.6 p.525*

Al Qaeda Now: Understanding Today's Terrorists. . *.v.4 p.659*

Al Smith and His America. . . . . *.v.3 p.458*

Alabama, a Bicentennial History. . . . . *.v.3 p.504*

Alabama Governors: A Political History of the State. *.v.3 p.505*

Alabama in the Twentieth Century. . . . *.v.3 p.504, v.4 p.541*

Alabama: The History of a Deep South State. . . . *.v.3 p.505*

Alabama's Response to the Penitentiary Movement, 1829-1865. . . . .*v.4 p.542*

Alabi's World. *v.4 p.41*

☐ ALADIN: Adult Learning Documentation and Information Network. *v.4 p.319*

Alain Chartier: The Quarrel of the Belle Dame Sans Mercy. *v.2 p.468*

The Alamo: An Illustrated History. *v.3 p.509*

Alan Jay Lerner: A Biography. *v.1 p.251, p.336*

Alan Lomax: Selected Writings, 1934-1997. . . . . .*v.1 p.296*

Al-Andalus: The Art of Islamic Spain. *v.1 p.673, p.686*

Alaska: A Bicentennial History. *v.3 p.533*

Alaska: A Guide to Alaska, Last American Frontier. . *v.3 p.533*

Alaska: A History of the 49th State. *v.3 p.533*

Alaska Anthology: Interpreting the Past. *v.3 p.533*

The Alaska Highway: A Geographical Discovery. . . *v.3 p.545*

The Alaska Purchase and Russian-American Relations. *v.3 p.437*

Alaska: Saga of a Bold Land. *v.3 p.533*

Alaska's Lost Frontier: Life in the Days of Homesteads, Dog Teams, and Sailboat Fisheries. *v.3 p.533*

Alban Berg: "Lulu". *v.1 p.216, p.230, p.309*

Alban Berg: Wozzeck. *v.1 p.216, p.230, p.309*

Albania at War, 1939-1945. . . . .*v.3 p.251, p.252*

Albania in Crisis: The Predictable Fall of the Shining Star. *v.3 p.252*

Albania in Transition: The Rocky Road to Democracy. *v.4 p.600*

Albanian Identities: Myth and History. *v.3 p.252*

Albanian Literature: A Short History. . . . *v.2 p.815, v.3 p.251*

The Albanians: A Modern History. *v.3 p.252*

The Albanians: An Ethnic History from Prehistoric Times to the Present. *v.3 p.252*

Albert Camus : une vie. *v.2 p.512*

Albert Camus: A Life. *v.2 p.512*

Albert Camus and the Literature of Revolt. *v.2 p.512*

Albert Einstein: A Biography. *v.3 p.46, v.5 p.542, p.543*

☐ Albert Ellis Institute. *v.5 p.666*

Albert Hadley: The Story of America's Preeminent Interior Designer. *v.1 p.802*

Albert J. Beveridge: American Nationalist. *v.3 p.456*

Albert Pinkham Ryder: Painter of Dreams. *v.1 p.741*

Alberta: A New History. *v.3 p.546*

Alberto Giacometti: The Complete Graphics, Catalogue Raisonné. *v.1 p.757*

Albertus Seba: Cabinet of Natural Curiosities. *v.5 p.224*

Albion's Fatal Tree: Crime and Society in Eighteenth-Century England. *v.3 p.107, p.108, p.109, p.124, p.131*

Album of Science: Antiquity and the Middle Ages. . *v.5 p.399*

Album of Science: From Leonardo to Lavoisier, 1450-1800. . . . .*v.5 p.390*

Album of Science: The Nineteenth Century. *v.5 p.391*

El Alcalde de Zalamea. *v.2 p.646*

Alcatraz: Indian Land Forever. *v.6 p.689, p.694*

Alcestis. *v.2 p.410*

The Alchemist: A Fable about Following Your Dream. *v.2 p.690*

The Alchemy of Culture: Intoxicants in Society. . . .*v.4 p.776*

The Alchemy of the Heavens: Searching for Meaning in the Milky Way. *v.5 p.71*

Alcohol and Public Policy: No Ordinary Commodity. *v.5 p.512, p.521*

Alcohol and Temperance in Modern History: An Global Encyclopedia. *v.5 p.663*

The Alcohol Fuel Handbook. *v.5 p.742*

Alcohol in Health and Disease. *v.5 p.512, p.521*

Alcohol Marketing and Advertising: A Report to Congress by the U. S. Federal Trade Commission. *v.4 p.153*

Alcohol Problems in Older Adults: Prevention and Management. *v.4 p.775, p.776*

Alcohol, Reform and Society: The Liquor Issue in Social Context, 83. . . . .*v.5 p.663*

The Alcoholic Family in Recovery: A Developmental Model. *v.5 p.672, p.673*

The Alcoholic Republic: An American Tradition. . . .*v.5 p.664*

Alcoholics Anonymous Comes of Age: A Brief History of Alcoholic Anonymous. *v.5 p.672*

Alcoholics Anonymous: The Story of How Many Thousands of Men and Women Have Recovered from Alcoholism. *v.5 p.672*

Alcoholics Anonymous. *v.5 p.669*

Alcoholism and Other Drug Problems. *v.4 p.776*

Alcools. *v.2 p.506*

Aldabonazo: Inside the Cuban Revolutionary Underground 1952-58, a participant's Account. *v.3 p.310*

Aldous Huxley: A Collection of Critical Essays. *v.2 p.354*

Aldous Huxley; Satire and Structure. *v.2 p.354*

Aldous Huxley, Satirist and Novelist. *v.2 p.353*

Aldous Huxley's Brave New World. *v.2 p.353*

Aldous Huxley. *v.2 p.354, p.355*

☐ Aldrich Catalog. *v.5 p.258*

The Aldrich Library of 13C and 1H FT-NMR Spectra, 3 vols. *v.5 p.272*

The Aldrich Library of FT-IR Spectra. *v.5 p.270*

The Aldrich Library of Infrared Spectra. *v.5 p.270*

The Aldrich Library of NMR Spectra. *v.5 p.272*

Aldrich/ACD Library of FT NMR Spectra. *v.5 p.272*

Alejandro Malaspina: Portrait of a Visionary. *v.3 p.73, p.240, p.241*

Alejo Carpentier: The Pilgrim at Home. *v.2 p.671*

Alejo Carpentier. *v.2 p.673*

Aleksandr Blok's Trilogy of Lyric Drama. *v.2 p.801*

Aleksandr Griboedov's 'Woe from Wit': A Commentary and Translation. *v.2 p.804*

Aleksandr Nikolaevich Engelgardt's Letters from the Country, 1872-1887. . . . .*v.3 p.217*

The Aleph and Other Stories. *v.2 p.677, p.678*

Alessandro Manzoni's the Count of Carmagnola and Adelchis. *v.2 p.712*

Alessandro Manzoni. *v.2 p.712*

Alessandro Scarlatti: His Life and Works. . . .*v.1 p.183, p.352*

Alessandro Stradella, 1639-1682: His Life and Music. *v.1 p.184, p.358*

Alex North, Film Composer: A Biography. . . .*v.1 p.256, p.346*

Alex Posey: Creek Poet, Journalist, and Humorist. . .*v.2 p.49*

Alexander Calder. *v.1 p.780*

Alexander H. Stephens, a Biography. *v.3 p.427*

Alexander Hamilton: A Biography. *v.3 p.415*

Alexander Hamilton. *v.4 p.517*

Alexander Herzen and the Birth of Russian Socialism, 1812-1855. . . . .*v.3 p.218*

Alexander I of Russia, the Man Who Defeated Napoleon. *v.3 p.218*

Alexander I: Tsar of War and Peace. *v.3 p.218*

Alexander II and the Modernization of Russia. . . .*v.3 p.219*

Alexander II: The Last Great Tsar. *v.3 p.219*

Alexander Kerensky: The First Love of the Revolution.*v.3 p.221*

Alexander of Macedon, 356-323 B.C.: A Historical Biography. *v.3 p.19*

The Alexander Plays. *v.1 p.121*

Alexander Pope: A Life. *v.2 p.257*

Alexander Pope: Selected Letters. *v.2 p.257*

Alexander Pope: The Genius of Sense. *v.2 p.257*

Alexander Pope: The Poetry of Allusion. *v.2 p.257*

Alexander Pope's The Rape of the Lock. *v.2 p.257*

Alexander Pope. *v.2 p.256, p.257*

Alexander Pushkin: Complete Prose Fiction. *v.2 p.807*

The Alexander Technique in Everyday Life. *v.1 p.50*

Alexander Technique: Original Writings of F. M. Alexander - Constructive Conscious Control. *v.1 p.52*

Alexander Technique. *v.1 p.52*

Alexander the Great: A New Life. *v.3 p.19*

Alexander the Great: A Reader. *v.3 p.20*

Alexander the Great: Historical Sources in Translation.*v.3 p.20*

Alexander the Great: Narrative. *v.3 p.20*

Alexander the Great: Sources and Studies, Vol. 2. . .*v.3 p.20*

Alexander the Great. *v.3 p.19, p.20*

Alexander to Actium: The Historical Evolution of the Hellenistic Age. *v.3 p.21*

Alexandre Dumas: Genius of Life. *v.2 p.489*

Alexandre Dumas, pere. *v.2 p.489*

Alexandria in Late Antiquity: Topography and Social Conflict. *v.3 p.10*

Alexej von Jawlensky, 1890-1938: Catalogue Raisonné of the Watercolours and Drawings. *v.1 p.722, p.734, p.735*

Alexej Von Jawlensky: Catalogue Raisonné of the Oil Paintings 1914-1933. . . . .*v.1 p.741*

Alexej Von Jawlensky: Catalogue Raisonné of the Oil Paintings, 1934-1937. . . . .*v.1 p.741*

Alexej Von Jawlensky: Catalogue Raisonné of the Oil Paintings. *v.1 p.741*

The Alexiad of the Princess Anna Comnena. *v.3 p.192*

The Alexiad. *v.3 p.63*

Alexis de Tocqueville and the Second Republic, 1848-1852: A Study in Political Practice and Principles. *v.3 p.154*

Alexis Lichine's New Encyclopedia of Wines and Spirits.*v.5 p.32*

Alexis. *v.6 p.400*

Alfalfa and Alfalfa Improvement. *v.5 p.21, p.25*

Alfred Binet. *v.5 p.574*

Alfred Cortot's Studies in Musical Interpretation. . .*v.1 p.397*

Alfred de Musset. *v.2 p.498*

Alfred de Vigny's Chatterton: A 3-Act Play. *v.2 p.502*

Alfred Döblin. *v.2 p.617*

Alfred E. Smith: The Happy Warrior. *v.3 p.458*

Alfred Einstein on Music: Selected Music Criticisms.*v.1 p.247*

Alfred H. Barr, Jr. and the Intellectual Origins of the Museum of Modern Art. *v.1 p.679*

Alfred Jarry: A Critical and Biographical Study. . . .*v.2 p.521*

Alfred Jarry: Nihilism and the Theatre of the Absurd.*v.2 p.521*

Alfred Kazin's America: Critical and Personal Writings.*v.2 p.91*

Alfred Lord Tennyson: A Memoir by His Son. *v.2 p.315*

Alfred Lord Tennyson. *v.2 p.313*

Alfred North Whitehead: An Anthology. *v.1 p.447*

The Alfred Russel Wallace Reader: A Selection of Writings from the Field. *v.5 p.197*

Alfred Schutz: An Intellectual Biography. *v.4 p.686*

Alfred Schutz on Phenomenology and Social Relations: Selected Writings. *v.4 p.685, p.686*

Alfred Stieglitz: The Key Set: The Alfred Stieglitz Collection of Photographs. *v.1 p.766*

Algae of the Western Great Lakes Area, with an Illustrated Key to the Genera of Desmids and Freshwater Diatoms.*v.5 p.208*

Algae. *v.5 p.208*

Algal Cultures, Analogues of Blooms and Applications.*v.5 p.208*

Algal Culturing Techniques. *v.5 p.207*

Algebra for College Students. *v.5 p.472*

Algebra for Review. *v.5 p.472*

Algebra, Vol. II. *v.5 p.474*

Algebra, Vol. I. *v.5 p.474*

Algebraic Combinatorics. *v.5 p.478*

The Algebraic Eigenvalue Problem. *v.5 p.473, p.492*

Algebraic Geometry: A First Course. *v.5 p.497*

Algebraic Geometry. *v.5 p.497*

Algebraic Graph Theory. *v.5 p.480*

Algebraic Number Theory. *v.5 p.476*

Algebraic Statistics for Computational Biology. *v.5 p.92, p.93, p.107*

Algebraic Topology. *v.5 p.499*

Algebra. *v.5 p.473*

Algeria, 1830-2000: A Short History. *v.6 p.61*

Algerian White. *v.6 p.642, p.643*

Algiers in the Age of the Corsairs. *v.6 p.642*

The Algorithmic Composer. *v.1 p.386*

Algorithmics: The Spirit of Computing. .*v.5 p.335, p.336, p.343*

Algorithms in Java: Graph Algorithms. *v.5 p.336, p.347*

Algorithms in Java, Pt. 1-4. . . . . . .*v.5 p.336, p.347*

Algunas Nubes/No Habra Final Feliz. *v.2 p.669*

Alice Doesn't: Feminism, Semiotics, Cinema. *v.6 p.474*

Alice Munro. *v.2 p.737*

Alice Schille. *v.1 p.739*

Alice's Adventures in Wonderland. *v.2 p.277*

Alice's Adventures: Lewis Carroll in Popular Culture.*v.2 p.277*

Alien Bodies: Representations of Modernity, "Race" and Nation in Early Modern Dance. *v.1 p.27*

Alien Invasion: America's Battle with Non-Native Animals and Plants. *v.5 p.166, p.182*

Alien Regimes and Border States, 907-1368. . .*v.6 p.186, p.204*

Alien Species and Evolution: The Evolutionary Ecology of Exotic Plants, Animals, Microbes, and Interacting Native Species. *v.5 p.186, p.191*

Alien Vision of Victorian Poetry: Sources of the Poetic Imagination in Tennyson, Browning and Arnold. *v.2 p.184, v.6 p.755*

Alien Wisdom: The Limits of Hellenization. *v.3 p.21*

Alien Zone 2: The Spaces of Science Fiction Cinema. *v.6 p.318, p.319*

Alien Zone: Cultural Theory and Contemporary Science Fiction Cinema. *v.6 p.318*

The Alienated Academy: Culture and Politics in Republican China, 1919-1937. . . . .*v.6 p.191*

Alienated Minority: The Jews of Medieval Latin Europe. *v.6 p.574*

Alienated Women: A Study on Polish Women's Fiction. .*v.2 p.788*

Alienation and Charisma: A Study of Contemporary American Communes. *v.4 p.740*

Alienation and Freedom. *v.1 p.505, p.506*

Alienation of Church Wealth in Mexico. *v.3 p.288*

Aliens and Dissenters: Federal Suppression of Radicals, 1903-1933. . . . .*v.3 p.444, p.449*

Aliens in the Backyard: Plant and Animal Imports into America. *v.5 p.187*

Aliens R Us: The Other in Science Fiction Cinema. . .*v.6 p.319*

Alif Baa: Introduction to Arabic Letters and Sounds. .*v.6 p.653*

Alkaloids: Nature's Curse or Blessing. *v.5 p.299*

al-Kitaab fii Ta'allum al-Arabiyya; with DVDs: A Textbook for Beginning Arabic. *v.6 p.653*

All about Art. *v.1 p.668*

All American: The Rise and Fall of Jim Thorpe. .*v.4 p.841, p.869*

All Around What Empties Out. *v.6 p.103*

All Backs Were Turned. *v.2 p.790*

All Deliberate Speed: Reflections on the First Half Century of Brown v. Board of Education. *v.6 p.12, p.21, p.22*

All Else Equal: Are Public and Private Schools Different? *v.4 p.296*

All for One: Terrorism, NATO and the United States. *v.4 p.564, p.631, p.660*

All Hallows' Eve. *v.2 p.387*

All His Jazz: The Life and Death of Bob Fosse. . .*v.1 p.8, p.31*

All I'm Asking for Is My Body. *v.6 p.101*

All in the Dances: A Brief Life of George Balanchine. .*v.1 p.13*

All Is Clouded by Desire: Global Banking, Money Laundering, and International Organized Crime. *v.6 p.251*

All Made of Tunes: Charles Ives and the Uses of Musical Borrowing. *v.1 p.210, p.333*

All Men Are Mortal. *v.2 p.509*

☐ All Movie Guide. *v.6 p.305*

All Music Guide to Classical Music: The Definitive Guide to Classical Music. *v.1 p.172, p.234, p.235, p.238, p.244*

All Music Guide to Country: The Definitive Guide to Country Music. *v.1 p.169, p.266*

All Music Guide to Electronica: The Expert's Guide to the Best Electronic Recordings. *v.1 p.169, p.170, p.266*

All Music Guide to Hip-Hop: The Definitive Guide to Rap and Hip-Hop. *v.1 p.170, p.266*

All Music Guide to Jazz: The Definitive Guide to Jazz. *v.1 p.170, p.257*

All Music Guide to Rock: The Definitive Guide to Rock, Pop and Soul. *v.1 p.170, p.266*

All Music Guide to the Blues: The Definitive Guide to the Blues. *v.1 p.170, p.257*

All My Relations: An Anthology of Contemporary Canadian Native Fiction. *v.2 p.732, v.6 p.698*

All of Us: The Collected Poems. *v.2 p.142*

All Our Kin: Strategies for Survival in a Black Community. *v.4 p.37*

All Our Relations: Native Struggles for Land and Life. .*v.6 p.681*

All Our Yesterdays. *v.2 p.717*

All over Creation. *v.6 p.101*

All Passion Spent. *v.2 p.380, p.381*

All Politics Is Local: Family, Friends, and Provincial Interests in the Creation of the Constitution. *v.4 p.542, p.543*

All Possible Worlds: A History of Geographical Ideas. *v.3 p.45, v.4 p.378*

All Quiet on the Western Front. *v.2 p.614*

All Roads Are Good: Native Voices on Life and Culture. .*v.6 p.678*

All Scientists Now: The Royal Society in the Nineteenth Century. *v.5 p.385*

All Shook Up: How Rock 'n' Roll Changed America. .*v.1 p.265*

All That Is Native and Fine: The Politics of Culture in an American Region. *v.3 p.498*

All That Is Solid Melts into Air: The Experience of Modernity. *v.6 p.709*

All That Remains: The Palestinian Villages Occupied and Depopulated by Israel in 1948. . . . .*v.6 p.618*

All the Conspirators. *v.2 p.355, p.356*

All the Days and Nights: The Collected Stories of William Maxwell. *v.2 p.97*

All the Essential Half-Truths about Higher Education. .*v.4 p.290*

All the Happy Endings: A Study of the Domestic Novel in America, the Women Who Wrote It, the Women Who Read It, in the Nineteenth Century. *v.2 p.8*

All the King's Men. *v.2 p.129*

All the Laws but One: Civil Liberties in Wartime. . . .*v.4 p.456*

All the News That's Fit to Sell: How the Market Transforms Information into News. *v.4 p.414*

All the Pasha's Men: Mehmed Ali, His Army and the Making of Modern Egypt. *v.6 p.639*

All the Poems: Collected Poems. *v.2 p.384*

All the Power in the World. *v.1 p.489*

All the President's Men. *v.3 p.465, v.4 p.404, p.405*

All the Pretty Horses. *v.2 p.149*

All the Rage: The Story of Gay Visibility in America. *v.6 p.366, p.369*

All the Shah's Men: An American Coup and the Roots of Middle East Terror. *v.4 p.654*

All the Stories of Muriel Spark. *v.2 p.383*

All the Women Are White, All the Blacks are Men, but Some of Us Are Brave: Black Women's Studies. *v.6 p.463*

All Things Are Possible: The Healing and Charismatic Revivals in Modern America. *v.1 p.648*

All Things Austen: An Encyclopedia of Austen's World. *v.2 p.268*

All Things Shakespeare: An Encyclopedia of Shakespeare's World, Vol. 1. . . . .*v.2 p.222*

All Things Shakespeare: An Encyclopedia of Shakespeare's World, Vol. 2. . . . .*v.2 p.222*

All Visitors Ashore. *v.2 p.749*

All Work and No Play....: How Educational Reforms Are Harming Our Preschoolers. *v.4 p.370*

All You Need to Know about the Music Business. . . .*v.1 p.385*

All Your Worth: The Ultimate Lifetime Money Plan. . *v.4 p.98*

Allah Is Not Obliged. *v.2 p.545*

Allah N'est Pas Oblige. *v.2 p.545*

All-American Girl: The Ideal of Real Womanhood in Mid-Nineteenth Century America. *v.2 p.9*

Allan Houser: An American Master - Chiricahua Apache 1914-1994. . . . .*v.1 p.781, v.6 p.679*

Allan Ramsay: A Study of His Life and Works. *v.2 p.258*

The Allegorical Dramas of Calderon: An Introduction to the Auto Sacramentales. *v.2 p.647*

Allegories of Contamination: Pier Paolo Pasolini's Trilogy of Life. *v.6 p.339*

Allegories of Empire: The Figure of Woman in the Colonial Text. *v.2 p.728*

Allegories of Love: Cervante's Persiles and Sigismunda. *v.2 p.650*

The Allegory of Love: A Study of Medieval Tradition. *v.2 p.164*

Allegory: The Theory of a Symbolic Mode. *v.2 p.572*

Alleluia pour une Femme-Jardin. *v.2 p.536*

Allen and Greenough's New Latin Grammar. *v.2 p.423*

Allen Tate: Orphan of the South. *v.2 p.125*

Allen's Astrophysical Quantities. *v.5 p.63*

Allergic Diseases: Diagnosis and Management. *v.5 p.517*

Allergic Diseases: Diagnosis and Treatment. . *v.5 p.517, p.518*

Alléluia pour une femme-jardin. *v.2 p.536*

Alliance Against Babylon: The US, Israel and Iraq. . *v.4 p.641*

An Alliance at Risk: The United States and Europe since September 11. . . . .*v.4 p.563*

Alliance Capitalism: The Social Organization of Japanese Business. *v.6 p.219*

The Alliance Israelite Universelle and the Jewish Communities of Morocco, 1862-1962. . . . .*v.6 p.597, p.643*

Allies and Adversaries: The Joint Chiefs of Staff, the Grand Alliance and U. S. Strategy in World War II. . . .*v.4 p.561*

Allies at Odds?: The United States and the European Union. *v.4 p.642*

Allies: The U. S. Britain, and Europe in the Aftermath of the Iraq War. *v.4 p.647*

The Alliterative Morte Arthure: A New Verse Translation. *v.2 p.206*

The Alliterative Revival. *v.2 p.551*

☐ Allmusic = All Music Guide. *v.1 p.169, p.265*

All's Well That Ends Well. *v.2 p.223*

The Allure of the Foreign: Imported Goods in Postcolonial Latin America. *v.3 p.272*

Allusion to the Poets. *v.2 p.180, p.181*

Allusions in Ulysses: An Annotated List. *v.2 p.360*

The Ally Who Came in from the Cold: A Survey of Icelandic Foreign Policy 1946-1956. . . . .*v.3 p.234*

The Allyn and Bacon Guide to Writing Center: Theory and Practice. *v.2 p.564*

Alma Mahler: Or the Art of Being Loved. *v.1 p.214, p.338, p.339, p.378, p.379*

Al-Ma'mun. *v.6 p.584*

The Almanac of American Employers 2006: The Only Complete Guide to America's Hottest, Fastest-Growing Corporate Employers. *v.4 p.170*

The Almanac of Canadian Politics. *v.4 p.586*

The Almanac of Federal PACs: 2006-2007. . . . . .*v.4 p.559*

The Almanac of Renewable Energy: The Complete Guide to Emerging Energy Technologies. *v.5 p.361*

al-Maqrizi's Book of Contention and Strife Concerning the Relations between the Banu Umayya and the Banu Hashim. *v.6 p.584*

Almayer's Folly. *v.2 p.339, p.340*

The Almighty Latin King and Queen Nation: Street Politics and the Transformation of a New York City Gang. . . .*v.6 p.547*

Almost a Gentleman: An Autobiography, 1955-1956. *v.2 p.376*

Almost a Woman: Combined with When I Was Puerto Rican. *v.2 p.155*

Almost a Woman. *v.6 p.490*

Almost NATO: Partner and Players in Central and Eastern European Security. *v.4 p.639, p.654, p.655*

Almost Shakespeare: Reinventing His Works for Cinema and Television. *v.6 p.326*

Aloft. *v.6 p.100, p.101*

Aloha Betrayed: Native Hawaiian Resistance to American Colonialism. *v.6 p.131*

Alone Before God: The Religious Origins of Modernity in Mexico. *v.3 p.264, p.288*

Alone in the Trenches: My Life As a Gay Player in the NFL. *v.4 p.839, p.860*

Alone of All Her Sex: The Myth and the Cult of the Virgin Mary. *v.6 p.573*

Along the Faultlines: Sex, Race and Nation in Australian Women's Writing. *v.2 p.741, p.742*

Along the Huron: The Natural Communities of the Huron River Corridor in Ann Arbor, Michigan. *v.5 p.233*

Along This Way: The Autobiography of James Weldon Johnson. *v.2 p.89, p.90, v.6 p.6, p.7, p.18*

Alonso de Zorita: Royal Judge and Christian Humanist, 1512-1585. . . . .*v.3 p.318*

Aloud!: Voices from the Nuyorican Poets Cafe. *v.6 p.505, p.509*

Les alouettes naïves : roman. *v.2 p.544*

Alphabet: Abeceda. *v.2 p.784*

Alphabet to Email: How Written English Evolved and Where It's Headed. *v.2 p.554*

Alphonse de Lamartine: A Political Biography. *v.2 p.495*

Alpine Biodiversity in Europe. *v.5 p.169*

The Alps: Europe's Mountain Heart. *v.3 p.245*

Al-Qaeda: Brotherhood of Terror. *v.4 p.662*

☐ Al's Notebook. *v.5 p.295*

Altazor. *v.2 p.680*

Alterations of Consciousness: An Empirical Analysis for Social
   Scientists. *v.5 p.612*

The Alteration. *v.2 p.328*

Altered Harvest: Agriculture, Genetics and the Fate of the
   World's Food Supply. *v.5 p.7*

Altered Lives, Enduring Community: Japanese Americans
   Remember Their World War II Incarceration. . . .*v.6 p.133*

Altered States of Consciousness and Mental Health: A
   Cross-Cultural Perspective. *v.5 p.638*

Altering American Consciousness: Essays on the History of
   Alcohol and Drug Use in the United States,
   1800-2000. . . . .*v.4 p.775, v.5 p.663*

Altering Party Systems: Strategic Behavior and the Emergence
   of New Political Parties in Western Democracies. *v.4 p.579*

Alternate Civilities: Democracy and Culture in China and
   Taiwan. *v.4 p.618, p.620, p.621*

Alternative Agriculture: A History: From the Black Death to the
   Present Day. *v.3 p.43, v.5 p.13*

Alternative Agriculture. *v.5 p.4, p.30, p.31*

An Alternative Approach to Allergies: The New Field of
   Clinical Ecology Unravels the Environmental
   Causes of Mental and Physical Ills. *v.5 p.365*

Alternative Cars in the 21st Century: A New Personal
   Transportation Paradigm. *v.4 p.154, v.5 p.701*

Alternative Construction: Contemporary Natural Building
   Methods. *v.1 p.796*

Alternative Energy: Facts, Statistics and Issues. . . .*v.5 p.452*

Alternative Europe: Eurotrash and Exploitation Cinema Since
   1945. . . . .*v.6 p.314*

Alternative Fuels and the
   Environment. *v.5 p.705, v.6 p.289, p.290*

☐ Alternative Press Index. *v.6 p.361*

Alternative Scriptwriting: Successfully Breaking the
   Rules. *v.6 p.352*

Alternative Teacher Certification, A State-by-State Analysis:
   1998-1999 Edition. *v.4 p.278*

Alternative Theatre in Poland: 1954-1989. . . . . .*v.2 p.788*

Alternative Transportation Fuels: An Environmental and Energy
   Solution. *v.5 p.742*

Alternatives to Hitler: German Resistance under the Third
   Reich. *v.3 p.173*

Alternatives to Independence: Explorations in Post-Colonial
   Relations. *v.4 p.583, p.584*

Altgeld's America: The Lincoln Ideal Versus Changing
   Realities. *v.3 p.515*

Alton Locke, Vol. 1. . . . .*v.2 p.296*

Altruism and Altruistic Love: Science, Philosophy, and Religion
   in Dialogue. *v.1 p.501, v.5 p.655*

The Altruistic Imagination: A History of Social Work and Social
   Policy in the United States. *v.4 p.757*

☐ Aluminium Industry Abstracts (AIA). *v.5 p.730*

Aluminum and Aluminum Alloys. *v.5 p.736*

Aluminum by Design. *v.5 p.736*

Alvar Aalto: A Critical Study. *v.1 p.794*

Alvar Aalto: Toward a Human Modernism. *v.1 p.794*

Alvar Aalto. *v.1 p.794, p.795*

Alvin Ailey: A Life in Dance. *v.1 p.7, v.6 p.414*

Always Astonished: Selected Prose. *v.2 p.688*

Always Now: The Collected Poems. *v.2 p.733*

Always Running: Gang Days in L. A. *v.4 p.714*

Always Running: La Vida Loca: Gang Days in L.
   A. *v.6 p.490, p.503, p.547*

Am I a Snob?: Modernism and the Novel. *v.2 p.191*

Am I Blue?: Coming Out from the Silence. *v.6 p.368*

Am I That Name?: Feminism and the Category of Women in
   History. *v.6 p.435*

Am I Thin Enough Yet?: The Cult of Thinness and the
   Commercialization of Identity. .*v.4 p.778, v.5 p.653, v.6 p.445*

Ama Ata Aidoo. *v.2 p.753*

AMA Dictionary of Marketing Terms. *v.4 p.134*

AMA Handbook for Customer Satisfaction: A Complete Guide
   to Research, Planning, and Implementation. . . .*v.4 p.136*

AMA Marketing Encyclopedia: Issues and Trends Shaping the
   Future. *v.4 p.134*

Amadis de Gaula, I. *v.2 p.646*

Amadis de Gaulle. *v.2 p.646*

Amadis of Gaul. *v.2 p.646*

Amalia. *v.2 p.678*

L' Amante Anglaise. *v.2 p.516*

L' Amant. *v.2 p.516*

Amartya Sen's Work and Ideas: A Gender Perspective. .*v.4 p.272*

The Amateur and the Professional: Antiquarians, Historians and
   Archaeologists in Victorian England
   1838-1886. . . . .*v.6 p.750, p.751, p.754*

☐ Amateur Athletic Foundation of Los
   Angeles. . . . *v.4 p.803, p.812, p.830, p.839, p.845, p.903*

Amateurs, Photography, and the Mid-Victorian
   Imagination. *v.6 p.738*

The Amazing Adventures of Kavalier and
   Clay. *v.2 p.142, v.6 p.395*

Amazing Grace: A Vocabulary of Faith. *v.1 p.650, p.651*

The Amazon and the Page: Natalie Clifford Barney and Renee
   Vivien. *v.6 p.402*

Amazon Conservation in the Age of Development: The Limits
   of Providence. *v.3 p.269*

The Amazon Rubber Boom, 1850-1920. . . . .*v.3 p.270, p.338*

Amazons and Military Maids: Women Who Dressed as Men in
   Pursuit of Life, Liberty and Happiness. *v.6 p.367*

The Ambassadors: An Authoritative Text, the Author on the
   Novel, Criticism. *v.2 p.45*

The Ambassadors and America's Soviet Policy. *v.3 p.390*

An Ambassador's Journey: An Exploration of People and
   Culture. *v.3 p.455*

The Ambassadors' Secret: Holbein and the World of the
   Renaissance. *v.1 p.744, p.745*

The Amber Spyglass. *v.2 p.373*

El Ambiente Nuestro: Chicano/Latino Homoerotic
   Writing. *v.6 p.498, p.506, p.512*

Ambiguities of Domination: Politics, Rhetoric, and Symbols in
   Contemporary Syria. *v.6 p.608*

Ambiguity and Choice in Organizations. *v.4 p.280*

The Ambiguity of Teaching to the Test: Standards, Assessment, and Educational Reform. *v.4 p.286*

Ambiguous Adventure. *v.2 p.545*

The Ambiguous Legacy: U. S. Foreign Relations in the "American Century". *v.3 p.452*

Ambiguous Loss: Learning to Live with Unresolved Grief. *v.5 p.651*

Ambition and Accommodation: How Women View Gender Relations. *v.4 p.746, v.6 p.430*

Ambivalent Allies?: A Study of South Korean Attitudes Toward the U. S. *v.3 p.390*

The Ambivalent Art of Katherine Anne Porter. *v.2 p.110*

Ambivalent Conquests: Maya and Spaniard in Yucatan, 1517-1570. . . . .*v.3 p.285*

Ambivalent Neighbors: The EU, NATO and the Price of Membership. *v.4 p.638*

The Ambivalent Revolution: Forging State and Nation in Chiapas, 1910-1945. . . . .*v.3 p.294*

Ambling into History: The Unlikely Odyssey of George W. Bush. *v.4 p.485*

Ambrose of Milan: Church and Court in a Christian Capital. *v.3 p.32*

AMC Guide to Outdoor Leadership. *v.4 p.786, p.787*

Amedeo Modigliani: Paintings, Sculptures, Drawings. *v.1 p.699*

▢ Amendments to the Constitution. *v.4 p.455*

AmeRícan. *v.6 p.507, p.510*

America Alone: The Neo-Conservatives and the Global Order. *v.4 p.516*

America and the Holy Land: With Eyes Toward Zion, IV. *v.6 p.610*

America and the World Revolution, and Other Lectures. *v.3 p.370*

America and the World. *v.3 p.384*

America As a Civilization: Life and Thought in the United States Today. *v.3 p.368*

America As a Military Power, 1775-1865: From the American Revolution to the Civil War. *v.3 p.382*

America As Second Creation: Technology and Narratives of New Beginnings. *v.3 p.381*

America Ascendant: From Theodore Roosevelt to FDR in the Century of American Power, 1901-1945. . . . . .*v.3 p.446*

America at the Polls 1920-1956: Harding to Eisenhower A Handbook of American Presidential Election Statistics. *v.4 p.555, p.556*

America at the Polls 1960-2004: Kennedy to George W. Bush - A Handbook of American Presidential Election Statistics, Vol. 2. . . . .*v.4 p.556*

America Begins: Early American Writings. *v.2 p.28*

America Beyond Capitalism: Reclaiming Our Wealth, Our Liberty, and Our Democracy. *v.4 p.493, p.502*

America Discovered: A Historical Atlas of North American Exploration. *v.4 p.379, p.382*

America Divided: The Civil War of the 1960s. *v.3 p.473*

America Encounters Japan: From Perry to MacArthur. *v.3 p.391*

America First!: Its History, Culture and Politics. *v.4 p.486*

America Goes to War: The Civil War and Its Meaning in American Culture. *v.3 p.430*

America in 1492: The World of the Indian Peoples Before the Arrival of Columbus. *v.6 p.685, p.703*

America in the 1990s. *v.3 p.477*

America in the Age of the Titans: From the Rise of Theodore Roosevelt to the Death of FDR. *v.3 p.394*

America in the Gilded Age: From Abraham Lincoln to Theodore Roosevelt. *v.3 p.435*

America in the Gilded Age: From the Death of Lincoln to the Rise of Theodore Roosevelt. *v.3 p.394*

America in the Modern World. *v.3 p.366, p.370*

America in the Twenties. *v.3 p.447*

America in the World: The Historiography of U. S. Foreign Relations since 1941. . . . .*v.3 p.452*

America in Vietnam: A Documentary History. *v.3 p.454, p.455*

America Is in the Heart. *v.6 p.93*

America Is West: An Anthology of Middle Western Life and Literature. *v.2 p.21*

America Moves West. *v.3 p.519*

America on Film: Hollywood and American History. *v.6 p.314*

America on Film: Modernism, Documentary, and a Changing America. *v.6 p.309*

America on Film: Representing Race, Class, Gender, and Sexuality at the Movies. *v.6 p.415*

America on Record: A History of Recorded Sound. . *v.1 p.387*

America, Past and Present: Primary Source Edition. . *v.3 p.379*

America Restored. *v.1 p.822*

America Right or Wrong: An Anatomy of American Nationalism. *v.3 p.368*

America Unbound: The Bush Revolution in Foreign Policy. *v.3 p.483, v.4 p.560*

America Unrivaled: The Future of the Balance of Power. *v.3 p.448*

America Views the Holocaust, 1933-1945: A Brief Documentary History. *v.3 p.82*

America Votes 26: 2003-2004, Election Returns by State. *v.4 p.547*

America Votes: A Handbook of Contemporary American Election Statistics, Vol. 24. . . . .*v.4 p.549*

America Without the Death Penalty: States Leading the Way. *v.6 p.247*

American Abstract Expressionism of the 1950s: An Illustrated Survey. *v.1 p.728*

The American Academic Profession: A Synthesis of Social Scientific Inquiry since World War II. *v.4 p.292*

The American Age: U. S. Foreign Policy at Home and Abroad, from 1750 to the Present. *v.3 p.453*

American Agriculture: A Brief History. *v.5 p.4*

American Agriculture and the Problem of Monopoly: The Political Economy of Grain Belt Farming, 1953-1980. *v.5 p.14*

American Agriculture in the Twentieth Century: How It Flourished and What It Cost. *v.5 p.4*

An American Album: One Hundred of Fifty Years of Harper's Magazine. *v.2 p.19, p.584*

American Alliance Policy in the Middle East, 1945-1992: Iran, Israel and Saudi Arabia. *v.3 p.391*

American Ambassador: Joseph C. Grew and the Development of the United States Diplomatic Tradition. *v.3 p.459*

American Anthem: Masterworks from the American Folk Art Museum. *v.1 p.800*

American Anthropology, 1921-1945: Papers from the American Anthropologist. *v.4 p.3*

American Anthropology in Micronesia: An Assessment. *v.4 p.4*

American Apartheid: Segregation and the Making of the Underclass. *v.4 p.730*

American Apocalypse: Yankee Protestants and the Civil War, 1860-1869. . . . .*v.1 p.606*

The American Approach to Foreign Policy: A Pragmatic Perspective. *v.3 p.385*

American Architecture: A Critical History. *v.1 p.789*

American Architecture: A History. *v.1 p.790*

American Art: A Cultural History. *v.1 p.681, p.682*

American Art and Architecture. *v.1 p.682*

American Art Directory 2005-2006. . . . .*v.1 p.667*

American Art: History and Culture. *v.1 p.682*

American Art since 1945. . . . .*v.1 p.679, p.682*

American Artists: Signatures and Monograms, 1800-1989. . . . .*v.1 p.663*

American Arts and Crafts Textiles. *v.1 p.715, p.809*

☐ American Association for Career Education. *v.5 p.576*

☐ American Association of Colleges for Teacher Education. *v.4 p.279*

☐ American Association of Community Colleges. . .*v.4 p.291*

☐ American Association of State Colleges and Universities. *v.4 p.291*

American Attitudes: Who Thinks What about the Issues That Shape Our Lives. *v.5 p.586*

American Attitutdes: What Americans Think about the Issues That Shape Their Lives. *v.4 p.138*

American Avant-Garde Theatre. *v.1 p.84, p.111*

The American Avant-Garde Tradition: William Carlos Williams, Postmodern Poetry, and the Politics of Cultural Memory. *v.2 p.136*

American Babylon: Race and the Struggle for Postwar Oakland. *v.6 p.719*

The American Ballet Theatre. *v.1 p.24*

The American Bar Association Legal Guide for Small Business: Everything a Small-Business Person Must Know, from Start-Up to Employment Laws to Financing and Selling a Business. *v.4 p.87, p.444*

☐ American Bibliography of Slavic and East European Studies. *v.2 p.773*

American Bison: A Natural History. *v.6 p.284*

☐ American Board of Professional Psychology. . . .*v.5 p.675*

American Broadcasting and the First Amendment. . .*v.4 p.459*

American Buffalo. *v.1 p.62, p.116*

American Bureaucracy: Public Choice and Public Law. .*v.4 p.463*

American Burlesque Show. *v.1 p.36*

The American Campaigns of Rochambeau's Army, 1780, 1781, 1782, 1783. . . . .*v.3 p.413*

American Capitalism: The Concept of Countervailing Power. *v.4 p.214*

American Catholic Biblical Scholarship: A History from the Early Republic to Vatican II. *v.1 p.573*

The American Catholic Experience: A History from Colonial Times to the Present. *v.1 p.572, p.573*

American Catholic Social Ethics: Twentieth-Century Approaches. *v.1 p.575*

American Catholics, American Culture: Tradition and Resistance. *v.4 p.721*

American Catholics and Slavery, 1789-1866: An Anthology of Primary Documents. *v.1 p.575*

The American Cause. *v.3 p.368*

The American Century: Consensus and Coercion in the Projection of American Power. *v.3 p.370*

American Ceramics: 1876 to the Present. *v.1 p.807*

American Character. *v.3 p.366*

American Chemists and Chemical Engineers. *v.5 p.261*

An American Childhood. *v.2 p.144*

American Children's Folklore. *v.2 p.16*

American Cinematographer Manual. *v.6 p.349*

The American City: What Works, What Doesn't. . . .*v.6 p.727*

The American Civil War. *v.3 p.432*

The American Class Structure in an Age of Growing Inequality: A New Synthesis. *v.4 p.724*

The American College: A Psychological and Social Interpretation of the Higher Learning. *v.4 p.290, p.291, p.332*

The American College and University: A History. . . .*v.4 p.332*

American College in the Nineteenth Century. *v.4 p.331*

☐ American College of Sports Medicine. *v.4 p.824, p.876, p.878*

American Colonial Wealth: Documents and Methods, Set. *v.3 p.405, p.406*

The American Colonies in the Eighteenth Century. *v.3 p.406, v.4 p.518*

American Colonies in the Seventeenth Century, Vol. 2. . . . .*v.3 p.406, v.4 p.518*

American Colonies: The Settling of North America. . .*v.3 p.407*

An American Colony: Regionalism and the Roots of Midwestern Culture. *v.3 p.506*

The American Community College. *v.4 p.291*

American Composers: Dialogues on Contemporary Music. *v.1 p.225*

American Confluence: The Missouri Frontier from Borderland to Border State. *v.3 p.512*

American Congressional Dictionary. *v.4 p.529*

The American Congress. *v.4 p.531*

☐ American Conifer Society. *v.5 p.36*

American Constitutional Law, Vol. I. *v.4 p.454*

American Corrections. *v.6 p.272*

American Costume, 1915-1970: A Source Book for the Stage Costumer. *v.1 p.151*

American Counties: Origins of County Names Dates of Creation and Population Data 1950-2000. . . . .*v.3 p.381*

American Couples: Money, Work, Sex. . . .*v.4 p.739, v.6 p.466*

American Couples. *v.4 p.731*

The American Cowboy: The Myth and the Reality. *v.3 p.521, v.6 p.324*

American Dark Comedy: Beyond Satire. *v.6 p.312*

American Datelines: Major News Stories from Colonial Times to the Present. *v.4 p.404*

American Decorative Arts and Paintings in the Bayou Bend Collection. *v.1 p.801*

American Democracy: A Commentary and an Interpretation. *v.3 p.368*

American Design in the 20th Century. *v.1 p.714*

American Destiny: Narrative of a Nation. *v.3 p.379*

The American Development of Biology. *v.5 p.80*

The American Dictionary of Criminal Justice: Key Terms and Major Court Cases. *v.4 p.677, v.6 p.246*

An American Dilemma: The Negro Problem and Modern Democracy. *v.4 p.730*

An American Dilemma. *v.4 p.730*

American Diplomacy: A History. *v.3 p.385*

American Diplomacy and the Narcotics Traffic, 1900-1939: A Study in International Humanitarian Reform. . . . *v.3 p.282*

American Diplomacy: The Twentieth Century. . . . *v.3 p.451*

American Diplomacy. *v.3 p.452*

The American Direct Primary: Party Institutionalization and Transformation in the American North. *v.4 p.550*

The American Discovery of Tradition, 1865-1942. . . . . *v.3 p.366, p.367*

The American Disease: Origins of Narcotic Control. . *v.3 p.282*

The American Doctrine of Judicial Supremacy. *v.4 p.454, p.455*

American Drama: From the Colonial to the Contemporary. *v.1 p.119*

American Drama of the Twentieth Century. *v.1 p.112*

American Drawings and Watercolors in the Metropolitan Museum of Art: A Catalogue of Works by Artists Born Before 1835. . . . . *v.1 p.721, p.730*

The American Dream and the Public Schools. *v.4 p.300, p.301*

The American Dream in the Great Depression. *v.3 p.367, p.368*

American Dreams, Rural Realities: Family Farms in Crisis. *v.5 p.29, p.30*

An American Dream. *v.2 p.99*

American Education: A History with the McGraw-Hill Foundations of Education Timeline. *v.4 p.329*

American Education and Vocationalism: A Documentary History, 1870-1970. . . . . *v.4 p.353*

American Educational History Revisited: A Critique of Progress. *v.4 p.326*

🖥 American Educational Research Association. . . . *v.5 p.571*

American Educators' Encyclopedia. *v.4 p.339*

The American Elections of 1984. . . . . *v.3 p.449*

American Elections: The Rules Matter. *v.4 p.548*

American Empire in the Pacific: Fron Trade to Strategic Balance, 1700-1922. . . . . *v.3 p.304*

American Empire: Roosevelt's Geographer and the Prelude to Globalization. *v.4 p.378*

American Empire: The Realities and Consequences of U. S. Diplomacy. *v.3 p.385*

An American Engineer in Stalin's Russia: The Memoirs of Zara Witkin, 1932-1934. . . . . *v.3 p.226*

American English: Dialects and Variation. *v.2 p.553*

American Engravers upon Copper and Steel, Set. . . *v.1 p.754*

The American Environment: Readings in the History of Conservation. *v.5 p.17, p.28*

ⓔ American Environmental Leaders: From Colonial Times to the Present. *v.6 p.285*

American Environmentalism: The U. S. Environmental Movement, 1970-1990. . . . . *v.6 p.295*

The American Essays of Henry James. *v.2 p.7*

The American Establishment and Other Reports, Opinions, and Speculations. *v.3 p.449, p.450*

American Evangelical Christianity: An Introduction. . *v.1 p.648*

The American Evangelical Story: A History of the Movement. *v.1 p.590*

The American Evasion of Philosophy: A Genealogy of Pragmatism. *v.1 p.513*

American Exceptionalism and Human Rights. *v.4 p.512*

The American Experiment: Vineyard of Liberty. . . . *v.3 p.379*

An American Family. *v.6 p.376*

American Federalism and Public Policy: How the System Works. *v.4 p.523*

American Federalism: Competition among Governments. *v.4 p.523*

American Feminist Playwrights. *v.1 p.120*

American Film and Society since 1945. . . . . *v.6 p.340*

American Film Genres: Approaches to a Critical Theory of Popular Film. *v.6 p.311*

American Film Institute Desk Reference: Complete Guide to Everything You Need to Know about the Movies. *v.6 p.305*

American Film Institute's Guide to Writing Great Screenplays for Film and TV, Set. *v.6 p.352*

American Film Music: Major Composers, Techniques, Trends, 1915-1990. . . . . *v.1 p.255*

American Film Musical Themes and Forms. *v.6 p.316*

The American Film Musical. *v.6 p.315*

American Film Studios: An Historical Encyclopedia. *v.6 p.306, p.341*

American Films of the 70s: Conflicting Visions. . . . *v.6 p.342*

American Folk Art Canes: Personal Sculpture. . . . *v.1 p.716*

American Folk Poetry: An Anthology. *v.2 p.22*

🖥 The American Folklife Center - Ethnographic Resources related to Folklore, Anthropology, Ethnomusicology, and the Humanities. *v.4 p.45*

American Folklore: An Encyclopedia. *v.2 p.16*

American Folklore Scholarship: A Dialogue of Dissent. *v.2 p.17*

American Folklore Studies: An Intellectual History. . *v.2 p.16*

American Foreign Policy: A History, Vol. I. *v.3 p.386*

American Foreign Policy and Process. *v.3 p.386*

American Foreign Policy: History, Politics, and Policy. *v.3 p.386*

American Foreign Policy in a New Era. *v.3 p.483*

American Foreign Policy in the Making, 1932-1940: A Study in Responsibilities. *v.3 p.465*

American Foreign Policy since World War II. *v.3 p.452, v.4 p.560*

American Foreign Policy: Theoretical Essays. *v.4 p.560, p.626*

American Forests: A History of Resiliency and Recovery. *v.5 p.38*

American Forests: Nature, Culture and Politics. . . . *v.5 p.39*

American Frontier Life: Early Western Painting and Prints. *v.1 p.733*

American Furniture of the 18th Century: History, Technique, and Structure. *v.1 p.804*

American Furniture: Understanding Styles, Construction and Quality. *v.1 p.804*

The American Game: Baseball and Ethnicity. *v.4 p.823, p.830, p.849*

American Gargoyles: Flannery O'Connor and the Medieval Grotesque. *v.2 p.106*

American Gay. *v.4 p.748, v.6 p.367*

American Generations: Who They Are, How They Live, What They Think. *v.4 p.138*

American Genesis: Captain John Smith and the Founding of Virginia. *v.3 p.500*

American Georgics: Economy and Environment in American Literature, 1580-1864. . . . .*v.6 p.288*

The American GI Forum: In Pursuit of the Dream, 1948-1983. . . . .*v.6 p.541*

American Global Strategy and the 'War on Terrorism'. .*v.4 p.563*

American Goddess at the Rape of Nanking: The Courage of Minnie Vautrin. *v.6 p.193, p.202*

American Governors and Gubernatorial Elections, 1775-1978. . . . .*v.4 p.557*

American Governors and Gubernatorial Elections, 1979-1987. . . . .*v.4 p.557*

American Green: Class, Crisis and the Deployment of Nature in Central Park, Yosemite and Yellowstone. . .*v.6 p.727, p.728*

American Gulag: Inside U. S. Immigration Prisons. *v.4 p.764, v.6 p.275*

American Gypsy: Six Native American Plays. *v.1 p.121, p.124,v.6 p.698*

American Hazardscapes: The Regionalization of Hazards and Disasters. *v.5 p.423*

American Heretic: Theodore Parker and Transcendentalism. *v.1 p.589*

The American Heritage History of the United States. .*v.3 p.365*

The American Heritage Illustrated History of the Presidents: More Than Two Centuries of American Leadership.*v.3 p.377*

The American Heritage Science Dictionary. *v.5 p.386*

The American High School Today: A First Report to Interested Citizens. *v.4 p.367*

American High: The Years of Confidence, 1945-1960. *v.3 p.477*

American Higher Education, a Documentary History. .*v.4 p.331*

American Higher Education: A Guide to Reference Sources, 12. . . . .*v.4 p.290*

American Higher Education: A History. *v.4 p.331*

American Higher Education in the Twenty-First Century: Social, Political, and Economic Challenges. *v.4 p.330*

The American Historian: A Social. *v.3 p.375*

American Historians, 1607-1865. . . . .*v.3 p.375*

American Historians, 1866-1912. . . . .*v.3 p.375*

American History and Contemporary Hollywood Film. *v.6 p.315, p.342*

American History on the Screen: Film and Video Resource. *v.3 p.375*

The American Horror Film: An Introduction. *v.6 p.318*

American Horrors: Essays on the Modern American Horror Film. *v.6 p.320*

American Horticultural Society Encyclopedia of Gardening. *v.5 p.44*

American Horticultural Society Plant Propagation: The Fully Illustrated Plant-by-Plant Manual of Practical Techniques. *v.5 p.45*

American House Designs: An Index to Popular and Trade Periodicals 1850-1915. . . . .*v.1 p.711, p.783*

American Household Botany: A History of Useful Plants, 1620-1900. . . . .*v.5 p.16*

American Humor: A Study of the National Character. .*v.2 p.586*

☐ American Hypertexts. *v.2 p.17*

American Ideals vs. the New Deal. *v.4 p.213*

American Images of China, 1931-1949. . . . .*v.6 p.215*

American Immigration and Ethnicity: A Reader. . . .*v.4 p.764*

American Imperialism: A Speculative Essay. *v.3 p.433*

American Impressionism. *v.1 p.727, p.731*

American Impressions: Prints since Pollock. *v.1 p.752*

American Indian Activism: Alcatraz to the Longest Walk. *v.6 p.694*

☐ American Indian and Alaska Native (AIAN) Data and Links (U.S. Census Bureau). *v.6 p.677*

The American Indian and the Problem of History. . .*v.6 p.682*

American Indian Ballerinas. *v.1 p.10*

American Indian Education: A History. . .*v.4 p.312, v.6 p.680*

American Indian Ethnic Renewal: Red Power and the Resurgence of Identity and Culture. . .*v.4 p.730, v.6 p.694*

☐ American Indian Health : An Informational Portal for and about the Health of Native Peoples of the United States. *v.6 p.702*

American Indian Health: Innovations in Health Care, Promotion, and Policy. *v.6 p.702*

The American Indian Integration of Baseball. *v.4 p.809, p.818, p.841, p.851*

American Indian Lacrosse: Little Brother of War. *v.4 p.810, p.841, p.842, p.863*

American Indian Law in a Nutshell. *v.6 p.691*

American Indian Literature, Environmental Justice, and Ecocriticism: The Middle Place. *v.6 p.287, p.697*

American Indian Medicine. *v.6 p.702*

The American Indian Parfleche: A Tradition of Abstract Painting. *v.6 p.679*

American Indian Policy in Crisis: Christian Reformers and the Indian, 1865-1900. . . . .*v.6 p.688, p.692, p.701*

American Indian Policy in the Jacksonian Era. *v.6 p.686, p.687, p.692*

American Indian Policy in the Twentieth Century. *v.3 p.440, p.446,v.6 p.689, p.691, p.695*

American Indian Politics and the American Political System. *v.6 p.693*

American Indian Sovereignty and the U. S. Supreme Court: The Masking of Justice. *v.4 p.465, v.6 p.697*

American Indian Theater in Performance: A Reader. . .*v.1 p.124*

American Indian Treaties: The History of a Political Anomaly. *v.4 p.465, p.573,v.6 p.683, p.696*

American Indian Women: Telling Their Lives. .*v.6 p.476, p.705*

American Indians, American Justice. *v.6 p.691*

The American Indians and Their Music. *v.1 p.295*

American Indians, Time and the Law: Historical Rights at the Bar of the Supreme Court. *v.4 p.465, p.540*

American Indians, Time, and the Law: Native Societies in a Modern Constitutional Democracy. *v.6 p.693*

American Individualisms: Child Rearing and Social Class in Three Neighborhoods. *v.4 p.733*

American Influence in Greece, 1917-1929. . . . . . .*v.3 p.195*

The American Inquisition: Justice and Injustice in the Cold War. *v.3 p.448*

American Insects: A Handbook of the Insects of America North of Mexico. *v.5 p.27*

The American Intellectual Tradition: 1630-1865. . .*v.3 p.368*

The American Intellectual Tradition: 1865 to the Present. *v.3 p.368*

American Intervention in Greece: 1943-1949. . . . .*v.3 p.196*

The American Irish: A History. *v.3 p.134, p.135*

The American Jew, 1545-1990: A History. *v.1 p.549*

American Jewish Fiction: A Century of Stories. . . .*v.2 p.27*

The American Jewish Woman: 1654-1980. . . .*v.6 p.434, p.435, p.452, p.454, p.459, p.465*

The American Jewish Woman: A Documentary History. *v.6 p.434, p.459, p.465*

American Journal of Sexuality Education. *v.6 p.361*

American Journalism 1690-1940, Set. *v.4 p.405*

American Journalism History: An Annotated Bibliography. *v.4 p.404*

American Journalism: History, Principles, Practices. . *v.4 p.404*

☐ American Journeys: Eyewitness Accounts of Early American Exploration and Settlement: A Digital Library and Learning Center. *v.3 p.404, p.407, p.410, p.414*

American Judaism: A History. *v.1 p.549*

The American Judicial Tradition: Profiles of Leading American Judges. *v.4 p.469*

The American Jury System. *v.6 p.270*

The American Jury. *v.4 p.473*

American Juvenile Justice. *v.6 p.249*

American Kinship: A Cultural Account. *v.4 p.32, p.734*

American Klezmer : Its Roots and Offshoots. *v.1 p.300*

American Knees. *v.6 p.102*

American Labor and the Cold War: Grassroots Politics and Postwar Political Culture. *v.4 p.120, p.121*

The American Language. *v.2 p.552*

The American Law Dictionary. *v.4 p.437*

American Law in the 20th Century. *v.4 p.109, p.441*

American Lawyers in a Changing Society, 1776-1876. .*v.4 p.440*

American Lawyers. *v.4 p.440*

American Lazarus: Religion and the Rise of African-American and Native American Literatures. *v.6 p.23, p.35*

American Left: Radical Political Thought in the Twentieth Century. *v.4 p.709*

American Legacy: Our National Forests. *v.5 p.18, p.41*

An American Life: The Autobiography. *v.3 p.478*

☐ American Literary Classics. *v.2 p.17*

ⓔ American Literary Realism and the Failed Promise of Contract. *v.2 p.5*

American Literary Realism and the Failed Promise of Contract. *v.2 p.5*

American Literary Scholarship: An Annual, 1995. . . .*v.2 p.5*

American Mafia: A History of Its Rise to Power. . . .*v.6 p.251*

American Magazine Journalists, 1741-1850. . . . . .*v.4 p.410*

American Magazine Journalists, 1850-1900. . . . . .*v.4 p.410*

American Manhood: Transformations in Masculinity from the Revolution to the Modern Era. *v.4 p.745, v.6 p.430, p.452, p.455*

The American Marketplace: Demographics and Spending Patterns. *v.4 p.138*

American Massacre: The Tragedy at Mountain Meadows, September 1857. . . . .*v.3 p.529*

☐ American Memory: A Century of Lawmaking for a New Nation. *v.4 p.481, p.517*

☐ American Memory. *v.1 p.661, p.710*

American Men and Women of Science, Set. *v.5 p.395*

American Men and Women of Science. *v.5 p.396*

The American Mercury Reader: A Selection of Distinguished Articles. *v.2 p.27*

American Military History, 1775-1902, Vol. 1. . . . .*v.3 p.383*

American Military History: 1902-1985. . . . .*v.3 p.383*

American Military History and the Evolution of Warfare in the Western World. *v.3 p.382*

☐ American Mineralogist Crystal Structure Database. .*v.5 p.283*

☐ American Model United Nations International (collegiate). *v.4 p.632*

The American Mosaic: An In-Depth Report on the Future of Diversity at Work. *v.4 p.131, p.132*

American Music: A Panorama. *v.1 p.278*

American Music in the Twentieth Century. *v.1 p.214*

The American Musical and the Formation of National Identity. *v.1 p.251*

The American Musical Film Song Encyclopedia. . .*v.6 p.316*

American Musical Theater: A Chronicle. *v.1 p.31, p.248*

The American Musical Theatre: A Complete Musical Theatre Course. *v.1 p.93, p.117*

American Musical Traditions. *v.1 p.297*

American Naive Paintings. *v.1 p.731*

American National Biography, Set. *v.3 p.376*

☐ American National Elections Studies (ANES). . .*v.4 p.547*

American National Security and Civil Liberties in an Era of Terrorism. *v.4 p.563, p.572*

American Naturalistic and Realistic Novelists: A Biographical Dictionary. *v.2 p.7*

American Naval History: An Illustrated Chronology of the U. S. Navy and Marine Corps, 1775-Present. *v.3 p.384*

American Negro Poetry. *v.2 p.22, v.6 p.23*

American Neo-Colonialism: Its Emergence in the Philippines and Asia. *v.6 p.180*

American Newspaper Journalists, 1926-1950. . . . .*v.4 p.410*

The American Northwest: A History of Washington and Oregon. *v.3 p.532*

American Notes; and The Uncommercial Traveler. by Charles Dickens. *v.2 p.282*

American Notes. *v.2 p.282, p.296, p.297*

☐ American Nuclear Society. *v.5 p.739*

American Nursing: A Biographical Dictionary. . . .*v.5 p.528*

American Nursing: A History. *v.5 p.527, p.529*

The American Occupation of Austria: Planning and Early Years. *v.3 p.185*

The American Occupation of Japan and Okinawa: Literature and Memory. *v.6 p.231, p.235*

The American Occupational Structure. *v.4 p.726*

American Opinion on World Affairs in the Atomic Age. .*v.3 p.451*

American Outpost: A Book of Reminiscences. *v.2 p.119*

The American Pageant: A Complete History of the Republic. *v.3 p.379*

American Paintings of the Eighteenth Century. . . . *v.1 p.732*

American Paintings of the Nineteenth Century, Pt. II. .*v.1 p.733*

American Paradise: The World of the Hudson River School. *v.1 p.730*

American Paradox: The Conflict of Thought and Action. .*v.3 p.367*

American Pastoral: A Novel. *v.2 p.154*

American Patriots: The Story of Blacks in the Military from the Revolution to Desert Storm. *v.4 p.717*

American Penology: A History of Control. *v.6 p.273*

The American People and Foreign Policy. *v.3 p.451*

The American People: Census 2000. . . . . *v.4 p.138*

The American People in the Twentieth Century. . . . *v.3 p.367*

American Pharaoh: Mayor Richard J. Daley: His Battle for Chicago and the Nation. *v.3 p.516*

American Philosophic Naturalism in the Twentieth Century. *v.1 p.516*

American Photographs: The First Century. . . *v.1 p.763, p.766*

American Photography. *v.1 p.764*

American Plastic: A Cultural History. *v.5 p.319*

American Plays and Musicals on Screen: 650 Stage Productions and Their Film and Televison Adaptations. *v.6 p.326*

American Playwrights, 1880-1945: A Research and Production Sourcebook. *v.1 p.58, p.113*

American Poetry - The Nineteenth Century: Freneau to Whitman. *v.2 p.23*

American Poetry: Melville to Stickney, American Indian Poetry, Folk Songs and Spirituals. *v.2 p.23, v.6 p.698*

American Poetry of the Seventeenth Century. *v.2 p.24*

American Poetry: The Modernist Ideal. *v.2 p.15*

American Poetry: The Nineteenth Century. *v.2 p.23*

American Poetry: The Twentieth Century: E. E. Cummings to May Swenson. *v.2 p.23, p.24*

American Poetry: The Twentieth Century: Henry Adams to Dorothy Parker. *v.2 p.23*

American Policy Toward Communist China, 1949-1969. . . . . *v.3 p.388*

American Political Writing During the Founding Era - 1780-1805, Vol. 1 and 2. . . . .*v.4 p.517*

American Politics and the African American Quest for Universal Freedom. *v.6 p.32*

American Popular Music and Its Business: The First Four Hundred Years, 1790-1909. . . . .*v.1 p.279, p.385*

American Popular Music and Its Business: The First Four Hundred Years, 1900-1984, Vol. 3. . . . .*v.1 p.279, p.385*

American Popular Music and Its Business: The First Four Hundred Years: From 1790 to 1909, Vol. II. .*v.1 p.279, p.385*

American Popular Music: From Minstrelsy to MTV. *v.1 p.274, p.275*

American Popular Song: The Great Innovators, 1900-1950. . . . . *v.1 p.276*

American Power and the New Mandarins. *v.3 p.451*

American Pragmatism and Education, an Interpretation and Criticism. *v.4 p.341*

American Pragmatism: Peirce, James and Dewey. . . *v.1 p.513*

The American Predicament: Apartheid and United States Foreign Policy. *v.3 p.393*

The American Presidency: A Glorious Burden. . . . *v.3 p.377*

The American Presidency: An Intellectual History. . . *v.3 p.378*

The American Presidency and Women: Promise, Performance, and Illusion. *v.4 p.527*

The American Presidency: Origins and Development, 1776-1993. . . . . *v.4 p.527*

The American Presidency: Principles and Problems. . *v.4 p.528*

The American Presidency. *v.3 p.377*

American Presidential Campaigns and Elections: A Reference Guide, Set. *v.4 p.550, p.556*

The American Presidents: Critical Essays. *v.3 p.379*

American Presidents: Year by Year. *v.4 p.528*

American Printer: The Graphic Arts Managers Magazine. *v.4 p.140*

American Printmakers, 1880-1945: An Index to Reproductions and Biocritical Information. *v.1 p.711, p.712, p.751*

American Printmakers, 1946-1996: An Index to Reproductions and Biocritical Information. *v.1 p.711, p.751*

American Printmakers of the Twentieth Century: A Bibliography. *v.1 p.751*

American Prisons: A History of Good Intentions. . . *v.6 p.273*

☐ American Probation and Parole Association. . . . *v.6 p.278*

American Professors: A National Resource Imperiled. *v.4 p.292*

An American Profile: Attitude and Behaviors of the American People, 1972-1989. . . . .*v.5 p.586, p.587*

American Progressive History: An Experiment in Modernization. *v.3 p.373*

American Pronunciation. *v.2 p.557*

☐ American Psychiatric Association. *v.5 p.662*

The American Psychiatric Press Textbook of Psychiatry. *v.5 p.517*

The American Psychiatric Publishing Textbook of Forensic Psychiatry. *v.5 p.593*

The American Psychiatric Publishing Textbook of Substance Abuse Treatment. *v.5 p.512, p.521*

☐ American Psychological Association (APA). . . . *v.5 p.593*

☐ American Psychological Association Education Directorate. *v.5 p.675*

☐ American Psychological Association of Graduate Students. *v.5 p.675*

American Psychology and Schools: A Critique. . . . *v.5 p.572*

American Public Life and the Historical Imagination. *v.3 p.384*

American Public School Law. *v.4 p.449*

The American Puritans: Their Prose and Poetry. . . . *v.2 p.29*

The American Quilt: A History of Cloth and Comfort 1750-1950. . . . . *v.1 p.809*

American Realism and American Drama, 1880-1940. . . . .*v.1 p.80, p.117*

American Realism. *v.1 p.682*

American Reformers, 1815-1860. . . . .*v.3 p.402*

American Regional Dialects: A Word Geography. . . .*v.2 p.551*

The American Response to Canada since 1776. . . . .*v.3 p.392*

The American Revisionists: The Lessons of Intervention in
World War I. *v.3 p.468*

The American Revolution 1775-1783: An
Encyclopedia. *v.3 p.407, p.413*

The American Revolution Considered As a Social
Movement. *v.3 p.409*

The American Revolution: Explorations in the History of
American Radicalism. *v.3 p.410, p.411*

The American Revolution in Georgia, 1763-1789. . . .*v.3 p.503*

The American Revolution, Set. *v.3 p.410*

American Revolution. *v.3 p.413*

American Rhetorical Discourse. *v.2 p.28*

☐ American Rhetoric. *v.4 p.422*

The American Roman Noir: Hammett, Cain and
Chandler. *v.2 p.65, p.82*

American: Russian Relations 1781. . . . . . .*v.3 p.393, p.454*

The American School, 1642-2004. . . . .*v.4 p.329*

☐ American School Counselor Association. *v.5 p.576*

☐ American School Health Association. *v.5 p.571*

American Science Fiction and the Cold War: Literature and
Film. *v.6 p.319, p.320*

American Science in the Age of Jefferson. . . .*v.5 p.388, p.393*

American Scream: Allen Ginsberg's Howl and the Making of
the Beat Generation. *v.2 p.79*

American Sculpture in the Metropolitan Museum of Art. *v.1 p.778*

The American Senator. *v.2 p.317, p.318*

American Sermons: The Pilgrims to Martin Luther King
Jr. *v.1 p.650, v.2 p.28*

American Shelf and Wall Clocks: A Pictorial History for
Collectors. *v.1 p.806*

American Short Stories since 1945. . . . .*v.2 p.26*

American Silent Film Comedies: An Illustrated Encyclopedia of
Persons, Studios and Terminology. . .*v.6 p.307, p.313, p.332*

American Silent Film: Discovering Marginalized
Voices. *v.6 p.332*

☐ American Slavery: A Composite Autobiography. .*v.6 p.33, p.37*

☐ American Soccer History Archives. *v.4 p.803, p.867*

☐ American Society of Agronomy. *v.5 p.15, p.19, p.48*

☐ American Society of Landscape Architects. . . .*v.1 p.811*

American Society: Problems of Structure. *v.4 p.707*

The American Soldier: Adjustment During Army Life, Vol.
1. . . . .*v.5 p.585*

The American Soldier: Combat and Its Aftermath, Vol.
2. . . . .*v.5 p.585*

American Soldiers: Ground Combat in the World Wars, Korea
and Vietnam. *v.3 p.383*

The American Son: A Novel. *v.6 p.102, p.130*

American Song, a Book of Poems. *v.2 p.71*

American Song: The Complete Musical Theatre Companion,
1877-1995, Vol. 1 & 2. . . . .*v.1 p.165, p.248*

The American South: A History. *v.3 p.493, p.494*

The American South: Portrait of a Culture. *v.3 p.494*

American Spirit in Literature: Chronicle. *v.2 p.6*

American Sports Empire: How the Leagues Breed
Success. *v.4 p.884, p.888, p.896*

American Sports: From the Age of Folk Games to the Age of
Televised Sports. *v.4 p.809, p.818*

The American Stage: Social and Economic Issues from the
Colonial Period to the Present. *v.1 p.113*

American Stage. *v.1 p.112, p.143*

American Stepfamilies. *v.5 p.639*

American Streamlined Design: The World of
Tomorrow. *v.1 p.713, p.714*

The American Street Gang: Its Nature, Prevalence, and
Control. *v.6 p.256*

American Studio Glass: 1960-1990. . . . .*v.1 p.810*

American Sugar Kingdom: The Plantation Economy of the
Spanish Caribbean, 1898-1934. . . . . . .*v.3 p.316, p.318*

American Superrealism: Nathanael West and the Politics of
Representation in the 1930's. *v.2 p.131*

The American Supreme Court. *v.4 p.466*

American Theaters: Performance Halls of the Nineteenth
Century. *v.1 p.113, p.154*

American Theatre: A Chronicle of Comedy and Drama,
1914-1930. . . . .*v.1 p.112*

American Theatre: A Chronicle of Comedy and Drama,
1969-2000. . . . .*v.1 p.115*

American Thought and Writing: The 1890's. *v.2 p.21*

The American Tintype. *v.1 p.764*

American Trade Politics. *v.4 p.57, p.567*

The American Tradition in Literature, Vol. 2. . . . . .*v.2 p.18*

American Tragedy: Kennedy, Johnson, and the Origins of the
Vietnam War. *v.3 p.442, v.4 p.486*

An American Tragedy. *v.2 p.70*

The American Transcendentalists: Their Prose and
Poetry. *v.2 p.20, p.21*

An American Travesty: Legal Responses to Adolescent Sexual
Offending. *v.6 p.255*

American Universities and Colleges. *v.4 p.330*

The American University: How It Runs, Where It Is
Going. *v.4 p.289, p.330*

American Urban Politics: The Reader. *v.6 p.728*

American Vanguard: The United Auto Workers During the
Reuther Years, 1935-1970. . . . .*v.4 p.124*

American Vaudeville As Seen by Its Contemporaries. . .*v.1 p.35*

American Vaudeville, Its Life and Times. *v.1 p.35*

An American Vein: Critical Readings in Appalachian
Literature. *v.2 p.12*

☐ American Verse Project. *v.2 p.22*

American Vineyards. *v.5 p.52*

American Violence and Public Policy: An Update of the
National Commission on the Causes and Prevention of
Violence. *v.6 p.254*

An American Vision: Henry Francis du Pont's Winterthur
Museum. *v.1 p.800*

American Visions: The Epic History of Art in America. *v.1 p.682*

An American Visitor. *v.2 p.337*

American Voices: How Dialects Differ from Coast to
Coast. *v.2 p.553*

The American Voter. *v.4 p.548*

The American War Film: History and Hollywood. . . .*v.6 p.323*

The American Way: A Geographical History of Crisis and
    Recovery. *v.3 p.380, p.381,v.4 p.381, p.382*

The American Way: Family and Community in the Shaping of
    the American Identity. *v.3 p.366*

The American Way of Death Revisited. *v.2 p.371*

The American Way of Spelling: The Structure and Origins of
    American English Orthography. *v.2 p.558*

The American Way of War: A History of United States Military
    Strategy and Policy. *v.3 p.384*

American West: A New Interpretive History. *v.3 p.518*

The American West: The Reader. *v.3 p.518, p.519*

The American West. *v.3 p.518*

The American West.Visions and Revisions. *v.3 p.519*

American Wits: An Anthology of Light Verse. *v.2 p.23*

American Woman: A Novel. *v.2 p.143*

The American Woman in Sport. *v.4 p.805, p.836*

American Women Civil Rights Activists: Biobibliographies of
    68 Leaders, 1825-1992. . . . .*v.6 p.431*

American Women in Mission: A Social History of Their
    Thought and Practice. *v.1 p.647*

📧 American Women in Science: 1950 to the Present - A
    Biographical Dictionary. *v.5 p.394*

American Women in Technology: An
    Encyclopedia. *v.5 p.679, p.680*

📖 American Women: Library of Congress Guide for the Study
    of Women's History and Culture in the United
    States. *v.6 p.432*

American Women Photographers: A Selected and Annotated
    Bibliography. *v.1 p.761*

American Women Playwrights from 1900 to 1950. . .*v.1 p.122*

American Women Regionalists: A Norton Anthology. . .*v.2 p.21*

American Women Sculptors: A History of Women Working in
    Three Dimensions. *v.1 p.777*

American Women Writers: A Biographical Dictionary. . .*v.2 p.7*

American Women Writers and the Nazis: Ethics and Politics in
    Boyle, Porter, Stafford and Hellman. . .*v.2 p.62, p.83, p.120*

American Women Writers and the Work of History,
    1790-1860. . . . .*v.6 p.477*

American Women Writers: From Colonial Times to the Present:
    A Critical Reference Guide. *v.2 p.8*

American Women's Autobiography: Fea(s)ts of
    Memory. *v.6 p.476*

📖 American Women's History: A Research Guide. . .*v.6 p.450*

American Women's Track and Field: A History, 1895 Through
    1980. . . . .*v.6 p.438*

American women's track and field:a history, 1895 through
    1980. . . . .*v.4 p.810, p.838, p.869*

American Workers, Colonial Power: Philippine Seattle and the
    Transpacific West, 1919-1941. . . . . . .*v.6 p.116, p.129*

American Writers, Set. *v.2 p.6, p.7*

The American Years: Chronologies of American History and
    Experience. *v.3 p.372*

American Youth Gangs at the Millennium. *v.4 p.714*

Americanization, Acculturation, and Ethnic Identity: The Nisei
    Generation in Hawaii. *v.6 p.132*

Americanization of the Common Law: The Impact of Legal
    Change on Massachusetts Society, 1760-1830. . . .*v.4 p.474*

The Americanization of West Virginia: Creating a Modern
    Industrial State, 1916-1925. . . . .*v.3 p.501*

Americans and Chinese: Passage to Differences. *v.6 p.182*

Americans and the California Dream, 1850-1915. . . .*v.3 p.531*

Americans and Their Forests: A Historical Geography. .*v.5 p.40*

Americans at Play: Demographics of Outdoor Recreation and
    Travel. *v.4 p.788, p.824*

Americans at War. *v.3 p.382*

Americans First: Chinese Americans and the Second World
    War. *v.6 p.116, p.128*

🖥 Americans for the Arts. *v.1 p.825*

Americans in Paris: A Literary Anthology. *v.2 p.19*

The Americans: The Colonial Experience. . . .*v.3 p.366, p.405*

The Americans: The Democratic Experience. *v.3 p.366*

The Americans: The National Experience. *v.3 p.366*

Americans with Disabilities Act Handbook. *v.4 p.447*

American-Soviet Relations: From Nineteen Forty-Seven to the
    Nixon-Kissinger Grand Design, 61. . . . .*v.3 p.387*

The American. *v.2 p.45*

America's 100th Meridian: A Plains Journey. *v.4 p.382*

America's Ailing Cities: Fiscal Health and the Design of Urban
    Policy. *v.4 p.544, v.6 p.724*

America's Alternative Religions. *v.1 p.544*

America's Ancient Forests: From the Ice Age to the Age of
    Discovery. *v.5 p.175, p.239*

America's Art: Masterpieces from the Smithsonian American Art
    Museum. *v.1 p.683*

America's Ascent: The United States Becomes a Great Power,
    1880-1914. . . . .*v.3 p.433*

America's Asia: Racial Form and American Literature,
    1893-1945. . . . .*v.4 p.485*

🖥 America's Best Graduate Schools. *v.4 p.295*

America's Best Newspaper Writing: A Collection of ASNE
    Prizewinners. *v.4 p.410*

🖥 America's Career InfoNet. *v.4 p.304*

America's Colony: The Political and Cultural Conflict Between
    the United States and Puerto Rico. *v.6 p.538*

America's Coming-of-Age. *v.2 p.7*

America's Communal Utopias. *v.4 p.499, p.500*

America's Constitution: A Biography. *v.4 p.452*

America's Corporate Families: The Billion Dollar
    Directory. *v.5 p.397*

America's Entry into World War I. *v.3 p.476*

America's Experiment with Capital Punishment: Reflections on
    the Past, Present, and Future of the Ultimate Penal
    Sanction. *v.4 p.567, v.6 p.247*

America's Failing Schools: How Parents and Teachers Can
    Cope with No Child Left Behind. *v.4 p.328*

America's Failure in China, Nineteen Forty-One to Nineteen
    Fifty, Vol. II. *v.6 p.204*

America's First Battles, 1776-1965. . . . .*v.3 p.383*

America's First Cuisines. *v.3 p.261, p.271*

America's First Families: An Inside View of 200 Years of
    Private Life in the White House. *v.3 p.377*

America's Forgotten Pandemic: The Influenza of 1918. .*v.6 p.291*

America's Frontier Heritage. *v.3 p.380*

America's Game: The Epic Story of How Pro Football Captured a Nation. *v.4 p.859, p.897*

America's Garden Book. *v.5 p.43*

America's Germany: John J. McCloy and the Federal Republic of Germany. *v.3 p.176*

America's God: From Jonathan Edwards to Abraham Lincoln. *v.1 p.605, p.606*

America's Golden Bough: The Science Advisory Intertwist. *v.5 p.394, p.412*

America's Hidden Wilderness: Lands of Seclusion. *v.5 p.179, p.233*

The Americas in the Age of Revolution, 1750-1850. . .*v.3 p.315*

The Americas in the Spanish World Order: The Justification for Conquest in the Seventeenth Century. *v.4 p.583*

America's Instrument: The Banjo in the Nineteenth Century. *v.1 p.277, p.389*

America's Longest War: The United States and Vietnam, 1950-1975. . . . .*v.6 p.168*

America's Miracle Man in Vietnam: Ngo Dinh Diem, Religion, Race, and U. S. Intervention in Southeast Asia. . .*v.3 p.389*

America's Music: From the Pilgrims to the Present. . .*v.1 p.277*

America's Musical Stage: Two Hundred Years of Musical Theatre. *v.1 p.32, p.252*

America's National Parks and Their Keepers. *v.5 p.18*

America's National Pastime: A Study of Race and Merit in Professional Baseball. *v.4 p.804, p.830, p.849, p.890*

America's National Wildlife Refuges: A Complete Guide. .*v.5 p.83*

America's New Allies: Poland, Hungary, and the Czech Republic in NATO. *v.4 p.639*

America's New Downtowns: Revitalization or Reinvention? *v.6 p.727*

America's Obsession: Sports and Society since 1945. .*v.4 p.805*

The Americas of Asian American Literature: Gendered Fictions of Nation and Transnation. *v.6 p.96, p.112*

America's Outward Thrust: Approaches to Foreign Affairs, 1865-1890. . . . .*v.3 p.433*

America's Prisoner: The Memoirs of Manuel Noriega. .*v.3 p.305*

America's Public Schools: From the Common School to "No Child Left Behind". *v.4 p.328*

America's Real Estate: Natural Resource, National Legacy. *v.4 p.159, p.166*

America's Response to China: A History of Sino-American Relations. *v.3 p.387, v.6 p.203, p.204, p.218*

America's Rise to World Power: 1898-1954. . . . .*v.3 p.451*

America's Road to Empire: The War with Spain and Overseas Expansion. *v.3 p.437*

America's Secret War: Inside the Hidden Worldwide Struggle Between the United States and Its Enemies. . . .*v.3 p.483*

America's Splendid Little Wars: A Short History of U. S. Engagements from the Fall of Saigon to Baghdad. .*v.3 p.304*

America's Sporting Heritage: 1850-1950. . . . . . .*v.4 p.803*

America's Struggle Against Poverty in the Twentieth Century. *v.4 p.758*

America's Unpatriot Acts: The Federal Government's Violation of Constitutional and Civil Rights. *v.4 p.561, p.562, p.563, p.572*

America's Untapped Resource: Low-Income Students in Higher Education. *v.4 p.294*

America's Vietnam War: A Narrative History. *v.6 p.168*

America's Welfare State: From Roosevelt to Reagan. .*v.4 p.754*

The Americas. *v.1 p.61, p.118, p.127*

Amerigo and the New World: The Life and Times of Amerigo Vespucci. *v.3 p.403*

L' Ameto. *v.2 p.701*

El Amigo Manso. *v.2 p.655*

Aminadab. *v.2 p.510*

Amino Acid and Peptide Synthesis. *v.5 p.328*

Amino Acids and Amines, v. 2. . . . .*v.5 p.300*

Amino Acids and Peptides. *v.5 p.328*

Aminta: A Pastoral Play. *v.2 p.710*

Aminta. *v.2 p.710*

Amir Khusraw: The Poets of Sultans and Sufis. . . .*v.6 p.673*

Amiri Baraka: The Politics and Art of a Black Intellectual. *v.2 p.142*

Amish Enterprise: From Plows to Profits. *v.1 p.586*

The Amish in the American Imagination. *v.1 p.586*

Ammianus Marcellinus: A Selection. *v.2 p.428*

Ammianus Marcellinus and the Representation of Historical Reality. *v.2 p.428, v.3 p.29*

▢ Amnesty International Library. *v.4 p.669*

Among the Jasmine Trees: Music and Modernity in Contemporary Syria. *v.1 p.287*

Among Women Only. *v.2 p.720*

Amor en los Tiempos del Colera. *v.2 p.682*

Amos: A New Translation. *v.1 p.622*

Amos Tutuola Revisited. *v.2 p.757*

Amour-- amours-- : roman. *v.2 p.528*

Amped: How Big Air, Big Dollars, and a New Generation Took Sports to the Extreme. *v.4 p.857, p.899*

Amphibian Declines: The Conservation Status of United States Species. *v.5 p.215*

Amphibians and Reptiles of the Great Lakes Region. *v.5 p.174, p.215, p.234*

Amphibians: The World of Frogs, Toads, Salamanders and Newts. *v.5 p.215*

Amphitryon. *v.2 p.475*

▢ Amputee Sport Resouces on the Net. *v.4 p.842*

The Amusements of the People and Other Papers: Reports, Essays and Reviews, 1834-1851. . . . . . .*v.6 p.754, p.756*

Amusing Ourselves to Death: Public Discourse in the Age of Show Business. *v.4 p.417*

Amy Beach, Passionate Victorian: The Life and Works of an American Composer, 1867-1944. . .*v.1 p.194, p.305, p.378*

Amy Lowell, American Modern. *v.2 p.95*

Amy Lowell: Selected Poems. *v.2 p.95*

The Amy Vanderbilt Complete Book of Etiquette. . . .*v.1 p.486*

The Anabaptists. *v.1 p.586*

Anabasis. *v.2 p.422*

Anabolic Steroids and the Athlete. *v.4 p.826*

Anabolic Steroids in Sport and Exercise. *v.4 p.826*

Anabolic Steroids. *v.4 p.826*

Anais Nin: A Biography. *v.2 p.105*

Anais Nin and the Remaking of Self: Gender, Modernism, and Narrative Identity. *v.2 p.105*

Anais Nin: Literary Perspectives. *v.2 p.105*

Anais Nin. *v.2 p.105*

Analects. *v.1 p.418*

The Analects. *v.6 p.184, p.207, p.208*

Analog and Digital Communication Systems. *v.5 p.726*

Analog and Digital Electronics: A First Course. . . .*v.5 p.722*

Analog Circuit Design. *v.5 p.721*

The Analogical Imagination. *v.1 p.637*

Analogy of Religion, Natural and Reveale. *v.1 p.645*

Analyses of Nineteenth- and Twentieth-Century Music, 1940-1985. . . . .*v.1 p.169, p.207, p.227*

Analysis and Behavior of Structures. *v.5 p.696*

Analysis and Control of Age-Dependent Population Dynamics. *v.5 p.167*

Analysis and Design of Analog Integrated Circuits. . *v.5 p.722*

The Analysis and Design of Linear Circuits: Laplace Early. *v.5 p.721*

Analysis and Design of Plated Structures Volume 1 Stability. *v.5 p.696*

Analysis and Metaphysics: An Introduction to Philosophy. *v.1 p.502*

Analysis of Biogeochemical Cycling Process in Walker Branch Watershed. *v.5 p.176*

Analysis of Faulted Power Systems. *v.5 p.723*

Analysis of Financial Time Series. . . *v.4 p.205, p.206, p.264*

The Analysis of Gene Expression Data: Methods and Software. *v.5 p.102*

Analysis of Genes and Genomes. *v.5 p.136*

Analysis of Geological Structures. *v.5 p.441*

Analysis of Microarray Gene Expression Data. . . .*v.5 p.102*

Analysis of Panel Data. *v.4 p.202, p.206*

Analysis of Tonal Music: A Schenkerian Approach. . *v.1 p.369*

Analysis of Vertebrate Structure. *v.5 p.157*

Analysis. *v.5 p.489*

Analytic Philosophy: An Anthology. *v.1 p.502*

Analytical Approaches to 20th Century Music. *v.1 p.371*

Analytical Atomic Absorption Spectroscopy: Selected Methods. *v.5 p.273*

Analytical Biogeography: An Integrated Approach to the Study of Animal and Plant Distributions. *v.5 p.169*

Analytical Chemistry for Technicians. *v.5 p.274*

Analytical Chemistry Handbook. *v.5 p.267*

☐ Analytical Chemistry Network. *v.5 p.274*

☐ Analytical Chemistry Springboard. *v.5 p.274*

Analytical Chemistry: The Approved Text to the FECS Curriculum Analytical Chemistry. *v.5 p.273*

☐ Analytical Chemistry--Subject Guide (Stanford University). *v.5 p.274*

☐ Analytical Chemistry--Web Links (Stanford University). *v.5 p.274*

Analytical Didactic: Translated from the Latin with Introd. and Notes. *v.4 p.341*

Analytical Electrochemistry. *v.5 p.273*

Analytical Gas Chromatography. *v.5 p.269*

ⓔ Analytical Instrumentation Handbook. *v.5 p.267*

Analytical Marxism: A Critique. *v.1 p.508*

Analytical Mechanics. *v.5 p.546*

Analytical Methods of Electroacoustic Music. *v.1 p.224, p.245, p.373*

Analytical Modelling of Structural Systems: An Entirely New Approach with Emphasis on Behaviour of Building Structures. *v.5 p.698*

Analytical Molecular Biology. *v.5 p.129, p.130*

Analytical Philosophy of History. *v.1 p.441*

☐ Analytical Sciences Digital Library. *v.5 p.274*

Analytical Solid-Phase Extraction. *v.5 p.268*

An Analytical Survey of the 15 Sinfonias: Three-Part Inventions by J. S. Bach. *v.1 p.184, p.240, p.303*

Analytical Techniques in DNA Sequencing. *v.5 p.136*

Analytical Tools for DNA, Genes and Genomes: Nuts and Bolts. *v.5 p.120, p.122, p.135*

Analyzing and Reporting Focus Group Results. . . .*v.4 p.136*

Analyzing Bach Cantatas. *v.1 p.183, p.235, p.303*

Analyzing Chromosomes. *v.5 p.132*

Analyzing Crime Patterns: Frontiers of Practice. . . .*v.6 p.251*

Analyzing English Grammar. *v.2 p.557*

Analyzing Freud: Letters of H. D., Bryher and Their Circle. *v.5 p.595*

Analyzing Microarray Gene Expression Data. . *v.5 p.102, p.141*

Analyzing Opera: Verdi and Wagner. *v.1 p.193, p.227, p.364, p.365*

Analyzing Performance: Theater, Dance, and Film. *v.1 p.43, p.46*

Analyzing Sentences: An Introduction to English Syntax. *v.2 p.556*

Analyzing Teaching Behavior. *v.4 p.347*

Analyzing Visual Data. *v.4 p.690*

Anandamath, or the Sacred Brotherhood. *v.6 p.151*

The Anarchical Society: A Study of Order in World Politics. *v.4 p.625, p.628*

Anarchism: A Collection of Revolutionary Writings. . *v.4 p.493*

Anarchism and Countercultural Politics in Early Twentieth-Century Cuba. *v.3 p.313*

Anarchism and the Mexican Revolution: The Political Trials of Ricardo Flores Magón in the United States. *v.6 p.536*

Anarchism in the Chinese Revolution. *v.6 p.190*

The Anarchist in the Library: How the Clash Between Freedom and Control Is Hacking the Real World and Crashing the System. *v.4 p.761*

The Anarchists of Casas Viejas. *v.4 p.42*

Anarchy, State, and Utopia. *v.1 p.501, v.4 p.511*

Anasazi and Pueblo Painting. *v.1 p.730, v.6 p.678*

Anatolian Tales. *v.6 p.667*

Anatomy: A Regional Atlas of the Human Body. *v.5 p.95, p.158*

Anatomy and Dissection of the Fetal Pig. *v.5 p.89, p.90*

Anatomy and Physiology. *v.5 p.164*

Anatomy of a Business Plan: A Step-by-Step Guide to Building a Business and Securing Your Company's Future. *v.4 p.174*

Anatomy of a Conflict: Identity, Knowledge, and Emotion in Old-Growth Forests. . . . . *.v.5 p.39, p.41,v.6 p.292*

Anatomy of a Controversy: The Debate over Essays and Reviews. . . . . *.v.6 p.758, p.763*

The Anatomy of a Game: Football, the Rules, and the Men Who Made the Game. . . . . *.v.4 p.808, p.859*

Anatomy of a Miracle: The End of Apartheid and the Birth of the New South Africa. . . . . *.v.6 p.79, p.80*

Anatomy of a Park: The Essentials of Recreation Area Planning and Design. . . . . *.v.5 p.17, p.18*

The Anatomy of a Party: The National CCF, 1932-1961. *.v.4 p.589*

Anatomy of a Power Elite: The Provincial Governors of Early Modern France. . . . . *.v.3 p.145*

Anatomy of a Rose: Exploring the Secret Life of Flowers. . . . . *.v.5 p.156*

The Anatomy of a Scientific Institution: The Paris Academy of Sciences, 1666-1803. . . . . *.v.5 p.385*

The Anatomy of American Popular Culture, 1840-1861. *.v.3 p.366*

Anatomy of Criticism: Four Essays. . . . . *.v.2 p.568*

The Anatomy of Dependence. . . . . *.v.6 p.221*

The Anatomy of Fascism. . . . . *.v.4 p.510*

Anatomy of Flowering Plants: An Introduction to Structure and Development. . . . . *.v.5 p.156*

Anatomy of Hatha Yoga: A Manual for Students, Teachers and Practitioners. . . . . *.v.4 p.793*

The Anatomy of Impact: What Makes the Great Works of Psychology Great. . . . . *.v.5 p.598*

The Anatomy of Inquiry: Philosophical Studies in the Theory of Science. . . . . *.v.5 p.404*

Anatomy of Love: The Tristan of Gottfried Von Strassburg. . . . . *.v.2 p.595*

The Anatomy of Melancholy: Text. . . . . *.v.2 p.213*

Anatomy of Movement. . . . . *.v.1 p.51*

The Anatomy of Power. . . . . *.v.4 p.773*

Anatomy of Reality: Merging of Intuition and Reason. *.v.5 p.404*

The Anatomy of Satire. . . . . *.v.2 p.427*

The Anatomy of Sports Forecasting: Modeling Parallels Between Sports Gambling and Financial Markets. . . . . *.v.4 p.203, p.207*

Anatomy of the Law. . . . . *.v.4 p.433*

Anatomy of Wonder: A Critical Guide to Science Fiction. *.v.2 p.580*

Ancestor Masks and Aristocratic Power in Roman Culture. *.v.3 p.23*

Ancestor of the West: Writing, Reasoning, and Religion in Mesopotamia, Elam, and Greece. . . . . *.v.3 p.5*

The Ancestor's Tale: A Pilgrimage to the Dawn of Evolution. . . . . *.v.5 p.191*

Ancestors. *.v.2 p.767*

The Anchor Anthology of French Poetry: From Nerval to Valery in English Translation. . . . . *.v.2 p.464*

The Anchor Bible Dictionary, Vol. 1. . . . . . . *.v.1 p.614*

The Anchor Bible Dictionary, Vol. 2. . . . . . . *.v.1 p.614*

The Anchor Bible Dictionary, Vol. 3. . . . . . . *.v.1 p.614*

The Anchor Bible Dictionary, Vol. 4. . . . . . . *.v.1 p.614*

The Anchor Bible Dictionary, Vol. 5. . . . . . . *.v.1 p.614*

The Anchor Bible Dictionary, Vol. 6. . . . . . . *.v.1 p.614*

The Anchored Angel: Selected Writings by Jose Garcia Villa. . . . . *.v.6 p.104, p.130*

Les Anciens Canadiens. . . . . *.v.2 p.538*

Ancient Angkor. . . . . *.v.6 p.170*

Ancient Borinquen: Archaeology and Ethnohistory of Native Puerto Rico. . . . . *.v.3 p.321*

Ancient Canada. . . . . *.v.4 p.11*

Ancient China in Transition: An Analysis of Social Mobility, 722-222 B. C. . . . . *.v.6 p.183, p.184*

Ancient China's Technology and Science. . . . . *.v.5 p.392*

Ancient Cities of the Indus Valley Civilization. . . . . *.v.4 p.9, v.6 p.150, p.713*

The Ancient City: A Study on the Religion, Laws, and Institutions of Greece and Rome. . . . . . . *.v.4 p.489*

Ancient Civilizations of Mesoamerica: A Reader. . . . *.v.4 p.10*

Ancient Damascus: A Historical Study of the Syrian City-State from Earliest Times until Its Fall to the Assyrians in 732 B.C. *.v.3 p.7*

Ancient Delhi. . . . . *.v.6 p.162*

Ancient DNA. . . . . *.v.5 p.121, p.122*

Ancient Earth, Ancient Skies: The Age of Earth and Its Cosmic Surroundings. . . . . *.v.5 p.446*

Ancient Economy. . . . . *.v.3 p.3*

Ancient Education and Its Meaning for Us. . . . . *.v.4 p.326*

Ancient Education. . . . . *.v.4 p.329*

Ancient Egypt: Anatomy of a Civilization. . . . . *.v.4 p.8*

The Ancient Egyptian Book of the Dead. . . . . . *.v.3 p.8*

The Ancient Egyptian Books of the Afterlife. . . . *.v.3 p.9*

Ancient Egyptian Literature: A Book of Readings: The New Kingdom. . . . . *.v.6 p.644*

Ancient Egyptian Literature: An Anthology. . . . . *.v.6 p.644*

Ancient Egyptian Literature: Late Period. . . *.v.3 p.9, v.6 p.644*

Ancient Egyptian Literature: New Kingdom. . . . . *.v.3 p.9*

Ancient Egyptian Literature: Old and Middle Kingdoms. *.v.3 p.9*

Ancient Egyptian Literature: The Old and the Middle Kingdoms. . . . . *.v.6 p.644*

The Ancient Egyptian "Tale of Two Brothers": The Oldest Fairy Tale in the World. . . . . *.v.6 p.644*

Ancient Egypt. . . . . *.v.3 p.9*

Ancient Environments. . . . . *.v.5 p.449*

Ancient Europe 8000 B.C.—A.D. 1000: An Encyclopedia of the Barbarian World. . . . . *.v.4 p.12*

The Ancient Gods Speak: A Guide to Egyptian Religion. . . . . *.v.1 p.543, v.3 p.9*

Ancient Greece: From Prehistoric to Hellenistic Times. *.v.3 p.12*

Ancient Greece: Social and Historical Documents from Archaic Times to Death of Socrates. . . . . *.v.3 p.13*

Ancient Greek Athletics. . . . . *.v.3 p.14*

Ancient Greek Literature and Society. . . . . . . *.v.2 p.400*

Ancient Greek Literature. . . . . *.v.2 p.401*

Ancient Greek Music. . . . . *.v.1 p.176*

Ancient Greek Novels - The Fragments: Introduction, Text, Translation, and Commentary. . . . . *.v.2 p.405*

Ancient Greek Religion. . . . . *.v.1 p.533*

Ancient Invertebrates and Their Living Relatives. . . . *.v.5 p.447*

Ancient Japan. . . . . *.v.4 p.9*

Ancient Lakes: Biodiversity, Ecology and
Evolution. *v.5 p.174, p.196*

Ancient Law: Its Connection with the Early History of Society,
and Its Relation to Modern Ideas. *v.4 p.33*

Ancient Law: Its Connection with the Early History of Society
and Its Relation to Modern Ideas. *v.4 p.433*

Ancient Literacy. *v.2 p.576, p.577*

The Ancient Mariners: Seafarers and Sea Fighters of the
Mediterranean in Ancient Times. *v.3 p.3*

Ancient Maya Commoners. *v.3 p.297*

The Ancient Maya of the Belize Valley: Half a Century of
Archaeological Research. *v.3 p.297*

Ancient Maya Women. *v.3 p.296*

The Ancient Maya. *v.4 p.10*

Ancient Medicine, Airs, Waters, Places, Epidemics 1 and 3, the
Oath, Precepts, Nutriment, Vol. 1. . . . . *v.2 p.404, v.5 p.510*

Ancient Menippean Satire. *v.2 p.427, p.428*

Ancient Mesoamerican Warfare. *v.3 p.296, p.297*

The Ancient Mesopotamian City. *v.3 p.6*

Ancient Mesopotamia. *v.3 p.6*

Ancient Mosaics. *v.1 p.811*

Ancient Mystery Cults. *v.1 p.530, p.531, p.532, v.3 p.13*

Ancient Natural History: Histories of Nature. *v.5 p.221*

Ancient Near East 3000-330 B. C. *v.3 p.4*

Ancient near East: Historical Sources in Translation. . . *v.3 p.4*

Ancient near East in Pictures Relating to the Old Testament
with Supplement. *v.1 p.619*

Ancient near Eastern Texts Relating to the Old Testament with
Supplement, Set. *v.1 p.619, v.3 p.4*

Ancient North America: The Archaeology of a Continent. *v.4 p.10*

The Ancient Olympics: A History. *v.3 p.15, v.4 p.810*

The Ancient Orient: An Introduction to the Study of the Ancient
Near East. *v.3 p.5*

Ancient Panama: Chiefs in Search of Power. *v.3 p.304*

Ancient Philosophy: A New History of Western
Philosophy. *v.1 p.420*

Ancient Philosophy: A Very Short Introduction. . . . *v.1 p.419*

Ancient Philosophy, Mystery, and Magic: Empedocles and
Pythagorean Tradition. *v.1 p.421*

Ancient Rain: Poems. 1956-1978. . . . . *v.2 p.91*

Ancient Records of Egypt: Historical Documents from the
Earliest Times to the Persian Conquest. . . *v.3 p.8, v.6 p.57*

Ancient Roman Villa Gardens. *v.1 p.819*

The Ancient Romances: A Literary-Historical Account of Their
Origins. *v.2 p.405*

Ancient Rome. *v.3 p.22*

Ancient Sichuan: Treasures from a Lost
Civilization. *v.1 p.669, p.692, v.4 p.8*

Ancient Sorceries and Other Weird Stories. *v.2 p.331*

Ancient South America. *v.4 p.11*

Ancient Texts for New Testament Studies: A Guide to the
Background Literature. *v.1 p.625*

The Ancient Traditions of the Virgin Mary's Dormition and
Assumption. *v.1 p.642*

Ancient Wine: The Search for the Origins of Viniculture. *v.5 p.52*

The Ancient World in the Cinema. *v.6 p.315*

Ancient World Mapping Center. *v.3 p.3*

Ancient Writers: Greece and Rome, Set. *v.2 p.399*

Ancilla to the Pre-Socratic Philosophers: A Complete Translation
of the Fragments in Diels, Fragmente Der
Vorsokratiker. *v.1 p.421*

Ancrene Wisse, Vol. 1. . . . . *v.2 p.204*

Ancrene Wisse/A Guide for Anchoresses: A Translation. *v.2 p.204*

Ancrene Wisse. *v.2 p.204*

And a Time for Hope: Americans in the Great
Depression. *v.3 p.475*

And a Time to Die: How American Hospitals Shape the End of
Life. *v.5 p.532*

And Be a Villain. *v.2 p.117*

And Here the World Ends: The Life of an Argentine
Village. *v.4 p.706*

And It Don't Stop: The Best American Hip-Hop Journalism of
the Last 25 Years. *v.1 p.267*

And Keep Your Powder Dry: An Anthropologist Looks at
America. *v.3 p.369*

And Now a Few Words from Me: Advertising's Leading Critic
Lays down the Law, Once and for All. *v.4 p.427*

And Other Neighborly Names: Social Process and Cultural
Image in Texas Folklore. *v.6 p.522*

And the Band Played On: Politics, People, and the AIDS
Epidemic. *v.6 p.379*

And the Crooked Places Made Straight: The Struggle for Social
Change in the 1960s. *v.3 p.468*

And the Mirror Cracked: Feminist Cinema and Film
Theory. *v.6 p.475*

And the Money Kept Rolling In (and Out): Wall Street, the
IMF, and the Bankrupting of Argentina. *v.4 p.94, p.98, p.99*

And the Poor Get Children: Sex, Contraception, and Family
Planning in the Working Class. . *v.4 p.775, v.6 p.465, p.471*

And the Russians Stayed...: A Personal Portrait of the
Sovietization of Cuba. *v.3 p.307*

And the Stars Were Shining: Poems. *v.2 p.57*

And the View from the Shore: Literary Traditions of
Hawaii. *v.6 p.98, p.131*

And the Walls Came Tumbling Down: The Basketball Game
That Changed American Sports. . . *v.4 p.831, p.853, p.893*

And the War Came: The North and the Secession Crisis,
1860-1861. . . . . *v.3 p.365, p.401, p.421*

And the Witnesses Were Silent: The Confessing Church and the
Persecution of the Jews. *v.3 p.84*

And Then: Natsume Soseki's Novel Sorekara. . . . *v.6 p.232*

And Then There Were None. *v.2 p.338*

And There Were Giants in the Land: The Life of William Heard
Kilpatrick. *v.4 p.340*

...And Well Tied Down: Chile's Press under Democracy. *v.3 p.354*

And Where Were You, Adam? *v.2 p.604*

Andean Journeys: Migration, Ethnogenesis and the State in
Colonial Quito. *v.3 p.332, p.333*

Andean Lives: Gregorio Condori Mamani and Asunta Quispe
Huamán. *v.3 p.332*

The Andean Past: Land Societies, and Conflicts. . . *v.3 p.328*

Andean Worlds: Indigenous History, Culture, and Consciousness
under Spanish Rule, 1532-1825. . . . . . *v.3 p.323, p.325*

Andersonville. *v.2 p.91*

The Andes Viewed from the City: Literary and Political
    Discourse on the Indian in Peru, 1848-1930. . . . . *v.3 p.327*

Andre Breton: Surrealism and Painting. *v.1 p.729*

Andre Breton. *v.2 p.511*

Andre Chenier. *v.2 p.479*

Andre Gide: A Life in the Present. *v.2 p.520*

Andre Gide: L insaisissable protee, etude critique de l oeuvre de
    Gide. *v.2 p.519*

Andre Gide Revisited. *v.2 p.519*

Andrea Palladio: The Complete Illustrated Works. . . . *v.1 p.793*

Andreas Gryphius/Catharina von Georgien: Sprachlich
    Modernisierter Text der Erstfassung von 1657/Herausgegeben
    von J. E. Oyler und A. H. Schulze. *v.2 p.595*

Andreas Gursky. *v.1 p.766*

Andrei Bely: The Major Symbolist Fiction. *v.2 p.801*

Andrei Bitov: The Ecology of Inspiration. . . . *v.2 p.797, p.802*

Andrei Platonov: Uncertainties of Spirit. *v.2 p.808*

Andres Bello: Venezuelan Author. *v.2 p.687*

Andrew Glassner's Notebook: Recreational Computer
    Graphics. *v.5 p.340*

Andrew Jackson: His Life and Times. . . *v.3 p.415, v.4 p.517*

Andrew Jackson, Symbol for an Age. *v.3 p.418*

Andrew Jackson: The Course of American Democracy,
    1833-1845. . . . . *v.3 p.418*

Andrew Jackson: The Course of American Empire,
    1767-1821. . . . . *v.3 p.417, p.418*

Andrew Jackson: The Course of American Freedom,
    1822-1832. . . . . *v.3 p.418*

Andrew Johnson: A Biography. *v.3 p.401, p.402*

Andrew Johnson and Reconstruction. *v.3 p.437*

Andrew Lloyd Webber. *v.1 p.254, p.337*

Andrew Marvell: A Biography. *v.2 p.253*

Andrew Marvell: A Reference Guide. *v.2 p.252*

An Andrew Marvell Companion. *v.2 p.252, p.253*

Andrew Marvell Revisited. *v.2 p.253*

Andrew Marvell. *v.2 p.252*

Andrew Marvel. *v.2 p.252*

Andrew Wyeth: Memory and Magic. *v.1 p.742*

André Breton : Le grand indésirable. *v.2 p.511*

André Breton: Selections. *v.2 p.510, p.511*

André Gide - Paul Valéry : correspondance,
    1890-1942. . . . . *v.2 p.520, p.528*

Andrés Bello: Scholarship and Nation-Building in
    Nineteenth-Century Latin America. *v.3 p.265*

Androids, Humanoids and Other Science Fiction Monsters:
    Science and Soul in Science Fiction. *v.6 p.319*

Andromache. *v.2 p.411, p.477*

Andy Warhol Prints. *v.1 p.756*

The Andy Warhol Show. *v.1 p.698*

Andy Warhol. *v.1 p.697, p.728*

Anecdotal Theory. *v.2 p.568*

Anecdotes of Destiny. *v.2 p.626*

An Angel at My Table: The Complete Autobiography. *v.2 p.745*

Angel Guerra, Vol. 1. *v.2 p.655*

The Angel of History. *v.2 p.145*

Angel Pavement. *v.2 p.378*

Angelic Monks and Earthly Men: Monasticism and Its Meaning
    to Medieval Society. *v.6 p.572*

Angels and Insects: Two Novellas. *v.2 p.331, p.332*

Angels in America: A Gay Fantasia on National
    Themes. *v.1 p.62, p.126, v.6 p.412*

Angels in America: Perestroika. *v.2 p.148*

Anger, Aggression and Violence: An Interdisciplinary
    Study. *v.5 p.656*

The Angevin Empire. *v.3 p.98, v.6 p.568*

Angkor Cambodia 16th Cent. *v.6 p.170*

Angkor Wat: Time, Space, and Kingship. . . . *v.1 p.692, p.777*

Angle of Ascent: New and Selected Poems. *v.2 p.81*

Anglicanism and the Christian Church: Theological Resources in
    Historical Perspective. *v.1 p.655*

Anglicko-Slovensky Slovnik. *v.2 p.777*

Angliisko-Bulgarski Frazeologichen Rechnik: Okolo 25 000
    Idioma: A-Z. *v.2 p.774*

Angliisko-Bulgarski I Bulgarsko-Angliiski Kartinen Rechnik
    Duden-Trud. *v.2 p.774*

Angliisko-Bulgarski Rechnik - English-Bulgarian
    Dictionary. *v.2 p.774*

Anglo-American Relations in the Twentieth Century: The
    Politics and Diplomacy of Friendly Superpowers. *v.3 p.388*

Anglo-American Relations with Greece: The Coming of the
    Cold War, 1942-47. . . . . *v.3 p.195*

The Anglo-Argentine Connection, 1900-1939. . . . . *v.3 p.348*

Anglo-Greek Attitudes: Studies in History. *v.3 p.195*

Anglo-Irish Literature. *v.2 p.163*

Anglo-Norman England, 1066-1166. *v.3 p.97, v.6 p.561, p.562*

Anglos and Mexicans in the Making of Texas,
    1836-1986. . . . . *v.6 p.532*

Anglo-Saxon Attitudes. *v.2 p.389*

Anglo-Saxon Charters. *v.4 p.436*

The Anglo-Saxon Chronicle. *v.3 p.96*

▢ Anglo-Saxon England: A Guide to Online
    Resources. *v.2 p.203*

Anglo-Saxon Oral Poetry: A Study of the Traditions. *v.2 p.168*

Anglo-Saxon Poetic Records: A Collectve Edition. . *v.2 p.196*

The Anglo-Saxon World. *v.2 p.196*

The Anglo-Saxons. *v.3 p.96, v.6 p.561*

Anglo-Welsh Poetry 1480-1990. . . . . *v.2 p.199*

Angola, Mozambique, and the West. *v.6 p.74*

Angola: Promises and Lies. *v.6 p.75*

Angola under the Portuguese: The Myth and the Reality. *v.6 p.75*

Angola. *v.6 p.75*

Angora Matta: Fatal Acts of North-South Translation = Actos
    Fatales de Traduccion Norte-Sur. *v.1 p.15, p.43*

The Angry Theatre; New British Drama. *v.2 p.189*

Angst. *v.2 p.529*

Angus Wilson: A Biography. *v.2 p.389*

Aniara: An Epic Science Fiction Poem. *v.2 p.630*

Anil's Ghost. *v.2 p.737*

Animal Anatomy and Physiology. *v.5 p.156*

Animal Architecture. *v.5 p.212*

Animal Attractions: Nature on Display in American
    Zoos. *v.5 p.83*

Animal Behaviour: Psychobiology, Ethology, and
    Evolution. *v.5 p.166, p.170*

Animal biomarkers as pollution indicators. *v.5 p.365*

Animal Cognition: An Introduction to Modern Comparative
    Psychology. *v.5 p.615, p.616*

Animal Cognition in Nature: The Convergence of Psychology
    and Biology in Laboratory and Field. *v.5 p.165*

Animal Diversity. *v.5 p.189, p.215*

Animal Ecology. *v.5 p.54, v.6 p.291*

The Animal Estate: The English and Other Creatures in the
    Victorian Age. *v.6 p.760, p.764*

Animal Farm: Centennial Edition. *v.2 p.376*

Animal Intelligence: Experimental Studies. *v.5 p.615*

Animal Locomotion. *v.5 p.212*

Animal Minds and Human Morals: The Origins of the Western
    Debate. *v.5 p.615*

Animal Minds. *v.6 p.291*

The Animal Mind. *v.5 p.616*

Animal Models of Human Emotion and Cognition. . .*v.5 p.614*

Animal Play: Evolutionary, Comparative and Ecological
    Perspectives. *v.5 p.614*

Animal Research and Human Health: Advancing Human
    Welfare Through Behavioral Science. *v.5 p.614*

The Animal Rights Debate. *v.6 p.288*

Animal Social Complexity: Intelligence, Culture, and
    Individualized Societies. *v.5 p.614*

Animals and Fishes in Aquaterrariums. *v.5 p.89*

Animals and Why They Matter. *v.1 p.486*

The Animals Came Dancing: Native American Sacred Ecology
    and Animal Kinship. *v.6 p.288*

Animals in Bronze Reference and Price Guide. . . .*v.1 p.776*

Animals, Property, and the Law. *v.4 p.448*

Animalwatch: Behavior, Biology and Beauty. *v.5 p.166*

The Animated Film Encyclopedia: A Complete Guide to
    American Shorts, Features and Sequences,
    1900-1979. . . . .*v.6 p.308*

Animating Culture: Hollywood Cartoons from the Sound
    Era. *v.6 p.308*

Animating the Letter: The Figurative Embodiment of Writing
    from Late Antiquity to the Renaissance. *v.1 p.719*

Animation and America. *v.6 p.308*

Animation: Genre and Authorship. *v.6 p.308*

Animation in Asia and the Pacific. *v.6 p.308*

Animation: The Whole Story. *v.6 p.348*

Anime Explosion!: The What? Why? and Wow! of Japanese
    Animation. *v.6 p.307*

Anime from Akira to Princess Mononoke: Experiencing
    Contemporary Japanese Animation. *v.6 p.308*

Anita Loos: A Biography. *v.2 p.94*

Anita Loos Rediscovered: Film Treatments and Fiction.*v.2 p.94*

An-My Le: Small Wars. *v.1 p.769*

Ann Petry: Critical Perspectives Past and
    Present. *v.2 p.109, v.6 p.25, p.43*

Ann Petry's Short Fiction: Critical Essays. *v.2 p.109*

Ann Veronica. *v.2 p.320*

▢ Anna Akhmatova. *v.2 p.795, p.800*

Anna Halprin: Experience as Dance. .*v.1 p.11, p.12, p.29, p.31*

Anna in the Tropics. *v.2 p.160*

Anna Karenina: Backgrounds and Sources Criticism. .*v.2 p.809*

Anna Karenina. *v.2 p.809*

Anna of the Five Towns. *v.2 p.334*

Anna Pavlova: Her Life and Art. *v.1 p.11*

Anna Sokolow: The Rebellious Spirit. *v.1 p.13, p.14*

Anna St. Ives A Novel. *v.2 p.245*

Annalen der Deutschen Literatur; eine Gemeinschaftsarbeit
    Zahlreicher Fachgelehrter. *v.2 p.589*

Annales, Vol. I-VI, Bks. XI-XVI. *v.2 p.444*

Annals of Imperial Rome. *v.2 p.444*

Annals of Opera, Fifteen Ninety-Seven to Nineteen Forty,
    Set. *v.1 p.161, p.231*

The Annals of Quintus Ennius. *v.2 p.434*

Annals of Roger De Hoveden. *v.3 p.98*

Annals of the Former World, Set. *v.5 p.432*

Annals of the French Stage from Its Origin to the Death of
    Racine. *v.1 p.59, p.105, p.106, p.140*

Annals of the New York Stage. . . .*v.1 p.4, p.55, p.117, p.137*

Annals of the Turkish Empire from 1591 to 1659 of the
    Christian Era. *v.6 p.591*

Annals. *v.2 p.445*

Anne Bradstreet Revisited. *v.2 p.29*

Anne Bradstreet, the Worldly Puritan: An Introduction to Her
    Poetry. *v.2 p.30*

Anne Conway: The Principles of the Most Ancient and Modern
    Philosophy. *v.1 p.448*

Anne Hebert: Collected Later Novels. *v.2 p.539*

Anne Hebert: Le Secret de Vie et de Mort. *v.2 p.538*

Anne Hebert. *v.2 p.540*

Anne of Green Gables. *v.2 p.736, p.737*

Anne Sexton: A Biography. *v.2 p.115*

Anne Sexton. *v.2 p.115*

Anne's Bohemia: Czech Literature and Society,
    1310-1420. . . . .*v.2 p.782*

The Annexation of Bosnia, 1908-1909. . . . . . .*v.3 p.249*

The Annie Dillard Reader. *v.2 p.144*

Annie Ernaux: An Introduction to the Writer and her
    Audience. *v.2 p.532*

Annie John: A Novel. *v.2 p.767*

Annie on My Mind. *v.6 p.396*

Annie's box: Charles Darwin, his daughter, and human
    evolution. *v.5 p.222*

Annihilation. *v.2 p.792*

Anniversaries: From the Life of Gesine Cresspahl. . .*v.2 p.618*

The Annotated Alice: Alice's Adventures in Wonderland and
    Through the Looking Glass. *v.2 p.277*

The Annotated Ancient Mariner. *v.2 p.279*

▢ Annotated Bibliography and Guide to Archival Resources on
    the History of Jewish Women in America. *v.6 p.459*

An Annotated Bibliography of Homosexuality. *v.6 p.359*

An Annotated Bibliography of Inuit Art. *v.1 p.662*

🄴 Annotated Bibliography of Southern American
  English. *v.2 p.552*

The Annotated Christmas Carol: A Christmas Carol in
  Prose. *v.2 p.284*

The Annotated Huckleberry Finn: Adventures of Huckleberry
  Finn (Tom Sawyer's Comrade). *v.2 p.35*

The Annotated Innocence of Father Brown. *v.2 p.277*

The Annotated Lolita. *v.2 p.104*

The Annotated She: A Critical Edition of H. Rider Haggard's
  Victorian Romance. *v.2 p.290*

Annotations to Finnegans Wake. *v.2 p.360*

Annual Book of ASTM Standards, Annual Compilation; 71 vols.
  in 16 sections. *v.5 p.318*

Annual Editions: Business Ethics 06/07. . . . . . .*v.4 p.53*

Annual Review of Astronomy and Astrophysics. . . .*v.5 p.64*

Annual Review of Physical Chemistry. *v.5 p.275*

▢ Annual Review of Sociology. *v.4 p.675*

The Annunciation. *v.2 p.145*

Annus Mirabilis 1905: Albert Einstein, and the Theory of
  Relativity. *v.5 p.539*

Anomalistic Psychology: A Study of Magical Thinking. *v.5 p.614*

Los Anos con Laura Diaz. *v.2 p.668*

Another America: The Politics of Race and Blame. . *v.4 p.573*

Another Birth. *v.6 p.670*

Another Century of War. *v.3 p.448*

Another City: Writing from Los Angeles. *v.2 p.584*

Another Fine Math You've Got Me Into. *v.5 p.469*

Another Life and The House on the Embankment. . . *v.2 p.809*

Another Mother Tongue: Gay Words, Gay Worlds. . *v.6 p.360*

Another Raft. *v.2 p.757*

Another Reason: Science and the Imagination of Modern
  India. *v.6 p.158*

Another Sea, Another Shore: Persian Stories of
  Migration. *v.6 p.673*

Another Such Victory: President Truman and the Cold War,
  1945-1953. . . . .*v.3 p.477*

Anouilh Plays, Vol. 1. . . . .*v.2 p.506*

Anouilh Plays, Vol. 2. . . . .*v.2 p.506*

Anrufung des grossen Bären: Gedichte. *v.2 p.603*

The Anschluss Movement, 1931-1938. . . . .*v.3 p.185*

Ansel Adams: A Biography. *v.1 p.765*

Ansel Adams at 100. . . . .*v.1 p.769*

Ansel Adams: Divine Performance. *v.1 p.766, p.767*

Anselm and Talking about God. *v.1 p.638*

Anselm Kiefer. *v.1 p.735*

Anselm's Discovery: A Re-Examination of the Ontological
  Proof for God's Existence. *v.1 p.432, p.639*

Answer to History. *v.6 p.631*

Answerable Style: Essays on Paradise Lost. *v.2 p.255*

Answering the "Virtuecrats": A Moral Conversation on
  Character Education. *v.4 p.306*

Ant. Lirica Renacentista (Anthology - Renaissance
  Poetry). *v.2 p.643*

The Antagonists: Hugo Black, Felix Frankfurter and Civil
  Liberties in Modern America. *v.4 p.469*

Antal and Her Path of Love: Poems of a Woman Saint from
  South India. *v.6 p.151*

Antaractica Ahoy!. *v.2 p.781*

Antarctic Communities: Species, Structure and
  Survival. *v.5 p.204*

Antarctic Ecosystems: Change and Conservation. *v.5 p.180, p.238*

Antarctic Marine Geology. *v.5 p.434*

Antarctica: An Encyclopedia from Abbott Ice Shelf to
  Zooplankton. *v.5 p.434*

Antarctica and the Arctic: The Complete Encyclopedia. *v.5 p.434*

Antarctica the Last Frontier. *v.5 p.176, p.238*

Ante-Bellum Kentucky: A Social History, 1800-1860. *v.3 p.511*

The Antecedents of Self-Esteem. *v.5 p.625, p.631*

Antecedents to Modern Rwanda: The Nyiginya
  Kingdom. *v.6 p.65*

The Ante-Nicene Fathers, Set. *v.1 p.591, p.592*

Antenna and EM Modeling with MatLab. *v.5 p.728*

Antenna Arraying Techniques in the Deep Space
  Network. *v.5 p.728*

Antenna Theory: Analysis and Design. *v.5 p.728*

Antenna Theory and Design. *v.5 p.728*

Antennas and Propagation for Wireless Communication
  Systems. *v.5 p.728*

Antennas for All Applications. *v.5 p.728*

Antennas for Multi-band RF Front-end Modules. . . *v.5 p.728*

Antennas. *v.5 p.728*

The Anther: Form, Function and Phylogeny. *v.5 p.155*

Anthologie de la littérature française de Belgique : entre réel et
  surréel. *v.2 p.535*

Anthologie de la Nouvelle Poesie Negre et Malgache de Langue
  Francaise: Avec: Sartre, Jean-Paul. Orphee Noir. . *v.2 p.535*

Anthologie de la poésie française, vol. 1. . . . . .*v.2 p.464*

Anthologie de la poésie française, vol. 2. . . . . .*v.2 p.464*

Anthologie du conte fantastique français. *v.2 p.465*

Anthologie thématique de la poésie française du Moyen Age:
  traductions, introduction, préface. *v.2 p.465, p.466*

An Anthology of African Art: The Twentieth Century. *v.1 p.690*

Anthology of American Jazz Dance. *v.1 p.31*

Anthology of Arabic Literature, Culture, and Thought from
  Pre-Islamic Times to the Present. *v.6 p.659*

An Anthology of Austrian Drama. . . *v.1 p.68, p.110,v.2 p.594*

An Anthology of Brazilian Modernist Poetry. *v.2 p.692*

An Anthology of Canadian Native Literature in English. *v.2 p.732*

An Anthology of Chinese Literature: Beginnings to
  1911. . . . .*v.6 p.208*

Anthology of Chinese Literature: From the Earliest Times to the
  Fourteenth Century. *v.6 p.207*

Anthology of Chinese Literature: From the Fourteenth Century
  to the Present Day, Vol. 2. . . . .*v.6 p.207*

Anthology of Contemporary Kurdish Poetry. *v.6 p.668*

An Anthology of Contemporary Russian Women Poets. *v.2 p.794*

An Anthology of Czech Literature: 1st Period: From the
  Beginnings until 1410. . . . .*v.2 p.781, p.782*

Anthology of Czech Poetry. *v.2 p.781*

Anthology of Danish Literature. *v.2 p.625, p.626*

An Anthology of Elizabethan Prose Fiction. *v.2 p.203*

An Anthology of Galician Short Stories: Asi Vai o Conto. *v.2 p.692*

Anthology of German Expressionist Drama. *v.1 p.69, p.83, p.85, p.86, p.110*

An Anthology of German Poetry from Hölderlin to Rilke in English Translation. *v.2 p.593*

An Anthology of Jewish-Russian Literature. *v.2 p.795*

An Anthology of Modern Albanian Poetry: An Elusive Eagle Soars. *v.2 p.815*

An Anthology of Modern Arabic Poetry. *v.6 p.661*

An Anthology of Modern Arabic Verse. *v.6 p.658*

Anthology of Modern Estonian Poetry. *v.2 p.781*

An Anthology of Modern French Poetry (1850-1950). .*v.2 p.463*

An Anthology of Modern Persian Poetry. *v.6 p.671*

An Anthology of Modern Turkish Short Stories. .*v.6 p.666, p.667*

An Anthology of New Zealand Poetry in English. . . .*v.2 p.742*

An Anthology of Old English Poetry. *v.2 p.197*

An Anthology of Old Spanish. *v.2 p.643*

An Anthology of Quevedo's Poetry. *v.2 p.651*

An Anthology of Renaissance Plays in Translation: Works from the Italian, Spanish, and Portuguese Traditions. *v.1 p.63, p.74, p.95*

An Anthology of Romanian Women Poets. *v.2 p.816*

An Anthology of Russian Literature from Earliest Writings to Modern Fiction: Introduction to a Culture. *v.2 p.795*

An Anthology of Scandinavian Literature, from the Viking Period to the Twentieth Century. *v.2 p.624*

An Anthology of Slovak Literature. *v.2 p.812*

The Anthology of Space and Place: Locating Culture. .*v.6 p.721*

An Anthology of Spanish Poetry: From the Beginnings to the Present Day, Including Both Spain and Spanish America. *v.2 p.643*

Anthology of Statistics in Sports. *v.4 p.871*

Anthology of the Provencal Troubadours. *v.2 p.463*

An Anthology of Twentieth Century New Zealand Poetry. *v.2 p.743*

An Anthology of Twentieth-Century Brazilian Poetry. .*v.2 p.689*

Anthology of Twentieth-Century British and Irish Poetry. *v.2 p.201*

An Anthology of Vietnamese Poems: From the Eleventh Through the Twentieth Centuries. *v.6 p.169*

An Anthology of Western Marxism: From Lukacs and Gramsci to Socialist-Feminism. *v.1 p.508*

Anthony Blunt: His Lives. *v.1 p.700, p.701*

Anthony Burgess: A Biography. *v.2 p.336*

Anthony Burgess Revisited. *v.2 p.336*

Anthony Caro: A Life in Sculpture. *v.1 p.778*

Anthony Caro: Explorations in Sculpture. *v.1 p.782*

Anthony Trollope: A Critical Study,. *v.2 p.316*

Anthony Trollope: A Victorian in His World. *v.2 p.317*

Anthony Trollope: His Art and Scope. *v.2 p.316*

Anthony Trollope. *v.2 p.316, p.317*

Anthropological Linguistics. *v.4 p.18*

Anthropological Locations: Boundaries and Grounds of a Field Science. *v.4 p.23*

The Anthropological Romance of Bali 1597-1972. . . . .*v.6 p.174, p.176*

Anthropological Theory Today. *v.4 p.24*

Anthropologies and Histories: Essays in Culture, History, and Political Economy. *v.4 p.24*

An Anthropologist at Work: Writings of Ruth Benedict. .*v.4 p.22*

Anthropologists in a Wider World: Essays on Field Research. *v.4 p.25*

e Anthropologizing Sri Lanka: A Eurocentric Misadventure. *v.6 p.154*

Anthropology and Cognitive Science: Essays on Cultural Transmission. *v.4 p.26, p.27*

Anthropology and Human Movement: Searching for Origins. *v.1 p.49*

Anthropology and the Colonial Encounter. *v.4 p.4*

Anthropology and the Dance: Ten Lectures. *v.1 p.49*

Anthropology and the Global Factory. *v.4 p.28*

Anthropology, by Comparison. *v.4 p.22*

Anthropology in Practice. *v.4 p.45*

Anthropology in Public Health: Bridging Differences in Culture and Society. *v.4 p.44*

Anthropology in the Margins of the State. *v.4 p.34*

Anthropology in Theological Perspective. *v.1 p.643*

The Anthropology of Anger: Civil Society and Democracy in Africa. *v.4 p.497, p.585, p.612*

Anthropology of Art: A Reader. *v.1 p.708, v.4 p.26*

The Anthropology of Buddhism and Hinduism: Weberian Themes. *v.4 p.721*

The Anthropology of Dance. *v.1 p.49*

The Anthropology of Development and Globalization: From Classical Political Economy to Contemporary Neoliberalism. *v.4 p.28*

The Anthropology of Europe: Identities and Boundaries in Conflict. *v.4 p.41, p.42*

The Anthropology of Language: An Introduction to Linguistic Anthropology. *v.4 p.18*

Anthropology of Law: A Comparative Theory. . .*v.4 p.33, p.34*

The Anthropology of Medicine: From Culture to Method. .*v.4 p.47*

The Anthropology of Peace and Nonviolence. *v.4 p.35*

Anthropology of Performing Arts: Artistry, Virtuosity, and Interpretation in a Cross-Cultural Perspective. *v.1 p.49, v.4 p.26*

The Anthropology of Politics: A Reader in Ethnography, Theory, and Critique. *v.4 p.35*

The Anthropology of Religious Conversion. *v.4 p.36*

The Anthropology of Slavery. *v.4 p.28*

Anthropology of the North Pacific Rim. *v.6 p.703*

The Anthropology of the State: A Reader. *v.4 p.34*

Anthropology, Sport, and Culture. *v.4 p.819*

Anthropology: The Basics. *v.4 p.23*

Anthropology: Theoretical Practice in Culture and Society. *v.4 p.24*

Anthropology Today: An Encyclopedic Inventory. *v.4 p.3*

Anthropology Toward History: Culture and Work in a 19th-Century Maine Town. *v.3 p.486*

Anthropomorphism, Anecdotes, and Animals. *v.5 p.615*

☐ AnthroSource. *v.4 p.45*

Anti-American Terrorism and the Middle East: A Documentary
Reader. *v.1 p.560*

Anti-Americanism in Russia: From Stalin to Putin. . .*v.3 p.212*

Anti-Asian Violence in North America: Asian American and
Asian Canadian Reflections on Hate, Healing and
Resistance. *v.6 p.123*

☐ Antibody Explorer. *v.5 p.328*

Antic Hay. *v.2 p.354*

Anti-Calvinists: The Rise of English Arminianism c.
1590-1640. . . . .*v.3 p.122*

Anticipating Madam President. *v.4 p.528*

Anticipations of the General Theory and Other Essays on
Keynes. *v.4 p.225*

Anticolonialism in British Politics: The Left and the End of
Empire 1918-1964. . . . .*v.3 p.125*

Anti-Communism and Popular Culture in Mid-Century
America. *v.4 p.712*

The Anti-Corn Law League 1838-1846. . . . .*v.3 p.113*

The Antifederalists. *v.4 p.518*

Antifungal Agents: Methods and Protocols. *v.5 p.112*

The Antigay Agenda: Orthodox Vision and the Christian
Right. *v.6 p.373*

Antigones: How the Antigone Legend Has Endured in Western
Literature, Art, and Thought. *v.2 p.421*

Antigone. *v.2 p.420*

Anti-Intellectualism in American Life. *v.3 p.368*

Antilyrik and Other Poems. *v.2 p.784*

The Anti-Marcos Struggle: Personalistic Rule and Democratic
Transition in the Philippines. *v.6 p.180*

Antioch and Rome: New Testament Cradles of Catholic
Christianity. *v.1 p.625*

Antiochos III and the Cities of Western Asia Minor: With New
Preface and Addenda. *v.3 p.21, v.6 p.714*

Antioqueno Colonization in Western Colombia. . . .*v.3 p.358*

The Antipeople. *v.2 p.546*

Antiphon and Andocides. *v.2 p.405*

The Antiquary. *v.2 p.307*

Antique Furniture of Quebec: Four Centuries of Furniture
Making. *v.1 p.804*

Antiques from the Garden. *v.1 p.819*

Antiquespeak: A Guide to the Styles, Techniques and Materials
of the Decorative Arts from the Renaissance to Art
Deco. *v.1 p.798*

Antiquity and the Middle Ages: From Ancient Greece to the
Middle Ages. *v.1 p.178*

Antisemitism: A Historical Encyclopedia of Prejudice and
Persecution. *v.3 p.60*

Antisemitism in the Modern World: An Anthology of
Texts. *v.3 p.60*

Antisemitism, Its History and Causes. *v.3 p.60*

The Antislavery Appeal: American Abolitionism after
1830. . . . .*v.3 p.421*

The Antislavery Origins of the Fourteenth Amendment. *v.3 p.421*

Antislavery Reconsidered: New Perspectives on the
Abolitionists. *v.3 p.421*

☐ Anti-Slavery Society. *v.4 p.727*

Antislavery Vanguard: New Essays on the Abolitionists. .*v.3 p.419*

Antisocial Behavior in Organizations. *v.4 p.130*

Antitrust and Competition Policy. *v.4 p.252*

The Antitrust Laws: A Primer. .*v.4 p.85, p.110, p.111, p.112, p.444*

The Antitrust Paradox. *v.4 p.444*

The Antitrust Revolution: Economics, Competition, and
Policy. *v.4 p.84, p.109*

Antoine and the Theatre Libre. *v.1 p.81, p.106, p.153*

Antoine Busnois: Method, Meaning, and Context in Late
Medieval Music. *v.1 p.180, p.314, p.315*

Antoine de Saint-Exupery. *v.2 p.526*

Antoine Lavoisier: Science, Administration and
Revolution. *v.5 p.262*

Antoine Watteau 1684-1721: Catalogue Raisonné des
Dessins. *v.1 p.724*

Antología de autores Españoles: Antiguos y Modernos. .*v.2 p.645*

Antología de la Literatura Española: Edad Media. . .*v.2 p.644*

Antología de la Poesía Cubana: Obra Completa. . . .*v.2 p.672*

Antología de la Poesía Latinoamericana de Vanguardia
(1916-1935). *v.2 p.666*

Antología. *v.2 p.675*

Antologia Critica de la Poesia Modernista
HispanoAmericana. *v.2 p.664*

Antologia de Autores Espanoles: Modernos. . .*v.2 p.643, 644*

Antologia de la Literatura Espanola, Renacimiento y Siglo de
Oro, Vol. 2. . . . .*v.2 p.644*

Antologia de la Literatura Espanola: Siglos XVIII y
XIX. *v.2 p.644*

Antologia de la Poesia del Romanticismo Hispanoamericano:
(1820-1890). *v.2 p.665, p.666*

Antologia de Literatura Hispanica Contemporanea, Vol.
1. . . . .*v.2 p.642*

Antologia Del Teatro Medieval. *v.2 p.642*

Antologia della Poesia Italiana, vol. 1. . . . .*v.2 p.700*

Antologia della Poesia Italiana, vol. 2. . . . .*v.2 p.700*

Antologia della Poesia Italiana, vol. 3. . . . .*v.2 p.700*

Antologia Personal de Alfredo Bryce Echenique. . . .*v.2 p.685*

Antologia Personal. *v.2 p.670*

Antologia Poetica: 1960-1994. . . . .*v.2 p.666*

Antologia Poetica del Romanticismo Espano (Poetic Anthology
of the Spanish Romanticism). *v.2 p.642*

Antologia Poetica. *v.2 p.655, p.660, p.662, p.687*

Antologia. *v.2 p.661*

Anton Chekhov's Short Stories. *v.2 p.802*

Anton Von Webern: A Chronicle of His Life and
Work. *v.1 p.219, p.367*

Antoni Gaudi. *v.1 p.795*

Antonia Merce, la Argentina: Flamenco and the Spanish Avant
Garde. *v.1 p.6*

ANTONIL, Mama Coca. *v.3 p.281*

Antonin Artaud: A Critical Reader. *v.2 p.507*

Antonin Artaud. *v.2 p.507*

The Antonines: The Roman Empire in Transition. .*v.3 p.27, p.28*

Antonio Machado: Selected Poems. *v.2 p.662*

Antonio Stradivari, His Life and Work
    (1644-1739). *v.1 p.184, p.358, p.359, p.389*

Antony and Cleopatra. *v.2 p.225*

Un an. *v.2 p.529, p.530*

Anuran Communication. *v.5 p.171*

Anvil of Victory: The Communist Revolution in
    Manchuria. *v.6 p.192, p.206*

Anxiety Veiled: Euripides and the Traffic in Women. *v.2 p.412*

The Anxious Decades: America in Prosperity and Depression
    1920-1941. . . . .*v.3 p.449*

Anxious Parents: A History of Modern Childrearing in
    America. *v.3 p.444*

Any Human Heart: A Novel. *v.2 p.335*

Any Old Iron. *v.2 p.335, p.336*

Anyan's Story: A New Guinea Woman in Two Worlds. *v.4 p.43*

Anyplace but Here. *v.6 p.23*

Anything but Mexican: Chicanos in Contemporary Los
    Angeles. *v.6 p.535, p.548*

Anything but Straight: Unmasking the Scandals and Lies Behind
    the Ex-Gay Myth. *v.6 p.372*

AP Success - Biology. *v.5 p.246*

Apache Odyssey: A Journey Between Two Worlds. . *v.6 p.704*

Aparajito: the Unvanquished. *v.6 p.150, p.151*

Apart from Modernism: Edith Wharton, Politics, and Fiction
    Before World War I. *v.2 p.131, p.132*

Apartheid, Imperialism and African Freedom. *v.3 p.391*

Apartheid in South Africa. *v.6 p.79*

Apartment in Athens. *v.2 p.128*

Apes and Angels: The Irishman in Victorian
    Caricature. *v.6 p.737, p.746, p.750*

Apes, Language, and the Human Mind. *v.4 p.19, p.20,v.5 p.615*

Apex of Power: The Prime Minister and Political Leadership in
    Canada. *v.4 p.588*

Aphra Behn (1640-1689): Selected Poems. *v.2 p.238*

Apocalypse and the Writings on Revelation. *v.2 p.363*

Apocalypse in Oklahoma: Waco and Ruby Ridge
    Revenged. *v.4 p.524*

The Apocalyptic Imagination: An Introduction to Jewish
    Apocalyptic Literature. *v.1 p.617, p.618, p.619*

Apocalyptic Literature and Testaments. *v.1 p.623*

Apocalyptic Spirituality. *v.1 p.645*

Apocolocyntosis. *v.2 p.443*

The Apocryphal New Testament: A Collection of Apocryphal
    Christian Literature in an English Translation. . . .*v.1 p.632*

Apocryphal Tales: With a Selection of Fables and Would-Be
    Tales. *v.2 p.783*

Apogee of Empire: Spain and New Spain in the Age of Charles
    III, 1759-1789. . . . .*v.3 p.288*

Apollinaire: Poet among the Painters. *v.2 p.507*

Apollodorus: The Library of Greek Mythology. *v.2 p.407*

The Apollonian Clockwork: On Stravinsky. . . .*v.1 p.208, p.359*

Apollo's Lyre: Greek Music and Music Theory in Antiquity and
    the Middle Ages. *v.1 p.175*

Apologia and Two Folk Plays: The Great Highway, the
    Crownbridge, and Swanwhite. *v.2 p.631*

Apologia Pro Vita Sua. *v.1 p.579*

Apologies to the Iroquois: The Iroquois and Their
    Neighbors. *v.6 p.684, p.704*

An Apology for the Life of Colley Cibber. *v.2 p.243*

Apology for the Woman Writing and Other
    Works. *v.2 p.469, p.470*

The Apostate Angel; a Critical Study of Gore Vidal. . *v.2 p.127*

Apostles and Agitators: Italy's Marxist Revolutionary
    Tradition. *v.3 p.202*

The Apostles' Creed in Light of Today's Questions. . .*v.1 p.646*

The Apostolic Church of the East: A History of the Nestorian
    Church. *v.1 p.569*

The Apostolic Fathers: Epistle of Barnabas, Papias and
    Quadratus, Epistle to Diognetus, the Shepherd of
    Hermas. *v.1 p.591*

The Apostolic Fathers: Greek Texts and English
    Translations. *v.1 p.591*

The Apostolic Fathers: I Clement. II Clement. Ignatius.
    Polycarp. Didache. *v.1 p.590*

Apostolic Fathers. *v.1 p.591*

The Apotheosis of Captain Cook: European Mythmaking in the
    Pacific. *v.4 p.43*

Appalachia: A History. *v.3 p.498*

Appalachia in the Making. *v.3 p.498*

Appalachia on Our Mind: The Southern Mountains and
    Mountaineers in the American Consciousness,
    1870-1920. . . . .*v.3 p.498*

The Appalachian Forest: A Search for Roots and
    Renewal. *v.5 p.36, p.37,v.6 p.297*

Appalachian Legacy. *v.3 p.497*

Appalachian Mountain Religion: A History. *v.3 p.498*

Appalachian Trail Design, Construction, and
    Maintenance. *v.5 p.229*

The Appalachians: America's First and Last
    Frontier. *v.3 p.489, p.490*

Appalachians and Race: The Mountain South from Slavery to
    Segregation. *v.3 p.497*

The Apparitional Lesbian: Female Homosexuality and Modern
    Culture. *v.6 p.392*

Apparitions of the Self: The Secret Autobiographies of a Tibetan
    Visionary. *v.6 p.241*

Appeal to Arms: A Military History of the American
    Revolution. *v.3 p.414*

Appearance and Reality: A Metaphysical Essay. *v.1 p.445, p.488*

Appeasement and Germany's Last Bid for Colonies. . .*v.3 p.74*

Appeasement in International Politics. *v.4 p.646*

Appendix Vergiliana. *v.2 p.447*

Appetites and Identities: An Introduction to Social Anthropology
    of Western Europe. *v.4 p.41*

Appetites: Food and Sex in Postsocialist China. . . .*v.6 p.193*

☐ APPIC Online Directory. *v.5 p.675*

The Applause-Best Plays Theater Yearbook, 1990-1991: The
    Complete Broadway and Off-Broadway
    Sourcebook. *v.1 p.65, p.114*

The Applause-Best Plays Theater Yearbook, 1991-1992:
    Featuring the Ten Best Plays of the Year. . . .*v.1 p.66, p.114*

Apple in the Dark. *v.2 p.691*

Apple of God: Constitutionalism in Israel and the United States. *v.6 p.614*

Apples: Botany, Production and Uses. *v.5 p.21*

Apples of Immortality: Folktales of Armenia. *v.6 p.665*

The Applications and Limitations of Taxonomy (in Classification of Organisms): An Anthology of Current Thought. *v.5 p.189*

Applications in Coordination, Organometallic and Bioinorganic Chemistry, Pt. B. *v.5 p.305*

Applications of Bioinformatics in Cancer Detection. . .*v.5 p.98*

Applications of Biological Anthropology to Human Affairs. *v.4 p.14*

Applications of Genomics and Proteomics for Analysis of Bacterial Biological Warfare Agents. *v.5 p.115, p.139, p.217*

Applications of Nonverbal Communication. *v.4 p.424*

Applications of Ultra Wide Band Wireless. *v.5 p.727*

Applied Abstract Algebra. *v.5 p.473*

Applied Animal Nutrition: Feeds and Feeding. *v.5 p.54*

Applied Anthropology: A Career-Oriented Approach. . *v.4 p.44*

The Applied Anthropology Reader. *v.4 p.45*

Applied Climatology: Principles and Practice. *v.5 p.427*

Applied Combinatorics. *v.5 p.479*

Applied Cryptography: Protocols, Algorithms, and Source Code in C. *v.5 p.335*

Applied Demography for Biologists: With Special Emphasis on Insects. *v.5 p.167, p.212*

Applied Digital Control: Theory, Design and Implementation. *v.5 p.711*

Applied Econometric Time Series. *v.4 p.206*

Applied Ethics. *v.1 p.486*

Applied Ethnobotany: People, Wild Plant Use and Conservation. *v.5 p.16, p.17*

Applied Functional Analysis. *v.5 p.493*

Applied Genetics. *v.5 p.135*

Applied Geomorphology: Theory and Practice. *v.5 p.423*

Applied Geophysics. *v.5 p.445*

Applied GIS and Spatial Analysis. *v.4 p.386*

Applied Linear Regression. *v.5 p.483*

Applied Linguistics as Social Science. *v.2 p.564, v.5 p.622, p.624*

Applied Mathematics: Body and Soul: Derivatives and Geometry in IR3. . . . .*v.5 p.500*

Applied Numerical Linear Algebra. *v.5 p.472*

Applied Plasticity. *v.5 p.688*

Applied Population Biology. *v.5 p.189*

Applied Population Ecology: A Supply-Demand Approach. *v.5 p.184, p.188*

Applied Population Ecology Using RAMAS Ecolab: Principles and Computer Exercises Using RAMAS EcoLab 2.0. . . . .*v.5 p.182, p.187, p.189*

▢ Applied Science & Technology Full Text. *v.5 p.406*

Applied Structural and Mechanical Vibrations: Theory Methods and Measuring Instrumentation. *v.5 p.694*

Applied Structural Steel Design. *v.5 p.696*

Applying Sociology: Making a Better World. *v.4 p.675*

Applying Sport Psychology: Four Perspectives. *v.5 p.583*

Applying Telecommunications and Technology from a Global Business Perspective. *v.4 p.420*

Appointment in Samarra. *v.2 p.106*

The Apprenticeship of Duddy Kravitz The Apprenticeship of Duddy Kravitz. *v.2 p.738*

An Approach to Community Mental Health. *v.5 p.670*

An Approach to Congreve. *v.2 p.244*

An Approach to Improving Decision Making in Wetland Restoration and Creation. *v.5 p.179*

Approaches to Academic Freedom and Related Issues. *v.4 p.298*

Approaches to Teaching Garcia Marquez's One Hundred Years of Solitude. *v.2 p.682*

Approaches to Teaching Lafayette's Princess of Cleves. *v.2 p.474*

Approaches to Teaching Melville's Moby Dick. *v.2 p.47*

Approaches to Teaching Stowe's Uncle Tom's Cabin. . .*v.2 p.51*

Approaches to Teaching the Dramas of Euripides. . . .*v.2 p.411*

Approaches to Teaching Vergil's Aeneid. *v.2 p.445, p.446*

Approaches to Teaching Wordsworth's Poetry. *v.2 p.323*

Approaches to the American Musical. *v.6 p.316*

Approaches to the Poetics of Derek Walcott. *v.2 p.770*

Approaches to the Study of Religion. *v.1 p.521*

Approaching Suharto's Indonesia from the Margins. *v.6 p.175, p.178*

Approaching the Land of Bliss: Religious Praxis in the Cult of Amitabha. *v.1 p.567*

Approaching the Millennium: Essays on Angels in America. *v.6 p.411*

Approaching the Qur'an. *v.1 p.556*

Appropriating Shakespeare: Contemporary Critical Quarrels. *v.2 p.232*

The Appropriation of Nature: Essays on Human Ecology and Social Relations. *v.4 p.29*

Approved Methods of the American Association of Cereal Chemists. *v.5 p.33*

April Blood: Florence and the Plot Against the Medici. *v.3 p.200*

Aprismo: The Ideas and Doctrines of Victor Raul Haya de la Torre. *v.3 p.328*

Apropos of Lady Chatterley's Lover. *v.2 p.362*

Apuleius: Cupid and Psyche. *v.2 p.428*

Apuleius: Rhetorical Works. *v.2 p.428*

Aquaculture: Farming Aquatic Animals and Plants. . . .*v.5 p.32*

Aquaculture: Principles and Practices. *v.5 p.32*

▢ AquaNIC: The Aquaculture Network Information Center. *v.5 p.32*

The Aquarium Encyclopedia. *v.5 p.56*

Aquariums of North America: A Guidebook to Appreciating North America's Aquatic Treasures. *v.5 p.83*

Aquariums: Windows to Nature. *v.5 p.85*

Aquatic Chemistry: Chemical Equilibria and Rates in Natural Waters. *v.5 p.313*

Aquatic Chemistry Concepts. *v.5 p.313*

Aquinas: Disputed Questions on the Virtues. *v.1 p.434*

Aquinas: God and Action. *v.1 p.638*

Aquinas: Moral, Political, and Legal Theory. *v.4 p.490*

Aquinas on Being and Essence: A Translation and Interpretation. *v.1 p.638*

Aquinas: Political Writings. *v.1 p.433, p.434, p.490, p.491, v.4 p.490*

Aquinas: Summa of Theology, Questions on
God. *v.1 p.434, p.575, p.595*

Aquinas: Summa Theologiae, Questions on God. . . .*v.1 p.434*

Aquinas's Shorter Summa: St. Thomas's Own Concise Version
of His Summa Theologica. *v.3 p.56*

Aquinas. *v.1 p.435*

The Arab Awakening: The Story of the Arab National
Movement. *v.6 p.582*

The Arab Conquest of Egypt and the Last Thirty Years of the
Roman Dominion. *v.6 p.635*

Arab Conquest of Spain: 710-797. . . . . .*v.3 p.237, v.6 p.562*

Arab Historians of the Crusades. *v.3 p.63, v.6 p.609*

Arab Human Development Report 2004: Towards Freedom in
the Arab World. *v.4 p.615*

The Arab Kingdom and Its Fall. *v.6 p.589*

The Arab Legion, 1923-1957. . . . .*v.6 p.621*

Arab Mass Media: Newspapers, Radio, and Television in Arab
Politics. *v.6 p.583*

Arab National Communism in the Jewish State. . . .*v.6 p.614*

Arab Nationalism: A Critical Enquiry. *v.6 p.583*

Arab Nationalism: A History:Nation and State in the Arab
World. *v.6 p.582*

Arab Nationalism in the Twentieth Century: From Triumph to
Despair. *v.6 p.582*

The Arab Predicament: Arab Political Thought and Practice
since 1967. . . . .*v.6 p.582*

The Arab Shi'a: The Forgotten Muslims. *v.1 p.560*

Arab Society: Class, Gender, Power, and Development. *v.4 p.703*

Arab Women Novelists: The Formative Years and
Beyond. *v.6 p.481*

The Arab World: 40 Years of Change. *v.6 p.583*

☐ Arab World and Islamic Resources. *v.4 p.311*

The Arab World: Society, Culture, and State. *v.6 p.591*

The Arab World. *v.1 p.60, p.129, p.130*

The Arabesk Debate: Music and Musicians in Modern
Turkey. *v.1 p.287*

🐟 Arabesques and Geometry. *v.5 p.494*

Arabesques. *v.6 p.651*

Arabia Before Muhammad. *v.6 p.625*

Arabian Love Poems. *v.6 p.661*

Arabian Nights: The Thousand and One Nights. . . .*v.6 p.661*

Arabic Historical Thought in the Classical Period. . .*v.6 p.585*

The Arabic Language and National Identity: A Study in
Ideology. *v.6 p.655*

Arabic Language Handbook. *v.6 p.653*

The Arabic Language in America. *v.6 p.654*

The Arabic Language Today. *v.6 p.653*

The Arabic Literary Heritage: The Development of its Genres
and Criticism. *v.6 p.657*

Arabic Literature in the Post-Classical Period. *v.6 p.657*

Arabic Literature to the End of the Umayyad Period. *v.6 p.658*

Arabic Made Easy. *v.6 p.654*

Arabic Poetry: A Primer for Students. *v.6 p.657*

Arabic Short Stories. *v.6 p.660*

Arabic Thought in the Liberal Age, 1798-1939. . . .*v.6 p.593*

Arabic Through the Qur'an. *v.6 p.654*

Arabidopsis Protocols. *v.5 p.89, p.129, p.146, p.206*

The Arab-Israeli Conflict. *v.6 p.619*

Arab-Israeli Relations in World Politics. *v.6 p.618*

The Arab-Israeli Wars: War and Peace in the Middle East from
the 1948 War of Independence to the Present. . . .*v.6 p.593*

Arab-Jewish Relations, 1921-1936. . . . .*v.6 p.612*

Arabs and Berbers: From Tribe to Nation in North
Africa. *v.6 p.61, p.600*

Arabs and Young Turks: Ottomanism, Arabism, and Islamism in
the Ottoman Empire, 1908-1918. . . . .*v.6 p.593*

The Arabs in History. *v.6 p.583*

Arab-Syrian Gentleman and Warrior in the Period of the
Crusades: Memoirs of Usamah Ibn-Munqidh. . . .*v.6 p.609*

Aracoeli. *v.2 p.719*

The Aran Islands. *v.2 p.306*

Arata Isozaki: Architecture, 1960-1990. . . . . . .*v.1 p.793*

Arbitrary and Capricious: The Supreme Court, the Constitution,
and the Death Penalty. *v.4 p.471, v.6 p.268*

Arbitration and Collective Bargaining. *v.4 p.447*

El Arbol de la Ciencia. *v.2 p.656*

El Arbol de la Cruz. *v.2 p.674*

The Arbor House Treasury of Great Western Stories. . *v.2 p.27*

Arboriculture: Care of Trees, Shrubs and Vines in the
Landscapes. *v.5 p.41*

Arboriculture: Integrated Management of Landscape Trees,
Shrubs, and Vines. *v.5 p.43*

Arc de Triomphe: Roman. *v.2 p.618*

Arc of Justice: A Saga of Race, Civil Rights, and Murder in the
Jazz Age. *v.4 p.438*

The Arcades Project. *v.3 p.158, v.6 p.709*

Arcadian Adventures with the Idle Rich. *v.2 p.736*

Arcangelo Corelli: New Orpheus of Our Times. *v.1 p.182, p.319*

Arch of Triumph. *v.2 p.618*

Arch: Selected Readings. *v.4 p.199*

The Archaebacteria: Biochemistry and
Biotechnology. *v.5 p.112, p.205*

Archaelogy of the Land of the Bible. *v.1 p.617*

Archaeological Chemistry: Organic, Inorganic, and Biochemical
Analysis. *v.5 p.263*

Archaeological Encyclopedia of the Holy Land. *v.1 p.617*

☐ Archaeological Resource Guide for Europe. *v.4 p.45*

Archaeological Theory: An Introduction. *v.4 p.6*

Archaeological Theory and Scientific Practice. *v.4 p.6*

Archaeological Theory: Who Sets the Agenda? *v.4 p.6*

Archaeology and Biblical Interpretation. *v.1 p.617*

Archaeology and the New Testament. *v.1 p.626*

Archaeology and World Religion. *v.1 p.524*

Archaeology As a Process: Processualism and Its Progeny. *v.4 p.6*

Archaeology at La Isabela: America's First European
Town. *v.3 p.316, v.4 p.13*

The Archaeology of Africa. *v.4 p.8*

The Archaeology of Ancient Greece. *v.3 p.19, v.4 p.13*

The Archaeology of Ancient Israel. *v.3 p.7*

The Archaeology of Ancient Judea and Palestine. . . .*v.4 p.9*

The Archaeology of Athens. *v.3 p.17*

The Archaeology of Benin: Excavations and Other Researches in and Around Benin City, Nigeria. *v.6 p.71*

The Archaeology of Central America. *v.4 p.9, p.10*

The Archaeology of Early Historic South Asia: The Emergence of Cities and States. *v.4 p.8, v.6 p.145*

Archaeology of Early Rome and Latium. *v.3 p.24*

The Archaeology of Elam: Formation and Transformation of an Ancient Iranian State. *v.3 p.6*

Archaeology of Knowledge. *v.1 p.458*

The Archaeology of Korea. *v.4 p.9*

The Archaeology of Mainland Southeast Asia: From 10,000 B. C. to the Fall of Angkor. *v.4 p.8*

The Archaeology of Medieval England. *v.6 p.555*

The Archaeology of Mesopotamia: Theories and Approaches. *v.3 p.6*

The Archaeology of Qumran and the Dead Sea Scrolls. .*v.1 p.546*

The Archaeology of Shakespeare: The Material Legacy of Shakespeare's Theatre. *v.2 p.228*

The Archaeology of Southern Africa. *v.4 p.8*

The Archaeology of Syria: From Complex Hunter-Gatherers to Early Urban Societies (C.16,000-300 BC). *v.4 p.8*

Archaeology of the Dreamtime: The Story of Prehistoric Australia and Its People. *v.4 p.13*

Archaeology of the Land of the Bible: The Assyrian, Babylonian, and Persian Periods (782-332 B. C. E.). .*v.1 p.618*

Archaeology of the Moundville Chiefdom. *v.4 p.11*

Archaeology of the Southeastern United States: Paleoindian to World War I. *v.4 p.10*

Archaeology of the Southwest. *v.4 p.10*

The Archaeology of Time. *v.4 p.6*

Archaeology: The Key Concepts. *v.4 p.6*

Archaeology: Theories, Methods and Practice. . . .*v.4 p.5, p.6*

Archaic and Classical Greece: A Selection of Ancient Sources in Translation. *v.3 p.13*

Archaic and Classical Greek Art. *v.1 p.670*

Archaic Latin Prose. *v.2 p.424*

Archaic Roman Religion, Vol. 2. . . . .*v.1 p.532*

Archbishop Romero: Memories and Reflections. . . .*v.3 p.299*

Archetypes and Ancestors: Palaeontology in Victorian London, 1850-1875. . . . .*v.6 p.750, p.759, p.762*

Archetypes in Japanese Film: The Sociopolitical and Religious Significance of the Principal Heroes and Heroines. .*v.6 p.335*

The Archidamian War. *v.3 p.18*

Archimedes: What Did He Do Beside Cry Eureka? .*v.5 p.468*

Archimedes. *v.5 p.465*

Archipelago: Portraits of Life in the World's Most Remote Island Sanctuary. *v.5 p.358, p.359*

The Architect of Genocide: Himmler and the Final Solution. *v.3 p.83*

The Architects and the City: Holabird and Roche of Chicago, 1880-1918. . . . .*v.1 p.792*

The Architect's Handbook of Professional Practice. .*v.1 p.796*

Architects of Political Change: Constitutional Quandaries and Social Choice Theory. *v.4 p.484, p.769*

Architects of the American Century: Individuals and Institutions in Twentieth-Century U.S. Foreign Policymaking. .*v.3 p.454*

Architectural Anthropology. *v.4 p.25*

Architectural Glass Art: Form and Technique in Contemporary Glass. *v.1 p.810, p.811*

Architectural Graphic Standards. *v.1 p.785*

Architectural Lighting Design. *v.1 p.803*

Architectural Principles in the Age of Humanism. . .*v.1 p.788*

The Architectural Theory of Viollet-le-Duc: Readings and Commentaries. *v.1 p.704, p.788*

Architecture after Modernism. *v.1 p.786*

Architecture and Art of the Deccan Sultanates. . . .*v.1 p.691*

Architecture and Arts 1900-2004: A Century of Creative Projects in Building, Design, Cinema, Painting, Photography, Sculpture. *v.1 p.712*

▢ Architecture and Building. *v.1 p.783*

Architecture and Feminism: Yale Publications on Architecture. *v.6 p.472*

Architecture and Ideology in Early Medieval Spain. .*v.3 p.236*

Architecture and Landscape: The Design Experiment of the Great European Gardens and Landscapes. *v.1 p.820*

Architecture and Planning of Graham, Anderson, Probst and White, 1912-1936: Transforming Tradition. . . .*v.1 p.792*

Architecture and Town Planning in Colonial North America. *v.6 p.713*

Architecture: From Prehistory to Postmodernism. . .*v.1 p.785*

Architecture in Britain: The Middle Ages. *v.6 p.556*

Architecture in France, 1800-1900. . . . .*v.1 p.790*

Architecture in France in the Eighteenth Century. .*v.1 p.676, p.689*

Architecture in Italy, 1400-1500. . . . .*v.1 p.786*

Architecture in Italy, 1500-1600. . . . .*v.1 p.787*

Architecture in the Age of Stalin: Culture Two. . . .*v.1 p.787*

Architecture in the Scandinavian Countries. *v.1 p.789*

Architecture in the United States, 1800-1850. . . .*v.1 p.790*

Architecture in the United States. *v.1 p.791*

Architecture: Nineteenth and Twentieth Centuries. . .*v.1 p.786*

The Architecture of Conquest: Building in the Viceroyalty of Peru, 1535-1635. . . . .*v.3 p.263*

Architecture of Fear. *v.6 p.727*

The Architecture of Global Governance: An Introduction to the Study of International Organizations. *v.4 p.629*

The Architecture of Landscape, 1940-1960. . . . . .*v.1 p.815*

Architecture of Mughal India. *v.1 p.788*

The Architecture of Philip Johnson. *v.1 p.793*

The Architecture of Prague and Bohemia. . .*v.3 p.190, p.191*

The Architecture of Reason: The Structure and Substance of Rationality. *v.1 p.513*

Architecture of Sports Facilities. *v.4 p.880, p.882*

Architecture of Thailand: A Guide to Traditional and Contemporary Forms. *v.1 p.791*

The Architecture of the 18th Century. *v.1 p.787*

Architecture of Yoshio Taniguchi. *v.1 p.795*

Architecture, Power, and National Identity. *v.6 p.726*

Architecture Sourcebook: A Guide to Resources on the History and Practice of Architecture. *v.1 p.783*

Architecture.com. *v.1 p.782*

An Archive of Famous Organic Chemists. *v.5 p.291*

Archives of the Universe: A Treasury of Astronomy's Historic
    Works of Discovery. *v.5 p.61*

Arctic and Alpine Biodiversity: Patterns, Causes, and Ecosystem
    Consequences. *v.5 p.167, p.168, p.175, p.238*

Arctic Climate Impact Assessment - Scientific Report. *v.4 p.393*

Arctic Dreams: Imagination and Desire in a Northern
    Landscape. *v.5 p.238*

The Arctic Grail: The Quest for the Northwest Passage and the
    North Pole, 1818-1909. . . . .*v.3 p.534, p.535*

Arctic National Wildlife Refuge: Seasons of Life and
    Land. *v.5 p.82*

Arctic National Wildlife Refuge. *v.5 p.83*

The Arctic Ocean Region. *v.5 p.434*

Arctic Revolution: A Political and Social History of the
    Northwest Territories, 1935-1993. . . . . *v.3 p.547*

Arctic Wilderness: The 5th World Wilderness
    Congress. *v.5 p.176, p.238*

The Arctic. *v.5 p.238*

The Arden Dictionary of Shakespeare Quotations. . . *v.2 p.226*

The Arden Shakespeare Complete Works. . . . *v.1 p.76, p.103*

The Ardis Anthology of Russian Futurism. *v.2 p.794*

The Ardis Anthology of Russian Romanticism. . . . *v.2 p.795*

Are Cops Racist?: How the War Against the Police Harms Black
    Americans. *v.6 p.264*

Are the World's Coral Reefs Threatened? *v.4 p.392*

Are We Still a Nation at Risk Two Decades Later? . *v.4 p.322*

Area Studies and Social Science: Strategies for Understanding
    Middle East Politics. *v.6 p.595*

The Arena of Masculinity: Sports, Homosexuality, and the
    Meaning of Sex. *v.4 p.839, v.6 p.384*

Arete: Greek Sports from Ancient Sources. *v.3 p.14*

Aretha Franklin: The Queen of Soul. . *v.1 p.265, p.324, p.325*

Aretino: Selected Letters. *v.2 p.707*

Aretino's Dialogues. *v.2 p.707*

Aretino's Satyr: Sexuality, Satire, and Self-Projection in
    Sixteenth-Century Literature and Art. *v.2 p.707*

Argentina, 1943-1987: The National Revolution and
    Resistance. *v.3 p.348*

Argentina and the United States: A Conflicted
    Relationship. *v.3 p.393*

Argentina, Fifteen-Sixteen to Nineteen Eighty-Two: From
    Spanish Colonization to the Falklands War. . . . *v.3 p.346*

The Argentine Labor Movement, 1930-1945: A Study in the
    Origins of Peronism. *v.3 p.349*

The Argentine Right: Its History and Intellectual Origins, 1910
    to the Present. *v.3 p.348*

The Argentine Tango as Social History, 1880-1955: The Soul of
    the People. *v.3 p.266*

The Argonautica of Apollonius. *v.2 p.406*

Argonautica. *v.2 p.406*

The Argonautika: The Story of Jason and the Quest for the
    Golden Fleece. *v.2 p.406*

Argonauts of the Western Pacific: An Account of Native
    Enterprise and Adventure in the Archipelagoes of
    Melanesian New Guinea. *v.1 p.17*

Argonauts of the Western Pacific. *v.4 p.28*

Argos and the Argolid. *v.3 p.19*

Arguing for Socialism. *v.4 p.506, p.507*

Arguing Revolution: The Intellectual Left in Post-War
    France. *v.3 p.157, p.158*

Arguing with the Crocodile: Gender and Class in
    Bangladesh. *v.4 p.31*

The Argument of "Ulysses". *v.2 p.360*

Arguments of Augustan Wit. *v.2 p.195*

Ariadne's Thread: Story Lines. *v.2 p.164*

The Arid Lands. *v.6 p.294*

Arid Zone Geomorphology: Process, Form and Change in
    Drylands. *v.5 p.424*

Ariel or the Life of Shelley. *v.2 p.311*

Ariel's Gift: Ted Hughes, Sylvia Plath, and the Story of the
    Birthday Letters. *v.2 p.353*

Ariel. *v.2 p.153, p.687*

Ariosto Today: Contemporary Perspectives. *v.2 p.707*

Arise, Arise. *v.2 p.139*

Aristide Maillol. *v.1 p.780*

Aristocracy and People: Britain, 1815-1865. . *v.3 p.111, p.130*

Aristocratic Century: The Peerage of Eighteenth-Century
    England. *v.3 p.127*

Aristocratic Government in the Age of Reform: Whigs and
    Liberals, 1830-1852. . . . . *v.3 p.113, p.131*

Aristophanes: Plays One. *v.1 p.70, p.89*

Aristophanes: Plays Two. *v.1 p.70, p.89*

Aristophanic Comedy. *v.2 p.423*

Aristotle and the Renaissance. *v.3 p.71*

Aristotle: De Anima. *v.1 p.427*

Aristotle: Fundamentals of the History of His
    Development. *v.1 p.426, v.2 p.408*

Aristotle on Comedy: Towards a Reconstruction of "Poetics
    II". *v.1 p.90*

Aristotle on Poetics. *v.1 p.56, p.70, p.88, p.89*

Aristotle on Teaching. *v.4 p.345*

Aristotle on the Necessity of Public Education. . . . *v.4 p.341*

Aristotle: Politics. *v.4 p.488*

Aristotle: The Desire to Understand. *v.1 p.426*

Aristotle the Philosopher. *v.1 p.425, p.426*

Aristotle Transformed: The Ancient Commentators and Their
    Influence. *v.1 p.427*

Aristotle's Ethics. *v.1 p.426*

Aristotle's Logic of Education. *v.4 p.340*

Aristotle's Nicomachean Ethics: An Introduction. . . *v.1 p.427*

Aristotle's Nicomachean Ethics. *v.1 p.426*

Aristotle's Philosophy of Biology: Studies in the Origins of Life
    Science. *v.5 p.80*

Aristotle's Physics: A Collection of Essays. *v.5 p.399*

Aristotle's Physics and Its Medieval Varieties. . . . *v.5 p.399*

Aristotle's Politics: A Critical Reader. *v.4 p.488*

Aristotle. *v.1 p.427, v.2 p.408, v.4 p.489*

Arius: Heresy and Tradition. *v.1 p.647*

Arizona: A History. *v.3 p.528*

Arizona: A State Guide. *v.3 p.528*

Arizona-Sonora Desert Museum Book of
Answers. *v.5 p.234, p.235, p.240*

The Ark in the Park: The Story of Lincoln Park Zoo. . .*v.5 p.85*

Arkansas, 1800-1860: Remote and Restless. *v.3 p.510*

Arkansas: A Narrative History. *v.3 p.511*

Arkansas: A People and Their Reputation. *v.3 p.511*

Arkansas and the New South, 1874-1929. . . . . . .*v.3 p.511*

Arkansas in Modern America, 1930-1999. . . . . .*v.3 p.510*

Arkansas. *v.3 p.510*

Arkham's Masters of Horror: A 60th Anniversary Anthology
Retrospective of the First 30 Years of Arkham House. *v.2 p.27*

Armadale. *v.2 p.281*

The Armada. *v.3 p.91, p.100*

Armageddon: The Battle for Germany,
1944-1945. . . . .*v.3 p.175, v.4 p.647*

Armaments and the Coming of War: Europe, 1904-1914. .*v.3 p.80*

Der Arme Heinrich. *v.2 p.595*

Armed and Dangerous: Memoirs of a Chicago
Policewoman. *v.6 p.259*

The Armed Forces and Democracy in Latin America. .*v.3 p.274*

Armed Martial Arts of Japan: Swordsmanship and
Archery. *v.4 p.863*

The Armed Nation: The Brazilian Corporate Mystique. .*v.3 p.274*

Armed Robbers in Action: Stickups and Street Culture. *v.6 p.253*

Armed Struggle and the Search for State: The Palestinian
National Movement, 1949-1993. . . . .*v.6 p.620*

The Armed Vision: A Study in the Methods of Modern Literary
Criticism. *v.2 p.575*

Armenia: Portraits of Survival and Hope. *v.6 p.633*

Armenian Communities in Syria Under Ottoman
Dominion. *v.6 p.608*

The Armenian Massacres in Ottoman Turkey: A Disputed
Genocide. *v.6 p.624*

Armenian People from Ancient to Modern Times, Set. *v.6 p.633*

Armies and Politics in Latin America. *v.3 p.275*

Armies and Warfare in the Middle Ages: The English
Experience. *v.3 p.68, v.6 p.567*

The Armies of the Caliphs: Military and Society in the Early
Islamic State. *v.6 p.585*

The Armies of the Night: History As a Novel - The Novel As
History. *v.2 p.99*

Armies Without Nations: Public Violence and State Formation
in Central America, 1821-1960. . . . .*v.4 p.659*

Armin Landeck: The Catalogue Raisonné of His Prints. *v.1 p.757*

Arming Against Hitler: France and the Limits of Military
Planning. *v.3 p.155*

Arminius: A Study in the Dutch Reformation. *v.1 p.583*

Arms Akimbo: African Women in Contemporary
Literature. *v.6 p.26, p.45*

Arms and Men: A Study in American Military
History. *v.3 p.383, p.453*

Arms and Politics in Latin America. *v.3 p.275*

Arms and Politics in the Dominican Republic. . . .*v.3 p.273*

Arms Control: The New Guide to Negotiations and Agreements
with New Supplement. *v.4 p.656*

Arms for the Horn: U. S. Security Policy in Ethiopia and
Somalia, 1953-1991. . . . .*v.3 p.390*

Arms Trade and Economic Development: Theory and Policy in
Offsets. *v.4 p.217, p.256, p.258*

Arms Uncontrolled. *v.4 p.655*

The Army and Politics in Argentina, 1928-1945: Yrigoyen to
Peron. *v.3 p.276, p.349,v.4 p.592*

The Army and Politics in Argentina, 1945-1962: Peron to
Frondizi. *v.3 p.276, p.349,v.4 p.592*

The Army and Politics in Argentina, 1962-1973: From
Frondizi's Fall to the Peronist
Restoration. *v.3 p.276, p.349,v.4 p.592*

The Army and Society, 1815-1914. . . . .*v.3 p.116*

An Army for Empire: The United States Army in the Spanish
American War. *v.3 p.435, p.436*

The Army in Bourbon Mexico, 1760-1810. . . . . .*v.3 p.273*

Army, Industry and Labour in Germany, 1914-1918. . .*v.3 p.164*

Army Life in a Black Regiment. *v.3 p.431*

The Army of Flanders and the Spanish Road, 1567-1659: The
Logistics of Spanish Victory and Defeat in the Low
Countries' Wars. *v.3 p.205, p.240*

The Army of the French Revolution: From Citizen-Soldiers to
Instrument of Power. *v.3 p.149*

Army Politics in Cuba, Eighteen Ninety-Eight to Nineteen
Fifty-Eight. *v.3 p.276*

Arna Bontemps-Langston Hughes Letters,
1925-1967. . . . .*v.6 p.16, p.23*

Arnheim's Principles of Athletic Training: A Competency-Based
Approach. *v.5 p.519*

Arnold and God. *v.2 p.265*

Arnold O. Beckman: One Hundred Years of Excellence. *v.5 p.262*

Arnold Schoenberg's Vienna. *v.1 p.217, p.353*

Arnold Zweig. *v.2 p.615*

Arnold. *v.2 p.265*

ℯ The Arnolfini Betrothal: Medieval Marriage and the Enigma
of Van Eyck's Double Portrait. *v.1 p.740*

Ar'n't I a Woman?: Female Slaves in the Plantation
South. *v.6 p.452*

Aromatic Chemistry. *v.5 p.292*

Aromatic Heterocyclic Chemistry. *v.5 p.298*

Around Jewish Art: Encyclopaedia of Painters, Photographers,
and Sculptors. *v.1 p.663*

Around the World in Eighty Days. *v.2 p.504*

Arranged Marriage: Stories. *v.2 p.764*

Array and Phased Array Antenna Basics. *v.5 p.729*

Arrest Discretion of Police Officers: The Impact of Varying
Organizational Structures. *v.6 p.263*

ℯ Arrest the Music!: Fela and His Rebel Art and
Politics. *v.1 p.286, p.335*

The Arrivants: A New World Trilogy. *v.2 p.767*

The Arrogance of Humanism. *v.1 p.507*

The Arrogance of Power. *v.3 p.451, p.452*

The Arrogant Capital: Washington, Wall Street, and the
Frustrations of American Politics. *v.4 p.486, p.572*

Ars Electronica 1979-2004: The Network for Art, Technology
and Society: the First 25 Years. *v.1 p.771*

Ars Rhetorica. *v.2 p.408*

Ars Sacra, 800-1200. . . . .*v.1 p.672*

Arsenic and Old Lace. *v.2 p.92*

Arsenic in the Environment: Human Health and Ecosystem
Effects, Vol. 2. . . . .*v.5 p.366*

Arshile Gorky: His Life and Work. *v.1 p.697, p.740*

Art Across America: Two Centuries of Regional Painting,
Set. *v.1 p.731*

Art across Time Combined. *v.1 p.667*

Art and Accounting. *v.1 p.826*

Art and Aesthetics in Nursing. *v.5 p.530*

Art and Agency: An Anthropological Theory. *v.4 p.26*

Art and Anger: Reading Like a Woman. *v.2 p.164*

Art and Answerability: Early Philosophical Essays. .*v.2 p.797*

Art and Anthropology: Directions in Theory and
Research. *v.4 p.25*

Art and Architecture in Canada: A Bibliography and Guide to
the Literature to 1981 (Art et Archtiecture au
Canada: Bibliographie et Guide de la Documentation
Jusqu'en 1981). *v.1 p.662*

Art and Architecture in France, 1500-1700. . . . . .*v.1 p.685*

Art and Architecture in Italy: 1250-1400. . . .*v.1 p.673, p.689*

Art and Architecture in Italy, 1600-1750. . . . . .*v.1 p.676*

Art and Architecture in Medieval France: Medieval Architecture,
Sculpture, Stained Glass, Manuscripts, the Art of the Church
Treasuries. *v.6 p.556*

The Art and Architecture of Ancient Egypt. *v.1 p.671*

Art and Architecture of Cambodia. *v.1 p.692*

The Art and Architecture of China. *v.1 p.693*

The Art and Architecture of Islam, 1250-1800. . . .*v.1 p.673*

The Art and Architecture of Japan. *v.1 p.694*

The Art and Architecture of Russia. *v.1 p.687*

The Art and Architecture of the Ancient Orient. *v.1 p.670, p.693*

Art and Architecture of the Indian Subcontinent. . .*v.1 p.692*

⬚ Art and Architecture Thesaurus Online. *v.1 p.661*

Art and Artists of Twentieth-Century China. . .*v.1 p.681, p.694*

Art and Artists. *v.1 p.665*

Art and Ceremony in Late Antiquity. *v.3 p.31*

Art and Commerce in the Dutch Golden Age: A Social History
of Seventeenth-Century Netherlandish Painting. . .*v.3 p.205*

Art and Copyright. *v.1 p.827*

The Art and Craft of Case Writing. *v.4 p.178*

The Art and Craft of Problem Solving. *v.4 p.197*

Art and Cultural Heritage: Law, Policy and Practice. .*v.1 p.827*

The Art and Culture of Early Greece: 1100-480 B. C. .*v.3 p.16*

Art and Faith in Mexico: The Nineteenth-Century Retablo
Tradition. *v.1 p.732, v.3 p.265, p.266*

The Art and Genius of Anne Hebert: Essays on Her Works:
Night and the Day Are One. *v.2 p.539*

Art and Illusion: A Study in the Psychology of Pictorial
Representation. *v.1 p.702*

Art and Money: Visual and Economic Representation. .*v.1 p.826*

Art and Patronage in Eighteenth-Century
Portugal. *v.1 p.674, p.686*

Art and Politics. *v.1 p.206, p.366*

The Art and Practice of Leadership Coaching: 50 Top Executive
Coaches Reveal Their Secrets. *v.4 p.65*

Art and Revolution in Latin America,
1910-1990. . . . .*v.1 p.684, v.3 p.266*

The Art and Science of Classroom Assessment: The Missing
Part of Pedagogy, 27. . . . .*v.4 p.285*

The Art and Science of Negotiation. *v.5 p.504*

The Art and Science of Ultra-Wideband
Antennas. *v.5 p.728, p.729*

The Art and Science of Victorian History. . . .*v.6 p.750, p.754*

Art and Social Theory: Sociological Arguments in
Aesthetics. *v.1 p.708*

Art and Socialism. *v.2 p.301*

Art and Substance in George Meredith: A Study in
Narrative. *v.2 p.300*

Art and the Industrial Revolution. . . . *v.6 p.737, p.763, p.765*

Art and the Victorian Middle Class: Money and the Making of
Cultural Identity. *v.6 p.737, p.744*

The Art and Thought of Heraclitus: A New Arrangement and
Translation of the Fragments with Literary and Philosophical
Commentary. *v.1 p.421*

Art and Visual Perception: A Psychology of the Creative
Eye. *v.5 p.618*

Art, Antiquity and the Law: Preserving Our Global Cultural
Heritage. *v.1 p.827*

Art As Politics in the Third Reich. *v.3 p.173*

Art Beyond the West: The Arts of Africa, India and Southeast
Asia, China, Japan and Korea, the Pacific, and the
Americas. *v.1 p.668*

Art Blakey: Jazz Messenger. *v.1 p.259, p.312*

Art, Cultural Heritage, and the Law. *v.1 p.827*

Art, Culture and National Identity in Fin-de-Siecle
Europe. *v.1 p.678, p.686*

Art Deco Painting. *v.1 p.728*

Art Diary International 2004-2005: The World Art
Directory. *v.1 p.667*

Art Direction for Film and Video. *v.6 p.349*

Art Forms in Nature: The Prints of Ernst Haeckel. . .*v.5 p.230*

Art from Africa: Long Steps Never Broke a
Back. *v.1 p.690, v.4 p.26*

⬚ Art Full Text. *v.1 p.661*

The Art Historian: National Traditions and Institutional
Practices. *v.1 p.701*

Art History: A Critical Introduction to Its Methods. . .*v.1 p.701*

Art History after Modernism. *v.1 p.700*

Art History in the Age of Bellori: Scholarship and Cultural
Politics in Seventeenth-Century Rome. . . .*v.1 p.674, p.685*

Art History Versus Aesthetics, Vol. 1. . . . .*v.1 p.702*

Art, Ideology, and Economics in Nazi Germany: The Reich
Chambers of Music, Theater, and the Visual Arts. .*v.3 p.174*

Art in a Season of Revolution: Painters, Artisans and Patrons in
Early America. *v.1 p.682*

Art in Action: Toward a Christian Aesthetic. *v.1 p.596*

Art in an Age of Bonapartism, 1800-1815. . . . . . .*v.1 p.707*

Art in an Age of Counterrevolution (1815-1848). . . .*v.1 p.707*

Art in an Age of Revolution, 1750-1800. . . . .*v.1 p.707, p.708*

Art in Australia: From Colonization to Postmodernism. *v.1 p.694*

Art in China. *v.1 p.693*

Art in Europe, 1700-1830. . . . .*v.1 p.686*

Art in France, 1900-1940. . . . .*v.1 p.678, p.687*

Art in Latin America: The Modern Era, 1820-1980. . . . .*v.1 p.676, p.683*

Art in Organic Synthesis. *v.5 p.293*

Art in Renaissance Italy: 1350-1500. . . . . . .*v.1 p.676, p.689*

Art in Renaissance Italy. *v.1 p.675, p.688*

Art in Rome in the Eighteenth Century. *v.1 p.674, p.685*

Art in the Making: Underdrawings in Renaissance Paintings. *v.1 p.721, p.750*

Art in the Modern Era: A Guide to Styles, Schools, and Movements. *v.1 p.663, p.677, p.678*

Art in Theory, 1648-1815: An Anthology of Changing Ideas. *v.1 p.704*

Art in Theory, 1815-1900: An Anthology of Changing Ideas. *v.1 p.704*

Art in Theory, 1900-2000: An Anthology of Changing Ideas. *v.1 p.703*

Art Incorporated: The Story of Contemporary Art. . .*v.1 p.681*

☐ Art Index Retrospective: 1929-1984. . . . . . .*v.1 p.661*

Art into Pop. *v.1 p.269*

Art Is Work: Graphic Design, Interiors, Objects and Illustration. *v.1 p.720*

Art Law Handbook: 2002 Supplement. *v.1 p.827*

Art Law Handbook. *v.1 p.827*

Art Looting and Nazi Germany: Records of the Fine Arts and Monuments Adviser, Ardelia Hall, 1945-1961. . .*v.1 p.827*

Art Marketing 101: A Handbook for the Fine Artist. . *v.1 p.826*

Art, Mind, and Education: Research from Project Zero. *v.5 p.618*

☐ Art Museum Image Gallery. *v.1 p.711*

Art Nouveau, 1890-1914. . . . .*v.1 p.799, p.800*

Art Nouveau Glass: The Gerda Koepff Collection. . .*v.1 p.811*

Art Nouveau. *v.1 p.678*

The Art of Accompaniment from a Thorough-Bass, Vol. 1. . . . .*v.1 p.182, p.399*

The Art of Accompaniment from a Thorough-Bass, Vol. 2. . . . .*v.1 p.182, p.399*

The Art of Accompanying: Master Lessons from the Repertoire. *v.1 p.399*

The Art of Adaptation: Turning Fact and Fiction into Film. *v.6 p.353*

The Art of Adolf Wolfli: St. Adolf-Giant-Creation. . .*v.1 p.724*

The Art of Aeschylus. *v.2 p.407*

Art of Africa. *v.1 p.777*

The Art of Aikido: Principles and Essential Techniques. *v.4 p.863*

The Art of Ama Ata Aidoo: Polylectics and Reading Against Neocolonialism. *v.2 p.753*

The Art of Ancient Greece: Sources and Documents. *v.1 p.670*

The Art of Art History: A Critical Anthology. *v.1 p.701*

The Art of Arts: Rediscovering Painting. *v.1 p.750*

The Art of Bacchylides. *v.2 p.409*

The Art of Being Kuna: Layers of Meaning among the Kuna of Panama. *v.3 p.305*

The Art of Beowulf. *v.2 p.204*

The Art of Biblical Narrative. *v.1 p.618*

Art of Biblical Poetry. *v.1 p.621*

The Art of Burning Bridges: A Life of John O'Hara. *v.2 p.107*

Art of Case Analysis: How to Improve Performance by Developing Better Case Analysis Skills. *v.4 p.178*

The Art of Ceramics: European Ceramic Design 1500-1830. . . . .*v.1 p.807*

The Art of Chinese Poetry. *v.6 p.210*

The Art of Colonial Latin America. . . .*v.1 p.676, p.677, p.683*

Art of Computer Programming: Fundamental Algorithms. *v.5 p.336*

The Art of Computer Programming: Seminumerical Algorithms. *v.5 p.336*

The Art of Computer Programming: Sorting and Searching. *v.5 p.336*

Art of Counterpoint: Part Three of "Le Institution Harmoniche", 1558. . . . .*v.1 p.181*

The Art of Courtly Love. *v.2 p.457*

The Art of Dance in Education. *v.1 p.48*

The Art of Dancing in Seventeenth-Century Spain: Juan de Esquivel Navarro and His World. *v.1 p.16, p.20*

The Art of Demosthenes. *v.2 p.409*

The Art of Editing: In the Age of Convergence. *v.4 p.411, p.412*

The Art of Fact: A Historical Anthology of Literary Journalism. *v.4 p.403*

The Art of Fiction. *v.2 p.578*

The Art of Film Acting: A Guide for Actors and Directors. *v.6 p.348*

The Art of Film Music. *v.1 p.255, v.6 p.351*

The Art of Flamenco. *v.1 p.21*

The Art of Frank Norris, Storyteller. *v.2 p.49*

The Art of French Fiction: Prevost, Standahl, Zola, Maupassant, Gide, Mauriac, Proust. *v.2 p.463*

The Art of Fugue: Bach Fugues for Keyboard, 1715-1750. . . . .*v.1 p.185, p.240, p.303*

The Art of Governance: Analyzing Management and Administration. *v.4 p.580*

The Art of Greece and Rome. *v.1 p.671, p.689*

The Art of History: African American Women Artists Engage the Past. *v.6 p.472*

The Art of Impressionism: Painting Technique and the Making of Modernity. *v.1 p.750*

The Art of James Joyce: Method and Design in Ulysses and Finnegans Wake. *v.2 p.359*

The Art of John Webster. *v.2 p.235*

Art of Kabuki: Five Famous Plays. *v.1 p.129, p.132, p.134, v.6 p.235*

The Art of Kate Greenaway: A Nostalgic Portrait of Childhood. *v.1 p.724*

The Art of Kula. *v.4 p.25, p.26*

The Art of la Celestina. *v.2 p.651*

The Art of Literary Research. *v.2 p.163*

Art of Love, Cosmetics, Remedies for Love, Ibis, Walnut-Tree, Sea Fishing, Consolation, Vol. 2. . . . .*v.2 p.439*

The Art of Loving. *v.5 p.611*

The Art of M&A Structuring. *v.4 p.84*

The Art of Managing Everyday Conflict: Understanding Emotions and Power Struggles. *v.5 p.647*

The Art of Margaret Atwood: Essays in Criticism. . . .*v.2 p.734*

The Art of Mathematics. *v.5 p.459*

The Art of Maurice Sendak: 1980 to the Present. . . *v.1 p.723*

The Art of MesoAmerica: From Olmec to Aztec. . . *v.1 p.670*

The Art of Mesoamerica: From Olmec to Aztec. . . *v.1 p.670*

The Art of MesoAmerica: From Olmec to Aztec. . . *v.1 p.684*

The Art of Mesoamerica: From Olmec to Aztec. . . *v.1 p.684*

The Art of Molecular Dynamics Simulation. . . *v.5 p.551, p.552*

The Art of Music Engraving and Processing; A Complete Manual, Reference and Text book on Preparing Music for Reproduction and Print. *v.1 p.387*

The Art of Native American Basketry: A Living Legacy. *v.1 p.806*

Art of Nature: Reflections on the Grand Design. . . *v.5 p.222*

The Art of Noises. *v.1 p.222, p.372*

The Art of Oscar Wilde. *v.2 p.321*

The Art of Pantomime. *v.1 p.93, p.143*

The Art of Parmigianino. *v.1 p.738*

The Art of Paul Verlaine. *v.2 p.503*

The Art of Persian Music. *v.1 p.286, p.287*

Art of Persuasion in Greece. *v.2 p.405*

The Art of Reading Scripture. *v.1 p.615*

The Art of Record: A Critical Introduction to Documentary. *v.6 p.309*

The Art of Renaissance Venice: Architecture, Sculpture, and Painting, 1460-1590. . . . . *v.1 p.675, p.687*

The Art of Revitalization: Improving Conditions in Distressed Inner City Neighborhoods. *v.6 p.727*

The Art of Rhetoric in the Roman World, 300 B.C.-A.D. 300. . . . . *v.2 p.427*

The Art of Rice: Spirit and Sustenance in Asia. . . . *v.1 p.692*

Art of Scientific Investigation. *v.5 p.408*

The Art of Southeast Asia: Cambodia, Vietnam, Thailand, Laos, Burma, Java and Bali. *v.1 p.692*

The Art of Sportscasting: How to Build a Successful Career. *v.4 p.906, p.907*

Art of Teaching Piano. *v.1 p.396*

The Art of Teaching. *v.4 p.348*

The Art of the Actor: The Essential History of Acting from Classical Times to the Present Day. *v.1 p.137, p.143, v.6 p.347, p.348*

The Art of the Aeneid. *v.2 p.445*

The Art of the American Musical: Conversations with the Creators. *v.1 p.249*

The Art of the Ancient near East. *v.3 p.4*

Art of the Andes: From Chavin to Inca. . . . *v.1 p.671, p.685*

The Art of the Basket: Traditional Basketry from Around the World. *v.1 p.806*

Art of the Byzantine Era. *v.1 p.672*

Art of the Celts: From 700 B.C. to the Celtic Revival. *v.1 p.670, p.688*

The Art of the Comic Book: An Aesthetic History. . *v.2 p.581*

The Art of the Commonplace: The Agrarian Essays of Wendell Berry. *v.5 p.3*

The Art of the Documentary: Ten Conversations with Leading Directors, Cinematographers, Editors, and Producers. *v.6 p.309*

The Art of the Dramatist: An Anthology of Writings on the Theatre. *v.2 p.378*

The Art of the Financial Statements: A Practical Handbook for Managers. *v.4 p.91*

Art of the First Cities: The Third Millennium B. C. from the Mediterranean to the Indus. *v.3 p.4*

Art of the First Cities: The Third Millennium B.C. from the Mediterranean to the Indus. *v.1 p.668, p.669*

Art of the Imperial Cholas. *v.1 p.691, p.777*

Art of the Middle Ages. *v.1 p.671, p.672, p.673*

Art of the Modern Age: Philosophy of Art from Kant to Heidegger. *v.1 p.480*

The Art of the Novel: Critical Prefaces. *v.2 p.4, p.45*

The Art of the Novel. *v.2 p.578*

The Art of the Personal Essay: An Anthology from the Classical Era to the Present. *v.2 p.584*

Art of the Postmodern Era: From the Late 1960s to the Early 1990s. *v.1 p.680*

The Art of the Pre-Raphaelites. *v.1 p.729*

The Art of the Print: Masterpieces, History, Techniques. *v.1 p.759*

The Art of the Renaissance. *v.1 p.675, p.688*

The Art of the Shoe. *v.1 p.715*

The Art of the Short Story: 52 Great Authors, Their Best Short Fiction, and Their Insights on Writing. *v.2 p.583*

The Art of the Short Story. *v.2 p.583*

The Art of the Song Recital. *v.1 p.395*

The Art of the Steal: Inside the Sotheby's-Christie's Auction House Scandal. *v.1 p.827*

The Art of the Storyboard: Storyboarding for Film, TV, and Animation. *v.6 p.350*

The Art of the Theatre. *v.1 p.105, p.143*

The Art of the Turkish Tale. *v.6 p.668*

The Art of Thomas Cole: Ambition and Imagination. *v.1 p.698*

The Art of Thomas Hardy. *v.2 p.292*

The Art of Thornton Wilder. *v.2 p.133*

Art of Throwing. *v.1 p.808*

Art of Tibet. *v.1 p.691*

The Art of Transition: Latin American Culture and the Neoliberal Crisis. *v.3 p.267*

The Art of Vase-Painting in Classical Athens. . *v.1 p.729, p.808*

The Art of Vergil: Image and Symbol in the "Aeneid". *v.2 p.446*

Art of Victorian Prose. *v.2 p.176, v.6 p.754*

The Art of Wonder: A History of Seeing. *v.1 p.668*

The Art of Worldly Wisdom. *v.2 p.650*

The Art of Writing Reasonable Organic Reaction Mechanisms. *v.5 p.295*

The Art of Writing. *v.2 p.578*

Art Past, Art Present. *v.1 p.668*

Art Performs Life: Merce Cunningham, Meredith Monk, Bill T. Jones. *v.6 p.414*

Art poétique : précédé de, Paroi ; et, suivi de, Le chant. *v.2 p.518*

Art since 1940: Strategies of Being. *v.1 p.678*

Art since 1960. . . . . *v.1 p.676*

The Art Song: A Reference and Information Guide. *v.1 p.169, p.236, p.396*

ART: The World of Art, from Aboriginal to American Pop, Renaissance Masters to Postmodernism. *v.1 p.667*

The Art Theatre: A Discussion of Its Ideals, Its Organization, and Its Promise As a Corrective for Present Evils in the Commercial Theatre. *v.1 p.81, p.95*

Art Today. *v.1 p.679*

Art under a Dictatorship. *v.3 p.172*

Art Without Boundaries: The World of Modern Dance. .*v.1 p.25*

The Art Work of the Future. *v.1 p.205, p.366*

Art Works: Money. *v.1 p.826*

Art Works: Perform. *v.1 p.679*

Art Works Place. *v.1 p.677*

Artaud for Beginners. *v.2 p.507, p.508*

El Arte Nuevo de Estudiar Comedias: Literary Theory and Spanish Golden Age Drama. *v.2 p.640*

Artemisia Gentileschi and the Authority of Art: Critical Reading and Catalogue Raisonné. *v.1 p.736*

Artemisia. *v.2 p.707, p.708*

Artful Leadership: Managing Stakeholder Problems in Nonprofit Arts Organizations. *v.1 p.825*

Arthritic Japan: The Slow Pace of Economic Reform. .*v.6 p.219*

Arthur and George. *v.2 p.332*

Arthur Harry Church: The Anatomy of Flowers. *v.5 p.155, p.156, p.232*

Arthur Hugh Clough: A Poet's Life. *v.2 p.278*

Arthur Hugh Clough: Selected Poems. *v.2 p.278*

Arthur Hughes: His Life and Works. *v.1 p.745*

Arthur Miller: A Critical Study. . . .*v.1 p.79, p.112,v.2 p.101*

Arthur Miller: Collected Plays, 1944-1961. .*v.1 p.117, v.2 p.102*

Arthur Miller: His Life and Work. *v.2 p.101*

Arthur Miller's America: Theater and Culture in a Time of Change. *v.2 p.101*

Arthur Miller. *v.2 p.102*

Arthur Rimbaud. *v.2 p.498, p.499*

Arthur Schnitzler. *v.2 p.615, p.616*

Arthur Wing Pinero. *v.2 p.302*

Arthurian Romance: A Short Introduction. *v.2 p.205*

Arthurian Romances. *v.2 p.466*

Arthur's Britain: History and Archaeology, AD 367-634. .*v.3 p.96*

Articles of Faith: The Story of British Intellectual Journalism. *v.4 p.403*

Articles on American Literature: 1900-1950. . . . . .*v.2 p.4*

Articles on American Literature: 1950-1967. . . . . .*v.2 p.4*

Articles on American Literature, 1968-1975. . . . .*v.2 p.4*

Articulate Silences: Hisaye Yamamoto, Maxine Hong Kingston, Joy Kogawa. *v.6 p.95, p.96*

The Articulated Peasant: Household Economies in the Andes. *v.3 p.326*

Articulation and Phonological Disorders. *v.5 p.665, p.673*

Articulos de Costumbres. *v.2 p.654*

Artificial Intelligence: A Modern Approach. *v.5 p.339*

Artificial Intelligence and Heuristic Methods in Bioinformatics, Vol. 183. . . . .*v.5 p.109*

Artificial Minds. *v.5 p.589*

Artisans and Cooperatives: Developing Alternative Trade for the Global Economy. *v.4 p.44*

Artist and Identity in Twentieth-Century America. . . .*v.1 p.681*

The Artist and the Garden. *v.1 p.820*

The Artist as Critic: Critical Writings of Oscar Wilde. .*v.2 p.322*

An Artist of the Floating World. *v.2 p.355*

Artistic Exchange and Cultural Translation in the Italian Renaissance City. *v.1 p.674, p.686*

An Artistic Exile: A Life of Feng Zikai (1898-1975). *v.1 p.735, v.6 p.199*

Artistic Gymnastics: A Comprehensive Guide to Performing and Teaching Skills for Beginners and Advanced Beginners. *v.4 p.797, p.862*

Artistic Theory in Italy. *v.1 p.730*

Artistic Truth: Aesthetics, Discourse and Imaginative Disclosure. *v.1 p.480*

Artists and Patrons in Colonial Latin America. . . .*v.3 p.264*

Artists and the Avant-Garde: Theatre in Paris, 1887-1900. . . . .*v.1 p.84, p.95*

Artists as Illustrators: An International Directory with Signatures and Monograms, 1800-Present. *v.1 p.663*

Artists' Books: A Critical Anthology and Sourcebook. *v.1 p.761*

Artists' Estates: Reputations in Trust. *v.1 p.827*

Artists from Latin American Cultures: A Biographical Dictionary. *v.1 p.663, p.684*

Artists in Glass: Late Twentieth Century Masters in Glass. *v.1 p.810*

Artists in the Audience: Cults, Camp, and American Film Criticism. *v.6 p.344*

Artists' Monograms and Indiscernible Signatures: An International Directory, 1800-1991. . . . . .*v.1 p.663*

The Artists of Poland: A Biographical Dictionary from the 14th Century to the Present. *v.1 p.666*

The Artists of the Ara Pacis: The Process of Hellenization in Roman Relief Sculpture. *v.1 p.775*

Artists of World War II. *v.1 p.680*

Artists' Pigments: A Handbook of Their History and Characteristics. *v.1 p.751*

The Artist's Reality: Philosophies of Art. *v.1 p.746*

Artist's Signatures and Monograms of the 19th and 20th Centuries. *v.1 p.726*

⬚ ArtLex - art dictionary. *v.1 p.661*

The Arts - Fitness Quality of Life Activities Program: Creative Ideas for Working with Older Adults in Group Settings. *v.4 p.785, p.786, p.790, p.841*

Arts Administration and Management: A Guide for Administrators and Their Staffs. *v.1 p.825*

Arts and Crafts Furniture: From Classic to Contemporary. *v.1 p.804*

The Arts and Crafts Movement in California: Living the Good Life. *v.1 p.800*

The Arts and Crafts Movement. *v.1 p.677, p.799*

The Arts at Black Mountain College. *v.1 p.682*

The Arts in Prehistoric Greece. *v.1 p.668, p.687*

Arts Management: A Guide to Finding Funds and Winning Audiences. *v.1 p.826*

Arts Management Reader. *v.1 p.825*

Arts of Africa: 7000 Years of African Art. *v.1 p.689*

The Arts of China to A.D. 900. . . . .*v.1 p.694*

The Arts of China. *v.1 p.694*

The Arts of Love: Five Studies in the Discourse of Roman Love Elegy. *v.2 p.426*

The Arts of Persia. *v.1 p.673, p.691*

Arts of Southeast Asia. *v.1 p.692*

The Arts of Spain: From Prehistory to Postmodernism. *v.1 p.688, v.3 p.236, p.237*

Arts of the Amazon. *v.1 p.683, p.684*

The Arts of the Beautiful. *v.1 p.479*

Artspeak: A Guide to Contemporary Ideas, Movements and Buzzwords, 1945 to the Present. *v.1 p.662*

☐ ARTstor. *v.1 p.711*

Arturo Islas: The Uncollected Works. *v.6 p.497*

Arturo, la Estrella Mas Brillante. *v.2 p.670*

Arturo's Island: A Novel. *v.2 p.719*

☐ Art. *v.1 p.661, p.683*

Arvo Part. *v.1 p.216, p.347*

Arya Dharm: Hindu Consciousness in Nineteenth-Century Punjab. *v.1 p.536*

Aryans and British India. *v.6 p.150*

As a Man Grows Older. *v.2 p.723, p.724*

As Eve Said to the Serpent: On Landscape, Gender, and Art. *v.1 p.707*

As for Me and My House. *v.2 p.738*

As He Saw It. *v.3 p.462*

As Her Whimsey Took Her: Critical Essays on the Work of Dorothy L. Sayers. *v.2 p.381*

As I Crossed the Bridge of Dreams: Recollections of a Woman in Eleventh-Century Japan. *v.6 p.233*

As I Saw It. *v.3 p.462*

As If Learning Mattered: Reforming Higher Education. .*v.4 p.332*

As Is. *v.6 p.378, p.379, p.412*

As It Was: An Inside View of Politics and Power in the Fifties and Sixties. *v.3 p.474*

As Nomadism Ends: The Israeli Bedouin of the Negev. .*v.6 p.596*

As Others See Chicago: Impressions of Visitors, 1673-1933. . . . .*v.3 p.516*

As Our Barrio Turns... Who the Yoke B On? *v.6 p.497*

As Sociology Meets History. *v.4 p.684*

As the Future Catches You: How Genomics and Other Forces Are Changing Your Life, Work, Health and Wealth. .*v.5 p.132*

As the Romans Did: A Sourcebook in Roman Social History. *v.3 p.24*

As Thousands Cheer: The Life of Irving Berlin. .*v.1 p.248, p.310*

As Through a Veil: Mystical Poetry in Islam. *v.6 p.663*

As We Forgive Our Debtors: Bankruptcy and Consumer Credit in America. *v.4 p.250*

As You Like It. *v.2 p.224*

Asad of Syria: The Struggle for the Middle East. . . .*v.6 p.608*

ASAE Standards: Standards, Engineering Practices and Data Adopted by the American Society of Agricultural Engineers. *v.5 p.3*

Asante in the Nineteenth Century. *v.6 p.70*

☐ ASCAP: The American Society of Composers, Authors and Publishers. *v.1 p.172, p.383*

ASCE/EWRI 45-05 (Standard Guidelines for the Design of Urban Stormwater Systems), ASCE/EWRI 46-05 (Standard Guidelines for the Installation of Urban Stormwater Systems), and ASCE/EWRI 47-05 (Standard Guidelines for the Operation and Maintenance of Urban Stormwater Systems). *v.5 p.685*

The Ascent of Man. *v.5 p.400*

The Ascent of Science. *v.5 p.391*

Asceticism and Eroticism in the Mythology of Siva. . .*v.1 p.537*

Asceticism. *v.1 p.531*

ASE Transit Bus Technician Certification H6: Electrical/Electronic Systems. *v.5 p.701*

Ashenden, or, The British Agent. *v.2 p.370*

Ashes and Diamonds. *v.2 p.787, p.789*

Ashes of Glory: Richmond at War. *v.3 p.499*

The Ashes of Gramsci. *v.2 p.721*

Ashes of Immortality: Widow-Burning in India. .*v.6 p.460, p.471*

Ashes of Izalco. *v.2 p.674*

Ashes to Ashes. *v.2 p.377*

Ashes. *v.2 p.717*

Ashford's Dictionary of Industrial Chemicals. *v.5 p.316*

Ashgate Handbook of Pesticides and Agricultural Chemicals. *v.5 p.312*

Asia in the Making of Europe: A Century of Advance: East Asia. *v.6 p.145, p.215*

Asia in the Making of Europe: A Century of Advance, South Asia. *v.6 p.145*

Asia in the Making of Europe: A Century of Advance: Trade, Missions, Literature. *v.6 p.215*

Asia in the Making of Europe: A Century of Advance. .*v.6 p.215*

Asia in the Making of Europe: A Century of Wonder: The Literary Arts. *v.6 p.145*

Asia in the Making of Europe: A Century of Wonder: The Visual Arts. *v.6 p.215*

Asia in the Making of Europe: The Century of Discovery, vol. 1. . . . .*v.6 p.145*

Asia in the Making of Europe: The Century of Discovery. *v.6 p.145*

Asia in the Making of Europe. *v.3 p.74, v.6 p.215*

Asian America: Chinese and Japanese in the United States Since 1850. . . . .*v.6 p.126, p.131*

Asian America Through the Lens: History, Representations and Identity. *v.6 p.89, p.90*

Asian American Autobiographers: A Bio-Bibliographical Critical Sourcebook. *v.6 p.86, p.93, p.94*

Asian American Children: A Historical Handbook and Guide. *v.6 p.87, p.110*

Asian American Drama: 9 Plays from the Multiethnic Landscape. *v.1 p.68, p.125, v.6 p.92, p.99*

☐ Asian American Drama. *v.6 p.85, p.90, p.98*

Asian American Dreams: The Emergence of an American People. *v.6 p.105*

The Asian American Educational Experience: A Sourcebook for Teachers and Students. *v.4 p.311, v.6 p.109*

The Asian American Encyclopedia, Set. *v.6 p.86, p.87*

Asian American Issues. *v.6 p.85*

Asian American Literature: A Brief Introduction and
  Anthology. *v.6 p.92*

Asian American Literature: An Annotated
  Bibliography. *v.6 p.86, p.90*

Asian American Literature: Reviews and Criticism of Works by
  American Writers of Asian Descent. *v.6 p.87, p.98*

The Asian American Movement: A Social
  History. *v.6 p.108, p.115*

Asian American Panethnicity: Bridging Institutions and
  Identities. *v.6 p.85, p.120, p.123*

Asian American Playwrights: A Bio-Bibliographical Critical
  Sourcebook. *v.1 p.60, p.125,v.6 p.86, p.99*

Asian American Poetry: The Next Generation. . . .*v.6 p.103*

Asian American Politics: Law, Participation, and
  Policy. *v.6 p.117, p.121*

Asian American Psychology: The Science of Lives in
  Context. *v.6 p.122*

Asian American Religions: The Making and Remaking of
  Borders and Boundaries. *v.6 p.105*

Asian American Sexualities: Dimensions of the Gay and Lesbian
  Experience. *v.6 p.92, p.112*

Asian American Short Story Writers: An A-to-Z
  Guide. *v.6 p.86, p.100*

Asian American Studies: An Annotated Bibliography and
  Research Guide. *v.6 p.86*

Asian American Women and Men: Labor, Laws and
  Love. *v.6 p.111, p.123*

Asian American Women and Men. *v.6 p.111, p.123*

Asian American X: An Intersection of Twenty-First Century
  Asian American Voices. *v.6 p.93, p.122, p.123*

Asian American Youth: Culture, Identity and
  Ethnicity. *v.6 p.85, p.110, p.123*

Asian America.Net: Ethnicity, Nationalism and
  Cyberspace. . . .*v.6 p.89, p.90, p.123, p.141, p.143, p.145*

The Asian Americans: An Interpretive History. . *v.6 p.85, p.113*

Asian Americans and Politics: Perspectives, Experiences,
  Prospects. *v.6 p.120*

Asian Americans: Comparative and Global Perspectives. .*v.6 p.85*

Asian Americans: Contemporary Trends and Issues. . .*v.6 p.85*

Asian Americans in Class: Charting the Achievement Gap
  among Korean American Youth. *v.6 p.109, p.136*

Asian Americans: Personality Patterns, Identity, and Mental
  Health. *v.6 p.122*

Asian Americans: The Movement and the
  Moment. *v.6 p.107, p.120*

Asian Americans: Vulnerable Populations, Model Interventions,
  Clarifying Agendas. *v.6 p.121, p.141*

Asian and Pacific Islander Americans: Issues and Concerns for
  Counseling and Psychotherapy. *v.6 p.122*

Asian Databook. *v.6 p.86*

Asian North American Identities: Beyond the
  Hyphen. *v.6 p.98, p.125, p.126*

The Asian Pacific American Heritage: A Companion to
  Literature and Arts. *v.6 p.86, p.96*

Asian Pacific Americans in the Workplace. *v.6 p.117*

Asian Religions in America: A Documentary History. .*v.6 p.106*

Asian Religions in Practice: An Introduction. *v.1 p.534*

Asian Theatre. *v.1 p.130*

Asian Traditions Modern Expressions: Asian American Artists
  and Abstraction, 1945-1970. . . . .*v.6 p.88*

Asian Voices: Asian and Asian American Health Educators
  Speak Out. *v.6 p.121, p.141*

Asian Voices in Christian Theology. *v.1 p.633*

Asian Voices in English. *v.2 p.759, p.760*

Asian Women Artists. *v.6 p.472*

Asian-American Education: Historical Background and Current
  Realities. *v.4 p.311, v.6 p.109*

Asian/American: Historical Crossings of a Racial
  Frontier. *v.6 p.114, p.124*

Asian-American Literature: An Anthology. *v.6 p.92*

Asian-American Literature: An Introduction to the Writings and
  Their Social Context. *v.6 p.96*

Asian-American Mental Health: Assessment Theories and
  Methods. *v.6 p.122*

Asian/Pacific Islander American Women: A Historical
  Anthology. *v.6 p.112, p.114*

Asia-Pacific Diplomacy: The Nongovernmental Approach to
  Regional Economic Cooperation. *v.4 p.640*

Asia/Pacific. *v.1 p.58, p.131*

Asia's Educational Edge: Current Achievements in Japan,
  Korea, Taiwan, China, and India. *v.4 p.334*

Asimov's Biographical Encyclopedia of Science and
  Technology: The Lives and Achievements of 1510 Great
  Scientists from Ancient Times to the Present,
  Chronologically Arranged. *v.5 p.394*

Asimov's Chronology of Science and Discovery. . . .*v.5 p.391*

Ask the Dust. *v.2 p.72*

AskART ; the American Artists Bluebook. *v.1 p.661*

Asking and Telling. *v.6 p.411*

Asking Questions: The Definitive Guide to Questionnaire
  Design — for Market Research, Political Polls,
  and Social and Health Questionnaires. *v.4 p.137*

ASL Arts & Sciences Libraries: Biodiversity. . . .*v.5 p.144*

ASL Arts & Sciences Libraries Genomics Research and
  Bioinformatics. *v.5 p.144*

ASM Desk Editions: Metals Handbook; Engineered Materials
  Handbook. *v.5 p.730*

ASM Engineered Materials Handbook: Desk Edition. .*v.5 p.688*

ASM Handbook. *v.5 p.690*

ASM Materials Engineering Dictionary. . . .*v.5 p.731, p.732*

ASM Metals Reference Book. *v.5 p.687, p.731*

Asoka and the Decline of the Mauryas: With a New Afterword
  Bibliography and Index. *v.6 p.155*

Gli Asolani. *v.2 p.708*

Aspects of Development and Underdevelopment. . . .*v.4 p.260*

Aspects of Early Visnuism. *v.1 p.536*

Aspects of Genre in Late Medieval French Drama. . .*v.2 p.462*

Aspects of Modern Poetry. *v.2 p.382*

Aspects of Multivariate Statistical Theory. . . .*v.5 p.482, p.483*

Aspects of Organic Chemistry: Structure. *v.5 p.293*

Aspects of Personal Faith: Personality and Religion in Western and Eastern Traditions. *v.5 p.632*

Aspects of Scientific Explanation. *v.1 p.499, v.5 p.402*

Aspects of Subjectivity: Society and Individuality from the Middle Ages to Shakespeare and Milton. *v.6 p.576*

Aspects of the Drama: A Handbook. *v.1 p.57, p.58*

Aspects of the Novel. *v.2 p.579*

Aspects of Twentieth-Century Theatre in French. .*v.1 p.105, p.127*

Aspirin Age 1919-1941. . . . .*v.3 p.368*

The Asrama System: The History and Hermeneutics of a Religious Institution. *v.1 p.537*

The Assassination of Gaitan: Public Life and Urban Violence in Columbia. *v.3 p.357*

Assata: An Autobiography. *v.6 p.19, p.46*

Assault on Paradise. *v.2 p.676*

Assault on Society: Satirical Literature to Film. . . .*v.6 p.313*

The Assault. *v.2 p.623, p.670*

Assembling for Development: The Maquila Industry in Mexico and the United States. *v.4 p.759*

Assembling the Absurd: Sculpture of George Fullard. .*v.1 p.782*

Assembling the Tree of Life. *v.5 p.191, p.198, p.201*

Assessing and Managing Earthquake Risk: Geo-Scientific and Engineering Knowledge for Earthquake Risk Mitigation: Developments, Tools, Techniques. .*v.5 p.695, p.696*

Assessing and Screening Preschoolers: Psychological and Educational Dimensions. *v.5 p.572*

Assessing Attention-Deficit/Hyperactivity Disorder. . .*v.4 p.318*

Assessing Career Development. *v.5 p.577*

Assessing Democracy Assistance: The Case of Romania. *v.4 p.584, p.585, p.600*

Assessing Rational Expectations: Eductive Stability in Economics. *v.4 p.201, p.250*

Assessing Site Significance: A Guide for Archaeologists and Historians. *v.4 p.7*

Assessing Student Performance: Exploring the Purpose and Limits of Testing. *v.4 p.287*

Assessing Students in Groups: Promoting Group Responsibility and Individual Accountability. *v.4 p.286*

Assessing the Business Environment: Guidelines for Strategists. *v.4 p.137*

☑ Assessment and Culture: Psychological Tests with Minority Populations. *v.5 p.600*

Assessment in the Block: The Link to Instruction. . . .*v.4 p.288*

Assessment: Issues and Challenges for the Millennium. .*v.5 p.602*

Assessment of Childhood Disorders. *v.5 p.663*

Assessment of Children: Behavioral and Clinical Applications. *v.5 p.603*

Assessment of Children: Cognitive Applications. .*v.5 p.602, p.603*

Assessment Strategies for Elementary Physical Education. *v.4 p.798*

Asset Accumulation and Economic Activity: Reflections on Contemporary Macroeconomic Theory. *v.4 p.239*

Assèze l'Africaine : roman. *v.2 p.544*

Assia Djebar : écrire, transgresser, résister. *v.2 p.544*

Assimilating Asians: Gendered Strategies of Authorship in Asian America. *v.6 p.96*

Assimilation and Association in French Colonial Theory, 1890-1914. . . . .*v.4 p.584*

Assimilation and Community: The Jews in Nineteenth-Century Europe. *v.3 p.59*

☑ Assimilation's Agent: My Life As a Superintendent in the Indian Boarding School System. . . .*v.4 p.755, v.6 p.680*

Associated Press Broadcast News Handbook. *v.4 p.414*

Associated Press Reporting Handbook. *v.4 p.414*

The Associated Press Stylebook: And Briefing on Media Law. *v.4 p.412*

☐ Association for Behavioral and Cognitive Therapies. .*v.5 p.666*

☐ Association for Computing Machinery. *v.5 p.344*

☐ Association for Consumer Research. *v.5 p.604*

☐ Association for Psychological Science (APS). . . .*v.5 p.593*

L' Assommoir. *v.2 p.505*

Astaire and Rogers. *v.6 p.316*

Astaire Dancing: The Musical Films. *v.1 p.37, p.46*

ASTD 2004 Competency Study: Mapping the Future: New Workplace Learning and Performance Competencies. *v.4 p.304*

The ASTD e-Learning Handbook: Best Practices, Strategies and Case Studies for an Emerging Field. *v.4 p.305*

The ASTD Training and Development Handbook: A Guide to Human Resource Development. *v.4 p.304*

✿ ASTM International Standards on Sustainability in Buildings. *v.5 p.684*

ASTM Standards on Building Economics. *v.5 p.685*

ASTM Standards Related to Environmental Site Characterization. *v.5 p.685*

Astrobiology: Future Perspectives. *v.5 p.242, p.243*

Astrobiology: Multi Disciplinary Approach. . . .*v.5 p.74, p.243*

Astrobiology, the Origin of Life, and the Death of Darwinism: Evolutionary Metamorphosis. *v.5 p.203, p.243*

Astrobiology: The Quest for the Conditions of Life. . .*v.5 p.243*

☐ Astrogeology Research Program. *v.5 p.435*

Astrology: A History. *v.5 p.62*

Astronomical Algorithms. *v.5 p.64*

Astronomical Almanac for the Year 2006 and Its Companion, the Astronomical Almanac Online: Data for Astronomy, Space Sciences, Geodesy, Surveying, Navigation and Other Applications. *v.5 p.63*

☐ Astronomical Applications Department. U.S. Naval Observatory. *v.5 p.63*

Astronomical Equipment for Amateurs. *v.5 p.65*

Astronomical Optics. *v.5 p.66*

The Astronomical Revolution: Copernicus - Kepler - Borelli. *v.3 p.47*

Astronomy Methods: A Physical Approach to Astronomical Observations. *v.5 p.65*

Astrophysical Concepts. *v.5 p.66*

The Astrophysical Context of Life. *v.5 p.243*

Astrophysical Formulae: Volume I: Radiation, Gas Processes and High Energy Astrophysics Volume II: Space, Time, Matter and Cosmology. *v.5 p.63*

Astrophysical Techniques. *v.5 p.65*

Astrophysics and Twentieth-Century Astronomy to 1950. .*v.5 p.61*

Title Index

Astrophysics E-Print Archive. *v.5 p.64*

Astrophysics of Gaseous Nebulae and Active Galactic
Nuclei. *v.5 p.67*

Astropolitik: Classical Geopolitics in the Space Age. *v.5 p.719*

Astrostatistics. *v.5 p.64*

The Asylum Dance. *v.2 p.331*

Asymmetric Catalysis in Organic Synthesis. *v.5 p.295*

The Asymmetric Society. *v.4 p.716*

Asymmetric Synthesis, Vol. 1: Analytical Methods. . *v.5 p.295*

Asymmetric Synthesis. *v.5 p.294, p.295*

Asymptotic Giant Branch Stars. *v.5 p.70*

Asymptotic Methods for Elastic Structures: Proceedings:
International Conference on Asymptotic Methods
for Elastic Structures (1993: Lisbon, Portugal). . . *v.5 p.693*

Asymptotic Theory for Econometricians. *v.4 p.205*

At America's Gates: Chinese Immigration During the Exclusion
Era, 1882-1943. . . . .*v.6 p.119, p.127*

At Home in Diaspora: South Asian Scholars and the
West. *v.6 p.145*

At Home in the Street: Street Children of Northeast
Brazil. *v.3 p.279*

At Home with the Marquis de Sade. *v.2 p.484*

At Lincoln's Side: John Hay's Civil War Correspondence and
Selected Writings. *v.3 p.434*

At Play in the Fields of the Lord. *v.2 p.149*

At Swim, Two Boys. *v.6 p.398*

At Swim-Two-Birds. *v.2 p.373*

At the Back of the North Wind. *v.2 p.299*

At the Crossroads: Indians and Empires on a Mid-Atlantic
Frontier, 1700-1763. . . . .*v.6 p.686*

At the Edge of Empire: The Terek Cossacks and the North
Caucasus Frontier, 1700-1860. . . . .*v.3 p.212*

At the Edge of the State: Indigenous Peoples and
Self-Determination. *v.4 p.33*

At the Elbow of Another: Learning to Teach by
Coteaching. *v.4 p.277*

At the Fringes of Science: Science, Science Contested and
Pseudo-Science. *v.5 p.388*

At the Highest Levels: The Inside Story of the End of the Cold
War. *v.4 p.643, p.645*

At the Origins of Mathematical Economics: The Contribution of
A. N. Isnard. *v.4 p.205*

At the Pleasure of the Mayor. *v.6 p.724*

At the Royal Court: 25 Years of the English Stage
Company. *v.1 p.98, p.143, p.149, p.154*

At the South-East Asian Table. *v.6 p.165*

At the Vanishing Point. *v.1 p.39*

At Weddings and Wakes. *v.2 p.150*

At Work with Grotowski on Physical
Actions. *v.1 p.110, p.145, p.153*

Atala and René. *v.2 p.488*

Ataturk: A Biography of Mustafa Kemal, Father of Modern
Turkey. *v.6 p.624*

Ataturk: The Biography of the Founder of Modern
Turkey. *v.6 p.624*

Ate It Anyway: Stories. *v.2 p.160*

The Athabaskan Languages: Perspectives on a Native American
Language Family. *v.6 p.690*

Athananius. *v.1 p.612*

Athanasius and Constantius: Theology and Politics in the
Constantinian Empire. *v.3 p.29, p.30*

Athanasius: The Life of Antony and the Letter to
Marcellinus. *v.1 p.591*

Atheism: A Philosophical Justification. *v.1 p.545*

Atheism from the Reformation to the Enlightenment. *v.1 p.545*

Atheist's Mass. *v.2 p.485*

Athenaeum. *v.6 p.741, p.751, p.752*

Athenagoras, Embassy for the Christians, the Resurrection of the
Dead. *v.1 p.590, p.591*

The Athenian Acropolis: History, Mythology, and Archaeology
from the Neolithic Era to the Present. *v.3 p.18*

The Athenian Agora: Excavations In The Heart of Classical
Athens. *v.3 p.17*

Athenian Democracy in the Age of Demosthenes: Structure,
Principles and Ideology. *v.4 p.500*

Athenian Democracy. *v.3 p.19, v.4 p.500*

Athenian Economy and Society: A Banking
Perspective. *v.3 p.13, p.14*

The Athenian Empire. *v.3 p.18*

Athenian Identity and Civic Ideology. *v.3 p.17*

Athenian Myths and Institutions: Words in Action. . .*v.3 p.15*

The Athenian Nation. *v.3 p.17*

Athenian Politics C. 800-500 B. C.: A Sourcebook. . .*v.3 p.13*

Athenian Red Figure Vases: The Classical
Period. *v.1 p.669, p.807*

The Athenian Revolution: Essays on Ancient Greek Democracy
and Political Theory. *v.3 p.18*

Athens: A Cultural and Literary History. . .*v.3 p.196, v.6 p.715*

Athens: A Portrait of the City in Its Golden Age. . . .*v.3 p.18*

Athens after the Peloponnesian War: Class, Faction and Policy,
403-386 B.C. *v.3 p.20*

Athens and Persia in the Fifth Century BC: A Study in Cultural
Receptivity. *v.3 p.18*

Athens from Alexander to Antony. *v.3 p.21*

Athens: From the Classical Period to the Present Day (5th
Century B. C. -A. D. 2000). *v.3 p.196*

Athlete's Guide to Career Planning. *v.4 p.904*

The Athletic Crusade: Sport and American Cultural
Imperialism. *v.3 p.319, p.320*

Athletic Intruders: Ethnographic Research on Women, Culture,
and Exercise. *v.4 p.814, p.834, p.835*

Athletic Training and Sports Medicine. *v.4 p.829*

The Athletic Woman's Survival Guide. *v.4 p.825*

Athletics and Academe: An Anatomy of Abuses and a
Prescription for Reform. *v.4 p.821*

Athletries: The Untold History of Ancient Greek Women
Athletes. *v.4 p.809, p.838*

ATLA Religion Database. *v.1 p.521*

Atlantic Canada: A Concise History. *v.3 p.543*

The Atlantic Frontier: Colonial American Civilization,
1607-1763. . . . .*v.3 p.407*

The Atlantic Migration, 1607-1860. . . . .*v.4 p.667*

The Atlantic Provinces in Confederation. *v.3 p.543*

The Atlantic Region to Confederation: A History. .*v.3 p.542, p.543*

Atlas and Dissection Guide for Comparative Anatomy. .*v.5 p.90*

Atlas and Glossary of Primary Sedimentary Structures. .*v.5 p.439*

Atlas of Allergic Diseases. *v.5 p.517*

Atlas of American Agriculture: The American Cornucopia. .*v.5 p.5*

Atlas of American History. *v.4 p.380*

Atlas of American Indian Affairs. *v.6 p.683, p.692*

Atlas of Ancient America. *v.4 p.10*

Atlas of Clinical Gross Anatomy. *v.5 p.95, p.158, p.214*

Atlas of Communism. *v.4 p.506*

Atlas of Early American History: The Revolutionary Era,
    1760-1790. . . . .*v.3 p.407*

Atlas of Egyptian Art. *v.1 p.669, p.690*

Atlas of Exploration. *v.4 p.379, p.381*

Atlas of Human Anatomy. *v.5 p.96, p.158*

Atlas of Human Chromosome Heteromorphisms. . . .*v.5 p.138*

Atlas of Igneous Rocks and Their Textures. *v.5 p.437*

An Atlas of Interpersonal Situations. *v.5 p.648*

Atlas of Invertebrate Anatomy. *v.5 p.95, p.156*

Atlas of Irish History. *v.3 p.134, p.135, p.140*

Atlas of Jewish History. *v.4 p.381*

The Atlas of Jewish History. *v.6 p.608*

Atlas of Medieval Jewish History. *v.6 p.573*

Atlas of Metamorphic Rocks and Their Textures. . . .*v.5 p.440*

Atlas of Microscopy of Medicinal Plants, Culinary Herbs, and
    Spices. *v.5 p.96, p.155*

The Atlas of Near Infrared Spectra. *v.5 p.270*

Atlas of Nearby Galaxies. *v.5 p.64*

The Atlas of North American Exploration: From the Norse
    Voyages to the Race to the Pole. *v.4 p.381*

Atlas of North America. *v.4 p.379*

Atlas of Poverty in America. *v.4 p.398*

Atlas of Rock-Forming Minerals in Thin Section. . . .*v.5 p.435*

Atlas of Sedimentary Rocks under the Microscope. . .*v.5 p.438*

Atlas of Sexually Transmitted Diseases and
    AIDS. *v.5 p.515, p.516*

Atlas of Spectral Data and Physical Constants for Organic
    Compounds. *v.5 p.297*

The Atlas of States: Global Change, 1900-2000. . . .*v.4 p.381*

Atlas of Stereochemistry: Absolute Configurations of Organic
    Molecules, I. *v.5 p.298*

Atlas of Stereochemistry: Absolute Configurations of Organic
    Molecules. *v.5 p.297*

Atlas of the Civil War, Month by Month: Major Battles and
    Troop Movements. *v.3 p.424*

Atlas of the Civil War. *v.4 p.381*

An Atlas of the Human Embryo and Fetus: A Photographic
    Review of Human Prenatal Development. *v.5 p.162*

Atlas of the Islamic World since 1500. . . . .*v.6 p.582*

Atlas of the Medieval World. *v.4 p.381*

Atlas of the Middle East. *v.6 p.593, p.594*

Atlas of the Moon. *v.5 p.64*

Atlas of the Ocean: The Deep Frontier. *v.5 p.428*

Atlas of the Pacific Northwest. *v.5 p.38*

Atlas of the World's Deserts. *v.4 p.381*

Atlas of the World's Religions. *v.1 p.525*

Atlas of the World. *v.4 p.380*

The Atlas of U. S. and Canadian Environmental
    History. *v.5 p.5, p.28, p.353*

Atlas of United States Environmental Issues. *v.4 p.159*

Atlas of Westward Expansion. *v.4 p.381*

An Atlas of World Affairs. *v.4 p.381*

Atlas of World Art. *v.1 p.665*

Atlas Shrugged: Centennial Edition. *v.2 p.113*

Atmospheric Chemistry and Physics: From Air Pollution to
    Climate Change. *v.5 p.313, p.363, p.371, p.427, p.705*

The Atmospheric Environment: Effects of Human
    Activity. *v.5 p.426*

The Atom and Its Nucleus. *v.5 p.554*

Atomic and Molecular Orbitals. *v.5 p.280*

Atomic Bomb Cinema: Apocalyptic Imagination on
    Film. *v.6 p.320*

Atomic Diplomacy: Hiroshima and Potsdam: The Use of the
    Atomic Bomb and the American Confrontation with Soviet
    Power. *v.3 p.464*

Atomic Physics: An Exploration through Problems and
    Solutions. *v.5 p.554*

Atomic Physics. *v.5 p.554*

Atomic Radii Tables. *v.5 p.280*

The Atomic Scientists: A Biographical History. *v.3 p.49*

Atomic Spectra and Atomic Structure. *v.5 p.562*

Atomic Theory and the Description of Nature. *v.5 p.554*

The Atomists: Leucippus and Democritus: Fragments. .*v.1 p.422*

Atoms in the Family: My Life with Enrico Fermi. . .*v.5 p.542*

The Atoms of Language: The Mind's Hidden Rules of
    Grammar. *v.2 p.559*

The Atonal Music of Anton Webern. *v.1 p.213, p.367*

The Atonal Music of Arnold Schoenberg,
    1908-1923. . . . .*v.1 p.224, p.353*

Atonement: A Novel. *v.2 p.367, p.368*

Atonement and Forgiveness: A New Model for Black
    Reparations. *v.6 p.22, p.36*

Attachment Disorganization. *v.5 p.669*

Attachment, Evolution, and the Psychology of Religion. .*v.5 p.634*

Attachment from Infancy to Adulthood: The Major Longitudinal
    Studies. *v.5 p.627, p.631*

Attack of the Leading Ladies: Gender, Sexuality and
    Spectatorship in Classic Horror Cinema. *v.6 p.317*

The Attack on the Mill and Other Stories. *v.2 p.505*

Attack upon Christendom. *v.1 p.593*

Attention Deficit Disorder: The Unfocused Mind in Children
    and Adults. *v.5 p.662*

Attention: Theory and Practice. *v.5 p.611*

Attention-Deficit Hyperactivity Disorder: A Handbook for
    Diagnosis and Treatment. *v.5 p.662*

The Attentive Brain. *v.5 p.617*

Attitude!: Eight Young Dancers Come of Age at the Ailey
    School. *v.1 p.18, p.28, p.30*

Attitudes, Chaos and the Connectionist Mind. *v.5 p.585*

Attitudes in and Around Organizations, Vol. 9. . . . .*v.5 p.578*

Attitudes, Personality, and Behavior. v.5 p.585, p.604

A. v.2 p.139

☐ ATTRA - National Sustainable Agriculture Information Service. v.5 p.30, p.45

Aubrey Beardsley: A Biography. v.1 p.720

Aucassin et Nicolette. v.2 p.466, p.467

Auctor and Actor: A Narratological Reading of Apuleius' "The Golden Ass". v.2 p.429

Audel Automated Machines and Toolmaking. v.5 p.714

Auden and Isherwood: The Berlin Years. v.2 p.330, p.356,v.6 p.403

Auden, MacNeice, Spender: The Thirties Poetry. v.2 p.329, p.330, p.369, p.384

Auden. v.2 p.329

The Audible Past: Cultural Origins of Sound Reproduction. v.1 p.377, p.388

The Audiencia of New Galicia in the Sixteeenth Century: A Study in Spanish Colonial Government. v.4 p.592

The Audio Dictionary. v.1 p.163, p.388

The Audio Recording Handbook. v.1 p.387

Audiology. v.5 p.523

Auditing and Tax Research. v.4 p.105, p.106, p.107

Auditory Scene Analysis: The Perceptual Organization of Sound. v.5 p.607

The Audubon Ark: A History of the National Audubon Society. v.6 p.293, p.295

Augmentative and Alternative Communication: Supporting Children and Adults with Complex Communication Needs. v.4 p.318

August Strindberg and the Other: New Critical Approaches. v.2 p.629

August Strindberg. v.2 p.630

August Wilson and Black Aesthetics. v.6 p.27, p.28

August Wilson and the African-American Odyssey. . . .v.6 p.27

Augustans and Romantics, Sixteen Eighty-Nine to Eighteen Thirty. v.2 p.166

Auguste Comte : The Foundation of Sociology. . . .v.4 p.685

Auguste Comte and Positivism. v.1 p.511, p.512

Auguste Comte and the Religion of Humanity: The Post-Theistic Program of French Social Theory. . .v.1 p.455

Augustine: A New Biography. v.1 p.430, v.2 p.430

Augustine: A Very Short Introduction. v.6 p.570

Augustine and Politics as Longing in the World. . . .v.4 p.490

The Augustine Catechism: The Enchiridion on Faith, Hope, and Love. v.1 p.592

Augustine: Confessions, Bks. I-IV. v.2 p.429

Augustine of Hippo: A Biography with a New Epilogue. v.1 p.430, v.2 p.430, v.3 p.56

Augustine of Hippo. v.1 p.612, v.6 p.570

Augustine: On the Trinity. v.1 p.430

Augustine through the Ages: An Encyclopedia. . . .v.1 p.592

Augustine to Galileo. v.6 p.575

The Augustinian Tradition. v.1 p.498

Augustus. v.3 p.28

Aunt Julia and the Scriptwriter. v.2 p.686

Aunt Safiyya and the Monastery: A Novel. v.6 p.664

Aunt Tula / la Tia Tula: A Dual-Language Book. . . .v.2 p.662

The Aunt's Story. v.2 p.750

Aurelia Followed by Sylvie. v.2 p.492

Aurelian and the Third Century. v.3 p.29

Aurora Leigh: Norton Critical Edition. v.2 p.271

Aurora: The Mysterious Northern Lights. v.5 p.73, p.427, p.444, p.445

The Aurora Watcher's Handbook. v.5 p.73

Aus dem Tagebuch Einer Schnecke. v.2 p.607

Auschwitz, 1270 to the Present. v.3 p.83

Ausgewaehlte Werke in Sechs Baenden. v.2 p.605

Ausgewahlte Gedichte. v.2 p.603

Ausgewanderten. v.2 p.618

Ausgewählte Werke. v.2 p.600

Austen, Eliot, Charlotte Bronte and the Mentor-Lover. .v.2 p.193

Austere Luminosity of Chinese Classical Furniture. . .v.1 p.804

Austerlitz. v.2 p.618

☐ AustLit Online Database : The Resource for Australian Literature. v.2 p.740

Australia and America Through 200 Years; 1776-1976. .v.3 p.387

Australia, Antarctica, and the Pacific. v.4 p.384, p.385

ⓔ Australia, Oceania, and Antarctica: A Continental Overview of Environmental Issues. v.4 p.385

Australian Art. v.1 p.695

Australian Gay and Lesbian Writing: An Anthology. . .v.2 p.742

An Australian Girl. v.2 p.747

☐ Australian Government and Politics Database. . . .v.4 p.624

☐ Australian Literary and Historical Texts. v.2 p.742

Australian Painting, 1788-2000. . . . . .v.1 p.733

Australian Politics and Government: The Commonwealth, States and Territories. v.4 p.624

Australian Short Fiction: A History. v.2 p.740

The Australian Short Story. v.2 p.743

Australians at Home: A Documentary History of Australian Domestic Interiors from 1788-1914. . . . . . .v.1 p.800

Australia. v.4 p.385

Austria and the Papacy in the Age of Metternich: Between Conflict and Cooperation, 1809-1830, Vol. 1. . . .v.3 p.182

Austria and the Papacy in the Age of Metternich II: Revolution and Reaction, 1830-1838. . . . . .v.3 p.182

Austria: Out of the Shadow of the Past. v.4 p.595

Austria-Hungary and the Origins of the First World War. v.3 p.80, p.185

Austrian and New Classical Business Cycle Theories: A Comparative Study Through the Method of Rational Reconstruction. v.4 p.233, p.234

Austrian Economics in America: The Migration of a Tradition. v.4 p.234

The Austrian Mind: An Intellectual and Social History, 1848-1938. . . . . .v.3 p.181

The Austrian Party System. v.4 p.579, p.595

Austrian Philosophy: The Legacy of Franz Brentano. .v.1 p.465

Austrian Poetry Today. v.2 p.591

The Austrians: A Thousand Year Odyssey. v.3 p.181

Austria's Eastern Question, 1700-1970. . . . . . .v.3 p.183

Austria's Wars of Emergence, 1683-1797. . . . . . .*v.3 p.182*

Austro-German Relations in the Anschluss Era. *v.3 p.185*

The Austro-Prussian War: Austria's War with Prussia and Italy
in 1866. . . . .*v.3 p.168, p.182*

Authenticities: Philosophical Reflections on Musical
Performance. *v.1 p.381, p.401*

Authenticity and Early Music: A Symposium. *v.1 p.401*

Authenticity and Fiction in the Russian Literary Journey,
1790-1840. . . . .*v.2 p.800*

Author and Printer in Victorian
England. *v.3 p.119, v.6 p.739, p.741*

The Authoritarian Personality. *v.4 p.767*

The Authoritarian Specter. *v.4 p.509*

Authoritarianism and Democratization: Soldiers and Workers in
Argentina, 1976-1983. . . . .*v.3 p.276*

Authoritarianism in Latin America Since
Independence. *v.3 p.260, p.343, p.344*

Authoritarianism in the Middle East: Regimes and
Resistance. *v.6 p.594*

Authoritative Guide to Self-Help Resources in Mental Health,
Revised Edition. *v.5 p.669*

Authority and Conflict: England,
1603-1658. . . . .*v.3 p.94, p.102, p.103, p.121*

Authority and Female Authorship in Colonial America. *v.2 p.8*

Authority and Freedom in Education: An Introduction to the
Philosophy of Education. *v.4 p.344*

Authority and Influence: Australian Literary Criticism
1950-2000. . . . .*v.2 p.740*

Authority and Power in the Free Church Tradition: A Social
Case Study of the American Baptist Convention. . *v.1 p.583*

Authority and Resistance in the Investiture Contest. . *v.1 p.574*

Authority and the Sacred: Aspects of the Christianisation of the
Roman World. *v.3 p.30*

Authority and Upheaval in Leipzig, 1910-1920: The Story of a
Relationship. *v.3 p.170*

Authority Without Power: Law and the Japanese
Paradox. *v.4 p.475, v.6 p.219*

Authority. *v.4 p.695*

Authors and Authority. *v.2 p.164*

Authors and Owners: The Invention of Copyright. . . .*v.3 p.37*

Author. *v.2 p.574*

Autism: Understanding the Disorder. *v.5 p.658*

Autobiographical Memory and the Construction of a Narrative
Self: Developmental and Cultural Perspectives. . . *v.5 p.657*

The Autobiographical Notes of Charles Evans Hughes. .*v.3 p.434*

An Autobiographical Novel. *v.2 p.114*

Autobiographical Voices: Race, Gender,
Self-Portraiture. *v.6 p.477*

Autobiographical Writings by Early Quaker Women. . *v.1 p.585*

Autobiographical Writings: Narrative. *v.3 p.419*

Autobiographies: Narrative of the Life, My Bondage and My
Freedom, Life and Times. *v.2 p.36, v.6 p.24*

The Autobiographies of Sean O'Casey. *v.2 p.373*

Autobiography and Authorship in Renaissance Verse: Chronicles
of the Self. *v.2 p.182*

Autobiography: I Wonder as I Wander. *v.2 p.87, p.88*

The Autobiography of a Brown Buffalo. . . .*v.6 p.488, p.497*

The Autobiography of a Curmudgeon. *v.3 p.459*

Autobiography of a Family Photo. *v.6 p.400*

Autobiography of a Geisha. *v.6 p.227*

Autobiography of a People: Three Centuries of African
American History Told by Those Who Lived It. . . *v.6 p.3*

The Autobiography of a Runaway Slave. *v.3 p.279*

The Autobiography of a Slave: A Bilingual Edition. . *v.3 p.279*

The Autobiography of Benvenuto Cellini. *v.3 p.200*

The Autobiography of Bertrand Russell. *v.1 p.447*

The Autobiography of Carl Schurz. *v.3 p.434*

The Autobiography of Chester Himes. *v.2 p.86*

The Autobiography of Eleanor Roosevelt. *v.3 p.462*

The Autobiography of Fukuzawa Yukichi. *v.6 p.229*

Autobiography of John Stuart Mill. *v.4 p.222*

The Autobiography of Karl Von Dittersdorf. . *v.1 p.192, p.321*

The Autobiography of Leroi Jones- Amiri Baraka. . . *v.2 p.140*

The Autobiography of Mark Twain. *v.2 p.33*

The Autobiography of Martin Van Buren. *v.3 p.418*

The Autobiography of Michel de Montaigne. *v.2 p.471*

The Autobiography of Miss Jane Pittman. *v.2 p.145*

Autobiography of Mother Jones. *v.4 p.126*

The Autobiography of My Mother. *v.2 p.767, p.768*

The Autobiography of Will Rogers. *v.1 p.90, p.117, p.118*

The Autobiography of William Butler Yeats: Consisting of
Reveries over Chilhood and Youth, the Trembling
of the Veil, and Dramatis Personae. *v.2 p.327*

Autobiography: The Big Sea. *v.2 p.87*

An Autobiography. *v.1 p.765*

Autobiography. *v.2 p.119*

An Autobiography. *v.2 p.318*

Automated People Movers VI: Creative Access for Major
Activity Centers: Proceedings of the Sixth International
Conference. *v.5 p.701*

Automatic Control of Aircraft and Missiles. *v.5 p.717*

Automatic Control Systems. *v.5 p.711*

The Automatic Muse: Surrealist Novels. *v.2 p.515*

Automation, Production Systems, and Computer-Integrated
Manufacturing. *v.4 p.116*

The Automobile Age. *v.4 p.154*

Automotive Electronics Handbook. *v.5 p.716*

Automotive Fuel Economy: How Far Can We
Go? *v.5 p.715, p.716*

The automotive industry and the environment : a technical,
business and social future. *v.5 p.716*

Autonomy and Power: The Dynamics of Class and Culture in
Rural Bolivia. *v.3 p.324*

Autopsy of a Suicidal Mind. *v.5 p.663*

Autosegmental and Metrical Phonology: An
Introduction. *v.2 p.560*

Autumn: A Season of Change. *v.5 p.222, p.223*

The Autumn of the Middle Ages. *v.1 p.600*

The Autumn of the Patriarch. *v.2 p.683*

Availability and Sale of Alcohol: Experiences from Canada and
the U. S. *v.4 p.153*

☐ The Avalon Project at Yale Law School: Documents in Law, History and Diplomacy. *v.4 p.451*

Avant Garde Drama: A Casebook. *v.1 p.84, p.96*

Avant Garde: The Experimental Theater in France. *v.1 p.85, p.106,v.2 p.462*

Avant-Garde Performance and the Limits of Criticism: Approaching the Living Theatre, Happenings/Fluxus and the Black Arts Movement. *v.1 p.85, p.118*

Avant-Garde Performance. *v.1 p.84, p.95*

Avant-Garde Theatre: 1892-1992. . . . . . .*v.1 p.85, p.96*

The Avenger. *v.2 p.281*

The Avenue Bearing the Initial of Christ into the New World: Poems: 1953-1964. . . . .*v.2 p.92*

Averting Extinction: Reconstructing Endangered Species Recovery. *v.6 p.290*

☐ Avery Index to Architectural Periodicals. *v.1 p.661, p.783, p.798, p.811, p.821*

Aves Sin Nido. *v.2 p.685*

Avez-vous lu Racine?: mise au point polémique. . . .*v.2 p.477*

Aviation Insecurity: The New Challenges of Air Travel. *v.5 p.718*

Avicenna, His Life and Works. *v.1 p.431*

Avicenna. *v.1 p.432*

The Avignon Papacy, 1305-1403. . . . .*v.1 p.574*

The Avionics Handbook. *v.5 p.718*

Le Avventure di Pinocchio. *v.2 p.710*

The Awakening and Selected Short Fiction. *v.2 p.32*

Awakening China: Politics, Culture, and Class in the Nationalist Revolution. *v.6 p.190*

Awakening of American Nationalism, 1815-1828. . . .*v.3 p.414*

The Awakening of Faith: Attributed to Asvaghosha. . .*v.1 p.563*

Awakenings: A Translation of Gabriel Marcel's Autobiography. *v.1 p.457*

Award Winning Films: A Viewer's Reference to 2700 Acclaimed Motion Pictures. *v.6 p.346*

Awareness Through Movement: Health Exercises for Personal Growth. *v.1 p.50*

Awash in a Sea of Faith: The Christianization of the American People 1550-1865. . . . .*v.1 p.543, p.606*

Away down South: A History of Southern Identity. . .*v.3 p.493*

Away from Home: American Indian Boarding School Experience, 1879-2000. . . . .*v.4 p.312*

Away. *v.2 p.739*

An Awfully Big Adventure. *v.2 p.330*

☐ AWIC: Animal Welfare Information Center. . .*v.5 p.56, p.57*

Awkward Years: American Foreign Relations Under Garfield and Arthur. *v.3 p.400, p.437*

Awo: The Nigerian Colossus. *v.6 p.71*

Axel's Castle: A Study of the Imaginative Literature of 1870-1930. . . . .*v.2 p.570*

Axel. *v.2 p.502, p.503*

The Axe. *v.2 p.784*

Axiomatic Concensus Theory in Group Choice and Biomathematics. *v.5 p.91*

Axis and Circumference: The Cylindrical Shape of Plants and Animals. *v.5 p.92, p.156*

Ayala's Angel. *v.2 p.317*

Ayer. *v.1 p.445*

Ayn Rand's Normative Ethics: The Virtuous Egoist. . .*v.1 p.510*

The Azande: History and Political Institutions. *v.6 p.59*

Azeotropic Data, Vol. 2. . . . .*v.5 p.282*

Azeotropic Data. *v.5 p.281*

The Azerbaijani Turks: Power and Identity under Russian Rule. *v.3 p.231*

Azorin (Jose Martinez Ruiz). *v.2 p.656*

Aztec and Maya World. *v.4 p.10*

Aztec Medicine, Health, and Nutrition. *v.3 p.261*

Aztec Thought and Culture: A Study of the Ancient Nahuatl Mind. *v.3 p.261*

Aztecs: An Interpretation. *v.3 p.285*

Aztecs, Moors, and Christians: Festivals of Reconquest in Mexico and Spain. *v.3 p.263*

Aztlan: Chicano Culture and Folklore. *v.6 p.515, p.524*

Aztlan: Essays on the Chicano Homeland. . . .*v.6 p.497, p.511*

B

The B. B. King Reader: Six Decades of Commentary. *v.1 p.261, p.335*

B. F. Skinner: A Life. *v.5 p.595*

B2B-Integration: Concepts and Architecture. *v.4 p.113*

Baal Babylone : roman. *v.2 p.507*

☐ The Baba and the Comrade: Gender and Politics in Revolutionary Russia. *v.3 p.55, p.225,v.6 p.443*

Baba: Men and Fatherhood in South Africa. . . .*v.4 p.734*

Babaylan: An Anthology of Filipina and Filipina American Writers. *v.6 p.91*

Babe: The Life and Legend of Babe Didrikson Zaharias. *v.4 p.835, p.860*

Babel Guide to Italian Fiction in Translation. *v.2 p.698*

Babel Tower. *v.2 p.332*

The Babi and Baha'i Religions: From Messianic Sh'ism to a World Religion. *v.1 p.561*

The Baburnama: Memoirs of Babur, Prince and Emperor. *v.6 p.644*

Baby Be-Bop. *v.6 p.394*

Baby Boom: Americans Born 1946 To 1964. *v.4 p.137, v.5 p.585*

Babyji. *v.6 p.395*

Babylon, Memphis, Persepolis: Eastern Contexts of Greek Culture. *v.3 p.12*

The Babylonian Story of the Deluge and the Epic of Gilgamesh with an Account of the Royal Libraries of Nineveh. *v.6 p.664*

The Babylonians: An Introduction. *v.3 p.5*

Baccaria: On Crimes and Punishments and Other Writings. *v.6 p.249*

Bacchae. *v.2 p.410*

Bacchylides: A Selection. *v.2 p.408, p.409*

Bach and the Patterns of Invention. *v.1 p.183, p.303*

Bach and the Riddle of the Number Alphabet. *v.1 p.187, p.304*

The Bach Family: Seven Generations of Creative Genius. *v.1 p.184, p.302, p.303*

Bach in Berlin: Nation and Culture in Mendelssohn' Revival of the St. Matthew Passion. *v.3 p.178*

Bach: Mass in B Minor. *v.1 p.183, p.235, p.303*

Bach: The Goldberg Variations. *v.1 p.187, p.244, p.304*

Bach: The Mass in B Minor. *v.1 p.187, p.237, p.304*

Bach: The Orgelbuchlein. *v.1 p.187, p.243, p.304*

Bachata: Social History of a Dominican Popular
Music. *v.1 p.293, v.3 p.267, p.317*

Bachelard: Science and Objectivity. *v.1 p.457, p.458*

Bachelors: Essays on Nine Women "Bachelors" Who Challenged
Masculinist Aesthetics. *v.1 p.706*

The Bachelors. *v.2 p.383*

Bach's Well-Tempered Clavier: The 48 Preludes and
Fugues. *v.1 p.185, p.241, p.303*

Bach's Works for Solo Violin: Style, Structure,
Performance. *v.1 p.185, p.241, p.303*

Bach. *v.1 p.182, p.302*

The Bachura Scandal: And Other Stories and Sketches. *v.2 p.783*

Back Door to War: The Roosevelt Foreign Policy
1933-1941. . . . .*v.3 p.480*

Back from Exile: Six Speeches upon His Return. . . .*v.2 p.433*

Back from the Future: Cuba under Castro. *v.3 p.308, v.4 p.508*

Back in the Saddle Again: New Essays on the Western. *v.6 p.323*

Back of the Yards: The Making of a Local Democracy. *v.4 p.707*

The Back Room. *v.2 p.661*

Back to Africa: George Ross and the Maroons: From Nova
Scotia to Sierra Leone. *v.6 p.70*

Back to Basics: Your Guide to Manufacturing
Excellence. *v.4 p.119*

Back to Middletown: Three Generations of Sociological
Reflections. *v.4 p.679*

Back to Nature: The Arcadian Myth in Urban
America. *v.3 p.369, p.370*

Backdoor to Eugenics. *v.5 p.152*

Backfire: Carly Fiorina's High-Stakes Battle for the Soul of
Hewlett-Packard. *v.4 p.84*

The Background of English Literature: Classical and Romantic,
and Other Collected Essays and Addresses. *v.2 p.166*

Background to a Coup: Civil Military Relations in Twentieth
Century Chile and the Overthrow of Salvador
Allende. *v.3 p.354*

Backgrounds of Early Christianity. *v.1 p.599*

Backgrounds to Augustan Poetry, Gallus, Elegy and
Rome. *v.2 p.427*

Backing Hitler: Consent and Coercion in Nazi Germany. *v.3 p.171*

Backlash: The Undeclared War Against American
Women. *v.6 p.433*

Back-of-the-Envelope Physics. *v.5 p.541*

Backpacking and Hiking. *v.4 p.788*

Backs to the Wall in Suriname: Forest Policy in a Country in
Crisis. *v.3 p.322, p.323*

Backward and Upward: The New Conservative Writing. *v.3 p.467*

Backwaters of Global Prosperity: How Forces of Globalization
and GATT/WTO Trade Regimes Contribute to the
Marginalization of the World's Poorest Nations. . .*v.4 p.664*

The Backwoods of Canada, No. 11. . . . .*v.2 p.733*

Bacterial Pathogenesis: Identification, Regulation and Function
of Virulence Factors. *v.5 p.166*

Bacterial Plant Pathology: Cell and Molecular Aspects. *v.5 p.47*

Bad Boy of Music. *v.1 p.208, p.301*

☐ The Bad Bug Book. *v.5 p.33*

Bad Habits: Drinking, Smoking, Taking Drugs, Gambling,
Sexual Misbehavior and Swearing in American
History. *v.4 p.709*

Bad: Infamy, Darkness, Evil, and Slime on Screen. . .*v.6 p.314*

Bad Kids: Race and the Transformation of the Juvenile
Court. *v.6 p.269*

Bad Language: Are Some Words Better than Others? *v.2 p.551*

Bad Language, Naked Ladies and Other Threats to the Nation:
A Political History of Comic Books in Mexico. . .*v.3 p.267*

Bad Leadership: What It Is, How It Happens, Why It
Matters. *v.4 p.697*

Bad Men Do What Good Men Dream: A Forensic Psychiatrist
Illuminates the Darker Side of Human
Behavior. *v.5 p.661, p.662*

Bad Music: The Music We Love to Hate. *v.1 p.383*

Bad Neighbor Policy: Washington's Futile War on Drugs in
Latin America. *v.6 p.246, p.247, p.262*

Badenheim 1939. . . . .*v.6 p.647*

A Badly Flawed Election: Debating Bush v. Gore, the Supreme
Court and the American Democracy. *v.4 p.536*

Badminton. *v.4 p.795, p.864*

Baghdad, Metropolis of the Abbasid Caliphate. . . .*v.6 p.602*

Bagombo Snuff Box: Uncollected Short Fiction. . . .*v.2 p.158*

The Baha'i Faith: A Short History. *v.1 p.561*

The Baha'i Faith: The Emerging Global Religion. . .*v.1 p.561*

Baha'i– World Faith: Selected Writings of Baha'u'llah and
'Abdu'l-Baha. *v.1 p.560, p.561*

A Bahian Counterpoint: Sugar, Tobacco, Cassava, and Slavery in
the Recôncavo, 1780-1860. . . . .*v.3 p.334*

Bailey's Industrial Oil and Fat Products, Vol. 1. . . .*v.5 p.742*

Bait and Switch: Human Rights and U. S. Foreign
Policy. *v.4 p.513*

Bait and Switch: The (Futile) Pursuit of the American
Dream. *v.4 p.265*

Baker Encyclopedia of Christian Apologetics. . *v.1 p.645, p.646*

Baker's Biographical Dictionary of Musicians: Centennial
Edition. *v.1 p.162*

Baker's Biographical Dictionary of Musicians, Vol. 1. *v.1 p.162*

Baker's Biographical Dictionary of Musicians, Vol. 2. *v.1 p.162*

Baker's Biographical Dictionary of Musicians, Vol. 3. *v.1 p.162*

Baker's Biographical Dictionary of Musicians, Vol. 4. *v.1 p.162*

Baker's Biographical Dictionary of Musicians, Vol. 5. *v.1 p.162*

Baker's Biographical Dictionary of Musicians, Vol. 6. *v.1 p.162*

Baker's Dictionary of Music. *v.1 p.162*

Baladi Women of Cairo: Playing with an Egg and a
Stone. *v.6 p.637*

Balanced Scorecard Diagnostics: Maintaining Maximum
Performance. *v.4 p.82*

Balanced Scorecard Step-by-Step: Maximizing Performance and
Maintaining Results. *v.4 p.73*

The Balanced Scorecard: Translating Strategy into
Action. *v.4 p.73, p.81, p.82*

Balanchine Pointework. *v.1 p.25*

Balanchine's Complete Stories of the Great Ballets. *v.1 p.3, p.228*

Balanchine's Tchaikovsky: Interviews with George
Balanchine. *v.1 p.46*

Balancing Acts: American Thought and Culture in the 1930s. *v.3 p.367*

Balancing Evils Judiciously: The Proslavery Writings Zephaniah Kingsley. *v.3 p.315*

Balancing Juvenile Justice. *v.6 p.248*

A Balcony over the Fakihani. *v.6 p.658*

The Balcony. *v.2 p.518, p.519*

Balinese Dance in Transition: Kaja and Kelod. *v.1 p.21*

Balkan Babel: Politics, Culture, and Religion in Yugoslavia. *v.3 p.247*

Balkan Blues: Writing Out of Yugoslavia. *v.2 p.818*

The Balkan Wars: Conquest, Revolution and Retribution from the Ottoman Era to the Twentieth Century. *v.3 p.245*

The Balkan Wars. *v.3 p.245, p.246*

The Balkans: From Constantinople to Communism. . .*v.3 p.246*

The Balkans since 1453. . . . .*v.3 p.246*

The Balkans since the Second World War. *v.3 p.246*

The Balkans. *v.4 p.383*

Ball, Bat and Bishop: The Origin of Ball Games. .*v.4 p.806, p.850*

Ball Pest and Disease Manual: Disease, Insect, and Mite Control on Flower and Foliage Crops. *v.5 p.44*

Ball Redbook, Vol. 1. . . . .*v.5 p.43*

Ball Redbook. *v.5 p.43*

The Ballad of Peckham Rye. *v.2 p.383*

The Ballad of Rocky Ruiz. *v.6 p.502*

Ballet 101: A Complete Guide to Learning and Loving the Ballet. *v.1 p.3, p.24*

Ballet: An Illustrated History. *v.1 p.23*

Ballet and Dance in the 1940's: An Historical Retrospective: The War Years and Beyond. *v.1 p.5*

Ballet and Modern Dance: A Concise History. *v.1 p.5*

Ballet and Opera in the Age of Giselle. *v.1 p.25*

The Ballet Called Giselle. *v.1 p.22, p.23*

The Ballet Called Swan Lake. *v.1 p.22*

Ballet in Leicester Square. *v.1 p.24*

The Ballet of the Enlightenment: The Establishment of the Ballet d'Action in France, 1770-1793. . . . . . .*v.1 p.24*

The Ballet of the Second Empire. *v.1 p.24*

Ballet or Ballyhoo: The American Careers of Maria Bonfanti, Rita Sangalli, and Giuseppina Morlacchi. *v.1 p.6*

Ballet-Maker's Handbook: Sources, Vocabulary, Styles. .*v.1 p.37*

The Ballets of Antony Tudor: Studies in Psyche and Satire. *v.1 p.6, p.7, p.23*

The Ballets Russes and Its World. *v.1 p.25*

The Ballets Russes: The Serge Lifar Collection of Theater Designs, Costumes, and Paintings at the Wadsworth Atheneum. *v.1 p.46*

Ballots and Barricades: Class Formation and Republican Politics in France, 1830-1871. . . . .*v.3 p.148*

Ballots for Freedom: Antislavery Politics in the United States, 1837-1860. . . . .*v.3 p.401, p.421*

Ballroom Dance Music: A Reference Guide. *v.1 p.34*

Balthasar. *v.2 p.344*

Balthus. *v.1 p.737*

The Baltic and the Outbreak of the Second World War. *v.3 p.255*

Baltic Drama: A Handbook and Bibliography. *v.2 p.781*

Baltic Literature: A Survey of Finnish, Estonian, Latvian, and Lithuanian Literatures. *v.2 p.780*

The Baltic Revolution: Estonia, Latvia, Lithuania and the Path to Independence. *v.3 p.256*

The Baltic States - Estonia, Latvia, Lithuania: The Years of Independence, 1917-1940. . . . .*v.3 p.256*

The Baltic States in World Politics. *v.4 p.641, p.644*

The Baltic States, Years of Dependence, 1940-1992. . *v.3 p.256*

The Baltic World, 1772-1993: Europe's Nothern Periphery in an Age of Change. *v.3 p.256*

Balzac: A Biography. *v.3 p.153*

Balzac: A Life. *v.2 p.487*

Balzac and the French Revolution. *v.2 p.486*

Balzac: Fiction and Melodrama. *v.2 p.487*

Balzac, James and the Realistic Novel. *v.2 p.487*

Balzac: Selected Short Stories. *v.2 p.486*

Balzac's Comedie Humaine. *v.2 p.486, p.487*

Balzac. *v.2 p.487*

Bambini: The Italian Approach to Infant/Toddler Care. .*v.4 p.368*

Bamboo among the Oaks: Contemporary Writing by Hmong Americans. *v.6 p.92, p.139, p.140*

The Banality of Denial: Israel and the Armenian Genocide. *v.4 p.651*

The Banalization of Nihilism: Twentieth-Century Responses to Meaninglessness. *v.1 p.509*

Banana Cultures: Agriculture, Consumption, and Environmental Change in Honduras and the United States. *v.3 p.270*

Banana Wars: Power, Production, and History in the Americas. *v.3 p.272*

Bananas and Plantains. *v.5 p.23, p.25*

Bananas, Beaches and Bases: Making Feminist Sense of International Politics. *v.6 p.440*

Banaras: City of Light. *v.1 p.535*

Band of Angels. *v.2 p.129*

The Band Plays. *v.6 p.411*

Banda: Mexican Musical Life Across Borders. *v.1 p.294*

Bandarshah. *v.6 p.663*

Bandido: The Death and Resurrection of Oscar Zeta Acosta. *v.6 p.503, p.516*

The Bandit King: Lampiao of Brazil. *v.3 p.339*

Bandits, Peasants, and Politics: The Case of la Violencia in Colombia. *v.3 p.359*

Bang the Drum Slowly. *v.2 p.80, p.81*

Banister Fletcher's A History of Architecture: Centenary Edition. *v.1 p.785*

Bankable Business Plans. *v.4 p.82*

Bankers and Bureaucrats: The Development of Capital and the Role of the State in Thailand. *v.6 p.171*

Bankers and Pashas: International Finance and Economic Imperialism in Egypt. *v.3 p.77*

Banned Films: Movies, Censors and the First Amendment. *v.4 p.451*

The Banquet in Blitva. *v.2 p.818*

Bantu Prophets in South Africa. *v.1 p.611*

Baptism in the New Testament. *v.1 p.657*

Baptist Heritage. *v.1 p.583*

Baptist Ways: A History. *v.1 p.583*

Barabbas. *v.2 p.630*

Barbara Hepworth. *v.1 p.780*

Barbara Morgan. *v.1 p.29, p.30, p.46*

Barbara Pym: A Reference Guide. *v.2 p.379*

Barbarian Virtues: The United States Encounters Foreign
    Peoples at Home and Abroad, 1876-1917. . . . .*v.4 p.571*

The Barbarian West: 400-1000. . . . .*v.3 p.67*

Barbarians and Politics at the Court of Arcadius. . . .*v.3 p.30*

Barbarians and Romans, A. D. 418-584: The Techniques of
    Accommodation. *v.3 p.31*

The Barbarians are Coming. *v.6 p.101*

Barbarians at the Gate: The Fall of R. J. R. Nabisco. . .*v.4 p.84*

The Barbarians Speak: How the Conquered Peoples Shaped
    Roman Europe. *v.3 p.29*

Barbarians Within the Gates of Rome: A Study of Roman
    Military Policy and the Barbarians, ca. 375-425 A. D. .*v.3 p.30*

The Barbary Coast: Algiers under the Turks, 1500 to
    1830. . . . .*v.6 p.61*

Barbary Legend. *v.6 p.60*

Barbed Wire and Mirrors: Essays on New Zealand
    Prose. *v.2 p.741*

The Barber of Seville and Moses. *v.1 p.203, p.232, p.352, p.409*

Barcelona and Its Rulers, 1096-1291. . . . .*v.6 p.577*

Barchester Towers. *v.2 p.318*

Barclays: The Business of Banking, 1690-1996. . . .*v.4 p.90*

Barefoot Boy with Cheek. *v.2 p.116*

Bare-Knuckle Negotiation: Savvy Tips and True Stories from
    the Master of Give-and-Take. *v.4 p.74*

Bareknuckles: A Social History of
    Prize-Fighting. *v.4 p.804, p.855*

Bargaining for Advantage: Negotiation Strategies for Reasonable
    People. *v.4 p.75*

Barley: Genetics, Biochemistry, Molecular Biology and
    Biotechnology. *v.5 p.9, p.23*

Barley. *v.5 p.23, p.25*

Barnaby Rudge. by Charles Dickens. (Boz.) with ... illustrations
    from designs by George Cattermole and H. K.
    Browne. *v.2 p.282*

Barnett Newman: A Catalogue Raisonné. *v.1 p.699*

Barnett Newman. *v.1 p.747*

Barney's Version. *v.2 p.738*

The Baron in the Trees. *v.2 p.714*

Baroque and Rococo: Art and Culture. *v.1 p.675*

Baroque and Rococo. *v.1 p.674*

Baroque Art: A Topical Dictionary. . . .*v.1 p.663, p.664, p.674*

Baroque Music. *v.1 p.184, p.186*

Baroques. *v.1 p.674*

Barren Ground. *v.2 p.79*

Barriers to Riches. *v.4 p.196, p.259, p.260*

Barrio Boy. *v.6 p.488, p.535*

Barrio Dreams: Puerto Ricans, Latinos, and the Neoliberal
    City. *v.6 p.548, p.717*

Barrio Gangs: Street Life and Identity in Southern
    California. *v.6 p.547, p.550, p.551*

Barrio Rhythm: Mexican American Music in Los
    Angeles. *v.6 p.518, p.549*

Barrio-Logos: Space and Place in Urban Chicano Literature and
    Culture. *v.6 p.504, p.516*

Barrios in Arms: Revolution in Santo Domingo. . . .*v.3 p.317*

Barrios Norteños: St. Paul and Midwestern Mexican
    Communities in the Twentieth Century. . . .*v.6 p.536, p.550*

Barron's ESL Guide to American Business
    English. *v.4 p.58, p.172*

Barron's How to Prepare for the AP Biology Exam. . .*v.5 p.245*

ⓔ Barry Goldwater: Native Arizonan. *v.3 p.459*

Barry Goldwater: Native Arizonan. *v.3 p.459*

Barry Goldwater. *v.3 p.458, v.4 p.486*

Barry Lyndon: The Memoirs of Barry Lyndon, Esq. . .*v.2 p.316*

The Barrytown Trilogy: The Commitments, the Snapper, the
    Van. *v.2 p.343*

Bartók: Concerto for Orchestra. *v.1 p.211, p.238, p.305*

Barthes: A Very Short Introduction. *v.2 p.570*

Bartholomew Fair. *v.2 p.220*

Bartok and His World. *v.1 p.217, p.305*

The Bartok Companion. *v.1 p.214, p.305*

Bartok: Concerto for Orchestra: Understanding Bartok's
    World. *v.1 p.225, p.243, p.305*

Bartok Perspectives: Man, Composer, and
    Ethnomusicologist. *v.1 p.208, p.304*

Bartok Remembered. *v.1 p.214, p.305*

Bartok's Viola Concerto: The Remarkable Story of His
    Swansong. *v.1 p.218, p.241, p.305*

Barton Mumaw, Dancer: From Denishawn to Jacob's Pillow and
    Beyond. *v.1 p.12*

Baruch: My Own Story. *v.3 p.455*

The Barye Bronzes: A Catalogue Raisonné. . . .*v.1 p.698, p.699*

Baryshnikov: From Russia to the West. *v.1 p.12*

La Bas (Down There). *v.2 p.495*

Baseball: A History of America's Game. *v.4 p.809, p.851*

Baseball: A Literary Anthology. *v.2 p.18, v.4 p.811, p.850*

Baseball: An Illustrated History. *v.4 p.810, p.852*

Baseball and the American Dream: Race, Class, Gender and the
    National Pastime. *v.4 p.815, p.830, p.850*

The Baseball Coaching Bible. *v.4 p.795, p.796, p.851*

Baseball in 1889: Players vs
    Owners. *v.4 p.808, p.851, p.885, p.889, p.892, p.897*

Baseball in Blue and Gray: The National Pastime During the
    Civil War. *v.4 p.807, p.851*

▢ Baseball Reference. *v.4 p.801, p.849, p.871*

Baseball with a Latin Beat: A History of the Latin American
    Game. *v.4 p.804, p.833, p.849, p.890*

Baseball's Great Experiment: Jackie Robinson and His
    Legacy. *v.4 p.810, p.833, p.852, p.898*

The Bases of Competence: Skills for Lifelong Learning and
    Employability. *v.4 p.303, p.304*

Basic Algebra II. *v.5 p.473*

Basic Algebra I. *v.5 p.473*

Basic and Clinical Biostatistics. *v.5 p.515*

Basic Atomic and Molecular Spectroscopy. *v.5 p.273*

Basic Atonal Theory. *v.1 p.372*

Basic Bioinformatics. *v.5 p.97*

Basic Biomechanics of the Musculoskeletal System. . .*v.4 p.908*

Basic Biomechanics with Dynamic Human and PowerWeb/OLC Bind-In Passcard. *v.4 p.908*

Basic Biophysics for Biology. *v.5 p.125*

Basic Biotechnology. *v.4 p.156*

The Basic Business Library: Core Resources. *v.4 p.180*

Basic Call to Consciouness. *v.6 p.691, p.700*

Basic Concepts in Embryology: A Student's Survival Guide. *v.5 p.161*

Basic Concepts in Medical Genetics. *v.5 p.149*

Basic Concepts of Criminal Law. *v.6 p.268*

Basic Concepts of Environmental Chemistry. *v.5 p.310*

Basic Conducting Techniques. *v.1 p.402*

Basic Corrosion Technology for Scientists and Engineers. *v.5 p.735*

A Basic Course in Iraqi Arabic. *v.6 p.653*

A Basic Course in Modern Kurmanji. *v.6 p.668*

A Basic Course in Moroccan Arabic. *v.6 p.654*

Basic Documents in American History. *v.3 p.372*

Basic Documents on Human Rights. *v.4 p.434*

Basic Econometrics. *v.4 p.201, p.205*

Basic Economics: A Citizen's Guide to the Economy. .*v.4 p.186*

Basic Elements of Earthquake Engineering. *v.5 p.694*

Basic Engineering Circuit Analysis. *v.5 p.721*

Basic Essentials Using GPS. *v.4 p.390*

Basic Facts about the United Nations. *v.4 p.632*

Basic Gas Chromatography. *v.5 p.269*

Basic Geological Mapping. *v.5 p.420, p.423*

A Basic Guide to Eschatology: Making Sense of the Millennium. *v.1 p.645*

Basic Guide to Pesticides: Their Characteristics and Hazards. *v.5 p.312*

Basic Hazardous Waste Management. *v.5 p.313*

Basic HPLC and CE of Biomolecules. *v.5 p.326*

Basic Ideas and Concepts in Nuclear Physics. *v.5 p.553*

Basic Introduction to Statistics for the Behavioral Sciences. *v.5 p.602*

Basic Judaism. *v.1 p.551*

Basic Laboratory and Industrial Chemicals: A CRC Quick Reference Handbook. *v.5 p.316*

Basic Linear Algebra. *v.5 p.472*

Basic Lubrication Theory. *v.5 p.708*

Basic Mathematics for Chemists. *v.5 p.267*

Basic Mathematics for Economists. *v.4 p.175*

Basic Methods in Microscopy: Protocols and Concepts from Cells. *v.5 p.86*

A Basic Music Library: Essential Scores and Sound Recordings. *v.1 p.166*

Basic Nature Projects: 101 Fun Explorations. *v.5 p.228*

Basic Neurochemistry: Molecular, Cellular and Medical Aspects. *v.5 p.516*

Basic One- and Two-Dimensional NMR Spectroscopy. *v.5 p.272*

Basic Organic Stereochemistry. *v.5 p.297, p.298*

Basic Partial Differential Equations. *v.5 p.487*

Basic Physics of Atoms and Molecules. *v.5 p.554*

Basic Plant Pathology Methods. *v.5 p.46*

Basic Polish: Grammar. *v.2 p.775*

Basic Political Writings. *v.4 p.492*

Basic Principles and Calculations in Chemical Engineering. *v.5 p.741*

Basic Principles of Curriculum and Instruction. . . .*v.4 p.366*

The Basic Principles of Effective Consulting. *v.4 p.65*

Basic Problems of Ethnopsychiatry. *v.4 p.35*

The Basic Problems of Phenomenology. . . .*v.1 p.468, p.511*

Basic Questions in Theology: Collected Essays, Vol. II. .*v.1 p.636*

Basic Questions in Theology: Collected Essays, Vol. I. .*v.1 p.636*

A Basic Reference Grammar of Slovene. *v.2 p.777*

Basic Set Theory. *v.5 p.471*

Basic Steps in Planning Nursing Research. *v.5 p.529*

Basic Techniques in Molecular Biology. *v.5 p.129*

Basic Topology. *v.5 p.498*

Basic Training in Chemistry. *v.5 p.264*

The Basic Works of Aristotle. *v.1 p.426, p.427*

Basic Writings of Bertrand Russell. *v.1 p.447*

Basic Writings of Existentialism. *v.1 p.505*

The Basic Writings of John Stuart Mill: On Liberty, the Subjection of Women and Utilitarianism. *v.1 p.445*

Basic Writings of Nietzsche. *v.1 p.467*

Basic Writings of Saint Thomas Aquinas. *v.1 p.434*

Basic Writings: Proslogium; Monologium; Gaunilo's "In Behalf of the Fool"; Cur Deus Homo. *v.1 p.433*

□ BasicBIOSIS. *v.5 p.325*

The Basics of Crystallography and Diffraction. *v.5 p.284, p.436*

Basics of Electroorganic Synthesis. *v.5 p.294, p.295*

Basics of Geographical Information Systems. *v.4 p.386*

Basics of Qualitative Research: Techniques and Procedures for Developing Grounded Theory. *v.4 p.688*

Basics of Selection. *v.5 p.190*

Basics of Vocal Pedagogy: The Foundations and Process of Singing. *v.1 p.396, p.406*

Basil of Caesarea. *v.1 p.613*

Basil. *v.2 p.280*

Basin Analysis: Principles and Applications. *v.5 p.438*

The Basis for Gene Therapy. *v.5 p.148*

Basketball Biographies: Four Hundred Thirty-Four U. S. Players, Coaches and Contributors to the Game, 1891-1990. . . . .*v.4 p.854*

Basketball Skills and Drills. *v.4 p.796, p.854, p.904*

Basque Dance. *v.1 p.33*

Bas-Relief with Heroes: Selected Poems, 1960-1982. .*v.2 p.817*

Bass Culture: When Reggae Was King. *v.1 p.291*

Bassoon and Contrabassoon. *v.1 p.390*

Bassoon. *v.1 p.392*

Bastard Out of Carolina. *v.6 p.394*

Bastardy and Its Comparative History: Studies in the History of Illegitimacy and Martial Nonconformism. *v.4 p.740*

La Batarde. *v.6 p.397*

Bates' Guide to Physical Examination and History Taking. *v.5 p.520*

Bathing in Public in the Roman World. *v.3 p.23*

The Battered Woman Syndrome. *v.4 p.743, p.759*

Battered Women and Feminist Lawmaking and the Struggle for Equality. *v.4 p.472*

Battle Cry of Freedom: The Era of the Civil War. . . .*v.3 p.399*

The Battle for North America. *v.3 p.538*

The Battle for Peace. *v.6 p.616*

The Battle for Public Opinion: The President, the Press and the Polls During Watergate. *v.3 p.474*

The Battle for Saudi Arabia: Royalty, Fundamentalism, and Global Power. *v.4 p.643, v.6 p.626*

Battle for Stalingrad: The 1943 Soviet General Staff Study. *v.3 p.227*

The Battle for the American Mind: A Brief History of a Nation's Thought. *v.3 p.369*

The Battle for the Soul of Capitalism. *v.4 p.88*

Battle for the Wilderness. *v.5 p.233*

The Battle of Blair Mountain: The Story of America's Largest Labor Uprising. *v.4 p.129*

The Battle of Britain: The Greatest Air Battle of World War II. *v.3 p.81*

The Battle of Hastings 1066. . . . .*v.3 p.97, p.98*

The Battle of Kosovo. *v.3 p.248*

The Battle of Salamis: The Naval Encounter That Saved Greece — and Western Civilization. *v.3 p.19*

The Battle of the Gods and Giants: The Legacies of Descartes and Gassendi, 1655-1715. . . . .*v.1 p.436*

ⓔ The Battle over Hetch Hetchy: America's Most Controversial Dam and the Birth of Modern Environmentalism. *v.6 p.296*

The Battle That Stopped Rome: Emperor Augustus Arminius and Slaughter of Legions in Teutoburg Forest. *v.3 p.29*

The Battlefield: Algeria 1988-2002: Studies in a Broken Polity. *v.6 p.60, p.61, p.642*

Battlefield and Classroom: Four Decades with the American Indian, 1867-1904. . . . .*v.6 p.680, p.683*

Battlefield and Classroom: Four Decades with the American Indian, 1876-1904. . . . .*v.3 p.400*

Battleground of Desire: The Struggle for Self Control in Modern America. *v.3 p.371*

The Battleground of the Curriculum: Liberal Education and American Experience. *v.4 p.294*

The Battles of Coxinga: Chikamatsu's Puppet Play, Its Background and Importance. *v.6 p.234, p.235*

Battles on the Bench: Conflict Inside the Supreme Court. *v.4 p.466, p.535*

Battling for American Labor: Wobblies, Craft Workers, and the Making of the Union Movement. *v.4 p.127*

Battling for Manassas: The Fifty-Year Preservation Struggle at Manassas National Battlefield Park. *v.1 p.824*

Battling for Peace: A Memoir. *v.6 p.615*

Baudelaire: Les Fleurs du Mal. *v.2 p.488*

Baudelaire the Damned. *v.2 p.488*

Baudelaire's World. *v.2 p.488*

Baudelaire. *v.2 p.488*

The Bauhaus and America: First Contacts, 1919-1936. . . . .*v.1 p.786, p.787*

Bauhaus: Crucible of Modernism. *v.1 p.679*

Bauhaus: Weimar, Dessau, Berlin, Chicago. *v.3 p.179*

Bauhaus. *v.1 p.713, p.788*

Baumgartner's Bombay. *v.2 p.764*

Bay Area Figurative Art: 1950-1965. . . . .*v.1 p.732*

Bay Cities and Water Politics: The Battle for Resources in Boston and Oakland. *v.4 p.543, v.6 p.722, p.723*

Bay of the North: The Struggle for Control of Hudson Bay, 1686-1713. . . . .*v.3 p.545*

The Bayeux Tapestry. *v.3 p.97*

Bayonets Before Bullets: The Imperial Russian Army, 1861-1914. . . . .*v.3 p.212*

Bayonets to Lhasa. *v.6 p.240*

Bayreuth: A History of the Wagner Festival. *v.3 p.179*

▢ BCIN, the Bibliographic Database of the Conservation Information Network. *v.1 p.820*

Be My Knife: A Novel. *v.6 p.648*

Beacham's Guide to Environmental Issues and Sources, Set. *v.4 p.159, p.160*

Beaches and Coasts. *v.4 p.391*

Beacons along a Naturalist's Trail: California Naturalists and Innovators. *v.5 p.233*

Bear and His Daughter. *v.2 p.156*

The Bear Boy. *v.2 p.151*

The Bear Watches the Dragon: Russia's Perceptions of China and the Evolution of Russian-Chinese Relations since the Eighteenth Century. *v.3 p.212*

Bearing Arms for His Majesty: The Free-Colored Militia in Colonial Mexico. *v.3 p.288*

Bearing the Cross: Martin Luther King, Jr., and the Southern Christian Leadership Conference. *v.1 p.581*

Bearing the Word: Language and Female Experience in Nineteenth-Century Women's Writing. *v.2 p.175*

Bearing Witness: Gay Men's Health Crisis and the Politics of AIDS. *v.4 p.779, v.6 p.379*

Beasts and Super Beasts. *v.2 p.381*

The Beat Book: Poems and Fiction from the Beat Generation. *v.2 p.20*

Beat Book: Poems and Fiction from the Beat Generation. .*v.2 p.21*

Beat down to Your Soul. *v.2 p.20*

The Beat Generation: A Gale Critical Companion. .*v.2 p.11, p.12*

The Beat of a Different Drummer: Essays on Educational Renewal in Honor of John I. Goodlad. *v.4 p.340*

The Beat of My Drum: An Autobiography. *v.1 p.11, p.14*

Beat Your Ticket: Go to Court and Win!. *v.4 p.444*

Beaten Down: A History of Interpersonal Violence in the West. *v.4 p.698*

Beating the Odds: Crime, Poverty and Life in the Inner City. *v.6 p.256*

Beating the System: The Underground Economy. *v.4 p.270, p.271*

The Beatles As Musicians: Revolver Through the Anthology. *v.1 p.268, p.305, p.306*

The Beatles Lyrics: The Songs of Lennon, McCartney, Harrison and Starr. *v.1 p.265, p.305, p.411*

The Beatles Reader: A Selection of Contemporary Views, News and Reviews of the Beatles in Their Heyday. *v.1 p.273, p.306*

The Beatles Recording Sessions. *v.1 p.170, p.306*

The Beatles. *v.1 p.271, p.306*

Beaton in the Sixties: The Cecil Beaton Diaries As He Wrote Them, 1965-1969. . . . .*v.1 p.765*

Beatrice Webb (1858-1943) - The Socialist with a Sociological Imagination. *v.4 p.270*

Beatrice Webb. *v.4 p.273*

The Beats: A Literary Reference. *v.2 p.11*

Beaumarchais: "Le Barbier de Seville". *v.2 p.478*

Beaumarchais: "Mariage de Figaro". *v.2 p.478, p.479*

Beaumarchais. *v.2 p.478*

The Beautiful and the Dangerous: Encounters with the Zuni Indians. *v.6 p.704*

Beautiful Losers. *v.2 p.734*

A Beautiful Mind: A Biography of John Forbes Nash, Jr. , Winner of the Nobel Prize for Economics 1994. . .*v.5 p.661*

Beautiful Mornin': The Broadway Musical in The 1940s. *v.1 p.252*

A Beautiful Pageant: African American Theatre, Drama, and Performance in the Harlem Renaissance, 1910-1927. . . . .*v.1 p.123, v.2 p.16*

The Beautiful Room Is Empty. *v.6 p.400*

Beautiful Senoritas and Other Plays. *v.6 p.508, p.518*

Beautiful Shadow: A Life of Patricia Highsmith. *v.2 p.86, v.6 p.404*

Beauty and Art 1750-2000. . . . .*v.1 p.703, p.704*

The Beauty and Complexity of the Mandelbrot Set: University Edition. *v.5 p.498*

Beauty and Holiness: The Dialogue Between Aesthetics and Religion. *v.1 p.524, p.525*

Beauty and Love/Seyh Galip; Translated from the Ottoman Turkish with an Introduction and Key by Victoria Rowe Holbrook. *v.6 p.667, p.668*

Beauty and Revolution in Science. *v.3 p.45*

Beauty and Sadness. *v.6 p.230*

Beauty Before Age: Growing Older in Gay Culture.*v.6 p.380*

The Beauty Myth: How Images of Beauty are Used Against Women. *v.6 p.436*

The Beauty of Fired Clay: Ceramics from Burma, Cambodia, Laos, and Thailand. *v.1 p.808*

The Beauty of Men, Vol. 1. . . . .*v.6 p.406*

The Beauty of Sport: A Cross-Disciplinary Inquiry. *v.4 p.811, p.812*

The Beauty of the Cross: The Passion of Christ in Theology and the Arts, from the Catacombs to the Eve of the Renaissance. *v.1 p.654*

The Beautyful Ones Are Not yet Born. *v.2 p.752, p.753*

Bebop to Cool: Context, Ideology, and Musical Identity. *v.1 p.261, p.262*

Because I Tell a Joke or Two: Comedy, Politics and Social Difference. *v.6 p.313*

Because It Is Bitter, and Because It Is My Heart. . .*v.2 p.152*

Because It's There: The Life of George Mallory. . .*v.4 p.789*

Because Writing Matters: Improving Student Writing in Our Schools. *v.4 p.364*

Beckett Remembering, Remembering Beckett: A Centenary Celebration. *v.1 p.91, p.94, v.2 p.333*

Becket. *v.2 p.506*

Becky and Her Friends. *v.6 p.499*

Become an Energy Addict: Simple, Powerful Ways to Energize Your Life. *v.5 p.163*

Becoming a Man: Half a Life Story. *v.6 p.379, p.403*

Becoming a Model Warden: Striving for Excellence. .*v.6 p.275*

Becoming a Poet: Elizabeth Bishop with Marianne Moore and Robert Lowell. *v.2 p.62, p.102*

Becoming a Strategic Leader: Your Role in Your Organization's Enduring Success. *v.4 p.71*

Becoming Adult Learners: Principles and Practices for Effective Development. *v.4 p.319, p.320*

Becoming an Effective Leader. *v.4 p.71*

Becoming Asian American: Second-Generation Chinese and Korean American Identities. *v.6 p.110, p.127, p.135*

Becoming Biliterate: A Study of Two-Way Bilingual Immersion Education. *v.6 p.494, p.527*

Becoming Brothers. *v.5 p.629, p.631, p.632*

Becoming Campesinos: Politics, Identity, and Agrarian Struggle in Postrevolutionary Michoacan, 1920-1935. . . .*v.3 p.290*

Becoming Europe: Immigration, Integration, and the Welfare State. *v.4 p.601*

Becoming Europeans?: Attitudes, Behaviour, and Socialization in the European Parliament. *v.4 p.603*

Becoming Evil: How Ordinary People Commit Genocide and Mass Killing. *v.4 p.654, v.6 p.257, p.258*

Becoming Gay: The Journey to Self-Acceptance. . . .*v.6 p.368*

Becoming Justice Blackmun: Harry Blackmun's Supreme Court Journey. *v.4 p.467, p.536*

Becoming Maya: Ethnicity and Social Inequality in Yucatan since 1500. . . . .*v.3 p.292*

Becoming National: A Reader. *v.3 p.61*

Becoming Partners. *v.4 p.739*

Becoming President: The Bush Transition, 2000-2003.*v.3 p.482*

Becoming Prominent: Regional Leadership in Upper Canada, 1791-1841. . . . .*v.3 p.544*

Becoming Roman: The Origins of Provincial Civilization in Gaul. *v.3 p.29, p.142*

Becoming Visible: Women in European History. *v.3 p.50, v.6 p.449*

Becoming Walata: A History of Saharan Social Formation and Transformation. *v.6 p.70*

Becoming Wordsworthian: A Performative Aesthetic.*v.2 p.323*

A Bed for the Night: Humanitarianism in Crisis. . .*v.4 p.671*

Bed of Sphinxes: Selected Poems. *v.2 p.94*

The Bedbug and Selected Poetry. *v.2 p.806*

Bede the Venerable. *v.6 p.570*

Bede's Historia Ecclesiastica. *v.2 p.448*

Das Bedeutungsbuch. *v.2 p.620*

Bedford Companion to Shakespeare: An Introduction with Documents. *v.2 p.222*

Bedford Critical Companion to Joyce's Ulysses. . . .*v.2 p.360*

The Bedford Introduction to Drama. *v.1 p.67*

The Bedouin of Cyrenaica: Studies in Personal and Corporate Power. *v.4 p.40*

Bedouin of the Negev. *v.6 p.596*

Bedouin Poetry from Sinai and the Negev: Mirror of a Culture. *v.6 p.658*

The Bedside, Bathtub and Armchair Companion to Agatha Christie. *v.2 p.339*

A Bedside Nature: Genius and Eccentricity in Science, 1869-1953. . . . .*v.5 p.230*

Beef Housing and Equipment Handbook. *v.5 p.55*

Beef Production and Management Decisions. *v.5 p.54*

Beethoven and the Creative Process. *v.1 p.196, p.306*

Beethoven As I Knew Him. *v.1 p.204, p.308*

The Beethoven Compendium. *v.1 p.196, p.306*

Beethoven Concertos: History, Style, Performance. *v.1 p.202, p.242, p.307*

Beethoven: Eroica Symphony. *v.1 p.204, p.243, p.308*

Beethoven: His Life, Work and World. *v.1 p.200, p.307*

Beethoven: Impressions by His Contemporaries. .*v.1 p.204, p.308*

Beethoven in German Politics, 1870-1989. . . . . . .*v.3 p.178*

Beethoven: Missa Solemnis. *v.1 p.197, p.235, p.306*

Beethoven "Symphony No. 9". *v.1 p.195, p.196, p.235, p.238, p.306*

Beethoven on Beethoven: Playing His Piano Music His Way. *v.1 p.201, p.307, p.401*

The Beethoven Quartet Companion. . .*v.1 p.207, p.244, p.308*

The Beethoven Reader. *v.1 p.193, p.306*

Beethoven, Sibelius and "The Profound Logic": Studies in Symphonic Analysis. .*v.1 p.202, p.221, p.241, p.242, p.307, p.356, p.357*

The Beethoven Sketchbooks: History, Reconstruction, Inventory. *v.1 p.198, p.199, p.307*

Beethoven; the Last Decade 1817-1827. . . .*v.1 p.196, p.306*

Beethoven: The 'Moonlight' and Other Sonatas, Op. 27 and Op. 31. . . . .*v.1 p.199, p.240, p.307*

Beethoven: The Music and the Life. *v.1 p.200, p.307*

Beethoven: The Ninth Symphony. *v.1 p.200, p.235, p.236, p.241, p.307*

Beethoven: The Pastoral Symphony. . .*v.1 p.199, p.240, p.307*

Beethoven: Violin Concerto. *v.1 p.205, p.243, p.308*

The Beethoven Violin Sonatas: History, Criticism, Performance. *v.1 p.200, p.241, p.307*

Beethoven's Anvil: Music in Mind and Culture. . . .*v.5 p.618*

Beethoven's Compositional Process. *v.1 p.199, p.307*

Beethoven's Critics: Aesthetic Dilemmas and Resolutions During the Composer's Lifetime. *v.1 p.206, p.308*

Beethoven's Diabelli Variations. *v.1 p.199, p.240, p.307*

Beethoven's Ninth Symphony: A Portrayal of Its Musical Content, with Running Commentary on Performance and Literature As Well. .*v.1 p.204, p.307, p.308*

Beethoven's Piano Sonatas: A Short Companion. *v.1 p.203, p.242, p.307*

Beethoven. *v.1 p.204, p.308*

Before Adam Smith: The Emergence of Political Economy 1662-1776. . . . .*v.4 p.215*

Before and after an Oil Spill: The Arthur Kill. . . .*v.5 p.363*

Before Colonialism: Theories on Asian-European Relations, 1500-1750. . . . .*v.6 p.147*

Before Color Prejudice: The Ancient View of Blacks. . .*v.3 p.3*

Before European Hegemony: The World System A.D. 1250-1350. . . . .*v.6 p.145*

Before France and Germany: The Creation and Transformation of the Merovingian World. *v.3 p.143, p.162, v.6 p.563*

Before Homosexuality in the Arab-Islamic World, 1500-1800. . . . .*v.6 p.392*

Before Internment: Essays in Prewar Japanese-American History. *v.6 p.134*

Before Mickey: The Animated Film, 1898-1928. . . .*v.6 p.307*

Before Night Falls: A Memoir. . . .*v.2 p.670, v.6 p.400, p.401*

Before Novels: The Cultural Contexts of Eighteenth Century English Fiction. *v.2 p.192*

Before Silent Spring: Pesticides in Pre-DDT America. *v.5 p.10, p.354*

Before Stalingrad: Barbarossa, Hitler's Invasion of Russia 1941. . . . .*v.3 p.174, p.175*

Before Stonewall: Activists for Gay and Lesbian Rights in Historical Context. *v.6 p.387*

Before Stonewall: The Making of a Gay and Lesbian Community. *v.6 p.366*

Before the Best Interests of the Child. *v.4 p.442*

Before the Closet: Same-Sex Love from Beowulf to Angels in America. *v.2 p.167, v.6 p.392*

Before the Deluge: A Portrait of Berlin in the 1920s. .*v.3 p.181*

Before the Echo: Essays on Nature. *v.5 p.226*

Before the Fall: An Inside View of the Pre-Watergate White House. *v.3 p.479*

Before the Five Frontiers: Panama from 1821-1903. . .*v.3 p.305*

Before the Horror: The Population of Hawai'i on the Eve of Western Contact. *v.6 p.131*

Before the Industrial Revolution: European Society and Economy, 1000-1700. . . . .*v.3 p.39*

Before the Mayflower: A History of Black America. . . .*v.6 p.3*

Before the Muses: An Anthology of Akkadian Literature. *v.6 p.664, p.665*

Before the Normans: Southern Italy in the Ninth and Tenth Centuries. *v.6 p.563*

Before the Revolution: The Vietnamese Peasants under the French. *v.4 p.704, v.6 p.167*

Before We Are Born: Essentials of Embryology and Birth Defects. *v.5 p.162*

Before We Were Free. *v.3 p.316*

The Beforelife. *v.2 p.159*

The Beggar and the Professor: A Sixteenth-Century Family Saga. *v.3 p.244*

The Beggar Maid: Stories of Flo and Rose. *v.2 p.737*

The Beggar, the Thief and the Dogs, Autumn Quail. .*v.6 p.661*

Beggar Your Neighbours: Apartheid Power in Southern Africa. *v.6 p.74*

Beggars and Choosers: How the Politics of Choice Shapes Adoption, Abortion, and Welfare in the United States. *v.4 p.769, v.6 p.471*

The Beggar's Opera. *v.1 p.250, p.407, p.408*

Beginners Bulgarian. *v.2 p.774*

A Beginner's Guide to Microarrays. *v.5 p.103, p.110*

Beginning Functional Analysis. *v.5 p.494*

The Beginning of Philosophy. *v.1 p.420*

The Beginning of the Great Game in Asia, 1828-1834. .*v.3 p.77*

Beginning Slovak: A Course for the Individual or Classroom Learner. *v.2 p.777*

Beginning to Read: Thinking and Learning about Print. *v.4 p.361*

Beginning with O. *v.2 p.141, v.6 p.404*

The Beginnings and Evolution of Algebra. . . .*v.5 p.465, p.472*

The Beginnings of English Literature to Skelton 1509. *v.2 p.167*

Beginnings of Modernization in the Middle East: The Nineteenth Century. *v.6 p.594*

Beginnings of Rome: Italy and Rome from the Bronze Age to the Punic Wars (c. 1000-264 B. C.). *v.3 p.24, v.4 p.12*

The Beginnings of Social Understanding. *v.5 p.626, p.631*

Beginnings. *v.2 p.736, v.5 p.77*

Begrimed and Black: Christian Traditions on Blacks and Blackness. *v.1 p.608*

Behan Complete Plays. *v.2 p.333*

Behavior: An Introduction to Comparative Psychology. .*v.5 p.616*

Behavior Analysis and Treatment. *v.5 p.667*

⬜ Behavior Analysis (APA Division 25). *v.5 p.662*

⬜ Behavior Analyst Certification Board. *v.5 p.666*

Behavior and Design of Aluminum Structures. .*v.5 p.697, p.736*

Behavior and Misbehavior: A Teacher's Guide to Action. *v.4 p.284*

Behavior Modification: Basic Principles. *v.5 p.667*

Behavior of Industrial Prices. *v.4 p.239*

The Behavior of the Laboratory Rat: A Handbook with Tests. *v.5 p.616*

A Behavior System: An Introduction to Behavior Theory Concerning the Individual Organism. *v.5 p.615*

Behavior Theory and Conditioning. *v.5 p.616*

Behavior Therapy Techniques: Guide to the Treatment of Neuroses. *v.5 p.667*

Behavioral and Emotional Disorders in Adolescents: Nature, Assessment, and Treatment. *v.5 p.663*

Behavioral Ecology and Conservation Biology. *v.5 p.165, p.166, p.178*

Behavioral, Social, and Emotional Assessment of Children and Adolescents. *v.5 p.602*

Behavioral Theory of the Firm. *v.4 p.72, p.83*

Behavior-Based Robotics. *v.5 p.710*

Behaviour and Conservation. *v.5 p.17, v.6 p.291*

Behavioural Approaches to Conservation in the Wild. .*v.5 p.178*

Behemoth: The Structure and Practice of National Socialism, 1933-1944. . . . .*v.3 p.173*

Behind a Mask: The Unknown Thrillers of Louisa May Alcott. *v.2 p.31*

Behind Bakke: Affirmative Action and the Supreme Court. *v.4 p.539*

Behind Closed Doors: Violence in the American Family. *v.4 p.743*

Behind Mud Walls: Seventy-Five Years in a North Indian Village. *v.4 p.40*

Behind the Burnt Cork Mask: Early Blackface Minstrelsy and Antebellum American Popular Culture. *v.1 p.281*

Behind the Curtains. *v.2 p.657*

Behind the Gates: Security and the New American Dream. *v.6 p.718*

Behind the Geometrical Method: A Reading of Spinoza's Ethics. *v.1 p.477*

Behind the Green Curtains: Figuro in the Night. *v.2 p.373, p.374*

Behind the Intifada: Labor and Women's Movements in the Occupied Territories. *v.6 p.454, p.617*

Behind the Lines: Gender and the Two World Wars. . *v.6 p.454*

Behind the Lines in the Southern Confederacy. *v.3 p.429*

Behind the Lines: The Oral History of Special Operations in World War II. *v.4 p.486*

Behind the Mask: My Double Life in Baseball. *v.6 p.384*

Behind the Mask of Innocence: Sex, Violence, Prejudice, Crime: Films of Social Conscience in the Silent Era. *v.6 p.320, p.321*

Behind the Mask: On Sexual Demons, Sacred Mothers, Transvestites, Gangsters and Other Japanese Cultural Heroes. *v.6 p.219*

Behind the Mule: Race and Class in African-American Politics. *v.6 p.4, p.31*

Behind the Oval Office: Getting Reelected Against All Odds. *v.3 p.476*

Behind the Razor Wire: Portrait of a Contemporary American Prison System. *v.6 p.275*

Behind the Screen: How Gays and Lesbians Shaped Hollywood, 1910-1969. . . . .*v.6 p.417*

Behind the Smoke and Mirrors: Research from the Mexican Migration Project. *v.6 p.529*

Behind the Trail of Broken Treaties: An Indian Declaration of Independence. *v.6 p.693, p.695*

Behind the Urals: An American Worker in Russias City of Steel. *v.3 p.224*

Behind the Veil in Arabia: Women in Oman. *v.4 p.40, v.6 p.628*

Behind the War on Terror: Western Secret Strategy and the Struggle for Iraq. *v.4 p.562*

Behn: Five Plays. *v.1 p.77, p.98,v.2 p.238*

⬜ Beilstein Dictionary. *v.5 p.289*

The Beilstein System: Strategies for Effective Searching. *v.5 p.288*

Beilstein's Index. *v.5 p.289*

Being and Becoming, the Cinemas of Asia. *v.6 p.334*

Being and Nothingness. *v.1 p.458, p.505*

Being and Some Philosophers. *v.1 p.489*

Being and Time. *v.1 p.470*

Being Buddhist in a Christian World: Gender and Community in a Korean American Temple. *v.6 p.106, p.136, p.137*

Being Extreme. *v.4 p.857*

Being Geniuses Together, 1920-1930. . . . .*v.2 p.63*

Being Human. *v.5 p.158*

Being Israeli: The Dynamics of Multiple Citizenship. *v.6 p.615, p.616*

Being Logical: A Guide to Good Thinking. *v.1 p.492*

Being Modern in Bali: Image and Change. . . .*v.6 p.175, p.178*

Being Muslim the Bosnian Way: Identity and Community in a Central Bosnian Village. *v.3 p.249*

Being Right: Conservative Catholics in America. .*v.1 p.574, p.575*

Beirut '75. . . . .*v.6 p.663*

Beirut Blues. *v.6 p.657*

The Beirut Massacre: The Complete Kahan Commission Report. *v.6 p.606*

Beirut Nightmares. *v.6 p.663*

Beisbol: Latin Americans and the Grand Old
    Game. *v.4 p.808, p.833, p.844, p.851, p.899*

The Bel Canto Operas: A Guide to the Operas of Rossini,
    Bellini, and Donizetti. *v.1 p.201, p.231, p.309, p.321, p.351*

Bela Bartok: A Guide to Research. .*v.1 p.163, p.208, p.304, p.305*

Bela Bartok Studies in Ethnomusicology. *v.1 p.297*

Bel-Ami. *v.2 p.497*

Belarus: At the Crossroads in History. *v.3 p.230*

Belfast Politics. *v.4 p.607*

Belgium: A History. *v.3 p.206*

Belgium's Return to Neutrality: An Essay in the Frustrations of
    Small Power Diplomacy. *v.3 p.206*

Belief and Knowledge: Mapping the Cognitive
    Landscape. *v.1 p.483*

Belief and Uncertainty in the Poetry of Robert Frost. . .*v.2 p.77*

Belief in God in an Age of Science. *v.1 p.526*

e Belief in Psychology: A Study in the Ontology of
    Mind. *v.5 p.593, p.594*

Beliefs, Behaviors, and Alcoholic Beverages: A Cross-Cultural
    Survey. *v.4 p.776*

The Bell Curve: Intelligence and Class Structure in American
    Life. *v.5 p.608, p.632, p.653*

A Bell for Adano. *v.2 p.81*

e Bell Hooks' Engaged Pedagogy: A Transgressive Education
    for Critical Consciousness. *v.4 p.342*

The Bell Jar. *v.2 p.153*

☐ BELL: the Business Ethics Links Library - Resources for
    Research in Business Ethics and Social
    Responsibility. *v.4 p.53*

☐ BELL: the business ethics links library. *v.4 p.146*

Belle de jour. *v.2 p.521*

Bellow: A Biography. *v.2 p.59, p.60*

The Bellwomen: The Story of the Landmark AT&T Sex
    Discrimination Case. *v.4 p.134, p.445*

The Belly Dance Book: Rediscovering the Oldest Dance. .*v.1 p.17*

Belly Dance: Orientalism, Transnationalism, and Harem
    Fantasy. *v.1 p.16, p.17*

Belmont Revisited: Ethical Principles for Research with Human
    Subjects. *v.5 p.674*

Belonging to the World: Women's Rights and American
    Constitutional Culture. *v.4 p.458*

Beloved Land: Mexican American Oral Histories from Southern
    Arizona. *v.6 p.489, p.523*

Beloved. *v.2 p.151*

Belzoni's Travels: Narrative of Ther Operations and Recent
    Discoveries in Egypt and Nubia. *v.3 p.11*

Ben and Jerry's: How Two Real Guys Built a Business with a
    Social Conscience and a Sense of Humor. *v.4 p.52*

Ben Hogan: An American Life. *v.4 p.860*

Ben Hogan's Five Lessons: The Modern Fundamentals of
    Golf. *v.4 p.861*

Ben Jonson: Authority Criticism. *v.2 p.219*

Ben Jonson: Dramatist. *v.2 p.219*

Ben Jonson: His Craft and Art. *v.2 p.220*

Ben Jonson Revised. *v.2 p.220*

Ben Jonson: To the First Folio. *v.2 p.219*

Ben Jonson's Plays and Masques. *v.2 p.219*

Ben Jonson's Poems, a Study of the Plain Style. . . .*v.2 p.220*

Ben Okri: Towards the Invisible City. *v.2 p.756*

Ben Shahn: An Artist's Life. *v.1 p.739*

Ben Shahn's New York: The Photography of Modern
    Times. *v.1 p.767*

The Bench and the Ballot; Southern Federal Judges and Black
    Voters. *v.4 p.461*

Bench Press. *v.4 p.817, p.869, p.870*

The Benchley Roundup: A Selection by Nathaniel Benchley of
    his Favorites. *v.2 p.58*

Benchmarks: Great Constitutional Controversies in the Supreme
    Court. *v.4 p.536*

A Bend in the River. *v.2 p.768, p.769*

Bending the Landscape: Fantasy. *v.6 p.406*

Bending the Landscape: Horror. *v.6 p.406*

Bending with the Winds: Kurt Waldheim and the United
    Nations. *v.4 p.633*

The Bends: Compressed Air in the History of Science, Diving,
    and Engineering. *v.4 p.870*

Beneath the American Renaissance: The Subversive Imagination
    in the Age of Emerson and Melville. *v.2 p.9, p.10*

Beneath the Cross: Catholics and Huguenots in
    Sixteenth-Century Paris. *v.3 p.145*

Beneath the Equator: Cultures of Desire, Male Homosexuality,
    and Emerging Gay Communities in Brazil. *v.4 p.31*

Beneath the Underdog. *v.1 p.262, p.341*

Benedetto Croce Reconsidered: Truth and Error in Theories of
    Art, Literature, and History. *v.1 p.473*

Benedictine Monachism: Studies in Benedictine Life and
    Rule. *v.1 p.577, v.3 p.56*

Benefits for the Workplace of the Future. *v.4 p.98, p.99*

Benet's Reader's Encyclopedia. *v.2 p.549*

Benevolent Assimilation: The American Conquest of the
    Philippines, 1899-1903. . . . .*v.6 p.180*

Benevolent Repression: Social Control and the American
    Reformatory-Prison Movement. *v.6 p.274*

Benezit Dictionary of Artists, Set. *v.1 p.664*

Bengal Divided: Hindu Communalism and Partition,
    1932-1947. . . . .*v.6 p.160*

Bengal Nights: A Novel. *v.2 p.817*

Bengal: The British Bridgehead: Eastern India
    1740-1828. . . . .*v.6 p.161*

Ben-Hur. *v.2 p.128*

Benin. *v.6 p.73*

Benito Perez Galdos. *v.2 p.655*

Benjamin Britten: A Biography. . . .*v.1 p.211, p.314, v.6 p.409*

Benjamin Constant: A Biography. *v.2 p.479*

Benjamin Franklin, an American Man of Letters. . . .*v.2 p.29*

Benjamin Franklin and Pennsylvania Politics. *v.3 p.492*

Benjamin Franklin: Autobiography, Poor Richard, and Later
    Writings. *v.2 p.29*

Benjamin Franklin: Silence Dogood, the Busy-Body, and Early
    Writings. *v.2 p.29*

Benjamin Franklin Tracy: Father of the Modern American
    Fighting Navy. *v.3 p.433*

Benjamin Harrison: Hoosier President: The White House and
    After 1889-1901. . . . .*v.3 p.438*

Benjamin Harrison: Hoosier Statesman. *v.3 p.438*

Benjamin Harrison: Hoosier Warrior. *v.3 p.438*

Benjamin Thompson, Count Rumford. *v.5 p.396*

Benjamin. *v.2 p.690*

Benny Carter: A Life in American Music, Set. .*v.1 p.257, p.316*

Benozzo Gozzoli. *v.1 p.734*

The Bent Lens: A World Guide to Gay and Lesbian
    Film. *v.6 p.416*

Bent: The Play. *v.6 p.413*

Bentham's Handbook of Political Fallacies. *v.4 p.574*

Bentham's Prison: A Study of the Panopticon
    Penitentiary. *v.3 p.115, p.129*

Bentham. *v.1 p.445*

Beowulf: A Dual-Language Edition. *v.2 p.203*

Beowulf: A New Verse Translation. *v.2 p.204, p.352*

Beowulf: A Translation and Commentary. *v.2 p.205*

Beowulf: An Imitative Translation. *v.2 p.204*

Beowulf: An Introduction to the Study of the Poem with a
    Discussion of the Stories of Offa and Finn,. . . .*v.2 p.204*

Beowulf and the Appositive Style. *v.2 p.205*

Beowulf and the Beowulf Manuscript. *v.2 p.205*

Beowulf and the Fight at Finnsburg: A Bibliography. *v.2 p.205*

Beowulf and the Fight at Finnsburg. *v.2 p.204*

Beowulf and the Medieval Proverb Tradition. *v.2 p.205*

Beowulf Scholarship: An Annotated Bibliography,
    1979-1990. . . . .*v.2 p.205*

Beowulf: The Donaldson Translation, Backgrounds and Sources,
    Criticism. *v.2 p.203*

Beowulf: The Poem and Its Tradition. *v.2 p.205*

Beowulf: With the Finnesburg Fragment. *v.2 p.203*

Beowulf. *v.2 p.204*

Berber Culture on the World Stage: From Village to
    Video. *v.6 p.600*

The Berbers and the Islamic State: The Marinid
    Experience. *v.6 p.586, p.601*

The Berbers of Morocco. *v.6 p.600, p.601*

Bereavement: Studies of Grief in Adult Life. *v.5 p.655*

The Berg Companion. *v.1 p.216, p.309*

Berg: Violin Concerto. *v.1 p.221, p.242, p.309*

Bergey's Manual of Systematic Bacteriology: The Archaea, and
    the Deeply Branching and Phototropic Bateria. . .*v.5 p.206*

Bergey's Manual of Systematic Bacteriology: The
    Proteobacteria. *v.5 p.206*

The Berg-Schoenberg Correspondence: Selected
    Letters. *v.1 p.215, p.309, p.353*

Bergson. *v.1 p.456*

Berio. *v.1 p.220, p.309, p.310*

Berkeley: An Interpretation. *v.1 p.450, p.451*

Berkeley at War: The 1960s. *v.3 p.531*

Berkeley's Principles and Dialogues: Background Source
    Materials. *v.1 p.449*

Berkeley. *v.1 p.450*

Berkshire Encyclopedia of World Sport. *v.4 p.848*

Berlin Alexanderplatz: Die Geschichte Von Franz
    Biberkopf. *v.2 p.606*

Berlin Cabaret. *v.3 p.178*

The Berlin Jewish Community: Enlightenment, Family and
    Crisis, 1770-1830. . . . .*v.3 p.180*

Berlin Journal, 1989-1990. . . . .*v.3 p.177*

The Berlin Novels of Theodor Fontane. *v.2 p.597*

Berlin: Spatial Structure of a Divided City. *v.3 p.181*

The Berlin Stories. *v.2 p.356*

Berlin. *v.3 p.181*

Berlioz and the Romantic Century. *v.1 p.193, p.310*

Berlioz: Romeo et Juliette. *v.1 p.203, p.236, p.311*

Berlioz's Orchestration Treatise: A Translation and
    Commentary. *v.1 p.393*

Berlioz. *v.1 p.198, p.310*

Bernadette of Lourdes: Her Life, Death and
    Visions. *v.3 p.54, p.154*

Bernanos. *v.2 p.508*

The Bernard Cohn Omnibus: An Anthropologist among the
    Historians and Other Essays, Colonialism and Its
    Forms of Knowledge, India: The Social Anthropology of a
    Civilization. *v.6 p.153*

Bernard Herrmann's the Ghost and Mrs. Muir: A Film Score
    Guide. *v.1 p.255, p.332*

Bernard Herrmann's Vertigo: A Film Score
    Handbook. *v.1 p.255, p.332*

Bernard Mandeville. *v.2 p.251*

Bernard Maybeck: Visionary Architect. *v.1 p.795, p.796*

Bernard Meadows: Sculpture and Drawings. *v.1 p.778*

Bernard of Clairvaux: Between Cult and History. . .*v.1 p.578*

Bernard of Clairvaux: Five Books on Consideration - Advice to
    a Pope. *v.1 p.572*

Bernard of Clairvaux: Selected Works. *v.3 p.56*

Bernard of Clairvaux. *v.1 p.579*

Bernard Shaw: A Life. *v.2 p.309*

Bernard Shaw and the Comic Sublime. *v.2 p.309*

Bernard Shaw and the Webbs. *v.2 p.309*

Bernard Shaw: The Ascent of the Superman. *v.2 p.309*

Bernard Shaw: The One-Volume Definitive Edition. . .*v.2 p.309*

Bernard Shaw, Vol. 1. . . . .*v.2 p.309*

Bernard Shaw's Remarkable Religion: A Faith That Fits the
    Facts. *v.2 p.309*

Bernard Shaw's the Quintessence of Ibsenism and Related
    Writings. *v.1 p.80, p.103*

Bernardino de Sahagun, First Anthropologist. *v.3 p.286*

Bernardo O'Higgins and the Independence of Chile. . *v.3 p.351*

Bernhard Riemann, 1826-1866: Turning Points in the
    Conception of Mathematics. *v.5 p.467*

Bernhardt. *v.6 p.649*

Bernini and the Art of Architecture. *v.1 p.794*

Berossos and Manetho, Introduced and Translated: Native
    Traditions in Ancient Mesopotamia and Egypt. . . .*v.3 p.11*

Beroul: The Romance of Tristan. *v.2 p.468*

Beroul's "Tristan" and the "Folie de Berne". *v.2 p.468*

Berta Hummel Catalogue Raisonné 1927-1931: Student Days in Munich. *v.1 p.698*

Berthe Morisot. *v.1 p.734*

Bertoldo di Giovanni, Sculptor of the Medici Household: Critical Reappraisal and Catalogue Raisonné. . . .*v.1 p.779*

Bertolt Brecht in America. *v.2 p.605*

Bertolt Brecht: The Plays. *v.2 p.605*

Bertolt Brecht. *v.2 p.605*

Bertrand Barere: A Reluctant Terrorist. *v.3 p.150*

Bertrand Russell. *v.1 p.447*

Besame Mucho: An Anthology of Gay Latino Fiction. *v.6 p.496*

Beside the Golden Door: Policy, Politics, and the Homeless. *v.4 p.751*

Beside the Golden Door: Policy, Politics and the Homeless. *v.4 p.769*

🄒 Besos Mágicos. *v.2 p.692*

Bessemer: A Sociological Perspective of a Chicano Barrio. *v.6 p.542, p.548*

Bessie Head. *v.2 p.756*

Bessie. *v.1 p.257, p.357,v.6 p.408*

The Best American Essays 2005. . . . .*v.2 p.28, p.584*

The Best American Essays of the Century. *v.2 p.28*

The Best American Gay Fiction. *v.6 p.406*

Best American Plays: Third Series, 1945-51. . . .*v.1 p.65, p.114*

The Best American Short Plays 1989. . . . . .*v.1 p.64, p.112*

The Best American Short Plays 1990. . . . .*v.1 p.69*

The Best American Short Stories 2005. . . . .*v.2 p.583*

The Best American Short Stories of the Century. . . .*v.2 p.27*

The Best American Sports Writing of the Century. . . .*v.2 p.19*

The Best and the Brightest. *v.3 p.472*

The Best Circles: Society Etiquette and the Season. *v.3 p.92, p.111, p.123*

The Best Circles. *v.6 p.744, p.747, p.761*

The Best Contemporary Jewish Writing. *v.2 p.19, p.20*

The Best Divisions for Knowledge of the Regions. . .*v.6 p.584*

Best Entry-Level Jobs, 2005-2006. . . . .*v.4 p.171*

Best Laid Schemes: The Psychology of the Emotions. .*v.5 p.655*

The Best Little Boy in the World. *v.6 p.403*

The Best Man. *v.2 p.127*

Best Mathematical Puzzles of Sam Loyd. *v.5 p.469*

The Best Men: Liberal Reformers in the Gilded Age with a New Preface. *v.3 p.438*

The Best Nature Writing of Joseph Wood Krutch. .*v.5 p.79, p.230*

The Best of Clarence Day. *v.2 p.69*

The Best of Faiz. *v.6 p.151*

The Best of Newspaper Design. *v.4 p.409*

The Best of Plays and Players 1953-1968, Vol. 1. .*v.1 p.68, p.117*

The Best of Plays and Players: 1969-1983, Vol. 2. .*v.1 p.68, p.117*

The Best of the Achaeans: Concepts of the Hero in Archaic Greek Poetry. *v.2 p.415*

The Best of Times: America in the Clinton Years. *v.3 p.442, p.473,v.4 p.486*

The Best Olympics Ever?: Social Impacts of Sydney 2000. . . . .*v.4 p.846, p.884, p.885, p.888, p.891*

The Best Pitcher in Baseball: The Life of Rube Foster, Negro League Giant. *v.4 p.831, p.850*

Best Plays, 1963-1964. . . . .*v.1 p.62, p.111*

Best Plays, 1964-1965. . . . .*v.1 p.62, p.111*

Best Plays, 1966-1967. . . . .*v.1 p.62, p.111*

The Best Plays of 1919-1920. . . . . .*v.1 p.68, p.116, p.117*

The Best Plays of 1929-1930. . . . .*v.1 p.68, p.117*

The Best Plays of 1932-1933. . . . .*v.1 p.62, p.111*

The Best Plays of 1987-1987. . . . .*v.1 p.66, p.114*

Best Plays of 1987-1988. . . . .*v.1 p.66, p.115*

The Best Plays of 1988-1989. . . . .*v.1 p.66, p.114*

The Best Plays of 1989-1990. . . . . .*v.1 p.66, p.114, p.115*

The Best Plays of 1998-1999: The Otis Guernsey-Burns Mantle Theatre Yearbook. *v.1 p.65, p.114*

The Best Plays of 1999-2000: The Otis Guernsey-Burns Mantle Theatre Yearbook, Set. *v.1 p.65, p.114*

The Best Plays of 2000-2001: The Otis Guernsey-Burns Mantle Theatre Yearbook. *v.1 p.67, p.115*

Best Plays of the Early American Theatre, 1787-1911. . . . .*v.1 p.65, p.114,v.2 p.25*

Best Plays of the Early American Theatre: From the Beginning to 1916. . . . .*v.2 p.25*

Best Plays Series. *v.1 p.62, p.111*

The Best Poems of the English Language: From Chaucer Through Frost. *v.2 p.582*

Best Practice: Ideas and Insights from the World's Foremost Business Thinkers. *v.4 p.71, p.72*

Best Practice in Inventory Management. *v.4 p.117*

Best Practices for Teaching Introduction to Psychology. .*v.5 p.675*

Best Practices in Planning and Management Reporting: From Data to Decisions. *v.4 p.81*

Best Resumes for College Students and New Grads. . .*v.4 p.170*

Best Russian Short Stories. *v.2 p.795*

The Best Short Plays: 1983. . . . .*v.1 p.64, p.112*

The Best Short Plays: 1984. . . . .*v.1 p.64, p.112*

The Best Short Plays: 1985. . . . .*v.1 p.64, p.113*

The Best Short Plays: 1987. . . . . .*v.1 p.64, p.112, p.113*

The Best Short Plays: 1988-1989. . . . .*v.1 p.64, p.112*

The Best Short Plays of 1986. . . . .*v.1 p.64, p.113*

Best Short Stories of J. G. Ballard. *v.2 p.330*

The Best Stories of Paul Laurence Dunbar. *v.2 p.36*

The Best Test Preparation for the CLEP Biology. . . .*v.5 p.244*

Bestiario: Varia Invención. *v.2 p.667*

Bestiario. *v.2 p.678*

Best's Review. *v.4 p.163*

Bestsellers: Popular Fiction since 1900. . . . .*v.2 p.190*

La Bete Humaine. *v.2 p.505*

Betrayal and Other Acts of Subversion: Feminism, Sexual Politics, Asian American Women's Literature. *v.6 p.95, p.111*

Betrayal: German Churches and the Holocaust. *v.1 p.609, p.610*

Betrayal of Science and Reason: How Anti-Environmental Rhetoric Threatens Our Future. *v.5 p.411*

The Betrayal of the Negro: From Rutherford B. Hayes to Woodrow Wilson, Vol. 1. . . . .*v.6 p.7*

Betrayal of Trust: The Collapse of Global Public Health. .*v.4 p.668*

Title Index

Betrayed: A History of Presidential Failure to Protect Black
Lives. *v.4 p.568*

The Betrothed: (I Promessi Sposi). *v.2 p.712*

The Betrothed. *v.2 p.307*

Better Angel: A Novel. *v.6 p.395*

Better Books! Better Readers!: How to Choose, Use and Level
Books for Children in the Primary Grades. *v.4 p.360*

A Better Class of Person: An Autobiography,
1929-1956. . . . . *v.2 p.376*

Better Environmental Policy Studies: How to Design and
Conduct More Effective Analysis. . . . *v.4 p.566, v.6 p.301*

The Better of Mcsweeney's Volume One: Issues 1-10, Vol.
1. . . . . *v.2 p.583*

A Better Place to Live: Reshaping the American Suburb. *v.6 p.718*

Better Together: Restoring the American Community. *v.4 p.719*

Betting the Line: Sports Wagering in American
Life. *v.4 p.715, p.899, p.900*

Betty Ford: Candor and Courage in the White House. *v.3 p.471*

Between Athens and Jerusalem: Jewish Identity in the
Hellenistic Diaspora. *v.1 p.547*

Between Ballots and Bullets: Algeria's Transition from
Authoritarianism. *v.6 p.642*

Between Bargaining and Politics: An Introduction to European
Labor Relations. *v.4 p.123*

Between Capitalism and Socialism: Essays in Political
Economics. *v.4 p.243, p.244*

Between Church and State: Religion and Public Education in a
Multicultural America, 1600-2000. . . . . *v.4 p.307*

Between Devotion and Design: The Architecture of John Cyril
Hawes. *v.1 p.795*

Between East and West: Polish and Russian Nineteenth-Century
Travel to the Orient. *v.2 p.778, p.779, p.789, p.798*

Between Facts and Norms: Contributions to a Discourse Theory
of Law and Democracy. *v.4 p.484, p.767*

Between Field and Cooking Pot: The Political Economy of
Marketwomen in Peru. *v.3 p.328*

Between Freedom and Subsistence: China and Human
Rights. *v.4 p.513, p.620*

Between Geography and History: Hellenistic Constructions of
the Roman World. *v.4 p.377*

Between God and Man: A Judgment on War Crimes; a Play in
Two Parts. *v.6 p.230, p.231*

Between God and the Party: Religion and Politics in
Revolutionary Cuba. *v.3 p.310*

Between Heaven and Earth: A History of Chinese
Writing. *v.1 p.719*

Between Home and the Diaspora: The Politics of Theorizing
Filipino and Filipino American Identities. *v.6 p.129*

Between Labor and Management. *v.4 p.121*

Between Landscape Architecture and Land Art. *v.1 p.815*

Between Man and Man. *v.1 p.467, p.468*

Between Marriage and the Market: Intimate Politics and
Survival in Cairo. *v.6 p.456, p.638*

Between Memory and Desire: The Middle East in a Troubled
Age. *v.6 p.593*

Between Memory and Vision: The Case for Faith-Based
Schooling. *v.4 p.308*

Between Men: English Literature and Male Homosocial
Desire. *v.2 p.192, v.6 p.760*

Between Montmartre and the Mudd Club: Popular Music and
the Avant-Garde. *v.1 p.269*

Between Necessity and Probability: Searching for the Definition
and Origin of Life. *v.5 p.243*

Between Philosemitism and Antisemitism: Defenses of Jews and
Judaism in Germany, 1871-1932. . . . . *v.3 p.180*

Between Prison and Probation: Intermediate Punishments in a
Rational Sentencing System. *v.6 p.271, p.275*

Between Promise and Policy: Ronald Reagan and Conservative
Reformism. *v.3 p.442*

Between Qur'an and Crown: The Challenge of Political
Legitimacy in the Arab World. *v.6 p.595*

Between Race and Empire: African-Americans and Cubans
Before the Cuban Revolution. *v.3 p.307*

Between Redemption and Revival: The Jewish Yishuv of
Jerusalem in the Nineteenth Century. *v.6 p.610*

Between Reform and Revolution: German Socialism and
Communism from 1840 to 1990. . . . . *v.3 p.159*

Between Reform and Revolution: Political Struggles in the
Peruvian Andes, 1969-1991. . . . . *v.3 p.331*

Between Salt Water and Holy Water. *v.3 p.197*

Between Science and Values. *v.5 p.410, p.411, p.412*

Between Silver and Guano: Commercial Policy and the State in
Postindependence Peru. *v.3 p.327*

Between Slavery and Free Labor: The Spanish-Speaking
Caribbean in the 19th Century. *v.3 p.317*

Between the Acts. *v.2 p.393, p.394*

Between the Eyes: Essays on Photography and Politics. *v.1 p.767*

Between the Fields and the City: Women, Work, and Family in
Russia, 1861-1914. . . . . *v.3 p.217*

Between the Flag and the Banner: Women in Israeli
Politics. *v.6 p.616*

Between the Lines: South Asians and
Postcoloniality. *v.2 p.759, v.6 p.137*

Between the Lines: Yeats's Poetry in the Making. . . *v.2 p.327*

Between the Sheets, in the Streets: Queer, Lesbian and Gay
Documentary. *v.6 p.416*

Between Tsar and People: Educated Society and the Quest for
Public Identity in Late Imperial Russia. *v.3 p.220*

Between Two Cultures: An Introduction to Economic
History. *v.3 p.39*

Between Two Empires: Race, History, and Transnationalism in
Japanese America. *v.4 p.570, p.572, v.6 p.131*

Between Two Empires: The Ordeal of the Philippines,
1929-1946. . . . . *v.6 p.179*

Between Two Fires: American Indians in the Civil War. *v.6 p.687*

Between Two Islands: Dominican International
Migration. *v.4 p.570, v.6 p.529*

Between Two Nations: The Political Predicament of Latinos in
New York City. *v.6 p.538, p.549, p.718*

Between Two Worlds: The Construction of the Ottoman
State. *v.6 p.590*

Between Two Worlds: The Inner Lives of Children of
Divorce. *v.5 p.640*

Between Two Worlds. *v.2 p.109, p.538*

Between Us Girls: A Novel. *v.2 p.374*

Between Voice and Silence: Women and Girls, Race and Relationships. . . . . *.v.4 p.737*

Between Warrior Brother and Veiled Sister: Islamic Fundamentalism and the Cultural Politics of Patriarchy in Iran. . . . . *.v.6 p.632*

Between Worlds: Contemporary Asian-American Plays. *.v.6 p.98*

Between Worlds: Women Writers of Chinese Ancestry. *.v.6 p.97*

Beware the People Weeping: Public Opinion and the Assassination of Abraham Lincoln. . . . . *.v.3 p.427*

Beware the Winner's Curse: Victories That Can Sink You and Your Company. . . . . *.v.4 p.84*

The Bewitchment of Silver: The Social Economy of Mining in Nineteenth-Century Peru. . . . . *.v.3 p.327*

Beyond 1492: Encounters in Colonial North America. *.v.6 p.685*

Beyond Amazement: New Essays on John Ashbery. . . *.v.2 p.58*

Beyond Belief: Essays on Religion in a Post-Traditionalist World. . . . . *.v.4 p.719*

Beyond Belief: Psychotherapy and Religion. . . . . *.v.5 p.636*

Beyond Bilateralism: U. S.- Japan Relations in the New Asia-Pacific. *.v.3 p.390*

Beyond Black and White: Race, Ethnicity, and Gender in the U. S. South and Southwest. . . . . *.v.3 p.498*

Beyond Boredom and Anxiety: Experiencing Flow in Work and Play. . . . . *.v.5 p.583*

Beyond Boundaries: Rereading John Steinbeck. . . . *.v.2 p.123*

Beyond Bullet Points: Using Microsoft PowerPoint to Create Presentations That Inform, Motivate, and Inspire. . *.v.4 p.171*

Beyond Classical Pedagogy: Teaching Elementary School Mathematic. *.v.4 p.366*

Beyond Cloning: Religion and the Remaking of Humanity. . . . . *.v.1 p.595*

Beyond College for All: Career Paths for the Forgotten Half. . . . . *.v.4 p.305, p.353,v.5 p.577, p.578*

Beyond Criminology: Taking Harm Seriously. . . . . *.v.6 p.249*

Beyond Culture. . . . . *.v.2 p.165, v.4 p.696*

Beyond Dance: Laban's Legacy of Movement Analysis. *.v.1 p.41*

Beyond Discipline: From Compliance to Community. *.v.4 p.284*

Beyond Discourse: Education, the Self, and Dialogue. *.v.4 p.345*

Beyond Diversity Day: A Q and A on Gay and Lesbian Issues in Schools. . . . . *.v.6 p.385*

Beyond Document: Essays on Nonfiction Film. . . . *.v.6 p.310*

Beyond Domination: New Perspectives on Women and Philosophy. *.v.6 p.461*

Beyond Earth Day: Fulfilling the Promise. . . . . . *.v.6 p.296*

Beyond Ebonics: Linguistic Pride and Racial Prejudice. *.v.2 p.551*

Beyond Empire and Nation: Postnational Arguments in the Fiction of Nuruddin Farah and B. Kojo Laing. . . *.v.2 p.755*

Beyond Empiricism: Institutions and Intentions in the Study of Crime. . . . . *.v.6 p.250*

Beyond Flesh: Queer Masculinities and Nationalism in Israeli Cinema. . . . . *.v.6 p.417*

Beyond French Feminisms: Debates on Women, Politics, and Culture in France, 1981-2001. . . . *.v.6 p.433, p.453, p.456*

Beyond Genetics: Putting the Power of DNA to Work in Your Life. . . . . *.v.5 p.122, p.135*

Beyond Glory: Joe Louis vs. Max Schmeling and a World on the Brink. . . . . *.v.4 p.808, p.855*

Beyond Greed and Fear: Understanding Behavioral Finance and the Psychology of Investing. *v.4 p.97, p.102, p.103,v.5 p.586*

Beyond Grey Pinstripes 2001: Preparing MBAs for Social and Environmental Stewardship. . . . . *.v.4 p.177*

Beyond Heterochrony: The Evolution of Development. *.v.5 p.198*

Beyond Hindu and Muslim: Multiple Identity in Narratives from Village India. . . . . *.v.6 p.154*

Beyond Idols: The Shape of a Secular Society. . . . *.v.1 p.545*

Beyond Imagined Communities: Reading and Writing the Nation in Nineteenth-Century Latin America. . . . . . *.v.3 p.264*

Beyond Individual and Group Differences: Human Individuality, Scientific Psychology, and William Stern's Critical Personalism. *.v.5 p.597*

Beyond Individual Choice: Teams and Frames in Game Theory. . . . . *.v.4 p.83*

Beyond Intifada: Narratives of Freedom Fighters in the Gaza Strip. . . . . *.v.6 p.617*

Beyond Knowledge Management. . . . . *.v.4 p.77*

Beyond Labor's Veil: The Culture of the Knights of Labor. . . . . *.v.4 p.130*

Beyond Left and Right: Insurgency and the Establishment. . . . . *.v.3 p.441*

Beyond Left and Right: The Future of Radical Politics. *.v.4 p.768*

Beyond Leveled Books: Supporting Transitional Readers in Grades 2-5. *.v.4 p.365*

Beyond Memory: The Crimean Tatars' Deportation and Return. . . . . *.v.3 p.213*

Beyond MIDI: The Handbook of Musical Codes. . . *.v.1 p.388*

Beyond Nationalism: A Social and Political History of the Habsburg Officer Corps, 1848-1918. . . . . . . *.v.3 p.182*

Beyond Natural Selection. . . . . *.v.5 p.197*

Beyond Naturalism: A New Realism in American Theatre. . . . . *.v.1 p.79, p.113*

Beyond Oil: The View from Hubbert's Peak. *.v.4 p.160, v.5 p.452*

Beyond Paradise: The Life of Ramon Novarro. . . . *.v.6 p.419*

Beyond Party: Cultures of Antipartisanship in Northern Politics Before the Civil War. . . . . *.v.4 p.552, p.553*

Beyond Persuasion: Organizational Efficiency and Presidential Power. . . . . *.v.4 p.527*

Beyond Positivism and Relativism: Theory, Method, and Evidence. . . . . *.v.5 p.400, p.403*

Beyond Positivism: Economic Methodology in the Twentieth Century. . . . . *.v.4 p.194, p.198*

Beyond Praetorianism: The Latin American Military in Transition. *.v.3 p.276*

Beyond Productivity: How Leading Companies Achieve Superior Performance by Leveraging Their Human Capital. . . . . *.v.4 p.72, p.78*

Beyond Reasonable Doubt and Probable Cause: Historical Perspectives on the Anglo-American Law of Evidence. *.v.6 p.270*

Beyond Remembering: The Collected Poems of Al Purdy. . . . . *.v.2 p.738*

Beyond Right and Left: Democratic Elitism in Mosca and Gramsci. . . . . *.v.4 p.491, p.501, p.502*

Beyond Silenced Voices: Class, Race, and Gender in United States Schools. . . . . *.v.4 p.302*

Beyond Silent Spring: Integrated Pest Management and Chemical Safety. *v.5 p.9*

Beyond Smoke and Mirrors: Mexican Immigration in an Era of Free Trade. *v.4 p.571, v.6 p.525, p.530*

Beyond Sovereignty: Issues for a Global Agenda. . . .*v.4 p.496*

Beyond Standardized Testing: Better Information for School Accountability and Management. *v.4 p.286*

Beyond Stereotypes: The Critical Analysis of Chicana Literature. *v.6 p.499, p.512, p.513*

Beyond Sweatshops: Foreign Direct Investment and Globalization in Developing Nations. *v.4 p.60*

Beyond Teams: Building the Collaborative Organization. *v.4 p.80*

Beyond the American Revolution: Explorations in the History of American Radicalism. *v.3 p.411*

Beyond the Area Studies Wars: Toward a New International Studies. *v.4 p.627*

Beyond the Aspen Grove. *v.5 p.235*

Beyond the Barricades: Nicaragua and the Struggle for the Sandinista Press, 1979-1998. . . . .*v.3 p.302*

Beyond the Best Interests of the Child. *v.4 p.757*

Beyond the Boundaries of Physical Education: Educating Young People for Citizenship and Social Responsibility. *v.4 p.798, p.799*

Beyond the Cheers: Race as Spectacle in College Sport. *v.4 p.817, p.822, p.830, p.894*

Beyond the Color Line and the Iron Curtain: Reading Encounters Between Black and Red, 1922-1963. *v.6 p.30, p.31*

Beyond the Constitution. *v.4 p.453*

Beyond the Coral Sea: Travels in the Old Empires of the South-West Pacific. *v.4 p.385*

Beyond the Crime Lab: The New Science of Investigation. *v.6 p.267*

Beyond the Down Low: Sex, Lies, and Denial in Black America. *v.6 p.368, p.375, p.378*

Beyond the Exotic: Women's Histories in Islamic Societies. *v.6 p.582*

Beyond the Frontier: Writers, Western Regionalism and a Sense of Place. *v.2 p.15*

Beyond the Glass. *v.2 p.386, p.387*

Beyond the Hundredth Meridian: John Wesley Powell and the Second Opening of the West. *v.5 p.397*

Beyond the Influence: Understanding and Defeating Alcoholism. *v.5 p.673*

Beyond the Ivory Tower: Social Responsibilities of the Modern University. *v.4 p.289*

Beyond the Ivory Tower: The Frontiers of Public and Private Science. *v.5 p.409*

Beyond the Killing Fields: Voices of Nine Cambodian Survivors in America. *v.6 p.139*

Beyond the Lines: Pictorial Reporting, Everyday Life, and the Crisis of Gilded-Age America. *v.4 p.409*

Beyond the Mainstream: Essays on Modern and Contemporary Art. *v.1 p.680*

Beyond the Metafictional Mode: Directions in the Modern Spanish Novel. *v.2 p.642*

Beyond the Molecular Frontier: Challenges for Chemistry and Chemical Engineering. *v.5 p.741*

Beyond the Mountains. *v.2 p.114*

Beyond the Nation-State: Functionalism and International Organization. *v.4 p.629*

Beyond the New Deal: Harry S. Truman and American Liberalism. *v.3 p.472*

Beyond the Open Door. *v.4 p.331*

Beyond the Pale: The Jewish Encounter with Late Imperial Russia. *v.3 p.60, p.218*

Beyond the Promised Land: Jews and Arabs on the Hard Road to a New Israel. *v.6 p.610*

Beyond the Ring: The Role of Boxing in American Society. *v.4 p.819, p.856*

Beyond the Rodney King Story: An Investigation of Police Conduct in Minority Communities. *v.6 p.261*

Beyond the Ruling Class: Strategic Elites in Modern Society. *v.4 p.724*

Beyond the Shadow of Camptown: Korean Military Brides in America. *v.6 p.116, p.137, p.237*

Beyond the Stream: Islam and Society in a West African Town. *v.6 p.69*

Beyond the Synagogue Gallery: Finding a Place for Women in American Judaism. *v.1 p.553*

Beyond the Third Dimension: Geometry, Computer Graphics and Higher Dimensions. *v.5 p.494*

Beyond the Veil: Male-Female Dynamics in Modern Muslim Society. *v.6 p.450*

Beyond the Walls: Selected Poems. *v.6 p.666*

Beyond the Welfare State: Economic Planning and Its International Implications. *v.4 p.256*

Beyond Time Out: A Practical Guide to Understanding and Serving Students with Behavioral Impairments in the Public Schools. *v.4 p.284*

Beyond Unions and Collective Bargaining. *v.4 p.123*

Beyond Utility: Liberal Education for a Technological Age. *v.4 p.303*

Beyond Victims and Villains: Contemporary Plays by Disabled Playwrights. *v.1 p.67*

Beyond Vocational Education: Career Majors, Tech Prep, Schools Within Schools, Magnet Schools and Academies. *v.4 p.305*

Beyond Walras, Keynes and Marx. *v.4 p.229, p.230*

Beyond Words: Images from America's Concentration Camps. *v.6 p.88, p.133*

Beyond Zero Tolerance: Discrimination in Military Culture. *v.4 p.717, p.718, v.6 p.390*

La bâtarde. *v.2 p.521*

The Bhagavad Gita. *v.1 p.534*

Bharata Natyam from Temple to Theatre. *v.1 p.15*

Bharati Mukherjee: Critical Perspectives. *v.2 p.765*

Bi Any Other Name: Bisexual People Speak Out. . . .*v.6 p.372*

Bi Lives: Bisexual Women Tell Their Stories. *v.6 p.372*

Bi Men: Coming Out Every Which Way. *v.6 p.368*

Biased Embryos and Evolution. *v.5 p.159*

The Bible: A Very Short Introduction. *v.1 p.615*

The Bible and the Future. *v.1 p.645*

The Bible As Literature: An Introduction. *v.1 p.616*

Bible Atlas. *v.4 p.379*

The Bible: Contemporary English Version. *v.1 p.613*

The Bible in English: Its History and Influence. *v.3 p.37*

The Bible Unearthed: Archaeology's New Vision of Ancient
    Israel and the Origin of Its Sacred Texts. *v.1 p.619*

The Biblical Drama of Medieval Europe. *v.1 p.73, p.97*

Biblical Hebrew for Students of Modern Israeli Hebrew. .*v.6 p.645*

Biblical Hebrew. *v.6 p.646*

A Biblical History of Israel. *v.1 p.619*

Biblical Interpretation. *v.1 p.616*

Biblical Subtexts and Religious Themes in Works of Anton
    Chekhov. *v.2 p.809*

Biblical Tradition in Blake's Early Prophecies: The Great Code
    of Art. *v.2 p.240*

Bibliographic Guide to Chicana and Latina
    Narrative. *v.6 p.500, p.507, p.514*

Bibliographic Guide to Gabriel Garcia Marquez,
    1986-1992. . . . .*v.2 p.682*

A Bibliographic Guide to Resources in Scientific Computing,
    1945-1975. . . . .*v.5 p.405, p.406*

A Bibliographical Guide to the History of Indian-White
    Relations in the United States. *v.6 p.683, p.692*

A Bibliographical History of the Study and Use of Color from
    Aristotle to Kandinsky. *v.1 p.662, p.710*

Bibliographies of New England History: Further Additions, to
    1994. . . . .*v.3 p.485*

Bibliography and the Sociology of Texts. *v.2 p.577*

Bibliography of African American Leadership: An Annotated
    Guide. *v.6 p.32, p.35*

Bibliography of American Literature. *v.2 p.6*

A Bibliography of Anton Chekhov in English. *v.2 p.805*

Bibliography of Business Ethics Articles, 1992 -
    present. *v.4 p.53*

A Bibliography of Female Economic Thought to
    1940. . . . .*v.4 p.214, p.274*

Bibliography of Slavic Literature. *v.2 p.779*

Bibliography of the Eddas: A Supplement to Bibliography of the
    Eddas (Islandica XIII) by Halldór Hermannsson. . .*v.2 p.624*

Bibliography of the Eddas. *v.2 p.624*

Bibliography of the History of American Education. .*v.4 p.327*

Bibliography of the History of Art (BHA). *v.1 p.661*

Bibliography of Ukrainian Literature in English and French:
    Translations and Critical Works, 1950-1986. . . . .*v.2 p.814*

Bibliophiling Tejano Scholarship: Secondary Sources on
    Hispanic Texas. *v.6 p.485*

La Biblioteca Italiana. *v.2 p.699*

Biblioteca Virtual Miguel de Cervantes. *v.3 p.259*

Bibliotheca Classica Selecta. *v.2 p.399*

Bicycle Citizens: The Political World of the Japanese
    Housewife. *v.6 p.219, p.441*

Bicycle: The History. *v.4 p.857*

The Bicycle. *v.4 p.857, p.870*

Bid Me to Live: A Madrigal. *v.2 p.89*

Bidding and Auctioning for Procurement and Allocation:
    Proceedings of a Conference at the Center for
    Applied Economics, New York University. *v.4 p.251*

Bifurcated Politics: Evolution and Reform in the National Party
    Convention. *v.4 p.551*

The Big Aiiieeeee!. *v.6 p.91*

The Big Banana. *v.6 p.508*

The Big Bang: A View from the 21st Century. . .*v.5 p.71, p.72*

The Big Bang. *v.5 p.72*

The Big Book of Ceramics: A Guide to the History, Materials,
    Equipment and Techniques of Hand-Building,
    Throwing, Molding, Kiln-Firing and Glazing Pottery and
    Other Ceramic Objects. *v.1 p.807*

The Big Book of Logos 3. . . . .*v.1 p.717*

The Big Book of Logos 4. . . . .*v.1 p.717*

The Big Book of Logos. *v.1 p.717*

Big Business in China: Sino-Foreign Rivalry in the Cigarette
    Industry, 1890-1930. . . . .*v.6 p.189, p.218*

Big Business, the State, and Free Trade: Constructing Coalitions
    in Mexico. *v.3 p.295*

Big Cartoon Database. *v.6 p.307*

The Big Change: America Transforms Itself:
    1900-1950. . . . .*v.3 p.365*

The Big Chill: Investigative Reporting in the Current Media
    Environment. *v.4 p.408*

Big City Boss in Depression and War: Mayor Edward J. Kelly
    of Chicago. *v.3 p.515*

The Big Clock. *v.2 p.73*

Big Dams of the New Deal Era: A Confluence of Engineering
    and Politics. *v.5 p.702*

Big Deal: 2000 and Beyond. *v.4 p.85, p.92*

Big Digs Around the World: Proceedings of Sessions of
    Geo-Congress 98, Sponsored by the Geo-Institute
    of the American Society of Civil Engineers, October 18-21,
    1998, Boston, Massachusetts. *v.5 p.422*

The Big Fellow: Michael Collins and the Irish
    Revolution. *v.2 p.374*

Big Five Assessment. *v.5 p.603*

The Big Fix: Inside the S&L Scandal: How an Unholy Alliance
    of Politics and Money Destroyed America's Banking
    System. *v.4 p.90*

Big Game, Small World: A Basketball Adventure. .*v.4 p.845, p.855*

The Big Hunger: Stories, 1932-1959. . . . .*v.2 p.72*

The Big Knife. *v.2 p.108*

The Big Outside: A Descriptive Inventory of the Big Wilderness
    Areas of the United States. *v.5 p.168, p.234*

The Big Picture: The New Logic of Money and Power in
    Hollywood. *v.6 p.344*

The Big Rock Candy Mountain. *v.2 p.121*

The Big Sky. *v.2 p.78*

Big Sur. *v.2 p.93*

The Big Test: The Secret History of the American
    Meritocracy. *v.4 p.286*

The Biggest Bangs: The Mystery of Gamma-Ray Bursts, the
    Most Violent Explosions in the Universe. *v.5 p.68*

The Biggest Game of All: The Inside Strategies, Tactics, and
    Temperaments That Make Great Dealmakers Great. .*v.4 p.84*

The Bigness Complex: Industry, Labor, and Government in the
    American Economy. *v.4 p.52, p.53, p.120, p.148*

The Bijak of Kabir. *v.6 p.151*

Bike Boys, Drag Queens and Superstars: Avant-Garde, Mass Culture and Gay Identities in the 1960s Underground Cinema. *v.6 p.417*

Biko. *v.6 p.80*

A Bilingual Anthology of Contemporary Spanish Poetry: The Generation of 1970. . . . . *v.2 p.644, p.645*

A Bilingual Anthology of Slovene Literature. *v.2 p.812*

A Bilingual Edition of Poems by St. John of the Cross: Spiritual Songs and Ballads. *v.2 p.646*

A Bilingual Edition of the Major Epics of Victor Hugo. *v.2 p.493*

Bilingual Education for Hispanic Students in the United States. *v.6 p.526*

Bilingual Encyclopedia of Japan. *v.6 p.219*

Bill Barrett: The Evolution of a Sculptor. *v.1 p.781*

Bill Brandt: Selected Texts and Bibliography. *v.1 p.769*

The Bill Clinton Story: Winning the Presidency. . . . *v.4 p.556*

Bill Evans: How My Heart Sings. *v.1 p.262, p.323*

The Bill Monroe Reader. *v.1 p.268, p.342*

The Bill of Rights and the Politics of Interpretation. . *v.4 p.456*

The Bill of Rights: Creation and Reconstruction. . . *v.4 p.455*

Bill of Rights Reader: Leading Constitutional Cases. *v.4 p.455, p.456*

Bill of Rights. *v.4 p.455*

Bill Reid. *v.1 p.699, v.6 p.679*

Bill Viola: Going Forth by Day. *v.1 p.773*

Bill Viola: The Passions. *v.1 p.773*

Billard Um Halbzehn. *v.2 p.604*

Billboard: Art on the Road. *v.1 p.714*

The Billboard Book of Number One Hits. . . *v.1 p.170, p.266*

The Billboard Guide to Tejano and Regional Mexican Music. *v.6 p.518*

Billiards at Half-Past Nine. *v.2 p.604*

The Billie Holiday Companion: 7 Decades of Commentary. *v.1 p.259, p.332*

Billy Bathgate. *v.2 p.144*

Billy Graham: A Parable of American Righteousness. *v.1 p.648*

Billy the Kid: His Life and Legend. *v.3 p.527, p.528*

Billy. *v.2 p.748*

Binchois Studies. *v.1 p.180, p.311*

Binding Cultures: Black Women Writers in Africa and the Diaspora. *v.6 p.29*

Bing Crosby: A Pocketful of Dreams - The Early Years, 1903-1940. . . . . *v.1 p.269, p.319*

Bingo Night at the Fire Hall: The Case for Cows, Orchards, Bake Sales and Fairs. *v.4 p.772*

The Bingo Palace. *v.2 p.144, p.145*

Bio2010: Transforming Undergraduate Education for Future Research Biologists. *v.5 p.246*

Bioarchaeology: Interpreting Behavior from the Human Skeleton. *v.4 p.14*

Bioassessment and Management of North American Freshwater Wetlands. *v.5 p.380, p.381*

The Biobased Economy of the Twenty-First Century: Agriculture Expanding into Health, Energy, Chemicals and Materials. *v.5 p.13*

A Biobibliographical Handbook of Bulgarian Authors. *v.2 p.780*

A Bio-Bibliography for the History of the Biochemical Sciences since 1800. . . . . *v.5 p.326*

Biocatalysis - From Discovery to Application. *v.5 p.327*

The Biochemical Approach to Life. *v.5 p.327*

The Biochemical Basis of Sports Performance. . . . *v.4 p.874*

Biochemical Cycling and Sediment Ecology. *v.5 p.171*

Biochemical Individuality. *v.5 p.115*

Biochemical Messengers: Hormones, Neurotransmitters and Growth Factors. *v.5 p.330*

Biochemical Methods: A Concise Guide for Students and Researchers. *v.5 p.89, p.114*

Biochemical Pathways: An Atlas of Biochemistry and Molecular Biology. *v.5 p.113, p.154*

The Biochemical Periodic Table. *v.5 p.331*

Biochemical, Physiological and Molecular Aspects of Human Nutrition. *v.5 p.513*

Biochemical Society Symposia: Proteases and the Regulation of Biological Processes, Vol. 70. . . . . *v.5 p.114*

Biochemistry and Molecular Biology of Plants. *v.5 p.78, p.111, p.112, p.124*

Biochemistry of Lipids, Lipoproteins and Membranes. *v.5 p.111*

The Biochemistry of Natural Pigments. *v.5 p.330*

Biochemistry of Plant Secondary Metabolism. *v.5 p.125*

The Biochemistry of the Nucleic Acids. . . . *v.5 p.121, p.328*

Biochemistry Primer for Exercise Science. *v.4 p.874*

Biochemistry: The Chemical Reactions of Living Cells. *v.5 p.113*

Biochemistry. *v.5 p.112, p.327, p.328, p.331, p.521*

Biochips: Technology and Applications. *v.5 p.130*

Biocomputing. *v.5 p.106, p.108*

Biocosm: The New Scientific Theory of Evolution: Intelligent Life Is the Architect of the Universe. . . . *v.5 p.192, p.243*

Biodegradation of cellulose: enzymology and biotechnology. *v.5 p.361, p.362*

Biodiversity: A Reference Handbook. *v.6 p.285*

Biodiversity and Pest Management in Agroecosystems. *v.5 p.9, p.10, p.26*

Biodiversity: Biomolecular Aspects of Biodiversity and Innovative Utilization. *v.5 p.185, p.200*

The Biodiversity Crisis: Losing What Counts. *v.5 p.84*

Biodiversity, Ecosystems, and Conservation in Northern Mexico. *v.5 p.178, p.183, p.233*

Biodiversity in British Columbia: Our Changing Environment. *v.5 p.179, p.234*

Biodiversity: Measurement and Estimation. *v.5 p.179*

Bioenergetics. *v.5 p.327*

BioEngagement: Making a Christian Difference Through Bioethics Today. *v.5 p.247*

Bioethics and Secular Humanism: The Search for a Common Morality. *v.5 p.247*

Bioethics and the Common Good. *v.5 p.247*

Bioethics: Asian Perspectives - A Quest for Moral Diversity. *v.5 p.248*

Bioethics for Scientists. *v.5 p.246*

Bioethics for the Biosciences: An Introduction. . . . *v.5 p.248*

Bioethics in a Small World. *v.5 p.250*

Bioethics in Complexity: Foundations and Evolutions. *v.5 p.247*

Bioethics in Europe. *v.5 p.248, p.249*

BioEvolution: How Biotech Is Changing Our World. .*v.5 p.217*

Bioexplorer.Net: History of Biology. *v.5 p.77*

Biogeochemical Cycles: A Computer-Interactive Study of Earth
System Science and Global Change. *v.5 p.112*

Biogeochemistry: An Analysis of Global Change. .*v.5 p.440, p.441*

Biogeochemistry of Environmentally Important Trace
Elements. *v.5 p.112*

Biogeochemistry of Forested Catchments in a Changing
Environment. *v.5 p.176*

Biogeography: An Ecological and Evolutionary
Approach. *v.4 p.394, v.5 p.168*

Biogeography: Introduction to Space, Time, and Life. .*v.5 p.168*

Biogeography of Mediterranean Invasions. . . .*v.5 p.168, p.237*

Biogeography of the West Indies: Patterns and
Perspectives. *v.3 p.316, v.5 p.169*

Biogeography. *v.4 p.394, v.5 p.169*

Biographia Literaria: Biographical Sketches of My Literary Life
and Opinions, Vol. 7. . . . .*v.2 p.279*

Biographic Dictionary of Chinese Communism, 1921-1965:
Volume 1, Ai Szu-ch'i - lo I-nung; Volume 2, lo
Jui-ch'ing—Yun Tai-ying, Set. *v.6 p.194, p.199*

A Biographical Dictionary of Actors, Actresses, Musicians,
Dancers, Managers and Other Stage Personnel in London,
1660-1800. . . . .*v.1 p.100, p.140, p.142*

Biographical Dictionary of Afro-American and African
Musicians. *v.1 p.162, p.282*

Biographical Dictionary of American and Canadian Naturalists
and Environmentalists. *v.5 p.231, p.232, p.233*

Biographical Dictionary of American Cult and Sect
Leaders. *v.1 p.544*

Biographical Dictionary of American Educators, Vol. 2. .*v.4 p.338*

Biographical Dictionary of American Educators, Vol. 3. .*v.4 p.338*

Biographical Dictionary of American Educators. . . .*v.4 p.338*

Biographical Dictionary of American Science: The Seventeenth
Through the Nineteenth Centuries. *v.5 p.395*

A Biographical Dictionary of British Architects,
1600-1840. . . . .*v.1 p.783*

Biographical Dictionary of Dance. *v.1 p.3*

A Biographical Dictionary of Dissenting Economists. .*v.4 p.193*

Biographical Dictionary of Evangelicals. *v.1 p.590*

The Biographical Dictionary of Hispanic
Americans. *v.6 p.485, p.490*

Biographical Dictionary of Hispanic Literature in the United
States: The Literature of Puerto Ricans, Puerto
Rican Americans, Cuban Americans, and Other Hispanic
Writers. *v.6 p.500, p.507, p.513*

Biographical Dictionary of Literary Influences: The Nineteenth
Century, 1800-1914. . . . .*v.2 p.176, p.184, p.188, p.193*

Biographical Dictionary of Mathematicians, Set. . . .*v.5 p.464*

Biographical Dictionary of Modern American
Educators. *v.4 p.338*

Biographical Dictionary of Modern Egypt. *v.6 p.637*

Biographical Dictionary of Psychology. *v.5 p.598, p.599*

Biographical Dictionary of Republican China, Vol.
3. . . . .*v.6 p.189, p.198*

The Biographical Dictionary of Scientists, Set. *v.5 p.62*

A Biographical Dictionary of Silent Film Western Actors and
Actresses. *v.6 p.324*

Biographical Dictionary of Social and Cultural
Anthropology. *v.4 p.3, p.4*

Biographical Dictionary of Social Welfare in
America. *v.4 p.758, p.759*

Biographical Dictionary of the Confederacy. *v.3 p.427*

Biographical Dictionary of Transcendentalism. . . .*v.1 p.515*

Biographical Dictionary of Twentieth-Century
Philosophers. *v.1 p.415*

A Biographical Dictionary of Women Economists. . . .*v.4 p.193*

A Biographical Dictionary of Women Healers: Midwives,
Nurses and Physicians. *v.6 p.444*

The Biographical Dictionary of Women in Science: Pioneering
Lives from Ancient Times to the Mid-20th Century,
Set. *v.5 p.395, v.6 p.439*

Biographical Directory of American Colonial and Revolutionary
Governors, 1607-1789. . . . .*v.3 p.377, p.406*

Biographical Directory of American Territorial
Governors. *v.3 p.376, p.377*

The Biographical Directory of Native American
Painters. *v.1 p.725, v.6 p.679*

Biographical Directory of the Governors of the United States,
1789-1978. . . . .*v.3 p.377*

Biographical Directory of the Governors of the United States,
1978-1983. . . . .*v.3 p.377*

Biographical Directory of the Governors of the United States,
1983-1988. . . . .*v.3 p.377*

Biographical Directory of the United States Congress,
1774-2003. . . . .*v.3 p.376*

The Biographical Encyclopedia of Astronomers. *v.5 p.62*

The Biographical Encyclopedia of Jazz. *v.1 p.159, p.258*

Biographical Encyclopedia of Scientists. *v.5 p.395*

Biographical Essays. *v.2 p.281*

A Biographical Handbook of Hispanics and United States
Film. *v.6 p.489, p.493*

The Biographical History of Basketball. *v.4 p.853*

Biographical Index of Artists in Canada. *v.1 p.665*

Biographical Index of Historic American Stained Glass
Makers. *v.1 p.810*

Biographical Memoirs. *v.5 p.395*

Biographical Snapshots of Famous Women and Minority
Chemists. *v.5 p.260*

Biographies of Famous Chemists. *v.5 p.260*

Biographies of Noble Hispanics. *v.3 p.526*

Biographies of Scientists: An Annotated Bibliography. .*v.5 p.396*

The Biography of a River Town: Memphis—Its Heroic
Age. *v.3 p.510*

The Biography of an Institution: The Civil Service Commission
of Canada, 1908-1967. . . . .*v.4 p.588*

A Biography of Distinguished Scientist Gilbert Newton
Lewis. *v.5 p.261*

A Biography of the English Language. *v.2 p.555, p.557*

Bioindustry Ethics. *v.5 p.217, p.247*

Bioinformatics: A Biologist's Guide to Biocomputing and the
Internet. *v.5 p.97, p.105*

Bioinformatics: A Practical Approach. *v.5 p.97*

Bioinformatics: A Practical Guide to the Analysis of Genes and Proteins. .*v.5 p.99, p.101, p.102, p.103, p.104, p.115, p.138, p.145*

Bioinformatics: An Introduction. *v.5 p.98*

Bioinformatics and Computational Biology Solutions Using R and Bioconductor. *v.5 p.99, p.341*

Bioinformatics and Functional Genomics. .*v.5 p.98, p.142, p.146*

Bioinformatics and Genome Analysis. . .*v.5 p.106, p.141, p.146*

Bioinformatics and Genomes. *v.5 p.105, p.107*

Bioinformatics Basics: Applications in Biological Science and Medicine. *v.5 p.97, p.98*

Bioinformatics Biocomputing and Perl: An Introduction to Bioinformatics Computing Skills and Practice. . . .*v.5 p.109*

Bioinformatics Computing. *v.5 p.107*

Bioinformatics for Dummies. *v.5 p.97*

Bioinformatics for Geneticists. *v.5 p.105, p.131*

Bioinformatics, Genomics, and Proteomics: Getting the Big Picture. *v.5 p.97, p.104, p.144, p.145, p.148*

Bioinformatics in the Post-Genomic Era: Genome, Transcriptome, Proteome, and Information-Based Medicine. *v.5 p.101, p.102, p.104, p.144*

Bioinformatics: Managing Scientific Data. *v.5 p.97*

Bioinformatics Methods and Protocols. *v.5 p.100*

Bioinformatics: New Research. *v.5 p.99*

Bioinformatics of Genome Regulation and Structure. *v.5 p.102, p.127, p.140*

Bioinformatics: Sequence and Genome Analysis. .*v.5 p.102, p.142*

Bioinformatics: Sequence, Structure and Databanks: A Practical Approach. *v.5 p.101, p.102*

Bioinformatics Software Engineering: Delivering Effective Applications. *v.5 p.109*

Bioinformatics Technologies. *v.5 p.107, p.108*

Bioinformatics: The Machine Learning Approach. . . .*v.5 p.107*

Bioinformatics Using Computational Intelligence Paradigms. *v.5 p.106, p.109*

Bioinformatics-From Genomes to Drugs, Set. *v.5 p.97, p.98, p.146, p.149, p.152*

Bioinformatics. *v.5 p.98*

☐ Biological Abstracts/RRM. *v.5 p.325*

Biological Abstracts. *v.5 p.325*

☐ Biological Abstracts. *v.5 p.325*

The Biological and Environmental Chemistry of Chromium. *v.5 p.313*

Biological Anthropology: An Introductory Reader. .*v.4 p.14, p.15*

Biological Anthropology of the Human Skeleton. . . .*v.4 p.14*

A Biological Assessment of the Aquatic Ecosystems of the Caura River Basin, Bolivar State, Venezuela: RAP Bulletin of Biological Assessment 28. .*v.5 p.172, p.185, p.236*

A Biological Assessment of the Aquatic Ecosystems of the Pantanal, Mato Grosso do Sul, Brasil. *v.5 p.172, p.186*

A Biological Assessment of the Aquatic Ecosystems of the Rio Paraguay Basin, Alto Paraguay, Paraguay. *v.5 p.175, p.235, p.236*

The Biological Basis of Human Behavior: A Critical Review. *v.4 p.15*

The Biological Chemistry of the Elements: The Inorganic Chemistry of Life. *v.5 p.327*

Biological Chemistry. *v.5 p.327, p.328*

Biological Complexity and Integrative Pluralism. . . .*v.5 p.170*

Biological Control: Benefits and Risks. *v.5 p.8*

Biological Effects of Radiation. *v.5 p.376*

Biological Exuberance: Animal Homosexuality and Natural Diversity. *v.6 p.419, p.420*

Biological Imaging and Sensing. *v.5 p.86*

Biological Indicators of Soil Health. *v.5 p.89*

Biological Indicators of Stress in Fish. *v.5 p.214*

Biological Invasions: A Global Perspective. *v.5 p.186*

Biological Invasions: Theory and Practice. *v.5 p.181*

Biological Invasions. *v.5 p.182*

Biological Mass Spectrometry. *v.5 p.87*

Biological Nitrogen Fixation. *v.5 p.24, p.51*

Biological Nomenclature. *v.5 p.96*

Biological Oceanography: An Early History, Eighteen Seventy to Nineteen Sixty. *v.4 p.392, v.5 p.431*

Biological Oceanography: An Introduction. .*v.4 p.392, v.5 p.431*

Biological Oceanography. *v.4 p.392, v.5 p.431*

Biological Physics: Energy, Information, Life. *v.5 p.564*

Biological Populations as Indicators of Environmental Change, Vol. 1. . . . .*v.5 p.182, p.187*

Biological Responses to DNA Damage. *v.5 p.120, p.130*

The Biological Roots of Human Nature: Forging Links Between Evolution and Behavior. *v.5 p.166, p.167, p.192*

Biological Sequence Analysis: Probabilistic Models of Proteins and Nucleic Acids. *v.5 p.121*

Biological Systematics: Principles and Applications. . .*v.5 p.171*

Biological Systematics: The State of the Art. *v.5 p.199*

The Biological Variation in Indian Populations. *v.6 p.155*

Biological Warfare and Disarmament: New Problems/New Perspectives. *v.4 p.657*

Biologically Inspired Robot Behavior Engineering. . .*v.5 p.710*

A Biologist's Guide to Analysis of DNA Microarray Data. *v.5 p.100, p.103, p.110*

Biology 2007. . . . .*v.5 p.245*

Biology: A Guide to the Natural World. *v.5 p.222*

Biology: A Self-Teaching Guide. *v.5 p.245*

☐ Biology and Biochemistry--Web Guide (Stanford University). *v.5 p.324*

Biology and Epistemology. *v.5 p.247*

Biology and Social Thought 1850-1914. . . . .*v.5 p.77*

Biology and the Mechanics of the Wave-Swept Environment. *v.5 p.356, p.368*

Biology as Ideology: The Doctrine of DNA. *v.5 p.122*

Biology at the Single Molecule Level. *v.5 p.128*

Biology Demystified. *v.5 p.245*

Biology Inquiries: Standards-Based Labs, Assessments, and Discussion Lessons; Grades 7-12. . . . . .*v.5 p.89, p.246*

Biology Made Simple. *v.5 p.245*

Biology of Aging. *v.5 p.164*

The Biology of Alcoholism: Pathogenesis of Alcoholism: Biological Factors. *v.5 p.512, p.521*

The Biology of Alcoholism: Pathogenesis of Alcoholism: Psychosocial Factors. *v.5 p.512, p.522*

Biology of Amphibians. *v.5 p.214*

Biology of Animal Behavior. *v.5 p.166*

The Biology of Animal Stress: Basic Principles and Implications
    for Animal Welfare. *v.5 p.166*

Biology of Fishes. *v.5 p.214*

The Biology of Freshwater Wetlands. *v.4 p.393*

Biology of Growth of Domestic Animals. *v.5 p.56*

Biology of Lakes and Ponds. *v.4 p.391, v.5 p.174*

The Biology of Lichens. *v.5 p.210*

Biology of Nonvascular Plants. *v.5 p.206, p.207*

The Biology of Numbers: The Correspondence of Vito Volterra
    on Mathematical Biology. *v.5 p.79, p.91*

Biology of Rarity: Causes and Consequences of Rare-Common
    Differences. *v.5 p.155*

Biology of Sharks and Their Relatives. *v.5 p.214*

The Biology of the Deep Ocean. *v.5 p.173*

Biology of the Red Algae. *v.5 p.208*

The Biology of the Southern Ocean. *v.5 p.431*

Biology of Women. *v.5 p.524*

Biology Takes Form: Animal Morphology and the German
    Universities, 1800-1900. . . . .*v.3 p.45*

Biology Teacher's Survival Guide: Tips, Techniques and
    Materials for Success in the Classroom. *v.5 p.245*

Biology: The Dynamics of Life Student Edition) 2004. .*v.5 p.245*

Biology Today: An Issues Approach. *v.5 p.245, p.246*

[BiologyLabs On-Line; EvolutionLab; Evolution Lab] Lab
    Manual for BiologyLabs On-Line: EvolutionLab. . .*v.5 p.88*

Biology. *v.5 p.246*

Biomass for Renewable Energy, Fuels, and
    Chemicals. *v.5 p.362, p.377*

Biomath: Problem Solving for Biology Students. . . .*v.5 p.91*

Biomeasurement: Understanding, Analysing and Communicating
    Data in the Biosciences. *v.5 p.90*

The Biomechanics and Motor Control of Human
    Movement. *v.4 p.875, p.876, p.908, p.910*

Biomechanics in Sports: Performance Improvement and Injury
    Prevention. *v.4 p.827, p.828, p.829, p.880, p.908*

Biomechanics: Motion, Flow, Stress, and Growth. . .*v.4 p.908*

Biomechanics of Distance
    Running. *v.4 p.874, p.879, p.907, p.909*

The Biomechanics of Sports Techniques. . . .*v.4 p.873, p.908*

Biomechanics of Women's Gymnastics. . . .*v.4 p.861, p.908*

Biomedia. *v.5 p.129, p.220*

Biomedical Applications of Proteomics. *v.5 p.104, p.105, p.118*

Biomedical Engineering Principles in Sports. *v.4 p.872*

Biomedical Ethics. *v.1 p.486, v.5 p.511*

Biometrika: One Hundred Years. *v.5 p.81, p.90*

Bioorganic Chemistry: A Chemical Approach to Enzyme
    Action. *v.5 p.119, p.327*

Bioorganic Chemistry: Nucleic Acids. *v.5 p.121*

Bioorganic Chemistry. *v.5 p.119, p.327*

☐ Biophysical Chemistry Online Resources (UW,
    Madison)--Databases. *v.5 p.324*

☐ Biophysical Chemistry Online Resources (UW,
    Madison)--Techniques. *v.5 p.269*

The Biophysical Foundations of Human Movement ent, Vol.
    2. . . . .*v.4 p.874, p.907, p.909*

Bio-Pics: How Hollywood Constructed Public
    History. *v.6 p.314, p.327*

Biopolis: Patrick Geddes and the City of Life. *v.6 p.716*

The Biopsychosocial Approach: Past, Present, and
    Future. *v.5 p.532*

☐ BIOSIS Previews. *v.5 p.325*

Biosocial Criminology: Challenging Environmentalism's
    Supremacy. *v.6 p.250*

Biostatistical Methods. *v.5 p.100*

Biostatistics: A Methodology for the Health
    Sciences. *v.5 p.90, p.93*

BioStats Basics: A Student Handbook. *v.5 p.92*

The Biosynthesis of Steroids, Terpenes, and
    Acetogenins. *v.5 p.330*

The Biotech Age: The Business of Biotech and How to Profit
    from It. *v.5 p.218, p.219*

Biotech Industry: A Global, Economic, and Financing
    Overview. *v.5 p.217*

Biotech Investing: Every Investor's Guide. *v.5 p.218*

The Biotech Investor: How to Profit from the Coming Boom in
    Biotechnology. *v.5 p.217*

The Biotech Investor's Bible. *v.5 p.220*

Biotechnology: An Introduction. *v.4 p.156*

Biotechnology and Biopharmaceuticals: Transforming Proteins
    and Genes into Drugs. *v.5 p.218*

Biotechnology and Genetic Engineering. *v.5 p.138, p.220*

Ⓔ Biotechnology and Integrated Pest Management. . . .*v.5 p.8*

Biotechnology Careers. *v.5 p.250*

Biotechnology Demystified. *v.4 p.156, p.157*

Biotechnology: Demystifying the Concepts. *v.5 p.217*

Biotechnology: DNA to Protein--A Laboratory Project in
    Molecular Biology. *v.5 p.129, p.220*

Biotechnology from A to Z. *v.5 p.7, p.325*

Biotechnology of Fruit and Nut Crops. *v.5 p.8, p.22*

Biotechnology: Science, Engineering, and Ethical Challenges for
    the 21st Century. *v.5 p.219, p.249*

Biotechnology Unzipped: Promises and Realities. . . .*v.4 p.156*

☐ Biotechnology--Subject Guide (Stanford
    University). *v.5 p.324*

Biotechnology. *v.5 p.122, p.218, p.219, p.220, p.742*

☐ Biotechnology--Web Guide (Stanford University).   *v.5 p.324*

Birch Browsings: A John Burroughs Reader. . .*v.5 p.80, p.226*

The Birch Grove and Other Stories. *v.2 p.791*

The Bird Almanac: A Guide to Essential Facts and Figures of
    the World's Birds. *v.5 p.157, p.214*

Bird in a Cage: Legal Reform in China after Mao. . .*v.4 p.475*

A Bird in the House. *v.2 p.736*

Bird Migration: A General Survey. *v.5 p.214, p.215*

Bird Populations Studies: Relevance to Conservation and
    Management. *v.5 p.216*

Birding Across North America: A Naturalist's
    Observations. *v.5 p.84, p.87, p.215, p.229*

Birds and Beasts of Ancient Latin America. *v.3 p.268*

Birds and Other Relations: Selected Poetry of Dezso
    Tandori. *v.2 p.786*

Bird's Eye View: Dancing with Martha Graham and on Broadway. *v.1 p.28, p.29, p.36*

Birds: The Art of Ornithology. *v.5 p.78, p.214*

Birds without a Nest: A Novel. . . .*v.2 p.685, v.3 p.283, p.327*

Birdy. *v.2 p.158, p.159*

Birth and Development of the Geological Sciences. . .*v.5 p.418*

The Birth of a Consumer Society: Commercialization of Eighteenth Century England. *v.3 p.123*

The Birth of a Consumer Society: The Commercialization of Eighteenth-Century England. *v.3 p.123, p.129*

Birth of a Salesman: The Transformation of Selling in America. *v.4 p.146, p.165*

The Birth of a Theater. *v.2 p.639*

The Birth of African-American Culture: An Anthropological Perspective. *v.4 p.41*

The Birth of Bebop: A Social and Musical History. . .*v.1 p.258*

The Birth of Botswana: A History of the Bechuanaland Protectorate from 1910 to 1966. . . . .*v.6 p.75*

The Birth of City Planning in the United States: 1840-1917. . . . .*v.1 p.797, v.6 p.729*

The Birth of Dirt: Origins of Mountain Biking. . . .*v.4 p.856*

Birth of Europe. *v.6 p.563*

Birth of Kumára. *v.6 p.151*

The Birth of Modern Mexico, 1780-1824. . . . . .*v.3 p.284*

The Birth of Modern Science. *v.5 p.391*

The Birth of Nobility: Constructing Aristocracy in England and France, 900-1300. . . . .*v.3 p.62*

The Birth of Opera. *v.1 p.187, p.233*

The Birth of Purgatory. *v.1 p.645*

The Birth of the Bill of Rights, 1776-1791. . . . . .*v.4 p.518*

Birth of the Bill of Rights: Encyclopedia of the Antifederalists. *v.4 p.526*

Birth of the Communist Manifesto. *v.4 p.507, p.509*

The Birth of the Despot: Venice and the Sublime Porte. .*v.6 p.623*

The Birth of the Messiah: A Commentary on the Infancy Narratives in the Gospels of Matthew and Luke. . .*v.1 p.628*

The Birth of the Middle Ages, 395-814. . . . .*v.3 p.66*

The Birth of the Modern World, 1780-1914: Global Connections and Comparisons. *v.3 p.35*

The Birth of the Orchestra: History of an Institution, 1650-1815. . . . .*v.1 p.186, p.187, p.192, p.394*

The Birth of the Palestinian Refugee Problem Revisited. .*v.6 p.619*

The Birth of the Penitentiary in Latin America: Essays on Criminology, Prison Reform, and Social Control, 1830-1940. . . . .*v.3 p.351*

The Birth of the Republic: 1763-89. . . . .*v.3 p.410*

The Birth of Tragedy. *v.1 p.56, p.57, p.88, p.89*

The Birth of Vietnam. *v.6 p.167*

The Birth of Western Canada: A History of the Riel Rebellions. *v.3 p.546*

The Birthday Boys. *v.2 p.330*

Birthday Letters: Poems. *v.2 p.353*

Birthing the Nation: Strategies of Palestinian Women in Israel. *v.6 p.618*

Bisexual Characters in Film: From Anais to Zee. . . .*v.6 p.415*

Bisexual Resource Center. *v.6 p.357*

Bisexual Resource Guide. *v.6 p.360*

Bisexualities: The Ideology and Practice of Sexual Contact with Both Males and Females. *v.4 p.750, v.6 p.370, p.372*

Bisexuality: A Critical Reader. *v.4 p.750, v.6 p.372*

Bisexuality and the Challenge to Lesbian Politics: Sex, Loyalty, and Revolution. *v.4 p.750, v.6 p.372, p.375, p.376*

Bisexuality and the Eroticism of Everyday Life. *v.6 p.368*

Bisexuality in the Ancient World. *v.6 p.364*

Bisexuality: The Psychology and Politics of an Invisible Minority. *v.6 p.371, p.372*

The Bishop of Broadway: The Life and Work of David Belasco. *v.1 p.81, p.138, p.141*

Bismarck: 1815-1871, Vol. 1. . . . .*v.3 p.164*

Bismarck and the Development of Germany: The Period of Consolidation, 1871-1880, Vol. 2. . . . .*v.3 p.164*

Bismarck and the Development of Germany: The Period of Fortification, 1880-1898, Vol. 3. . . . .*v.3 p.164*

Bismarck and the Development of Germany: The Period of Unification, 1815-1871, Vol. 1. . . . .*v.3 p.164*

Bismarck: White Revolutionary 1815-1871, Vol. 2. . .*v.3 p.164*

A Bit off the Map, and Other Stories. *v.2 p.389*

Bitita's Diary: The Childhood Memoirs of Carolina Maria de Jesus. *v.3 p.336*

Bitter Fruit: The Politics of Black-Korean Conflict in New York City. *v.6 p.123, p.135*

Bitter Fruits of Bondage: The Demise of Slavery and the Collapse of the Confederacy, 1861-1865. . . . .*v.4 p.521*

Bitter Harvest: A History of California Farmworkers, 1870-1941. . . . .*v.6 p.525*

Bitter Harvest: FDR, Presidential Power and the Growth of the Presidential Branch. *v.3 p.440*

A Bitter Harvest: U.S. Foreign Policy and Afghanistan. *v.3 p.390*

Bitter Milk: Women and Teaching. *v.4 p.282*

Bitter Music: Collected Journals, Essays, Introductions and Librettos. *v.1 p.221, p.347*

The Bitter Smell of Almonds: Selected Fiction. *v.2 p.784*

Bitter Waters: Life and Work in Stalin's Russia. *v.3 p.224*

Bitter Winds: A Memoir of My Years in China's Gulag. *v.6 p.203*

Bix: The Definitive Biography of Jazz Legend Leon "Bix" Beiderbecke. *v.1 p.261, p.308*

The Biz: The Basic Business, Legal, and Financial Aspects of the Film Industry. *v.6 p.345*

Black '47 and Beyond: The Great Irish Famine in History, Economy, and Memory. *v.3 p.138*

The Black Abolitionist Papers: The British Isles, 1830-1865. . . . .*v.3 p.421*

Black Abolitionists. *v.3 p.400, p.421*

Black African Cinema. *v.6 p.334*

Black African Literature in English, 1982-1986. . . .*v.2 p.751*

Black African Literature in English, 1987-1991. . . .*v.2 p.751*

Black African Literature in English, 1992-1996. . . .*v.2 p.751*

Black American Cinema: Aesthetics and Spectatorship. *v.6 p.329, p.341*

Black American Poets and Dramatists of the Harlem Renaissance. *v.6 p.22*

Black American Short Stories. *v.6 p.24*

Black American Women in Olympic Track and Field: A Complete Illustrated Reference. *v.6 p.41, p.42, p.43*

Black and Blue: Policing in South Africa. *v.4 p.774*

Black and Blues. *v.2 p.767*

Black and Brown: African Americans and the Mexican Revolution, 1910-1920. . . . . *v.3 p.293*

Black and White Identity Formation. *v.5 p.627*

Black and White Women of the Old South: The Peculiar Sisterhood in American Literature. *v.6 p.478*

Black Apollo of Science: The Life of Ernest Everett Just. *v.6 p.18, p.48*

Black April. *v.2 p.109*

Black Art: A Cultural History. *v.1 p.705*

Black Art and Culture in the 20th Century. *v.1 p.705*

The Black Artist in America: An Index to Reproductions. *v.1 p.711*

The Black Arts Movement: Literary Nationalism in the 1960s and 1970s. *v.6 p.13, p.28*

Black Athena Revisited. *v.3 p.12*

Black Athena: The Afroasiatic Roots of Classical Civilization: The Fabrication of Ancient Greece, 1785-1985. . . *v.3 p.12*

Black Athena: The Afroasiatic Roots of Classical Civilization: The Linguistic Evidence. *v.3 p.12, v.6 p.10, p.19*

Black Athena: The Archaeological and Documentary Evidence. *v.3 p.12*

Black Athena Writes Back: Martin Bernal Responds to His Critics. *v.3 p.12*

Black Atlantic Writers of the Eighteenth Century: Living the New Exodus in England and the Americas. . *v.2 p.9, p.172*

Black Australian Literature: A Bibliography of Fiction, Poetry, Drama, Oral Traditions and Non-Fiction, Including Critical Commentary, 1900-1991. . . . . *v.2 p.741*

Black Baseball Entrepreneurs, 1860-1901: Operating by Any Means Necessary. *v.4 p.807, p.832, p.851, p.885, p.888, p.897*

The Black Book of Communism: Crimes, Terror, Repression. *v.4 p.658*

The Black Book. *v.6 p.667*

Black Bostonians: Family Life and Community Struggle in the Antebellum North. *v.3 p.488*

Black Box. *v.6 p.650*

Black Brown and Red: The Movement for Freedom among Black, Chicano, Latino, and Indian. *v.6 p.693*

Black, Brown, Yellow, and Left: Radical Activism in Los Angeles. *v.6 p.108, p.116, p.117, p.124*

Black Canadians: History, Experience, Social Conditions. *v.3 p.542*

Black Characters in the Brazilian Novel. *v.2 p.692*

Black Children: Their Roots, Culture, and Learning Styles. *v.4 p.310*

Black Christians: The Untold Lutheran Story. *v.1 p.585*

Black Church in America: African American Christian Spirituality. *v.1 p.607, p.608*

The Black Church in the African American Experience. *v.1 p.608, v.6 p.7, p.36*

Black City Cinema: African American Urban Experiences in Film. *v.6 p.330, p.342*

The Black Cloth: A Collection of African Folk Tales. *v.2 p.541, p.542*

Black Congressmen During Reconstruction: A Documentary Sourcebook. *v.6 p.7, p.31*

Black Cuban, Black American: A Memoir. . . *v.6 p.489, p.542*

Black Dance: An Annotated Bibliography. *v.1 p.17*

Black Dance: From 1619 to Today. *v.1 p.14, p.18, p.19, p.31, p.34*

Black Dance in America: A History Through Its People. *v.1 p.18*

The Black Dancing Body: A Geography from Coon to Cool. *v.1 p.18*

The Black Death, 1346-1353: The Complete History. . *v.3 p.42*

The Black Death and the Transformation of the West. . *v.3 p.43*

The Black Death in Egypt and England: A Comparative Study. *v.3 p.42*

The Black Death in the Middle East. *v.6 p.584*

The Black Death Transformed: Disease and Culture in Early Renaissance Europe. *v.3 p.42, p.43, p.70*

Black Death, White Medicine: Bubonic Plague and the Politics of Public Health in Colonial Senegal, 1914-1945. . *v.6 p.72*

The Black Death. *v.3 p.68, p.69*

Black Death. *v.6 p.576*

Black Demons: The Media's Depiction of the African American Male Criminal Stereotype. *v.6 p.256*

Black Dionysus: Greek Tragedy and African American Theatre. *v.1 p.72, p.123*

Black Directors in Hollywood. *v.6 p.329, p.341*

▢ Black Drama 1850 to Present. *v.1 p.57, p.122, p.139, p.140*

Black Drama Anthology. *v.2 p.25*

Black Drama in America: An Anthology. *v.2 p.25*

▢ Black Drama. *v.6 p.28, p.29, p.30*

The Black Dwarf. *v.2 p.307*

Black Earth: A Journey Through Russia after the Fall. *v.3 p.229*

Black Education: A Transformative Research and Action Agenda for the New Century. *v.4 p.301, p.310, p.355*

Black Elk Speaks: Being the Life Story of a Holy Man of the Oglala Sioux. *v.2 p.31, v.6 p.701*

Black Enterprise Guide to Building Your Career. . . . *v.4 p.167*

Black Families at the Crossroads: Challenges and Prospects. *v.4 p.734*

Black Families in Therapy: Understanding the African American Experience. *v.5 p.667*

🄴 Black Female Playwrights: An Anthology of Plays Before 1950. . . . . . . *v.1 p.68, p.121, p.123, v.6 p.15, p.18, p.34*

Black Feminist Anthropology: Theory, Politics, Praxis and Poetics. *v.4 p.31, v.6 p.435*

Black Feminist Criticism: Perspectives on Black Women Writers. *v.6 p.478*

The Black Feminist Reader. *v.6 p.26, p.44*

Black Feminist Thought: Knowledge, Consciousness and Politics of Empowerment. *v.6 p.31, p.42*

🄴 Black Feminist Thought: Knowledge, Consciousness, and the Politics of Empowerment. *v.6 p.427*

Black Film, White Money. *v.6 p.330*

Black Filmmakers. *v.6 p.330, p.342*

Black, French, and African: A Life of Leopold Sedar Senghor. *v.2 p.543*

Black Garden: Armenia and Azerbaijan Through Peace and War. *v.3 p.231*

Black Gay Man. *v.6 p.27, p.40, p.367*

The Black Heralds: Los Heraldos Negros. *v.2 p.685*

The Black Hole at the Center of Our Galaxy. *v.5 p.71*

Black Holes and Baby Universes and Other
Essays. *v.5 p.555, p.556, p.557*

Black Holes and Time Warps: Einstein's Outrageous
Legacy. *v.5 p.73, p.557*

The Black Holocaust for Beginners. *v.6 p.11*

Black in America. *v.1 p.768*

Black in Blue: African American Police Officers and
Racism. *v.6 p.259*

Black into White: Race and Nationality in Brazilian
Thought. *v.3 p.280*

Black into White; Race and Nationality in Brazilian
Thought. *v.3 p.342*

Black Jack: The Life and Times of John J. Pershing,
Set. *v.3 p.384, p.463, p.481*

The Black Jacobins: Toussaint L'Ouverture and the San
Domingo Revolution. *v.6 p.6, p.18*

Black Knights: The Story of the Tuskegee Airmen. *v.6 p.6, p.17*

Black Labor on a White Canal: Panama, 1904-1981. . *v.3 p.304*

Black Lamb and Grey Falcon: A Journey Through
Yugoslavia. *v.3 p.247, p.248*

Black Lenses, Black Voices: African American Film
Now. *v.6 p.330, p.343*

Black Liberation in Conservative America. *v.4 p.573*

The Black Lights: Inside the World of Professional
Boxing. *v.4 p.855, p.896*

Black Like Me. *v.4 p.730*

Black Literature Criticism, Set. *v.6 p.24, p.33*

Black Macho and the Myth of the Superwoman. *v.6 p.41, p.47*

Black Magic: A Pictorial History of the African-American in the
Performing Arts. *v.1 p.34, p.35*

Black Magic: White Hollywood and African American
Culture. *v.6 p.329, p.341*

ℯ The Black Man, His Antecedents, His Genius, and His
Achievements. *v.6 p.4*

The Black Man in Slavery and Freedom in Colonial
Brazil. *v.3 p.335*

Black Man of the Nile and His Family. *v.6 p.9, p.10*

Black Manhood in James Baldwin, Ernest J. Gaines, and August
Wilson. *v.6 p.23, p.24*

The Black Man's Burden: Africa and the Curse of the
Nation-State. *v.6 p.54*

Black Margins: Sa'adat Hasan Manto Stories. *v.6 p.152*

Black Metropolis: A Study of Negro Life in a Northern
City. *v.6 p.711*

The Black Mind: A History of African Literature. . . *v.6 p.80*

Black Mischief. *v.2 p.388*

Black Mondays: Worst Decisions of the U. S. Supreme
Court. *v.4 p.537*

Black Music in America: A Bibliography. . . .*v.1 p.169, p.282*

Black Music of Two Worlds: African, Caribbean, Latin, and
African-American Traditions. *v.1 p.282, p.294*

Black Musical Theatre: From Coontown to
Dreamgirls. *v.1 p.254, p.283*

Black Music. *v.1 p.280*

The Black Muslims in America. *v.1 p.560, v.6 p.7, p.36*

Black Narcissus. *v.2 p.347*

Black Nationalism in American Politics and Thought. *v.4 p.573*

Black Nationalists: Reconsidering Du Bois, Garvey, Booker T.
and Nkrumah. *v.6 p.13*

Black Noise: Rap Music and Black Culture in Contemporary
America. *v.1 p.274*

Black on Black: Twentieth-Century African American Writing
about Africa. *v.6 p.25*

Black Panther Party Reconsidered. *v.6 p.12, p.13*

Black Paris: The African Writers' Landscape. *v.2 p.542*

Black Physicians Struggle for Civil Rights: Edward C. Mazique,
M. D. *v.6 p.19, p.48*

Black Picket Fences: Privilege and Peril among the Black
Middle Class. *v.4 p.725, p.730*

Black Police in America. *v.6 p.259*

A Black Political Theology. *v.1 p.636*

Black Power-White Control: The Struggle of the Woodlawn
Organization in Chicago. *v.4 p.702*

The Black Presence. *v.3 p.93*

ℯ Black Presidential Politics in America: A Strategic
Approach. *v.4 p.556, p.573, p.574*

Black Presidential Politics in America: A Strategic
Approach. *v.4 p.555, p.556*

The Black Press: New Literary and Historical Essays. *v.4 p.411*

The Black Prince. *v.2 p.372*

Black Prophets of Justice: Activist Clergy Before the Civil
War. *v.1 p.607*

Black Protest and the Great Migration: A Brief History with
Documents. *v.6 p.3*

Black Protest: Issues and Tactics, 14. . . . .*v.3 p.419*

Black Rain. *v.6 p.229*

Black Rebels: African-Caribbean Freedom Fighters in
Jamaica. *v.6 p.9*

Black Reconstruction in America 1860-1880: An Essay Toward
a History of the Part Which Black Folk Played in the
Attempt to Reconstruct Democracy in
America. *v.3 p.436, v.6 p.4*

Black Religions in the New World. *v.1 p.544, v.4 p.37*

Black Roadways: A Study of Jamaican Folk Life. . .*v.4 p.40*

The Black Room at Longwood: Napoleon's Exile on Saint
Helena. *v.3 p.152*

Black Saga: The African American Experience: A
Chronology. *v.6 p.4*

Black Salt: Poems. *v.2 p.537*

Black Sexual Politics: African Americans, Gender, and the New
Racism. *v.4 p.743, v.6 p.31, p.42*

The Black Sheep. *v.2 p.486*

▢ Black Short Fiction. *v.6 p.22, p.28, p.29*

Black Short Story Anthology. *v.2 p.26*

Black Sister: Poetry by Black American Women,
1746-1980. . . . .*v.2 p.24*

Black Skins, French Voices: Caribbean Ethnicity and Activism
in Urban France. *v.4 p.40*

Black Slaveowners: Free Black Slave Masters in South
Carolina, 1790-1860. . . . .*v.4 p.727*

Black Song: The Forge and the Flame. *v.1 p.281*

Black Spark, White Fire: Did African Explorers Civilize Ancient Europe? *v.6 p.10, p.20*

☐ Black Studies Center: Schomburg Studies on the Black Experience. *v.6 p.14, p.34*

The Black Studies Reader. *v.6 p.13*

Black Sun: Aryan Cults, Esoteric Nazism and the Politics of Identity. *v.4 p.768*

The Black Swan. *v.2 p.612*

Black Theater, U. S. A.: Forty-Five Plays by Black Americans, 1847-1974. . . . .*v.2 p.25*

Black Then: Blacks and Montreal, 1780-1880's. *v.3 p.544*

Black Theology: A Documentary History, 1966-1979. . . . .*v.1 p.635, v.6 p.31, p.35*

Black Theology: A Documentary History, 1980-1992. . . . .*v.1 p.635, v.6 p.31, p.35*

Black Theology and Black Power. .*v.1 p.642, p.643,v.6 p.31, p.35*

Black Theology of Liberation: Twentieth Anniversary with Critical Responses. *v.1 p.635*

☐ Black Thought and Culture. *v.6 p.14*

Black Thunder: Gabriel's Revolt: Virginia 1800. .*v.2 p.58, v.6 p.23*

Black Tradition in American Dance. *v.1 p.32*

Black Trials: Citizenship from the Beginnings of Slavery to the End of Caste. *v.4 p.723*

The Black Tulip. *v.2 p.489*

Black Voices: An Anthology of African-American Literature. *v.2 p.18, v.6 p.23*

Black Votes Count: Political Empowerment in Mississippi after 1965. . . . .*v.4 p.555, p.573, p.579*

Black Water. *v.2 p.152*

Black Wealth/White Wealth: A New Perspective on Racial Inequality. *v.4 p.730*

The Black West: A Documentary and Pictoral History of the African American Role in the Westward Expansion of the United States. *v.6 p.7*

Black, White, and in Color: Essays on American Literature and Culture. *v.6 p.28*

Black Women Abolitionists: A Study in Activism, 1828-1860. . . . .*v.6 p.37, p.38, p.47*

Black Women As Cultural Leaders. *v.6 p.329, p.340*

Black Women Film and Video Artists. *v.6 p.329, p.340*

Black Women, Identity, and Cultural Theory: (Un)becoming the Subject. *v.6 p.45*

Black Women in America: An Historical Encyclopedia. *v.6 p.5, p.44*

Black Women in America: Confronting Gender, Race, and Class. *v.6 p.450*

Black Women in America, Set. *v.6 p.434, p.449, p.450*

Black Women in the Academy: Promises and Perils. *v.6 p.21, p.41, p.42*

Black Women in the Labor Force. *v.4 p.271*

Black Women in White America: A Documentary History. *v.6 p.450*

Black Women in White: Racial Conflict and Cooperation in the Nursing Profession, 1890-1950. . . . .*v.5 p.529*

Black Women Playwrights: Visions on the American Stage. *v.6 p.15, p.45*

Black Women Poets of Harlem Renaissance. . . .*v.6 p.24, p.43*

Black Women Scientists in the United States. *v.5 p.396*

Black Women Writers, 1950-1980: A Critical Evaluation. *v.6 p.24, p.25, p.43*

Black Women Writing Autobiography: A Tradition Within a Tradition. *v.6 p.476*

Black Women's Activism: Reading African American Women's Historical Romances. *v.6 p.4, p.42*

Black Women's Blues: A Literary Anthology: 1934-Present. *v.2 p.18*

Black Women/White Men: The Sexual Exploitation of Female Slaves in the Danish West Indies. *v.4 p.727*

Black Words White Page: Aboriginal Literature 1929-1988. . . . .*v.2 p.742*

Black Writers Abroad: A Study of Black American Writers in Europe and Africa. *v.6 p.29*

Black Writers and the Hispanic Canon. *v.2 p.664*

Black Writers in French: An Interpretive History. . . .*v.2 p.535*

Black Writers of America: A Comprehensive Anthology. .*v.2 p.18*

Black Zodiac: Poems. *v.2 p.159*

Blackberry Winter: My Earlier Years. *v.4 p.23*

Blackbird: The Life and Times of Paul McCartney. *v.1 p.269, p.340*

Black-Brown Relations and Stereotypes. *v.6 p.542*

Blacker the Berry. *v.2 p.124*

Blackfoot Musical Thought: Comparative Perspectives. *v.1 p.296, p.297*

Blacking Up: The Minstrel Show in Nineteenth-Century America. *v.1 p.35*

Black-Korean Encounter: Toward Understanding and Alliance. *v.6 p.115, p.125, p.137*

Blackness and Race Mixture: The Dynamics of Racial Identity in Colombia. *v.3 p.281, p.359*

Blackness in Latin America and the Caribbean, Social Dynamics and Cultural Transformations: Central America, Northern, and Western South America. *v.3 p.281*

Blackness in Latin America and the Caribbean, Social Dynamics and Cultural Transformations: Eastern South America and the Caribbean. *v.3 p.280*

Blackness Without Ethnicity: Constructing Race in Brazil. *v.3 p.280*

Blackout: The Untold Story of Jackie Robinson's First Spring Training. *v.4 p.807, p.832, p.851*

The Blacks: A Clown Show. *v.2 p.519*

Blacks and Whites in Sao Paulo, Brazil, 1888-1988. . .*v.3 p.338*

Blacks, Coloureds and National Identity in Nineteenth-Century Latin America. *v.3 p.337*

Blacks in American Film and Television: An Encyclopedia. *v.6 p.329, p.340*

Blacks in Black and White: A Source Book on Black Films. *v.6 p.330*

Blacks in Blackface: A Source Book on Early Black Musical Shows. *v.1 p.35, p.282*

The Blacks in Canada: A History. *v.3 p.542*

Blacks in Science: Ancient and Modern. .*v.6 p.9, p.48, p.49, p.51*

Blacks in Science and Medicine. *v.6 p.22, p.34, p.48*

Black's Law Dictionary, Deluxe. *v.4 p.436*

Blacks on John Brown. *v.3 p.432*

Black's Veterinary Dictionary. *v.5 p.54, p.56*

Blackshirts and Reds: Rational Fascism and the Overthrow of Communism. *v.4 p.509, p.510*

The Blackwell City Reader. *v.6 p.709*

The Blackwell Companion to Christian Spirituality. . .*v.1 p.650*

The Blackwell Companion to Philosophy. *v.1 p.415*

The Blackwell Companion to Protestantism. *v.1 p.580*

The Blackwell Companion to Social Movements. . .*v.4 p.710*

The Blackwell Companion to the Sociology of Families. .*v.4 p.732*

The Blackwell Dictionary of Eastern Christianity. .*v.1 p.569, p.570*

Blackwell Dictionary of Social Policy. *v.4 p.676*

The Blackwell Dictionary of Sociology: A User's Guide to Sociological Language. *v.4 p.677*

The Blackwell Dictionary of Western Philosophy. . .*v.1 p.415*

The Blackwell Encyclopedia of Modern Christian Thought. *v.1 p.594*

The Blackwell Encyclopedia of Social Psychology. .*v.5 p.646*

Blackwell Encyclopedia of the American Revolution. *v.3 p.409*

The Blackwell Encyclopedia of Writing Systems. *v.2 p.560, v.4 p.18*

The Blackwell Guide to Aesthetics. *v.1 p.479, p.480*

The Blackwell Guide to American Philosophy. . . .*v.1 p.439*

The Blackwell Guide to Ancient Philosophy. . .*v.1 p.420, p.421*

The Blackwell Guide to Continental Philosophy. . .*v.1 p.511*

The Blackwell Guide to Descartes' Meditations. . . .*v.1 p.453*

The Blackwell Guide to Metaphysics. *v.1 p.488*

The Blackwell Guide to Philosophical Logic. *v.1 p.492*

Blackwell Guide to Philosophy of Language. *v.1 p.490*

The Blackwell Guide to Philosophy of Mind. *v.1 p.498*

The Blackwell Guide to Plato's Republic. *v.1 p.425*

The Blackwell Guide to Recorded Jazz. . . .*v.1 p.170, p.260*

The Blackwell Guide to Soul Recordings. . .*v.1 p.171, p.273*

Blackwell Guide to the Modern Philosophers: Descartes to Nietzsche. *v.1 p.436*

The Blackwell Guide to the Philosophy of Education. *v.4 p.323, p.338*

Blackwell Guide to the Philosophy of Law and Legal Theory. *v.1 p.491*

The Blackwell Guide to the Philosophy of Religion. .*v.1 p.498*

The Blackwell Guide to the Philosophy of the Social Sciences. *v.1 p.501*

Blackwell Handbook of Adolescence. *v.5 p.625, p.640*

Blackwell Handbook of Childhood Cognitive Development. *v.5 p.626, p.630*

The Blackwell Handbook of Organizational Learning and Knowledge Management. *v.4 p.79*

Blackwell Reader in Pastoral and Practical Theology. *v.1 p.649*

Blades of Glory: The True Story of a Young Team Bred to Win. *v.4 p.819, p.840, p.862*

The Blair Effect, 2001-5: A Wasted Term? *v.4 p.605*

The Blair Effect: The Blair Government, 1997-2001. .*v.4 p.605*

Blaise Cendrars - Complete Poems. *v.2 p.512*

Blaise Cendrars : l'or d'un poète. *v.2 p.513*

Blaise Pascal. *v.1 p.452, v.2 p.476*

Blake: A Biography. *v.2 p.238*

Blake and the Idea of the Book. *v.2 p.240*

Blake and the Language of Art. *v.2 p.240*

☐ The Blake Archive. *v.2 p.239*

Blake as an Artist. *v.2 p.238, p.239*

A Blake Dictionary: The Ideas and Symbols of William Blake. *v.2 p.239*

☐ Blake Digital Text Project. *v.2 p.239*

Blake: Prophet Against Empire. *v.2 p.239*

Blake's Apocalypse; a Study in Poetic Argument. . .*v.2 p.239*

Blake's Composite Art: A Study of the Illuminated Poetry. *v.2 p.240*

Blake's Poetry and Designs. *v.2 p.239*

Blake's Prophetic Psychology. *v.2 p.240*

Blake's Therapy. *v.2 p.680*

Blake's Visionary Forms Dramatic. *v.2 p.239*

Blaming the Victims. *v.6 p.619*

Blaming the Victim. *v.4 p.706*

Blandings Castle. *v.2 p.390*

The Blank Slate: The Modern Denial of Human Nature. *v.5 p.628, p.650, p.658*

Blast One. *v.2 p.367*

Blasters' Handbook. *v.5 p.738*

BLAST. *v.5 p.103*

☐ BLAST. *v.5 p.103, p.108*

Blazing the Trail: The Early History of Spacecraft and Rocketry. *v.5 p.719*

Bleak House. by Charles Dickens. (Boz.) with ... illustrations, from designs by Phiz [pseud.] and Cruikshank. . .*v.2 p.282*

Bleak House. *v.2 p.284*

Bless Me, Ultima. *v.6 p.497*

Blessed Anastacia: Women, Race and Popular Christianity in Brazil. *v.3 p.338*

Blessed Rage for Order: The New Pluralism in Theology. *v.1 p.634*

Blessing the Boats: New and Selected Poems, 1988-2000. . . . .*v.2 p.143*

Blessings in Disguise: Or, the Morality of Evil. . . .*v.2 p.456*

The Blessing. *v.2 p.371*

Blind Ambition: The White House Years. *v.3 p.469*

The Blind Assassin. *v.2 p.734*

Blind Memory: Visual Representations of Slavery in England and America. *v.1 p.705*

The Blind Owl. *v.6 p.671*

Blind Rider. *v.2 p.658*

Blind Spot: The Secret History of American Counterterrorism. *v.4 p.565*

Blind Watchers of the Sky: The People and Ideas That Shaped Our View of the Universe. *v.5 p.62*

The Blind Watchmaker: Why the Evidence of Evolution Reveals a Universe Without Design. *v.5 p.191*

The Blinded Eye: Thucydides and the New Written Word. *v.2 p.421*

Blindenschrift. *v.2 p.606*

Blindfold and Alone: British Military Executions in the Great War. *v.3 p.79*

The Blindfold Horse: Memories of a Persian Childhood. .*v.6 p.631*

Blindness and Insight: Essays in the Rhetoric of Contemporary
  Criticism. *v.2 p.570*

Blink: The Power of Thinking Without Thinking. *v.4 p.83*

The Blithedale Romance. *v.2 p.41*

A Bloc of One: The Political Career of Hiram W.
  Johnson. *v.3 p.460*

Block by Block: Neighborhoods and Public Policy on Chicago's
  West Side. *v.6 p.715*

The Block Scheduling Handbook. *v.4 p.288*

Blok: Selected Poems. *v.2 p.810*

Blonde: A Novel. *v.2 p.152*

The Blonde on the Street Corner. *v.2 p.80*

Blood and Belonging: Journeys into the New
  Nationalism. *v.4 p.494*

Blood and Debt: War and the Nation-State in Latin
  America. *v.3 p.274, v.4 p.591*

Blood and Fire: La Violencia in Antioquia, Colombia,
  1946-1953. . . . .*v.3 p.358*

Blood and Religion: The Conscience of Henri IV,
  1553-1593. . . . .*v.3 p.145*

Blood Brook. *v.5 p.222*

Blood Feud and Other Stories. *v.6 p.663*

Blood in the Sand: Imperial Fantasies, Right-Wing Ambitions,
  and the Erosion of American Democracy. *v.3 p.446*

Blood Knot and Other Plays. *v.2 p.754, p.755*

Blood Memory: An Autobiography. *v.1 p.8*

The Blood of Government: Race, Empire, the United States, and
  the Philippines. *v.6 p.180*

Blood of Kings: Dynasty and Ritual in Maya Art. . . .*v.1 p.684*

The Blood of Our Sons: Men, Women, and the Renegotiation of
  British Citizenship During the Great
  War. *v.3 p.53, p.79, v.4 p.604*

Blood of the Prophets: Brigham Young and the Massacre at
  Mountain Meadows. *v.1 p.587, v.3 p.529*

The Blood Oranges. *v.2 p.82, p.83*

Blood Pact and Other Stories. *v.2 p.675, p.686*

Blood Revenge: Family, Honor, Mediation and
  Outcasting. *v.6 p.596*

Blood Road: The Mystery of Shen Dingyi in Revolutionary
  China. *v.6 p.191, p.202, p.203*

Blood Sacrifice and the Nation: Totem Rituals and the American
  Flag. *v.4 p.767*

Blood Sisters: The French Revolution in Women's
  Memory. *v.3 p.55, p.151, p.152, p.158*

Blood Sport: A Social History of Spanish
  Bullfighting. *v.4 p.808, p.856*

Blood Struggle: The Rise of Modern Indian
  Nations. *v.6 p.690, p.693*

Blood, Sweat and Cheers: Sport and the Making of Modern
  Canada. *v.4 p.807*

Blood Ties: Life and Violence in Rural Mexico. *v.4 p.772*

Blood Wedding and Yerma. *v.2 p.659*

Blood Wedding, Yerma, and The House of Bernard Alba: Garcia
  Lorca's Tragic Trilogy. *v.2 p.660*

The Bloodaxe Book of Modern Australian Poetry. . . .*v.2 p.743*

A Blood-Dimmed Tide: Dispatches from the Middle
  East. *v.6 p.610*

The Bloody Chamber. *v.2 p.336*

Bloody Mary in the Mirror: Essays in Psychoanalytic
  Folkloristics. *v.2 p.584*

Bloody Murder: From the Detective Story to the Crime
  Novel. *v.2 p.580*

The Bloomsbury Group: A Collection of Memoirs, Commentary,
  and Criticism. *v.3 p.117, p.127*

Blowback: Linguistic Nationalism, Institutional Decay, and
  Ethnic Conflict in Sri Lanka. *v.6 p.163*

Blowback: The Costs and Consequences of American
  Empire. *v.6 p.145*

Blowing Bubbles in the Cosmos: Astronomical Winds, Jets, and
  Explosions. *v.5 p.66*

Blown to Bits: How the New Economics of Information
  Transforms Strategy. *v.4 p.77*

Blows and Bombs: Antonin Artaud: The Biography. . .*v.2 p.507*

The Blue Afternoon, Vol. 1. . . . .*v.2 p.335*

Blue and Brown Books: Preliminary Studies for the
  Philosophical Investigations. *v.1 p.473*

The Blue and the Gray: From the Nomination of Lincoln to the
  Eve of Gettysburg. *v.3 p.428*

Blue and the Gray on the Silver Screen: More Than 80 Years of
  Civil War Movies. *v.6 p.322*

Blue Blood: How Rebekah Harkness, One of the Richest
  Women in the World, Destroyed a Great American
  Family. *v.1 p.13*

Blue Collar Marriage. *v.4 p.739*

Blue Dreams: Korean Americans and the Los Angeles
  Riots. *v.4 p.713, v.6 p.113, p.135*

The Blue Estuaries: Poems: 1923-1968. . . . .*v.2 p.58*

Blue Frontier: Dispatches from America's Ocean
  Wilderness. *v.5 p.430*

Blue Gold: The Fight to Stop the Corporate Theft of the
  World's Water. *v.6 p.299*

Blue Highways: A Journey into America. *v.2 p.146*

The Blue Mountain. *v.6 p.651*

The Blue Nile. *v.6 p.51*

Blue Nippon: Authenticating Jazz in Japan. *v.6 p.218*

The Blue Planet: A Natural History of the
  Oceans. *v.5 p.172, p.241*

Bluebeard's Egg. *v.2 p.734*

The Bluebook: A Uniform System of Citation. *v.4 p.439*

Bluegrass: A History. *v.1 p.274*

The Bluegrass Reader. *v.1 p.269*

Blueprint for a Sustainable Economy. *v.5 p.13, v.6 p.298*

Blueprint for Black Power: A Moral, Political and Economic
  Imperative for the Twenty-First Century.   *v.6 p.9, p.20, p.32*

A Blueprint for Corporate Governance: Strategy, Accountability,
  and the Preservation of Shareholder Value. *v.4 p.86*

Blueprints: Solving the Mystery of Evolution. *v.5 p.191*

The Blues Aesthetic and the Making of American Identity in the
  Literature of the South. *v.2 p.3*

Blues All Around Me: The Autobiography of B. B.
  King. *v.1 p.260, p.335*

Blues Basics. *v.1 p.264*

Blues Fell This Morning: Meaning in the Blues. . . .*v.1 p.262*

Blues for Mister Charlie: A Play. *v.2 p.59*

The Blues: From Robert Johnson to Robert Cray. . . .*v.1 p.263*

The Blues in Gray: The Civil War Journal of William Daniel Dixon and the Republican Blues Daybook. *v.4 p.520*

Blues Legacies and Black Feminism: Gertrude "Ma" Rainey, Bessie Smith, and Billie Holiday. *v.6 p.29, p.42, p.474*

The Blues Makers. *v.1 p.258*

Blues of a Lifetime: The Autobiography of Cornell Woolrich. *v.2 p.128*

Blues People: Negro Music in White America. *v.1 p.280, v.6 p.3, p.29*

The Bluest Eye. *v.2 p.151*

Bluestown Mockingbird Mambo. *v.6 p.506, p.510*

Blunders in International Business. *v.4 p.70*

Blurred Boundaries: Questions of Meaning in Contemporary Culture. *v.6 p.309*

Blu's Hanging. *v.6 p.102*

□ BMI = Broadcast Music Inc. *v.1 p.172, p.383*

The Boat of Longing. *v.2 p.629*

The Boat People and Achievement in America: A Study of Economic and Educational Success. *v.4 p.763, p.764,v.6 p.140*

Bob Dylan Companion: Four Decades of Commentary. *v.1 p.265, p.266, p.322*

Bobbed Hair and Bathtub Gin: Writers Running Wild in the Twenties. *v.2 p.11*

Boccaccio: Decameron. *v.2 p.702*

Boccaccio: The Man and His Works. *v.2 p.701, p.702*

Boccaccio. *v.2 p.701*

Boccioni's Materia: A Futurist Masterpiece and the European Avant-Garde. *v.1 p.736*

Bodies and Souls: A Novel. *v.2 p.154*

Bodies of the Text: Dance As Theory, Literature As Dance. *v.1 p.45*

Bodies Out of Bounds: Fatness and Transgression. . .*v.6 p.445*

Body Against Body: The Dance and Other Collaborations of Bill T. Jones and Arnie Zane. *v.1 p.9*

Body Alchemy: Transsexual Portraits. *v.6 p.370, p.407*

Body and Mature Behavior: A Study of Anxiety, Sex, Gravitation, and Learning. *v.1 p.51*

Body and Sacred Place in Medieval Europe, 1100-1389. *v.6 p.571*

The Body and Society: Men, Women, and Sexual Renunciation in Early Christianity. *v.1 p.598, p.652,v.3 p.30*

Body and Soul: Jazz, Blues, and Race in American Film, 1927-63. . . . .*v.6 p.316*

Body Awareness As Healing Therapy: The Case of Nora. .*v.1 p.52*

Body Blows: Six Performances. *v.6 p.412*

The Body Can Speak: Essays on Creative Movement Education with Emphasis on Dance and Drama. *v.1 p.47*

The Body, Dance and Cultural Theory. *v.1 p.44*

Body Ego Technique: An Educational and Therapeutic Approach to Body Image and Self Identity. *v.1 p.51*

The Body in Late-Capitalist U. S. A. *v.4 p.775*

Body in Question: Exploring the Cutting Edge in Forensic Science. *v.6 p.266*

The Body in the Library. *v.2 p.338*

▣ Body, Movement, and Culture: Kinesthetic and Visual Symbolism in a Philippine Community. *v.1 p.17, p.49*

Body Movement: Coping with the Environment. .*v.1 p.50, p.51*

The Body of Life. *v.1 p.52*

Body of Power, Spirit of Resistance: The Culture and History of a South African People. *v.1 p.610*

The Body of the Artisan: Art and Experience in the Scientific Revolution. *v.5 p.392, p.411*

The Body Project: An Intimate History of American Girls. *v.6 p.466*

Body Snatcher. *v.2 p.687*

Body Work: Beauty and Self-Image in American Culture. *v.6 p.436*

The Boer War. *v.3 p.77, v.6 p.79*

Boesman and Lena and Other Plays. *v.2 p.755*

Boethius Is "De topicis Differentilis". *v.1 p.430*

▣ Boethius, the Consolations of Music, Logic, Theology, and Philosophy. *v.1 p.430, v.6 p.567*

Boethius. *v.1 p.579*

Bogolan: Shaping Culture Through Cloth in Contemporary Mali. *v.4 p.26*

Bohemia in History. *v.3 p.191*

Bohemian Fifths: An Autobiography. *v.1 p.215, p.331*

The Bohemian Grove and Other Retreats: A Study in Ruling-Class Cohesiveness. *v.4 p.719, p.726*

A Bohemian Youth. *v.2 p.783*

The Boilerplate Rhino: Nature in the Eye of the Beholder. *v.5 p.223*

Bois d'ébène ; suivi de Madrid. *v.2 p.537*

Bol (Ferdinand), a Catalogue Raisonné of the Graphic Work. *v.1 p.757*

Bold Endeavors: Lessons from Polar and Space Exploration. *v.5 p.392*

A Bold Stroke for a Wife. *v.2 p.243*

Bold Words: A Century of Asian American Writing. *v.2 p.20, v.6 p.92*

The Bolero School: an illustrated history of the Bolero, the Seguidillas and the Escuela Bolera : syllabus and dances. *v.1 p.20*

Bolingbroke and His Circle: The Politics of Nostalgia in the Age of Walpole. *v.3 p.107*

The Bolivarian Presidents: Conversations and Correspondence with Presidents of Bolivia, Peru, and Ecuador. . . .*v.3 p.333*

Bolivia: Land, Location and Politics since 1825. . . .*v.3 p.323*

Bolshevik Women. *v.3 p.53, p.222,v.6 p.440, p.453*

The Bolsheviks: The Intellectual and Political History of the Triumph of Communism in Russia. *v.3 p.223*

Bomber Crew: Taking on the Reich. *v.6 p.743, p.760*

Le Bon usage : grammaire française. *v.2 p.453*

Bonanza West: The Story of the Western Mining Rushes 1848-1900. . . . .*v.3 p.518*

Bonaventure: The Soul's Journey into God: the Tree of Life, the Life of Francis. *v.1 p.571*

Bonaventure. *v.1 p.432, p.579*

The Bondage of the Will. *v.3 p.57*

Bonds of Affection: Americans Define Their Patriotism.*v.3 p.366*

Bone: A Novel. *v.6 p.101*

The Bone People. *v.2 p.746*

Bone Voyage: A Journey in Forensic Anthropology. . . .*v.4 p.15*

The Bone Woman: A Forensic Anthropologist's Search for Truth in Rwanda, Bosnia, and Kosovo. *v.4 p.33*

The Bonehunters' Revenge: Dinosaurs, Greed, and the Greatest Scientific Feud of the Gilded Age. *v.3 p.46*

Bones, Bodies, Behavior: Essays in Behavioral Anthropology. *v.4 p.5*

Bones, Stones, and Buddhist Monks: Collected Papers on the Archaeology, Epigraphy, and Texts of Monastic Buddhism in India. *v.1 p.566*

The Bonfire of the Vanities. *v.2 p.159*

Bonheur d'Occasion. *v.2 p.539*

Bonjour Tristesse. *v.2 p.526*

Bonnard. *v.1 p.741*

The Book and the Brotherhood. *v.2 p.372*

The Book Before Printing: Ancient, Medieval and Oriental. *v.3 p.37*

Book Business: Publishing: Past, Present and Future. *v.4 p.149*

The Book for My Brother. *v.2 p.813*

The Book History Reader. *v.2 p.576*

Book Illumination in the Middle Ages: An Introduction. *v.1 p.672*

The Book in Japan: A Cultural History from the Beginnings to the Nineteenth Century. *v.6 p.225*

The Book Nobody Read: Chasing the Revolutions of Nicolaus Copernicus. *v.3 p.47*

The Book of Alternative Photographic Processes. *v.1 p.769, p.770*

The Book of American Windsor Furniture: Styles and Technologies. *v.1 p.804*

The Book of Blam. *v.2 p.812*

Book of Common Prayer. *v.1 p.582*

The Book of Concord: The Confessions of the Evangelical Lutheran Church. *v.1 p.585*

Book of Confessions: Study Edition. *v.1 p.588*

The Book of Count Lucanor and Patronio: A Translation of Don Juan Manuel's El Conde Lucanor. *v.2 p.651*

The Book of Dance. *v.1 p.5*

The Book of Daniel. *v.1 p.622*

A Book of Danish Ballads. *v.2 p.626*

Book of Dede Korkut: A Turkish Epic. *v.6 p.668*

The Book of Disquiet. *v.2 p.689*

Book of Exodus. *v.1 p.620*

The Book of Gay and Lesbian Quotations: A Collection of 3,000 Thoughts, Insights, Views, and Perceptions from Antiquity to the Present. *v.6 p.360*

The Book of Good Love: Of the Archpriest of Hita, Juan Ruiz. *v.2 p.652*

The Book of Hard Things: A Novel. *v.2 p.160*

The Book of Hebrew Script: History, Palaeography, Script Styles, Calligraphy and Design. *v.6 p.646*

The Book of Illusions: A Novel. *v.2 p.139*

The Book of Korean Shijo. *v.6 p.238*

A Book of Latin Letters. *v.2 p.426*

Book of Man. *v.5 p.131*

Book of Margery Kempe. *v.1 p.653*

The Book of Margery Kempe. *v.2 p.206, p.207, v.3 p.57*

A Book of Middle English. *v.2 p.550, p.551*

The Book of Misers: al-Bukhala. *v.6 p.656*

The Book of Mormon: Another Testament of Jesus Christ. *v.1 p.587*

Book of My Nights. *v.6 p.103*

The Book of Naturalists: An Anthology of the Best Natural History. *v.5 p.77, p.225, p.226*

Book of Negro Folklore. *v.6 p.16, p.23*

The Book of Numbers. *v.5 p.475*

The Book of Pearl: Its History, Art, Science and Industry. *v.1 p.715*

Book of Poems / Libro de Poemas: A Dual-Language Book. *v.2 p.658*

The Book of Revelation. *v.1 p.632*

The Book of Risk. *v.4 p.92*

The Book of Salt: A Novel. *v.6 p.102, p.399*

The Book of Secrets: A Novel. *v.2 p.759*

The Book of Secrets. *v.2 p.747*

The Book of Songs. *v.6 p.210*

The Book of Ten Nights and a Night: Eleven Stories. *v.2 p.142*

The Book of the Acts. *v.1 p.629, p.630*

The Book of the City of Ladies. *v.2 p.469*

Book of the Courtier. *v.2 p.708*

The Book of the Dead: Egyptian Literature. *v.6 p.644*

The Book of the Goddess Past and Present: An Introduction to Her Religion. *v.1 p.529*

Book of the It. *v.5 p.619*

The Book of the Virgins. *v.2 p.716*

The Book of World-Famous Music: Classical, Popular and Folk. *v.1 p.160*

The Book on the Bookshelf. *v.2 p.577*

The Book Publishing Industry. *v.4 p.149*

Booker Tropical Soil Manual: A Handbook for Soil Survey and Agriculture and Evaluation in the Tropics and Subtropics. *v.5 p.50*

Books and Readers in the Early Church: A History of Early Christian Texts. *v.1 p.599*

Books and Their Readers in Eighteenth-Century England: New Essays. *v.2 p.172*

The Books at the Wake: A Study of Literary Allusions in James Joyce's "Finnegans Wake". *v.2 p.357*

The Books in My Life. *v.2 p.102*

The Books of Songs: The Ancient Chinese Classic of Poetry. *v.6 p.210*

The Bookshop; The Gate of Angels; The Blue Flower. *v.2 p.344*

The Boom in Contemporary Israeli Fiction. *v.6 p.650*

Booms and Depressions. *v.4 p.199, p.243*

Bootleg: The Rise and Fall of the Secret Recording History. *v.1 p.384*

Bootlegging: Romanticism and Copyright in the Music Industry. *v.1 p.384*

Boots of Leather, Slippers of Gold: The History of a Lesbian Community. *v.6 p.365*

The Bop Apocalypse: The Religious Visions of Kerouac, Ginsberg, and Burroughs. *v.2 p.64, p.79, p.93*

Borden: His Life and World. *v.3 p.539*

The Border and the Revolution: Clandestine Activities of the Mexican Revolution, 1910-1920. . . . . *v.3 p.293*

Border Correspondent: Selected Writings, 1955-1970. *v.6 p.494*

☐ Border Cultures: Conjunto Music. *v.6 p.487, p.519*

The border finder: a border studies bibliography. . . .*v.6 p.677*

Border Games: Policing the U.S.- Mexico Divide. *v.6 p.486, p.537*

Border Identifications: Narratives of Religion, Gender, and Class on the U. S. -Mexico Border. *v.4 p.727*

Border Matters: Remapping American Cultural Studies. *v.6 p.487, p.491, p.515*

Border Oasis: Water and the Political Ecology of the Colorado River Delta, 1940-1975. . . . .*v.3 p.270*

Border of a Dream: Selected Poems of Antonio Machado. *v.2 p.661*

The Border Patrol Ate My Dust. *v.4 p.763*

Border People: Life and Society in the U.S.-Mexico Borderlands. *v.6 p.487, p.522*

Border State. *v.2 p.781*

Border Visions: Mexican Cultures of the Southwest United States. *v.3 p.528, v.4 p.770, v.6 p.488, p.533*

A Border Within: National Identity, Cultural Plurality and Wilderness. *v.3 p.534*

The Borderers. *v.2 p.325*

Bordering Fires: The Vintage Book of Contemporary Mexican and Chicana and Chicano Literature. *v.2 p.19*

Bordering the Future: The Impact of Mexico on the United States. *v.4 p.382, p.383*

Borderlands - La Frontera: The New Mestiza. *v.2 p.14, v.6 p.477, p.543, p.545, p.546*

Borderlands of Western Civilization: A History of East Central Europe. *v.3 p.206*

Borderlands Sourcebook: A Guide to the Literature on Northern Mexico and the American Southwest. *v.6 p.677*

Borderless Borders: U. S. Latinos, Latin Americans, and the Paradox of Interdependence. *v.6 p.521*

The Borderless World: Power and Strategy in the Interlinked Economy. *v.4 p.70*

BorderLine: A Bibliography of the United States-Mexico Borderlands. *v.6 p.684, p.693*

Borders and Boundaries: Women in India's Partition. *v.6 p.159, p.454, p.455*

Borders. *v.2 p.150, v.6 p.501, p.510*

Boreal Ecosystems and Landscapes: Structures, Processes and Conservation of Biodiversity. *v.5 p.177, p.181*

Boredom. *v.2 p.720*

Borges: A Life. *v.2 p.679*

Borges and His Fiction: A Guide to His Mind and Art. *v.2 p.677*

Borges Revisited (Argentina). *v.2 p.679*

Boricua Literature: A Literary History of the Puerto Rican Diaspora. *v.6 p.506, p.512*

Boricua Pop: Puerto Ricans and American Culture from West Side Story to Jennifer Lopez. *v.4 p.712, v.6 p.493*

Boricuas in Gotham: Puerto Ricans in the Making of New York City. *v.6 p.544, p.549*

Boricuas: Influential Puerto Rican Writings - An Anthology. *v.2 p.20, v.6 p.496, p.509*

Boris Godunov. *v.1 p.201, p.231, p.345, p.409, v.3 p.215*

Born and Bred: Idioms of Kinship and New Reproductive Technologies in England. *v.4 p.31*

Born for Liberty. *v.6 p.449*

Born for the Muses: The Life and Masses of Jacob Obrecht. *v.1 p.181, p.346*

Born in Bondage: Growing up Enslaved in the Antebellum South. *v.4 p.706*

Born in Exile. *v.2 p.289*

Born in Seattle: The Campaign for Japanese American Redress. *v.6 p.134, p.135*

Born in the U. S. A.: A Story of Japanese America: 1889-1947. . . . .*v.6 p.131, p.133*

Born in the U. S. A.: The Myth of America in Popular Music from Colonial Times to the Present. *v.1 p.274*

Born in Tibet. *v.6 p.242*

Born Losers: A History of Failure in America. . . .*v.4 p.706*

Born of the Poor: The Latin American Church Since Medellin. *v.1 p.572*

Born on the Fourth of July. *v.6 p.168, p.169*

Born Red: A Chronicle of the Cultural Revolution. *v.6 p.195, p.200*

Born to Buy: The Commercialized Child and the New Consumer Culture. *v.5 p.587*

Born to Crime: Cesare Lombroso and the Origins of Biological Criminology. *v.6 p.254*

Born to Run: Origins of the Political Career. . .*v.4 p.550, p.551*

Born to Win: The Authorized Biography of Althea Gibson. *v.4 p.832, p.836, p.864*

Born Yesterday. *v.2 p.91*

Borneo in Transition: People, Forests, Conservation, and Development. *v.5 p.39*

The Borough. *v.2 p.281*

Borror and DeLong's Introduction to the Study of Insects. *v.5 p.27*

A Borrowed Place: The History of Hong Kong. *v.6 p.206, p.207*

Borrowed Time: An AIDS Memoir. *v.6 p.379, p.403*

Borrowed Words: Translation, Imitation and the Making of the Nineteenth-Century Novel in Spain. *v.2 p.641*

Borstal Boy. *v.2 p.333*

The Borzoi Anthology of Latin American Literature, Vol. 1. . . . .*v.2 p.666*

The Borzoi Anthology of Latin American Literature, Vol. 2. . . . .*v.2 p.666*

Borzoi Book of Modern Dance. *v.1 p.26*

BOSCH Automotive Handbook. *v.5 p.715*

Bosch. *v.1 p.738, p.743*

Bosnia: A Short History. *v.3 p.249*

Bosnia and Hercegovina: A Tradition Betrayed. . . .*v.3 p.249*

The Bosnian Chronicle. *v.2 p.819*

Boss: Richard J. Daley of Chicago. *v.3 p.516*

Boss Tweed: The Rise and Fall of the Corrupt Pol Who Conceived the Soul of Modern New York. *v.3 p.490*

Boston: A Topographical History. . .*v.3 p.489, v.6 p.721, p.722*

Boston Adventure. *v.2 p.120*

Boston Marathon: The First Century of the World's Premier Running Event. *v.4 p.843, p.866*

Boston Riots: Three Centuries of Social Violence. *v.4 p.713, v.6 p.715*

Boston, Seventeen Hundred to Nineteen Eighty: The Evolution of Urban Politics. *v.3 p.488, v.6 p.712*

The Bostonians. *v.2 p.44, v.6 p.397*

Boston's Immigrants, 1790-1880: A Study in Acculturation. *v.3 p.487, p.488,v.6 p.712*

Boston's "Changeful Times": Origins of Preservation and Planning in America. *v.1 p.822, v.6 p.726*

Boswell, Laird of Auchinleck: 1778-1782: The Yale Editions of the Private Papers of James Boswell. *v.2 p.240, p.241*

Boswell's Life of Johnson: Together with Boswell's Journal of a Tour to the Hebrides, and Johnson's Diary of a Journey into North Wales. *v.2 p.240*

The Botanical Garden: Perennials and Annuals. . . .*v.5 p.84*

The Botanical Garden: Trees and Shrubs. *v.5 p.84*

The Botanical Gardens at the Huntington. *v.5 p.83*

Botanical Latin. *v.5 p.207*

The Botanist and the Vintner: How Wine Was Saved for the World. *v.5 p.52*

The Botany of Desire: A Plant's-Eye View of the World. *v.5 p.16, p.45*

Botero: Catalogue Raisonné: Paintings 1975-1990. . .*v.1 p.748*

Botero: Drawings. *v.1 p.723*

Botero Mujeres. *v.2 p.668*

Both Gains and Gaps: Feminist Perspectives on Women's Leisure. *v.4 p.784, p.836*

Both Right and Left Handed: Arab Women Talk about Their Lives. *v.6 p.583*

Both Sides of the Mirror: The Science and Art of Ballet. *v.1 p.49, p.50*

Botswana: a Short Political History. *v.6 p.75*

Botticelli: From Lorenzo the Magnificent to Savonarola.*v.1 p.737*

Botticelli: Life and Work. *v.1 p.698*

The Bottle Factory Outing. *v.2 p.330*

Bottom Dogs. *v.2 p.69*

Bottom Line Writing: Reporting the Sense of Dollars. *v.4 p.406, p.407*

Bottom-Line Automation. *v.4 p.117*

Boule de Suif. *v.2 p.497*

Les boulevards de ceinture. *v.2 p.532*

Boulez on Music Today. *v.1 p.209, p.312*

Bound by Law: Tales from the Public Domain: by Day a Filmmaker, by Night She Fought for Fair Use!. . .*v.4 p.445*

e Bound by Our Constitution: Women, Workers, and the Minimum Wage. *v.6 p.456, p.469*

Bound by Recognition. *v.4 p.513, p.514*

Bound for Santa Fe: The Road to New Mexico and the American Conquest, 1806-1848. . . . .*v.3 p.528*

Bound for the Promised Land: Harriet Tubman, Portrait of an American Hero. *v.6 p.7, p.18, p.44, p.45*

Bound Man, and Other Stories. *v.2 p.602*

Bound to Bond: Gender, Genre and the Hollywood Romantic Comedy. *v.6 p.313, p.317, p.328, p.329, p.343*

Bound to Please: An Extraordinary One-Volume Literary Education. *v.2 p.573*

Bound to Sin: Abuse, Holocaust and the Christian Doctrine of Sin. *v.1 p.643*

Boundaries and Belonging: States and Societies in the Struggle to Shape Identities and Local Practices. . . *v.4 p.495, p.496*

The Boundaries of the Canadian Confederation. *v.3 p.536, p.537*

Boundaries: The Making of France and Spain in the Pyrenees. *v.3 p.243*

Boundary Element Methods. *v.5 p.491*

The Boundaryless Organization: Breaking the Chains of Organizational Structure. *v.4 p.85*

The Boundless Frontier: America from Christopher Columbus to Abraham Lincoln. *v.3 p.382*

The Bounds of Sense: An Essay on Kant's Critique of Pure Reason. *v.1 p.462*

Bourbon Democracy of the Middle West, 1865-1896. .*v.3 p.506*

Bourbon Peru 1750-1824. . . . .*v.3 p.325, p.326*

Bourbons and Brandy: Imperial Reform in Eighteenth-Century Arequipa. *v.3 p.325*

The Bourbons of Naples. *v.3 p.201*

Bourgeois Society in 19th Century Europe. *v.3 p.74, p.75*

Bourgeoisie in Eighteenth Century France. *v.4 p.723*

Bournonville and Ballet Technique: Studies and Comments on August Bournonville's Etudes Choregraphiques. . . *v.1 p.23*

Bouvard and Pecuchet. *v.2 p.491*

Bowen's Court and Seven Windows. *v.2 p.334*

The Bowie Companion. *v.1 p.275, p.313*

The Bowker Annual Library and Book Trade Almanac 2005-2006. . . . .*v.4 p.148*

Bowker's Guide to Characters in Fiction, 2006. . . . .*v.2 p.549*

Bowling Alone: The Collapse and Revival of American Community. *v.4 p.706*

Bowling Fundamentals. *v.4 p.796, p.848*

Boxing and Society: An International Analysis. *v.4 p.820, p.844, p.856*

The Boxing Register: International Boxing Hall of Fame Official Record Book. *v.4 p.856*

Boy Crazy: Remembering Adolescence, Memories and Dreams. *v.5 p.629, p.631*

The Boy in the Bush. *v.2 p.363*

Boy Soldier: A German Teenager at the Nazi Twilight. *v.3 p.175*

The Boy Who Would Be a Helicopter. *v.4 p.370*

The Boy Without a Flag: Tales of the South Bronx. . .*v.6 p.508*

Boyhood: Scenes from Provincial Life. *v.2 p.753*

Boys and Girls Together: A Novel. *v.2 p.118*

Boys Together: English Public Schools 1800-1864. . .*v.6 p.745*

Boys Will Be Boys. *v.6 p.739, p.757*

Boys Will Be Girls: The Feminine Ethic and British Children's Fiction, 1857-1917. . . . .*v.2 p.176, v.6 p.748, p.756, p.765*

Boy-Wives and Female-Husbands: Studies in African Homosexualities. *v.6 p.372, p.421*

Bracebridge Hall, Tales of a Traveller and the Alhambra. *v.2 p.42*

The Bracero Experience: Elitelore vs. Folklore. *v.6 p.523*

The Bradbury Chronicles: The Life of Ray Bradbury. . *v.2 p.63*

Bradford's History of Plymouth Plantation, 1606-1646. *v.3 p.487*

The Bradlaugh Case: Atheism, Sex, and Politics among the Late Victorians. *v.3 p.110, p.120*

Bradley's Arnold Latin Prose Composition. *v.2 p.423*

Brahms: A German Requiem. *v.1 p.201, p.236, p.313*

Brahms and the Principle of Developing Variation. *v.1 p.197, p.313, p.370*

A Brahms Reader. *v.1 p.201, p.313*

Brahms: The Four Symphonies. *v.1 p.197, p.239, p.313*

Brahms. *v.1 p.200, p.313*

Braid of Feathers: American Indian Law and Contemporary Tribal Life. *v.6 p.692*

Braided Lives. *v.2 p.153*

Brain and Visual Perception: The Story of a 25-Year Collaboration. *v.5 p.617*

Brain, Culture and the Human Spirit: Essays from an Emergent Evolutionary Perspective. *v.5 p.632*

Brain Maps: Structure of the Rat Brain. *v.5 p.618*

Brain Stem Cells. *v.5 p.165*

Brain Storm: Tap into Your Creativity to Generate Awesome Ideas and Remarkable Results. *v.4 p.67*

Brain Tattoos: Creating Unique Brands That Stick in Your Customers' Minds. *v.4 p.142*

Brainstorms: Philosophical Essays on Mind and Psychology. *v.1 p.496*

Bramble Bush: On Our Law and Its Study. *v.4 p.439*

Branching Processes in Biology. *v.5 p.154*

Branching Processes: Variation, Growth, and Extinction of Populations. *v.5 p.184, p.188*

Brancusi. *v.1 p.781*

Brand Failures: The Truth about the 100 Biggest Branding Mistakes of All Time. *v.4 p.142*

Brand Hijack: Marketing Without Marketing. *v.4 p.142*

☐ Brand Name Lookup. *v.4 p.141*

Brand New Memory. *v.6 p.507, p.508*

Brand Royalty: How the World's Top 100 Brands Thrive and Survive. *v.4 p.142*

Brandeis Modern Hebrew. *v.6 p.646*

The Brandeis-Frankfurter Connection: The Secret Political Activities of Two Supreme Court Justices. *v.4 p.468*

Brand-Name Bullies: The Quest to Own and Control Culture. *v.4 p.773*

Brands and Their Companies. *v.4 p.141*

Brands, Consumers, Symbols and Research: Sidney J Levy on Marketing. *v.4 p.135, v.5 p.587*

Brands: The Logos of the Global Economy. *v.4 p.261*

Brands. *v.4 p.141*

Brandung: Roman. *v.2 p.619*

Brandweek: The Newsweekly of Marketing Communications. *v.4 p.140, p.141, p.150*

Branle-bas en noir et blanc : roman. *v.2 p.544*

Braque: The Late Works. *v.1 p.739*

The Brass Check: A Study of American Journalism. . .*v.4 p.404*

Brass Instruments: Their History and Development. . .*v.1 p.388*

Brassaï: The Monograph. *v.1 p.768*

Brasseys' Guide to War Films. *v.6 p.322*

Braunwald's Heart Disease: A Textbook of Cardiovascular Medicine. *v.5 p.520*

The Brave Bulls. *v.2 p.94*

Brave New Families: Stories of Domestic Upheaval in Late-Twentieth-Century America. *v.4 p.732*

Brave New Neighborhoods: The Privatization of Public Space. *v.6 p.723*

Brave New World and Brave New World Revisited. . .*v.2 p.354*

Brave New World Revisited. *v.4 p.696*

Braving a New World: Cambodian (Khmer) Refugees in an American City. *v.6 p.118, p.139*

The Brawn Drain: Foreign Student Athletes in American Universities. *v.4 p.821, p.893, p.898*

Brazil and the Quiet Intervention, 1964. . . . . . .*v.3 p.342*

Brazil and the Struggle for Rubber: A Study in Environmental History. *v.3 p.268, p.339*

Brazil Built: The Architecture of the Modern Movement in Brazil. *v.1 p.789*

Brazil: Empire and Republic, 1822-1930. . . . . . .*v.3 p.335*

Brazil: Five Centuries of Change. *v.3 p.342*

Brazil Is Not for Amateurs: Patterns of Governance in the Land of Jeitinho. *v.3 p.339*

Brazil since 1980. . . . .*v.3 p.341*

The Brazilian Empire: Myths and Histories. *v.3 p.336*

Brazilian Literature: 1500-1880. . . . .*v.2 p.691*

Brazilian Literature: 1880-1920, Vol. 2. . . . .*v.2 p.691*

Brazilian Literature: 1920-1960, Vol. 3. . . . .*v.2 p.691*

Brazilian Literature: An Outline. *v.2 p.693*

Brazilian Music: Northeastern Traditions and the Heartbeat of a Modern Nation. *v.1 p.291*

Brazilian Narrative Traditions in a Comparative Context. *v.2 p.690*

Brazilian Party Politics and the Coup of 1964. . . . .*v.3 p.341*

The Brazilian People: The Formation and Meaning of Brazil. *v.3 p.342*

Brazilian Poetry (1950-1980). *v.2 p.689*

Brazilian Popular Music and Globalization. *v.1 p.293*

Brazilian Portuguese. *v.2 p.638*

Brazilian Women Speak: Contemporary Life Stories. . .*v.3 p.342*

Brazil's Second Chance: En Route Toward the First World. *v.3 p.340*

Brazzaville Beach. *v.2 p.335*

Bread, Hashish and Moon: Four Modern Arab Poets. *v.6 p.655*

Bread, Knowledge and Freedom: A Study of Nineteenth-Century Working Class Autobiography. *v.3 p.116, p.132, v.6 p.739, p.743*

The Bread Loaf Anthology of Contemporary American Short Stories. *v.2 p.26*

The Bread of Salt and Other Stories. *v.6 p.179*

The Bread of Those Early Years. *v.2 p.604*

Break of Day. *v.2 p.510*

Breakdancing. *v.1 p.18*

Breakfast at Tiffany's: A Short Novel and Three Stories. *v.2 p.66*

Breakfast of Champions. *v.2 p.158*

Breakfast Served Any Time All Day: Essays on Poetry New and Selected. *v.2 p.4, p.82*

Breaking Boundaries: Latina Writing and Critical
Readings. *v.6 p.500, p.506, p.513*

Breaking Bounds: The Dance Photography of Lois
Greenfield. *v.1 p.45*

Breaking Bread: Insurgent Black Intellectual Life. . . .*v.6 p.26*

Breaking into Baseball: Women and the National
Pasttime. *v.4 p.813, p.834, p.849*

Breaking New Ground. *v.3 p.434, v.5 p.39*

Breaking Out: VMI and the Coming of Women. *v.6 p.462*

The Breaking Point: Sedan and the Fall of France, 1940. .*v.3 p.156*

Breaking Silence: The Case That Changed the Face of Human
Rights. *v.3 p.345*

Breaking Story: South African Press. *v.4 p.410*

Breaking the Abortion Deadlock: From Choice to
Consent. *v.4 p.472*

Breaking the Bargain: Public Servants, Ministers and
Parliament. *v.4 p.588*

Breaking the Brass Ceiling: Women Police Chiefs and Their
Paths to the Top. *v.6 p.260*

Breaking the Chains: African-American Slave Resistance. .*v.6 p.7*

Breaking the Codes: Female Criminality in Fin-de-Siecle
Paris. *v.3 p.54, p.155,v.6 p.471*

Breaking the Glass Ceiling: Sexism and Racism in Corporate
America: the Myths, the Realities and the Solutions. .*v.4 p.134*

Breaking the Heart of the World: Woodrow Wilson and the
Fight for the League of Nations. . .*v.3 p.468, p.469,v.4 p.631*

Breaking the Land: The Transformation of Cotton, Tobacco, and
Rice Cultures since 1880. . . . .*v.4 p.771*

Breaking the Maya Code. *v.4 p.22*

Breaking the Rules: The NCAA and Recruitment in America's
High Schools. *v.4 p.822, p.895*

Breaking the Silence: The Redress Movement in Seattle. .*v.6 p.135*

Breaking the Spell: Religion as a Natural Phenomenon. .*v.1 p.545*

Breaking Through Bureaucracy: A New Vision for Managing in
Government. *v.4 p.529*

Breaking Through Culture Shock: What You Need to Succeed in
International Business. *v.4 p.56*

Breakthrough International Negotiation: How Great Negotiators
Transformed the World's Toughest Post-Cold War
Conflicts. *v.4 p.646*

Breakthrough Swimming. *v.4 p.868, p.879*

Breast Cancer: Society Shapes an Epidemic: The Social
Construction of an Illness. *v.6 p.443*

Breath on the Mirror: Mythic Voices and Visions of the Living
Maya. *v.2 p.677*

Breath: Poems. *v.2 p.149*

Breathing Lessons: A Novel. *v.2 p.157*

Brecht: A Biography. *v.2 p.605*

Brecht; A Collection of Critical Essays. *v.2 p.605*

Brecht on Theatre: The Development of an
Aesthetic. *v.1 p.55, p.56, p.138, p.149, p.152*

Breeding Field Crops. *v.5 p.8, p.15, p.23*

▢ Breeds of Livestock. *v.5 p.54*

▢ Breeds of Poultry. *v.5 p.53*

Bref séjour chez les vivants : roman. *v.2 p.529*

Brendan Behan: A Life. *v.2 p.333, p.334*

Brendan Behan: Cultural Nationalism and the Revisionist
Writer. *v.2 p.333*

Brennan vs. Rehnquist: The Battle for the
Constitution. *v.4 p.470, p.537*

The Brenner Debate: Agrarian Class Structure and Economic
Development in Pre-Industrial Europe. *v.3 p.42*

Brentano and Intrinsic Value. *v.1 p.464*

Brer Rabbit, Uncle Remus and the 'Cornfield Journalist': The
Tale of Joel Chandler Harris. *v.2 p.40*

Bret Harte, Argonaut and Exile. *v.2 p.40*

Bret Harte: Opening the American Literary West. . . .*v.2 p.40*

Bretherick's Handbook of Reactive Chemical Hazards,
Set. *v.5 p.312*

Bretherick's Handbook of Reactive Chemical
Hazards. *v.5 p.312, p.682*

Brethren of the Net: American Entomology,
1840-1880. . . . .*v.5 p.81, p.213*

The Bretons. *v.3 p.158*

Brewer's Dictionary of Phrase and Fable. *v.2 p.549*

Brezhnev Reconsidered. *v.3 p.228*

Brian Eno: His Music and the Vertical Color of
Sound. *v.1 p.275, p.323, p.324*

Brick: A World History. *v.1 p.796*

The Brick People. *v.2 p.150, v.6 p.502*

Brickyards to Graveyards: From Production to Genocide in
Rwanda. *v.4 p.652*

The Bridal Canopy. *v.6 p.646*

Bride of Acacias: Selected Poems of Forugh
Farrokhzad. *v.6 p.670*

Brideshead Revisited: The Past Redeemed. *v.2 p.387*

Brideshead Revisited. *v.2 p.388, v.6 p.399, p.400*

The Bridge of Beyond. *v.2 p.538*

Bridge-Makers and Cross-Bearers: Korean-American Women
and the Church. *v.6 p.105, p.112, p.135*

The Bridges at Toko-Ri. *v.2 p.98*

Bridges to Cuba/Puentes a Cuba. . .*v.3 p.306, v.6 p.495, p.505*

Bridging Cultures: An Introduction to Chicano/Latino
Studies. *v.6 p.486*

Bridging Cultures Between Home and School: A Guide for
Teachers with Special Focus on Immigrant Latino
Families. *v.4 p.311, p.312,v.6 p.528*

Bridging Differences: Effective Intergroup
Communication. *v.5 p.647*

Bridging the European Divide: Middle Power Politics and
Regional Security Dilemmas. *v.4 p.397*

Bridging the Literacy Achievement Gap, Grades 4-12. .*v.4 p.365*

Bridgings: Readings in Australian Women's Poetry. . .*v.2 p.741*

Bridled Ambition: Why Countries Constrain Their Nuclear
Capabilities. *v.4 p.656*

A Brief Course in Business Statistics. *v.4 p.179*

Brief Encounters: Lesbians and Gays in British Cinema,
1930-1971. . . . .*v.6 p.415*

A Brief Guide to Sources of Metals Information. . . .*v.5 p.732*

A Brief History of Ancient Greece: Politics, Society, and
Culture. *v.3 p.13*

A Brief History of Argentina. *v.3 p.346, p.347*

A Brief History of Chinese and Japanese Civilizations. .*v.6 p.181*

A Brief History of Cocaine. *v.3 p.281*

A Brief History of Heaven. *v.1 p.645*

A Brief History of Heresy. *v.1 p.646*

Brief History of the Czech Lands To 2004. . . . . .*v.3 p.187*

A Brief History of the Paradox: Philosophy and the Labyrinths of the Mind. *v.1 p.495*

A Brief History of the Presbyterians. *v.1 p.588*

A Brief History of Time: From the Big Bang to Black Holes. *v.5 p.72, p.556, p.557*

A Brief on Tensor Analysis. *v.5 p.486*

Brief Psychotherapy with the Latino Immigrant Client. *v.6 p.541, p.551*

A Brief Stay with the Living. *v.2 p.529*

A Brief Tour of Human Consciousness: From Impostor Poodles to Purple Numbers. *v.5 p.617*

Briefe an Goethe. *v.2 p.597, p.598*

Briefe. *v.2 p.613*

Briefing for a Descent into Hell. *v.2 p.364*

Brigands with a Cause: Brigandage and Irredentism in Modern Greece 1821-1912. . . . .*v.3 p.195*

Brigham Young: American Moses. *v.1 p.587*

Bright Balkan Morning: Romani Lives and the Power of Music in Greek Macedonia. *v.1 p.298*

Bright Boulevards, Bold Dreams: The Story of Black Hollywood. *v.1 p.18, p.32, p.36*

Bright Earth: Art and the Invention of Color. *v.1 p.710*

Bright Existence. *v.2 p.147*

Bright Promises, Dismal Performance: An Economist's Protest. *v.4 p.231, p.232*

The Bright Star Catalogue. *v.5 p.64*

The Bright Work Grows: Women Writers of the Romantic Age. *v.2 p.173*

A Brighter Tomorrow: Fulfilling the Promise of Nuclear Energy. *v.5 p.739*

Brighton Rock. *v.2 p.349*

Bright's Old English Grammar. *v.2 p.205, p.550*

Brill's Companion to Cicero: Oratory and Rhetoric. .*v.2 p.433*

Bringing Chemistry to Life: From Matter to Man. . . .*v.5 p.264*

Bringing Equity Back: Research for a New Era in American Educational Policy. *v.4 p.299, p.302*

Bringing Life to Ethics: Global Bioethics for a Humane Society. *v.5 p.247*

Bringing Peace Home: Feminism, Violence, and Nature. .*v.6 p.471*

Bringing Ritual to Mind: Psychological Foundations of Cultural Forms. *v.5 p.635*

Bringing the Empire Back Home: France in the Global Age. *v.4 p.608, p.609*

Bringing the Mountain Home. *v.5 p.175*

Bringing the War Home: The Weather Underground, the Red Army Faction, and Revolutionary Violence in the Sixties and Seventies. *v.3 p.445*

Bringing Them under Subjection: California's Tejon Indian Reservation and Beyond, 1852-1864. . .*v.4 p.542, v.6 p.687*

Bringing Transformative Learning to Life. *v.4 p.320*

The Brink of Peace: The Israeli-Syrian Negotiations. .*v.4 p.650*

Britain and Europe since 1945: Historiographical Perspectives on Integration. *v.3 p.87*

Britain and Germany in Africa: Imperial Rivalry and Colonial Rule. *v.3 p.76, v.6 p.56*

Britain and Indian Nationalism: The Imprint of Ambiguity, 1929-1942. . . . .*v.6 p.157*

Britain and Poland, 1939-1943: The Betrayed Ally. . .*v.3 p.81*

Britain and the Continent 1000-1300: The Impact of the Norman Conquest. *v.3 p.97*

Britain and the Onset of Modernization in Brazil, 1850-1914. . . . .*v.3 p.336*

Britain and the Origins of Canadian Confederation, 1837-1867. . . . .*v.3 p.539*

Britain and the War for the Union, Vol. 2. . . . . .*v.3 p.433*

Britain Between the Wars, 1918-1940. . . . .*v.3 p.118*

Britain in China: Community, Culture and Colonialism, 1900-49. . . . . . .*v.6 p.203, p.214, p.217, p.218*

Britain, Kenya and the Cold War: Imperial Defence, Colonial Security and Decolonisation. *v.6 p.65*

Britain, Poland and the Eastern Front 1939. . . . . .*v.3 p.254*

Britain: Travellers' Nature Guide. *v.5 p.237*

Britain's Imperial Century 1815-1914: A Study of Empire and Expansion. *v.3 p.125*

Britain's Informal Empire in the Middle East: A Case Study of Iraq 1929-1941. . . . .*v.6 p.603*

Britannicus; Phaedra; Athaliah. *v.2 p.477*

British Art since 1900. . . . .*v.1 p.680, p.681, p.689*

The British Book Trade and Spanish American Independence: Education and Knowledge Transmission in Transcontinental Perspective. *v.3 p.265*

The British Cinema Book. *v.6 p.339*

British Cinema in the 1950s: An Art in Peacetime. . .*v.6 p.339*

British Colonial Rule and the Resistance of the Malay Peasantry, 1900-1957. . . . .*v.6 p.172, p.173*

The British Communist Party and the Trade Unions, 1933-45. . . . .*v.4 p.604, p.606*

British Diplomats and Diplomacy, 1660-1800. . . .*v.4 p.645*

The British Documentary Film Movement, 1926-1946.*v.6 p.310*

British Drama, 1660-1779: A Critical History. *v.2 p.187*

British Drama, 1950 to Present. *v.2 p.189*

British Drama Beginnings to Sixteen Hundred Sixty. *v.2 p.185, p.186*

British Drama, Eighteen Ninety to Nineteen Fifty. . .*v.2 p.188*

British Economic Growth During the Industrial Revolution. *v.3 p.122*

The British Electorate, 1963-1992: A Compendium of Data from the British Election Studies. *v.4 p.606*

The British Empire, 1558-1995. . . . .*v.3 p.89, p.125*

The British Empire, Fifteen Fifty-Eight to Nineteen Eighty-Three. *v.3 p.89*

The British Empire. *v.3 p.90*

A British Enterprise in Brazil: The St. John d'el Rey Mining Company and the Morro Velho Gold Mine, 1830-1960. . . . .*v.3 p.340*

The British Experience in Iraq: Lessons for U.S. Policymakers. *v.4 p.561, p.643, p.644*

The British Folk Revival: 1944-2002. . . . .*v.1 p.298*

The British Folklorists: A History. *v.2 p.584*

British Foreign Policy in the Age of the American Revolution. *v.4 p.583*

British Foreign Policy in the Age of Walpole. . .*v.3 p.90, p.106*

The British Foreign Service and the American Civil War. *v.4 p.565*

The British General Elections, 1945-1992, Set. *v.4 p.606*

British Historical and Political Orations, from the 12th to the 20th Century. *v.2 p.197*

British History, 1815-1906. . . . .*v.3 p.113*

British Honduras: Colonial Dead End, 1859-1900. . . .*v.3 p.297*

British Imperial Policy and Decolonization, 1938-64: 1938-51, Vol. 1. . . . .*v.3 p.125*

British Imperial Policy and Decolonization, 1938-64: Nineteen Fifty-One to Nineteen Sixty-Four, Vol. 2. . . . .*v.3 p.125*

British Imperialism: 1688-2000. . . . .*v.4 p.583*

The British in Palestine: The Mandatory Government and the Arab-Jewish Conflict 1917-1929. . . . .*v.6 p.613*

The British Industrial Revolution: An Economic Perspective. *v.3 p.123*

British Industrial Revolution: An Economic Perspective. .*v.4 p.212*

British Labor and the American Civil War. . . .*v.3 p.396, p.433*

British Literary Magazines: The Romantic Age, 1789-1836. . . . .*v.6 p.736, p.742, p.753*

British Literary Magazines: The Victorian and Edwardian Age, 1837-1913. . . . .*v.6 p.736, p.742, p.753*

British Literary Publishing Houses, 1881-1965. . . .*v.6 p.742*

British Literature, 1640-1789: An Anthology. *v.2 p.196*

British Merchants and Chilean Development, 1851-1886, Vol. 22. . . . .*v.3 p.351*

The British Moralists and the Internal "Ought": 1640-1740. . . . .*v.1 p.450*

British Painting: The Golden Age. *v.1 p.733*

British Philosophy: Hobbes to Hume, Vol. 5. . . . .*v.1 p.450*

British Philosophy in the Age of Enlightenment. .*v.1 p.449, p.450*

The British Political Tradition, Set. *v.4 p.607*

British Politics in the Age of Anne. *v.3 p.94, p.106*

The British Presidency: Tony Blair and the Politics of Public Leadership. *v.4 p.605*

British Printmakers 1855-1955: A Century of Printmaking from the Etching Revival to St. Ives. *v.1 p.754*

British Prints: Dictionary and Price Guide. *v.1 p.752*

British Radio Drama. *v.1 p.94, p.99*

British Realist Theatre: The New Wave in Its Context, 1956-1965. . . . .*v.1 p.80, p.101*

British Regime in Wisconsin and the Northwest. . . .*v.3 p.517*

British Sculptors of the Twentieth Century. *v.1 p.774*

British Social Movements since 1945: Sex, Colour, Peace and Power. *v.4 p.711*

British Society since 1945. . . . .*v.4 p.705*

British Theatre Design. *v.1 p.100, p.154*

British Women Poets of the Romantic Era: An Anthology. *v.2 p.199*

British Women's Autobiographics: A Comprehensive Guide to Research. *v.6 p.476, p.477*

The British Working Class Reader, 1790-1848; Literacy and Social Tension. *v.3 p.116, p.132*

British Writers of the Thirties. *v.2 p.178*

Britons: Forging the Nation, 1707-1837. . . . .*v.6 p.757, p.763*

Britten: War Requiem. *v.1 p.211, p.235, p.314*

Broadax and Bayonet: The Role of the United States Army in the Development of the Northwest, 1815-1860. . .*v.6 p.686*

Broadband Planar Antennas: Design and Applications. .*v.5 p.729*

Broadband Satellite Communications for Internet Access. *v.5 p.726, p.727*

Broadband Telecommunications Handbook. .*v.4 p.115, v.5 p.726*

Broadcast Journalism. *v.4 p.413*

A Broadcast News Manual of Style. *v.4 p.414*

Broadcast News. *v.4 p.414*

Broadcast Talk, Vol. 5. . . . .*v.4 p.412*

Broadcasting and Cable Yearbook. *v.4 p.157*

Broadcasting Freedom: Radio War and the Politics of Race, 1938-1948. . . . .*v.4 p.487, p.573*

Broadcasting in the Arab World: A Survey of the Electronic Media in the Middle East. *v.4 p.412*

Broadcasting in the Third World: Promise and Performance. *v.4 p.412*

The Broadview Anthology of Restoration and Early Eighteenth-Century Drama. *v.2 p.202*

The Broadview Anthology of Romantic Drama. *v.1 p.64, p.78, p.99*

The Broadview Anthology of Seventeenth-Century Verse and Prose. *v.2 p.197, p.201*

Broadway Boogie Woogie: Damon Runyon and the Making of New York City Culture. *v.2 p.114, v.6 p.731*

The Broadway Musical: A Critical and Musical Survey. .*v.1 p.254*

Broadway, the Golden Years: Jerome Robbins and the Great Choreographer-Directors, 1940 to the Present. *v.1 p.36*

Broadway. *v.1 p.111, p.112*

The Brock Bibliography of Published Canadian Plays in English, 1766-1978. . . . .*v.2 p.731*

Broken Bottles, Broken Dreams: Understanding and Helping the Children of Alcoholics. *v.4 p.776, v.5 p.663*

Broken Churches, Broken Nation: Denominational Schism and the Coming of the American Civil War. *v.1 p.606*

The Broken Commandment. *v.6 p.233*

The Broken Compass: A Study of the Major Comedies of Ben Jonson. *v.2 p.220*

The Broken Covenant: American Civil Religion in a Time of Trial. *v.3 p.366*

The Broken Covenant: American Civil Religion in Time of Trial. *v.3 p.365, p.366*

Broken Covenant. *v.6 p.609*

The Broken Eagle: The Politics of Austrian Literature from Empire to Anschluss. *v.2 p.590*

The Broken Mirror: A Collection of Writings from Contemporary Poland,. *v.2 p.787*

Broken Promise: The Subversion of U. S. Labor Relations, 1947-1994. . . . .*v.4 p.121, p.122*

Broken Promises: Evaluating the Native American Health Care System. *v.6 p.702*

The Broken Spears: The Aztec Account of the Conquest of Mexico. *v.3 p.286*

Broken Star: The Story of the League of Nations (1919-1939). *v.4 p.631*

The Broken Tower: A Life of Hart Crane. *v.2 p.68*

Brokenburn: The Journal of Kate Stone, 1861-1868. . .*v.3 p.427*

Brokered Homeland: Japanese Brazilian Migrants in Japan. *v.6 p.119, p.132*

Bronislava Nijinska: Early Memoirs. *v.1 p.11*

Bronislaw Malinowski: Collected Works, Set. *v.4 p.3*

The Bronte Sisters: Selected Poems of Charlotte, Emily and Anne Bronte. *v.2 p.270*

The Brontes: A Life in Letters. *v.2 p.269*

The Brontes A to Z. *v.2 p.271*

The Brontes (Authors in Context). *v.2 p.271*

Brontes. *v.2 p.269*

The Bronx: A History. *v.3 p.491*

El Bronx Remembered. *v.6 p.507*

The Bronze Age and Early Iron Age Peoples of Eastern Central Asia. *v.4 p.9*

The Bronze Age of Southeast Asia. *v.4 p.8, p.9*

Bronzes of the 19th Century: Dictionary of Sculptors. .*v.1 p.774*

Das Brot der Fruhen Jahre: Erzahlung. *v.2 p.604*

Brother Enemy: The War after the War. *v.6 p.167*

Brother Ray: Ray Charles' Own Story. .*v.1 p.267, p.316, p.317*

Brother to Brother: New Writings by Black Gay Men. .*v.6 p.406*

Brother to Dragons: A Tale in Verse and Voices. . . .*v.2 p.129*

Brotherhood: Gay Life in College Fraternities. *v.6 p.386*

Brotherhood in Rhythm: The Jazz Tap Dancing of the Nicholas Brothers. *v.1 p.32*

Brotherhood of the Bomb: The Tangled Lives and Loyalties of Robert Oppenheimer, Ernest Lawrence, and Edward Teller. *v.5 p.543*

Brothers and Keepers: A Memoir. . .*v.6 p.19, p.28, p.254, p.255*

The Brothers and Sisters Learn to Write: Popular Literacies in Childhood and School Cultures. *v.4 p.360*

Brothers and Strangers: The East European Jew in German and German Jewish Consciousness, 1800-1923. . . . .*v.3 p.59*

Brothers in Arms: The Rise and Fall of the Sino-Soviet Alliance, 1945-1963. . . . .*v.3 p.212*

The Brothers Karamazov: Norton Critical Edtion. . . .*v.2 p.803*

The Brothers Mann: The Lives of Heinrich and Thomas Mann, 1871-1950 and 1875-1955. . . . .*v.2 p.612*

Brothers of Light, Brothers of Blood: The Penitentes of the Southwest. *v.1 p.578*

The Brothers. *v.2 p.691*

Brought to You By: Postwar Television Advertising and the American Dream. *v.4 p.426*

Brown Girl, Brownstones. *v.2 p.768*

Brown, Jones and Robinson. *v.2 p.318*

Brown, Not White: School Integration and the Chicano Movement in Houston. *v.6 p.527, p.528, p.550*

Brown River, White Ocean: An Anthology of Twentieth-Century Philippine Literature in English. *v.2 p.760, v.6 p.179*

Brown Tide Rising: Metaphors of Latinos in Contemporary American Public Discourse. *v.6 p.494, p.522*

Brown v. Board of Education: A Civil Rights Milestone and Its Troubled Legacy. *v.4 p.450*

Brown vs. Board of Education: A Brief History with Documents. *v.4 p.439*

Brown vs. Board of Education: A Documentary History. .*v.4 p.451*

Brown vs. Board of Education: Caste, Culture, and the Constitution. *v.4 p.449, p.450*

The Brown-Driver-Briggs Hebrew and English Lexicon: Coded to Strong's Numbering System. *v.6 p.645*

Browning: The Critical Heritage. *v.2 p.272*

Browning's Beginnings: The Art of Disclosure. *v.2 p.272*

Browning's Characters: A Study in Poetic Technique. .*v.2 p.272*

Browning's Hatreds. *v.2 p.272*

Browning's Major Poetry. *v.2 p.272*

The Brownings. *v.2 p.272*

Brownsville, Brooklyn: Blacks, Jews, and the Changing Face of the Ghetto. *v.6 p.725*

Bruce Beasley: Sculpture. *v.1 p.779*

Bruce Davidson: Time of Change: Civil Rights Photographs, 1961-1965. . . . .*v.6 p.12, p.16*

Bruce Nauman. *v.1 p.773*

Bruce Springsteen: Two Hearts. *v.1 p.272, p.358*

Bruckner: Symphony No. 8. . . . . .*v.1 p.199, p.240, p.314*

Bruckner. *v.1 p.206, p.314*

Bruegel. *v.1 p.747*

Brunel: The Man Who Built the World. *v.1 p.720*

Brunelleschi's Dome: How a Renaissance Genius Reinvented Architecture. *v.1 p.787, v.3 p.200*

Brunner And Suddarth's Textbook of Medical-Surgical Nursing. *v.5 p.522*

Brush with Death: A Social History of Lead Poisoning. *v.5 p.363, p.372,v.6 p.297*

Brushes: A Handbook for Artists and Artisans. *v.1 p.751*

Brushes with Power: Modern Politics and the Chinese Art of Calligraphy. *v.1 p.719*

Brushing Back Jim Crow: The Integration of the Minor Leagues in the American South. *v.4 p.813, p.830, p.849*

Brutality Garden: Tropicalia and the Emergence of a Brazilian Counterculture. *v.1 p.292, v.3 p.266, p.267*

Brute New World: The Rediscovery of Latin America in the Early 19th Century. *v.3 p.265*

Bryophyte Biology. *v.5 p.209, p.210*

Bryophytes and Lichens in a Changing Environment. .*v.5 p.210*

Buckdancer's Choice: Poems. *v.2 p.143*

Buckle at the Ballet: Selected Ballet Writings. *v.1 p.38*

Buckminster Fuller: Designing for Mobility. *v.1 p.793*

Budapest 1900: A Historical Portrait of a City and Its Culture. *v.3 p.186*

Budapest: A Novel. *v.2 p.690*

Buddenbrooks. *v.2 p.612*

The Buddha of Suburbia. *v.2 p.360, p.361*

Buddhacarita or Acts of the Buddha. *v.1 p.563*

The Buddha. *v.1 p.692, p.693, p.710*

Buddhism: A Modern Perspective. *v.1 p.565*

Buddhism: A Short History. *v.1 p.564*

Buddhism after Patriarchy: A Feminist History, Analysis, and Reconstruction of Buddhism. *v.6 p.459*

Buddhism and Society: A Great Tradition and Its Burmese Vicissitudes. *v.1 p.562*

Buddhism and the State in Sixteenth Century Japan. . . *v.1 p.562*

Buddhism in China: A Historical Survey. *v.1 p.561*

Buddhism in Chinese History. *v.1 p.563, v.6 p.185*

Buddhism in Chinese Society: An Economic History from the Fifth to the Tenth Centuries. *v.1 p.561*

Buddhism in Contemporary Tibet: Religious Revival and Cultural Identity. *v.6 p.240, p.241*

Buddhism in Practice. *v.1 p.565*

Buddhism in the Modern World: Adaptations of an Ancient Tradition. *v.1 p.561*

Buddhism in the Sung. *v.1 p.561*

Buddhism in Translations: Passages Selec. *v.1 p.564*

The Buddhism of Tibet and the Key to the Middle Way. *v.1 p.566*

Buddhism Transformed: Religious Change in Sri Lanka. *v.1 p.540*

Buddhism under Mao. *v.1 p.563*

Buddhist Art and Architecture. *v.1 p.691, p.692, p.693*

Buddhist Backgrounds of the Burmese Revolution. . . *v.1 p.562*

The Buddhist Conquest of China. The Spread and Adaptation of Buddhism in Early Medieval China. *v.1 p.563*

Buddhist Mahayana Texts: The Sacred Books of the East Part Forty-Nine. *v.1 p.564*

Buddhist Meditation. *v.1 p.564, p.565*

Buddhist Monastic Discipline: Sanskrit Pratimoksa Sutras of the Mahasamghikas and Mulasarvastivadins. *v.1 p.564*

Buddhist Philosophy: A Historical Analysis. *v.1 p.565*

The Buddhist Poetry of the Great Kamo Priestess: Daisaiin Senshi and "Hosshin Wakashu". *v.6 p.230*

Buddhist Scriptures. *v.1 p.563*

Buddhist Suttas. *v.1 p.564*

Buddhist Texts Through the Ages. *v.1 p.563*

Buddhist Thought: Complete Introduction to the Indian Tradition. *v.1 p.565*

Buddhist Thought in India: Three Phases of Buddhist Philosophy. *v.1 p.561*

The Buddhist Tradition: In India, China and Japan. . *v.1 p.563*

Buddhist Wisdom: The Diamond Sutra and the Heart Sutra. *v.1 p.564*

Buddhist Women Across Cultures: Realizations. *v.6 p.436, p.460*

Buddhists, Hindus, and Sikhs in America. *v.6 p.106*

The Budget Book for Film and Television. *v.6 p.345*

The Budget of the United States Government Fiscal Year 2006. . . . . *v.4 p.248*

☐ Budget of the United States Government. *v.4 p.481*

Budweisers into Czechs and Germans: A Local History of Bohemian Politics. *v.3 p.190*

Buena Vista: Life and Work on a Puerto Rican Hacienda, 1833-1904. . . . . *v.3 p.318*

Buenos Aires: Plaza to Suburb Eighteen Seventy to Nineteen Ten. *v.4 p.706*

Buffalo Bill Cody: The Man Behind the Legend. . . *v.3 p.519*

The Buffalo Hunters: The Story of the Hide Men. . . *v.3 p.521*

Buffalo Nickel. *v.6 p.503*

The Buffalo Soldiers: A Narrative of the Negro Cavalry in the West. *v.4 p.718*

Buffett: The Making of an American Capitalist. *v.4 p.96, p.147, p.148*

The Bugatti Queen: In Search of a French Racing Legend. *v.4 p.838, p.848*

Builders of Ohio: A Biographical History. . . *v.3 p.513, p.514*

Builders of the Bay Colony. *v.3 p.487*

Building a Better World: An Introduction to Trade Unionism in Canada. *v.4 p.124*

Building a Bridge to 18th Century. *v.4 p.323*

Building a Character. *v.1 p.145*

Building a Knowledge-Driven Organization. *v.4 p.77*

Building a Palestinian State: The Incomplete Revolution. *v.6 p.619*

Building Bodies. *v.4 p.818, p.844, p.855*

Building Character in the American Boy: The Boy Scouts, YMCA and Their Forerunners, 1870-1920. . . . *v.4 p.719*

Building Code Requirements and Specification for Masonry Structures - 2005, ACI 530/ASCE 5-05/TMS 402 and ACI 530.1/ASCE 6-05/TMS 602. . . . . . *v.5 p.686*

Building Community in Schools. *v.4 p.281*

Building Construction Cost Data. *v.5 p.686*

Building Democracy in South Asia: India, Nepal, Pakistan. *v.4 p.617*

Building Diaspora: Filipino Community Formation on the Internet. *v.6 p.89, p.129, p.141*

Building Effective Afterschool Programs. *v.4 p.288*

Building Effective Evaluation Capacity: Lessons from Practice. *v.4 p.580*

Building European Union: A Documentary History and Analysis. *v.3 p.88*

Building Global Biobrands: Taking Biotechnology to Market. *v.5 p.219*

Building Great Customer Experiences. *v.4 p.143*

Building Inside Nature's Envelope: How New Construction and Landscape Preservation Can Work Together. . . *v.1 p.824*

Building Models for Conservation and Wildlife Management. *v.5 p.223*

Building Public Trust: The Future of Corporate Reporting. *v.4 p.92, p.105, p.106, p.111*

Building San Francisco's Parks, 1850-1930. . . . . *v.1 p.820*

Building Smart Teams: A Roadmap to High Performance. *v.4 p.79, p.80*

Building Strong Brands. *v.4 p.141*

Building Suburbia: Green Fields and Urban Growth, 1820-2000. . . . . *v.6 p.726*

Building the Bank of England: Money, Architecture and Society, 1694-1942. . . . . *v.4 p.90*

Building the Continental Empire: American Expansion from the Revolution to the Civil War. *v.3 p.382*

Building the Fourth Estate: Democratization and the Rise of a Free Press in Mexico. *v.4 p.409*

Building the National Parks: The Historic Landscape Design and Construction. *v.1 p.819, v.6 p.295*

Building the Next Ark: How NGOs Work to Protect Biodiversity. *v.4 p.640, p.666*

Building the Union: Skilled Workers and Anglo-Gaelic Immigrants in the Rise of the UAW. *v.4 p.124*

🄔 Building Virtual Communities: Learning and Change in Cyberspace. *v.4 p.762*

Building Virtual Communities: Learning and Change in Cyberspace. *v.4 p.762*

Building Wealth: The New Rules for Individuals, Companies, and Nations in a Knowledge-Based Economy. *v.4 p.78*

Building with Light: An International History of Architectural Photography. *v.1 p.762*

Building with Our Hands: Directions in Chicana Studies. *v.6 p.486, p.546*

💻 BuildingGreen.com. *v.1 p.782*

Buildings of Alaska. *v.1 p.789*

Buildings of Colorado. *v.1 p.790*

Buildings of Iowa. *v.1 p.789*

Buildings of Louisiana. *v.1 p.790*

Buildings of Michigan. *v.1 p.789*

Buildings of Nevada. *v.1 p.790*

Buildings of Rhode Island. *v.1 p.789, p.790*

Buildings of the District of Columbia. *v.1 p.790, p.791*

Buildings of Virginia: Tidewater and Piedmont. . . . *v.1 p.791*

Buildings of West Virginia: With support from the West Virginia Humanities Council. *v.1 p.788*

Build-Up. *v.2 p.136*

💻 Built in America; Historic American Buildings Survey/Historic American Engineering Record, 1933-Present. *v.1 p.711, p.820*

Built to Last: Successful Habits of Visionary Companies. .*v.4 p.67*

Built to Win: The Female Athlete As Cultural Icon. *v.4 p.816, p.836*

Bukharin and the Bolshevik Revolution: A Political Biography, 1888-1938. . . . .*v.3 p.222*

Bulgaria During the Second World War. *v.3 p.251*

Bulgaria in Transition: Politics, Economics, Society and Culture after Communism. *v.3 p.251*

The Bulgarian Economy in Transition. *v.3 p.251*

Bulgarian Urban Culture in the Eighteenth and Nineteenth Centuries. *v.3 p.251*

Bulgaria's Road to the First World War. *v.3 p.251*

Bulgarsko-Angliiski Rechnik - Bulgarian-English Dictionary. *v.2 p.774*

Bullet Park. *v.2 p.67*

Bulletproof Buddhists and Other Essays. *v.6 p.104*

Bulozi under the Luyana Kings; Political Evolution and State Formation in Pre-Colonial Zambia. *v.6 p.77*

Bunny. *v.2 p.351*

🦋 Bunraku: Masters of Japanese Puppet Theater. .*v.1 p.132, p.134*

Buppies, B-Boys, Baps, and Bohos: Notes on Post-Soul Black Culture. *v.1 p.269*

The Burden of Egypt: An Interpretation of Ancient Egyptian Culture. *v.6 p.57*

The Burden of Memory, the Muse of Forgiveness. . .*v.2 p.758*

The Burden of Southern History. *v.3 p.494*

💻 Bureau of Justice Statistics. *v.6 p.246*

Bureaucracy and Bureaucrats in Mexico City, 1742-1835. . . . .*v.3 p.284*

Bureaucracy and Society in Modern Egypt: A Study of the Higher Civil Service. *v.6 p.636, p.637*

Bureaucracy, Aristocracy, and Autocracy. *v.3 p.167*

Bureaucracy, Economy, and Leadership in China: The Institutional Origins of the Great Leap Forward. . .*v.4 p.619*

Bureaucracy of Repression: The Iraqi Government in Its Own Words. *v.6 p.603*

Bureaucratic and Political Corruption in Africa: The Public Choice Perspective. *v.4 p.612*

Bureaucratic Reform in the Ottoman Empire: The Sublime Porte, 1789-1922. . . . .*v.4 p.614, v.6 p.589*

Bureaucratic Representation: Civil Servants and the Future of Capitalist Democracies. *v.4 p.546*

Bureaucrats and Politicians in Western Democracies. .*v.4 p.601*

The Bureaucrats of Buenos Aires, 1769-1810: Amor al Real Servicio. *v.3 p.347*

Bureaucrats, Planters, and Workers: The Making of the Tobacco Monopoly in Bourbon Mexico. *v.3 p.285*

Bureaucrats, Politics, and the Environment. .*v.4 p.546, v.6 p.301*

The Burger Court, 1968-1984, Vol. 9. . . . .*v.4 p.536*

The Burger Court: Counter-Revolution or Confirmation? *v.4 p.539*

The Burger Court: The Counter-Revolution That Wasn't. *v.4 p.470*

Burglars on the Job: Streetlife and Residential Break-Ins. *v.6 p.253*

Buridans Esel: Roman. *v.2 p.616, p.617*

Buried by the Times: The Holocaust and America's Most Important Newspaper. *v.4 p.411*

Buried Child. *v.2 p.155*

The Buried Mirror: Reflections on Spain and the New World. *v.3 p.73, p.74*

Burlesque and the New Bump-N-Grind. *v.1 p.36*

Burma at the Turn of the Twenty-First Century. *v.6 p.165, p.166*

Burma in Revolt: Opium and Insurgency since 1948. .*v.6 p.166*

Burma: Military Rule and the Politics of Stagnation. *v.6 p.165, p.166*

Burma: Political Economy under Military Rule. *v.6 p.165, p.166*

Burma, the State of Myanmar. *v.6 p.165, p.166*

Burmese Dance and Theatre. *v.1 p.16, p.133*

Burmese Days. *v.2 p.375*

Burmese Nationalist Movements, 1940-1949. . . . . .*v.6 p.166*

The Burmese Polity, 1752-1819: Politics, Administration, and Social Organization in the Early Kon-baung Period. *v.6 p.166*

Burn Before Reading: Presidents, CIA Directors, and Secret Intelligence. *v.4 p.562*

Burning and Building: Schooling and State Formation in Japan, 1750-1890. . . . .*v.4 p.336*

Burning Questions: America's Fight with Nature's Fire. *v.5 p.31, v.6 p.290*

The Burning Tigris: The Armenian Genocide and America's Response. *v.4 p.651*

Burning Your Boats: The Collected Short Stories. . . .*v.2 p.336*

Burnout in Probation and Corrections. *v.6 p.276*

A Burns Companion. *v.2 p.272*

Burns Mantle Best Plays of Nineteen Forty-Nine to Nineteen Fifty. *v.1 p.63, p.112*

Burnt Sugar Cana Quemada: Contemporary Cuban Poetry in English and Spanish. *v.2 p.671*

A Burnt-Out Case. *v.2 p.349*

Burr. *v.2 p.127*

The Burt Affair. *v.5 p.596*

Burundi: Ethnic Conflict and Genocide. . . .*v.4 p.653, v.6 p.63*

Bury My Heart at Wounded Knee: An Indian History of the American West.   .*v.3 p.394, v.4 p.572, p.573, p.646,v.6 p.682*

Burying Mao: Chinese Politics in the Age of Deng Xiaoping. *v.6 p.196*

Bush at War: Inside the Bush White House. .*v.3 p.484, v.4 p.565*

The Bush Garden: Essays on the Canadian Imagination. .*v.2 p.729*

The Bush Presidency: First Appraisals. *v.3 p.467*

Bush Studies. *v.2 p.744*

The Bushes: Portrait of a Dynasty. *v.3 p.484*

Bushman Myth: The Making of a Namibian Underclass. .*v.6 p.76*

Bushmanders and Bullwinkles: How Politicians Manipulate Electronic Maps and Census Data to Win Elections. .*v.4 p.385*

The Bushmen of Southern Africa: A Foraging Society in Transition. *v.6 p.76*

Bush's War for Reelection: Iraq, the White House, and the People. *v.3 p.484*

The Bushwhacked Piano. *v.2 p.150*

Business Across Cultures. *v.4 p.59*

Business and Industry in Nazi Germany. *v.3 p.173*

Business and Its Environment. *v.4 p.51*

The Business and Practice of Coaching: Finding Your Niche, Making Money and Attracting Ideal Clients. *v.4 p.64*

Business and Society: A Reader in the History, Sociology, and Ethics of Business. *v.4 p.52*

Business and Society: Corporate Strategy, Public Policy, and Ethics with PowerWeb and Enron Case. *v.4 p.52*

Business and the Environment: A Resource Guide. . . .*v.4 p.62*

Business as a Calling: Work and the Examined Life. *v.4 p.55, p.167*

Business As War: Battling for Competitive Advantage. .*v.4 p.70*

Business Calculus Demystified. *v.4 p.175*

Business Civilization in Decline. *v.4 p.214*

Business, Commerce, and Social Responsibility: Beyond Agenda. *v.4 p.145*

Business Consulting: A Guide to How It Works and How to Make It Work. *v.4 p.65*

Business Creativity: Breaking the Invisible Barriers. . *v.4 p.66*

The Business Cycle: Theories and Evidence, Proceedings of the Sixteenth Annual Economic Policy Conference of the Federal Reserve Bank of St. Louis. *v.4 p.242, p.243*

Business Cycle Theory. *v.4 p.244*

Business Cycles: A Theoretical, Historical, and Statistical Analysis of the Capitalist Process. *v.4 p.230, p.245*

Business Ethics: A Reference Handbook. . .*v.4 p.53, p.55, p.180*

Business Ethics and the Natural Environment.   . .*v.4 p.61, p.64*

Business Ethics with CD-ROM. *v.1 p.485*

Business Ethics. *v.4 p.54, p.55, p.181*

Business, Government and Society. *v.4 p.52*

Business Information: Finding and Using Data in the Digital Age. *v.4 p.181, p.183, p.185*

Business Information: How to Find It, How to Use It. .*v.4 p.180*

Business Information Sources. *v.4 p.180*

Business Interest Groups in Nineteenth-Century Brazil. .*v.3 p.342*

Business Law. *v.4 p.109*

Business Letters Ready to Go!. *v.4 p.171*

Business Library and How to Use It: A Guide to Sources and Research Strategies for Information on Business and Management. *v.4 p.180*

Business Math Demystified. *v.4 p.174*

Business Math. *v.4 p.175*

Business, Not Politics: The Making of the Gay Market. .*v.6 p.383*

The Business of Alchemy: Science and Culture in the Holy Roman Empire. *v.3 p.48*

The Business of Art Unveiled: New York Art Dealers Speak Up. *v.1 p.826*

Business of Baseball. *v.4 p.849, p.880, p.881, p.886, p.890, p.895*

The Business of Books: How the International Conglomerates Took over Publishing and Changed the Way We Read. *v.4 p.149*

The Business of Genocide: The SS, Slave Labor and the Concentration Camps. *v.3 p.171*

The Business of Lobbying in China. *v.4 p.145*

The Business of Sports Agents. *v.4 p.905*

The Business of Sport. *v.4 p.884, p.891, p.896*

The Business of the Supreme Court: A Study in the Federal Judicial System. *v.4 p.470*

The Business of Theatrical Design. *v.1 p.147, p.150*

Business on Trial: The Civil Jury and Corporate Responsibility. *v.4 p.109, p.112*

Business Plans and Profiles Index: A Subject Guide to Sample Business Plans and Profiles for Specific Business Types. *v.4 p.172*

Business Plans Handbook, Vol. 11. . . . .*v.4 p.174*

Business Politics and the State in Twentieth-Century Latin America. *v.3 p.260*

Business Ratios and Formulas: A Comprehensive Guide. *v.4 p.174, p.175*

Business Simulations, Games and Experiential Learning in International Business Education. *v.4 p.177*

Business Statistics Demystified. *v.4 p.179*

The Business Style Handbook: An A-to-Z Guide for Writing on the Job with Tips from Communications Experts at the Fortune 500. . . . .*v.4 p.172*

Business Tax Stories 2005. . . .*v.4 p.106, p.107, p.109, p.112*

Business: The Ultimate Resource. *v.4 p.180, p.181*

The Business Writer's Handbook. *v.4 p.171*

Business Writing for Results: How to Create a Sense of Urgency and Increase Response to Your E-Mails, Letters, Proposals, Reports, Newsletters and Websites. *v.4 p.172*

BusinessWeek Guide to the Best Business Schools. . .*v.4 p.176*

Busting the Mob: The United States vs. Cosa Nostra. .*v.4 p.438*

But First a School: The First Fifty Years of the School of American Ballet. *v.1 p.23, p.47*

But Is It Science?: The Philosophical Question in the Creation/Evolution Controversy. *v.5 p.81, p.196*

But Is It Science?: The Philosophical Question in the Evolution-Creation Controversy. *v.5 p.196*

But Still, Like Air, I'll Rise: New Asian American Plays. *v.1 p.67, p.125,v.6 p.91, p.98*

But the Irish Sea Betwixt Us: Ireland, Colonialism and Renaissance Literature. *v.2 p.170*

But... The Lord Is Silent. *v.2 p.813*

But There Was No Peace: The Role of Violence in the Politics of Reconstruction. *v.3 p.400*

Butcher: The Duke of Cumberland and the Suppression of the Forty-Five. *v.3 p.133*

Butcher's Copy-Editing: The Cambridge Handbook for Editors, Proofreaders and Copy-Editors. *v.2 p.574*

The Butcher's Tale: Murder and Anti-Semitism in a German Town. *v.3 p.169*

Butler's Lives of the Saints. *v.1 p.578*

Butler. *v.1 p.450*

Butoh: Dance of the Dark Soul. *v.1 p.15*

Butor en perspective. *v.2 p.511*

Butterfield 8. . . . .*v.2 p.107*

Butterfly Burning: A Novel. *v.2 p.759*

Butterfly on Rock: A Study of Themes and Images in Canadian Literature. *v.2 p.729*

Butting Out: Reading Resistive Choreographies Through Works by Jawole Willa Jo Zollar and Chandralekha. *v.1 p.28, p.30, p.40*

Der Butt. *v.2 p.608*

BuyersGuideChem. *v.5 p.317*

Buzzwords: A Scientist Muses on Sex, Bugs, and Rock 'n' Roll. *v.5 p.413*

By Different Paths to Common Outcomes. *v.4 p.368*

By Himself. *v.2 p.275*

By Honor Bound: State and Society in Early Modern Russia. *v.3 p.215*

By Love Possessed. *v.2 p.65*

By Order of the President: FDR and the Internment of Japanese Americans. *v.6 p.134*

By Order of the President: The Use and Abuse of Executive Direct Action. *v.4 p.461*

By Reason or Force: Chile and the Balancing of Power in South America, 1830-1905. . . . .*v.3 p.350*

By Sheer Pluck A Tale of the Ashanti War. *v.2 p.290*

By the Banks of the Neva: Chapters from the Lives and Careers of the British in Eighteenth-Century Russia. *v.3 p.215*

By the Light of the Glow-Worm Lamp: Three Centuries of Reflections on Nature. *v.5 p.232*

By the Numbers: Using Facts and Figures to Get Your Projects, Plans and Ideas Approved. *v.4 p.173, p.175*

By the Rivers of Babylon and Other Stories. *v.2 p.688*

By Their Blood: Christian Martyrs from the Twentieth Century and Beyond. *v.1 p.612*

By with to and From: A Lincoln Kirstein Reader. *v.1 p.42, v.6 p.414*

By-Line Ernest Hemingway: Selected Articles and Dispatches of Four Decades. *v.2 p.85*

Byron and Romanticism. *v.2 p.172, p.183, p.274*

Byron and the Victorians. . . .*v.6 p.739, p.740, p.755, p.763*

Byron, Poetics and History. *v.2 p.274*

Byron, the Last Journey, April 1823-April 1824. . . .*v.2 p.274*

The Byronic Hero: Types and Prototypes. *v.2 p.274*

Byron's Letters and Journals: 'In My Hot Youth', 1798-1810, Vol. 1. . . . .*v.2 p.273, p.274*

The Byzantine and Early Islamic near East: Problems in the Literary Source Material. *v.6 p.581, p.584*

Byzantine Art and Architecture: An Introduction. . . .*v.1 p.672*

Byzantine Art. *v.1 p.671*

The Byzantine Commonwealth: Eastern Europe, 500-1453. . . . .*v.3 p.193*

Byzantine Court Culture from 829 To 1204. . . . .*v.3 p.193*

Byzantine Garden Culture. *v.1 p.819*

Byzantine Monuments of Istanbul. *v.1 p.788*

The Byzantine Revival, 780-842. . . . .*v.3 p.193*

The Byzantine Theocracy: The Weil Lectures, Cincinatti. *v.1 p.570*

Byzantine Theology: Historical Trends and Doctrinal Themes. *v.1 p.570*

The Byzantine Tradition after the Fall of Constantinople. *v.3 p.191*

Byzantium and the Arabs in the Fifth Century. *v.6 p.581, p.586*

Byzantium and the Arabs in the Fourth Century. *v.6 p.581, p.583*

Byzantium and the Arabs in the Sixth Century. *v.6 p.581, p.583, p.584*

Byzantium and the Crusades. *v.3 p.193*

Byzantium and the Early Islamic Conquests. . *v.6 p.581, p.585*

Byzantium Endures. *v.2 p.368*

Byzantium: Faith and Power (1261-1557). *v.1 p.671, p.672, p.686*

Byzantium in the Seventh Century: The Transformation of a Culture. *v.3 p.193*

Byzantium Rediscovered. *v.1 p.671, p.686*

Byzantium: The Apogee. *v.3 p.193*

Byzantium: The Decline and Fall. *v.3 p.193*

Byzantium: The Early Centuries. *v.3 p.193*

Byzantium Viewed by the Arabs. *v.6 p.581, p.584*

C

C. Ben Ross and the New Deal in Idaho. *v.3 p.525, p.526*

C. P. E. Bach. *v.1 p.191, p.302*

C++ Primer. *v.5 p.347*

The C Programming Language: ANSI C Version. . . .*v.5 p.347*

The C# Programming Language. *v.5 p.346*

The C Puzzle Book. *v.5 p.346*

C. S. Lewis: A Biography. *v.2 p.366*

C. S. Lewis. *v.2 p.366*

The C++ Standard Template Library: A Definitive Approach to C++ Programming Using Stl. *v.5 p.347, p.349*

C. Vann Woodward: A Southern Historian and His Critics. *v.3 p.374*

C. Wright Mills: An American Utopian. *v.4 p.685*

C. Wright Mills and the Ending of Violence. . *v.4 p.690, p.766*

C-13 and Proton Chemical Shifts. *v.5 p.296, p.297*

A Cab at the Door and Midnight Oil. *v.2 p.378*

Caballero: A Historical Novel. *v.6 p.499*

Cabaret: The Illustrated Book and Lyrics. .*v.1 p.252, p.408, p.409*

Cabell's Directory of Publishing Opportunities in
Accounting. *v.4 p.148, p.149*

Cabell's Directory of Publishing Opportunities in Economics
and Finance. *v.4 p.149*

Cabell's Directory of Publishing Opportunities in
Management. *v.4 p.149*

La Cabeza de Cordero. *v.2 p.656*

Cabinets and Counselors: The President and the Executive
Branch. *v.4 p.526*

Cabinets and First Ministers. *v.4 p.588*

ⓔ Cable Communications: Building the Information
Infrastructure. *v.4 p.421*

CAD-CAM Handbook. *v.4 p.116*

The Caddo Nation: Archaeological and Ethnohistoric
Perspectives. *v.6 p.704*

Caddy for Life: The Bruce Edwards Story. *v.4 p.860*

Cadres and Corruption: The Organizational Involution of the
Chinese Communist Party. *v.4 p.620*

Caesar Augustus: Seven Aspects. *v.3 p.28*

Caesar: Gallic War I. *v.2 p.428*

Caesar: Politician and Statesman. *v.2 p.428*

Caesar. *v.2 p.428*

Caetana Says No: Women's Stories from a Brazilian Slave
Society. *v.3 p.279, p.341*

Caetana's Sweet Song. *v.2 p.692*

Cafe Con Leche: Race, Class, and National Image in
Venezuela. *v.3 p.281*

Cafe con Leche: Race, Class, and National Image in
Venezuela. *v.3 p.360, p.361*

Cafe Nostalgia. *v.2 p.673*

La Cage aux Folles. *v.6 p.411*

Cages of Reason: The Rise of the Rational State in France,
Japan, the United States, and Great Britain. .*v.4 p.545, p.581*

Cahier d'un Retour au Pays Natal. *v.2 p.536*

Les cahiers et les poésies d'André Walter : avec des fragments
inédits du Journal. *v.2 p.520*

Cahiers Suzanne Lilar. *v.2 p.521, p.522*

Cahokia and the Hinterlands: Middle Mississippian Cultures of
the Midwest. *v.4 p.10*

Cahokia: Mirror of the Cosmos. *v.4 p.10*

Cain: The Biography of James M. Cain. *v.2 p.65*

The Caine Mutiny. *v.2 p.129*

Cairo: One Thousand-One Years of the City
Victorious. *v.6 p.56, p.634*

Cairo. *v.6 p.57, p.635*

Cakes and Ale. *v.2 p.370*

Calamus: Male Homosexuality in Twentieth Century Literature:
An International Anthology. *v.6 p.406*

Calculated Risks: How to Know When Numbers Deceive
You. *v.5 p.481*

Calculations for Molecular Biology and Biotechnology: A Guide
to Mathematics in the
Laboratory. *v.5 p.90, p.107, p.108, p.129*

Calculus and Analytic Geometry. *v.5 p.485*

Calculus: Early Transcendentals. *v.5 p.485*

Calculus for Biology and Medicine. . . .*v.5 p.91, p.485, p.502*

Calculus for Business, Economics, and the Social and Life
Sciences. *v.5 p.503*

Calculus: Multi-Variable Calculus and Linear Algebra with
Applications. *v.5 p.486*

Calculus of Variations. *v.5 p.493*

The Calculus of Variations. *v.5 p.493*

Calculus on Manifolds: A Modern Approach to Classical
Theorems of Advanced Calculus. . . .*v.5 p.486, p.499, p.500*

Calculus: One-Variable Calculus with an Introduction to Linear
Algebra. *v.5 p.486*

Calculus: The Elements. *v.5 p.485*

Calculus. *v.5 p.485*

The Calcutta Chromosome: A Novel of Fevers, Delirium and
Discovery. *v.2 p.764*

Calderon: Plays One. *v.1 p.74, p.107*

Caleb Williams: Or Things As They Are. *v.2 p.288*

Caliban's Curse: George Lamming and the Revisioning of
History. *v.2 p.768*

Calidore. *v.2 p.302*

California: A Guide to the Golden State. *v.3 p.531*

California: A History. *v.3 p.531, p.532*

ⓔ California Agricultural Research Priorities: Pierce's
Disease. *v.5 p.46*

California: An Interpretive History. *v.3 p.531*

The California Condor: A Saga of Natural History and
Conservation. *v.6 p.292*

California Conquered: The Annexation of a Mexican Province,
1846-1850. . . . .*v.3 p.531*

California: Land of New Beginnings. *v.3 p.531*

California School of Professional Psychology Handbook of
Juvenile Forensic Psychology. *v.5 p.593*

The California School of Professional Psychology: Handbook of
Multicultural Education, Research, Intervention, and
Training. *v.5 p.636, p.637*

California's Prodigal Sons: Hiram Johnson and the Progressives,
1911-1917. . . . .*v.3 p.531*

Caligula: The Corruption of Power. *v.3 p.27*

The Caliphate, Its Rise, Decline, and Fall: From Original
Sources. *v.6 p.585*

Call and Response: The Riverside Anthology of the African
American Literary Tradition. *v.6 p.5, p.26*

The Call Heard 'Round the World: VoIP and the Quest for
Convergence. *v.4 p.422*

Call It Sleep: A Novel. *v.2 p.114*

The Call of Service. *v.4 p.719*

Call of the Game: What Really Goes on in the Broadcast
Booth. *v.4 p.408, p.906*

The Call of the Toad. *v.2 p.608*

A Call to Action: Reconnecting College Sports and Higher
Education. *v.4 p.821, p.894*

Call to Order: Floor Politics in the House and Senate. .*v.4 p.534*

The Call to Personhood: A Christian Theory of the Individual in
Social Relationships. *v.1 p.643*

Callaham's Russian-English Dictionary of Science and
Technology. *v.5 p.258, p.386*

Calligrammes: Poems of Peace and War, 1913-1916. .*v.2 p.506*

Calligraphy and Illumination: A History and Practical Guide. *v.1 p.719*

The Call. *v.6 p.218*

Calo Orbis: Semiotic Aspects of a Chicano Language Variety. *v.6 p.494*

Calvert Casey: The Collected Stories. *v.2 p.671*

Calvet's Web: Enlightenment and the Republic of Letters in Eighteenth-Century France. *v.3 p.146, p.147*

Calvin: A Biography. *v.1 p.602*

Calvin: An Introduction to His Thought. *v.1 p.589*

Calvin and the Consolidation of the Genevan Reformation. *v.1 p.604*

Calvin Coolidge: The Quiet President. *v.3 p.475*

Calvin: Institutes of the Christian Religion. *v.1 p.589*

Calvin: Theological Treatises. *v.1 p.589*

Calvino Revisited. *v.2 p.715*

Calypso Calaloo: Early Carnival Music of Trinidad. . *v.1 p.292*

Cambodge: The Cultivation of a Nation, 1860-1945. . *v.6 p.170*

Cambodia after the Khmer Rouge: Inside the Politics of Nation Building. *v.6 p.170*

Cambodia, Pol Pot, and the United States: The Faustian Pact. *v.3 p.389*

Cambodian Buddhism: History and Practice. *v.6 p.170*

Cambodian Culture since Nineteen Seventy-Five: Homeland and Exile. *v.6 p.170*

Cambodian Refugees' Pathways to Success: Developing a Bi-Cultural Identity. *v.6 p.138*

Cambodia. *v.6 p.170*

The Cambrdige History of Scandinavia: Prehistory to 1520. . . . . *v.3 p.232, p.233*

The Cambridge Aerospace Dictionary. *v.5 p.717, p.718*

The Cambridge Ancient History, Set. *v.3 p.3*

The Cambridge Apostles, 1820-1914: Liberalism, Imagination, and Friendship in British Intellectual and Professional Life. *v.6 p.745, p.751*

The Cambridge Bibliography of English Literature: 1800-1900. . . . . *v.2 p.177, v.6 p.753*

The Cambridge Biography of D. H. Lawrence: Dying Game, 1922-1930. . . . .*v.2 p.362*

☐ Cambridge Center for Behavioral Studies. *v.5 p.666*

The Cambridge Companion to Adorno. *v.1 p.506, p.507*

The Cambridge Companion to American Modernism. . *v.2 p.11*

The Cambridge Companion to American Women Playwrights. *v.1 p.60, p.121, v.2 p.16*

The Cambridge Companion to Anselm. *v.1 p.432*

The Cambridge Companion to Aphra Behn. *v.1 p.59, p.77, p.78, p.101, v.2 p.238*

The Cambridge Companion to Aquinas. *v.1 p.434*

The Cambridge Companion to Aristotle. . *v.1 p.426, v.2 p.408*

The Cambridge Companion to Arthur Miller. *v.2 p.101*

The Cambridge Companion to Augustine. *v.1 p.431, p.592, p.593, v.2 p.430*

The Cambridge Companion to Australian Literature. . *v.2 p.742*

The Cambridge Companion to Bach. *v.1 p.183, p.303*

The Cambridge Companion to Bacon. *v.1 p.448*

The Cambridge Companion to Bartók. *v.1 p.209, p.305*

The Cambridge Companion to Baudelaire. *v.2 p.488*

The Cambridge Companion to Beethoven. . . *v.1 p.204, p.308*

The Cambridge Companion to Benjamin Britten. *v.1 p.211, p.314*

The Cambridge Companion to Berg. *v.1 p.221, p.309*

The Cambridge Companion to Berlioz. *v.1 p.194, p.310*

The Cambridge Companion to Bertrand Russell. . . *v.1 p.447*

The Cambridge Companion to Biblical Interpretation. *v.1 p.615, p.618*

The Cambridge Companion to Blues and Gospel Music. *v.1 p.262*

The Cambridge Companion to Brahms. . . . *v.1 p.201, p.313*

The Cambridge Companion to Brass Instruments. . . *v.1 p.389*

The Cambridge Companion to Brentano. *v.1 p.465*

The Cambridge Companion to Bruckner. . . . *v.1 p.207, p.314*

The Cambridge Companion to Canadian Literature. . *v.2 p.730*

The Cambridge Companion to Cervantes. *v.2 p.647*

The Cambridge Companion to Charles Dickens. . . .*v.2 p.285*

The Cambridge Companion to Chaucer. . . *v.2 p.207, v.6 p.564*

The Cambridge Companion to Chekhov. *v.2 p.804*

The Cambridge Companion to Chopin. *v.1 p.204, p.317*

The Cambridge Companion to Christian Doctrine. . . *v.1 p.635*

The Cambridge Companion to Conducting. *v.1 p.402*

The Cambridge Companion to Crime Fiction. . *v.2 p.191, p.580*

The Cambridge Companion to Critical Theory. *v.1 p.502, p.503*

The Cambridge Companion to D. H. Lawrence. . . .*v.2 p.362*

The Cambridge Companion to Dante. . . . *v.2 p.704, v.6 p.565*

The Cambridge Companion to David Mamet. . *v.1 p.58, p.112*

The Cambridge Companion to Debussy. . . . *v.1 p.226, p.321*

The Cambridge Companion to Descartes. *v.1 p.453*

The Cambridge Companion to Dostoevsky. *v.2 p.805*

The Cambridge Companion to Early Greek Philosophy. *v.1 p.421, p.422*

The Cambridge Companion to Edgar Allan Poe. . . .*v.2 p.50*

The Cambridge Companion to Edith Wharton. . . .*v.2 p.131*

The Cambridge Companion to Elgar. *v.1 p.197, p.323*

The Cambridge Companion to English Literature, 1500-1600. . . . .*v.2 p.169*

The Cambridge Companion to English Literature, 1650-1740. . . . . *v.2 p.170, p.171, p.173*

The Cambridge Companion to English Literature, 1740-1830. . . . .*v.2 p.172*

The Cambridge Companion to English Poetry, Donne to Marvell. *v.2 p.181, p.182*

The Cambridge Companion to English Renaissance Drama. *v.1 p.58, p.74, p.98, v.2 p.185*

The Cambridge Companion to English Restoration Theatre. *v.1 p.59, p.77, p.100, v.2 p.186*

The Cambridge Companion to Eugene O'Neill. *v.1 p.60, p.116, v.2 p.107*

The Cambridge Companion to Ezra Pound. *v.2 p.112*

The Cambridge Companion to F. Scott Fitzgerald. . . *v.2 p.77*

The Cambridge Companion to Feminism in Philosophy. *v.6 p.461*

The Cambridge Companion to Flaubert. . . . *v.2 p.491, p.492*

The Cambridge Companion to Foucault. *v.1 p.459*

The Cambridge Companion to Friedrich Schleiermacher. *v.1 p.581*

The Cambridge Companion to Gadamer. *v.1 p.468*

The Cambridge Companion to George Bernard Shaw. *v.2 p.309*

The Cambridge Companion to George Eliot. *v.2 p.287*

The Cambridge Companion to German Idealism. . . .*v.1 p.508*

The Cambridge Companion to Giovanni Bellini. . . .*v.1 p.741*

The Cambridge Companion to Grand Opera. *v.1 p.229*

The Cambridge Companion to Greek and Roman
Philosophy. *v.1 p.428*

The Cambridge Companion to Greek
Tragedy. *v.1 p.59, p.71, p.88,v.2 p.401*

The Cambridge Companion to Habermas. *v.1 p.469*

The Cambridge Companion to Handel. *v.1 p.183, p.328*

The Cambridge Companion to Hannah Arendt. . . .*v.4 p.493*

The Cambridge Companion to Harold
Pinter. *v.1 p.60, p.92, p.103,v.2 p.377*

The Cambridge Companion to Haydn. *v.1 p.188, p.330*

The Cambridge Companion to Hegel. . . .*v.1 p.463, v.3 p.167*

The Cambridge Companion to Heidegger. *v.1 p.470*

The Cambridge Companion to Hemingway. *v.2 p.84*

The Cambridge Companion to Henry David Thoreau. . .*v.2 p.52*

The Cambridge Companion to Henry James. *v.2 p.43*

The Cambridge Companion to Herodotus. *v.2 p.412*

The Cambridge Companion to Historical Archaeology. *v.4 p.14*

The Cambridge Companion to Hobbes. . . .*v.1 p.448, p.449*

The Cambridge Companion to Homer. *v.2 p.413*

The Cambridge Companion to Hume. *v.1 p.451*

The Cambridge Companion to Husserl. *v.1 p.470*

The Cambridge Companion to James Joyce. *v.2 p.357*

The Cambridge Companion to Jane Austen. *v.2 p.267*

The Cambridge Companion to Jazz. *v.1 p.258*

The Cambridge Companion to John
Cage. *v.1 p.219, p.220, p.315,v.6 p.408*

The Cambridge Companion to John Calvin. *v.1 p.589*

The Cambridge Companion to John Dryden. *v.2 p.247*

The Cambridge Companion to Joseph Conrad. . . .*v.2 p.342*

The Cambridge Companion to Kant and Modern
Philosophy. *v.1 p.461*

The Cambridge Companion to Karl Barth. *v.1 p.581*

The Cambridge Companion to Keats. *v.2 p.296*

The Cambridge Companion to Keynes. *v.4 p.226*

The Cambridge Companion to Kierkegaard. *v.1 p.581*

The Cambridge Companion to Leibniz. *v.1 p.459*

The Cambridge Companion to Liszt. *v.1 p.198, p.336*

The Cambridge Companion to Locke's Essay Concerning
Human Understanding. *v.4 p.196*

The Cambridge Companion to Locke. *v.1 p.448*

The Cambridge Companion to Malebranche. *v.1 p.452*

The Cambridge Companion to Margaret Atwood. . . .*v.2 p.734*

The Cambridge Companion to Martin Luther. *v.3 p.166*

The Cambridge Companion to Marx. *v.1 p.464*

The Cambridge Companion to Mary Shelley. *v.2 p.310*

The Cambridge Companion to Masaccio. *v.1 p.734*

The Cambridge Companion to Medieval English
Theatre. *v.1 p.58, p.73, p.98,v.6 p.564*

The Cambridge Companion to Medieval Philosophy. .*v.1 p.433*

The Cambridge Companion to Medieval
Romance. *v.2 p.168, v.6 p.565*

The Cambridge Companion to Medieval Women's
Writing. *v.2 p.168, v.6 p.564*

The Cambridge Companion to
Mendelssohn. *v.1 p.200, p.340, p.341*

The Cambridge Companion to Merleau-Ponty. *v.1 p.456*

The Cambridge Companion to Mill. *v.1 p.445*

The Cambridge Companion to Milton. *v.2 p.253*

The Cambridge Companion to Modern British Women
Playwrights. *v.1 p.57, p.98*

The Cambridge Companion to Modern Russian Culture. *v.3 p.210*

The Cambridge Companion to
Modernism. *v.2 p.175, p.179, p.572*

The Cambridge Companion to Montaigne. *v.2 p.470*

The Cambridge Companion to Mozart. *v.1 p.190, p.344*

The Cambridge Companion to Nabokov. *v.2 p.104*

The Cambridge Companion to Native American
Literature. *v.6 p.699*

The Cambridge Companion to Newton. *v.5 p.542*

The Cambridge Companion to Old English
Literature. *v.2 p.167, v.6 p.565*

The Cambridge Companion to Oscar Wilde. *v.2 p.321*

The Cambridge Companion to Ovid. *v.2 p.438*

The Cambridge Companion to Pascal. . .*v.1 p.452, v.2 p.476*

The Cambridge Companion to Peirce. *v.1 p.440*

The Cambridge Companion to Piero Della Francesca. *v.1 p.750*

The Cambridge Companion to
Plato. *v.1 p.424, v.2 p.417, v.4 p.489*

The Cambridge Companion to Pop and Rock. *v.1 p.269*

The Cambridge Companion to Postcolonial Literary
Studies. *v.4 p.485*

The Cambridge Companion to Postmodernism. . . .*v.1 p.512*

The Cambridge Companion to Proust. *v.2 p.523*

The Cambridge Companion to Quine. *v.1 p.443*

The Cambridge Companion to Ralph Waldo Emerson. *v.2 p.38*

The Cambridge Companion to Raphael. *v.1 p.697*

The Cambridge Companion to Ravel. *v.1 p.218, p.350*

The Cambridge Companion to Robert Frost. *v.2 p.77*

The Cambridge Companion to Roman Satire. *v.2 p.427*

The Cambridge Companion to Rossini. *v.1 p.204, p.352*

The Cambridge Companion to Rousseau. *v.1 p.454*

The Cambridge Companion to Sam Shepard. . .*v.1 p.61, p.118*

The Cambridge Companion to Samuel Johnson. . . .*v.2 p.250*

The Cambridge Companion to Sartre. *v.1 p.458*

The Cambridge Companion to Schopenhauer. *v.1 p.465*

The Cambridge Companion to Schubert. . . .*v.1 p.197, p.354*

The Cambridge Companion to Shakespeare on Film. *v.6 p.326*

The Cambridge Companion to Shakespeare on
Stage. *v.1 p.61, p.77, p.104, p.105,v.2 p.232, p.233*

The Cambridge Companion to Shakespearean Comedy. *v.2 p.233*

The Cambridge Companion to Shakespearean
Tragedy. *v.1 p.76, v.2 p.235*

The Cambridge Companion to Shakespeare's History Plays. *v.2 p.233, p.234*

The Cambridge Companion to Shakespeare. . .*v.2 p.228, p.229*

The Cambridge Companion to Shelley. *v.2 p.311*

The Cambridge Companion to Sibelius. *v.1 p.215, p.356*

The Cambridge Companion to Singing. *v.1 p.236, p.396*

The Cambridge Companion to Spinoza. *v.1 p.477*

The Cambridge Companion to St. Paul. *v.1 p.630*

The Cambridge Companion to Stravinsky. . . .*v.1 p.212, p.360*

The Cambridge Companion to T. S. Eliot. *v.2 p.72*

The Cambridge Companion to Tennessee Williams. . .*v.2 p.134*

Cambridge Companion to the African American Novel. .*v.6 p.25*

The Cambridge Companion to the Age of Augustus. . .*v.3 p.27*

The Cambridge Companion to the Age of Constantine. *v.3 p.31, p.192*

The Cambridge Companion to the Age of Justinian. *v.3 p.31, p.192*

The Cambridge Companion to the Bible. *v.1 p.615*

The Cambridge Companion to the Brontës. *v.2 p.270*

The Cambridge Companion to the Cello. . . .*v.1 p.391, p.392*

The Cambridge Companion to the Clarinet. *v.1 p.390*

The Cambridge Companion to the Classic Russian Novel. *v.2 p.793, p.798*

The Cambridge Companion to the Concerto. *v.1 p.240*

The Cambridge Companion to the Eighteenth-Century Novel. *v.2 p.172, p.192*

The Cambridge Companion to the French Novel: From 1800 to the Present. *v.2 p.463*

The Cambridge Companion to the Guitar. *v.1 p.389*

The Cambridge Companion to the Hellenistic World. . .*v.3 p.20*

The Cambridge Companion to the Italian Novel. . . .*v.2 p.697*

The Cambridge Companion to the Latin American Novel. *v.2 p.664*

The Cambridge Companion to the Lied. *v.1 p.236, p.246*

The Cambridge Companion to the Musical. .*v.1 p.59, p.92, p.249*

The Cambridge Companion to the Orchestra. *v.1 p.393*

The Cambridge Companion to the Organ. *v.1 p.392*

The Cambridge Companion to the Piano. *v.1 p.391*

The Cambridge Companion to the Recorder. *v.1 p.392*

The Cambridge Companion to the Saxophone. . . .*v.1 p.390*

The Cambridge Companion to the Spanish Novel: From 1600 to the Present. *v.2 p.639, p.642*

The Cambridge Companion to the Stoics. . .*v.1 p.428, p.429*

The Cambridge Companion to the String Quartet. . .*v.1 p.243*

The Cambridge Companion to the Victorian Novel. *v.2 p.194, v.6 p.755, p.756*

The Cambridge Companion to the Violin. *v.1 p.392*

The Cambridge Companion to Theodore Dreiser. . . .*v.2 p.70*

The Cambridge Companion to Thomas Reid. . . .*v.1 p.450*

The Cambridge Companion to Tolstoy. *v.2 p.797, p.806*

The Cambridge Companion to Tom Stoppard. .*v.2 p.384, p.385*

The Cambridge Companion to Twentieth-Century Opera. *v.1 p.211, p.229*

The Cambridge Companion to Velázquez. *v.1 p.748*

The Cambridge Companion to Verdi. . .*v.1 p.193, p.228, p.364*

The Cambridge Companion to Vermeer. *v.1 p.738*

The Cambridge Companion to Victorian and Edwardian Theatre. . .*v.1 p.60, p.79, p.80, p.103,v.2 p.176, p.188, p.189*

The Cambridge Companion to Victorian Poetry. *v.2 p.174, p.184,v.6 p.755*

The Cambridge Companion to Virgil. *v.2 p.446*

The Cambridge Companion to W. H. Auden. *v.2 p.330*

The Cambridge Companion to William Blake. . . .*v.2 p.239*

The Cambridge Companion to William Faulkner. . . .*v.2 p.75*

The Cambridge Companion to Wittgenstein. *v.1 p.472*

The Cambridge Companion to Wordsworth. *v.2 p.323*

The Cambridge Dictionary of Human Biology and Evolution. *v.4 p.15*

The Cambridge Dictionary of Philosophy. *v.1 p.415*

The Cambridge Dictionary of Space Technology. . . .*v.5 p.720*

The Cambridge Economic History of Europe from the Decline of the Roman Empire: Economic Organisation and Policies in the Middle Ages. *v.3 p.41, v.6 p.558*

The Cambridge Economic History of Europe from the Decline of the Roman Empire: The Agrarian Life of the Middle Ages. *v.3 p.41, v.6 p.558, p.575*

The Cambridge Economic History of Europe from the Decline of the Roman Empire: The Economic Organization of Early Modern Europe. *v.3 p.42*

The Cambridge Economic History of Europe from the Decline of the Roman Empire: The Industrial Economies: Capital, Labour and Enterprise, the United States, Japan and Russia. *v.3 p.40*

The Cambridge Economic History of Europe: The Economy of Expanding Europe in the 16th and 17th Centuries, Vol. 4. . . . .*v.3 p.42*

The Cambridge Economic History of Europe: The Industrial Economies: Capital Labour and Enterprise, Part 1, Britain, France, Germany and Scandinavia. *v.3 p.40*

The Cambridge Economic History of Europe: The Industrial Economies: The Development of Economic and Social Policies, Vol. 8. . . . .*v.3 p.41*

The Cambridge Economic History of Europe: Trade and Industry in the Middle Ages. *v.3 p.41, v.6 p.558*

Cambridge Economic History of Europe. *v.3 p.38*

The Cambridge Encyclopedia of Africa. *v.6 p.51*

The Cambridge Encyclopedia of China. *v.6 p.183*

The Cambridge Encyclopedia of Hunters and Gatherers. .*v.4 p.3*

The Cambridge Encyclopedia of Meteorites. *v.5 p.69*

The Cambridge Encyclopedia of Ornithology. . .*v.5 p.95, p.214*

The Cambridge Encyclopedia of Russia: And the Former Soviet Union. *v.3 p.209*

The Cambridge Encyclopedia of Space: Missions, Applications and Exploration. *v.5 p.720*

The Cambridge Encyclopedia of the English Language. *v.2 p.551, p.552*

The Cambridge Encyclopedia of the Middle East and North Africa. *v.6 p.60*

Cambridge Essays, 1888-99. . . . .*v.1 p.447*

The Cambridge Gazetteer of the USA and Canada: A Dictionary of Places. *v.4 p.374*

The Cambridge Grammar of the English Language. . .*v.2 p.556*

The Cambridge Guide to African and Caribbean
Theatre. *v.1 p.57, p.128, p.130*

The Cambridge Guide to Asian Theatre.   *v.1 p.58, p.130, p.131*

The Cambridge Guide to English Literature. *v.2 p.167*

The Cambridge Guide to English Usage. *v.2 p.558*

The Cambridge Guide to the Arts in Britain: Renaissance and
Reformation. *v.3 p.128*

The Cambridge Guide to the Arts in Britain: The Augustan
Age. *v.3 p.128*

The Cambridge Guide to the Arts in Britain: The Seventeenth
Century. *v.3 p.128*

The Cambridge Guide to Theatre. . .*v.1 p.57, p.61, p.128, p.134*

▢ Cambridge Healthtech Institute BioPharmaceutical Glossary,
Taxonomies and Guide to 21st Century Therapeutics,
Technologies and Trends. *v.5 p.126, p.139*

The Cambridge History of Africa, Set. *v.6 p.52*

The Cambridge History of African and Caribbean Literature,
Set. *v.2 p.751*

The Cambridge History of American Foreign Relations: America
in the Age of Soviet Power, 1945-1991. . . . . .*v.3 p.385*

The Cambridge History of American Foreign Relations: The
American Search for Opportunity, 1865-1913. *v.3 p.385, p.386*

The Cambridge History of American Foreign Relations: The
Creation of a Republican Empire, 1776-1865. . . .*v.3 p.386*

Cambridge History of American Foreign Relations: The
Globalizing of America, 1913-1945. . . . .*v.3 p.385*

The Cambridge History of American Literature, Set. . . .*v.2 p.5*

The Cambridge History of American Music. *v.1 p.279*

The Cambridge History of American Theatre:
1870-1945. . . . .*v.1 p.119*

The Cambridge History of American Theatre: Beginnings to
1870. . . . .*v.1 p.119*

The Cambridge History of American Theatre: Post-World War II
to The 1990s. *v.1 p.119*

The Cambridge History of Ancient China: From the Origins of
Civilization to 221 BC. *v.4 p.9*

The Cambridge History of British Theatre,
1660-1895. . . . .*v.2 p.186, p.187, p.188*

The Cambridge History of British Theatre: Origins to
1660. . . . .*v.2 p.185, p.186, p.187*

The Cambridge History of British Theatre: Since 1895.*v.2 p.188*

The Cambridge History of China. *v.6 p.188*

Cambridge History of Christianity: Enlightenment, Reawakening
and Revolution 1660-1815. . . . .*v.1 p.611*

Cambridge History of Christianity: Origins to
Constantine. *v.1 p.600*

Cambridge History of Christianity: World Christianities C.
1815-C. 1914. . . . .*v.1 p.611*

The Cambridge History of Classical Literature: Latin
Literature. *v.2 p.425*

The Cambridge History of Early Christian Literature. *v.1 p.593*

The Cambridge History of Early Inner Asia: From Earliest
Times to the Rise of the Mongols. *v.6 p.239*

The Cambridge History of Early Modern English
Literature. *v.2 p.170*

The Cambridge History of Egypt. 2 vols. *v.6 p.635*

The Cambridge History of Eighteenth-Century Philosophy,
Set. *v.1 p.437*

The Cambridge History of English Literature,
1660-1780. . . . .*v.2 p.170, p.172*

The Cambridge History of Hellenistic Philosophy. . .*v.1 p.427*

The Cambridge History of Iran, Set. *v.6 p.629*

The Cambridge History of Iran: The Seleucid, Parthian and
Sasanid Periods. *v.6 p.630*

The Cambridge History of Iran. *v.6 p.629*

The Cambridge History of Irish Literature, Set. *v.2 p.163*

The Cambridge History of Islam. *v.6 p.581, p.582*

The Cambridge History of Italian Literature. *v.2 p.697*

The Cambridge History of Later Greek and Early Medieval
Philosophy. *v.1 p.430*

The Cambridge History of Later Medieval Philosophy: From the
Rediscovery of Aristotle to the Disintegration of
Scholasticism, 1100-1600. . . . .*v.1 p.432*

The Cambridge History of Medicine. *v.3 p.50*

The Cambridge History of Medieval English
Literature. *v.2 p.169, v.6 p.566*

The Cambridge History of Medieval Political Thought C. 350-C.
1450. . . . .*v.4 p.490, p.501*

The Cambridge History of Nineteenth-Century
Music. *v.1 p.203, v.6 p.757*

The Cambridge History of Political Thought,
1450-1700. . . . .*v.3 p.106, p.108, p.123, p.127*

The Cambridge History of Renaissance
Philosophy. *v.1 p.435, v.3 p.71*

The Cambridge History of Russian Literature. *v.2 p.799*

The Cambridge History of Science: Early Modern
Science. *v.3 p.44*

The Cambridge History of Seventeenth-Century Philosophy,
Set. *v.1 p.436, p.437*

The Cambridge History of Southeast Asia Set. . . .*v.6 p.165*

The Cambridge History of Spanish Literature. .*v.2 p.638, p.639*

The Cambridge History of the Bible: From the Beginnings to
Jerome, Vol. 1. . . . .*v.1 p.614*

The Cambridge History of the English Language:
1776-1997. . . . .*v.2 p.555*

The Cambridge History of the English Language, Set. *v.2 p.554*

The Cambridge History of the Native Peoples of the Americas,
Set. *v.6 p.683, p.684*

The Cambridge History of the Pacific
Islanders. *v.4 p.42, v.6 p.130*

The Cambridge History of Twentieth-Century English
Literature. *v.2 p.179*

The Cambridge History of Twentieth-Century Music. .*v.1 p.211*

The Cambridge History of Western Music Theory. . .*v.1 p.369*

The Cambridge History of Western Textiles,
Set. *v.1 p.809, v.3 p.40*

The Cambridge Illuminations: Ten Centuries of Book
Production. *v.1 p.672*

The Cambridge Illustrated Dictionary of Natural
History. *v.5 p.225*

The Cambridge Illustrated History of Ancient Greece. *v.3 p.12*

The Cambridge Illustrated History of Astronomy. . . .*v.5 p.61*

The Cambridge Illustrated History of British Theatre. *v.2 p.185*

The Cambridge Illustrated History of China. *v.6 p.183*

The Cambridge Illustrated History of Prehistoric Art. *v.1 p.668*

The Cambridge Illustrated History of the British Empire. *v.3 p.89, p.125*

The Cambridge Illustrated History of the Middle Ages, Set. *v.6 p.562*

The Cambridge Illustrated History of the Roman World. .*v.3 p.22*

The Cambridge Introduction to French Poetry. *v.2 p.461*

The Cambridge Introduction to Modern British Fiction, 1950-2000. . . . .*v.2 p.194*

The Cambridge Introduction to Russian Poetry. *v.2 p.793*

The Cambridge Introduction to Spanish Poetry: Spain and Spanish America. *v.2 p.639, p.640*

The Cambridge Introduction to Twentieth-Century American Poetry. *v.2 p.15*

The Cambridge Old English Reader. *v.2 p.206, p.550*

The Cambridge Shakespeare Library: Shakespeare's Times, Texts, and Stages; Shakespeare Criticism; Shakespeare Performance, Set. *v.1 p.57, p.75, p.98*

The Cambridge Social History of Britain, 1750-1950: People and Their Environment. *v.6 p.736, p.762*

The Cambridge Social History of Britain, 1750-1950: Regions and Communities. *v.6 p.736, p.762*

The Cambridge Social History of Britain, 1750-1950: Social Agencies and Institutions, Vol. 3. . . . . . .*v.6 p.736, p.762*

Cambridge Structural Database--Tutorial. *v.5 p.283*

Cambridge Translations of Renaissance Philosophical Texts: Moral and Political Philosophy. *v.1 p.435*

The Cambridge World History of Food, Set. *v.5 p.34*

Cambridge-Signorelli Italian-English-English-Italian Dictionary. *v.2 p.699*

The Camel and the Wheel. *v.6 p.294*

Camel Lot: The True Story of a Zoo-Illogical Farm. . .*v.5 p.85*

Camera Indica: The Social Life of Indian Photographs. .*v.6 p.154*

Camera Obscura. *v.2 p.611, p.612*

Cameroon: Politics and Society in Critical Perspectives. .*v.4 p.612*

The Cameroons from Mandate to Independence. *v.6 p.62*

Camilla. *v.2 p.242*

Camille Claudel: A Life. *v.1 p.778*

Camille Claudel: A Sculpture of Interior Solitude. . .*v.1 p.779*

Camille Pissarro. *v.1 p.743*

Camille. *v.2 p.489*

Camilo Jose Cela Revisited: Later Novels. *v.2 p.657*

Camino de Perfección. *v.2 p.656*

CAMIO ; Catalog of Art Museum Images Online. .*v.1 p.711*

Camisa English Spoken - S. Garcia. *v.2 p.663*

Camouflage Isn't Only for Combat: Gender, Sexuality, and Women in the Military. *v.4 p.717*

Camp David: Peacemaking and Politics. *v.6 p.594*

Camp Notes and Other Poems. *v.6 p.104*

Campaign Contributions and Legislative Voting: A New Approach. *v.4 p.530*

Campaign Finance Information Center. *v.4 p.558*

Campaign Warriors: Political Consultants in Elections. .*v.4 p.558*

Campaigning for Hearts and Minds: How Emotional Appeals in Political Ads Work. *v.4 p.424*

Campaigns and Conscience: The Ethics of Political Journalism. *v.4 p.406*

Campaigns and Elections: Issues, Concepts, Cases. . .*v.4 p.552*

Campaigns and the Court: The U. S. Supreme Court in Presidential Elections. *v.4 p.540*

Campaigns, Congress and the Courts: The Making of Federal Campaign Finance Laws. *v.4 p.525*

The Campaigns of Napoleon: The Mind and Method of History's Greatest Soldier. *v.3 p.152*

Campaigns of the American Revolution: An Atlas of Manuscript Maps. *v.3 p.413*

La Campana. *v.2 p.668*

Campaspe and Sappho and Phao: John Lyly. *v.2 p.213*

The Camphor Flame: Popular Hinduism and Society in India. *v.1 p.535*

Campion's Work. *v.2 p.213*

Campus Climate for Gay, Lesbian, Bisexual, and Transgender People: A National Perspective. *v.6 p.386*

Campus Hate Speech on Trial. *v.4 p.459*

Campus Life: Undergraduate Cultures from the End of the Eighteenth Century to the Present. *v.4 p.290, p.331*

Camus: A Collection of Critical Essays. *v.2 p.511*

Camus: The Stranger. *v.2 p.512*

Can Ethics Be Taught?: Perspectives, Challenges, and Approaches at the Harvard Business School. *v.4 p.53, p.177*

Can God and Caesar Coexist?: Balancing Religious Freedom and International Law. *v.1 p.656*

Can Gun Control Work? *v.6 p.266*

Can Jane Eyre Be Happy?: More Puzzles in Classic Fiction. *v.2 p.192*

Can Japan Compete? *v.6 p.220*

Can Regional Integration Arrangements Enforce Trade Discipline?: The Story of EU Enlargement. *v.4 p.60*

Can Somebody Shout Amen!: Inside Tents and Tabernacles of American Revivalists. *v.1 p.649*

Can You Forgive Her? *v.2 p.317*

Can You Hear, Bird: Poems. *v.2 p.57*

Canaan Land: A Religious History of African Americans. *v.1 p.608*

Canaanite Myth and Hebrew Epic: Essays in the History of the Religion of Israel. *v.3 p.7*

Canaanites. *v.3 p.7*

Canada 1874-1896: Arduous Destiny. *v.3 p.540*

Canada, 1957-1967: The Years of Uncertainty and Innovation. *v.3 p.541*

Canada: A Millennium Portrait. *v.3 p.535*

Canada and Imperialism, 1896-1899. . . . .*v.3 p.540*

Canada and Quebec: One Country, Two Histories. .*v.3 p.535*

Canada and Quebec: One Country, Two Histories. . .*v.3 p.535*

Canada and the Age of Conflict: A History of Canadian External Policies, 1867-1921. . . . .*v.3 p.540*

Canada and the Age of Conflict: A History of Canadian External Policies, 1921-1948 - The Mackenzie King Era. . .*v.3 p.540*

Canada and the Age of Conflict: A History of Canadian External Policies. *v.3 p.537*

Canada and the British Army, 1846-1871: A Study in the Practice of Responsible Government. *v.3 p.540*

Canada and the French-Canadian Question. *v.3 p.536*

Canada and the Idea of North. *v.3 p.547*

Canada and the United States: Differences That Count. .*v.4 p.587*

Canada and World Order: The Multilateralist Tradition in
Canadian Foreign Policy. *v.3 p.541*

Canada at the Polls, 1984: A Study of the Federal General
Elections. *v.4 p.590, p.591*

Canada Before Conferation: A Study in Historical Geography,
No. 166. . . . .*v.3 p.536*

Canada in World Affairs, the Pre-War Years. *v.3 p.537*

Canada in World Affairs. *v.3 p.541*

Canada since 1945: Power, Politics, and Provincialism. .*v.3 p.540*

Canada: the State of the Federation: Reconfiguring
Aboriginal-State Relations. *v.4 p.587*

Canada: The Story of the Yukon and Northwest
Territories. *v.3 p.545, p.546*

Canada Votes, 1935-1989. . . . .*v.4 p.590*

Canada's Boreal Forest. . *v.5 p.176, p.211, p.234, p.239, p.240*

Canada's Diverse Peoples: A Reference Sourcebook. .*v.3 p.542*

☐ Canada's Early Women Writers. *v.2 p.729*

Canada's Founding Debates. *v.3 p.538*

Canada's Religions. *v.1 p.543*

Canadian Art: From Its Beginnings to 2000. . . . .*v.1 p.682*

☐ The Canadian Association for Commonwealth Literature and
Language Studies. *v.2 p.728*

Canadian Boundary. *v.3 p.536*

The Canadian Brothers: or The Prophecy Fulfilled: A Tale of the
Late American War. *v.2 p.733*

Canadian Canons: Essays in Literary Value. *v.2 p.730*

Canadian Culture: International Dimensions. *v.3 p.537*

Canadian Drama and the Critics. *v.2 p.729*

Canadian Dualism: Studies of French-English
Relations. *v.3 p.536*

Canadian Federalism and Quebec Sovereignty. . . .*v.4 p.581*

Canadian Foreign Policy, 1945-2000: Major Documents and
Speeches. *v.3 p.540*

The Canadian Frontier, 1534-1760. . . . .*v.3 p.538*

The Canadian Identity. *v.3 p.537*

The Canadian Indian: A History Since 1500. . . . .*v.6 p.682*

Canadian Indian Bibliography Nineteen Sixty to Nineteen
Seventy. *v.6 p.688*

Canadian Indian Policy: A Critical Bibliography. .*v.6 p.683, p.693*

The Canadian Legal System. *v.4 p.436*

☐ Canadian Literature & Culture in the Postcolonial and
Postimperial Literature in English. *v.2 p.728*

☐ The Canadian Literature Archive. *v.2 p.731*

Canadian Military Heritage: 1000-1754. . . . . . .*v.3 p.537*

Canadian Military Heritage: 1755-1871. . . . . . .*v.3 p.537*

☐ Canadian Poetry. *v.2 p.731*

☐ Canadian Poets Online: Writing Canada into the
Millenium. *v.2 p.731*

Canadian Political Party Systems. *v.4 p.588*

Canadian Politics in the 21st Century. *v.4 p.587*

Canadian Politics. *v.4 p.586*

The Canadian Postmodern: A Study of Contemporary Canadian
Fiction. *v.2 p.729*

The Canadian Prairies: A History. *v.3 p.546, v.6 p.682*

Canadian Provincial Politics. *v.4 p.589*

The Canadian Public Service: A Physiology of Government,
1867-1970. . . . .*v.4 p.588*

Canadian Science Fiction and Fantasy. *v.2 p.729, p.730*

Canadian Theatre History: Selected Readings. *v.1 p.127*

Canadian Writers, 1890-1920. . . . .*v.2 p.730*

Canadian Writers and Their Works: Dennis Cooley, Christopher
Dewdney, Steve McCaffery, Fred Wah and Tom
Wayman, Vol. XII. *v.2 p.730*

Canadian Writers and Their Works: Fiction. *v.2 p.730*

Canadian Writers and Their Works: Neil Bissoondath, Austin
Clarke, Joy Kogawa, Rohinton Mistry and Josef
Skvorecky, Vol. 11. . . . .*v.2 p.730*

Canadian Writers and Their Works: Roo Borson, Lorna Crozier,
Mary di Michele, Erin Moure and Sharon Thesen. .*v.2 p.730*

Canadian Writers and Their Works: Sandra Birdsell, Timothy
Findley, W. P. Kinsella and David Adams Richards. .*v.2 p.730*

Canadian Writers since 1960, First Series. *v.2 p.730*

Canadian Writers since 1960, Second Series. *v.2 p.730*

Canadian-American Relations in Wartime: From the Great War
to the Cold War. *v.3 p.387*

The Canadianization Movement: Emergence, Survival, and
Success. *v.3 p.535*

Canadians in the Making: A Social History of Canada. .*v.3 p.535*

Canaletto's Etchings: Catalogue Raisonné. *v.1 p.755*

Canaletto. *v.1 p.743*

Cancer in Two Voices. *v.6 p.377*

Cancer: Principles and Practice of Oncology. *v.5 p.520*

Cancer Treatment. *v.5 p.520*

Cancer Ward. *v.2 p.808*

Canciones (1921-1924). *v.2 p.658*

Canciones y Poemas para Ninos. *v.2 p.658*

Candid Science: Conversations with Famous Chemists. .*v.5 p.261*

Candid Science II: Conversations with Famous Biomedical
Scientists. *v.5 p.326*

Candide and Other Stories. *v.2 p.484, p.485*

Candide. *v.3 p.148*

Cane Fires: The Anti-Japanese Movement in Hawaii,
1865-1945. . . . .*v.6 p.132*

Cane Ridge: America's Pentecost. *v.1 p.648*

Cane. *v.2 p.126*

Cannery Women, Cannery Lives: Mexican Women,
Unionization, and the California Food Processing Industry,
1930-1950. . . . .*v.6 p.526, p.546, p.547*

Cannibal Tours and Glass Boxes: The Anthropology of
Museums. *v.4 p.47*

Cannibals All!, or, Slaves Without Masters. . . .*v.3 p.396, p.419*

The Cannibal. *v.2 p.83*

The Canoe: A Living Tradition. *v.4 p.789*

The Canon of Scripture. *v.1 p.614*

The Canon of the New Testament: Its Origin, Development, and
Significance. *v.1 p.624*

Canons and Decrees of the Council of Trent. . .*v.1 p.570, p.571*

Can't Find My Way Home: America in the Great Stoned Age,
1945-2000. . . . .*v.4 p.777*

The Cantatas of J. S. Bach. *v.1 p.183, p.184, p.235, p.303*

The Canterbury Tales: A Facsimile and Transcription of the Hengwrt Manuscript with Variants from the Ellesmere Manuscript. *v.2 p.208*

The Canterbury Tales: Nine Tales and the General Prologue. *v.2 p.208*

The Canterbury Tales, Vol. 1. . . . .*v.2 p.208*

The Canterbury Tales. *v.2 p.207, p.208, p.210*

The Canti with a Selection of His Prose: The Centenary Edition. *v.2 p.711, p.712*

Canticle for Leibowitz. *v.2 p.98*

Cantique des Plaines: Roman. *v.2 p.540*

Canto General. *v.2 p.681*

Canton under Communism: Programs and Politics in a Provincial Capital, 1949-1968. . . . . . .*v.6 p.195, p.206*

Cantonese: A Comprehensive Grammar. *v.6 p.207*

The Cantos of Ezra Pound, Nos. 1-117. . . . . . .*v.2 p.112*

Canzoniere: Rerum Vulgarium Fragmenta. *v.2 p.706*

Canzoniere. *v.2 p.706*

The Capacity to Budget. *v.4 p.543*

The Capacity to Judge: Public Opinion and Deliberative Democracy in Upper Canada, 1791-1854. . . . .*v.3 p.544*

Cape Dorset Sculpture. *v.1 p.777, v.6 p.679*

Capetian France 987-1328. . . . .*v.3 p.143, v.6 p.568*

The Capetian Kings of France: Monarchy and Nation, 987. . . . .*v.3 p.142*

Capillary Electrochromatography. *v.5 p.269*

Capillary Electrophoresis of Nucleic Acids: The Capillary Electrophoresis System as an Analytical Tool. . . .*v.5 p.120*

Capillary Electrophoresis of Nucleic Acids, Vol. II: Practical Applications of Capillary Electrophoresis. *v.5 p.120*

Capillary Electrophoresis of Proteins and Peptides. . .*v.5 p.89*

Capital: A Critique of Political Economy. *v.4 p.215*

Capital and Collusion: The Political Logic of Global Economic Development. *v.4 p.260, p.261*

Capital and Growth. *v.4 p.209*

Capital and Interest. *v.4 p.233*

Capital and Its Earnings. *v.4 p.223*

Capital and Time: A Neo-Austrian Theory. *v.4 p.214*

A Capital Case in America: How Today's Justice System Handles Death Penalty Cases, from Crime Scene to Ultimate Execution of Sentence. *v.6 p.269*

Capital Ideas: The Improbable Origins of Modern Wall Street. *v.4 p.91, p.93, p.94, p.99*

Capital, Labor, and State: The Battle for American Labor Markets from the Civil War to the New Deal. . . .*v.4 p.123*

Capital of the Tycoon: A Narrative of a Three Years' Residence in Japan. *v.6 p.223*

Capital Punishment in the United States: A Documentary History. *v.4 p.487, p.568*

Capital Punishment. *v.4 p.471*

Capital: Theories of Surplus Value, Vol. 4. . . . . .*v.4 p.236*

Capital Theory and the Rate of Return. *v.4 p.245*

Capitalism and Freedom. *v.4 p.214, p.231*

Capitalism and Material Life, 1400-1800. . . . . . .*v.3 p.38*

Capitalism and Modern Social Theory: An Analysis of the Writings of Marx, Durkheim and Max Weber. . . .*v.4 p.679*

Capitalism and Slavery. *v.6 p.20, p.37*

Capitalism and Social Democracy. *v.4 p.507*

Capitalism As a Moral System: Adam Smith's Critique of the Free Market Economy. *v.4 p.219*

Capitalism in Colonial Puerto Rico: Central San Vicente in the Late Nineteenth Century. *v.3 p.320*

Capitalism, Politics and Railroads in Prussia, 1830-1870. . . . .*v.3 p.168*

Capitalism, Socialism, and Democracy Revisited. .*v.4 p.214, p.235*

ⓔ Capitalism, Socialism and Democracy. . . .*v.4 p.230, p.235*

Capitalism, Socialism and Democracy. . .*v.4 p.500, p.505, p.507*

Capitalism. *v.4 p.214, p.215*

ⓔ Capitalist Development in the Twentieth Century: An Evolutionary-Keynesian Analysis. *v.4 p.241, p.242*

Capitalist Development in the Twentieth Century: An Evolutionary-Keynesian Analysis. *v.4 p.214*

Capitalist Diversity and Change: Recombinant Governance and Institutional Entrepreneurs. *v.4 p.67*

Capitalist Punishment: Prison Privatization and Human Rights. *v.6 p.276*

Los Capitalistas: Hispano Merchants on the Santa Fe Trade. *v.6 p.524, p.533*

Capitalists, Caciques, and Revolution: The Native Elite and Foreign Enterprise in Chihuahua, Mexico, 1854-1911. . . . .*v.3 p.296*

Capitol Accumulation in Thailand, 1855-1985. . . .*v.6 p.171*

Capote: A Biography. *v.6 p.401*

Capriccio for Goya. *v.2 p.780*

Capsicum y Cultura: La Historia del Chilli. *v.3 p.271*

Captain Alatriste. *v.2 p.663*

The Captain and the Enemy. *v.2 p.350*

Captain John Smith: A Select Edition of His Writings. .*v.3 p.500*

Captain John Smith: Jamestown and the Birth of the American Dream. *v.3 p.499*

Captain John Smith. *v.3 p.499*

Captain Sam Grant, 1822-1861. . . . .*v.3 p.437*

Captain Swing. *v.3 p.112, p.131*

Captains Courageous. *v.2 p.297*

Captains of Consciousness: Advertising and the Social Roots of the Consumer Culture. *v.4 p.52*

The Captive and the Free. *v.2 p.337, p.338*

The Captive Mind. *v.3 p.255*

A Captive of the Caucasus. *v.2 p.801*

Captive University: The Sovietization of East German, Czech and Polish Higher Education, 1945-1956. . . . . .*v.3 p.207*

Captives: Selected Short Stories. *v.2 p.794*

Captured Heritage: The Scramble for the Northwest Coast Artifacts. *v.6 p.678, p.702*

Capturing Sound: How Technology Has Changed Music. *v.1 p.387*

Capturing the Revolution: The United States, Central America and Nicaragua, 1961-1972. . . . .*v.3 p.301*

Car Emblems: The Ultimate Guide to Automotive Logos Worldwide. *v.1 p.717*

The Caracas Company, 1728-1784: Study in the History of Spanish Monopolistic Trade. *v.3 p.359*

Caracol Beach. *v.2 p.670*

Les Caracteres. *v.2 p.474*

Les caractères de Théophraste traduits du grec avec Les caractères ou Les moeurs de ce siècle. *v.2 p.474*

Caramelo. *v.6 p.498*

Caravaggio and His Two Cardinals: Method and Meaning. *v.1 p.739*

Caravaggio. *v.1 p.744*

Carbanions in Organic Synthesis. *v.5 p.295*

The Carbohydrates: Chemistry and Biochemistry, Vol. 2A. *v.5 p.330*

Carbohydrates: The Sweet Molecules of Life. *v.5 p.330*

Carbon and Nitrogen Cycling in European Forest Ecosystems. *v.5 p.185*

Carbon Sequestration in the Biosphere: Processes and Prospects. *v.5 p.183, p.186*

The Carbon War: Global Warming and the End of the Oil Era. *v.6 p.300*

Carbon-13 NMR spectroscopy: high-resolution methods and applications in organic chemistry and biochemistry. .*v.5 p.272*

Carbonate Sediments and Their Diagenesis. *v.5 p.439*

The Card: A Story of Adventure in the Five Towns. . .*v.2 p.334*

Cardano's Cosmos: The Worlds and Works of a Renaissance Astrologer. *v.3 p.47*

A Cardboard Castle?: An Inside History of the Warsaw Pact, 1955-1991. . . . .*v.4 p.630*

The Cardiovascular System. *v.5 p.163*

Cardozo. *v.4 p.468*

Care and Conservation of Natural History Collections. .*v.5 p.221*

The Care and Education of America's Young Children: Obstacles and Opportunities. *v.4 p.369*

The Care and Feeding of Ideas. *v.4 p.428*

The Care of Antiques and Historical Collections. . . .*v.1 p.824*

The Care of Strangers: The Rise of America's Hospital System. *v.5 p.513*

The Career and Legend of Vasco da Gama. *v.3 p.73*

Career as a biochemist: cutting edge scientific research, practical applications in industry, new specialties: biotechnology and bioengineering, many top professional positions in medicine, pharmaceuticals, nutrition. . .*v.5 p.251*

Career as A Biochemist: Cutting Edge Scientific Research, Practical Applications in Industry, New Specialties: Biotechnology and Bioengineering, Many Yop Professional Positions in Medicine, Pharmaceuticals, Nutrition. *v.5 p.218, p.251*

A Career as An Environmental Engineer: Using Technology to Help Save the Planet. *v.5 p.250, p.251*

Career Burnout: Causes and Cures. *v.5 p.580*

Career Choice and Development. *v.5 p.577*

Career Development and Counseling: Putting Theory and Research to Work. *v.5 p.576, p.577*

Career Development and Vocational Behavior of Racial and Ethnic Minorities. *v.5 p.577, p.578*

Career Directions. *v.4 p.168*

Career Experiences of African American Police Executives: Black in Blue Revisited. *v.6 p.259, p.260*

The Career Guide: The Employment Opportunities Directory. *v.4 p.168*

Career Imprints: Creating Leaders Across an Industry. .*v.4 p.71*

Career Insights: Presidents/GMs from the NFL, MLB, NHL and MLS on Achieving Personal and Professional Success: Landing a Job with a Sports Team. *v.4 p.905*

Career Opportunities for Bilinguals and Multilinguals: A Directory of Resources in Education, Employment, and Business. *v.4 p.168*

Career Opportunities in Aviation and the Aerospace Industry. *v.4 p.151*

Career Opportunities in Television, Cable, Video and Multimedia: A Comprehensive Guide to More Than 100 Exciting Careers in Television, Video, and New Media. *v.6 p.347*

Career Opportunities in the Publishing Industry: A Guide to Careers in Newspapers, Magazines, and Books. . .*v.4 p.150*

Career Paths in Psychology: Where Your Degree Can Take You. *v.5 p.676*

Career Planning and Adult Development Network. .*v.5 p.577*

The Career Psychology of Women. *v.5 p.577*

Career Transitions in Sport: International Perspectives. .*v.4 p.903*

CareerPreneurs: Lessons from Leading Women Entrepreneurs on Building a Career Without Boundaries. *v.4 p.68*

Careers for Environmental Types and Others Who Respect the Earth. *v.5 p.250*

Careers for Number Crunchers and Other Quantitative Types. *v.4 p.167*

Careers for Sports Nuts and Other Athletic Types. . .*v.4 p.903*

Careers in Bioinformatics: Fusing High-Powered Computing and Biology to Revolutionize Healthcare. *v.5 p.251*

Careers in Biotech Pharmaceuticals: WetFeet Insider Guide. *v.5 p.251*

Careers in Biotechnology, Bolecular Biology: Genetic Engineering-- Gene Therapy. *v.5 p.218, p.251*

Careers in biotechnology, molecular biology: genetic engineering-- gene therapy. *v.5 p.251*

Careers in Criminal Justice and Related Fields: From Internship to Promotion. *v.6 p.245*

Careers in Genetics Research: Cell Biology. *v.5 p.251*

Careers in Government. *v.4 p.546*

Careers in Health, Physical Education, and Sports. *v.4 p.794, p.903*

Careers in Industrial Hygiene: Occupational and Environmental Health and Safety. *v.5 p.251*

Careers in Sports Fitness and Recreation. *v.4 p.785, p.904*

Careers with Animals. *v.5 p.251*

Cargo, Cult, and Culture Critique. *v.4 p.711*

The Caribbean after Grenada: Revolution, Conflict, and Democracy. *v.3 p.320*

Caribbean Art. *v.1 p.684*

The Caribbean as Columbus Saw It. *v.3 p.404*

Caribbean Creolization: Reflections on the Cultural Dynamics of Language, Literature, and Identity. *v.3 p.314*

Caribbean Currents: Caribbean Music from Rumba to Reggae. *v.1 p.293*

Caribbean Life in New York City: Sociocultural Dimensions. *v.6 p.542, p.550*

The Caribbean Novel in English: An Introduction. . . .*v.2 p.767*

Caribbean Popular Music: An Encyclopedia of Reggae, Mento, Ska, Rocksteady, and Dancehall. *v.1 p.161, p.293*

Caribbean Revolutions and Revolutionary Theory: An Assessment of Cuba, Nicaragua and Grenada. .*v.3 p.302, p.320*

The Caribbean Slave: A Biological History. *v.3 p.271*

Caribbean Spanish in the Metropolis: Spanish Language among Cubans, Dominicans and Puerto Ricans in the New York City Area. *v.6 p.494*

Caribbean Transformations. *v.4 p.41*

Caribbean Waves: Relocating Claude Mckay and Paule Marshall. *v.2 p.767*

Caribbean Women Writers: Fiction in English. *v.2 p.767*

Caribbean Women Writers. *v.2 p.767*

□ CARINDEX. *v.3 p.259*

Caring Classrooms/Intelligent Schools: The Social Emotional Education of Young Children. *v.4 p.362*

Caring for Sexuality in Health and Illness. *v.5 p.530*

Caring Jurisprudence: Listening to Patients at the Supreme Court. *v.4 p.535*

Carissimi. *v.1 p.183, p.316*

Carl B. Stokes and the Rise of Black Political Power. .*v.3 p.513*

Carl Maria Von Weber. *v.1 p.206, p.367*

Carl Menger and His Legacy in Economics. . .*v.4 p.194, p.195*

Carl Menger and the Origins of Austrian Economics. .*v.4 p.233*

Carl Nielsen. *v.1 p.218, p.345*

Carl Sandburg: A Biography. *v.2 p.115*

Carl Schurz: A Biography. *v.3 p.434, p.435*

Carl Zuckmayer. *v.2 p.615*

Carlo Goldoni and Eighteenth-Century Theatre. *v.1 p.107*

Carlo Goldoni. *v.2 p.711*

Carlo Scarpa: The Complete Works. *v.1 p.792*

Carlos Fuentes. *v.2 p.668*

Carlos Saura: Interviews. *v.1 p.21, p.36*

Carlyle and German Thought: 1819-1834. . . . . .*v.2 p.276*

Carlyle and the Idea of the Modern: Studies in Carlyle's Prophetic Literature and Its Relation to Blake, Nietzsche, Marx and Others. *v.2 p.277*

A Carlyle Reader: Selections from the Writings of Thomas Carlyle. *v.2 p.276*

Carlylye and Scottish Thought. *v.2 p.276, p.277*

Carmen and Other Stories. *v.2 p.498*

Carmen. *v.1 p.194, p.228, p.312, p.407*

Carmina. *v.2 p.430*

Carminum Libri Tres. *v.2 p.445*

Carnal Knowing: Female Nakedness and Religious Meaning in the Christian West. *v.1 p.643*

The Carnegie Atlas of Galaxies. *v.5 p.64*

Le carnet du chat sauvage. *v.2 p.513*

Carnets : 1995-1998. . . . .*v.2 p.530, p.531*

Carnival and Culture: Sex, Symbol, and Status in Spain. .*v.3 p.242*

Carnival and the Formation of a Caribbean Transnation. .*v.4 p.44*

Carnival Music In Trinidad: Experiencing Music, Expressing Culture. *v.1 p.291, p.292*

A Carnival of Revolution: Central Europe 1989. . . . .*v.3 p.208*

Carnival Theater: Uruguay's Popular Performers and National Culture. *v.3 p.267*

Carnivals, Rogues, and Heroes: An Interpretation of the Brazilian Dilemma. *v.3 p.266*

Carolan: The Life Times and Music of an Irish Harper. *v.1 p.298, p.316*

Caroline Feller Bauer's New Handbook for Storytellers. .*v.4 p.362*

Carolingian and Romanesque Architecture: 800-1200. .*v.1 p.786*

The Carolingians: A Family Who Forged Europe. .*v.3 p.143, p.162*

The Carolingians and the Written Word. *v.3 p.143, p.162*

The Carpathians. *v.2 p.745*

The Carpenter's Pencil. *v.2 p.692, p.693*

Carry On, Jeeves!. *v.2 p.390*

Cars and Culture: The Life Story of a Technology. . .*v.4 p.154*

Carson McCullers: A Life. *v.2 p.100*

Carson McCullers: Complete Novels. *v.2 p.100*

Carson McCullers. *v.2 p.100*

Cartas Antologia. *v.2 p.660*

Cartas Marruecas. *v.2 p.654*

The Carter Presidency: A Re-Evaluation. *v.3 p.470*

The Carter Presidency: Policy Choices in the Post-New Deal Era. *v.3 p.471*

Cartesian Linguistics: A Chapter in the History of Rationalist Thought. *v.2 p.559*

Cartesian Meditations, 1. . . . .*v.1 p.469*

Carthage Mosaic of Ancient Tunisia. *v.6 p.59*

Cartographic Design Using Arcview GIS. . . .*v.4 p.385, p.387*

Cartographic Mexico: A History of State Fixations and Fugitive Landscapes. *v.4 p.383*

Cartographies of Desire: Captivity, Race and Sex in the Shaping of an American Nation. *v.2 p.3*

Cartography: Thematic Map Design with Arcview GIS Software. *v.4 p.385*

The Cartoon Guide to Physics. *v.5 p.540*

Cartoon Monickers: An Insight Into the Animation Industry. *v.6 p.307*

Cartoons: One Hundred Years of Cinema Animation. .*v.6 p.307*

Cartucho and My Mother's Hands. *v.2 p.667*

Cartucho: Relatos de la Lucha en el Norte de Mexico. .*v.2 p.667*

□ CAS, a Division of the American Chemical Society. .*v.5 p.256*

□ CAS DDS Title Search. *v.5 p.256*

□ CAS Standard Abbreviations and Acronyms. . . .*v.5 p.257*

La Casa de Bernarda Alba. *v.2 p.659*

Casa de Campo. *v.2 p.679, p.680*

La Casa de Mis Suenos: Dreams of Home in a Transnational Migrant Community. *v.6 p.529*

Casarett and Doull's Essentials of Toxicology. *v.5 p.514*

The Case Against Punishment: Retribution, Crime Prevention, and the Law. *v.6 p.275*

The Case Against Q: Studies in Markan Priority and the Synoptic Problem. *v.1 p.629*

The Case Against Standardized Testing: Raising the Scores, Ruining the Schools. *v.4 p.286*

The Case for African Freedom, and Other Writings on Africa. *v.2 p.338*

The Case for Change: Rethinking the Preparation of Educators. *v.4 p.277*

The Case for Classical Christian Education. *v.4 p.308*

A Case for Conservatism. *v.4 p.511*

A Case for Nuclear-Generated Electricity, or, Why I Think Nuclear Power Is Cool and Why It Is Important That You Think So Too. *v.5 p.709, p.739, p.740*

The Case for Same-Sex Marriage: From Sexual Liberty to Civilized Commitment. *v.6 p.388, p.389*

The Case for Shakespeare: The End of the Authorship Question. *v.2 p.231*

Case in Point: Complete Case Interview Preparation. *v.4 p.169*

The Case of Charles Dexter Ward. *v.2 p.94*

The Case of Ezra Pound. *v.2 p.112*

The Case of Sergeant Grischa. *v.2 p.616*

The Case of the Sulky Girl. *v.2 p.78*

Case Studies in Music Therapy. *v.1 p.406*

Case Studies in Organizational Communication: Ethical Perspectives and Practices. *v.4 p.53, p.173*

Case Studies of City-County Consolidation: Reshaping the Local Government Landscape. *v.4 p.542, p.544*

Case Studies of Existing Human Tissue Repositories: Best Practices for a Biospecimen Resource for the Genomic and Proteomic Era. *v.5 p.112, p.148*

Case Studies of Teacher Development: An In-Depth Look at How Thinking about Pedagogy Develops over Time. *v.4 p.277*

Case Study Research: Design and Methods. *v.4 p.688*

Cases for Teacher Development: Preparing for the Classroom. *v.4 p.277*

Cases in the Environment of Business: International Perspectives. *v.4 p.69*

Casey at the Bat: A Centennial Edition. *v.2 p.51*

Cash: The Autobiography. *v.1 p.267, p.316*

Casino Royale. *v.2 p.344*

Caspar David Friedrich. *v.1 p.740*

Caspar Schwenckfeld, Reluctant Radical. *v.1 p.603*

Cass Gilbert, Architect. *v.1 p.793*

Cass Gilbert: Life and Work. *v.1 p.792*

Cass Timberlane. *v.2 p.95*

Cassandra: A Novel and Four Essays. *v.2 p.620*

The Cassava Transformation: Africa's Best-Kept Secret.*v.5 p.22*

Cassell Companion to Cinema. *v.6 p.307*

Cassell's Encyclopedia of Queer Myth, Symbol and Spirit: Gay, Lesbian, Bisexual and Transgender Lore. *v.6 p.358, p.372, p.373*

Cassell's German English Dictionary. *v.2 p.620*

Cassell's History of English Literature. *v.2 p.166*

Cassell's Latin Dictionary: Latin-English, English-Latin. *v.2 p.424*

Cassell's New Dutch Dictionary: English-Dutch, Dutch-English. *v.2 p.620*

Cassell's Spanish-English English-Spanish Dictionary. *v.2 p.636*

Cast a Cold Eye. *v.2 p.99*

Casta Painting: Images of Race in Eighteenth-Century Mexico. *v.3 p.263*

Caste and Capitalism in Colonial India: The Nattukottai Chettiars. *v.6 p.154*

Caste and Class in a Southern Town. *v.3 p.496*

Caste, Class and Power: Changing Patterns of Stratification in a Tanjore Village. *v.6 p.149*

Caste, Conflict and Ideology: Mahatma Jotirao Phule and Low Caste Protest in Nineteenth-Century Western India. *v.6 p.149*

Caste, Culture and Hegemony: Social Dominance in Colonial Bengal. *v.6 p.149*

Caste, Nationalism, and Communism in South India: Malabar, 1900-1948. . . . .*v.6 p.161*

Caste, Society and Politics in India from the Eighteenth Century to the Modern Age. *v.4 p.722, p.723, v.6 p.149*

Caste Today. *v.6 p.149*

The Caste War of Yucatan. *v.3 p.289*

Castello Branco: The Making of a Brazilian President. *v.3 p.340*

The Castells Reader on Cities and Social Theory. . . *v.6 p.717*

Castes of Mind: Colonialism and the Making of Modern India. *v.6 p.149*

The Castilian Crisis of the Seventeenth Century: New Perspectives on the Economic and Social History of Seventeenth-Century Spain. *v.3 p.240*

Castle Corner. *v.2 p.338*

The Castle Diaries 1964-70. . . . .*v.3 p.93, p.119*

Castle Keep. *v.2 p.70, p.71*

The Castle of Crossed Destinies. *v.2 p.714*

Castle of Fratta. *v.2 p.712*

The Castle of Otranto. *v.2 p.264*

Castle Rackrent. *v.2 p.286*

Castlereagh and Adams: England and the United States, 1812-1823. . . . .*v.3 p.417*

Castles in the Air. *v.1 p.6*

Castles of Our Conscience: Social Control and the American State, 1800-1985. . . . .*v.4 p.773*

The Castle. *v.2 p.610, p.611*

The Castrati in Opera. *v.1 p.230*

Castro, the Blacks, and Africa. *v.3 p.311*

Castro's Daughter: An Exile's Memoir of Cuba.*v.3 p.308, p.309*

Castro's Final Hour. *v.3 p.312*

Casualties of Privilege: Essays on Prep Schools' Hidden Culture. *v.4 p.296*

Casualty of War: The Bush Administration's Assault on a Free Press. *v.4 p.563*

Casualty Report. *v.6 p.509*

Cat and Mouse. *v.2 p.608*

The Cat Fanciers' Association Complete Cat Book. . . *v.5 p.56*

Catalan Nationalism: Past and Present. *v.4 p.608*

Catalina. *v.2 p.370*

Catalog Handbook of Fine Chemicals. *v.5 p.259*

Catalog of American Political Prints in the Library of Congress, 1766-1876. . . . .*v.1 p.754*

🔲 Catalog of U.S. Government Publications. *v.4 p.482*

Catalogue: Foster and Partners. *v.1 p.791*

Title Index

A Catalogue of Crime. *v.2 p.579, p.580*

Catalogue Raisonné de l'Oeuvre Lithographie de Honoré
    Daumier. *v.1 p.756*

Catalogue Raisonné: Friedensreich Hundertwasser,
    1928-2000. . . . .*v.1 p.699*

Catalogué Raisonne Friedensreich Hundertwasser. . . .*v.1 p.699*

Catalysis and Zeolites: Fundamentals and Applications.*v.5 p.278*

Catalytic Chemistry: An Introductory Text. *v.5 p.278*

Catalyzing Inquiry at the Interface of Computing and
    Biology. *v.5 p.108*

Catarino Garza's Revolution on the Texas-Mexico
    Border. *v.3 p.296*

Catastrophe Remembered: Palestine, Israel and the Internal
    Refugees. *v.6 p.618*

Catastrophe Survived: Euripides' Plays of Mixed
    Reversal. *v.2 p.409, p.410*

Catastrophes and Lesser Calamities: The Causes of Mass
    Extinctions. *v.5 p.450*

Catawba Indian Pottery: The Survival of a Folk
    Tradition. *v.1 p.807, v.6 p.678*

Catch a Fire: The Life of Bob Marley. *v.1 p.276, p.340*

Catch-22: A Novel. *v.2 p.146*

The Catcher in the Rye. *v.2 p.118*

Catechism of the Catholic Church. *v.1 p.576*

Categorical Data Analysis with SAS and SPSS
    Applications. *v.4 p.690*

The Categorical Imperative: A Study in Kant's Moral
    Philosophy. *v.1 p.462*

Categorical Perception: The Groundwork of Cognition.*v.5 p.605*

Categories and Modules with K-Theory in View. . . .*v.5 p.473*

Categories of Medieval Culture. *v.6 p.563*

Category Killers: The Retail Revolution and Its Impact on
    Consumer Culture. *v.4 p.165*

Catfish and Mandala: A Two-Wheeled Voyage Through the
    Landscape and Memory of Vietnam. . *v.6 p.94, p.95, p.141*

The Cathars: Dualist Heretics in Languedoc in the High Middle
    Ages. *v.3 p.142*

The Cathedral and the Bazaar: Musings on Linux and Open
    Source by an Accidental
    Revolutionary. *v.5 p.342, p.343, p.348*

The Cathedrals of England. *v.1 p.608, p.609, p.789*

Cathedrals of Europe. *v.6 p.555, p.572*

Cathedral. *v.2 p.142, p.494*

Cather: Later Novels: A Lost Lady; the Professor's House;
    Death Comes for the Archbishop; Shadows on the
    Rock; Lucy Gayheart; Sapphira and the Slave Girl. *v.2 p.67*

Cather: Stories, Poems, and Other Writings. *v.2 p.67*

Catherine of Aragon. *v.3 p.100*

Catherine the Great: A Short History. *v.3 p.217*

Catherine the Great: Life and Legend. *v.3 p.217*

The Catherine Wheel. *v.2 p.120*

The Catholic Church: A Short History. *v.1 p.573*

The Catholic Church and Democracy in Chile and
    Peru. *v.3 p.329, p.353*

The Catholic Church and Nazi Germany. *v.1 p.573, p.574,v.3 p.85*

The Catholic Church and Social Change in Nicaragua. *v.3 p.301*

🄔 The Catholic Church and the Holocaust, 1930-1965. .*v.3 p.86*

Catholic Colonialism: A Parish History of Guatemala,
    1524-1821. . . . .*v.3 p.298*

Catholic Feminism and the Social Question in Chile, 1910-1917:
    The Liga de Damas Chilenas. *v.3 p.355, p.356*

Catholic Philosophy of Education. *v.4 p.345*

The Catholic Rediscovery of Protestantism. *v.1 p.576*

Catholic Reform from Cardinal Ximenes to the Council of
    Trent, 1495-1563: An Essay with Illustrative
    Documents and a Brief Study of St. Ignatius Loyola. .*v.1 p.612*

Catholic Revival in the Age of the Baroque: Religious Identity
    in Southwest Germany, 1550-1750. . . . .*v.3 p.166*

Catholic Schools and the Common Good. *v.4 p.307*

Catholic Social Teaching: Our Best Kept Secret. . .*v.1 p.575*

Catholic Social Thought: The Documentary Heritage. *v.1 p.572*

Catholicism: A Study of Dogma in Relation to the Corporate
    Destiny of Mankind. *v.1 p.575*

Catholicism and American Freedom: A History from Slavery to
    Abortion. *v.4 p.486*

Catholicism in South Florida, 1868-1968. . . .*v.6 p.520, p.532*

Catholicism. *v.1 p.575*

Catholics and American Culture: Fulton Sheen, Dorothy Day
    and the Notre Dame Football
    Team. *v.1 p.574, v.4 p.817, p.818, p.859, p.894*

Catholics and Sultans: The Church and the Ottoman Empire
    1453-1923. . . . .*v.6 p.589*

Catholics in Western Democracies: A Study in Political
    Behavior. *v.1 p.575*

Catilina, Iugurtha, Historiarum Fragmenta Selecta; Appendix
    Sallustiana. *v.2 p.443*

Cato the Censor. *v.3 p.24*

Cat's Eye. *v.2 p.734*

Cats' Paws and Catapults: Mechanical Worlds of Nature and
    People. *v.5 p.564*

Cats: The Book of the Musical. *v.1 p.249, p.337, p.407*

Cattle Bring Us to Our Enemies: Turkana Ecology, Politics, and
    Raiding in a Disequilibrium System. *v.4 p.30*

Cattle, Horses and Men of the Western Range. . . .*v.3 p.527*

The Cattle Kings. *v.3 p.422, p.510, p.524*

The Cattle on a Thousand Hills: Southern California,
    1850-1880. . . . .*v.3 p.531*

The Cattle Towns. *v.3 p.521*

Catullan Provocations: Lyric Poetry and the Drama of
    Position. *v.2 p.430*

The Catullan Revolution. *v.2 p.430*

Catullus and His World: A Reappraisal. *v.2 p.431*

Catullus and the Traditions of Ancient Poetry. . . .*v.2 p.431*

Catullus: Poems. *v.2 p.430*

Catullus, Vol. 34. . . . .*v.2 p.430*

Catullus. *v.2 p.430*

Caucasians Only: The Supreme Court, the NAACP, and the
    Restrictive Covenant Cases. *v.4 p.443*

Caudillos y Caciques: Antonio Lopez de Santa Anna y Juan
    Alvarez. *v.3 p.289*

Caught in the Middle: Contradictions in the Lives of
    Sociologists from Working Class
    Backgrounds. *v.4 p.682, p.683*

Caught in the Middle: Korean Merchants in America's
    Multiethnic Cities. *v.6 p.106, p.114, p.116, p.136*

La Causa: Civil Rights, Social Justice and the Struggle for
    Equality in the Midwest. *v.6 p.539, p.540*

Causal Models in the Social Sciences. *v.4 p.687*

Causality and Chance in Modern Physics. *v.5 p.556*

Causality and Determinism. *v.1 p.503, p.504*

Causality and Explanation. *v.5 p.400, p.404, p.409*

Causality in Macroeconomics. *v.4 p.240*

Causality: Models, Reasoning, and Inference. *v.5 p.339*

Cause and Correlation in Biology: A User's Guide to Path
    Analysis, Structural Equations and Causal Inference. .*v.5 p.90*

Cause and Meaning in the Social Sciences. *v.4 p.700*

The Cause Lost: Myths and Realities of the
    Confederacy. *v.3 p.395*

Cause Marketing. *v.4 p.145*

Causes and Consequences of Feelings. *v.5 p.611*

Causes of Conduct Disorder and Juvenile Delinquency. .*v.5 p.662*

Causes of Delinquency. *v.6 p.255*

Causes of Evolution: A Paleontological Perspective. . .*v.5 p.196*

Causes of International War. *v.4 p.647, p.649*

The Causes of the English Civil War. *v.3 p.103, p.104*

The Causes of the English Revolution 1529-1642. . . .*v.3 p.104*

The Causes of the War of 1812. . . . .*v.3 p.417*

Cavalcade of Journalists 1900-2000. . . . .*v.4 p.404*

Cavalier and Yankee: The Old South and American National
    Character. *v.3 p.494*

Cavalleria Rusticana and Other Stories. *v.2 p.713*

Cavalli. *v.1 p.184, p.316*

Cave of Lascaux: The Final Photographs. *v.1 p.669*

Caveat. *v.3 p.472*

Caves: Processes, Development, Management. *v.5 p.424*

The Cave. *v.2 p.129*

Cavour. *v.3 p.201*

☐ CAWP: Center for American Women and Politics. .*v.6 p.439*

Caxton's Malory: A New Edition of Sir Thomas Malory's Le
    Mort d'Arthur, Based on the Pierpont Morgan Copy
    of William Caxton's Edition of 1485, Vol. Set. . . .*v.2 p.212*

☐ CBOE, Chicago Board Options Exhange. . . .*v.4 p.93, p.101*

The CBOT Handbook of Futures and
    Options. *v.4 p.94, p.101, p.162*

☐ CCIIM (Clearinghouse for Chemical Information
    Instructional Materials). *v.5 p.266*

CCTV and Policing: Public Area Surveillance and Police
    Practices in Britain. *v.6 p.265*

☐ CDA: Copper.org. *v.5 p.730*

☐ CE (Chemical Engineering) Buyer's Guide. *v.5 p.317*

Ce qui fut sans lumière ; suivi de Début et fin de la neige et de
    Là où retombe la flèche. *v.2 p.510*

Cebu. *v.6 p.99*

The Cecchetti Method of Classical Ballet Theory and
    Technique. *v.1 p.23*

Cecil Textbook of Medicine. *v.5 p.515*

Cecilia, or Memoirs of an Heiress. *v.2 p.241, p.242*

Cecilia Reclaimed: Feminist Perspectives on Gender and
    Music. *v.1 p.378, v.6 p.474*

Cecilia Valdes or el Angel Hill. *v.2 p.673*

☐ CEDES (Centro de Estudios de Estado y Sociedad). .*v.3 p.259*

Cela s'appelle l'aurore : roman. *v.2 p.526*

Celebrated Cases of Judge Dee: An Authentic Eighteenth
    Century Chinese Detective Novel. *v.6 p.212*

Celebrating Irving Fisher: The Legacy of a Great
    Economist. *v.4 p.200, p.225*

Celebrating Jesus Christ in Africa: Liturgy and
    Inculturation. *v.1 p.573*

Celebrating Moore: Works from the Collection of the Henry
    Moore Foundation. *v.1 p.780*

Celebrating the Family: Ethnicity, Consumer Culture, and
    Family Rituals. *v.4 p.705, p.706, p.734*

Celebrating the Land: Women's Nature Writings,
    1850-1991. . . . .*v.5 p.79*

Celebrating Women Coaches: A Biographical
    Dictionary. *v.4 p.836*

The Celebration of the Eucharist: The Origin of the Rite and the
    Development of Its Interpretation. *v.1 p.657*

☐ A Celebration of Women Writers. *v.6 p.475*

Celestial Encounters: The Origins of Chaos and
    Stability. *v.5 p.66, p.488*

Celestial Sirens: Nuns and Their Music in Early Modern
    Milan. *v.1 p.184, p.185, p.379*

La Celestina: Tragicomedia de Calisto y Melibea: Edicion
    Critica. *v.2 p.652*

La Celestina: Tragicomedia de Calisto y Melibea:
    Introduccion. *v.2 p.652*

La Celestina: Tragicomedia de Calisto y Melibea. .*v.2 p.651, p.652*

Celestina. *v.2 p.260, p.643*

La Celestina. *v.2 p.651*

Celia: My Life. *v.1 p.294, p.319*

The Cell: A Molecular Approach. *v.5 p.154*

Cell Behaviour: Control and Mechanism of Motility, Vol.
    65. . . . .*v.5 p.153*

Cell Biological Applications of Confocal Microscopy, Vol.
    70. . . . .*v.5 p.86*

Cell Biology and Biotechnology in Space. . . .*v.5 p.153, p.217*

Cell Biology, Set. *v.5 p.154*

Cell Culture for Biochemists. *v.5 p.87*

The Cell: Evolution of the First Organism. *v.5 p.154*

Cell Imaging Techniques: Methods and Protocols. . . .*v.5 p.86*

Cell Immortalization. *v.5 p.152*

Cellini and the Principles of Sculpture. *v.1 p.775*

Cells, Embryos and Evolution: Toward a Cellular and
    Developmental Understanding of Phenotypic Variation and
    Evolutionary Adaptability. *v.5 p.160, p.192*

Cellular Computing. *v.5 p.105*

Cellular Pathology as Based upon Physiological and
    Pathological Histology. *v.5 p.514*

Cellular Responses to Stress, Vol. 64. . . . .*v.5 p.153*

The Celluloid Closet: Homosexuality in the Movies. .*v.6 p.417*

The Celluloid Closet. *v.6 p.417*

Celluloid Gaze. *v.6 p.416*

Celluloid Heroes down Under: Australian Film,
1970-2000. . . . .*v.6 p.337*

Celluloid Indians: Native Americans and Film. *v.6 p.700*

Celluloid Jukebox: Popular Music and the Movies since the
50s. *v.6 p.316*

Celluloid Skyline: New York and the Movies. *v.6 p.730*

Celluloid Wars: A Guide to Film and the American Experience
of War. *v.6 p.323*

Celtic Britain. *v.3 p.96*

Celtic Christianity: Making Myths and Chasing
Dreams. *v.1 p.608*

Celtic Modern: Music at the Global Fringe. *v.1 p.299*

Celtic Music: The Complete Guide. *v.1 p.298, p.299*

Celtic Spirituality. *v.1 p.609*

Cement. *v.2 p.803, v.3 p.224, p.225*

Cena Trimalchionis. *v.2 p.440*

Censorship in Canadian Literature. *v.2 p.729*

Censorship, Inc.: The Corporate Threat to Free Speech in the
United States. *v.4 p.515*

Censorship of the Movies: The Social and Political Control of a
Mass Medium. *v.4 p.451*

The Centennial Anthology of North Dakota History: Journal of
the Northern Plains. *v.3 p.523*

Centennial Essays for Robinson Jeffers. *v.2 p.91*

☐ Center for American Women and
Politics. *v.4 p.547, p.548, p.568*

☐ Center for Customer Driven Quality, Purdue
University. *v.5 p.585, p.604*

☐ Center for Gifted Education, College of William and
Mary. *v.5 p.575*

☐ Center for History and New Media. *v.4 p.419*

☐ Center for Psychology in Schools. *v.5 p.571*

☐ Center for Research and Data, Child Welfare League of
America. *v.5 p.671*

☐ Center for Research on Education, Diversity & Excellence
(CREDE). *v.4 p.302, p.346*

☐ Center for Talented Youth, Johns Hopkins
University. *v.5 p.575*

☐ Center for the Study of Sexual Minorities in the
Military. *v.4 p.717, v.6 p.390*

The Center Holds: The Power Struggle Inside the Rehnquist
Court. *v.4 p.539*

☐ Center on Urban Poverty and Social Change, Case Western
Reserve University. *v.5 p.671, v.6 p.717*

Center Stage: An Anthology of Twenty-One Contemporary
Black-American Plays. *v.1 p.68, p.123*

Center Stage: Helen Gahagan Douglas - A Life. *v.3 p.462*

Central African Republic: The Continent's Hidden Heart. .*v.6 p.62*

Central America and the Middle East: The Internationalization
of the Crises. *v.3 p.301*

Central American Refugees and U. S. High Schools: A
Psychosocial Study of Motivation and Achievement. .*v.6 p.528*

Central and Eastern European Agriculture in an Expanding
European Union. *v.5 p.15*

Central and Flexible Staging: A New Theater in the
Making. *v.1 p.154*

Central and Local Government Relations: A Comparative
Analysis of West European Unitary States. *v.4 p.582*

Central Asia at the End of the Transition. . . .*v.4 p.599, p.624*

Central Asia in World History. *v.6 p.238*

Central Asia's Second Chance. *v.3 p.231*

Central Europe: Enemies, Neighbors, Friends. *v.3 p.206*

Central Ideas in the Development of American Journalism: A
Narrative History. *v.4 p.404*

The Central Philosophy of Buddhism: A Study of the
Madhyamika System. *v.1 p.566*

Central Planning. *v.4 p.235*

The Central Questions of Philosophy. *v.1 p.416*

Centralization and Decentralization in Economic Policy. .*v.4 p.237*

Centralizing and Decentralizing Trends in Federal
States. *v.4 p.523*

Centre of Things: Political Fiction in Britain from Disraeli to
the Present. *v.6 p.756, p.758*

Centres of Learning: Learning and Location in Pre-Modern
Europe and the Near East. *v.4 p.334*

☐ Centro de Estudios Puertorriqueños. *v.6 p.485*

Los Centroamericanos. *v.2 p.668*

Centrosomes in Development and Disease. *v.5 p.152*

Centuries of Childhood: A Social History of Family
Life. *v.4 p.735*

A Century of Advance: Southeast Asia. *v.6 p.145*

A Century of Advance: Trade, Missions, Literature. . .*v.6 p.145*

A Century of American Printmaking, 1880-1980. . . .*v.1 p.754*

A Century of Artists Books. *v.1 p.754, p.761*

A Century of British Geography. *v.4 p.374, p.378*

A Century of British Painters. *v.1 p.733*

A Century of Chemistry: The Role of Chemists and the
American Chemical Society. *v.5 p.263*

A Century of Chicano History: Empire, Nations and
Migration. *v.6 p.531*

A Century of Cuban Writers in Florida: Selected Prose and
Poetry. *v.6 p.496, p.507*

A Century of Genocide: Utopias of Race and Nation. .*v.4 p.715*

☐ A Century of Lawmaking for a New Nation: U.S.
Congressional Documents and Debates,
1774-1875. . . . .*v.4 p.516, p.517*

☐ A Century of Lawmaking. *v.4 p.437, p.440*

A Century of Movie Posters: From Silent to Art House. .*v.1 p.718*

A Century of Musicals in Black and White: An Encyclopedia of
Musical Stage Works by, About, or Involving Black
Americans. *v.1 p.60, p.93*

A Century of Nobel Prize Recipients: Chemistry, Physics, and
Medicine. *v.5 p.389*

A Century of Organized Labor in France: A Union Movement
for the Twenty-First Century?. *v.4 p.129*

A Century of Posters. *v.1 p.718*

A Century of Psychology As Science. *v.5 p.597*

A Century of Recorded Music: Listening to Musical
History. *v.1 p.383, p.386*

The Century of Revolution,
1603-1714. . . . .*v.3 p.102, p.103, p.130, p.131*

A Century of Separation Science. *v.5 p.274*

A Century of Sonnets: The Romantic-Era Revival 1750-1850. . . . .*v.2 p.199*

Century of Struggle: The Woman's Rights Movement in the United States. *v.6 p.430*

The Century of the Gene. *v.5 p.134*

A Century of the Scottish People: 1830-1950. .*v.3 p.132, p.133*

Century of the Tiger: One Hundred Years of Korean Culture in America. *v.6 p.87, p.135*

A Century of Women's Basketball: From Frailty to Final Four. *v.4 p.807, p.836, p.837, p.854*

A Century of Wonder: The Scholarly Disciplines, Vol. 2..*v.6 p.145*

A Century of Wonder: The Visual Arts. *v.6 p.215*

Century's Ebb: The Thirteenth Chronicle. *v.2 p.69*

Ceramic Trees of Life: Popular Art from Mexico..*v.1 p.684, p.777*

Ceramics: A Potter's Handbook. *v.1 p.808*

Ceramics from Islamic Lands. *v.1 p.801*

Ceramics of the Islamic World. *v.1 p.800*

▢ Ceramics WebBook. *v.5 p.305*

▢ CeramicsWeb. *v.1 p.774*

Ceremonial Animal: A New Portrait of Anthropology. .*v.4 p.22*

Ceremonies: Prose and Poetry. *v.6 p.397, p.405*

The Ceremony and Other Stories. *v.2 p.91*

Ceremony in Lone Tree. *v.2 p.103*

Ceremony. *v.2 p.155, v.6 p.699*

The Cerrados of Brazil: Ecology and Natural History of a Neotropical Savanna. *v.5 p.236, v.6 p.292*

A Certain Idea of Europe. *v.4 p.638*

Certain Solitudes: On the Poetry of Donald Justice. . . .*v.2 p.90*

Certain Trumpets: The Nature of Leadership. *v.4 p.72*

A Certain Woman. *v.6 p.229*

Certainty of Justice: Reform in the Crime Victim Movement. *v.4 p.754*

▢ Certification Requirements for 50 States. *v.4 p.278*

Cervantes: A Biography. *v.2 p.647*

Cervantes: A Collection of Critical Essays. *v.2 p.649*

Cervantes and the Comic Mind of His Age. *v.2 p.648*

Cervantes and the Humanist Vision: A Study of Four Exemplary Novels. *v.2 p.649*

Cervantes and the Mystery of Lawlessness: A Study of el Casamiento Enganoso y El Coloquio de los Perros. .*v.2 p.649*

Cervantes' Don Quixote: A Casebook. *v.2 p.649*

Cervantes' Don Quixote: A Reference Guide. *v.2 p.649*

The Cervantes Encyclopedia. *v.2 p.649*

Cervantes' Exemplary Fictions: A Study of the Novelas Ejemplares. *v.2 p.649*

Cervantes; His Life, His Times, His Works. *v.2 p.647*

Cervantes in Algiers: A Captive's Tale. *v.2 p.649*

Cervantes: "Don Quixote". *v.2 p.648*

Cervante's Novel of Modern Times: A New Reading of Don Quijote. *v.2 p.649*

Cervantes, the Novel, and the New World. *v.2 p.648*

Cervantes. *v.2 p.645, p.647, p.648, p.649, p.650*

Ces Enfants de Ma Vie. *v.2 p.539, p.540*

Cesar Birotteau. *v.2 p.485*

Cesar Chavez: A Biography. *v.4 p.124*

Cesar Chávez: A Triumph of Spirit. .*v.4 p.126, v.6 p.489, p.526*

Cesar Vallejo: An Anthology of Poetry. *v.2 p.685*

Cesare Pavese: A Study of the Major Novels and Poems..*v.2 p.721*

Cesare Pavese. *v.2 p.720*

C'Etait Avant la Guerre a l'Anse-a-Gilles. *v.2 p.540*

Cette aveuglante absence de lumière : roman. *v.2 p.543*

Ceuvre Poetique 1950-1990. . . . .*v.2 p.539*

Ceuvre Poetique, 1957-1996. . . . .*v.2 p.538*

Cezanne and Provence: The Painter in His Culture. . .*v.1 p.735*

Cezanne in Provence. *v.1 p.737*

Cezanne. *v.1 p.700, p.746*

César Vallejo: Autógrafos Olvidados. *v.2 p.685*

Cézanne: The Self-Portraits. *v.1 p.745*

Chaco Canyon: Archeologists Explore the Lives of an Ancient Society. *v.4 p.10*

The Chaco Mission Frontier: The Guaycuruan Experience, 1700-1800. . . . .*v.3 p.343*

The Chaco War: Bolivia and Paraguay, 1932-1935. . .*v.3 p.274*

Chain and Round Dance Patterns. *v.1 p.16*

Chain of Command: The Road from 9/11 to Abu Ghraib. *v.3 p.483, v.4 p.659*

Chainbreaker: The Revolutionary War Memoirs of Governor Blacksnake As Told to Benjamin Williams. *v.6 p.685*

The Chained Boy: ORC and Blake's Idea of Revolution. .*v.2 p.240*

Chairing the Academic Department: Leadership among Peers. *v.4 p.294*

Chairman Mao Would Not Be Amused: Fiction from Today's China. *v.6 p.212*

Chaiyo! King Vajiravudh and the Development of Thai Nationalism. *v.6 p.172*

Chaiyol, King Vajiravudh and the Development of Thai Nationalism. *v.6 p.172*

Chalet. *v.1 p.772*

Challenge and Change in Education: The Experience of the Baltic States in the 1990's. *v.4 p.335*

The Challenge for Geography: A Changing World, a Changing Discipline. *v.4 p.378*

The Challenge of Basic Christian Communities. *v.1 p.578*

The Challenge of Community Policing: Testing the Promises. *v.6 p.263, p.264*

The Challenge of Crime: Rethinking Our Response. . .*v.6 p.250*

The Challenge of Global Capitalism: The World Economy in the 21st Century. *v.4 p.55*

The Challenge of Jesus: Rediscovering Who Jesus Was and Is. *v.1 p.642*

Challenge of Local Feminisms: Women's Movements in Global Perspective. *v.6 p.430*

The Challenge of Restructuring: North American Labor Movements Respond. *v.4 p.122*

The Challenge of Same-Sex Marriage: Federalist Principles and Constitutional Protections. *v.4 p.570, v.6 p.389*

Challenge of World Poverty: A World Poverty Program in Outline. *v.4 p.259*

Challenge to Affluence. *v.4 p.214*

The Challenge to Isolation: The World Crisis of 1937-1940 and American Foreign Policy. *v.3 p.453*

Challenges and Opportunities for further Improving the Transit Systems and Economic Development of Landlocked and Transit Developing Countries. *v.5 p.701*

Challenges for Rural America in the 21st Century. . . .*v.4 p.771*

Challenges of Teaching with Technology Across the Curriculum: Issues and Solutions. *v.4 p.352*

Challenging Art: Artforum 1962-1974. . . . .*v.1 p.703*

Challenging Lesbian and Gay Inequalities in Education. .*v.6 p.385*

Challenging the Boundaries of Slavery. *v.3 p.395*

Challenging the Incumbent: An Underdog's Undertaking. *v.4 p.550*

Challenging Traditional Views of Russian History. . . .*v.3 p.209*

Chamber Music: A Research and Information Guide. *v.1 p.165, p.238*

Chamber Music. *v.2 p.358, p.359*

Chamberlain and Appeasement: British Policy and the Coming of the Second World War. *v.3 p.79*

Chamberlain, Germany, and Japan. *v.3 p.78*

Chambers Nuclear Energy and Radiation Dictionary. *v.5 p.360, p.740*

Chambre sourde : l'antiesthétique de Malraux. . . . *v.2 p.522*

Champion Joe Louis: A Biography. . . *v.4 p.832, p.855, p.856*

Champions of Charity: War and the Rise of the Red Cross. *v.3 p.36*

Champlain: The Birth of French America. *v.3 p.538*

Champlain, the Founder of New France. *v.3 p.538*

Champlain, the Life of Fortitude. *v.3 p.537*

Chance: A Tale in Two Parts. *v.2 p.340*

Chance in Biology: Using Probability to Explore Nature. .*v.5 p.92*

Chance in the House of Fate: A Natural History of Heredity. *v.5 p.130*

Chance or Destiny: Turning Points in American History. .*v.3 p.376*

Chandler - Later Novels and Other Writings: The Lady in the Lake; The Little Sister; The Long Goodbye; Playback; Double Indemnity; Essays and Letters. *v.2 p.64, p.65*

Chandler - Stories and Early Novels: Pulp Stories; The Big Sleep; Farewell, My Lovely; The High Window. . .*v.2 p.65*

Change and Continuity in Indian Religion. *v.1 p.540*

Change and Decline: Roman Literature in the Early Empire. *v.2 p.425*

Change at Work. *v.4 p.85*

The Change Makers: From Carnegie to Gates, How the Great Entrepreneurs Transformed Ideas into Industries. . .*v.4 p.66*

Change Masters. *v.4 p.76*

Changes: A Love Story. *v.2 p.752*

Changes and Conflicts: Korean Immigrant Families in New York. *v.6 p.110, p.119, p.136*

Changes in Scenery: Contemporary Landscape Architecture in Europe. *v.1 p.814*

Changes in the Land: Indians, Colonists, and the Ecology of New England. *v.6 p.294, p.295*

The Changing American Presidency. *v.4 p.528*

Changing Authoritarian Rule and Public Policy in Argentina, 1930-1970. . . . .*v.3 p.348*

The Changing Bedouin. *v.6 p.596*

The Changing Borders of Juvenile Justice: Transfer of Adolescents to the Criminal Court. *v.6 p.269*

Changing Corporate America from Inside Out: Lesbian and Gay Workplace Rights. *v.6 p.382*

Changing Course: The International Boundary, U. S. and Mexico, 1848-1963. . . . .*v.3 p.528*

Changing Economic Geography Of Globalization. *v.4 p.398, p.399*

The Changing Experience of Childhood: Families and Divorce. *v.4 p.735*

Changing Face of Christianity. *v.1 p.611*

The Changing Face of Economics: Conversations with Cutting Edge Economists. *v.4 p.185*

The Changing Face of Empire: Charles V, Philip II, and Habsburg Authority, 1551-1559. . . . .*v.3 p.240*

The Changing Geography of Africa. *v.6 p.51*

The Changing Geography of Asia. *v.4 p.384*

Changing History: Afro-Cuban Cabildos and Societies of Color in the Nineteenth Century. *v.3 p.310*

Changing Images of Pictorial Space: A History of Spatial Illusion in Painting. *v.1 p.727*

Changing India: Bourgeois Revolution on the Subcontinent. *v.6 p.158*

Changing Kids' Games. *v.4 p.304, p.364*

Changing Life: Genomes, Ecologies, Bodies and Commodities. *v.5 p.249, p.250*

The Changing Light at Sandover: A Poem. *v.6 p.405*

The Changing Light at Sandover: Including the Whole of the Book of Ephraim, Mirabell's Books of Number, Scripts for the Pageant, and a New Coda, The Higher Keys. *v.2 p.100*

Changing Lives: Delinquency Prevention as Crime-Control Policy. *v.6 p.255*

Changing Lives of Refugee Hmong Women. . .*v.6 p.111, p.139*

Changing Meanings of Citizenship in Modern China. .*v.4 p.619*

Changing Military Doctrine: Presidents and Military Power in Fifth Republic France, 1958-2000. . . . .*v.3 p.141*

Changing National Identities at the Frontier: Texas and New Mexico, 1800-1850. . . . .*v.6 p.534*

A Changing of the Guard: Anglo-American Relations, 1941-1946. . . . .*v.3 p.393*

The Changing of the Guard: Lesbian and Gay Elders, Identity, and Social Change. *v.6 p.367, p.380, p.387*

Changing Ones: Third and Fourth Genders in Native North America. *v.4 p.746, v.6 p.371, p.705, p.707, p.709*

The Changing People: A History of the Canadian Indians. *v.6 p.682, p.683*

Changing Places. *v.2 p.361*

Changing Plant Life of la Frontera: Observations on Vegetation in the United States/Mexico Borderlands. . .*v.6 p.488, p.551*

The Changing Politics of Foreign Policy. *v.4 p.628*

Changing Race: Latinos, the Census, and the History of Ethnicity in the United States. *v.6 p.545*

The Changing Role of the Embryo in Evolutionary Thought: Roots of Evo-Devo. *v.5 p.159, p.162, p.190*

The Changing Same: Black Women's Literature, Criticism, and Theory. *v.6 p.27, p.45, p.479*

The Changing Shape of Church History. *v.1 p.598*

The Changing Social Structure of England and Wales
    1871-1961. . . . .*v.4 p.704, p.705*

Changing Structure of Mexico: Political, Social, and Economic
    Prospects. *v.4 p.383, p.593*

Changing the Atmosphere: Expert Knowledge and
    Environmental Governance. *v.4 p.666, p.667*

Changing the Guard: Developing Democratic Police
    Abroad. *v.6 p.262*

Changing the Odds: Open Admissions and the Life Chances of
    the Disadvantaged. *v.4 p.294*

Changing the Story: Feminist Fiction and the Tradition. *v.6 p.478*

Changing Times: Work and Leisure in Postindustrial
    Society. *v.4 p.761*

Changing Tropical Forests: Historical Perspectives on Today's
    Challenges in Central and South America. *v.3 p.270*

A Changing United Nations: Multilateral Evolution and the
    Quest for Global Governance. *v.4 p.634*

The Changing Wildlife of Great Britain and Ireland. . *v.5 p.237*

The Changing World of Bali: Religion, Society and
    Tourism. *v.4 p.39*

The Changing World of Mongolia's Nomads. *v.4 p.28, v.6 p.240*

Channelized Rivers: Perspectives for Environmental
    Management. *v.5 p.704*

The Chan's Great Continent: China in Western Minds. *v.6 p.216*

La Chanson de Roland: Oxford Text and English
    Translation. *v.2 p.466*

La chanson de Roland. *v.2 p.468*

Chants for Socialists. *v.2 p.301*

Chants. *v.2 p.150, v.6 p.501, p.510*

Chaos: An Introduction to Dynamical Systems. *v.5 p.489*

Chaos and Fractals: New Frontiers of Science. .*v.5 p.488, p.489*

Chaos and Life: Complexity and Order in Evolution and
    Thought. *v.5 p.190*

Chaos in Classical and Quantum Mechanics. *v.5 p.546*

Chaos in Real Data: Analysis of Non-Linear Dynamics in Short
    Ecological Space. *v.5 p.171*

Chaos of the Senses. *v.6 p.662*

Chaos: The Making of a New Science. *v.5 p.488*

Chaotic Elections!: A Mathematician Looks at Voting. *v.5 p.504*

▢ Chapin Hall Center for Children, University of
    Chicago. *v.5 p.671*

Chaplin in the Sound Era: An Analysis of the Seven
    Talkies. *v.6 p.332*

Chapters in Brazil's Colonial History, 1500-1800. . . .*v.3 p.334*

Character and Characterization in Shakespeare: Essays. *v.2 p.230*

The Character of a Genius: Beethoven in
    Perspective. *v.1 p.196, p.306*

The Character of American Higher Education and Intercollegiate
    Sport. *v.4 p.289, p.290, p.821, p.893*

The Character of Credit: Personal Debt in English Culture,
    1740-1914. . . . .*v.6 p.745, p.761*

The Character of Physical Law. *v.5 p.541*

The Character of Swift's Satire: A Revised Focus. . . *v.2 p.263*

Character Strengths and Virtues: A Handbook and
    Classification. *v.5 p.670*

Characteristic Raman Frequencies of Organic
    Compounds. *v.5 p.297*

▢ Characteristics of Public School Teachers' Professional
    Development Activities: 1999-2000. . . . .*v.4 p.278*

Characterization of Polymers: Surfaces, Interfaces, Thin
    Films. *v.5 p.323*

Characters of Shakespeare's Plays. *v.2 p.229, p.230*

Characters. *v.2 p.473*

The Charioteer. *v.6 p.398*

Charitable Choices: Religion, Race, and Poverty in the
    Post-Welfare Era. *v.5 p.670*

Charlemagne and France: A Thousand Years of
    Mythology. *v.3 p.140, p.141*

Charlemagne: Father of a Continent. *v.3 p.142, p.162*

Charlemagne. *v.3 p.142, p.162*

Charles Baudelaire: A Lyric Poet in the Era of High
    Capitalism. *v.2 p.488*

Charles Brasch Collected Poems. *v.2 p.744*

Charles Bukowski. *v.2 p.141*

Charles Churchill. *v.2 p.243*

Charles Darwin: A New Life. *v.3 p.48*

Charles Darwin: The Power of Place. *v.3 p.48*

Charles Darwin: Voyaging. *v.3 p.48*

Charles Darwin's Zoology Notes and Specimen Lists from H.
    M. S. Beagle. *v.5 p.231*

Charles Dickens: A Critical Study. *v.2 p.284*

Charles Dickens, a Pictorial Biography. *v.2 p.285*

Charles Dickens A to Z: The Essential Reference to His Life
    and Work. *v.2 p.282*

Charles Dickens and His Publishers. .*v.3 p.120, v.6 p.741, p.742*

Charles Dickens' Book of Memoranda: A Photographic and
    Typographic Facsimile of the Notebook Begun in January
    1855. . . . .*v.2 p.284*

Charles Dickens, His Tragedy and Triumph. . .*v.2 p.284, p.285*

Charles Dickens in Cyberspace: The Afterlife of the Nineteenth
    Century in Postmodern Culture. *v.2 p.282, v.6 p.752*

Charles Dickens. *v.2 p.285*

Charles d'Orleans. *v.2 p.469*

Charles d'Orléans poésies. *v.2 p.468*

Charles E. Ives: Memos. *v.1 p.217, p.333*

Charles Eliot, Landscape Architect. *v.1 p.816*

Charles Evans Hughes and American Democratic
    Statesmanship. *v.3 p.461*

Charles Francis Adams, 1807-1886. . . . . .*v.3 p.424, p.425*

Charles Francis Adams 1835-1915: An Autobiography. *v.3 p.433*

Charles G. Finney and the Spirit of American
    Evangelicalism. *v.1 p.584*

Charles Gleyre, 1806-1874: Biography and Catalogue
    Raisonné. *v.1 p.740*

Charles I of Anjou: Power, Kingship and State-Making in
    Thirteenth-Century Europe. *v.3 p.198*

Charles Ives and His World. *v.1 p.210, p.333*

Charles Ives: Guide to Research. *v.1 p.164, p.223, p.333*

Charles Ives Remembered: An Oral History. . .*v.1 p.221, p.333*

Charles Lamb and the Theatre. *v.2 p.298*

Charles Lamb: Prose and Poetry. *v.2 p.298*

Charles Lamb: Selected Writings. *v.2 p.298*

Charles Lamb: The Evolution of Elia. *v.2 p.298*

Charles Lamb. v.2 p.298

Charles Laughton, a Difficult Actor. v.6 p.418

Charles Olson's Reading: A Biography. v.2 p.108

Charles Rennie Mackintosh. v.1 p.792

Charles S. Peirce: Selected Writings. v.1 p.441

Charles Sanders Peirce: A Life. v.1 p.440

Charles Simic: Selected Early Poems. v.2 p.155

Charles Stewart Parnell. v.3 p.135, p.136

Charles Sumner and the Coming of the Civil
War. v.3 p.422, p.423, p.428

Charles Sumner and the Rights of Man. .v.3 p.422, p.423, p.428

Charles T. Griffes: A Life in Music. . . .v.1 p.208, p.327, p.328

Charles T. Griffes: The Life of an American Composer. .v.6 p.409

Charles the First and the Popish Plot. v.3 p.102, p.120

Charles W. Chesnutt and the Fictions of Race. v.2 p.32

Charlie Chan at the Movies: History, Filmography, and
Criticism. v.6 p.330

Charlie Chan Is Dead: At Home in the World an Anthology of
Contemporary Asian American Fiction. v.6 p.91

Charlie Parker and Thematic Improvisation. . .v.1 p.261, p.346

The Charlie Parker Companion: Six Decades of
Commentary. v.1 p.265, p.346, p.347

Charlie Parker: His Music and Life. . . .v.1 p.264, p.265, p.346

Charlotte and Emily Bronte: Literary Lives. v.2 p.271

Charlotte Bronte and Victorian Psychology. v.2 p.271

Charlotte Bronte: The Novels. v.2 p.270

Charlotte Brontë's Jane Eyre: A Casebook. v.2 p.271

Charlotte Perriand: An Art of Living. v.1 p.802

Charlotte Smith. v.2 p.260

Charlotte Temple. v.2 p.30

The Charm of Physics. v.5 p.552

A Charmed Life. v.2 p.99

Charon's Ferry: Fifty Poems. v.2 p.786

Charred Lullabies: Chapters in an Anthropography of
Violence. v.6 p.153

Charter of the New Urbanism. v.1 p.797

☐ Charter of the United Nations and Statute of the International
Court of Justice. v.4 p.635

Charter of the United Nations: Report to the President on the
Results of the San Francisco Conference. v.4 p.635

The Charter School Challenge: Avoiding the Pitfalls, Fulfilling
the Promise. v.4 p.280

Charter Schools: Another Flawed Educational Reform? .v.4 p.281

Chartered Schools: Two Hundred Years of Independent
Academies in United States, 1727-1925. . . . . .v.4 p.296

The Charterhouse of Parma. v.2 p.502

The Chartists: Popular Politics in the Industrial
Revolution. v.3 p.116, p.123

Chasidic Dance. v.1 p.16

Chasing Hubble's Shadows: The Search for Galaxies at the
Edge of Time. v.5 p.71

The Chastening: Inside the Crisis That Rocked the Global
Financial System and Humbled the IMF. v.4 p.99

Chateaubriand: "Atala" and "Rene". v.2 p.488

Chateaubriand: The Longed-for Tempests, 1768-93, Vol.
1. .v.2 p.488

Chateaubriand. v.2 p.488

The Chatham House Version: And Other Middle Eastern
Studies. v.4 p.614

Chaucer: An Introduction. v.2 p.209

Chaucer: An Oxford Guide. v.2 p.209

Chaucer and Boccaccio: Antiquity and
Modernity. v.2 p.209, p.702

Chaucer and His World. v.2 p.207

Chaucer and Medieval Estates Satire: The Literature of Social
Classes and the General Prologue to the Canterbury
Tales. v.2 p.210

Chaucer and the Canterbury Tales: A Short Introduction. .v.2 p.209

Chaucer and the Fictions of Gender. v.2 p.209

Chaucer and the French Tradition: A Study in Style and
Meaning. v.2 p.210

Chaucer and the Imagery of Narrative: The First Five
Canterbury Tales. v.2 p.209

Chaucer and the Late Medieval World. v.6 p.564

Chaucer and the Subject of History. v.2 p.210

Chaucer, Boccaccio and the Debate of Love: A Comparative
Study of the Decameron and the Canterbury Tales. .v.2 p.210

Chaucer Criticism: An Anthology,. v.2 p.210

A Chaucer Glossary. v.2 p.209

Chaucer: His Life, His Works, His World. v.2 p.209

Chaucer: The Canterbury Tales. v.2 p.209

Chaucer to Shakespeare, 1337-1580. . . . . . . .v.2 p.169

Chaucerian Polity: Absolutist Lineages and Associational Forms
in England and Italy. v.2 p.210, p.211

Chaucer's Drama of Style: Poetic Variety and Contrast in the
Canterbury Tales. v.2 p.207

Chaucer's Knight: The Portrait of a Medieval
Mercenary. v.2 p.209

Chaucer's Sexual Poetics. v.2 p.209

Chaucer's Troilus and Criseyde. v.2 p.207

Chaucer's Women: Nuns, Wives and Amazons. v.2 p.210

Chaucer. v.2 p.207

The Chautauqua Moment: Protestants, Progressives, and the
Culture of Modern Liberalism, 1874-1920. . . . .v.4 p.721

Chauvet Cave: The Art of Earliest Times. . .v.1 p.668, v.4 p.16

Chavin and the Origins of Andean Civilization. v.4 p.11

Chavin: And the Origins of the Andean Civilization. . .v.3 p.260

☐ CHC Digital: Online Resources for Cuban and
Cuban-American Studies from the Cuban Heritage
Collection. v.6 p.485

☐ CHEA web site. v.4 p.289

Cheap Bibles: Nineteenth-Century Publishing and the British
and Foreign Bible Society. . . .v.3 p.37, v.6 p.741, p.759

Cheap Print and Popular Piety, 1550-1640. .v.3 p.102, p.122, p.130

Cheap Rooms and Restless Hearts: A Study of Formula in the
Urban Tales of William Sydney Porter. v.2 p.50

The Cheapest Nights. v.6 p.660

Chechnya: Life in a War-Torn Society. v.3 p.229

Checklist of CITES Species: A Reference to the Appendices to the Convention on International Trade in Endangered Species of Wild Fauna and Flora. *v.5 p.224*

A Checklist of Painters from c.1200. . . . .*v.1 p.725*

Checklist of Writings on American Music, 1640-1992, Vols. 1-3. . . . . *v.1 p.168, p.278*

Cheerleader!: An American Icon. *v.4 p.847*

The Cheers and the Tears: A Healthy Alternative to the Dark Side of Youth Sports Today. *v.4 p.818, p.840*

The Cheese and the Worms: The Cosmos of a Sixteenth-Century Miller. *v.1 p.610, v.3 p.200, p.201*

☐ Chem Soc Timeline. *v.5 p.262*

☐ Chem Tutor. *v.5 p.266*

☐ ChemACX Pro. *v.5 p.317*

☐ ChemCats (STN or SciFinder/SciFinder Scholar). .*v.5 p.317*

☐ Chemcyclopedia. *v.5 p.317*

☐ ChemExper.com. *v.5 p.317*

☐ ChemFinder.com Database & Internet Searching. . .*v.5 p.258*

Chemical Abstracts Service Source Index (CASSI). . .*v.5 p.256*

Chemical Abstracts. *v.5 p.256*

Chemical Achievers: The Human Face of the Chemical Sciences. *v.5 p.260*

Chemical Analysis in Complex Matrices. *v.5 p.268, p.269*

Chemical Analysis in the Laboratory: A Basic Guide. .*v.5 p.268*

Chemical Analysis: Modern Instrumental Methods and Techniques. *v.5 p.268*

☐ Chemical and Engineering News Safety Letters (1993+). *v.5 p.265*

Chemical and Functional Properties of Food Components. *v.5 p.329*

Chemical Applications of Group Theory. *v.5 p.548*

The Chemical Bond: Structure and Dynamics. .*v.5 p.282, p.283*

Chemical Concepts in Pollutant Behavior. . . .*v.5 p.363, p.375*

Chemical Creativity: Ideas from the Work of Woodward, Hückel, Meerwein, and Others. *v.5 p.262*

☐ Chemical Education--Web Guide (Stanford University). *v.5 p.266*

Chemical Elements and Their Compounds. *v.5 p.301*

Chemical Engineering Data Sources. *v.5 p.741*

Chemical Engineering: Design. *v.5 p.318, p.741*

Chemical Engineering: Fluid Flow, Heat Transfer and Mass Transfer. *v.5 p.318*

Chemical Engineering Process Design and Economics : A Practical Guide. *v.5 p.743*

Chemical Engineering: Solutions to the Problems in Chemical Engineering. *v.5 p.318*

Chemical Engineering, Vol. 3. . . . .*v.5 p.741*

Chemical engineering, Vol. 4, Solutions to the problems in Chemical engineering, vol. 1. . . . .*v.5 p.741*

Chemical Engineers' Portable Handbook. *v.5 p.741*

Chemical Equilibria and Kinetics in Soils. *v.5 p.51*

Chemical Evolution: Origins of the Elements, Molecules, and Living Systems. *v.5 p.263*

The Chemical Formulary. *v.5 p.407*

Chemical Genomics. *v.5 p.139, p.147*

A Chemical History Tour: Picturing Chemistry from Alchemy to Modern Molecular Science. *v.5 p.262, p.263*

The Chemical Industry at the Millenium: Maturity, Restructuring and Globalization. *v.4 p.157*

Chemical Information: A Practical Guide to Utilization. .*v.5 p.256*

Chemical Information Manual. *v.5 p.312*

Chemical Information Sources. *v.5 p.256*

☐ Chemical Information System. *v.5 p.315*

Chemical Kinetics and Catalysis. *v.5 p.279*

Chemical Kinetics and Mechanism. *v.5 p.279*

Chemical Kinetics and Process Dynamics in Aquatic Systems. *v.5 p.378*

Chemical Kinetics and Transport. *v.5 p.279*

☐ Chemical Laboratory Safety (Stanford University). *v.5 p.265*

Chemical Manufacturers Directory of Trade Name Products. *v.5 p.317*

Chemical Metallurgy: Principles and Practice. *v.5 p.732*

Chemical Micro Process Engineering: Fundamentals, Modelling and Reactions. *v.5 p.743*

Chemical Misconceptions: Prevention, Diagnosis and Cure. *v.5 p.264, p.265*

Chemical Modeling: From Atoms to Liquids. *v.5 p.277*

Chemical Periodicity. *v.5 p.304*

The Chemical Philosophy. *v.3 p.46*

Chemical Process: Design and Integration. *v.5 p.743*

Chemical Process Equipment: Selection and Design. *v.5 p.742, p.743*

Chemical Process Safety: Fundamentals with Applications. *v.5 p.681, p.682*

Chemical Processes in Soils. *v.5 p.51*

Chemical Property Estimation: Theory and Application. *v.5 p.280, p.281*

Chemical Publications. *v.5 p.255*

Chemical Safety in the Laboratory. *v.5 p.266*

Chemical Safety Matters: Safe Use and Disposal of Chemicals in Laboratories. *v.5 p.314*

☐ Chemical Safety--Web Guide (Stanford University). *v.5 p.265*

Chemical Sciences in the Modern World. *v.5 p.263*

Chemical Separations: Principles, Techniques and Experiments. *v.5 p.274*

Chemical Technicians' Ready Reference Handbook. . .*v.5 p.259*

Chemical Thermodynamics. *v.5 p.278*

☐ Chemical Week buyer's guide. *v.5 p.317*

Chemicals in the Human Food Chain. *v.5 p.310*

☐ ChemiCool Periodic Table. *v.5 p.259*

☐ ChemIDplus. *v.5 p.259*

☐ Chemie.de Information Service. *v.5 p.320*

Le chemin de longue étude. *v.2 p.469*

Chemin d'Europe. *v.2 p.543*

☐ ChemIndustry.com. *v.5 p.317, p.320*

☐ CHEMINFO, Chemical Information Sources from Indiana University. *v.5 p.255*

Chemisches Zentralblatt. *v.5 p.256*

Chemistry, 1901-1995 [electronic resource]. *v.5 p.260*

Chemistry: An Industry-Based Introduction with CD-ROM. *v.5 p.267*

Chemistry and Ecotoxicology of Pollution: Environmental Science and Technology. *v.5 p.705*

☐ Chemistry and Environmental Dictionary. *v.5 p.310*

Chemistry and the Chemical Industry: A Practical Guide for Non-Chemists. *v.5 p.317*

Chemistry and the Human Genome. . . .*v.5 p.140, p.141, p.328*

Chemistry at the Beginning of the Third Millennium: Molecular Design, Supramolecules, Nanotechnology and Beyond. *v.5 p.265*

Chemistry Connections: The Chemical Basis of Everyday Phenomena. *v.5 p.264*

Chemistry for Environmental Engineering. *v.5 p.310*

Chemistry, Health and Environment. *v.5 p.315*

☐ Chemistry Hypermedia Project--Analytical Chemistry Cross-Index. *v.5 p.267*

☐ Chemistry Hypermedia Project--Encyclopedia of Analytical Instrumentation. *v.5 p.268*

☐ Chemistry Hypermedia Project--General Chemistry Cross-Index. *v.5 p.256*

☐ Chemistry Index. *v.5 p.255*

The Chemistry Maths Book. *v.5 p.267*

Chemistry of Advanced Materials: An Overview. .*v.5 p.318, p.319*

Chemistry of Carbon Compounds: a Modern Comprehensive Treatise, Various Vols., 1951-1989. . . . .*v.5 p.292*

The Chemistry of Fireworks. *v.5 p.320*

The Chemistry of Fragrances. *v.5 p.319*

Chemistry of Hypervalent Compounds. *v.5 p.308*

Chemistry of Iron. *v.5 p.309*

Chemistry of Marine Water and Sediments. *v.5 p.429*

The Chemistry of Nanomaterials: Synthesis, Properties and Applications. *v.5 p.319*

Chemistry of Non-Stoichiometric Compounds. *v.5 p.304*

Chemistry of Organic Flourine Compounds. *v.5 p.296*

Chemistry of Organic Fluorine Compounds II: A Critical Review. *v.5 p.296*

Chemistry of Particles, Fogs and Rains. *v.5 p.363*

The Chemistry of Soil Analysis. *v.5 p.51*

The Chemistry of Soils. *v.5 p.51*

The Chemistry of the Actinide Elements, Vol. 2. . .*v.5 p.308*

The Chemistry of the Actinide Elements, Vol. I. . .*v.5 p.308*

Chemistry of the Elements. *v.5 p.303*

The Chemistry of the Fullerenes. *v.5 p.306*

Chemistry of the Solid-Water Interface: Processes at the Mineral-Water and Particle-Water Interface in Natural Systems. *v.5 p.313*

☐ Chemistry Resources on the Internet. *v.5 p.255*

Chemistry Today and Tomorrow: The Central, Useful, and Creative Science. *v.5 p.264*

☐ Chemistry.org. *v.5 p.259*

Chemistry. *v.5 p.264*

The Chemist's Companion: A Handbook of Practical Data, Techniques, and References. *v.5 p.259*

Chemist's Electronic Book of Orbitals. *v.5 p.279*

The Chemist's Ready Reference Handbook. *v.5 p.259*

Chemometrics: A Practical Guide. *v.5 p.273, p.274*

Chemometrics: Statistics and Computer Applications in Analytical Chemistry. *v.5 p.274*

Chemoton Theory: Theory of Living Systems. *v.5 p.248*

✦ ChemPrep [Electronic Resource]. *v.5 p.288*

ChemReact41/InfoChem: Reaction Database/Reaction Display File. *v.5 p.288*

☐ Chemsoc: The RSC's Chemical Science Network. .*v.5 p.260*

☐ ChemSpy.com. *v.5 p.321*

Chen Duxiu, Founder of the Chinese Communist Party. *v.6 p.192, p.200*

Chen Village under Mao and Deng: The Recent History of a Peasant Community in Mao's China. . .*v.4 p.701, v.6 p.193*

Le chercheur d'or. *v.2 p.531*

Cherishing Men from Afar: Qing Guest Ritual and the Macartney Embassy of 1793. . . . .*v.6 p.204*

Chernobyl: Catastrophe, Consequences and Solutions. .*v.5 p.364*

The Cherokee Cases: Two Landmark Federal Decisions in the Fight for Sovereignty. *v.4 p.465*

Cherokee Dance and Drama. *v.1 p.15*

Chesapeake Invader: Discovering America's Giant Meteorite Crater. *v.5 p.441*

Chester Himes: A Life. *v.2 p.86*

Chester Himes. *v.2 p.86*

The Chester Mystery Cycle: A Casebook. *v.2 p.185*

The Chevalier Noverre: Father of Modern Ballet, a Biography. *v.1 p.10*

Cheyenne Way: Conflict and Case Law in Primitive Jurisprudence. *v.6 p.691, p.692, p.703*

Chéri. *v.2 p.514*

The Chiapas Rebellion: The Struggle for Land and Democracy. *v.4 p.711*

Chibaro: African Mine Labour in Southern Rhodesia 1900-1933. . . . .*v.6 p.77*

Chicago '68. . . . .*v.3 p.515*

☐ Chicago Board of Trade. *v.4 p.93, p.101, p.102*

Chicago: City on the Make. *v.3 p.515*

Chicago Divided: The Making of a Black Mayor. *v.3 p.515, p.516*

Chicago: Growth of a Metropolis. *v.3 p.516*

The Chicago Guide to Writing about Multivariate Analysis. *v.5 p.681*

The Chicago Guide to Writing about Numbers. *v.4 p.173, p.179, v.5 p.681*

The Chicago Homer. *v.2 p.414*

Chicago: Race, Class, and the Response to Urban Decline. *v.4 p.544*

The Chicago Renaissance in American Letters: A Critical History. *v.2 p.14, p.15*

La Chicana and the Intersection of Race, Class and Gender. *v.6 p.546*

Chicana Creativity and Criticism: New Frontiers in American Literature. *v.6 p.499, p.513*

Chicana Critical Issues. *v.6 p.497, p.511, p.545*

Chicana Feminisms: A Critical Reader. *v.6 p.546*

Chicana Feminist Thought: The Basic Historical
    Writings. *v.6 p.427, p.486, p.546*
The Chicana Feminist. *v.6 p.546*
Chicana Lesbians: The Girls Our Mothers Warned Us
    About. *v.6 p.547*
Chicana Literary and Artistic Expressions: Culture and Society
    in Dialogue. *v.6 p.499, p.512*
Chicana Lives and Criminal Justice: Voices from el
    Barrio. *v.6 p.469*
La Chicana: The Mexican-American Woman. *v.6 p.546*
Chicana Traditions: Continuity and Change. . .*v.6 p.433, p.546*
Chicana Voices: Intersections of Class, Race, and
    Gender. *v.6 p.546*
Chicana Ways: Conversations with Ten Chicana
    Writers. *v.6 p.500, p.513*
Chicana/o Cultural Studies Reader. *v.6 p.486, p.491*
Chicanas - Chicanos at the Crossroads: Social, Economic, and
    Political Change. *v.6 p.521*
Chicanas - Latinas in American Theatre: A History of
    Performance. *v.1 p.122, p.125*
Chicanas and Chicanos in School: Racial Profiling, Identity
    Battles, and Empowerment. *v.4 p.301*
Chicanas and Latin American Women Writers Exploring the
    Realm of the Kitchen as a Self-Empowering Site. *v.2 p.663*
Chicano: A Novel. *v.6 p.504*
Chicano Art Digital Image Collection. *v.6 p.492*
Chicano Art for Our Millennium: Collected Works from the
    Arizona State University Community. *v.6 p.492*
Chicano Art Inside/Outside the Master's House: Cultural Politics
    and the CARA Exhibition. *v.6 p.492*
Chicano Art: Resistance and Affirmation, 1965-1985. *v.6 p.492*
Chicano Controversy: Oscar Acosta and Richard
    Rodriguez. *v.6 p.499, p.512*
Chicano Detective Fiction: A Critical Study of Five
    Novelists. *v.6 p.503, p.516*
Chicano Discourse: Socio-Historic Perspectives. . . .*v.6 p.494*
Chicano Drama: Performance, Society and Myth. *v.6 p.513, p.517*
Chicano Education in the Era of Segregation. *v.6 p.527*
Chicano English in Context. *v.6 p.494*
Chicano Ethnicity. *v.6 p.544*
The Chicano Experience: An Alternative Perspective. *v.6 p.522*
The Chicano Experience in the Northwest. *v.6 p.521*
Chicano Folklore: A Guide to the Folktales, Traditions, Rituals
    and Religious Practices of Mexican Americans. . *v.6 p.523*
Chicano Literature: A Reference Guide. *v.6 p.501, p.514*
A Chicano Manual on How to Handle Gringos. . . .*v.6 p.540*
Chicano Narrative: The Dialectics of Difference. *v.6 p.503, p.515*
Chicano Poetry: A Response to
    Chaos. *v.6 p.497, p.509, p.510, p.511*
Chicano Politics and Society in the Late Twentieth
    Century. *v.6 p.538*
Chicano Politics: Reality and Promise, 1940-1990. .*v.6 p.538*
Chicano Popular Culture: Que Hable el Pueblo. *v.6 p.491, p.494*
Chicano Psychology. *v.6 p.541*
The Chicano Renaissance: Contemporary Cultural
    Trends. *v.6 p.491*

Chicano Research Collection. *v.6 p.486, p.520*
Chicano Satire: A Study in Literary Culture. . *v.6 p.499, p.512*
Chicano School Failure and Success: Past, Present, and
    Future. *v.4 p.311, v.6 p.528*
Chicano Sketches: Short Stories. *v.6 p.503*
The Chicano Studies Reader: An Anthology of Aztlan
    1970-2000. . . . .*v.6 p.487*
Chicano!: The History of the Mexican American Civil Rights
    Movement. *v.6 p.541*
Chicano Timespace: The Poetry and Politics of Ricardo
    Sanchez. *v.6 p.501, p.514*
Chicano Visions: American Painters on the Verge. . . *v.6 p.492*
Chicano Workers and the Politics of Fairness: The FEPC in the
    Southwest, 1941-1945. . . . .*v.6 p.525*
Chicano Writers. *v.6 p.501, p.514*
Chicano/Latino Homoerotic Identities. . *v.6 p.498, p.506, p.512*
Chicanos and Film: Essays on Chicano Representation and
    Resistance. *v.6 p.493*
The Chicanos: As We See Ourselves. *v.6 p.545*
Chicanos in a Changing Society: From Mexican Pueblos to
    American Barrios in Santa Barbara and Southern California,
    1848-1930. . . . .*v.6 p.530, p.548*
Chickencoop Chinaman and Year of the Dragon: Two
    Plays. *v.6 p.98*
Chief Contemporary Dramatists, Second Series: Eighteen Plays
    from the Recent Drama of England, Ireland, America,
    France, Germany, Austria, Italy, Spain, Russia, and
    Scandinavia. *v.1 p.64, p.79, p.82, p.96, p.113*
Chief Contemporary Dramatists: Twenty-Two Plays from the
    Recent Drama of England, Ireland, America,
    Germany, France, Belgium, Norway, Sweden and
    Russia. *v.1 p.64, p.79, p.82, p.95, p.113*
Chief Contemporary
    Dramatists. *v.1 p.64, p.79, p.82, p.95, p.96, p.113*
The Chief European Dramatists: Twenty-One Plays from the
    Drama of Greece, Rome, Spain, France, Italy,
    Germany, Denmark, and Norway from 500 B. C. to 1879 A.
    D. *v.1 p.68, p.97*
The Chief Governors: The Rise and Fall of Reform Government
    in Tudor Ireland 1536-1588. . . . .*v.3 p.136*
Chief Justice: Leadership and the Supreme Court. . . *v.4 p.540*
A Chief Justice's Progress: John Marshall from Revolutionary
    Virginia to the Supreme Court. *v.4 p.538*
The Chief Justiceship of Melville W. Fuller, 1888-1910. *v.4 p.467*
Chief Justiceship of Warren Burger, 1969-1986: A Provocative
    Interpretation of the Burger Court. . *v.4 p.468, p.537, p.538*
Chief of Staff: Lyndon Johnson and His Presidency. . *v.4 p.528*
Chief Plays. *v.1 p.63, p.78, p.105,v.2 p.473*
Chief Sources of English Legal History. *v.4 p.433*
The Chief: The Life of William Randolph Hearst. *v.4 p.149, p.411*
Chiefs Know Their Boundaries: Essays on Property, Power, and
    the Past in Asante, 1896-1996. . . . .*v.6 p.69*
Chiefship and Cosmology: An Historical Study of Political
    Competition. *v.6 p.63*
Chihuly Projects. *v.1 p.810*
Chihuly. *v.1 p.802, p.810*
Chikamatsu: Five Late Plays. *v.6 p.234*
The Child and Adolescent Athlete. . .*v.4 p.828, p.874, p.878*

The Child and Society. *v.4 p.735*

The Child and the Curriculum and the School and
Society. *v.4 p.356*

Child by Child: The Comer Process for Change in
Education. *v.4 p.280*

Child Care and the Growth of Love. *v.4 p.735*

Child Development and Education: A Piagetian
Perspective. *v.4 p.342*

☐ Child Development Institute, University of North
Carolina. *v.5 p.571*

Child Language. *v.4 p.356*

Child Neurology. *v.5 p.516*

Child of All Nations. *v.6 p.178*

The Child of Exile: A Poetry Memoir. . .*v.6 p.506, p.507, p.510*

The Child of Pleasure. *v.2 p.716*

Child of the Dark: The Diary of Carolina Maria de
Jesus. *v.3 p.278, p.283, p.336,v.6 p.29*

Child of War, Woman of Peace. *v.6 p.93, 140*

A Child on Her Mind: The Experience of Becoming a
Mother. *v.5 p.640*

Child Rearing in America: Challenges Facing Parents with
Young Children. *v.5 p.641*

The Child, the State and the Victorian Novel. . *v.2 p.174, p.190*

Child Welfare: Major Themes in Health and Social
Welfare. *v.4 p.757*

A Child Went Forth: Reflective Teaching with Young Readers
and Writers. *v.4 p.360*

Child Witnesses: Fragile Voices in the American Legal
System. *v.4 p.473*

Childe Hassam, American Impressionist. *v.1 p.749*

Childe Hassam: Impressionist in the West. *v.1 p.736*

Childe Hassam, Impressionist. *v.1 p.734*

Childhood and Adolescence: Cross-Cultural Perspectives and
Applications. *v.5 p.626*

Childhood and Society. *v.4 p.735, v.5 p.513, p.658*

The Childhood and Youth of Charles Dickens. . . .*v.2 p.285*

Childhood, Culture, and Class in Britain: Margaret McMillan,
1860-1931. . . . .*v.4 p.346*

Childhood in Contemporary Cultures. *v.4 p.735*

Childhood in the Promised Land: Working-Class Movements
and the Colonies de Vacances in France, 1880-1960. *v.4 p.711*

Childhood Stress in Contemporary Society. *v.5 p.627*

Childhood's End. *v.2 p.337*

Children above One Hundred Eighty IQ Stanford-Binet: Origins
and Development. *v.5 p.575*

Children and Grief: When a Parent Dies. *v.5 p.629*

Children and Youth in Sport. *v.4 p.824, p.840*

Children Are Civilians Too. *v.2 p.604*

Children, Cinema and Censorship: From Dracula to Dead
End. *v.6 p.312*

Children Communicating: The First Five Years (& a Little Bit
Beyond...). *v.5 p.627*

Children Exploring Their World: Theme Teaching in Elementary
School. *v.5 p.229, p.246*

Children in Changing Families: Life after Parental
Seperation. *v.4 p.740*

Children in Exile: Poems 1968-1984. . . . .*v.2 p.344*

Children in Foster Care: A Longitudinal Investigation. *v.4 p.756*

The Children of Abraham: Judaism, Christianity, Islam. *v.1 p.547*

Children of Alcoholism. *v.5 p.664*

The Children of Athena: Athenian Ideas about Citizenship and
the Division Between the Sexes. *v.3 p.14*

Children of Bondage: A Social History of the Slave Society at
the Cape of Good Hope, 1652-1838. . . . . .*v.6 p.79*

Children of Colonial Despotism: Press, Politics and Culture in
Cuba 1790-1840. . . . .*v.3 p.310*

Children of Global Migration: Transnational Families and
Gender Woes. *v.6 p.116, p.119, p.129, p.130*

Children of Global Migration: Transnational Families and
Gendered Woes. *v.4 p.44, v.6 p.110, p.113, p.129*

Children of God's Fire: A Documentary History of Black
Slavery in Brazil. *v.3 p.278, p.335, p.336*

The Children of NAFTA: Labor Wars on the U. S.-Mexico
Border. *v.4 p.726*

Children of Sanchez. *v.4 p.733*

Children of the Alley: A Novel. *v.6 p.662*

Children of the Dragonfly: Native American Voices on Child
Custody and Education. *v.4 p.755, v.6 p.680*

The Children of the Dream. *v.4 p.735*

Children of the Enemy: Oral Histories of Vietnamese
Amerasians and Their Mothers. *v.6 p.93, p.140*

Children of the Father King: Youth, Authority, and Legal
Minority in Colonial Lima. *v.3 p.326*

Children of the Mire: Modern Poetry from Romanticism to the
Avant-Garde. *v.2 p.669*

Children of the New World: A Novel of the Algerian
War. *v.2 p.544, p.545*

Children of the Night: The Best Short Stories by Black Writers,
1967 to the Present. *v.2 p.26*

Children of the Night: The Six Archetypal Characters of Classic
Horror Films. *v.6 p.319*

Children of the Revolution: A Yankee Teacher in the Cuban
Schools. *v.4 p.335*

Children of the Storm: Black Children and American Child
Welfare. *v.4 p.755*

The Children of the Sun: Mexican-Americans in the Literature
of the United States. *v.6 p.503, p.515*

Children of the Waters. *v.6 p.663*

Children of the Western Plains: The Nineteenth-Century
Experience. *v.3 p.521*

Children on the Streets of the Americas: Globalization,
Homelessness Education in Brazil, Cuba and the United
States. *v.4 p.335*

Children, School, and Society in Nineteenth-Century
England. *v.4 p.334*

Children Who Murder: A Psychological Perspective. . *v.5 p.592*

Children with Special Needs: Lessons for Early Childhood
Professionals. *v.4 p.316*

Children with Specific Language Impairment. . *v.5 p.665, p.673*

Children's Exercise Physiology, Vol. 2. . . . .*v.4 p.875*

Children's Films: History, Ideology, Pedagogy, Theory. *v.6 p.312*

Children's Friendships: The Beginnings of
Intimacy. *v.5 p.626, p.631*

The Children's Hour. *v.6 p.411*

ⓔ Children's Inquiry: Using Language to Make Sense of the
    World. *v.4 p.423*

Children's Interpersonal Trust: Sensitivity to Lying, Deception
    and Promise Violations. *v.5 p.628, p.631*

Children's Lifeworlds: Gender, Welfare and Labour in the
    Developing World. *v.4 p.40*

Children's Literature in Canada. *v.2 p.731*

Children's Literature in Hitler's Germany: The Cultural Policy
    of National Socialism. *v.3 p.172*

Children's Literature in the Elementary School with
    Litlinks. *v.4 p.364*

ⓔ Children's Literature of the Harlem Renaissance. . *v.6 p.28*

Children's Mathematics: Cognitively Guided
    Instruction. *v.5 p.462*

Children's Minds, Talking Rabbits and Clockwork: Changes -
    Essays on Education. *v.4 p.339*

Children's Minds. *v.4 p.356*

Children's Peer Relations and Social Competence: A Century of
    Progress. *v.5 p.627, p.631*

Children's Play: The Roots of Reading. *v.4 p.304, p.354, p.359*

Children's Psychological Testing: A Guide for
    Nonpsychologists. *v.5 p.603*

Children's Reading Comprehension and Assessment. *v.4 p.365*

Children's Rights: Caribbean Realities. *v.4 p.755*

A Child's Christmas in Wales: And Five Poems. . .*v.2 p.386*

The Child's Conception of Geometry. *v.4 p.358*

The Child's Conception of Language. *v.5 p.624*

The Child's Conception of Number. *v.5 p.628, p.630*

The Child's Conception of Physical Causality. *v.5 p.628, p.630*

Child's Conception of Space, Vol. 1. . . . . .*v.5 p.628, p.630*

The Child's Conception of the World: A 20th-Century Classic of
    Child Psychology. *v.5 p.628, p.630*

Child's Play. *v.5 p.627*

Child's Talk: Learning to Use Language. *v.5 p.622*

Chile - The Other September 11: An Anthology of Reflections
    on the 1973 Coup. *v.3 p.351, p.352*

Chile and the United States: Empires in Conflict. . . .*v.3 p.392*

Chile and the War of the Pacific. *v.3 p.277, p.355*

Chile from Within, 1973-1988. . . . .*v.3 p.353*

Chile in the Nitrate Era: The Evolution of Economic
    Dependence, 1880-1930. . . . .*v.3 p.351*

Chile, Peru and the California Gold Rush of Eighteen
    Forty-Nine. *v.3 p.327, p.328, p.351*

Chile: Prospects for Democracy. *v.3 p.353*

Chile since Independence. *v.3 p.350*

Chile: The Legacy of Hispanic Capitalism. *v.3 p.350*

Chilean Politics, 1920-1931: The Honorable Mission of the
    Armed Forces. *v.3 p.276*

The Chilean Press During the Allende Years,
    1970-1973. . . . .*v.3 p.354*

Chilean Theater, 1973-1985: Marginality, Power,
    Selfhood. *v.3 p.352*

Chile's Days of Terror: Eyewitness Accounts of the Military
    Coup. *v.3 p.356*

Chile. *v.3 p.350*

Chilies to Chocolate: Foods the Americas Gave the
    World. *v.3 p.271*

Chimalpahin and the Kingdoms of Chalco. *v.3 p.287*

Chimayo Weaving: The Transformation of a
    Tradition. *v.6 p.489, p.492, p.523*

Chimeras. *v.2 p.492*

Les Chimeres. *v.2 p.492*

The Chimney of the World: A History of Smoke Pollution in
    Victorian and Edwardian Manchester. *v.6 p.289, p.296*

Chimpanzee Cultures. *v.5 p.616*

Ch'in and Han Empires, 221 BC-AD 220, Vol. 1. . . .*v.6 p.184*

China, 1898-1912: The Xinzheng Revolution and Japan.*v.6 p.188*

China: A Journey into Its Musical Art. *v.1 p.290*

ⓔ China: A Macro History. *v.6 p.183*

China: A New History. *v.3 p.388, v.6 p.183*

China: A Short Cultural History. *v.6 p.183*

China among Equals: The Middle Kingdom and Its Neighbors,
    10th-14th Centuries. *v.6 p.204*

China and Charles Darwin. *v.6 p.191*

China and Christianity: The Missionary Movement and the
    Growth of Chinese Anti-Foreignism,
    1860-1870. . . . .*v.6 p.188, p.203, p.218*

China and Democracy: Reconsidering Prospects for a
    Democratic China. *v.4 p.621*

China and Japan in the Global Setting. *v.6 p.181*

China and the Origins of the Pacific War,
    1931-1941. . . . .*v.6 p.193, p.204*

China and the Search for Happiness: Recurring Themes in Four
    Thousand Years of Chinese Cultural History. . . .*v.6 p.181*

China and the Vietnam Wars, 1950-1975. . . . . . .*v.6 p.169*

China Confidential: American Diplomats and Sino-American
    Relations, 1945-1996. . .*v.3 p.393, v.4 p.561, p.566, p.644*

China Cross Talk: The American Debate over China Policy
    since Normalization, a Reader. *v.3 p.390*

China During the Cultural Revolution, 1966-1976: A Selected
    Bibliography of English Language Works. *v.6 p.195*

China Facts and Figures Annual, Vol. 23. . . . . . .*v.6 p.197*

China, Hong Kong, Taiwan, Inc. *v.6 p.206*

China in Revolution: The First Phase, 1900-1913. . .*v.6 p.189*

China in Revolution: The Yenan Way Revisited. . . .*v.6 p.192*

China in World History. *v.6 p.183*

China, Inc: How the Rise of the Next Superpower Challenges
    America and the World. *v.6 p.196, p.197*

China, Korea and Japan: The Rise of Civilization in East
    Asia. *v.4 p.8, v.6 p.183*

China Marches West: The Qing Conquest of Central
    Eurasia. *v.6 p.239*

The China Mystique: Pearl S. Buck, Anna May Wong, Mayling
    Soong, and the Transformation of American
    Orientalism. *v.6 p.88, p.89, p.90, p.94, p.96, p.97, p.112, p.215*

China off Center: Mapping the Margins of the Middle
    Kingdom. *v.6 p.181, p.196*

China on Screen: Cinema and Nation. *v.6 p.207*

China on the Eve of Communist Takeover. *v.6 p.189*

ⓔ China Reporting: An Oral History of American Journalism in
    the 1930's and 1940's. *v.6 p.215*

China Reporting: An Oral History of American Journalism in
the 1930's and 1940's. *v.6 p.190, p.215, p.216*

China Scapegoat, the Diplomatic Ordeal of John Carter
Vincent. *v.3 p.460*

China Shakes the World. *v.6 p.192, p.214*

China since Tiananmen: The Politics of Transition. . .*v.4 p.619*

The China Station: War and Diplomacy 1830-1860. . . .*v.3 p.76*

China, the United Nations, and Human Rights: The Limits of
Compliance. *v.4 p.513*

China Transformed: Historical Change and the Limits of
European Experience. *v.6 p.182, p.183, p.204*

Chinabound: A Fifty Year Memoir. *v.6 p.201, p.214*

e China. *v.6 p.182*

Chinaman Pacific and Frisco R. R. Co. *v.6 p.99*

A Chinaman's Chance: The Chinese on the Rocky Mountain
Mining Frontier. *v.6 p.115, p.129*

China's Bitter Victory: The War with Japan, 1937-1945..*v.6 p.193*

China's Cultural Heritage: The Qing Dynasty,
1644-1912. . . . .*v.6 p.187*

China's Cultural Revolution, 1966-1969: Not a Dinner
Party. *v.6 p.196*

China's Environmental Crisis: An Inquiry into the Limits of
National Development. *v.6 p.197*

China's Intellectuals: Advise and Dissent. *v.6 p.194*

China's Leadership in the Twenty-first Century: The Rise of the
Fourth Generation. *v.4 p.619*

China's New Nationalism: Pride, Politics, and
Diplomacy. *v.6 p.197, p.204*

China's New Voices: Popular Music, Ethnicity, Gender, and
Politics, 1978-1997. . . . .*v.1 p.288*

China's One-Child Family Policy. *v.4 p.731*

China's Ownership Transformation: Process, Outcomes,
Prospects. *v.4 p.86*

China's Past, China's Future: Energy, Food,
Environment. *v.6 p.195*

China's Peasants: The Anthropology of a Revolution. . .*v.4 p.40*

China's Place in Global Geopolitics: Domestic, Regional and
International Challenges. *v.4 p.400*

China's Political System: Modernization and Tradition..*v.4 p.619*

China's Republican Revolution: The Case of Kwangtung,
1895-1913. . . . .*v.6 p.188, p.189*

China's Response to the West: A Documentary Survey,
1839-1923. . . . .*v.6 p.183, p.187, p.191*

China's Trade Unions and Management. *v.4 p.128*

China's Universities, 1895-1995: A Century of Cultural
Conflict. *v.4 p.334, p.335*

China's Universities and the Open Door. *v.4 p.334*

China's Urban Transition. *v.6 p.723*

China's Western Development: The Role of the State in
Historical and Regional Perspective. *v.4 p.397*

Chinatown Family. *v.6 p.94*

Chinatown Gangs: Extortion, Enterprise, and Ethnicity..*v.6 p.126*

Chinatown: Most Time, Hard Time. *v.6 p.127*

Chinatown, N. Y.: Labor and Politics,
1930-1950. . . . .*v.6 p.116, p.120, p.127*

Chinese American Literature since the 1850s. . .*v.6 p.98, p.128*

Chinese American Transnationalism: The Flow of People,
Resources, and Ideas Between China and America
During the Exclusion Era. *v.6 p.118, p.126*

Chinese American Voices: From the Gold Rush to the
Present. *v.6 p.115, p.128*

Chinese Americans and Their Immigrant Parents: Conflict,
Identity and Values. *v.6 p.110, p.128*

The Chinese Americans. *v.6 p.128*

Chinese Art. *v.1 p.694*

Chinese Capitalists in Japan's New Order: The Occupied Lower
Yangzi, 1937-1945. . . . .*v.6 p.193*

Chinese Characteristics. *v.6 p.187, p.216*

Chinese Christians in America: Conversion, Assimilation and
Adhesive Identities. *v.1 p.608, v.6 p.106, p.128*

The Chinese Classics: With a Translation, Critical and
Exegetical Notes, Prolegomena, and Copious Indexes,
Set. *v.6 p.184, p.208*

The Chinese Conception of the Theatre. .*v.1 p.56, p.131,v.6 p.209*

The Chinese Cultural Revolution Reconsidered: Beyond Purge
and Holocaust. *v.6 p.195*

Chinese Democracy. *v.6 p.194*

Chinese Dialectics: From Yijing to
Marxism. *v.1 p.476, p.508, p.509*

The Chinese Diaspora: Space, Place, Mobility and
Identity. *v.4 p.765, v.6 p.119, p.127*

Chinese Education: Problems, Policies, and Prospects. .*v.4 p.334*

Chinese Elites and Political Change: Zheijang Province in the
Early Twentieth Century. *v.6 p.189, p.206*

The Chinese Emperor. *v.6 p.215*

Chinese Encounters. *v.6 p.197, p.216*

Chinese Femininities/Chinese Masculinities. . .*v.6 p.451, p.453*

Chinese Gentry: Studies on Their Role in 19th-Century Chinese
Society. *v.4 p.701*

Chinese History: A Manual. *v.6 p.182*

The Chinese Journalist: Mediating Information in the World's
Most Populous Country. *v.4 p.403*

The Chinese Language: Fact and Fantasy. *v.6 p.207*

The Chinese Laundryman: A Study of Social Isolation.*v.6 p.128*

Chinese Lineage and Society: Fukien and Kwantung. . .*v.4 p.39*

e Chinese Local Elites and Patterns of Dominance. . .*v.6 p.187*

Chinese Maps: Images of All under Heaven. *v.6 p.182*

Chinese Music and Orchestration: A Primer on Principles and
Practice. *v.1 p.289, p.290*

Chinese Music in the 20th Century. *v.1 p.290*

Chinese Musical Instruments. *v.1 p.288, p.290*

A Chinese Odyssey: The Life and Times of a Chinese
Dissident. *v.6 p.203*

Chinese on the American Frontier. *v.6 p.113, p.126*

Chinese Opera: Images and Stories. *v.1 p.15, p.288*

Chinese Poems. *v.6 p.210*

Chinese Religion: An Anthology of Sources. *v.1 p.539*

Chinese Religion and Society: The Transformation of a
Field. *v.1 p.539*

Chinese Religions. *v.1 p.539*

The Chinese Revolution in Historical Perspective. . . .*v.6 p.183*

Chinese Rhyme-Prose: Poems in the Fu Form from the Han and Six Dynasties Period. *v.6 p.210*

Chinese San Francisco, 1850-1943: A Trans-Pacific Community. *v.6 p.126*

Chinese Sculpture. *v.1 p.777*

Chinese Shadow Theatre. *v.1 p.131, v.6 p.209*

Chinese Society in the Eighteenth Century. . . .*v.6 p.187, p.188*

Chinese Technology in the 17th Century: T'Ien-Kung K'Ai-Wu. *v.6 p.198*

Chinese Theatre and the Actor in Performance. .*v.1 p.132, p.145*

Chinese Theories of Theater and Performance from Confucius to the Present. *v.1 p.56, p.131,v.6 p.209*

Chinese Thought from Confucius to Mao Tse-Tung. . .*v.1 p.475*

A Chinese Village in Early Communist Transition. . .*v.4 p.708*

Chinese Village, Socialist State. *v.6 p.193, p.194*

Chinese Women in a Century of Revolution, 1850-1950. .*v.6 p.454*

Chinese Women Through Chinese Eyes. . . .*v.6 p.199, p.217*

The Chinese. *v.6 p.181, p.196*

Chinese. *v.6 p.207*

Le Chinois vert d'Afrique. *v.2 p.545*

Chinook Jargon: The Hidden Language of the Pacific Northwest. *v.6 p.690*

The Chinua Achebe Encyclopedia. *v.2 p.753*

Chinua Achebe's Things Fall Apart: A Casebook. . .*v.2 p.753*

The Chivalrous Society. *v.4 p.682, v.6 p.556*

Chivalry. *v.6 p.556*

Chiwaya War: Malawians in the First World War. . .*v.6 p.76*

Chloe Plus Olivia: An Anthology of Lesbian Literature from the Seventh Century to the Present. *v.6 p.364, p.406*

Chocolat: A Novel. *v.2 p.351*

The Chocolate Deal. *v.6 p.648*

Choice and Chance: An Introduction to Inductive Logic. .*v.1 p.495*

Choice and Coercion: Birth Control, Sterilization, and Abortion in Public Health and Welfare. *v.4 p.756*

Choice: Current Reviews for College Libraries. . . .*v.5 p.405*

A Choice of Kipling's Verse. *v.2 p.297*

Choice Theory: A New Psychology of Personal Freedom. *v.5 p.647*

Choice, Welfare, and Measurement. *v.4 p.266*

☐ Choices III. *v.4 p.139, p.142*

Choices in Vichy France: The French under Nazi Occupation. *v.3 p.156*

Choices, Values, and Frames. *v.4 p.272*

The Choice. *v.3 p.482*

Chomsky's Universal Grammar: An Introduction. *v.2 p.559, p.560*

Choosing a President: The Electoral College and Beyond. *v.4 p.527*

Choosing an Electoral System: Issues and Alternatives. .*v.4 p.576*

Choosing and Using Statistics: A Biologist's Guide. . .*v.5 p.92*

Choosing Your Battles: American Civil-Military Relations and the Use of Force. *v.4 p.561*

Chopin at the Boundaries: Sex, History, and Musical Genre. *v.1 p.199, p.317, p.379*

Chopin: The Four Ballades. *v.1 p.204, p.242, p.317*

Chopin: The Piano Concertos. *v.1 p.202, p.242, p.317*

Chopin. *v.1 p.203, p.317*

Choral Music: A Research and Information Guide. *v.1 p.169, p.236, p.237, p.396*

Choral Performance: A Guide to Historical Practice. *v.1 p.396, p.402*

Choreographic Politics: State Folk Companies, Representation and Power. *v.1 p.17, p.43*

Choreo-Graphics: A Comparison of Dance Notation Systems from the Fifteenth Century to the Present. *v.1 p.38*

Choreographing History. *v.1 p.41*

Choreography Observed. *v.1 p.38*

Choreophobia: Solo Improvised Dance in the Iranian World. *v.1 p.17*

Choro: A Social History of a Brazilian Popular Music. *v.1 p.292, p.293*

A Chorus Line: The Complete Book of the Musical. *v.1 p.251, p.408*

Chorus of Stones: The Private Life of War. *v.5 p.584*

Chosen Peoples: Sacred Sources of National Identity. *v.1 p.525, v.3 p.62*

The Chosen Species: The Long March of Human Evolution. *v.4 p.15*

Chosen Voices: The Story of the American Cantorate. *v.1 p.300, p.301*

Les choses : une histoire des années soixante. .*v.2 p.532, p.533*

Choshu in the Meiji Restoration. *v.6 p.223*

The Chouans. *v.2 p.485*

Choura: The Memoirs of Alexandra Danilova. *v.1 p.7*

Chretien de Troyes: A Study of the Arthurian Romances. .*v.2 p.468*

Chretien de Troyes Revisited. *v.2 p.468*

Chretien de Troyes: The Man and His Work. *v.2 p.467*

Christ and Culture. *v.1 p.596*

Christ, Faith and History. *v.1 p.641*

Christ in a Pluralistic Age. *v.1 p.641*

Christ in Christian Tradition: From the Apostolic Age to Chalcedon (451). *v.1 p.640*

Christ in Christian Tradition: From the Concil of Chalcedon (451) to Gregory the Great (590-604), Vol. 2. . . .*v.1 p.640*

Christ in Christian Tradition: From the Council of Chalcedon (451) to Gregory the Great (590-604), Part 4: The Church of Alexandria with Nubia and Ethiopia after 451. . . . .*v.1 p.640*

Christ in Christian Tradition: From the Council of Chalcedon (451) to Gregory the Great (590-604). *v.1 p.640*

Christ in Concrete. *v.2 p.69*

Christ in Eastern Christian Thought. *v.1 p.640*

Christ in the Light of the Christian-Jewish Dialogue. .*v.1 p.642*

Christ on the Rue Jacob. *v.2 p.673*

Christ Outside the Gate: Mission Beyond Christendom. .*v.1 p.647*

Christ Stopped at Eboli: The Story of a Year. . . .*v.3 p.197*

Christ: The Experience of Jesus as Lord. *v.1 p.641*

Christ the Sacrament of the Encounter with God. . .*v.1 p.577*

The Christensen Brothers: An American Dance Epic. . .*v.1 p.9*

A Christian America: Protestant Hopes and Historical Realities. *v.1 p.605*

The Christian Burial Case: An Introduction to Criminal and Judicial Procedure. *v.6 p.269*

Christian Community in History. *v.1 p.655*

Christian Dietrich Grabbe. *v.2 p.596*

Christian Doctrine and Modern Culture (Since 1700), Vol. 5. . . . .*v.1 p.634*

The Christian Faith. *v.1 p.636*

Christian Love. *v.1 p.651*

Christian Marclay: The First ICP Triennial of Photography and Video. *v.1 p.773*

Christian Missionary Enterprise in the Niger Delta, 1864-1918. . . . .*v.6 p.72*

Christian Morgenstern's Galgenlieder (Gallows Songs), Bilingual Edition. *v.2 p.614*

Christian Morgenstern. *v.2 p.613, p.614*

Christian Origins: A People's History of Christianity. .*v.1 p.599*

The Christian Philosophy of Saint Augustine. *v.1 p.430*

The Christian Philosophy of St. Thomas Aquinas: Philosophy. *v.1 p.434, v.6 p.567, p.571*

Christian Pluralism in the United States: The Indian Immigrant Experience. *v.6 p.106, p.138*

Christian Political Theory and Church Politics in the Mid-Twelfth Century: The Ecclesiology of Gratian's Decretum. *v.1 p.572*

Christian Prayer Through the Centuries. *v.1 p.654*

Christian Rite and Christian Drama in the Middle Ages: Essays in the Origin and Early History of Modern Drama. *v.1 p.577*

Christian Rossetti and the poetry of discovery. . . .*v.2 p.304*

Christian Slaves, Muslim Masters: White Slavery in the Mediterranean, the Barbary Coast and Italy, 1500-1800. . . . .*v.4 p.727*

Christian Spirituality: An Introduction. *v.1 p.650*

Christian Spirituality: High MiddleAges and Reformation. *v.6 p.572*

Christian Theology: An Introduction to Its Traditions and Tasks. *v.1 p.636*

The Christian Tradition: A History of the Development of Doctrine: Reformation of Church and Dogma (1300-1700). *v.1 p.634*

The Christian Tradition: A History of the Development of Doctrine: The Emergence of the Catholic Tradition (100-600), Vol. 1. . . . .*v.1 p.634*

The Christian Tradition and the Unity We Seek. . . .*v.1 p.568*

Christianity: A Short Introduction. *v.1 p.597*

Christianity among the Arabs in Pre-Islamic Times. *v.6 p.584, p.601*

Christianity among the Nomads: The Catholic Church in Northern Kenya. *v.1 p.574*

Christianity: An Introduction. *v.1 p.597*

Christianity and Paganism in the Fourth to Eighth Centuries. *v.3 p.31*

Christianity and Politics in Doe's Liberia. *v.6 p.70*

Christianity and Revolution: Radical Christian Testimonies, 1520-1650. . . . .*v.1 p.602*

Christianity and the Kikuyu: Religious Divisions and Social Conflict. *v.1 p.611*

Christianity and the Mass Media in America: Toward a Democratic Accommodation. *v.1 p.656*

Christianity and the Religions: From Encounter to Dialogue. *v.1 p.597*

Christianity and the Rhetoric of Empire: The Development of Christian Discourse. *v.1 p.598, p.599*

Christianity and the Social Crisis. *v.1 p.643, p.644*

Christianity and the Superpowers: Religion, Politics and History in U. S. - U. S. S. R. Relations. *v.3 p.388*

Christianity at the Religious Roundtable: Evangelicalism in Conversation with Hinduism, Buddhism, and Islam. *v.1 p.597*

Christianity in China: From the Eighteenth Century to the Present. *v.6 p.187, p.189*

Christianity in Relation to Jews, Greeks and Romans. *v.1 p.597*

Christianity in the Caribbean: Essays on Church History. *v.3 p.315*

Christianity, Islam and the Negro Race. *v.6 p.35, p.70*

Christianity, Social Change and Globalization in the Americas. *v.3 p.299*

Christianity, Social Tolerance, and Homosexuality: Gay People in Western Europe from the Beginning of the Christian Era to the Fourteenth Century. . . .*v.6 p.363, p.364, p.373*

Christianity with an Asian Face: Asian-American Theology in the Making. *v.1 p.608*

The Christianization of Scandinavia. *v.3 p.236*

ⓔ Christianizing the Roman Empire: (A. D. 100-400). *v.3 p.28*

Christian-Muslim Dialogue in the Twentieth Century. *v.1 p.558, p.559*

Christians and Chiefs in Zimbabwe: A Social History of the Hwesa People. *v.6 p.77*

ⓔ Christians and Jews in the Ottoman Arab World: The Roots of Sectarianism. *v.6 p.590, p.597, p.601*

Christians and Jews in the Ottoman Empire: The Functioning of a Plural Society. *v.6 p.589, p.596, p.600*

Christians and Muslims in Ottoman Cyprus and the Mediterranean World, 1571-1640. . . . .*v.6 p.601*

Christians and the American Revolution. *v.3 p.410*

The Christians As the Romans Saw Them. *v.1 p.600*

Christians in Asia Before 1500. . . . .*v.1 p.610*

Christians Versus Muslims in Modern Egypt: The Century-Long Struggle for Coptic Equality. *v.6 p.637, p.638*

Christina Rossetti: A Divided Life. *v.2 p.303*

Christina Rossetti: A Literary Biography. *v.2 p.303, p.304*

Christina Rossetti: A Writer's Life. *v.2 p.304*

Christina Rossetti and Illustration: A Publishing History. *v.2 p.303*

Christina Rossetti and the Poetry of Discovery. . . .*v.2 p.304*

Christina Rossetti: Faith, Gender and Time. *v.2 p.303*

Christina Rossetti, Revisited. *v.2 p.305*

Christina Rossetti's Feminist Theology. *v.2 p.304*

Christina Rossetti. *v.2 p.303*

Christina Stead's Politics of Place. *v.2 p.748*

Christina Stead. *v.2 p.748*

Christine de Pizan: A Casebook. *v.2 p.468*

Christine Jorgensen: A Personal Autobiography. *v.6 p.370, p.402*

A Christmas Garland. *v.2 p.331*

Christmas Stories. by Charles Dickens. (Boz.) with ... illustrations. from designs by J. Leech and D. Maclise. *v.2 p.282*

Christo and Jeanne-Claude: On the Way to the Gates, Central
Park, New York City. *v.1 p.772, p.773*

The Christological Controversy. *v.1 p.640*

Christology at the Crossroads: A Latin American
Approach.. . . . .*v.1 p.641*

Christology of the Later Fathers. *v.1 p.640*

Christoph Martin Wieland: Gesammelte Schriften. . . .*v.2 p.615*

Christoph Martin Wieland. *v.2 p.615*

Christopher and His Kind. *v.2 p.356, v.6 p.402*

Christopher Columbus Encyclopedia, Vol. II. . .*v.3 p.403, p.405*

Christopher Columbus Encyclopedia, Vol. I. *v.3 p.403*

Christopher Isherwood Encyclopedia.. . . . .*v.2 p.356*

Christopher Isherwood: His Era, His Gang, and the Legacy of
the Truly Strong Man. *v.2 p.356*

Christopher Isherwood. *v.2 p.356*

Christopher Marlowe: A Renaissance Life. *v.2 p.221*

Christopher Marlowe: A Study of His Thought, Learning, and
Character.. . . . .*v.2 p.221*

Christopher Marlowe and the Renaissance of Tragedy,
63. . . . .*v.2 p.220, p.221*

Christopher Smart: Scholar of the University. *v.2 p.259*

Christopher Smart Selected Poems. *v.2 p.259, p.260*

Christopher Wilmarth: Light and Gravity. *v.1 p.780*

Christ's Churches Purely Reformed: A Social History of
Calvinism. *v.1 p.588, p.601*

Christus Victor: An Historical Study of the Three Main Types of
the Idea of Atonement. *v.1 p.641, p.642*

Chromatic Transformations in Nineteenth-Century
Music.. . . . .*v.1 p.371*

Chromatin and Chromatin Remodeling Enzymes, Pt. C. .*v.5 p.143*

Chromatography: A Laboratory Handbook of Chromatographic
and Electrophoretic Methods. *v.5 p.269*

Chromatography for Organic Chemistry. *v.5 p.309*

Chromatography: Fundamentals and Applications of
Chromatography and Related Differential Migration
Methods. *v.5 p.269*

Chronic Viral Hepatitis: Diagnosis and Therapeutics. .*v.5 p.515*

▢ Chronicle Careers.. . . . .*v.4 p.292*

Chronicle in Stone. *v.2 p.815*

Chronicle of a Death Foretold. *v.2 p.683*

A Chronicle of American Music, 1700-1995. . . . .*v.1 p.277*

A Chronicle of Damascus, 1389-1397: The Unique Bodleian
Library Manuscript Al-Durra Al Mudi a Fi L-Dawla
Al-Zahiriya.. . . . .*v.6 p.607*

The Chronicle of James I, King of Aragon, Surnamed the
Conqueror, (Written by Himself). with an
Historical Introduction, Notes, Appendix, Glossary, and
General Index, by Pascual de Gayangos, Vol. 2. . . .*v.3 p.65*

Chronicle of the Abbey of Bury St. Edmunds. *v.3 p.66*

The Chronicle of the Lodz Ghetto, 1941-1944.. . . .*v.3 p.83*

The Chronicler of Barsetshire: A Life of Anthony
Trollope. *v.2 p.317*

Chronicles II. *v.1 p.620*

The Chronicles of Clovis. *v.2 p.381*

The Chronicles of Froissart. *v.3 p.69*

The Chronicles of Narnia: The Magician's Nephew; The Lion,
the Witch and the Wardrobe; The Horse and His Boy;
Prince Caspian; The Voyage of the Dawn Treader; The Silver
Chair; The Last Battle. *v.2 p.366*

The Chronicles of Panchita Villa and Other Guerrilleras: Essays
on Chicana/Latina Literature and
Criticism. *v.6 p.502, p.508, p.515*

Chronicles of the Canongate. *v.2 p.308*

Chronicles of the Crusades.. . . . .*v.3 p.63*

Chronicles, Vol. 1. . . . .*v.1 p.268, p.322*

Chronicling Cultures: Long-Term Field Research in
Anthropology. *v.4 p.25*

Chronobiology: Biological Timekeeping. *v.5 p.616*

Chronological History of U. S. Foreign Relations,
Set. *v.4 p.560, p.627*

Chronologisch-thematisches Verzeichnis sämtlicher Tonwerke
Wolfgang Amadé Mozarts: nebst Angabe der
verlorengegangenen, angefangenen, von fremder Hand
bearbeiteten, zweifelhaften und unterschobenen
Kompositionen. *v.1 p.164, p.190, p.344*

A Chronology of American Musical Theater, Set. . . .*v.1 p.253*

Chronology of Communication in the United States. . .*v.4 p.424*

A Chronology of Geological Thinking from Antiquity to
1899. . . . .*v.5 p.418*

The Chronology of Oral Tradition: Quest for a Chimera. .*v.6 p.53*

Chronology of the Ancient World. *v.3 p.3*

Chronology of Western Classical Music, 1751-2000,
Set.. . . . .*v.1 p.174*

Chronology of Women Worldwide: People, Places, and Events
That Shaped Women's History. *v.6 p.425*

Chronology of Women's History. *v.6 p.426*

The Chrysanthemum and the Sword: Patterns of Japanese
Culture.. . . . .*v.6 p.221*

Chrysler: The Life and Times of an Automotive Genius. .*v.4 p.153*

Chuck Berry: The Autobiography. *v.1 p.266, p.311*

Chuck Close: A Retrospective.. . . . .*v.1 p.700*

Chuck Close Prints: Process and Collaboration. . . .*v.1 p.758*

The Church and Clergy in Sixteenth-Century Mexico. .*v.3 p.287*

The Church and Economic Activity in the Middle
Ages. *v.6 p.558, p.571*

The Church and Politics in Chile: Challenges to Modern
Catholicism.. . . . .*v.3 p.355*

Church and Politics in Latin America. *v.3 p.300, p.344*

The Church and Politics in the Chilean Countryside.. .*v.3 p.355*

Church and Society in Byzantium under the Comneni,
1081-1261. . . . .*v.1 p.568, p.569, v.3 p.192*

Church and Society in England, 1000-1500. .*v.3 p.96, v.6 p.570*

Church and Society in England, 1770-1970: A Historical
Survey. *v.1 p.609*

Church and State Education in Revolutionary Mexico
City. *v.4 p.336*

Church and State in America. *v.1 p.604*

Church and State in Bourbon Mexico: The Diocese of
Michoacan, 1749-1810. . . . .*v.3 p.284*

Church and State in Ethiopia, 1270-1527. . . . . . .*v.1 p.611*

Church and State in Soviet Russia: Russian Orthodoxy from
World War II to the Khrushchev Years. *v.3 p.222*

Church and State in the Modern Age: A Documentary History. *v.1 p.611*

Church and State in Yugoslavia since 1945. . . . . . .*v.3 p.246*

Church and State in Yugoslavia since Nineteen Forty-Five. *v.3 p.247*

Church and State Through the Centuries. *v.3 p.56*

The Church and the Churches: Toward an Ecumenical Ecclesiology. *v.1 p.655*

The Church and the Churches. *v.1 p.655*

The Church and the Homosexual. *v.6 p.373*

The Church and the Jews in the Thirteenth Century: 1254-1314. . . . .*v.6 p.571, p.573*

The Church and the Second Sex. *v.1 p.655, v.6 p.459*

Church and Worship Music: A Research and Information Guide. *v.1 p.166*

The Church at the Grassroots in Latin America: Perspectives on Thirty Years of Activism. *v.3 p.298, p.301*

The Church, Dictatorships and Democracy in Latin America. *v.3 p.260*

Church Dogmatics. *v.1 p.634*

The Church Faces Death: Ecclesiology in a Post-Modern Context. *v.1 p.655*

Church History: An Introduction to Research, Reference Works, and Methods. *v.1 p.597, p.598*

The Church in Anglo-Saxon England. *v.6 p.571*

The Church in Brazil. *v.1 p.572*

The Church of Solitude. *v.2 p.717*

Church, Religion and Society in Early Modern Italy. .*v.3 p.200*

Church, State and Christian Society at the Time of the Investiture Contest. *v.1 p.576*

A Church That Can and Cannot Change. *v.1 p.574*

Church, World and the Christian Life: Practical-Prophetic Ecclesiology. *v.1 p.655*

Churches and the Working Classes in Victorian England. *v.3 p.112, p.121*

Churchill and America. *v.4 p.485, p.644*

Churchill's Cold War: The Politics of Personal Diplomacy. *v.4 p.645*

Churching of America, 1776-2005: Winners and Losers in Our Religious Economy. *v.4 p.720*

Church-State Relations. *v.1 p.656, v.4 p.486*

Chushingura: The Treasury of Loyal Retainers. *v.6 p.230*

Chymia. *v.5 p.263*

☐ CIA Declassified Documents. *v.4 p.481*

☐ CIA World Fact Book. *v.4 p.60, p.61*

☐ CIAO (Columbia International Affairs Online). . . .*v.4 p.624*

The CIA's Secret War in Tibet. *v.6 p.240*

Cicero: A Political Biography. *v.2 p.434*

Cicero: A Portrait. *v.2 p.434*

Cicero Brutus, Orator: Rhetorical Treatises. *v.2 p.431*

Cicero: Cato Maior de Senectute. *v.2 p.432*

Cicero: De Natura Deorum. *v.2 p.431*

Cicero: De Re Publica, Selections. *v.2 p.433*

Cicero: In Catilinam I and II. *v.2 p.431*

Cicero: Laelius on Friendship and the Dream of Scipio. .*v.2 p.432*

Cicero: Letters to Atticus. *v.2 p.432*

Cicero: On Moral Ends. *v.1 p.428, v.2 p.431*

Cicero: On Old Age. *v.2 p.431*

Cicero: On the Commonwealth and on the Laws. . . .*v.2 p.433*

Cicero on the Emotions: Tusculan Disputations 3 and 4. .*v.2 p.431*

Cicero: Philippics I-II. *v.2 p.432*

Cicero Pro Archia Poeta Oratio: A Syntactic Analysis of the Speech and Companion to the Commentary. . . .*v.2 p.431*

Cicero Pro Archia. *v.2 p.431*

Cicero: Rhetorica ad Herennium, A. Rhetorical Treatises. *v.2 p.427*

Cicero: Select Letters. *v.2 p.433*

Cicero: Selected Political Speeches. *v.2 p.431*

Cicero the Advocate. *v.2 p.434*

Cicero the Politician. *v.2 p.433*

Cicero: The Senior Statesman. *v.2 p.433, p.434*

Cicero: Tusculan Didputations I. *v.2 p.431*

Cicero: Tusculan Disputations II and V. *v.2 p.431*

Cicero: Verrine V. *v.2 p.431, p.432*

Cicero: Verrines II.1. . . . .*v.2 p.432*

Cicero's Caesarian Speeches: A Stylistic Commentary. .*v.2 p.431*

Cicero's Correspondence: A Literary Study. *v.2 p.433*

Cicero's Elegant Style: An Analysis of the Pro Archia. .*v.2 p.433*

Cicero. *v.2 p.433*

Le Cid: A Translation in Rhymed Couplets. *v.2 p.473*

The Cid and His Spain. *v.3 p.65*

The Cid, Cinna, the Theatrical Illusion. *v.2 p.473*

The Cider House Rules. *v.2 p.147*

Ciel!, Blake! = Sky!, Mortimer! : dictionnaire français-anglais des expressions courantes. *v.2 p.453*

Cien Sonetos de Amor. *v.2 p.681*

The Cigar Roller: A Novel. *v.6 p.507*

CIGR Handbook of Agricultural Engineering: Agro Processing Engineering. *v.5 p.3*

CIGR Handbook of Agricultural Engineering: Animal Production and Aquacultural Engineering. *v.5 p.3*

CIGR Handbook of Agricultural Engineering: Energy and Biomass Engineering. *v.5 p.5*

CIGR Handbook of Agricultural Engineering: Land and Water Engineering. *v.5 p.6*

CIGR Handbook of Agricultural Engineering: Plant Production Engineering. *v.5 p.6, p.45*

Cimabue. *v.1 p.695*

Cimarron. *v.2 p.73*

☐ CIMMYT International Maize and Wheat Improvement Center. *v.5 p.19*

☐ CINAHL®. *v.5 p.509*

Cinco Obras de Teatro. *v.2 p.663*

Cinco Tratados. *v.2 p.651*

Cinderella and Her Sisters: The Envied and the Envying. *v.5 p.657*

Cinderella Man: James J. Braddock, Max Baer, and the Greatest Upset in Boxing History. *v.4 p.856*

Cinema and Cultural Identity: Reflections on Films from Japan, India and China. *v.6 p.334*

Cinema and Culture: Independent Film in the United States, 1980-2001. . . . .*v.6 p.343*

Cinema and Desire: Feminist Marxism and Cultural Politics in the Works of Dai Jinhua. *v.6 p.335*

Cinema and Nation. *v.6 p.331*

Cinema and Soviet Society: From the Revolution to the Death of Stalin. *v.3 p.222*

Cinema and the City: Film and Urban Societies in a Global Context. *v.6 p.730*

Cinema and the Great War. *v.6 p.322*

Cinema and the Invention of Modern Life. *v.6 p.321*

Cinema and the Second Sex. *v.6 p.329*

Cinema East: A Critical Study of Major Japanese Films. .*v.6 p.336*

Cinema in Australia: A Documentary History. *v.6 p.337*

The Cinema of Generation X: A Critical Study of Films and Directors. *v.6 p.332*

Cinema of Japan and Korea. *v.6 p.334*

The Cinema of Spain and Portugal. *v.6 p.339*

Cinema Studies Key Concepts E3. . . . .*v.6 p.306, p.307*

Cinemas of the World: Film and Society from 1895 to the Present. *v.6 p.331*

The Cinematic City. *v.6 p.730*

Cinematic Landscapes: Observations on the Visual Arts and Cinema of China and Japan. *v.6 p.327, p.334*

Cinematic Uses of the Past. *v.6 p.331*

Cinematography. *v.6 p.349*

Cinnamon Gardens: A Novel. *v.2 p.761*

The Cinnamon Peeler: Selected Poems. *v.2 p.737*

Cinq grandes odes : suivies d'un Processionnal pour saluer le siècle nouveau. *v.2 p.513*

Cinq Grandes Odes, Processional Pour Saluer le Siecle Nouveau, la Cantate a Trois Voix. *v.2 p.513*

The CIO, 1935-1955. . . . .*v.4 p.130*

The CIO Challenge to the AFL: A History of the American Labor Movement. *v.4 p.126*

Circa, 1492: Art in the Age of Exploration. *v.3 p.73*

The Circle Game. *v.2 p.734*

The Circle of Baal Shem Tov: Studies in Hasidism. . .*v.1 p.552*

The Circle of Innovation: You Can't Shrink Your Way to Greatness. *v.4 p.67*

Circle of Paradox: Time and Essence in the Poetry of Juan Ramon Jimenez. *v.2 p.661*

Circle of Protest: Political Ritual in the Tibetan Uprising, 1987-1992. . . . .*v.6 p.241*

A Circle of Quiet, Set. *v.2 p.148*

Circles and Lines: The Shape of Life in Early America. .*v.4 p.702*

Circles of Recovery: Self-Help Organizations for Addictions. *v.5 p.669*

Circuit Analysis: A Systems Approach. *v.5 p.721*

Circuit Analysis Essentials: A Signal Processing A. . .*v.5 p.720*

Circuit Analysis: Theory and Practice. *v.5 p.721*

Circuit Analysis with Devices: Theory and Practice. . .*v.5 p.721*

Circuit Chautauqua: From Rural Education to Popular Entertainment in Early Twentieth Century America. .*v.4 p.321*

The Circuit Rider: A Tale of the Heroic Age. *v.2 p.37*

Circuits and Networks: Analysis and Synthesis. . . .*v.5 p.721*

Circulating Nucleic Acids in Plasma or Serum, Vol. 906. . . . .*v.5 p.119, p.120*

Circulating Nucleic Acids in Plasma/Serum III and Serum Proteomics. *v.5 p.116, p.120*

The Circus in the Attic and Other Stories. *v.2 p.129*

The Cistercians: Ideals and Reality. *v.6 p.572*

The Citadel of Learning. *v.4 p.290, p.331*

The Citadel. *v.2 p.337*

☐ Citas Latinoamericanas en Ciencias Sociales y Humanidades (CLASE). *v.3 p.259*

Cities and Fiscal Choices: A New Model of Urban Public Investment. *v.4 p.544, v.6 p.724, p.725*

Cities and Race: America's New Black Ghetto. *v.6 p.722*

Cities and Society. *v.6 p.718*

Cities and the Arts: A Handbook for Renewal. *v.1 p.826*

Cities and the Rise of States in Europe, A. D. 1000-1800. .*v.3 p.44*

Cities, Classes, and the Social Order. *v.4 p.37, v.6 p.722*

Cities in a Globalizing World: Global Report on Human Settlements. *v.4 p.544, p.545*

Cities in a Globalizing World. *v.6 p.726*

Cities in a World Economy. *v.6 p.719*

Cities in the International Marketplace: The Political Economy of Urban Development in North America and Western Europe. *v.6 p.725*

Cities of Europe: Changing Contexts, Local Arrangements and the Challenge to Urban Cohesion. *v.6 p.723*

Cities of God: The Religion of the Italian Communes, 1125-1325. . . . .*v.3 p.199*

Cities of Ladies. *v.6 p.561, p.573*

The Cities of Paul: Images from the Harvard New Testament Archaeology Project. *v.1 p.625*

Cities of Salt. *v.6 p.656*

Cities of the Interior. *v.2 p.105*

Cities of the World: A History in Maps. *v.6 p.716*

Cities of Tomorrow: An Intellectual History of Urban Planning and Design in the Twentieth Century. *v.6 p.712, p.726*

Cities, Politics, and Policy: A Comparative Analysis. .*v.6 p.725*

Cities, Sin, and Social Reform in Imperial Germany. .*v.3 p.164*

Cities, War, and Terrorism: Towards an Urban Geopolitics. *v.4 p.659, v.6 p.723*

Cities Without Suburbs: A Census 2000 Edition. . . .*v.6 p.709*

Citizen and Subject: Contemporary Africa and the Legacy of Late Colonialism. *v.6 p.55*

Citizen Emperor: Pedro II and the Making of Brazil, 1825-1891. . . . .*v.3 p.335*

The Citizen Factory: Schooling and Cultural Production in Bolivia. *v.3 p.324*

Citizen Hearst, a Biography of William Randolph Hearst. *v.4 p.411*

Citizen Hobo: How a Century of Homelessness Shaped America. *v.4 p.757*

Citizen in Court: Litigant, Witness, Juror, Judge. . .*v.4 p.465*

Citizen Politics: Public Opinion and Political Parties in Advanced Industrial Democracies. *v.4 p.578, p.579*

Citizens and Politics: Perspectives from Political Psychology. *v.5 p.643*

Citizens, Cops, and Power: Recognizing the Limits of Community. *v.4 p.774, v.6 p.264*

Citizens of Zion: Social Origins of Camp Meeting Revivalism. *.v.1 p.648*

Citizenship and Governance in the European Union. . . . . *.v.4 p.602, p.636*

Citizenship and Nationhood in France and Germany. . . . . *.v.3 p.61, v.4 p.608, p.609*

Citizenship and the State: A Comparative Study of Citizenship Legislation in Israel, Jordan, Palestine, Syria and Lebanon. *.v.6 p.592*

[c] Citizenship in the Western Tradition: Plato to Rousseau. *.v.4 p.578*

Citizenship: The Civic Ideal in World History, Politics and Education. . . . . *.v.4 p.577*

Citizens. . . . . *.v.4 p.586*

The City: A Global History. . . . . *.v.4 p.772, v.6 p.713*

City Against Suburb: The Culture Wars in an American Metropolis. *.v.6 p.719*

City and Nation: Rethinking Place and Identity. . . . . *.v.6 p.719*

The City and the House. . . . . *.v.2 p.717*

The City and the Pillar. . . . . *.v.2 p.127, v.6 p.399*

The City and the Theatre: The History of New York Playhouses: A 250 Year Journey from Bowling Green to Times Square. . . . . *.v.1 p.115, p.154*

City Art: New York's Percent for Art Program. . . . *.v.1 p.825*

The City As Subject: Seki Hajime and the Reinvention of Modern Osaka. . . . . *.v.6 p.224*

The City Assembled: The Elements of Urban Form Through History. *.v.1 p.797*

City Assembled: The Elements of Urban Form Through History. *.v.6 p.713*

The City at Stake: Secession, Reform, and the Battle for Los Angeles. . . . . *.v.3 p.444, v.4 p.544*

The City Beautiful Movement. . . . . *.v.6 p.729*

The City Builders: Property Development in New York and London, 1980-2000. . . . . *.v.6 p.723*

City Codes: Reading the Modern Urban Novel. *.v.6 p.731, p.733*

A City Divided: The Racial Landscape of Kansas City, 1900-1960. . . . . *.v.3 p.512*

City Games: The Evolution of American Urban Society and the Rise of Sports. . . . . *.v.4 p.819*

The City in History: Its Origins, Its Transformations and Its Prospects. . . . . *.v.4 p.771, v.6 p.714*

City in the Sky: The Rise and Fall of the World Trade Center. . . . . *.v.1 p.792, p.793*

The City in Time and Space. . . . . *.v.6 p.719*

The City in Which I Love You. . . . . *.v.6 p.103*

City Life: Urban Expectations in a New World. *.v.6 p.715, p.729*

[c] City Making: Building Communities Without Building Walls. *.v.6 p.723*

City of Angels. . . . . *.v.1 p.250, p.408*

City of Ash. *.v.2 p.781*

City of Bits: Space, Place, and the Infobahn. . . . . *.v.6 p.730*

The City of Dickens. . . . . *.v.2 p.285*

City of Dreadful Delight: Narratives of Sexual Danger in Late-Victorian London. . . . . . *.v.3 p.54, p.55,v.6 p.749*

City of God Against the Pagans, Bks. 12-15. . . . . *.v.2 p.429*

City of God Against the Pagans, Bks. 16-18. 35. . . *.v.2 p.429*

City of God Against the Pagans, Bks. 18. 36-20. . . *.v.2 p.429*

City of God Against the Pagans, Bks. 21-22. . . . . *.v.2 p.429*

City of God Against the Pagans, Bks. 4-7. . . . . . *.v.2 p.429*

City of God Against the Pagans, Bks. 8-11. . . . . . *.v.2 p.430*

City of God Against the Pagans, Vol. 1. . . . . . . *.v.2 p.429*

City of God. . . . . *.v.1 p.592, v.2 p.429, v.3 p.56*

City of Light: The Story of Fiber Optics. . . . . . . *.v.5 p.701*

City of Lingering Splendour: A Frank Account of Old Peking's Exotic Pleasures. . . . . *.v.6 p.205*

City of Love and Ashes. . . . . *.v.6 p.660*

City of Many Days: A Novel. . . . . *.v.6 p.648, p.649*

The City of Mexico in the Age of Díaz. . . . . *.v.3 p.289*

The City of Musical Memory: Salsa, Record Grooves, and Popular Culture in Cali, Colombia. . . . . *.v.3 p.268*

City of Night. . . . . *.v.6 p.398, p.502*

City of Quartz: Excavating the Future in Los Angeles. *.v.6 p.717*

City of Sacrifice: Violence from the Aztec Empire to the Modern Americas. . . . . *.v.3 p.261*

City of Saffron. . . . . *.v.6 p.656*

City of the Dead: Thebes in Egypt. . . . . *.v.3 p.9*

City of the Living and Other Stories. . . . . *.v.2 p.121*

City of Walls: Crime, Segregation and Citizenship in São Paulo. *.v.4 p.773*

City of Wrong: A Friday in Jerusalem. . . . . *.v.6 p.660*

City on a Hill: A History of Ideas and Myths in America. *.v.3 p.365*

City on the Edge: The Transformation of Miami. . . *.v.3 p.505*

City Poet: The Life and Times of Frank O'Hara. . . *.v.6 p.401*

City Politics and Public Policy. . . . . *.v.6 p.726*

City Politics: The Political Economy of Urban America. *.v.6 p.723*

City Politics. *.v.6 p.722*

City Politiques. . . . . *.v.2 p.243*

The City Reader. . . . . *.v.1 p.797*

City Room. . . . . *.v.4 p.412*

City Schools and the American Dream: Reclaiming the Promise of Public Education. . . . . *.v.4 p.315*

The City Shaped: Urban Patterns and Meanings Through History. *.v.6 p.728*

City, Sister, Silver. . . . . *.v.2 p.784*

City Trenches: Urban Politics and the Patterning of Class in the United States. . . . . *.v.6 p.723*

City: Urbanism and Its End. . . . . *.v.6 p.719*

City Voices: Hong Kong Writing in English, 1945-Present. . . . . *.v.2 p.761*

City Walls: The Urban Enceinte in Global Perspective. *.v.4 p.771*

Cityscapes and Capital: The Politics of Urban Development. . . . . *.v.6 p.724*

The City. . . . . *.v.6 p.718, p.719, p.720*

Ciudades Desiertas (Deserted Cities). . . . . *.v.2 p.666*

Civic Agriculture: Reconnecting Farm, Food, and Community. . . . . *.v.5 p.14*

The Civic Culture: Political Attitudes and Democracy in Five Nations. *.v.5 p.642*

Civic Engagement in American Democracy. . *.v.4 p.547, p.555*

The Civic Tradition and Roman Athens. *v.3 p.21*

Civil and Structural Engineering: Design of Reinforced Concrete
Structures. *v.5 p.696, p.697*

Civil and Uncivil Violence in Lebanon: A History of the
Internationalization of Communal Conflict. *v.6 p.605*

Civil Commitment of Sexual Predators: A Study in Policy
Implementation. *v.6 p.247*

Civil Disobedience and Other Essays. *v.1 p.501*

Civil Disobedience: Theory and Practice. *v.4 p.497*

'Civil Disorder Is the Disease of Ibadan': Chieftaincy and Civic
Culture in a Colonial City. *v.6 p.72*

Civil Engineering Formulas: Pocket Guide. *v.5 p.685*

The Civil Engineering Handbook. *v.5 p.685*

Civil Engineering Practice in the Twenty-First Century:
Knowledge and Skills for Design and Management. .*v.5 p.685*

Civil Engineering Practice: vol. 5: Water
Resources/Environmental. *v.5 p.705*

Civil Engineering Reference Manual for the PE
Exam. *v.5 p.685, p.686*

ⓔ Civil Engineer's Illustrated Sourcebook. *v.5 p.686*

Civil Islam: Muslims and Democratization in
Indonesia. *v.6 p.174, p.176*

Civil Liberties and the Vinson Court. *v.4 p.456*

The Civil Rights Act of 1964: The Passage of the Law That
Ended Racial Segregation. *v.4 p.457*

The Civil Rights Era: Origins and Development of National
Policy, 1960-1972. . . . .*v.4 p.486*

Civil Servants and Their Constitutions. *v.4 p.546*

Civil Society: A Reader in History, Theory, and Global
Politics. *v.4 p.498*

Civil Society and Government. *v.4 p.499*

Civil Society and Political Change in Asia: Expanding and
Contracting Democratic Space. *v.4 p.616*

Civil Society, Democracy and Civic Renewal. *v.4 p.547*

Civil Society in Japan: The Growing Role of NGOs in Tokyo's
Aid and Development Policy. *v.4 p.640, p.663*

Civil Society in the Information Age. *v.4 p.640*

Civil Society in the Yemen: The Political Economy of Activism
in Modern Arabia. *v.4 p.614, v.6 p.628*

The Civil War and Reconstruction. *v.3 p.432*

Civil War Command and Strategy: The Process of Victory and
Defeat. *v.3 p.398*

The Civil War Dictionary. *v.3 p.429, p.430*

Civil War in China: The Political Struggle,
1945-1949. . . . .*v.6 p.190, p.191*

The Civil War in Nicaragua: Inside the Sandinistas. . .*v.3 p.303*

Civil War in Poland, 1942-1948. . . . .*v.3 p.254*

Civil War in the American West. *v.6 p.687*

The Civil War (Pharsalia). *v.2 p.436*

Civil War Prisons: A Study in War Psychology. .*v.3 p.398, p.425*

Civil War Treasury of Tales, Legends and Folklore. . .*v.3 p.394*

Civil War Treasury. *v.3 p.424*

The Civil War: With the Anonymous Alexandrian, African, and
Spanish Wars. *v.2 p.428*

The Civil War Years: Canada and the United States. . .*v.3 p.433*

The Civil Wars in Chile, or, the Bourgeois Revolutions That
Never Were. *v.3 p.350*

Civilian and the Military: A History of the American
Anti-Militarist Tradition. *v.3 p.382*

The Civilian Elite of Cairo in the Later Middle Ages. .*v.6 p.635*

Civilising Subjects: Metropole and Colony in the English
Imagination 1830-1867. . . . .*v.6 p.746*

Civility in the City: Blacks, Jews, and Koreans in Urban
America. *v.6 p.106, p.123, p.136*

Civilization and Capitalism, 15th-18th Century: The Wheels of
Commerce. *v.3 p.38*

Civilization at the Crossroads: Social and Human Implications
of the Scientific and Technological
Revolution. *v.5 p.410, p.412*

The Civilization of Ancient Crete. *v.3 p.16*

The Civilization of Angkor. *v.6 p.170*

Civilization of Europe in the Renaissance. *v.3 p.70*

The Civilization of Medieval Europe. *v.6 p.563*

Civilization of the Ancient Mediterranean: Greece and Rome,
Set. *v.3 p.3*

The Civilization of the Goddess: The World of Old
Europe. *v.1 p.531*

Civilization of the Middle Ages. *v.3 p.66, v.6 p.561*

Civilization of the Old Northwest. *v.3 p.512*

The Civilization of the Renaissance in Italy. . .*v.3 p.70, p.200*

Civilization or Barbarism: An Authentic Anthropology. .*v.6 p.10*

Civilization Without Sexes: Reconstructing Gender in Postwar
France, 1917-1927. . . . . . .*v.3 p.54, p.79, p.80, p.155*

The Civilizations of Africa: A History to 1800. . . . .*v.6 p.52*

Civilizations of the Ancient Near East, set. *v.1 p.619*

Civilizing Rio: Reform and Resistance in a Brazilian City,
1889-1930. . . . .*v.3 p.341*

Civilizing the Machine: Technology and Republican Values in
America, 1776-1900. . . . .*v.3 p.409*

Civil-Military Relations: Building Democracy and Regional
Security in Latin America, Southern Asia, and Central
Europe. *v.3 p.275*

Civil-Military Relations in Latin America: New Analytical
Perspectives. *v.3 p.276*

Civil-Military Relations in Russia and Eastern Europe. .*v.4 p.597*

Civil-Military Relations in South Asia: Pakistan, Bangladesh and
India. *v.4 p.617, p.618*

▢ CLACSO (Consejo Latinoamericano de Ciencias
Sociales). *v.3 p.259*

▢ CLACSO. *v.3 p.259*

Cladistic Biogeography: Interpreting Patterns of Plant and
Animal Distributions. *v.5 p.170, p.201*

Cladistics: A Practical Course in Systematics. *v.5 p.205*

Cladistics: A Practical Primer. *v.5 p.202*

Cladistics: The Theory and Practice of Parsimony
Analysis. *v.5 p.199, p.201*

Claiming America: Constructing Chinese American Identities
During the Exclusion Era. *v.6 p.115, p.128*

Claiming Kin: Confronting the History of an African American
Family. *v.6 p.11, p.40*

The Claims of Kinfolk: African American Property and
Community in the Nineteenth-Century South. . . .*v.4 p.705*

Clan Leaders and Colonial Chiefs in Lango: The Political History of an East African Stateless Society C. 1800-1939. . . . .*v.6 p.67*

Clandestine Poems (Poemas Clandestinos). *v.2 p.675*

Clandestine Poems--Poemas Clandestinos: Bilingual Edition. *v.2 p.675*

Clara Schumann: The Artist and the Woman. . .*v.1 p.202, p.354*

Clarence Thomas: A Biography. *v.4 p.540*

Clarendon and the English Revolution. *v.3 p.103, p.105*

Clarice Lispector: A Bio-Bibliography, 2. . . . . . .*v.2 p.692*

Clarice Lispector. *v.2 p.690*

Claridad Errante: Poesia y Prosa. *v.2 p.668*

The Clarinet and Clarinet Playing. *v.1 p.391, p.398*

Clarissa's Ciphers: Meaning and Disruption in Richardson's Clarissa. *v.2 p.258*

Clarissa. *v.2 p.259*

Claros Varones de Belken: Fair Gentlemen of Belken County, Bilingual Edition. *v.6 p.499, p.500*

The Clash of Empires: The Invention of China in Modern World Making. *v.6 p.204*

The Clash of Gods: A Reinterpretation of Early Christian Art. *v.1 p.599*

Class Act: The Jazz Life of Choreographer Cholly Atkins. *v.1 p.6, p.31, p.32*

Class Action: The Landmark Case That Changed Sexual Harassment Law. *v.4 p.130*

Class Actions: Teaching for Social Justice in Elementary and Middle School. *v.4 p.361*

Class and Class Conflict in Industrial Society. *v.4 p.724*

Class and Class Consciousness in the Industrial Revolution, 1780-1850. . . . .*v.3 p.114, p.131*

Class and Conformity: A Study in Values. . .*v.4 p.695, p.724*

Class and Party in American Politics. *v.4 p.552*

Class and Power in Sudan: The Dynamics of Sudanese Politics, 1898-1985. . . . .*v.6 p.640*

Class, Ethnicity, and Community in Southern Mexico: Oaxaca's Peasantries. *v.4 p.771*

Class Ethnicity and Politics in Liberia: A Class Analysis of Power Struggles in the Tubman and Tolbert Administrations from 1944-1975. . . . . .*v.4 p.703, v.6 p.70*

Class: Image and Reality in Britain, France and the U. S. A. since 1930. . . . .*v.4 p.724*

Class, Language, and American Film Comedy. . . .*v.6 p.312*

Class Mates: Male Student Culture and the Making of a Political Class in Nineteenth-Century Brazil. . . .*v.3 p.337*

Class Notes: Posing as Politics and Other Thoughts on the American Scene. *v.4 p.484*

[e] The Class of 2000: The Definitive Survey of the New Generation. *v.4 p.288*

A Class of Their Own: When Children Teach Children. .*v.4 p.349*

Class, Sect and Party: The Making of the British Middle Class, Leeds, 1820-1850. . . . .*v.3 p.114, p.131*

Class, Sports, and Social Development. *v.4 p.816*

Class, Status and Power: A Reader in Social Stratification. *v.4 p.723*

The Class Structure of the Advanced Societies. . . .*v.4 p.724*

Class Struggle in Hollywood, 1930-1950: Moguls, Mobsters, Stars, Reds, and Trade Unionists. *v.6 p.328, p.341*

Class Warfare in the Information Age. *v.4 p.698*

Classic African American Women's Narratives. .*v.2 p.18, v.6 p.41*

Classic American Popular Song: The Second Half-Century, 1950-2000. . . . .*v.1 p.270*

Classic and Romantic German Aesthetics. *v.1 p.480*

Classic Art: An Introduction to the Italian Renaissance. .*v.1 p.676*

Classic Asian Philosophy: A Guide to the Essential Texts. *v.1 p.475*

Classic Chinese Cuisine. *v.6 p.182*

Classic Drama Plays by Greek, Spanish, French, German and English Dramatists, Vol. 1. . . . .*v.1 p.63, p.95*

Classic Drama Plays by Greek, Spanish, French, German and English Dramatists, Vol. 2. . . . .*v.1 p.69, p.97*

Classic Essays on the Culture of Cities. *v.6 p.719*

Classic Essays on Twentieth-Century Music : A Continuing Symposium. *v.1 p.217*

Classic Experiments in Psychology. *v.5 p.597*

Classic Fiction of the Harlem Renaissance. . . .*v.2 p.25, p.26*

The Classic French Cinema, 1930-1960. . . . .*v.6 p.337, p.338*

Classic Irish Short Stories. *v.2 p.374*

Classic Music: Expression, Form and Style. *v.1 p.191*

The Classic Noh Theatre of Japan. *v.1 p.132, p.134*

Classic Operating Systems: from Batch Processing to Distributed Systems. *v.5 p.348*

[□] Classic Organic Reactions. *v.5 p.295*

Classic Readings in Urban Planning. .*v.1 p.797, p.798,v.6 p.729*

The Classic Slum: Salford Life in the First Quarter of the Century. *v.4 p.706*

Classic Texts in Mission and World Christianity. . .*v.1 p.647*

The Classical Age of German Literature, 1740-1815. .*v.2 p.590*

Classical and Christian Ideas in English Renaissance Poetry: A Student's Guide. *v.2 p.182*

Classical and Modern Fourier Analysis. *v.5 p.493, p.494*

Classical and Neoclassical Theories of General Equilibrium. *v.4 p.206, p.218, p.224, p.271*

Classical and Romantic Performing Practice 1750-1900. . . . . . .*v.1 p.188, p.194, p.195, p.399, p.400*

Classical and Vernacular Chinese Furniture in the Living Environment. *v.1 p.804*

Classical Architecture: An Introduction to Its Vocabulary and Essentials, with Special Terms Glossary. *v.1 p.783*

Classical Art: From Greece to Rome. *v.1 p.669, p.685*

The Classical Athenian Democracy. *v.4 p.501*

The Classical Background of English Literature. . .*v.2 p.165*

Classical Ballet: The Flow of Movement. *v.1 p.24*

Classical Black Nationalism: From the American Revolution to Marcus Garvey. *v.6 p.13*

Classical Bronzes: The Art and Craft of Greek and Roman Statuary. *v.1 p.775*

Classical Christianity and Rabbinic Judaism: Comparing Theologies. *v.1 p.549*

Classical Comedy - Greek and Roman: Six Plays. *v.1 p.64, p.69, p.70, p.71, p.72, p.90*

Classical Dance and Theatre in South-East Asia. .*v.1 p.133, p.134*

The Classical Drama of France. *v.2 p.459*

Classical Dynamics: A Contemporary Approach. . . .*v.5 p.546*

Classical Dynamics of Particles and Systems. *v.5 p.547*

Classical Economics and Modern Theory: Studies in
 Long-Period Analysis. *v.4 p.218*

Classical Economics. *v.4 p.217*

The Classical Economists Revisited. *v.4 p.218*

Classical Electricity and Magnetism. *v.5 p.565*

Classical Electrodynamics. *v.5 p.564, p.565*

Classical Electromagnetic Radiation. *v.5 p.565*

The Classical Epic Tradition. *v.2 p.402*

The Classical Era: From the 1740's to the End of the 18th
 Century. *v.1 p.192, p.193*

Classical Fighting Arts of Japan: A Complete Guide to Koryeu
 Jeujutsu. *v.4 p.863*

Classical Film Violence: Designing and Regulating Brutality in
 Hollywood Cinema, 1930-1968. . . . .*v.6 p.321*

Classical Hindu Mythology: A Reader in the Sanskrit
 Puranas. *v.1 p.537, p.538*

The Classical Hollywood Cinema: Film Style and Mode of
 Production to 1960. . . . .*v.6 p.345*

Classical Hollywood Comedy. *v.6 p.312, p.313*

Classical Horizons: The Origins of Sociology in Ancient
 Greece. *v.4 p.683*

Classical Indian Philosophy: An Introductory Text. . .*v.1 p.419*

A Classical Introduction to Modern Number Theory. . .*v.5 p.476*

Classical Literary Criticism. *v.2 p.399*

Classical Mechanics: Transformations, Flows, Integrable and
 Chaotic Dynamics. *v.5 p.547*

Classical Mechanics. *v.5 p.64, p.546*

Classical Modern Philosophy. *v.1 p.436*

Classical Moment: Studies of Corneille, Moliere, and
 Racine. *v.2 p.462*

Classical Music and Postmodern Knowledge. *v.1 p.381*

Classical Music: The Era of Haydn, Mozart, and
 Beethoven. *v.1 p.189*

Classical Mythology in Shakespeare. *v.2 p.231*

Classical Persian Literature. *v.6 p.670*

The Classical Roman Reader: New Encounters with Ancient
 Rome. *v.2 p.424*

The Classical Roots of Ethnomethodology: Durkheim, Weber,
 and Garfinkel. *v.4 p.688*

Classical Scholarship: An Annotated Bibliography. . .*v.2 p.399*

Classical Social Theory. *v.4 p.677, p.678*

Classical Sociological Theory. *v.4 p.677*

Classical Studies: A Guide to the Reference Literature. .*v.2 p.399*

Classical Style: Haydn, Mozart,
 Beethoven. *v.1 p.191, p.307, p.330, p.331, p.344*

Classical Taste in America, 1800-1840. . . . .*v.1 p.682*

Classical Telugu Poetry: An Anthology. *v.6 p.152*

The Classical Theatre of China. *v.1 p.132, p.134*

The Classical Theory of Fields. *v.5 p.564, p.565*

Classical Theory of the Gains from Trade: The Origins of
 International Economics. *v.4 p.256, p.257*

Classical Thought. *v.1 p.420*

Classical Tragedy Greek and Roman: Eight Plays with Critical
 Essays. *v.1 p.64, p.69, p.71, p.72, p.88*

The Classical Utilitarians: Bentham and Mill. . .*v.1 p.515, p.516*

Classical Voices: Studies of Corneille, Racine, Molière, Mme de
 Lafayette. *v.2 p.458*

Le Classicisme. *v.2 p.459*

Classics: A Treasury of Investment Literature. *v.4 p.94*

Classics and Feminism: Gendering the
 Classics. *v.2 p.399, v.6 p.463*

Classics and the Uses of Reception. *v.2 p.399*

Classics in Hydrocarbon Chemistry: Syntheses, Concepts,
 Perspectives. *v.5 p.291*

Classics in Management. *v.4 p.116*

Classics in Movement Science. *v.4 p.873, p.908, p.909*

Classics in the History of Psychology. *v.5 p.596*

Classics in the Theory of Chemical Combination. . . .*v.5 p.262*

Classics of Analytic Philosophy. *v.1 p.501, p.502*

Classics of Practicing Anthropology, 1978-1998. .*v.4 p.44, p.45*

The Classics Page at Ad Fontes Academy. *v.2 p.399*

Classics: The Most Interesting Ideas and Concepts from the
 Literature of Investing. *v.4 p.94*

Classification, Evolution, and the Nature of Biology. . .*v.5 p.201*

The Classified Directory of Artists' Signatures, Symbols and
 Monograms: International and American
 Editions. *v.1 p.662, p.663*

Classroom Assessment Techniques: A Handbook for College
 Teachers. *v.4 p.285*

Classroom Killers? Hallway Hostages?: How Schools Can
 Prevent and Manage School Crises. *v.4 p.281*

Classroom Life as Civic Education: Individual Achievement and
 Student Cooperation in Schools. *v.4 p.362*

A Classroom of One: How Online Learning Is Changing Our
 Schools and Colleges. *v.4 p.322*

Classroom Power Relations: Understanding Student-Teacher
 Interaction. *v.4 p.349, p.350*

Classroom Teacher's Survival Guide: Practical Strategies,
 Management Techniques, and Reproducibles for
 New and Experienced Teachers. *v.4 p.284*

Classrooms That Work: They Can All Read and Write. .*v.4 p.362*

Claude Debussy: A Guide to Research. .*v.1 p.163, p.210, p.320*

Claude Debussy: Pelléas et
 Mélisande. *v.1 p.220, p.231, p.320, p.321*

Claude Levi-Strauss: The Formative Years. *v.4 p.24*

Claude Monet: The Color of Time. *v.1 p.747*

Claude Pepper and Ed Ball: Politics, Purpose and
 Power. *v.3 p.504*

Claudio Monteverdi: A Guide to Research. .*v.1 p.164, p.185, p.342*

Claudio Monteverdi: Orfeo. . . .*v.1 p.187, p.234, p.342, p.343*

Claudius: The Corruption of Power. *v.3 p.28*

The Claverings. *v.2 p.318*

The Claws of the Dragon: Kang Sheng - the Evil Genius Behind
 Mao - and His Legacy of Terror in People's China. .*v.6 p.199*

Clay and Star: Contemporary Bulgarian Poets. *v.2 p.780*

Clay Walls. *v.6 p.100*

Clayey Barrier Systems for Waste Disposal Facilities. .*v.5 p.377*

Clayhanger. *v.2 p.334*

Clays, Muds, and Shales. *v.5 p.439*

Clean Air Act Handbook. *v.6 p.300*

The Clean Air Act Handbook. *v.6 p.300*

Clean Air Act of 1990: A Primer on
Consensus-Building. *v.5 p.355*

Clean Coastal Waters: Understanding and Reducing the Effects
of Nutrient Pollution. *v.5 p.353, p.357, p.379*

Clean Electricity from Photovoltaics. *v.5 p.362*

Clean Slate: New and Selected Poems. *v.2 p.677*

Clean Water Act Handbook. *v.6 p.301*

Clean Water Act Thirty-Year Retrospective: History and
Documents Related to the Federal Statute. *v.6 p.294*

Cleanth Brooks and Allen Tate: Collected Letters,
1933-1976. . . . .*v.2 p.125*

Cleanth Brooks and Robert Penn Warren: A Literary
Correspondence. *v.2 p.12*

Cleanth Brooks and the Rise of Modern Criticism. *v.2 p.5*

A Clear Eye for Branding: Straight Talk on Today's Most
Powerful Business Concept. *v.4 p.138*

Clear Light of Day. *v.2 p.764*

A Clearing in the Distance: Frederick Law Olmsted and
America in the 19th Century. *v.1 p.816, v.6 p.715*

☐ Clearinghouse on Educational Policy and
Management. *v.4 p.280*

Clea. *v.2 p.344*

Clemens Brentano. *v.2 p.596*

Clement Marot. *v.2 p.470*

Clement of Alexandria. *v.1 p.613*

Clementi: His Life and Music. *v.1 p.191, p.317*

Clementine Hunter: American Folk Artist. *v.1 p.750*

Cleopatra and Rome. *v.3 p.10*

Cleopatra. *v.3 p.10*

A Clergyman's Daughter. *v.2 p.375*

Clerical Celibacy: The Heritage. *v.1 p.649*

Cleveland: A Concise History, 1796-1996. . . . . .*v.3 p.513*

Clever Hans (The Horse of Mr. Von Osten). *v.5 p.615*

The Clicking of Cuthbert. *v.2 p.390*

Clifford Odets and American Political Theatre. . . .*v.2 p.108*

Clifford Odets: Playwright-Poet. *v.2 p.108*

Clifford Sifton: A Lonely Eminence, 1901-1929, Vol. 2. *v.3 p.539*

Clifford Sifton: Young Napoleon, 1861-1900. . . . .*v.3 p.539*

Cligés. *v.2 p.466*

Climate Change 1994: Radiative Forcing of Climate Change and
an Evaluation of the IPCC 1992 IS92 Emission
Scenarios. *v.5 p.371*

Climate Change and Africa. *v.4 p.394*

Climate Change and Biodiversity. *v.4 p.394*

Climate Change and Society: Consequences of Increasing
Atmospheric Carbon Dioxide. *v.5 p.355, p.371*

Climate Change and the Global Harvest: Potential Impacts of
the Greenhouse Effect on Agriculture. *v.5 p.28*

Climate Change: Causes, Effects, and Solutions. . . .*v.5 p.426*

Climate Change: Critical Concepts in the Environment and
Physical Geography. *v.4 p.393*

Climate Change Policy: A Survey. *v.6 p.301*

Climate Process and Change. *v.5 p.425*

Climates and Constitutions: Health, Race, Environment and
British Imperialism in India, 1600-1850. . . . . .*v.6 p.157*

Climatic Geomorphology. *v.4 p.391*

Climatology: An Atmospheric Science. *v.5 p.426*

The Climb: Tragic Ambitions on Everest. *v.4 p.789*

Climbing Free: My Life in the Vertical World. *v.4 p.789, p.836*

Climbing in North America. *v.4 p.789*

Climbing Mount Improbable. *v.5 p.191*

Climbing Parnassus: A New Apologia for Greek and
Latin. *v.4 p.303*

Climbing: The Complete Reference. *v.4 p.789*

Climbing the Ladder: An Update on the Status of Doctoral
Women Scientists and Engineers. *v.5 p.398*

Climbing the Mountain: The Scientific Biography of Julian
Schwinger. *v.5 p.543*

Clinical Anatomy. *v.5 p.158*

Clinical Behavior Therapy: Adults and Children. . . .*v.5 p.666*

Clinical embryology: a color atlas and text. *v.5 p.162*

Clinical Genetics: A Short Course. *v.5 p.152*

Clinical Genetics in Nursing Practice, Third Edition. . *v.5 p.149*

Clinical Gynecologic Endocrinology and Infertility. . *v.5 p.524*

Clinical Hypertension. *v.5 p.520*

Clinical Management of Infections in Immunocompromised
Infants and Children. *v.5 p.518*

Clinical Measurement of Speech and Voice. *v.5 p.518*

Clinical Neuroanatomy. *v.5 p.516*

Clinical Nursing Skills and Techniques. *v.5 p.528*

Clinical Pathology. *v.5 p.521, p.522*

The Clinical Practice of Career Assessment: Abilities, Interests,
and Personality. *v.5 p.578*

Clinical Practice of Sports Injury Prevention and Care. *v.4 p.827*

Clinical Procedures for Medical Assistants. *v.5 p.534*

Clinical Textbook of Addictive Disorders. . . .*v.5 p.512, p.521*

Clinical Toxicology. *v.5 p.514*

Clinically Oriented Anatomy. *v.5 p.158*

Clinton and Congress, 1993-1996: Risk, Restoration, and
Reelection. *v.4 p.532*

Clinton in Haiti: The 1994 US Invasion of Haiti. *v.3 p.314, p.315*

The Clinton Legacy. *v.3 p.467*

The Clinton Presidency: First Appraisals. *v.3 p.467*

The Clinton Scandal and the Future of American
Government. *v.3 p.479*

The Clinton Scandals and the Politics of Image
Restoration. *v.3 p.466*

The Clinton Wars. *v.3 p.466*

Clinton's World: Remaking American Foreign Policy. *v.3 p.473*

Clio Unbound: Perception of the Social and Cultural Past in
Renaissance England. *v.3 p.100*

Clio's Cosmetics. *v.2 p.426*

Clio's Favorites: Leading Historians of the U. S.,
1945-2000. . . . .*v.3 p.374, p.375*

Clive Barker Sculpture: Catalogue Raisonné,
1958-2000. . . . .*v.1 p.779*

Clive: Inside the Record Business. *v.1 p.383*

The Cloaking of Power: Montesquieu, Blackstone, and the Rise of Judicial Activism. *v.4 p.541*

Clocks and Culture, 1300-1700. . . . .*v.3 p.39*

The Clocks of Columbus: The Literary Career of James Thurber. *v.2 p.125*

A Clockwork Orange. *v.2 p.336*

Clog and Character Dances. *v.1 p.33*

The Cloister and the Hearth A Tale of the Middle Ages. .*v.2 p.303*

Cloning and the Future of Human Embryo Research. .*v.5 p.162*

Close Calls: New Lesbian Fiction. *v.2 p.26*

Close Encounters: Film, Feminism, and Science Fiction. .*v.6 p.319*

Close Quarters. *v.2 p.347*

Close Reading: The Reader. *v.2 p.164*

Close Relationships: A Sourcebook. *v.5 p.647, p.648*

Close to the Knives: A Memoir of Disintegration. . .*v.6 p.408*

Close to the Land: Reflections on Re-Connecting. . .*v.5 p.173*

Close Up: Iranian Cinema, Past, Present and Future. .*v.6 p.333*

Closed Chambers: The First Eyewitness Account of the Epic Struggles Inside the Supreme Court. *v.4 p.537*

Closed-face Tunnelling Machines and Ground Stability: A Guideline for Best Practice. *v.5 p.698*

Closely Watched Trains. *v.2 p.783*

Closer. *v.6 p.395*

Close-Up: How to Read the American City. *v.6 p.717*

Closing an Era: Historical Perspectives on Modern Archives and Records Management. *v.4 p.115*

Closing of the American Mind. *v.3 p.366, v.4 p.289*

Closing the Gate: Race, Politics and the Chinese Exclusion Act. *v.6 p.118, p.123, p.126, p.127*

Clotel, or, the President's Daughter. *v.6 p.23*

Clothes for a Summer Hotel. *v.2 p.135*

The Cloud of Danger: Current Realities of American Foreign Policy. *v.3 p.473*

The Cloud of Unknowing. *v.1 p.653*

The Cloud People: The Divergent Evolution of the Zapotic and Mixte Civilizations. *v.4 p.9*

Clouded Sky. *v.2 p.786*

Clouds of Witness. *v.2 p.381*

Cloudsplitter: A Novel. *v.2 p.140*

Cloudstreet: A Novel. *v.2 p.749*

Clouds. *v.2 p.423*

Clough: The Critical Heritage. *v.2 p.278*

The Clown. *v.2 p.604*

Club Cultures: Music, Media, and Subcultural Capital. .*v.1 p.34*

Club Date Musicians: Playing the New York Party Circuit. *v.1 p.384*

🄮 Clubbing: Dancing, Ecstasy and Vitality. *v.1 p.34*

The Clubwomen's Daughters: Collectivist Impulses in Progressive-Era Girls' Fiction. *v.2 p.10*

Cluster Analysis for Social Scientists. *v.4 p.689*

Clyfford Still: Paintings 1944-1960. . . . .*v.1 p.737*

CMOS Analog Circuit Design. *v.5 p.721*

CMOS Digital Integrated Circuits Analysis and Design. .*v.5 p.722*

CNN Effect: Myth of News Media Foreign Policy and Intervention. *v.4 p.407, p.408, p.415*

Coach: The Life of Paul Bear Bryant. *v.4 p.858, p.893*

Coaching Basketball. *v.4 p.854, p.904*

Coaching Tennis Successfully. *v.4 p.864*

Coaching Volleyball: Building a Winning Team. *v.4 p.869, p.904, p.905*

Coaching Volleyball Successfully. . . .*v.4 p.794, p.869, p.904*

Coaching Women's Soccer: A Revolutionary Approach to Putting the Play Back into Practice. *v.4 p.800, p.838, p.868, p.905*

Coaching Youth Baseball. *v.4 p.794, p.849*

Coaching Youth Hockey. *v.4 p.794, p.862*

Coaching Youth Soccer. *v.4 p.794, p.839, p.867, p.904*

Coaching Youth Tennis. . .*v.4 p.794, p.795, p.839, p.863, p.864*

Coaching Youth Volleyball. *v.4 p.839, p.869, p.904*

Coaching Youth Wrestling. *v.4 p.795, p.839, p.870*

Coal: A Human History. . . .*v.4 p.146, p.160, v.5 p.450, p.737*

Coal Camp Justice: Two Wrongs Make a Right. . . .*v.2 p.160*

Coal Energy Systems. *v.5 p.361*

Coal Geology. *v.5 p.450, p.451, p.738*

Coal: The Energy Source of the Past and Future. . .*v.5 p.738*

Coast Guard's House. *v.2 p.719*

Coast of Dreams: California on the Edge, 1990-2003. .*v.3 p.532*

Coastal and Estuarine Environments: Sedimentology, Geomorphology and Geoarchaeology. *v.4 p.392*

Coastal Evolution: Late Quaternary Shoreline Morphodynamics. *v.5 p.366*

Coastal Geomorphology: An Introduction. . . .*v.5 p.423, p.424*

Coastal Maine: A Maritime History. *v.3 p.486*

Coastal Planning and Management. *v.6 p.283*

Coasts: Form, Process and Evolution. *v.4 p.393, v.5 p.424*

The Coasts of Bohemia: A Czech History. *v.3 p.191*

Cobbler in Congress: The Life of Henry Wilson, 1812-1875. . . . .*v.3 p.422, p.423, p.427*

Cobden and Bright: a Victorian Political Partnership. *v.3 p.95, p.114, p.115*

Cobra and Maitreya. *v.2 p.673*

The Coca Boom and Rural Social Change in Bolivia. .*v.3 p.282*

Coca Exotica. *v.3 p.281, p.282*

The Coca Leaf and Cocaine Papers. *v.3 p.281*

La Coca Liberal: Producción y Circulación a Principios del Siglo XX. *v.3 p.282*

Coca Prohibition in Peru: The Historical Debates. .*v.3 p.281, p.329*

Cocaine: A Drug and Its Social Evolution. *v.3 p.281*

Cocaine Addiction: Theory, Research and Treatment. *v.5 p.664, p.673*

Cocaine: From Medical Marvel to Modern Menace in the United States, 1884-1920. . . . .*v.3 p.282*

Cocaine: Global Histories. *v.3 p.281*

Cocaine: Its History, Uses and Effects. *v.3 p.281*

Cocaine Nights. *v.2 p.330*

Cocaine: White Gold Rush in Peru. *v.3 p.282, p.330*

Cochabamba, 1550-1900: Colonialism and Agrarian Transformation in Bolivia. *v.3 p.324*

Cochrane: Brittania's Last Sea King. *v.3 p.91*

La Cocina Cotidiana y Festiva de Los Limeños en el Siglo XIX. *v.3 p.272*

La Cocina en el Virreinato del Peru. *v.3 p.272*

The Cockatoos: Shorter Novels and Stories. *v.2 p.750*

A Cock-Eyed Comedy. *v.2 p.658*

Cocktail Time. *v.2 p.390*

Cocteau: A Biography. *v.1 p.13, v.6 p.419*

Coctel de Frutas: Yuja'n Uwach Che'. *v.2 p.676*

Cod: A Biography of the Fish That Changed the World. .*v.6 p.291*

📖 CODATA Key Values for Thermodynamics. *v.5 p.285*

Code Breaking: A History and Exploration. *v.5 p.408*

Code Complete. *v.5 p.346, p.348*

Code Name Ginger: The Story Behind Segway and Dean Kamen's Quest to Invent a New World. *v.5 p.716*

📖 Code of Federal Regulations (CFR). *v.4 p.481*

The Code of Leke Dukagjini. *v.2 p.815*

The Code of Maimonides, Bks. 5-6 & 8-14. . . . . *v.1 p.550*

The Code of Maimonides (Mishneh Torah): The Book of Love. *v.1 p.550*

The Code of Maimonides: The Book of Seasons. . . *v.1 p.550*

Code of Medical Ethics, Current Opinions with Annotations 2004-2005. . . . . *v.5 p.511*

Code of the Streets: Decency, Violence and the Moral Life of the Inner City. *v.4 p.723*

The Code of the Woosters. *v.2 p.390*

Coercion and Control in Communist Society: The Visible Hand in a Command Economy. *v.4 p.708*

Coercion and Governance: The Declining Political Role of the Military in Asia. *v.4 p.616*

Coercion and Market: Silver Mining in Colonial Potosi, 1692-1826. . . . . *v.3 p.325*

Coercion, Capital, and European States, AD 990-1990. . . . . *v.3 p.62, v.4 p.501, p.602*

The Coevolution of Human Potential and Converging Technologies. *v.5 p.589*

The Coevolutionary Process. *v.5 p.197*

Co-Existence in Wartime Lebanon: Death of a State and Birth of a Nation. *v.4 p.614, p.616*

Coffee and Capitalism in the Venezuelan Andes. . . *v.3 p.361*

Coffee and Conflict in Colombia 1886-1910. . . . . *v.3 p.357*

Coffee and Power: Revolution and the Rise of Democracy in Central America. *v.3 p.303*

Coffee and the Growth of Agrarian Capitalism in Nineteenth-Century Puerto Rico. *v.3 p.318*

Coffee, Cocoa and Tea. *v.5 p.24, p.35, p.36*

A Coffee Frontier in Latin America: Land, Society, and Politics in Duaca, Venezuela, 1830-1936. . . *v.3 p.361, p.363, p.365*

Coffee in Colombia, Eighteen Hundred to Nineteen Hundred Seventy: An Economic, Social and Political History. .*v.3 p.358*

A Coffin for Dimitrios. *v.2 p.328*

Coffins on Our Shoulders: The Experience of the Palestinian. *v.6 p.619*

Cognition and Curriculum Reconsidered. *v.4 p.362*

Cognition and the Visual Arts. *v.5 p.609, p.619*

Cognition in Practice: Mind, Mathematics and Culture in Everyday Life. *v.4 p.27*

The Cognitive Bases of Interpersonal Communication. .*v.5 p.621*

Cognitive Bases of Musical Communication. *v.1 p.375*

Cognitive Developments in Economics. *v.4 p.272*

Cognitive Development. *v.5 p.626, p.629, p.630*

Cognitive Dimensions of Social Science: The Way We Think about Politics, Economics, Law, and Society. . . . *v.4 p.272*

Cognitive Dissonance: Progress on a Pivotal Theory in Social Psychology. *v.5 p.650*

📱 Cognitive Economics: An Interdisciplinary Approach. *v.4 p.272*

Cognitive Economics: An Interdisciplinary Approach. *v.4 p.272*

Cognitive Economics. *v.4 p.272*

Cognitive Foundations of Musical Pitch. *v.1 p.376*

Cognitive Foundations of Natural History: Towards an Anthropology of Science. *v.4 p.26*

Cognitive Models of Psychological Time. *v.5 p.604*

Cognitive Neuroscience of Attention. *v.5 p.611*

Cognitive Neuroscience of Emotion. *v.5 p.612*

The Cognitive Neuroscience of Music. *v.1 p.376*

The Cognitive Neurosciences. *v.5 p.617*

Cognitive Pragmatism: The Theory of Knowledge in Pragmatic Perspective. *v.1 p.513*

Cognitive Processes and Economic Behaviour. *v.4 p.249, p.250, p.272*

Cognitive Psychology: An Overview for Cognitive Scientists. *v.5 p.608*

Cognitive Science: A Philosophical Introduction. . . *v.1 p.497*

Cognitive Science and Concepts of Mind: Toward a General Theory of Human and Artificial Intelligence. .*v.5 p.590, p.591*

Cognitive Sociology. *v.4 p.692*

Cognitive Technology: In Search of a Humane Interface. *v.5 p.589*

Cognitive Therapy of Personality Disorders. *v.5 p.665*

Cognitive Therapy of Schizophrenia. . .*v.5 p.660, p.661, p.665*

Cognitive-Behavioral Assessment and Therapy with Adolescents. *v.5 p.666*

Cognitive-Behavioral Therapies with Lesbian, Gay and Bisexual Clients. *v.5 p.665, v.6 p.381*

Cohabitation, Marriage, Divorce, and Remarriage in the United States. *v.4 p.739*

The Coherence of Theism. *v.1 p.639, p.640*

The Cohesion of Oppression: Clientship and Ethnicity in Rwanda, 1860-1960. . . . .*v.4 p.582, p.584, p.612*

The Cohesion of Saudi Arabia: Evolution of Political Identity. *v.6 p.626*

Coinage and History of the Roman Empire, C. 82 B.C.—A.D. 480, Set. *v.3 p.22*

📖 Colby College. Chemistry Department. *v.5 p.269*

Cold Peace: Stalin and the Soviet Ruling Circle, 1945-1953. . . . . *v.3 p.225*

The Cold War: A New History. *v.3 p.388, v.4 p.628*

The Cold War and Soviet Insecurity: The Stalin Years. *v.3 p.87, p.226*

The Cold War Comes to Main Street: America in 1950. .*v.3 p.479*

Cold War, Cool Medium: Television, McCarthyism, and American Culture. *v.4 p.418*

Cold War Culture: Media and the Arts, 1945-1990. . . *v.3 p.444*

Cold War Diplomacy: American Foreign Policy,
   1945-1975. . . . . *v.3 p.452*

Cold War Fantasies: Film, Fiction and Foreign
   Policy. *v.6 p.322, p.323*

The Cold War on the Periphery: The United States, India, and
   Pakistan. *v.3 p.391*

Cold War Statesmen Confront the Bomb: Nuclear Diplomacy
   since 1945. . . . . *v.4 p.645, p.647*

Cold War Strategist: Stuart Symington and the Search for
   National Security. *v.3 p.461*

Cold Warriors: Eisenhower's Generation and American Foreign
   Policy. *v.3 p.466*

The Cold War. *v.4 p.485*

A Colder Eye: The Modern Irish Writers. *v.2 p.178*

Cole Porter: A Biography. *v.1 p.252, p.347, v.6 p.409*

Colegio Cesar Chavez, 1973-1983: A Chicano Struggle for
   Educational Self-Determination. *v.6 p.527*

Coleridge and Wordsworth: A Lyrical Dialogue. *v.2 p.280, p.324*

Coleridge: Poems. *v.2 p.280*

Coleridge the Visionary. *v.2 p.278*

Coleridge, Wordsworth and the Language of Allusion. *v.2 p.324*

Coleridge's Criticism of Shakespeare. *v.2 p.279*

Collaboration in Belgium: Leon Degrelle and the Rexist
   Movement, 1940-1944. . . . . *v.3 p.206*

Collaboration: Japanese Agents and Local Elites in Wartime
   China. *v.6 p.193*

Collaborative Analysis of Student Work: Improving Teaching
   and Learning. *v.4 p.286*

Collaborative Entrepreneurship: How Communities of
   Networked Firms Use Continuous Innovation to Create
   Economic Wealth. *v.4 p.68*

Collaborative Learning: Higher Education, Interdependence, and
   the Authority of Knowledge. *v.4 p.349*

Collaborative Manufacturing: Using Real-Time Information to
   Support the Supply Chain. *v.4 p.118*

Collaborative Planning for Wetlands and Wildlife: Issues and
   Examples. *v.5 p.177, p.181*

Collaborative Public Management: New Strategies for Local
   Governments. *v.4 p.542, p.543*

The Collaborator: The Trial and Execution of Robert
   Brasillach. *v.3 p.156*

Collages of John Evans. *v.1 p.696*

Collapse: How Societies Choose to Fail or Succeed. . *v.4 p.760*

The Collapse of British Power. . . *v.3 p.88, p.90, p.117, p.118*

The Collapse of Canada? *v.4 p.587*

The Collapse of Communist Power in Poland: Strategic
   Misperceptions and Unanticipated Outcomes. . . *v.3 p.255*

The Collapse of State Socialism: The Case of
   Poland. *v.4 p.506, p.508, p.596*

The Collapse of the Confederacy. *v.3 p.397*

The Collapse of the Kyoto Protocol and the Struggle to Slow
   Global Warming. *v.6 p.299, p.301*

The Collapse of the Tokugawa Bakufu, 1862-1868: Eighteen
   Sixty-Two to Eighteen Sixty-Eight. *v.6 p.226*

Collapsed States: The Disintegration and Restoration of
   Legitimate Authority. *v.4 p.613*

Collected Ancient Greek Novels. *v.2 p.405*

The Collected Books of Jack Spicer. *v.2 p.156*

The Collected Correspondence and London Notebooks of Joseph
   Haydn. *v.1 p.189, p.330*

The Collected Dialogues of Plato: Including the
   Letters. *v.1 p.424, p.425, v.2 p.418*

Collected Early Poems, 1950-1970. . . . . *v.2 p.115*

Collected Economic Essays: Essays on Economic Stability and
   Growth. *v.4 p.209*

Collected Economic Essays: Essays on Value and
   Distribution. *v.4 p.209*

Collected Economic Papers of Joan Robinson -
   Index. *v.4 p.251, p.252*

Collected Economic Papers. *v.4 p.196*

Collected Editions, Historical Series and Sets, and Monuments
   of Music: A Bibliography. *v.1 p.167*

Collected Essays in Literary Criticism. *v.2 p.379*

The Collected Essays, Journalism and Letters of George Orwell:
   An Age Like This, 1920-1940. . . . . *v.2 p.375*

The Collected Essays, Journalism and Letters of George Orwell:
   As I Please, 1943-1945. . . . . *v.2 p.375, p.376*

The Collected Essays, Journalism and Letters of George Orwell:
   In Front of Your Nose, 1945-1950. . . . . . . *v.2 p.375*

The Collected Essays, Journalism and Letters of George Orwell:
   My Country Right or Left, 1940-1943. . . . . . *v.2 p.375*

The Collected Essays of Christopher Hill: Writing and
   Revolution in Seventeenth-Century England, Vol.
   1. . . . . *v.3 p.102, p.103, p.131*

The Collected Essays of Milton Babbitt. . . . *v.1 p.209, p.302*

Collected Essays. *v.2 p.125, p.576*

The Collected Fables of Ambrose Bierce. *v.2 p.31*

The Collected Fiction of Kenneth Koch. *v.2 p.92*

Collected Fictions, Vol. 3. . . . . *v.2 p.677*

Collected Later Poems. *v.2 p.146*

Collected Letters, 1911-1925. . . . . . . *v.2 p.309, p.310*

Collected Letters of Harriet Martineau. *v.4 p.195*

The Collected Letters of Katherine Mansfield:
   1888-1917. . . . . *v.2 p.369*

The Collected Letters of Katherine Mansfield: 1918-September
   1919. . . . . *v.2 p.369*

The Collected Letters of Katherine Mansfield:
   1919-1920. . . . . *v.2 p.369*

The Collected Letters of Thomas Hardy, 1893-1901, Vol.
   2. . . . . *v.2 p.292*

The Collected Letters of Thomas Hardy: 1902-1908, Vol.
   3. . . . . *v.2 p.292*

The Collected Letters of Thomas Hardy: 1914-1919, Vol.
   5. . . . . *v.2 p.292*

The Collected Letters of Thomas Hardy: 1920-1925, Vol.
   6. . . . . *v.2 p.292*

The Collected Letters of Thomas Hardy: 1926-1927 (with
   Addenda, Corrigenda, and General Index), Vol. 7. *v.2 p.292*

Collected Letters. *v.2 p.248*

Collected Narrative and Lyrical Poetry. *v.2 p.807*

Collected Novellas. *v.2 p.683*

Collected Novels and Plays: James
   Merrill. *v.2 p.101, v.6 p.398, p.412*

Collected Novels: Fanshawe, the Scarlet Letter, the House of the Seven Gables, the Blithedale Romance, the Marble Faun. *v.2 p.41*

Collected Novels of Conrad Aiken. *v.2 p.56*

Collected Papers of Franco Modigliani: Essays in Macroeconomics. *v.4 p.210*

Collected Papers. *v.1 p.446, v.4 p.514*

Collected Philosophical Papers. *v.1 p.456*

Collected Plays: Hay Fever; the Vortex, Fallen Angels; Easy Virtue. *v.2 p.342*

Collected Plays in Translation. *v.1 p.129, p.131,v.6 p.153*

Collected Plays I. *v.2 p.378*

The Collected Plays of Edward Albee, 1966-1977, Vol. 2. . . . .*v.1 p.86, p.91, p.111*

The Collected Plays of Edward Albee: 1978-2003. . . . .*v.1 p.86, p.91, p.111*

The Collected Plays of Edward Albee, Vol. 1.*v.1 p.86, p.91, p.111*

The Collected Plays of Neil Simon, Vol. 1. . . . . . .*v.2 p.116*

The Collected Plays of Neil Simon, Vol. 2. . . . . . .*v.2 p.116*

The Collected Plays of Neil Simon, Vol. 3. . . . . . .*v.2 p.116*

The Collected Plays of Neil Simon, Vol. 4. . . . . . .*v.2 p.116*

The Collected Plays of Terence Rattigan: The Early Plays 1936-1952. . . . .*v.2 p.379*

The Collected Plays of Terence Rattigan: The Later Plays, 1953-1977. . . . .*v.2 p.379*

Collected Plays of William Butler Yeats. *v.2 p.327*

Collected Plays: Six Characters in Search of an Author, All for the Best, Clothe the Naked and Limes from Sicily, Vol. 2. . . . .*v.2 p.723*

Collected Plays Two. *v.2 p.378*

The Collected Plays, Vol. 1. . . . .*v.2 p.750*

Collected Plays, Vol. 1. . . . .*v.2 p.758*

Collected Plays, Vol. 2. . . . .*v.2 p.750, p.758*

Collected plays, vol. 3: The rules of the game, Each in his own way, Grafted, The other son. *v.2 p.722*

Collected Plays, Vol. 3. . . . .*v.2 p.342*

Collected Plays, Vol. 4. . . . .*v.2 p.342*

Collected Plays, Vol. 5. . . . .*v.2 p.342*

Collected Plays. *v.2 p.349, p.527, p.605*

Collected Poems: 1909-1962. . . . .*v.2 p.71*

Collected Poems 1912-1944. . . . .*v.2 p.88*

Collected Poems, 1916-1970. . . . .*v.2 p.56*

Collected Poems 1917 to 1982. . . . .*v.2 p.98, p.99*

Collected Poems, 1919-1976. . . . .*v.2 p.125*

Collected Poems 1920-1954: Bilingual Edition. . . .*v.2 p.719*

Collected Poems, 1928-1985. . . . .*v.2 p.384*

Collected Poems, 1930-1976. . . . .*v.2 p.71*

Collected Poems, 1930-1983. . . . .*v.2 p.98*

Collected Poems, 1931-1974. . . . .*v.2 p.344*

Collected Poems, 1943-2004. . . . .*v.2 p.128*

Collected Poems 1947-1980. . . . .*v.6 p.404*

Collected Poems 1947-1997. . . . .*v.2 p.79*

Collected Poems, 1948-1984. . . . .*v.2 p.770*

Collected Poems, 1953-93. . . . .*v.2 p.157*

The Collected Poems: 1956-1998. . . . .*v.2 p.790*

Collected Poems, 1975. . . . .*v.2 p.348*

The Collected Poems: A Bilingual Edition. *v.2 p.659*

Collected Poems and Other Verse. *v.2 p.496*

Collected Poems and Prose. *v.2 p.377*

Collected Poems by Vachel Lindsay. *v.2 p.94*

The Collected Poems of Audre Lorde. . .*v.2 p.149, v.6 p.405*

Collected Poems of Charles Olson: Excluding the Maximus Poems. *v.2 p.108*

The Collected Poems of Dylan Thomas: 1934-1952. .*v.2 p.386*

The Collected Poems of Frank O'Hara. . . .*v.2 p.106, v.6 p.405*

The Collected Poems of George Oppen. *v.2 p.106*

The Collected Poems of Howard Nemerov. *v.2 p.105*

The Collected Poems of James Agee. *v.2 p.55*

The Collected Poems of James K. Baxter. *v.2 p.744*

The Collected Poems of Jean Toomer. *v.2 p.126*

The Collected Poems of John Ciardi. *v.2 p.65*

The Collected Poems of Joseph Hall, Bishop of Exeter and Norwich. *v.2 p.214*

The Collected Poems of Kenneth Koch. *v.2 p.92*

Collected Poems of Kenneth Patchen. *v.2 p.110*

The Collected Poems of Muriel Rukeyser. *v.2 p.114*

The Collected Poems of Octavio Paz, 1957-1987: Bilingual Edition. *v.2 p.669*

The Collected Poems of Paul Blackburn. *v.2 p.58*

The Collected Poems of Robert Creeley, 1945-1975. .*v.2 p.65*

The Collected Poems of Robert Louis Stevenson. . .*v.2 p.312*

Collected Poems of Robert Penn Warren. *v.2 p.129*

Collected Poems of Rolfe Humphries. *v.2 p.81*

The Collected Poems of Rupert Brooke. *v.2 p.335*

The Collected Poems of Sara Teasdale. *v.2 p.124*

The Collected Poems of Sarton, 1930-1993. . . . .*v.2 p.119*

The Collected Poems of Stanley Kunitz. *v.2 p.92*

Collected Poems of Stephane Mallarme. *v.2 p.496*

The Collected Poems of Sterling A. Brown. *v.2 p.58*

The Collected Poems of Stevie Smith [I. *v.2 p.382, p.383*

Collected Poems of Ted Hughes. *v.2 p.353*

The Collected Poems of Tennessee Williams. *v.2 p.135*

The Collected Poems of Theodore Roethke. *v.2 p.114*

The Collected Poems of Weldon Kees. *v.2 p.91*

The Collected Poems of Wendell Berry, 1957-1982. .*v.2 p.141*

The Collected Poems of William Carlos Williams, 1909-1939, Vol. 1. . . . .*v.2 p.136*

The Collected Poems of William Carlos Williams, 1939-1962, Vol. 2. . . . .*v.2 p.136, p.137*

Collected Poems. .*v.2 p.62, p.63, p.90, p.96, p.98, p.101, p.129, p.139, p.153, p.291, p.331, p.337, p.358, p.361, p.362, p.368*

The Collected Poems. *v.2 p.380*

Collected Poems. . .*v.2 p.382, p.499, p.659, p.660, p.732, p.733, p.739, p.744, p.749, p.753, p.756,v.6 p.404, p.405*

Collected Poetry and Prose. *v.2 p.305*

Collected Poetry of Aldous Huxley. *v.2 p.354*

The Collected Poetry of Nikki Giovanni: 1968-1998. . . . .*v.2 p.146, v.6 p.25, p.43*

Collected Prose: Autobiographical Writings, True Stories, Critical Essays, Prefaces, and Collaborations with Artists. *v.2 p.139*

The Collected Prose. *v.2 p.61*

Collected Prose. *v.2 p.65, p.100, p.606*

The Collected Scientific Papers of Paul A. Samuelson. *v.4 p.196*

The Collected Scientific Papers of Paul Samuelson, Vol. 1. . . . .*v.4 p.196*

The Collected Scientific Papers of Paul Samuelson, Vol. 2. . . . .*v.4 p.196*

The Collected Scientific Papers of Paul Samuelson, Vol. 3. . . . .*v.4 p.196*

The Collected Scientific Papers of Paul Samuelson, Vol. 4. . . . .*v.4 p.196*

The Collected Scientific Papers of Paul Samuelson, Vol. 5. . . . .*v.4 p.197*

Collected Short Stories of Julia Peterkin. *v.2 p.109*

The Collected Short Stories of W. Somerset Maugham, Vol. 1. . . . .*v.2 p.370*

The Collected Short Stories of W. Somerset Maugham, Vol. 2. . . . .*v.2 p.370*

The Collected Short Stories of W. Somerset Maugham, Vol. 3. . . . .*v.2 p.370*

The Collected Short Stories of W. Somerset Maugham, Vol. 4. . . . .*v.2 p.370*

Collected Short Stories. *v.2 p.354*

The Collected Short Stories. *v.2 p.769*

The Collected Shorter Fiction, Vol. II. *v.2 p.809*

Collected Shorter Fiction, Vol. I. *v.2 p.809*

The Collected Stories of Angus Wilson. *v.2 p.389*

The Collected Stories of Arthur C. Clarke. *v.2 p.337*

Collected Stories of Carson McCullers. *v.2 p.100*

The Collected Stories of Chester Himes. *v.2 p.86*

The Collected Stories of Colette. *v.2 p.514*

The Collected Stories of Elizabeth Bowen. *v.2 p.334*

Collected Stories of Henry Lawson. *v.2 p.747*

The Collected Stories of Jean Stafford. *v.2 p.120*

The Collected Stories of Jessamyn West. *v.2 p.130*

The Collected Stories of Katherine Anne Porter. . . .*v.2 p.109*

The Collected Stories of Maria Cristina Mena. . . .*v.6 p.501*

The Collected Stories of Moacyr Scliar. *v.2 p.693*

The Collected Stories of Moacyr Scliar. *v.2 p.693*

The Collected Stories of Peter Taylor. *v.2 p.157*

The Collected Stories of Reynolds Price. *v.2 p.153*

The Collected Stories of Richard Yates. *v.2 p.159*

The Collected Stories of Wallace Stegner. *v.2 p.121*

The Collected Stories of William Carlos Williams. . .*v.2 p.137*

Collected Stories of William Faulkner. *v.2 p.73*

The Collected Stories. *v.2 p.78*

Collected Stories. *v.2 p.135*

The Collected Stories. *v.2 p.152*

Collected Stories. *v.2 p.374*

The Collected Stories. *v.2 p.386*

Collected Stories. *v.2 p.683, v.6 p.400*

Collected Tales, Sketches, Speeches and Essays, 1852-1890, Vol. 1. . . . .*v.2 p.34*

Collected Tales, Sketches, Speeches and Essays. . . .*v.2 p.34*

Collected Travel Writings: Great Britain and America. *v.2 p.45*

Collected Verse of Henry Lawson. *v.2 p.747*

Collected Verse of Rudyard Kipling. *v.2 p.297*

Collected Verse. *v.2 p.342*

The Collected Works of Abraham Lincoln. *v.3 p.425*

The Collected Works of Billy the Kid. *v.2 p.737*

The Collected Works of C. G. Jung, Set. *v.5 p.659*

The Collected Works of Dante Gabriel Rossetti, Vol. 1. .*v.2 p.305*

The Collected Works of Eric Voegelin. *v.1 p.469*

The Collected Works of James Mill, Set. *v.1 p.445*

The Collected Works of John Dewey, 1882-1953: (Windows). *v.4 p.342*

Collected Works of John Locke: Collected Works. . . .*v.1 p.449*

The Collected Works of L. S. Vygotsky: Child Psychology. *v.5 p.572*

The Collected Works of L. S. Vygotsky: Fundamentals of Defectology (Abnormal Psychology and Learning Disabilities). *v.5 p.573*

The Collected Works of L. S. Vygotsky: Problems of General Psychology, Including the Volume "Thinking and Speech". *v.4 p.695, v.5 p.573, p.622, p.624*

The Collected Works of L. S. Vygotsky: Problems of the Theory and History of Psychology. *v.5 p.572*

The Collected Works of L. S. Vygotsky: Scientific Legacy. *v.5 p.573*

The Collected Works of L. S. Vygotsky: The History of the Development of Higher Mental Functions. *v.5 p.572, p.621, p.623, p.624*

The Collected Works of Langston Hughes, Vol. 11. . .*v.2 p.87*

The Collected Works of Ralph Waldo Emerson: The Conduct of Life, Vol. VI. *v.2 p.38*

The Collected Works of Samuel Taylor Coleridge: Aids of Reflection. *v.2 p.278*

The Collected Works of Spinoza, Vol. 1. . . . . . .*v.1 p.478*

The Collected Works of St. John of the Cross. *v.1 p.571*

The Collected Works of St. Teresa of Avila: The Book of Her Life, Spiritual Testimonies, Soliloquies. . . *v.1 p.571, p.572*

The Collected Works of St. Teresa of Avila, Vol. 2. . *v.1 p.571*

The Collected Works of St. Teresa of Avila, Vol. 3. . *v.1 p.571*

The Collected Works of St. Thomas Aquinas. *v.1 p.571*

The Collected Works of Thomas Muntzer. *v.3 p.166*

Collected Works of Velimir Khlebnikov: Letters and Theoretical Writings, Vol. I. *v.2 p.805*

Collected Works of Velimir Khlebnikov: Prose, Plays, and Supersagas, Vol. II. *v.2 p.805*

The Collected Works of William Howard Taft: Taft Papers on League of Nations. *v.4 p.632*

The Collected Writings of Ambrose Bierce. *v.2 p.31*

The Collected Writings of John Maynard Keynes. . .*v.4 p.228*

The Collected Writings of Robert Motherwell. *v.1 p.744*

The Collected Writings of Wallace Thurman: A Harlem Renaissance Reader. *v.2 p.124*

Collecting Visible Evidence. *v.4 p.413, v.6 p.309*

Collection of Short Stories. *v.2 p.329*

A Collection of the Moral and Instructive Sentiments, Maxims, Cautions and Reflections, Contained in the Histories of Pamela, Clarissa, and Sir Charles Grandison. *v.2 p.258*

Collective Action and Community: Public Arenas and the Emergence of Communalism in North India. *v.6 p.160*

The Collective and the Public in Latin America: Cultural Identities and Political Order. *v.3 p.260*

Collective Bargaining in the Public Sector: The Experience of Eight States. *v.4 p.123*

Collective Barganing in the Private Sector. *v.4 p.121*

Collective Behavior and Public Opinion: Rapid Shifts in Opinion and Communication. *v.4 p.713, v.5 p.586, p.622, p.625*

Collective Choice and Social Welfare. *v.4 p.266*

Collective Memory, National Identity, and Ethnic Conflict: Greece, Bulgaria and the Macedonian Question. . .*v.3 p.250*

Collector's History of English Pottery. *v.1 p.808*

The Collector. *v.2 p.346*

College Algebra: Concepts and Models. *v.5 p.472*

☐ College and University Rankings. *v.4 p.289*

College Athletes for Hire: The Evolution and Legacy of the NCAA's Amateur Myth. *v.4 p.822, p.889, p.894*

College Costs and Financial Aid Handbook. *v.4 p.293*

College Football: History, Spectacle, Controversy. *v.4 p.810, p.860, p.895*

College Grad Job Hunter. *v.4 p.170*

A College Grammar of English. *v.2 p.556*

The College Handbook. *v.4 p.294*

College Majors and Careers: A Resource Guide for Effective Life Planning. *v.4 p.167, p.168*

College Majors Handbook with Real Career Paths and Payoffs: The Actual Jobs, Earnings, and Trends for Graduates of 60 College Majors. *v.4 p.167*

College Mathematics for Business, Economics, Life Sciences and Social Sciences. *v.5 p.503*

College Physics, Vol. 2. . . . .*v.5 p.539*

College: The Undergraduate Experience in America. *v.4 p.289, p.330*

The College Transfer Student in America: The Forgotten Student. *v.4 p.294*

The Collegeville Atlas of the Bible. *v.1 p.617*

Collegeville Bible Commentary. *v.1 p.615*

Colley Cibber. *v.2 p.242*

Collins Atlas of 20th Century History. *v.4 p.380*

Collins Atlas of Military History. *v.4 p.380*

Collins Dicionario Ingles-Portugues, Portugues-Ingles. *v.2 p.637*

Collins Robert comprehensive French dictionary. . . .*v.2 p.453*

Collins Spanish-English, English-Spanish Dictionary = Collins Diccionario Español-Inglés, Inglés-Español. *v.2 p.635*

Collision Course: NATO, Russia, and Kosovo. *v.4 p.644*

Collision Course: The Strange Convergence of Affirmative Action and Immigration Policy in America. . . .*v.4 p.570*

Collision Theory. *v.5 p.553*

The Colloidal Domain: Where Physics, Chemistry, Biology, and Technology Meet. *v.5 p.283*

Colloquial Albanian: The Complete Course for Beginners. *v.2 p.778*

Colloquial Arabic (Levantine). *v.6 p.654*

Colloquial Hungarian: The Complete Course for Beginners. *v.2 p.775*

Colloquial Lithuanian: A Complete Language Course. *v.2 p.773, p.774*

Colloquial Persian: The Complete Course for Beginners. *v.6 p.669*

Colloquial Polish: The Complete Course for Beginners.*v.2 p.775*

Colloquial Ukrainian. *v.2 p.777*

The Colloquies and Selected Letters. *v.2 p.715*

Colombia and the United States: Hegemony and Interdependence. *v.3 p.391*

Colombia Before Independence: Economy, Society and Politics under Bourbon Rule. *v.3 p.356*

Colombia: Territorial Rule and The Llanos Frontier. . *v.3 p.358*

Colombia: The Genocidal Democracy. *v.3 p.274*

The Colombian Caribbean: A Regional History, 1870-1950. . . . .*v.3 p.358*

The Colombian Novel, 1844-1987. . . . .*v.2 p.684*

The Colometry of Latin Prose. *v.2 p.424*

The Colonel: The Life and Legend of Robert R. McCormick, 1880-1955. . . . .*v.3 p.462, p.463*

Colonel: The Life and Legend of Robert R. McCormick, 1880-1955. . . . .*v.4 p.411*

The Colonel: The Life and Wars of Henry Stimson, 1867-1950. . . . .*v.3 p.459*

Colonial America on Film and Television: A Filmography. *v.6 p.315*

Colonial and Postcolonial Fiction: An Anthology. . . .*v.2 p.728*

Colonial and Postcolonial Literature. *v.2 p.727*

The Colonial Background of the American Revolution: Four Essays in American Colonial History. *v.3 p.407*

Colonial Brazil. *v.3 p.334*

Colonial Cakchiquels: Highland Maya Adaptations to Spanish Rule, 1600-1700. . . . .*v.3 p.298*

Colonial Connecticut: A History. *v.3 p.489*

Colonial Crisis, Community, and Andean Self-Rule: Aymara Politics in the Age of Insurgency: Eighteenth Century La Paz. *v.3 p.325*

Colonial Dilemma: Critical Perspectives on Contemporary Puerto Rico. *v.6 p.522*

Colonial Discourse: PostColonial Theory. *v.2 p.727*

The Colonial Elite of Caracas: Formation and Crisis, 1567-1767. . . . .*v.3 p.359*

Colonial Fantasies: Towards a Feminist Reading of Orientalism. *v.6 p.595, p.596*

Colonial Georgia: A History. *v.3 p.503*

Colonial Habits: Convents and the Spiritual Economy of Cuzco, Peru. *v.3 p.282, p.325*

Colonial Idiom. *v.2 p.28*

Colonial Lives: Documents on Latin American History, 1550-1850. . . . .*v.3 p.284*

Colonial Maryland: A History. *v.3 p.493*

Colonial Massachusetts: A History. *v.3 p.487*

Colonial Massachusetts Silversmiths and Jewelers: A
    Biographical Dictionary Based on the Notes of Francis Hill
    Bigelow and John Marshall Phillips. *v.1 p.798*

The Colonial Metamorphoses in Rhode Island: A Study of
    Institutions in Change. *v.3 p.489*

Colonial Migrants and Racism: Algerians in France,
    1900-62. . . . .*v.3 p.157*

Colonial Modernity in Korea. *v.6 p.237*

Colonial Narratives/Cultural Dialogues: Discoveries of India in
    the Language of Colonialism. *v.2 p.165, p.762, p.763*

Colonial New Hampshire: A History. *v.3 p.486*

Colonial New York: A History. *v.3 p.490*

Colonial North Carolina; a History. *v.3 p.502*

Colonial Odysseys: Empire and Epic in the Modernist
    Novel. *v.2 p.190*

Colonial Pennsylvania: A History. *v.3 p.492*

The Colonial Period of American History. . .*v.3 p.405, v.4 p.517*

Colonial Placer Mining in Colombia. *v.3 p.357, p.359*

Colonial Policy and Practice: A Comparative Study of Burma
    and Netherlands India. *v.6 p.165, p.166, p.174, p.176*

The Colonial Present: Afghanistan, Palestine, and
    Iraq. *v.6 p.603, p.610, p.634*

Colonial Rule and Crisis in Equatorial Africa: Southern Gabon,
    C. 1850-1940. . . . .*v.6 p.63*

Colonial Rule and the Kamba: Social Change in the Kenya
    Highlands, 1889-1939. . . . .*v.6 p.65*

Colonial Situations: Essays on the Contextualization of
    Ethnographic Knowledge. *v.4 p.5*

Colonial South Africa and the Origins of the Racial
    Order. *v.6 p.79*

Colonial South Carolina: A History. *v.3 p.502*

Colonial South Carolina: A Political History,
    1663-1763. . . . .*v.3 p.502*

The Colonial South Carolina Scene: Contemporary Views
    1697-1774. . . . .*v.3 p.502*

The Colonial Spanish-American City: Urban Life in the Age of
    Atlantic Capitalism. *v.3 p.286*

Colonial Subjects: Puerto Ricans in a Global
    Perspective. *v.3 p.320, v.6 p.529, p.536*

Colonial to Global: Malaysian Women's Writing in English,
    1940s-1990s. *v.2 p.760*

Colonial Travelers in Latin America. *v.3 p.403, p.404*

Colonial Virginia. *v.3 p.500*

Colonial Williamsburg. *v.3 p.500*

Colonialism: A Theoretical Overview. *v.4 p.583*

Colonialism and Its Forms of Knowledge: The British in
    India. *v.6 p.146*

Colonialism and Resistance in Belize: Essays in Historical
    Sociology. *v.3 p.296*

Colonialism and Revolution in the Middle East: Social and
    Cultural Origins of Egypt's 'Urabi Movement. . . .*v.6 p.637*

Colonialism, Catholicism, and Contraception: A History of Birth
    Control in Puerto Rico. *v.3 p.321*

Colonialism/Postcolonialism. *v.2 p.572*

Colonias and Public Policy in Texas and Mexico: Urbanization
    by Stealth. *v.6 p.551*

Colonising Egypt. *v.6 p.638*

Colonization As Exploitation in the Amazon Rain Forest,
    1758-1911. . . . .*v.3 p.334*

Colonizing Hawai'i: The Cultural Power of Law. .*v.6 p.130, p.131*

Colonizing Nature: The Tropics in British Arts and Letters,
    1760-1820. . . . .*v.2 p.173*

The Colonnade of Teeth: Modern Hungarian
    Poetry. *v.2 p.785, p.786*

Color: An Introduction to Practice and Principles. . . .*v.1 p.710*

Color and Light in Nature. *v.5 p.73*

Color Atlas of Anatomy: A Photographic Study of the Human
    Body. *v.5 p.158*

Color Atlas of Anatomy of Small Laboratory Animals, Vol.
    1. . . . .*v.5 p.157*

Color Atlas of Anatomy of Small Laboratory Animals, Vol.
    2. . . . .*v.5 p.157*

Color Atlas of Clinical Embryology. *v.5 p.162, p.163*

Color Atlas of Histology. *v.5 p.159*

Color Atlas of Livestock Breeds. *v.5 p.56*

Color Codes: Modern Theories of Color in Philosophy, Painting
    and Architecture, Literature, Music, and Psychology. .*v.1 p.710*

El Color de Agosto. *v.2 p.638*

Color for Interior Design. *v.1 p.803*

A Color Guide to the Petrography of Carbonate Rocks: Grains,
    Textures, Porosity, Diagenesis. *v.5 p.439, p.440*

Color Handbook of Biological Control in Plant
    Protection. *v.5 p.27*

Color Naming in Human Languages. *v.4 p.27*

The Color of Angels: Cosmology, Gender and the Aesthetic
    Imagination. *v.5 p.612*

Color of Darkness. *v.2 p.110*

The Color of Guilt and Innocence: Racial Profiling and Police
    Practices in America. *v.6 p.264*

The Color of Justice: Race, Ethnicity, and Crime in
    America. *v.6 p.257*

The Color of Melancholy: The Uses of Books in the Fourteenth
    Century. *v.6 p.564, p.568, p.569*

The Color of Privilege: Three Blasphemies on Race and
    Feminism. *v.6 p.434*

The Color of School Reform: Race, Politics and the Challenge
    of Urban Education. *v.4 p.315*

The Color of Summer: Or the New Garden of Earthly
    Delight. *v.2 p.670*

The Color Purple. *v.2 p.158, v.6 p.28, p.399*

Color Space and Its Divisions: Color Order from Antiquity to
    the Present. *v.1 p.710*

Colorado: A Guide to the Highest State. *v.3 p.526*

Colorado: A History of the Centennial State. *v.3 p.526*

Colorado: Bicentennial and History Guide. *v.3 p.526*

A Colorado History. *v.3 p.526*

Colorado Profiles: Men and Women Who Shaped the Centennial
    State. *v.3 p.526*

Colorado: The Story of a Western Commonwealth. . .*v.3 p.526*

Colorado's Great Gardens: Plains, Mountains and
    Plateaus. *v.1 p.812*

The Colorblind Career: What Every African-American,
    Hispanic-American and Asian-American Needs to Succeed in
    Today's Tough Job Market. *v.4 p.168*

The Color-Blind Constitution. *v.4 p.457*

Colorblind Injustice: Minority Voting Rights and the Undoing of the Second Reconstruction. *v.4 p.555, p.573, p.579*

Colored Contradictions: An Anthology of Contemporary African-American Plays. *v.1 p.65, p.122*

Colored Lights: Forty Years of Words and Music, Show Biz, Collaboration, and All That Jazz. *v.6 p.412*

Colorful Impressions: The Printmaking Revolution in Eighteenth-Century France. *v.1 p.753*

Colorimetric Chemical Analytical Methods. *v.5 p.269*

Color-Line to Borderlands: The Matrix of American Ethnic Studies. *v.6 p.108*

The Colors of Violence: Cultural Identities, Religion, and Conflict. *v.6 p.149*

Colors Passing Through Us: Poems. *v.2 p.153*

Color. *v.1 p.710, v.2 p.65*

Colossians and Philemon. *v.1 p.631*

Colossus Reborn: The Red Army at War: 1941-1943. *v.3 p.227*

Colossus: The Price of America's Empire. *v.4 p.560*

Colour: Art and Science. *v.5 p.607*

Colour Chemistry. *v.5 p.320*

Colour, Class and the Victorians: English Attitudes Toward the Negro in the Mid-Nineteenth Century. *v.3 p.92*

The Colour of Metal Compounds. *v.5 p.303*

The Colours of Life: An Introduction to the Chemistry of Porphyrins and Related Compounds. *v.5 p.330*

The Columbia Anthology of Gay Literature: Readings from Western Antiquity to the Present Day. *v.6 p.406*

The Columbia Anthology of Modern Chinese Literature. *v.6 p.208, p.212, p.213*

The Columbia Anthology of Traditional Chinese Literature. *v.6 p.208*

The Columbia Book of Chinese Poetry: From Early Times to the Thirteenth Century. *v.6 p.210*

The Columbia Book of Later Chinese Poetry: Yuan, Ming, and Ch'ing Dynasties (1279-1911). *v.6 p.209*

The Columbia Comedy Shorts: Two-Reel Hollywood Film Comedies, 1933-1958. . . . . *v.6 p.313*

The Columbia Companion to Modern East Asian Literature. *v.6 p.181*

The Columbia Dictionary of Shakespeare Quotations. *v.2 p.226*

The Columbia Documentary History of the Asian American Experience. *v.6 p.87, p.119*

The Columbia Gazetteer of North America. *v.3 p.372, v.4 p.374*

The Columbia Gazetteer of the World. *v.4 p.374*

e The Columbia Guide to America in the 1960s. . . *v.3 p.470*

The Columbia Guide to American Environmental History. *v.6 p.286*

The Columbia Guide to American Indian Literatures of the United States since 1945. . . . . *v.6 p.697*

The Columbia Guide to American Indians of the Northeast. *v.6 p.702*

The Columbia Guide to Asian American History. *v.6 p.87, p.114*

The Columbia Guide to Asian American Literature since 1945. . . . . *v.6 p.86, p.90*

e The Columbia Guide to Contemporary African American Fiction. *v.6 p.24*

The Columbia Guide to the Cold War. *v.3 p.442*

The Columbia Guide to the Literatures of Eastern Europe Since 1945. . . . . *v.2 p.779*

Columbia Guides to American History and Culture. . *v.6 p.681*

The Columbia History of American Poetry. *v.2 p.15*

The Columbia History of British Poetry. *v.2 p.180*

The Columbia History of Latinos in the United States Since 1960. . . . . *v.6 p.521, p.536*

The Columbia History of the British Novel. *v.2 p.189*

The Columbia History of Western Philosophy. . . . *v.1 p.417*

The Columbia Literary History of the United States. . *v.2 p.6*

Columbia River Basketry: Gift of the Ancestors, Gift of the Earth. *v.1 p.806*

Columbia University Libraries Biological Sciences Library Biology Internet Resources. *v.5 p.94*

The Columbian Exchange: Biological and Cultural Consequences of 1492. . . . . *v.3 p.268, p.271*

Combating Corporate Crime: Local Prosecutors at Work. *v.4 p.472*

Combinatorial Chemistry. *v.5 p.328*

Combinatorial Geometry. *v.5 p.479, p.498*

Combinatorial Group Theory: Presentations of Groups in Terms of Generators and Relations. *v.5 p.475, p.479*

A Combinatorial Introduction to Topology. . . *v.5 p.478, p.499*

Combinatorial Mathematics. *v.5 p.479*

Combinatorial Miscellany. *v.5 p.478*

Combinatorial Problems and Exercises. *v.5 p.479*

Combinatorial Theory. *v.5 p.478*

Combinatorics: A Problem Oriented Approach. . . . *v.5 p.479*

Combinatorics and Graph Theory. *v.5 p.480*

Combined Chemical Dictionary. *v.5 p.259*

The Combined New Persian-English and English-Persian Dictionary. *v.6 p.669*

Combined-Cycle Gas and Steam Turbine Power Plants. *v.5 p.708*

Combustion and Flames: Chemical and Physical Principles. *v.5 p.279*

Combustion. *v.5 p.279*

Come Dance with Me, a Memoir 1898: 1956. . . . . . *v.1 p.7*

Come into My Time: Lithuania in Prose Fiction, 1970-90. . . . . *v.2 p.781*

Comeback Cities: A Blueprint for Urban Neighborhood Revival. *v.6 p.728*

Comeback: The Fall and Rise of the American Automobile Industry. *v.4 p.154*

The Comedians. *v.2 p.349*

Comedias de Capa y Espada: La Dama Duende; No Hay Cosa Como Callar. *v.2 p.646*

Comedies and Proverbs. *v.2 p.498*

Comedies: Aspis - Georgos - Dis Exapaton - Dyskolos - Encheiridion - Epitrepontes. *v.2 p.416*

The Comedies of Ariosto. *v.2 p.707*

The Comedies of Goldoni. *v.2 p.711*

The Comedies of Machiavelli: The Woman from Andros, The Mandrake, Clizia. *v.2 p.709*

Comedy - Cinema - Theory. *v.6 p.312*

Comedy: A Geographic and Historical Guide. *v.1 p.58, p.89, p.90*

Comedy and America: The Lost World of Washington
  Irving. *v.2 p.42*

Comedy and Culture: England, 1820-1900. . . . . .*v.6 p.752*

Comedy and Society from Congreve to Fielding. . .*v.2 p.187*

Comedy and the Woman Writer: Woolf, Spark, and
  Feminism. *v.2 p.393*

Comedy Is a Man in Trouble: Slapstick in American
  Movies. *v.6 p.312*

The Comedy of Errors. *v.2 p.223*

Comets II. *v.5 p.69*

La comédie de Charleroi. *v.2 p.515, p.516*

Comédie et actes divers. *v.2 p.509*

La comédie humaine, vol. 10. . . . .*v.2 p.485*

La comédie humaine, vol. 11. . . . .*v.2 p.485*

La comédie humaine, vol. 12. . . . .*v.2 p.485*

La comédie humaine, vol. 1. . . . .*v.2 p.485*

La comédie humaine, vol. 2. . . . .*v.2 p.485*

La comédie humaine, vol. 3. . . . .*v.2 p.485*

La comédie humaine, vol. 4. . . . .*v.2 p.485*

La comédie humaine, vol. 5. . . . .*v.2 p.485*

La comédie humaine, vol. 6. . . . .*v.2 p.485*

La comédie humaine, vol. 7. . . . .*v.2 p.485*

La comédie humaine, vol. 8. . . . .*v.2 p.485*

La comédie humaine, vol. 9. . . . .*v.2 p.485*

The Comfort of Strangers. *v.2 p.368*

Comfort Woman. *v.6 p.100*

The Comforters. *v.2 p.383*

The Comforts of Home: Prostitution in Colonial
  Nairobi. *v.6 p.455*

Comic Faith: The Great Tradition from Austen to
  Joyce. *v.2 p.176, p.191*

The Comic Mind: Comedy and the Movies. *v.6 p.313*

Comic Politics: Gender in Hollywood Comedy after the New
  Right. *v.6 p.313*

Comic Transactions: Literature, Humor, and the Politics of
  Community in Twentieth-Century Britain. *v.2 p.195*

Comics and Sequential Art. *v.2 p.581*

The Comics Before 1945. . . . .*v.1 p.702*

Comics, Comix and Graphic Novels: A History of Comic
  Art. *v.2 p.582*

The Coming Age of Scarcity: Preventing Mass Death and
  Genocide in the Twenty-First Century. . . .*v.4 p.662, p.663*

Coming Apart: An Informal History of America in the
  1960's. *v.4 p.486*

The Coming Biotech Age: The Business of
  Bio-Materials. *v.5 p.219*

The Coming Crisis of Western Sociology. *v.4 p.682*

The Coming Democracy: New Rules for Running a New
  World. *v.4 p.498*

Coming of Age as a Poet: Milton, Keats, Eliot,
  Plath. *v.2 p.181, p.295*

Coming of Age in Samoa. *v.4 p.43*

Coming of Age in the Milky Way. *v.5 p.61*

Coming of Age in U.S. High Schools: Economic, Kinship,
  Religious, and Political Crosscurrents. *v.4 p.29*

Coming of Age: The United States During the 1920s and
  1930s. *v.3 p.448, p.449*

The Coming of Age. *v.2 p.509*

The Coming of Christianity to Anglo-Saxon England. .*v.6 p.572*

Coming of Post-Industrial Society: A Venture in Social
  Forecasting. *v.4 p.769*

The Coming of the Book: The Impact of Printing,
  1450-1800. . . . .*v.2 p.576, v.3 p.37*

The Coming of the Civil War. *v.3 p.414*

The Coming of the Devi: Adivasi Assertion in Western
  India. *v.6 p.157*

The Coming of the French Revolution: By Georges Lefebvre:
  Translated and with a Preface by R. R. Palmer. . .*v.3 p.150*

The Coming of the Friars. *v.6 p.570*

The Coming of the Greeks: Indo-European Conquests in the
  Aegean and the near East. *v.3 p.15*

The Coming of the New Deal: 1933-1935, the Age of
  Roosevelt. *v.3 p.479, v.4 p.522*

The Coming of the New Deal, 1933-1935. . . .*v.3 p.444, p.450*

The Coming of the New Deal. *v.3 p.479*

The Coming of the Night. *v.2 p.154*

The Coming of the Revolution, 1763-1775. . . . . .*v.3 p.409*

The Coming of Winter. *v.2 p.738*

Coming on Strong: Gender and Sexuality in Twentieth-Century
  Women's Sports. *v.4 p.804, p.835,v.6 p.437*

Coming Out: Homosexual Politics in Britain from the 19th
  Century to the Present. *v.6 p.363, p.422*

Coming Out of Cancer: Writings from the Lesbian Cancer
  Epidemic. *v.6 p.377*

Coming Out to Parents: A Two-Way Survival Guide for
  Lesbians and Gay Men and Their Parents. *v.6 p.368*

Coming Out under Fire: The History of Gay Men and Women
  in World War Two. *v.6 p.364, p.365, p.389*

The Coming Plague: Newly Emerging Diseases in a World Out
  of Balance. *v.6 p.283*

The Coming Race War?: And Other Apocalyptic Tales of
  America after Affirmative Action and Welfare. . . .*v.4 p.729*

Coming Soon!!!: A Narrative. *v.2 p.142*

The Coming Storm: A Novel. *v.6 p.398, p.399*

Coming Through the Swamp: The Nature Writings of Gene
  Stratton Porter. *v.5 p.80, p.232*

Coming to Light: American Women Poets in the Twentieth
  Century. *v.2 p.8*

Coming to Terms: South Africa's Search for Truth. . .*v.6 p.78*

Coming to Terms with Security: A Lexicon for Arms Control,
  Disarmament and Confidence-Building. *v.4 p.657*

Coming to the Edge of the Circle: A Wiccan Initiation
  Ritual. *v.1 p.529, p.530*

Coming up for Air. *v.2 p.375*

Coming up Roses: The Broadway Musical in the 1950s. .*v.1 p.252*

Coming up Short: The Challenge of 401(K) Plans. .*v.4 p.97, p.99*

The Comintern: A History of International Communism from
  Lenin to Stalin. *v.4 p.509*

Command of Office: How War, Secrecy and Deception
  Transformed the Presidency, from Theodore Roosevelt to
  George W. Bush. *v.3 p.441*

Command or Control: Command, Training and Tactics in the German and British Armies, 1888-1918. . . . . . *v.3 p.80*

Commandant of Auschwitz: The Autobiography of Rudolf Hess. *v.3 p.84*

The Commanders of the Civil War. *v.3 p.395*

The Commanders. *v.3 p.482*

The Commanding Heights: The Battle for the World Economy. *v.4 p.56, p.58*

The Commedia Dell'arte from the Renaissance to Dario Fo: The Italian Origins of European Theatre VI. . . . *v.1 p.91, p.106*

The Commedia Dell'Arte in the Twentieth Century. *v.1 p.91, p.135*

🅔 Commedia Dell'Arte Performance: Context and Contents. *v.1 p.91, p.106*

Commedia, vol. 1: Inferno. *v.2 p.702*

Commedia, vol. 2: Purgatorio. *v.2 p.702*

Commedia, vol. 3: Paradiso. *v.2 p.702*

Commemorating Poussin: Reception and Interpretation of the Artist. *v.1 p.746, p.747*

Comment c'est. *v.2 p.509*

Commentaries on American Law. *v.4 p.441*

Commentaries on the Laws of England: In Four Books, 2. . . . . *v.4 p.435*

Commentarii: Bello Gallico Cum A. Hirti Supplemento, Vol. I. *v.2 p.428*

Commentarii: De Bello Civili Cum Libris Incertorum Auctorum de Bello Alexandrino Africo Hispaniensi. *v.2 p.428*

A Commentary on Aristotle's De Anima. *v.1 p.434*

Commentary on Aristotle's Metaphysics. *v.1 p.434*

Commentary on Aristotle's Nicomacheau Ethics. . . *v.1 p.434*

A Commentary on Book I of the Epigrams of Martial. *v.2 p.437*

A Commentary on Cicero, De Officiis. *v.2 p.433*

A Commentary on Heidegger's Being and Time. . . *v.1 p.470*

A Commentary on Herodotus, Vol. 2. . . . . *v.2 p.412*

A Commentary on Horace: Odes, Bk. 1. . . . . . . *v.2 p.435*

A Commentary on Horace: Odes, Book II. *v.2 p.435*

A Commentary on Horace: Odes. *v.2 p.435*

A Commentary on Kant's Critique of Practical Reason. *v.1 p.460, p.461*

A Commentary on Livy, Bks. I-V. *v.2 p.436*

A Commentary on Malthus' 1798 Essay on Population As Social Theory. *v.4 p.221*

A Commentary on the Aristotelian Athenaion Politeia. *v.4 p.489*

A Commentary on the Collected Poems of W. B. Yeats. *v.2 p.326*

A Commentary on the Complete Greek Tragedies: Aeschylus. *v.2 p.407*

Commentary on the Complete Poems of Gerard Manley Hopkins. *v.2 p.294*

A Commentary on the Creed of Islam. *v.1 p.557*

A Commentary on the General Prologue to the Canterbury Tales. *v.2 p.207*

A Commentary on the Plays of Sophocles. *v.2 p.419*

A Commentary on Virgil Eclogues. *v.2 p.446*

A Commentary to Kant's Critique of Pure Reason. . *v.1 p.462*

Commerce and Capitalism in Chinese Societies: Organisation of Chinese Economics. *v.4 p.214, p.257, p.259*

The Commerce of Everyday Life: Selections from the Tatler and the Spectator (Bedford Cultural Editions). . *v.2 p.202, p.236*

Commercial Chicken Meat and Egg Production. *v.5 p.56*

🖥 Commercial Closet. *v.6 p.382*

Commercial Nuclear Power: Assuring Safety for the Future. *v.5 p.709, p.740*

The Commercialization of American Culture: New Advertising, Control and Democracy. *v.4 p.697*

The Commissariat of Enlightenment: Soviet Organization of Education and the Arts under Lunacharsky, October 1917-1921. . . . . *v.4 p.334*

Commitment in the Workplace: Theory, Research and Application. *v.5 p.579*

Committed Journalism: An Ethic for the Profession. . *v.4 p.405*

The Committee and Its Critics: A Calm Review of the House Committee on Un-American Activities. *v.3 p.446*

The Committee. *v.6 p.660*

Committing to Peace: The Successful Settlement of Civil Wars. *v.4 p.651*

Commodifying Bodies. *v.5 p.249*

Commodities and Capabilities. *v.4 p.266*

The Commodities Price Locator. *v.4 p.178*

The Commodity Culture of Victorian England: Advertising and Spectacle, 1851-1914. . . . . . *v.6 p.745, p.762, p.764*

Common and Scientific Names of Fishes from the United States and Canada. *v.5 p.216*

The Common Asphodel. *v.2 p.181*

Common Bodies: Women, Touch and Power in Seventeenth-Century England. *v.3 p.52*

The Common but Less Frequent Loon and Other Essays. *v.5 p.226, p.227, p.231*

🖥 Common Cause. *v.4 p.516*

Common Destiny: Dictatorship, Foreign Policy, and War in Fascist Italy and Nazi Germany. *v.3 p.81*

Common Faith. *v.1 p.521*

Common Fossil Plants of Western North America. . . *v.5 p.449*

The Common Good and Christian Ethics. *v.1 p.575*

The Common Good. *v.4 p.185*

Common Ground: A Turbulent Decade in the Lives of Three American Families. *v.3 p.488*

Common Ground: Reimagining American History. *v.3 p.376, v.6 p.105, p.114, p.124*

Common Human Needs. *v.4 p.755, p.758*

Common Knowledge: How Companies Thrive by Sharing What They Know. *v.4 p.78*

The Common Law. *v.4 p.434, p.435*

Common LISP: The Language. *v.5 p.347*

Common Man, Mythic Vision: The Paintings of Ben Shahn. *v.1 p.736*

The Common Peace: Participation and the Criminal Law in Seventeenth-Century England. *v.3 p.123, p.124*

Common Poisonous Plants and Mushrooms of North America. *v.5 p.209*

Common Problems - Proper Solutions: Avoiding Error in Quantitative Research. *v.4 p.689*

🖥 Common Reactive Intermediates in Organic Chemistry. *v.5 p.288*

The Common Reader, Vol. 1. . . . .*v.2 p.576*

The Common Reader, Vol. 2. . . . .*v.2 p.576*

The Common Reader. *v.2 p.394*

Common Sense Business: Starting, Operating, and Growing
    Your Small Business—in Any Economy!. *v.4 p.87*

The Common Sense of Science. *v.5 p.400*

Common Sense on Mutual Funds: New Imperatives for the
    Intelligent Investor. *v.4 p.94*

Common Sense School Reform. *v.4 p.280*

Common Stocks and Uncommon Profits and Other
    Writings. *v.4 p.95*

Common Threads: Stories from the Quilt. *v.6 p.378*

The Common Writer: Life in Nineteenth-Century Grub
    Street. *v.3 p.119, v.6 p.739*

Commoners, Tribute, and Chiefs: The Development of
    Algonquian Culture in the Potomac Valley. *v.4 p.11*

Commonsense and Nuclear Warfare. *v.4 p.656*

Common-Sense Classroom Management for Middle and High
    School Teachers: Surviving September and Beyond in
    the Secondary Classroom. *v.4 p.284*

Common-Sense Pest Control: Least-Toxic Solutions for Your
    Home, Garden, Pets and Community. *v.5 p.44*

The Commonwealth and Restoration
    Stage. *v.1 p.77, p.101, p.144, p.145*

Commonwealth Literature Periodicals: A Bibliography, Including
    Periodicals of Former Commonwealth Countries, with
    Locations in the United Kingdom. *v.2 p.728*

Commonwealth Secretariat. *v.4 p.605*

Commonwealth to Protectorate. *v.3 p.104, p.105*

Communal Riots in Bengal, 1905-1947. . . . . . .*v.6 p.153*

Communalism in India: History, Politics and Culture. *v.4 p.705*

The Communards of Paris, 1871. . . . .*v.3 p.154*

Communicable Disease Epidemiology and Control. . .*v.5 p.365*

Communicate: Independent British Graphic Design since the
    Sixties. *v.1 p.714, p.715*

Communicating Across Cultures at Work. *v.4 p.132*

Communicating Effectively. *v.4 p.423*

Communicating Emotion: Social, Moral, and Cultural
    Processes. *v.5 p.648*

Communicating in Geography and the Environmental
    Sciences. *v.4 p.376*

Communicating Racism: Ethnic Prejudice in Thought and
    Talk. *v.4 p.21*

Communicating Science Handbook. *v.5 p.407*

Communicating When Your Company Is under Siege. *v.4 p.174*

Communication and Culture in War and Peace. . . .*v.4 p.766*

Communication and Litigation: Case Studies of Famous
    Trials. *v.4 p.438*

Communication and Personal Relationships. *v.5 p.647*

Communication and Persuasion: Psychological Studies of
    Opinion Change,. *v.4 p.423*

Communication and Persuasion: Psychological Studies of
    Opinion Change. *v.5 p.586*

Communication and Persuasion: Psychological Studies of
    Opinion Change,. *v.5 p.624, p.625*

Communication and the Evolution of Society. *v.4 p.696*

Communication Consultants in Political Campaigns: Ballot Box
    Warriors. *v.4 p.550*

Communication Disability in Aging: Prevention to
    Intervention. *v.5 p.665*

Communication Ethics and Universal Values. *v.4 p.405*

Communication Ethics, Media, and Popular Culture. . *v.4 p.417*

Communication for Rural Innovation: Rethinking Agricultural
    Extension. *v.5 p.3*

Communication in History: Technology, Culture,
    Society. *v.3 p.37, v.4 p.415, p.416*

Communication in the Age of Virtual Reality.   *v.5 p.620, p.624*

Communication Skills: A Guide for Engineering and Applied
    Science Students. *v.5 p.680*

Communication Systems: Analysis and Design. *v.5 p.726*

Communication Systems Engineering. *v.5 p.726*

Communication Systems. *v.4 p.422, v.5 p.725*

Communication, Technology and Cultural
    Change. *v.4 p.760, p.761*

Communication Technology. *v.4 p.590*

Communications and Power: Propaganda and the Press in the
    Indian National Struggle, 1920-1947. . . . .*v.6 p.157*

Communications Systems and Networks. *v.4 p.115*

A Communicative Grammar of English. *v.2 p.557*

Communion of Immigrants: A History of Catholics in
    America. *v.1 p.573*

Communion. *v.6 p.501, p.510*

Communism: A History. *v.4 p.509*

Communism, Anticommunism, and the CIO, 91. . . .*v.4 p.127*

The Communist Controversy in Washington: From the New
    Deal to McCarthy. *v.3 p.448*

The Communist Manifesto: Karl Marx and Friedrich Engels:
    Edited and Translated by L.M. Findlay. .*v.4 p.507, p.508, p.509*

The Communist Manifesto. *v.4 p.236*

The Communist Movement in Egpyt, 1920-1988. . . .*v.6 p.638*

Communist Neo-Traditionalism: Work and Authority in Chinese
    Industry. *v.6 p.195*

The Communist Road to Power in Vietnam. .*v.6 p.167, p.168*

Communist Subversion of Czechoslovakia, 1938-1948: The
    Failure of Coexistence. *v.3 p.189, p.190*

Communists, Cowboys, and Queers: The Politics of Masculinity
    in the Work of Arthur Miller and Tennessee
    Williams. *v.2 p.102, p.134, p.135*

Communists in Harlem During the Depression. *v.4 p.552, p.554*

Communities and Ecosystems: Linking the Aboveground and
    Belowground Components. *v.6 p.292*

Communities in Motion: Dance, Community and Tradition in
    America's Southeast and Beyond. *v.1 p.33*

Communities in Transition: Bedford and Lincoln, Massachusetts,
    1729-1850. . . . .*v.4 p.703*

Communities of Journalism: A History of American Newspapers
    and Their Readers. *v.4 p.149*

Community and Consensus in Islam: Muslim Representation in
    Colonial India 1860-1947. . . . .*v.6 p.158*

Community and Public Health Nursing. *v.5 p.531*

Community and Revolution in Modern Vietnam. . . .*v.6 p.168*

Community and Social Change in America. *v.4 p.770*

Community and Society in Roman Italy. *v.3 p.198*

Community and Society. *v.4 p.686*

Community As Partner: Theory and Practice in Nursing. .*v.5 p.531*

Community Besieged: The Anglophone Minority and the Politics of Quebec. *v.4 p.581*

Community by Design: New Urbanism for Suburbs and Small Communities. *v.1 p.797, v.6 p.728*

The Community Called Church. *v.1 p.575, p.576*

Community Corrections and Human Dignity. *v.6 p.278*

e Community, Empire and Migration: South Asians in Diaspora. *v.6 p.118, p.137*

Community Forestry in the United States: Learning from the Past, Crafting the Future. *v.5 p.36*

The Community Forests of Mexico: Managing for Sustainable Landscapes. *v.3 p.268*

Community, Gender and Violence: Subaltern Studies XI. *v.6 p.146*

Community Geography: GIS in Action. *v.4 p.387*

Community Health Nursing: Promoting and Protecting the Public's Health. *v.5 p.530, p.531*

Community in a Black Pentecostal Church: An Anthropological Study. *v.1 p.587*

The Community of Rights. *v.4 p.512*

Community of the Cross: Moravian Piety in Colonial Bethlehem. *v.1 p.590*

The Community of the Holy Spirit: A Movement of Change in a Covent of Nuns in Puerto Rico. *v.3 p.321*

Community Organizing and Community Building for Health. *v.4 p.778*

Community Policing: A Handbook for Beat Cops and Supervisors. *v.6 p.264*

Community Policing: Can It Work? *v.6 p.264*

Community Policing-Origins, Elements, Implementation, Assessment. *v.6 p.264*

Community Psychology: In Pursuit of Liberation and Well-Being. *v.5 p.672*

Community Psychology: Linking Individuals and Communities. *v.5 p.671*

Community, Religion and Literature: Essays. *v.2 p.3*

Community Stability in Forest-Based Economies. *v.5 p.36, v.6 p.297, p.298*

Community Studies: An Introduction to the Sociology of the Local Community. *v.4 p.770*

A Community Transplanted: The Trans-Atlantic Experience of a Swedish Immigrant Settlement in the Upper Middle West, 1835-1915. . . . .*v.4 p.571*

A Community under Siege: A Chronicle of Chicanos East of the Los Angeles River, 1945-1975. . . . . . .*v.6 p.535, p.548*

Community Without Unity: A Politics of Derridean Extravagance. *v.4 p.501*

Commutative Algebra, Vol. 2. . . . .*v.5 p.474*

Commutative Algebra, Volume 1. . . . .*v.5 p.474*

The Commuter Nation: Perspectives on Puerto Rican Migration. *v.6 p.528*

Commwealth Games Federation. *v.4 p.842, p.898*

Como Agua para Chocolate. *v.2 p.667*

Como Escribir Bien en Espanol. *v.2 p.636*

Compact and Broadband Microstrip Antennas. *v.5 p.729*

The Compact Dictionary of Exact Science and Technology: English - German. *v.5 p.387*

The Compact Dictionary of Exact Science and Technology: German - English, Vol. 2. . . . .*v.5 p.387*

Compact Handbook of Computational Biology. .*v.5 p.90, p.107*

The Compact NASA Atlas of the Solar System. *v.5 p.63, p.64, p.68, p.69*

Companeras: Latina Lesbians: An Anthology. *v.6 p.496*

Companion Eencyclopedia of the History of Medicine. .*v.3 p.50*

Companion Encyclopedia of Asian Philosophy. . . .*v.1 p.474*

Companion Encyclopedia of Geography: The Environment and Humankind. *v.4 p.373*

Companion Encyclopedia of Middle Eastern and North African Film. *v.6 p.333*

Companion Encyclopedia of the History and Philosophy of the Mathematical Sciences, Vol. 2. . . . .*v.5 p.466*

A Companion to 20th-Century Poetry. *v.2 p.184*

Companion to a Sand County Almanac: Interpretive and Critical Essays. *v.5 p.357, p.369*

Companion to African American History. *v.6 p.6, p.14*

The Companion to African Literatures. *v.2 p.750*

A Companion to African Philosophy. *v.1 p.476, p.477*

A Companion to African-American Philosophy. . . .*v.1 p.442*

A Companion to American Foreign Relations. *v.3 p.386*

Companion to American Indian History. *v.6 p.683*

A Companion to Analytic Philosophy. *v.1 p.502*

Companion to Ancient Philosophy. *v.1 p.420*

A Companion to Anglo-Saxon Literature. *v.2 p.168*

Companion to Baroque Music. *v.1 p.186*

A Companion to Beowulf. *v.2 p.205*

A Companion to Bioethics. *v.1 p.486*

A Companion to California Wine: An Encyclopedia of Wine and Winemaking from the Mission Period to the Present. .*v.5 p.53*

A Companion to Chaucer. *v.2 p.207*

A Companion to Chritien de Troyes. *v.2 p.467*

Companion to Continental Philosophy. *v.1 p.510*

A Companion to Early Modern Philosophy. . .*v.1 p.436, p.437*

A Companion to Eighteenth-Century Poetry. .*v.2 p.171, p.183*

A Companion to Epistemology. *v.1 p.482*

A Companion to Ethics. *v.1 p.485*

Companion to European Romanticism. *v.2 p.171, p.572*

Companion to Gender Studies. .*v.6 p.360, p.370, p.425, p.429*

A Companion to Gower. *v.2 p.211*

A Companion to Greek Tragedy. *v.1 p.71, v.2 p.401*

A Companion to Heidegger. *v.1 p.471*

The Companion to Hispanic Studies. *v.2 p.638*

A Companion to Homer's Odyssey. *v.2 p.415*

A Companion to Homer. *v.2 p.415*

A Companion to Indian Music and Dance. *v.1 p.15*

Companion to Irish Traditional Music. *v.1 p.163, p.299*

A Companion to Joyce Studies. *v.2 p.357*

A Companion to Latin Literature. *v.2 p.424, p.425*

A Companion to Linguistic Anthropology. . .*v.2 p.560, v.4 p.18*

Companion to Literary Myths: Heroes and Archetypes. *v.1 p.526, p.527, v.2 p.549*

A Companion to Literature from Milton to Blake. .*v.2 p.170, p.173*

A Companion to Malory. *v.2 p.212*

Companion to Medieval and Renaissance Music. . . .*v.1 p.177*

A Companion to Metaphysics. *v.1 p.488, p.489*

A Companion to "Ancrene Wisse". *v.2 p.204*

A Companion to Modern Spanish American Fiction. . .*v.2 p.665*

Companion to Modernist Literature and Culture. .*v.2 p.178, p.572*

A Companion to Mozart's Piano
    Concertos. *v.1 p.190, p.240, p.344*

A Companion to Old and Middle English
    Literature. *v.2 p.167, p.168*

A Companion to Petronius. *v.2 p.440*

Companion to Phenomenology and Existentialism. . .*v.1 p.510*

A Companion to Philosophical Logic. *v.1 p.492*

A Companion to Piers Plowman. *v.2 p.211*

A Companion to Plato's Republic. *v.1 p.425, v.4 p.490*

A Companion to Restoration Drama. *v.2 p.187*

A Companion to Romanticism. *v.2 p.173*

A Companion to Science Fiction. *v.2 p.581*

A Companion to Shakespeare Studies. *v.2 p.227*

A Companion to Shakespeare's Works: Shakespeare's
    Histories. *v.2 p.234*

A Companion to Shakespeare's Works: The Comedies. .*v.2 p.233*

A Companion to Shakespeare's Works: The Poems, Problem
    Comedies, Late Plays. *v.2 p.225*

A Companion to Shakespeare's Works: The
    Tragedies. *v.2 p.234, p.235*

Companion to Shakespeare's Works, Vols. 1-4. . . .*v.2 p.229*

Companion to Socrates. *v.1 p.422*

The Companion to Southern Literature: Themes, Genres, Places,
    People, Movements and Motifs. *v.2 p.13*

A Companion to Spanish-American Literature. . . .*v.2 p.664*

A Companion to the Ancient near East. *v.3 p.4*

Companion to the Anthropology of American Indians. . .*v.4 p.3*

A Companion to the British and Irish Novel
    1945-2000. . . . .*v.2 p.179, p.194, p.195*

A Companion to the Concerto. *v.1 p.241*

A Companion to the Eighteenth-Century English Novel and
    Culture. *v.2 p.171, p.189*

A Companion to the Gawain-Poet. *v.2 p.206*

A Companion to the Greek Lyric Poets. *v.2 p.403*

Companion to the History of Modern Science. *v.3 p.45*

A Companion to the Literature and Culture of the American
    South. *v.2 p.13*

A Companion to the Middle English Lyric. .*v.2 p.168, v.6 p.564*

A Companion to the "Iliad". *v.2 p.416*

A Companion to the Nibelungenlied. *v.2 p.595*

A Companion to the Philosophers. *v.1 p.415*

A Companion to the Philosophy of Mind. . . .*v.1 p.496, p.497*

The Companion to the Scottish Enlightenment. *v.3 p.71*

A Companion to the Victorian
    Novel. *v.2 p.177, p.192, p.193, v.6 p.755*

Companion to Theatre in Australia. *v.2 p.741*

A Companion to Theoretical Econometrics. *v.4 p.198*

A Companion to Thomas Mann's Magic Mountain. . .*v.2 p.612*

The Companion to Titian. *v.1 p.744*

A Companion to Tragedy. *v.1 p.58, p.88*

A Companion to Twentieth Century American Drama. .*v.1 p.116*

A Companion to Victorian Literature and
    Culture. *v.2 p.177, v.6 p.736*

A Companion to Victorian Poetry. *v.2 p.174, p.184*

A Companion to Wittgenstein's Tractatus. *v.1 p.471*

A Companion to World Philosophies. *v.1 p.474*

Companions in Crime: The Social Aspects of Criminal
    Conduct. *v.6 p.256, p.257*

Company: Music and Lyrics by Stephen
    Sondheim. *v.1 p.249, p.357, p.407*

The Company She Keeps. *v.2 p.99*

The Company They Kept: Migrants and the Politics of Gender
    in Caribbean Costa Rica, 1870-1960. . . . . . .*v.3 p.280*

The Company We Keep: An Ethics of Fiction. . . .*v.2 p.568*

ⓔ Comparable Worth: New Directions for Research. .*v.4 p.254*

Comparable Worth: Theories and Evidence. *v.4 p.133*

A Comparative Analysis of Capital Punishment: Statutes,
    Policies, Frequencies and Public Attitudes the World
    Over. *v.6 p.247*

A Comparative Analysis of Complex Organizations. . .*v.4 p.716*

Comparative Anatomy of the Vertebrates. *v.5 p.157*

Comparative Biochemistry: A Comprehensive Treatise, 7
    Vols. *v.5 p.327*

Comparative Biomechanics: Life's Physical
    World. *v.4 p.908, v.5 p.564*

Comparative Constitutional Engineering: An Inquiry into
    Structures, Incentives, and Outcomes. *v.4 p.574*

Comparative Cultural Studies and Michael Ondaatje's
    Writing. *v.2 p.738*

Comparative Economics in a Transforming World
    Economy. *v.4 p.237*

Comparative Education: The Dialectic of the Global and the
    Local. *v.4 p.313, p.338*

Comparative Federalism: The Territorial Dimension of
    Politics. *v.4 p.491*

Comparative Genomics: Recomb 2004 International Workshop,
    Rcg 2004, Bertinoro, Italy, October 16-19, 2004,
    Revised Selected Papers. *v.5 p.140*

Comparative Genomics. *v.5 p.139*

The Comparative Guide to American Elementary and Secondary
    Schools 2004. . . . .*v.4 p.280*

Comparative Higher Education: Knowledge, the University, and
    Development. *v.4 p.313*

A Comparative History of World Philosophy: From the
    Upanishads to Kant. *v.1 p.417*

Comparative Industrial Relations: An Introduction to
    Cross-National Perspectives. *v.4 p.120*

Comparative Law: The Role of Law and the Legal Process in
    Japan. *v.6 p.220*

The Comparative Method in Evolutionary
    Biology. *v.5 p.192, p.193*

Comparative Patterns of Economic Development,
    1850-1914. . . . .*v.4 p.237, p.259*

Comparative Psychology of Mental
    Development. *v.5 p.594, p.595*

The Comparative Reception of Darwinism. . . .*v.5 p.79, p.203*

A Comparative Sociology of World Religions: Virtuosi, Priests, and Popular Religion. *v.1 p.525, v.4 p.722*

Comparative Stylistics of French and English: A Methodology for Translation. *v.2 p.454*

Comparative Women's Rights and Political Participation in Europe. *v.4 p.601*

Comparing Asian Politics: India, China, and Japan. . .*v.4 p.616*

Comparing Empires: European Colonialism from Portuguese Expansion to the Spanish-American War. *v.3 p.76*

Comparing Financial Systems. *v.4 p.88*

Comparing Postcolonial Literatures: Dislocations. . . .*v.2 p.727*

Comparison and History: Europe in Cross National Perspective. *v.3 p.35*

Compassing the Vast Glove of the Earth. *v.4 p.378*

▣ Compassion Fatigue: How the Media Sell Disease, Famine, War, and Death. *v.4 p.407*

The Compassionate Satirist. *v.2 p.219*

Compelled to Excel: Immigration, Education, and Opportunity among Chinese Americans. *v.6 p.109, p.127*

Compelling Belief: The Culture of American Schooling. *v.4 p.297*

A Compelling Interest: Examining the Evidence on Racial Dynamics in Colleges and Universities. *v.4 p.295, p.308, p.309, p.355*

Compendium and Description of the West Indies. .*v.3 p.404, p.405*

Compendium of Alfalfa Diseases. *v.5 p.46*

▣ Compendium of Analytical Nomenclature. *v.5 p.274*

Compendium of Barley Diseases. *v.5 p.46*

Compendium of Bean Diseases. *v.5 p.47*

Compendium of Corn Diseases. *v.5 p.47*

A Compendium of Geochemistry: From Solar Nebula to the Human Brain. *v.5 p.440*

Compendium of Modern Instrumental Techniques. *v.1 p.393, p.398*

Compendium of Organic Synthetic Methods, Vol. 1. . .*v.5 p.294*

Compendium of Pea Diseases. *v.5 p.46*

Compendium of Rice Diseases. *v.5 p.47*

The Compendium of Safety Data Sheets for Research and Industrial Chemicals: Flavors and Fragrances, Vol. 7. .*v.5 p.744*

The Compendium of Safety Data Sheets for Research and Industrial Chemicals, Set, Vols. 1-6. . . . .*v.5 p.744*

Compendium of Sorghum Diseases. *v.5 p.46*

Compendium of Soybean Diseases. *v.5 p.46*

Compendium of Sweet Potato Diseases. *v.5 p.46*

Compendium of Tourism Statistics. *v.4 p.162*

Compere General Soleil. *v.2 p.535*

Competence in Performance: The Creativity of Tradition in Mexicano Verbal Art. *v.2 p.16*

Competency-Based Human Resource Management. . . .*v.4 p.76*

The Competent Classroom: Aligning High School Curriculum, Standards and Assessment - A Creative Teaching Guide. *v.4 p.304*

Competing Against Time: How Time-Based Competition Is Reshaping Global Markets. *v.4 p.119*

Competing by Design: The Power of Organizational Architecture. *v.4 p.86*

Competing Devotions: Career and Family among Women Executives. *v.5 p.578*

Competing for the Future. *v.4 p.81*

Competing on the Edge: Strategy As Structured Chaos. *v.4 p.81*

Competition among States and Local Governments: Efficiency and Equity in American Federalism. *v.4 p.524*

Competition and Chaos: U. S. Telecommunications since the 1996 Telecom ACT. *v.4 p.419*

Competition for Empire, 1740-1763. . . . .*v.3 p.73*

The Competitive Advantage: Creating and Sustaining Superior Performance. *v.4 p.51, p.64*

Competitive Advantage: Creating and Sustaining Superior Performance. *v.4 p.73*

The Competitive Advantage of Nations and Their Firms. *v.4 p.51, p.57, p.59*

The Competitive Advantage of Nations. *v.4 p.51, p.665*

The Competitive City: The Political Economy of Suburbia. *v.4 p.543*

⌨ The Competitive Disadvantage: Teacher Compensation in Rural America. *v.4 p.278*

Competitive Intelligence: A Framework for Web-based Analysis and Decision Making. *v.4 p.83*

Competitive Intelligence and Global Business. . .*v.4 p.69, p.82*

Competitive Solutions: The Strategist's Toolkit. . . . *v.4 p.83*

Competitive Strategy: Techniques for Analyzing Industries and Competitors. *v.4 p.81*

Competitor or Ally?: Japan's Role in American Educational Debates. *v.4 p.335, v.6 p.221, p.222*

Compilation of EPA's Sampling and Analysis Methods. *v.5 p.268*

Compilers: Principles, Techniques, and Tools. . *v.5 p.346, p.348*

The Compleat Belly Dancer. *v.1 p.16, p.17*

The Compleat Brahms: A Guide to the Musical Works of Johannes Brahms. *v.1 p.194, p.313*

The Compleat Cladist: A Primer of Phylogenetic Procedures. *v.5 p.205*

The Compleat Conductor. *v.1 p.403*

The Compleat Mozart: A Guide to the Musical Works of Wolfgang Amadeus Mozart. *v.1 p.193, p.345*

The compleat naturalist: a life of Linnaeus. *v.5 p.231*

The Compleat Strategyst: Being a Primer on the Theory of Games of Strategy. *v.5 p.505, p.507*

Complementary Methods for Research in Education. . *v.4 p.355*

Complementary Sports Medicine: Balancing Traditional and Nontraditional Treatments. *v.4 p.827, p.829*

Complementary/Alternative Therapies in Nursing. . . .*v.5 p.531*

The Complete Annotated Gilbert and Sullivan. *v.1 p.248, p.361, p.407*

The Complete Aspects of Love. *v.1 p.250, p.337, p.407*

The Complete Black Book of Russian Jewry. *v.3 p.86*

Complete Book of Ballets: A Guide to the Principal Ballets of the Nineteenth and Twentieth Centuries. *v.1 p.3*

Complete Book of Ballets: Ballets Past and Present. . .*v.1 p.3*

The Complete Book of Ballroom Dancing. *v.1 p.34*

The Complete Book of Baseball's Negro Leagues: The Other Half of Baseball History. *v.6 p.41*

Complete Book of Drills for Winning Football. *v.4 p.858, p.904*

The Complete Book of Running for Women: Everything You Need to Know about Training, Nutrition, Injury Prevention, Motivation, Racing and Much, Much More. . . . . *.v.4 p.837, p.866*

The Complete Book of Scriptwriting. *v.6 p.353*

Complete Book of Shaker Furniture. *v.1 p.804*

The Complete Book of Square Dancing and Round Dancing. *v.1 p.33*

The Complete Book of Swimming. *v.4 p.869*

The Complete Breast Book: Everything You Need to Know about Breast Disease. *v.6 p.443*

The Complete Canterbury Tales of Geoffrey Chaucer. . .*v.3 p.68*

The Complete Claudine: Claudine at School - Claudine in Paris - Claudine Married - Claudine and Annie. *v.6 p.395*

Complete Collected Essays. *v.2 p.378*

Complete Collected Stories. *v.2 p.378*

A Complete Concordance to the Poems of John Donne. .*v.2 p.213*

Complete Conditioning for Rugby. *v.4 p.865, p.879*

Complete Conditioning for Tennis. *v.4 p.864*

Complete Critical Edition: The Poems; The Prose Works, Vol. 8. . . . .*v.2 p.219*

Complete Critical Guide to D. H. Lawrence. *v.2 p.362*

The Complete Critical Guide to Robert Browning. . .*v.2 p.272*

The Complete Critical Guide to Samuel Beckett. *v.1 p.92, p.97,v.2 p.333*

The Complete Critical Prose and Letters. . . .*v.2 p.805, p.806*

The Complete Dead Sea Scrolls in English. .*v.1 p.546, p.620*

A Complete Dictionary of Furniture. *v.1 p.805*

The Complete Dictionary of Symbols. *v.1 p.710*

The Complete Directory to Prime Time Network TV Shows, 1946-Present. *v.4 p.418*

The Complete Dog Book. *v.5 p.53*

Complete Dublin Diary of Stanislaus Joyce. *v.2 p.358*

The Complete Elegies of Sextus Propertius. .*v.2 p.441, p.442*

The Complete Enderby. *v.2 p.336*

The Complete English Poems. *v.2 p.213*

The Complete English Works: Poems and Other Writings. *v.2 p.249*

Complete Essays, 1920-1925, Vol. I. *v.2 p.354*

Complete Essays, 1926-1930, Vol. II. *v.2 p.354*

Complete Essays, 1930-1935. . . . .*v.2 p.354*

Complete Essays, 1936-1938, Vol. IV. *v.2 p.354*

Complete Essays, 1938-1956, Vol. 5. . . . .*v.2 p.354*

The Complete Fables of La Fontaine. *v.2 p.474*

The Complete Fairy Tales of the Brothers Grimm. . .*v.2 p.593*

Complete Film Dictionary. *v.6 p.307*

The Complete Film Production Handbook. *v.6 p.347*

The Complete German Commission E Monographs: Therapeutic Guide to Herbal Medicines. *v.5 p.531*

The Complete Gods and Goddesses of Ancient Egypt. .*v.1 p.543*

A Complete Guide to Brass: Instruments and Techniques. *v.1 p.392, p.399*

A Complete Guide to Chi-Gung. *v.4 p.793*

The Complete Guide to Digital Photography. *v.1 p.769*

Complete Guide to Film Scoring: The Art and Business of Writing Music for Movies and TV. *v.6 p.351*

The Complete Guide to Modern Dance. *v.1 p.4, p.27*

A Complete Guide to Scientific and Common Names of Reptiles and Amphibians of the World. *v.5 p.95, p.215*

The Complete Guide to Software Testing. *v.5 p.346*

Complete Guide to Sport Education: Teacher Resources. .*v.4 p.797*

The Complete Guide to Sports Injuries. .*v.4 p.827, p.828, p.829*

The Complete Handbook of the Internet. *v.4 p.115*

The Complete Hebrew Dictionary in Three Volumes. .*v.6 p.646*

The Complete Hebrew-English/English-Hebrew Dictionary. *v.6 p.645*

The Complete Henry Bech. *v.2 p.157*

The Complete Idiot's Guide to Finance for Small Business. *v.4 p.87*

The Complete Idiot's Guide to Reptiles and Amphibians. *v.5 p.216*

The Complete IEP Guide: How to Advocate for Your Special Ed Child. *v.4 p.451*

The Complete Independent Movie Marketing Handbook: Promote, Distribute and Sell Your Film or Video. *v.6 p.345*

A Complete Introduction to Modern NMR Spectroscopy. *v.5 p.272*

The Complete Jacob Lawrence: Painting, Drawings, and Murals (1935-1999), A Catalogue Raisonné. *v.1 p.744*

The Complete Learning Disabilities Directory 2005. . .*v.4 p.318*

Complete Learning Disabilities Handbook: Ready-to-Use Strategies and Activities for Teaching Students with Learning Disabilities. *v.4 p.318*

The Complete Lesbian and Gay Parenting Guide. . . .*v.6 p.377*

The Complete Letters of Lady Mary Wortley Montagu. *v.2 p.256, v.3 p.107, p.129*

Complete Letters of Vincent Van Gogh. *v.1 p.749*

The Complete Love Poems of May Swenson. *v.2 p.117*

The Complete Lyrics of Cole Porter. *v.1 p.253, p.347, p.348, p.409, p.412*

The Complete Lyrics of Frank Loesser. .*v.1 p.251, p.408, p.412*

The Complete Lyrics of Ira Gershwin. *v.1 p.250, p.325, p.408, p.411*

Complete Lyrics of Irving Berlin. .*v.1 p.251, p.310, p.408, p.412*

The Complete Lyrics of Lorenz Hart. *v.1 p.250, p.329, p.408, p.411*

The Complete Major Prose Plays. .*v.1 p.80, p.82, p.83, p.109*

The Complete Make-up Artist: Working in Film, Television, and Theatre. *v.6 p.351*

The Complete "Beyond the Fringe". *v.2 p.331*

Complete Mondrian. *v.1 p.695*

The Complete Narrative Prose of Conrad Ferdinand Meyer. *v.2 p.599*

The Complete Notebooks of Henry James. *v.2 p.44*

The Complete Oil Paintings of Edward Hopper. . . .*v.1 p.743*

The Complete Operas of Richard Wagner. .*v.1 p.201, p.231, p.366*

The Complete Phantom of the Opera. .*v.1 p.253, p.337, p.409*

Complete Physical Education Plans for Grades 7-12: 366 Lesson Plans for 14 Sports and Activities. *v.4 p.798, p.799*

The Complete Plain Words. *v.2 p.550*

The Complete Plant Selection Guide for Landscape
Design. *v.1 p.817*

Complete Plays and Poems. *v.2 p.221*

Complete Plays of Frances Burney. *v.2 p.242*

The Complete Plays of Henry James. *v.2 p.44*

The Complete Plays of Synge. *v.2 p.306*

The Complete Plays of T. S. Eliot. *v.2 p.71*

Complete Plays of William Congreve. *v.2 p.244*

The Complete Plays. *v.1 p.108, v.2 p.374, p.802*

The Complete Poems, 1904-1962. . . . . *v.2 p.68*

The Complete Poems, 1927-1979. . . . . *v.2 p.61*

The Complete Poems and Major Prose. *v.2 p.255*

The Complete Poems and Selected Letters and Prose of Hart
Crane. *v.2 p.68*

The Complete Poems: Anne Sexton. *v.2 p.115, p.116*

Complete Poems by Ingeborg Bachmann: Bilingual
Edition. *v.2 p.603*

Complete Poems: Charles Baudelaire. *v.2 p.487*

Complete Poems: Francois Villon. *v.2 p.469*

The Complete Poems: Jonson. *v.2 p.220*

The Complete Poems of Anna Akhmatova. . . *v.2 p.800, p.801*

Complete Poems of Anne Bronte. *v.2 p.270*

Complete Poems of Basil Bunting. *v.2 p.331*

The Complete Poems of C. Day Lewis. . . . *v.2 p.342, p.343*

The Complete Poems of Carl Sandburg. *v.2 p.115*

Complete Poems of Charlotte Bronte. *v.2 p.269*

Complete Poems of Christina Rossetti: A Variorum Edition, Vol.
III. *v.2 p.304*

Complete Poems of Christina Rossetti: A Variorum Edition, Vol.
II. *v.2 p.304*

Complete Poems of Christina Rossetti: A Variorum Edition, Vol.
I. *v.2 p.304*

The Complete Poems of Emily Jane Brontë. *v.2 p.270*

The Complete Poems of Hugh MacDiarmid, Vol. 3. . *v.2 p.368*

The Complete Poems of John Crowe Ransom. . . . *v.2 p.113*

The Complete Poems of John Wilmot, Earl of
Rochester. *v.2 p.259*

The Complete Poems of Kenneth Rexroth. *v.2 p.114*

The Complete Poems of Michelangelo. *v.2 p.708*

The Complete Poems of Paul Laurence Dunbar. . . . *v.2 p.36*

The Complete Poems of Sarah Orne Jewett. *v.2 p.46*

The Complete Poems: Sir Thomas Wyatt. *v.2 p.217*

Complete poems. *v.2 p.51*

Complete Poems. *v.2 p.73*

The Complete Poems. *v.2 p.90*

Complete Poems. *v.2 p.110, p.216, p.343, p.363*

The Complete Poems. *v.2 p.702*

The Complete Poetical Works of Byron: Childe Harold's
Pilgrimage. *v.2 p.274*

The Complete Poetical Works of James Russell Lowell. *v.2 p.95*

Complete Poetical Works of Lucian Blaga. *v.2 p.816*

The Complete Poetical Works of Oliver Goldsmith. . *v.2 p.248*

Complete Poetical Works of Thomas Campbell. . . . *v.2 p.243*

The Complete Poetical Works of Thomas Hood. . . . *v.2 p.291*

Complete Poetical Works. *v.2 p.271*

The Complete Poetical Works. *v.2 p.274*

Complete Poetry and Prose: A Bilingual Edition. . . *v.2 p.470*

The Complete Poetry and Prose of William Blake. . *v.2 p.239*

The Complete Poetry of Percy Bysshe Shelley, Vol.
1. . . . . *v.2 p.311, p.312*

The Complete Poetry of Percy Bysshe Shelley, Vol. 2. *v.2 p.311*

The Complete Poetry of Richard Crashaw. *v.2 p.243*

The Complete Poetry of Teresa of Avila: A Bilingual
Edition. *v.2 p.646*

The Complete Prefaces: 1889-1913. . . . . . . *v.2 p.310*

The Complete Prefaces: 1914-1929. . . . . . . *v.2 p.310*

The Complete Prefaces: 1930-1950. . . . . . . *v.2 p.310*

The Complete Presidential Press Conferences of Franklin
Delano Roosevelt 1933-1945. . . . . *v.3 p.478*

The Complete Printmaker: Techniques - Traditions -
Innovations. *v.1 p.760*

The Complete Prose of Marianne Moore. *v.2 p.103*

The Complete Prose Works of John Milton. *v.2 p.254*

Complete Prose Works. *v.2 p.265*

The Complete Resume and Job Search Book for College
Students: The A-Z Career Guide for College
Students. *v.4 p.168*

The Complete Romances of Chretien de Troyes. . . *v.2 p.468*

The Complete Sherlock Holmes, Pack. *v.2 p.285*

The Complete Short Novels. *v.2 p.802*

The Complete Short Prose of Samuel Beckett,
1929-1989. . . . . *v.2 p.333, p.509, p.510*

Complete Short Stories of D. H. Lawrence, Vol. 2. . *v.2 p.362*

The Complete Short Stories of H. G. Wells. *v.2 p.319*

The Complete Short Stories of Thomas Wolfe. . . . *v.2 p.137*

The Complete Short Stories, Vol. I. *v.2 p.317*

Complete Short Stories. *v.2 p.350, p.351, p.383*

The Complete Shorter Fiction of Victoria Woolf. . . *v.2 p.394*

The Complete Shorter Fiction of Virginia Woolf. . . *v.2 p.394*

The Complete Small Business Guide: A Sourcebook for New
and Small Businesses. *v.4 p.87*

The Complete Small Business Start-up Guide. . . . *v.4 p.88*

The Complete Stalky and Co. *v.2 p.297*

The Complete Stories of Erskine Caldwell. *v.2 p.66*

The Complete Stories of Evelyn Waugh. *v.2 p.388*

Complete Stories. *v.2 p.110*

The Complete Stories. *v.2 p.611*

The Complete Tales in Verse: Jean de la Fontaine. . *v.2 p.474*

The Complete Tales of Uncle Remus. *v.2 p.40*

Complete Transcripts of the Clarence Thomas-Anita Hill
Hearings: October 11, 12, 13, 1991. . . . . . *v.4 p.538*

A Complete Treatise on the Art of Singing : Complete and
Unabridged. *v.1 p.395, p.400*

The Complete Walker IV. *v.4 p.787*

The Complete Wartime Correspondence of Tsar Nicholas II and
the Empress Alexandra: April 1914-March 1917. . *v.3 p.220*

The Complete Watercolors of Edward Hopper. . . . *v.1 p.743*

The Complete Who's Who in the Bible. . . . *v.1 p.616, p.617*

Complete Works: Betrayal. . . *v.1 p.92, p.102, p.103, v.2 p.377*

Complete Works: Birthday Party. .v.1 p.62, p.92, p.102,v.2 p.377

Complete Works in Prose and Verse. v.2 p.256

The Complete Works of Aphra Behn: Love-Letters Between and Nobleman and His Sister. v.2 p.238

Complete Works of Aristotle: The Revised Oxford Translation, Set.. . . . . .v.2 p.408

Complete Works of Aristotle: The Revised Oxford Translation. v.1 p.426

The Complete Works of Chuang Tzu. . .v.1 p.417, p.418, p.475

The Complete Works of Francois Rabelais. v.2 p.472

The Complete Works of Isaac Babel. v.2 p.801

Complete Works of John Lyly. v.2 p.215

Complete Works of John Webster, Set. v.2 p.236

The Complete Works of Kate Chopin. v.2 p.32, p.33

The Complete Works of Michael Drayton, Now First Collected, Vol. 3. . . . . .v.2 p.214

Complete Works of O. Henry. v.2 p.51

The Complete Works of Oscar Wilde: De Profundis; Epistola: In Carcere et Vinculis. v.2 p.321

The Complete Works of Oscar Wilde: Poems and Poems in Prose. v.2 p.322

The Complete Works of Oscar Wilde: The Picture of Dorian Gray: the 1890 and 1891 Texts. v.2 p.320

The Complete Works of Oscar Wilde. . . .v.2 p.321, v.6 p.400

The Complete Works of Ralph Waldo Emerson.v.2 p.37, p.38

Complete Works of Robert and James Adam and Unbuilt Adam. v.1 p.793

The Complete Works of Robert Burns, Vol. 1. . . .v.2 p.273

The Complete Works of Robert Burns, Vol. 2. . . .v.2 p.272

The Complete Works of Robert Burns, Vol. 3. . . .v.2 p.272

The Complete Works of Robert Burns, Vol. 4. .v.2 p.272, p.273

The Complete Works of Robert Burns, Vol. 5. . . .v.2 p.272

The Complete Works of Samuel Taylor Coleridge, Vol. 7. .v.2 p.280

The Complete works of Samuel Taylor Coleridge. with an introductory essay upon his philosophical and theological opinions. Ed. by Professor Shedd. the Friend. v.2 p.279

The Complete Works of Shakespeare. v.1 p.77, p.103

The Complete Works of Shelley. v.2 p.311

The Complete Works of Thomas Chatterton: A Bicentenary Edition. v.2 p.243

The Complete Works of Thomas Lodge. v.2 p.215

The Complete Works of W. H. Auden: Prose, 1939-1948. . . . . .v.2 p.329

The Complete Works of W H Auden: Prose and Travel Books in Prose and Verse, 1926-1938. . . . . .v.2 p.329

The Complete Works of Washington Irving: Journals and Notebooks, 1807-1822. . . . . .v.2 p.42

The Complete Works of William Congreve, Vol. 2. .v.2 p.244

Complete Works, Set. v.2 p.214

Complete Works: The Caretaker, Vol. 2..v.1 p.92, p.102,v.2 p.377

Complete Works: The Homecoming, Vol. 3. . . . . .v.1 p.92, p.102,v.2 p.377

Complete Works. v.2 p.263

The Complete Works. v.2 p.471

Complete World of Human Evolution. v.4 p.16

The complete writings and pictures of Dante Gabriel Rossetti : A hypermedia research archive. v.2 p.304

The Complete Writings and Pictures of Dante Gabriel Rossetti. v.2 p.304, p.305

Completely Queer: The Gay and Lesbian Encyclopedia.v.6 p.358

Completing the Union: Alaska, Hawai'i, and the Battle for Statehood. v.3 p.533

Complex Algebraic Curves. v.5 p.491, p.497

Complex Analysis: The Geometric Viewpoint. .v.5 p.491, p.495

Complex Analysis. v.5 p.490, p.491

Complex Fate: Hawthorne, Henry James and Some American Writers. v.2 p.7

Complex Information Processing: The Impact of Herbert A. Simon. v.5 p.590

Complex Population Dynamics: A Theoretical/Empirical Synthesis. v.5 p.186

The Complex Roles of the Teacher: An Ecological Perspective. v.4 p.278

Complex Variables and Applications. v.5 p.490

Complexities: Beyond Nature and Nurture. v.4 p.24

Complicated Women: Sex and Power in Pre-Code Hollywood. v.6 p.328, p.332

Complying with the Americans with Disabilities Act: A Guidebook for Management and People with Disabilities. v.4 p.131

Components of Scientific Instruments and Applications of Computers to Chemical Research, Vol. 1. . . . .v.5 p.276

Composers at Work: The Craft of Musical Composition 1450-1600. . . . . .v.1 p.180

Composers on Modern Music Culture: An Anthology of Source Readings on Twentieth-Century Music. v.1 p.224

Composers on Music: An Anthology of Composers Writings from Palestrina to Copland. v.1 p.174, p.247

Composing a World: Lou Harrison, Musical Wayfarer. v.1 p.219, p.329

Composing for the Films. v.1 p.254, v.6 p.351

Composing for Voice: A Guide for Composers, Singers, and Teachers. v.1 p.369

Composing the Soul: Reaches of Nietzsche's Psychology. v.5 p.597

Composite Index for CRC Handbooks, Version 1.1..v.5 p.259

Composite Materials for Aircraft Structures. v.5 p.717

Composite Materials Handbook. v.5 p.691

Composite Steel and Concrete Structural Members: Fundamental Behaviour. v.5 p.695, p.697

Composites Engineering Handbook, Vol. 11. . . . .v.5 p.690

Composites Manufacturing: Materials, Product and Process Engineering. v.5 p.690

Composition Chemistry, and Climate of the Atmosphere. v.5 p.355

Composition with Pitch-Classes: A Theory of Compositional Design. v.1 p.372

Compositional and Failure Analysis of Polymers: A Practical Approach. v.5 p.691

The Compositional Process of J. S. Bach. . . .v.1 p.185, p.303

Compositional Subjects: Enfiguring Asian/American Women. *v.6 p.96, p.112*

Compositional Theory in the 18th Century. . . *v.1 p.191, p.371*

Comprehending Cults: The Sociology of New Religious Movements. *v.4 p.721*

Comprehending Suicide: Landmarks in 20th-Century Suicidology. *v.5 p.663*

Comprehensive Analytical Chemistry. *v.5 p.273*

Comprehensive Biochemistry (Set). *v.5 p.327*

☐ Comprehensive Chemistry Sites. *v.5 p.255*

Comprehensive Choral Music Education. *v.1 p.395*

Comprehensive Clinical Psychology, Set. *v.5 p.667*

Comprehensive Coordination Chemistry II: From Biology to Nanotechnology, Set. *v.5 p.299*

Comprehensive Coordination Chemistry: The Synthesis, Reactions, Properties and Applications of Coordination Compounds, Set. *v.5 p.300*

Comprehensive Dictionary of Physical Chemistry. . . *v.5 p.275*

A Comprehensive French Grammar. *v.2 p.454*

The Comprehensive Gazetteer of England and Wales, Set. *v.4 p.374*

A Comprehensive Grammar of the English Language. *v.2 p.558*

A Comprehensive Guide to the Hazardous Properties of Chemical Substances. *v.5 p.312*

Comprehensive Handbook of Psychological Assessment, Personality Assessment, Vol. 2. . . . . *v.5 p.603*

Comprehensive Heterocyclic Chemistry II: An Extended and Updated Review of the Literature (1982-1995), Set. *v.5 p.298*

Comprehensive Heterocyclic Chemistry: The Structure, Reactions, Synthesis and Uses of Heterocyclic Compounds. *v.5 p.298*

The Comprehensive High School Today. *v.4 p.327*

Comprehensive Inorganic Chemistry, Set. *v.5 p.302*

Comprehensive Inorganic Chemistry. *v.5 p.303*

A Comprehensive Introduction to Differential Geometry, Vol. 1. . . . . *v.5 p.497*

A Comprehensive Introduction to Differential Geometry, Vol. 2. . . . . *v.5 p.496*

A Comprehensive Introduction to Differential Geometry, Vol. 3. . . . . *v.5 p.497*

A Comprehensive Introduction to Differential Geometry, Vol. 4. . . . . *v.5 p.497*

A Comprehensive Introduction to Differential Geometry, Vol. 5. . . . . *v.5 p.496, p.497*

Comprehensive Medicinal Chemistry. *v.5 p.330*

Comprehensive Natural Products Chemistry, Set. . . *v.5 p.299*

Comprehensive Organic Functional Group Transformations, Set. *v.5 p.294*

Comprehensive Organic Synthesis, Set. *v.5 p.294*

Comprehensive Organic Transformations: A Guide to Functional Group Preparations. *v.5 p.294*

Comprehensive Organometallic Chemistry II: A Review of the Literature 1982-1994. . . . . *v.5 p.307*

Comprehensive Organometallic Chemistry: The Synthesis, Reactions and Structures of Organometallic Compounds. *v.5 p.307*

Comprehensive Perinatal and Pediatric Respiratory Care. *v.5 p.536*

Comprehensive Persian-English Dictionary: Including the Arabic Words and Phrases to Be Met with in Persian Literature. *v.6 p.669*

Comprehensive Polymer Science Series: The Synthesis, Characterization, Reactions and Applications of Polymers, Set. *v.5 p.322*

Comprehensive Respiratory Care. *v.5 p.536*

A Comprehensive Russian Grammar. *v.2 p.776*

Comprehensive Supramolecular Chemistry, Set. . . . *v.5 p.300*

Comprehensive Toxicology. *v.5 p.314, p.315, p.365*

A Comprehensive Treatise on Inorganic and Theoretical Chemistry, 16 v. *v.5 p.303*

A Compromise of Principle: Congressional Republicans and Reconstruction 1863-1869. . . . . *v.3 p.394, p.435*

Compromised Compliance: Implementation of the 1965 Voting Rights Act, 66. . . . . *v.4 p.461*

Compulsory Compassion: A Critique of Restorative Justice. *v.4 p.754*

Compulsory Happiness. *v.2 p.817*

Compulsory Mis-Education. *v.4 p.347*

Computability and Unsolvability. *v.5 p.471*

Computability, Complexity, and Languages: Fundamentals of Theoretical Computer Science. *v.5 p.336, p.471*

Computation and Human Experience. *v.5 p.590*

Computational Analysis of Biochemical Systems: A Practical Guide for Biochemists and Molecular Biologists. *v.5 p.92, p.94, p.114, p.115*

Computational and Statistical Approaches to Genomics. *v.5 p.93, p.130, p.147, p.148*

Computational Biology and Genome Informatics. *v.5 p.98, p.143, p.147*

Computational Biology: First International Conference on Biology, Informatics, and Mathematics, JOBIM 2000: Selected Papers. *v.5 p.97*

Computational Biology. *v.5 p.106*

The Computational Brain. *v.5 p.591*

☐ Computational Chemistry Comparison and Benchmark Database. *v.5 p.280*

☐ Computational Chemistry List (CCL Links). . . . *v.5 p.266*

Computational Complexity. *v.5 p.336*

Computational Economics. *v.4 p.202*

Computational Fluid Dynamics. *v.5 p.547*

Computational Genomics: Theory and Application. *v.5 p.106, p.108, p.140*

Computational Geometry in C. *v.5 p.337, p.340*

Computational Learning Theory. *v.5 p.339, p.340*

Computational Modeling of Genetic and Biochemical Networks. *v.5 p.111, p.145*

Computational Models in the Economics of Environment and Development. *v.4 p.207, p.267*

Computational Models in the Economics of Environment And. *v.5 p.14*

Computational Molecular Biology: An Algorithmic Approach. *v.5 p.107, p.123, p.128*

Computational Molecular Biology: An Introduction. *v.5 p.105, p.341, p.501, p.502*

Computational Molecular Biology. *v.5 p.106, p.127*

Computational Organometallic Chemistry. *v.5 p.299*

Computational Physics: Fortran Version. *v.5 p.551*

Computational Physics: Problem Solving with Computers. *v.5 p.551*

Computational Physics. *v.5 p.551*

Computational Systems Biology. *v.5 p.97, p.105, p.108*

Computational Text Analysis: For Functional Genomics and Bioinformatics. *v.5 p.106, p.142, p.146, p.341*

Computer: A History of the Information Machine. *v.3 p.366, v.4 p.114, v.5 p.342, p.343*

Computer Algorithms: Introduction to Design and Analysis. *v.5 p.336*

☐ Computer Almanac: Interesting and Useful Numbers About Computers. *v.5 p.343, p.344, p.348*

Computer and Internet Use on Campus: A Legal Guide to Issues of Intellectual Property, Free Speech, and Privacy. *v.4 p.441*

Computer Applications in Music: A Bibliography, Supplement 1. . . . .*v.1 p.166, p.386*

Computer Applications in Music: A Bibliography. *v.1 p.165, p.166, p.386*

Computer Architecture: A Quantitative Approach. *v.5 p.344, p.345, p.730*

Computer Architecture: From Microprocessors to Supercomputers. *v.5 p.344, p.345, p.730*

Computer Control of Machines and Processes. . . .*v.5 p.710*

The Computer Engineering Handbook. *v.5 p.730*

Computer Graphics: Principles and Practices. *v.5 p.340*

The Computer Industry. *v.4 p.158*

Computer Music: Synthesis, Composition, and Performance. *v.1 p.386*

The Computer Music Tutorial. *v.1 p.387*

Computer Networking: A Top-down Approach Featuring the Internet. *v.5 p.727*

Computer Networking with Internet Protocols. . . .*v.5 p.727*

Computer Networks: A Systems Approach. . . .*v.5 p.345, p.727*

Computer Networks and Internets with Internet Applications. *v.5 p.345*

Computer Networks. *v.4 p.422, v.5 p.727, p.728*

Computer Processing of Remotely-Sensed Images: An Introduction. *v.4 p.389*

Computer Resources for People with Disabilities: A Guide to Assistive Technologies, Tools, and Resources for People of All Ages. *v.4 p.317*

Computer Science and Computing: A Guide to the Literature. *v.5 p.344*

Computer Security Fundamentals. *v.4 p.113*

Computer Simulation in Chemical Physics. *v.5 p.551*

Computer Simulation Methods in Theoretical Physics. *v.5 p.551*

Computer Software Applications in Chemistry. *v.5 p.267*

Computer Solution of Linear Programs. *v.5 p.683*

Computer Systems Design and Architecture. *v.5 p.730*

Computer Systems That Learn: Classification and Prediction Methods from Statistics, Neural Nets, Machine Learning and Expert Systems. *v.5 p.339, p.408*

Computer Visualization for the Theatre: 3D Modelling for Designers. *v.1 p.148*

Computer-Assisted Investigative Reporting. *v.4 p.408*

Computer-Assisted Reporting: A Practical Guide. . . *v.4 p.414*

Computerized Data Acquisition and Analysis for the Life Sciences: A Hands-on Guide. . . *v.5 p.92, p.93, p.94, p.99*

Computers and Art. *v.1 p.771*

Computers and Intractability: A Guide to the Theory of NP-Completeness. *v.5 p.336, p.471*

Computers and Thought. *v.5 p.590*

Computers and Writing: The Cyborg Era. *v.2 p.565*

Computers As Cognitive Tools: No More Walls. . . . *v.5 p.590*

Computers in Manufacturing. *v.5 p.684*

Computers in Railways X: Computer System Design and Operation in the Railway and Other Transit Systems. *v.5 p.699, p.700*

Computers Ltd: What They Really Can't Do. *v.5 p.343*

Computer-Supported Collaborative Learning in Higher Education. *v.4 p.350*

Comrade Chiang Ch'ing. *v.6 p.196, p.200, p.217*

Comrades Against Apartheid: The ANC and the South African Communist Party in Exile, 1966-1990. . . . . . .*v.4 p.613*

Comrade. *v.2 p.720*

Comstockery in America: Patterns of Censorship and Control. *v.4 p.472*

Comte after Positivism. *v.1 p.455*

Con barro del Corazon: Ruk' Kach' Ulew Re Uk'Ux Jun. *v.2 p.674*

Concentration Camps USA: Japanese Americans and World War II. *v.6 p.133*

Concept and Controversy: Sixty Years of Taking Ideas to Market. *v.4 p.559*

The Concept and Method of Cultural Ecology. *v.4 p.30*

The Concept of Anxiety. *v.1 p.643*

The Concept of Biblical Theology: An Old Testament Perspective. *v.1 p.618*

The Concept of Constituency: Political Representation, Democratic Legitimacy, and Institutional Design. . *v.4 p.576*

The Concept of Dance Education. *v.1 p.43, p.47*

The Concept of Irony, with Continual Reference to Socrates/Notes of Schelling's Berlin Lectures. . . *v.1 p.478*

The Concept of Jacksonian Democracy: New York As a Test Case. *v.3 p.490*

The Concept of Law. *v.4 p.434*

The Concept of Liberty in the Age of the American Revolution. *v.4 p.452*

The Concept of Logical Consequence. *v.1 p.494*

The Concept of Man in Early China. *v.1 p.418*

The Concept of Mind. *v.1 p.497*

The Concept of Nature: Tarner Lectures. *v.5 p.404*

The Concept of Representation. *v.4 p.576*

The Concept of Utopia. *v.4 p.499*

The Concept of Woman: The Aristotelian Revolution, 750 B. C. -A. D. 1250. . . . .*v.6 p.433, p.460*

The Conception of God: A Philosophical Discussion Concerning the Nature of the Divine Idea as a Demonstrable Reality. *v.1 p.639*

Conceptions of Giftedness. *v.5 p.576*

Concepts and Methods in Evolutionary Biology. . . . *v.5 p.191*

Concepts and Theories of Human Development. . . . *v.5 p.627*

Concepts in Biological Oceanography: An Interdisciplinary
Primer. *v.4 p.392, v.5 p.431*

Concepts in Fitness Programming. *v.4 p.791, p.903*

Concepts in Integrated Pest Management. *v.5 p.10, p.27*

Concepts of Cleanliness: Changing Attitudes in France since the
Middle Ages. *v.3 p.141*

Concepts of Genetics. *v.5 p.134*

Concepts of God in Africa. *v.1 p.525, p.526*

Concepts of Modern Art. *v.1 p.681*

Concepts of Modern Physics. *v.5 p.547*

Concepts of Particle Physics, Vol. I. *v.5 p.552*

Concepts of Science: A Philosophical
Analysis. *v.1 p.499, v.5 p.400*

Concepts of Symbiogenesis: A Historical and Critical Study of
the Research of Russian Botanists. *v.5 p.193*

Concepts, Theories and the Mind-Body Problem. . . *v.5 p.401*

Conceptual Art and the Politics of Publicity. *v.1 p.825*

Conceptual Art. *v.1 p.680*

Conceptual Foundations for Therapeutic
Recreation. *v.4 p.783, p.829, p.842*

Conceptual Foundations of Human Factors
Measurement. *v.5 p.587*

Conceptual Mathematics: A First Introduction to
Categories. *v.5 p.473*

Conceptual Physics. *v.5 p.539, p.540*

The Conceptual Practices of Power: A Feminist Sociology of
Knowledge. *v.4 p.744*

Conceptual Roots of Mathematics. *v.5 p.470*

Conceptualization and Measurement in the Social
Sciences. *v.4 p.689*

Concerning the Angels. *v.2 p.655*

Concerning the Spiritual in Art. *v.1 p.703*

Concert Life in Haydn's Vienna: Aspects of a Developing
Musical and Social Institution. *v.1 p.191, p.330*

The Concerto: A Listener's Guide. *v.1 p.243*

El Concierto de San Ovidio; El Tragaluz. *v.2 p.656*

A Concise Anglo-Saxon Dictionary. *v.2 p.206, p.550*

Concise Atlas of World History. *v.4 p.381*

The Concise Cambridge History of English Literature. *v.2 p.167*

Concise Chemical and Technical Dictionary. *v.5 p.257*

A Concise Companion to Chaucer. *v.2 p.210*

A Concise Companion to Contemporary British
Fiction. *v.2 p.178, p.194*

A Concise Companion to Modernism. *v.2 p.178, p.184*

A Concise Companion to Postwar American Literature and
Culture. *v.3 p.441*

Concise Companion to the Restoration and the Eighteenth
Century. *v.2 p.173*

A Concise Companion to the Victorian Novel. .*v.2 p.176, p.193*

Concise Dictionary of American Biography, Set. . . *v.3 p.377*

A Concise Dictionary of Literary Terms. *v.2 p.549*

Concise Dictionary of Modern Japanese History. . . *v.6 p.224*

Concise Dictionary of Scientific Biography. . *v.5 p.394, p.395*

A Concise Economic History of the World: From Paleolithic
Times to the Present. *v.3 p.38*

Concise Encyclopaedia of Metallurgy. *v.5 p.732*

Concise Encyclopedia Biochemistry and Molecular
Biology. *v.5 p.114, p.325*

Concise Encyclopedia of Corrosion Technology. . . .*v.5 p.735*

The Concise Encyclopedia of English and American Poets and
Poetry. *v.2 p.15, p.16, p.180*

The Concise Encyclopedia of Foods and Nutrition. . .*v.5 p.329*

A Concise Encyclopedia of Hinduism. *v.1 p.536*

Concise Encyclopedia of Latin American Literature. . *v.2 p.665*

Concise Encyclopedia of Plant Pathology. *v.5 p.47*

Concise Encyclopedia of Polymer Science and
Engineering. *v.5 p.321*

Concise Encyclopedia of Special Education: A Reference for the
Education of the Handicapped and Other Exceptional
Children and Adults. *v.4 p.316*

A Concise Encyclopedia of the Baha'i Faith. *v.1 p.561*

Concise Encyclopedia of Traffic and Transportation
Systems. *v.5 p.700, p.701*

The Concise Encyclopedia of Western Philosophy and
Philosophers. *v.1 p.416*

A Concise Glossary of Feminist Theory. *v.6 p.426, p.427*

A Concise Guide to Technical Communication. *v.5 p.680*

Concise Handbook of Experimental Methods for the Behavioral
and Biological Sciences. *v.5 p.88*

🄴 A Concise Handbook of Movie Industry Economics. *v.6 p.345*

A Concise Historical Grammar of the Albanian Language:
Reconstruction of Proto-Albanian. *v.2 p.778*

Concise History of American Painting and Sculpture. .*v.1 p.681*

A Concise History of Brazil. *v.3 p.340*

A Concise History of Greece. *v.3 p.194*

A Concise History of Hungary. *v.3 p.185*

Concise History of Irish Art. *v.1 p.685*

A Concise History of Mathematics. *v.5 p.468*

A Concise History of Mining. *v.5 p.738*

Concise History of Modern Painting. *v.1 p.729*

A Concise History of Ornithology. *v.5 p.81, p.82, p.216*

A Concise History of Poland. *v.3 p.252*

A Concise History of Portugal. *v.3 p.243*

A Concise History of the Arab-Israeli Conflict. .*v.6 p.616, p.617*

A Concise History of the Armenian People. .*v.3 p.231, v.6 p.633*

A Concise History of the Common Law [1956]. . . .*v.4 p.436*

A Concise History of the Italian Theatre. *v.1 p.107*

Concise History of the Middle East. *v.6 p.581*

A Concise Hungarian-English Dictionary. . .*v.2 p.774, p.775*

🄴 A Concise Introduction to Econometrics: An Intuitive
Guide. *v.4 p.200*

A Concise Introduction to Econometrics: An Intuitive
Guide. *v.4 p.200*

Concise Introduction to Pure Mathematics. *v.5 p.459*

A Concise Introduction to the Theory of
Integration. *v.5 p.489, p.490*

Concise Manual of Chemical and Environmental Safety in Schools and Colleges. *v.5 p.266*

The Concise Oxford Companion to African American Literature. *v.6 p.22, p.33*

The Concise Oxford Companion to Canadian Literature. .*v.2 p.731*

The Concise Oxford Dictionary of Art Terms. *v.1 p.663*

The Concise Oxford Dictionary of English Place-Names. *v.3 p.126*

The Concise Oxford Dictionary of French Literature. .*v.2 p.456*

The Concise Oxford Dictionary of Politics. *v.4 p.482*

The Concise Oxford Dictionary of Zoology. *v.5 p.211*

Concise Polymeric Materials Encyclopedia. *v.5 p.321*

Concluding Unscientific Postscripts to Philosophical Fragments, Vol. II. *v.1 p.595*

Concluding Unscientific Postscripts to Philosophical Fragments, Vol. I. *v.1 p.478, p.595*

Concord and Conflict: The United States and Russia, 1867-1914. . . . .*v.3 p.392*

Concord in Discord: The Plays of John Ford, 1586-1986. . . . .*v.2 p.218*

A Concordance of the Qur'an. *v.1 p.556*

A Concordance to Finnegans Wake (1963). *v.2 p.358*

A Concordance to the Anglo-Saxon Poetic Records. . .*v.2 p.203*

Concordance to the Complete Poetical Works of Sir Thomas Wyatt. *v.2 p.214*

A Concordance to the Novels of Virginia Woolf. . .*v.2 p.392*

Concordance to the Poems of Edmund Spenser. *v.2 p.215*

A Concordance to the Poems of W. B. Yeats. *v.2 p.328*

Concrete and Clay: Reworking Nature in New York City. *v.6 p.727*

Concrete Mathematics: A Foundation for Computer Science. *v.5 p.337*

Concrete Structures: Materials, Maintenance and Repair. *v.5 p.697*

Concrete Structures: Stresses and Deformations. . . .*v.5 p.694*

Concrete. *v.5 p.692*

Le Conde Lucanor: A Collection of Mediaeval Spanish Stories. *v.2 p.661*

The Condemned Apple: Selected Poetry. *v.2 p.815*

Condensed Encyclopedia of Polymer Engineering Terms. *v.5 p.321*

Condensed Matter Physics. *v.5 p.555*

Condillac: Essay on the Origin of Human Knowledge. .*v.1 p.454*

⌨ Condition of Education. *v.4 p.322*

Conditions in Occupational Therapy: Effect on Occupational Performance. *v.5 p.535*

Conditions in Occupational Therapy. *v.5 p.535*

Conditions of Knowledge: An Introduction to Epistemology and Education. *v.4 p.345*

Conditions of Liberty: Civil Society and Its Rivals. . .*v.4 p.515*

The Condor Years: How Pinochet and His Allies Brought Terrorism to Three Continents. *v.3 p.353*

Conduct Disorders in Childhood and Adolescence. . .*v.5 p.662*

The Conduct of the Chaco War. *v.3 p.278*

Conduct Unbecoming: Gays and Lesbians in the U. S. Military. *v.6 p.390*

Conducting Choral Music. *v.1 p.402*

Conducting School-Based Assessments of Child and Adolescent Behavior. *v.5 p.572*

Conducting Technique: For Beginners and Professionals. *v.1 p.402, p.403*

Conduction of Heat in Solids. *v.5 p.560*

Conductors in Conversation: Fifteen Contemporary Conductors Discuss Their Lives and Profession. *v.1 p.403*

A Coney Island of the Mind. *v.2 p.75*

Coney Island: The People's Playground. *v.3 p.491*

The Confederacy As a Revolutionary Experience. . . .*v.3 p.401*

A Confederacy of Dunces: A Novel. *v.2 p.157*

The Confederacy. *v.3 p.429*

The Confederate Constitutions. *v.4 p.474*

A Confederate General from Big Sur; Dreaming of Babylon; The Hawkline Monster. *v.2 p.141*

Confederate Leaders in the New South. *v.3 p.425*

Confederate Nation 1861-1865. . . . .*v.3 p.429*

Confederate Navy in Europe. *v.3 p.432*

The Confederate Republic: A Revolution Against Politics. *v.3 p.400, v.4 p.521*

Confederate Settlements in British Honduras. *v.3 p.297*

The Confederate War: How Popular Will Nationalism, and Millitary Strategy Could Not Stave off Defeat. . . .*v.4 p.520*

Confederates in the Attic: Dispatches from the Unfinished Civil War. *v.4 p.521*

The Confederation Debates in the Province of Canada 1865. . . . .*v.4 p.587*

The Conference of Birds. *v.6 p.670*

Conference on the Introductory Physics Course: On the Occasion of the Retirement of Robert Resnick. . . .*v.5 p.564*

ⓔ Confessio Amantis or Tales of the Seven Deadly Sins. *v.2 p.211*

Confessio Amantis, Vol. 2. . . . .*v.2 p.211*

Confessio Amantis, Vol. 3. . . . .*v.2 p.211, p.212*

Confessio Amantis. *v.2 p.212*

La confession anonyme. *v.2 p.521*

Le confessioni d'un italiano. *v.2 p.712*

The Confessions and Correspondence, Including the Letters to Malesherbes. *v.2 p.482*

Confessions, Bks. 1-8. . . . .*v.2 p.429*

Confessions, Bks. 9-13. . . . .*v.2 p.430*

Confessions: Commentary. *v.2 p.429, p.430*

Confessions of a Mask. *v.6 p.231, p.398*

Confessions of A Young Man. *v.2 p.300*

Confessions of an English Opium Eater. *v.2 p.281*

Confessions of Felix Krull, Confidence Man: The Early Years. *v.2 p.613*

The Confessions of Fitz-Boodle; and Some Passages in the Life of Major Gahagan. by W. M. Thackeray. *v.2 p.315*

The Confessions of Lady Nijo. *v.6 p.229*

Confessions of Lord Byron. *v.2 p.273*

The Confessions of Nat Turner. *v.2 p.156*

Confessions: Text and Prolegomena. *v.2 p.429, p.430*

Confessions. *v.1 p.592, v.2 p.429*

Title Index

Confidence Men and Painted Women: Study of Middle Class Culture in America, 1830-70. . . . .*v.4 p.724*

Confidences de gargouille. *v.2 p.508*

The Confident Coach's Guide to Teaching Lacrosse: From Basic Fundamentals to Advanced Player Skills and Team Strategies. *v.4 p.862*

The Confidential Agent. *v.2 p.349*

Confidential Informant: Law Enforcement's Most Valuable Tool. *v.6 p.267*

Configurations of Exile: The South Asian Writers and Their World. *v.2 p.760*

Configuring Gender: Explorations in Theory and Politics. *v.6 p.441*

Confinement and Ethnicity: An Overview of World War II Japanese American Relocation Sites. *v.6 p.133*

Confirmation Trials: Causes and Consequences of Judicial Selection Battles. *v.4 p.541*

Conflict and Change in Cuba. *v.3 p.311*

Conflict and Coexistence: Archbishop Rodrigo and the Muslims and Jews of Medieval Spain. *v.6 p.572, p.574*

Conflict and Competition: The Latin American Church in a Changing Environment. *v.3 p.259*

Conflict and Consensus in Switzerland. *v.4 p.706*

Conflict and Control in the World Economy: Contemporary Economic Realism and Neo-Mercantilism. *v.4 p.260*

Conflict and Crisis: The Presidency of Harry S. Truman, 1945-1948. . . . .*v.3 p.469*

Conflict and Violence in Singapore and Malaysia 1945-1983. . . . .*v.6 p.172*

Conflict and War in the Middle East: From Interstate War to New Security. *v.6 p.595*

Conflict, Cleavage, and Change in Central Asia and the Caucasus. *v.4 p.623*

Conflict in Afghanistan: An Encyclopedia. *v.6 p.634*

The Conflict in Education in a Democratic Society. . .*v.4 p.343*

The Conflict in Modern Culture and Other Essays. . .*v.4 p.766*

Conflict in the Cosmos: Fred Hoyle's Life in Science. .*v.5 p.62*

Conflict in the Southern Cone: The Argentine Military and the Boundary Dispute with Chile, 1870-1902. . . . .*v.3 p.276*

The Conflict of European and Eastern Algonkian Cultures 1504-1700: A Study in Canadian Civilization. *v.3 p.534, v.6 p.684*

Conflict of Light and Wind: The Spanish Generation of 1927 and the Ideology of Poetic Form. *v.2 p.640*

Conflict or Codetermination: The Congress, the President, and the Power to Make War. *v.4 p.528*

Conflict Resolution in Uganda. *v.4 p.497, p.613*

Conflict, Social Capital, and Managing Natural Resources: A West African Case Study. *v.4 p.268, v.5 p.13, p.17, p.18, v.6 p.297*

Conflict Sociology : Toward an Explanatory Science. .*v.4 p.681*

Conflict Unending: India-Pakistan Tensions Since 1947. .*v.6 p.159*

The Conflict with the Arabs in Israeli Politics and Society. *v.6 p.618*

Conflicting Missions: Havana, Washington and Africa, 1959-1976. . . . .*v.3 p.309*

Conflicting Paradigms in Adult Literacy Education: In Quest of a U.S. Democratic Politics of Literacy. . . .*v.4 p.298, p.304*

Conflicting Stories: American Women Writers at the Turn into the Twentieth Century. *v.2 p.8*

Conflicts and Conspiracies: Brazil and Portugal, 1750-1808. . . . .*v.3 p.335*

Conflicts in Feminism. *v.6 p.427*

Conflicts of Empires: Spain, the Low Countries and the Struggle for World Supremacy, 1585-1713. . . . .*v.3 p.205, p.239*

Confluences. *v.6 p.25*

Confocal and Two-Photon Microscopy: Foundations, Applications and Advances. *v.5 p.88*

Confocal Microscopy for Biologists. *v.5 p.86*

Conformal Array Antenna Theory and Design. *v.5 p.728*

Conformational Analysis. *v.5 p.297*

Conformational Proteomics of Macromolecular Architecture: Approaching the Structure of Large Molecular Assemblies and Their Mechanisms of Action. *v.5 p.104, p.115*

The Conformist. *v.2 p.719*

Confronting Catastrophe: New Perspectives on Natural Disasters. *v.4 p.394, p.395*

Confronting Change, Challenging Tradition: Women in Latin American History. *v.3 p.296*

Confronting Climate Change: Risks, Implications and Responses. *v.5 p.371*

Confronting Race: Women and Indians on the Frontier, 1815-1915. . . . .*v.3 p.521*

Confronting Silence: Selected Writings. .*v.1 p.225, p.226, p.362*

Confronting the Enemy Within: Security Intelligence, the Police, and Counterterrorism in Four Democracies. . . .*v.4 p.658*

Confronting the German Question: Germans on the East-West Divide. *v.3 p.179*

Confronting the Third World: United States Foreign Policy, 1945-1980. . . . .*v.3 p.453*

Confucian China and Its Modern Fate: The Problem of Intellectual Continuity. *v.6 p.190*

Confucian Gentlemen and Barbarian Envoys: The Opening of Korea, 1875-1885. . . . .*v.6 p.236*

The Confucian Kingship in Korea: Yôngjo and the Politics of Sagacity. *v.6 p.236*

Confucianism and Human Rights. *v.4 p.513*

Confucius and the Chinese Way. *v.6 p.184, p.199*

The Confusions of Pleasure: Commerce and Culture in Ming China. *v.6 p.185, p.186*

The Confusions of Young Torless. *v.2 p.614*

Congo Diary and Other Uncollected Pieces. *v.2 p.340*

Congo, My Country. *v.6 p.18, p.29, p.62*

Congo-Paris: Transnational Traders on the Margins of the Law. *v.4 p.44*

The Congo-Zaire Experience, 1960-98. . . . . .*v.6 p.62, p.63*

Congregational Communion: Clerical Friendship in the Anglo-American Puritan Community, 1610-1692. .*v.1 p.588*

Congress and Law-Making: Researching the Legislative Process. *v.4 p.439*

Congress and the Constitution. *v.4 p.531*

Congress and the Governance of the Nation's Capital: The Conflict of Federal and Local Interests. *v.4 p.524*

Congress and the Presidency. *v.4 p.527*

Congress: Games and Strategies. *v.4 p.529, p.530*

Congress Makes a Law: The Story Behind the Employment Act of 1946. . . . . *v.4 p.446*

The Congress of Vienna: A Study in Allied Unity, 1812-1822. . . . . *v.3 p.152*

Congress, Parliament and Defence: The Impact of Legislative Reform on Defence Accountability in Britain and America. *v.4 p.531*

Congress, Progressive Reform, and the New American State. *v.3 p.441, v.4 p.531*

Congress Reconsidered. *v.4 p.529*

Congress Resurgent: Foreign and Domestic Policy on Capitol Hill. *v.4 p.531*

Congress, the President, and Policymaking: A Historical Analysis. *v.4 p.527, p.528, p.531, p.532*

Congress, the President, and Public Policy. *v.4 p.527*

Congress, the Press, and Political Accountability. . . *v.4 p.406*

Congress, the Press, and the Public. *v.4 p.530*

Congressional Abdication on War and Spending. . . *v.4 p.531*

Congressional Careers: Contours of Life in the U. S. House of Representatives. *v.4 p.533*

Congressional Conservatism and the New Deal: The Growth of the Conservative Coalition in Congress, 1933 to 1939. . . . . *v.3 p.478, v.4 p.522*

☐ The Congressional Directory. *v.4 p.481*

Congressional Districts in the 2000s: A Portrait of America. *v.4 p.557*

☐ Congressional Election Statistics 1920 - 2004. . . *v.4 p.557*

Congressional Elections, 1946-1996. . . . . *v.4 p.557*

Congressional Elections: Campaigning at Home and in Washington. *v.4 p.549*

Congressional Politics in the Second World War. . . *v.3 p.482*

Congressional Politics: The Evolving Legislative System. *v.4 p.531*

Congressional Procedures and the Policy Process. . . *v.4 p.532*

☐ Congressional Record Index. *v.4 p.481*

☐ Congressional Record. *v.4 p.481*

Congreve's Plays on the Century Stage. *v.2 p.244*

Congreve. *v.2 p.244*

Conifers: The Illustrated Encyclopedia, Vol. 2. . . . . *v.5 p.37*

Coningsby: Or, the New Generation. *v.2 p.275*

Conjecture and Proof. *v.5 p.470*

Conjectures and Refutations: The Growth of Scientific Knowledge. *v.1 p.499*

Conjectures of Order: Intellectual Life and the American South, 1810-1860. . . . . *v.3 p.495*

The Conjure Woman, and Other Conjure Tales. *v.6 p.23*

ⓔ The Conjure Woman. *v.2 p.32*

Conjuring the Folk: Forms of Modernity in African America. *v.2 p.5*

Connected Places: Region, Pilgrimage, and Geographical Imagination in India. *v.1 p.540*

The Connected School: Technology and Learning in High School. *v.4 p.351, p.352*

Connecticut: A Guide to Its Roads, Lore and People. *v.3 p.489*

Connecticut. *v.3 p.489*

Connecting Girls and Science: Constructivism, Feminism, and Science Education Reform. *v.4 p.367*

Connecting: How We Form Social Bonds and Communities in the Internet Age. *v.4 p.772*

Connecting Special Education and Technology for the 21st Century. *v.4 p.350, p.351*

Connecting Spheres: European Women in a Globalizing World, 1500 to the Present. *v.3 p.50, v.6 p.451, p.453*

The Connection Gap: Why Americans Feel So Alone. *v.4 p.694*

Connections: A Broadcast History Reader. *v.4 p.417*

Conn's Biological Stains. *v.5 p.88*

Conquering Goliath: Cesar Chávez at the Beginning. *v.4 p.128, p.129*

Conquering Nature: The Environmental Legacy of Socialism in Cuba. *v.3 p.268*

The Conquerors: Roosevelt, Truman and the Destruction of Hitler's Germany, 1941-1945. . . . *v.3 p.439, p.455, p.465*

The Conquerors. *v.2 p.522, v.6 p.216*

Conquest and Colonisation: The Normans in Britain, 1066-1100. . . . . *v.3 p.97*

Conquest and Empire: The Reign of Alexander the Great. *v.3 p.19*

Conquest and survival in colonial Guatemala: A historical geography of the Cuchumatan highlands, 1500-1821. . . . . *v.3 p.298*

Conquest by Law. *v.6 p.692*

Conquest, coexistence, and change: Wales, 1063-1415. *v.3 p.132*

The Conquest of a Continent: Siberia and the Russians. *v.3 p.214*

The Conquest of America. *v.3 p.404*

The Conquest of Happiness. *v.1 p.485*

Conquest of Lisbon: De Expugnatione Lyxbonesi. *v.3 p.63, p.238, p.244*

The Conquest of Mexico: The Incorporation of the Indian Societies into the Western World. *v.3 p.263*

The Conquest of Morocco. *v.6 p.61*

The Conquest of Nature: Water, Landscape, and the Making of Modern Germany. *v.3 p.159*

The Conquest of the Last Maya Kingdom. *v.3 p.286*

The Conquest of the Philippines by the United States, 1898-1925. . . . . *v.6 p.180*

The Conquest of the Reich: D-Day to VE Day - A Soldier's History. *v.3 p.81*

Conquests and Historical Identities in California, 1769-1936. . . . . *v.6 p.531*

Conquista y Comida: Consecuencias del Encuentro de Dos Mundos. *v.3 p.271*

Conrad and Empire. *v.2 p.341*

Conrad and Impressionism. *v.2 p.341*

Conrad Ferdinand Meyer. *v.2 p.598*

Conrad in Perspective: Essays on Art and Fidelity. . *v.2 p.341*

Conrad in the Nineteenth Century. *v.2 p.342*

Conrad in the Twenty-First Century: Contemporary Approaches and Perspectives. *v.2 p.341*

Conrad on Film. *v.6 p.326*

Conrad under Familial Eyes. *v.2 p.340*

Conrad's Eastern World. *v.2 p.341, p.342*

Conrad's Prefaces to His Works. *v.2 p.340*

Conrad's Western World. *v.2 p.342*

Conscience in Politics: Adlai E. Stevenson in the
1950's. *v.3 p.515*

The Conscience of a Conservative. *v.3 p.458*

The Conscience of the Court: Selected Opinions of Justice
William J. Brennan, Jr. on Freedom and Equality. *v.4 p.539*

The Conscience of Words. *v.2 p.606*

The Conscious Mind: In Search of a Fundamental
Theory. *v.1 p.496*

Consciousness: A User's Guide. *v.5 p.618*

Consciousness and Class Experience in 19th Century
Europe. *v.4 p.705*

Consciousness and Culture: Emerson and Thoreau
Reviewed. *v.2 p.38, p.52*

Consciousness and the Mind of God. *v.1 p.504*

Consciousness and the Novel: Connected Essays. . . .*v.2 p.169*

Consciousness Explained. *v.1 p.496, v.5 p.612*

Consciousness in Action. *v.1 p.497, v.5 p.613*

Consciousness Reconsidered. *v.1 p.496*

Consciousness-Raising: A Primer for Multicultural
Counseling. *v.5 p.637*

The Conscription Society: Administered Mass
Organizations. *v.4 p.510*

The Consecration of the Writer, 1750-1830. . . . . .*v.2 p.458*

Consensus and Disunity: The Lloyd George Coalition
Government, 1918-1922. . . . .*v.3 p.94, p.95, p.118*

Consequences of Class and Color: West Indian
Perspectives. *v.4 p.704*

The Consequences of Mr. Keynes: An Analysis of the Misuse of
Economic Theory for Political Profiteering, with
Proposals for Constitutional Disciplines. *v.4 p.226*

Consequences of Pragmatism: Essays 1972-1980. . . .*v.1 p.513*

Conservancy. *v.6 p.298*

Conservation and Restoration of Glass. *v.1 p.824*

Conservation and the Gospel of Efficiency: The Progressive
Conservation Movement, 1890-1920. *v.5 p.4, p.17,v.6 p.283*

Conservation and the Law. *v.4 p.463*

Conservation Biology: For the Coming Decade. *v.5 p.179*

Conservation Directory: The Guide to Worldwide Environmental
Organizations. *v.5 p.18, v.6 p.286*

Conservation, Ecology, and Management of African Fresh
Waters. *v.5 p.178, p.179, p.236, p.241*

Conservation Farming in the United States: The Methods and
Accomplishments of the STEEP Program. . . .*v.5 p.17, p.30*

Conservation of Biodiversity for Sustainable
Development. *v.5 p.181*

Conservation on Private Lands: An Owner's Manual. .*v.5 p.179*

Conservation Skills: Judgement, Method and Decision
Making. *v.1 p.822*

Conservatism in Early American
History. *v.3 p.406, v.4 p.553, p.554*

Conservative Century: The Conservative Party since
1900. . . . .*v.4 p.607*

The Conservative Intellectual Movement in America since
1945. . . . .*v.3 p.449*

Conservative Judaism: The New Century. *v.1 p.551*

The Conservative Party from Peel to Thatcher. *v.4 p.606*

The Conservative Tradition in America. *v.4 p.516*

Conservatives in an Age of Change: The Nixon and Ford
Administrations. *v.3 p.478*

Conservatives in Court. *v.4 p.536*

Considering the Bush Presidency. *v.3 p.483*

Considering the Radiance. *v.2 p.55*

Consilience: The Unity of Knowledge. *v.1 p.483*

The Consolation of Philosophy. . .*v.1 p.430, v.2 p.448, v.3 p.66*

Consolidated Index of Selected Property Values: Physical
Chemistry and Thermodynamics. *v.5 p.281*

Conspiracy Nation: The Politics of Paranoia in Postwar
America. *v.3 p.371*

Conspiracy of Fools: A True Story. *v.4 p.103*

A Conspiracy of Optimism: Management of the National Forests
since World War Two. *v.5 p.37*

A Conspiracy So Immense: The World of Joe Mccarthy. .*v.3 p.461*

Conspiracy to Murder: The Rwanda
Genocide. *v.4 p.653, v.6 p.257*

Constable and His Drawings. *v.1 p.723*

Constable. *v.1 p.746*

Constancia y Otras Novelas para Virgenes. *v.2 p.668*

Constant: Adolphe. *v.2 p.479*

A Constant Journey: The Fiction of Monique Wittig. *v.2 p.532*

Constantine and Eusebius. *v.3 p.30*

Constantine and Rome. *v.1 p.670, p.687*

Constantine: History Historiography and Legend. . . .*v.3 p.31*

Constantine the Great and the Christian Revolution. . *v.3 p.191*

Constantinople: City of the World's Desire, 1453-1924. .*v.6 p.622*

Constantinople in the Early Eighth Century. *v.6 p.622*

Constantly Risking Absurdity: The Writings of Lawrence
Ferlinghetti. *v.2 p.75*

Constitution and Criminal Procedure: First
Principles. *v.4 p.473, v.6 p.268*

The Constitution and Race. *v.4 p.457*

The Constitution and the Regulation of Society. . . .*v.4 p.463*

The Constitution and the States: The Role of the Original
Thirteen in the Framing and Adoption of the Federal
Constitution. *v.4 p.523*

The Constitution As Political Structure. *v.4 p.525*

▢ A Constitution for Europe. *v.4 p.636*

A Constitution for the European Union. *v.4 p.636*

The Constitution in Conflict. *v.4 p.462*

Constitution in Crisis Times, 1918-1969. . . . . . .*v.4 p.452*

The Constitution in the Courts: Law or Politics? *v.4 p.455, p.538*

The Constitution in the Supreme Court: The First Hundred
Years, 1789-1888. . . . .*v.4 p.453, p.536*

The Constitution in the Supreme Court: The Second Century,
1888-1986. . . . .*v.4 p.453, p.536*

The Constitution in Wartime: Beyond Alarmism and
Complacency. *v.4 p.462*

The Constitution of Iran: Politics and the State in the Islamic
Republic. *v.6 p.633*

The Constitution of Society: Outline of the Theory of
Structuration. *v.4 p.679, p.680*

Constitution of the Islamic Republic of Iran. *v.6 p.632*

The Constitution of the Roman Republic. . .*v.3 p.25, v.4 p.501*

Constitution of the United States. *v.4 p.451*

The Constitution of Tyranny: Regimes of Exception in Spanish
America. ***v.3 p.275, v.4 p.592***

The Constitution, the Courts, and Human Rights: An Inquiry
into the Legitimacy of Constitutional Policymaking by the
Judiciary. *v.4 p.456*

Constitutional Amendment in Canada. *v.4 p.586*

Constitutional Brinksmanship: Amending the Constitution by
National Convention. *v.4 p.454*

Constitutional Conflicts Between Congress and the
President. *v.4 p.454, p.528, p.531*

Constitutional Deliberation in Congress: The Impact of Judicial
Review in a Separated System. *v.4 p.538*

Constitutional Democracy. *v.4 p.504*

Constitutional Dialogues: Interpretation As Political
Process. *v.4 p.453, p.454*

Constitutional Dictatorship: Crisis Government in the Modern
Democracies. *v.4 p.575*

Constitutional Fate. *v.4 p.454*

Constitutional History of the American Revolution: The
Authority of Law. *v.4 p.456*

Constitutional History of the American Revolution: The
Authority of Rights. *v.4 p.456*

Constitutional History of the American Revolution: The
Authority to Legislate. *v.4 p.456*

Constitutional History of the American Revolution: The
Authority to Tax. *v.4 p.456*

Constitutional Options for A Democratic South Africa: A
Comparative Perspective. *v.4 p.614*

Constitutional Politics in the Progressive Era: Child Labor and
the Law. *v.4 p.447*

Constitutional Politics: The Republic Referendum and the
Future. *v.4 p.624*

Constitutional Predicament: Canada after the Referendum of
1992. . . . .*v.4 p.586*

Constitutional Process: A Social Choice Analysis of Supreme
Court Decision Making. *v.4 p.540*

Constitutional Revolution: The Link Between Constitutionalism
and Progress. *v.4 p.576*

Constitutional Rights of Prisoners. *v.6 p.276*

The Constitutional System: The Group Character of the Elected
Institutions. *v.4 p.532*

The Constitutional Underclass: Gays, Lesbians, and the Failure
of Class-Based Equal Protection. *v.4 p.457, v.6 p.469*

Constitutionalism and American Culture: Writing the New
Constitutional History. *v.4 p.453*

Constitutionalism and the Separation of Powers. . . .*v.4 p.576*

The Constitutionalist: Notes on the First Amendment. .*v.4 p.458*

Constitutions of the World. *v.4 p.435, p.574*

Constraints of Desire: The Anthropology of Sex and Gender in
Ancient Greece. ***v.6 p.364, p.422, p.423, p.425***

A Constructed Peace: The Making of the European Settlement,
1945-1963. . . . .***v.4 p.629, p.647, p.648***

Constructing a Sociology of the Arts. *v.1 p.708*

Constructing Boundaries: Jewish and Arab Workers in
Mandatory Palestine. *v.6 p.612*

Constructing Democracy: Human Rights, Citizenship and
Society in Latin America. *v.4 p.512*

Constructing Gendered Bodies. *v.6 p.369*

Constructing Masculinity. *v.6 p.428*

Constructing Public Opinion: How Political Elites Do What
They Like and Why We Seem to Go along with It. .*v.4 p.425*

Constructing Socialism at the Grass-Roots: The Transformation
of East Germany, 1945-1965. . . . .*v.3 p.177*

Constructing the Black Masculine: Identity and Ideality in
African American Men's Literature and Culture,
1775-1995. . . . .*v.6 p.41*

Constructing the Canon of Children's Literature: Beyond
Library Walls and Ivory Towers. *v.2 p.582*

Constructing the Heartland: Television News and Natural
Disaster. *v.4 p.414*

Constructing the New York Area Hispanic Mosaic: A
Demographic Portrait of Colombians and Dominicans in New
York. ***v.6 p.537, p.547***

constructing the new. ***v.6 p.528, p.536, p.539***

Constructing the Political Spectacle. ***v.5 p.642, p.643***

Constructing the World Polity: Essays on International
Institutionalization. *v.4 p.625*

Construction and Housing Publications. *v.4 p.159*

Construction Business Development: Meeting New Challenges,
Seeking Opportunities. *v.4 p.159*

Construction Funding: The Process of Real Estate Development,
Appraisal, and Finance. *v.4 p.158*

Construction Industry Compliance Assistance Portal. *v.4 p.159*

Construction of Christian Poetry in Old English. . . .*v.2 p.167*

The Construction of Communalism in Colonial North
India. *v.6 p.161*

The Construction of Social Reality. *v.1 p.501*

Construction Statistics. *v.4 p.159*

Construction WebLinks Portal. *v.4 p.159*

Constructional Morphology and Evolution. . . .***v.5 p.196, p.205***

Constructive Combinatorics. *v.5 p.479*

Constructive Education for Children. *v.4 p.359*

Consuelo. *v.2 p.499*

Consultant: A Diagnostic Support System for Veterinary
Medicine. ***v.5 p.56, p.57, p.59, p.61***

Consultative Group on International Agricultural Research
(CGIAR). *v.5 p.3*

Consultative Selling: The Hanan Formula for High-Margin Sales
at High Levels. ***v.4 p.142, p.143***

Consumer Behavior and Marketing Strategy. *v.4 p.139*

Consumer Behavior II: The Meaning of Consumption. *v.5 p.586*

Consumer Behavior: Research and Influences. .***v.5 p.586, p.604***

Consumer Behavior. *v.4 p.249*

Consumer Boycotts: Effecting Change Through the Marketplace
and the Media. *v.4 p.759*

Consumer Economics after Keynes: Theory and Evidence of the
Consumption Function. ***v.4 p.232, p.245, p.250***

Consumer Economics Issues in America. *v.4 p.250*

A Consumers' Republic: The Politics of Mass Consumption in
Postwar America. *v.6 p.711*

Consuming Angels: Advertising and Victorian
Women. ***v.6 p.739, p.748***

Consuming Citizenship: Children of Asian Immigrant
Entrepreneurs. *v.6 p.107, p.110, p.127, p.136*

Consuming Fiction. *v.2 p.193, v.6 p.756*

A Consuming Fire: The Fall of the Confederacy in the Mind of
the White Christian South. *v.4 p.520*

Consuming Habits: Drugs in History and Anthropology. .*v.3 p.281*

Consuming Modernity: Public Culture in a South Asian
World. *v.2 p.759, v.6 p.150*

Consuming Pleasures: Active Audiences and Serial Fictions
from Dickens to Soap Opera. *v.2 p.284*

Consuming the Past: The Medieval Revival in Fin-De-Siecle
France. *v.3 p.155*

Consumption As an Investment. *v.4 p.246, p.250*

Consumption Intensified: The Politics of Middle-Class Daily
Life in Brazil. *v.3 p.341*

Consumption Takes Time: Implications for Economic
Theory. *v.4 p.246*

Contagious Divides: Epidemics and Race in San Francisco's
Chinatown. *v.6 p.128, p.141*

Contagious Success. *v.4 p.79*

Containing the Poor: The Mexico City Poor House,
1774-1871. . . . .*v.3 p.284, p.288*

Containment Culture: American Narratives, Postmodernism, and
the Atomic Age. *v.3 p.371*

Contaminated Sites and Environmental Cleanup: International
Approaches to Prevention, Remediation, and Reuse. .*v.5 p.706*

Contemplating Music: Challenges to Musicology. . . .*v.1 p.173*

Contemplating the People's Branch: Legislative Dynamics in the
Twenty First Century. *v.4 p.530, p.531*

The Contemplative Poetry of Edwin Arlington Robinson, Robert
Frost, and Yvor Winters. *v.2 p.77*

Contemporary African American Cinema. . . .*v.6 p.329, p.340*

Contemporary African American Female Playwrights: An
Annotated Bibliography. *v.6 p.15, p.16, p.35, p.47*

Contemporary African American Novelists: A
Bio-Bibliographical Critical Sourcebook. . . .*v.6 p.18, p.34*

Contemporary African Art. *v.1 p.679, p.690*

Contemporary African Plays. *v.1 p.129, p.130*

Contemporary Albanian Literature. *v.2 p.815*

Contemporary American Playwrights. *v.1 p.112*

Contemporary American Poetry. *v.2 p.23*

Contemporary American Public Discourse: A Collection of
Speeches and Critical Essays. *v.2 p.28*

Contemporary American Reform Responsa. *v.1 p.552*

The Contemporary American Short Story. *v.2 p.26*

Contemporary American Women Sculptors. *v.1 p.774*

Contemporary Archaeology in Theory: A Reader. . . .*v.4 p.6*

Contemporary Architects. *v.1 p.784*

[e] Contemporary Argentinean Women Writers: A Critical
Anthology. *v.2 p.678*

The Contemporary Arranger. *v.1 p.394*

Contemporary Art and Anthropology. *v.4 p.26*

Contemporary Artists. *v.1 p.665, p.680*

Contemporary Asian American Communities: Intersections and
Divergences. *v.6 p.120*

The Contemporary Asian American Experience: Beyond the
Model Minority. *v.6 p.85*

The Contemporary Atlas of China. *v.6 p.182*

Contemporary Australian Cinema: An Introduction. . .*v.6 p.337*

Contemporary Australian Plays. *v.1 p.128, v.2 p.743*

Contemporary Belarus: Between Democracy and
Dictatorship. *v.3 p.230*

Contemporary Black Men's Fiction and Drama. . . .*v.6 p.24*

Contemporary Black Thought: Alternative Analyses in Social
and Behavioral Science. *v.6 p.38*

Contemporary British and Irish Fiction: An Introduction
Through Interviews. *v.2 p.194*

Contemporary British Dramatists. *v.2 p.188*

Contemporary British Philosophy: Personal Statements First
Series. *v.1 p.446*

Contemporary British Philosophy: Personal Statements Fourth
Series. *v.1 p.446*

Contemporary British Philosophy: Personal Statements Second
Series. *v.1 p.446*

Contemporary British Philosophy: Personal Statements Third
Series. *v.1 p.446*

Contemporary Caribbean Cultures and Societies in a Global
Context. *v.4 p.40, p.41*

Contemporary Chicana and Chicano Art: Artists, Works, Culture,
and Education. *v.6 p.492*

[e] Contemporary Chicana Poetry: A Critical Approach to an
Emerging Literature. *v.6 p.480, p.503, p.511, p.516*

Contemporary Chicano and Chicana Art: Artists, Works, Culture,
and Education, Vol. 2. . . . .*v.6 p.492*

Contemporary Chicano Fiction: A Critical
Survey. *v.6 p.500, p.514*

Contemporary Chicano Theatre. *v.2 p.25*

Contemporary Composers on Contemporary Music. . .*v.1 p.223*

Contemporary Continental Philosophy. *v.1 p.438*

The Contemporary Contrabass. *v.1 p.394, p.399*

Contemporary Critical Theorists: From Lacan to Said. .*v.1 p.503*

Contemporary Cuban Writers. *v.2 p.673, v.6 p.509, p.516*

Contemporary Danish Poetry. *v.2 p.626*

Contemporary Danish Prose. *v.2 p.625*

Contemporary Democracies: Participation, Stability and
Violence. *v.4 p.577*

Contemporary Designers. *v.1 p.712*

Contemporary Directions: Korean Folk Music Engaging the
Twentieth Century and Beyond. *v.1 p.288*

Contemporary Europe: A Geographic Analysis. . . .*v.4 p.383*

Contemporary French Literature: 1945 and after. .*v.2 p.459, p.460*

Contemporary French Philosophy: Modernity and the
Persistence of the Subject. *v.1 p.458, p.515*

Contemporary Gay American Novelists: A Bio-Bibliographical
Critical Sourcebook. *v.6 p.391, p.393*

Contemporary Gay American Poets and Playwrights: An A-to-Z
Guide. *v.6 p.391*

Contemporary Influences in Early Childhood
Curriculum. *v.4 p.369*

Contemporary Intellectual Assessment: Theories, Tests and
Issues. *v.5 p.602*

Contemporary International Glass. *v.1 p.811*

Contemporary Issues in Behavior Therapy: Improving the
Human Condition. *v.5 p.666*

Contemporary Issues in Mathematics Education. .*v.5 p.462, p.463*

Contemporary Italy: Politics, Economy and Society Since
   1945. . . . .*v.4 p.594*

Contemporary Japanese Film. *v.6 p.336*

Contemporary Japanese Sculpture. *v.1 p.777*

Contemporary Jewish Writing in Hungary: An
   Anthology. *v.2 p.785*

Contemporary Jewish Writing in Poland: An Anthology. .*v.2 p.788*

Contemporary Labor Economics. *v.4 p.253*

Contemporary Latvian Poetry. *v.2 p.780*

Contemporary Lesbian Writers of the United States: A
   Bio-Bibliographical Critical Sourcebook. *v.6 p.391*

Contemporary Linguistics: An Introduction. *v.2 p.563*

Contemporary Literary Critics. *v.2 p.3*

Contemporary Literature of Asia. *v.2 p.759*

Contemporary Macedonian Poetry. *v.2 p.787*

Contemporary Masterworks. *v.1 p.665*

Contemporary Materialism: A Reader. *v.1 p.509*

Contemporary Mental Health Issues among African
   Americans. *v.6 p.21*

Contemporary New Mexico, 1940-1990. . . . . . .*v.3 p.528*

The Contemporary Novel in German: A Symposium. .*v.2 p.592*

Contemporary Parenting: Challenges and Issues, Vol. 9. .*v.5 p.638*

Contemporary Perspectives on the Native Peoples of Pampa,
   Patagonia, and Tierra del Fuego: Living on the Edge. .*v.3 p.352*

Contemporary philosophy, a New Survey. *v.1 p.438*

☐ Contemporary Philosophy of Mind: An Annotated
   Bibliography. *v.1 p.496*

Contemporary Philosophy: Studies of Logical Positivism and
   Existentialism. *v.1 p.511*

Contemporary Photographers. *v.1 p.762*

Contemporary Plays by Women of Color: An
   Anthology. *v.1 p.68, p.121, p.122, p.123, p.124, p.125,v.2 p.25*

Contemporary Portugal. *v.3 p.244*

Contemporary Portuguese Poetry: An Anthology in
   English. *v.2 p.687, p.688*

Contemporary Postcolonial Theory: A Reader. . . .*v.2 p.728*

The Contemporary Print: Pre-Pop to Postmodernism. .*v.1 p.754*

Contemporary Psychometrics: A Festschrift for Roderick P.
   Mcdonald. *v.5 p.601*

Contemporary Quebec and the United States,
   1960-1985. . . . .*v.4 p.581*

Contemporary Russian Politics: A Reader. *v.4 p.597*

Contemporary Russian Satire: A Genre Study. *v.2 p.800*

Contemporary Scottish Fictions—Film, Television, and the
   Novel. *v.6 p.339*

The Contemporary Spanish Theater, 1949-1972. . . .*v.2 p.640*

Contemporary Spanish Theatre: Seven One-Act Plays. .*v.2 p.644*

Contemporary Sport Management. *v.4 p.885, p.889*

Contemporary Strategy Analysis: Concepts, Techniques,
   Applications. *v.4 p.51*

Contemporary Studies in Combat Psychiatry. *v.5 p.583*

Contemporary Swedish Poetry. *v.2 p.629*

Contemporary Theatre Architecture: An Illustrated
   Survey. *v.1 p.155*

Contemporary Theatre, Film and Television: A Biographical
   Guide Featuring Performers, Directors, Writers,
   Producers, Designers, Managers, Choreographers, Technicians,
   Composers, Executives, Dancers, and Critics in the
   United States, Canada, Great Britain and the World, Vol.
   65. . . . .*v.1 p.141*

Contemporary Theatre, Film, and Television, Vol. 71. . .*v.1 p.57*

Contemporary Turkish Literature: Fiction and Poetry. .*v.6 p.666*

Contemporary Turkish Politics: Challenges to Democratic
   Consolidation. *v.4 p.616, v.6 p.624*

Contemporary U. S. Tax Policy. *v.4 p.108*

Contemporary Urban Planning. *v.1 p.797, v.6 p.728*

The Contemporary Violin: Extended Performance
   Techniques. *v.1 p.394, p.399*

Contemporary West African States. *v.6 p.68*

Contemporary Women Artists. *v.1 p.664, p.706,v.6 p.473*

Contemporary Women Writers in Italy: A Modern
   Renaissance. *v.2 p.697*

Contemporary Women Writers of Spain. *v.2 p.639*

☐ Contemporary Women's Issues. *v.6 p.432*

Contemporary World Regional Geography: Global Connections,
   Local Voices. *v.4 p.396*

The Contempt Power. *v.4 p.472*

Contempt. *v.2 p.720*

The Contender: Richard Nixon: The Congress Years,
   1946-1952. . . . .*v.4 p.485*

Contending with Change: African Food Systems in
   Crisis. *v.4 p.45*

Contending with Modernity: Catholic Higher Education in the
   Twentieth Century. *v.4 p.291*

Content Area Reading: Literacy and Learning Across the
   Curriculum, MyLabSchool Edition. *v.4 p.366*

☐ Content Knowledge: A Compendium of Standards and
   Benchmarks for K-12 Education. *v.4 p.359*

Contentious Republicans: Popular Politics, Race, and Class in
   Nineteenth-Century Colombia. *v.3 p.280, p.358*

The Contentious Senate: Partisanship, Ideology and the Myth of
   Cool Judgement. *v.4 p.533*

Contes d'Amadou Koumba. *v.2 p.544*

Contes et Nouvelles, Tome 1. . . . .*v.2 p.497*

Contes et Nouvelles, Tome 2. . . . .*v.2 p.497*

Contest for Constitutional Authority: The Abortion and War
   Powers Debates. *v.4 p.531, p.535*

The Contest of Christian and Muslim Spain: 1031-1157. .*v.3 p.238*

The Contested City. *v.6 p.724*

Contested Closets: The Politics and Ethics of
   Outing. *v.6 p.368, p.386, p.387*

Contested Communities: Class, Gender and Politics in Chile's
   El Teniente Copper Mine, 1904-1948. . . . . . .*v.3 p.354*

Contested Hierarchies: A Collaborative Ethnography of Caste
   among the Newars of the Kathmandu Valley, Nepal. .*v.6 p.164*

The Contested Homeland: A Chicano History of New
   Mexico. *v.6 p.531*

Contested Identities: Gender and Kinship in Modern
   Greece. *v.3 p.195*

Contested Metropolis: Six Cities at the Beginning of the 21st
   Century. *v.6 p.729*

Contested Mountains: Nature, Development and Environment in the Cairngorms Region of Scotland, 1880-1980. . . . .*v.5 p.79, p.237*

A Contested Nation: History, Memory and Nationalism in Switzerland, 1761-1891. . . . .*v.3 p.245*

The Contested Plains: Indians, Goldseekers and the Rush to Colorado. *v.6 p.687*

Contested Policy: The Rise and Fall of Federal Bilingual Education in the United States, 1960-2001. . . . .*v.6 p.528*

Contested Power in Angola, 1840s to the Present. . . .*v.6 p.75*

Contested Territory: Whites, Native Americans and African Americans in Oklahoma. *v.3 p.524, v.6 p.688*

Contested Tongues: Language Politics and Cultural Correction in Ukraine. *v.4 p.20, p.21*

Contesting Castro: The United States and the Triumph of the Cuban Revolution. *v.3 p.312*

Contesting Ireland: Irish Voices Against England in the Eighteenth-Century. *v.3 p.137*

Contesting Postcolonialisms. *v.2 p.760*

Contesting the Boundaries of Liberal and Professional Education: The Syracuse Experiment. *v.4 p.295*

Contesting the Nation: Religion, Community, and the Democracy in India. *v.6 p.149*

Contes. *v.2 p.476*

Conteurs français du XVIe siècle. *v.2 p.465*

Context and Beyond: Reframing the Theory and Practice of Education. *v.4 p.336*

The Context of Ethnicity: Sikh Identity in a Comparative Perspective. *v.6 p.154*

The Contexts of Acadian History, 1686-1784. . . . . .*v.3 p.543*

The Contexts of Juvenile Justice Decision Making: When Race Matters. *v.6 p.271*

Contexts of Kinship: An Essay in the Family Sociology of the Gonja of Northern Ghana. *v.4 p.32*

Contextual Teaching and Learning: What It Is and Why It's Here to Stay. *v.4 p.348*

Continent of Hunter-Gatherers: New Perspectives in Australian Prehistory. *v.4 p.13*

Continent of Mystery: A Thematic History of Australian Crime Fiction. *v.2 p.741*

A Continent Revealed: The European Geotraverse, Structure and Dynamic Evolution. *v.5 p.432*

The Continental Aesthetics Reader. *v.1 p.479*

Continental Crossroads: Remapping U. S.-Mexico Borderlands History. *v.6 p.488, p.533*

Continental Deformation. *v.5 p.441*

Continental Divide: The Values and Institutions of the United States and Canada. *v.3 p.368, v.4 p.586, p.587, p.591*

Continental Drift. *v.2 p.140*

Continental Philosophy in the 20th Century. *v.1 p.438*

Continental Philosophy of Science. *v.5 p.402*

The Continental Renaissance, 1500-1600. . . . .*v.2 p.458*

Continental Stagecraft. *v.1 p.80, p.83, p.97*

The Continental System, an Economic Interpretation. .*v.3 p.152*

Continents and Supercontinents. *v.5 p.442, p.443*

Continents in Motion. *v.5 p.443*

Contingency and Freedom: John Duns Scotus Lectura 139. . . . .*v.1 p.433, p.503*

Continual Permutations of Action. *v.4 p.682*

The Continuing Silence of a Poet: The Collected Stories of A. B. Yehoshua. *v.6 p.652*

Continuities in Popular Culture: The Present in the Past and the Past in the Present and Future. *v.4 p.701*

Continuity and Change in House Elections. *v.4 p.548*

Continuity and Change in Medieval Persia: Aspects of Administrative, Economic and Social History, 11th-144th Century. *v.6 p.630*

Continuity and Change on the United States Courts of Appeals. *v.4 p.470*

Continuity and Disruption: Essays in Public Administration. *v.4 p.545, p.580*

Continuous Replay: The Photographs of Arnie Zane. . .*v.1 p.46*

Continuous -Time Finance. *v.4 p.238*

Continuum Companion to Twentieth Century Theatre. *v.1 p.58, p.140*

The Continuum Complete International Encyclopedia of Sexuality. *v.4 p.677, p.747, p.748*

The Continuum Encyclopedia of Native Art. *v.1 p.667*

Continuum Encyclopedia of Native Art. *v.6 p.680*

Continuum Encyclopedia of Popular Music of the World: Media, Industry and Society, Vol. 1. . . . . .*v.1 p.162, p.274, p.284*

Continuum Encyclopedia of Popular Music of the World: Performance and Production, Vol. 2. .*v.1 p.162, p.274, p.284*

The Continuum of Inductive Methods. *v.1 p.495*

Continuum Political Encyclopedia of the Middle East. .*v.6 p.595*

Continuum Studies in Geography Education: Continuum Guide to Geography Education. *v.4 p.376*

Contour in Time: The Plays of Eugene O'Neill. *v.2 p.107*

Contours of Canadian Thought. *v.3 p.535*

Contours of the Heart: South Asians Map North America. *v.6 p.92, p.137*

Contours of the Theatrical Avant-Garde: Performance and Textuality. *v.1 p.85, p.96*

Contra Dance Choreography: A Reflection of Social Change. *v.1 p.33*

Contracts in a Nutshell. *v.4 p.443*

Contradiction and Conflict: The Popular Church in Nicaragua. *v.3 p.303*

The Contradictions of American Capital Punishment. .*v.6 p.248*

The Contradictory College: The Conflicting Origins, Impacts, and Futures of the Community College. . . .*v.4 p.291, p.292*

Contrarian Investment Strategies, the Next Generation: Beat the Market Going Against the Crowd. *v.4 p.94*

Contrary Music: The Prose Style of John Donne. . . .*v.2 p.216*

Contrary Neighbors: Southern Plains and Removed Indians in Indian Territory. *v.6 p.687*

The Contras, 1980-1989: A Special Kind of Politics. .*v.3 p.303*

Contrast: A Comedy. *v.2 p.30*

Contrasting the French and Italian Communist Parties: Comrades and Culture. *v.4 p.594, p.609*

Contre Sainte-Beuve. *v.2 p.524*

The Contributions of John Maynard Keynes to Foreign Trade Theory and Policy, 1909-1946. . . . .*v.4 p.226*

Contributions to Modern Econometrics: From Data Analysis to Economic Policy. *v.4 p.202*

Contributions to Modern Economics. *v.4 p.270*

Contributions to Philosophy: From Enowning. *v.1 p.470*

Contributions to the Theory and Practice of Public Finance. *v.4 p.199, p.247*

Contributions to Urban Sociology. *v.4 p.770, v.6 p.716*

Control: A History of Behavioral Psychology. *v.5 p.667*

Control in Robotics and Automation: Sensor Based Integration. *v.5 p.710*

Control of Communicable Diseases Manual. *v.5 p.532*

Control of Human Movement. *v.4 p.908, p.909*

Control of Induction Motors. *v.5 p.725*

The Control of the Arms Race: Disarmament and Arms Control in the Missile Age,. *v.4 p.655*

Control: Sociology's Central Notion. *v.4 p.773*

Control System Design Guide: Using Your Computer to Understand and Diagnose Feedback Controllers. . *v.5 p.710*

Control Systems Theory with Engineering Applications. *v.5 p.711*

The Controller's Function: The Work of the Managerial Accountant. *v.4 p.106*

Controlling Knowledge: Religion, Power and Schooling in a West African Muslim Society. *v.6 p.73*

Controlling Strategy: Management, Accounting, and Performance Measurement. *v.4 p.81*

Controversiae - Suasoriae, Fragments, Vol. 2. . . . .*v.2 p.443*

Controversial Issues in Policing. *v.6 p.262*

A Controversial Spirit: Evangelical Awakenings in the South. *v.1 p.607*

Controversies and Commanders of the Civil War: Dispatches from the Army of the Potomac. *v.3 p.401*

Controversies in Minority Voting: The Voting Rights Act in Perspective. *v.4 p.461*

Controversies in Victimology. *v.6 p.258*

The Controversy over German Industrialization, 1890-1902. . . . .*v.3 p.163*

Conundrums for the Long Weekend: England, Dorothy L. Sayers and Lord Peter Wimsey. *v.2 p.381*

Conundrum. *v.6 p.371, p.403*

Convective Heat and Mass Transfer. *v.5 p.560*

Convention: A Philosophical Study. *v.1 p.502*

Conventional Wisdom: The Content of Musical Form. *v.1 p.247*

Conventions Against Terrorism. *v.4 p.662*

Conventions of Form and Thought in Early Greek Epic Poetry. *v.2 p.402*

Convergence Culture. *v.4 p.422*

Convergence Marketing: Strategies for Reaching the New Hybrid Consumer. *v.4 p.135*

Converging Cultures: Art and Identity in Spanish America. *v.3 p.263*

Converging Movements: Modern Dance and Jewish Culture at the 92nd Street Y. *v.1 p.26*

Converging Stories: Race, Ecology, and Environmental Justice in American Literature. *v.2 p.4, p.5*

Conversation in the Cathedral. *v.2 p.686*

Conversation with Spinoza: A Cobweb Novel. *v.2 p.787*

Conversational Borderlands: Talk with Troubled Teens in an Urban School. *v.4 p.315*

Conversations about Bernstein. *v.1 p.210, p.311*

Conversations in Natural Philosophy, 1826. . . . . .*v.4 p.218*

Conversations on Growth, Stability and Trade: An Historical Perspective. *v.4 p.245, p.258*

Conversations with Amiri Baraka. *v.2 p.142*

Conversations with Chester Himes. *v.2 p.86*

Conversations with Chinua Achebe. *v.2 p.753*

Conversations with Christopher Isherwood. *v.2 p.355*

Conversations with Cuba. *v.3 p.313*

Conversations with Derek Walcott. *v.2 p.770*

Conversations with Economists: New Classical Economists and Opponents Speak Out on the Current Controversy in Macroeconomics. *v.4 p.233*

Conversations with Eugene O'Neill. *v.2 p.107*

Conversations with F. Scott Fitzgerald. *v.2 p.76*

Conversations with Gabriel Garcia Marquez. *v.2 p.681*

Conversations with Goethe. *v.2 p.597*

Conversations with Gore Vidal. *v.2 p.127*

Conversations with Graham Greene. *v.2 p.349*

Conversations with Gwendolyn Brooks. *v.2 p.63, p.64*

Conversations with Igor Stravinsky. *v.1 p.225, p.360*

Conversations with Indian Economists. *v.4 p.255*

Conversations with Jack Kerouac. *v.2 p.92*

Conversations with James Baldwin. *v.6 p.28*

Conversations with James Thurber. *v.2 p.125*

Conversations with John Cheever. *v.2 p.67, p.68*

Conversations with John Steinbeck. *v.2 p.122, p.123*

Conversations with Leading Economists: Interpreting Modern Macroeconomics. *v.4 p.240, p.241*

Conversations with Margaret Walker. *v.6 p.47*

Conversations with Mary McCarthy. *v.2 p.99*

Conversations with May Sarton. *v.2 p.119*

Conversations with Paul Bowles. *v.2 p.62*

Conversations with Ralph Ellison. *v.6 p.25*

Conversations with Richard Wilbur. *v.2 p.128*

Conversations with Robert Graves. *v.2 p.348*

Conversations with Robert Penn Warren. *v.2 p.129*

Conversations with S. J. Perelman. *v.2 p.111*

Conversations with Salman Rushdie. *v.2 p.766*

Conversations with Saul Bellow. *v.2 p.60*

Conversations with Thornton Wilder. *v.2 p.134*

Conversations with Toni Morrison. *v.6 p.27, p.45*

Conversations with Ulrich Beck. *v.4 p.261, p.267*

Conversations with William S. Burroughs. *v.2 p.64*

Conversations with Wole Soyinka. *v.2 p.757*

Conversing with Cage. *v.1 p.217, p.315*

Conversion Factors. *v.5 p.280*

The Conversion of Henri the Fourth: Politics, Power and Religious Belief in Early Modern France. *v.3 p.146*

Conversion Tables of Units in Science & Engineering. *v.5 p.407*

Converting Women: Gender and Protestant Christianity in Colonial South India. *v.6 p.459*

The Convert. *v.2 p.113, p.114*

Convex Sets and Their Applications. *v.5 p.498*

Convict Criminology. *v.6 p.276*

Convicted but Innocent: Wrongful Conviction and Public
Policy. *v.4 p.567*

Los Convidados de Piedra. *v.2 p.680*

Cook: The Extraordinary Sea Voyages of Captain James
Cook. *v.4 p.385*

Cool Season Forage Grasses. *v.5 p.50*

Coolidge: An American Enigma. . . .*v.3 p.480, v.4 p.487, p.528*

Cooperative Learning: Research and Theory. *v.4 p.350*

Coordinating Technology: Studies in the International
Standardization of Telecommunications. *v.4 p.420*

Coordination Chemistry of Aluminum. *v.5 p.300*

The Copernican Revolution: Planetary Astronomy in the
Development of Western Thought. *v.5 p.61*

Copernicus and His Successors. *v.3 p.48*

Coping with an Oiled Sea: An Analysis of Oil Spill Response
Technologies. *v.6 p.289*

Coping with Life Crises: An Integrated Approach. . .*v.4 p.699*

Coping with Loss. *v.5 p.655*

Coping with Stress: Effective People and Processes. .*v.5 p.656*

Copland: 1900 Through 1942. . . . .*v.1 p.211, p.318*

Copland on Music. *v.1 p.211, p.318*

Copland: Since 1943. . . . .*v.1 p.211, p.212, p.318*

Copper Crucible: How the Arizona Miners' Strike of 1983
Recast Labor-Management Relations. *v.4 p.128*

Copper into Gold: Prints by John Raphael Smith
(1751-1812). *v.1 p.755, p.756*

Copper, Silver, Gold, Zinc, Cadmium, and Mercury, Vol.
5. . . . .*v.5 p.306*

Cops Across Borders: The Internationalization of U. S. Criminal
Law Enforcement. *v.3 p.282*

The Copts in Egyptian Politics 1918 - 1952. . .*v.6 p.600, p.637*

Copy Writer's Bible. *v.4 p.427*

The Copyeditor's Handbook: A Guide for Book Publishing and
Corporate Communications. *v.4 p.149*

☐ Copyright and Fair Use in the Classroom, on the Internet,
and the World Wide Web. *v.4 p.289*

The Copyright Book: A Practical Guide. *v.4 p.446*

☐ Copyright for Music Librarians. . . .*v.1 p.384, p.385, p.406*

Copyright in Cyberspace 2: Questions and Answers for
Librarians. *v.4 p.446*

Copyright Your Software. *v.4 p.446*

Copyright's Highway: From Gutenberg to the Celestial
Jukebox. *v.4 p.109, p.110, p.446*

The Coquette; or, The History of Eliza Wharton: Founded on
Fact by a Lady of Massachusetts. *v.2 p.29*

Coral: A Play. *v.2 p.611*

Coral Fish. *v.5 p.216*

The Coral Island. *v.2 p.264*

Coral Reef Conservation. *v.4 p.391*

Coral Reef Fishes: Dynamics and Diversity in a Complex
Ecosystem. *v.4 p.393*

The Corbaccio. *v.2 p.701*

Le Corbusier: Architect of the Twentieth Century. . .*v.1 p.792*

Le Corbusier: The Creative Search. *v.1 p.791*

Le Corbusier. *v.1 p.792*

Cordilleran Section Field Guide. *v.5 p.432*

The Core Business Web: A Guide to Key Information
Resources. *v.4 p.181*

Core Concepts in Biological Anthropology. *v.4 p.14*

Core Concepts of Management. *v.4 p.73*

☐ Core Documents of U.S. Democracy. *v.4 p.481*

☐ The Core Historical Literature of Agriculture (CHLA). .*v.5 p.3*

☐ The Core Historical Literature of
Agriculture. *v.4 p.151, p.163, p.164*

Core Java(TM) 2 Advanced Features, Vol. II. *v.5 p.347*

Core Java(TM) 2: Fundamentals. *v.5 p.346, p.347*

☐ Core Journals Covered in CAplus. *v.5 p.256*

Core List of Books and Journals in Education. .*v.4 p.339, p.340*

The Core of Japanese Democracy: Latent Interparty
Politics. *v.4 p.622*

Corea the Hermit Nation. *v.6 p.236*

Corinne, or Italy. *v.2 p.501*

Corinne, ou, L'Italie. *v.2 p.501*

Coriolanus. *v.2 p.223*

Corn and Capitalism: How a Botanical Bastard Grew to Global
Dominance. *v.3 p.273, v.5 p.24*

Corn and Corn Improvement. *v.5 p.24*

Corn Is Our Blood: Culture and Ethnic Identity in a
Contemporary Aztec Indian Village. *v.3 p.272*

Corn: Origin, History, Technology and Production. .*v.5 p.23, p.25*

Corneille: His Heroes and Their Worlds. *v.2 p.473*

Corneille: "Rodogune" and "Nicomede". *v.2 p.473*

Corneille's Tragedies: The Role of the Unexpected. .*v.2 p.473*

The Cornel West Reader. *v.6 p.20, p.41*

The Cornelius Quartet: The Final Program; A Cure for Cancer;
The English Assassin; The Condition of Muzak. .*v.2 p.368*

The Corner That Held Them. *v.2 p.387*

Cornered: Big Tobacco at the Bar of Justice. *v.4 p.439*

Le cornet à dés. *v.2 p.521*

The Cornish Trilogy: The Rebel Angels; What's Bred in the
Bone; The Lyre of Orpheus. *v.2 p.735*

Corona de Luz. *v.2 p.669*

El Coronel No Tiene Quien le Escriba. *v.2 p.683*

Corot. *v.1 p.745*

Corporate Art. *v.1 p.826*

The Corporate Closet: The Professional Lives of Gay Men in
America. *v.6 p.382*

Corporate Environmentalism and Public
Policy. *v.4 p.61, p.63, p.64*

Corporate Financing and Governance in Japan: The Road to the
Future. *v.6 p.224*

Corporate Governance: Accountability, Enterprise and
International Comparisons. *v.4 p.86*

Corporate Governance at the Crossroads: A Book of
Readings. *v.4 p.54*

Corporate Governance. *v.4 p.85, p.86, p.87*

The Corporate Ideal in the Liberal State:
1900-1918. . . . .*v.3 p.445, p.450*

Corporate Integrity: A Toolkit for Managing Beyond Compliance. . . . . *.v.4 p.86*

Corporate Integrity: Rethinking Organizational Ethics and Leadership. . . . . *.v.4 p.697*

Corporate Power, American Democracy, and the Automobile Industry. . . . . *.v.4 p.154*

Corporate Responsibility and Labour Rights: Codes of Conduct in the Global Economy. . . . . *.v.4 p.131*

Corporate Social Responsibility: Doing the Most Good for Your Company and Your Cause. . . . . *.v.4 p.54*

Corporate Social Responsibility in the Mining Industries. . . . . *.v.6 p.297*

Corporate Statements: The Official Missions, Goals, Principles and Philosophies of over 900 Countries. . . . . . *.v.4 p.173*

Corporate Taxes 2005—2006: Worldwide Summaries. . . . . *.v.4 p.92, p.107*

Corporate Tides: The Inescapable Laws of Organizational Structure. . . . . *.v.4 p.86*

Corporation Be Good!: The Story of Corporate Social Responsibility. . . . . *.v.4 p.53*

Corporatism and Comparative Politics: The Other Great Ism. . . . . *.v.4 p.510*

Corporatist Ideology in Kemalist Turkey. . . . . . . *.v.6 p.624*

Les corps étrangers : roman. . . . . *.v.2 p.512*

Corps Lesbien. . . . . *.v.2 p.534*

Corpus Christi: The Eucharist in Late Medieval Culture. *.v.1 p.657*

Corpus of Early Arab Sources for West African History. *.v.6 p.68*

Correcting the Blueprint of Life: An Historical Account of the Discovery of DNA Repair Mechanisms. . . . . . *.v.5 p.133*

Correctional Boot Camps: Military Basic Training or a Model for Corrections? . . . . *.v.6 p.274*

☐ Correctional Education Association. . . . . *.v.6 p.274*

Correctional Law for the Correctional Officer. . . . . *.v.6 p.273*

Correctional Leadership: A Cultural Perspective. . . *.v.6 p.275*

Correctional Mental Health Handbook. . . . . . . *.v.6 p.277*

Corrections: A Humanistic Approach. . . . . *.v.6 p.272*

The Corrections: A Novel. . . . . *.v.2 p.160*

Correggio. . . . . *.v.1 p.696*

☐ Correlates of War (COW) Project. . . . . *.v.4 p.625*

Correspondance choisie. . . . . *.v.2 p.484*

Correspondance: Juillet 1675 - Septembre 1680, Vol. II. *.v.2 p.477*

Correspondance: Mars 1646 - Juillet 1675, Vol. I. . . *.v.2 p.478*

Correspondance. . . . . *.v.2 p.477, p.478*

The Correspondence of Alfred Marshall, Economist, Set. . . . . *.v.4 p.224*

The Correspondence of Charles Darwin: 1860, Vol. 8. . . . . *.v.3 p.48, p.49*

The Correspondence of Charles Darwin: 1861. . . . . *.v.3 p.48*

The Correspondence of Emerson and Carlyle. . *.v.2 p.38, p.276*

The Correspondence of Henry and Sarah Fielding. . . . . *.v.2 p.247, p.248*

Correspondence of Leon Walras. . . . . *.v.4 p.215*

A Correspondence of Renaissance Musicians. . . . . *.v.1 p.179*

The Correspondence of William James. . . . . . . *.v.1 p.439*

Correspondence: Yale Edition of Horace Walpole's Correspondence. . . . . . . *.v.3 p.108, p.109, p.110, p.130*

Correspondence. . . . . *.v.1 p.459, v.2 p.249*

Corrosion and Corrosion Control, No. 3. . . . . *.v.5 p.735, p.736*

Corrosion and Corrosion Protection Handbook, Vol. 1. *.v.5 p.735*

Corrosion and Protection. . . . . *.v.5 p.687, p.734*

Corrosion Chemistry. . . . . *.v.5 p.734*

Corrosion Engineering Handbook, Vol. 11. . . . . . *.v.5 p.735*

Corrosion Engineering. . . . . *.v.5 p.734*

Corrosion for Students of Science and Engineering. . *.v.5 p.735*

☐ Corrosion Information Server: Internet resources in Corrosion & Materials. . . . . *.v.5 p.734*

Corrosion of Aluminium-Based Metal Matrix Composites. . . . . *.v.5 p.734, p.735*

The Corrosion of Character: The Personal Consequences of Work in the New Capitalism. . . . . *.v.4 p.717*

Corrosion of Metals. . . . . *.v.5 p.689, p.734*

Corrosion of Stainless Steels. . . . . *.v.5 p.735*

Corrosion Resistance Tables: Metals, Nonmetals, Coatings, Mortars, Plastics, Elastomers and Linings, and Fabrics. . . . . *.v.5 p.691, p.735*

Corrosion Resistance Tables, Part A. . . . . *.v.5 p.735*

Corrosion Science and Technology. . . . . *.v.5 p.735*

Corrosion Testing and Evaluation: Silver Anniversary Volume. . . . . *.v.5 p.734*

Corrosion Tests and Standards: Application and Interpretation. . . . . *.v.5 p.734*

Corrosion: Understanding the Basics. . . . . *.v.5 p.734*

Corrosion. . . . . *.v.5 p.735*

Corruption and Development in Africa: Lessons from Country Case-Studies. . . . . *.v.4 p.611, p.664*

Corruption and Market in Contemporary China. . . . *.v.4 p.620*

Corruption and Politics in Contemporary Mexico. . . *.v.3 p.294*

Corruption and Reform in the Teamsters Union. . . . *.v.4 p.130*

Corruption and State Politics in Sierra Leone. . . . . *.v.4 p.612, p.613, v.6 p.73*

Corruption and the Decline of Rome. . . . . . . *.v.3 p.28*

Corruption by Design: Building Clean Government in Mainland China and Hong Kong. . . . . *.v.4 p.620*

☐ Corruption Perceptions Index. . . . . *.v.4 p.55*

☐ Corvinus Library Hungarian History. . . . . . . *.v.3 p.185*

Corydon. . . . . *.v.2 p.519, p.520, v.6 p.362*

Cosa Facil. . . . . *.v.2 p.669*

Cosima. . . . . *.v.2 p.717*

Cosmic Canticle. . . . . *.v.2 p.675*

Cosmic Catastrophes: Supernovae, Gamma-ray Bursts, and Adventures in Hyperspace. . . . . *.v.5 p.67*

The Cosmic Century: A History of Astrophysics and Cosmology. . . . . *.v.5 p.62*

The Cosmic Dance: Science Discovers the Mysterious Harmony of the Universe. . . . . *.v.5 p.401*

The Cosmic Dancers: Exploring the Physics of Science Fiction. . . . . *.v.5 p.399*

Cosmic Dragons: Life and Death on Our Planet. . . *.v.5 p.243*

Cosmic Gamma-Ray Sources. . . . . *.v.5 p.68*

The Cosmic Perspective. . . . . *.v.5 p.64, p.65*

Cosmicomics. . . . . *.v.2 p.714*

The Cosmological Eye. *v.2 p.102*

Cosmological Physics. *v.5 p.72*

Cosmology in Antiquity. *v.1 p.500*

Cosmology: The Science of the Universe. *v.5 p.72*

Cosmopolitan Urbanism. *v.4 p.395*

The Cosmopolitan World of Henry James: An Intertextual
Study. *v.2 p.46*

Cosmos and Pornografia. *v.2 p.787*

Cosmos and Tragedy: An Essay on the Meaning of
Aeschylus. *v.2 p.407*

The Cossack Hero in Russian Literature: A Study in Cultural
Mythology. *v.2 p.798, p.799*

Cost and Choice: An Inquiry in Economic Theory. . .*v.4 p.194*

Cost Benefit Analysis: Concepts and Practice. . . .*v.4 p.82, p.83*

The Cost of Discipleship. *v.1 p.642*

The Cost of Living. *v.2 p.765, p.766*

Cost-Benefit Analysis and Water Resources
Management. *v.5 p.702*

Cost-Benefit Analysis: With Reference to Environment and
Ecology. *v.4 p.83*

Cost-Effective Marketing Research: A Guide for Marketing
Managers. *v.4 p.136*

The Costs of Crime and Justice. *v.6 p.247*

Costume and Cinema: Dress Codes in Popular Film. . .*v.6 p.350*

Costume and Fashion: A Concise History. *v.1 p.715*

Costume Design in the Movies: An Illustrated Guide to the
Work of 157 Great Designers. *v.6 p.349, p.350*

Costume Design: Techniques of Modern Masters. . .*v.1 p.37*

The Costume Designer's Handbook: A Complete Guide for
Amateur and Professional Costume Designers. . . .*v.6 p.349*

Costume Design. *v.6 p.349*

The Costume Technician's Handbook. *v.6 p.349*

Costumes and Settings for Historical Plays: The Classical
Period: Ancient Through Early Middle Ages. .*v.1 p.146, p.150*

Costuming for Opera: Who Wears What and
Why. *v.1 p.234, p.404*

Le cotne fantastique en France de Nodier a Maupassant. .*v.2 p.458*

Cotnoir. *v.2 p.540*

Cotton, Colonialism, and Social History in Sub-Saharan
Africa. *v.6 p.53*

The Cotton Kingdom: A Chronicle of the Old South. .*v.3 p.495*

The Cotton Kingdom: A Traveller's Observations on Cotton and
Slavery in the American Slave States, 1853-1861. .*v.3 p.495*

Cotton Mather's Verse in English. *v.2 p.29*

Cotton Mather. *v.2 p.29*

Cotton: Origin, History, Technology, and
Production. *v.5 p.20, p.24, p.25*

Cotton. *v.5 p.19, p.24*

Coulomb and the Evolution of Physics and Engineering in
Eighteenth Century France. *v.5 p.396*

▢ Council for Exceptional Children. *v.5 p.574*

Counseling Across Cultures. *v.5 p.637*

Counseling and Psychotherapy with Religious Persons: A
Rational Emotive Behavior Therapy Approach. . . .*v.5 p.665*

Counseling Diverse Populations. *v.5 p.636*

Counseling for Diversity: A Guide for School Counselors and
Related Professionals. *v.4 p.353*

Counseling the Alzheimer's Caregiver: A Resource for
Healthcare Professionals. *v.5 p.519*

Counseling the Culturally Diverse: Theory and Practice. .*v.5 p.638*

Counseling to End Violence Against Women: A Subversive
Model. *v.4 p.751, v.6 p.446, p.471, p.472*

Counselling in a Multicultural Society. *v.5 p.637*

Count and Bishop in Medieval Germany: A Study of Regional
Power, 1100-1350. . . . .*v.3 p.161*

Count Belisarius. *v.2 p.348*

Count Down: Six Kids Vie for Glory at the World's Toughest
Math Competition. *v.5 p.459*

The Count of Monte Cristo. *v.2 p.489*

Countdown to Rebellion: British Policy in Cyprus, 1939-1955,
27. . . . .*v.3 p.197*

The Count-Duke of Olivares: The Statesman in an Age of
Decline. *v.3 p.238*

Counter-Examples in Differential Equations and Related
Topics. *v.5 p.487*

Counterexamples in Probability and Statistics. *v.5 p.481*

Counterfactuals. *v.1 p.493*

The Counterfeiters. *v.2 p.519, v.6 p.396*

Countering Terrorism: Dimensions of Preparedness. . .*v.4 p.564*

Countering the Counterculture: Rereading Postwar American
Dissent from Jack Kerouac to Tomás Rivera. .*v.6 p.501, p.514*

Counterintuitive Marketing: Achieve Great Results Using
Uncommom Sense. *v.4 p.134*

Counterpoint: A Translation of Kontrapunkt. *v.1 p.373*

Counterpoint in Composition: The Study of Voice
Leading. *v.1 p.373*

Counterpoint: Perspectives on Asian America. . . .*v.6 p.85, p.96*

Counterpoint: The Polyphonic Vocal Style of the 16th
Century. *v.1 p.371*

Counterpoint. *v.1 p.371, p.372*

Counterrealism and Indo-Anglian Fiction. *v.2 p.762*

The Counter-Reformation in the Villages: Religion and Reform
in the Bishopric of Speyer, 1560-1720. . . . . . .*v.3 p.166*

The Counter-Reformation: The Essential Readings. . .*v.3 p.57*

Counterrevolution in Argentina, 1900-1932: The Argentine
Patriotic League. *v.3 p.347, p.348*

The Counterrevolution of Slavery: Politics and Ideology in
Antebellum South Carolina. *v.3 p.502*

Counter-Statement. *v.2 p.568*

Countervisions: Asian American Film Criticism. . .*v.6 p.89, p.97*

The Countess of Pembroke's Arcadia: (The Old
Arcadia). *v.2 p.215, p.216*

Counting and Probability. *v.5 p.484*

Counting on Frameworks: Mathematics to Aid the Design of
Rigid Structures. *v.5 p.501, p.683*

Counting Votes: Lessons from the 2000 Presidential Election in
Florida. *v.4 p.550*

Counting What Counts: Turning Corporate Accountability to
Competitive Advantage. *v.4 p.85*

Countries of the Mind: The Poetry of William Carlos
Williams. *v.2 p.136*

Country: A Regional Exploration. *v.1 p.275*

Country and Court: England, Sixteen Fifty-Eight to Seventeen Fourteen. *v.3 p.105, p.107*

The Country and the City. . . .*v.2 p.173, p.177,v.6 p.288, p.763*

The Country Dance Book. *v.1 p.33, p.34*

Country Doctor: Quest of the Absolute and Other Novels. *v.2 p.485*

The Country Girls. *v.2 p.372, p.373*

The Country Girl. *v.2 p.108*

The Country House in English Renaissance Poetry. . .*v.2 p.182*

The Country House Poem: A Cabinet of Seventeenth-Century Estate Poems and Related Items. *v.2 p.199*

Country Life, City Life: Five Theories of Community. .*v.4 p.770*

Country Music Sources: A Biblio-Discography of Commercially Recorded Traditional Music. . .*v.1 p.168, p.170, p.171, p.272*

Country Music, U. S. A. *v.1 p.271*

The Country of Pointed Firs and Other Stories: Centennial Edition. *v.2 p.46*

The Country of Streams and Grottoes: Expansion, Settlement, and the Civilizing of the Sichuan Frontier in Song Times. *v.6 p.186, p.187, p.206*

Country People. *v.2 p.117*

Country Reports on Human Rights Practices. . . .*v.4 p.670*

A Country Study [Afghanistan, Algeria, Bahrein, Egypt, Iran, Iraq, Israel, Jordan, Kuwait, Lebanon, Libya, Oman, Qatar, Saudi Arabia, Sudan, Syria, UAE, and Turkey]. *v.6 p.582*

A Country Study: Kazakhstan. *v.4 p.623*

A Country Study: Kyrgyzstan. *v.4 p.623*

A Country Study: Mongolia. *v.4 p.623*

A Country Study: Tajikistan. *v.4 p.623*

A Country Study: Turkmenistan. *v.4 p.623*

A Country Study: Uzbekistan. *v.4 p.623*

The Country under My Skin: A Memoir of Love and War. *v.3 p.301*

The Country Waif. *v.2 p.500*

The Country Wife and Other Plays: Love in a Wood; The Gentleman Dancing-Master; The Country Wife; The Plain Dealer. *v.2 p.264*

Country Wild. *v.5 p.233*

The Countryside in Colonial Latin America. *v.3 p.286*

The Countryside in the Age of the Modern State: Political Histories of Rural America. *v.5 p.6*

Coup!: The Last Day of Allende. *v.3 p.356*

Couple Therapy with Gay Men. *v.6 p.381*

Couples Coping with Stress: Emerging Perspectives on Dyadic Coping. *v.5 p.668*

Coups and Army Rule in Africa: Motivations and Constraints. *v.6 p.55*

Coups from Below: Armed Subalterns and State Power in West Africa. *v.4 p.498, p.611*

Courage in a Dangerous World: The Political Writings of Eleanor Roosevelt. *v.3 p.462*

Courage in a Dangerous World: The Political Writings of Eleanor Roosevelt. *v.4 p.487, p.569*

The Courage of Their Convictions: Sixteen Americans Who Fought Their Way to the Supreme Court. . .*v.4 p.455, p.537*

Courage Tastes of Blood: The Mapuche Community of Nicolas Ailío and the Chilean State, 1906-2001. . . . . . .*v.3 p.354*

Courage, the Adventuress and the False Messiah. . . .*v.2 p.596*

The Courage to Be. *v.1 p.581*

The Courage to Create. *v.5 p.654*

Courage under Siege: Starvation, Disease and Death in the Warsaw Ghetto. *v.3 p.86*

Cours sur la rive sauvage. *v.2 p.542*

A Course in Arithmetic. *v.5 p.477*

A Course in Combinatorics. *v.5 p.479*

A Course in Computational Number Theory. *v.5 p.475*

A Course in Convexity. *v.5 p.497*

A Course in Econometrics. *v.4 p.200*

A Course in Functional Analysis. *v.5 p.493*

A Course in Game Theory. *v.4 p.207, v.5 p.504, p.505*

Course in General Linguistics. *v.2 p.564*

A Course in Mathematical Modeling. *v.5 p.500*

A Course in Mathematical Physics, Vol II. *v.5 p.548*

A Course in Modern Linguistics. *v.2 p.561*

Course in Phonetics. *v.2 p.562*

A Course in Phonology. *v.2 p.563, p.564*

A Course in Public Economics. *v.4 p.247*

The Course of American Democratic Thought. . . .*v.3 p.367*

The Course of German Nationalism: From Frederick the Great to Bismarck, 1763-1867. . . . .*v.3 p.179*

The Course of Irish History. *v.3 p.135, p.136*

A Course of Modern Analysis. *v.5 p.490*

Course of Modern Jewish History. *v.1 p.548, 549*

A Course of Pure Mathematics. *v.5 p.489*

A Course of Their Own: A History of African American Golfers. *v.6 p.41*

Course of Theoretical Physics: The Classical Theory of Fields, Vol. 2. . . . .*v.5 p.548*

A Course of Time. *v.2 p.623*

The Course of Tolerance: Freedom of the Press in Nineteenth-Century America. *v.4 p.458*

Courses Toward Urban Life: Archeological Considerations of Some Cultural Alternates. Subscribers Ed. *v.4 p.37*

Court and the Country: The Beginning of the English Revolution. *v.3 p.102, p.105*

Court, Cloister, and City: The Art and Culture of Central Europe, 1450-1800. . . . .*v.1 p.687*

A Court Divided: The Rehnquist Court and the Future of Constitutional Law. *v.4 p.540*

Court, Kirk and Community: Scotland, 1470-1625. . . . .*v.3 p.122, p.133*

The Court of France 1789-1830. . . . .*v.3 p.149*

Court of Richard II. *v.6 p.556*

Court Patronage and Corruption in Early Stuart England. *v.3 p.95, p.102*

The Court Society. *v.4 p.726*

Courtesans and Fishcakes: The Consuming Passions of Classical Athens. *v.3 p.14*

A Courtesan's Day. *v.1 p.754*

Courtesan's Quarter. *v.6 p.152*

Courting Democracy in Mexico: Party Strategies and Electoral Institutions. *v.3 p.292*

Courting Disaster: The Supreme Court and the Unmaking of American Law. *v.4 p.536*

Courting Justice: Gay Men and Lesbians vs. the Supreme Court. *v.6 p.388*

Courtly Culture and Political Life in Early Medieval India. *v.6 p.150*

Courtly Love Songs of Medieval France. *v.2 p.457*

Courts and Conflict in Twelfth-Century Tuscany. . . .*v.3 p.199*

Courts and Congress. *v.4 p.537*

Courts and the Public Schools. *v.4 p.450*

Courts, Corrections, and the Constitution: The Impact of Judicial Intervention on Prisons and Jails. *v.6 p.273*

Courts, Judges, and Politics. *v.4 p.465, p.466*

The Courts of Babylon: Tales of Greed and Glory in the Harsh New High-Stakes World of Professional Tennis. *v.4 p.814, p.864, p.887*

Courts under Constraints: Judges, Generals, and Presidents in Argentina. *v.3 p.274, p.348*

Cousin Bazilio. *v.2 p.689*

Cousin Bette. *v.2 p.486*

Cousin Henry. *v.2 p.318*

Le Cousin Pons: Poor Relations. *v.2 p.486*

Cousin Rosamund. *v.2 p.389*

Cousins and Strangers: America, Britain, and Europe in a New Century. *v.4 p.642*

The Covenant Sealed: The Development of Puritan Sacramental Theology in Old and New England, 1570-1720. . .*v.1 p.657*

A Covenant with Power: America and World Order from Wilson to Reagan. *v.3 p.452*

The Covent-Garden Journal. *v.2 p.247*

Covering Congress. *v.4 p.406*

Covering the Courts: A Handbook for Journalists. . . .*v.4 p.406*

Covering the Courts: Free Press, Fair Trials and Journalistic Performance. *v.6 p.270*

Covering the Plague: AIDS and the American Media. .*v.6 p.379*

Covering Violence: A Guide to Ethical Reporting about Victims and Trauma. *v.4 p.407*

Covert Operations: Medieval Uses of Secrecy. *v.6 p.567*

The Cowards. *v.2 p.784*

Cowboy Songs and Other Frontier Ballads. *v.2 p.20*

Cowboy Way: An Exploration of History and Culture. .*v.3 p.521*

Cowboys As Cold Warriors: The Western and U. S. History. *v.6 p.323, p.324*

Cowboys, Gentlemen and Cattle Thieves: Ranching on the Western Frontier. *v.3 p.545*

Cowgirls of the Rodeo: Pioneer Professional Athletes. *v.4 p.837, p.865*

Co-wives and Calabashes. *v.4 p.41*

Cows, Pigs, Wars, and Witches: The Riddles of Culture.*v.4 p.22*

Coyotes and Town Dogs: Earth First! and the Environmental Movement. *v.6 p.288*

CQ: Developing Cultural Intelligence at Work. . .*v.4 p.58, p.172*

CQ Electronic Library. *v.4 p.516*

CQ's Desk Reference on the Economy: Over 600 Answers to Questions That Will Help You Understand News, Trends and Issues. *v.4 p.566, p.567*

Crabgrass Frontier: The Suburbanization of the United States. *v.6 p.718*

Crabwalk. *v.2 p.608*

Crack and the Evolution of Anti-Drug Policy. *v.4 p.568*

Crack in America: Demon Drugs and Social Justice. .*v.4 p.777*

A Crack in the Edge of the World: America and the Great California Earthquake of 1906. . . . .*v.3 p.532*

Cracking Cases: The Science of Solving Crimes. . . .*v.6 p.266*

Cracking India: A Novel. *v.2 p.766*

Cracking the AP Biology Exam, 2006-2007 Edition. . .*v.5 p.246*

Cracking the Genome: Inside the Race to Unlock Human DNA. *v.5 p.121, p.132*

Cracking the GRE Biology Test. *v.5 p.246*

Cracking the SAT II Biology E/M Subject Test: 2005-2006. . . . .*v.5 p.246*

Cracking Your Retirement Nest Egg (Without Scrambling Your Finances): 25 Things You Must Know Before You Tap Your 401(K), IRA, or Other Retirement Savings Plan. *v.4 p.96, p.109*

A Crackling of Thorns. *v.2 p.87*

Crackpot. *v.2 p.739*

Cracks in the Monolith: Party Power in the Brezhnev Era. *v.4 p.598, p.599, p.600*

Cracks in the Wall: Nadine Gordimer's Fiction and the Irony of Apartheid. *v.2 p.755*

The Crack-Up. *v.2 p.76, p.77*

Cradle of Conflict: Iraq and the Birth of the Modern U. S. Military. *v.4 p.647*

The Cradle of Culture and What Children Know about Writing and Numbers Before Being Taught. *v.4 p.369*

Cradle of Life: The Discovery of Earth's Earliest Fossils. *v.5 p.447, p.449*

Cradle of the Middle Class: The Family in Oneida County, New York, 1790-1865. . . . .*v.4 p.734*

Cradle to Cradle: Remaking the Way We Make Things. *v.5 p.319, v.6 p.298*

The Craft and Art of Clay. *v.1 p.808*

The Craft of Justice: Politics and Work in Criminal Court Communities. *v.6 p.267, p.268*

The Craft of Musical Composition. *v.1 p.371*

The Craft of Piano Playing: A New Approach to Piano Technique. *v.1 p.397*

The Craft of Religious Studies. *v.1 p.522*

The Craft of Research. *v.2 p.564, p.566*

The Craft of Scientific Presentations: Critical Steps to Succeed and Critical Errors to Avoid. *v.5 p.267*

Crafting a Legacy: Contemporary American Crafts at the Philadelphia Museum of Art. *v.1 p.800, p.801*

Crafting Civilian Control of the Military in Venezuela: A Comparative Perspective. *v.3 p.361*

Crafting Gender: Women and Folk Art in Latin America and the Caribbean. *v.1 p.705*

Crafting Selves: Power, Gender, and Discourses of Identity in a Japanese Workplace. *v.4 p.39, v.6 p.221*

Crafting the Republic: Lima's Artisans and Nation-Building in Peru, 1221-1879. . . . .*v.3 p.327*

The Crafts in Britain in the Twentieth Century. . . . *v.1 p.800*

The Crafty Reader. *v.2 p.165*

Cranford. *v.2 p.289*

Cranial Guitar. *v.2 p.147*

Crash: A Novel. *v.2 p.330*

Crashaw and the Baroque. *v.2 p.242*

Crashing the Gate: Netroots, Grassroots, and the Rise of People-Powered Politics. *v.4 p.554*

Crashing Thunder: The Autobiography of an American Indian. *v.6 p.704*

Crazy Like a Fox: The Inside Story of How Fox News Beat CNN. *v.4 p.414*

Crazy Love. *v.6 p.508*

CRC Concise Encyclopedia of Mathematics. *v.5 p.460, p.461, p.462*

CRC Desk Reference for Nutrition. *v.5 p.329*

CRC Handbook of Basic Tables for Chemical Analysis. *v.5 p.267*

CRC Handbook of Chemistry and Physics: A Ready-Reference Book of Chemical and Physical Data. *v.5 p.259*

CRC Handbook of Chromatography. *v.5 p.269*

CRC Handbook of Laboratory Safety. *v.5 p.266*

CRC Handbook of Mathematical Sciences. *v.5 p.460*

CRC Handbook of Pesticides. *v.5 p.312*

CRC Handbook of Tables for Organic Compound Identification. *v.5 p.291*

CRC Handbook of Thermophysical and Thermochemical Data. *v.5 p.275*

CRC Handbook of Thermophysical and Thermochemical Data. *v.5 p.275*

CRC Materials Science and Engineering Handbook. *v.5 p.316, p.322*

CRC Standard Mathematical Tables and Formulas. . .*v.5 p.462*

CRC Standard Probability and Statistics Tables and Formulae. *v.5 p.460, p.480*

La Creacion (The Creation). *v.2 p.670*

Created Equal? The Complete Lincoln: Douglas Debates of 1858. . . . . *v.3 p.425*

Creating a Democratic Civil Society in Eastern Germany: The Case of the Citizen Movements and Alliance 90. . *v.4 p.610*

Creating a Role. *v.1 p.139, p.145, p.146*

Creating Alternative Discourses in the Education of Latinos and Latinas: A Reader. *v.4 p.301*

Creating Artists' Books. *v.1 p.759*

Creating Black Americans: African American History and Its Meanings, 1619 to the Present. *v.6 p.8*

Creating Born Criminals. *v.6 p.254*

Creating Brand Loyalty: The Management of Power Positioning and Really Great Advertising. *v.4 p.427*

Creating Campus Community: In Search of Ernest Boyer's Legacy. *v.4 p.333*

Creating Change: Public Policy, Civil Rights and Sexuality. *v.4 p.569, v.6 p.388*

Creating Chinese Ethnicity: Subei People in Shanghai, 1850-1980. . . . . *v.6 p.194*

Creating Connections: The CEFPI Guide for Educational Facility Planning. *v.4 p.288*

Creating Country Music: Fabricating Authenticity. . . *v.1 p.273*

Creating G. I. Jane: Sexuality and Power in the Women's Army Corps During World War II. *v.4 p.766, v.6 p.465*

Creating High Performance Classroom Groups. . . . *v.4 p.349*

Creating Independent Readers: Developing Word Recognition Skills in K-12 Classrooms. *v.4 p.364*

Creating Judaism: History, Tradition, Practice. *v.1 p.545, p.546, p.552*

Creating Literacy Instruction for All Students. *v.4 p.363*

Creating New Schools: How Small Schools Are Changing American Education. *v.4 p.280*

Creating Parliamentary Government: The Transition to Democracy in Bulgaria. *v.4 p.585, p.600*

Creating Public Value: Strategic Management in Government. *v.4 p.545, p.546*

Creating Spaces and Finding Voices: Teachers Collaborating for Empowerment. *v.4 p.279*

Creating the Big Game: John W. Heisman and the Invention of American Football, 34. . . . . . .*v.4 p.810, p.860, p.895*

Creating the Corporate Soul: The Rise of Public Relations and Corporate Imagery in American Big Business. *v.4 p.144, p.145, p.429*

Creating the Entrepreneurial Organization. *v.4 p.65*

Creating the Florentine State: Peasants and Rebellion, 1348-1434. . . . . *v.3 p.199*

Creating the Judicial Branch: The Unfinished Reform. *v.4 p.535*

Creating the Nation in Provincial France: Religion and Political Identity in Brittany. *v.3 p.154, p.155*

Creating the National Pastime: Baseball Transforms Itself, 1903-1953. . . . . *v.4 p.852*

Creating the New Egyptian Woman: Consumerism, Education, and National Identity, 1863-1922. . . . . *v.6 p.58*

Creating the West: Historical Interpretations, 1890-1990. . . . . *v.3 p.518*

Creating Their Own Image: The History of African-American Women Artists. . . . *v.1 p.704, p.706,v.6 p.16, p.43, p.472*

Creating Through Dance. *v.1 p.47*

Creating Tropical Yankees: Social Science Textbooks and U. S. Ideological Control in Puerto Rico, 1898-1908. . *v.3 p.320*

Creating Unforgettable Characters. *v.6 p.353*

Creating Value through Corporate Restructuring: Case Studies in Bankruptcies, Buyouts, and Breakups. *v.4 p.76, p.84*

Creating Women's Networks: A How-to-Guide for Women and Companies. *v.4 p.57*

Creation: Life and How to Make It. *v.5 p.218*

The Creation of America: Through Revolution to Empire. *v.4 p.517*

The Creation of Confederate Nationalism: Ideology and Identity in the Civil War South. *v.4 p.520*

The Creation of Feminist Consciousness: From the Middle Ages to Eighteen-Seventy. *v.3 p.51, v.6 p.434, p.450*

The Creation of Iraq, 1914-1921. . . . . *v.6 p.604*

The Creation of Meaning in Clinical Social Work. . . *v.4 p.758*

The Creation of Modern Athens: Planning the Myth. *v.3 p.194*

The Creation of Modern Georgia. *v.3 p.503*

The Creation of Patriarchy. *v.3 p.51, v.6 p.467*

The Creation of the American Republic,
1776-1787. . . . .*v.3 p.410, v.4 p.517*

The Creation of the Future: The Role of the American
University. *v.4 p.332*

The Creation of the Modern World: The Untold Story of the
British Enlightenment. *v.1 p.450, v.3 p.72*

The Creation of Tribalism in Southern Africa. *v.6 p.75*

Creation, Use, and Deployment of Digital
Information. *v.5 p.621, p.625*

Creation's Journey: Native American Identity and
Belief. *v.6 p.678*

Creations of Fire: Chemistry's Lively History from Alchemy to
the Atomic Age. *v.3 p.44, v.5 p.262*

Creative Advertising: Ideas and Techniques from the World's
Best Campaigns. *v.4 p.427*

A Creative Approach to Music Fundamentals. *v.1 p.370*

Creative Arts Marketing. *v.1 p.826*

Creative Business: Achieving Your Goals Through Creative
Thinking and Action. *v.4 p.65*

Creative Collaboration: Simple Tools for Inspired
Teamwork. *v.4 p.66*

Creative Conflict in African American Thought: Frederick
Douglass, Alexander Crummell, Booker T.
Washington, W. E. B. Du Bois, and Marcus Garvey. .*v.6 p.31*

Creative Consulting: Innovative Perspectives on Management
Consulting. *v.4 p.64*

Creative Dance: Experience for Learning. *v.1 p.47*

The Creative Destruction of Manhattan, 1900-1940. . .*v.6 p.714*

Creative Destruction: Why Companies That Are Built to Last
Underperform the Market - And How to
Successfully Transform Them. *v.4 p.67*

The Creative Elite in America. *v.3 p.370*

Creative Evolution. *v.1 p.456*

Creative Fidelity. *v.1 p.523*

Creative Fitness: Applying Health Psychology and Exercise
Science to Everyday Life. *v.5 p.581*

The Creative Habit: Learn It and Use It for Life. *v.1 p.37, p.44*

Creative Industries: Contracts Between Art and
Commerce. *v.1 p.826*

Creative Jazz Improvisation. *v.1 p.403*

Creative Movement and Dance in Groupwork. *v.1 p.51*

Creative Politics: Taxes and Public Goods in a Federal
System. *v.4 p.523*

Creative Tensions: An Introduction to Seventeenth-Century
French Literature. *v.2 p.459*

Creative Type: A Sourcebook of Classic and Contemporary
Letterforms. *v.1 p.719*

The Creative Vision of Bessie Head. *v.2 p.756*

Creative Women in Medieval and Early Modern Italy: A
Religious and Artistic Renaissance. . . .*v.3 p.201, v.6 p.560*

[e] Creativity Across the Primary Curriculum: Framing and
Developing Practice. *v.4 p.360*

Creativity and Intelligence: Explorations with Gifted
Students,. *v.5 p.626, p.630*

[e] Creativity at Work: Developing the Right Practices to Make
Innovation Happen. *v.4 p.66*

Creativity: From Potential to Realization. *v.5 p.657*

Creativity in Education and Learning: A Guide for Teachers and
Educators. *v.4 p.356*

Creativity in Virtual Teams: Key Components for
Success. *v.4 p.67*

Creativity: The Magic Synthesis. *v.5 p.651*

Creatures of Darkness: Raymond Chandler, Detective Fiction
and Film Noir. *v.2 p.65*

Creatures of Empire: How Domestic Animals Transformed Early
America. *v.5 p.54, v.6 p.684*

Creatures of Habit and Creatures of Change: Essays on Art,
Literature and Society, 1914-1956. . . . .*v.2 p.575*

Credibility: How Leaders Gain and Lose It, Why People
Demand It. *v.4 p.71*

Crediting Poetry: The Nobel Lecture. *v.2 p.352*

Creeds and Confessions of Faith in the Christian
Tradition. *v.1 p.646*

Creeds, Councils, and Controversies. *v.1 p.599, p.600*

Creole Identity in the French Caribbean Novel. . . .*v.2 p.537*

Creoles and Cajuns: French Louisiana - La Louisiane
Francaise. *v.3 p.507*

The Crescent and the Rising Sun. *v.6 p.173, p.174*

The Crest of the Peacock: The Non-European Roots of
Mathmatics. *v.3 p.47, v.5 p.466*

Cretan Cults and Festivals. *v.1 p.533*

Crete: Its Past, Present and People. *v.3 p.196*

Le Creuset des Cultures: La Litterature Antillaise. . .*v.2 p.537*

Cricket and England: A Cultural and Social History of Cricket
of the Inter-War Years. *v.4 p.811, p.856*

Cricket and Race. *v.4 p.820, p.856*

Crime Against Nature. *v.6 p.405*

Crime and Coercion: An Integrated Theory of Chronic
Criminality. *v.6 p.254*

Crime and Crime Control: A Global View. *v.6 p.262*

Crime and Law in Media Culture. *v.6 p.256*

Crime and Local Television News: Dramatic, Breaking, and
Live from the Scene. *v.4 p.407*

Crime and Politics: Big Government's Erratic Campaign for
Law and Order. *v.6 p.247*

Crime and Punishment in American History. *v.4 p.471*

Crime and Punishment in Contemporary Culture. . .*v.6 p.247*

Crime and Punishment in Late Colonial Mexico City,
1692-1810. . . . .*v.3 p.285*

Crime and Punishment in Western Countries, 1980/1999, Vol.
33. . . . .*v.6 p.273*

Crime and Punishment. *v.2 p.803*

Crime and Technology: New Frontiers for Regulation, Law
Enforcement and Research. *v.6 p.253*

Crime and the Courts in England, 1660-1800. . . . .*v.3 p.123*

Crime and the Justice System in America: An
Encyclopedia. *v.4 p.676*

Crime As Play: Delinquency in a Middle Class Suburb. *v.4 p.753*

Crime Control and Social Justice: The Delicate
Balance. *v.6 p.248, p.263*

The Crime Drop in America. *v.6 p.251*

CRIME FICTION IV: A Comprehensive Bibliography,
1749-2000. . . . .*v.2 p.580*

Crime, Justice, History. *v.6 p.245*

Crime, Madness and Politics in Modern France: The Medical
    Concept of National Decline. *v.4 p.705*

Crime Novels: American Noir of the 1930s and '40s. . .*v.2 p.20*

Crime Novels: American Noir of the 1950s. *v.2 p.21*

The Crime of Father Amaro. *v.2 p.688*

Crime on Campus: Legal Issues and Campus
    Administration. *v.4 p.451*

Crime, Policy and Criminal Behavior in America: Criminology
    Studies. *v.6 p.248*

Crime: Public Policies for Crime Control. *v.6 p.263*

Crime, Punishment, and Policing in China. . . .*v.6 p.261, p.262*

Crime Science: Methods of Forensic Detection. .*v.6 p.266, p.267*

The Crimean Tatars: Studies of Nationalities in the U. S. S.
    R. *v.3 p.213*

The Crimean Tatars: The Diaspora Experience and the Forging
    of a Nation. *v.3 p.213, p.214*

Crimes Against Nature: Squatters, Poachers, Thieves, and the
    Hidden History of American Conservation. . . .*v.6 p.297*

Crimes of Conscience: Selected Short Stories. *v.2 p.755*

The Crimes of Love. *v.2 p.483*

Crimes of the Heart. *v.2 p.146*

Crimes of War; a Legal, Political-Documentary, and
    Psychological Inquiry into the Responsibility of Leaders,
    Citizens, and Soldiers for Criminal Acts in Wars. . .*v.4 p.477*

Crimes of War: What the Public Should Know. *v.4 p.652*

The Crimes Women Commit: The Punishments They
    Receive. *v.6 p.258, p.471*

Criminal Interrogation and Confessions. *v.6 p.267*

☐ Criminal Justice Abstracts (Database). *v.6 p.245*

Criminal Justice and Criminology: A Career Guide to Local,
    State, Federal, and Academic Positions. *v.6 p.245*

Criminal Justice and Criminology: Concepts and Terms. .*v.4 p.676*

Criminal Justice and Drugs: The Unresolved
    Connection. *v.5 p.664*

Criminal Justice and Political Culture: National and International
    Dimensions of Crime Control. *v.6 p.247*

Criminal Justice in Colonial America, 1606-1660. . .*v.6 p.245*

☐ Criminal Justice Periodicals (Database). *v.6 p.245*

Criminal Justice Policy Making: Federal Roles and
    Processes. *v.6 p.247*

Criminal Justice Technology in the 21st Century. . . .*v.6 p.248*

The Criminal Law Handbook: Know Your Rights, Survive the
    System. *v.4 p.473*

Criminal Law. *v.6 p.268*

Criminal Man: According to the Classification of Cesare
    Lombroso. *v.4 p.752, v.6 p.254*

Criminal Procedure: A Contemporary Perspective. . . .*v.6 p.269*

The Criminal Process in the People's Republic of China,
    1949-1963: An Introduction. *v.4 p.475*

The Criminality of Women. *v.4 p.752*

The Criminalization of the State in Africa. *v.4 p.611*

The Criminals of Lima and Their Worlds: The Prison
    Experience, 1850-1935. . . . .*v.3 p.327*

Criminal. *v.6 p.254*

Criminological Theories: Introduction, Evaluation, and
    Application. *v.6 p.249*

Criminological Theories: Traditional and Non-Traditional Voices
    and Themes. *v.6 p.250*

Criminological Theories: Understanding Crime in
    America. *v.6 p.249*

Criminology: Theories, Patterns, and Typologies. . . .*v.6 p.249*

Crises of the Republic: Lying in Politics, Civil Disobedience, on
    Violence, Thoughts on Politics and Revolution. . .*v.4 p.497*

Crisis and Catharsis: The Power of the Apocalypse. . .*v.1 p.632*

Crisis and Change: The Church in Latin America Today. .*v.1 p.572*

Crisis and Confrontation: Ronald Reagan's Foreign
    Policy. *v.3 p.476*

Crisis and Transformation in China's Hong Kong. . . .*v.6 p.205*

Crisis Communications: A Casebook
    Approach. *v.4 p.429, p.431, p.433*

Crisis in Allende's Chile: New Perspectives. *v.3 p.354*

Crisis in Blanc and White: Urbanization and Ethnic Identity in
    French Canada. *v.3 p.543*

Crisis in Europe, 1560-1660: Essays from "Past and
    Present". *v.3 p.38*

Crisis in Identity and Contemporary Japanese Novels. .*v.6 p.230*

The Crisis in Kashmir: Portents of War, Hopes of Peace. .*v.6 p.160*

A Crisis in Swiss Pluralism: The Romans and Their Relations
    with the German- and Italian-Swiss in the Perspective of a
    Millennium. *v.3 p.244*

Crisis in U. S. Foreign Policy: An International History
    Reader. *v.3 p.452*

Crisis Intervention in the Schools. *v.4 p.353*

Crisis Management in the Food and Drinks Industry: A Practical
    Approach. *v.4 p.160*

The Crisis of Argentine Capitalism. *v.3 p.348*

The Crisis of Austrian Socialism: From Red Vienna to Civil
    War, 1927-1934. . . . .*v.3 p.185*

The Crisis of Church and State
    1050-1300. . . . .*v.1 p.656, v.3 p.58, p.68*

The Crisis of Democracy in Spain: Centrist Politics under the
    Second Republic (1931-1936). *v.3 p.242*

Crisis of European Sciences and Transcendental
    Phenomenology: An Introduction to Phenomenological
    Philosophy. *v.1 p.469*

The Crisis of German Ideology: Intellectual Origins of the Third
    Reich. *v.3 p.179*

The Crisis of Parliaments: English History,
    1509-1660. . . . .*v.3 p.95, p.101, p.122*

The Crisis of Russian Autocracy: Nicholas II and the 1905
    Revolution. *v.3 p.221*

The Crisis of the Aristocracy, 1558 to
    1641. . . . .*v.3 p.101, p.102, p.131*

Crisis of the House Divided: An Interpretation of the Issues in
    the Lincoln-Douglas Debates. *v.3 p.425*

The Crisis of the Negro Intellectual: A Historical Analysis of the
    Failure of Black Leadership. *v.6 p.24*

The Crisis of the Old Order, 1919-1933. .*v.3 p.372, p.444, p.450*

The Critic and Society: From Matthew Arnold to the New
    Historicism. *v.2 p.265*

A Critic Writes: Essays by Reyner Banham. *v.1 p.702*

A Critical Analysis of Bell Hooks' Engaged Pedagogy: A
  Transgressive Education for the Development of Critical
  Consciousness. *v.4 p.310*

Critical and Miscellaneous Essays: The W, Vol. 1. . . .*v.2 p.275*

Critical and Miscellaneous Essays: The W, Vol. 2. . . .*v.2 p.275*

Critical and Miscellaneous Essays: The W, Vol. 3. . . .*v.2 p.275*

Critical Anthology of Spanish Verse. *v.2 p.644*

A Critical Companion to 'Beowulf'. *v.2 p.205*

Critical Companion to John Steinbeck: A Literary Reference to
  His Life and Work. *v.2 p.123*

Critical Companion to the Russian Revolution,
  1914-1921. . . . .*v.3 p.221*

Critical Companion to William Shakespeare: A Literary
  Reference to His Life and Work. *v.2 p.222*

Critical Corporate Communications: A Best Practice
  Blueprint. *v.4 p.173*

Critical Criminology: Issues, Debates, Challenges. . .*v.4 p.752*

Critical Data of Pure Substances, Set, Vol. 2, Pts. 1 &
  2. . . . .*v.5 p.281, p.741*

Critical Dictionary of Film and Television Theory. . .*v.6 p.307*

A Critical Dictionary of Sociology. *v.4 p.676*

A Critical Dictionary of the French Revolution. *v.3 p.150, p.158*

A Critical, Dual-Language Edition of Quadras Ao Gosta
  Popular/Quatrains in the Popular Style. . . .*v.2 p.688, p.689*

Critical Edition of "The Jealous Wife" and "Polly Honeycombe"
  by George Colman the Elder (1732-1794). *v.2 p.243*

Critical Elections and Critical Coups: State, Society and the
  Military in the Processes of Latin American
  Development. *v.3 p.278, v.4 p.593*

Critical Elections and the Mainsprings of American
  Politics. *v.4 p.548*

Critical Entertainments: Music Old and New. . .*v.1 p.247, p.248*

Critical Essay on George Bernard Shaw. *v.2 p.308, p.309*

Critical Essays: Ancient Orators, Lysias, Isocrates, Isaeus,
  Demosthenes, Thucydides. *v.2 p.405*

Critical Essays of Enzensberger. *v.2 p.607*

Critical Essays on A. R. Ammons. *v.2 p.55*

Critical Essays on Aldous Huxley. *v.2 p.354, p.355*

Critical Essays on Alexander Pope. *v.2 p.257*

Critical Essays on Alfred Lord Tennyson. *v.2 p.315*

Critical Essays on Angus Wilson. *v.2 p.389*

Critical Essays on Anne Bradstreet. *v.2 p.28*

Critical Essays on Anne Sexton. *v.2 p.117*

Critical Essays on Carson McCullers. *v.2 p.100*

Critical Essays on Cervantes. *v.2 p.650*

Critical Essays on Charles Chesnutt. *v.2 p.32*

Critical Essays on Charlotte Bronte. *v.2 p.270*

Critical Essays on Chaucer's Troilus and Criseyde and His
  Major Early Poems. *v.2 p.207*

Critical Essays on Clifford Odets. *v.2 p.108*

Critical Essays on D. H. Lawrence. *v.2 p.362*

Critical Essays on Daniel Defoe. *v.2 p.246*

Critical Essays on Dante. *v.2 p.705*

Critical Essays on Doris Lessing. *v.2 p.366*

Critical Essays on E. B. White. *v.2 p.133*

Critical Essays on E. M. Forster. *v.2 p.346*

Critical Essays on Edna St. Vincent Millay. *v.2 p.98*

Critical Essays on Elizabeth Barrett Browning. . . .*v.2 p.271*

Critical Essays on Eudora Welty. *v.2 p.130*

Critical Essays on Eugene O'Neill. *v.2 p.107*

Critical Essays on F. Scott Fitzgerald's "The Great
  Gatsby". *v.2 p.76*

Critical Essays on Finnegans Wake. *v.2 p.360*

Critical Essays on Frank Norris. *v.2 p.49*

Critical Essays on Gabriel Garcia Marquez. . *v.2 p.683, p.684*

Critical Essays on Gabriel Rossetti. *v.2 p.304*

Critical Essays on Geoffery Chaucer. *v.2 p.210*

Critical Essays on Gerard Manley Hopkins. *v.2 p.294*

Critical Essays on Henry David Thoreau's Walden. . . .*v.2 p.52*

Critical Essays on Henry Fielding. *v.2 p.248*

Critical Essays on Honore de Balzac. *v.2 p.487*

Critical Essays on Isaac Bashevis Singer. *v.2 p.120*

Critical Essays on Ivan Turgenev. *v.2 p.805*

Critical Essays on J. M. Coetzee. *v.2 p.754*

Critical Essays on James Joyce's "Ulysses". *v.2 p.357*

Critical Essays on James Joyce. *v.2 p.357*

Critical Essays on James Merrill. *v.2 p.101*

Critical Essays on John Greenleaf Whittier. *v.2 p.55*

Critical Essays on John O'Hara. *v.2 p.106*

Critical Essays on Joyce's Portrait of the Artist As a Young
  Man. *v.2 p.357*

Critical Essays on Katherine Anne Porter. *v.2 p.110*

Critical Essays on Kay Boyle. *v.2 p.63*

Critical Essays on Kurt Vonnegut. *v.2 p.157, p.158*

Critical Essays on Laurence Sterne. *v.2 p.262*

Critical Essays on Lord Byron. *v.2 p.274*

Critical Essays on Louisa May Alcott. *v.2 p.30, p.31*

Critical Essays on Louis-Ferdinand Celine. *v.2 p.515*

Critical Essays on Mark Twain, 1910-1980. . . . . .*v.2 p.33*

Critical Essays on Maxine Hong Kingston. *v.6 p.97*

Critical Essays on Melville's "Billy Budd". *v.2 p.48*

Critical Essays on Muriel Spark. *v.2 p.383*

Critical Essays on Nathanael West. *v.2 p.131*

The Critical Essays on Ngugi wa Thiong'o. . *v.2 p.758, p.759*

Critical Essays on Ralph Waldo Emerson. *v.2 p.37*

Critical Essays on Randall Jarrell. *v.2 p.90*

Critical Essays on Robert Burns. *v.2 p.273*

Critical Essays on Robert Lowell. *v.2 p.96*

Critical Essays on Robinson Jeffers. *v.2 p.91*

Critical Essays on Rudyard Kipling. *v.2 p.297*

Critical Essays on Sherwood Anderson. *v.2 p.56*

Critical Essays on Sir Walter Scott. *v.2 p.308*

Critical Essays on Tennessee Williams. . .*v.2 p.134, v.6 p.393*

Critical Essays on the Prose and Poetry of Modern Slavic
  Women Writers. *v.2 p.778, p.779*

Critical Essays on Thornton Wilder. *v.2 p.133*

Critical Essays on Vàiclav Havel. *v.2 p.783*

Critical Essays on W. D. Howells, 1866-1920. . *v.2 p.41, p.42*

Critical Essays on Wallace Stevens. *v.2 p.123*

Critical Essays on Willa Cather. *v.2 p.67*

Critical Essays on William Carlos Williams. *v.2 p.136*

Critical Essays on William Saroyan. *v.2 p.118*

Critical Essays on William Wordsworth. *v.2 p.323*

Critical Essays on Zora Neale Hurston. *v.2 p.80*

Critical Essays. *v.2 p.345*

Critical Fictions: The Literary Criticism of Jean-Paul
Sartre. *v.2 p.527*

Critical Gestures: Writings on Dance and Culture. . . *v.1 p.39*

A Critical Handbook of Children's Literature. *v.2 p.582*

Critical, historical, and miscellaneous essays and poems, by
Lord Macaulay; with a memoir and Index. *v.2 p.299*

A Critical History of Early Rome: From Prehistory to the First
Punic War. *v.3 p.24, p.25*

Critical History of English Literature. *v.2 p.166*

Critical History of French Poetry. *v.2 p.460*

Critical Introduction to the New Testament. *v.1 p.624*

Critical Issues in Child Welfare. *v.4 p.756*

Critical Issues in China's Growth and Development. . *v.4 p.398*

Critical Issues in Police Training. *v.6 p.263*

Critical Issues in Qualitative Research Methods. . . . *v.5 p.529*

Critical Issues in Restorative Justice. *v.6 p.279*

A Critical Legal Study of Solutions to Domestic Violence
among Black Male-Female Couples. *v.6 p.259*

Critical Lessons in Slavery and the Slavetrade: Essential Studies
and Commentaries on Slavery, in General and the African
Slavetrade, in Particular. *v.6 p.10, p.37*

Critical Mappings of Arturo Islas's Fictions. . *v.6 p.497, p.511*

Critical Mass: How One Thing Leads to Another. . . *v.4 p.691*

Critical Medical Anthropology. *v.4 p.47*

Critical Moves: Dance Studies in Theory and Politics. *v.1 p.43*

Critical Path Analysis in Practice: Collected Papers on Project
Control. *v.4 p.116*

Critical Perspectives in Politics and Socio-Economic
Development in Ghana. *v.4 p.613*

Critical Perspectives on Amos Tutuola. *v.2 p.757*

Critical Perspectives on Calderon de la Barca. . . . *v.2 p.647*

Critical Perspectives on Christopher Okigbo. *v.2 p.756*

Critical Perspectives on Classicism in Japanese Painting,
1600-1700. . . . . *v.1 p.732*

Critical Perspectives on Gabriel Garcia Marquez. . . *v.2 p.684*

Critical Perspectives on Leon Gontran Damas. . . . *v.2 p.538*

Critical Perspectives on Leopold Sedar Senghor. . . *v.2 p.543*

Critical Perspectives on Mongo Beti. *v.2 p.543*

Critical Problems in the History of Science: Proceedings of the
Institute for the History of Science 1957. . . . . *v.5 p.388*

[Critical] Properties of Various Gases. *v.5 p.280*

Critical Race Counterstories along the Chicana/Chicano
Educational Pipeline. *v.6 p.528*

Critical Race Feminism: A Reader. *v.6 p.436, p.472*

Critical Race Theory: The Cutting Edge. *v.4 p.456*

The Critical Reception of Edith Wharton. *v.2 p.131*

The Critical Response to Anais Nin. *v.2 p.105*

The Critical Response to Erskine Caldwell. *v.2 p.66*

The Critical Response to Eugene O'Neill. *v.2 p.107*

The Critical Response to George Eliot. *v.2 p.287*

The Critical Response to H. G. Wells. *v.2 p.319*

The Critical Response to Jack London. *v.2 p.95, p.96*

The Critical Response to John Cheever. *v.2 p.67*

The Critical Response to Kamau Brathwaite. *v.2 p.768*

The Critical Response to Robert Lowell. *v.2 p.96*

The Critical Response to Samuel Beckett. *v.2 p.332*

The Critical Response to Saul Bellow. *v.2 p.60*

The Critical Response to Tennessee Williams. *v.2 p.134*

The Critical Response to Thomas Carlyle's Major
Works. *v.2 p.277*

The Critical Response to Truman Capote. *v.2 p.66*

Critical Social Theory in Public Administration. *v.4 p.545, p.580*

Critical Stability Constants. *v.5 p.302*

A Critical Study of Beethoven's Nine
Symphonies. *v.1 p.194, p.306*

A Critical Study of the Fiction of Patricia Highsmith--from the
Psychological to the Political. *v.2 p.86*

Critical Study of the Novels of R. K. Narayan. . . . *v.2 p.765*

A Critical Survey of Indian Philosophy. . . . *v.1 p.475, p.476*

Critical Survey of Long Fiction. *v.2 p.165, p.569*

Critical Survey of Mystery and Detective Fiction, 4
vols. *v.2 p.580*

Critical Survey of Poetry, Revised Edition, Vol. 8. . *v.2 p.180*

Critical Terms for Art History. *v.1 p.665*

Critical Theories of the State: Marxist, Neo-Marxist,
Post-Marxist. *v.4 p.491*

Critical Theory and Methodology, Vol. 3. . . . . . *v.4 p.680*

Critical Theory and Performance. *v.1 p.56, p.139*

Critical Theory since 1965. . . . . *v.2 p.566, p.573*

Critical Theory since Plato. *v.2 p.566, p.573*

Critical Theory: The Essential Readings. *v.1 p.502*

Critical Thinking and Learning: An Encyclopedia for Parents
and Teachers. *v.4 p.366*

Critical Traditions in Contemporary Archaeology. . . *v.4 p.6*

The Critical Waltz: Essays on the Work of Dorothy
Parker. *v.2 p.110*

Critical Works. *v.2 p.258*

Critical Writings of James Joyce. *v.2 p.359*

Critical Year: A Study of Andrew Johnson and
Reconstruction. *v.3 p.394, p.435*

Critical Years in Immigration: Canada and Australia Compared,
Vol. 2. *v.4 p.667*

Criticism and Fiction, and Other Essays. *v.2 p.578*

Criticism and the Growth of Knowledge: Proceedings of the
International Colloquium in the Philosophy of
Science, London 1965. . . . . *v.5 p.403*

Criticism in America: An Account of the Development of
Critical Techniques from the Early Period of the
Republic to the Middle Years of the Twentieth Century. *v.2 p.5*

Criticism in America: Its Functions and Status. . . . *v.2 p.3*

Criticism in the Borderlands: Studies in Chicano Literature,
Culture, and Ideology. *v.6 p.497, p.498, p.511*

Criticism: Major Statements. *v.2 p.568*

Criticisms on Paradise Lost. *v.2 p.236*

Critics, Values, and Restoration Comedy. *v.2 p.186*

Critique of Dialectical Reason, Vol. 1. . . . .*v.1 p.508*

Critique of Everyday Life, Vol. 1. . . . .*v.4 p.680*

The Critique of Judgment: Containing Kant's Critique of Aesthetic Judgement and Critique of Teleological Judgement. *v.1 p.462, p.481*

A Critique of Keynesian Economics. *v.4 p.226*

A Critique of Modern Textual Criticism. *v.2 p.164, p.569*

Critique of Practical Reason. *v.1 p.461*

Critique of Pure Reason. *v.1 p.462*

Critique of Scientific Reason. *v.5 p.402*

Critique of the Power of Judgment. *v.1 p.462*

A Critique of the Study of Kinship. *v.4 p.32*

Croatia: A Nation Forged in War. *v.3 p.248, p.249*

Croatia: between Europe and the Balkans. *v.3 p.248*

Crome Yellow. *v.2 p.354*

☐ Crony Capitalism: Corruption and Development in South Korea and the Philippines. *v.4 p.621*

Crony Capitalism: Corruption and Development in South Korea and the Philippines. *v.4 p.621*

Crop Ecology: Productivity and Management in Agricultural Systems. *v.5 p.22*

Crop Evolution, Adaptation and Yield. *v.5 p.21*

Crop Improvement: Quality Characters. *v.5 p.21*

Crop Improvement: Stress Tolerance. *v.5 p.21*

Crop Production: Evolution, History, and Technology. .*v.5 p.23*

Crop Production, Vol. 2. . . . .*v.5 p.43*

Crop Variety Improvement and Its Effect on Productivity: The Impact of International Agricultural Research. . . .*v.5 p.21*

Crops and Environmental Change: An Introduction to Effects of Global Warming, Increasing Atmospheric CO2 and O3 Concentrations, and Soil Salinization on Crop Physiology and Yield. *v.5 p.23, p.28*

Crops As Enhancers of Nutrient Use. *v.5 p.20*

Cross and Sword: An Eyewitness History of Christianity in Latin America. *v.1 p.608*

The Cross and the Cinema: The Legion of Decency and the National Catholic Office for Motion Pictures, 1933-1970. . . . .*v.6 p.328, p.343*

The Cross and the Scroll: 1,000 Years of Jewish-Hispanic Literature. *v.2 p.665*

The Cross and the Serpent: Religious Repression and Resurgence in Colonial Peru. *v.3 p.263, p.326*

Cross Channel. *v.2 p.332*

Cross Cultural Perspectives in Medical Ethics: Readings. *v.5 p.511*

Cross Currents in the International Women's Movement, 1848-1948. . . . .*v.6 p.430*

Cross Dressing, Sex, and Gender. *v.6 p.370*

A Cross of Iron: Harry S. Truman and the Origins of the National Security State, 1945-1954. . . .*v.3 p.472, v.4 p.486*

Cross-Cultural Business-Behaviour: Negotiating, Selling, Sourcing and Managing Across Cultures. *v.4 p.56*

Cross-Cultural Communication: The Essential Guide to International Business. *v.4 p.59*

Cross-Cultural Encounters and Conflicts. *v.6 p.582*

Cross-Cultural Filmmaking: A Handbook for Making Documentary and Ethnographic Films and Videos. .*v.6 p.310*

Cross-Cultural Perspectives on Youth and Violence. . .*v.4 p.752*

The Cross-Cultural Process in Christian History: Studies in the Transmission and Reception of Faith. *v.1 p.648*

Crosscurrents of Children's Literature: An Anthology of Texts and Criticism. *v.2 p.582*

Cross-Currents of Jungian Thought: An Annotated Bibliography. *v.5 p.596*

☐ CrossFire Beilstein. *v.5 p.289*

☐ CrossFire Gmelin. *v.5 p.302*

Crossfire: Philosophy and the Novel in Spain, 1900-1934. . . . .*v.2 p.641*

Crossing: A Memoir. *v.4 p.185, v.6 p.402*

Crossing Borders: An American Woman in the Middle East. *v.6 p.592*

Crossing Borders: An Autobiography. *v.2 p.676*

Crossing Borders, Reinforcing Borders: Social Categories, Metaphors, and Narrative Identities on the U.S.-Mexico Frontier. *v.6 p.488, p.522*

Crossing Borders: Re-mapping Women's Movements at the Turn of the 21st Century. *v.6 p.434*

Crossing Boundaries: Comparative History of Black People in Diaspora. *v.3 p.320*

Crossing Cultures in Mental Health. *v.5 p.637*

Crossing over the Line: Legislating Morality and the Mann Act. *v.4 p.473*

Crossing Paths: Schubert, Schumann, and Brahms. *v.1 p.196, p.313, p.353, p.354*

Crossing Sidelines, Crossing Cultures: Sport and Asian Pacific American Cultural Citizenship. *v.4 p.834, v.6 p.125*

Crossing Swords: Politics and Religion in Mexico. . .*v.3 p.291*

Crossing the 49th Parallel: Migration from Canada to the United States, 1900-1930. . . . .*v.4 p.571*

Crossing the Color Line: Readings in Black and White. *v.2 p.26*

Crossing the Next Meridian: Land, Water, and the Future of the West. *v.4 p.463*

Crossing the Snow Bridge. *v.6 p.104*

Crossing Vines: A Novel. *v.6 p.499*

Crossings: The Great Transatlantic Migrations, 1870-1914. . . . .*v.4 p.571, p.765*

Crossroads and Conflict: Security and Foreign Policy in the Caucasus and Central Asia. *v.4 p.623*

Crossroads, and Other Plays by Carlos Solorzano. *v.2 p.676, p.677*

Crossroads Between Culture and Mind: Continuities and Change in Theories of Human Nature. *v.4 p.35*

Crossroads of Power. *v.3 p.107, p.109*

Crossroads to Israel 1917-1948. . . . . . .*v.6 p.612, p.613*

Cross-Talk in Comp Theory: A Reader. *v.2 p.565*

Crosstown Traffic: Jimi Hendrix and Post-War Pop. *v.1 p.272, p.273, p.331*

Crosswinds: An Anthology of Black Dramatists in the Diaspora. *v.1 p.63, p.95, p.122, p.127, p.130*

Crow Dog's Case: American Indian Sovereignty, Tribal Law, and United States Law in the Nineteenth Century. *v.4 p.464, v.6 p.688, p.696*

The Crowd: A Study of the Popular Mind. *v.4 p.713*

The Crowd and the Public: And Other Essays. *v.4 p.713*

Crowd in History. *v.4 p.713*

The Crowd in Rome in the Late Republic. *v.3 p.26*

The Crowded Prairie: American National Identity in the Hollywood Western. *v.6 p.324*

Crowded Years. *v.3 p.460, p.461*

Crowds and Riots: A Study in Social Organization. . *v.4 p.713*

Crowell's Handbook of Elizabethan and Stuart Literature. *v.2 p.170*

Crown and Calumet: British-Indian Relations, 1783-1815. . . . .*v.6 p.685, p.691*

Crown and Nobility: England, 1272-1461. . . . . .*v.6 p.568*

Crown and Ritual: The Royal Insignia of Ngoyo. . . *v.4 p.708*

Crown and the Turban: Muslims and West African Pluralism. *v.1 p.554*

The Crown of Life: Essays in Interpretation of Shakespeare's Final Plays. *v.2 p.230*

The Crowned Cannibals. *v.6 p.631*

The Crowning Privilege. *v.2 p.181*

The Crucial Decade: America, 1945-1955. . . .*v.3 p.447, p.471*

The Crucial Era: The Great Depression and WWII, 1929-1945. . . . .*v.3 p.477*

Crucible of Power: A History of American Foreign Relations to 1913. . . . .*v.3 p.385*

Crucible of War: The Seven Years' War and the Fate of Empire in British North America, 1754-1766. . . . . . .*v.3 p.405*

Crucibles: The Lives and Achievements of the Great Chemists. *v.5 p.261*

Crucibles: The Story of Chemistry from Ancient Alchemy to Nuclear Fission. *v.5 p.261*

The Crucified God: The Cross of Christ as the Foundation and Criticism of Christian Theology. *v.1 p.641*

Crude Chronicles: Indigenous Politics, Multinational Oil, and Neoliberalism in Ecuador. *v.4 p.711*

Crude: The Story of Oil. *v.5 p.738*

Cruel and Unusual Punishment: The U. S. Blockade of Cuba. *v.3 p.312*

Cruel and Unusual: The Supreme Court and Capital Punishment. *v.4 p.471*

Cruel Compassion: Psychiatric Control of Society's Unwanted. *v.4 p.775*

Cruel Tales. *v.2 p.503*

Cruelty and Civilization: The Roman Games. *v.3 p.22*

Cruelty and Companionship: Conflict in Nineteenth Century Married Life. *v.6 p.765*

Cruelty and Utopia. *v.1 p.790, v.6 p.728*

Cruising Modernism: Class and Sexuality in American Literature and Social Thought. *v.2 p.11*

The Crusade Against Heretics in Bohemia, 1418-1437: Sources and Documents for the Hussite Crusades. *v.3 p.188*

Crusade Against Slavery: Friends, Foes, and Reforms 1820-1860. . . . .*v.3 p.396, p.419*

Crusade and Conversation on the Baltic Frontier 1150-1500. . . . .*v.3 p.232*

Crusade and Mission. *v.6 p.556*

The Crusade for Justice: Chicano Militancy and the Government's War on Dissent. *v.6 p.541*

Crusade: The Untold Story of the Persian Gulf War. . *v.6 p.604*

Crusader Archaeology: The Material Culture of the Latin East. *v.6 p.555, p.556, p.566*

Crusader Art in the Holy Land, from the Third Crusade to the Fall of Acre, 1187-1291. . . . .*v.1 p.672*

Crusader Nation: The United States in Peace and the Great War, 1898-1920. . . . .*v.3 p.450, p.481*

The Crusader States and their Neighbours: 1098-1291. . . . .*v.3 p.64, v.6 p.609*

Crusaders and Compromisers: Essays on the Relationship of the Antislavery Struggle to the Antebellum Party System. *v.3 p.420*

Crusaders and Pragmatists: Movers of Modern American Foreign Policy. *v.3 p.454*

The Crusades and the Expansion of Catholic Christendom, 1000-1714. . . . .*v.1 p.573*

The Crusades: Islamic Perspectives. *v.3 p.63*

Crusades: The Illustrated History. *v.6 p.556*

The Crusades Through Arab Eyes. *v.6 p.556*

The Crusades. *v.6 p.556, p.557*

Crustal Heat Flow: A Guide to Measurement and Modelling. *v.5 p.444*

The Cry and the Dedication. *v.6 p.99*

Cry for Justice: An Anthology of the Literature of Social Protest. *v.4 p.751*

The Cry Was Unity: Communists and African Americans, 1917-1936. . . . .*v.4 p.509, p.554*

Crying Hands: Eugenics and Deaf People in Nazi Germany. *v.3 p.171*

The Crying of Lot 49. . . . .*v.2 p.153*

Crying: The Natural and Cultural History of Tears. . *v.5 p.654*

Cryptogams: Algae. *v.5 p.208*

Cryptogams: Ferns and Fern Allies. *v.5 p.210*

Cryptography and Network Security. *v.5 p.335, p.345*

Cryptological Mathematics. *v.5 p.476*

The Crystal Desert: Summers in Antarctica. *v.5 p.175, p.238, p.240*

Crystal Palaces: American Garden Conservatories. *v.1 p.818, v.5 p.83*

Crystal Spirit: A Study of George Orwell. *v.2 p.376*

Crystal Structure Analysis for Chemists and Biologists. .*v.5 p.284*

Crystal Structure Determination. *v.5 p.284*

Crystal Structures, Lattices and Solids in Stereoview. *v.5 p.284*

The Crystal World. *v.2 p.330*

Crystallization Technology Handbook. *v.5 p.284*

Crystallography: An Introduction. *v.5 p.284*

Crystallography in Modern Chemistry: A Resource Book of Crystal Structures. *v.5 p.284*

⬚ Crystallography Links. *v.5 p.283*

Crystallography Made Crystal Clear: A Guide for Users of Macromolecular Models. *v.5 p.328, p.329*

⬚ Crystallography Online. *v.5 p.283*

⬚ Crystallography Open Database. *v.5 p.283*

⬚ Crystallography Subject Guide (Stanford University). *v.5 p.283*

Crystals: Growth, Morphology and Perfection. *v.5 p.436, p.437*

⬚ CS: UCLA Chicano Studies Research Center. *v.6 p.486, p.520*

C'ta ton Tour, Laura Cadieux. *v.2 p.541*

☐ C/T/A/H/R College of Tropical Agriculture and Human
Resources University of Hawaii at Manoa: The Noni
Website. *v.5 p.25, p.45*

Cuba, 1753-1815: Crown, Military and
Society. *v.3 p.275, p.310, p.311*

Cuba, 1933: Students, Yankees, and Soldiers. *v.3 p.307*

Cuba: A Different America. *v.3 p.307*

Cuba: A New History. *v.3 p.309*

Cuba: A Short History. *v.3 p.307*

Cuba after Communism. *v.3 p.307*

Cuba after the Cold War. *v.3 p.311*

Cuba and Its Music: From the First Drums to the
Mambo. *v.1 p.295*

Cuba and the Autonomists in the Politics of the First Spanish
Restoration, 1878-1898. . . . .*v.3 p.311*

Cuba and the Caribbean: Regional Issues and Trends in the
Post-Cold War Era. *v.3 p.313*

Cuba and the Future. *v.3 p.313*

Cuba and the Politics of Passion. *v.3 p.309*

Cuba and the United States: Intervention and Militarism,
1868-1933. . . . .*v.3 p.310*

Cuba: Confronting the U. S. Embargo. *v.3 p.313*

Cuba: Dilemmas of a Revolution. *v.3 p.308*

Cuba: From Conquistador to Castro. *v.3 p.313*

Cuba in the 1850's: Through the Lens of Charles DeForest
Fredricks. *v.3 p.311*

Cuba in the International System: Normalization and
Integration. *v.3 p.313*

Cuba in Transition: Crisis and Transformation. . . .*v.3 p.310*

Cuba Libre: Poems. *v.2 p.672*

Cuba on My Mind: Journeys to a Severed
Nation. *v.3 p.308, v.6 p.488, p.543*

Cuba or the Pursuit of Freedom. *v.3 p.313*

The Cuba Reader: History, Culture, Politics. *v.3 p.307*

Cuba, the Elusive Nation: Interpretations of National
Identity. *v.3 p.309*

Cuba: The Revolution in Peril. *v.3 p.309*

Cuba: The Shaping of Revolutionary Consciousness. . .*v.3 p.311*

Cuba Today and Tomorrow: Reinventing Socialism. . .*v.3 p.306*

Cuba—Going Back. *v.3 p.311*

Cuban American Fiction in English: An Annotated Bibliography
of Primary and Secondary Sources. . .*v.6 p.505, p.511, p.512*

Cuban American Theater. *v.6 p.495, p.505, p.517*

The Cuban Americans. *v.3 p.309, v.6 p.521*

Cuban and Cuban-American Women: An Annotated
Bibliography. *v.6 p.547*

The Cuban Condition: Translation and Identity in Modern
Cuban Literature. *v.2 p.671*

Cuban Democratic Experience: The Autentico Years,
1944-1952. . . . .*v.3 p.306*

The Cuban Economy at the Start of the Twenty-First
Century. *v.3 p.308*

The Cuban Economy: Measurement and Analysis of Socialist
Performance. *v.3 p.314*

The Cuban Economy. *v.3 p.312, p.313*

The Cuban Filmography: 1897 Through 2001. .*v.6 p.339, p.340*

Cuban Fire: The Saga of Salsa and Latin Jazz. . . .*v.6 p.518*

Cuban Fire: The Story of Salsa and Latin Jazz. . . .*v.1 p.292*

The Cuban Military under Castro. *v.3 p.277*

The Cuban Missile Crisis 1962: A National Security Archive
Documents Reader. *v.3 p.468*

The Cuban Missile Crisis: International Crises and the Role of
Law Published under the Auspices of the American
Society of International Law. *v.3 p.468*

Cuban Music: From Son and Rumba to the Buena Vista Social
Club and Timba Cubana. *v.1 p.294*

Cuban Politics: The Revolutionary Experiment. . . .*v.3 p.312*

☐ Cuban Research Institute. *v.6 p.486*

The Cuban Revolution into the 1990s: Cuban
Perspectives. *v.3 p.307*

The Cuban Revolution: Origins, Course, and Legacy. .*v.3 p.312*

Cuban Rural Society in the Nineteenth Century: The Social and
Economic History of Monoculture in Matanzas. . .*v.3 p.306*

The Cuban Slave Market, 1790-1880. . . . . .*v.3 p.306, p.307*

Cuban Socialism in a New Century. *v.3 p.306, v.4 p.506*

Cuban Theater in the United States: A Critical
Anthology. *v.6 p.496, p.512, p.517*

Cubana: Contemporary Fiction by Cuban Women. . .*v.2 p.673*

Cuban-American Art in Miami: Exile, Trauma, Postmodernism
and the Neo-Baroque. *v.6 p.491*

The Cuban-American Experience: Culture, Images and
Perspectives. *v.6 p.543*

Cuban-American Literature of Exile: From Person to
Persona. *v.6 p.505, p.511*

Cubanas en la Posguerra (1898-1902): Acercamiento a la
Reconstrucción de una Etapa Olvidada. *v.3 p.314*

Cubanisimo!: The Vintage Book of Contemporary Cuban
Literature. *v.2 p.671, p.672, v.6 p.495, p.506*

The Cubans: Voices of Change. *v.3 p.309*

The Cubans. *v.6 p.489, p.531*

CubanTime: A Celebration of Cuban Life in
America. *v.6 p.491, p.521*

Cuba's Foreign Relations in a Post-Soviet World. . .*v.3 p.308*

Cuba's Second Economy: From Behind the Scenes to Center
Stage. *v.3 p.312*

Cuba's Sugar Industry. *v.3 p.306*

Cubism: A History and Analysis, Nineteen Hundred Seven to
Nineteen Fourteen. *v.1 p.727*

Cubism and Culture. *v.1 p.676*

The Cubist Painters. *v.1 p.726*

Cuentos Completos. *v.2 p.666, p.685, p.686*

Cuentos de Amor de Locura y de Muerte. *v.2 p.687*

Cuentos de Eva Luna. *v.2 p.679*

Cuentos Negros de Cuba. *v.2 p.671*

Cuentos para Adultos Ninos y Retrasados Mentales. .*v.2 p.671*

Cuentos: Stories by Latinas. *v.6 p.495, p.496*

Cuentos. *v.2 p.669, p.673*

The Cult Experience: An Overview of Cults, Their Traditions
and Why People Join Them. *v.5 p.633*

The Cult of Ivan the Terrible in Stalin's Russia. . . .*v.3 p.226*

The Cult of Personality: How Personality Tests Are Leading Us to Miseducate Our Children, Mismanage Our Companies, and Misunderstand Ourselves. *v.5 p.603, p.655*

The Cult of Remembrance and the Black Death: Six Renaissance Cities in Central Italy. *v.3 p.199*

The Cult of Saint Thecla: A Tradition of Women's Piety in Late Antiquity. *v.1 p.599*

The Cult of the Court. *v.4 p.535*

Cult of the Dead in a Chinese Village. *v.1 p.527*

The Cult of the Saints: Its Rise and Function in Latin Christianity. *v.1 p.577, p.598,v.6 p.570*

Cultivated Landscapes: Chinese Paintings from the Collection of Marie-Helene and Guy Weill. *v.1 p.732*

Cultivated Plants of the Tropics and Subtropics: Cultivation, Economic Value, Utilization. *v.5 p.25, p.26*

Cultivated Power: Flowers, Culture, and Politics in the Reign of Louis XIV. *v.1 p.813*

Cultivating Crisis: The Human Cost of Pesticides in Latin America. *v.3 p.269*

Cultivating the Ground on Which We Stand: African-American Theater. *v.1 p.123*

Cultivating the Sociological Imagination: Concepts and Models for Service-Learning in Sociology. *v.4 p.675, p.676*

The Cultivation of Body and Mind in Nineteenth-Century American Delsartism. *v.1 p.48*

The Cults of the Roman Empire. *v.1 p.533*

The Cultural Analysis of Kinship: The Legacy of David M. Schneider. *v.4 p.32*

The Cultural Animal. *v.5 p.645*

Cultural Anthropology and the Old Testament. . . . *v.1 p.619*

Cultural Atlas of Africa. *v.6 p.51*

Cultural Atlas of Ancient Egypt. *v.6 p.56, p.57*

Cultural Atlas of China. *v.6 p.181*

The Cultural Background of Personality. *v.4 p.695*

Cultural Capital and Black Education: African American Communities and the Funding of Black Schooling, 1860 to the Present. *v.6 p.21, p.38*

Cultural Capital: The Problem of Literary Canon Formation. *v.2 p.163*

Cultural Compass: Ethnographic Explorations of Asian America. *v.6 p.105, p.123, p.124*

Cultural Competence in Substance Abuse Prevention. *v.4 p.758*

The Cultural Context of Medieval Learning: Proceedings of the 1st International Colloquium on Philosophy, Science and Theology in the Middle Ages, Boston, Sept. 1973, No.76. . . . . *v.6 p.576*

The Cultural Contradictions of Capitalism: 20th Anniversary Edition. *v.3 p.370*

Cultural Critique and Abstraction: Marianne Moore and the Avant-Garde. *v.2 p.102*

Cultural Diversity in the Workplace: Issues and Strategies. *v.4 p.132*

The Cultural Dynamics of Democratization in Spain. *v.4 p.608*

Cultural Foundations of Political Psychology. . . . *v.5 p.644*

Cultural Geography: Critical Concepts in the Social Sciences. *v.4 p.399*

Cultural Geography in Practice. *v.4 p.399*

Cultural Geography. *v.4 p.399*

Cultural Hegemony and African American Development. *v.4 p.700*

A Cultural History of Modern Science in China. *v.5 p.392, p.410*

A Cultural History of the American Novel, 1890-1940: Henry James to William Faulkner. *v.2 p.11*

A Cultural History of the English Language. *v.2 p.554*

Cultural Identity and Social Liberation in Latin American Thought. *v.4 p.685*

Cultural Imperialism and the Indo-English Novel: Genre and Ideology in the Novels of R. K. Narayan, Anita Desai, Kamala Markandaya, and Salman Rushdie. *v.2 p.761*

Cultural Intelligence: A Guide to Working with People from Other Cultures. *v.4 p.59*

Cultural Intelligence: People Skills for Global Business. *v.4 p.59*

Cultural Models in Language and Thought. *v.4 p.27*

The Cultural Origins of Human Cognition. . . *v.5 p.638, p.650*

The Cultural Origins of the French Revolution. . . . *v.3 p.149*

Cultural Pasts: Essays in Early Indian History. . . . *v.6 p.155*

Cultural Politics and Education. *v.4 p.300*

Cultural Politics in Greater Romania: Regionalism, Nation Building, and Ethnic Struggle, 1918-1930. . . . . *v.3 p.250*

Cultural Politics of Food and Eating. *v.4 p.46*

Cultural Psychology: Essays on Comparative Human Development. *v.4 p.36*

Cultural Residues: Chile in Transition. *v.3 p.355*

Cultural Resources Management. *v.1 p.822*

The Cultural Revolution: A Bibliography, 1966-1996. *v.6 p.196*

Cultural Secrets As Narrative Form: Storytelling in Nineteenth-Century America. *v.2 p.9*

The Cultural Studies Reader. *v.2 p.570*

Cultural Study of Work. *v.4 p.717*

Cultural Sutures: Medicine and Media. *v.4 p.774*

The Cultural Territories of Race: Black and White Boundaries. *v.4 p.728*

Cultural Transformation and Human Rights in Africa. *v.4 p.33*

The Cultural Unity of Black Africa. *v.6 p.10*

Culture: A Problem That Cannot Be Solved. *v.4 p.35*

Culture Across Borders: Mexican Immigration and Popular Culture. *v.6 p.493, p.529*

Culture Against Man. *v.4 p.22*

Culture and Anarchy: Landmarks in the History of Education. *v.2 p.265*

Culture and Anomie: Ethnographic Imagination in the Nineteenth Century. *v.6 p.756, p.763*

Culture and Clinical Care. *v.5 p.530*

Culture and Commitment: The New Relationships Between the Generations in the 1970s. *v.4 p.700*

Culture and Conquest in Mongol Eurasia. *v.4 p.623, v.6 p.238*

Culture and Customs of Argentina. *v.3 p.346*

Culture and Customs of Cuba. *v.3 p.311*

Culture and Customs of Egypt. *v.6 p.634*

Culture and Customs of Israel. *v.6 p.608*

Culture and Customs of the Dominican Republic. . . *v.3 p.316*

Culture and Customs of Zimbabwe. *v.6 p.77*

Culture and Entertainment in Wartime Russia. . . . *v.3 p.227*

Culture and Experience. *v.4 p.35*

Culture and Identity in Early Modern Europe (1500-1800): Essays in Honor of Natalie Zemon Davis. *v.1 p.601*

Culture and Identity: Selected English Writings of Faiz Ahmad Faiz. *v.6 p.151, p.162*

Culture and Imperialism. *v.2 p.572, v.6 p.746, p.757*

Culture and National Identity in Republican Rome. . . *v.3 p.25*

Culture and Pedagogy: International Comparisons in Primary Education. *v.4 p.312, p.313, p.338*

Culture and Political Crisis in Vienna: Christian Socialism in Power, 1897-1918. . . . . *v.3 p.183*

Culture and Politics in Indonesia. *v.6 p.174, p.175*

Culture and Power in Banaras: Community, Performance, and Environment, 1800-1980. . . . . *v.6 p.160*

Culture and Power: The Sociology of Pierre Bourdieu. *v.4 p.682*

Culture and Society, 1780-1950. *v.2 p.173, p.177, p.179, v.3 p.93, p.117, p.130, v.6 p.736*

Culture and Society in Italy, 1290-1420. . . . . . . *v.3 p.199*

Culture and Subjective Well-Being. *v.5 p.670*

Culture and the Media in the U. S. S. R. Today. . . . *v.3 p.228*

Culture and the State in Late Choson Korea. *v.6 p.236*

Culture As History: The Transformation of American Society in the Twentieth Century. *v.3 p.370*

Culture as Praxis. *v.4 p.699*

Culture, Behavior, and Personality. *v.4 p.35*

The Culture Business: Management Strategies for the Arts-Related Business. *v.1 p.825*

Culture Care Diversity and Universality: A Worldwide Nursing Theory. *v.5 p.530*

Culture Clash in America. *v.6 p.517*

Culture Clash: Law and Science in America. *v.4 p.451*

Culture Clash: Life, Death and Revolutionary Comedy. *v.6 p.517*

Culture, Class, and Work among Arab-American Women. *v.4 p.763*

Culture, Environment, and Conservation in the Appalachian South. *v.1 p.822*

Culture, History and Ideology in the Formation of Ba'thist Iraq, 1968-1989. . . . . *v.6 p.602*

Culture in Mind: Cognition, Culture, and the Problem of Meaning. *v.4 p.24, p.25*

Culture in Practice: Selected Essays. *v.4 p.24*

Culture in Special Education: Building Reciprocal Family-Professional Relationships. *v.4 p.316*

Culture, Leadership, and Organizations: The GLOBE Study of 62 Societies. *v.4 p.69, p.71*

Culture Matters: How Values Shape Human Progress. *v.4 p.269, p.700*

The Culture of Ancient Egypt. *v.3 p.10*

The Culture of Bureaucracy. *v.4 p.527*

The Culture of Christina Rossetti: Female Poetics and Victorian Contexts. *v.2 p.303*

The Culture of Cities. *v.6 p.714*

The Culture of Conflict in Modern Cuba. *v.3 p.313*

The Culture of Conformism: Understanding Social Consent. *v.4 p.695*

The Culture of Control: Crime and Social Order in Contemporary Society. *v.4 p.752, p.773, v.6 p.248*

A Culture of Corruption?: Coping with Government in Post-Communist Europe. *v.4 p.582*

The Culture of Craft. *v.1 p.702*

The Culture of Defeat: On National Trauma, Mourning, and Recovery. *v.4 p.706*

A Culture of Desert Survival: Bedouin Proverbs from Sinai and the Negev. *v.6 p.596*

Culture of Education. *v.4 p.347, p.356*

Culture of Eloquence: Oratory and Reform in Antebellum America. *v.2 p.14*

Culture of Honor: The Psychology of Violence in the South. *v.5 p.637*

Culture of Misfortune: An Interpretive History of Textile Unionism in the United States. *v.4 p.125*

The Culture of Narcissism: American Life in an Age of Diminishing Expectations. *v.4 p.704*

The Culture of Oklahoma. *v.3 p.524*

The Culture of Profession in Late Renaissance Italy. . *v.3 p.200*

The Culture of Protestantism in Early Modern Scotland. *v.1 p.581, p.582*

The Culture of Queers. *v.6 p.416*

The Culture of Sectarianism: Community, History, and Violence in Nineteenth-Century Ottoman Lebanon. *v.6 p.605*

The Culture of Sentiment: Race, Gender, and Sentimentality in 19th-Century America. *v.2 p.10*

The Culture of the High Renaissance: Ancients and Moderns in Sixteenth-Century Rome. *v.3 p.71*

The Culture of the Mathematics Classroom: Analyses and Changes. *v.5 p.464*

Culture on the Margins: The Black Spiritual and the Rise of American Cultural Interpretation. *v.1 p.281*

Culture on Tour: Ethnographies of Travel. *v.4 p.44*

Culture Shock! Living and Working Abroad: A Practical Guide. *v.4 p.168*

Culture, Technology, and the Creation of America's National Parks. *v.1 p.818, v.5 p.18, v.6 p.297*

Culture Wars in Brazil: The First Vargas Regime, 1930-1945. . . . . *v.3 p.343*

Culture Wars: School and Society in the Conservative Restoration 1969-1984. . . . . *v.4 p.300*

The Cultured Chimpanzee: Reflections on Cultural Primatology. *v.5 p.615*

Cultures and Organizations: Software for the Mind. *v.4 p.58, p.59, p.75*

Cultures and Societies of Africa. *v.4 p.38*

Culture's Consequences: Comparing Values, Behaviors, Institutions and Organizations Across Nations. . . *v.4 p.718*

Cultures in Conflict: Christians, Muslims, and Jews in the Age of Discovery. *v.6 p.582*

Cultures in Conflict: Social Movements and the State in Peru. *v.3 p.332*

The Cultures of Cities. *v.6 p.720*

Cultures of Commerce: Representation and American Business Culture, 1877-1960. . . . . *v.4 p.141*

Cultures of Darkness: Night Travels in the Histories of Transgression. *v.4 p.709*

Cultures of Human Development and Education: Challenge to Growing up African. *v.4 p.335*

Cultures of Letters: Scenes of Reading and Writing in Nineteenth-Century America. *v.2 p.9*

Cultures of Natural History. *v.5 p.222*

Cultures of Relatedness: New Approaches to the Study of Kinship. *v.4 p.31*

Cultures of the Jews: Diversities of Diaspora. *v.1 p.546*

Cultures of the Jews: Mediterranean Origins. *v.1 p.546*

Cultures of the Jews: Modern Encounters. *v.1 p.546*

Cultures of Transnational Adoption. *v.4 p.708*, **v.6** *p.110, p.111, p.125*

Cumbe Reborn: An Andean Ethnography of History. . *v.3 p.358*

The Cumulated Index to the U. S. Department of State Papers Relating to the Foreign Relations of the United States, 1939-1945, Set. *v.4 p.627*

A Cumulative Bibliography of Medieval Military History and Technology. *v.6 p.566*

Cumulative Record: Definitive Edition. *v.5 p.615, p.646*

The Cunning of Reason. *v.1 p.492*

Cunningham's Manual of Practical Anatomy: Head, Neck and Brain. *v.5 p.158*

Cunningham's Manual of Practical Anatomy: Thorax and Abdomen. *v.5 p.158*

Cunningham's Manual of Practical Anatomy: Upper and Lower Limbs. *v.5 p.158*

A Cup of Tears: A Diary of the Warsaw Ghetto. *v.3 p.85*

Curanderismo: Mexican American Folk Healing. *v.6 p.524, p.551, p.552*

Curanderismo: Mexican-American Folk Psychiatry. *v.6 p.523, p.551*

Curandero: A Life in Mexican Folk Healing. . *v.6 p.524, p.551*

Curators of the Buddha: The Study of Buddhism under Colonialism. *v.1 p.561, p.562*

Curbing the Courts: The Constitution and the Limits of Judicial Power. *v.4 p.538*

Cures: A Gay Man's Odyssey. *v.6 p.381, p.401*

The Curious Cook: More Kitchen Science and Lore. *v.5 p.34, p.35*

Curious Fragments: Jack London's Tales of Fantasy Fiction. *v.2 p.95*

The Curious Incident of the Dog in the Night-Time: A Novel. *v.2 p.351*

Curious Land: Jesuit Accommodation and the Origins of Sinology. *v.6 p.186, p.216, p.218*

The Curious Life of Robert Hooke: The Man Who Measured London. *v.3 p.47*

The Curious Naturalist: Nature's Everyday Mysteries. .*v.5 p.223*

The Curious Perspective. *v.2 p.171*

Curious Wine. *v.6 p.396*

☐ The Curran Index. *v.6 p.739*

Current Approaches in Drama Therapy. *v.1 p.94*

Current Approaches in the Cognitive Science of Religion. *v.5 p.635*

Current Care of Women: Diagnosis and Treatment. . *v.5 p.523*

⚙ Current Chemical Reactions. *v.5 p.288*

⚙ Current Facts [Computer File]; (Beilstein Current Facts in Chemistry). *v.5 p.288*

☐ Current Industrial Reports. *v.4 p.150*

Current Issues in Linguistic Theory. *v.2 p.559*

Current Issues in Natural Resource Policy. *v.4 p.62*

Current Issues in Nursing. *v.5 p.527*

Current Land Policy in Latin America: Regularing Land Tenure under Neo-Liberalism. *v.3 p.300*

Current Medical Diagnosis and Treatment. *v.5 p.515*

Current Paleoethnobotany: Analytical Methods and Cultural Interpretations of Archaeological Plant Remains. . . *v.4 p.7*

Current Pediatric Diagnosis and Treatment. *v.5 p.525*

Current Perspectives in Forensic Psychology and Criminal Justice. *v.5 p.591*

Current Protocols in Bioinformatics. *v.5 p.87, p.99, p.101, p.102, p.110*

Current Protocols in Neuroscience. *v.5 p.88*

Current Protocols in Nucleic Acid Chemistry. *v.5 p.120*

Current Themes in Theoretical Biology: A Dutch Perspective. *v.5 p.114*

Current Therapy in Obstetrics and Gynecology. . . .*v.5 p.524*

Current Topics in Computational Molecular Biology. .*v.5 p.127*

Currents in the Contemporary Argentine Novel: Arlt, Mallea, Sabato, and Cortazar. *v.2 p.678*

Curriculum: A Comprehensive Introduction. *v.4 p.364*

Curriculum and Assessment. *v.4 p.286, p.287*

Curriculum as Conversation: Transforming Traditions of Teaching and Learning. *v.4 p.294, p.361*

Curriculum Development and Evaluation in Nursing. .*v.5 p.529*

Curriculum Development and Teaching Strategies for Gifted Learners. *v.4 p.317*

Curriculum Development: Theory into Practice. .*v.4 p.365, p.366*

Curriculum for Gifted and Talented Students. . *v.4 p.317, p.318*

Curriculum Improvement: Decision Making and Process. *v.4 p.362*

The Curriculum: Purpose, Substance, Practice. . . .*v.4 p.363*

The Curriculum Studies Reader. *v.4 p.366*

Curriculum Studies: The Reconceptionalization (Curriculum Theorizing:The Reconceptualists). *v.4 p.361*

The Curriculum Vitae Handbook: How to Present and Promote Your Academic Career. *v.4 p.168*

The Cursed Poets. *v.2 p.503*

Cursing in America: A Psycholinguistic Study of Dirty Language in the Courts, in the Movies, in the Schoolyards, and on the Streets. *v.2 p.552*

Curtains and Draperies: History, Design and Inspiration. .*v.1 p.809*

The Curved Planks: Poems / A Bilingual Edition. . . *v.2 p.510*

Custer Died for Your Sins: An Indian Manifesto. *v.6 p.693, p.694, p.700, p.701*

Customer Mania!: It's Never Too Late to Build a Customer-Focused Company. *v.4 p.143*

Customs in Common. *v.3 p.124*

The Cutting Edge: An Encyclopedia of Advanced Technologies. *v.5 p.679*

Cutting Edge: Art-Horror and the Horrific Avant-Garde. .*v.6 p.318*

Cutting Edge Chemistry. *v.5 p.265*

The Cutting Edge: Conserving Wildlife in Logged Tropical Forests. *v.5 p.37, p.41, p.353,* **v.6** *p.291*

Cutting the Edge: Current Perspectives in Radical and Critical Criminology and Criminal Justice. *v.6 p.250*

Cutting the Lion's Tail: Suez Through Egyptian Eyes. .*v.6 p.639*

Cutting the Wire: Gambling Prohibition and the Internet. *v.6 p.253*

Cuttlefish Bones. *v.2 p.719*

Cy Twombly: A Monograph. *v.1 p.697*

Cy Young: A Baseball Life. *v.4 p.849*

Cybercartography: Theory and Practice. *v.4 p.386*

The Cybercities Reader. *v.6 p.729, p.730*

Cybercrime: A Reference Handbook. *v.6 p.253*

The Cyberiad. *v.2 p.790*

Cybernetics or Control and Communication in the Animal and the Machine. *v.5 p.408*

Cyberpsychology. *v.5 p.589*

Cyberspace and the Law: Your Rights and Duties in the on-Line World. *v.4 p.444*

Cyburbia ; the Planning Portal. *v.1 p.783, p.798*

Cycles and Events in Stratigraphy. *v.5 p.446*

Cycles of Conquest: The Impact of Spain, Mexico, and the United States on the Indians of the Southwest 1533. .*v.6 p.683*

Cycles of Soils: Carbon, Nitrogen, Phosphorus, Sulfur, Micronutrients. *v.5 p.51*

Cycles, Trends, and Turning Points: Practical Marketing and Sales Forecasting Techniques. *v.4 p.137*

Cycling Past 50. . . . .*v.4 p.787, p.841, p.857*

Cyclopedia of American Agriculture: A Popular Survey of Agricultural Conditions, Practices and Ideals in the United States and Canada, Set. *v.5 p.3*

Cyclopedia of World Authors, Fourth Revised Edition, Volume 3: Joel Chandler Harris--Alessandro Manzoni. . .*v.2 p.575*

Cyclops. *v.2 p.411*

Cymbeline. *v.2 p.223*

Cynewulf. *v.2 p.203*

The Cynical Society: The Culture of Politics and the Politics of Culture in American Life. *v.3 p.367, p.371*

Cynics: The Cynic Movement in Antiquity and Its Legacy. *v.1 p.428*

A Cynthia Ozick Reader. *v.2 p.151*

Cyprus: A Modern History. *v.6 p.601*

Cyprus and Its People: Nation, Identity, and Experience in an Unimaginable Community, 1955-1997. . .*v.3 p.197, v.6 p.601*

The Cyprus Conspiracy: America, Espionage and the Turkish Invasion. *v.3 p.197*

Cyprus: The Impact of Diverse Nationalism on a State. .*v.6 p.601*

Cyprus: The Search for a Solution. *v.3 p.197*

Cyprus under British Rule. *v.6 p.601*

Cyrano de Bergerac: A Heroic Comedy in Five Acts. .*v.2 p.498*

Cyrano de Bergerac: Heroic Comedy in Five Acts. . .*v.2 p.498*

Cyrano de Bergerac. *v.2 p.336*

Cyril of Alexandria. *v.1 p.593*

Cyril of Jerusalem. *v.1 p.593*

Cyropaedia, Bks. 1-4. . . . .*v.2 p.422*

Cyropaedia, Bks. 5-8. . . . .*v.2 p.422*

Czech & Germans : A Study of the Struggle in the Historic Provinces of Bohemia and Moravia. *v.3 p.190*

Czech: An Essential Grammar. *v.2 p.774*

The Czech and Slovak Republics. *v.3 p.190*

Czech Drama since World War II. *v.2 p.782*

Czech Literature. *v.2 p.782*

Czech Photographic Avant-Garde, 1918-1948. . . . .*v.1 p.763*

Czech Plays: Modern Czech Drama. *v.1 p.64, p.108*

Czech Prose: An Anthology. *v.2 p.781*

The Czech Revolution of 1848. . . . .*v.3 p.188*

The Czech Romantics. *v.2 p.782*

Czech Writers and Politics, 1945-1969. . . . . . .*v.2 p.782*

Czechoslovak New Wave. *v.6 p.337*

Czechoslovakia, 1918-88: Seventy Years from Independence. *v.3 p.188*

Czechoslovakia: Anvil of the Cold War. *v.3 p.187, p.188*

Czechoslovakia Between Stalin and Hitler: The Diplomacy of Edvard Benes in the 1930s. *v.3 p.189*

Czechoslovakia: Crossroads and Crises, 1918-88. . .*v.3 p.188*

Czechoslovakia: The Short Goodbye. *v.3 p.190*

Czechoslovakia: The Velvet Revolution and Beyond. .*v.3 p.190*

The Czechs under Nazi Rule: The Failure of National Resistance, 1939-42. . . . .*v.3 p.189*

Czech. *v.2 p.774*

D

D and B/Gale Industry Reference Handbook: Electronics and Software. *v.5 p.317*

D and B/Gale Industry Reference Handbook: Health and Medical Services. *v.5 p.317*

D and B/Gale Industry Reference Handbook: Telecommunications. *v.5 p.317*

d- and f- Block Chemistry. *v.5 p.303*

D. H. Lawrence: A Literary Life. *v.2 p.364*

D. H. Lawrence and Italy: Twilight in Italy, Sea and Sardinia, Etruscan Places. *v.2 p.363*

D. H. Lawrence: Late Essays and Articles. *v.2 p.363*

D. H. Lawrence: New Worlds. *v.2 p.362*

D. H. Lawrence: The Cambridge Biography of D. H. Lawrence. *v.2 p.362*

D. H. Lawrence: The Early Years, 1885-1912, Vol. 1. .*v.2 p.364*

D. H. Lawrence: The Life of an Outsider. *v.2 p.364*

D. H. Lawrence: The Novels. *v.2 p.364*

D. H. Lawrence's Women in Love: A Casebook. . .*v.2 p.362*

D. H. Lawrence. *v.2 p.362*

Dada: Art and Anti-Art. *v.1 p.680*

Daddy's Roommate. *v.6 p.400*

Dahomey and Neighbours. *v.6 p.73*

Dahomey: Between Tradition and Modernity. *v.6 p.74*

Daidalos and the Origins of Greek Art. *v.1 p.670*

Daily Life in Ancient Rome: The People and the City at the Height of the Empire. *v.3 p.23*

Daily Life in China on the Eve of the Mongol Invasion, 1250-1276. . . . .*v.6 p.186*

Daily Life in Colonial Mexico: The Journey of Friar Ilarione da Bergamo, 1761-1768. . . . .*v.3 p.286*

Daily Life in Colonial New England. *v.3 p.485*

Daily Life in Johnson's London. *v.3 p.109, p.129*

Daily Life in Portugal in the Late Middle
    Ages. *v.3 p.244, v.6 p.557*

Daily Life in Rembrandt's Holland. *v.3 p.205*

Daily Life in the World of Charlemagne. *v.6 p.557*

Daily Life in Victorian England. *v.6 p.761, p.762*

Daily Life of the Nubians. *v.4 p.701, v.6 p.59*

Daily Liturgical Prayer: Origins and Theology. . . .*v.1 p.655*

Daily Living in the Twelfth Century: Based on the Observations
    of Alexander Neckam in London and
    Paris. *v.6 p.557, p.577, p.713*

The Daily Newspaper in America: The Evolution of a Social
    Instrument, Set. *v.4 p.410, p.411*

Dairy Cattle Science. *v.5 p.56*

Dairy Freestall Housing and Equipment, MWPS-7. . . .*v.5 p.54*

Dakota: A Spiritual Geography. *v.3 p.523*

Dakota Grammar: With Texts and Ethnography. *v.6 p.690*

Dakota Territory, 1861-1889: A Study of Frontier
    Politics. *v.3 p.523*

The Dalai Lama's Secret Temple: Tantric Wall Paintings from
    Tibet. *v.1 p.730*

Dalcroze Today: An Education Through and into Music. .*v.1 p.404*

Dali. *v.1 p.695*

Dam Engineering 2004. . . . .*v.5 p.703*

La Dama Duende. *v.2 p.646, p.647*

Damascus Between Democracy and Dictatorship. . . .*v.6 p.607*

The Damascus Chronicle of the Crusades. *v.6 p.609*

Damascus under the Mamluks. *v.6 p.607*

La Dame aux Camelias. *v.2 p.489*

La Dame aux Camélias : le roman, le drame, La
    Traviata. *v.2 p.489*

Damming the Past: Dams and Cultural Heritage
    Management. *v.5 p.702*

Damn You, England: Collected Prose. *v.2 p.376*

The Damnation of Theron Ware. *v.2 p.37*

Damned: An Illustrated History of the Devil. *v.1 p.709*

The Damned (La-Bas). *v.2 p.494*

Damned to Fame: The Life of Samuel Beckett. *v.2 p.333*

The Damned Yard and Other Stories. *v.2 p.819*

A Damsel in Distress. *v.2 p.390*

Dan Emmett and the Rise of Early Negro Minstrelsy. . .*v.1 p.35*

Dan Flavin: The Complete Lights, 1961-1996. . . . .*v.1 p.773*

Dan Graham: Catalogue Raisonné. *v.1 p.779*

Dana's New Mineralogy: The System of Mineralogy of James
    Dwight Dana and Edward Salisbury Dana. *v.5 p.435*

Dance: A Basic Educational Technique. *v.1 p.48*

Dance: A Creative Art Experience. *v.1 p.47*

Dance: A Short History of Classic Theatrical
    Dancing. *v.1 p.5, p.24*

Dance and Music: A Guide to Dance Accompaniment for
    Musicians and Dance Teachers. *v.1 p.44, p.47, p.397*

Dance and Other Expressive Art Therapies: When Words Are
    Not Enough. *v.1 p.51*

Dance and Photography. *v.1 p.45*

Dance and the Body Politic in Northern Greece. .*v.1 p.16, p.48*

Dance and the Lived Body. *v.1 p.41*

Dance and the Music of J. S. Bach. . . .*v.1 p.45, p.185, p.303*

Dance and the Performative: A Choreological Perspective :
    Laban and Beyond. *v.1 p.43*

Dance and the Specific Image: Improvisation. *v.1 p.43*

Dance Anecdotes: Stories from the Worlds of Ballet, Broadway,
    the Ballroom, and Modern Dance. *v.1 p.44*

The Dance, Art, and Ritual of Africa. *v.1 p.21*

Dance As a Theatre Art: Source Readings in Dance History
    from 1851 to Present. *v.1 p.41*

Dance As an Element of Life. *v.1 p.47, p.48*

Dance As Education. *v.1 p.46, p.47*

Dance As Religious Studies. *v.1 p.21*

Dance As Text: Ideologies of the Baroque Body. .*v.1 p.41, p.42*

A Dance Autobiography. *v.1 p.10*

Dance Beat: Selected Views and Reviews, 1967-1976. .*v.1 p.39*

Dance Between Two Cultures: Latino Caribbean Literature
    Written in the United States. *v.6 p.507, p.514*

Dance Education and Training in Britain. *v.1 p.47*

The Dance Encyclopedia. *v.1 p.3*

Dance for Export: Cultural Diplomacy and the Cold
    War. *v.1 p.29, p.31*

Dance, Gender, and Culture. *v.1 p.44*

Dance Has Many Faces. *v.1 p.44*

Dance History: Introduction. *v.1 p.5, p.46*

The Dance in Ancient Greece. *v.1 p.16*

Dance in Elementary Education: A Program for Boys and
    Girls. *v.1 p.48*

Dance in Hispanic Cultures. *v.1 p.20, p.21*

The Dance in Mind: Profiles and Reviews, 1977-83. . .*v.1 p.39*

Dance in Psychotherapy. *v.1 p.51*

The Dance in Spain. *v.1 p.20*

Dance in the City. *v.1 p.44*

Dance in the Field: Theory, Methods and Issues in Dance
    Ethnography. *v.1 p.48*

Dance in the Hollywood Musical. *v.1 p.37*

Dance in the Musical Theater: Jerome Robbins and His Peers,
    1934-1965, A Guide. *v.1 p.4, p.37*

Dance in the Shadow of the Guillotine. *v.1 p.5*

The Dance in Theory. *v.1 p.39*

Dance Injuries. *v.1 p.49*

Dance Jamaica: Cultural Definition and Artistic Discovery, the
    National Dance Theatre Company of Jamaica
    1962-1983. . . . .*v.1 p.19*

Dance Kinesiology. *v.1 p.49*

Dance Magazine College Guide, 1998-1999. . . . . .*v.1 p.3*

Dance Medicine: A Comprehensive Guide. *v.1 p.50*

Dance, Modernity and Culture: Explorations in the Sociology of
    Dance. *v.1 p.44*

Dance Movement Therapy: A Healing Art. *v.1 p.51*

Dance Movement Therapy: Theory and Practice. *v.1 p.51*

Dance Movement Therapy: Theory, Research and
    Practice. *v.1 p.51*

Dance Notation: The Process of Recording Movement on
    Paper. *v.1 p.38*

Dance of Court and Theater: Selected Writings of Wendy
    Hilton. *v.1 p.22*

The Dance of Death: Nigerian History and Christopher Okigbo's Poetry. *v.2 p.756*

The Dance of Death. *v.2 p.631*

The Dance of Legislation. *v.4 p.461*

Dance of the Dialectic: Steps in Marx's Method. . . .*v.4 p.507*

Dance of the Millions: Military Rule and the Social Revolution in Colombia, 1930-1956. . . . .*v.3 p.357*

The Dance of the Rose and the Nightingale. . . .*v.1 p.11, p.17*

Dance of the Sleepwalkers: The Dance Marathon Fad. .*v.1 p.40*

Dance on Camera: A Guide to Dance Films and Videos. .*v.1 p.4*

Dance on Screen: Genres and Media from Hollywood to Experimental Art. *v.1 p.36, p.37*

Dance Pathologies: Performance, Poetics, Medicine. . .*v.1 p.49*

Dance, Power, and Difference: Critical and Feminist Perspectives on Dance Education. *v.1 p.48*

Dance Rhythms of the French Baroque: A Handbook for Performance. *v.1 p.22, p.185, p.401*

Dance: Rituals of Experience. *v.1 p.42*

Dance, Sex, and Gender: Signs of Identity, Dominance, Defiance, and Desire. *v.1 p.48, **v.6** p.474*

Dance Spectrum: Critical and Philosophical Enquiry. . .*v.1 p.44*

Dance Technique and Injury Prevention. *v.1 p.49*

The Dance Technique of Lester Horton. *v.1 p.27*

Dance: The Art of Production. *v.1 p.37, p.38*

Dance Therapy and Depth Psychology: The Moving Imagination. *v.1 p.50*

Dance Therapy Redefined: A Body Approach to Therapeutic Dance. *v.1 p.50*

Dance Therapy: Theory and Application. *v.1 p.50*

A Dance to Music of Time: Second Movement. . . .*v.2 p.377*

A Dance to the Music of Time: First Movement. .*v.2 p.377, p.378*

A Dance to the Music of Time: Fourth Movement. . .*v.2 p.377*

A Dance to the Music of Time: Third Movement. . .*v.2 p.377*

Dance to the Piper and Promenade Home: A Two-Part Autobiography. *v.1 p.7*

A Dance with Death: Soviet Airwomen in World War II. .*v.3 p.227*

Dance Words. *v.1 p.4*

Dance Writings and Poetry. *v.1 p.39*

The Dance Writings of Carl Van Vechten. *v.1 p.40*

Dance-Movement Therapy: Mirror of Ourselves: The Psychoanalytic Approach. *v.1 p.51*

Dancer: A Novel. *v.1 p.46*

The Dancer and the Dance: Merce Cunningham in Conversation with Jacqueline Lesschaeve. *v.1 p.7*

The Dancer Defects: The Struggle for Cultural Supremacy During the Cold War. *v.3 p.87*

Dancer from the Dance: A Novel. *v.6 p.397*

A Dancer Takes Flight: Psychological Concerns in the Development of the American Male Dancer. . . .*v.1 p.50*

The Dancer's Foot Book. *v.1 p.50*

Dancers Talking Dance: Critical Evaluation in the Choreography Class. *v.1 p.47*

The Dances of Haiti. *v.1 p.19*

The Dances of India: A General Guide and a Users' Handbook. *v.1 p.15, p.16*

The Dances of Shakespeare. *v.1 p.45*

Dances of Spain and Italy from 1400-1600. . . . . .*v.1 p.20*

The Dances of the Processions of Seville in Spain's Golden Age. *v.1 p.20*

Dances That Describe Themselves: The Improvised Choreography of Richard Bull. *v.1 p.41*

Dance. *v.1 p.45*

Dancin' in the Streets!: Anarchists, IWWs, Surrealists, Situationists and Provos in the 1960s As Recorded in the Pages of the Rebel Worker and Heatwave. *v.4 p.554*

Dancing Arabs. *v.6 p.649*

Dancing at the Dawn of Agriculture: Dance and Display at the Beginning of Farming. *v.4 p.26*

Dancing at the Dead Sea: Tracking the World's Environmental Hot Spots. *v.6 p.292*

Dancing by the Book: a Catalogue of Books, 1531-1804, in the Collection of Mary Ann O'Brian Malkin. *v.1 p.4*

Dancing Desires: Choreographing Sexualities on and off the Stage. *v.1 p.41, **v.6** p.414*

Dancing Female: Lives and Issues of Women in Contemporary Dance. *v.1 p.42*

Dancing for Balanchine. *v.1 p.6*

Dancing Gods: Indian Ceremonials of New Mexico and Arizona. *v.1 p.14*

Dancing Identity: Metaphysics in Motion. *v.1 p.41*

Dancing in Montreal: Seeds of a Choreographic History. .*v.1 p.15*

Dancing in the Distraction Factory: Music Television and Popular Culture. *v.1 p.255*

Dancing in the Inns of Court. *v.1 p.21, p.22*

Dancing in the Street: Motown and the Cultural Politics of Detroit. *v.1 p.385*

Dancing in the Sun: Hollywood Choreographers, 1915-1937. . . . .*v.1 p.11, p.37*

Dancing in the Vortex: The Story of Ida Rubinstein. . .*v.1 p.14*

Dancing into Darkness: Butoh, Zen, and Japan. . .*v.1 p.15, p.26*

Dancing Longer, Dancing Stronger: A Dancer's Guide to Improving Technique and Preventing Injury. . . .*v.1 p.50*

Dancing Many Drums: Excavations in African American Dance. *v.1 p.18, p.41*

Dancing Modernism - Performing Politics. .*v.1 p.28, p.30, p.42*

The Dancing Mouse A Study in Animal Behavior. . . .*v.5 p.616*

Dancing on My Grave. *v.1 p.9*

Dancing Revelations: Alvin Ailey's Embodiment of African American Culture. *v.1 p.18, p.41*

Dancing Skeletons: Life and Death in West Africa. . . .*v.4 p.45*

Dancing Spirit: An Autobiography. *v.1 p.9*

Dancing Spirits: Rhythms and Rituals of Haitian Vodun, the Rada Rite. *v.1 p.21, p.292,v.3 p.314*

Dancing till Dawn: A Century of Exhibition Ballroom Dance. *v.1 p.34*

Dancing to Different Tunes: Sexuality and Its Misconceptions. *v.4 p.749, v.6 p.447*

Dancing with Cuba: A Memoir of the Revolution. *v.1 p.20, p.28, p.30,v.3 p.309*

Dancing with Data to Improve Learning. *v.4 p.287*

Dancing with Demons: The Authorized Biography of Dusty Springfield. *v.6 p.410*

Dancing with Ghosts: A Critical Biography of Arturo
    Islas. *v.6 p.488, p.497, p.511*

Dancing with Goddesses: Archetypes, Poetry, and
    Empowerment. *v.6 p.460*

Dancing with the Devil: Society and Cultural Poetics in
    Mexican-American South Texas. *v.6 p.523*

Dancing Women: Female Bodies on Stage. *v.6 p.473*

Dancing Wu Li Masters: An Overview of the New
    Physics. *v.5 p.541*

Dandelion Wine. *v.2 p.63*

Dandies and Desert Saints: Styles of Victorian
    Masculinity. *v.2 p.173, p.190,v.6 p.477*

Dandil: Stories from Iranian Life. *v.6 p.672*

Daneshvar's Playhouse: A Collection of Stories. *v.6 p.670*

Danger and Beauty: Dangerous Music, Pet Food and Tropical
    Apparitions and New Writings. *v.6 p.103*

Danger in the Field: Ethics and Risk in Social Research. .*v.4 p.690*

Dangerous Border Crossers: Artist Talks Back. *v.6 p.492*

Dangerous Company: The Consulting Powerhouses and the
    Businesses They Save and Ruin. *v.4 p.65*

Dangerous Enthusiasm: William Blake and the Culture of
    Radicalism in the 1790s. *v.2 p.240*

Dangerous Liaisons: Blacks, Gays and the Struggle for
    Equality. *v.6 p.386*

Dangerous Men: The Sociology of Parole. *v.6 p.278*

Dangerous Pleasures: Prostitution and Modernity in
    Twentieth-Century Shanghai. *v.6 p.217*

Dangerous Schools: What We Can Do about the Physical and
    Emotional Abuse to Our Children. *v.4 p.284*

Dangerous Strait: The U.S.—Taiwan—China
    Crisis. *v.3 p.393, v.6 p.214*

The Dangerous Summer. *v.2 p.84*

Dangerous Women: Gender and Korean
    Nationalism. *v.6 p.112, p.135*

Daniel Boone: An American Life. *v.3 p.511*

Daniel Brush Gold Without Boundaries. *v.1 p.801, p.802*

Daniel Defoe: Ambition and Innovation. *v.2 p.245*

Daniel Defoe: His Life and Ideas. *v.2 p.246*

Daniel Defoe: His Life. *v.2 p.245*

Daniel Defoe. *v.2 p.246*

Daniel Dennett. *v.1 p.441*

Daniel Deronda. *v.2 p.287*

Daniel H. Burnham: Visionary Architect and Planner. .*v.6 p.715*

Daniel Webster. *v.3 p.415*

The Danish Girl. *v.6 p.396*

Danny Elfman's Batman: A Film Score Guide. *v.1 p.255*

Dante: A Life in Works. *v.2 p.704*

Dante Alighieri: His Life and Works. *v.2 p.705*

Dante Alighieri's Divine Comedy: Inferno, Commentary, Vol.
    2. . . . .*v.2 p.704*

Dante Alighieri's Divine Comedy: Inferno, Italian Text and
    Translation, Vol. 1. . . . .*v.2 p.703*

Dante Alighieri's Divine Comedy, Vol. 3: Purgatory. Italian Text
    and Verse Translation. *v.2 p.702*

Dante Alighieri's Divine Comedy, vol. 4: Purgatory.
    Commentary. *v.2 p.704*

Dante Alighieri's Divine Comedy, Vol. 5. Paradise: Italian Text
    with Verse Translation. *v.2 p.702*

Dante Alighieri's Divine Comedy, Vol. 6. Paradise: Notes and
    Commentary. *v.2 p.704*

Dante Alighieri. *v.2 p.704*

Dante: An Introduction to the Minor Works. *v.2 p.705*

Dante and His Circle: With the Italian Poets Preceding Him. a
    Collection of Lyrics. *v.2 p.304, p.700*

Dante and Philosophy. *v.2 p.704*

Dante: Contemporary Perspectives. *v.2 p.704*

Dante: De Vulgari Eloquentia. *v.2 p.448, p.449, p.702*

The Dante Encyclopedia. *v.2 p.705*

Dante Gabriel Rossetti: An Alien Victorian. *v.2 p.303*

Dante Gabriel Rossetti Revisited. *v.2 p.304*

Dante Gabriel Rossetti. *v.1 p.695*

Dante: Monarchia. *v.2 p.703*

Dante Now. *v.2 p.704*

Dante, Poet of the Desert: History and Allegory in the Divine
    Comedy. *v.2 p.705*

Dante: Poet of the Secular World. *v.2 p.703*

Dante: The Divine Comedy. *v.2 p.704, p.705*

Dante: The Poet, the Political Thinker, the Man. . . .*v.2 p.705*

Dante: The Poetics of Conversion. *v.2 p.704*

Dante's Divine Comedy: The Inferno. *v.2 p.704*

Dante's 'Divine Comedy'. *v.2 p.703, p.704*

Dante's II Convivio. *v.2 p.703*

Dante's Inferno. *v.2 p.703*

Dante's Italy and Other Essays. *v.3 p.199*

Dante's Lyric Poetry. *v.2 p.702*

Dante's Poets: Textuality and Truth in the Comedy. . .*v.2 p.703*

Dante's Vision and the Circle of Knowledge. *v.2 p.705*

Dante. *v.2 p.704, p.705,v.6 p.564*

Danwei: The Changing Chinese Workplace in Historical and
    Comparative Perspective. *v.6 p.194*

The Danzig Trilogy of Gunter Grass: A Study of the Tin Drum,
    Cat and Mouse, and Dog Years. *v.2 p.608, p.609*

Dao de Jing: The Book of the Way. *v.1 p.418*

Daoism and Chinese Culture. *v.1 p.539*

Daredevils of Sassoun: The Armenian National Epic. .*v.6 p.665*

Darfur: The Ambiguous Genocide. *v.4 p.653, v.6 p.59*

Daring to Be Bad: Radical Feminism in America,
    1967-1975. . . . .*v.6 p.427, p.433, p.453*

Daring to Find Our Names: The Search for Lesbigay Library
    History. *v.6 p.383*

A Daring Young Man: A Biography of William Saroyan. .*v.2 p.118*

The Daring Young Man on the Flying Trapeze. *v.2 p.118*

Dario Fo: Revolutionary Theatre. *v.2 p.724*

Dario Fo: Stage, Text and Tradition. *v.2 p.724*

Dark Back of Time. *v.2 p.661*

Dark Blue Suit: And Other Stories. *v.6 p.99*

The Dark Child. *v.2 p.542, p.543,v.6 p.28, p.29*

Dark Continent of Our Bodies: Black Feminism and the Politics
    of Respectability. *v.6 p.9, p.47*

The Dark Glass. *v.2 p.303*

Dark God of Eros: A William Everson Reader. *v.2 p.71*

Dark Horse: A Biography of Wendell Wilkie. *v.3 p.461*

Dark Humor and Social Satire in the Modern British Novel. *v.2 p.195*

Dark Lanterns: Secret Political Societies, Conspiracies and Treason Trials in the Civil War. *v.3 p.398, p.428*

Dark Laughter. *v.2 p.56, p.57*

Dark Lover: The Life and Death of Rudolph Valentino. .*v.6 p.418*

A Dark Night's Passing. *v.6 p.233*

Dark Paradise: A History of Opiate Addiction in America. *v.3 p.281, v.4 p.776, v.5 p.663*

Dark Passage. *v.2 p.80*

Dark Romance: Sexuality in the Horror Film. *v.6 p.318*

The Dark Side of Behaviour at Work: Understanding and Avoiding Employees Leaving, Thieving and Deceiving. *v.4 p.130*

The Dark Side of Democracy: Explaining Ethnic Cleansing. *v.4 p.660, p.715*

The Dark Side of Families: Current Family Violence Research. *v.6 p.464, p.469*

The Dark Side of Paradise: Political Violence in Bali. *v.6 p.175, p.177*

Dark Side of the Dream: Australian Literature and the Postcolonial Mind. *v.2 p.741*

Dark Sweat, White Gold: California Farm Workers, Cotton, and the New Deal. *v.6 p.525*

Dark Symphony. *v.2 p.19*

Dark Thoughts: Philosophic Reflections on Cinematic Horror. *v.6 p.319*

Dark Victory: America's Second War Against Iraq. *v.4 p.561, v.6 p.604*

The Darkening Glass. *v.2 p.305*

The Darker Side of Genius: Richard Wagner's Anti-Semitism. *v.1 p.199, p.300, p.365, v.3 p.178*

Darkling I Listen: Robert E. Lee's Army of Northern Virginia. *v.2 p.296*

The Darkness and the Light: Poems. *v.2 p.146*

The Darkness Around Us Is Deep: Selected Poems of William Stafford. *v.2 p.117*

Darkness at Noon. *v.3 p.226*

Darsan: Seeing the Divine Image in India. .*v.1 p.535, p.539, p.540*

Dartmouth Atlas of Health Care in the United States. .*v.5 p.513*

Darwin and Design: Does Evolution Have a Purpose? .*v.5 p.203*

Darwin and the Barnacle: The Story of the One Tiny Creature and History's Most Spectacular Scientific Breakthrough. *v.5 p.231*

Darwin and the Novelists: Patterns of Science in Victorian Fiction. *v.2 p.175, p.176, p.191*

Darwin in the Genome: Molecular Strategies in Biological Evolution. *v.5 p.145, p.202*

Darwin on Trial. *v.5 p.203*

The Darwin Wars: How Stupid Genes Became Selfish Gods. *v.5 p.78, p.202*

The Darwin Wars: The Scientific Battle for the Soul of Man. *v.5 p.78, p.202*

Darwinian Dynamics: Evolutionary Transitions in Fitness and Individuality. *v.5 p.203*

Darwinian Myths: The Legends and Misuses of a Theory. *v.5 p.78, p.202*

The Darwinian Paradigm: Essays on Its History, Philosophy and Religious Implications. *v.5 p.203, p.226*

The Darwinian Revolution: Science Red in Tooth and Claw. *v.5 p.203, p.204*

Darwinism and the Study of Society: A Centenary Symposium. *v.3 p.48*

Darwinism Evolving: Systems Dynamics and the Genealogy of Natural Selection. *v.5 p.202*

Darwinism's Struggle for Survival: Heredity and the Hypothesis of Natural Selection. *v.5 p.203*

Darwinism. *v.5 p.202*

Darwin's Athletes: How Sport has Damaged Black America and Preserved the Myth of Race. *v.4 p.802, p.816, p.832*

Darwin's Black Box: The Biochemical Challenge to Evolution. *v.5 p.111, p.199, p.202*

Darwin's Blind Spot: Evolution Beyond Natural Selection. *v.5 p.204*

Darwin's Cathedral: Evolution, Religion, and the Nature of Society. *v.4 p.720*

Darwin's Dangerous Idea: Evolution and the Meanings of Life. *v.1 p.516, v.5 p.202*

Darwin's Ghost: The Origin of the Species Updated. .*v.5 p.203*

Darwin's Leap of Faith: Exposing the False Religion of Evolution. *v.5 p.77, p.202*

Darwin's Metaphor: Nature's Place in Victorian Culture. *v.3 p.117*

Darwin's Plots: Evolutionary Narrative in Darwin, George Eliot and Nineteenth-Century Fiction. *v.2 p.286, v.6 p.759*

Darwin's Spectre: Evolutionary Biology in the Modern World. *v.5 p.203*

Dashiell Hammett: Crime Stories and Other Writings. .*v.2 p.80*

Dashiell Hammett: Five Complete Novels. *v.2 p.80*

The Dastgah Concept in Persian Music. *v.1 p.287*

Dat: Tackling Life and the NFL. *v.4 p.834, p.859*

☐ Data & Property Calculation Websites. *v.5 p.280*

Data Analysis and Classification for Bioinformatics. *v.5 p.106, p.108, p.110*

Data Analysis and Visualization in Genomics and Proteomics. *v.5 p.93, p.104, p.105, p.108, p.115, p.126*

Data Analysis in Molecular Biology and Evolution. *v.5 p.106, p.200*

Data Analysis Methods in Physical Oceanography. . .*v.5 p.430*

Data Analysis: Statistical and Computational Methods for Scientists and Engineers. *v.5 p.562*

Data Analysis Techniques for High-Energy Physics. .*v.5 p.562*

Data Analysis Tools for DNA Microarrays. *v.5 p.121*

Data and Computer Communications. *v.4 p.422, v.5 p.727*

Data Communications and Networking. *v.5 p.726*

Data Communications Networking. *v.5 p.727*

☐ Data Compilation of Pure Compound Properties Database. *v.5 p.275*

Data Compilation Tables of Properties of Pure Compounds. *v.5 p.280*

Data Compression: The Complete Reference. . .*v.5 p.335, p.348*

Data Driven Differentiation in the Standards-Based Classroom. *v.4 p.349*

The Data Game: Controversies in Social Science Statistics. *v.4 p.690*

Data, Instruments and Theory: A Dialectical Approach to Understanding Science. *v.5 p.406*

Data Mining: Concepts and Techniques. *v.5 p.337*

Data Mining in Bioinformatics. *v.5 p.98*

Data Reduction and Error Analysis for the Physical Sciences. *v.5 p.64, p.562*

Data Wise: A Step-by-Step Guide to Using Assessment Results to Improve Teaching and Learning. *v.5 p.600*

Database Annotation in Molecular Biology: Principles and Practice. *v.5 p.128*

Database Design for Smarties: Using UML for Data Modeling. *v.5 p.337*

Database Modeling and Design. *v.5 p.337*

Database Nation: The Death of Privacy in the 21st Century. *v.4 p.515*

Database of African-American Poetry, 1760-1900. . .*v.2 p.22*

Database of Gas Explosion Hazards. *v.5 p.320*

A Daughter of Han: The Autobiography of a Chinese Working Woman. *v.6 p.203, p.217*

A Daughter of Isis: the Autobiography of Nawal el Saadawi. *v.6 p.657*

Daughter of Persia: A Woman's Journey from Her Father's Harem Through the Islamic Revolution. *v.6 p.631*

A Daughter of the Middle Border. *v.2 p.39*

Daughters of Abraham: Feminist Thought in Judaism, Christianity and Islam. *v.1 p.558*

Daughters of Isis: Women of Ancient Egypt. *v.6 p.57*

Daughters of Joy, Sisters of Misery: Prostitutes in the American West, 1865-90. . . . .*v.4 p.747*

Daughters of the Dust: The Making of an African Woman's Film. *v.6 p.24, 42*

Daughters of the Great Depression: Women, Work, and Fiction in the American 1930s. *v.2 p.8*

Daughters of Thunder: Black Women Preachers and Their Sermons, 1850-1979. . . . .*v.6 p.35, p.42*

Daughters of Tunis: Women, Family, and Networks in a Muslim City. *v.4 p.38, v.6 p.641*

The Daughter's Seduction: Feminism and Psychoanalysis. *v.2 p.571*

Daumier: 1808-1879. . . . .*v.3 p.153*

Dave Pelz's Short Game Bible: Master the Finesse Swing and Lower Your Score. *v.4 p.861*

Davenport's Art Reference and Price Guide 2006/2007 Book. *v.1 p.708, p.709*

David, and Other Poems. *v.2 p.733*

David Copperfield. by Charles Dickens. (Boz.) with ... illustrations from designs by H. K. Browne. *v.2 p.282, p.283*

David Copperfield. *v.2 p.282*

David Crockett: The Man and the Legend. *v.3 p.511*

David d'Angers: Sculptural Communication in the Age of Romanticism. *v.1 p.779*

David Duke and the Politics of Race in the South. .*v.3 p.507*

David Garrick: A Critical Biography. . *v.1 p.104, p.141, p.153*

David Garrick, Director. *v.1 p.99, p.152*

David Glasgow Farragut. *v.3 p.425*

David Hackett Souter: Traditional Republican on the Rehnquist Court. *v.4 p.540*

David Hare: Fanshen; A Map of the World; Saigonp; The Bay at Nice; The Secret Rapture. *v.1 p.100*

David Hare: Slag, Teeth 'n' Smiles, Knuckle, Licking Hitler, Plenty. *v.1 p.100*

David Harum. *v.2 p.53*

David Harvey: A Critical Reader. *v.6 p.709, p.710*

David Hockney. *v.1 p.698*

David Hume: An Introduction to His Philosophical System. *v.1 p.452*

David Kimhi's Hebrew Grammar: Mikhlol: Systematically Presented and Critically Annotated. *v.6 p.645*

David Kopay Story. *v.6 p.384*

David Livingstone: The Dark Interior. *v.6 p.74*

David Malouf: Johnno, Short Stories, Poems, Essays and Interviews. *v.2 p.747*

David Walker's Appeal: To the Coloured Citizens of the World but in Particular, and Very Expressly, to Those of the United States of America. *v.6 p.9, p.37*

David Wojnarowicz: Memories That Smell Like Gasoline. *v.6 p.408*

David. *v.1 p.743*

Davis and Lee at War. *v.4 p.522*

The Dawes Act and the Allotment of Indian Lands. . .*v.6 p.696*

Dawkins vs. Gould: Survival of the Fittest. *v.5 p.197*

Dawn and the Darkest Hour: A Study of Aldous Huxley. *v.2 p.355*

The Dawn of Canadian History: A Chronicle of Aboriginal Canada and the Coming of the White Man. *v.4 p.379, v.6 p.685*

The Dawn of Modern Geography: A History of Exploration and Geographical Science. *v.4 p.377*

Dawn of Modern Science: From the Arabs to Leonardo Da Vinci. *v.5 p.390*

The Dawn of the Floating World: Early Ukiyo-E Treasures from the Museum of Fine Arts, Boston. *v.1 p.754*

Dawn of the Golden Age: Northern Netherlandish Art, 1580-1620. . . . .*v.1 p.685, p.686*

The Dawn of the Roman Empire, Bks. 31-40. . . . .*v.2 p.436*

Dawn Powell: A Biography. *v.2 p.112, p.113*

Dawn Powell: Novels 1930-1942. . . . .*v.2 p.113*

Dawn Powell: Novels 1944-1962. . . . .*v.2 p.113*

Dawn Powell. *v.2 p.113*

A Day for the Hunter, a Day for the Prey: Popular Music and Power in Haiti. *v.1 p.291*

The Day I Was Older: Writings on the Poetry of Donald Hall. *v.2 p.82*

A Day in a Medieval City. *v.6 p.577*

A Day in the Country and Other Stories. *v.2 p.497*

The Day of Maysalun: A Page from the Modern History of the Arabs. *v.6 p.591*

The Day of the Carpetbagger: Republican Reconstruction in Mississippi. *v.3 p.504, p.505*

The Day the Presses Stopped: A History of the Pentagon Papers Case. *v.4 p.439*

Dayananda Sarasvati: His Life and Ideas. *v.1 p.536*

Daybreak of Freedom: The Montgomery Bus Boycott. .*v.3 p.504*

Daydreams and Nightmares: Czech Communist and
Ex-Communist Literature 1917-1987. . . . .*v.2 p.782*

Daylight in Nightclub Inferno : Czech Fiction from the
Post-Kundera generation. *v.2 p.781*

Daylighting Performance and Design. *v.1 p.803*

Days of Anger. *v.2 p.530*

Days of Dust. *v.6 p.658*

Days of H. L. Mencken: Three Volumes in One: Happy Days,
Newspaper Days, and Heathen Days. *v.2 p.97*

The Days of Henry Thoreau: A Biography. *v.2 p.52*

Days of Hope: Race and Democracy in the New Deal. .*v.3 p.444*

Days of Sadness, Years of Triumph: The American People,
1939-1945. . . . .*v.3 p.478*

The Days of the Consuls. *v.2 p.819*

Days on Earth: The Dance of Doris Humphrey. . . .*v.1 p.12*

Days with Ulanova. *v.1 p.9*

The Day's Work. *v.2 p.297*

Dayspring in Darkness: Sacrament in Hopkins. . . .*v.2 p.294*

The Day-Star of Liberty: William Hazlitt's Radical
Style. *v.2 p.293*

The Days. *v.6 p.659, p.660*

Dazzled. *v.6 p.102*

DC Confidential: The Controversial Memoirs of Britain's
Ambassador at the Time of 9/11 and the Iraq
War. *v.4 p.645, p.646*

The DC Guide to Writing Comics. *v.4 p.140*

DDT: Scientists, Citizens, and Public Policy. . .*v.5 p.9, p.354*

Los De Abajo: Novela de la Revolucion Mexicana. . .*v.2 p.667*

De Anima, Bks. II-III. *v.1 p.426*

De Anima. *v.2 p.408*

De Arte Poetica Liber. *v.2 p.408*

De Chateaubriand à Baudelaire, 1820-1869. . . . .*v.2 p.459*

De Gaulle: The Rebel, 1890-1944. . . . .*v.3 p.155*

De Gaulle: The Ruler 1945-1970, Vol. II. *v.3 p.157*

De Generatione et Corruptione. *v.5 p.399*

De Imperatoribus Romanis. *v.3 p.27, p.29*

De Kooning: An American Master. *v.1 p.700*

De l'Encyclopédie aux Méditations. *v.2 p.458*

De los Otros: Intimacy and Homosexuality among Mexican
Men. *v.6 p.421*

De Miseria Condicionis Humane. *v.1 p.643*

De Montaigne à Corneille. *v.2 p.458*

De Nerval: Selected Writings. *v.2 p.492*

De Officiis. *v.2 p.433*

De Profundis. *v.2 p.321, p.322*

De Re Metallica. *v.5 p.731*

De Rerum Natura: The Latin Text of Lucretius. . . .*v.2 p.437*

De Rerum Natura: The Poem of Nature. *v.2 p.437*

De Rerum Natura: Titi Lucreti Cari de Rerum Natura: Libri
Sex. *v.2 p.437*

De Valera: The Man and the Myths. *v.3 p.138*

De Valera. *v.3 p.134, p.138*

De Villon à Ronsard : XVe-XVIe siècles. *v.2 p.457*

De Zola à Guillaume Apollinaire, 1869-1920. . . . .*v.2 p.457*

The Dead and Their Possessions: Repatriation in Principle,
Policy, and Practice. *v.4 p.47*

Dead End Kids: Gang Girls and the Boys They
Know. *v.4 p.714, v.6 p.464, p.466*

The Dead Father. *v.2 p.140*

Dead Man Walking. *v.6 p.247*

Dead Right: The End of the Conservativism of Hope and the
Rise of the Conservativism of Fear. *v.3 p.440*

The Dead Sea Scrolls Today. *v.1 p.619, p.620*

The Dead Secret. A Novel. *v.2 p.280*

Dead Sociologists' Society. *v.4 p.675*

Dead Souls. *v.2 p.803*

Deadeye Dick. *v.2 p.158*

Deadliest Enemies: Law and Making the Race Relations on and
off Rosebud Reservation. *v.4 p.33*

Deadlock or Decision: The U. S. Senate and the Rise of
National Politics. *v.4 p.530*

Deadly Arsenals: Nuclear, Biological and Chemical
Threats. *v.4 p.655*

The Deadly Bet: LBJ, Vietnam, and the 1968 Election. .*v.3 p.474*

Deadly Connections: States that Sponsor Terrorism. . .*v.4 p.658*

Deadly Consequences. *v.4 p.775*

Deadly Embrace: Hitler, Stalin and the Nazi-Soviet Pact,
1939-1941. . . . .*v.3 p.226*

Deadly Encounters: Two Victorian Sensations. . . .*v.6 p.744*

The Deadly Ethnic Riot. *v.4 p.713*

Deadly Gambits: The Reagan Administration and the Stalemate
in Nuclear Arms Control. *v.4 p.562, p.657*

Deaf in America: Voices from a Culture. *v.4 p.700*

Deaf Sport: The Impact of Sports Within the Deaf
Community. *v.4 p.830*

The Deaf Way: Perspectives from the International Conference
on Deaf Culture. *v.4 p.709*

Deaf World: A Historical Reader and Primary
Sourcebook. *v.4 p.699*

The Deal Decade: What Takeovers and Leveraged Buyouts
Mean for Corporate Governance. *v.4 p.84*

Dealing Crack: The Social World of Streetcorner
Selling. *v.6 p.253*

Dealing in Diversity: America's Market for Nature
Conservation. *v.5 p.179*

Dealing with Alcohol: Indigenous Usage in Australia, New
Zealand and Canada. *v.4 p.46, v.5 p.664*

Dealing with Difference: Opening Dialogue about Lesbian, Gay
and Straight Issues. *v.6 p.385*

Dealing with Difficult People: How to Deal with Nasty
Customers, Demanding Bosses and Annoying
Co-Workers. *v.4 p.130*

Dealing with Difficult People. *v.4 p.73*

Dealing with Financial
Risk. *v.4 p.90, p.93, p.97, p.100, p.102, p.103*

Dealing with Terrorism. *v.4 p.659*

Dealing with the Visual: Art History, Aesthetics and Visual
Culture. *v.1 p.702*

Deals of the Century: Wall Street, Mergers, and the Making of
Modern America. *v.4 p.84, p.89, p.155*

Dean Acheson and the Making of U. S. Foreign Policy. .*v.3 p.456*

Dean Acheson: The Cold War Years, 1953-71. . . . .*v.3 p.456*

Dean LeBaron's Treasury of Investment Wisdom: 30 Great
Investing Minds. *v.4 p.95*

Dean's Handbook of Organic Chemistry. *v.5 p.290*

Dear Miye: Letters Home from Japan,
1939-1946. . . . .*v.6 p.95, p.114, p.115, p.133*

Dear Mr. Darwin: Letters on the Evolution of Life and Human
Nature. *v.5 p.202, p.203*

Dear Mr. Kawabata. *v.6 p.656*

Dear Rafe/Mi Querido Rafa. *v.6 p.500*

Dear Reader: The Conscripted Audience in Nineteenth-Century
British Fiction. *v.2 p.177, p.193,v.6 p.739, p.757*

Dear Sisters: Dispatches from the Women's Liberation
Movement. *v.6 p.433, p.440*

Dearest Chums and Partners: Joel Chandler Harris's Letters to
His Children: A Domestic Biography. *v.2 p.40*

Death and Burial in Ancient Egypt. *v.6 p.57*

Death and Deliverance: "Euthansasia" in Germany c.
1900-1945. . . . .*v.3 p.171*

Death and Life in the Tenth Century. *v.6 p.557*

Death and Life of Dith Pran. *v.6 p.170*

The Death and Life of Great American Cities. . . .*v.6 p.718*

The Death and Rebirth of the Seneca. *v.4 p.37, v.6 p.684, p.704*

Death and Renewal: Sociological Studies in Roman
History. *v.4 p.501*

Death and Salvation in Ancient Egypt. *v.3 p.8*

Death and the Dervish. *v.2 p.812*

Death and the Future Life in Victorian Literature and
Theology. *v.6 p.753, p.759, p.764*

Death and the King's Horseman. *v.2 p.758*

Death and the Right Hand. *v.4 p.24*

Death As a Way of Life: Israel Ten Years after Oslo. .*v.6 p.614*

Death Before Dying: The Sufi Poems of Sultan Bahu. .*v.6 p.153*

Death by a Thousand Cuts: The Fight over Taxing Inherited
Wealth. *v.4 p.107*

Death, Dissection and the Destitute. *v.3 p.115, p.124*

Death in Beirut. *v.6 p.658*

Death in Danzig. *v.2 p.789*

A Death in Texas: A Story of Race, Murder and a Small Town's
Struggle for Redemption. *v.6 p.257*

Death in the Afternoon. *v.2 p.84*

Death in the Everglades: The Murder of Guy Bradley, America's
First Martyr to Environmentalism. *v.6 p.295, p.296*

Death in the Woods and Other Stories. *v.2 p.57*

Death in Troy. *v.6 p.667*

Death in Venice. *v.6 p.397*

Death Is a Festival: Funeral Rites and Rebellion in
Nineteenth-Century Brazil. *v.3 p.265, p.342*

Death of a Lake. *v.2 p.749*

Death of a Nation: American Culture and the End of
Exceptionalism. *v.3 p.443*

Death of a Rat: Understandings and Appreciations of
Science. *v.5 p.249*

Death of a Red Heroine: An Inspector Chen
Investigation. *v.6 p.207, p.213*

Death of a River Guide. *v.2 p.745*

The Death of a Thousand Cuts: Corporate Campaigns and the
Attack on the Corporation. *v.4 p.52, p.54, p.145*

The Death of Adam: Evolution and Its Impact on Western
Thought. *v.5 p.79, p.192*

The Death of Character: Moral Education in an Age Without
Good or Evil. *v.4 p.306*

Death of Christopher Marlowe. *v.2 p.221*

The Death of Common Sense: How Law Is Suffocating
America. *v.4 p.441*

Death of Dignity: Angola's Civil War. *v.6 p.75*

The Death of God and the Meaning of Life. *v.1 p.509*

Death of Innocence: The Story of the Hate Crime That Changed
America. *v.6 p.8, p.40*

The Death of Nature: Women, Ecology, and the Scientific
Revolution. *v.5 p.398*

The Death of Our Planet's Species: A Challenge to Ecology and
Ethics. *v.5 p.358, p.369*

The Death of Outrage: Bill Clinton and the Assault on American
Ideals. *v.3 p.465*

The Death of Ramon Gonzalez: The Modern Agricultural
Dilemma. *v.3 p.270*

The Death of Rhythm and Blues. *v.1 p.269*

The Death of the Heart. *v.2 p.334*

The Death of the Messiah: From Gethsemane to the Grave: A
Commentary on the Passion Narratives in the Four
Gospels. *v.1 p.628*

The Death of Tragedy. *v.1 p.89*

The Death of Virgil. *v.2 p.603*

The Death of Vishnu: A Novel. *v.2 p.766*

The Death of White Sociology. *v.4 p.683, v.6 p.39*

The Death of Woman Wang. *v.6 p.203, p.217*

Death on the Fourth of July: The Story of a Killing, a Trial, and
Hate Crime in America. *v.6 p.252, p.253*

Death on the Installment Plan. *v.2 p.515*

Death Penalties: The Supreme Court's Obstacle Course. .*v.4 p.471*

The Death Penalty: An American History. *v.6 p.247*

Death Penalty Cases. *v.6 p.268*

The Death Penalty in America: Current Controversies. .*v.4 p.471*

Death Sentence. *v.2 p.510*

Death, Sex, and Fertility: Population Regulation in Pre-Industrial
and Developing Societies. *v.4 p.736, p.737*

Death Squad: The Anthropology of State Terror. .*v.4 p.34, p.35*

Death to the Death of Poetry: Essays, Reviews, Notes,
Interviews. *v.2 p.82*

Death Without Weeping: The Violence of Everyday Life in
Brazil. *v.3 p.280, v.4 p.46*

The Deathly Embrace: Orientalism and Asian American
Identity. *v.6 p.97*

Deathquest II: An Introduction to the Theory and Practice of
Capital Punishment in the United States. *v.6 p.247*

Deathtraps: The Postmodern Comedy Thriller. . .*v.1 p.86, p.89*

La Debacle. *v.2 p.505*

The Debate on the English
Revolution. *v.3 p.88, p.104, p.121, p.122*

The Debate on the French Revolution, 1789-1800. . . .*v.3 p.91*

Debates about Canada's Future, 1868-1896. . . . . . .*v.3 p.540*

Debating Design: From Darwin to DNA. *v.5 p.202*

Debating Human Kind's Place in Nature; 1860-2000: The Nature of Paleoanthropology. *v.4 p.14*

Debating Sexual Correctness: Pornography, Sexual Harassment, Date Rape and the Politics of Sexual Equality. . . .*v.6 p.471*

Debating the Death Penalty: Should America Have Capital Punishment? The Experts on Both Sides Make Their Best Case. *v.4 p.567*

Debating the Past: Music, Memory, and Identity in the Andes. *v.1 p.294*

The Debris of Ham: Ethnicity, Regionalism, and the 1994 Rwandan Genocide. *v.4 p.654*

Debt Management: A Practitioner's Guide. *v.4 p.91*

The Debt to Pleasure. *v.2 p.361*

The Debtors: Whites Respond to the Call for Black Reparations. *v.6 p.20, p.30*

Debt's Dominion: A History of Bankruptcy Law in America. *v.4 p.97, p.110, p.444*

Debunking the Middle-Class Myth: Why Diverse Schools Are Good for All Kids. *v.4 p.309*

Debussy and His World. *v.1 p.213, p.320*

Debussy in Proportion: A Musical Analysis. . .*v.1 p.216, p.320*

Debussy: La Mer. *v.1 p.226, p.243, p.321*

Debussy Remembered. *v.1 p.220, p.320*

Debussy's Iberia. *v.1 p.210, p.320*

DEC Recommended Practices: A Comprehensive Guide for Practical Application. *v.4 p.316, p.317*

Decade of Betrayal: Mexican Repatriation in the 1930s. *v.6 p.528, p.535*

The Decade of Destruction Series. . .*v.5 p.353, p.357, p.370*

The Decade of Destruction: The Crusade to Save the Amazon Rain Forest. *v.5 p.40, p.353, p.356, p.363, p.364*

The Decadent Reader: Fiction, Fantasy, and Perversion from Fin-de-Siècle France. *v.2 p.494*

Decadent Vision in Leopoldo Alas. *v.2 p.655*

The Decameron, Its Sources and Analogues. *v.2 p.702*

Decameron: The John Payne Translation, Set. *v.2 p.701*

Decameron. *v.2 p.701*

The Decameron. *v.2 p.701*

Decameron. *v.3 p.69*

The Decanter: An Illustrated History 1650-1950. . . .*v.1 p.810*

The Decapitated Chicken and Other Stories. *v.2 p.687*

The Decay of the Angel. *v.6 p.231*

Deceit, Desire, and the Novel: Self and Other in Literary Structure. *v.2 p.462, p.578*

Decentralization, Democratic Governance, and Civil Society in Comparative Perspective: Africa, Asia, and Latin America. *v.4 p.585, p.586, p.613*

Decentralizing the State: Elections, Parties, and Local Power in the Andes. *v.4 p.582*

The Deception. *v.2 p.616*

Deciding to Decide: Agenda Setting in the United States Supreme Court. *v.4 p.466, p.538*

Deciding to Intervene: The Reagan Doctrine and American Foreign Policy. *v.3 p.479, p.480*

Deciding to Leave: The Politics of Retirement from the United States Supreme Court. *v.4 p.540*

Decision Analysis: An Integrated Approach. *v.4 p.83*

Decision Analysis, Game Theory, and Information. . . .*v.4 p.83*

Decision and Organization. *v.4 p.269*

Decision at Sea: Five Naval Battles That Shaped American History. *v.3 p.384*

Decision: How the Supreme Court Decides Cases. *v.4 p.466, p.539*

Decision Making Using Game Theory: An Introduction for Managers. *v.4 p.83*

Decisions at Yalta: An Appraisal of Summit Diplomacy. *v.4 p.565, p.566*

🄴 Decisions, Uncertainty, and the Brain: The Science of Neuroeconomics. *v.4 p.272*

Declaration of Independence: A Study in the History of Political Ideas. *v.4 p.518*

The Declaration of Independent Filmmaking: An Insider's Guide to Making Movies Outside of Hollywood. *v.6 p.347*

The Declaration of Rights, 1689. . . . .*v.3 p.107*

The Declaration of Rights, Sixteen Eighty-Nine. . . .*v.3 p.107*

Declaration on the Relation of the Church to Non-Christian Religions. *v.1 p.571*

The Declared Enemy: Texts and Interviews. *v.2 p.518*

The Decline and Fall of the British Aristocracy. *v.3 p.110, p.111, p.130, v.6 p.744*

The Decline and Fall of the Habsburg Empire, 1815-1918. . . . .*v.3 p.182*

The Decline and Fall of the Income Tax: How to Make Sense of the American Tax Mess and the Flat-Tax Cures That Are Supposed to Fix It. *v.4 p.107*

The Decline and Fall of the Supreme Court: Living Out the Nightmare of the Federalists. *v.4 p.470*

Decline and Fall. *v.2 p.388*

Decline and Growth in English Towns, 1400-1640. . . .*v.3 p.99*

Decline and Obsolescence of Logical Empiricism: Carnap vs. Quine and the Critics. *v.1 p.512*

Decline in History: The European Experience. *v.3 p.71*

Decline of American Liberalism. *v.3 p.384*

The Decline of Constitutional Democracy in Indonesia. *v.6 p.174*

The Decline of Medieval Hellenism in Asia Minor and the Process of Islamization from the Eleventh Through the Fifteenth Century. *v.3 p.194, v.6 p.588*

The Decline of Politics: The Conservatives and the Party System, 1901-1920. . . . .*v.4 p.588*

The Decline of Power, Nineteen Fifteen to Nineteen Sixty-Four. *v.3 p.90, p.91*

The Decline of the Californios: A Social History of the Spanish-Speaking Californians, 1846-1890. . . . .*v.6 p.535*

The Decline of the Copper Industry in Chile and the Entrance of North American Capital, 1870 to 1916. . . . . . .*v.3 p.351*

The Decline of the German Mandarins: The German Academic Community, 1890-1933. . . . .*v.3 p.179, v.4 p.336*

The Decline of the Progressive Movement in Wisconsin, 1890-1920. . . . .*v.3 p.517*

The Decline of Urban Politics: Political Theory and the Crisis of the Local State. *v.6 p.723*

Declining by Degrees: Higher Education at Risk. . . .*v.4 p.331*

The Declining Economic Status of Black Children. .*v.6 p.20, p.40*

The Declining Significance of Race: Blacks and Changing
American Institutions. *v.4 p.730, p.731*

Decoding the Ethics Code: A Practical Guide for
Psychologists. *v.5 p.674*

The Decolonial Imaginary: Writing Chicanas into
History. *v.6 p.546*

ⓔ Decolonial Voices: Chicana and Chicano Cultural Studies in
the 21st Century. *v.6 p.487, p.493, p.494*

Decolonisation and the British Empire, 1775-1997. . .*v.4 p.583*

Decolonising the Mind: The Politics of Language in African
Literature. *v.2 p.759*

Decolonization and African Independence: The Transfers of
Power 1960-1980. . . . .*v.4 p.582, p.583,v.6 p.54*

Decolonization in Africa. *v.4 p.583, p.584,v.6 p.53*

The Decolonization of Portuguese Africa: Metropolitan
Revolution and the Dissolution of Empire. .*v.4 p.584, v.6 p.56*

Decolonization since 1945: Collapse of European Overseas
Empires. *v.4 p.583*

Decolonizing Anthropology: Moving Further Toward an
Anthropology of Liberation. *v.4 p.27*

Deconstructing Public Relations: Public Relations
Criticism. *v.4 p.429*

Deconstruction and Criticism. *v.2 p.566, p.570*

Deconstruction in a Nutshell: A Conversation with Jacques
Derrida. *v.1 p.512*

Decorative Art, 1950's. *v.1 p.799*

Decorative Art, 1960's. *v.1 p.799*

Decorative Art 1970s. *v.1 p.799*

Decorative Arts 1900s-1910s. *v.1 p.799*

Decorative Arts, 1920s. *v.1 p.799*

Decorative Arts, 1930s-1940s. *v.1 p.799*

Decrees of the Ecumenical Councils: From Nicea I to Vatican
II. *v.1 p.571, v.3 p.58*

✦ Dective and Mystery Fiction: An International Bibliography
of Secondary Sources. *v.2 p.579*

Dedans. *v.2 p.529*

The Deeds of Frederick Barbarossa. *v.3 p.163*

The Deeds of God in Rddhipur. *v.1 p.535*

Deep down in the Jungle: Negro Narrative Folklore from the
Streets of Philadelphia. *v.2 p.16*

Deep Ecology and World Religions: New Essays on Sacred
Ground. *v.6 p.288*

Deep River Talk: Collected Poems. *v.2 p.749*

Deep Rivers. *v.3 p.328*

Deep South: A Social Anthropological Study of Caste and
Class. *v.4 p.701, p.702*

Deep Symbols: Their Postmodern Effacement and
Reclamation. *v.1 p.635*

Deep Time: Cladistics, the Revolution in
Evolution. *v.5 p.201, p.205*

Deepening Democracy: Global Governance and Political Reform
in Latin America. *v.4 p.584, p.640*

Deepening Democracy: Institutional Innovations in Empowered
Participatory Governance, Vol. 4. . . . .*v.4 p.504*

Deepening Fiction: A Practical Guide for Intermediate and
Advanced Writers. *v.2 p.579*

The Deeper Dimension of Yoga: Theory and Practice. .*v.1 p.475*

Deeper Reading: Comprehending Challenging Texts,
4-12. . . . .*v.4 p.363*

Deeply into the Bone: Re-Inventing Rites of Passage. .*v.1 p.530*

Deeps of Deliverance. *v.2 p.623*

The Deerslayer; or, The First War-Path: A Tale. *v.2 p.35*

Def Jam, Inc.: Russell Simmons, Rick Rubin, and the Rise of
Def Jam Records. *v.1 p.384*

The Defeat of the German U-Boats: The Battle of the
Atlantic. *v.3 p.81*

Defeated Flesh: Medicine, Society and the Birth of Modern
France. *v.3 p.155*

Defeating Darwinism by Opening Minds. *v.5 p.203*

The Defence of Guenevere, and Other Poems. *v.2 p.301*

The Defence of Lawino. *v.2 p.757*

Defence of Socrates, Euthyphro, Crito. *v.1 p.422, p.423*

Defence of Usury. *v.4 p.194*

Defenders of the Holy Land: Relations Between the Latin East
and the West, 1119-1187. . . . .*v.3 p.64*

Defending Evolution in the Classroom: A Guide to the
Creation/Evolution Controversy. *v.5 p.202, p.244*

Defending Illusions: Federal Protection of Ecosystems. .*v.5 p.179*

Defending Mother Earth: Native American Perspectives on
Environmental Justice. *v.6 p.681*

Defending Pornography. *v.4 p.748, p.749,v.6 p.471*

Defending the Land of the Jaguar: A History of Conservation in
Mexico. *v.3 p.270*

A Defense of Abortion. *v.1 p.485, v.4 p.775*

The Defense of Community in Peru's Central Highlands:
Peasant Struggle and Capitalist Transition,
1860-1940. . . . .*v.3 p.330*

The Defense of Gracchus Babeuf. *v.3 p.151*

A Defense of Poetry: Reflections on the Occasion of
Writing. *v.2 p.180*

Defensible Policies: Developing, Writing and Implementing
Valid Policies for Problem Oriented Policing. . . .*v.6 p.265*

Deference and Defiance in Monterrey: Workers, Paternalism,
and Revolution in Mexico, 1890-1950. . . . . . .*v.3 p.295*

Deferrals of Domain: Contemporary Women Novelists and the
State. *v.2 p.343*

Defiant Children: A Clinician's Manual for Assessment and
Parent Training. *v.5 p.662*

Defining America Through Immigration Policy. *v.4 p.571*

Defining Americans: The Presidency and National
Identity. *v.3 p.370*

Defining British Citizenship: Empire Commonwealth and
Modern Britain. *v.4 p.605, p.667*

Defining Cult Movies: The Cultural Politics of Oppositional
Tastes. *v.6 p.313, p.314*

Defining Germany: The 1848 Frankfurt Parliamentarians and
National Identity. *v.3 p.168*

The Defining Moment: The Great Depression and the American
Economy in the Twentieth Century. *v.4 p.213*

Defining Moments: When Managers Must Choose Between
Right and Right. *v.4 p.145*

Defining Music Therapy. *v.1 p.406*

Defining Nations:Iimmigrants and Citizens in Early Modern Spain and Spanish America. *v.3 p.239*

Defining Russia Musically: Historical and Hermeneutical Essays. *v.1 p.247, v.3 p.210, p.211*

Defining Russian Federalism. *v.4 p.598*

Defining the Family: Law, Technology, and Reproduction in an Uneasy Age. *v.4 p.448*

Defining the Victorian Nation: Class, Race, Gender and the British Reform Act of 1867. . . . .*v.6 p.758*

Definitions in Political Economy: Preceded by an Inquiry into the Rules Which Ought to Guide Political Economists in the Definition and Use of Their Terms. *v.4 p.218*

Definition. *v.1 p.494*

The Definitive Journals of Lewis and Clark, Vol. 7. .*v.3 p.520*

Deforestation and Land Use in the Amazon. *v.5 p.40*

Deforesting the Earth: From Prehistory to Global Crisis. *v.5 p.40, v.6 p.296, p.301*

Deformation and Fracture Behavior of Polymers. .*v.5 p.688, p.689*

Deformation and Fracture Mechanics of Engineering Materials. *v.5 p.689*

The Degaev Affair: Terror and Treason in Tsarist Russia. .*v.4 p.661*

Degas and the Dance. *v.1 p.23, p.45*

Degas Dancers. *v.1 p.45*

Degas Pastels. *v.1 p.722*

Degas's Complete Sculpture: A Catalogue Raisonné. .*v.1 p.781*

Degas. *v.1 p.695*

DeGowin's Diagnostic Examination. *v.5 p.520, p.521*

The Degradation of the Academic Dogma. . . .*v.4 p.290, p.332*

Degrees of Control: A Sociology of Educational Expansion and Occupational Credentialism. *v.4 p.295*

Degrees of Freedom: Louisiana and Cuba after Slavery. .*v.3 p.280*

Degrees. *v.2 p.511*

The Dehumanization of Art: And Other Essays on Art, Culture, and Literature. *v.1 p.481*

The Deindustrialization of America : Plant Closings, Community Abandonment, and the Dismantling of Basic Industry. *v.4 p.722*

Dekker Encyclopedia of Nanoscience and Nanotechnology, 10. . . . .*v.5 p.679*

Dekker Encyclopedia of Nanoscience and Nanotechnology, Vol. 1. . . . .*v.5 p.679*

Dekker Encyclopedia of Nanoscience and Nanotechnology. *v.5 p.275*

Del Amor y Otros Demonios. *v.2 p.682*

Delacroix - The Graphic Work: Catalogue Raisonné. .*v.1 p.756*

Delacroix, Art and Patrimony in Post-Revolutionary France. *v.1 p.738, p.739*

Delacroix. *v.1 p.741*

Delaware, a Bicentennial History. *v.3 p.493*

Delaware: A Guide to the First State. *v.3 p.493*

The Delaware Indians: A History. *v.6 p.704*

Delectus ex Iambis et Elegis Graecis. *v.2 p.403*

Delegation and Accountability in Parliamentary Democracies. *v.4 p.576*

The Delhi Sultanate: A Political and Military History. .*v.6 p.156*

Delhi Through the Ages: Essays in Urban History, Culture and Society. *v.6 p.160, p.712*

Deliberate Prose: Selected Essays, 1952-1995. . . . .*v.2 p.79*

Delie. *v.2 p.472*

Delights and Shadows: Poems. *v.2 p.148*

Delight. *v.2 p.378*

Delinquency in a Birth Cohort. *v.4 p.753, p.754,v.6 p.255*

Delinquent Daughters: Protecting and Policing Adolescent Female Sexuality in the United States, 1885-1920. . . . .*v.4 p.736, v.6 p.467*

Delirious New York: A Retroactive Manifesto for Manhattan. *v.1 p.797*

Deliverance. *v.2 p.143*

Delmore Schwartz: The Life of an American Poet. . .*v.2 p.119*

Delmore Schwartz. *v.2 p.119*

The Delphic Boat: What Genomes Tell Us. *v.5 p.139*

Delphine. *v.2 p.501*

Delta of Venus. *v.2 p.105*

The Deluge: British Society and the First World War. .*v.3 p.118*

Delusions of Grandeur: The United Nations and Global Intervention. *v.4 p.633*

Demand and Supply of Public Goods, Vol. 5. . . . .*v.4 p.247*

Demand Forcasting and Inventory Control: A Computer Aided Learning Approach. *v.4 p.117*

Demian. *v.2 p.609, p.610*

The Demise of Communist East Europe: 1989 in Context. *v.4 p.509, p.596, p.600*

Democracies at the Turning Point: Britain, France and the End of the Postware Order, 1928-1933. . . . .*v.3 p.75*

Democracy Adrift : Caudillo Politics in Nicaragua. . .*v.3 p.301*

The Democracy Advantage: How Democracies Promote Prosperity and Peace. *v.4 p.505*

Democracy after Liberalism: Pragmatism and Deliberative Politics. *v.4 p.505, p.506, p.511*

Democracy after Slavery: Black Publics and Peasant Rebels in Haiti and Jamaica. *v.3 p.316*

Democracy: An American Novel. *v.2 p.30*

Democracy and America's War on Terror. *v.4 p.564*

Democracy and Authoritarianism in Peru: Political Coalitions and Social Change. *v.3 p.329, v.4 p.591*

Democracy and Deliberation: New Directions for Democratic Reform. *v.4 p.503, p.504*

Democracy and Development: Political Institutions and Well-Being in the World, 1950-1990. . . . . . .*v.4 p.505*

Democracy and Dictatorship in Ghana and Tanzania. *v.4 p.576, p.612*

Democracy and Diplomacy: The Impact of Domestic Politics in U. S. Foreign Policy, 1789-1994. . . . .*v.3 p.386*

Democracy and Disagreement. *v.4 p.504*

Democracy and Disorder: Protest and Politics in Italy, 1965-1975. . . . .*v.4 p.594*

Democracy and Education. *v.4 p.342*

Democracy and Elections: Electoral Systems and Their Political Consequences. *v.4 p.577*

Democracy and Human Rights. *v.4 p.503*

Democracy and Its Critics. *v.4 p.503*

Democracy and Participation in Athens. *v.4 p.501*

Democracy and Public Management Reform: Building the
Republican State. *v.4 p.545*

Democracy and Redistribution. *v.4 p.503*

Democracy and Social Ethics. *v.4 p.769*

Democracy and the Global Order: From the Modern State to
Cosmopolitan Governance. *v.4 p.504*

Democracy and the Market: Political and Economic Reforms in
Eastern Europe and Latin America. *v.4 p.592*

Democracy and the Welfare State. *v.4 p.524*

Democracy at Gunpoint: the Greek Front. *v.3 p.196*

Democracy at Risk: How Political Choices Undermine Citizen
Participation, and What We Can Do about It. . . .*v.4 p.547*

A Democracy at War: America's Fight at Home and Abroad in
World War II. *v.3 p.443*

Democracy Betrayed: The Wilmington Race Riot of 1898 and
Its Legacy. *v.3 p.501*

Democracy, Citizenship and the Global City: Rights, Democracy
and Place. *v.4 p.544, v.6 p.723*

Democracy Defended. *v.4 p.505*

ℰ Democracy Delayed: The Case of Castro's Cuba. .*v.3 p.311*

Democracy Derailed in Russia: The Failure of Open
Politics. *v.4 p.597*

Democracy, Diamonds and Oil: Politics in Today's
Africa. *v.4 p.398*

Democracy, Empire, and the Arts in Fifth-Century
Athens. *v.3 p.17*

Democracy, Governance and Economic Performance: East and
Southeast Asia. *v.4 p.618, p.622*

Democracy: History, Theory, Practice. *v.4 p.504*

Democracy in Alberta: Social Credit and the Party
System. *v.4 p.590*

Democracy in America. *v.4 p.517*

Democracy in Europe. *v.4 p.603, p.638*

Democracy in Immigrant America: Demographics and Political
Participation. *v.4 p.571*

Democracy in India: A Hollow Shell. *v.6 p.158*

Democracy in Japan. *v.4 p.621*

Democracy in Jonesville: A Study in Quality and
Inequality. *v.4 p.708*

Democracy in Latin America: Political Change in Comparative
Perspective. *v.4 p.593*

Democracy in Modern Spain. *v.4 p.608*

Democracy in Plural Societies: A Comparative
Exploration. *v.4 p.502, p.504*

Democracy in Poland. *v.4 p.506, p.597*

Democracy in Translation: Understanding Politics in an
Unfamiliar Culture. *v.4 p.505, p.585, p.613*

Democracy, Italian Style. *v.4 p.594*

Democracy Matters: Winning the Fight Against
Imperialism. *v.6 p.32*

A Democracy of Chameleons: Politics and Culture in the New
Malawi. *v.4 p.611*

Democracy, Security, and Development in India. . . .*v.4 p.618*

Democracy, Sovereignty and the European Community. .*v.4 p.603*

Democracy, the Threshold of Freedom. *v.4 p.577*

Democracy vs. National Security: Civil-Military Relations in
Latin America. *v.4 p.593*

Democracy without Associations: Transformation of the Party
System and Social Cleavages in India. *v.4 p.617*

Democracy Without Citizens: Media and the Decay of American
Politics. *v.4 p.558*

Democracy Without Competition in Japan: Opposition Failure in
a One-Party Dominant State. *v.4 p.622*

Democracy's Body: Judson Dance Theater,
1962-1964. . . . .*v.1 p.25, p.40*

Democracy's College: The Land-Grant Movement in the
Formative Stage. *v.4 p.332*

Democracy's Dilemma: Environment, Social Equity, and the
Global Economy. *v.4 p.505, p.667*

Democracy's Discontent: America in Search of a Public
Philosophy. *v.4 p.555*

Democracy's Feast: Elections in America. *v.4 p.531*

Democracy. *v.4 p.503*

The Democratic Century. *v.4 p.505*

Democratic Changes and Authoritarian Reactions in Russia,
Ukraine, Belarus and Moldova. *v.4 p.585, p.597*

Democratic Development and Political Terrorism: The Global
Perspective. *v.4 p.503, p.658*

Democratic Distributive Justice. *v.4 p.515*

Democratic Equality: What Went Wrong? *v.4 p.514*

The Democratic Experience and Political Violence. . .*v.4 p.497*

The Democratic Experiment: New Directions in American
Political History. *v.3 p.384, p.385*

Democratic Experiments in Africa: Regime Transitions in
Comparative Perspective. *v.4 p.503, p.584, p.611*

Democratic Governance and Social Inequality. *v.4 p.506*

Democratic Government in Poland: Constitutional Politics since
1989. . . . .*v.4 p.505, p.596*

Democratic Legislative Institutions: A Comparative
View. *v.4 p.575*

Democratic Miners: Work and Labor Relations in the Anthracite
Coal Industry, 1875-1925. . . . .*v.4 p.124*

The Democratic Party Heads North. 1877-1962. . . .*v.4 p.553*

▢ The Democratic Party. *v.4 p.553*

Democratic Phoenix: Reinventing Political Activism. .*v.4 p.577*

Democratic Politics and Economic Reform in India. . .*v.4 p.617*

Democratic Promise: The Populist Moment in
America. *v.3 p.397, p.436*

The Democratic Question. *v.4 p.504*

The Democratic Republic, 1801-1815. . . . .*v.3 p.415*

The Democratic Republicans of New York: The Origins,
1763-1797. . . . .*v.3 p.411*

Democratic Subjects: The Self and the Social in
Nineteenth-Century England. *v.6 p.742, p.743, p.758*

Democratic Teacher Education: Programs, Processes, Problems,
and Prospects. *v.4 p.277*

The Democratic Wish: Popular Participation and the Limits of
American Government. *v.4 p.555, p.579*

Democratization and Revolution in the U. S. S. R.,
1985-91. . . . .*v.4 p.598*

Democratization and the Jews: Munich, 1945-1965. . .*v.3 p.59*

Democratization in Africa: The Theory and Dynamics of Political Transitions. *v.4 p.503, p.585, p.611*

Democratization in South Africa: The Elusive Social Contract. *v.4 p.614*

The Democratization of American Christianity. *v.1 p.605*

Democratizing Higher Education Policy: Constraints of Reform in Post-Apartheid South Africa. *v.4 p.336*

Democratizing the Enemy: The Japanese American Internment. *v.6 p.133, p.134*

Demographic Collapse: Indian Peru, 1520-1620. . . .*v.3 p.323*

Demographic Methods and Concepts. *v.4 p.376*

Demographic Vistas: Television in American Culture. *v.4 p.418*

Demographic Yearbook 2001. . . . .*v.4 p.763*

Demography Through Problems. *v.5 p.502*

The Demon, and Other Poems. *v.2 p.805*

The Demon in the Aether: The Story of James Clerk Maxwell. *v.5 p.543*

Demon Lovers: Witchcraft, Sex, and the Crisis of Belief. *v.6 p.569*

Demonology of the Early Christian World. *v.1 p.628*

Demons of Disorder: Early Blackface Minstrels and Their World. *v.1 p.119, p.120, p.281*

Demosthenes and His Time: A Study in Defeat. . . .*v.3 p.20*

Demosthenes: On the Crown. *v.2 p.409*

Demosthenes: Selected Private Speeches. *v.2 p.409*

Demosthenes: Six Private Speeches. *v.2 p.409*

Demosthenes, Speeches 18 and 19. . . . .*v.2 p.409*

Demosthenes, Speeches 27-38. . . . .*v.2 p.409*

Demosthenes, Speeches 50-59. . . . .*v.2 p.409*

Demosthenes: Statesman and Orator. *v.2 p.409*

Den of Thieves: The Untold Story of the Men Who Plundered Wall Street and the Chase That Brought Them Down. *v.4 p.100, p.101, p.110, p.147*

Denali: Reflection of a Naturalist. *v.5 p.235*

Deng Xiaoping and the Chinese Revolution: A Political Biography. *v.6 p.197, p.200*

Deng Xiaoping Shakes the World: An Eyewitness Account of China's Party Work Conference and the Third Plenum. *v.6 p.198*

The Denial of Bosnia. *v.3 p.249*

Denis Glover: Selected Poems. *v.2 p.746*

Denise Uyehara: Maps of City and Body. *v.6 p.90*

Denmark: A Troubled Welfare State. *v.4 p.594*

Density-Functional Theory of Atoms and Molecules. *v.5 p.551*

The Dent Dictionary of Symbols in Christian Art. *v.1 p.666, p.710*

Dental Anatomy: Its Relevance to Dentistry. . *v.5 p.525, p.526*

Dentistry: An Illustrated History. *v.5 p.525*

Dentistry, Dental Practice, and the Community. . . .*v.5 p.525*

Denying Evolution: Creationism, Scientism, and the Nature of Science. *v.5 p.195*

Denying History: Who Says the Holocaust Never Happened and Why Do They Say It? *v.3 p.86*

Department of Education: Efforts by the Office for Civil Rights to Resolve Asian-American Complaints. . . .*v.6 p.107, p.108*

Department of Energy New Technology: Sharing New Frontiers. *v.5 p.359*

Dependency and Development in Latin America. . . .*v.3 p.339*

The Dependent Empire, 1900-1948: Colonies, Protectorates and Mandates Select Documents on the Constitutional History of the British Empire and Commonwealth, Vol. 7. . . . .*v.4 p.435*

The Dependent Empire and Ireland, 1840-1900: Advance and Retreat in Representative Self-Government - Select Documents on the Constitutional History of the British Empire and Commonwealth, Vol. V. *v.4 p.436*

Dependent Rational Animals: Why Human Beings Need the Virtues. *v.6 p.288*

Depositional Sedimentary Environments with Reference to Terrigenous Classics. *v.5 p.438, p.439*

Depression and Aggression in Family Interaction. *v.5 p.660, p.662*

Depression and Other Mental Health Issues: The Filipino American Experience. *v.6 p.122, p.130*

Depression in New Mothers: Causes, Consequences, and Treatment Alternatives. *v.5 p.660*

Depression: The Evolution of Powerlessness. *v.5 p.659*

Depression: Theories and Treatments: Psychological, Biological, and Social Perspectives. *v.5 p.660*

The Deptford Trilogy. *v.2 p.735*

The Deputy. *v.2 p.617, p.618*

Derbys Dugan's Depression Funnies: A Novel. *v.2 p.143*

Derek Jarman. *v.6 p.419*

Derek Walcott. *v.2 p.770*

Derivatives: A Comprehensive Resource for Options, Futures, Interest Rate Swaps and Mortgage Securities. *v.4 p.92, p.93, p.101, p.103*

des Belles-soeurs à Marcel poursuivi par les chiens. . *v.2 p.540*

Des Minnesangs Fruhling: A Complete Reference Work. *v.2 p.595*

Des Romans de Tradition Haitienne: Sur un Recit Tragique. *v.2 p.537*

Des Teufels General. *v.2 p.616*

Descartes Against the Skeptics. *v.1 p.453*

Descartes: An Intellectual Biography. *v.1 p.453, p.454*

Descartes and His Contemporaries: Meditations, Objections, and Replies. *v.1 p.453*

Descartes' Cogito: Saved from the Great Shipwreck. *v.1 p.454*

A Descartes Dictionary. *v.1 p.453*

Descartes' Dualism. *v.1 p.504*

Descartes: His Life and Thought. *v.1 p.454*

Descartes' Natural Philosophy. *v.1 p.454, p.498*

Descartes' Philosophy of Science. *v.5 p.401*

Descartes Reinvented. *v.1 p.454*

Descartes: The Project of Pure Enquiry. *v.1 p.454*

Descartes to Derrida: An Introduction to European Philosophy. *v.1 p.436*

Descartes's Metaphysical Reasoning. *v.1 p.453*

Descartes's Rules for the Direction of the Mind. . . .*v.1 p.454*

Descartes. *v.1 p.453, p.454*

The Descent of Darwin: The Popularization of Darwinism in Germany, 1860-1914. . . . .*v.3 p.49, p.164*

Deschooling Society: Social Questions. *v.4 p.327*

Describing Species: Practical Taxonomic Procedure for Biologists. *v.5 p.199, p.205*

A Description of Millenium Hall, and the Country Adjacent, 1762. . . . .*v.2 p.259*

A Description of Spoken Prague Czech. *v.2 p.774*

Descriptions of Old Siam. *v.6 p.172*

Descriptive Physical Oceanography: An Introduction. .*v.5 p.430*

Desert Christians: An Introduction to the Literature of Early Monasticism. *v.1 p.577*

Desert Ecology: An Introduction to Life in the Arid Southwest. *v.5 p.177, p.240*

Desert Exile: The Uprooting of a Japanese-American Family. *v.6 p.95, p.115, p.135*

Desert Frontier: Ecological and Economic Change along the Western Sahel, 1600-1850. . . . .*v.6 p.69*

Desert Geomorphology. *v.5 p.424*

Desert Immigrants: The Mexican of el Paso, 1880-1920. . . . .*v.3 p.508, v.6 p.531, p.549*

Desert of the Heart. *v.6 p.398*

Desert People: A Study of the Walbiri Aborigines of Central Australia. *v.4 p.43*

Desert Run: Poems and Stories. *v.6 p.104*

Desert Tracings: Six Classic Arabian Odes by 'Alqama, Shanfara, Labid, 'Antara, Al-A'sha, and Dhu Al-Rumma. *v.6 p.663*

Deserts: Miracle of Life. *v.5 p.175, p.240*

The deserts of Bohemia: Czech Ffiction and Its Social Context. *v.2 p.782*

The Deserts of Bohemia: Czech Fiction and Its Social Context. *v.3 p.188*

Deserts of the Earth. *v.5 p.176, p.240*

The Deserts of the Southwest: A Sierra Club Naturalist's Guide. *v.5 p.234, p.240*

Deserts: The Living Drylands. *v.5 p.240*

Deserts. *v.5 p.174, p.240*

Desesperanto: Poems, 1999-2002. . .*v.2 p.146, v.6 p.404, p.405*

Design and Analysis of DNA Microarray Investigations. *v.5 p.101, p.123*

Design and Analysis of Ecological Experiments. . . .*v.5 p.171*

Design and Analysis of Integrated Manufacturing Systems. *v.5 p.684*

The Design and Implementation of Geographic Information Systems. *v.4 p.387*

The Design and Management of Effective Distance Learning Programs. *v.4 p.321*

Design and the Decorative Arts: Britain 1500-1900. . .*v.1 p.801*

Design Art: Functional Objects from Donald Judd to Rachel Whiteread. *v.1 p.712*

The Design Art of Nicos Zographos. *v.1 p.801*

Design As a Catalyst for Learning. *v.4 p.356*

Design Discourse: History, Theory, Criticism. . .*v.1 p.703, p.713*

Design for Ballet. *v.1 p.37*

Design for Victory: World War II Posters on the American Home Front. *v.1 p.718*

Design History: An Anthology. *v.1 p.712*

Design in the USA. *v.1 p.714*

The Design in the Wax: The Structure of the Divine Comedy and Its Meaning. *v.2 p.704, v.6 p.564*

Design Issues: How Graphic Design Informs Society. .*v.4 p.140*

Design of Aircraft. *v.5 p.717*

Design of Automatic Machinery. *v.5 p.714*

The Design of Building Structures. *v.5 p.698*

Design of Buildings and Bridges for Wind: A Practical Guide for ASCE-7 Standard Users and Designers of Special Structures. *v.5 p.686, p.696*

Design of Concrete Structures. *v.5 p.695*

The Design of Development. *v.4 p.245*

Design of Experiments in Chemical Engineering: A Practical Guide. *v.5 p.743*

Design of Machine Elements. *v.5 p.715*

Design of Machinery: An Introduction to the Synthesis and Analysis of Mechanisms and Machines. . . .*v.5 p.714, p.715*

Design of Wood Structures - ASD. *v.5 p.685*

Design Patterns: Elements of Reusable Object-Oriented Software. *v.5 p.346, p.348, p.349*

Design Sensitivity: Statistical Power for Experimental Research. *v.4 p.686*

Design since 1945. . . . .*v.1 p.712, p.713*

Design Standards for Recreation Facilities. . . .*v.4 p.792, p.881*

Design with Culture: Claiming America's Landscape Heritage. *v.1 p.817, p.822*

Design Within: Psychoanalytic Approaches to Shakespeare. *v.2 p.229*

Designer Food: Mutant Harvest or Breadbasket of the World? *v.5 p.370, v.6 p.294*

Designer's Guide to Furniture Styles. *v.1 p.805*

Designers on Designers. *v.1 p.799*

Designing Across Cultures: How to Create Effective Graphics for Diverse Ethnic Groups. *v.1 p.721*

Designing America's Waste Landscapes. *v.1 p.813*

Designing and Conducting Survey Research: A Comprehensive Guide. *v.4 p.691*

Designing and Developing Programs for Gifted Students. *v.4 p.317*

Designing and Drawing for the Theater. *v.1 p.147*

Designing Better Maps: A Guide for GIS Users. . . .*v.4 p.386*

Designing Brand Identity: A Complete Guide to Creating, Building, and Maintaining Strong Brands. *v.4 p.142*

Designing Crops for Added Value. *v.5 p.8, p.22*

Designing Dead Souls: An Anatomy of Disorder in Gogol. *v.2 p.803*

Designing Early Literacy Programs: Strategies for at-Risk Preschool and Kindergarten Children. *v.4 p.368*

Designing for Newspapers and Magazines. *v.4 p.409*

Designing for Older Adults: Principles and Creative Human Factors Approaches. *v.5 p.587*

Designing for Virtual Communities in the Service of Learning. *v.4 p.761*

Designing Instruction for Technology-Enhanced Learning. *v.4 p.352*

Designing Judicial Review: Interest Groups, Congress and Communications Policy. *v.4 p.539*

Designing Qualitative Research. *v.4 p.687*

Designing Resistance Training Programs. . . .*v.4 p.790, p.879*

Designing Safer Chemicals: Green Chemistry for Pollution Prevention. *v.5 p.310*

Designing Social Inquiry: Scientific Inference in Qualitative Research. *v.4 p.483*

Designing Sound for Animation. *v.6 p.348*

Designing State Higher Education Systems for a New Century. *v.4 p.295*

Designing Surveys: A Guide to Decisions and Procedures. *v.4 p.137*

Designing the Life of Johnson. *v.2 p.256*

Designing the Molecular World: Chemistry at the Frontier. *v.5 p.291*

Designing the User Interface: Strategies for Effective Human-Computer Interaction. *v.5 p.339*

Designing Web Usability: The Practice of Simplicity. *v.5 p.338, p.339*

Designing with Illustration. *v.1 p.716*

Design-Oriented Analysis of Structures: A Unified Approach. *v.5 p.695*

Designs for Life: Molecular Biology after World War II. *v.5 p.126*

Designs, Graphs, Codes and Their Links. *v.5 p.478*

Desirable Daughters. *v.2 p.765, v.6 p.101*

Desirada : roman. *v.2 p.536*

Desirada. *v.2 p.536*

Desire and Delusion: Three Novellas. *v.2 p.615*

Desire and Domestic Fiction: A Political History of the Novel. *v.2 p.174, p.190, p.192, p.578,v.6 p.746, p.755, p.764*

Desire and Excess: The Nineteenth-Century Culture of Art. *v.1 p.680*

Desire in Language: A Semiotic Approach to Literature and Art. *v.2 p.571*

Desire: Poems. *v.2 p.141*

Desis in the House: Indian American Youth Culture in New York City. *v.4 p.704, v.6 p.110, p.137*

Desktop Encyclopedia of Telecommunications. . . . *v.4 p.420*

Desmond. *v.2 p.261*

Desolate Angel: Jack Kerouac, the Beat Generation, and America. *v.2 p.93*

Desolation Angels. *v.2 p.93*

Desperately Seeking the Audience. *v.4 p.418*

Dessert, Appetizer and Related Flavored Wines. . . *v.5 p.52*

e Destination Culture: Tourism, Museums, and Heritage. *v.4 p.47*

Destination Europe: The Political and Economic Growth of a Continent. *v.4 p.638*

Destined to Witness: Growing up Black in Nazi Germany. *v.6 p.29*

The Destruction of Black Civilization. *v.6 p.11*

The Destruction of Brazilian Slavery, 1850-1888. . . *v.3 p.336*

Destruction of Hazardous Chemicals in the Laboratory. *v.5 p.313, p.314*

The Destruction of Pompeii and Other Stories. . . . *v.2 p.801*

The Destruction of the European Jews. *v.1 p.548*

Destruction or Love: La Destruccibon O el Amor. . . *v.2 p.656*

Destructive Messages: How Hate Speech Paves the Way for Harmful Social Movements. *v.4 p.423, p.424*

Detecting the Nation: Fictions of Detection and the Imperial Venture, 1788-1927. . . . . *v.2 p.191*

Detection of Light: From the Ultraviolet to the Submillimeter. *v.5 p.65, p.66*

Detective and Mystery Fiction: An International Bibliography of Secondary Sources. *v.2 p.579*

Detente and the Nixon Doctrine: American Foreign Policy and the Pursuit of Stability, 1969-1976. . . . . . . *v.3 p.474*

Determinants of Economic Growth: A Cross-Country Empirical Study. *v.4 p.242*

Determination of Chemical Composition and Molecular Structure. *v.5 p.276, p.277*

The Determination of Ionization Constants: A Laboratory Manual. *v.5 p.309*

Determinations: Critical Essays. *v.2 p.164*

Determined Survivors: Community Life among the Urban Elderly. *v.4 p.742*

Deterrence in American Foreign Policy: Theory and Practice. *v.3 p.452*

Deterring Democracy. *v.3 p.468*

La Detresse et l'Enchantement: Autobiographie. . . . *v.2 p.539*

Detroit: City of Race and Class Violence. *v.3 p.517*

Deuteronomy 1-11. . . . . *v.1 p.621*

Deuteronomy: A Commentary. *v.1 p.621*

Das deutsche Drama vom Barock bis zur Gegenwart: Interpretationen. *v.2 p.592*

Deutsche Hochsprache; Bühnenaussprache. *v.2 p.621*

Deutsche Literatur der Gegenwart; Themen, Stile, Tendenzen. *v.2 p.590, p.591*

Deutsche Literatur Im Burgerlichen Realismus, 1848-1898. . . . . *v.2 p.590*

Deutsche Literaturgeschichte in Tabellen. *v.2 p.589*

Deutsche Literaturgeschichte: Von Den Anfangen Bis Zur Gegenwart. *v.2 p.589*

Der deutsche Roman vom Barock bis zur Gegenwart; Struktur und Geschichte. *v.2 p.592*

Deutsche Romantik. *v.2 p.590*

Deutsches Woerterbuch, Set. *v.2 p.621*

Deutsches Woerterbuch. *v.2 p.622*

Deutschland: A Winter's Tale. *v.3 p.168*

Deutschstunde: Roman. *v.2 p.612*

Developing a Chemical Hygiene Plan. *v.5 p.266*

Developing a Lifelong Contract in the Sports Marketplace. *v.4 p.883, p.905*

Developing Adult Learners: Strategies for Teachers and Trainers. *v.4 p.321*

Developing Affordable Housing: A Practical Guide for Nonprofit Organizations. *v.4 p.158*

Developing Arts Loving Readers: Top 10 Questions Teachers Are Asking about Integrated Arts Education. . . . *v.4 p.364*

Developing Bioinformatics Computer Skills. *v.5 p.108*

Developing Constructivist Early Childhood Curriculum: Practical Principles and Activities. *v.4 p.368*

Developing Critical Thinkers: Challenging Adults to Explore Alternative Ways of Thinking and Acting. *v.4 p.319*

Developing Cross-Cultural Competence: A Guide for Working with Children and Their Families. *v.4 p.316*

▢ Developing Educational Standards. *v.4 p.287*

Developing Effective Safety Systems. *v.5 p.682*

The Developing Human: Clinically Oriented
    Embryology. *v.5 p.162*

The Developing Human. *v.5 p.154, p.160*

Developing in Two Languages: Korean Children in
    America. *v.6 p.109, p.136*

Developing Innovation in Online Learning: An Action Research
    Framework. *v.4 p.322*

Developing Innovation Systems: Mexico in a Global
    Context. *v.4 p.383*

Developing Learning in Early Childhood. *v.4 p.368*

Developing More Curious Minds. *v.4 p.346*

Developing Personal, Social and Moral Education Through
    Physical Education: A Practical Guide for Teachers. *v.4 p.796*

Developing Questions for Focus Groups. *v.4 p.136*

Developing Talent in Young People. *v.5 p.575, p.625*

Developing the Core Curriculum. *v.4 p.363*

Developing the Leaders Around You: How to Help Others
    Reach Their Full Potential. *v.4 p.71*

Developing the Physical Education Curriculum: An
    Achievement-Based Approach. *v.4 p.795*

Developing the Teacher Workforce. *v.4 p.278*

Developing Variations: Style and Ideology in Western
    Music. *v.1 p.382*

Developing Wind Power Projects: Theory and Practice.*v.5 p.709*

Development and Change in Highland Yemen. *v.6 p.628*

Development and Communication in Africa. *v.4 p.398*

Development and Crisis of the Welfare State: Parties and
    Policies in Global Markets. *v.4 p.594*

Development and Education of Mind. *v.4 p.343, p.356*

Development and the Developing World. *v.4 p.259*

[Development and Underdevelopment] Rich Lands and Poor:
    The Road to World Prosperity. *v.4 p.244*

Development as Freedom. *v.4 p.515*

ⓔ Development, Change, and Gender in Cairo: A View from
    the Household. *v.6 p.638*

Development Economics. *v.4 p.258, p.259, p.268*

Development in the Land of Contrasts. *v.4 p.398*

The Development of a Gay Latino Identity. *v.6 p.367*

The Development of African American English. . . .*v.2 p.555*

The Development of Biological Systematics: Antoine-Laurent de
    Jussieu, Nature, and the Natural System. . .*v.5 p.171, p.197*

Development of Chemistry. *v.5 p.263*

The Development of Cognitive Anthropology. *v.4 p.27*

The Development of Commonsense Psychology. . . .*v.5 p.630*

Development of Economic Analysis. *v.4 p.196*

Development of Education in the Twentieth Century. .*v.4 p.328*

The Development of English Drama in the Late Seventeenth
    Century. *v.2 p.187*

The Development of Greek Biography. *v.2 p.401*

Development of Islam in West Africa. . . .*v.1 p.554, v.6 p.68*

The Development of Language: Acquisition, Change and
    Evolution. *v.2 p.562*

The Development of Logic. *v.1 p.494*

The Development of Mexico's Tourism Industry: Pyramids by
    Day, Martinis by Night. *v.3 p.290*

The Development of Modern Chemistry. *v.5 p.263*

Development of Modern Education in the Gulf. . . .*v.4 p.335*

The Development of Realism in the Fiction of Tsubouchi
    Shoyo. *v.6 p.233*

Development of Secularism in Turkey. *v.6 p.623*

Development of Shakespeare as a Dramatist. *v.2 p.228*

The Development of Social Cognition and
    Communication. *v.5 p.621*

The Development of Southern Sectionalism,
    1819-1848. . . . .*v.3 p.495, p.496*

The Development of Standard English, 1300-1800: Theories,
    Descriptions, Conflicts. *v.2 p.555*

Development of the Colombian Labor Movement. . .*v.3 p.359*

The Development of the English Playhouse. . *v.1 p.101, p.155*

The Development of the Family and Marriage in
    Europe. *v.6 p.557*

Development of the Industrial United States (1878-1899), Vol.
    8. . . . .*v.3 p.370*

The Development of the Person: The Minnesota Study of Risk
    and Adaptation from Birth to Adulthood. *v.5 p.629*

Development of Transjordan 1929-1939: A History of the
    Hashemite Kingdom of Jordan. *v.6 p.620*

Development of Western Music. *v.1 p.174*

Developmental Biology of Ascidians. *v.5 p.162*

Developmental Biology of Fern Gametophytes. *v.5 p.161, p.210*

Developmental Biology of Flowering Plants. *v.5 p.161*

Developmental Biology Protocols, 3 Vol. Set. *v.5 p.161*

Developmental Biology. *v.5 p.154, p.160, p.161*

Developmental Genetics of Higher Organisms: A Primer in
    Developmental Biology. *v.5 p.160*

Developmental Movement Therapy. *v.1 p.51*

Developmental Sport and Exercise Psychology: A Lifespan
    Perspective. *v.4 p.878, v.5 p.583*

Developmental States: Relevancy, Redundancy or
    Reconfiguration? *v.4 p.398*

Developmental/Adapted Physical Education: Making Ability
    Count. *v.4 p.800, p.801*

Developments in Central and East European Politics 3.*v.3 p.207*

Developments in International Trade Theory: The Origins of
    International Economics. *v.4 p.257*

Developments in Pressure Equipment: Where to
    Next? *v.5 p.702, p.703*

Devi: Goddesses of India. *v.1 p.540*

Deviance and Identity. *v.4 p.696*

Deviant Conduct in World Politics. *v.4 p.626*

Deviant Eyes, Deviant Bodies: Sexual Re-Orientation in Film
    and Video. *v.6 p.417*

Deviant Knowledge: Criminology, Politics and
    Policy. *v.6 p.246, p.247*

Devices and Desires: A History of Contraceptives in
    America. *v.4 p.775*

Devices and Desires. *v.2 p.355*

The Devil and Daniel Webster. *v.2 p.60*

The Devil and the Jews: The Medieval Conception of the Jew
    and Its Relation to Modern Anti-Semitism. *v.6 p.574*

The Devil and the Land of the Holy Cross: Witchcraft, Slavery,
    and Popular Religion in Colonial Brazil. . *v.3 p.264, p.335*

Devil in the Mountain: A Search for the Origin of the Andes. *v.5 p.432*

The Devil in the New World: The Impact of Diabolism in New Spain. *v.3 p.262, p.284, p.285*

The Devil: Perceptions of Evil from Antiquity to Primitive Christianity. *v.1 p.529*

Devil Take the Hindmost: A History of Financial Speculation. *v.4 p.88, p.99, p.101*

A Devil's Chaplain: Reflections on Hope, Lies, Science, and Love. *v.5 p.191*

The Devil's Dictionary. *v.2 p.31*

The Devil's Disciples: The Makers of the Salem Witchcraft Trials. *v.4 p.474*

The Devil's Highway: A True Story. *v.4 p.765, v.6 p.530*

The Devil's Own Work: The Civil War Draft Riots and the Fight to Reconstruct America. *v.4 p.713*

The Devil's Pool and Other Stories. *v.2 p.499, p.500*

The Devil's Race-Track: Mark Twain's Great Dark Writings. *v.2 p.34*

Devils. *v.2 p.803*

Devolution and Black State Legislators: Challenges and Choices in the 21st Century. *v.4 p.530*

A Devotion to Their Science: Pioneer Women of Radioactivity. *v.3 p.49, v.5 p.261*

Devotions upon Emergent Occasions and Death's Duel. .*v.1 p.652*

Devotion. *v.2 p.619*

Devouring Whirlwind: Terror and Transcendence in the Cinema of Cruelty, 21. . . . .*v.6 p.319*

The Devs of Cincvad: A Lineage and State in Maharashtra. *v.6 p.161*

Dew on the Thorn. *v.6 p.499*

Dewey, Pragmatism and Economic Methodology. . . .*v.4 p.195*

Dewey. *v.1 p.443*

Déconnection. *v.2 p.532*

Le désert mauve. *v.2 p.540*

The Dévotes: Women and Church in Seventeenth-Century France. *v.3 p.147, p.148*

☐ DGR Web 2005 (Directory of Graduate Research). *v.5 p.260*

D.H. Lawrence's Sons and Lovers: A Casebook. . . .*v.2 p.364*

The Dharma Bums. *v.2 p.93*

Dharma Lion: A Biography of Allen Ginsberg. .*v.2 p.79, v.6 p.403*

Dharmasutras: The Law Codes of Ancient India. . . .*v.1 p.537*

La Diabla a Pie: Women's Tales from the New Mexico WPA. *v.6 p.496, p.502, p.524*

Le diable au corps ; suivi de, Le bal du comte d'Orgel : romans : texte intégral. *v.2 p.525*

Diaghilev's Ballets Russes. *v.1 p.23*

Diaghilev. *v.1 p.6*

The Diagnosis and Correction of Vocal Faults: A Manual for Teachers of Singing and for Choir Directors. *v.1 p.395, p.405*

Diagrammatica: The Path to Feynman Diagrams. . . .*v.5 p.553*

Dialectic of Duration. *v.1 p.455*

Dialectic of Enlightenment. *v.1 p.468*

The Dialectic of Sex: The Case for Feminist Revolution. *v.4 p.724, p.744, p.747*

Dialectical Materialism. *v.1 p.508*

The Dialectics of Oppression in Zaire. *v.4 p.513*

The Dialectics of Seeing: Walter Benjamin and the Arcades Project. *v.6 p.709*

Dialoghi, vol. 1. . . . .*v.2 p.709, p.710*

Dialoghi, vol. 2. . . . .*v.2 p.710*

The Dialogic Imagination: Four Essays. *v.2 p.570*

The Dialogic Sign: Essays on the Major Novels of Dostojefsky. *v.2 p.802*

Dialogue and History: Constructing South India, 1795-1895. . . . .*v.6 p.161*

Dialogue Concerning the Two Chief World Systems. . .*v.5 p.61*

Dialogue Education at Work: A Case Book. *v.4 p.321*

Dialogue on Ancient and Modern Music. *v.1 p.179*

Dialogue on the Infinity of Love. *v.1 p.435*

Dialogue: Theorizing Difference in Communication Studies. *v.4 p.422, v.5 p.620*

Dialogues Concerning Natural Religion and the Natural History of Religion. *v.1 p.451*

Dialogues Concerning Two New Sciences. *v.5 p.546*

Dialogues of Alfred North Whitehead. *v.1 p.447*

The Dialogues of Plato: Ion, Hippias Minor, Laches, Protagoras. *v.1 p.424*

The Dialogues of Plato: The Symposium. *v.1 p.424*

Dialogues with Leuco. *v.2 p.720*

Dialogues. *v.1 p.225, p.360, p.456*

Diamond Classics: Essays on 100 of the Best Baseball Books Ever Published. *v.4 p.812, p.852*

Diamonds Are Forever: The Business of Baseball. *v.4 p.852, p.886, p.889, p.897*

Diamonds around the Globe: The Encyclopedia of International Baseball. *v.3 p.316*

Diana of the Crossways. *v.2 p.300*

The Diana. *v.2 p.650*

Diane Arbus: An Aperture Monograph. *v.1 p.766*

Diane Arbus: Family Albums. *v.1 p.767*

Diaries 1920-1922. . . . .*v.2 p.605*

Diaries, 1939-1960, Vol. 1. . . . .*v.2 p.356*

The Diaries of a Cabinet Minister. *v.3 p.93, p.119*

The Diaries of Beatrice Webb. *v.4 p.193*

The Diaries of Evelyn Waugh. *v.2 p.387*

The Diaries of Hannah Cullwick, Victorian Maidservant. *v.6 p.743, p.747*

The Diary and Life of Samuel Sewall. *v.3 p.488*

The Diary and Life of William Byrd II of Virginia, 1674-1744. . . . .*v.3 p.500*

Diary in America. *v.2 p.299*

A Diary in the Strict Sense of the Term. *v.4 p.4*

The Diary of a Country Priest. *v.2 p.508*

Diary of a Madman, the Government Inspector and Selected Stories. *v.2 p.804*

Diary of a Man in Despair: A Masterpiece about the Comprehension of Evil. *v.3 p.173*

Diary of a Newlywed Poet: A Bilingual Edition of Diario de un Poeta Reciencasado. *v.2 p.660*

Diary of an Arctic Year. *v.5 p.238*

Diary of Cotton Mather Vol. 1: 1681-1709. . . . . .*v.3 p.487*

Diary of Cotton Mather Vol. 2: 1709-1724. . . . . . .*v.3 p.487*

The Diary of Dawid Sierakowiak: Five Notebooks from the
Lodz Ghetto. *v.3 p.86*

The Diary of James A. Garfield, Vols. I-IV. *v.3 p.435*

The Diary of John Evelyn. *v.3 p.105*

Diary of John Quincy Adams: 1794-1845. . . . . .*v.3 p.416*

The Diary of Lady Murasaki. *v.6 p.233*

The Diary of Samuel Pepys: A New and Complete
Transcription. *v.3 p.105*

Diary of the Civil War 1860: 1865. . . . .*v.3 p.426*

Diary of the Sinai Campaign. *v.6 p.613*

The Diary of Vaslav Nijinsky. *v.1 p.11*

The Diary of Virginia Woolf. *v.2 p.394*

The Diary of W. M. Rossetti 1870-1873. . . . . .*v.2 p.305*

Diary. *v.3 p.422, p.423, p.424, p.429*

Dias de Combate. *v.2 p.669*

Diaspora: Jews Amidst Greeks and Romans. *v.3 p.21*

The Diatoms of the United States (Exclusive of Alaska and
Hawaii), Vol. 2, Pt. 1. . . . .*v.5 p.208*

The Diblos Notebook. *v.2 p.100, p.101*

Diccionario Avanzado de Sinonimos Yantonimos de la Lengua
Española. *v.2 p.635*

Diccionario de Argot Espanol. *v.2 p.636*

Diccionario de Dudas y Diflcultades. *v.2 p.637*

Diccionario de Dudas. *v.2 p.635*

Diccionario de Escritores Hispanoamericanos del Siglo XVI al
Siglo XX. *v.2 p.664*

Diccionario de Literatura Espanola e
Hispanoamericana. *v.2 p.639*

Diccionario de Sinonimos y Antonimos. *v.2 p.635*

Diccionario de Uso del Español. *v.2 p.636*

Diccionario Panhispanico de Dudas. *v.2 p.637*

Diccionario Practico de la Lengua Española del Nuevo
Mundo. *v.2 p.637*

Dichter der Neueren Schweiz. *v.2 p.620*

Das dichterische Werk. *v.2 p.603*

Dichtungen, Briefe, Reden; eine Auswahl. *v.2 p.602*

Dichtungen und Briefe. *v.2 p.615*

Dickens: A Biography. *v.2 p.285*

Dickens and Crime. *v.2 p.282, v.6 p.744*

Dickens and the Eighteen Thirties. *v.2 p.282, v.6 p.739*

Dickens and the Grown-Up Child. *v.2 p.282*

Dickens, Dali and Others. *v.2 p.375*

Dickens' Fictions: Tapestries of Conscience. *v.2 p.284*

Dickens, Novel Reading, and the Victorian Popular
Theatre. *v.2 p.285*

Dickens on America and the Americans. *v.2 p.284*

Dickens on Screen. *v.6 p.326*

▢ The Dickens Project. *v.2 p.282*

Dickens: Public Life and Private Passion. *v.2 p.282*

Dickens Redressed: The Art of Bleak House and Hard
Times. *v.2 p.285*

Dickens: The Critical Heritage. *v.2 p.282*

The Dickens World. *v.2 p.284*

Dickens's Villains: Melodrama, Character, Popular
Culture. *v.2 p.284*

Dickinson: Strategies of Limitation. *v.2 p.37*

Dickinson: The Modern Idiom. *v.2 p.37*

The Dickinsons of Amherst. *v.2 p.37*

Dictating Demography: The Problem of Population in Fascist
Italy. *v.3 p.203*

The Dictator Next Door: The Good Neighbor Policy and the
Trujillo Regime in the Dominican Republic,
1930-1945. . . . .*v.3 p.317, p.391*

Dictatorship and Political Police: International Library of
Sociology C: Political Sociology. *v.4 p.768*

Dictatorship, Development and Disintegration: Politics and
Social Change in the Dominican Republic, Vol. 3. .*v.3 p.318*

Dictee. *v.6 p.95, p.102, p.104, p.122, p.123*

Dictionar englez-roman: b 70,000 cuvinte. *v.2 p.778*

Dictionar roman-englez: 60,000 de cuvinte. *v.2 p.778*

Dictionary and Thesaurus of the Hebrew Language, Set.*v.6 p.645*

Dictionary, Corrosion and Corrosion Control: English-German,
German-English. *v.5 p.734*

Dictionary for Theological Interpretation of the Bible. .*v.1 p.616*

The Dictionary of 19th Century British Book
Illustrators. *v.1 p.712*

The Dictionary of 20th Century British Book
Illustrators. *v.1 p.712*

Dictionary of Agriculture and Environmental
Science. *v.5 p.6, p.28*

Dictionary of Agriculture. *v.5 p.6*

Dictionary of Albanian Literature. *v.2 p.815*

Dictionary of Alkaloids. *v.5 p.299*

Dictionary of American Biography, Set. *v.3 p.377*

Dictionary of American Negro Biography. *v.6 p.14, p.33*

Dictionary of American Nursing Biography. . .*v.5 p.527, p.529*

Dictionary of American Regional English. . . .*v.2 p.552, p.554*

Dictionary of American Religious Biography. *v.1 p.525*

Dictionary of American Sculptors: Eighteenth Century to the
Present. *v.1 p.774*

A Dictionary of Ancient History. *v.3 p.3, p.4*

A Dictionary of Ancient Near Eastern Architecture. . .*v.1 p.784*

The Dictionary of Anthropology. *v.4 p.3*

Dictionary of Anthropology. *v.4 p.3*

Dictionary of Architectural and Building Technology. .*v.1 p.783*

Dictionary of Architecture and Construction. . .*v.1 p.783, p.784*

Dictionary of Architecture and Landscape
Architecture. *v.1 p.783, p.811, p.812*

A Dictionary of Architecture. *v.1 p.783*

A Dictionary of Art Titles: The Origins of the Names and Titles
of 3,000 Works of Art. *v.1 p.666*

Dictionary of Artists' Models. *v.1 p.664*

Dictionary of Art. *v.1 p.663*

The Dictionary of Art. *v.1 p.666, p.667*

A Dictionary of Asian Christianity. *v.1 p.610*

Dictionary of Automotive Engineering. *v.5 p.716*

The Dictionary of Bible and Religion. *v.1 p.614*

Dictionary of Biblical Interpretation. *v.1 p.616*

Dictionary of Biochemistry and Molecular Biology. . . *v.5 p.114*

Dictionary of Bioinformatics and Computational Biology. *v.5 p.97*

Dictionary of Bird Artists of the World. *v.1 p.664*

The Dictionary of Blue and White Printed Pottery, 1780-1880. . . . . *v.1 p.798, p.807*

Dictionary of Brazilian Literature. *v.2 p.693*

The Dictionary of British Art: 20th Century Painters and Sculptors. *v.1 p.666*

The Dictionary of British Art: British 18th Century Painters, Vol. 2. . . . . *v.1 p.726*

The Dictionary of British Art: British Artists 1880-1940. . . . . *v.1 p.664, p.665*

The Dictionary of British Art: Victorian Painters. *v.1 p.667, p.724, p.726*

Dictionary of British Cartoonists and Caricaturists. *v.1 p.701, p.721*

Dictionary of British Comic Artists, Writers and Editors. .*v.1 p.701*

Dictionary of Buddhist and Hindu Iconography: Objects, Devices, Concepts, Rites and Related Terms. . . . *v.1 p.709*

Dictionary of Building Preservation. *v.1 p.821*

A Dictionary of Business and Management. . .*v.4 p.173, p.174*

Dictionary of Business Terms. *v.4 p.172*

Dictionary of Canadian Biography, 1901-1910 - Dictionnaire Biographique du Canada, 1901-1910, Vol. 13. . . .*v.3 p.534*

Dictionary of Canadian Biography: 1921 to 1930, Vol. 15. . . . .*v.3 p.534*

Dictionary of Canadian Biography, Vol. 14. . . . .*v.3 p.534*

Dictionary of Canadian Biography, Vols. I-XII. . . .*v.3 p.534*

Dictionary of Chemical Names and Synonyms. . . .*v.5 p.258*

Dictionary of Chemical Terminology. *v.5 p.258*

A Dictionary of Chemistry. *v.5 p.257, p.258*

Dictionary of Christian Art. *v.1 p.665*

The Dictionary of Christian Biography. *v.1 p.613*

Dictionary of Christian Denominations. *v.1 p.598*

Dictionary of Christianity in America: A Comprehensive Resource on the Religious Impulse That Shaped a Continent. *v.1 p.606*

Dictionary of Classical Ballet in Labanotation. *v.1 p.38*

Dictionary of Classical Ballet Terminology: Royal Academy of Dancing. *v.1 p.4*

Dictionary of Common Names = Trivialnamen-Handbuch. *v.5 p.258*

Dictionary of Concepts in Recreation and Leisure Studies, 9. . . . .*v.4 p.785*

The Dictionary of Cricket. *v.4 p.856*

Dictionary of Criminal Justice. *v.6 p.246*

Dictionary of Deities and Demons in the Bible. . . .*v.1 p.618*

Dictionary of Demography: Terms, Concepts, and Institutions. *v.4 p.678*

Dictionary of Developmental Biology and Embryology. *v.5 p.95, p.160*

Dictionary of Developmental Disabilities Terminology. .*v.4 p.318*

A Dictionary of Econometrics. *v.4 p.188, p.199*

Dictionary of Economics. *v.4 p.191*

Dictionary of Enamelling. *v.1 p.798*

Dictionary of Energy. *v.5 p.708*

Dictionary of Engineering Materials. *v.5 p.679*

Dictionary of Engineering. *v.5 p.679*

The Dictionary of English Furniture, Set. *v.1 p.805*

The Dictionary of English Furniture, Vol. 1. . . . .*v.1 p.805*

The Dictionary of English Furniture, Vol. 2. . . . .*v.1 p.805*

The Dictionary of English Furniture, Vol. 3. . . . .*v.1 p.805*

A Dictionary of Entomology. *v.5 p.96, p.213*

Dictionary of Environment and Development: People, Places, Ideas, and Organizations. *v.5 p.353*

Dictionary of Environmental & Civil Engineering. . .*v.5 p.707*

Dictionary of Environmentally Important Chemicals. *v.5 p.310, p.311, p.706*

A Dictionary of Ethology. *v.5 p.96, p.166*

Dictionary of Existentialism. *v.1 p.505*

Dictionary of Feminist Theologies. *v.6 p.460*

The Dictionary of Feminist Theory. *v.6 p.427, p.428*

Dictionary of Film Terms: The Aesthetic Companion to Film Art. *v.6 p.306*

A Dictionary of Finance and Banking. *v.4 p.91, p.95, p.102, p.103, p.155, p.162*

A Dictionary of Food and Nutrition. *v.5 p.33*

Dictionary of Food Science and Technology. *v.5 p.34*

Dictionary of French Language Literature: Dictionnaire des Litteratures de Langue Francaise. *v.2 p.455*

Dictionary of French Literature. *v.2 p.455*

Dictionary of Furniture. *v.1 p.805*

Dictionary of Gems and Gemology. *v.5 p.435, p.452*

The Dictionary of Gene Technology: Genomics, Transcriptomics, Proteomics. *v.5 p.116, p.140*

A Dictionary of Genetics. *v.5 p.134*

A Dictionary of Geography. *v.4 p.373*

Dictionary of Geological Terms. *v.6 p.285, p.293*

Dictionary of Geology and Mineralogy. *v.6 p.286*

Dictionary of Geophysics, Astrophysics, and Astronomy. *v.5 p.63, p.443*

Dictionary of German Synonyms. *v.2 p.621*

ⓔ Dictionary of Global Climate Change. *v.5 p.371*

Dictionary of Historical and Comparative Linguistics. *v.2 p.564, v.5 p.622, p.624*

Dictionary of Holland Occupational Codes. *v.5 p.577*

The Dictionary of Human Geography. *v.4 p.373*

Dictionary of Inorganic and Organometallic Compounds: Version 6.1. . . . .*v.5 p.302*

Dictionary of Inorganic Compounds. *v.5 p.302*

Dictionary of Insurance Terms. *v.4 p.163*

Dictionary of International and Comparative Law. . .*v.4 p.434*

Dictionary of International Human Rights Law. . . .*v.4 p.434*

Dictionary of Irish Artists: 20th Century. *v.1 p.666*

Dictionary of Irish Literature. *v.2 p.163*

Dictionary of Islamic Architecture. *v.1 p.784*

Dictionary of Italian Literature. *v.2 p.697*

Dictionary of Jesus and the Gospels: A Compendium of Contemporary Biblical Scholarship. *v.1 p.629*

A Dictionary of Linguistics and
    Phonetics. *v.2 p.560, v.5 p.620, p.623*

Dictionary of Literary Biography, Vol. 307. . . . . . .*v.2 p.692*

The Dictionary of Marketing Communications. *v.4 p.134*

Dictionary of Mathematical Games, Puzzles, and
    Amusements. *v.5 p.469*

Dictionary of Media and Communication Studies. . . .*v.4 p.424*

Dictionary of Medical Acronyms and Abbreviations. . .*v.5 p.509*

Dictionary of Medical Sociology. *v.4 p.677*

Dictionary of Medical Syndromes. *v.5 p.509*

Dictionary of Metallurgy. *v.5 p.731*

Dictionary of Mexican American History. *v.6 p.532*

Dictionary of Microscopy. *v.5 p.86*

@ Dictionary of Midwestern Literature: The Authors, Vol.
    1. . . . .*v.2 p.15*

Dictionary of Ming Biography,
    1364-1644. . . . .*v.6 p.186, p.198, p.199*

Dictionary of Mining, Mineral and Related Terms. . .*v.5 p.450*

Dictionary of Mining, Mineral, and Related Terms. . .*v.5 p.737*

Dictionary of Mining, Mineral and Related Terms. . .*v.5 p.739*

Dictionary of Mining, Mineral, and Related Terms. . .*v.6 p.283*

The Dictionary of Minton. *v.1 p.798, p.807*

A Dictionary of Modern Design. *v.1 p.712*

Dictionary of Modern Expressions and Phrases. *v.2 p.635*

Dictionary of Modern French Literature: From the Age of
    Reason Though Realism. *v.2 p.458*

A Dictionary of Modern Legal Usage. *v.4 p.436*

The Dictionary of Modern Politics. *v.4 p.482*

A Dictionary of Modern Written Arabic. *v.6 p.655*

The Dictionary of Multimedia Terms and Acronyms. .*v.1 p.770*

Dictionary of Music Business Terms. *v.1 p.163, p.386*

Dictionary of Music Production and Engineering
    Terminology. *v.1 p.163, p.388*

A Dictionary of Musical Quotations. *v.1 p.159*

Dictionary of Musical Technology. *v.1 p.159, p.386*

A Dictionary of Musical Themes. *v.1 p.159*

⚡ Dictionary of Natural Products on CD-ROM. . . .*v.5 p.298*

Dictionary of Nature Myths: Legends of the Earth, Sea, and
    Sky. *v.1 p.527*

The Dictionary of Nineteenth-Century American Artists in Italy,
    1760-1914. . . . .*v.1 p.666*

The Dictionary of Occupational Titles. *v.5 p.578*

Dictionary of Opera and Song Themes. .*v.1 p.159, p.228, p.235*

⚡ Dictionary of Organic Compounds on CD-ROM. . .*v.5 p.290*

Dictionary of Organic Compounds, Set. *v.5 p.290*

Dictionary of Pastoral Care and Counseling. *v.1 p.649*

Dictionary of Paul and His Letters: A Compendium of
    Contemporary Biblical Scholarship. *v.1 p.631*

Dictionary of Petroleum Exploration, Drilling and
    Production. *v.5 p.451*

A Dictionary of Philosophy. *v.1 p.415*

Dictionary of Philosophy. *v.1 p.415*

Dictionary of Photography and Digital Imaging: The Essential
    Reference for the Modern Photographer. . .*v.1 p.761, p.770*

The Dictionary of Physical Geography. . . .*v.4 p.373, v.5 p.417*

A Dictionary of Physics. *v.5 p.545*

Dictionary of Physics. *v.5 p.545*

A Dictionary of Plant Pathology. *v.5 p.46*

Dictionary of Polish Literature. *v.2 p.788*

The Dictionary of Portrait Painters in Britain up to
    1920. . . . .*v.1 p.725, p.726*

A Dictionary of Psychology. *v.5 p.593*

Dictionary of Public Policy and Administration. .*v.4 p.482, p.483*

Dictionary of Qualitative Inquiry. *v.4 p.689*

Dictionary of Quotations in Sociology. *v.4 p.676*

Dictionary of Received Ideas. *v.2 p.491*

A Dictionary of Russian and Soviet Artists, 1420-1970. .*v.1 p.665*

Dictionary of Russian Literature since 1917. . . . .*v.2 p.796*

Dictionary of Russian Women Writers. . .*v.2 p.793, p.796, p.797*

Dictionary of Scandinavian History. *v.3 p.232, p.233*

Dictionary of Science and Technology: English-French. .*v.5 p.387*

Dictionary of Science and Technology:
    German-English. *v.5 p.387*

Dictionary of Science and Technology. *v.5 p.387*

Dictionary of Scientific Biography, Set. *v.5 p.395*

A Dictionary of Scientific Units Including Dimensionless
    Numbers and Scales. *v.5 p.63, p.567, p.569, p.571*

Dictionary of Scottish Art and Architecture. *v.1 p.665*

The Dictionary of Scottish Painters, 1600 to the Present. .*v.1 p.725*

Dictionary of Scottish Painters 1600-1960. . . . . .*v.1 p.725*

The Dictionary of Sculptors in Bronze. *v.1 p.774*

The Dictionary of Sea Painters of Europe and America. .*v.1 p.725*

Dictionary of Serbian, Croatian, and Bosnian New
    Words. *v.2 p.774, p.776, p.778*

A Dictionary of Shakespeare. *v.2 p.226*

A Dictionary of Social Science Methods. *v.4 p.687*

Dictionary of South and Southeast Asian Art. . .*v.1 p.663, p.691*

Dictionary of Spanish Literature. *v.2 p.639*

Dictionary of Special Education and Rehabilitation. . .*v.4 p.317*

A Dictionary of Spectroscopy. *v.5 p.270*

Dictionary of Sporting Artists. *v.1 p.667*

Dictionary of Sports: A Complete Guide to the Vocabulary of
    the World's Leading Speakers. *v.4 p.848*

A Dictionary of Stage Directions in English Drama,
    1580-1642. . . . .*v.1 p.140*

Dictionary of Statistics and Methodology: A Nontechnical Guide
    for the Social Sciences. *v.4 p.679*

The Dictionary of Substances and Their Effects. . . .*v.5 p.311*

Dictionary of Terrorism. *v.4 p.662*

Dictionary of the Ancient Near East. *v.3 p.4*

A Dictionary of the Bible. *v.1 p.614*

Dictionary of the Black Theatre: Broadway, Off-Broadway, and
    Selected Harlem Theatre. *v.1 p.61, p.123, p.124*

A Dictionary of the Characters and Proper Names in the Works
    of Shakespeare. *v.2 p.226*

A Dictionary of the Characters and Scenes in the Stories and
    Poems of Rudyard Kipling, 1886-1911. . . . . .*v.2 p.298*

Dictionary of the Dance. *v.1 p.4*

Dictionary of the Ecumenical Movement. *v.1 p.568*

A Dictionary of the European Union. *v.4 p.603, p.638*

Dictionary of the History of Science. *v.5 p.390*

Dictionary of the Khazars: Female Edition. *v.2 p.811*

Dictionary of the Khazars: Male Edition. *v.2 p.811*

Dictionary of the Middle Ages, Set. *v.6 p.555*

Dictionary of the Middle Ages: Supplement I. *v.6 p.555*

Dictionary of the Modern Politics of Japan. *v.6 p.220*

Dictionary of the Political Thought of the People's Republic of
China. *v.4 p.620*

Dictionary of the Presbyterian and Reformed Tradition in
America. *v.1 p.587, p.588*

Dictionary of the Social Sciences. *v.4 p.373, p.677*

Dictionary of the Theatre: Terms, Concepts, and
Analysis. *v.1 p.60*

Dictionary of the Theatre: Terms, Concepts and Analysis. .*v.1 p.60*

A Dictionary of Theatre Anthropology: The Secret Art of the
Performer. *v.1 p.151*

Dictionary of Theology. *v.1 p.594*

Dictionary of Today's Landscape Designers. *v.1 p.812*

Dictionary of Toxicology. *v.5 p.311*

Dictionary of Travel, Tourism and Hospitality. . . .*v.4 p.161*

A Dictionary of Turkish Verbs: In Context and by
Theme. *v.6 p.665*

Dictionary of Twentieth-Century British Cartoonists and
Caricaturists. *v.1 p.701, p.721*

Dictionary of Twentieth-Century Cuban
Literature. *v.2 p.672, v.6 p.507, p.514*

Dictionary of Victorian Engravers, Print Publishers and Their
Works. *v.1 p.752*

Dictionary of Victorian London. *v.6 p.763*

Dictionary of Victorian Wood Engravers. . . .*v.1 p.751, p.752*

A Dictionary of Vocal Terminology. *v.1 p.161, p.396*

Dictionary of Water and Waste
Management. *v.5 p.379, p.380, p.707*

The Dictionary of Watercolour Artists: Up to 1920, Vol.
2. . . . .*v.1 p.725*

The Dictionary of Watercolour Artists: Up to 1920. . .*v.1 p.725*

A Dictionary of Weights, Measures, and Units. . . .*v.5 p.567*

Dictionary of Women Artists, Set. .*v.1 p.664, p.706, v.6 p.472*

Dictionary of Women's Art Before 1900. . . . .*v.1 p.662, p.705*

The Dictionary of Worcester Porcelain, 1751-1851, Vol.
1. . . . .*v.1 p.798, p.808*

Dictionary of Word Roots and Combining Forms. . . .*v.5 p.225*

Dictionary of World Philosophy. *v.1 p.415*

A Dictionary of Zoology. *v.5 p.211, p.212*

Dictionnaire de Diderot. *v.2 p.480*

Dictionnaire de Jean-Jacques Rousseau. *v.2 p.483*

Dictionnaire de la langue française. *v.2 p.454*

Dictionnaire de l'ancien français. *v.2 p.453*

Dictionnaire de l'argot français et de ses origines. . .*v.2 p.453*

Dictionnaire de Stendhal. *v.2 p.501*

Dictionnaire des lettres françaises, vol. 1. . . . . .*v.2 p.455*

Dictionnaire des lettres françaises, vol. 2. . . .*v.2 p.455, p.456*

Dictionnaire des lettres françaises, vol. 3. . . . . .*v.2 p.456*

Dictionnaire des littératures de langue française, vol. 1.*v.2 p.454*

Dictionnaire des littératures de langue française, vol. 2.*v.2 p.454*

Dictionnaire des littératures de langue française, vol. 3.*v.2 p.454*

Dictionnaire des littératures de langue française, vol. 4.*v.2 p.454*

Dictionnaire des Oeuvres Littéraires du Québec, Vols.
1-7. . . . .*v.2 p.538*

Dictionnaire du moyen français. *v.2 p.453*

Dictionnaire général de Voltaire. *v.2 p.484*

Dictionnaire québécois français. *v.2 p.454*

Did Darwin Get It Right? *v.5 p.204*

Did the Greeks Believe in Their Myths?: An Essay on the
Constitutive Imagination. *v.1 p.533*

Did They Mention the Music?: The Autobiography of Henry
Mancini. *v.1 p.256, p.339*

The Didache, the Epistle of Barnabas, the Epistle and
Martyrdom of St. Polycarp, the Fragments of Papias, the
Epistle of Diognetus. *v.1 p.591*

Diderot on Art. *v.2 p.479*

A Diderot Pictorial Encyclopedia of Trades and Industry:
Manufacturing and the Technical Arts in Plates
Selected from "L'Encyclopedie, ou Dictionnaire Raisonne
des Sciences, des Arts et des Metiers". *v.2 p.479*

Diderot: Political Writings. *v.2 p.480*

Diderot's Letters to Sophie Volland: A Selection. . .*v.2 p.479*

Diderot. *v.2 p.480*

Die Angst des Tormanns beim Elfmeter. *v.2 p.617*

Die Aufzeichnungen des Malte Laurids Brigge. . . .*v.2 p.614*

Die Blechtrommel. *v.2 p.607, p.608*

Die Blendung. *v.2 p.605*

Die Deutsche Lyrik Seit Herder, Vol. 1. . . . . . .*v.2 p.591*

Die Deutsche Lyrik Seit Herder, Vol. 2. . . . . . .*v.2 p.591*

Die Deutsche Lyrik Seit Herder, Vol. 3. . . . . . .*v.2 p.591*

Die Deutsche Rechtschreibung. *v.2 p.621*

Die deutsche Tragödie von Lessing bis Hebbel. . . .*v.2 p.592*

Die Dramen. *v.2 p.616*

Die Erzahlungen. *v.2 p.616*

Die Fackel Im Ohr: Lebensgeschichte 1921-1931. . .*v.2 p.605*

Die Gerettete Zunge: Geschichte Einer Jugend. .*v.2 p.605, p.606*

Die Hexe Im Landhaus: Gesprach in Solothurn. . . .*v.2 p.618*

Die Jugend des Königs Henri Quatre. *v.2 p.614*

Die Linkshandige Frau: Erzahlung. *v.2 p.617*

Die Rattin. *v.2 p.608*

Die Stunde der Wahren Empfindung. *v.2 p.617*

Die Verlorene Ehre der Katharina Blum: Oder, Wie Gewalt
Entstehen und Wohin Sie Fuhren Kann: Erzahlung. *v.2 p.604*

Die Verwirrungen des Zoglings Torless. *v.2 p.614*

Die Welt von Gerstern: Erinnerungen eines Europäers. *v.2 p.616*

Die Widmung: Eine Erzahlung. *v.2 p.619*

The Dies Committee: A Study of the Special House Committee
for the Investigation of Un-American Activities,
1938-1944. . . . .*v.3 p.449*

Dies Committee, a Study of the Special House Committee for
the Investigation of Un-American Activities,
1938-1944. . . . .*v.3 p.449*

Dies Irae: A Guide to Requiem Music. *v.1 p.235*

Diet for a New America: How Your Food Choices Affect Your
Health, Happiness, and the Future of Life on
Earth. *v.5 p.33, p.35*

Dieter Kienast. . . . .*.v.1 p.815*

Dieter Roth: Books + Multiples: Catalogue Raisonné. *.v.1 p.696*

Dietrich Buxtehude: Organist in Lubeck. . . . .*.v.1 p.186, p.315*

Diez Siglos de Poesia Castelana. . . . .*.v.2 p.643*

Difference and Repetition. . . . .*.v.1 p.415, p.456*

The Difference of Man and the Difference It Makes. . *.v.1 p.495*

Different Games, Different Rules: Why Americans and Japanese
   Misunderstand Each Other. . . . .*.v.4 p.20*

Different Hours: Poems. . . . .*.v.2 p.144*

A Different Mirror: A History of Multicultural America. .*.v.4 p.707*

A Different Nature: The Paradoxical World of Zoos and Their
   Uncertain Future. . . . .*.v.5 p.83*

Different Worlds: A Sociological Study of Taste, Choice and
   Success in Art. . . . .*.v.1 p.708*

Differential and Integral Calculus. . . . .*.v.5 p.486*

Differential Diagnosis for the Orthopedic Physical
   Therapist. . . . .*.v.5 p.535*

Differential Diagnosis of Common Complaints. . . .*.v.5 p.521*

Differential Equations and Mathematical Biology. . . *.v.5 p.91*

Differential Equations, Dynamical Systems, and an Introduction
   to Chaos. . . . .*.v.5 p.488*

Differential Equations. . . . .*.v.5 p.486, p.487*

Differential Geometry: A Geometric Introduction. . .*.v.5 p.496*

Differential Geometry of Curves and Surfaces. . . .*.v.5 p.496*

Differentiated Assessment Strategies: One Tool Doesn't Fit
   All. . . . .*.v.4 p.285*

The Differentiated Classroom: Responding to the Needs of All
   Learners. . . . .*.v.4 p.350*

Differentiated Instruction: Meeting the Educational Needs of All
   Students in Your Classroom. . . . .*.v.4 p.316, p.350*

Differentiated Instructional Strategies: One Size Doesn't Fit
   All. . . . .*.v.4 p.349*

The Difficult Flowering of Surinam: Ethnicity and Politics in a
   Plural Society. . . . .*.v.3 p.322*

Difficult Lives: Jim Thompson, David Goodis, Chester
   Himes. . . . .*.v.2 p.80, p.86, p.87, p.124*

Difficult Loves. . . . .*.v.2 p.715*

Difficulties of a Bridegroom: Stories. . . . .*.v.2 p.353*

Diffusing Geography: Essays for Peter Haggett. . . .*.v.4 p.373*

Diffusion and Ecological Problems: Mathematical
   Models. . . . .*.v.5 p.502*

Diffusion of Innovations. . . . .*.v.4 p.761*

Dig up My Heart: Selected Poems 1952-83. . . . . .*.v.2 p.733*

Digest for the Successful Terrarium. . . . .*.v.5 p.229*

🔲 Digest of Education Statistics. . . . .*.v.4 p.322*

Digging the Africanist Presence in American Performance:
   Dance and Other Contexts. . . . .*.v.1 p.18*

Digging up the Mountains: Selected Stories. . . . .*.v.2 p.733*

Digital and Analog Communication Systems. . . . .*.v.5 p.725*

Digital Art for the 21st Century: Renderosity. . . .*.v.1 p.770*

Digital Art History: Computers and the History of
   Art. . . . .*.v.1 p.770, p.771*

Digital Art. . . . .*.v.1 p.772*

Digital Code of Life: How Bioinformatics Is Revolutionizing
   Science, Medicine, and Business. . . . .*.v.5 p.98*

Digital Communications: Fundamentals and
   Applications. . . . .*.v.5 p.726*

Digital Communication. . . . .*.v.5 p.725*

Digital Concepts: The Cultural Context Of New Information
   Technologies. . . . .*.v.4 p.419*

Digital Control: A State-Space Approach. . . . . . .*.v.5 p.712*

Digital Control of Dynamic Systems. . . . .*.v.5 p.710*

Digital Control System Analysis and Design. . *.v.5 p.711, p.712*

Digital Control Systems. . . . .*.v.5 p.711*

Digital Crime and Digital Terrorism. . . . .*.v.6 p.253*

Digital Crossroads: American Telecommunications Policy in the
   Internet Age. . . . . *.v.4 p.52, p.111, p.166, p.420*

Digital Currents: Art in the Electronic Age. . . . . .*.v.1 p.771*

Digital Design: Principles and Practices. . . . . . .*.v.5 p.730*

Digital Design with CPLD Applications and VHDL. . *.v.5 p.729*

Digital Design. . . . .*.v.5 p.730*

The Digital Dilemma: The Future of Intellectual Property in the
   Information Infrastructure. . . . .*.v.4 p.110, p.111*

Digital Economics: How Information Technology Has
   Transformed Business Thinking. . . . .*.v.4 p.82*

Digital Electronics: A Practical Approach. . . . . .*.v.5 p.722*

Digital Electronics: Principles and Applications, Student Text
   with MultiSIM CD-ROM. . . . .*.v.5 p.723*

Digital Evidence and Computer Crime. . . . .*.v.6 p.270*

Digital Filmmaking 101: An Essential Guide to Producing
   Low-Budget Movies. . . . .*.v.6 p.347*

The Digital Hand: How Computers Changed the Work of
   American Manufacturing, Transportation, and Retail
   Industries. . . . .*.v.4 p.146, p.149*

The Digital Hand, Volume 2: How Computers Changed the
   Work of American Financial, Telecommunications,
   Media, and Entertainment
   Industries. . . . . . .*.v.4 p.146, p.155, p.157, p.158, p.165*

Digital Integrated Circuits. . . . .*.v.5 p.722*

The Digital Photographer's Pocket Encyclopedia: 3000 Terms
   Explained. . . . .*.v.1 p.762, p.770*

Digital Signal Processing: Principles, Algorithms and
   Applications. . . . .*.v.5 p.336, p.341*

The Digital Sublime: Myth, Power, and Cyberspace. .*.v.4 p.425*

Dilemma of a Ghost and Anowa. . . . .*.v.2 p.752*

The Dilemma of Access: Minorities in Two Year
   Colleges. . . . .*.v.4 p.312*

Dilemma of Mexico's Development: The Roles of the Private
   and Public Sectors. . . . .*.v.3 p.296*

The Dilemmas of an Upright Man: Max Planck and the
   Fortunes of German Science. . . . .*.v.5 p.543*

The Dilemmas of Corrections: Multidisciplinary
   Perspectives. . . . .*.v.6 p.274*

Dilemmas of Democracy and Political Parties in Sectarian
   Societies: The Case of the PSP in Lebanon. . . . .*.v.4 p.616*

🔳 Dilemmas of Pluralist Democracy: Autonomy Vs.
   Control. . . . .*.v.4 p.503*

Dilemmas of Pluralist Democracy: Autonomy vs.
   Control. . . . .*.v.4 p.503*

Dilemmas of Political Change in Mexico. . . . . . .*.v.3 p.294*

The Dilemmas of Presidential Leadership: Of Caretakers and
   Kings. . . . .*.v.4 p.527*

Dilemmas of State-Led Nation Building in
 Ukraine. . . . . *.v.4 p.585, p.598*

Dilthey: Philosopher of the Human Studies. . . . . . *.v.1 p.464*

The Dimension of Music in Islamic and Jewish Culture. *.v.1 p.287*

⬜ Dimension Stone: Statistics and Information. *.v.5 p.451, p.452*

Dimensions of Literacy: A Conceptual Base for Teaching
 Reading and Writing in School Settings. . *.v.4 p.354, p.364*

Dimensions of Musical Learning and Teaching: A Different Kind
 of Classroom. . . . . *.v.1 p.404, p.405*

The Dimensions of Regional Trade Integration in Southeast
 Asia. . . . . *.v.4 p.61*

Dimensions of the Sacred: An Anatomy of the World's
 Beliefs. *.v.1 p.521*

Dimensions of United States-Mexican Relations. 5 vols. *.v.3 p.292*

Dimensions of U.S. Role in Conflict Resolution: Four Case
 Studies in Post-Colonial Africa. . . . . *.v.6 p.56*

Diminished Democracy: From Membership to Management in
 American Civic Life. . . . . *.v.4 p.547, p.555*

Dimitrov and Stalin, 1934-1943: Letters from the Soviet
 Archives. *.v.3 p.225*

Dimitry's Shade: A Reading of Alexander Pushkin's Boris
 Godunov. *.v.2 p.802*

Dinner at the Homesick Restaurant. . . . . *.v.2 p.157*

Dinner with Friends. . . . . *.v.2 p.149*

Dinners and Nightmares. . . . . *.v.2 p.143*

Dinosaur in a Haystack: Reflections in Natural
 History. . . . . *.v.5 p.192, p.221*

Dinosaur Tracks and Traces. . . . . *.v.5 p.448, p.450*

Dinosaur Tracks. . . . . *.v.5 p.448, p.450*

The Dinosauria. . . . . *.v.5 p.448*

Dionysius and "The History of Archaic Rome". . . . *.v.3 p.24*

Dionysos: Archetypal Image of Indestructible Life. . *.v.1 p.532*

Dionysus in Paris: A Guide to Contemporary French
 Theatre. . . . . *.v.1 p.105, v.2 p.461*

Dionysus: Myth and Cult. . . . . *.v.1 p.533*

⬜ Diotima: Materials for the Study of Women and Gender in
 the Ancient World. . . . . . . *.v.2 p.399, v.3 p.3, v.6 p.450*

The Diplomacies of New Small States: The Case of Slovenia
 with Some Comparison from the Baltics. . *.v.4 p.641, p.644*

Diplomacy and Diplomats in Nineteenth Century Asante. *.v.6 p.69*

Diplomacy for a Next Century. . . . . *.v.4 p.645*

Diplomacy of Fear: Canada and the Cold War,
 1941-1948. . . . . *.v.3 p.541, p.542*

A Diplomacy of Hope: Canada and Disarmament,
 1945-1988. . . . . *.v.4 p.644, p.656*

The Diplomacy of Hope: The United Nations since the Cold
 War. . . . . *.v.4 p.633*

The Diplomacy of Ideas: U. S. Foreign Policy and Cultural
 Relations, 1938-1950. . . . . *.v.3 p.477*

The Diplomacy of India: Indian Foreign Policy in the United
 Nations,. . . . . *.v.4 p.632, p.633*

The Diplomacy of Involvement: American Economic Expansion
 across the Pacific, 1784-1900. . . . . . *.v.3 p.381, p.433*

The Diplomacy of the American Revolution. . . . . *.v.3 p.413*

The Diplomacy of the Crucial Decade: American Foreign
 Relations During the 1960s. . . . . *.v.3 p.473*

The Diplomacy of Trade and Investment: American Economic
 Expansion in the Hemisphere,
 1865-1900. . . . . *.v.3 p.381, p.400, p.433*

Diplomacy, Pt. 2. . . . . *.v.3 p.453*

Diplomacy: Theory and Practice. . . . . *.v.4 p.645*

Diplomacy. *.v.4 p.645*

Diplomat in Carpet Slippers: Abraham Lincoln Deals with
 Foreign Affairs. . . . . *.v.3 p.433*

A Diplomat in Japan. . . . . *.v.6 p.228*

Diplomatic Departures: The Conservative Era in Canadian
 Foreign Policy, 1984-1993. . . . . *.v.3 p.541*

The Diplomatic History of British Honduras, 1638 to
 1901. . . . . *.v.3 p.297*

A Diplomatic History of the American Revolution. . *.v.3 p.413*

The Diplomatic History of the Canadian Boundary,
 1749-1763. . . . . *.v.3 p.538*

A Diplomatic Revolution: Algeria's Fight for Independence and
 the Origins of the Post-Cold War Era. . . . . . . *.v.6 p.60*

Diplomatic Theory from Machiavelli to Kissinger. . . *.v.4 p.645*

Direct Democracy in Switzerland. . . . . *.v.3 p.244*

Direct Energy Conversion: Fundamentals of Electric Power
 Production. . . . . *.v.5 p.360*

Direct Energy Conversion. . . . . *.v.5 p.359*

Direct from Dell: Strategies That Revolutionized an
 Industry. . . . . *.v.4 p.157, p.158*

Direct Legislation: Voting on Ballot Propositions in the United
 States. . . . . *.v.4 p.460*

Direct Phasing in Crystallography: Fundamentals and
 Applications. . . . . *.v.5 p.284*

Direct Wood Sculpture: Technique, Innovation,
 Creativity. . . . . *.v.1 p.782*

Directed by Dorothy Arzner. . . . . *.v.6 p.418, p.419*

⬜ DirectGov. . . . . *.v.4 p.604*

Directing Actors: Creating Memorable Performances for Film
 and Television. . . . . *.v.6 p.350*

Directing: Film Techniques and Aesthetics. . . . . *.v.6 p.350*

Directing the Documentary. . . . . *.v.6 p.309, p.310*

Directions in Sociolinguistics: The Ethnography of
 Communication. . . . . *.v.4 p.19*

Directions of Change in Rural Egypt. . . . . *.v.6 p.639*

The Director: And Other Stories from Morocco. . . . *.v.6 p.655*

Director and the Stage. . . . . *.v.1 p.137, p.152*

A Director Prepares: Seven Essays on Art and Theatre. *.v.1 p.152*

Directors in Rehearsal: A Hidden World. . . . . . *.v.1 p.152*

Directors on Directing: A Source Book of the Modern
 Theatre. *.v.1 p.152*

The Directory for Exceptional Children: A Listing of
 Educational and Training Facilities. . . *.v.4 p.316, v.5 p.574*

Directory of Adult and Juvenile Correctional Departments,
 Institutions, Agencies and Probation and Parole. . *.v.6 p.272*

Directory of African Film-Makers and Films. . . . . *.v.6 p.334*

Directory of American Philosophers. . . . . *.v.1 p.416*

Directory of Blacks in the Performing Arts. . . . . . *.v.1 p.4*

Directory of Chemistry Software, 1992. . . . . . . *.v.5 p.260*

Directory of Graduate Research. . . . . *.v.5 p.260*

The Directory of Jobs and Careers Abroad. . . . . *.v.4 p.170*

Directory of Music Faculties in Colleges and Universities, U.S. and Canada. *v.1 p.172, p.405*

Directory of Research Grants 2005. . . . . *v.4 p.293*

Directory of Theatre Training Programs, 2003-05. . . . . *v.1 p.141, p.142*

Dirksen of Illinois: Senatorial Statesman. *v.3 p.462*

Dirt and Deity: A Life of Robert Burns. *v.2 p.273*

Dirt Music: A Novel. *v.2 p.749*

The Dirt She Ate: Selected and New Poems. *v.6 p.405*

A Dirty Filthy Book: The Writings of Charles Knowlton and Annie Besant on Birth Control and Reproductive Physiology and an Account of the Bradlaugh-Besant Trial. *v.4 p.736*

Disability and Contemporary Performance: Bodies on Edge. *v.1 p.86, p.87, p.135*

Disability Matters: Legal and Pedagogical Issues of Disability in Education. *v.4 p.450*

Disability Sport and Recreation Resources. *v.4 p.784, p.801, p.842*

Disability Sport. *v.4 p.800, p.842*

☐ Disabled Sport USA. *v.4 p.787, p.789, p.842, p.843*

Disaffections: Complete Poems 1930-1950. . . . . . *v.2 p.720*

The Disappearance of God: Five Nineteenth-Century Writers. *v.2 p.176*

The Disappearance of Telecommunications. *v.4 p.420*

Disappearance of the Dowry: Women, Families, and Social Change in São Paulo, Brazil, 1600-1900. . . . . *v.3 p.337*

Disappearing Witness: Change in Twentieth-Century American Photography. *v.1 p.764*

Disarmament Without Order: The Politics of Disarmament at the United Nations. *v.4 p.655*

Disarming Iraq: Monitoring Power and Resistance. . . *v.4 p.656*

Disarming Iraq. *v.4 p.655*

Disarming Strangers: Nuclear Diplomacy with North Korea. *v.4 p.566, p.644, p.657*

Disarming the Nation: Women's Writing and the American Civil War. *v.2 p.10, v.6 p.481*

Disaster and the Millennium. *v.1 p.645*

Disasters by Design: A Reassessment of Natural Hazards in the United States. *v.5 p.423*

The Discarded Image: An Introduction to Medieval and Renaissance Literature. *v.2 p.164, v.6 p.565*

Discerning Spirits: Divine and Demonic Possession in the Middle Ages. *v.6 p.570*

Disciples of Passion. *v.6 p.658*

Discipline and Punish: The Birth of the Prison. *v.4 p.752, p.753, v.6 p.275*

The Discipline of Market Leaders: Choose Your Customers, Narrow Your Focus, Dominate Your Market. . . . *v.4 p.135*

Discipline of Power: The Conservative Interlude and the Liberal Restoration. *v.3 p.541*

A Disciplined Intelligence: Critical Inquiry and Canadian Thought in the Victorian Era. *v.3 p.535*

The Disciplined Mind: Beyond Facts and Standardized Tests, the K-12 Education That Every Child Deserves. . . . *v.4 p.343*

Disciplining Foucault: Feminism, Power and the Body. *v.6 p.461*

Disconnected America: The Consequences of Mass Media in a Narcissistic World. *v.5 p.622, p.625*

Disconnected Rivers: Linking Rivers to Landscapes. *v.5 p.172, p.242*

Disconnection. *v.2 p.532*

Discontented America: The United States in the 1920s. *v.3 p.372, p.441, p.447*

Discordant Voices: The Non-Russian Soviet Literatures, 1952-1973. . . . . *v.2 p.814*

Discourse: A Critical Introduction. *v.4 p.21*

Discourse and Ideology in Nabokov's Prose. *v.2 p.104*

The Discourse of Character Education: Culture Wars in the Classroom. *v.4 p.306*

The Discourse of Enclosure: Representing Women in Old English Literature. *v.2 p.167*

The Discourse of Race in Modern China. . . *v.6 p.189, p.190*

A Discourse of Trade, from England unto the East-Indies. *v.4 p.257*

Discourse on Free Will. *v.1 p.644*

A Discourse on Inequality. *v.3 p.148*

Discourse on Metaphysics and Other Essays. *v.1 p.459*

A Discourse on Method and Meditations on First Philosophy. *v.1 p.453, p.482*

Discourse on the Origin of Inequality, Polemics, and Political Economy. *v.2 p.483*

Discourse on the Sciences and Arts and Polemics. . . *v.2 p.482*

Discourses in America. *v.2 p.265*

Discourses on Livy. *v.2 p.709, v.4 p.492, p.502*

Discoveries and Opinions of Galileo. *v.5 p.62*

Discoveries in the Human Brain: Neuroscience Prehistory, Brain Structure, and Function. *v.5 p.617*

Discoveries in the Ruins of Nineveh and Babylon. . . . *v.3 p.5*

Discovering Ancient Egypt. *v.3 p.11*

Discovering Aquinas: An Introduction to His Life, Work, and Influence. *v.1 p.579*

Discovering Fossil Fishes: Your Guide to the Wonders of Prehistoric Ocean Life. *v.5 p.215, p.216*

Discovering Genomics, Proteomics, and Bioinformatics. *v.5 p.97, p.103, p.104, p.145*

Discovering Grammar: An Introduction to English Sentence Structure. *v.2 p.557*

Discovering History in China: American Historical Writing on the Recent Chinese Past. *v.6 p.183*

Discovering Islam: Making Sense of Muslim History and Society. *v.1 p.553*

Discovering Latino Religion: A Comprehensive Social Science Bibliography. *v.6 p.520*

Discovering Modernism: T. S. Eliot and His Context. *v.2 p.72*

Discovering Reality: Feminist Perspectives on Epistemology, Metaphysics, Methodology, and Philosophy of Science. *v.6 p.461, p.462, p.463*

Discovering Sexuality in Dostoevsky. *v.2 p.803*

Discovering the American Past: A Look at the Evidence: To 1877. . . . . *v.3 p.375*

Discovering the Chesapeake: The History of an Ecosystem. *v.5 p.169, p.233, p.234*

Discovering the Roman Family: Studies in Roman Social History. *v.3 p.23*

The Discovery and Conquest of Peru: Chronicles of the New World Encounter. *v.3 p.325*

The Discovery of America. *v.3 p.403*

The Discovery of Evolution. *v.5 p.82, p.198*

The Discovery of Freedom in Ancient Greece. . .*v.3 p.18, p.19*

The Discovery of Global Warming. *v.5 p.427*

The Discovery of Poetry: A Field Guide to Reading and Writing Poems. *v.2 p.578*

The Discovery of South America. *v.3 p.404*

The Discovery of Subatomic Particles. *v.5 p.544, p.553*

The Discovery of the Asylum: Social Order and Disorder in the New Republic. *v.6 p.273*

Discovery of the Child. *v.4 p.344*

Discovery of the Elements. *v.5 p.264*

The Discovery of the Greek Bronze Age. *v.3 p.15, p.191*

The Discovery of Time. *v.1 p.500*

Discovery: Windows of the Life Sciences. *v.5 p.80*

◻ DiscoveryGate. *v.5 p.256*

Discrete Algorithmic Mathematics. *v.5 p.478*

Discrete Chaos. *v.5 p.477*

Discrete Mathematics: Elementary and Beyond. . . .*v.5 p.478*

Discrete Mathematics. *v.5 p.337*

Discrimination at Work: The Psychological and Organizational Bases. *v.4 p.133*

Discrimination by Design: A Feminist Critique of the Man-Made Environment. *v.1 p.707, p.800,v.6 p.473*

Discrimination, Harassment and the Failure of Diversity Training: What to Do Now. *v.4 p.132*

Discussion as a Way of Teaching: Tools and Techniques for Democratic Classrooms. *v.4 p.292, p.347*

Discussions of the Canterbury Tales. *v.2 p.210*

Disease and Death in Early Colonial Mexico: Simulating Amerindian Depopulation, Vol. 28. . . . .*v.3 p.288*

Diseases of Poultry. *v.5 p.56, p.57*

Diseases of the Human Body. *v.5 p.514*

Diseases of the Liver and Biliary System in Children. .*v.5 p.519*

Diseases of Trees and Shrubs. *v.5 p.47*

Diseasing of America: How We Allowed Recovery Zealots and the Treatment Industry to Convince Us We Are out of Control. *v.4 p.777*

The Disenchanted Self: Representing the Subject in the Canterbury Tales. *v.2 p.209*

The Disenchanted. *v.2 p.115*

Dishonest Broker: America's Role in Israel and Palestine. *v.4 p.560, p.565, p.641*

Disilicates and Ring Silicates. *v.5 p.436*

Disintegrating the Musical: Black Performance and American Musical Film. *v.6 p.316, p.330, p.342*

Dislocating Cultures: Identities, Traditions and Third World Feminism. *v.6 p.435*

Disloyalty in the Confederacy. *v.3 p.429*

Dismantling Democratic States. *v.4 p.581*

Dismantling Desegregation: The Quiet Reversal of Brown vs. Board of Education. *v.4 p.301*

Dismantling the Universe: The Nature of Scientific Discovery. *v.5 p.409*

Dismembering Lahui: A History of the Hawaiian Nation to 1887. . . . .*v.6 p.131*

Disney Discourse: Producing the Magic Kingdom. . .*v.6 p.308*

The Disobedient Generation: Social Theorists in the Sixties. *v.4 p.684*

Disorder and Progress: Bandits, Police, and Mexican Development. *v.3 p.289*

The Disordered Couple. *v.5 p.661, p.667, p.668*

Disordered Eating among Athletes: A Comprehensive Guide for Health Professionals. *v.4 p.801, p.824, p.825, p.876*

Disorderly Women: Sexual Politics and Evangelicalism in Revolutionary New England. *v.1 p.583*

Disorders of Learning in Childhood. *v.5 p.574, p.575*

The Disorders of War: The Revolution in South Carolina. *v.3 p.410*

Disorientations: Cultural Praxis in Theatre: Asia, Pacific, and Australia. *v.1 p.128, p.133*

Disoriented: Asian Americans, Law and the Nation State. *v.4 p.456, v.6 p.107, p.117*

Dis-Orienting Rhythms: The Politics of the New Asian Dance Music. *v.4 p.26*

Disowning Knowledge: In Seven Plays of Shakespeare.*v.2 p.228*

La disparition. *v.2 p.533*

Dispatches from the Ebony Tower: Intellectuals Confront the African American Experience. *v.6 p.7, p.21*

The Dispersion of Egyptian Jewry: Culture, Politics, and the Formation of a Modern Diaspora. . .*v.6 p.596, p.634, p.635*

Displacing Homophobia: Gay Male Perspectives in Literature and Culture. *v.6 p.392*

Displacing Natives: The Rhetorical Production of Hawaii. *v.6 p.131*

Displaying Women: Spectacles of Leisure in Edith Wharton's New York. *v.2 p.131*

Disposable Domestics: Immigrant Women Workers in the Global Economy. *v.6 p.456*

Disposable People: New Slavery in the Global Economy. *v.4 p.27, p.28*

The Dispossessed: America's Underclasses from the Civil War to the Present. *v.4 p.708*

Disraeli Gears: Cream. *v.1 p.273, p.319*

Disraeli. *v.2 p.275, v.3 p.93, p.110,v.6 p.757*

The Disruption of American Democracy. . . .*v.3 p.399, p.421*

Disruption: Overturning Conventions and Shaking up the Marketplace. *v.4 p.428*

Disruptive Acts: The New Woman in Fin-de-Siecle France. *v.3 p.54, p.155*

Disruptive Divas: Feminism, Identity, and Popular Music. *v.1 p.378*

Dissection Guide and Atlas of the Fetal Pig. *v.5 p.89*

Dissections: Plane and Fancy. *v.5 p.469*

Dissent and Reform in the Early Middle Ages. . . .*v.6 p.573*

Dissent in the Years of Krushchev: Nine Stories about Disobedient Russians. *v.3 p.228*

Dissent on Development: Studies and Debates in Development Economics. *v.4 p.242*

Dissenting Knowledges, Open Futures: The Multiple Selves and Strange Destinations of Ashis Nandy. *v.6 p.150*

Dissociation Constants of Organic Acids in Aqueous Solution. *v.5 p.300*

Dissociation Constants of Organic Bases in Aqueous Solution. *v.5 p.300*

The Dissolution of the Habsburg Monarchy. *v.3 p.183*

Dissolution of the Monasteries. *v.1 p.578*

Dissolution: The Crisis of Communism and the End of East Germany. *v.3 p.177*

Distance Education: The Complete Guide to Design, Delivery, and Improvement. *v.4 p.321, p.322*

Distance Sampling: Estimating Abundance of Biological Populations. *v.5 p.92, p.188*

A Distant City: Images of Urban Experience in the Medieval World. *v.6 p.577, p.712*

Distant Dances. *v.1 p.11*

Distant Friends: The United States and Russia, 1763-1867. . . . .*v.3 p.392*

A Distant Heritage: The Growth of Free Speech in Early America. *v.4 p.459*

Distant Lands: The Genesis and Evolution of Romanian-American Relations. *v.3 p.392*

The Distant Magnet; European Emigration to the U. S. A. *v.4 p.668*

Distant Star. *v.2 p.679*

A Distant Technology: Science Fiction Film and the Machine Age. *v.6 p.320*

A Distant Trumpet. *v.2 p.81*

Distant View of a Minaret and Other Stories. *v.6 p.663*

Distinction: A Social Critique of the Judgement of Taste. .*v.4 p.726*

Distinguished Asian American Business Leaders. .*v.6 p.87, p.107*

Distinguished Asian American Political and Governmental Leaders. *v.6 p.86, p.94, p.120, p.121*

Distinguished Asian Americans: A Biographical Dictionary. *v.6 p.86*

Distinguished Women Economists. *v.4 p.193*

The Distorted Past: A Re-Interpretation of Europe. . .*v.3 p.35*

Distributed Algorithms. *v.5 p.345*

Distributed Power Generation: Planning and Evaluation, Vol. 10. . . . .*v.5 p.724, p.725*

Distributed Systems. *v.5 p.345*

Distributed Work. *v.4 p.69*

The Distribution of Wealth: A Theory of Wages, Interest and Profits. *v.4 p.223, p.252*

The Distribution of Wealth and Universal Economic Laws. *v.4 p.223*

The Distribution of Wealth. *v.4 p.266*

Distribution: Planning and Control—Managing in the Era of Supply Chain Management. *v.4 p.118*

District and Circle: Poems. *v.2 p.352*

District of Columbia: A Bicentennial History. *v.3 p.493*

Disturbance and Recovery in Arctic Lands: An Ecological Perspective: Proceedings of the NATO Advanced Research Workshop on Disturbance and Recovery of Arctic Terrestrial Ecosystems, Rovaniemi, Finland, 24-30 Sept. 1995. . . . .*v.5 p.175, p.183, p.238*

Disturbed Soil Properties and Geotechnical Design. . .*v.5 p.699*

The Disturbed Violent Offender. *v.6 p.277*

Disturbing the Universe. *v.5 p.542*

Ditte. *v.2 p.627*

Div, Grad, Curl, and All That: An Informal Text on Vector Calculus. *v.5 p.486*

The Divan-I-Hafiz. *v.6 p.671*

Diva. *v.6 p.404*

Divergent Series. *v.5 p.490*

Diverse Sexuality and Schools: A Reference Handbook. .*v.6 p.385*

Diversified Health Occupations. *v.5 p.533*

Diversifying the Los Angeles Area Latino Mosaic: Salvadoran and Guatemalan Leaders' Assessments of Community Public Policy Needs. *v.6 p.537, p.547*

Diversifying the New York Area Hispanic Mosaic: Colombian and Dominican Leaders' Assessments of Community Public Policy Needs. *v.6 p.537, p.547, p.548*

Diversity: A Biography of a Concept. *v.4 p.709*

Diversity and Citizenship Education: Global Perspectives. *v.4 p.313*

Diversity and Developmentally Appropriate Practice in Early Childhood Education: Challenges for Early Childhood Education. *v.4 p.369*

Diversity and Distrust: Civic Education in a Multicultural Democracy. *v.4 p.328*

Diversity and Interactions in a Temperate Forest Community: Ogawa Forest Reserve of Japan. *v.5 p.176*

Diversity and Public Administration: Theory, Issues, and Perspectives. *v.4 p.545, p.580, p.581*

Diversity in Advertising: Broadening the Scope of Research Directions. *v.4 p.426*

Diversity in Counseling. *v.5 p.636*

Diversity in the Power Elite: Have Women and Minorities Reached the Top? *v.4 p.133*

Diversity in the Work Force. *v.4 p.132*

The Diversity of Amphibians and Reptiles: An Introduction. *v.5 p.214*

A Diversity of Creatures and Letters of. *v.2 p.297*

The Diversity of Human Relationships. *v.5 p.646*

Diversity of Life: The Illustrated Guide to the Five Kingdoms. *v.5 p.205*

The Diversity of Life. *v.5 p.359*

The Diversity of Living Organisms. *v.5 p.204*

The Diverted Dream: Community Colleges and the Promise of Educational Opportunity in America, 1900-1985. . . . .*v.4 p.291, p.330, p.331*

Divide and Dissent: Kentucky Politics, 1930-1963. . .*v.3 p.511*

Divide and Rule: The Partition of Africa, 1880-1914. . . . .*v.3 p.77, v.4 p.583, v.6 p.11*

The Divided Academy. *v.4 p.292*

Divided Arrival: Narratives of the Puerto Rican Migration, 1920-1950. . . . .*v.6 p.529*

Divided Borders: Essays on Puerto Rican Identity. . .*v.6 p.543*

The Divided City: On Memory and Forgetting in Ancient Athens. *v.3 p.20*

Divided Countries, Separated Cities. *v.6 p.159*

Divided Cyprus: Modernity, History, and an Island in Conflict. *v.6 p.601*

Divided Democrats: Ideological Unity, Party Reform, and Presidential Elections. *v.4 p.551, p.553*

Divided Empire: Milton's Political Imagery. *v.2 p.253*

Divided Families: What Happens to Children When Parents Part. *v.4 p.739, p.740,v.5 p.640*

The Divided Ground: Indians, Settlers, and the Northern Borderland of the American Revolution. *v.4 p.581, v.6 p.686*

Divided Hearts: Britain and the American Civil War. *v.4 p.519*

The Divided Heritage: Themes and Problems in German Modernism. *v.1 p.680, p.688*

A Divided Legacy: The Partition in Selected Novels of India, Pakistan, and Bangladesh. *v.2 p.761*

Divided Loyalties: Canadian Concepts of Federalism. *v.4 p.586*

Divided Loyalties: Nationalism and Mass Politics in Syria at the Close of Empire. *v.6 p.607*

Divided Memory: The Nazi Past in the Two Germanys. *v.3 p.178*

Divided We Fail: Issues of Equity in American Schools. *v.4 p.302*

Divided We Fall: Gambling with History in the Nineties. *v.3 p.473*

Divided We Fought: A Pictorial History of the War 1861. . . . . *v.3 p.429*

Divided We Govern: Party Control, Lawmaking and Investigations, 1946-1990. . . . . *v.3 p.443*

Divided We Govern: Party Control, Lawmaking, and Investigations, 1946-2002. . . . . *v.4 p.551, p.552*

Dividend Policy: Its Impact on Firm Value. . . . *v.4 p.91, p.95*

La Divina Commedia. *v.2 p.703*

Divine and Human Action: Essays in the Metaphysics of Theism. *v.1 p.499*

The Divine Comedy of Dante Alighieri: Inferno, Vol. 1. *v.2 p.703*

The Divine Comedy of Dante Alighieri: Purgatorio. . *v.2 p.703*

The Divine Comedy: The Inferno, the Purgatorio and the Paradiso. *v.2 p.702*

The Divine Comedy. *v.2 p.702, p.703*

The Divine Consort: R-adh-a and the Goddesses of India. *v.1 p.536*

Divine Dancer: A Biography of Ruth St. Denis. . . . *v.1 p.12*

The Divine Dramatist: George Whitefield and the Rise of Modern Evangelicalism. *v.1 p.586, p.587, p.607, p.649*

Divine Empathy: A Theology of God. *v.1 p.635*

The Divine Hierarchy: Popular Hinduism in Central India. *v.1 p.534, p.539*

The Divine Nine: The History of African-American Fraternities and Sororities in America. *v.4 p.289*

Divine Passions: The Social Construction of Emotion in India. *v.6 p.154*

Divine Player: A Study of Krsna Lila. *v.1 p.536*

The Divine Relativity: A Social Conception of God. . *v.1 p.525*

Divine Sovereignty: The Origins of Modern State Power. *v.4 p.491, p.496, p.498*

Divine Utterances: The Performance of Afro-Cuban Santeria. *v.1 p.292*

The Divine Virginia: A Biography of Virginia Zucchi. . *v.1 p.8*

The Diviners. *v.2 p.736*

Diving Deep and Surfacing: Women Writers on Spiritual Quest. *v.1 p.528*

Divining Desire: Tennyson and the Poetics of Transcendence. *v.2 p.313*

Division and Discord: The Supreme Court under Stone and Vinson, 1941-1953. . . . . *v.4 p.469*

☐ Division of Child, Youth, and Family Services (APA Division 37). *v.5 p.671*

The Division of Labor in Society. *v.4 p.722*

The Division of Literature: Or the University in Deconstruction. *v.2 p.456*

☐ Division of School Psychology (APA Division 16). *v.5 p.576*

Divisions on a Ground: Essays on Canadian Culture. *v.3 p.535*

Divorce: An American Tradition. *v.5 p.640*

Divorce: Causes and Consequences. *v.5 p.639*

Divorce: Crisis, Challenge or Relief? *v.4 p.739*

Divorce in Psychosocial Perspective: Theory and Research. *v.5 p.640*

Divorce Talk: Women and Men Make Sense of Personal Relationships. *v.6 p.467*

Divorced in America: Marriage in an Age of Possibility. *v.4 p.739*

Divus Julius Caesar. *v.2 p.444*

The Dixie Frontier: A Social History of the Southern Frontier from the First Transmontaine Beginnings to the Civil War. *v.3 p.510*

Dixie Rising: How the South Is Shaping American Values, Politics, and Culture. *v.3 p.496*

Dizionario critico della letteratura italiana del Novecento. *v.2 p.698*

Django: The Life and Music of a Gypsy Legend. *v.1 p.258, p.350*

Djinn : un trou rouge entre les pavés disjoints. . . . *v.2 p.525*

Djuka Society and Social Change: History of an Attempt to Develop a Bush Negro Community in Surinam, 1917-1926. . . . . *v.3 p.322*

Djuna: The Life and Work of Djuna Barnes. *v.6 p.402*

DLB 147: South Slavic Writers Before World War II. *v.2 p.779*

☐ DLESE: Digital Library for Earth System Education. *v.5 p.419*

DNA Analysis. *v.5 p.134*

DNA and Destiny: Nature and Nurture in Human Behavior. *v.5 p.612, p.658*

DNA and RNA Binders, from Small Molecules to Drugs, Vol. 1. . . . . *v.5 p.121, p.124*

DNA and the Criminal Justice System: The Technology of Justice. *v.6 p.266, p.270*

DNA Arrays: Methods and Protocols. *v.5 p.103*

DNA Arrays: Technologies and Experimental Strategies. *v.5 p.121*

DNA Fingerprinting: An Introduction. *v.5 p.122*

DNA Methylation: Approaches, Methods, and Applications. *v.5 p.132*

DNA Microarrays: A Molecular Cloning Manual. . . *v.5 p.110*

DNA Microarrays: A Practical Approach. *v.5 p.110*

DNA Microarrays and Gene Expression: From Experiments to Data Analysis and Modeling. *v.5 p.109, p.110, p.120, p.130*

DNA Microarrays and Related Genomic Techniques: Statistical Design, Analysis, and Interpretation of Experiments. *v.5 p.109, p.120*

DNA Microarrays: Gene Expression
    Applications. v.5 p.102, p.122

DNA Pioneers and Their Legacy. v.5 p.122

DNA Repair and Mutagenesis. v.5 p.121, p.133

DNA Repair, Pt. A. v.5 p.131

DNA Replication. v.5 p.122

DNA Science: A First Course. v.5 p.122

DNA Sequencing. v.5 p.131

DNA Structure and Function. v.5 p.123

DNA Technology: The Awesome Skill. v.5 p.130

DNA: The Double Helix: Perspective and Prospective at Forty
    Years. v.5 p.131

DNA: The Secret of Life. v.5 p.123

DNA, Words and Models: Statistics of Exceptional
    Words. v.5 p.107, p.123, p.146, p.219

Do Animals Think? v.5 p.616

Do Conventions Matter?: Choosing National Party Leaders in
    Canada. .v.4 p.588

Do Oxen Low When Mangers Are Full?: Novel. . . .v.2 p.815

Do You Hear Them? v.2 p.527

Doctor Fausti Weheklag; die Volksbücher von D. Johann Faust
    und Christoph Wagner. Nach den Erstdrucken neu
    bearb. und eingeleitet von Helmut Wiemken. v.2 p.593

Doctor Faustus: The Life of the German Composer, Adrian
    Leverkuhn, As Told by a Friend. v.2 p.613

Doctor Sax. .v.2 p.93

Doctor Thorne. v.2 p.318

Doctor Zhivago. v.2 p.806

The Doctor's House. v.2 p.140

Doctors: The Biography of Medicine. v.5 p.510

□ Doctors Without Borders/ Medecins Sans Frontieres. .v.4 p.668

Doctrine and Argument in Indian Philosophy. v.1 p.476

Doctrine and Covenants of the Church of Jesus Christ of
    Latter-Day Saints: Containing the Revelations
    Given to Joseph Smith, Jun, the Prophet, for the Building up
    of the Kingdom of God in the Last Days. v.1 p.587

The Doctrine of Being in the Aristotelian Metaphysics: A Study
    in the Greek Background of Mediaeval Thought. . .v.1 p.427

The Doctrine of the Sufis. v.1 p.559

Doc. v.2 p.738

Documentary: A History of the Non-Fiction Film. . .v.6 p.308

Documentary Archaeology in the New World. v.4 p.6

Documentary Film Classics. v.6 p.310

The Documentary Film Movement: An Anthology. . .v.6 p.308

Documentary Filmmakers Speak. v.6 p.310

A Documentary History of Art: Michelangelo and the
    Mannerists, the Baroque and the Eighteenth Century. .v.1 p.675

A Documentary History of Art: The Middle Ages and the
    Renaissance. v.1 p.672, p.675

A Documentary History of Banking and Currency in the United
    States. .v.4 p.246

A Documentary History of Communism in Russia: From Lenin
    to Gorbachev. v.3 p.222

Documentary History of Hong Kong: Economy. . . .v.6 p.205

A Documentary History of Hong Kong: Society. . . .v.6 p.205

A Documentary History of Indian South Africans. . .v.6 p.78

Documentary History of Reconstruction: Political, Military,
    Social, Religious, Educational and Industrial. . .v.3 p.436

A Documentary History of Religion in America since
    1877. . . . . .v.1 p.543

□ The Documentary History of the Ratification of the
    Constitution. v.4 p.451

Documentary Screens: Non-Fiction Film and
    Television. v.4 p.413, v.6 p.308, p.309

Documentary Storytelling for Video and Filmmakers. .v.6 p.309

Documenting America, 1935-1943. . . . . .v.1 p.763

Documenting Ourselves: Film, Video, and Culture. . .v.6 p.310

Documenting the Documentary: Close Readings of Documentary
    Film and Video. v.6 p.309

□ Documents from the Continental Congress and the
    Constitutional Convention, 1774-1789. . . . . .v.4 p.518

□ Documents from the Women's Liberation Movement: An
    On-line Archival Collection. v.6 p.432

Documents in Medieval Latin. v.2 p.450

Documents of American Constitutional and Legal History: From
    the Age of Industrialization to the Present. v.4 p.440

Documents of American Constitutional and Legal History: From
    the Founding Through the Age of
    Industrialization. v.4 p.440, p.441

Documents of American Indian Diplomacy: Treaties,
    Agreements, and Conventions,
    1775-1979. . . . . .v.4 p.464, v.6 p.695

Documents of Ancient Greek Music: The Extant Melodies and
    Fragments. v.1 p.176

Documents of Texas History (1528-1993). v.3 p.509

Documents of the American Revolution, Vol. 10. . . .v.3 p.408

Documents of the American Revolution, Vol. 11. . . .v.3 p.408

Documents of the American Revolution, Vol. 12. . . .v.3 p.408

Documents of the American Revolution, Vol. 13. . . .v.3 p.408

Documents of the American Revolution, Vol. 14. . . .v.3 p.408

Documents of the American Revolution, Vol. 15. .v.3 p.408, p.409

Documents of the American Revolution, Vol. 16. . . .v.3 p.408

Documents of the American Revolution, Vol. 17. . . .v.3 p.408

Documents of the American Revolution, Vol. 18. . . .v.3 p.408

Documents of the American Revolution, Vol. 19. . . .v.3 p.408

Documents of the American Revolution, Vol. 20. . . .v.3 p.408

Documents of the American Revolution, Vol. 21. . . .v.3 p.408

Documents of the American Revolution, Vol. 2. . . .v.3 p.408

Documents of the American Revolution, Vol. 3. . . .v.3 p.408

Documents of the American Revolution, Vol. 4. . . .v.3 p.408

Documents of the American Revolution, Vol. 5. . . .v.3 p.409

Documents of the American Revolution, Vol. 6. . . .v.3 p.408

Documents of the American Revolution, Vol. 7. . . .v.3 p.408

Documents of the American Revolution, Vol. 8. . . .v.3 p.408

Documents of the American Revolution, Vol. 9. . . .v.3 p.408

Documents of the American Revolution. v.3 p.408

Documents of the Christian Church. v.1 p.597, v.3 p.56

Documents of the Coronado Expedition, 1539-1542: They Were
    Not Familiar with His Majesty, nor Did They Wish to Be His
    Subjects. v.3 p.403

Documents of the Vatican Council. v.1 p.570

Documents of United States Indian Policy. v.6 p.692

The Documents of Vatican II. *v.1 p.570*

Documents on the French Revolution 1848. . .*v.3 p.153, p.154*

Documents on the Holocaust: Selected Sources on the
Destruction of the Jews of Germany and Austria, Poland, and
the Soviet Union. *v.3 p.82*

Documents on the Rape of Nanking. *v.6 p.193*

Documents on the Suez Crisis, 26 July to 6 November
1956. . . . .*v.4 p.628*

Documents Relating to the Sentimental Agents in the Volyen
Empire. *v.2 p.364*

Doers of the Word: African-American Women Speakers and
Writers in the North (1830-1880). *v.6 p.8, p.45*

Does America Need a Foreign Policy?: Toward a Diplomacy for
the 21st Century. *v.3 p.452, p.453*

Does Atlas Shrug?: The Economic Consequences of Taxing the
Rich. *v.4 p.107, p.108*

Does Foreign Direct Investment Promote Development. .*v.4 p.60*

Does God Belong in Public Schools? *v.4 p.298, p.307*

Does God Exist?: An Answer for Today. *v.1 p.639*

Does God Exist?: The Craig-Flew Debate. *v.1 p.498*

Does Jane Compute?: Preserving Our Daughters' Place in the
Cyber Revolution. *v.6 p.438, p.439*

Does Your Mama Know?: An Anthology of Black Lesbian
Coming Out Stories. *v.6 p.369, p.407*

Doña Inés: Historia de Amor. *v.2 p.656*

The Dog: Its Behavior, Nutrition and Health. . .*v.5 p.54, p.56*

Dog Years. *v.2 p.608*

Dogeaters. *v.6 p.100*

Dogma in Medieval Jewish Thought: From Maimonides to
Abravanel. *v.1 p.552*

Doing Business In 2006: Creating Jobs. . .*v.4 p.58, p.110, p.112*

Doing Business in the Middle East: Politics and Economic
Crisis in Jordan and Kuwait. *v.6 p.594*

Doing Business Internationally: The Guide to Cross-Cultural
Success. *v.4 p.59*

Doing Business Internationally: The Resource for Business and
Social Etiquette. *v.4 p.57*

Doing Business with the Government: Federal, State, Local and
Foreign Purchasing Practices for Every Business and Public
Institution. *v.4 p.524, p.525*

Doing Daily Battle: Interviews with Moroccan Women. .*v.6 p.643*

Doing Our Own Thing: The Degradation of Language and
Music and Why We Should, Like, Care. *v.2 p.552*

Doing Science: Design, Analysis, and Communication of
Scientific Research. *v.5 p.399, p.409*

Doing Social Life: The Qualitative Study of Human Interaction
in Natural Settings. *v.4 p.692*

Doing Their Bit: Wartime American Animated Short Films,
1939-1945. . . . .*v.6 p.308*

Doing Theology in a Revolutionary Situation. *v.1 p.637*

Doing Time on the Outside: Incarceration and Family Life in
Urban America. *v.6 p.276*

Doing Women's Work: Men in Nontraditional
Occupations. *v.6 p.458*

Dok Suni: Recipes from My Mother's Korean Kitchen. .*v.6 p.235*

The Dollar and the Policy Mix: 1971. . . . . . .*v.4 p.247*

The Doll. *v.2 p.791*

Dolly City. *v.6 p.648*

Dom Casmurro. *v.2 p.691*

Dombey and Son. by Charles Dickens. (Boz). with ...
illustrations. from designs of Phiz [pseud.] and
Cruikshank. *v.2 p.283*

The Dome and the Rock: Structure in the Poetry of Wallace
Stevens. *v.2 p.123*

The Dome of Silence: Sexual Harrassment and Abuse in
Sport. *v.4 p.817, p.840*

Domenico Scarlatti: Master of Music. *v.1 p.182, p.352*

Domenico Scarlatti. *v.1 p.185, p.352*

Domenico Tiepolo: Master Draftsman. *v.1 p.723*

Domesday Book: A Complete Translation. *v.3 p.96, p.97*

Domesday Book: A Survey of the Counties of England. *v.3 p.97*

☐ Domesday Book Online. *v.6 p.561*

Domesday Gazetteer. *v.3 p.126*

Domestic and Foreign Finance in Modern Peru, 1850-1950:
Financing Visions of Development. *v.3 p.331*

Domestic Animal Behavior for Veterinarians and Animal
Scientists. *v.5 p.55, p.57*

Domestic Architecture and Power: The Historical Archaeology
of Colonial Ecuador. *v.4 p.14*

The Domestic Dog: Its Evolution, Behaviour and Interactions
with People. *v.5 p.166*

Domestic Government: Kinship, Community, and Polity in
North Yemen. *v.6 p.628*

Domestic Individualism: Imagining Self in Nineteenth-Century
America. *v.2 p.9*

Domestic Interiors: The British Tradition 1500-1850. *v.1 p.800*

The Domestic Life of a Medieval City: Women, Children and
the Family in Fourteenth-Century Ghent. . .*v.6 p.560, p.577*

Domestic Society in Medieval Europe: A Select
Bibliography. *v.6 p.557*

Domestic Sources of International Environmental Policy:
Industry, Environmentalists, and U. S.
Power. *v.5 p.29, v.6 p.299*

Domestic Tyranny: The Making of Social Policy Against Family
Violence from Colonial Times to the Present. .*v.4 p.742, p.743*

Domesticating Drink: Women, Men, and Alcohol in America,
1870-1940. . . . .*v.5 p.664, v.6 p.470*

Domestication of Plants in the Old World: The Origin and
Spread of Cultivated Plants in West Asia, Europe,
and the Nile Valley. *v.5 p.24, p.45*

The Domestication of the Human Species. *v.4 p.17*

Doméstica: Immigrant Workers Cleaning and Caring in the
Shadows of Affluence. *v.6 p.524, p.525, p.546*

Dominance Without Hegemony: History and Power in Colonial
India. *v.6 p.157*

Dominant Beliefs and Alternative Voices: Discourse, Belief and
Gender in American Study Abroad. *v.6 p.462*

Domination and Cultural Resistance: Authority and Power
among Andean People. *v.3 p.324, p.331*

The Dominican Americans. *v.6 p.522*

The Dominican Diaspora: From the Dominican Republic to New
York City, Villagers in Transition. *v.6 p.529, p.549*

The Dominican People: A Documentary History. *v.3 p.317, p.318*

The Dominican Republic: A National History. *v.3 p.317*

Dominican Studies Institute. *v.6 p.486*

The Dominicans. *v.1 p.577*

The Dominion of War: Empire and Liberty in North America 1500-2000. . . . .*v.3 p.382*

The Dominions and India since 1900: Select Documents on the Constitutional History of the British Empire and Commonwealth. *v.4 p.435, p.436*

Dominique, Vol. 1. . . . .*v.2 p.490*

Dominique, Vol. 2. . . . .*v.2 p.490*

Dominique. *v.2 p.490*

Dominoes and Other Stories from the Puerto Rican. *v.6 p.495, p.504, p.505*

Dominoes. *v.2 p.489*

Don Giovanni. *v.1 p.192, p.232, p.344*

Don Juan: And Other Plays. *v.2 p.475*

Don Juan de Onate, Colonizer of New Mexico 1595: 1628. . . . .*v.3 p.528*

Don Juan. *v.2 p.273, p.475*

Don Markstein's Toonopedia. *v.6 p.308*

Don Quixote de la Mancha. *v.2 p.648*

Don Quixote in Exile. *v.3 p.317*

Don Quixote. *v.2 p.648, p.649, p.650*

Don Segundo Sombra. *v.2 p.678*

Dona Barbara: Translated into English. *v.2 p.687*

Dona Flor and Her Two Husbands. *v.2 p.689*

Dona Luz. *v.2 p.655*

Donald Davidson: Meaning, Truth, Language, and Reality. *v.1 p.442*

Donald Davidson. *v.1 p.442*

Donald Davie: Collected Poems. *v.2 p.342*

Donald Judd. *v.1 p.773*

A Donald Justice Reader: Selected Poetry and Prose. . *v.2 p.90*

Donatello: Sculptor. *v.1 p.781*

Donating and Exploiting DNA: Social and Ethical Aspects of Public Participation in Genetic Databases. *v.5 p.121*

The Donatist Church: A Movement of Protest in Roman North Africa. *v.1 p.646*

Done into Dance: Isadora Duncan in America. . . .*v.1 p.7, p.26*

Donizetti. *v.1 p.193, p.228, p.321*

The Donkey, the Carrot, and the Club: William C. Bullitt and Soviet-American Relations, 1917-1948. . . . . . .*v.3 p.456*

Don't: A Reader's Guide to the Military's Anti-Gay Policy. *v.6 p.389*

Don't Ask, Don't Tell: Debating the Gay Ban in the U. S. Military. *v.4 p.569, v.6 p.389*

Don't Breathe the Air: Air Pollution and U. S. Environmental Politics, 1945-1970. . . . .*v.4 p.566, v.6 p.299*

Don't Call It Night. *v.6 p.650*

Don't Call Us Out of Name: The Untold Lives of Women and Girls in Poor America. *v.6 p.469*

Don't Look Back: Satchel Paige on the Shadows of Baseball. *v.4 p.809, p.833, p.852*

Don't Look Now. *v.2 p.343*

Don't Make Me Think: A Common Sense Approach to the Web Usability. *v.5 p.338, p.339*

Don't Tell Alfred. *v.2 p.371*

Don't Think Pink: What Really Makes Women Buy -- and How to Increase Your Share of This Crucial Market. . . .*v.5 p.587*

Don't You Know There's a War On?: The American Home Front, 1941-1945. . . . .*v.3 p.474*

Doo-Dah!: Stephen Foster and the Rise of American Popular Culture. *v.1 p.277, p.324*

Doomed to Fail: The Built-in Defects of American Education. *v.4 p.340*

The Doorman: A Novel. *v.2 p.670*

The Doorman. *v.6 p.505*

The Doors Companion: Four Decades of Commentary. *v.1 p.273, p.321, p.322*

The Door. *v.2 p.786*

Doping in Elite Sport: The Politics of Drugs in the Olympic Movement. *v.4 p.826, p.846, p.847*

Dorian's Dictionary of Science and Technology: German - English. *v.5 p.387*

Dorian's Dictionary of Science and Technology, Vol. II. .*v.5 p.387*

Doris Humphrey: An Artist First. *v.1 p.9*

Doris Lessing: A Biography. *v.2 p.364*

The Doris Lessing Reader. *v.2 p.364*

Doris Lessing: The Poetics of Change. *v.2 p.364*

Doris Lessing. *v.2 p.365, p.366*

Dorland's Illustrated Medical Dictionary. *v.5 p.325, p.509*

Dorothy Hodgkin: A Life. *v.5 p.262*

Dorothy L. Sayers: A Literary Biography. *v.2 p.381*

Dorothy Parker: What Fresh Hell Is This? *v.2 p.110*

Dorothy Wordsworth and Romanticism. *v.2 p.322*

Dorothy Wordsworth. *v.2 p.322*

Do's and Taboos Around the World for Women in Business. *v.4 p.57*

Do's and Taboos around the World. *v.4 p.56, p.58*

Dos Passos: A Collection of Critical Essays. *v.2 p.69*

The Dose Makes the Poison: A Plain-Language Guide to Toxicology. *v.5 p.314*

Dossier Secreto: Argentina's Desaparecidos and the Myth of the "Dirty War". *v.3 p.347*

Dostoevsky and the Christian Tradition. *v.2 p.806, p.807*

A Dostoevsky Dictionary. *v.2 p.796*

The Dostoevsky Encyclopedia. *v.2 p.805*

Dostoevsky's the Devils: A Critical Companion. . . .*v.2 p.805*

Dostoyevsky and the Process of Literary Creation. *v.2 p.797, p.802*

Dostoyevsky: The Brothers Karamazov. *v.2 p.805*

A Dot on the Map: Selected Stories and Poems. . . .*v.6 p.666*

Double Agency: Acts of Impersonation in Asian American Literature and Culture. *v.6 p.95, p.123*

Double Consciousness - Double Bind: Theoretical Issues in Twentieth-Century Black Literature. *v.6 p.22*

The Double Helix: A Personal Account of the Discovery of the Structure of DNA. *v.3 p.463, v.5 p.123*

The Double Life of George Sand. *v.2 p.500*

Double or Nothing?: Jewish Families and Mixed Marriage. *v.4 p.721*

A Double Singleness: Gender and the Writings of Charles and Mary Lamb. *v.2 p.298*

Double Vision: Four Slovene Poets. *v.2 p.812*

Double-Chain Silicates. *v.5 p.436*

The Double-Edged Helix: Social Implications of Genetics in a
Diverse Society. *v.5 p.130*

The Double-Edged Sword: How Character Makes and Ruins
Presidents, from Washington to Clinton. *v.3 p.378*

Doubt: A Parable. *v.2 p.155*

Doubt and Dogmatism: Studies in Hellenistic
Epistemology. *v.1 p.517*

The Doubtful Strait. *v.2 p.675*

Doughboy War: The American Expeditionary Force in World
War I. *v.3 p.472*

Douglas Gordon. *v.1 p.772*

Douglas Jerrold: A Life (1803-1857). *v.6 p.754, p.755*

The Douglas Opinions. *v.4 p.437*

Douglas Southall Freeman. *v.3 p.374*

Doves of War: Four Women of Spain. *v.3 p.241, p.242*

Dowland: Lachrimae (1604). . .*v.1 p.180, p.239, p.240, p.322*

Down and Dirty: Hollywoods Exploitation Filmmakers and
Their Movies. *v.6 p.314*

Down and Out in Paris and London. *v.2 p.375*

Down by the Lemonade Springs: Essays on Wallace
Stegner. *v.2 p.121*

Down by the River: Drugs, Money, Murder, and Family. *v.4 p.764*

Down from Olympus: Archaeology and Philhellenism in
Germany, 1750-1970. . . . .*v.3 p.178, p.179, p.191*

Down from the Shimmering Sky: Masks of the Northwest
Coast. *v.1 p.777, v.6 p.679*

Down on Their Luck: A Study of Homeless Street
People. *v.4 p.751*

Down the Nights and down the Days: Eugene O'Neill's
Catholic Sensibility. *v.2 p.108*

Down There on a Visit. *v.2 p.356*

Down These Mean Streets. *v.6 p.491, p.509*

Down to Earth: Nature's Role in American History. . *v.6 p.296*

Down with Big Brother: The Fall of the Soviet Empire. *v.3 p.228*

The Downfall of the Anti-Semitic Political Parties in Imperial
Germany. *v.4 p.609, p.610*

Downsizing Prisons: How to Reduce Crime and End Mass
Incarceration. *v.6 p.274*

Downstream. *v.2 p.494*

Downtown America: A History of the Place and the People Who
Made It. *v.6 p.713*

Downtown: Its Rise and Fall, 1880-1950. . . . . . .*v.6 p.712*

Dow's Fire and Explosion Index Hazard Classification
Guide. *v.5 p.743*

Doxology: The Praise of God in Worship, Doctrine and Life: A
Systematic Theology. *v.1 p.637*

A Dozen French Farces from the 15th to the 20th
Centuries. *v.2 p.464, p.465*

Dr. Ambedkar and Untouchability: Fighting the Indian Caste
System. *v.6 p.159*

Dr. Fischer of Geneva or the Bomb Party. *v.2 p.349*

Dr. Fisher's Life on the Ark: Green Alligators, Bushman, and
Other. *v.5 p.83*

Dr. Lavendar's People. *v.2 p.36*

Dr. Strangelove: Or How I Learned to Stop Worrying and Love
the Bomb. *v.2 p.347*

Dracula: Authoritative Text, Contexts, Reviews and Reactions,
Criticism, Dramatic and Film Variations. *v.2 p.306*

The Drafting of the Covenant. *v.4 p.631*

Dragon Bone Hill: An Ice-Age Saga of Homo Erectus. *v.4 p.16*

Dragon Country, Eight Plays: In the Bar of a Tokyo Hotel,
Mutilated, Gnadiges Fraulein, I Rise in Flames
Cried the Phoenix, I Can't Imagine Tomorrow, Confessional,
Frosted Glass Coffin and Perfect Analysis Given by a
Parrot. *v.2 p.135*

The Dragon Empress. *v.6 p.189, p.203, p.217*

The Dragon in the Land of Snows: A History of Modern Tibet
Since 1947. . . . .*v.6 p.241*

Dragon Ladies: Asian American Feminists Breathe
Fire. *v.6 p.108, p.113, p.435*

Dragon Seed. *v.2 p.58*

The Dragon Seekers: How an Extraordinary Circle of Fossilists
Discovered the Dinosaurs and Paved the Way for
Darwin. *v.3 p.49*

The Dragon, the Lion and the Eagle: Chinese-British-American
Relations, 1949-1958. . . . .*v.3 p.393*

A Dragonfly in the Sun: An Anthology of Pakistani Writing in
English. *v.2 p.761*

Dragons and Tigers: A Geography of South, East, and Southeast
Asia. *v.4 p.384, p.399*

Dragons Entangled: Indochina and the China-Vietnam
War. *v.6 p.168*

Dragon's Teeth I. *v.2 p.119*

Drama + Theory: Critical Approaches to Modern British
Drama. *v.2 p.188*

Drama Contemporary: Czechoslovakia. *v.1 p.65, p.109*

Drama Contemporary: France. *v.1 p.69, p.106*

Drama Contemporary: Germany. *v.1 p.69, p.110, p.111*

Drama Contemporary: Hungary. *v.1 p.63, p.108*

Drama Contemporary: India. *v.1 p.129, p.131, v.6 p.148*

Drama Contemporary: Scandinavia. . .*v.1 p.69, p.110, v.2 p.624*

Drama Contemporary: Spain. *v.1 p.66, p.67, p.108*

Drama for a New South Africa: Seven Plays. *v.2 p.752*

Drama, Its Costume and Decor. *v.1 p.151*

Drama of a Nation: Public Theater in Renaissance England and
Spain. *v.1 p.74, p.95*

The Drama of Everyday Life. *v.5 p.594*

The Drama of Gender: Feminist Theater by Women of the
Americas. *v.1 p.121, p.127*

The Drama of Medieval England. *v.1 p.74, p.105*

The Drama of Power. *v.2 p.234*

The Drama of Revolt: A Critical Study of Georg
Büchner. *v.2 p.596*

The Drama of Russian Political History: System Against
Individuality. *v.3 p.209*

The Drama of Sensibility: A Sketch of the History of English
Comedy and Domestic Tragedy. *v.2 p.187*

The Drama of the Gifted Child: The Search for the True
Self. *v.5 p.628*

Drama of the Storm and Stress. *v.2 p.591, p.592*

Drama Stage and Audience. *v.1 p.55*

Dramas from the American Theatre, 1762-1909. . . . .*v.2 p.25*

The Dramas of Lord Byron, a Critical Study. *v.2 p.274*

Dramas of Nationhood: The Politics of Television in
    Egypt. *v.6 p.639*

Dramatic Art in Aeschylus's Seven Against Thebes. . .*v.2 p.407*

🄮 The Dramatic Art of Athol Fugard: From South Africa to the
    World. *v.2 p.755*

Dramatic Design in the Chester Cycle. *v.2 p.185*

The Dramatic Festivals of Athens. *v.2 p.402*

The Dramatic Imagination: Reflections and Speculations on the
    Art of the Theatre. *v.1 p.139, p.147*

Dramatic Technique. *v.1 p.55*

Dramatic Theory and Criticism. *v.1 p.56*

The Dramatic Use of Bawdy in Shakespeare. *v.2 p.228*

Dramatic Works and Dialogues, Vol. 2. . . . . . .*v.1 p.91, p.94*

Dramatic Works and Poems, with Notes by William
    Gifford. *v.2 p.222*

The Dramatic Works in the Beaumont and Fletcher
    Canon. *v.2 p.217*

The Dramatic Works of George Lillo: Including Silvia.*v.2 p.251*

The Dramatic Works of Gerhart Hauptmann. *v.2 p.609*

Dramatic Works of Richard Brome. *v.2 p.217*

The Dramatic Works of Samuel Beckett: Volume III of the
    Grove Centenary Editions. . *v.1 p.91, p.94,v.2 p.332, p.509*

Dramatic Works of William D'Avenant. *v.2 p.217*

Dramatic Works. *v.2 p.470*

Dramatic Writings. *v.2 p.222*

Dramatists in Perspective: Spanish Theatre in the Twentieth
    Century. *v.2 p.640*

La dramaturgie classique en France. *v.2 p.462*

Dramen. *v.2 p.609, p.619*

Drame. *v.2 p.533*

Dramma per Musica: Italian Opera Seria of the Eighteenth
    Century. *v.1 p.192, p.233, p.246*

Drammi per musica, vol. 1. . . . .*v.2 p.712*

Drammi per musica, vol. 2. . . . .*v.2 p.712*

Drawing for the Absolute and Utter Beginner. *v.1 p.724*

A Drawing Manual by Thomas Eakins. *v.1 p.724*

Drawing the Human Body: An Anatomical Guide. . .*v.1 p.724*

Drawing the Line: Art and Cultural Identity in Contemporary
    Latin America. *v.3 p.266*

Drawing the Line: The American Decision to Divide Germany,
    1944-1949. . . . .*v.3 p.388*

Drawing the Line. *v.6 p.103*

Drawn by the Brush: Oil Sketches by Peter Paul
    Rubens. *v.1 p.748*

Drawn from Nature: The Plant Lithographs of Ellsworth
    Kelly. *v.1 p.755*

Drawn to Extremes: The Use and Abuse of Editorial Cartoons in
    the United States. *v.4 p.409, p.417*

The Dread Disease: Cancer and Modern American
    Culture. *v.4 p.778, p.779*

The Dread of Difference: Gender and the Horror Film. *v.6 p.318*

Dream a Little: Land and Social Justice in Modern
    America. *v.6 p.287*

The Dream and the Dialogue: Adrienne Rich's Feminist
    Poetics. *v.2 p.115*

Dream Boy: A Novel. *v.6 p.396*

Dream Catchers: How Mainstream America Discovered Native
    Spirituality. *v.1 p.543*

The Dream Endures: California Enters the 1940s. . . .*v.3 p.532*

The Dream Job: Sports Publicity, Promotion and
    Marketing. *v.4 p.906*

Dream Jungle. *v.6 p.100*

The Dream Life: Movies, Media, and the Mythology of the
    Sixties. *v.6 p.321*

Dream Makers, Dream Breakers: The World of Justice Thurgood
    Marshall. *v.4 p.538, p.539*

Dream Nation: Enlightenment, Colonization, and the Institution
    of Modern Greece. *v.3 p.194*

The Dream of a Common Language: Poems,
    1974-1977. . . . .*v.2 p.115*

The Dream of a New Social Order: Popular Magazines in
    America, 1893-1914. . . . .*v.4 p.410*

The Dream of Arcady: Place and Time in Southern
    Literature. *v.2 p.14*

A Dream of John Ball and A King's Lesson. *v.2 p.301*

A Dream of Order: The Medieval Ideal in Nineteenth-Century
    English Literature. *v.6 p.750, p.752, p.763*

Dream on Monkey Mountain and Other Plays. *v.2 p.770*

The Dream Palace of the Arabs: A Generation's
    Odyssey. *v.6 p.582*

The Dream Shattered: Vietnamese Gangs in
    America. *v.6 p.140, p.141*

Dream Song: The Life of John Berryman. *v.2 p.61*

The Dream Songs. *v.2 p.61*

Dream Story. *v.2 p.615*

A Dreamer for the People. *v.2 p.656*

Dreaming Equality: Color, Race and Racism in Urban
    Brazil. *v.3 p.280, p.342,v.4 p.37*

Dreaming Gardens: Landscape Architecture and the Making of
    Modern Israel. *v.1 p.813*

Dreaming in Cuban. *v.2 p.145, v.6 p.506*

Dreaming in Pictures: The Photography of Lewis
    Carroll. *v.1 p.764*

Dreaming of Change: Young Middle-Class Women and Social
    Transformation in Jordan. *v.6 p.621*

Dreaming of Gold, Dreaming of Home: Transnationalism and
    Migration Between the United States and South China,
    1882-1943. . . . .*v.6 p.118, p.127*

Dreaming on a Sunday in the Alameda and Other
    Plays. *v.6 p.502, p.517*

Dreaming Suburbia: Detroit and the Production of Postwar
    Space and Culture. *v.6 p.713*

Dreaming with His Eyes Open: A Life of Diego Rivera. *v.1 p.744*

Dreamings: The Art of Aboriginal Australia. *v.1 p.694*

The Dreamkeepers: Successful Teachers of African-American
    Children. *v.4 p.310*

Dreams and Nightmares: The Origin and Meaning of
    Dreams. *v.5 p.613*

Dreams and Stones. *v.2 p.792*

Dreams in the Mirror: A Biography of E. E. Cummings. *v.2 p.68*

Dreams of a Final Theory: The Scientist's Search for the Ultimate Laws of Nature. *v.5 p.541, p.553*

Dreams of Development: Colombia's National School of Mines and Its Engineers, 1887-1970. . . . .*v.3 p.358*

Dreams of Exile: Robert Louis Stevenson, a Biography. *v.2 p.312*

Dreams of Power: The Role of the Organization of African Unity in the Politics of Africa, 1963-1993. . . . . .*v.4 p.631*

Dreams of Trespass: Tales of a Harem Girlhood. . . .*v.6 p.643*

Dred: A Tale of the Great Dismal Swamp. *v.2 p.52*

The Dred Scott Case: Its Significance in American Law and Politics. *v.3 p.396, v.4 p.453*

Dred Scott V. Sandford: A Brief History with Documents. *v.4 p.453*

Dresden: Tuesday, February 13 1945. . . . .*v.3 p.175*

The Dreyfus Affair: J'accuse and Other Writings. . . .*v.2 p.505*

The Dreyfus Affair: J'Accuse and Other Writings. *v.3 p.155, p.156*

Drieu La Rochelle, ou, le bal des maudits. *v.2 p.517*

Drift and Mastery. *v.4 p.768*

Drink: A Social History of America. *v.4 p.699*

Drink and the Victorians: The Temperance Question in England, 1815-1872. . . . .*v.3 p.112, p.123, v.6 p.761*

Drink Cultura: Chicamismo. *v.6 p.497*

Drinking: Anthropological Approaches. *v.4 p.45*

Drinking in America: A History. *v.4 p.700, v.5 p.664*

Drinking Water Quality: Problems and Solutions. *v.5 p.368, p.379*

Drinking with the Moon: A Guide to Classical Chinese Poetry. *v.6 p.209*

Dripping Dry: Literature, Politics and Water in the Desert Southwest. *v.6 p.287*

Drive: The First Quartet; New Poems 1980-2005. . . .*v.2 p.142*

Driven into Paradise: The Musical Migration from Nazi Germany to the United States. *v.1 p.245, p.299*

Driven Patriot: The Life and Times of James Forrestal. *v.3 p.459*

Driven Wild: How the Fight Against Automobiles Launched the Modern Wilderness Movement. *v.6 p.296*

Driving Emissions to Zero: Are the Benefits of California's Zero Emission Vehicle Program Worth the Costs? *v.5 p.716*

Driving Force. *v.5 p.191*

Driving Miss Daisy. *v.2 p.157*

Drogas y Política en el Perú: La Connección Norteamericana. *v.3 p.281*

Droll Stories, Vol. 1. . . . .*v.2 p.485*

Droll Stories, Vol. 2. . . . .*v.2 p.485, p.486*

Droll Stories, Vol. 3. . . . .*v.2 p.486*

Dropouts in America: Confronting the Graduation Rate Crisis. *v.4 p.299*

Droughts, Food, and Culture: Ecological Change and Food Security in Africa's Later Prehistory. *v.4 p.7, p.8*

The Drowned and the Saved. *v.3 p.85*

Drowning in Fire. *v.6 p.699*

Drown. *v.6 p.506*

Drug and Crime Deviant Pathways. *v.6 p.255*

Drug Calculations: Process and Problems for Clinical Practice. *v.5 p.526*

Drug Carrier Systems. *v.5 p.219*

Drug Control in the Americas. *v.3 p.282*

Drug Diplomacy in Twentieth Century: International History. *v.3 p.282*

Drug Discovery Handbook. *v.5 p.95, p.104, p.113, p.145, p.217, p.218*

Drug Legalization: For and Against. *v.4 p.448, p.449*

Drug War Heresies: Learning from Other Vices, Times, and Places. *v.4 p.777*

Drug War Politics: The Price of Denial. *v.4 p.568*

□ DrugBank. *v.5 p.290*

Drugs, Alcohol and Criminality in American Society. *v.6 p.255*

Drugs and Doping in Sport: Socio-Legal Perspectives. *v.4 p.826, p.901*

Drugs in Sport. *v.4 p.826*

Drugs, Labor, and Colonial Expansion. *v.3 p.281*

The Druids. *v.1 p.534*

Drums along the Mohawk. *v.2 p.71*

The Drums of Father Ned. *v.2 p.374*

A Drunk Man Looks at the Thistle. *v.2 p.368*

Drunkard's Progress: Narratives of Addiction, Despair, and Recovery. *v.5 p.663, p.673*

Drunken Comportment: A Social Explanation. *v.4 p.776*

Druze Faith. *v.1 p.539*

The Druze in the Middle East: Their Faith, Leadership, Identity and Status. *v.6 p.600*

The Druzes: A New Study of Their History, Faith and Society. *v.6 p.600*

Dryden in Revolutionary England. *v.2 p.246*

Dryden the Public Writer, 1660-1685. . . . .*v.2 p.246*

Dryden's Heroic Plays. *v.2 p.246*

Dryden's Poetry. *v.2 p.246*

DSM-IV-TR Diagnostic and Statistical Manual of Mental Disorders: Text Revision. *v.5 p.516*

Du Bois on Education. *v.4 p.345*

Du Bois: Writings. *v.2 p.36*

Du domaine, suivi de Euclidiennes. *v.2 p.518*

The du Mauriers. *v.2 p.343*

Du surréalisme à l'empire de la critique. *v.2 p.459*

Dual Attraction: Understanding Bisexuality. *v.6 p.367*

Dual Diagnosis: Substance Misuse and Psychiatric Disorders. *v.5 p.512, p.522*

Dual Mandate in British Tropical Africa. *v.6 p.56*

The Dual-Image of the Japanese Emperor. *v.4 p.622*

Duane Hanson: Virtual Reality. *v.1 p.780*

Dubliners: Text and Criticism. *v.2 p.359*

Dubliners. *v.2 p.359*

Dublin's Joyce. *v.2 p.359*

The Duchess of Malfi and Other Plays: The White Devil; The Duchess of Malfi; The Devil's Law-Case; A Cure for a Cuckold. *v.2 p.236*

The Duchess of Malfi: Eight Masterpieces of Jacobean Drama. *v.1 p.67, p.74, p.75*

The Duchess of Malfi: Sources, Themes, Characters. *v.2 p.235*

The Duchess of Malfi. *v.2 p.235*

La Duchesse et le Roturier. *v.2 p.541*

Duden Aussspracheworterbuch. *v.2 p.620*

Duden Bildwörterbuch der deutschen Sprache. . . . *v.2 p.620*

Duden: das Synonymwörterbuch : ein Wörterbuch
  sinnverwandter Wörter. *v.2 p.621*

Duden Fremdwörterbuch. *v.2 p.620*

Duden, Grammatik der deutschen Gegenwartssprache. *v.2 p.621*

Due Process. *v.4 p.458*

Duel Between the First Ironclads. *v.3 p.430*

A Duel of Giants: Bismarck, Napoleon III, and the Origins of
  the Franco-Prussian War. *v.3 p.168*

Dueling: The Cult of Honor in Fin-de-Siecle Germany. *v.3 p.169*

Duelling Idiots and Other Probability Puzzlers. *v.5 p.469, p.484*

The Duel. *v.2 p.805*

Dufay. *v.1 p.179, p.322*

Duke Ellington: A Listener's Guide. *v.1 p.261, p.323*

Duke Ellington, Jazz Composer. *v.1 p.263, p.323*

The Duke Ellington Reader. *v.1 p.264, p.323*

The Duke of Alba. *v.3 p.239*

The Duke of Havana: Baseball, Cuba, and the Search for the
  American Dream. *v.6 p.552*

Dukes' Physiology of Domestic Animals. *v.5 p.54*

Dulcinea in the Factory: Myths, Morals, Men and Women in
  Colombia's Industrial Experiment, 1905-1960. . . .*v.3 p.357*

Dulcitius, a Mediaeval Comedy. *v.1 p.62, p.73, p.109*

Dulles: A Biography of Eleanor, Allen and John Foster Dulles
  and Their Family Network. *v.3 p.461*

Dumbarton Oaks: The Origins of the United Nations and the
  Search for Postwar Security. *v.4 p.654*

Dumbarton Oaks. *v.1 p.820*

Dun and Bradstreet/Gale Industry Reference
  Handbooks. *v.5 p.317*

Dun and Bradstreet's Guide to Doing Business Around the
  World. *v.4 p.56*

Dune. *v.2 p.146, p.147*

Duns Scotus. *v.1 p.579*

Dunstaple. *v.1 p.179, p.322*

Dunyazad. *v.6 p.664*

Duras: A Biography. *v.2 p.517*

Duras: Two Plays. *v.2 p.516*

Duras, Writing, and the Ethical: Making the Broken
  Whole. *v.2 p.515*

Durer to Veronese: Sixteenth-Century Painting in the National
  Gallery. *v.1 p.727*

The Durham Report: An Abridged Version with an Introduction
  and Notes by Sir Reginald Coupland. *v.3 p.539*

Durkheim on Religion. *v.1 p.521*

Durkheim's Ghosts: Cultural Logics and Social Things. *v.4 p.683*

Durrenmatt: A Study in Plays, Prose, Theory. *v.2 p.607*

The Dust Bowl: An Agricultural and Social History. . . .*v.5 p.4*

Dust Bowl: The Southern Plains in the 1930s. *v.3 p.528, v.6 p.297*

The Dust of Empire: The Race for Mastery in the Asian
  Heartland. *v.4 p.642*

Dust Tracks on a Road: An Autobiography. *v.2 p.81, v.6 p.6, p.17*

Dutch Art and Architecture: 1600-1800. . . . . . .*v.1 p.688*

Dutch Calvinism in Modern America: A History of a
  Conservative Subculture. *v.1 p.588, p.589*

Dutch Civilization in the Seventeenth Century. *v.3 p.204*

Dutch Garden in the Seventeenth Century. *v.1 p.818*

The Dutch in Brazil, 1624-1654. . . . .*v.3 p.334*

The Dutch in the Caribbean and in Surinam,
  1791/5-1942. . . . .*v.3 p.322*

Dutch Interior: Postwar Poetry of the Netherlands and
  Flanders. *v.2 p.622*

The Dutch Language: A Survey. *v.2 p.620*

Dutch Painting, 1600-1800. . . . .*v.1 p.729, p.733*

Dutch Painting. *v.1 p.731*

The Dutch Republic: Its Rise, Greatness, and Fall
  1477-1806. . . . .*v.3 p.204, p.205*

The Dutch Revolt. *v.3 p.205*

Dutch, the Language of Twenty Million Dutch and Flemish
  People. *v.2 p.622*

The Dutch under German Occupation, 1940-1945. . . .*v.3 p.205*

Dutra's World: Wealth and Family in Nineteenth-Century Rio de
  Janeiro. *v.3 p.340*

Duveen: A Life in Art. *v.1 p.709*

Dvorak and His World. *v.1 p.193, p.322*

Dvorák: Cello Concerto. *v.1 p.204, p.243, p.322*

Dwarf Bamboo. *v.6 p.103*

The Dwarf. *v.2 p.630*

Dwelling in the Archive: Women Writing House, Home, and
  History in Late Colonial India. *v.2 p.761*

Dwight D. Eisenhower. *v.4 p.528, p.529*

The Dyer's Hand and Other Essays. *v.2 p.574, p.575*

A Dying Colonialism. *v.6 p.642*

Dying to Kill: The Allure of Suicide Terror. *v.4 p.658, v.6 p.251*

Dying to Teach: The Educator's Search for Immortality. *v.4 p.346*

Dying Well: Peace and Possibilities at the End of Life. *v.5 p.531*

Dylan Thomas: A New Life. *v.2 p.385*

Dylan Thomas: His Life and Work. *v.2 p.385*

Dylan Thomas: The Complete Screenplays. *v.2 p.386*

Dynamic Alignment Through Imagery. *v.1 p.51*

Dynamic Biogeography. *v.5 p.168*

The Dynamic Constitution: An Introduction to American
  Constitutional Law. *v.4 p.453*

Dynamic Cover Letters for New Graduates. . .*v.4 p.169, p.170*

Dynamic Earth: Plates, Plumes and Mantle
  Convection. *v.5 p.442, p.443*

Dynamic Economics: Quantitative Methods and
  Applications. *v.4 p.197*

Dynamic Energy and Mass Budgets in Biological
  Systems. *v.5 p.113*

The Dynamic Genome: Barbara McClintock's Ideas in the
  Century of Genetics. *v.5 p.132*

Dynamic Modeling of Monetary and Fiscal Cooperation among
  Nations. *v.4 p.203, p.240*

The Dynamic of Mexican Nationalism. *v.3 p.295*

Dynamic Physical Education for Elementary School
  Children. *v.4 p.798*

Dynamic Sociology. *v.4 p.684*

Dynamic State Variable Models in Ecology: Methods and
Applications. *v.5 p.501*

The Dynamic Structure of the Deep Earth: An Interdisciplinary
Approach. *v.5 p.442, p.443*

Dynamic Testing: The Nature and Measurement of Learning
Potential. *v.4 p.287*

Dynamical Cognitive Science. *v.5 p.609*

Dynamical Models in Biology. *v.5 p.90*

Dynamical Systems and Their Applications in
Biology. *v.5 p.91, p.92*

Dynamical Systems in Population Biology. *v.5 p.171*

Dynamical Systems in Social Psychology. . . *v.5 p.586, p.622*

A Dynamical Theory of the Electromagnetic Field. . *v.5 p.565*

Dynamics and Income Distribution: Selected Essays of Irma
Adelman, Vol. 2. . . . .*v.4 p.252, p.264*

Dynamics and Modelling of Ocean Waves. *v.5 p.430*

The Dynamics of Biological Invasions. *v.5 p.184*

The Dynamics of Business Cycles: A Study in Economic
Fluctuations. *v.4 p.245*

Dynamics of Character. *v.5 p.658, p.661*

The Dynamics of Conflict in Northern Ireland: Power, Conflict
and Emancipation. *v.3 p.140, v.4 p.607*

The Dynamics of Conflict Resolution: A Practitioner's
Guide. *v.4 p.74*

The Dynamics of Deforestation and Economic Growth in the
Brazilian Amazon. *v.4 p.267*

The Dynamics of Deterrence. *v.4 p.657*

The Dynamics of Divorce: A Life Cycle Perspective. *v.5 p.640*

Dynamics of Faith. *v.1 p.644*

Dynamics of Family Development: A Theoretical
Perspective. *v.4 p.735, v.5 p.639*

Dynamics of Flight: Stability and Control. *v.5 p.717*

The Dynamics of Folklore. *v.2 p.585*

The Dynamics of Global Dominance: European Overseas
Empires, 1415-1980. . . . .*v.3 p.73*

Dynamics of International Relations. *v.4 p.626*

The Dynamics of Leadership: Theory and
Practice. *v.4 p.546, p.698*

Dynamics of Machinery. *v.5 p.715*

Dynamics of nutrient cycling and food webs. *v.5 p.163*

The Dynamics of Persuasion: Communication and Attitudes in
the 21st Century. *v.5 p.646*

Dynamics of Physical Circuits and Systems. *v.5 p.711*

The Dynamics of Polyandry: Kinship, Domesticity, and
Population on the Tibetan Border. *v.6 p.164*

Dynamics of Russian Politics: Putin's Federal-Regional
Reforms. *v.4 p.582, p.598*

Dynamics of Structures: Theory and Applications to Earthquake
Engineering. *v.5 p.693*

The Dynasts: An Epic Drama of the War with Napoleon Parts
One and Two. *v.2 p.291*

E

E. B. White: A Biography. *v.2 p.133*

E. B. White: Charlotte's Web, Stuart Little, and the Trumpet of
the Swan, Set. *v.2 p.133*

E. B. White: The Children's Books. *v.2 p.133*

E. B. White: The Emergence of an Essayist. *v.2 p.133*

E. B. White. *v.2 p.133*

E. Franklin Frazier Reconsidered. *v.4 p.683*

E. J. Pratt: Complete Poems, Pts. I & II. *v.2 p.738*

E. M. Forster: A Biography of the Novelist E. M.
Forster. *v.2 p.345, v.6 p.401*

E. M. Forster: A Human Exploration: Centenary Essays. *v.2 p.346*

E. M. Forster: A Literary Life. *v.2 p.346*

E. M. Forster: A Passage to India. *v.2 p.345*

E. M. Forster and the Politics of Imperialism. . . .*v.2 p.346*

E. M. Forster: The Novels. *v.2 p.345*

E M Forster: The Perils of Humanism. *v.2 p.345*

E. M. Forster's Modernism. *v.2 p.346*

E. M. Forster. *v.2 p.346*

E Pluribus Unum: The Formation of the American Republic,
1776-1790. . . . .*v.4 p.517*

E. T. A. Hoffmann's Musical Writings: Kreisleriana, The Poet
and the Composer, Music Criticism. *v.1 p.198*

E. W. Godwin: Aesthetic Movement Architect and
Designer. *v.1 p.793*

E. W. Scripps and the Business of Newspapers. . . .*v.4 p.148*

Eager to Learn: Educating Our Preschoolers. *v.4 p.370*

Eagle and Sword: The Federalists and the Creation of the
Military Establishment in America, 1783-1802. . .*v.3 p.383*

The Eagle and the Crow: Modern Polish Short Stories. *v.2 p.788*

The Eagle and the Lion: The Tragedy of American-Iranian
Relations. *v.6 p.631*

Eagle and the Virgin. *v.3 p.296*

An Eagle Nation. *v.6 p.699*

Eagle Rules?: Foreign Policy and American Primacy in the
Twenty-First Century. *v.4 p.641, p.642*

Eakins and the Photograph: Works by Thomas Eakins and His
Circle in the Collection of the Pennsylvania Academy
of the Fine Arts. *v.1 p.766*

Eakins Revealed. *v.1 p.734*

Ear Training: A Technique for Listening. *v.1 p.404*

Ear Training for the Body: A Dancer's Guide to Music. *v.1 p.404*

Earl Warren: A Public Life. *v.4 p.469*

Earl Warren: The Judge Who Changed America. . . .*v.4 p.469*

The Earliest Christian Heretics: Readings from Their
Opponents. *v.1 p.646*

Earliest Christianity: A History of the Period A.D.
30-150. . . . .*v.1 p.627*

The Earliest Semitic Pantheon: A Study of the Semitic Deities
Attested in Mesopotamia Before Ur III. *v.1 p.539*

The Early Abbasid Caliphate: A Political History. . .*v.6 p.585*

Early America Revisited. *v.6 p.9*

Early American Decorative Arts, 1620-1860: A Handbook for
Interpreters. *v.1 p.800*

Early American Music, 1620-1820: A Research and Information
Guide. *v.1 p.166, p.167, p.277*

Early American Wars and Military Institutions. . . .*v.3 p.382*

Early American Women Dramatists, 1780-1860. . . .*v.1 p.121*

Early American Writings. *v.2 p.21*

Early Americas Digital Archive. *v.3 p.404, p.406, p.409, p.414*

Early and Late Papers Hitherto Uncollected. by William
Makepeace Thackeray. *v.2 p.315*

ⓔ Early Anthropology in the Sixteenth and Seventeenth
Centuries. *v.4 p.4*

The Early Arrival of Dreams: A Year in
China. *v.6 p.197, p.202, p.216*

Early Art and Architecture of Africa. *v.1 p.690*

Early Art of the Southeastern Indians: Feathered Serpents and
Winged Beings. *v.1 p.683, v.6 p.679*

Early Auden. *v.2 p.329*

The Early Baroque Era. *v.1 p.186*

Early Black American Playwrights and Dramatic Writers: A
Biographical Directory and Catalog of Plays, Films
and Broadcasting Scripts. *v.6 p.18, p.34*

Early Buddhist Discourses. *v.1 p.418*

Early Buddhist Metaphysics: The Making of a Philosophical
Tradition. *v.1 p.418*

The Early Career of Alexander Pope. *v.2 p.257, p.258*

Early Ch'an in China and Tibet. *v.1 p.568*

Early Childhood Assessment. *v.5 p.602*

Early Childhood Curriculum: A Review of Current
Research. *v.4 p.369*

Early Childhood Curriculum Resource Handbook. . .*v.4 p.369*

Early Childhood Education: Policy Issues for the 1990s.*v.4 p.369*

Early Chinese Literature. *v.6 p.208*

Early Christian and Byzantine Architecture. *v.1 p.599*

Early Christian Creeds. *v.1 p.646*

The early Christian doctrine of God. *v.1 p.639*

Early Christian Doctrines. *v.1 p.633*

Early Christian Fathers. *v.1 p.591*

Early Christian Ireland: Introduction to the Sources. .*v.6 p.563*

Early Christian Lives. *v.1 p.612*

Early Christian Rhetoric: The Language of the Gospel.*v.1 p.626*

Early Christian Writings: The Apostolic Fathers. . . .*v.3 p.58*

Early Christianity and Its Sacred Literature. *v.1 p.624*

The Early Church to the Reformation. *v.1 p.598*

The Early Church. *v.1 p.599*

The Early Colombian Labor Movement: Artisans and Politics in
Bogota, 1832-1919. . . . .*v.3 p.358, p.359*

The Early Commedia Dell'arte (1550-1621): The Mannerist
Context. *v.1 p.91*

Early Coptic Papacy: The Egyptian Church and Its Leadership
in Late Antiquity. *v.1 p.569*

Early Critical Essays, Eighteen Twenty to Eighteen
Twenty-Two. *v.2 p.35*

Early Days Yet: New and Collected Peoms 1941-1997.*v.2 p.744*

Early Downhome Blues: A Musical and Cultural
Analysis. *v.1 p.264, p.297*

Early Dynastic Egypt: Strategies, Society and Security. *v.6 p.58*

Early Dynastic Egypt. *v.3 p.10*

The Early Economic Writings of Alfred Marshall,
1867-1890. . . . .*v.4 p.224*

Early Education in the Public Schools: Lessons from a
Comprehensive Birth-to-Kindergarten
Program. *v.4 p.368, p.369*

Early Embryonic Development of Animals. . . .*v.5 p.161, p.162*

The Early English Carols. *v.2 p.199*

Early English Drama: An Anthology. *v.1 p.63, p.73, p.99*

Early English Stages, 1300 To 1660. . . . . . .*v.1 p.105, p.155*

Early Essays on Social Philosophy. *v.4 p.679*

The Early Flute: A Practical Guide. *v.1 p.389, p.400*

The Early French Explorers of North America. *v.4 p.378, p.379*

Early French Tristan Poems, Vol. II. *v.2 p.467*

Early Georgian Interiors. *v.1 p.799*

Early German Philosophy: Kant and His
Predecessors. *v.1 p.460, p.461*

Early Germans. *v.3 p.161*

Early Greece. *v.3 p.17*

Early Greek Myth: A Guide to Literary and Artistic
Sources. *v.1 p.532, v.2 p.400*

Early Greek Philosophy. *v.1 p.421*

Early Greek Science: Thales to Aristotle. . .*v.2 p.404, v.5 p.392*

Early Greek States Beyond the Polis. *v.3 p.16, p.17*

Early Greek Vase Painting: 11th to 6th Centuries B.C. *v.1 p.726*

The Early Growth of the European Economy: Warriors and
Peasants from the Seventh to the Twelfth Century. *v.6 p.557*

✦ Early History of Mathematics. *v.5 p.465*

The Early History of the Church of Canterbury. . . .*v.1 p.582*

The Early Horn: A Practical Guide. *v.1 p.390, p.400*

Early Human Behaviour in the Global Context: The Rise and
Diversity of the Lower Paleolithic Period. *v.4 p.17*

Early Humans and Their World. *v.4 p.16, p.17*

Early in the Summer of Nineteen Seventy. *v.6 p.652*

Early Intervention: The Essential Readings. *v.4 p.316*

Early Ionian Historians. *v.3 p.17*

The Early Irish Stage, the Beginnings to 1720. . . .*v.1 p.108*

Early Islamic Art, 650-1100: Constructing the Study of Islamic
Art. *v.1 p.673*

The Early Islamic Conquests. *v.6 p.584*

Early Jazz: Its Roots and Musical Development. . . .*v.1 p.263*

Early Keyboard Instruments: A Practical Guide. *v.1 p.391, p.402*

Early Kings of Norway. *v.2 p.275*

Early Korean Literature: Selections and Introductions. *v.6 p.238*

Early Latin Theology. *v.1 p.591*

Early Latino Ballplayers in the United States: Major, Minor and
Negro Leagues, 1901-1949. . *v.6 p.491, p.552, p.553, p.555*

Early Life: Evolution on the PreCambrian Earth. . . .*v.5 p.194*

The Early Life of Thomas Hardy: 1840-1891. . . . .*v.2 p.291*

Early Literacy. *v.4 p.360, p.361*

Early Lives of Charlemagne. *v.3 p.66*

Early Madhyamika in India and China. *v.1 p.565*

The Early Mallarme: Parentage, Early Years and
Juvenilia. *v.2 p.496*

Early Medieval Architecture. *v.1 p.787*

Early Medieval Art. *v.1 p.671, p.672*

Early Medieval Europe, 300-1000. . . . .*v.6 p.562*

Early Medieval Ireland, 400-1200. . . . .*v.3 p.137*

Early Medieval Italy: Central Power and Local Society
400-1000. . . . .*v.3 p.199*

Early Medieval Philosophy, 480-1150. . . . .*v.1 p.433*

Early Medieval Spain: Unity in Diversity,
400-1000. . . . .*v.3 p.65, p.243, v.6 p.562*

Early Modern Capitalism: Economic and Social Change in Europe 1400-1800. . . . .*v.3 p.41, p.42*

The Early Modern City, 1450-1750. . . . .*v.3 p.44*

Early Modern English Drama: A Critical Companion. *v.1 p.75, p.104,v.2 p.186*

Early Modern English. *v.2 p.553*

The Early Modern European Economy. *v.3 p.41, p.70*

Early Modern European Society. *v.3 p.40, p.70*

Early Modern Ireland, 1534-1691. . . . . . .*v.3 p.136, p.137*

Early Modern Italy: 1550-1796. . . . .*v.3 p.201*

Early Modern Russian Writers: Late Seventeenth and Eighteenth Centuries. *v.2 p.796*

Early Modern Women Database. *v.6 p.432*

Early Narratives of the Northwest, 1634-1699. . . .*v.3 p.512*

Early Native American Writing: New Critical Essays. . .*v.2 p.4*

Early Netherlandish Painting. *v.1 p.727, p.728*

Early New Zealand Books. *v.2 p.742*

Early Novels and Stories: The Troll Garden; O Pioneers!; The Song of the Lark; My Antonia; One of Ours. *v.2 p.67*

Early Novels and Stories. *v.2 p.59*

The Early Origins of the Social Sciences. *v.4 p.683*

The Early Pianoforte. *v.1 p.391*

Early Poems, 1947-1959. . . . .*v.2 p.510*

Early Poems and Fragments, 1785-1797. . . . . . .*v.2 p.325*

The Early Poetic Manuscripts and Notebooks of Gerard Manley Hopkins. *v.2 p.294*

The Early Poetry of Robert Graves: The Goddess Beckons. *v.2 p.348*

Early Protestant Educators. *v.4 p.339*

Early Psychological Thought: Ancient Accounts of Mind and Soul. *v.5 p.596*

The Early Public Theatre in France. *v.1 p.106*

Early Quaker Writings. *v.1 p.585*

Early Reading Assessment: A Practitioner's Handbook.*v.4 p.361*

Early Recordings and Musical Style: Changing Tastes in Instrumental Performance, 1900-1950. . . .*v.1 p.387, p.401*

The Early Reformation in Europe. *v.1 p.602*

The Early Reformation on the Continent. *v.1 p.601*

The Early Roman Period. *v.1 p.547*

The Early Romantic Era. *v.1 p.202*

Early Russian Cinema and Its Cultural Reception. . .*v.6 p.339*

Early Short Stories. *v.2 p.318*

Early Spanish American Narrative. *v.2 p.664*

The Early Stories, 1953-1975. . . . .*v.2 p.157*

Early Tales and Sketches: 1851-1864. . . . .*v.2 p.34*

Early Tales and Sketches: 1864-1869. . . . .*v.2 p.34*

The Early Universe. *v.5 p.72*

The Early Upper Paleolithic Beyond Western Europe. *v.4 p.15, p.16*

Early Victorian Government, 1830-1870. . . . . . .*v.3 p.113*

The Early Violin and Viola: A Practical Guide.*v.1 p.392, p.402*

The Early Works of John Dewey, 1882-1898. . . . .*v.1 p.443*

Early Writings of Gustave Flaubert. *v.2 p.491*

The Early Years, 1770-1803, Vol. 1. . . . .*v.2 p.324*

Early-Modern England: A Social History, 1550-1760. .*v.4 p.707*

The Earnest Men: Republicans of the Civil War Senate.*v.3 p.427*

Earning and Learning: How Schools Matter. . .*v.4 p.265, p.266*

Earshot. *v.6 p.100*

Earth: An Intimate History. *v.5 p.445*

Earth House Hold. *v.2 p.156*

Earth in the Balance: Ecology and the Human Spirit. .*v.6 p.291*

The Earth Machine: The Science of a Dynamic Planet.*v.5 p.419*

Earth Negotiations: Analyzing Thirty Years of Environmental Diplomacy. *v.5 p.29, v.6 p.299*

Earth Observatory. *v.5 p.420, p.421*

Earth Odyssey: Around the World in Search of Our Environmental Future. *v.5 p.358, p.370, p.371*

Earth Power Coming: Short Fiction in Native American Literature. *v.2 p.26, v.6 p.698*

Earth Report 2000. . . . .*v.6 p.285*

Earth Science World Image Bank. *v.5 p.417*

Earth Story: The Forces That Have Shaped Our Planet. *v.5 p.419, p.445*

Earth Structure: An Introduction to Structural Geology and Tectonics. *v.5 p.442*

The Earth, Student's Companion: An Introduction to its Physical and Human Geography. *v.4 p.374, p.376*

Earth Surface Processes. *v.5 p.423*

Earth System Science: From Biogeochemical Cycles to Global Changes. *v.5 p.168, p.426*

The Earth System. *v.5 p.248*

Earthly and Heavenly Journey of Simone Martini. *v.2 p.715, p.716*

Earthly Paradise - Colette: An Autobiography Drawn from Her Lifetime Writings. *v.2 p.514, p.515*

Earthly Powers. *v.2 p.336*

Earthly Signs: Moscow Diaries, 1917-1922. . . . . .*v.2 p.810*

Earthquake Engineering. *v.5 p.693*

Earthquakes in Human History: The Far-Reaching Effects of Seismic Disruptions. *v.5 p.442*

Earthquakes. *v.5 p.442*

The Earthquake. *v.6 p.664*

Earth's Dynamic Systems. *v.4 p.390, v.5 p.418, p.419*

Earth's Pre-Pleistocene Glacial Record. *v.5 p.425*

The Earthscan Reader in Environment, Development and Rural Livelihoods. *v.4 p.268, v.5 p.28*

The Earthscan Reader in Sustainable Agriculture. . . .*v.5 p.13*

Earthshaking Science: What We Know (and Don't Know) about Earthquakes. *v.5 p.442*

Earthshine. *v.6 p.379, p.398*

Earthshock: Hurricanes, Volcanoes, Earthquakes, Tornadoes, and Other Forces of Nature. *v.5 p.426, p.427*

The Earth. *v.2 p.505*

Earth. *v.5 p.419*

Earthworks: Art and the Landscape of the Sixties. . .*v.1 p.775*

Earthworm Ecology. *v.5 p.49*

The Earthy paradise, a poem. by William Morris. . . .*v.2 p.301*

Easier Fatherland: Germany in the Twenty-First Century. *v.3 p.159*

East Africa: Portuguese Encounters with the World in the Age of Discoveries. *v.6 p.63*

The East African Coast. *v.6 p.63*

East African Expressions of Christianity. *v.6 p.63*

East and West. *v.2 p.40*

East Asia: A Cultural, Social, and Political History. . *v.6 p.181*

East Asia at the Center: Four Thousand Years of Engagement with the World. *v.6 p.180, p.182*

The East Asian Miracle: Economic Growth and Public Policy. *v.6 p.181*

East Central Europe Between the Two World Wars. . . *v.3 p.207*

East German Poetry: An Anthology. *v.2 p.593*

East German Short Stories: An Introductory Anthology. *v.2 p.594*

East Goes West: The Making of an Oriental Yankee. . . *v.6 p.94*

East into Upper East: Plain Tales from New York and New Delhi. *v.2 p.355*

East London for Mosley: The Membership and Branches of the British Union of Fascists in East London and South-West Essex, 1933-40. . . . . *v.4 p.582*

East Los Angeles: History of a Barrio. *v.6 p.536, p.550*

East Lynne. *v.2 p.319*

East Meets West in Dance: Voices in the Cross-Cultural Dialogue. *v.1 p.49*

East of Byzantium: Syria and Armenia in the Formative Period. *v.1 p.569*

East Timor, Australia and Regional Order: Intervention and Its Aftermath in Southeast Asia. *v.6 p.174, p.176*

East to America: Korean American Life Stories. *v.6 p.94, p.135*

East, West: Stories. *v.2 p.766*

Easter 1916: The Irish Rebellion. *v.3 p.135, p.139*

Eastern Arabic: With MP3 Files; An Introduction to Palestinian Arabic. *v.6 p.654*

Eastern Christianity. *v.1 p.569*

Eastern Europe, 1939-2000. . . . . *v.3 p.207*

Eastern Europe Between the Wars: 1918-1941. . . . *v.3 p.207*

Eastern Europe in the Twentieth Century and After. . *v.3 p.207*

Eastern Europe in Transformation: The Impact on Sociology. *v.4 p.683*

Eastern Europe, Russia and Central Asia 2005. *v.4 p.396, p.397*

Eastern Europe Since 1945. . . . . *v.3 p.208*

Eastern European Journalism: Before, During and after Communism. *v.4 p.403*

The Eastern Front, 1914-1917. . . . . *v.3 p.80*

The Eastern Front, 1941-1945: German Troops and the Barbarisation of Warfare. *v.3 p.174*

The Eastern Origins of Western Civilisation. *v.3 p.74*

Eastern Philosophy: The Key Readings. *v.1 p.475*

Eastern Poland on the Eve of the Holocaust: Shtetl Jews under Soviet Rule 1939-1941. . . . . *v.3 p.86*

The Eastern Question 1774-1923. . . . . *v.3 p.246*

The Eastern Schism: A Study of the Papacy and the Eastern Churches During the XIth and XIIth Centuries. *v.3 p.57, p.58*

Eastern Science: An Outline of Its Scope and Contribution. *v.5 p.405*

Eastman Johnson : painting America. *v.1 p.736*

Easy Outline of Genetics. *v.5 p.137*

Easy Way to Kurdish. *v.6 p.668*

Eat a Bowl of Tea. *v.6 p.99*

Eat the Rich: A Treatise on Economics. *v.4 p.185, p.196, p.251*

Eating Disorder among Athletes: Theory, Issues and Research. *v.5 p.581*

Eating Disorders: Anatomy of a Social Epidemic. *v.4 p.777, p.778*

Eating Korean: From Barbecue to Kimchi, Recipes from My Home. *v.6 p.235*

The Ebb-Tide: A Trio and Quartette. *v.2 p.312*

Ebla: A New Look at History. *v.3 p.7*

Ⓔ Ebonics: The Urban Education Debate. *v.6 p.21*

E-Business Implementation: A Guide to Web Services, EAI, BPI, E-Commerce, Content Management, Portals, and Supporting Technologies. *v.4 p.113*

Eca de Queiros and European Realism. *v.2 p.688*

Ecce Homo: How One Becomes What One Is. . . . *v.1 p.467*

Eccentrics of Comedy. *v.6 p.313*

Ecclesiastes: A New Translation with Introduction and Commentary. *v.1 p.622*

Ecclesiastical Authority and Spiritual Power in the Church of the First Three Centuries. *v.1 p.638*

Ecclesiastical History - Lives of the Abbots, Letter to Egbert, Bks. 4-5, Vol. 2. . . . . *v.2 p.448*

Ecclesiastical History, Bks. 1-3. . . . . *v.2 p.448*

Ecclesiastical History, Bks. 6-10. . . . . *v.2 p.448, v.3 p.67*

The Ecclesiastical History of the English People; The Greater Chronicle; Bede's Letter to Egbert. *v.1 p.608*

Ecclesiastical History of the English People. *v.3 p.66*

The Echo of War: Home Front Propaganda and the Wartime BBC 1939-1945. . . . . *v.4 p.413*

Echoes and Moving Fields: Structure and Subjectivity in the Poetry of W. S. Merwin and John Ashbery. . *v.2 p.57, p.58*

Echoes from the Dead Zone: Across the Cyprus Divide. *v.3 p.197*

Echoes of Discontent: Jesse Jackson, Pat Robertson, and the Resurgence of Populism. *v.3 p.447*

Echoes of History: Naxi Music in Modern China. . . *v.1 p.289*

Echoes of Scripture in the Letters of Paul. *v.1 p.625*

Echoes of the Marseillaise: Two Centuries Look Back on the French Revolution. *v.3 p.158*

Echoes upon Echoes: New Korean American Writings. *v.6 p.91, p.135*

▢ ECLAC/CEPAL: Economic Commission for Latin America. *v.3 p.259*

The Eclipse of Biblical Narrative: A Study in Eighteenth and Nineteenth-Century Hermeneutics. *v.1 p.635*

Eclipse of Empire. *v.3 p.87*

Eclipse of God: Studies in the Relation Between Religion and Philosophy. *v.1 p.522*

Eclipse of Reason. *v.1 p.468*

Eclogues and Georgics of Virgil. *v.2 p.447*

Ecocide of Native America: Environmental Destruction of Indian Lands and Peoples. *v.6 p.681*

The Ecocriticism Reader: Landmarks in Literary Ecology. *v.2 p.4*

Ecocriticism. *v.2 p.572, v.6 p.287*

Ecodesign: A Manual for Ecological Eesign. *v.5 p.367*

Ecofeminism: Women, Animals, Nature. . . . *v.6 p.433, p.434*

The Ecological Basis of Conservation: Heterogeneity, Ecosystems, and Biodiversity. *v.5 p.180, p.181, p.185*

Ecological Census Techniques: A Handbook. *v.5 p.171*

Ecological Economics: Principles and Applications. . . .*v.5 p.14*

Ecological Entomology. *v.5 p.170, p.213*

Ecological Golf Course Management. *v.4 p.788, p.872, p.881, p.886*

Ecological Imperialism: The Biological Expansion of Europe, 900-1900. . . . .*v.3 p.73, v.6 p.295*

Ecological Indian: Myth and History. *v.6 p.295, p.681*

Ecological Integrity: Integrating Environment, Conservation and Health. *v.6 p.289*

Ecological Management of Agricultural Weeds. *v.5 p.5, p.11, p.12, p.13*

Ecological Methodology. *v.5 p.170*

Ecological Morphology: Integrative Organismal Biology. *v.5 p.197*

Ecological Orbits: How Planets Move and Populations Grow. *v.5 p.184, p.188*

Ecological Planning: A Historical and Comparative Synthesis. *v.1 p.813, p.814*

The Ecological principles of nature conservation: applications in temperate and boreal environments. *v.5 p.179*

The Ecological Risks of Engineered Crops. *v.5 p.8, p.11*

Ecological Stewardship: A Common Reference for Ecosystem Management. *v.5 p.184*

Ecological Stoichiometry: The Biology of Elements from Molecules to the Biosphere. *v.5 p.114, p.185, p.186, p.200, p.201*

Ecology: A Pocket Guide. *v.6 p.293*

Ecology and Conservation of Amphibians. *v.5 p.214*

Ecology and Man in Mexico's Central Volcanoes Area. *v.5 p.177, p.178, p.223*

The Ecology and Management of Grazing Systems. . .*v.5 p.42*

Ecology, Genetics and Evolution of Metapopulations. *v.5 p.133, p.184, p.188*

Ecology, Law and Economics: The Simple Analytics of Natural Resource and Environment Economics. *v.4 p.62*

Ecology of a Glacial Flood Plain. *v.5 p.178*

Ecology of Arctic Environments. *v.5 p.178*

The Ecology of Human Development: Experiments by Nature and Design. *v.5 p.625*

The Ecology of Invasions by Animals and Plants. . .*v.6 p.291*

The Ecology of Malnutrition in Western South America, Vol. 14. . . . .*v.3 p.271, p.272*

The Ecology of Power: Culture, Place and Personhood in the Southern Amazon, AD 1000-2000. . . . . .*v.4 p.11, p.12*

Ecology of Teleost Fishes. *v.5 p.217*

The Ecology of the Cambrian Radiation. *v.5 p.449*

The Ecology of Tropical Food Crops. .*v.5 p.11, p.23, p.26, p.28*

Ecology WWW page. *v.5 p.169*

E-Commerce and the Digital Economy. *v.4 p.113*

Econometric Analysis of Cross Section and Panel Data. *v.4 p.205, p.206*

Econometric Analysis of Financial and Economic Time Series Part A. *v.4 p.200*

Econometric Analysis of Panel Data. *v.4 p.198, p.206*

The Econometric Analysis of Seasonal Time Series. . .*v.4 p.200*

Econometric Analysis. *v.4 p.201*

Econometric Exploration and Diagnosis. *v.4 p.201*

Econometric Foundations. *v.4 p.203*

Econometric Methods and Applications. *v.4 p.203*

Econometric Methods with Applications in Business and Economics. *v.4 p.201*

Econometric Models and Economic Forecasts. .*v.4 p.203, p.207*

Econometrics: A Modern Introduction. *v.4 p.203*

Econometrics: Alchemy or Science? *v.4 p.201*

Econometrics and Economic Theory: Essays in Honour of Jan Tinbergen. *v.4 p.204*

Econometrics and the Cost of Capital, Vol. 2. . . . .*v.4 p.202*

Econometrics and the Philosophy of Economics: Theory-Data Confrontations in Economics. *v.4 p.204*

Econometrics: Econometric Modeling of Producer Behavior. *v.4 p.207*

Econometrics: Economic Growth in the Information Age. *v.4 p.202*

The Econometrics of Corporate Governance Studies. .*v.4 p.198*

The Econometrics of Financial Markets. *v.4 p.198*

The Econometrics of Macroeconomic Modelling. .*v.4 p.202, p.240*

Econometrics of Qualitative Dependent Variables. . .*v.4 p.200*

Econometrics. *v.4 p.201, p.205*

Economic Analysis and Policy in Underdeveloped Countries, 4. . . . .*v.4 p.242*

Economic Analysis of Law. *v.4 p.442*

Economic and Financial Decisions under Risk. .*v.4 p.207, p.263*

Economic and Housing Data. *v.4 p.159*

The Economic and Philosophic Manuscripts of 1844 and the Communist Manifesto: With Friedrich Engels. . . .*v.1 p.465*

Economic and Political Change in Tunisia: From Bourguiba to Ben Ali. *v.6 p.641*

The Economic and Social Growth of Early Greece: 800-500 B.C. *v.3 p.15*

Economic and Social History of Medieval Europe. . .*v.3 p.69*

An Economic and Social History of the Ottoman Empire, 1300-1914, Set. *v.6 p.590*

Economic Backwardness in Historical Perspective. . .*v.3 p.40*

The Economic Borders of the State. *v.4 p.227*

Economic Botany: Principles and Practices. *v.5 p.16*

Economic Botany. *v.5 p.44*

Economic Change and Rural Resistance in Southern Bolivia, 1880-1930. . . . .*v.3 p.324*

Economic Change in Thailand, 1850-1970. . . . . .*v.6 p.171*

Economic Crisis and State Reform in Brazil: Toward a New Interpretation of Latin America. *v.3 p.338*

The Economic Decline of Empires. *v.3 p.39*

Economic Development and Planning: Essays in Honour of Jan Tinbergen. *v.4 p.260*

Economic Development in Saudi Arabia. *v.6 p.626*

Economic Development in the Long Run. *v.3 p.42*

The Economic Dimensions of Globalization. *v.4 p.664*

The Economic Doctrines of Karl Marx. *v.4 p.214*

Economic Dynamics and General Equilibrium: Time and Uncertainty. *v.4 p.206*

The Economic Emergence of Women. *v.4 p.273*

Economic Essays. *v.4 p.220*

Economic Freedom of the World, 2005. . . . . . .*v.4 p.189*

Economic Geography. *v.4 p.398*

Economic Growth and Resources: Proceedings of the Fifth World Congress of the International Economic Association held in Tokyo, Japan, 1977. . . . . . .*v.4 p.256*

Economic Growth and Social Equity in Developing Countries. *v.4 p.253, p.258*

Economic Growth in Prewar China. *v.6 p.191*

Economic Heresies: Some Old-Fashioned Questions in Economic Theory. *v.4 p.185, p.186*

Economic History Colombia. *v.3 p.357, p.358*

The Economic History of Britain since 1700: 1700-1860. . . . .*v.3 p.122*

The Economic History of Britain since 1700: 1860-1939. . . . .*v.3 p.122, p.123*

The Economic History of Britain since 1700: 1939-1992. . . . .*v.3 p.122*

The Economic History of Britain since 1700, Set. . . .*v.3 p.111*

An Economic History of Central Niger. *v.6 p.70*

An Economic History of Film. *v.6 p.345*

An Economic History of Imperial Madagascar, 1750-1895: The Rise and Fall of an Island Empire. *v.6 p.67*

An Economic History of Ireland since 1660. . . . . .*v.3 p.135*

An Economic History of Malaysia, C. 1800-1990: The Transition to Modern Economic Growth. *v.6 p.172*

Economic History of Puerto Rico: Institutional Change and Capitalist Development. *v.3 p.319*

An Economic History of Sweden. *v.3 p.235*

An Economic History of the Baltic Countries. .*v.3 p.255, p.256*

An Economic History of the Middle East and North Africa. *v.6 p.582*

An Economic History of West Africa. *v.6 p.68*

An Economic History of Women in America: Women's Work, the Sexual Division of Labor and the Development of Capitalism. *v.6 p.457*

The Economic History of World Population. *v.3 p.42*

Economic History of World Trade. . . . *v.4 p.57, p.147, p.180*

Economic Imperialism: A Book of Readings. *v.4 p.208*

Economic Integration and Development in Africa. . .*v.4 p.384*

An Economic Interpretation of the Constitution of the United States. *v.4 p.518*

The Economic Legacy of Robert Lucas, Jr. *v.4 p.233*

Economic Losses from Marine Pollution: A Handbook for Assessment. *v.6 p.298*

Economic Management and Economic Development in Peru and Colombia. *v.3 p.332*

Economic Nationalism and Development: Central and Eastern Europe Between the Two World Wars. *v.3 p.207*

Economic Perspectives: Further Essays on Money and Growth. *v.4 p.209*

The Economic Philosophy of David Ricardo As a Textbook Which Far Surpasses Anything Employed in Our Schools Today. *v.4 p.220*

Economic Philosophy. *v.4 p.196*

Economic Policy and Projects: The Development of a Consumer Society in Early Modern England. . *v.3 p.101, p.102, p.123*

Economic Policy: Principles and Design. *v.4 p.197*

Economic Policy Reform in Egypt. *v.6 p.639*

Economic Politics: The Costs of Democracy. *v.4 p.214*

Economic Principles for Education: Theory and Evidence. *v.4 p.297*

☐ Economic Report of the President. *v.4 p.481*

Economic Report on Africa 2004: Unlocking Africa's Trade Potential. *v.4 p.664*

The Economic Rise of the Hapsburg Empire 1750-1914. .*v.3 p.181*

Economic Sentiments: Adam Smith, Condorcet, and the Enlightenment. *v.3 p.72*

Economic Sociology of Capitalism. . . *v.4 p.215, p.271, p.272*

Economic Sociology. *v.4 p.718*

Economic Sophisms. *v.4 p.187*

The Economic Status of Black Women: An Exploratory Investigation. *v.6 p.20, p.21, p.47, p.48*

Economic Theories of Peace and War. *v.4 p.268*

An Economic Theorist's Book of Tales: Essays That Entertain the Consequences of New Assumptions in Economic Theory. *v.4 p.194*

Economic Theory and Cognitive Science: Microexplanation. *v.4 p.272*

Economic Theory in Retrospect. *v.4 p.194, p.208*

An Economic Theory of Democracy. . *v.4 p.503, p.545, p.580*

Economic Thought since Keynes: A History and Dictionary of Major Economists. *v.4 p.187, p.188, p.208*

The Economic Transformation of American Cities. . .*v.6 p.724*

The Economic Transformation of the Soviet Union, 1913-1945. . . . .*v.3 p.222*

Economic Trends in U. S. Agriculture and Food Systems since World War II. *v.5 p.14*

The Economic Writings of Sir William Petty. *v.4 p.216*

The Economical Table: An Attempt Toward Ascertaining and Exhibiting the Source, Progress and Employment of Riches. *v.4 p.217*

The Economical Table. *v.4 p.217*

Economical Writing. *v.3 p.41*

Economics: An Awkward Corner. *v.4 p.270*

Economics, an Examination of Scarcity: Adam Smith's Micro to Current U. S. Macro. *v.4 p.219*

Economics and Politics in the Weimar Republic. . . .*v.3 p.169*

The Economics and Politics of Sports Facilities. *v.4 p.881, p.885, p.886, p.889, p.892*

Economics and Sociology: Conversations with Economists and Sociologists. *v.4 p.271*

Economics and the Art of Controversy. *v.4 p.213*

Economics as a Moral Science: The Political Economy of Adam Smith. *v.4 p.220*

Economics as Worldly Philosophy: Essays in Political and Historical Economics in Honour of Robert Heilbroner. *v.4 p.208, p.240*

Economics, Bounded Rationality and the Cognitive Revolution. *v.4 p.250, p.272*

Economics Essays: A Festschrift for Werner Heldenbrand. *v.4 p.201*

Economics for Humans. *v.4 p.196, p.270*

Economics for the Common Good: Two Centuries of Social
  Economic Thought in the Humanistic
  Tradition. *v.4 p.207, p.208, p.209*

Economics from the Heart: A Samuelson
  Sampler. *v.4 p.196, p.197*

Economics in Practice: Six Lectures on Current Issues. .*v.4 p.210*

The Economics of a Disaster: The Exxon Valdez Oil
  Spill. *v.6 p.298*

The Economics of Adam Smith. *v.4 p.211, p.212, p.219*

The Economics of Altruism. *v.4 p.267*

The Economics of Biological Invasions. *v.5 p.180*

The Economics of Biotechnology. *v.4 p.156, v.5 p.218*

The Economics of Collective Action. *v.4 p.208*

Economics of College Sports. *v.4 p.887, p.893*

The Economics of Common Currencies. *v.4 p.238*

The Economics of Comparable Worth. *v.4 p.253*

The Economics of David Ricardo. *v.4 p.212, p.220*

The Economics of Discrimination. *v.4 p.133, p.253*

The Economics of Education: Human Capital, Family
  Background and Inequality. *v.4 p.297*

The Economics of Environmental Degradation: Tragedy for the
  Commons? *v.6 p.298, p.299*

Economics of European Integration. *v.4 p.638*

The Economics of F. A. Hayek. *v.4 p.234*

The Economics of Francois Quesnay. *v.4 p.217*

The Economics of Health and Health Care. .*v.4 p.163, v.5 p.511*

The Economics of Imperfect Competition. *v.4 p.239*

Economics of Imperfect Competition. *v.4 p.252, p.270*

Economics of Industry: 1879 Edition. *v.4 p.224*

The Economics of International Security: Essays in Honour of
  Jan Tinbergen. *v.4 p.262*

The Economics of Irving Fisher: Reviewing the Scientific Work
  of a Great Economist. *v.4 p.200, p.225*

The Economics of John Stuart Mill, Set. *v.4 p.217, p.222*

Economics of Marketing. *v.4 p.134*

The Economics of Natural and Environmental
  Resources. *v.4 p.268*

The Economics of Natural Environments: Studies in the
  Valuation of Commodity and Amenity Resources. . .*v.4 p.62*

The Economics of Organic Farming: An International
  Perspective. *v.5 p.30, p.31*

The Economics of Professional Team
  Sports. *v.4 p.883, p.896, p.899*

The Economics of Recreation, Leisure and
  Tourism. *v.4 p.785, p.889, p.890*

Economics of Resources, Agriculture and
  Food. *v.4 p.152, p.160, p.164*

The Economics of Slavery, and Other Studies in Econometric
  History. *v.4 p.208*

Economics of Sport and Recreation. *v.4 p.884, p.888*

The Economics of Sport, Set. *v.4 p.890*

The Economics of Sports. *v.4 p.888*

Economics of Staging the Olympics: A Comparison of the
  Games 1972-2008. . . . .*v.4 p.846, p.889*

The Economics of Taxation. *v.4 p.107*

The Economics of the British Stage,
  1800-1914. . . . .*v.6 p.745, p.754, p.762*

The Economics of the Family: Marriage, Children, and Human
  Capital. *v.4 p.266*

The Economics of the Trade Union. *v.4 p.124*

Economics of the U. S. Commercial Airline Industry:
  Productivity, Technology and Deregulation. . . .*v.4 p.152*

The Economics of Time and Ignorance. *v.4 p.270*

The Economics of Under-Developed Countries. . . .*v.4 p.242*

Economics of Vilfredo Pareto. *v.4 p.195*

The Economics of Welfare. *v.4 p.252*

The Economics of Women, Men, and Work. *v.4 p.273*

The Economics of World War II: Six Great Powers in
  International Comparison. *v.3 p.81*

Economics: Principles and Policy, 2004 Update. . . .*v.4 p.187*

Economics: The Basics. *v.4 p.185*

Economics Uncut: A Complete Guide to Life, Death and
  Misadventure. *v.4 p.185*

Economics. *v.4 p.186, p.195*

The Economies of Mexico and Peru During the Late Colonial
  Period, 1760-1810. . . . .*v.3 p.326*

Economist Guide to the European Union. *v.4 p.638*

The Economist: Henry Thoreau and Enterprise. . . .*v.2 p.52*

Economist Intelligence Unit (EIU). *v.3 p.259*

Economy and Society: A Study in the Integration of Economic
  and Social Theory, Vol. 26. . . . .*v.4 p.270*

Economy and Society in Early Modern Europe; Essays from
  Annales. *v.3 p.38*

Economy and Society of Ancient Greece. *v.3 p.14*

Economy and Society. *v.4 p.718*

An Economy of Abundant Beauty: Fortune Magazine and
  Depression America. *v.4 p.409*

The Economy of Early Renaissance Europe, 1300-1460. .*v.3 p.41*

The Economy of Europe in an Age of Crisis, 1600-1750. .*v.3 p.42*

Economy of Literary Form: English Literature and the
  Industrialization of Publishing, 1800-1850. . . .*v.3 p.119*

The Economy of Literary Form: English Literature and the
  Industrialization of Publishing, 1800-1850. . . .*v.6 p.741*

The Economy of the Later Renaissance Europe,
  1460-1600. . . . .*v.3 p.41*

Eco-Physiology of Fungi. *v.5 p.209*

Ecoregion-Based Design for Sustainability. *v.6 p.293*

The Ecosystem Approach in Anthropology: From Concept to
  Practice. *v.4 p.30*

Ecosystem Dynamics in a Polar Desert: The McMurdo Dry
  Valleys, Antarctica. *v.5 p.185, p.187*

Ecosystem Geography. *v.5 p.356*

Ecosystem Management: Applications for Sustainable Forest and
  Wildlife Resources. *v.5 p.11, p.28, p.29, p.40, p.356*

Ecosystem Management in the United States: An Assessment of
  Current Experience. *v.5 p.186, p.235*

Ecosystem Management: Sustaining the Nation's Natural
  Resources Trust : Majority Staff Report of the
  Committee on Natural Resources of the U.S. House of
  Representatives, One Hundred Third Congress, Second
  Session. *v.5 p.181, p.182, p.186*

Ecotourism and Sustainable Development: Who Owns Paradise? . . . . *.v.6 p.283*

The Ecozones of the World: The Ecological Divisions of the Geosphere. . . . . *.v.5 p.185*

Ecritures littéraires : dictionnaire critique des oeuvres africaines de langue française, vol. 1. . . . . *.v.2 p.542*

Ecstasy and Demon: The Dances of Mary Wigman. . *.v.1 p.10*

Ecstasy and the Demon: Feminism and Nationalism in the Dances of Mary Wigman. . . . . *.v.1 p.26, p.27*

Ecstasy: The Complete Guide - A Comprehensive Look at the Risks and Benefits of MDMA. . . . . *.v.4 p.776*

Ecstatic Occasions, Expedient Forms: 85 Leading Contemporary Poets Select and Comment on Their Poems. . . . *.v.2 p.578*

Ecstatic Religion: An Anthropological Study of Spirit Possession and Shamanism. . . . . *.v.4 p.36*

Ecuador: An Andean Enigma. . . . . *.v.3 p.333*

Ecuador vs. Peru: Peacemaking Amid Rivalry. . . . *.v.4 p.649*

eCultural Resources ; Cultural Resource Network. *.v.1 p.821*

The ecumenical revolution; an interpretation of the Catholic-Protestant dialogue. . . . . *.v.1 p.568*

Ed Delahanty in the Emerald Age of Baseball. *.v.4 p.804, p.850*

Ed Ruscha. . . . . *.v.1 p.698*

Edda: A Collection of Essays. . . . . *.v.2 p.624*

Eden, Eden, Eden. . . . . *.v.2 p.530*

The Eden-Eisenhower Correspondence, 1955-1957. . *.v.4 p.560*

The Edens of Florida: A Guide to Florida's Gardens, Preserves and Nature Centers. . . . . *.v.1 p.812*

Edgar Allan Poe: A Study of the Short Fiction. . . . . *.v.2 p.50*

Edgar Allan Poe A to Z: The Essential Reference to His Life and Work. . . . . *.v.2 p.50*

Edgar Allan Poe: Poems and Poetics. . . . . . . *.v.2 p.50*

EDGAR: SEC Filings & Forms. . . . *.v.4 p.90, p.93, p.111*

The Edge City: Life on the New Frontier. . . . . *.v.4 p.770, p.771,v.6 p.717*

Edge of Empires: Chinese Elites and British Colonials in Hong Kong. . . . . *.v.6 p.205*

The Edge of Everything: Reflections on Curatorial Practice. . . . . *.v.1 p.829*

The Edge of Life: Human Dignity and Contemporary Bioethics. . . . . *.v.5 p.248*

Edge of Midnight: The Life of John Schlesinger: The Authorized Biography. . . . . *.v.6 p.418*

Edge of Midnight: The Life of John Schlesinger. . . *.v.6 p.418*

Edge of Objectivity: An Essay in the History of Scientific Ideas. . . . . *.v.5 p.390*

The Edge of the Alphabet. . . . . *.v.2 p.745*

The Edge of the South: Life in Nineteenth-Century Virginia. . . . . *.v.3 p.498, p.499*

The Edges of the Civilized World: A Journey in Nature and Culture. . . . . *.v.5 p.78*

edHelper.com. . . . . *.v.4 p.346, p.349, p.359*

Edinburgh Book of Twentieth-Century Scottish Poetry. *.v.2 p.200*

Edith Head: The Life and Times of Hollywood's Celebrated Costume Designer. . . . . *.v.6 p.418*

Edith Wharton: A Biography. . . . . *.v.2 p.131*

Edith Wharton: A Study of the Short Fiction. . . . . *.v.2 p.132*

Edith Wharton A to Z: The Essential Guide to the Life and Work. . . . . *.v.2 p.132, p.133*

Edith Wharton and the Politics of Race. . . . . . . *.v.2 p.131*

Edith Wharton: Collected Stories 1891-1910. . . . . *.v.2 p.132*

Edith Wharton: Collected Stories 1911-1937. . . . . *.v.2 p.132*

Edith Wharton: Early Critical Responses. . . . . . . *.v.2 p.132*

Edith Wharton: Four Novels. . . . . *.v.2 p.132*

Edith Wharton in Context: Essays on Intertextuality. . *.v.2 p.132*

Edith Wharton: New Critical Essays. . . . . *.v.2 p.131*

Edith Wharton: Selected Poems. . . . . *.v.2 p.132*

Edith Wharton: The Uncollected Critical Writings. . . *.v.2 p.132*

Edith Wharton's New York Quartet. . . . . *.v.2 p.132*

Edith Wharton's Travel Writings: The Making of a Connoisseur. . . . . *.v.2 p.133*

Editing and Postproduction. . . . . *.v.6 p.350*

Editing Virginia Woolf: Interpreting the Modernist Text. *.v.2 p.392*

Editor's Study: A Comprehensive Edition of William Dean Howell's Column. . . . . *.v.2 p.42*

Edizione nazionale delle opere di Pietro Aretino, vol. 1. *.v.2 p.706*

Edizione nazionale delle opere di Pietro Aretino, vol. 2. *.v.2 p.706*

Edizione nazionale delle opere di Pietro Aretino, vol. 3. *.v.2 p.706*

Edizione nazionale delle opere di Pietro Aretino, vol. 4. *.v.2 p.706*

Edizione nazionale delle opere di Pietro Aretino, vol. 5. *.v.2 p.706*

Edizione nazionale delle opere di Pietro Aretino, vol. 6. . . . . *.v.2 p.706, p.707*

Edizione nazionale delle opere di Pietro Aretino, vol. 7. *.v.2 p.707*

Edizione nazionale delle opere di Pietro Aretino, vol. 8. *.v.2 p.707*

Edizione nazionale delle opere di Pietro Aretino, vol. 9. *.v.2 p.707*

Edmund Burke: A Philosophical Inquiry into the Origin of Our Ideas of the Sublime and Beautiful. . . . *.v.1 p.450, p.480*

Edmund C. Tarbell: Poet of Domesticity. . . . . . . *.v.1 p.736*

Edmund Kean. . . . . *.v.1 p.100, p.144*

Edmund Spenser and The Faerie Queene. . . . . . *.v.2 p.213*

Edmund Spenser: Selected Short Poems. . . . . . *.v.2 p.216*

Edmund Waller. . . . . *.v.2 p.264*

Edmund Wilson: A Biography. . . . . *.v.2 p.137*

Edmund Wilson: A Critic for Our Time. . . . . . . *.v.2 p.137*

Edmund Wilson: A Life in Literature. . . . . *.v.2 p.137*

Edmund Wilson's America. . . . . *.v.2 p.137*

Edmund Wilson. . . . . *.v.2 p.137*

Edna St. Vincent Millay: Selected Poems. . . . . . *.v.2 p.98*

Edna St. Vincent Millay. . . . . *.v.2 p.97*

Edo: Art in Japan, 1615-1868. . . . . *.v.1 p.693, p.694*

Edo Culture: Daily Life and Diversions in Urban Japan, 1600-1868. . . . . *.v.6 p.225*

Edouard Manet: Rebel in a Frock Coat. . . . . . . *.v.1 p.736*

Edouard Vuillard. . . . . *.v.1 p.696*

EDSITEment. . . . . *.v.4 p.303, p.348, p.350*

The Educated Mind: How Cognitive Tools Shape Our Understanding. . . . . *.v.4 p.339*

Educating African American Males: Voices from the Field. . . . . *.v.6 p.21, p.32*

Educating Children with Emotional and Behavioural Difficulties: Inclusive Practice in Mainstream Schools. . . . . *.v.4 p.319*

Educating Children with Multiple Disabilities: A Collaborative Approach. *v.4 p.318, p.319*

Educating Deaf Students: From Research to Practice. *v.4 p.318*

Educating Exceptional Children. *v.4 p.316*

Educating for Freedom: The Paradox of Pedagogy. . *v.4 p.339*

Educating for Intelligent Belief or Unbelief. *v.4 p.307*

Educating for OSHA Savvy Chemists. *v.5 p.315*

Educating Hearts and Minds: A Comprehensive Character Education Framework. *v.4 p.370*

Educating Hearts and Minds: Reflections on Japanese Preschool and Elementary Education. *v.4 p.364, p.370*

Educating Immigrant Children: What We Need to Know to Meet the Challenges. *v.6 p.109*

Educating Latino Students: A Guide to Successful Practice. *v.4 p.311, v.6 p.527*

Educating Middle Class Daughters: Private Girls Schools in Copenhagen 1790-1820. . . . . *v.3 p.233, p.234*

Educating Minds and Hearts: Social Emotional Learning and the Passage into Adolescence: A Guide for Educators. *v.4 p.303, p.356, p.362*

Educating Moral People: A Caring Alternative to Character Education. *v.4 p.306*

Educating Professional Psychologists: History and Guiding Conception. *v.5 p.676*

Educating Professionals: Responding to New Expectations for Competence and Accountability. *v.4 p.295*

Educating Republicans: The College in the Era of the American Revolution, 1750-1800. . . . . *v.4 p.332*

Educating Students from Other Nations: American Colleges and Universities in International Educational Interchange. *v.4 p.290*

Educating Women: Cultural Conflict and Victorian Literature. *v.2 p.175, p.190*

Education Abstracts. *v.5 p.571*

Education and a Radical Humanism: Notes Toward a Theory of the Educational Crisis. *v.4 p.343*

Education and Citizenship in Liberal-Democratic Societies: Teaching for Cosmopolitan Values and Collective Identities. *v.4 p.323*

Education and Cultural Process: Anthropological Approaches. *v.4 p.29, p.303*

Education and Culture in the Barbarian West: Sixth Through Eighth Centuries. *v.6 p.559*

Education and Democracy: The Meaning of Alexander Meiklejohn, 1872-1964. . . . . *v.4 p.344*

Education and Democratic Citizenship in America. *v.4 p.505, p.547*

Education and Ecstasy: With the Great School Reform Hoax. *v.4 p.327, p.328*

Education and Human Relations. *v.4 p.344*

Education and Identity in Rural France: The Politics of Schooling. *v.4 p.29*

Education and Imperialism: The Puerto Rican Experience in Higher Education, 1898-1986. . . . . *v.6 p.527*

Education and Income: Inequalities of Opportunity in Our Public Schools. *v.4 p.329*

Education and Jobs: The Great Training Robbery. . . *v.4 p.297*

Education and Mind in the Knowledge Age. *v.4 p.356*

Education and Nationalism: An Historical Interpretation of American Education. *v.4 p.298*

Education and Power. *v.4 p.300*

Education and Social Change: Themes in the History of American Schooling. *v.4 p.297, p.328, p.329, p.762*

Education and Social Mobility in the Soviet Union 1921-1934. . . . . *v.4 p.334*

Education and the Cult of Efficiency: A Study of the Social Forces That Have Shaped the Administration of the Public Schools. *v.4 p.325*

Education and the Good Life. *v.4 p.345*

Education and the Law: A Dictionary. *v.4 p.451*

e Education and the Rise of the Global Economy. *v.4 p.313, p.314*

Education and the Scottish People, 1750-1918. . . . *v.4 p.333*

Education and the Social Order. *v.4 p.345*

Education and Training in a Knowledge Based Economy. *v.4 p.297*

Education and Warfare in Europe. *v.4 p.333*

Education As Cultural Imperialism. *v.4 p.325*

Education, Assumptions vs. History: Collected Papers. *v.4 p.310*

Education at the Crossroads. *v.4 p.344*

▯ Education Atlas: History of Education. *v.4 p.326*

Education Between Two Worlds. *v.4 p.344*

Education by Choice: The Case for Family Control. . *v.4 p.280*

Education East and West: The Influence of Mao Zedong and John Dewey. *v.4 p.344*

Education for Critical Consciousness. *v.4 p.300*

Education for Cultural Diversity: Convergence and Divergence. *v.4 p.309*

Education for Everyone: Agenda for Education in a Democracy. *v.4 p.326*

Education for Extinction: American Indians and the Boarding School Experience, 1875-1928. . . . . *v.4 p.311, p.763, v.6 p.680, p.681*

Education for Judgment: The Artistry of Discussion Leadership. *v.4 p.177*

Education for the Emerging Age. *v.4 p.341*

Education for the New Europe. *v.4 p.333*

Education for Transformation: Implications in Lewis Mumford's Ecohumanism. *v.4 p.341*

The Education Gap: Vouchers and Urban Schools. *v.4 p.298, p.299*

The Education Gospel: The Economic Power of Schooling. *v.4 p.305*

Education in a Divided World: The Function of the Public Schools in Our Unique Society. *v.4 p.325*

Education in Ancient Rome: From the Elder Cato to the Younger Pliny. *v.3 p.23*

Education in Central America and the Caribbean. . . *v.4 p.333*

Education in Contemporary Japan: Inequality and Diversity. *v.4 p.335, p.336, v.6 p.222*

Education in England and Wales. *v.4 p.334*

Education in Exile: SOMAFCO, the African National Congress School in Tanzania, 1978-1992. . . . . *v.4 p.335*

Education in the Forming of American Society: Needs and Opportunities for Study. *v.4 p.324*

Education in the Rural American Community: A Lifelong
Process. *v.4 p.315*

Education in the West of England, 1066-1548. . . . .*v.4 p.336*

Education in Violence: The Life of George H. Thomas and the
History of the Army of the Cumberland. *v.3 p.426*

Education: Intellectual, Moral, and Physical. . .*v.4 p.345, p.346*

Education, Literacy, and Humanization: Exploring the Work
of Paulo Freire. *v.4 p.345*

The Education of a Coach. *v.4 p.858, p.896*

The Education of a Public Man: My Life and Politics. .*v.3 p.459*

The Education of a Senator. *v.3 p.457*

The Education of a True Believer. *v.3 p.224*

The Education of Black Folk: The Afro-American Struggle for
Knowledge in White America. *v.4 p.309*

The Education of Children, How the Young Man Should Study
Poetry, on Listening to Lectures, How to Tell a Flatterer
from a Friend, How a Man May Become Aware
of His Progress in Virtue. *v.2 p.418*

The Education of Henry Adams: An Autobiography. . .*v.3 p.373*

Education of the Senses: The Bourgeois Experiance - Victoria to
Freud. *v.6 p.760, p.761*

Education on the Wild Side: Learning for the Twenty-First
Century. *v.4 p.303*

Education Policy: Issues Affecting Lesbian, Gay, Bisexual
and Transgender Youth. *v.6 p.384, p.385*

Education Policy-Making in England and Wales: The Crucible
Years, 1895-1911. . . . .*v.4 p.333, p.334*

Education Reform in Postwar Japan: The 1946 U. S.
Educational Mission. *v.6 p.222*

Education, Religion, and the Common Good: Advancing a
Distinctly American Conversation about
Religion's Role in Our Shared Life. *v.4 p.307, p.486*

Education Resource Organizations Directory
(EROD). *v.4 p.323*

Education Resources Information Center. *v.5 p.573*

Education, Society, and Economic Opportunity: A Historical
Perspective on Persistent Issues. *v.4 p.329, p.330*

Education Through Art. *v.4 p.345*

Education Through Cooperative Extension. *v.5 p.12*

Education Today. *v.4 p.342*

Education, Training and the New Vocationalism: Experience and
Policy. *v.4 p.353*

Education under Mao: Class and Competition in Canton
Schools, 1960-1980. . . . .*v.4 p.337*

Education, Work and Social Capital: Towards a New Conception
of Vocational Training. *v.4 p.306*

Educational Assessment. *v.5 p.601*

Educational Design and Cognitive Science. *v.5 p.573*

Educational Facilities. *v.4 p.288*

The Educational Imagination: On the Design and Education of
School Programs. *v.4 p.362*

Educational Leadership: Policy Dimensions in the 21st Century,
1. . . . .*v.4 p.281, p.282*

Educational Measurement. *v.5 p.604*

Educational Media and Technology Yearbook: 2006. .*v.4 p.352*

Educational Opportunity Guide: A Directory of Programs for
the Gifted. *v.5 p.575*

Educational Philosophy: A History from the Ancient World to
Modern America. *v.4 p.323, p.340*

Educational Psychology: A Century of Contributions: A Project
of Division 15 (educational Psychology) of the
American Psychological Society. *v.4 p.359, v.5 p.573*

Educational Psychology. *v.4 p.359, v.5 p.571*

Educational Reform: A Self Scrutinizing Memoir. . .*v.4 p.329*

Educational Reform in the Commonwealth Caribbean. *v.4 p.335*

Educational Renewal: Better Teachers, Better Schools. *v.4 p.279*

Educational Research, Methodology and Measurement: An
International Handbook. *v.4 p.286, p.355*

Educational Roots and Routes in Western Europe. . .*v.4 p.333*

Educational Strategies among Muslims in the Context of
Globalization: Some National Case Studies. . . .*v.4 p.308*

Educational Technology: The Development of a
Concept. *v.4 p.351*

Educational Theory of Immanuel Kant. *v.4 p.343*

Educational Theory of Jean Jacques Rousseau. . . .*v.4 p.341*

Educational Thought and Ideology in Modern Japan: State
Authority and Individual Freedom. *v.6 p.224*

The Educational Thought and Influence of Matthew Arnold, Vol.
223. . . . .*v.4 p.341*

Educational Views of Benjamin Franklin. *v.4 p.342*

An Educational War on Poverty: American and British
Policy-Making 1960-1980. . . . .*v.4 p.337*

Educational Wastelands: The Retreat from Learning in Our
Public Schools. *v.4 p.340*

Educative Assessment: Designing Assessments to Inform and
Improve Student Performance. *v.4 p.287*

The Educator's Desk Reference: (EDR) A Sourcebook of
Educational Information and Research. *v.4 p.355*

Educator's Reference Desk. *v.4 p.338*

Edutopia: Success Stories for Learning in the Digital
Age. *v.4 p.351*

Edvard Grieg: The Man and the Artist. *v.1 p.194, p.327*

Edvard Munch: Behind the Scream. *v.1 p.699*

Edvard Munch: The Complete Graphic Works. . . .*v.1 p.758*

Edward Albee: A Casebook. *v.1 p.87, p.92, p.116*

Edward Frankland: Chemistry, Controversy and Conspiracy in
Victorian England. *v.5 p.261*

Edward Gordon Craig: A Vision of Theatre. .*v.1 p.83, p.101, p.147*

The Edward Hopper: A Catalogue Raisonné. *v.1 p.697*

Edward Hopper: Portraits of America. *v.1 p.746*

Edward Hopper. *v.1 p.747*

Edward MacDowell: An American Master. . .*v.1 p.200, p.338*

Edward Preble: A Naval Biography, 1761-1807. . . .*v.3 p.412*

Edward Ruscha: Catalogue Raisonné of the Paintings. *v.1 p.741*

Edward S. Corwin's, Constitution and What It Means
Today. *v.4 p.453*

Edward Sapir: Linguist, Anthropologist, Humanist. . .*v.4 p.4*

Edward Steichen: The Early Years. *v.1 p.769*

Edward Weston: A Legacy. *v.1 p.769*

Edward Weston: The Last Years in Carmel. *v.1 p.769*

Edward Wilmot Blyden: Pan-Negro Patriot, 1832-1912. *v.6 p.70*

Edwardian Architecture. *v.1 p.787*

Edwardian Fiction: An Oxford Companion. *v.2 p.194*

Edwardian Fiction. *v.2 p.194*

The Edwardian Theatre: Essays on Performance and the
   Stage. *v.2 p.188*

The Edwardian Turn of Mind. *v.3 p.117*

The Edwardians. *v.2 p.381*

An Edwin Arlington Robinson Encyclopedia. *v.2 p.113*

E.E. Cummings: A Biography. *v.2 p.68, p.69*

E-Economy: Rhetoric or Business Reality? *v.4 p.263*

EEO Law and Personnel Practices. *v.4 p.131*

Eerdmans Commentary on the Bible. *v.1 p.615*

Eero Saarinen : an architecture of multiplicity. . . .*v.1 p.795*

Eero Saarinen. *v.1 p.794*

☐ EEVL: Computing. *v.5 p.343, p.344*

The E-Factor: Turning Environmental Responsibility into Good,
   Green Profits. *v.4 p.63*

The Effect of Gamma Rays on Man-in-the-Moon
   Marigolds. *v.2 p.159, p.160*

Effective and Responsible Teaching: The New
   Synthesis. *v.4 p.348*

The Effective Board of Trustees. *v.4 p.293*

Effective Consultancies in Development and Humanitarian
   Programmes: A Practical Guide. *v.4 p.65*

The Effective Corrections Manager: Correctional Supervision for
   the Future. *v.6 p.275*

The Effective Executive: The Definitive Guide to Getting the
   Right Things Done. *v.4 p.72*

Effective Leadership in Adventure Programming. .*v.4 p.788, p.789*

Effective Legal Research. *v.4 p.439*

Effective Partnering for School Change: Improving Early
   Childhood Education in Urban Classrooms. . . .*v.4 p.368*

The Effective Presentation: Talk Your Way to Success. .*v.4 p.423*

Effective Prison Leadership. *v.6 p.275*

Effective Public Relations. *v.4 p.172*

Effects of Acid Rain on Forest Processes. *v.5 p.38*

The Effects of Noise on Man. *v.5 p.364, p.365, p.374*

The Effects of Violence on Peace Processes. *v.4 p.648*

Effeminate England: Homoerotic Writing after
   1885. . . . .*v.2 p.174, p.178*

Effeminism: The Economy of Colonial Desire. . . .*v.6 p.157*

Effi Briest. *v.2 p.596*

Efficient Conservation of Crop Genetic Diversity: Theoretical
   Approaches and Empirical Studies. *v.5 p.9, p.24*

The Efficient Secret: The Cabinet and the Development of
   Political Parties in Victorian England. *v.4 p.604*

Effort and Excellence in Urban Classrooms: Expecting, and
   Getting, Success with All Students. *v.4 p.314*

Effort at Speech: New and Selected Poems. . . .*v.2 p.97, p.98*

Efforts to Improve the Quality of Vocational Education in
   Secondary Schools: Impact of Federal and State
   Policies. *v.4 p.305*

Effort-Shape Analysis of Movement: The Unity of Expression
   and Function. *v.1 p.50*

☐ Efunda: Engineering Fundamentals. *v.5 p.679*

Efuru. *v.2 p.756*

Egan's Fundamentals of Respiratory Care. *v.5 p.536*

Egeria, Diary of a Pilgrimage. *v.1 p.591*

Egg Incubation: Its Effects on Embryonic Development in Birds
   and Reptiles. *v.5 p.161*

Egil's Saga. *v.2 p.625*

The Egoist. *v.2 p.300*

Egon Schiele: Landscapes. *v.1 p.743*

Egon Schiele. *v.1 p.699*

E-Government 2003. . . . .*v.4 p.546*

Egypt after the Pharaohs, 332 BC-AD 642: From Alexander to
   the Arab Conquest. *v.3 p.10*

Egypt and Syria under the Circassian Sultans, 1382-1468 A.D.:
   Systematic Notes to Ibn Taghri Birdi's Chronicles of
   Egypt. *v.6 p.607, p.636*

Egypt and the Fertile Crescent, 1516-1922: A Political
   History. *v.6 p.583*

Egypt As a Woman: Nationalism, Gender, and Politics. .*v.6 p.634*

Egypt Before the Pharaohs. *v.3 p.8, p.9*

Egypt, Canaan, and Israel in Ancient Times. *v.3 p.7, p.9*

Egypt from Alexander the Great to the Arab Conquest. .*v.6 p.635*

Egypt from Alexander to the Early Christians: An
   Archaeological and Historical Guide. *v.3 p.10*

Egypt, Greece and Rome: Civilizations of the Ancient
   Mediterranean. *v.3 p.3*

Egypt in Late Antiquity. *v.3 p.10, v.6 p.58, p.635*

Egypt in the Age of Cleopatra: History and Society under the
   Ptolemies. *v.3 p.10, v.6 p.58*

Egypt in the Reign of Muhammad Ali. *v.6 p.58, p.639*

Egypt, Islam and Democracy: Critical Essays. *v.6 p.639*

Egypt, Islam, and the Arabs: The Search for Egyptian
   Nationhood, 1900-1930. . . . .*v.6 p.637*

Egypt: Music in the Age of the Pyramids. *v.1 p.176*

The Egypt of Nasser and Sadat: the Political Economy of Two
   Regimes. *v.6 p.640*

Egypt of the Pharaohs: An Introduction. *v.3 p.8*

Egypt: Politics and Society, 1945-1990. . . . . . .*v.6 p.58*

Egyptian Art in the Age of the Pyramids. *v.1 p.669, p.689*

Egyptian Art. *v.1 p.669, p.689*

The Egyptian Book of the Dead: The Papyrus of Ani. .*v.1 p.542*

Egyptian Earth. *v.6 p.657*

Egyptian Mummies. *v.3 p.8*

Egyptian Nubians: Resettlement and Years of
   Coping. *v.6 p.58, p.635*

Egyptian One-Act Plays. *v.6 p.660*

Egyptian Politics: The Dynamics of Authoritarian
   Rule. *v.4 p.500, p.611*

Egyptian Politics under Sadat: The Post-Populist Development
   of an Authoritarian-Modernizing State. *v.6 p.638*

Egyptian Sculpture: Cairo and Luxor. *v.1 p.776*

Egyptian Society under Ottoman Rule, 1517-1798. .*v.6 p.58, p.59*

The Egyptian, Syrian, and Iraqi Revolutions: Some Observations
   on Their Underlying Causes and Social
   Character. *v.6 p.602, p.607, p.639*

Egyptian Tales and Legends: Pagan, Christian, and
   Muslim. *v.6 p.644, p.645, p.659*

Egyptian Treasures from the Egyptian Museum in
   Cairo. *v.1 p.671*

Egyptian Women in a Changing Society, 1899-1987. .*v.6 p.636*

The Egyptians. *v.3 p.8*

Egyptology: The Missing Millennium - Ancient Egypt in
   Medieval Arabic Writings. *v.6 p.58*

Egypt's Liberal Experiment, 1922-1936. . . . . .*v.6 p.57, p.636*

☐ EH.Net Encyclopedia of Economic and Business
   History. *v.4 p.146, p.179*

Ehrengard. *v.2 p.626*

☐ EIA - Energy Data and Analysis Publications, Reports,
   Articles, and brochures. *v.5 p.452*

☐ EIA Energy Information Administration: Official Energy
   Statistics from the U. S. Government. *v.5 p.737*

Eichmann in Jerusalem: A Report on the Banality of Evil. .*v.3 p.82*

Eight Centuries of Troubadours and Trouvéres: The Changing
   Identity of Medieval Music. *v.1 p.177*

Eight Expressionist Plays. *v.2 p.631*

Eight Men Out: The Black Sox and the 1919 World
   Series. *v.4 p.849*

Eight Men: Short Stories. *v.2 p.138*

Eight Novellas. *v.2 p.658*

Eight Philosophers of the Italian Renaissance. *v.1 p.435*

Eight Stories. *v.2 p.386*

Eight Theories of Religion. *v.1 p.521*

Eight Twentieth-Century Russian Plays. .*v.1 p.67, p.109,v.2 p.794*

Eight Urban Musical Cultures: Tradition and Change. .*v.1 p.283*

Eight Words for the Study of Expressive Culture. .*v.2 p.584, p.585*

Eight Years with Wilson's Cabinet, 1913 to 1920. .*v.3 p.472, p.473*

Eighteen Forty-Eight: The Making of a Revolution. .*v.3 p.75, p.76*

Eighteenth and Nineteenth Century American Drama. . .*v.2 p.25*

The Eighteenth Century, 1715-1789. . . . . . .*v.2 p.456, p.459*

Eighteenth Century Economics. *v.4 p.215*

The Eighteenth Century French Novel: Techniques of
   Illusion. *v.2 p.462*

The Eighteenth Century in Indian History: Revolution or
   Evolution? *v.6 p.156*

Eighteenth Century Keyboard Music. *v.1 p.191, p.241*

Eighteenth Century Plays. *v.1 p.62, p.98*

The Eighteenth Century Revolution in Spain. *v.3 p.240*

Eighteenth Century Russian Literature Culture and Thought: A
   Bibliography of English-Language Scholarship and
   Translations. *v.2 p.795*

Eighteenth Century Satire: Essays on Text and Context from
   Dryden to Peter Pindar. *v.2 p.195*

Eighteenth Century Women Poets: An Oxford
   Anthology. *v.2 p.200*

Eighteenth-Century Fiction on Screen. *v.6 p.326*

Eighteenth-Century French Drawings in New York
   Collections. *v.1 p.722*

An Eighteenth-Century Musical Chronicle: Events 1750-1799,
   25. . . . .*v.1 p.189*

Eighteenth-Century Poetry: An Annotated Anthology. .*v.2 p.199*

Eighteenth-Century Women Dramatists. *v.2 p.202*

The Eighth Day: A Novel. *v.2 p.133, p.134*

The Eighth Day of the Week. *v.2 p.790*

The Eighties: America in the Age of Reagan. *v.3 p.470*

Eighty Exemplary Ethics Statements. *v.4 p.173*

Eighty-Sixed. *v.6 p.378, p.396*

Eileen Gray. *v.1 p.792*

Eilhard Mitscherlich: Prince of Prussian
   Chemistry. *v.5 p.261, p.262*

Das Einhorn. *v.2 p.619*

Einstein, History and Other Passions. .*v.3 p.46, v.5 p.390, p.395*

Einstein's Greatest Blunder?: The Cosmological Constant and
   Other Fudge Factors in the Physics of the Universe. .*v.5 p.71*

Einstein's Miraculous Year: Five Papers That Changed the Face
   of Physics. *v.5 p.539*

Eisenhauer and the American Crusades. *v.3 p.477*

Eisenhower: A Soldier's Life. *v.3 p.469*

Eisenhower and Israel: United States-Israeli Relations,
   1953-1960. . . . .*v.3 p.386*

Eisenhower and the Cold War. *v.3 p.469*

Eisenhower at War, 1943-1945. . . . .*v.3 p.470*

The Eisenhower Court and Civil Liberties. *v.4 p.540*

The Eisenhower Diaries. *v.3 p.470*

Eisenhower: The Inside Story. *v.3 p.469*

Eisenhower. *v.3 p.464, p.478*

Eisenstein, Cinema, and History. *v.6 p.339*

Elaborations on Emptiness: Uses of the Heart
   Sutra. *v.1 p.563, p.564*

ELAS: Greek Resistance Army. *v.3 p.195*

Elbow Room: Stories. *v.2 p.150*

ⓔ Elbow Room: The Varieties of Free Will Worth
   Wanting. *v.1 p.503*

Eleanor of Aquitaine and the Four Kings. *v.3 p.98*

Eleanor of Castile: Queen and Society in Thirteenth Century
   England. *v.6 p.560*

Eleanor Roosevelt: 1884-1933. . . . .*v.6 p.390*

Eleanor Roosevelt: The Defining Years, 1933-1938. . .*v.6 p.390*

Eleanor: The Years Alone. *v.3 p.460*

E-Learning: Technology and the Development of Learning and
   Teaching. *v.4 p.352*

Electing Jimmy Carter: The Campaign of 1976. . . .*v.3 p.465*

Electing Justice: Fixing the Supreme Court Nomination
   Process. *v.4 p.536*

The Election of 2000: Reports and Interpretations. . .*v.4 p.531*

Elections and Conflict Management in Africa. .*v.4 p.578, p.613*

Elections and Democratization in Ukraine. .*v.4 p.577, p.584, p.597*

Elections and Voters: A Comparative Introduction. . .*v.4 p.577*

Elections and Voters in Post-Communist Russia. .*v.4 p.578, p.599*

Elections and War: The Electoral Incentive in the Democratic
   Politics of War and Peace. *v.4 p.504*

Elections as Instruments of Democracy: Majoritarian and
   Proportional Visions. *v.4 p.577*

Elections in Africa: A Data Handbook. *v.4 p.612*

The Elections in Israel 1992. . . . .*v.4 p.615*

Elections in the French Revolution: An Apprenticeship in
   Democracy, 1789-1799. . . . .*v.4 p.608*

Elections Without Order: Russia's Challenge to Vladimir
   Putin. *v.4 p.578, p.599*

Elections. *v.4 p.586*

Electoral Engineering: Voting Rules and Political
   Behavior. *v.4 p.577*

[e] Electoral Laws and Their Political Consequences.   *.v.4 p.576*

Electoral Realignments: A Critique of an American
Genre.   *.v.4 p.551*

The Electoral System in Britain.   *.v.4 p.606*

Electoral Systems: A Theoretical and Comparative
Introduction.   *.v.4 p.577, p.578*

The Electorate, the Campaign, and the Office: A Unified
Approach to Senate and House Elections.   *.v.4 p.533, p.534*

Electra.   *.v.2 p.410*

Electric Circuit Analysis.   *.v.5 p.721*

Electric Circuits: Analysis and Design.   *.v.5 p.721*

Electric Circuits.   *.v.5 p.721*

The Electric Guitar: A History of an American Icon.   *.v.1 p.390*

The Electric Kool-Aid Acid Test.   *.v.2 p.159*

Electric Ladyland: Women and Rock Culture,
1965-1975.   *.v.1 p.379, p.380*

Electric Light: Poems.   *.v.2 p.352*

Electric Machinery and Transformers.   *.v.5 p.723*

Electric Machinery.   *.v.5 p.725*

Electric Motors and Motor Controls.   *.v.5 p.725*

Electric Motors.   *.v.5 p.725*

Electric power distribution handbook.   *.v.5 p.360*

Electric Power Distribution Handbook.   *.v.5 p.724*

Electric Power Distribution.   *.v.5 p.724*

Electric Power Generation: A Nontechnical Guide.   *.v.5 p.723*

Electric Power Systems: A Conceptual Introduction.   *.v.5 p.724*

Electric Power Systems: Analysis and
Control.   *.v.5 p.360, p.369, p.724*

Electric Power Systems Manual.   *.v.5 p.724*

Electric Sound: The Past and Promise of Electronic
Music.   *.v.1 p.211, p.244*

Electric Universe: How Electricity Switched on the Modern
World.   *.v.5 p.390, p.391, p.409*

Electric Vehicle Technology Explained.   *.v.5 p.716*

Electrical Power and Controls.   *.v.5 p.724*

Electrical Power Engineering.   *.v.5 p.724*

Electrical Researches of the Honourable Henry
Cavendish.   *.v.5 p.543*

Electrical Safety Handbook.   *.v.5 p.681*

Electricity and Magnetism.   *.v.5 p.564*

Electrochemical Data.   *.v.5 p.285*

Electrochemical Methods: Fundamentals and
Applications.   *.v.5 p.284*

[□] Electrochemical Science and Technology Information
Resource (ESTIR).   *.v.5 p.284*

Electrochemistry for Chemists.   *.v.5 p.285*

Electrochemistry.   *.v.5 p.285*

Electrodynamics of Continuous Media, Vol. 8.   *.v.5 p.565*

Electromagnetic Theory: Including an Account of Heaviside'
Unpublished Notes, Set.   *.v.5 p.564*

Electromechanical Energy Devices and Power Systems.   *.v.5 p.725*

Electron: A Centenary Volume.   *.v.5 p.541*

Electronic and Computer Music.   *.v.1 p.218, p.244, p.245*

Electronic and Experimental Music: Pioneers in Technology and
Composition.   *.v.1 p.216, p.244*

[⊘] Electronic Beowulf.   *.v.2 p.204*

Electronic Collaboration in Science.   *.v.5 p.589*

Electronic Communication Systems.   *.v.4 p.422*

Electronic Communication Techniques.   *.v.5 p.726*

Electronic Design: From Concept to Reality.   *.v.5 p.722*

Electronic Devices: A Design Approach.   *.v.5 p.721, p.722*

Electronic Devices and Circuit Theory.   *.v.5 p.722*

Electronic Devices and Circuits: Discrete and
Integrated.   *.v.5 p.722*

Electronic Devices and Circuits.   *.v.5 p.722*

Electronic Devices (Conventional Current Version).   *.v.5 p.722*

Electronic Interpretation of Organic Chemistry: A
Problems-Oriented Text.   *.v.5 p.301*

Electronic Learning Communities: Issues and Practices.   *.v.4 p.322*

Electronic Materials Information Service (EMIS)
database.   *.v.5 p.275*

The Electronic Media and the Transformation of Law.   *.v.4 p.445*

Electronic Music: A Listener's Guide.   *.v.1 p.223, p.245*

Electronic Properties of Engineering Materials.   *.v.5 p.732*

[□] Electronic Review of Computer Books.   *.v.5 p.344*

Electronic Structure and Optical Properties of
Semiconductors.   *.v.5 p.555*

Electronics: A Top-down Approach.   *.v.5 p.722*

Electronics and Circuit Analysis Using MATLAB.   *.v.5 p.720*

Electrons and Phonons: The Theory of Transport Phenomena in
Solids.   *.v.5 p.555*

Electrons and Valence: Development of the Theory,
1900-1925.   *.v.5 p.282*

Electrophoresis in Practice: A Guide to Methods and
Applications of DNA and Protein
Separations.   *.v.5 p.90, p.103, p.104*

Electroplating and Electroless Plating of Copper and Its
Alloys.   *.v.5 p.737*

Elegant Debts: The Social Art of Wen Zhengming.   *.v.1 p.693*

The Elegant Universe: Superstrings, Hidden Dimensions, and
the Quest for the Ultimate Theory.   *.v.5 p.552*

Elegia di madonna Fiammetta.   *.v.2 p.701*

Elegies and the Songs and Sonnets.   *.v.2 p.213*

Elegies, I-IV: Propertius.   *.v.2 p.442*

Elegies.   *.v.2 p.343*

Elegy and Paradox: Testing the Conventions.   *.v.2 p.180*

Elegy for an Age: The Presence of the Past in Victorian
Literature.   *.v.2 p.184*

Elegy for Iris.   *.v.2 p.371*

Elegy for Kosovo: Stories.   *.v.2 p.815*

Elegy for the Southern Drawl.   *.v.2 p.147*

Elementary Algebraic Geometry.   *.v.5 p.497*

Elementary and Middle School Mathematics: Teaching
Developmentally.   *.v.5 p.464*

Elementary Bayesian Statistics.   *.v.4 p.197, p.198*

Elementary Chemical Engineering.   *.v.5 p.743*

Elementary Differential Equations: With Solutions
Manual.   *.v.5 p.486*

Elementary Differential Geometry.   *.v.5 p.496*

Elementary Education: A Reference Handbook.   *.v.4 p.363*

Elementary Engineering Fracture Mechanics. *v.5 p.687*

Elementary Fluid Dynamics. *v.5 p.547*

Elementary Labanotation. *v.1 p.38*

Elementary Lessons in Logic: Deductive and Inductive. .*v.4 p.231*

Elementary Logic. *v.1 p.492*

Elementary Mathematical Models: Order Aplenty and a Glimpse
of Chaos. *v.5 p.500*

Elementary Mathematics from an Advanced Standpoint:
Geometry. *v.5 p.495*

An Elementary Middle English Grammar. *v.2 p.551*

Elementary Modern Standard Arabic. *v.6 p.653*

Elementary Nuclear Theory. *v.5 p.553*

The Elementary Particles. *v.2 p.530*

Elementary Persian Grammar. *v.6 p.669*

Elementary Principles of Economics. *v.4 p.195, p.199*

Elementary Principles of Statistical Mechanics. . . .*v.5 p.558*

Elementary Probability Theory: With Stochastic Processes and
an Introduction to Mathematical Finance. . .*v.5 p.483, p.503*

Elementary School Objectives: A Report Prepared for the
Mid. *v.4 p.364*

Elementary School Science and How to Teach It. . . .*v.4 p.362*

Elementary Solid State Physics: Principles and
Applications. *v.5 p.555*

Elementary Structures for Architects and Builders. . .*v.5 p.696*

Elementary Survey Sampling. *v.5 p.482*

Elementary Surveying: An Introduction to Geomatics. .*v.4 p.389*

Elementary Teacher's Discipline Problem Solver: A Practical
A-Z Guide for Managing Classroom Behavior
Problems. *v.4 p.284*

Elementary Topics in Differential Geometry. *v.5 p.497*

Elementary Training for Musicians. *v.1 p.404*

Elements of Algebra: Geometry, Numbers, Equations. *v.5 p.472*

Elements of Computer Music. *v.1 p.387*

The Elements of Drama. *v.1 p.55*

Elements of Econometrics. *v.4 p.202*

Elements of Economics of Industry. *v.4 p.224*

Elements of Environmental Engineering: Thermodynamics and
Kinetics. *v.5 p.705, p.712*

The Elements of Graphing Data. *v.5 p.480*

Elements of Hebrew by an Inductive Method. *v.6 p.646*

The Elements of Learning. *v.4 p.356*

Elements of Mathematical Ecology. *v.5 p.91, p.170*

Elements of Modern X-Ray Physics. *v.5 p.560, p.561*

The Elements of Moral Philosophy. *v.1 p.485*

Elements of Music. *v.1 p.374*

Elements of Petroleum Geology. *v.5 p.451, p.738*

Elements of Practical Coal Mining. *v.5 p.737*

Elements of Pure Economics, or the Theory of Social
Wealth. *v.4 p.213, p.217*

The Elements of San Joaquin. *v.6 p.503, p.511*

Elements of Semiology. *v.2 p.559*

Elements of Soil Mechanics. *v.5 p.699*

Elements of Space Technology. *v.5 p.720*

The Elements of Statistical Learning: Data Mining, Inference,
and Prediction. *v.5 p.408*

Elements of Strength of Materials. *v.5 p.691*

The Elements of Style. *v.2 p.565*

The Elements of Teaching. *v.4 p.346*

Elements of the Nature and Properties of Soils. . . .*v.5 p.48*

Elements of the p Block. *v.5 p.303*

The Elements on Earth: Inorganic Chemistry in the
Environment. *v.5 p.303*

The Elements. *v.5 p.264*

Eleonora Duse: A Biography. *v.1 p.141, p.145*

Elephant: The Animal and Its Ivory in African
Culture. *v.1 p.690, v.4 p.707, p.710*

Elevator Music: A Surreal History of Muzak, Easy-Listening,
and Other Moodsong; Revised and Expanded
Edition. *v.1 p.376*

The Eleventh Amendment and Sovereign Immunity. . .*v.4 p.443*

The Eleventh Hour: The Eightieth Anniversary of Armistice
Day. *v.3 p.79*

The Eleventh Plague: The Politics of Biological and Chemical
Warfare. *v.4 p.655, p.656*

The Elgar Companion to Classical Economics, Set. . .*v.4 p.218*

The Elgar Companion to Consumer Research and Economic
Psychology. *v.5 p.604*

The Elgar Companion to Feminist Economics. *v.6 p.457*

The Elgar Companion to Law and Economics. *v.4 p.187*

The Elgar Companion to Post Keynesian Economics. *v.4 p.232*

The Elgar Dictionary of Economic Quotations. *v.4 p.191*

Elgar: Enigma Variations. *v.1 p.203, p.242, p.323*

Elias Portolu. *v.2 p.717*

☐ e-Library @ Iowa State University: Materials Science
Resources on the Web. *v.5 p.731*

Elihu Root and the Conservative Tradition. *v.3 p.434*

Elihu Root, Set. *v.3 p.434*

Elihu Root. *v.3 p.398*

Elijah P. Lovejoy, Abolitionist Editor. *v.3 p.419*

Eliot: Selected Essays, Poems and Others Writings. . *v.2 p.287*

Eliot's Dark Angel: Intersections of Life and Art. *v.2 p.72*

Elisabeth Anderson-Ivantsova: A Bolshoi Ballerina
Abroad. *v.1 p.13*

Elite Accommodation in Canadian Politics. *v.4 p.591*

Elite Discourse and Racism. *v.4 p.731*

Elite MBA Programs at Public Universities: How a Dozen
Innovative Schools Are Redefining Business
Education. *v.4 p.177*

The Elite of the Elite: Permanent Secretaries in the British
Higher Civil Service. *v.4 p.605*

Elite Theatre in Ming China, 1368-1644. . . .*v.1 p.132, p.134*

Elizabeth and After: A Novel. *v.2 p.734*

Elizabeth Barrett Browning: The Origins of a New
Poetry. *v.2 p.272*

Elizabeth Barrett Browning. *v.2 p.272*

Elizabeth Bishop and Her Art. *v.2 p.62*

Elizabeth Bishop and Marianne Moore: The Psychodynamics of
Creativity. *v.2 p.61, p.102*

Elizabeth Bishop: Her Poetics of Loss. *v.2 p.62*

Elizabeth Bishop: Life and the Memory of It. *v.2 p.62*

Elizabeth Bishop: The Biography of a Poetry. . . .*v.2 p.61, p.62*

Elizabeth Bishop: The Geography of Gender. *v.2 p.62*

Elizabeth Bishop: The Restraints of Language. *v.2 p.61*

Elizabeth Bowen: The Shadow Across the Page. . . .*v.2 p.335*

Elizabeth Bowen. *v.2 p.335*

Elizabeth Gaskell: A Habit of Stories. *v.2 p.289*

Elizabeth Gaskell: A Portrait in Letters. *v.2 p.288*

Elizabeth Gaskell: The Early Years. *v.2 p.288*

Elizabeth Gaskell. *v.2 p.289*

Elizabeth I and Her Parliaments, 1584-1601. . . .*v.3 p.95, p.100*

Elizabeth I. *v.3 p.100*

Elizabeth Tudor: Portrait of a Queen. *v.3 p.101*

Elizabethan and Jacobean Playwrights. *v.2 p.186*

The Elizabethan Courtier Poets: The Poems and Their
Contexts. *v.2 p.182*

Elizabethan Lyric. *v.2 p.182*

The Elizabethan Puritan Movement. . .*v.1 p.588, v.3 p.99, p.120*

Elizabethan Theatre. *v.1 p.75, p.102, v.2 p.186*

The Elizabethans and America. *v.3 p.406*

Elkouri and Elkouri: How Arbitration Works. *v.4 p.447*

The Ella Fitzgerald Companion: Seven Decades of
Commentary. *v.1 p.259, p.324*

Ellen Gilchrist: Collected Stories. *v.2 p.145*

Ellen Glasgow: A Biography. *v.2 p.80*

Ellen Glasgow: New Perspectives. *v.2 p.80*

Ellen Terry. *v.1 p.102, p.145*

Ellenberg and Rifkin's Diabetes Mellitus: Theory and
Practice. *v.5 p.518*

Elles: A Bilingual Anthology of Modern French Poetry by
Women. *v.2 p.464*

Elliott Carter: Collected Essays and Lectures,
1937-1995. . . . .*v.1 p.211, p.316*

Elmer Bischoff: The Ethics of Paint. *v.1 p.743*

Eloquent Images: Word and Image in the Age of New
Media. *v.1 p.703, p.771*

The Eloquent Oboe: A History of the Hautboy from
1640-1760. . . . .*v.1 p.389*

Elsevier's Dictionary of Nature and Hunting: In English, French,
Russian, German and Latin. *v.5 p.225*

Elsevier's Dictionary of Nuclear Science and Technology: In
English-American (with Definitions), French,
Spanish, Italian, Dutch and German. *v.5 p.739*

Elsevier's Dictionary of Soil Science: Definitions in English
with French, German, and Spanish Word
Translations. *v.5 p.49, v.6 p.285*

Elsevier's Dictionary of the Genera of Life: In English (with
Definitions). *v.5 p.246*

Elsevier's Dictionary of Water and Hydraulic
Engineering. *v.5 p.703*

Elsevier's Encyclopedic Dictionary of Measures: In English
(with Definitions). *v.5 p.567*

Elsewhere Perhaps. *v.6 p.650, p.651*

The Elusive Agenda: Mainstreaming Women in
Development. *v.6 p.457*

Elusive Citizenship: Immigration, Asian Americans, and the
Paradox of Civil Rights. *v.6 p.107, p.108, p.117*

The Elusive Eden: A New History of California. . . .*v.3 p.531*

The Elusive Mr. Wesley. *v.1 p.586*

Elusive Obvious. *v.1 p.50, p.51*

The Elusive Quest for Growth: Economists' Adventures and
Misadventures in the Tropics. *v.4 p.243*

The Elusive Republic: Political Economy in Jeffersonian
America. *v.6 p.295*

An Elusive Science: The Troubling History of Education
Research. *v.4 p.355*

Elusive Stability: Essays in the History of International Finance,
1919-1939. . . . .*v.4 p.255*

Elvis Culture: Fans, Faith, and Image. *v.1 p.268, p.348*

Elvis in Jerusalem: Post-Zionism and the Americanization of
Israel. *v.6 p.615*

The Elvis Reader: Texts and Sources on the King of Rock 'n'
Roll. *v.1 p.273, p.348*

Elvis. *v.1 p.272, p.348*

Elwina, le roman fée : roman. *v.2 p.528*

The Emancipated. *v.2 p.289*

Emancipating the Female Sex: The Struggle for Women's Rights
in Brazil, 1850-1940. . . . .*v.3 p.336*

Emancipation of the Polish Peasantry. *v.3 p.253*

The Emancipation Proclamation. *v.3 p.430*

The Emancipatory Promise of Charter Schools: Toward a
Progressive Politics of School Choice. *v.4 p.281*

The Embarrassment of Riches: An Interpretation of Dutch
Culture in the Golden Age. *v.3 p.205*

Embarrassment: Poise and Peril in Everyday
Life. *v.5 p.648, p.655*

Embattled Confederacy: The Image of War, 1861-1865. .*v.3 p.431*

Embattled Courage: The Experience of Battle in the American
Civil War. *v.3 p.398, p.399*

Embattled Dreams: California in War and Peace,
1940-1950. . . . .*v.3 p.532*

Embattled Reason: Essays on Social Knowledge, Vol. 2. .*v.4 p.682*

Embattled Reason, Vol. 1. . . . .*v.4 p.682*

The Embedded Corporation: Corporate Governance and
Employment Relations in Japan and the United States. .*v.4 p.86*

Embers. *v.2 p.786*

Emblem and Expression: Meaning in English Art of the
Eighteenth Century. *v.3 p.129*

Emblems of Desire: Selections from "Delie". *v.2 p.472*

Emblems of Mind: The Inner Life of Music and
Mathematics. *v.5 p.460*

Embodied Image. *v.1 p.732*

Embodied Spirituality in a Sacred World. *v.5 p.636*

The Embodiment of the National: Politics, Race, and Gender in
Late Nineteenth-Century Mexican Painting. . . .*v.3 p.265*

Embodying Bioethics: Recent Feminist Advances. . . .*v.5 p.247*

Embodying Morality: Growing up in Rural Northern
Vietnam. *v.4 p.772*

Embodying the Spirit: New Perspectives on North American
Revivalism. *v.1 p.648*

Embrace Tiger, Return to Mountain: The Essence of Tai
Ji. *v.4 p.793*

Embracing a Gay Identity: Gay Novels As Guides. . .*v.6 p.393*

Embracing America: A Cuban Exile Comes of
Age. *v.6 p.490, p.508*

Embracing Cyprus: The Path to Unity in the New
    Europe. *v.4 p.637*

Embracing Defeat: Japan in the Wake of World War II. .*v.6 p.223*

Embracing the East: White Women and American
    Orientalism. *v.6 p.98, p.115*

Embroidery: A History. *v.1 p.716, p.809*

Embryo Experimentation: Ethical, Legal and Social
    Issues. *v.5 p.160, p.249*

Embryology: Constructing the Organism. *v.5 p.161*

Embryology, Epigenesis and Evolution: Taking Development
    Seriously. *v.5 p.160*

The Embryology of Behavior. *v.5 p.626*

Embryos: Color Atlas of Development. *v.5 p.159*

Embryos, Galaxies, and Sentient Beings: How the Universe
    Makes Life. *v.5 p.243*

Emendatio Vitae: Orationes ad Honorem Nominis
    Ihesu. *v.2 p.449, p.450*

Emergence of a Free Press. *v.4 p.459*

☐ Emergence of Advertising in America: 1850-1920. *v.4 p.426*

The Emergence of Agricultural Science: Justus Liebig and the
    Americans, 1840-1880. . . . .*v.5 p.5*

The Emergence of Agriculture. *v.4 p.6*

The Emergence of Arab Nationalism: With a Background Study
    of Arab-Turkish Relations in the Near East. *v.6 p.583*

The Emergence of Bangladesh: Class and Political Struggles in
    East Pakistan, 1947-1958. . . . .*v.6 p.148*

The Emergence of German as a Literary Language,
    1700-1775. . . . .*v.2 p.620*

The Emergence of Insurgency in El Salvador: Ideology and
    Political Will. *v.3 p.299*

The Emergence of Liberation Theology: Radical Religion and
    Social Movement Theory. *v.4 p.721*

The Emergence of Life on Earth: A Historical and Scientific
    Overview. *v.5 p.192*

The Emergence of Lincoln: Prologue to Civil War, 1859-1861,
    Vol. 4. . . . .*v.3 p.426*

The Emergence of Logical Empiricism: From 1900 to the
    Vienna Circle. *v.1 p.512*

The Emergence of Modern Ireland 1600-1900. . . .*v.3 p.135*

The Emergence of Modern Southeast Asia: A New
    History. *v.6 p.165*

The Emergence of Modern Turkey. *v.6 p.624*

The Emergence of Private Authority in Global
    Governance. *v.4 p.663*

The Emergence of Richard Wright. *v.2 p.138*

The Emergence of Russia, 750-1200. . . . .*v.3 p.215*

The Emergence of State Government: Parties and New Jersey
    Politics, 1950-1999. . . . .*v.4 p.552, p.553, p.554*

The Emergence of the African-American Artist: Roberts S.
    Duncanson, 1821-1872. . . . .*v.1 p.705*

The Emergence of the American University. *v.4 p.333*

Emergence of the Catholic Tradition, 100-600. . . . .*v.3 p.57*

The Emergence of the Cinema: The American Screen to 1907,
    Vol. 1. . . . .*v.6 p.332, p.343*

Emergence of the Modern Mexican Woman, 1910-1940: Her
    Participation in Revolution and Struggle for
    Equality. *v.6 p.432, p.436*

Emergence of the New South,
    1913-1945. . . . .*v.3 p.444, p.445, p.450, p.497*

The Emergence of the Palestinian Arab National Movement,
    1918-1929. . . . .*v.6 p.612*

The Emergence of the Playwright-Director in American Theatre,
    1960-1983. . . . .*v.1 p.113, p.114, p.137, p.152*

Emergency Care and Transportation of the Sick and
    Injured. *v.5 p.534*

Emergency Law in Ireland, 1918-1925. . . . .*v.3 p.138*

Emergency Nursing Procedures. *v.5 p.531*

Emergent Issues in Education: Comparative
    Perspectives. *v.4 p.313*

Emerging Complexity: The Later Prehistory of South-East
    Spain, Iberia and the West Mediterranean. *v.4 p.12*

Emerging Needs and Opportunities for Human Factors
    Research. *v.5 p.588*

Emerging Perspectives of Buchi Emecheta. *v.2 p.754*

Emerging Perspectives on Ama Ata Aidoo. *v.2 p.753*

Emerging Perspectives on Bessie Head. *v.2 p.756*

Emerging Perspectives on Chinua Achebe: ISINKA, the Artistic
    Purpose: Chinua Achebe and the Theory of African
    Literature, Vol. 2. . . . .*v.2 p.753*

Emerging Perspectives on Mariama Ba: Postcolonialism,
    Feminism, and Postmodernism. *v.2 p.543*

Emerging Perspectives on Maryse Conde: A Writer of Her
    Own. *v.2 p.535*

Emerging Perspectives on Nuruddin Farah. *v.2 p.755*

Emerging Technologies in Plastics Recycling. . *v.5 p.376, p.377*

Emerging Themes in Mexican American
    Research. *v.6 p.486, p.531*

Emerging Visions of the Aesthetic Process: In Psychology,
    Semiology, and Philosophy. *v.5 p.618*

Emerson As Poet. *v.2 p.38*

Emerson: Collected Poems and Translations. *v.2 p.38*

Emerson's 'Nature': Origin, Growth, Meaning. *v.2 p.38*

Emery's Elements of Medical Genetics: With Student Consult
    Access. *v.5 p.152*

Emics and Etics: The Insider/Outsider Debate. . *v.4 p.18, p.19*

The Emigrants. *v.2 p.618, p.619, p.628*

Emigrants. *v.2 p.630*

The Emigrants. *v.2 p.768*

Emil Nolde: Catalogue Raisonné of the Oil Paintings: Volume
    Two 1915-1951, Vol. 2. . . . .*v.1 p.748, p.749*

Emil W. Haury's Prehistory of the American Southwest. .*v.4 p.11*

Emile de Antonio: Radical Filmmaker in Cold War
    America. *v.6 p.342*

Emile Durkheim: Ethics and the Sociology of Morals. .*v.4 p.681*

Emile Durkheim on the Family. *v.4 p.681*

Emile Durkheim: Selected Writings. *v.4 p.684, p.685*

Emile Durkheim. *v.4 p.685*

Emile: Or on Education. *v.3 p.148*

Emile Zola, an Introductory Study of His Novels. . .*v.2 p.504*

Emile Zola. *v.2 p.504*

Emilio's Carnival: Or Senilita. *v.2 p.723*

Emily Brontë: A Biography. *v.2 p.270*

Emily Carr: New Perspectives. *v.1 p.748*

Emily Dickinson: A Biography. *v.2 p.37*

Emily Dickinson's Poetry: Stairway of Surprise. .*v.2 p.36, p.37*

Emily Post's the Etiquette Advantage in Business: Personal Skills for Professional Success. *v.4 p.57, p.174*

Eminent Chinese of the Ch'ing Period, 1644-1912. . . . .*v.6 p.187, p.199*

Eminent Maricones: Arenas, Lorca, Puig, and Me. . . .*v.6 p.402*

Eminent Victorians Definitive Edition. *v.3 p.116, p.129*

Eminent Victorians. *v.2 p.380, v.6 p.735, p.736*

Emissions Trading: Principles and Practice. *v.4 p.63*

Emma: Critical Edition. *v.2 p.266*

Emma Goldman: A Documentary History of the American Years. *v.4 p.506, p.553*

Emmeline Pankhurst. *v.4 p.604*

Emmeline: The Orphan of the Castle. *v.2 p.260, p.261*

Emmy Noether, 1882-1935. . . . .*v.5 p.465*

☐ Emory Women Writers Resource Project. *v.6 p.476*

Emotion and Adaptation. *v.5 p.612, p.654*

Emotion and Consciousness. *v.5 p.611*

Emotion and Meaning in Music. *v.1 p.382*

Emotion and Motivation. *v.5 p.611, p.612*

Emotion and Peace of Mind: From Stoic Agitation to Christian Temptation. *v.1 p.498*

Emotion and Religion: A Critical Assessment and Annotated Bibliography. *v.5 p.633*

Emotion Concepts. *v.5 p.654*

Emotional Branding: The New Paradigm for Connecting Brands to People. *v.4 p.142*

Emotional Decisions: Trade off Difficulty and Coping in Consumer Choice. *v.4 p.203*

Emotional Design: Why We Love (or Hate) Everyday Things. *v.5 p.588*

The Emotional Development of Young Children: Building an Emotion-Centered Curriculum. *v.4 p.369*

Emotional Intelligence: Science and Myth. *v.5 p.654*

Emotional Life of the Toddler. *v.5 p.642*

Emotionally Focused Couple Therapy with Trauma Survivors: Strengthening Attachment Bonds. *v.5 p.668*

The Emotions: A Philosophical Exploration. *v.1 p.496*

Emotions and Beliefs: How Feelings Influence Thoughts. *v.5 p.611*

Emotions and Social Movements. *v.4 p.694*

Emotions in Finance: Distrust and Uncertainty in Global Markets. *v.4 p.250, p.261*

Emotions in Humans and Artifacts. *v.5 p.590*

Emotions in Sport. *v.4 p.877*

Emotions, Stress, and Health. *v.4 p.699*

Emperor and Aristocracy in Japan, 1467-1680: Resilience and Renewal. *v.4 p.726*

Emperor and Priest: The Imperial Office in Byzantium. .*v.1 p.569*

The Emperor and the Roman Army: Thirty-One B.C. to A.D. Two Hundred Thirty-Five. *v.3 p.27*

Emperor and the Wolf: The Lives and Films of Akira Kurosawa and Toshiro Mifune. *v.6 p.226, p.335, p.336*

Emperor Charles V: The Growth and Destiny of a Man and of a World-Empire. *v.3 p.182, p.183*

Emperor Francis Joseph, King of the Hungarians. . . .*v.3 p.186*

Emperor Francis Joseph of Austria; A Biography. . . .*v.3 p.184*

The Emperor in the Roman World. *v.3 p.28*

Emperor Nicholas the First of Russia: The Apogee of Autocracy, 1825-1855. . . . .*v.3 p.219*

Emperor of China. *v.6 p.188, p.203*

Emperor of Japan: Meiji and His World, 1852-1912. .*v.6 p.227*

The Emperor's Beard: Dom Pedro II and the Tropical Monarchy of Brazil. *v.3 p.337*

Emperors in the Jungle: The Hidden History of the U. S. in Panama. *v.3 p.269, p.305*

The Emperor's New Clothes: Biological Theories of Race at the Millennium. *v.4 p.17*

Empire and Aftermath: Yoshida Shigeru and the Japanese Experience, 1878-1954. . . . . . .*v.6 p.223, p.226*

Empire and Antislavery: Spain, Cuba and Puerto Rico, 1833-1874. . . . .*v.3 p.241*

Empire and Commonwealth. *v.4 p.587, p.605*

Empire and Elites after the Muslim Conquest: The Transformation of Northern Mesopotamia. *v.6 p.602*

Empire and Inequality (H): America and the World Since 9/11. . . . .*v.3 p.484*

Empire and Islam: Punjab and the Making of Pakistan. .*v.6 p.160*

Empire and Liberty: American Resistance to British Authority, 1755-1763. . . . .*v.3 p.406*

Empire and Order: The Concept of Empire, 800-1800. . . . .*v.3 p.74, v.4 p.501*

Empire and Revolution: The Americans in Mexico since the Civil War. *v.3 p.293*

Empire Boys: Adventures in a Man's World. *v.6 p.477*

Empire by Integration: The United States and European Integration, 1945-1997. . . . .*v.4 p.638, p.642*

Empire Can Wait: American Opposition to Hawaiian Annexation, 1893 - 1898. . . . .*v.3 p.534*

Empire Falls. *v.2 p.154*

Empire Families: Britons and Late Imperial India. . . .*v.6 p.156*

Empire: How Spain Became a World Power, 1492-1763. . . . .*v.3 p.74, p.239*

Ⓔ An Empire Nowhere: England, America, and Literature from Utopia to the Tempest. *v.2 p.163, p.164*

Empire of Care: Nursing and Migration in Filipino American History. *v.6 p.111, p.116, p.118, p.129, p.141*

Empire of Conspiracy: The Culture of Paranoia in Postwar America. *v.4 p.709*

Empire of Debt: The Rise of an Epic Financial Crisis. *v.4 p.246, p.267*

Empire of Dreams. *v.6 p.491*

Empire of Knowledge: Academy of Sciences of the U. S. S. R. (1917-1970). *v.3 p.45, p.46, p.223*

The Empire of Manuel I Komnenos, 1143-1180. . . .*v.3 p.193*

Empire of Nations: Ethnographic Knowledge and the Making of the Soviet Union. *v.3 p.213*

The Empire of Reason: How Europe Imagined and America Realized the Enlightenment. *v.3 p.365*

The Empire of the Seas: A Biography of Rear Admiral Robert Wilson Shufeldt, USN. *v.3 p.382*

The Empire of the St. Lawrence: A Study in Commerce and Politics. *v.3 p.536*

Empire of the Stars: Obsession, Friendship, and Betrayal in the Quest for Black Holes. *v.5 p.62*

The Empire of the Steppes: A History of Central Asia. .*v.3 p.230*

Empire of the Sun. *v.2 p.330, v.6 p.214*

Empire of Words: The Reign of the O. E. D. *v.2 p.553*

Empire on the English Stage 1660-1714. . . . . . .*v.2 p.187*

Empire on the Pacific: A Study in American Continental Expansion. *v.3 p.381*

The Empire State: A History of New York. *v.3 p.490*

Empire Statesman: The Rise and Redemption of Al Smith. *v.3 p.462*

Empire Strikes Back: The Impact of Imperialism on Britain from the Mid-Nineteenth Century. *v.3 p.90, p.126*

Empire: The British Imperial Experience from 1765 to the Present. *v.3 p.77, p.89, p.125*

Empire to Commonwealth: Consequences of Monotheism in Late Antiquity. *v.3 p.192*

Empire to Umpire: Canada and the World to the 1990s. .*v.3 p.541*

Empire to Welfare State: English History, 1906-1985. .*v.3 p.119*

Empire, Welfare State, Europe: History of the United Kingdom, 1906-2001. . . . .*v.3 p.89, p.125*

Empire Without Tears: America's Foreign Relations, 1921-1933. . . . .*v.3 p.440, p.446*

The Empire Writes Back: Theory and Practice in Post-Colonial Literatures. *v.2 p.571, p.727*

Empires: Europe and Globalization, 1492-1788. . . . .*v.3 p.74*

Empires in Conflict: Armenia and the Great Powers, 1912-1920. . . . .*v.3 p.231*

Empires of the Atlantic World: Britain and Spain in America 1492-1830. . . . .*v.3 p.73*

Empires of the Monsoon. *v.4 p.378*

Empires of the Sand: The Struggle for Mastery in the Middle East, 1789-1923. . . . .*v.6 p.593*

Empires of the Word: A Language History of the World. .*v.2 p.563*

ⓔ Empirical Modeling in Economics: Specification and Evaluation. *v.4 p.201, p.207*

Empirical Modeling in Economics: Specification and Evaluation. *v.4 p.200, p.201, p.207*

Empirical Musicology: Aims, Methods, Prospects. . . .*v.1 p.173*

Empirical Stance. *v.1 p.504*

The Empirical Stance. *v.1 p.504*

An Empirically-Based Microeconomics. *v.4 p.248*

Empiricism and the Philosophy of Mind. *v.1 p.497*

The Empiricists: Critical Essays on Locke, Berkeley, and Hume. *v.1 p.449*

The Empiricists. *v.1 p.504, p.505*

Employee Involvement: Methods for Improving Performance and Work Attitudes. *v.5 p.578, p.579*

The Employee Recruitment and Retention Handbook. . .*v.4 p.75*

Employer's Guide to Workplace Privacy. *v.4 p.131*

Employment and Equilibrium: A Theoretical Discussion. *v.4 p.210*

Employment, Disability, and the Americans with Disabilities Act: Issues in Law, Public Policy, and Research. . .*v.4 p.446*

Employment Discrimination Law. *v.4 p.134*

Employment Dispute Resolution and Worker Rights in the Changing Workplace. *v.4 p.121*

Employment Relations in France: Evolution and Innovation. *v.4 p.122*

Employment Relations in Non-Union Firms. *v.4 p.121*

Employment Relations in the Asia Pacific: Changing Approaches. *v.4 p.120*

Employment Relations in the United States: Law, Policy, and Practice. *v.4 p.109, p.122, p.126*

Emplumada. *v.6 p.498, p.510*

Empowering Collaborations: Writing Partnerships Between Religious Women and Scribes in the Middle Ages. *v.6 p.569, p.570*

Empowering Ourselves and Transforming Schools: Educators Making a Difference. *v.4 p.283*

The Empress Matilda: Queen Consort, Queen Mother and Lady of the English. *v.6 p.559, p.568*

Empress Taytu and Menilek II: Ethiopia, 1883-1910. . .*v.6 p.64*

The Empress, the Queen, and the Nun: Women and Power at the Court of Philip III of Spain. *v.3 p.240*

The Empress Theodora: Partner of Justinian. *v.3 p.192*

The Empty Cradle: Infertility in America from Colonial Times to the Present. *v.6 p.470*

Empty Pastures: Confined Animals and the Transformation of the Rural Landscape. *v.6 p.290*

Empty Phantoms: Interviews and Encounters with Jack Kerouac. *v.2 p.93*

ⓔ Empty Without You: The Intimate Letters of Eleanor Roosevelt and Lorena Hickok. *v.6 p.404*

Empty Words: Writings, '73 -'78. . . . . . .*v.1 p.210, p.315*

The E-Myth Revisited. *v.4 p.67, p.68*

En attendant le vote des bêtes sauvages : roman. . .*v.2 p.545*

En la mirilla del Jaguar: Biografia novelada de monsenor Gerardi. *v.2 p.675*

En Las Orillas Del Sar. *v.2 p.654*

En Route. *v.2 p.494*

Enabling Knowledge Creation: How to Unlock the Mystery of Tacit Knowledge and Release the Power of Innovation. *v.4 p.79*

An Enchanted Modern: Gender and Public Piety in Shi'i Lebanon. *v.6 p.605*

The Enchanted Wanderer: Selected Tales. *v.2 p.805*

ⓔ The Enchantments of Love: Amorous and Exemplary Novels. *v.2 p.653*

The Enchantments of Love: Amorous and Exemplary Novels. *v.2 p.653*

Enciclopedia de El Salvador, Set. *v.3 p.299*

Enclave. *v.6 p.507, p.510*

Enclosure Three: Harry Partch. *v.6 p.408, p.409*

The Encomenderos of New Spain, 1521-1555. . . . .*v.3 p.286*

Encomienda Politics in Early Colonial Guatemala, 1524-1544: Dividing the Spoils. *v.3 p.298*

Encomium of Ptolemy Philadelphus. *v.2 p.421*

Encountering Children's Literature: An Arts Approach. .*v.4 p.360*

Encountering Student Texts: Interpretive Issues in Reading Student Writing. *v.2 p.565*

Encountering the West: Christianity and the Global Cultural Process. *v.1 p.596*

Encounters in Modern Hebrew, Level 1. . . . . *v.6 p.645*

Encounters: The Meeting of Asia and Europe 1500 - 1800. . . . . *v.1 p.693*

Encounters with Ancient Egypt. *v.3 p.10*

Encounters with Lise and Other Stories. *v.2 p.802, p.803*

Encounters with Nationalism. *v.4 p.494*

Encounters with Nature: Essays by Paul Shepard. . . *v.5 p.226*

Encounters with Paradise: Views of Hawaii and Its People, 1778-1941. . . . . *v.1 p.682, p.694*

Encouraging Diversity: The Conversation and Development of Plant Genetic Resources. *v.5 p.182*

Encumbered Cuba: Capital Markets and Revolt, 1878-1895. . . . . *v.3 p.309*

Encyclopaedia of Indian Literature, Vol. 2. . . . . . *v.6 p.147*

Encyclopaedia of Islam: Historical Atlas of Islam, and Index of Subjects, Set. *v.6 p.581*

Encyclopaedia of Mathematics. *v.5 p.458, p.461*

An Encyclopaedia of Metallurgy and Materials. . . . *v.5 p.733*

Encyclopaedia of Midrash: Biblical Interpretation in Formative Judaism. *v.1 p.551*

Encyclopaedia of Occupational Health and Safety. . . *v.5 p.365*

Encyclopaedia of Scientific Units, Weights, and Measures: Their SI Equivalences and Origins. *v.5 p.386, p.413*

Encyclopaedia of the History of Science, Technology, and Medicine in Non-Western Cultures. *v.5 p.389*

The Encyclopaedia of Women and Islamic Cultures. . *v.6 p.459*

The Encyclopaedic Dictionary of Environmental Change. *v.6 p.284, p.286*

Encyclopedia Iranica: Ab-Abd-Al-Hamid. *v.6 p.630*

Encyclopedia Judaica. *v.1 p.546*

Encyclopedia Latina: History, Culture, and Society in the United States. *v.6 p.485*

Encyclopedia of 20th Century Sculpture. *v.1 p.774*

Encyclopedia of 20th-Century Architecture. *v.1 p.784*

Encyclopedia of 20th-Century Technology. *v.5 p.679*

Encyclopedia of Adult Development. *v.5 p.627*

Encyclopedia of Aesthetics, Set. *v.1 p.479*

Encyclopedia of African Art. *v.1 p.663, p.689, p.690*

Encyclopedia of African History, Set. *v.6 p.54*

Encyclopedia of African Literature. *v.2 p.750, v.6 p.80*

Encyclopedia of African-American Religions. *v.1 p.544*

Encyclopedia of Aging. *v.4 p.751*

Encyclopedia of Agricultural, Food, and Biological Engineering. *v.5 p.4*

Encyclopedia of AIDS: A Social, Political, Cultural, and Scientific Record of the HIV Epidemic. *v.6 p.379*

Encyclopedia of Allergy and Environmental Illness. . *v.5 p.365*

Encyclopedia of America in the Twentieth Century, 1. *v.3 p.442*

Encyclopedia of America in the Twentieth Century, 2. *v.3 p.442*

Encyclopedia of America in the Twentieth Century, 3. *v.3 p.442*

Encyclopedia of American Agricultural History. . . . *v.5 p.6*

The Encyclopedia of American Art Before 1914. . . *v.1 p.667*

The Encyclopedia of American Catholic History. . . *v.1 p.571*

Encyclopedia of American Cultural and Intellectual History. *v.3 p.368*

Encyclopedia of American Economic History, Set. . . *v.4 p.567*

Encyclopedia of American Education, Set. *v.4 p.340*

Encyclopedia of American, English, and European Earthenware, Ironstone, Stoneware, 1780-1980: Makers, Marks, and Patterns in Blue and White, Historic Blue, Flow Blue, Mulberry, Romantic Transferware, Tea Leaf, and White Ironstone. *v.1 p.798*

The Encyclopedia of American Facts and Dates. . . *v.3 p.372*

Encyclopedia of American Farm Implements and Antiques. *v.5 p.6, p.30*

Encyclopedia of American Folk Art. *v.1 p.667*

Encyclopedia of American Foreign Policy, Set. *v.3 p.386, v.4 p.561, p.628*

Encyclopedia of American Gospel Music. . . *v.1 p.161, 296*

Encyclopedia of American History, Set. *v.3 p.373*

Encyclopedia of American Indian Civil Rights. . . . *v.4 p.465*

Encyclopedia of American Indian Costume. *v.1 p.716, v.6 p.679*

Encyclopedia of American Industries. . *v.4 p.148, p.150, p.179*

Encyclopedia of American Parties, Campaigns and Elections. *v.4 p.547*

The Encyclopedia of American Political History. *v.3 p.384, v.4 p.485*

The Encyclopedia of American Prisons. *v.4 p.678*

The Encyclopedia of American Religions. *v.1 p.527, p.528, p.544, p.605*

The Encyclopedia of American Soccer History. . . . *v.4 p.867*

Encyclopedia of American Social History, Set. . . . *v.4 p.677*

Encyclopedia of American Social Movements. . . . *v.4 p.678*

ⓔ Encyclopedia of American Women and Religion. . *v.6 p.458*

Encyclopedia of American Women in Business: From Colonial Times to the Present [Two Volumes], Vol. 2. . . . *v.4 p.57*

Encyclopedia of Analytical Chemistry: Applications, Theory, and Instrumentation, Vol. 1-15. . . . . *v.5 p.267*

Encyclopedia of Analytical Science, 10 vols. *v.5 p.267*

The Encyclopedia of Ancient Egyptian Architecture. . *v.1 p.783*

Encyclopedia of Animal Behavior. . *v.5 p.54, v.6 p.285, p.290*

Encyclopedia of Animal Science. *v.5 p.56*

Encyclopedia of Animals: Mammals, Birds, Reptiles, Amphibians. *v.5 p.212*

The Encyclopedia of Animated Cartoons. . . . *v.6 p.307, p.308*

Encyclopedia of Antarctica and the Southern Oceans. *v.5 p.434*

Encyclopedia of Anthropology. *v.4 p.3*

The Encyclopedia of Apocalypticism: Apocalypticism in the Modern Period and the Contemporary Age, Vol. 3. *v.1 p.529*

The Encyclopedia of Apocalypticism: Apocalypticism in Western History and Culture, Vol. 2. . . . . *v.1 p.529*

The Encyclopedia of Apocalypticism: The Origins of Apocalypticism in Judaism and Christianity, Vol. 1. *v.1 p.529*

Encyclopedia of Appalachia. *v.3 p.497*

Encyclopedia of Applied Ethics, Set. *v.1 p.485*

ⓔ The Encyclopedia of Applied Geology. *v.5 p.417*

Encyclopedia of Applied Physics. *v.5 p.545*

Encyclopedia of Aquaculture. *v.5 p.32*

Encyclopedia of Arabic Literature. *v.6 p.663, p.664*

Encyclopedia of Archaeology: History and Discoveries. *v.4 p.5*

Encyclopedia of Arms Control and Disarmament, Set. *v.4 p.655*

Encyclopedia of Artists' Signatures, Symbols and Monograms: North American, European Plus More. Old Masters to Modern. *v.1 p.663*

The Encyclopedia of Arts and Crafts. *v.1 p.798*

Encyclopedia of Asian Philosophy. *v.1 p.475*

Encyclopedia of Associations. *v.5 p.397*

Encyclopedia of Astronomy and Astrophysics, Set. *v.5 p.63*

The Encyclopedia of Australian Art. *v.1 p.665*

Encyclopedia of Behavior Modification and Cognitive Behavior Therapy:Volume I: Adult Clinical Applications Volume II: Child Clinical Applications Volume III: Educational Applications. *v.5 p.665, p.666, p.667*

Encyclopedia of Bioprocess Technology, Set. *v.5 p.325*

Encyclopedia of Black Studies. *v.6 p.13*

Encyclopedia of British Football. *v.4 p.867*

Encyclopedia of British Humorists: Geoffrey Chaucer to John Cleese, Set. *v.2 p.195*

Encyclopedia of Business Information Sources. *v.4 p.181*

The Encyclopedia of Business Letters, Fax Memos, and E-Mail. *v.4 p.172*

The Encyclopedia of California: A Reference Guide to the Golden State. *v.3 p.530*

Encyclopedia of Canada's Peoples. *v.3 p.534*

Encyclopedia of Careers and Vocational Guidance, Set. *v.5 p.576, p.578*

Encyclopedia of Caribbean Literature. *v.2 p.767*

Encyclopedia of Catalysis, Set. *v.5 p.278*

Encyclopedia of Caves and Karst Science. *v.5 p.424*

Encyclopedia of Chemical Reactions, 8 v. *v.5 p.304*

The Encyclopedia of Chicago. *v.3 p.515*

Encyclopedia of Chinese Philosophy. *v.1 p.475*

The Encyclopedia of Christianity: (A-D). *v.1 p.594*

Encyclopedia of Christianity: E-I, Vol. 2. *v.1 p.594*

The Encyclopedia of Christianity: (J-O). *v.1 p.594*

The Encyclopedia of Christianity, Vol. 4. *v.1 p.594*

Encyclopedia of Christianity. *v.1 p.593, p.594*

Encyclopedia of Chromatography. *v.5 p.269*

Encyclopedia of Classical Philosophy. *v.1 p.421*

Encyclopedia of Coastal Science. *v.5 p.429, v.6 p.284*

Encyclopedia of Cognitive Science. *v.5 p.609*

Encyclopedia of Communication and Information. *v.4 p.423*

Encyclopedia of Comparative Iconography: Themes Depicted in Works of Art, Set. *v.1 p.666, p.709*

Encyclopedia of Computational Chemistry, Set. *v.5 p.275*

Encyclopedia of Computer Science. *v.5 p.343, p.344*

Encyclopedia of Conflicts since World War II. *v.4 p.485*

Encyclopedia of Constitutional Amendments: Proposed Amendments, and Amending Issues, 1789-2002. *v.4 p.454*

Encyclopedia of Consumer Brands. *v.4 p.142*

Encyclopedia of Contemporary American Culture. *v.3 p.443*

Encyclopedia of Contemporary Christian Music. *v.1 p.161, p.273*

The Encyclopedia of Country Music: The Ultimate Guide to the Music. *v.1 p.160, p.270, p.271*

Encyclopedia of Crime and Justice, Set. *v.4 p.677, p.752,v.6 p.245*

Encyclopedia of Crime and Punishment, Set. *v.6 p.245*

Encyclopedia of Criminology and Deviant Behaviour, Set. *v.4 p.676, p.677,v.6 p.249*

Encyclopedia of Criminology. *v.4 p.678*

Encyclopedia of Cuban-United States Relations. *v.3 p.390*

Encyclopedia of Dairy Sciences, Set. *v.5 p.34, p.54*

The Encyclopedia of Dance and Ballet. *v.1 p.3*

Encyclopedia of Democratic Thought. *v.4 p.482, p.503*

Encyclopedia of Deserts. *v.5 p.424*

Encyclopedia of Diagnostic Proteomics and Genomics. *v.5 p.116, p.139*

The Encyclopedia of Diderot and d'Alembert: A Collaborative Translation Project. *v.2 p.479*

Encyclopedia of Dinosaurs. *v.5 p.448*

Encyclopedia of Distance Learning, Vol. 1. *v.4 p.321*

Encyclopedia of Distributed Learning. *v.4 p.321*

Encyclopedia of Drugs, Alcohol and Addictive Behavior, Set. *v.4 p.678, p.777,v.5 p.664*

Encyclopedia of Early Childhood Education, Set. *v.4 p.369*

Encyclopedia of Early Christianity. *v.1 p.599*

Encyclopedia of Early Cinema. *v.6 p.332*

Encyclopedia of Earth Science. *v.5 p.417*

Encyclopedia of Earth System Science, 4. *v.5 p.417*

Encyclopedia of Earthquakes and Volcanoes. *v.5 p.437, p.442*

Encyclopedia of Eastern Europe: From the Congress of Vienna to the Fall of Communism. *v.3 p.206*

Encyclopedia of Ecological and Environmental Toxicology. *v.5 p.366*

The Encyclopedia of Ecology and Environmental Management. *v.5 p.28*

The Encyclopedia of Ecotourism. *v.4 p.161, p.162*

Encyclopedia of Educational Research. *v.4 p.338, p.354, p.355,v.5 p.571*

The Encyclopedia of Education. *v.4 p.322*

Encyclopedia of Electrochemistry, Vol. 1. *v.5 p.284*

Encyclopedia of Electrochemistry. *v.5 p.285*

Encyclopedia of Empiricism. *v.1 p.504*

Encyclopedia of Endangered Species. *v.5 p.221, p.225*

Encyclopedia of Energy Conservation Technology. *v.5 p.361*

Encyclopedia of Energy, Set. *v.5 p.359, p.360, p.708*

Encyclopedia of Energy Technology and the Environment, Set. *v.5 p.359*

Encyclopedia of Entomology. *v.5 p.9, p.212*

Encyclopedia of Environmental Biology, Set. *v.5 p.357*

Encyclopedia of Environmental Science and Engineering. *v.5 p.353, p.355, p.368, p.377, p.379*

Encyclopedia of Environmental Studies. *v.5 p.707, v.6 p.286*

Encyclopedia of Ephemera: A Guide to the Fragmentary Documents of Everyday Life for the Collector, Curator and Historian. *v.1 p.798*

Encyclopedia of Ethics, Set. *v.1 p.483*

Encyclopedia of European and Asian Regional Geology. *v.5 p.432*

Encyclopedia of European Social History: From 1350 to 2000, Set. *v.4 p.699, p.707*

Encyclopedia of Evolution, Set. *v.5 p.195*

Encyclopedia of Exploration: The Explorers. *v.4 p.379*

The Encyclopedia of Fantastic Film: Ali Baba to
Zombies. *v.6 p.320*

The Encyclopedia of Fantasy. *v.2 p.581*

Encyclopedia of Feminist Literature. *v.6 p.480*

Encyclopedia of Feminist Theories. *v.6 p.427*

ⓔ The Encyclopedia of Field and General Geology. . *v.5 p.417*

The Encyclopedia of Figure Skating. *v.4 p.866*

An Encyclopedia of Film Festivals. *v.6 p.346*

Encyclopedia of Film Themes, Settings and Series. . *v.6 p.311*

Encyclopedia of Fishes. *v.5 p.216*

Encyclopedia of Folk Heroes. *v.2 p.585*

Encyclopedia of Food and Culture. *v.5 p.34*

Encyclopedia of Food and Drink in America. *v.5 p.35*

Encyclopedia of Food Sciences and Nutrition, Set. . . *v.5 p.35*

Encyclopedia of Forensic Sciences, Set. *v.4 p.678*

Encyclopedia of Frontier Biography, Set. *v.3 p.521, p.522*

Encyclopedia of Furniture Materials, Trades and
Techniques. *v.1 p.805*

Encyclopedia of Gardens: History and Design,
Set. *v.1 p.812, p.819, p.820, v.5 p.44*

Encyclopedia of Genetics, Genomics, Proteomics and
Bioinformatics. *v.5 p.115, p.116, p.139*

Encyclopedia of Genetics, Revised Edition, Vol. 2. . *v.5 p.136*

Encyclopedia of Genocide and Crimes Against
Humanity. *v.4 p.653, p.654*

Encyclopedia of Geochemistry. *v.5 p.440*

Encyclopedia of Geomorphology. *v.4 p.391, v.5 p.417*

Encyclopedia of Geophysics. *v.5 p.443*

Encyclopedia of Global Environmental Change: A CBT
Workbook for Young People. *v.6 p.286*

Encyclopedia of Global Environmental Change, Causes and
Consequences of Global Environmental Change, Vol.
3. *v.4 p.677*

Encyclopedia of Global Environmental Change, Social and
Economic Dimensions of Global Environmental Change, Vol.
5. . . . . *v.4 p.375, p.678, p.679*

Encyclopedia of Global Industries. *v.4 p.150*

The Encyclopedia of Global Population and Demographics,
Two-Vol. Set. *v.4 p.678*

Encyclopedia of Government and Politics, Set. . . . *v.4 p.482*

Encyclopedia of Graphics File Formats: The Complete
Reference on CD-ROM with Links to Internet
Resources. *v.5 p.340*

Encyclopedia of Greece and the Hellenic Tradition, Set. . *v.3 p.13*

Encyclopedia of Gun Control and Gun Rights. . . . *v.4 p.449*

Encyclopedia of Hair: A Cultural History. *v.1 p.716*

Encyclopedia of Historical Treaties and Alliances. . . *v.4 p.476*

The Encyclopedia of HIV and AIDS. *v.4 p.669*

Encyclopedia of Homelessness. *v.4 p.678*

The Encyclopedia of Housing. *v.6 p.709*

The Encyclopedia of Human Ecology. *v.5 p.358*

Encyclopedia of Human Emotions, Vol. 2. . . . . . *v.5 p.654*

Encyclopedia of Human Geography. *v.4 p.396*

Encyclopedia of Human Intelligence, Vol. 1. . . . . *v.5 p.656*

Encyclopedia of Human Rights Issues since 1945. . . *v.4 p.513*

Encyclopedia of Hydrology and Water Resources. . . *v.6 p.283*

The Encyclopedia of Igneous and Metamorphic
Petrology. *v.5 p.437*

The Encyclopedia of Ignorance, Vol. 1 & 2. . . . . *v.5 p.399*

Encyclopedia of Immigration and Migration in the American
West. *v.4 p.570*

Encyclopedia of Indian Philosophies: Nyaya-Vaisesika from
Gangesa to Raghunatha Siromani. *v.1 p.419*

Encyclopedia of Inorganic Chemistry, Set. *v.5 p.302*

Encyclopedia of Insects. *v.5 p.27, p.28*

Encyclopedia of International Development. . *v.4 p.192, p.373*

The Encyclopedia of International Games. *v.4 p.843*

Encyclopedia of International Media and Communications,
Set. *v.4 p.415*

Encyclopedia of International Relations and Global
Politics. *v.4 p.626*

Encyclopedia of International Sports Studies. *v.4 p.812*

Encyclopedia of Islam and the Muslim World. . . . *v.1 p.554*

▢ Encyclopedia of Islam Online. *v.1 p.553*

The Encyclopedia of Jazz in the Seventies. . . *v.1 p.159, p.258*

Encyclopedia of Jazz in the Sixties. *v.1 p.159, p.258*

Encyclopedia of Jazz. *v.1 p.159*

An Encyclopedia of Keynesian Economics. *v.4 p.192*

The Encyclopedia of Latin American and Caribbean
Art. *v.1 p.667*

Encyclopedia of Latin American Politics. *v.4 p.592*

Encyclopedia of Latin American
Theater. *v.1 p.58, p.127, v.2 p.663*

Encyclopedia of Latinos and Latinas in the United
States. *v.6 p.485*

Encyclopedia of Law Enforcement. *v.6 p.261*

The Encyclopedia of Learning Disabilities. *v.4 p.319*

Encyclopedia of Leisure and Outdoor
Recreation. *v.4 p.784, p.787, p.823*

Encyclopedia of Lesbian, Gay, Bisexual and Transgendered
History in America. *v.6 p.358, p.363*

Encyclopedia of Line Dances: The Steps that Came and
Stayed. *v.1 p.4*

Encyclopedia of Linguistics. *v.2 p.564*

Encyclopedia of Literature in Canada. *v.2 p.730*

An Encyclopedia of Macroeconomics. *v.4 p.192, p.193*

The Encyclopedia of Mass Spectrometry: Biological
Applications: Carbohydrates, Nucleic Acids
and Other Biological Compounds. *v.5 p.271*

The Encyclopedia of Mass Spectrometry: Biological
Applications. *v.5 p.271*

The Encyclopedia of Mass Spectrometry: Fundamentals of and
Applications to Organic (and Organometallic)
Compounds. *v.5 p.271*

The Encyclopedia of Mass Spectrometry: Hyphenated
Methods. *v.5 p.271*

The Encyclopedia of Mass Spectrometry: Methods of Mass
Analysis and Associated Instrumentation. *v.5 p.271*

The Encyclopedia of Mass Spectrometry: Theory and Ion
Chemistry. *v.5 p.271*

Encyclopedia of Materials, Parts, and Finishes. *v.5 p.679*

Encyclopedia of Media and Politics in America. *v.4 p.559*

Encyclopedia of Medical Anthropology: Health and Illness in the World's Cultures. *v.4 p.46*

Encyclopedia of Medieval Literature. *v.6 p.565*

Encyclopedia of Mental Health, Set. *v.5 p.666*

The Encyclopedia of Michigan: A Reference Guide to the Wolverine State, Set. *v.3 p.516*

Encyclopedia of Middle Ages, Set. *v.6 p.555*

The Encyclopedia of Mineralogy. *v.5 p.435*

Encyclopedia of Minerals. *v.5 p.435*

Encyclopedia of Minorities in American Politics: African Americans and Asian Americans. *v.6 p.87, p.121*

Encyclopedia of Minorities in American Politics, Set. .*v.4 p.573*

Encyclopedia of Modern Asia, Set. *v.6 p.145*

Encyclopedia of Modern Separatist Movements. . . .*v.4 p.628*

The Encyclopedia of Molecular Biology. *v.5 p.325*

Encyclopedia of Molecular Cell Biology and Molecular Medicine, Index, Vol. 16. . . . .*v.5 p.141, p.150*

Encyclopedia of Molecular Cell Biology and Molecular Medicine, Proteasomes to Receptor, Transporter and Ion Channel Diseases, Vol. 11. . . . .*v.5 p.141, p.150*

Encyclopedia of Molecular Cell Biology and Molecular Medicine, Recombination and Genome Rearrangements to Serial Analysis of Gene Expression, Vol. 12. . . . .*v.5 p.141, p.142, p.150*

Encyclopedia of Molecular Cell Biology and Molecular Medicine, Sex Hormones (Male): Analogs and Antagonists to Synchrotron Infrared Microspectroscopy, Vol. 13. . . . .*v.5 p.142, p.150*

Encyclopedia of Molecular Cell Biology and Molecular Medicine, Syngamy and Cell Cycle Control to Triacylglyerol Storage and Mobilization, Regulation Of, Vol. 14. . . . .*v.5 p.142, p.150*

Encyclopedia of Molecular Cell Biology and Molecular Medicine, Triplet Repeat Diseases to Zebrafish (Danio rerio) Genome and Genetics, Vol. 15. . . . . .*v.5 p.142, p.150*

Encyclopedia of Molecular Cell Biology and Molecular Medicine, Vol. 10. . . . .*v.5 p.141, p.150*

Encyclopedia of Molecular Cell Biology and Molecular Medicine, Vol. 1. . . . .*v.5 p.141, p.150*

Encyclopedia of Molecular Cell Biology and Molecular Medicine, Vol. 2. . . . .*v.5 p.141, p.150*

Encyclopedia of Molecular Cell Biology and Molecular Medicine, Vol. 3. . . . .*v.5 p.141, p.149, p.150*

Encyclopedia of Molecular Cell Biology and Molecular Medicine, Vol. 4. . . . .*v.5 p.141, p.150*

Encyclopedia of Molecular Cell Biology and Molecular Medicine, Vol. 5. . . . .*v.5 p.141, p.149*

Encyclopedia of Molecular Cell Biology and Molecular Medicine, Vol. 6. . . . .*v.5 p.141, p.150*

Encyclopedia of Molecular Cell Biology and Molecular Medicine, Vol. 7. . . . .*v.5 p.141, p.150*

Encyclopedia of Molecular Cell Biology and Molecular Medicine, Vol. 8. . . . .*v.5 p.141, p.150*

Encyclopedia of Molecular Cell Biology and Molecular Medicine, Vol. 9. . . . .*v.5 p.141, p.150*

Encyclopedia of Monasticism, Set. *v.1 p.531*

Encyclopedia of Mongolia and the Mongol Empire. . .*v.6 p.239*

Encyclopedia of Mosaics: Techniques, Materials and Designs. *v.1 p.803*

The Encyclopedia of Motion Picture Sound. . .*v.6 p.351, p.352*

Encyclopedia of Movie Special Effects. *v.6 p.352*

Encyclopedia of Musical Theater. *v.1 p.160, p.249, p.250*

Encyclopedia of Nanoscience and Nanotechnology. . .*v.5 p.275*

Encyclopedia of Nationalism, Set. *v.4 p.494, p.495*

The Encyclopedia of Native American Economic History. *v.4 p.192, v.6 p.682*

The Encyclopedia of Native American Legal Tradition. *v.4 p.464, p.465,v.6 p.691, p.703*

The Encyclopedia of Native Music: More Than a Century of Recordings from Wax Cylinder to the Internet. . . .*v.6 p.699*

The Encyclopedia of Natural Insect and Disease Control. *v.5 p.370, p.381, p.383*

Encyclopedia of New Media: An Essential Reference Guide to Communication and Technology. *v.4 p.419, v.5 p.621, p.625*

Encyclopedia of New York: A Reference Guide to the Empire State. *v.3 p.490*

Encyclopedia of New York City. *v.3 p.491, v.6 p.713*

Encyclopedia of North American Indians: Native American History, Culture, and Life from Paleo-Indians to the Present. *v.6 p.682*

The Encyclopedia of North American Trees. *v.5 p.36*

Encyclopedia of North Carolina: A Reference Guide to the Tar Heel State. *v.3 p.501*

The Encyclopedia of Novels into Film. *v.6 p.327*

Encyclopedia of Ocean Sciences, Set. *v.5 p.429*

Encyclopedia of Opera on Screen: A Guide to More Than 100 Years of Opera Films, Videos, and DVDs. . *v.6 p.316, p.317*

Encyclopedia of Operations Research and Management Science: Centennial Edition. *v.4 p.119*

Encyclopedia of Paleontology, Set. *v.5 p.447*

Encyclopedia of Pest Management. *v.5 p.10, p.27*

Encyclopedia of Phenomenology. *v.1 p.510, p.511*

Encyclopedia of Philosophy, Set. *v.1 p.416*

Encyclopedia of Physical Science and Technology, Set. *v.5 p.387, p.388*

Encyclopedia of Physics. *v.5 p.545*

Encyclopedia of Plant and Crop Science. *v.5 p.21*

Encyclopedia of Plant Pathology. *v.5 p.46*

Encyclopedia of Police Science. *v.4 p.676*

Encyclopedia of Political Economy. *v.4 p.192*

The Encyclopedia of Political Revolutions. *v.4 p.486*

Encyclopedia of Polymer Science and Engineering, A to Amorphous Polymers, Vol. 1. . . . .*v.5 p.321*

Encyclopedia of Polymer Science and Technology, Vol. 14, Pt. 1. . . . .*v.5 p.321*

Encyclopedia of Popular Music of the World, Vols 3-7. . . . .*v.1 p.162, p.274, p.284*

The Encyclopedia of Popular Music, Set. *v.1 p.160, p.161, p.271*

Encyclopedia of Post-Colonial Literatures in English. *v.2 p.727, p.759*

Encyclopedia of Postcolonial Studies. *v.2 p.727*

Encyclopedia of Postmodernism. *v.1 p.512*

The Encyclopedia of Precolonial Africa: Archaeology, History, Languages, Cultures and Environments. *v.4 p.8*

Encyclopedia of Presidential Campaigns, Slogans, Issues, and Platforms. *v.4 p.556*

The Encyclopedia of Printmaking Techniques: A Comprehensive Visual Guide to Traditional and Contemporary Techniques. *v.1 p.752, p.759, p.760*

Encyclopedia of Prisons and Correctional Facilities. . .*v.6 p.272*

Encyclopedia of Protestantism. *v.1 p.580*

Encyclopedia of Psychology. *v.5 p.594*

Encyclopedia of Public Choice. *v.4 p.192*

Encyclopedia of Public Relations. *v.4 p.428*

Encyclopedia of Racism in the United States. . .*v.6 p.86, p.124*

Encyclopedia of Radio, Set. *v.4 p.413*

Encyclopedia of Rainforests: Diane Jukofsky for the Rainforest Alliance. *v.5 p.176, p.211, p.225, p.239*

Encyclopedia of Reagents for Organic Synthesis, Set. .*v.5 p.289*

Encyclopedia of Reagents for Organic Synthesis. . . .*v.5 p.289*

The Encyclopedia of Record Producers. .*v.1 p.161, p.273, p.387*

Encyclopedia of Recorded Sound. *v.1 p.160, p.387*

Encyclopedia of Recreation and Leisure in America. *v.4 p.783, p.823*

Encyclopedia of Religion and Society. *v.4 p.678, p.720*

Encyclopedia of Religion in American Politics. .*v.4 p.487, p.560*

Encyclopedia of Religion. *v.1 p.522*

Encyclopedia of Religious and Spiritual Development. *v.1 p.650*

Encyclopedia of Religious Freedom. *v.1 p.656*

Encyclopedia of Reptiles and Amphibians. . . .*v.5 p.95, p.214*

Encyclopedia of Russian and Slavic Myth and Legend. *v.1 p.534*

The Encyclopedia of Schizophrenia and Other Psychotic Disorders. *v.5 p.661*

The Encyclopedia of Science Fiction Movies: From 1897 to the Present. *v.6 p.318*

The Encyclopedia of Science Fiction. *v.2 p.581*

Encyclopedia of Sediments and Sedimentary Rocks. . *v.5 p.438*

The Encyclopedia of Shaker Furniture. *v.1 p.805*

Encyclopedia of Singapore. *v.6 p.173*

Encyclopedia of Small Business. *v.4 p.88*

Encyclopedia of Smart Materials. *v.5 p.679, p.691*

Encyclopedia of Social and Cultural Anthropology. . . .*v.4 p.3*

Encyclopedia of Social Measurement, Set. *v.4 p.677*

Encyclopedia of Social Theory. *v.4 p.678, p.680*

Encyclopedia of Social Welfare History in North America. *v.4 p.754*

Encyclopedia of Social Work, 1997 Supplement. . .*v.4 p.677*

Encyclopedia of Social Work: Supplement 2003. . .*v.4 p.677*

Encyclopedia of Social Work. *v.4 p.677*

Encyclopedia of Sociology, Set. *v.4 p.676*

Encyclopedia of Soils in the Environment, Set. *v.5 p.49*

Encyclopedia of Special Education: A Reference for the Education of the Handicapped and Other Exceptional Children and Adults. *v.4 p.316, v.5 p.572*

Encyclopedia of Spectroscopy and Spectrometry, Set. *v.5 p.270*

Encyclopedia of Spectroscopy. *v.5 p.270*

The Encyclopedia of Sports Medicine. *v.4 p.825*

The Encyclopedia of Stage Plays into Film. *v.6 p.327*

Encyclopedia of Statistical Sciences: Including Supplements and Updates, Set. *v.5 p.481*

Encyclopedia of Student and Youth Movements. . . .*v.4 p.325*

The Encyclopedia of Suicide. *v.4 p.677, v.5 p.662*

ⓔ Encyclopedia of Support Services and Distance Education. *v.4 p.321*

Encyclopedia of Surface and Colloid Science. *v.5 p.283*

The Encyclopedia of Surfing. *v.4 p.788, p.868*

The Encyclopedia of Taxation and Tax Policy. . . .*v.4 p.107*

Encyclopedia of Television. *v.4 p.415, p.418*

Encyclopedia of Terrorism. *v.4 p.678*

Encyclopedia of the Alamo and the Texas Revolution. *v.3 p.508, p.509*

Encyclopedia of the American Civil War: A Political Social and Military History. *v.3 p.424*

Encyclopedia of the American Constitution, Set. . . .*v.4 p.454*

Encyclopedia of the American Judicial System: Studies of the Principal Institutions, Set. *v.4 p.437*

Encyclopedia of the American Legislative System, Set. *v.4 p.575*

Encyclopedia of the American Presidency. *v.3 p.378*

Encyclopedia of the American West, Vol. 4. . . . . .*v.3 p.519*

Encyclopedia of the Antebellum South. *v.3 p.496*

Encyclopedia of the Arctic. *v.6 p.284*

Encyclopedia of the Blues. *v.1 p.160, p.261*

The Encyclopedia of the Chemical Elements. *v.5 p.257*

Encyclopedia of the City. *v.6 p.709*

Encyclopedia of the Confederacy, Set. . .*v.3 p.424, v.4 p.520*

Encyclopedia of the Consumer Movement. *v.5 p.585*

Encyclopedia of the Dead Sea Scrolls, Set. *v.1 p.546*

Encyclopedia of the Documentary Film. .*v.4 p.413, v.6 p.308*

Encyclopedia of the Enlightenment 1670-1815, Set. . .*v.3 p.72*

Encyclopedia of the Enlightenment, Set. *v.3 p.71, p.72*

Encyclopedia of the Enlightenment, Vol. 1. . . . . .*v.1 p.437*

Encyclopedia of the Enlightenment, Vol. 2. . .*v.1 p.437, p.438*

Encyclopedia of the Enlightenment, Vol. 3. . . . . .*v.1 p.437*

Encyclopedia of the Enlightenment, Vol. 4. . . . . .*v.1 p.437*

Encyclopedia of the European Union. *v.4 p.602, p.637*

Encyclopedia of the Global Economy: A Guide for Students and Researchers. *v.4 p.192*

Encyclopedia of the Great Depression. *v.3 p.443*

Encyclopedia of the Great Plains. *v.3 p.519*

Encyclopedia of the Harlem Literary Renaissance: The Essential Guide to the Lives and Works of the Harlem Renaissance Writers. *v.6 p.23*

Encyclopedia of the Harlem Renaissance. *v.6 p.22, p.28, p.33, p.35*

The Encyclopedia of the Jewish Religion. *v.1 p.546*

Encyclopedia of the JFK Assassination. *v.3 p.465*

Encyclopedia of the Mexican American Civil Rights Movement. *v.6 p.540*

The Encyclopedia of the Midwest. *v.3 p.506*

Encyclopedia of the Modern Middle East. . .*v.6 p.591, p.592*

The Encyclopedia of the Musical Theatre. .*v.1 p.59, p.92, p.160*

The Encyclopedia of the New York Stage, 1920-1930,
Set. *v.1 p.60, p.116*

The Encyclopedia of the New York Stage, 1920-1930, Vol.
1. . . . .*v.1 p.60, p.116*

The Encyclopedia of the New York Stage,
1930-1940. . . . .*v.1 p.59, p.116*

The Encyclopedia of the New York Stage,
1940-1950. . . . . *v.1 p.59, p.60, p.116*

Encyclopedia of the North American Colonies,
Set. *v.3 p.405, v.4 p.517*

Encyclopedia of the Palestinians. *v.6 p.608*

Encyclopedia of the Scientific Revolution from Copernicus to
Newton. *v.5 p.386, p.391*

Encyclopedia of the Sea. *v.5 p.428*

The Encyclopedia of the South (To 1984). *v.3 p.494*

The Encyclopedia of the Stone-Campbell Movement. .*v.1 p.584*

The Encyclopedia of the Supreme Court. *v.4 p.539*

Encyclopedia of the U. S. Census. *v.4 p.676*

Encyclopedia of the United Nations: And International
Agreements, Set. *v.4 p.635*

Encyclopedia of the United Nations. *v.4 p.634*

Encyclopedia of the Victorian Era. *v.6 p.735*

An Encyclopedia of the Violin. . .*v.1 p.159, p.388, p.396, p.397*

Encyclopedia of the World's Zoos,
Set. *v.5 p.82, p.83, p.95, p.224, p.225*

Encyclopedia of Tourism. *v.4 p.161*

Encyclopedia of Twentieth-Century Latin American and
Caribbean Literature, 1900-2003. . . . .*v.2 p.663*

Encyclopedia of Twentieth-Century Photography. . . .*v.1 p.762*

Encyclopedia of Twentieth-Century Technology. . . .*v.5 p.387*

Encyclopedia of U. S. Foreign Relations, Set. *v.4 p.628*

🄴 Encyclopedia of Urban America: The Cities and
Suburbs. *v.6 p.709*

Encyclopedia of Urban Cultures: Cities and Cultures Around the
World. *v.6 p.717*

Encyclopedia of Urban Legends. *v.2 p.16, p.17*

Encyclopedia of Vernacular Architecture of the
World. *v.1 p.784, p.821*

Encyclopedia of Violence, Peace and Conflict, Set. . .*v.4 p.679*

Encyclopedia of Virginia Biography, Set. *v.3 p.500*

Encyclopedia of Vitamins, Minerals, and Supplements. .*v.5 p.329*

Encyclopedia of Volcanoes. *v.5 p.438, v.6 p.286*

The Encyclopedia of War Movies: Wars 1900 to the
Present. *v.6 p.322*

Encyclopedia of Water. *v.6 p.284*

The Encyclopedia of Westerns. *v.6 p.324*

Encyclopedia of Wireless Telecommunications. *v.4 p.419*

Encyclopedia of Women & Islamic Cultures. *v.6 p.582*

Encyclopedia of Women and Gender: Sex Similarities and
Differences and the Impact of Society on Gender, Vol.
1. . . . .*v.4 p.679*

Encyclopedia of Women and Gender: Sex Similarities and
Differences and the Impact of Society on Gender, Vol.
2. . . . .*v.4 p.679*

Encyclopedia of Women and Gender: Sex Similarities and
Differences and the Impact of Society on Gender. .*v.6 p.426*

Encyclopedia of Women and Religion in North
America. *v.1 p.528*

The Encyclopedia of Women and Religion in North
America. *v.1 p.543, p.544, p.605*

Encyclopedia of Women and Sport in America. *v.6 p.438*

Encyclopedia of Women and World Religion, Vol. 1. .*v.6 p.460*

Encyclopedia of Women and World Religion, Vol. 2. .*v.6 p.460*

Encyclopedia of Women and World Religions, Set. . .*v.1 p.529*

Encyclopedia of Women in American Politics. *v.4 p.569*

Encyclopedia of Women in the Middle Ages. *v.6 p.451*

Encyclopedia of Women's Associations Worldwide. . .*v.6 p.425*

Encyclopedia of Women's Autobiography, Vol. 1. . . .*v.6 p.477*

Encyclopedia of Women's Autobiography. *v.6 p.476*

Encyclopedia of World Cities, Set. *v.6 p.709*

The Encyclopedia of World Climatology. . .*v.5 p.426, v.6 p.284*

Encyclopedia of World Terrorism, 1996-2002 and Encyclopedia
of World Terrorism, Documents, Set. *v.4 p.661, p.662*

The Encyclopedia of World Theater: With 420 Illustrations and
an Index of Play Titles. *v.1 p.57, p.61, p.128*

Encyclopedia of World Writers, Beginnings to the Twentieth
Century. *v.2 p.575*

Encyclopedia: Selections. *v.2 p.479*

Encyclopedic Dictionary of Applied Geophysics. . . .*v.5 p.445*

Encyclopedic Dictionary of Chemical Technology. . . .*v.5 p.316*

Encyclopedic Dictionary of Genetics, Genomics, and
Proteomics. *v.5 p.96, p.104, p.106, p.146*

Encyclopedic Dictionary of Mathematics. *v.5 p.461*

Encyclopedic Dictionary of Semiotics, Media and
Communication. *v.4 p.423*

An Encyclopedic Dictionary of Women in Early American
Films: 1895-1930. . . . .*v.6 p.332*

⬚ Encyclopédie ou Dictionnaire raisonné des sciences, des arts
et des métiers. *v.2 p.479*

The Encylopedia of Environmental Pollution and Cleanup,
Set. *v.5 p.311*

The Encylopedia of Hasidism. *v.1 p.547*

Encylopedia of Molecular Cell Biology and Molecular
Medicine, Set. *v.5 p.96, p.150, p.153*

The End: Hamburg 1943. . . . .*v.3 p.175*

The End of American Exceptionalism: Frontier Anxiety from the
Old West to the New Deal. *v.3 p.382*

The End of American Innocence: A Study of the First Years of
Our Own Time, 1912-1917. . . . .*v.3 p.369*

The End of an Era: The Image of War, 1861-1865. . .*v.3 p.431*

End of Arcadia: Gordon Browning and Tennessee
Politics. *v.3 p.511*

The End of Art. *v.1 p.679*

The End of Baseball As We Knew It: The Players Union,
1960-81. . . . .*v.4 p.851, p.888, p.891*

The End of Capitalism (As We Knew It): A Feminist Critique of
Political Economy. *v.4 p.273*

The End of Democracy?: The Judicial Usurpation of
Politics. *v.4 p.525*

The End of Education: Redefining the Value of Schools. .*v.4 p.323*

The End of Empire: Dependencies since 1948: The West Indies, British Honduras, Hong Kong, Fiji, Cyprus, Gibraltar and the Falklands Select Documents on the Constitutional History of the British Empire and Commonwealth. *v.4 p.435*

The End of Empire in French West Africa: France's Successful Decolonization? *v.4 p.584, v.6 p.68*

The End of Empire?: The Transformation of the U.S.S.R. in Comparative Perspective. *v.4 p.508*

The End of Globalization: Lessons from the Great Depression. *v.4 p.664*

The End of Ideology: On the Exhaustion of Political Ideas in the Fifties, with the Resumption of History in the New Century. *v.4 p.701*

End of Kaunda Era. *v.6 p.77*

The End of Laissez Faire and the Economic Consequences of the Peace. *v.3 p.79*

The End of Laissez-Faire: National Purpose and the Global Economy after the Cold War. *v.4 p.665*

The End of Obscenity: The Trials of Lady Chatterley, Tropic of Cancer and Fanny Hill. *v.4 p.472, p.473*

The End of Oil: On the Edge of a Perilous New World. .*v.6 p.298*

The End of Philosophy. *v.1 p.471*

The End of Poverty: Economic Possibilities for Our Time. *v.4 p.266*

The End of Realignment?: Interpreting American Electoral Eras. *v.4 p.548, p.552*

The End of Reform: New Deal Liberalism in Recession and War. *v.3 p.466*

The End of Roman Britain. *v.3 p.63*

The End of Slavery in Africa. *v.6 p.53*

The End of the Absolute Monarchy in Siam. *v.6 p.171*

The End of the Affair. *v.2 p.349*

The End of the Age of Innocence: Edith Wharton and the First World War. *v.2 p.132*

The End of the American Era: U. S. Foreign Policy and the Geopolitics of the Twenty-First Century. *v.4 p.642*

The End of the Bronze Age: Changes in Warfare and the Catastrophe Ca. 1200 B. C. *v.3 p.15*

The End of the Chinese 'Middle Ages': Essays in Mid-Tang Literary Culture. *v.6 p.210, p.212*

The End of the Cold War: Its Meaning and Implications. .*v.4 p.486*

The End of the Keynesian Era. *v.4 p.229*

End of the Line: The Rise and Coming Fall of the Global Corporation. *v.4 p.665*

The End of the Old Order in Rural Europe. *v.4 p.701*

The End of the Old Regime in Europe, 1776-1789: The Great States of the West, Pt. I, Vols. I & II. *v.3 p.75*

The End of the Palestine Mandate. *v.6 p.610*

The End of the Peace Process: Oslo and After. *v.4 p.630, p.650,v.6 p.619*

End of the Peasantry: The Rural Labor Movement in Northeast Brazil, 1961-1988. . . . .*v.3 p.342*

The End of the World News: An Entertainment. *v.2 p.336*

The End of Utopia: A Study of Aldous Huxley's Brave New World. *v.2 p.353*

End to Torment: A Memoir of Ezra Pound. *v.2 p.111*

Endangered Dreams: The Great Depression in California. *v.3 p.532*

Endangered Languages in Africa. *v.6 p.80*

Endangered Lives: Public Health in Victorian Britain. .*v.3 p.117*

Endangered Mexico: An Environment on the Edge. . .*v.3 p.270*

Endangered Oceans. *v.5 p.430*

Endangered Self: Identity and Social Risk. .*v.4 p.779, v.6 p.378*

Endangered Spaces, Enduring Places: Change, Identity, and Survival in Rural America. *v.4 p.702*

The Endangered Species Act at Thirty: Conserving Biodiversity in Human-Dominated Landscapes. *v.6 p.292, p.296*

The Endangered Species Act at Thirty: Renewing the Conservation Promise. *v.6 p.291, p.295*

The Endangered Species Act: History, Conservation Biology and Public Policy. *v.4 p.463*

Endangered Species: Health, Illness, and Death among Madagascar's People of the Forest. *v.4 p.46*

Endangered Species: Must They Disappear? *v.5 p.204*

Endgame in Ireland. *v.3 p.135, p.140*

Ending Hunger in Our Lifetime: Food Security and Globalization. *v.4 p.665*

Ending Neglect: The Elimination of Tuberculosis in the United States. *v.5 p.532*

Ending the Cold War at Home: From Militarism to a More Peaceful World Order. *v.4 p.561*

Ending the Vietnam War: A History of America's Involvement in and Extrication from the Vietnam War. *v.3 p.453*

Endings. *v.6 p.655*

Endless Forms Most Beautiful: The New Science of Evo Devo and the Making of the Animal Kingdom. *v.5 p.131, p.159, p.160*

Endless Forms: Species and Speciation. *v.5 p.199*

Endocrine Disruption: Biological Basis for Health Effects in Wildlife and Humans. *v.5 p.366*

Endocrine Pathology. *v.5 p.518*

The Endocrine System in Sports and Exercise, Vol. XI. *v.4 p.826, p.875*

Endocrinology and Metabolism. *v.5 p.518*

Endorsements in Advertising: A Social History. .*v.4 p.140, p.141*

Ends and Means: An Inquiry into the Nature of Ideals and into the Methods Employed for Their Realization. . . .*v.4 p.750*

Endurance in Sport. *v.4 p.826, p.875, p.880*

Endurance Sports Nutrition: Eating Plans for Optimal Training, Racing and Recovery. *v.4 p.825, p.876*

Enduring Issues in American Nursing. *v.5 p.527*

Enduring Love. *v.2 p.368*

The Enduring Memory: Time and History in a French Village. *v.4 p.708*

Enduring, Surviving and Thriving As a Law Enforcement Executive. *v.6 p.265*

Enemies of Civilization: Attitudes Toward Foreigners in Ancient Mesopotamia, Egypt, and China. *v.4 p.644*

Enemies of Freedom: Understanding Right-Wing Authoritarianism. *v.4 p.767*

Enemies of the Enlightenment: The French Counter-Enlightenment and the Making of Modernity. .*v.3 p.72*

Enemies of the Roman Order: Treason Unrest and Alienation in the Empire. *v.3 p.28*

The Enemy: A Biography of Wyndham Lewis. *v.2 p.367*

The Enemy: A Review of Art and Literature, Vol. 1. . *v.2 p.367*

The Enemy: A Review of Art and Literature, Vol. 2. . *v.2 p.367*

Enemy Aliens: Double Standards and Constitutional Freedoms in the War on Terrorism. *v.4 p.460*

Energy: A Guidebook. *v.5 p.361*

Energy: A Historical Perspective and 21st Century Forecast. *v.5 p.450, p.452*

Energy Addict®: 101 Physical, Mental, and Spiritual Ways to Energize Your Life. *v.5 p.163*

Energy and Security: Toward a New Foreign Policy Strategy. *v.4 p.62*

Energy and the Evolution of Life. *v.5 p.192*

Energy and the Imagination: A Study of the Development of Blake's Thought. *v.2 p.240*

Energy at the Crossroads: Global Perspectives and Uncertainties. *v.4 p.667*

Energy Atlas, United States. *v.5 p.360, p.361*

The Energy Balance of Corn Ethanol : An Update. . .*v.5 p.742*

An Energy Field More Intense Than War: The Nonviolent Tradition and American Literature. *v.2 p.5*

Energy for Animal Life. *v.5 p.111*

Energy from Heaven and Earth. *v.5 p.360*

Energy Information Administration: EIA : eia.doe.gov: Official Energy Statistics from the U. S. Government. *v.5 p.452*

Energy: Management, Supply and Conservation. . . .*v.5 p.361*

Energy Methods in Structural Mechanics. *v.5 p.694*

Energy or Extinction. *v.5 p.358, p.360*

Energy Risk Assessment. *v.5 p.360, p.368*

Energy: Supplies, Sustainability, and Costs. *v.5 p.359*

Energy Supply. *v.5 p.710*

Une enfance gantoise. *v.2 p.521*

Les enfants terribles : roman. *v.2 p.514*

Les Enfants Terribles. *v.2 p.514*

Enforced Disarmament: From the Napoleonic Campaigns to the Gulf War. *v.4 p.657*

Engaged in Reading: Processes, Practices and Policy Implications. *v.4 p.354*

Engagement with the Past: The Lives and Works of the World War II Generation of Historians. *v.3 p.374*

Engaging All Families: Creating a Positive School Culture by Putting Research into Practice. *v.4 p.303*

Engaging India: Diplomacy, Democracy, and the Bomb. *v.3 p.392, p.393,v.4 p.644, p.646*

Engaging Young Children in Mathematics: Standards for Pre-School and Kindergarten Mathematics Education. *v.4 p.360*

Engaging Young Readers: Promoting Achievement and Motivation. *v.4 p.363*

Engels after Marx. *v.4 p.509*

Engels on Capital: Synopsis, Reviews, and Supplementary Material. *v.4 p.207*

Engendered Lives: A New Psychology of Women's Experience. *v.6 p.446*

Engendered Lives: A New Psychology of Women's Lives. *v.6 p.446*

Engendering African American Archaeology: A Southern Perspective. *v.6 p.4, p.16*

Engendering Archaeology: Women and Prehistory. . . *v.6 p.450*

Engendering Democracy in Brazil: Women's Movements in Transition Politics. *v.3 p.282, p.338,v.6 p.439*

Engendering Democracy in Chile. *v.3 p.352*

Engendering Economics: Conversations with Women Economists in the United States. *v.4 p.185, p.274*

Engendering International Health: The Challenge of Equity. *v.6 p.444*

(En)Gendering Knowledge: Feminists in Academe. . .*v.6 p.463*

Engendering Origins: Critical Feminist Readings in Plato and Aristotle. *v.1 p.506*

Engendering Rome: Women in Latin Epic. . . .*v.2 p.425, p.426*

Engendering the Chinese Revolution: Radical Women, Communist Politics, and Mass Movements in the 1920s. *v.6 p.192, p.217*

The Engine of Reason, the Seat of the Soul: A Philosophical Journey into the Brain. *v.1 p.496, v.5 p.616*

The Engineer of Human Souls. *v.2 p.784*

Engineering and Product Development Management: The Holistic Approach. *v.4 p.118, p.119*

An Engineering Approach to Optimal Control and Estimation Theory. *v.5 p.712*

Engineering Circuit Analysis. *v.5 p.721*

Engineering, Ethics, and the Environment. *v.5 p.705*

Engineering Geology: An Environmental Approach. . .*v.5 p.422*

Engineering Geology and Construction. *v.5 p.421*

Engineering Geology and Geotechnics for Infrastructure Development in Europe. *v.5 p.698*

Engineering Geology: Rock in Engineering Construction. *v.5 p.421*

Engineering Library Resources in Nuclear Engineering. *v.5 p.739*

Engineering Materials 1: An Introduction to Properties, Applications and Design. *v.5 p.687*

Engineering Materials: Properties and Selection. .*v.5 p.687, p.688*

Engineering Materials Science: Properties, Uses, Degradation, Remediation. *v.5 p.732*

Engineering Mechanics of Composite Materials. . . .*v.5 p.688*

Engineering Polymer Sourcebook. *v.5 p.323*

Engineering Properties of Foods. *v.5 p.5, p.35*

Engineering Properties of Soils and Rocks. *v.5 p.421*

Engineering Properties of Steel. *v.5 p.689*

Engineering Reliability and Risk in Water Resources. .*v.5 p.702*

Engineering the Farm: The Social and Ethical Aspects of Agricultural Biotechnology. *v.5 p.7*

Engineering the Human Germline: An Exploration of the Science and Ethics of Altering the Genes We Pass to Our Children. *v.5 p.152*

Engineering the Revolution: Arms and Enlightenment in France, 1763-1815. . . . .*v.3 p.146*

Engineering. *v.5 p.741, p.742*

The Engineers and the Price System. *v.4 p.214, p.250*

Engineers' Guide to Technical Writing. *v.5 p.680*

Engineers of the Renaissance. *v.3 p.70*

England, 1868-1914: The Age of Urban
Democracy. *v.3 p.92, p.95, p.115*

England and the Discovery of America, 1481-1620. . .*v.3 p.404*

England and the German Hanse, 1157-1611: A Study of Their
Trade and Commercial Diplomacy. . .*v.3 p.96, p.161, p.162*

England, England. *v.2 p.332*

England in Shakespeare's Day. *v.2 p.196, p.197, p.227*

England in the Age of Hogarth. *v.3 p.108, p.109, p.128*

England in the Age of the American Revolution. . . .*v.3 p.109*

England in the Eighteen-Eighties: Toward a Social Basis for
Freedom. *v.4 p.704*

England in the Later Middle Ages. *v.6 p.568*

England Made Me. *v.2 p.349*

England, My England. *v.2 p.362*

England, Spain and the Grand Armada, 1585-1604. . .*v.3 p.240*

England under the Angevin Kings. *v.3 p.98*

England under the Norman and Angevin Kings,
1075-1225. . . . .*v.3 p.97*

England under the Tudors. *v.3 p.99*

England's Dreaming: Anarchy, Sex Pistols, Punk Rock, and
Beyond. *v.1 p.274, p.356*

England's Sea Empire. *v.3 p.100, p.101, p.102*

England's Treasure by Forraign Trade. *v.4 p.216*

Englisch-Deutsches, Deutsch-Englishes Woerterbuch: English -
German. *v.2 p.622*

English Albanian Dictionary of Idioms. *v.2 p.773*

The English Alehouse: A Social History,
1200-1830. . . . .*v.3 p.92, p.123*

English and Italian Literature from Dante to Shakespeare: A
Study of Sources, Analogy and
Divergence. *v.2 p.168, p.169, p.230*

The English and Scottish Popular Ballads, Vol. 1. . .*v.2 p.198*

The English and Scottish Popular Ballads, Vol. 2. . .*v.2 p.198*

The English and Scottish Popular Ballads, Vol. 3. . .*v.2 p.198*

The English and Scottish Popular Ballads, Vol. 4. . .*v.2 p.198*

The English and Scottish Popular Ballads, Vol. 5. . .*v.2 p.198*

English Architecture. *v.1 p.788*

English Around the World: Sociolinguistic Perspectives. .*v.2 p.551*

English as a Global Language. *v.2 p.552*

The English Atlantic, 1675-1740: An Exploration of
Communication and Community. *v.3 p.106, p.107*

English, August: An Indian Story. *v.2 p.764*

English Canadian Theatre, 1765-1826, Vol. 27. . . .*v.1 p.126*

The English Catholic Community,
1570-1850. . . . .*v.1 p.572, v.3 p.120*

The English Church, 1000-1066: A History of the Later
Anglo-Saxon Church. *v.1 p.608*

The English Church, 1066-1154: A History of the
Anglo-Norman Church. *v.1 p.608, v.3 p.96, p.97*

The English Common People: A Social History from the
Norman Conquest to the Present. *v.3 p.90, v.4 p.703*

The English Common Reader: A Social History of the Mass
Reading Public, 1800-1900. .*v.2 p.576, v.3 p.36, p.37,v.6 p.738*

The English Constitution. *v.4 p.604*

English Critical Essays: Nineteenth Century. *v.2 p.175*

English Critical Essays: Sixteenth, Seventeenth and Eighteenth
Centuries. *v.2 p.169, p.170, p.172*

English Critical Essays: Twentieth Century. *v.2 p.178*

English Culture and the Decline of the Industrial Spirit,
1850-1980. .*v.3 p.93, p.117, p.123, p.130,v.6 p.745, p.751, p.766*

The English Dancing Master (Sixteen Fifty-One). . . .*v.1 p.22*

English Discovery of America To 1585. . . . . . .*v.3 p.404*

The English Drama, 1485-1585. . . . .*v.2 p.185*

English Drama, 1660-1700. . . . .*v.2 p.186, p.187*

English Drama: A Cultural History. *v.2 p.185*

English Drama: The Beginnings of the Modern Period,
1900-1930. . . . .*v.2 p.188*

English Eccentrics. *v.2 p.382*

The English Elegy: Studies in the Genre from Spenser to
Yeats. *v.2 p.180*

The English Epic and Its Background. *v.2 p.165*

The English Garden and National Identity: The Competing
Styles of Garden Design, 1870-1914. . . . . . .*v.1 p.818*

English Grammar for Students of French: The Study Guide for
Those Learning French. *v.2 p.557, p.558*

English Grammar for Students of German: A Study Guide for
Those Studying German. *v.2 p.558*

English Grammar for Students of Spanish: The Study Guide for
Those Learning Spanish. *v.2 p.558*

English Grammar: Principles and Facts. *v.2 p.557*

English Historical Documents, 1042-1189. . . . . .*v.3 p.97*

English Historical Economics, 1870-1926: The Rise of
Economic History and Neo-Mercantilism. . .*v.4 p.212, p.215*

English History, 1914-1945. . . . .*v.3 p.117, p.118, p.119*

The English History of African American English. . .*v.2 p.555*

The English Hymn: A Critical and Historical Study. . .*v.1 p.655*

English in Britain and Overseas: Origins and
Development. *v.2 p.554*

English in North America. *v.2 p.553*

English Is Broken Here: Notes on Cultural Fusion in the
Americas. *v.6 p.492*

English Journey: Jubilee Edition. *v.3 p.126*

English Landed Society in the Eighteenth Century. . .*v.4 p.705*

English Landed Society in the Nineteenth
Century. *v.3 p.116, p.132*

English Language: A Guided Tour of the
Language. *v.2 p.552, p.554*

The English Language: A Linguistic History. *v.2 p.554*

The English Language: Structure and
Development. *v.2 p.556, p.557*

The English Language. *v.2 p.551*

English Lessons: The Pedagogy of Imperialism in
Nineteenth-Century China. *v.6 p.204*

English Literature, 1815-1832: Scott, Byron, and
Keats. *v.2 p.175, p.274, p.295, p.307*

English Literature, 1832-1890, Excluding the Novel. .*v.2 p.177*

English Literature and the Russian Aesthetic
Renaissance. *v.2 p.164, p.165*

English Literature Before Chaucer. *v.2 p.169*

The English Literature Set: Consisting of the Oxford
Chronology of English Literature and the Oxford Companion
to English Literature. *v.2 p.163*

The English Literatures of America: 1500-1800. . . . .*v.2 p.20*

English Lyric Poetry: The Early Seventeenth Century. *v.2 p.182*

English Madrigal. *v.2 p.199*

The English Mail Coach and Joan of Arc. *v.2 p.281*

English Mediaeval Architects: A Biographical Dictionary to 1550. . . . .*v.1 p.784*

English Money and Irish Land; The Adventurers in the Cromwellian settlement of Ireland. *v.3 p.137*

English Nobility in the Late Middle Ages. *v.6 p.576*

The English Novel: An Introduction. *v.2 p.189*

English Novel from Dickens to Lawrence. *v.2 p.194*

English Novel. *v.2 p.189, p.190*

English Old Eng. Old Eng. Dictionary. *v.2 p.206, p.550*

English Painting: A Concise History. *v.1 p.731*

English Passengers: A Novel. *v.2 p.360*

English Pastoral Poetry, from the Beginnings to Marvell. *v.2 p.200*

The English Patient. *v.2 p.737*

The English People and the English Revolution, 1640-1649. . . . .*v.3 p.92, p.104*

English People on the Eve of Colonization: 1603-1630. . . . .*v.3 p.104, p.121*

English Philosophy Since Nineteen Hundred. *v.1 p.447*

English Phonology: An Introduction. *v.2 p.556*

English Poems, Original and Translated from the Norse and Welsh. *v.2 p.249*

English Poetry of the Eighteenth Century, 1700-1789. *v.2 p.183*

English Poets of the Eighteenth Century. *v.2 p.198*

English Politics in the Thirteenth Century. *v.3 p.98*

The English Poor in the Eighteenth Century: A Study in Social and administrative History. *v.3 p.107, p.109*

The English Poor Law, 1531-1782. . . . .*v.3 p.120*

English Population History from Family Reconstitution 1580-1837. . . . .*v.3 p.43*

English Postcoloniality: Literatures from Around the World. *v.2 p.727, p.728*

English Provincial Society from the Reformation to the Revolution: Religion, Politics and Society in Kent, 1500-1640. . . . .*v.3 p.126*

The English Reformation Revised. *v.3 p.100, p.120*

English Reformations: Religion, Politics, and Society under the Tudors. *v.1 p.604, p.609*

The English Reformation. *v.1 p.604, p.609, v.3 p.99, p.120*

English Renaissance Drama: A Norton Anthology. *v.1 p.63, p.74, p.98, v.2 p.202*

The English Revolution, 1688-1689. . . . .*v.3 p.108*

The English Romance in Time: Transforming Motifs from Geoffrey of Monmouth to the Death of Shakespeare. *v.2 p.168*

English Romantic Poetry: An Anthology. *v.2 p.198*

English Romantic Poetry. *v.2 p.183*

The English Romantic Poets. *v.2 p.183*

English Sacred Music 1549-1649. . . . .*v.1 p.181*

English Seignorial Agriculture, 1250-1450. . . . . . .*v.3 p.96*

English Society, 1688-1832: Ideology, Social Structure and Political Practice During the Ancien Regime. *v.3 p.93, p.106, p.108, p.127*

English Society in the Eighteenth Century. *v.3 p.90, p.92*

English Spelling and Spelling Reform. *v.2 p.557*

The English Stage: A History of Drama and Performance. *v.1 p.104*

English Syntax: A Grammar for English Language Professionals. *v.2 p.557*

English Syntax: An Introduction. *v.2 p.558*

English Syntax. *v.2 p.555*

English Theatre: A Short History. *v.1 p.102, v.2 p.185*

English Thought in the Nineteenth Century. . . .*v.3 p.115, p.129*

English to Hungarian Classical Comprehensive Dictionary. *v.2 p.775*

The English Traditional Ballad: Theory, Method, and Practice. *v.1 p.297*

The English Utilitarians. *v.1 p.516*

English Vernacular Furniture, 1750-1900. . . . . . .*v.1 p.804*

English Victorian Poetry: An Anthology. *v.2 p.200*

English with an Accent. *v.2 p.552, v.4 p.21*

The English Works of Thomas Hobbes, Set. *v.1 p.448*

English Works. *v.2 p.212, p.213*

English-Albanian Comprehensive Dictionary. *v.2 p.778*

English-Arabic Dictionary. *v.6 p.654, p.655*

English-Deutsches, Deutsch-Englisches Woerterbuch, Vol. 2. . . . .*v.2 p.622*

☐ English-German and French-German Dictionary. . *v.5 p.386*

English-Hungarian Comprehensive Dictionary. *v.2 p.775*

English-Italian, Italian-English. *v.2 p.699*

The Englishman's Boy. *v.2 p.739*

The English-Only Question: An Official Language for Americans. *v.2 p.553, p.554*

English-Persian / Persian-English Dictionary Smaller. .*v.6 p.669*

English-Russian Dictionary of Science and Technology. *v.5 p.386*

English-Serbian and Serbian-English Dictionary and Grammar. *v.2 p.776, p.777*

English-Serbian and Serbian-English Dictionary. . . .*v.2 p.776*

An Englishwoman in India: The Memoirs of Harriet Tyler 1828-1858. . . . .*v.6 p.158*

Engraving in England in the Reign of James I: A Catalogue Raisonné. *v.1 p.753*

Engraving in England in the Tudor Period: A Catalogue Raisonné. *v.1 p.753*

☐ Enhanced NMR Periodic Table. *v.5 p.272, p.280*

Enigma: How the Poles Broke the Nazi Code. *v.3 p.254*

Enigma of 1989: The U. S. S. R. and the Liberation of Eastern Europe. *v.3 p.208, p.222*

The Enigma of Felix Frankfurter. *v.4 p.467*

The Enigma of Japanese Power: People and Politics in a Stateless Nation. *v.4 p.622*

Enigma of Piero: Piero Della Francesca. *v.1 p.739*

The Enigmatic Body: Essays on the Arts. *v.1 p.704*

The Enjoyment of Music: An Introduction to Perceptive Listening. *v.1 p.174*

The Enlargement of the European Union and NATO: Ordering from the Menu in Central Europe. . *v.4 p.585, p.603, p.637*

Enlarging NATO: The National Debates. *v.4 p.630, p.639*

Enlightened Nationalism: The Transformation of Prussian
Political Culture, 1806-1848. . . . .*v.3 p.168*

Enlightened Power: How Women Are Transforming the Practice
of Leadership. *v.4 p.70*

The Enlightenment - An Interpretation: The Science of
Freedom. *v.3 p.72*

The Enlightenment: A Comparative Social History,
1721-1794. . . . .*v.3 p.72*

The Enlightenment: A Comparative Social History
1721-1794. . . . .*v.3 p.72*

Enlightenment Against Empire. *v.3 p.72*

Enlightenment and Reform in Eighteenth-Century
Europe. *v.3 p.71*

The Enlightenment and the Birth of Modern Nationhood: Polish
Political Thought from Noble Republicanism to Tadeusz
Kosciuszko. *v.3 p.253*

The Enlightenment As Social Criticism: Iosipos Moisiodax and
Greek Culture in the Eighteenth Century. *v.3 p.194*

Enlightenment Geography: The Political Languages of British
Geography, 1650-1850. . . . .*v.4 p.375*

The Enlightenment in America. *v.3 p.406*

Enlightenment Phantasies: Cultural Identity in France and
Germany, 1750-1914. . . . .*v.3 p.72*

Enlightenment, Revolution, and Romanticism: The Genesis of
Modern German Political Thought,
1790-1800. . . . .*v.3 p.166, p.167*

Enlightenment Science in the Romantic Era: The Chemistry of
Berzelius and Its Cultural Setting. *v.5 p.263*

The Enlightenment: The Rise of Modern Paganism. . .*v.3 p.72*

The Enlightenment. *v.3 p.72*

Ennin's Diary: The Record of a Pilgrimage to China in Search
of the Law. *v.6 p.185*

Ennin's Travels in Tang China. *v.6 p.185, p.216, p.218*

Ennio Morricone's the Good, the Bad and the Ugly: A Film
Score Guide. *v.1 p.255, p.256*

Enoch Arden, andc. by Alfred Tennyson. *v.2 p.314*

The Enormous Room. *v.2 p.68*

The Enormous Vogue of Things Mexican: Cultural Relations
Between the United States and Mexico, 1920-1935. .*v.3 p.264*

Enough for One Lifetime: Wallace Carothers, Inventor of
Nylon. *v.5 p.316, p.317*

An Enquiry Concerning Human Understanding. . . .*v.1 p.451*

The Enragés: Socialists of the French Revolution?. . .*v.3 p.151*

Enrico Dandolo and the Rise of Venice. *v.3 p.199*

Ensayo Cubano del Siglo XX: Antología. *v.2 p.672*

Enser's Filmed Books and Plays: A List of Books and Plays
from Which Films Have Been Made, 1928-2001. .*v.6 p.325*

Ensor: Catalogue Raisonné of the Oil Paintings. . . .*v.1 p.748*

Ensuring Inequality: The Structural Transformation of the
African American Family. *v.4 p.729*

Entangled Edens: Visions of the Amazon. *v.4 p.707*

Entangling Relations: American Foreign Policy in Its
Century. *v.3 p.453*

Enter the Dragon: China's Undeclared War Against the U. S. in
Korea, 1950-51. . . . .*v.6 p.237*

Enter the New Negroes: Images of Race in American
Culture. *v.2 p.11*

Entering the Watershed: A New Approach to Save America's
River Ecosystems. *v.5 p.174, p.234, p.241, p.242*

Enterprise and American Law, 1836-1937. . . . . .*v.4 p.444*

Enterprise and Secular Change: Readings in Economic
History. *v.3 p.40*

Enterprise Knowledge Portals: Next Generation Portal Solutions
for Dynamic Information Access, Better Decision Making
and Maximum Results. *v.4 p.77*

The Enterprise of Florida: Pedro Menendez de Aviles and the
Spanish Conquest of 1565-1568. . . . .*v.3 p.505*

Enterprise Unionism in Japan. *v.4 p.126*

Enterprising Images: The Goodridge Brothers, African American
Photographers, 1847-1922. . . . . .*v.1 p.704, p.705, p.767*

Enterprising Women: 250 Years of American Business. .*v.6 p.456*

Entertaining Tsarist Russia: Tales, Songs, Plays, Movies, Jokes,
Ads, and Images from Russian Urban Life,
1779-1917. . . . .*v.2 p.793*

Entertainment Awards: A Music, Cinema, Theatre and
Broadcasting Guide, 1928 Through 2003. . . . .*v.6 p.346*

Entertainment Law and Business. *v.1 p.150*

Enthalpies of Vaporization of Organic Compounds: A Critical
Review and Data Compilation. *v.5 p.300*

Entitlement Politics: Medicare and Medicaid,
1995-2001. . . . .*v.4 p.756, p.757*

Entomology: A Guide to Information Sources. . . .*v.5 p.213*

Entomology: High-School Science Fair
Experiments. *v.5 p.228, p.229, p.244*

Entomology. *v.5 p.26, p.27, p.212*

Entre el Taco Mazahua y el Mundo: La Comida de las
Relaciones de Poder, Resistencia e Identidades. . .*v.3 p.273*

Entre Nous: Essays on Thinking-of-the-Other. .*v.1 p.456, p.457*

Entrepreneurial Mindset: Strategies for Continuously Creating
Opportunity in an Age of Uncertainty. *v.4 p.68*

The Entrepreneurial Shift: Americanization in European
High-Technology Management Education. *v.4 p.176*

Entrepreneurs and Politics in Twentieth-Century
Mexico. *v.3 p.291*

The Entrepreneur's Guide to Business Law. .*v.4 p.67, p.108, p.109*

Entrepreneurship and Self-Help among Black Americans: A
Reconsideration of Race and Economics. *v.6 p.20*

Entrepreneurship and Small Business. *v.4 p.87*

Entrepreneurship, Geography, and American Economic
Growth. *v.4 p.381*

Entrepreneurship, the New Economy and Public Policy:
Schumpeterian Perspectives. *v.4 p.230, p.234, p.235*

Entrepreneurship. *v.4 p.67*

Entretiens sur la poesie 1972-1990. . . . .*v.2 p.510*

⬜ Entrez Genome. .*v.5 p.102, p.103, p.104, p.108, p.109, p.144*

⬜ Entrez, the Life Science Search Engine. *v.5 p.328*

Entropy and its Physical Meaning. *v.5 p.277*

Entropy, Information, and Evolution: New Perspectives on
Physical and Biological Evolution. *v.5 p.197*

Entry into the Inconceivable: An Introduction to Hua-yen
Buddhism. *v.1 p.567*

Enumerative Combinatorics, Vol. 1. . . . .*v.5 p.479*

Enumerative Combinatorics, Vol. 2. . . . .*v.5 p.479*

⬜ Envirofacts Data Warehouse. *v.5 p.315*

Environment and Animal Development: Genes, Life Histories and Plasticity. *v.5 p.161*

Environment and Ethnicity in India, 1200-1991. . . . *v.6 p.161*

Environment and the City. *v.4 p.395, v.6 p.721*

Environment As a Focus for Public Policy. *v.4 p.566*

The Environment As Hazard. *v.4 p.395*

The Environment: Between Theory and Practice. *v.5 p.28, v.6 p.299*

Environment, Subsistence and System: The Ecology of Small-Scale Social Formations. *v.4 p.29*

Environment under Fire: Imperialism and the Ecological Crisis in Central America. *v.3 p.268, p.269*

Environmental and Engineering Geophysics. *v.5 p.445*

Environmental Anthropology: A Reader. *v.6 p.290*

Environmental Biogeography. *v.4 p.394*

Environmental Biology for Engineers and Scientists. . *v.5 p.705*

Environmental Biology of Fishes. *v.5 p.215*

Environmental Biotechnology: Concepts and Applications. *v.5 p.704*

Environmental Biotechnology: Principles and Applications. *v.5 p.703*

Environmental Biotreatment: Technologies for Air, Water, Soil, and Waste. *v.5 p.706*

Environmental Chemistry. *v.5 p.310, p.704*

Environmental Conservation. *v.5 p.17, p.29*

The Environmental Debate: A Documentary History. *v.4 p.566, v.6 p.301*

Environmental Design: An Introduction for Architects and Engineers. *v.5 p.705*

Environmental Disasters in Global Perspective. . . . *v.4 p.760*

Environmental Dividends: Cutting More Chemical Wastes. *v.5 p.363, p.373, p.378, p.705*

Environmental Effects of Mining. *v.5 p.706*

Environmental Effects of Off-Road Vehicles: Impact and Management in Arid Regions. *v.6 p.290*

Environmental Encyclopedia, 1998. . . . . *v.5 p.353*

Environmental Engineering and Sanitation, Vol. 1121. . . . . *v.5 p.704, p.705*

Environmental Engineering and Science: An Introduction. *v.5 p.704*

Environmental Engineering Dictionary. *v.5 p.707*

Environmental Engineers' Handbook. *v.5 p.707*

Environmental Engineers' Handbook. *v.5 p.368, p.707*

Environmental engineer's mathematics handbook. . . *v.5 p.707*

Environmental Epidemiology and Risk Assessment. *v.5 p.364, p.365*

Environmental Epidemiology: Public Health and Hazardous Wastes. *v.5 p.365*

Environmental Epidemiology: Use of the Gray Literature and Other Data in Environmental Epidemiology. . . . *v.5 p.364*

Environmental Ethics: An Anthology. *v.1 p.486*

Environmental Ethics Today. *v.1 p.486, v.6 p.289*

Environmental Evolution: Effects of the Origin and Evolution of Life on Planet Earth. *v.5 p.185, p.187, p.194*

Environmental Fate and Effects of Pesticides. *v.5 p.9*

Environmental Geology. *v.5 p.423*

The Environmental Guidebook: A Selective Reference Guide to Environmental Organizations and Related Entities. *v.5 p.707, v.6 p.286*

Environmental Hazards: Assessing Risk and Reducing Disaster. *v.4 p.395*

Environmental Hydrology and Hydraulics: Eco-Technological Practices for Sustainable Development. *v.5 p.702*

The Environmental Imagination: Thoreau, Nature Writing, and the Formation of American Culture. *v.2 p.52*

Environmental Impact Analysis. *v.5 p.367*

Environmental Impact Assessment: Issues, Trends and Practice. *v.5 p.367*

Environmental Impact Assessment. *v.5 p.367*

Environmental Injustice in the U. S.: Myth and Realities. *v.4 p.566*

Environmental Justice in South Africa. *v.6 p.300*

Environmental Justice: Law, Policy and Regulation. . *v.5 p.374*

The Environmental Justice Reader Politics, Poetics, and Pedagogy. *v.6 p.287*

Environmental Law. *v.6 p.300*

Environmental Management and Decision Making for Business. *v.4 p.62, p.64*

Environmental Management and Pollution Prevention. *v.5 p.706*

Environmental Management Handbook. *v.5 p.707*

Environmental Management on North America's Borders. *v.3 p.269*

Environmental Management Tools on the Internet: Accessing the World of Environmental Information. *v.5 p.707*

Environmental Marketing: Positive Strategies for Reaching the Green Consumer. *v.4 p.63*

Environmental Microbiology. . . . *v.5 p.355, p.356, p.377, p.379*

Environmental Molecular Microbiology: Protocols and Applications. *v.5 p.153*

Environmental Organic Chemistry. *v.5 p.310*

Environmental Physiology of Animals. *v.5 p.357*

Environmental Physiology of the Amphibians. *v.5 p.163, p.164, p.184, p.214*

Environmental Policy in the European Union. *v.4 p.602, v.6 p.297, p.299*

Environmental Policy-Making in Britain, Germany and the European Union: The Europeanisation of Air and Water Pollution Control. . *v.4 p.604, v.6 p.301, p.303, p.305*

Environmental Pollution and Plant Responses. . . . *v.6 p.290*

Environmental Problems in Eastern Europe. *v.5 p.705*

The Environmental Protection Agency: Structuring Motivation in a Green Bureaucracy: the Conflict Between Regulatory Style and Cultural Identity. *v.6 p.300, p.301*

Environmental Psychology: Behaviour and Experience in Context. *v.5 p.587*

Environmental Psychology. *v.5 p.587*

Environmental Radioactivity from Natural, Industrial and Military Sources: From Natural, Industrial and Military Sources. *v.5 p.706*

Environmental Regulation in the New Global Economy: The Impact on Industry and Competitiveness. *v.4 p.267, v.5 p.28*

Environmental Remote Sensing. *v.4 p.389*

Environmental, Safety, and Health Engineering. *v.5 p.682, p.683*

Environmental Science and Engineering. *v.5 p.704*

Environmental Science: Physical Principles and
Applications. *v.5 p.564*

Environmental Soil and Water Chemistry: Principles and
Applications. *v.5 p.313*

Environmental Soil Biology. *v.5 p.90*

Environmental Soil Chemistry. *v.5 p.51*

Environmental Technologies Handbook. *v.5 p.367*

Environmental Technology Resources
Handbook. *v.5 p.706, p.707*

Environmental Toxicants: Human Exposures and Their Health
Effects. *v.5 p.365, p.366*

Environmental Toxicology and Chemistry. *v.5 p.314*

Environmental Transport Processes. *v.5 p.704*

Environmental Values in American Culture. *v.4 p.30*

Environmentalism and Cultural Theory: Exploring the Role of
Anthropology in Environmental Discourse. *v.4 p.30*

Environmentalism and Economic Justice: Two Chicano
Struggles in the Southwest. *v.6 p.525, p.551*

Environmentalism and the New Logic of Business: How Firms
Can Be Profitable and Leave Our Children a Living
Planet. *v.4 p.61, p.63*

Environmentalism in Landscape Architecture: History of
Landscape Architecture Colloquium. *v.1 p.818*

Environment. *v.5 p.704*

Envisioning Africa: Racism and Imperialism in Conrad's Heart
of Darkness. *v.2 p.341*

Envisioning Human Geographies. *v.4 p.396*

Envisioning Information. *v.1 p.721*

Envisioning Power: Ideologies of Dominance and Crisis. *v.4 p.25*

Envisioning the City: Six Studies in Urban Cartography. *v.6 p.720*

The Envoy from Mirror City: An Autobiography. . . .*v.2 p.745*

Envy. *v.2 p.806*

Enzyme Kinetics: A Modern Approach. *v.5 p.119*

Enzyme Nomenclature 1984 Z Cth. *v.5 p.325*

Enzyme Nomenclature 1992. . . . .*v.5 p.119, p.325*

Enzyme Technology. *v.5 p.119*

Enzymes: A Practical Introduction to Structure, Mechanism, and
Data Analysis. *v.5 p.119*

Enzymes in Synthetic Organic Chemistry. . . .*v.5 p.119, p.295*

Enzymes. *v.5 p.119*

☐ EPA Estimation Program Interface (EPI) Suite. . . .*v.5 p.311*

Ephesians 1-3. . . . .*v.1 p.630*

Ephesians: Translation and Commentary on Chapters
4-6. . . . .*v.1 p.630*

Epic and Folk Plays from the Yiddish Theatre. . *v.1 p.67, p.126*

Epic Films: Casts, Credits, and Commentary on over 300
Historical Spectacle Movies. *v.6 p.315*

The Epic History of Biology. *v.5 p.81*

Epic Journeys of Freedom. *v.6 p.11, p.37*

Epic Lives: One Hundred Black Women Who Made a
Difference. *v.6 p.19, p.34, p.46*

Epic Mythology. *v.1 p.536*

The Epic of Gilgamesh. *v.1 p.539, v.6 p.665*

The Epic of New York City: A Narrative History. . . .*v.3 p.490*

The Epic of Sheik Bedreddin and Other Poems. *v.6 p.666*

Epic of the Dispossessed: Derek Walcott's Omeros. . .*v.2 p.770*

The Epic of the Kings: Shah-nama, the National Epic of
Persia. *v.6 p.671*

The Epic Successors of Virgil: A Study in the Dynamics of a
Tradition. *v.2 p.425*

Epictetus: A Stoic and Socratic Guide to Life. *v.1 p.429*

Epicurean Ethics: Katastematic Hedonism. . . .*v.1 p.429, p.430*

The Epicurean Tradition. *v.1 p.429*

☐ Epicurious. *v.5 p.32*

Epicurus: An Introduction. *v.1 p.430, v.2 p.409*

Epicurus and His Philosophy. *v.1 p.429*

Epicurus in Lycia: The Second-Century World of Diogenes of
Oenoanda. *v.1 p.429*

The Epicurus Reader: Selected Writings and
Testimonia. *v.1 p.429, v.2 p.409*

Epicurus' Scientific Method. *v.1 p.429*

Epidemiology of Sports Injuries. *v.4 p.827*

Epigenetics, Vol. 69. . . . .*v.5 p.143*

Epigrams - Spectacles: Bks. 1-5, Vol. 1. . . . . .*v.2 p.438*

Epigrams: Bks. 11-14, Vol. 2. . . . .*v.2 p.437*

Epigrams: Bks. 11-14, Vol. 3. . . . .*v.2 p.437, p.438*

Epigraphic Evidence: Ancient History from Inscriptions. *v.3 p.13*

Epinician Odes and Dithyrambs: Bacchylides. *v.2 p.409*

Episcopal Power and Florentine Society, 1000-1320. . *v.3 p.198*

Episcopal Women: Gender, Spirituality, and Commitment in an
American Mainline Denomination. *v.1 p.582*

Episodic Memory: New Directions in Research. *v.5 p.609*

☐ Episteme Links. *v.1 p.415*

Epistemic Justification: Internalism vs. Externalism, Foundations
vs. Virtues. *v.1 p.481*

Epistemological Problems of Economics. *v.4 p.212, p.213*

Epistemology of the Closet. *v.2 p.572, p.573, v.6 p.393*

Epistemology: The Big Questions. *v.1 p.481*

Epistle to the Philippians. *v.1 p.630*

The Epistle to the Romans. *v.1 p.630*

Epistole. *v.2 p.706*

Epistulae Ad Familiares: 62-47 B. C., Vol. 1. . . . .*v.2 p.432*

Epistulae Ad Familiares:47-43 B. C., Vol. 2. . . . .*v.2 p.432*

Epistulae Ad Quintum Fratrem et M. Brutum. *v.2 p.432*

Epitaph for a Spy. *v.2 p.328*

The Epithalamions, Anniversaries and Epicedes. . . .*v.2 p.213*

Epochs of Greek and Roman Biography. *v.2 p.401*

Epodes. *v.2 p.434*

🄴 An Eponymous Dictionary of Economics: A Guide to Laws
and Theorems Named after Economists. *v.4 p.192*

La Epopeya Castellana a Través de la Literatura
Española. *v.2 p.640*

Equal Educational Opportunity for Blacks in U. S. Higher
Education: An Assessment. *v.4 p.310*

Equal in Monastic Profession: Religious Women in Medieval
France. *v.3 p.51, p.143*

Equal Justice in the Balance: America's Legal Responses to the
Emerging Terrorist Threat. *v.4 p.564*

Equal Pay in the Office. *v.4 p.253*

Equal Protection and the African-American Constitutional Experience: A Documentary History. *v.6 p.5*

Equality and Partiality. *v.4 p.514*

Equality by Statute. *v.4 p.456*

Equality of Educational Opportunity. *v.4 p.301*

The Equality of the Human Races: Positivist Anthropology. *v.4 p.17*

The Equations of Love. *v.2 p.739*

Equilibrium and Disequilibrium: From Adam Smith to Robert Lucas. *v.4 p.214*

Equity and Science Education Reform. *v.4 p.367*

The Equity Culture: The Story of the Global Stock Market. *v.4 p.97, p.102, p.162, p.163*

The Era of Charlemagne: Frankish State and Society. . .*v.3 p.66*

The Era of Good Feelings. *v.3 p.416*

Era of Reconstruction, 1865-1877. . . . .*v.3 p.401, p.438*

The Era of Reform, 1830-1860. . . . .*v.3 p.416*

The Era of the Muckrackers. *v.3 p.449*

The Era of the Muckrakers. *v.3 p.444*

Era of the Oath: Northern Loyalty Tests During the Civil War and Reconstruction. *v.3 p.428*

The Erasers. *v.2 p.525*

Erasmus of Rotterdam. *v.1 p.603*

Erasmus of the Low Countries. *v.1 p.603*

Erec and Enide. *v.2 p.466*

Erec et Enide. *v.2 p.466*

Erect Men/Undulating Women: The Visual Imagery of Gender, "Race" and Progress in Reconstructive Illustrations of Human Evolution. *v.4 p.31*

Erec. *v.2 p.595*

Erewhon and Erewhon Revisited. *v.2 p.273*

Ergonomics for Therapists. *v.5 p.535*

Eric Dolphy: A Musical Biography and Discography. *v.1 p.263, p.321*

☐ ERIC (Education Resources Information Center). . .*v.4 p.322*

☐ Eric Weisstein's World of Astronomy. *v.5 p.63*

☐ Eric Weisstein's World of Chemistry. *v.5 p.256*

☐ Eric Weisstein's World of Mathematics. . . .*v.5 p.460, p.461*

Erich Lessing: Arresting Time - Reportage Photography 1948-1973. . . . .*v.1 p.762*

Erich Maria Remarque. *v.2 p.613*

Erik Bruhn: Danseur Noble. *v.1 p.8*

Erik Dorn. *v.2 p.81*

Erik Satie. *v.1 p.214, p.352*

Eritrea: Even the Stones Are Burning. *v.6 p.67*

Ernest Hemingway: A Reconsideration. *v.2 p.86*

Ernest Hemingway A to Z: The Essential Reference to His Life and Work. *v.2 p.85*

Ernest Hemingway: An Introduction and Interpretation. .*v.2 p.83*

Ernest Hemingway Life Story. *v.2 p.83*

Ernest Hemingway: Machismo and Masochism. *v.2 p.84*

Ernest Hemingway: Seven Decades of Criticism. . . .*v.2 p.85*

Ernest Thayer's "Casey at the Bat": Background and Characters of Baseball's Most Famous Poem. *v.2 p.51*

Ernst and Young's Personal Financial Planning Guide. *v.4 p.94, p.95*

Ernst Meissonier and Art for the French Bourgeoisie: Master in His Genre. *v.1 p.741*

Eroding Military Influence in Brazil: Politicians Against Soldiers. *v.3 p.274, p.341, v.4 p.592*

☐ EROS Image Gallery Collections. *v.5 p.421*

Eros Plus Massacre: An Introduction to the Japanese New Wave Cinema. *v.6 p.335*

Eros: The Myth of Ancient Greek Sexuality. . .*v.6 p.364, p.422*

Eroshima, Vol. 132. . . . .*v.2 p.540, p.541*

An Erotic Beyond: Sade. *v.2 p.484*

Erotic Distance. *v.2 p.160*

The Erotic History of Advertising. *v.4 p.426*

The Erotic Whitman. *v.2 p.54*

Eroticism and Art. *v.1 p.706*

☐ Erratic Impact: Philosophy Research Base. *v.1 p.415*

Errors and Expectations: A Guide for the Teacher of Basic Writing. *v.2 p.565*

Erskine Caldwell: A Biography. *v.2 p.66*

Erskine Caldwell Reconsidered. *v.2 p.65, p.66*

Erskine Caldwell. *v.2 p.66*

Erzahlungen. *v.2 p.610, p.611*

Erzählende Schriften. *v.2 p.612*

Erzählungen, Hörspiele, Aufsätze. *v.2 p.604*

Esau and Jacob. *v.2 p.691, p.692*

Esau's Plant Anatomy: Meristems, Cells, and Tissues of the Plant Body: Their Structure, Function, and Development. *v.5 p.156*

The Escape and Other Stories of 1947. . . . .*v.6 p.148*

Escape Attempts: The Struggle of Resistance in Everyday Life. *v.4 p.774, p.775*

Escape from Freedom. *v.4 p.768, v.5 p.645*

Escape from Violence: Conflict and the Refugee Crisis in the Developing World. *v.4 p.765*

Escape into War?: The Foreign Policy of Imperial Germany. *v.3 p.80, p.161*

Escaping the Delta: Robert Johnson and the Invention of the Blues. *v.1 p.264, p.334*

La Escuela Del Dolor Humano de Sechuan. *v.2 p.667*

Esdras I and II. *v.1 p.623*

The Eskimos and Aleuts. *v.4 p.10*

Espasa Diccionario de Sinonimos y Antonimos. . . .*v.2 p.635*

El Espejo Indígena. El Discurso Indigenista en Bolivia, 1900-1956. . . . .*v.3 p.324*

ESPN: The Uncensored History. *v.4 p.805, p.902*

The ESRI Guide to GIS Analysis: Geographic Patterns and Relationships. *v.4 p.387, p.388*

The ESRI Guide to GIS Analysis: Spatial Measurements and Statistics. *v.4 p.388*

Essais critiques. *v.2 p.520*

Essais. *v.2 p.511, p.523*

An Essay Concerning Human Understanding, Set. . .*v.4 p.216*

An Essay Concerning Human Understanding. *v.1 p.448, p.482, v.4 p.195*

An Essay in Aid of a Grammar of Assent. *v.1 p.595*

An Essay on African Philosophical Thought: The Akan Conceptual Scheme. *v.6 p.36*

An Essay on Anaxagoras. *v.1 p.422*

An Essay on Economic Growth and Planning. . . . *v.4 p.243*

An Essay on Free Will. *v.1 p.503*

An Essay on French Verse - for Readers of English Poetry. *v.2 p.460*

Essay on Gardens: A Chapter in the French Picturesque Translated into English for the First Time. *v.1 p.820*

An Essay on Man: An Introduction to a Philosophy of Human Culture. *v.1 p.495*

An Essay on Marxian Economics. *v.4 p.236, p.241, p.270*

An Essay on Metaphysics. *v.1 p.488*

An Essay on Nature. *v.1 p.498*

An Essay on Philosophical Method. *v.1 p.416*

Essay on the Origin of Languages and Writings Related to Music. *v.2 p.483*

An Essay on the Principle of Population, or a View of Its Past and Present Effects on Human Happiness: With an Inquiry into Our Prospects Respecting the Future Removal or Mitigation of the Evils Which it Occasions. . . . *v.4 p.222*

An Essay on the Principle of Population. .*v.4 p.221, p.222, p.763*

Essay on the True Art of Playing Keyboard Instruments. *v.1 p.188, 399*

Essays and Aphorisms. *v.1 p.465*

Essays and Introductions. *v.2 p.327*

Essays and Leaves from a Note-Book. *v.2 p.286*

Essays and Lectures on Social and Political Subjects. *v.4 p.209, p.269*

Essays and Lectures. *v.2 p.38*

Essays and Reviews. *v.2 p.50*

Essays and Uncollected Papers. *v.2 p.286*

The Essays, Articles and Reviews of Evelyn Waugh. .*v.2 p.388*

Essays, Biographical, Critical, and Historical, Illustrative of the Tatler, Spectator, and Guardian, Vol. 3. . . . .*v.2 p.202*

Essays in Biochemistry: Molecular Motors, Vol. 35. . .*v.5 p.113*

Essays in Biochemistry: Regulation of Gene Expression, Vol. 37. . . . .*v.5 p.101, p.112*

Essays in Biography, Vol. 10. . . . .*v.4 p.193*

Essays in Constructive Mathematics. *v.5 p.470*

Essays in Criticism: Second Series. *v.2 p.265*

Essays in Development Economic: Dependence and Interdependence. *v.4 p.243*

Essays in Developmental Economics: Wealth and Poverty. *v.4 p.243*

Essays in Econometrics: Collected Papers of Clive W. J. Granger. *v.4 p.200*

Essays in Economic History: Reprints,. *v.3 p.38*

Essays in Economic Sociology. *v.4 p.681*

Essays in Economics: Consumption and Econometrics. .*v.4 p.205*

Essays in Economics: Macroeconomics. *v.4 p.239*

Essays in Economics: National and International. . . .*v.4 p.239*

Essays in Economics: Theory and Policy. *v.4 p.239*

Essays in European Economic History 1500-1800. . . .*v.3 p.39*

Essays in German and Comparative Literature. *v.2 p.590*

Essays in Idleness: The Tsurezuregusa of Kenko. . . .*v.6 p.230*

Essays in International Economic Theory: The International Factor Mobility. *v.4 p.255*

Essays in International Economic Theory: The Theory of Commercial Policy. *v.4 p.255*

Essays in Jewish Thought. *v.1 p.547*

Essays in Linguistics: Dialectology, Grammar, and Lexicography in Honor of James B. McMillan. *v.2 p.553*

Essays in Literary Criticism of George Santayana. . . .*v.2 p.576*

Essays in Ottoman and Turkish History, 1774-1923: The Impact of the West. *v.6 p.623*

Essays in Our Changing Order: A Posthumous Collection of Papers from Periodicals. *v.4 p.251*

Essays in Our Changing Order. *v.4 p.197*

Essays in Panel Data Econometrics. *v.4 p.203*

Essays in Persuasion. *v.4 p.228*

Essays in Positive Economics. *v.4 p.231*

Essays in Psychical Research. *v.5 p.613, p.614*

Essays in Quantitative Economic History. *v.3 p.40*

Essays in Radical Empiricism. *v.1 p.439*

Essays in Science and Philosophy. *v.5 p.400, p.404*

Essays in Social History. *v.3 p.40*

Essays in Socio-Economics. *v.4 p.269*

Essays in Sociological Theory. *v.4 p.680*

Essays in Swedish History. *v.3 p.235*

Essays in the History of Economics. *v.4 p.210, p.223*

Essays in the History of Ideas. *v.1 p.442*

Essays in the History of Linguistic Anthropology. . . .*v.4 p.18*

Essays in the Theory of Economic Fluctuations. *v.4 p.244*

Essays in the Theory of Economic Growth. *v.4 p.260*

Essays in the Theory of Employment. *v.4 p.253, p.270*

Essays in the Theory of Society. *v.4 p.679*

Essays, Mainly Shakespearean. *v.2 p.228*

Essays of E. B. White. *v.2 p.133*

Essays of Elia: The Works of Charles Lamb, Vol. 1. . .*v.2 p.298*

Essays of Joseph Addison. *v.2 p.236*

Essays of Three Decades. *v.2 p.612*

The Essays of Virginia Woolf: 1912-1918. . . . . .*v.2 p.393*

Essays of Virginia Woolf: 1912-8. . . . .*v.2 p.394*

The Essays of Virginia Woolf: 1919-1924. . . . . .*v.2 p.393*

Essays of Virginia Woolf: 1925-1928. . . . .*v.2 p.395*

The Essays of Virginia Woolf, Vol. 1. . . . .*v.2 p.395*

The Essays of Warren Buffett: Lessons for Corporate America. *v.4 p.94*

Essays on Actions and Events: Philosophical Essays Volume 1. . . . .*v.1 p.441*

Essays on Actions and Events. *v.1 p.441, p.495*

Essays on Adam Smith. *v.4 p.219*

Essays on Aristotle's de Anima. *v.1 p.427*

Essays on Aristotle's Ethics. *v.1 p.427*

Essays on Aristotle's Poetics. *v.2 p.408*

Essays on Art, Race, Politics and World Affairs, Vol. 9. .*v.2 p.87*

Essays on Brecht: Theatre and Politics. *v.2 p.605*

Essays on Conrad. *v.2 p.342*

Essays on Czech Literature. *v.2 p.782*

Essays on Developing Economies. *v.4 p.259, p.269*

Essays on Economic Policy. *v.4 p.244*

Essays on Fielding's Miscellanies: A Commentary on Volume One. *v.2 p.248*

Essays on Goldsmith. *v.2 p.249*

Essays on Heidegger and Others: Philosophical Papers, Vol. 2. . . . . *v.1 p.442*

Essays on la Mujer. *v.6 p.547*

Essays on Latin Lyric, Elegy, and Epic. *v.2 p.426*

e Essays on Life, Art and Science. *v.2 p.273*

Essays on Mankind and Political Arithmetic. . . . *v.4 p.254*

Essays on Music. *v.1 p.380*

Essays on New Testament Themes. *v.1 p.625*

Essays on Philosophical Subjects, with Dugald Stewart's Account of Adam Smith. *v.4 p.220*

Essays on Political Economy. *v.4 p.208*

Essays on Realism. *v.2 p.572*

Essays on Religion. *v.1 p.525*

Essays on Sex Equality. *v.6 p.452*

Essays on Sociology and Social Psychology. *v.4 p.692*

Essays on Some Unsettled Questions of Political Economy. *v.4 p.222*

Essays on the Active Powers of Man. *v.1 p.450*

Essays on the American Revolution. *v.3 p.409*

Essays on the Civil War and Reconstruction. *v.3 p.436*

Essays on the Dramatic Works of Polish Poet Zbigniew Herbert. *v.2 p.789*

Essays on the Great Depression. *v.4 p.213*

Essays on the History of Organic Chemistry in the United States, 1875-1955. . . . . *v.5 p.291*

Essays on the History of Organic Chemistry. *v.5 p.291*

Essays on the Law of Nature: The Latin Text with a Translation, Introduction and Notes, Together with Transcripts of Locke's Shorthand in His Journal for 1676. . . . *v.1 p.448*

Essays on the Making of the Constitution. *v.4 p.452*

Essays on the Moral Philosophy of Mengzi. *v.1 p.418*

Essays on the Nature of Commerce in General. . . . *v.4 p.215*

Essays on the Origins of Kurdish Nationalism. . . . *v.6 p.600*

Essays on the Price History of Eighteenth-Century Latin America. *v.3 p.286*

Essays on the Sociology of Knowledge. *v.4 p.762*

Essays, reviews, and reports; previously uncollected writings. *v.4 p.212*

Essays, Speeches and Public Letters. *v.2 p.74*

Essays. *v.2 p.375*

The Essays. *v.2 p.471*

Essays. *v.2 p.584, p.612*

The Essence of Bruckner. *v.1 p.204, p.314*

The Essence of Christianity. *v.1 p.464, p.498*

Essence of Decision: Explaining the Cuban Missile Crisis. *v.3 p.386, p.464*

Essence of Judaism. *v.1 p.551*

Essence of Line: French Drawings from Ingres to Degas. *v.1 p.722*

The Essential Aldo Leopold: Quotations and Commentaries. *v.5 p.370*

The Essential Alfred Chandler: Essays Toward a Historical Theory of Big Business. *v.4 p.147, p.148*

Essential Arabic Grammar: Colloquial Cairo Dialect. *v.6 p.653*

The Essential Bach Choir. *v.1 p.186, p.304, p.401*

Essential Bioinformatics. *v.5 p.99*

The Essential Brecht. *v.2 p.605*

Essential Cell Biology. *v.5 p.154*

Essential Components of Cognitive-Behavior Therapy for Depression. *v.5 p.665, p.666*

The Essential Conversation: What Parents and Teachers Can Learn from Each Other. *v.4 p.353*

Essential Cowell: Selected Writings on Music. *v.1 p.212, p.319*

The Essential Davidson. *v.1 p.441*

The Essential Dewey: Ethics, Logic, Psychology. . . *v.1 p.443*

The Essential Dewey: Pragmatism, Education, Democracy. *v.1 p.443*

Essential Entomology: An Order-by-Order Introduction. *v.5 p.213*

The Essential Erasmus. *v.1 p.593*

The Essential Frankfurt School Reader. *v.4 p.699*

The Essential Gay Mystics: Shiva's Dancing Ground. *v.6 p.374*

Essential Genetics: A Genomic Perspective. . *v.5 p.133, p.134*

The Essential Guide to Vitamins and Minerals. . . . *v.5 p.329*

The Essential Gunnar Myrdal. *v.4 p.269, p.270*

The Essential Gwendolyn Brooks. *v.2 p.63*

The Essential Handbook of Offender Assessment and Treatment. *v.6 p.277*

The Essential Kierkegaard. *v.1 p.478*

Essential Mathematical Biology. *v.5 p.91*

Essential Medical Physiology. *v.5 p.164*

The Essential Monster Movie Guide. *v.6 p.318*

The Essential Montessori: An Introduction to the Woman, the Writings, the Method and the Movement. *v.4 p.343*

The Essential Neruda: Selected Poems. *v.2 p.681*

Essential Papers on Depression. *v.5 p.659*

Essential Papers on Literature and Psychoanalysis. . *v.2 p.570*

The Essential Peirce: Selected Philosophical Writings, 1867-1893. . . . . *v.1 p.440*

The Essential Piaget: An Interpretive Reference and Guide. *v.5 p.627, p.630*

The Essential Pinter: Selections from the Work of Harold Pinter. *v.2 p.377*

The Essential Pritchett: Selected Writings. *v.2 p.378*

Essential Quantitative Methods for Business, Management and Finance. *v.4 p.179*

Essential Readings in Juvenile Justice. *v.6 p.248*

Essential Readings in World Politics. *v.4 p.625*

The Essential Salvador Dali. *v.1 p.739*

The Essential Samuel Beckett: An Illustrated Biography. *v.2 p.333*

Essential Saroyan. *v.2 p.118*

The Essential Shakespeare: An Annotated Bibliography of Major Modern Studies. *v.2 p.228*

Essential Sources in the Scientific Study of Consciousness. *v.5 p.612*

The Essential Soyinka: A Reader. *v.2 p.758, v.6 p.29*

Essential Substances: A Cultural History of Intoxicants in
    Society. *v.3 p.282*

The Essential Tension: Selected Studies in Scientific Tradition
    and Change. *v.5 p.403*

Essential Tibetan Buddhism. *v.6 p.241*

The Essential Tillich: An Anthology of the Writings of Paul
    Tillich. *v.1 p.632, p.633*

Essential Transcendentalists. *v.1 p.515*

Essential Trends in Inorganic Chemistry. *v.5 p.301*

The Essential Trudeau. *v.3 p.542*

The Essential Vedanta: A New Source Book of Advaita
    Vedanta. *v.1 p.419*

The Essential Victor Hugo. *v.2 p.493*

The Essential Wallerstein. *v.4 p.759*

The Essential Writings of B. R. Ambedkar. *v.6 p.158*

The Essential Writings of Christian Mysticism. . . .*v.1 p.653*

The Essential Writings of Jawaharlal Nehru, Vol. II. . .*v.6 p.159*

The Essential Writings of Netaji Subhas Chandra Bose. *v.6 p.158*

The Essential Writings of Raja Rammohan Ray. . . .*v.6 p.158*

The Essential Writings of Ralph Waldo Emerson. *v.1 p.439, p.515*

Essentials of Anatomy and Physiology. *v.5 p.164*

Essentials of Animal Behaviour. *v.5 p.166*

Essentials of Athletic Injury Management. .*v.4 p.827, p.828, p.829*

Essentials of Balanced Scorecard. *v.4 p.82*

Essentials of Carbohydrate Chemistry. *v.5 p.330*

Essentials of Circuit Analysis. *v.5 p.720*

Essentials of Complementary and Alternative Medicine. *v.5 p.531*

Essentials of Computer Architecture. *v.5 p.729*

Essentials of Conservation Biology. . . .*v.5 p.18, 358, p.359*

Essentials of Econometrics. *v.4 p.201*

Essentials of Economic Theory as Applied to Modern Problems
    of Industry and Public Policy. *v.4 p.208, p.223*

Essentials of Economics. *v.4 p.194*

Essentials of English Grammar. *v.2 p.557*

Essentials of Forensic Psychological Assessment. . .*v.5 p.591*

Essentials of Forestry Practice. *v.5 p.40, p.354*

Essentials of Genetics. *v.5 p.134, p.135*

Essentials of Genomics and
    Bioinformatics. *v.5 p.98, p.142, p.143, p.147*

Essentials of Genomics. *v.5 p.138*

Essentials of Human Anatomy and Physiology. . . .*v.5 p.164*

Essentials of International Management: A Cross-Cultural
    Perspective. *v.4 p.70*

Essentials of Lean Six Sigma. *v.4 p.117*

Essentials of Managed Health Care. *v.5 p.509*

🄔 Essentials of Mass Communication Theory. . . .*v.4 p.422*

Essentials of Mass Communication Theory. *v.4 p.416*

Essentials of Mechatronics. *v.5 p.714*

Essentials of Medical Genomics. *v.5 p.148*

Essentials of Modern Research Methods in Health, Physical
    Education and Recreation. *v.4 p.795*

Essentials of Modern Telecommunications Systems. . .*v.4 p.115*

Essentials of Molecular Biology. *v.5 p.128*

Essentials of Nursing Research: Methods, Appraisal, and
    Utilization. *v.5 p.529*

Essentials of Person-Environment-Correspondence
    Counseling. *v.5 p.578*

Essentials of Production and Operations Management. *v.4 p.119*

🄔 Essentials of Psychological Testing. *v.5 p.602*

Essentials of Respiratory Care. *v.5 p.518*

Essentials of Soil Mechanics and Foundations: Basic
    Geotechnics. *v.5 p.699*

Essentials of Sports Law. *v.4 p.449, p.901*

Essentials of Stage Management. *v.1 p.150*

Essentials of Stochastic Processes. *v.5 p.483, p.484*

Essentials of the Theory of Fiction. *v.2 p.578*

Establishment of Communist Regimes in Eastern Europe,
    1944-1949. . . . .*v.3 p.207*

The Establishment of the Balkan National States,
    1804-1920. . . . .*v.3 p.246*

Estado Boliviano y Ayllu Andino. Tierra y Tributo en el Norte
    de Potosí. *v.3 p.324*

Esteemed Colleagues: Civility and Deliberation in the U. S.
    Senate. *v.4 p.534*

Estes Kefauver: A Biography. *v.3 p.458*

Esther: A Novel. *v.2 p.30*

Esther Waters. *v.2 p.300, p.301*

Esther. *v.1 p.621*

Esthetics of Music. *v.1 p.380*

Estimated Withdrawals from Principal Aquifers in the United
    States, 2000. . . . .*v.6 p.294*

Estimation and Inference in Econometrics. *v.4 p.199*

Estonia and the Estonians. *v.3 p.256*

Estonian Dictionary and Phrasebook. *v.2 p.773*

Estonian Short Stories. *v.2 p.781*

Estonian-English Dictionary. *v.2 p.773*

Estrada?!: Grand Narratives and the Philosophy of the Russian
    Popular Song since Perestroika. *v.1 p.298*

Estuaries: A Physical Introduction. *v.4 p.391, p.392*

Estuaries, Vol. 5, Pts. H. *v.4 p.393*

Estuarine Shores: Evolution, Environments, and Human
    Alterations. *v.4 p.392*

E-Supply Chain Management: Foundations for Maximizing
    Technology and Achieving Breakthrough
    Performance. *v.4 p.118*

ETA and Basque Nationalism: The Fight for Euskadi,
    1890-1986. . . . .*v.4 p.608*

Etcetera: The Unpublished Poems of e e cummings. . .*v.2 p.68*

Etchings of Wilfred Fairclough: A Catalogue Raisonné. *v.1 p.757*

The Eternal Darkness: A Personal History of Deep-Sea
    Exploration. *v.6 p.293*

Eternal Egypt: Masterworks of Ancient Art from the British
    Museum. *v.1 p.670, p.671, p.690*

The Eternal Frontier: An Ecological History of North America
    and Its Peoples. *v.5 p.168, v.6 p.295*

Eternal Hope. *v.1 p.645*

Eternal Life?: Life after Death As a Medical, Philosophical, and
    Theological Problem. *v.1 p.529*

Eternal Moment. *v.2 p.786, p.787*

The Eternally Wounded Woman: Women, Exercise, and Doctors in the Late Nineteenth Century. *v.4 p.810, p.838*

Ethan Allen: Frontier Rebel. *v.3 p.411*

Ethcaste: PanAfrican Communalism and the Black Middleclass. *v.4 p.724*

Etherege and the Seventeenth-Century Comedy of Manners. *v.2 p.245*

Ethica Eudemia. *v.2 p.408*

Ethica Nicomachea. *v.2 p.408*

The Ethical Brain. *v.5 p.617*

Ethical Conflicts in Psychology. *v.5 p.674*

Ethical Decisions in Sport: Interscholastic, Intercollegiate, Olympic and Professional. . . .*v.4 p.797, p.803, p.822, p.840*

Ethical Dilemmas in Social Service: A Guide for Social Workers. *v.4 p.758*

Ethical Dimensions of Diversity, Vol. 5. . . . . . .*v.4 p.132*

The Ethical Dimensions of the Biological and Health Sciences. *v.5 p.246, p.247*

The Ethical Dimensions of the Biological Sciences. . .*v.5 p.247*

The Ethical Imperative: Why Moral Leadership Is Good Business. *v.4 p.70, p.71*

Ethical Issues in Archaeology. *v.1 p.829*

⬜ Ethical Issues in Food and Agriculture. *v.5 p.7, p.32*

Ethical Issues in Policing: Contemporary Problems and Perspectives: Contemporary Problems and Perspectives. *v.6 p.263*

Ethical Journalism: A Guide for Students, Practitioners and Consumers. *v.4 p.405, p.406*

The Ethical Primate: Humans, Freedom and Morality. .*v.1 p.503*

⬜ Ethical Principles of Psychologists and Code of Conduct. *v.5 p.674*

Ethical Standards of the American Educational Research Association: Cases and Commentary. *v.4 p.354*

Ethical Systems and Legal Ideals: An Essay on the Foundations of Legal Criticism. *v.4 p.433, p.434*

Ethical Theory and Business. *v.1 p.485*

Ethical Theory: The Problems of Normative and Critical Ethics. *v.1 p.483*

Ethical Writings: The Complete Texts of Ethics and Dialogue Between a Philosopher, a Jew, and a Christian. *v.1 p.431, v.3 p.55, p.56*

Ethico-Religious Concepts in the Qur'an. *v.1 p.556*

Ethics: An Essay on the Understanding of Evil. . . .*v.1 p.483*

Ethics and Airpower in World War II: The British Bombing of German Cities. *v.3 p.80, p.81*

Ethics and College Sports: Ethics, Sports, and the University. *v.4 p.715, p.802, p.821, p.893, p.894*

Ethics and Issues in Contemporary Nursing. . .*v.5 p.511, p.530*

Ethics and Law for School Psychologists. *v.5 p.576*

Ethics and Morality in Sport Management. *v.4 p.786, p.883, p.900*

Ethics and Narrative in the English Novel, 1880-1914. .*v.2 p.189*

Ethics and Society in England: The Revolution in the Social Sciences, 1870-1914. . . . .*v.3 p.115, p.129*

Ethics and Spiritual Care: A Guide for Pastors, Chaplains, and Spiritual Directors. *v.1 p.649*

Ethics and the Limits of Philosophy. *v.1 p.487, p.488*

Ethics and the Rule of Law. *v.1 p.487*

Ethics and the Urban Ethos; an Essay in Social Theory and Theological Reconstruction. *v.1 p.644*

Ethics at Work: Basic Readings in Business Ethics. .*v.4 p.54, p.55*

Ethics, Computing, and Genomics. .*v.5 p.106, p.129, p.147, p.249*

Ethics for Behavior Analysts: A Practical Guide to the Behavior Analyst Certification Board Guidelines for Responsible Conduct. *v.5 p.674*

Ethics for Life Scientists. *v.5 p.248*

Ethics in a Multicultural Context. *v.5 p.674, p.675*

Ethics in International Affairs: Theories and Cases. *v.4 p.484, p.627*

Ethics in Marketing. *v.4 p.146*

Ethics in Marriage and Family Therapy. *v.5 p.675*

Ethics in Media Communications: Cases and Controversies. *v.4 p.417*

Ethics in Plain English: An Illustrative Casebook for Psychologists. *v.5 p.674*

Ethics in Psychiatric Research: A Resource Manual on Human Subjects Research. *v.5 p.675*

The Ethics of Destruction: Norms and Force in International Relations. *v.4 p.484*

The Ethics of Identity. *v.4 p.693*

The Ethics of Killing: Problems at the Margins of Life. .*v.1 p.486*

The Ethics of Life. *v.5 p.250*

Ethics on the Ark: Zoos, Animal Welfare, and Wildlife Conservation. *v.5 p.83, p.84, p.179, p.248*

Ethics, the Heart of Leadership. *v.4 p.697*

⬜ Ethics Updates. *v.1 p.484*

Ethics with Aristotle. *v.1 p.426*

Ethics Without God. *v.1 p.487*

Ethics. *v.1 p.446, p.477, p.483, p.484, p.485, p.487*

Ethiopia and Eritrea: A Documentary Study. *v.6 p.64*

Ethiopia at Bay: A Personal Account of the Haile Sellassie Years. *v.6 p.64*

Ethiopia, Great Britain and the United States, 1941-1974: The Politics of Empire. *v.6 p.64*

Ethiopia since the DERG: A Decade of Democratic Pretension and Performance. *v.4 p.612, v.6 p.64*

The Ethiopian Revolution 1974-1987: A Transformation from an Aristocratic to a Totalitarian Autocracy. *v.6 p.64*

Ethnic America: The South Central States. *v.3 p.510*

Ethnic Chicago: A Multicultural Portrait. *v.3 p.515*

Ethnic Conflict and Civic Life: Hindus and Muslims in India. *v.6 p.149, p.150*

Ethnic Conflict and Reconciliation in Sri Lanka. . .*v.6 p.163*

The Ethnic Eye: Latino Media Arts. *v.6 p.493*

Ethnic Futures: The State and Identity Politics in Asia. *v.6 p.147*

Ethnic Groups and Population Changes in Twentieth-Century Central-Eastern Europe : History, Data, and Analysis. *v.3 p.207*

Ethnic Identity and Social Negotiation: A Study of a Filipino Community in California. *v.6 p.129*

Ethnic Identity in Greek Antiquity. *v.3 p.14*

The Ethnic Image in Modern American Literature: 1900-1950, Set. *v.2 p.18*

Ethnic Labels, Latino Lives: Identity and the Politics of (Re) Presentation. *v.6 p.539, p.544*

Ethnic Music on Records - A Discography of Ethnic Recordings Produced in the United States, 1893-1942: Artist Index, Title Index. *v.1 p.171, p.280*

Ethnic Music on Records - A Discography of Ethnic Recordings Produced in the United States, 1893-1942: Eastern Europe. *v.1 p.171, p.279*

Ethnic Music on Records - A Discography of Ethnic Recordings Produced in the United States, 1893-1942: Middle East, Far East, Scandinavian, English Language, American Indian, International. *v.1 p.171, p.280*

Ethnic Music on Records - A Discography of Ethnic Recordings Produced in the United States, 1893-1942: Record Number Index, Matrix Number Index. . . .*v.1 p.171, p.279*

Ethnic Music on Records - A Discography of Ethnic Recordings Produced in the United States, 1893-1942: Slavic. *v.1 p.171, p.280*

Ethnic Music on Records - A Discography of Ethnic Recordings Produced in the United States, 1893-1942: Spanish, Portuguese, Philippines, Basque. *v.1 p.171, p.279*

Ethnic Music on Records - A Discography of Ethnic Recordings Produced in the United States, 1893-1942: Western Europe. *v.1 p.171, p.279, p.280*

Ethnic Nationalism and State Power: The Rise of Irish Nationalism, Afrikaner Nationalism and Zionism. *v.4 p.495*

☐ Ethnic Newswatch. *v.6 p.86*

The Ethnic Origins of Nations. *v.3 p.62*

Ethnic Origins: The Adaptation of Cambodian and Hmong Refugees in Four American Cities. *v.6 p.139*

The Ethnic Phenomenon. *v.4 p.729*

Ethnic Revival And Religious Turmoil: Identities and Representatons in the Himalayas. *v.6 p.161*

Ethnic Stratification: A Comparative Approach. . . .*v.4 p.725*

Ethnic Theatre in the United States. *v.1 p.87, p.120*

Ethnicity and Family Therapy. *v.5 p.668*

Ethnicity and Nationalism: Anthropological Perspectives. *v.4 p.34*

Ethnicity and Nation-Building in the Nordic World. *v.3 p.232, p.233*

Ethnicity and Sport in North American History and Culture. *v.4 p.805, p.830*

Ethnicity in the Mainstream: Three Studies of English Canadian Culture in Ontario. *v.3 p.544*

Ethnicity in the Sunbelt: A History of Mexican Americans in Houston. *v.6 p.531, p.548*

Ethnicity, Markets, and Migration in the Andes: At the Crossroads of History and Anthropology. *v.3 p.324*

Ethnicity on the Great Plains. *v.3 p.521*

Ethnicity, Security, and Separatism in India. *v.6 p.158*

Ethnicity Versus Nationalism: The Devolution Discourse in Sri Lanka. *v.6 p.163*

Ethnicity. *v.4 p.731*

Ethnobiological Classification: Principles of Categorization of Plants and Animals in Traditional Societies. *v.4 p.26*

Ethnobotany: A Methods Manual. *v.5 p.16*

Ethnobotany: Principles and Applications. *v.5 p.15, p.16*

Ethnobotany: The Evolution of a Discipline. *v.5 p.16*

Ethnocultural Factors in Substance Abuse Treatment. *v.4 p.777, v.5 p.512, p.522, p.673*

Ethnodrama: An Anthology of Reality Theatre. *v.2 p.25*

The Ethnographer's Magic: And Other Essays in the History of Anthropology. *v.4 p.5*

Ethnographic Bibliography of North America. *v.6 p.703, p.704*

Ethnographic Presents: Pioneering Anthropologists in the Papua New Guinea Highlands. *v.4 p.4*

Ethnography at the Border. *v.3 p.528*

Ethnography for Marketers : A Guide to Consumer Immersion. *v.4 p.139*

Ethnography, Linguistics, Narrative Inequality: Toward an Understanding of Voice. *v.4 p.19*

The Ethnography of Communication: An Introduction. *v.4 p.19*

The Ethnography of Reading. *v.4 p.22*

☐ Ethnologue: Languages of the World. *v.2 p.560*

Ethnomathematics: A Multicultural View of Mathematical Ideas. *v.5 p.457, p.465*

Ethnomathematics: Challenging Eurocentrism in Mathematics Education. *v.5 p.464*

Ethnomethodology's Program: Working Out Durkheim's Aphorism. *v.4 p.688*

The Ethnomusicologist. *v.1 p.173*

Ethnomusicology : An Introduction. *v.1 p.173*

Ethnomusicology: A Contemporary Reader. *v.4 p.26*

Ethnomusicology: A Guide to Research. *v.1 p.169, p.283, p.284*

Ethnonational Identities. *v.4 p.767*

Ethnonationalism: The Quest for Understanding. *v.3 p.61, v.4 p.494*

Ethnosyntax: Explorations in Grammar and Culture. . *v.4 p.20*

Etier ; suivi de Autres. *v.2 p.518*

Etruscan Art. *v.1 p.669, p.671, p.685*

Etruscan Cities and Rome. *v.3 p.24, v.6 p.715*

The Etruscan Cities and Their Culture. *v.3 p.24, v.6 p.710*

☐ ETS TestLink. *v.5 p.576, p.577*

☐ ETS. *v.4 p.286*

Etymologisches Worterbuch der Deutschen Sprache. . *v.2 p.621*

☐ EU at a Glance. *v.4 p.636*

The Eucharistic Words of Jesus. *v.1 p.657*

Euclidean and Non-Euclidean Geometry: An Analytic Approach. *v.5 p.495*

Eudemian Ethics. *v.1 p.426*

Eudora Welty: A Biography. *v.2 p.130*

Eudora Welty: A Form of Thanks. *v.2 p.129*

Eudora Welty: A Study of the Short Fiction. *v.2 p.129, p.130*

Eudora Welty: A Writer's Life. *v.2 p.130*

Eudora Welty: Seeing Black and White. *v.2 p.130*

Eudora Welty: The Contemporary Reviews. *v.2 p.130*

Eudora Welty: The Robber Bridegroom; Delta Wedding; The Ponder Heart; Losing Battles; The Optimist's Daughter. *v.2 p.130*

Eudora Welty's Chronicle: A Story of Mississippi Life. *v.2 p.129*

Eugene Atget. *v.1 p.767*

Eugene Fromentin: A Life in Art and Letters. *v.2 p.490*

Eugene Ionesco. *v.1 p.91, p.92, p.96*

Eugene Labiche and Georges Feydeau. *v.2 p.517*

Eugene Onegin: A Novel in Verse. *v.2 p.807*

Eugene O'Neill: A Playwright's Theatre. . *v.1 p.81, p.83, p.118*

Eugene O'Neill and His Eleven-Play Cycle: A Tale of
    Possessors Self-Dispossessed. . . . . *.v.2 p.107*

Eugene O'Neill and the Tragic Tension. . . . . . . *.v.2 p.107*

Eugene O'Neill: Beyond Mourning and Tragedy. . . *.v.2 p.107*

Eugene O'Neill's Creative Struggle: The Decisive Decade,
    1924-1933. . . . . *.v.1 p.79, p.81, p.111*

Eugene O'Neill's Last Plays: Separating Art from
    Autobiography. . . . . *.v.2 p.107*

Eugenie Grandet. . . . . *.v.2 p.486*

Eugenio Barba. . . . . *.v.1 p.87, p.107, p.153*

Eugenio Montale: Poet on the Edge. . . . . . . *.v.2 p.719*

Eugenio Montale's Poetry: A Dream in Reason's
    Presence. . . . . *.v.2 p.718*

Eugenio Montale. . . . . *.v.2 p.718*

Euler: The Master of Us All, Vol. 22. . . . . . . *.v.5 p.465*

Eulogy for a Brown Angel: A Mystery Novel. . . . *.v.6 p.498*

Euripidean Drama: Myth, Theme and Structure. . . . *.v.2 p.410*

Euripides' Alcestis: A New Translation. . . . . . *.v.2 p.353*

Euripides' Alcestis. . . . . *.v.2 p.411*

Euripides and Dionysus: An Interpretation of the
    "Bacchae". . . . . *.v.2 p.411*

Euripides and the Instruction of the Athenians. . . . *.v.2 p.411*

Euripides and the Poetics of Sorrow: Art, Gender, and
    Commemoration in "Alcestis," "Hippolytus," and
    "Hecuba". . . . . *.v.2 p.412*

Euripides: Bacchae, Iphigenia at Aulis, Rhesus. . . . *.v.2 p.411*

Euripides: Children of Heracles, Hippolytus, Andromache,
    Hecuba. . . . . *.v.2 p.410*

Euripides: Cyclops, Alcestis, Medea. . . . . *.v.2 p.411*

Euripides' Hecuba: Introduction, Text and Commentary. *.v.2 p.410*

Euripides: Helen, Phoenician Women, Orestes. . . . *.v.2 p.410*

Euripides: Helen. . . . . *.v.2 p.410*

Euripides: Heraclidae. . . . . *.v.2 p.411*

Euripides: Ion. . . . . *.v.2 p.411*

Euripides: Medea. . . . . *.v.2 p.411*

Euripides: Orestes. . . . . *.v.2 p.411*

Euripides: Phoenecian Women. . . . . *.v.2 p.410*

Euripides: Suppliant Women, Electra, Heracles. *.v.2 p.410, p.411*

Euripides: Suppliant Women. . . . . *.v.2 p.411*

Euripides: Troades. . . . . *.v.2 p.411*

Euripides: Trojan Women. . . . . *.v.2 p.410*

Euripides, Vol. 3. . . . . *.v.2 p.410*

Euripides, Vol. 4. . . . . *.v.2 p.410*

▢ EurLex. . . . . *.v.4 p.474, p.475*

Euro on Trial: To Reform or Split Up? . . . . . . *.v.4 p.636*

▢ Eurobarometer. . . . . *.v.4 p.637*

The Eurogang Paradox: Street Gangs and Youth Groups in the
    U. S. and Europe. . . . . *.v.6 p.256*

Eurojargon: A Dictionary of the European Union. *.v.4 p.603, p.638*

▢ Europa: Gateway to the European Union. . *.v.4 p.482, p.603*

Europa World Year Book 2005. . . . . *.v.4 p.601*

▢ Europa—Gateway to the European Union. . . . . *.v.4 p.637*

Europe 1715-1919: From Enlightenment to World War. *.v.3 p.74*

Europe: A Concise Encyclopedia of the European Union from
    Aachen to Zollverein. . . . . . . *.v.4 p.603, p.637, p.638*

Europe: A Cultural History. . . . . *.v.3 p.50*

Europe and Scandinavia : Aspects of the Process of Integration
    in the 17th Century. . . . . *.v.3 p.235*

Europe and the People Without History. . . . *.v.3 p.35, v.4 p.35*

Europe As an Idea and an Identity. . . . . *.v.3 p.35*

Europe in 1848: Revolution and Reform. . . . . . . *.v.3 p.75*

▢ Europe in Figures—Eurostat Yearbook 2005. *.v.4 p.601, p.636*

Europe in the 18th Century: Aristocracy and the Bourgeois
    Challenge. . . . . *.v.4 p.706*

Europe in the Central Middle Ages, 962-1154. . . . *.v.6 p.561*

Europe in the Era of Two World Wars: From Militarism and
    Genocide to Civil Society, 1900-1950. . . . . . . *.v.4 p.497*

Europe in the High Middle Ages, 1150-1309. . . . . *.v.6 p.564*

Europe in the Neolithic: The Creation of New Worlds. *.v.4 p.13*

The Europe of 1500-1815 on Film and Television: A Worldwide
    Filmography of over 2550 Works, 1895 Through
    2000. . . . . *.v.6 p.314, p.315*

Europe Reconsidered: Perceptions of the West in
    Nineteenth-Century Bengal. . . . . *.v.6 p.161*

Europe, the World's Banker 1870-1914. . . . . . . *.v.3 p.76*

Europe Unites: The E. U.'s Eastern Enlargement. . . *.v.4 p.638*

Europe, Vol. 1. . . . . *.v.1 p.61, p.97*

Europe Without Borders: Remapping Territory, Citizenship, and
    Identity in a Transnational Age. . . . . *.v.4 p.383*

European Approaches to International Relations Theory: A
    House with Many Mansions. . . . . *.v.4 p.626*

European Architecture 1750-1890. . . . . *.v.1 p.788*

European Armies and the Conduct of War. . . *.v.4 p.627, p.647*

European Artists: Signatures and Monograms, 1800-1990
    Including Selected Artists from Other Parts of the
    World. . . . . *.v.1 p.663*

The European Automobile Industry. . . . . *.v.4 p.154*

European Banks and the American Challenge: Competition and
    Cooperation in International Banking Under Bretton
    Woods. . . . . *.v.4 p.88*

▢ European Bibliography of Slavic and East European
    Studies. . . . . *.v.2 p.773*

European Cities in the Knowledge Economy: The Cases of
    Amsterdam, Dortmund, Eindhoven, Helsinki,
    Manchester, Munich, Munster, Rotterdam and
    Zaragoza. . . . . *.v.6 p.726*

The European Colonial Empires, 1815-1919. . . . . . *.v.3 p.77*

European Community Integration: From Community to
    Unity. . . . . *.v.4 p.603*

European Constitutionalism Beyond the State. . . . . *.v.4 p.639*

European Crisis Management in the 1980s. . . . . . *.v.3 p.322*

European Culture in the Great War: The Arts, Entertainment and
    Propaganda, 1914-1918. . . . . *.v.3 p.80*

European Dimensions: Education, Training and the European
    Union. . . . . *.v.4 p.334*

The European Discovery of America: The Southern Voyages, A.
    D. 1492 - 1616. . . . . *.v.3 p.404*

The European Discovery of America, Vol. 1. . . . . *.v.3 p.404*

European Economic History: From Mercantilism to Maastricht
    and Beyond. . . . . *.v.4 p.211, p.215*

European Encounter with the New World: From Renaissance to
    Romanticism. . . . . *.v.3 p.74*

The European Family. *v.4 p.32*

European Imperialism in the Nineteenth and Twentieth
  Centuries. *v.3 p.77*

European Iron Age. *v.4 p.12*

European Literature and the Latin Middle Ages. *v.2 p.448*

The European Mind, the Critical Years 1680: 1715. . . .*v.3 p.72*

The European Miracle: Environments, Economies and
  Geopolitics in the History of Europe and Asia. . . .*v.3 p.40*

The European Mosaic: Contemporary Politics, Economics, and
  Culture. *v.4 p.383*

European Naval and Maritime History, 300-1500: Archibald R.
  Lewis and Timothy J. Runyan. *v.6 p.567*

European of Yesterday: A Biography of Stefan Zweig. *v.2 p.615*

European Paganism: Realities of Cult from Antiquity to Middle
  Ages. *v.1 p.531, v.6 p.569*

European Peasants and Their Markets: Essays in Agrarian
  Economic History. *v.3 p.41*

European Perspectives on Exercise and Sport
  Psychology. *v.4 p.812, p.876*

The European Philosophers from Descartes to
  Nietzsche. *v.1 p.435*

European Political Facts, 1648-1789. . . . .*v.4 p.601*

European Political Facts of the 20th Century. *v.4 p.601*

European Post-Baroque Neoclassical Theatre
  Architecture. *v.1 p.96, p.97, p.155*

The European Reformations. *v.1 p.601, p.602*

The European Reformation. *v.1 p.601*

The European Revolutions, 1848-1851. . . . .*v.3 p.76*

The European Revolutions of 1848 and the Americas. *v.3 p.260*

The European Ritual: Football in the New
  Europe. *v.4 p.817, p.844, p.867*

The European Settlement of North America
  (1492-1754). *v.4 p.382*

European Social Class: Stability and
  Change. *v.4 p.700, p.701, p.723*

European Socialists and Spain: The Transition to Democracy,
  1959-1977. . . . .*v.3 p.242*

European Societies in the Bronze Age. *v.4 p.12*

European Treaty Series (ETS). *v.4 p.474*

The European Union: A Polity of States and
  Peoples. *v.4 p.604, p.638, p.639*

European Union A to Z Index. *v.4 p.474*

The European Union and the Cyprus Conflict: Modern Conflict,
  Postmodern Union. *v.4 p.602, p.637*

European Union: Dilemmas of Regional Integration. . *v.4 p.602*

European Union Foreign Policy: What It Is and What It
  Does. *v.4 p.603, p.604, p.638*

The European Union Handbook. *v.4 p.602, p.636*

The European Union: Readings on the Theory and Practice of
  European Integration. *v.3 p.87, p.88*

European Union—A Guide for Americans. *v.4 p.603, p.637*

European Universities from the Enlightenment to 1914. *v.4 p.333*

European Urbanization: 1500-1800. . . . .*v.3 p.43, p.44*

The European Women's Almanac. *v.6 p.426*

European Writers: The Middle Ages and the
  Renaissance. *v.2 p.576*

The Europeanisation of Industrial Relations: National and
  European Processes in Germany, UK, Italy and
  France. *v.4 p.121*

The Europeans: A Geography of People, Culture, and
  Environment. *v.4 p.397*

Europe's Foreign and Security Policy: The Institutionalization of
  Cooperation. *v.4 p.638*

Europe's Last Red Terrorists: The Revolutionary Organization
  17 November. *v.4 p.659*

Europe's Reformations, 1450-1650: Doctrine, Politics, and
  Community. *v.1 p.602*

Europol and Police Cooperation in Europe. . . .*v.6 p.262, p.263*

Euros and Europeans: Monetary Integration and the European
  Model of Society. *v.4 p.212*

Eurydice Street: A Place in Athens. *v.3 p.196*

Eusebius' Ecclesiastical History: A Third Century Historian
  Looks at the Early Church. *v.1 p.591, v.3 p.57*

The Eustace Diamonds. *v.2 p.318*

Euthanasia and Physician-Assisted Suicide. . . .*v.1 p.485, p.486*

Euthyphro, Apology of Socrates, and Crito. *v.2 p.417*

E.V. Komarek Fire Ecology Database. *v.5 p.31, p.32*

The EVA Challenge: Implementing Value-Added Change in an
  Organization. *v.4 p.92*

Eva Peron: A Biography. *v.3 p.349*

Eva Trout. *v.2 p.334*

Evaluated Kinetic Data for High Temperature
  Reactions. *v.5 p.285, p.286*

Evaluating E-Learning. *v.4 p.321*

Evaluating Gun Policy: Effects on Crime and Violence. *v.6 p.266*

Evaluation and Assessment for Conservation. *v.5 p.359*

Evaluation for Continuing Education: A Comprehensive Guide
  to Success. *v.4 p.320*

Evaluation of R&D Processes: Effectiveness Through
  Measurements. *v.4 p.118*

Evaluation of the Inter-Lok Retaining Wall System. . *v.5 p.698*

Evaluation of the Versa-Lok/Miragrid Reinforced Soil Wall
  System. *v.5 p.698*

Evaluative Research in Recreation, Park and Sport Settings:
  Searching for Useful Information. *v.4 p.786*

Evan Harrington, Pt. 1. . . . .*v.2 p.300*

Evan Harrington, Pt. 2. . . . .*v.2 p.300*

The Evangelical Church in Boston's Chinatown: A Discourse of
  Language, Gender, and Identity. *v.6 p.106, p.127*

Evangelical Feminism: A History. *v.1 p.590*

Evangelical Theology: An Introduction. *v.1 p.634, p.635*

Evangelicalism and Modern America. *v.1 p.605*

Evangelicalism and the Stone-Campbell
  Movement. *v.1 p.584, p.585*

The Evangelicals: A Historical, Thematic and Biographical
  Guide. *v.1 p.648*

Evaporites and Hydrocarbons. *v.5 p.451*

Evaporites: Sedimentology, Resources and
  Hydrocarbon. *v.5 p.451*

Eve and the New Jerusalem: Socialism and Feminism in the
  Nineteenth Century. *v.3 p.54, p.116, v.6 p.442, p.749*

Evelina: The History of a Young Lady's Entrance into the
  World. *v.2 p.242*

Evelyn Waugh: A Biography. *v.2 p.387*

Evelyn Waugh: The Critical Heritage. *v.2 p.388*

Evelyn Waugh: The Early Years, 1903-1939. . . . .*v.2 p.388*

Evelyn Waugh: The Later Years, 1939-1966. . . . .*v.2 p.388*

Evelyn Waugh. *v.2 p.387*

Even Mountains Vanish: Searching for Solace in an Age of
Extinction. *v.5 p.186*

Even the Children of Strangers: Equality under the U. S.
Constitution. *v.4 p.458*

Even the Rat Was White: A Historical View of
Psychology. *v.5 p.596*

An Evening Walk. *v.2 p.325*

Evenings with the Orchestra: A Norton Companion for
Concert-Goers. *v.1 p.240*

Evenings with the Orchestra. *v.1 p.194, p.310*

Event Landscape?: Contemporary German Landscape
Architecture. *v.1 p.812*

Event, Metaphor, Memory: Chauri Chaura, 1922-1992. .*v.6 p.160*

Event Planning: The Ultimate Guide to Successful Meetings,
Corporate Events, Fundraising Galas, Conferences,
Conventions, Incentives, and Other Special Events. .*v.4 p.161*

Eventline. *v.5 p.405*

Event. *v.2 p.534*

Ever Closer Union: An Introduction to European
Integration. *v.4 p.602, p.603, p.637*

Ever Green Is...: Selected Prose. *v.2 p.812*

Ever since Darwin: Reflections in Natural History. . .*v.5 p.221*

Everett Dirksen and His Presidents: How a Senate Giant Shaped
American Politics. *v.3 p.459*

Everlasting Flower: A History of Korea. *v.6 p.237*

Every Farm a Factory: The Industrial Ideal in American
Agriculture. *v.5 p.4, p.14, p.29*

Every Little Movement: A Book about Delsarte. .*v.1 p.27, p.43*

Every Little Thing Gonna Be Alright: The Bob Marley
Reader. *v.1 p.266, p.291, p.340*

Every Man a King: The Autobiography of Huey P.
Long. *v.3 p.460*

Every Man in His Humour. *v.2 p.220*

Every Minute Counts: Making Your Math Class Work. .*v.5 p.463*

Every Teacher's Guide to Working with Parents. . . .*v.4 p.353*

Everybody Belongs: Changing Negative Attitudes Towards
Classmates with Disabilities. *v.4 p.317*

Everybody Counts: A Report to the Nation on the Future of
Mathematics Education. *v.5 p.463*

Everybody Who Was Anybody: A Biography of Gertrude
Stein. *v.2 p.121*

Everybody Wins!: A Life in Free Enterprise. *v.5 p.316*

Everyday Cognition in Adulthood and Late Life. .*v.5 p.628, p.630*

Everyday Genius: Self-Taught Art and the Culture of
Authenticity. *v.1 p.826*

Everyday Life and Politics in Nineteenth Century Mexico: Men,
Women, and War. *v.3 p.265, p.289, p.290*

Everyday Life in Ancient Egypt. *v.3 p.8*

Everyday Life in Ancient Mesopotamia. *v.3 p.5*

Everyday Life in Byzantium. *v.3 p.193*

Everyday Life in Ottoman Turkey. *v.6 p.590*

Everyday Politics: The Power of Public Work. *v.4 p.547*

Everyday Stalinism: Ordinary Life in Extraordinary Times:
Soviet Russia in the 1930s. *v.3 p.225*

Everyday Talk: Building and Reflecting Identities. . .*v.4 p.423*

The Everyman Book of Victorian Verse: The
Post-Romantics. *v.2 p.201*

The Everyman Book of Victorian Verse: The Pre-Raphaelites to
the Nineties. *v.2 p.201*

Everyman's Dictionary of Literary Biography. *v.2 p.163*

Everynight Life: Culture and Dance in Latino
America. *v.1 p.19, p.20, v.3 p.266*

Everything in its Path: Destruction of Community in the Buffalo
Creek Flood. *v.4 p.760*

Everything Is Pickrick: The Life of Lester Maddox. . .*v.3 p.503*

Everything Was Forever, until It Was No More: The Last Soviet
Generation. *v.3 p.223*

Everything Within the Revolution: Cuban Strategies for Social
Development since 1960. . . . .*v.3 p.308*

Eve's Herbs: A History of Contraception and Abortion in the
West. *v.4 p.778*

Evidence and Faith: Philosophy and Religion since the 17th
Century. *v.1 p.526*

The Evidence for Quality: Strengthening the Tests of Academic
and Administrative Effectiveness. *v.4 p.289*

Evidence of Things Unseen. *v.2 p.159*

Evidence-Based Practice in Nursing and Healthcare: A Guide to
Best Practice. *v.5 p.528*

The Evidential Argument from Evil. *v.1 p.594*

Evil God of Love. *v.1 p.639*

Evil in Modern Thought: An Alternative History of
Philosophy. *v.1 p.484, p.485*

Evita, First Lady: A Biography of Eva Peron. *v.3 p.347*

Evita. *v.1 p.252, p.337, p.408*

Evitez le franglais, parlez français!. *v.2 p.454*

Evolution: A Case of Stating the Obvious. *v.5 p.193*

Evolution: An Oxford Reader. *v.5 p.195, p.226*

Evolution and Adaptation of Crops: Cereals. . . .*v.5 p.20, p.24*

Evolution and Environment. *v.4 p.493*

The Evolution and Extinction of the Dinosaurs. . . .*v.5 p.448*

Evolution and Structure of the Internet: A Statistical Physics
Approach. *v.5 p.338, p.345*

Evolution and the Myth of Creationism: A Basic Guide to the
Facts in the Evolution Debate. *v.5 p.190*

Evolution and the Recognition Concept of Species: Collected
Writings. *v.5 p.199*

Evolution As Entropy: Toward a Unified Theory of
Biology. *v.5 p.191*

Evolution As Natural History: A Philosophical
Analysis. *v.5 p.197, p.249*

Evolution, Creationism, and Other Modern Myths: A Critical
Inquiry. *v.6 p.701*

The Evolution Explosion: How Humans Cause Rapid
Evolutionary Change. *v.5 p.195*

Evolution!: Facts and Fallacies. *v.5 p.196*

The Evolution from Protein Chemistry to Proteomics: Basic
Science to Clinical Application. *v.5 p.117*

Evolution in Four Dimensions: Genetic, Epigenetic, Behavioral, and Symbolic Variation in the History of Life. . . .*v.5 p.193*

Evolution in Hawaii: A Supplement to Teaching about Evolution and the Nature of Science. *v.5 p.195, p.235*

Evolution in Perspective: The Science Teacher's Compendium. *v.5 p.191, p.244*

The Evolution of a Manufacturing System at Toyota. .*v.5 p.716*

The Evolution of Agency and Other Essays. *v.5 p.197*

The Evolution of American Educational Technology. . .*v.4 p.352*

The Evolution of American Investigative Journalism. .*v.4 p.408*

Evolution of Biological Systems in Random Media: Limit Theorems. *v.5 p.92, p.171*

The Evolution of Communication Systems: A Comparative Approach. *v.5 p.166, p.195*

The Evolution of Communication. *v.5 p.621, p.623*

The Evolution of Complexity by Means of Natural Selection. *v.5 p.190*

The Evolution of Cooperation. *v.4 p.625*

The Evolution of Crises and Underdevelopment in Africa. *v.4 p.384*

Evolution of Crop Plants. *v.5 p.23*

The Evolution of Darwinism: Selection, Adaptation and Progress in Evolutionary Biology. *v.5 p.204*

Evolution of Domesticated Animals. *v.5 p.55*

The Evolution of Greek Prose Style. *v.2 p.400*

The Evolution of Homo Erectus: Comparative Anatomical Studies of an Extinct Human Species. *v.4 p.16*

The Evolution of Igneous Rocks. *v.5 p.437*

Evolution of International Human Rights: Visions Seen. .*v.4 p.513*

The Evolution of Life Histories. *v.5 p.196, p.197*

The Evolution of Love. *v.5 p.654*

The Evolution of Mental Health Law. . . .*v.4 p.448, v.5 p.592*

The Evolution of National Wildlife Law. *v.4 p.463*

The Evolution of North America. *v.5 p.432*

The Evolution of Physics: The Growth of Ideas from Early Concepts to Relativity and Guanta. *v.5 p.541*

The Evolution of Plants. *v.5 p.449*

The Evolution of Presidential Polling. *v.4 p.526*

The Evolution of Reason: Logic as a Branch of Biology. .*v.5 p.78*

The Evolution of Retirement: An American Economic History, 1880-1990. . . . .*v.4 p.741*

The Evolution of Social Insurance, Eighteen Eighty-One to Nineteen Eighty-One: Studies of Great Britain, France, Switzerland, Austria, and Germany. *v.4 p.247*

The Evolution of Species. *v.5 p.199*

The Evolution of the Cuban Military, 1492-1986. . . .*v.3 p.308*

Evolution of the Earth. *v.5 p.445*

The Evolution of the French Novel, 1641-1782. .*v.2 p.462, p.463*

Evolution of the Genetic Code. *v.5 p.200*

The Evolution of the Genome. *v.5 p.140*

Evolution of the Global Biogeochemical Sulphur Cycle. .*v.5 p.111*

The Evolution of the Igneous Rocks: Fiftieth Anniversary Perspectives. *v.5 p.437*

The Evolution of the Liberal Democratic State with a Case Study of Latinos in San Antonio, Texas. . .*v.6 p.537, p.548*

Evolution of the Market Process. *v.4 p.233, p.246*

The Evolution of the Slave Society and Economy of Saao Paulo, from the 1760s to the 1850s. . . .*v.3 p.334, p.335*

The Evolution of the Trade Regime: Politics, Law and Economics of the Gatt and the Wto. *v.4 p.61*

The Evolution of the US Airline Industry: Theory, Strategy and Policy. *v.4 p.151, p.152*

Evolution of the Vertebrates: A History of the Backboned Animals Through Time. *v.5 p.448*

The Evolution of U. N. Peacekeeping: Case Studies and Comparative Analysis. *v.4 p.649*

The Evolution of Western Private Law. *v.4 p.433*

Evolution on Planet Earth: Impact of the Physical Environment. *v.5 p.196*

Evolution: The History of an Idea. *v.5 p.77, p.190*

Evolution: The Remarkable History of a Scientific Theory. *v.5 p.79, p.80, p.193*

Evolution: The Triumph of an Idea. *v.5 p.198*

The Evolution Wars: A Guide to the Debates. *v.5 p.196*

Evolutionary and Neo-Schumpeterian Approaches to Economics. *v.4 p.233*

Evolutionary and Neurocognitive Approaches to Aesthetics, Creativity, and the Arts. *v.5 p.619*

The Evolutionary Biology of Plants. *v.5 p.449*

Evolutionary Biology. *v.5 p.192*

Evolutionary Catastrophes: The Science of Mass Extinction. *v.5 p.449, p.450*

Evolutionary Computation in Bioinformatics. . .*v.5 p.107, p.108*

Evolutionary Developmental Biology. *v.5 p.160*

Evolutionary Economics: Post-Schumpeterian Contributions. *v.4 p.233*

Evolutionary Genetics: From Molecules to Morphology. .*v.5 p.200*

Evolutionary Genetics. *v.5 p.194, p.200*

Evolutionary Naturalism: Selected Essays. *v.1 p.516*

Evolutionary Paleoecology: The Ecological Context of Macroevolutionary Change. *v.5 p.449*

Evolutionary Patterns and Processes. *v.5 p.193*

Evolutionary Playwork and Reflective Analytic Practice. *v.4 p.784, p.795*

Evolutionary Progress. *v.5 p.195*

Evolutionary Systems: Biological and Epistemological Perspectives on Selection and Self-Organization. . .*v.5 p.197*

An Evolutionary Theory of Economic Change. *v.4 p.233*

Evolutionary Wars. *v.5 p.193*

Evolutionism in Cultural Anthropology: A Critical History. *v.4 p.23*

Evolution's Rainbow: Diversity, Gender, and Sexuality in Nature and People. *v.4 p.744, p.746,v.6 p.420*

Evolution's Workshop: God and Science on the Galapagos Islands. *v.5 p.193, p.236*

Evolution. *v.5 p.195*

The Evolving American Family: New Policies for a New Century. *v.4 p.733*

Evolving Perspectives on the History of Psychology. .*v.5 p.598*

The Evolving Self: Problem and Process in Human Development. *v.5 p.627*

Evolving Technology and Market Structure: Studies in Schumpeterian Economics. *v.4 p.230, p.235*

The Evolving World: Evolution in Everyday Life. . . . *.v.5 p.194*

Exactly Solvable Models of Biological
Invasion. . . . . *.v.5 p.169, p.185, p.187*

Examination of Musculoskeletal Injuries. .*v.4 p.827, p.828, p.829*

An Examination of the Place of Reason in Ethics. . . .*v.1 p.487*

Excavations and Foundations in Soft Soils. *v.5 p.699*

Excavation. *v.4 p.7*

Excel for Chemists: A Comprehensive Guide. *v.5 p.267*

Excellent Women. *v.2 p.379*

Exceptional C++: 47 Engineering Puzzles, Programming
Problems, and Solutions. . . .*v.5 p.347, p.349, p.351, p.353*

Exceptional Child Education Resources (database). .*v.5 p.574*

Exceptional Children and Youth: An Introduction to Special
Education. *v.4 p.316*

Exceptional Fossil Preservation: A Unique View on the
Evolution of Marine Life. *v.5 p.446*

The Excesses of God: Robinson Jeffers As a Religious
Figure. *v.2 p.91*

The Exchange and Other Stories. *v.2 p.809, p.810*

Exchange Rates and International Finance Markets: An
Asset-Theoretic Perspective with Schumpeterian
Innovation. *v.4 p.258, p.264*

Exchange Rates, Capital Flows and Policy. . . .*v.4 p.257, p.263*

Exchange-Rate Veriability and Trade: Essays on the Impact of
Exchange-Rate Variability on Trade Policy and Trade
Flows. *v.4 p.257*

Excited States and Photochemistry of Organic
Molecules. *v.5 p.297*

Excursions in Modern Mathematics. *v.5 p.460*

Excursions in World Music. *v.1 p.283*

The Excursion. *v.2 p.237*

Executing the Constitution: Putting the President Back into the
Constitution. *v.4 p.527*

The Execution of Mayor Yin and Other Stories from the
Great Proletarian Cultural Revolution. *v.6 p.212*

Executioner's Song. *v.2 p.99*

Executive Governance: Presidental Administrations and Policy
Change in the Federal Bureaucracy. *v.4 p.527*

Executive Intelligence: What All Great Leaders Have. .*v.4 p.71*

Executive Privilege: A Constitutional Myth. *v.4 p.454*

The Exegetical Imagination: On Jewish Thought and
Theology. *v.1 p.551*

The Exemplary Middle School. *v.4 p.367*

The Exemplary Novels, Vol. 3. . . . .*v.2 p.648*

The Exemplary Novels, Vol. 4. . . . .*v.2 p.648*

The Exemplary Novels, Vol. I. *v.2 p.648*

Exercise Physiology: Energy, Nutrition, and Human
Performance. *v.4 p.875, v.5 p.519*

Exercise Physiology: People and Ideas. *v.4 p.810, p.874*

Exercise Physiology. *v.5 p.519*

Exercise Psychology. *v.4 p.876, p.877, v.5 p.581*

Exercises for Weather and Climate. *v.4 p.393*

Exercises in Number Theory. *v.5 p.477*

Exercises in Psychological Testing. *v.5 p.600*

Exercises in Synthetic Organic Chemistry. *v.5 p.301*

Exhumations in Panama: Breaking the Silence, Commission of
Defense the Human Rights in Central America. . .*v.3 p.304*

Exhumations. *v.2 p.356*

Exile and Cultural Hegemony: Spanish Intellectuals in Mexico,
1939 - 1975. . . . .*v.3 p.292*

The Exile: Cuba in the Heart of Miami. *v.6 p.542*

Exile on a Peppercorn: The Poetry of Mircea Dinescu. .*v.2 p.816*

Exile on Main Street: Rolling Stones. *v.1 p.273, p.351*

Exile, Ostracism and Democracy: The Politics of Expulsion in
Ancient Greece. *v.3 p.17*

Exile Within: The Schooling of Japanese
Americans. *v.6 p.108, p.134*

Exiled at Home: Comprising at the Edge of Psychology, the
Intimate Enemy and Creating a Nationality. *v.6 p.157*

Exiled in the Land of the Free: Democracy, Indian Nations and
the U. S. Constitution. *v.6 p.692*

Exiled Memories: A Cuban Childhood. . . .*v.3 p.311, v.6 p.489*

Exiles, Allies, Rebels: Brazil's Indianist Movement, Indigenist
Politics and the Imperial Nation-State. *v.3 p.343*

Exiles and Emigres: The Flight of European Artists from
Hitler. *v.1 p.677*

Exiles and Marriage. *v.2 p.82*

The Exiles and Other Stories. *v.2 p.687*

Exiles. *v.2 p.359*

The Exile. *v.6 p.200*

Existence and Utopia: The Social and Political Thought of
Martin Buber. *v.4 p.768*

The Existence of God. *v.1 p.523, p.595, p.640*

Existentialism: A Reconstruction. *v.1 p.505*

Existentialism and Humanism. *v.1 p.505*

Existentialism from Dostoevsky to Sartre. *v.1 p.505*

Existentialism. *v.1 p.506*

Existentialists. *v.1 p.505*

Exiting Iraq: Why the U. S. Must End the Military Occupation
and Renew the War Against Al Qaeda. *v.4 p.565*

Exits and Entrances. *v.2 p.755*

Exodus 1-18: A New Translation with Notes and
Comments. *v.1 p.621*

Exorcising History: Argentine Theater under
Dictatorship. *v.1 p.127*

The Exotic in Western Music. *v.1 p.247*

Exotics at Home: Anthropologies, Others, and American
Modernity. *v.4 p.34*

Expanding Discourse: Feminism and Art
History. *v.1 p.706, v.6 p.472*

Expanding Horizons in Bioethics. *v.5 p.247, p.248*

Expansion and American Indian Policy, 1783-1812. . .*v.6 p.686*

Expansion and Coexistence. *v.3 p.393*

The Expansion of Islam in the Middle Periods. . . .*v.1 p.555*

Expansionists of 1898: The Acquisition of Hawaii and the
Spanish Islands. *v.3 p.400, p.438*

Expansionists of Eighteen Twelve. *v.3 p.417*

Expansive Soils: Problems and Practice in Foundation and
Pavement Engineering. *v.5 p.422*

ExPASy Proteomics Server. *v.5 p.104, p.105*

▢ Expectations of Excellence: Curriculum Standards for Social Studies. *v.4 p.359, p.360*

Expected Utility, Fair Gambles and Rational Choice. *v.4 p.201*

The Expedient Utopian: Bandaranaike and Ceylon. . *v.6 p.163*

The Expedition of Humphry Clinker. *v.2 p.261*

The Expendable Future: U. S. Politics and the Protection of Biological Diversity. *v.5 p.181*

An Expenditure Tax. *v.4 p.248*

Experience and Education. *v.4 p.342, v.5 p.571*

Experience and Prediction: An Analysis of the Foundations and the Structure of Knowledge. *v.1 p.482*

The Experience Economy: Work Is Theatre and Every Business a Stage. *v.4 p.144*

Experience Marketing: Strategies for the New Millenium. *v.4 p.786, p.787, p.885*

The Experience of Buddhism: Sources and Interpretations. *v.1 p.562*

The Experience of Defeat: Milton and Some Contemporaries. *v.3 p.103*

Experiences of Depression: Theoretical, Clinical, and Research Perspectives. *v.5 p.659*

Experiencing Dewey: Insights for Today's Classroom. *v.4 p.341*

Experiencing Dominion: Culture, Identity and Power in the British Mediterranean. *v.3 p.194, p.195*

Experiencing Music Technology. *v.1 p.388*

Experiencing Music Video: Aesthetics and Cultural Context. *v.1 p.256*

Experiential Marketing: How to Get Customers to Sense, Feel, Think, Act and Relate to Your Company and Brand. *v.4 p.135*

Experiment Optimization in Chemistry and Chemical Engineering. *v.5 p.743*

The Experimental Arabic Novel: Postcolonial Literary Modernism in the Levant. *v.6 p.662*

Experimental Chemical Thermodynamics, v. 1: Combustion Calorimetry. *v.5 p.286*

Experimental Cognitive Psychology and Its Applications. *v.5 p.608*

The Experimental College. *v.4 p.290*

Experimental Economics: How We Can Build Better Financial Markets. *v.4 p.264, p.272*

Experimental Ethnography: The Work of Film in the Age of Video. *v.6 p.311*

The Experimental Impulse in George Meredith's Fiction. *v.2 p.300*

Experimental Methods in Psychology. *v.5 p.605*

Experimental Music: Cage and Beyond. *v.1 p.220*

Experimental Nuclear Physics, Vol. 1. . . . . . . *v.5 p.553*

Experimental Physical Chemistry. *v.5 p.287*

Experimental Physics: Modern Methods. *v.5 p.563*

The Experimental Psychology of Alfred Binet: Selected Papers. *v.5 p.574*

Experimental Researches in Electricity. *v.5 p.564*

Experimental Stress Analysis. *v.5 p.688*

Experimental Techniques in High-Pressure Research: W. F. Sherman and A. A. Stadmuller. *v.5 p.563*

Experimental Techniques in Low-Temperature Physics. *v.5 p.563*

Experimental Television, Test Films, Pilots and Trial Series, 1925 Through 1995: Seven Decades of Small Screen Almosts. *v.6 p.333*

Experimental Theatre: From Stanislavsky to Peter Brook. *v.1 p.80, p.83, p.85, p.87, p.137, p.138*

Experimental Thermochemistry: Measurement of Heats of Reaction, 2v. *v.5 p.286*

Experimentation in Mathematics: Computational Paths to Discovery. *v.5 p.457*

Experimenters, Rebels and Disparate Voices: The Theatre of the 1920s Celebrates American Diversity. . *v.1 p.82, p.84, p.114*

Experimenting with Nature Study. *v.5 p.223, p.224*

Experiments: Design and Analysis. *v.5 p.409*

Experiments in Consilience: Integrating Science and Social Process to Save Endangered Species. . . . *v.6 p.284*

Experiments in Family Planning: Lessons from the Developing World. *v.4 p.736*

Experiments in Modern Physics. *v.5 p.563*

Experiments in Physical Chemistry. *v.5 p.287*

Experiments in Polymer Science. *v.5 p.322, p.323*

Expert Political Judgment: How Good Is It? How Can We Know? *v.5 p.645*

Explaining Congressional-Presidential Relations: A Multiple Perspective Approach. *v.4 p.527*

Explaining Long-Term Economic Change. *v.3 p.38*

Explaining Music: Essays and Explorations. *v.1 p.382*

Explaining NATO Enlargement. *v.4 p.639*

Explaining the History of American Foreign Relations. *v.3 p.385*

An Explanation of the Birds: A Novel. *v.2 p.688*

Explanatory Supplement to the Astronomical Almanac. *v.5 p.66*

Explicit and Authentic Acts: Amending the U. S. Constitution, 1776-1995. . . . . *v.4 p.454*

Exploding Metropolis. *v.6 p.729*

Exploding Poetry: Baudelaire-Rimbaud. *v.2 p.461*

Exploration and Analysis of DNA Microarray and Protein Array Data. *v.5 p.120*

Exploration and Contestation in the Study of World Politics: A Special Issue of International Organization. *v.4 p.624, p.629*

The Exploration Diaries of H M Stanley, Now First Published from the Original Manuscripts. *v.6 p.52*

The Exploration of Northern Canada, 500 to 1920: A Chronology. *v.3 p.546*

The Exploration of the Colorado River and Its Canyons. *v.3 p.527*

Explorations in Connected History: Mughals and Franks. *v.6 p.156*

Explorations in Indian Philosophy: Indian Philosophy, Vol. 1. . . . . *v.1 p.419*

▢ Explorations in Learning & Instruction: The Theory Into Practice Database. *v.4 p.357*

Explorations in Political Psychology. *v.5 p.643*

Explorations in Quantum Computing. *v.5 p.552*

Explorations in the Ethnography of Speaking. . . . *v.4 p.18*

Explorations. *v.2 p.327*

The Explorer's Eye: First-Hand Accounts of Adventure and Exploration. *v.4 p.378*

The Explorers of North America, Fourteen Ninety-Two to Eighteen Hundred Six. *v.3 p.403, p.405*

Exploring an Islamic Empire: Fatimid History and Its
   Sources. *v.6 p.588*

Exploring Ancient Skies: An Encyclopedic of
   Archaeoastronomy. *v.5 p.63*

Exploring Cognitive Development: The Child As Problem
   Solver. *v.5 p.626, p.630*

Exploring Corrections in America. *v.6 p.272*

Exploring Drawing for Animation. *v.6 p.348*

Exploring Environments, Grades K-6. . . . .*v.5 p.229*

The Exploring Expedition to the Rocky Mountains. . .*v.3 p.520*

Exploring Genomes: Web-Based Bioinformatic
   Excercises. *v.5 p.99, p.143, p.147*

Exploring Lewis and Clark: Reflections on Men and
   Wilderness. *v.3 p.520*

Exploring Medical Anthropology. *v.5 p.536*

Exploring Mercury: The Iron Planet. . . .*v.5 p.69, p.434, p.435*

Exploring Nature in Winter. *v.5 p.227*

Exploring Package Design. *v.1 p.718*

Exploring Phenomenology: A Guide to the Field and Its
   Literature. *v.1 p.511*

Exploring Reality: The Intertwining of Science and
   Religion. *v.1 p.526, p.596*

Exploring Sport and Exercise
   Psychology. *v.4 p.878, p.904, v.5 p.583*

Exploring the Heritage of American Higher Education: The
   Evolution of Philosophiy and Policy. *v.4 p.330*

Exploring the Musical Mind: Cognition, Emotion, Ability,
   Function. *v.1 p.376, v.5 p.619*

Exploring the Number Jungle: A Journey into Diophantine
   Analysis. *v.5 p.475*

Exploring the Ocean: The Physical Ocean; Life in the Ocean;
   Uses of the Ocean; Index. *v.4 p.391*

Exploring the Religious Life. *v.1 p.525*

Exploring the United States with the Five Themes of
   Geography. *v.4 p.382*

Exploring the Urban Community: A GIS Approach. . .*v.6 p.723*

Exploring Twentieth-Century Music: Tradition and
   Innovation. *v.1 p.227*

Exploring Twentieth-Century Vocal Music: A Practical Guide to
   Innovations in Performance and Repertoire. . . .*v.1 p.395*

Exploring Visual Culture: Definitions, Concepts,
   Contexts. *v.1 p.704*

Exploring Water Resources: GIS Investigations for the Earth
   Sciences. *v.4 p.387*

Explosion in a Cathedral. *v.2 p.671*

The Explosive Child: A New Approach for Understanding and
   Parenting Easily Frustrated, Chronically Inflexible
   Children. *v.4 p.283, p.284*

The Explosive World of Tatyana N. Tolstaya's Fiction. .*v.2 p.804*

Exporters - Alcoholic Beverages Worldwide. *v.4 p.153*

☐ Export.gov. *v.4 p.60*

Exporting America: Why Corporate Greed Is Shipping American
   Jobs Overseas. *v.4 p.252, p.261*

Exposing Prejudice: Puerto Rican Experiences of Language,
   Race, and Class. *v.6 p.494, p.542*

Expositions and Developments. *v.1 p.225, p.360*

Exposure Assessment in Occupational and Environmental
   Epidemiology. *v.5 p.365*

Expounding the Doubtful Points. *v.6 p.104*

The Expression of the Emotions in Man and Animals. .*v.5 p.611*

Expressionism and Modernism in the American Theatre: Bodies,
   Voices, Words. *v.1 p.83, p.84, p.86, p.118, p.119*

The Expressionists. *v.1 p.678*

Expressive Politics: Issue Strategies of Congressional
   Challengers. *v.4 p.548*

Expulsion and the Nineteenth-Century Novel: The Scapegoat in
   English Realist Fiction. *v.2 p.191*

The Expulsion of the Jews from Spain. *v.3 p.58, p.238*

Exquisite Rebel: The Essays of Voltairine de Cleyre —
   Anarchist, Feminist, Genius. *v.4 p.500*

The Extant Remains. *v.2 p.409*

The Extended Phenotype: The Long Reach of the
   Gene. *v.5 p.143, p.145*

Extending the Supply Chain: How Cutting-Edge Companies
   Bridge the Critical Last Mile into Customers Homes. .*v.4 p.117*

Extension du domaine de la lutte : roman. *v.2 p.530*

Extinct Lands, Temporal Geographies: Chicana Literature and
   the Urgency of Space. *v.6 p.497, p.511*

Extinction: Bad Genes or Bad Luck?. *v.5 p.181*

Extinction Rates. *v.5 p.170*

Extracellular Regulators of Differentiation. *v.5 p.127*

Extradition, Politics and Human Rights. *v.4 p.473*

Extraordinary Child: Poems from a South Indian Devotional
   Genre. *v.6 p.152*

Extraordinary Furniture. *v.1 p.804*

Extraordinary Measures: Afrocentric Modernism and
   Twentieth-Century American Poetry. *v.6 p.28*

The Extraordinary Mr. Wilkes: His Life and
   Times. *v.3 p.94, p.109*

An Extraordinary Woman: Selected Writings of Germaine de
   Stael. *v.2 p.501*

Extreme Beauty: The Body Transformed. *v.1 p.715*

Extreme Exposure: An Anthology of Solo Performance Texts
   from the 20th Century. *v.2 p.24*

Extreme Science: Chasing the Ghost Bat: Extreme Science and
   Other Mysteries of Nature. *v.5 p.215, p.222*

Extreme Stars: At the Edge of Creation. *v.5 p.70*

Exuberance: The Passion for Life. *v.5 p.653*

The Eye in the Door. *v.2 p.330*

The Eye of Duncan Phillips: A Collection in the
   Making. *v.1 p.709*

The Eye of Heaven: Ptolemy, Copernicus,
   Kepler. *v.3 p.47, v.5 p.61*

The Eye of the Lynx: Galileo, His Friends, and the Beginnings
   of Modern Natural History. *v.5 p.396*

The Eye of the Storm: How John Chambers Steered Cisco
   Through the Technology Collapse. *v.4 p.157*

The Eye of the Storm. *v.2 p.750*

Eye to I: The Autobiography of a Photographer. . . .*v.1 p.765*

Eyeless in Gaza. *v.2 p.354*

The Eyes of Discovery: The Pageant of North America as Seen
   by the First Explorers. *v.3 p.403*

Eyes on the Prize: America's Civil Rights Years, 1954-1965. . . . .*v.6 p.12*

The Eyes on the Prize Civil Rights Reader: Documents, Speeches, and Firsthand Accounts from the Black Freedom Movement, 1954-1990. . . . . . .*v.6 p.12*

Eyes Toward Zion: Western Societies and the Holy Land. *v.6 p.610*

Eyeshot. *v.2 p.150*

Eyewitness: A Filmmaker's Memoir of the Chicano Movement. *v.6 p.541*

An Eye-Witness Account of the French Revolution by Helen Maria Williams: Letters Containing a Sketch of the Politics of France. *v.2 p.264*

Eyewitness Accounts of the Thirty Years War 1618-48. .*v.3 p.166*

Eyewitness Auschwitz: Three Years in the Gas Chambers. *v.3 p.85*

Eyewitness Memory. *v.5 p.610*

Eyewitness Testimony. *v.4 p.473*

Eyewitness to a Genocide: The United Nations and Rwanda. *v.4 p.632, p.651*

Eyewitness to America: 500 Years of American History in the Words of Those Who Saw It Happen. *v.3 p.371, p.372*

Ezekiel 1-20. . . . .*v.1 p.622*

Ezekiel 21-37: A New Translation. *v.1 p.622*

Ezra and Nehemiah. *v.1 p.621*

Ezra Pound: A Literary Life. *v.2 p.112*

Ezra Pound and China. *v.2 p.112*

Ezra Pound and Confucianism: Remaking Humanism in the Face of Modernity. *v.2 p.111*

Ezra Pound As Critic. *v.2 p.112*

The Ezra Pound Encyclopedia. *v.2 p.112*

Ezra Pound: Poems and Translations. *v.2 p.112*

Ezra Pound: The Last Rower: A Political Profile. . .*v.2 p.111*

Ezra Pound: Voice of Silence. *v.2 p.112*

Ezra Pound's Cantos: A Casebook. *v.2 p.112*

Ezra Pound. *v.2 p.111*

F

F. A. Hayek As a Political Economist: Economic Analysis and Values. *v.4 p.243*

F. D. R.: Into the Storm, 1937-1940. . . . . . .*v.3 p.440, p.457*

F. D. R.: The New Deal Years, 1933-1937. . . . . .*v.3 p.457*

F. D. R.: The New York Years, 1928-1933. . . . . .*v.3 p.457*

F. Holland Day: Selected Texts and Bibliography. . . .*v.1 p.766*

À la lumière d'hiver : précédé de Leçons et de Chants d'en bas. *v.2 p.531*

F. O. B. and Other Plays. *v.6 p.99*

F. P. Ramsey: Philosophical Papers. *v.1 p.446*

F. R. Leavis: Essays and Documents. *v.2 p.164*

F. Scott Fitzgerald A to Z: The Essential Reference to His Life and Work. *v.2 p.77*

F. Scott Fitzgerald: Critical Assessments, Set. *v.2 p.76*

An F. Scott Fitzgerald Encyclopedia. *v.2 p.77*

F. Scott Fitzgerald in the 21st Century. *v.2 p.76*

F. Scott Fitzgerald: New Perspectives. *v.2 p.76*

F. Scott Fitzgerald: Novels and Other Stories 1920-1922. .*v.2 p.76*

F. Scott Fitzgerald. *v.2 p.76, p.77*

F. Y. Edgeworth: Writings in Probability, Statistics and Economics, Set. *v.4 p.203*

The Faber Book of Pop. *v.1 p.271*

The Fable of the Bees and Other Writings. *v.1 p.484*

Fables of Aggression: Wyndham Lewis, the Modernist As Fascist. *v.2 p.367*

Fables of Identity: Studies in Poetic Mythology. .*v.2 p.180, p.181*

Fables of la Fontaine. *v.2 p.473, p.474*

The Fables of Marie de France: An English Translation. .*v.2 p.467*

Fables of Subversion: Satire and the American Novel. .*v.2 p.16*

Fables of the East: Selected Tales 1662-1785. . . . .*v.2 p.196*

Fables. *v.2 p.808*

Fabric of Freedom, 1763-1800. . . . .*v.3 p.410*

The Fabric of the Cosmos: Space, Time, and the Texture of Reality. *v.5 p.557*

Fabricating Israeli History: The "New Historians". . .*v.6 p.614*

Fabricating the Keynesian Revolution: Studies of the Inter-War Literature on Money, the Cycle and Unemployment. *v.4 p.225, p.238*

Fabrics and Wallpapers for Historic Buildings. . . .*v.1 p.824*

The Fabulous Sylvester: The Legend, the Music, the 70s in San Francisco. *v.6 p.409*

Fabulous voyager: James Joyce's Ulysses. *v.2 p.359*

The Face Behind the Face. *v.2 p.810*

A Face Beside the Fire: Memories of Dawn Grey Owl-Richardson. *v.5 p.230*

Face of an Angel. *v.6 p.498*

The Face of Battle. *v.3 p.36, v.6 p.567*

The Face of Nature: Wit, Narrative, and Cosmic Origins in Ovid's Metamorphoses. *v.2 p.439*

The Face of New Testament Studies: A Survey of Recent Research. *v.1 p.625, p.626*

The Face of Our Past: Images of Black Women from Colonial America to the Present. *v.6 p.11, p.47*

Face to Face: Gay and Lesbian Clergy on Holiness and Life Together. *v.1 p.650*

Face Zion Forward: First Writers of the Black Atlantic, 1785-1798. . . . .*v.6 p.23*

Faceless Men: And Other Macedonian Stories. *v.2 p.787*

Faces in the Water. *v.2 p.745*

The Faces of Honor: Sex, Shame, and Violence in Colonial Latin America. *v.3 p.263, p.283*

The Faces of Janus: Marxism and Fascism in the Twentieth Century. *v.4 p.510*

Faces of Jesus: Latin American Christologies. *v.1 p.641*

Faces of Lebanon: Sects, Wars and Global Expansion. .*v.6 p.604*

Faces of Power: Alexander's Image and Hellenistic Politics. *v.3 p.20*

The Faces of Power: Constancy and Change in United States Foreign Policy from Truman to Reagan. *v.3 p.451*

The Faces of Power: United States Foreign Policy from Truman to Clinton. *v.3 p.451*

Fachwörterbuch, Chemie und Chemische Technik: Deutsch-Englisch, mit etwa 62 000 Wortstellen=Technical Dictionary of Chemistry and Chemical Technology; German English: with About : 62,000 Entries. . . .*v.5 p.316*

Facilitating the Development and Use of Interactive Learning Environments. *v.5 p.589*

Facilities Management and the Business of Space. . . .*v.4 p.113*

Facilities Management Handbook. *v.4 p.113*

Facilities Management. *v.4 p.112, p.113*

Facing East from Indian Country: A Native History of Early America. *v.6 p.686*

Facing Japan: Chinese Politics and Japanese Imperialism, 1931-1937. . . . .*v.6 p.193*

Facing Mount Kenya. *v.6 p.65*

Facing Shadows. *v.6 p.103*

Facing the Holocaust: Selected Israeli Fiction. *v.6 p.651*

Facing the Mirror: Lesbian Writing from India. *v.2 p.763*

Facing the Ocean: The Atlantic and Its Peoples 8000 BC-AD 1500. . . . .*v.4 p.12*

Facing the Unexpected: Disaster Preparedness and Response in the United States. *v.5 p.423*

Facing West: The Metaphysics of Indian-Hating and Empire-Building. *v.6 p.682*

☐ FACT (Facility for the Analysis of Chemical Thermodynamics). *v.5 p.280*

Fact, Fiction, and Forecast. *v.1 p.493*

The Fact of a Doorframe: selected poems, 1950-2001. *v.2 p.115*

The Fact of a Doorframe: Selected Poems, 1950-2001.*v.6 p.405*

A Factious People: Politics and Society in Colonial New York. *v.3 p.405*

Factor Analysis in Chemistry. *v.5 p.280*

Factories in the Field: The Story of Migratory Farm Labor in California. *v.5 p.5, p.30*

Factorization and Primality Testing. *v.5 p.475*

Factors of Soil Formation: A System of Quantitative Pedology. *v.5 p.49, p.52,v.6 p.293*

Factory and Community in Stalin's Russia: The Making of an Industrial Working Class. *v.3 p.226*

Factory Physics. *v.4 p.119*

Facts about the Presidents. *v.3 p.378*

Facts About the World's Languages: An Encyclopedia of the World's Major Languages, Past and Present. *v.2 p.549, p.550, p.560*

Facts and Mysteries in Elementary Particle Physics. . *v.5 p.553*

The Facts of Life: The Creation of Sexual Knowledge in Britain, 1650-1950. . . . .*v.3 p.55*

The Facts on File Atlas of American Military History. *v.3 p.383, p.384*

The Facts on File Biology Handbook. *v.5 p.95*

The Facts on File Dictionary of American Politics. . .*v.4 p.516*

The Facts on File Dictionary of Astronomy. . . .*v.5 p.62, p.63*

The Facts on File Dictionary of Biochemistry. *v.5 p.112*

The Facts on File Dictionary of Biology. *v.5 p.225*

The Facts on File Dictionary of Biotechnology and Genetic Engineering. *v.5 p.96, p.220*

The Facts on File Dictionary of Cell and Molecular Biology. *v.5 p.154*

Facts on File Dictionary of Chemistry. *v.6 p.285*

The Facts on File Dictionary of Earth Science. *v.6 p.285*

The Facts on File Dictionary of Environmental Science.*v.5 p.707*

Facts on File Dictionary of Human Geography. *v.4 p.396*

Facts on File Encyclopedia of Art, Set. *v.1 p.664*

The Facts on File Encyclopedia of Science, Set. *v.5 p.387*

The Facts on File Encyclopedia of Science, Technology and Society, Set. *v.5 p.388*

The Facts on File Encyclopedia of World Mythology and Legend. *v.1 p.527*

The Facts on File Marine Science Handbook. . .*v.5 p.428, p.429*

Faded Mosaic: The Emergence of Post-Cultural America. *v.4 p.764*

Fading Footsteps of the Issei: An Annotated Checklist of the Manuscript Holdings of the Japanese. *v.6 p.87, p.132*

Fado Alexandrino. *v.2 p.688*

Fads and Foibles in Modern Sociology and Related Sciences. *v.4 p.683*

The Faerie Queene; a Companion for Readers. *v.2 p.214*

The Faerie Queene. *v.2 p.216*

Faggots. *v.6 p.397*

Fagin's Children: Criminal Children in Victorian England. *v.6 p.744*

El Águila y la Serpiente. *v.2 p.668*

Fahrenheit 451. . . . .*v.2 p.63*

Fail Safe. *v.2 p.59*

Failed Crusade: America and the Tragedy of Post-Communist Russia. *v.3 p.387*

The Failed Promise of the American High School, 1890-1995. . . . .*v.4 p.324*

Failing at Fairness: How America's Schools Cheat Girls. *v.4 p.302*

Failing the Future: A Dean Looks at Higher Education in the 21st Century. *v.4 p.331*

Failure of Empire: Valens and the Roman State in the Fourth Century A.D. *v.3 p.31*

The Failure of Multi-Culturalism in One Country: Literature and Literary Politics in the Rise and Fall of Yugoslavia. *v.2 p.819*

The Failure of the Founding Fathers: Jefferson, Marshall, and the Rise of Presidential Democracy. *v.4 p.522, p.523, p.535*

Fair and Tender Ladies. *v.2 p.155*

Fair and Varied Forms: Visual Textuality in Medieval Illuminated Manuscripts. *v.6 p.556*

Fair Greece, Sad Relic. *v.2 p.165*

The Fair Maid of Perth. *v.2 p.308*

Fair Play: The Ethics of Sport. *v.4 p.803*

Fair Representation: Meeting the Ideal of One Man, One Vote. *v.5 p.503*

Fair, Square and Legal: Safe Hiring, Managing, and Firing Practices to Keep You and Your Company Out of Court. *v.4 p.447*

Fair Trade for All: How Trade Can Promote Development. *v.4 p.53, p.56, p.665*

Fair Trial Rights of the Accused: A Documentary History. *v.6 p.271*

Fair Trial: Rights of the Accused in American History. *v.6 p.271*

The Fair Voice: A Study of Indian Women Poets in English. *v.2 p.761, p.762*

Fairfield Porter: A Catalogue Raisonné of the Paintings, Watercolors, and Pastels. *v.1 p.743*

Fairfield Porter: A Life in Art. *v.1 p.747*

A Fairly Honourable Defeat. *v.2 p.372*

⬜ FairTest. *v.4 p.286*

The Fairy Queen. *v.2 p.216*

Fairy Tales: Traditional Stories Retold for Gay Men. .*v.6 p.406*

The Faith and Fiction of Muriel Spark. *v.2 p.384*

Faith and Freedom: Women's Human Rights in the Middle
   East. *v.6 p.591*

Faith and Health: Psychological Perspectives. *v.5 p.635*

Faith and Knowledge. *v.1 p.523*

Faith and Meaning in the Southern Uplands. . .*v.3 p.497, p.498*

Faith and Rationality: Reason and Belief in God. . . .*v.1 p.523*

Faith and Understanding. *v.1 p.632*

Faith and Violence: Christian Teaching and Christian
   Practice. *v.1 p.643*

Faith in Nation: Exclusionary Origins of Nationalism. .*v.4 p.494*

Faith in the Byzantine World. *v.1 p.569*

The Faith of George W. Bush. *v.3 p.483*

The Faith of the Christian Church. *v.1 p.634*

Faith on Earth: An Inquiry into the Structure of Human
   Faith. *v.1 p.644*

Faith, Science and Understanding. *v.1 p.596*

Faith: Stories: Short Fiction on the Varieties and Vagaries of
   Faith. *v.2 p.583*

Faithful and Fearless: Moving Feminist Protest Inside the
   Church and Military. *v.4 p.745, p.746,v.6 p.431*

Faithful Generations: Race and New Asian American
   Churches. *v.6 p.105*

The Faithful River. *v.2 p.792, v.3 p.253*

The Faithful Shepherd: A History of the New England Ministry
   in the Seventeenth Century, with a New
   Introduction. *v.1 p.584*

The Faithful Shepherd: A Translation of Battista Guarini's Il
   Pastor Fido. *v.2 p.709*

Falange: A History of Spanish Fascism. *v.3 p.241*

Falconer. *v.2 p.67, v.6 p.395*

Fall: A Comparative Study of the End of Communism in
   Czechoslovakia, East Germany, Hungary and
   Poland. *v.3 p.208, v.4 p.509, p.596, p.600*

The Fall and Recovery of the Cuban Economy in the 1990s:
   Mirage or Reality?. *v.3 p.310*

Fall and Rise of the Irish Nation: The Catholic
   Question,1690-1830. . . . .*v.3 p.134, p.137*

The Fall and Rise of the Stately Home. *v.6 p.744*

The Fall of Berlin 1945. . . . .*v.3 p.174*

The Fall of Constantinople 1453. . . . . .*v.3 p.193, v.6 p.581*

The Fall of France: The Nazi Invasion of 1940. . .*v.3 p.156*

The Fall of Hong Kong: Britain, China, and the Japanese
   Occupation. *v.6 p.206*

The Fall of New France: How the French Lost a North
   American Empire. *v.3 p.537, p.538*

The Fall of Rome: And the End of Civilization. . . .*v.3 p.32*

The Fall of the Athenian Empire. *v.3 p.18*

The Fall of the Bell System: A Study in Prices and
   Politics. *v.4 p.421*

The Fall of the House of Habsburg. *v.3 p.184*

The Fall of the Ivory Tower: Government Funding, Corruption
   and the Bankrupting of Higher Education. *v.4 p.525*

The Fall of the Roman Empire: A New History of Rome and the
   Barbarians. *v.3 p.31*

The Fall of the Romanovs: Political Dreams and Personal
   Struggles in a Time of Revolution. *v.3 p.220, p.221*

The Fall of the Royal Government in Peru. *v.3 p.273*

Fallen Blue Knights: Controlling Police Corruption. .*v.6 p.260*

Fallen Is Babylon: The Revelation to John. *v.1 p.632*

Fallen Soldiers: Reshaping the Memory of the World
   Wars. *v.5 p.584*

Falling from Grace: Downward Mobility in the Age of
   Affluence. *v.4 p.725*

Falling in Old Age: Prevention and Management. . .*v.5 p.519*

The Falling Sickness: A History of Epilepsy from the Greeks to
   the Beginnings of Modern Neurology. *v.5 p.516*

Falling Terrorism and Rising Conflicts: The Afghan Contribution
   to Polarization and Confrontation in West and South
   Asia. *v.4 p.661*

Fallingwater Rising: Frank Lloyd Wright, E. J. Kaufmann, and
   America's Most Extraordinary House. *v.1 p.795*

The Falls: A Novel. *v.2 p.152*

Der falsche Nero: Roman. *v.2 p.607*

False Alarm: The Truth about the Epidemic of Fear. .*v.4 p.694*

The False Dawn. *v.3 p.76*

False Mystics: Deviant Orthodoxy in Colonial Mexico.*v.3 p.286*

False Promises: The Shaping of American Working Class
   Consciousness. *v.4 p.726*

Falsettos: In Trousers, Falsettoland and March of the
   Falsettos. *v.1 p.249, p.407*

Álvar Núñez Cabeza de Vaca; The Journey and Route of the
   First European to Cross the Continent of North America,
   1534-1536. . . . .*v.3 p.403*

Famed for Dance. *v.1 p.22*

La Familia: Chicano Families in the Urban Southwest, 1848 to
   the Present. *v.3 p.527, v.6 p.531, p.545*

La Familia de Pascual Duarte. *v.2 p.657*

Familia: Migration and Adaptation in Baja and Alta California,
   1880-1975. . . . .*v.6 p.528, p.545*

Familiar Faces, Hidden Lives: The Story of Homosexual Men in
   America Today. *v.6 p.365*

Familiar Spirits: A Memoir of James Merrill and David
   Jackson. *v.6 p.402*

Families Against the City: Middle Class Homes of Industrial
   Chicago, 1872-1890. . . . .*v.4 p.734*

⬜ Families and Work Institute. *v.5 p.580*

Families in Classical and Hellenistic Greece: Representations
   and Realities. *v.3 p.14*

Families Like Mine: Children of Gay Parents Tell It Like It
   Is. *v.4 p.740, v.6 p.376*

Families of a New World: Gender, Politics, and State
   Development In a Global Context. *v.3 p.260*

Families, Violence and Social Change. *v.6 p.259*

Families We Choose: Lesbians, Gays,
   Kinship. *v.4 p.33, p.740,v.6 p.375*

Family Album: Three Novellas. *v.2 p.674*

A Family and a Fortune. *v.2 p.339*

Family and Community: Italian Immigrants in Buffalo, 1880-1930. . . . .*v.3 p.491*

Family and Fortune: Studies in Aristocratic Finance in the Sixteenth and Seventeenth Centuries. *v.3 p.131*

Family and Frontier in Colonial Brazil: Santana de Parnaiba, 1580-1822. . . . .*v.3 p.335*

Family and Kinship: A Study of the Pandits of Rural Kashmir. *v.6 p.154*

Family and Kinship in East London. *v.4 p.37, p.38*

Family and Kinship in England, 1450-1800. . . . .*v.4 p.708*

Family Bonds: Adoption, Infertility, and the New World of Child Production. *v.4 p.737*

Family Business: Two Lives in Letters and Poetry. . . *v.2 p.79*

Family Constellation: Its Effects on Personality and Social Behavior. *v.5 p.629, p.631*

Family, Dependence, and the Origins of the Welfare State: Britain and France, 1914-1945. . . . .*v.3 p.54*

Family Diversity and Well-Being. *v.4 p.731*

The Family Estate in Africa: Studies in the Role of Property in Family Structure and Lineage Continuity. *v.4 p.32*

Family Fortunes: Men and Women of the English Middle Class, 1780-1850. . . . .*v.3 p.111, p.130, v.6 p.743, p.765*

Family, Friends and Followers: Political and Social Bonds in Early Medieval Europe. *v.4 p.501*

The Family Herds: A Study of Two Pastoral Tribes in East Africa: The Jie and Turkana. *v.4 p.38*

Family History in the Middle East: Household, Property, and Gender. *v.6 p.592*

Family Identity and the State in the Bamako Kafu, c. 1800-c.1900. . . . .*v.4 p.705*

The Family in America: An Encyclopedia, Set. *v.5 p.638*

The Family in Bahia, Brazil, 1870-1945. . . . . . .*v.3 p.338*

The Family in Greek History. *v.3 p.14*

The Family in the American Economy. *v.4 p.265*

Family Involvement in Treating Schizophrenia: Models, Essential Skills, and Process. *v.5 p.661*

The Family Letters of Christina Georgina Rossetti. . .*v.2 p.304*

Family Life and Illicit Love in Earlier Generations: Essays in Historical Sociology. *v.4 p.737*

Family Life and School Achievement: Why Poor Black Children Succeed or Fail. *v.4 p.309, p.310*

📧 Family Life in a Northern Thai Village: A Study in the Structural Significance of Women. *v.4 p.40*

Family, Love and Work in the Lives of Victorian Gentlewomen. *v.6 p.744, p.748, p.762, p.765*

A Family Madness. *v.2 p.746*

Family Man: Fatherhood, Housework, and Gender Equity. *v.4 p.745*

Family Matters: Secrecy and Disclosure in the History of Adoption. *v.4 p.737*

Family Memories: An Autobiographical Journey. . . .*v.2 p.389*

Family Nursing: Research, Theory, and Practice. .*v.5 p.525, p.529*

The Family of Pascual Duarte. *v.2 p.657*

Family Problem Solving. *v.4 p.758*

Family Psychology: The Art of the Science. *v.5 p.639*

The Family Romance of the French Revolution. . . .*v.3 p.150*

The Family Secret: Domestic Violence in America. . .*v.4 p.743*

Family Secrets: William Butler Yeats and His Relatives. *v.2 p.326, p.327*

Family, Sex and Marriage in England, Fifteen Hundred to Eighteen Hundred. *v.4 p.734*

The Family, Sex and Marriage. *v.3 p.92, p.124*

Family Socialization and Interaction Process. *v.4 p.738*

Family Therapy: Concepts and Methods. *v.5 p.668*

Family Therapy Techniques. *v.5 p.668*

Family Therapy: Theory and Practice. *v.5 p.668*

Family Tightrope: The Changing Lives of Vietnamese Americans. *v.6 p.140*

Family Values and the New Society: Dilemmas of the 21st Century. *v.4 p.738*

Family Violence Across the Lifespan: An Introduction. .*v.6 p.259*

Family Violence and Police Response: Learning from Research, Policy and Practice in European Countries. .*v.6 p.259, p.265*

The Family. *v.6 p.212*

Famine, Disease and the Social Order in Early Modern Society. *v.3 p.43*

Famine in Zimbabwe, 1890-1960. . . . .*v.6 p.77*

Famine, Land and Politics: British Government and Irish Society, 1843-1850. . . . .*v.3 p.138*

The Famished Road. *v.2 p.756, p.757*

Famous in My Time, 1810-1812, Vol. 2. . . . . . .*v.2 p.274*

Famous Italian Opera Arias: A Dual-Language Book. *v.1 p.394, p.411*

▢ Famous Trials. *v.4 p.438*

Famous Women. *v.2 p.701*

The Fan of Swords. *v.6 p.656*

Fanny and Anna Parnell: Ireland's Patriot Sisters. . .*v.3 p.138*

Fanny Burney. *v.2 p.242*

Fanny Cerrito: The Life of a Romantic Ballerina. . . .*v.1 p.8*

Fanny Elssler. *v.1 p.8*

Fanny Hill: Or Memoirs of a Woman of Pleasure. . . .*v.2 p.243*

Fanny Mendelssohn. *v.1 p.205, p.331*

Fans: From the 18th to the Beginning of the 20th Century. *v.1 p.807*

Fanshen: A Documentary of Revolution in a Chinese Village. *v.6 p.192*

Fantabulosa: The Dictionary of Polari and Gay Slang. .*v.6 p.358*

Fantasia. *v.2 p.544*

Fantastic Tales: Visionary and Everyday. *v.2 p.714*

The Fantasticks. *v.1 p.253, p.409*

Fantasy and Feeling in Education. *v.4 p.357*

Fantasy and Horror: A Critical and Historical Guide to Literature, Illustration, Film, T.V., Radio and the Internet. *v.2 p.580, p.581*

Fantasy City: Pleasure and Profit in the Postmodern Metropolis. *v.6 p.712*

Fantasy Femmes of Sixties Cinema: Interviews with 20 Actresses from Biker, Beach, and Elvis Movies. . .*v.6 p.332*

Fantasy Pieces: Metrical Dissonance in the Music of Robert Schumann. *v.1 p.200, p.354, p.355*

FAO Statistical Yearbook, Vol. 1. . . . .*v.4 p.151, p.164*

FAO/Unesco: Soil Map of the World: Revised Legend. .*v.5 p.48*

Far and Wide: Cultural Diversity in American Boarding Schools. *v.4 p.296*

A Far Cry from Kensington. *v.2 p.383*

Far from Denmark. *v.1 p.10*

Far from the Madding Crowd. *v.2 p.291*

The Far Southwest, 1846-1912: A Territorial History. *v.3 p.527*

Far Tortuga: A Novel. *v.2 p.149*

Far Valley: Four Years in Japanese Village. *v.4 p.39, p.40*

Far Western Frontier, 1830-1860. . . . .*v.3 p.518*

ÁRaza Sí! ÁGuerra No!: Chicano Protest and Patriotism during the Viet Nam War Era. *v.6 p.539, p.541*

Farce: A History from Aristophanes to Woody Allen. . .*v.1 p.89*

La Farce de maître. *v.2 p.469*

Farce. *v.1 p.90*

Farewell Espana: The World of the Sephardim Remembered. *v.6 p.598*

Farewell, My Nation: The American Indian and the United States in the Nineteenth Century. *v.3 p.402, v.6 p.687*

Farewell, Revolution: Disputed Legacies, France, 1789 - 1989. . . . .*v.3 p.150*

Farewell, Revolution: The Historian's Feud, France, 1789-1989. . . . .*v.3 p.150*

The Farewell Symphony. *v.6 p.400*

Farewell to an Idea: Episodes from a History of Modernism. *v.1 p.702*

A Farewell to Arms. *v.2 p.84*

Farewell to Manzanar. *v.6 p.93, p.134*

Farewell to Matyora: A Novel. *v.2 p.807*

Farewell to the Bloody Shirt: Northern Republicans and the Southern Negro 1877. . . . .*v.3 p.436, p.437*

Farewell to the Sea: A Novel of Cuba. *v.2 p.670*

Farewells to Plasma. *v.2 p.790*

Farm to Factory: A Reinterpretation of the Soviet Industrial Revolution. *v.4 p.267, v.5 p.3*

Farmers' and Farm Workers' Movements. *v.5 p.5, p.30*

Farmers' Bounty: Locating Crop Diversity in the Contemporary World. *v.5 p.20*

Farmers, Cooperatives, and USDA: A History of Agricultural Cooperative Service. *v.5 p.5*

Farmers' Frontier, 1865-1900. . . . .*v.3 p.396*

Farmers, Kings, and Traders: The People of Southern Africa, 200-1860. . . . .*v.6 p.74*

Farmers of Forty Centuries or Permanent Agriculture in China, Korea and Japan. *v.5 p.5, v.6 p.198, p.295*

Farmers of Forty Centuries: Permanent Agriculture in China, Korea and Japan. *v.6 p.181*

Farming the Home Place: A Japanese American Community in California, 1919-1982. . . . .*v.6 p.132*

Faroe: The Emergence of a Nation. *v.3 p.234*

☐ FASB: Financial Accounting Standards Board. *v.4 p.104, p.105*

Fascinating Rhythm: The Collaboration of George and Ira Gershwin. *v.1 p.253, p.325, p.326*

Fascism in Popular Memory: The Cultural Experience of the Turin Working Class. *v.3 p.203*

Fascism in Spain, 1923-1977. . . . .*v.3 p.241, p.242*

Fascism: Past, Present, Future. *v.4 p.510*

Fascist Modernities: Italy, 1922-1945. . . . .*v.3 p.202*

The Fascist Revolution: Toward a General Theory of Fascism. *v.4 p.510*

Fashioning Sapphism: The Origins of a Modern English Lesbian Culture. *v.6 p.392*

Fashioning the Female Subject: The Intertextual Networking of Dickinson, Moore, and Rich. *v.2 p.37*

Fashioning the More Ethical Representative: The Impact of Ethics Reforms in the U. S. House of Representatives. *v.4 p.533*

Fashion. *v.1 p.715*

The Fashoda Incident of 1898: An Encounter on the Nile. .*v.3 p.76*

Fassbinder: The Life and Work of a Provocative Genius. .*v.6 p.418*

Fast Cars, Clean Bodies: Decolonization and the Reordering of French Culture. *v.3 p.157*

Fast Food, Fast Track: Immigrants, Big Business, and the American Dream. *v.6 p.107, p.117, p.126*

Fast Food Nation: The Dark Side of the All American Meal. *v.5 p.35*

The Fast Forward MBA in Business Math. *v.4 p.175*

Fasti. *v.2 p.439*

Fast-Talking Dames. *v.6 p.312, p.328, p.341*

The Fatal Eggs. *v.2 p.801*

The Fatal Environment: The Myth of the Frontier in the Age of Industrialization, 1800-1890. . . . .*v.3 p.381*

Fatal Glory: Narciso López and the First Clandestine U. S. War Against Cuba. *v.3 p.307*

The Fatal Knot: The Guerrilla War in Navarre and the Defeat of Napoleon in Spain. *v.3 p.75, p.241*

The Fate of America: An Inquiry into National Character. *v.3 p.367*

The Fate of Carmen. *v.2 p.497, p.498*

Fate of Organic Chemicals in the Aquatic Environment. *v.5 p.10, p.379*

The Fate of Reason: German Philosophy from Kant to Fichte. *v.3 p.167*

The Fate of the Earth and the Abolition. *v.4 p.656, p.657*

The Fate of the Forest: Developers, Destroyers and Defenders of the Amazon. *v.3 p.269*

The Fate of the Mammoth: Fossils, Myth, and History. .*v.3 p.44*

Fate of the Rain Forest, Classroom Set. *v.3 p.268*

Fateful Decisions: Inside the National Security Council. .*v.4 p.562*

Fateful Harvest: The True Story of a Small Town, a Global Industry, and a Toxic Secret. *v.5 p.353, p.355, p.375, p.377*

A Fateful Time: Background and Legislation of the Indian Reorganization Act. *v.6 p.692*

Fateful Triangle: The United States, Israel, and the Palestinians. *v.3 p.387, v.6 p.617*

Fateless. *v.2 p.786*

Father and Son. *v.6 p.758, p.765*

Father Brown: The Essential Tales. *v.2 p.277, p.278*

The Father of Frankenstein. *v.6 p.394, p.395*

The Father of Spin: Edward L. Bernays and the Birth of Public Relations. *v.4 p.429*

Father of the Blues: An Autobiography. *v.1 p.260, p.329, v.6 p.17, p.25, p.26, p.29, p.30*

Father-Daughter Incest. *v.4 p.737*

Fathers and Sons. *v.2 p.810*

Fathers Work for Their Sons: Accumulation, Mobility, and Class
    Formation in an Extended Yorùbá Community. . . .*v.6 p.71*

The Fathers. *v.2 p.125*

Fathoming the Ocean: The Discovery and Exploration of the
    Deep Sea. *v.5 p.429*

Fatigue Data Book: Light Structural Alloys. *v.5 p.697*

Fatigue Failure of Metals. *v.5 p.689*

The Fatimids and Their Traditions of Learning. . . .*v.6 p.636*

Fatma: A Novel of Arabia. *v.6 p.657*

Fats Waller: The Cheerful Little Earful. *v.1 p.263, p.367*

Faubus: The Life and Times of an American Prodigal. *v.3 p.511*

Faulkner: A Biography, Vol. 1. . . . .*v.2 p.73*

Faulkner and Modernism: Revision and Rewriting. *v.2 p.74, p.75*

Faulkner and the Discourses of Culture. *v.2 p.74*

Faulkner's Heroic Design: The Yoknapatawpha Novels. *v.2 p.74*

Fault Lines: A Memoir. *v.6 p.92*

Fault Lines of Democracy in Post-Transition Latin
    America. *v.3 p.273, v.4 p.591*

Fauré and French Musical Aesthetics. . *v.1 p.195, p.210, p.324*

Faust: Parts One and Two. *v.1 p.62, p.78, p.79, p.108*

The Faustian Bargain: The Art World in Nazi Germany. *v.3 p.173*

A Faustian Bargain: U.S. Intervention in the Nicaraguan
    Elections and American Foreign Policy in the Post-Cold War
    Era. *v.3 p.303*

Faust's Metropolis: A History of Berlin. *v.3 p.181*

Fauvism. *v.1 p.729*

Favored Strangers: Gertrude Stein and Her
    Family. *v.2 p.122, v.6 p.404*

The Favorite Uncle Remus. *v.2 p.40*

Fay Jones. *v.1 p.793*

The FBI and American Democracy: A Brief Critical
    History. *v.6 p.261*

FDI and Industrial Organization in Developing Countries: The
    Challenge of Globalization in India. *v.4 p.60*

FDR: The Beckoning of Destiny, 1882-1928: A History. *v.3 p.457*

FDR: The War President, 1940-1943: A History. . . *v.3 p.457*

The FDR Years: On Roosevelt and His
    Legacy. *v.3 p.442, p.448, p.474*

Fear and Memory in the Brazilian Army and Society,
    1889-1954. . . . .*v.3 p.277, p.342*

Fear and Temptation: The Image of the Indigene in Canadian,
    Australian and New Zealand Literatures. . *v.2 p.729, p.740*

Fear and Trembling: Repetition. *v.1 p.478*

Fear and Trembling. *v.1 p.594, p.595, v.6 p.672, p.673*

Fear at the Edge: State Terror and Resistance in Latin
    America. *v.4 p.515*

Fear Itself: Enemies Real and Imagined in American
    Culture. *v.3 p.370*

Fear of Crime among Inner-City African Americans. . *v.6 p.258*

Fear of Intimacy. *v.5 p.652*

Fear of Judging: Sentencing Guidelines in the Federal
    Courts. *v.6 p.272*

Fear: The History of a Political Idea. . . . *v.4 p.484, v.5 p.644*

A Fearful Freedom: Women's Flight from Equality. . *v.4 p.458*

Fearful Symmetry: A Study of William Blake. *v.2 p.239*

Fearful Symmetry: India-Pakistan Crises in the Shadow of
    Nuclear Weapons. *v.6 p.159*

Fearless Women in the Mexican Revolution and the Spanish
    Civil War. *v.3 p.294*

A Feast in the Mirror: Stories by Contemporary Iranian
    Women. *v.6 p.671*

A Feast of Creatures: Anglo-Saxon Riddle Songs. . . *v.2 p.204*

The Feast of the Goat: A Novel. *v.2 p.686*

Feasts and Riot: Revelry, Rebellion, and Popular Consciousness
    on the Swahili Coast. *v.6 p.63*

Feasts of Fear and Agony. *v.2 p.623*

A Feather on the Breath of God: A Novel. *v.6 p.101*

The Feathered Onion: Creation of Life in the Universe. *v.5 p.243*

Feathers from the Green Crow, Sean O'Casey 1905:
    1925. . . . .*v.2 p.374*

The Feature Film Distribution Deal: A Critical Analysis of the
    Single Most Important Film Industry Agreement. . *v.6 p.345*

Feature Films, 1950-1959: A United States
    Filmography. *v.6 p.341*

Fed Up: Women and Food in America. . . *v.4 p.778, v.6 p.446*

Éden, Éden, Éden. *v.2 p.530*

The Federal Budget in Brief, July 1950/June 1951. . *v.4 p.248*

The Federal Budget: Politics, Policy, Process. *v.4 p.567*

Federal Censorship: Obscenity in the Mail. *v.4 p.445*

Federal Communications Commission: The Ups and Downs of
    Radio-TV Regulation. *v.4 p.445*

The Federal Courts. *v.4 p.465, p.534*

Federal Drug Control: The Evolution of Policy and
    Practice. *v.4 p.448*

⬚ Federal Election Commission Campaign Finance Reports and
    Data. *v.4 p.557*

⬚ Federal Election Commission. *v.4 p.548*

The Federal Government and Urban Housing: Ideology and
    Change in Public Policy. *v.4 p.524*

The Federal Government Subject Guide. *v.4 p.529*

The Federal Impeachment Process: A Constitutional and
    Historical Analysis. *v.4 p.461*

⬚ Federal Register. *v.4 p.481*

Federal regulatory directory. *v.4 p.463*

The Federal Reserve System: A History. *v.4 p.90*

The Federal Reserve System: An Encyclopedia. . . .*v.4 p.155*

⬚ Federal School Code List. *v.4 p.293*

Federal Tax Research. *v.4 p.107*

Federal Taxation in America: A Short History. *v.4 p.107*

The Federal Theatre Project: A Case
    Study. *v.1 p.119, p.146, p.150*

Federalism: A Dialogue. *v.4 p.455*

Federalism and the Role of the State. *v.4 p.586*

Federalism: The Politics of Intergovernmental
    Relations. *v.4 p.525*

Federalism, the Supreme Court and the Seventeenth
    Amendment: The Irony of Constitutional
    Democracy. *v.4 p.525, p.534*

Federalism. *v.4 p.587*

⬚ The Federalist. *v.4 p.518*

Federal-Provincial Diplomacy. *v.4 p.587*

☐ Federation of Gay Games. *v.4 p.839, p.843*

Federico Garcia Lorca: A Life. *v.2 p.660*

Federico Garcia Lorca: Impossible Theater: Five Plays and
    Thirteen Poems. *v.2 p.660*

FedEx Delivers: How the World's Leading Shipping Company
    Keeps Innovating and Outperforming the
    Competition. *v.4 p.165*

Feedback Control Systems. *v.5 p.711*

Feedback Optimal Control. *v.5 p.710*

Feedback: The Video Data Bank Catalog of Video Art and Artist
    Interviews. *v.1 p.770*

Feeding Ecology of Fish. *v.5 p.215*

Feeding Mexico: The Political Uses of Food since 1910. .*v.3 p.272*

Feeding the Fear of Crime: Crime-Related Media and Support
    for Three Strikes. *v.6 p.258*

Feeding the World: An Economic History of Agriculture,
    1800-2000. . . . .*v.5 p.4*

A Feel for the Game: To Brookline and Back. *v.4 p.860*

Feeling and Form. *v.1 p.441*

Feeling and Thinking: The Role of Affect in Social
    Cognition. *v.4 p.694, v.5 p.649, p.653*

Feelings and Emotions: The Amsterdam Symposium. .*v.5 p.612*

Fei Xiaotong and Sociology in Revolutionary
    China. *v.6 p.189, p.199*

Fela: From West Africa to West Broadway. . . .*v.1 p.286, p.335*

The Feldenkrais Method: Teaching by Handling, A Technique
    for Individuals. *v.1 p.52*

Felix Frankfurter Reminisces. *v.4 p.467*

Felix Holt, the Radical. *v.2 p.287*

Felix Mendelssohn Bartholdy: Guide to Research with
    Introduction to Research Concerning
    Fanny. *v.1 p.163, p.196, p.340*

Felix S. Cohen's Federal Indian Law. *v.6 p.691*

Felix S. Cohen's Handbook of Federal Indian
    Law. *v.4 p.465, v.6 p.695*

Felix Teynard, Calotypes of Egypt: A Catalogue
    Raisonné. *v.1 p.700*

Fellah and Townsman in the Middle East: Studies in Social
    History. *v.4 p.700*

The Fellowship of the Ring: Being the First Part of the Lord of
    the Rings. *v.2 p.386*

Felony Justice: An Organizational Analysis of Criminal
    Courts. *v.6 p.267*

Felony Probation: Problems and Prospects. *v.6 p.278*

Female Adolescent Development. *v.5 p.629*

The Female Athlete's Body: How to Prevent and Treat Sports
    Injuries in Women and Girls. *v.4 p.827, p.874, p.878*

The Female Body and the Law. *v.4 p.458*

The Female Body in Western Culture: Contemporary
    Perspectives. *v.6 p.437, p.473*

The Female Bridegroom: A Comparative Study in Life-Crisis
    Rituals in South India and Sri Lanka. *v.6 p.154*

Female Citizens, Patriarchs, and the Law in Venezuela,
    1786-1904. . . . .*v.3 p.360*

Female Desires: Same-Sex Relations and Transgender Practices
    Across Cultures. *v.4 p.750, v.6 p.371, p.375, p.420*

The Female Dramatists: Profiles of Women Playwrights from the
    Middle Ages to the Contemporary Times. *v.1 p.60*

The Female Experience in Eighteenth and Nineteenth-Century
    America: A Guide to the History of American
    Women. *v.6 p.453*

Female Fitness on Foot: Walking, Jogging, Running and
    Orienteering. *v.4 p.788, p.793*

Female Gangs in America: Essays on Girls, Gangs and
    Gender. *v.6 p.256, p.468*

Female Genital Mutilation: A Practical Guide to Worldwide
    Laws and Policies. *v.6 p.444*

Female Gladiators: Gender, Law, and Contact Sport in
    America. . . .*v.4 p.835, p.836, p.893, p.896, p.900, v.6 p.437*

The Female Hero in English Renaissance Tragedy. . .*v.2 p.186*

Female Masculinity. *v.6 p.368, p.429*

The Female Offender: Girls, Women and
    Crime. *v.6 p.255, p.258, p.468*

Female Playwrights and Eighteenth-Century Comedy:
    Negotiating Marriage on the London Stage. *v.2 p.187*

Female Playwrights of the Restoration: Five
    Comedies. *v.1 p.67, p.78, p.90, p.101*

Female Power and Male Dominance: On the Origins of Sexual
    Inequality. *v.4 p.744, v.6 p.430*

The Female Quixote: Or the Adventures of Arabella. .*v.2 p.251*

Female Revolt: Women's Movements in World and Historical
    Perspective. *v.6 p.430*

Female Rule in Chinese and English Literary Utopias. *v.6 p.481*

☐ Feminae: Medieval Women and Gender Index. . . .*v.6 p.451*

The Feminine and the Sacred. *v.1 p.528*

Feminine Endings: Music, Gender, and
    Sexuality. *v.1 p.379, v.6 p.475*

The Feminine Gaze: A Canadian Compendium of Non-Fiction
    Women Authors and Their Books, 1836-1945. . . .*v.2 p.731*

The Feminine: In Jungian Psychology and in Christian
    Theology. *v.6 p.460*

The Feminine Middlebrow Novel, 1920s to 1950s: Class,
    Domesticity and Bohemianism. *v.2 p.191*

The Feminine Mystique. *v.6 p.433*

Feminine Psychology. *v.6 p.445*

Feminism - Postmodernism. *v.6 p.428, p.461*

Feminism and Anthropology. *v.4 p.31*

Feminism and Art History: Questioning the Litany. . .*v.6 p.472*

Feminism and Christian Tradition: An Annotated Bibliography
    and Critical Introduction to the Literature. *v.6 p.460*

🄴 Feminism and Disability. *v.6 p.443*

Feminism and Documentary. *v.6 p.310*

Feminism and Epistemology: An Introduction. *v.1 p.506*

Feminism and Film Theory. *v.6 p.475*

Feminism and History of Philosophy. *v.1 p.506*

Feminism and Islamic Fundamentalism: The Limits of
    Postmodern Analysis. *v.6 p.435, p.460, p.465*

Feminism and Linguistic Theory. *v.5 p.622*

Feminism and Masculinities. *v.6 p.367, p.429*

Feminism and Methodology: Social Science Issues. . .*v.4 p.690*

Feminism and Modern Philosophy. *v.1 p.506*

Feminism and Motherhood in Germany,
1800-1914. . . . . *.v.3 p.52, p.159*

Feminism and Political Theory. . . . .*.v.6 p.442*

ⓔ Feminism and Psychoanalytic Theory. . . . . . .*.v.6 p.445*

Feminism and Religion: An Introduction. . . . . . .*.v.1 p.528*

ⓔ Feminism and Science. . . . .*.v.6 p.439*

Feminism and Science. . . . .*.v.6 p.439*

Feminism and Social Change: Bridging Theory and
Practice. . . . .*.v.6 p.427*

The Feminism and Socialism of Lily Braun. . . . . .*.v.3 p.54*

Feminism and Sociological Theory. . . . . .*.v.4 p.744, p.745*

Feminism and Sporting Bodies: Essays on Theory and
Practice. . . . .*.v.4 p.806, p.813, p.836,v.6 p.437*

Feminism and Suffrage: The Emergence of an Independent
Women's Movement in America 1848-1869. . . . .*.v.3 p.396*

Feminism and World
Religions. . . . . .*.v.1 p.528, p.529,v.6 p.435, p.460, p.466*

Feminism in France: From May '68 to Mitterand. .*.v.6 p.433, p.453*

Feminism in Modern Japan: Citizenship, Embodiment and
Sexuality. . . . .*.v.6 p.434*

Feminism in Twentieth-Century Science, Technology, and
Medicine. . . . .*.v.6 p.438*

Feminism, Marriage and the Law in Victorian England,
1850-1895. . . . .*.v.6 p.748*

Feminism, Multiculturalism, and the Media: Global
Diversities. . . . .*.v.6 p.448, p.449*

Feminism on the Border: Chicana Gender Politics and
Literature. . . . .*.v.6 p.480, p.503, p.515*

Feminism Without Borders: Decolonizing Theory, Practicing
Solidarity. . . . .*.v.6 p.428, p.457*

Feminism Without Women: Culture and Criticism in a
"Postfeminist" Age. . . . .*.v.6 p.475*

Feminisms: An Anthology of Literary Theory and
Criticism. . . . .*.v.2 p.569, v.6 p.480*

Feminisms at a Millennium. . . . .*.v.6 p.434*

Feminist and Womanist Pastoral Theology. . . . . .*.v.1 p.649*

The Feminist Classroom: Dynamics of Gender, Race and
Privilege. . . . .*.v.6 p.463*

The Feminist Companion to Literature in English: Women
Writers from the Middle Ages to the Present. . . .*.v.6 p.476*

A Feminist Companion to
Shakespeare. . . . . . .*.v.1 p.75, p.76, p.86, p.99,v.2 p.228*

Feminist Economics and the World Bank: History, Theory, and
Policy. . . . .*.v.4 p.274*

Feminist Economics: Interrogating the Masculinity of Rational
Economic Man. . . . .*.v.4 p.273*

Feminist Economics Today: Beyond Economic Man. .*.v.4 p.273*

The Feminist Encyclopedia of Spanish Literature, Vol.
1. . . . .*.v.2 p.639*

Feminist Epistemologies. . . . .*.v.6 p.426, p.460, p.462*

Feminist Ethics and Natural Law: The End of the
Anathemas. . . . .*.v.1 p.576*

Feminist Ethics. . . . .*.v.6 p.460*

Feminist Film Theory: A Classical Reader. . . . . .*.v.6 p.475*

Feminist Frameworks: Alternative Theoretical Accounts of the
Relations Between Women and Men. . . . . . .*.v.6 p.470*

Feminist Frontiers. . . . .*.v.6 p.436*

Feminist Genealogies, Colonial Legacies, Democratic
Futures. . . . .*.v.6 p.439*

Feminist Hollywood: From Born in Flames to Point
Break. . . . .*.v.6 p.328, p.342*

Feminist Interpretation of the Bible. . . . .*.v.1 p.617*

Feminist Interpretations and Political Theory. . . . .*.v.6 p.442*

A Feminist Introduction to Romanticism. . . . . . .*.v.2 p.171*

Feminist Literary Criticism and Social Change. . . . .*.v.2 p.8*

Feminist Literary Studies: An Introduction. . . . . .*.v.2 p.165*

▣ Feminist Majority Foundation. . . . .*.v.6 p.432*

Feminist Methods in Social Research. . . .*.v.4 p.688, v.6 p.426*

Feminist Philosophy of Science: An Introduction. .*.v.1 p.499, p.506*

Feminist Philosophy. . . . .*.v.1 p.506, v.4 p.744*

Feminist Politics and Human Nature. . . . .*.v.4 p.744, v.6 p.441*

Feminist Postcolonial Theory: A Reader. . . . .*.v.6 p.428, p.434*

A Feminist Reader in Early Cinema. . . . . . .*.v.6 p.328, p.332*

Feminist Science Education. . . . .*.v.6 p.462*

▣ Feminist Science Fiction, Fantasy and Utopia. . . .*.v.6 p.476*

Feminist Sociology. . . . .*.v.4 p.743*

The Feminist Spectator As Critic. . . . .*.v.1 p.56, p.121*

The Feminist, the Housewife, and the Soap Opera. . .*.v.6 p.447*

Feminist Theory and Christian Theology: Cartographies of
Grace. . . . .*.v.1 p.636*

Feminist Theory and International Relations in a Postmodern
Era. . . . .*.v.6 p.442*

Feminist Theory and the Body: A Reader. . .*.v.6 p.436, p.437*

Feminist Theory and the Classics. . . . .*.v.2 p.399*

Feminist Theory: From Margin to Center. . . . . . .*.v.6 p.427*

Feminist Theory Reader: Local and Global
Perspectives. . . . .*.v.6 p.428*

▣ Feminist Theory. . . . .*.v.6 p.426*

Feminist Thought: A More Comprehensive
Introduction. . . . .*.v.6 p.428*

Feminist Views on the English Stage: Women Playwrights,
1990-2000. . . . .*.v.1 p.98*

Feminist Writers. . . . .*.v.6 p.479*

Feminists Doing Ethics. . . . .*.v.1 p.483, v.6 p.461*

Feminists, Islam and Nation: Gender and the Making of Modern
Egypt. . . . .*.v.6 p.634*

Feminists Rethink the Self. . . . .*.v.6 p.461*

Feminization Debate in Eighteenth-Century Britain: Literature,
Commerce and Luxury. . . . .*.v.2 p.171*

The Feminization of American Culture. . . . .*.v.2 p.8*

Feminizing Chaucer. . . . .*.v.2 p.210*

La femme en rouge : et autres nouvelles. . . . . . .*.v.2 p.529*

La Femme Gelee. . . . .*.v.2 p.530*

Femmes : roman. . . . .*.v.2 p.533*

Femmes d'Alger dans leur appartement : nouvelles. . .*.v.2 p.544*

Les Femmes Savantes. . . . .*.v.2 p.475*

Fences: A Play. . . . .*.v.1 p.123, v.2 p.159*

Fenelon. . . . .*.v.2 p.473*

Feral Children and Clever Animals: Reflections on Human
Nature. . . . .*.v.5 p.595, p.614*

Feral Future: The Untold Story of Australia's Exotic
Invaders. . . . .*.v.5 p.185*

Ferdinand I of Austria. *v.3 p.183*

Ferdydurke. *v.2 p.790*

Ferlinghetti: The Artist in His Time. *v.2 p.145*

Fermat's Enigma: The Quest to Solve the World's Greatest
Mathematical Problem. *v.5 p.468, p.477*

Fernand Leger, 1911-1924: The Rhythm of Modern
Life. *v.1 p.742*

Fernando de Rojas. *v.2 p.651*

Fernando Pessoa and Co.: Selected Poems. *v.2 p.689*

Fernando Rojas: Celestina. *v.2 p.652*

Ferns of Britain and Ireland. *v.5 p.210*

Ferruccio Vitale: Landscape Architect of the Country Place
ERA. *v.1 p.817*

Fervent Years: The Group Theatre and the
Thirties. *v.1 p.112, p.143*

Festival and Events Management: An International Arts and
Culture Perspective. *v.1 p.825*

Festival Night. *v.2 p.721*

The Festival of the Greasy Pole. *v.2 p.536*

Festivals of the Jewish Year: A Modern Interpretation and Guide
Theodor H. Gaster. *v.1 p.552*

The Festive State: Race, Ethnicity and Nationalism as Cultural
Performance. *v.3 p.267, p.360*

Fetal Pig Dissection: A Laboratory Guide. *v.5 p.87*

Fetish, Recognition, Revolution. *v.6 p.175, p.178*

Le feu follet : suivi de Adieu à Gonzague. *v.2 p.516*

Feudal Monarchy in the Latin Kingdom of Jerusalem,
1100-1291. . . . .*v.3 p.64*

The Feudal Nobility and the Kingdom of Jerusalem,
1174-1277. . . . .*v.3 p.64*

Feudal Society, Vol. 1. . . . .*v.3 p.67, v.6 p.561*

Feudal Society, Vol. 2. . . . .*v.3 p.67, v.6 p.561*

The Feudal Transformation, 900-1200. . . . .*v.3 p.143*

Feudalism in History. *v.4 p.490, p.501*

Feudalism. *v.3 p.67*

Fever: Twelve Stories. *v.2 p.159*

Feydeau, théâtre. *v.2 p.517*

The Feynman Lectures on Physics, the Definitive Edition
Volume 1. . . . .*v.5 p.539*

The Feynman Lectures on Physics, the Definitive Edition
Volume 2. . . . .*v.5 p.539*

The Feynman Lectures on Physics, the Definitive Edition
Volume 3. . . . .*v.5 p.539*

The Feynman Processor: Quantum Entanglement and the
Computing Revolution. *v.5 p.552*

☐ FIAF Directory. *v.6 p.346*

Fiber. *v.2 p.140*

Ficciones. *v.2 p.678*

Fichte: The System of Ethics. *v.1 p.460*

Fiction Against History: Scott As Storyteller. . . .*v.2 p.307*

Fiction for the Working Man. *v.6 p.743, p.754, p.756*

The Fiction of Josef Skvorecky. *v.2 p.784*

The Fiction of Leroi Jones - Amiri Baraka. *v.2 p.140*

Fiction of Nathanael West: No Redeemer, No Promised
Land. *v.2 p.131*

The Fiction of Paule Marshall: Reconstructions of History,
Culture, and Gender. *v.2 p.767*

Fiction Refracts Science: Modernist Writers from Proust to
Borges. *v.5 p.406, p.411*

Fictions of Empire: Heart of Darkness, The Man Who Would Be
King and The Beach at Falesá. *v.2 p.297, p.312, p.341*

Fictions of Feminine Desire: Disclosures of Heloise. .*v.2 p.456*

Fictions of Romantic Tourism. *v.2 p.306, p.307*

Fictions. *v.2 p.678*

A Fictive People: Antebellum Economic Development and the
American Reading Public. *v.2 p.10*

The Fictive World of Conrad Aiken: A Celebration of
Consciousness. *v.2 p.56*

Fidalgos and Philanthropists: The Santa Casa de Misericordia of
Bahia, 1550-1755. . . . .*v.3 p.335*

Fiddler on the Roof: Based on Sholom Aleichem's
Stories. *v.1 p.254, p.410*

Fiddling for Norway: Revival and Identity. *v.1 p.298*

Fidel Castro: A Biography. *v.3 p.311*

Fidel Castro and the Quest for a Revolutionary Culture in
Cuba. *v.3 p.307*

Fidel Castro. *v.3 p.312*

Fidelio. *v.1 p.194, p.228, p.306, p.407*

Fiefs and Vassals: The Medieval Evidence Reinterpreted. .*v.3 p.68*

Field Archaeology: An Introduction. *v.4 p.7*

The Field Description of Igneous Rocks. *v.5 p.420, p.437*

The Field Description of Metamorphic Rocks. .*v.5 p.420, p.440*

Field Engineer's Manual. *v.5 p.686*

Field Geology Illustrated. *v.5 p.420*

Field Guide to Fossils: North America. *v.5 p.417, p.447*

The Field Guide to Geology. *v.5 p.419*

Field Guide to Liverwort General of Pacific North
America. *v.5 p.209*

A Field Guide to Reptiles and Amphibians: Eastern and Central
North America. *v.5 p.214*

A Field Guide to Rocks and Minerals. *v.5 p.436*

A Field Guide to the Ecology of Western Forests. . . .*v.5 p.38*

Field Guide. *v.2 p.146*

Field Hockey: Steps to Success. *v.4 p.795, p.857*

Field Hockey Techniques and Tactics. *v.4 p.796, p.857*

A Field Manual of the Ferns and Fern-Allies of the United
States and Canada. *v.5 p.210*

Field Methods in Remote Sensing. *v.4 p.389*

Field Notes from a Catastrophe: Man, Nature, and Climate
Change. *v.5 p.371*

The Field of Adult Services: Social Work Practice and
Administration. *v.4 p.758*

The Field of Cultural Production: Essays on Art and
Literature. *v.1 p.825*

Field of Honor: A Novel. *v.6 p.697*

The Field of Social Work. *v.4 p.757*

The Field of Vision. *v.2 p.103*

Field of Vision. *v.5 p.222*

Field Techniques in Glaciology and Glacial
Geomorphology. *v.4 p.391*

Field Theory: A Path Integral Approach - Lecture Notes in
    Physics, Vol. 52. . . . . *.v.5 p.550*

Field Theory and Its Classical Problems. . . . . . . *.v.5 p.473*

Fieldnotes: The Makings of Anthropology. . . . . *.v.4 p.24*

Fields, Forest, and Family: Women's Work and Power in Rural
    Laos. . . . . *.v.6 p.454, p.456, p.457*

Fields of Faith: Theology and Religious Studies for the
    Twenty-First Century. . . . . *.v.1 p.521*

Fields of Honor: The Golden Age of College Football and the
    Men Who Created It. . . . . . . *.v.4 p.809, p.859, p.894*

Fields of Wheat, Hills of Blood: Passages to Nationhood in
    Greek Macedonia, 1870-1990. . . . . *.v.3 p.195*

Fields on the Hoof: Nexus of Tibetan Nomadic
    Pastoralism. . . . . *.v.4 p.39*

Fields Watered with Blood: Critical Essays on Margaret
    Walker. . . . . *.v.6 p.25, p.43*

Fieldwork and Footnotes: Studies in the History of European
    Anthropology. . . . . *.v.4 p.5*

Fieldwork. . . . . *.v.4 p.690*

The Fierce and Beautiful World. . . . . *.v.2 p.807*

A Fierce Discontent: The Rise and Fall of the Progressive
    Movement in America, 1870-1920. . . . . *.v.4 p.552*

Fierce Gods: Inequality, Ritual, and the Politics of Dignity in a
    South Indian Village. . . . . *.v.6 p.154*

FIFA and the Contest for World Football: Who Rules the
    Peoples Game. . . . . *.v.4 p.845, p.847, p.868*

Fifteen Modern Polish Short Stories: An Annotated Reader and
    a Glossary. . . . . *.v.2 p.788*

Fifteen-Eighty-Seven, a Year of No Significance: The Ming
    Dynasty in Decline. . . . . *.v.6 p.186*

The Fifteenth Century, 1399-1485. . . . . *.v.6 p.563*

Fifth Chinese Daughter. . . . . *.v.6 p.95*

The Fifth Column: And Four Stories of the Spanish Civil
    War. . . . . *.v.2 p.84*

The Fifth Discipline: The Art and Practice of the Learning
    Organization. . . . . *.v.4 p.79, p.80*

The Fifth Miracle: The Search for the Origin and Meaning of
    Life. . . . . *.v.5 p.112, p.242*

The Fifth Monarchy Men; A Study in Seventeenth-Century
    English Millenarianism. . . . . *.v.3 p.103*

Fifth-Century Gaul: A Crisis of Identity? . . . . . *.v.3 p.142*

Fifty Best American Short Stories, 1915-1939. . . . . *.v.2 p.26*

Fifty Contemporary Choreographers. . . . . . *.v.1 p.3, p.6*

Fifty Key Contemporary Thinkers: From Structuralism to
    Postmodernity. . . . . *.v.1 p.512*

Fifty Key Eastern Thinkers. . . . . *.v.1 p.475*

Fifty Key Thinkers in International Relations. . . . . *.v.4 p.628*

Fifty Key Thinkers in Psychology. . . . . *.v.5 p.598*

Fifty Letters of Pliny. . . . . *.v.2 p.441*

Fifty Major Economists: A Reference Guide. . . . . *.v.4 p.185*

Fifty Major Economists. . . . . *.v.4 p.185, p.208*

Fifty Major Thinkers on Education: From Confucious to
    Dewey. *.v.4 p.340*

Fifty Modern Thinkers on Education: From Piaget to the Present
    Day. . . . . *.v.4 p.340*

Fifty Poems of Hafiz. . . . . *.v.6 p.671*

Fifty Stories. . . . . *.v.2 p.63*

Fifty Years of Anthropology and Education, 1950-2000: A
    Spindler Anthology. . . . . *.v.4 p.29*

Fifty Years of Fashion: From New Look to Now. . . *.v.1 p.716*

Fifty-Five Short Stories from the New Yorker. . . . . *.v.2 p.26*

The Fifty-Year Wound: How America's Cold War Victory
    Shapes Our World. . . . . *.v.3 p.453*

The Figaro Plays. . . . . *.v.2 p.478*

The Figaro Trilogy: The Barber of Seville, the Marriage of
    Figaro, the Guilty Mother. . . . . *.v.2 p.478*

The Fight for Conservation. . . . . *.v.5 p.17, p.39*

Fight for Freedom and Other Writings on Civil Rights. *.v.2 p.87*

The Fight in the Fields: Cesar Chavez and the Farmworkers
    Movement. . . . . *.v.6 p.488, p.540*

The Fight of the Century: Jack Johnson, Joe Louis, and the
    Struggle for Racial Equality. . . . . *.v.4 p.816, p.832, p.855*

Fighting Against the Odds: A History of Southern Labor since
    World War II. . . . . *.v.4 p.127*

Fighting Angel. . . . . *.v.6 p.200*

Fighting Bob la Follette: The Righteous Reformer. . *.v.3 p.402*

Fighting Dirty: The Inside Story of Covert Operations from Ho
    Chi Minh to Osama Bin Laden. . . . . . *.v.4 p.561, p.659*

Fighting Fans: Football Hooliganism as a World
    Phenomenon. . . . . *.v.4 p.715, p.815, p.843, p.867*

Fighting for America: Black Soldiers—The Unsung Heroes of
    World War II. . . . . *.v.6 p.8*

Fighting for Canada: Seven Battles, 1758-1945. . . . *.v.3 p.537*

Fighting for Time: The Image of War, 1861-1865. . . *.v.3 p.431*

Fighting Napoleon: Guerrillas, Bandits, and Adventurers in
    Spain, 1808-1814. . . . . *.v.3 p.75, p.240*

Fighting Poverty: What Works and What
    Doesn't. . . . . *.v.4 p.253, p.264, p.265*

Fighting Slavery in the Caribbean: The Life and Times of a
    British Family in Nineteenth-Century Havana. . . *.v.3 p.311*

Fighting Spirit: A Study of Psychological Factors in
    War. . . . . *.v.5 p.584*

Fighting Sprawl and City Hall: Resistance to Urban Growth in
    the Southwest. . . . . *.v.4 p.544*

Fighting to Learn: Popular Education and Guerrilla War in El
    Salvador. . . . . *.v.3 p.299*

Fighting Two Colonialisms: Women in Guinea-Bissau. *.v.6 p.74*

Fighting Warsaw: The Story of the Polish Underground State,
    1939-1945. . . . . *.v.3 p.254*

Fighting Windmills: Encounters with Don Quixote. . *.v.2 p.648*

Fighting Words: Individuals, Communities, and Liberties of
    Speech. *.v.4 p.459*

Figuration/Abstraction: Strategies for Public Sculpture in Europe
    1945-1968. . . . . *.v.1 p.776*

The Figure in Clay: Contemporary Sculpting Techniques by
    Master Artists. . . . . *.v.1 p.782*

The Figure of Beatrice: A Study in Dante. . . . . . *.v.2 p.705*

The Figure of Dante: An Essay on the Vita Nuova. . *.v.2 p.705*

Figure Work: The Nude and Life Modelling in New Zealand
    Art. . . . . *.v.1 p.750*

Figured Harmony at the Keyboard, Pt. 1. . . . . . . *.v.1 p.372*

Figured Harmony at the Keyboard, Pt. 2. . . . . . . *.v.1 p.372*

The Figured Wheel: New and Collected Poems,
    1966-1996. . . . . *.v.2 p.153*

Figures and Figurations. *v.2 p.668, p.669*

Figures Traced in Light: On Cinematic Staging. *v.6 p.350*

Figuring the Sacred: Religion, Narrative and
Imagination. *v.2 p.572*

Filipino American Lives. *v.6 p.93, p.129*

Filipino Americans: Transformation and
Identity. *v.4 p.706, v.6 p.130*

The Filipino Americans. *v.6 p.130*

Filipino Immigration to the Continental United States and to
Hawaii. *v.6 p.119, p.129*

Filipino Women Writers in English: Their Story:
1905-2002. . . . .*v.2 p.761*

Film, an International Bibliography. *v.6 p.305*

Film and Literature: A Comparative Approach to
Adaptation. *v.6 p.325*

Film and Nationalism. *v.6 p.321*

Film and Politics in America: A Social Tradition. . . .*v.6 p.343*

Film and Television: A Guide to the Reference
Literature. *v.6 p.305*

Film and Television Acting: From Stage to Screen. .*v.6 p.348*

The Film Anthologies Index. *v.6 p.305*

The Film Book Bibliography, 1940-1975. . . . . . .*v.6 p.305*

Film Choreographers and Dance Directors: An Illustrated
Biographical Encyclopedia, with a History and
Filmographies, 1893 Through 1995. . . . . . .*v.1 p.3, p.37*

Film Directing Shot by Shot: Visualizing from Concept to
Screen. *v.6 p.347*

Film Editing: History, Theory and Practice: Looking at the
Invisible. *v.6 p.350*

Film Editing Room Handbook: How to Manage the near Chaos
of the Cutting Room. *v.6 p.350*

Film Editing: The Art of the Expressive. *v.6 p.350*

The Film Encyclopedia: The Most Comprehensive Encyclopedia
of World Cinema in a Single Volume. *v.6 p.307*

The Film Factory: New Approaches to Russian and Soviet
Cinema. *v.6 p.339*

The Film Festival Guide: For Filmmakers, Film Buffs and
Industry Professionals. *v.6 p.346*

Film Finance and Distribution: A Dictionary of Terms. .*v.6 p.345*

Film Genre 2000: New Critical Essays. *v.6 p.311*

Film Genre Reader III. *v.6 p.311*

Film Index: A Bibliography: The Film As Art, Vol. 1. .*v.6 p.305*

The Film Industry in Argentina: An Illustrated Cultural
History. *v.6 p.344*

Film It with Music: Encyclopedic Guide to the American Movie
Musical. *v.6 p.316*

Film Literature Index. *v.6 p.305*

Film Music: A Neglected Art. *v.1 p.256*

Film Nation: Hollywood Looks at U. S. History. .*v.6 p.314, p.340*

Film Noir: An Encyclopedic Reference to the American
Style. *v.6 p.307, p.314, p.343*

Film Policy: International, National, and Regional
Perspectives. *v.6 p.345*

Film Production Theory. *v.6 p.346*

Film Sound: Theory and Practice. *v.6 p.352*

The Film Studies Dictionary. *v.6 p.306*

Film Study: An Analytical Bibliography, Vol. 3. . . . .*v.6 p.305*

☐ Filmbug. *v.6 p.305*

Film/Genre. *v.6 p.311*

Filming Shakespeare's Plays: The Adaptations of Laurence
Olivier, Orson Welles, Peter Brook and Akira
Kurosawa. *v.6 p.325*

The Filmmaker's Guide to Production Design. .*v.6 p.348, p.349*

The Filmmaker's Handbook: A Comprehensive Guide for the
Digital Age. *v.6 p.346*

Filmmaking on the Fringe: The Good, the Bad and the Deviant
Directors. *v.6 p.314*

Filmography of American History. *v.6 p.315*

Filmography of Social Issues: A Reference Guide. . . .*v.6 p.321*

Films by Genre: 775 Categories, Styles, Trends and Movements
Defined, with a Filmography for Each. *v.6 p.311*

The Films of Akira Kurosawa. *v.6 p.336*

The Films of Derek Jarman. *v.6 p.417*

Films of Makhmalbaf: Cinema, Politics and Culture in
Iran. *v.6 p.333*

The Films of Nagisa Oshima: Images of a Japanese
Iconoclast. *v.6 p.337*

The Films of the Eighties: A Complete, Qualitative Filmography
to over 3400 Feature-Length English Language Films,
Theatrical and Video-Only, Released Between Janaury 1, 1980,
and December 31, 1989. . . . .*v.6 p.333*

The Films of the Nineties: A Complete, Qualitative Filmography
to over 3000 Feature-Length English Language Films,
Theatrical and Video-Only, Released Between January 1, 1990,
and December 31, 1999. . . . .*v.6 p.332, p.333*

The Films of the Seventies: A Filmography of American, British
and Canadian Films 1970-1979. . . . .*v.6 p.333*

Films Without Images: Three Radio Plays. *v.2 p.513*

Filostrato. *v.2 p.701*

Filthy Fictions: Asian American Literature by Women. .*v.6 p.96*

The Final Days. *v.3 p.465*

Final Del Juego. *v.2 p.678*

Final Exam: A Study of the Perpetual Scrutiny of American
Education: Historical Perspectives on Assessment,
Standards, Outcomes, and Criticism of U. S.
Schools. *v.4 p.285*

Final Freedom: The Civil War, the Abolition of Slavery, and the
Thirteenth Amendment. *v.4 p.453*

Final Gifts: Understanding the Special Awareness, Needs, and
Communications of the Dying. *v.5 p.531, p.532*

A Final Promise: The Campaign to Assimilate the Indians,
1880-1920. . . . .*v.6 p.688, p.689*

The Final Sack of Nineveh: The Discovery, Documentation, and
Destruction of Sennacherib's Palace at Nineveh, Iraq. *v.3 p.6*

Final Solution: Nazi Population Policy and the Murder of the
European Jew. *v.3 p.82*

Final Solutions: Mass Killing and Genocide in the 20th
Century. *v.4 p.654, p.715,v.6 p.257*

Finance and Financiers in European History, 1880-1960. *v.4 p.91*

Finance and Government under Maria Theresa, 1740-1780, Vol.
II Finance and Credit. *v.3 p.183*

Finance and Government under Maria Theresia, 1740-1780. Vol.
1 Society and Government. *v.3 p.183*

Finance and Investment
Handbook. *v.4 p.94, p.101, p.102, p.103, p.162*

Finance, Governance, and Competitiveness in Japan. *v.6 p.218*

☐ Finance Site List. *v.4 p.88*

☐ Finance, Wikipedia, the free encyclopedia. *v.4 p.88*

Finance. *v.4 p.104*

Financial Calculus: An Introduction to Derivative
Pricing. *v.5 p.503*

Financial Crime Investigation and Control. *v.6 p.267*

Financial Crises and Recession in the Global
Economy. *v.4 p.242, p.260*

Financial Derivatives. *v.4 p.89, p.95, p.100, p.102*

Financial Econometrics: Problems, Models, and
Methods. *v.4 p.200*

Financial Founding Fathers: The Men Who Made America
Rich. *v.4 p.90, p.148*

A Financial History of Modern U S Corporate
Scandals. *v.4 p.89, p.104, p.109, p.147*

A Financial History of the United States. . . . *v.4 p.89, p.247*

The Financial Numbers Game: Detecting Creative Accounting
Practices. *v.4 p.96, p.97, p.102, p.105, p.106, p.111*

Financial Shenanigans: How to Detect Accounting Gimmicks
and Fraud in Financial
Reports. *v.4 p.92, p.97, p.105, p.106, p.111*

Financial Statement Analysis: A Practitioner's
Guide. *v.4 p.91, p.95, p.105, p.106, p.175*

The Financier. *v.2 p.70*

Financing Education in a Climate of Change. *v.4 p.280*

Financing Education: The Struggle Between Governmental
Monopoly and Parental Control. *v.4 p.280*

Financing Sport: Winning Strategies. *v.4 p.884, p.888*

Financing Sport. *v.4 p.888, p.891*

Financing the Sport
Enterprise. *v.4 p.886, p.889, p.892, p.897, p.899*

Find it Online: The Complete Guide to Online
Research. *v.5 p.679*

Finders Keepers: Selected Prose 1971-2001. . . . . *v.2 p.352*

Fin-de-siècle Vienna: Politics and Culture. *v.3 p.184*

Finding an Ending: Reflections on Wagner's
Ring. *v.1 p.199, p.231, p.365*

Finding Balance: Fitness, Training, and Health for a Lifetime in
Dance. *v.1 p.50*

Finding George Orwell in Burma: Travels in a Police
State. *v.2 p.374, p.375*

Finding Groups in Data: An Introduction to Cluster
Analysis. *v.4 p.689, p.690*

Finding Her Voice: Women in Country Music,
1800-2000. . . . . *v.1 p.267, p.378*

Finding Order in Nature: The Naturalist Tradition from Linnaeus
to E. O. Wilson. *v.3 p.44*

☐ Finding Physical and Chemical Properties. *v.5 p.280*

Finding the Law 2005. . . . . *v.4 p.439*

Finding the Mean: Theory and Practice in Aristotelian Political
Philosophy. *v.4 p.489*

Finding the Muse: A Sociopsychological Inquiry into the
Conditions of Artistic Creativity. *v.1 p.702*

Finding the Walls of Troy: Frank Calvert and Heinrich
Schliemann at Hisarlik. *v.3 p.15*

Finding Time: How Corporations, Individuals, and Families Can
Benefit from New Work Practices. *v.5 p.579*

Finding Time: New Work Practice. *v.5 p.580*

☐ FindLaw. *v.4 p.108*

The Fine Art of Advertising : Irreverent, Irrepressible,
Irresistibly Ironic. *v.4 p.140, p.141*

The Fine Art of Advertising. *v.1 p.714, p.715*

Fine Art of the West. *v.1 p.683*

Fine Art Publicity: The Complete Guide for Galleries and
Artists. *v.1 p.825*

A Fine Balance: A Novel. *v.2 p.765*

The Fine-Arts Etchings of James David Smillie, 1833-1909: A
Catalogue Raisonné. *v.1 p.758*

Fingers Pointing Somewhere Else. *v.2 p.783*

Fingersmith. *v.6 p.399*

The Finishing School: A Novel. *v.2 p.383*

The Finishing School. *v.2 p.383*

Finite Element Analysis with Error Estimators: An Introduction
to the FEM and Adaptive Error Analysis for Engineering
Students. *v.5 p.692*

Finite Element Method: The Basis, Vol. 1. . . . . . *v.5 p.697*

Finite Element Model Updating in Structural Dynamics. *v.5 p.693*

Finite Element Programs in Structural Engineering and
Continuum Mechanics. *v.5 p.696*

Finite Element Techniques in Structural Mechanics. . *v.5 p.696*

Finite Elements: Theory, Fast Solvers, and Applications in Solid
Mechanics. *v.5 p.491, p.500*

Finite Mathematics and Its Applications. *v.5 p.477*

Finite-Dimension Vector Spaces. *v.5 p.472*

Finland : Myth and Reality. *v.3 p.236*

Finland: People, Nation State. *v.4 p.594*

Finnish Modern Design: Utopian Ideals and Everyday Realities,
1930-97. . . . . *v.1 p.712, p.800*

Fins de Siècle: English Poetry in 1590, 1690, 1790, 1890,
1990. . . . . *v.2 p.181*

Fire: A Brief History. *v.5 p.31*

Fire Across the Sea: The Vietnam War and Japan,
1965-1975. . . . . *v.6 p.168, p.224*

Fire and Iron; Critical Approaches to Njals Saga. . . *v.2 p.624*

The Fire and the Sun: Why Plato Banished the Artists. *v.1 p.424*

Fire and Vegetation Dynamics: Studies from the North American
Boreal Forest. *v.5 p.38*

Fire in America: A Cultural History of Wildland and Rural
Fire. *v.5 p.31, v.6 p.284*

Fire in the City: Savonarola and the Struggle for the Soul of
Renaissance Florence. *v.3 p.200*

Fire in the Rain...Singer in the Storm: An
Autobiography. *v.6 p.409*

Fire in the Sky: Comets and Meteors, the Decisive Centuries, in
British Art and Science. *v.1 p.688*

Fire in Tropical Savannas: The Kapalga
Experiment. *v.5 p.182, p.240*

The Fire Next Time. *v.2 p.59*

Fire, Snow & Honey: Voices from Kurdistan: Essays, Life
Stories, Poems, Short Fiction and Fables. *v.6 p.668*

The Fire Stays in Red: Poems. *v.6 p.651, p.652*

Fire This Time: The Watts Uprising and the
1960's. *v.3 p.531, v.6 p.713*

The Fire This Time: U. S. War Crimes in the Gulf. . .*v.4 p.652*

A Fire to Win: The Life and Times of Woody
Hayes. *v.4 p.859, p.894*

Fire under the Sea: The Discovery of the Most Extraordinary
Environment on Earth - Volcanic Hot Springs on the Ocean
Floor. *v.5 p.428*

The Fire Within the Eye: A Historical Essay on the Nature and
Meaning of Light. *v.5 p.540*

The Firebrand: William Lyon Mackenzie and the Rebellion in
Upper Canada. *v.3 p.539*

The Firefly Encyclopedia of Astronomy. *v.5 p.63*

Firefly Encyclopedia of Reptiles and Amphibians. .*v.5 p.95, p.214*

Fires on the Plain. *v.6 p.232*

Fires Were Started: British Cinema and Thatcherism. .*v.6 p.339*

Firewall: The Iran-Contra Conspiracy and
Cover-Up. *v.3 p.445, p.481*

Fireweed: A Political Autobiography. *v.3 p.374*

First Across the Continent: Sir Alexander Mackenzie. .*v.3 p.545*

First Aid Manual for Chemical Accidents. *v.5 p.266*

The First Amendment, Democracy, and Romance. . .*v.4 p.459*

The First Amendment in Schools. *v.4 p.450*

The First America: The Spanish Monarchy, Creole Patriots and
the Liberal State, 1492-1866. . . . .*v.3 p.262, p.284*

The First American Frontier: Transition to Capitalism in
Southern Appalachia, 1700-1860. . . . .*v.3 p.497*

The First American Revolution: The American Colonies on the
Eve of Independence. *v.4 p.518*

The First Americans, 1607-1690. . . . .*v.3 p.407*

First among Equals: The Supreme Court in American
Life. *v.4 p.540*

First among Friends: George Fox and the Creation of
Quakerism. *v.1 p.585*

The First and Second Lady Chatterley Novels. *v.2 p.363*

The First Austrian Republic Nineteen Eighteen to Nineteen
Thirty-Eight: A Study Based on British and Austrian
Documents. *v.3 p.184*

First, Break All the Rules: What the World's Greatest Managers
Do Differently. *v.4 p.70, p.72*

The First Canadians: A Profile of Canada's Native People
Today. *v.6 p.688, p.689, p.691*

The First Casualty: The War Correspondent as Hero and
Myth-Maker from the Crimea to Iraq. *v.4 p.403*

The First Circle. *v.2 p.808*

First City: Philadelphia and the Forging of Historical
Memory. *v.3 p.492*

A First Class Temperament: The Emergence of Franklin
Roosevelt. *v.3 p.463*

A First Course in Abstract Algebra: Rings, Groups, and
Fields. *v.5 p.473*

First Course in Chaotic Dynamical Systems. *v.5 p.488*

A First Course in Database Systems. *v.5 p.337, p.338*

A First Course in Design and Analysis of Experiments. .*v.5 p.482*

A First Course in Discrete Dynamical
Systems. *v.5 p.477, p.478, p.488*

A First Course in Discrete Mathematics. *v.5 p.477*

A First Course in General Relativity. *v.5 p.72, p.73, p.558*

The First Course in Mathematical Logic. *v.5 p.471*

A First Course in Optimization Theory. *v.4 p.207*

A First Course in Partial Differential Equations with Complex
Variables and Transform Methods. *v.5 p.488, p.491*

A First Course in the Numerical Analysis of Differential
Equations. *v.5 p.486, p.492*

First Course on Wavelets. *v.5 p.494*

First Crossing: Alexander Mackenzie, His Expedition Across
North America and the Opening of the Continent. .*v.4 p.379*

The First Crusade and the Idea of Crusading. *v.3 p.63*

First Cut: Conversations with Film Editors. *v.6 p.350*

The First Day and Other Stories. *v.6 p.647, p.648*

The First Days of Class: A Practical Guide for the Beginning
Teacher. *v.4 p.279*

The First Days of School: How to Be an Effective
Teacher. *v.4 p.278*

The First Dynasty of Islam: The Umayyad Caliphate, AD
661-750. . . . .*v.6 p.584*

The First Emperor of China. *v.6 p.184, p.202*

First Encyclopedia of Our World. *v.5 p.225*

First English Feminist: Reflections upon Marriage and Other
Writings. *v.2 p.237*

The First Epistle to the Corinthians. *v.1 p.631*

The First European Revolution: 970-1215. . . . . . .*v.3 p.68*

First Farmers: The Origins of Agricultural Societies. . .*v.4 p.5*

The First Four Books of Poems: Including a Mask for Janus, the
Dancing Bear, Green with Beasts, the Drunk in the
Furnace. *v.2 p.101*

The First Four Books of Poems. *v.2 p.101, p.146*

The First Four Georges. *v.3 p.107, p.109*

The First French Republic, Seventeen Ninety-Two to Eighteen
Four. *v.3 p.151*

The First Gentlemen of Virginia: Intellectual Qualities of the
Early Colonial Ruling Class. *v.3 p.501*

The First Golden Age of the Viennese Symphony: Haydn,
Mozart, Beethoven and
Schubert. .*v.1p.188,p.194,p.238,p.306,p.329,p.330,p.343,p.353*

First Hollywood Musicals: A Critical Filmography of 171
Features, 1927 Through 1932. . . . .*v.6 p.315*

The First Idea: How Symbols, Language, and Intelligence
Evolved in Early Primates and Humans. . .*v.5 p.620, p.623*

The First Immigrants from Asia: A Population History of the
North American Indian. *v.4 p.764*

The First Imperial Age: European Overseas Expansion
1400-1715. . . . .*v.3 p.74*

First in His Class: A Biography of Bill Clinton. *v.3 p.475*

The First Industrial Nation: An Economic History of Britain,
1700-1914. . . . .*v.3 p.113*

The First Jesuits. *v.1 p.578*

First Language Acquisition. *v.5 p.620, p.623*

The First Liberty: America's Foundation in Religious
Freedom. *v.1 p.657*

First Love and The Diary of a Superfluous Man. . . .*v.2 p.810*

The First Men in the Moon. *v.2 p.320*

The First Modern Comedies: The Significance of Etherege, Wycherley and Congreve. *v.2 p.244*

The First Modern Economy: Success, Failure, and Perseverance of the Dutch Economy, 1500-1815. . . . .*v.3 p.204*

The First New Nation: The United States in Historical and Comparative Perspective. *v.3 p.368, p.369*

First Nights at the Opera. *v.1 p.230*

First Nights: Five Musical Premieres. *v.1 p.174*

First Omnibus. *v.2 p.339*

First One Hundred Years of American Geology. *v.5 p.418*

First Person Singular: Writers on Their Craft. *v.2 p.7*

First Photographs: William Henry Fox Talbot and the Birth of Photography. *v.1 p.765*

First Principles: The Jurisprudence of Clarence Thomas. .*v.4 p.467*

The First Punic War. *v.3 p.25*

The First Russian Revolution, 1825: The Decembrist Movement. *v.3 p.218*

The First Scientific Exploration of Russian America and the Purchase of Alaska. *v.3 p.533*

First Signals: The Evolution of Multicellular Development. *v.5 p.159*

First Son: George W. Bush and the Bush Family Dynasty. *v.3 p.509*

The First South Americans: The Peopling of a Continent from the Earliest Evidence to High Culture. *v.4 p.12*

The First South. *v.3 p.494*

The First Suburban Chinatown: The Remaking of Monterey Park, California. *v.6 p.126, p.712*

First the Seed: The Political Economy of Plant Biotechnology. *v.5 p.8, p.47*

First They Killed My Father: A Daughter of Cambodia Remembers. *v.6 p.95, p.139*

First Things to Hand: Poems. *v.2 p.153*

The First Third and Other Writings. *v.2 p.64*

The First Time I Met Frank O'Hara: Reading Gay American Writers. *v.2 p.106*

The First Universities: Studium Generale and the Origins of University Education in Europe. *v.4 p.336*

The First Urban Christians: The Social World of the Apostle Paul. *v.1 p.627*

First Use of Nuclear Weapons: Under the Constitution, Who Decides? *v.4 p.532*

First We Take Manhattan: Four American Women and the New York School of Dance Criticism. *v.1 p.40*

The First Well: A Bethlehem Boyhood. *v.6 p.660*

First with the News: A History of W. H. Smith and Son since 1792-1972. . . . .*v.6 p.742*

First Word Philosophy: Wittgenstein-Austin-Cavell, Writings on Ordinary Language. *v.1 p.510*

First World Third Class and Other Tales of the Global Mix. *v.2 p.692*

The First World War and British Military History. . . .*v.3 p.78*

The First World War and Popular Cinema: 1914 to the Present. *v.6 p.323*

The First World War: Germany and Austria-Hungary 1914-1918. . . . . . .*v.3 p.79, p.160, p.161, p.184, p.185*

The First World War, Vol. 1: To Arms. *v.3 p.80*

The First World War. *v.3 p.79, p.80*

FirstGov.gov: The U.S. Government's Official Web Portal. *v.4 p.546*

First-Job Survival Guide: How to Thrive and Advance in Your New Career. *v.4 p.167*

Fiscal Disobedience: An Anthropology of Economic Regulation in Central Africa. *v.4 p.260*

Fiscal Policy and Business Cycles. *v.4 p.243, p.246*

Fiscal Theory and Political Economy: Selected Essays. .*v.4 p.208*

The Fischer-Dieskau Book of Lieder. *v.2 p.593*

Fish Diseases and Disorders: Protozoan and Metazoan Infections. *v.5 p.32*

Fish Ecology. *v.5 p.216, p.217*

Fish Head Soup and Other Plays. *v.6 p.98*

A Fish in the Water: A Memoir. *v.2 p.686, v.3 p.332*

The Fisher King: A Novel. *v.2 p.768*

The Fisher King. *v.2 p.378*

Fisheries Conservation and Management. *v.5 p.18, p.32*

Fisher's Capital and Income. *v.4 p.250*

Fishes: An Introduction to Ichthyology. *v.5 p.216*

Fishes of the Central United States. *v.5 p.216*

Fishes of the Great Lakes Region. *v.5 p.215*

Fishing the Great Lakes: An Environmental History, 1783-1933. . . . .*v.5 p.77, v.6 p.294*

Fists and Flowers: A Social Psychological Interpretation of Student Dissent. *v.4 p.326*

Fit to Teach: Same-Sex Desire, Gender, and School Work in the Twentieth Century. *v.4 p.309, v.6 p.384*

Fitness Aquatics. *v.4 p.792*

Fitness in American Culture: Images of Health, Sport and the Body, 1830-1940. . . . .*v.4 p.791, p.806*

Fitness Programming and Physical Disability. *v.4 p.784, p.791, p.801*

Fitness Running. *v.4 p.866*

Fitness Through Aerobics and Step Training. *v.4 p.793*

Fitness Weight Training. *v.4 p.792, p.878*

Fits, Trances, and Visions: Experiencing Religion and Explaining Experience from Wesley to James. . . .*v.5 p.636*

Fitting Models to Biological Data Using Linear and Nonlinear Regression: A Practical Guide to Curve Fitting. . .*v.5 p.101*

Fitzgerald, Hemingway and the Twenties. *v.2 p.75, p.83*

The Five Biggest Unsolved Problems in Science. *v.5 p.82*

Five Centuries of British Painting: From Holbein to Hodgkin. *v.1 p.734*

Five Centuries of Hannukah Lamps from the Jewish Museum: A Catalogue Raisonné. *v.1 p.806*

Five Comedies: Bacchides, Menaechmi, Miles Gloriosus, Hecyra, and Adelphoe. *v.2 p.440*

Five Comedies from the Italian Renaissance. *v.2 p.699*

Five Comedies. *v.2 p.500*

The Five C's of Cinematography: Motion Picture Filming Techniques. *v.6 p.349*

Five Easy Lessons: Strategies for Successful Physics Teaching. *v.5 p.563*

Five Empresses: Court Life in Eighteenth-Century Russia. *v.3 p.215*

Five Families: Mexican Case Studies in the Culture of Poverty. *v.4 p.733*

Five Golden Rules: Great Theories of 20th-Century Mathematics-and Why They Matter. *v.5 p.457*

Five Hundred Thirty-Six Puzzles and Curious Problems. .*v.5 p.469*

Five Hundred Years of Chinese Poetry, 1150-1650: The Chin, Yuan, and Ming Dynasties. *v.6 p.209, p.210*

Five Hundred Years of Printing. *v.2 p.577*

Five Hungarian Writers. *v.2 p.785*

Five Italian Renaissance Comedies. *v.2 p.700*

Five Kingdoms: An Illustrated Guide to the Phyla of Life on Earth. *v.5 p.205*

Five Lectures. *v.5 p.644*

Five Modern No Plays. *v.6 p.235*

Five Novels of Ronald Firbank: Valmouth, Artificial Princess, Flower Beneath the Foot, Prancing Nigger and Cardinal Pirelli. *v.6 p.396*

The Five People You Meet in Heaven. *v.2 p.160*

Five Plays by Langston Hughes. *v.2 p.88*

Five Plays: Comedies and Tragicomedies. *v.2 p.659*

Five Plays: Cyprian's Prayer, the Crime in the Whistler Room, This Room and This Gin and These Sandwiches, Beppo An. *v.2 p.137*

The Five Red Herrings. *v.2 p.381*

Five Roads to Nordic Security. *v.3 p.235*

Five Romantic Plays, 1768-1821. . . . . . .*v.1 p.63, p.78, p.98*

Five Screenplays: The Servant; The Pumpkin Eater; The Quiller Memorandum; Accident; The Go-Between. *v.2 p.377*

Five Seasons. *v.6 p.652*

Five Sisters: Women Against the Tsar. *v.3 p.219*

Five Stories of Ferrara. *v.2 p.713*

Five Tales for the Theatre: The Raven, The King Stag, Turandot, The Serpent Woman, and The Green Bird. .*v.2 p.710, p.711*

The Five Ways: St. Thomas Aquinas' Proofs of God's Existence, Vol. 5. . . . .*v.1 p.639*

Five Women Who Loved Love. *v.6 p.233*

The Five-Factor Model of Personality: Theoretical Perspectives. *v.5 p.658*

Fixed Broadband Wireless System Design. *v.5 p.726*

The Fixer. *v.2 p.149*

Fixin' to Git: One Fan's Love Affair with NASCAR's Winston Cup. *v.4 p.820, p.848, p.849*

Flag Burning and Free Speech: The Case of Texas vs. Johnson. *v.4 p.438*

A Flag for Sunrise. *v.2 p.156*

Flags Through the Ages and Across the World. . . .*v.4 p.499*

Flame of Love: Poems of the Spanish Mystics. . . .*v.2 p.646*

Flamenco: Gypsy Dance and Music from Andalusia. *v.1 p.21, p.299*

Flamenco!. *v.1 p.20*

Flames Across the Border, 1813-1814. . . . .*v.3 p.416*

Flame. *v.2 p.716*

Flaming Classics: Queering the Film Canon. *v.6 p.416*

The Flaming Heart. *v.2 p.165*

The Flamingo in the Garden: American Yard Art and the Vernacular Landscape. *v.1 p.777, p.778*

Flammable Australia: The Fire Regimes and Biodiversity of a Continent. *v.5 p.31, p.167, v.6 p.293*

A Flann O'Brien Reader. *v.2 p.373*

Flann O'Brien. *v.2 p.373*

Flannery O'Connor and the Mystery of Love. *v.2 p.106*

Flannery O'Connor, Hermit Novelist -- Richard Giannone. *v.2 p.106*

Flash and Crash Days: Brazilian Theater in the Post-Dictatorship Period. *v.1 p.127*

The Flash of Capital: Film and Geopolitics in Japan. *v.6 p.328, p.335*

Flash of the Cathode Rays: A History of J. J. Thomson's Electron. *v.5 p.542*

Flash!: The Hunt for the Biggest Explosions in the Universe. *v.5 p.67*

Flat Broke with Children: Women in the Age of Welfare Reform. *v.6 p.466, p.467, p.469, p.470*

Flatland: A Romance of Many Dimensions. *v.5 p.494*

Flatlining on the Field of Dreams: Cultural Narratives in the Films of President Reagan's America. *v.6 p.343*

Flatterland: Like Flatland, Only More So. . . .*v.5 p.495, p.496*

Flaubert: A Biography. *v.2 p.490*

Flaubert and Madame Bovary. *v.2 p.491*

Flaubert and Turgenev: A Friendship in Letters: The Complete Correspondence. *v.2 p.491*

Flaubert: Madame Bovary. *v.2 p.491*

Flaubert's Parrot. *v.2 p.332*

Flaubert-Sand: The Correspondence. *v.2 p.491, p.499*

Flaubert. *v.2 p.490*

Flavian Rome: Culture, Image, Text. *v.3 p.27*

Flawed Giant: Lyndon Johnson and His Times, 1961-1973. . . . .*v.3 p.469*

Flawed Victory: A New Perspective on the Civil War. .*v.3 p.429*

A Flea in Her Rear: or Ants in Her Pants: And Nine Other French Farces. *v.2 p.465*

Fledgling: A Novel. *v.6 p.23, p.42*

Fleet Walker's Divided Heart: The Life of Baseball's First Black Major Leaguer. *v.4 p.811, p.833, p.853*

Fleeting Moments: Nature and Culture in American History. *v.3 p.365*

Flemish Art and Architecture, 1585-1700. . . .*v.1 p.676, p.689*

The Flemish Movement: A Documentary History 1780-1980. . . . .*v.3 p.206*

Flemish Tapestry. *v.1 p.809*

Flesh and Blood. *v.6 p.395*

The Flesh Is Frail, 1818-1819. . . . .*v.2 p.274*

Fletcher, Beaumont and Company. *v.2 p.217*

Fletcher Benton. *v.1 p.780*

Fletcher Steele, Landscape Architect: An Account of the Gardenmaker's Life, 1885-1971. . . . .*v.1 p.816*

Les Fleurs du Mal. *v.2 p.487*

Flexagons Inside Out. *v.5 p.469*

Flexible Citizenship: The Cultural Logics of Transnationality. *v.6 p.107, p.119*

Ein Fliehendes Pferd: Novelle. *v.2 p.619*

Flight Against Time. *v.6 p.662*

Flight among the Tombs: Poems. *v.2 p.146*

Flight Dynamics Principles. *v.5 p.717*

Flight in America: From the Wrights to the Astronauts. .*v.5 p.717*

Flight International World Aircraft and Systems
    Directory. *v.4 p.151*

Flight Maps: Adventures with Nature in Modern
    America. *v.5 p.235*

The Flight of the 'Eagle': A Documentary
    Novel. *v.2 p.631, p.633, p.635*

The Flight of the Mind: Virginia Woolf's Art and
    Manic-Depressive Illness. *v.5 p.659*

Flight of the Skylark: The Development of Shelley's
    Reputation. *v.2 p.311*

Flight Stability and Automatic Control. *v.5 p.718*

Flight to the Future: Human Factors in Air Traffic
    Control. *v.5 p.588, p.718*

Flinders Petrie: A Life in Archaeology. *v.3 p.11*

Flippin': Filipinos on America. *v.6 p.91*

The Floating Borderlands: Twenty-Five Years of U. S. Hispanic
    Literature. *v.2 p.19*

The Floating World in Japanese Fiction. *v.6 p.229*

The Floating World. *v.6 p.100*

Flood Tide of Empire: Spain and the Pacific Northwest,
    1543-1819. . . . .*v.3 p.530*

Floor Coverings for Historic Buildings: A Guide to Selecting
    Reproductions. *v.1 p.824, p.825*

Flora: A Gardener's Encyclopedia, Vol. 2. . . . . . .*v.5 p.43*

Flora: A Gardener's Encyclopedia. *v.5 p.43*

Floral Biology: Studies on Floral Evolution in Animal-Pollinated
    Plants. *v.5 p.206*

Flora's Orchids. *v.5 p.43*

Florence and Its Church in the Age of Dante. *v.3 p.199*

Florence Nightingale: Mystic, Visionary,
    Reformer. *v.5 p.527, p.528, p.529*

Florence Nightingale. *v.5 p.527, p.529*

Florence: The Golden Age,
    1138-1737. . . . .*v.3 p.197, p.199, p.203, p.204*

The Florentine Camerata: Documentary Studies and
    Translations. *v.1 p.180*

The Florentine Magnates: Lineage and Faction in a Medieval
    Commune. *v.3 p.199*

Florentine Villas in the Fifteenth-Century: An Architectural and
    Social History. *v.1 p.790*

Floricanto Si!: A Collection of Latina Poetry. . .*v.6 p.495, p.510*

Florida: A Guide to the Southern-Most State. *v.3 p.504*

Florida: A Short History. *v.3 p.504*

Florida: Bicentennial and History Guide. *v.3 p.505*

Florida Politics in the Gilded Age, 1877-1893. . . .*v.3 p.505*

The Flounder. *v.2 p.608*

Flourescence Microscopy of Living Cells in Culture: Quantitaive
    Flourescence Microscopy-Imaging and Spectroscopy. *v.5 p.86*

Flourishing: Positive Psychology and the Life
    Well-Lived. *v.5 p.670*

Flow Cytometry in Biotechnology. *v.5 p.219*

Flow in Sports: The Keys to Optimal Experiences and
    Performances. *v.4 p.802, p.877*

Flower and Fruit Prints of the 18th and Early 19th Centuries:
    Their History, Makers and Uses, with a Catalogue
    Raisonné of the Works in Which They Are Found. *v.1 p.753*

The Flower Drum Song. *v.6 p.101*

Flowering in the Shadows: Women in the History of Chinese
    and Japanese Painting. *v.6 p.473*

The Flowering of Mysticism. *v.1 p.653*

The Flowering of New England, 1815-1865. . . . . .*v.2 p.12*

Flowering of the Cumberland. *v.3 p.510*

Flowering of the Landscape Garden: English Pleasure Grounds,
    1720-1800. . . . .*v.1 p.819*

Flowering Plant Origin, Evolution & Phylogeny. .*v.5 p.155, p.190*

Flowering Wilderness. *v.2 p.347*

Flowers for Algernon. *v.2 p.148*

Flowers from the Royal Gardens of Kew: Two Centuries of
    Curtis's Botanical Magazine. *v.5 p.85*

Flowers in the Mirror. *v.6 p.211*

The Flowers of Evil. *v.2 p.487, p.488*

Flowers of Fire: Twentieth-Century Korean Stories. . .*v.6 p.238*

Flu: The Story of the Great Influenza Pandemic of 1918 and the
    Search for the Virus That Caused It. *v.5 p.510, p.532, p.533*

Fluctuations and Scaling in Biology. *v.5 p.92*

Fludd: A Novel. *v.2 p.367*

Fluent Hebrew. *v.6 p.645*

Fluid Borders: Latino Power, Identity, and Politics in Los
    Angeles. *v.6 p.538, p.549*

Fluid Boundaries: Forming and Transforming Identity in
    Nepal. *v.6 p.163, p.164*

Fluid Dynamics and Heat Transfer of Turbomachinery. *v.5 p.713*

Fluid Dynamics for Physicists. *v.5 p.547*

Fluid Exchanges: Artists and Critics in the AIDS Crisis. .*v.6 p.407*

Fluid Mechanics, Vol. 6. . . . .*v.5 p.547*

Fluid Mechanics. *v.5 p.547*

⦿ Fluid Power Design Handbook. *v.5 p.709, p.710*

Fluorine Chemistry at the Millennium: Fascinated by
    Fluorine. *v.5 p.308*

Flush. *v.2 p.394*

The Flute Book: A Complete Guide for Students and
    Performers. *v.1 p.392, p.399*

Flutes of Fire: Essays on California Indian
    Languages. *v.6 p.690, p.691*

The Flute. *v.1 p.391*

Fluvial Forms and Processes: A New Perspective. . . .*v.5 p.427*

Fluvial Processes and Environmental Change. *v.4 p.391*

Fluvial Processes in Geomorphology. *v.5 p.427*

The Fluvial System. *v.5 p.427*

Fluxes of Carbon, Water and Energy of European
    Forests. *v.5 p.178*

Fly and the Fly: Bottle. *v.1 p.446*

Fly Fishing for the Compleat Idiot: A No-Nonsense Guide to
    Fly Casting. *v.5 p.251*

Fly Pushing: The Theory and Practice of Drosophila
    Genetics. *v.5 p.133*

▢ FlyBase. *v.5 p.109, p.138, p.144*

The Flying Circus of Physics. *v.5 p.541*

Flying Dragons, Flowing Streams: Music in the Life of San Francisco's Chinese. *v.1 p.297*

Focal Encyclopedia of Photography. *v.1 p.762*

The Focus Group Guidebook. *v.4 p.137*

Focus Groups: A Practical Guide for Applied Research. .*v.4 p.686*

Focus Groups: A Step-by-Step Guide. *v.4 p.136*

Focus Groups as Qualitative Research. *v.4 p.687*

Focus Groups: Theory and Practice. *v.4 p.687*

Focus on African Films. *v.6 p.334*

Focus on Genome Research. *v.5 p.143, p.147*

Focus. *v.2 p.101*

Foe. *v.2 p.753*

Foiglman. *v.6 p.650*

Foil, Saber and Epee Fencing: Skills, Safety, Operations, and Responsibilities. *v.4 p.857*

Fokine: Memoirs of a Ballet Master. *v.1 p.8*

The Folded Leaf. *v.2 p.97*

Folded, Spindled and Mutilated: The Economics of U. S. vs IBM. *v.4 p.438, p.439*

Folding Star. *v.6 p.397*

☐ FOLDOC: Free Online Dictionary of Computing. .*v.5 p.344*

Folk and Blues: The Premier Encyclopedia of American Roots Music. *v.1 p.162, p.163, p.264, p.297*

Folk and Traditional Music of the Western Continents. *v.1 p.287, p.293*

Folk Art in American Life. *v.1 p.681*

The Folk Art of Java. *v.1 p.800*

Folk Buddhist Religion: Dissenting Sects in Late Traditional China. *v.1 p.562*

Folk Dances of Latin America. *v.1 p.19, p.20, p.33*

Folk Groups and Folklore Genres: An Introduction. .*v.2 p.585*

The Folk Healer: The Mexican-American Tradition of Curanderismo. *v.6 p.524, p.551*

Folk Music: A Regional Exploration. *v.1 p.295*

Folk Music in America: A Reference Guide. *v.1 p.168, p.169, p.296*

Folk Music of China: Living Instrumental Traditions. .*v.1 p.288*

Folk Music of the Hungarians. *v.1 p.299*

Folk Music U. S. A.: The Changing Voice of Protest. .*v.1 p.296*

Folk Nation: Folklore in the Creation of American Tradition. *v.2 p.16*

Folk Religion in Japan: Continuity and Change. . . .*v.1 p.541*

Folk Roots and Mythic Wings in Sarah Orne Jewett and Toni Morrison: The Cultural Function of Narrative. .*v.2 p.46, p.150*

Folk Song Style and Culture. *v.1 p.296*

Folk Tale, Fiction and Saga in the Homeric Epics. . .*v.2 p.413*

Folklore and Culture on the Texas-Mexican Border. *v.6 p.487, p.524*

Folklore and Folklife: A Guide to English-Language Sources. *v.1 p.4*

Folklore and Folklife: An Introduction. *v.2 p.584*

The Folklore and Folklife of New Jersey. *v.2 p.17*

Folklore in Utah: A History and Guide to Resources. . .*v.2 p.17*

Folklore, Memoirs, and Other Writings. *v.2 p.81, v.6 p.16, p.17, p.18, p.26, p.39*

The Folklore of Spain in the American Southwest: Traditional Spanish Folk Literature in Northern New Mexico and Southern Colorado. *v.6 p.523*

The Folklore Text: From Performance to Print. . . .*v.2 p.585*

Folkloristics: An Introduction. *v.2 p.585*

Folktales in Homer's Odyssey. *v.2 p.415*

Folkways Records: Moses Asch and His Encyclopedia of Sound. *v.1 p.385*

La Follette and the Rise of the Progressives in Wisconsin. *v.3 p.434*

La Follette's Autobiography: A Personal Narrative of Political Experiences. *v.3 p.434*

Follies: New Stories. *v.2 p.140*

Follies. *v.1 p.254, p.357, p.410*

☐ Follow the Money. *v.4 p.558*

Follow the Music. *v.1 p.384*

Follow the Rabbit-Proof Fence. *v.2 p.748*

Follow This Path: How the World's Greatest Organizations Drive Growth by Unleashing Human Potential. . . .*v.4 p.76*

Following Balanchine. *v.1 p.23*

Following Tradition: Folklore in the Discourse of American Culture. *v.2 p.16*

Fonética y fonología Españolas: Teoría y Práctica. . .*v.2 p.635*

La Fontaine. *v.2 p.474*

The Fontana Economic History of Europe: The Middle Ages. *v.3 p.39*

The Fontana Economic History of Europe: The Twentieth Century. *v.3 p.39*

The Fontana Economic History of Europe. *v.3 p.39*

Fontanka 16: The Tsars' Secret Police. *v.3 p.218*

Fonteyn and Nureyev: The Story of a Partnership. . . .*v.1 p.6*

Fonteyn: The Making of a Legend. *v.1 p.11*

Fonvizin: The Minor. *v.2 p.803*

Food, Agriculture and Rural Policy into the Twenty-First Century: Issues and Trade-Offs. *v.5 p.12*

Food Aid after Fifty Years: Recasting its Role. .*v.4 p.259, p.265*

☐ The Food and Agriculture Organization of the United Nations: WAICENT Information Finder. *v.5 p.3*

Food and Beverage Market Place: Suppliers Guide, 2000-01. . . . .*v.4 p.160*

Food and Culture: A Reader. *v.4 p.45*

Food and Culture. *v.5 p.34*

Food and Gender: Identity and Power. *v.4 p.45*

☐ Food and Nutrition Information Center at the National Agricultural Library. *v.5 p.32*

Food Biotechnology: Current Issues and Perspectives. .*v.5 p.34*

Food Biotechnology in Ethical Perspective. *v.5 p.35*

Food Biotechnology: Microorganisms. *v.5 p.34*

Food Biotechnology. *v.5 p.33*

Food, Conquest and Colonization in Sixteenth-Century Spanish America. *v.3 p.270, p.272*

Food Culture in China. *v.5 p.35, v.6 p.182*

Food Culture in Italy. *v.5 p.35*

Food Culture in Mexico. *v.3 p.272, p.273, v.5 p.35*

Food, Gender, and Poverty in the Ecuadorian Andes. .*v.3 p.273*

Food in Chinese Culture: Anthropological and Historical
  Perspectives. *v.6 p.181*

Food in Medieval Times. *v.5 p.32, v.6 p.557*

Food in the USA: Reader. *v.4 p.45*

The Food Industry Wars: Marketing Triumphs and
  Blunders. *v.4 p.160*

Food Microbiology: Fundamentals and Frontiers. .*v.5 p.33, p.34*

Food, Nutrition and Sports Performance II: The IOC Consensus
  Conference on Sports Nutrition. *v.4 p.825, p.876*

The Food of China. *v.6 p.181*

The Food of the Gods and How It Came to Earth. . .*v.2 p.319*

Food Plants of the World. *v.5 p.24, p.44, p.45*

Food, Politics and Society in Latin America. *v.3 p.272*

Food Quality and Consumer Value: Delivering Food That
  Satisfies. *v.4 p.160*

The Food System: A Guide. *v.4 p.152*

Food: The Chemistry of Its Components. *v.5 p.329*

Food Values of Portions Commonly Used. *v.5 p.35, p.513*

Foods: A Scientific Approach. *v.5 p.33*

Foods and Food Production Encyclopedia. *v.5 p.33*

Foods: Experimental Perspectives. *v.5 p.35*

☐ FoodSafety.gov: Gateway to Government Food Safety
  Information. *v.5 p.32*

The Fool of Quality; or, The History of Henry, Earl of
  Moreland. by Henry Brooke. *v.2 p.238*

☐ Fool.com: To Educate, Amuse and Enrich. . .*v.4 p.93, p.101*

Fools and Philosophers: A Gallery of Com. *v.2 p.378*

Fools of Fortune. *v.2 p.385*

Fools Rush In: Steve Case, Jerry Levin, and the Unmaking of
  AOL Time Warner. *v.4 p.84, p.85*

A Foot in the Door: Networking Your Way into the Hidden Job
  Market. *v.4 p.170*

Football: A College History. *v.4 p.808, p.859*

Football: A Sociology of the Global
  Game. *v.4 p.815, p.843, p.867*

Football and American Identity. *v.4 p.805, p.858*

Football and Fascism: The National Game under
  Mussolini. *v.4 p.808, p.817, p.867, p.891, p.892*

Football and Its Fans: An Account of Supporters and Their
  Relations. *v.4 p.820, p.868*

Football Hooligans: Knowing the Score. *v.4 p.813, p.867*

Football: The Ivy League Origins of an American
  Obsession. *v.4 p.803, p.858*

Football U.: Spectator Sports in the Life of the American
  University. . . .*v.4 p.716, p.820, p.822, p.859, p.860, p.895*

Footbinding, Feminism and Freedom: The Liberation of
  Women's Bodies in Modern China. *v.4 p.835*

Footlights Across the Border: A History of Spanish-Language
  Professional Theatre on the Texas Stage. *v.6 p.518*

Footnotes: A Memoir. *v.6 p.415*

Footprints: The Life and Music of Wayne
  Shorter. *v.1 p.262, p.356*

Footsteps in the Jungle: Adventures in the Scientific Exploration
  of the American Tropics. *v.5 p.236, p.239*

Footsteps. *v.6 p.178*

For a Crust of Bread. *v.2 p.813*

For a New Novel: Essays on Fiction. *v.2 p.525, p.579*

For Adult Users Only: The Dilemma of Violent
  Pornography. *v.4 p.748*

For All the Peoples of Asia: Federation of Asian Bishops'
  Conferences Documents from 1970 to 1991. . . . .*v.1 p.574*

For Better and for Worse: Welfare Reform and the Well-Being
  of Children and Families. *v.4 p.755, p.756*

For Better or for Worse: Divorce Reconsidered. . . .*v.5 p.640*

For Better or for Worse: The Marriage of Science and
  Government in the United States. *v.4 p.525*

For Better or Worse?: Same Sex Marriages, Pro and Con: A
  Reader. *v.4 p.570, v.6 p.389*

For Cause and Comrades: Why Men Fought in the Civil
  War. *v.4 p.521*

For Democracy's Sake: Foundations and Democracy Assistance
  in Central Europe. *v.4 p.585, p.640*

For Every Sin. *v.6 p.647*

For Freedom's Battle, 1823-1824, Vol. XI. *v.2 p.274*

For Fun and Profit: The Transformation of Leisure into
  Consumption. *v.4 p.783, p.887*

For Girls Only: Making a Case for Single-Sex
  Schooling. *v.6 p.464*

For God, Country and Coca-Cola: The Definitive History of the
  Great American Soft Drink and the Company That Makes
  It. *v.3 p.282*

For Health and Beauty: Physical Culture for Frenchwomen,
  1880s-1930s. *v.3 p.54*

For la Patria: Politics and the Armed Forces in Latin
  America. *v.3 p.275, v.4 p.592*

For Lizzie and Harriet. *v.2 p.96*

For Love Alone. *v.2 p.749*

For My People. *v.2 p.128*

For Pride, Profit and Patriarchy: Football and the Incorporation
  of American Cultural Values. . . .*v.4 p.805, p.858, p.881*

For Social Peace in Brazil: Industrialists and the Remaking of
  the Working Class in Sao Paulo, 1920-1964. . . . .*v.3 p.343*

For the Baptism of Our Fragments. *v.2 p.716*

For the Common Defense: A Military History of the United
  States of America. *v.3 p.383*

For the Common Good: A Critical Examination of Law and
  Social Control. *v.4 p.773, p.774*

For the End of Time: The Story of the Messiaen
  Quartet. *v.1 p.222, p.242, p.341*

For the Future of Israel. *v.6 p.615*

For the Geography of a Soul: Emerging Perspectives on Kamau
  Brathwaite. *v.2 p.768*

For the Glory: College Football Dreams and Realities Inside
  Paterno's Program. *v.4 p.858, p.893*

For the Love of Enzymes: The Odyssey of a Biochemist. .*v.5 p.119*

For the Love of Pleasure: Women, Movies, and Culture in
  Turn-of-the-Century Chicago. *v.6 p.343*

For the Public Record: A Documentary History of the League of
  Women Voters. *v.4 p.519, p.569*

For the Record: A Documentary History of America, Vol.
  2. . . . .*v.3 p.372*

For the Record: From Wall Street to Washington. . .*v.4 p.529*

For the Soul of the People: Protestant Protest Against
  Hitler. *v.1 p.581, v.3 p.82, p.171*

For the Survival of Democracy: Franklin Roosevelt and the World Crisis of the 1930's. *v.3 p.472, v.4 p.522*

For the Union of Evangelical Christendom: The Irony of the Reformed Episcopalians. *v.1 p.582*

For the Wild Places: Profiles in Conservation. *v.5 p.17, p.178,v.6 p.293*

For We are Sold, I and My People: Women and Industry in Mexico's Frontier. *v.4 p.729*

For Weber: Essays on the Sociology of Fate. *v.4 p.686*

For Whom the Bell Tolls. *v.2 p.84*

For Women and the Nation: Funmilayo Ransome-Kuti of Nigeria. *v.6 p.28, p.44*

Foragers and Farmers: Population Interaction and Agricultural Expansion in Prehistoric Europe. *v.4 p.12*

Forages: An Introduction to Grassland Agriculture. *v.5 p.20, p.24*

Forages: The Science of Grassland Agriculture. . . . *v.5 p.42*

Forbidden Acts: Pioneering Gay and Lesbian Plays of the Twentieth Century. *v.1 p.100, p.126,v.6 p.411, p.412*

Forbidden Animation: Censored Cartoons and Blacklisted Animators in America. *v.6 p.307*

The forbidden best-sellers of pre-revolutionary France. *v.3 p.147*

The Forbidden Forest. *v.2 p.817*

Forbidden Grounds: The Case Against Employment Discrimination Laws. *v.4 p.133*

Forbidden Matter: Religion in the Drama of Shakespeare and His Contemporaries. *v.2 p.186, p.231*

The Forbidden Modern: Civilization and Veiling. . . *v.6 p.623*

The Forbidden Stitch: An Asian-American Women's Anthology. *v.6 p.91, p.111, p.112*

Forbidden Territory and Realms of Strife: The Memoirs of Juan Goytisolo. *v.2 p.658*

Forbidden Workers: Illegal Chinese Immigrants and American Labor. *v.6 p.106, p.114, p.116*

Force and Ideas: The Early Writings. *v.3 p.474*

La force de l'âge. *v.2 p.508*

La force des choses. *v.2 p.508*

A Force for Change: How Leadership Differs from Management. *v.4 p.71*

The Force of Knowledge. *v.5 p.411, p.412, p.413*

The Force of Poetry. *v.2 p.180*

Forced Choices: Class, Community, and Worker Ownership. *v.4 p.727*

Forced Justice: School Desegregation and the Law. *v.4 p.300, p.449*

Forced Migration Online. *v.4 p.667*

Forced Sexual Intercourse in Intimate Relationships. . *v.4 p.742*

Forces of Deviance: Understanding the Dark Side of Policing. *v.6 p.261*

The Forces of Economic Growth: A Time Series Perspective. *v.4 p.243*

Forces of Habit: Drugs and the Making of the Modern World. *v.3 p.281, v.4 p.776*

Forces of Labor: Workers' Movements and Globalization Since 1870. . . . . *v.4 p.129*

Ford: Five Plays. *v.2 p.218*

A Ford, Not a Lincoln. *v.3 p.478*

Fordson, Farmall and Poppin' Johnny: A History of the Farm Tractor and Its Impact on America. *v.5 p.6, p.30*

Forecasting and Market Analysis Techniques: A Practical Approach. *v.4 p.137*

Forecasting Economic Time Series. *v.4 p.206*

Foreign Affairs. *v.2 p.149*

Foreign Attachments: The Power of Ethnic Groups in the Making of American Foreign Policy. *v.3 p.454*

Foreign Clientele, Two Hundred Sixty-Four to Seventy BC. *v.3 p.25*

Foreign Devils on the Silk Road: The Search for the Lost Treasures of Central Asia. *v.6 p.204*

A Foreign Exchange Primer. . *v.4 p.89, p.90, p.97, p.98, p.100*

Foreign Films in America: A History. *v.6 p.343*

Foreign Government Resources on the Web. . . . *v.4 p.482*

Foreign in a Domestic Sense: Puerto Rico, American Expansion and the Constitution. *v.3 p.319*

Foreign Language Learning: Psycholinguistic Studies on Training and Retention. *v.5 p.610*

The Foreign Legion. *v.2 p.691*

Foreign News: Exploring the World of Foreign Correspondents. *v.4 p.407*

The Foreign Policies of Herbert Hoover 1929-1933. . *v.3 p.476*

Foreign Policies of Lyndon Johnson: Beyond Vietnam. *v.3 p.466*

The Foreign Policies of Northern Europe. . . *v.3 p.235, p.236*

Foreign Policy and the American Spirit. *v.3 p.386*

The Foreign Policy of George W. Bush: Values, Strategy and Loyalty. *v.3 p.484*

The Foreign Policy of Victorian England, 1830-1902. . . . . *v.3 p.91, p.110*

Foreign Policy, War and Racial Extermination: A Documentary Reader. *v.3 p.173*

Foreign Relations of the United States. *v.4 p.482, p.561, p.566, p.643*

The Foreign Service of the United States: First Line of Defense. *v.4 p.529*

Foreign Shakespeare: Contemporary Performance. *v.1 p.76, p.101, p.135*

Foreigners in Their Native Land: Historical Roots of the Mexican Americans. *v.6 p.533*

Forensic and Criminal Psychology. *v.5 p.592*

Forensic Mental Health Assessment: A Casebook. . . *v.5 p.592*

The Forensic Psychologist's Casebook: Psychological Profiling and Criminal Investigation. *v.5 p.591*

Forensic Psychology: Concepts, Debates and Practice. *v.5 p.591*

Forensic Psychology: From Classroom to Courtroom. *v.5 p.593*

Forensic Psychology. *v.5 p.593*

Forensic Structural Engineering Handbook. *v.5 p.686*

Forerunners of the Reformation: The Shape of Late Medieval Thought. *v.1 p.632*

Foreshortened Time: Andrew Marvell and 17th-Century Revolutions. *v.2 p.252*

Foresight and Understanding: An Enquiry into the Aims of Science. *v.5 p.404*

Forest and Garden: Traces of Wildness in a Modernizing Land, 1897-1949. . . . . *v.1 p.814*

Forest and Range Policy. *v.5 p.37*

The Forest and the Sea: A Look at the Economy of Nature and the Ecology of Man. *v.6 p.293*

Forest and Wildlife Science in America: A History. . . . *v.5 p.39*

Forest Decline Concepts. *v.5 p.38*

Forest Diversity and Function: Temperate and Boreal Systems. *v.5 p.176, p.180*

Forest Ecology: A Foundation for Sustainable Forest Management and Environmental Ethics in Forestry. *v.5 p.38*

Forest Fires: An Introduction to Wildland Fire Behavior, Management, Firefighting, and Prevention. *v.5 p.32, p.358, p.373*

Forest for the Trees?: Government Policies and the Misuse of Forest Resources. *v.5 p.39*

Forest Giants of the Pacific Coast. *v.5 p.40*

The Forest History Society. *v.5 p.36*

Forest Measurements. *v.5 p.36*

Forest Mensuration. *v.5 p.38*

A Forest of Kings: The Untold Story of the Ancient Maya. *v.3 p.262*

The Forest of Symbols: Aspects of Ndembu Ritual. *v.4 p.37, v.6 p.77*

The Forest People. *v.4 p.39, v.6 p.63*

Forest Primeval: The Natural History of an Ancient Forest. *v.5 p.38*

The Forest Ranger: A Study in Administrative Behavior. *v.5 p.38*

Forest Resource Management: Decision-Making Principles and Cases. *v.5 p.41*

The Forest Service: A Study in Public Land Management. *v.5 p.18, p.39, v.6 p.296*

The Forest Service and the greatest good: a centennial history. *v.5 p.38*

Forestry Education in America Today and Tomorrow. . *v.5 p.40*

Forestry Handbook. *v.5 p.40*

Forests: A Journey into North America's Vanishing Wilderness. *v.5 p.175, p.234, p.239*

Forests and Livelihoods: Social Dynamics of Deforestation in Developing Countries. *v.5 p.36*

Forests for Whom and for What? *v.5 p.37*

Forests in Time: The Environmental Consequences of 1,000 Years of Change in New England. *v.5 p.357*

Forests of Gold: Essays on the Akan and the Kingdom of Asante. *v.6 p.70*

Forever Flowing. *v.2 p.804*

Forever Foreigners or Honorary Whites: The Asian Ethnic Experience Today. *v.6 p.124, p.125*

Forever Free: The Story of Emancipation and Reconstruction. *v.3 p.436, v.4 p.485*

Forever in the Shadow of Hitler?: The Dispute about the Germans' Understanding of Hisotry: Original Documents of the Historikerstreit, the Controversy Concerning the Singularity of the Holocaust. *v.3 p.178*

Forever valley : roman. *v.2 p.533*

Forever Valley. *v.2 p.533*

Forex Revolution: An Insider's Guide to the Real World of Foreign Exchange Trading. . . . *v.4 p.89, p.97, p.98, p.100*

Forge of Progress, Crucible of Revolt: The Origins of the Mexican Revolution in La Comarca Lagunera, 1880-1911. . . . . *v.3 p.294*

The Forge of the Spirit: Structure, Motion and Meaning in the Japanese Martial Tradition. *v.4 p.863*

Forging a Community: The Latino Experience in Northwest Indiana, 1919-1975. . . . . *v.6 p.536*

Forging Democracy: A Comparative Study of the Effects of U.S. Foreign Policy on Central American Democratization. *v.3 p.303*

Forging Democracy from Below: Insurgent Transitions in South Africa and el Salvador. *v.4 p.614*

Forging Freedom: The Formation of Philadelphia's Black Community, 1720-1840. . . . . *v.3 p.492, v.6 p.714*

Forging Mexico, 1821-1835. . . . . *v.3 p.288*

The Forging of a Black Community: Seattle's Central District, from 1870 Through the Civil Rights Era. *v.6 p.715*

The Forging of an Aristocracy. *v.4 p.707*

The Forging of the American Empire: From the Revolution to Vietnam: A History of American Imperialism. . . *v.3 p.386*

The Forging of the Ring: Richard Wagner's Composition Sketches for Der Ring des Nibelungen. *v.1 p.205, p.234, p.366*

Forging Stalin's Army: Marshal Tukhachevsky and the Politics of Military Innovation. *v.3 p.212*

Forging the Tortilla Curtain: Cultural Drift and Change along the United States-Mexico Boarderlands from the Spanish Conquest to the Present. *v.3 p.527, v.6 p.487, p.488, p.533*

Forgiveness and Mercy. *v.1 p.651*

Forgotten Armies: The Fall of British Asia, 1941-1945. *v.6 p.164*

Forgotten Children: Parent-Child Relations from 1500 to 1900. . . . . *v.3 p.92, v.4 p.735*

Forgotten Families: Ending the Growing Crisis Confronting Children and Working Parents in the Global Economy. *v.4 p.759, p.760*

Forgotten Females: Women of African and Indian Descent in Colonial Chile, 1535-1800. . . . . *v.3 p.350*

The Forgotten Few: The Polish Air Force in World War II. *v.3 p.255*

The Forgotten Front: The British Campaign in Italy 1917-18. . . . . *v.3 p.78*

The Forgotten Frontier: A History of the Sixteenth Century Ibero-African Frontier. *v.6 p.60*

The Forgotten Holocaust: The Poles under German Occupation, 1939-1944. . . . . *v.3 p.254*

The Forgotten Naturalist: In Search of Alfred Russel Wallace. *v.5 p.231, p.232*

The Forgotten North: A History of Canada's Provincial North. *v.3 p.546*

Forgotten People: A Study of New Mexicans. . . *v.6 p.533*

Forgotten Readers: Recovering the Lost History of African-American Literary Societies. *v.6 p.27*

A Forgotten Voice: A Biography of Leta Stetter Hollingworth. *v.4 p.337, v.5 p.575, p.597*

Form and Transformation in Asian American Literature. *v.6 p.98*

Form Follows Finance: Skyscrapers and Skylines in New York and Chicago. *v.6 p.729*

Form in Music. *v.1 p.369*

The Form of Faust: The Work of Art and Its Intrinsic Structures. *v.2 p.598*

Formaciones Económicas y Políticas en el Mundo
Andino. *v.3 p.324*

Formal Arabic. *v.6 p.654*

Formal Logic: Its Scope and Limits. *v.1 p.492*

Formal Organizations: A Comparative Approach. . . *v.4 p.717*

The Formal Semantics of Programming Languages: An
Introduction. *v.5 p.336, p.347, p.348, p.349*

Formal Sociology: The Work of Georg Simmel. *v.4 p.196*

Formal Spoken Arabic Basic Course. *v.6 p.654*

Formalized Music: Thought and Mathematics in
Composition. *v.1 p.227, p.368, p.374*

The Formation of a Colonial Society: Belize, from Conquest to
Crown Colony. *v.3 p.296*

The Formation of Campaign Agendas: A Comparative Analysis
of Party and Media Roles in Recent American and British
Elections. *v.4 p.549, p.550, p.558, p.559*

The Formation of Christendom. *v.6 p.563*

The Formation of Econometrics: A Historical
Perspective. *v.4 p.204*

The Formation of English Common Law: Law and Society in
England from the Norman Conquest to Magna Carta. .*v.3 p.98*

The Formation of Islam: Religion and Society in the near East,
600-1800. . . . .*v.4 p.721, v.6 p.581*

The Formation of National Party Systems: Federalism and Party
Competition in Canada, Great Britain, India, and the United
States. *v.4 p.578*

The Formation of National States in Western Europe. .*v.4 p.602*

The Formation of Q: Trajectories in Ancient Wisdom
Collections. *v.1 p.629*

The Formation of the Christian Bible. *v.1 p.615*

Formation of the Modern State: The Ottoman Empire, Sixteenth
to Eighteenth Centuries. *v.6 p.589*

The Formation of Turkey: The Seljukid Sultanate of Reum:
Eleventh to Fourteenth Century. *v.6 p.622*

The Formative Era of American Law. *v.4 p.440*

The Formative Period in Alabama, 1815-1828. . . . .*v.3 p.504*

The Formative Period of Islamic Thought. *v.1 p.558*

The Formative Years of Plant Pathology in the United
States. *v.5 p.45, p.46*

Forms of Discovery: Critical and Historical Essays on the Forms
of the Short Poem in English. *v.2 p.180*

Forms of Hope: Essays. *v.2 p.781*

Forms of Speech in Victorian Fiction: Studies in 18th and 19th
Century Literature. *v.6 p.751, p.755*

Forms of Talk. *v.4 p.423, v.5 p.623*

Formula Index to NMR Literature Data, Vol. 1. . . . .*v.5 p.287*

Formula Index to NMR Literature Data, Vol. 2. . . . .*v.5 p.287*

Formulas for Stress, Strain, and Structural Matrices. .*v.5 p.696*

Fornalutx: Selected Poems, 1928-1990. . . . .*v.2 p.736*

The Forsyte Saga. *v.2 p.347*

Fort Mose: Colonial America's Black Fortress of
Freedom. *v.4 p.13*

Fort Sumter to Perryville. *v.3 p.396*

The Forties: From Notebooks and Diaries of the Period. .*v.2 p.137*

Fortran 95/2003 Explained. *v.5 p.347, p.349*

Fortress America: Gated Communities in the United
States. *v.6 p.716*

Fortress America: The American Military and the Consequences
of Peace. *v.4 p.561*

Fortress Introduction to Lutheranism. *v.1 p.585*

Fortress Introduction to the Lutheran Confessions. . .*v.1 p.585*

The Fortress. *v.2 p.812*

Fortunata and Jacinta: Two Stories of Married Women. .*v.2 p.654*

Fortunata and Jacinta. *v.2 p.655*

The Fortune at the Bottom of the Pyramid: Eradicating Poverty
Through Profits. *v.4 p.665*

Fortune, My Foe and Eros at Breakfast: Two Plays. . *v.2 p.735*

Fortunes of Falstaff. *v.2 p.233*

Fortunes of Nigel. *v.2 p.308*

Fortunes of Richard Mahoney. *v.2 p.746*

The Fortunes of Richard Mahony. *v.2 p.748*

Fortune's Wheel: Dickens and the Iconography of Women's
Times. *v.2 p.282*

Fortuny. *v.1 p.720*

The Forty Days of Musa Dagh. *v.2 p.616*

The Forum of Trajan in Rome: A Study of the Monuments in
Brief. *v.3 p.29*

Forward Ever!: Three Years of the Grenadian
Revolution. *v.3 p.318*

The Fossil Hunters: In Search of Ancient Plants. . . *v.5 p.449*

Fossil Hydrocarbons: Chemistry and Technology. . . *v.5 p.320*

Fossil Invertebrates. *v.5 p.447*

Fossil Plants. *v.5 p.449*

The Fossil Trail: How We Know What We Think We Know
about Human Evolution. *v.4 p.16*

Fossils, Finches, and Fuegians: Darwin's Adventures and
Discoveries on the Beagle. *v.5 p.233*

Fossils in the Field: Information Potential and Analysis. *v.5 p.447*

Fossils: The Evolution and Extinction of Species. . . *v.5 p.447*

Fossils: The Key to the Past. *v.5 p.447*

Foster Children in the Life Course Perspective: The Casey
Family Program Experience. *v.4 p.757*

Fostering Algebraic Thinking: A Guide for Teachers, Grades
6-10. . . . .*v.5 p.462*

Foucault: A Critical Reader. *v.1 p.459*

Foucault and Education: Disciplines and Knowledge. *v.4 p.340*

The Foucault Reader: An Introduction to Foucault's
Thought. *v.1 p.458, p.459*

Foucault's Challenge: Discourse, Knowledge, and Power in
Education. *v.4 p.345*

Foucault's Critical Project: Between the Transcendental and the
Historical. *v.1 p.459*

Foucault's Nietzschean Genealogy: Truth, Power, and the
Subject. *v.1 p.459*

Foul Play: Drug Abuse in Sports. *v.4 p.802, p.826*

Found Tribe: Jewish Coming Out Stories. . . .*v.6 p.369, p.374*

Foundation Analysis and Design. *v.5 p.421*

Foundation Engineering Handbook. *v.5 p.421*

The Foundation of Rome: Myth and History. *v.3 p.24*

The Foundation Pit. *v.2 p.807*

Foundation Vibration Analysis: A Strength of Materials
Approach. *v.5 p.697*

Foundational Fictions: The National Romances of Latin
 America. *v.3 p.265*

Foundational Theology: Jesus and the Church. *v.1 p.635*

Foundations and Practices in the Use of Distance
 Education. *v.4 p.321*

Foundations for Microwave Engineering. *v.5 p.729*

Foundations for the Future: The AICPA from
 1980-1995. . . . .*v.4 p.104*

Foundations in Singing. *v.1 p.396*

The Foundations of American Constitutionalism [1932]. *v.4 p.518*

Foundations of American Constitutionalism. *v.4 p.454*

Foundations of Analog and Digital Electronic Circuits. *v.5 p.721*

Foundations of Animal Behavior: Classic Papers with
 Commentaries. *v.5 p.166, p.167, p.614*

Foundations of Applied Mathematics. *v.5 p.501*

Foundations of Biogeography: Classic Papers with
 Commentaries. *v.4 p.394, v.5 p.168, p.226*

The Foundations of Buddhism. *v.1 p.565*

Foundations of Casualty Actuarial Science. *v.5 p.504*

Foundations of Chemical Analysis. *v.5 p.268*

Foundations of Christian Faith: An Introduction to the Idea of
 Christianity. *v.1 p.575, p.636*

Foundations of Cognitive Psychology: Core Readings. *v.5 p.608*

The Foundations of Contemporary and Historical
 Sociology. *v.4 p.248*

Foundations of Crusader Valencia: Revolt and Recovery,
 1257-1263. . . . .*v.3 p.65*

Foundations of Cryptography: Basic Applications. . . *v.5 p.335*

Foundations of Cryptography: Basic Tools, Vol. 1. . . *v.5 p.335*

Foundations of Cyclopean Perception. *v.5 p.605*

Foundations of Despotism: Peasants, the Trujillo Regime, and
 Modernity in Dominican History. *v.3 p.318*

Foundations of Dialogue in Science and Religion. . . *v.1 p.526*

Foundations of Dynamic Economic Analysis: Optimal Control
 Theory and Applications. *v.4 p.198*

The Foundations of Early Modern Europe, 1460-1559, Vol.
 1. . . . .*v.1 p.602*

The Foundations of Econometric Analysis. *v.4 p.201*

Foundations of Economic Analysis. *v.4 p.197, p.204*

Foundations of Economic Value Added. *v.4 p.89*

The Foundations of Economics: History and Theory in the
 Analysis of Economic Reality. *v.4 p.209*

Foundations of Electromagnetic Theory. *v.5 p.565*

Foundations of Engineering Geology. *v.5 p.422*

Foundations of Environmental Engineering. *v.5 p.704*

Foundations of Ethics: The Gifford Lectures Delivered in the
 University of Aberdeen, 1935-1936. . . . . . .*v.1 p.487*

Foundations of Exercise Psychology. *v.5 p.581*

The Foundations of Fuzzy Control. *v.5 p.711*

The Foundations of Geometry. *v.5 p.466, p.495*

Foundations of Geotechnical Engineering. *v.5 p.698*

Foundations of Inventory Management. *v.4 p.117*

Foundations of Language: Brain, Meaning, Grammar,
 Evolution. *v.2 p.550, p.561*

The Foundations of Latin. *v.2 p.423*

Foundations of Mathematical Genetics. *v.5 p.143, p.144*

Foundations of Modern Econometrics: The Selected Essays of
 Ragnar Frisch. *v.4 p.198*

Foundations of Multidimensional and Metric Data
 Structures. *v.5 p.335, p.340*

Foundations of Music Education. *v.1 p.404*

Foundations of Music History. *v.1 p.173*

The Foundations of Mysticism: Origins to the Fifth
 Century. *v.1 p.653*

The Foundations of New Testament Christology. . . .*v.1 p.640*

The Foundations of Paul Samuelson's Revealed Preference
 Theory: A Study by the Method of Rational
 Reconstruction. *v.4 p.197*

Foundations of Paul Samuelson's Revealed Preference
 Theory. *v.4 p.251*

Foundations of Physical Education, Exercise Science, and Sport
 with PowerWeb. *v.4 p.797*

Foundations of Physical Therapy: A 21st Century-Focused
 View. *v.5 p.535, p.536*

Foundations of Post-Keynesian Economic
 Analysis. *v.4 p.232, p.233*

Foundations of Probability, Econometrics and Economic Games,
 Vols. 1-10. . . . .*v.4 p.201*

Foundations of Program Evaluation: Theories of
 Practice. *v.4 p.690*

Foundations of Psychological Testing. *v.5 p.601*

The Foundations of Science. *v.5 p.403*

The Foundations of Scientific Inference. *v.5 p.404*

Foundations of Scientific Method: The Nineteenth
 Century. *v.5 p.401*

Foundations of Social Behavior. *v.5 p.649, p.650*

Foundations of Social Evolution. *v.5 p.192*

The Foundations of Socratic Ethics. *v.1 p.422*

Foundations of Sport and Exercise Psychology. *v.5 p.583*

Foundations of Systems Biology. *v.5 p.106, p.127, p.146, p.149*

Foundations of the Economics of Innovation: Theory,
 Measurement and Practice. *v.4 p.241*

Foundations of the Unity of Science: Toward an International
 Encyclopedia of Unified Science, 1. . . . .*v.5 p.388*

Foundations of the Unity of Science: Toward an International
 Encyclopedia of Unified Science. *v.5 p.388*

Foundations of Vacuum Science and Technology. . . .*v.5 p.563*

Foundations of World Order: The Legalist Approach to
 International Relations, 1898-1921. . . . .*v.4 p.627*

The Founder: Cecil Rhodes and the Pursuit of Power. *v.3 p.126*

The Founder of Modern Egypt. *v.6 p.639*

The Founders of Geology. *v.5 p.418*

Founding Brothers: The Revolutionary Generation. . *v.4 p.485*

Founding Fathers: The Puritans in England and
 America. *v.3 p.484*

Founding Mothers and Others: Women Educational Leaders
 During the Progressive Era. *v.6 p.463, p.464*

Founding Mothers: The Women Who Raised Our
 Nation. *v.4 p.487, p.517, p.569*

The Founding of a Nation: A History of the American
 Revolution, 1763-1776. . . . . .*v.3 p.405, v.4 p.517, p.518*

The Founding of Israeli Democracy, 1948-1967. . . .*v.4 p.615*

The Founding of New England. *v.3 p.405, v.4 p.517*

The Founding of Russia's Navy: Peter the Great and the Azov Fleet, 1688-1714. . . . .*v.3 p.217*

The Founding of the Kamakura Shogunate, 1880-1885. with Selected Translations from the Azuma Kagami. *v.6 p.225, p.226*

The Fountain of Age. *v.6 p.445*

Fountain of Discontent: The Trent Affair and Freedom of the Sea. *v.3 p.433*

The Fountainhead: Centennial Edition. *v.2 p.113*

Four Adaptations of Effort Theory in Research and Teaching. *v.1 p.50*

The Four Adventures of Richard Hannay: The Thirty-Nine Steps; Greenmantle; Mr. Standfast; The Three Hostages. *v.2 p.331*

Four Against the Odds: The Struggle to Save Our Environment. *v.5 p.230*

Four Billion Years: An Essay on the Evolution of Genes and Organisms. *v.5 p.193, p.194*

Four British Women Novelists: Anita Brookner, Margaret Drabble, Iris Murdoch, Barbara Pym: An Annotated and Critical Secondary Bibliography. . .*v.2 p.379*

Four by Sondheim: Wheeler, Lapine, Shevelove, Gelbart. *v.1 p.254, p.357, p.410*

Four Centuries of Ballet: Fifty Masterworks. *v.1 p.24*

Four Centuries of Modern Iraq. *v.6 p.603*

Four Colors Suffice: How the Map Problem Was Solved. *v.5 p.468, p.480*

Four Comedies: Lysistrata, the Congresswomen, the Acharnians, the Frogs. *v.2 p.423*

Four Days with Dr. Deming: A Strategy for Modern Methods of Management. *v.4 p.73*

Four Decades of Polish Essays. *v.2 p.787*

Four Essays on Gulliver's Travels. *v.2 p.262*

The Four Faces of Nuclear Terrorism. *v.4 p.658, p.659*

Four French Renaissance Plays: In Translation with Introduction and Notes, Preceded by an Essay on French Renaissance Drama. *v.2 p.465*

Four Generations: Population, Land, and Family in Colonial Andover, Massachusetts. *v.3 p.488*

Four German Poets: Gunter Eich, Hilde Domin, Erich Fried and Gunter Kunert. *v.2 p.594*

The four Gospels; a study of origins, treating of the manuscript tradition, sources, authorship, & dates. *v.1 p.629*

The Four Gospels and the One Gospel of Jesus Christ. .*v.1 p.629*

Four Greek Plays: Andromache, Iphigenia, Phaedra, Athaliah. *v.2 p.476, p.477*

Four Hundred Million Customers: The Experiences - Some Happy, Some Sad - of an American in China and What They Taught Him. *v.6 p.214*

Four in Hand: A Quartet of Novels. *v.2 p.387*

The Four Just Men. *v.2 p.386*

The Four Little Dragons: The Spread of Industrialization in East Asia. *v.6 p.181, p.206*

The Four Loves. *v.1 p.651*

Four Major Plays. *v.1 p.84, p.107, p.108,v.2 p.658, p.659*

Four Musical Minimalists: La Monte Young, Terry Riley, Steve Reich, Philip Glass. *v.1 p.221*

Four Novels: Collected Works II. *v.2 p.521*

Four Parts, No Waiting: A Social History of American Barbershop Harmony. *v.1 p.265, p.295*

Four Plays: Come Back Little Sheba; Picnic; Bus Stop; The Dark at the Top of the Stairs. *v.2 p.89*

Four plays: Romulus the Great. The Marriage of Mr. Mississippi. An Angel Comes to Babylon. The Physicists. *v.2 p.606*

Four Plays. *v.2 p.516, p.715*

Four Playwrights and a Postscript: Brecht, Ionesco, Beckett, Genet. *v.1 p.82, p.85, p.92, p.96*

Four Renaissance Comedies. *v.1 p.69, p.75, p.103*

Four Renaissance Tragedies. *v.2 p.465*

Four Restoration Libertine Plays. . .*v.1 p.65, p.77, p.90, p.100*

Four Roman Comedies: The Haunted House, Casina, or A Funny Thing Happened on the Way to the Wedding, the Eunuch, Brothers. *v.1 p.72, p.90*

Four Screenplays of Ingmar Bergman. *v.2 p.629*

Four Souls: A Novel. *v.2 p.145*

Four Stories. *v.2 p.628, p.629*

Four Theories of the Press: The Authoritarian, Libertarian, Social Responsibility and Soviet Communist Concepts of What the Press Should Be. *v.4 p.406*

The Four Wise Men. *v.2 p.534*

The Four-Gated City. *v.2 p.364*

Fourier Analysis: An Introduction. *v.5 p.494*

Fourier Descriptors and Their Applications in Biology. *v.5 p.91, p.94*

Fourier Series and Boundary Value Problems. *v.5 p.487*

The Fourier Transform and Its Applications. *v.5 p.64*

Fourscore Classics of Music Literature. *v.1 p.174*

Fourteen Byzantine Rulers: The Chronographia of Michael Psellus. *v.3 p.193*

The Fourteen-Book Prelude. *v.2 p.325*

The Fourteenth Amendment: From Political Principle to Judicial Doctrine. *v.4 p.457*

Fourth Crusade: The Conquest of Constantinople. . . .*v.3 p.63*

The Fourth Estate and the Constitution: Freedom of the Press in America. *v.4 p.459*

The Fourth Great Awakening and the Future of Egalitarianism: The Political Realignment of the 1990s and the Fate of Egalitarianism. *v.4 p.514*

☐ Fourth World Documentation Project. *v.4 p.482*

Les Fous des Bassan. *v.2 p.539*

Fowler's Modern English Usage. *v.2 p.550, p.556*

The Fox from up Above and the Fox from down Below. .*v.2 p.685*

The Fox, the Captain's Doll, the Ladybird. *v.2 p.363*

Foxe's Book of Martyrs. *v.1 p.612*

Foxfire: Confessions of a Girl Gang. *v.2 p.152*

Fra Angelico at San Marco. *v.1 p.741*

Fra Angelico. *v.1 p.742, p.747*

Fra Filippo Lippi: The Carmelite Painter. *v.1 p.740*

The Fractal Geometry of Nature. *v.5 p.498, p.502*

Fractal Horizons: The Future Uses of Fractals. .*v.5 p.411, p.498*

Fractals and Chaos in Geology and Geophysics. *v.5 p.420*

Fractals, Chaos and Power Laws: Minutes from an Infinite Paradise. *v.5 p.498*

Fractals: Form, Chance, and Dimension. *v.5 p.498*

The Fractional Quantum Hall Effect: A Survey of the Incompressible Quantum Fluid Including the Integer Quantum Hall Effect. *v.5 p.565*

The Fractious Nation?: Unity and Division in Contemporary American Life. *v.3 p.371*

Fracture and Fatigue Control in Structures: Applications of Fracture Mechanics. *v.5 p.687*

Fracture Mechanics: Fundamentals and Application. . *v.5 p.687*

Fracture Mechanics of Polymers. *v.5 p.692*

Fracture Mechanics Testing Methods for Polymers, Adhesives and Composites. *v.5 p.690*

A Fractured Society: The Politics of London in the First Age of Party, 1688-1715. . . . .*v.3 p.93, p.105, p.106*

Fragile Evidence: A Critique of Reading Assessment. *v.4 p.354*

The Fragile Middle Class: Americans in Debt. *v.4 p.271*

Fragility and Goodness: Why Bulgaria's Jews Survived the Holocaust. *v.3 p.251*

The Fragility of Goodness: Luck and Ethics in Greek Tragedy and Philosophy. *v.1 p.420*

The Fragmentary Latin Poets: Edited with Commentary. *v.2 p.424*

The Fragmentation of Afghanistan: State Formation and Collapse in the International System. *v.6 p.634*

The Fragmented Forest: Island Biogeography Theory and the Preservation of Biotic Diversity. *v.5 p.37, p.40, p.41, p.358, p.373*

The Fragmented Metropolis: Los Angeles, 1850-1930. . . . .*v.3 p.531, v.6 p.712*

Fragmented Ties: Salvadoran Immigrant Networks in America. *v.6 p.530*

Fragments of a Poetics of Fire. *v.1 p.455*

Fragments of Culture: The Everyday of Modern Turkey. *v.6 p.624*

Fragments of Memory: A Story of a Syrian Family. . .*v.6 p.662*

Fragments of the Artwork. *v.2 p.518*

Fragonard: Art and Eroticism. *v.1 p.747*

Frame by Frame II: A Filmography of the African American Image, 1978-1994. . . . .*v.6 p.330, p.342*

Framed! Labor and the Corporate Media. *v.4 p.127*

Frames of Mind: The Theory of Multiple Intelligences. *v.5 p.571*

Frames of Reference: A Resource Guide from the National Initiative to Preserve America's Dance. *v.1 p.52*

Frameworks for Sport Psychologists: Enhancing Sport Performance. *v.4 p.877*

Framing ADHD Children: A Critical Examination of the History, Discourse, and Everyday Experience of Attention Deficit/Hyperactivity Disorder. *v.4 p.319*

Framing America: A Social History of American Art. *v.1 p.682, p.683, p.708*

Framing Dropouts: Notes on the Politics of an Urban High School. *v.6 p.526, p.548*

Framing Feminism: Art and the Women's Movement, 1970-1985. . . . .*v.6 p.473*

Framing Latin American Cinema: Contemporary Critical Perspectives. *v.6 p.344*

The Framing of the Constitution of the United States. *v.4 p.452*

Framing Our Past: Constructing Canadian Women's History in the Twentieth Century. *v.6 p.453*

Framing Shakespeare on Film. *v.6 p.326*

Framing the Victim: Domestic Violence, Media, and Social Problems. *v.6 p.447, p.468*

Framing the Victorians: Photography and the Culture of Realism. *v.6 p.737, p.750*

Framley Parsonage. *v.2 p.317*

France, 1943-1945. . . . .*v.3 p.156*

France and Algeria: A History of Decolonization and Transformation. *v.4 p.584, v.6 p.642*

France and America During the Revolutionary Era: The Life of Jacques-Donatien Leray de Chaumont, 1725-1803. *v.3 p.151*

France and Britain 1900-1940. . . . . . .*v.3 p.141, v.4 p.643*

France and Britain, 1940-1994: The Long Separation. *v.3 p.141, v.4 p.643*

France and Britain in Africa: Imperial Rivalry and Colonial Rule. *v.3 p.76, v.6 p.56*

France and Europe in 1848: A Study of French Foreign Affairs in Time of Crisis. *v.3 p.76, p.153*

France and Panama: The Unknown Years, 1894-1908. *v.3 p.306*

France and the Dreyfus Affair: A Documentary History. *v.3 p.59*

France and the French: A Modern History. *v.3 p.140*

France and the Great War. *v.3 p.155*

France and the Nazi Threat 1932-1939: The Collapse of French Diplomacy. *v.3 p.154*

France and the Origins of the First World War. . . .*v.3 p.141*

France and the Origins of the Second World War. *v.3 p.82, p.141, p.156*

France and the South Pacific since, 1940. . . . . . .*v.4 p.583*

France and the United States: The Cold Alliance since World War II. *v.3 p.387*

France and the United States; Their Diplomatic Relation, 1789-1914. . . . .*v.3 p.387*

France and the World since 1870. . . . .*v.3 p.141*

France in Greece in World War I: A Study in the Politics of Power. *v.3 p.196*

France in the Age of Henry IV: The Struggle for Stability. *v.3 p.145*

France in the Making 843-1180. . . . .*v.3 p.142*

France in the Middle Ages, 987-1460: From Hugh Capet to Joan of Arc. *v.3 p.67, v.6 p.562*

France in the Sixteenth Century. *v.3 p.144*

France on the Eve of Revolution: British Travellers' Observations, 1763-1788. . . . .*v.3 p.147*

France Restored: Cold War Diplomacy and the Quest for Leadership in Europe, 1944-1954. . . . . . .*v.3 p.79, p.157*

France Seventeen Eighty-Nine to Eighteen Fifteen: Revolution and Counterrevolution. *v.3 p.151*

France since 1870: Culture, Politics and Society. . . *v.3 p.141*

France since 1945. . . . .*v.3 p.156, p.157*

France, the Cold War and the Western Alliance, 1944-1949: French Foreign Policy and Post-War Europe. *v.3 p.157*

France: Travellers' Nature Guide. *v.5 p.237*

Frances Burney: The Life in the Works. *v.2 p.242*

Frances Elkins - Interior Design. *v.1 p.802*

France's Overseas Frontier: Les Departements et Territoires d'Outre-Mer. *v.3 p.157*

Frances Power Cobbe: Victorian Feminist, Journalist, Reformer. *v.6 p.740, p.748*

Francesca Da Rimini. *v.2 p.716*

Francesco Clemente: Three Worlds. *v.1 p.723*

The Franchise: A History of Sports Illustrated Magazine. *v.4 p.807, p.902, p.907*

Franchising Dreams: The Lure of Entrepreneurship in America. *v.4 p.164*

Francis and Clare: The Complete Works. *v.1 p.571*

Francis Bacon and the Loss of Self. *v.1 p.749*

Francis Bacon and the Transformation of Early-Modern Philosophy. *v.1 p.448*

Francis Bacon: The Major Works. . .*v.1 p.447, p.448,v.2 p.213*

Francis Bacon, the State and the Reform of Natural Philosophy. *v.3 p.129*

Francis Bacon. *v.1 p.449, p.746,v.3 p.48*

Francis Crick: Discoverer of the Genetic Code. *v.5 p.136*

Francis Joseph. *v.3 p.183*

Francis Parkman Reader. *v.3 p.538*

Francis Place, 1771-1854: The Life of a Remarkable Radical. *v.3 p.114, p.131*

Francis Poulenc. *v.1 p.218, p.348,v.6 p.409*

Francis Trilogy: Life of Saint Francis... . . . .*v.1 p.580*

Francisco de Miranda: A Transatlantic Life in the Age of Revolution. *v.3 p.359*

Francisco de Quevedo: Dreams and Discourses. *v.2 p.650*

Francisco Goya y Lucientes, 1746-1828. . . . .*v.1 p.700*

Francisco Pizarro and His Brothers: The Illusion of Power in Sixteenth-Century Peru. *v.3 p.326*

Franco: A Biography. *v.3 p.242*

The Franco Regime, 1936-1975. . . . . .*v.3 p.242, v.4 p.608*

Francois Couperin and the French Classical Tradition. *v.1 p.185, p.319*

Francois Couperin. *v.1 p.182, p.319*

Francois Quesnay, (1694-1774), Vols. 1 & 2. . . . . .*v.4 p.215*

Francois Villon Revisited. *v.2 p.469*

Francoise Gilot: Monograph, 1940-2000. . . . .*v.1 p.696*

Francoise Sagan. *v.2 p.526*

The Franco-Peron Alliance: The Relations Between Spain and Argentina, 1946-1955. . . . .*v.3 p.242*

Francophone African Women Writers: Destroying the Emptiness of Silence. *v.2 p.542*

Francophone Literatures: An Introductory Survey. . . .*v.2 p.535*

Francophone Post-Colonial Cultures: Critical Essays. .*v.2 p.535*

Francophone Sub-Saharan Africa, 1880-1995. . . . . .*v.6 p.56*

The Franco-Prussian War: The German Conquest of France in 1870-1871. . . . .*v.3 p.154, p.168*

Frank Auerbach. *v.1 p.741*

Frank B. Kellogg and American Foreign Relations 1925-1929. . . . .*v.3 p.372, p.446*

The Frank Family That Survived. *v.3 p.205*

Frank Gehry, Architect. *v.1 p.792, p.794*

The Frank Lloyd Wright Companion. *v.1 p.795*

Frank Lloyd Wright. *v.1 p.793, p.794*

Frank Norris: A Life. *v.2 p.49*

Frank Norris Revisited. *v.2 p.49*

Frank Norris. *v.2 p.49*

Frank O'Hara: Poet among Painters. *v.2 p.106*

Frank Sinatra: A Complete Recording History of Technqiues, Songs, Composers, Lyricists, Arrangers, Sessions and First-Issue Albums, 1939-1984. .*v.1 p.169, p.265, p.357*

The Frank Sinatra Reader. *v.1 p.273, p.357*

Frank Wedekind: Four Major Plays. *v.2 p.616*

Frank Wedekind. *v.2 p.615*

The Frank Zappa Companion: Four Decades of Commentary. *v.1 p.217, p.271, p.369*

Frankenstein: Or, the Modern Prometheus: The 1818 Text. *v.2 p.310*

Frankenstein. *v.2 p.310, p.311*

Frankenthaler: A Catalog Raisonné, Prints 1961-1994. .*v.1 p.756*

The Frankfurt Parliament. *v.3 p.168*

Frankfurt School. *v.4 p.675*

Franklin D. Roosevelt and American Foreign Policy, 1932-1945: With a New Afterword. *v.3 p.469*

Franklin D. Roosevelt and Congress: The New Deal and Its Aftermath. *v.3 p.482*

Franklin D. Roosevelt and the New Deal 1932-1940. . . . .*v.3 p.442, p.448, p.474*

Franklin D. Roosevelt and the Search for Security: American-Soviet Relations, 1933-1939. . . . . . .*v.3 p.387*

Franklin D. Roosevelt and the Transformation of the Supreme Court. *v.3 p.444, v.4 p.539*

Franklin D. Roosevelt: Rendezvous with Destiny. *v.3 p.440, p.447, p.458*

The Franks in the Aegean, 1204-1500. . . . .*v.3 p.193*

Franny and Zooey. *v.2 p.118*

A Franz Boas Reader: The Shaping of American Anthropology, 1883-1911. . . . .*v.4 p.3*

Franz Boas: The Early Years, 1858-1906. . . . .*v.4 p.4*

Franz Grillparzer. *v.2 p.597*

Franz Joseph Haydn: A Guide to Research. *v.1 p.163, p.164, p.189, p.330*

Franz Kafka: Literature As Corrective Punishment. .*v.2 p.611*

Franz Kafka: Parable and Paradox. *v.2 p.611*

Franz Kafka. *v.2 p.611*

Franz Kline (1910-1962). *v.1 p.737*

Franz Liszt: A Guide to Research. . . .*v.1 p.164, p.203, p.336*

Franz Liszt: The Final Years, 1861-1886. . . . .*v.1 p.206, p.336*

Franz Liszt: The Virtuoso Years, 1811-1847. .*v.1 p.206, p.336*

Franz Liszt: The Weimar Years, 1848-1861. .*v.1 p.206, p.336*

Franz Marc: The Retrospective. *v.1 p.740*

Fraser Gold 1858!: The Founding of British Columbia. .*v.3 p.547*

The Fraser Valley: A History. *v.3 p.546*

Fraternal Organizations. *v.4 p.719*

Frauen: German Women Recall the Third Reich. *v.3 p.54, p.86, p.173*

Fray Angelico Chavez: Poet, Priest, and Artist. .*v.6 p.491, p.514*

Freakonomics: A Rogue Economist Explores the Hidden Side of Everything. *v.4 p.185, p.271*

The Fred Astaire and Ginger Rogers Book. *v.1 p.31*

Frederic Chopin: A Guide to
  Research. *v.1 p.164, p.165, p.204, p.317*

Frederic Edwin Church: Catalogue Raisonné of Works of Art at
  Olana State Historic Site.. . . . .*v.1 p.695*

Frederic Le Play on Family, Work, and Social Change. .*v.4 p.685*

Frederic Remington: A Catalogue Raisonné of Paintings,
  Watercolors and Drawings. *v.1 p.697*

Frederic Remington: The Color of Night. *v.1 p.735*

Frederic Remington: The Hogg Brothers Collection of the
  Museum of Fine Arts, Houston.. . . . .*v.1 p.744*

Frederick Ashton and His Ballets. *v.1 p.13, p.25*

Frederick Delius: Music, Art and
  Literature. *v.1 p.210, p.211, p.321*

The Frederick Douglass Papers: Autobiographical
  Writings. *v.3 p.395, p.396,v.6 p.4, p.17, p.24*

Frederick Douglass.. . . . .*v.3 p.400*

Frederick H. Evans: Selected Texts and Bibliography. .*v.1 p.767*

Frederick Sandys: A Catalogue Raisonné. *v.1 p.696*

Frederick Second: A Medieval Emperor. *v.3 p.163, p.198*

Frederick Sommer: Selected Texts and Bibliography. .*v.1 p.766*

Frederick the Great: A Historical Profile. *v.3 p.167*

Frederick the Second, 1194-1250. . . . .*v.3 p.163*

Fredericksburg to Meridian. *v.3 p.396*

Free and Other Stories.. . . . .*v.2 p.70*

Free at Last?: U. S. Policy Toward Africa and the End of the
  Cold War. *v.6 p.56*

Free Coloreds in the Slave Societies of St. Kitts and Grenada,
  1763-1833. . . . .*v.3 p.319*

Free Composition: New Musical Theories and Fantasies = Der
  freie Satz.. . . . .*v.1 p.373*

Free Culture: How Big Media Uses Technology and the Law to
  Lock down Culture and Control Creativity. *v.4 p.446*

The Free Fantasia and the Musical Picturesque. *v.1 p.191*

The Free Germany Movement: A Case of Patriotism or
  Treason? *v.3 p.175*

Free in the Forest: Ethnohistory of the Vietnamese Central
  Highlands, 1954-1976, Vol. 2. . . . .*v.6 p.168*

Free Jazz and Free Improvisation: An
  Encyclopedia.. . . . .*v.1 p.160, p.260*

Free Jazz: The Roots of Jazz. *v.1 p.260*

Free Markets and Social Justice. *v.4 p.434*

Free Men All: The Personal Liberty Laws of the North,
  1780-1861.. . . . .*v.4 p.453*

Free Press - Free People: The Best Cause. *v.4 p.405*

Free Press vs. Fair Trial: Supreme Court Decisions since
  1807.. . . . .*v.6 p.269, p.270*

Free Radicals and Oxidative Stress: Environment, Drugs and
  Food Additives. *v.5 p.163*

Free Radicals: Enzymology, Signalling and Disease. . .*v.5 p.112*

Free Radicals in Exercise and Aging.. . . . .*v.4 p.875*

Free Soil, Free Labor, Free Men: The Ideology of the
  Republican Party Before the Civil War. . . .*v.3 p.396, p.420*

Free Speech in Its Forgotten Years, 1870-1920. . . .*v.4 p.459*

Free Time and Leisure Participation: International
  Perspectives. *v.4 p.785, p.899*

Free to Choose: A Personal Statement. *v.4 p.232*

Free to Die for Their Country: The Story of the Japanese
  American Draft Resisters in World War II.   *v.6 p.107, p.134*

Free Trade Between the United States and Canada: The
  Potential Economic Effects.. . . . .*v.4 p.258*

Free Trade for the Americas?: The United States' Push for the
  FTAA Agreement. *v.4 p.61*

Free Trade?: Informal Economies at the U.S.-Mexican
  Border.. . . . .*v.6 p.487, p.525*

Free Trade Today. *v.4 p.256*

Free Trade under Fire. *v.4 p.55, p.257, p.261, p.664*

Free Voices in Russian Literature, 1950s-1980s: A
  Bio-Bibliographical Guide to over 900
  Authors. *v.2 p.795, p.796*

Free Will. *v.1 p.503*

Free World: America, Europe, and the Surprising Future of the
  West.. . . . .*v.4 p.628*

Freedom and After. *v.6 p.65*

Freedom and Beyond.. . . . .*v.4 p.343*

Freedom and Civilization. *v.4 p.700*

Freedom and Culture. *v.4 p.503*

Freedom and Determinism. *v.1 p.503*

Freedom and Development, Uhuru Na Maendeleo: A Selection
  from Writings and Speeches, 1968-73. . . . . . .*v.6 p.66*

Freedom and Its Limitations in American Life. *v.4 p.695*

Freedom and Reason.. . . . .*v.1 p.484, p.487*

Freedom and Religion in the Nineteenth Century. . . .*v.1 p.656*

Freedom and Responsibility.. . . . .*v.1 p.503*

Freedom and the Court: Civil Rights and Liberties in the United
  States. *v.4 p.455*

Freedom at Risk: Secrecy, Censorship, and Repression in the
  1980s.. . . . .*v.4 p.458*

Freedom by a Hair's Breadth: Tsimihety in Madagascar..*v.4 p.39*

Freedom Evolves. *v.1 p.503*

Freedom from Fear: The American People in Depression and
  War, 1929-1945.. . . . .*v.3 p.448*

Freedom in Fulani Social Life: An Introspective
  Ethnography.. . . . .*v.4 p.38*

Freedom in This Village: Twenty-Five Years of Black Gay
  Men's Writing. *v.6 p.406*

Freedom Is an Endless Meeting: Democracy in American Social
  Movements.. . . . .*v.4 p.711*

Freedom Is Not Enough: Black Voters, Black Candidates, and
  American Presidential Politics. *v.4 p.519, p.555,v.6 p.9, p.32*

Freedom of French Classicism. *v.2 p.455*

Freedom of the Press 2004: A Global Survey of Media
  Independence.. . . . .*v.4 p.409*

Freedom of the Press for Whom?: The Right of Access to Mass
  Media.. . . . .*v.4 p.458*

Freedom of the Press from Hamilton to the Warren
  Court. *v.4 p.459*

Freedom of the Press from Zenger to Jefferson. . . .*v.4 p.459*

Freedom on My Mind: The Columbia Documentary History of
  the African American Experience. *v.6 p.7, p.33*

Freedom or Security: The Consequences for Democracies Using
  Emergency Powers to Fight Terror. *v.4 p.659*

The Freedom Principle: Jazz after 1958. . . . . . .*v.1 p.261*

Freedom Song: Three Novels. *v.2 p.764*

Freedom, the Individual and the Law. *v.4 p.436*

Freedom to Learn. *v.4 p.358*

The Freedom to Remember: Narrative, Slavery and Gender in Contemporary Black Women's Fiction. . .*v.6 p.37, p.40, p.45*

Freedom with Responsibility: The Social Market Economy in Germany, 1918-1963. . . . .*v.3 p.177*

Freedom's Daughters: The Unsung Heroines of the Civil Rights Movement from 1830 to 1970. . . . .*v.6 p.12, p.45*

Freedom's Ferment. *v.3 p.402*

Freedoms Given, Freedoms Won: Afro-Brazilians in Post-Abolition Sao Paolo and Salvador. . . .*v.3 p.278, p.339*

Freedom's Law: The Moral Reading of the American Constitution. *v.4 p.453*

Freedom's Ordeal: The Struggle for Human Rights and Democracy in Post-Soviet States. *v.4 p.512, p.513*

Freedom's Soldiers: The Black Military Experience in the Civil War. *v.3 p.429*

The Freeholder: Or, Political Essays. *v.2 p.236*

Freeing Intelligence Through Teaching: A Dialectic of the Rational and the Personal. *v.4 p.358*

Freemasonry and American Culture, 1880-1930. . . . .*v.4 p.719*

Freer Markets, More Rules: Regulatory Reform in Advanced Industrial Countries. *v.6 p.220, p.221*

Frege: A Critical Introduction. *v.1 p.468, p.469*

Frege. *v.1 p.469*

Frei Otto: The Complete Works. *v.1 p.794*

Fremont: Explorer for a Restless Nation. .*v.3 p.422, p.423, p.428*

French Achievement in Literature. *v.2 p.456*

French African Verse. *v.2 p.542*

The French and Their Revolution: Selected Writings. *v.3 p.149, p.150*

French Anti-Slavery: The Movement for the Abolition of Slavery in France, 1802-1848. . . . .*v.3 p.149*

French Architectural and Ornament Drawings of the Eighteenth Century. *v.1 p.722*

French Baroque Music from Beaujoyeulx to Rameau. .*v.1 p.182*

French Baroque Opera: A Reader. . . .*v.1 p.186, p.233, p.246*

The French Book: Religion, Absolutism and Readership, 1585-1715. . . . .*v.3 p.144*

French, Cajun, Creole, Houma: A Primer on Francophone Louisiana. *v.3 p.507*

French Cinema from the Liberation to the New Wave, 1945-1958. . . . .*v.6 p.337*

French Cinema in The 1970s: The Echoes of May. . .*v.6 p.338*

French Cinema in the 1980s: Nostalgia and the Crisis of Masculinity. *v.6 p.338*

French Cinema since 1950. . . . .*v.6 p.338*

French Cinema: The First Wave, 1915-1929. . . . . .*v.6 p.340*

French Cities in the Nineteenth Century: Class, Power, and Urbanization. *v.3 p.149*

The French Civil Wars, 1562-1598. . . . .*v.3 p.145*

French Classical Literature, an Essay. *v.2 p.458*

French 'Classical' Theatre Today: Teaching, Research, Performance. *v.1 p.106*

French Colonial Rule and the Baule Peoples: Resistance and Collaboration, 1889-1911. . . . .*v.6 p.69*

French Comic Drama from the Sixteenth to the Eighteenth Century. *v.2 p.461*

French Connections: Hemingway and Fitzgerald Abroad. *v.2 p.77, p.85*

French Court Dance and Music: A Guide to Primary Source Writings 1643-1789. . . . .*v.1 p.22*

French Empire at War, 1940-1945. . . . . . .*v.3 p.81, p.156*

The French Empire Between the Wars: Imperialism, Politics and Society. *v.3 p.157*

The French Encounter with Africans: White Response to Blacks, 1530-1880. . . . .*v.6 p.56*

French Erotic Fiction: Women's Desiring Writing, 1880-1990. . . . .*v.2 p.459*

The French Experience in Mexico, 1821-1861: A History of Constant Misunderstanding. *v.3 p.141*

French Fiction Revisited. *v.2 p.462*

French Film: Text and Contexts. *v.6 p.338*

French Flower Painters: Eighteen Hundred to Nineteen Hundred - A Dictionary. *v.1 p.725*

French Fur Traders and Voyageurs in the American West. *v.3 p.520*

The French Generation of 1820. . . . .*v.3 p.153*

A French Genocide: The Vendee. *v.4 p.653*

French Gothic Architecture of the Twelfth and Thirteenth Centuries. *v.6 p.555*

French Grammar and Usage. *v.2 p.453*

French Higher Education in the Seventeenth and Eighteenth Centuries: A Cultural History. *v.4 p.333*

The French in Central America: Culture and Commerce, 1820-1930. . . . .*v.3 p.305, p.306*

French Language Today: Linguistic Introduction. . . .*v.2 p.453*

The French Lieutenant's Woman. *v.2 p.346*

French Literature and Its Background, Vol. 3. . . . .*v.2 p.455*

French Literature and Its Background, Vol. 4. . . . .*v.2 p.455*

French Literature and Its Background, Vol. 5. . . . .*v.2 p.455*

French Literature and Its Background, Vol. 6. . . . .*v.2 p.455*

French Literature and Its Background. *v.2 p.455*

French Master Drawings from the Collection of Muriel Butkin. *v.1 p.722*

French Motets in the Thirteenth Century: Music, Poetry and Genre. *v.1 p.177*

French Negotiating Behavior: Dealing with la Grande Nation. *v.4 p.643, p.645*

The French New Novel: Claude Simon, Michel Butor, Alain Robbe-Grillet. *v.2 p.511, p.526*

The French New Novel. *v.2 p.463*

French Painting in the Golden Age. *v.1 p.730*

French Peasantry, Fourteen Fifty to Sixteen Fifty. . .*v.3 p.145*

French Peasants in Revolt: The Insurrection of 1851. .*v.3 p.153*

French Philosophers and New England Transcendentalism. *v.1 p.515*

French Philosophy in the Twentieth Century. *v.1 p.456*

French Poetry: The Renaissance Through 1915. . . . .*v.2 p.460*

French Poets and Novelists. *v.2 p.456*

French Policy and the American Alliance of, 1778. . .*v.3 p.413*

The French Pre-Revolution, 1787-1788. . . . .*v.3 p.150*

French Presence in Cochinchina and Cambodia: Rule and
    Response 1859-1905. . . . .*v.6 p.167, p.170*

The French Presence in the South Pacific,
    1842-1940. . . . .*v.4 p.583, p.584*

French Prose and Criticism 1790 to World War II. . . .*v.2 p.457*

French Prose and Criticism Through, 1789. . . . . .*v.2 p.462*

The French Reformation. *v.1 p.604*

The French Regime in Prince Edward Island. *v.3 p.543*

French Renaissance Comedy, 1552-1630. . . . .*v.2 p.457, p.458*

The French Republic, 1879-1992. . . . .*v.3 p.140*

The French Revolution: A Document Collection. . . .*v.3 p.151*

The French Revolution and First Empire: An Historical Sketch.
    by William O'Connor Morris. with an appendix upon
    the bibliography of the subject and a course of study by Hon.
    Andrew D. White. *v.2 p.302*

The French Revolution and the Church. *v.3 p.151*

The French Revolution in Germany: Occupation and Resistance
    in the Rhineland 1792-1802. . . . .*v.3 p.167*

The French Revolution: The Works of Thom, Vol.
    1. . . . .*v.2 p.275, p.276*

The French Revolution: The Works of Thom, Vol. 2. .*v.2 p.275*

The French Revolutionary Wars, 1787-1802. . . . .*v.3 p.149*

The French Revolution. *v.3 p.150*

French Rural History: An Essay on Its Basic
    Characteristics. *v.3 p.140*

The French Second Empire: An Anatomy of Political
    Power. *v.3 p.154*

French Social Theory. *v.4 p.679*

French Society, Seventeen Eighty-Nine to Nineteen
    Seventy. *v.4 p.702*

A French Song Companion. *v.1 p.395, p.411, p.412*

The French Stage in the Eighteenth Century. *v.1 p.106*

French Theater since 1968. . . . .*v.2 p.462*

French Theatre, 1918-1939. . . . .*v.2 p.462*

French Theatre in the Neo-Classical Era:
    1550-1789. . . . .*v.1 p.78, p.106*

The French Tradition and the Literature of Medieval
    England. *v.6 p.564*

French Tragic Drama in the Sixteenth and Seventeenth
    Centuries. *v.2 p.461*

The French Wars of Religion, 1562-1629. . .*v.1 p.610, v.3 p.145*

The French Wars of Religion: Selected Documents. . .*v.1 p.610*

French Women Philosophers: A Contemporary Reader. .*v.1 p.506*

French Writers and Their Society, 1715-1800. . . . .*v.2 p.459*

French-Canadian Civilization. *v.3 p.535*

The French-Canadian Idea of Confederation,
    1864-1900. . . . .*v.3 p.536*

The French-Canadian Outlook: A Brief Account of the Unknown
    North Americans. *v.3 p.536*

French-English Dictionary for Chemists. *v.5 p.258*

French-English Science and Technology Dictionary. . .*v.5 p.387*

Frenchman's Creek. *v.2 p.343*

Frenchmen into Peasants: Modernity and Tradition in the
    Peopling of French Canada. *v.3 p.537*

French. *v.2 p.465*

The French. *v.3 p.141*

Frequent Flyers: Developing Global Executives. .*v.4 p.59, p.120*

Fresco: Selected Poetry of Luljeta Lleshanaku. . . .*v.2 p.815*

Fresh Girls and Other Stories. *v.2 p.736*

Fresh Talk/Daring Gazes: Conversations on Asian American
    Art. *v.6 p.88*

Fresh Wounds: Early Narratives of Holocaust
    Survival. *v.3 p.85, p.86*

Freshwater Algae of North America: Ecology and
    Classification. *v.5 p.208*

The Freshwater Algal Flora of the British Isles: An Identification
    Guide to Freshwater and Terrestrial Algae. .*v.5 p.208, p.209*

Freshwater Ecoregions of North America: A Conservation
    Assessment. *v.5 p.174, p.233, p.241,v.6 p.290*

Freshwater Fishes of the Carolinas, Virginia, Maryland, and
    Delaware. *v.5 p.216*

Freshwater Wetlands: Ecological Processes and Management
    Potential. *v.5 p.53, p.379*

Freud and Jung on Religion. *v.5 p.635*

Freud and the Child Woman: The Memoirs of Fritz
    Wittels. *v.5 p.598*

Freud: Darkness in the Midst of Vision. *v.5 p.595*

Freud in the Pampas: The Emergence and Development of a
    Psychoanalytic Culture in Argentina. *v.3 p.349*

Freud: Living and Dying. *v.5 p.598*

Freud, Psychoanalysis and Symbolism. *v.5 p.598*

Freud: Standard Edition. *v.5 p.658*

The Freud-Jung Letters: The Correspondence Between Sigmund
    Freud and C. G. Jung. *v.5 p.596, p.658, p.659*

Freud's Theory and Its Use in Literary and Cultural Studies: An
    Introduction. *v.2 p.570*

Freud's Women. *v.5 p.595*

Friction: An Enthography of Global Connection. . . .*v.4 p.27*

Friction, Lubrication, and Wear Technology. . .*v.5 p.707, p.708*

Frida Kahlo. *v.1 p.742*

Friday Night Lights: A Town, a Team, and a
    Dream. *v.4 p.814, p.840, p.858*

Friday. *v.2 p.534, v.6 p.288*

Frieda Lawrence: Including Not I but the Wind by Frieda
    Lawrence. *v.2 p.362*

Friedel Crafts and Related Reactions. *v.5 p.296*

Friedlaender's Etchings, 1988-1992: Catalogue
    Raisonné. *v.1 p.756*

Friedrich Durrenmatt: Selected Writings - Essays. . .*v.2 p.606*

Friedrich Durrenmatt: Selected Writings - Plays. . . .*v.2 p.606*

Friedrich Durrenmatt: Selected Writings. *v.2 p.606*

Friedrich Froebel. *v.4 p.342*

Friedrich Hebbel: A Study of His Life and Work. . .*v.2 p.601*

Friedrich Hölderlin. *v.2 p.602*

Friedrich Miescher and the Story of Nucleic Acid. .*v.5 p.81, p.120*

Friedrich Schiller. *v.2 p.601, p.602*

Friedrich Von Gentz, Defender of the Old Order. . . .*v.3 p.184*

Friend of My Youth. *v.2 p.737*

The Friend, Vol. 4. . . . .*v.2 p.280*

A Friendly Introduction to Number Theory. *v.5 p.477*

The Friendly Persuasion. *v.2 p.130*

☐ Friends & Partners Russian Literature Site. .*v.2 p.792, p.793*

Friends and Apostles: The Correspondence of Rupert Brooke and James Strachey, 1905-1914. . . . .*v.2 p.335*

Friends and Enemies: The United States, China, and the Soviet Union, 1948-1972. . . . .*v.3 p.387*

Friends and Foes: How Congress and the President Really Make Foreign Policy. *v.4 p.528, p.531, p.532*

Friends and Lovers: Gay Men Write about the Families They Create. *v.6 p.375*

Friends, Brothers and Informants: Fieldwork Memoirs of Banaras. *v.6 p.154*

Friends of Friends. *v.4 p.693*

The Friends of Liberty: The English Democratic Movement in the Age of the French Revolution. . . .*v.3 p.94, p.108, p.128*

Friends, You Drank Some Darkness: Three Swedish Poets, Harry Martinson, Gunnar Ekelof, and Tomas Transtromer. *v.2 p.629*

Friendship Matters: Communication, Dialectics, and the Life Course. *v.4 p.697, v.5 p.621*

The Friendship of Nature: A New England Chronicle of Birds and Flowers. *v.5 p.235*

Friendship Processes, Vol. 12. . . . .*v.5 p.647, p.652*

Friendship under Stress: U. S.-Swiss Relations, 1900-1950. . . . .*v.3 p.245*

Frightening the Horses: The Rise and Rise of Gay Cinema. *v.6 p.415*

Frigid Embrace: Politics, Economics, and Environment in Alaska. *v.6 p.300*

Fritz Pollard: Pioneer in Racial Advancement. *v.4 p.814, p.831, p.858*

Frogs, Flies, and Dandelions: Speciation--The Evolution of New Species. *v.5 p.199*

Frogs. *v.2 p.423*

From 1865: Portrait of America. *v.3 p.380*

From '9-11' to the 'Iraq War 2003': International Law in an Age of Complexity. *v.4 p.655, p.660*

From a Biological Point of View: Essays in Evolutionary Philosophy. *v.1 p.516*

From a Crooked Rib. *v.2 p.754*

From a Logical Point of View: Nine Logico-Philosophical Essays. *v.1 p.493, p.510*

From Abacus to Zeus: A Handbook of Art History. . .*v.1 p.665*

From Alchemy to IPO: The Business of Biotechnology. .*v.5 p.219*

From Alien to the Matrix: Reading Science Fiction Film. *v.6 p.318*

From Altoids to Zima: The Surprising Stories Behind 125 Famous Brand Names. *v.4 p.142*

From Aristotle to Augustine. *v.1 p.419*

From Babel to Dragomans: Interpreting the Middle East. *v.4 p.614, p.615*

From Baltic Shores: Short Stories from Denmark, Estonia, Finland, Latvia, Lithuania, Sweden. *v.2 p.781*

From Bandwagon to Balance-of-Power Politics: Structural Constraints and Politics in China, 1949-1978. .*v.4 p.619, p.620*

From Barbie to Mortal Kombat: Gender and Computer Games. *v.6 p.438*

From Barter to Slavery: The Economic Relations of Portuguese and Indians in the Settlement of Brazil, 1500-1580. .*v.3 p.335*

From Baudelaire to Surrealism. *v.2 p.461*

From Beirut to Jerusalem. *v.6 p.592*

From Belasco to Brook: Representative Directors of the English-Speaking Stage. *v.1 p.97, p.116, p.153*

From Bench to Market: The Evolution of Chemical Synthesis. *v.5 p.740, p.741*

From Blackjacks to Briefcases: A History of Commercialized Strikebreaking and Unionbusting in the United States. *v.4 p.129*

From Bomba to Hip-Hop: Puerto Rican Culture and Latino Identity. *v.6 p.543*

From Book to Screen: Modern Japanese Literature in Films. *v.6 p.327, p.336*

From Boston to Beijing: Managing with a World View. *v.4 p.58, p.69*

From Boycott to Annihilation: The Economic Struggle of German Jews, 1933-1943. . . . .*v.3 p.179*

From Breakpoint to Advantage: A Practical Guide to Optimal Tennis Health and Performance. *v.4 p.828, p.864, p.875, p.879, p.880*

From British Peasants to Colonial American Farmers. . *v.5 p.5*

From Building and Loans to Bail Outs: A History of the American Savings and Loan Industry, 1831-1995. . . . .*v.4 p.147, p.155*

From Caveman to Chemist: Circumstances and Achievements. *v.5 p.263*

From Cells to Souls and Beyond: Changing Portraits of Human Nature. *v.1 p.526*

From Chance to Choice: Genetics and Justice. *v.5 p.131*

From Chemical Philosophy to Theoretical Chemistry: Dynamics of Matter and Dynamics of Disciplines, 1800-1950. .*v.5 p.263*

From Chicago to L. A.: Making Sense of Urban Theory. *v.6 p.709*

From Chivalry to Terrorism: War and the Changing Nature of Masculinity. *v.6 p.440*

From Clay to Bronze: A Studio Guide to Figurative Sculpture. *v.1 p.782*

From Coastal Wilderness to Fruited Plain: A History of Environmental Change in Temperate North America from 1500 to the Present. *v.6 p.284*

From Coello to Inorganic Chemistry: A Lifetime of Reactions. *v.5 p.260*

ⓔ From Colonia to Community: The History of Puerto Ricans in New York City. *v.6 p.533, p.550*

From Colonization to Democracy: A New Historical Geography of South Africa. *v.6 p.78*

From Colony to Country: The Revolution in American Thought, 1750-1820. . . . .*v.3 p.368*

From Colony to Empire: Essays in the History of American Foreign Relations. *v.3 p.454*

From Columbus to ConAgra: The Globalization of Agriculture and Food. *v.4 p.151*

From Comrade to Citizen: The Struggle for Political Rights in China. *v.4 p.619*

From Concentration Camp to Campus: Japanese American Students and World War II. *v.6 p.133*

From Concept to Wall Street: A Complete Guide to Entrepreneurship and Venture Capital. . .*v.4 p.89, p.91, p.95*

From Confederation to Nation: The American Constitution, 1835-1877. . . . .*v.4 p.452*

From Confrontation to Negotiation: U. S. Relations with Cuba. *v.3 p.307*

From Constantine to Julian: A Source History. *v.3 p.31*

From Cooperation to Complicity: Degussa in the Third Reich. *v.3 p.172*

From Cuba with a Song. *v.2 p.673*

From Cubism to Surrealism in French Literature. . . .*v.2 p.459*

From Cuenca to Queens: An Anthropological Story of Transnational Migration. *v.4 p.44*

From Cyrus to Alexander: A History of the Persian Empire. *v.3 p.11*

From Darwin to Hitler: Evolutionary Ethics, Eugenics, and Racism in Germany. *v.3 p.78, p.165*

From Dictatorship to Democracy: Rebuilding Political Consensus in Chile. *v.3 p.355*

From Direct Action to Affirmative Action: Fair Employment Law and Policy in America, 1933-1972. . . .*v.4 p.133, p.447*

From DNA to Diversity: Molecular Genetics and the Evolution of Animal Design. *v.5 p.131, p.200*

From Drawing to Painting: Poussin, Watteau, Fragonard, David, and Ingres. *v.1 p.722*

From Dust to Stars: Studies of the Formation and Early Evolution of Stars. *v.5 p.70*

From East Germans to Germans?: The New Postcommunist Elites. *v.4 p.610*

From Egg to Embryo: Regional Specification in Early Development. *v.5 p.160, p.161*

From Emperor to Citizen. *v.6 p.188, p.191, p.200*

From Empire to Community: A New Approach to International Relations. *v.4 p.262, p.626, p.628, p.629*

From Empire to Republic: Essays on Ottoman and Turkish Social History. *v.6 p.590, p.622*

From Empire to Republic: Turkish Nationalism and the Armenian Genocide. *v.4 p.651*

From Epic to Canon: History and Literature in Ancient Israel. *v.3 p.7*

From Error Correcting Codes through Sphere Packings to Semigroups. *v.5 p.479*

From Euclid to Eddington: A Study of Conceptions of the External World. *v.5 p.404*

From Eudoxus to Einstein: A History of Mathematical Astronomy. *v.5 p.62*

From Exile to Diaspora: Versions of the Filipino Experience in the United States. *v.6 p.119, p.130*

From Exile to Redemption: The Fiction of Isaac Bashevis Singer. *v.2 p.120*

From Falling Bodies to Radio Waves: Classical Physicists and Their Discoveries. *v.5 p.544*

From Fanatics to Folk: Brazilian Millenarianism and Popular Culture. *v.3 p.265, p.342*

From Father's Property to Children's Rights: The History of Child Custody in the United States. *v.4 p.442, p.740,v.6 p.467*

From Field to Factory: Community Structure and Industrialization in West Bengal. *v.4 p.704*

From Fontainebleau to the Louvre: French Drawing from the Seventeenth Century. *v.1 p.722*

From Fort Laramie to Wounded Knee: In the West That Was. *v.3 p.521*

From Frontier to Plantation in Tennessee: A Study in Frontier Democracy. *v.3 p.510*

From Furmanov to Sholokhov: An Anthology of the Classics of Socialist Realism. *v.2 p.794*

From Garrison State to Nation-State: Political Power and the Russian Military under Gorbachev and Yeltsin. . . .*v.4 p.598*

From Gautier to Eliot: The Influence of France on English Literature, 1851-1939. . . . .*v.2 p.165*

From Gene to Animal: An Introduction to the Molecular Biology of Animal Development. *v.5 p.161*

From Genes to Genomes: Concepts and Applications of DNA Technology. *v.5 p.132*

From Genesis to Genetics: The Case of Evolution and Creationism. *v.5 p.135*

From Genome to Proteome: Advances in the Practice and Application of Proteomics. *v.5 p.104, p.115, p.145*

From Genome to Therapy: Integrating New Technologies with Drug Development. *v.5 p.218*

From Georges Sorel: Essays in Socialism and Philosophy, Vol. I. *v.4 p.507*

From Giotto to Cezanne: A Concise History of Painting. .*v.1 p.726*

From Global to Metanational: How Companies Win in the Knowledge Economy. *v.4 p.69*

From Glory to Glory: Texts from Gregory of Nyssa's Mystical Writings. *v.1 p.653*

From Grandmother to Granddaughter: Salvadoran Women's Stories. *v.3 p.299*

From Grierson to the Docu-Soap: Breaking the Boundaries. *v.6 p.309*

From Guerrillas to Government: The Eritrean People's Liberation Front. *v.6 p.67*

From Hanoi to Hollywood: The Vietnam War in American Film. *v.6 p.322*

From Hayes to McKinley: National Party Politics, 1877-1896. . . . .*v.3 p.437*

From Heart to Heart. *v.2 p.813*

From Hegel to Existentialism. *v.1 p.506*

From Hegel to Marx: Studies in the Intellectual Development of Karl Marx. *v.1 p.468*

From Here to Eternity. *v.2 p.90*

From Heresy to Dogma: An Institutional History of Corporate Environmentalism. *v.4 p.61, p.63,v.6 p.298*

From Hiroshima to the Iceman: The Development and Applications of Accelerator Mass Spectrometry. . .*v.5 p.540*

From Household to Empire: Society and Economy in Early Colonial New Mexico. *v.4 p.383*

From Identity to Politics: The Lesbian and Gay Movements in the United States. *v.4 p.570, v.6 p.387*

From Imperial Myth to Democracy: Japan's Two Constitutions, 1889-2001. . . . .*v.6 p.223*

From Ink Lake: Canadian Stories. *v.2 p.732*

From Insurrection to Revolution in Mexico: Social Bases of Agrarian Violence, 1750-1940. . . . . . .*v.3 p.295, p.296*

From Ireland Coming: Irish Art from the Early Christian to the Late Gothic Period and Its European Context. *v.1 p.672, p.687*

From Isolation to Conversation: Supporting New Teachers' Development. *v.4 p.279*

From Isolation Towards Integration: The Surinam Maroons and Their Colonial Rulers : Official Documents Relating to the Djukas (1845-1863). *v.3 p.322*

From Jacobin to Liberal: Marc-Antoine Jullien, 1775-1848. . . . . *v.3 p.149*

From Jim Crow to Civil Rights: The Supreme Court and the Struggle for Racial Equality. *v.4 p.457, p.537*

From Joseph Second to the Jacobin Trials: Government Policy and Public Opinion in the Habsburg Dominions in the Period of the French Revolution. *v.3 p.183*

From Knowledge to Intelligence: Creating Competitive Advantage in the Next Economy. *v.4 p.77, p.83*

From Kostenki to Clovis: Upper Paleolithic-Paleo-Indian Adaptations. *v.4 p.17*

From Latin to Spanish. *v.2 p.636*

From Learning to Earning: Yahoo! HotJobs Success Strategies for New Grads. *v.4 p.169*

From Liberal to Revolutionary Oaxaca: The View from the South, Mexico 1867-1911. . . . . *v.3 p.291*

From Lord to Patron: Lordship in Late Medieval England. *v.3 p.68*

From Love Field: Our Final Hours with President John F. Kennedy. *v.4 p.485*

From Madrid to Purgatory: The Art and Craft of Dying in Sixteenth-Century Spain. *v.3 p.238*

From Mammy to Miss America and Beyond: Cultural Images and the Shaping of U. S. Social Policy. . . . *v.6 p.39, p.44*

From Many, One: The Process of Political Integration. *v.4 p.628*

From Martyrdom to Power: The Partido Accion Nacional in Mexico. *v.3 p.294*

From Max Weber: Essays in Sociology. *v.4 p.681*

From Medical Chemistry to Biochemistry: The Making of a Biomedical Discipline. *v.5 p.326*

From Memory to Written Record: England 1066-1307. *v.6 p.569*

From Migrant to Acadian: A North American Border People, 1604-1755. . . . . *v.3 p.543*

From Migrants to Ethnic Minorities: The Settlement of Refugees from Vietnam, Laos, and Cambodia in the United States. *v.4 p.571, p.763, p.764, v.6 p.118, p.138*

From Military Rule to Liberal Democracy in Argentina. *v.3 p.277, v.4 p.593*

From Milton to McLuhan: The Ideas Behind American Journalism. *v.4 p.403*

From Mineralogy to Geology: The Foundations of a Science, 1650-1830. . . . . *v.5 p.418*

From "Fair Sex" to Feminism: Sport and the Socialization of Women in the Industrial and Post-Industrial Eras. *v.4 p.818, p.837, v.6 p.438*

From "Good Order" to Glorious Revolution: Salem, Massachusetts, 1628-1689. . . . . *v.3 p.489*

From Modernism to Postmodernism: American Poetry and Theory in the Twentieth Century. *v.2 p.3*

From Monuments to Traces: Artifacts of German Memory, 1870-1990. . . . . *v.3 p.159*

From Moon Goddesses to Virgins: The Colonization of Yucatecan Maya Sexual Desire. *v.3 p.264*

From Moonshine to Madison Avenue: A Cultural History of the NASCAR Winston Cup Series. *v.4 p.848, p.888*

From Moscow to Madrid: European Cities, Postmodern Cinema. *v.6 p.337*

From Mouse to Mermaid: The Politics of Film, Gender, and Culture. *v.6 p.311*

From Muslim Fortress to Christian Castle: Social and Cultural Change in Medieval Spain. *v.3 p.237*

From Myth to Modern Mind: A Study of the Origins and Growth of Scientific Thought, Vol. I. *v.5 p.389*

From Myth to Modern Mind: From Copernicus to Quantum Mechanics. *v.3 p.45, v.5 p.389*

From Myth to the Modern Mind: A Study of the Origins and Growth of Scientific Thought: Animism to Archimedes. *v.3 p.45*

From Needs Assessment to Action: Transforming Needs into Solution Strategies. *v.4 p.81*

From Neurons to Neighborhoods: The Science of Early Childhood Development. *v.5 p.513*

From Neuroscience to Neurology: Neuroscience, Molecular Medicine and the Therapeutic Transformation of Neurology. *v.5 p.165*

From New Era to New Deal: Herbert Hoover, the Economists, and American Economic Policy, 1921-1933. . . . . *v.3 p.439, v.4 p.522*

From Noon to Starry Night: A Life of Walt Whitman. *v.2 p.53*

From Obstruction to Moderation: The Transformation of Senate Conservatism, 1938-1952. . . . . *v.4 p.534*

From Origin to Ecology: Nature and the Poetry of W. S. Merwin. *v.2 p.101*

From Oslo to Iraq and the Road Map: Essays. *v.6 p.619, p.620*

From Out of the Shadows: Mexican Women in Twentieth-Century America. *v.6 p.450, p.455, p.547*

From Page to Screen: Adaptations of the Classic Novel. *v.6 p.325, p.326*

From Page to Stage: How Theatre Designers Make Connections Between Scripts and Images. *v.1 p.147*

From Panthers to Promise Keepers: Rethinking the Men's Movement. *v.4 p.711*

From Paracelsus to Newton: Magic and the Making of Modern Science. *v.3 p.48*

From Parchment to Power: How James Madison Used the Bill of Rights to Save the Constitution. *v.4 p.452*

From Peasant to Petersburger. *v.3 p.220*

From People's War to People's Rule: Insurgency, Intervention, and the Lessons of Vietnam. *v.6 p.169*

From Petipa to Balanchine: Classical Revival and the Modernization of Ballet. *v.1 p.24, p.25*

From Philosophy To Poetry: T. S. Eliot's Study of Knowledge and Experience. *v.2 p.71*

From Physico-Theology to Bio-Technology: Essays in the Social and Cultural History of Biosciences: A Festschrift for Mikul'as Teich. *v.5 p.77*

From Poliziano to Machiavelli: Florentine Humanism in the High Renaissance. *v.2 p.698*

From Popular Sovereignty to the Sovereignty of Law: Law, Society, and Politics in Fifth Century Athens. . . *v.4 p.501*

From Prejudice to Persecution: A History of Austrian Anti-Semitism. *v.3 p.60, p.185*

From Primitive to Postcolonial in Melanesia and Anthropology. *v.4 p.43*

From Progressivism to Prosperity: World War I and American
Society. *v.3 p.482*

From Protein Folding to New Enzymes, Vol. 68. . . .*v.5 p.115*

From Psalm to Symphony: A History of Music in New
England. *v.1 p.280*

From Puerto Rico to Philadelphia: Puerto Rican Workers and
Postwar Economies. *v.3 p.321, p.322*

From Puritan to Yankee: Character and the Social Order in
Connecticut, 1690-1765. . . . .*v.3 p.489*

From Rebellion to Independence in the Andes: Soundings from
Southern Peru, 1750-1830. . . . .*v.3 p.325*

From Reform to Revolution: The Demise of Communism in
China and the Soviet Union. *v.6 p.197*

From Reformation to Restoration: Ireland
1534-1660. . . . .*v.3 p.134, p.136*

From Reformation to Restoration: Ireland,
1534-1660. . . . .*v.3 p.136, p.137*

From Reich to Revolution: German History 1600-1806. .*v.3 p.165*

From 'Reich' to State: The Rhineland in the Revolutionary Age,
1780-1830. . . . .*v.3 p.168*

From Religion to Philosophy: A Study in the Origins of Western
Speculation. *v.1 p.421*

From Renaissance to Baroque: Essays on Literature and
Art. *v.2 p.182*

From Resistance to Revolution: Colonial Radicals and the
Development of American Opposition to Britain,
1765-1776. . . . .*v.3 p.409*

From Reverence to Rape: The Treatment of Women in the
Movies. *v.6 p.474*

From Revolution to Constitution: Connecticut, 1763 to 1818,
Vol. 2. . . . .*v.3 p.489*

From Revolutionary Cadres to Party Technocrats in Socialist
China. *v.4 p.620*

From Ritual to Record: The Nature of Modern
Sports. *v.4 p.806, p.816*

From Ritual to Theatre: The Human Seriousness of
Play. *v.1 p.55, p.136*

From Romanticism to Modernismo in Latin America. .*v.2 p.664*

From Romanticism to Surrealism: Seven Spanish Poets. .*v.2 p.643*

From Russia with Love: Costumes for the Ballets Russes,
1909-1933. . . . .*v.1 p.45*

From Samarkhand to Sardis: A New Approach to the Seleucid
Empire. *v.3 p.21*

From Sand Creek: Rising in This Heart Which Is Our
America. *v.2 p.151*

From Sangha to Laity: Nationalist Movements of Burma,
1920-1940. . . . .*v.6 p.166*

From Savage to Negro: Anthropology and the Construction of
Race, 1896-1954. . . . .*v.4 p.4*

From Savage to Nobleman: Images of Native Americans in
Film. *v.6 p.700*

From Scarcity to Visibility: Gender Differences in the Careers of
Doctoral Scientists and Engineers. *v.5 p.398*

From School to Salon: Reading Nineteenth-Century American
Women's Poetry. *v.2 p.8*

From Script to Screen: The Collaborative Art of
Filmmaking. *v.6 p.347*

From Seance to Science: A History of the Profession and
Practice of Psychology in America. *v.5 p.595*

From Secession to Reinvention: Art, Design, and Architecture in
Central Europe 1890-1920. . . . .*v.1 p.677, p.686*

From Self to Society, 1919-1941. . . . .*v.3 p.367*

From Set Shot to Slam Dunk: The Glory Days of Basketball in
the Words of Those Who Played It. *v.4 p.854, p.897*

From Settler to Citizen: New Mexican Economic Development
and the Creation of Vecino Society,
1750-1820. . . . .*v.6 p.524, p.531*

From Shell Shock to Combat Stress: A Comparative History of
Military Psychiatry. *v.5 p.583*

From Skisport to Skiing: One Hundred Years of an American
Sport, 1840-1940. . . . .*v.4 p.866, p.867*

From Slave to Pharaoh: The Black Experience of Ancient
Egypt. *v.3 p.9, p.10,v.6 p.57*

From Slavery to Freedom: A History of Negro Americans. .*v.6 p.4*

From Slavery to Vagrancy in Brazil: Crime and Social Control
in the Third World. *v.3 p.336*

From Slogans to Mantras: Social Protest and Religious
Conversion in the Late Vietnam Era. *v.4 p.710*

From So Simple a Beginning: Darwin's Four Great
Books. *v.3 p.49*

From So Simple a Beginning: The Book of
Evolution. *v.5 p.197, p.198*

From Solar Energy to Mechanical Power. *v.5 p.708*

From Solon to Socrates: Greek History and Civilization During
the 6th and 5th Centuries B.C. *v.3 p.17*

From Soul to Self. *v.1 p.526*

From Space to Earth: The Story of Solar Electricity. . .*v.5 p.362*

From Spirituals to Symphonies: African-American Women
Composers and Their Music. .*v.1 p.282, p.283,v.6 p.30, p.47*

From Squaw Tit to Whorehouse Meadow: How Maps Name,
Claim, and Inflame. *v.4 p.386*

From Stalinism to Pluralism: A Documentary History of Eastern
Europe since 1945. . . . .*v.3 p.208*

From Stimulus to Science. *v.1 p.443, p.444*

From Subjects to Citizens: Honor, Culture and Politics in
Arequipa, Peru, 1780-1854. . . . . .*v.3 p.283, p.325, p.327*

From Teaching to Mentoring in Adult Education: The
Integration of Principle and Practice. *v.4 p.320*

From Technological to Virtual Art. *v.1 p.772*

From Tejano to Tango: Latin American Popular Music. .*v.1 p.291*

From Television to the Internet: Postmodern Visions of
American Media Culture in the Twentieth Century. .*v.4 p.418*

From Texas to the World and Back: Essays on the Journeys of
Katherine Anne Porter. *v.2 p.108, p.109*

From the American System to Mass Production, 1800-1932: The
Development of Manufacturing Technology in the United
States. *v.3 p.368*

From the Ballroom to Hell: Grace and Folly in
Nineteenth-Century Dance. *v.1 p.34*

From the Baltic to the Black Sea: Studies in Medieval
Archaeology. *v.6 p.555*

From the Barrel of a Gun: The United States and the War
Against Zimbabwe, 1965-1980. . . . .*v.3 p.389*

From the Beginning to Plato. *v.1 p.421*

From the Cables of Genocide: Poems on Love and
Hunger. *v.2 p.142, v.6 p.498, p.510*

From the Center of the Earth: The Search for the Truth about
China. *v.6 p.196*

From the Center to the Edge: The Politics and Policies of the
Clinton Presidency. *v.3 p.465*

From the Classicists to the Impressionists: Art and Architecture
in the Nineteenth Century. *v.1 p.679, p.687*

From the Closed World to the Infinite Universe. *v.1 p.488*

From the Communal Reformation to the Revolution of the
Common Man. *v.3 p.165*

From the Country of Eight Islands: An Anthology of Japanese
Poetry. *v.6 p.235*

From the Crash to the Blitz, 1929-1939. . . . . . .*v.3 p.369*

From the Diary of a Snail. *v.2 p.608*

From the Earth to the Moon. *v.2 p.503*

From the Easy Chair, Vol. 1. . . . .*v.2 p.32*

From the Enlightenment to the Police State: The Public Life of
Johann Anton Pergen. *v.3 p.182*

From the Gracchi to Nero: A History of Rome from 133 B. C.
to A. D. 68. . . . .*v.3 p.26*

From the Idyll to the Novel: Karamzin's Sentimentalist
Prose. *v.2 p.793, p.804*

From the Land of Morning Calm: The Koreans in
America. *v.6 p.119, p.120, p.137*

From the Land of Sheba: Tales of the Jews of
Yemen. *v.6 p.597, p.628*

From the Maccabees to the Mishnah. *v.1 p.547, v.3 p.7*

From the Margin: Writings in Italian Americana. . . .*v.2 p.20*

From the Mountain, from the Valley: New and Collected
Poems. *v.2 p.117*

From the Notebooks of Melanin Sun. *v.6 p.376, p.400*

From the Puritans to the Projects: Public Housing and Public
Neighbors. *v.4 p.757*

From the Terrace. *v.2 p.106, p.107*

From the Velvets to the Voidoids: The Birth of American Punk
Rock. *v.1 p.270*

ⓔ From the Wireless to the Web: The Evolution of
Telecommunications, 1901-2001. . . . .*v.4 p.420*

From These Beginnings: A Biographical Approach to American
History. *v.3 p.380*

From Three Worlds: New Ukrainian Writing. *v.2 p.813*

From Tinfoil to Stereo: The Acoustic Years of the Recording
Industry, 1877-1929. . . . .*v.1 p.386, p.388*

From Tobacco Road to Route 66: The Southern Poor White in
Fiction. *v.2 p.13*

From Tradition to Gospel. *v.1 p.628, p.629*

From Trickster to Badman: The Black Folk Hero in Slavery and
Freedom. *v.2 p.17*

From Trucial States to United Arab Emirates: A Society in
Transisition. *v.6 p.628*

From Tsar to Soviets: The Russian People and Their Revolution,
1917-1921. . . . .*v.3 p.221*

From Two Republics to One Divided: Contradictions of
Postcolonial Nationmaking in Andean Peru. .*v.3 p.265, p.328*

From Van Eyck to Bruegel: Early Netherlandish Painting in the
Metropolitan Museum of Art. *v.1 p.731*

From Versailles to London, 1919-1920, Vol. 2. . . . .*v.6 p.633*

From Versailles to Pearl Harbor: The Origins of the Second
World War in Europe and Asia. *v.6 p.164*

From Viracocha to the Virgin of Copacabana: Representation of
the Sacred at Lake Titicaca. *v.3 p.264*

From Vital Force to Structural Formulas. *v.5 p.291*

From Voting to Violence: Democratization and Nationalist
Conflict. *v.4 p.505*

From War to Cold War : Anglo-Finnish Relations in the 20th
Century. *v.3 p.236*

From Welcomed Exiles to Illegal Immigrants: Cuban Migration
to the U. S., 1959-1995. . . . .*v.3 p.311*

From William Morris: Building Conservation and the Arts and
Crafts Cult of Authenticity, 1877-1939. . . . . .*v.1 p.823*

From Witches to Crack Moms: Women, Drug Law, and
Policy. *v.6 p.258*

From Writer to Reader: Studies in Editorial Method. .*v.2 p.574*

From X-Rays to Quarks: Modern Physicists and Their
Discoveries. *v.5 p.544*

From Yalta to Berlin: The Cold War Struggle over
Germany. *v.3 p.177*

The Fronde: A French Revolution, 1648-1652. . . . .*v.3 p.146*

Front Page: Covers of the Twentieth-Century. *v.1 p.719*

The Front Runner: 20th Anniversary Edition. *v.6 p.399*

Front Stage, Backstage: The Dramatic Structure of Labor
Negotions. *v.4 p.121*

La Frontera de Cristal. *v.2 p.668*

Fronteras No Mas: Toward Social Justice at the U. S. - Mexico
Border. *v.4 p.560, p.640*

Fronteras No Mas: Toward Social Justice at the U. S.-Mexico
Border. *v.6 p.487, p.541*

Frontier Army in the Settlement of the West. *v.3 p.521*

Frontier Expansion and Peasant Protest in Columbia,
1850-1936. . . . .*v.3 p.357*

The Frontier in American History. *v.3 p.381*

Frontier Indiana. *v.3 p.514*

Frontier Passages: Ethnopolitics and the Rise of Chinese
Communism, 1921-1945. . . . .*v.4 p.620*

Frontier Regulars: The United States Army and the Indian,
1866-1891. . . . .*v.3 p.402, v.6 p.688*

The Frontier Republic: Ideology and Politics in the Ohio
Country, 1780-1825. . . . .*v.3 p.513*

Frontier Settlements. *v.3 p.380*

The Frontier Thesis: Valid Interpretation of American
History? *v.3 p.380*

Frontiers in Computational Genomics: Functional
Genomics. *v.5 p.139*

Frontiers of Asian American Studies: Writing, Research, and
Commentary. *v.6 p.90, p.91, p.109*

Frontiers of Biogeography: New Directions in the Geography of
Nature. *v.4 p.394, v.5 p.168*

Frontiers of Cognitive Therapy. *v.5 p.666*

Frontiers of Heresy: The Spanish Inquisition from the Basque
Lands to Sicily. *v.1 p.612*

Frontiers of Human-Centered Computing, Online Communities
and Virtual Environments. *v.4 p.772*

The Frontiers of Love. *v.6 p.99*

Frontiers of Population Ecology. *v.5 p.184, p.188*

Frontiers of the Roman Empire: A Social and Economic
Study. *v.3 p.29*

Frontiers of the State in the Late Ottoman Empire: Transjordan,
1850-1921. . . . .*v.6 p.621*

Frontiers of Theology in Latin America. *v.1 p.638*

Frontiers of X-Ray Astronomy. *v.5 p.67*

Frontiers: Territory and State Formation in the Modern
World. *v.4 p.487, p.495*

Frontiersmen in Blue: The United States Army and the Indian,
1848-1865. . . . .*v.6 p.687*

Frontline Nationalism in Angola and Mozambique. . . .*v.6 p.74*

The Front-Loading Problem in Presidential
Nominations. *v.4 p.549*

Frontsoldaten: The German Soldier in World War II. . *v.3 p.174*

Frost: A Literary Life Reconsidered. *v.2 p.78*

Frost: Collected Poems, Prose, and Plays. *v.2 p.77*

A Frozen Hell: The Russo-Finnish Winter War of,
1939-1940. . . . .*v.3 p.236*

A Frozen Woman. *v.2 p.530*

The Fruit Machine: Twenty Years of Writings on Queer
Cinema. *v.6 p.417*

The Fruited Plain: The Story of American Agriculture. . *v.5 p.4*

Fruitful Sites: Garden Culture in Ming Dynasty China. .*v.6 p.186*

Fruitless Trees: Portuguese Conservation and Brazil's Colonial
Timber. *v.3 p.269*

Fruits of Capitalism: Modernisation of Chilean Agriculture
1950-2000. . . . .*v.3 p.355*

Fruits of Her Plume: Essays on Contemporary Russian Women's
Culture. *v.2 p.798*

Fruits of Propaganda in the Tyler Administration. . . .*v.3 p.417*

Fruits of Warm Climates. *v.5 p.25*

Frustration Theory: An Analysis of Dispositional Learning and
Memory. *v.5 p.614*

Fu Manchu Omnibuses: The Island of Fu Manchu; the Wrath of
Fu Manchu and Other Stories, Vol. 5. . . . . . .*v.2 p.379*

Fuel Cell Systems Explained. *v.5 p.742*

Fuel Cell Technology Handbook. *v.5 p.362*

Fuels and Engines: Technology, Energy, Environment. .*v.5 p.742*

Fuenteovejuna. *v.2 p.653*

The Fuero Militar in New Spain 1764: 1800. . . . .*v.3 p.275*

A Fugitive from Utopia: The Poetry of Zbigniew
Herbert. *v.2 p.788*

The Fugitive Legacy: A Critical History. *v.2 p.12, p.13*

Fugitive Light: A Novel. *v.6 p.658*

Fugitive Pieces. *v.2 p.273, p.736*

Fugitive Writings. *v.4 p.493*

The Fugitives. *v.2 p.13*

Fugue: History and Practice. *v.1 p.371*

Fulbright: A Biography. *v.3 p.464*

Fulfilling the Promise: Biology Education in the Nation's
Schools. *v.5 p.246*

Fulfillment in the Promised Land, 1917-1937. . . . .*v.6 p.612*

Full Bloom: The Art and Life of Georgia O'Keeffe. . .*v.1 p.738*

Full Employment and Growth: Further Keynesian Essays on
Policy. *v.4 p.239*

Full House: The Spread of Excellence from Plato to
Darwin. *v.5 p.79*

Full of Life: UNESCO Biosphere Reserves, Model Regions for
Sustainable Development. *v.5 p.233*

Full of Life. *v.2 p.72*

Fullerenes: Chemistry, Physics, and Technology. *v.5 p.306*

Fun and Games in Twentieth-Century America: A Historical
Guide to Leisure. *v.4 p.784*

Fun with GPS. *v.4 p.389*

Fun Without Fatigue. *v.4 p.784, p.801, p.830*

The Function of Dance in Human Society. . . . *v.1 p.46, p.48*

The Function of Newspapers in Society: A Global
Perspective. *v.4 p.411, p.417*

Functional Analysis. *v.5 p.494*

Functional Anatomy of Vertebrates: An Evolutionary
Perspective. *v.5 p.157, p.190*

Functional Chordate Anatomy. *v.5 p.157*

Functional Exercise Progressions. . . . *v.4 p.793, p.794, p.880*

Functional Genomics: Methods and Protocols. *v.5 p.138*

Functional Genomics. *v.5 p.147*

Functional Microbial Genomics, Vol. 33. . . . .*v.5 p.132, p.153*

Functional Morphology in Vertebrate Paleontology. . .*v.5 p.448*

Functional Movement Development Across the Life
Span. *v.4 p.907, p.908, p.909*

A Functional Past: The Uses of History in Nineteenth-Century
Chile. *v.3 p.351*

Functional Performance in Older Adults. *v.5 p.535*

Functional Training for Sports. *v.4 p.790, p.878*

Functional Ultrastructure: An Atlas of Tissue Biology and
Pathology. *v.5 p.159*

Functionalism Historicized: Essays on British Social
Anthropology. *v.4 p.5*

Functionalized Polymers: Synthesis, Properties and
Applications. *v.5 p.322*

Functions of One Complex Variable II. *v.5 p.490*

Functions of One Complex Variable I. *v.5 p.490*

Functions of Social Conflict. *v.4 p.766*

The Functions of the Executive. *v.4 p.64*

Fundamental Astronomy. *v.5 p.65*

Fundamental Bacterial Genetics. *v.5 p.137*

Fundamental Concepts of Bioinformatics. *v.5 p.97*

Fundamental Finite Element Analysis and Applications: With
Mathematica and Matlab Computations. *v.5 p.693*

Fundamental Genetics. *v.5 p.136*

Fundamental Groups and Covering
Spaces. *v.5 p.474, p.475, p.499*

Fundamental Principles of Polymeric Materials. *v.5 p.690, p.691*

The Fundamental Questions of Philosophy. *v.1 p.417*

Fundamentalism and American Culture: The Shaping of
Twentieth-Century Evangelicalism,
1870-1925. . . . .*v.1 p.606, p.636*

Fundamentalisms Comprehended. *v.4 p.722*

Fundamentals and Applications of Solar Energy, Pt. II. *v.5 p.742*

Fundamentals of Acoustics. *v.5 p.567*

Fundamentals of Analytical Flame Spectroscopy. . . .*v.5 p.273*

Fundamentals of Aquatic Toxicology: Methods and Applications. . . . . *.v.5 p.704*

Fundamentals of Athletic Training. . . . . *.v.4 p.828*

Fundamentals of Biogeography. . . . . *.v.5 p.168*

Fundamentals of Biostatistics. . . . . *.v.5 p.93*

Fundamentals of Building Construction: Materials and Methods. . . . . *.v.1 p.796*

Fundamentals of Building Energy Dynamics. . . . . *.v.5 p.360, p.361, p.362, p.368*

Fundamentals of Business Marketing Education: A Guide for University-Level Faculty and Policy Makers. . . . *.v.4 p.176*

Fundamentals of Business Marketing Research: A Guide for University-Level Faculty and Policymakers. . . . *.v.4 p.136*

Fundamentals of Celestial Mechanics. . . . . *.v.5 p.66*

Fundamentals of Complementary and Integrative Medicine. . . . . *.v.5 p.531*

The Fundamentals of Corrosion. . . . . *.v.5 p.691*

Fundamentals of Cyclic Stress and Strain. . . . . . *.v.5 p.691*

Fundamentals of Digital Logic and Microcomputer Design. . . . . *.v.5 p.344, p.730*

Fundamentals of Ecotoxicology. . . . . *.v.5 p.704*

Fundamentals of Electric Circuits. . . . . *.v.5 p.720*

Fundamentals of Electrochemical Corrosion. . . . *.v.5 p.735*

Fundamentals of Electronic Circuit Design. . . . . *.v.5 p.722*

Fundamentals of Entomology. . . . . *.v.5 p.212*

Fundamentals of Enzyme Kinetics. . . . . *.v.5 p.119*

Fundamentals of Exercise Physiology: For Fitness, Performance, and Health. . . . . *.v.4 p.875*

Fundamentals of Fluid Film Lubrication, Vol. 169. . *.v.5 p.708*

⊜ Fundamentals of Fluid Film Lubrication. . . . . *.v.5 p.708*

Fundamentals of Forensic Practice: Mental Health and Criminal Law. . . . . *.v.5 p.593, v.6 p.270*

Fundamentals of Geographic Information Systems. . . . . *.v.4 p.386, p.387*

Fundamentals of Ground Water. . . . . *.v.5 p.428*

Fundamentals of Heat and Mass Transfer. . . . . *.v.5 p.560*

Fundamentals of Heat Transfer for Process Engineering. *.v.5 p.742*

Fundamentals of Infrastructure Engineering: Civil Engineering Systems, Vol. 7. . . . . *.v.5 p.686*

Fundamentals of Language. . . . . *.v.2 p.550, p.561*

Fundamentals of Learning. . . . . *.v.4 p.359*

Fundamentals of Light Microscopy and Electronic Imaging. . . . . *.v.5 p.86*

Fundamentals of Local Arts Management. . . . . . *.v.1 p.825*

Fundamentals of Machine Component Design. . . . *.v.5 p.714*

Fundamentals of Manufacturing for Engineers. . . . *.v.5 p.684*

Fundamentals of Metal Fatigue Analysis. . . . . . *.v.5 p.687*

Fundamentals of Metal Forming. . . . . *.v.5 p.692*

Fundamentals of Metal-Matrix Composites. . . . . *.v.5 p.690*

Fundamentals of Mobile and Pervasive Computing. . *.v.4 p.114*

Fundamentals of Modern Manufacturing: Materials, Processes and Systems. . . . . *.v.4 p.116*

Fundamentals of Modern Physics. . . . . *.v.5 p.547*

Fundamentals of Molecular Evolution. . . . . . . *.v.5 p.113*

Fundamentals of Musical Composition. . . . . . . *.v.1 p.373*

Fundamentals of Music. . . . . *.v.1 p.176*

Fundamentals of Network Security. . . . . *.v.4 p.114*

Fundamentals of Optics. . . . . *.v.5 p.73, p.561*

Fundamentals of Physics: EGrade Plus Stand-Alone Access. . . . . *.v.5 p.539*

Fundamentals of Physics. . . . . *.v.5 p.546*

Fundamentals of Pipe Flow. . . . . *.v.5 p.713*

Fundamentals of Plasma Physics. . . . . *.v.5 p.566*

Fundamentals of Polymer Science: An Introductory Text. . . . . *.v.5 p.322*

Fundamentals of Portland Cement Concrete - A Quantitative Approach: Fresh Concrete, Vol. 1. . . . . . . *.v.5 p.690*

Fundamentals of Private Pensions. . . . . *.v.4 p.98*

Fundamentals of Protein NMR Spectroscopy. . . . . *.v.5 p.118*

Fundamentals of Queueing Theory. . . . . *.v.5 p.481*

Fundamentals of Radiochemistry. . . . . *.v.5 p.307*

Fundamentals of Renewable Energy Processes. . . . *.v.5 p.361*

Fundamentals of Reservoir Engineering. . . . . . . *.v.5 p.451*

Fundamentals of Robotics: Analysis and Control. . . *.v.5 p.712*

Fundamentals of Sales Management for the Newly Appointed Sales Manager. . . . . *.v.4 p.143*

Fundamentals of Soil Behavior. . . . . *.v.5 p.422*

Fundamentals of Soil Science. . . . . *.v.5 p.49*

Fundamentals of Soils. . . . . *.v.5 p.424*

Fundamentals of Sport Marketing. . . . . . *.v.4 p.786, p.885*

Fundamentals of Sports Injury Management. *.v.4 p.827, v.5 p.519*

Fundamentals of Statistical and Thermal Physics. . . *.v.5 p.559*

Fundamentals of Structural Analysis. . . . . *.v.5 p.693*

Fundamentals of Superconductivity. . . . . *.v.5 p.565*

Fundamentals of Supply Chain Management: Twelve Drivers of Competitive Advantage. . . . . *.v.4 p.118*

Fundamentals of Track and Field. . . . . . . *.v.4 p.794, p.869*

Fundamentals of Transportation Engineering: A Multimodal Systems Approach. . . . . *.v.5 p.700*

Fundamentals of Vasistadvaita Vedanta: A Study Based on Vedanta Desika's Tattva-Mukta-Kalapa. . . . . *.v.1 p.535*

Fundamentals of Wireless Networking. . . . . *.v.5 p.727*

Fundamentals of World Regional Geography. . . . . *.v.4 p.397*

The Funding of Higher Education: International Perspectives. . . . . *.v.4 p.295*

Funeral en Teruel. . . . . *.v.2 p.672, p.673*

The Funeral Party: A Novel. . . . . *.v.2 p.810*

Funeral Rites. . . . . *.v.2 p.519, v.6 p.396*

Fungal Disease Resistance in Plants: Biochemistry, Molecular Biology, and Genetic Engineering. . . . . . *.v.5 p.46, p.47*

Fungal Ecology. . . . . *.v.5 p.209*

Fungal Morphogenesis. . . . . *.v.5 p.161*

Fungal Populations and Species. . . . . *.v.5 p.209*

Fungi: Experimental Methods in Biology. . . . . . . *.v.5 p.209*

Funk and Wagnall's Standard Dictionary of Folklore, Mythology, and Legend. . . . . *.v.2 p.585*

Funny Boy: A Novel in Six Stories. . . . *.v.2 p.766, v.6 p.399*

Funny, It Doesn't Sound Jewish: How Yiddish Songs and Synagogue Melodies Influenced Tin Pan Alley, Broadway, and Hollywood. . . . . *.v.1 p.299*

Funny Ladies: 100 Years of Great Comediennes. . . .*v.6 p.313*

The Fur Trade in Canada. *v.3 p.545, v.6 p.684*

Fur Traders, Trappers and Mountain Men of the Upper
 Missouri. *v.3 p.522*

Furnishing the Mind: Concepts and Their Perceptual
 Basis. *v.1 p.504*

Furniture and Interiors of the 1940s. *v.1 p.799*

Furniture and Interiors of the 1960s. *v.1 p.799*

Furniture: From Rococo to Art Deco. *v.1 p.805*

The Furniture of Sam Maloof. *v.1 p.720, p.803*

Further Considerations Concerning Raising the Value of
 Money. *v.4 p.215*

Further Contributions to Modern Economics. . .*v.4 p.196, p.270*

Further Essays on Capital and Interest, Vol. 3. .*v.4 p.233, p.234*

Further Fridays: Essays, Lectures and Other Nonfiction,
 1984-1994. . . . .*v.2 p.142*

Further Letters of Gerard Manley Hopkins, Including His
 Correspondence with Coventry Patmore. *v.2 p.293*

Further Voices in Vergil's Aeneid. *v.2 p.446*

The Fus Fixico Letters. *v.2 p.49*

The Fusion Quest. *v.5 p.362*

Future Developments in Soil Science Research. . . .*v.5 p.48*

Future Drive: Electric Vehicles and Sustainable
 Transportation. *v.5 p.701*

Future Evolution: An Illuminated History of Life to
 Come. *v.5 p.197*

The Future for Investors: Why the Tried and the True Triumph
 over the Bold and the New. *v.4 p.97, p.100*

A Future for Marxism?: Althusser, the Analytical Turn and the
 Revival of Socialist Theory. *v.4 p.507*

Future Indefinite, Vol. 2. . . . .*v.2 p.342*

Future Iraq: US Policy in Reshaping the Middle East. .*v.4 p.560*

Future Jazz. *v.1 p.261*

The Future of Academic Freedom. *v.4 p.298*

The Future of Advertising: New Media, New Clients, New
 Consumers in the Post-Television Age. . . .*v.4 p.140, p.426*

The Future of Air Traffic Control: Human Operators and
 Automation. *v.5 p.718*

The Future of American Democratic Politics: Principles and
 Practices. *v.4 p.555*

The Future of an Illusion. *v.1 p.524, v.5 p.634*

The Future of Anthropology: Its Relevance to the Contemporary
 World. *v.4 p.27*

Future of Children: Marriage and Child Well-Being. . .*v.4 p.756*

The Future of Christianity. *v.1 p.597*

The Future of Foreign Investment in Southeast Asia. . .*v.4 p.60*

The Future of Higher Education: Rhetoric, Reality, and the
 Risks of the Market. *v.4 p.332*

The Future of Human Nature. *v.1 p.495*

The Future of Human Resource Management: 64 Thought
 Leaders Explore the Critical HR Issues of Today and
 Tomorrow. *v.4 p.76*

The Future of Ice: A Journey into the Cold. *v.6 p.293*

The Future of Ideas: The Fate of the Commons in a Connected
 World. *v.4 p.435*

The Future of Imprisonment. *v.6 p.272*

The Future of Kurdistan in Iraq. *v.6 p.603*

Future of Law in a Multicultural World. *v.4 p.477*

The Future of Leadership: Today's Top Leadership Thinkers
 Speak to Tomorrow's Leaders. *v.4 p.70*

The Future of Life. *v.6 p.292*

The Future of Marketing: Critical 21st Century
 Perspectives. *v.4 p.137*

The Future of Marriage. *v.4 p.738*

The Future of Money. *v.4 p.246, p.261*

The Future of NATO: Enlargement, Russia and European
 Security. *v.4 p.639*

The Future of NATO Expansion: Four Case Studies. . .*v.4 p.639*

The Future of North America: Canada, the United States and
 Quebec Nationalism. *v.4 p.589*

The Future of Northern Ireland. *v.4 p.607*

The Future of Political Science. *v.4 p.483*

The Future of Religious Colleges. *v.4 p.307*

The Future of Ritual: Writings on Culture and
 Performance. *v.1 p.135, p.136*

The Future of Roman Catholic Theology. *v.1 p.570*

The Future of School Choice. *v.4 p.450*

Future of Social Security: A Feminist Economics
 Perspective. *v.4 p.274*

The Future of the American Labor Movement. *v.4 p.130*

The Future of the Environment: The Social Dimensions of
 Conservation and Ecological Alternatives. *v.5 p.223*

The Future of the Novel: Essays on the Art of Fiction. .*v.2 p.578*

Future of the Olympic Games. *v.4 p.846*

The Future of the Past. *v.1 p.823, p.824*

The Future of the United Nations System: Potential for the
 Twenty-First Century. *v.4 p.632*

The Future of the World Economy: A United Nations
 Study. *v.4 p.259*

The Future of Turkish Foreign Policy. *v.6 p.624*

The Future of U. S. Nuclear Weapons Policy. *v.4 p.561*

The Future Role of Pesticides in U. S. Agriculture. . .*v.5 p.10*

Future Shock. *v.4 p.769*

The Future U. S. Healthcare System: Who Will Care for the
 Poor and Uninsured? *v.4 p.778*

FutureNatural: Nature, Science, Culture. *v.5 p.248*

The Futures Game: Who Wins, Who Loses, and
 Why. *v.4 p.98, p.102*

Futurism. *v.1 p.681*

The Futurist Cookbook. *v.2 p.718*

Fuzzy Logic: A Practical Approach. *v.5 p.711*

Fuzzy Logic and Neural Network Handbook. *v.5 p.710*

Fuzzy Logic: Implementation and Applications. . . .*v.5 p.711*

☐ FyodorDostoevsky.com. *v.2 p.796, p.800*

G

G. A. Bredero, the Spanish Brabanter: A Seventeenth-Century
 Dutch Social Satire in Five Acts. *v.2 p.622*

G. E. Moore: Essays in Retrospect. *v.1 p.445*

G. E. Moore: Selected Writings. *v.1 p.446*

G. F. Handel: A Guide to Research. . . .*v.1 p.164, p.186, p.329*

G. Howard Ferguson: Ontario Tory. *v.3 p.545*

G Proteins and Signal Transduction. *v.5 p.117*

G. W. Leibniz's Monadology: An Edition for Students. *v.1 p.459, p.460*

The G7/G8 System: Evolution, Role and Documentation. *v.4 p.630*

Gabon: Beyond the Colonial Legacy. *v.6 p.63*

Gabriel Fauré: A Musical Life. *v.1 p.219, p.324*

Gabriel García Márquez. *v.2 p.682*

Gabriel Garcia Marquez: A Critical Companion. *v.2 p.684*

Gabriel Garcia Marquez: A Study of the Short Fiction. .*v.2 p.684*

Gabriel Garcia Marquez: An Annotated Bibliography, 1947-1979. . . . .*v.2 p.682*

Gabriel Garcia Marquez and His Magical Universe. . .*v.2 p.682*

Gabriel Garcia Marquez and the Powers of Fiction. . .*v.2 p.684*

Gabriel Garcia Marquez: His Life and Works. *v.2 p.681*

Gabriel Garcia Marquez: New Readings. *v.2 p.683*

Gabriel Garcia Marquez's Love in the Time of Cholera: A Reader's Guide. *v.2 p.682*

Gabriel Garcia Marquez's One Hundred Years of Solitude: A Casebook. *v.2 p.681, p.682*

Gabriel Garcia Marquez's One Hundred Years of Solitude. *v.2 p.682*

Gabriel Garcia Marquez. *v.2 p.682, p.684*

Gabriela, Clove and Cinnamon. *v.2 p.689*

A Gabriela Mistral Reader. *v.2 p.681*

Gabriela Mistral: Selected Poems. *v.2 p.680, p.681*

Gabriele D'Annunzio: Defiant Archangel. . . .*v.2 p.716, p.717*

Gabriele D'Annunzio: The Dark Flame. *v.2 p.716*

Gabriele D'Annunzio. *v.2 p.716*

Gabrielle Roy: Creation and Memory. *v.2 p.538*

Gabrielle Roy: Une Vie. *v.2 p.539*

Gaelic Ireland, C 1250-C 1650: Land, Lordship and Settlement. *v.3 p.134*

Gaelic Ireland C.1350-1600: Land, Lordship and Settlement. *v.3 p.134, p.136*

Gaffers, Grips and Best Boys: From Producer-Director to Gaffer and Computer Special Effects Creator, a Behind-the-Scenes Look at Who Does What in the Making of a Motion Picture. *v.6 p.347*

The Gag Family: German-Bohemian Artists in America. .*v.1 p.720*

Gaia: A New Look at Life on Earth. *v.5 p.248*

Gaia's Body: Toward a Physiology of Earth. *v.5 p.250*

Gaiety Transfigured: Gay Self-Representation in American Literature. *v.6 p.392*

Gaining Access: A Practical and Theoretical Guide for Qualitative Researchers. *v.4 p.690*

Gainsborough. *v.1 p.749*

Gaitan of Colombia: A Political Biography. *v.3 p.358*

Gaitanismo, Left Liberalism, and Popular Mobilization in Colombia. *v.3 p.357*

Gal: A True Life. *v.6 p.23, p.42*

Galactic Astronomy. *v.5 p.71*

Galactic Dynamics. *v.5 p.71*

Galapagos. *v.2 p.158*

Galatians: A New Translation with Introduction and Commentary. *v.1 p.631*

Galatians. *v.1 p.630*

Galaxies in the Universe: An Introduction. *v.5 p.71*

Galaxy Formation and Evolution. *v.5 p.71*

Galdos and the Art of the European Novel. *v.2 p.654*

Gale Encyclopedia of Childhood and Adolescence. . .*v.4 p.676*

The Gale Encyclopedia of Childhood and Adolescence. .*v.5 p.627*

Gale Encyclopedia of E-Commerce. *v.4 p.113*

Galen on Food and Diet. *v.2 p.404*

Galenism: Rise and Decline of a Medical Philosophy. .*v.2 p.405*

La galeria. *v.2 p.708*

Galileo: A Very Short Introduction. *v.3 p.46*

Galileo, Courtier: The Practice of Science in the Culture of Absolutism. *v.3 p.46, v.5 p.396*

Galileo: For Copernicanism and for the Church. . . .*v.3 p.46*

Galileo's Instruments of Credit: Telescopes, Images, Secrecy. *v.5 p.62*

Gallegos: "Dona Barbara". *v.2 p.687*

Gallery of Best Resumes. *v.4 p.170*

The Gallery. *v.6 p.395*

Gallica Classique. *v.2 p.463*

The Gallup Poll Cumulative Index: Public Opinion, 1935-1997. . . . .*v.5 p.585, p.586*

The Gallup Poll: Public Opinion, 1935-1971, Set. . . .*v.4 p.697*

The Gallup Poll: Public Opinion 2003. . . . .*v.5 p.586*

Galois Theory. *v.5 p.474*

The Galton Case: A Lew Archer Novel. *v.2 p.97*

The Gambia, a Cultural Profile. *v.6 p.69*

The Gambler. *v.2 p.803*

Gambling in America: An Encyclopedia of History, Issues, and Society. *v.4 p.777, p.899, p.900*

Gambling with Truth: An Essay on Induction and the Aims of Science. *v.5 p.400, p.409*

Gambling with Virtue: Japanese Women and the Search for Self in a Changing Nation. *v.6 p.446*

Game for Dancers: Performing Modernism in the Postwar Years, 1945-1960. . . . .*v.1 p.29, p.30, p.31, p.43*

The Game of Death in Ancient Rome: Arena Sport and Political Suicide. *v.3 p.23*

The Game of Life: College Sports and Educational Values. *v.4 p.293, p.294, p.822, p.895*

The Game Planners: Transforming Canada's Sport System. *v.4 p.891, p.898, p.899*

Game Theory: A Critical Introduction. *v.4 p.688, p.689*

Game Theory and Economics. *v.4 p.84*

Game Theory and Politics. *v.4 p.83*

Game Theory at Work: How to Use Game Theory to Outthink and Outmaneuver Your Competition. *v.4 p.83, p.84*

Game Theory in Economics. *v.4 p.207*

Game Theory in the Social Sciences: Concepts and Solutions. *v.4 p.689*

Gamelan: Cultural Interaction and Musical Development in Central Java. *v.1 p.290*

Gamelan Gong Kebyar : The Art of Twentieth-Century Balinese Music. *v.1 p.290*

Games and Decisions: Introduction and Critical Survey. .*v.5 p.504*

Games and Sanctuaries in Ancient Greece: Olympia, Delphi, Isthmia, Nemea, Athens. *v.3 p.15*

Games and Sets: The Changing Face of Sport on Television. *v.4 p.803, p.813, p.886, p.901*

Games at Twilight. *v.2 p.764*

Games Businesses Play: Cases and Models. *v.4 p.177*

Games Colleges Play: Scandal and Reform in Intercollegiate Athletics. *v.4 p.291, p.822, p.895*

Games Criminals Play: How You Can Profit by Knowing Them. *v.6 p.276*

The Games Must Go On: Avery Brundage and the Olympic Movement. *v.4 p.845, p.846*

Games of Terror: Halloween, Friday the 13th and the Films of the Stalker Cycle. *v.6 p.317, p.318*

Games That Teach: Experiential Activities for Reinforcing Training. *v.4 p.84*

The Game. *v.4 p.862*

Gandhi in His Time and Ours: The Global Legacy of His Ideas. *v.6 p.159*

Gandhi: Pan-Islamism, Imperialism and Nationalism in India. *v.6 p.157*

Gandhi: Prisoner of Hope. *v.6 p.158*

Gandhi: Selected Writings. *v.1 p.475*

Gandhi: The South African Experience. *v.6 p.79*

Gandhi's Body: Sex, Diet and the Politics of Nationalism. *v.6 p.156*

Gandhi's Passion: The Life and Legacy of Mahatma Gandhi. *v.6 p.160*

Gandhi's Pilgrimage of Faith: From Darkness to Light. *v.6 p.159*

Gandhi. *v.6 p.159*

The Gang: A Study of 1,313 Gangs in Chicago. *v.4 p.752, v.6 p.256*

The Gang: Coleridge, the Hutchinsons and Wordsworths in 1802. . . . . *v.2 p.280, p.325, p.326*

Gang Nation: Delinquent Citizens in Puerto Rican, Chicano, and Chicana Narratives. *v.6 p.495, p.511, p.547*

The Gang That Wouldn't Write Straight: Wolfe, Thompson, Didion and the New Journalism Revolution. *v.4 p.403*

▢ Gangresearch.net. *v.4 p.753*

Gangs and Delinquency in Developmental Perspective. *v.6 p.256*

Gangs and Society: Alternative Perspectives. *v.4 p.714*

The Gangs of New York: An Informal History of the Underworld. *v.4 p.714*

Ganymede in the Renaissance: Homosexuality in Art and Society. *v.6 p.407*

▢ GAO Reports. *v.4 p.481*

Gao Village. *v.6 p.195*

Gap Creek: The Story of a Marriage. *v.2 p.151*

Garbage in the Cities: Refuse, Reform, and the Environment. *v.5 p.706*

Garcia Marquez in 90 Minutes. *v.2 p.684*

Garcia Marquez: "One Hundred Years of Solitude". *v.2 p.684, p.685*

Garcia Marquez: The Man and His Work. *v.2 p.682*

Garcia Marquez: Writer of Colombia. *v.2 p.684*

Garcia Marquez. *v.2 p.682*

Garcilaso de la Vega and the Italian Renaissance. *v.2 p.652, p.653*

Garcilaso de la Vega. *v.2 p.652*

Garden and the City: Retirement and Politics in the Later Poetry of Pope, 1731-1743. . . . . *v.2 p.257*

The Garden and the Workshop: Essays on the Cultural History of Vienna and Budapest. *v.3 p.186*

Garden, Ashes. *v.2 p.811*

Garden History: Issues, Approaches, Methods. . . . *v.1 p.818*

The Garden: New and Selected Poetry. *v.2 p.800*

The Garden of Eden. *v.2 p.84, p.85*

Garden of the Departed Cats. *v.6 p.667*

The Garden of the Finzi-Continis. *v.2 p.713*

The Garden Party and Other Plays. *v.2 p.783*

The Garden Plants of China. *v.5 p.44*

Gardens Across America: The American Horticultural Society's Guide to American Public Gardens and Arboreta. . *v.1 p.812*

Gardens Across America, Vol. 2. . . . . *v.1 p.812*

Gardens and Historic Plants of the Antebellum South. *v.1 p.818*

Gardens and the Picturesque: Studies in the History of Landscape Architecture. *v.1 p.818, p.819*

Gardens in the Dunes. *v.2 p.155, v.6 p.699*

Gardens, Landscape and Vision in the Palaces of Islamic Spain. *v.1 p.674, p.814*

Gardens of Gertrude Jekyll. *v.1 p.815*

The Gardens of Japan. *v.6 p.221*

Gardens of the Arts and Crafts Movement: Reality and Imagination. *v.1 p.820*

Gardens of the Roman World. *v.1 p.818*

Gardens of the World: Two Thousand Years of Garden Design. *v.1 p.819*

Gardenwalks in the Pacific Northwest: Beautiful Gardens along the Coast from Oregon to British Columbia. . . . *v.1 p.812*

▢ GardenWeb : the internets garden community. . . *v.1 p.811*

Gardner's Art Through the Ages: A Concise History. *v.1 p.667, p.668*

Gardner's Chemical Synonyms and Trade Names. . . *v.5 p.259*

Gardner's Photographic Sketch Book of the Civil War. *v.3 p.431*

Garfield. *v.3 p.399, p.400, p.437*

Garfinkel and Ethnomethodology. *v.4 p.688*

Gargantua and Pantagruel. *v.2 p.472*

The Garland Companion to Vladimir Nabakov. *v.2 p.103, p.104*

The Garland Encyclopedia of World Music Set. *v.1 p.161, p.283*

The Garland Handbook of African Music. *v.1 p.286*

The Garland Handbook of Latin American Music. . . *v.1 p.293*

Garner's Modern American Usage. *v.2 p.552, p.556*

Garrett Eckbo: Modern Landscapes for Living. . . *v.1 p.817*

The Garrick Year. *v.2 p.343*

Garrick. *v.1 p.98, p.151, p.152*

Gary Hill: Language Willing. *v.1 p.773*

Gary Snyder Reader: Prose, Poetry, and Translations. *v.2 p.156*

Gary Snyder. *v.2 p.154, p.155*

Gas Chromatography in Forensic Science. *v.5 p.269*

Gas One: A Play. *v.2 p.611*

Gas Two: A Play. *v.2 p.611*

Gases, Liquids and Solids: And Other States of Matter. *v.5 p.277*

Gaspar! A Spanish Poet-Priest in the Nicaraguan Revolution. *v.3 p.302*

Gaspard, Melchior & Balthazar. *v.2 p.534*

Gas-Phase Ion and Neutral Thermochemistry. *v.5 p.282*

Gassendi's Ethics: Freedom in a Mechanistic
    Universe. *v.1 p.452, p.453*

Gastrointestinal Pathology: An Atlas and Text. *v.5 p.519*

La Gastronomia en Potosí y Charcas: Siglos XVIII y XIX, 800
    Recetas de la Cocina Criolla. *v.3 p.272*

Gastrulation: From Cells to Embryo. *v.5 p.161*

The Gate of Heavenly Peace: The Chinese and Their
    Revolution, 1895-1980. . . . .*v.6 p.193*

The Gate of Heavenly Peace. *v.6 p.197*

Gate of the Sun: Bab al-Shams. *v.6 p.661*

Gateless Gate: The Classic Book of Zen Koans. .*v.6 p.223, p.235*

Gates: How Microsoft's Mogul Reinvented an Industry - and
    Made Himself the Richest Man in America. *v.4 p.158*

Gates of Bronze. *v.6 p.649*

Gates of Freedom: Voltairine de Cleyre and the Revolution of
    the Mind. *v.4 p.493*

The Gates of Horn: A Study of Five French Realists. .*v.2 p.462*

The Gates of Ivory. *v.2 p.343*

The Gateway to the Middle Ages: Monasticism. *v.3 p.56*

Gateways to the Global Economy. *v.4 p.256, p.260*

Gathering Evidence: A Memoir. *v.2 p.616*

A Gathering of Fugitives. *v.2 p.165*

Gathering Power: The Future of Progressive Politics in
    America. *v.4 p.555*

Gathering the Tribes. *v.2 p.145*

Gaudy Night. *v.2 p.381*

Gauge Fields and Strings. *v.5 p.550*

Gaugin: Catalogue Raisonné of the Paintings,
    1873-1888. . . . .*v.1 p.749*

Gauguin and Impressionism. *v.1 p.736*

Gauguin. *v.1 p.739*

Gauss: Titan of Science. *v.5 p.465*

Gautier on Dance. *v.1 p.39*

Gautrek's Saga, and Other Medieval Tales. . . .*v.2 p.624, p.625*

Gavarni. Catalogue Raisonné of the Graphic Work: L'oeuvre de
    Gavarni. *v.1 p.755*

Gaviotas: A Village to Reinvent the World. *v.3 p.270*

Gay & Lesbian Alliance Against Defamation
    (GLAAD). *v.6 p.357*

Gay & Lesbian Alliance Against Defamation. . .*v.6 p.387*

Gay & Lesbian Review Worldwide. *v.6 p.361*

The Gay 100: A Ranking of the Most Influential Gay Men and
    Lesbians, Past and Present. *v.6 p.358*

The Gay Almanac: The Most Comprehensive Reference Source
    of Its Kind. *v.6 p.360*

Gay American History: Lesbians and Gay Men in the
    U.S.A. *v.6 p.357*

Gay and Gray: The Older Homosexual Man. *v.6 p.380*

Gay and Lesbian Aging: Research and Future
    Directions. *v.6 p.380*

Gay and Lesbian Almanac. *v.6 p.360*

Gay and Lesbian American Plays: An Annotated
    Bibliography. *v.6 p.359, p.411*

Gay and Lesbian Americans and Political Participation: A
    Reference Handbook. *v.4 p.570, v.6 p.360, p.387*

Gay and Lesbian Educators: Personal Freedoms - Public
    Constraints. *v.4 p.309, v.6 p.383, p.385*

Gay and Lesbian Families: A Bibliography. *v.6 p.359*

The Gay and Lesbian Liberation Movement. *v.6 p.386*

Gay and Lesbian Library Service. *v.6 p.383*

Gay and Lesbian Literary Heritage: A Reader's Companion to
    the Writers and Their Works, from Antiquity to the
    Present. *v.6 p.360, p.361, p.391*

Gay and Lesbian Literature, Vol. 1. . . . .*v.6 p.391*

Gay and Lesbian Literature, Vol. 2. . . . .*v.6 p.391*

The Gay and Lesbian Movement: References and
    Resources. *v.6 p.363*

Gay and Lesbian Parenting. *v.6 p.376*

Gay and Lesbian Plays Today. *v.6 p.411*

Gay and Lesbian Poetry in Our Time: An Anthology. .*v.6 p.405*

Gay and Lesbian Rights in the United States: A Documentary
    History. *v.6 p.388*

Gay and Lesbian Students: Understanding Their
    Needs. *v.4 p.309, v.6 p.384*

The Gay and Lesbian Theatrical Legacy: A Biographical
    Dictionary of Major Figures in American Stage
    History in the Pre-Stonewall
    Era. *v.1 p.126, v.6 p.358, p.359, p.413*

A Gay Bibliography: Eight Bibliographies on Lesbian and Male
    Homosexuality: an Original Anthology. *v.6 p.359*

Gay Comics. *v.6 p.407*

Gay Cops. *v.6 p.383*

Gay Couples and the Law: A Bibliography. *v.6 p.359*

The Gay Detective Novel: Lesbian and Gay Main Characters
    and Themes in Mystery Fiction. *v.6 p.391*

Gay Fandom and Crossover Stardom: James Dean, Mel Gibson,
    and Keanu Reeves. . .*v.6 p.327, p.328, p.340, p.341, p.416*

Gay Fiction Speaks: Conversations with Gay Novelists. .*v.6 p.392*

Gay Fictions: Studies in a Male Homosexual Literary
    Tradition. *v.6 p.393, p.394*

Gay Histories and Cultures. *v.4 p.748, v.6 p.358, p.363*

Gay Hollywood Film & Video Guide: Over 75 Years of Male
    Homosexuality in the Movies. *v.6 p.417*

Gay Identity: The Self under Ban. *v.6 p.366*

Gay, Lesbian, and Transgender Issues in Education: Programs,
    Policies, and Practices. *v.6 p.386*

Gay, Lesbian, Bisexual and Transgender Public Policy Issues: A
    Citizen's and Administrator's Guide to the New Cultural
    Struggle. *v.6 p.372*

Gay Lesbian Straight Education Network. .*v.4 p.309, v.6 p.384*

Gay Lives: Homosexual Autobiography from John Addington
    Symonds to Paul Monette. *v.6 p.393*

Gay Love Poetry. *v.6 p.405*

Gay Marriage and Democracy: Equality for All. . . .*v.6 p.389*

Gay Men and Aging. *v.6 p.380*

Gay Men and Women Who Enriched the World. . .*v.6 p.357*

Gay Men's Friendships: Invincible Communities. . .*v.6 p.375*

Gay Midlife and Maturity. *v.6 p.380*

The Gay Mystique: The Myth and Reality of Male
    Homosexuality. *v.6 p.366, p.367*

Gay New York: Gender, Urban Culture, and the Making of the Gay Male World 1890-1940. . . . .*v.6 p.362, p.717*

The Gay Nineties in America: A Cultural Dictionary of the 1890s. *v.6 p.358*

The Gay Novel: The Male Homosexual Image in America. *v.6 p.393*

Gay Olympian: The Life and Death of Dr. Tom Waddell. *v.4 p.839, v.6 p.384*

Gay Rebel of the Harlem Renaissance: Selections from the Work of Richard Bruce Nugent. *v.6 p.27, p.403*

Gay Rights and American Law. *v.4 p.457*

Gay Rights, Military Wrongs: Political Perspectives on Lesbians and Gays in the Military. *v.6 p.390*

Gay Rights on Trial: A Handbook with Cases, Laws, and Documents. *v.6 p.388*

Gay Rights. *v.6 p.360, p.388*

Gay Science: The Ethics of Sexual Orientation Research. *v.6 p.420*

The Gay Science: With a Prelude in Rhymes and an Appendix of Songs. *v.1 p.466*

Gay Talk: A (Sometimes Outrageous) Dictionary of Gay Slang. *v.6 p.358*

Gay Voices of the Harlem Renaissance. *v.6 p.393*

Gay Warriors: A Documentary History from the Ancient World to the Present. *v.6 p.389*

Gay Widowers: Life after the Death of a Partner. .*v.6 p.376, p.382*

Gaylaw: Challenging the Apartheid of the Closet. *v.4 p.457, v.6 p.388*

Gaylord Music Library Necrology. *v.1 p.159*

Gays and Lesbians in the Democratic Process: Public Policy, Public Opinion and Political Representation. *v.4 p.569, p.570*

Gays, Lesbians and Consumer Behavior: Theory, Practice and Research Issues in Marketing. *v.6 p.383*

The Gazelle: Medieval Hebrew Poems on God, Israel and the Soul. *v.6 p.566, p.574*

Gc/Ms: A Practical User's Guide. *v.5 p.271*

Gear Motor Handbook. *v.5 p.715*

Gedichte - Dramen I, (1891 - 1898). *v.2 p.609*

Gedichte und Interpretationen. *v.2 p.591*

Gedichte. *v.2 p.609*

Geeks and Geezers: How Era, Values, and Defining Moments Shape Leaders. *v.4 p.262, p.263*

Geigy Scientific Tables, 4 vols.. . . . .*v.5 p.326*

Geisha, Gangster, Neighbor, Nun: Scenes from Japanese Lives. *v.6 p.228*

Geist der Goethezeit: Versuch einer Ideellen Entwicklung der klassisch-romantischen Literaturgeschichte. *v.2 p.590*

Gel Electrophoresis: Nucleic Acids. *v.5 p.326*

Gel Electrophoresis of Nucleic Acids: A Practical Approach. *v.5 p.123*

Gemini. *v.2 p.534*

Gems. *v.5 p.452*

Gendarmes and the State in Nineteenth-Century Europe. .*v.3 p.74*

Gender - Body - Knowledge: Feminist Reconstruction of Being and Knowing. *v.6 p.463*

Gender and Assimilation in Modern Jewish History: The Roles and Representations of Women. *v.6 p.454, p.459*

Gender and Citizenship in the Middle East. *v.6 p.593*

Gender and Class in Modern Europe. *v.3 p.53*

Gender and Consumer Culture Reader. *v.6 p.458*

Gender and Crime: Patterns in Victimization and Offending. *v.6 p.258, p.259*

Gender and Development. *v.4 p.259, p.273*

Gender and Discourse. *v.4 p.21*

Gender and Emotion: Social Psychological Perspectives. *v.4 p.694*

Gender and Empire. *v.3 p.89, p.125*

Gender and Fair Assessment. *v.4 p.287*

Gender and French Cinema. *v.6 p.327, p.338*

Gender and Genre in Gertrude Stein. *v.2 p.121*

Gender and Governance. *v.4 p.512*

Gender and Health: An International Perspective. . . .*v.4 p.47*

Gender and History in Western Europe. *v.3 p.55*

Gender and International Relations. *v.6 p.441, p.442*

Gender and Modernity in Andean Bolivia. *v.3 p.325*

Gender and Modernization in the Spanish Realist Novel. *v.2 p.641*

Gender and Nation in the Spanish Modernist Novel. .*v.2 p.641*

Gender and Nationalism in Colonial Cuba: The Travels of Santa Cruz y Montalvo, Condesa de Merlin. *v.3 p.313*

Gender and Nationalism in Colonial Cuba: the Travels of Santa Cruz y Montalvo. *v.3 p.311*

Gender and Physical Education: Contemporary Issues and Future Directions. *v.4 p.796*

Gender and Policing: Comparative Perspectives. . . .*v.6 p.260*

Gender and Power in the Japanese Visual Field. . . .*v.6 p.473*

Gender and Religion in Old and New Worlds. *v.1 p.655*

Gender and Representation: Women in Spanish Realist Fiction. *v.2 p.641*

Gender and Rhetoric in Plato's Political Thought. . .*v.4 p.489*

Gender and Romance in Chaucer's Canterbury Tales. .*v.2 p.209*

Gender and Russian Literature: New Perspectives. . .*v.2 p.799*

The Gender and Science Reader. *v.5 p.398, v.6 p.439*

Gender and Sexuality in Weimar Modernity: Film, Literature and New Objectivity. *v.6 p.338*

Gender and Stratification. *v.4 p.722*

Gender and the Israeli-Palestinian Conflict: The Politics of Women's Resistance. *v.6 p.620*

Gender and the Politics of History. *v.3 p.54, v.6 p.450*

Gender and the Social Construction of Illness. *v.6 p.443, p.444*

Gender at the Crossroads of Knowledge: Feminist Anthropology in the Postmodern Era. *v.4 p.30*

Gender, Colonialism and Education: The Politics of Experience. *v.6 p.462*

Gender, Conflict, and Peacekeeping. *v.4 p.650*

Gender, Crime, and Punishment. *v.6 p.257*

Gender Differences in Science Careers: The Project Access Study. *v.5 p.398, v.6 p.439*

Gender Dimensions of Alcohol Consumption and Alcohol-Related Problems in Latin America and the Caribbean. *v.4 p.776*

Gender, Emotion, and the Family. *v.4 p.694, v.5 p.651, p.657, v.6 p.445, p.466*

Gender Equality in the Philosophy of Education: Catharine Macaulay's Forgotten Contribution. *v.4 p.346*

Gender Equity: An Integrated Theory of Stability and Change. *v.4 p.723*

Gender equity in Sports. *v.4 p.820, p.834, p.890*

Gender Fantasy and Realism in American Literature. . . .*v.2 p.4*

Gender, Identity and Representation in Spain's Golden Age. *v.2 p.640*

Gender Ideology and Psychological Reality: An Essay on Cultural Reproduction. *v.4 p.36*

Gender in African Women's Writing: Identity, Sexuality and Difference. *v.6 p.479, p.480*

Gender in Crisis: Women and the Palestinian Resistance Movement. *v.6 p.455, p.619*

Gender in History. *v.3 p.51, v.6 p.450*

Gender in Latin America. *v.6 p.429*

Gender in Performance: The Presentation of Difference in the Performing Arts. *v.6 p.475*

Gender in Policy and Practice: Perspectives on Single-Sex and Coeducational Schooling. *v.4 p.301*

Gender in the Early Medieval World: East and West, 300-900. . . . .*v.3 p.51*

Gender in the Mirror: Cultural Imagery and Women's Agency. *v.6 p.446, p.461*

Gender in the Workplace: A Case Study Approach. *v.4 p.253, p.273*

Gender Injustice: An International Comparative Analysis of Equality in Employment. *v.4 p.133*

The Gender Knot: Unraveling Our Patriarchal Legacy. .*v.6 p.429*

The Gender Line: Men, Women, and the Law. .*v.4 p.442, v.6 p.470*

Gender Nonconformity, Race, and Sexuality: Charting the Connections. *v.6 p.371*

Gender on the Market: Moroccan Women and the Revoicing of Tradition. *v.4 p.31*

Gender Outlaw: On Men, Women and the Rest of Us. .*v.6 p.369*

Gender Perspectives on Vocational Education: Historical, Cultural, and Policy Aspects. *v.4 p.305*

Gender Play: Girls and Boys in School. *v.6 p.464*

Gender, Politics, and Allegory in the Art of Rubens. *v.1 p.707, p.746*

Gender, Politics and Fiction: Twentieth Century Australian Women's Novels. *v.2 p.740*

Gender, Politics, and Islam. *v.6 p.460*

Gender, Practice and Faith in Nicaragua. *v.3 p.302*

Gender, Race, and the National Education Association: Professionalism and Its Limitations. *v.4 p.283*

Gender Roles in Development Projects: A Case Book. .*v.6 p.457*

Gender Shifts in the History of English. *v.2 p.554*

Gender, Social Inequalities and Aging. *v.6 p.444, p.445*

Gender Talk: The Struggle for Women's Equality in African American Communities. *v.4 p.743, v.6 p.4, p.42*

Gender Trouble: Feminism and the Subversion of Identity. *v.2 p.572, v.6 p.370*

Gender Vertigo: American Families in Transition. . . .*v.6 p.467*

A Gendered Collision: Sentimentalism and Modernism in Dorothy Parker's Poetry and Fiction. *v.2 p.110*

Gendered Community: Rousseau, Sex and Politics. . .*v.6 p.462*

Gendered Compromises: Political Cultures and the State in Chile, 1920-1950. . . . .*v.3 p.355*

Gendered Fields: Rural Women, Agriculture, and Environment. *v.4 p.772, v.6 p.458*

Gendered Freedoms: Race, Rights, and the Politics of Household in the Delta, 1861-1875. . . . .*v.6 p.453*

The Gendered Society: Identities, Behaviors, and Society. *v.4 p.744, v.6 p.429*

Gendered Strife and Confusion: The Political Culture of Reconstruction. *v.6 p.452*

The Gendered Worlds of Latin American Women Workers: From Household and Factory to the Union Hall and Ballot Box. *v.3 p.283, v.6 p.456*

Gendering Government: Feminist Engagement with the State in Australia and Canada. *v.6 p.440*

Gendering Politics: Women in Israel. *v.6 p.614*

Gendering the Master Narrative: Women and Power in the Middle Ages. *v.6 p.559*

Gendering World Politics: Issues and Approaches in the Post-Cold War Era. *v.6 p.443*

GenderInn. *v.6 p.476*

GenderQueer: Voices from Beyond the Sexual Binary. .*v.6 p.371*

Genders and Sexualities in Japan. *v.6 p.421*

Genders, Races, and Religious Cultures in Modern American Poetry, 1908-1934. . . . .*v.2 p.15*

The Gender/Sexuality Reader: Culture, History, Political Economy. *v.6 p.428, p.436*

Gender. *v.4 p.743, v.6 p.429*

GenderWatch. *v.6 p.432*

Gene Avatars: Neo-Darwinian Theory of Evolution. . .*v.5 p.200*

Gene Banks and the World's Food. *v.5 p.370*

Gene Biotechnology. *v.5 p.219*

Gene Expression Regulation at the RNA and Protein Levels. *v.5 p.115, p.123, p.130, p.131*

Gene Genealogies, Variation and Evolution: A Primer in Coalescent Theory. *v.5 p.140*

The Gene Hunters: Biotechnology and the Scramble for Seeds. *v.5 p.218*

The Gene Illusion: Genetic Research in Psychiatry and Psychology under the Microscope. *v.5 p.658*

Gene Kelly: A Life of Dance and Dreams. *v.1 p.14, p.32*

Gene Kelly. *v.1 p.9*

The Gene Masters: How a New Breed of Scientific Entrepeneurs Raced for the Biggest Prize in Biology. . . .*v.5 p.82, p.220*

Gene Regulation and Metabolism: Post-Genomic Computational Approaches. *v.5 p.101, p.139, p.148*

Gene Silencing by RNA Interference: Technology and Application. *v.5 p.137*

The Gene Wars: Science, Politics and the Human Genome. *v.5 p.132*

A Genealogical Chart of Greek Mythology. *v.1 p.533*

A Genealogy of Nihilism: Philosophies of Nothing and the Difference of Theology. *v.1 p.509*

A Genealogy of Sovereignty. *v.4 p.496*

La Generacion de 1898 Ante Espana: Antologia de Literatura Moderna de Temas Nacionales y Universales. . . .*v.2 p.643*

Generacion del 27. . . . .*v.2 p.639*

General Chemistry Virtual Textbook (Stephen Lower). *v.5 p.266*

General Competitive Analysis. *v.4 p.198*

The General Councils: A History of the Twenty-One Church Councils from Nicaea to Vatican II. *v.1 p.570*

The General Crisis of the Seventeenth Century. *v.3 p.41, v.6 p.165*

General Economic History. *v.4 p.725*

General Education in a Free Society. *v.4 p.290, p.294*

El General en Su Laberinto. *v.2 p.682*

General Equilibrium in International Trade: The Origins of International Economics. *v.4 p.206, 257*

The General Factor of Intelligence: How General Is It? *v.5 p.572, p.573*

General Gage in America: Being Principally a History of His Role in the American Revolution. *v.3 p.411*

General George B. McClellan: Shield of the Union. . *v.3 p.425*

General Guide for Chemists and Chemical Engineers. *v.5 p.260*

A General History of Music, from the Earliest Ages to the Present Period (1789). *v.1 p.174*

A General History of the Science and Practice of Music. *v.1 p.174*

General Horatio Gates: A Biography. *v.3 p.412*

The General in His Labyrinth. *v.2 p.682*

General Issues in Literacy - Illiteracy in the World: A Bibliography. *v.4 p.300*

General James Longstreet: The Confederacy's Most Controversial Soldier. *v.4 p.522*

General Motors and the Nazis: The Struggle for Control of Opel, Europe's Biggest Carmaker. *v.3 p.174*

General of the Army: George C. Marshall, Soldier and Statesman. *v.3 p.457*

General Physics: Mechanics and Molecular Physics. . *v.5 p.546*

General Principles of Criminal Law. *v.4 p.434*

The General Prologue. *v.2 p.207*

General Science Full Text. *v.5 p.406*

The General Strike of 1926. . . . .*v.4 p.127*

General Sun, My Brother. *v.2 p.535*

A General Theory of Love. *v.4 p.738, v.5 p.650, p.654*

The General Theory of Transformational Growth: Keynes after Sraffa. *v.4 p.228*

General Topology and Homotopy Theory. *v.5 p.499*

General Topology. *v.5 p.500*

General Viticulture. *v.5 p.36*

The Generalissimo's Son: Chiang Ching-kuo and the Revolutions in China and Taiwan. *v.6 p.200, p.214*

Generalization in Ethics: An Essay in the Logic of Ethics, with the Rudiments of a System of Moral Philosophy. . *v.1 p.487*

The Generalization of the General Theory and Other Essays. *v.4 p.270*

Generalized Musical Intervals and Their Transformations. *v.1 p.371*

Generals Die in Bed: A Story from the Trenches. . . *v.2 p.735*

Generals in Blue and Gray. *v.4 p.521*

Generals in Blue: Lives of the Union Commanders. . *v.3 p.427*

Generals in Gray: Lives of the Confederate Commanders. *v.3 p.427*

Generals vs. Presidents: Neo-Militarism in Latin America. *v.3 p.275*

Generating Functionology. *v.5 p.478*

Generation Ecstasy: Into the World of Techno and Rave Culture. *v.1 p.273*

The Generation of 1898 and After: An Anthology for Students of Spanish. *v.2 p.644*

The Generation of 2000: Contemporary American Poets. *v.2 p.23*

Generation of Vipers. *v.3 p.370*

Generation X: Americans Born 1965 to 1976. . . . .*v.4 p.137*

Generation X: Americans Born 1965 To 1976. . . . *v.5 p.585*

Generations and Geographies in the Visual Arts: Feminist Readings. *v.6 p.473*

Generations and Identity: Japanese Americans. . . . *v.6 p.132*

Generations at Work: Managing the Clash of Veterans, Boomers, Xers, Nexters in Your Workplace. *v.4 p.132, p.133*

Generations of Winter. *v.2 p.801*

Generative Processes in Music: The Psychology of Performance, Improvisation, and Composition. *v.1 p.376, v.5 p.619*

A Generative Theory of Tonal Music. *v.1 p.371*

Genes: A Philosophical Inquiry. *v.5 p.133*

Genes and DNA: A Beginner's Guide to Genetics and Its Applications. *v.5 p.123, p.136*

Genes and Embryos: Frontiers in Molecular Biology. *v.5 p.160*

Genes and the Agents of Life: The Individual in the Fragile Sciences Biology. *v.5 p.138*

Genes, Categories, and Species: The Evolutionary and Cognitive Causes of the Species Problem. . . *v.5 p.134, p.198, p.199*

Genes, Crops and the Environment. *v.5 p.8, p.22, p.45*

Genes, Girls and Gamow: After the Double Helix. *v.5 p.82, p.137*

Genes, Trade, and Regulation: The Seeds of Conflict in Food Biotechnology. *v.5 p.7*

Genes VIII. *v.5 p.122, p.135*

The Genes We Share with Yeast, Flies, Worms, and Mice: New Clues to Human Health and Disease. *v.5 p.126*

Genes, Women, Equality. *v.5 p.80, p.135,v.6 p.444*

Genescapes: The Ecology of Genetic Engineering. . . *v.6 p.284*

Genesis A: A New Edition. *v.2 p.203, p.204*

Genesis and Structure of Hegel's Phenomenology of Spirit. *v.1 p.463*

Genesis: Ideas of Origin in African Sculpture. *v.1 p.777*

Genesis of a Music: An Account of a Creative Work, Its Roots, and Its Fulfillments. *v.1 p.220, p.221, p.347*

The Genesis of Doctrine: A Study in the Foundation of Doctrinal Criticism. *v.1 p.632*

The Genesis of German Conservatism. *v.3 p.167*

The Genesis of Heidegger's Being and Time. *v.1 p.471*

Genesis of the Pharaohs. *v.3 p.10*

Genesis, Structure, and Meaning in Gary Snyder's Mountains and Rivers Without End. *v.2 p.154*

Genesis: The Evolution of Biology. *v.5 p.81*

Genesis, Vol. 1. . . . .*v.1 p.621*

Genet: A Biography. . *v.1 p.61, p.92, p.106,v.2 p.519, v.6 p.404*

Genetic and Ecological Diversity: The Sport of Nature. *v.5 p.169*

The Genetic Basis of Common Diseases. *v.5 p.149*

The Genetic Basis of Human Cancer. *v.5 p.520*

The Genetic Code and the Origin of Life. *v.5 p.200*

Genetic Destinies. *v.5 p.135*

Genetic Disorders and the Fetus: Diagnosis, Prevention, and
Treatment. *v.5 p.533*

Genetic Dissection of Complex Traits, Vol. 42. . . .*v.5 p.133*

Genetic Engineering. *v.5 p.133*

Genetic Epistemology. *v.5 p.628, p.630*

Genetic Politics. *v.5 p.140*

Genetically Modified Athletes: The Ethical Implications of
Genetic Technologies in
Sport. *v.4 p.802, p.803, p.825, p.872, p.875*

Genetically Modified Crops: Their Development, Uses, and
Risks. *v.5 p.8, p.16, p.22*

Genetically Modified Crops. *v.5 p.7, p.8, p.21*

Genetically Modified Foods: Debating Biotechnology. *v.5 p.219*

Genetically Modified Language. *v.5 p.20*

Genetically Modified Organisms in Agriculture: Economics and
Politics. *v.5 p.8*

The Geneticist Who Played Hoops with My DNA: And Other
Masterminds from the Frontiers of Research. . . .*v.5 p.121*

Genetics: A Beginner's Guide. *v.5 p.133*

Genetics: Analysis of Genes and Genomes. *v.5 p.99, p.133, p.134*

Genetics and Criminal Behavior. *v.6 p.254*

Genetics and Evolution: The Molecules of Inheritance. *v.5 p.130*

Genetics and Heredity. *v.5 p.132*

Genetics and Society. *v.5 p.140*

Genetics and the Extinction of Species: DNA and the
Conservation of Biodiversity. *v.5 p.122*

Genetics and the Logic of Evolution. *v.5 p.137*

Genetics and the Search for Modern Human Origins. *v.5 p.201*

Genetics Demystified. *v.5 p.137, p.138*

Genetics for Dummies. *v.5 p.131, p.132*

Genetics for Healthcare Professionals: A Lifestage
Approach. *v.5 p.151*

Genetics: From Genes to Genomes. *v.5 p.134*

Genetics in Obstetrics and Gynecology. *v.5 p.151*

Genetics in the Clinic: Clinical, Ethical, and Social Implications
for Primary Care. *v.5 p.149, p.533*

Genetics of Populations. *v.5 p.134*

Genetics, Paleontology and Macroevolution. *v.5 p.193*

Genetics: The Nutrition Connection. *v.5 p.148*

Geneva and the Coming of the Wars of Religion in France,
1555-1563. . . . .*v.3 p.145*

Genghis Khan and the Making of the Modern World. *v.6 p.239*

Genius and the Mind: Studies of Creativity and
Temperament. *v.5 p.656*

Genius Denied: How to Stop Wasting Our Brightest Young
Minds. *v.5 p.575*

The Genius of American Education. *v.4 p.325*

The Genius of China: Three Thousand Years of Discovery,
Invention and Science. *v.6 p.198*

The Genius of John Henry Newman: Selections from His
Writings. *v.1 p.572*

The Genius of John Ruskin: Selections from His
Writings. *v.2 p.306, v.6 p.738, p.755*

The Genius of the German Lyric: An Historic Survey of Its
Formal and Metaphysical Values. *v.2 p.591*

The Genius of Wilhelm Busch. *v.2 p.603*

Genius: The Life and Science of Richard Feynman. .*v.5 p.543*

Genius: The Natural History of Creativity. . . .*v.5 p.612, p.652*

The Genius. *v.2 p.70*

Genoa and the Genoese, 958-1528. . . . . .*v.3 p.199, v.6 p.562*

Genocide and Democracy in Cambodia: The Khmer Rouge, the
U. N. and the International Community. *v.4 p.653*

Genocide and Millennialism in Upper Peru: The Great Rebellion
of 1780-1782. . . . .*v.3 p.326*

Genocide and the Global Village. *v.4 p.651*

Genocide and the Modern Age: Etiology and Case Studies of
Mass Death, 3. . . . .*v.4 p.654*

Genocide in Bosnia: The Policy of "Ethnic Cleansing". *v.4 p.652*

Genocide in International Law: The Crimes of Crimes. *v.4 p.653*

Genocide in Our Time: An Annotated Bibliography with
Analytical Introductions. *v.4 p.652*

Genocide in Paraguay. *v.3 p.344*

Genocide in Rwanda: Complicity of the Churches. . *v.4 p.653*

Genocide: Its Political Use in the Twentieth Century. *v.4 p.435*

Genocide, War Crimes and the West: History and
Complicity. *v.4 p.652, v.6 p.257*

The Genome of Homo Sapiens. . *v.5 p.147, p.151, p.152, p.201*

Genome: The Autobiography of a Species in 23
Chapters. *v.5 p.123*

[e] Genome Transcriptome and Proteome
Analysis. *v.5 p.101, p.103, p.138*

Genome Visualization by Classic Methods in Light
Microscopy. *v.5 p.139*

The Genome War: How Craig Venter Tried to Capture the Code
of Life and Save the World. *v.5 p.81, p.129, p.137*

Genomes and Databases on the Internet: A Practical Guide to
Functions and
Applications. . . .*v.5 p.95, p.96, p.105, p.106, p.108, p.127*

Genomes. *v.5 p.131, p.147, p.148*

Genome. *v.5 p.131*

The Genomic Environment and Niche-Experience. . .*v.5 p.138*

Genomic Regulatory Systems: In Development and
Evolution. *v.5 p.132*

The Genomic Revolution: Unveiling the Unity of Life. *v.5 p.132*

Genomic Technologies: Present and Future. *v.5 p.139*

Genomics and Proteomics: Functional and Computational
Aspects. *v.5 p.106, p.118, p.147*

Genomics and Proteomics in Nutrition. *v.5 p.104, p.117, p.146*

Genomics and Proteomics
Technologies. *v.5 p.104, p.117, p.118, p.146*

[e] Genomics and World Health: Report of the Advisory
Committee on Health Research. *v.5 p.148*

Genomics, Health and Society: Emerging Issues for Public
Policy. *v.5 p.149*

Genomics of Plants and Fungi, Vol. 18. . . . .*v.5 p.125, p.136*

Genomics, Proteomics, and Clinical Bacteriology: Methods and
Reviews. *v.5 p.105, p.119, p.143, p.147*

Genomics, Proteomics and Vaccines. . . .*v.5 p.116, p.140, p.149*

Genomics: The Science and Technology Behind the Human Genome Project. *v.5 p.145*

Genre and Contemporary Hollywood. *v.6 p.311*

Genre and Hollywood. *v.6 p.327, p.343*

Genre. *v.2 p.577*

Genteel Rhetoric: Writing High Culture in 19th Century Boston. *v.2 p.6, p.9, p.12*

A Gentle Introduction to Game Theory. *v.5 p.505*

Gentleman Boss: The Life of Chester Alan Arthur. . .*v.3 p.438*

The Gentleman from San Francisco. *v.2 p.802*

Gentleman Junkie: The Life and Legacy of William S. Burroughs. *v.6 p.401*

A Gentleman of Leisure. *v.2 p.390*

Gentleman Spy: The Life of Allen Dulles. *v.3 p.458*

Gentlemen and Freeholders: Electoral Politics in Colonial Virginia. *v.3 p.500*

Gentlemen Callers: Tennessee Williams, Homosexuality, and Mid-Twentieth-Century Drama. *v.2 p.134, v.6 p.412*

Gentlemen of Science: Early Years of the British Association for the Advancement of Science. *v.3 p.114, v.5 p.385*

Gentlemen Prefer Blondes and but Gentlemen Marry Brunettes: The Illuminating Diary of a Professional Lady. . . .*v.2 p.94*

Gentlemen, Scholars and Scoundrels: A Treasury of the Best of Harper's Magazine; from 1850 to the Present. *v.2 p.19*

The Gentlemen Theologians: American Theology in Southern Culture, 1795-1860. . . . .*v.1 p.607*

Gentrification in a Global Context: The New Urban Colonialism. *v.6 p.716*

Gentrification of the City. *v.6 p.721*

Gentry and Common Folk: Political Culture on a Virginia Frontier, 1740-1789. . . . .*v.3 p.500*

The Gentry: The Rise and Fall of a Ruling Class. . .*v.4 p.726*

Geochemical Thermodynamics. *v.5 p.440*

Geochemistry, Groundwater and Pollution. *v.5 p.440*

Geochemistry of Hydrothermal Ore Deposits. *v.5 p.450*

The Geochemistry of Natural Waters: Surface and Groundwater Environments. *v.5 p.441*

Geochemistry: Pathways and Processes. *v.5 p.440*

The Geochronology and Evolution of Africa. *v.5 p.433*

Geodata.Gov U.S. maps and Data. *v.4 p.373*

GeoDestinies: The Inevitable Control of Earth Resources over Nations and Individuals. *v.5 p.739*

Geodesy? What's That?: My Personal Involvement in the Age-Old Quest for the Size and Shape of the Earth.*v.4 p.389*

Geodesy. *v.5 p.443*

Geodetic and Topographic Surveying. *v.4 p.390*

Geodynamics. *v.5 p.443*

Geoenvironmental engineering: contaminated soils, pollutant fate, and mitigation. *v.5 p.422, p.423*

Geoenvironmental Engineering: Site Remediation, Waste Containment, and Emerging Waste Management Technologies. *v.5 p.369, p.377, p.422*

Geoenvironmental Mapping: Method, Theory and Practice. *v.4 p.376, v.5 p.423*

Geoffrey Chaucer: 1837-1933. . . . .*v.2 p.207*

Geoffrey Chaucer of England. *v.2 p.208*

The Geoffrey Hartman Reader. *v.2 p.568*

Geoffrey Holder: A Life in Theater, Dance and Art.*v.1 p.18, p.45*

Geographic Databases and GIS. *v.4 p.388*

Geographic Information Systems: An Introduction. . .*v.4 p.386*

Geographic Information Systems and Science. . . .*v.4 p.387*

Geographic Information Systems: Applications in Forestry and Natural Resources Management. *v.4 p.386, v.5 p.36*

Geographic Information Systems for the Social Sciences: Investigating Space and Place. *v.4 p.388, v.6 p.721*

Geographic Information Systems in Business. *v.4 p.388*

Geographic Literacy: Maps for Memorization. . . .*v.4 p.375*

The Geographic Mosaic of Coevolution. *v.5 p.197*

A Geographical History of United States City-Systems: From Frontier to the Urban Transformation. . .*v.4 p.382, v.6 p.721*

The Geographical Imagination in America, 1880-1950.*v.4 p.378*

Geographical Information Systems in Archaeology. *v.4 p.6, p.7, p.386*

Geographical Information Systems: Principles, Techniques, Management and Applications. *v.4 p.387*

A Geographical Introduction to History: An Introduction to Human Geography. *v.4 p.375*

Geographical Thought: A Contextual History of Ideas.*v.4 p.377*

The Geographical Tradition: Episodes in the History of a Contested Enterprise. *v.4 p.374, p.375*

Geographie Generale. *v.4 p.377*

Geographies and Moralities: International Perspectives on Justice, Development and Place. *v.4 p.398*

Geographies of Agriculture: Globalisation, Restructuring, and Sustainability. *v.4 p.395, p.396*

Geographies of Development. *v.4 p.398*

Geographies of Global Change: Remapping the World.*v.4 p.373*

Geographies of Home. *v.6 p.508*

Geographies of Learning: Theory and Practice, Activism and Performance. *v.1 p.125, p.135*

Geographies of Muslim Women: Gender, Religion, and Space. *v.4 p.399, v.6 p.581*

Geography and Economy. *v.4 p.398*

Geography and Ethics: Journeys in a Moral Terrain. .*v.4 p.375*

Geography and Geographers: Anglo-American Human Geography since 1945. . . . .*v.4 p.374, p.378*

Geography and History: Bridging the Divide. .*v.4 p.375, p.377*

Geography and Imperialism, 1820-1940. . . . . .*v.4 p.502*

Geography and Revolution. *v.4 p.375*

Geography and Technology. *v.4 p.387*

Geography, Culture and Education. *v.4 p.377*

Geography in America at the Dawn of the 21st Century.*v.4 p.382*

Geography in Early Judaism and Christianity: The Book of Jubilees. *v.4 p.377*

Geography into the Twenty-First Century. *v.4 p.378*

Geography of Canada. *v.3 p.535*

The Geography of Ethnic Violence: Identity, Interests, and the Indivisibility of Territory. . .*v.4 p.488, p.496, p.497, p.498*

A Geography of Norden. *v.3 p.232, p.233*

The Geography of Nowhere: The Rise and Decline of America's Man-Made Landscape. *v.4 p.771*

The Geography of Opportunity: Race and Housing Choice in Metropolitan America. *v.4 p.381, v.6 p.720*

The Geography of Presidential Elections in the United States, 1868-2004. . . . .*v.4 p.382*

The Geography of South Africa in a Changing World. *v.4 p.384*

Geography of the Heart: A Memoir. *v.6 p.379, p.402*

The Geography of Thought: How Asians and Westerners Think Differently... and Why. *v.5 p.637*

The Geography of War and Peace: From Death Camps to Diplomats. *v.4 p.495*

Geography's Inner Worlds: Pervasive Themes in Contemporary American Geography. *v.4 p.377*

☐ Geologic Guidebooks of North America Database. *v.5 p.419, p.431*

☐ The Geologic History of the Moon (USGS Professional Paper 1348). *v.5 p.435*

Geologic Map of North America, Decade of North American Geology Project. Continental-Scale Map. *v.5 p.432*

☐ Geologic Names Lexicon: GEOLEX. *v.5 p.417*

Geologic Population Analysis: Tools for the Analysis of Biodiversity. *v.5 p.100*

The Geologic Story Of National Parks and Monuments. *v.5 p.419*

A Geologic Time Scale 2004. . . . .*v.5 p.444, p.446*

Geological Atlas of Africa: With Notes on Stratigraphy, Tectonics, Economic Geology, Geohazards and Geosites of Each Country. *v.5 p.433*

Geological Atlas of Western and Central Europe. . .*v.5 p.432*

The Geological Evolution of Australia and New Zealand. *v.5 p.433*

Geological Hazards: A Sourcebook. *v.5 p.423*

Geological Hazards: Their Assessment, Avoidance and Mitigation. *v.5 p.423*

Geological Structures and Maps: A Practical Guide. . *v.5 p.441*

Geologists and Ideas: A History of North American Geology. *v.5 p.418, p.431*

Geology, 2 vols. *v.5 p.419*

Geology: An Introduction to Physical Geology. . . .*v.4 p.390*

Geology and Mineralogy of Radioactive Waste Repositories. *v.5 p.367, p.376, p.378*

Geology in the Field. *v.5 p.419, p.420*

Geology in the Nineteenth Century: Changing Views of a Changing World. *v.5 p.418*

Geology of Australia. *v.5 p.433*

Geology of Deltas. *v.4 p.392*

Geology of Earthquakes. *v.5 p.442*

The Geology of Fluvial Deposits: Sedimentary Facies, Basin Analysis and Petroleum Geology. *v.5 p.427*

Geology of Gems. *v.5 p.452*

Geology of Japan. *v.5 p.432*

Geology of North America: An Overview. *v.5 p.431*

The Geology of Ore Deposits. *v.5 p.436, p.450*

The Geology of the Mexican Republic. *v.5 p.432*

Geology of the U. S. S. R. *v.5 p.432, p.433*

Geology of U. S. Parklands. *v.5 p.419*

Geomatics. *v.4 p.389*

Geometric Differentiation: For the Intelligence of Curves and Surfaces. *v.5 p.496*

Geometric Fundamentals of Robotics. *v.5 p.715*

Geometric Greece: 900-700 BC. *v.3 p.16*

Geometric Inequalities. *v.5 p.498*

Geometric Morphometrics for Biologists. *v.5 p.155*

Geometrical Methods in the Theory of Ordinary Differential Equations. *v.5 p.487, p.494*

Geometrical Vectors. *v.5 p.496*

Geometry and Billiards. *v.4 p.855, p.871*

Geometry and Interpolation of Curves and Surfaces. . *v.5 p.497*

Geometry and the Imagination. *v.5 p.495*

Geometry Civilized: History, Culture, and Technique. *v.5 p.466, p.495*

Geometry: Euclid and Beyond. *v.5 p.466, p.495*

The Geometry of Numbers. *v.5 p.477*

The Geometry of Physics: An Introduction. . . .*v.5 p.496, p.501*

Geometry Revisited. *v.5 p.495*

Geometry. *v.5 p.494, p.495*

Geomodernisms: Race, Modernism, Modernity. . . .*v.3 p.314*

Geomorphic Systems of North America. *v.5 p.431*

Geomorphological Techniques. *v.4 p.390*

Geomorphology: A Systematic Analysis of Late Cenozoic Landforms. *v.5 p.424*

Geomorphology: Critical Concepts in Geography. *v.4 p.390, p.391*

Geomorphology, Vol. 3. . . . .*v.4 p.391*

The Geonim of Babylonia and the Shaping of Medieval Jewish Culture. *v.6 p.573*

Geons, Black Holes and Quantum Foam: A Life in Physics. *v.5 p.544*

Geophysical Data Analysis. *v.5 p.443*

Geopolitical Reader. *v.4 p.400, p.401, p.403*

Geopolitical Traditions: Critical Histories of Century of Political Thought. *v.4 p.488, p.495*

Geopolitics and the Post-Colonial: Rethinking North-South Relations. *v.4 p.400*

Geopolitics of East Asia. *v.4 p.400*

The Geopolitics of Euro-Atlantic Intergration. . .*v.4 p.383, p.400*

Geopolitics of Globalization: The Consequences for Development. *v.4 p.400*

Geopolitics of Resource Wars: Resource Dependence, Governance and Violence. *v.4 p.400*

Geopolitics of the World System. . . .*v.4 p.487, p.488, p.495*

The Geopolitics Reader. *v.4 p.488, p.496*

Georg Buchner and Birth of Modern Drama. *v.2 p.597*

Georg Buchner: Complete Plays and Prose. *v.2 p.596*

Georg Buchner. *v.2 p.597*

Georg Kaiser. *v.2 p.612*

Georg Lukacs: Life, Thought and Politics. *v.3 p.187*

Georg Simmel on Individuality and Social Forms. . .*v.6 p.719*

George and Rue. *v.2 p.733*

George B. McClellan: The Young Napoleon. *v.3 p.401*

George B. Post, Architect: Picturesque Designer and Determined Realist. *v.1 p.793*

George Balanchine: Ballet Master. *v.1 p.6*

George Balanchine: The Ballet Maker. *v.1 p.8, p.23, p.24*

George Balanchine. *v.1 p.10*

George Bancroft: The Intellectual As Democrat. *v.3 p.415*

George Bellows and Urban America. *v.1 p.738*

George Bellows, the Lithographs: Catalogue Raisonné. .*v.1 p.757*

George Bernard Shaw's Plays: Mrs. Warren's Profession,
Pygmalion, Man and Superman, Major Barbara:
Contexts and Criticism. *v.2 p.309*

George Bush and the Guardianship Presidency. *v.3 p.475*

George Bush: The Life of a Lone Star Yankee. .*v.3 p.477, p.478*

George C. Marshall: Soldier-Statesman of the American
Century. *v.3 p.463*

George C. Marshall: Statesman, 1945-1959. . . . . .*v.3 p.461*

George Colman, the Elder. *v.2 p.243*

George Crabbe. *v.2 p.281*

George Cruikshank's Life, Times and Art:
1792-1835. . . . .*v.1 p.758, v.6 p.737, p.738*

George Cruikshank's Life, Times and Art:
1835-1878. . . . .*v.1 p.758, v.6 p.737*

George Cukor: A Double Life: A Biography of the Gentleman
Director. *v.6 p.419*

George Eliot - Voice of a Century: A Biography. . . .*v.2 p.287*

George Eliot: A Bibliographical History. *v.2 p.286*

George Eliot, Adam Bede, the Mill on the Floss, Middlemarch:
Essays, Articles and Reviews. *v.2 p.286*

George Eliot and the British Empire. *v.2 p.287*

George Eliot Poetry. *v.2 p.288*

George Eliot's Life As Related in Her Letters and
Journals. *v.2 p.287*

George Eliot's Originals and Contemporaries: Essays in
Victorian Literary History and Biography. *v.2 p.287*

George Eliot. *v.2 p.286*

George Elton Mayo: Critical Evaluations in Business and
Management. *v.5 p.580*

George F. Hoar and the Half-Breed Republicans. . . .*v.3 p.435*

George F. Kennan and the Making of American Foreign Policy,
1947-1950. . . . .*v.3 p.461*

George F. Kennan: Cold War Iconoclast. *v.3 p.459*

George Gershwin: A New Biography. *v.1 p.216, p.325*

The George Gershwin Reader. *v.1 p.227, p.254, p.325*

George Gissing. *v.2 p.289, p.290*

George Grosz - The Graphic Work: Catalogue Raisonné. .*v.1 p.756*

George Herbert: A Literary Life. *v.2 p.249*

George Herbert: His Religion and Art. *v.2 p.249*

George Herbert Mead and Human Conduct. . .*v.4 p.682, p.692*

George Herbert: The Critical Heritage. *v.2 p.249*

George Herbert Walker Bush: A Penguin Life. .*v.3 p.481, p.482*

George Herbert's Lyrics. *v.2 p.249*

George III and the Historians. *v.3 p.108*

George Innes and the Visionary Landscape. *v.1 p.735*

George Inness and the Science of Landscape. *v.1 p.737*

George Meany and His Times. *v.4 p.128*

George Meredith. *v.2 p.300*

George Moore, 1852-1933. . . . .*v.2 p.300*

George Nelson: The Design of Modern Design. *v.1 p.720*

George Oppen: A Radical Practice. *v.2 p.106*

George Orwell: A Literary Life. *v.2 p.374*

George Orwell: The Politics of Literary Reputation. . .*v.2 p.376*

George Orwell. *v.2 p.376*

George Peele. *v.2 p.221*

George Pierce Baker and the American Theatre. *v.1 p.116*

George Russell's Lydian Chromatic Concept of Tonal
Organization: The Art and Science of Tonal Gravity. .*v.1 p.403*

George S. Counts and Charles A. Beard: Collaborators for
Change. *v.4 p.341*

George S. Counts: Educator for a New Age. . .*v.4 p.341, p.342*

George Sand: A Biography. *v.2 p.499*

George Sand: Writing for Her Life. *v.2 p.499*

George Sand-in Her Own Words. *v.2 p.499*

George Sand. *v.2 p.499*

George Soros on Globalization. *v.4 p.665*

George the First, Elector and King. *v.3 p.106*

The George W. Bush Presidency: An Early Assessment. .*v.3 p.483*

The George W. Bush Presidency: Appraisals and
Prospects. *v.3 p.482, p.483*

George W. Norris: The Making of a Progressive, 1861 to
1912. . . . .*v.3 p.460*

George W. Norris: The Persistence of a Progressive,
1913-1933. . . . .*v.3 p.460*

George W. Norris: The Triumph of a Progressive,
1933-1944. . . . .*v.3 p.460*

George Washington: From the Original Manuscript Sources,
1745-1799. . . . .*v.2 p.30*

George Washington Gómez. *v.6 p.502*

George Washington's Generals and Opponents: Their Exploits
and Leadership. *v.3 p.411*

Georges Bataille: Essential Writings. *v.1 p.457*

Georges Bizet: Carmen. *v.1 p.200, p.231, p.312*

Georges Bizet: His Life and Work. *v.1 p.196, p.312*

Georges Braque: A Bio-Bibliography. *v.1 p.662, p.696*

Georges Clemenceau: A Political Biography. *v.3 p.155*

Georges Cuvier, Fossil Bones, and Geological Catastrophes:
New Translations and Interpretations of the Primary
Texts. *v.5 p.418*

Georges Perec, a Life in Words: A Biography. *v.2 p.532*

Georgia Governors in an Age of Change: From Ellis Arnall to
George Busbee. *v.3 p.503*

Georgia in Antiquity: A History of Colchis and Transcaucasian
Iberia, 550 BC-AD 562. . . . .*v.3 p.230*

Georgia O'Keeffe and New Mexico: A Sense of Place. .*v.1 p.743*

Georgia O'Keeffe: Catalogue Raisonne. *v.1 p.695*

Georgia O'Keeffe: Library of American Art. *v.1 p.738*

Georgia O'Keeffe: The Poetry of Things. *v.1 p.741*

Georgia O'Keeffe. *v.1 p.744*

Georgia: The WPA Guide to Its Towns and Countryside. .*v.3 p.503*

The Georgics of Virgil: A Critical Survey. *v.2 p.448*

Georgics. *v.2 p.447*

Geosciences, Environment and Man. *v.5 p.423*

Geostatistics and Petroleum Geology. *v.5 p.420*

Geotechnical and Geoenvironmental Engineering Handbook. *v.5 p.367, p.422*

Geotechnical Earthquake Engineering Handbook. . . .*v.5 p.421*

Geotechnical Engineering for Transportation Infrastructure -Theory and Practice, Planning and Design, Construction and Maintenance: Proceedings of the XIIth ECSMGE Conference, Amsterdam, 7-10 June 1999/Additional Volume. *v.5 p.698*

Geotechnical Engineering Investigation Handbook. . .*v.5 p.421*

Geotechnical Engineering: Principles and Practices of Soil Mechanics and Foundation Engineering, Vol. 10. . .*v.5 p.422*

Geotechnical Engineering: Principles and Practices. . .*v.5 p.421*

Geotechnical Modelling. *v.5 p.699*

Geothermal Energy: It's Past, Present and Future Contributions to the Energy Needs of Man. *v.5 p.362*

Geothermal Energy: Utilization and Technology. . . .*v.5 p.362*

Gerald Ford and the Challenges of The 1970s. .*v.3 p.475, p.476*

Gerald Manley Hopkins and His Contemporaries: Liddon, Newman, Darwin, and Pater. *v.2 p.294*

Gerald R. Ford's Date with Destiny: A Political Biography. *v.3 p.479*

Gerard de Nerval. *v.2 p.492*

Gerard Manley Hopkins (1844-1889): New Essays on His Life, Writing and Place in English Literature. *v.2 p.293*

Gerard Manley Hopkins: A Very Private Life. *v.2 p.294*

Gerard Manley Hopkins and Critical Discourse. . . .*v.2 p.293*

Gerard Manley Hopkins and the Language of Mystery. .*v.2 p.293*

Gerard Manley Hopkins: Selected Letters. *v.2 p.294*

Gerard Manley Hopkins. *v.2 p.294*

Gerard Ter Borch. *v.1 p.749*

Gerhard Richter: Catalogue Raisonné. *v.1 p.745*

Gerhard Richter: Forty Years of Painting. . . .*v.1 p.747, p.748*

Gerhart Hauptmann. *v.2 p.609*

Geriatric Medicine: An Evidence-Based Approach. . .*v.5 p.518*

Geriatric Medicine and Gerontology. *v.5 p.518*

Geriatric Respiratory Care. *v.5 p.536*

Germaine de Stael, Revisited. *v.2 p.500*

The German Aesthetic Tradition. *v.1 p.480*

The German Army and Nazi Policies in Occupied Russia. *v.3 p.86, p.175*

German Atrocities, 1914: A History of Denial. . .*v.3 p.79, p.161*

The German Baroque Novel. *v.2 p.592*

German Baroque Poetry, 1618-1723. . . . .*v.2 p.591*

German Big Business and the Rise of Hitler. *v.3 p.170*

The German Bildungsroman from Weiland to Hesse. .*v.2 p.592*

The German Bildungsroman: History of a Genre. . .*v.2 p.592*

German Bourgeoisie: Essays on the Social History of the German Middle Class. *v.3 p.180*

German Catastrophe: Reflections and Recollections. .*v.3 p.178*

German Chemical Abbreviations. *v.5 p.258*

The German Churches under Hitler: Background, Struggle and Epilogue. *v.1 p.610*

The German Cinema Book. *v.6 p.338*

The German Colonial Empire. *v.4 p.584*

German Drama of the 18th Century: Lessing - Goethe - Lenz - Schiller - Kleist. *v.2 p.590*

German Drama of the Baroque. *v.2 p.594*

The German Empire, 1871-1918. . . . .*v.3 p.165*

The German Experience of Professionalization: Modern Learned Professions and Their Organizations from the Early Nineteenth Century to the Hitler Era. *v.3 p.160*

German Expressionist Drama. *v.2 p.592*

German Expressionist Plays. *v.1 p.68, p.85, p.110*

German Expressionist Poetry. *v.2 p.591*

German Expressionist Prints and Drawings. *v.1 p.721, p.722, p.753*

German Generals Talk. *v.3 p.81, p.175*

The German Greens: Paradox Between Movement and Party. *v.4 p.610*

German History, 1770-1866. . . . .*v.3 p.165*

The German Home Front in World War II: A Documentary Reader. *v.3 p.173*

German Humanism. *v.2 p.589*

The German Ideology Including Theses on Feuerbach and Introduction to the Critique of Political Economy: With Friedrich Engels. *v.1 p.465*

German Imperialism in Africa: From the Beginnings until the Second World War. *v.6 p.56*

German Intonation: An Outline. *v.2 p.621*

The German language. *v.2 p.621*

German Lesson. *v.2 p.612*

German Liberalism in the 19th Century. *v.3 p.160*

German Lieder. *v.1 p.236, p.246, p.412*

A German Life in the Age of Revolution: Joseph Gorres, 1776-1848. . . . .*v.3 p.168*

German Literature: A Critical Survey. *v.2 p.589*

German Literature of the Nineteenth Century, 1832-1899. . . . .*v.2 p.590*

German Literature under National Socialism. *v.2 p.591*

The German Lyric of the Baroque in English Translation. *v.2 p.593, p.594*

German Medieval Tales. *v.2 p.594*

German National Cinema. *v.6 p.338*

German Nationalism and Religious Conflict: Culture, Ideology, Politics, 1870-1914. . . . .*v.3 p.165*

The German Novel: Studies. *v.2 p.592*

The German Novelle. *v.2 p.592*

The German Occupation of Belgium 1940-1944. . . .*v.3 p.206*

German Opera: From the Beginnings to Wagner. .*v.1 p.234, p.247*

The German People and the Reformation. *v.1 p.604*

German Plays 2. . . . .*v.1 p.64, p.108*

German Plays. *v.1 p.64, p.65, p.82, p.108*

German Poetic Realism. *v.2 p.590*

German Poetry, 1910-1975: An Anthology. *v.2 p.593*

German Poetry: A Guide to Free Appreciation. . . .*v.2 p.591*

German Poetry in the Age of the Enlightenment: From Brockes to Klopstock. *v.2 p.591*

German Politics and the Jews: Dusseldorf and Nuremberg, 1910-1933. . . . .*v.3 p.180*

German Professions, 1800-1950. . . . .*v.3 p.159*

German Pronunciation and Phonology. *v.2 p.620*

The German Reformation: The Essential Readings. . .*v.3 p.165*

The German Reformation. *v.1 p.604*

German Resistance Against Hitler: The Search for Allies
    Abroad, 1938-1945. . . . .*v.3 p.174*

German Rule in Russia 1941-1945. . . . . .*v.3 p.174, p.226*

German Scholars and Ethnic Cleansing,
    1920-1945. . . . .*v.3 p.84, p.171*

German Sculpture, 1430-1540: A Catalogue of the Collection in
    the Victoria and Albert Museum. *v.1 p.777*

German Social Democracy, 1905-1917: The Development of the
    Great Schism. *v.4 p.610*

German Sociology. *v.4 p.684*

German Strategy and the Path to Verdun: Erich von Falkenhayn
    and the Development of Attrition, 1870-1916. . . .*v.3 p.160*

The German Sturm und Drang. *v.2 p.590*

The German Transfer Problem and International Capital
    Movements: The Origins of International
    Economics. *v.4 p.261, p.263*

German Twentieth Century Philosophy: The Frankfurt
    School. *v.1 p.506*

The German Way: Aspects of Behavior, Attitudes and Customs
    in the German-Speaking World. *v.3 p.159*

The German Way of War: From the Thirty Years' War to the
    Third Reich. *v.3 p.160*

A German Women's Movement: Class and Gender in Hanover,
    1880-1933. . . . .*v.3 p.54, p.160*

German/English Dictionary of Idioms. *v.2 p.621*

German-English Technical and Engineering Dictionary. .*v.5 p.387*

Germania. *v.3 p.67*

The German-Jewish Economic Elite, 1820-1935: A
    Socio-Cultural Profile. *v.3 p.180*

German-Jewish History in Modern Times: Emancipation and
    Acculturation, 1870-1871. . . . .*v.3 p.180*

German-Jewish History in Modern Times: Renewal and
    Destruction, 1918-1945. . . . .*v.3 p.179*

German-Jewish History in Modern Times: Tradition and
    Enlightenment 1600-1780. . . . .*v.3 p.180*

The Germans and the Final Solution: Public Opinion under
    Nazism. *v.3 p.82*

The Germans in Chile: Immigration and Colonization,
    1849-1914. . . . .*v.3 p.351*

Germans in the Cameroons, Eighteen Eighty-Four to Nineteen
    Fourteen: A Case Study in Modern Imperialism. . . .*v.6 p.62*

Germans into Nazis. *v.3 p.170*

Germans, Jews and the Claims of Modernity. *v.3 p.180*

The Germans. *v.3 p.159*

Germany, 1866-1945. . . . .*v.3 p.163, p.164*

Germany: A New History. *v.3 p.160*

Germany: A New Social and Economic History, 1450-1630, Vol.
    1. . . . .*v.3 p.164, p.165*

Germany: A New Social and Economic History 1630-1800, Vol.
    2. . . . .*v.3 p.164*

Germany: A New Social and Economic History, since 1800, Vol.
    3. . . . .*v.3 p.164*

Germany after the First World War. *v.3 p.169*

Germany and the European East in the Twentieth
    Century. *v.3 p.161*

Germany and the Second World War: Germany's Initial
    Conquests in Europe, Vol. II. *v.3 p.175*

Germany and the Second World War: The Build-Up of German
    Aggression, Vol. I. *v.3 p.174*

Germany and the Second World War: The Mediterranean,
    South-East Europe, and North Africa 1939-1941
    (from Italy's Declaration of Non-Belligerence to the Entry of
    the United States into the War). *v.3 p.175*

Germany Divided: From the Wall to Reunification. . .*v.4 p.610*

Germany from Napoleon to Bismarck, 1800-1866. . .*v.3 p.164*

Germany? Germany!: A Kurt Tucholsky Reader. . . .*v.2 p.616*

Germany, Hitler, and World War II: Essays in Modern German
    and World History. *v.3 p.175*

Germany in the Age of Absolutism. *v.3 p.167*

Germany in the Eighteenth Century. *v.3 p.167*

Germany in the High Middle Ages: C.
    1050-1200. . . . .*v.3 p.161, v.6 p.563*

Germany in the Later Middle Ages. *v.3 p.163*

Germany under the Old Regime, 1600-1790. . . . .*v.3 p.164*

Germany Under the Salian and Hohenstaufen Emperors. .*v.3 p.161*

Germany's Cold War: The Global Campaign to Isolate East
    Germany, 1949-1969. . . . .*v.3 p.177*

Germany's Transient Pasts: Preservation and National Memory
    in the Twentieth Century. *v.1 p.822*

Germany. *v.3 p.159*

Germinal. *v.2 p.505*

The Germination of Seeds. *v.5 p.47, p.48*

Gerontological Nursing. *v.5 p.518, p.519*

Gershwin: A Biography. *v.1 p.216, p.325*

Gershwin: Rhapsody in Blue. *v.1 p.223, p.242, p.325*

The Gershwin Style: New Looks at the Music of George
    Gershwin. *v.1 p.223, p.325*

The Gershwin Years: George and Ira. . .*v.1 p.251, p.325, p.326*

Gertrude and Alice. *v.6 p.403*

Gertrude Stein and Richard Wright: The Poetics and Politics of
    Modernism. *v.2 p.122, p.138*

Gertrude Stein and the Essence of What Happens. . . .*v.2 p.122*

Gertrude Stein and the Making of Literature. *v.2 p.122*

Gertrude Stein and Wallace Stevens: Performance of Modern
    Consciousness. *v.2 p.121, p.124*

Gertrude Stein in Pieces. *v.2 p.121*

Gertrude Stein: Modernism and the Problem of Genius. .*v.2 p.122*

Gertrude Stein: Study of Short Fiction. *v.2 p.122*

Gerusalemme liberata. *v.2 p.710*

Gesammelte Erzählungen. *v.2 p.612*

Gesammelte Hörspiele. *v.2 p.606*

Gesammelte Schriften. *v.2 p.609*

Gesammelte schriften. *v.2 p.610*

Gesammelte Werke: In 10 Bd. *v.2 p.615*

Gesammelte Werke in einem Band. *v.2 p.614*

Gesammelte Werke in Funf Banden. *v.2 p.606*

Gesammelte Werke: [Supplementbände]. *v.2 p.605*

Gesammelte Werke. *v.2 p.597, p.600, p.603, p.605*

Gesammelte Werke... . . . .*v.2 p.606*

Gesammelte Werke. *v.2 p.612, p.613*

Gesammelte werke. . . . . *.v.2 p.615*

Gesammelte Werke. . . . . *.v.2 p.615*

Das Gesamtwerk des Zeichners und Dichters. . . . . *.v.2 p.603*

Das Gesamtwerk. . . . . *.v.2 p.603*

Geschichte der deutschen literatur bis zum ausgang des mittelalters. *.v.2 p.589*

Geschichte der Deutschen Literatur Von Den Anfangen Bis Zur Gegenwart. . . . . *.v.2 p.589*

Geschichte der Deutschen Sprache. . . . . *.v.2 p.621*

Gesellschaftsethik und Romantheorie: Studien zu Grimmelshausen, Weise und Beer. . . . . *.v.2 p.596*

Gesta Principum Polonorum: The Deeds of the Princes of the Poles. . . . . *.v.3 p.252*

Gestalt Psychology in German Culture, 1890-1967: Holism and the Quest for Objectivity. . . . . *.v.5 p.595*

Gestalt Psychology. . . . . *.v.5 p.606*

The Gestalts of War. . . . . *.v.5 p.584*

The Gestapo and German Society: Enforcing Racial Policy, 1933-1945. . . . . *.v.3 p.84, p.171*

Gestundete Zeit. . . . . *.v.2 p.602, p.603*

A Gesture Life. . . . . *.v.6 p.101*

Gesture: Visible Action as Utterance. . . . . *.v.4 p.22*

Gesualdo: The Man and His Music. . . . . . *.v.1 p.181, p.326*

Get A Job! Interview Survival Skills for College Students. . . . . *.v.4 p.169*

Get a Life: A Novel. . . . . *.v.2 p.755*

Get 'Em All! Kill 'Em!: Genocide, Terrorism, Righteous Communities. . . . . *.v.4 p.662*

The Getaway. . . . . *.v.2 p.125*

Getting Absent Workers Back on the Job: An Analytical Approach. *.v.4 p.130*

Getting Ahead: Economic and Social Mobility in America. . . . . *.v.4 p.266*

Getting an Academic Job: Strategies for Success, Vol. 17. . . . . *.v.4 p.170*

Getting Choice Right: Ensuring Equity and Efficiency in Education Policy. . . . . *.v.4 p.302*

Getting God's Ear: Women, Islam and Healing in Saudi Arabia and the Gulf. . . . . *.v.6 p.625*

Getting Home Alive. . . . . *.v.6 p.496, p.507*

Getting It Right the First Time: How Innovative Companies Anticipate Demand. . . . . *.v.4 p.82*

Getting Justice and Getting Even: Legal Consciousness among Working-Class Americans. . . . . *.v.4 p.33*

Getting Married. *.v.2 p.630*

Getting Results with Curriculum Mapping. . . . . . . *.v.4 p.364*

Getting Rich: America's New Rich and How They Got That Way. . . . . *.v.4 p.245, p.265*

Getting Started in Entrepreneurship. . . . . *.v.4 p.68*

Getting Them to Give a Damn: How to Get Your Front Line to Care about Your Bottom Line. . . . . *.v.4 p.72*

Getting to Know ArcGIS Desktop: The Basics of ArcView, ArcEditor, and ArcInfo Updated for ArcGIS 9. . . *.v.4 p.388*

Getting to Yes: Negotiating Agreement Without Giving In. . . . . *.v.4 p.74*

Getting up and Down: How to Save Strokes from Forty Yards and In. *.v.4 p.861*

Getting Wiser to Teens: More Insights into Marketing to Teenagers. . . . . *.v.5 p.587*

Getting Wiser to Teens. . . . . *.v.4 p.139*

☐ The Getty Provenance Index. . . . . *.v.1 p.661, p.708*

Das Gewicht der Welt: Ein Journal (Nov. . . . . . . *.v.2 p.617*

Gödel, Escher, Bach: An Eternal Golden Braid. . . . *.v.5 p.470*

Ghana and the Ivory Coast; Perspectives on Modernization. . . . . *.v.6 p.69*

Ghana's New Christianity: Pentecostalism in a Globalising African Economy. . . . . *.v.1 p.611*

Gharbzadegi: Weststruckness. . . . . *.v.6 p.632*

The Ghaznavids: Their Empire in Afghanistan and Eastern Iran, 994-1040. . . . . *.v.6 p.630, p.634*

Ghetto Schooling: A Political Economy of Urban Educational Reform. . . . . *.v.4 p.314*

The Ghost Dance: The Origins of Religion. . . . . . . *.v.4 p.36*

Ghost Dancing the Law: The Wounded Knee Trials. . . . . *.v.6 p.690, p.694, p.695*

Ghost of Lucrece. . . . . *.v.2 p.215*

The Ghost of the Executed Engineer: Technology and the Fall of the Soviet Union. . . . . *.v.3 p.222*

Ghost Road. . . . . *.v.2 p.330*

The Ghost Stories of Muriel Spark. . . . . *.v.2 p.383*

The Ghost with Trembling Wings: Science, Wishful Thinking, and the Search for Lost Species. . . . . *.v.6 p.292*

The Ghost Writer. . . . . *.v.2 p.154*

The Ghost-Dance Religion and the Sioux Outbreak of 1890. . . . . *.v.4 p.37, v.6 p.688, p.701, p.703*

The Ghostly Lover. . . . . *.v.2 p.80*

Ghosts along Cumberland: Deathlore in the Kentucky Foothills. *.v.2 p.17*

Ghosts, Demons and Henry James: The Turn of the Screw at the Turn of the Century. . . . . *.v.2 p.43*

Ghosts in the Mirror. . . . . *.v.2 p.526*

The Ghosts of Berlin: Confronting German History in the Urban Landscape. . . . . . . *.v.3 p.181, v.4 p.582, v.6 p.726*

Ghosts of Slavery: A Literary Archaeology of Black Women's Lives. . . . . *.v.3 p.322*

Ghosts of the Confederacy: Defeat, the Lost Cause and the Emergence of the New South, 1865 to 1913. . . . *.v.4 p.520*

Giacomo Leopardi, Poems: Poems: Bilingual. . . . . *.v.2 p.712*

Giacomo Leopardi. . . . . *.v.2 p.711*

Giacomo Puccini: La Bohème. . *.v.1 p.197, p.229, p.230, p.349*

Giacomo Puccini: Tosca. . . . . *.v.1 p.195, p.228, p.229, p.349*

Giambattista Tiepolo: A Catalogue Raisonné, Paintings. *.v.1 p.739*

The Giant Jellybean Jar. . . . . *.v.1 p.62, p.63, p.107*

The Giant O'Brien. . . . . *.v.2 p.367*

Giant of the Grand Siècle: The French Army, 1610-1715. . . . . *.v.3 p.145*

Giant Pandas. . . . . *.v.5 p.85*

Giant Steps: The New Generation of African American Writers. . . . . *.v.6 p.28*

Giant Telescopes: Astronomical Ambition and the Promise of Technology. . . . . *.v.5 p.65*

Giants in the Earth: A Saga of the Prairie. . . . . . . *.v.2 p.629*

Gideon Mantell and the Discovery of Dinosaurs. . . . *.v.3 p.44*

Gideon Welles: Lincoln's Secretary of the Navy. . . .*v.3 p.426*

Gideon's Trumpet. *v.4 p.473, v.6 p.269*

Gide. *v.2 p.519*

Gifford Pinchot and the Making of Modern
Environmentalism. *v.5 p.39*

Gifford Pinchot: Forester-Politician. *v.3 p.434*

A Gift Imprisoned: The Poetic Life of Matthew Arnold. *v.2 p.265*

The Gift in Sixteenth-Century France. *v.3 p.144, p.145*

The Gift of a Cow: A Translation of the Hindi Novel,
Godaan. *v.6 p.152*

A Gift of Fire: Social, Legal, and Ethical Issues for Computers
and the Internet. *v.5 p.342, p.343*

The Gift of Good Land: Further Essays Cultural and
Agricultural. *v.5 p.29*

The Gift: The Form and Reason for Exchange in Archaic
Societies. *v.4 p.28*

The Gifted Child Grows Up: Twenty-Five Years' Follow-Up of
a Superior Group. *v.5 p.576*

Gifted Children: Myths and Realities. *v.5 p.576*

Gifted Education: Promising Practices. *v.4 p.317*

The Gifted Group at Mid-Life: Thirty-Five Years' Follow-Up of
the Superior Child. *v.5 p.576*

The Gifted Group in Later Maturity. *v.5 p.575*

Gifted Hands: The Ben Carson Story. *v.6 p.17, p.48*

The Gifts of Civilization: Germs and Genocide in
Hawai'I. *v.6 p.130*

The Gifts of the Body. *v.6 p.378, p.395*

Gifts to the Tzars 1500-1700: Treasures from the
Kremlin. *v.1 p.801*

Gifts. *v.2 p.754*

The Gift. *v.2 p.89*

Gil Vicente: Three Discovery Plays: Auto da Barca do Inferno,
Exortacao da Guerra, Auto da India. *v.2 p.689*

Gilbert and Sullivan: A Dual Biography. *v.1 p.248, p.361*

Gilbert Keith Chesterton. *v.2 p.278*

Gilbert Stuart. *v.1 p.735*

The Gilda Stories. *v.6 p.396*

The Gilded Age and Later Novels. *v.2 p.34*

The Gilded Age Press, 1865-1900. . . . .*v.4 p.411*

The Gilded Dome: The U. S. Senate and Campaign Finance
Reform. *v.4 p.534*

Gildersleeve's Latin Grammar. *v.2 p.423*

Gilead: A Novel. *v.2 p.154*

Giles and Phineas Fletcher - Poetical Works. . . .*v.2 p.214*

Giles Goat-Boy. *v.2 p.142*

Gilgamesh: A New English Version. *v.6 p.665*

Gilgamesh Epic and Old Testament Parallels. *v.6 p.665*

Gilles. *v.2 p.516*

Gillray Observed: The Earliest Account of His Caricatures in
London and Paris. *v.1 p.701, p.722*

The Ginger Man. *v.2 p.69*

Ginsberg: A Biography. *v.2 p.79*

Giordano Bruno and the Hermetic Tradition. *v.3 p.48*

Giorgio Morandi: The Art of Silence. *v.1 p.734*

Giotto to Durer: Early Renaissance Painting in the National
Gallery. *v.1 p.727*

Giovanni and Lusanna: Love and Marriage in Renaissance
Florence. *v.4 p.738*

Giovanni Batista Piranesi: The Complete Etchings. . *v.1 p.756*

Giovanni Bellini. *v.1 p.739*

Giovanni Boccaccio: Il Filostrato. *v.2 p.701*

Giovanni Boccaccio: The Life of Dante. *v.2 p.704*

Giovanni Boccaccio: Theseid of the Nuptials of Emilia. *v.2 p.701*

Giovanni Gabrieli and the Music of the Venetian High
Renaissance. *v.1 p.179, p.325*

Giovanni Pierluigi da Palestrina: A Research
Guide. *v.1 p.164, p.180, p.346*

Giovanni Verga. *v.2 p.712, p.713*

Giovanni's Room. *v.6 p.394*

Giraffes, Black Dragons, and Other Pianos: A Technological
History from Cristofori to the Modern Concert
Grand. *v.1 p.389*

The Girl and the Game: A History of Women's Sport in
Canada. *v.4 p.806, p.836*

The Girl from the Coast: A Novel. *v.6 p.178*

Girl on the Magazine Cover: The Origins of Visual Stereotypes
in American Mass Media. *v.4 p.141*

The Girl on the Magazine Cover: The Origins of Visual
Stereotypes in American Mass
Media. *v.4 p.416, p.697,v.5 p.621, p.625*

The Girl Problem: Female Sexual Delinquency in New York,
1900-1930. . . . .*v.4 p.753, v.6 p.468*

Girl Talk: Adolescent Magazines and Their Readers. . *v.6 p.448*

The Girl Who Fell Down: A Biography of Joan
Mccracken. *v.1 p.12*

Girlfriend: Men, Women and Drag. *v.6 p.370*

Girls and Boys in School: Together or Separate? *v.4 p.301, p.302*

Girls, Boys and Junior Sexualities: Exploring Childrens' Gender
and Sexual Relations in the Primary School. *v.4 p.748*

Girls, Boys, Books, Toys: Gender in Children's Literature and
Culture. *v.2 p.582*

Girls, Delinquency, and Juvenile Justice. *v.6 p.255, p.258*

Girls Growing up in Late Victorian and Edwardian
England. *v.3 p.111, v.6 p.747, p.765*

Girls of Alexandria. *v.6 p.656*

Girls Who Went Wrong: Prostitutes in American Fiction,
1885-1917. . . . .*v.2 p.4*

Girolamo Frescobaldi. *v.1 p.184, p.325*

The Girondins of Chile: Reminiscences of an
Eyewitness. *v.3 p.351*

Gis: A Short Introduction. *v.4 p.388*

GIS and Crime Mapping. *v.4 p.386, v.6 p.251*

GIS and Remote Sensing Applications in Biogeography and
Ecology. *v.5 p.87, p.88, p.89, p.94, p.169, p.185*

GIS for Ecologists and Environmental
Scientists. *v.4 p.387, v.5 p.28*

GIS for Everyone: Exploring Your Neighborhood and Your
World with a Geographic I. *v.4 p.386*

GIS for the Urban Environment. *v.4 p.387, v.6 p.721*

GIS Technology, Maps, Society. *v.4 p.386*

Gis Tutorial: A Workbook for Arcview 9. 0. . . . . .*v.4 p.387*

Gisants : poèmes III, 1980-1995. . . . .*v.2 p.529*

Giulio Romano, Master Designer: An Exhibition of Drawings in Celebration of the 500th Anniversary of His Birth. .*v.1 p.723*

Giuseppe Verdi: A Guide to Research. . .*v.1 p.164, p.198, p.364*

Giuseppe Verdi: Falstaff. *v.1 p.198, p.230, p.364*

Giuseppe Verdi: Otello. *v.1 p.198, p.230, p.364*

The Give and Take of Everyday Life: Language Socialization of Kaluli Children. *v.4 p.20*

Give Me Liberty!: An American History. *v.3 p.379, p.380*

Give My Regards to Eighth Street: Collected Writings of Morton Feldman. *v.1 p.213, p.324*

Give or Take a Day: Contemporary Hungarian Short Stories. *v.2 p.785*

Given Giving: Selected Poems of Michel Deguy. . . .*v.2 p.529*

Giving a Voice to the Voiceless: Four Pioneering Black Women Journalists. *v.6 p.3, p.4, p.42*

Giving Preservation a History: Histories of Historic Preservation in the United States. *v.1 p.823*

Giving up the Gun: Japan's Reversion to the Sword, 1543-1879. . . . .*v.6 p.225*

Glacial and Quaternary Geology. *v.5 p.425*

Glacial Environments. *v.5 p.425*

Glacial Geology: Ice Sheets and Landforms. *v.5 p.425*

Glaciers and Glaciation. *v.5 p.424, p.425*

Glaciers. *v.5 p.425*

The Gladiators: History's Most Deadly Sport. *v.3 p.23*

Gladstone 1809-1898. . . . .*v.3 p.113, v.6 p.758*

Gladstone and the Bulgarian Agitation, 1876. . . . .*v.3 p.115*

The Glamour Factory: Inside Hollywood's Big Studio System. *v.6 p.340*

The Glamour of Grammar: Orality and Politics and the Emergence of Sean O'Casey. *v.2 p.373*

The Glasgow Edition of the Works and Correpondence of Adam Smith, Set. *v.4 p.218*

Glasnost: An Anthology of Russian Literature under Gorbachev. *v.2 p.794*

The Glass Air: Poems Selected and New. *v.2 p.738*

Glass Art: Reflections of the Centuries. *v.1 p.811*

Glass Art. *v.1 p.810*

The Glass Bead Game: Magister Ludi. *v.2 p.610*

Glass Ceilings and Asian Americans: The New Face of Workplace Barriers. *v.4 p.134, v.6 p.107*

Glass Ceilings and Bottomless Pits: Women's Work, Women's Poverty. *v.4 p.272, v.6 p.455*

The Glass Enclosure: The Life of Bud Powell. .*v.1 p.259, p.348*

Glass: From Sassanian Antecedents to European Imitations. *v.1 p.810*

The Glass House: The Life of Theodore Roethke. . . .*v.2 p.114*

Glass of the Sultans: Twelve Centuries of Islamic Masterworks. *v.1 p.673, p.810*

The Glass Palace. *v.2 p.764*

Glass Throughout Time: The History and Technology of Glassmaking from the Ancient World to the Present.*v.1 p.810*

A Glastonbury Romance. *v.2 p.373*

⬜ GLBT Life with Full Text. *v.6 p.361*

⬜ glbtq: The Online Encyclopedia of Gay, Lesbian, Bisexual, Transgender, and Queer Culture. *v.6 p.358*

Glengarry Glen Ross. *v.1 p.62, p.80, p.116,v.2 p.149*

The Glenn Gould Reader. *v.1 p.214, p.215, p.247*

Glenn Murcutt: A Singular Architectural Practice. . .*v.1 p.791*

Glenn Murcutt: Buildings and Projects, 1962-2003. .*v.1 p.792*

Glenway Wescott Personally: A Biography. *v.6 p.403*

Gliding: A Handbook on Soaring Flight. .*v.4 p.787, p.788, p.848*

A Glimpse of Sion's Glory: Puritan Radicalism in New England, 1620-1660. . . . .*v.3 p.485*

Glimpses of Glory: John Bunyan and English Dissent. .*v.2 p.241*

Global Acquisitions: Strategic Integration and the Human Factor. *v.4 p.84*

Global Analysis of Seismic-Resistant Steel Structures. .*v.5 p.694*

Global Banking. . .*v.4 p.92, p.98, p.102, p.103, p.156, p.163*

Global Bioethics: Building on the Leopold Legacy. . .*v.5 p.248*

Global Biogeochemical Cycles. *v.5 p.167, p.183*

Global Biogeography. *v.5 p.167*

Global Business Etiquette: A Guide to International Communication and Customs. *v.4 p.56*

Global Capitalism: Its Fall and Rise in the Twentieth Century. *v.4 p.664*

The Global Casino: An Introduction to Environmental Issues. *v.4 p.159*

Global Change and Challenge: Geography for the 1990s. *v.4 p.377*

Global Cities: Cinema, Architecture and Urbanism in a Digital Age. *v.6 p.730*

Global Cities Reader. *v.6 p.716, p.720*

The Global City: New York, London, Tokyo. . .*v.6 p.719, p.721*

Global City-Regions: Trends, Theory, Policy. *v.6 p.725*

Global Civil Society: An Answer to War. *v.4 p.498*

Global Civil Society?. *v.4 p.498*

Global Climate Change and Tropical Ecosystems: Cold. .*v.5 p.187*

The Global Coastal Ocean: Interdisciplinary Regional Studies and Syntheses. *v.4 p.392*

The Global Coffee Economy in Africa, Asia and Latin America, 1500-1989. . . . .*v.3 p.271, p.303*

Global Community: The Role of International Organizations in the Making of the Contemporary World. *v.4 p.640*

⬜ Global Corruption Report. *v.4 p.54*

Global Covenant: The Social Democratic Alternative to the Washington Consensus. *v.4 p.659*

Global Culture, Island Identity: Continuity and Change in the Afro-Caribbean Community of Nevis. *v.4 p.41*

Global Currents: Media and Technology Now. . . .*v.4 p.419*

Global Decisions, Local Collisions: Urban Life in the New World Order. *v.6 p.725*

Global Directory of Private Banking. *v.4 p.179*

Global Divas: Filipino Gay Men in the Diaspora. .*v.6 p.112, p.129*

Global Dynamical Properties of Lotka-Volterra Systems. *v.5 p.98, p.197*

Global Earth Physics: A Handbook of Physical Constants. *v.5 p.443*

Global Economics: A History of the Theater Business, the Chamberlain's/King's Men, and Their Plays, 1599-1642. . . . .*v.1 p.149*

☐ Global Edge. *v.4 p.59*

Global Education: A Study of School Change. *v.4 p.314*

The Global Eighteenth Century. *v.2 p.172*

The Global Environment in the Twenty-First Century: Prospects for International Cooperation. *v.4 p.666*

The Global Environment in the Twenty-First Century: Prospects for International Co-operation. *v.6 p.299*

☐ Global Environment Outlook 3: Past, Present, and Future Perspectives. *v.5 p.353*

Global Environment: Water, Air, and Geochemical Cycles. *v.5 p.312*

Global Feminisms: A Survey of Issues and Controversies. *v.6 p.428, p.435, p.436*

Global Financial Crime: Terrorism, Money Laundering, and Off Shore Centres. *v.6 p.253*

Global Financial Turmoil and Reform: A United Nations Perspective. *v.4 p.664*

Global Formation: Structures of the World Economy. *v.4 p.723*

Global Games. *v.4 p.845*

The Global Genome: Biotechnology, Politics, and Culture. *v.5 p.220*

Global Geological Record of Lake Basins, Vol. 1. . . .*v.5 p.438*

Global Geopolitical Flashpoints: An Atlas of Conflict. *v.4 p.487, p.495*

Global Geopolitics: A Critical Introduction. *v.4 p.400*

Global Governance of Financial Systems: The Legal and Economic Regulation of Systemic Risk. *v.4 p.90*

Global Health Leadership and Management. *v.4 p.668*

The Global Impact of the Great Depression, 1929-1939. *v.5 p.15*

Global Impact of the Portuguese Language. *v.2 p.687*

Global Integrated Supply Chain Systems. *v.4 p.69*

The Global Jukebox: The International Music Industry. *v.1 p.383*

Global Lab - An Integrated Science Program: Becoming a Global Community, Unit I. *v.5 p.223*

Global Lab - An Integrated Science Program: Extended Investigations, Unit V. *v.5 p.227, p.228*

Global Lab - An Integrated Science Program: Investigating Our Earth: Land, Unit II. *v.5 p.228*

Global Lab - An Integrated Science Program: Investigating Our Earth, Unit IV. *v.5 p.228*

Global Lab - An Integrated Science Program: Investigating Our Earth: Water, Unit III. *v.5 p.223*

Global Lab: An Integrated Science Program. *v.5 p.228*

☐ The Global Language Monitor. *v.2 p.549, p.558, p.559*

☐ Global Legal Information Network GLIN. *v.4 p.474, p.475, p.476*

The Global Market: Developing a Strategy to Manage Across Borders. *v.4 p.73*

Global Marketing and Advertising: Understanding Cultural Paradoxes. *v.4 p.427*

Global Money, Capital Restructuring and the Changing Patterns of Labour. *v.4 p.261, p.262*

The Global Negotiator: Making, Managing and Mending Deals Around the World in the Twenty-First Century. *v.4 p.59, p.74, p.75*

Global Networks Linked Cities. *v.6 p.725*

Global Noise: Rap and Hip Hop Outside the U. S. A. *v.1 p.272*

Global Operations Management. *v.4 p.119*

Global Order and Global Disorder: Globalization and the Nation-State. *v.4 p.640, p.663*

Global Outrage: The Origins and Impact of World Opinion from the 1780s to the 21st Century. *v.4 p.425*

Global Patterns: Climate, Vegetation and Soils. *v.5 p.48*

Global Perspectives on Agroecology and Sustainable Agricultural Systems: Proceedings of the Sixth International Scientific Conference of the International Federation of Organic Agriculture Movements. *v.5 p.12*

Global Physical Climatology. *v.5 p.426*

Global Positioning System: A Field Guide for the Social Sciences. *v.4 p.390*

Global Positioning System: Theory and Practice. . . *v.5 p.719*

Global Prescriptions: Gendering Health and Human Rights. *v.4 p.669*

The Global Public Relations Handbook: Theory, Research, and Practice. *v.4 p.428*

The Global Reach of Empire: Britain's Maritime Expansion in the Indian and Pacific Oceans, 1764-1814. . . . . .*v.4 p.385*

Global Semiotics. *v.2 p.571, v.4 p.424*

Global Sex Workers: Rights, Resistance and Redefinition. *v.6 p.457, p.470*

Global Sex. *v.4 p.746*

Global Smarts: The Art of Communicating and Deal Making Anywhere in the World. *v.4 p.56*

Global Spin: The Corporate Assault on Environmentalism. *v.6 p.298*

Global Studies: Europe. *v.4 p.383*

Global Studies: The Middle East. *v.6 p.595*

Global Supply Chain Management. *v.4 p.118*

Global Television and Film: An Introduction to the Economics of the Business. *v.6 p.344, p.345*

Global Terrorism: A Beginner's Guide. *v.4 p.662*

Global Trading System at Crossroads: A Post-Seattle Perspective. *v.4 p.664*

The Global Transformations Reader: An Introduction to the Globalization Debate. *v.4 p.663*

The Global Underworld: Transnational Crime and the United States. *v.6 p.251*

A Global View of Instructional Technology for the 21st Century. *v.4 p.351*

Global Warming: The Complete Briefing. *v.5 p.426*

Global Warming: The Science of Climate Change. *v.5 p.425, v.6 p.294*

The Global Water Cycle: Geochemistry and Environment. *v.5 p.441*

Global Woman: Nannies, Maids, and Sex Workers in the New Economy. *v.6 p.456*

The Global World of Indian Merchants, 1750-1947: Traders of Sind from Bukhara to Panama. *v.3 p.305*

Globalism: The New Market Ideology. *v.4 p.665*

Globalization: A Very Short Introduction. *v.4 p.55, p.56*

Globalization and Cross-Border Labor Solidarity in the Americas: The Anti-Sweatshop Movement and the Struggle for Social Justice. *v.4 p.262*

Globalization and Culture Change in the Pacific Islands. .*v.4 p.385*

Globalization and Its Discontents. . .*v.4 p.56, p.58, p.262, p.665*

Globalization and Resistance: Transnational Dimensions of Social Movements. *v.4 p.640, p.663*

🄴 Globalization and Strategic Alliances: The Case of the Airline Industry. *v.4 p.152*

Globalization and Terrorism: The Migration of Dreams and Nightmares. *v.4 p.660, p.661, p.663*

Globalization and the International Financial System: What's Wrong and What Can Be Done. *v.4 p.261, p.263*

Globalization and the Nation State: The Impact of the IMF and the World Bank. *v.4 p.262*

Globalization and the Politics of Development in the Middle East. *v.6 p.595*

Globalization: Capatalism and Its Alternatives. *v.4 p.760*

Globalization: Encyclopedia of Trade, Labor, and Politics. *v.4 p.56, p.58, p.181*

Globalization, Europeanization, and the End of Scandinavian Social Democracy? *v.3 p.232, p.233*

Globalization, Governmentiality and Global Politics: Regulation for the Rest of Us? *v.4 p.261, p.262*

Globalization, Marginalization, and Development. . . .*v.3 p.300*

The Globalization Reader. *v.4 p.55*

Globalization: What's New. *v.4 p.663*

Globalizations and Social Movements: Culture, Power and the Transnational Public Sphere. *v.3 p.302*

▢ Globalization. *v.4 p.56*

The Globalized Woman: Reports from a Future of Inequality. *v.4 p.666*

Globalizing Capital: A History of the International Monetary System. *v.3 p.39, p.40*

Globalizing Cities: A New Spatial Order? . . .*v.6 p.721, p.728*

Globalizing Feminist Bioethics: Crosscultural Perspectives. *v.5 p.250*

Globalizing the Sacred: Religion Across the Americas. .*v.4 p.720*

Globular Cluster Systems. *v.5 p.70*

The Glorious Cause: The American Revolution, 1763-1789. . . . .*v.3 p.409, p.410*

The Glorious Revolution in America. *v.3 p.406*

The Glory and the Dream: A Narrative History of America, 1932-1972. . . . .*v.3 p.475*

Glory Bound: Black Athletes in a White America. *v.4 p.822, p.833*

The Glory of Byzantium: Art and Culture of the Middle Byzantine Era, A.D. 843-1261. . . . .*v.1 p.672*

The Glory of Venice: Art in the Eighteenth Century. *v.1 p.675, p.688*

Glory Road. *v.3 p.430*

▢ Glossary of Acronyms. *v.5 p.319*

▢ Glossary of Basic Terms in Polymer Science. . . .*v.5 p.321*

Glossary of Biochemistry and Molecular Biology. *v.5 p.325, p.326*

Glossary of Biotechnology and Nanobiotechnology Terms. *v.4 p.156*

Glossary of Chemical Terms. *v.5 p.258*

▢ Glossary of Class Names of Organic Compounds and Reactive Intermediates Based on Structuresbased on structure. *v.5 p.288*

▢ Glossary of Class Names of Organic Compounds and Reactive Intermediates Based on Structures. . . .*v.5 p.288*

Glossary of Crop Science Terms. *v.5 p.20*

A Glossary of Cultural Theory. *v.4 p.676*

A Glossary of Feminist Theory. *v.4 p.676, v.6 p.427*

Glossary of Geology. *v.5 p.417*

A Glossary of Literary Terms. *v.2 p.549*

Glossary of Meteorology. *v.5 p.425, p.426*

Glossary of Organic Chemistry, Including Physical Organic Chemistry. *v.5 p.289*

Glossary of Reliability and Maintenance Terms. . . .*v.5 p.679*

▢ Glossary of Terms Used in Bioinorganic Chemistry. .*v.5 p.301*

▢ Glossary of Terms Used in Physical Organic Chemistry. *v.5 p.288, p.289*

Glowing Genes: A Revolution in Biotechnology. *v.5 p.96, p.220, p.227*

GLQ: A Journal of Lesbian and Gay Studies. *v.6 p.361*

The GLSEN Workbook: A Developmental Model for Assessing, Describing and Improving Schools for Lesbian, Gay, Bisexual and Transgender (LGBT) People. *v.6 p.385*

Gluck: An Eighteenth-Century Portrait in Letters and Documents. *v.1 p.190, p.326*

Gluck and the Opera: A Study in Musical History. *v.1 p.191, p.231, p.326*

Glycogenomics: The Impact of Genomics and Informatics in Glycobiology. *v.5 p.112, p.139*

Gmelins Handbuch der Anorganischen Chemie, 590 vols. *v.5 p.302*

▢ GNIS Geographic Names Information System: Digital Gazetteer. *v.4 p.374*

Gnosis. *v.1 p.647*

The Gnostic Scriptures: A New Translation with Annotations and Introductions. *v.1 p.646*

Go Tell It on the Mountain. *v.2 p.59*

Go the Way Your Blood Beats. *v.6 p.407*

The Goalie's Anxiety at the Penalty Kick. *v.2 p.617*

Goat and the Butcher: Turkey, Kurdistan-Iraq, and Iraq Relations. *v.6 p.599*

Goat Production: Breeding and Management. *v.5 p.54*

Go-Betweens and the Colonization of Brazil: 1500-1600. . . . .*v.3 p.335*

God Alone Is King: Islam and Emancipation in Senegal: The Wolf Kingdoms of Kajour and Bawol, 1859-1914. . .*v.6 p.72*

God and Caesar at the Rio Grande: Sanctuary and the Politicization of Religion in the United States. .*v.6 p.519, p.540*

God and Contemporary Science. *v.1 p.526*

God and Creation in Christian Theology. *v.1 p.636, p.637*

God and Design: The Teleological Argument and Modern Science. *v.1 p.596*

God and General Longstreet: The Lost Cause and the Southern Mind. *v.3 p.395*

God and Mammon: Protestants, Money, and the Market, 1790-1860. . . . .*v.1 p.606, p.607*

God and Man at Yale: The Superstitions of "Academic Freedom". *v.4 p.292*

God and Other Minds: A Study of the Rational Justification of Belief in God. *v.1 p.639*

God and Philosophy. *v.1 p.638, p.639*

God and Skepticism. *v.1 p.517*

God and the Big Bang: Discovering Harmony Between Science and Spirituality. *v.1 p.500*

God and the Constitution: Christianity and American Politics. *v.1 p.605*

God and the Embryo: Religious Voices on Stem Cells and Cloning. *v.1 p.526*

God and the Rhetoric of Sexuality. *v.1 p.619*

God and Time: Essays on the Divine Nature. *v.1 p.594*

God Bless You, Mr. Rosewater. *v.2 p.158*

The God Boy. *v.2 p.744*

God, Death and Time. *v.1 p.456*

God Dies by the Nile. *v.6 p.657*

The God Gene: How Faith Is Hardwired into Our Genes. *v.5 p.634*

God, Guilt and Death: An Existential Phenomenology of Religion. *v.1 p.523, p.524*

God in Chinatown: Religion and Survival in New York's Evolving Immigrant Community. *v.6 p.105, p.126*

God in Search of Man: A Philosophy of Judaism. . . .*v.1 p.551*

God in the Details: American Religion in Popular Culture. *v.4 p.712*

God Is Red: A Native View of Religion. . .*v.4 p.721, v.6 p.701*

God, Man and the World: Lectures and Essays. *v.1 p.551*

The God of Modernity: The Development of Nationalism in Western Europe. *v.3 p.61*

The God of Small Things. *v.2 p.766*

God of the Oppressed. *v.6 p.31, p.35*

God on the Hill: Temple Poems from Tirupati. *v.6 p.153*

The God Particle: If the Universe Is the Answer, What Is the Question? *v.5 p.541*

God, Power, and Evil: A Process Theodicy. *v.1 p.639*

The God That Failed. *v.4 p.508*

God the Future of Man. *v.1 p.638*

God the Problem. *v.1 p.639*

God-Apes and Fossil Men: Paleoanthropology of South Asia. *v.4 p.15*

The Goddess and the Bull: Catalhöyük: An Archaeological Journey to the Dawn of Civilization. *v.4 p.12*

Goddess: Martha Graham's Dancers Remember. *v.1 p.27*

Goddesses and Gods of Old Europe, 7000 to 3500 B. C.: Myths, Legends, and Cult Images. *v.1 p.527*

Goddesses and Monsters: Women, Myth, Power, and Popular Culture. *v.6 p.447, p.448, p.458, p.459*

The Goddesses' Henchmen: Gender in Indian Hero Worship. *v.6 p.161*

Goddesses, Whores, Wives and Slaves: Women in Classical Antiquity. *v.3 p.14, v.6 p.451*

Godel's Proof. *v.5 p.470*

Godhead and the Nothing. *v.1 p.637*

ⓔ Godiva's Ride: Women of Letters in England, 1830-1880. . . . .*v.6 p.740, p.748*

Godless Communists: Atheism and Society in Soviet Russia, 1917-1932. . . . .*v.3 p.222*

The Godless Constitution: A Moral Defense of the Secular State. *v.1 p.656*

Godliness and Good Learning: Four Studies on a Victorian Ideal. *v.3 p.114, p.121, v.6 p.745, p.759*

Godric: A Novel. *v.2 p.141*

Gods and Heroes in Art. *v.1 p.664*

Gods and Heroes in Late Archaic Greek Art. *v.1 p.671*

Gods and Men in Egypt: 3000 B. C. E. to 395 C. E. . .*v.6 p.57*

Gods and Vampires: Return to Chipaya. *v.3 p.325*

The Gods Are Not to Blame. *v.2 p.757*

God's Assassins: State Terrorism in Argentina in the 1970s. *v.3 p.348, v.4 p.660*

God's Bits of Wood. *v.2 p.545*

God's Caliph: Religious Authority in the First Centuries of Islam. *v.1 p.557*

God's Chinese Son: The Taiping Heavenly Kingdom of Hong Xiaquan. *v.6 p.189, p.200*

God's Choice: The Total World of a Fundamentalist Christian School. *v.4 p.308*

Gods, Demons, and Others. *v.2 p.765*

God's Englishman: Oliver Cromwell and the English Revolution. *v.3 p.103*

God's Funeral: The Decline of Faith in Western Civilization. *v.1 p.526*

God's Human Face: The Christ Icon. *v.1 p.654*

God's Little Acre. *v.2 p.66*

God's Man for the Gilded Age: D. L. Moody and the Rise of Modern Mass Evangelism. *v.1 p.648*

Gods of Flesh/Gods of Stone: The Embodiment of Divinity in India. *v.1 p.538*

Gods of the City: Religion and the American Urban Landscape. *v.6 p.718*

The Gods of the Greeks. *v.1 p.532*

God's Playground: A History of Poland in Two Volumes. *v.3 p.252*

God's Rule: Government and Islam, Six Centuries of Medieval Islamic Political Thought. *v.6 p.584*

The Gods Will Have Blood. *v.2 p.490*

God's World: An Anthology of Short Stories. *v.6 p.662*

The Godwits Fly. *v.2 p.746*

Goethe: A Critical Introduction. *v.2 p.598*

Goethe and the Novel. *v.2 p.597*

Goethe: Faust I and II, Vol. 2. . . . .*v.2 p.598*

Goethe Set, Vol 1-10. . . . .*v.2 p.598*

Goethe's Autobiography. *v.2 p.598*

Goethes Briefe. *v.2 p.598*

Goethe's Plays. *v.2 p.598*

Goethe. *v.2 p.597, p.598*

Going All the Way: Christian Warlords, Israeli Adventurers and the War in Lebanon. *v.6 p.606*

Going Alone: The Case for Relaxed Reciprocity in Freeing Trade. *v.4 p.256*

Going Digital: The Practice and Vision of Digital Artists. *v.1 p.772*

Going down to the Barrio: Homeboys and Homegirls in Change. *v.6 p.547, p.549, p.550*

Going Public: Women and Publishing in Early Modern France. *v.2 p.457*

Going South: Jewish Women in the Civil Rights Movement. *v.6 p.432*

Going the Other Way: Lessons from a Life in and out of Major League Baseball. *v.6 p.383, p.384*

ⓔ Going to College: How Social, Economic, and Educational Factors Influence the Decisions Students Make. . .*v.4 p.294*

Going to Meet the Man. *v.2 p.59*

Going to the Dance. *v.1 p.39*

Going Under. *v.6 p.509*

Gold and Spices: The Rise of Commerce in the Middle Ages. *v.6 p.558*

Gold: Chemistry, Biochemistry, and Technology. . . .*v.5 p.309*

Gold of the Akan from the Glassell Collection. *v.1 p.746*

Gold of the Pharaohs. *v.1 p.806*

The Golden Age Comedia: Text, Theory and Performance. *v.2 p.640*

The Golden Age: Dutch Painters of the Seventeenth Century. *v.1 p.731, p.732*

The Golden Age of Amateur Basketball: The AAU Tournament, 1921-1968. . . . .*v.4 p.854*

The Golden Age of Black Nationalism, 1850-1925. . .*v.6 p.13*

The Golden Age of Brazil 1695: 1750. . . . .*v.3 p.334*

The Golden Age of Dutch Art: Painting, Sculpture, Decorative Art. *v.1 p.732*

The Golden Age of Dutch Painting in Historical Perspective. *v.1 p.731*

The Golden Age of Painting in Spain. *v.1 p.731*

The Golden Age of Persian Art, 1501-1722. . . . . .*v.1 p.691*

The Golden Age of Zen: Zen Masters of the T'Ang Dynasty. *v.1 p.568*

The Golden Ass. *v.2 p.428, p.429*

The Golden Bowl Be Broken: Peasant Life in Four Cultures. *v.4 p.39*

The Golden Bowl. *v.2 p.45*

The Golden Compass. *v.2 p.373*

The Golden Droplet. *v.2 p.534*

Golden Fetters: The Gold Standard and the Great Depression, 1919-1939. . . . .*v.4 p.213*

The Golden Fruits. *v.2 p.527*

The Golden Grove: Selected Passages from the Sermons and Writings of Jeremy Taylor. *v.2 p.263*

The Golden Horns: Mythic Imagination and the Nordic Past. *v.2 p.624*

The Golden Legend: Readings on the Saints. *v.1 p.579*

Golden Men: The Power of Gay Midlife. *v.6 p.380*

Golden Mouth: The Story of John Chrysostom - Ascetic, Preacher, Bishop. *v.1 p.613*

The Golden Notebook: Perennial Classics Edition. . .*v.2 p.364*

The Golden Peaches of Samarkand. *v.6 p.185, p.204*

The Golden Ratio: The Story of Phi, the World's Most Astonishing Number. *v.5 p.467, p.476*

Golden Road to Modernity. *v.6 p.166*

Golden UFOs: The Indian Poems Los Ovnis de Oro: Poemas Indios. *v.2 p.675*

Gold-Hall and Earth-Dragon: Beowulf as Metaphor. . .*v.2 p.205*

Goldoni, Vol. 1. . . . .*v.1 p.107*

Goldoni, Vol. 2. . . . .*v.1 p.107*

Goldsmith: The Critical Heritage. *v.2 p.249*

The Golem: What Everyone Should Know about Science. *v.5 p.401*

Golf and the American Country Club. *v.4 p.716*

Golf Course Architecture: Design, Construction and Restoration. *v.4 p.881*

Golf Handbook for Women: The Complete Guide to Improving Your Game. *v.4 p.838, p.861*

Golf Magazine's Complete Book of Golf Instruction. .*v.4 p.861*

Golf My Way: The Instructional Classic. *v.4 p.861*

Golf's Golden Age: Robert T. Jones, Jr. and the Legendary Players of the '10s, '20s and '30s. *v.4 p.861*

The Golovyov Family. *v.2 p.808*

Les gommes. *v.2 p.525*

Goncourt Journals, 1851-1870. . . . .*v.2 p.492*

Gone to Texas: A History of the Lone Star State. . .*v.3 p.508*

Gone with the Wind. *v.2 p.98*

Gonzales/Rodriguez: Uncut and Uncensored. *v.6 p.521*

Good and Evil: Interpreting a Human Condition. . .*v.1 p.635*

The Good Apprentice. *v.2 p.372*

Good Behaviour. *v.2 p.360*

Good Cop, Bad Cop: Racial Profiling and Competing Views of Justice. *v.4 p.573, v.6 p.264*

Good Cops: The Case for Preventative Policing. . . .*v.6 p.263*

Good Courts: The Case for Problem-Solving Justice. *v.6 p.269*

Good Dirt: Confessions of a Conservationist. . .*v.5 p.180, p.230*

The Good Earth. *v.2 p.58, v.6 p.214*

Good Faith and Truthful Ignorance: A Case of Transatlantic Bigamy. *v.3 p.285*

The Good Father: On Men, Masculinity, and Life in the Family. *v.5 p.639*

A Good Man in Africa: A Novel. *v.2 p.335*

Good Morning! and Other Stories. *v.6 p.659*

Good Morning Blues: An Autobiography of Count Basie. *v.1 p.257, p.305*

Good Morning, Midnight. *v.2 p.769*

Good Morning, Revolution: Uncollected Writings of Social Protest. *v.2 p.87*

Good Natured: The Origins of Right and Wrong in Humans and Other Animals. *v.5 p.614*

The Good Neighbor Policy and Authoritarianism in Paraguay: United States Economic Expansion and Great - Power Rivalry in Latin America During World War II. . .*v.3 p.344*

The Good Neighbors: America, Panama and the 1977 Canal Treaties. *v.3 p.306*

Good Night, Sweet Prince. *v.1 p.144*

The Good Old Days: The Holocaust As Seen by Its Perpetrators and Bystanders. *v.3 p.85*

Good Poems for Hard Times. *v.2 p.23*

Good Poems. *v.2 p.23*

The Good Regiment: The Carignan-Salihres Regiment in
    Canada, 1665-1668. . . . . *v.4 p.581*

Good Samaritan and Other Stories. *v.2 p.107*

A Good Scent from a Strange Mountain: Stories. *v.2 p.141, p.142*

The Good Soldier: A Tale of Passion. *v.2 p.345*

The Good Soldier Svejk: And His Fortunes in the World
    War. *v.2 p.783*

The Good Teacher Mentor: Setting the Standard for Support and
    Success. *v.4 p.278*

The Good Terrorist. *v.2 p.364*

Good to Great: Why Some Companies Make the Leap... and
    Others Don't. *v.4 p.70*

Good Wives: Image and Reality in the Lives of Women in
    Northern New England, 1650-1750. . . . . *v.3 p.487*

Good Woman: Poems and a Memoir, 1969-1980. . . . *v.2 p.143*

Good Work: When Excellence and Ethics
    Meet. *v.4 p.53, p.54, p.55*

Goodbye, Mr. Chips. *v.2 p.351*

Good-Bye, Samizdat: Twenty Years of Czechoslovak
    Underground Writing. *v.2 p.781*

Good-Bye to All That: An Autobiography. *v.2 p.348*

The Good-Bye Window: A Year in the Life of a Day-Care
    Center. *v.4 p.735*

Goodbyes and Stories. *v.2 p.687*

Goodman and Gilman's the Pharmacological Basis of
    Therapeutics. *v.5 p.526*

Goods, Power, History: Latin America's Material
    Culture. *v.3 p.271*

☐ Google Directory : Astronomy. *v.5 p.61*

☐ Google Directory: Biological Laboratories. *v.5 p.82*

☐ Google Directory: Biology Associations. *v.5 p.94*

☐ Google Directory: Biology, Biochemistry and Molecular
    Biology. *v.5 p.110*

☐ Google Directory: Biology, Biogeochemistry. . . . *v.5 p.111*

☐ Google Directory: Biology Bioinformatics. *v.5 p.96*

☐ Google Directory: Biology, Biomechanics. . *v.5 p.155, p.163*

☐ Google Directory: Biology, Biophysics. *v.5 p.111*

☐ Google Directory: Biology, Biotechnology. *v.5 p.217*

☐ Google Directory: Biology, Botany. *v.5 p.206*

☐ Google Directory: Biology, Cell Biology. *v.5 p.152*

☐ Google Directory: Biology, Developmental Biology. *v.5 p.159*

☐ Google Directory: Biology Directories. . . . *v.5 p.94, p.95*

☐ Google Directory: Biology, Ecology. *v.5 p.169*

☐ Google Directory: Biology Education. *v.5 p.244*

☐ Google Directory: Biology, Evolution. . . *v.5 p.189, p.190*

☐ Google Directory: Biology, Flora and Fauna. . . . *v.5 p.169*

☐ Google Directory: Biology, Genetics, Genomics. . *v.5 p.144*

☐ Google Directory: Biology, Genetics. *v.5 p.130*

☐ Google Directory: Biology, Histology. *v.5 p.158*

☐ Google Directory: Biology Humor. *v.5 p.244*

☐ Google Directory: Biology, Immunology. *v.5 p.165*

☐ Google Directory: Biology Meetings. *v.5 p.94, p.95*

☐ Google Directory: Biology, Microbiology. *v.5 p.205*

☐ Google Directory: Biology Museums. *v.5 p.85*

☐ Google Directory: Biology, Mycology. *v.5 p.206*

☐ Google Directory: Biology, Neurobiology. *v.5 p.164*

☐ Google Directory: Biology, Physiology. *v.5 p.163*

☐ Google Directory: Biology Products and
    Services. *v.5 p.94, p.95*

☐ Google Directory: Biology, Taxonomy. *v.5 p.204*

☐ Google Directory: Biology, Zoology, Chordates, Ornithology
    [Birds]. *v.5 p.211*

☐ Google Directory: Biology, Zoology. *v.5 p.211*

☐ Google Directory: Biology. *v.5 p.94*

☐ Google Directory: Biotechnology and Pharmaceuticals
    Employment. *v.5 p.244*

☐ Google Directory: History of Biology. *v.5 p.77*

☐ Google Directory: Zoos and Aquariums. *v.5 p.82*

The Google Story: Inside the Hottest Business, Media, and
    Technology Success of Our Time. *v.4 p.68, p.69*

The Gorbachev Phenomenon: A Historical
    Interpretation. *v.3 p.228*

Gordon's Photography Price Annual International
    2005. . . . . *v.1 p.708, p.762*

Gordon's Print Price Annual 2005. . . . . . . *v.1 p.708, p.752*

Gore Vidal: A Biography. *v.2 p.127, v.6 p.402*

Gore Vidal: A Critical Companion. *v.2 p.126, p.127*

Gore Vidal: Writer Against the Grain. *v.2 p.127*

Gore Vidal's Historical Novels and the Shaping of American
    Political Consciousness. *v.2 p.127*

Gore Vidal. *v.2 p.127*

Gorgias. *v.1 p.425, v.2 p.418*

The Gormenghast Novels: Titus Groan, Gormenghast, Titus
    Alone. *v.2 p.373*

Gospel Figures in Art. *v.1 p.710*

The Gospel in a Pluralist Society. *v.1 p.596*

Gospel of Disunion: Religion and Separatism in the Antebellum
    South. *v.3 p.401*

The Gospel of Gentility: American Women Missionaries in
    Turn-of-the-Century China. *v.6 p.201, p.218*

Gospel of John: A Commentary. *v.1 p.628*

The Gospel of John. *v.1 p.629*

The Gospel of Luke. *v.1 p.629*

The Gospel of Mark. *v.1 p.629*

The Gospel of Matthew. *v.1 p.629*

Gospel Women: Studies of the Named Women in the
    Gospels. *v.1 p.628*

The Gossamer Years: The Diary of a Noblewoman of Heian
    Japan. *v.6 p.233*

Gosta Berling's Saga. *v.2 p.630*

Gotham: A History of New York City to 1898. *v.3 p.490, v.6 p.711*

Gothic Architecture. *v.1 p.786*

Gothic Art. *v.1 p.672*

The Gothic Enterprise: A Guide to Understanding the Medieval
    Cathedral. *v.1 p.787*

The Gothic History of Jordanes: In English Version with an Introduction and a Commentary. *v.3 p.63*

The Gothic Idol: Ideology and Image-Making in Medieval Art. *v.1 p.654, p.671*

The Gothic Revival. *v.1 p.787*

Gothic Sculpture, 1140-1300. . . . .*v.1 p.776*

The Gothic Tales of the Marquis de Sade. *v.2 p.483*

Gothic Traditions and Narrative Technique in the Fiction of Eudora Welty. *v.2 p.130*

Goths and Romans AD 332-489. . . . .*v.3 p.31, p.62*

The Goths. *v.3 p.31*

Gottfried Benn: The Unreconstructed Expressionist. *v.2 p.603, p.604*

Gottfried Keller: Life and Works. *v.2 p.600*

Gottfried Semper: Architect of the Nineteenth Century: A Personal and Intellectual Biography. *v.1 p.794*

Go. *v.2 p.81*

Gould's Book of Fish: A Novel in Twelve Fish. . . .*v.2 p.745*

La goutte d'or : roman. *v.2 p.534*

Gouverneurs de la rosée : roman. *v.2 p.537*

Governance, Accountability, and the Future of the Catholic Church. *v.1 p.576*

Governance and Opportunity in Metropolitan America: Governmental Arrangements and Individual Life Chances in Urban America. *v.4 p.542, p.543,v.6 p.724*

Governance and Policy in Sport Organizations. *v.4 p.844, p.891, p.898*

Governance and Society in Colonial Mexico: Chihuahua in the Eighteenth Century. *v.3 p.286*

Governance in China. *v.4 p.620*

Governance, Multinationals, and Growth. .*v.4 p.243, p.261, p.263*

The Governance of Ethnic Communities: Political Structures and Processes in Canada, 26. . . . .*v.3 p.542*

The Governess: [the Little Female Academy]. *v.2 p.248*

Governing American Cities: Inter-Ethnic Coalitions, Competition, and Conflict. *v.4 p.544*

Governing China's Multiethnic Frontiers. *v.4 p.620*

Governing Complex Societies: Trajectories and Scenarios. *v.4 p.580*

Governing Europe. *v.4 p.603, p.637*

Governing from Below: Urban Regions and the Global Economy. *v.4 p.543*

Governing from the Center: Politics and Policy-Making in the Netherlands. *v.4 p.601*

Governing from the Centre: The Concentration of Power in Canadian Politics. *v.4 p.587*

Governing Independent Colleges and Universities: A Handbook for Trustees, Chief Executives and Other Campus Leaders. *v.4 p.291*

Governing Israel: The Chosen People, the Promised Land, and the Prophetic Tradition. *v.6 p.616*

Governing Italy: The Politics of Bargained Pluralism. .*v.4 p.594*

Governing Metropolitan Indianapolis. *v.4 p.543*

Governing Mexico, 1976-88: The Statecraft of Crisis Management. *v.3 p.290*

Governing Middle-Sized Cities: Studies in Mayoral Leadership. *v.4 p.543*

Governing New York City: Politics in the Metropolis. .*v.6 p.725*

Governing Ourselves?: The Politics of Canadian Communities. *v.4 p.581, p.587*

Governing Paradoxes of Restorative Justice. *v.4 p.754*

Governing Pleasures: Pornography and Social Change in England, 1815-1914. . . . .*v.6 p.739, p.742, p.760, p.764*

Governing Prisons. *v.6 p.275*

Governing Public Colleges and Universities: A Handbook for Trustees, Chief Executives and Other Campus Leaders. *v.4 p.291*

Government and Change in Lesotho, 1800-1966. .*v.6 p.75, p.76*

Government and Environmental Politics: Essays on Historical Developments since World War II. *v.5 p.369, p.370, p.371, p.374*

Government and Politics in Africa. *v.4 p.613*

Government and Politics in Hungary. *v.4 p.595*

Government and Politics in Revolutionary China: Selected Documents, 1949-1979. . . . .*v.6 p.194*

The Government and Politics of France. *v.4 p.609*

The Government and Politics of Ireland. *v.4 p.607, p.608*

The Government and Politics of Israel. *v.6 p.615*

Government and Politics of Singapore. *v.6 p.173*

The Government and Politics of Spain. *v.4 p.608*

Government and Politics of the Middle East and North Africa. *v.6 p.594*

Government and Politics of Uruguay. *v.4 p.593*

Government and Society in Malaysia. *v.4 p.622*

Government and the Arts: Debates over Federal Support of the Arts in America from George Washington to Jesse Helms. *v.4 p.524*

Government by Judiciary: The Transformation of the Fourteenth Amendment. *v.4 p.462*

Government Coalitions in Western Democracies. .*v.4 p.574, p.575*

Government for the People: The Federal Role: What It Is, What It Should Be. *v.4 p.523*

Government Job Finder. *v.4 p.170*

Government Lawyers: The Federal Legal Bureaucracy and Presidential Politics. *v.4 p.523*

▢ Government of Canada, Gouvernement du Canada. *v.4 p.586*

▢ Government of Canada: Provinces and Territories. *v.4 p.587*

The Government of Canada. *v.4 p.587, p.588*

The Government of Edward Schreyer: Democratic Socialism in Manitoba. *v.3 p.546*

The Government of Manitoba. *v.4 p.589*

Government of Nova Scotia. *v.4 p.589*

A Government of Our Own: The Making of the Confederacy. *v.4 p.520*

The Government of Philip Augustus: Foundations of French Royal Power in the Middle Ages. *v.3 p.142*

The Government of Prince Edward Island. *v.4 p.590*

The Government of Scotland: Public Policy Making after Devolution. *v.4 p.607*

The Government of the Ottoman Empire in the Time of Suleiman the Magnificent. *v.6 p.590*

The Government of the Tongue: Selected Prose, 1978-1987. . . . .*v.2 p.352*

The Government Party: Organizing and Financing the Liberal
Party of Canada, 1930-58. . . . . *v.4 p.589*

Government Research Directory. *v.5 p.397*

Government Views of Iraq. *v.4 p.642*

Governments as Interest Groups: Intergovernmental Lobbying
and the Federal System. *v.4 p.523*

Governments, Citizens and Genocide: A Comparative and
Interdisciplinary Analysis. *v.4 p.651*

The Governor and the Rebel: A History of Bacon's Rebellion in
Virginia. *v.3 p.500*

Governor Philip F. LaFollette: The Wisconsin Progressives, and
the New Deal. *v.3 p.517*

The governors and judges of Egypt. *v.6 p.635*

Governors and Legislatures: Contending Powers. . . *v.4 p.541*

Governors of Louisiana. *v.3 p.507*

Gower Handbook of Supply Chain Management. *v.4 p.117, p.118*

Goya: Drawings from His Private Albums. *v.1 p.724*

Goya's Caprichos: Aesthetics, Perception, and the Body. *v.1 p.758*

Goya. *v.1 p.697*

GPS Satellite Surveying. *v.4 p.390*

The Gracchi. *v.3 p.26*

Grace - W. R. Grace and Co.: The Formative Years:
1850-1930. . . . . *v.3 p.329*

Grace Abounding to the Chief of Sinners. *v.2 p.241*

Grace and Glory: A Century of Women in the
Olympics. *v.4 p.824, p.837, p.838, p.846*

Grace and Gratitude: The Eucharistic Theology of John
Calvin. *v.1 p.589*

A Grace Disguised: How the Soul Grows Through Loss. *v.1 p.652*

Grace King: a southern destiny. *v.2 p.43*

Grace King of New Orleans; a selection of her writings. *v.2 p.43*

Grace under Pressure: Passing Dance Through
Time. *v.1 p.37, p.52, p.53, p.55*

Graduate Medical Education Directory 2004-2005. . *v.5 p.509*

Graduate Study in Psychology: 2007 Edition. . . . *v.5 p.675*

Graduate to Your Perfect Job in 6 Easy Steps. . . . *v.4 p.169*

Gradus II: The Second Year and After. *v.1 p.371*

Graecia Capta: The Landscapes of Roman Greece. . *v.3 p.191*

Grafter and Goo Goos: Corruption and Reform in Chicago,
1833-2003. . . . . *v.3 p.516*

Graham Greene: A Literary Life. *v.2 p.351*

Graham Greene: A Study of Four Dramas. *v.2 p.351*

Graham Greene: A Study of the Short Fiction. . . . *v.2 p.351*

Graham Greene's Thrillers and the 1930s. *v.2 p.349*

Graham Greene. *v.2 p.349*

Graham's Electroplating Handbook. *v.5 p.737*

Grain Legumes: Evolution and Genetic Resources. *v.5 p.23, p.45*

Grainger on Music. *v.1 p.215, p.247*

Grains of Sand. *v.5 p.175*

Gramatica Didactica del Espanol. *v.2 p.636*

A Grammar of Classical Arabic. *v.6 p.653*

The Grammar of Conducting: A Comprehensive Guide to Baton
Technique and Interpretation. *v.1 p.403*

A Grammar of Contemporary English. *v.2 p.558*

A Grammar of Contemporary Polish. *v.2 p.775*

A Grammar of Contemporary Slovak. *v.2 p.777*

A Grammar of Late Modern English, Vol. 4, Pt. 2. . *v.2 p.558*

A Grammar of Motives. *v.1 p.489*

The Grammar of Science. *v.5 p.403*

A Grammar of the Arabic Language. *v.6 p.655*

Grammar of the Edit. *v.6 p.351*

Grammar of the Shot. *v.6 p.349*

Grammars of Creation: Originating in the Gifford Lectures of
1990. . . . . *v.2 p.569*

Grammatical Man: Information, Entropy, Language and
Life. *v.5 p.408*

Grammatical Theory in the United States: From Bloomfield to
Chomsky. *v.2 p.562, p.563*

Grammaticalization. *v.2 p.561*

Gramsci, Culture and Anthropology. *v.4 p.23*

Gramsci's Politics. *v.4 p.492*

La Gran Linea: Mapping the United States - Mexico Boundary,
1849-1857. . . . . *v.6 p.487, p.535*

Granada: A Novel. *v.6 p.655*

The Grand Babylon Hotel: A Fantasia on Modern
Themes. *v.2 p.334*

Grand Delusion: Stalin and the German Invasion of
Russia. *v.3 p.227*

Grand Design: Hollywood As a Modern Business Enterprise,
1930-1939. . . . . *v.6 p.345*

Grand Designs and Visions of Unity: The Atlantic Powers and
the Reorganization of Western Europe,
1955-1963. . . . . *v.4 p.637, p.654*

The Grand Illusion: The Prussianization of the Chilean
Army. *v.3 p.274, p.351*

Grand Master Workman: Terence Powderly and the Knights of
Labor. *v.4 p.128*

Le Grand Meaulnes. *v.2 p.506, p.515*

The Grand Prize and Other Stories. *v.2 p.816*

Le grand Robert de la langue française. *v.2 p.454*

The Grand Scribe's Records: The Basic Annals of Pre-Han
China, Vol. 7. . . . . *v.6 p.184*

The Grand Slam: Bobby Jones, America, and the Story of
Golf. *v.4 p.823, p.860*

Grand Strategies in War and Peace. *v.3 p.36*

Grand Strategy in the War Against
Terrorism. *v.4 p.564, p.565, p.660*

The Grand Strategy of Philip II. *v.3 p.240*

The Grand Strategy of the Roman Empire: From the First
Century A. D. to the Third. *v.3 p.28*

The Grand Strategy of the Russian Empire, 1650-1831. *v.3 p.212*

Le Grand Tango: The Life and Music of Astor
Piazzolla. *v.1 p.291, p.347*

The Grand Titration; Science and Society in East and
West. *v.5 p.392*

The Grand Titration. *v.6 p.198*

The Grand Tour: A Traveler's Guide to the Solar System. *v.5 p.68*

Grande Dicionário da Língua Portuguesa. *v.2 p.637*

Grande dizionario italiano dell'uso. *v.2 p.698, p.699*

Grande Maison. *v.2 p.542*

La grande ourse. *v.2 p.513*

Les grandes doctrines littéraires en France. *v.2 p.458*

Grandeur and Illusion: French Literature and Society, 1600-1715. . . . .*v.2 p.458*

The Grandissimes. *v.2 p.32*

Grandma Moses in the Twenty-First Century. *v.1 p.742*

The Grandmothers: A Family Portrait. *v.2 p.128*

The Grandmothers: Four Short Novels. *v.2 p.364, p.365*

Les grands désordres : roman. *v.2 p.528*

The Granite Landscape: A Natural History of America's Mountain Domes, from Acadia to Yosemite. *v.5 p.235*

The Granite State: New Hampshire, an Illustrated History. *v.3 p.486*

Granny: Scenes from Country Life. *v.2 p.784*

Grant: A Biography. *v.3 p.399, p.437*

Grant and Hackh's Chemical Dictionary. *v.5 p.258*

Grant and Lee: A Study in Personality and Generalship. *v.3 p.397, p.430*

Grant Moves South. *v.3 p.435*

Grant Takes Command. *v.3 p.435*

Grant Wood's Studio: Birthplace of American Gothic. .*v.1 p.744*

Grantland Rice and His Heroes: The Sportswriter As Mythmaker in the 1920s. *v.4 p.811, p.907*

Grant's Atlas of Anatomy. *v.5 p.158*

Grant's Dissector: Essentials of Pulmonary and Critical Care Medicine. *v.5 p.89*

The Grants Register 2005: The Complete Guide to Postgraduate Funding Worldwide, Twenty-Third Edition. . . .*v.4 p.293*

The Grape Grower: A Guide to Organic Viticulture. . .*v.5 p.53*

Graph Theory with Applications. *v.5 p.480*

Graphic Agitation 2: Social and Political Graphics in the Digital Age. *v.1 p.713*

Graphic Arts Monthly: Applied Technology for the Printing Industry. *v.4 p.140*

Graphic Communications Today. © 20.04 . . . . .*v.1 p.713*

Graphic Design History. *v.1 p.713*

Graphic Design in America: A Visual Language History. .*v.1 p.713*

Graphic Design in Germany 1890-1945. . . . . . .*v.1 p.713*

Graphic Design in the Mechanical Age: Selections from the Merrill C. Berman Collection. *v.1 p.718*

Graphic Design Inspirations and Innovations. *v.1 p.721*

Graphic Wit: The Art of Humor in Design. *v.1 p.701*

The Graphic Work of Dame Laura Knight: Including a Catalogue Raisonné of Her Prints. *v.1 p.755*

The Graphite Page. *v.5 p.305*

Graphs, Algorithms and Optimization. *v.5 p.480*

Graphs and Digraphs. *v.5 p.480*

The Grasmere and Alfoxden Journals. *v.2 p.322*

The Grass Genera of the World. *v.5 p.42*

The Grass Harp: Including a Tree of the Night and Other Stories. *v.2 p.66*

The Grass Is Singing: A Novel. *v.2 p.365*

Grass: Its Production and Utilization. *v.5 p.42*

Grass on the Wayside. *v.6 p.232*

Grassland Dynamics: Long-Term Ecological Research in Tallgrass Prairie. *v.5 p.170, p.240*

Grasslands, Systems Analysis and Man. *v.5 p.42, p.358*

Grassroots Pacifism in Post-War Japan: The Rebirth of a Nation. *v.4 p.712*

The Grateful Dead Reader. *v.1 p.268, p.327*

Grave Injustice: The American Indian Repatriation Movement and NAGPRA. *v.4 p.464, v.6 p.694, p.704*

The Gravest Show on Earth: America in the Age of AIDS. *v.6 p.378*

Gravitation and Cosmology: Principles and Applications of the General Theory of Relativity. *v.5 p.73, p.557*

Gravitational Lenses. *v.5 p.67*

Gravitation. *v.5 p.72, p.556, p.557*

Gravity's Fatal Attraction: Black Holes in the Universe. .*v.5 p.72*

Gravity's Rainbow. *v.2 p.153*

Gravy Training: Inside the Shadowy World of Business Schools. *v.4 p.176*

Gray: Poetry and Prose. *v.2 p.249*

The Graying of America: An Encyclopedia of Aging, Health, Mind and Behavior. *v.4 p.677*

Gray's Anatomy Edition: The Anatomical Basis of Clinical Practice. *v.5 p.158*

Gray's Anatomy for Students. *v.5 p.158*

The Graywolf Annual: Short Stories. *v.2 p.27*

Grazia Deledda : a legendary life. *v.2 p.717*

Grazing Management: An Ecological Perspective. . . .*v.5 p.42*

Grazing Management. *v.5 p.42, p.43*

Greasers and Gringos: Latinos, Law, and the American Imagination. *v.4 p.456*

The Great Age of Chinese Poetry: The High T'ang. . .*v.6 p.210*

Great American Battles. *v.3 p.383*

The Great American History Fact-Finder: The Who, What, Where, When, and Why of American History. . . .*v.3 p.373*

The Great American Playwrights on the Screen: A Critical Guide to Film, TV, Video and DVD. *v.6 p.327*

Great American Trials. *v.4 p.438*

The Great Art of Government: Locke's Use of Consent. *v.4 p.491, p.497*

Great Ascent: The Struggle for Economic Development in Our Time. *v.4 p.244*

The Great Awakening and American Education: A Documentary History. *v.4 p.329*

The Great Barrier Reef: Finding the Right Balance. . .*v.5 p.173*

The Great Barrier Reef: History, Science, Heritage. . .*v.5 p.172*

The Great Belzoni: The Circus Strongman Who Discovered Egypt's Ancient Treasures. *v.3 p.11*

The Great Beyond: Higher Dimensions, Parallel Universes and the Extraordinary Search for a Theory of Everything. .*v.5 p.557*

The Great Black Jockeys: The Lives and Times of the Men Who Dominated America's First National Sport. *v.4 p.832, p.847, p.848*

Great Black Leaders: Ancient and Modern. *v.6 p.9, p.19*

Great Britain and the American Civil War. .*v.3 p.393, p.394, p.432*

Great Britain: The Lion at Home; a Documentary History of Domestic Policy, 1689-1973. . . . .*v.3 p.110*

The Great Campaigns: Reform and War in America, 1900-1928. . . . .*v.3 p.441, p.447*

The Great Cat Massacre: And Other Episodes in French Cultural History. *v.3 p.147*

The Great Chain of Being: A Study of the History of an Idea. *v.1 p.488*

Great Chemists. *v.5 p.260*

The Great Chicago Fire and the Myth of Mrs. O'Leary's Cow. *v.3 p.515*

The Great Chief Justice: John Marshall and the Rule of Law. *v.4 p.467, p.468*

The Great Church in Captivity: A Study of the Patriarchate of Constantinople from the Eve of the Turkish Conquest to the Greek War of Independence. . . .*v.3 p.194*

The Great Columbia Plain: A Historical Geography, 1805-1910. . . . .*v.3 p.530*

Great Comedians Talk About Comedy. *v.6 p.313*

Great Conductors. *v.1 p.403*

The Great Crash 1929. . . . . . .*v.3 p.440, p.447,v.4 p.95, p.99, p.100, p.243*

Great Debates at the United Nations: An Encyclopedia of Fifty Key Issues, 1945-2000. . . . .*v.4 p.633*

The Great Deception: The Secret History of the European Union. *v.4 p.602, p.636*

The Great Departure: The United States and World War I, 1914-1920. . . . .*v.3 p.480*

The Great Depression: America, 1929-1941. . . . .*v.3 p.475*

The Great Depression: An International Disaster of Perverse Economic Policies. *v.4 p.213*

The Great Depression and the Culture of Abundance: Kenneth Fearing, Nathanael West and Mass Culture in the 1930s. *v.2 p.131*

Great Depression. *v.4 p.210*

The Great Dinosaur Controversy: A Guide to the Debates. *v.5 p.448*

The Great Disorder: Politics, Economics, and Society in the German Inflation, 1914-1924. . . . .*v.3 p.170*

The Great Divergence: China, Europe and the Making of the Modern World Economy. *v.6 p.181*

The Great Divide: The Rocky Mountains in the American Mind. *v.3 p.525*

The Great Divorce. *v.1 p.484, v.2 p.366*

The Great Earthquake and Firestorms of 1906: How San Francisco Nearly Destroyed Itself. *v.6 p.712*

Great Economists Before Keynes: An Introduction to the Lives and Works of One Hundred Great Economists of the Past. *v.4 p.208*

Great Economists since Keynes: An Introduction to the Lives and Works of One Hundred Modern Economists. *v.4 p.188, p.194, p.208*

Great Esquire Fiction: The Finest Stories from the First Fifty Years. *v.2 p.26*

The Great Exhibition of 1851: A Nation on Display. . .*v.6 p.763*

Great Expectations. by Charles Dickens ... with ... illustrations. from original designs by John Mclenan. *v.2 p.283*

Great Expectations: Norton Critical Editions. *v.2 p.283*

Great Expectations. *v.2 p.283*

The Great Famine and Beyond: Irish Immigrants in Britain in the Nineteenth and Twentieth Centuries. *v.3 p.135*

The Great Famine: Northern Europe in the Early Fourteenth Century. *v.3 p.43, p.69*

The Great Father: The United States Government and the American Indians, Set. *v.6 p.683, p.696*

The Great Fear. *v.3 p.446*

The Great Festivals of Colonial Mexico City: Performing Power and Identity. *v.3 p.262, p.263*

Great Fortune: The Epic of Rockefeller Center. . . .*v.1 p.790*

Great Game of Genocide: Imperialism, Nationalism, and the Destruction of the Ottoman Armenians. *v.4 p.651*

The Great Game: The Emergence of Wall Street as a World Power, 1653-2000. . . . . .*v.4 p.100, p.147, p.155, p.162*

The Great Gatsby: A Documentary. *v.2 p.75, p.76*

The Great Gatsby. *v.2 p.76*

The Great German Mystics: Eckhart, Tauler and Suso. .*v.6 p.570*

Great German Short Stories. *v.2 p.594*

The Great God Pan and the Hill of Dreams. *v.2 p.367*

The Great Hollywood Musical Pictures. *v.6 p.316*

The Great Hunger: Ireland, 1845-1849. . . . .*v.3 p.139*

The Great Ideas of Biology: The Romanes Lecture for 2003. . . . .*v.5 p.80*

The Great Indian Novel. *v.2 p.766, p.767*

The Great Instauration: Science, Medicine and Reform, 1626-1660. . . . .*v.5 p.393, p.404*

The Great Irish Potato Famine. *v.3 p.138*

The Great Island. *v.3 p.196, p.197*

Great Jazz Day. *v.1 p.259*

Great Jobs for Accounting Majors. *v.4 p.169*

Great Jobs for Biology Majors. *v.5 p.250*

Great Jobs for Business Majors. *v.4 p.170*

Great Jobs for Economics Majors. *v.4 p.168, p.169*

Great Jobs for Math Majors. *v.5 p.459*

Great Lakes Archaeology. *v.4 p.11*

The Great Lakes of Africa: Two Thousand Years of History. *v.6 p.63*

The Great Law and the Longhouse: A Political History of the Iroquois Confederacy. *v.6 p.682, p.691*

Great Masters of Mexican Folk Art. *v.1 p.684*

The Great Mayor: Fiorello La Guardia and the Making of the City of New York. *v.3 p.456, v.6 p.710, p.711*

The Great Meadow. *v.2 p.113*

The Great "Red Menace": United States Prosecution of American Communists, 1947-1952. . . . .*v.3 p.450*

The Great Mortality: An Intimate History of the Black Death, the Most Devastating Plague of All Time. *v.5 p.532*

Great Musicals of the American Theatre. . . .*v.1 p.253, p.409*

The Great Nation: France from Louis XV to Napoleon. *v.3 p.147*

Great Observatories of the World. *v.5 p.65*

The Great Peace of Montreal of 1701: French-Native Diplomacy in the Seventeenth Century. *v.4 p.630, v.6 p.685*

Great Pianists on Piano Playing: Godowsky, Hofmann, Lhevinne, Paderewski and 24 Other Legendary Pianists. *v.1 p.397*

The Great Pianists. *v.1 p.391*

A Great Place to Work: What Makes Some Employers So Good - And Most So Bad. *v.5 p.579*

The Great Plains in Transition. *v.3 p.518*

The Great Plains. *v.3 p.518, p.519*

Great Planned Communities. *v.1 p.797*

Great Possessions: An Amish Farmer's Journal. *v.5 p.79*

Great Power Rivalries. *v.4 p.628*

Great Psychologists and Their Times: Scientific Insights into
Psychology's History. *v.5 p.598*

The Great Reforms: Autocracy, Bureaucracy, and the Politics of
Change in Imperial Russia. *v.3 p.219*

Great River: The Rio Grande in North American History. Vol. 1,
Indians and Spain. Vol. 2, Mexico and the United
States. *v.3 p.509*

The Great Road: The Life and Times of Chu Teh. .*v.6 p.192, p.203*

The Great Rock Discography: Complete Discographies Listing
Every Track Recorded by More Than 1,200
Artists. *v.1 p.171, p.275*

Great Rock Musicals. *v.1 p.253, p.409*

A Great Russia: Russia and the Triple Entente,
1905-1914. . . . .*v.3 p.221*

The Great Salt Lake. *v.3 p.529, p.530*

Great Scientific Experiments: Twenty Experiments That
Changed Our View of the World. *v.5 p.409*

The Great Silent Army of Abolitionism: Ordinary Women in the
Antislavery Movement. *v.6 p.454*

The Great Singers: From the Dawn of Opera to Our Own
Time. *v.1 p.232*

The Great Song Thesaurus. *v.1 p.168, p.251, p.271*

The Great Sophists in Periclean Athens. *v.1 p.427*

Great Spanish Plays: 16th-20th Century. *v.2 p.643*

The Great Tamaulipan Natural Province. *v.5 p.179, p.234*

The Great Tax Wars: Lincoln to Wilson - The Fierce Battles
over Money and Power That Transformed the
Nation. *v.4 p.108, p.147*

The Great Telecom Meltdown. *v.4 p.111, p.165, p.166*

The Great Terror: A Reassessment. *v.3 p.225*

The Great Terror War. *v.4 p.563*

Great Time Coming: The Life of Jackie Robinson from Baseball
to Birmingham. *v.4 p.805, p.831, p.850*

Great Tours!: Thematic Tours and Guide Training for Historic
Sites. *v.1 p.823, p.828*

Great Tranquillity: Questions and Answers. *v.6 p.647*

The Great Transformation: The Beginning of Our Religious
Traditions. *v.1 p.527*

The Great Transformation: The Political and Economic Origins
of Our Time. *v.3 p.41, v.4 p.196, p.210*

Great Transformations: Economic Ideas and Institutional Change
in the Twentieth Century. *v.4 p.487, p.664*

The Great Treks: The Transformation of Southern Africa,
1815-1854. . . . .*v.6 p.79*

A Great Trial in Chinese History: The Trial of the Lin Biao and
Jiang Qing Counter-Revolutionary Cliques, Nov. 1980-Jan.
1981. . . . .*v.4 p.475*

The Great War and Modern Memory. *v.2 p.178*

The Great War and the British People. *v.3 p.93, p.118*

The Great War and the Language of Modernism. *v.2 p.11, p.179*

The Great War and the Search for a Modern Order. . *v.3 p.441*

The Great Wells of Democracy: The Meaning of Race in
American Life. *v.4 p.573*

The Great World. *v.2 p.747, v.3 p.94, p.112*

The Great Zoo and Other Poems. *v.2 p.672*

Greater France: A History of French Overseas
Expansion. *v.3 p.157*

Greater Game: India's Race with Destiny and China. .*v.6 p.160*

The Greater Roman Historians. *v.2 p.426*

The Greater Trumps. *v.2 p.387*

The Greatest Benefit to Mankind: A Medical History of
Humanity from Antiquity to the Present. .*v.3 p.50, v.5 p.510*

The Greatest Good: 100 Years of Forestry in America. .*v.5 p.39*

The Greatest Taboo: Homosexuality in Black
Communities. *v.6 p.38*

The Greatest Threat: Iraq, Weapons of Mass Destruction, and
the Crisis of Global Security. *v.4 p.655*

The Greatness of Flaubert. *v.2 p.491*

El Greco. *v.1 p.737*

Greece, 1941-1949: From Resistance to Civil War: The Strategy
of the Greek Communist Party. *v.3 p.196*

Greece and the Inter-War Economic Crisis. *v.3 p.196*

Greece in the 1940s: A Nation in Crisis. *v.3 p.195*

Greece in the Bronze Age. *v.3 p.16*

Greece Since 1945: Politics, Economy and Society. .*v.3 p.195*

Greece: The Modern Sequel. *v.3 p.194*

Greek and Latin in Scientific Terminology. *v.5 p.406*

Greek and Latin Letters: An Anthology with
Translation. *v.2 p.426*

Greek Architecture. *v.1 p.787*

Greek Art. *v.1 p.669, p.670, p.685, p.687*

Greek Athletes and Athletics. *v.4 p.806*

Greek Athletics and the Genesis of Sport. *v.4 p.809*

Greek Biography and Panegyric in Late Antiquity. . .*v.2 p.401*

The Greek Cities of Magna Graecia and Sicily. *v.3 p.16, v.6 p.711*

The Greek City: From Homer to Alexander. *v.3 p.13*

The Greek City States: A Source Book. *v.3 p.19*

The Greek Cosmologists: The Formation of the Atomic Theory
and Its Earliest Critics. *v.1 p.419, p.420, p.500*

Greek Elegiac Poetry: From the Seventh to the Fifth Centuries
B. C. - Tyrtaeus, Solon, Theognis, and Others. . . .*v.2 p.403*

Greek Federal States: Their Institutions and History. .*v.3 p.21*

Greek Grammar of the New Testament and Other Early
Christian Literature. *v.2 p.399, p.400*

A Greek Grammar. *v.2 p.400*

Greek Grammar. *v.2 p.400*

The Greek Heritage in Victorian
Britain. *v.3 p.116, p.129, v.6 p.751, p.753, p.764*

The Greek Historians of the West: Timaeus and His
Predecessors. *v.2 p.402, p.403, v.3 p.21*

The Greek Historians. *v.2 p.402*

Greek Historians. *v.2 p.402*

Greek Historical Inscriptions, 404-323 BC. *v.3 p.20*

Greek Historiography. *v.2 p.402*

Greek Homosexuality: Updated and with a New
Postscript. *v.3 p.14, v.6 p.364, p.421*

A Greek Island Cosmos: Kinship and Community on Meganisi. *v.4 p.42*

The Greek Language. *v.2 p.400*

Greek Literature, Vol. 1. . . . .*v.2 p.400*

Greek Lyric - Anacreon, Anacreontea, Choral Lyric from Olympus to Alcman, Vol. 2. . . . .*v.2 p.403*

Greek Lyric - Sappho and Alcaeus, Vol. I. *v.2 p.403*

Greek Lyric: Bacchylides, Corinna, and Others. . . .*v.2 p.403*

Greek Lyric Poetry: A Commentary on Selected Larger Pieces (Alcman, Stesichorus, Sappho, Alcaeus, Ibycus, Anacreon, Simonides, Bacchylides, Pindar, Sophocles, Euripides). *v.2 p.403*

Greek Lyric Poetry: A Selection of Early Greek Lyric, Elegiac and Iambic Poetry. *v.2 p.403*

Greek Lyric Poetry from Alcman to Simonides. . . .*v.2 p.403*

Greek Lyric Poetry: The Poems and Fragments of the Greek Iambic, Elegiac, and Melic Poets, Excluding Pindar and Bacchylides, down to 450 BC. *v.2 p.403, p.404*

Greek Lyric Poetry. *v.2 p.403*

Greek Lyric: The New School of Poetry and Anonymous Songs and Hymns. *v.2 p.403*

Greek Manuscripts of the Ancient World. *v.2 p.401*

Greek Medicine: From the Heroic to the Hellenistic Age: A Source Book. *v.2 p.404, p.405*

Greek Musical Writings: Harmonic and Acoustic Theory. *v.1 p.175*

Greek Musical Writings: The Musician and His Art. . .*v.1 p.175*

The Greek Nation, 1453-1669. . . . .*v.3 p.191*

Greek Nymphs: Myth, Cult, Lore. *v.1 p.532, p.533*

Greek Painted Pottery. *v.1 p.807*

Greek Philosophy. *v.1 p.421*

Greek Political Theory, Plato and His Predecessors. . .*v.4 p.488*

Greek Popular Morality in the Time of Plato and Aristotle. *v.1 p.483, v.3 p.14*

Greek Rational Medicine: Philosophy and Medicine from Alcmaeon to the Alexandrians. *v.2 p.405*

Greek Religion: Archaic and Classical. *v.1 p.532, v.3 p.13*

A Greek Roman Empire: Power and Belief under Theodosius II. *v.3 p.32*

Greek Science after Aristotle. *v.2 p.404, v.5 p.392*

Greek Science: Greece and Rome, New Surveys in the Classics, Vol. 29. . . . .*v.2 p.405*

Greek Science in Antiquity. *v.5 p.390*

Greek Science: Its Meaning for Us. *v.5 p.392*

Greek Science of the Hellenistic Era: A Sourcebook. .*v.2 p.404*

Greek Sculpture: An Exploration. *v.1 p.776*

Greek Sculpture: Function, Materials, and Techniques in the Archaic and Classical Periods. *v.1 p.776*

Greek Sculpture: The Late Classical Period and Sculpture in Colonies and Overseas. *v.1 p.775*

Greek society in the making, 1863-1913 : realities, symbols, and visions. *v.3 p.194*

The Greek Struggle for Independence, 1821-1833. . .*v.3 p.194*

Greek Theatre of the Fifth Century Before Christ. .*v.1 p.70, p.154*

Greek Theatre Performance: An Introduction. . .*v.1 p.72, p.138*

Greek Tragedy in Action. *v.2 p.402*

Greek Tragedy. *v.2 p.402*

Greek Tragic Theatre. *v.1 p.71, p.137*

The Greek Tyrants. *v.3 p.16*

Greek Word Order. *v.2 p.400*

The Greek World after Alexander: 323-30 B. C. *v.3 p.21*

A Greek-English Lexicon: With a Revised Supplement 1996. . . . .*v.2 p.400*

The Greeks: A Portrait of Self and Others. *v.3 p.17*

The Greeks and Greek Civilization. *v.3 p.12, p.191*

The Greeks and the Irrational. *v.2 p.400*

The Greeks and Their Gods. *v.1 p.532*

Greeks in Bactria and India. *v.3 p.21, p.22*

Greeks in Ptolemaic Egypt: Case Studies in the Social History of the Hellenistic World. *v.3 p.10*

The Greeks Overseas: Their Early Colonies and Trade. .*v.3 p.16*

Green Against Green: The Irish Civil War. *v.3 p.138*

A Green and Permanent Land: Ecology and Agriculture in the Twentieth Century. *v.5 p.10, p.11*

Green Architecture: The Art of Architecture in the Age of Ecology. *v.1 p.788*

◻ The Green Book: Background Material and Data on Programs Within the Jurisdiction of the House Committee on Ways and Means. *v.4 p.481*

The Green Book of Language Revitalization in Practice: Toward a Sustainable World. *v.4 p.19, v.6 p.690*

Green Book of Language Revitalization in. *v.6 p.691*

The Green Book of Songs by Subject: The Thematic Guide to Popular Music. *v.1 p.160, p.170*

Green Building Guidelines: Meeting the Demand for Low-Energy, Resource-Efficient Homes. *v.1 p.796*

Green Building Materials: A Guide to Product Selection and Specification. *v.1 p.785*

Green Building: Project Planning and Cost Estimating. *v.4 p.63, p.158,v.5 p.685*

Green Cathedrals: A Wayward Traveler in the Rainforest. *v.5 p.182, p.238*

Green Chemistry: An Introductory Text. *v.5 p.310*

Green Chemistry: Frontiers in Benign Chemical Syntheses and Processes. *v.5 p.310*

Green Chemistry: Theory and Practice. *v.5 p.310*

◻ Green Chemistry. *v.5 p.309*

Green Guerrillas: Environmental Conflicts and Intiatives in Latin America and the Caribbean. *v.3 p.268*

Green Halo: A Bird's-Eye View of Ecological Ethics. .*v.6 p.288*

The Green House. *v.2 p.685, p.686*

Green Ink: An Introduction to Environmental Journalism. *v.4 p.407*

The Green Man. *v.2 p.328*

Green Parties and Political Change in Contemporary Europe: New Politics, Old Predicaments. *v.4 p.602*

Green Pastures. *v.2 p.65*

Green Plastics: An Introduction to the New Science of Biodegradable Plastics. *v.5 p.320, v.6 p.294*

The Green Republic: A Conservation History of Costa Rica. *v.3 p.268*

Green River: New and Selected Poems. *v.2 p.151*

Green Roofs: Ecological Design and Construction. . . *v.1 p.817*

Green Screen: Environmentalism and Hollywood
Cinema. *v.6 p.300*

The Green Skyscraper: The Basis for Designing Sustainable
Intensive Buildings. *v.5 p.361, p.374*

Green Thoughts, Green Shades: Essays by Contemporary Poets
on the Early Modern Lyric. *v.2 p.182*

Green Writing: Romanticism and Ecology. . . *v.3 p.45, v.6 p.287*

Greene and Greene: Creating a Style. *v.1 p.802*

Greene: Collected Essays. *v.2 p.349*

☐ Greener Education Materials. *v.5 p.315*

Greener Pastures: Politics, Markets and Community Among a
Migrant Pastoral People. *v.6 p.153*

Greenhouse Operation and Management. *v.5 p.43*

Greening the Americas: NAFTA's Lessons for Hemispheric
Trade. *v.6 p.283, p.298*

Greening the College Curriculum: A Guide to Environmental
Teaching in the Liberal Arts. *v.5 p.369*

Greening the Corporation: Management Strategy and the
Environmental Challenge. *v.4 p.63*

Greening the Firm: The Politics of Corporate
Environmentalism. *v.4 p.63*

Greening the Industrial Facility: Perspectives, Approaches, and
Tools. *v.5 p.373, p.376, p.377*

Greening Trade and Investment: Environmental Protection
Without Protectionism. *v.4 p.63*

Greenspan's Basic and Clinical Endocrinology. . . . *v.5 p.518*

Greenwich Village, 1963: Avant-Garde Performance and the
Effervescent Body. *v.1 p.25, p.40*

The Greenwood Dictionary of Education. *v.4 p.322*

The Greenwood Encyclopedia of African American
Literature. *v.2 p.6, v.6 p.27, p.34*

The Greenwood Encyclopedia of American Regional
Cultures. *v.3 p.444*

The Greenwood Encyclopedia of Science Fiction and Fantasy:
Themes, Works, and Wonders. *v.2 p.581*

The Greenwood Encyclopedia of Women's Issues
Worldwide. *v.4 p.679, v.6 p.426*

The Greenwood Library of American War Reporting. . *v.4 p.406*

A Gregarious Culture: Topical Writings of Miles
Franklin. *v.2 p.745*

Gregarious Saints: Self and Community in American
Abolitionism, 1830-1870. . . . . *v.3 p.420*

The Gregg Reference Manual: A Manual of Style, Grammar,
Usage, and Formatting. *v.4 p.174*

Gregorius: A Medieval Oedipus Legend. *v.2 p.595*

Gregory of Nyssa. *v.1 p.593*

Gregory of Tours : the Merovingians. *v.3 p.162*

Gregory: Selected Writings. *v.2 p.288*

Gregory the Great and His World. *v.1 p.579*

Gregory the Great. *v.1 p.593*

Grenada: A History of Its People. *v.3 p.321*

Grenada: A Study in Politics and the Limits of International
Law. *v.3 p.319*

Grenada and Soviet-Cuban Policy: Internal Crisis and U. S.
OECS Intervention. *v.3 p.321*

The Grenada Documents: Window on Totalitarianism. *v.3 p.319*

The Grenada Invasion: Politics, Law, and Foreign Policy
Decision Making. *v.3 p.318*

Grenada Morning: A Memoir of the "Revo". *v.3 p.321*

The Grenada Papers. *v.3 p.321*

Grenada: The Jewel Despoiled. *v.3 p.320*

Grenada. *v.3 p.319*

The Grenadian Peasantry and Social Revolution,
1930-50. . . . . *v.3 p.318, p.319*

Grendel. *v.2 p.145*

Grettir's Saga. *v.2 p.624*

Grey Area. *v.2 p.380*

La grève des bàttu, ou, Les dèchets humains : roman. *v.2 p.545*

Grief Observed. *v.1 p.652*

The Grifters. *v.2 p.125*

Grignard Reactions of Nonmetallic Substances. . . . *v.5 p.295*

Grillparzer: A Critical Introduction. *v.2 p.597*

The Grim Smile of the Five Towns. *v.2 p.334*

The Grimke Sisters from South Carolina. . . . *v.3 p.398, p.420*

☐ GRIN Taxonomy for Plants. *v.5 p.206, p.207, p.211*

The Gringo's Hawk. *v.3 p.269*

Groovin' High: The Life of Dizzy Gillespie. . *v.1 p.263, p.326*

Groping for Ethics in Journalism. *v.4 p.406*

La Grosse Femme d'a Cote Est Enceinte: Roman. . . *v.2 p.541*

Grossere Hoffnung. *v.2 p.602*

The Grotowski Sourcebook. *v.1 p.111, p.146*

Ground Anchors and Anchored Structures. *v.5 p.697*

Ground Rules: Baseball and Myth. *v.4 p.812, p.852*

☐ Ground Water Atlas of the United States. *v.5 p.428*

Ground Work: Before the War/In the Dark. *v.2 p.144*

Groundbreaking Scientific Experiments, Inventions and
Discoveries of the 17th Century. . *v.3 p.46, v.5 p.389, p.390*

Groundbreaking Scientific Experiments, Inventions and
Discoveries of the 18th Century. *v.3 p.45, v.5 p.389*

Groundbreaking Scientific Experiments, Inventions and
Discoveries of the 19th Century. *v.3 p.46, v.5 p.390*

Groundbreaking Scientific Experiments, Inventions, and
Discoveries of the Ancient World. . . . *v.3 p.45, v.5 p.389*

Groundbreaking Scientific Experiments, Inventions, and
Discoveries of the Middle Ages and the
Renaissance. . . *v.3 p.45, v.5 p.388, p.389, v.6 p.575, p.576*

The Grounding of American Poetry: Charles Olson and the
Emersonian Tradition. *v.2 p.108*

The Grounding of Modern Feminism. . . . *v.4 p.723, v.6 p.433*

Groundswell: Constructing the Contemporary
Landscape. *v.1 p.814*

Groundwater Chemicals Desk Reference. *v.5 p.313*

Groundwater Contamination by Organic Pollutants: Analysis and
Remediation. *v.5 p.368, p.375, p.379*

Groundwater Contamination from Hazardous
Wastes. *v.5 p.369, p.380*

Groundwater Geomorphology: The Role of Subsurface Water in
Earth-Surface Processes and Landforms. *v.5 p.428*

Groundwater Hydraulics and Pollutant
Transport. *v.5 p.379, v.6 p.289*

Groundwater Hydrology. *v.5 p.428*

Groundwater in Geologic Processes. *v.5 p.428*

Groundwater. *v.5 p.428*

Groundwork: Charles Hamilton Houston and the Struggle for Civil Rights. *v.6 p.12, p.21, p.22*

Groundwork for the Metaphysics of Morals. *v.1 p.462*

Groundwork of the Metaphysics of Morals. *v.1 p.461, p.462, p.484*

Group Creativity: Innovation through Collaboration. . .*v.5 p.648*

The Group of Seven and Tom Thomson. *v.1 p.747*

Group Performance and Interaction. *v.5 p.648*

Group Portrait with Lady. *v.2 p.604*

Group Processes: Dynamics Within and Between Groups. *v.4 p.692*

Group Processes in the Classroom. *v.4 p.350*

Group Psychology and Political Theory. . .*v.4 p.483, v.5 p.642*

Group Rights: Reconciling Equality and Difference. . .*v.4 p.576*

Group Theory and Its Application to Physical Problems. .*v.5 p.548*

Group Theory in Chemistry and Spectroscopy. *v.5 p.280*

Group Theory in Physics: An Introduction to Symmetry Principles, Group Representations, and Special Functions. *v.5 p.548*

Group Theory in Physics: An Introduction. *v.5 p.548*

Groups and Symmetry. *v.5 p.474, p.494*

Groups in Harmony and Tension: An Integration of Studies on Intergroup Relations. *v.4 p.717*

Groups, Interests, and U. S. Public Policy. *v.4 p.559*

The Group. *v.2 p.99*

Groupwork in Diverse Classrooms: A Casebook for Educators. *v.4 p.350*

▢ Grove Art Online. *v.1 p.661, p.662*

The Grove Companion to Samuel Beckett: A Reader's Guide to His Works, Life, and Thought. *v.2 p.332*

▢ Grove Music Online. *v.1 p.159, p.227, p.256, p.257*

Grover Cleveland: A Study in Character. *v.3 p.394*

Grover Cleveland: A Study in Courage, Vol. 2. . . .*v.3 p.437*

The Groves of Academe. *v.2 p.99*

Grow Long, Blessed Night: Love Poems from Classical India. *v.6 p.148*

Growing Minds. *v.4 p.337*

Growing Old in El Barrio. *v.4 p.741, p.742,v.6 p.542, p.543, p.548*

Growing Old Is Not for Sissies 2: Portraits of Senior Athletes. *v.4 p.841*

Growing Prosperity: The Battle for Growth with Equity in the Twenty-First Century. *v.4 p.722*

Growing Through the Ugly. *v.6 p.504*

Growing Together: Personal Relationships Across the Life Span. *v.4 p.741, v.5 p.648*

Growing up American: How Vietnamese Children Must Adapt to Life in the United States. *v.6 p.109, p.110, p.141*

Growing up American: Schooling and the Survival of Community. *v.4 p.303, p.315, p.367*

Growing up Asian American: Stories of Childhood, Adolescence and Coming of Age. *v.6 p.91*

Growing up Bilingual: Puerto Rican Children in New York. *v.4 p.21*

Growing up Ethnic in America: Contemporary Fiction about Learning to Be American. *v.2 p.26*

Growing up Fast. *v.4 p.759*

Growing up Forgotten. *v.4 p.736*

Growing Up Gay/Growing Up Lesbian: A Literary Anthology. *v.6 p.407*

Growing up in a Lesbian Family: Effects on Child Development. *v.6 p.376*

Growing up in the People's Republic: Conversations between Two Daughters of China's Revolution. .*v.6 p.196, p.203, p.217*

Growing up Literate: Learning from Inner-City Families. *v.4 p.762*

Growing up Nisei: Race, Generation and Culture among Japanese Americans of California, 1924-49. .*v.6 p.115, p.133*

Growing up Palestinian: Israeli Occupation and the Intifada Generation. *v.6 p.617*

Growing up Puerto Rican: 20 Puerto Rican Authors Write in Fiction and Essay about Childhood. *v.6 p.495, p.505, p.506*

Growing up Teaching: Kay's Journey. *v.4 p.277*

Growing up to Be Violent: A Longitudinal Study of the Development of Aggression. *v.5 p.627*

Growing up with a Single Parent: What Hurts, What Helps. *v.4 p.739*

Growing up Working Class: Continuity and Change among Viennese Youth 1890-1938. . . . .*v.3 p.185*

Growing Young. *v.4 p.737*

Growth Against Development: The Economic Impact of Railroads in Porfirian Mexico. *v.3 p.288, p.289*

Growth and Mineral Nutrition of Field Crops, Vol. 57. . . . .*v.5 p.21, p.25*

Growth and Structure of the English Language. . . .*v.2 p.554*

Growth Company: Dow Chemical's First Century. . .*v.5 p.316*

Growth of American Thought. *v.3 p.367*

Growth of Cities in the Nineteenth Century. *v.6 p.716*

The Growth of Islam among the Yoruba, 1841-1908. . .*v.6 p.71*

The Growth of Leaves of Grass: The Organic Tradition in Whitman Studies. *v.2 p.53*

The Growth of Logical Thinking from Childhood to Adolescence. *v.5 p.628, p.630*

Growth of Medieval Theology (600-1300), Vol. 3. . .*v.1 p.634*

The Growth of Mysticism: From Gregory the Great Through the 12th Century, Vol. 2. . . . .*v.1 p.653*

The Growth of Papal Government in the Middle Ages; a Study in the Ideological Relation of Clerical to Lay Power. *v.1 p.574, v.3 p.58*

Growth of Political Stability. *v.3 p.93, p.101, p.106*

The Growth of Scientific Ideas. *v.5 p.389*

The Growth of Social Knowledge: Theory, Simulation, and Empirical Research in Group Processes. *v.4 p.690*

Growth of Southern Civilization, 1790-1860. . . . .*v.3 p.495*

The Growth of Southern Nationalism, 1848-1861. . . . .*v.3 p.395, p.495*

The Growth of the American Republic, Vol. II. . . .*v.3 p.380*

The Growth of the American Republic, Vol. I. . . .*v.3 p.380*

The Growth of the Law. *v.4 p.433*

Growth of the Medieval City: From Late Antiquity to the Early Fourteenth Century. *v.3 p.44*

Growth of the Soil. *v.2 p.628*

The Growth of Victorian London. *v.3 p.114*

Growth Recurring: Economic Change in World History. *v.4 p.209*

Growth Theory: An Exposition. *v.4 p.245*

Growth Triumphant: The Twenty-First Century in Historical
Perspective. *v.4 p.243*

Grub Street and the Ivory Tower: Literary Journalism and
Literary Scholarship from Fielding to the Internet. *v.4 p.403*

☐ Grubb & Ellis Real Estate Forecast. *v.4 p.158*

Grueze the Draftsman. *v.1 p.723*

Gruppe 47 [I. E. Siebenundvierzig], ein Querschnitt: An
Anthology of Contemporary German Literature. . .*v.2 p.593*

Gruppenbild Mit Dame. *v.2 p.604*

Grzimek's Animal Life Encyclopedia, Set. . . .*v.6 p.285, p.291*

Guaman Poma: Writing and Resistance in Colonial
Peru. *v.3 p.262*

Guanxi (the Art of Relationships): Microsoft, China, and Bill
Gates's Plan to Win the Road Ahead. *v.4 p.157*

The Guarani under Spanish Rule in the Rio de la
Plata. *v.3 p.343, p.344*

Guarantee Clause of the U. S. Constitution. *v.4 p.455*

Guard of Honor. *v.2 p.65*

Guardians of the Dynasty: A History of the U. S. Created
Guardia Nacional De Nicaragua and the Somoza
Family. *v.3 p.275, p.276*

Guardians of the Nation?: Economists, Generals, and Economic
Reform in Latin America. *v.3 p.273*

Guarding Greensboro: A Confederate Company in the Making
of a Southern Community. *v.4 p.521*

Guarding the Golden Door: American Immigration Policy and
Immigrants since 1882. . . . .*v.4 p.570, v.6 p.118, p.120*

Guatemala in the Spanish Colonial Period. *v.3 p.298*

The Guatemalan Military Project: A Violence Called
Democracy. *v.3 p.277*

Gubernatorial Elections, 1787-1997. . . . .*v.4 p.557*

Gubernatorial Transitions: The 1983 and 1984
Elections. *v.4 p.548, p.557*

Guerilla Documentary Film Makers Handbook. . . .*v.6 p.347*

Guerilla Film Makers. *v.6 p.347*

Les Guerilleres. *v.2 p.534*

Guerilleres. *v.2 p.534*

Les Guerilleres. *v.6 p.400*

The Guermantes Way: In Search of Lost Time. . . .*v.2 p.524*

Guernica and Other Plays: The Labyrinth, The Tricycle, Picnic
on the Battlefield, and They Put Handcuffs on the
Flowers, The Architect and the Emperor of Assyria, Garden
of Delights. *v.2 p.507*

La Guerra del Fin del Mundo. *v.2 p.686*

La Guerre, Yes Sir!. *v.2 p.540*

La Guerre. *v.2 p.531*

Guerrilla Prince: The Untold Story of Fidel Castro. . *v.3 p.309*

The Guerrilla Wars of Central America: Nicaragua, El Salvador
and Guatemala. *v.3 p.299, p.302*

Guerrillas and Generals: The "Dirty War" in
Argentina. *v.3 p.275, p.348, v.4 p.592*

Guerrillas and Revolution in Latin America: A Comparative
Study of Insurgents and Regimes since 1956. . . .*v.4 p.498*

Guerrillas. *v.2 p.769*

A Guest for the Night. *v.6 p.646, p.647*

Guests of the Sheik: An Ethnography of an Iraqi
Village. *v.6 p.602*

☐ La Guia:Internet Resources for Latin America. . .*v.3 p.260*

The Guide: A Novel. *v.2 p.765*

Guide for the Care and Use of Laboratory Animals. . *v.5 p.674*

The Guide for the Perplexed. *v.1 p.433*

Guide Through the District of the Lakes in the North of
England: With a Description of the Scenery for
the Use of Tourists and Residents. *v.3 p.110, p.127*

Guide to Aesthetics. *v.1 p.473, p.480, v.2 p.566*

A Guide to African Cinema. *v.6 p.334*

A Guide to American Zoos and Aquariums. *v.5 p.83*

Guide to Analysis of DNA Microarray
Data. *v.5 p.100, p.110, p.122*

Guide to Basic Information Sources in Chemistry. . . .*v.5 p.255*

Guide to British Poetry Explication: Old English -
Medieval. *v.6 p.565*

Guide to Business Modelling. *v.4 p.179*

The Guide to Careers in Sports. *v.4 p.903*

Guide to Chamber Music. *v.1 p.238*

A Guide to Chaucer's Meter. *v.2 p.209*

A Guide to Chicago's Murals. *v.1 p.731*

Guide to Chinese Prose. *v.6 p.212*

A Guide to Collections on Paraguay in the United
States. *v.3 p.344*

A Guide to Conducting Prevention Research in the Community:
First Steps. *v.5 p.671*

A Guide to Contemporary Italian Literature, from Futurism to
Neorealism. *v.2 p.698*

A Guide to Copyright for Museums and Galleries. . .*v.1 p.827*

Guide to Corporate Giving in the Arts 4. . . . . .*v.1 p.825*

Guide to Dance in Film. *v.1 p.36*

🄴 A Guide to Econometrics. *v.4 p.202*

A Guide to Econometrics. *v.4 p.202*

Guide to Economic Indicators. *v.4 p.178*

Guide to Effective Coaching: Principles and Practices with
PowerWeb: Health and Human Performance. *v.4 p.904*

Guide to Electric Power Generation. *v.5 p.724*

Guide to Electrical Power Distribution Systems. . . .*v.5 p.724*

A Guide to Experiments in Quantum Optics. *v.5 p.562*

Guide to Ezra Pound's Selected Cantos. *v.2 p.111*

A Guide to Films on the Korean War. *v.6 p.322*

Guide to Financial Markets. *v.4 p.96, p.102, p.103*

A Guide to Folktales in the English Language: Based on the
Aarne-Thompson Classification System. *v.2 p.584*

A Guide to Food Laws and Regulations. . . .*v.4 p.151, p.165*

A Guide to French Literature: Early Modern to
Postmodernism. *v.2 p.457*

Guide to French Poetry Explication. *v.2 p.460*

☐ Guide to Geoscience Careers and Employers. . .*v.5 p.417*

☐ Guide to Geoscience Departments. . *v.5 p.417, p.418, p.419*

A Guide to Golf Course Irrigation System Design and
Drainage. *v.4 p.872, p.881, p.906*

Guide to Graduate Business Schools. *v.4 p.176*

Guide to Greek Theatre and Drama. *v.1 p.71*

Guide to Information Sources in Engineering. *v.5 p.679*

Guide to Internet Job Searching 2006-2007. . . . . .*v.4 p.169*

A Guide to Jewish Religious Practice. *v.1 p.552*

A Guide to Lasers in Chemistry. *v.5 p.278*

Guide to LaTeX. *v.5 p.461*

Guide to Managerial Communication. *v.4 p.173*

Guide to Materials Engineering Data and Information. *v.5 p.731*

Guide to Metallurgical Information. *v.5 p.732*

🄴 A Guide to Modern Econometrics. *v.4 p.205*

A Guide to Modern Econometrics. *v.4 p.205*

Guide to Modern Japanese Woodblock Prints,
1900-1975. . . . .*v.1 p.753*

A Guide to Monte Carlo Simulations in Statistical
Physics. *v.5 p.551*

A Guide to Musical Analysis. *v.1 p.370*

Guide to Nonprofit Corporate Governance in the Wake of
Sarbanes-Oxley. *v.4 p.85*

A Guide to Old English. *v.2 p.206, p.550*

A Guide to Organophosphorus Chemistry. *v.5 p.296*

Guide to Political Campaigns in America. *v.4 p.548*

🄳 Guide to Polymer Abbreviations/Tradenames. . .*v.5 p.321*

A Guide to Post-Keynesian Economics. *v.4 p.232*

Guide to Programs in Geography in the United States and
Canada 2001-2002. . . . .*v.4 p.373*

Guide to Protein Purification, Vol. 182. . . . . . .*v.5 p.115*

Guide to Record Retention Requirements as of August
2005. . . . .*v.4 p.115*

Guide to Reference Books: Covering Materials from 1985-1990,
Supplement to the Tenth Edition. *v.5 p.405*

Guide to Reference Books. *v.5 p.405*

A Guide to Research in Music Education. *v.1 p.173, p.174, p.406*

Guide to Rocks and Minerals. *v.5 p.435*

A Guide to Russian Words and Expressions That Cause
Difficulties. *v.2 p.776*

A Guide to Schenkerian Analysis. *v.1 p.372*

A Guide to Silent Westerns. *v.6 p.324*

A Guide to Sociological Thinking. *v.4 p.676*

Guide to Sonatas: Music for One or Two Instruments. *v.1 p.238*

Guide to Spectroscopic Identification of Organic
Compounds. *v.5 p.300*

A Guide to Statistical Sources in Money, Banking, and
Finance. *v.4 p.88*

Guide to Sustainable Development and Environmental
Policy. *v.6 p.286*

A Guide to Taijiquan: Twenty-Four and Forty-Eight Postures
with Applications. *v.4 p.793*

Guide to Teaching Brass. *v.1 p.396*

A Guide to the Culture of Science, Technology, and
Medicine. *v.5 p.410, p.411*

A Guide to the Gamelan. *v.1 p.290*

A Guide to the History of Florida. *v.3 p.504*

A Guide to the History of Illinois: Reference Guides to State
History and Research. *v.3 p.515*

A Guide to the History of Pennsylvania: Reference Guides to
State History and Research. *v.3 p.491*

Guide to the Literature of Art History, Vol. 2. . . . .*v.1 p.662*

Guide to the Literature of Art History. *v.1 p.661, p.662*

Guide to the National Wildlife Refuges. . .*v.5 p.84, p.85, p.235*

A Guide to the Oriental Classics. *v.6 p.208*

🄴 Guide to the Pianist's Repertoire. . .*v.1 p.167, p.239, p.398*

Guide to the Poetry of William Carlos Williams. . . .*v.2 p.136*

Guide to the Practical Study of Harmony. *v.1 p.374*

A Guide to the Preventative Conservation of Photograph
Collections. *v.1 p.824*

A Guide to the Sacraments. *v.1 p.657*

A Guide to the Sculpture Parks and Gardens of
America. *v.1 p.774, p.812*

A Guide to the Selected Poems of T. S. Eliot. *v.2 p.72*

Guide to the Silent Years of American Cinema. *v.6 p.332*

A Guide to the Sources of United States Military History,
Supplement III. *v.3 p.383*

A Guide to the Sources of United States Military History,
Supplement II. *v.3 p.383*

A Guide to the Sources of United States Military History,
Supplement I. *v.3 p.383*

A Guide to the Sources of United States Military History,
Supplement IV. *v.3 p.383*

A Guide to the Sources of United States Military
History. *v.3 p.383*

Guide to the U.S. Supreme Court. *v.4 p.466, p.539*

Guide to the Use of the Wind Load Provisions of ASCE
7-02. . . . .*v.5 p.686*

Guide to the Works of John Dewey. *v.4 p.341*

A Guide to Trollope. *v.2 p.316*

Guide to U. S. Elections. *v.4 p.547, p.548*

The Guide to United States Popular Culture. *v.3 p.366*

A Guide to Vocational Assessment. *v.4 p.305, p.353*

Guide to Wetlands: A Comprehensive and Fascinating Guide to
the Wetlands of the World. *v.5 p.53, v.6 p.293*

Guide to Writing and Publishing in the Social and Behavioral
Sciences Cloth. *v.4 p.675*

A Guide to Writing as an Engineer. *v.5 p.680*

Guide to Yeast Genetics and Molecular and Cell Biology, Vol.
351, Pt. C. *v.5 p.153*

Guide to Yeast Genetics and Molecular Cell Biology, Vol. 350,
Pt. B. *v.5 p.153*

Guidebook for Selecting Appropriate Technology Systems for
Small Urban and Rural Public Transportation
Operators. *v.5 p.701*

A Guidebook to Mechanism in Organic Chemistry. . .*v.5 p.292*

🄳 Guidelines for Ethical Conduct in the Care and Use of
Animals. *v.5 p.674*

Guidelines for Fire Protection in Chemical, Petrochemical, and
Hydrocarbon Processing Facilities. *v.5 p.743*

Guidelines for Institutional Policies and Planning in Natural
History Collections. *v.5 p.220*

Guidelines for Investigating Chemical Process
Incidents. *v.5 p.743*

Guidelines for Mechanical Integrity Systems. *v.5 p.743*

Guidelines for Safe and Reliable Instrumented Protective Systems. *v.5 p.742*

Guidelines for Safe Handling of Powders and Bulk Solids. *v.5 p.743, p.744*

Guidelines for Style Analysis. *v.1 p.371*

☐ GuideStar.org. *v.4 p.545*

Guidée par le songe : nouvelles (texte intégral). *v.2 p.508*

Guido Cavalcanti: The Other Middle Ages. *v.2 p.702*

Guillaume Apollinaire. *v.2 p.507*

Guillaume de Machaut: A Guide to Research. *v.1 p.163, p.177, p.338*

Guillaume de Machaut and Reims: Context and Meaning in His Musical Works. *v.1 p.178, p.338*

Guillaume de Machaut. *v.1 p.178, p.338*

Guillen on Guillen: The Poetry and the Poet. *v.2 p.658*

Guillermo Cabrera Infante. *v.2 p.673*

The Guinea Pig: Healing, Food, and Ritual in the Andes. .*v.3 p.272*

The Guinea Pigs. *v.2 p.784*

Guinea-Bissau: Politics, Economics, and Society. *v.6 p.73*

The Guitar: A Guide for Students and Teachers. *v.1 p.391*

The Guitar and Its Music. *v.1 p.392*

The Guitar: The History, the Music, the Players. . . .*v.1 p.390*

The Gulag Archipelago, 1918-1956. . . . .*v.2 p.808, v.4 p.753*

The Gulf of Years: Letters from John Ruskin to Kathleen Olander. *v.2 p.306*

Gulf States. *v.4 p.382*

The Gulistan; or Rose-Garden or Shekh Muslihu'd-Din Sadi of Shiraz: Trubner's Oriental Series. *v.6 p.672*

Gullivers Travels. *v.2 p.263*

The Gull's Hornbook. *v.2 p.217, p.218*

The Gun and the Olive Branch: The Roots of Violence in the Middle East. *v.6 p.617*

Gun Control and Gun Rights: A Reader and Guide. . .*v.6 p.266*

Gun Control and Gun Rights. *v.6 p.266*

Gun Control and the Constitution: Sources and Explorations on the Second Amendment. *v.4 p.449*

The Gun Control Debate: You Decide. *v.6 p.266*

A Gun for Sale. *v.2 p.350*

Gun Violence: Opposing Viewpoints. *v.6 p.266*

Gunboats, Corruption, and Claims: Foreign Intervention in Venezuela, 1899-1908. . . . .*v.3 p.361*

Gunfighter Nation: The Myth of the Frontier in Twentieth-Century America. *v.6 p.324, p.325*

Gunga Din Highway. *v.6 p.99*

The Gunpower Empires and Modern Times, Vol. 3. . .*v.1 p.555*

Guns, Crime, and Punishment in America. *v.6 p.266*

Guns, Germs, and Steel: The Fates of Human Societies. *v.4 p.627, p.628*

Guns in American Society: An Encyclopedia of History, Politics, Culture, and the Law, Set. *v.4 p.485*

e Guns in American Society: An Encyclopedia of History, Politics, Culture, and the Law. *v.6 p.266*

The Guns of '62: The Image of War, 1861-1865. . . .*v.3 p.431*

Gunslinger. *v.2 p.144*

Gunter Grass: The Writer in a Pluralist Society. . . .*v.2 p.608*

Guru Nanak and the Sikh Religion. *v.1 p.540, p.541*

Gurus, Hired Guns, and Warm Bodies: Itinerant Experts in a Knowledge Economy. *v.4 p.268*

Gus Van Sant: An Unauthorized Biography. *v.6 p.419*

Gustav Mahler: Songs and Symphonies of Life and Death - Interpretations and Annotations. *v.1 p.219, p.339*

Gustav Mahler: The Early Years. *v.1 p.219, p.339*

Gustav Mahler: the Wunderhorn Years: Chronicles and Commentaries. *v.1 p.219, p.339*

Gustav Mahler: Vienna: The Years of Challenge (1897-1904). *v.1 p.212, p.339*

Gustav Mahler: Vienna: Triumph and Disillusion (1904-1907). *v.1 p.212, p.339*

Gustav Stresemann: Weimar's Greatest Statesman. *v.3 p.170, p.171*

Gustave Flaubert's Madame Bovary. *v.2 p.490*

Gustave Flaubert. *v.2 p.490*

Gustave Stickley's Craftsman Farms: The Quest for an Arts and Crafts Utopia. *v.1 p.793*

Gustavus Adolphus and the Rise of Sweden. *v.3 p.235*

Gut Reactions: A Perceptual Theory of Emotion. .*v.5 p.655, p.656*

Gutcheck!: An Anthropologist's Wild Ride into the Heart of College Football. *v.4 p.819, p.859, p.894, p.895*

The Gutenberg Galaxy: The Making of Typographic Man. *v.2 p.577*

Guts and Glory: The Making of the American Military Image in Film. *v.6 p.323*

Guts: Legendary Black Rodeo Cowboy Bill Pickett. *v.4 p.832, p.865*

Guy de Maupassant Revisited. *v.2 p.497*

Guy Mannering. *v.2 p.307*

Guys and Dolls. *v.2 p.114*

Guys Like Us: Citing Masculinity in Cold War Poetics. .*v.6 p.478*

Guzman de Alfarache: The Unrepentant Narrator. . .*v.2 p.650*

Gyn/Ecology: The Metaethics of Radical Feminism. . .*v.6 p.461*

Gyorgy Ligeti: Contemporary Composer. *v.1 p.215, p.336*

Gyorgy Ligeti: Music of the Imagination. . . .*v.1 p.224, p.336*

Gyorgy Ligeti. *v.1 p.226, p.336*

The Gypsies and Other Narrative Poems. *v.2 p.807*

Gypsy Ballads. *v.2 p.659*

Gypsy. *v.1 p.36, p.254, p.410*

H

H. D. and Sapphic Modernism 1910-1950. . .*v.2 p.88, v.6 p.392*

H. D. and the Image. *v.2 p.88*

H. D. and the Victorian Fin de Siècle: Gender, Modernism, Decadence. *v.2 p.89*

H. D.: The Poetics of Childbirth and Creativity. . . .*v.2 p.89*

H. D.'s Freudian Poetics: Psychoanalysis in Translation. *v.2 p.88*

H. D.'s Poetry: "The Meanings That Words Hide": Essays. *v.2 p.88*

H. G. Wells and the Culminating Ape: Biological Imperatives and Imaginative Obsessions. *v.2 p.319*

An H. G. Wells Companion: A Guide to the Novels, Romances, and Short Stories. *v.2 p.319*

H. G. Wells: Traversing Time. *v.2 p.319*

H. G. Wells. *v.2 p.319*

H. H. Richardson: The Architect, His Peers, and Their
Era. *v.1 p.794*

H. L. Mencken and the American Mercury Adventure. *v.4 p.410*

H. L. Mencken's Smart Set Criticism. *v.2 p.4*

H. M. Pulham, Esq. *v.2 p.97*

H. N. Werkman. *v.1 p.720*

H. P. Lovecraft: Tales. *v.2 p.94, p.95*

Habakkuk: A New Translation with Introduction and
Commentary. *v.1 p.622*

Habeas Corpus: Rethinking the Great Writ of Liberty. .*v.4 p.524*

The Habermas Reader. *v.4 p.770*

Habib Bourguiba, Islam and the Creation of Tunisia. .*v.6 p.642*

Habitat, Economy and Society: A Geographical Introduction to
Ethnology. *v.4 p.29*

Habitations of Modernity: Essays in the Wake of Subaltern
Studies. *v.6 p.146*

Habitats and Ecosystems: An Encyclopedia of Endangered
America. *v.5 p.178, p.356*

The Habits of Legality: Criminal Justice and the Rule of the
Law. *v.6 p.268*

Habits of the Heart: Individualism and Commitment in
American Life. *v.3 p.366, p.370,v.4 p.720*

Habits: Their Making and Unmaking. *v.5 p.666*

The Habsburg Monarchy 1490-1848: Attributes of
Empire. *v.3 p.181*

The Habsburg Monarchy, 1618-1815. . . . .*v.3 p.181*

The Habsburg Monarchy, 1809-1918: A History of the Austrian
Empire and Austria-Hungary. *v.3 p.182*

The Habsburg Monarchy among the Great Powers,
1815-1918. . . . .*v.3 p.182*

The Habsburg Monarchy, C. 1765-1918: From Enlightenment to
Eclipse. *v.3 p.181, p.182*

Haciendas and Ayllus: Rural Society in the Bolivian Andes in
the Eighteenth and Nineteenth Centuries. *v.3 p.324*

Hacker Culture. *v.4 p.709*

The Hacker Ethic: And the Spirit of the Information
Age. *v.4 p.761*

A Hacker Manifesto. *v.4 p.761*

Hadrian and the Cities of the Roman Empire.*v.3 p.27, v.6 p.710*

Hadrian and the City of Rome. *v.3 p.27*

Hadrian: The Restless Emperor. *v.3 p.27*

Hadriana dans tous mes rêves : roman. *v.2 p.536, p.537*

Hadriana in My Dreams. *v.2 p.535*

Haeckel's Art Forms from Nature. *v.5 p.230*

Haggai, Zechariah 1-8. . . . .*v.1 p.623*

Hagiography and the Cult of Saints: The Diocese of Orléans,
800-1200. . . . .*v.6 p.571*

The Haider Phenomenon in Austria. *v.4 p.595, p.596*

The Haider Phenomenon. *v.4 p.595*

A Haiku Journey: Basho's Narrow Road to a Far
Province. *v.6 p.234*

Hail and Farewell!, Vol. 1. . . . .*v.2 p.300*

Hail and Farewell!, Vol. 2. . . . .*v.2 p.300*

Hail to the Chief: The Making and Unmaking of American
Presidents. *v.3 p.377, p.378*

Hailey: A Study in British Imperialism, 1872-1969. .*v.3 p.124*

Hair in African Art and Culture. *v.1 p.716*

Hair Raising: Beauty, Culture, and African American
Women. *v.6 p.40, p.46, p.448*

Hair Story: Untangling the Roots of Black Hair in
America. *v.6 p.38, p.42*

Hair: The American Tribal Love-Rock Musical. *v.1 p.252, p.408*

Haiti and the Dominican Republic. *v.3 p.317*

Haiti, History and the Gods. *v.3 p.314*

Haiti in the New World Order: The Limits of the Democratic
Revolution. *v.3 p.314*

The Haiti Issue: 1804 and Nineteenth-Century French
Studies. *v.3 p.315*

Haiti Singing. *v.1 p.291*

🄴 Haitian Revolutionary Studies. *v.3 p.314*

The Haitian Trilogy: Plays: Henri Christophe, Drums and
Colours, and The Haytian Earth. *v.2 p.770*

Haitian-Dominican Counterpoint. *v.3 p.315, p.317*

Haitians and African Americans: A Hertiage of Tragedy and
Hope. *v.3 p.315*

Halakhic Man. *v.1 p.552*

Halcyon. *v.2 p.716*

Half a Life. *v.2 p.769*

Half Bitter, Half Sweet; an Excursion into Italian-American
History. *v.3 p.387, p.388*

Half Brother, Half Son: The Letters of Louis D. Brandeis to
Felix Frankfurter. *v.4 p.469*

A Half Caste and Other Writings. *v.6 p.102*

Half Past Autumn: A Retrospective. *v.1 p.768*

Halfway Home. *v.6 p.379, p.398*

Hall of Mirrors: Power, Witchcraft, and Caste in Colonial
Mexico. *v.3 p.263, p.286*

The Hall of Three Pines: An Account of My Life. . . .*v.6 p.200*

Hallaj: Mystic and Martyr. *v.1 p.555*

Halldor Laxness. *v.2 p.625*

Halliday: System and Function in Language: Selected
Papers. *v.2 p.561*

Hallmarks of Effective Outcomes Assessment: Assessment
Update Collections. *v.4 p.285*

Hallucinogens and Culture. *v.4 p.776, v.5 p.663*

Halogen Chemistry, 3 v. *v.5 p.309*

The Halt in the Mud: French Strategic Planning from Waterloo
to Sedan. *v.3 p.141*

Ham on Rye. *v.2 p.141*

Hamilton Fish: The Inner History of the Grant
Administration. *v.3 p.434*

Hamlet in Purgatory. *v.2 p.229*

Hamlet on the Holodeck: The Future of Narrative in
Cyberspace. *v.5 p.341, p.342*

Hamletmachine and Other Texts for the Stage. . . .*v.2 p.618*

Hamlet's Perfection. *v.2 p.230*

Hamlet. *v.2 p.225*

Hammer and Hoe: Alabama Communists During the Great
Depression. *v.4 p.508, p.553*

The Hammer and the Flute: Women, Power, and Spirit
Possession. *v.1 p.527*

Hammer Blows. *v.2 p.544*

The Hammon and the Beans and Other Stories. *v.2 p.109, v.6 p.502*

Hamp: An Autobiography. *v.1 p.260, p.328*

The Han Dynasty. *v.6 p.185*

Han Social Structure. *v.4 p.701, v.6 p.185*

Han Sorya and North Korean Literature: The Failure of Socialist Realism in the DPRK. *v.6 p.238*

Handbook for AOAC members. *v.5 p.267*

A Handbook for Classroom Instruction That Works. .*v.4 p.364*

A Handbook for Classroom Management That Works. .*v.4 p.284*

A Handbook for Developing Multicultural Awareness. .*v.5 p.637*

Handbook for Enhancing Undergraduate Education in Psychology. *v.5 p.676*

A Handbook for Geography Teachers. *v.4 p.376, p.377*

Handbook for Measurement and Evaluation in Early Childhood Education. *v.4 p.356*

A Handbook for Modern Educational Dance. *v.1 p.48*

A Handbook for Museum Trustees. *v.1 p.828*

Handbook for Preparing Engineering Documents: From Concept to Completion. *v.5 p.681*

Handbook for Restoring Tidal Wetlands. *v.5 p.241, p.242*

Handbook for the Treatment of Abused and Neglected Children. *v.4 p.756*

Handbook for Working with Children and Youth: Pathways to Resilience Across Cultures and Contexts. *v.5 p.629*

Handbook of Adolescent Behavioral Problems: Evidence-Based Approaches to Prevention and Treatment. *v.5 p.625*

Handbook of Adolescent Psychology. *v.5 p.642*

Handbook of Adult Development. *v.5 p.626*

The Handbook of Advanced Materials: Enabling New Designs. *v.5 p.692*

Handbook of Advanced Materials Testing, Vol. 9. . . .*v.5 p.688*

Handbook of Affect and Social Cognition. .*v.5 p.649, p.652, p.653*

Handbook of Affective Sciences. *v.5 p.611*

The Handbook of African American Literature. . .*v.6 p.24, p.35*

Handbook of Aging and the Family. *v.5 p.638*

Handbook of Aging and the Social Sciences. *v.4 p.741*

Handbook of Agricultural Economics, Vol. 1. . . . .*v.4 p.189*

Handbook of Agricultural Economics, Vol. 2. . . . .*v.4 p.189*

Handbook of Agricultural Meteorology. *v.5 p.49*

Handbook of Aluminum: Alloy Production and Materials Manufacturing. *v.5 p.736*

Handbook of Aluminum: Physical Metallurgy and Processes, Vol. 1. . . . .*v.5 p.736*

Handbook of American Film Genres. *v.6 p.311*

Handbook of American Folklore. *v.2 p.17*

Handbook of American Popular Culture, Vol. 3. . . .*v.3 p.368*

Handbook of American Women's History. *v.6 p.450*

Handbook of Analytical Techniques, Set. *v.5 p.267, p.268*

Handbook of Antisocial Behavior. *v.5 p.661*

Handbook of Applied Behavior Analysis. *v.5 p.666*

Handbook of Applied Econometrics: Microeconomics. *v.4 p.191, p.203*

The Handbook of Applied Linguistics. *v.2 p.560, v.5 p.620, p.623*

Handbook of Applied Mathematics: Selected Results and Methods. *v.5 p.461, p.500*

Handbook of Aqueous Electrolyte Solutions: Physical Properties, Estimation and Correlation Methods. *v.5 p.282*

The Handbook of Art and Design Terms. *v.1 p.712*

Handbook of Asian American Psychology. *v.6 p.87, p.122*

Handbook of Asset and Liability Management: Theory and Methodology. *v.4 p.192*

The Handbook of Astronomical Image Processing. . . .*v.5 p.65*

Handbook of Attachment: Theory, Research, and Clinical Applications. *v.5 p.625, p.631, p.651*

The Handbook of Attitudes. *v.5 p.651*

Handbook of Autism and Pervasive Developmental Disorders. *v.5 p.663*

Handbook of Behavioral Economics: Behavioral Decision Making, Vol. 1, Pt. A: Behavioral Microeconomics. *v.4 p.190*

Handbook of Biblical Chronology: Principles of Time Reckoning in the Ancient World and Problems of Chronology in the Bible. *v.1 p.617*

Handbook of Black American Health: The Mosaic of Conditions, Issues, Policies, and Prospects. . .*v.6 p.22, p.39*

Handbook of Canadian Foreign Policy. *v.3 p.537*

Handbook of Career Counseling for Women. . .*v.4 p.306, p.354*

Handbook of Career Counseling Theory and Practice. *v.5 p.578*

Handbook of Career Theory. *v.5 p.577*

ⓔ Handbook of Ceramics and Composites. *v.5 p.688*

Handbook of Cereal Science and Technology, Vol. 99. . . . .*v.5 p.22, p.32, p.33*

▢ Handbook of Chemistry and Physics. *v.5 p.259*

The Handbook of Chicana/o Psychology and Mental Health. *v.5 p.638, v.6 p.541, p.542*

Handbook of Child Behavior Therapy in the Psychiatric Setting. *v.5 p.666*

Handbook of Child Behavior Therapy. *v.5 p.667*

Handbook of Child Psychology, Set. *v.5 p.625, p.626, p.641, p.642*

Handbook of Children and the Media. *v.4 p.417*

Handbook of Christian Apologetics. *v.1 p.646*

Handbook of Christianity in China, 635-1800, Vol. 1. *v.1 p.610*

Handbook of Christianity in Japan. *v.1 p.610*

Handbook of Chromatography: Amino Acids and Amines. *v.5 p.300*

Handbook of Chromatography, Set. *v.5 p.330*

Handbook of Classical Rhetoric in the Hellenistic Period (330 B.C.-A.D. 400). *v.2 p.405*

Handbook of Classroom Management: Research, Practice, and Contemporary Issues. *v.4 p.283*

Handbook of Climbing. *v.4 p.789*

Handbook of Clinical Sociology. *v.4 p.692*

The Handbook of Clinically Tested Herbal Remedies. *v.5 p.211*

Handbook of Closeness and Intimacy. *v.5 p.648, p.654*

Handbook of Coastal and Ocean Engineering, vol. 1: Wave Phenomena and Costal Structures. *v.5 p.702*

Handbook of Coastal and Ocean Engineering, vol. 2: Offshore Structures, Marine Foundations, Sediment Processes, and Modeling. *v.5 p.702*

Handbook of Coastal and Ocean Engineering, vol. 3: Harbors, Navigational Channels, Estuaries, Environmental Effects. *.v.5 p.702*

Handbook of Cognition and Emotion. . . . . *.v.5 p.605*

Handbook of Cognition. . . . .*.v.5 p.649, p.650*

Handbook of Cognitive Task Design. . . . . *.v.5 p.587*

Handbook of Communication and Emotion: Research, Theory, Applications, and Contexts. . . . . *.v.5 p.646*

Handbook of Community Psychology. . . . . .*.v.5 p.650, p.672*

Handbook of Comparative Genomics: Principles and Methodology. . . . .*.v.5 p.96, p.146*

Handbook of Complex Variables. . . . . *.v.5 p.491*

Handbook of Computational Economics: Agent-Based Computational Economics. . . . . *.v.4 p.190*

Handbook of Computational Economics. . . .*.v.4 p.186, p.197*

Handbook of Computer Crime Investigation: Forensic Tools and Technology. . . . .*.v.5 p.341, p.343*

The Handbook of Conflict Resolution: Theory and Practice. *.v.5 p.647*

Handbook of Consumer Behavior. . . . . *.v.5 p.586*

Handbook of Corrosion Engineering. . . . . *.v.5 p.735*

Handbook of Counseling and Psychotherapy with Lesbian, Gay and Bisexual Clients. . . . . *.v.5 p.637*

Handbook of Counseling Psychology. . . . . *.v.5 p.576*

Handbook of Creativity. . . . . *.v.5 p.656*

The Handbook of Crime and Punishment. . . . . . *.v.6 p.250*

Handbook of Crisis Counseling, Intervention, and Prevention in the Schools. . . . . *.v.4 p.353*

The Handbook of Critical Theory. . . . . *.v.1 p.502*

Handbook of Cross-Cultural and Multicultural Personality Assessment. *.v.5 p.603*

Handbook of Cross-Cultural Counseling and Therapy. *.v.5 p.637*

Handbook of Data Analysis. . . . . *.v.4 p.178*

Handbook of Data on Common Organic Compounds, 3 v. . . . . *.v.5 p.290*

Handbook of Data on Organic Compounds, 7 v. . . . .*.v.5 p.290*

Handbook of Data on Organic Compounds (HODOC), Vol. 1. . . . . *.v.5 p.291*

Handbook of Data Structures and Applications. *.v.5 p.335, p.344*

Handbook of Defense Economics, Vol. 1. . . . . . . *.v.4 p.189*

Handbook of Denominations in the United States. . . . .*.v.1 p.544, p.605*

Handbook of Depression. . . . . *.v.5 p.659*

Handbook of Design, Manufacturing and Automation. *.v.5 p.684*

Handbook of Development Economics, Vol. 3A. . . *.v.4 p.188*

Handbook of Development Economics, Vol. 3B. . . *.v.4 p.188*

Handbook of Development Economics, Vols. 3A & 3B. *.v.4 p.192*

A Handbook of Diction for Singers: Italian, German, French. *.v.1 p.394*

Handbook of Differential Equations. . . . . . *.v.5 p.462, p.487*

Handbook of Discrete and Computational Geometry. . . . . *.v.5 p.337, p.340*

Handbook of Disruptive Behavior Disorders. . *.v.5 p.662, p.663*

Handbook of Distance Education. . . . . *.v.4 p.322*

Handbook of Drug Abuse Prevention: Theory, Science, and Practice. . . . . *.v.5 p.512, p.522*

Handbook of Drug Screening, Vol. 114. . . . . *.v.5 p.219*

Handbook of Dynamics in Parent-Child Relations. . . *.v.5 p.641*

Handbook of Early Childhood Literacy. . . . . . . *.v.4 p.368*

Handbook of Early Literacy Research, Vol. 1. *.v.4 p.358, p.369*

Handbook of Early Literacy Research, Vol. 2. *.v.4 p.300, p.368*

Handbook of Ecological Restoration: Restoration in Practice, Vol. 2. . . . . *.v.6 p.284*

Handbook of Econometrics, Vol. 2. . . . . . *.v.4 p.189, p.201*

Handbook of Econometrics, Vol. 4. . . . . *.v.4 p.199*

Handbook of Econometrics, Vol. 5. . . . . .*.v.4 p.189, p.201*

Handbook of Econometrics, Vol. 6. . . . . *.v.4 p.189*

Handbook of Economic Growth. . . . . . . *.v.4 p.186, p.194*

The Handbook of Economic Sociology. . . . . *.v.4 p.718*

Handbook of Ecotoxicology. . . . .*.v.5 p.311, v.6 p.283*

Handbook of Electoral System Choice. . . . . *.v.4 p.577*

Handbook of Electric Motors. . . . . *.v.5 p.725*

Handbook of Engineering Polymeric Materials. . . . *.v.5 p.688*

Handbook of Enology, the Chemistry of Wine: Stabilization and Treatments. . . . . *.v.5 p.53*

Handbook of Environmental Acoustics. *.v.5 p.367, p.368, p.374*

Handbook of Environmental and Resource Economics. *.v.4 p.62*

Handbook of Environmental Data on Organic Chemicals, Set. . . . . *.v.5 p.312, p.363*

Handbook of Environmental Economics: Economywide and International Environmental Issues. . . . . *.v.4 p.191*

Handbook of Environmental Economics: Environmental Degradation and Institutional Responses. . . . . *.v.4 p.192*

Handbook of Environmental Economics: Valuing Environmental Changes. . . . . *.v.4 p.191*

Handbook of Environmental Fate and Exposure Data for Organic Chemicals: Solvents, Vol. 2. . . . .*.v.5 p.311*

Handbook of Environmental Fate and Exposure Data for Organic Chemicals, Vol. 1. . . . . *.v.5 p.311*

Handbook of Environmental Health, Vol. 1. . *.v.5 p.358, p.364*

Handbook of Environmental Management and Technology. . . . . *.v.5 p.706*

Handbook of Environmental Psychology. . . . . . . *.v.5 p.587*

Handbook of Environmental Sociology. . . . . *.v.4 p.760*

Handbook of Ethological Methods. . . . . *.v.5 p.615*

Handbook of European History, 1400-1600: Late Middle Ages, Renaissance, and Reformation. . . . . . . *.v.1 p.600, p.601*

Handbook of European History, 1400-1600: Late Middle Ages Renaissence and Reformation. . . . . *.v.3 p.38*

Handbook of European Union. . . . . *.v.4 p.603, p.638*

Handbook of Experimental Psychology. . . . . . . *.v.5 p.605*

Handbook of Extractive Metallurgy, Set. . . . . . . *.v.5 p.732*

Handbook of Family Communication. . . . . *.v.5 p.622, p.639*

Handbook of Family Development and Intervention. . *.v.5 p.639*

Handbook of Family Diversity. . . . . *.v.5 p.638*

Handbook of Fermented Functional Foods. . . . . . . *.v.5 p.34*

The Handbook of Fish Biology and Fisheries, Vol. 2. *.v.5 p.215*

The Handbook of Fixed Income Securities. . . . . . *.v.4 p.103*

Handbook of Fluid Dynamics and Fluid Machinery, Set. *.v.5 p.713*

Handbook of Food Analytical Chemistry, Water, Proteins, Enzymes, Lipids, and Carbohydrates, Vol. 1. . . . . *.v.5 p.36*

Handbook of Forensic Psychology: Resource for Mental Health and Legal Professionals. *v.5 p.592*

The Handbook of Forensic Psychology. *v.5 p.593*

Handbook of Game Theory with Economic Applications, Vol. 1. . . . .*v.4 p.187, v.5 p.504*

Handbook of Game Theory with Economic Applications, Vol. 3. . . . .*v.4 p.187, v.5 p.504*

Handbook of Game Theory with Economic Applications. *v.4 p.187, v.5 p.504*

Handbook of Gender and Women's Studies. *v.6 p.425*

Handbook of Genome Research: Genomics, Proteomics, Metabolomics, Bioinformatics, Ethical and Legal Issues. . .*v.5 p.105, p.106, p.108, p.118, p.143, p.147, p.249*

Handbook of Geographic Information Science. *v.4 p.388*

The Handbook of Geographical Information Science. *v.4 p.388*

Handbook of Geometrical Tolerancing: Design, Manufacturing and Inspection. *v.5 p.684*

Handbook of Geothermal Energy. *v.5 p.360, p.362*

Handbook of Gifted Education. *v.5 p.575*

Handbook of Girls' and Women's Psychological Health. .*v.5 p.642*

Handbook of Glass in Construction. *v.5 p.687*

A Handbook of Greek Constitutional History. *v.4 p.489*

A Handbook of Greek Literature: From Homer to the Age of Lucian. *v.2 p.401*

Handbook of Green Chemistry and Technology. . . .*v.5 p.311*

Handbook of Groundwater Engineering. *v.5 p.702*

Handbook of Health Economics, Vol. 1A. *v.4 p.188, p.199, p.264*

Handbook of Health Economics, Vol. 1B. .*v.4 p.188, p.199, p.264*

Handbook of Health Economics. *v.4 p.188, v.5 p.511*

Handbook of Heat and Mass Transfer: Advances in Reactor Design and Combustion Science, Vol. 4. . . . . .*v.5 p.713*

Handbook of Heat and Mass Transfer: Catalysis, Kinetics and Reactor Engineering, Vol. 3. . . . .*v.5 p.713*

Handbook of Heat and Mass Transfer, Vol. 1. . . . .*v.5 p.713*

Handbook of Heat and Mass Transfer, Vol. 2. . . . .*v.5 p.713*

Handbook of Heat Transfer. *v.5 p.713*

Handbook of Heterocyclic Chemistry. *v.5 p.298*

Handbook of Hispanic Cultures of the U. S., Set. . . .*v.6 p.485*

The Handbook of Historical Linguistics. *v.2 p.561, v.5 p.621, p.623*

Handbook of Human Factors and Ergonomics. . . .*v.5 p.588*

Handbook of Human Factors in Web Design. *v.5 p.588*

Handbook of Human Factors Testing and Evaluation. *v.5 p.587*

Handbook of Hydrology. *v.5 p.703*

Handbook of Incentive Measures for Niodiversity: Design and Implementation. *v.5 p.223*

Handbook of Income Distribution, Vol. 1. . . . . .*v.4 p.187*

Handbook of Indigenous Fermented Foods, Vol. 73. . .*v.5 p.35*

Handbook of Industrial and Hazardous Waste Treatment: Second Edition, Revised and Expanded. *v.5 p.707*

Handbook of Industrial Chemistry. *v.5 p.315, p.740*

Handbook of Industrial Engineering: Technology and Operations Management. *v.4 p.119*

Handbook of Industrial Organization, Set, Vols. 1 & 2. .*v.4 p.191*

Handbook of Industrial Organization, Vol. 1. . . . .*v.4 p.191*

Handbook of Industrial Organization, Vol. 2. . . . .*v.4 p.191*

Handbook of Industrial Organization. *v.4 p.186*

Handbook of Industrial Robotics. *v.4 p.116*

Handbook of Industrial Surfactants: An International Guide to More Than 21,000 Products by Trade Name, Composition, Function and Manufacturer. *v.5 p.318*

Handbook of Infant Development. *v.5 p.626*

Handbook of Infant, Toddler, and Preschool Mental Health Assessment. *v.5 p.602*

Handbook of Infrared and Raman Spectra of Inorganic Compounds and Organic Salts, Set. *v.5 p.305*

Handbook of Infrared Astronomy. *v.5 p.67*

Handbook of Inorganic Chemicals. *v.5 p.302*

Handbook of Inorganic Compounds. *v.5 p.302*

Handbook of Institutional Advancement: A Modern Guide to Executive Management, Institutional Relations, Fund Raising, Alumni Administration, Government Relations, Publications, Periodicals, and Enrollment Management. *v.4 p.293*

Handbook of Instrumental Techniques for Analytical Chemistry. *v.5 p.268*

The Handbook of Intelligent Control. *v.5 p.712*

Handbook of International Economics: International Monetary Economics and Finance. *v.4 p.190*

Handbook of International Economics: International Trade. *v.4 p.190*

Handbook of International Economics, Vol. 3. . . . .*v.4 p.189*

A Handbook of International Human Rights Terminology. *v.4 p.669*

A Handbook of International Law. *v.4 p.477*

Handbook of International Psychology. *v.5 p.594*

Handbook of Interpersonal Communication. *v.5 p.648*

Handbook of Japanese Popular Culture. *v.6 p.222, p.232*

Handbook of Labor Economics, Vol. 3A. *v.4 p.187*

Handbook of Labor Economics, Vol. 3C. *v.4 p.187*

Handbook of Labor Economics, Vol. 3. . . . .*v.4 p.187*

Handbook of Labor Economics. *v.4 p.186, p.187*

Handbook of Laboratory Health and Safety. *v.5 p.266*

The Handbook of Language and Gender. *v.2 p.563*

Handbook of Language and Social Interaction. *v.5 p.647*

Handbook of Latin American Studies (HLAS). *v.3 p.259, v.4 p.591*

A Handbook of Latin Literature. *v.2 p.425*

Handbook of Learning Disabilities. *v.5 p.575*

Handbook of Lichenology. *v.5 p.210*

The Handbook of Linguistics. *v.2 p.559*

A Handbook of Literary Feminisms. *v.2 p.567, v.6 p.477*

Handbook of Machinery Dynamics, Vol. 132. . . . .*v.5 p.714*

Handbook of Machinery Dynamics. *v.5 p.714*

Handbook of Macroeconomics, Vol. 15. . . . . . .*v.4 p.192*

Handbook of Macroeconomics, Vol. 1B. *v.4 p.192*

Handbook of Macroeconomics. *v.4 p.192*

Handbook of Market Creation for Biodiversity: Issues in Implementation. *v.5 p.223*

Handbook of Marketing and Society. *v.4 p.145*

Handbook of Materials Behavior Models: Nonlinear Models and Properties. *v.5 p.689*

Handbook of Materials Selection for Engineering
   Applications. *v.5 p.690*

Handbook of Materials Selection. *v.5 p.689*

Handbook of Mathematical Economics, Set. *v.4 p.186*

Handbook of Mathematical Economics, Vol. 1. *v.4 p.186, p.198*

Handbook of Mathematical Economics, Vol. 3. *v.4 p.186, p.198*

Handbook of Mathematical Economics, Vol. 4. . . *v.4 p.189*

Handbook of Mathematical Functions with Formulas, Graphs
   and Mathematical Tables. *v.5 p.460, p.493*

Handbook of Mathematical Logic. *v.5 p.470*

Handbook of Medical Anthropology: Contemporary Theory and
   Method. *v.4 p.47*

Handbook of Medieval Sexuality: A Book of Essays.   *v.6 p.559*

Handbook of Mental Health Interventions in Children and
   Adolescents: An Integrated Developmental
   Approach. *v.5 p.513*

Handbook of Mental Retardation and Development. . *v.5 p.517*

Handbook of Micro/Nanotribology, Vol. 1. . . . . . *v.5 p.707*

The Handbook of Microwave Technology, Vol. 109. . *v.5 p.729*

A Handbook of Middle English. *v.2 p.551*

Handbook of Military Psychology, Vol. 1. . . . . . *v.5 p.584*

Handbook of Mineralogy: Borates, Carbonates,
   Sulfates. *v.5 p.435*

Handbook of Mineralogy: Silica, Silicates. *v.5 p.435*

Handbook of Modern British Painting and Printmaking,
   1900-1990. . . . . *v.1 p.734, p.754*

Handbook of Molecular and Cellular Methods in Biology and
   Medicine. *v.5 p.126*

Handbook of Monetary Economics, Vol. 1. . . . *v.4 p.188, p.189*

Handbook of Monetary Economics, Vol. 2. . . . . . *v.4 p.189*

Handbook of Multicultural Competencies in Counseling and
   Psychology. *v.5 p.637*

Handbook of Multicultural Perspectives on Stress and
   Coping. *v.4 p.699*

Handbook of Multimethod Measurement in
   Psychology. *v.5 p.599, p.600*

Handbook of Nanophase and Nanostructured Materials: Volume
   I: SynthesisVolume II: CharacterizationVolume III:
   Materials Systems and Applications IVolume IV: Materials
   Systems and Applications II. *v.5 p.692*

Handbook of Nanostructured Materials and Nanotechnology,
   Set. *v.5 p.690*

Handbook of Natural Resource and Energy Economics:
   Handbooks in Economics, Six, 2. . . . . . . *v.4 p.190*

Handbook of Natural Resource and Energy Economics:
   Handbooks in Economics, Six, Set. *v.4 p.190*

Handbook of Natural Resource and Energy Economics, Vol.
   1. *v.4 p.190*

Handbook of Natural Resource and Energy Economics, Vol.
   2. *v.4 p.190*

Handbook of Natural Resource and Energy, Vol. 3. . *v.4 p.190*

The Handbook of Negotiation: Theoretical Advances and
   Cross-Cultural Perspectives. *v.4 p.74, p.698*

Handbook of Norse Mythology. *v.1 p.533, p.534*

Handbook of North American Indians: Arctic. . . . *v.6 p.677*

Handbook of North American Indians, California, Vol.
   8. *v.6 p.677*

Handbook of North American Indians: Great Basin, Vol.
   11. . . . . *v.6 p.677*

Handbook of North American Indians: Northeast, Vol.
   15. . . . . *v.6 p.677*

Handbook of North American Indians: Northwest Coast. *v.6 p.677*

Handbook of North American Indians: Plains,
   Set. *v.6 p.677, p.678*

Handbook of North American Indians: Plateau. . . . *v.6 p.677*

Handbook of North American Indians: Southeast, Vol.
   14. . . . . *v.6 p.677*

Handbook of North American Indians: Southwest. . . *v.6 p.677*

Handbook of North American Indians: Subarctic, Vol. 6. *v.6 p.677*

Handbook of North American Indians, Vol. 17:
   Languages. *v.6 p.690*

Handbook of North American Indians. *v.6 p.678*

Handbook of Nuclear Chemistry, 5 vols. *v.5 p.308*

Handbook of Occupational Health Psychology. . . . *v.5 p.581*

Handbook of Optics. *v.5 p.73, p.545, p.561*

A Handbook of Organic Analysis. *v.5 p.300*

Handbook of Organic Analytical Reagents. *v.5 p.291*

Handbook of Organic Chemistry. *v.5 p.290*

Handbook of Organic Solvents. *v.5 p.290*

Handbook of Organizational Learning and Knowledge. *v.4 p.78*

Handbook of Organopalladium Chemistry for Organic
   Synthesis. *v.5 p.299, p.300*

Handbook of OSHA Construction Safety and Health. *v.5 p.686*

Handbook of Package Engineering. *v.4 p.116*

Handbook of Parenting: Being and Becoming a Parent. *v.5 p.641*

Handbook of Parenting: Biology and Ecology of
   Parenting. *v.5 p.641*

Handbook of Parenting: Children and Parenting. . . *v.5 p.641*

Handbook of Parenting: Practical Issues in Parenting. *v.5 p.641*

Handbook of Parenting: Social Conditions and Applied
   Parenting. *v.5 p.640, p.641*

The Handbook of Parenting: Theory, Research and
   Practice. *v.5 p.641*

Handbook of Pediatric Psychology. *v.5 p.642*

Handbook of Personality Disorders: Theory and
   Practice. *v.5 p.661*

Handbook of Personality Disorders: Theory, Research, and
   Treatment. *v.5 p.661*

Handbook of Personality Psychology. *v.5 p.657, p.658*

The Handbook of Phonological Theory. *v.2 p.560*

Handbook of Photography. *v.1 p.769*

Handbook of Physical Properties of Organic Chemicals. *v.5 p.318*

Handbook of Physical-Chemical Properties and Environmental
   Fate for Organic Chemicals. *v.5 p.293*

Handbook of Physics. *v.5 p.275, p.545*

The Handbook of Pidgins and Creoles. *v.2 p.562*

Handbook of Plant Biotechnology. *v.5 p.7*

Handbook of Plastics, Elastomers and Composites. . *v.5 p.319*

Handbook of Political Science Research on the Middle East and
   North Africa. *v.4 p.615, v.6 p.594*

Handbook of Polymer Degradation. *v.5 p.324*

Handbook of Population and Family Economics, Vol. IA. *v.4 p.191*

Handbook of Population and Family Economics, Vol. IB. *v.4 p.191*

Handbook of Population and Family Economics, Vols. 1A & 1B. *v.4 p.191*

Handbook of Positive Psychology. *v.5 p.670*

Handbook of Powder Metallurgy. *v.5 p.732*

Handbook of Practical Gear Design. *v.5 p.714*

The Handbook of Pragmatics. *v.4 p.424*

Handbook of Print Media: Technologies and Production Methods. *v.4 p.417*

The Handbook of Private Schools: An Annual Descriptive Survey of Independent Education. *v.4 p.297*

Handbook of Processes and Modeling in the Soil-Plant System. *v.5 p.48*

Handbook of Professional Ethics for Psychologists: Issues, Questions, and Controversies. *v.5 p.594, p.674*

Handbook of Property Estimation Methods for Chemicals: Enviornmental and Health Sciences. *v.5 p.293*

Handbook of Proteomic Methods. *v.5 p.115*

Handbook of Psychoeducational Assessment: A Practical Handbook. *v.4 p.285, v.5 p.602*

Handbook of Psychological and Educational Assessment of Children: Intelligence, Aptitude, and Achievement. *v.5 p.602*

Handbook of Psychological and Educational Assessment of Children: Personality, Behavior and Context. . . .*v.5 p.602*

Handbook of Psychological Anthropology. *v.4 p.35*

Handbook of Psychology and Law. *v.5 p.592*

Handbook of Psychology, Assessment Psychology, Vol. 10. . . . .*v.5 p.599*

Handbook of Psychology: Biological Psychology. . . .*v.5 p.617*

Handbook of Psychology, Educational Psychology, Vol. 7. . . . .*v.4 p.357, v.5 p.571*

Handbook of Psychology, History of Psychology, Vol. 1. .*v.5 p.596*

Handbook of Psychology in Legal Contexts. . .*v.5 p.591, p.592*

Handbook of Psychology, Set. *v.5 p.594*

Handbook of Psychotherapy and Religious Diversity. .*v.5 p.635*

Handbook of Public Administration. *v.4 p.545, p.580*

Handbook of Public Economics, Vol. 1, June 1985. . .*v.4 p.187*

Handbook of Public Economics, Vol. 2. . . . .*v.4 p.187*

Handbook of Public Economics, Vol. 4. . . . .*v.4 p.187*

Handbook of Public Economics, Vol. I. *v.4 p.187*

Handbook of Public Economics. *v.4 p.187*

Handbook of Racial and Ethnic Minority Psychology, Vol. 4. . . . .*v.5 p.636, v.6 p.121*

Handbook of Reading Research. *v.4 p.354*

Handbook of Reagents for Organic Synthesis, Acidic and Basic Reagents, Vol. 2. . . . .*v.5 p.291*

Handbook of Regional and Urban Economics: Applied Urban Economics. *v.4 p.188*

Handbook of Regional and Urban Economics: Cities and Geography, Vol. 4. . . . .*v.4 p.189*

Handbook of Regional and Urban Economics: Urban Economics. *v.4 p.191*

Handbook of Regional and Urban Economics: Volumes One and Two. *v.4 p.191*

Handbook of Rehabilitation Psychology. *v.5 p.672*

Handbook of Religion and Mental Health. *v.5 p.634*

Handbook of Research Design and Social Measurement. *v.4 p.686, p.687*

Handbook of Research for Educational Communications and Technology: A Project of the Association for Educational Communications and Technology. . . .*v.4 p.351*

Handbook of Research Methods in Social and Personality Psychology. *v.5 p.646*

Handbook of Research Methods in Work and Organizational Psychology. *v.5 p.579*

Handbook of Research on Curriculum. *v.4 p.355, p.361*

Handbook of Research on Educational Psychology. *v.4 p.356, v.5 p.571*

Handbook of Research on Multicultural Education. *v.4 p.300, p.308*

Handbook of Research on Sport Psychology. *v.5 p.583*

Handbook of Research on Teaching Literacy Through the Communicative and Visual Arts: Sponsored by the International Reading Association. *v.4 p.300*

Handbook of Research on Teaching the English Language Arts: Sponsored by the International Reading Association and the National Council of Teachers of English. . . .*v.4 p.363*

Handbook of Research on Teaching. *v.4 p.355*

Handbook of Research on Urban Politics and Policy in the United States, Vol. 28, no. 13. . . . .*v.4 p.544, v.6 p.709*

Handbook of Resilience in Children. *v.5 p.626*

Handbook of Russian Literature. *v.2 p.797*

The Handbook of Sailing Techniques: Professional Tips, Expert Advice, Essential Skills. *v.4 p.866*

The Handbook of School Psychology. . . .*v.4 p.358, v.5 p.577*

Handbook of School-Based Interventions: Resolving Student Problems and Promoting Healthy Educational Environments. *v.4 p.352, p.353*

Handbook of Schooling in Urban America. *v.4 p.315*

Handbook of Seed Physiology: Applications to Agriculture. *v.5 p.20, p.47*

Handbook of Slope Stabilisation. *v.5 p.699*

Handbook of Social Choice and Welfare, Vol. 1. . . .*v.4 p.186*

Handbook of Social Cognition, Set. *v.4 p.692, p.693*

The Handbook of Social Policy. *v.4 p.769*

The Handbook of Social Psychology, Set. *v.4 p.691, p.692,v.5 p.645, p.646*

Handbook of Social Psychology. *v.5 p.645*

The Handbook of Sociolinguistics. *v.4 p.18*

Handbook of Soil Science. *v.5 p.50*

Handbook of South American Geology: An Explanation of the Geologic Map of South America. *v.5 p.432*

Handbook of Spectroscopy. *v.5 p.270*

ⓔ Handbook of Sport Psychology. *v.4 p.877, p.878*

Handbook of Sport Psychology. *v.5 p.583*

Handbook of Stainless Steels. *v.5 p.736*

Handbook of Structural Concrete. *v.5 p.689*

Handbook of Superconductivity. *v.5 p.565*

Handbook of Surface and Colloid Chemistry. *v.5 p.283*

Handbook of Surfaces and Interfaces of Materials, Set. *v.5 p.690*

Handbook of Technical Writing. *v.5 p.680*

Handbook of Telecommunications Economics: Technology
Evolution and the Internet. *v.4 p.190, p.191*

Handbook of Test Development. *v.5 p.600*

Handbook of the Economics of Finance: Corporate
Finance. *v.4 p.188*

Handbook of the Economics of Finance: Financial Markets and
Asset Pricing. *v.4 p.188*

Handbook of the Economics of Finance. *v.4 p.188*

Handbook of the Economics of Giving, Altruism and
Reciprocity: Applications. *v.4 p.190*

Handbook of the Economics of Giving, Altruism and
Reciprocity: Foundations. *v.4 p.189*

Handbook of the Indians of California. *v.6 p.703*

Handbook of the International Phonetic Association: A Guide to
the Use of the International Phonetic Alphabet. . .*v.2 p.561*

Handbook of the Life Course. *v.5 p.628, p.632*

Handbook of the Media in Asia. *v.4 p.415*

Handbook of the Psychology of Religion and
Spirituality. *v.5 p.635*

Handbook of the Psychology of Women and Gender. *v.6 p.446*

Handbook of the Sociology of the Military. *v.4 p.717*

Handbook of the Teaching of Psychology. *v.5 p.675*

A Handbook of the Troubadours. *v.2 p.453*

Handbook of Toxic and Hazardous Chemicals and
Carcinogens. *v.5 p.315, p.682,v.6 p.286*

Handbook of Toxicogenomics: Strategies and
Applications. *v.5 p.125, p.138, p.145, p.183*

Handbook of Training Technologies: An Introductory Guide to
Facilitating Learning with Technology — From Planning to
Evaluation. *v.4 p.352*

Handbook of Transportation Engineering. *v.5 p.700*

Handbook of Tribology: Materials, Coatings, and Surface
Treatments. *v.5 p.707*

Handbook of Twentieth-Century Literatures of India. *.v.2 p.762*

Handbook of Typography for the Mathematical
Sciences. *v.5 p.461*

Handbook of Urban and Regional Economics. *v.4 p.191*

Handbook of Vegetable Pests. *v.5 p.3, p.20, p.26*

Handbook of Vocational Psychology: Theory, Research, and
Practice. *v.4 p.306, v.5 p.578*

Handbook of Warnings. *v.5 p.588, p.589*

Handbook of Water Use and Conservation: Homes, Landscapes,
Businesses, Industries, Farms. .*v.5 p.19, p.380,v.6 p.286, p.287*

Handbook of Weather, Climate and Water: Dynamics, Climate,
Physical Meteorology, Weather Systems and
Measurements. *v.5 p.426*

Handbook of Women's Health: An Evidence-Based
Approach. *v.6 p.444*

Handbook of Work and Organizational Psychology. . .*v.5 p.579*

Handbook of Work Stress. *v.5 p.580*

Handbook of Workplace Diversity. *v.4 p.132*

Handbook of Workplace Violence. *v.4 p.130, p.131*

Handbook of World Philosophy: Contemporary Developments
since 1945. . . . .*v.1 p.438*

Handbook of Writing for the Mathematical
Sciences. *v.5 p.458, p.461*

Handbook on Architectures of Information Systems. . .*v.4 p.114*

Handbook on Data Management in Information
Systems. *v.4 p.114*

Handbook on Economics of Sport. *v.4 p.186*

Handbook on Geographic Information Systems and Digital
Mapping. *v.4 p.388*

Handbook on Nondestructive Testing of
Concrete. *v.5 p.689, p.690*

Handbook on the Globalization of the World Economy. *v.4 p.261*

Handbook on the Physics and Chemistry of Rare Earths, Vol.
15. . . . .*v.5 p.308*

Handbook on the Physics and Chemistry of Rare Earths. *.v.5 p.308*

Handbook on the Physics and Chemistry of the Actinides, Pt. 1:
Physics, Vol. 2. . . . .*v.5 p.308*

Handbook on the Physics and Chemistry of the Actinides, Vol.
1. . . . .*v.5 p.308*

Handbook on the Physics and Chemistry of the Actinides, Vol.
3. . . . .*v.5 p.307*

Handbook on the Physics and Chemistry of the Actinides, Vol.
4. . . . .*v.5 p.307, p.308*

Handbook on the Physics and Chemistry of the Actinides, Vol.
6. . . . .*v.5 p.307*

Handbook on the Physics and Chemistry of the
Actinides. *v.5 p.308*

Handbook on U. S. Relations with Greece and Cyprus. *.v.3 p.392*

Handbook on Undergraduate Curriculum: Prepared for the
Carnegie Council on Policy Studies in Higher
Education. *v.4 p.294*

Handbook Series in Organic Electrochemistry, Set. . *v.5 p.290*

A Handbook to Appalachia: An Introduction to the
Region. *v.3 p.497*

A Handbook to English Romanticism. . . . .*.v.2 p.172*

The Handbook to Life in Ancient Egypt. . . . .*.v.3 p.8*

Handbook to Life in Ancient Greece. *v.3 p.12*

Handbook to Life in Ancient Rome. *v.3 p.22*

A Handbook to Literature. *v.2 p.549*

Handbook to the Palace of Minos at Knoss. . . . . .*.v.3 p.16*

Handbuch der Organischen Chemie, Various Vols. & Eds.,1918 -
Present. *v.5 p.290*

Handel: A Documentary Biography. *v.1 p.183, p.329*

Handel As Orpheus: Voice and Desire in the Chamber
Cantatas. *v.6 p.408*

Handel: Messiah. *v.1 p.183, p.235, p.328*

Handel: The Orchestral Music. *v.1 p.185, p.241, p.329*

Handel's Dramatic Oratorios and
Masques. *v.1 p.183, p.235, p.328, p.329*

Handel's Messiah: Origins, Composition,
Sources. *v.1 p.185, p.235, p.329*

Handel's Operas Seventeen Four to Seventeen
Twenty-Six. *v.1 p.183, p.229, p.329*

Handel. *v.1 p.182, p.183, p.184, p.328, p.329*

A Handful of Authors: Essays on Books and Writers. *v.2 p.575*

A Handful of Dust. *v.2 p.388*

Handke Plays One. *v.1 p.109*

Handless Maiden: Moriscos and the Politics of Religion in Early
Modern Spain. *v.3 p.240*

A Handlist to James Joyce's Ulysses: A Complete Alphabetical Index to the Critical Reading Text. *v.2 p.360*

The Handmaid's Tale. *v.2 p.734*

Hands and Hearts: A History of Courtship in America. *v.4 p.738*

Hands Behind My Back: Selected Poems. *v.2 p.817*

Handwriting: Poems. *v.2 p.737*

The Handy Biology Answer Book. *v.5 p.95*

Hanford Site Historic District: History of the Plutonium Production Facilities, 1943-1990. . . . . . *v.5 p.375, p.391, p.413, p.415, p.417*

Hanging in and Dropping Out: Voices of At-Risk High School Students. *v.4 p.299*

Hangman's Knot: Lynching, Legal Execution, and America's Struggle with the Death Penalty. *v.6 p.247, p.248*

Hank Williams: The Biography. *v.1 p.268, p.368*

Hannibal: Rome's Greatest Enemy. *v.3 p.25*

Hannibal's Dynasty: Power and Politics in the Western Mediterranean, 247-183 BC. *v.3 p.25*

Hannibal's War: A Military History of the Second Punic War. *v.3 p.25*

Hannibal's War. *v.2 p.436*

Hanns Eisler: Political Musician. *v.1 p.209, p.323*

Hanoverian London, Seventeen Fourteen to Eighteen Eight. *v.3 p.107, p.109, p.126, p.127*

Hans Christian Andersen: The Story of His Life and Work 1805-75. . . . . *v.2 p.626*

Hans Christian Andersen. *v.2 p.626*

Hans Hofmann. *v.1 p.741*

Hans Holbein the Younger: Painter at the Court of Henry VIII. *v.1 p.736*

Hans Memling: The Complete Oeuvre. *v.1 p.737*

Hans Staden, the True History of His Captivity 1557. *v.3 p.334*

Hansberry's Drama: Commitment amid Complexity. . *v.2 p.80*

Hansen Solubility Parameters: A User's Handbook. . *v.5 p.282*

Hanslick's Music Criticisms. *v.1 p.198*

Hanya Holm: The Biography of an Artist. *v.1 p.12*

The Happiest Corpse I've Ever Seen: The Last Twenty-Five Years of the Broadway Musical. *v.1 p.252*

Happiness and Education. *v.4 p.339*

The Happiness Hypothesis: Finding Modern Truth in Ancient Wisdom. *v.5 p.670*

The Happiness Paradox. *v.5 p.654*

Happiness, Pleasure, and Judgment: The Contextual Theory and Its Applications. *v.5 p.655*

Happy Death. *v.2 p.512*

Happy Ending: The Collected Lyrics of Louise I. Guiney. *v.2 p.39*

Hard at Play: Leisure in America, 1840-1940. *v.4 p.716, p.784*

Hard Bodies: Hollywood Masculinity in the Reagan Era. *v.6 p.328, p.341, p.474*

Hard Cash. *v.2 p.303*

Hard Choices, Easy Answers: Values, Information, and American Public Opinion. *v.4 p.425, p.559*

Hard Choices: Four Critical Years in Managing America's Foreign Policy. *v.3 p.481*

Hard Choices, Lost Voices: How the Abortion Conflict Has Divided America, Distorted Constitutional Rights, and Damaged the Courts. *v.4 p.448*

Hard Core: Power, Pleasure, and the Frenzy of the Visible. *v.6 p.317*

The Hard Hand of War: Union Military Policy Toward Southern Civilians, 1861-1865. . . . . *v.3 p.397*

The Hard Life. *v.2 p.373*

Hard Pressed: 600 Years of Prints and Process. . . . *v.1 p.760*

A Hard Road to Glory, 1619-1918, Vol. 1. . . . . . *v.4 p.831*

A Hard Road to Glory: 1919-1945, Vol. 2. . . . *v.4 p.830, p.831*

A Hard Road to Glory: A History of the African American Athlete, 1946-1969, Vol. 3, 3rd Edition, Vol. 3. . *v.4 p.831*

A Hard Road to Glory: A History of the African American Athlete, 1970-Present, Vol. 4. . . . . *v.4 p.831*

Hard Time: Understanding and Reforming the Prison. *v.6 p.274*

Hard Times: An Oral History of the Great Depression in America. *v.3 p.480*

Hard Times and New Deal in Kentucky, 1929-1939. . *v.3 p.511*

Hard Times: Force of Circumstance: The Autobiography of Simone de Beauvoir, 1952-1962. . . . . *v.2 p.508*

Hard Times. *v.2 p.283*

Hardball: The Education of a Baseball Commissioner. *v.4 p.807, p.851, p.884*

Hardboiled: An Anthology of American Crime Stories. *v.2 p.26, p.27*

Harding Era: Warren G. Harding and His Administration. *v.3 p.443, p.449*

The Harding Era: Warren G. Harding and His Administration. *v.3 p.476*

Hardware and Computer Organization. . . *v.4 p.114, v.5 p.345*

Hardwired Behavior: What Neuroscience Reveals about Morality. *v.5 p.618*

The Hare Krishna Movement: The Postcharismatic Fate of a Religious Transplant. *v.1 p.535*

Harland's Half Acre. *v.2 p.747*

Harlem - The Making of a Ghetto: Negro New York, 1890-1930. . . . . *v.6 p.714*

Harlem Gallery: And Other Poems. *v.2 p.124*

Harlem: Lost and Found. *v.1 p.788*

Harlem: Negro Metropolis. *v.3 p.491, v.6 p.714*

The Harlem Reader: A Celebration of New York's Most Famous Neighborhood, from the Renaissance Years to the 21st Century. *v.3 p.490, v.6 p.710*

The Harlem Renaissance: A Gale Critical Companion. *v.2 p.11*

Harlem Renaissance and Beyond: Literary Biographies of One Hundred Black Women Writers, 1900-1945. . . . . *v.6 p.19, p.27, p.34*

Harlem Renaissance: Art of Black America. *v.6 p.15*

The Harlem Renaissance. *v.6 p.22, p.23*

Harlem Voices from the Soul of Black America. . . . *v.6 p.24*

Harlem's Glory: Black Women Writing, 1900-1950. . *v.2 p.20*

Harlem's Hell Fighters: The African-American 369th Infantry in World War I. *v.6 p.5*

Harlequin Britain: Pantomime and Entertainment, 1690-1760. . . . . *v.1 p.94, p.102*

A Harlot High and Low. *v.2 p.486*

Harlot's Ghost. *v.2 p.99*

Harlow and Harrar's Textbook of Dendrology. *v.5 p.41*

Harm Reduction: Pragmatic Strategies for Managing High-Risk
Behaviors. *v.4 p.779, p.781, p.783*

Harmonic Function in Chromatic Music: A Renewed Dualist
Theory and an Account of Its Precedents. *v.1 p.370*

The Harmonic Organization of the Rite of
Spring. *v.1 p.213, p.239, p.360*

Harmonic Practice in Tonal Music. *v.1 p.370*

Harmony and Voice Leading. *v.1 p.369*

Harmony Book. *v.1 p.369*

The Harmony of the Spheres: The Pythagotean Tradition in
Music. *v.1 p.381*

Harmony. *v.1 p.372, p.373*

Harnessing Solar Power: The Photovoltaics
Challenge. *v.5 p.362, p.363*

Harold Arlen: Rhythm, Rainbows, and
Blues. *v.1 p.251, p.301, p.302,v.6 p.409*

Harold Macmillan: A Biography. *v.3 p.93, p.94, p.119*

Harold Prince and the American Musical Theater. *v.1 p.251, p.348*

Harold: The People's Mayor. *v.3 p.516*

HarperCollins Bible Commentary. *v.1 p.615*

The HarperCollins Bible Dictionary. *v.1 p.614*

The HarperCollins Dictionary of Religion. *v.1 p.522*

HarperCollins Italian-English, English-Italian
Dictionary. *v.2 p.698*

Harper's Illustrated Biochemistry. *v.5 p.111*

Harps and Harpists. *v.1 p.391*

Harrap English/French Dictionary, Vol. 2. . . . . . *v.2 p.454*

Harrap's French and English Science Dictionary. . . *v.5 p.387*

Harrap's Portuguese Compact Dictionary. *v.2 p.637*

Harrap's Unabridged French-English Dictionary. . . *v.2 p.453*

Harriet Beecher Stowe: A Life. *v.2 p.51*

Harriet Beecher Stowe. *v.2 p.51*

Harriet Brooks: Pioneer Nuclear Scientist. *v.5 p.544*

Harriet Hosmer, American Sculptor, 1830-1908. . . . *v.1 p.781*

Harriet Jacobs: A Life. *v.6 p.19, p.38, p.47*

Harriet Martineau: Theoretical and Methodological
Perspectives. *v.4 p.690*

Harriet Martineau's Autobiography, Vol. 2. . . . . *v.4 p.193*

Harriet Martineaus's Autobiography, Vol.
1. . . . . . . *v.2 p.299, v.4 p.209, v.6 p.740, p.748, p.764*

Harriet Martineaus's Autobiography, Vol.
2. . . . . *v.2 p.299, v.6 p.740, p.748, p.764*

Harriet Tubman: The Life and the Life Stories. . . *v.6 p.6, p.17*

Harriet Wilson's 'Our Nig': A Cultural Biography of a
'Two-Story' African American Novel. *v.2 p.53*

Harrison Birtwistle: Man, Mind, Music. . . . *v.1 p.212, p.312*

Harry Benson's America. *v.1 p.765*

Harry Byrd and the Changing Face of Virginia Politics,
1945-1966. . . . . *v.3 p.501*

Harry Hooper: An American Baseball Life. *v.4 p.853*

Harry Hopkins: Ally of the Poor and Defender of
Democracy. *v.3 p.461*

Harry Partch: A Biography. *v.1 p.214, p.347*

Harry S. Truman: A Life. *v.3 p.470*

Harry S. Truman and the Fair Deal. *v.3 p.472*

Harry S. Truman and the Founding of Israel. *v.3 p.465*

Harry Seidler. *v.1 p.792*

Hart Crane: A Life. *v.2 p.68*

Hart Crane and the Homosexual Text: New Thresholds, New
Anatomies. *v.2 p.68, v.6 p.394*

Hart Crane Revisited. *v.2 p.68*

Hartmann and Kester's Plant Propagation: Principles and
Practices. *v.5 p.15, p.16, p.43*

Haruko's World: A Japanese Farm Woman and Her
Community. *v.6 p.226*

The Harvard Biographical Dictionary of Music. . . . *v.1 p.161*

Harvard Business Review on Advances in Strategy. . . *v.4 p.73*

Harvard Business Review on Corporate Ethics. *v.4 p.53*

Harvard Business Review on Corporate
Responsibility. *v.4 p.52, p.54*

Harvard Business Review on Corporate Strategy. . . . *v.4 p.81*

Harvard Business Review on Developing Leaders: Ideas with
Impact. *v.4 p.176*

The Harvard Business School Guide to Careers in
Finance. *v.4 p.167*

The Harvard Business School Guide to Careers in Management
Consulting. *v.4 p.167*

The Harvard Concordance to Shakespeare. *v.2 p.226*

The Harvard Dictionary of Music. *v.1 p.161*

Harvard University Department of Molecular and Cellular
Biology - Biology Links. *v.5 p.125, p.152, p.153*

The Harvest - La Cosecha. *v.6 p.503*

Harvest of Despair: Life and Death in Ukraine under Nazi
Rule. *v.3 p.229*

Harvest of Empire: A History of Latinos in America. *v.6 p.531*

Harvest of Hellenism. *v.3 p.21*

The Harvest of Medieval Theology: Gabriel Biel and Late
Medieval Nominalism. *v.1 p.634*

The Harvest of Mysticism in Medieval Germany
(1300-1500). *v.1 p.653*

The Harvest of Sorrow: Soviet Collectivization and the
Terror-Famine. *v.3 p.225*

Harvest of Want: Hunger and Food Security in Central America
and Mexico. *v.3 p.273*

Harvesting Pa Chay's Wheat: The Hmong and America's Secret
War in Laos. *v.6 p.171*

The Harvey Milk Institute Guide to Lesbian, Gay, Bisexual,
Transgender and Queer Internet Research. *v.6 p.360*

Has Man a Future? *v.4 p.656*

Hasidic Prayer. *v.1 p.552*

Hastening Toward Prague: Power and Society in the Medieval
Czech Lands. *v.3 p.188*

The Hatchet: The Life of Stephen the Great. *v.2 p.817*

Hate Crimes: A Reference Handbook. *v.4 p.568*

Hate Crimes: Confronting Violence Against Lesbians and Gay
Men. *v.4 p.568, p.751,v.6 p.386*

Hate Crimes: Criminal Law and Identity
Politics. *v.4 p.472, p.568,v.6 p.252*

Hate Speech, Sex Speech, Free Speech. . . . *v.4 p.460, p.749*

Hate Speech: The History of an American Controversy. .*v.4 p.472*

Hateship, Friendship, Courtship, Loveship, Marriage:
Stories. *v.2 p.737*

Hatred in the Hallways: Violence and Discrimination Against
Lesbian, Gay, Bisexual, and Transgender Students in U.S.
Schools. *v.6 p.384*

Hatred: The Psychological Descent into Violence. . . .*v.5 p.653*

Hats in the Ring: An Illustrated History of American
Presidential Campaigns. *v.3 p.377*

Hatshepsut: From Queen to Pharaoh. . .*v.1 p.670, p.690,v.3 p.10*

Hauling up the Morning: Writings and Art by Political Prisoners
and Prisoners of War in the U. S. *v.6 p.23*

The Haunted Bookshop. *v.2 p.98*

Haunted House and Other Short Stories. *v.2 p.394*

The Haunted Land: Facing Europe's Ghosts after
Communism. *v.3 p.208*

Haunted Media: Electronic Presence from Telegraphy to
Television. *v.4 p.419*

The Haunted Study: A Social History of the English Novel
1875-1914. . . . .*v.6 p.740, p.741*

Haunted Weather: Resonant Spaces, Silence and
Memory. *v.1 p.226*

The Haunting of Hill House. *v.2 p.90*

Hausa Women in the Twentieth Century. *v.6 p.71*

Havana Dreams: A Story of a Cuban Family. *v.3 p.309*

Havana: History and Architecture of a Romantic City. .*v.1 p.790*

Havana: The Making of Cuban Culture. *v.3 p.310*

Havana U. S. A.: Cuban Exiles and Cuban Americans in South
Florida, 1959-1994. . . . .*v.6 p.543, p.544*

Haven and Home: A History of the Jews in America. .*v.1 p.549*

Having a Good Cry: Effeminate Feelings and Pop-Culture
Forms. *v.4 p.695*

Havoc. *v.2 p.627*

The Haw Lantern. *v.2 p.352*

Hawaii: A History, from Polynesian Kingdom to American
State. *v.3 p.534*

Hawaii, America's Sugar Territory 1898-1959. . . . .*v.3 p.534*

Hawaii: Bicentennial and History Guide. *v.3 p.534*

Hawaii Pono: An Ethnic and Political History. . . .*v.4 p.702*

Hawaii: The Past, Present, and Future of Its Island-Kingdom:
An Historic Account of the Sandwich Islands of
Polynesia. *v.3 p.534*

Hawaiian Cowboys. *v.6 p.104*

The Hawaiian Kingdom: Foundation and Transformation,
1778-1854. . . . .*v.3 p.534*

Hawaiian Music and Musicians: An Illustrated
History. *v.1 p.288, p.296*

The Hawaiian Republic, 1894-98: And Its Struggle to Win
Annexation. *v.3 p.534*

Hawaii's Ferns and Fern Allies. *v.5 p.210*

Hawley's Condensed Chemical Dictionary, Set. *v.5 p.258*

Hawthorne and the Historical Romance of New England.*v.2 p.40*

Hawthorne, Melville and the Novel. *v.2 p.40, p.47*

Hawthorne: Tales and Sketches. *v.2 p.41*

Hawthorne: The Critical Heritage. *v.2 p.41*

Hawthorne's Mad Scientists: Pseudoscience and Social Science
in Nineteenth-Century Life and Letters. *v.2 p.41*

Haydn and the Enlightenment: The Late Symphonies and Their
Audience. *v.1 p.192, p.242, p.331*

Haydn at Eszterhaza, 1766-1790. . . . .*v.1 p.190, p.330*

Haydn: His Life and Music. *v.1 p.191, p.330*

Haydn in England, 1791-1795. . . . .*v.1 p.190, p.330*

Haydn, Mozart and the Viennese School
1740-1780. . . . .*v.1 p.189, p.190, p.330, p.343*

Haydn: The Creation. .*v.1 p.191, p.192, p.236, p.237, p.330, p.331*

Haydn: The Early Years, 1732-1765. . . . . . .*v.1 p.190, p.330*

Haydn: The Late Years, 1801-1809. . . . . . .*v.1 p.190, p.330*

Haydn: The 'Paris' Symphonies. *v.1 p.189, p.239, p.330*

Haydn: The Years of Creation, 1796-1800. . . .*v.1 p.190, p.330*

Haydn's Ingenious Jesting with Art: Contexts of Musical Wit
and Humor. *v.1 p.192, p.331*

Haydn's Symphonic Forms: Essays in Compositional
Logic. *v.1 p.189, p.239, p.330*

Haydn. *v.1 p.192, p.331*

Hayek on Liberty. *v.4 p.211*

Hayri the Barber Surname. *v.6 p.667*

Hayseeds, Moralizers, and Methodists: The Twentieth Century
Image of Kansas. *v.3 p.524*

Hazard and Choice Perception in Flood Plain
Management. *v.4 p.395*

Hazard Assessment of Chemicals: Vol. 1, Current
Developments. *v.5 p.363, p.376*

Hazard Assessment of Chemicals, Vol. 2. .*v.5 p.369, p.375, p.376*

Hazard Assessment of Chemicals, Vol. 4. . . . . . .*v.5 p.373*

Hazard Assessment of Chemicals, Vol. 6. .*v.5 p.363, p.369, p.376*

Hazardous Chemicals Desk Reference. *v.5 p.311*

Hazardous Laboratory Chemicals Disposal Guide. . . .*v.5 p.266*

Hazardous Materials Chemistry for Emergency
Responders. *v.5 p.313*

Hazardous Materials Dictionary. *v.5 p.311*

☐ Hazardous Substances Data Bank (HSDB). *v.5 p.311*

Hazardous Waste Chemistry: Toxicology and
Treatment. *v.5 p.314*

Hazardous Waste Management. *v.5 p.314, p.705, p.706*

Hazards in the Chemical Laboratory. *v.5 p.266*

Hazlitt: A Life: From Winterslow to Frith Street. . . .*v.2 p.293*

Hazlitt on Theatre: Selections from the View of the English
Stage and Criticisms and Dramatic Essays. *v.2 p.292*

☐ HazMap: Occupational Exposure to Hazardous
Materials. *v.5 p.311*

Hazmat. *v.2 p.149, p.150,v.6 p.405*

He Is the Sun, She Is the Moon: Women in Early Modern
Germany. *v.3 p.52, p.165*

He Knew He Was Right. *v.2 p.318*

He Knew She Was Right: The Independent Woman in the
Novels of Anthony Trollope. *v.2 p.317*

He Shall Go Out Free: The Lives of Denmark
Vesey. *v.3 p.501, p.502*

Head Hunters: The Making of Jazz's First Platinum
Album. *v.1 p.262, p.328*

Headfirst: The Olympic Success Story of Skeleton. . .*v.4 p.846*

Headlong Hall. *v.2 p.302*

Heads by Harry. *v.6 p.102*

The Heads of Religious Houses: England and Wales, 940-1216. . . . .*v.1 p.578*

The Healers: A Novel. *v.2 p.753*

The Healer. *v.6 p.647*

Healing Communities in Conflict: International Assistance in Complex Emergencies. *v.4 p.671*

The Healing of Nations: The Promise and Limits of Political Forgiveness. *v.4 p.483, p.624*

Healing Wound: Experiences and Reflections, Germany, 1938-2001. . . . .*v.3 p.178*

Health and Human Rights: Basic International Documents. *v.4 p.668, p.669, p.670*

Health and Medicine in the Christian Science Tradition. .*v.1 p.583*

Health and Slavery in Colonial Colombia. *v.3 p.356*

Health Care Administration: Planning, Implementing, and Managing Organized Delivery Systems. *v.5 p.514*

Health Care Ethics for Psychologists: A Casebook. . .*v.5 p.674*

Health Care in Colombia, c. 1920-c. 1950: A Preliminary Analysis. *v.3 p.357*

Health Care in the Black Community: Empowerment, Knowledge, Skills and Collectivism. *v.6 p.22*

Health Care in the Parisian Countryside, 1800-1914. . .*v.3 p.148*

Health Care Systems in Transit. *v.5 p.700*

Health Care, USA: Understanding Its Organization and Delivery. *v.5 p.514*

Health Care Worker's Primer on Professionalism. . . .*v.5 p.533*

Health Clubs: Architecture and Design. . . .*v.4 p.792, p.881*

Health Economics. *v.5 p.511*

Health Fitness Instructor's Handbook. *v.4 p.791, p.906*

Health Fitness Management: A Comprehensive Resource for Managing and Operating Programs and Facilities. *v.4 p.792, p.906*

Health Insurance: Current Issues and Background. . .*v.4 p.163*

Health Movement in America: Promoting Fitness. *v.4 p.790, p.791, p.805*

Health Promotion in Nursing Practice. *v.5 p.528*

Health Promotion Throughout the Life Span. *v.5 p.527*

The Health Status of Latinos in California. *v.6 p.551*

Healthcare Reform in America: A Reference Handbook. *v.4 p.160, p.161*

Healthcare Trends and Forecasts in 2006: Performance Expectations for the Healthcare Industry. *v.4 p.160*

The Healthy Body and Victorian Culture. *v.6 p.763*

The Healthy Dancer: Dance Medicine for Dancers. . .*v.1 p.50*

Healthy Runner's Handbook. *v.4 p.866, p.879*

Healthy Women, Healthy Lives: A Guide to Preventing Disease, from the Landmark Nurses' Health Study. *v.5 p.523*

Healthy Work: Stress, Productivity, and the Reconstruction of Working Life. *v.5 p.580*

Heard on the Street: Quantitative Questions from Wall Street Job Interviews. *v.4 p.169*

Hearing Bach's Passions. *v.1 p.185, p.236, p.303, p.304*

Hearing in Children. *v.5 p.523*

Hearing the Motet: Essays on the Motet of the Middle Ages and Renaissance. *v.1 p.178*

Hearing the Past : Essays in Historical Ethnomusicology and the Archaeology of Sound. *v.1 p.175*

Hearing. *v.5 p.607*

Hearst Castle: The Biography of a Country House. .*v.1 p.793*

The Hearsts: An American Dynasty. *v.4 p.149, p.411*

Heart and Head: Black Theology—Past, Present, and Future. *v.6 p.6, p.36*

A Heart at Fire's Center: The Life and Music of Bernard Herrmann. *v.1 p.256, p.332*

Heart Disease in Women. *v.5 p.520*

The Heart Is Katmandu: Novel. *v.6 p.649*

Heart of a Dog. *v.2 p.801*

The Heart of Change: Real Life Stories of How People Change Their Organizations. *v.4 p.73*

The Heart of Confederate Appalachia: Western North Carolina in the Civil War. *v.4 p.521*

Heart of Darkness: An Authoritative Text, Backgrounds and Sources, Criticism. *v.2 p.340*

Heart of Darkness and the Secret Sharer. *v.2 p.340*

Heart of Darkness. *v.2 p.340*

The Heart of Islam: Enduring Values for Humanity. . .*v.1 p.557*

The Heart of Mathematics: A Guide to Effective Thinking. *v.5 p.457, p.465*

The Heart of Midlothian. *v.2 p.307, p.308*

The Heart of Redness: A Novel. *v.2 p.756*

The Heart of the Matter. *v.2 p.349, p.350*

Heart of the Rock: The Indian Invasion of Alcatraz. *v.6 p.689, p.694*

The Heart of the Serpent: Soviet Science Fiction. . . .*v.2 p.810*

A Heart So White. *v.2 p.661*

The Heart Sutra Explained: Indian and Tibetan Commentaries. *v.6 p.241*

Heartbeat of Struggle: The Revolutionary Life of Yuri Kochiyama. *v.6 p.93, p.107, p.131*

Heartbeat of the People: Music and Dance of the Northern Pow-Wow. *v.1 p.14*

Heartbreak and Vine: Hardboiled Writers in Hollywood. .*v.6 p.326*

Hearths of Darkness: The Family in the American Horror Film. *v.6 p.320*

Heartland: Comparative Histories of the Midwestern States. *v.3 p.506*

Heartland Excursions: Ethnomusicological Reflections on Schools of Music. *v.1 p.406*

Heart's Needle. *v.2 p.116*

Hearts of Darkness: White Women Write Race. *v.2 p.191*

Hearts of Sorrow: Vietnamese-American Lives. *v.6 p.140*

Heartwood: The First Generation of Theravada Buddhism in America. *v.6 p.105*

Heat and Dust. *v.2 p.355*

Heat and Thermodynamics: An Intermediate Textbook. .*v.5 p.560*

Heat Capacities and Entropies of Organic Compounds in the Condensed Phase. *v.5 p.286*

Heat Exchangers: Selection, Rating, and Thermal Design. *v.5 p.713*

The Heat Is On: The Climate Crisis, the Cover-Up, the
    Prescription. *v.6 p.293*

The Heat of the Day. *v.2 p.334*

The Heat of the Hearth: The Process of Kinship in a Malay
    Fishing Community. *v.4 p.31*

Heat Transfer Essentials: A Textbook. *v.5 p.713*

Heat Transfer Handbook. *v.5 p.740*

Heat Transfer in Single and Multiphase Systems. . . .*v.5 p.713*

Heat Transfer Solver. *v.5 p.713*

Heat Transfer. *v.5 p.560, p.713*

Heather Has Two Mommies. *v.6 p.398*

Heaven and Earth: Unseen by the Naked Eye. *v.5 p.223*

Heaven Below: Early Pentecostals and American
    Culture. *v.1 p.587*

Heaven, Hell, and the Victorians. *v.2 p.177*

Heaven on Earth: The Rise and Fall of Socialism. . .*v.4 p.507*

Heavenly City of the Eighteenth-Century Philosophers. *v.3 p.71*

Heaven's Coast: A Memoir. *v.6 p.378, p.401*

Heaven's My Destination: A Novel. *v.2 p.134*

The Heavy Elements: Chemistry, Environmental Impact and
    Health Effects. *v.5 p.310*

Heavy Lifting: The Job of the American Legislature. *v.4 p.531*

Heavy Metals in the Environment: Origin, Interaction and
    Remediation. *v.5 p.354, p.355, p.371, p.372, p.373*

Heavy Metals in the Environment: Using Wetlands for Their
    Removal. *v.5 p.53, p.368, p.372, p.379*

Heavy Water and the Wartime Race for Nuclear Energy. *v.5 p.739*

Heavy Weather. *v.2 p.390*

Hebbel's Prose Tragedies. *v.2 p.599*

Hebrew and Modernity. *v.6 p.645*

The Hebrew Bible and Its Modern Interpreters. . . .*v.1 p.619*

Hebrew in America: Perspectives and Prospects. . . .*v.6 p.646*

Hebrew Literature in the Wake of the Holocaust. . . .*v.6 p.652*

Hebrew Novel in Czarist Russia: A Portrait of Jewish Life in the
    Nineteenth Century. *v.2 p.799*

Hebrew Scholarship and the Medieval World. *v.6 p.645*

Hebrews. *v.1 p.630*

Hecho a Mano: The Traditional Arts of Tucson's Mexican
    American Community. *v.6 p.492, p.523*

Hecho en Tejas: Texas-Mexican Folk Arts and
    Crafts. *v.6 p.492, p.523*

Hector Berlioz: "Les Troyens". *v.1 p.199, p.230, p.310*

The Hedgehog, the Fox, and the Magister's Pox: Mending the
    Gap Between Science and the Humanities. *v.5 p.410*

Hedgehogging. *v.4 p.94, p.99, p.162*

Hedonics of Taste. *v.5 p.606*

Hedonism and Naturalistic Ethics. *v.1 p.507*

The Hedonistic Approach to Life. *v.1 p.507*

⌨ H-Education. *v.4 p.327*

Hedwig and the Angry Inch. *v.1 p.252, p.379, p.409*

Hegel: A Biography. *v.3 p.168*

Hegel: A Re-Examination. *v.1 p.463*

Hegel: A Very Short Introduction. *v.1 p.464*

Hegel: An Intellectual Biography. *v.1 p.463*

Hegel and After: Studies in Continental Philosophy Between
    Kant and Sartre. *v.1 p.438*

A Hegel Dictionary. *v.1 p.464*

Hegel: Political Writings. *v.4 p.491, p.502*

Hegel's Educational Theory and Practice. . . .*v.4 p.343, p.344*

Hegel's Lectures in the History of Philosophy, Vols. 1-3. .*v.1 p.463*

Hegel's Logic: Being Part One of the Encyclopaedia of the
    Philosophical Sciences (1830). *v.1 p.463*

Hegel's Phenomenology of Spirit. *v.1 p.463*

Hegel's Philosophy of Politics: Idealism, Identity, and
    Modernity. *v.4 p.491*

Hegel. *v.1 p.464*

Hegemony and Culture: Politics and Change among the
    Yoruba. *v.6 p.71*

Heidegger: A Very Short Introduction. *v.1 p.471*

A Heidegger Dictionary. *v.1 p.471*

Heidegger, Education and Modernity. *v.4 p.345*

Heidegger: Through Phenomenology to Thought. . . .*v.1 p.471*

Heidegger's Philosophy of Science. *v.1 p.470*

The Heidi Chronicles and Other Plays. . . .*v.1 p.122, v.2 p.158*

Heimatmuseum: Roman. *v.2 p.612*

Heimskringla : History of the Kings of Norway. . . .*v.3 p.234*

Heimskringla: Sagas of the Norse Kings. *v.2 p.625*

Heimskringla: The Norse King Sagas. *v.2 p.625*

The Heinemann Book of African Women's Writing. . .*v.2 p.752*

The Heinemann Book of Caribbean Poetry. *v.2 p.768*

Heinous Crime: Cases, Causes, and Consequences. . .*v.6 p.252*

Heinrich Boll. *v.2 p.604, p.605*

Heinrich Heine: An Interpretation. *v.2 p.599*

Heinrich Heine. *v.2 p.601, p.602*

Heinrich Pestalozzi. *v.4 p.342*

Heinrich Schenker: A Guide to Research. . . .*v.1 p.163, p.369*

Heinrich Von Kleist. *v.2 p.599*

Heir to the Glimmering World. *v.2 p.151, p.152*

Heisenberg Probably Slept Here: The Lives, Times, and Ideas of
    the Great Physicists of the 20th Century. *v.5 p.542*

Heisenberg's War: The Secret History of the German
    Bomb. *v.3 p.49*

Heitor Villa-Lobos: A Life (1887-1959). *v.1 p.208, p.364*

Helen in Egypt. *v.2 p.88*

Helena. *v.2 p.388*

Helene Cixous. *v.2 p.531, p.532*

Helene Cixous: A Politics of Writing. *v.2 p.532*

The Helene Cixous Reader. *v.2 p.532*

Helen. *v.2 p.410*

Hell Without Fire: Conversion in Slave Religion. *v.6 p.36, p.37*

Hell Without Fires: Slavery, Christianity, and the Antebellum
    Spiritual Narrative. *v.6 p.36*

Hellenica, Bks. 1-4. . . . .*v.2 p.422*

Hellenica, Bks. 5-7. . . . .*v.2 p.422*

Hellenism and Homosexuality in Victorian Oxford. . .*v.6 p.760*

Hellenism in Late Antiquity. *v.3 p.30*

Hellenism in the East: The Interaction of Greek and Non-Greek
    Civilizations from Syria to Central Asia After
    Alexander. *v.3 p.21*

The Hellenistic Age, Vol. 2. . . . .*v.1 p.547*

Hellenistic and Early Modern Philosophy. *v.1 p.436*

Hellenistic and Roman Sparta. *v.3 p.21*

Hellenistic Civilization and the Jews. *v.3 p.22*

Hellenistic Civilization. *v.3 p.22*

Hellenistic Constructs: Essays in Culture, History, and
    Historiography. *v.3 p.20, p.21*

Hellenistic Economies. *v.3 p.13*

Hellenistic History and Culture. *v.3 p.21*

The Hellenistic Period: Historical Sources in Translation..*v.3 p.20*

The Hellenistic Philosophers: Translations of the Principal
    Sources with Philosophical Commentary, Vol. 1. . .*v.1 p.428*

Hellenistic Philosophy: Introductory Readings. . . .*v.1 p.428*

Hellenistic Philosophy of Mind. *v.1 p.427, p.428, p.496*

Hellenistic Philosophy: Stoics, Epicureans, Sceptics. .*v.1 p.428*

Hellenistic Science and Culture in the Last Three
    Centuries. *v.5 p.393*

Hellenistic Sculpture I: The Styles of ca. 331-200 B.C.*v.1 p.776*

Hellenistic Sculpture II: The Styles of ca. 200-100 B.C.*v.1 p.776*

Hellenistic Sculpture III: The Styles of ca. 100-31 B.C.*v.1 p.776*

Hellenistic Sculpture. *v.1 p.776*

The Hellenistic World and the Coming of Rome. . . .*v.3 p.25*

The Hellenistic World from Alexander to the Roman Conquest:
    A Selection of Ancient Sources in Translation. . .*v.3 p.20*

Hello, Hello Brazil: Popular Music in the Making of Modern
    Brazil. *v.1 p.293, v.3 p.267*

Help! My Job Interview Is Tomorrow!: How to Use the Library
    to Research an Employer. *v.4 p.171*

Help or Hindrance?: The Economic Implications of Immigration
    for African Americans. *v.4 p.570, p.571*

Helping at-Risk Youth Through Physical Fitness
    Programming. *v.4 p.795*

Helping Children Left Behind: State Aid and the Pursuit of
    Educational Equity. *v.4 p.302*

Helping the Dreamer: New and Selected Poems,
    1966-1988. . . . .*v.2 p.158*

Helsinki of the Czars Finland's Capital, 1808-1918. . .*v.3 p.236*

Hematology of Infancy and Childhood. *v.5 p.521*

Hemingway: A Biography. *v.2 p.85*

Hemingway: A Life Without Consequences. *v.2 p.85*

Hemingway and His Conspirators: Hollywood, Scribners, and
    the Making of the American Dream. *v.2 p.85*

Hemingway and the Movies. *v.2 p.85*

Hemingway and The Natural World. *v.2 p.84*

Hemingway and Women: Female Critics and the Female
    Voice. *v.2 p.83*

Hemingway: Essays of Reassessment. *v.2 p.85*

Hemingway: The 1930s. *v.2 p.85*

Hemingway: The Critical Heritage. *v.2 p.85*

Hemingway: The Final Years. *v.2 p.85*

Hemingway: The Paris Years. *v.2 p.85*

Hemingway: The Postwar Years and the Posthumous
    Novels. *v.2 p.83*

Hemingway vs. Fitzgerald: The Rise and Fall of a Literacy
    Friendship. *v.2 p.76, p.84*

Hemingway's Genders: Rereading the Hemingway
    Text. *v.2 p.83, p.84*

Hemingway's Theaters of Masculinity. *v.2 p.85*

Hemlock and After. *v.2 p.389, v.6 p.400*

Henderson the Rain King. *v.2 p.60*

Henderson's Dictionary of Biological Terms. *v.5 p.225*

Henley's Twentieth Century Book of Formulas, Processes, and
    Trade Secrets. *v.5 p.407*

Henning Kronstam: Portrait of a Danish Dancer. . . .*v.1 p.13*

Henri Cartier-Bresson: The Biography. *v.1 p.765*

Henri Dutilleux: His Life and Works. *v.1 p.221, p.322*

Henri Matisse: A Bio-Bibliography. *v.1 p.662, p.696*

Henri Matisse: A Retrospective. *v.1 p.696*

Henri Matisse: Catalogue Raisonné de l'Oeuvre Sculpte Etabli
    avec la Collaboration de Wanda de Guebriant. . .*v.1 p.779*

Henri Michaux : la poésie comme destin : biographie. .*v.2 p.522*

Henri Rousseau. *v.1 p.734*

Henrik Ibsen. *v.2 p.628*

Henry A. Wallace and American Foreign Policy. . . .*v.3 p.463*

Henry A. Wallace: His Search for a New World Order. .*v.3 p.464*

A Henry Adams Reader. *v.2 p.30*

Henry Adams: The Historian as Political Theorist. . . .*v.3 p.375*

Henry and Cato. *v.2 p.372*

Henry Cabot Lodge and the Search for an American Foreign
    Policy. *v.3 p.402, p.435*

Henry Clay and the Art of American Politics. *v.3 p.415*

Henry Cowell, Bohemian. . . .*v.1 p.215, p.216, p.319,v.6 p.409*

Henry Darger: Art and Selected Writings. *v.1 p.696*

Henry David Thoreau and the Moral Agency of
    Knowing. *v.2 p.52*

Henry David Thoreau: Collected Essays and Poems. . .*v.2 p.53*

Henry Fielding and the Augustan Ideal under Stress. .*v.2 p.248*

Henry Fielding: Plays, 1728-1731. . . . . . .*v.2 p.247, p.248*

Henry Fielding. *v.2 p.247, p.248*

Henry Fox Talbot: Selected Texts and Bibliography. . .*v.1 p.769*

Henry Handel Richardson: The Getting of Wisdom, Stories,
    Selected Prose and Correspondence. *v.2 p.748*

Henry Highland Garnet: A Voice of Black Radicalism in the
    19th Century. *v.3 p.421*

Henry II: King of France 1547-1559. . . . .*v.3 p.144*

Henry III and the Jesuit Politicians. *v.3 p.146*

Henry II. *v.3 p.99*

Henry I. *v.3 p.97, p.98*

Henry IV of Germany 1056-1106. . . . .*v.3 p.162*

Henry James - Complete Stories 1892-1898, Vol. I..*v.2 p.44, p.45*

Henry James - Complete Stories, 1898-1910, Vol. 2. . .*v.2 p.44*

Henry James: A Reference Guide. *v.2 p.43*

Henry James: A Study of the Short Fiction. *v.2 p.43, p.44*

Henry James and Homo-Erotic Desire. *v.2 p.43*

Henry James and the 'Woman Business'. *v.2 p.43*

Henry James' Apprenticeship: The Tales, 1864-1882. . .*v.2 p.45*

Henry James: Autobiography. *v.2 p.44*

A Henry James Chronology. *v.2 p.43*

Henry James Collected Travel Writings: The Continent: A Little Tour in France; Italian Hours; Other Travels. *v.2 p.45*

Henry James: Complete Stories 1864-1874. . . . . . .*v.2 p.45*

Henry James: Complete Stories, 1874-1884. . . . . . .*v.2 p.45*

A Henry James Encyclopedia. *v.2 p.43*

Henry James Goes to the Movies. *v.2 p.43, v.6 p.326*

Henry James: Literary Criticism: Essays, American and English Writers. *v.2 p.44*

Henry James: Novels, 1896-1899. . . . .*v.2 p.45*

Henry James: Novels, 1901-1902. . . . .*v.2 p.44*

Henry James on Stage and Screen. *v.2 p.43*

Henry James: The Contemporary Reviews. *v.2 p.43*

Henry James: The Later Novels. *v.2 p.45*

Henry James. *v.2 p.43*

Henry, King of France. *v.2 p.614*

◙ Henry Kissinger: Doctor of Diplomacy. *v.3 p.479*

Henry L. Stimson: The First Wise Man. *v.3 p.444, p.462*

Henry Lawson. *v.2 p.747*

Henry Mayhew. *v.2 p.298, p.299*

The Henry Miller Reader. *v.2 p.102*

Henry Moore, Complete Drawings: A Catalogue Raisonné, 1916-83. . . . .*v.1 p.723*

Henry Moore: Sculpting the Twentieth Century. *v.1 p.780*

Henry Morgan's Raid on Panama: Geopolitics and Colonial Ramifications, 1669-1674. . . . .*v.3 p.305*

Henry Norris Russell: Dean of American Aastronomers. .*v.5 p.62*

Henry Ossawa Tanner. *v.1 p.699*

Henry Purcell: A Guide to Research. *v.1 p.165, p.187, p.188, p.349, p.350*

Henry Purcell and the London Stage. . .*v.1 p.186, p.232, p.349*

Henry Purcell. *v.1 p.184, p.349*

Henry R. Luce and the Rise of the American News Media. *v.4 p.409*

Henry Shaw's Victorian Landscapes: The Missouri Botanical Garden and Tower Grove Park. *v.1 p.813*

Henry Steele Commager: Midcentury Liberalism and the History of the Present. *v.3 p.374*

Henry V, War Criminal?: And Other Shakespeare Puzzles. *v.2 p.222*

Henry Vaughan: A Life and Interpretation. *v.2 p.264*

Henry VIII. *v.3 p.101*

Henry Von Ofterdingen. *v.2 p.601*

Henry W. Grady, Spokesman of the New South. . . .*v.3 p.434*

Henry Wadsworth Longfellow: His Poetry and Prose. .*v.2 p.47*

Henry Wadsworth Longfellow: Poems and Other Writings. *v.2 p.47*

▢ Henryk Sienkiewicz. *v.2 p.789*

The Heptameron. *v.2 p.470*

Heptaméron. *v.2 p.470*

Her Body Knows: Two Novellas. *v.6 p.648*

Her Dream of Dreams: The Rise and Triumph of Madam C. J. Walker. *v.6 p.7, p.18, p.45*

Her Eyes. *v.6 p.669*

Her Husband: Hughes and Plath: Portrait of a Marriage.*v.2 p.353*

Her Husband. *v.2 p.722*

Her Kind of Want. *v.2 p.160*

Her Own Life: Autobiographical Writings by 17th Century Englishwomen. *v.2 p.196*

Her Privates We. *v.2 p.747*

Her Voice, Her Faith: Women Speak on World Religions. *v.1 p.529*

Her Wild American Self. *v.6 p.100*

Heracleitus - On the Universe: Nature of Man, Regimen in Health, Humours, Amorphisms, Regimen 1-3, Dreams., Vol. 4. . . . .*v.2 p.404, v.5 p.510*

Heracles. *v.2 p.410*

Heraclitus - Fragments: A Text and Translation with a Commentary. *v.1 p.422*

Heraclitus. *v.1 p.422*

Herbarium. *v.5 p.85*

Herbert Hoover: Forgotten Progressive. *v.3 p.482*

Herbert Hoover: The Great War and Its Aftermath, 1914-23. . . . .*v.3 p.471*

Herbert Hoover: The Postpresidential Years, 1933-1964, Set. *v.3 p.465, p.466*

Herbert Hoover: The Public Life. *v.3 p.439, p.467*

Herbert Hoover. *v.3 p.474*

Herbert List: The Monograph. *v.1 p.768*

Herbert Spencer on Education. *v.4 p.346*

Herbicides in War: The Long Term Ecological and Human Consequences. *v.5 p.10, p.354, p.355*

Herculean Ferrara: Ercole d'Este (1471-1505) and the Invention of a Ducal Capital. *v.3 p.200*

Hercules, My Shipmate. *v.2 p.348*

Herculine Barbin: Being the Recently Discovered Memoirs of a Nineteenth-Century French Hermaphrodite. *v.6 p.370*

Herder and the Beginnings of Comparative Literature. .*v.2 p.600*

Herder: His Life and Thought. *v.2 p.598*

Here and Elsewhere: The Collected Fiction of Kenneth Burke. *v.2 p.59*

Here at Eagle Pond. *v.2 p.82*

Here Beneath Low-Flying Planes. *v.2 p.160*

Here I Stand: A Life of Martin Luther. *v.1 p.602*

Here I Stand. *v.6 p.19*

Here to Stay: American Families in the Twentieth Century. *v.4 p.732*

Here to Stay: Five Plays from the Women's Project. *v.1 p.68, p.121*

Here Today Vanishing Species. *v.5 p.180*

Herencia: The Anthology of Hispanic Literature of the United States. *v.2 p.19, v.6 p.496*

Herero Heroes: A Socio-Political History of the Herero of Namibia, 1890-1923. . . . .*v.6 p.76*

Here's New England: A Guide to Vacationland. . . .*v.3 p.485*

Here's Where I Stand: A Memoir. *v.4 p.486*

Heresy and Authority in Medieval Europe. . . .*v.1 p.646, p.647*

Heresy in the University: The Black Athena Controversy and the Responsibilities of American Intellectuals. . .*v.6 p.3, p.21*

Heretics and Scholars in the High Middle Ages, 1000-1200. . . . .*v.6 p.570*

Hereward the Wake. *v.2 p.296*

Heritage and Hellenism. v.3 p.21

The Heritage Encyclopedia of Band Music: Composers and
Their Music, Set. v.1 p.161

Heritage, Museums and Galleries: An Introductory
Reader. v.1 p.827

The Heritage of China: Contemporary Perspectives on Chinese
Civilization. v.6 p.182

Heritage of Engineering Geology - The First 100
Years. v.5 p.421, p.422

The Heritage of Experimental Embryology: Hans Spemann and
the Organizer. v.5 p.160

The Heritage of Giotto's Geometry: Art and Science on the Eve
of the Scientific Revolution. v.3 p.70

The Heritage of Persia. v.6 p.629

The Heritage of Vietnamese Poetry. v.6 p.169

The Heritage. v.2 p.612

Das Herkunftswoerterbuch, Vol. 7. . . . . . .v.2 p.620

Herman Melville: A Biography, 1819-1851. . . . . .v.2 p.48

Herman Melville: A Biography, 1851-1891. . . . . .v.2 p.48

Herman Melville A to Z: The Essential Reference to His Life
and Work. v.2 p.48

A Herman Melville Encyclopedia. v.2 p.47, p.48

Herman Melville: Moby-Dick, Billy Budd and Other
Writings. v.2 p.48

Herman Melville. v.2 p.48

Herman Miller: The Purpose of Design. v.1 p.801

Hermanitos Comanchitos: Indo-Hispano Rituals of Captivity and
Redemption. v.6 p.523

Hermann Hesse: Life and Art. v.2 p.610

Hermaphrodites and the Medical Invention of Sex. . .v.4 p.746

The Hermeneutic Tradition: From Ast to Ricoeur. . . .v.1 p.507

Hermeneutics and Education. v.4 p.323, p.339

@ Hermeneutics and Modern Philosophy. v.1 p.507

Hermeneutics and the Human Sciences: Essays on Language,
Action and Interpretation. v.1 p.457, p.507

Hermetic Definition. v.2 p.88, p.89

The Hermit in Paris: Autobiographical Writings. . . .v.2 p.714

The Hermit of Peking: The Hidden Life of Sir Edmund
Backhouse. v.6 p.201, p.216

Hernani: Victor Hugo. v.2 p.494

The Hero and the Outlaw: Building Extraordinary Brands
Through the Power of Archetypes. v.4 p.144

The Hero in Scandinavian Literature: From Peer Gynt to the
Present. v.2 p.624

The Hero in the Earthly City: A Reading of Beowulf. .v.2 p.205

A Hero of Our Time. v.2 p.805

The Hero of the Waverley Novels: With New Essays on
Scott. v.2 p.308

The Hero with a Thousand Faces. v.1 p.527

Herodotus, Bk. 1. . . . . .v.2 p.412

Herodotus: Histories. v.2 p.412

Herodotus in Context: Ethnography, Science and the Art of
Persuasion. v.2 p.412, p.413

Herodotus, Vol. 8. . . . . .v.2 p.412

Herodotus. v.2 p.412

Heroes of the French Epic: A Selection of Chansons de
Geste. v.2 p.464, p.466

The Heroes of the Greeks. v.1 p.532

Heroes of Their Own Lives: The Politics and History of Family
Violence: Boston, 1880-1960. . . . . .v.4 p.742

Heroic Defeats: The Politics of Job Loss. v.4 p.121

Heroic Diplomacy: Sadat, Kissinger, Carter, Begin and the
Quest for Arab-Israeli Peace. .v.4 p.566, p.642, p.646, p.650

The Heroic Image in Chile: Arturo Prat, Secular Saint. .v.3 p.277

The Heroic Temper: Studies in Sophoclean Tragedy. . .v.2 p.419

Heroides and Amores, Vol. 1. . . . . .v.2 p.439

Herpetology: An Introductory Biology of Amphibians and
Reptiles. v.5 p.217

Herself Surprised, Vol. I. v.2 p.338

Herself Surprised. v.2 p.338

Her. v.2 p.75, v.6 p.398

Herzog. v.2 p.60

He's a Rebel: Phil Spector - Rock and Roll's Legendary
Producer. v.1 p.273

Hesiod and the Language of Poetry. v.2 p.413

Hesiod: Theogony, Works and Days, Shield. v.2 p.413

The Hesiodic Catalogue of Women: Constructions and
Reconstructions. v.2 p.413

Hesiod's Cosmos. v.2 p.413

Hesiod. v.2 p.413

Hesse Companion. v.2 p.610

The Hesse-Mann Letters: The Correspondence of Hermann
Hesse and Thomas Mann, 1910-1955. . . . . . .v.2 p.609

Hester Lynch Piozzi. v.2 p.256

Heterochrony in Evolution: A Multidisciplinary
Approach. v.5 p.194

Heterochrony: The Evolution of Ontogeny. v.5 p.194

▢ Heterocycles (Natural Products) Databases (1975+). .v.5 p.299

Heterocyclic Chemistry. v.5 p.298

Heterogeneous Reaction Dynamics. v.5 p.275

Hetty Dorval. v.2 p.739

Heuristics and Biases: The Psychology of Intuitive
Judgment. v.4 p.195

Hevajra Tantra. v.1 p.564

Hey's Mineral Index: Mineral Species, Varieties and
Synonyms. v.5 p.435

▢ HFA = Harry Fox Agency. v.1 p.172, p.384

▢ HHMI Howard Hughes Medical Institute: Blazing a Genetic
Trail. v.5 p.144

The Hiawatha Man: The Life and Music of Samuel
Coleridge-Taylor. v.1 p.204, p.282, p.318

Hibakusha Cinema: Hiroshima, Nagasaki, and the Nuclear
Image in Japanese Film. v.6 p.335

The Hidden Cost of Being African American. . . .v.6 p.20, p.40

Hidden Depths: The Story of Hypnosis. v.5 p.613

The Hidden Face of Eve: Women in the Arab World. .v.6 p.583

The Hidden Foundation: Cinema and the Question of
Class. v.6 p.321

Hidden from History: Reclaiming the Gay and Lesbian
Past. v.6 p.362

Title Index

The Hidden Genius of Emotion: Lifespan Transformations of Personality. .v.5 p.654

Hidden Hands: An Anthology of American Women Writers, 1790 to 1870. . . . . .v.2 p.29

The Hidden Hippopotamus: Reappraisal in African History, the Early Colonial Experience. v.6 p.77

Hidden Histories of Gender and the State in Latin America. v.3 p.283, p.303

The Hidden History of the Korean War, 1950-1951. . .v.6 p.237

A Hidden Holocaust: Lesbian and Gay Persecution in Germany, 1933-1945. . . . . .v.3 p.84, v.6 p.365

The Hidden Law: The Poetry of W. H. Auden. v.2 p.329

A Hidden Love: Art and Homosexuality. v.1 p.706

Hidden Messages: Representation and Resistance in Andean Colonial Drama. v.3 p.262

The Hidden Power of Social Networks: Understanding How Work Really Gets Done in Organizations. v.4 p.120

The Hidden Room. v.2 p.738

Hidden Scholars: Women Anthropologists and the Native American Southwest. v.4 p.4

Hidden Springs (Medieval Religious Women), Set. v.6 p.560, p.572

Hidden Treasures Revealed: Impressionist Masterpieces and Other Important French Paintings Preserved by the State Hermitage Museum, St. Petersburg. v.1 p.728

The Hidden Wordsworth: Poet, Lover, Rebel, Spy. . .v.2 p.323

The Hidden-Hand Presidency: Eisenhower as Leader. .v.3 p.472

Hideous Dream: Special Operations, Racism and Imperialism in the Haiti Invasion of 1994. . . . . .v.3 p.315

Hideyoshi. v.6 p.226

Hiding from Humanity: Disgust, Shame, and the Law. .v.1 p.491

Hierarchical Structures and Social Value: The Creation of Black and Irish Identities in the United States. v.4 p.730

The Hieroglyphics of Space: Understanding the City. .v.6 p.728

Hieronymus Bosch - The Complete Prints: Catalogue Raisonné. v.1 p.757

Hieronymus Bosch: Garden of Earthly Delights. .v.1 p.735, p.736

High and Dry: The Texas-New Mexico Struggle for the Pecos River. .v.6 p.300

High and Low: Modern Art and Popular Culture. . . .v.1 p.681

High and Mighty SUV's: The World's Most Dangerous Vehicles and How They Got That Way. v.5 p.715

High and Mighty: The Dangerous Rise of the SUV. . .v.4 p.153

High Comedy in American Movies: Class Humor from the 1920's to the Present. v.6 p.313

High Culture Fever: Politics, Aesthetics, and Ideology in Deng's China. v.6 p.198, p.208

High Energy Astrophysics: Particles, Photons and Their Detection, Vol. 1. . . . . .v.5 p.66, p.67

High Energy Astrophysics: Stars, the Galaxy and the Interstellar Medium. v.5 p.66

High Frequency Techniques: An Introduction to RF and Microwave Engineering. v.5 p.729

High Hopes: The Clinton Presidency and the Politics of Ambition. v.3 p.478

High Literacy and Ethnic Identity: Dominican American Schooling in Transition. v.6 p.527

The High Lonesome: Epic Solo Climbing Stories. . . .v.4 p.789

High Lonesome: Stories 1966-2006. . . . . .v.2 p.152

High Middle Ages: Hebrew Language and Letters. . .v.6 p.645

High Mountains Rising: Appalachia in Place and Time. .v.3 p.498

High Noon in the Cold War: Kennedy, Khrushchev, and the Cuban Missile Crisis. v.3 p.440, p.471

High Performance Networks. v.5 p.726

High Performance: The Culture and Technology of Drag Racing, 1950-2000. . . . . .v.4 p.848

The High Price of Bullion: A Proof of Depreciation of Bank Notes. v.4 p.220

The High Price of Materialism. v.5 p.586

High Renaissance and Mannerism: Italy, the North and Spain, 1500-1600. . . . . .v.1 p.675, p.688

High Resolution Spectroscopy. v.5 p.273

High Risk and Big Ambition: The Presidency of George W. Bush. v.3 p.484

The High Road to Pyrrhonism. v.1 p.517

The High Status Track: Studies of Elite Schools and Stratification. v.4 p.296, p.297

High Tech and High Heels in the Global Economy: Women, Work and Pink-Collar Identities in the Caribbean. . .v.4 p.28

High Tech Harvest: Understanding Genetically Modified Food Plants. v.5 p.8, p.370

High Tech Hot Shots: Careers in Sports Engineering. v.4 p.870, p.903

The High Tide of Prophecy. . .v.4 p.488, p.490, p.493, p.517

High Times and Hard Times: Sketches and Tales by George Washington Harris. v.2 p.39

Higher Education and Opinion Making in Twentieth-Century England. v.4 p.336, p.337

Higher Education As a Moral Enterprise. v.4 p.290

Higher Education in a Maturing Democracy. v.4 p.331

Higher Education in Ireland: North and South. . . .v.4 p.336

Higher Education in Transition: A History of American Colleges and Universities. v.4 p.331

Higher Education under Fire: Politics, Economics and the Crisis of the Humanities. v.4 p.330

Higher Goals: Women's Ice Hockey and the Politics of Gender. v.4 p.820, p.838, p.862, v.6 p.438

Higher Learning in America, 1980-2000. . . . . . .v.4 p.331

The Higher Learning in America: A Memorandum on the Conduct of Universities by Business Men. v.4 p.250

The Higher Learning in America. v.4 p.290

Higher Learning. v.4 p.295, p.330

The Highest Apple: Sappho and the Lesbian Poetic Tradition. v.6 p.393

The Highland Lute: The Albanian National Epic. v.2 p.815, v.3 p.252

High-Tech Cycling. v.4 p.856, p.870, p.871

Highway 61 Revisited: The Tangled Roots of American Jazz, Blues, Rock, and Country Music. v.1 p.274

El hijo de Casa. v.2 p.676

Hilary Putnam. v.1 p.441

Hilbert. .v.5 p.467

Hildegard of Bingen: A Visionary Life. v.1 p.177, p.332, v.6 p.570, p.571

The Hill of Evil Counsel. *v.6 p.650*

Hillbilly: A Cultural History of an American Icon. . . .*v.4 p.709*

The Hills Beyond. *v.2 p.137, p.138*

Hills of Conflict: Basque Nationalism in France. . . .*v.3 p.158*

Him with His Foot in His Mouth and Other Stories. . .*v.2 p.60*

Himalaya: Life on the Edge of the World. *v.6 p.162*

Himalayan Architecture. *v.1 p.788*

Himalayan Households: Tamang Demography and Domestic
  Processes. *v.6 p.164*

Himalayan Traders: Economy, Society, and Culture in Northwest
  Nepal. *v.6 p.163*

Himalayan Voices: An Introduction to Modern Nepali
  Literature. *v.6 p.151, p.164*

Hindu Art and Architecture. *v.1 p.692*

Hindu Bioethics for the Twenty-First Century. *v.5 p.247*

The Hindu Caste System: The Sacralization of a Social
  Order. *v.4 p.703*

Hindu Goddesses: Vision of the Divine Feminine in the Hindu
  Religious Tradition. *v.1 p.536*

Hindu Monastic Life: The Monks and Monasteries of
  Bhubaneswar. *v.1 p.537*

Hindu Myths: A Sourcebook Translated from the
  Sanskrit. *v.1 p.535*

Hindu Nationalism and Indian Politics: The Origins and
  Development of the Bharatiya Jana Sangh. *v.4 p.617*

The Hindu Nationalist Movement in India. .*v.1 p.540, v.6 p.157*

Hindu Nationalists in India: The Rise of the Bharatiya Janata
  Party. *v.4 p.618*

Hindu Places of Pilgrimage in India: A Study in Cultural
  Geography. *v.1 p.535*

Hindu Tantric and Sakta Literature. *v.1 p.536*

The Hindu Tradition: Readings in Oriental Thought. . .*v.1 p.535*

Hindu Writings: A Short Introduction to the Major
  Sources. *v.1 p.536, p.537*

Hinduism: A Cultural Perspective. *v.1 p.536*

Hinduism: A Very Short Introduction. *v.1 p.537*

Hinduism: New Essays in the History of Religions. . .*v.1 p.534*

The Hinduism Omnibus. *v.1 p.537*

Hip Hop America. *v.1 p.269*

Hip Hoptionary (TM): The Dictionary of Hip Hop
  Terminology. *v.1 p.163, p.276*

HIPAA Policies and Procedures Desk Reference. . . .*v.5 p.513*

Hippocrates: Affections, Diseases 1, Diseases 2. . . .*v.5 p.510*

Hippocrates: Diseases 3, Internal Affections, Regimen in Acute
  Diseases. *v.2 p.404, v.5 p.510*

Hippocrates: Epidemics 2, 4-6. . . . . . .*v.2 p.404, v.5 p.510*

Hippocrates in a World of Pagans and Christians. . . .*v.1 p.525*

Hippocrates: Places in Man - Glands, Fleshes. Prorrhetic 1-2,
  Physician, Use of Liquids, Ulcers, Haemorrhoids and
  Fistulas. *v.2 p.404*

Hippocrates: Places in Man. *v.2 p.404*

Hippocratic Writings. *v.2 p.404*

Hippolytus. *v.2 p.410*

Hiram Johnson: Political Revivalist. *v.3 p.463, p.464*

Hiro: Photographs. *v.1 p.765*

Hirohito and the Making of Modern Japan. *v.6 p.226*

Hiroshi Hara: The 'Floating World' of his Architecture. .*v.1 p.791*

Hiroshige's Journey in the 60 Odd Provinces. *v.1 p.757*

Hiroshima Mon Amour. *v.2 p.516*

Hirschfeld on Line: Over 400 Drawings, Paintings and
  Photos. *v.1 p.701*

☐ Hirshhorn Museum and Sculpture Garden. *v.1 p.774*

His Current Woman. *v.2 p.791*

His Daughter. *v.6 p.649*

His Exits and His Entrances, the Story of Shakespeare's
  Reputation. *v.2 p.231*

His Invention So Fertile: A Life of Christopher Wren. .*v.1 p.795*

His Song: The Musical Journey of Elton John. *v.6 p.410*

His Very Self and Voice: Collected Conversations of Lord
  Byron. *v.2 p.273*

Hispanas de Queens: Latino Panethnicity in a New York City
  Neighborhood. *v.6 p.545, p.550*

The Hispanic American Almanac: A Reference Work on
  Hispanics in the United States. *v.6 p.485*

Hispanic American Firsts: 500 Years of Extraordinary
  Achievement. *v.6 p.485*

☐ Hispanic American Periodicals Index (HAPI). . . .*v.3 p.259*

The Hispanic Condition: Reflections on Culture and Identity in
  America. *v.6 p.522, p.545*

Hispanic Culture in the Southwest. *v.6 p.530*

The Hispanic Databook: Statistics for All U.S. Counties and
  Cities with over 10,000 Population. *v.6 p.485*

Hispanic Education in the United States: Raices y
  Alas. *v.4 p.311, v.6 p.527*

Hispanic Folk Music of New Mexico and the Southwest: A
  Self-Portrait of the People. *v.6 p.519, p.524*

Hispanic Furniture: An American Collection. *v.1 p.804*

The Hispanic Image on the Silver Screen: An Interpretive
  Filmography from Silents into Sound, 1898-1935. .*v.6 p.330*

Hispanic Literature Criticism, Set. *v.2 p.665*

Hispanic Literature of the United States: A Comprehensive
  Reference. *v.6 p.500, p.507, p.513*

The Hispanic Market Handbook. *v.4 p.136*

Hispanic Nation: Culture, Politics and the Constructing of
  Identity. *v.6 p.537, p.543*

Hispanic Periodicals in the U. S., Origins To 1960: A Brief
  History and Comprehensive Bibliography. *v.6 p.485*

Hispanic Spaces, Latino Places: Community and Cultural
  Diversity in Contemporary America. *v.4 p.381*

Hispanic Theatre in the United States. *v.1 p.124*

Hispanic Writers: A Selection of Sketches from Contemporary
  Authors. *v.6 p.501, p.507, p.514, p.515*

Hispanic-American Material Culture: A Directory of Collections,
  Sites, Archives and Festivals in the United States and
  Canada. *v.6 p.485*

Hispanic/Latino Identity: A Philosophical Perspective. .*v.6 p.544*

Hispanics in Congress: A Historical and Political
  Survey. *v.6 p.539*

Hispanics in Hollywood: An Encyclopedia of Film and
  Television. *v.6 p.490, p.493*

ⓔ Hispanics in the American West. *v.3 p.521*

Hispanics in the American West. *v.3 p.518*

Hispanics in the Mormon Zion, 1912-1999. . . . . .*v.6 p.536*

Hispanics in the United States. *v.6 p.522*

Hispanics/Latinos in the United States: Ethnicity, Race, and Rights. *v.6 p.540, p.544*

The Hispano Homeland. *v.6 p.532*

História da Alimentação no Brasil, 2 vols. *v.3 p.271*

Histoire de la littérature belge francophone : 1830-2000. .*v.2 p.535*

Histoire de la littérature française au XVIIe siècle, vol. 1. . . . .*v.2 p.458*

Histoire de la littérature française au XVIIe siècle, vol. 2. . . . .*v.2 p.458*

Histoire de la littérature française au XVIIe siècle, vol. 3. . . . .*v.2 p.458*

Histoire de la Louisiane Francaise. *v.3 p.507*

Histoire d'O. *v.2 p.533*

Histoire Generale des Sciences. *v.5 p.389*

Histology and Cell Biology: An Introduction to Pathology. *v.5 p.153, p.159*

Historia de Cuba: 1492 1898: Formación y Liberación de la Nación. *v.3 p.313*

Historia de la Alimentación en Venezuela. *v.3 p.271*

Historia de la Literatura Española obra Completa. . .*v.2 p.639*

Historia de la Literatura Espanola: Edad Media y Renacimiento, Vol. 1. . . . .*v.2 p.638*

Historia de la Literatura Espanola: El Romanticismo, Vol. 4. . . . .*v.2 p.638*

Historia de la Literatura Espanola: El Siglo XVIII, Vol. 3. . . . .*v.2 p.638*

Historia de la Literatura Espanola: Epoca Barroca, Vol. 2. . . . .*v.2 p.638*

Historia de la Literatura Hispanoamericana: Tomo I. Época Colonial. *v.2 p.665*

Historia de la Literatura Hispanoamericana: Tomo II. Del Neoclasicismo Al Modernismo. *v.2 p.664, p.665*

Historia de la Literatura HispanoAmericana. *v.2 p.639*

Historia de la Lituratura Espanola. *v.2 p.638*

Historia de la Nueva Mexico, 1610: A Critical and Annotated Spanish/English Edition. *v.6 p.510, p.533*

Historia de una Escalera (Story of Stairway - Meninas): Las Meninas. *v.2 p.656*

Historia Del Hambre en México. *v.3 p.271*

La Historia del Helado en México. *v.3 p.271*

Historia Del Teatro Español: (Desde Sus Orígenes Hasta 1900). *v.2 p.640*

Historia Del Teatro Español: Siglo XX. *v.2 p.640*

Historia: Empiricism and Erudition in Early Modern Europe. *v.5 p.80*

Historia Moderna de México, 10 vols. *v.3 p.289*

Historia Patria: Politics, History, and National Identity in Spain, 1875-1975. . . . .*v.3 p.243*

Historia: The Literary Making of Chicana and Chicano History. *v.6 p.514, p.532*

Historia von Doctor Johann Fausten. English. The Historie of the Damnable Life and Deserved Death of Doctor John Faustus. Modernized, edited, and introduced by William Rose. *v.2 p.593*

Historiae, Vol. I, Bks. I-IV. *v.2 p.422*

Historiae, Vol. II, Bks. V-VIII. *v.2 p.422*

The Historian L. Calpurnius Piso Frugi and the Roman Annalistic Tradition. *v.2 p.426*

Historians Against History: The Frontier Thesis and the National Covenant in American Historical Writing since 1830. .*v.3 p.376*

Historians and Africanist History: A Critique. *v.6 p.54*

Historians in Public: The Practice of American History, 1890-1970. . . . .*v.3 p.375*

The Historians of Ancient Rome: An Anthology of the Major Writings. *v.3 p.22*

Historians of Economics and Economic Thought: The Construction of Disciplinary Memory. . . .*v.4 p.209, p.210*

Historias del Comer y del Beber en Buenos Aires: Arqueología Histórica de la Vajilla de Mesa. *v.3 p.272*

Historias para Ser Contadas - Stories for the Theatre. .*v.2 p.678*

☐ Historic American Buildings Survey / Historic American Engineering Survey. *v.1 p.711, p.782, p.821*

Historic Cities and Sacred Sites: Cultural Roots for Urban Futures. *v.1 p.823, v.6 p.729*

Historic Cities of the Americas: An Illustrated Encyclopedia. *v.6 p.709*

Historic Costume for the Stage. *v.1 p.150*

Historic Delhi: An Anthology. *v.6 p.161*

The Historic Imaginary: Politics of History in Fascist Italy. *v.3 p.203*

Historic Louisiana: An Illustrated History. *v.3 p.507*

Historic Millwork: A Guide to Restoring and Re-Creating Doors, Windows, and Moldings of the Late Nineteenth Through Mid-Twentieth Centuries. . . .*v.1 p.824*

Historic Preservation for a Living City: Historic Charleston Foundation, 1947-1997. . . . .*v.1 p.824*

Historic Storms of the North Sea, British Isles and Northwest Europe. *v.6 p.293*

Historic U. S. Court Cases: An Encyclopedia, Set. . .*v.4 p.441*

Historical and Cultural Atlas of African Americans. .*v.6 p.3, p.33*

An Historical and Historiographical Commentary on Suetonius' Life of C. Caligula. *v.2 p.443, p.444*

Historical and Multicultural Encyclopedia of Women's Reproductive Rights in the United States. *v.4 p.676*

An Historical Anthology of Select British Speeches. . .*v.2 p.197*

Historical Archaeology in Africa: Representation, Social Memory, and Oral Traditions. *v.4 p.14*

The Historical Archaeology of the Ottoman Empire: Breaking New Ground. *v.4 p.13*

Historical Archaeology. *v.4 p.14*

Historical Atlas of Africa. *v.6 p.51*

Historical Atlas of Central America. *v.3 p.298, v.4 p.399*

An Historical Atlas of Central Asia. *v.4 p.384*

Historical Atlas of Central Europe. *v.3 p.206, p.207*

Historical Atlas of Empires: From 4000 BC to the 21st Century. *v.4 p.380*

Historical Atlas of Indonesia. *v.6 p.174, p.176*

A Historical Atlas of Iraq. *v.6 p.602*

A Historical Atlas of North America Before Columbus. *v.4 p.380, v.6 p.685*

The Historical Atlas of the American Revolution. . . .*v.3 p.413*

Historical Atlas of the Crusades. *v.4 p.380*

The Historical Atlas of the Earth: A Visual Exploration of the Earth's Physical Past. *v.5 p.445, p.446*

Historical Atlas of the Middle East. *v.6 p.581*

Historical Atlas of the Napoleonic Era. *v.4 p.383*

Historical Atlas of the North Pacific Ocean: Maps of Discovery and Scientific Exploration, 1500-2000. . . . . *v.4 p.379*

Historical Atlas of the Rise of Islam. *v.4 p.380*

Historical Atlas of World War Two. *v.4 p.380, p.381*

The Historical Austen. *v.2 p.267*

Historical Biogeography: An Introduction. *v.5 p.168*

Historical Chemistry--Full Text and Miscellaneous Sites. *v.5 p.262*

Historical Commentary on Polybius. *v.2 p.406*

A Historical Commentary on Sallust's Bellum Jugurthinum. *v.2 p.442*

The Historical Development of the Calculus. . *v.5 p.465, p.485*

Historical Dictionary of Afghan Wars, Revolutions and Insurgencies. *v.6 p.633, p.634*

Historical Dictionary of Afghanistan. *v.6 p.633*

The Historical Dictionary of Algeria. *v.6 p.642*

Historical Dictionary of Armenia. *v.6 p.633*

Historical Dictionary of Arms Control and Disarmament. *v.4 p.656*

Historical Dictionary of Australian and New Zealand Cinema. *v.6 p.337*

Historical Dictionary of Burma (Myanmar). *v.6 p.166*

Historical Dictionary of Cambodia. *v.6 p.170*

Historical Dictionary of Canada. *v.3 p.534*

Historical Dictionary of Cyprus. *v.6 p.601*

Historical Dictionary of Descartes and Cartesian Philosophy. *v.1 p.436*

Historical Dictionary of Egypt. *v.6 p.635*

Historical Dictionary of European Imperialism. . . . *v.4 p.583*

Historical Dictionary of Feminism. *v.6 p.433*

Historical Dictionary of Guangzhou (Canton) and Guangdong. *v.6 p.205*

Historical Dictionary of Hinduism. *v.1 p.537*

Historical Dictionary of Human Rights and Humanitarian Organizations. *v.4 p.670*

Historical Dictionary of Iran. *v.6 p.629*

Historical Dictionary of Iraq. *v.6 p.601*

Historical Dictionary of Israel. *v.6 p.608*

Historical Dictionary of Japanese Traditional Theatre. *v.1 p.60, p.132*

Historical Dictionary of Kant and Kantianism. *v.1 p.460, p.461*

Historical Dictionary of Kyrgyzstan. *v.3 p.230*

Historical Dictionary of Laos. *v.6 p.171*

Historical Dictionary of Law Enforcement. *v.6 p.261*

Historical Dictionary of Lebanon. *v.6 p.604*

Historical Dictionary of Libya. *v.6 p.640*

Historical Dictionary of Malaysia. *v.6 p.172*

Historical Dictionary of Mongolia. *v.6 p.240*

Historical Dictionary of Morocco. *v.6 p.643*

Historical Dictionary of Multinational Peacekeeping. *v.4 p.650*

Historical Dictionary of North Korea. *v.6 p.236*

Historical Dictionary of Organized Labor. *v.4 p.125*

Historical Dictionary of Palestine. *v.6 p.608*

Historical Dictionary of Paraguay. *v.3 p.344*

Historical Dictionary of Refugee and Disaster Relief Organizations. *v.4 p.667*

Historical Dictionary of Saudi Arabia. *v.6 p.625*

Historical Dictionary of Sikhism. *v.1 p.541*

Historical Dictionary of Sweden. *v.3 p.235*

Historical Dictionary of Syria. *v.6 p.606*

Historical Dictionary of Taiwan (Republic of China). *v.6 p.213*

Historical Dictionary of Terrorism. *v.4 p.657*

The Historical Dictionary of the 1960s. *v.3 p.477*

Historical Dictionary of the Bahai Faith. *v.1 p.560*

Historical Dictionary of the Berbers (Iimazighen). . . *v.6 p.600*

Historical Dictionary of the Dirty Wars. . . . *v.3 p.348, p.354*

Historical Dictionary of the Druzes. *v.6 p.601*

Historical Dictionary of the Friends (Quakers). . . . *v.1 p.585*

Historical Dictionary of the Gay Liberation Movement: Gay Men and the Quest for Social Justice. . . . *v.6 p.358, p.363*

Historical Dictionary of the Hong Kong SAR and the Macao SAR. *v.6 p.205*

Historical Dictionary of the Kurds. *v.6 p.598*

Historical Dictionary of the Lesbian Liberation Movement: Still the Rage. *v.6 p.358, p.363, p.387*

Historical Dictionary of the Modern Olympic Movement. *v.4 p.805, p.845*

Historical Dictionary of the Mongol World Empire. *v.6 p.238, p.239*

Historical Dictionary of the Olympic Movement. *v.4 p.807, p.846*

Historical Dictionary of the Ottoman Empire. *v.6 p.591*

Historical Dictionary of the Philippines. *v.6 p.179*

Historical Dictionary of the Republic of Korea. . . . *v.6 p.237*

Historical Dictionary of the United Nations. *v.4 p.632*

Historical Dictionary of Tunisia. *v.6 p.641*

Historical Dictionary of Turkey. *v.6 p.621*

Historical Dictionary of Turkmenistan. *v.3 p.231*

Historical Dictionary of U. S. -Latin American Relations. *v.4 p.641*

Historical Dictionary of Unitarian Universalism. . . . *v.1 p.589*

Historical Dictionary of Utopianism. *v.4 p.678*

Historical Dictionary of Vietnam. *v.6 p.167*

Historical Dictionary of Women's Education in the United States. *v.6 p.462*

Historical Dictionary of Yemen. *v.6 p.628*

Historical Ecology: Cultural Knowledge and Changing Landscapes. *v.4 p.29*

Historical Encyclopedia of American Labor. *v.4 p.123*

Historical Essay on the Colony of Surinam, 1788. . . *v.3 p.322*

Historical Essays. *v.2 p.276*

The Historical Film: History and Memory in Media. . *v.6 p.315*

Historical Gazetteer of the United States. *v.4 p.374*

An Historical Geography of Europe. *v.3 p.35*

An Historical Geography of Iran. *v.6 p.629*

An Historical Geography of Scandinavia. . . . *v.3 p.232, p.233*

Historical German Phonology and Morphology. . . . *v.2 p.621*

A Historical Guide to Edith Wharton. *v.2 p.132*

A Historical Guide to Emily Dickinson. *v.2 p.37*

A Historical Guide to Ernest Hemingway. . . . *v.2 p.85, p.86*

A Historical Guide to F. Scott Fitzgerald. *v.2 p.76*

A Historical Guide to Henry David Thoreau. *v.2 p.52*

A Historical Guide to Herman Melville. *v.2 p.48*

A Historical Guide to Langston Hughes. *v.2 p.88*

A Historical Guide to the U. S. Government. *v.4 p.517*

The Historical Jesus: A Foundational Anthology. . . .*v.1 p.627*

The Historical Jesus in Recent Research. *v.1 p.627*

The Historical Jesus: The Life of a Mediterranean Jewish Peasant. *v.1 p.627*

Historical Linguistics: An Introduction. *v.2 p.559*

Historical Linguistics. *v.2 p.559, p.562, p.564*

The Historical Method of Herodotus. *v.2 p.412*

Historical Modules for the Teaching and Learning of Mathematics. *v.5 p.463, p.467*

Historical Painting Techniques, Materials and Studio Practice: University of Leiden, Netherlands, June 1995 Preprints. *v.1 p.751*

The Historical Performance of Music: An Introduction.*v.1 p.401*

Historical Perspectives on the Education of Black Children. *v.4 p.310*

The Historical Present: Uses and Abuses of the Past. .*v.3 p.376*

Historical Problems of Imperial Africa. *v.6 p.52*

Historical Reason. *v.1 p.474*

Historical Romances: The Prince and the Pauper; A Connecticut Yankee in King Arthur's Court; Personal Recollections of Joan of Arc. *v.2 p.35*

Historical Sets, Collected Editions, and Monuments of Music: A Guide to Their Contents. *v.1 p.167*

Historical Statistics of the United States. *v.4 p.676*

The Historical Study of African Religion: With Special Reference to East and Central Africa. *v.1 p.543*

An Historical Study of English: A Dynamic Approach.*v.2 p.555*

The Historical Study of the Mother Tongue: An Introduction to Philological Method. *v.2 p.555*

Historical Survey of Pre-Christian Education. *v.4 p.327*

An Historical Syntax of the English Language: Syntactical Units with One Verb; Syntactical Units with Two Verbs; Syntactical Units with Two and More Verbs. . . .*v.2 p.555*

An Historical Syntax of the English Language. . . .*v.2 p.555*

The Historical Theory of the Ruling Class. *v.4 p.248*

Historical Thinking in South Asia: A Handbook of Sources from Colonial Times to the Present. *v.6 p.150*

The Historical Times Illustrated Encyclopedia of the Civil War. *v.3 p.430*

The Historical Trek of the Land Grant College of Agriculture: Past, Present and Future. *v.5 p.5*

Historical Writing on American Science: Perspectives and Prospects. *v.5 p.388, p.393, p.394*

Historical Writing on American Science, Vol. 1. .*v.5 p.388, p.394*

The Historical-Critical Method. *v.1 p.616*

Historicizing Milton: Spectacle, Power and Poetry in Restoration England. *v.2 p.254*

Histories and Annals, Vols. II-V. *v.2 p.444*

Histories, Bks. 1-2. . . . .*v.2 p.406*

Histories, Bks. 28-39. . . . .*v.2 p.406*

Histories, Bks. 3-4. . . . .*v.2 p.406*

Histories, Bks. 9-15,Vol. 4. . . . .*v.2 p.406*

Histories: French Constructions of the Postwar French Thought. *v.3 p.157*

The Histories of Brazil. *v.3 p.339*

Histories of Leisure. *v.4 p.716, p.784*

Histories of Sexually Transmitted Diseases and HIV/AIDS in Sub-Saharan Africa. *v.6 p.55*

Histories of the Hanged: The Dirty War in Kenya and the End of Empire. *v.6 p.64*

Histories, Vol. 3. . . . .*v.2 p.406*

Histories, Vol. 5. . . . .*v.2 p.406*

Historiography in the Middle Ages. *v.3 p.62*

The Historiography of the Holocaust. *v.3 p.87*

Historisch-Kritische Gesamtausgabe der Werke. . . .*v.2 p.599*

History: A Novel. *v.2 p.719*

History and Archival Resources in Higher Education. *v.4 p.332*

History and Beyond: Interpreting Early India, Time as a Metaphor of History, Cultural Transaction and Early India and from Lineage to State. *v.6 p.155*

The History and Character of Calvinism. *v.1 p.589*

The History and Characteristics of Human Factors-Ergonomics. *v.5 p.587*

History and Critique of Interest Theories, Vol. 1. . . .*v.4 p.234*

The History and Culture of Iroquois Diplomacy: An Interdisciplinary Guide to the Treaties of the Six Nations and Their League. *v.6 p.684, p.685, p.696*

A History and Dictionary of British Flower Painters 1650-1950. . . . .*v.1 p.726*

History and Documentation of Human Rights in Iran. .*v.6 p.629*

History and Feminism: A Glass Half Full. . . .*v.6 p.436, p.450*

The History and Growth of Vocational Education in America. *v.4 p.305*

History and Literature in Contemporary Russia. *v.2 p.799*

History and Memory in the Age of Enslavement: Becoming Merina in Highland Madagascar, 1770-1822. . . . .*v.6 p.67*

History and Memory in the Carolingian World. .*v.3 p.143, p.162*

History and Overview of Solar Heat Technologies. *v.5 p.712, p.713*

History and Power in the Study of Law: New Directions in Legal Anthropology. *v.4 p.34*

The History and Power of Writing. *v.3 p.37*

The History and Practice of Ancient Astronomy. . . .*v.5 p.61*

The History and Remarkable Life of the Truly Honourable Colonel Jacque, Commonly Called Colonel Jack. .*v.2 p.245*

History and Social Theory. *v.4 p.682, p.699*

The History and Sociology of Genocide: Analyses and Case Studies. *v.4 p.651, p.652, p.767*

History and the Historians of Medieval Spain. *v.3 p.243*

History and the Homeric Iliad. *v.2 p.415*

History and the Shaping of Irish Protestantism, Vol. 4. *v.1 p.581*

The History and Use of Our Earth's Chemical Elements: A Reference Guide. *v.5 p.263*

History Begins at Sumer: Thirty-Nine "Firsts" in Man's
   Recorded History. *v.3 p.5*

History by Hollywood: The Use and Abuse of the American
   Past. *v.6 p.315*

History Central Africa, Vol. 2. . . . .*v.6 p.61*

History Comes Home: Family Stories Across the
   Curriculum. *v.4 p.366*

History in Ovid. *v.2 p.439*

History in Three Keys: The Boxers as Event, Experience, and
   Myth. *v.6 p.188, p.203*

History Lessons: Teaching, Learning, and Testing in U. S. High
   School Classrooms. *v.4 p.367*

☐ History Matters. *v.4 p.366*

The History of a Myth: Pacariqtambo and the Origin of the
   Inkas. *v.3 p.262*

History of Accountancy in the United States: The Cultural
   Significance of Accounting. *v.4 p.104*

The History of Accounting: An Encyclopedia. *v.4 p.104*

A History of Afghanistan. *v.6 p.633*

A History of African American Theatre. .*v.1 p.123, v.6 p.15, p.30*

History of African Cities South of the Sahara: From Origins to
   Colonization. *v.6 p.52*

A History of African Higher Education from Antiquity to the
   Present: A Critical Synthesis. *v.4 p.335*

A History of African-American Artists: From 1792 to the
   Present. *v.6 p.15, p.16*

A History of Africa. *v.6 p.52*

History of Africa. *v.6 p.54*

The History of Agricultural Science and Technology: An
   International Annotated Bibliography. *v.5 p.5*

History of Albanian Literature. *v.2 p.815*

The History of Alberta. *v.3 p.546*

The History of Al-Tabari: 'Abbasid Authority Affirmed: The
   Early Years of Al-Mansur A. D. 753-763/A. H.
   136-145. . . . .*v.6 p.587, p.588*

The History of Al-Tabari: Al-Mansur and Al-Mahdi, A. D.
   763-786/A. H. 146-169. . . . .*v.6 p.587*

The History of Al-Tabari: Between Civil Wars: the Caliphate of
   Mu'Awiyah, A. D. 661-680/A. H. 40-60. . . . . .*v.6 p.588*

The History of Al-Tabari: Biographies of the Prophet's
   Companions and Their Successors: Al-Tabari's Supplement to
   His History. *v.6 p.587*

The History of Al-Tabari: General Introduction and from the
   Creation to the Flood. *v.6 p.588*

The History of Al-Tabari: Incipient Decline: The Caliphates of
   Al-Wathiq, Al-Mutawakkil, and Al-Muntasir, A.D.
   841-863/A. H. 227-248. . . . .*v.6 p.587*

The History of Al-Tabari: Muhammad at Mecca. . . .*v.6 p.588*

The History of Al-Tabari: Prophets and Patriarchs. . .*v.6 p.586*

The History of Al-Tabari: Storm and Stress along the Northern
   Frontiers of the 'Abbasid Caliphate: The Caliphate of
   Al-Mu'Tasim A. D. 833-842/A. H. 218-227. . . . .*v.6 p.586*

The History of Al-Tabari: The 'Abbasid Caliphate in
   Equilibrium: The Caliphates of Musa Al-Hadi and Harun
   Al-Rashid, A. D. 785-809/A. H. 169-193. . . . . .*v.6 p.586*

The History of Al-Tabari: The 'Abbasid Recovery: The War
   Against the Zanj Ends, A. D. 879-893/A. H.
   266-279. . . . .*v.6 p.586, p.587*

The History of Al-Tabari: The 'Abbasid Revolution, A. D.
   743-750/A. H. 126-132. . . . .*v.6 p.588*

The History of Al-Tabari: The Ancient Kingdoms. . . .*v.6 p.588*

The History of Al-Tabari: The Battle of Al-Qadisiyyah and the
   Conquest of Syria and Palestine, A. D. 635-637/A. H.
   14-15. . . . .*v.6 p.587*

The History of Al-Tabari: The Caliphate of Yazid B.
   Mu'awiyah, A. D. 680-683/A. H. 60-64. . . . . . .*v.6 p.587*

The History of Al-Tabari: The Challenge to the Empires, A. D.
   633-635/A. H. 12-13. . . . .*v.6 p.586*

The History of Al-Tabari: The Children of Israel. . . .*v.6 p.586*

The History of Al-Tabari: The Collapse of Sufyanid Authority
   and the Coming of the Marwanids: The Caliphates of
   Mu'Awiyah II and Marwan I and the Beginning of the
   Caliphate of 'Abd Al-Malik, A. D. 683-685/A.H.
   64-66. . . . .*v.6 p.587*

The History of Al-Tabari: The Community Divided: The
   Caliphate of 'Ali I, A. D. 656-657/A. H. 35-36. . .*v.6 p.586*

The History of Al-Tabari: The Conquest of Arabia: The Riddah
   Wars, A. D. 632-633/A. H. 11. . . . .*v.6 p.586*

The History of Al-Tabari: The Conquest of Iran, A. D.
   641-643/A. H. 21-23. . . . .*v.6 p.586*

The History of Al-Tabari: The Conquest of Iraq, Southwestern
   Persia, and Egypt: The Middle Years of 'Umar's
   Caliphate, A .D. 636-642/A. H. 15-21. . . . . . .*v.6 p.587*

The History of Al-Tabari: The Crisis of the 'Abbasid Caliphate
   -The Caliphates of Al-Musta'In and Al-Mu'Tazz, A. D.
   862-869/A. H. 24-255. . . . .*v.6 p.588*

The History of Al-Tabari: The Crisis of the Early Caliphate: The
   Reign of 'Uthman, A. D. 644-656/A. H. 24-35. . . .*v.6 p.587*

The History of Al-Tabari: The Empire in Transition: The
   Caliphates of Sulayman, 'Umar, and Yazid, A. D.
   715-724/A. H. 97-105. . . . .*v.6 p.588*

The History of Al-Tabari: The End of Expansion: The Caliphate
   of Hisham, A. D. 724-738/A. H. 105-120. . . . . .*v.6 p.586*

The History of Al-Tabari: The First Civil War: From the Battle
   of Siffin to the Death of 'Ali, A. D. 656-661/A. H.
   36-40. . . . .*v.6 p.587*

The History of Al-Tabari: The Foundation of the Community:
   Muhammad at Al-Madina, A. D. 622-626/ijrah-4 A.
   H. *v.6 p.588*

The History of Al-Tabari: The Last Years of the Prophet: the
   Formation of the State, A. D. 630-632/A. H. 8-11. .*v.6 p.588*

The History of Al-Tabari: The Marwanid Restoration: the
   Caliphate of 'Abd Al-Malik: A. D. 693-701/A. H.
   74-81. . . . .*v.6 p.588*

The History of Al-Tabari: The Return of the Caliphate to
   Baghdad: The Caliphate of Al-Mu'Tadid,
   Al-Muktafi and Al-Muqtadir, A. D. 892-915/A. H.
   279-302. . . . .*v.6 p.588*

The History of Al-Tabari: The Reunification of the 'Abbasid
   Caliphate: The Caliphate of Al-Ma'Mun, A. D.
   813-833/A. H. 198-218. . . . .*v.6 p.586*

The History of Al-Tabari: The Revolt of the Zanj, A. D.
   869-879/A. D. 255-265. . . . .*v.6 p.588*

The History of Al-Tabari: The Sasanids, the Lakhmids and
   Yemen. *v.6 p.586*

The History of Al-Tabari: The Victory of Islam: Muhammad at
   Medina, A. D. 626-630/A. H. 5-8. . . . .*v.6 p.587*

The History of Al-Tabari: The Victory of the Marwanids, A. D. 685-693/A. H. 66-73. . . . . *v.6 p.587*

The History of Al-Tabari: The Waning of the Umayyad Caliphate: Prelude to Revolution, A. D. 738-745/A. H. 121-127. . . . . *v.6 p.587*

The History of Al-Tabari: The War Between Brothers: The Caliphate of Muhammad al-Amin A. D. 809-813/A. H. 193-198. . . . . *v.6 p.587*

The History of Al-Tabari: The Zenith of the Marwanid House: The Last Years of 'Abd Al-Malik and the Caliphate of Al-Walid A. D. 700-715/A. H. 81-96. . . . . . *v.6 p.587*

The History of American Catholic Women. . . . *v.1 p.573, p.605*

History of American Church Music. *v.1 p.277*

The History of American Foregn Policy. *v.3 p.385*

A History of American Higher Education. *v.4 p.332*

A History of American Law. *v.4 p.440*

A History of American Magazines: 1885-1905. . . . *v.4 p.409*

A History of American Music Education. *v.1 p.405*

History of American Physical Education and Sport. . *v.4 p.797*

History of American Presidential Elections, 1789-2001, Set. *v.3 p.384*

History of American Theatre from Its Origins to 1832. *v.1 p.113*

History of American Wars: From 1745-1918. . . . . *v.3 p.384*

A History of Analytical Chemistry. *v.5 p.274*

History of Ancient Egypt: An Introduction. *v.3 p.9*

History of Ancient Israel and Judah. *v.1 p.619, v.3 p.7*

The History of Ancient Palestine. *v.3 p.6*

A History of Ancient Philosophy I: From the Origins to Socrates. *v.1 p.420*

A History of Ancient Philosophy II: Plato and Aristotle. *v.1 p.420*

A History of Ancient Philosophy III: Systems of the Hellenistic Age. *v.1 p.420*

A History of Ancient Philosophy IV: The Schools of the Imperial Age. *v.1 p.420*

A History of Antarctic Science. *v.4 p.378, v.5 p.434*

A History of Anthropological Theory. *v.4 p.23*

The History of Anti-Semitism. *v.3 p.60*

A History of Appalachia. *v.3 p.497*

A History of Arabian Music to the XIIIth Century. . *v.1 p.287*

A History of Archaeological Thought. *v.4 p.6*

History of Architectural Conservation. *v.1 p.822*

A History of Architecture: Settings and Rituals. . . . *v.1 p.785*

A history of Argentina in the Twentieth Century. . . *v.3 p.349*

A History of Argentine Political Thought. *v.4 p.592*

A History of Argos to 500 B. C. *v.3 p.16*

A History of Art in Africa. *v.1 p.689*

History of Art. *v.1 p.668*

A History of Asian American Theatre. *v.1 p.125*

History of Astronomy: An Encyclopedia. *v.5 p.61, p.62*

A History of Australian Literature. *v.2 p.740*

A History of Baroque Music: Music in the Seventeenth and First Half of the Eighteenth Centuries. *v.1 p.182*

History of Beauty. *v.1 p.702*

A History of Bel Canto. *v.1 p.229*

History of Belize. *v.3 p.297*

A History of Bisexuality. *v.6 p.362, p.371*

History of Black Americans: From the Compromise of 1850 to the End of the Civil War. *v.3 p.396, p.420*

The History of Black Catholics in the United States. . *v.1 p.572*

History of Botswana. *v.6 p.75*

A History of Brazil. *v.3 p.339, p.341*

A History of British Industrial Relations, 1939-1979: Industrial Relations in a Declining Economy. *v.4 p.213*

The History of British Journalism, from the Foundation of the Newspaper Press in England, to the Repeal of the Stamp Act in 1855. . . . . *v.4 p.403*

A History of British Publishing. *v.2 p.576, v.3 p.119*

History of British Publishing. *v.6 p.741*

A History of British Trade Unionism, 1700-1998. . . *v.4 p.126*

The History of Broadcasting in the United Kingdom. *v.4 p.413*

History of Buddhist Thought. *v.1 p.565*

A History of Bulgarian Literature 865-1944. . . . . *v.2 p.780*

A History of Business in Medieval Europe, 1200-1550. . . . . *v.3 p.40, p.62*

History of Byzantine Music and Hymnography. . . . *v.1 p.178*

A History of Byzantium. *v.3 p.193*

A History of Cambodia. *v.6 p.169, p.170*

History of Canada Before 1867. . . . . *v.3 p.538*

History of Canada, or New France, Vol. 1. . . . . . *v.3 p.538*

History of Canada since 1867. . . . . . . *v.3 p.538, p.539*

A History of Canadian Architecture, Set. *v.1 p.790*

A History of Canadian Literature. *v.2 p.730*

History of Central Africa: The Contemporary Years. . *v.6 p.61*

History of Central Africa, Vol. 1. . . . . *v.6 p.61*

A History of Central Banking in Great Britain and the United States. *v.4 p.156*

The History of Chemical Technology: An Annotated Bibliography. *v.5 p.317*

The History of Chemistry. *v.5 p.263*

History of Chemistry. *v.5 p.263*

History of Chemistry. *v.5 p.262*

A History of Chile, 1808-2002. . . . . *v.3 p.350*

The History of Chile. *v.3 p.350*

A History of Chinese Architecture. *v.1 p.789*

A History of Chinese Civilization. *v.6 p.183*

History of Chinese Philosophy, Set. *v.6 p.182*

History of Chinese Philosophy: The Period of the Philosophers (from the Beginnings to Circa 100 B. C.). . . . *v.1 p.418*

A History of Christian Doctrine. *v.1 p.633*

A History of Christian Missions. *v.1 p.647*

History of Christian Philosophy in the Middle Ages. *v.1 p.432, v.3 p.56, v.6 p.567*

A History of Christian Theology: An Introduction. . . *v.1 p.634*

A History of Christianity in Africa: From Antiquity to the Present. *v.1 p.611*

A History of Christianity in Asia: 1500 to Present. . *v.1 p.610*

A History of Christianity in Asia: Beginnings to 1500. *v.1 p.610*

A History of Christianity in Belize 1776-1838. . . . *v.3 p.297*

A History of Christianity in India: 1707-1858. . . . *v.1 p.610*

A History of Christianity in India: The Beginnings to AD 1707. . . . .*v.1 p.610*

A History of Christianity in the United States and Canada. *v.1 p.606*

A History of Christianity. *v.1 p.598*

ℰ A History of Christian-Latin Poetry from the Beginnings to the Close of the Middle Ages. *v.2 p.449, v.6 p.566*

History of Civilizations of Central Asia, Set. *v.4 p.8*

History of Classical Scholarship from 1300 to 1850. . .*v.2 p.399*

A History of Classical Scholarship from the Sixth Century B. C. to the 19th Century. *v.2 p.399*

The History of Congo. *v.6 p.62*

A History of Contemporary Italy: Society and Politics, 1943-1988. . . . .*v.3 p.204, v.4 p.594*

History of Criminal Justice. *v.6 p.245*

History of Criminology: A Philosophical Perspective. *v.6 p.245, p.250*

The History of Cuba. *v.3 p.313*

A History of Cynicism, from Diogenes to the 6th Century A. D. *v.1 p.428*

The History of Dance. *v.1 p.5*

A History of Danish Literature. *v.2 p.626*

History of Delaware. *v.3 p.493*

History of Denmark. *v.3 p.234*

The History of Doctor Johann Faustus. *v.2 p.593*

History of Dogma. *v.1 p.633, v.3 p.56*

The History of Doing: The Women's Movement in India. *v.6 p.431*

A History of Early Chinese Buddhism: From Its Introduction to the Death of Hui-Yuan, Set. *v.1 p.562, p.563*

History of Eastern Arabia: Rise and Development of Bahrain, Kuwait and Wahhabi Saudi Arabia. *v.6 p.626, p.627*

The History of Econometric Ideas. *v.4 p.203*

The History of Economic Analysis: Selected Essays by John Creedy. *v.4 p.195, p.208*

History of Economic Analysis: With a New Introduction. *v.4 p.210, p.230, p.235*

A history of economic theories. *v.4 p.236*

A History of Economic Theory and Method. *v.4 p.195*

A History of Education Before the Middle Ages. . .*v.4 p.326*

A History of Education During the Middle Ages and the Transition of Modern Times. *v.4 p.326*

⬚ History of Education: Selected Moments of the 20th Century. *v.4 p.329*

History of Egypt, 1382-1469 A. D. *v.6 p.636*

History of Egypt from the Earliest Time. *v.6 p.58*

The History of Egypt. *v.6 p.57, p.58, p.635*

History of Elections in Bohemia and Moravia. *v.4 p.574, p.577, p.596*

The History of Emily Montague. *v.2 p.237, p.238*

History of England from the Accession of James II. . .*v.3 p.105*

A History of English Criticism. *v.2 p.165*

A History of English Law and Its Administration from 1750: Victorian and Edwardian England: The Emergence of Penal Policy. *v.4 p.436*

The History of English Law Before the Time of Edward I 1898, Set. *v.3 p.98, v.4 p.436*

History of English Literature, Set. *v.2 p.167*

A History of English Literature. *v.2 p.166*

A History of English Opera. *v.1 p.234, p.247*

A History of English Phonology. *v.2 p.557*

A History of English Poetry. *v.2 p.179*

A History of English Words. *v.2 p.554*

History of Engraving and Etching: From the 15th Century to the Year 1914. . . . .*v.1 p.753*

A History of Environmental Politics. *v.4 p.566, v.6 p.300*

A History of Ethiopia. *v.6 p.64*

History of European Drama and Theatre. *v.1 p.55, p.96*

A History of European Folk Music. *v.1 p.298*

A History of European Puppetry from Its Origins to the End of the 19th Century. *v.1 p.93, p.96*

A History of European Puppetry: The Twentieth Century. *v.1 p.93, p.96*

The History of Exercise and Sport Science. . .*v.4 p.808, p.873*

History of Experimental Psychology. *v.5 p.595*

History of Fanny Burney. *v.2 p.242*

History of Far Eastern Art. *v.1 p.693*

A History of Farming Systems Research. *v.5 p.4, p.29*

A History of Fascism, 1914-1945. . . . .*v.4 p.510*

A History of Federal Crime Control Initiatives, 1960-1993. . . . .*v.4 p.567*

The History of Fencing: Foundations of Modern European Swordplay. *v.4 p.857*

A History of Finland. *v.3 p.236*

A History of Florida. *v.3 p.505*

A History of France, 1460-1560: The Emergence of a Nation-State. *v.3 p.146*

History of Friedrich the Second Called F. *v.2 p.276*

A History of Georgia. *v.3 p.503*

A History of German Literary Criticism, 1730-1980. . .*v.2 p.589*

A History of German Literature. *v.2 p.589*

History of Germany, 1780-1918: The Long Nineteenth Century. *v.3 p.159, p.163*

History of Germany in the Nineteenth Century. . . .*v.3 p.165*

The History of Germany. *v.3 p.160*

A History of Greece to 322 B. C. *v.3 p.12, p.17*

History of Greece. *v.3 p.191*

History of Greek Literature. *v.2 p.400, p.401*

A History of Greek Literature. *v.2 p.401*

History of Greek Mathematics, Vol. 1. . . . .*v.5 p.466*

A History of Greek Mathematics, Vol. 2. . . . . . .*v.5 p.466*

A History of Greek Philosophy: Aristotle: An Encounter. *v.1 p.420*

A History of Greek Philosophy: Plato: The Man and His Dialogues: Earlier Period. *v.1 p.420*

A History of Greek Philosophy: The Earlier Presocratics and the Pythagoreans. *v.1 p.420*

A History of Greek Philosophy: The Fifth Century Enlightenment: The Sophists. *v.1 p.427*

A History of Greek Philosophy: The Fifth Century Enlightenment. *v.1 p.420*

A History of Greek Philosophy: The Later Plato and the Academy. *v.1 p.420*

A History of Greek Philosophy: The Presocratic Tradition from Parmenides to Democritus, Vol. 2. . . . .*v.1 p.420*

A History of Haiku: From Issa up to the Present. . . .*v.6 p.234*

History of Henry Esmond. *v.2 p.316*

A History of Hispanic Theatre in the United States: Origins to 1940. . . . .*v.6 p.513, p.517*

A History of Hispanics in Southern Nevada. *v.6 p.532*

The History of History: Politics and Scholarship in Modern India. *v.6 p.146*

The History of Holland. *v.3 p.204*

A History of Homosexuality in Europe, 1919-1939. . . . .*v.3 p.55, v.6 p.421, p.422*

The History of Human Rights: From Ancient Times to the Globalization Era. *v.4 p.512*

A History of Hungarian Literature. *v.2 p.785*

A History of Hungarian Music. *v.1 p.245*

A History of Hungary: Millennium in Central Europe. .*v.3 p.185*

A History of Hungary. *v.3 p.185*

A History of Hypnotism. *v.5 p.612, p.613*

History of Iberian Civilization. *v.3 p.243*

History of Icelandic Prose Writers, 1800-1940. . . . .*v.2 p.625*

The History of Iceland. *v.3 p.234*

History of Idaho. *v.3 p.525*

A History of Ideas in American Psychology. . .*v.5 p.596, p.597*

A History of Illuminated Manuscripts. *v.3 p.37*

A History of Indian Buddhism: From Sakyamuni to Early Mahayana. *v.1 p.561*

History of Indian Buddhism. *v.1 p.561*

A History of Indian English Literature. *v.2 p.762*

History of Indian Literature in English. *v.2 p.762*

History of Indian Literature. *v.1 p.541*

History of Indian-White Relations. *v.6 p.683*

History of Industrial Gases. *v.5 p.391*

e A History of Industrial Power in the United States, 1780-1930. . . . .*v.5 p.406*

A History of Inner Asia. *v.6 p.239*

History of Interest Rates. *v.4 p.155*

History of Interior Design and Furniture: From Ancient Egypt to Nineteenth-Century Europe. *v.1 p.799*

A History of Interior Design. *v.1 p.799*

History of Iowa. *v.3 p.522*

History of Iranian Literature. *v.6 p.672*

A History of Irish Theatre, 1601-2000. . . . .*v.1 p.109, p.110*

The History of Islam in Africa. *v.6 p.53*

A History of Islamic Legal Theories: An Introduction to Sunni Usul Al-fiqh. *v.1 p.556*

History of Islamic Philosophy. *v.1 p.432*

The History of Islamic Political Thought: From the Prophet to the Present. *v.1 p.556, p.557*

A History of Islamic Societies. *v.1 p.554*

A History of Islamic Spain. *v.6 p.588*

A History of Israel and the Holy Land. *v.6 p.608*

A History of Israel: From the Rise of Zionism to Our Time. *v.1 p.549, v.6 p.611*

History of Italian Literature. *v.2 p.698*

A History of Italian Literature. *v.2 p.698*

History of Italian Renaissance Art. *v.1 p.675, p.687*

The History of Japan, Together with a Description of the Kingdom of Siam, 1690-92. . . . .*v.6 p.224, p.225*

History of Japanese Art. *v.1 p.693, v.6 p.219, p.220*

The History of Japanese Photography. *v.1 p.765*

A History of Japanese Religion. *v.1 p.541*

History of Japan. *v.6 p.226*

The History of Java. *v.6 p.177*

The History of Jazz. *v.1 p.259*

The History of Jerusalem: The Early Muslim Period, 638-1099. . . . .*v.6 p.609*

A History of Jewish Literature. *v.6 p.566, p.574*

A History of Jewish Philosophy in the Middle Ages. *v.6 p.568, p.574*

A History of Jordan. *v.6 p.621*

History of Judaism. *v.1 p.547*

A History of Key Characteristics in the 18th and Early 19th Centuries. *v.1 p.192, p.374*

A History of Keyboard Literature: Music for the Piano and Its Forerunners. *v.1 p.239*

The History of King Richard III and Selections from the English and Latin Poems. *v.2 p.215*

A History of Korean Literature. *v.6 p.238*

History of Latvian Jews. *v.3 p.256*

A History of Law in Japan until 1868. . . . .*v.6 p.226*

A History of Lay Judges, 1960. . . . .*v.4 p.435*

History of Literary Criticism: From Plato to the Present. *v.2 p.573*

A History of Literature in the Caribbean: Hispanic and Francophone Regions. *v.2 p.535*

A History of Macedonia. *v.3 p.19*

A History of Madagascar. *v.6 p.67*

A History of Malaysia, Singapore and Brunei. *v.6 p.173*

A History of Malaysia. *v.6 p.172*

The History of Marketing Thought. *v.4 p.134*

History of Mathematics: A Reader. *v.5 p.466*

A History of Mathematics. *v.5 p.465*

History of Mathematics. *v.5 p.466, p.467*

A History of Medieval Austria. *v.6 p.563*

A History of Medieval Spain. *v.3 p.238*

The History of Men: Essays on the History of American and British Masculinities. *v.4 p.745, v.6 p.429*

A History of Militarism: Civilian and Military. *v.3 p.36*

History of Missouri, Vol. 4. . . . .*v.3 p.512*

History of Missouri, Vol. 5. . . . .*v.3 p.512*

History of Modern Art: Painting, Sculpture, Architecture, Photography. *v.1 p.676*

A History of Modern Burma. *v.6 p.165*

A History of Modern Chinese Fiction. *v.6 p.208*

History of Modern Computing. *v.5 p.342*

A History of Modern Criticism, 1750-1950: French, Italian, and Spanish Criticism, 1900-1950. . . . .*v.2 p.573*

A History of Modern Criticism, 1750-1950: German, Russian, and East European Criticism, 1900-1950. . . . . .*v.2 p.573*

A History of Modern Criticism, 1750-1950: The First Half of the Twentieth Century: English and American. . . .*v.2 p.573*

History of Modern Design. *v.1 p.713*

A History of Modern Economic Analysis. *v.4 p.194*

The History of Modern Egypt: From Muhammad Ali to Mubarak. *v.6 p.638, p.639*

A History of Modern Ethiopia, 1855-1991. . . . . . .*v.6 p.64*

History of Modern France: 1715-1799. . . . .*v.3 p.140*

History of Modern France: 1871-1962. . . . .*v.3 p.140*

A History of Modern France: From the First Empire to the Second Empire. *v.3 p.140*

A History of Modern Germany since 1815. . . . . .*v.3 p.165*

History of Modern Hungary, 1867-1986. . . . . . .*v.3 p.185*

A History of Modern Indonesia since c. 1200. . . .*v.6 p.177*

A History of Modern Indonesia. *v.6 p.178*

A History of Modern Libya. *v.6 p.641*

A History of Modern Norway, 1814-1972. . . . . .*v.3 p.234*

A History of Modern Palestine: One Land, Two Peoples. .*v.6 p.611*

A History of Modern Planetary Physics: Transmuted Past: The Age of the Earth and the Evolution of the Elements from Lyell to Patterson. *v.5 p.446*

A History of Modern Psychology. *v.5 p.597*

A History of Modern Russia: From Nicholas II to Vladimir Putin. *v.3 p.209*

A History of Modern Tibet, 1913-1951: The Demise of the Lamaist State. *v.6 p.240*

A History of Modern Tunisia. *v.6 p.641, p.642*

A History of Modern Yemen. *v.6 p.628*

A History of Molecular Biology. *v.5 p.80, p.128*

A History of Mountain Climbing. *v.4 p.789*

A History of Mozambique. *v.6 p.76*

The History of Mr Polly. *v.2 p.320*

A History of Music in Pictures. *v.1 p.174*

History of My Heart: Poems. *v.2 p.153*

A History of Narrative Film. *v.6 p.331*

A History of NATO: The First Fifty Years, Set. *v.4 p.639*

The History of Natural History: An Annotated Bibliography. *v.5 p.224*

History of Nature. *v.5 p.404*

A History of N'cobra and the Reparations Movement: The Demand for Black Reparations. *v.6 p.30*

History of Nebraska. *v.3 p.524, p.525*

A History of Neglect: Health Care for Southern Blacks and Mill Workers in the Twentieth-Century South. *v.4 p.774*

A History of Negro Education in the South: From 1619 to the Present. *v.4 p.309*

A History of Nepal. *v.6 p.164*

History of Nevada. *v.3 p.529*

History of New Testament Research: From Deism to Tubingen. *v.1 p.624, p.625*

History of New Testament Research: From Jonathan Edwards to Rudolf Bultmann. *v.1 p.625*

A History of News: From Oral Culture to the Information Age. *v.4 p.403*

A History of Newspapers in the United States Through 250 Years, 1690-1940, Set. *v.4 p.411*

A History of Niger, Eighteen Fifty to Nineteen Sixty. *v.6 p.70, p.71*

History of Nineteenth-Century Russian Literature. . . .*v.2 p.800*

History of North Dakota. *v.3 p.523*

A History of Northern Ireland, 1920-1996. . . .*v.3 p.139, p.140*

History of Norway. *v.3 p.234*

History of Norwegian Literature. *v.2 p.627*

A History of Nursing Ideas. *v.5 p.527, p.529*

A History of Ohio. *v.3 p.513*

A History of Old English Literature. *v.2 p.167, v.6 p.565*

The History of Ophelia. *v.2 p.248*

The History of Orchestral Conducting: In Theory and Practice. *v.1 p.402*

The History of Orchestration. *v.1 p.393*

A History of Organized Labor in Uruguay and Paraguay. .*v.3 p.346*

A History of Palestine, 634-1099. . . . . . .*v.6 p.608, p.609*

The History of Panama. *v.3 p.304*

A History of Pantomime. *v.1 p.93*

A History of Pastoral Care. *v.1 p.649*

The History of Pendennis. His Fortunes and Misfortunes, His Friends and His Greatest Enemy. by William Maekpeace Thackeray. with illustrations on wood by the Author. *v.2 p.315*

History of Pennsylvania. *v.3 p.492*

A History of Performing Pitch: The Story of "A". . . .*v.1 p.375*

A History of Persia. *v.6 p.630*

History of Philosophy: Bentham to Russell. *v.1 p.438*

History of Philosophy: Descartes to Leibniz. *v.1 p.437*

History of Philosophy: Fichte to Nietzsche. *v.1 p.508*

History of Philosophy: Greece and Rome. *v.1 p.428*

A History of Philosophy in America, 1720-2000. . . .*v.1 p.439*

A History of Philosophy in America, Vol. 1. . . . .*v.1 p.439*

History of Philosophy: Maine de Bira to Sartre. . . .*v.1 p.455*

History of Philosophy: Ockham to Suarez. *v.1 p.431*

History of Philosophy: Wolff to Kant. *v.1 p.437*

A History of Philosophy. *v.1 p.417*

History of Photography: A Bibliography of Books, Vol. 2. . . . .*v.1 p.761*

History of Photography: A Bibliography of Books. . .*v.1 p.761*

The History of Photography: As Seen Through the Spira Collection. *v.1 p.763*

The History of Poland. *v.3 p.252*

History of Polish Culture. *v.3 p.252*

The History of Polish Literature. *v.2 p.789*

History of Political Philosophy. *v.4 p.488*

A History of Popular Women's Magazines in the United States, 1792-1995. . . . .*v.4 p.410*

A History of Portugal: From Lusitania to Empire. . . .*v.3 p.244*

The History of Portugal. *v.3 p.243*

A History of Post Keynesian Economics since 1936. . .*v.4 p.269*

A History of Postwar Britain, 1945-1974. . . . . . .*v.3 p.119*

A History of Prison and Confinement in Africa. *v.6 p.273*

A History of Private Life: From Pagan Rome to Byzantium, Vol. 1. . . . .*v.4 732*

A History of Private Life: From Pagan Rome to Byzantium, Vol. I. *v.6 p.557*

A History of Private Life: From the Fires of Revolution to the Great War. *v.4 p.734*

A History of Private Life: Passions of the Renaissance. *v.3 p.70, v.4 p.732*

A History of Private Life: Revelations of the Medieval World, Vol. 2. . . . .*v.4 p.733, v.6 p.557*

A History of Private Life: Riddles of Identity in Modern Times, Vol. 5. . . . .*v.4 p.732*

A History of Progress: Selected U. S. Papers in Geotechnical Engineering. *v.5 p.422*

A History of Prophecy in Israel. *v.1 p.622*

A History of Psychology: Ancient and Patristic, Vol. 1..*v.5 p.595*

A History of Psychology in Autobiography, Vol. 6. . .*v.5 p.597*

A History of Psychology in Autobiography, Vol. VIII. .*v.5 p.597*

A History of Psychology in Autobiography, Vol. VII. .*v.5 p.597*

A History of Psychology in Letters. *v.5 p.595*

A History of Psychology: Mediaeval and Early Modern Period, Vol. 2. . . . .*v.5 p.595*

A History of Psychology: Modern Psychology, Vol. 3. .*v.5 p.595*

History of Psychology. *v.5 p.596*

▢ History of Psychology. *v.5 p.595*

A History of Puerto Ricans in the United States of America, Vol. I. *v.6 p.535*

A History of Quebec Nationalism. *v.3 p.543*

The History of Rasselas, Prince of Abissinia. *v.2 p.250*

A History of Reading in the West. *v.2 p.573*

A History of Reading. *v.2 p.573, v.3 p.37*

History of Regional Science and the Regional Science Association International: The Beginnings and Early History. *v.4 p.397*

History of Roman: Summaries, Fragments, Julius Obsequens, General Index. *v.2 p.435*

History of Romanian Literature. *v.2 p.816*

History of Rome: Books 1-2, Vol. 1. . . . .*v.2 p.436*

History of Rome: Books 23-25, Vol. 6. . . . .*v.2 p.436*

History of Rome: Books 28-30, Vol. 8. . . . .*v.2 p.436*

History of Rome: Books 3-4, Vol. 2. . . . .*v.2 p.436*

History of Rome: Books 38-39, Vol. 11. . . . .*v.2 p.435*

History of Rome: Books 40-42, Vol. 12. . . . .*v.2 p.436*

History of Rome: Books 43-45, Vol. 13. . . . .*v.2 p.435*

History of Rome: Books 5-7, Vol. 3. . . . .*v.2 p.435*

History of Rome: Books 8-10, Vol. 4. . . . .*v.2 p.435, p.436*

History of Rome, Vol. 10. . . . .*v.2 p.436*

History of Rome, Vol. 5. . . . .*v.2 p.435*

History of Rome, Vol. 7. . . . .*v.2 p.435*

History of Rome, Vol. 9. . . . .*v.2 p.435*

A History of Russia: Medieval, Modern, Contemporary, c. 882-1996. . . . .*v.3 p.209*

A History of Russia since 1855. . . . .*v.3 p.209*

History of Russia: To 1917. . . . .*v.3 p.209*

A History of Russian Architecture. *v.1 p.788*

A History of Russian Economic Thought. .*v.4 p.211, p.235, p.255*

History of Russian Literature: From Its Beginnings to 1900. . . . .*v.2 p.799*

A History of Russian Painting. *v.1 p.730*

A History of Russian Philosophy, Set. *v.1 p.474*

A History of Russian Poetry. *v.2 p.797*

A History of Russian Theatre. *v.1 p.109*

A History of Russian Thought: From the Enlightenment to Marxism. *v.3 p.211*

A History of Russian Women's Writing 1820-1992. .*v.2 p.798*

The History of Russia. *v.3 p.209*

A History of Saudi Arabia. *v.6 p.625*

A History of Scandinavian Literature: 1870 to 1980. .*v.2 p.624*

A History of Scandinavia. *v.3 p.232, p.233*

The History of Scepticism: From Savonarola to Bayle. .*v.1 p.517*

A History of Science and its Relations with Philosophy and Religion. *v.5 p.390*

History of Scottish Literature. *v.2 p.164*

🅮 A History of Secular Latin Poetry in the Middle Ages. *v.2 p.449, v.6 p.566*

A History of Sexuality: An Introduction, Vol. 1. . . . .*v.3 p.55, v.4 p.747, v.6 p.364, p.429, p.447*

The History of Sexuality: The Care of the Self, Vol. 3. . . . .*v.4 p.747, v.6 p.364*

The History of Sexuality: The Use of Pleasure, Vol. 2. . . . .*v.4 p.747, v.6 p.364*

A History of Shakespeare on Screen: A Century of Film and Television. *v.2 p.231, v.6 p.327*

A History of Siam, from the Earliest Times to the Year A. D. 1781. . . . .*v.6 p.172*

A History of Sicily. *v.3 p.197*

A History of Sierra Leone. *v.6 p.72, p.73*

A History of Singapore, Eighteen Nineteen to Nineteen Eighty-Five. *v.6 p.173*

The History of Sir George Ellison. *v.2 p.259*

A History of Sixteenth-Century France, 1483-1598: Renaissance, Reformation, and Rebellion. *v.3 p.145*

A History of Slovak Literature. *v.2 p.812*

A History of Slovakia: The Struggle for Survival. . . .*v.3 p.190*

A History of Small Business in America. *v.4 p.87, p.146*

A History of Song. *v.1 p.237*

A History of South African Literature. *v.6 p.80*

A History of South Africa. *v.6 p.79*

History of South American Colonial Art and Architecture: Spanish South American and Brazil. *v.1 p.683*

History of South Dakota, Vol. 2. . . . .*v.3 p.523*

History of South Dakota. *v.3 p.523*

A History of South-East Asia. *v.6 p.164*

History of Southern Africa. *v.6 p.74*

The History of Southern Literature. *v.2 p.14*

The History of Southern Women's Literature. *v.2 p.14*

A History of Spaces: Cartographic Reason, Mapping, and the Geo-Coded World. *v.4 p.375*

A History of Spanish Golden Age Drama. *v.2 p.641*

History of Spanish Literature, Vol. II. *v.2 p.639*

A History of Spanish Literature. *v.2 p.638*

The History of Statistics: The Measurement of Uncertainty
    Before 1900. . . . .*v.5 p.468, p.481*

History of Structuralism. *v.1 p.515*

The History of Surrealism. *v.2 p.458*

The History of Sweden. *v.3 p.235*

History of Swedish Literature. *v.2 p.629*

History of Switzerland: From Before the Beginnings to the Days
    of the Present. *v.3 p.245*

History of Syria, Including Lebanon and
    Palestine. *v.6 p.604, p.606, p.608*

The History of Syriac Literature and Sciences. . . .*v.6 p.652*

History of Telecommunications Technology: An Annotated
    Bibliography. *v.4 p.421*

A History of Telegraphy: Its Technology and
    Application. *v.4 p.421*

A History of Thailand. *v.6 p.171*

The History of That Ingenious Gentleman, Don Quijote de la
    Mancha. *v.2 p.648*

A History of the Adult Education Movement in the United
    States. *v.4 p.320*

The History of the Adventures of Joseph Andrews and of His
    Friend Mr. Abraham Adams; and, an Apology for
    the Life of Mrs. Shamela Andrews. *v.2 p.247*

History of the African Methodist Episcopal Church. . .*v.1 p.586*

History of the American Association of Cereal Chemists. .*v.5 p.6*

A History of the American Bar. *v.4 p.440*

History of the American Cinema, Set. *v.6 p.344*

A History of the American Theatre 1700: 1950. . . .*v.1 p.115*

History of the American Theatre. *v.1 p.118*

A History of the Ancient near East, c. 3000-323 BC. . .*v.3 p.5*

A History of the Ancient World. *v.3 p.4*

A History of the Arab Peoples. *v.6 p.583*

A History of the Arab State of Zanzibar. *v.6 p.66*

History of the Arabs. *v.6 p.583*

History of the Archbishops of Hamburg-Bremen. . . .*v.3 p.162*

A History of the Art of War in the Middle Ages. . . .*v.3 p.69*

History of the Art of War Within the Framework of Political
    History: The Middle Ages. *v.3 p.35*

History of the Art of War Within the Framework of Political
    History: The Modern Era. *v.3 p.35*

A History of the Ayyubid Sultans of Egypt. *v.6 p.635*

History of the Balkans: Eighteenth and Nineteenth Centuries,
    Vol. 1. . . . .*v.3 p.246*

History of the Balkans, Vol. 2. . . . .*v.3 p.246*

History of the Balkans. *v.3 p.246*

The History of the Baltic States. *v.3 p.256*

A History of the Behavioral Therapies: Founders' Personal
    Theories. *v.5 p.667*

A History of the Bemba: Political Growth and Change in
    North-Eastern Zambia Before 1900. . . . . . .*v.6 p.77*

History of the Bible in English. *v.1 p.614, p.615*

A History of the Black Press. *v.4 p.404*

History of the Blues: The Roots, the Music, the People.*v.1 p.258*

The History of the Boston Theatre, 1854-1901. . . .*v.1 p.118*

History of the Byzantine Empire, 324-1453, Vol. 1. . .*v.3 p.194*

History of the Byzantine Empire, 324-1453, Vol. 2. . .*v.3 p.194*

History of the Byzantine Empire, 324-1453. . . . . .*v.3 p.67*

A History of the Byzantine State and Society. .*v.3 p.193, p.194*

History of the Byzantine State. *v.3 p.66, p.193*

A History of the Catholic Church in Belize. *v.3 p.297*

History of the Christian Church, Set. *v.1 p.598, v.3 p.58*

A History of the Church in England. *v.1 p.582, p.609*

History of the Church in Latin America. *v.1 p.608*

A History of the Church of Ireland. *v.1 p.608*

History of the Colony of Massachusetts Bay. *v.3 p.487*

History of the Commonwealth and Protectorate,
    1649-1656. . . . .*v.3 p.103*

A History of the Concerto. *v.1 p.242*

A History of the Confederate Navy. *v.4 p.521*

The History of the Conquest of Egypt, North Africa and Spain
    Known As the Futuh Misr of Ibn'abd
    Al-Hakan. *v.6 p.584, p.585*

A History of the Crusades: Fourteenth and Fifteenth
    Centuries. *v.3 p.64*

A History of the Crusades, Set. *v.3 p.63*

A History of the Crusades: The Art and Architecture of the
    Crusader States, Vol. 4. . . . .*v.3 p.64*

A History of the Crusades: The First Hundred Years. . .*v.3 p.64*

A History of the Crusades: The Impact of the Crusades on
    Europe. *v.3 p.64, v.6 p.557*

A History of the Crusades: The Impact of the Crusades on the
    near East. *v.3 p.64, v.6 p.557*

A History of the Crusades: The Later Crusades,
    1189-1311. . . . .*v.3 p.64*

A History of the Dalit Christians in India. *v.6 p.155*

The History of the Damnable Life and Deserved Death of
    Doctor John Faustus. *v.2 p.593*

A History of the Dance in Art and Education. . . .*v.1 p.5, p.47*

The History of the Decline and Fall of the Roman Empire,
    Set. *v.3 p.31*

A History of the Development of Japanese Thought: From 1592
    to 1868. . . . .*v.1 p.476*

History of the Discovery and Conquest of Costa Rica. .*v.3 p.303*

A History of the Earth. *v.5 p.445*

A History of the Ecumenical Movement: 1517 to 1948.*v.1 p.568*

A History of the Ecumenical Movement: 1948 to 1968.*v.1 p.568*

A History of the Ecumenical Movement: 1968 to 2000.*v.1 p.568*

The History of the English Language: A Source Book.*v.2 p.554*

History of the English Language. *v.2 p.555*

A History of the English People in the Nineteenth
    Century. *v.3 p.112*

A History of the English-Canadian Literature to the
    Confederation: Its Relation to the Literature of Great Britain
    and the United States. *v.2 p.728*

History of the Franciscan Order: From Its Origins to the Year
    1517. . . . .*v.6 p.572*

A History of the Franks. *v.3 p.66*

A History of the French Language. *v.2 p.454*

A History of the French New Wave Cinema. *v.6 p.338*

History of the French Revolution. *v.3 p.158*

A History of the German Language. . . . . *.v.2 p.622*

A History of the German Novelle. . . . . *.v.2 p.592*

History of the German Novel. . . . . *.v.2 p.592*

The History of the German Resistance, 1933-1945. . . *.v.3 p.172*

History of the Goths. . . . . *.v.3 p.63*

History of the Great Civil War, 1642-1649. . . . . . *.v.3 p.103*

The History of the Greek and Roman Theater. *.v.1 p.69, p.70, p.72*

A History of the Greek City States, 700-338 BC. . . . *.v.3 p.13*

The History of the Gulag: From Collectivization to the Great
Terror. . . . . *.v.3 p.226*

A History of the Habsburg Empire, 1526-1918. . . . *.v.3 p.181*

A History of the Harpsichord. . . . . *.v.1 p.390*

A History of the Hebrew Language. . . . . . . *.v.6 p.646*

A History of the Holocaust. . . . . *.v.3 p.82*

History of the Hour: Clocks and Modern Temporal
Orders. *.v.3 p.44*

History of the Idea of Progress. . . . . *.v.4 p.700*

The History of the Illustrated Book: The Western
Tradition. . . . . *.v.1 p.716*

History of the Imams and Seyyids of Oman: From A.D. 661 to
1856. *.v.6 p.627*

History of the Inca Realm. . . . . *.v.3 p.326*

History of the Internet: A Chronology, 1843 to the
Present. . . . . *.v.5 p.679*

History of the Islamic Peoples: Orientalism. . . . *.v.6 p.581*

A History of the Israeli-Palestinian Conflict. . . . . *.v.6 p.620*

A History of the Jews in Baghdad. . . . . . . *.v.6 p.598, p.602*

A History of the Jews in Christian Spain, Vol. I. . . . *.v.3 p.65*

A History of the Jews in England. . . . . *.v.6 p.574*

History of the Jews in Russia and Poland. . . . . . *.v.1 p.548*

A History of the Kikuyu, 1500-1900. . . . . *.v.6 p.65*

The History of the Kings of Britain. . . . . . . *.v.3 p.95, p.96*

History of the Labor Movement in the United States:
1914-1918, Vol. 7. . . . . *.v.4 p.125*

A History of the Labor Movement in the United States:
1915-1916, on the Eve of America's Entrance into World War
I, Vol. 6. . . . . *.v.4 p.125*

History of the Labor Movement in the United States: From
Colonial Times to the Founding of the American
Federation of Labor, Vol. 1. . . . . *.v.4 p.125*

History of the Labor Movement in the United States: From the
Founding of the American Federation of Labor to the
Emergence of American Imperialism, Vol. 2. . . . *.v.4 p.125*

History of the Labor Movement in the United States: Postwar
Struggles, 1918-1920, Vol. 8. . . . . *.v.4 p.125*

History of the Labor Movement in the United States: The AFL
in the Progressive Era, 1910-1913. . . . . . . *.v.4 p.125*

History of the Labor Movement in the United States: The
Industrial Workers of the World. . . . . *.v.4 p.125*

History of the Labor Movement in the United States: The
Policies and Practices of the AFL, 1900-1909, Vol. 3. *.v.4 p.125*

History of the Labor Movement in the United States: The TUEL
to the End of the Gompers Era, Vol. 9. . . . . . *.v.4 p.125*

History of the Labor Movement: The TUEL, 1925-1929, Vol.
10. . . . . *.v.4 p.125*

History of the Later Roman Empire: From the Death of
Theodosius I to the Death of Justinian. . . . *.v.3 p.30, p.192*

A History of the League of Nations. . . . . *.v.4 p.632*

A History of the Life Sciences. . . . . *.v.5 p.80*

History of the Low Countries. . . . . *.v.3 p.204*

A History of the Lute from Antiquity to the
Renaissance. . . . . *.v.1 p.391*

The History of the Maghrib: An Interpretive
Essay. . . . . *.v.6 p.641, p.642, p.643*

A History of the Maghrib in the Islamic
Period. . . . . *.v.6 p.59, p.640, p.641, p.642, p.643*

History of the Mass Media in the United States: An
Encyclopedia. . . . . *.v.4 p.415*

⦿ A History of the Mexican-American People. . . . *.v.6 p.532*

A History of the Middle East. . . . . *.v.6 p.582*

A History of the Minstrel Show. . . . . *.v.1 p.120*

A History of the Modern Middle East. . . . . . . *.v.6 p.592*

A History of the Modern World, with PowerWeb. . . *.v.3 p.35*

The History of the Organ in the United
States. . . . . *.v.1 p.279, p.390, p.391*

A History of the Ostrogoths. . . . . *.v.3 p.30*

History of the Ottoman Empire and Modern
Turkey. . . . . *.v.6 p.591, p.625*

History of the Ottoman Empire to 1730. . . . . . *.v.6 p.589*

History of the Ottoman Turks: From the Beginning of Their
Empire to the Present Time. . . . . *.v.6 p.589*

A History of the Pacific Northwest. . . . . *.v.3 p.530*

A History of the Peoples of Siberia: Russia's North Asian
Colony, 1581-1990. . . . . *.v.3 p.214*

History of the Persian Empire. . . . . . . *.v.3 p.12, v.6 p.630*

History of the Persian Wars, 4. . . . . *.v.2 p.412*

History of the Persian Wars, Bks. 1-2. . . . . . . *.v.2 p.412*

History of the Persian Wars, Bks. 3-4. . . . . . . *.v.2 p.412*

History of the Persian Wars, Bks. 5-7. . . . . . . *.v.2 p.412*

A History of the Portuguese Fado. . . . . *.v.1 p.299*

A History of the Post in England from the Romans to the
Stuarts. . . . . *.v.3 p.119*

History of the Poster. . . . . *.v.1 p.718*

The History of the Primitive Church, Vol. 3. . . . . *.v.3 p.57*

History of the Ptolemaic Empire. . . . . *.v.6 p.58*

A History of the Puerto Ricans in the United States of America,
Vol. II. . . . . *.v.6 p.535*

The History of the Rebellion and Civil Wars in England Begun
in the Year 1641, Set. . . . . *.v.3 p.103, p.104*

A History of the Roman World 753 to 146 BC. . . . *.v.3 p.25*

A History of the Romanians. . . . . *.v.3 p.250*

The History of the Rugby World Cup. . . . . *.v.4 p.847, p.865*

A History of the Russian Church to 1448. . *.v.1 p.569, v.3 p.215*

A History of the Scottish People, 1560-1830. . . . . *.v.3 p.133*

History of the Seljuq Turks: The Saljuq-Nama of Zahir Al-Din
Nishapuri. . . . . *.v.6 p.622*

The History of the Sierra Club, 1892-1970. . . . . *.v.5 p.78*

A History of the Southern Confederacy. . . . . . . *.v.3 p.428*

A History of the Southwest: The Land and Its People. *.v.3 p.527*

A History of the Spanish Language. . . . . *.v.2 p.637*

History of the Standard Oil Company. . . . . *.v.4 p.147, p.148*

A History of the Sudan: From the Coming of Islam to the Present Day. *v.6 p.640*

A History of the Supreme Court. *v.4 p.466, p.539*

History of the Surrealist Movement. *v.1 p.678*

A History of the Swedish People: From Prehistory to the Renaissance. *v.3 p.235*

A History of the Swedish People: From Renaissance to Revolution. *v.3 p.235*

A History of the Synoptic Problem: The Canon, the Text, the Composition, and the Interpretation of the Gospels. *v.1 p.629*

History of the Synoptic Tradition. *v.1 p.628*

A History of the Theatre in America from Its Beginnings to the Present Time. *v.1 p.115*

History of the Theatre. *v.1 p.55, p.137*

A History of the Theories of Production and Distribution in English Political Economy from 1776 To 1848. . .*v.4 p.211*

History of the Thirteen. *v.2 p.485*

History of the United States Army. *v.3 p.384*

History of the United States from the Compromise of 1850. . . . .*v.3 p.400*

History of the United States of America from the Discovery of the Continent, Vol. 1. . . . .*v.3 p.379*

History of the United States of America from the Discovery of the Continent, Vol. 2. . . . .*v.3 p.379*

History of the United States of America from the Discovery of the Continent, Vol. 3. . . . .*v.3 p.379*

History of the United States of America from the Discovery of the Continent, Vol. 4. . . . .*v.3 p.379*

History of the United States of America from the Discovery of the Continent, Vol. 5. . . . .*v.3 p.379*

History of the United States of America from the Discovery of the Continent, Vol. 6. . . . .*v.3 p.379*

A History of the United States. *v.3 p.379*

A History of the University in Europe: Universities in Early Modern Europe (1500-1800). *v.4 p.326*

A History of the University in Europe: Universities in the Middle Ages. *v.4 p.325, p.326, v.6 p.558*

A History of the University in Europe: Universities in the Nineteenth and Early Twentieth Centuries (1800-1945). *v.4 p.329*

A History of the Upper Guinea Coast, 1545-1800. . .*v.6 p.69*

A History of the Vikings. *v.3 p.62, p.63, p.235, p.236*

History of the Wars. Secret History. *v.3 p.67*

A History of the Western Educational Experience. *v.4 p.326, p.327*

History of the World Christian Movement: Earliest Christianity to 1453. . . . .*v.1 p.598*

A History of the World in Six Glasses. *v.4 p.710*

A History of the World in Ten and a Half Chapters. . .*v.2 p.332*

The History of the Yorubas. *v.6 p.71*

A History of Theatre in Africa. *v.1 p.130*

A History of Their Own: Women in Europe from Prehistory to the Present, Vol. 1. . . . .*v.3 p.50, v.6 p.449*

A History of Their Own: Women in Europe from Prehistory to the Present. *v.3 p.50, v.6 p.449, p.559*

The History of Trade Unionism. *v.4 p.212, p.254*

A History of Twelfth-Century Western Philosophy. . .*v.1 p.432*

A History of Twentieth-Century African Literatures. *v.2 p.752, v.6 p.80, p.81*

History of Twentieth-Century Philosophy of Science. .*v.1 p.499*

A History of Ukrainian Literature: From the 11th to the End of the 19th Century. *v.2 p.814*

A History of Ulster. *v.3 p.139*

History of Universities. *v.4 p.334*

A History of Venetian Architecture. *v.1 p.789*

The History of Venezuela. *v.3 p.361*

The History of Violin Playing from Its Origins to 1761: And Its Relationship to the Violin and Violin Music. *v.1 p.389, p.397, p.399*

A History of West Africa: An Introductory Survey. . .*v.6 p.68*

History of West Africa, Vol. 1. . . . .*v.6 p.67*

History of West Africa, Vol. 2. . . . .*v.6 p.67, p.68*

A History of West Germany, Vol. I: From Shadow to Substance, 1945-1963. . . . .*v.3 p.176*

A History of West Germany, Vol. II: Democracy & Its Discontents, 1963-1988. . . . .*v.3 p.176*

A History of Western Architecture. *v.1 p.788*

A History of Western Educational Ideas. *v.4 p.339*

History of Western Education—Civilization of Europe: 6th to 16th Century, Vol. 2. . . . .*v.4 p.324*

History of Western Education—The Ancient World: Orient and Mediterranean 2000 B. C.-A. D. 1054, Vol. 1. . . .*v.4 p.324*

History of Western Education—The Modern West: Europe and the New World, Vol. 3. . . . .*v.4 p.324*

The History of Western Education. *v.4 p.324, p.325*

A History of Western Musical Aesthetics. *v.1 p.382*

A History of Western Music. *v.1 p.174*

History of Western Philosophy. *v.1 p.417*

The History of Wisconsin. *v.3 p.517*

A History of Women: From Ancient Goddesses to Christian Saints. *v.3 p.51, v.6 p.559*

A History of Women in the United States: State-By-State Reference. *v.6 p.426*

A History of Women in the West: Silences of the Middle Ages. *v.6 p.560*

A History of Women Photographers. .*v.1 p.707, p.764, v.6 p.473*

A History of Women's Football: Gender, Power and the Rise of a Global Game. *v.4 p.811, p.845, p.868*

e A History of Women's Writing in Russia. *v.2 p.797*

A History of Women's Writing in Russia. *v.6 p.477*

History of Wyoming. *v.3 p.526*

A History of Yugoslav Literature. *v.2 p.818*

A History of Zambia. *v.6 p.77*

History of Zanzibar, from the Middle Ages to 1856. . .*v.6 p.66*

A History of Zionism: From the French Revolution to the Establishment of the State of Israel. *v.1 p.549*

A History Reclaimed: An Annotated Bibliography of Chinese Language Materials on the Chinese of America. *v.6 p.86, p.127*

History, Tales and Sketches: The Sketch Book, A History of New York, Salmagundi, Letters of Jonathan Goldstyle, Gent. *v.2 p.42*

History's Mysteries: Bizarre Beings. *v.5 p.77*

The History. *v.2 p.412*

Hit Men: Power Brokers and Fast Money Inside the Music
Business. *v.1 p.383*

Hitler, 1889-1936: Hubris. *v.3 p.84, p.172*

Hitler, 1936-1945: Nemesis. *v.3 p.84, p.85, p.172*

Hitler and His Generals: Military Conferences,
1942-1945. . . . .*v.3 p.175*

Hitler and His Generals: Miltary Conferences 1942-1945: The
First Complete Stenographic Record of the Military
Conferences from Stalingrad to Berlin. *v.3 p.81*

Hitler and Spain: The Nazi Role in the Spanish Civil War,
1936-1939. . . . .*v.3 p.174, p.242*

Hitler and the Collapse of Weimar Germany. . .*v.3 p.169, p.170*

Hitler and the Jews: The Genesis of the Holocaust. . .*v.3 p.83*

Hitler, Germans, and the Jewish Question. *v.3 p.59*

The Hitler Kiss: A Memoir of the Czech Resistance. .*v.3 p.189*

The Hitler State: The Foundation and Development of the
Internal Structure of the Third Reich. *v.3 p.171*

Hitler Strikes Poland: Blitzkrieg, Ideology, and Atrocity. .*v.3 p.254*

Hitler Youth. *v.3 p.172*

Hitler's Austria: Popular Sentiment in the Nazi Era,
1938-1945. . . . .*v.3 p.83, p.185*

Hitler's Exiles: The German Cultural Resistance in America and
Europe. *v.3 p.179*

Hitler's Foreign Policy: The Road to World War II
1933-1939. . . . .*v.3 p.81*

Hitler's Foreign Workers: Enforced Foreign Labor in Germany
under the Third Reich. *v.3 p.172*

Hitler's Generals. *v.3 p.80, p.174*

Hitler's Germany: Origins, Interpretations, Legacies. . .*v.3 p.174*

Hitler's Heroines: Stardom and Womanhood in Nazi
Cinema. *v.6 p.328, p.338*

Hitler's Hometown: Linz, Austria, 1908-1945. . . . .*v.3 p.184*

Hitler's Prisons: Legal Terror in Nazi Germany. *v.3 p.174*

Hitler's Second Book: The Unpublished Sequel to Mein
Kampf. *v.3 p.172*

Hitler's Secret War in South America, 1939-1945: German
Military Espionage and Allied Counterespionage in
Brazil. *v.3 p.340, p.341*

Hitler's Social Revolution: Class and Status in Nazi Germany,
1933-1939. . . . .*v.3 p.173*

Hitler's Vienna: A Dictator's Apprenticeship. *v.3 p.183*

Hitotsubashi on Knowledge Management. . . .*v.4 p.77, p.78*

The Hittites: And Their Contemporaries in Asia
Minor. *v.3 p.6, v.4 p.9*

The Hittites. *v.3 p.6*

HIV Infection in Primary Care. *v.5 p.515*

☐ HIV InSite: HIV Policy. *v.4 p.668*

HIV Nursing and Symptom Management. *v.5 p.515*

HIV/AIDS in Russia and Eurasia, Vol. 1. . . . . .*v.4 p.669*

The Hive. *v.2 p.657*

Hmong Means Free: Life in Laos and America. . . .*v.6 p.139*

The Hmong Refugees Experience in the United States: Crossing
the River. *v.6 p.139*

☐ H-Net Women: Internet Links. *v.6 p.432*

Ho Chi Minh: A Life. *v.6 p.167, p.168*

Ho Chi Minh. *v.6 p.168, p.169*

Hobbes on Civil Association. *v.4 p.492, p.493*

Hobbes. *v.1 p.448, p.449*

The Hobbit: Or There and Back Again. *v.2 p.386*

Hobomok. *v.2 p.32*

Hoe and Wage: A Social History of a Circular Migration System
in West Africa. *v.6 p.73*

Hoffa. *v.4 p.129*

Hofmannsthal's Festival Dramas. *v.2 p.609*

Hokusai and His Age. *v.1 p.692, p.693, p.695*

Hokusai: Prints and Drawings. *v.1 p.723, p.756*

Holabird and Roche and Root: An Illustrated Catalogue of
Works, 1880-1940. . . . .*v.1 p.792*

Holbein and England. *v.1 p.686, p.687, p.738*

The Hold Life Has: Coca and Cultural Identity in an Andean
Community. *v.4 p.36, p.700*

Holdfast: At Home in the Natural World. *v.5 p.226*

Holding Accountability Accountable: What Ought to Matter in
Public Education. *v.4 p.281*

Holding Corporations Accountable: Corporate Conduct,
International Codes and Citizen Action. *v.4 p.145*

Holding on to the Air: An Autobiography. *v.1 p.7*

Holding the Line: The Eisenhower Era, 1952-1961. .*v.3 p.464*

Holding up More Than Half the Sky: Chinese Women Garment
Workers in New York City, 1948-92. *v.6 p.111, p.116, p.126*

The Holiday Trilogy. *v.2 p.711*

The Holiness of the Real: The Short Verse of Kenneth
Rexroth. *v.2 p.114*

The Holiness-Pentecostal Tradition: Charismatic Movements in
the Twentieth Century. *v.1 p.587*

Holism and Reductionism in Biology and Ecology: The Mutual
Dependence of Higher and Lower Level Research
Programmes. *v.5 p.184, p.185*

Holism and the Understanding of Science: Integrating the
Analytical, Historical and Sociological. *v.5 p.401*

Holland and the Dutch Republic in the Seventeenth Century:
The Politics of Particularism. *v.3 p.205*

Holland under Habsburg Rule, 1506-1566: The Formation of a
Body Politic. *v.3 p.205*

Holler If You Hear Me: Searching for Tupac
Shakur. *v.6 p.29, p.38*

The Hollow Crown: Ethnohistory of an Indian
Kingdom. *v.6 p.160*

Hollywood Androgyny. *v.6 p.415*

Hollywood As Historian: American Film in a Cultural
Context. *v.6 p.315*

Hollywood Bedlam: Classic Screwball Comedies. . .*v.6 p.312*

Hollywood Behind the Wall: The Cinema of East
Germany. *v.6 p.338*

Hollywood Blue: The Tinseltown Pornographers. . .*v.6 p.317*

Hollywood Economics: How Extreme Uncertainty Shapes the
Film Industry. *v.6 p.344*

Hollywood Fantasies of Miscegenation: Spectacular Narratives
of Gender and Race. *v.6 p.321*

Hollywood Gays. *v.6 p.416*

Hollywood Genres: Formulas, Filmmaking, and the Studio
System. *v.6 p.311*

Hollywood Goes Shopping. *v.6 p.344*

Hollywood Lesbians. *v.6 p.416*

Hollywood Modernism: Film and Politics in the Age of the New
Deal. *v.6 p.321*

Hollywood Musicals, the Film
Reader. *v.1 p.249, p.255,v.6 p.315, p.316*

Hollywood Musicals Year by Year. *v.6 p.316*

The Hollywood Musical. *v.6 p.316*

Hollywood Renaissance: The Cinema of Democracy in the Era
of Ford, Capra and Kazan. *v.6 p.341*

Hollywood Rhapsody: The Story of Movie Music,
1900-1975. . . . .*v.6 p.342*

Hollywood Sings: An Inside Look at Sixty Years of Academy
Award-Nominated Songs. *v.6 p.316*

Hollywood Song: The Complete Film and Musical
Companion. *v.1 p.165, p.248, p.254, p.255,v.6 p.315*

Hollywood Songsters: Singers Who Act and Actors Who Sing,
Set. *v.6 p.316*

The Hollywood Standard: The Complete and Authoritative
Guide to Script Format and Style. *v.6 p.353*

Hollywood Surf and Beach Movies: The First Wave,
1959-1969. . . . .*v.6 p.342*

Hollywood Theory, Non-Hollywood Practice: Cinema
Soundtracks in the 1980s and 1990s. *v.1 p.255*

Hollywood vs. America. *v.6 p.321*

Hollywood War Films, 1937-1945: An Exhaustive Filmography
of American Feature-Length Motion Pictures Relating
to World War II. *v.6 p.323*

Hollywood's America: Social and Political Themes in Motion
Pictures. *v.6 p.343*

Hollywood's Indian: The Portrayal of the Native American in
Film. *v.6 p.700*

Hollywood's New Deal. *v.6 p.343*

Hollywood's Overseas Campaign: The North Atlantic Movie
Trade, 1920-1950. . . . .*v.6 p.341*

Hollywood's Road to Riches. *v.6 p.345*

Hollywood's White House: The American Presidency in Film
and History. *v.6 p.315*

Hollywood's World War I: Motion Picture Images. . .*v.6 p.323*

Holman Bible Atlas: A Complete Guide to the Expansive
Geography of Biblical History. *v.1 p.617*

Holmes' Principles of Physical Geology. *v.5 p.418*

Holmes-Laski Letters, the Correspondence of Justice Oliver
Wendell Holmes and Harold J. Laski, 1916-1935, 2.*v.4 p.468*

Holmes-Pollock Letters: The Correspondence of Mr. Justice
Holmes and Sir Frederick Pollock, 1874-1932. . . .*v.4 p.468*

The Holocaust and the Literary Imagination. *v.2 p.572*

The Holocaust Encyclopedia. *v.3 p.85*

The Holocaust Film Sourcebook. *v.6 p.315*

The Holocaust in American Life. *v.3 p.86*

The Holocaust in History. *v.3 p.85*

The Holocaust in Latvia, 1941-1944: The Missing
Center. *v.3 p.83, p.256*

The Holocaust in Romania: The Destruction of Jews and
Gypsies under the Antonescu Regime,
1940-1944. . . . .*v.3 p.84, p.250*

Holocaust in the Ukraine. *v.3 p.87, p.230*

Holocaust Justice: The Battle for Restitution in America's
Courts. *v.4 p.464*

Holocaust Testimonies: The Ruins of Memory. *v.3 p.85*

The Holocaust, the French, and the Jews. *v.3 p.156*

Holocene Settlement of the Egyptian Sahara. *v.4 p.8*

Holst: The Planets. *v.1 p.215, p.239, p.332*

The Holy Bible, English Standard Version: Classic Reference -
Hardcover, Black Letter. *v.1 p.613*

Holy Feast and Holy Fast: The Religious Significance of Food
to Medieval Women. *v.1 p.600, v.3 p.51*

The Holy Household: Women and Morals in Reformation
Augsburg. *v.3 p.52*

Holy Johnson: Pioneer of African Nationalism,
1836-1917. . . . .*v.6 p.72*

Holy Land Pilgrimage in the Later Roman Empire: AD
312-460. . . . .*v.6 p.608*

The Holy Land. *v.2 p.630*

Holy Leisure: Recreation and Religion in God's Square
Mile. *v.4 p.720*

Holy Radishes. *v.6 p.506*

The Holy Reich: Nazi Conceptions of Christianity,
1919-1945. . . . .*v.3 p.174*

The Holy Sinner. *v.2 p.613*

The Holy Teaching of Vimalakirti: Mahayana Scripture.*v.1 p.564*

Holy Terrors: Thinking about Religion after September
11. . . . .*v.4 p.564, p.660*

Holy Terror. *v.1 p.524*

The Holy War. *v.2 p.241*

Holy Women of the Syrian Orient. . . .*v.1 p.569, p.612, p.613*

Holy Writ or Holy Church: The Crisis of the Protestant
Reformation. *v.1 p.638*

Homage to Catalonia. *v.2 p.375, v.3 p.241*

Hombre que Amaba el Sol. *v.2 p.666*

Hombres de Maize. *v.2 p.674*

Home and Away: A Collection of Kannada Short
Stories. *v.6 p.152*

Home and Exile. *v.2 p.753*

Home and Homeland: The Dialectics of Tribal and National
Identities in Jordan. *v.6 p.620*

Home at Grasmere. *v.2 p.325*

Home Before Dark. *v.2 p.65*

Home Bound: Filipino Lives Across Cultures, Communities, and
Countries. *v.6 p.129*

Home, Family and Kinship in Maharashtra. *v.6 p.154*

Home Fires Burning: Food, Politics and Everyday Life in World
War I Berlin. *v.3 p.164*

Home Fronts: Controversies in Nontraditional
Parenting. *v.6 p.377*

Home Girls: Chicana Literary Voices. *v.6 p.480*

The Home: Its Work and Influence. *v.4 p.737, v.6 p.466*

Home Orchid Growing. *v.5 p.43, p.44*

Home Schooling: Political, Historical, and Pedagogical
Perspectives. *v.4 p.296*

Home Team: Professional Sports and the American
Metropolis. *v.4 p.883, p.887, p.896*

Home to Stay: Asian American Fiction by Women. .*v.6 p.92, p.102*

Home Town News: William Allen White and the Emporia Gazette. *v.4 p.410*

Home Town. *v.4 p.704*

Home Truths: Fictions of the South Asian Diaspora in Britain. *v.2 p.760*

Homebase. *v.6 p.102*

The Homecoming Game: A Novel. *v.2 p.105*

Homecoming: The Story of African-American Farmers. .*v.6 p.20*

Homecoming. *v.6 p.232*

Homelands and Diasporas: Holy Lands and Other Places. *v.6 p.614*

Homeland. *v.4 p.767*

Homelessness, AIDS, and Stigmatization: The NIMBY Syndrome in the United States at the End of the Twentieth Century. *v.4 p.722*

The Homeless. *v.4 p.750, p.751*

Homemakers, the Forgotten Workers. *v.4 p.736, v.6 p.466*

Homeplace Geography: Essays for Appalachia. . . .*v.4 p.381*

Homer: His Art and His World. *v.2 p.414*

Homer: Iliad I-XII. *v.2 p.414*

Homer: Iliad XIII-XXIV. *v.2 p.414*

Homer: Odyssey I-XII. *v.2 p.414*

Homer: Odyssey XIII-XXIV. *v.2 p.414*

Homer on Life and Death. *v.2 p.413, p.414*

Homer: The Iliad. *v.2 p.414*

Homer: The Odyssey. *v.2 p.413*

Homeric Dictionary. *v.2 p.413*

Homeric Greek. *v.2 p.415*

The Homeric Hymns: A Translation, with Introduction and Notes. *v.2 p.415*

Homeric Hymns, Homeric Apocrypha, Lives of Homer. *v.2 p.415, p.416*

The Homeric Hymns. *v.2 p.414*

Homeric Moments: Clues to Delight in Reading the Odyssey and the Iliad. *v.2 p.413*

Homeric Questions. *v.2 p.415*

Homeric Responses. *v.2 p.415*

Homeric Soundings: The Shaping of the Iliad. . . .*v.2 p.415*

Homeric Vocabularies: Greek and English Word-Lists for the Study of Homer. *v.2 p.413*

Homer's Traditional Art. *v.2 p.413*

Homer. *v.2 p.415*

Homeschooling in Full View: A Reader. *v.4 p.296*

The Homewood Books. *v.2 p.159*

L' Homme Rapaille: Poemes. *v.2 p.541*

Les hommes de bonne volonté, Vol. 1. . . . . . .*v.2 p.526*

Les hommes de bonne volonté, Vol. 2. . . . . . .*v.2 p.526*

Les hommes de bonne volonté, Vol. 3. . . . . . .*v.2 p.526*

Les hommes de bonne volonté, Vol. 4. . . . . . .*v.2 p.526*

Homo Economics: Capitalism, Community and Lesbian and Gay Life. *v.6 p.382*

Homo Faber. *v.2 p.607*

Homo Hierarchicus; an Essay on the Caste System. .*v.4 p.723*

Homo Necans: The Anthropology of Ancient Greek Sacrificial Ritual and Myth. *v.1 p.532*

The Homoerotics of Early Modern Drama. *v.6 p.411*

Homophobia: A History. *v.6 p.362*

The Homosexual and Society: An Annotated Bibliography, 18. . . . .*v.6 p.359*

The Homosexual in America: A Subjective Approach. *v.6 p.362, p.381*

Homosexual: Oppression and Liberation. *v.6 p.386*

Homosexual Themes in Literary Studies, 8. . . . .*v.6 p.392*

The Homosexual Tradition in American Poetry. . . .*v.6 p.393*

Homosexualities: A Study of Diversity Among Men and Women. *v.6 p.371*

Homosexualities in the English Theatre: From Lyly to Wilde, 79. . . . .*v.6 p.411*

Homosexualities. *v.6 p.372*

Homosexuality: A History. *v.4 p.749, v.6 p.362*

Homosexuality: A Research Guide. *v.6 p.360*

Homosexuality: A Selective Bibliography of Over Three Thousand Items. *v.6 p.359*

Homosexuality: An Annotated Bibliography. *v.6 p.359*

Homosexuality and American Psychiatry: The Politics of Diagnosis. *v.6 p.380*

Homosexuality and Civilization. *v.4 p.747, v.6 p.364*

Homosexuality and the Bible: Two Views. *v.1 p.618*

Homosexuality and the Judeo-Christian Tradition: An Annotated Bibliography. *v.6 p.359, p.373*

Homosexuality and the Law: A Dictionary. *v.4 p.457*

Homosexuality and the Western Christian Tradition. *v.6 p.362, p.373*

Homosexuality and World Religions. *v.6 p.373*

Homosexuality Bibliography: Second Supplement, 1976-1982. . . . .*v.6 p.359*

Homosexuality Bibliography: Supplement, 1970-1975. .*v.6 p.359*

Homosexuality in French History and Culture. . . .*v.6 p.421*

Homosexuality in Greece and Rome: A Sourcebook of Basic Documents. *v.3 p.14*

Homosexuality in Renaissance England. *v.6 p.364, p.421*

Homosexuality in the Priesthood and Religious Life. .*v.6 p.373*

Homosexuality: Lesbians and Gay Men in Society, History and Literature. *v.6 p.363*

The Homosexuality of Men and Women. *v.4 p.748, v.6 p.381, p.420*

The Homosexualization of America: The Americanization of the Homosexual. *v.6 p.362*

The Hon. Alexander MacKenzie, His Life and Times. .*v.3 p.539*

Honduras: Caudillo Politics and Military Rulers. . .*v.3 p.276*

Honen's Senchakushu: Passages on the Selection of the Nembutsu in the Original Vow. *v.6 p.221*

Honest Numbers and Democracy: Social Policy Analysis in the White House, Congress and the Federal Agencies. .*v.4 p.526*

Honest Numbers and Democracy: Social Policy Analysis in the White House, Congress, and the Federal Agencies. *v.4 p.567, p.770*

Honest Whore. *v.2 p.218*

An Honest Writer: The Life and Times of James T. Farrell. *v.2 p.73*

Honey and Vinegar: Incentives, Sanctions and Foreign Policies. *v.4 p.642*

Honey for the Bears. *v.2 p.336*

Honey, Honey, Miss Thang: Being Black, Gay, and on the
  Streets. *v.6 p.371*

Hong Kong Cinema: A Cross-Cultural View. *v.6 p.335*

Hong Kong: Stability and Change: A Collection of
  Essays. *v.6 p.206*

Hong Kong's Embattled Democracy: A Societal
  Analysis. *v.4 p.618*

Hong Kong. *v.6 p.206*

Les honneurs perdus : roman. *v.2 p.544*

Honor and Grace in Anthropology. *v.4 p.42*

The Honor Plays of Lope De Vega. *v.2 p.652*

Honor, Status, and Law in Modern Latin America. . .*v.3 p.283*

An Honorable Defeat: The Last Days of the Confederate
  Government. *v.4 p.520*

Honorable Justice: The Life of Oliver Wendell Holmes. .*v.4 p.469*

Honorable Lives: Lawyers, Families and Politics in Colombia,
  1780-1850. . . . .*v.3 p.356, p.357*

The Honorary Consul. *v.2 p.350*

Honore d'Urfe, Astrea. *v.2 p.474, p.475*

Honoré Daumier. *v.1 p.697*

Honoré Lannuier, Cabinet Maker from Paris: The Life and Work
  of a French Ebeniste in Federal New York. .*v.1 p.802, p.804*

The Honors Class: Hilbert's Problems and Their
  Solvers. *v.5 p.468*

Honor. *v.6 p.596*

The Honourable Schoolboy: A Novel. *v.2 p.361*

Hons and Rebels. *v.2 p.371*

Honus Wagner: A Biography. *v.4 p.850*

The 'Hood Comes First: Race, Space, and Place in Rap and
  Hip-Hop. *v.1 p.268*

The Hood River Issei: An Oral History of Japanese Settlers in
  Oregon's Hood River Valley. *v.6 p.114, p.132, p.133*

Hoodlums: Black Villains and Social Bandits in American
  Life. *v.6 p.40, p.41, p.256*

Hood's Own or Laughter from Year to Year. *v.2 p.290*

Hood. *v.6 p.395*

Hoofing on Broadway: A History of Show Dancing. .*v.1 p.31, p.32*

The Hoosier School-Master. *v.2 p.37*

Hoover, Conservation and Consumerism: Engineering the Good
  Life. *v.3 p.440, v.6 p.298*

Hoover's Dominican Diplomacy and the Origins of the Good
  Neighbor Policy. *v.3 p.316*

▢ Hoover's Online. *v.4 p.93, p.101, p.148*

Hope Against Hope: A Memoir. *v.2 p.806*

Hope Dies Last: The Autobiography of Alexander
  Dubcek. *v.3 p.189*

Hope Is the Thing with Feathers: A Personal Chronicle of
  Vanished Birds. *v.6 p.290*

Hope Leslie: Or, Early Times in the Massachusetts. . .*v.2 p.51*

Hopeful Girls Troubled Boys: Race and Gender Disparity in
  Urban Education. *v.4 p.315*

Hopes and Fears for Art. *v.2 p.301*

The Hopi Way: By Laura Thompson and Alice Joseph. .*v.6 p.704*

Hopkins; A Collection of Critical Essays. *v.2 p.293*

Hopkins: A Literary Biography. *v.2 p.294*

A Hopkins reader. *v.2 p.293*

Hopkins, the Self and God. *v.2 p.294*

Hoplites: Classical Greek Battle Experience. *v.3 p.17*

Horace: Epistles Book II and Ars Poetica. . .*v.2 p.434, p.435*

Horace: Epistles. *v.2 p.434*

Horace Mann, a Biography. *v.4 p.344*

Horace Odes I: Carpe Diem. *v.2 p.434*

Horace Odes II: Vatis Amici. *v.2 p.434*

Horace Odes III Dulce Periculum: Text, Translation, and
  Commentary. *v.2 p.434*

Horace, the Odes: New Translations by Contemporary
  Poets. *v.2 p.434*

Horace Walpole's, Miscellany 1786-1795. . . . . . .*v.2 p.264*

Horace White, Nineteenth Century
  Liberal. *v.3 p.422, p.423, p.428, p.429*

Horace's Compromise: The Dilemma of the American High
  School. *v.4 p.329*

Horace's School: Redesigning the American High
  School. *v.4 p.329*

Horace. *v.2 p.434*

Horizons West: The Western from John Ford to Clint
  Eastwood. *v.6 p.324*

The Horizontal Organization: What the Organization of the
  Future Actually Looks Like and How It Delivers Value to
  Customers. *v.4 p.80*

Hormonal Chaos: The Scientific and Social Origins of the
  Environmental Endocrine Hypothesis. .*v.5 p.355, p.366, p.375*

The Horn Handbook. *v.1 p.391, p.398*

Horns, Strings and Harmony. *v.1 p.374*

Horn. *v.1 p.392*

Horowitz: A Musical Biography. *v.1 p.332, p.333*

Horror: A Thematic History in Fiction and Film. . . .*v.6 p.318*

Horror Film: Creating and Marketing Fear. *v.6 p.318*

Horror Film Reader. *v.6 p.320*

The Horror Film. *v.6 p.319*

Horror in Silent Films: A Filmography, 1896-1929. .*v.6 p.318*

Horrors of the Half-known Life: Male Attitudes Toward Women
  and Sexuality in 19th Century America. *v.4 p.743*

The Horrors of the Half-Known Life: Male Attitudes Toward
  Women and Sexuality in Nineteenth-Century
  America. *v.6 p.428*

Horse Facilities Handbook. *v.5 p.56*

Horse Has Six Legs: Contemporary Serbian Poetry. . .*v.2 p.811*

The Horse in West African History: The Role of the Horse in
  the Societies of Pre-Colonial West Africa. *v.6 p.68*

Horses in the Air and Other Poems. *v.2 p.658*

The Horse's Mouth. *v.2 p.338*

The Horses of San Marco and The Quadriga of the
  Lord. *v.1 p.775*

The Horse. *v.5 p.54*

Horspiele: Aichinger, Bachmann, Boll, Eich, Hildesheimer
  Etc. *v.2 p.602*

Horta. *v.1 p.791*

Horticultural Science. *v.5 p.44*

Hortus Third: A Concise Dictionary of Plants Cultivated in the
  United States and Canada. *v.5 p.44*

Hosea. *v.1 p.622*

The Hospice Handbook: A Complete Guide. *v.5 p.531*

Hospital Costs and Health Insurance. *v.4 p.247*

Hospital Epidemiology and Infection Control. *v.5 p.533*

Hospitality Facilities Management and Design. . . .*v.4 p.161*

Hospitality World!: An Introduction. *v.4 p.161*

Host-Parasite Interactions. *v.5 p.167*

Hot Jazz and Jazz Dance: Roger Pryor Dodge Collected
    Writings 1929-1964. . . . .*v.1 p.31*

Hot Potato: How Washington and New York Gave Birth to
    Black Basketball and Changed America's Game
    Forever. *v.4 p.807, p.832, p.854*

Hot Water. *v.2 p.390*

Hotei Encyclopedia of Japanese Woodblock
    Prints. *v.1 p.752, p.754*

Hotel and Lodging Management: An Introduction. . .*v.4 p.161*

Hotel and Restaurant Industries: A Bibliography and
    Sourcebook. *v.4 p.161*

Hotel du Lac. *v.2 p.331*

Hotel Lautreamont. *v.2 p.57*

Hotel Rwanda: Bringing the True Story of an African Hero to
    Film. *v.6 p.333*

Hotel Splendid. *v.2 p.533*

The Hothouse Effect: Intensify Creativity in Your Organization
    Using Secrets from History's Most Innovative
    Communities. *v.4 p.66*

The Hothouse. *v.2 p.377*

Hotspots Revisited: Earth's Biologically Richest and Most
    Endangered Terrestrial
    Ecoregions. *v.5 p.356, p.357,v.6 p.286, p.292*

ⓔ The Houghton Mifflin Dictionary of Geography: Places and
    Peoples of the World. *v.4 p.373*

The Hour and the Woman: Harriet Martineau's "Somewhat
    Remarkable" Life. *v.2 p.299*

An Hour Before Dawn: Stories of the Outdoors. . . .*v.5 p.227*

The Hour of Eugenics: Race, Gender and Nation in Latin
    America. *v.3 p.280*

The Hour of the Star. *v.2 p.691*

Hourglass. *v.2 p.811*

The Hours: A Novel. *v.2 p.143, v.6 p.395*

The Hours of Henry VIII: A Renaissance Masterpiece by Jean
    Poyet. *v.1 p.729, p.730, p.749*

A House and Its Head. *v.2 p.339*

The House and Senate Explained: The People's Guide to
    Congress. *v.4 p.533*

House and Senate. *v.4 p.529, p.533*

House and Society in the Ancient Greek World. . . .*v.3 p.14*

House and Street: The Domestic World of Servants and Masters
    in Nineteenth-Century Rio de Janeiro. *v.3 p.337*

The House by the Church-Yard. *v.2 p.361*

The House by the Medlar Tree. *v.2 p.713*

A House Divided: Argentina, 1880-1980. . . . . . .*v.3 p.347*

A House Divided: Catholics, Socialists, and Flemish Nationalists
    in Nineteenth Century Belgium. *v.3 p.206*

A House Divided: Sectionalism and Civil War,
    1848-1865. . . . .*v.3 p.401*

A House for Mr. Biswas: A Novel. *v.2 p.769*

The House Gun. *v.2 p.755*

A House in Bali. *v.6 p.175, p.177*

The House in Paris. *v.2 p.334*

House Made of Dawn. *v.2 p.150, v.6 p.698*

House of All Nations. *v.2 p.749*

House of Bernarda Alba. *v.2 p.658*

The House of Blackwood: Author-Publisher Relations in the
    Victorian Era. *v.6 p.741*

The House of Breath. *v.2 p.78*

House of Bush, House of Saud: The Secret Relationship
    Between the World's Two Most Powerful Dynasties. .*v.3 p.484*

House of Dolls. *v.6 p.649*

House of Glass: A Novel. *v.6 p.178*

House of Incest. *v.2 p.105*

The House of Joshua: Meditations on Family and Place. .*v.5 p.608*

The House of Lim: A Study of a Chinese Family. . . .*v.6 p.214*

A House of Many Mansions: The History of Lebanon
    Reconsidered. *v.6 p.604*

The House of Morgan: An American Banking Dynasty and the
    Rise of Modern Finance. *v.4 p.91*

The House of Morgan: An American Banking Family and the
    Rise of Modern Finance. . . .*v.4 p.146, p.148, p.154, p.155*

A House of My Own: Social Organization in the Squatter
    Settlements of Lima, Peru. *v.3 p.330*

The House of Rothschild: Money's Prophets,
    1798-1848. . . . .*v.4 p.146, p.155*

The House of Rothschild: The World's Banker,
    1849-1999. . . . .*v.4 p.147, p.155*

House of Sand and Fog. *v.2 p.144*

The House of Si Abd Allah: The Oral History of a Moroccan
    Family. *v.6 p.643, p.644*

House of Splendid Isolation. *v.2 p.373*

The House of the Spirits. *v.2 p.679*

The House of Ulloa: A Novel by Emilia Pardo Bazan. .*v.2 p.662*

The House on Mango Street. *v.6 p.498*

The House on the Canal. *v.2 p.622*

⬚ The House Practice: A Guide to the Rules, Precedents and
    Procedures of the House. *v.4 p.532*

House with Wisteria: Memoirs of Halide Edib. . . .*v.6 p.623*

The House You Pass on the Way. *v.6 p.400*

Houseboat Days: Poems. *v.2 p.57*

Houseboy. *v.2 p.543*

Household and Class Relations: The Peasant Economy of the
    Northern Peruvian Highlands, 1900-1980. . . . .*v.3 p.327*

Household Interests: Property, Marriage Strategies, and Family
    Dynamics in Ancient Athens. *v.3 p.14*

⬚ Household Products Database. *v.5 p.311*

Household Spending: Who Spends How Much on What. .*v.4 p.138*

Household Words: A Weekly Journal 1850-1859, Conducted by
    Charles Dickens. Table of Contents, List of
    Contributors and Their Contributions Based on the
    Household Words Office Book in the Morris L. Parrish
    Collection of Victorian Novelists, Princeton
    Uni. *v.6 p.741, p.754*

Households, Employment and Gender: A Social, Economic and
    Demographic View. *v.4 p.724, p.733,v.6 p.456*

Housekeeping: A Novel. *v.2 p.154*

Houses behind the Trees. *v.6 p.655, p.656*

Houses in the Rain Forest: Ethnicity and Inequality among
    Farmers and Foragers in Central Africa. *v.4 p.772*

The Houses of Belgrade. *v.2 p.811, p.812*

Houses of Worship: An Identification Guide to the History and
    Style of American Religious Architecture. *v.1 p.784*

Housing Desegregation and Federal Policy. *v.4 p.524*

Housing in the Twenty-First Century: Achieving Common
    Ground. *v.4 p.158, v.6 p.722*

Housing, Space and Quality of Life. *v.6 p.727*

How America Goes to War. *v.3 p.384*

How Bosnia Armed: The Birth and Rise of the Bosnian
    Army. *v.3 p.249*

How Bosnia Armed. *v.3 p.249*

How Boston Played: Sport, Recreation, and Community,
    1865-1915. . . . .*v.4 p.806, p.816*

How Brains Make up Their Minds. *v.5 p.616, p.617*

How Britain Works: From Ideology to Output Politics. *v.4 p.582*

How Can I Keep from Singing: Pete Seeger. . .*v.1 p.296, p.355*

How Children Fail. *v.4 p.364*

How Children Learn the Meanings of Words. *v.5 p.574*

How Children Learn. *v.4 p.357*

How Cities Work: Suburbs, Sprawl, and the Roads Not
    Taken. *v.4 p.771, v.6 p.728*

How Class Works: Power and Social Movement. . .*v.4 p.710*

How CNN Fought the War: A View from the Inside. *v.4 p.407*

How College Affects Students: A Third Decade of
    Research. *v.4 p.332*

How College Affects Students: Findings and Insights from
    Twenty Years of Research. *v.4 p.290*

How Communities Build Stonger Schools: Stories, Strategies,
    and Promising Practices for Educating Every Child. *v.4 p.303*

How Customers Think: Essential Insights into the Mind of the
    Markets. *v.5 p.587*

How Democracies Vote. *v.4 p.577*

How Democratic Is the American Constitution? . . . *v.4 p.453*

How Did This Happen?: Terrorism and the New War. *v.4 p.564*

How Did You Get to Be Mexican?: A White/Brown Man's
    Search for Identity. *v.6 p.489, p.544*

How Do I Look?: Queer Film and Video. *v.6 p.415*

How Do Judges Decide?: The Search for Fairness and Justice in
    Punishment. *v.6 p.271, p.272*

How Economics Became a Mathematical Science. . . *v.4 p.176*

How Economists Model the World into Numbers. *v.4 p.198, p.240*

How Educational Ideologies Are Shaping Global Society:
    Intergovernmental Organizations, NGO's, and the
    Decline of the Nation-State. *v.4 p.314*

How Europe Underdeveloped Africa. *v.6 p.55*

How Far from Austerlitz?: Napoleon 1805-1815. . . .*v.3 p.152*

How Fascism Ruled Women: Italy, 1922-1945. .*v.3 p.53, p.203*

How Fra Angelico and Signorelli Saw the End of the
    World. *v.1 p.739*

How France Votes. *v.4 p.609*

How Free Are You?: The Determinism Problem. . . .*v.1 p.503*

How Free Can the Press Be? *v.4 p.458*

How Full Is Your Bucket?: Positive Strategies for Work and
    Life. *v.4 p.83*

How Golf Clubs Really Work and How to Optimize Their
    Designs. *v.4 p.861, p.870, p.871, p.872*

How Green Was My Valley. *v.2 p.361*

How Homo Became Sapiens: On the Evolution of
    Thinking. *v.5 p.649*

How Humans Relate: A New Interpersonal Theory. . *v.5 p.646*

How I Learned to Drive. *v.1 p.62, p.122,v.2 p.157*

How Industries Evolve: Understanding the Critical Link
    Between Strategy and Innovation. *v.4 p.81, p.149*

How Israel Was Won: A Concise History of the Arab-Israeli
    Conflict. *v.6 p.611*

How It All Began: The Prison Novel. *v.3 p.222*

How Landscapes Change: Human Disturbance and Ecosystem
    Fragmentation in the Americas. . . .*v.5 p.167, p.178, p.186*

How Late It Was, How Late. *v.2 p.360*

How Latin American Fell Behind: Essays on the Economic
    Histories of Brazil and Mexico, 1800-1914. . . . .*v.3 p.285*

How Milton Works. *v.2 p.253*

How Monetary Policy Works. *v.4 p.246*

How Much Is That in Real Money?: A Historical Commodity
    Price Index for Use As a Deflator of Money Values
    in the Economy of the United States. *v.4 p.175*

How Much Risk?: A Guide to Understanding Environmental
    Health Hazards. *v.6 p.285*

The How of WOW: A Guide to Giving a Speech That Will
    Positively Blow 'Em Away. *v.4 p.172*

⬚ How Our Laws Are Made. *v.4 p.461*

How Our Lives Become Stories: Making Selves. . . *v.4 p.693*

How People Learn: Brain, Mind, Experience and
    School. *v.5 p.572*

How Poets See the World: The Art of Description in
    Contemporary Poetry. *v.2 p.578, p.583*

How Popular Musicians Learn: A Way Ahead for Music
    Education. *v.1 p.405*

How Products Are Made: An Illustrated Guide to Product
    Manufacturing, Vol. 1. . . . .*v.5 p.684*

How Products Are Made: An Illustrated Guide to Product
    Manufacturing. *v.5 p.684*

How Russia Votes. *v.4 p.599*

How Schools Change: Lessons from Three
    Communities. *v.4 p.330*

How Scripts Are Made. *v.6 p.352*

How Sex Changed: A History of Transsexuality in the United
    States. *v.4 p.744, v.6 p.363, p.371*

How Societies Are Born: Governance in West Central Africa
    Before 1600. . . . .*v.6 p.61*

How Students Learn: History, Math, and Science in the
    Classroom. *v.5 p.574*

How Students Learn: Reforming Schools Through
    Learner-Centered Education. *v.5 p.574*

How Sweet the Sound: Music in the Spiritual Lives of
    Americans. *v.1 p.280*

How Teachers Taught: Constancy and Change in American Classrooms, 1890-1990. . . . . *v.4 p.325*

How the Dead Live. *v.2 p.380*

How the Garcia Girls Lost Their Accents. *v.6 p.505*

How the Great Pyramid Was Built. *v.6 p.57*

How the Human Genome Works. *v.5 p.135, p.141*

How the Indians Lost Their Land: Law and Power on the Frontier. *v.6 p.681, p.691*

How the Leopard Changed Its Spots: The Evolution of Complexity. *v.5 p.192*

How the News Makes Us Dumb: The Death of Wisdom in an Information Society. *v.4 p.418*

How the North Won: A Military History of the Civil War. *v.3 p.398*

How the Other Half Lives. *v.4 p.755*

How the Other Half Worships. *v.1 p.656*

How the War Was Remembered: Hollywood and Vietnam. *v.6 p.321, p.322*

How Things Work: The Physics of Everyday Life. . *v.5 p.539*

How to Ace Calculus: The Streetwise Guide. *v.5 p.485*

How to Ace the Rest of Calculus: The Streetwise Guide - Including Multi-Variable Calculus. *v.5 p.485*

How to Adapt Anything into a Screenplay. *v.6 p.326*

How to Build a Great Screenplay: A Master Class in Storytelling for Film. *v.6 p.352*

How to Build a Successful Consulting Practice. . . . *v.4 p.65*

How to Cook and Eat in Chinese. *v.6 p.181, p.182*

How to Create Interest-Evoking, Sales-Inducing, Non-Irritating Advertising. *v.4 p.428*

How to Cure a Fanatic. *v.6 p.615*

How to Do Theory. *v.2 p.567*

How to Do Things with Words. *v.1 p.445, p.489, p.510*

How To Encourage Girls in Math and Science: Strategies for Parents and Educators. *v.5 p.407*

How to Find Chemical Information: A Guide for Practicing Chemists, Educators, and Students. *v.5 p.255*

How to Find Information - Chemistry: A Guide to Searching in Published Sources. *v.5 p.255*

How to Find Out about Iron and Steel. *v.5 p.733*

☐ How to Find Out in Environmental Engineering. . *v.5 p.706*

How to Get an MBA. *v.4 p.177*

How to Get into the Top MBA Programs. *v.4 p.177*

How to Have Theory in an Epidemic: Cultural Chronicles of AIDS. *v.4 p.779*

How to Identify Prints. *v.1 p.752, p.759*

How to Increase Reading Ability: A Guide to Developmental and Remedial Methods. *v.4 p.363*

How to Keep Your Language Alive: A Commonsense Approach to One-on-One Language Learning. *v.6 p.691*

How to Know the Lichens. *v.5 p.210*

How to Lie with Maps. *v.4 p.375, p.385, p.386*

How to Live/What to Do: H. D. 's Cultural Poetics. . *v.2 p.89*

How to Make Dances in an Epidemic: Tracking Choreography in the Age of AIDS. . . *v.1 p.28, p.30, p.37, p.42, v.6 p.414*

How to Negotiate Like a Child: Unlease the Little Monster Within to Get Everything You Want. *v.4 p.74*

How to Plan Advertising. *v.4 p.427*

How to Play Drums. *v.1 p.397*

How to Prevent Genocide: A Guide for Policymakers, Scholars, and the Concerned Citizen. *v.4 p.652*

How to Promote Children's Social and Emotional Competence. *v.4 p.354*

How to Prosper as an Interior Designer: A Business and Legal Guide. *v.1 p.802, p.803*

How to Put Your Book Together and Get a Job in Advertising: 21st Century Edition. *v.4 p.428*

How to Read a Book. *v.2 p.573*

How to Read a Financial Report: Wringing Vital Signs Out of the Numbers. *v.4 p.92, p.98, p.105, p.176*

How to Read and Do Proofs: An Introduction to Mathematical Thought Processes. *v.5 p.471*

How to Read and Why. *v.2 p.566, p.573*

How to Read Egyptian Hieroglyphs: A Step-by-Step Guide to Teach Yourself. *v.3 p.8*

How to Read Sade. *v.2 p.484*

How to Read Superhero Comics and Why. . . *v.2 p.581, p.582*

How to Read the Bible for All Its Worth. *v.1 p.616*

How to Research Congress. *v.4 p.530*

How to Research the Supreme Court. *v.4 p.466*

How to Run a Company: Lessons from Top Leaders of the CEO Academy. *v.4 p.85*

How to Say It at Work: Putting Yourself Across with Power Words, Phrases, Body Language and Communication Secrets. *v.4 p.173*

How to Solve It: A New Aspect of Mathematical Method. *v.5 p.460*

How to Speak, Read and Write Persian (farsi). . . . *v.6 p.669*

How to Survive and Thrive As a Therapist: Information, Ideas, and Resources for Psychologists in Practice. . . . *v.5 p.676*

How to Use Biological Abstracts, Chemical Abstracts and Index Chemicus. *v.5 p.255*

How to Write a Selling Screenplay. *v.6 p.352, p.353*

How to Write and Present Technical Information. . . *v.5 p.681*

How to Write and Publish a Scientific Paper. *v.5 p.680*

How to Write the History of the New World: Histories, Epistemologies, and Identities in the Eighteenth-Century Atlantic World. *v.3 p.71, p.262*

How Using Pr Can Boost Your Business Public Relations for the Small Business. *v.4 p.87*

How We Became Human: New and Selected Poems, 1975-2001. . . . . *v.2 p.146*

How We Believe: The Search for God in an Age of Science. *v.5 p.636*

How We Die: Reflections on Life's Final Chapter. . . *v.5 p.532*

How We Grieve: Relearning the World. *v.5 p.651*

How We Have Changed: America since 1950. . . . . *v.3 p.369*

How We Think They Think: Anthropological Approaches to Cognition, Memory and Literacy. *v.4 p.27*

Howard Carter: The Path to Tutankhamun. *v.3 p.11*

Howard Hodgkin Prints: A Catalogue Raisonné. . . . *v.1 p.756*

A Howard Nemerov Reader. *v.2 p.105*

Howard Zinn: A Radical American Vision. *v.3 p.374*

Howards End: Authoritative Text, Textual Appendix,
    Backgrounds and Contexts, Criticism. *v.2 p.346*

The Howe Brothers and the American Revolution. . . .*v.3 p.411*

Howells Novels, 1886-1888: The Minister's Charge; April
    Hopes; Annie Kilburn. *v.2 p.42*

Howling Near Heaven: Twyla Tharp and the Reinvention of
    Modern Dance. *v.1 p.12, p.29, p.31*

HPLC, a Practical User's Guide. *v.5 p.269*

HPLC and CE: Principles and Practice. *v.5 p.269*

The HPLC Solvent Guide. *v.5 p.269*

HR Best Practices: Top Human Resources Executives from
    Prudential Financial, Northrop Grumman, and More
    on Hiring the Right People and Enhancing Corporate
    Culture. *v.4 p.75, p.76*

The HR Scorecard: Linking People, Strategy, and
    Performance. *v.4 p.76*

The HR Value Proposition. *v.4 p.77*

HRD in the Age of Globalization: A Practical Guide to
    Workplace Learning in the Third Millennium. . . .*v.4 p.79*

Hrotsvitha Dulcitius and Paphnutius. *v.2 p.449*

☐ HSLDA: Home School Legal Defense Association. *v.4 p.296*

Hsun Tzu: Basic Writings. *v.6 p.184, p.208, p.209*

HTML and XHTML: The Definitive Guide. . .*v.5 p.338, p.347*

H. *v.2 p.533*

Huanuco Pampa: An Inca City and Its Hinterland. . .*v.3 p.261*

Huasipungo. *v.2 p.685*

The Hub: Boston Past and Present. . .*v.3 p.487, p.488,v.6 p.714*

Hubbert's Peak: The Impending World Oil
    Shortage. *v.5 p.451, p.737*

Hubert Humphrey: A Biography. *v.3 p.463*

Hubert Humphrey: A Political Biography. *v.3 p.463*

Huck Finn and Tom Sawyer among the Indians and Other
    Unfinished Stories. *v.2 p.34*

The Huddled Masses Myth: Immigration and Civil
    Rights. *v.4 p.460*

The Huddled Masses: The Immigrant in American Society,
    1880-1921. . . . .*v.3 p.442, v.4 p.667, p.668*

Hudibras: And Selected Other Writings. *v.2 p.242*

Huellas de las literaturas Hispanoamericanas. *v.2 p.664*

Huey Long's Louisiana: State Politics, 1920-1952. . .*v.3 p.507*

Huey Long. *v.3 p.464*

Huge Dreams: San Francisco and Beat Poems. *v.2 p.150*

Hugh Johnson's Modern Encyclopedia of Wine. *v.5 p.32*

Hugh MacDiarmid; a Critical Survey. *v.2 p.368*

The Hugh MacDiarmid Anthology: Poems in Scots and
    English. *v.2 p.368*

Hugh of St. Victor: On the Sacraments of the Christian
    Faith. *v.1 p.577*

Hugh Primas and the Archpoet. *v.2 p.448*

Hugh S. Johnson and the New Deal. *v.3 p.461*

Hugh Wynne, Free Quaker; Sometime Brevet
    Lieutenant-Colonel on the Staff of His Excellency General
    Washington. *v.2 p.46*

Hugo Black: A Biography. *v.4 p.468, p.538*

Hugo Grotius and International Relations. *v.4 p.625*

Hugo L. Black: Cold Steel Warrior. *v.4 p.467*

Hugo Von Hofmannsthal. *v.2 p.609*

Hugo Wolf: The Vocal Music. *v.1 p.207, p.238, p.368*

The Huguenot Struggle for Recognition. *v.3 p.146*

Huitzil Uan Tuxtli: Colibri y Conejo - Medio Siglo de
    Poesia. *v.2 p.676*

The Huk Rebellion: A Study of Peasant Revolt in the
    Philippines. *v.6 p.179, p.180*

Hula Pahu: Hawaiian Drum Dances: Ha'a and Hula Pahu Sacred
    Movements. *v.1 p.17*

Huldrych Zwingli: His Life and Work. *v.1 p.603*

Human Action: A Treatise on Economics. *v.4 p.212*

Human, All-Too-Human, Vol. 2, Pts. 1&2. . . . . .*v.1 p.467*

Human Anatomy for Artists: The Elements of Form. . *v.1 p.722*

☐ Human and Constitutional Rights. *v.4 p.476*

Human and Machine Thinking. *v.5 p.590*

The Human Animal: Personal Identity Without
    Psychology. *v.1 p.495*

Human Behavior and Public Policy - Political
    Psychology. *v.5 p.645*

Human Biodiversity: Genes, Race and History. *v.4 p.17*

Human Biological Variation. *v.4 p.17, v.5 p.164*

Human Brain Proteome, Vol. 61. . . . .*v.5 p.117*

Human Cancer: Epidemiology and Environmental
    Causes. *v.5 p.364, p.375*

The Human Career: Human Biological and Cultural
    Origins. *v.4 p.15*

Human Cargo: A Journey among Refugees. *v.4 p.765*

Human Chromosomes. *v.5 p.142*

Human Comedy. *v.2 p.118*

Human Communication Disorders: An
    Introduction. *v.5 p.664, p.665, p.673*

The Human Condition. *v.4 p.718*

The Human Core of Spirituality: Mind as Psyche and
    Spirit. *v.5 p.634*

Human Development Report 2002: Deepening Democracy in a
    Fragmented World. *v.4 p.586*

Human Development Report 2005: International Cooperation at
    a Crossroads: Aid, Trade and Security in an Unequal
    World. *v.4 p.258, p.262, p.666*

Human Differences. *v.5 p.593*

Human Dignity in the Biotech Century: A Christian Vision for
    Public Policy. *v.1 p.595*

Human Ecology As Human Behavior: Essay in Environmental
    and Development Anthropology. *v.4 p.29*

Human Embryo Experimentation. *v.5 p.162, p.247*

Human Embryology and Developmental Biology: With Student
    Consult Access. *v.5 p.162*

Human Embryology and Developmental Biology. . . .*v.5 p.162*

Human Embryology. *v.5 p.162*

Human Embryonic Stem Cells: An Introduction to the Science
    and Therapeutic Potential. *v.5 p.162*

Human Embryonic Stem Cells. *v.5 p.159*

Human Error. *v.5 p.588, p.609*

Human Ethology. *v.5 p.616*

Human Evolutionary Genetics. *v.5 p.134*

The Human Face of Warfare: Killing, Fear and Chaos in Battle. *v.5 p.583, p.584*

Human Factors and Web Development. *v.5 p.588, p.589*

Human Factors for Highway Engineers. *v.5 p.716*

Human Factors in System Design. *v.5 p.587, p.588*

The Human Factor. *v.2 p.350*

Human Families. *v.4 p.708*

The Human Fossil Record, Set. *v.4 p.16*

Human Genetics: A Problem Based Approach. . . . *v.5 p.135*

Human Genetics: A Problem-Based Approach. . . . *v.5 p.533*

Human Genetics for the Social Sciences, Vol. 4. . . . *v.5 p.131*

Human Genetics. *v.5 p.135*

The Human Genome: A Beginner's Guide to the Chemical Code of Life. *v.5 p.138, p.139*

The Human Genome: A User's Guide. *v.5 p.134, p.140*

The Human Genome: Biology and Medicine. *v.5 p.142, p.146, p.151*

Human Genome Evolution: Human Molecular Genetics. *v.5 p.140, p.145, p.149, p.201*

The Human Genome Project: Cracking the Code Within Us. *v.5 p.135*

The Human Genome Project: Cracking the Genetic Code of Life. *v.5 p.135*

☐ The Human Genome Project: Exlporing the Genomic Landscape. *v.5 p.144*

☐ The Human Genome Project: Exploring our Molecular Selves. *v.5 p.140, p.145, p.149, p.245*

☐ The Human Genome Project Information DOE HGP Genomics Primers. *v.5 p.144*

☐ The Human Genome Project Publications. *v.5 p.144*

☐ The Human Genome Project Resources. *v.5 p.144*

The Human Genome Project. *v.5 p.132*

The Human Genome. *v.5 p.139*

Human Geography: An Introduction. *v.4 p.396*

Human Geography of East-Central Europe. *v.3 p.207*

Human Geography of the UK. *v.4 p.373*

Human Geography: People, Place, and Culture. . . . *v.4 p.396*

Human Geography. *v.4 p.396*

The Human Group. *v.4 p.692*

Human Heredity: Principles and Issues. *v.5 p.132*

The Human Image and Postmodern America. *v.5 p.598*

Human Immunology: Patient-Based Research. . . . *v.5 p.165*

Human Institutions: A Theory of Societal Evolution. . *v.4 p.718*

The Human Journalist: Reporters, Perspectives, and Emotions. *v.4 p.412*

Human Landscapes. *v.6 p.666*

Human Lead Exposure. *v.5 p.372*

Human Liberation in a Feminist Perspective: A Theology. *v.1 p.644*

Human Molecular Biology: An Introduction to the Molecular Basis of Health and Disease. *v.5 p.126*

Human Molecular Biology. *v.5 p.129*

Human Molecular Genetics. *v.5 p.143*

Human Motives and Cultural Models. *v.4 p.27*

Human Motor Control. *v.5 p.608*

Human Motor Development: A Lifespan Approach with PowerWeb/OLC Bind-In Card. *v.4 p.910*

Human Movement Potential: Its Ideokinetic Facilitation. *v.1 p.51, p.52*

Human Nature and the Social Order. *v.4 p.692, p.693*

Human Nature, Cultural Diversity, and the French Enlightenment. *v.3 p.148*

Human Nature in American Thought: A History. . . *v.3 p.367*

Human Nature in Politics: The Dynamics of Political Behavior. *v.4 p.483, v.5 p.642*

Human Natures: Genes, Cultures and the Human Prospect. *v.5 p.652*

Human Past. *v.4 p.6*

Human Performance and Ergonomics: Perceptual and Cognitive Principles. *v.5 p.587*

The Human Person in Science and Theology. *v.1 p.526*

The Human Potential for Peace: An Anthropological Challenge to Assumptions about War and Violence. *v.4 p.766*

The Human Problems of an Industrial Civilization, Vol. 6. . . . . *v.5 p.579*

☐ Human Protein Atlas. *v.5 p.328*

Human Resource Development: Strategy and Tactics. . *v.4 p.77*

Human Resource Management: Essential Perspectives. *v.4 p.76*

Human Resource Management in Public Service: Paradoxes, Processes, and Problems. *v.4 p.76*

Human Resource Management in Sport and Recreation. *v.4 p.883, p.900*

Human Resource Management in the Knowledge Economy: New Challenges, New Roles, New Capabilities. . . *v.4 p.76*

Human Resource Management. *v.4 p.119, p.120, p.180*

Human Rights and Diversity: Area Studies Revisited. *v.4 p.669*

Human Rights and Gender Violence: Translating International Law into Local Justice. *v.4 p.33*

Human Rights and Military Intervention. *v.4 p.513*

Human Rights and Social Policy in the 21st Century: A History of the Idea of Human Rights and Comparison of the United Nations Universal Declaration of Human Rights with United States Federal and State Constitutions. . . *v.4 p.670*

Human Rights and Societies in Transition: Causes, Consequences, Responses. *v.4 p.670*

Human Rights as Politics and Idolatry. *v.4 p.512*

Human Rights: Beyond the Liberal Vision. *v.4 p.768*

☐ Human Rights Campaign. *v.6 p.357, p.387*

Human Rights: Concept and Context. *v.4 p.513*

Human Rights Horizons: The Pursuit of Justice in a Globalizing World. *v.4 p.512*

Human Rights in Commonwealth Africa. . . *v.4 p.512, v.6 p.55*

Human Rights in Global Perspective: Anthropological Studies of Rights, Claims and Entitlements. *v.4 p.34*

Human Rights in Iran. *v.4 p.512*

Human Rights in the West Bank and Gaza: Legacy and Politics. *v.6 p.619*

Human Rights of Indigenous Peoples. *v.4 p.34*

The Human Rights of Women: International Instruments and African Experiences. *v.6 p.440*

Human Rights of Women: National and International Perspectives. *v.6 p.440*

Human Rights: The Essential Reference. .*v.4 p.436, p.437, p.669*

Human Rights: The Scholar as Activist. *v.4 p.45*

☐ Human Rights Watch Publications. *v.4 p.670*

☐ Human Services Policy Center, University of
   Washington. *v.5 p.671*

Human Sexuality. *v.4 p.748*

The Human Side of Enterprise. *v.4 p.120*

Human Skills. *v.5 p.605*

Human Types, an Introduction to Social Anthropology. *v.4 p.22*

Human Universals. *v.4 p.23*

Human Use of Human Beings: Cybernetics and Society. *v.5 p.408*

Human Variation, Races, Types, and Ethnic Groups. . *v.4 p.17*

Human Walking. *v.4 p.791, p.910*

The Human Zoo. *v.5 p.617*

Human-Computer Interaction: Ergonomics and User
   Interfaces. *v.5 p.589*

Human-Computer Interaction, Vol. 1. . . . .*v.5 p.589*

Humanism in Italian Renaissance Musical
   Thought. *v.1 p.180, p.181*

Humanism of the Other. *v.1 p.508*

Humanists and Reformers: A History of the Renaissance and
   Reformation. *v.1 p.602*

Humanitarian Intervention and International Relations. *v.4 p.671*

Humanitarian Intervention: Ethical, Legal and Political
   Dilemmas. *v.4 p.669, p.670, p.671*

Humanity: A Moral History of the Twentieth Century. *v.4 p.652*

Humanity of God. *v.1 p.633*

Human-Powered Vehicles. *v.5 p.715*

Humans: An Introduction to Four-Field
   Anthropology. *v.4 p.22, p.23*

Humboldt's Gift. *v.2 p.60*

☐ Humbul Humanities Hub. *v.2 p.549*

Hume: A Very Short Introduction. *v.1 p.451*

Hume and the Problem of Causation. *v.1 p.451*

Hume's Moral Theory. *v.1 p.451*

Hume's Philosophical Development: A Study of His
   Methods. *v.1 p.451, p.452*

Hume's Philosophy of Belief: A Study of His First
   Inquiry. *v.1 p.451*

Hume's Philosophy of Common Life. *v.1 p.451*

Hume. *v.1 p.452, v.3 p.129*

The Hummingbird's Daughter: A Novel. *v.6 p.504*

Humor as an Instructional Defibrillator: Evidence-Based
   Techniques in Teaching and Assessment. *v.4 p.346*

Humor in Early Islam. *v.6 p.663*

Humor in Eighteenth and Nineteenth-Century British Literature:
   A Reference Guide. *v.2 p.195*

Humor of the Old Southwest. *v.2 p.21*

Humor: The Psychology of Living Buoyantly. *v.5 p.654*

Humorous Poems by Thomas Hood. *v.2 p.290, p.291*

Humour in Society: Resistance and Control. *v.4 p.773*

Humphrey Repton: Landscape Gardening and the Geography of
   Georgian England. *v.1 p.815*

Humphry Davy: Science and Power. *v.5 p.261*

Humps and Wings: Polish Poetry Since '68. . . . .*v.2 p.787*

Humus Chemistry: Genesis, Composition, Reactions. . .*v.5 p.51*

The Hunchback of Notre Dame. *v.2 p.494*

The Hunchback's Tailor: Giovanni Giolitti and Liberal Italy
   from the Challenge of Mass Politics to the Rise of Fascism,
   1882-1922. . . . .*v.3 p.202*

Hundejahre. *v.2 p.608*

The Hundred Thousand Fools of God: Musical Travels in
   Central Asia (& Queens, New York). *v.1 p.300*

The Hundred Yard Lie: The Corruption of College Football and
   What We Can Do to Stop It. *v.4 p.822, p.895*

A Hundred Years of Japanese Film: A Concise History, with a
   Selective Guide to DVDs and Videos. *v.6 p.336*

A Hundred Years of Philosophy. *v.3 p.129*

The Hundred Years War: England and France at War c.1300 -
   c.1450. . . . .*v.3 p.68, v.6 p.566*

The Hundred Years War: Trial by Battle. *v.3 p.144*

The Hundred Years War. . . .*v.3 p.143, v.4 p.641, p.643, p.647*

Hungarian: An Essential Grammar. *v.2 p.775*

Hungarian Cinema: A Concise History. *v.6 p.337*

Hungarian Parliament, 1867-1918: A Mirage of Power. *v.3 p.186*

Hungarian Plays. *v.1 p.69, p.110*

The Hungarian Revolution of 1956 in Retrospect. . .*v.3 p.187*

Hungarian Short Stories. *v.2 p.785*

☐ Hungarian texts in translation. *v.2 p.785*

The Hungarians: A Thousand Years of Victory in
   Defeat. *v.3 p.185*

Hungary and the Habsburgs, 1765-1800. . . . .*v.3 p.185, p.186*

Hungary and the Soviet Bloc. *v.3 p.187*

Hungary and the Victor Powers, 1945-1950. . . . .*v.3 p.187*

Hungary in the Cold War: 1945-1956. . . . .*v.3 p.187*

Hungary's Admiral on Horseback: Miklo's Horthy,
   1918-1944. . . . .*v.3 p.187*

Hungary's Negotiated Revolution: Economic Reform, Social
   Change and Political Succession. *v.4 p.595*

Hunger and Public Action. *v.4 p.265*

Hunger and Work in a Savage Tribe: A Functional Study of
   Nutrition among the Southern Bantu. *v.4 p.46*

Hunger of Memory: The Education of Richard
   Rodriguez. *v.6 p.490, p.527*

Hunger Trilogy. *v.6 p.213*

Hunger. *v.2 p.628, v.6 p.99*

The Huns. *v.3 p.63*

Hunter-Gatherers: An Interdisciplinary Perspective. . .*v.4 p.28*

Hunters and Gatherers: Property, Power and
   Ideology. *v.4 p.29, p.30*

Hunters and Herders of Southern Africa: A Comparative
   Ethnography of the Khoisan Peoples. . . .*v.4 p.38, v.6 p.74*

Hunters in a Narrow Street. *v.6 p.660*

The Hunter's Vision: The Prehistoric Rock Art of
   Zimbabwe. *v.1 p.690*

Hunting Terrorists: A Look at the Psychopathology of
   Terror. *v.6 p.252*

☐ Huntsman World Senior Games. *v.4 p.840, p.847*

Hurd's Letters on Chivalry and Romance. *v.2 p.245*

The Hurrians: Ancient Near East. *v.3 p.7, p.8*

☐ Hurricanes. *v.5 p.426*

Hurried Child: Growing up Too Fast Too Soon. .*v.5 p.626, p.641*

Husbands and Wives: The Dynamics of Married
Living. *v.4 p.732, v.6 p.464, p.466*

Husserl and the Search for Certitude. *v.1 p.469*

Husserl: Shorter Works. *v.1 p.470*

Husserlian Meditations: How Words Present Things. .*v.1 p.470*

Husserl's Transcendental Phenomenology. *v.1 p.470*

Husserl. *v.1 p.469*

The Hussite Revolution: 1424-1437. . . . .*v.3 p.188*

Hustlers, Beats and Others. *v.4 p.706*

Hutcheson: Two Texts on Human Nature. *v.1 p.450*

Hutterite Society. *v.1 p.586*

Huxley: From Devil's Disciple to Evolution's High
Priest. *v.5 p.396*

Hybridization of Crop Plants. *v.5 p.21*

Hydraulic Canals Design, Construction, Regulation And
Maintenance. *v.5 p.703*

Hydraulic Design of Hydraulic Machinery. *v.5 p.714*

Hydraulic Machines: Turbines and Pumps. *v.5 p.714*

Hydraulic Modelling. *v.5 p.703*

Hydraulics of Open Channel Flow: An Introduction: Basic
Principles, Sediment Motion, Hydraulic Modelling,
Design of Hydraulic Structures. *v.5 p.378, p.379*

Hydroboration. *v.5 p.296*

Hydrocarbon Chemistry. *v.5 p.292*

Hydrodynamics, mass and heat transfer in chemical
engineering. *v.5 p.743*

The Hydrogen Economy: The Creation of the Worldwide Energy
Web and the Redistribution of Power on Earth. .*v.5 p.709*

Hydrogen fuel for surface transportation. *v.5 p.700*

Hydrogen: The Essential Element. *v.5 p.309*

Hyman's Comparative Vertebrate Anatomy. *v.5 p.157*

Hymen's Triumph. *v.2 p.217*

A Hymn to Him: The Lyrics of Alan Jay
Lerner. *v.1 p.252, p.336, p.408*

Hymns to the Night. *v.2 p.601*

Hypatia of Alexandria. *v.1 p.430*

Hyperscapes in the Poetry of Frank O'Hara: Difference,
Homosexuality, Topography. *v.6 p.393*

Hypersea: Life on the Land. *v.5 p.176*

Hyperspace: A Scientific Odyssey Through Parallel Universes,
Time Warps, and the Tenth Dimension. *v.5 p.557*

Hypnosis and Suggestibility: An Experimental
Approach. *v.5 p.613*

Hysterical Fictions: The "Woman's Novel" in the Twentieth
Century. *v.2 p.191*

Hystories: Hysterical Epidemics and Modern Media. .*v.4 p.714*

I

I Am a Memory Come Alive: Autobiographical
Writings. *v.2 p.611*

I Am Aztlan: The Personal Essay in Chicano
Studies. *v.6 p.490, p.544*

I Am My Own Wife: A Play. *v.2 p.159, v.6 p.413*

I Am No One You Know: Stories. *v.2 p.152*

I Am One of You Forever. *v.2 p.142, p.143*

I Am Snowing: The Confessions of a Woman of
Prague. *v.2 p.783, p.784*

I Am the Blues: The Willie Dixon Story. *v.1 p.263, p.321*

I and Thou. *v.1 p.468*

I Begin My Life All Over: The Hmong and the American
Immigrant Experience. *v.6 p.93, p.139*

I Can't Go on, I'll Go On: A Samuel Beckett
Reader. *v.2 p.332, p.509*

The I Ching: Or Book of Changes. *v.6 p.183, p.207*

I Chose Freedom: The Personal and Political Life of a Soviet
Official. *v.3 p.224*

I Chronicles 10-29: A New Translation with Introduction and
Commentary. *v.1 p.620*

I Chronicles: A New Translation with Introduction and
Commentary. *v.1 p.620*

I, Claudius and Claudius the God. *v.2 p.348*

I Didn't Do It for You: How the World Betrayed a Small
African Nation. *v.6 p.67*

I Die with My Country: Prespectives on the Paraguayan War,
1864-1870. . . . .*v.3 p.274, p.275, p.344, p.345*

I Don't Need You Any More. *v.2 p.101*

I Gave You All I Had. *v.2 p.673*

I Had a Hammer: The Hank Aaron Story. . .*v.4 p.830, p.849*

I Have a Photographic Memory. *v.5 p.466*

I Have Chosen to Stay and Fight. *v.6 p.93*

I Have What I Gave: The Fiction of Janet Frame. .*v.2 p.745, p.746*

I Heard It Through the Grapevine: Rumor in African-American
Culture. *v.2 p.17*

I Kings: A New Translation with Introduction and
Commentary. *v.1 p.620*

I Knew a Phoenix: Sketches for an Autobiography. .*v.2 p.119*

I Know Why the Caged Bird Sings. *v.2 p.139*

I, Koch: A Decidedly Unauthorized Biography of the Mayor of
New York City. *v.3 p.490*

I, Lars Hard. *v.2 p.629*

I. M. Pei: A Profile in American Architecture. *v.1 p.795*

I Maccabees. *v.1 p.623*

I Malavoglia. *v.2 p.713*

I Never Had It Made: An Autobiography of Jackie
Robinson. *v.4 p.833, p.852*

I, Orhan Veli. *v.6 p.668*

I Passed This Way. *v.2 p.743*

I Peter: A New Translation with Introduction and
Commentary. *v.1 p.631*

I, Pierre Riviere, Having Slaughtered My Mother, My Sister,
and My Brother. *v.4 p.751*

I Remember Balanchine: Recollections of the Ballet Master by
Those Who Knew Him Best. *v.1 p.10*

I, Rhoda Manning, Go Hunting with My Daddy: And Other
Stories. *v.2 p.145, p.146*

I, Rigoberta Menchu: An Indian Woman in Guatemala. .*v.2 p.676*

I Romanzi. *v.2 p.712*

I Served the King of England. *v.2 p.783*

I Sweep the Sun off Rooftops: Stories. *v.6 p.657*

I, the Jury. *v.2 p.117*

I Thought of Daisy. *v.2 p.137*

I, Tituba, Black Witch of Salem. *v.2 p.536*

I Too Am Here: Selections from the Letters of Jane Welsh
    Carlyle. *v.2 p.275*

I Was a Communist for the F. B. I.: The Unhappy Life and
    Times of Matt Cvetic. *v.4 p.524*

I Was Loneliness: The Complete Graphic Works of John
    Muafangejo, A Catalogue Raisonné, 1968-1987. . .*v.1 p.757*

I Watched a Wild Hog Eat My Baby!: A Colorful History of
    Tabloids and Their Cultural Impact. *v.4 p.411*

I Will Be Heard 1822-1835, Vol. 1. . . . .*v.3 p.397*

I Will Wear No Chain!: A Social History of African American
    Males. *v.6 p.449*

I Wouldn't Have Missed It: Selected Poems of Ogden
    Nash. *v.2 p.103*

I Write What I Like: Selected Writings. *v.6 p.78*

□ IASB: International Accounting Standards
    Board. *v.4 p.106, p.111*

□ IAWM = International Alliance for Women in
    Music. *v.1 p.172, p.379*

Iberia and the Americas: Culture, Politics, and History.*v.4 p.591*

Iberia Before the Iberians: The Stone Age Prehistory of
    Cantabrian Spain. *v.4 p.17*

Ibn Battuta in Black Africa: Expanded Edition for the 700th
    Anniversary of Ibn Batutta's Birth. *v.6 p.63*

Ibsen and the Temper of Norwegian Literature. . . .*v.2 p.627*

Ibsen: The Complete Major Prose Plays. *v.2 p.628*

Ibsen: The Man and His Work. *v.2 p.627, p.628*

Ibsen's Dramatic Method: A Study of the Prose Dramas.*v.2 p.628*

Ibsen's Selected Plays. *v.1 p.80, p.82, p.109*

Ibsen. *v.2 p.628*

Les Icariens: The Utopian Dream in Europe and
    America. *v.4 p.500*

The Ice Age: A Collection of Poems. *v.2 p.344*

Ice Age Peoples of North America: Environments, Origins, and
    Adaptations of the First Americans. *v.4 p.10*

The Ice Age. *v.2 p.343*

Ice Core Studies of Global Biogeochemical Cycles. .*v.5 p.112*

An Ice Cream War. *v.2 p.335*

An Iceland Fisherman. *v.2 p.496*

The Icelandic Family Saga; An Analytic Reading. . .*v.2 p.624*

Icelandic Poems and Stories. *v.2 p.625*

The Icelandic Saga. *v.2 p.624*

The Icon and the Axe: An Interpretive History of Russian
    Culture. *v.1 p.609, v.3 p.210*

The Icon: Window on the Kingdom. *v.1 p.570*

Iconography of Power: Soviet Political Posters under Lenin and
    Stalin. *v.3 p.221, p.222*

Icons of Evolution: Science or Myth? *v.5 p.197*

□ ICRISAT: International Crops Research Institute for the
    Semi-arid Tropics. *v.5 p.19*

Ida B. Wells-Barnett and American Reform,
    1880-1930. . . . .*v.6 p.8, p.19, p.46*

Idaho - Collected Works of Federal Writers Project. .*v.3 p.525*

The Idea and Practice of World Government. *v.4 p.629*

The Idea of a Liberal Theory. *v.4 p.493, p.511*

The Idea of a University. *v.4 p.290*

The Idea of Absolute Music. *v.1 p.380*

The Idea of Comedy: History, Theory, Critique. . .*v.1 p.56, p.90*

The Idea of Democracy in the Modern ERA. *v.4 p.504*

The Idea of Europe. *v.3 p.88*

The Idea of France. *v.3 p.140*

The Idea of History in Early Stuart England: Erudition,
    Ideology, and the Light of Truth from the Accession of James
    I to the Civil War. *v.3 p.88, p.102, p.104*

The Idea of Japan: Western Images, Western Myths. .*v.6 p.219*

The Idea of Pakistan. *v.4 p.643, p.645*

Idea of Phenomenology. *v.1 p.468, p.511*

The Idea of Poverty: England in the Early Industrial
    Age. . . .*v.3 p.112, v.4 p.754, v.6 p.743, p.745, p.758, p.766*

The Idea of Propaganda: A Reconstruction. *v.4 p.425*

The Idea of the American South: 1920-1941. . . . .*v.3 p.497*

The Idea of the Book in the Middle Ages: Language Theory,
    Mythology, and Fiction. *v.6 p.565, p.569*

The Idea of the Gentleman in the Victorian
    Novel. *v.2 p.190, v.6 p.747, p.756, p.761*

The Idea of the Holy. *v.1 p.521*

The Idea of the Middle Class: White-Collar Workers and
    Peruvian Society. *v.3 p.331*

The Idea of the University: A Reexamination. *v.4 p.303*

Ideal Citizens: The Legacy of the Civil Rights
    Movement. *v.4 p.710*

Ideal Government and the Mixed Constitution in the Middle
    Ages. *v.4 p.490, p.501,v.6 p.568*

The Ideal of the Practical: Colombia's Struggle to Form a
    Technical Elite. *v.3 p.358*

Ideals and Realities in Russian Literature. . . .*v.2 p.799, p.805*

I-Deals: Idiosyncratic Deals Employees Bargain for
    Themselves. *v.4 p.74*

Ideals, Varieties, and Algorithms: An Introduction to
    Computational Algebraic Geometry and Commutative
    Algebra. *v.5 p.473, p.474, p.497*

Ideas about Illness: An Intellectual and Political History of
    Medical Sociology. *v.4 p.778*

Ideas and Forms of Tragedy from Aristotle to the Middle
    Ages. *v.1 p.56, p.70, p.71, p.72, p.73, p.88*

Ideas and Realities of Emotion. *v.5 p.612*

Ideas: General Introduction to Pure Phenomenology. .*v.1 p.469*

Ideas in America. *v.2 p.7*

Ideas in Chemistry: A History of the Science. . . .*v.5 p.263*

Ideas of Greatness; Heroic Drama in England. . . .*v.2 p.187*

Ideas of Social Order in the Ancient World. *v.4 p.773*

Ideas of Space: Euclidean, Non-Euclidean, and
    Relativistic. *v.5 p.466, p.495*

Ideas of Theatre: The Five Directorial Perspectives of the
    American Stage. *v.1 p.118, p.153*

Ideas That Shaped Buildings. *v.1 p.703, p.786*

The Identification and Analysis of Chicano
    Literature. *v.6 p.500, p.513*

Identification of Freshwater Diatoms from Live
    Material. *v.5 p.208*

Identification of Learning Disabilities: Research to
    Practice. *v.4 p.318*

Identifying Marine Phytoplankton. *v.5 p.208*

Identities in Motion: Asian American Film and
Video. *v.6 p.88, p.89, p.329, p.341*

Identity and Community in the Gay World. *v.6 p.367*

Identity and Development: An Interdisciplinary
Approach. *v.5 p.651*

Identity and Difference. *v.1 p.470, p.471*

Identity and Global Politics: Theoretical and Empirical
Elaborations. *v.4 p.483, v.5 p.643*

Identity and Story: Creating Self in Narrative. *v.5 p.655*

Identity Mania: Fundamentalism and the Politicization of
Cultural Differences. *v.4 p.766*

The Identity of Jesus Christ. *v.1 p.635*

The Identity of Yeats. *v.2 p.326*

Identity Politics and Women: Cultural Reassertions and
Feminisms in International Perspective. . . .*v.6 p.429, p.435*

Identity Politics on the Israeli Screen. *v.6 p.333, p.334*

Identity Youth and Crisis. *v.5 p.513*

Ideologies in Action: Language Politics on Corsica. . .*v.4 p.21*

Ideologies of Liberation in Black Africa,
1856-1970. . . . .*v.6 p.10, p.31, p.36*

Ideologies of the Raj. *v.6 p.157*

Ideologies of Violence. *v.4 p.497*

Ideology: A Very Short Introduction. *v.1 p.501*

Ideology: An Introduction. *v.1 p.501*

Ideology and Crime: A Study of Crime in Its Social and
Historical Context. *v.4 p.752, v.6 p.250*

Ideology and Curriculum. *v.4 p.300*

Ideology and Experience: Antisemitism in France at the Time of
the Dreyfus Affair. *v.3 p.61*

Ideology and National Identity in Post-Communist Foreign
Policy. *v.4 p.494*

Ideology and Popular Protest. *v.4 p.710, p.713*

Ideology and Pre-Columbian Civilizations. *v.4 p.11*

Ideology and U. S. Foreign Policy. *v.3 p.385*

Ideology and Utopia: An Introduction to the Sociology of
Knowledge. *v.4 p.685*

Ideology, Legitimacy and the New State: Yugoslavia, Serbia and
Croatia. *v.3 p.247, v.4 p.600*

The Ideology of the Aesthetic. *v.1 p.479*

The Ideology of the Sandinistas and the Nicaraguan
Revolution. *v.3 p.303*

The Ides of March: A Novel. *v.2 p.134*

Idi Amin Dada: Hitler in Africa. *v.6 p.66*

Idolatry and Its Enemies: Colonial Andean Religion and
Extirpation, 1640-1750. . . . .*v.3 p.326*

Idolatry. *v.1 p.527*

Idols of Perversity: Fantasies of Feminine Evil in Fin-de-Sìecle
Culture. *v.2 p.175, p.190*

Idylls of the King and a Selection of Poems. *v.2 p.314*

Idylls of the Marketplace: Oscar Wilde and the Victorian
Public. *v.2 p.321, v.6 p.740, p.754*

Idylls. *v.2 p.421*

Idyls of the King. by Alfred Tennyson, D. C. L., poet
Laureate. *v.2 p.314*

▢ IEEE Computer Society. *v.5 p.344*

If All the World Were a Blackbird: Poems. *v.2 p.786*

If All We Did Was to Weep at Home: A History of White
Working-Class Women in America. *v.6 p.454*

If Beale Street Could Talk. *v.2 p.59*

If Each Comes Halfway: Meeting Tamang Women in
Nepal. *v.6 p.164*

If He Hollers Let Him Go: A Novel. *v.6 p.26*

If He Hollers Let Him Go. *v.2 p.86*

If I Don't Know. *v.2 p.337*

If It Die: An Autobiography. *v.2 p.519*

If on a Winter's Night a Traveler. *v.2 p.714*

If Only the Sea Could Sleep: Love Poems. *v.6 p.655*

If P Then Q: Conditionals and the Foundations of
Reasoning. *v.1 p.494*

If the Workers Took a Notion: The Right to Strike and
American Political Development. *v.4 p.127*

If They Come in the Morning: Voices of
Resistance. *v.4 p.751, p.752, v.6 p.277*

If You Don't Go, Don't Hinder Me: The African American
Sacred Song Tradition. *v.6 p.30*

If You Poison Us: Uranium and Native Americans. . .*v.6 p.681*

The IFILM Digital Video Filmmaker's Handbook. . .*v.6 p.346*

Igbo Art and Culture, and Other Essays. *v.4 p.38*

I-Genetics. *v.5 p.136, p.137*

The Ignation Personality of Gerard Manley Hopkins. .*v.2 p.293*

Ignatius Donnelly: The Portrait of a Politican. *v.3 p.434*

Ignatius Loyola. *v.1 p.578*

Ignazio Silone: Beyond the Tragic Vision. *v.2 p.723*

Igneous and Metamorphic Petrology. *v.5 p.437*

Igneous Petrology. *v.5 p.437*

Igneous Rocks: A Classification and Glossary of Terms:
Recommendations of the International Union of
Geological Sciences Subcommission on the Systematics of
Igneous Rocks. *v.5 p.437*

Ignorant Armies: Sliding into War in Iraq. *v.3 p.483*

Iguana Dreams: New Latino Fiction. *v.6 p.496*

II Corinthians. *v.1 p.631*

Il Corbaccio. *v.2 p.701*

Il Duecento e il Trecento. *v.2 p.697*

Il était une fois-- Marcel Pagnol. *v.2 p.523*

Il libro del cortegiano. *v.2 p.708*

Il Morgante. *v.2 p.708*

Il Novecento. *v.2 p.697*

Il pastor fido. *v.2 p.708*

Il Quattrocento e il Cinquecento. *v.2 p.697*

Il Seicento. *v.2 p.697*

Il Settecento. *v.2 p.697*

Iliad Book IX. *v.2 p.414*

The Iliad, the Odyssey, and the Epic Tradition. *v.2 p.402*

The Iliad. *v.2 p.414*

Ilios: City of the Trojans. *v.3 p.16*

I'll Get There: It Better Be Worth the Trip. *v.6 p.396*

Illiberal Education: The Politics of Race and Sex on
Campus. *v.4 p.331*

Illinois - Collected Works of Federal Writers Project,
Set. *v.3 p.515*

Illinois: A History of the Land and Its People. *v.3 p.514*

Illinois: A History. *v.3 p.515*

Illness As Metaphor and Aids and Its
  Metaphors. *v.4 p.778, v.6 p.378, p.379*

The Illuminated Blake: William Blake's Complete Illuminated
  Works with a Plate-by-Plate Commentary. *v.2 p.239*

Illuminating Life: Selected Papers from Cold Spring Harbor,
  1903-1969. . . . .*v.5 p.82*

Illuminating the Renaissance: The Triumph of Flemish
  Manuscript Painting in Europe. *v.1 p.732, p.734*

Illuminating Video: An Essential Guide to Video Art.   *v.1 p.771*

Illumination and Night Glare: The Unfinished Autobiography of
  Carson McCullers. *v.2 p.100*

Illuminations. *v.2 p.575*

The Illusion of Conscious Will. *v.5 p.619, p.657*

The Illusion of Control: Force and Foreign Policy in the 21st
  Century. *v.3 p.446*

The Illusion of Cultural Identity. *v.4 p.699*

The Illusion of Life: Disney Animation. *v.6 p.308*

The Illusion of Neutrality. *v.3 p.469*

Illusion of Order: The False Promise of Broken Windows
  Policing. *v.6 p.263*

The Illusion of Power: Political Theater in the English
  Renaissance. *v.1 p.78, p.102*

The Illusion of Victory: America in World War I. . . .*v.3 p.471*

Illusions of a Revolving Door. *v.6 p.496, p.508, p.517*

Illusions of Influence: The Political Economy of United
  States-Philippines Relations, 1942-1960. . . . . .*v.6 p.179*

The Illusions of Postmodernism. *v.1 p.512*

The Illusions of Progress. *v.4 p.759*

Illustrated Chemistry Laboratory Terminology. *v.5 p.259*

An Illustrated Chinese-English Guide for Biomedical
  Scientists. *v.5 p.96*

The Illustrated Chronicles of Matthew Paris: Observations of the
  Thirteenth-Century Life. *v.3 p.99*

Illustrated Dictionary and Resource Directory of Environmental
  and Occupational Health. *v.5 p.682*

Illustrated Dictionary of Architectural Preservation. . *v.1 p.821*

An Illustrated Dictionary of British Steel Engravers. . *v.1 p.752*

Illustrated Dictionary of Building Design and
  Construction. *v.1 p.783, v.4 p.158*

Illustrated English Social History. *v.3 p.90, p.92, p.93*

Illustrated Field Guide to Ferns and Allied Plants of the British
  Isles. *v.5 p.210*

An Illustrated Glossary of Early Southern Architecture and
  Landscape. *v.1 p.784*

An Illustrated History of American Psychology. *v.5 p.598*

An Illustrated History of Boxing. *v.4 p.855*

The Illustrated History of Canada. *v.3 p.535*

An Illustrated History of Hong Kong. *v.6 p.205*

An Illustrated History of New Mexico. *v.3 p.528*

The Illustrated Lark Rise to Candleford: A
  Trilogy. *v.6 p.759, p.762*

The Illustrated Petroleum Reference Dictionary. *v.5 p.738*

Illustrated Theatre Production Guide. *v.1 p.147*

The Illustrated Zuleika Dobson. *v.2 p.331*

The Illustrations from the Works of Andreas Vesalius of
  Brussels: With Annotations and Translations, a
  Discussion of the Plates and Their Background, Authorship
  and Influence, and a Biographical Sketch of
  Vesalius. *v.5 p.510, p.511*

Illustrations of Political Economy: Selected
  Tales. *v.4 p.218, p.269*

Illustrations of the English Stage,
  1580-1642. . . . .*v.1 p.76, p.100, p.154*

Illustrator in America, 1860-2000. . . . .*v.1 p.716*

Illywhacker. *v.2 p.744*

Ilongot Headhunting, 1883-1974: A Study in Society and
  History. *v.6 p.180*

The Ilse: First-Generation Korean Immigrants in Hawaii,
  1903-1973. . . . .*v.6 p.114, p.121, p.136*

Ilya Kabakov - Installations: Catalogue Raisonné,
  1983-2000. . . . .*v.1 p.772*

I'm Going to Have a Little House: The Second Diary of
  Carolina Maria de Jesus. *v.3 p.336*

I'm Gone. *v.2 p.530*

Im Krebsgang. *v.2 p.608*

I'm Not Stiller. *v.2 p.607*

Im Querschnitt Volker Braun: Gedichte, Prosa, Stücke,
  Aufsätze. *v.2 p.616*

I'm the One That I Want. *v.6 p.90, p.93*

I'm the Teacher, You're the Student: A Semester in the
  University Classroom. *v.4 p.337*

Im Western Nichts Neues. *v.2 p.618*

Image and Idea: Fourteen Essays on Literary Themes. *v.2 p.569*

The Image and Influence of the Oklahoma Prairie in Washington
  Irving's Tour of the West. *v.2 p.42, p.43*

Image and Memory: Photography from Latin America,
  1866-1994. . . . .*v.1 p.763, p.764*

Image and Reality of the Israel-Palestine Conflict. . . *v.6 p.617*

Image and Representation: Stories of Muslim Lives in
  India. *v.6 p.146, p.148*

Image and Word: The Interaction of Twentieth-Century
  Photographs and Texts. *v.1 p.763*

Image Ethics: The Moral Rights of Subjects in Photographs,
  Film, and Television. *v.4 p.412*

Image Interpretation in Geology. *v.5 p.420*

Image Library of Biological Macromolecules. . . *v.5 p.328*

Image Marketing: Using Public Perceptions to Create Awareness
  and Build Market Share. *v.4 p.145*

The Image of America in Montaigne, Spenser and Shakespeare:
  Renaissance Ethnography and Literary Reflection. *v.2 p.169*

The Image of the Black in Western Art: From the American
  Revolution to World War I, Vol. IV, Pt. 2: Black
  Models & White Myths. *v.1 p.704*

The Image of the City. *v.6 p.726*

The Image of the Medieval Peasant as Alien and
  Exemplary. *v.6 p.575*

Image of Women in Indo-Anglian Novel. *v.2 p.761*

Image Processing and Data Analysis: The Multiscale
  Approach. *v.5 p.501*

The Imagery and Poetry of Lucretius. *v.2 p.437*

The Imagery of Euripides. *v.2 p.409*

Images and Identities: The Puerto Rican in Two World Contexts. *v.6 p.506, p.512*

Images from the Underworld: Naj Tunich and the Tradition of Maya Cave Painting. *v.3 p.262*

Images: Iconography of Music and Musicians in African-American Culture 1770s-1920s. . *v.1 p.282, v.6 p.30*

Images in the Dark: An Encyclopedia of Gay and Lesbian Film and Video. *v.6 p.358, p.417*

Images of Community in Old English Poetry. *v.2 p.168*

Images of Contemporary African American Artists. . . .*v.6 p.16*

Images of English: A Cultural History of the Language. .*v.2 p.553*

Images of Kinship in "Paradise Lost": Milton's Politics and Christian Liberty. *v.2 p.253*

Images of Materials. *v.5 p.692*

Images of Mind. *v.5 p.617*

Images of Myths in Classical Antiquity. *v.1 p.671*

Images of Terror: What We Can and Can't Know about Terrorism. *v.4 p.659*

Images of the American City. *v.6 p.719*

Images of the Gods: Khmer Mythology in Cambodia, Laos and Thailand. *v.1 p.692*

Images of the Ohio Valley: A Historical Geography of Travel. *v.3 p.513*

Images of Victorian Womanhood in English Art. .*v.6 p.737, p.746*

Images That Injure: Pictorial Stereotypes in the Media. .*v.4 p.416*

Images: The Piano Music of Claude Debussy. *v.1 p.222, p.242, p.321*

Imaginary Homelands: Essays and Criticism 1981-1991. . . . .*v.2 p.165, p.569, p.766*

The Imaginary Museum of Musical Works: An Essay in the Philosophy of Music. *v.1 p.381*

The Imaginary Puritan: Literature, Intellectual Labor, and the Origins of Personal Life. *v.2 p.3*

An Imaginary Tale: The Story of (The Square Root of Minus One). *v.5 p.476*

The Imaginary Voyage: With Theodor Herzl in Israel. .*v.6 p.615*

An Imaginative Approach to Teaching. *v.4 p.347*

Imagine Nation: The American Counterculture of the 1960s and 1970s. *v.4 p.712*

Imagined Cities: Urban Experience and the Language of the Novel. *v.6 p.730*

Imagined Communities: Reflections on the Origin and Spread of Nationalism. *v.3 p.61, v.4 p.493, p.494*

The Imagined Island: History, Identity, and Utopia in Hispaniola. *v.3 p.315, p.316, p.318*

Imaging in Biological Research, Part B, Vol. 386. . . .*v.5 p.86*

Imaging in Biological Research, Vol. 385, Pt. A. *v.5 p.86*

Imaging Japanese America: The Visual Construction of Citizenship, Nation, and the Body. *v.6 p.87, p.88, p.89, p.131*

Imaging of Nucleic Acids and Quantitation in Photonic Microscopy. *v.5 p.120*

Imaging Techniques in Biology and Medicine. *v.5 p.86*

Imagining America at War: Politics, War and Film. . .*v.6 p.323*

Imagining Baseball: America's Pastime and Popular Culture. *v.4 p.818, p.851*

Imagining Development: Economic Ideas in Peru's "Fictitious Prosperity" of Guano, 1840-1880. . . . .*v.3 p.330*

Imagining God: Theology and Religious Imagination. .*v.1 p.635*

Imagining Miami: Ethnic Politics in a Postmodern World. *v.3 p.504, v.6 p.537, p.548*

Imagining New England: Explorations of Regional Identity from the Pilgrims to the Mid-Twentieth Century. *v.3 p.484*

Imagining Numbers: (Particularly the Square Root of Minus Fifteen). *v.5 p.476*

Imagining Shakespeare. *v.1 p.76, p.102, v.2 p.231*

Imagining the African American West. *v.2 p.14*

Imagining the Balkans. *v.3 p.246*

Imagining the Filipino American Diaspora: Transnational Relations, Identities, and Communities. . . .*v.6 p.119, p.129*

Imagining the Middle Class: The Political Representation of Class in Britain, C. 1780-1840. . . . .*v.6 p.744*

Imagining the Nation: Asian American Literature and Cultural Consent. *v.6 p.97*

Imagining Vietnam and America: The Making of Postcolonial Vietnam, 1919-1950. . . . .*v.6 p.168*

Imagining War: French and British Military Doctrine Between the Wars. *v.3 p.74*

Imaginization: New Mindsets for Seeing, Organizing and Managing. *v.4 p.66, p.67*

The Imamate Tradition of Oman. *v.6 p.628*

□ i-mass.com (Mass spectrometry Web address). . . .*v.5 p.271*

Imitation and Politics: Redesigning Modern Germany. .*v.4 p.609*

Imitation in Animals and Artifacts. *v.5 p.589*

The Imitation of Christ. *v.1 p.593, p.652*

Imlil, a Moroccan Mountain Community in Change. *v.6 p.601, p.643*

Immaculate and Powerful: The Female in Sacred Image and Social Reality. *v.1 p.528*

Immanuel Kant. *v.1 p.461*

The Immaterial Self: A Defence of the Cartesian Dualist Conception of the Mind. *v.1 p.504*

Immersed in Great Affairs: Allan Nevins and the Heroic Age of American History. *v.3 p.374*

Immigrant Acts: On Asian American Cultural Politics. .*v.6 p.97*

The Immigrant Church: New York's Irish and German Catholics, 1815-1865. . . . .*v.1 p.573*

Immigrant Entrepreneurs: Koreans in Los Angeles, 1965-1982. . . . .*v.6 p.106, p.136*

The Immigrant Experience in Wisconsin. *v.3 p.517*

Immigrants and the American City. *v.4 p.571, v.6 p.714*

Immigrants and the American Dream: Remaking the Middle Class. *v.4 p.764*

Immigrants and the City: Ethnicity and Mobility in a 19th Century Midwestern City. *v.3 p.514, v.6 p.711, p.712*

Immigrants in the Lands of Promise: Italians in Buenos Aires and New York City, 18701914. . .*v.4 p.763, p.764, v.6 p.716*

Immigrants on the Land: Coffee and Society in Sao Paulo, 1886-1934. . . . .*v.3 p.341*

Immigrants, Unions, and the New U. S. Labor Market. .*v.4 p.128*

Immigration and Politics in the New Europe: Reinventing Borders. *v.4 p.637, p.668*

Immigration Research for a New Century: Multidisciplinary Perspectives. *v.4 p.764*

An Immodest Agenda: Rebuilding America Before the 21st
Century. *v.4 p.213*

The Immoralist: A Dual-Language Book. *v.2 p.519*

The Immoralist. *v.6 p.396*

The Immortal Bartfuss. *v.6 p.647*

Immortal Boy: A Portrait of Leigh Hunt. *v.2 p.290*

Immortal River: The Upper Mississippi in Ancient and Modern
Times. *v.3 p.506*

Immortal Rose: An Anthology of Persian Lyrics. . . .*v.6 p.670*

Immortality. *v.2 p.784*

Immunology for Medical Students. *v.5 p.518*

Imogen Cunningham: Portraiture. *v.1 p.766*

Imogen Cunningham: Selected Texts and Bibliography. .*v.1 p.768*

Imogen Cunningham. *v.1 p.767*

Impact Cratering: A Geologic Process. *v.5 p.434*

The Impact of Intervention: The Dominican Republic During the
U. S. Occupation Of 1916-1924. . . . .*v.3 p.316*

The Impact of Keynes on Economics in the 20th
Century. *v.4 p.227*

The Impact of Migration on the Metropolitan and Folk Society
of Carriacou, Grenada. *v.3 p.320*

The Impact of Napoleon: Prussian High Politics, Foreign Policy
and the Crisis of the Executive, 1797-1806. . . .*v.3 p.167*

The Impact of Public Opinion on U. S. Foreign Policy since
Vietnam: Constraining the Colossus. *v.3 p.454*

The Impact of Public Opinion on U. S. Foreign Policy since
Vietnam. *v.3 p.454*

Impact of Science on Society. *v.5 p.404*

Impact of Strikes: Their Social and Economic Costs. .*v.4 p.124*

The Impact of Taxes on the American Economy. . . .*v.4 p.248*

Impact of the Civil War and Reconstruction on Arkansas:
Persistence in the Midst of Ruin. *v.4 p.521*

The Impact of the Gene: From Mendel's Peas to Designer
Babies. *v.5 p.533*

The Impact of the Haitian Revolution in the Atlantic
World. *v.3 p.314*

The Impact of the Internet on Our Moral Lives. . . .*v.4 p.761*

The Impact of Women in Public Office. *v.6 p.440*

Impasses of Divorce: The Dynamics and Resolution of Family
Conflict. *v.5 p.668*

Impeachable Offenses: A Documentary History from 1787 to the
Present. *v.4 p.462*

Impeachment: A Handbook. *v.4 p.461*

The Impeachment and Trial of Andrew Johnson. . . .*v.3 p.435*

Impeachment in America, 1635-1805. . . . .*v.4 p.461*

Impeachment of a President: Andrew Johnson, the Blacks and
Reconstruction. *v.3 p.401*

Impeachment: The Constitutional Problems, Enlarged
Edition. *v.4 p.461*

The Impending Crisis of the South: How to Meet
It. *v.3 p.398, p.420*

Impending Crisis. *v.3 p.400, p.429*

The Impenitent Confession of Guzman de Alfarache. .*v.2 p.646*

Imperialism in Southeast Asia: A Fleeting Passing Phase.*v.6 p.165*

The Imperative of Freedom: A Philosophy of Journalistic
Autonomy. *v.4 p.405*

Imperatores Victi: Military Defeat and Aristocratic Competition
in the Middle and Late Republic. *v.3 p.26*

Imperfect Garden: The Legacy of Humanism. *v.1 p.508*

The Imperfect Panacea: American Faith in Education. .*v.4 p.328*

An Imperfect Union: Slavery, Federalism, and Comity. .*v.4 p.453*

Imperial Borderland: Bobrikov and the Attempted Russification
of Finland, 1898-1904. . . . .*v.3 p.213, 236*

The Imperial Challenge: Quebec and Britain in the Age of the
American Revolution. *v.3 p.539*

Imperial China, 900-1800. . . . .*v.6 p.185*

Imperial Cities and the Reformation. *v.1 p.602*

Imperial City: Rome, Romans and Napoleon,
1796-1815. . . . .*v.3 p.201*

Imperial Cults and the Apocalypse of John: Reading Revelation
in the Ruins. *v.1 p.632*

Imperial Culture in Germany, 1871-1918. . . . . . .*v.3 p.169*

Imperial Encounters: Religion and Modernity in India and
Britain. *v.1 p.541*

The Imperial Experience: From Carlyle to Forster. .*v.3 p.88, p.124*

Imperial Footprints. *v.6 p.51, p.52*

Imperial Germany 1867-1918: Politics, Culture, and Society in
an Authoritarian State. *v.3 p.164*

Imperial Germany 1871-1918: Economy, Society, Culture and
Politics. *v.3 p.169*

Imperial Germany and the Great War, 1914-1918. . .*v.3 p.163*

Imperial Germany and the Industrial Revolution. . .*v.4 p.251*

The Imperial Harem: Women and Sovereignty in the Ottoman
Empire. *v.6 p.591*

The Imperial Idea and Its Enemies: A Study in British
Power. *v.3 p.126*

Imperial Ideology and Provincial Loyalty in the Roman
Empire. *v.3 p.27*

The Imperial Imagination: Magic and Myth in Kipling's
India. *v.2 p.298*

The Imperial Intellect: A Study of Newman's Educational
Ideal. *v.4 p.341*

Imperial Israel and the Palestinians: The Politics of Expansion,
1967-2000. . . . .*v.6 p.618*

The Imperial Legacy: The Ottoman Imprint on the Balkans and
the Middle East. *v.3 p.245, v.6 p.589*

Imperial Legend: The Mysterious Disappearance of Tsar
Alexander I. *v.3 p.218*

Imperial Meridian: The British Empire and the World
1780-1830. . . . .*v.3 p.124*

Imperial Overstretch: Germany in Soviet Policy from Stalin to
Gorbachev: an Analysis Based on New Archival
Evidence, Memoirs, and Interviews. *v.3 p.211*

Imperial Panama: Commerce and Conflict in Isthmian America,
1550-1800. . . . .*v.3 p.306*

Imperial Policies and Perspectives Towards Georgia,
1760-1819. . . . .*v.3 p.213*

The Imperial Republic; the United States and the World,
1945-1973. . . . .*v.3 p.451*

Imperial Rome and Christian Triumph: The Art of the Roman
Empire AD 100-450. . . . .*v.1 p.669, p.686*

Imperial Rule. *v.3 p.213*

Imperial Russia 1682-1825: The Coming of Age of Modern
Russia. *v.3 p.216*

Imperial Russian Foreign Policy. *v.3 p.212*

Imperial Russia's Jewish Question, 1855-1881. . . . .*v.3 p.219*

The Imperial Screen: Japanese Film Culture in the Fifteen Years War of 1931-1945. . . . .*v.6 p.336*

Imperial Simla: The Political Culture of the Raj. . . .*v.6 p.161*

Imperial Spain 1469-1716. . . . .*v.3 p.238*

The Imperial Tense: Prospects and Problems of American Empire. *v.3 p.482*

Imperial Texas; an Interpretive Essay in Cultural Geography. *v.3 p.509*

Imperial Theme: Further Interpretations of Shakespeare's Tragedies, Inlcuding the Roman Plays. . . .*v.2 p.235*

Imperialism and Colonialism: Essays on the History of European Expansion. *v.3 p.77, v.4 p.583*

Imperialism and Internationalism in the Discipline of International Relations. *v.4 p.625*

Imperialism and Orientalism: A Documentary Sourcebook. *v.6 p.592*

Imperialism and Popular Culture. *v.3 p.89, p.125*

Imperialism and Theatre: Essays on World Theatre, Drama and Performance. *v.1 p.86, p.128, p.135*

Imperialism: The Idea and Reality of British and French Colonial Expansion, 1880-1914. . . . .*v.3 p.76*

Imperialism: The Robinson and Gallagher Controversy. *v.3 p.77*

Imperialism's New Clothes: The Repartition of Tropical Africa, 1914-1919. . . . .*v.6 p.56*

The Imperialist Imagination: German Colonialism and Its Legacy. *v.4 p.584*

The Imperiled Union: Essays on the American Civil War. *v.3 p.429*

Implementation and Performance in New American Schools: Three Years into Scale Up. *v.4 p.280*

Implementing E-Commerce Strategies: A Guide to Corporate Success after the Dot. Com Bust. *v.4 p.113*

Implementing Standards-Based Education. *v.4 p.286*

Implementing the Constitution. *v.4 p.536*

The Implications of Literacy: Written Language and Models of Interpretation in the 11th and 12th Centuries. . . .*v.2 p.564*

The Implicit Genome. *v.5 p.145, p.200*

The Implosion of American Federalism. *v.4 p.525*

The Importance of Chaucer. *v.6 p.564, p.565*

The Importance of Living. *v.6 p.208*

c Importing Diversity: Inside Japan's JET Program. *v.6 p.220*

Imposing Decency: The Politics of Sexuality and Race in Puerto Rico, 1870-1920. . . . .*v.3 p.283, p.319*

Imposing Wilderness: Struggles over Livelihood and Nature Preservation in Africa. *v.5 p.18, p.19*

The Impossible Art of Golf: An Anthology of Golf Writing. *v.4 p.812, p.861*

The Impossible Exchange. *v.1 p.455, p.509*

Impossible Purities: Blackness, Femininity and Victorian Culture. *v.6 p.477*

Impossible Subjects: Illegal Aliens and the Making of Modern America. . . *v.4 p.460, p.571,v.6 p.119, p.124, p.125, p.126*

Impossible Women: Lesbian Figures and American Literature. *v.2 p.5, v.6 p.393*

The Impostor: A Play for Demagogues. *v.2 p.669*

The Impostor. *v.6 p.395*

Impressionism: Art, Leisure and Parisian Society. . . .*v.1 p.728*

Impressionism in America: The Ten American Painters.*v.1 p.728*

Impressionism. *v.1 p.729*

The Impressionist Print. *v.1 p.753*

Impressionist Still Life. *v.1 p.729*

Impressionist Subjects: Gender, Interiority and Modernist Fiction in England. *v.2 p.191*

The Impressionists at First Hand. *v.1 p.726, p.727*

Impressions of Cuba in the Nineteenth Century: The Travel Diary of Joseph J. Dimock. *v.3 p.308*

Impressions of Light: The French Landscape from Corot to Monet. *v.1 p.733*

Imprisoning America: The Social Effects of Mass Incarceration. *v.6 p.272*

Imprisonment of African American Women: Causes, Conditions and Future Implications. *v.6 p.38, p.42, p.277, p.469*

The Improbable Era: The South since World War II. .*v.3 p.497*

Improper Bostonians: Lesbian and Gay History from the Puritans to Playland. *v.6 p.362, p.363*

The Improved Binoculars. *v.2 p.736*

Improvement of Mankind: The Social and Political Thought of John Stuart Mill. *v.3 p.115, p.129,v.4 p.223*

Improving Care for the End of Life: A Sourcebook for Health Care Managers and Clinicians. *v.5 p.532*

Improving Customer Satisfaction, Loyalty, and Profit: An Integrated Measurement and Management System. *v.4 p.139*

Improving Intergroup Relations. *v.5 p.648, p.649*

Improving Inventory Record Accuracy: Getting Your Stock Information Right. *v.4 p.117*

Improving Primary Education in Developing Countries. .*v.4 p.314*

Improving Safety in the Chemical Laboratory: A Practical Guide. *v.5 p.266*

Improving Schools from Within: Teachers, Parents, and Principals Can Make the Difference. *v.4 p.324*

Improving Teaching in the High School Block Period. *v.4 p.287, p.288*

Improving the Sustainability of Rice-Wheat Systems: Issues and Impacts. *v.5 p.12*

Improving Undergraduate Education Through Faculty Development: An Analysis of Effective Programs and Practices. *v.4 p.292*

Improving Vegetatively-Propagated Crops. *v.5 p.19*

Improvisation in the Arts of the Middle Ages and Renaissance. *v.1 p.177*

Improvisational Models of Music Therapy. *v.1 p.406*

Improvisations on a Missing String. *v.6 p.664*

Improvisations on Butor: Transformation of Writing, by Michel Butor. *v.2 p.511*

Improvised Dialogue: Emergence and Creativity in Conversation. *v.4 p.423*

Imps of the Perverse: Gay Monsters in Film. *v.6 p.417*

Impure Cultures: University Biology and the World of Commerce. *v.5 p.218*

Impure Science: AIDS, Activism, and the Politics of Knowledge. *v.6 p.378*

In a Cold Crater: Cultural and Intellectual Life in Berlin, 1945-1948. . . . .*v.3 p.176*

In a Different Voice: Psychological Theory and Women's Development. *v.4 p.692, v.6 p.445*

In a Foreign Harbor: Essays in Honor of Vasa D. Mihailovich. *v.2 p.778*

In a Little Kingdom: The Tragedy of Laos, 1960-1980. .*v.3 p.392*

In a Lonely Street: Film Noir, Genre and Masculinity. *v.6 p.314, p.328, p.342*

In a Persian Mirror: Images of the West and Westerners in Iranian Fiction. *v.6 p.671*

In a Queer Time and Place: Transgender Bodies, Subcultural Lives. *v.6 p.370*

In Amazonia: A Natural History. *v.3 p.269*

In Another Country: Colonialism, Culture, and the English Novel in India. *v.2 p.191, p.762*

In Arden: Editing Shakespeare - Arden Shakespeare. . .*v.2 p.232*

In Black and White: Race and Sports in America. *v.4 p.819, p.833,v.6 p.41*

In Black and White: The Life of Sammy Davis, Jr. *v.1 p.8, p.9, p.36*

In Code: A Mathematical Journey. *v.5 p.476*

In Custody. *v.2 p.764*

In Defence of British India: Great Britain in the Middle East, 1775-1842. . . . .*v.3 p.77*

In Defence of Canada: From the Great War to Thegreat Depression. *v.3 p.541*

In Defence of Globalisation. *v.4 p.262*

In Defense of a Political Court. *v.4 p.538*

In Defense of American Higher Education. *v.4 p.330*

In Defense of Anarchism. *v.4 p.511*

In Defense of Animals: The Second Wave. .*v.1 p.486, v.6 p.289*

In Defense of Congress. *v.4 p.530*

In Defense of Globalization. *v.4 p.55, p.663*

In Defense of History. *v.3 p.35*

In Defense of Honor: Sexual Morality, Modernity and Nation in Early Twentieth Century Brazil. . . .*v.3 p.282, p.283, p.339*

In Defense of Neutral Rights; the United States Navy and the Wars of Independence in Chile and Peru. . .*v.3 p.327, p.350*

In Defense of Prisons. *v.6 p.274*

In Defense of Reason. *v.2 p.7*

In Defense of the National Interest: A Critical Examination of American Foreign Policy. *v.3 p.453*

In Defense of Wildlife: Preserving Communities and Corridors. *v.5 p.179*

In Defense of Winters: The Poetry and Prose of Yvor Winters. *v.2 p.128*

In Defiance of Oligarchy: The Tory Party 1714-60. .*v.3 p.93, p.106*

In Defiance: The Battle Against General Noriega Fought from Panama's Embassy. *v.3 p.306*

In Divers Tones. *v.2 p.738*

In Face of Mystery: A Constructive Theology. . . .*v.1 p.639*

In Focus - Doris Ulmann: Photographs from the J. Paul Getty Museum. *v.1 p.767*

In Focus - Lészló Moholy-Nagy: Photographs from the J. Paul Getty Museum. *v.1 p.768*

In Focus: Photographs from the J. Paul Getty Museum. .*v.1 p.766*

In Front of the Children: Screen Entertainment and Young Audiences. *v.6 p.311*

In Gods We Trust: The Evolutionary Landscape of Religion. *v.4 p.36, v.5 p.632*

In Good Faith: Schools, Religion and Public Funding. .*v.4 p.308*

In Griot Time: An American Guitarist in Mali. . . .*v.1 p.285*

In His Image, but: Racism in Southern Religion, 1780-1910. . . . .*v.1 p.644*

In Hitler's Germany: Everyday Life in the Third Reich. .*v.3 p.171*

In Hitler's Shadow: West German Historians and the Attempt to Escape from the Nazi Past. *v.3 p.83, p.178*

In Its Own Image: How Television Has Transformed Sports. *v.4 p.809, p.818, p.819, p.902*

In Labor's Cause: Main Themes on the History of the American Worker. *v.4 p.124*

In Memoriam. *v.2 p.313, p.314*

In Memory of Her: A Feminist Theological Reconstruction of Christian Origins. *v.1 p.599*

In Ole Virginia: Or, Marse Chan and Other Stories. . .*v.2 p.49*

In or Out: Hollywood Gays and Straights Talk about Themselves and Each Other. *v.6 p.416*

In Other Words: Literatures of Latinas of the United States. *v.2 p.19, v.6 p.495*

In Other Words: New Writing by Indian Women. . . .*v.2 p.763*

In Other Worlds: Essays in Cultural Politics. .*v.2 p.761, v.6 p.97*

In Our Defense: The Bill of Rights in Action. *v.4 p.455*

In Our Own Voices: Four Centuries of American Women's Religious Writings. *v.1 p.605*

In Our Own Words: Extraordinary Speeches of the American Century. *v.2 p.28*

In Our Time. *v.2 p.84*

In Plain Arabic: A Play in Two Acts. *v.6 p.656*

In Praise of Books: A Cultural History of Cairo's Middle Class, Sixteenth to the Eighteenth Century. . . .*v.4 p.726, v.6 p.637*

In Praise of Commercial Culture. *v.1 p.826*

In Praise of Education. *v.4 p.326*

In Praise of Later Roman Emperors: The Panegyrici Latini. *v.3 p.32*

In Praise of the Stepmother. *v.2 p.686*

In Pursuit of a Scientific Culture: Science, Art, and Society in the Victorian Age. *v.6 p.737, p.759*

In Pursuit of Excellence: How to Win in Sport and Life Through Mental Training. *v.4 p.877*

In Pursuit of Peace: A History of the Israeli Peace Movement. *v.6 p.613*

In Pursuit of Privacy: Law, Ethics, and the Rise of Technology. *v.4 p.443*

In Pursuit of the Past: Decoding the Archaeological Record: With a New Afterword. *v.4 p.6*

In Quest of Community. *v.4 p.684*

In Search of a Beginning: My Life with Graham Greene. *v.2 p.349*

In Search of a Character. *v.2 p.350*

In Search of an American Catholicism: A History of Religion and Culture in Tension. *v.1 p.573, p.604*

In Search of Authenticity: Existentialism from Kierkegaard to Camus. *v.1 p.505*

In Search of Blandings: An Investigation into the Sources That Inspired P. G. Wodehouse. *v.2 p.390*

In Search of Buddy Bolden: First Man of Jazz. .*v.1 p.261, p.312*

In Search of Chinese Democracy: Civil Opposition in Nationalist China, 1929-1949. . . . .*v.4 p.619*

In Search of Critical Social Theory in the Interests of Black Folk. *v.6 p.40*

In Search of Dreamtime: The Quest for the Origin of Religion. *v.1 p.521*

In Search of Equality: The Chinese Struggle Against Discrimination in Nineteenth-Century America. . .*v.4 p.457*

In Search of Excellence: Lessons from America's Best-Run Companies. *v.4 p.81, p.148*

In Search of God the Mother: The Cult of Anatolian Cybele. *v.1 p.533*

In Search of Homo Sapiens: Twenty-Five Contemporary Slovak Short Stories. *v.2 p.812*

In Search of Human Nature: The Decline and Revival of Darwinism in American Social Thought. *v.4 p.682*

In Search of Identity. *v.6 p.639*

In Search of J. D. Salinger. *v.2 p.118*

In Search of Lost Time, Set. *v.2 p.524*

In Search of Muhammad. *v.1 p.555*

In Search of Myself. *v.2 p.732*

In Search of Old Peking. *v.6 p.205*

In Search of Prosperity: Analytic Narratives on Economic Growth. *v.4 p.240*

In Search of Respect: Selling Crack in el Barrio. . .*v.4 p.776*

In Search of Schrodinger's Cat: Quantum Physics and Reality. *v.5 p.540*

In Search of Self: An Exploration of the Role of the School in Promoting Self-Understanding. *v.4 p.357*

In Search of Southeast Asia: A Modern History. . . .*v.6 p.165*

In Search of Swampland: A Wetland Sourcebook and Field Guide. *v.4 p.393*

In Search of the Ivory-Billed Woodpecker. *v.6 p.291*

In Search of the Light: The Adventures of a Parapsychologist. *v.5 p.613*

In Search of the Promised Land: Paintings by Frederic Edwin Church. *v.1 p.736*

In Search of the Rain Forest. *v.5 p.177*

In Search of the Silent South: Southern Liberals and the Race Issue. *v.3 p.497*

In Search of the Ultimate Building Blocks. *v.5 p.544*

In Search of Wealth and Power: Yen Fu and the West. *v.6 p.191, p.203*

In September, the Light Changes: The Stories of Andrew Holleran. *v.6 p.397*

In Sickness and in Health: Disease As Metaphor in Art and Popular Wisdom. *v.1 p.709*

In Sickness and in Wealth: American Hospitals in the Twentieth Century. *v.5 p.514*

'In Silico' Simulation of Biological Processes, No. 247. .*v.5 p.113*

In Small Things Forgotten: The Archaeology of Early American Life. *v.3 p.484, p.485*

In Sorcery's Shadow: A Memoir of Apprenticeship among the Songhay of Niger. *v.4 p.37*

In Spite of Innocence: Erroneous Convictions in Capital Cases. *v.6 p.268*

In Stalin's Time: Middleclass Values in Soviet Fiction. .*v.2 p.798*

In Struggle: SNCC and the Black Awakening of the Nineteen Sixties. *v.6 p.12*

In the Absence of Don Porfirio: Francisco Leon de la Barra and the Mexican Revolution. *v.3 p.293*

In the Absence of Power: Governing America. *v.3 p.473*

In the Adopted Land: Abused Immigrant Women and the Criminal Justice System. *v.6 p.111, p.117, p.259*

In the Aftermath of Genocide: Armenians and Jews in Twentieth Century France. *v.4 p.653*

In the Afternoon of Time: An Autobiography. *v.6 p.150*

In the Arms of Africa: The Life of Colin M. Turnbull. . *v.4 p.4*

In the Barrios: Latinos and the Underclass Debate. *v.6 p.522, p.525*

In the Beginning: A Short History of the Hebrew Language. *v.6 p.646*

In the Belly of the Beast: Letters from Prison. *v.6 p.276*

In the Belly of the River: Tribal Conflicts over Development in the Narmada Valley. *v.6 p.153*

In the Blink of an Eye: A Perspective on Film Editing. .*v.6 p.350*

In the Castle of My Skin. *v.2 p.768*

In the Company of Educated Women: A History of Women and Higher Education in America. *v.4 p.302*

In the Company of Light. *v.5 p.221, p.222*

In the Company of Mushrooms: A Biologist's Tale. . .*v.5 p.209*

In the Country of Last Things. *v.2 p.139*

In the Course of Performance: Studies in the World of Musical Improvisation. *v.1 p.283*

In the Dark Before Dawn: New Selected Poems of Thomas Merton. *v.2 p.98*

In the Dark Body of Metamorphosis and Other Poems. .*v.2 p.716*

In the Days of McKinley: William McKinley. .*v.3 p.398, p.437*

In the Devil's Shadow: U. N. Special Operations During the Korean War. *v.4 p.634*

In the Eye of the Beholder: Tales of Egyptian Life from the Writings of Yusuf Idris. *v.6 p.660*

In the Eye of the Storm: Growing up Jewish in Germany, 1918-1943, a Memoir. *v.3 p.180*

In the Eye of the Storm: Women in Postrevolutionary Iran. *v.6 p.631, p.632*

In the Fascist Bathroom: Punk in Pop Music, 1977-1992. . . . .*v.1 p.271*

In the Feminine Mode: Essays on Hispanic Women Writers. *v.2 p.639*

In the Flesh: The Cultural Politics of Body Modification. .*v.4 p.26*

In the Footsteps of Orpheus: The Life and Times of Miklbos Radnboti. *v.2 p.785*

In the Forbidden City: An Anthology of Erotic Fiction by Italian Women. *v.2 p.699*

In the Game: Gay Athletes and the Cult of Masculinity. *v.4 p.839, v.6 p.383*

In the Grip of Disease: Studies in the Greek Imagination. *v.2 p.404*

In the Heart of the Country. *v.2 p.753, p.754*

In the Heart of the Seas: A Story of a Journey to the Land of Israel. *v.6 p.647*

In the House of Osubgo: Critical Essays on Wole Soyinka. *v.2 p.757, v.6 p.28*

In the House of the Law: Gender and Islamic Law in Ottoman Syria and Palestine. *v.6 p.608, p.611, p.612*

In the Houses of the Holy: Led Zeppelin and the Power of Rock Music. *v.1 p.268, p.335*

In the Land of Dreamy Dreams: Short Fiction. *v.2 p.146*

In the Land of Israel. *v.6 p.615*

In the Land of Mirrors: Cuban Exile Politics in the United States. *v.6 p.539*

In the Land of Orpheus: Rural Livelihoods and Nature Conservation in Post-Socialist Bulgaria. *v.3 p.251*

In the Life: A Black Gay Anthology. *v.6 p.406*

In the Matter of Color: Race and the American Legal Process: The Colonial Period, Vol. 1. . . . .*v.4 p.457*

In the Maw of the Earth Monster: Studies of Mesoamerican Ritual Cave Use. *v.3 p.296*

In the Mind's Eye: Enhancing Human Performance. . .*v.5 p.605*

In the Mind's Eye: Julian Hochberg on the Perception of Pictures, Films, and the World. *v.5 p.605*

In the Mind's Eye: Visual Thinkers, Gifted People with Dyslexia and Other Learning Difficulties, Computer Images and the Ironies of Creativity. *v.5 p.607*

In the Miro District and Other Stories. *v.2 p.157*

In the Money. *v.2 p.136*

In the Mouth of the Dragon. *v.5 p.320*

In the Name of Civil Society: From Free Election Movements to People Power in the Philippines. *v.6 p.179*

In the Name of Hawaiians: Native Identities and Cultural Politics. *v.6 p.130*

In the Name of Osama Bin Laden: Global Terrorism and the Bin Laden Brotherhood. *v.4 p.659*

In the Name of Salome. *v.6 p.505*

In the Name of Terrorism: Presidents on Political Violence in the Post-World War II Era. *v.4 p.565*

In the Name of the People: Prophets and Conspirators in Prerevolutionary Russia. *v.3 p.219*

In the News: American Journalists View Their Craft. .*v.4 p.412*

In the Path of Hizbullah. *v.4 p.616*

In the Rapids: New South African Stories. . . .*v.2 p.623, p.624*

In the Realm of Eight Deer: The Archaeology of the Mixtec Codices. *v.3 p.260, p.261*

In the Red: On Contemporary Chinese Culture. . . .*v.6 p.196*

In the Rings of Saturn. *v.4 p.154*

In the Room of Never Grieve: New and Selected Poems, 1985-2003. . . . .*v.2 p.158*

In the Shade of Spring Leaves: The Life and Writings of Higuchi Ichiyo, with Nine of Her Best Short Stories. .*v.6 p.229*

In the Shadow of Catastrophe: German Intellectuals Between Apocalypse and Enlightenment. *v.3 p.170*

In the Shadow of FDR: From Harry Truman to Ronald Reagan. *v.3 p.378, p.448*

In the Shadow of Marriage: Gender and Justice in an African Community. *v.4 p.32*

In the Shadow of Power: States and Strategies in International Politics. *v.4 p.498, p.625*

In the Shadow of Slavery: African Americans in New York City, 1626-1863. . . . .*v.6 p.712, p.713*

In the Shadow of the Garrison State: America's Anti-Statism and Its Cold War Grand Strategy. *v.4 p.498*

In the Shadow of the Han: Literati Thought and Society at the Beginning of the Southern Dynasties. *v.6 p.185*

In the Shadow of the Mexican Revolution: Contemporary Mexican History, 1910-1989. . . . .*v.3 p.290*

In the Shadow of the Poorhouse: A Social History of Welfare in America. *v.4 p.758*

In the Shadow of Vesuvius : A Cultural History of Naples. *v.3 p.197*

In the Shadow of Vesuvius: A Cultural History of Naples. *v.3 p.204*

In the Shadow of Young Girls in Flower: In Search of Lost Time. *v.2 p.524*

In the Shadows of State and Capital: The United Fruit Company, Popular Struggle and Agrarian Restructuring in Ecuador, 1900-1995. . . . .*v.3 p.333, p.334*

In the Skin of a Lion: A Novel. *v.2 p.737*

In the Spirit of Crazy Horse. *v.6 p.689, p.694*

In the Tavern of Life and Other Stories. *v.6 p.656*

In the Tennessee Mountains. *v.2 p.32, p.46*

In the Time of the Americans: FDR, Truman, Eisenhower, Marshall, MacArthur - The Generation That Changed America's Role in the World. *v.3 p.451*

In the Twilight of Revolution: The Political Theory of Amilcar Cabral. *v.6 p.74*

In the Vineyard: Working in African American Studies. *v.6 p.5, p.14*

In the Wake of 9/11: The Psychology of Terror. . . .*v.5 p.632*

In the Wake of Terror: Medicine and Morality in a Time of Crisis. *v.4 p.660, p.669*

In the Wake of the Goddesses: Women, Culture and the Biblical Transformation of Pagan Myth. *v.1 p.529*

In the Wake of the Plague: The Black Death and the World It Made. *v.4 p.742*

In the Wake of War: The Reconstruction of German Cities after World War II. *v.3 p.176*

In the Year of Jubilee. *v.2 p.289*

In the Zone: Epic Survival Stories from the Mountaineering World. *v.4 p.789*

In Theory: Nations, Classes, Literature. *v.2 p.759*

In This House of Brede. *v.2 p.347*

In This Our Life. *v.2 p.79*

In Time of Plague: The History and Social Consequences of Lethal Epidemic Disease. *v.4 p.778*

In Times of Challenge: Chicanos and Chicanas in American Society. *v.6 p.521*

In Transit: The Transport Workers Union in New York City, 1933-1966: With a New Epilogue. *v.4 p.126*

In Your Eyes: Quotations on Gay Love. *v.6 p.360*

Inanna: Queen of Heaven and Earth. *v.1 p.539*

The Inarticulate Society: Eloquence and Culture in America. *v.4 p.423*

Inattentional Blindness. *v.5 p.611*

Inbreeding, Incest, and the Incest Taboo: The State of
Knowledge at the Turn of the Century. *v.4 p.738*

Inca Architecture and Construction at Ollantaytambo. .*v.3 p.262*

Inca Cosmology and the Human Body. *v.3 p.261*

Incapacitation: Penal Confinement and the Restraint of
Crime. *v.4 p.753, v.6 p.272*

Incarcerating White-Collar Offenders: The Prison Experience
and Beyond. *v.6 p.276*

The Incas. *v.4 p.11*

Incentive Pay and Career Ladders for Today's Teachers: A Study
of Current Programs and Practices. *v.4 p.282*

Incentives to Improve Education: A New Perspective. .*v.4 p.280*

Incident at Vichy. *v.2 p.101, p.102*

Incidents in the Life of a Slave Girl. *v.2 p.43*

Incipient Feminists: Women Writers in the Slovak National
Revival. *v.2 p.812*

Incipient Industrialization in an Underdeveloped Country: The
Case of Chile, 1845-1879. . . . .*v.3 p.351*

Including Students with Severe and Multiple Disabilities in
Typical Classrooms: Practical Strategies for
Teachers. *v.4 p.318*

The Inclusion Breakthrough: Unleashing the Real Power of
Diversity. *v.4 p.132*

Inclusion: Including People with Disabilities in Parks and
Recreation Opportunities. *v.4 p.787, p.842*

Inclusion Through Sports: A Guide to Individualizing Sport
Experiences. *v.4 p.800*

Inclusive Physical Activity: A Lifetime of
Opportunities. *v.4 p.801*

The Incoherence of the Philosophers. *v.1 p.431*

Income Differences. *v.4 p.249*

Income Distribution in Macroeconomic Models. .*v.4 p.252, p.253*

Income Distribution. *v.4 p.249*

Income Inequality in America: An Analysis of
Trends. *v.4 p.133, p.134*

Income Security: Statutory History of the United States. .*v.4 p.447*

The Incompleat Folksinger. *v.1 p.297*

Incomplete Transition: Military Power and Democracy in
Argentina. *v.3 p.275*

Incorporating Women: A History of Women and Business in the
United States. *v.4 p.57*

The Incorporation of America: Culture and Society in the Gilded
Age. *v.3 p.401, p.438*

Increase Mather, the Foremost American Puritan. . . .*v.3 p.487*

Increasing Human Efficiency in Business. *v.5 p.581*

Independence and Democracy in Burma, 1945-1952: The
Turbulent Years. *v.6 p.166*

Independence Day. *v.2 p.145*

The Independence Movements in Arab North
Africa. *v.6 p.60, p.592*

The Independence of Spanish America. *v.4 p.583*

Independent Counsel: The Law and the Investigations. .*v.4 p.462*

Independent Feature Film Production: A Complete Guide from
Concept Through Distribution. *v.6 p.346, p.347*

Independent Iraq, Nineteen Thirty-Two to Nineteen Fifty-Eight:
A Study in Iraqi Politics. *v.6 p.603*

Independent Justice: The Federal Special Prosecutor in
American Politics. *v.4 p.524*

Independent Schools, Independent Thinkers. *v.4 p.296*

Independent Women: Work and Community for Single Women,
1850-1920. . . . .*v.4 p.738, v.6 p.466, p.468, p.749*

The Indeterminate World: A Study of the Novels of Joyce
Cary. *v.2 p.337*

An Index Dictionary of Chinese Artist, Collectors and
Connoisseurs, with Character Identification by Modified Stroke
Count: Including over 5,000 Chinese Names and
Biographies from the T'ang Dynasty Through the Modern
Period. *v.1 p.666*

⌨ Index Islamicus Online. *v.1 p.553*

Index of American Print Exhibitions, 1882-1940. . . .*v.1 p.751*

Index of American Watercolor Exhibitions, 1900-1945. .*v.1 p.725*

An Index of Early Chinese Painters and Paintings: T'ang, Sung,
Yuan. *v.1 p.725*

Index of Majors and Graduate Degrees. *v.4 p.295*

⌨ Index of Native American Resources on the Internet (WWW
Virtual Library American Indians). *v.6 p.677*

Index of Paintings Sold in the British Isles During the
Nineteenth Century: 1801-1805, Vol. 1. . . . . .*v.1 p.708*

Index to Artistic Biography, Set. *v.1 p.662*

Index to Crime and Mystery Anthologies. *v.2 p.580*

⌨ The Index to Current Urban Documents (ICUD). . .*v.6 p.709*

Index to "The London Stage, 1660-1800". . . .*v.1 p.103, p.141*

⌨ Index to Physical, Chemical and Other Property
Data. *v.5 p.280*

Index to Poetry in Music. *v.1 p.165*

An Index to Reproductions of Paintings by Twentieth-Century
Chinese Artists. *v.1 p.711*

An Index to the Advocate: The National Gay Newsmagazine
1967-1982. . . . .*v.6 p.361*

Index to 'The Elizabethan Stage' and 'William Shakespeare' by
Sir Edmund Chambers. *v.2 p.227*

Index to the Ladder, Vols I-XVI, 1956-1972. . . . .*v.6 p.361*

Index to the Prose Writings. *v.2 p.263*

India Against Itself: Assam and the Politics of
Nationality. *v.6 p.160*

India and Pakistan: The First Fifty Years. *v.6 p.159*

India and Pakistan. *v.6 p.159, p.160*

India and the China Crisis. *v.6 p.159*

India and the Indian Ocean - 1500 to 1800. . .*v.6 p.155, p.156*

India and the United States in a Changing
World. *v.3 p.390, v.4 p.642, p.644*

India Before Europe. *v.6 p.155*

India: Government and Politics in a Developing Nation. .*v.4 p.617*

India in the World Order: Searching for Major-Power
Status. *v.6 p.146, p.147*

India: Pioneering Photographers, 1850-1900. . . . .*v.1 p.763*

The India-China Relationship: What the United States Needs to
Know. *v.6 p.155*

Indian Affairs: Laws and Treaties, Set. *v.6 p.696*

Indian Affairs. Laws and Treaties, Vol. 5. . . . . .*v.6 p.693*

⌨ Indian Affairs: Laws and Treaties. . . .*v.4 p.465, v.6 p.696*

Indian Agriculture in America: Prehistory to the
    Present. *v.5 p.4, p.5,v.6 p.681*

Indian Art. *v.1 p.691, p.692*

Indian Buddhism. *v.1 p.563*

The Indian Child Welfare Act Handbook: A Legal Guide to the
    Custody and Adoption of Native American Children. .*v.6 p.691*

Indian Clothing Before Cortes: Mesoamerican Costumes from
    the Codices. *v.3 p.260, v.6 p.684*

Indian Country, God's Country: Native Americans and the
    National Parks. *v.6 p.299, p.680, p.691*

Indian Dances of North America: Their Importance to Indian
    Life. *v.6 p.700*

Indian Democracy: Meanings and Practices. *v.4 p.618*

Indian English Drama: Critical Perspectives. *v.2 p.762*

Indian English Poetry: Since Nineteen Fifty: An
    Anthology. *v.2 p.763*

Indian Esoteric Buddhism: A Social History of the Tantric
    Movement. *v.1 p.567*

The Indian Frontier of the American West,
    1846-1890. . . . .*v.3 p.402, v.6 p.687*

Indian Games and Dances with Native Songs: Arranged from
    American Indian Ceremonies and Sports. . . .*v.1 p.14, p.15*

Indian Gaming: Tribal Sovereignty and American
    Politics. *v.4 p.465, v.6 p.696*

☐ Indian Health Service. *v.6 p.702*

The Indian Imagination: Critical Essays on Indian Writing in
    English. *v.2 p.763*

The Indian in Latin American History: Resistance, Resilience,
    and Acculturation. *v.3 p.298*

Indian Integration in Peru: A Half Century of Experience,
    1900-1948. . . . .*v.3 p.329*

Indian Killer. *v.2 p.139*

Indian Life in the Upper Great Lakes, 11,000 B C to a D
    1800. . . . .*v.6 p.704*

Indian Literature in English: Longman Literature in English
    Series. *v.2 p.763*

Indian Medicine in Highland Guatemala: The Pre-Hispanic and
    Colonial Periods. *v.3 p.298*

Indian Music and the West. *v.1 p.288*

Indian Ocean: Five Island Countries. *v.6 p.67*

Indian Philosophy: A Very Short Introduction. *v.1 p.475*

Indian Philosophy: An Introduction to Hindu and Buddhist
    Thought. *v.1 p.419*

The Indian Princes and Their States. *v.6 p.161*

ⓔ The Indian Reorganization Act: Congresses and
    Bills. *v.6 p.695*

Indian Reserved Water Rights: The Winters Doctrine in Its
    Social and Legal Context, 1880s-1930s. . . .*v.6 p.681, p.697*

Indian Running: Native American History and
    Tradition. *v.4 p.841, v.6 p.682*

Indian Self-Rule: First-Hand Accounts of Indian-White Relations
    from Roosevelt to Reagan. *v.6 p.689, p.692*

Indian Society and the Making of the British Empire. .*v.6 p.156*

Indian, Soldier and Settler: Experiences in the Struggle for the
    American West. *v.6 p.684*

Indian Survival in Colonial Nicaragua. *v.3 p.302, p.303*

The Indian Tribes of North America. *v.6 p.683, p.704*

Indian Women of Early Mexico. *v.3 p.287*

Indian Writing in English. *v.2 p.763*

Indiana, 1816 to 1850: The Pioneer Period. *v.3 p.514*

Indiana: A Guide to the Hoosier State. *v.3 p.514*

Indiana: A History. *v.3 p.514*

The Indiana Companion to Traditional Chinese Literature, Vol.
    1. . . . .*v.6 p.208*

The Indiana Companion to Traditional Chinese Literature, Vol.
    2. . . . .*v.6 p.208*

Indiana in the Civil War Era, 1850-1880. . . . . . .*v.3 p.514*

Indiana in Transition, 1880-1920. . . . .*v.3 p.514*

Indiana Politics During the Civil War. *v.3 p.514*

Indiana Territory, 1800-2000: A Bicentennial
    Perspective. *v.3 p.514*

Indiana Through Tradition and Change: A History of the
    Hoosier State and Its People, 1920-1945. . . . .*v.3 p.514*

Indiana to Eighteen Sixteen: The Colonial Period. . .*v.3 p.514*

☐ Indiana University Chemistry Library Acronyms
    Database. *v.5 p.257*

Indiana. *v.2 p.500*

The Indianized States of South-East Asia. *v.6 p.164*

Indian-Religious Relations in Colonial Spanish
    America. *v.3 p.345*

Indians and Anthropologists: Vine Deloria, Jr., and the Critique
    of Anthropology. *v.4 p.27, v.6 p.702*

Indians and English: Facing Off in Early
    America. *v.6 p.685, p.686*

Indians at Work: An Informal History of Native Labour in
    British Columbia 1858-1930. . . . .*v.6 p.688, p.689*

The Indians in American Society: From the Revolutionary War
    to the Present. *v.4 p.729, v.6 p.683, p.692*

Indians in the Fur Trade: Their Roles as Trappers, Hunters and
    Middlemen in the Lands Southwest. *v.6 p.685*

The Indians of Canada. *v.6 p.703*

Indians of North America. *v.6 p.702*

Indians of the Greater Southeast: Historic Archaeology and
    Ethnohistory. *v.4 p.11, v.6 p.703*

Indians of the High Plains: From the Prehistoric Period to the
    Coming of Europeans. *v.6 p.703*

The Indians of the Paraguayan Chaco: Identity and
    Economy. *v.3 p.344*

Indians, Oil and Politics: A Recent History of Ecuador. .*v.3 p.333*

Indians, Settlers, and Slaves in a Frontier Exchange Economy:
    The Lower Mississippi Valley Before 1783. . . .*v.3 p.506*

Indian-White Relations: A Persistent Paradox. .*v.6 p.683, p.692*

Indian-White Relations in the United States: A Bibliography of
    Works Published 1975-1980. . . . .*v.6 p.683, p.692*

☐ Indianz.com. *v.6 p.677*

India-Pakistan: The History of Unsolved Conflicts. . .*v.6 p.158*

India's Communities A-Z, Set. *v.6 p.155*

India's Democracy: An Analysis of Changing State-Society
    Relations. *v.4 p.617, p.618*

India's Democracy: New Challenges. *v.4 p.617*

India's Interaction with China, Central and West Asia. *v.6 p.155*

India's Islamic Traditions: 711-1750. . . . .*v.6 p.150*

India's Partition: Process, Strategy and Mobilization. .*v.6 p.159*

India's Silent Revolution: The Rise of the Lower Castes in North Indian Politics. *v.6 p.149*

Indigenizing the Academy: Native Scholars and Scholarship on Natives. *v.4 p.312, v.6 p.680*

Indigenous American Women: Decolonization, Empowerment, Activism. *v.6 p.435, p.705*

Indigenous Australian Voices: A Reader. *v.2 p.743*

Indigenous Literature of Oceania: A Survey of Criticism and Interpretation. *v.2 p.740*

Indigenous Mestizos: The Politics of Race and Culture in Cuzco, 1919-1991. . . . .*v.3 p.329*

Indigenous People of the Caribbean. *v.4 p.41*

Indigenous Peoples and Environmental Issues: An Encyclopedia. *v.4 p.30*

Indigenous Religious Musics. *v.1 p.284*

Indigenous Rulers: An Ethnohistory of Town Governments in Colonial Cuernavaca. *v.3 p.285*

Indigenous Struggle at the Heart of Brazil: State Policy, Frontier Expansion and the Xavante Indians, 1937-1988. . .*v.3 p.340*

Indigo. *v.5 p.320*

Indirect Perception. *v.5 p.607*

The Indiscreet Jewels. *v.2 p.479, p.480*

The Indispensable Enemy: Labor and the Anti-Chinese Movement in California. *v.6 p.117, p.121, p.128*

Individual and Community: The Rise of the Polis, 800-500 B.C. *v.3 p.17*

The Individual and the Cosmos in Renaissance Philosophy. *v.1 p.435*

The Individual and the Social Self: Unpublished Work of George Herbert Mead. *v.4 p.693*

The Individual in a Social World: Essays and Experiments. *v.5 p.646*

The Individual, Society, and Education: A History of American Educational Ideas. *v.4 p.327*

Individual Taxes 2005—2006: Worldwide Summaries. .*v.4 p.107*

Individual-based models and approaches in ecology: populations, communities, and ecosystems. . .*v.5 p.183*

Individualism and Economic Order. *v.4 p.248*

Individuals. *v.1 p.489*

Indo-Anglian Literature, 1880-1970: A Survey. . . .*v.2 p.763*

The Indochina Tangle: China's Vietnam Policy, 1975-1979. . . . .*v.6 p.169*

Gli indomabili : con un'antologia di scritti futuristi sull'arte meccanica e d'avanguardia. *v.2 p.718*

Indonesia: A Country Study. *v.6 p.174*

Indonesia: A Profile. *v.6 p.175*

Indonesia Beyond Suharto: Polity Economy Society Transition. *v.4 p.622*

Indonesian Cinema: Framing the New World Order. .*v.6 p.175*

Indonesian Destinies. *v.6 p.174, p.176*

Indonesian Economic History of the Dutch Colonial Era. *v.6 p.174, p.176*

Indonesian Education: Teachers, Schools, and Central Bureaucracy. *v.4 p.333*

The Indonesian National Revolution 1945-1950. . . .*v.6 p.177*

Indonesian Political Thinking, 1945-1965. . . . . .*v.6 p.174*

Indonesian Politics under Suharto: The Rise and Fall of the New Order. *v.6 p.175, p.178*

The Indonesian Presidency: The Shift from Personal Toward Constitutional Rule. *v.6 p.175, p.177*

Indoor Air Pollution and Health, Vol. 9. . . . . . .*v.5 p.354*

Indoor Air Pollution: Problems and Priorities. *v.5 p.372*

Indoor Air Pollution. *v.5 p.355, v.6 p.292*

Indoor Air Quality and Human Health. .*v.5 p.366, p.372, p.373*

Indoor Air Quality Engineering: Environmental Health and Control of Indoor Pollutants. .*v.5 p.354, p.368, p.372, p.376*

Indoor Air Quality Handbook. *v.5 p.372*

Indoor Environment Quality. *v.5 p.705*

Indoor Pollution: A Reference Handbook. . . .*v.5 p.313, p.707*

Induction Probability and Causation: Selected Papers. .*v.1 p.495*

La Industria de la Masa y la Tortilla: Desarrollo y Tecnología. *v.3 p.272*

Industrial Archaeology: Future Directions. *v.4 p.13*

Industrial Chemical Thesaurus: Chemical to Tradename Reference and Tradename to Chemical Cross Reference and Manufacturers Directory. *v.5 p.316*

Industrial Design Techniques and Materials. *v.1 p.717*

Industrial Design. *v.1 p.717*

Industrial Dynamics. *v.4 p.119*

Industrial Ecology. *v.5 p.706*

The Industrial Economies: Capital, Labour and Enterprise: The United States, Japan and Russia, Vol. 7, Pt. 2. .*v.3 p.40, p.41*

The Industrial History of the United States. *v.4 p.248*

Industrial Landscapes. *v.1 p.765*

Industrial Marketing: An Analytical Approach to Planning and Execution. *v.4 p.144*

Industrial Marketing Research. *v.4 p.135*

Industrial Mathematics: A Course in Solving Real-World Problems. *v.5 p.500*

Industrial Minerals & Rocks: Commodities, Markets, and Uses. *v.5 p.450*

The Industrial Muse: A Study of Nineteenth Century British Working-Class Literature. *v.2 p.177, p.194*

Industrial Organic Chemicals. *v.5 p.318*

Industrial Pollution Prevention Handbook. .*v.5 p.368, p.373, p.376*

Industrial Process Control Systems. *v.4 p.116*

Industrial Proteomics: Applications for Biotechnology and Pharmaceuticals. *v.4 p.156, v.5 p.217*

The Industrial Reformation of English Fiction: Social Discourse and Narrative Form, 1832-1867. . . . . .*v.2 p.193, v.6 p.756, p.761, p.765, p.766*

Industrial Relations and European State Traditions. . .*v.4 p.121*

The Industrial Revolution, 1700 - 1914. . . . .*v.3 p.39*

The Industrial Revolution, 1760-1830. . . . .*v.3 p.122*

▢ Industrial Solvents Handbook. *v.5 p.318*

Industrial Strength Design: How Brooks Stevens Shaped Your World. *v.1 p.717*

Industrialization, Family Life, and Class Relations: Saint Chamond, 1815-1914. . . . .*v.3 p.148*

The Industrialization of Sao Paulo, 1880-1945. . . . .*v.3 p.339*

▢ Industries Statistics. *v.4 p.150*

Industry and Empire: The Birth of the Industrial
  Revolution. *v.3 p.77, p.89, p.123, p.125*

Industry and Ideology: I. G. Farben in the Nazi
  Era. *v.3 p.84, p.172*

Industry and Trade: A Study of Industrial Technique and
  Business Organization; and of Their Influences
  on the Conditions of Various Classes and Nations - Volume
  I, Vol. 1. . . . . *v.4 p.224*

Industry and Trade: A Study of Industrial Technique and
  Business Organization; and of Their Influences
  on the Conditions of Various Classes and Nations. *v.4 p.224*

Industry and Trade, Textile, Apparel, Footwear, U. S. A. *v.4 p.153*

Industry and Underdevelopment: The Industrialization of
  Mexico, 1890-1940. . . . . *v.3 p.289*

Industry Reference Handbooks, Set. *v.5 p.317*

Industry Reference Handbooks. *v.5 p.317, p.318*

☐ Industry Research Portal. *v.4 p.159*

Industry Research Using the Economic Census: How to Find It,
  How to Use It. *v.4 p.148, p.178, p.180*

Industry, State, and Society in Stalin's Russia,
  1926-1934. . . . . *v.3 p.226*

Industry Studies. *v.4 p.149*

Inebriety and the Candidate. *v.2 p.281*

Inefficient Markets: An Introduction to Behavioral
  Finance. *v.4 p.97, p.100*

Inequalities from Complex Analysis. *v.5 p.490, p.491*

Inequalities. *v.5 p.489*

Inequality and Social Mobility in Brazil. *v.4 p.705*

Inequality at Work: Hispanics in the U. S. Labor Force. *v.6 p.524*

Inequality in an Age of Decline. *v.4 p.718*

Inequality Reexamined. *v.4 p.514*

The Inevitable Domination by Man: An Evolutionary Detective
  Story. *v.5 p.193*

Inextricably Bonded: Israeli, Arab, and Jewish Writers
  Re-Visioning Culture. *v.6 p.648*

Infallible?: An Unresolved Enquiry. *v.1 p.655*

Infant Chimpanzee and Human Child: A Classic 1935
  Comparative Study of Ape Emotions and
  Intelligence. *v.5 p.615*

Infante's Inferno. *v.2 p.672*

Infants of the Spring. *v.2 p.124*

The Infection of Thomas De Quincey: The Psychopathology of
  Imperialism. *v.2 p.281*

Infections and Inequalities: The Modern Plagues. . . *v.4 p.778*

Infectious Diseases of Humans: Dynamics and Control. *v.5 p.501*

Infectious Diseases of Livestock, Set. *v.6 p.283*

Infectious Diseases of the Fetus and the Newborn
  Infant. *v.5 p.533*

Infectious Greed: Restoring Confidence in America's
  Companies. *v.4 p.87*

☐ infed. *v.4 p.319*

The Infernal Machine and Other Plays. *v.2 p.514*

Inferno: Alone and Other Writings. *v.2 p.631*

Inferno, Esolen Translation. *v.3 p.69*

Inferno. *v.2 p.703*

The Inferno. *v.2 p.703*

Inferring Phylogenies. *v.5 p.204, p.205*

Infertility and Patriarchy: The Cultural Politics of Gender and
  Family Life in Egypt. *v.6 p.639*

Infertility Around the Globe: New Thinking on Childlessness,
  Gender, and Reproductive Technologies. *v.6 p.443*

Infiltration: A Novel. *v.6 p.649*

Infinitas Gracias: Contemporary Mexican Votive
  Painting. *v.1 p.733*

Infinite Divisions: An Anthology of Chicana
  Literature. *v.6 p.496, p.502*

Infinite Thought: Truth and the Return of Philosophy. *v.1 p.455*

Infinite Tropics: An Alfred Russel Wallace Anthology. *v.5 p.197*

The Inflation -Targeting Debate. *v.4 p.246*

Inflation Targeting: Lessons from the International
  Experience. *v.4 p.246*

Inflation, Unemployment and Monetary Policy. . . . *v.4 p.245*

The Inflationary Universe: The Quest for a New Theory of
  Cosmic Origins. *v.5 p.71*

Influence of Beaumont and Fletcher on the Restoration
  Stage. *v.2 p.217*

The Influence of Cattle Grazing and Grass Seeding on
  Coniferous Regeneration after Shelterwood Cutting in Eastern
  Oregon. *v.5 p.42*

The Influence of Islam on Medieval Europe. *v.6 p.575*

The Influence of Sea Power upon History,
  1660-1783. . . . . *v.3 p.36, p.383, p.417*

Influence: Science and Practice. *v.4 p.139, v.5 p.586*

Influence Without Authority. *v.4 p.70, p.172*

The Influentials: One American in Ten Tells the Other Nine
  How to Vote, Where to Eat, and What to Buy. . . *v.4 p.145*

Informal Logic: A Handbook for Critical Argument. . *v.1 p.493*

Informal Politics in East Asia. *v.4 p.618*

Informatics in Proteomics. *v.5 p.103*

Information Ages: Literacy, Numeracy and the Computer
  Revolution. *v.5 p.406*

Information and Communication Technology and the Teacher of
  the Future. *v.4 p.351*

Information and Control in the Living Organism: An Elementary
  Introduction. *v.5 p.408*

Information and Coordination: Essays in Macroeconomic
  Theory. *v.4 p.240*

Information and Its Role in Nature. *v.5 p.224*

Information and Management Systems for Product
  Customization. *v.4 p.117*

Information Communication Technology: Changing
  Education. *v.4 p.350*

Information Highways and Byways: From the Telegraph to the
  21st Century. *v.4 p.420*

The Information Mosaic. *v.4 p.106*

Information Processing and Living Systems. . . *v.5 p.96, p.97*

Information Retrieval: SciFinder and SciFinder
  Scholar. *v.5 p.255, p.256*

Information Rules: A Strategic Guide to the Network
  Economy. *v.4 p.51*

Information Security Management Handbook, Vol. 2. *v.4 p.114*

Information Security Management Handbook, Vol. 3. *v.4 p.114*

Information Security Management Handbook. *v.4 p.114*

Information Sources in Chemistry. *v.5 p.256*

Information Sources in Metallic Materials. *v.5 p.733*

Information Sources in Music. *v.1 p.166*

Information Sources in Political Science. *v.4 p.482*

Information Sources in Polymers and Plastics. . . .*v.5 p.321*

Information Sources in Science and Technology. . .*v.5 p.405*

Information Sources in the History of Science and
Medicine. *v.5 p.401*

Information Sources in the Life Sciences. *v.5 p.325*

The Information Systems Security Officer's Guide: Establishing
and Managing an Information Protection
Program. *v.4 p.113, p.114*

Information: The New Language of
Science. *v.5 p.405, p.407, p.408*

Information Theory and Coding. *v.5 p.391, p.408*

Information Theory and Evolution. *v.5 p.190*

Information Theory, Evolution and the Origin of Life. .*v.5 p.198*

Informational Biopolymers of Genes and Gene
Expression. *v.5 p.138*

The Informed Student Guide to Management Science. .*v.4 p.119*

The Informed Vision: Essays on Learning and Human
Nature. *v.4 p.339*

⬚ Infoshare Online. *v.6 p.709*

Inframundo: El Mexico de Juan Rulfo. *v.2 p.669*

Infrared Absorption Spectra, 1959-1964, 2 vols. . . .*v.5 p.270*

Infrared and Raman Spectra of Inorganic and Coordination
Compounds, Pts. A&B, Set. *v.5 p.305*

The Infrared Spectra Atlas of Monomers and Polymers. .*v.5 p.323*

The Infrared Spectra Building Blocks of Polymers. . .*v.5 p.323*

Infrared Spectra Handbook of Common Organic
Solvents. *v.5 p.297*

Infrared Spectra Handbook of Inorganic Compounds. .*v.5 p.305*

Infrared Spectra Handbook of Intermediates. *v.5 p.297*

Infrared Spectra of Complex Molecules, Vol. 2. . . .*v.5 p.270*

Infrared Spectral Interpretation: A Systematic
Approach. *v.5 p.270, p.271*

Infrastructure Risk Management Processes: Natural, Accidental,
and Deliberate Hazards. *v.5 p.686*

Ingeld and Christ: Heroic Conceptions and Values in Old
English Christian Poetry. *v.2 p.167*

El Ingenioso Hidalgo Don Quijote de la Mancha. . . .*v.2 p.646*

Ingenious Mechanisms for Designers and Inventors, Vol.
14. . . . .*v.5 p.714*

Ingenious Pursuits: Building the Scientific Revolution. .*v.3 p.47*

L' Ingratitutde: Roman. *v.2 p.540*

Ingres. *v.1 p.746, p.749*

The Inheritance. *v.6 p.661*

The Initiative and Referendum Almanac: A Comprehensive
Reference Guide to the Initiative and Referendum
Process. *v.4 p.460*

'Injuns!': Native Americans in the Movies. *v.6 p.700*

Injurious to Public Morals: Writers and the Meiji State. .*v.6 p.233*

Injury Prevention and Rehabilitation for Active Older
Adults. *v.4 p.826, p.875, p.880*

Ink into Bits: A Web of Converging
Media. *v.4 p.418, p.419, p.422*

Inka Bodies and the Body of Christ: Corpus Christi in Colonial
Cusco, Peru. *v.3 p.263, p.325*

The Inklings: C. S. Lewis, J. R. R. Tolkien, Charles Williams,
and Their Friends. *v.2 p.366*

The Inland Ground: An Evocation of the American Middle
West. *v.3 p.506*

The Innate Capacity: Mysticism, Psychology, and
Philosophy. *v.5 p.634*

Inner Asian Frontiers of China. *v.6 p.239*

The Inner Civil War: Northern Intellectuals and the Crisis of the
Union. *v.3 p.397, p.430*

The Inner Courtyard: Stories by Indian Women. . . .*v.2 p.763*

The Inner Game of Fencing: Excellence in Strategy and
Spirit. *v.4 p.857, p.877*

Inner Lives and Social Worlds: Readings in Social
Psychology. *v.5 p.646*

Inner Lives: Profiles of African American Women in
Prison. *v.6 p.277*

The Inner Man. *v.2 p.619*

The Inner Opium War. *v.6 p.188*

The Inner Quarters: Marriage and the Lives of Chinese Women
in the Sung Period. *v.6 p.186, p.217, p.452*

Inner Rhythm: Dance Training for the Deaf. *v.1 p.46*

Innocent Blood. *v.2 p.355*

Innocent Erendira: And Other Stories. *v.2 p.682*

Innocent III. *v.6 p.568, p.573*

The Innocent Traveller. *v.2 p.739*

L' Innocente (The Victim). *v.2 p.716*

The Innocents Abroad and Roughing It. *v.2 p.34*

Innovation and Entrepreneurship in State and Local
Government. *v.4 p.542*

Innovation and Entrepreneurship: Practice and Principles. .*v.4 p.67*

Innovation and Growth: Schumpeterian
Perspectives. *v.4 p.230, p.235*

Innovation in Ethnographic Film: From Innocence to
Self-Consciousness, 1955-1985. . . . .*v.6 p.310*

Innovation Patterns in Crisis and Prosperity: Schumpeter's Long
Cycle Reconsidered. *v.4 p.235*

Innovations in Educational Ethnography: Theories, Methods and
Results. *v.4 p.29*

Innovations in E-Government: The Thoughts of Governors and
Mayors. *v.4 p.546*

The Innovative Individual. *v.4 p.67*

Innovative Management: Best Practice Guidelines and Templates
for Team Planning and Learning in Action. *v.4 p.80*

Innovative Relevance: Realigning the Organization for
Profit. *v.4 p.66*

Innovators and Preachers: The Role of the Editor in Victorian
England. *v.6 p.740, p.753*

The Innovator's Dilemma: When New Technologies Cause
Great Firms to Fail. *v.4 p.51*

The Innovator's Solution: Creating and Sustaining Successful
Growth. *v.4 p.65*

Inorganic Biochemistry: An Introduction. *v.5 p.112, p.327*

Inorganic Chemical Nomenclature: Principles and
Practice. *v.5 p.301*

Inorganic Chemistry: A Modern Introduction. *v.5 p.301*

Inorganic Chemistry: An Industrial and Environmental
Perspective. .v.5 p.303

The Inorganic Chemistry of Materials: How to Make Things
Out of Elements. v.5 p.303

Inorganic Crystal Structures. v.5 p.304

Inorganic Electronic Structure and Spectroscopy, 2 v. .v.5 p.304

Inorganic Electronic Structure and Spectroscopy, Applications
and Case Studies, Vol. 2. . . . . .v.5 p.304

Inorganic Electronic Structure and Spectroscopy, Applications
and Case Studies. v.5 p.304

Inorganic Electronic Structure and Spectroscopy, Methodology,
Vol. 1. .v.5 p.304

Inorganic Electronic Structure and Spectroscopy,
Methodology. v.5 p.304

Inorganic Mass Spectrometry: Fundamentals and Applications,
Vol. 23. .v.5 p.305

Inorganic Polymers. v.5 p.301

Inorganic Preparations: A Laboratory Manual. v.5 p.304

Inorganic Reactions and Methods: Formation of Bonds to
Transition and Inner-Transition Metals, Set. v.5 p.305

Inorganic Reactions and Structure. v.5 p.304

Inorganic Syntheses. v.5 p.304

Inorganics. v.5 p.309

Input-Output Economics. v.4 p.213

Inquieta Compania. v.2 p.668

The Inquiring Organization: Tacit Knowledge, Conversation, and
Knowledge Creation Skills for 21st-Century
Organizations. v.4 p.79

Inquiring Organizations: Moving from Knowledge Management
to Wisdom. v.4 p.77

Inquiring Spirit: A New Presentation of Coleridge from His
Published and Unpublished Writings. v.2 p.279

Inquiry and Education: John Dewey and the Quest for
Democracy. v.4 p.337

Inquiry and Essays. v.1 p.450

Inquiry into the Nature and Progress of Rent and the Principles
by Which It Is Regulated: A Greenwood Archival
Edition. v.4 p.221, p.222

An Inquiry into the Nature and Progress of Rent and the
Principles by Which It Is Regulated. v.4 p.221

An Inquiry into the Nature of Peace: And the Terms of Its
Perpetuation. v.4 p.250, p.251

An Inquiry into the Nature of Peace and the Terms of its
Perpetuation. v.4 p.651

An Inquiry into the Original of Our Ideas of Beauty and Virtue:
In Two Treatises. v.1 p.450, p.484

An Inquiry into the Principles of Political Economy, Vol.
1. . . . . .v.4 p.217

Inquisition. v.3 p.57

The Inquisitive Problem Solver. v.5 p.460, p.469, p.470

The Inquisitors' Manual. v.2 p.688

Insatiability: A Novel. v.2 p.792

Insatiable Appetite: The U. S. and the Ecological Degradation of
the Tropical World. v.6 p.299

Insect Pest Management: Field and Protected
Crops. v.5 p.22, p.27

Insect Pest Management: Techniques for Environmental
Protection. v.5 p.10

Insect Pest Management. v.5 p.9, p.26

Insect Physiology and Biochemistry. v.5 p.213

Insect-Plant Biology. v.5 p.27

The Insects: An Outline of Entomology. v.5 p.213

The insects: an outline of entomology. v.5 p.213

Inside Black Australia: An Anthology of Aboriginal
Poetry. v.2 p.742, p.743

Inside Bureaucracy. v.4 p.545, p.580

Inside Charter Schools: The Paradox of Radical
Decentralization. v.4 p.298

Inside Cisco: The Real Story of Sustained M&A Growth. .v.4 p.85

Inside College: Undergraduate Education for the Future. .v.4 p.291

Inside Deaf Culture. v.4 p.709

Inside Game-Outside Game: Winning Strategies for Saving
Urban America. v.6 p.725

Inside Guzman De Alfarache. v.2 p.651

Inside Hitler's Greece: The Experience of
Occupation,1941-1944. . . . . .v.3 p.196

Inside Japanese Ceramics. v.6 p.223

Inside Lincoln's Cabinet: The Civil War Diaries of Salmon P.
Chase. v.3 p.422, p.423, p.427, p.428

Inside Lincoln's Cabinet. v.3 p.394

Inside Multi-Media Case Based Instruction. v.5 p.590

Inside Nazi Germany: Conformity, Opposition, and Racism in
Everyday Life. v.3 p.173

Inside Soviet Film Satire. v.6 p.312

Inside Sports: Using Sociology to Understand Athletes and Sport
Experiences. v.4 p.814

Inside Stalin's Secret Police: NKVD Politics,
1936-1939. . . . . .v.3 p.225

The Inside Story of the Teacher Revolution in America. .v.4 p.124

Inside Subculture: The Postmodern Meaning of Style. .v.4 p.709

Inside Sudan: Political Islam, Conflict, and Catastrophe. .v.6 p.640

Inside Tap: Technique and Improvisation for Today's Tap
Dancer. .v.1 p.32

Inside Teams: How 20 World-Class Organizations Are Winning
Through Teamwork. v.4 p.80

Inside Terrorism. v.4 p.659

Inside the Cuban Revolution: Fidel Castro and the Urban
Underground. v.3 p.313

Inside the Great House: Planter Family Life in
Eighteenth-Century Chesapeake Society. v.4 p.734

Inside the Jury (1983). v.4 p.471

Inside the Minstrel Mask: Readings in Nineteenth-Century
Blackface Minstrelsy. v.1 p.119

Inside the Mirage: America's Fragile Partnership with Saudi
Arabia. .v.3 p.390

Inside the Nuremberg Trial: A Prosecutor's Comprehensive
Account. v.3 p.87, v.4 p.477

Inside the Olympics: A Behind-the-Scenes Look at the Politics,
the Scandals, and the Glory of the
Games. v.4 p.846, p.885, p.889, p.892

Inside the Revolution: Everyday Life in Socialist Cuba. .v.4 p.41

Inside the Royal Shakespeare Company: Creativity and the
Institution. v.1 p.76, p.99, p.136, p.149

Inside the Sports Pages: Work Routines, Professional Ideologies, and the Manufacture of Sports News. *v.4 p.407*

Inside the State: The Bracero Program, Illegal Immigrants, and the INS. *v.4 p.570, v.6 p.525, p.528, p.529*

Inside the Victorian Home: A Portrait of Domestic Life in Victorian England. *v.3 p.53, v.6 p.747, p.761, p.765*

Inside the Yield Book: The Classic That Created the Science of Bond Analysis. *v.4 p.103*

The Inside-Out Stomach: An Introduction to Animals without Backbones. *v.5 p.156*

The Insider/Outsider Problem in the Study of Religion: A Reader. *v.1 p.521*

Inside. *v.2 p.529*

Insights and Illusions of Philosophy, Vol. 5. . . . . . *v.1 p.417*

Insights from Film into Violence and Oppression: Shattered Dreams of the Good Life. *v.6 p.321*

La Insolacion. *v.2 p.661*

Inspection and Monitoring Techniques for Bridges and Civil Struct. *v.5 p.693, p.694*

Inspiring Science: Jim Watson and the Age of DNA. *v.5 p.134*

Installation Art in the New Millennium: The Empire of the Senses. *v.1 p.771*

Installation Art. *v.1 p.770, p.771*

Instant Case Studies: How to Design, Adapt, and Use Case Studies in Training. *v.4 p.177*

Instant Messaging Rules: A Business Guide to Managing Policies, Security, and Legal Issues for Safe IM Communication. *v.4 p.172*

Instant Notes in Animal Biology. *v.5 p.212*

Instant Notes in Bioinformatics. *v.5 p.98, p.99*

Instant Notes in Inorganic Chemistry. *v.5 p.303*

Instant Notes in Molecular Biology. *v.5 p.128*

Instant Notes in Physical Chemistry. *v.5 p.288*

The Instinct of Workmanship and the State of the Industrial Arts. *v.4 p.251*

☐ Institute for Urban and Minority Education. . . . *v.4 p.308*

Institutional Change and Globalization. *v.4 p.261*

Institutional Design in New Democracies: Eastern Europe and Latin America. *v.4 p.504, p.505*

Institutional Investors. *v.4 p.99, p.155, p.162*

Institutions and Ethnic Politics in Africa. *v.4 p.612*

Institutions and Organizations. *v.4 p.716, p.717*

Institutions and Reform in Africa: The Public Choice Perspective. *v.4 p.612*

Institutions for Environmental Aid: Pitfalls and Promise. *v.4 p.666*

Institutions, Information and International Capital: A Political Economy of Foreign Direct Investment. . . . *v.4 p.59, p.60*

Institutions, Institutional Change and Economic Performance. *v.4 p.248*

Institutions of Advanced Societies. *v.4 p.718*

Institutions of American Democracy: The Judicial Branch. *v.4 p.534, p.535*

Institutions of Modern Spain: A Political and Economic Guide. *v.4 p.582, p.608*

Institutions of the English Novel: From Defoe to Scott. *v.2 p.189*

Institutions, Parties, and Coalitions in Argentine Politics. *v.3 p.348*

Instruction of Students with Severe Disabilities. . . . *v.4 p.318*

Instructional Design: Principles and Applications. . . *v.4 p.346*

☐ Instructional Intranet—Chicago Public Schools—Assessments. *v.4 p.285*

Instructional Models for Physical Education. *v.4 p.796*

Instructional Strategies for Secondary School Physical Education with NASPE: Moving into the Future. *v.4 p.797*

Instructional Technologies: Cognitive Aspects of Online Programs. *v.4 p.351*

Instrumental Methods for Determining Elements: Selection and Applications. *v.5 p.269*

Instrumentation Reference Book. *v.5 p.563*

Instruments and Experimentation in the History of Chemistry. *v.5 p.263*

Instruments for Clinical Health-Care Research. . . . *v.5 p.529*

Instruments in Church: A Collection of Source Documents. *v.1 p.390*

Instruments of Desire: The Electric Guitar and the Shaping of Musical Experience. *v.1 p.275, p.377, p.392*

Insult to Injury: Libel, Slander and Invasion of Privacy. *v.4 p.443*

Insurance Dictionary Illustrated. *v.4 p.163*

Insurance: From Underwriting to Derivatives. *v.4 p.163*

Insurgency and Terrorism: Inside Modern Revolutionary Warfare. *v.4 p.661*

Insurgent Collective Action and Civil War in el Salvador. *v.3 p.300*

Insurgent Cuba: Race, Nation, and Revolution, 1868-1898. . . . . *v.3 p.278, p.279, p.309*

Insurrection and Revolution: Armed Struggle in Cuba, 1952-1959. . . . . *v.3 p.309*

Integer and Combinatorial Optimization. *v.5 p.479, p.493*

Integral Equations. *v.5 p.488*

Integral Psychology: Consciousness, Spirit, Psychology, Therapy. *v.5 p.636*

The Integral Years: Poems, 1966-1994. . . . . *v.2 p.71*

Integrated Broadband Networks: TCP/IP, ATM, SDH/SONET, and WDM/Optics. *v.5 p.727*

Integrated Developmental and Life-Course Theories of Offending. *v.6 p.254*

Integrated Pest Management in the Global Arena. . . *v.5 p.10*

Integrated Pest Management: Potential, Constraints, and Challenges. *v.5 p.9*

Integrated Production, Control Systems: Management, Analysis and Design. *v.4 p.117*

Integrated Production Systems: Design, Planning, Control, and Scheduling. *v.4 p.116*

Integrated Public Lands Management: Principles and Applications to National Forests, Parks, Wildlife Refuges, and BLM Lands. *v.5 p.38*

Integrated Strategies for Drug Discovery Using Mass Spectrometry. *v.5 p.88, p.218*

An Integrated System of Classification of Flowering Plants. *v.5 p.207*

Integrating Complementary Medicine into Health Systems. *v.5 p.531*

Integrating Conventional and Alternative Therapies: Holistic Care for Chronic Conditions. *v.5 p.531*

Integrating Educational Technology into Teaching. . . .*v.4 p.352*

Integrating Human Services: Understanding the Past to Shape the Future. *v.4 p.754, p.755*

Integrating Psychology and Spirituality? *v.5 p.634*

Integrating Technology: Effective Tools for Collaboration. *v.4 p.351*

Integration of Modern Iraq. *v.6 p.603*

Integrative Assessment of Adult Personality. *v.5 p.603*

Integrative Physiology in the Proteomics and Post-Genomics Age. *v.5 p.118, p.119, p.163*

The Intellectual Adventure of Ancient Man: An Essay of Speculative Thought in the Ancient Near East. *v.3 p.4*

The Intellectual Capital of Michal Kalecki: A Study in Economic Theory and Policy. *v.4 p.211*

Intellectual Foundations of China. *v.6 p.182, p.184*

Intellectual Freedom: A Reference Handbook. *v.4 p.459*

Intellectual Growth in Young Children. *v.4 p.357*

The Intellectual Hero: Studies in the French Novel 1880. . . . .*v.2 p.462*

An Intellectual History of Islamic India. *v.1 p.553*

An Intellectual History of Psychology. *v.5 p.598*

The Intellectual Legacy of Milton Friedman, Set. . .*v.4 p.232*

Intellectual Life in the Colonial South, 1585-1763, Set. .*v.3 p.495*

The Intellectual Life of Colonial New England. *v.3 p.485*

The Intellectual Life of the British Working Classes. *v.3 p.120, v.4 p.726, v.6 p.739*

The Intellectual Life of Western Europe in the Middle Ages. *v.6 p.562*

Intellectual Origins of the English Revolution—Revisited. *v.3 p.103, p.120*

Intellectual Property Rights in Agricultural Biotechnology. .*v.5 p.7*

Intellectual Women and Victorian Patriarchy: Harriet Martineau, Elizabeth Barrett Browning, George Eliot. *v.2 p.286, v.6 p.747, p.750*

Intellectuals and the State in Modern China. *v.6 p.190*

Intellectuals and the State in Twentieth-Century Mexico. *v.3 p.291*

Intelligence and Technology: The Impact of Tools on the Nature and Development of Human Abilities. *v.5 p.588*

Intelligence, Genes and Success: Is It All in the Genes?: Scientists Respond to the Bell Curve. *v.5 p.652*

Intelligence Intervention in the Politics of Democratic States: The United States, Israel, and Britain. *v.6 p.613*

Intelligence of Apes and Other Rational Beings. . . .*v.5 p.615*

The Intelligence of Evil or the Lucidity Pact. *v.1 p.455*

Intelligence Power in Peace and War. *v.4 p.546, p.580*

Intelligence Reframed: Multiple Intelligences for the 21st Century. *v.4 p.303, v.5 p.608, p.653*

The Intelligent Ear: On the Nature of Sound and Perception. *v.5 p.607, p.608*

The Intelligent Investor: The Definitive Book on Value Investing. *v.4 p.89, p.95*

Intelligent Life in the Universe: Principles and Requirements Behind Its Emergence. *v.5 p.243*

Intelligent Vehicle Technologies. *v.5 p.716*

Intended Consequences: Birth Control, Abortion and the Federal Government in Modern America. *v.4 p.523*

Intensive Agriculture and Sustainability: A Farming Systems Analysis. *v.5 p.12*

Intensive Care: Selected and New Poems. *v.2 p.783*

Intensive Care. *v.2 p.745*

Intensive Scheduling: Restructuring America's Secondary Schools Through Time Management. *v.4 p.287*

Intentionality: An Essay in the Philosophy of Mind. . .*v.1 p.497*

Intentions and Intentionality: Foundations of Social Cognition. *v.5 p.650*

Intention. *v.1 p.491*

Interaction and the Standardized Survey Interview: The Living Questionnaire. *v.4 p.691*

Interaction Between Structural and Geotechnical Engineers. *v.5 p.698, p.699*

The Interaction of Ocean Waves and Wind. *v.5 p.430*

Interaction of the. *v.3 p.192*

Interaction Process Analysis. *v.4 p.695*

Interaction Ritual Chains. *v.4 p.694*

Interaction Ritual: Essays in Face-to-Face Behavior. . .*v.4 p.697*

Interactions: A Journey Through the Mind of a Particle Physicist and the Matter of This World. *v.5 p.543*

Interactions: The Biological Context of Social Systems. .*v.5 p.167*

Interactive Operations Research with Maple: Methods and Models. *v.5 p.683*

Interactive Storytelling: Techniques for 21st Century Fiction. *v.5 p.340, p.341*

☐ Interactive Tutorial about Diffraction. *v.5 p.283*

☐ Inter-American Development Bank-IADB. *v.3 p.259*

☐ Interbrand's Brand Glossary: The Resource for Branding and Brand Management. *v.4 p.142*

☐ Intercollegiate Atheletics Four-Year Colleges' Experiences Adding and Discontinuing Teams. . .*v.4 p.820, p.890, p.893*

Intercollegiate Athletics and the American University: A University President's Perspective. *v.4 p.821, p.893*

Intercolonial Aspects of American Culture on the Eve of the Revolution: With Special Reference to the Northern Towns. *v.3 p.368*

Intercountry Adoption from China: Examining Cultural-Heritage and Other Postadoption Issues. .*v.6 p.110, p.125, p.127, p.128*

Intercultural Communication: A Discourse Approach. . .*v.4 p.20*

Intercultural Utopias: Public Intellectuals, Cultural Experimentation, and Ethnic Pluralism in Colombia. .*v.3 p.358*

Interdisciplinary Encyclopedia of Marine Sciences. *v.5 p.429, v.6 p.284*

☐ InterDok. *v.5 p.385*

Interest and Prices: A Study of the Causes Regulating the Value of Money. *v.4 p.239, p.241*

ⓔ Interest Groups and Political Change in Israel. . .*v.4 p.615*

The Interesting Narrative of the Life of Olaudah Equiano: Written by Himself. *v.2 p.28, p.29*

An Interethnic Companion to Asian American Literature. .*v.6 p.95*

Interferometry and Synthesis in Radio Astronomy. . . .*v.5 p.67*

Interferon, or On Theater. *v.2 p.783*

Intergenerational Communication Across the Lifespan. .*v.5 p.622*

Title Index

Interim Report: On the Books Jesus & Christ. *v.1 p.641*

The Interior Castle: The Art and Life of Jean Stafford. *v.2 p.120*

The Interior Design Business Handbook: A Complete Guide to Profitability. *v.1 p.803*

Interior Design in the 20th Century. *v.1 p.800*

The Interior Distance. *v.2 p.456*

Interior Lighting for Designers. *v.1 p.803*

The Interlingual Critic: Interpreting Chinese Poetry. .*v.6 p.208*

An Intermediate Course in Probability. *v.5 p.484*

An Intermediate Greek-English Lexicon: Founded upon the 7th Edition of Liddell and Scott's Greek-English Lexicon 1889. . . . .*v.2 p.400*

Intermediate Microeconomics: A Modern Approach. .*v.4 p.249*

Intermediate Quantum Mechanics. *v.5 p.549*

Intermediate Statistics and Econometrics: A Comparative Approach. *v.4 p.203, p.204*

Internal Displacement: A Global Overview of Trends and Developments in 2005. . . . .*v.4 p.667*

Internal Factors. *v.2 p.562*

Internal Labor Markets and Manpower Analysis. . .*v.4 p.717*

Internally Displaced People: A Global Survey. *v.4 p.667, p.765*

International Advertising: Realities and Myths. . . .*v.4 p.426*

International Agreements. *v.4 p.437, p.476*

The International Almanac of Electoral History. . . .*v.4 p.577*

International and Interregional Payments Adjustment: A Synthetic View. *v.4 p.264*

International and Multicultural Organizational Communication. *v.4 p.132*

International Architecture Database. *v.1 p.711, p.782*

International Arms Control: Issues and Agreements. .*v.4 p.657*

International Assignments: An Integration of Strategy, Research, and Practice. *v.4 p.70*

International Atomic Energy Agency (IAEA). . . .*v.5 p.739*

International Bibliography of Anthropology. *v.4 p.3*

International Building Code 2006: Softcover Version. *v.1 p.785, v.5 p.685*

International Business and Society. *v.4 p.145*

International Business Information: How to Find It, How to Use It. *v.4 p.180*

International Business: the Challenge of Global Competition. *v.4 p.69*

International Code of Botanical Nomenclature (St. Louis Code): Adopted by the 16th International Botanical Congress, St. Louis August 1999. . . . .*v.5 p.207*

International Code of Botanical Nomenclature. . . .*v.5 p.207*

International Corporate Governance after Sarbanes-Oxley. *v.4 p.85*

The International Corrosion Council (ICC). . . .*v.5 p.734*

International Council of Sport Science and Physical Education. . .*v.4 p.794, p.824, p.872, p.903, p.907, p.909*

International Criminal Law. *v.6 p.268*

International Dictionary Miniature Painters, Porcelain Printers, and Silhouettists. *v.1 p.725*

International Dictionary of Adult and Continuing Education. *v.4 p.320*

International Dictionary of Architects and Architecture, Set. *v.1 p.784*

International Dictionary of Ballet, Set. *v.1 p.3*

International Dictionary of Black Composers, Set. *v.1 p.159, p.281*

International Dictionary of Broadcasting and Film. . .*v.6 p.306*

International Dictionary of Insurance and Finance. . .*v.4 p.163*

International Dictionary of Modern Dance. *v.1 p.4*

International Dictionary of Theatre: Actors, Directors and Designers. *v.1 p.141, p.145, p.147, p.153*

An International Dictionary of Theatre Language. . . .*v.1 p.59*

International Dictionary of Theatre, Set. *v.1 p.57*

International Dimensions of Organizational Behavior. *v.4 p.58, p.75*

International directory of art libraries. *v.1 p.667*

International Directory of Gay and Lesbian Periodicals. *v.6 p.361*

International Directory of Importers - Drugs and Pharmaceuticals. *v.4 p.156*

International Economic Accounts. *v.4 p.59*

International Economic Integration. *v.4 p.256*

International Education in Practice: Dimensions for Schools and International Schools. *v.4 p.313*

International Education: Its History and Promise for Today. *v.4 p.314*

International Education: Principles and Practice. . . .*v.4 p.313*

The International Education Quotations Encyclopedia. *v.4 p.339*

International Encyclopaedia of Indian Literature: Assamese. *v.6 p.148*

International Encyclopaedia of Indian Literature: Kannada. *v.6 p.147*

International Encyclopaedia of Indian Literature: Oriya. *v.6 p.148*

International Encyclopaedia of Indian Literature: Sindhi. *v.6 p.147, p.148*

International Encyclopaedia of Indian Literature: Urdu. *v.6 p.147*

International Encyclopaedia of Indian Literature, Vol. 2: Tamil. *v.6 p.147*

International Encyclopaedia of Indian Literature, Vol. VI. *v.6 p.148*

International Encyclopaedia of Indian Literature, Vol. V. *v.6 p.147*

International Encyclopedia for Women and Sports, Vol. 1. . . . .*v.4 p.834, p.843*

International Encyclopedia for Women and Sports, Vol. 2. . . . .*v.4 p.834, p.843*

International Encyclopedia for Women and Sports, Vol. 3. . . . .*v.4 p.834, p.843*

International Encyclopedia of Adult Education. *v.4 p.320*

International Encyclopedia of Composites, Set. *v.5 p.689*

International Encyclopedia of Dance. *v.1 p.3*

International Encyclopedia of Economic Sociology. . .*v.4 p.193*

The International Encyclopedia of Education, Set. *v.4 p.313, p.322*

International Encyclopedia of Environmental Politics. *v.4 p.666, v.5 p.29, v.6 p.285*

International Encyclopedia of Ergonomics and Human Factors, Set. *v.5 p.679*

International Encyclopedia of Hospitality Management. *v.4 p.161*

International Encyclopedia of Linguistics,
Set. *v.2 p.560, v.5 p.620, p.623*

International Encyclopedia of Marriage and Family,
Set. *v.5 p.638, p.639*

International Encyclopedia of National Systems of
Education. *v.4 p.313*

The International Encyclopedia of Physical Chemistry and
Chemical Physics (22 v.). *v.5 p.275*

The International Encyclopedia of Secret Societies and Fraternal
Orders. *v.4 p.719*

International Encyclopedia of Social and Behavioral
Sciences. *v.4 p.678*

International Encyclopedia of Sociology of Education. *v.4 p.762*

International Encyclopedia of Women and Sports, Set. *v.6 p.437*

International Encyclopedia of Women's Suffrage. . . *v.6 p.431*

International Environmental Law, Policy and Ethics. . *v.4 p.434*

International Exchange Rates: The Origins of International
Economics, Vol. 8. . . . .*v.4 p.255*

☐ International Federation of Sports
Medicine. *v.4 p.824, p.872, p.907, p.909*

International Finance and Accounting
Handbook. *v.4 p.88, p.104, p.155, p.162*

International Financial Economics: Corporate Decisions in
Global Markets. *v.4 p.256, p.263*

International Financial Reporting Standards Desk Reference:
Overview, Guide and Dictionary. *v.4 p.91, p.106*

The International Financial Statistics Locator: A Research and
Information Guide. *v.4 p.178, p.179, p.180*

International Fire Code 2006: Softcover
Version. *v.1 p.785, v.5 p.685*

International Folkloristics: Classic Contributions by the
Founders of Folklore. *v.2 p.584*

☐ International Gender Studies Resources. *v.6 p.436*

International Governance of War-Torn Territories: Rule and
Reconstruction. *v.4 p.628*

International Government Information and Country Information:
A Subject Guide. *v.4 p.60*

International Handbook of Behavior Modification and
Therapy. *v.5 p.666*

International Handbook of Curriculum Research. . . *v.4 p.365*

International Handbook of Early Childhood
Education. *v.4 p.314, p.359, p.369, p.370*

International Handbook of Earthquake and Engineering
Seismology. *v.5 p.442*

International Handbook of Educational Policy. . . . *v.4 p.297*

International Handbook of Educational Reform. . . . *v.4 p.325*

International Handbook of Giftedness and Talent. . . *v.4 p.317*

The International Handbook of Market Research
Techniques. *v.4 p.135*

International Handbook of Personality and Intelligence. *v.5 p.656*

International Handbook of Research and Development of
Giftedness and Talent. *v.5 p.575*

International Handbook of Trade Unions. *v.4 p.123*

International Handbook of Women's
Education. *v.4 p.301, p.313, p.314*

International Handbook on Geographical Education. . *v.4 p.377*

International Historical Statistics: Africa, Asia and Oceania,
1750-2002. . . . .*v.4 p.385*

An International History of the Recording Industry. . .*v.1 p.384*

International Human Resource Management: A Critical
Text. *v.4 p.77*

International Human Resource Management. *v.4 p.77*

International Human Rights and Authoritarian Rule in
Chile. *v.3 p.353, v.4 p.512*

☐ International Index to Black Periodicals Full Text
(IIBP). *v.6 p.14, p.34*

International Index to Film Periodicals. *v.6 p.305*

☐ International Index to Music Periodicals: IIMP Full
Text. *v.1 p.163*

International Information: Doc, Pub and Electronic Information
of International Organizations. *v.4 p.630*

International Intervention in the Greek Civil War: The United
Nations Special Committee on the Balkans,
1947-1952. . . . .*v.4 p.647, p.650*

International Investments. *v.4 p.96*

International Job Finder: Where the Jobs Are
Worldwide. *v.4 p.170*

International Journal of Transgenderism: The Official Journal of
the Harry Benjamin International Gender Dysphoria
Association. *v.6 p.361*

International Labour Migration: Historical Perspectives. *v.3 p.322*

International Law: A Dictionary. *v.4 p.476*

International Law and the Use of Force by National Liberation
Movements. *v.4 p.478, p.479, p.481*

International Law in the 21st Century: Rules for Global
Governance. *v.4 p.477*

International Logistics: Global Supply Chain Management
-. *v.4 p.118*

International Management: Culture, Strategy, and
Behavior. *v.4 p.69*

International Management. *v.4 p.57, p.64, p.180*

International Maoism in the Developing World. . . . *v.4 p.508*

International Maritime Dictionary. *v.6 p.285*

International Marketing: Strategy, Planning, Market Entry and
Implementation. *v.4 p.134*

International Mathematical Olympiads, 1986-1999. . *v.5 p.459*

International Migration and Economic Development: Lessons
from Low-Income Countries. *v.4 p.259, p.265*

International Mission Bibliography, 1960-2000. . . . *v.1 p.647*

The International Monetary System. *v.4 p.239*

The International Movie Industry. *v.6 p.345*

International Negotiation: Analysis, Approaches, Issues. *v.4 p.645*

International News and Foreign Correspondents. . . *v.4 p.414*

International News in the 21st Century. *v.4 p.407*

International Organization and Integration, Vols. 1a &
1b. *v.4 p.634*

☐ International Organization for Migration
(IOM). *v.4 p.763, p.764*

International Organizations: A Comparative Approach to the
Management of Cooperation. *v.4 p.629*

International Organizations and the Analysis of Economic
Policy, 1919-1950. . . . .*v.4 p.630*

☐ International Paralympic Comittee. *v.4 p.842, p.845*

International Personality Item Pool. *v.5 p.603*

International Perspectives in Rural Sociology. *v.4 p.772*

International Perspectives on Intercultural Education. *v.4 p.313*

International Police Cooperation: A World Perspective. *v.6 p.262*

International Political Economy and Mass Communication in Chile: National Intellectuals and Transnational Hegemony. *v.3 p.352*

International Politics: Enduring Concepts and Contemporary Issues. *v.4 p.625*

The International Politics of Eurasia: Political Culture and Civil Society in Russia and the New States of Eurasia. . *v.4 p.599*

The International Politics of Quebec Secession: State Making and State Breaking in North America. *v.3 p.543*

The International Politics of Sport in the 20th Century. *v.4 p.844, p.892, p.899*

The International Politics of the Middle East. *v.6 p.593*

International Potato Center: Centro Internacional de la Papa. *v.5 p.19*

International Psychology: Views from Around the World. *v.5 p.594*

International Radio Broadcasting: The Limits of the Limitless Medium. *v.4 p.413*

International Radio Journalism. *v.4 p.413*

International Regions and the International System: A Study in Political Ecology. *v.4 p.629*

International Relations: A Concise Companion. . . . *v.4 p.627*

International Relations in the Ancient near East, 1600-1100 B. C. *v.3 p.4*

The International Relations of the Middle East in the 21st Century: Patterns of Continuity and Change. . . . *v.6 p.593*

International Relations: The Key Concepts. *v.4 p.626*

International Residential Code 2006: Softcover Version. *v.1 p.785, v.5 p.685*

International Resources Guide to Hazardous Chemicals: Manufacturers, Agencies. Organizations, and Useful Sources of Information. *v.5 p.707*

International Sculpture Center. *v.1 p.774*

The International Secretariat: A Great Experiment in International Administration. *v.4 p.632*

International Society: Diverse Ethical Perspectives. *v.4 p.766*

International Society of Biomechanics in Sports. *v.4 p.824, p.872, p.907, p.909*

International Sports Economics Comparisons. *v.4 p.843, p.884, p.891, p.898*

International Stratigraphic Guide: A Guide to Stratigraphic Classification, Terminology, and Procedure. . . . *v.5 p.446*

International Trade and Finance: Essays in Honour of Jan Tinbergen. *v.4 p.258*

International Tribunal for the Law of the Sea. . . *v.4 p.476*

The International Tribunal for the Law of the Sea. *v.4 p.478*

An International Vocabulary of Technical Theatre Terms, in Eight Languages: American, Dutch, English, French, German, Italian, Spanish, Swedish. . . . *v.1 p.141*

International Who's Who in Classical Music. *v.1 p.172*

International Who's Who in Popular Music. *v.1 p.172*

Internationally Yours: Writing and Communicating Successfully in Today's Global Marketplace. *v.4 p.58, p.172*

The Internet and the First Amendment: Schools and Sexually Explicit Expressions. *v.4 p.449*

Internet Art. *v.1 p.771*

Internet Broadway Database. *v.1 p.57, p.92, p.111*

The Internet Challenge to Television. *v.4 p.422*

Internet Classics Archive. *v.2 p.399*

The Internet Encyclopedia of Philosophy. *v.1 p.416*

The Internet for Cell and Molecular Biologists. *v.5 p.97, p.126*

The Internet Galaxy: Reflections on the Internet, Business and Society. *v.4 p.761*

Internet Guide to International Fisheries Law. . . *v.4 p.478*

Internet Millenium Edition. *v.5 p.679*

Internet Modern History Sourcebook. *v.3 p.259*

Internet Movie Database: IMDb. *v.6 p.305*

The Internet Movie Database. *v.4 p.415*

Internet Newspapers: The Making of a Mainstream Medium. *v.4 p.417*

The Internet Public Library Online literary criticism collection. *v.2 p.163*

Internet Resources for Physical Anthropology. *v.4 p.45*

Internet Resources for Social and Cultural Anthropology. *v.4 p.45*

Internet Sources on Each U. S. State: Selected Sites for Classroom and Library. *v.3 p.484*

Internet Telephony. *v.4 p.421*

Internet Women's History Sourcebook. *v.6 p.449*

Internet4Classrooms Gateway - Biology. *v.5 p.228, p.229, p.244*

The Internship Bible. *v.4 p.170, p.171*

Internship Success: Real-World, Step-by-Step Advice on Getting the Most Out of Internships. *v.4 p.169*

Internships in Psychology: The APAGS Workbook for Writing Successful Applications and Finding the Right Match. *v.5 p.676, p.677, p.679*

Internships, Jobs and Careers in Sports Industry. . . *v.4 p.904*

Interpersonal Communication. *v.5 p.647*

The Interpersonal Context. *v.5 p.650*

Interpersonal World of the Infant: A View from Psychoanalysis and Developmental Psychology. *v.5 p.629, p.631*

Interpolation and Approximation. *v.5 p.491, p.492*

The Interpretation and Use of Rate Data: The Rate Concept. *v.5 p.743*

Interpretation of Airphotos and Remotely Sensed Imagery. *v.4 p.388*

The Interpretation of Caste. *v.4 p.723*

An Interpretation of Christian Ethics. *v.1 p.485*

Interpretation of Cultures. *v.4 p.22*

An Interpretation of Existence. *v.1 p.488*

Interpretation of Mass Spectra. *v.5 p.271*

The Interpretation of Music: Philosophical Essays. *v.1 p.381*

Interpretation of Pulmonary Function Tests: A Practical Guide. *v.5 p.518*

An Interpretation of Religion: Human Responses to the Transcendent. *v.1 p.597*

The Interpretation of Scripture in Early Judaism and
    Christianity: Studies in Language and
    Tradition. *v.1 p.615, p.616*

The Interpretation of the Fourth Gospel. *v.1 p.629*

The Interpretation of the New Testament, 1861-1986. . *v.1 p.626*

The Interpretation of Topographic Maps: A Laboratory Manual
    for Use in Connection with the Topographic Maps of
    the United States Geological Survey. to Accompany Courses
    in Physiography. *v.4 p.390*

The Interpretation of Vapor-Phase Infrared Spectra. . *v.5 p.270*

Interpretations of Conflict: Ethics, Pacifism, and the Just-War
    Tradition. *v.1 p.486*

Interpretations of Legal History. *v.4 p.433*

Interpretations of the Two Germanies,
    1945-1990. . . . . *v.3 p.176, p.177*

Interpreter of Maladies. *v.2 p.148, v.6 p.100*

The Interpreters. *v.2 p.758*

Interpreting Astronomical Spectra. *v.5 p.65*

Interpreting Infrared, Raman, and Nuclear Magnetic Resonance
    Spectra. *v.5 p.270*

Interpreting Irish History: The Debate on Historical
    Revisionism. *v.3 p.134*

Interpreting Macroeconomics: Explorations in the History of
    Economic Thought. *v.4 p.239*

Interpreting Personality Tests: A Clinical Manual for the
    MMPI-2, MCMI-III, CPI-R, And 16PF. *v.5 p.603*

Interpreting Plato. *v.4 p.490*

Interpreting Popular Music. *v.1 p.266*

Interpreting Quantitative Data with SPSS. *v.4 p.689*

Interpreting Shakespeare on Screen. *v.6 p.325*

Interpreting the Theatrical Past: Essays in the Historiography of
    Performance. *v.1 p.55, p.56, p.117, p.137*

Interpreting Women's Lives: Feminist Theory and Personal
    Narratives. *v.6 p.477*

Interracial Intimacies: Sex, Marriage, Identity, and
    Adoption. *v.4 p.442*

Interracial Intimacy: The Regulation of Race and
    Romance. *v.4 p.457, p.737, p.738*

Interracial Justice: Conflict and Reconciliation in Post-Civil
    Rights America. *v.6 p.117, p.125*

Interrelations Between the Social Environment and Psychiatric
    Disorders: Papers Presented at the 1952 Annual
    Conference of the Milbank Memorial Fund. . . . *v.5 p.671*

Interrogating Caribbean Masculinities: Theoretical and Empirical
    Analyses. *v.3 p.297*

Interrogation: Achieving Confessions Using Permissible
    Persuasion. *v.6 p.267*

Interrogations: The Nazi Elite in Allied Hands 1945. . *v.3 p.176*

Intersections Lithography: Lithography, Photography, and the
    Traditions of Printmaking. *v.1 p.760*

Intersex and Identity: The Contested Self. *v.6 p.371*

Intertextual Persuits: Literary Mediations in Modern Spanish
    Narrative. *v.2 p.641*

☐ Inter-university Consortium for Political and Social Research
    (ICPSR). *v.4 p.483, p.689*

Intervention and Underdevelopment: Greece During the Cold
    War. *v.3 p.195*

Intervention: How America Became Involved in
    Vietnam. *v.6 p.168*

Interviewing for Social Scientists: An Introductory Resource
    with Examples. *v.4 p.691*

Interviews with John Kenneth Galbraith. *v.4 p.193*

Interviews/Entrevistas. *v.6 p.400*

Interwoven Lives: Adolescent Mothers and Their
    Children. *v.4 p.735*

Intifada: The Palestinian Uprising - Israel's Third Front. *v.6 p.620*

Intifada: The Palestinian Uprising. *v.6 p.619*

Intimacy and Exclusion: Religious Politics in Pre-Revolutionary
    Baden. *v.3 p.168*

Intimacy and Terror: Soviet Diaries of The 1930s. . . *v.3 p.225*

The Intimacy Dance: A Guide to Long-Term Success in Gay
    and Lesbian Relationships. *v.6 p.374*

The Intimacy Paradox: Personal Authority in the Family
    System. *v.5 p.669*

Intimate Companions: A Triography of George Platt Lynes, Paul
    Cadmus, Lincoln Kirstein, and Their Circle. . . . *v.6 p.414*

Intimate Enemies: Jews and Arabs in a Shared Land. . *v.6 p.609*

The Intimate Enemy: Loss and Recovery of Self under
    Colonialism. *v.2 p.760*

An Intimate History of Killing: Face-to-Face Killing in
    Twentieth Century Warfare. *v.3 p.78*

Intimate Intrusions. *v.4 p.752*

Intimate Journalism: The Art and Craft of Reporting Everyday
    Life. *v.4 p.408*

Intimate Journals. *v.2 p.487*

Intimate Matters: A History of Sexuality in America. . *v.6 p.362*

Intimate Terrorism: The Crisis of Love in an Age of
    Disillusion. *v.5 p.655*

The Intimate World of Abraham Lincoln. *v.6 p.390*

Intimate Worlds: Life Inside the Family. *v.5 p.639*

Into Our Own Hands: The Women's Health Movement in the
    United States, 1969-1990. . . . . *v.5 p.524*

Into That Darkness: An Examination of Conscience. . *v.3 p.86*

Into the Land of Bones: Alexander the Great in
    Afghanistan. *v.3 p.20*

Into the Light: The Projected Image in American Art,
    1964-1977. . . . . *v.1 p.771*

Into the Porcupine Cave and Other Odysseys: Adventures of an
    Occasional Naturalist. *v.5 p.231*

Into the Woods. *v.1 p.251, p.357, p.408*

Into Thin Air: A Personal Account of the Mount Everest
    Disaster. *v.4 p.789*

Into Unknown England, 1866-1913: Selections from the Social
    Explorers. *v.6 p.742, p.761*

Intramural Recreation: A Step-by-Step Guide to Creating an
    Effective Program. *v.4 p.800*

Intrigue: Espionage and Culture. *v.2 p.191*

Introducción a la Lingüística Española. *v.2 p.635*

Introducción a la lingüistica hispánica. *v.2 p.635*

Introduccion a la Poesia de Gomez Manrique. *v.2 p.651*

Introduced Mammals of the World: Their History, Distribution
    and Influence. *v.6 p.283, p.284*

Introduced Species. *v.5 p.180*

Introducing American Folk Music: Ethnic and Grassroot Traditions in the United States. *v.1 p.296*

Introducing Camus. *v.2 p.512*

Introducing Einstein's Relativity. *v.5 p.556*

Introducing Genetics: From Mendel to Molecules. . . *v.5 p.137*

Introducing Geographic Information Systems with ArcGIS. *v.4 p.387*

Introducing Human Geographies. *v.4 p.396*

Introducing Latino/a Theologies. *v.6 p.520*

Introducing Marquis de Sade. *v.2 p.484*

Introducing Romanticism. . . . *v.2 p.171, p.172, p.183, p.568*

Introducing Sartre. *v.2 p.528*

Introducing Shakespeare. *v.2 p.227*

Introducing Social Geographies. *v.4 p.399*

Introducing Structures: Civil and Structural Engineering, Building and Architecture. *v.5 p.697*

Introducing the Apocrypha: Message, Context, and Significance. *v.1 p.623*

Introduction aux littératures francophones : Afrique, Caraïbe, Maghreb. *v.2 p.535*

Introduction à la linguistique française. *v.2 p.453*

Introduction: The Persian Period. *v.1 p.547*

Introduction to a Philosophy of Music. *v.1 p.381*

An Introduction to Aesthetics. *v.1 p.480*

Introduction to African Civilizations. *v.6 p.10*

An Introduction to African Languages. *v.6 p.80*

Introduction to African Oral Literature and Performance. *v.2 p.751, p.752*

An Introduction to African Philosophy. *v.1 p.476*

Introduction to African Religion. *v.1 p.542, v.6 p.36*

Introduction to Agricultural Economics. *v.5 p.15*

An Introduction to Agricultural Engineering. . . . *v.5 p.5, p.6*

An Introduction to Agricultural Geography. *v.4 p.395, v.5 p.4, p.12*

Introduction to AI Robotics. *v.5 p.711*

Introduction to Aircraft Design. *v.5 p.717*

Introduction to Algorithms. *v.5 p.335, p.336*

Introduction to American Music. *v.1 p.277*

Introduction to Analytic Number Theory. *v.5 p.475*

An Introduction to Applied Biogeography. *v.5 p.169*

Introduction to Applied Mathematics. *v.5 p.500*

Introduction to Approximation Theory. *v.5 p.491*

An Introduction to Arabic Literature. *v.6 p.657*

An Introduction to Astrobiology. *v.5 p.74*

Introduction to Athletic Training. *v.4 p.828*

An Introduction to Atmospheric Physics. *v.5 p.425*

Introduction to Audiology. *v.5 p.523*

Introduction to Audio. *v.1 p.388*

Introduction to Autonomous Mobile Robots. *v.5 p.339, p.342, p.712*

An Introduction to Bach Studies. . . . *v.1 p.164, p.185, p.304*

Introduction to Bayesian Statistics. *v.5 p.480*

Introduction to Biocatalysis Using Enzymes and Microorganisms. *v.5 p.119*

Introduction to Bioethics. *v.5 p.246*

Introduction to Bioinformatics: A Theoretical and Practical Approach. *v.5 p.97*

An Introduction to Bioinformatics Algorithms. *v.5 p.107, p.336, p.341*

Introduction to Bioinformatics. *v.5 p.98, p.502*

An Introduction to Biological Control. *v.5 p.27*

Introduction to Biophotonics. *v.5 p.219*

An Introduction to Biostatistics. *v.5 p.99*

Introduction to Black Studies. *v.6 p.14*

An Introduction to Book History. *v.2 p.576*

An Introduction to Botanical Nomenclature. *v.5 p.207*

Introduction to Bryology. *v.5 p.209*

An Introduction to Buddhism: Teachings, History and Practices. *v.1 p.565*

An Introduction to Buddhist Psychology. *v.5 p.633*

Introduction to Business Statistics. *v.4 p.179*

An Introduction to C. S. Peirce: Philosopher, Semiotician, and Ecstatic Naturalist. *v.1 p.440*

An Introduction to Caribbean Francophone Writing: Guadeloupe and Martinique. *v.2 p.537*

Introduction to Chemical Exposure and Risk Assessment. *v.5 p.365, p.375*

Introduction to Christian Worship. *v.1 p.655*

Introduction to Classical and Modern Optics. *v.5 p.561*

An Introduction to Classical Econometric Theory. . . *v.4 p.204*

An Introduction to Classical Korean Literature: From Hyangga to P'ansori. *v.6 p.238*

Introduction to Classical Mechanics. *v.5 p.546*

An Introduction to Coastal Processes and Geomorphology. *v.5 p.424*

An Introduction to Coding and Information Theory. . *v.5 p.335*

Introduction to Colloquial Arabic. *v.6 p.654*

Introduction to Commercial Recreation and Tourism: An Entrepreneurial Approach. *v.4 p.786, p.883*

Introduction to Communication Science and Disorders. *v.5 p.665*

Introduction to Communication Systems Simulation. . *v.5 p.724*

An Introduction to Complex Function Theory. *v.5 p.491, p.494*

Introduction to Composite Materials Design. *v.5 p.687*

An Introduction to Composite Materials. *v.5 p.689*

Introduction to Computational Biology: Maps, Sequences and Genomes. *v.5 p.342, p.502*

Introduction to Computational Earthquake Engineering. *v.5 p.694*

Introduction to Computer-Intensive Methods of Data Analysis in Biology. *v.5 p.101*

An Introduction to Confucianism. *v.1 p.418*

Introduction to Connectionist Modelling of Cognitive Proce. *v.5 p.591*

An Introduction to Contemporary Metaphysics. . . . *v.1 p.488*

An Introduction to Criminological Theory. *v.6 p.249*

An Introduction to Cultural Ecology. *v.4 p.30*

An Introduction to Database Systems. *v.5 p.337*

Introduction to Design for Civil Engineers. *v.5 p.686*

Introduction to Designing and Conducting Research. . *v.5 p.409*

Introduction to Development Economics. *v.4 p.258, p.259*

Introduction to Difference Equations: With Illustrative Examples from Economics, Psychology and Sociology. .*v.5 p.486, p.503*

An Introduction to Digital and Analog Communications. *v.5 p.725, p.726*

Introduction to Digital Astrophotography: Imaging the Universe with a Digital Camera. *v.5 p.65*

Introduction to Digital Audio. *v.1 p.388*

An Introduction to Digital Communications. *v.5 p.726*

Introduction to Documentary. *v.6 p.309*

Introduction to Dramatherapy: Ariadne's Ball of Thread. .*v.1 p.94*

Introduction to Dramatherapy: Person and Threshold. . .*v.1 p.94*

Introduction to Early Modern English. *v.2 p.552, p.554*

Introduction to Econometrics. *v.4 p.204, p.205*

An Introduction to Egyptian Colloquial Arabic. *v.6 p.654*

An Introduction to Eighteenth Century Drama, 1700-1780. . . . .*v.2 p.187*

Introduction to Electric Circuits. *v.5 p.720, p.721*

Introduction to Electrodynamics. *v.5 p.564*

Introduction to Electronic Circuit Design. . . .*v.5 p.722, p.723*

Introduction to Elementary Particles. *v.5 p.552*

Introduction to Elliptic Curves and Modular Forms. *v.5 p.476, p.497*

Introduction to Engineering Communication. *v.5 p.680*

Introduction to Engineering Materials: Behavior, Properties, and Selection, Vol. 2. . . . .*v.5 p.319, p.732*

An Introduction to English Grammar. *v.2 p.556*

An Introduction to English Poetry. *v.2 p.179, p.180*

An Introduction to Environmental Biophysics. *v.5 p.49*

An Introduction to Environmental Chemistry. *v.5 p.423*

Introduction to Environmental Management. *v.5 p.704*

Introduction to Environmental Soil Physics. *v.5 p.49*

Introduction to Environmental Toxicology. . . .*v.5 p.330, p.704*

An Introduction to Error Analysis: The Study of Uncertainties in Physical Measurements. *v.5 p.64, p.563*

Introduction to Exercise Science. *v.4 p.873*

[e] An Introduction to Fernando Pessoa: Modernism and the Paradoxes of Authorship. *v.2 p.689*

Introduction to Finite Mathematics. *v.5 p.478*

Introduction to Flight. *v.5 p.717*

An Introduction to Fluid Dynamics. *v.5 p.547*

Introduction to Food Engineering. *v.5 p.6, p.35*

Introduction to Foodservice. *v.4 p.165*

An Introduction to Forensic DNA Analysis. *v.5 p.326*

Introduction to Forensic Psychology: Clinical and Social Psychological Perspectives. *v.5 p.593*

Introduction to Forensic Psychology: Issues and Controversies in Crime and Justice. *v.5 p.591*

Introduction to Forensic Psychology: Research and Application. *v.5 p.591*

Introduction to Forest and Renewable Resources. . . .*v.4 p.164*

Introduction to Forest Resource Management. *v.5 p.38, p.41, p.354*

Introduction to French Linguistics. *v.2 p.454*

An Introduction to French Pronunciation. *v.2 p.454*

An Introduction to Fuzzy Control. *v.5 p.710*

An Introduction to Fuzzy Sets: Analysis and Design. *v.5 p.470, p.471*

An Introduction to General Systems Thinking: Silver Anniversary Edition. *v.5 p.407*

An Introduction to Genetic Analysis. *v.5 p.99, p.133*

An Introduction to Genetic Engineering. *v.5 p.136, p.218*

Introduction to Genetics. *v.5 p.136*

Introduction to Geochemistry. *v.5 p.440*

Introduction to Geodesy: The History and Concepts of Modern Geodesy. *v.5 p.443*

Introduction to Geological Data Analysis. . . .*v.5 p.419, p.420*

An Introduction to Geological Structures and Maps. *v.4 p.375, p.376,v.5 p.441*

Introduction to Geomagnetic Fields. *v.5 p.443*

Introduction to Geometry. *v.5 p.495*

An Introduction to Geophysical Exploration. *v.5 p.445*

Introduction to Geopolitics. *v.4 p.400*

Introduction to Geotechnical Engineering. *v.5 p.421*

An Introduction to Global Financial Markets. *v.4 p.58, p.98, p.102, p.103*

[e] Introduction to GPS: The Global Positioning System. *v.4 p.389, p.390*

Introduction to Graph Theory (reprint). *v.5 p.480*

Introduction to Graph Theory. *v.5 p.480*

Introduction to Green Chemistry. *v.5 p.310*

An Introduction to Gregorian Chant. *v.1 p.176, p.177*

Introduction to Health Occupations: Today's Health Care Worker. *v.5 p.533*

Introduction to Hebrew. *v.6 p.646*

An Introduction to Hegel's Logic. *v.1 p.463*

Introduction to Hegel's Philosophy of History. . . .*v.1 p.463*

Introduction to High Energy Physics. *v.5 p.552*

An Introduction to Hinduism. *v.1 p.535*

An Introduction to Historical Linguistics. *v.2 p.560*

Introduction to Homological Algebra, No. 85. . . . .*v.5 p.474*

An Introduction to Human Disease: Pathology and Pathophysiology Correlations. *v.5 p.514*

Introduction to Human Factors Engineering. *v.5 p.588*

Introduction to Human Geography: A World-Systems Approach. *v.4 p.396*

An Introduction to Human Molecular Genetics: Mechanisms of Inherited Diseases. *v.5 p.151*

An Introduction to Hydrogen Bonding. *v.5 p.277*

An Introduction to Igneous and Metamorphic Petrology. .*v.5 p.437*

Introduction to Insect Biology and Diversity. *v.5 p.26*

Introduction to Insect Pest Management. *v.5 p.10, p.27*

An Introduction to Interferometry. *v.5 p.561*

Introduction to Islamic Theology and Law. *v.1 p.557*

Introduction to Italian Poetry. *v.2 p.698*

An Introduction to Japanese Society. *v.6 p.220*

An Introduction to Kant's Ethics. *v.1 p.462, p.487*

Introduction to Kinesiology: Studying Physical Activity. *v.4 p.873, p.903*

An Introduction to Knot Theory. *v.5 p.499*

An Introduction to Koranic and Classical Arabic: An Elementary Grammar of the Language. *v.6 p.655*

An Introduction to Labor Arbitration. *v.4 p.122*

Introduction to Landscape Design. *v.1 p.817*

Introduction to Languages, Machines and Logic: Computable Machines, Abstract Machines and Formal Logic. . .*v.5 p.471*

Introduction to Lattices and Order. *v.5 p.478*

An Introduction to Legal Reasoning. *v.4 p.441*

Introduction to Leisure Services: Career Perspectives. *v.4 p.784, p.903*

Introduction to Lie Algebras and Representation Theory. *v.5 p.473*

Introduction to Limnology. *v.4 p.391*

An Introduction to Linear and Nonlinear Finite Element Analysis: A Computational Approach. *v.5 p.695*

An Introduction to Literary Studies. *v.2 p.163*

An Introduction to Logic and Scientific Method. . . .*v.1 p.492*

Introduction to Logic. *v.1 p.492, p.493*

Introduction to Machine Learning. *v.5 p.407*

Introduction to Macromolecular Science. *v.5 p.322*

Introduction to Magnetism and Magnetic Materials. . *v.5 p.566*

An Introduction to Magnetohydrodynamics. . .*v.5 p.547, p.566*

An Introduction to Malory. *v.2 p.212*

An Introduction to Materials Engineering and Science: For Chemical and Materials Engineers. *v.5 p.732*

Introduction to Mathematical Control Theory. *v.5 p.492*

Introduction to Mathematical Methods in Bioinformatics. *v.5 p.107*

Introduction to Mathematical Models in the Social and Life Sciences. *v.5 p.503*

Introduction to Mathematical Thinking: The Formation of Concepts in Modern Mathematics. *v.5 p.464, p.468*

Introduction to Mechatronics and Measurement Systems. *v.5 p.707, p.714*

Introduction to Medicinal Chemistry: How Drugs Act and Why. *v.5 p.329, p.330*

Introduction to Medieval Logic. *v.1 p.494*

Introduction to Metamathematics. *v.5 p.470*

An Introduction to Metamorphic Petrology. *v.5 p.440*

An Introduction to Metaphysics. *v.1 p.456*

Introduction to Metaphysics. *v.1 p.470*

An Introduction to Metaphysics. *v.1 p.488*

Introduction to Microelectromechanical Microwave Systems. *v.5 p.729*

Introduction to Middle English. *v.2 p.551*

An Introduction to Middle English. *v.2 p.551*

An Introduction to Mill's Utilitarian Ethics. *v.1 p.516*

An Introduction to Modern Astrophysics. *v.5 p.66*

Introduction to Modern Biochemistry. *v.5 p.327*

Introduction to Modern Bulgarian Literature: An Anthology of Short Stories. *v.2 p.779, p.780*

An Introduction to Modern Cosmology. *v.5 p.72*

Introduction to Modern Inorganic Chemistry. *v.5 p.301*

An Introduction to Modern Literary Arabic. *v.6 p.653*

Introduction to Modern Optics. *v.5 p.561*

Introduction to Modern Polish Literature. *v.2 p.787*

Introduction to Modern Statistical Mechanics. *v.5 p.558*

Introduction to Molecular Biology. *v.5 p.125*

Introduction to Molecular Biophysics. *v.5 p.125*

An Introduction to Molecular Biotechnolo: From Molecular Biological Fundmentals to Methoda and Applications in Modern Biotechnology. *v.4 p.157*

An Introduction to Molecular Medicine and Gene Therapy. *v.5 p.149, p.152*

Introduction to Molecular Medicine. *v.5 p.151*

An Introduction to Molecular Orbitals. *v.5 p.304*

Introduction to Mongolian History and Culture. *v.6 p.240*

An Introduction to Mormonism. *v.1 p.587*

An Introduction to Morse Theory. *v.5 p.499*

Introduction to Multicultural Counseling. *v.5 p.637*

Introduction to Multidimensional Scaling: Theory, Methods, and Applications. *v.5 p.599*

An Introduction to Music Therapy: Theory and Practice.*v.1 p.406*

Introduction to Neural and Cognitive Modeling. *v.5 p.591*

Introduction to Newton's Principia. . .*v.5 p.546, p.555, p.556*

An Introduction to Nietzsche as Political Thinker: The Perfect Nihilist. *v.4 p.490, p.491*

☑ Introduction to Nondestructive Testing: A Training Guide. *v.5 p.690*

Introduction to Nonlinear Differential and Integral Equations. *v.5 p.486, p.488*

Introduction to Non-Linear Optimization. *v.5 p.493*

Introduction to Nuclear Engineering. *v.5 p.740*

An Introduction to Nuclear Physics. *v.5 p.553*

An Introduction to Ocean Remote Sensing. .*v.4 p.389, v.5 p.428*

An Introduction to Old French. *v.2 p.453, p.454*

Introduction to Operations Research. *v.5 p.493*

Introduction to Optical Engineering. *v.5 p.702*

Introduction to Optics and Lasers in Engineering. .*v.5 p.701, p.730*

Introduction to Optics. *v.5 p.561*

Introduction to Ore-Forming Processes. *v.5 p.450*

An Introduction to Ottoman Poetry. *v.6 p.666*

Introduction to Palaeoecology. *v.5 p.449*

Introduction to Percolation Theory. *v.5 p.559*

An Introduction to Persian Literature. *v.6 p.672*

Introduction to Phase Transitions and Critical Phenomena. *v.5 p.559*

Introduction to Phenomenology. *v.1 p.511*

Introduction to Philosophical Hermeneutics. *v.1 p.507*

An Introduction to Philosophical Logic. *v.1 p.492*

An Introduction to Phonetics and Phonology. *v.2 p.559*

Introduction to Phosphorus Chemistry. *v.5 p.296*

Introduction to Physical Education and Sport: Foundations and Trends with Introduction to Careers in Health, Physical Education and Sport. *v.4 p.794, p.903*

Introduction to Physical Oceanography. . .*v.4 p.392, v.5 p.430*

Introduction to Physical Therapy. *v.5 p.535*

Introduction to Plant Pathology. *v.5 p.47*

Introduction to Plasma Physics and Controlled Fusion: Plasma and Physics. *v.5 p.566*

Introduction to Plasma Physics: With Space and Laboratory Applications. . . . . *.v.5 p.566*

Introduction to Plasma Theory. . . . . *.v.5 p.566*

An Introduction to Plato's Laws. . . . . . . *.v.4 p.489, p.490*

An Introduction to Plato's Republic. . . . *.v.1 p.423, v.4 p.488*

Introduction to Political Psychology. . . . *.v.4 p.483, v.5 p.642*

Introduction to Population Biology. . . . . *.v.5 p.170*

Introduction to Positive Philosophy. . . . . . *.v.1 p.455, p.511*

An Introduction to Postcommunist Bulgaria: Political, Economic and Social Transformation. . . . . *.v.3 p.251*

Introduction to Post-Tonal Theory. . . . . *.v.1 p.374*

Introduction to Practical Linear Programming. . . . *.v.5 p.683*

An Introduction to Probability and Inductive Logic. . . . . *.v.5 p.470, p.484*

An Introduction to Probability Theory and Its Applications, Vol. 1. . . . . *.v.5 p.484*

An Introduction to Probability Theory and Its Applications, Vol. 2. . . . . *.v.5 p.484*

Introduction to Probability Theory. . . . . *.v.5 p.484*

Introduction to Proteomics: Tools for the New Biology. *.v.5 p.117*

Introduction to Quantum Field Theory. . . . . . . *.v.5 p.550*

Introduction to Quantum Mechanics in Chemistry. . . *.v.5 p.279*

Introduction to Quantum Mechanics with Applications to Chemistry. . . . . *.v.5 p.550*

Introduction to Quantum Mechanics. . . . . *.v.5 p.549*

An Introduction to Quantum Physics. . . . . *.v.5 p.549*

Introduction to Queueing Theory. . . . . *.v.5 p.683*

Introduction to Rabbinic Literature. . . . . *.v.1 p.550*

An Introduction to Radio Astronomy. . . . . *.v.5 p.67*

Introduction to Radiologic Sciences and Patient Care. *.v.5 p.534*

Introduction to Recreation Services for People with Disabilities: A Person-Centered Approach. . . . *.v.4 p.785, p.829, p.842*

An Introduction to Regression Graphics. . . . . . . *.v.5 p.483*

Introduction to Remote Sensing. . . . . *.v.4 p.388*

An Introduction to Rights. . . . . *.v.4 p.512, p.669*

Introduction to Risk Management and Insurance. . . *.v.4 p.163*

Introduction to Robotics: Analysis, Systems, Applications. . . . . *.v.5 p.711*

Introduction to Robotics in CIM Systems. . . . . . *.v.5 p.712*

Introduction to Robotics: Mechanics and Control. . . *.v.5 p.710*

An Introduction to Roman Religion. . . . . *.v.1 p.533, v.3 p.24*

Introduction to Schenkerian Analysis: Form and Content in Tonal Music. . . . . *.v.1 p.370*

Introduction to Seismology, Earthquakes and Earth Structure. . . . . *.v.5 p.442, p.443, p.444*

An Introduction to Shakespeare's Poems. . . . . . *.v.2 p.230*

Introduction to Shell Structures: The Art and Science of Vaulting. . . . . *.v.5 p.698*

Introduction to Soil Chemistry: Analysis and Instrumentation. . . . . *.v.5 p.49*

Introduction to Solid State Physics. . . . . *.v.5 p.554*

Introduction to Solid-State Theory. . . . . . *.v.5 p.554, p.555*

Introduction to Space Flight. . . . . *.v.5 p.719*

An Introduction to Spanish Literature. . . . . . . *.v.2 p.639*

Introduction to Spanish Poetry. . . . . *.v.2 p.643*

An Introduction to Spanish-American Literature. . . . *.v.2 p.664*

Introduction to Special Relativity. . . . . *.v.5 p.558*

Introduction to Stage Lighting: The Fundamentals of Theatre Lighting Design. . . . . *.v.1 p.149*

Introduction to Statistical Theory. . . . . *.v.5 p.482*

Introduction to Stellar Astrophysics: Basic Stellar Observations and Data, Vol. 1. . . . . *.v.5 p.70*

Introduction to Stellar Astrophysics, Vol. 2. . . . . . *.v.5 p.70*

Introduction to Stellar Astrophysics, Vol. 3. . . . . . *.v.5 p.70*

Introduction to Stereochemistry and Conformational Analysis. *.v.5 p.298*

An Introduction to Stochastic Processes with Biology Applications. . . . . *.v.5 p.501*

Introduction to Stochastic Processes. . . . . *.v.5 p.484*

Introduction to Structural Analysis and Design. . . . *.v.5 p.696*

Introduction to Structural Biology. . . . . *.v.5 p.115*

Introduction to Structural Dynamics and Aeroelasticity. *.v.5 p.718*

An Introduction to Structured Population Dynamics. . . . . *.v.5 p.183, p.188*

Introduction to Superconductivity. . . . . *.v.5 p.565*

An Introduction to Support Vector Machines and Other Kernel-Based Learning Methods. . . . . *.v.5 p.407*

Introduction to Supramolecular Chemistry. . . . . . *.v.5 p.299*

Introduction to Symbolic Logic and Its Applications. . . . . *.v.1 p.491, p.492*

Introduction to Syriac: An Elementary Grammar with Readings from Syriac Literature. . . . . *.v.6 p.652, p.653*

Introduction to Systems Biology and the Design Principles of Biological Circuits. . . . . . *.v.5 p.125, p.138, p.144, p.148*

[e] Introduction to Telecommunications Network Engineering. . . . . *.v.4 p.115*

Introduction to Telecommunications Networks. . . . *.v.5 p.726*

Introduction to Telecommunications. . . . . *.v.5 p.724*

Introduction to the Algae. . . . . *.v.5 p.208*

An Introduction to the Analysis of Spin-Spin Splitting in High-Resolution Nuclear Magnetic Resonance Spectra. *.v.5 p.272*

An Introduction to the Anthropology of Melanesia: Culture and Tradition. . . . . *.v.4 p.43*

Introduction to the Art of Playing on the Piano Forte; Containing the Elements of Music, Preliminary Notions on Fingering, and Fifty Fingered Lessons. . . *.v.1 p.397, p.400*

Introduction to the Art of Singing by Johann Friedrich Agricola. . . . . *.v.1 p.182, p.394, p.399*

Introduction to the Biology of Marine Life. . . . . . *.v.5 p.172*

Introduction to the Bootstrap. . . . . *.v.5 p.482*

An Introduction to the Canterbury Tales: Fiction, Writing, Context. . . . . *.v.2 p.210*

An Introduction to the Christian Orthodox Churches. *.v.1 p.569*

Introduction to the Code of Maimonides (Mishneh Torah). *.v.1 p.550*

Introduction to the Dance. . . . . *.v.1 p.5*

Introduction to the Devout Life. . . . . *.v.1 p.576*

An Introduction to the French Caribbean Novel. . . . *.v.2 p.537*

An Introduction to the French Poets: Villon to the Present Day. . . . . *.v.2 p.460*

An Introduction to the Gospel of John. . . . . *.v.1 p.628*

An Introduction to the Grammar of English: Syntactic
Arguments and Socio-Historical Background. . . . *v.2 p.552*

An Introduction to the Greek Theatre. *v.1 p.70, p.88, p.89*

Introduction to the Health Professions. *v.5 p.533, p.534*

Introduction to the Hebrew Bible. *v.1 p.619*

Introduction to the History of African Civilization: Colonial and
Post-Colonial Africa. *v.6 p.53*

Introduction to the History of African Civilization: Precolonial
Africa. *v.6 p.53*

Introduction to the History of Christianity. *v.1 p.598*

An Introduction to the History of English Medieval
Towns. . . . . *.v.6 p.577*

An Introduction to the History of Mathematics. *.v.5 p.465, p.466*

An introduction to the history of structural mechanics: Pt. 1:
Statics and resistance of solids. *v.5 p.693*

An Introduction to the History of Structural Mechanics: Vaulted
Structures and Elastic Systems. *v.5 p.693*

Introduction to the Human Sciences: An Attempt to Lay a
Foundation for the Study of Society and History. . *v.1 p.464*

An Introduction to the International Criminal Court. . *v.6 p.268*

An Introduction to the Logic of the Sciences. *v.5 p.402*

An Introduction to the Mathematical Theory of Waves. *v.5 p.501*

An Introduction to the Mathematics of Biology: With Computer
Algebra Models. *v.5 p.502, p.503*

An Introduction to the Music of Milton Babbit. *v.1 p.218, p.302*

Introduction to the New Testament: History and Literature of
Early Christianity. *v.1 p.627*

Introduction to the New Testament: History, Culture, and
Religion of the Hellenistic Age. *v.1 p.626*

An Introduction to the New Testament. *v.1 p.624*

Introduction to the New Testament. *v.1 p.624*

Introduction to the Old Testament As Scripture. . . . *v.1 p.618*

Introduction to the Old Testament: The Canon and the Christian
Imagination. *v.1 p.618*

An Introduction to the Philosophy of Art. *v.1 p.479*

An Introduction to the Philosophy of Law [1922]. . . *v.4 p.434*

An Introduction to the Philosophy of Mind. *v.1 p.497*

Introduction to the Philosophy of Science: Cutting Nature at Its
Seams. *v.5 p.403*

An Introduction to the Physical Chemistry of Biological
Organization. *v.5 p.114*

An Introduction to the Physics of Particle Accelerators. *v.5 p.552*

An Introduction to the Principles of Morals and
Legislation. *v.1 p.444, p.445, p.491*

Introduction to the Reading of Hegel: Lectures on the
Phenomenology of Spirit. *v.1 p.464*

Introduction to the Science of Sociology. *v.4 p.680*

Introduction to the Sociology of Music. *v.1 p.376*

An Introduction to the Structure of Biological
Molecules. *v.5 p.326*

An Introduction to the Study of Medieval Latin
Versification. *v.2 p.449*

Introduction to the Talmud and Midrash. *v.1 p.551*

Introduction to the Theory of Computation. *v.5 p.337*

Introduction to the Theory of Employment. . . *v.4 p.253, p.270*

Introduction to the Theory of Error-Correcting Codes. *v.5 p.477*

An Introduction to the Theory of Groups. . . . . . . *.v.5 p.475*

An Introduction to the Theory of Mental and Social
Measurements. . . . . *.v.5 p.599*

Introduction to the Theory of Numbers. *v.5 p.476*

An Introduction to the Theory of Numbers. . . *v.5 p.476, p.477*

Introduction to the Thought of Karl Popper. *v.1 p.445*

Introduction to the U. S. Latina and Latino Religious
Experience. *v.1 p.607, v.6 p.519*

An Introduction to the World's Oceans. *v.5 p.429*

Introduction to Theoretical Ecology. *v.5 p.503*

Introduction to Theoretical Mechanics. *v.5 p.546*

Introduction to Theoretical Organic Chemistry and Molecular
Modelling. *v.5 p.293*

Introduction to Thermal Physics. *v.5 p.560*

Introduction to Topology and Modern Analysis. *v.5 p.489, p.499*

Introduction to Topology. *v.5 p.499*

An Introduction to Toxicogenomics. *v.5 p.126*

Introduction to Transportation Engineering: A Multimodal
Integration. *v.5 p.700*

An Introduction to Twentieth-Century Czech Fiction: Comedies
of Defiance. *v.2 p.782*

An Introduction to Twentieth-Century French
Literature. *v.2 p.459*

An Introduction to Twentieth-Century Poetry in
English. *v.2 p.184*

An Introduction to Ultra Wideband Communication
Systems. *v.5 p.727*

An Introduction to Virgil's Aeneid. *v.2 p.446*

Introduction to VLSI Circuits and Systems. *v.5 p.723*

Introduction to Voltammetic Analysis. *v.5 p.273*

Introduction to Wildland Fire. *v.5 p.31*

Introduction to World Peace Through World Law. . . *v.4 p.635*

Introduction to World Religions. *v.1 p.525*

Introductory Biostatistics. *v.5 p.100*

Introductory Chemistry for the Environmental Sciences. *v.5 p.310*

Introductory Circuit Analysis. *v.5 p.720*

Introductory Combinatorics. *v.5 p.478*

Introductory Discrete Mathematics. *v.5 p.477*

Introductory Dynamical Oceanography. *v.5 p.430*

Introductory Econometrics: A Modern Approach. . . *v.4 p.205*

Introductory Econometrics for Finance. *v.4 p.198*

Introductory Econometrics with Applications. *v.4 p.204*

☐ Introductory Guide to Critical Theory. . . *v.2 p.163, p.567*

Introductory Mathematical Analysis for Business, Economics
and the Life and Social Sciences. . . . *v.4 p.175, v.5 p.503*

Introductory Mining Engineering. *v.5 p.738*

Introductory Modern Algebra: A Historical
Approach. *v.5 p.468, p.474*

Introductory Mycology. *v.5 p.209*

Introductory Nuclear Physics. *v.5 p.554*

Introductory Polymer Chemistry. *v.5 p.322*

Introductory Quantum Mechanics. *v.5 p.550*

Introductory Statistical Mechanics. *v.5 p.558*

Introductory Structural Analysis. *v.5 p.696*

The Intruders: Unreasonable Searches and Seizures from King
John to John Ashcroft. *v.4 p.473*

Intuition and Science. *v.5 p.400, p.401*

Intuition: Its Powers and Perils. *v.5 p.608, p.609*

Intuitive Topology. *v.5 p.499*

An Invariant Approach to Statistical Analysis of Shapes. .*v.5 p.100*

Invasion Ecology. *v.5 p.186, p.187*

The Invasion of America: Indians, Colonialism, and the Cant of
Conquest. *v.3 p.485, v.6 p.684, p.686*

[e] The Invasion of Indian Country in the Twentieth Century:
American Capitalism and Tribal Natural Resources. .*v.6 p.295*

Invasions of the Land: The Transitions of Organisms from
Aquatic to Terrestrial Life. *v.5 p.198*

Invasive Alien Species: A New Synthesis. *v.5 p.180*

Invasive Exotic Species in the Sonoran Region. *v.5 p.181*

Invasive Plant Species of the World: A Reference Guide to
Environmental Weeds. *v.5 p.6, v.6 p.287*

Invasive Species in a Changing World. . . .*v.5 p.180, v.6 p.292*

Invasive Species: Vectors and Management Strategies. .*v.5 p.181*

Invectives. *v.2 p.706*

Invented Lives: The Marriage of F. Scott and Zelda
Fitzgerald. *v.2 p.77*

Invented Truth: Soviet Reality and the Literary Imagination of
Iurii Trifonov. *v.2 p.810*

Inventing AIDS. *v.6 p.379*

Inventing America: Jefferson's Declaration of
Indepedence. *v.3 p.410*

Inventing America: Spanish Historiography and the Formation
of Eurocentrism. *v.3 p.264*

Inventing Black-on-Black Violence: Discourse, Space, and
Representation. *v.6 p.257*

Inventing Boundaries: Gender, Politics and the Partition of
India. *v.6 p.157*

Inventing Champagne: The Worlds of Lerner and
Loewe. *v.1 p.251, p.252, p.336, p.337, p.338*

Inventing Criminology: Essays on the Rise of 'Homo
Criminalis'. *v.6 p.249*

Inventing Eastern Europe: The Map of Civilization on the Mind
of the Enlightenment. *v.3 p.72, p.207*

Inventing High and Low: Literature, Mass Culture and Uneven
Modernity in Spain. *v.2 p.642*

Inventing Home: Emigration, Gender, and the Middle Class in
Lebanon, 1870-1920. . . . .*v.6 p.605*

Inventing Iraq: The Failure of Nation-Building and a History
Denied. *v.4 p.643, v.6 p.602*

Inventing Modern: Growing up with X-Rays, Skyscrapers, and
Tailfins. *v.5 p.406, p.410*

Inventing Personality: Gordon Allport and the Science of
Selfhood. *v.5 p.597*

Inventing Polymer Science: Staudinger, Carothers, and the
Emergence of Macromolecular Chemistry. *v.5 p.322*

Inventing the Business of Opera: The Impresario and His World
in Seventeenth-Century Venice. . . .*v.1 p.184, p.229, p.384*

Inventing the Dream: California Through the Progressive
Era. *v.3 p.532*

Inventing the French Revolution: Essays on French Political
Culture in the Eighteenth Century. *v.3 p.149*

Inventing the Modern Artist: Art and Culture in Gilded Age
America. *v.1 p.682*

Inventing the Victorians. *v.6 p.749*

Inventing Vietnam: The War in Film and Television. . .*v.6 p.321*

Inventing Wonderland: Victorian Childhood as Seen Through the
Lives and Fantasies of Lewis Carroll, Edward Lear, J. M.
Barrie, Kenneth Grahame, and A. A. Milne. . . .*v.2 p.177*

Inventing Wyatt Earp: His Life and Many Legends. . .*v.3 p.526*

The Invention of Art: A Cultural History. *v.1 p.704*

The Invention of Heterosexuality. *v.6 p.372*

The Invention of Journalism Ethics: The Path to Objectivity and
Beyond. *v.4 p.406*

The Invention of Liberty, 1700-1789. . . . .*v.2 p.459*

The Invention of Painting in America. *v.1 p.729, p.733*

The Invention of Peace: Reflections on War and International
Order. *v.4 p.647, p.649*

The Invention of Racism in Classical Antiquity. *v.3 p.3*

The Invention of the Italian Renaissance Printmaker. .*v.1 p.753*

The Invention of the Modern Hospital, Boston,
1870-1930. . . . .*v.5 p.514*

The Invention of the United States Senate. *v.4 p.534*

The Invention of the West: Joseph Conrad and the
Double-Mapping of Europe and Empire. *v.2 p.341*

The Invention of the Western Film: A Cultural History of the
Genre's First Half Century. *v.6 p.324*

The Invention of the White Race: Racial Oppression and Social
Control. *v.4 p.731*

The Invention of the White Race: The Origins of Racial
Oppression in Anglo-America, Vol. II. *v.4 p.729*

The Invention of Tradition. *v.3 p.61*

Inventions and Inventors, Vol. 2. . . . . . .*v.5 p.683, p.684*

Inventions of Teaching: A Genealogy. *v.4 p.339*

Inventory and Supply Chain Management with Forecast
Updates. *v.4 p.118*

Inventory Classification Innovation: Paving the Way for
Electronic Commerce and Vendor Managed
Inventory. *v.4 p.116, p.117*

Inventory of Longitudinal Studies in the Social
Sciences. *v.4 p.689*

Inventory of World Topographic Mapping: The International
Cartographic Association. *v.4 p.390*

Inverse Problems in the Mathematical Sciences. *v.5 p.488*

Invertebrate Palaeontology and Evolution. *v.5 p.447*

Invertebrate Zoology: A Functional Evolutionary
Approach. *v.5 p.156, p.157, p.196, p.213*

Invertebrate Zoology. *v.5 p.212, p.213*

The Invertebrates: An Illustrated Glossary. . . .*v.5 p.96, p.157*

Invertebrates as Webmasters in Ecosystems. *v.5 p.212*

Investigated Reporting: Muckrakers, Regulators and the Struggle
over Television Documentary. *v.4 p.408*

Investigating Disease Patterns: The Science of
Epidemiology. *v.5 p.365*

Investigating Gender: Contemporary Perspectives in
Education. *v.4 p.301*

Investigating Linguistic Acceptability. *v.2 p.553*

Investigations in Currency and Finance. *v.4 p.231*

Investigations into the Method of the Social Sciences. .*v.4 p.234*

Investigations. *v.5 p.127*

Investigative Journalism: Context and Practice. *v.4 p.408*

The Investigative Reporter's Handbook: A Guide to Documents, Databases and Techniques. *v.4 p.408*

Investigative Reporting for Print and Broadcast. *v.4 p.408*

Investing by the Numbers. *v.4 p.205*

Investing in Biotechnology Stocks. *v.5 p.218*

Investing Online for Dummies®. *v.4 p.97*

The Investiture Controversy: Church and Monarchy from the Ninth to the Twelfth Century. *v.1 p.572*

Investment and Production: A Study in the Theory of the Capital-Using Enterprise. *v.4 p.248*

Investment in Learning: The Individual and Social Value of American Higher Education. *v.4 p.289, p.330*

Investment Management. *v.4 p.94, p.162*

Investment Statistics Locator. *v.4 p.178*

▢ Investopedia - Your Source for Investment Education. *v.4 p.93, p.101, p.102*

Investor Capitalism: How Money Managers Are Changing the Face of Corporate America. *v.4 p.90*

The Investor's Anthology: Original Ideas from the Industry's Greatest Minds. *v.4 p.94*

▢ The Investor's Clearinghouse. *v.4 p.93*

▢ InvestorWords.com. *v.4 p.93, p.101, p.102*

The Invisible Art of Film Music: A Comprehensive History. *v.1 p.256*

Invisible Bride: Poems. *v.2 p.160, p.161, p.163*

Invisible Cities. *v.2 p.714, v.6 p.730*

The Invisible Code: Honor and Sentiment in Postrevolutionary France, 1814-1848. . . . .*v.3 p.153*

The Invisible Continent: Four Strategic Imperatives of the New Economy. *v.4 p.70*

Invisible Farmers: Women in Agricultural Production. . *v.5 p.13*

Invisible Genealogies: A History of Americanist Anthropology. *v.4 p.4*

The Invisible Heart: An Economic Romance. *v.4 p.185*

The Invisible Heart: Economics and Family Values. . .*v.4 p.273*

Invisible Lives: Social Worlds of the Aged. *v.4 p.742*

Invisible Lives: The Erasure of Transsexual and Transgendered People in the Cultural and Institutional World. . . .*v.6 p.371*

The Invisible Man: The Life and Liberties of H. G. Wells. *v.2 p.319*

Invisible Man. *v.2 p.144*

The Invisible Man. *v.2 p.320*

Invisible Man. *v.6 p.24*

The Invisible Medium: Commercial, Public and Community Radio. *v.4 p.413*

Invisible Natives: Myth and Identity in the American Western. *v.6 p.324, p.700*

The Invisible People: How the U. S. Has Slept Through the Global AIDS Pandemic, the Greatest Humanitarian Catastrophe of Our Time. *v.4 p.769, p.770*

Invisible Punishment: The Collateral Consequences of Mass Imprisonment. *v.6 p.249*

Invisible Relations: Representations of Female Intimacy in the Age of Enlightenment. *v.2 p.173*

An Invisible Spectator: A Biography of Paul Bowles. . .*v.2 p.62*

The Invisible Woman: Gender, Crime, and Justice. . .*v.6 p.260*

An Invitation to Algebraic Geometry. *v.5 p.497*

An Invitation to Ethnomethodology: Language, Society and Interaction. *v.4 p.688*

Invitation to Sociology: A Humanistic Perspective. . .*v.4 p.679*

Invitation to the Mathematics of Fermat-Wiles. *v.5 p.476*

Invitation to Vernacular Architecture: A Guide to the Study of Ordinary Buildings and Landscapes. *v.1 p.822*

Invitations to Love: Literacy, Love Letters, and Social Change in Nepal. *v.6 p.163*

Invoking the Past: The Uses of History in South Asia. *v.6 p.145*

Involvement by Invitation: American Strategies of Containment in Iran. *v.3 p.392*

Involving Community Members in Focus Groups. . . *v.4 p.136*

Inward Bound: Of Matter and Forces in the Physical World. *v.5 p.540*

Iola Leroy, or Shadows Uplifted. *v.2 p.39*

The IOMA Handbook of Logistics and Inventory Management. *v.4 p.118*

Ion and Hippias Major: Two Comic Diaglogues. . . *v.1 p.425*

Ion Barbu. *v.2 p.816*

Ion Exchange in Analytical Chemistry. *v.5 p.269*

Ionian Vision: Greece in Asia Minor, 1919-1922. . .*v.3 p.196*

Ionic Equilibrium: Solubility and pH Calculations. . .*v.5 p.281*

Ionization Constants of Inorganic Acids and Bases in Aqueous Solution, No.29. . . . .*v.5 p.302*

Ionization Constants of Organic Acids in Aqueous Solution. *v.5 p.300*

Ion-Molecule Reactions. *v.5 p.279*

Ions in Solution. *v.5 p.281*

Ion. *v.2 p.817*

Iowa: A Guide to the Hawkeye State. *v.3 p.522*

Iowa Interiors. *v.2 p.117*

Iowa: The Middle Land. *v.3 p.522*

Iowa. *v.3 p.522*

IP Convergence: The Next Revolution in Telecommunications. *v.4 p.422*

Iphigenia in Tauris. *v.2 p.411*

IPM for Gardeners: A Guide to Integrated Pest Management. *v.5 p.43*

IR and NMR spectral data-structure correlations for the carbonyl group. *v.5 p.270*

Ira Aldridge, the Negro Tragedian. *v.1 p.123, p.145*

Ira Gershwin: The Art of the Lyricist. *v.1 p.249, p.325*

Iracema. *v.2 p.689*

Iran and the Rise of Reza Shah: From Qajar Collapse to Pahlavi Power. *v.6 p.631*

Iran Between Two Revolutions. *v.6 p.630*

Iran: From Religious Dispute to Revolution. *v.6 p.631*

Iran, Saudi Arabia and the Gulf: Power Politics in Transition. *v.4 p.640, p.641*

Iran-Contra: The Final Report. *v.3 p.481*

The Iranian Constitutional Revolution, 1906-1911: Grassroots Democracy, Social Democracy, and the Origins of Feminism. *v.4 p.616, v.6 p.630*

Iranian History and Politics: State and Society in Perpetual
    Conflict. *v.6 p.629*

Iranian Jewry's Hour of Peril and
    Heroism. *v.6 p.597, p.598, p.629*

The Iranian Revolution: Its Global Impact. *v.6 p.632*

Iraq after the Muslim Conquest. *v.6 p.602*

Iraq Between the Two World Wars: The Militarist Origins of
    Tyranny. *v.6 p.603, p.604*

Iraq from Monarchy to Tyranny: from the Hashemites to the
    Rise of Saddam. *v.6 p.602*

☐ Iraq Index. *v.4 p.616*

Iraq: Sanctions and Beyond. *v.6 p.604*

Iraq since 1958: From Revolution to Dictatorship. . . .*v.6 p.602*

The Iraq War: Hidden Agendas and Babylonian Intrigue: The
    Regional Impact on Shi'ites, Kurds, Sunnis and
    Arabs. *v.6 p.604*

Iraqi Jews: A History of the Mass Exodus. . . .*v.6 p.598, p.603*

Iraqi Kurdistan: Political Development and Emergent
    Democracy. *v.6 p.604*

Iraqi Revolution of 1958: The Old Social Classes
    Revisited. *v.6 p.602*

Iraq's Crime of Genocide: The Anfal Campaign Against the
    Kurds. *v.6 p.598, p.599, p.603*

Iraq's Road to War. *v.6 p.604*

Ireland, 1912-1985: Politics and Society. *v.3 p.139*

Ireland and the Great War. *v.3 p.138*

Ireland and the Jacobite Cause, 1685-1766: A Fatal
    Attachment. *v.3 p.137*

Ireland and the Vatican. *v.3 p.138*

Ireland Before and after the Famine: Explorations in Economic
    History, 1800-1925. . . . .*v.3 p.139*

Ireland in the Age of the Tudors, 1447-1603: English Expansion
    and the End of Gaelic Rule. *v.3 p.136*

Ireland since the Famine. *v.3 p.135*

Ireland's Painters, 1600-1940. . . . .*v.1 p.731*

Ireland. *v.5 p.237*

Irenaeus of Lyons. *v.1 p.612*

Iris Murdoch: A Life. *v.2 p.372*

Iris Murdoch Revisited. *v.2 p.372*

Iris Murdoch. *v.2 p.371, p.372*

Irish Art. *v.1 p.685*

The Irish Counter-Revolution, 1921-36: Treatyite Politics and
    Settlement in Independent Ireland. *v.3 p.139*

The Irish Countryman: An Anthropological Study. . . .*v.4 p.41*

The Irish Diaspora: A Primer. *v.3 p.133*

Irish Emigration and Canadian Settlement: Patterns, Links, and
    Letters. *v.3 p.542*

The Irish Famine: A Documentary History. *v.3 p.139*

Irish Folk-History Plays. *v.2 p.288*

Irish Home Rule, 1867-1921. . . . .*v.3 p.139*

The Irish in Philadelphia: Ten Generations of Urban
    Experience. *v.3 p.492, v.6 p.711*

ⓔ The Irish in the South, 1815-1877. . . . .*v.3 p.498*

The Irish in the South, 1815-1877. . . . .*v.3 p.498*

Irish Jesus, Roman Jesus: The Formation of Early Irish
    Christianity. *v.1 p.609*

Irish Journal. *v.2 p.604*

The Irish Republican Brotherhood: From the Land League to
    Sinn Fein. *v.3 p.139*

Irish Stories. *v.2 p.334*

Irish Travellers: Racism and the Politics of Culture. . .*v.4 p.731*

Irish Troubles: A Generation of
    Violence,1967-92. . . . .*v.3 p.134, p.139*

Irish Voters Decide: Voting Behaviour in the Republic of
    Ireland. *v.4 p.608*

The Irish War of Independence. *v.3 p.134, p.138*

Irish-American Diaspora Nationalism: The Friends of Irish
    Freedom, 1916-35. . . . .*v.3 p.134*

Iron and Silk: In Which a Young American Encounters
    Swordsmen, Bureaucrats and Other Citizens of Contemporary
    China. *v.6 p.197, p.216*

Iron Cages: Race and Culture in 19th-Century America. .*v.2 p.10*

The Iron Giant. *v.2 p.353*

Iron John: A Book about Men. *v.4 p.745*

Iron Man: The Defiant Reign of Jean Chrétien. . . .*v.3 p.541*

The Iron Wall: Israel and the Arab World. *v.6 p.616*

The Iron Wedge - (L'Appel de la Race), No. 136. . .*v.2 p.539*

The Iron-Blue Vault: Selected Poems. *v.2 p.786*

The Ironic World of Evelyn Waugh: A Study of Eight
    Novels. *v.2 p.387*

Ironies of Imprisonment. *v.6 p.272*

Ironweed. *v.2 p.147*

ⓔ The Irony of Vietnam: The System Worked. *v.3 p.388*

The Iroquois and the New Deal. *v.6 p.689*

The Iroquois Book of Rites. . . .*v.6 p.682, p.690, p.701, p.703*

The Iroquois in the American Revolution. *v.6 p.685*

The Iroquois in the Civil War: From Battlefield to
    Reservation. *v.6 p.687*

Iroquois Land Claims. *v.6 p.684, p.697*

Iroquois Music and Dance: Ceremonial Arts of Two Seneca
    Longhouses. *v.1 p.15*

The Iroquois Struggle for Survival: World War II to Red
    Power. *v.6 p.689*

The Iroquois. *v.4 p.11*

Iroquois. *v.6 p.704*

ⓔ Irrational Exuberance. *v.4 p.245, p.250*

Irrational Exuberance. *v.4 p.97, p.100, p.264*

Irrational Forces Contributing to the Ondulatory and Neurotic
    Course of History: The Theory of the Residues and of the
    Derivations. *v.4 p.248, p.249*

Irrational Man: A Study in Existential Philosophy. . . .*v.1 p.505*

Irrational Numbers. *v.5 p.476*

The Irreducible Needs of Children: What Every Child Must
    Have to Grow, Learn and Flourish. *v.5 p.641*

The Irrepressible Conflict, 1850-1865. . . . . .*v.3 p.394, p.395*

The Irresistible Theatre. *v.1 p.98, p.99*

The Irreversible Decline of Eddie Socket: A
    Novel. *v.6 p.380, p.400*

☐ IRRI: International Rice Research Institute. *v.5 p.19*

Irrigation with Treated Sewage Effluent: Management for
    Environmental Protection. *v.5 p.353, p.379*

☐ IRS: Internal Revenue Service. *v.4 p.106*

Irvine's Writing about Music. *v.1 p.173*

Irving Berlin: American Troubadour. *v.1 p.251, p.310*

Irving Fisher (1867-1947), Arthur Hadley (1856-1930), Ragnar Frisch (1895-1973), Friedrich von Hayek (1899-1992), Allyn Young (1876-1929), Ugo Mazzola (1863-1899). *v.4 p.194*

The Irwin Guide to Using the Wall Street Journal. . . .*v.4 p.96*

The Irwin Handbook of Telecommunications Management. *v.4 p.115*

Is Communism Dead Forever? *v.4 p.509*

Is Geography Destiny?: Lessons from Latin America. .*v.4 p.397*

Is He Dead?: A Comedy in Three Acts. *v.2 p.34*

Is Heathcliff a Murderer?: Great Puzzles in Nineteenth-Century Fiction. *v.2 p.192*

Is It in Your Genes?: How Genes Influence Common Disorders and Diseases That Affect You and Your Family. . .*v.5 p.151*

Is Japan Really Changing Its Ways?: Regulatory Reform and the Japanese Economy. *v.6 p.219*

IS Management Handbook. *v.4 p.114, p.115*

Is Taiwan Chinese?: The Impact of Culture, Power, and Migration on Changing Identities. *v.6 p.213*

Is the Fetus a Person?: A Comparison of Policies Across the Fifty States. *v.4 p.569, v.6 p.471*

Is the Goddess a Feminist?: The Politics of South Asian Goddesses. *v.1 p.540*

Is the Homosexual My Neighbor?: A Positive Christian Response. *v.6 p.373*

Is There a Text in This Class?: The Authority of Interpretive Communities. *v.2 p.568*

Is There an Engineer Inside You?: A Comprehensive Guide to Career Decisions in Engineering. *v.5 p.740*

Isaac Albeniz: Portrait of a Romantic. *v.1 p.195, p.301*

Isaac Bashevis Singer: A Life. *v.2 p.120*

Isaac Bashevis Singer: A Study of the Short Fiction. .*v.2 p.120*

Isaac Bashevis Singer: Collected Stories. *v.2 p.120*

Isaac Newton: Adventurer in Thought. *v.3 p.47*

Isaac Witkin. *v.1 p.782*

Isabel Allende: A Critical Companion. *v.2 p.679*

Isabel Allende: Award-Winning Latin American Author. .*v.2 p.680*

Isabel Allende. *v.2 p.680*

Isabelle Greene: Shaping Place in the Landscape. . . .*v.1 p.816*

Isadora: A Sensational Life. *v.1 p.10, v.6 p.414*

Isadora: Portrait of the Artist As a Woman. *v.1 p.6*

Isaiah 1-39: A New Translation with Introduction and Commentary. *v.1 p.622*

Isaiah 40-55: A New Translation with Introduction and Commentary. *v.1 p.622*

Isaiah 56-66: A New Translation with Introduction and Commentary. *v.1 p.622*

Isak Dinesen: The Life of a Storyteller. *v.2 p.627*

Isara, a Voyage Around. *v.6 p.19, p.29*

Isherwood: A Life Revealed. *v.2 p.356, v.6 p.403*

The Isherwood Century: Essays on the Life and Work of Christopher Isherwood. *v.2 p.355*

Ishiwara Kanji and Japan's Confrontation with the West. *v.6 p.228*

Ishmael: An Adventure of the Mind and Spirit. .*v.6 p.287, p.288*

ISI Proceedings. Science & Technology edition. *v.5 p.405*

Isis and Osiris, the E at Delphi, the Oracles at Delphi No Longer Given in Verse, the Obsolescence of Oracles. .*v.2 p.418*

I--Six Non-Lectures: The Charles Eliot Norton Lectures. .*v.2 p.68*

La isla de las Navajas: Ri Utukel Ulew Re Ri Ch'ich'. .*v.2 p.676*

Islam and Christian Spain. *v.3 p.65, p.237*

Islam and Democracy: The Failure of Dialogue in Algeria. *v.4 p.586, p.613*

Islam and Democracy. *v.4 p.500*

Islam and Gender: The Religious Debate in Contemporary Iran. *v.6 p.632*

Islam and Human Rights: Tradition and Politics. . . .*v.1 p.559*

Islam and Imperialism in Senegal: Sine-Saloum, 1847-1914. . . . .*v.6 p.72*

Islam and Mammon: The Economic Predicaments of Islamism. *v.4 p.207, p.237*

Islam and Modernity. *v.1 p.557*

Islam and Politics in Kenya. *v.6 p.65*

Islam and Resistance in Afghanistan. *v.6 p.634*

Islam and Social Order in Mauritania: A Case Study from the Nineteenth Century. *v.6 p.70*

Islam and Social Policy. *v.4 p.721*

Islam and the Myth of Confrontation: Religion and Politics in the Middle East. *v.6 p.592, p.593*

Islam and the West: Conflict or Cooperation? *v.4 p.642*

Islam and the West: The Making of an Image. *v.1 p.558*

Islam: Continuity and Change in the Modern World. . *v.1 p.554*

Islam, Democracy and the State in North Africa. .*v.1 p.553, p.554*

Islam from Within: Anthology of a Religion. *v.1 p.557*

Islam, Gender, and Social Change. *v.6 p.592*

Islam in a World of Nation-States. *v.4 p.500*

Islam in East Africa. *v.1 p.554, v.6 p.63*

Islam in History: Ideas, People and Events in the Middle East. *v.6 p.582*

Islam in Revolution. *v.6 p.632*

Islam in South-East Asia. *v.1 p.553*

Islam in the African-American Experience. *v.6 p.36*

Islam in the Political Process. *v.1 p.558*

Islam in the Soviet Union: From the Second World War to Gorbachev. *v.3 p.231*

Islam, Kurds and the Turkish Nation State. .*v.6 p.598, p.621, p.622*

Islam Obscured: The Rhetoric of Anthropological Representation. *v.4 p.37*

Islam Observed: Religious Development in Morocco and Indonesia. *v.1 p.554, v.6 p.174, p.176*

Islam: The Religious and Political Life of a World Community. *v.1 p.557*

Islam: The Straight Path Updated with New Epilogue. .*v.1 p.557*

Islam Today: A Short Introduction to the Muslim World. .*v.1 p.553*

Islam under the Double Eagle: The Muslims of Bosnia and Hercegovina, 1878-1914. . . . .*v.3 p.249*

🄴 Islamic Activism: A Social Movement Theory Approach. *v.4 p.712*

Islamic Art and Architecture, 650-1250. . . . .*v.1 p.673, p.691*

Islamic Art and Architecture. *v.1 p.674, p.691*

Islamic Art in the 19th Century: Tradition, Innovation and
   Eclecticism. *v.1 p.673*

Islamic Art V: Studies on the Art and Culture of the Muslim
   World. *v.1 p.673, p.674, p.691*

Islamic Art. *v.1 p.673*

Islamic Courts in Indonesia: A Study in the Political Bases of
   Legal Institutions. *v.6 p.175*

The Islamic Dynasties. *v.1 p.556*

Islamic Economics and Finance: A Glossary. *v.4 p.190*

Islamic Education, Diversity and National Identity: Dini Madaris
   in India Post 9/11. . . . .*v.4 p.308, p.334*

Islamic Education: Its Traditions and Modernization into the
   Arab National Systems. *v.4 p.337*

Islamic Fundamentalism in the West Bank and Gaza: Muslim
   Brotherhood and Islamic Jihad. *v.6 p.616*

Islamic Historiography. *v.6 p.574, p.575, p.585*

Islamic History: A. D. 600 - 750 (Ah 132). *v.6 p.586*

Islamic History: A Framework for Inquiry. *v.6 p.584*

Islamic History: A New Interpretation: AD 750-1055 (Ah
   132-448). *v.6 p.586*

Islamic Homosexualities: Culture, History, and
   Literature. *v.6 p.374, p.421*

Islamic Identity, Postcoloniality, and Educational Policy:
   Schooling and Ethno-Religious Conflict in the Southern
   Philippines. *v.4 p.335*

Islamic Law and the Challenges of Modernity. . . .*v.1 p.556*

Islamic Messianism. *v.1 p.558*

The Islamic Movement in North Africa. *v.6 p.59, p.60*

Islamic Perspectives on Management and Organization. .*v.4 p.718*

Islamic Philosophy and Theology. *v.1 p.558, v.3 p.66*

Islamic Political Ethics: Civil Society, Pluralism, and
   Conflict. *v.4 p.500*

Islamic Society and State Power in Senegal: Disciples and
   Citizens in Fatick, Senegal. *v.6 p.72*

Islamic Society and the West: A Study of the Impact of Western
   Civilization on Moslem Culture in the Near East. .*v.6 p.589*

Islamic Spain, 1250 to 1500. . . . .*v.3 p.237, v.6 p.584*

Islamic State Practices, International Law and the Threat from
   Terrorism: A Critique of the 'Clash of Civilizations'
   in the New World Order. *v.4 p.661*

Islamic Visual Culture, 1100-1800, Vol. 2. . . . . .*v.1 p.673*

The Islamic World: Past and Present, Set. *v.1 p.555*

Islamism, Secularism and Human Rights in the Middle
   East. *v.4 p.513*

Islam. *v.1 p.557*

The Island at the Center of the World: The Epic Story of Dutch
   Manhattan and the Forgotten Colony That Shaped
   America. *v.3 p.491, v.6 p.715*

The Island Edge of America: A Political History of
   Hawaii. *v.3 p.533, p.534,v.6 p.130*

Island Lives: Historical Archaeologies of the
   Caribbean. *v.4 p.13, p.14*

The Island Melanesians. *v.4 p.13*

The Island of Cuba: A Political Essay. *v.3 p.310*

The Island of Formosa: Past and Present. . . .*v.6 p.213, p.214*

The Island of Lost Luggage. *v.6 p.698*

Island: Poetry and History of Chinese Immigrants on Angel
   Island, 1910 to 1949. . . . . .*v.6 p.103, p.118, p.119, p.127*

Island Possessed. *v.1 p.19*

Island Refuge: Britain and Refugees from the Third Reich,
   1933-1939. . . . .*v.4 p.668*

The Island: Three Tales. *v.2 p.790*

Islands in the Stream: A Novel. *v.2 p.84*

Islands in the Street: Gangs and American Urban
   Society. *v.4 p.714*

Islands of Discontent: Okinawan Responses to Japanese and
   American Power. *v.6 p.235*

The Isle Full of Noises: Modern Chinese Poetry from
   Taiwan. *v.6 p.211, p.213*

Isle of Discord: Nationalism, Imperialism, and the Making of
   the Cyprus Problem. *v.6 p.601*

Isle of the Saints: Monastic Settlement and Christian
   Community in Early Ireland. *v.1 p.577*

ISO 9000 Quality Systems Handbook. *v.4 p.117*

ISO 9000:2000: An A-Z Guide. *v.4 p.117*

Isolationism in America, 1935-1941. . . . .*v.3 p.452*

Isolationist Impulse: Its Twentieth Century Reaction. .*v.3 p.451*

Isotopes: Principles and Applications. *v.5 p.444*

ⓔ Israel after Begin. *v.4 p.615, v.6 p.614*

Israel: Challenges to Identity, Democracy, and the State. .*v.6 p.614*

Israel, Egypt, and the Palestinians: From Camp David to
   Intifada. *v.6 p.618, p.639*

Israel in Egypt: The Evidence for the Authenticity of the Exodus
   Tradition. *v.3 p.7*

Israel in Search of Identity: Reading The Formative
   Years. *v.6 p.615*

Israel in the Begin Era. *v.6 p.613*

Israel in the Next Century. *v.6 p.614*

Israel: Land of Tradition and Conflict. *v.6 p.615*

Israel on the Road to Peace: Accepting the
   Unacceptable. *v.6 p.613*

Israel, Palestine and Peace: Essays. *v.6 p.611*

The Israel Palestine Question. *v.6 p.619*

The Israel-Arab Reader: A Documentary History of the Middle
   East Conflict. *v.6 p.618*

Israeli Cinema: East-West and the Politics of
   Representation. *v.6 p.334*

Israeli Family and Community: Women's Time. .*v.6 p.614, p.615*

Israeli Film: A Reference Guide. *v.6 p.333*

Israeli Holocaust Drama. *v.6 p.652*

Israeli Painting: From Post-Impressionism to Post
   Zionism. *v.1 p.731*

Israeli Politics in the 1990s: Key Domestic and Foreign Policy
   Factors. *v.4 p.615*

Israeli Writers Consider the "Outsider". *v.6 p.652*

Israelis: Founders and Sons. *v.6 p.613*

Israelites: Introduction. *v.3 p.7*

The Israel-Palestine Conflict: One Hundred Years of
   War. *v.6 p.617*

Israel/Palestine: The Black Book. *v.6 p.619*

Israel's First Fifty Years. *v.6 p.613, p.614*

Israel's Holocaust and the Politics of Nationhood. . . .*v.6 p.616*

Israel's Lebanon War. . . . . *.v.6 p.606, p.615*

Israel's National Security Towards the 21st Century. . . *.v.6 p.613*

Israel's Place in the Middle East: A Pluralist Perspective. . . . . *.v.6 p.611*

Issei, Nisei, War Bride: Three Generations of Japanese American Women in Domestic Service. . . . . *.v.6 p.112, p.131*

The Issei: The World of the First-Generation Japanese Immigrants, 1885-1924. . . . . *.v.6 p.131, p.132*

The Issues: An Overview of Primary Prevention. . . .*v.5 p.670*

Issues and Dilemmas of Biotechnology: A Reference Guide. . . . . *.v.5 p.219, p.249*

Issues and Problems in Teacher Education: An International Handbook. . . . . *.v.4 p.277, p.313*

Issues in Geography Teaching. . . . . *.v.4 p.376*

Issues in Physical Education. . . . . *.v.4 p.795*

Issues in the Economics of Aging. . . . . *.v.4 p.267*

Issues in Transnational Policing. . . . . *.v.6 p.263*

Issues in Wetlands Protection: Background Papers Prepared for the National Wetlands Policy Forum. . . . . *.v.5 p.176, p.177*

☐ Issues: School Choice. . . . . *.v.4 p.299*

Istanbul and the Civilization of the Ottoman Empire. *.v.6 p.622, p.623*

Istanbul Boy: The Autobiography of Aziz Nesin. . . *.v.6 p.667*

Istanbul: Memories and the City. . . . . *.v.6 p.624*

IT and Organizational Learning: Managing Change through Technology and Education. . . . . *.v.4 p.79*

It Began with a Stone: A History of Geology from the Stone Age to the Age of Plate Tectonics. . . . . *.v.5 p.418*

It Can't Happen Here. *.v.2 p.95*

It Depends: A Poet's Notebook. . . . . *.v.2 p.719*

It Didn't Happen Here: Why Socialism Failed in the United States. . . . . *.v.4 p.507, p.554*

It Seems to Me: Selected Letters of Eleanor Roosevelt. *.v.3 p.462*

It Sure Looks Different from the Inside. . . . . . . *.v.3 p.477*

It Takes a Nation: A New Agenda for Fighting Poverty. . . . . *.v.4 p.264, p.754*

Italian Anarchism, 1864-1892. . . . . *.v.3 p.202*

Italian Architecture: From Michelangelo to Borromini. *.v.1 p.786*

Italian Baroque Sculpture. . . . . *.v.1 p.775*

Italian Etchers of the Renaissance and Baroque. . . . *.v.1 p.754*

Italian Fables. . . . . *.v.2 p.697*

Italian Fascism: Its Origins and Development. . . . . *.v.3 p.203*

Italian Fascisms from Pareto to Gentile. . . . . *.v.3 p.202*

Italian Folktales in America: The Verbal Art of an Immigrant Woman. . . . . *.v.2 p.17*

Italian Folktales. . . . . *.v.2 p.714*

Italian Frescoes: High Renaissance to the Baroque, 1510-1600. . . . . *.v.1 p.728, p.732*

Italian Futurist Poetry. . . . . *.v.2 p.699*

Italian Futurist Theatre, 1909-1944. . . . . . . *.v.1 p.84, p.106*

Italian Grotesque Theater. . . . . *.v.2 p.697*

Italian Horror Films of the 1960s: A Critical Catalog of 62 Chillers. . . . . *.v.6 p.338, p.339*

Italian Illuminated Manuscripts in the J. Paul Getty Museum. . . . . *.v.1 p.672, p.716*

The Italian Language Today. . . . . *.v.2 p.699*

Italian Language. . . . . *.v.2 p.699*

The Italian Madrigal. *.v.1 p.179*

Italian Master Drawings at the Philadelphia Museum of Art. . . . . *.v.1 p.721*

The Italian "Trio" Sonata: From Its Origins until Corelli. *.v.1 p.182*

Italian Opera. . . . . *.v.1 p.231, p.246*

Italian Paintings, 1250-1450, in the John G. Johnson Collection and the Philadelphia Museum of Art. . . . . . . *.v.1 p.733*

Italian Paintings of the Fifteenth Century. . . *.v.1 p.726, p.730*

Italian Renaissance Sculpture. . . . . *.v.1 p.776*

Italian Resistance: An Anthology: Manchester New Italian Texts. . . . . *.v.3 p.203*

The Italian Risorgimento: State, Society and National Unification. . . . . *.v.3 p.201*

The Italian Solo Concerto, 1700-1760: Rhetorical Strategies and Style History. . . . . *.v.1 p.185*

Italian Straw Hat. . . . . *.v.2 p.495*

Italian Tales: An Anthology of Contemporary Italian Fiction. . . . . *.v.2 p.700*

The Italian Theater of the Grotesque: A New Theater for the Twentieth Century: An Anthology. . . . . *.v.1 p.107*

The Italian Tragedy in the Renaissance: Cultural Realities and Theatrical Innovations. . . . . *.v.1 p.74, p.106, p.107*

Italian Villas and Gardens. . . . . *.v.1 p.820*

Italian Women Poets of the Twentieth Century. . . . *.v.2 p.700*

Italian Women Poets. *.v.2 p.700*

Italian Women's Writing, 1860-1994. . . . . *.v.2 p.698*

The Italians in Chicago, 1880-1930: A Study in Ethnic Mobility. . . . . *.v.3 p.516*

Italians Then, Mexicans Now: Immigrant Origins and Second-Generation Progress, 1890 to 2000. . . . *.v.4 p.765*

Italo Calvino and the Compass of Literature. . . . . *.v.2 p.714*

Italo Calvino. . . . . *.v.2 p.715*

Italo Svevo. . . . . *.v.2 p.724*

Italy: A Short History. . . . . *.v.3 p.198*

Italy and Its Invaders. . . . . *.v.4 p.643*

Italy and Its Monarchy. . . . . *.v.3 p.202*

Italy and the Approach of the First World War. . . . *.v.3 p.202*

Italy: Fiction, Theater, Poetry, Film Since 1950. . . . *.v.2 p.698*

Italy: From Revolution to Republic, 1700 to the Present. *.v.3 p.197, p.198*

Italy in the Age of Dante and Petrarch, 1216-1380. . . . . *.v.3 p.199, p.200*

Italy in the Central Middle Ages, 1000-1300. . . . . *.v.3 p.198*

Italy in the Early Middle Ages, 476-1000. . . . . . . *.v.3 p.198*

Item Generation for Test Development. . . . . *.v.5 p.601*

It's a Battlefield. . . . . *.v.2 p.350*

It's a Print!: Detective Fiction from Page to Screen. . . . . *.v.6 p.326, p.327*

It's about Time: America's Imprisonment Binge. . . *.v.6 p.274*

It's about Time: The Dave Brubeck Story. . . *.v.1 p.260, p.314*

It's All about Service: How to Lead Your People to Care for Your Customers. . . . . *.v.4 p.143*

It's All about the Client: Consulting for Results. . . . *.v.4 p.65*

It's Hard to Talk about Yourself. . . . . *.v.2 p.718*

It's Hardly Sportin': Stadiums, Neighborhoods, and the New Chicago. *v.6 p.729*

Its Not the Media: The Truth about Pop Culture's Influence on Children. *v.4 p.712, p.713*

It's Only a Game. *v.4 p.858*

It's Raining in Mango. *v.2 p.743, p.744*

Itsuka. *v.2 p.735, v.6 p.100*

☐ IUCN The World Conservation Union. *v.5 p.16, p.17*

☐ IUPAC Nomenclature of Organic Chemistry (Recommendations 1979/1993). *v.5 p.289*

☐ IUPAC-NIST Solubility Data Series Database. . . .*v.5 p.281*

☐ IUPLR: Inter-University Program for Latino Research. *v.6 p.486*

Iustitia Dei: A History of the Christian Doctrine of Justification. *v.1 p.644*

☐ Ivan Franko. *v.2 p.814*

The Ivan R. Dee Guide to Plays and Playwrights. . . .*v.1 p.59*

Ivan the Terrible: First Tsar of Russia. *v.3 p.214*

Ivan the Terrible. *v.3 p.215*

Ivanhoe. *v.2 p.308*

Ivan's War: Life and Death in the Red Army, 1939-1945. . . . .*v.3 p.227*

I've a Feeling We're Not in Kansas Anymore. . . .*v.6 p.398*

Ives, Concord Sonata: Piano Sonata No. 2. . . .*v.1 p.209, p.333*

Ivor Novello: Screen Idol. *v.6 p.419*

Ivy Compton-Burnett. *v.2 p.339*

Ivy When Young: The Early Life of I. Compton-Burnett, 1884-1919. . . . .*v.2 p.339*

Iwein: The Knight with the Lion. *v.2 p.595*

Iznik: The Artistry of Ottoman Ceramics. *v.1 p.673*

J

J. B.: A Play in Verse. *v.2 p.98*

J. Craig Annan: Selected Texts and Bibliography. *v.1 p.765, p.766*

J. D. Salinger: A Study of the Short Fiction. *v.2 p.118*

J. D. Salinger, Revisited. *v.2 p.117, p.118*

J. G. Frazer: His Life and Work. *v.4 p.3*

J Hillis Miller Reader. *v.2 p.164*

J. J. P. Oud and the International Style: A Bio-Bibliography. *v.1 p.783, p.793*

J. L. Austin. *v.1 p.447*

J. M. Barrie and the Lost Boys. *v.2 p.269*

J. M. Barrie: Glamour of Twilight. *v.2 p.269*

J. M. Coetzee: South Africa and the Politics of Writing.*v.2 p.753*

J. M. Coetzee. *v.2 p.754*

J. M. Keynes in Retrospect: The Legacy of the Keynesian Revolution. *v.4 p.227, p.228*

J. M. Synge: Literary Companion. *v.2 p.306*

J. R. Jayewardene of Sri Lanka: A Political Biography: from 1956 to His Retirement, Vol. 2. . . . .*v.6 p.163*

J. R. Jayewardene of Sri Lanka: A Political Biography: The First Fifty Years. *v.6 p.163*

J. Robert Oppenheimer: Shatterer of Worlds. *v.5 p.543*

J. S. Bach: The Complete Cantatas. *v.1 p.411*

J. S. Bach's "The Art of the Fugue": The Work and Its Interpretation. *v.1 p.184, p.239, p.303*

J. S. Bach's Musical Offering: History, Interpretation and Analysis. *v.1 p.183, p.238, p.303*

J. W. Waterhouse. *v.1 p.748*

J. William Fulbright: Advice and Dissent. *v.3 p.456*

Jabberwocky and Other Nonsense Verse. *v.2 p.277*

Jack: A Life Like No Other. *v.3 p.478*

Jack: A Life of C. S. Lewis. *v.2 p.366*

Jack Kerouac: A Biography. *v.2 p.92*

Jack Kerouac: Selected Letters, 1957-1969. . . . . . .*v.2 p.93*

Jack Kerouac's Duluoz Legend: The Mythic Form of an Autobiographical Fiction. *v.2 p.92, p.93*

Jack Kerouac. *v.2 p.92*

Jack London. *v.2 p.96*

Jack: Straight from the Gut. *v.4 p.72*

Jack the Ripper and the London Press. *v.6 p.744*

Jack: The Struggles of John F. *v.3 p.478*

Jackets Required: An Illustrated History of the American Book Jacket 1920-1950. . . . .*v.1 p.719*

Jackie Robinson: A Biography. *v.4 p.832, p.833, p.851*

Jackie Robinson: Race, Sports and the American Dream. *v.4 p.805, p.831, p.850, p.887, p.896*

Jack's Book: An Oral Biography of Jack Kerouac. . . .*v.2 p.92*

☐ The Jackson Laboratory. *v.5 p.82, p.87, p.111, p.125*

Jackson Pollock: A Biography. *v.1 p.747*

Jackson Pollock: An American Saga. *v.1 p.744*

Jackson Pollock: Supplement Number 1 to a Catalogue Raisonné of Paintings, Drawings, and Other Works. .*v.1 p.698*

Jackson Pollock. *v.1 p.747, p.749*

Jacksonian America: Society, Personality, and Politics. *v.3 p.414, p.415*

The Jacksonian Persuasion: Politics and Belief. *v.3 p.414*

Jacksonians vs. the Banks: Politics in the States after the Panic of 1837. . . . .*v.3 p.418*

Jacksonville: The Consolidation Story, from Civil Rights to the Jaguars. *v.4 p.543*

Jacob Burckhardt and the Crisis of Modernity. *v.3 p.244*

Jacob Lawrence: The Complete Prints (1963-2000) - A Catalogue Raisonné. *v.1 p.757, p.758*

Jacob Van Ruisdael: A Complete Catalogue of His Paintings, Drawings, and Etchings. *v.1 p.699*

Jacob Van Ruisdael: Master of Landscape. *v.1 p.747*

Jacobean Ppageant; or, The Court of King James I. . .*v.3 p.101*

Jacobite Ireland, 1685-91. . . . .*v.3 p.138*

The Jacobite Risings in Britain, 1689-1746. . . . . .*v.3 p.133*

Jacobitism and the English People, 1688-1788. .*v.3 p.107, p.109*

Jacob's Children in the Land of the Mahdi: Jews of the Sudan. *v.6 p.597, p.640*

Jacob's Dream. *v.2 p.603*

Jacob's Ladder: The History of the Human Genome. .*v.5 p.133*

Jacob's Room. *v.2 p.394, p.395*

Jacqueline Kennedy: First Lady of the New Frontier. *v.3 p.443, p.444, p.461*

A Jacques Barzun Reader: Selections from His Works. *v.2 p.575*

Jacques Lacan: His Life and Work. *v.5 p.598*

Jacques the Fatalist. *v.2 p.479*

Jacques-Louis David and Jean-Louis Prieur, Revolutionary Artists: The Public, the Populace, and Images of the French Revolution. *v.1 p.745, p.746*

Jadwiga of Anjou and the Rise of East Central Europe. .*v.3 p.206*

The Jahangirnama: Memoirs of Jahangir, Emperor of India. *v.6 p.156*

Jahrestage: aus dem Leben von Gesine Cresspahl. . . .*v.2 p.618*

Jaina Sutras, Pt. 1. . . . .*v.1 p.538*

Jaina Sutras, Pt. 2. . . . .*v.1 p.538*

The Jains. *v.1 p.538*

Jake's Thing. *v.2 p.328*

La Jalousie. *v.2 p.525*

Jamaica Inn. *v.2 p.343*

Jamaica Kincaid: A Critical Companion. *v.2 p.768*

Jamaica Kincaid: Writing Memory, Writing Back to the Mother. *v.2 p.767*

James Abbott McNeill Whistler: Pastels. *v.1 p.723*

James Agee: A Biography. *v.2 p.55, p.56*

James Agee and the Legend of Himself: A Critical Study. .*v.2 p.56*

James Agee: Film Writing and Selected Journalism. . .*v.2 p.55*

James Agee: Let Us Now Praise Famous Men, a Death in the Family, and Shorter Fiction. *v.2 p.55*

James Agee Rediscovered: The Notebooks for Let Us Now Praise Famous Men, and Other New Manuscripts. . .*v.2 p.56*

James Agee. *v.2 p.56*

James B. Hunt: A North Carolina Progressive. *v.3 p.502*

James Baldwin: A Biography. *v.6 p.26, p.402*

James Baldwin: Collected Essays. *v.2 p.59, v.6 p.22*

James Baldwin Now. *v.2 p.59, v.6 p.26, p.27*

James Boswell's Life of Johnson: An Edition of the Original Manuscript. *v.2 p.240*

James Boswell's Life of Samuel Johnson. *v.2 p.240*

James Brown: The Godfather of Soul. *v.1 p.266, p.314*

James Fenimore Cooper: New Critical Essays. *v.2 p.35*

James Fenimore Cooper. *v.2 p.35*

James Henry Hammond and the Old South: A Design for Mastery. *v.3 p.502*

James Hutton and the History of Geology. *v.5 p.418*

James Ivory in Conversation: How Merchant Ivory Makes Its Movies. *v.6 p.416*

James Joyce: A Critical Introduction. *v.2 p.359*

James Joyce: A Study of the Short Fiction. *v.2 p.357*

James Joyce A to Z: The Essential Reference to His Life and Writings. *v.2 p.358*

A James Joyce Miscellany: Second Series. . . .*v.2 p.359, p.360*

A James Joyce Miscellany. Third series. *v.2 p.360*

A James Joyce Miscellany. *v.2 p.360*

James Joyce's Dublin: A Topographical Guide to the Dublin of Ulysses. *v.2 p.358*

James Joyce's Early Fiction: The Biography of a Form. *v.2 p.357*

James Joyce's Ulysses: A Casebook. *v.2 p.357*

James Joyce's Ulysses: Critical Essays. *v.2 p.358*

James Joyce's Ulysses. *v.2 p.358*

James Joyce. *v.2 p.358*

James K. Polk, Jacksonian, 1795-1843. . . . .*v.3 p.421*

James Laughlin, New Directions Press, and the Remaking of Ezra Pound. *v.2 p.111*

James: Literary Criticism: European Writers and Prefaces to the New York Edition. *v.2 p.44*

James M. Cain. *v.2 p.65*

James Madison: A Biography. *v.3 p.417*

James McBey - Etchings and Drypoints: A Catalogue Raisonné. *v.1 p.756*

James McNeill Whistler: Watercolors, Pastels, and Drawings: A Catalogue Raisonné¡. *v.1 p.723*

James Merrill's Poetic Quest, 81. . . . .*v.2 p.100*

James Monroe: The Quest for National Identity. . . .*v.3 p.416*

James P. Johnson: A Case of Mistaken Identity. *v.1 p.257, p.334*

James Russell Lowell: Portrait of a Many-Sided Man. *v.2 p.47*

James Shepherd Pike: Republicanism and the American Negro 1850-1882. . . . .*v.3 p.422, p.423, p.428*

James Shirley. *v.2 p.221, p.222*

James Stirling and Michael Wilford: Buildings and Projects, 1975-1992. . . . .*v.1 p.794*

James T. Farrell: Studs Lonigan a Trilogy. *v.2 p.72, p.73*

James the Just and Christian Origins. *v.1 p.626*

James Thurber: His Life and Times. *v.2 p.125*

James Thurber: Writings and Drawings. *v.2 p.126*

James Weldon Johnson: Writings. *v.2 p.89*

James Whale: A New World of Gods and Monsters. . .*v.6 p.418*

James Woodforde: The Diary of a Country Parson, 1758-1802. . . . .*v.3 p.106, p.108*

Jamestown, 1544 to 1699. . . . .*v.3 p.499*

James. *v.1 p.439, p.630*

Jammin' at the Margins: Jazz and the American Cinema. *v.6 p.316*

Janacek and His World. *v.1 p.194, p.209, p.333*

Janacek: Glagolitic Mass. *v.1 p.227, p.237, p.333*

The Janacek Opera Libretti: Kat'a Kabanova Translations and Pronunciation. *v.1 p.211, p.229, p.333, p.407*

The Janacek Opera Libretti: Translations and Pronunciation. *v.1 p.216, p.230, p.333, p.408*

Janacek Operas. *v.1 p.226, p.233, p.333*

JANAF Thermodynamical Tables. *v.5 p.286, p.287*

Jane Austen, 1811-1870, Vol. 1. . . . .*v.2 p.268*

Jane Austen, 1870-1940, Vol. 2. . . . .*v.2 p.268*

Jane Austen: A Collection of Critical Essays. . . .*v.2 p.269*

Jane Austen: A Companion. *v.2 p.268*

Jane Austen: A Literary Life. *v.2 p.267*

Jane Austen, a Study of Her Artistic Development. . .*v.2 p.268*

Jane Austen and Co.: Remaking the Past in Contemporary Culture. *v.2 p.268*

Jane Austen and Discourses of Feminism. *v.2 p.268*

Jane Austen and Her Art. *v.2 p.267*

Jane Austen and the Clergy. *v.2 p.267*

Jane Austen and the Enlightenment. *v.2 p.267*

Jane Austen and the Fiction of Her Time. *v.2 p.269*

Jane Austen and the Morality of Conversation. . . .*v.2 p.269*

Jane Austen and the Province of Womanhood. .*v.2 p.268, p.269*

Jane Austen and the War of Ideas. *v.2 p.267*

Jane Austen: Facts and Problems. *v.2 p.267*

Jane Austen Handbook. *v.2 p.268*

Jane Austen: Her Life. *v.2 p.267*

Jane Austen in Hollywood. *v.6 p.327, p.344*

Jane Austen: Irony As Defense and Discovery. . . . *v.2 p.268*

Jane Austen on Film and Television: A Critical Study of the
    Adaptations. *v.2 p.268, v.6 p.326*

Jane Austen, or the Secret of Style. *v.2 p.268*

Jane Austen: Women, Politics, and the Novel. *v.2 p.267*

Jane Austen's Beginnings: The Juvenilia and "Lady
    Susan". *v.2 p.267*

Jane Austen's Letters. *v.2 p.266*

Jane Austen's Novels: The Fabric of Dialogue. . . . *v.2 p.267*

Jane Austen's Novels. *v.2 p.269*

Jane Austen. *v.2 p.267*

Jane Carlyle: Newly Selected Letters. *v.2 p.276*

Jane Eyre: Critical Edition. *v.2 p.269*

Jane Eyre. *v.2 p.269, p.270*

Janeites: Austen's Disciples and Devotees. *v.2 p.268*

Jane's Urban Transport Systems 2005-2006. . . . . *v.5 p.701*

Janet Frame: Subversive Fictions. *v.2 p.745*

Janet Guthrie: A Life at Full Throttle. *v.4 p.836, p.848*

Janáček. *v.1 p.227, p.333, p.334*

Janus Identities and Forked Tongues: Two Caribbean Writers in
    the United States. *v.6 p.508, p.515*

Japan 1945: A U.S. Marine's Photographs from Ground
    Zero. *v.1 p.768*

🄴 Japan: A Documentary History. *v.6 p.225*

Japan: A Short Cultural History. *v.6 p.225*

Japan as a Low-Crime Nation. *v.6 p.250*

Japan As Number One: Lessons for America. *v.6 p.220*

Japan at War: An Oral History. *v.6 p.223*

Japan Before Perry: A Short History. *v.6 p.226*

Japan: East Asia: A Cultural, Social and Political
    History. *v.6 p.223, p.224*

Japan: Its Architecture, Art and Art Manufacturers. . *v.6 p.221*

Japan: Spirit and Form. *v.6 p.221*

Japan Statistical Yearbook 2004. . . . .*v.6 p.218*

Japan: Who Governs?: The Rise of the Developmental
    State. *v.6 p.224*

🄴 Japan. *v.6 p.220*

Japanese American Celebration and Conflict: A History of
    Ethnic Identity and Festival, 1934-1990. . . . . *v.6 p.132*

Japanese American Ethnicity: The Persistence of
    Community. *v.4 p.764, v.6 p.131*

The Japanese American Experience. *v.6 p.132*

Japanese American Internment During World War II: A History
    and Reference Guide. *v.6 p.115, p.116, p.134*

Japanese Americans: Evolution of a Subculture. . . . *v.6 p.132*

Japanese Americans: From Relocation to Redress. . . *v.6 p.133*

Japanese Americans. *v.6 p.132*

The Japanese and Peru, 1873-1973. . . . . *v.3 p.329*

Japanese Art after 1945: Scream Against the Sky. . . *v.6 p.222*

Japanese Art. *v.1 p.694*

The Japanese Automobile Industry: A Business History. .*v.4 p.154*

The Japanese Bon Dance in Hawaii. *v.1 p.17*

Japanese Buddhism. *v.1 p.561*

Japanese Cinema: An Introduction. *v.6 p.336*

The Japanese Community in Brazil, 1908-1940: Between
    Samurai and Carnival. *v.3 p.341*

The Japanese Constitution: Documents and Analysis. .*v.6 p.224*

Japanese Court Poetry. *v.6 p.234*

Japanese Culture. *v.6 p.220*

Japanese Design: A Survey since 1950. . . . *v.1 p.713, p.714*

Japanese Documentary Films: The Meiji Era Through
    Hiroshima. *v.6 p.309*

The Japanese Economic System and Its Historical
    Origins. *v.6 p.220*

The Japanese Family Storehouse, or, the Millionaire's Gospel
    Modernised = Nippon Eitai: Gura, or, Daifuku Shin
    Choja Kyo (1688). *v.6 p.229, p.230*

The Japanese Film: Art and Industry. *v.6 p.335*

Japanese Film Directors. *v.6 p.335*

Japanese Films: A Filmography and Commentary,
    1921-1989. . . . .*v.6 p.305, p.335*

Japanese Frames of Mind: Cultural Perspectives on Human
    Development. *v.5 p.598*

Japanese High School: Silence and Resistance. . . . *v.6 p.223*

Japanese Horror Cinema. *v.6 p.319, p.336*

Japanese Immigrant Clothing in Hawaii,
    1885-1941. . . . .*v.6 p.87, p.132*

Japanese Law in Context: Readings in Society, the Economy,
    and Politics. *v.6 p.220*

Japanese Law. *v.6 p.220*

Japanese Linked Poetry. *v.6 p.231*

The Japanese Main Bank System: Its Relevance for Developing
    and Transforming Economies. *v.6 p.220*

The Japanese Mind: The Goliath Explained. *v.6 p.219*

Japanese Model of Schooling: Comparisons with the U.
    S. *v.6 p.222*

Japanese Musical Instruments. *v.1 p.288*

The Japanese Novel of the Meiji Period and the Ideal of
    Individualism. *v.6 p.234*

Japanese Patterns of Behavior. *v.6 p.221*

Japanese Philosophy. *v.1 p.476*

The Japanese Police System Today: A Comparative
    Study. *v.6 p.262*

Japanese Policymaking -: The Politics Behind Politics, Informal
    Mechanisms and the Making of China Policy. . . *v.4 p.622*

Japanese Religion and Society: Paradigms of Structure and
    Change. *v.6 p.219*

The Japanese School: Lessons for Industrial America. .*v.4 p.334*

Japanese Schooling: Patterns of Socialization, Equality, and
    Political Control. *v.6 p.222*

The Japanese Seizure of Korea, 1868-1910. . . . . .*v.6 p.236*

Japanese Sense of Self. *v.4 p.693*

Japanese Society. *v.4 p.705*

Japanese Sports: A History. *v.4 p.806, p.834*

The Japanese Theatre: From Shamanistic Ritual to
    Contemporary Pluralism. *v.1 p.133*

Japanese Things: Being Notes on Various Subjects Connected with Japan. *v.6 p.219*

A Japanese View of Nature: The World of Living Things by Kinji Imanishi. *v.5 p.237*

Japanese Woodblock Printing. *v.1 p.754, p.755*

The Japanese. *v.6 p.220*

Japan's Comfort Women: The Military and Involuntary Prostitution During War and Occupation. *v.6 p.455*

Japan's Dysfunctional Democracy: The Liberal Democractic Party and Structural Corruption. *v.4 p.621*

Japan's Economic Dilemma: The Institutional Origins of Prosperity and Stagnation. *v.6 p.219*

Japan's Emergence as a Modern State: Political and Economic Problems of the Meiji Period. *v.6 p.225*

Japan's Failed Revolution: Koizumi and the Politics of Economic Reform. *v.6 p.225*

Japan's Golden Age: Momoyama. *v.1 p.693*

Japan's Modern Myths: Ideology in the Late Meiji Period. *v.6 p.224*

Japan's Modern Prophet: Uchimura Kanzo, 1861-1930. .*v.6 p.227*

e Japan's New Middle Class; the Salary Man and His Family in a Tokyo Suburb. *v.4 p.725*

Japan's Orient: Rendering Pasts into History. *v.6 p.220*

Japan's Postwar Party Politics. *v.4 p.621, p.622*

Japan's Reluctant Realism: Foreign Policy Challenges in an Era of Uncertain Power. *v.6 p.224*

Un Jardin au Bout du Monde. *v.2 p.539*

El Jardin de la Senora Murakami. *v.2 p.667*

Jasmine. *v.2 p.765, v.6 p.101*

Jasper Johns: A Print Retrospective. *v.1 p.755*

Java in a Nutshell. *v.5 p.346*

Java in a Time of Revolution. *v.6 p.175*

The Java Programming Language. *v.5 p.346*

The Java(tm) Language Specification. *v.5 p.346*

Jawaharlal Nehru: Rebel and Statesman. *v.6 p.159*

Jawetz, Melnick, and Adelberg's Medical Microbiology. .*v.5 p.515*

Jazz: A Regional Exploration. *v.1 p.265*

Jazz Arranging and Orchestration: A Concise Introduction with Interactive CD-ROM. *v.1 p.394, p.403*

The Jazz Bass Book: Technique and Tradition. . . .*v.1 p.403*

Jazz cleopatra Rose: Josephine Baker in Her Time. . . .*v.1 p.11*

Jazz Composition and Arranging. *v.1 p.393, p.403*

Jazz Composition and Orchestration. *v.1 p.394, p.403*

Jazz Dance Class: Beginning Thru Advanced. *v.1 p.31*

Jazz Dance: The Story of American Vernacular Dance. *v.1 p.19, p.33*

Jazz Dance Today. *v.1 p.32*

The Jazz Guitar. *v.1 p.264*

Jazz Improvisation. *v.1 p.403*

Jazz in the Bittersweet Blues of Life. *v.1 p.264, p.340*

A Jazz Odyssey: The Life of Oscar Peterson. . .*v.1 p.262, p.347*

Jazz on Film: The Complete Story of the Musicians and Music Onscreen. *v.6 p.317*

Jazz Performers: An Annotated Bibliography of Biographical Materials. *v.1 p.165, p.257*

Jazz Piano: A Jazz History. *v.1 p.264*

The Jazz Piano Book. *v.1 p.403*

The Jazz Poetry Anthology. *v.2 p.583*

Jazz Scholarship and Pedagogy: A Research and Information Guide. *v.1 p.168, p.262, p.405*

Jazz Singing: America's Great Voices from Bessie Smith to Bebop and Beyond. *v.1 p.258, p.259*

Jazz Styles: History and Analysis. *v.1 p.259*

Jazz. *v.1 p.806, p.807*

JCE (Journal of Chemical Education) Digital Library. *v.5 p.266*

JCE LivTexts: Physical Chemistry [Quantum States of Atoms and Molecules]. *v.5 p.278*

JCE Online: Journal of Chemical Education. . . .*v.5 p.266*

Je vivrai l'amour des autres : roman. *v.2 p.512*

Jealousy and In the Labyrinth. *v.2 p.525*

Jean Cocteau. *v.2 p.514*

Jean de la Bruyere. *v.2 p.473*

Jean Dubuffet: Trace of an Adventure. *v.1 p.696*

Jean François Lyotard: Critical Evaluations in Cultural Theory. *v.1 p.457*

Jean Genet, le poète travesti : Portrait d'une oeuvre. .*v.2 p.519*

Jean Genet. *v.2 p.519*

Jean Jacques Rousseau. *v.2 p.481*

Jean Jacques: The Early Life and Work of Jean-Jacques Rosseau, 1712-1754. . . . .*v.2 p.481, p.482*

Jean Lurcat: Monograph and Catalogue Raisonné, 1910-1965. . . . .*v.1 p.737, p.738*

Jean Paul. *v.2 p.599*

Jean Price Mars, the Haitian Elite and the American Occupation, 1915-1935. . . . .*v.3 p.316*

Jean Racine Revisited. *v.2 p.477*

Jean Rhys. *v.2 p.769, p.770*

Jean Santeuil. *v.2 p.524*

Jean Sibelius. *v.1 p.222, p.357*

Jean Stafford: A Study of the Short Fiction. . .*v.2 p.120, p.121*

Jean Stafford: Life of a Writer. *v.2 p.120*

Jean Toomer and the Harlem Renaissance. *v.2 p.126*

Jean Toomer, Artist: A Study of His Literary Life and Work, 1894-1936. . . . .*v.2 p.126*

A Jean Toomer Reader: Selected Unpublished Writings. .*v.2 p.126*

Jean Toomer: Selected Essays and Literary Criticism. .*v.2 p.126*

Jean-Baptiste Say and the Classical Canon in Economics: The British Connection in French Classicism. *v.4 p.223*

Jean-Christophe. *v.2 p.526*

Jean-Francois Millet: Drawn into the Light. . .*v.1 p.723, p.724*

Jean-Jacques Rousseau, Political Writings. *v.2 p.482*

Jean-Jacques Rousseau: Restless Genius. *v.3 p.147*

Jean-Jacques Rousseau: Transparency and Obstruction. .*v.2 p.483*

Jean-Jacques Rousseau. *v.2 p.482*

Jean-Jacques: The Early Life and Work of Jean-Jacques Rousseau, 1712-1754. . . . .*v.3 p.147*

Jean-Paul Sartre: A Literary and Political Study. . . .*v.2 p.528*

Jean-Paul Sartre: Basic Writings. *v.1 p.458*

Jean-Paul Sartre: The Philosopher As a Literary Critic. .*v.2 p.528*

Jean-Philippe Rameau: His Life and Work. . . .*v.1 p.184, p.350*

Jeeves and the Feudal Spirit. . . . . *.v.2 p.390*

Jeeves in the Offing. . . . . *.v.2 p.390*

Los Jefes, los Cachorros. . . . . *.v.2 p.686*

Jefferson and His Time. . . . . *.v.3 p.412*

Jefferson and Madison and the Making of Constitutions. *.v.3 p.412*

Jefferson and the Ordeal of Liberty. . . . . *.v.3 p.412*

Jefferson and the Revolutionary Mind. . . . . . . *.v.3 p.412*

Jefferson and the Rights of Man. . . . . *.v.3 p.412*

Jefferson Davis, American. . . . . *.v.4 p.520*

Jefferson Davis and His Cabinet. . . . . . *.v.3 p.399, p.429*

Jefferson Davis, Confederate
President. . . . . *.v.3 p.398, v.4 p.520, p.521*

Jefferson Davis: Private Letters, 1823-1889. . . . . . *.v.3 p.424*

Jefferson Davis: The Sphinx of the Confederacy. *.v.3 p.396, p.425*

Jefferson Davis. . . . . *.v.3 p.395, p.424*

The Jefferson Image in the American Mind. . . . . . *.v.3 p.412*

Jefferson the President, First Term, 1801-1805. . . . *.v.3 p.412*

Jefferson the President, Second Term, 1805-1809. . . *.v.3 p.412*

Jefferson the Virginian. . . . . *.v.3 p.412*

Jeffersonian America. . . . . *.v.4 p.525*

The Jeffersonian Crisis: Courts and Politics in the Young
Republic. . . . . *.v.4 p.462*

Jefferson's English Crisis, 1803-1809: Commerce, Embargo, and
the Republican Revolution. . . . . *.v.3 p.412*

Jefferson's Vision for Education, 1760-1845. . . . . *.v.4 p.340*

Jeffrey. . . . . *.v.6 p.414*

Jekyll on Trial: Multiple Personality Disorder and Criminal
Law. . . . . *.v.5 p.593*

Jenny Saville. . . . . *.v.1 p.739*

Jens Peter Jacobsen. . . . . *.v.2 p.627*

Jeremiah 1-20: A New Translation with Introduction and
Commentary. . . . . *.v.1 p.623*

Jeremiah 21-36. . . . . *.v.1 p.623*

Jeremiah 37-52: A New Translation with Introduction and
Commentary By. . . . . *.v.1 p.623*

Jeremias Gotthelf: An Introduction to the Swiss
Novelist. . . . . *.v.2 p.620*

Jeremy Bentham: His Life and Work. . . . . *.v.1 p.444*

Jeremy Bentham's Economic Writings. *.v.4 p.217, p.230, p.231*

Jernigan. . . . . *.v.2 p.145*

Jero Plays. . . . . *.v.1 p.128, p.130*

Jerome: His Life Writings and Controversies. . . . . *.v.6 p.571*

Jerome Kern: His Life and Music. . . . *.v.1 p.248, p.334, p.335*

Jerome Robbins: His Life, His Theater, His
Dance. . . . . *.v.1 p.9, p.36, v.6 p.414*

Jerome Robbins: That Broadway Man. . . . . *.v.1 p.7*

Jerome. . . . . *.v.1 p.613*

Jerry Herman: Poet of the
Showtune. . . . . *.v.1 p.248, p.249, p.331, v.6 p.413*

The Jerusalem Bible: Reader's Edition. . . . . . . *.v.1 p.613*

Jerusalem Delivered (Gerusalemme Liberata). . . . . *.v.2 p.710*

Jerusalem in the Mind of the Western World, 1800-1948,
V. . . . . *.v.6 p.609*

Jerusalem in the Twentieth Century. . . . . *.v.6 p.610*

Jerusalem: The Future of a Contested City. . . . . . *.v.6 p.713*

Jerusalem. . . . . *.v.2 p.630*

Jessamyn West. . . . . *.v.2 p.130*

Jesse Jackson's 1984 Presidential Campaign: Challenge and
Change in American Politics. . . . . *.v.3 p.445*

Jesse Owens: An American Life. . . . . . *.v.4 p.831, p.869*

A Jesse Stuart Reader: Stories and Poems. . . . . *.v.2 p.117*

A Jest of God. . . . . *.v.2 p.736*

Jest, Satire, Irony and Deeper Significance. . . . . . *.v.2 p.597*

The Jesuit and the Incas: The Extraordinary Life of Padre Blas
Valera, S. J. . . . . *.v.3 p.326*

The Jesuit Myth: Conspiracy Theory and Politics in
Nineteenth-Century France. . . . . *.v.3 p.148*

Jesuit Ranches and the Agrarian Development of Colonial
Argentina, 1650-1767. . . . . *.v.3 p.347*

Jesuits and Jacobins: Enlightenment and Enlightened Despotism
in Austria. . . . . *.v.3 p.182*

The Jesuits in North America in the Seventeenth
Century. . . . . *.v.3 p.538*

The Jesuits: Their Spiritual Doctrine and Practice. . . *.v.1 p.577*

Jesus - God and Man. . . . . *.v.1 p.641*

Jesus: An Experiment in Christology. . . . . *.v.1 p.641*

Jesus and Freedom. . . . . *.v.1 p.641*

Jesus and Judaism. . . . . *.v.1 p.627*

Jesus and the Ossuaries. . . . . *.v.1 p.617*

Jesus and the Word. . . . . *.v.1 p.627*

Jesus As Mother: Studies in the Spirituality of the High Middle
Ages. . . . . *.v.1 p.650*

Jesus Christ Liberator: A Critical Christology for Our
Time. . . . . *.v.1 p.640, p.641*

Jesus, Humanity and the Trinity: A Brief Systematic
Theology. . . . . *.v.1 p.636*

Jesus in the Qur'an. . . . . *.v.1 p.558*

Jesus of Nazareth. . . . . *.v.1 p.627*

The Jesus Quest: The Third Search for the Jew of
Nazareth. . . . . *.v.1 p.627, p.628*

Jesus, Symbol of God. . . . . *.v.1 p.635, p.636*

Jesus the Christ. . . . . *.v.1 p.641*

Jesus; the classic article from RGG expanded and
updated. . . . . *.v.1 p.641*

Jesus the Jew: A Historian's Reading of the Gospels. *.v.1 p.641*

Jesus Through the Centuries: His Place in the History of
Culture. . . . . *.v.1 p.640*

Jet Propulsion: A Simple Guide to the Aerodynamic and
Thermodynamic Design and Performance of Jet
Engines. . . . . *.v.5 p.717*

Le Jeu de L'amour et du Hasard and les Fausses
Confidences. . . . . *.v.2 p.481*

La jeune fille au balcon : roman. . . . . *.v.2 p.545*

Jew in the Medieval World: A Source Book, 315-1791. *.v.1 p.548*

The Jew in the Modern World: A Documentary
History. . . . . *.v.1 p.548, v.3 p.60*

A Jew in the New Germany. . . . . *.v.3 p.179*

Jew or Juif? Jews, French Canadians, and Anglo-Canadians,
1759-1914. . . . . *.v.3 p.542*

Jewel of the Desert: Japanese American Internment at
Topaz. . . . . *.v.6 p.135*

Jewelry: From Antiquity to the Present. *v.1 p.716*

Jewish American Literature: A Norton Anthology. . . .*v.2 p.18*

The Jewish Confederates. *v.3 p.498, v.4 p.521, p.522*

Jewish Daily Life in Germany, 1618-1945. . . . . . .*v.3 p.180*

Jewish Detroit. *v.3 p.516*

Jewish Education in the United States: A Documentary
History. *v.4 p.308*

The Jewish Enlightenment. *v.3 p.179*

Jewish Life in Muslim Libya: Rivals and
Relatives. *v.6 p.597, p.640*

Jewish Living: A Guide to Contemporay Reform
Practice. *v.1 p.552, p.553*

Jewish Music in Its Historical Development. *v.1 p.300*

Jewish Musical Traditions. *v.1 p.300*

Jewish Mystical Testimonies. *v.1 p.552*

The Jewish Nation in Surinam: Historical Essays. . .*v.3 p.322*

Jewish Policies and Right-Wing Politics in Imperial
Russia. *v.3 p.60*

A Jewish Renaissance in Fifteenth-Century
Spain. *v.3 p.58, p.59, p.239*

Jewish Scholarship and Culture in Nineteenth-Century Germany:
Between History and Faith. *v.3 p.180*

ⓔ Jewish State or Israeli Nation? *v.6 p.613*

Jewish Texts on the Visual Arts. *v.1 p.703*

Jewish Theology. *v.1 p.551, p.552*

Jewish Thought and Scientific Discovery in Early Modern
Europe. *v.3 p.48*

The Jewish Woman: New Perspectives. *v.1 p.553*

Jewish Women in America: An Historical Encyclopedia,
Set. *v.1 p.553, v.6 p.459*

Jewish Women in Historical Perspective. *v.1 p.553*

Jewish Worship. *v.1 p.552*

Jewish Writings of the Second Temple Period: Apocrypha,
Pseudepigrapha, Qumran, Sectarian Writings, Philo,
Josephus. *v.1 p.546*

Jews among Muslims: Communities in the Precolonial Middle
East. *v.6 p.597*

Jews and Arabs, Their Contacts Through the Ages. . .*v.6 p.597*

Jews and Muslims: Images of Sephardi and Easter Jewries in
Modern Times. *v.6 p.598*

The Jews and the Crusaders: The Hebrew Chronicles of the
First and Second Crusades. *v.6 p.597, p.609*

Jews and the German State: The Political History of a Minority,
1848-1933. . . . .*v.3 p.60, p.160*

Jews for Sale?: Nazi-Jewish Negotiations, 1939-1945. .*v.3 p.82*

Jews in an Arab Land: Libya, 1835-1970. . . .*v.6 p.597, p.640*

Jews in an Iberian Frontier Kingdom: Society, Economy, and
Politics in Morvedre, 1248-1391. *v.3 p.58, p.59, p.239, p.240*

Jews in Another Environment: Surinam in the Second Half of
the Eighteenth Century. *v.3 p.322*

Jews in Eastern Poland and the U. S. S. R., 1939-46. . .*v.3 p.86*

The Jews in Egypt and in Palestine Under the Fatimid
Caliphs. *v.6 p.597, p.609, p.636*

Jews in France During World War II. *v.3 p.156*

Jews in Islamic Countries in the Middle Ages. .*v.6 p.573, p.574*

The Jews in Modern Egypt, 1914-1952. . . . .*v.6 p.597, p.638*

Jews in Nineteenth Century Egypt. *v.6 p.597, p.638*

The Jews in Palestine, 1800-1882. . . . .*v.6 p.611*

Jews in Post-Holocaust Germany, 1945-1953. . .*v.3 p.179, p.180*

Jews in Russian Literature after the October Revolution: Writers
and Artists between Hope and Apostasy. *v.2 p.800*

The Jews in the Renaissance. *v.1 p.548*

The Jews in the Soviet Union since 1917. . . . . . .*v.3 p.222*

Jews in Weimar Germany. *v.3 p.60, p.180*

The Jews of Arab Lands: A History and Source Book. .*v.1 p.548*

The Jews of Arab Lands in Modern Times. *v.6 p.598*

The Jews of Bohemia and Moravia: A Historical Reader. .*v.3 p.190*

The Jews of Chicago: From Shtetl to Suburb. *v.3 p.515*

The Jews of Egypt, 1920-1970: In the Midst of Zionism,
Anti-Semitism, and the Middle East Conflict. *v.6 p.597, p.638*

The Jews of Islam. *v.1 p.558, v.6 p.573, p.574, p.597*

The Jews of Modern France. *v.3 p.155*

The Jews of Moslem Spain. *v.6 p.584, p.596*

The Jews of Palestine: A Political History from the Bar Kokhba
War to the Arab Conquest. *v.3 p.6, p.7*

The Jews of Spain: A History of the Sephardic
Experience. *v.1 p.548, v.3 p.243*

Jews of the Middle East (1860-1972). *v.6 p.596*

The Jews of the Middle East and North Africa in Modern
Times. *v.6 p.598*

The Jews of the Ottoman Empire and the Turkish
Republic. *v.6 p.598, p.622*

Jews, Turks, and Ottomans: A Shared History, Fifteenth to
Twentieth Centuries. *v.6 p.590, p.597*

Jews, Visigoths, and Muslims in Medieval Spain: Cooperation
and Conflict. *v.3 p.66*

JFK and LBJ: The Influence of Personality upon
Prejudice. *v.3 p.482*

JFK: Reckless Youth. *v.3 p.472*

Jig Cook and the Provincetown Players: Theatre in
Ferment. *v.1 p.80, p.83, p.118*

Jihad: From Qu'ran to Bin Laden. *v.1 p.560*

Jihad in Classical and Modern Islam: Documentary
History-Updated Edition with a Section on Jihad in the 21st
Century. *v.1 p.559, p.560*

Jihad: The Origin of Holy War in Islam. *v.1 p.560*

Jihad: The Trail of Political Islam. *v.6 p.593*

Jill the Reckless. *v.2 p.390*

Jill. *v.2 p.361*

Jim Crow's Children: The Broken Promise of the Brown
Decision. *v.4 p.450*

Jim Dine Prints, 1985-2000: A Catalogue Raisonné. . .*v.1 p.755*

Jim Thompson: Sleep with the Devil. *v.2 p.124*

The Jimi Hendrix Companion: Three Decades of
Commentary. *v.1 p.273, p.331*

Jimmy Carter: An American Moralist. *v.3 p.476*

Jimmy Carter: In Search of the Great White House. . .*v.3 p.471*

J-K Huysmans and the Fin-de-Siecle Novel, Vol. 3. . .*v.2 p.495*

Joan Jonas: Five Works. *v.1 p.773*

Joan Makes History. *v.2 p.746*

Joan Miró. *v.1 p.697*

Joan of Arc and Richard III: Sex, Saints, and Government in the
  Middle Ages. *v.3 p.96, p.144*

Joan of Arc and Spirituality. *v.3 p.143*

Joan of Arc: The Early Debate. *v.3 p.143, p.144*

Joan of Arc: The Legend and the Reality. *v.3 p.144*

Joan Robinson and the Americans. *v.4 p.271*

Joan Robinson: Economic Writings. *v.4 p.270*

The Joan Robinson Legacy. *v.4 p.270*

Joaquin Murieta: The Life and Adventures of Joaquin Murieta,
  the Celebrated California Bandit. *v.2 p.49, v.6 p.699*

Job Descriptions for Film, Video and CGI: Responsibilities and
  Duties for the Cinematic Craft Categories and
  Classifications. *v.6 p.347*

Job Hunting on the Internet. *v.4 p.168*

Job Queues, Gender Queues: Explaining Women's Inroads into
  Male Occupations. *v.4 p.725*

Job Satisfaction: Application, Assessment, Causes, and
  Consequences, Vol. 3. . . . .*v.5 p.579*

Job Surfing: Working Abroad. *v.4 p.171*

Job-Hunting for the So-Called Handicapped: Or People Who
  Have Disabilities. *v.4 p.168*

Jobless Pay and the Economy. *v.4 p.247*

Job. *v.1 p.621*

Jocks 2: Coming Out to Play. *v.4 p.839, v.6 p.384*

Jocks: True Stories of America's Gay Male
  Athletes. *v.4 p.839, v.6 p.384*

Jodo Shinshu: Shin Buddhism in Medieval Japan. . . .*v.6 p.219*

Joe DiMaggio: The Hero's Life. *v.4 p.850*

Joe McCarthy and the Press. *v.3 p.455*

Joe Tumulty and the Wilson Era. *v.3 p.456*

Joel: A New Translation with Notes. *v.1 p.622*

Joel Barlow. *v.2 p.29*

Joel Chandler Harris: A Biography and Critical Study. .*v.2 p.40*

Joel Whitburn Presents a Century of Pop Music: Year-by-Year
  Top 40 Rankings of the Songs and Artists That
  Shaped a Century: Compiled from America's Popular Music
  Charts, Surveys, and Record Listings 1900-1939, and
  Billboard's Pop Singles Charts, 1940-1999. *v.1 p.171, p.276*

Joel Whitburn Presents Top 10 Singles Charts: Chart Data
  Compiled from Billboard's Best Sellers in Stores
  and Hot 100 Charts, 1955-2000. . . .*v.1 p.171, p.172, p.276*

Joel Whitburn Presents Top R & B/Hip-Hop Singles,
  1942-2004. . . . .*v.1 p.172, p.276*

Joel Whitburn's Top Pop Albums, 1955-2001. .*v.1 p.172, p.276*

The Joffrey Ballet: Robert Joffrey and the Making of an
  American Dance Company. *v.1 p.5, p.22, v.6 p.414*

Johann Sebastian Bach: The Learned Musician. .*v.1 p.187, p.304*

Johann Strauss: A Nineteenth Century Pop-Idol. .*v.1 p.200, p.359*

Johann Strauss and Vienna: Operetta and the Politics of Popular
  Culture. *v.1 p.196, p.359*

Johannes Bobrowski. *v.2 p.603*

Johannes Brahms: A Biography. *v.1 p.313*

Johannes Brahms: Life and Letters. *v.1 p.194, p.313*

Johannes Brahms. *v.1 p.164, p.202, p.313*

Johannes Vermeer. *v.1 p.749*

The Johannine Letters: A Commentary on 1, 2, and 3
  John. *v.1 p.631*

John A. MacDonald: The Young Politician and the Old
  Chieftain. *v.3 p.539*

John Adams and the Diplomacy of the American
  Revolution. *v.3 p.413*

John Adams and the Spirit of Liberty. *v.4 p.515, p.516*

John Adams. *v.3 p.415*

John Ashbery and American Poetry. *v.2 p.57*

John Bale. *v.2 p.214*

John Berryman: A Critical Commentary. *v.2 p.61*

John Berryman: Collected Poems, 1937-1971. . . . .*v.2 p.61*

John Berryman: Selected Poems. *v.2 p.61*

John Bright. *v.3 p.95, p.115*

John Brown, 1800-1859: Biography Fifty Years After. .*v.3 p.432*

John Brown and the Legend of Fifty-Six, Set. *v.3 p.524*

John Brown's Body. *v.2 p.60, p.61*

John Bull's Island: Immigration and British society,
  1871-1971. . . . .*v.3 p.112*

John Bunyan, Mechanick Preacher. *v.2 p.241*

John Bunyan. *v.2 p.241*

John C. Calhoun, Opportunist: A Reappraisal. *v.3 p.415*

John C. Calhoun. *v.3 p.416*

John Calvin: A Sixteenth-Century Portrait. . . .*v.1 p.580, p.602*

John Cassian: The Conferences. *v.1 p.591, p.653*

John Cheever: A Biography. *v.2 p.68, v.6 p.401*

John Cheever: A Study of the Short Fiction. *v.2 p.68*

John Christian Bach: Mozart's Friend and
  Mentor. *v.1 p.189, p.302*

John Chrysostom. *v.1 p.593*

John Clare: A Biography. *v.2 p.278*

John Clare by Himself. *v.2 p.278*

John Clare in Context. *v.2 p.278*

John Clare. *v.2 p.278*

John Coltrane: A Discography and Musical
  Biography. *v.1 p.170, p.259, p.318*

John Coltrane and the Jazz Revolution of The
  1960s. *v.1 p.261, p.318*

John Coltrane Companion: Four Decades of
  Commentary. *v.1 p.265, p.318*

John Coltrane: His Life and Music. *v.1 p.262, p.318*

John Davidson, Poet of Armageddon. *v.2 p.275*

John Dewey and American Democracy. *v.4 p.493*

John Dewey and the Art of Teaching: Toward Reflective and
  Imaginative Practice. *v.4 p.345*

John Dewey and the Challenge of Classroom Practice. .*v.4 p.342*

John Dewey and the Paradox of Liberal Reform. .*v.4 p.344, p.345*

John Dewey in Perspective. *v.1 p.443*

John Dewey: Rethinking Our Time. *v.1 p.443*

John Dewey. *v.1 p.443*

John Donne - the Major Works: Including Songs and Sonnets
  and Sermons. *v.1 p.582*

John Donne and the Seventeenth-Century Metaphysical
  Poets. *v.2 p.182*

John Donne: Life, Mind and Art. *v.2 p.213*

John Donne: Selected Poems. *v.2 p.213*

John Donne: The Critical Heritage.. . . . .*v.2 p.216*

John Donne's Lyrics: The Eloquence of Action. *v.2 p.216*

John Donne's Sermons on the Psalms and Gospels: With a Selection of Prayers and Meditations. *v.2 p.213*

John Dos Passos: Novels, 1920-1925. . . . .*v.2 p.69*

John Dos Passos Revisited. *v.2 p.70*

ⓔ John Dos Passos: The Critical Heritage. *v.2 p.69, p.70*

John Dos Passos: Travel Books and Other Writings 1916 to 1941. . . . .*v.2 p.69*

John Dowland.. . . . .*v.1 p.181, p.322*

John Dryden and His World.. . . . .*v.2 p.247*

John Dryden: Dramatist, Satirist, Translator. *v.2 p.246*

John Edward Bruce: The Legacy of a Politician, Journalist, and Self-Trained Historian of the African Diaspora. *v.6 p.4, p.17*

John Elliot Cairnes: Collected Works. *v.4 p.217*

John Everett Millais: A Biography.. . . . .*v.1 p.738*

John Everett Millais: Beyond the Pre-Raphaelite Brotherhood. *v.1 p.743*

John F. Kennedy: A Biography. *v.3 p.477*

John F. Kennedy: Commander in Chief: A Profile in Leadership. *v.3 p.479*

John F. Kennedy: The Man, the Politician, the President. .*v.3 p.478*

The John Fante Reader. *v.2 p.72*

John Ford and the Caroline Theatre. *v.2 p.218*

John Foster Dulles: Piety, Pragmatism and Power in U. S. Foreign Policy. *v.3 p.459*

John Galsworthy: A Biography. *v.2 p.347*

John Galsworthy: A Reassessment.. . . . .*v.2 p.347*

John Galsworthy. *v.2 p.348*

John Greenleaf Whittier: Selected Poems. *v.2 p.55*

John Greenleaf Whittier's Poetry: An Appraisal and a Selection. *v.2 p.55*

John Grierson: Life, Contributions, Influence. *v.6 p.309*

John Hedgecoe's Complete Guide to Black and White Photography. *v.1 p.769*

John Henry Days: A Novel. *v.2 p.159*

John Henry Newman: The Challenge to Evangelical Religion. *v.1 p.580*

John Henry Twachtman, American Impressionist Painter as Printmaker: A Catalogue Raisonné of His Prints. . *v.1 p.755*

John Heywood's Works and Miscellaneous Short Poems. *v.2 p.219*

John Hopkins's Notions on Political Economy. *v.4 p.195*

John J. Crittenden: The Struggle for the Union. *v.3 p.415*

John James Audubon: The Making of an American. . .*v.1 p.745*

John Keats and the Culture of Dissent. *v.2 p.295*

John Keats: Complete Poems. *v.2 p.295*

John Keats: The Major Works: Including Endymion, the Odes and Selected Letters. *v.2 p.295*

John Keats: The Making of a Poet. *v.2 p.296*

John Keats. *v.2 p.294, p.295*

John Knox. *v.1 p.588*

John L. Sullivan and His America. . . .*v.4 p.807, p.816, p.855*

John Leech and the Victorian Scene. *v.6 p.737*

John Leighton Stuart and Twentieth-Century Chinese-American Relations. *v.6 p.201, p.204, p.205, p.218*

John Locke and the Way of Ideas. *v.1 p.449*

John Lyly. *v.2 p.216*

John Marshall: A Life in Law. *v.4 p.467*

John Marshall and the Heroic Age of the Supreme Court. *v.4 p.468*

John Marshall: Definer of a Nation. *v.4 p.469*

John Marshall Harlan: The Last Whig Justice.. . . . .*v.4 p.467*

John Marston, Satirist. *v.2 p.221*

John Marston's Plays: Theme, Structure and Performance. *v.2 p.222*

John Marston's Theatrical Drama. *v.2 p.221*

John Maynard Keynes, 1883-1946, Set.. . . . . . .*v.4 p.226*

John Maynard Keynes: A Study in the Psychology of Original Work. *v.4 p.228*

John Maynard Keynes: Critical Assessments, Vol. 38115. . . . .*v.4 p.229*

John Maynard Keynes: Critical Responses. *v.4 p.228*

John Maynard Keynes: Father of Modern Economics. .*v.4 p.229*

John Maynard Keynes: Fighting for Freedom 1937-1946. . . . .*v.4 p.229*

John Maynard Keynes: Hopes Betrayed, 1883-1920. . .*v.4 p.229*

John Maynard Keynes: Language and Method. *v.4 p.228*

John Maynard Keynes: Life, Ideas, Legacy. *v.4 p.226*

John Maynard Keynes: The Economist As Savior, 1920-1937. . . . .*v.4 p.229*

John Maynard Keyness: Keynesianism into the Twenty-First Century. *v.4 p.229*

John Maynard Keynes. *v.4 p.212*

John McGraw. *v.4 p.849*

John Millington Synge: A Biography. *v.2 p.306*

John Milton and the English Revolution: A Study in the Sociology of Literature. *v.2 p.254*

John Milton: Poetry. *v.2 p.254*

John Milton: Selected Prose. *v.2 p.255*

John Milton: The Inner Life. *v.2 p.255*

John Milton: The Self and the World. *v.2 p.255*

John Muir: Nature Writings: The Story of My Boyhood and Youth; My First Summer in the Sierra; The Mountains of California; Stickeen; Essays. *v.6 p.287*

John Nash: A Complete Catalogue. *v.1 p.794*

John of the Cross. *v.1 p.579*

John O'Hara: A Study of the Short Fiction. *v.2 p.106*

John O'Hara's Hollywood: Stories.. . . . .*v.2 p.106*

John Oldham. *v.2 p.252*

John Osborne Plays 1: Look Back in Anger; Epitaph for George Dillion; the World of Paul... . . . .*v.1 p.80, p.102,v.2 p.376*

John Osborne: The Entertainer-Hotel in Amsterdam-West of Suez. *v.2 p.376*

John Osborne: Vituperative Artist. *v.2 p.376*

John P. Hale and the Politics of Abolition. *v.3 p.422, p.423, p.429*

John Paul Jones: A Sailor's Biography. *v.3 p.383*

John Philip Kemble: The Actor in His Theatre. .*v.1 p.98, p.143*

John Philip Sousa: American Phenomenon. . . .*v.1 p.276, p.358*

John Quincy Adams: A Public Life, a Private Life. *v.3 p.415, p.416*

John Quincy Adams and American Global Empire. . .*v.3 p.505*

John Quincy Adams and the Foundations of American Foreign Policy. *v.3 p.416*

John Quincy Adams and the Union. *v.3 p.416*

John Quincy Adams Ward. *v.1 p.781*

John Rollin Ridge: His Life and Works. . . .*v.2 p.49, v.6 p.698*

John Ruskin: A Reference Guide. *v.2 p.305*

John Ruskin and the Victorian Eye. *v.2 p.305*

John Ruskin and Victorian Architecture. *v.1 p.791, p.792*

John Ruskin: The Early Years. *v.2 p.305*

John Ruskin: The Later Years. *v.2 p.305*

John Searle. *v.1 p.441, p.442, p.443*

John Singer Sargent: Portraits of the 1890s Complete Paintings. *v.1 p.745*

John Singer Sargent: The Early Portraits. *v.1 p.745*

John Singer Sargent: The Sensualist. *v.1 p.738*

John Skelton (1460-1529): Selected Poems. *v.2 p.216*

John Skelton's Poetry. *v.2 p.214*

John Sloan's Oil Paintings: A Catalogue Raisonné. .*v.1 p.738*

John Sloan's Prints: A Catalogue Raisonné of the Etchings, Lithographs and Posters. *v.1 p.757*

John Smibert: Colonial America's First Portrait Painter. .*v.1 p.746*

John Soane: An Accidental Romantic. *v.1 p.792*

John Soane, Architect: Master of Space and Light. . .*v.1 p.794*

John Steinbeck, 1936-1941: The Long Valley; the Grapes of Wrath; the Log from the Sea of Cortez; the Harvest Gypsies. *v.2 p.123*

John Steinbeck: A Biography. *v.2 p.123*

John Steinbeck: A Centennial Tribute. *v.2 p.123*

John Steinbeck Novels 1942-1952, Vol. 3. . . . .*v.2 p.123*

John Steinbeck. *v.2 p.123*

John Steuart Curry: Inventing the Middle West. . . .*v.1 p.742*

John Stuart and the Struggle for Empire on the Southern Frontier. *v.3 p.495*

John Stuart Mill: A Biography. *v.1 p.445*

John Stuart Mill: A Mind at Large. *v.1 p.444*

John Stuart Mill and Harriet Taylor: Their Correspondence and Subsequent Marriage. *v.4 p.211*

John Stuart Mill and India. *v.6 p.158*

John Stuart Mill and the Harriet Taylor Myth. *v.4 p.212*

John Stuart Mill on Education. *v.4 p.344*

John the Valiant. *v.2 p.786*

John Von Neumann: The Scientific Genius Who Pioneered the Modern Computer, Game Theory, Nuclear Deterrence and Much More. *v.5 p.397*

John Von Neumann. *v.5 p.397*

John Webster: A Critical Anthology. *v.2 p.235*

John Webster. *v.2 p.235*

John Winthrop: America's Forgotten Founding Father. *v.1 p.580, v.3 p.487*

John Wooden: An American Treasure. *v.4 p.853*

John Wycliffe and the Beginnings of English Nonconformity. *v.6 p.572*

John XXIII: Pope of the Century. *v.1 p.573*

Johnny the Partisan. *v.2 p.715*

Johns Hopkins Consumer Guide to Drugs 2005. . . .*v.5 p.526*

Johnson, Grant, and the Politics of Reconstruction. .*v.3 p.437*

Johnson on Shakespeare. *v.2 p.230*

Johnson the Poet: The Poetic Career of Samuel Johnson.*v.2 p.251*

Johnson, Writing, and Memory. *v.2 p.250*

The Johnson Years: Foreign Policy, the Great Society, and the White House. *v.3 p.469*

The Johnson Years: LBJ at Home and Abroad. . . .*v.3 p.469*

The Johnson Years: Vietnam, the Environment, and Science. *v.3 p.440, 469*

Johnson's Critical Presence: Image, History, Judgment. .*v.2 p.251*

Johnson's Journey to the Western Islands of Scotland and Boswell's Journal of a Tour to the Hebrides with Samuel Johnson. *v.3 p.133*

Johnson's Moral Comedy. *v.2 p.219*

A Joint Element for the Nonlinear Dynamic Analysis of Arch Dams. *v.5 p.694*

Jokes and Their Relationship to the Unconscious. .*v.2 p.585, p.586*

Jokes: Philosophical Thoughts on Joking Matters. . .*v.2 p.585*

The Joke. *v.2 p.784*

Jonah. *v.1 p.623*

Jonas and Kovner's Health Care Delivery in the United States. *v.5 p.513*

Jonathan Edwards: A Life. *v.1 p.581, p.584*

Jonathan Edwards, Religious Tradition, and American Culture from the Second Great Awakening to the Twentieth Century. *v.1 p.584*

Jonathan Edwards. *v.1 p.584*

Jonathan Sewall: Odyssey of an American Loyalist. . .*v.3 p.407*

Jonathan Strange and Mr. Norrell: A Novel. *v.2 p.337*

Jonathan Swift, a Critical Biography. *v.2 p.263*

Jonathan Swift and Ireland. *v.2 p.263*

Jonathan Swift and Popular Culture: Myth, Media and the Man. *v.2 p.263*

Jonathan Swift: Political Writer. *v.2 p.262*

Jonathan Wild. *v.2 p.247*

Jones Very: Selected Poems. *v.2 p.53*

The Joni Mitchell Companion: Four Decades of Commentary. *v.1 p.271, p.342*

Jonson and Elizabethan Comedy: Essays in Dramatic Rhetoric. *v.2 p.219*

Jookin': The Rise of Social Dance Formations in African-American Culture. *v.1 p.31*

Joos Van Cleve: The Complete Paintings. *v.1 p.740*

Joothan: An Untouchable's Life. *v.6 p.149, p.153*

Jordan in the 1967 War. *v.6 p.621*

Jordan, the United States and the Middle East Peace Process, 1974-1991. . . . .*v.3 p.391*

The Jordanian - Palestinian - Israeli Triangle: Smoothing the Path to Peace. *v.6 p.617*

The Jordanian-Israeli War 1948-1951: A History of the Hashemite Kingdom of Jordan. *v.6 p.620*

Jorge Amado (Brazi). *v.2 p.690*

Jorge Amado: New Critical Essays. *v.2 p.690*

Jorge Luis Borges: Argentine Writer. *v.2 p.679*

Jorge Luis Borges. *v.2 p.677, p.678*

Jose, Can You See?: Latinos on and off
Broadway. *v.6 p.493, p.515, p.516, p.518*

Jose Carlos Mariategui and the Rise of Modern Peru,
1890-1930. . . . .*v.3 p.329*

Jose Clemente Orozco in the United States. *v.1 p.744*

Jose Donoso. *v.2 p.680*

Jose Lezama Lima: Selections. *v.2 p.672*

Jose Limon: An Unfinished Memoir. *v.1 p.10*

Jose M. Arguedas: Los Rios Profundos. *v.2 p.685*

Jose Maria de Pereda. *v.2 p.654, p.655*

Jose Marti and the Emigre Colony in Key West: Leadership and
State Formation. *v.3 p.313*

Jose Marti in the United States: The Florida Experience.*v.3 p.312*

Jose Marti: Major Poems. *v.2 p.672*

Josef and Anni Albers: Designs for Living. *v.1 p.720*

Josef Hoffmann Designs: MAK- Austrian Museum of Applied
Arts. *v.1 p.720*

Joseph Addison and His Time. *v.2 p.236*

Joseph Addison and Richard Steele: A Reference Guide,
1730-1991. . . . .*v.2 p.236, p.237, p.261, p.262*

Joseph Addison's Sociable Animal: In the Market Place, on the
Hustings, in the Pulpit. *v.2 p.236*

Joseph Addison. *v.2 p.237*

Joseph and His Brothers. *v.2 p.613*

Joseph and the Amazing Technicolor
Dreamcoat. *v.1 p.253, p.337, p.409*

Joseph Andrews. *v.2 p.266*

Joseph Beuys - The Multiples: Catalogue Raisonné of Multiples
and Prints. *v.1 p.758*

Joseph Chamberlain: A Political Study. *v.3 p.94, p.113*

Joseph Conrad: A Biography. *v.2 p.341*

Joseph Conrad and the Anthropological Dilemma: 'Bewildered
Traveller'. *v.2 p.341*

Joseph Conrad As I Knew Him. *v.2 p.339*

Joseph Conrad: His Moral Vision. *v.2 p.341*

Joseph Conrad: Notes on Life and Letters. . . .*v.2 p.340, p.341*

Joseph Conrad's Heart of Darkness: A Casebook. . . .*v.2 p.340*

Joseph Conrad. *v.2 p.339*

Joseph Cornell: Shadowplay . . . Eterniday. *v.1 p.697*

Joseph E. Brown of Georgia. *v.3 p.434*

Joseph E. Davies: Envoy to the Soviets. *v.3 p.460*

Joseph Howe: Conservative Reformer, 1804-1848. . .*v.3 p.542*

Joseph II: In the Shadow of Maria Theresa, 1741-1780, Vol.
1. . . . .*v.3 p.182*

Joseph II. *v.3 p.182*

Joseph McCarthy: The Politics of Chaos. *v.3 p.460*

Joseph Pennell - the Lithographs and Etchings: A Catalogue
Raisonné. *v.1 p.758*

Joseph Pulitzer. *v.4 p.410*

Joseph Smith: Rough Stone Rolling. *v.1 p.580, p.581*

Joseph Story and the American Constitution: A Study in
Political and Legal Thought. *v.4 p.468*

Joseph von Eichendorff. *v.2 p.597*

Josephine: The Hungry Heart. *v.1 p.6*

Josh Gibson: The Power and the Darkness. . . .*v.4 p.833, p.852*

Joshua. *v.1 p.620*

Josiah Walls: Florida's Black Congressman of
Reconstruction. *v.3 p.434*

The Josquin Companion. *v.1 p.181, p.334*

The Jossey-Bass Reader on School Reform. *v.4 p.327*

Journal, 1955-1962: Reflections on the French-Algerian
War. *v.6 p.60*

Journal Citation Reports. *v.5 p.256*

Journal en miettes. *v.2 p.520*

Journal of a Residence in Chile During the Year 1822: And, a
Voyage from Chile to Brazil in 1823. . . . .*v.3 p.350, p.351*

Journal of a Voyage to Siam, 1685-1686. . . . . . .*v.6 p.171*

The Journal of Albion Moonlight. *v.2 p.110*

Journal of Bisexuality. *v.6 p.361*

Journal of Chemical Education Chemical Education Resource
Shelf. *v.5 p.267*

Journal of Delacroix. *v.1 p.696*

Journal of G L B T Family Studies. *v.6 p.361*

Journal of G L B T Issues in Counseling. *v.6 p.361*

Journal of Gay & Lesbian Issues in Education: An International
Quarterly Devoted to Research, Theory, and
Practice. *v.6 p.361*

Journal of Gay & Lesbian Psychotherapy. *v.6 p.361*

Journal of Gay & Lesbian Social Services. *v.6 p.361*

Journal of Heterocyclic Chemistry (search). *v.5 p.298*

Journal of Homosexuality. *v.6 p.361*

The Journal of John Gabriel Stedman, 1744-1797, Soldier and
Author, Including an Authentic Account of His
Expedition to Surinam in 1772. . . . .*v.3 p.323*

The Journal of John Winthrop, 1630-1649. . . . . . .*v.2 p.28*

Journal of Katherine Mansfield. *v.2 p.369*

Journal of L G B T Health Research. *v.6 p.361*

Journal of Lesbian Studies. *v.6 p.362*

The Journal of Madame Knight. *v.2 p.29*

Journal of Physical and Chemical Reference Data. . .*v.5 p.274*

Journal of the History of Sexuality. *v.6 p.362*

A Journal of the Plague Year: Being Observations or Memorials
of the Mosst Remarkable Occurence. *v.2 p.245*

Journal, vol. 1. . . . .*v.2 p.520*

The Journal, Vol. 1. . . . .*v.3 p.422, p.423, p.428*

Journal, vol. 2. . . . .*v.2 p.520*

Journalism in the United States from 1690 to 1872, Set.*v.4 p.405*

A Journalist's Guide to the Internet: The Net As a Reporting
Tool. *v.4 p.413, p.414*

The Journalist's Moral Compass: Basic Principles. . .*v.4 p.405*

Journals, 1889-1913, Vol. 1. . . . .*v.2 p.520*

Journals, 1914-1927, Vol. 2. . . . .*v.2 p.520*

Journals, 1928-1939, Vol. 3. . . . .*v.2 p.520*

Journals, 1939-1949, Vol. 4. . . . .*v.2 p.520*

Journals, 1939-1983. . . . .*v.2 p.384*

Journals and Letters. *v.2 p.242*

Journals of Dorothy Wordsworth. *v.2 p.322*

The Journals of George Eliot. *v.2 p.287*

The Journals of Lewis and Clark. *v.3 p.520*

The Journals, Vol. 1. . . . .*v.2 p.346*

Journals. *v.2 p.334*

A Journey for All Seasons: A Nature Conservancy
    Book. *v.5 p.222*

Journey from Petersburg to Moscow. *v.2 p.807, v.3 p.216*

Journey from Prince of Wales's Fort in Hudson's Bay to the
    Northern Ocean in the Years 1769-1772. . . . . . .*v.3 p.545*

Journey into Darkness: Genocide in Rwanda. . .*v.4 p.653, p.715*

Journey into Fear. *v.2 p.328*

A Journey into Gravity and
    Spacetime. *v.5 p.73, p.556, p.557, p.558*

Journey into the Whirlwind. *v.2 p.803, v.3 p.224*

Journey of Hope: The Back to Africa Movement in Arkansas in
    the Late 1800s. *v.4 p.764*

The Journey of Life: A Cultural History of Aging in
    America. *v.4 p.741*

The Journey of Little Gandhi. *v.6 p.661*

The Journey of Niels Klim to the World Underground. .*v.2 p.627*

The Journey of the Mind to God. *v.1 p.433*

The Journey Out: A Guide for and about Lesbian, Gay, and
    Bisexual Teens. *v.6 p.369*

A Journey Through Life. *v.3 p.354*

A Journey Through Other Spaces: Essays and Manifestos,
    1944-1990. . . . .*v.1 p.109, p.152*

A Journey Through Texas: Or a Saddle-Trip on the
    Southwestern Frontier. *v.3 p.509*

Journey to Oneself. *v.2 p.780*

Journey to the End of the Night. *v.2 p.515*

The Journey to the West, Vol. 1. . . . .*v.6 p.212*

Journey to the West, Vol. 2. . . . .*v.6 p.212*

Journey Without Maps. *v.2 p.351*

Journeying: Children Responding to Literature. .*v.4 p.363, p.364*

Journeys and Arrivals: On Being Gay and Jewish. . .*v.6 p.374*

Journeys of Women in Science and Engineering: No Universal
    Constants. *v.5 p.394, p.398, v.6 p.438*

Journeys to Selfhood: Hegel and Kierkegaard. . . .*v.1 p.436*

Joy in the Morning. *v.2 p.390*

Joy Is Not My Profession. *v.6 p.656*

The Joy Luck Club. *v.2 p.156, p.157, v.6 p.102*

The Joy of Digital Photography. *v.1 p.770, p.772*

The Joy of Hiking: Hiking the Trailmaster Way. . . .*v.4 p.788*

The Joy of Insight: Passions of a Physicist. *v.5 p.544*

The Joy of Music. *v.1 p.247, p.311*

The Joy of Sports: Endzones, Bases, Baskets, Balls, and the
    Consecration of the American Spirit. *v.4 p.803*

Joyce: A Collection of Critical Essays. *v.2 p.357*

Joyce Annotated: Notes for Dubliners and a Portrait of the Artist
    As a Young Man. *v.2 p.358*

Joyce Cary and Lawrence Durrell: A Reference
    Guide. *v.2 p.338, p.344*

Joyce Cary and the Dimensions of Order. *v.2 p.338*

Joyce Cary: Liberal Principles. *v.2 p.338*

Joyce Cary's Trilogies: Pursuit of the Particular Real. *v.2 p.337*

Joyce in the Hibernian Metropolis: Essays. *v.2 p.357*

Joyce, the Man, the Work, the Reputation. *v.2 p.360*

Joyce's Dublin: A Walking Guide to Ulysses. *v.2 p.360*

Joyce's "Portrait": Criticisms and Critiques. *v.2 p.357*

Joyce's Voices. *v.2 p.359*

Joyous Greetings: The First International Women's Movement,
    1830-1860. . . . .*v.3 p.52, v.4 p.710, v.6 p.430*

The Joys of Hebrew. *v.6 p.646*

The Joys of Motherhood. *v.2 p.754*

Joysprick: An Introduction to the Language of James
    Joyce. *v.2 p.357*

Juan Carlos Onetti: Selected Short Stories. *v.2 p.687*

Juan Carlos: Steering Spain from Dictatorship to
    Democracy. *v.3 p.242, p.243*

Juan Gris. *v.1 p.739*

Juan Melendez Valdes. *v.2 p.654*

Juan Ramon Jimenez. *v.2 p.660*

Juan Valera. *v.2 p.654*

Juan Vicente Gsmez and the Oil Companies in Venezuela,
    1908-1935. . . . .*v.3 p.360, p.361*

Juarez and Diaz: Machine Politics in Mexico. *v.3 p.289*

Judaic Religion in the Second Temple Period: Belief and
    Practice from the Exile to Yavneh. *v.1 p.547*

Judaism: A Historical Presentation. *v.1 p.546, p.547*

Judaism and Christian Beginnings. *v.1 p.550*

Judaism Eternal. *v.1 p.545*

Judaism in the Beginning of Christianity. *v.1 p.549*

Judaism in the First Centuries of the Christian Era: The Age of
    the Tannaim. *v.1 p.548*

Judas at the Jockey Club and Other Episodes of Porfirian
    Mexico. *v.3 p.264*

Jude the Obscure, Pride and Prejudice, Sons and Lovers, The
    Warden, Wuthering Heights, Vol. 2, Level 5. . . . .*v.2 p.292*

Jude the Obscure. *v.2 p.292*

Judenrat: The Jewish Councils in Eastern Europe under Nazi
    Occupation. *v.3 p.87*

Judeo-Christian Perspectives on Psychology: Human Nature,
    Motivation, and Change. *v.5 p.635*

Judge and Jury: The Life and Times of Judge Kenesaw
    Mountain Landis. *v.4 p.851, p.885, p.889, p.892*

Judge Not. *v.2 p.520*

Judge on Trial. *v.2 p.783*

Judges and the Cities: Interpreting Local Autonomy. . *v.4 p.543*

☐ Judges of the United States Courts Biographical Directory of
    Federal Judges. *v.4 p.467*

Judges. *v.1 p.620*

Judging Thomas: The Life and Times of Clarence
    Thomas. *v.4 p.536*

The Judgment of Paris: The Revolutionary Era that Gave the
    World Impressionism. *v.1 p.732*

Judgment under Uncertainty: Heuristics and
    Biases. *v.4 p.195, v.5 p.608*

Judgment without Trial: Japanese American Imprisonment
    during World War II. *v.6 p.115, p.134*

The Judicial Branch of Government. *v.4 p.534*

The Judicial Branch of State Government: People, Process, and
    Politics. *v.4 p.541*

The Judicial Branch. *v.4 p.534*

Judicial Branch. *v.4 p.534*

The Judicial Branch. *v.4 p.534*

The Judicial Development of Presidential War Powers. *v.4 p.539*

Judicial Dictatorship. *v.4 p.538*

Judicial Policies: Implementation and Impact. *v.4 p.465*

Judicial Policy Making and the Modern State: How the Courts Reformed America's Prisons. *v.6 p.268, p.273*

Judicial Power and American Character: Censoring Ourselves in an Anxious Age. *v.4 p.462*

The Judicial Process: An Introductory Analysis of the Courts of the United States, England, and France. *v.4 p.434*

Judicial Process in America. *v.4 p.534*

Judith Sargent Murray: A Brief Biography with Documents. *v.2 p.30*

Judith. *v.1 p.623, p.624,v.2 p.739*

Judson Dance Theater: 1962-1966. . . . .*v.1 p.11*

Judy Chicago: An American Vision. *v.1 p.698*

Judy Chicago. *v.1 p.700*

The Jugurthine War and the Conspiracy of Catiline. *v.2 p.442, p.443*

Juice: The Creative Fuel That Drives World-Class Inventors. *v.4 p.67*

Juju: A Social History and Ethnography of an African Popular Music. *v.1 p.286*

Jules Henry on Education. *v.4 p.343*

Jules LaForgue and Poetic Innovation. *v.2 p.495*

Jules Michelet. *v.2 p.498*

Jules Perrot: Master of the Romantic Ballet. *v.1 p.8*

Jules Renard. *v.2 p.526*

Jules Verne: An Exploratory Biography. *v.2 p.503*

Jules Verne, Five Complete Novels. *v.2 p.503*

Jules Verne, Inventor of Science Fiction. *v.2 p.503*

Jules Verne. *v.2 p.503*

Julia Alvarez: A Critical Companion. *v.6 p.509, p.516*

Julia Alvarez: Writing a New Place on the Map. *v.6 p.507, p.513*

Julia Kristeva: Speaking the Unspeakable. *v.2 p.532*

Julia Margaret Cameron: The Complete Photographs. *v.1 p.766*

Julia Morgan, Architect. *v.1 p.791*

The Julian Samora Research Institute. *v.6 p.520*

Julian Schnabel. *v.1 p.699*

Julian the Apostate. *v.3 p.30*

Julian Trevelyan: Catalogue Raisonné of Prints. . . .*v.1 p.758*

Julian. *v.2 p.127*

Julie: Or the New Heloise: Letters of Two Lovers Who Live in a Small Town at the Foot of the Alps. *v.2 p.483*

Julio Cortazar: A Study of the Short Fiction. *v.2 p.679*

Julio Cortazar. *v.2 p.677*

Julio Larraz. *v.1 p.743*

Julius Caesar. *v.2 p.223*

Jullien's Plan for Comparative Education 1816-1817. *v.4 p.342*

July, 1914: The Long Debate, 1918-1990. . . . . . .*v.3 p.79*

July, July: A Novel. *v.2 p.151*

July Monarchy. *v.3 p.153*

July's People. *v.2 p.755*

Jump Start Your Career in Bio Science. *v.5 p.251*

Jumpin' Jim Crow: Southern Politics from Civil War to Civil Rights. *v.3 p.496*

Jumping into Plyometrics. *v.4 p.793*

Jumpstarting Your Career: An Internship Guide for Criminal Justice. *v.6 p.245*

Jung: A Biography. *v.5 p.595*

Jung: A Feminist Revision. *v.6 p.435, p.446*

The Jung Cult: Origins of a Charismatic Movement. . .*v.5 p.597*

Jung on Christianity. *v.1 p.594*

Jungian Reflections Within the Cinema: A Psychological Analysis of Sci-Fi and Fantasy Archetypes. *v.6 p.318*

The Jungle Books. *v.2 p.297*

The Jungle. *v.2 p.120*

Jungle. *v.5 p.168, p.175, p.176*

Junky. *v.2 p.64*

Jupiter: The Planet, Satellites and Magnetosphere. *v.5 p.68, p.69*

Jura Separation in Switzerland. *v.3 p.245*

Juran's Quality Handbook. *v.5 p.685*

Jurgen. *v.2 p.64*

Jurors' Stories of Death: How America's Death Penalty Invests in Inequality. *v.6 p.270*

Juscelino Kubitschek and the Development of Brazil. *v.3 p.338*

Just an Ordinary Day: The Uncollected Stories of Shirley Jackson. *v.2 p.90*

The Just and the Lively: The Literary Criticism of John Dryden. *v.2 p.246*

Just Another Poster?: Chicano Graphic Arts in California. *v.6 p.492*

Just As I Am: The Autobiography of Billy Graham. . .*v.1 p.581*

Just as I Am: The Autobiography of Billy Graham. . .*v.1 p.648*

Just Cause: Marine Operations in Panama, 1988-1990. *v.3 p.305*

Just Chairs: Over 600 Designs from Around the World. *v.1 p.803*

Just Do It: The Nike Spirit in the Corporate World. *v.4 p.884, p.888*

Just for Fun: The Story of AAU Women's Basketball. *v.4 p.837, p.854, p.884*

Just Intonation Explained. *v.1 p.374*

A Just Measure of Pain: The Penitentiary in the Industrial Revolution, 1750-1850. . . . .*v.4 p.753*

Just Passing Through. *v.2 p.669*

Just Six Numbers: The Deep Forces That Shape the Universe. *v.5 p.541*

Just So Stories: For Little Children. *v.2 p.297*

Just Talk: Gossip, Meetings, and Power in a Papua New Guinea Village. *v.4 p.42*

Just the Facts. *v.4 p.404*

The Just War in the Middle Ages. *v.1 p.644*

Justice: Alternative Political Perspectives. *v.4 p.514*

Justice and the Politics of Difference. *v.4 p.506, p.514, p.515*

Justice Antonin Scalia and the Conservative Revival. *v.4 p.467, p.535*

Justice Antonin Scalia and the Supreme Court's Conservative Moment. *v.4 p.539, p.540*

Justice as Fairness: A Restatement. *v.4 p.514*

Justice at Nuremberg. *v.4 p.477*

Justice at War: The Story of the Japanese-American Internment Cases. *v.4 p.464, v.6 p.115, p.134*

Justice by Lottery. *v.4 p.514*

Justice Delayed: The Record of the Japanese American Internment Cases. *v.6 p.134*

Justice Denied: Clemency Appeals in Death Penalty Cases. *v.6 p.272*

Justice for Children: The Right to Counsel and the Juvenile Court. *v.6 p.271*

Justice for the Poor: A Study of Criminal Defense Work. .*v.6 p.267*

The Justice Juggernaut: Fighting Street Crime, Controlling Citizens. *v.6 p.263*

Justice Lewis F. Powell, Jr. *v.4 p.468*

Justice, Morality, and Education: A New Focus in Ethics in Education. *v.4 p.300*

Justice of Shattered Dreams: Samuel Freeman Miller and the Supreme Court During the Civil War Era. . *v.4 p.469, p.538*

Justice Oliver Wendell Holmes: The Proving Years, 1870-1882. . . . . *v.4 p.468*

Justice Oliver Wendell Holmes: The Shaping Years, 1841-1870. . . . . *v.4 p.468*

Justice Sandra Day O'Connor: Strategist on the Supreme Court. *v.4 p.468*

Justices and Presidents: A Political History of Appointments to the Supreme Court. *v.4 p.535*

Justices Black and Frankfurter: Conflict in the Court. .*v.4 p.470*

The Justices of the United States Supreme Court, 1789-1995: Their Lives and Major Opinions. *v.4 p.467*

Justices, Presidents and Senators: A History of the U. S. Supreme Court Appointments from Washington to Clinton. *v.4 p.466, p.535*

Justice. *v.4 p.514*

Justification: The Doctrine of Karl Barth and a Catholic Reflection. *v.1 p.644*

Justificatory Liberalism: An Essay on Epistemology and Political Theory. *v.4 p.511*

Justifying Legal Punishment. *v.6 p.275*

Justine, Philosophy in the Bedroom and Other Writings. *v.2 p.483, p.484*

Justine. *v.2 p.344*

Justinian: The Last Roman Emperor. *v.3 p.191*

Just-in-Time Teaching: Blending Active Learning with Web Technology. *v.5 p.564*

The Just. *v.1 p.491*

Juvenal and Persius. *v.2 p.435*

Juvenal: Satires. *v.2 p.435*

Juvenal the Satirist: A Study. *v.2 p.435*

Juvenile Crime, Juvenile Justice. *v.6 p.248*

Juvenile Delinquency: Prevention, Assessment, and Intervention. *v.6 p.248*

Juvenile Drug Courts and Teen Substance Abuse. . . *v.6 p.267*

Juvenile Justice in the Making. *v.6 p.249*

Juvenile Justice Sourcebook: Past, Present, and Future. *v.6 p.248, p.249*

Juvenile Offenders with Mental Health Disorders: Who Are They and What Do We Do with Them? *v.6 p.278*

Juvenilia: Poems, 1922-1928. . . . . *v.2 p.329*

K

Kabbalah. *v.1 p.551*

Kabir: the Weaver's Songs. *v.6 p.151*

Kabir. *v.6 p.153*

ⓔ Kabuki: Five Classic Plays. *v.6 p.234*

Kabuki Plays on Stage: Brilliance and Bravado, 1697-1766. . . . . *v.6 p.234*

Kabuki Plays on Stage: Darkness and Desire, 1804-1864. . . . . *v.6 p.234*

Kabuki Plays on Stage: Restoration and Reform, 1872-1905, Vol. 4. . . . . *v.6 p.234*

Kabuki Plays on Stage: Villainy and Vengeance, 1773-1799. . . . . *v.6 p.234*

The Kabuki Theatre of Japan. *v.1 p.133, p.134*

ⓔ The Kabuki Theatre. *v.1 p.132, p.134*

Kaddish for Kovno: Life and Death in a Lithuanian Ghetto, 1941-1945. . . . . *v.3 p.85, p.256*

ⓔ Kaempfer's Japan: Tokugawa Culture Observed. . *v.6 p.225*

Kaffir Boy in America: An Encounter with Apartheid. .*v.4 p.731*

Kafr El-Elow: Continuity and Change in an Egyptian Community. *v.4 p.702*

Kafu the Scribbler: The Life and Writings of Nagai Kafu, 1879-1959. . . . . *v.6 p.228*

The Kaiser and His Court: Wilhelm II and the Government of Germany. *v.3 p.164*

Kaiser Wilhelm II. *v.3 p.169*

The Kaiser's Army: The Politics of Military Technology in Germany during the Machine Age, 1870-1918. .*v.3 p.78, p.160*

Kaiso!: Writings by and about Katherine Dunham. .*v.1 p.18, p.19*

Kakungulu and the Creation of Uganda, 1868-1928. . *v.6 p.67*

Kalahari Hunter-Gatherers: Studies of the !Kung San and Their Neighbors. *v.4 p.38*

Kamasutra. *v.6 p.153*

Kamikaze Biker: Parody and Anomy in Affluent Japan. .*v.4 p.753*

Kamouraska. *v.2 p.539*

Kandinsky: The Complete Writings on Art. *v.1 p.697*

Kandinsky Watercolours: Catalogue Raisonné, 1900-1921. . . . . *v.1 p.735*

Kandinsky Watercolours: Catalogue Raisonné, 1922-1944. . . . . *v.1 p.735*

Kandinsky. *v.1 p.739, p.740, p.744*

Kangaroo Dreaming: An Australian Wildlife Odyssey. .*v.5 p.233*

Kangaroo. *v.2 p.363*

Kansas: A Bicentennial History. *v.3 p.524*

Kansas Governors. *v.3 p.525*

Kansas: The History of the Sunflower State, 1854-2000. .*v.3 p.524*

Kant: A Biography. *v.3 p.167*

Kant and the Problem of Metaphysics. *v.1 p.461*

Kant: Anthropology from a Pragmatic Point of View. .*v.1 p.462*

Kant: Political Writings. *v.3 p.167*

Kant: The Philosophy of Right. *v.1 p.462*

Kanthapura. *v.2 p.765*

Kant's Aesthetic Theory: An Introduction. *v.1 p.481*

Kant's First Critique: An Appraisal of the Permanent Significance of Kant's Critique of Pure Reason. . *v.1 p.461*

Kant's Inaugural Dissertation and Early Writings on
Space. *v.1 p.462*

Kant's Life and Thought. *v.1 p.461*

Kant's "Critique of Pure Reason". *v.1 p.460*

Kant's Moral Theory. *v.1 p.462*

Kant's Politics: Provisional Theory for an Uncertain
World. *v.4 p.491*

Kant's Theory of Justice. *v.4 p.514*

Kant's Theory of Mind: An Analysis of the Paralogisms of Pure
Reason. *v.1 p.460*

Kant. *v.1 p.462*

The Kapalikas and Kalamukhas: Two Lost Saivite
Sects. *v.1 p.537*

The Kapetanios. *v.3 p.195*

Kaplan and Sadock's Comprehensive Textbook of
Psychiatry. *v.5 p.517*

Kaplan AP Biology 2006. . . . .*v.5 p.245*

Karaite Anthology: Excerpts from the Early
Literature. *v.6 p.566, p.573, p.574*

A Karamazov Companion: Commentary on the Genesis,
Language, and Style of Dostoevsky's Novel. . . .*v.2 p.809*

Karaoke Around the World: Global Technology, Local
Singing. *v.1 p.272, p.283, p.387*

Karel Capek: Life and Work. *v.2 p.783*

Karl Fischer Titration. *v.5 p.268*

Karl Friedrich Schinkel: A Universal Man. *v.1 p.795*

Karl Kraus. *v.2 p.612*

Karl Marx: A Biography. *v.4 p.236*

Karl Marx: A Life. *v.4 p.237*

Karl Marx and Friedrich Engels on Literature and Art: A
Selection of Writings. *v.2 p.569*

Karl Marx and the Close of His System: Bohm-Bawerk's
Criticism of Marx. *v.4 p.234*

Karl Marx: His Life and Work. *v.4 p.236*

Karl Marx on Society and Social Change: With Selections by
Friedrich Engels. *v.4 p.681*

Karl Marx Selected Writings in Sociology and Social
Philosophy. *v.4 p.681*

Karl Marx. *v.1 p.465*

Karl Pearson: The Scientific Life in a Statistical Age. *v.5 p.467*

Karl Rahner in Dialogue. *v.1 p.579*

Karl Shapiro: Selected Poems. *v.2 p.116*

The Karma of Brown Folk. *v.6 p.124, p.137*

Karol Szymanowski: His Life and Work. *v.1 p.227, p.362*

Karst Geomorphology. *v.5 p.424*

Karst Hydrogeology and Geomorphology. . .*v.4 p.391, v.5 p.424*

The Kashf Al-Mahjub "The Revelation of the Veiled": An Early
Persian Treatise on Sufism. *v.1 p.559*

Kashmir 1947: Rival Versions of History. *v.6 p.161*

Kashmir and the British Raj 1847-1947. . . . . .*v.6 p.161*

Kassandra. *v.2 p.619*

Kate Chopin: A Critical Biography. *v.2 p.33*

Kate Chopin. *v.2 p.33*

Katerina: A Novel. *v.6 p.647*

Katharina Sieverding: Close-Ups. *v.1 p.769*

Kathe Kollwitz. *v.1 p.695*

Katherine Anne Porter: A Life. *v.2 p.109*

Katherine Anne Porter: A Sense of the Times. *v.2 p.110*

Katherine Anne Porter: The Life of an Artist. *v.2 p.110*

Katherine Anne Porter's Poetry. *v.2 p.109, p.110*

Katherine Dunham: A Biography. *v.1 p.6*

Katherine Dunham: Dancer and Choreographer. *v.1 p.7*

Katherine Dunham: Dancing a Life. *v.1 p.5, p.6, p.14, p.17, p.19*

Katherine Dunham: Reflections on the Social and Political
Contexts of Afro-American Dance. *v.1 p.17, p.18*

Katherine Dunham. *v.1 p.8*

Katherine Mansfield: A Darker View. *v.2 p.369*

Katherine Mansfield: A Literary Life. *v.2 p.369*

Katherine Mansfield: A Secret Life. *v.2 p.369, p.370*

Katherine Mansfield and the Origins of Modernist
Fiction. *v.2 p.369*

Katherine Mansfield and Virginia Woolf: A Public of
Two. *v.2 p.369, p.393*

The Katherine Mansfield Notebooks. *v.2 p.369*

Katherine Mansfield's New Zealand Stories. *v.2 p.369*

Katherine Mansfield's Short Stories. *v.2 p.369*

Katschen and The Book of Joseph. *v.6 p.649*

Katsura: Imperial Villa. *v.1 p.789*

Katutura: A Place Where We Stay: Life in a Post-Apartheid
Towns. *v.6 p.76*

Katyn and the Soviet Massacre of 1940: Truth, Justice and
Memory. *v.3 p.254, p.255*

Katz und Maus. *v.2 p.608*

Kazakhstan: Unfulfilled Promise. *v.3 p.231*

Keats' Craftsmanship: A Study in Poetic Development. *v.2 p.295*

Keats. *v.2 p.294, p.295*

Keep Moving!: Fitness Through Aerobics and Step. . .*v.4 p.793*

Keep the Aspidistra Flying. *v.2 p.375*

Keep the Change. *v.2 p.150*

Keep Your Eye on the Ball: Curve Balls, Knuckleballs, and
Fallacies of Baseball. *v.4 p.848, p.871*

Keepers of the Central Fire: Issues in Ecology for Indigenous
Peoples. *v.6 p.681*

Keepers of the Frame: The Film Archives. *v.6 p.346*

Keepers of the Kingdom: The New American Zoo. . . .*v.5 p.84*

Keepers of the Morning Star: An Anthology of Native Women's
Theater. *v.1 p.121, p.124, v.6 p.697*

Keepers of the Wilderness. *v.3 p.269, v.5 p.222*

Keeping Faith: Memoirs of a President. *v.3 p.467*

☐ Keeping Faith update of Call to
Action. *v.4 p.821, p.822, p.884, p.894*

Keeping House in Lusaka. *v.4 p.37, p.703*

Keeping Patients Safe: Transforming the Work Environment of
Nurses. *v.5 p.530*

Keeping Score: Film and Television Music, 1980-1988 (with
Additional Coverage of 1921-1979). *v.1 p.168, p.256*

Keeping Score: Film and Television Music,
1988-1997. . . . .*v.1 p.168, p.256*

Keeping Score: Film Music, 1972-1979. . . . .*v.1 p.168, p.256*

Keeping Score: The Economics of Big-Time Sports. *v.4 p.889, p.897*

Keeping the Faith: A Cultural History of the U. S. Supreme Court. *v.4 p.466, p.467, p.539*

Keeping the Tablets: Modern American Conservative Thought. *v.3 p.446*

Keeping Them Out of the Hands of Satan: Evangelical Schooling in America. *v.4 p.308*

Keeping Time: Readings in Jazz History. *v.1 p.264*

Keeping Time: The History and Theory of Preservation in America. *v.1 p.823, v.6 p.728*

Kefauver: A Political Biography. *v.3 p.458*

Kegan Paul - a Victorian Imprint: Publishers, Books, and Cultural History. *v.6 p.741*

Keith Haring - Short Messages: Posters Catalogue Raisonné. *v.1 p.720*

Keith Haring: The Authorized Biography. *v.6 p.407*

Keith Jarrett: The Man and His Music. *v.1 p.257, p.334*

Kelly's Dimensions of Professional Nursing. *v.5 p.527*

Kemet and the African Worldview: Research, Rescue and Restoration. *v.6 p.14, p.15*

Ken Smith Landscape Architects. *v.1 p.815*

Kendall's Advanced Theory of Statistics, Set. . .*v.5 p.64, p.482*

Kenilworth. *v.2 p.307*

Kenkyusha's New English-Japanese Dictionary. . . .*v.6 p.231*

Kenkyusha's New Japanese-English Dictionary. . . .*v.6 p.231*

Kenkyusha's New Little English-Japanese Dictionary. *v.6 p.230*

Kennan and the Art of Foreign Policy. *v.3 p.463*

Kennedy and Nixon: The Rivalry That Shaped Postwar America. *v.3 p.475*

Kennedy and Roosevelt: The Uneasy Alliance. *v.3 p.455, p.456*

The Kennedy Assassination. *v.3 p.467*

The Kennedy Imprisonment: A Meditation on Power. *v.3 p.464*

Kennedy, Khrushchev, and the Berlin-Cuba Crisis, 1961-1964: The 1961-64 Wall. *v.3 p.386*

The Kennedy Tapes: Inside the White House During the Cuban Missile Crisis. *v.3 p.443, p.475*

The Kennedy Tapes. *v.3 p.482*

Kennedy Versus Lodge: The 1952 Massachusetts Senate Race. *v.4 p.534*

The Kennedys: America's Emerald Kings: A Five-Generation History of the Ultimate Irish-Catholic Family. . . .*v.3 p.455*

Kennedy's Quest for Victory: American Foreign Policy, 1961-1963. . . . .*v.3 p.478*

Kennedy. *v.3 p.480*

Kenneth Fearing: Selected Poems. *v.2 p.72*

Kenneth MacMillan: The Man and the Ballets. *v.1 p.13*

Kenneth Patchen: A Collection of Essays. *v.2 p.110*

Kenneth Patchen: Rebel Poet in America. *v.2 p.111*

A Kentucky Cardinal, Aftermath, and Other Selected Works. *v.2 p.30*

The Kentucky Cycle. *v.2 p.155*

Kentucky: Land of Tomorrow. *v.3 p.511*

Kentucky's Governors. *v.3 p.511*

Kenya's Past. *v.6 p.65*

Kenyatta. *v.6 p.65*

Kepler's Somnium: The Dream: or Posthumous Work on Lunar Astronomy. *v.5 p.61*

Kernel Methods for Pattern Analysis. *v.5 p.340*

Kernel Methods in Computational Biology. *v.5 p.107, p.109, p.339, p.341, p.342*

The Kerner Report: The 1968 Report of the National Advisory Commission on Civil Disorders. *v.6 p.254*

Kerouac: A Biography. *v.2 p.92*

Kerouac: The Definitive Biography. *v.2 p.93*

Kerouac, the Word and the Way: Prose Artist As Spiritual Quester. *v.2 p.92*

Kerouac's Spontaneous Poetics. *v.2 p.94*

Kerry James Marshall. *v.1 p.748*

The Key and Diary of a Mad Old Man. *v.6 p.233*

Key Concepts in Adult Education and Training. . . .*v.4 p.321*

Key Concepts in Chinese Philosophy. *v.1 p.475*

Key Concepts in Eastern Philosophy. *v.1 p.475*

Key Concepts in Geography. *v.4 p.376*

Key Concepts in Language and Linguistics. *v.2 p.564, v.5 p.622, p.624*

Key Concepts in Leisure Studies. *v.4 p.716, p.784*

Key Concepts in Political Communication. *v.4 p.425*

Key Concepts in Postcolonial Literature. *v.2 p.728*

Key Concepts in the Philosophy of Education. *v.4 p.324, p.340*

Key Concepts in Urban Studies. *v.6 p.717*

Key Contemporary Social Theorists. *v.4 p.677*

Key Debates in Anthropology. *v.4 p.24*

Key Events in African History: A Reference Guide. . .*v.6 p.51*

Key Issues in Bioethics: A Guide for Teachers. . . .*v.5 p.248*

Key Pittman. *v.3 p.458*

Key Quotations in Sociology. *v.4 p.678*

Key Thinkers in Christianity. *v.1 p.632*

The Key to Earth History: An Introduction to Stratigraphy. *v.5 p.446*

A Key to Uncle Tom's Cabin (large Facsimile): Presenting the Original Facts and Documents upon which the Story Is Founded. *v.2 p.51*

☐ Key Topics Portal. *v.4 p.152*

The Key West Reader: The Best of Key West's Writers, 1830-1990. . . . .*v.2 p.13*

☐ The Key Work of School Boards. *v.4 p.280*

The Keyboard Music of J. S. Bach. *v.1 p.186, p.242, p.243, p.304*

The Keyboard Sonatas of Domenico Scarlatti and Eighteenth-Century Musical Style. *v.1 p.187, p.243, p.352, p.353*

Keynes and After. *v.4 p.229*

Keynes and Hayek: Money Economy. *v.4 p.229*

Keynes and His Contemporaries. *v.4 p.227*

Keynes and His Critics: Treasury Responses to the Keynesian Revolution, 1925-1946. . . . .*v.4 p.228*

Keynes and International Monetary Relations: The Second Keynes Seminar Held at University of Kent at Canterbury, 1974. . . . .*v.4 p.229*

Keynes and Philosophy: Essays on the Origins of Keyne's Thought. *v.4 p.226*

Keynes and Public Policy after Fifty Years: Economics and Policy, Vol. 1. . . . .*v.4 p.227*

Keynes and Public Policy after Fifty Years: Theories and Method, Vol. 2. . . . .*v.4 p.227*

Keynes: Aspects of the Man and His Work. *v.4 p.228*

Keynes, Cambridge and the General Theory. *v.4 p.223, p.224, p.225, p.226*

Keynes, Chicago and Friedman. *v.4 p.225, p.228, p.232*

Keynes: Contemporary Responses to the General Theory. *v.4 p.226*

Keynes, Coordination and Beyond: The Development of Macroeconomic and Monetary Theory since 1945. .*v.4 p.227*

Keynes, Knowledge and Uncertainty. *v.4 p.227*

Keynes' Monetary Thought: A Study of Its Development. *v.4 p.225*

Keynes on Population. *v.4 p.229*

Keynes: Philosophy, Economics and Politics: The Philosophical Foundations of Keynes's Thought and Their Influence on His Economics. *v.4 p.228*

Keynes, Pigou and Cambridge Keynesians: Authenticity and Analytical Perpective in the Keynes-Classics Debate. *v.4 p.226*

Keynes: The Instability of Capitalism. *v.4 p.229*

Keynes, the Treasury and British Economic Policy. . .*v.4 p.228*

Keynes, Uncertainty and the Global Economy: Beyond Keynes, Vol. 2. . . . .*v.4 p.227*

Keynesian Economics: The Permanent Revolution. *v.4 p.226, p.229*

Keynesian Economics: The Search for First Principles. .*v.4 p.226*

The Keynesian Revolution and Its Economic Consequences: Selected Essays by Peter Clarke. *v.4 p.226*

Keynes's General Theory: A Retrospective View. . . .*v.4 p.228*

Keynes's General Theory and Accumulation. *v.4 p.226*

Keynes's Monetary Theory: A Different Interpretation. .*v.4 p.228*

Keynes's Philosophical Development. *v.4 p.226*

The Keys of Egypt: The Obsession to Decipher Egyptian Hieroglyphs. *v.3 p.11*

Keys to Happiness. *v.2 p.810*

Keys to Life: Philosophy and New Mechanism of Evolution and Development. *v.5 p.250*

Keys to Reading an Annual Report. *v.4 p.175*

Keys to Soil Taxonomy. *v.5 p.51*

Keys to the Garden: New Israeli Writing. *v.6 p.647*

Keystone: The American Occupation of Okinawa and U. S.-Japanese Relations. *v.6 p.235*

Keywords and Concepts in Evolutionary Developmental Biology. *v.5 p.160*

KGB: The Inside Story of Its Foreign Operations from Lenin to Gorbachev. *v.3 p.211*

KGID: Konstantin Grcic Industrial Design. *v.1 p.720*

Khmer American: Identity and Moral Education in a Diasporic Community. *v.6 p.139*

Khrushchev: The Man and His Era. *v.3 p.228*

Khubilai Khan: His Life and Times. . .*v.6 p.186, p.201, p.239*

Khul-Khaal: Five Egyptian Women Tell Their Stories. *v.6 p.634*

Khyal: Creativity Within North India's Classical Music Tradition. *v.1 p.290*

The Kibbutz: Awakening from Utopia. *v.4 p.703*

Kicking the Carbon Habit: Global Warming and the Case for Renewable Energy. *v.5 p.356, p.361, p.371*

The Kid on the Sandlot: Congress and Professional Sports, 1910-1992. . . . .*v.4 p.885, p.891, p.897*

Kidnapped. *v.2 p.312*

The Kidnapping of Edgardo Mortara: The Extraordinary Story of How a Jewish Child, Made a Prisoner of the Vatican in 1858, Ended the Rule of the Popes in Italy. *v.3 p.59, p.201*

Kienast Vogt: Parks and Cemeteries. *v.1 p.813*

Kierkegaard Anthology. *v.1 p.580*

Kierkegaard's Fragments and Postscript: The Religious Philosophy of Johannes Climacus. *v.1 p.478*

Kierkegaard's Journals and Notebooks: Journals AA-DD. *v.1 p.478*

Kierkegaard. *v.1 p.478*

Kievan Russia. *v.3 p.215*

Killer Algae: The True Story of a Biological Invasion. *v.5 p.208*

The Killer Angels: A Novel of the Civil War. *v.2 p.155*

Killer Cover Letters and Resumes! The WetFeet Insider Guide 2004. . . . .*v.4 p.170*

The Killers Within: The Deadly Rise of Drug-Resistant Bacteria. *v.5 p.526*

Killing As Punishment: Reflection on the Death Penalty in America. *v.6 p.247*

Killing Custer: The Battle of the Little Big Horn and the Fate of the Plains Indians. *v.6 p.688*

The Killing Fields. *v.6 p.169*

The Killing of Reinhard Heydrich: The Ss Butcher of Prague. *v.3 p.189*

Killing Rage: Ending Racism. *v.4 p.730*

Killing Spanish: Literary Essays on Ambivalent U. S. Latino/a Identity. *v.6 p.508, p.515*

The Killing State: Capital Punishment in Law, Politics, and Culture. *v.4 p.471*

Killing the Black Body: Race, Reproduction, and the Meaning of Liberty. *v.6 p.40, p.46, p.447, p.471*

Killing the Second Dog. *v.2 p.790*

Killing Us Quietly: Native Americans and HIV/AIDS. *v.6 p.702*

The Kill. *v.2 p.505*

Kilvert, the Victorian: A New Selection from Kilvert's Diaries. *v.6 p.759, p.761*

☐ Kim Allen's Fullerene Page. *v.5 p.305*

Kim. *v.2 p.297*

Kin of Place: Essays on New Zealand Writers. *v.2 p.748*

Kin Recognition. *v.5 p.614*

The Kin Who Count: Family and Society in Ottoman Aleppo, 1770-1840. . . . .*v.6 p.607*

Kind of Blue: The Making of the Miles Davis Masterpiece. *v.1 p.260, p.262, p.320*

A Kind of Grace: A Treasury of Sportswriting by Women. *v.4 p.812, p.837*

The Kind of Schools We Need: Personal Essays. . . .*v.4 p.342*

A Kinder, Gentler Racism?: The Reagan-Bush Civil Rights Legacy. *v.3 p.444*

Kinder- und Hausmärchen, gesammelt durch die Brüder Grimm: vollständige Ausgabe auf der Grundlage der dritten Auflage (1837). *v.2 p.592, p.593*

Kindergartens and Cultures: The Global Diffusion of an Idea. *v.4 p.368*

Kindheitsmuster: Roman. *v.2 p.619*

Kindling Spirit: Lucy Maud Montgomery's Anne of Green Gables. *v.2 p.737*

Kindness in a Cruel World: The Evolution of Altruism. .*v.5 p.651*

The Kindness of Strangers: The Abandonment of Children in Western Europe from Late Antiquity to the Renaissance. *v.4 p.755*

Kindness of Strangers: The Life of Tennessee Williams. .*v.2 p.135*

Kindred Strangers: The Uneasy Relationship Between Politics and Business in America. *v.4 p.52, p.112*

Kinematic Wave Modeling in Water Resources, Set. *v.5 p.369, p.379*

Kinematics, Dynamics, and Design of Machinery. . . .*v.5 p.715*

Kinetic Theory: Classical, Quantum, and Relativistic Descriptions. *v.5 p.560*

Kinetics of Human Motion. *v.4 p.908, p.910*

King Abdullah, Britain and the Making of Jordan. . . *v.6 p.621*

A King and No King. *v.2 p.217*

The King and the Adultress: A Psychoanalytical and Literary Reinterpretation of Madame Bovary and King Lear. .*v.2 p.232*

King Arthur's Death: The Middle English Stanzaic Morte Arthur and Alliterative Morte Arthur. *v.2 p.206*

King Cotton Diplomacy: Foreign Relations of the Confederate States of America. *v.3 p.399, p.429*

King Football: Sport and Spectacle in the Golden Age of Radio and Newsreels, Movies and Magazines, the Weekly and the Daily Press. .*v.4 p.808, p.823, p.824, p.859, p.885, p.894, p.897, p.902*

King George III and the Politicians. . . . *v.3 p.88, p.95, p.109*

King Hammurabi of Babylon: A Biography. *v.3 p.6*

King Harald's Saga: Harald Hardradi of Norway: from Snorri Sturluson's Heimskringla. *v.2 p.625*

King Henry IV, Part 1. . . . .*v.2 p.225*

King Henry IV, Part 2. . . . .*v.2 p.224, p.225*

King Henry IV, Pt. 1. . . . .*v.2 p.225*

King Henry VI - Arden Shakespeare, Pt. 1. . . . . .*v.2 p.223*

King Henry VI, part 2. . . . .*v.2 p.223*

King Henry VI, Part 3. . . . .*v.2 p.223*

King Henry VIII. *v.2 p.224*

King Henry V. *v.2 p.224*

King Husain and the Kingdom of Hejaz. *v.6 p.626*

The King in Yellow and Other Horror Stories. *v.2 p.32*

King John: New Interpretations. *v.3 p.98*

King John. *v.2 p.224, v.3 p.99*

King Khama, Emperor Joe, and the Great White Queen: Victorian Britain Through African Eyes. *v.6 p.75*

King Lear. *v.2 p.224*

King Leopold's Congo: Aspects of the Development of Race Relations in the Congo Independent State. *v.6 p.63*

King Leopold's Ghost: A Story of Greed, Terror, and Heroism in Colonial Africa. *v.3 p.206*

King Leopold's Ghost. *v.3 p.77*

The King of Children: A Portrait of Janusz Korczak. .*v.4 p.343*

King of Flesh and Blood. *v.6 p.651*

King of Ragtime: Scott Joplin and His Era. . .*v.1 p.257, p.334*

The King of Romance: A Portrait of Alexandre Dumas. .*v.2 p.489*

King of the Mountain: The Nature of Political Leadership. *v.4 p.483, p.484, v.5 p.643*

King of the Night: Juan Jose Flores and Ecuador, 1824-1864. *v.3 p.333*

King of the World: Muhammad Ali and the Rise of an American Hero. *v.4 p.833, p.856*

The King of Time: Selected Writings of the Russian Futurian. *v.2 p.805*

King Richard III. *v.2 p.223*

King Richard II. *v.2 p.224*

King Solomon's Mines. *v.2 p.290*

King William IV. *v.3 p.117*

King Zog of Albania: Europe's Self-Made Muslim King. *v.3 p.252*

Kingdom and Colony: Ireland in the Atlantic World, 1560-1800. . . . .*v.3 p.136, p.137*

Kingdom of Children: Culture and Controversy in the Homeschooling Movement. *v.4 p.296*

The Kingdom of Cyprus and the Crusades, 1191-1374. .*v.6 p.601*

The Kingdom of God and Primitive Christianity. . . .*v.1 p.638*

The Kingdom of God in America. *v.1 p.638*

The Kingdom of God in the Teaching of Jesus. *v.1 p.638*

The Kingdom of Ireland, 1641-1760. . .*v.3 p.133, p.134, p.137*

The Kingdom of Kush: The Napatan and Meroitic Empires. *v.6 p.59*

The Kingdom of Leon-Castilla under King Alfonso VI, 1065-1109. . . . . *v.3 p.65, p.238*

Kingdom of Leon-Castilla under King Alfonso VII, 1126-1157. . . . . *v.3 p.65, p.66, p.238*

Kingdom of Quito in the Seventeenth Century: Bureaucratic Politics in the Spanish Empire. *v.3 p.332*

The Kingdom of Saudi Arabia. *v.6 p.626*

The Kingdom of Strangers. *v.6 p.661*

Kingdom of the Hittites. *v.3 p.6*

The Kingdom of This World: A Novel. *v.2 p.671*

Kingdoms of the Crusaders: From Jerusalem to Cyprus. .*v.3 p.64*

Kingfish: The Reign of Huey P. Long. *v.3 p.464*

Kings and Lords in Conquest England. *v.3 p.97*

Kings and Vikings: Scandinavia and Europe, A. *v.3 p.236*

The King's Army: Warfare, Soldiers and Society During the Wars of Religion in France, 1562-76. . . . .*v.3 p.146*

Kings, Commoners and Concessionaires: The Evolution and Dissolution of the Nineteenth-Century Swazi State. *v.6 p.78*

Kings II. *v.1 p.620*

Kings of the Ice: A History of World Hockey. .*v.4 p.844, p.862*

King's Peace 1637-1641. . . . .*v.3 p.104*

The King's Servants: The Civil Service of Charles I, 1625-1642. . . . .*v.3 p.101*

The King's Trial: Louis XVI vs. the French Revolution. .*v.3 p.150*

The King's Two Bodies: A Study in Mediaeval Political Theology. *v.3 p.69*

King's War: 1641. . . . .*v.3 p.104*

Kingship and Favoritism in the Spain of Philip III, 1598-1621. . . . . *.v.3 p.238, p.239*

Kingship and the Gods: A Study of Ancient near Eastern Religion as the Integration of Society and Nature. . . *.v.3 p.4*

Kingship, Conquest, and Patria. . . . . *.v.6 p.566*

Kingship of God. . . . . *.v.1 p.638*

Kingsley Amis Poems. . . . . *.v.2 p.328*

The King. . . . . *.v.2 p.140*

Kinship and Community in Two Chinese Villages. . . *.v.4 p.705*

Kinship and Family: An Anthropological Reader. . . . *.v.4 p.32*

Kinship and Politics: The Making of the Muscovite Political System, 1345-1547. . . . . *.v.3 p.215*

Kinship, Law and the Unexpected: Relatives Are Always a Surprise. . . . . *.v.4 p.33*

Kipling, Auden and Company: Essays and Reviews, 1935-1964. . . . . *.v.2 p.90, p.91*

Kipling's Hidden Narratives. . . . . *.v.2 p.296*

Kipps. *.v.2 p.320*

Kirk-Othmer Concise Encyclopedia of Chemical Technology, 2 vols. . . . . *.v.5 p.257*

☐ Kirk-Othmer encyclopedia of chemical technology [electronic resource]. . . . . *.v.5 p.257*

[Kirk-Othmer] Encyclopedia of chemical technology. *.v.5 p.257*

Kirk-Othmer Encyclopedia of Chemical Technology. . *.v.5 p.257*

[Kirk-Othmer] Encyclopedia of chemical technology. *.v.5 p.257*

Kirk-Othmer Encyclopedia of Chemical Technology. . *.v.5 p.741*

Kiss, Bow or Shake Hands: How to Do Business in Sixty Countries. . . . . *.v.4 p.56*

Kiss, Bow, or Shake Hands: The Bestselling Guide to Doing Business in More Than 60 Countries. . . . . . *.v.4 p.173*

Kiss of the Spider Woman and Two Other Plays. *.v.2 p.678, p.679*

Kiss of the Spider Woman. . . . . *.v.6 p.398*

Kiss the Hand You Cannot Bite: The Rise and Fall of the Ceausescus. . . . . *.v.3 p.250*

Kissing the Mango Tree: Puerto Rican Women Rewriting American Literature. . . . . *.v.6 p.508, p.515*

Kissing the Witch: Old Tales in New Skins. . *.v.6 p.395, p.396*

The Kitchen Spoon's Handle: Transnationalism and Sri Lanka's Migrant Households. . . . . *.v.6 p.154*

Kitchener: An Illustrated History. . . . . *.v.3 p.544*

Kitchener: Portrait of an Imperialist. . . . . . *.v.3 p.89, p.125*

Kitchen. . . . . *.v.6 p.234*

The Kite Runner. . . . . *.v.2 p.160*

KJV Bible 1611 Edition. . . . . *.v.1 p.613*

Klail City. . . . . *.v.6 p.499*

Klee Wyck. . . . . *.v.2 p.733*

Kleiner Mann, was nun?: Roman. . . . . *.v.2 p.606*

Kleiner Mann, Was Nun? . . . . *.v.2 p.607*

Klezmer!: Jewish Music from Old World to Our World. *.v.1 p.300*

Klimt. *.v.1 p.749*

Kline Guide to the U.S. Chemical Industry. . . . . *.v.5 p.318*

Klingsor's Last Summer. . . . . *.v.2 p.610*

The Klondike Fever: The Life and Death of the Last Great Gold Rush. . . . . *.v.3 p.533*

Klopstock, Friedrich Gottlieb: Werke und Briefe Historisch-Kritische Ausgabe. . . . . *.v.2 p.600*

The Knight of Olmedo/El Caballero de Olmedo. . . *.v.2 p.653*

Knight of Onions and Knight of Garlic. . . . . . *.v.6 p.648*

The Knight, the Lady and the Priest: The Making of Modern Marriage in Medieval France. . . . . *.v.4 p.733*

Knights at Court: Courtliness, Chivalry, and Courtesy from Ottonian Germany to the Italian Renaissance. . . *.v.3 p.162*

Knight's Foodservice Dictionary. . . . . *.v.4 p.165*

The Knights of Labor and the Haymarket Riot: The Fight for an Eight-Hour Workday. . . . . *.v.4 p.124*

Knights of the Plow: Oliver H. Kelley and the Origins of the Grange in Republican Ideology. . . . . *.v.5 p.6*

The Knight's Tale. . . . . *.v.2 p.208*

Knights Unhorsed: Internal Conflict in a Gilded Age Social Movement. . . . . *.v.4 p.130*

Knock 'Em Dead: The Ultimate Job Seeker's Guide. *.v.4 p.171*

Knock Your Socks Off Prospecting: How to Cold Call, Get Qualified Leads, and Make More Money. . . . . *.v.4 p.143*

Knocking on Heaven's Door: American Religion in the Age of Counterculture. . . . . *.v.4 p.720, p.721*

Knock. *.v.2 p.526*

The Knot Book: An Elementary Introduction to the Mathematical Theory of Knots. . . . . *.v.5 p.498*

A Knot into the Thread: The Life and Work of Jacques Roumain. . . . . *.v.2 p.537*

Knot Theory. . . . . *.v.5 p.499*

The Knotted Thong: Structures of Mimesis in Persius. . . . . *.v.2 p.439, p.440*

Knott's Handbook for Vegetable Growers. . . . *.v.5 p.22, p.26*

☐ Knovel Critical Tables. . . . . *.v.5 p.406, p.740*

☐ Knovel solvents : a properties database. . . . . . *.v.5 p.741*

Know Your Market: How to Do Low-Cost Market Research. . . . . *.v.4 p.135*

Knowing and Teaching Elementary Mathematics: Teachers' Understanding of Fundamental Mathematics in China and the United States. . . . . *.v.4 p.364*

Knowing the Enemy: Jihadist Ideology and the War on Terror. . . . . *.v.4 p.659*

Knowing the Score : Notes on Film Music. . . . . . *.v.1 p.254*

Knowing the Score: Film Composers Talk about the Art, Craft, Blood, Sweat, and Tears of Writing. . . . . . *.v.6 p.351*

Knowing What Students Know: The Science and Design of Educational Assessment. . . . . *.v.4 p.285*

Knowledge Accumulation and Industry Evolution: The Case of Pharma-Biotech. . . . . *.v.4 p.156*

Knowledge and Human Interests. . . . . *.v.1 p.482*

Knowledge and Passion. . . . . *.v.4 p.35*

Knowledge and Social Practice in Medieval Damascus, 1190-1350. . . . . *.v.6 p.607*

Knowledge and Wonder: The Natural World As Man Knows It. *.v.5 p.399*

Knowledge Capital: How Knowledge-Based Enterprises Really Get Built. . . . . *.v.4 p.77*

Knowledge Cities: Approaches, Experiences, and Perspectives. . . . . *.v.6 p.711*

Knowledge Discovery in Proteomics. . . . . *.v.5 p.116*

Knowledge, Gender, and Schooling: The Feminist Educational Thought of Jane Roland Martin. . . . . *.v.4 p.344*

Knowledge in Perspective: Selected Essays in Epistemology. *v.1 p.483*

Knowledge, Inequality and Growth in the New Economy. *v.4 p.254, p.259*

Knowledge Leadership: The Art and Science of the Knowledge-Based Organization. *v.4 p.77*

Knowledge Management in Theory and Practice. *v.4 p.77*

The Knowledge of Childhood in the German Middle Ages, 1100-1350. . . . .*v.3 p.55, p.162*

Knowledge, Possibility and Consciousness. *v.1 p.497*

Knowledge Puzzles: An Introduction to Epistemology. .*v.1 p.482*

A Known Scribbler: Frances Burney on Literary Life. .*v.2 p.242*

The Known World: A Novel. *v.2 p.147*

The Known World of Broadcast News: International News and the Electronic Media. *v.4 p.412*

Knut Hamsun. *v.2 p.628*

Knut Wicksell: Essays in Economics. *v.4 p.241*

Kodak and the Lens of Nostalgia. *v.4 p.427*

The Kodaly Method I: Comprehensive Music Education. *v.1 p.405*

The Kodaly Method II: Folksong to Masterwork. . . .*v.1 p.405*

Kodokan Judo: The Essential Guide to Judo by Its Founder. *v.4 p.863*

Koji Nakanishi: A Wandering Natural Products Chemist. *v.5 p.299*

Kojiki. *v.6 p.225*

Kokoro. *v.6 p.232*

Kolyma Tales. *v.2 p.808*

Komödien. *v.2 p.606*

Komodo Dragons: Biology and Conservation. *v.5 p.84*

Koneman's Color Atlas and Textbook of Diagnostic Microbiology. *v.5 p.515*

Konjaku Monogatari-Shu. *v.6 p.230*

Konoe Fumimaro: A Political Biography. *v.6 p.228*

Konrad Adenauer: From the German Empire to the Federal Republic, 1876-1952. . . . .*v.3 p.177*

Konrad Adenauer: The Statesman, 1952-1967. . . .*v.3 p.177*

The Koran Interpreted: A Translation. *v.1 p.556*

Korea: Art and Archaeology. *v.1 p.693, v.4 p.9*

Korea at the Center: Dynamics of Regionalism in Northeast Asia. *v.6 p.236*

Korea Between Empires, 1895-1919. . . . .*v.6 p.237*

The Korean American Dream: Immigrants and Small Business in New York City. *v.6 p.106, p.107, p.136*

Korean American Women: From Tradition to Modern Feminism. *v.6 p.112, p.113, p.136*

Korean Americans and Their Religions: Pilgrims and Missionaries from a Different Shore. *v.6 p.105, p.106, p.136*

Korean Endgame: A Strategy for Reunification and U. S. Disengagement. *v.6 p.236*

Korean Music: Historical and Other Aspects. *v.1 p.290*

Korean Music: Its History and Performance. *v.1 p.289*

Korean Musical Instruments. *v.1 p.288*

Korean War Filmography: 93 English Language Features through 2000. . . . .*v.6 p.322*

The Korean War in World History. *v.6 p.237*

Korean-American Relations: 1866-1997. . . . . . .*v.3 p.390*

Koreans in the Hood: Conflict with African Americans. *v.6 p.123, p.135, p.136*

Korea's Place in the Sun: A Modern History. *v.6 p.236*

Koreas. *v.6 p.236*

Kori: The Beacon Anthology of Korean American Fiction. *v.6 p.91, p.100*

Kosovo: A Short History. *v.3 p.249*

Kosovo: Contending Voices on Balkan Interventions. *v.3 p.249*

Kosovo: War and Revenge. *v.3 p.249*

Kotik Letaev. *v.2 p.801*

Kotoku Shusui: Portrait of a Japanese Radical. *v.6 p.225, p.228*

Kremlin Gold: 1000 Years of Russian Gems and Jewels. *v.1 p.715*

Kremlin Rising: Vladimir Putin's Russia and the End of Revolution. *v.3 p.229*

The Krio of Sierra Leone: An Interpretive History. . . .*v.6 p.73*

The Kristeva Critical Reader. *v.2 p.456*

Kristin Lavransdatter. *v.2 p.628*

Krugman's Infectious Diseases of Children. *v.5 p.532*

Krzysztof Penderecki: His Life and Work. . . .*v.1 p.223, p.347*

Kuan-yin: The Chinese Transformation of Avalokitesvara. *v.1 p.566*

Kuhn vs. Popper: The Struggle for the Soul of Science. *v.1 p.499, v.5 p.401*

Kukai: Major Works, Translated with an Account of His Life and a Study of His Thought. *v.6 p.221*

The Kurdish Conflict in Turkey: Obstacles and Chances for Peace and Democracy. *v.6 p.599, p.622*

Kurdish Culture and Identity. *v.6 p.598*

Kurdish Culture and Society: An Annotated Bibliography. *v.6 p.599, p.668*

Kurdish Dialect Studies 1-2. . . . .*v.6 p.668*

Kurdish Ethno-Nationalism Versus Nation-Building States: Collected Articles. *v.6 p.598*

Kurdish Kurmanji Modern Texts: Introduction, Selection and Glossary. *v.6 p.668*

The Kurdish National Movement: Its Origins and Development. *v.6 p.599*

Kurdish Nationalism and Political Islam in Turkey: Kemalist Identity in Transition. *v.6 p.599, p.600, p.625*

Kurdish Nationalism in Mam u Zin of Ahmad-i Khani. *v.6 p.669*

The Kurdish Nationalist Movement: Opportunity, Mobilization and Identity. *v.6 p.599*

The Kurdish Political Struggle in Iran, Iraq, and Turkey: A Critical Analysis. *v.6 p.599*

The Kurdish Question in Iraq. *v.6 p.598, p.601, p.602*

The Kurdish Question in U. S. Foreign Policy: A Documentary Sourcebook. *v.6 p.599*

Kurdish Short Stories. *v.6 p.668*

The Kurdish Tragedy. *v.6 p.598*

The Kurdish Woman's Life. *v.6 p.598*

Kurdish-Arabic Dictionary: Al-Hadiyati 'l-Hamidiyah. *v.6 p.668*

Kurdish-English Dictionary. *v.6 p.668*

Kurdish-English English-Kurdish Dictionary. *v.6 p.669*

Kurdish-English, English-Kurdish (Kurmanci) Dictionary. *v.6 p.668, p.669*

Kurdish-English/English-Kurdish Dictionary and
  Phrases. *v.6 p.668*

The Kurds: A Concise Handbook. *v.6 p.599*

The Kurds: A Contemporary Overview. *v.6 p.599*

The Kurds: A People in Search of Their Homeland. . *v.6 p.599*

Kurds and Ethnicity in Iran. *v.6 p.600, p.630*

The Kurds and the State: Evolving National Identity in Iraq,
  Turkey, and Iran. *v.6 p.599*

The Kurds in Iraq: The Past, Present and Future. .*v.6 p.600, p.602*

The Kurds in Turkey: EU Accession and Human
  Rights. *v.6 p.600, p.622*

The Kurds. *v.6 p.600*

Kurozumikyo and the New Religions of Japan. . . .*v.1 p.541*

Kurt Schwitters: Catalogue Raisonné 1905-1922. . .*v.1 p.699*

Kurt Vonnegut: A Critical Companion. *v.2 p.157*

Kurt Weill: A Life in Pictures and
  Documents. *v.1 p.213, p.249, p.368*

Kurt Weill: An Illustrated Life. *v.1 p.223, p.253, p.368*

Kurt Weill: "The Threepenny Opera". . *v.1 p.250, p.251, p.368*

Kuru Sorcery: Disease and Danger in the New Guinea
  Highlands. *v.4 p.46, p.47*

Kurusu: The Price of Progress in a Japanese Village,
  1951-1975. . . . .*v.4 p.707*

Kuwait: Dependency and Class in a Rentier State. . .*v.6 p.627*

Kuwait: Recovery and Security after the Gulf War. .*v.6 p.627*

Kuwait: Social Change in Historical Perspective. . .*v.6 p.627*

Kwaio Religion: The Living and the Dead in a Solomon Island
  Society. *v.1 p.544*

The Kwakiutl: Indians of British Columbia. *v.6 p.704*

Kwame Nkrumah's Contribution to Pan-African Agency: An
  Afrocentric Analysis. *v.6 p.13, p.18*

The Kwangju Uprising: Shadows over the Regime in South
  Korea. *v.6 p.236*

Kwanzaa and Me: A Teacher's Story. *v.4 p.310, p.365*

L

L. A. Noir: The City as Character. *v.6 p.730*

A la Deriva y Otros Cuentos. *v.2 p.687*

The La Follettes of Wisconsin: Love and Politics in Progressive
  America. *v.3 p.455*

☐ LAB SAFETY--Online Safety Course. *v.5 p.265*

Labanotation or Kinetography Laban: The System of Analyzing
  and Recording Movement. *v.1 p.38*

La-Bas, Lower Depths. *v.2 p.495*

Labeling Deviant Behavior: Its Sociological
  Implications. *v.4 p.697*

Labeling Women Devlant. *v.6 p.446*

El Laberinto de la Soledad. *v.2 p.668*

☐ LabGuide Online. *v.5 p.260*

Labor and Community: Mexican Citrus Worker Villages in a
  Southern California County, 1900-1950. . . . . .*v.6 p.525*

Labor and Desire: Women's Revolutionary Fiction in Depression
  America. *v.2 p.8*

Labor and Employment Arbitration in a Nutshell. . .*v.4 p.123*

Labor and Politics in Panama: The Torrijos Years. . .*v.3 p.304*

Labor and the Wartime State: Labor Relations and Law During
  World War II. *v.4 p.120*

Labor Arbitration in America: The Profession and
  Practice. *v.4 p.120*

Labor, Autonomy and the State in Latin America. . . *v.4 p.121*

Labor Economics. *v.4 p.253*

Labor in Cross-Cultural Perspective. *v.4 p.28*

Labor in Latin America: Comparative Essays on Chile,
  Argentina, Venezuela, and
  Colombia. *v.3 p.346, p.349, p.350, p.356, p.359*

Labor in the Puerto Rican Economy: Postwar Development and
  Stagnation. *v.3 p.321*

Labor Law, Industrial Relations and Employee Choice: The
  State of the Workplace in the 1990's. *v.4 p.120*

Labor Movements and Dictatorships: The Southern Cone in
  Comparative Perspective. *v.3 p.345, p.346, p.353*

The Labor of Life: Selected Plays. *v.6 p.650*

Labor of Love, Labor of Sorrow: Black Women, Work and the
  Family from Slavery to the Present. . . *v.6 p.7, p.44, p.457*

Labor Relations in Education: An International
  Perspective. *v.4 p.121*

Labor Relations in Europe: A History of Issues and
  Developments, 29. . . . .*v.4 p.123*

Labor Relations: Striking a Balance. *v.4 p.120*

Labor Relations. *v.4 p.121*

Labor Rights Are Civil Rights: Mexican American Workers in
  Twentieth-Century America. *v.4 p.255*

Labor Standards in the United States and
  Canada. *v.4 p.109, p.111, p.112, p.120*

Labor Unions, Partisan Coalitions, and Market Reforms in Latin
  America. *v.4 p.128*

The Labor Wars in Cordoba, 1955-1976: Ideology, Work, and
  Labor Politics in an Argentine Industrial Society. . *v.3 p.347*

Labor Will Rule: Sidney Hillman and the Rise of American
  Labor. *v.4 p.126*

Le laboratoire central. *v.2 p.521*

Laboratory Anatomy of the White Rat. *v.5 p.87*

Laboratory and Diagnostic Tests with Nursing
  Implications. *v.5 p.527, p.528*

The Laboratory Companion: A Practical Guide to Materials,
  Equipment, and Technique. *v.5 p.259*

Laboratory Course in Physical Chemistry. *v.5 p.287*

Laboratory Experiences in Group Theory. *v.5 p.475*

Laboratory Fume Hoods: A User's Manual. *v.5 p.266*

Laboratory Methodology in Biochemistry: Amino Acid Analysis
  and Protein Sequencing. *v.5 p.326*

Laboratory of Justice: The Supreme Court's 200-Year Struggle
  to Integrate Science and the Law. *v.4 p.536*

Laboratory Waste Management: A Guidebook. .*v.5 p.265, p.266*

☐ Labordoc. *v.5 p.580*

Laboring and Dependent Classes in Colonial America,
  1607-1783. . . . .*v.4 p.724*

Labor-Management Relations in a Changing
  Environment. *v.4 p.120*

Labors Appropriate to Their Sex: Gender, Labor, and Politics in
  Urban Chile, 1900-1930. . . . .*v.3 p.353, p.354*

Labor's Power and Industrial Performance: Automobile
  Production Regimes in the U. S., Germany, and
  Japan. *v.4 p.121*

Labor's Story in the United States. *v.4 p.128*

Labor's Text: The Worker in American Fiction. *v.2 p.4*

Labor's War at Home: The CIO in World War II. . . .*v.4 p.127*

The Labour Governments, 1945-51. . . . .*v.3 p.95, p.119*

Labour in Power, 1945-1951. . . . .*v.3 p.95, p.119*

Labour Legislation and Trade Unions in India and
    Pakistan. *v.4 p.120*

The Labour Party since 1979: Crisis and
    Transformation. *v.4 p.607*

Labour Relations in the Global Fast-Food Industry. .*v.4 p.123*

Labour Relations in Transition in Eastern Europe. . .*v.4 p.123*

Labour, Science and Technology in France,
    1500-1620. . . . .*v.3 p.49, p.145*

Labour Theory of Value. *v.4 p.195, p.253*

Labour's Turning Point, 1880-1900: Extracts from
    Contemporary Sources. *v.4 p.703*

The Labyrinth of Solitude: The Other Mexico and Return to the
    Labyrinth of Solitude and The U. S. A. and The
    Philanthropic Ogre. *v.2 p.668, v.3 p.294*

The Labyrinth of the Word: Truth and Representation in Czech
    Literature. *v.2 p.782*

Labyrinths of Power: Political Recruitment in Twentieth-Century
    Mexico. *v.3 p.295*

Lacrosse: A History of the Game. *v.4 p.805, p.841, p.862*

Lacrosse: Technique and Tradition, the Second Edition of the
    Bob Scott Classic. *v.4 p.862*

Lac. *v.2 p.530*

Der Laden: Roman. *v.2 p.615*

Ladies Almanack. *v.6 p.394*

Ladies and Gentlemen, the Bronx Is Burning: 1977, Baseball,
    Politics, and the Battle for the Soul of a City. . . .*v.6 p.714*

Ladies in the Laboratory? American and British Women in
    Science, 1800-1900: A Survey of Their Contributions to
    Research. *v.5 p.395, v.6 p.438*

Ladies in the Laboratory II: West European Women in Science,
    1800-1900: A Survey of Their Contributions to
    Research. *v.5 p.395, v.6 p.438*

Ladies' Pages: African American Women's Magazines and the
    Culture That Made Them. *v.6 p.40, p.46*

The Ladies' Paradise. *v.2 p.506*

Ladies, Please Don't Smash These Windows: Women's Writing,
    Feminist Consciousness and Social Change
    1918-1938. . . . .*v.6 p.479*

L'Adone. *v.2 p.708*

Lads, Citizens and Ordinary Kids: Working Class Youth
    Lifestyles in Belfast. *v.4 p.736*

The Lady and the Virgin: Image, Attitude, and Experience in
    Twelfth-Century France. *v.6 p.451, p.560*

Lady Anna. *v.2 p.318*

Lady Audley's Secret. *v.2 p.265*

Lady Bird: A Biography of Mrs. Johnson. *v.3 p.462*

Lady Chatterley's Lover. *v.2 p.363*

Lady Gregory: The Woman Behind the Irish
    Renaissance. *v.2 p.288*

Lady Gregory's Journals 1916 to 1930. . . . .*v.2 p.288*

Lady Gregory. *v.2 p.288*

Lady Luck: The Theory of Probability. *v.5 p.484, p.485*

Lady Mary Wortley Montagu: Essays and Poems and Simplicity,
    a Comedy. *v.2 p.256*

Lady Susan. *v.2 p.266*

The Lady Tasting Tea: How Statistics Revolutionized Science in
    the Twentieth Century. *v.5 p.467, p.481*

Lafayette in the Age of the American Revolution, Selected
    Letters and Papers, 1776-1790: April 10th, 1778-March 20th,
    1780. . . . .*v.3 p.411*

Lafayette in the Age of the American Revolution, Selected
    Letters and Papers, 1776-1790: April 27th, 1780-March 29th,
    1781. . . . .*v.3 p.411*

Lafayette in the Age of the American Revolution, Selected
    Letters and Papers, 1776-1790: December 7th,
    1776-March 30th, 1778. . . . .*v.3 p.411, p.412*

Lafayette in the Age of the American Revolution, Selected
    Letters and Papers, 1776-1790: January 4th,
    1782-December 29th, 1785. . . . .*v.3 p.411*

Lafayette in the Age of the American Revolution, Selected
    Letters and Papers, 1776-1790, Vol. IV: April 1st,
    1781-December 23rd, 1781. . . . .*v.3 p.411*

L'Africain. *v.2 p.531*

Le Lagarde et Michard (set). *v.2 p.463*

L'Age d'homme : précédé de De la Littérature considérée
    comme une tauromachie. *v.2 p.521*

Lais de Marie de France. *v.2 p.467*

The Lais of Marie de France. *v.2 p.467*

Lake Baikal: A Mirror in Time and Space for Understanding
    Global Change
    Processes. *v.5 p.174, p.187, p.237, p.238, p.242*

A Lake Beyond the Wind. *v.6 p.664*

Lake Erie: A Pictorial History. *v.3 p.516*

Lake Wobegon Days. *v.2 p.147, p.148*

Lakes: Chemistry, Geology, Physics. *v.5 p.427*

Lakes Handbook, Vol. 1,Set. *v.5 p.174*

Lake. *v.2 p.530*

The Lake. *v.6 p.230*

Lakota Dictionary: Lakota-English/English-Lakota, New
    Comprehensive Edition. *v.6 p.690*

LaLoie: The Life and Art of Loie Fuller. *v.1 p.12*

L'Amante anglaise. *v.2 p.516*

Lamb As Critic. *v.2 p.298*

Lambda Book Report. *v.6 p.362*

▢ Lambda Legal Defense. *v.6 p.387*

Lament for a Son. *v.1 p.652*

Lament for Agnes. *v.2 p.623*

Lamentations: A New Translation with Introduction and
    Commentary. *v.1 p.622, p.623*

L'amour, la fantasia : roman. *v.2 p.544*

The Lamp at Noon and Other Stories. *v.2 p.738, p.739*

The Lamp of Umm Hashim and Other Stories. *v.6 p.659*

The Lamps of Louis Comfort Tiffany. *v.1 p.810*

The Lance and the Shield: The Life and Times of Sitting
    Bull. *v.6 p.688*

Lancelot: The Knight of the Cart. *v.2 p.466*

Lancelot-Grail: The Old French Arthurian Vulgate and
    Post-Vulgate in Translation. *v.2 p.467*

Land and Environmental Art. *v.1 p.679*

Land and Labor in China. *v.6 p.191*

Land and Power in Latin America: Agrarian Economics and Social Process in the Andes. *v.4 p.28*

Land and Power: The Zionist Resort to Force, 1881-1948. . . . .*v.6 p.611*

Land and Society in Edwardian Britain. *v.4 p.399*

Land and Sovereignty in India: Agrarian Society and Politics under the Eighteenth Century Maratha Svarajya. . .*v.6 p.162*

Land Application of Agricultural, Industrial and Municipal By-Products. *v.5 p.50*

A Land As God Made It: Jamestown and the Birth of America. *v.3 p.499*

Land, Custom and Practice in the South Pacific. . . .*v.4 p.43*

Land Development Handbook. *v.4 p.158*

Land Hunger: David L. Payne and the Oklahoma Boomers. *v.3 p.524*

Land!: Irish Pioneers in Mexican and Revolutionary Texas. *v.3 p.291*

Land, Law, and Lordship in Anglo-Norman England. *v.3 p.97, p.98*

The Land Looks after Us: A History of Native American Religion. *v.1 p.544*

The Land Looks After Us: A History of Native American Religion. *v.6 p.701*

Land of a Thousand Dances: Chicano Rock 'n' Roll from Southern California. *v.6 p.519*

The Land of Bliss. *v.6 p.104*

Land of Childhood. *v.2 p.676*

Land of Hope: Chicago, Black Southerners, and the Great Migration. *v.6 p.712*

The Land of Iran. *v.6 p.629*

Land of Savagery, Land of Promise: The European Image of the American Frontier. *v.3 p.521*

The Land of the Lamas: Notes of a Journey Through China, Mongolia and Tibet. *v.6 p.241*

Land of the Lost. *v.2 p.748*

Land or Death: The Peasant Struggle in Peru. *v.3 p.328*

Land Resources: Now and for the Future. *v.5 p.370, p.371, p.374*

A Land the Size of Binoculars. *v.2 p.814, p.815*

Land Use and Society: Geography, Law, and Public Policy. *v.4 p.382, p.464*

Land Use and Watersheds: Human Influence on Hydrology and Geomorphology in Urban and Forest Areas. *v.5 p.703, p.704*

Land Use Problems and Conflicts: Causes, Consequences and Solutions. *v.4 p.267, v.5 p.17*

Land, Water, and Culture: New Perspectives on Hispanic Land Grants. *v.6 p.533*

The Land Where the Blues Began. *v.1 p.261*

The Land Where Two Streams Flow: Music in the German-Jewish Community of Israel. *v.1 p.299*

Land, Wind, and Hard Words: A Story of Navajo Activism. *v.6 p.695*

Land Without Justice. *v.3 p.247, p.248*

The landed estates of the Esterházy princes : Hungary during the reforms of Maria Theresia and Joseph II. . . .*v.3 p.186*

Landed Obligation: The Practice of Power in Buganda. *v.6 p.66*

Landessprache. *v.2 p.606*

Land-Grant Universities and Extension into the 21st Century: Renegotiating or Abandoning a Social Contract. . . .*v.5 p.5*

Landing Light: Poems. *v.2 p.373*

Landlocked. *v.2 p.365*

Landlords and Strangers: Ecological Adjustment. . . .*v.6 p.68*

Landmark Decisions of the United States Supreme Court. *v.4 p.453*

Landmark Essays on Voice and Writing. *v.2 p.566*

Landmark Legislation, 1774-2002: Major U. S. Acts and Treaties. *v.4 p.560, p.630*

Landmark Supreme Court Cases: A Reference Guide. *v.4 p.537*

Landmark Yiddish Plays: A Critical Anthology. *v.1 p.63, p.126*

Landmarks of French Classical Drama. *v.1 p.63, p.64, p.78, p.105, v.2 p.465*

Landon of Kansas. *v.3 p.461*

Landprints: Reflections on Place and Landscape. *v.1 p.814, v.6 p.294*

Landry: The Legend and the Legacy. *v.4 p.859*

Lands of Memory. *v.2 p.686, p.687*

The Lands of Partitioned Poland 1795-1918. . . . .*v.3 p.253*

The Lands of St. Peter. *v.3 p.199*

The Lands of the Eastern Caliphate. *v.6 p.585*

Landscape and Englishness. *v.4 p.399*

Landscape and Memory. *v.1 p.814*

The Landscape and the Looking Glass: Willa Cather's Search for Value. *v.2 p.67*

Landscape and Western Art. *v.1 p.702*

The Landscape Approach. *v.1 p.813*

Landscape Architecture: A Manual of Site Planning and Design. *v.1 p.817*

Landscape Architecture in Scandinavia: Projects from Denmark, Sweden, Norway, Finland and Iceland. *v.1 p.814*

Landscape Architecture Sourcebook: A Guide to Resources on the History and Practice of Landscape Architecture. *v.1 p.811*

Landscape Design: A Cultural and Architectural History. *v.5 p.44*

Landscape Ecology - A Widening Foundation: A Holistic Unifying Approach. *v.6 p.291*

Landscape, Literature, and English Religious Culture, 1660-1800: Samuel Johnson and Languages of Natural Description. *v.2 p.251*

The Landscape of Reform: Civic Pragmatism and Environmental Thought in America. *v.6 p.289*

Landscape Painted with Tea. *v.2 p.811*

Landscape Stories. *v.1 p.814*

Landscape Turned Red: The Battle of Antietam. *v.3 p.401, p.432*

Landscape with Human Figure. *v.6 p.404, p.505, p.510*

Landscapes of Devils: Tensions of Place and Memory in the Argentinean Chaco. *v.3 p.267*

Landscapes of Learning. *v.4 p.302*

Landscapes of Loss: The National Past in Postwar French Cinema. *v.6 p.338*

Landscapes of Power: From Detroit to Disney World. *v.6 p.720*

Landscapes of Race in United States. *v.4 p.382*

Landscapes of Settlement: Prehistory to the Present. . *v.4 p.395*

Landscapes of Struggle: Politics, Society, and Community in El Salvador. *v.3 p.299*

Landscapes of the Jihad: Militancy, Morality,
Modernity. *v.4 p.658*

Landscape. *v.4 p.399*

Landslide Hazard and Risk. *v.4 p.395*

Landslides in Practice: Investigation, Analysis, and
Remedial/Preventative Options in Soils. . . .*v.5 p.421, p.698*

Landslides: Investigation and Mitigation. *v.5 p.422*

Land. *v.2 p.381*

Land-Use Planning for Sustainable
Development. *v.5 p.373, p.374, p.377*

Lane Kirkland: Champion of American Labor. *v.4 p.128*

Langdon Cheves of South Carolina. *v.3 p.417*

Langenscheidt Routledge German Dictionary of Chemistry and
Chemical Technology: Germanenglish, Vol. 1. . . .*v.5 p.258*

Langenscheidt Routledge German Dictionary of Chemistry and
Chemical Technology, Vol. 2. . . . .*v.5 p.258*

Langenscheidt 's New Muret-Sanders Encyclopedic Dictionary
of the English and German Languages. . . .*v.2 p.621, p.622*

Lange's Handbook of Chemistry. *v.5 p.259*

Langman's Medical Embryology. *v.5 p.160*

Langsame Heimkehr: Erzahlung. *v.2 p.617*

Langston Hughes and the Blues. *v.2 p.88*

Langston Hughes: Critical Perspectives Past and
Present. *v.2 p.87, v.6 p.25*

A Langston Hughes Encyclopedia. *v.2 p.88*

The Langston Hughes Reader. *v.2 p.87*

Language Alive in the Classroom. *v.2 p.553*

Language an Introduction to the Study of
Speech. *v.4 p.20, v.5 p.624*

Language and Class in Victorian
England. *v.6 p.742, p.743, p.751, p.752*

Language and Gender: A Reader. *v.6 p.476*

Language and Gender. *v.4 p.21*

Language and Identity: National, Ethnic, Religious. . .*v.4 p.694*

The Language and Imagery of the Bible. *v.1 p.616*

Language and Learning: The Debate Between Jean Piaget and
Noam Chomsky. *v.2 p.563*

Language and Literacy Learning in Schools. *v.4 p.365*

Language and Literary Structure: The Linguistic Analysis of
Form in Verse and Narrative. *v.2 p.552*

Language and Mind. *v.2 p.559, v.5 p.622*

Language and Philosophy: Studies in Method. *v.1 p.489*

Language and Power: Exploring Indonesian Political
Culture. *v.6 p.173, p.175, p.176*

Language and Sexuality. *v.4 p.21*

Language and Silence: Essays on Language, Literature, and the
Inhuman. *v.2 p.576*

Language and Social Identity. *v.5 p.623*

Language and Society in la Vida de Lazarillo de
Tormes. *v.2 p.652*

Language and Symbolic Power. *v.4 p.21*

Language and the Comedia: Theory and Practice. . . .*v.2 p.640*

Language and Thought in Humans and Computers: Theory and
Research in Psychology, Artificial Intelligence and Neural
Science. *v.5 p.589, p.590*

Language and Woman's Place: Text and
Commentaries. *v.2 p.557, p.562, v.4 p.21*

Language As Cultural Practice: Mexicanos en el Norte. .*v.6 p.494*

Language Change and Linguistic Reconstruction. . . .*v.2 p.561*

Language Change: Progress or Decay? *v.2 p.553, p.559*

Language Contact. *v.4 p.20*

Language, Culture, and Society: A Book of
Readings. *v.4 p.17, p.18*

Language Death. *v.2 p.549, p.560, v.4 p.19*

Language Decline and Death in Africa: Causes, Consequences
and Challenges. *v.6 p.80*

Language, Discourse and Power in African American
Culture. *v.4 p.21*

Language Disorders Across the Lifespan. *v.5 p.665, p.674*

Language Diversity and Thought: A Reformulation of the
Linguistic Relativity Hypothesis. *v.4 p.20*

Language Diversity in the Classroom: From Intention to
Practice. *v.2 p.565*

Language, Gender and Society. *v.5 p.624*

Language Ideologies: Practice and Theory. *v.4 p.21*

Language in Action: Psychological Models of
Conversation. *v.5 p.622, p.624*

Language in the Americas. *v.6 p.690*

Language in the U. S. A.: Themes for the Twenty-First
Century. *v.2 p.552*

The Language Instinct: How the Mind Creates
Language. *v.2 p.563, v.5 p.621, p.623*

Language Loyalties: A Source Book on the Official English
Controversy. *v.2 p.554*

Language Matters: A Guide to Everyday Questions about
Language. *v.2 p.550, p.563*

Language, Memory, and Aging. *v.5 p.627, p.630, p.632*

Language, Music, and Mind. *v.1 p.382*

Language Myths. *v.2 p.550, p.564*

A Language Not to Be Betrayed. *v.2 p.385*

The Language of Art History. *v.1 p.703*

The Language of Biotechnology: A Dictionary of
Terms. *v.5 p.96, p.220*

The Language of Blood: A Memoir. *v.6 p.95, p.137*

The Language of Canaan: Metaphor and Symbol in New
England from the Puritans to the Transcendentalists. *v.2 p.12*

The Language of Cinema. *v.6 p.307*

Language of Fiction: Essays in Criticism and Verbal Analysis of
the English Novel. *v.2 p.189*

The Language of Genes: Unraveling the Mysteries of Human
Genetics. *v.5 p.134*

The Language of Humour. *v.2 p.195*

The Language of Landscape. *v.1 p.814*

Language of Liberty: Political. *v.3 p.397*

The Language of Morals. *v.1 p.487*

The Language of Movement. *v.1 p.47*

The Language of New Media. *v.4 p.419*

Language of Ornament. *v.1 p.713*

The Language of School Design: Design Patterns for 21st
Century Schools. *v.4 p.288*

The Language of Shakespeare's Plays. *v.2 p.229*

The Language of Spanish Dance. *v.1 p.21*

The Language of the Birds. *v.6 p.667*

The Language of the Goddess. *v.1 p.529*

The Language of Theatre. *v.1 p.59, p.140*

Language, Politics, and Social Interaction in an Inuit Community. *v.4 p.21*

Language, Proof and Logic. *v.1 p.493*

Language, Race, and Negotiation of Identity: A Study of Dominican Americans. *v.6 p.494, p.543*

Language, Religion, and Ethnic Assertiveness: The Growth of Sinhalese Nationalism in Sri Lanka. *v.6 p.163*

The Language Revolution. *v.2 p.560, v.4 p.19*

Language Shift and Cultural Reproduction: Socialization, Self and Syncretism in a Papua New Guinean Village. . *v.4 p.19*

Language Shock: Understanding the Culture of Conversation. *v.4 p.18*

Language Skills in Elementary Education. *v.4 p.361*

Language Socialization across Cultures. *v.4 p.20*

The Language That Rises, 1923-1934. . . . .*v.2 p.121*

Language, Thought, and Reality: Selected Writings. *v.4 p.20, v.5 p.624*

Language, Truth and Logic. *v.1 p.445*

Language Universals and Linguistic Typology: Syntax and Morphology. *v.4 p.18*

Language Variation in North American English: Research and Teaching. *v.2 p.552, p.556*

Languages of Africa. *v.6 p.80*

Languages of Art. *v.1 p.479*

Languages of Belonging: Islam, Regional Identity, and the Making of Kashmir. *v.6 p.162*

The Languages of China. *v.6 p.207*

Languages of Class: Studies in English Working Class History 1832-1982. . . . .*v.3 p.116, p.131, v.6 p.743*

Languages of Community: The Jewish Experience in the Czech Lands. *v.3 p.190*

The Languages of Italy. *v.2 p.699*

Languages of Labor and Gender: Female Factory Work in Germany, 1850-1914. . . . .*v.3 p.52, p.163*

The Languages of Learning: How Children Talk, Write, Dance, Draw and Sing Their Understanding of the World. *v.4 p.360*

The Languages of Native North America. *v.6 p.690*

Languages of the Lash: Corporal Punishment and Identity in Imperial Russia. *v.3 p.218*

Language. *v.2 p.559*

LANIC (Latin American Network Information Center). *v.3 p.259, v.4 p.591*

Lankavatara Sutra. *v.1 p.564*

L'anté-peuple : roman. *v.2 p.546*

Lanthanides and Actinides. *v.5 p.307*

Laocoon: An Essay on the Limits of Painting and Poetry. *v.1 p.481*

Laos. *v.6 p.171*

Lao-Tzu and the Tao-Te-Ching. *v.1 p.418*

The Lapita Peoples: Ancestors of the Oceanic World. . *v.4 p.13*

L'appel des arènes. *v.2 p.545*

Large Antennas of the Deep Space Network. *v.5 p.728*

The Large Sutra on Perfect Wisdom: With the Divisions of the Abhisamayalankara. *v.1 p.563*

Large-Scale Structure of the Universe. *v.5 p.72*

Lark in the Morning: The Verses of the Troubadours. *v.2 p.466*

Lark Rise to Candleford: A Trilogy. .*v.3 p.92, p.109, p.116, p.127*

Larkin's Jazz: Essays and Reviews, 1940-1984. . . . .*v.2 p.361*

Larousse Diccionario Standard: Espanol-Ingles - English-Spanish. *v.2 p.635*

Larousse Unabridged Dictionary: Spanish-English / English-Spanish. *v.2 p.636*

L'arrêt de mort. *v.2 p.510*

Lars Gyllensten. *v.2 p.629*

Lartigue: Album of a Century. *v.1 p.768*

Larvae and Evolution: Toward A New Zoology. *v.5 p.213*

Las Derechas: The Extreme Right in Argentina, Brazil, and Chile, 1890-1939. . . . .*v.3 p.334, p.346, p.350*

Las Hermanas: Chicana/Latina Religious-Political Activism in the U. S. Catholic Church. *v.6 p.435, p.459, p.460, p.465, p.520, p.546*

Las Meninas: A Fantasia in Two Parts. *v.2 p.657*

Las Obreras: Chicana Politics of Work and Family. . *v.6 p.547*

Las Tejanas: 300 Years of History. *v.3 p.508*

Las Tierras Flacas. *v.2 p.670*

Laser Capture Microdissection: Methods and Protocols. *v.5 p.89*

Laser Spectroscopy: Basic Concepts and Instrumentation. *v.5 p.562*

Lasers and Optical Engineering. *v.5 p.701, p.730*

L'asphyxie. *v.2 p.521*

Last Actor-Managers. *v.1 p.102, p.145, p.150*

Last Alternatives: Allen Tate. *v.2 p.125*

Last among Equals: Hawaiian Statehood and American Politics. *v.3 p.533*

Last and Lost Poems. *v.2 p.119*

The Last Best Hope of Earth: Abraham Lincoln and the Promise of America. *v.3 p.399*

The Last Cacique: Leadership and Politics in a Puerto Rican City. *v.3 p.320*

The Last Caravan. *v.6 p.61*

The Last Centuries of Byzantium, 1261-1453. . . . .*v.3 p.193*

Last Chance High: How Girls and Boys Drop in and Out of Alternative Schools. *v.4 p.299*

The Last Chronicle of Barset. *v.2 p.317*

The Last Closet: The Real Lives of Lesbian and Gay Teachers. *v.4 p.283, p.309, v.6 p.383, p.385*

The Last Confucian: Liang Shu-ming and the Chinese Dilemma of Modernity. *v.6 p.199*

Last Dance: Behind the Scenes at the Final Four. *v.4 p.853, p.893, p.902*

The Last Days of the Jerusalem of Lithuania: Chronicles from the Vilna Ghetto and the Camps, 1939-1944. . . . .*v.3 p.85*

The Last Days of the Renaissance: The March to Modernity. *v.3 p.71*

Last Days of the Sioux Nation. *v.3 p.402, v.6 p.687*

Last Diary of Tsaritsa Alexandra. *v.3 p.219*

The Last Emperors: A Social History of Qing Imperial Institutions. *v.6 p.187*

The Last Empire: Britain and the Commonwealth. . . .*v.4 p.605*

The Last Empire: Essays, 1992-2000. . . . .*v.2 p.127*

Last Essays. *v.2 p.590*

Last Evenings on Earth. *v.2 p.679*

Last Exit to Brooklyn. *v.2 p.155*

The Last Frontier: The Social Meaning of Growing Old. .*v.4 p.741*

The Last Generation of the Roman Republic. *v.3 p.26*

Last Giant of Beringia: The Mystery of the Bering Land
    Bridge. *v.5 p.434*

A Last Glass of Tea. *v.6 p.656*

The Last Governor: Chris Patten and the Handover of Hong
    Kong. *v.6 p.201, p.205*

The Last Great American Picture Show: New Hollywood
    Cinema in the 1970s. *v.6 p.341*

The Last Great Frenchman: A Life of General de Gaulle. .*v.3 p.155*

The Last Half-Century: Societal Change and Politics in
    America. *v.4 p.704, p.759*

The Last Human: A Guide to 19 Species of Extinct
    Humans. *v.4 p.16*

The Last Imaginary Place: A Human History of the Arctic
    World. *v.4 p.379*

The Last Jew: A Novel. *v.6 p.649*

The Last Jews in Baghdad: Remembering a Lost
    Homeland. *v.6 p.598, p.603*

The Last King of Poland. *v.3 p.253*

The Last King of Scotland. *v.2 p.345*

The Last Knight: The Twilight of the Middle Ages and the Birth
    of the Modern Era. *v.6 p.561*

Last Laughs: Perspectives on Women and Comedy. . .*v.2 p.585*

The Last Letter Home. *v.2 p.630*

Last Letters of Jacopo Ortis. *v.2 p.710*

The Last Lion: Winston Churchill Visions of Glory,
    1874-1932. . . . .*v.3 p.118, p.119*

Last Night a DJ Saved My Life: The History of the Disc
    Jockey. *v.1 p.266*

Last Night on Earth. *v.1 p.9*

The Last Oasis: Facing Water Scarcity. *v.5 p.357, p.380*

The Last of Chéri. *v.2 p.515*

The Last of the Menu Girls. *v.6 p.498*

The Last of the Mohicans. A narrative of 1757. by J. Fenimore
    Cooper. *v.2 p.35*

Last Orders. *v.2 p.380*

The Last Partnerships: Inside the Great Wall Street
    Dynasties. *v.4 p.89, p.100, p.155, p.162*

The Last Picture Show: A Novel. *v.2 p.150*

Last Poems, 1821-1850. . . . .*v.2 p.325*

Last Rights: Revisiting Four Theories of the Press. . .*v.4 p.405*

The Last Samurai: The Life and Battles of Saigo
    Takamori. *v.6 p.228*

The Last September. *v.2 p.334*

The Last Soviet Avant-Garde: OBERIU - Fact, Fiction,
    Metafiction. *v.2 p.799, p.800*

Last Stand: America's Virgin Lands. *v.5 p.234*

The Last Stand of Chinese Conservatism: The T'ung-Chih
    Restoration, 1862-1874. . . . .*v.6 p.189*

Last Stand of the Tallgrass Prairie. *v.5 p.240, p.241*

The Last Tasmanian Tiger: The History and Extinction of the
    Thylacine. *v.6 p.292*

The Last Things. *v.1 p.645*

The Last Titan: A Life of Theodore Dreiser. *v.2 p.70*

Last Train to Memphis: The Rise of Elvis
    Presley. *v.1 p.270, p.348*

The Last Tsar: The Life and Death of Nicholas II. . . .*v.3 p.220*

Last Witnesses: Reflections on the Wartime Internment of
    Japanese Americans. *v.6 p.133*

The Last Word. *v.1 p.514*

The Last Worthless Evening: Four Novellas and Two
    Stories. *v.2 p.144*

Lasting Impressions: Lithography as Art. *v.1 p.754*

L'astragale: roman. *v.2 p.533*

Late Antiquity: A Guide to the Postclassical
    World. *v.3 p.30, p.191, p.192*

The Late Baroque Era: From the 1680s to 1740. . .*v.1 p.182*

Late Ch'ing 1800-1911. . . . .*v.6 p.188*

Late Ch'ing, 1800-1911. . . . .*v.6 p.188*

A Late Divorce. *v.6 p.652*

The Late George Apley: A Novel. *v.2 p.97*

Late Harvest: Essays and Addresses in American Literature and
    Culture. *v.2 p.7*

The Late Medieval Age of Crisis and Renewal, 1300-1500: A
    Biographical Dictionary. *v.6 p.562*

Late Medieval and Renaissance Philosophy: Ockham, Francis
    Bacon and the Beginning of the Modern World, Vol.
    3. . . . .*v.1 p.431, p.432*

The Late Medieval Balkans: A Critical Survey from the Late
    Twelfth Century to the Ottoman Conquest. *v.3 p.246*

Late Medieval Ireland, 1370-1541. . . . . . .*v.3 p.134, p.136*

The Late Medieval Scottish Parliament: Politics and the Three
    Estates, 1424-1488. . . . .*v.6 p.566*

Late Modernism: Politics, Fiction, and the Arts Between the
    World Wars. *v.2 p.11*

The Late Roman West and the Vandals. *v.3 p.62*

The Late Romantic Era. *v.1 p.203*

Late Ruskin. *v.2 p.305*

Latent Heat Transfer: An Introduction to Fundamentals. *v.5 p.713*

Later Auden. *v.2 p.329*

The Later Career of Tobias Smollett. *v.2 p.261*

The Later Crusades, 1274-1580: From Lyons to Alcazar. *v.6 p.556*

Later Diaries of Ned Rorem: 1961-1972. . . . . . .*v.6 p.410*

The Later Ghaznavids: Splendour and Decay: The Dynasty in
    Afghanistan and Norther India, 1040-1186. *v.6 p.634, p.644*

The Later Marxism. *v.4 p.250*

The Later Medieval City 1300-1500. . . . .*v.3 p.44*

Later Medieval Europe: 1250-1520. . . . .*v.3 p.70*

Later Medieval France: The Polity. *v.4 p.704*

The Later Middle Ages, 1272-1485. . . . .*v.3 p.69*

The Later Middle Ages: From the Norman Conquest to the Eve
    of the Reformation. *v.6 p.570*

Later Nineteenth and Early Twentieth Century English and
    European Novelists: H. G. Wells. *v.2 p.319*

Later Nineteenth and Early Twentieth Century English and
    European Novelists: Rudyard Kipling. *v.2 p.296*

The Later Poetic Manuscripts of Gerard Manley Hopkins: From "The Wreck of the Deutschland" to the Final Dublin Sonnets in Facsimile. *v.2 p.293, p.294*

The Later Roman Empire, 284-602: A Social, Economic, and Administrative Survey, Vol. 1. . . . .*v.3 p.31, p.192*

The Later Roman Empire, 284-602: A Social, Economic, and Administrative Survey, Vol. 2. . . . .*v.3 p.31, p.192*

The Later Roman Empire A. D. 354-378. . . . . . .*v.2 p.428*

The Later Roman Empire. *v.3 p.30*

Later Short Stories. *v.2 p.318*

The Later Years, 1803-1850, Vol. 2. . . . .*v.2 p.324*

The Later Years of Thomas Hardy, 1892-1928. . . .*v.2 p.291*

LaTeX: A Document Preparation System. *v.5 p.461*

Latin: A Historical and Lingusitic Handbook. *v.2 p.423*

Latin America and Postmodernity: A Contemporary Reader. *v.1 p.444*

▢ Latin America Data Base (LADB). *v.3 p.259*

Latin America in the 1940's: War and Postwar Transitions. *v.3 p.346*

Latin America: Regions and People. *v.4 p.397*

Latin America since 1930: Spanish South America. . .*v.3 p.345*

Latin America: The Hegemonic Crisis and the Military Coup. *v.3 p.276*

Latin American and Caribbean Artists of the Modern Era: A Biographical Dictionary of over 10,000 Persons. *v.1 p.666, p.684, p.685*

Latin American Art: Ancient to Modern. *v.1 p.684*

Latin American Art of the 20th Century. *v.1 p.679, p.684*

Latin American Artists' Signatures and Monograms: Colonial Era to 1996. . . . .*v.1 p.663*

▢ Latin American Bureau. *v.3 p.259*

Latin American Dramatists: First Series. *v.2 p.665*

Latin American Journalism. *v.4 p.404*

The Latin American Left: From the Fall of Allende to Perestroika. *v.3 p.352*

▢ Latin American Periodicals Tables of Contents (LAPTOC). *v.3 p.259*

Latin American Philosophy: Currents, Issues, Debates. .*v.1 p.444*

Latin American Philosophy in the Twentieth Century: Man, Values and the Search for Philosophical Identity. . .*v.1 p.444*

Latin American Politics and Development. *v.4 p.593*

Latin American Popular Culture: An Introduction. . . .*v.3 p.266*

Latin American Religion in Motion: Tracking Innovation, Unexpected Change, and Complexity. *v.1 p.544*

Latin American Social Thought. *v.4 p.684*

Latin American Spanish. *v.2 p.636*

Latin American Sport: An Annotated Bibliography, 1988-1998. . . . .*v.4 p.812, p.813, p.833*

ⓔ Latin American Theatre in Translation: An Anthology of Work from Mexico, the Caribbean and the Southern Cone. *v.1 p.127, p.128*

Latin American Thought: Philosophical Problems and Arguments. *v.1 p.444*

Latin American Urbanization: Historical Profiles of Major Cities. *v.3 p.260*

Latin American Women Artists, Kahlo and Look Who Else: A Selective, Annotated Bibliography. *v.6 p.473, p.475*

Latin American Women: Historical Perspectives. . . .*v.3 p.283*

Latin American Writers on Gay and Lesbian Themes: A Bio-Critical Sourcebook. *v.6 p.392*

Latin Americanism. *v.2 p.663, p.664*

Latin America's Wars: The Age of Caudillo, 1791-1899. .*v.3 p.277*

Latin America's Wars: The Age of the Professional Soldier, 1900-2001. . . . .*v.3 p.277*

The Latin Beat: The Rhythms and Roots of Latin Music, from Bossa Nova to Salsa and Beyond. *v.1 p.293, v.3 p.317*

A Latin Dictionary: Founded on Andrews' Edition of Freund's Latin Dictionary. *v.2 p.424*

Latin Erotic Elegy: An Anthology and Reader. *v.2 p.426*

Latin Historians. *v.2 p.426*

Latin Jazz : The First of the Fusions, 1880s to Today. *v.1 p.294*

Latin Jazz: The First of the Fusions, 1900-Today. . . .*v.6 p.519*

Latin Jazz: The Perfect Combination - La Combinacion Perfecta. *v.1 p.258, p.292*

Latin Jazz. *v.6 p.509*

Latin Journey: Cuban and Mexican Immigrants in the United States. *v.4 p.571, v.6 p.530*

ⓔ Latin Language and Latin Culture: From Ancient to Modern Times. *v.2 p.423*

The Latin Language. *v.2 p.424*

Latin Literature: A History. *v.2 p.424*

Latin Literature of the Fourth Century. *v.2 p.424*

Latin Literature. *v.2 p.424*

Latin Looks: Images of Latinas and Latinos in the U.S. Media. *v.6 p.493, p.494*

The Latin Love Elegy. *v.2 p.426*

Latin Lyric and Elegiac Poetry: An Anthology of New Translations. *v.2 p.426, p.427*

Latin Moon in Manhattan: A Novel. *v.6 p.507*

Latin Palaeography: Antiquity and the Middle Ages. . .*v.6 p.555*

Latin Poetry and the Classical Tradition: Essays in Medieval and Renaissance Literature. *v.2 p.449*

Latin Politics, Global Media. *v.4 p.415*

The Latin Tinge: The Impact of Latin American Music on the United States. *v.1 p.294*

Latin Verse Satire: An Anthology and Critical Reader. *v.2 p.427*

Latina Health in the United States: A Public Health Reader. *v.5 p.523*

A Latina in the Land of Hollywood and Other Essays on Media Culture. *v.6 p.449, p.494*

Latina Legacies: Identity, Biography, and Community. *v.6 p.490, p.547*

Latina Performance: Traversing the Stage. . . .*v.6 p.516, p.517*

▢ Latindex: Sistema Regional de Información en línea para Revistas Científicas de América Latina,, el Caribe, España y Portugal. *v.3 p.259*

Latino Americans and Political Participation: A Reference Handbook. *v.6 p.539*

Latino and African American Athletes Today: A Biographical Dictionary. *v.4 p.832, p.833, p.834*

Latino and Latina Writers. *v.6 p.504, p.509, p.516*

Latino Boom: An Anthology of U.S. Latino Literature. *v.6 p.495*

Latino College Students. *v.6 p.527*

Latino Crossings: Mexicans, Puerto Ricans and the Politics of Race and Citizenship. *v.6 p.542*

Latino Cultural Citizenship: Claiming Identity, Space and Rights. *v.6 p.540, p.543*

Latino Culture: A Dynamic Force in the Changing American Workplace. *v.6 p.524*

The Latino Encyclopedia, Set. *v.6 p.485*

Latino Ethnic Consciousness: The Case of Mexican Americans and Puerto Ricans in Chicago. *v.6 p.544*

The Latino Family and the Politics of Transformation. .*v.6 p.545*

Latino Fiction and the Modernist Imagination: Literature of the Borderlands. *v.6 p.512*

Latino Gay Men and HIV: Culture, Sexuality and Risk Behavior. *v.6 p.378*

Latino Language and Literacy in Ethnolinguistic Chicago. *v.6 p.494, p.548*

Latino Literature in the Classroom: The Politics of Transformation. *v.6 p.502, p.508, p.515*

Latino Los Angeles: Transformations, Communities, and Activism. *v.6 p.544, p.550*

Latino Politics in America: Community, Culture, and Interests. *v.6 p.538*

Latino Politics in Massachusetts: Struggles, Strategies and Prospects. *v.6 p.538*

The Latino Reader: An American Literary Tradition from 1542 to the Present. *v.2 p.18, v.6 p.495*

Latino Social Movements: Historical and Theoretical Perspectives. *v.6 p.539*

The Latino Studies Reader: Culture, Politics and Society. *v.6 p.486*

Latino Voices: Mexican, Puerto Rican, and Cuban Perspectives on American Politics. *v.6 p.537*

The Latino/a Condition: A Critical Reader. . . .*v.6 p.521, p.540*

Latino/a Popular Culture. *v.6 p.493*

Latino/a Rights and Justice in the United States: Perspectives and Approaches. *v.6 p.540, p.541*

Latino/a Thought: Culture, Politics and Society. *v.6 p.522*

Latinos: A Biography of the People. . .*v.6 p.490, p.491, p.533*

Latinos and Education: Critical Reader. *v.6 p.526*

Latinos and the U. S. Political System: Two-Tiered Pluralism. *v.6 p.538*

Latinos and U. S. Foreign Policy: Representing the Homeland? *v.6 p.537*

Latinos in a Changing U. S. Economy: Comparative Perspectives on Growing Inequality. *v.6 p.525*

Latinos in New York: Communities in Transition. .*v.6 p.542, p.549*

Latinos in the United States: An Original Anthology. *v.6 p.521*

Latinos, Inc.: The Marketing and Making of a People. *v.4 p.132, p.138*

Latinos, Inc: The Marketing and Making of a People. *v.6 p.526*

Latinos: Remaking America. *v.6 p.522*

Latinos Unidos: From Cultural Diversity to the Politics of Solidarity. *v.4 p.311, v.6 p.545*

A Latter Day Confucian: Reminiscences of William Hung, 1893-1980. . . . .*v.6 p.199*

Latvia in Transition. *v.3 p.256*

Latvian-English - English-Latvian Practical Dictionary. *v.2 p.773*

The Latvians: A Short History. *v.3 p.256*

Laude. *v.2 p.701*

Laughable Loves. *v.2 p.784*

Laughing Gas. *v.2 p.390*

Laughing Hysterically: American Screen Comedy of the 1950s. *v.6 p.313*

Laughing Screaming: Modern Hollywood Horror and Comedy. *v.6 p.313, p.319*

Laughing to Keep from Crying. *v.2 p.87*

The Laughing Tradition: Stage Comedy in Garrick's Day. *v.2 p.187*

Laughter: A Scientific Investigation. *v.5 p.656*

Laughter: An Essay on the Meaning of the Comic. . *v.2 p.585*

Laughter in Interaction. *v.4 p.423*

The Laughter of Foxes: A Study of Ted Hughes. . . .*v.2 p.353*

The Laughter of My Father. *v.6 p.93, p.129*

Laughter Out of Place: Race, Class, Violence, and Sexuality in a Rio Shantytown. *v.3 p.279*

Laughter, Pain, and Wonder: Shakespeare's Comedies and the Audience in the Theater. *v.2 p.231*

Launching Democracy in South Africa: The First Open Election, April 1994. . . . .*v.4 p.613, p.614*

Launching into Cyberspace: Internet Development and Politics in Five World Regions. *v.4 p.624*

Laura Riding: Selected Poems in Five Sets. *v.2 p.89*

Laurence Sterne: A Life. *v.2 p.262*

Laurence Sterne: Riddles and Mysteries. *v.2 p.262*

Laurence Sterne's Tristram Shandy: A Casebook. . . *v.2 p.262*

Laurence Sterne. *v.2 p.262*

Laurie Anderson. *v.1 p.214, p.301*

Lautreamont and Sade. *v.2 p.483*

L'Avalée des avalés. *v.2 p.540*

Lavender Mansions: 40 Contemporary Lesbian and Gay Short Stories. *v.2 p.27, v.6 p.407*

Lavender Road to Success: The Career Guide for the Gay Community. *v.4 p.168, v.6 p.382*

The Lavender Scare: The Cold War Persecution of Gays and Lesbians in the Federal Government. .*v.6 p.365, p.383, p.388*

The Lavender Screen: The Gay and Lesbian Films - Their Stars, Directors, Characters and Critics. *v.6 p.416*

L'aventure ambiguë : récit. *v.2 p.545*

Lavish Self-Divisions: The Novels of Joyce Carol Oates. *v.2 p.152*

Lavoisier: Chemist, Biologist, Economist. *v.5 p.261*

Law and Community in Three American Towns. . . .*v.4 p.33*

Law and Ecology: The Rise of the Ecosystem Regime. *v.5 p.374*

Law and Economic Growth: The Legal History of the Lumber Industry in Wisconsin, 1836-1915. . .*v.5 p.37, p.38,v.6 p.295*

Law and Economic Organization: A Comparative Study of Preindustrial Studies. *v.4 p.33*

Law and Economic Policy in America: The Evolution of the Sherman Antitrust Act. *v.4 p.444*

Law and Empire in the Pacific: Fiji and Hawaii. . . .*v.4 p.43*

Law and Evidence: A Primer for Criminal Justice, Criminology, Law, and Legal Studies. *v.6 p.270*

Law and Identity in Mandate Palestine. *v.6 p.612*

Law and Industrial Relations: China and Japan after World War II. *v.4 p.122*

Law and People in Colonial America. *v.4 p.440*

Law and Psychology: The Broadening of the Discipline. *v.5 p.592*

Law and Psychology. *v.5 p.592*

Law and Revolution II: The Impact of the Protestant Reformations on the Western Legal Tradition. . . *v.4 p.433*

Law and Revolution: The Formation of the Western Legal Tradition. *v.4 p.433*

Law and Social Change in Postwar Japan. *v.6 p.220*

Law and Society in Byzantium, 9th-12th Centuries. . *v.3 p.193*

Law and Society in Contemporary Cuba. *v.3 p.308*

Law and Society in Puritan Massachusetts: Essex County, 1629-1692. . . . . *v.4 p.474*

Law and Society in Traditional China. *v.4 p.475*

Law and the American Indian: Readings, Notes and Cases. *v.6 p.696*

Law and the Shaping of the American Labor Movement. *v.4 p.125, p.126*

Law and the Transformation of Aztec Culture, 1500-1700. *v.3 p.286*

Law and Warfare: Studies in the Anthropology of Conflict. *v.4 p.433*

Law at the End of Life: The Supreme Court and Assisted Suicide. *v.4 p.448, p.539*

Law by Source: Global. *v.4 p.474, p.475, p.476*

The Law Code of Manu. *v.1 p.537*

Law, Crime and Sexuality: Essays in Feminism. . . . *v.6 p.269*

Law Enforcement in the 21st Century. *v.6 p.261*

Law for Global Commerce: A Tour. *v.4 p.57, p.110*

Law for Recreation and Sport Managers. *v.4 p.783, p.883, p.900*

The Law in America. *v.4 p.440*

The Law in Classical Athens. *v.4 p.433*

Law in Culture and Society. *v.4 p.33, p.433*

The Law in Plain English for Crafts. *v.1 p.827*

Law, Justice, and Power: Between Reason and Will. . *v.1 p.491*

Law, Labor, and Ideology in the Early American Republic. *v.4 p.447*

Law, Land, and Family: Aristocratic Inheritance in England, 1300 to 1800. . . . . *v.3 p.52*

Law, Liberty, and Psychiatry: An Inquiry into the Social Uses of Mental Health Practices. *v.6 p.269*

The Law of Agency and Partnership. *v.4 p.75*

Law of Her Own: The Reasonable Woman as a Measure of Man. *v.4 p.472*

The Law of Higher Education. *v.4 p.450*

The Law of Love. *v.2 p.667*

The Law of Mass Action: And Its Statistical Mechanical Basis. *v.5 p.278*

The Law of Mergers and Acquisitions. *v.4 p.85*

The Law of Nations: An Introduction to the International Law of Peace. *v.4 p.477*

The Law of Peoples. *v.4 p.625*

The Law of Primitive Man: A Study in Comparative Legal Dynamics. *v.4 p.433*

The Law of the Sea in a Nutshell. *v.4 p.478*

The Law of the Workplace: Rights of Employers and Employees. *v.4 p.131*

Law, Sex, and Christian Society in Medieval Europe. *v.3 p.51, v.6 p.568, p.570*

Law, Society and Culture in the Maghrib, 1300-1500. . . . . *v.6 p.641, p.642, p.643*

The Law under Swastika: Studies on Legal History in Nazi Germany. *v.3 p.174*

Lawful Order: A Case Study of Correctional Crisis and Reform. *v.6 p.274*

The Lawful Revolution: Louis Kossuth and the Hungarians, 1848-1849. . . . . *v.3 p.186*

The Lawless Liberators: Political Banditry and Cuban Independence. *v.3 p.313*

The Lawless Roads. *v.2 p.351*

Lawlessness and Economics: Alternative Modes of Governance. *v.4 p.248, p.252*

The Lawn: A History of an American Obsession. . . *v.1 p.813*

Lawrence and His Laboratory: A History of the Lawrence Berkeley Laboratory. *v.5 p.543*

Lawrence Durrell: A Biography. *v.2 p.344*

Lawrence Durrell: Comprehending the Whole. . . . *v.2 p.344*

Lawrence Ferlinghetti: Poet-at-Large. *v.2 p.75*

Lawrence Kohlberg's Approach to Moral Education. . *v.5 p.572*

Lawrence of Arabia: The Life, the Legend. *v.3 p.78*

Lawrence's England: The Major Fiction 1913-20. . . *v.2 p.362*

Lawrie's Meat Science. *v.5 p.34*

Laws and Models: Science, Engineering, and Technology. *v.5 p.407*

Laws and Order in Eighteenth-Century Chemistry. . *v.5 p.262*

Laws and Symmetry. *v.1 p.498*

Law's Empire. *v.4 p.434*

Laws of the Game: How the Principles of Nature Govern Chance. *v.5 p.401*

Laws of the Landscape: How Policies Shape Cities in Europe and America. *v.6 p.724*

The Laws of the Salian Franks. *v.3 p.142, p.162*

The Laws of Thought. *v.1 p.491*

Law's Promise, Law's Expression: Visions of Power in the Politics of Race, Gender, and Religion. *v.4 p.455*

Lay Buddhism in Contemporary Japan. *v.1 p.567*

The Lay of the Land: Metaphor As Experience and History in American Life and Letters. *v.2 p.6*

Lay People in the Church: A Study for a Theology of the Laity. *v.1 p.576*

Layers of Time: A History of Ethiopia. *v.6 p.64*

Laying down the Law: A Study of the Theodosian Code. *v.3 p.32*

Lazarillo de Tormes. *v.2 p.650*

Lazaro en el Laberinto. *v.2 p.657*

LBJ: A Life. *v.3 p.481*

The Leader of the Future. *v.4 p.71*

Leaders and Their Followers in a Dangerous World: The Psychology of Political Behavior. *v.4 p.512, p.698, v.5 p.644*

The Leader's Companion: Insights on Leadership Through the Ages. *v.4 p.72*

Leaders in the Study of Animal Behavior. *v.5 p.614*

Leadership and Community in Late Ancient Gaul. . . .*v.3 p.32*

Leadership and Governance from the Inside Out. *v.4 p.71, p.86*

Leadership and Groups in Recreational Service. *v.4 p.786*

Leadership and the New Science: Discovering Order in a Chaotic World. *v.4 p.72*

Leadership for Differentiating Schools and Classrooms. .*v.4 p.350*

Leadership for the Emerging Age: Transforming Practice in Adult and Continuing Education. *v.4 p.319*

Leadership for the Schoolhouse: How Is It Different? Why Is It Important? *v.4 p.282*

Leadership in Committee: A Comparative Analysis of Leadership Behavior in the U. S. Senate. *v.4 p.533*

Leadership in International Business Education and Research. *v.4 p.177*

Leadership in the Modern Presidency. *v.3 p.378*

The Leadership Pipeline: How to Build the Leadership-Powered Company. *v.4 p.70*

Leadership: Succeeding in the Private, Public, and Not-For-Profit Sectors. *v.4 p.698*

Leadership Theory and Research: Perspectives and Directions. *v.5 p.647*

Leading at the Edge of Chaos: How to Create the Nimble Organization. *v.4 p.72*

Leading Biotechnology Alliances: Right from the Start. .*v.5 p.219*

Leading by Example: Partisan Fighters and Leaders of New France, 1660-1760. . . . .*v.3 p.537*

Leading Change. *v.4 p.71*

Leading for Innovation: And Organizing for Results. . *v.4 p.71*

Leading in Prayer: A Workbook for Worship. *v.1 p.654*

Leading Minds: An Anatomy of Leadership. *v.5 p.647*

Leading Teams. *v.4 p.80*

Leading the Cheers. *v.2 p.336*

Leading the Revolution. *v.4 p.66, p.71, p.73*

Leading the Way: Asian American Artists of the Older Generation. *v.1 p.683, v.6 p.88*

Leading to Change: The Challenge of the New Superintendency. *v.4 p.281*

Leaf Storm: And Other Stories. *v.2 p.682, p.683*

The League Committees and World Order. *v.4 p.631*

The League of Nations: Its Life and Times, 1920-1946. . . . .*v.4 p.631, p.632*

The League of the Iroquois. *v.6 p.703*

Lean Enterprise Systems: Using IT for Continuous Improvement. *v.4 p.117*

Lean Six SIGMA Logistics: Strategic Development to Operational Success. *v.4 p.117*

Learn from the Masters. *v.5 p.468*

Learn How to Die the Easy Way. *v.1 p.773, p.774*

Learn to Write the Hebrew Script: Aleph Through the Looking Glass. *v.6 p.646*

Learned Girls and Male Persuasion: Gender and Reading in Roman Love Elegy. *v.2 p.426*

Learned Hand: The Man and the Judge. *v.4 p.441*

Learned Hand's Court. *v.4 p.470*

The Learned King: The Reign of Alfonso X of Castile. .*v.3 p.65*

Learning a Field Language. *v.4 p.18*

Learning: A Survey of Psychological Interpretations. . .*v.4 p.357*

Learning about Learning Disabilities. *v.4 p.319*

Learning and Behavior Therapy. *v.5 p.667*

Learning and Intelligence: Conversations with Skinner and Wheeler. *v.4 p.357*

Learning and Not Learning English: Latino Students in American Schools. *v.4 p.311, p.312,v.6 p.528*

Learning and Teaching Number Theory: Research in Cognition and Instruction. *v.5 p.462*

Learning and Work: An Exploration in Industrial Ethnography. *v.4 p.39, p.44*

Learning as Transformation: Critical Perspectives on a Theory in Progress. *v.4 p.320*

Learning by Heart. *v.4 p.324*

Learning Capoeira: Lessons in Cunning from an Afro-Brazilian Art. *v.1 p.14*

Learning, Creating, and Using Knowledge: Concept Maps As Facilitative Tools in Schools and Corporations. *v.4 p.358, v.5 p.572*

Learning Democracy: Citizen Engagement and Electoral Choice in Nicaragua, 1990-2001. . . . .*v.3 p.300, p.301*

Learning Democracy: Democratic and Economic Values in Unified Germany. *v.4 p.610*

Learning Disabilities: Theories, Diagnosis, and Teaching Strategies. *v.4 p.318*

Learning from Disaster: Risk Management after Bhopal. *v.5 p.364, p.373*

Learning from Museums: Visitor Experiences and the Making of Meaning. *v.1 p.828*

Learning from Our Mistakes: A Reinterpretation of Twentieth-Century Educational Theory. *v.4 p.328*

Learning from Six Philosophers: Descartes, Spinoza, Leibniz, Locke, Berkeley, Hume, Vol. 1. . . . . . .*v.1 p.435, p.436*

Learning from Six Philosophers: Descartes, Spinoza, Leibniz, Locke, Berkeley, Hume, Vol. 2. . . . .*v.1 p.435*

Learning from the Past: What History Teaches Us about School Reform. *v.4 p.330*

Learning How to Ask: A Sociolinguistic Appraisal of the Role of the Interview in Social Science Research. . . .*v.4 p.691*

Learning How to Read. *v.2 p.365*

Learning in Action: A Guide to Putting the Learning Organization to Work. *v.4 p.78*

Learning in Adulthood: A Comprehensive Guide. . . .*v.4 p.320*

Learning in Likely Places: Varieties of Apprenticeship in Japan. *v.6 p.222*

Learning in Small Moments: Life in an Urban Classroom. *v.4 p.315*

Learning Later. *v.4 p.320*

Learning Nature by a Country Road. *v.5 p.227*

The Learning of Liberty: The Educational Ideas of the American Founders. *v.4 p.328*

☐ The Learning Page—American Memory Collection. *v.4 p.367*

Learning, Remembering, Believing: Enhancing Human Performance. *v.5 p.605*

Learning Sequences in Music. *v.1 p.405*

The Learning Society Revisited. *v.4 p.327*

Learning Theories: A to Z. *v.5 p.571*

Learning Theory and Behavior. . . .*v.4 p.358, v.5 p.571, p.572*

Learning Theory and the Symbolic Processes. *v.4 p.358*

Learning to Be Adolescent: Growing up in U. S. and Japanese Middle Schools. *v.6 p.219*

Learning to Be Modern: Pound, Eliot and the American University. *v.2 p.72, p.112*

Learning to Be Old: Gender, Culture, and Aging. *v.5 p.625, p.632,v.6 p.445*

Learning to Draw: Studies in the Cultural History of a Polite and Useful Art. *v.1 p.724*

Learning to Go to School in Japan: The Transition from Home to Preschool Life. *v.6 p.222*

Learning to Labour. *v.4 p.42*

Learning to Legislate. *v.4 p.533*

Learning to Listen, Learning to Teach: The Power of Dialogue in Educating Adults. *v.4 p.321*

Learning to Read: Lessons from Exemplary First-Grade Classrooms. *v.4 p.360*

Learning to Read: The Great Debate. *v.4 p.362*

Learning to Read. *v.4 p.361*

Learning to Rock Climb. *v.4 p.789*

Learning to Swim and Other Stories. *v.2 p.380*

Learning to Teach in an Age of Accountability. . . .*v.4 p.277*

Learning to Use Statistical Skills in Psychology. . . .*v.5 p.600*

Learning to Win: Sports, Education and Social Change in Twentieth-Century North Carolina. *v.4 p.815, p.816, p.821, p.894*

Learning Together: Children and Adults in a School Community. *v.4 p.348*

Learning under the Sun. *v.5 p.222*

ⓔ The Least Dangerous Branch?: Consequences of Judicial Activism. *v.4 p.535*

The Least Dangerous Branch?: Consequences of Judicial Activism. *v.4 p.535, p.541*

The Least Developed Countries Report. *v.4 p.666*

Leave It to Psmith. *v.2 p.390, p.391*

Leaves of Grass. *v.2 p.54*

Leaving No Child Behind?: Options for Kids in Failing Schools. *v.4 p.347, p.348*

Leaving the Bench: Supreme Court Justices at the End. .*v.4 p.535*

Leaving the Land. *v.2 p.157*

Leaving Yuba City: Poems. *v.6 p.103*

The Lebanese and the World: A Century of Emigration. .*v.6 p.605*

The Lebanese Civil War. *v.6 p.606*

Lebanon: A Shattered Country. *v.6 p.605*

Lebanon in History: From the Earliest Times to the Present. *v.6 p.604*

Lebanon in Strife: Student Preludes to the Civil War. .*v.6 p.606*

The Lebanon in Turmoil: Syria and the Powers in 1860. .*v.6 p.604*

Lecture Notes on Elementary Topology and Geometry. .*v.5 p.495*

Lecture Notes on Molecular Medicine. *v.5 p.125, p.126*

Lectures, 1795: On Politics and Religion, Vol. 1. . . .*v.2 p.279*

Lectures, 1808-1819 on Literature. *v.2 p.279*

Lectures, 1818-1819: On the History of Philosophy. *v.2 p.279, p.280*

Lectures and Notes on Shakespeare and Other English Poets. *v.2 p.228*

Lectures on Economic Growth. *v.4 p.233, p.238*

Lectures on Elementary Number Theory. *v.5 p.477*

Lectures on International Trade. *v.4 p.256*

Lectures on Metaphysics. *v.1 p.461*

Lectures on Nuclear Theory. *v.5 p.553*

Lectures on Ordinary Differential Equations. *v.5 p.487*

Lectures on Partial Differential Equations. *v.5 p.487*

Lectures on Philosophical Theology. *v.1 p.462*

Lectures on Philosophy. *v.1 p.458*

Lectures on Political Economy: Money. *v.4 p.241*

Lectures on Rhetoric and Belles Lettres. *v.2 p.564, p.565*

Lectures on Russian Literature. *v.2 p.799*

Lectures on the dramatic literature of the age of Elizabeth. by William Hazlitt. *v.2 p.181*

Lectures on the English Comic Writers. *v.2 p.166*

Lectures on the Philosophy of Religion: One-Volume Edition. The Lectures of 1827. . . . .*v.1 p.522*

Lectures on the Philosophy of World History: Reason in History. *v.1 p.463*

Leddy and Pepper's Conceptual Bases of Professional Nursing. *v.5 p.528*

Lee Krasner: A Catalogue Raisonné. *v.1 p.742, p.743*

Lee Krasner. *v.1 p.740*

Lee Kuan Yew: The Beliefs Behind the Man. *v.6 p.173*

Lee Miller: Portraits from a Life. *v.1 p.766*

Lee's Lieutenants: A Study in Command, Cedar Mountain to Chancellorsville. *v.3 p.430*

Lee's Lieutenants: A Study in Command, Gettysburg to Appomattox. *v.3 p.430*

Lee's Lieutenants: A Study in Command Manassas to Malvern Hill. *v.3 p.430*

Lee's Lieutenants. *v.3 p.397, p.430*

Left Back: A Century of Battles over School Reform. .*v.4 p.328*

A Left Hand Like God: A History of Boogie Woogie Piano. *v.1 p.263*

The Left Hand of Darkness. *v.2 p.148*

The Left Hand of Eden: Meditations on Nature and Human Nature. *v.6 p.288*

Left Out: A Political Journey. *v.6 p.390*

Left Out: Reds and America's Industrial Unions. . . .*v.4 p.123*

The Left-Handed Woman. *v.2 p.617*

Legacies: A Chinese Mosaic. *v.6 p.201, p.217*

The Legacies of Communism in Eastern Europe. . . .*v.4 p.508*

The Legacies of Liberalism: Path Dependence and Political Regimes in Central America. *v.3 p.300, p.302*

Legacies of Twentieth-Century Dance. *v.1 p.23*

Legacy: New Perspectives on the Battle of the Little Bighorn. *v.6 p.688*

Legacy of Alexander: Politics, Warfare, and Propaganda under the Successors. *v.3 p.20*

The Legacy of Christopher Columbus: The Historic Litigations Involving His Discoveries, His Will, His Family, and His Descendants. *v.3 p.404, p.406*

The Legacy of Exile: Cubans in the United
   States. *v.6 p.538, p.544*

The Legacy of Genghis Khan: Courtly Art and Culture in
   Western Asia, 1256-1353. . . . .*v.1 p.674, p.691*

The Legacy of Keynes and Friedman: Economic Analysis,
   Money, and Ideology. *v.4 p.227*

The Legacy of Malthus: The Social Costs of the New Scientific
   Racism. *v.4 p.728*

The Legacy of Mesopotamia. *v.3 p.5*

The Legacy of Muslim Spain. *v.3 p.236*

The Legacy of Rousseau. *v.4 p.492*

The Legacy of Sacco and Vanzetti. *v.4 p.471*

Legacy of the Disinherited: Popular Culture in Latin America:
   Modernity, Globalisation, Hybridity and
   Authenticity. *v.3 p.268*

The Legacy of the Mexican and Spanish-American Wars: Legal,
   Literacy, and Historical Perspectives. *v.6 p.534*

The Legacy of Woodrow Wilson: American War Aims in World
   War I. *v.3 p.470*

Legacy to Liberation: Politics and Culture of Revolutionary
   Asian/Pacific. *v.6 p.107, p.120*

Legal and Ethical Considerations for Dental Hygienists and
   Assistants. *v.5 p.525*

Legal Aspects of Geology. *v.4 p.444*

Legal Concepts in Sport: A Primer. . . .*v.4 p.785, p.882, p.900*

Legal Controls of International Conflict: A Treatise on the
   Dynamics of Disputes. *v.4 p.478*

The Legal Culture of Northern New Spain, 1700-1810. .*v.3 p.285*

Legal Environment of Business: A Critical Thinking
   Approach. *v.4 p.51*

Legal Forms for Starting and Running a Small Business. .*v.4 p.88*

Legal Guide for Starting and Running a Small Business. .*v.4 p.444*

Legal Information: How to Find It, How to Use It. . .*v.4 p.439*

Legal Reasoning and Political Conflict. *v.4 p.434*

Legal Research: How to Find and Understand the
   Law. *v.4 p.109, p.180, p.439*

Legal Rights of Teachers and Students. *v.4 p.450*

Legal Systems of the World: A Political, Social, and Cultural
   Encyclopedia, Set. *v.4 p.433*

Legal Traditions of the World: Sustainable Diversity in
   Law. *v.4 p.434*

The Legalization of Drugs. *v.6 p.253*

Legalizing Gender Inequality: Courts, Markets and Unequal Pay
   for Women in America. *v.4 p.447*

Legalizing Marijuana: Drug Policy Reform and Prohibition
   Politics. *v.4 p.568, v.6 p.253*

Legally Wed: Same-Sex Marriage and the
   Constitution. *v.4 p.442, v.6 p.389*

The Legend of John Brown. *v.3 p.430*

The Legend of Maya Deren: A Documented Biography and
   Collected Works, Vol. 1, Part II. *v.1 p.44*

The Legend of Maya Deren: A Documented Biography and
   Collected Works: Vol. 1, Signatures (1917-42). .*v.1 p.44, p.45*

The Legend of the Mutilated Victory: Italy, the Great War, and
   the Paris Peace Conference, 1915-1919, 38. .*v.3 p.78, p.202*

A Legend of the Wars of Montrose. *v.2 p.307*

Legende Vom Gluck Ohne Ende. *v.2 p.618*

Legends from Camp. *v.6 p.103, p.134*

The Legends of the Jews, Vol. 1. . . . .*v.1 p.550*

The Legends of the Saints. *v.1 p.579*

Legends of the Samurai. *v.6 p.225*

Legislating Revolution: The Contract with America in Its First
   100 Days. *v.4 p.530*

Legislating Together: The White House and Capitol Hill from
   Eisenhower to Reagan. *v.3 p.444, v.4 p.532*

☐ Legislation Into Law. *v.4 p.532*

Legislative Entrepreneurship in the U.S. House of
   Representatives. *v.4 p.533*

Legislative Labyrinth: Congress and Campaign Finance
   Reform. *v.4 p.548*

☐ Legislative Observatory. *v.4 p.474*

Legislative Strategy: Shaping Public Policy. *v.4 p.531*

Legislative Term Limits: Public Choice Perspectives. .*v.4 p.530*

Legislators, Leaders, and Lawmaking: The U. S. House of
   Representatives in the Postreform Era. *v.4 p.533*

Legislatures. *v.4 p.575, p.588*

Legitimacy and Power Politics: The American and French
   Revolutions in International Political
   Culture. *v.4 p.496, p.591, p.608*

Legitimate Histories: Scott, Gothic, and the Authorities of
   Fiction. *v.2 p.307*

Lehninger Principles of Biochemistry. *v.5 p.327*

Leibniz: An Introduction to His Philosophy. *v.1 p.460*

Leibniz and the Rational Order of Nature. *v.1 p.460*

Leibniz: New Essays on Human Understanding. . . .*v.1 p.459*

Leibniz's Philosophy of Logic and Language. *v.1 p.459*

Leigh Hunt: Selected Writings. *v.2 p.291*

Leisure and Class in Victorian England: Rational Recreation and
   the Contest for Control,
   1830-1885. . . . . . .*v.3 p.91, p.110, p.130,v.6 p.743*

Leisure and Ethics: Reflections on the Philosophy of Leisure,
   Vol. II. *v.4 p.783, p.802*

Leisure and Feminist Theory. *v.4 p.785, p.838*

Leisure and Society in Colonial Brazzaville. *v.6 p.62*

Leisure Education: Theory and Practice. *v.4 p.784*

Leisure in Your Life: An Exploration. *v.4 p.784*

Leisure Industries. *v.4 p.786*

Leisure: The Basis of Culture. *v.4 p.784, p.785*

Lelia. *v.2 p.500*

L'enchanteur réticent : essai sur Julien Gracq. *v.2 p.518*

Lend Me Your Ear: Rhetorical Constructions of
   Deafness. *v.4 p.708*

L'enfant de sable ; la nuit sacrée. *v.2 p.543, p.544*

L'enfant noir : roman. *v.2 p.542*

L'Enfant's Legacy: Public Open Spaces in Washington,
   D.C. *v.6 p.727*

Lenin: A Biography. *v.3 p.223*

Lenin: A New Biography. *v.3 p.224*

Lenin and Philosophy and Other Essays. *v.1 p.473*

The Lenin Anthology. *v.3 p.225*

Lenin: The Practice and Theory of Revolution. *v.3 p.224*

Lenin's Tomb: The Last Days of the Soviet Empire. *v.3 p.228, p.229*

Lenin. *v.3 p.223*

The Lennon Companion: Twenty-Five Years of Comment. *v.1 p.275, p.335*

La Lenta Emergencia de la Comida Mexicana, Ambigüedades Criollas 1750-1800. . . . . *v.3 p.271*

Leo Melamed: Escape to the Futures. *v.4 p.89, p.148*

Leo Tolstoy: an annotated bibliography of English language sources from 1978-2003. . . . . *v.2 p.803*

Leon Bakst: The Theater Art. *v.1 p.46*

Leon Trotsky and World War One: August 1914 - February 1917. . . . . *v.3 p.221*

Leonard and Virginia Woolf As Publishers, 1917-1941: The Hogarth Press. *v.2 p.393*

Leonard Bernstein: A Life. *v.1 p.223, p.311,v.6 p.410*

Leonard Bernstein. *v.1 p.210, p.219, p.311*

Leonard Bourdon: The Career of a Revolutionary, 1754-1807. . . . . *v.3 p.151*

Leonardo da Vinci: Artist - Scientist - Inventor. . . . *v.5 p.397*

Leonardo Da Vinci: Flights of the Mind. *v.1 p.698*

Leonardo da Vinci, Master Draftsman. *v.1 p.723*

Leonardo da Vinci: Origins of a Genius. *v.1 p.736*

Leonardo da Vinci: The Complete Paintings. *v.1 p.742*

Leonardo da Vinci. *v.1 p.749*

Leonardo: The First Scientist. *v.5 p.397*

Leonardo, the Last Supper. *v.1 p.736*

Leonardo the Scientist. *v.5 p.397*

Leonardo's Incessant Last Supper. *v.1 p.747*

Leonardo's Laptop: Human Needs and the New Computing Technologies. *v.5 p.343, p.344*

Leonardo's Mountain of Clams and the Diet of Worms: Essays on Natural History. *v.5 p.226*

Leonardo. *v.1 p.742*

A Leopardi Reader. *v.2 p.711*

Leopardi: Selected Poems. *v.2 p.711*

The Leopard. *v.2 p.723*

Leopold Sedar Senghor: The Collected Poetry. . . . *v.2 p.543*

Leopold Sedar Senghor. *v.2 p.543*

Leopold the First of Austria. *v.3 p.183*

🄴 Leopoldo Alas (Clarin). *v.2 p.655*

Leopoldo Lugones, Cuento, Poesia y Ensayo. *v.2 p.678*

Leos Janacek: Kat'a Kabanova. *v.1 p.226, p.233, p.333*

The Leper King and his Heirs: Baldwin IV and the Crusader Kingdom of Jerusalem. *v.3 p.64*

Lermontov's A Hero of Our Time: A Critical Companion. *v.2 p.801*

The LeRoi Jones - Amiri Baraka Reader. *v.2 p.140*

Lesbian and Bisexual Identities: Constructing Communities, Constructing Selves. *v.6 p.366, p.374, p.375*

Lesbian and Gay Families: Redefining Parenting in America. *v.6 p.377*

Lesbian and Gay Families Speak Out: Understanding the Joys and Challenges of Diverse Family Life. *v.6 p.376*

Lesbian and Gay Psychology: New Perspectives. . . *v.6 p.381*

Lesbian and Gay Studies: An Introductory, Interdisciplinary Approach. *v.6 p.357*

Lesbian and Gay Studies Reader. *v.6 p.357*

Lesbian and Gay Voices: An Annotated Bibliography and Guide to Literature for Children and Young Adults. *v.6 p.359, p.391*

The Lesbian Body. *v.2 p.534, p.535*

Lesbian Desire in the Lyrics of Sappho. . *v.2 p.419, v.6 p.393*

Lesbian Empire: Radical Crosswriting in the Twenties. *v.2 p.179, p.192*

Lesbian Epiphanies: Women Coming Out in Later Life. *v.6 p.368*

Lesbian, Gay, and Bisexual Identities over the Lifespan: Psychological Perspectives. *v.6 p.366, p.381*

Lesbian Gothic: Transgressive Fictions. *v.6 p.393*

Lesbian Health. *v.6 p.377, p.378*

🖵 Lesbian Herstory Archives. *v.6 p.357*

Lesbian Histories and Cultures. . . . *v.4 p.749, v.6 p.358, p.363*

Lesbian Images. *v.6 p.393*

The Lesbian in Literature: A Bibliography. . . . *v.6 p.359, p.391*

Lesbian Lifestyles: Women's Work and the Politics of Sexuality. *v.6 p.382*

Lesbian Mothers: Accounts of Gender in American Culture. *v.6 p.375*

Lesbian Nuns: Breaking Silence. *v.6 p.373*

The Lesbian Periodicals Index. *v.6 p.361*

The Lesbian Postmodern. *v.6 p.368*

Lesbian Psychologies: Explorations and Challenges. *v.4 p.750, v.6 p.380, p.381*

Lesbian Rabbis: The First Generation. *v.6 p.374*

Lesbian Sources: A Bibliography of Periodical Articles, 1970-1990. . . . . *v.6 p.359*

Lesbian Women and Sexual Health: The Social Construction of Risk and Susceptibility. *v.6 p.377*

Lesbianism: An Annotated Bibliography and Guide to the Literature, 1976-1986. . . . . *v.6 p.359*

🖵 Lesbians and Gays in the Newsroom: 10 Years Later. *v.6 p.383*

Lesbians in Germany, 1890's-1920's. *v.6 p.362, p.421*

Lesbian/Woman. *v.6 p.367*

Leslie Stephen: The Godless Victorian. *v.6 p.739, p.749, p.758*

L'espace de Vivre: Poemes 1968-2002. . . . . *v.2 p.541*

Less Is Better: Laboratory Chemical Management for Waste Reduction. *v.5 p.265*

Less Than Angels. *v.2 p.379*

The Lesser Evil?: Debates on the Democratic Party and Independent Working-Class Politics. *v.4 p.553*

The Lesser Evil: Political Ethics in an Age of Terror. *v.4 p.659*

The Lesser of Two Evils: Eastern European Jewry under Soviet Rule 1939-1941. . . . . *v.3 p.85, p.226*

Lessing: His Life and Achievements. *v.2 p.601*

Lessing, the Founder of Modern German literature. . *v.2 p.599*

A Lesson Before Dying. *v.6 p.25*

The Lesson of the Master: On Borges and His Work. *v.2 p.678*

Lessons from Amazonia: The Ecology and Conservation of a Fragmented Forest. *v.5 p.175, p.235, p.239*

Lessons from Mount Kilimanjaro: Schooling, Community and Gender in East Africa. *v.4 p.29*

Lessons from the Edge: Survival Skills for Starting and
    Growing a Company. *v.4 p.68*

Lessons from the Great Depression. *v.4 p.214*

Lessons from the Living Cell: The Culture of Science and the
    Limits of Reductionism. *v.5 p.159, p.163*

Lessons from the Past. *v.4 p.404*

Lessons of the Locker Room: The Myth of School
    Sports. *v.4 p.822, p.840, p.885*

The Lessons of the Past: The Use and Misuse of History in
    American Foreign Policy. *v.3 p.453*

Lester Frank Ward: Selections from His Work. *v.4 p.686*

Lester Horton: Modern Dance Pioneer. *v.1 p.13*

A Lester Young Reader. *v.1 p.263, p.369*

Lester Young. *v.1 p.262, p.263, p.369*

Let It Rain Coffee. *v.6 p.505*

Let Jasmine Rain Down: Song and Remembrance among Syrian
    Jews. *v.1 p.300*

Let Me Tell You a Story: A Lifetime in the Game. .*v.4 p.823, p.853*

Let My People Go. *v.6 p.79*

Let Newton Be!. *v.3 p.46, p.47*

Let Shepherding Endure: Applied Anthropology and the
    Preservation of a Cultural Tradition in Israel and the Middle
    East. *v.6 p.596*

Let the River Stand. *v.2 p.747, p.748*

Let the Words: Selected Poems. *v.6 p.652*

Let Them Eat Prozac: The Unhealthy Relationship Between the
    Pharmaceutical Industry and Depression. *v.5 p.659*

Lethal Judgments: Assisted Suicide and American Law. .*v.4 p.448*

Let's Dance: Social, Ballroom and Folk Dancing. . . .*v.1 p.33*

Let's Fix It!: Overcoming the Crisis in Manufacturing. .*v.4 p.119*

Let's Go!. *v.2 p.675*

Let's Murder the Moonshine: Selected Writings. . . .*v.2 p.718*

Let's Talk about the Weather. *v.2 p.817*

A Letter from India: Contemporary Short Stories from
    Pakistan. *v.6 p.152, p.153*

Letter from India: Contemporary Short Stories from
    Pakistan. *v.6 p.162*

The Letter of James: A New Translation with Introduction and
    Commentary. *v.1 p.631*

Letter to Beaumont, Letters Written from the Mountain, and
    Related Writings. *v.2 p.482*

Letter to the Spanish Americans: A Facsimile of the Second
    English Edition. *v.3 p.288*

Letteratura dell'Italia unità : 1861-1968. . . . .*v.2 p.697, p.698*

Letteratura Italiana del Novecento Rizzoli Larousse, Vol. 1: La
    Nascita del Moderno, dalla Crisi del Naturalismo alle
    Avanguardie, 1900-1930. . . . .*v.2 p.697*

Letteratura Italiana del Novecento Rizzoli Larousse, Vol. 2: Le
    Forme del Realismo, dal Realismo Magico al Neorealismo,
    1930-1960. . . . .*v.2 p.697*

Letteratura Italiana del Novecento Rizzoli Larousse, Vol. 3:
    Sperimentalismo e Tradizione del Nuovo dalla
    Contestazione al Postmoderno, 1960-2000. . . . .*v.2 p.697*

The Letter-bag of the Great Western. *v.2 p.732*

Letters, 1831-1857, Vols. 1 & 2. . . . .*v.3 p.419*

Letters and Dispatches 1924-1944. . . . .*v.3 p.187*

Letters and Journals, Vols. 3 & 4. . . . .*v.2 p.35*

Letters and Panegyricus, Vol. 2, Bks. 8-10. . . . . .*v.2 p.441*

Letters and Papers of Alfred Thayer Mahan. *v.3 p.383*

Letters Between Katherine Mansfield and John Middleton
    Murry. *v.2 p.369*

Letters Concerning the English Nation. *v.2 p.484*

Letters Concerning the Love of God. *v.2 p.237*

Letters from Africa, 1914-1931. . . . .*v.2 p.626*

Letters from America, 1776-1779. . . . .*v.3 p.410*

Letters from America. *v.2 p.335*

Letters from an American Farmer. *v.2 p.30*

Letters from the Desert: The Correspondence of Flinders and
    Hilda Petrie. *v.3 p.11*

Letters in Gold: Ottoman Calligraphy from the Sakip Sabanci
    Collection, Istanbul. *v.1 p.673, p.719*

Letters of a Javanese Princess by Raden Adjeng Kartini. *v.6 p.177*

Letters of a Portuguese Nun: Uncovering the Mystery Behind a
    Seventeenth Century Forbidden Love. *v.2 p.458*

Letters of Abelard and Heloise. *v.2 p.448*

Letters of Aldous Huxley. *v.2 p.354*

The Letters of Alfred Lord Tennyson, 1821-1850. . . .*v.2 p.314*

The Letters of Alfred Lord Tennyson, 1851-1870, Vol.
    II. *v.2 p.314*

The Letters of Alfred Lord Tennyson: 1871-1892, Vol.
    3. . . . .*v.2 p.314*

The Letters of Anthony Trollope, Set. *v.2 p.317*

The Letters of Beethoven. *v.1 p.193, p.306*

The Letters of Brendan Behan. *v.2 p.333*

The Letters of Charles Dickens, Set. *v.2 p.284*

The Letters of Claudio Monteverdi. *v.1 p.187, p.342*

Letters of Composers Through Six Centuries. *v.1 p.175*

Letters of David Ricardo to Thomas Robert Malthus,
    1810-1823. . . . .*v.4 p.221*

Letters of Edgar Allan Poe, Set. *v.2 p.50*

Letters of Emily Dickinson. *v.2 p.37*

Letters of Emma and Florence Hardy. *v.2 p.291*

The Letters of George Gissing to Eduard Bertz,
    1887-1903. . . . .*v.2 p.289*

Letters of George Gissing to Members of His Family. *v.2 p.289*

Letters of George Meredith. *v.2 p.300*

The Letters of Gerard Manley Hopkins to Robert
    Bridges. *v.2 p.293*

Letters of Giacomo Puccini. *v.1 p.202, p.349*

Letters of Grover Cleveland, 1850-1908. . . . . . .*v.3 p.435*

The Letters of Gustave Flaubert, 1857-1880, Vol. II. .*v.2 p.491*

The Letters of Heloise and Abelard: A Translation of Their
    Complete Correspondence. *v.3 p.68*

The Letters of Henry James, 1843-1875, Vol. 1. . . .*v.2 p.44*

The Letters of Henry James, 1875-1883, Vol. 2. . . .*v.2 p.44*

The Letters of Henry James, 1883-1895, Vol. 3. . . .*v.2 p.44*

The Letters of Henry James, 1895-1916, Vol. 4. . . .*v.2 p.44*

Letters of James R. Lowell. *v.2 p.47*

The Letters of John Clare. *v.2 p.278*

The Letters of John Greenleaf Whittier, Set. *v.2 p.55*

The Letters of John Keats, 1814-1821. . . . .*v.2 p.295*

The Letters of John Keats. *v.2 p.295*

Letters of Joseph Addison. *v.2 p.236*

The Letters of Katherine Mansfield. *v.2 p.369*

Letters of Love and Duty: The Correspondence of Susanna and
John Moodie. *v.2 p.731*

Letters of Mary W. Shelley. *v.2 p.310*

The Letters of Matthew Arnold, 1848-1888, Set. . . .*v.2 p.265*

Letters of Mistress Henley Published by Her Friend. .*v.2 p.478*

The Letters of Philip Dormer Stanhope, 4th Earl of
Chesterfield. *v.3 p.106, p.127*

Letters of Ralph Waldo Emerson, Set. *v.2 p.38*

The Letters of Robert Browning and Elizabeth Barrett
Browning, 1845-1846, Vol. 2. . . . .*v.2 p.271*

The Letters of Robert Browning and Eliza. *v.2 p.271*

The Letters of Samuel Johnson: Volume I: 1731-1772, Volume
II: 1773-1776, Volume III: 1777-1781. . . . . .*v.2 p.251*

Letters of Sir Walter Scott. *v.2 p.307*

The Letters of St. Bernard of Clairvaux. *v.1 p.578*

The Letters of Stephen a Douglas. *v.3 p.422, p.423, p.428*

Letters of the Great Kings of the Ancient near East: The Royal
Correspondence of the Late Bronze Age. *v.3 p.4*

Letters of the Lewis and Clark Expedition, with Related
Documents, 1783-1854. . . . .*v.3 p.520*

The Letters of Thomas Mann, 1889-1955. . . . . .*v.2 p.613*

The Letters of Virginia Woolf, 1888-1912, Vol. I. . . .*v.2 p.395*

The Letters of Virginia Woolf, 1911-1922, Vol. II. . . .*v.2 p.395*

The Letters of Virginia Woolf, 1929-1931, Vol. IV. . .*v.2 p.395*

The Letters of Virginia Woolf, 1932-1935, Vol. V. . . .*v.2 p.395*

The Letters of Virginia Woolf, 1936-1941, Vol. VI. . .*v.2 p.395*

The Letters of Vita Sackville-West and Virginia Woolf.*v.2 p.392*

The Letters of William Wordsworth: A New Selection.*v.2 p.325*

The Letters of Wyndham Lewis. *v.2 p.367*

Letters on Demonology and Witchcraft. *v.2 p.308*

Letters on Literature and Politics, 1912-1972. . . . .*v.2 p.137*

Letters on Sweden, Norway and Denmark. *v.2 p.318*

Letters on the American Revolution, 1774-1776. . . .*v.3 p.410*

Letters on Turkey. *v.6 p.623*

Letters Papers from Prison. *v.1 p.580*

Letters to a Young Doubter. *v.1 p.650*

Letters to Alice: On First Reading Jane Austen. . . .*v.2 p.269*

Letters to Atticus: Indexes 1-6. . . . .*v.2 p.432, p.433*

Letters to Atticus. *v.2 p.432*

Letters to Friends, Family and Editors. *v.2 p.610*

Letters to Montgomery Clift. *v.6 p.394*

Letters to Olga: June 1979-September 1982. . . . .*v.2 p.782*

Letters to the Thessalonians. *v.1 p.631*

Letters, Vol. 3. . . . .*v.2 p.279*

The Letters. *v.1 p.477*

Letters. *v.2 p.246, p.358*

Letting the People Decide: The Dynamics of a Canadian
Election. *v.4 p.590*

Lettres : 1879-1922. . . . .*v.2 p.524*

Lettres a Sophie Volland. *v.2 p.479*

Lettres de Mistriss Henley Publiees par son Amie. . . .*v.2 p.478*

Lettres d'un voyageur. *v.2 p.499*

Lettres d'un Voyageur. *v.2 p.500*

Lettres d'une vie. *v.2 p.499*

Lettres à Sartre, vol. 1. . . . .*v.2 p.508*

Lettres à Sartre, vol. 2. . . . .*v.2 p.508*

Lettres portugaises. *v.2 p.473*

Leurres et lueurs : poèmes. *v.2 p.544*

The Levant: A Fractured Mosaic. *v.6 p.583*

Leveling Crowds: Ethno-Nationalist Conflicts and Collective
Violence in South Asia. *v.4 p.713, p.714*

The Leveller Tracts: 1647-1653. . . . .*v.3 p.103*

The Levellers and the English Revolution. . . .*v.3 p.102, p.103*

Levels of Selection in Evolution. *v.5 p.193*

The Lever of Riches: Technological Creativity and Economic
Progress. *v.3 p.41*

Leverage: How to Get It and How to Keep It in Any
Negotiation. *v.4 p.75*

The Leverage of Labor: Managing the Cortes Haciendas in
Tehuantepec, 1588-1688. . . . .*v.3 p.284*

Leviathan and the Air-Pump: Hobbes, Boyle, and the
Experimental Life. *v.3 p.48*

e The Leviathan. *v.1 p.448*

Leviathan's Choice: Capital Punishment in the Twenty-First
Century. *v.4 p.567, p.568*

The Leviathan. *v.4 p.491*

Leviticus 1-16, Vol. 3. . . . .*v.1 p.620*

Leviticus 17-22: A New Translation with Introduction and
Commentary. *v.1 p.620, p.621*

Leviticus 23-27: A New Translation with Introduction and
Commentary. *v.1 p.621*

The Levittowners: Ways of Life and Politics in a New Suburban
Community. *v.4 p.702, v.6 p.717*

Lewis Acids and Selectivity in Organic Synthesis. . . .*v.5 p.295*

Lewis and Clark among the Indians. *v.6 p.686*

The Lewis and Clark Companion: An Encyclopedic Guide to the
Voyage of Discovery. *v.3 p.520*

Lewis and Clark: Legacies, Memories, and New
Perspectives. *v.3 p.520*

Lewis: Arrowsmith, Elmer Gantry, Dodsworth. *v.2 p.95*

Lewis Carroll: A Biography. *v.2 p.277*

Lewis M. Terman: Pioneer in Educational Testing. . . .*v.5 p.597*

Lewis Morris, 1671-1746: A Study in Early American
Politics. *v.3 p.491*

Lewis Tappan and the Evangelical War Against Slavery. *v.3 p.422*

The Lexicon of Labor: More Than 500 Key Terms, Biographical
Sketches, and Historical Insights Concerning Labor in
America. *v.4 p.122, p.123*

Lexicon of Musical Invective: Critical Assaults on Composers
since Beethoven's Time. *v.1 p.248*

A Lexicon to Herodotus. *v.2 p.412*

LexisNexis Academic. *v.4 p.516*

LexisNexis Congressional. *v.4 p.529*

The Lexus and the Olive Tree: Understanding
Globalization. *v.4 p.55*

La Ley del Amor. *v.2 p.667*

Leyendas de Guatemala. *v.2 p.674*

Leyendas. *v.2 p.653, p.654*

La Lezarde: Roman. *v.2 p.537*

L'éclair au front : la vie de René Char. *v.2 p.513*

L'écriture du désastre. *v.2 p.510*

Léon Morin, prêtre. *v.2 p.508*

Léon-Gontran Damas : l'homme et l'oeuvre. *v.2 p.537*

Léonide Massine and the 20th Century Ballet. *v.1 p.24*

Léopold Sédar Senghor : genèse d'un imaginaire francophone ;
    suivi d'un entretien avec Aimé Césaire. *v.2 p.542*

Léopold Sédar Senghor and the Politics of Negritude. . .*v.6 p.72*

L'étoile des amants : roman. *v.2 p.534*

La Lézarde : roman. *v.2 p.537*

Li, Qi and Shu: An Introduction to Science and Civilization in
    China. *v.6 p.198*

Li Ta-Chao and the Origins of Chinese Marxism. .*v.6 p.192, p.200*

Les Liaisons Dangereuses, Laclos: Critical Monographs in
    English. *v.2 p.481*

Les Liaisons Dangereuses. *v.2 p.480*

Liang and Lin: Partners in Exploring China's Architectural
    Past. *v.6 p.199, p.200*

Liang Ch'i-Ch'ao and Intellectual Transition in China,
    1890-1907. . . . .*v.6 p.189, p.199*

Liar's Poker: Rising Through the Wreckage on Wall
    Street. *v.4 p.89, p.92, p.96, p.100, p.103*

The Liar. *v.2 p.626, p.627*

Liberace: An American Boy. *v.6 p.410*

Liberace. *v.6 p.409*

Liberal: Adolf A. Berle and the Vision of an American
    Era. *v.3 p.462*

Liberal and fascist Italy : 1900-1945. . . . .*v.3 p.202*

Liberal and Fascist Italy: 1900-1945. . . . .*v.3 p.202*

The Liberal and Technical in Teacher Education: A Historical
    Survey of American Thought. *v.4 p.277*

Liberal Arts Colleges: Thriving, Surviving, or
    Endangered? *v.4 p.291*

Liberal Democracy: A Critique of Its Theory. *v.4 p.504*

The Liberal Ideal and the Demons of Empire: Theories of
    Imperialism from Adam Smith to Lenin. *v.3 p.77*

The Liberal Imagination: Essays on Literature and Society. .*v.2 p.5*

Liberal Islam: A Sourcebook. *v.1 p.557*

The Liberal Mind in a Conservative Age: American Intellectuals
    in the 1940s and 1950s. *v.3 p.371*

The Liberal Party: Triumph and Disintegration,
    1886-1929. . . . .*v.4 p.604, p.605, p.607*

The Liberal Persuasion: Arthur Schlesinger, Jr., and the
    Challenge of the American Past. *v.3 p.374*

Liberal Purposes: Goods, Virtues, and Diversity in the Liberal
    State. *v.4 p.511*

The Liberal Self: John Stuart Mill's Moral and Political
    Philosophy. *v.1 p.445*

The Liberal Tradition in America: An Interpretation of American
    Political Thought Since the Revolution. *v.3 p.376*

Liberalism Against Populism: A Confrontation Between the
    Theory of Democracy and the Theory of Social
    Choice. *v.4 p.505*

Liberalism Ancient and Modern. *v.4 p.511*

Liberalism and Empire: A Study in Nineteenth-Century British
    Liberal Thought. *v.4 p.511, p.583*

Liberalism and Its Challengers: From F. D. R. to Bush. .*v.3 p.447*

Liberalism and Its Discontents. *v.3 p.446*

Liberalism and Liberal Politics in Edwardian England. .*v.3 p.117*

Liberalism and the Origins of European Social Theory. .*v.4 p.686*

Liberalism Divided: Freedom of Speech and the Many Uses of
    State Power. *v.4 p.515*

Liberalism in the Bedroom: Quarreling Spouses in
    Nineteenth-Century Lima. *v.3 p.327*

Liberalism in the South. *v.3 p.494*

Liberalism's Crooked Circle: Letters to Adam Michnik. .*v.4 p.511*

Liberalization Against Democracy: The Local Politics of
    Economic Reform in Tunisia. .*v.4 p.585, p.611, p.612, v.6 p.641*

Liberals, Politics, and Power: State Formation in
    Nineteenth-Century Latin America. *v.3 p.345*

The Liberated Bride. *v.6 p.652*

Liberating Culture: Cross-Cultural Perspectives on Museums,
    Curation, and Heritage Preservation. *v.4 p.47, p.48*

Liberating Cyberspace: Civil Liberties, Human Rights and the
    Internet. *v.5 p.342, p.343*

Liberating Economics: Feminist Perspectives on Families, Work,
    and Globalization. *v.4 p.273, v.6 p.455*

Liberating Minds: The Stories and Professional Lives of Gay,
    Lesbian and Bisexual Librarians and Their
    Advocates. *v.6 p.383*

Liberation Biology: The Scientific and Moral Case for the
    Biotech Revolution. *v.5 p.77*

Liberation Management: Necessary Disorganization for the
    Nanosecond Nineties. *v.4 p.73*

The Liberation of Theology. *v.1 p.638*

The Liberation of Tolstoy: A Tale of Two Writers. .*v.2 p.797, p.802*

The Liberation of Women: A Document in the History of
    Egyptian Feminism. *v.6 p.636*

Liberation Sociology. *v.4 p.680*

Liberation Theology and Class Struggle in Latin
    America. *v.3 p.301*

Liberation Theology. *v.1 p.644*

Liberia and Sierra Leone: Anarchy or Peace in West
    Africa? *v.6 p.70*

Liberia: The Quest for Democracy. *v.6 p.70*

Libertad Bajo Palabra: Obras Poetica, 1935-1957. . .*v.2 p.668*

Libertarianism: For and Against. *v.4 p.510*

Libertas: The Life of Leigh Hunt. *v.2 p.291*

Liberté, Égalité and Fraternité at Work: Changing French
    Employment Relations and Management. *v.4 p.122*

Liberté. *v.2 p.543*

The Libertine Reader: Eroticism and Enlightenment in
    Eighteenth-Century France. *v.2 p.465*

Liberty, a Better Husband: Single Women in America: The
    Generations of 1780-1840. . . . .*v.4 p.735, p.736*

Liberty and Equality in Caribbean Colombia,
    1770-1835. . . . .*v.3 p.279, p.356, p.357*

Liberty and Power: A Dialogue on Religion and U. S. Foreign
    Policy in an Unjust World. *v.4 p.515, p.641, p.642*

Liberty and Sexuality: The Right to Privacy and the Making of
    Roe vs. Wade. *v.4 p.447*

Liberty and Slavery: Southern Politics to 1860. .*v.3 p.494, p.495*

Liberty and Union. *v.3 p.414*

Liberty, Charity, Fraternity: Lay Religious Confraternities at Bergamo in the Age of the Commune. *v.6 p.572*

Liberty in Absolutist Spain: The Hapsburg Sale of Towns, 1516-1700. . . . .*v.3 p.240*

Liberty: Incorporating Four Essays on Liberty. *v.4 p.515*

Liberty, Justice and Equality: How These Constitutional Guarantees Have Been Shaped by United States Supreme Court Decisions since 1789. . . . .*v.4 p.537*

Liberty Lane: A Ballad Play of Dublin in Two Acts with a Prologue. *v.2 p.337*

The Liberty Line: The Legend of the Underground Railroad. *v.3 p.397, p.430, p.431*

Liberty, Retrenchment and Reform: Popular Liberalism in the Age of Gladstone, 1860-1880. . . . .*v.3 p.74*

The Libidinal Economy. *v.1 p.457*

Le Libraire. *v.2 p.540*

▢ Librarians' Internet Index : Astronomy. *v.5 p.61*

Libraries in the Ancient World. *v.3 p.3*

Libraries, the First Amendment and Cyberspace: What You Need to Know. *v.4 p.451*

The Library of Alexandria: Centre of Learning in the Ancient World. *v.3 p.21*

The Library of Babel. *v.2 p.677*

▢ Library of Congress Country Studies: Africa. . . .*v.4 p.612*

▢ Library of Congress Country Studies. *v.4 p.574*

▢ Library of Congress Poetry Center. *v.2 p.577, p.582*

The Library of Leonard and Virginia Woolf: A Short-Title Catalog. *v.2 p.392*

▢ Library of Southern Literature. *v.2 p.21*

▢ Library Resources for Communication Studies. . . .*v.4 p.415*

▢ Library Resources for Identifying Unknowns (Stanford University). *v.5 p.300*

Library Resources for Singers, Coaches and Accompanists: An Annotated Bibliography, 1970-1997. . . . .*v.1 p.168, p.395*

The Library's Legal Answer Book. *v.4 p.451*

El Libro de Buen Amor. *v.2 p.652*

El Libro de las Emociones: Son de la Razon Sin Corazon. *v.2 p.667*

Libro de Poemas. *v.2 p.659*

El Libro del Arcipreste, Tambien Llamado Libro de Buen Amor: Edicion Sinoptica. *v.2 p.652*

Libya: A Modern History. *v.6 p.60, p.641*

Libya since Independence: Oil and State-Building. . .*v.6 p.641*

Libya's Qaddafi: The Politics of Contradiction. *v.6 p.640, p.641*

A License to Steal: The Forfeiture of Property. *v.4 p.473*

The Lichen Symbiosis. *v.5 p.210*

Lichens of North America. *v.5 p.210*

A Lie and a Libel: The History of the Protocols of the Elders of Zion. *v.3 p.60, p.61*

Lie Down in Darkness. *v.2 p.156*

Lie Groups: An Introduction Through Linear Groups. *v.5 p.475*

The Lie That Tells a Truth: A Guide to Writing Fiction. *v.2 p.574*

Liebe Hanya: Mary Wigman's Letters to Hanya Holm. *v.1 p.16, p.28, p.30*

Lies: A Diary 1986-1999. . . . .*v.6 p.410*

Life: A Natural History of the First Four Billion Years of Life on Earth. *v.5 p.192*

Life: A User's Manual. *v.2 p.533*

The Life, Adventures, and Piracies of the Famous Captain Singleton. *v.2 p.245*

Life after Death in the World Religions. *v.1 p.529*

Life among Indian Tribes: The Autobiography of an Anthropologist. *v.6 p.155*

The Life and Adventures of Lyle Clemens. *v.2 p.154*

The Life and Adventures of Martin Chuzzlewit. by Chas. Dickens. *v.2 p.283*

The Life and Adventures of Nicholas Nickleby. by Charles Dickens ... with Illustrations. *v.2 p.283*

The Life and Adventures of Sir Launcelot Greaves. . .*v.2 p.261*

Life and Art of Edwin Booth. *v.1 p.119, p.146*

The Life and Ballets of Lev Ivanov: Choreographer of the Nutcracker and Swan Lake. *v.1 p.14, p.25*

Life and Death in Early Colonial Equador. *v.3 p.332*

Life and Death in Shanghai. *v.6 p.195, p.199*

Life and Death in the Templo Mayor. *v.3 p.261*

Life and Death: Moral Implications of Biotechnology. *v.5 p.218, 248*

The Life and Death of Anna Mae Aquash. . . .*v.6 p.688, p.693*

The Life and Death of Carolina Maria de Jesus. *v.3 p.279*

Life and Death of Carthage: A Survey of Punic History and Culture from Its Birth to the Final Tragedy. *v.6 p.60*

The Life and Death of Industrial Languedoc, 1700-1920. . . . .*v.3 p.158*

The Life and Death of Jason. A poem by William Morris. *v.2 p.301*

The Life and Death of Mr. Badman: Presented to the World in a Familiar Dialogue Between Mr. Wiseman and Mr. Attentive. *v.2 p.241*

Life and Death of St Thomas More. *v.2 p.214*

Life and Environment in the Mediterranean. *v.5 p.237*

Life and Fate. *v.2 p.804, v.3 p.227*

Life and Health Insurance. *v.4 p.163*

Life and Labor in the Old South. *v.3 p.494*

The Life and Legacy of Annie Oakley. *v.4 p.838, p.866*

The Life and Legacy of G. I. Taylor. *v.5 p.396*

Life and Legend of Leadbelly. *v.1 p.297, p.335*

Life and Leisure in Ancient Rome. *v.3 p.22*

Life and Letters of Charles Russell Lowell. *v.2 p.37*

Life and Letters of James Abram Garfield. *v.3 p.438*

The Life and Letters of James MacPherson. *v.2 p.252*

The Life and Letters of Joel Chandler Harris. *v.2 p.40*

The Life and Letters of John Donne. *v.2 p.214*

The Life and Letters of Maria Edgeworth, Vol. 1. . . .*v.2 p.286*

The Life and Letters of Maria Edgeworth, Vol. 2. . . .*v.2 p.286*

Life and Letters of Sir Wilfrid Laurier. *v.3 p.540*

Life and Letters of Vasco Nunez De Balboa. *v.3 p.304*

Life and Letters of Washington Irving, Set. *v.2 p.42*

Life and Miracles of St. Benedict. *v.1 p.579*

The Life and Music of Bela Bartok. *v.1 p.224, p.305*

The Life and Opinions of Tristram Shandy, Gentleman. *v.2 p.262*

The Life and Photography of Doris Ulmann. . . . . *.v.1 p.767*

The Life and Poetical Works of the Reverend George
Crabbe. *.v.2 p.281*

Life and Practice in the Early Church: A Documentary
Reader. . . . . *.v.1 p.655, p.656*

Life and Society in the Hittite World. . . . . *.v.3 p.6*

The Life and Thought of Michael Sattler. . . . . . *.v.1 p.603*

The Life and Times of Alexander Humboldt. . . . *.v.5 p.396*

The Life and Times of Confederation, 1864-1867: Politics,
Newsapers and the Union of British North America. *.v.3 p.540*

The Life and Times of Constantine the Great: The First
Christian Emperor. . . . . *.v.3 p.192*

The Life and Times of Cotton Mather. . . *.v.1 p.581, v.3 p.488*

The Life and Times of Emile Zola. . . . . *.v.2 p.504*

The Life and Times of Joe McCarthy: A Biography. . *.v.3 p.462*

The Life and Times of Menelik II: Ethiopia 1844-1913. *.v.6 p.64*

The Life and Times of Pancho Villa. . . . . *.v.3 p.293*

The Life and Times of Porgy and Bess: The Story of an
American Classic. . . . . *.v.1 p.228, p.248, p.325*

The Life and Times of William Lyon MacKenzie: With an
Account of the Canadian Rebellion of 1837, Vol.
2. . . . . *.v.3 p.539, p.540*

The Life and Times of Willie Velasquez: Su Voto Es Su
Voz. . . . . *.v.6 p.490, p.541*

Life and Work in Medieval Europe. . . . . *.v.3 p.67*

The Life and Work of Harold Pinter. . . . . *.v.2 p.376*

The Life and Work of Martin Johnson Heade: A Critical
Analysis and Catalogue Raisonné. . . . . *.v.1 p.700, p.747*

The Life and Works of George Peele. . . . . *.v.2 p.222*

The Life and Works of John Weaver: An Account of His Life,
Writings and Theatrical Productions, with an
Annotated Reprint of His Complete
Publications. . . . . *.v.1 p.14, p.22*

Life and Works of Phillis Wheatley. . . . . *.v.2 p.30*

The Life and Writings of Frederick Douglass, Vol. 1. *.v.3 p.419*

The Life and Writings of Frederick Douglass, Vol. 2. *.v.3 p.419*

The Life and Writings of Frederick Douglass, Vol. 3. *.v.3 p.419*

The Life and Writings of Frederick Douglass, Vol. 4. *.v.3 p.419*

A Life Apart: The English Working Class,
1890-1914. . . . . *.v.3 p.113, p.114, p.131*

Life As We Have Known It. . . . . *.v.3 p.53*

Life at the Zoo: Behind the Scenes with the Animal
Doctors. . . . . *.v.5 p.85, p.251*

Life Chemistry and Molecular Biology: An Introduction
Text. *.v.5 p.129*

Life Chemistry and Molecular Biology. . . . . . . *.v.5 p.129*

The Life Cycle of Copper, Its Co-Products and
Byproducts. . . . . *.v.5 p.736*

Life, Death and Bialys: A Father/Son Baking Story. . *.v.2 p.734*

Life, Death, and Entertainment in the Roman
Empire. . . . . *.v.3 p.23, p.24*

Life, Death, and Subjectivity: Moral Sources in
Bioethics. . . . . *.v.5 p.248*

The Life Divine. . . . . *.v.1 p.534*

Life Everywhere: The New Science of
Astrobiology. . . . . *.v.5 p.183, p.242*

Life Evolving: Molecules, Mind, and Meaning. . . . *.v.5 p.200*

A Life for Dance: The Autobiography of Rudolf
Laban. . . . . *.v.1 p.10, p.47*

Life History Evolution. . . . . *.v.5 p.195, p.196*

Life in a Cold Climate: A Portrait of a Contradictory
Woman. . . . . *.v.2 p.371*

Life in a Coral Reef. . . . . *.v.4 p.391*

Life in a Medieval City. . . . . *.v.4 p.703*

Life in Ancient Egypt. . . . . *.v.6 p.57*

Life in Egypt under Roman Rule. . . . *.v.3 p.10, p.11, v.6 p.58*

Life in Lesu: The Study of a Melanesian Society in New
Ireland. . . . . *.v.4 p.43*

Life in Mexico. . . . . *.v.3 p.289*

A Life in Our Times: Memoirs. . . . . *.v.4 p.209, p.211*

A Life in Ragtime: A Biography of James Reese
Europe. . . . . *.v.1 p.280, p.323*

Life in Schools: An Introduction to Critical Pedagogy in the
Foundations of Education. . . . . *.v.4 p.297*

Life in Search of Readers: Reading in Chicano: A
Literature. . . . . *.v.6 p.501, p.514*

Life in Shakespeare's England: A Book of Elizabethan
Prose. *.v.2 p.203*

Life in the Ancient near East, 3100-332 B. C. E. . . *.v.3 p.4, p.5*

Life in the Country. . . . . *.v.2 p.713*

Life in the English Country House: A Social and Architectural
History. . . . . *.v.4 p.726*

Life in the Gang: Family, Friends, and Violence. . . *.v.6 p.256*

Life in the Iron Mills. . . . . *.v.2 p.36*

Life in the Middle: Psychological and Social Development in
Middle Age. . . . . *.v.4 p.741*

Life in the Pueblos. . . . . *.v.6 p.704*

A Life in the Theatre. . . . . *.v.1 p.140, p.152*

A Life in the Twentieth Century: Innocent Beginnings,
1917-1950. . . . . *.v.3 p.375*

Life in the Universe: Expectations and Constraints. . *.v.5 p.243*

Life in the Universe: From the Miller Experiment to the Search
for Life on Other Worlds. . . . . *.v.5 p.243*

Life in the Universe. . . . . *.v.5 p.73, p.74, p.190, p.242*

Life into Art: Isadora Duncan and Her World. . . . . *.v.1 p.26*

Life Isn't All Ha Ha Hee Hee. . . . . *.v.2 p.766*

Life Itself. *.v.2 p.669*

Life, Learning, and Community: Concepts and Models for
Service-Learning in Biology. . . . . *.v.5 p.78, p.82*

The Life, Letters and Journals of Lord Byron. . . . *.v.2 p.274*

Life, Liberty, and Defense of Dignity: The Challenge for
Bioethics. . . . . *.v.5 p.248*

Life Lines: Community, Family, and Assimilation among Asian
Indian Immigrants. . . . . *.v.6 p.110, p.138*

ℯ The Life of a Russian Woman Doctor: A Siberian Memoir,
1869-1954. . . . . *.v.3 p.224*

The Life of a Simple Man. . . . . *.v.3 p.155*

Life of Adam Smith. . . . . *.v.4 p.219*

The Life of Adam Smith. . . . . *.v.4 p.219*

The Life of Bellini. . . . . *.v.1 p.203, p.309*

The Life of Billy Yank: The Common Soldier of the
Union. . . . . *.v.3 p.402, p.432*

The Life of Buddha: According to Pali Canon. . . . *.v.1 p.562*

The Life of Buddha As Legend and History. *v.1 p.562*

The Life of Celine: A Critical Biography. *v.2 p.515*

Life of Charlemagne. *v.6 p.562*

The Life of Charles Ives. *v.1 p.213, p.333*

The Life of Charlotte Bronte. *v.2 p.270, p.288*

Life of Constantine. *v.3 p.30, p.31*

The Life of D. H. Lawrence: An Illustrated Biography. .*v.2 p.364*

Life of David Belasco, Set. .*v.1 p.81, p.119, p.142, p.153, p.154*

The Life of David Hume. *v.1 p.451*

The Life of Debussy. *v.1 p.220, p.320*

Life of Edwin Forrest with Reminiscences and Personal
Recollections. *v.1 p.141, p.145*

The Life of Elgar. *v.1 p.199, p.323*

The Life of Emily Dickinson. *v.2 p.37*

The Life of Emma Willard. *v.4 p.338*

The Life of Evelyn Waugh: A Critical Biography. *v.2 p.387, p.388*

The Life of Geoffrey Chaucer: A Critical Biography. .*v.2 p.210*

The Life of Goethe: A Critical Biography. *v.2 p.598*

Life of Gotthold Ephraim Lessing. *v.2 p.601*

The Life of Graham Greene, 1904-1939, Vol. I. . . .*v.2 p.351*

The Life of Graham Greene, 1939-1955, Vol. II. . . .*v.2 p.351*

The Life of Graham Greene: 1955-1991. . . . . . .*v.2 p.351*

A Life of Gwendolyn Brooks. *v.2 p.64*

The Life of Harriot Stuart, Written by Herself. . . .*v.2 p.251*

The Life of Henry Brulard. *v.2 p.502*

A Life of Her Own: The Transformation of a Countrywoman in
20th-Century France. *v.3 p.154*

The Life of Herbert Hoover: Master of Emergencies,
1917-1918. . . . .*v.3 p.477*

The Life of Herbert Hoover: The Engineer, 1874-1914. .*v.3 p.477*

The Life of Herbert Hoover: The Humanitarian, 1914-1917, Vol.
2. . . . .*v.3 p.476, p.477*

Life of Ibsen. *v.2 p.628*

The Life of Insects: A Novel. *v.2 p.807*

The Life of Isaac Newton. *v.3 p.48, v.5 p.468*

The Life of Isamu Noguchi: Journey Without
Borders. *v.1 p.779, v.6 p.87, p.88, p.93*

The Life of Jane Austen. *v.2 p.267*

The Life of Jesus. *v.1 p.642*

The Life of J-K Huysmans. *v.2 p.494*

The Life of John Dryden. *v.2 p.247*

The Life of John Maynard Keynes. *v.4 p.211, p.227*

The Life of John Milton: A Critical Biography. . . .*v.2 p.254*

The Life of John Ruskin, 1819-1860: Volume I, Vol. 1. .*v.2 p.305*

The Life of John Ruskin, 1860-1900: Volume II, Vol. 2. .*v.2 p.305*

The Life of John Sterling; Latter Day Pamphlets: The Works of
Thomas Carlyle. *v.2 p.276*

The Life of Johnny Reb: The Common Soldier of the
Confederacy. *v.3 p.402, p.427*

Life of Johnson. *v.2 p.240*

The Life of Joseph Addison. *v.2 p.237*

The Life of Joseph Conrad: A Critical Biography. . . .*v.2 p.339*

A Life of Kenneth Rexroth. *v.2 p.114*

The Life of Langston Hughes, Set. . .*v.2 p.88, v.6 p.19, p.27*

The Life of Lazarillo de Tormes: A Critical Edition Including
the Original Spanish Text. *v.2 p.651*

Life of Lord Byron. *v.2 p.274*

A Life of Magic Chemistry: Autobiographical Reflections of a
Nobel Prize Winner. *v.5 p.261*

The Life of Mahatma Gandhi. *v.1 p.540*

The Life of Mahler. *v.1 p.213, p.339*

The Life of Miguel de Cervantes Saavedra: A Biographical,
Literary and Historical Study. *v.2 p.649*

The Life of Mozart. *v.1 p.191, p.192, p.344*

The Life of Muhammad. *v.1 p.555*

The Life of Musorgsky. *v.1 p.197, p.345*

The Life of Niccolo Machiavelli. *v.2 p.709*

The Life of Oscar Wilde. *v.2 p.321*

The Life of Percy Bysshe Shelley. *v.2 p.311*

Life of Petrarch. *v.2 p.706*

The Life of Reason. *v.1 p.440*

The Life of Richard Steele. *v.2 p.261*

The Life of Richard Strauss. *v.1 p.214, p.359*

The Life of Richard Wagner. *v.1 p.201, p.366*

The Life of Robert Baldwin, a Study in the Struggle for
Responsible Government. *v.3 p.540*

The Life of Robert Browning: A Critical Biography. . .*v.2 p.272*

Life of Ruskin. *v.2 p.305*

The Life of Schubert. *v.1 p.197, p.354*

Life of Science: Essays in the History of
Civilization. *v.5 p.400, p.410, p.411*

The Life of St Anselm, Archbishop of Canterbury. . .*v.1 p.579*

The Life of the Buddha. *v.1 p.562*

The Life of the Law: Anthropological Projects. *v.4 p.33*

Life of the Mind in America: From the Revolution to the Civil
War. *v.3 p.369*

The Life of Titian. *v.1 p.745*

The Life of Walter Scott: A Critical Biography. . . .*v.2 p.308*

The Life of Webern. *v.1 p.209, p.367*

The Life of William Ewart Gladstone, Set. *v.3 p.95, p.114*

Life of William Pitt. by Lord Macaulay. Preceded by the life of
the Earl of Chatham. *v.2 p.299*

Life on a Mediaeval Barony: A Picture of a Typical Feudal
Community in the Thirteenth Century. *v.3 p.67*

Life on a Young Planet: The First Three Billion Years of
Evolution on Earth. *v.5 p.193, p.445, p.447*

Life on the Hyphen: The Cuban-American Way. *v.6 p.493*

Life on the Mississippi (1883). *v.3 p.506*

Life on the Run. *v.4 p.853*

Life on the Russian Country Estate: A Social and Cultural
History. *v.3 p.211*

Life Out of Bounds: Bioinvasion in a Borderless World. .*v.5 p.178*

Life Outside: The Signorile Report on Gay Men: Sex, Drugs,
Muscles, and the Passages of Life. *v.6 p.372, p.382*

Life Records of John Milton, 1608-1674, Set. .*v.2 p.253, p.254*

Life Roles, Values, and Careers: International Findings of the
Work Importance Study. *v.5 p.578*

Life Science Ethics. *v.5 p.78, p.247*

Life Script: How the Human Genome Discoveries Will Transform Medicine and Enhance Your Health. *v.5 p.137, p.143, p.152*

Life Sentences: Writers, Artists, and AIDS. *v.1 p.707*

Life Situations: Essays Written and Spoken by Jean-Paul Sartre. *v.2 p.527*

Life Span Motor Development. *v.4 p.909*

Life Studies and for the Union Dead. *v.2 p.96*

A Life: The Humble Truth. *v.2 p.497*

Life Through Time: Evolutionary Activities for Grades 5-8. . . . .*v.5 p.190, p.244*

Life under a Cloud: American Anxiety about the Atom. .*v.5 p.740*

A Life under Russian Serfdom: The Memoirs of Savva Dmitrievich Purlevskii, 1800-1868. . . . .*v.3 p.211*

A Life Wild and Perilous: Mountain Men and the Path to the Pacific. *v.3 p.520, p.521*

Life with a Star. *v.2 p.784*

Life with an Idiot. *v.2 p.803*

Life with History. *v.3 p.373*

Life Without Genes. *v.5 p.138*

Life Without Parole: Living in Prison Today. *v.6 p.276*

Life Work. *v.2 p.82*

Lifeline of the Confederacy: Blockade Running During the Civil War. *v.4 p.522*

Lifelines: The Case for River Conservation. *v.5 p.180*

Lifelong Learning: Concepts and Contexts. *v.4 p.319*

Lifelong Leisure Skills and Lifestyles for Persons with Developmental Disabilities. *v.4 p.785, p.801*

Life's a Dream. *v.2 p.647*

Life's Dominion: An Argument about Abortion, Euthanasia, and Individual Freedom. *v.4 p.472*

Life's Handicap. *v.2 p.297*

Life's Matrix: A Biography of Water. *v.5 p.313*

Life's Origin: The Beginnings of Biological Evolution. *v.5 p.81, p.196*

Life's Solution: Inevitable Humans in a Lonely Universe. *v.5 p.183, p.242*

Life's Splendid Drama: Evolutionary Biology and the Reconstruction of Life's Ancestry, 1860-1940. . . . .*v.5 p.77, p.190, p.191*

Lifestyle Market Analyst. *v.4 p.138, p.139*

The Life-Threatened Elderly. *v.5 p.532*

Lifetime Allocation of Work and Income: Essays in the Economics of Aging. *v.4 p.265*

Lifetime of Color. *v.4 p.303, p.349*

The Lifted Veil and Brother Jacob. *v.2 p.287*

Lifting a Ton of Feathers: A Woman's Guide to Surviving in the Academic World. *v.4 p.292*

Ligand Field Theory and Its Applications. . . .*v.5 p.303, p.304*

Ligand Substitution Processes. *v.5 p.304*

Ligand-Receptor Energetics: A Guide for the Perplexed. .*v.5 p.327*

Light and Darkness. *v.6 p.232*

Light and Shadows: Selected Poems and Prose of Juan Ramon Jimenez. *v.2 p.660, p.661*

Light from Light: An Anthology of Christian Mysticism. *v.1 p.653*

The Light in the Forest. *v.2 p.113*

The Light in the Piazza and Other Italian Tales. .*v.2 p.116, p.117*

Light: Laser Light Dynamics. *v.5 p.561*

Light Rail Service: Pedestrian and Vehicular Safety. . .*v.5 p.700*

Light Such a Candle: Chapters in the History of Science and Technology. *v.5 p.391*

The Light that Failed. *v.2 p.297*

Light Through Darkness: The Orthodox Tradition. . . .*v.1 p.569*

The Lighter Side of Gravity. *v.5 p.556, p.557*

The Light-Green Society: Ecology and Technological Modernity in France, 1960-2000. . . . .*v.3 p.156*

Lighting and Sound. *v.1 p.148*

Lighting Design on Broadway: Designers and Their Credits, 1915-1990. . . . .*v.1 p.141, p.147, p.148*

Lighting for Energy Efficient Luminous Environments. *v.5 p.723, p.724*

Lightning Wires: The Telegraph and China's Technological Modernization, 1860-1890, 6. . . . .*v.4 p.421*

Lights On!: The Wild Century-Long Saga of Night Baseball. . . .*v.4 p.808, p.809, p.851, p.885, p.897, p.902*

Like a Hurricane: The Indian Movement from Alcatraz to Wounded Knee. *v.6 p.690, p.695*

Like Bread on the Seder Plate: Jewish Lesbians and the Transformation of Tradition. *v.6 p.373*

Like People in History: A Gay American Epic. .*v.6 p.379, p.398*

Like People You See in a Dream: First Contact in Six Papuan Societies. *v.4 p.43*

Like Sex with Gods: An Unorthodox History of Flying. .*v.5 p.718*

Lila: An Inquiry into Morals. *v.2 p.153*

Lilian's Story. *v.2 p.746*

Lillian Hellman: A Life with Foxes and Scoundrels. . .*v.2 p.83*

L'image. *v.2 p.509*

L'imaginaire métaphysique. *v.2 p.510*

Lime Creek Odyssey. *v.5 p.230*

The Lime Twig. *v.2 p.83*

Limited Government: A Comparison. *v.4 p.574*

Limits and Lies of Human Genetic Research: Dangers for Social Policy. *v.5 p.140*

Limits and Possibilities: The Crisis of Yugoslav Socialism and State Socialist Systems. *v.4 p.506, p.508*

The Limits of Agrarian Radicalism: Western Populism and American Politics. *v.3 p.519*

Limits of Anarchy: Intervention and State Formation in Chad. *v.6 p.62*

The Limits of Convergence: Globalization and Organizational Change in Argentina, South Korea, and Spain. . . .*v.3 p.348*

The Limits of Dissent: Clement L. Vallandigham and the Civil War. *v.3 p.398*

The Limits of Enlightenment: Joseph II and the Law. .*v.3 p.182*

The Limits of Family Influence: Genes, Experience, and Behavior. *v.5 p.656*

The Limits of Hegemony: United States Relations with Argentina and Chile During World War II. .*v.3 p.348, p.353*

The Limits of Illusion: A Critical Study of Calderon. .*v.2 p.647*

The Limits of Judicial Power: The Supreme Court in American Politics. *v.4 p.537*

The Limits of Participation: Women and the Civic Life in the Greek East in the Hellenistic and Roman Periods. *v.6 p.451*

The Limits of Power: The Nixon and Ford Administrations. *v.3 p.472*

The Limits of Power: The World and United States Foreign Policy, 1945-1954. *v.3 p.453*

The Limits of Privacy. *v.4 p.515*

The Limits of Racial Domination: Plebeian Society in Colonial Mexico City, 1660-1720. *v.3 p.285*

The Limits of Science. *v.5 p.400, p.403*

The Limits of Scientific Reasoning. *v.5 p.401*

The Limits of State Autonomy: Post-Revolutionary Mexico. *v.3 p.292*

ⓔ Limits: The Role of the Law in Bioethical Decision Making. *v.4 p.448*

The Limits to Growth; A Report for the Club of Rome's Project on the Predicament of Mankind. *v.4 p.763*

The Limits to Growth: The 30-Year Update. *v.4 p.763*

The Limits to Union: Same-Sex Marriage and the Politics of Civil Rights. *v.4 p.569*

Limnology: Lake and River Ecosystems. *v.5 p.172, p.427, p.428*

Limnology. *v.5 p.173, p.174, p.427*

Linajudos and Conversos in Seville: Greed and Prejudice in Sixteenth and Seventeenth Century Spain. *v.3 p.240*

Lincoln: A Novel. *v.2 p.127*

Lincoln, Abraham, Pres. U. S.: Collected Works Supplement, 1832-1865. *v.3 p.425, p.426*

Lincoln and Black Freedom: A Study in Presidential Leadership. *v.3 p.395, p.424*

Lincoln and His Generals. *v.3 p.403, p.432*

Lincoln and His Party in the Secession Crisis. *v.3 p.365, p.400, p.421*

Lincoln and the Civil War. *v.3 p.434*

Lincoln and the Negro. *v.3 p.426*

Lincoln and the Party Divided. *v.3 p.403, p.429*

Lincoln and the Radicals. *v.3 p.403*

Lincoln and the Tools of War. *v.3 p.430*

Lincoln As They Saw Him. *v.3 p.426*

The Lincoln Encyclopedia: The Spoken and Written Words of A. Lincoln Arranged for Ready Reference. *v.3 p.426*

The Lincoln Nobody Knows. *v.3 p.424*

The Lincoln Reader. *v.3 p.424*

Lincoln Reconsidered: Essays on the Civil War Era. *v.3 p.424*

Lincoln the President: Last full Measure. *v.3 p.400, p.426*

Lincoln's Generals. *v.3 p.396*

Lincoln's Quest for Union: Public and Private Meanings. *v.3 p.426*

Lincoln's War Cabinet. *v.3 p.425*

Lincoln. *v.3 p.395, v.4 p.517*

The Line of Beauty: A Novel. *v.2 p.352, v.6 p.397*

Linear Algebra and Its Applications. *v.5 p.472, p.473*

Linear Algebra and Matrix Theory. *v.5 p.472*

Linear Algebra Done Right. *v.5 p.472*

Linear Algebra. *v.5 p.472*

Linear Circuit Analysis, Set. *v.5 p.720*

Linear Integral Equations. *v.5 p.488*

Linear Programming and Economic Analysis. *v.4 p.199, p.243*

Linear Programming and Its Applications. *v.5 p.683*

Linear Programming: Introduction. *v.5 p.493*

Linear Programming: Theory and Extensions. *v.5 p.492, p.493*

Linear Programming. *v.5 p.492, p.683*

Linear Programs and Related Problems. *v.5 p.683*

Linguistic Anthropology: A Reader. *v.4 p.18*

Linguistic Archaeology of South Asia. *v.6 p.147, p.148*

Linguistic Change: An Introduction to the Historical Study of Language. *v.2 p.555, p.564*

Linguistic Diversity in the South: Changing Codes, Practices, and Ideology. *v.4 p.20*

Linguistic Fieldwork. *v.4 p.19*

A Linguistic History of Italian. *v.2 p.699*

Linguistic Theory in America. *v.2 p.563*

The Linguistic Turn: Essays in Philosophical Method. *v.1 p.490*

Linguistic Variation and Change: On the Historical Sociolinguistics of English. *v.2 p.555*

The Linguistics Encyclopedia. *v.2 p.562*

Linguistics in America, 1769-1924: A Critical History. *v.2 p.559*

Linguistics: Linguistic Theory: Extensions and Implications. *v.2 p.563*

Linguistics: Linguistic Theory: Foundations. *v.2 p.563*

The Linguistics of Punctuation. *v.2 p.558*

Linguistics: The Cambridge Survey: Language: Psychological and Biological Aspects. *v.2 p.563*

Linguistics: The Cambridge Survey: Language: the Socio-Cultural Context. *v.2 p.563*

The Linguistics Wars. *v.2 p.561, v.4 p.18, v.5 p.621, p.623*

Linkage of Effects to Tissue Residues: Development of a Comprehensive Database for Aquatic Organisms Exposed to Inorganic and Organic Chemicals. *v.5 p.366, p.368, p.380*

Linking Arms Together: American Indian Treaty Visions of Law and Peace, 1600-1800. *v.4 p.574, v.6 p.693*

Linking the Americas: Race, Hybrid Discourses, and the Reformulation of Feminine Identity. *v.6 p.476, p.478*

▯ Links for Chemists, the Chemistry Section of the WWW Virtual Library. *v.5 p.255*

Links. *v.2 p.754*

Linnaeus: Nature and Nation. *v.5 p.231*

Linnaeus' Philosophia Botanica. *v.5 p.207*

Linnaeus: The Compleat Naturalist. *v.5 p.231*

Linnaeus: The Man and His Work. *v.5 p.231*

L'innommable. *v.2 p.509*

Linocuts of the Machine Age: Claude Flight and His Followers. *v.1 p.755*

L'inquisitoire. *v.2 p.523*

Linus Pauling: A Life in Science and Politics. *v.5 p.260, p.261*

L'invitée. *v.2 p.508*

The Lion and the Honeycomb: Essays in Solicitude and Critique. *v.2 p.7*

The Lion and the Star: Gentile-Jewish Relations in Three Hessian Towns, 1919-1945. *v.3 p.84*

A Lion for Love: A Critical Biography of Stendhal. *v.2 p.501*

The Lioness and the Little One. *v.2 p.499*

Lions and Shadows: An Education in the Twenties. . . *.v.2 p.356*

Lions of the Punjab. . . . . *.v.6 p.160*

The Lion's Roar of Queen Srimala. . . . . *.v.1 p.564*

The Lion's Share: A Short History of British Imperialism, 1850-1995. . . . . *.v.6 p.746*

The Lion's Share: A Short History of British Imperialism, 1850-2004. . . . . . *.v.3 p.89, p.90, p.125, p.126,v.6 p.746*

Le lion. . . . . *.v.2 p.521*

The Lipid Handbook. . . . . *.v.5 p.329*

Lippincott Manual of Nursing Practice. . . . . *.v.5 p.528*

Lippincott Williams and Wilkins' Comprehensive Medical Assisting. *.v.5 p.534*

Liptako Speaks: History from Oral Tradition in Africa. *.v.6 p.73*

Liquid Metal: The Science Fiction Film Reader. . . . *.v.6 p.319*

Liquidation of Empire: The Decline of the British Empire. . . . . *.v.3 p.88, p.124, p.126*

Lira Espanola: Representative Spanish Lyric Poets, 15th to 20th Centuries. . . . . *.v.2 p.644*

Lisbon in the Renaissance. . . . . *.v.3 p.243*

Lise Meitner: A Life in Physics. . . . . *.v.5 p.544*

The Lisle Letters: An Abridgement. . . . . . . *.v.3 p.92, p.99*

List of Standard Abbreviations, (Symbols) for Synthetic Polymers and Polymeric Materials: Basic Definitions of Terms Relating to Polymers. . . . *.v.5 p.321*

Listen to the Music: A Self-Guided Tour Through the Orchestral Repertoire. . . . . *.v.1 p.240, p.241*

Listen Up: Voices from the Next Feminist Generation. *.v.6 p.433*

Listening in Paris: A Cultural History. . . . . *.v.1 p.245, p.246*

Listening to Classic American Popular Songs. . *.v.1 p.268, p.269*

Listening to Movies: Film Lover's Guide to Film Music. *.v.1 p.255*

Listening to Salsa: Gender, Latin Popular Music, and Puerto Rican Cultures. . . . . *.v.1 p.291, v.3 p.266*

Listening to the Sea: The Politics of Improving Environmental Protection. . . . . *.v.5 p.430, p.431*

Listening to the Sirens: Musical Technologies of Queer Identity from Homer to Hedwig. . . . . *.v.1 p.379, v.6 p.408*

Liszt: Sonata in B Minor. . . . . *.v.1 p.198, p.239, p.336*

Literacy and Bilingualism: A Handbook for All Teachers. . . . . *.v.4 p.299, p.300, p.312*

Literacy and Motivation: Reading Engagement in Individuals and Groups. . . . . *.v.4 p.354*

Literacy and Popular Culture: England, 1750-1914. . . *.v.2 p.577, v.3 p.116, p.129, p.130,v.6 p.738*

Literacy and Power in the Ancient World. . . . . . . *.v.3 p.3*

Literacy and the Social Order: Reading and Writing in Tudor and Stuart England. . . . . . *.v.3 p.99, p.102, p.105, p.127*

Literacy and Written Culture in Early Modern Central Europe. *.v.4 p.337*

Literacy and Young Children: Research-Based Practices. . . . . *.v.4 p.368*

Literacy as Social Exchange: Intersections of Class, Gender, and Culture. *.v.4 p.29*

Literacy Before Schooling. . . . . *.v.4 p.368*

Literacy Development of Students in Urban Schools: Research and Policy. . . . . *.v.4 p.360*

Literacy, Emotion and Authority: Reading and Writing on a Polynesian Atoll. . . . . *.v.4 p.21, p.22*

Literacy in America: Historic Journey and Contemporary Solutions. . . . . *.v.4 p.762*

Literacy in Early Modern Europe: Its Growth, Uses and Impact, 1500-1800. . . . . *.v.4 p.335*

▢ Literacy Web. . . . . *.v.4 p.299, p.338, p.346, p.354*

Literacy with an Attitude: Educating Working-Class Children in Their Own Self-Interest. . . . . *.v.4 p.302*

Literary Adaptations in Black American Cinema: From Micheaux to Morrison. . . . . . . *.v.6 p.326, p.330, p.342*

Literary Aftershocks: American Writers, Readers, and the Bomb. *.v.2 p.11*

Literary Amazonia: Modern Writing by Amazonian Authors. . . . . *.v.2 p.692*

The Literary Book of Economics. . . . . *.v.4 p.186*

Literary Capital and the Late Victorian Novel. *.v.2 p.193, v.6 p.756*

The Literary Career of Mark Akenside, Including an Edition of His Non-Medical Prose. . . . . *.v.2 p.237*

Literary Criticism and the Gospels: The Theoretical Challenge. . . . . *.v.1 p.626*

Literary Criticism for New Testament Critics. . . . . *.v.1 p.626*

Literary Criticism of Alexander Pope. . . . . *.v.2 p.257*

The Literary Critics. . . . . *.v.2 p.165*

Literary Cultures in History: Reconstructions from South Asia. . . . . *.v.2 p.761*

Literary Cultures of Latin America: A Comparative History: Configurations of Literary Culture. . . . . . . *.v.2 p.665*

Literary Cultures of Latin America: A Comparative History: Institutional Modes and Cultural Modalities. . . . *.v.2 p.665*

Literary Cultures of Latin America: A Comparative History: Latin American Literary Culture. . . . . *.v.2 p.665*

Literary Essays. . . . . *.v.2 p.575*

The Literary Guide to the Bible. . . . . *.v.1 p.616*

A Literary History of America. . . . . *.v.2 p.6*

Literary History of Canada: Canadian Literature in English. *.v.2 p.730*

Literary History of England. . . . . *.v.2 p.166*

A Literary History of Kentucky. . . . . *.v.2 p.14*

The Literary History of Meistergesang. . . . . *.v.2 p.589*

A Literary History of New England. . . . . *.v.2 p.12*

A Literary History of Persia, Set. . . . . *.v.6 p.670*

A Literary History of Rome: From the Origins to the Close of the Golden Age. . . . . *.v.2 p.424*

A Literary History of Rome in the Silver Age: From Tiberius to Hadrian. *.v.2 p.424*

A Literary History of the Arabs. . . . . *.v.6 p.662, p.663*

A Literary History of the English People, Set. *.v.2 p.166, p.167*

Literary History of the United States. . . . . *.v.2 p.7*

The Literary Humor of the Urban Northeast, 1830-1890. *.v.2 p.12*

Literary Language and Its Public in Late Latin Antiquity and in the Middle Ages. . . . . *.v.2 p.424, p.448*

Literary Lapses. . . . . *.v.2 p.736*

Literary Market Place 2004: The Directory of the American Book Publishing Industry. . . . . *.v.4 p.149*

Literary Market Place 2005: The Directory of the American Book Publishing Industry. . . . . *.v.2 p.573, p.574*

Literary Masterpieces: One Hundred Years of Solitude. .*v.2 p.684*

Literary Masters: Gabriel Garcia Marquez. *v.2 p.684*

The Literary Mind. *v.2 p.573*

Literary Occasions: Essays. *v.2 p.769*

Literary Origins of Surrealism: A New Mysticism in French
Poetry. *v.2 p.460*

Literary Outlaw: The Life and Times of William S.
Burroughs. *v.2 p.64*

Literary Pan-Africanism: History, Context and
Criticism. *v.6 p.13, p.28*

Literary Research Guide: An Annotated Listing of Reference
Sources in English Literary Studies. *v.2 p.549, p.566*

Literary Reviews and Essays on American, English and French
Literature. *v.2 p.4, p.45*

Literary Studies (Miscellaneous Essays). *v.2 p.166*

Literary Texts and the Roman Historian. *v.2 p.426*

Literary Theory: A Very Short Introduction. . .*v.2 p.566, p.567*

Literary Theory: An Introduction. *v.2 p.567*

The Literary Underground of the Old Regime. . . .*v.3 p.147*

The Literary Vision of Gabrielle Roy. *v.2 p.539*

The Literary Works of Ou-Yang Hsiu (1007-72). . .*v.6 p.211*

Literate Education in the Hellenistic and Roman Worlds. .*v.3 p.23*

Literatura Chicana, 1965-1995: An Anthology in Spanish,
English, and Calo. *v.6 p.495, p.498*

Literatura Espanola: Una Antologia: De 1700 Hasta la
Actualidad. *v.2 p.643*

Literatura Espanola: Una Antologia: De los Origenes Hasta
1700. . . . .*v.2 p.643*

Literature and Dissent in Milton's England. *v.2 p.170*

Literature and Film: A Guide to the Theory and Practice of Film
Adaptation. *v.6 p.327*

Literature and Nation: Britain and India 1800-1990. . .*v.2 p.761*

Literature and Nationalism in Partitioned Poland,
1795-1918. . . . .*v.2 p.789*

Literature and Religion at Rome: Cultures, Contexts, and
Beliefs. *v.1 p.532*

Literature and Revolution. *v.2 p.800*

Literature and Sincerity. *v.2 p.456*

Literature and Society in Germany, 1918-1945. . . .*v.2 p.591*

Literature and the Aborigine in Australia. *v.2 p.740, p.741*

Literature As Exploration. *v.2 p.571*

Literature As Opera. *v.1 p.233*

A Literature Guide to the Hospitality Industry. . . .*v.4 p.161*

Literature in medieval Germany. *v.2 p.589*

Literature in Post-Communist Russia and Eastern Europe: The
Russian, Czech and Slovak Fiction of the Changes,
1988-98. . . . .*v.2 p.778, p.797*

Literature in the Greek World. *v.2 p.401*

Literature in the Marketplace: Nineteenth-Century British
Publishing and Reading
Practices. *v.6 p.738, p.739, p.741, p.752*

Literature in the Roman World. *v.2 p.425*

Literature into Film: Theory and Practical Approaches. *v.6 p.325*

The Literature Machine: Essays. *v.2 p.714*

The Literature of Adult Education: A Bibliographic
Essay. *v.4 p.320*

The Literature of Al-Andalus. *v.6 p.662*

Literature of American Music III, 1983-1992. . .*v.1 p.168, p.278*

The Literature of American Music in Books and Folk Music
Collections: A Fully Annotated Bibliography.*v.1 p.167, p.278*

The Literature of Ancient Sumer. *v.3 p.5, v.6 p.664*

The Literature of Chamber Music. *v.1 p.238*

The Literature of Chemistry: Recommended Titles for
Undergraduate Chemistry Library Collections. . .*v.5 p.255*

The Literature of Crop Science. *v.5 p.22, p.23*

Literature of East Germany. *v.2 p.590*

The Literature of Forestry and
Agroforestry. *v.4 p.164, v.5 p.38, p.39*

The Literature of Lesbianism: A Historical Anthology from
Ariosto to Stonewall. *v.6 p.392*

The Literature of Rock, 1954-1978. . . . . .*v.1 p.167, p.270*

The Literature of Rock II: Including an Exhaustive Survey of
the Literature from 1979-1983 and Incorporating
Supplementary Material from 1954-1978 Not Covered in the
First Volume. *v.1 p.167, p.270*

The Literature of Rock III, 1984-1990: With Additional Material
for the Period 1954-1983. . . . .*v.1 p.167, p.270*

The Literature of Satire. *v.2 p.195*

The Literature of Soil Science. *v.5 p.50*

Literature of the American West. *v.2 p.21*

The Literature of the Anglo: Saxons. *v.2 p.167*

Literature of the Early Republic. *v.2 p.28*

Literature of the Hundred Flowers, Vol. 1. . . . . .*v.6 p.213*

Literature of the Lost Home: Kobayashi Hideo—Literary
Criticism, 1924-1939. . . . .*v.6 p.231*

Literature of the Low Countries. *v.2 p.622*

The Literature of the Middle Western Frontier. *v.2 p.15*

Literature of the Piano: A Guide for Amateur and
Student. *v.1 p.240, p.398*

The Literature of the Political Economy. *v.4 p.217*

A Literature of Their Own: British Women Novelists from
Brontë to Lessing. *v.2 p.169, v.6 p.748, p.749, p.757*

Literature, Satire and the Early Stuart State. *v.2 p.195*

Literature, Science and Exploration in the Romantic Era: Bodies
of Knowledge. *v.2 p.175*

Literature Through Film: Realism, Magic, and the Art of
Adaptation. *v.6 p.327*

Literature, Travel, and Colonial Writing in the English
Renaissance, 1545-1625. . . . .*v.2 p.169*

Literatures of Latin America: From Antiquity to the
Present. *v.2 p.663*

The Literatutre of Ancient Egypt: An Anthology of Stories,
Instructions, and Poetry. *v.6 p.645*

The Lithographs of James McNeill Whistler: A Catalogue
Raisonné; Correspondence and Technical Studies. *v.1 p.758*

The Lithographs of Prentiss Taylor: A Catalogue
Raisonné. *v.1 p.746*

The Lithographs of Thomas Hart Benton: Catalogue
Raisonné. *v.1 p.756*

Lithography Primer. *v.1 p.761*

Lithuania Ascending: A Pagan Empire Within East-Central
Europe, 1295-1345. . . . .*v.3 p.256*

Lithuania in Crisis: Nationalism to Communism, 1939-1940. . . . .*v.3 p.256*

Lithuania in European Politics: The Years of the First Republic, 1918-1940. . . . .*v.3 p.256*

Lithuania: Stepping Westward. *v.3 p.256*

Lithuanian Dictionary: English-Lithuanian, Lithuanian-English. *v.2 p.773*

Lithuanian Social Democracy in Perspective, 1893-1914. . . . .*v.3 p.256, p.257, p.259*

Lithuanian-English Dictionary and Phrasebook. *v.2 p.773*

Litigating in the Shadow of Death: Defense Attorneys in Capital Cases. *v.6 p.270*

The Litigious Society. *v.4 p.441*

Littérature engagée. *v.2 p.520*

Littérature et sensation. *v.2 p.459*

Littératures nationales d'écriture française : Afrique noire, Caraïbes, océan Indien : histoire littéraire et anthologie. *v.2 p.535*

Little Big Men: Bodybuilding Subculture and Gender Construction. *v.4 p.817, p.855*

The Little Black Fish and Other Modern Persian Stories. *v.6 p.670*

The Little Book of Planet Earth. *v.5 p.419*

The Little Clay Cart: An English Translation of the Mrcchakatika of Sudraka, As Adapted for the Stage. *v.1 p.128, p.129, p.131*

A Little Commonwealth: Family Life in Plymouth Colony. *v.4 p.733*

The Little Death: A Henry Rios Mystery. *v.6 p.502*

Little Dorrit. by Charles Dickens. (Boz.) with ... illustrations. from designs by Phiz [pseud.] and Cruikshank. . *v.2 p.283*

Little Dorrit. *v.2 p.284*

Little Flower: The Life and Times of Fiorello la Guardia. *v.3 p.457*

The Little Flowers of St. Francis of Assisi. . . .*v.1 p.579, p.580*

Little Germany: German Refugees in Victorian Britain. *v.6 p.749, p.760, p.761*

Little Girls in Pretty Boxes: The Making and Breaking of Elite Gymnasts and Figure Skaters. *v.4 p.819, p.838*

The Little Girls. *v.2 p.334*

Little Green Men, Meowing Nuns and Head-Hunting Panics: A Study of Mass Psychogenic Illnesses and Social Delusion. *v.4 p.714*

Little Havana Blues: A Cuban-American Literature Anthology. *v.6 p.496, p.509*

The Little Hotel. *v.2 p.749*

Little Ice Age: How Climate Made History 1300-1850. .*v.5 p.425*

Little Ice Ages: Ancient and Modern. .*v.4 p.393, p.394,v.5 p.426*

Little Ironies: Stories of Singapore. *v.2 p.760*

Little Labels - Big Sound. *v.1 p.384*

The Little Lavender Book: Quotations on Gays and Lesbians. *v.6 p.360*

The Little Man and Other Satires. *v.2 p.347*

Little Mountain. *v.6 p.661*

Little Novels of Sicily. *v.2 p.713*

A Little Primer of Tu Fu. *v.6 p.209*

The Little Prince. *v.2 p.526*

Little Stones at My Window: Selected Poems. *v.2 p.686*

A Little Tea, a Little Chat. *v.2 p.749*

The Little Virtues. *v.2 p.717*

Little Wilson and Big God. *v.2 p.336*

Liturgical Dance: An Historical, Theological, and Practical Handbook. *v.1 p.21*

Liu Shaoqi and the Chinese Cultural Revolution. .*v.6 p.195, p.199*

Live and Work in the U. S. A. and Canada. *v.4 p.169*

Live, Direct and Biased?: Making Television News in the Satellite Age. *v.4 p.415*

Livelihood and Resistance: Peasants and the Politics of Land in Peru. *v.3 p.331*

The Lives and Times of Archy and Mehitabel. *v.2 p.97*

The Lives and Times of the Patriots: An Account of the Rebellion in Upper Canada, 1837-1838, and of the Patriot Agitation in the United States, 1837-1842. .*v.3 p.539*

Lives and Voices: Sources in European Women's History. *v.3 p.50, p.51*

Lives at Risk: Single-Payer National Health Insurance in Countries Around the World. *v.4 p.768*

Lives in Between: Assimilation and Marginality in Austria, Brazil, and West Africa, 1780-1945. . . .*v.3 p.343, v.6 p.73*

Lives in Education: A Narrative of People and Ideas. .*v.4 p.338*

Lives in Transit: A Collection of Recent Russian Women's Writing. *v.2 p.794, v.6 p.478*

The Lives of Cleopatra and Octavia. *v.2 p.248*

The Lives of Dr. John Donne, Sir Henry Wotton, Mr. Richard Hooker, Mr. George Herbert: 1670. . . . .*v.3 p.90*

Lives of Dust and Water: An Anthropology of Change and Resistance in Northwestern Mexico. *v.4 p.28*

Lives of Girls and Women. *v.2 p.737*

Lives of Great 20th Century Artists. *v.1 p.679*

The Lives of Jean Toomer: A Hunger for Wholeness. .*v.2 p.126*

The Lives of Lesbians, Gays and Bisexuals: Children to Adults. *v.6 p.382*

The Lives of Michel Foucault. *v.6 p.402*

Lives of the Bigamists: Marriage, Family, and Community in Colonial Mexico. *v.3 p.262, p.284*

Lives of the Caesars, 2. . . . .*v.2 p.444*

Lives of the Caesars. *v.2 p.444*

Lives of the Poets. *v.2 p.180*

Lives of the Popes: The Pontiffs from St. Peter to Benedict XVI. *v.1 p.574*

Lives of the Saints: From Mary and St. Francis of Assisi to John XXIII and Mother Teresa. *v.1 p.579*

Lives of the Saints. *v.2 p.738*

Lives of Their Own: Blacks, Italians, and Poles in Pittsburgh, 1900-1960. . . . .*v.3 p.492*

The Lives of Thomas Becket. *v.3 p.98*

Lives of Victorian Literary Figures I: George Eliot, Charles Dickens and Alfred, Lord Tennyson by Their Contemporaries, Set. *v.6 p.753*

Lives of Victorian Literary Figures II: The Brownings, the Brontes and the Rossettis by Their Contemporaries, Set. *v.2 p.271, p.272, p.304,v.6 p.753*

Lives of Victorian Literary Figures III: The Carlyles, John Ruskin and Elizabeth Gaskell by their Contemporaries. *v.2 p.277, p.289, p.305, v.6 p.753*

Lives of Victorian Literary Figures IV: Henry James, Edith Wharton and Oscar Wilde by Their Contemporaries. .*v.6 p.753*

Lives of Victorian Literary Figures V: Mary Elilzabeth Braddon, Wilkie Collins, William Thackeray by Their Contemporaries. *v.2 p.281, p.315, v.6 p.752, p.753*

Lives on the Boundary: A Moving Account of the Struggles and Achievements of America's Educationally Underprepared. *v.2 p.565*

Lives on the Line: Dispatches from the U. S.-Mexican Border. *v.6 p.486, p.521*

Lives Together - Worlds Apart: Mothers and Daughters in Popular Culture. *v.4 p.738, v.6 p.436, p.449, p.468*

Lives Together - Worlds Apart: Quechua Colonization in Jungle and City. *v.4 p.763*

Livestock Waste Facilities Handbook. *v.5 p.55*

Livia: First Lady of Imperial Rome. *v.3 p.27*

Living a Life: Absurd Tales. *v.2 p.808*

Living and Dying in the USA: Behavioral, Health, and Social Differentials of Adult Mortality. *v.4 p.742*

The Living and the Dead. *v.3 p.227*

Living at the Edge: A Biography of D. H. Lawrence and Frieda Von Richthofen. *v.2 p.364*

A Living Bay: The Underwater World of Monterey Bay. .*v.5 p.84*

Living by the Pen. *v.2 p.192*

Living Chicana Theory. *v.6 p.428, p.547*

The Living Company. *v.4 p.78*

Living Dangerously: A Memoir of Political Change in Malawi. *v.6 p.76*

Living Dangerously in Korea: The Western Experience, 1900 - 1950. . . . .*v.6 p.236*

Living Downtown: The History of Residential Hotels in the United States. *v.4 p.771*

The Living Earth: The Coevolution of the Planet and Life. *v.5 p.191, p.192*

The Living Eye. *v.2 p.456*

The Living Fields: Our Agricultural Heritage. *v.5 p.4*

Living Folklore: An Introduction to the Study of People and Their Traditions. *v.2 p.585*

Living for Change: An Autobiography. *v.6 p.107, p.126*

Living History: A Memoir. *v.6 p.614*

Living History. *v.3 p.457*

Living in a Patchy Environment. *v.5 p.223*

Living in Hope and History: Notes from Our Century. *v.2 p.755*

Living in Praise. *v.1 p.652*

Living in Prison: A History of the Correctional System with an Insider's View. *v.6 p.273*

Living in Prison: The Ecology of Survival. . . .*v.6 p.276, p.277*

Living in the Shadow of the Second Coming: American Premillennialism, 1875-1982. . . . .*v.1 p.607*

Living in the Tenth Century: Mentalities and Social Orders. *v.6 p.576*

Living in Time: The Poetry of C. Day Lewis. *v.2 p.343*

Living Is What I Wanted: Last Poems. *v.2 p.89*

The Living Marine Resource of the Western Central Atlantic: Bony Fishes (Opistognathidae to Molidae), Sea Turtles and Marine Mammals, Vol. 3, Pt. 2. . . . .*v.5 p.213*

The Living Marine Resources of the Western Central Atlantic: Introduction, Molluscs, Crustaceans, Hagfishes, Sharks, Batoid Fishes and Chimaeras, Vol. 1. . . . .*v.5 p.172, p.212, p.213, p.215*

The Living Marine Resources of the Western Central Atlantic: Vol. 2, Pt. 1, Bony fishes., Acipenseridae to Grammatidae. *v.5 p.172, p.241*

Living Martyrs: Individuals and Revolution in Nepal. .*v.6 p.163*

A Living Minstrelsy: The Poetry and Music of Sidney Lanier. *v.2 p.47*

The Living of Charlotte Perkins Gilman: An Autobiography. *v.2 p.39*

The Living on the Dead. *v.6 p.650*

Living on the Lake in Prehistoric Europe: 150 Years of Lake-Dwelling Research. *v.4 p.12*

Living Pictures: The Origins of the Movies. *v.6 p.331*

Living Poor: A Peace Corps Chronicle. *v.4 p.707*

The Living Principle: "English" As a Discipline of Thought. *v.2 p.164*

The Living Rock: The Story of Metals since Earliest Time and Their Impact on Civilization. *v.6 p.290*

Living Room War. *v.4 p.414*

The Living Soil: Fundamentals of Soil Science and Soil Biology. *v.5 p.49*

The Living Temple: George Herbert and Catechizing. .*v.2 p.249*

Living the Ethnographic Life. *v.4 p.25*

Living the Faith Community: The Church That Makes a Difference. *v.1 p.656*

Living to Tell the Tale. *v.2 p.683*

Living Together: An Ethnography of a Retirement Hotel. *v.4 p.742*

Living Traditions: Studies in the Ethnoarchaeology of South Asia. *v.4 p.8*

The Living Universe: NASA and the Development of Astrobiology. *v.5 p.183, p.184, p.242*

The Living Unknown Soldier: A Story of Grief and the Great War. *v.3 p.79*

Living Wage Movements: Global Perspectives. *v.4 p.250, p.252, p.253, p.265*

Living Wages, Equal Wages: Gender and Labour Market Policies in the United States. *v.4 p.273*

Living Walden Two: B. F. Skinner's Behaviorist Utopia and Experimental Communities. *v.4 p.499*

Living with Contradictions: Controversies in Feminist Social Ethics. *v.6 p.461*

Living with Florida's Atlantic Beaches: Coastal Hazards from Amelia Island to Key West. *v.5 p.373*

Living with Karst: A Fragile Foundation. *v.5 p.424*

Living with Polio: The Epidemic and Its Survivors. . .*v.5 p.533*

Living Within Limits: Ecology, Economics and Population Taboos. *v.4 p.763*

Living World Encyclopedia. *v.5 p.225*

Le livre de la cité des dames. *v.2 p.469*

Le Livre de l'advision Cristine. *v.2 p.469*

Le Livre des questions, vol. 1. . . . .*v.2 p.521*

Le Livre des questions, vol. 2. . . . .*v.2 p.521*

Le livre du Graal. *v.2 p.468*

Livy: Ab Urbe Condita. *v.2 p.436*

Livy, Bk. 1. . . . .*v.2 p.435*

Livy: His Historical Aims and Methods. *v.2 p.436*

Livy: Reconstructing Early Rome. *v.2 p.436*

Livy: The Composition of His History. *v.2 p.436*

Livy XXXIX. *v.2 p.436*

Liza of Lambeth. *v.2 p.370*

Llamas, Weavings and Organic Chocolate: Multicultural
  Grassroots Development in the Andes and Amazon of
  Bolivia. *v.3 p.324*

El Llano en Llamas. *v.2 p.669*

The Llanos Frontier in Colombian History, 1830-1930. .*v.3 p.358*

La Llorona's Children: Religion, Life, and Death in the U.
  S.-Mexican Borderlands. *v.6 p.487, p.520*

Lloyd George and the Generals. *v.3 p.80*

Lloyd George: From Peace to War, 1912-1916. . .*v.3 p.94, p.118*

Lloyd George: The People's Champion,
  1902-1911. . . . .*v.3 p.94, p.117*

Loans and Legitimacy: The Evolution of Soviet-American
  Relations, 1919-1933. . . . .*v.3 p.392*

Loba. *v.2 p.143*

Lobbying for Higher Education: How Colleges and Universities
  Influence Federal Policy. *v.4 p.295*

Lobbyists and Legislators: A Theory of Political
  Markets. *v.4 p.575*

Loca Motion: The Travels of Chicana and Latina Popular
  Culture. *v.6 p.491, p.512*

Local Algebra. *v.5 p.474*

Local Anaesthetic. *v.2 p.608*

Local Government and Thatcherism. *v.4 p.582*

Local Government in China under the Ch'ing. *v.6 p.187*

Local Government in the New Europe. *v.4 p.581, p.582*

The Local Historians of Attica. *v.3 p.18*

Local Markets and Regional Trade in Medieval
  Exeter. *v.6 p.558, p.577*

Local Meanings, Global Schooling: Anthropology and World
  Culture Theory. *v.4 p.313*

☐ LocalHarvest. *v.5 p.30*

Locating Filipino Americans: Ethnicity and Cultural Politics of
  Space. *v.6 p.89, p.129*

Locke: A Very Short Introduction. *v.1 p.448*

Locke, Berkeley, Hume: Central Themes. *v.1 p.449*

Locke on Human Understanding. *v.1 p.448*

Locke on Money, Vol. 1. . . . .*v.4 p.216*

Locke on Money, Vol. 2. . . . .*v.4 p.216*

Locke: Two Treatises of Government. *v.4 p.492*

Locke's Second Treatise of Civil Government: An Essay
  Concerning the True Original, Extent, and End of Civil
  Government. *v.4 p.216*

Locke. *v.1 p.447, p.448,v.3 p.106*

A Loftier Flight. *v.1 p.13*

Logging the Globe. *v.4 p.164*

Logic and Existence. *v.1 p.463, p.464*

Logic and Knowledge. *v.1 p.483*

Logic Made Easy: How to Know When Language Deceives
  You. *v.1 p.491*

The Logic of Chemistry Synthesis. *v.5 p.294*

The Logic of Divine Love: A Critical Analysis of the
  Soteriology of Peter Abailard. *v.1 p.644*

The Logic of Japanese Politics: Leaders, Institutions and the
  Limits of Change. *v.4 p.621, v.6 p.223*

The Logic of Political Survival. *v.4 p.575*

The Logic of Provability. *v.1 p.495*

The Logic of Real Arguments. *v.1 p.492*

The Logic of Renewal. *v.1 p.655*

The Logic of Scientific Discovery: 14th
  Printing. *v.1 p.499, v.5 p.409*

The Logic of Social Control. *v.5 p.649*

The Logic of the Humanities. *v.1 p.468*

The Logic of Tragedy: Morals and Integrity in Aeschylus'
  Oresteia. *v.2 p.407*

Logic, Semantics, Metamathematics. *v.1 p.494*

The Logical Basis of Metaphysics. *v.1 p.488*

Logical Empiricism: Historical and Contemporary
  Perspectives. *v.1 p.512*

Logical Investigations. *v.1 p.469*

Logical Positivism. *v.1 p.511*

Logical Syntax of Language. *v.1 p.494*

The Logical Universe: The Real Universe. *v.1 p.500*

Logico-Linguistic Papers. *v.1 p.446, p.447, p.490*

Logistical Management: A Systems Integration of Physical
  Distribution Management and Materials
  Management. *v.4 p.143*

Logit Models from Economics and Other Fields. . . .*v.4 p.199*

The Logos Reader: Rational Radicalism and the Future of
  Politics. *v.4 p.510*

L'ogre; roman. *v.2 p.529*

Lohengrin. *v.1 p.206, p.234, p.366, p.410*

Loie Fuller: Goddess of Light. *v.1 p.7*

L'oiseau bleu : théâtre. *v.2 p.522*

Loitering with Intent. *v.2 p.383, p.384*

Lola Montez: A Life. *v.1 p.12*

Lolly Willowes: Or the Loving Huntsman. *v.2 p.387*

Lombard Street: A Description of the Money
  Market. *v.4 p.99, p.146, p.154*

The Lombards. *v.3 p.62*

London, 1808-1870: The Infernal wen. *v.3 p.115*

London: A History. *v.6 p.715*

London and Paris As International Finance Centres,
  1890-2000. . . . .*v.6 p.711*

London Assurance and Other Victorian Comedies. . .*v.2 p.202*

A London Child of the 1870s. *v.6 p.765*

London: City of the Romans. *v.3 p.96, p.126*

London Crowds in the Reign of Charles II: Propaganda and
  Politics from the Restoration until the Exclusion
  Crisis. *v.3 p.94, p.105*

London in the Age of Chaucer. . . .*v.3 p.96, p.126,v.6 p.577*

London Labour and the London Poor, Vol.
  2. . . . .*v.6 p.743, p.744, p.761*

London Labour and the London Poor. *v.2 p.299*

London Life in the Eighteenth Century. *v.3 p.106, p.108*

The London Novels. *v.2 p.367*

e The London Stage, 1660-1800: A Calendar of Plays,
Entertainments and Afterpieces Together with
Casts, Box-Receipts and Contemporary
Comment. *v.1 p.101, p.140*

The London Stage, 1890-1899: A Calendar of Plays and
Players. *v.1 p.104, p.142*

The London Stage, 1900-1909: A Calendar of Plays and Players,
Set. *v.1 p.104, p.142*

The London Stage, 1910-1919: A Calendar of Plays and Players,
Set. *v.1 p.104, p.142*

The London Stage, 1920-1929: A Calendar of Plays and Players,
Set. *v.1 p.104, p.142*

The London Stage, 1930-1939: A Calender of Plays and Players,
Set. *v.1 p.104, p.142*

The London Stage, 1940-1949: A Calendar of Plays and
Players. *v.1 p.104, p.142*

The London Stage, 1950-1959: A Calendar of Plays and
Players. *v.1 p.104, p.142*

The London Underworld in the Victorian Period: Authentic
First-Person Accounts by Beggars, Thieves and
Prostitutes. *v.2 p.299, v.6 p.743*

The Lone Ranger and Tonto Fistfight in Heaven. . . .*v.6 p.697*

Lone Star Justice: The First Century of the Texas
Rangers. *v.3 p.509*

Lone Star Nation: The Epic Story of the Battle for Texas
Independence. *v.3 p.508*

Lone Star Rising: Lyndon Johnson and His Times, 1908-1960,
Vol. 1. . . . .*v.3 p.469*

Lone Star Rising: The Revolutionary Birth of the Texas
Republic. *v.3 p.508*

Lone Star: The Story of Texas. *v.3 p.508*

Lone Wolf vs. Hitchcock: Treaty Rights and Indian Law at the
End of the Nineteenth Century. . . .*v.6 p.687, p.688, p.695*

The Loneliest Campaign: The Truman Victory of 1948. .*v.3 p.479*

The Loneliness of the Long Distance Writer: The Works of
Love and the Huge Season. *v.2 p.103*

The Loneliness of the Long-Distance Runner. *v.2 p.380*

The Lonely Hunter: A Biography of Carson McCullers. .*v.2 p.100*

Lonely Hunters: An Oral History of Lesbian and Gay Southern
Life, 1948-1968. . . . .*v.6 p.366*

Lonely in America. *v.4 p.694*

The Lonely Voice: A Study of the Short Story. *v.2 p.579*

A Lonely Woman: Forugh Farrokhzad and Her Poetry. *v.6 p.671*

Lonesome Dove: A Novel. *v.2 p.150*

A Long and Happy Life. *v.2 p.153*

The Long Argument: English Puritanism and the Shaping of
New England Culture, 1570-1700. . . . .*v.3 p.485*

The Long Day Wanes: A Malayan Trilogy. *v.6 p.172*

A Long, Deep Furrow: 3 Centuries of Farming in New
England. *v.3 p.485*

The Long Detour: The History and Future of the American
Left. *v.4 p.493*

The Long Entanglement: The United States and NATO after
Fifty Years. *v.3 p.452*

The Long Gestation: Irish Nationalist Life 1891-1918. .*v.3 p.139*

The Long March: How the Cultural Revolution of the 1960's
Changed America. *v.3 p.371*

Long Memory: The Black Experience in America. *v.6 p.3*

The Long Night. *v.2 p.95*

Long Passage to Korea: Black Sailors and the Integration of the
U. S. Navy. *v.6 p.8*

The Long Peace: Inquiries into the History of the Cold
War. *v.3 p.388*

The Long Peace: Ottoman Lebanon, 1861-1920. . . .*v.6 p.604*

The Long Pretense: Soviet Treaty Diplomacy from Lenin to
Gorbachev. *v.3 p.387*

The Long Recessional: The Imperial Life of Rudyard
Kipling. *v.2 p.296*

The Long Revolution. *v.2 p.169, v.3 p.130*

A Long Shadow: Jefferson Davis and the Final Days of the
Confederacy. *v.4 p.519*

Long Shadows: Truth, Lies and History. *v.4 p.767*

Long Steel Rail: The Railroad in American Folksong. *v.1 p.295*

The Long Surrender. *v.4 p.520*

Long Walk to Freedom: The Autobiography of Nelson
Mandela. *v.6 p.78*

The Long War: Dictatorship and Revolution in El
Salvador. *v.3 p.299*

The Long War for Freedom: The Arab Struggle for Democracy
in the Middle East. *v.4 p.615, v.6 p.594, p.595*

The Long Week-End: A Social History of Great Britain,
1918-1939. . . . .*v.3 p.118*

The Longest War: Israel in Lebanon. *v.6 p.606, p.616*

The Longest War: The Iran-Iraq Military
Conflict. *v.6 p.603, p.632*

Longevity Records: Life Spans of Mammals, Birds, Amphibians,
Reptiles, and Fish. *v.5 p.212*

Longfellow: A Rediscovered Life. *v.2 p.47*

The Longing for a Form: Essays on the Fiction of C. S.
Lewis. *v.2 p.366*

A Longing for the Light. *v.2 p.656*

Longitude and Empire: How Captain Cook's Voyages Changed
the World. *v.4 p.379*

Longitudinal Analysis of Labor Market Data. *v.4 p.254*

Longitudinal Research. *v.4 p.686*

Longman Anthology of American Drama. *v.2 p.25*

Long-Run Economic Relationships: Readings in
Cointegration. *v.4 p.199*

Long-Term Environmental Change in Arctic and Antarctic
Lakes. *v.5 p.174, p.187*

Long-Term Imprisonment: Policy, Science, and Correctional
Practice. *v.6 p.273*

Longtime Californ': A Documentary Study of an American
Chinatown. *v.6 p.127*

Look Away!: A History of the Confederate States of
America. *v.4 p.520*

A Look Beyond the Model Minority Image: Critical Issues in
Asian America. *v.6 p.108*

Look Homeward: A Life of Thomas Wolfe. *v.2 p.137*

Look Homeward, Angel. *v.2 p.138*

Look Me in the Eye: Old Women, Aging, and Ageism. *v.6 p.380*

Look to the Mountain: An Ecology of Indigenous
Education. *v.4 p.311, p.312,v.6 p.680*

Looking Ahead: Independent School Issues and
Answers. *v.4 p.296*

Looking at Atget. *v.1 p.765*

Looking at Ballet: Ashton and Balanchine, 1926-1936. .*v.1 p.25*

Looking at Cuba: Essays on Culture and Civil Society. .*v.3 p.310*

Looking at Greek Vases. *v.1 p.670, p.808*

Looking at Italian Renaissance Sculpture. .*v.1 p.774, p.775, p.777*

Looking at Life Magazine. *v.4 p.409*

Looking at Looking: An Introduction to the Intelligence of
Vision. *v.5 p.607*

Looking at Old Prints. *v.1 p.759*

Looking at Photographs: A Guide to Technical Terms. .*v.1 p.761*

Looking at Prints, Drawings and Watercolours: A Guide to
Technical Terms. *v.1 p.664, p.721, p.752*

Looking at the Words of Our People: An Anthology of First
Nation Literary Criticism. *v.2 p.728*

Looking at Totem Poles. *v.1 p.778*

Looking Back and Thinking Forward: Reexaminations of
Teaching and Schooling. *v.4 p.346*

Looking Back at Francis Bacon. *v.1 p.748*

Looking Back in Wonder: Diary of a Dance Critic. .*v.1 p.39, p.40*

Looking Back on the Reagan Presidency. *v.3 p.465*

Looking Backward: 2000-1887. . . . .*v.2 p.31*

Looking Backward, Moving Forward: Confronting the Armenian
Genocide. *v.6 p.623, p.624*

Looking for Eagles: Reflections of a Classical
Naturalist. *v.5 p.222*

Looking for God in Brazil: The Progressive Catholic Church in
Urban Brazil's Religious Arena. *v.3 p.338, p.339*

Looking for Life, Searching the Solar System. .*v.5 p.183, p.242*

Looking for Longleaf. *v.5 p.37*

Looking for Native Ground: Contemporary Appalachian
Poetry. *v.2 p.12*

Looking for the Other: Feminism, Film and the Imperial
Gaze. *v.6 p.474*

Looking Good: College Women and Body Image,
1875-1930. . . . .*v.6 p.446, p.463*

Looking Good: Male Body Image in Modern America. .*v.6 p.446*

Looking into Pictures: An Interdisciplinary Approach to Pictorial
Space. *v.5 p.606*

Looking into the Abyss: Essays on Scenography. . .*v.1 p.146*

Looking North: Royal Canadian Mounted Police Illustrations,
the Potlach Collection. *v.1 p.714*

Looking on Darkness: A Novel. *v.2 p.623*

Looking Out: Perspectives on Dance and Criticism in a
Multicultural World. *v.1 p.39, p.42*

Looking Outward: Years of Crisis at the United Nations. .*v.4 p.635*

Looking Queer: Body Image and Identity in Lesbian, Bisexual,
Gay, and Transgender Communities. *v.6 p.366*

Looking Toward Ararat: Armenia in Modern History. .*v.3 p.231*

The Loom and Other Stories. *v.6 p.102*

Loop the Loop: Posters of Flight. *v.1 p.718, p.719*

Loot: And Other Stories. *v.2 p.755*

The Looting of the Iraq Museum, Baghdad: The Lost Legacy of
Ancient Mesopotamia. *v.1 p.823*

Lope de Vega Carpio: Fuente Ovejuna. *v.2 p.653*

L'opoponax. *v.2 p.534*

Lorca: A Dream of Life. *v.2 p.660, v.6 p.403, p.404*

Lorca and Jimenez: Selected Poems. *v.2 p.659, p.660*

Lord and Peasant in Russia: From the 9th to the 19th
Century. *v.3 p.211, v.4 p.723*

Lord Byron's Correspondence, Set. *v.2 p.273*

Lord Chesterfield and His World. *v.3 p.107, p.129*

Lord Emsworth. *v.2 p.391*

Lord Jesus Christ: Devotion to Jesus in Earliest
Christianity. *v.1 p.626*

Lord Jim: A Tale. *v.2 p.340*

Lord John Russell. *v.3 p.95, p.114*

Lord Liverpool: The Life and Political Career of Robert Banks
Jenkinson, Second Earl of Liverpool,
1770-1828. . . . .*v.3 p.94, p.108*

Lord North. *v.3 p.109*

Lord of the Dance: My Story. *v.1 p.7, p.8*

Lord of the Flies. *v.2 p.347*

Lord Peter: A Collection of All the Lord Peter Wimsey
Stories. *v.2 p.381, p.382*

Lord Randolph Churchill. *v.3 p.93, p.111*

Lord Rochester's Monkey. *v.2 p.350*

Lord Russell's Canadian Policy, a Study in British Heritage and
Colonial Freedom. *v.3 p.539*

The Lord Won't Mind. *v.6 p.397, p.398*

Lords of All the World: Ideologies of Empire in Spain, Britain,
and France, 1492-1830. . . . .*v.3 p.74*

Lords of Creation: The Origins of Sacred Maya
Kingship. *v.1 p.669, p.670, p.684*

The Lords of Human Kind: European Attitudes to Other
Cultures in the Imperial Age. *v.3 p.78*

Lords of Parliament: Manners, Rituals and Politics. . .*v.4 p.606*

Lords of the Atlas: The Rise and Fall of the House of Glaoua,
1893-1956. . . . .*v.6 p.61*

Lords of the Lebanese Marches: Violence and Narrative in an
Arab Society. *v.6 p.605*

Lords of the Tiger Spirit : A History of the Caribs in Colonial
Venezuela and Guyana, 1498-1820. . . . . .*v.3 p.359, p.360*

Lords of Things: The Fashioning of the Siamese Monarchy's
Modern Image. *v.6 p.171*

Lordship, Kingship, and Empire: The Idea of Monarchy,
1400-1525 (The Carlyle Lectures 1988). *v.4 p.502*

Lordship, Reform, and the Development of Civil Society in
Medieval Italy: The Bishopric of Orvieto,
1100-1250. . . . .*v.3 p.198, v.6 p.577*

Lordship to Patronage: Scotland 1603 - 1745. . . . .*v.3 p.133*

Lordship to Patronage: Scotland 1603-1745. . . . .*v.3 p.133*

Lore and Science in Ancient Pythagoreanism. *v.1 p.421*

The Lore of New Mexico. *v.2 p.17*

Lore of Running. *v.4 p.866, p.875, p.879*

Lorenz Hart: A Poet on Broadway. . .*v.1 p.329, v.6 p.409, p.410*

The Los Angeles Barrio, 1850-1890: A Social
History. *v.6 p.534, p.549*

The Los Angeles Riots. *v.4 p.713*

Loser Takes All. *v.2 p.350*

The Losers: Gang Delinquency in an American Suburb.*v.4 p.753*

Losing Control?: Sovereignty in the Age of
   Globalization. *v.4 p.496*

Losing Generations: Adolescents in High-Risk
   Settings. *v.5 p.671, p.672*

Losing Matt Shepard: Life and Politics in the Aftermath of
   Anti-Gay Murder. *v.6 p.387*

Loss Within Loss: Artists in the Age of
   AIDS. *v.1 p.708, v.6 p.390, p.391*

Losses in the Los Angeles Civil Unrest, April 29-May 1, 1992:
   Lists of the Damaged Properties and Korean
   Merchants and the L. A. Riot -
   Rebellion. *v.6 p.106, p.124, p.136*

The Lost Apple: Operation Pedro Pan, Cuban Children in the U.
   S., and the Promise of a Better Future. *v.6 p.539*

Lost Childhood and Other Stories. *v.2 p.166*

The Lost Children of Wilder: The Epic Struggle to Change
   Foster Care. *v.4 p.757*

The Lost Chord: Essays on Victorian Music. *v.6 p.757*

Lost Christianities: The Battles for Scripture and the Faiths We
   Never Knew. *v.1 p.599*

Lost Cities of Africa. *v.6 p.52*

The Lost Colony of the Confederacy. *v.3 p.340*

Lost Debate: German Socialist Intellectuals and
   Totalitarianism. *v.4 p.510*

Lost Gay Novels: A Reference Guide to Fifty Works from the
   First Half of the Twentieth Century. *v.6 p.391*

The Lost Girl. *v.2 p.363*

Lost Ground: Welfare Reform, Poverty, and Beyond. .*v.4 p.754*

The Lost Grove: Autobiography of a Spanish Poet in
   Exile. *v.2 p.655*

Lost Harvests: Prairie Indian Reserve Farmers and Government
   Policy, No. 3. . . . .*v.5 p.14*

The Lost Honor of Katharina Blum. *v.2 p.604*

Lost Horizon. *v.2 p.351, p.352, v.6 p.215*

Lost Illusions: Latin American's Struggle for Democracy, as
   Recounted by Its Leaders. *v.3 p.352*

Lost Illusions. *v.2 p.486*

Lost in the Funhouse. *v.2 p.142*

The Lost Italian Renaissance: Humanists, Historians, and Latin's
   Legacy. *v.3 p.199*

The Lost Kingdom of Burgundy. *v.3 p.158*

Lost Knowledge: Confronting the Threat of an Aging
   Workforce. *v.4 p.78*

The Lost Land: The Chicano Image of the
   Southwest. *v.3 p.526, p.527, v.6 p.531*

The Lost Language of Cranes: A Novel. *v.6 p.397*

Lost Liberties: Ashcroft and the Assault on Personal
   Freedom. *v.4 p.515*

Lost Modernities: China, Vietnam, Korea, and the Hazards of
   World History. *v.6 p.167, p.237*

Lost Names: Scenes from Korean Boyhood. *v.2 p.760*

The Lost Painting: The Quest for a Caravaggio
   Masterpiece. *v.1 p.740*

Lost Prophet: The Life and Times of Bayard Rustin. .*v.6 p.390*

Lost Puritan: A Life of Robert Lowell. *v.2 p.96*

Lost Scriptures: Books That Did Not Make It into the New
   Testament. *v.1 p.599*

Lost Sounds: Blacks and the Birth of the Recording Industry,
   1890-1919. . . . .*v.1 p.280, p.281*

The Lost Steps. *v.2 p.671*

Lost Time: On Remembering and Forgetting in Late Modern
   Culture. *v.5 p.610*

Lost White Tribes: The End of Privilege and the Last Colonials
   in Sri Lanka, Jamaica, Brazil, Haiti, Namibia and
   Guadeloupe. *v.3 p.315*

Lost Woods: The Discovered Writing of Rachel Carson. .*v.5 p.78*

Lost Words: Narratives of Language and the Brain,
   1825-1926. . . . .*v.5 p.621, p.623, p.665, p.673*

The Lost World: Being an Account of the Recent Amazing
   Adventures of Professor George E. Challenger,
   Lord John Roxton, Professor Summerlee, and Mr E. D.
   Malone of the Daily Gazette. *v.2 p.285*

Lost World Illustrated. *v.2 p.503*

Lost Years: A Memoir, 1945-1951. . . . .*v.2 p.356*

Lothair. *v.2 p.275*

Lots of Parking: Land Use in a Car Culture. *v.1 p.797*

Lotte in Weimar: The Beloved Returns. *v.2 p.613*

The Lottery. *v.2 p.90*

L'Ottocento. *v.2 p.697*

Loud Hawk: The United States vs. the American Indian
   Movement. *v.4 p.438, v.6 p.695*

Louis: A Life of Robert Louis Stevenson. *v.2 p.312*

Louis and Bebe Barron's Forbidden Planet: A Film Score
   Guide. *v.1 p.245, p.256*

Louis Andriessen: De Staat. *v.1 p.207, p.208, p.301*

Louis Armstrong and Paul Whiteman: Two Kings of
   Jazz. *v.1 p.257, p.302, p.368*

The Louis Armstrong Companion: Eight Decades of
   Commentary. *v.1 p.257, p.302*

Louis Armstrong, in His Own Words: Selected
   Writings. *v.1 p.257, p.302*

Louis Comfort Tiffany at Tiffany and Co. *v.1 p.802*

Louis D. Brandeis: Justice for the People. *v.4 p.469*

Louis Horst: Musician in a Dancer's World. *v.1 p.12*

Louis I. Kahn. *v.1 p.794*

Louis Kahn's Situated Modernism. *v.1 p.793*

Louis Kahn. *v.1 p.795*

Louis MacNeice. *v.2 p.369*

Louis Moreau Gottschalk. *v.1 p.204, p.327*

Louis Pasteur: Free Lance of Science. *v.5 p.396*

Louis Pasteur. *v.5 p.396*

Louis Sullivan: The Poetry of Architecture. *v.1 p.795*

Louis the Fourteenth: A Profile. *v.3 p.146*

Louis Wirth on Cities and Social Life. *v.6 p.720*

Louis XIV and the Origins of the Dutch War. *v.3 p.146*

Louis XIV and Twenty Million Frenchmen. *v.3 p.145*

Louis XIV. *v.3 p.146*

Louis XVI: The Silent King. *v.3 p.147*

Louisa May: A Modern Biography of Louisa May Alcott.*v.2 p.31*

Louisa May Alcott: A Biography. *v.2 p.31*

Louisa May Alcott and "Little Women": Biography, Critique, Publications, Poems, Songs, and Contemporary Relevance. *v.2 p.31*

Louisa May Alcott: Little Women, Little Men, Jo's Boys. .*v.2 p.31*

Louise de la Valliere. *v.2 p.489*

Louise Farrenc, 1804-1875: Composer, Performer, Scholar. *v.1 p.197, p.324*

Louise Labe. *v.2 p.469*

Louise Nevelson: A Passionate Life. *v.1 p.780*

Louis-Ferdinand Celine. *v.2 p.515*

Louisiana, 1682-1803. . . . .*v.3 p.508*

Louisiana: A Bicentennial History. *v.3 p.507*

Louisiana: A History. *v.3 p.507*

Louisiana Governors: From Iberville to Edwards. . . .*v.3 p.507*

Louisiana in the Age of Jackson: A Clash of Cultures and Personalities. *v.3 p.508*

Louisiana Politics and the Paradoxes of Reaction and Reform, 1877-1928. . . . .*v.3 p.507*

Louisiana Reconstructed, 1863-1877. . . . . .*v.3 p.507, p.508*

Lourdes Portillo: The Devil Never Sleeps and Other Films. *v.6 p.493*

Love and Death in Medieval French and Occitan Courtly Literature: Martyrs to Love. *v.2 p.457*

Love and Ethics in Gower's Confessio Amantis. . .*v.2 p.212*

Love and Friendship: And Other Early Works. .*v.2 p.266, p.267*

Love and Longing in Bombay. *v.2 p.764*

Love and Loss: Selected Poems of Charles d'Orleans. .*v.2 p.469*

Love and Other Stories. *v.2 p.785*

Love and Pedagogy. *v.2 p.663*

Love and Politics: Women Politicans and the Ethics of Care. *v.6 p.441*

Love and Saint Augustine. *v.1 p.651*

Love and the American Delinquent: The Theory and Practice of "Progressive" Juvenile Justice, 1825-1920. . .*v.4 p.473, p.474*

Love and the Law in Cervantes. *v.2 p.649*

Love and Theft: Blackface Minstrelsy and the American Working Class. *v.1 p.281*

Love and Toil: Motherhood in Outcast London, 1870-1918. . . . .*v.3 p.54, v.6 p.748*

Love Between Women: Early Christian Responses to Female Homoeroticism. *v.6 p.364, p.373*

Love, Death, and Exile. *v.6 p.658*

Love, Death and the Ladies' Drill Team. *v.2 p.130, p.131*

Love Disconsoled: Meditations on Christian Charity. .*v.1 p.651*

Love, Ellen: A Mother/Daughter Journey. *v.6 p.419*

Love, Human and Divine: The Heart of Christian Ethics. *v.1 p.651*

Love in a Dark Time: And Other Explorations of Gay Lives and Literature. *v.6 p.394*

Love in the Kingdom of Oil. *v.6 p.656*

Love in the Ruins. *v.2 p.152*

Love in the Time of Cholera. *v.2 p.682, p.683*

Love in the Western World. *v.2 p.526*

Love Is Hard Work: Memorias de Loisaida/Poems. *v.6 p.505, p.509*

Love Known: Theology and Experience in George Herbert's Poetry. *v.2 p.249*

The Love Letters of William and Mary Wordsworth. . *v.2 p.325*

Love Makes a Family: Portraits of Lesbian, Gay, Bisexual and Transgendered Parents and Their Families. *v.6 p.368, p.369, p.372, p.376, p.377*

Love Medicine. *v.2 p.145*

The Love Nest and Other Stories. *v.2 p.94*

Love of Learning and Desire for God: A Study of Monastic Culture. *v.1 p.578, v.3 p.57*

The Love of Learning and the Desire for God: A Study of Monastic Culture. *v.6 p.572*

The Love of Nature and the End of the World: The Unspoken Dimensions of Environmental Concern. *v.6 p.287*

The Love of the Last Tycoon: The Authorized Text. . .*v.2 p.76*

Love on the Rocks: Men, Women, and Alcohol in Post-World War II America. *v.5 p.664*

The Love Poems. *v.2 p.439*

The Love Poetry of Francisco de Quevedo: An Aesthetic and Existential Study. *v.2 p.651*

Love, Power, and Justice: Ontological Analysis and Ethical Applications. *v.1 p.651*

Love Saves the Day: A History of American Dance Music Culture 1970-1979. . . . .*v.1 p.271*

Love Saves the Day: A History of American Dance Music Culture, 1970-1979. . . . .*v.1 p.271*

Love Song of the Dark Lord: Jayadeva's Gitagovinda. *v.6 p.152*

Love Speaks Its Name: Gay and Lesbian Love Poems. *v.6 p.405*

Love Stories: Sex Between Men Before Homosexuality. *v.6 p.363*

A Love Supreme: The Story of John Coltrane's Signature Album. *v.1 p.260, p.318*

Love the One You're With: A B-Boy Blues Novel. . *v.6 p.397*

Love! Valour! Compassion!. *v.6 p.412*

The Love Wife. *v.6 p.100*

Love Works, Vol. 2. . . . .*v.6 p.104*

The Loved One. *v.2 p.388*

Lovelock and Gaia: Signs of Life. *v.5 p.250*

The Lovely Treachery of Words: Essays Selected and New. *v.2 p.730*

Loverboys. *v.6 p.498*

Lovers and Beloveds: Sexual Otherness in Southern Fiction, 1936-1961. . . . .*v.2 p.14*

The Lover's Watch. *v.2 p.238*

The Lover. *v.2 p.516*

Lover. *v.6 p.397*

The Lover. *v.6 p.652*

Love's Body. *v.5 p.658*

Love's Labour's Lost. *v.2 p.223*

Love's Madness: Medicine, the Novel, and Female Insanity, 1800-1865. . . . .*v.6 p.749, p.757, p.760*

The Loves of Judith. *v.6 p.651*

Love's Perplexing Obsession, Experienced by Two Geniuses: Heinrich Heine and Percy Bysshe Shelley. *v.2 p.602*

Love's Redeeming Work: The Anglican Quest for Holiness. *v.1 p.582, p.583*

Love's Remedies: Recantation and Renaissance Lyric Poetry. . . . . *.v.2 p.182*

Lovesick: Modernist Plays of Same-Sex Love, 1894-1925. . . . . *.v.6 p.413*

Love. . . . . *.v.2 p.502*

The Loving Friends: A Portrait of Bloomsbury. *.v.3 p.117, p.128*

Loving Her. . . . . *.v.6 p.399*

Loving in the War Years: Lo Que Nunca Paso por Sus Labios. . . . . *.v.6 p.501, p.502, p.510*

Loving Pedro Infante. . . . . *.v.6 p.498*

Loving to Survive: Sexual Terror, Men's Violence and Women's Lives. . . . . *.v.4 p.742*

Lovis Corinth, the Paintings, a Catalogue Raisonné¡: Die Gemaelde, Werkverzeichnis. . . . . *.v.1 p.736*

The Low Countries, 1780-1940. . . . . *.v.3 p.205*

Low Intensity Conflict: Old Threats in a New World. *.v.3 p.298*

Low Pay High Profile: The Global Push for Fair Labor. . . . . *.v.4 p.254, p.261*

Lowden of Illinois - The Life of Frank O. Lowden: City and State. . . . . *.v.3 p.459*

Lowden of Illinois - The Life of Frank O. Lowden: Nation and Countryside, Vol. 2. . . . . *.v.3 p.459*

The Lower Depths. . . . . *.v.2 p.804*

Lower Silesia from Nazi Germany to Communist Poland, 1942-1949. . . . . *.v.3 p.255*

Lowly Origin: Where, When, and Why Our Ancestors First Stood Up. . . . . *.v.4 p.15*

The Loyal, True and Brave: America's Civil War Soldiers. . . . . *.v.4 p.522*

The Loyalists in Revolutionary America, 1760-1781. *.v.3 p.407*

The Loyalists of Revolutionary Delaware: A University of Delaware Bicentennial Book. . . . . *.v.3 p.409*

Loyalty and Leadership in an Early Islamic Society. . *.v.6 p.585*

LPGA's Guide to Every Shot. . . . . . . *.v.4 p.837, p.861*

LSAT: The Best Test Preparation for the Law School Admission Test with Software. . . . . *.v.4 p.440*

Lu Xun and His Legacy. . . . . *.v.6 p.200, p.213*

Lubrication: A Tribology Handbook. . . . . . . *.v.5 p.708*

Lubrication and Reliability Handbook. . . . . . . *.v.5 p.708*

Lubrication Fundamentals, Vol. 137. . . . . . . *.v.5 p.708*

Luca Marenzio: The Career of a Musician Between the Renaissance and the Counter-Reformation. . . . . *.v.1 p.179, p.339, p.340*

Lucan: An Introduction. . . . . *.v.2 p.436*

Lucan: De Bello Civili, Bk. II. . . . . *.v.2 p.436, p.437*

Lucan: De Bello Civili I. . . . . *.v.2 p.437*

Luce Irigaray: Key Writings. . . . . *.v.1 p.456*

Luces de Bohemia: Bohemian Lights. . . . . . . *.v.2 p.663*

La Lucha for Cuba: Religion and Politics on the Streets of Miami. . . . . *.v.4 p.543, v.6 p.519, p.520, p.537*

Luchino Visconti. . . . . *.v.6 p.419*

Lucia Joyce: To Dance in the Wake. . . . . . *.v.1 p.12, p.46*

Lucian: A Selection. . . . . *.v.2 p.416*

Lucian and His Influence in Europe. . . . . *.v.2 p.416*

Lucian Freud. . . . . *.v.1 p.738*

Lucian: Satirical Sketches. . . . . *.v.2 p.416*

Lucian: Seventy Dialogues. . . . . *.v.2 p.416*

Lucien Leuwen. . . . . *.v.2 p.502*

Lucifer: The Devil in the Middle Ages. . . . . . . *.v.1 p.529*

Lucinda Brayford. . . . . *.v.2 p.744*

The Luck of Nineveh. . . . . *.v.3 p.5*

The Luck of Roaring Camp and Other Sketches. . . . *.v.2 p.40*

The Luck of the Bodkins. . . . . *.v.2 p.391*

Luckiest Man: The Life and Death of Lou Gehrig. . *.v.4 p.850*

Lucknow: Memories of a City. . . . . *.v.6 p.161*

The Lucky Chance. . . . . *.v.2 p.238*

Lucky Child: A Daughter of Cambodia Reunites with the Sister She Left Behind. . . . . *.v.6 p.95, p.139*

Lucky in the Corner: A Novel. . . . . *.v.6 p.394*

Lucky Jim. . . . . *.v.2 p.328, p.329*

Lucky Kristoffer. . . . . *.v.2 p.626*

Lucky Poet: A Self-Study in Literature and Political Ideas Being the Autobiography of Hugh MacDiarmid. . . . *.v.2 p.368*

Lucrecia's Dreams: Politics and Prophecy in Sixteenth-Century Spain. . . . . *.v.3 p.237*

Lucretius and Epicurus. . . . . *.v.2 p.437*

Lucretius and the Transformation of Greek Wisdom. . *.v.2 p.437*

Lucretius: De Rerum Natura. . . . . *.v.2 p.437*

Lucretius in the Modern World. . . . . *.v.2 p.437*

Ludovico Carracci and the Art of Drawing. . . *.v.1 p.722, p.723*

Ludvig Holberg. . . . . *.v.2 p.627*

Ludwig Boltzmann: The Man Who Trusted Atoms. . *.v.5 p.542*

Ludwig Van Beethoven: Fidelio. *.v.1 p.202, p.203, p.232, p.307*

Ludwig Wittgenstein: A Memoir. . . . . *.v.1 p.472*

Ludwig Wittgenstein and the Vienna Circle. . . . . . *.v.1 p.472*

Ludwig Wittgenstein: Philosophy and Language. . . *.v.1 p.471*

The Luftwaffe's Way of War: German Air Force Doctrine, 1911-1945. . . . . *.v.3 p.175*

Lugbara Religion. . . . . *.v.4 p.36, p.37*

Luigi Pirandello: Contemporary Perspectives. . . . . *.v.2 p.722*

Luigi's Jazz Warm Up: An Introduction to Jazz Style and Technique. . . . . *.v.1 p.32*

Luis Barragan's Gardens of El Pedregal. . . . *.v.1 p.815, p.816*

Luis Leal: An Auto/Biography. . . . . *.v.6 p.488, p.512*

Luis Muñoz Marín Puerto Rico's Democratic Revolution. . . . . *.v.3 p.320*

Luis Valdez - Early Works: Actos, Bernabe and Pensamiento Serpentino. . . . . *.v.6 p.504, p.518*

Luisa in Realityland: A Novel. . . . . *.v.2 p.674*

Luke 1: A Commentary on the Gospel of Luke 1:1-9:50. *.v.1 p.628*

☐ LULAC: League of United Latin American Citizens. . . . . *.v.6 p.528, p.537, p.539*

Lully Studies. . . . . *.v.1 p.184, p.338*

Lully. . . . . *.v.6 p.408, p.412*

Lumumba Speaks: Speeches and Writings, 1958-1961. *.v.6 p.62*

Luna. . . . . *.v.6 p.398*

The Lunda-Ndembu: Style, Change and Social Transformation in South Central Africa. . . . . *.v.4 p.38, v.6 p.77*

La Lupa. . . . . *.v.2 p.713*

Lupercal. . . . . *.v.2 p.353*

The Lure of Africa: American Interests in Tropical Africa, 1919-1939. . . . .*v.6 p.56*

The Lure of God: A Biblical Background for Process Theism. *v.1 p.637, p.638*

Lure of Perfection: Fashion and Ballet, 1780-1830. .*v.1 p.23, p.44*

Lush Life: A Biography of Billy Strayhorn. *v.1 p.259, p.260, p.361, v.6 p.409*

The Lusiad, by Luis de Camoens, Translated by Richard Fanshawe. *v.2 p.688*

The Lustre of Our Country: The American Experience of Religious Freedom. *v.1 p.657*

Luther: An Introduction to His Thought. *v.1 p.602, p.603*

Luther and the False Brethren. *v.1 p.603*

Luther: Lectures on Romans. *v.1 p.631*

Luther: Man Between God and the Devil. *v.1 p.581, p.603, v.3 p.166*

Luther the Reformer: The Story of the Man and His Career. *v.3 p.166*

Lutheran Letters. *v.2 p.721*

The Lutherans, 9. . . . .*v.1 p.585*

Lutherans in North America. *v.1 p.585, p.586*

Lutherans Today: American Lutheran Identity in the Twenty-First Century. *v.1 p.585*

Luther's Ninety-Five Theses. *v.3 p.57*

Luther's Works, Set. *v.1 p.603*

Luxuriance and Economy: Cicero and the Alien Style. .*v.2 p.433*

Lying about Hitler: History, Holocaust and the David Irving Trial. *v.3 p.83*

Lying up a Nation: Race and Black Music. *v.1 p.282*

The Lymphatic Continuum: Lymphatic Biology and Disease. *v.5 p.163*

Lynching in America: A History in Documents. . . .*v.6 p.252*

The Lynching of Emmett Till: A Documentary Narrative. *v.3 p.505*

Lyndon: An Oral Biography. *v.3 p.476*

Lyndon Johnson and the American Dream. *v.3 p.471*

Lyndon Johnson Confronts the World: American Foreign Policy, 1963-1968. . . . .*v.3 p.468*

Lyndon Johnson's War: America's Cold War Crusade in Vietnam, 1945-1965: a Critical Issue. *v.6 p.168*

Lynwood Kreneck, Printmaker. *v.1 p.756, p.757*

The Lyotard Reader. *v.1 p.456*

Lyric and Dramatic Poems. *v.2 p.103*

Lyric and Dramatic Poetry, 1946-82. . . . . . .*v.2 p.535, p.536*

Lyric Poems and Ballads. *v.2 p.599*

Lyric Poetry of the Italian Renaissance: An Anthology with Verse Translations. *v.2 p.700*

Lyrica Graeca Selecta. *v.2 p.403*

Lyrical Ballads, 1798. . . . .*v.2 p.280, p.325*

Lyrical Ballads and Other Poems, 1797-1800. . . . .*v.2 p.325*

Lyrics: 1962-2001. . . . .*v.1 p.268, p.322, p.411*

Lyrics by Oscar Hammerstein II. .*v.1 p.250, p.328, p.408, p.411*

Lyrics of the Afro-American Spiritual: A Documentary Collection. *v.1 p.281, p.412*

Lyrics of the French Renaissance: Marot, du Bellay and Ronsard. *v.2 p.464, p.472*

Lyrics of the Troubadours and Trouveres: An Anthology and a History. *v.1 p.177, p.411*

Lysias and the Corpus Lysiacum. *v.2 p.407*

Lysias: Selected Speeches. *v.2 p.407, p.408*

Lysias. *v.2 p.408*

Lysistrata. *v.2 p.423*

Lysosomes. *v.5 p.114*

M

M. Butterfly: With an Afterword by the Playwright. *v.2 p.147, v.6 p.98, p.99*

M. C. Escher: Visions of Symmetry. *v.5 p.460*

M: The Man Who Became Carravagio. *v.1 p.745*

M: Writings '67-'72. . . . .*v.1 p.210, p.315*

Mabel Dwight: A Catalogue Raisonné of the Lithographs. *v.1 p.758*

MacArthur and the American Century: A Reader. . . .*v.3 p.460*

Macaulay and the Whig Tradition. *v.3 p.88*

Macaulay: The Shaping of the Historian. *v.3 p.88*

Macbeth. *v.2 p.223*

Maccabees II. *v.1 p.623*

Macdonald: His Life and World. *v.3 p.540*

Macedonia: Its People and History. *v.3 p.250*

Macedonia: Warlords and Rebels in the Balkans. . . .*v.3 p.250*

Macedonian: A Course for Beginning and Intermediate Students. *v.2 p.775*

The Macedonian Conflict: Ethnic Nationalism in a Transnational World. *v.3 p.250*

The Macedonian State: Origins, Instititions, and History. .*v.3 p.19*

Machado de Assis: Reflections on a Brazilian Master Writer. *v.2 p.690, p.691*

Machado de Assis: The Brazilian Master and His Novels. *v.2 p.690*

Machado de Assis. *v.2 p.690*

Machaut's Mass: An Introduction. . . .*v.1 p.177, p.235, p.338*

Machers and Rockers: Chess Records and the Business of Rock and Roll. *v.1 p.267, p.383*

Machete Season: The Killers in Rwanda Speak. . . .*v.6 p.65*

Machiavelli's Children: Leaders and Their Legacies in Italy and Japan. *v.4 p.622, v.6 p.225*

Machiavelli's Virtue. *v.4 p.492*

The Machine in the Garden: Technology and the Pastoral Ideal in America. *v.3 p.369*

Machine Learning. *v.5 p.339, p.408*

Machine Models of Music. *v.1 p.388*

Machine Musicianship. *v.1 p.388*

Machine Vision: Theory, Algorithms, Practicalities. . .*v.5 p.340*

The Machinery Question and the Making of Political Economy, 1815-1848. . . . .*v.6 p.749, p.750*

Machinery's Handbook Guide. *v.5 p.714*

Machinery's Handbook. *v.5 p.715, p.732, p.733*

Machos, Maricones, and Gays: Cuba and Homosexuality. *v.6 p.421*

MacKenzie King and the Prairie West. *v.3 p.546*

Mackenzie King: His Life and World. *v.3 p.539*

Mackenzie King of Canada: A Biography. *v.3 p.539*

The Macmillan Dictionary of Canadian Biography. . .*v.3 p.534*

Macmillan Encyclopedia of Chemistry, Set. *v.5 p.257*

Macmillan Encyclopedia of Death and Dying, Set. . *v.4 p.678*

Macmillan Encyclopedia of Earth Sciences, Set. *v.5 p.417*

Macmillan Encyclopedia of Energy. *v.5 p.360, p.361, p.453, p.455, p.457*

Macmillan's Magazine, 1859-1907: No Flippancy or Abuse Allowed. *v.6 p.740, p.742*

Maconochie's Gentlemen: The Story of Norfolk Island and the Roots of Modern Prison Reform. *v.6 p.273*

Macroeconometrics: Developments, Tensions and Prospects. *v.4 p.202*

Macroeconomic Instability and Coordination: Selected Essays of Axel Leijonhufvud. *v.4 p.240*

Macroeconomics and the Real World: Econometric Techniques and Macroeconomic, Vol. 1. . . . .*v.4 p.198*

Macroeconomics and the Real World: Keynesian Economics, Unemployment, and Policy, Vol. 2. . . . . .*v.4 p.198, p.225*

The Macroeconomics of Open Economies: An Introduction to Aggregate Behavior and Policy. *v.4 p.238*

Macroeconomics Policies and Poverty. *v.4 p.240, p.266*

Macroevolutionary Dynamics: Species, Niches and Adaptive Peaks. *v.5 p.198*

The Macrogalleria; A Cyberland of Polymer Fun. .*v.5 p.321*

MacTutor History of Mathematics Archive. *v.5 p.467*

The Maculate Muse: Obscene Language in Attic Comedy. *v.2 p.401, p.402*

Mad As Hell: Revolt at the Ballot Box, 1992. . . . . .*v.3 p.447*

Mad Mary Lamb: Lunacy and Murder in Literary London. *v.2 p.298*

The Mad Potter of Biloxi: The Art and Life of George E. Ohr. *v.1 p.807*

Mad Seasons: The Story of the First Women's Professional Basketball League, 1978-1981. . . . .*v.4 p.809, p.837, p.854*

Mad Shadows. *v.2 p.538*

Mad to Be Saved: The Beats, the '50s, and Film. .*v.6 p.343, p.344*

Madagascar: Conflicts of Authority in the Great Island. .*v.6 p.67*

Madagascar: Politics, Economics, and Society. *v.6 p.67*

Madam President: Women Blazing the Leadership Trail. .*v.4 p.526*

Madame Bovary. *v.2 p.490, p.491*

Madame Chiang Kai-Shek and Her China. .*v.6 p.189, p.202, p.217*

Madame de Lafayette. *v.2 p.474*

Madame de Stael, Novelist: The Emergence of the Artist As Woman. *v.2 p.500, p.501*

Madame Mao: The White-Boned Demon. . . .*v.6 p.200, p.217*

Made from This Earth: American Women and Nature. .*v.5 p.230*

Made in China: What Western Managers Can Learn from Trailblazing Chinese Entrepreneurs. *v.4 p.59, p.68*

Made in Texas: George W. Bush and the Southern Takeover of American Politics. *v.3 p.509*

Made in the Philippines: Gendered Discourses and the Making of Migrants. *v.6 p.117, p.120, p.130*

Madeleine L'Engle Herself: Reflections on a Writing Life. *v.2 p.149*

Madeline Hunter's Mastery Teaching: Increasing Instructional Effectiveness in Elementary and Secondary Schools. .*v.4 p.343*

Mademoiselle de Maupin. *v.2 p.492*

Mademoiselle Fifi and Other Stories. *v.2 p.497*

Madhumalati: An Indian Sufi Romance. *v.6 p.152*

Madison: A History of the Formative Years. *v.3 p.517*

The Madman and the Nun and the Crazy Locomotive: Three Plays (Including "The Water Hen"). *v.2 p.792*

A Madman's Defense. *v.2 p.631*

The Madman's Middle Way: Reflections on Reality of a Tibetan Monk Gendun Chopel. *v.6 p.241*

Madmen and Specialists. *v.2 p.758*

Madness and Lust: A Psychoanalytic Approach to Don Quixote. *v.2 p.649*

The Madonna Companion: Two Decades of Commentary. *v.1 p.272, p.338*

The Madonna of 115th Street: Faith and Community in Italian Harlem, 1880-1950. . . . .*v.1 p.544, p.607*

The Madonna of Excelsior: A Novel. *v.2 p.756*

Madonna's Drowned Worlds: New Approaches to Her Subcultural Transformations, 1983-2003. . .*v.1 p.269, p.338*

La Madre: The Woman and the Priest. *v.2 p.717*

Madrid: A Cultural and Literary Companion. *v.3 p.237*

The Madrigal. *v.1 p.181*

The Madwoman Can't Speak: or Why Insanity Is Not Subversive. *v.6 p.477, p.478*

The Madwoman in the Attic: The Woman Writer and the Nineteenth-Century Literary Imagination. *v.2 p.175, v.6 p.478, p.747, p.752*

Maestro: Greenspan's Fed and the American Boom. *v.4 p.90, p.156*

Maestros of the Pen: A History of Classical Music Criticism in America. *v.1 p.277*

Mafarka the Futurist. *v.2 p.718*

The Mafia in Havana: A Caribbean Mob Story. .*v.3 p.307, p.308*

The Mafia of a Sicilian Village, 1860-1960: A Study of Violent Peasant Entrepreneurs. *v.4 p.751*

Le maître de chasse : roman. *v.2 p.542*

Maître pathelin. *v.2 p.469*

Magazine Covers. *v.1 p.719*

The Magazine in America, 1741-1990. . . . .*v.4 p.410*

Magazine Publishers of America. *v.4 p.409*

Magazines in the Twentieth Century. *v.4 p.410*

Maggie: A Girl of the Streets. *v.2 p.36*

A Maggot. *v.2 p.346*

Magic and Medicine of Plants. *v.5 p.526*

Magic and Ritual in Tibet: The Cult of Tara. . .*v.1 p.565, p.566*

The Magic Behind the Voices: A Who's Who of Cartoon Voice Actors. *v.6 p.307*

The Magic Curtain: The Mexican-American Border in Fiction, Film, and Song. *v.6 p.488, p.491*

Magic in Medieval Manuscripts. *v.6 p.569*

Magic in the Middle Ages. *v.6 p.569*

The Magic Lantern: The Revolution of '89 Witnessed in Warsaw, Budapest, Berlin and Prague. *v.3 p.208*

The Magic Mirror: Law in American History. *v.4 p.440*

The Magic Mountains: Hill Stations and the British Raj. .*v.6 p.157*

The Magic of Blood. *v.6 p.499*

Magic of M. C. Escher. *v.1 p.757*

The Magic of Numbers and Motion: The Scientific Career of Rene Descartes. *v.5 p.391, p.395, p.396*

The Magic of Prayer: An Introduction to the Psychology of Faith. *v.5 p.633*

The Magic of Ritual: Our Need for Liberating Rites That Transform Our Lives and Our Communities. *v.1 p.530*

Magic, Reason, and Experience: Studies in the Origins and Development of Greek Science. *v.2 p.404*

Magic Seeds. *v.2 p.769*

The Magical Maze: Seeing the World Through Mathematical Eyes. *v.5 p.460*

Magical Muse: Millennial Essays on Tennessee Williams. *v.2 p.135*

Magical Mushrooms, Mischievous Molds. *v.5 p.209*

Magical Sites: Women Travelers in 19th Century Latin America. *v.3 p.350*

The Magical State: Nature, Money, and Modernity in Venezuela. *v.3 p.360*

Magical Urbanism: Latinos Reinvent the U. S. Big City. *v.6 p.548, p.717*

The Magicians. *v.2 p.378*

The Magician. *v.2 p.370*

Magill's Survey of Cinema: English Language Films, First Series, Set. *v.6 p.306*

Magill's Survey of Cinema: English Language Films, Second Series, Set. *v.6 p.306*

Magill's Survey of Cinema, Foreign Language Films, 8 vols. *v.6 p.306*

Magill's Survey of Cinema: Silent Films, Set. *v.6 p.306*

Magistrates of the Sacred: Priests and Parishioners in Eighteenth-Century Mexico. *v.3 p.264, p.288*

Magna Carta and Medieval Government. *v.3 p.68*

Magna Carta. *v.3 p.98, p.99*

Magnalia Christi Americana;. *v.3 p.485*

The Magnetic Era: Video Art in the Netherlands 1970-1985. . . . . *v.1 p.770*

The Magnetic Field of the Earth: Paleomagnetism, the Core, and the Deep Mantle. *v.5 p.444*

Magnetic Los Angeles: Planning the Twentieth-Century Metropolis. *v.6 p.728*

Magnetic Mountain: Stalinism as a Civilization. . . . *v.3 p.226*

Magnetism: Principles and Applications. *v.5 p.566*

The Magnificent Ambersons. *v.2 p.124*

The Magnificent Mughals. *v.6 p.156*

The Magnificent Ride: The First Reformation in Hussite Bohemia. *v.3 p.188*

Magnificent Tiffany Silver. *v.1 p.806*

Magnus : roman. *v.2 p.530*

Magnus Hirschfeld: A Portrait of a Pioneer in Sexology. *v.6 p.404*

Magomero: Portrait of an Africa Village. *v.6 p.76*

Magritte, 1898-1967. . . . . *v.1 p.745*

Magritte, 1898-1998. . . . . *v.1 p.749*

Magritte. *v.1 p.740*

The Magus. *v.2 p.346*

The Magyars in the Ninth Century. *v.3 p.63*

The Mahabharata: A Shortened Modern Prose Version of the Indian Epic. *v.2 p.765*

Mahan on Sea Power. *v.3 p.383*

Maharaja's Jewels. *v.1 p.716*

Mahatma Gandhi: A Biography. *v.6 p.159*

Mahayana Buddhism: The Doctrinal Foundations. . . *v.1 p.566*

Mahayana Buddhism. *v.1 p.566*

Mahayana Buddhist Meditation: Theory and Practice. *v.1 p.566*

Mahler and His World. *v.1 p.220, p.339*

The Mahler Companion. *v.1 p.219, p.339*

Mahler: Das Lied Von der Erde (The Song of the Earth). *v.1 p.215, p.235, p.339*

Mahler's Fourth Symphony. *v.1 p.227, p.244, p.339*

Mahler. *v.1 p.217, p.339*

Mahogany in Belize: A Historical Perspective. *v.3 p.297, p.298*

Maias. *v.2 p.688*

Maid in Waiting. *v.2 p.347*

Maid Marian. *v.2 p.302*

Maids and Deathwatch. *v.2 p.519*

Mailer: A Biography. *v.2 p.99*

A Maimonides Reader. *v.1 p.551*

⬚ Main Bodies [of the United Nations]. *v.4 p.635*

Main Currents in American Thought: Beginnings of Critical Realism in America, 1860-1920. . . . . *v.2 p.6*

Main Currents in American Thought: The Colonial Mind, 1620-1800. *v.2 p.6*

Main Currents in American Thought: The Romantic Revolution in America, 1800-1860. . . . . *v.2 p.6*

Main Currents in Sociological Thought: Durkheim, Pareto, Weber. *v.4 p.682*

Main Currents in Sociological Thought: Montesquieu, Comte, Marx, Tocqueville, and the Sociologists and the Revolution of 1848. . . . . *v.4 p.682*

Main Currents of Marxism: The Founders the Golden Age the Breakdown. *v.1 p.508*

Main d'oeuvre : 1913-1949. . . . . *v.2 p.525*

Main Group Chemistry. *v.5 p.303*

La main sèche. *v.2 p.545, p.546*

Main Street and Babbitt. *v.2 p.95*

Main Street on the Middle Border. *v.3 p.505*

Maine in the Early Republic: From Revolution to Statehood. *v.3 p.486*

Mainlines, Blood Feasts, Bad Taste: A Lester Bangs Reader. *v.1 p.265*

Mainstream Music of Early Twentieth Century America: The Composers, Their Times, and Their Works, 28. . . *v.1 p.280*

Mainstreaming Biodiversity in Agricultural Development: Toward Good Practice. *v.5 p.13*

Maintaining Diversity in Higher Education. *v.4 p.289*

Main-Travelled Roads. *v.2 p.39*

La Maison de Rendez-Vous and Djinn. *v.2 p.525, p.526*

La Maison de rendez-vous. *v.2 p.525*

Maitreya. *v.2 p.673*

Maize and Grace: Africa's Encounter with a New World Crop, 1500-2000. . . . . *v.5 p.22*

The Majesty of the Law: Reflections of a Supreme Court Justice. *v.4 p.466*

The Majesty That Was Islam: The Islamic World, 661-1100. . . . .*v.6 p.588, p.589*

Major Acts of Congress. *v.4 p.532*

Major Canadian Authors: A Critical Introduction to Canadian Literature in English. *v.2 p.731*

The Major Critics: The Development of English Literary Criticism. *v.2 p.163*

Major Events in the History of Life. *v.5 p.81*

Major International Treaties, 1914-1945: A History and Guide with Texts. *v.4 p.629*

The Major Languages of Eastern Europe. *v.2 p.773*

Major League Losers: The Real Cost of Sports and Who's Paying for It. *v.4 p.886, p.889, p.892, p.897*

Major Peace Treaties of Modern History, 1648-2001. *v.4 p.629*

The Major Plays of Chikamatsu. *v.6 p.234*

Major Problems in the History of Imperial Russia. .*v.3 p.209*

Major Psychological Assessment Instruments. *v.5 p.601*

Major Themes of the Qur'an. *v.1 p.556*

Major Theories of Personality Disorder. *v.5 p.661*

The Major Transitions in Evolution. *v.5 p.194*

Major Trends and Issues in Early Childhood Education: Challenges, Controversies, and Insights. *v.4 p.369*

Major Trends in Jewish Mysticism. *v.1 p.552*

Major Violation: A Balancing Act: Sports and Education. *v.4 p.821, p.894*

The Major Works of Heinrich von Kleist. *v.2 p.599*

The Major Works. *v.2 p.246, p.263, p.271, p.272*

Major Works. *v.2 p.278*

Majority Rule or Minority Will: Adherence to Precedent on the U. S. Supreme Court. *v.4 p.540*

Makbara. *v.2 p.657, p.658*

Make It Bigger. *v.1 p.713*

Make it Happen: Small business Start-up. *v.4 p.87*

Make It New: Essays. *v.2 p.569, p.575*

Make Love, Not War: The Sexual Revolution: an Unfettered History. *v.4 p.746*

Make No Law: The Sullivan Case and the First Amendment. *v.4 p.405, p.443*

Make Your Life Tax Deductible: Easy Techniques to Reduce Your Taxes and Start Building Wealth Immediately. *v.4 p.68*

Make-Believe: The Broadway Musical in the 1920s. . *v.1 p.252*

The Maker's Hand: American Studio Furniture 1940-1990. . . . .*v.1 p.803*

Makers of American Diplomacy, from Benjamin Franklin to Henry Kissinger. *v.3 p.386*

The Makers of Modern Economics, Vol. 2. .*v.4 p.215, p.217, p.223*

The Makers of Modern Economics, Vol. 3. . . . . .*v.4 p.193*

The Makers of Modern Economics, Vol. 4. . . . . .*v.4 p.193*

The Makers of Modern Economics. *v.4 p.193*

Makers of Modern Strategy: From Machiavelli to the Nuclear Age. *v.3 p.36*

Make-up, Hair and Costume for Film and Television. *v.6 p.351*

Makiko's Diary: A Merchant Wife in 1910 Kyoto. . .*v.6 p.227*

Making a Good Script Great. *v.6 p.353*

Making a Living: Changing Livelihoods in Rural Africa. *v.4 p.772*

Making a Living in the Middle Ages: The People of Britain 850-1520. . . . .*v.4 p.702, v.6 p.557, p.558*

Making a Place for Ourselves: The Black Hospital Movement, 1920-1945. . . . .*v.5 p.513*

Making a Place for Pleasure in Early Childhood Education. *v.4 p.369*

Making a Scene: The Contemporary Drama of Jewish-American Women. *v.2 p.24, p.25*

Making a Social Body: British Cultural Formation, 1830-1864. . . . .*v.6 p.751*

Making Agreements in Medieval Catalonia: Power, Order, and the Written Word, 1000-1200. . . . .*v.3 p.238*

Making American Foreign Policy: President - Congress Relations from the Second World War to the Post-Cold War Era. *v.3 p.451*

Making Americans: Jews and the Broadway Musical. *v.1 p.253, p.300*

Making and Marketing Arms. *v.4 p.608*

Making and Remaking Asian America Through Immigration Policy, 1850-1990. . . . .*v.6 p.118, p.121*

Making and Remaking Italy : The Cultivation of National Identity Around the Risorgimento. *v.3 p.201*

Making and Remaking Italy: The Cultivation of National Identity Around the Risorgimento. *v.3 p.201*

Making and Unmaking of Empires: Britain, India, and America c.1750-1783. . . . .*v.3 p.74*

Making and Using Terrariums and Planters. *v.5 p.229*

Making Art Safely: Alternatives in Drawing, Painting, Printmaking, Graphic Design, and Photography. *v.1 p.751, p.760*

Making Babies, Making Families: What Matters Most in an Age of Reproductive Technologies, Surrogacy, Adoption, and Same-Sex and Unwed Parents' Rights. *v.4 p.734, v.6 p.376, p.377*

Making Beats: The Art of Sample-Based Hip-Hop. *v.1 p.274, p.388*

Making Better Environmental Decisions: An Alternative to Risk Assessment. *v.6 p.301*

Making Callaloo: 25 years of Black Literature. . .*v.6 p.27, p.29*

Making Canadian Indian Policy: The Hidden Agenda, 1968-1970. . . . .*v.6 p.690, p.693*

Making Certain It Goes On: The Collected Poems of Richard Hugo. *v.2 p.81*

Making China Policy: From Nixon to G. W. Bush. .*v.3 p.388*

Making Civil Rights Law: Thurgood Marshall and the Supreme Court, 1936-1961. . . . .*v.4 p.457, p.458*

Making Connections: Brain, Mind, and Culture in a Social Anthropology. *v.4 p.27*

Making Constitutional Law: Thurgood Marshall and the Supreme Court, 1961-1991. . . . .*v.4 p.469*

Making Creativity Practical: Innovation That Gets Results. *v.4 p.66*

Making Democracy: Leadership, Class, Gender, and Political Participation in Thailand. *v.4 p.622*

Making Democracy Work: Civic Traditions in Modern Italy. *v.3 p.204, v.4 p.594*

Making Ecopreneurs: Developing Sustainable
Entrepreneurship. *v.4 p.51, p.52, p.54*

Making Ends Meet: How Single Mothers Survive Welfare and
Low-Wage Work. *v.6 p.466*

Making Ethnic Choices: California's Punjabi Mexican
Americans. *v.6 p.110, p.123, p.137*

Making Ethnic Ways: Communities and Their Transformations
in Taita, Kenya, 1800-1950. . . . . *v.6 p.64*

Making European Space: Mobility, Power and Territorial
Identity. *v.4 p.397*

Making Face, Making Soul - Haciendo Caras: Creative and
Critical Perspectives by Feminists of Color. . . . *v.6 p.477*

Making Gay History: The Half-Century Fight for Lesbian and
Gay Equal Rights. *v.6 p.365, p.387*

Making Girls into Women: American Women's Writing and the
Rise of Lesbian Identity. *v.2 p.6, p.11*

Making Good: How Ex-Convicts Reform and Rebuild Their
Lives. *v.6 p.279*

Making Good: How Young People Cope with Moral Dilemmas
at Work. *v.4 p.55*

Making History: An Oral History of the Struggle for Gay and
Lesbian Civil Rights, 1945-1990. . . . . . *v.6 p.365, p.366*

Making History Matter. *v.3 p.376*

Making Israel. *v.6 p.614*

Making It Whole: A Victorian Circle and the Shape of Their
World. *v.6 p.751, p.756, p.757*

Making Latino News: Race, Language, Class. *v.6 p.494*

Making Laws and Making News: Media Strategies in the U. S.
House of Representatives. *v.4 p.533*

Making Midwives Legal: Childbirth, Medicine, and the
Law. *v.4 p.445*

Making Monsters: False Memories, Psychotherapy, and Sexual
Hysteria. *v.4 p.714*

Making More Waves: New Writing by Asian American
Women. *v.6 p.91, p.92*

Making Movies. *v.6 p.347*

Making Museums Matter. *v.1 p.829*

Making Music in the Arab World: The Culture and Artistry of
Tarab. *v.1 p.287*

Making Music Modern: New York in the 1920s. *v.1 p.220, p.279*

Making Music on the Organ. *v.1 p.398*

Making Musicals: An Informal Introduction to the World of
Musical Theater. *v.1 p.404*

The Making of a Chicano Militant: Lessons from
Cristal. *v.6 p.489, p.538*

The Making of a Christian Aristocracy: Social and Religious
Change in the Western Roman Empire. *v.3 p.32*

The Making of a Continent. *v.5 p.432*

The Making of a Court Society: Kings and Nobles in Late
Medieval Portugal. *v.3 p.243*

Making of a Gay Asian Community: An Oral History of
Pre-AIDS Los Angeles. . . . *v.6 p.113, p.115, p.366, p.367*

The Making of a Musical. *v.1 p.404*

The Making of a Myth: The United States and China,
1897-1912. . . . . *v.3 p.393*

The Making of a Name: The Inside Story of the Brands We
Buy. *v.4 p.142*

The Making of a Nation in the Balkans: Bulgaria: from History
to Historiography. *v.3 p.251*

The Making of a Nation in the Balkans: Historiography of the
Bulgarian Revival. *v.3 p.251*

The Making of a Scientist. *v.5 p.395*

The Making of a Teacher: Teacher Knowledge and Teacher
Education. *v.4 p.279*

The Making of Americans: An Opera and a Play from the Novel
by Gertrude Stein. *v.2 p.122*

The Making of an Arab Nationalist: Ottomanism and Arabism in
the Life and Thought of Sati' al-Husri. *v.6 p.582*

The Making of an Artist, 1803-1832. . . . . *v.1 p.195, p.310*

The Making of an Enterprise: The Society of Jesus in Portugal,
Its Empire, and Beyond, 1540-1750. . . . . . *v.3 p.334*

The Making of an Industrial Society: Whickham,
1560-1765. . . . . *v.3 p.100, p.123*

The Making of an Inmate. *v.6 p.276*

The Making of Anthropology in East and Southeast Asia. *v.4 p.39*

The Making of Asian America Through Political
Participation. *v.6 p.120*

The Making of Byzantium, 600-1025. . . . . *v.3 p.194*

The Making of Cabaret. *v.1 p.250*

The Making of Chaucer's English: A Study of Words. *v.2 p.207*

The Making of Czech Jewry: National Conflict and Jewish
Society in Bohemia, 1870-1918. . . . . *v.3 p.188*

The Making of Economic Society. *v.4 p.209*

The Making of Economics: The Foundation. *v.4 p.185*

The Making of England: To 1399. . . . . . . *v.3 p.97, p.98*

The Making of Environmental Law. *v.4 p.448*

The Making of Europe: An Introduction to the History of
European Unity. *v.3 p.66*

The Making of Europe: Conquest, Colonization, and Cultural
Change, 9500-1350. . . . . *v.3 p.67*

The Making of Geology: Earth Science in Britain,
1660-1815. . . . . *v.5 p.418*

The Making of Green Knowledge: Environmental Politics and
Cultural Transformation. *v.6 p.300*

The Making of Guys and Dolls. *v.1 p.250, p.337*

The Making of Gypsy. *v.1 p.250*

The Making of Homeric Verse: The Collected Papers of Milman
Parry. *v.2 p.415*

The Making of Iran's Islamic Revolution: From Monarchy to
Islamic Republic. *v.6 p.631*

The Making of Ireland: A History. *v.3 p.135*

The Making of Jewish and Christian Worship. *v.1 p.653, p.654*

The Making of Latin London: Salsa Music, Place and
Identity. *v.3 p.267*

The Making of Marx's Capital. *v.4 p.236*

The Making of Masculinities: The New Men's
Studies. *v.6 p.369, p.428, p.429*

The Making of Meander's Comedy. *v.2 p.416*

Making of Michigan, 1820-1860: A Pioneer Anthology. *v.3 p.516*

The Making of Modern British Politics,
1867-1939. . . . . *v.3 p.95, p.114*

The Making of Modern Burma. *v.6 p.165, p.166*

Making of Modern Colombia: A Nation in Spite of
Itself. *v.3 p.357*

The Making of Modern Drama: A Study of Bhuchner, Ibsen, Strindberg, Chekhov, Pirandello, Brecht, Handke. . .*v.1 p.82*

The Making of Modern Irish History: Revisionism and the Revisionist Controversy. *v.3 p.135*

The Making of Modern Japan. *v.6 p.224*

The Making of Modern Lebanon. *v.6 p.605*

The Making of Modern Libya: State Formation, Colonization, and Resistance, 1830-1932. . . . .*v.4 p.582, v.6 p.60, p.640*

The Making of Modern Poetry in Canada: Essential Articles on Contemporary Canadian Poetry in English. *v.2 p.729*

The Making of Modern South Africa: Conquest, Segregation and Apartheid. *v.6 p.80*

The Making of Modern Switzerland, 1848-1998. . .*v.3 p.244*

The Making of Modern Tibet. *v.6 p.241*

The Making of Modern Turkey. *v.6 p.623*

The Making of Modern Woman. *v.3 p.55*

The Making of Moral Theology: A Study of the Roman Catholic Tradition. *v.1 p.574*

The Making of My Fair Lady. *v.1 p.250, p.337*

The Making of Piers Plowman. *v.2 p.211*

The Making of Portuguese Democracy. . . .*v.3 p.244, v.4 p.608*

The Making of Psychological Anthropology. . . .*v.4 p.35, p.36*

The Making of Revolutionary Paris. .*v.3 p.147, p.158,v.6 p.712*

The Making of Russian Absolutism, 1613-1801. .*v.3 p.215, p.216*

The Making of Saudi Arabia, 1916-1936: From Chieftancy to Monarchical State. *v.6 p.626*

The Making of Sikh Scripture. *v.1 p.540*

The Making of Telecommunication Policy. *v.4 p.420*

The Making of the Cold War Enemy: Culture and Politics in the Military-Intellectual Complex. *v.3 p.454*

The Making of the Creeds. *v.1 p.646*

Making of the English Landscape. *v.3 p.126*

The Making of the English Landscape. *v.6 p.575*

Making of the English Landscape. *v.6 p.575*

The Making of the English Middle Class: Business, Society and Family Life in London 1660-1730. . .*v.3 p.105, p.106, p.130*

The Making of the English Working Class. *v.3 p.116, p.131,v.4 p.725*

The Making of the Filipino Nation and Republic: From Barangays, Tribes, Sultanates and Colony (Ang Pagbubuo Ng Bansa at Republika Ng Pilipinas: Mula sa Mga Barangay, Tribu, Sultanato at Kolonya. . . .*v.6 p.178, p.179*

The Making of the Georgian Nation. *v.3 p.230*

The Making of the Hapsburg Monarchy, 1550-1700: An Interpretation. *v.3 p.181*

The Making of the Jewish Middle Class: Women, Family, and Identity in Imperial Germany. *v.3 p.164, p.180*

The Making of the Magdalen: Preaching and Popular Devotion in the Later Middle Ages. *v.6 p.571*

Making of the Mexican Mind: A Study in Recent Mexican Thought. *v.3 p.295*

The Making of the Middle Ages. *v.3 p.68, v.6 p.564*

The Making of the "Poema de Mio Cid". *v.2 p.646*

The Making of the Modern Body: Sexuality and Society in the Nineteenth-Century. *v.6 p.760*

The Making of the Modern Family. *v.4 p.739*

Making of the Modern Gulf States: Kuwait, Bahrain, Qatar, the United Arab Emirates and Oman. *v.6 p.626, p.627, p.628, p.629*

The Making of the Modern University: Intellectual Transformation and the Marginalization of Morality. .*v.4 p.332*

The Making of the Monroe Doctrine. *v.3 p.417*

The Making of the Mosaic: A History of Canadian Immigration Policy. *v.4 p.764, p.765*

The Making of the National Labor Relations Board: A Study in Economics, Politics, and the Law, 1933-1937. . .*v.4 p.446*

The Making of the National Poet: Shakespeare, Adaptation and Authorship, 1660-1769. . . . .*v.2 p.229*

The Making of the President, 1960. . . . .*v.3 p.450*

The Making of the Representative for Planet 8. . . . .*v.2 p.365*

The Making of the Roman Army: From Republic to Empire. *v.3 p.28*

The Making of the Second Reform Bill. *v.3 p.115*

The Making of the Slavs: History and Archaeology of the Lower Danube Region, c. 500-700. . .*v.3 p.62, p.192, p.214*

The Making of Urban Europe, 1000-1994. . .*v.3 p.44, v.6 p.713*

The Making of Victorian Drama. *v.2 p.188*

The Making of Victorian England. *v.3 p.111, p.113, p.127,v.6 p.735*

The Making of Victorian Sexuality. *v.6 p.760*

The Making of West Side Story. *v.1 p.250, p.311*

Making PCR: Story of Biotechnology. *v.5 p.219*

Making Peace: A First Hand Account of the Arab-Israeli Peace Process. *v.4 p.648*

Making Peace Pay: A Bibliography on Disarmament and Conversion. *v.4 p.656*

Making Places Special: Stories of Real Places Made Better by Planning. *v.6 p.726*

Making Plays: Interviews with Contemporary British Dramatists and Directors. *v.2 p.189*

Making Policy in Europe. *v.4 p.636*

Making Political Geography. *v.4 p.487, p.495*

Making Sense: A Student's Guide to Research and Writing: Geography and Environmental Sciences. *v.4 p.376*

Making Sense of Children's Drawings. *v.5 p.629*

Making Sense of Cities. *v.4 p.395, v.6 p.720*

Making Sense of Intellectual Capital: Designing a Method for the Valuation of Intangibles. *v.4 p.72*

Making Sense of Methods in the Classroom: A Pedagogical Presence. *v.4 p.348*

Making Sense of the Bible: Literary Type As an Approach to Understanding. *v.1 p.617*

Making Sense of the Molly Maguires. *v.4 p.126, p.127*

Making Sense of the Organization. *v.4 p.174*

Making Shapely Fiction. *v.2 p.579*

The Making, Shaping, and Treating of Steel: Ironmaking Volume. *v.5 p.736*

The Making, Shaping and Treating of Steel: Steelmaking and Refining Volume. *v.5 p.687, p.736*

Making Silent Stones Speak: Human Evolution and the Dawn of Technology. *v.4 p.17*

Making Space in the Early Modern Atlantic World. . .*v.4 p.399*

Making Space: Property Development and Urban Planning. *v.6 p.728*

Making Sweatshops: The Globalization of the U. S. Apparel Industry. *v.4 p.665*

Making the American Self: Jonathan Edwards to Abraham Lincoln. *v.4 p.694*

Making the American Team: Sport, Culture, and the Olympic Experience. *v.4 p.815, p.845, p.891, p.898*

Making the Corn Belt: A Geographical History of Middle-Western Agriculture. *v.3 p.506, v.5 p.4*

Making the Fascist Self: The Political Culture of Interwar Italy. *v.3 p.202, p.203*

Making the Foreign Serve China: Managing Foreigners in the People's Republic. *v.6 p.203*

Making the Grade: Reinventing America's Schools. . *v.4 p.330*

Making the Majors: The Transformation of Team Sports in America. *v.4 p.851, p.888, p.891, p.896*

Making the Right Connections: A Guide for Nature Writers. *v.5 p.232*

Making the Rugby World: Race, Gender, Commerce. *v.4 p.814, p.865*

Making the White Man's Indian: Native Americans and Hollywood Movies. *v.6 p.700*

Making Things Perfectly Queer: Interpreting Mass Culture. *v.6 p.390*

Making Tough Decisions: Tactics for Improving Managerial Decision Making. *v.4 p.83*

Making Transcendence Transparent: An Intuitive Approach to Classical Transcendental Number Theory. *v.5 p.475*

Making Trouble: Essays on Gay History, Politics, and the University. *v.6 p.386*

Making Urban Transport Sustainable. *v.6 p.728*

Making Vancouver, 1863-1913. . . . . . *v.6 p.714*

Making Visible the Invisible: An Anthology of Original Essays on Film Acting. *v.6 p.348*

Making Vocational Choices: A Theory of Vocational Personalities and Work Environments. *v.5 p.577*

Making Votes Count: Strategic Coordination in the World's Electoral Systems. *v.4 p.577, p.578*

Making Waves: An Anthology of Writings by and about Asian American Women. *v.6 p.91*

Making Waves: Essays. *v.2 p.686*

Making Waves. *v.5 p.544*

Making Whiteness: The Culture of Segregation in the South, 1890-1940. . . . . . *v.3 p.496*

Making Women Pay: The Hidden Costs of Fetal Rights. *v.4 p.442, p.774, v.6 p.471*

Making Workers Soviet: Power, Class, and Identity. . *v.3 p.223*

The Makioka Sisters. *v.6 p.233*

Mala Yerba/Esa Sangre. *v.2 p.667*

Malachi: A New Translation with Introduction and Commentary. *v.1 p.622*

The Malagasy and the Europeans. *v.6 p.67*

Malan to de Klerk: Leadership in the Apartheid State. *v.4 p.614*

Malawi: Foreign Policy and Development. *v.6 p.76*

Malawi: The History of the Nation. *v.6 p.76*

Malawi: The Politics of Despair. *v.6 p.76*

Malay Fishermen. *v.4 p.39*

Malcolm Lowry: A Biography. *v.2 p.367*

Malcolm Lowry. *v.2 p.367*

Malcolm X: A Research Site. *v.6 p.12, p.16*

Malcolm X and African American Self-Consciousness. *v.6 p.16, p.32*

Malcolm. *v.2 p.110, v.6 p.398*

The Malcontent and Other Plays. *v.2 p.222*

Male and Female: The Classic Study of the Sexes. . *v.4 p.748*

The Male Body: A New Look at Men in Public and in Private. *v.6 p.369, p.428, p.447*

Male Call: Becoming Jack London. *v.2 p.95*

The Male Dancer: Bodies, Spectacle and Sexualities. . *v.1 p.40*

Male Desire: The Homoerotic in American Art. *v.1 p.707, v.6 p.407*

Male Homosexual Behavior and the Effects of AIDS Education: A Study of Behavior and Safer Sex in New Zealand and South Australia. *v.4 p.779*

The Male Homosexual in Literature: A Bibliography. *v.6 p.359, p.360, p.391*

Male Prostitution. *v.4 p.749*

Male to Male: Sexual Feelings Across the Boundaries of Identity. *v.4 p.750, v.6 p.372*

Malebranche: Dialogues on Metaphysics and on Religion. *v.1 p.452*

Malebranche: The Search after Truth: With Elucidations of the Search after Truth. *v.1 p.452*

Malebranche. *v.1 p.452*

Malgudi Days. *v.2 p.765*

Malign Neglect: Race, Crime, and Punishment in America. *v.6 p.277*

Maligned Master: The Real Story of Antonio Salieri. *v.1 p.188, p.352*

Malinche Spanish Version: Novela. *v.2 p.667*

Malinche. *v.2 p.667, p.668*

Malinowski: Odyssey of an Anthropologist, 1884-1920. *v.4 p.5*

Malinowski, Rivers, Benedict and Others: Essays on Culture and Personality. *v.4 p.5*

Mallarme in the Twentieth Century. *v.2 p.496*

Mallarme: The Poet and His Circle. *v.2 p.496*

Mallarme's Divagations: A Guide and Commentary. . *v.2 p.496*

Mallarme's Prose Poems: A Critical Study. *v.2 p.496*

Mallarme. *v.2 p.496*

Mallarmé in Prose. *v.2 p.496*

Mallarmé, Poésies. *v.2 p.496*

Malolos: The Crisis of the Republic. *v.6 p.179*

Malone meurt. *v.2 p.509*

Malory's Morte d'Arthur: A 15th Century Chivalric Romance. *v.2 p.212*

Malory. *v.2 p.212*

Malraux: A Life. *v.2 p.522*

A Maltese Anthology. *v.6 p.657*

Malthus' Essay on Population. *v.4 p.221*

Malthus. *v.4 p.222*

Ma'luf: Reflections on the Arab Andalusian Music of Tunisia. *v.1 p.286*

Mama Dada: Gertrude Stein's Avant-Garde Theater. . . *v.2 p.121*

Mama Lola: A Vodou Priestess in Brooklyn. *v.1 p.542*

Maman a un amant : roman. *v.2 p.544*

Mambisas. *v.3 p.312*

Mambo Kingdom: Latin Music in New York,
1926-1990. . . . . *v.1 p.294, v.6 p.519*

The Mambo Kings Play Songs of Love. . . *v.2 p.147, v.6 p.506*

Mambo Montage: The Latinization of New York
City. *v.6 p.542, p.549*

The Mamluks in Egyptian Politics and Society. . . . *v.6 p.636*

Mammals from the Age of Dinosaurs: Origins, Evolution and
Structure. *v.5 p.448*

A Mammal's Notebook: Collected Writings of Erik
Satie. *v.1 p.222, p.223, p.352*

Mammary Development and Cancer. *v.5 p.165*

Mammies No More: The Changing Image of Black Women on
Stage and Screen. *v.6 p.15, p.41*

Mammon and the Pursuit of Empire: The Political Economy of
British Imperialism, 1860-1912. . . . . . *v.6 p.745, p.746*

The Mammoth Encyclopedia of Modern Crime Fiction. *v.2 p.579*

Mammoths, Sabertooths, and Hominids: 65 Million Years of
Mammalian Evolution in Europe. *v.5 p.448*

Man Against Mass Society. *v.1 p.457*

Man Alone. *v.2 p.747*

Man and Nature in the Renaissance. *v.5 p.391*

Man and Nature, or, Physical Geography As Modified by
Human Action. *v.5 p.354, p.355, p.370*

Man and Wife in America: A History. *v.4 p.442, p.739*

Man Awakened from Dreams: One Man's Life in a North China
Village, 1857-1942. . . . . *v.6 p.190, p.200*

Man Crazy: A Novel. *v.2 p.152*

Man Descending: Selected Stories. *v.2 p.739*

Man Discovers the Galaxies. *v.5 p.71*

A Man for All Seasons: A Play in Two Acts. *v.2 p.331*

Man for Himself: An Inquiry into the Psychology of
Ethics. *v.1 p.484*

The Man from Snowy River and Other Verse. *v.2 p.748*

Man in Revolt: A Christian Anthropology. *v.1 p.642*

Man in Society: A Biosocial View. *v.4 p.684*

The Man in the Gray Flannel Suit. *v.2 p.128*

Man in the Holocene: A Story. *v.2 p.607*

The Man in the Iron Mask. *v.2 p.489*

The Man in the Panther's Skin: A Romantic Epic. . . *v.6 p.665*

The Man in the Principal's Office. *v.4 p.282*

The Man in the Red Velvet Dress: Inside the World of Cross
Dressing. *v.6 p.369*

The Man In The Street. *v.3 p.385*

Man Is Not Alone: A Philosophy of Religion. . *v.1 p.522, p.523*

The Man of Feeling. *v.2 p.251, p.661*

Man of La Mancha. *v.1 p.249, p.407*

Man of the House: The Life and Political Memoirs of Speaker
Tip O'Neill. *v.3 p.461*

Man of the People: A Life of Harry S. Truman. . . . *v.3 p.472*

The Man on Horseback: The Role of the Military in
Politics. *v.4 p.575*

The Man on the Spot: Essays on British Empire History,
31. . . . . *v.3 p.89, p.125*

The Man Outside. *v.2 p.603*

Man Ray's Montparnasse. *v.1 p.767*

The Man Versus the State: With Four Essays on Politics and
Society. *v.4 p.484, p.511*

The Man Who Changed China: The Life and Legacy of Jiang
Zemin. *v.6 p.197, p.200*

The Man Who Could Fly and Other Stories. *v.6 p.497*

The Man Who Knew Infinity. *v.5 p.466*

The Man Who Knew Too Much: Alan Turing and the Invention
of the Computer. *v.5 p.590*

The Man Who Listens to Horses. *v.4 p.848*

The Man Who Lived Alone. *v.2 p.82*

The Man Who Lost His Shadow. *v.6 p.659*

The Man Who Loved Children. *v.2 p.749*

The Man Who Loved Only Numbers: The Story of Paul Erdos
and the Search for Mathematical Truth. *v.5 p.466*

The Man Who Mistook His Wife for a Hat: And Other Clinical
Tales. *v.5 p.516*

The Man Who Once Was Whizzer White. *v.4 p.468*

The Man Who Saved Kabuki: Faubion Bowers and Theatre
Censorship in Occupied Japan. *v.6 p.228*

The Man Who Shocked the World: The Life and Legacy of
Stanley Milgram. *v.5 p.645*

The Man Who Would Be King and Other Stories. . . *v.2 p.297*

The Man Who Would Be Queen: The Psychology of
Gender-Bending and Transsexualism. *v.6 p.380*

The Man Who Would Dam the Amazon and Other Accounts
from Afield. *v.5 p.230*

The Man Who Would Marry Susan Sontag: And Other Intimate
Portraits of the Bohemian Era. *v.2 p.10*

The Man with the Black Coat: Russia's Literature of the
Absurd. *v.2 p.794*

The Man with the Golden Arm. *v.2 p.56*

The Man with the Heart in the Highlands and Other Early
Stories. *v.2 p.118*

The Man Within. *v.2 p.351*

The Man Without Qualities. *v.2 p.614*

Managed Care: What It Is and How It Works. *v.5 p.509*

Management and the Arts. *v.1 p.825, p.826*

Management Communication. *v.4 p.171*

Management Consulting: Emergence and Dynamics of a
Knowledge Industry. *v.4 p.64, p.65*

Management Consulting Today. *v.4 p.65*

Management Control: Theories, Issues and Performance. *v.4 p.72*

Management of Infections in Immunocompromised
Patients. *v.5 p.517*

Management of Lakes and Ponds. *v.5 p.32*

The Management of Sport: Its Foundation and Application with
PowerWeb Bind-In Card. *v.4 p.786, p.885*

Management Research: An Introduction. *v.4 p.119*

Management Strategies in Athletic Training. *v.4 p.829*

Managerial Presidency. *v.4 p.527*

Managers and the Legal Environment: Strategies for the 21st
Century. *v.4 p.51*

The Manager's Guide to Strategy. *v.4 p.81*

Managers Not MBAs: A Hard Look at the Soft Practice of Managing and Management Development. . .*v.4 p.176, p.177*

Managers of Innovation: Insights into Making Innovation Happen. *v.4 p.67*

Managers of Virtue: Public School Leadership in America, 1820-1980. . . . .*v.4 p.282*

Managing Across Borders: The Transnational Solution. *v.4 p.58, p.64*

Managing Agricultural Biotechnology: Addressing Research Program Needs and Policy Implications. *v.5 p.7*

Managing Arsenic in the Environment: From Soil to Human Health. *v.5 p.379*

e Managing Business Support Services: Strategies for Outsourcing and Facilities Management. *v.4 p.113*

Managing Cities: The New Urban Context. .*v.4 p.543, v.6 p.723*

Managing Customer Relationships on the Internet. . . *v.4 p.143*

Managing Customers as Investments: The Strategic Value of Customers in the Long Run. *v.4 p.143*

Managing Democracy in Central America, a Case Study: United States Election Supervision in Nicaragua, 1927-1933. . . . .*v.3 p.301*

Managing Diversity: Toward a Globally Inclusive Workplace. *v.4 p.132*

Managing Egypt's Poor and the Politics of Benevolence, 1800-1952. . . . .*v.6 p.637*

Managing E-Learning: Design, Delivery, Implementation, and Evaluation. *v.4 p.322*

Managing E-Mail and Internet Use: A Practical Guide to Employer's Obligations and Employee's Rights. . .*v.4 p.131*

Managing Fiscal Strain in Major American Cities: Understanding Retrenchment in the Public Sector, 247. . . . .*v.4 p.544*

Managing Gender: Affirmative Action and Organizational Power in Australian, Canadian, and New Zealand Sport. . *v.4 p.837*

Managing Gigabytes: Compressing and Indexing Documents and Images. *v.5 p.341, p.342*

Managing Globalization in Developing Countries and Transition Economies: Building Capacities for a Changing World. *v.4 p.665*

Managing in a Time of Great Change. *v.4 p.72*

Managing in the Global Economy. *v.4 p.70*

Managing Innovation in the Arts: Making Art Work. . .*v.1 p.826*

Managing Interactively: Executing Business Strategy, Improving Communication, and Creating a Knowledge-Sharing Culture. *v.4 p.172*

Managing Knowledge for Sustained Competitive Advantage: Designing Strategies for Effective Human Resource Management. *v.4 p.76*

Managing Mathematical Projects - With Success!. . .*v.5 p.458*

Managing Mobility in African Rangelands: The Legitimization of Transhumance. *v.6 p.294*

Managing New Industry Creation: Global Knowledge Formation and Entrepreneurship in High Technology. . .*v.4 p.69, p.70*

Managing Organizational Deviance. *v.4 p.131*

Managing Product Development. *v.4 p.118*

Managing Service in Food and Beverage Operations. *v.4 p.165*

Managing Socialism: From Old Cadres to New Professionals in Revolutionary Cuba. *v.3 p.309*

Managing Sport and Risk Management Strategies. *v.4 p.882, p.886, p.900*

Managing Sport Organizations. *v.4 p.882*

Managing the Academic Enterprise: Case Studies for Deans and Provosts. *v.4 p.293*

Managing the Construction Process: Estimating, Scheduling, and Project Control. *v.4 p.158*

Managing the Environmental Crisis: Incorporating Competing Values in Natural Resource Administration. *v.4 p.62*

Managing the Modern Herbarium: An Interdisciplinary Approach. *v.5 p.85, p.86*

Managing the Nonprofit Organization. *v.4 p.72, p.73*

Managing the Organizational Melting Pot: Dilemmas of Workplace Diversity. *v.4 p.132*

Managing the President's Program: Presidential Leadership and Legislative Policy Formulation. *v.4 p.527*

Managing to Make a Difference: Making an Impact on the Careers of Men and Women Scientists. *v.5 p.77, p.244*

Managing Uncertainty in the House of Representatives: Adaptation and Innovation in Special Rules. *v.4 p.532, p.533*

Managing White Supremacy: Race, Politics, and Citizenship in Jim Crow Virginia. *v.3 p.500*

Managing with Power: Politics and Influence in Organizations. *v.4 p.73*

Manchus and Han: Ethnic Relations and Political Power in Late Qing and Early Republican China, 1861-1928. . . . .*v.4 p.623, p.624,v.6 p.191*

The Manchus. *v.6 p.239*

The Manciple's Tale. *v.2 p.208*

Mandarins of the Future: Modernization Theory in Cold War America. *v.3 p.371*

Les Mandarins. *v.2 p.508*

Les mandarins. *v.2 p.508*

Mandate Days: British Lives in Palestine, 1918-1948. .*v.6 p.612*

Mandated Reporting of Suspected Child Abuse: Ethics, Law and Policy. *v.4 p.756*

Mandates and Empire: The League of Nations and Africa, 1914-1931. . . . .*v.4 p.631*

Mande Music: Traditional and Modern Music of the Maninka and Mandinka of Western Africa. *v.1 p.285*

Mandela: The Authorized Biography. *v.6 p.78*

Mandelshtam: Selected Poems. *v.2 p.806*

Mandrakes from the Holy Land. *v.6 p.650*

The Man-Eater of Malgudi. *v.2 p.765*

Manet and the Family Romance. *v.1 p.743*

Manet: And the Painters of Contemporary Life. . . .*v.1 p.742*

Manet: The Still Life Paintings. *v.1 p.744*

Manet's Silence and the Poetics of Bouquets. *v.1 p.746*

Manet. *v.1 p.737*

Manet/Velazquez: The French Taste for Spanish Painting. *v.1 p.733*

Maneuvers: The International Politics of Militarizing Women's Lives. *v.6 p.464*

The Mangle of Practice: Time, Agency, and Science. *v.5 p.403*

Manhood in America. *v.4 p.745, v.6 p.429*

Manias, Panics, and Crashes: A History of Financial Crises. *v.4 p.95, p.100, p.147, p.244, p.263*

Manic Depression and Creativity. *v.5 p.659*

Manic-Depressive Illness. *v.5 p.517*

Manichaeism in the Later Roman Empire and Medieval China. *v.1 p.646*

Manifest Design: America Exceptionalism and Empire. .*v.3 p.381*

Manifest Destiny: A Primary Source History of the Settlement of the American Heartland in the Late 19th Century. .*v.3 p.381*

Manifest Destiny and Mission in American History. . .*v.3 p.381*

Manifest Manhood and the Antebellum American Empire. *v.3 p.381*

Manifestations of Discontent in Germany on the Eve of the Reformation: A Collection of Documents Selected, Translated, and Introduced by Gerald Strauss. . . .*v.3 p.163*

Manifesto for Philosophy. *v.1 p.455*

Manifestoes of Surrealism. *v.1 p.480*

Manifestos Manifest. *v.2 p.680*

The Manikin: A Novel. *v.2 p.155*

The Manipulators: Personality and Politics in Multiple Perspectives. *v.5 p.643*

Manitoba: The Keystone Province: An Illustrated History. *v.3 p.546*

Manitoba. *v.3 p.546*

Mankiller: A Chief and Her People. *v.6 p.690, p.693*

Manliness and Morality: Middle-Class Masculinity in Britain and America, 1800-1940. . . . .*v.4 p.817*

Manliness and the Boys' Story Paper in Britain: A Cultural History, 1855-1940. . . . .*v.6 p.746*

The Manly Art: Bare-Knuckle Prize Fighting in America. *v.4 p.805, p.806, p.855*

Manly States: Masculinities, International Relations, and Gender Politics. *v.6 p.441*

Man-Made Medicine: Women's Health, Public Policy and Reform. *v.6 p.444*

Mann Ohne Eigenschaften. *v.2 p.614*

Mannerism and Anti-Mannerism in Italian Painting. . .*v.1 p.727*

Mann's "Der Untertan". *v.2 p.613*

Manon Lescaut. *v.2 p.481*

Man's Fate. *v.2 p.522, v.6 p.192, p.216*

Man's Most Dangerous Myth: The Fallacy of Race. . .*v.4 p.729*

A Man's Place: Masculinity and the Middle-Class Home in Victorian England. *v.6 p.749*

A Man's Place. *v.2 p.530*

A Man's Reach: The Philosophy of Judge Jerome Frank. *v.4 p.437*

Man's Role in Changing the Face of the Earth. . . .*v.6 p.297*

Man's Search for Meaning. *v.5 p.619*

A Man's World?: Changing Men's Practices in a Globalized World. *v.4 p.744, v.6 p.430*

Manservant and Maidservant. *v.2 p.339*

Mansfeld's World Manual of Agricultural and Horticultural Crops. *v.5 p.21, p.25*

Mansfield Park and Persuasion. *v.2 p.268*

A Mansion in the Sky: And Other Short Stories. . . .*v.6 p.673*

The Mansions and the Shanties (Sobrados E Mucambos): The Making of Modern Brazil. *v.3 p.340*

Mantle Convection: Plate Tectonics and Global Dynamics. *v.5 p.442*

The Mantle of the Prophet: Religion and Politics in Iran. .*v.6 p.632*

Manual de Español Correcto. *v.2 p.636*

Manual de Gramática Histórica Española. *v.2 p.636*

Manual de Pronunciacion Espanola. *v.2 p.636*

Manual of Antibiotics and Infectious Diseases: Treatment and Prevention. *v.5 p.526*

Manual of Mineralogy *v.5 p.436*

The Manual of Museum Exhibitions. *v.1 p.828*

The Manual of Museum Management. *v.1 p.828*

A Manual of New Mineral Names, 1892-1978. . . .*v.5 p.435*

Manual of Nutritional Therapeutics. *v.5 p.512, p.513*

A Manual of Old English Prose. *v.2 p.168*

Manual of Organic Chemistry for Advanced Students. .*v.5 p.292*

Manual of political economy. *v.4 p.212*

Manual of Pteridology. *v.5 p.210, p.211*

Manual of Sixteenth-Century Italian Dance Steps. . .*v.1 p.22*

Manual of Soil Analysis: Monitoring and Assessing Soil Bioremediation. *v.5 p.50*

Manual of Steel Construction Allowable Stress Design. .*v.5 p.692*

Manual of Steel Construction, Load and Resistance Factor Design, 3rd Edition. *v.5 p.684, p.692*

Manual of Transportation Engineering Studies. . . .*v.5 p.701*

Manual of Voice Treatment: Pediatrics Through Geriatrics. *v.5 p.518*

The Manufacture of Madness: A Comparative Study of the Inquisition and the Mental Health Movement. . .*v.4 p.770*

The Manufactured Crisis: Myths, Fraud and the Attack on America's Public Schools. *v.4 p.324*

Manufacturing Culture: Vindications of Early Victorian Industry. *v.6 p.765*

Manufacturing Engineering Handbook. *v.5 p.684*

Manufacturing Engineer's Reference Book, Vol. 13. . .*v.5 p.684*

Manufacturing Facilities Design and Material Handling. .*v.4 p.116*

Manufacturing Handbook of Best Practices: An Innovation, Productivity, and Quality Focus. *v.4 p.119*

Manufacturing Hope and Despair: The School and Kin Support Networks of U. S.-Mexican Youth. *v.6 p.528*

Manufacturing Militance: Workers' Movements in Brazil and South Africa, 1970-1985. . . . .*v.3 p.342*

Manufacturing Montreal: The Making of an Industrial Landscape, 1850 to 1930. . . . .*v.6 p.714*

Manufacturing Processes Reference Guide. *v.5 p.684*

The Manuscript Found in Saragossa. *v.2 p.791*

Manuscrits de Pauline Archange: Vivre! Vivre! - Les Apparences. *v.2 p.538*

The Many Costs of Racism. *v.6 p.38*

The Many Faces of Defeat: The German People's Experience in 1945. . . . .*v.3 p.176*

The Many Faces of Realism. *v.1 p.514*

The Many Hands of My Relations: French and Indians on the Lower Missouri. *v.3 p.522*

The Many Landfalls of John Cabot. *v.4 p.379*

Many Lives Intertwined: A Memoir. *v.6 p.93, p.110*

The Many Lives of Academic Presidents: Association of
Governing Boards and Universities and Colleges. .*v.4 p.293*

Many Tender Ties: Women in Fur-Trade Society,
1670-1870. . . . .*v.3 p.546*

Many Thousands Gone: The First Two Centuries of Slavery in
North America. *v.6 p.3, p.37*

Many Unhappy Returns: One Man's Quest to Turn Around the
Most Unpopular Organization in America. *v.4 p.107*

Many Ways to Be Deaf. *v.4 p.22*

The Manyfaced Glass: Tennyson's Dramatic
Monologues. *v.2 p.313*

Many-Particle Physics. *v.5 p.546, p.547*

Many-Valued Logic. *v.1 p.492, p.493*

The Manzoni Family. *v.2 p.717, p.718*

Manzoni. *v.2 p.712*

Mao: A Biography. *v.6 p.202*

Mao: A Life. *v.6 p.202*

Mao: A Reinterpretation. *v.6 p.201*

Mao II: A Novel. *v.2 p.143*

Mao: The Unknown Story. *v.6 p.201*

Mao Zedong: A Penguin Life. *v.6 p.202*

Mao Zedong and China's Revolutions: A Brief History with
Documents. *v.6 p.192, p.201*

Maori Music. *v.1 p.289*

Mao's China and After: A Histroy of the People's
Republic. *v.6 p.194*

Mao's People: Sixteen Portraits of Life in Revolutionary
China. *v.4 p.702*

Mao's Road to Power - Revolutionary Writings, 1912-1949: The
Pre-Marxist Period, 1912-1920, Vol. I. *v.6 p.202*

Mao's Road to Power: Revolutionary Writings, 1912-1949 - The
Pre-Marxist Period, 1912-1920. . . . .*v.6 p.202*

Mao's Road to Power: Revolutionary Writings, 1912-1949:
From the Jinggangshan to the Establishment of the
Jiangxi. *v.6 p.202*

Mao's Road to Power: Revolutionary Writings, 1912-1949:
National Revolution and Social Revolution. . . .*v.6 p.202*

Mao's Road to Power: Revolutionary Writings, 1912-1949: The
Rise and Fall of the Chinese Soviet Republic,
1931-1934. . . . .*v.6 p.202*

Mao's War Against Nature: Politics and the Environment in
Revolutionary China. *v.6 p.194, p.195*

A Map of Australian Verse: The Twentieth Century. . .*v.2 p.741*

A Map of Glass. *v.2 p.739*

A Map to the Next World. *v.2 p.146*

Maple by Example. *v.5 p.460*

Mapping Biology Knowledge. *v.5 p.245*

Mapping Cultural Spaces: Postcolonial Indian Literature in
English: Essays in Honour of Nissim Ezekiel. . . .*v.2 p.762*

Mapping Early Modern Japan: Space, Place, and Culture in the
Tokugawa Period, 1603-1868. . . . .*v.6 p.226*

Mapping Global Cities: GIS Methods in Urban
Analysis. *v.4 p.388, v.6 p.721*

Mapping Men and Empire: A Geography of Adventure. .*v.2 p.246*

The Mapping of Geological Structures. *v.5 p.420*

The Mapping of New Spain: Indigenous Cartography and the
Maps of the Relaciones Geograficas. *v.3 p.287*

Mapping Our Genes: The Genome Project and the Future of
Medicine. *v.5 p.138*

Mapping the Code: The Human Genome Project and the
Choices of Modern Science. *v.5 p.132*

Mapping the Deep: The Extraordinary Story of Ocean
Science. *v.5 p.428*

Mapping the Future of America's National Parks: Stewardship
Through Geographic Information Systems. *v.4 p.382*

Mapping the Godzone: A Primer on New Zealand Literature and
Culture. *v.2 p.741*

Mapping the Nation. *v.3 p.61*

Mapping the Victorian Social Body. *v.6 p.750, p.759*

◻ Mapping the World of Women's Information
Services. *v.6 p.432*

Mapping Yorùbá Networks: Power and Agency in the Making of
Transnational Communities. *v.4 p.44*

Mappings: Feminism and the Cultural Geographies of
Encounter. *v.6 p.433, p.462*

Mapplethorpe: A Biography. *v.1 p.768, v.6 p.407, p.408*

Maps and the Internet. *v.4 p.386*

Maps, Myths, and Men: The Story of the Vinland Map. .*v.4 p.399*

Maps with the News: The Development of American
Journalistic Cartography. *v.4 p.386*

Maqroll. *v.2 p.684*

Mara and Dann: An Adventure. *v.2 p.365*

Maracatu Atomico: Traditional Modernity and Postmodernity in
the Mangue Movement and the New Music Scene of
Recife Pernambuco, Brazil. *v.3 p.267*

The Marathas 1600-1818. . . . .*v.6 p.160, p.161*

Marathon: The Pursuit of the Presidency, 1972-1976. .*v.3 p.482*

The Marble Man: Robert E. Lee and His Image in American
Society. *v.3 p.395*

Marbury vs. Madison: The Origins and Legacy of Judicial
Review. *v.4 p.455, p.538*

Marc Bloch: A Life in History. *v.3 p.154*

Marc Bloch, Sociology and Geography: Encountering Changing
Disciplines. *v.4 p.682*

Marc Chagall, 1887-1985. . . . .*v.1 p.735*

Marc Chagall and His Times: A Documentary Narrative. .*v.1 p.695*

Marc Chagall: The Lithographs; La Collection Sorlier. .*v.1 p.755*

Marc-Antoine Charpentier. *v.1 p.183, p.317*

Marcel Breuer, Architect: The Career and the Buildings. .*v.1 p.793*

Marcel Duchamp: The Bachelor Stripped Bare: A
Biography. *v.1 p.698*

Marcel Duchamp. *v.1 p.695, p.698, p.700*

Marcel Proust: A Life. *v.2 p.523, p.524, p.525*

Marcel Proust on Art and Literature, 1896-1919. . . .*v.2 p.524*

Marcel Proust: Selected Letters, 1880-1903. . . . . .*v.2 p.524*

Marcel Proust. *v.2 p.524*

A March of Liberty: A Constitutional History of the United
States: From 1877 to the Present, Vol. II. . .*v.4 p.452, p.453*

A March of Liberty: A Constitutional History of the United
States: From the Founding to 1890, Vol. I. *v.4 p.452*

The March of Spare Time: The Problem and Promise of Leisure
in the Great Depression. *v.4 p.783, p.823*

March to Zion: United States Policy and the Founding of Israel. *v.3 p.386*

Marching As to War: Canada's Turbulent Years, 1899-1953. . . . .*v.3 p.537*

Marching in Place: The Status Quo Presidency of George Bush. *v.3 p.470*

Marching Men. *v.2 p.57*

Marching to Glory: The History of the Salvation Army in the United States, 1880-1992. . . . .*v.1 p.589*

Marco Polo and the Discovery of the World. . .*v.6 p.215, p.563*

Marcovaldo: Or the Seasons in the City. *v.2 p.714*

Marcus Alonzo Hanna: His Life and Work. *v.3 p.436*

Marcus Aurelius. *v.3 p.27*

Marcus Crassus and the Late Roman Republic. . .*v.3 p.26, p.27*

Margaret Atwood: Vision and Forms. *v.2 p.734, p.735*

Margaret Atwood. *v.2 p.734*

Margaret Bourke-White: Photographer. *v.1 p.769*

Margaret Fuller, American Romantic: A Selection of Her Writings and Correspondence. *v.2 p.39*

Margaret Fuller, An American Romantic Life. . .*v.2 p.38, p.39*

Margaret Fuller: The Public Years. *v.2 p.38*

Margaret Fuller: Visionary of the New Age. *v.2 p.39*

Margaret Sanger's Eugenic Legacy: The Control of Female Fertility. *v.4 p.775*

Margaret Webster: A Life in the Theater. *v.6 p.413*

Marge Schott . . . Unleashed!. *v.4 p.849*

La marge. *v.2 p.523*

A Marginal Jew: Mentor, Message and Miracles. . . .*v.1 p.627*

A Marginal Jew: Rethinking the Historical Jesus. . . .*v.1 p.627*

A Marginal Jew: Roots of the Problem and the Person. .*v.1 p.627*

Margins and Mainstreams: Asians in American History and Culture. *v.6 p.85, p.114*

The Margins of City Life: Explorations on the French Urban Frontier, 1815-1851. . . . .*v.3 p.149*

Margins of Erasure: Purdah in the Subcontinental Novel in English. *v.2 p.762*

Margot Fonteyn: Autobiography. *v.1 p.8*

Margot Fonteyn Biography: A Life. *v.1 p.23*

Marguerite de Navarre's Heptameron: Themes, Language, and Structure. *v.2 p.470*

Marguerite Duras: Apocalyptic Desires. *v.2 p.517*

Marguerite Duras. *v.2 p.516*

Marguerite Yourcenar: Inventing a Life. *v.6 p.403*

Maria Amparo Ruiz de Burton: Critical and Pedagogical Perspectives. *v.6 p.501, p.514*

Maria Callas: A Musical Biography. *v.1 p.315, p.316*

Maria Edgeworth: A Literary Biography. *v.2 p.286*

Maria Montessori: A Biography. *v.4 p.343*

Maria: Novela Americana. *v.2 p.683*

Maria or the Wrongs of Woman. *v.2 p.319*

Maria Tallchief: America's Prima Ballerina. *v.1 p.13*

Maria Theresa and the House of Austria. *v.3 p.183*

Mariachi Bishop: The Life of Patrick Flores, First Mexican-American Bishop in the U.S. . . .*v.6 p.489, p.520*

Mariachi Music in America: Experiencing Music, Expressing Culture. *v.1 p.294, v.6 p.519*

Mariana Pineda. *v.2 p.659*

Marianna Sirca. *v.2 p.717*

Marianne in the Market: Envisioning Consumer Society in Fin-de-Siècle France. *v.3 p.54*

Marianne Moore, Elizabeth Bishop, and May Swenson: The Feminist Poetics of Self-Restraint. *v.2 p.62, p.103*

Marianne Moore: Questions of Authority. . . .*v.2 p.102, p.103*

Marianne Moore. *v.2 p.102*

Marianne. *v.2 p.500*

Marie Antoinette: The Last Queen of France. *v.3 p.147*

Marie de France: Fables. *v.2 p.468*

Marie de France. *v.2 p.468*

Marie Grubbe. *v.2 p.627*

Marie Taglioni (1804-1884). *v.1 p.10*

Marilynn Webb: Prints and Pastels. *v.1 p.758*

Marimekko: Fabrics, Fashion, Architecture. *v.1 p.809*

Marina Abramovic´: Installations and Objects 1965-2001. . . . .*v.1 p.772*

Marine and Coastal Geographical Information Systems. *v.4 p.393*

Marine Bioinvasions: Patterns, Processes, and Perspectives. *v.5 p.180*

Marine Biology: An Ecological Approach. . . .*v.5 p.171, p.172*

Marine Biology. *v.5 p.171*

Marine Chemistry. *v.4 p.393*

Marine Climate Change: Ocean Waves, Storms and Surges in the Perspective of Climate Change. *v.4 p.394*

Marine Flora and Fauna of Hong Kong and Southern China, Vol. 5. . . . .*v.5 p.171*

Marine Geochemistry. *v.5 p.429*

Marine Geology: Exploring the New Frontiers of the Ocean. *v.5 p.428*

Marine Life of the Pacific and Indian Oceans. *v.5 p.172*

Marine Realms Information Bank. *v.5 p.428*

Marinero en Tierra (Sailman at Shore). *v.2 p.655*

Marino Faliero Doge of Venice: An Historical Tragedy and the Prophecy of Dante A Poem. *v.2 p.273*

Marino Marini: Catalogue Raisonné of the Graphic Work, 1919-1980. . . . .*v.1 p.756*

Mario Botta: Light and Gravity. *v.1 p.792*

Mario de Andrade: The Creative Works. *v.2 p.693*

Mario Vargas Llosa. *v.2 p.685, p.686*

Maritime Empires: British Imperial Maritime Trade in the Nineteenth Century. *v.3 p.297*

A Maritime History of the Pacific Coast, 1540-1980. .*v.3 p.530*

The Maritime Provinces. *v.3 p.543*

The Maritime Rights Movement, 1919-1927: A Study in Canadian Regionalism. *v.3 p.543*

Marius the Epicurean: His Sensations and Ideas. . . .*v.2 p.303*

Marivaux, la Vie de Marianne and le Paysan Parvenu. *v.2 p.480*

Marivaux Plays. *v.2 p.481*

Marivaux: Three Plays. *v.2 p.481*

Marivaux. *v.2 p.480*

Mark 1-8: A New Translation with Introduction and Commentary. *v.1 p.629*

Mark Akenside: A Reassessment. *v.2 p.237*

Mark and Method: New Approaches in Biblical Studies. .*v.1 p.628*

Mark Di Suvero: At Storm King Art Center. *v.1 p.781*

Mark Morris's L'Allegro, il Pensorosco, ed il Moderato: A Celebration. *v.1 p.28, p.30*

Mark Morris. *v.1 p.5, v.6 p.414*

Mark Rothko: The Works on Canvas: A Catalogue Raisonné. *v.1 p.735*

Mark the Music: The Life and Work of Marc Blitzstein. *v.1 p.214, p.312,v.6 p.409*

Mark Twain : Mississippi Writings: Tom Sawyer; Life on the Mississippi; Huckleberry Finn; Pudd'Nhead Wilson. .*v.2 p.34*

Mark Twain, a Biography: The Personal and Literary Life of Samuel Langhorne Clemens. *v.2 p.33*

Mark Twain among the Scholars: Reconsidering Contemporary Twain Criticism. *v.2 p.33*

Mark Twain and the South. *v.2 p.33*

Mark Twain: The Critical Heritage. *v.2 p.33*

Mark Twain: The Essential Reference to His Life and Writings. *v.2 p.33*

Mark Twain-Howells Letters: The Correspondence of Samuel L. Clemens and William D. Howells, 1872-1910. . . .*v.2 p.35*

Mark Twain's America. *v.2 p.33*

Mark Twain's Helpful Hints for Good Living: A Handbook for the Damned Human Race. *v.2 p.33, p.34*

Mark Twain's Letters, 1853-1886, Vol. 1. . . . . . .*v.2 p.34*

Mark Twain's Letters, 1870-1871, Vol. 4. . . . . . .*v.2 p.34*

Mark Twain's Letters, 1872-1873. . . . .*v.2 p.35*

Mark Twain's Letters, 1874-1875, Vol. 6. . . . .*v.2 p.34, p.35*

Mark Twain's Notebooks and Journals, 1877-1883, Vol. 2. . . . .*v.2 p.34*

Mark Twain's Satires and Burlesques. *v.2 p.35*

Marked Women: Prostitutes and Prostitution in the Cinema. *v.6 p.321*

▢ Market and Trade Data: Statistical Market Information. *v.4 p.152, p.164*

The Market Economy and Christian Ethics. *v.1 p.596*

Market Efficiency: Stock Market Behavior in Theory and Practice. *v.4 p.263*

The Market for Virtue: The Potential and Limits of Corporate Social Responsibility. *v.4 p.54*

Market Research in Practice: A Guide to the Basics. *v.4 p.135, p.136*

Market Research Matters: Tools and Techniques for Aligning Your Business. *v.4 p.135*

The Market Research Toolbox: A Concise Guide for Beginners. *v.4 p.136*

Market Signaling: Informational Transfer in Hiring and Related Screening Processes. *v.4 p.254, p.255*

Market Structure and Innovation. *v.4 p.269*

The Market, the State, and the Export-Import Bank of the United States, 1934-2000. . . . .*v.4 p.88*

Marketer's Guide to Media. *v.4 p.140, p.150, p.157*

Marketing: A Complete Guide in Pictures. *v.4 p.135*

Marketing for Hospitality and Tourism. *v.4 p.161*

Marketing for Non-Profit Organizations. *v.4 p.135*

Marketing Imagination. *v.4 p.135*

Marketing of Olympic Sport Organisations. *v.4 p.845, p.887, p.891*

The Marketing of Rebellion: Insurgents, Media and International Activism. *v.4 p.497*

Marketing Plans That Work. *v.4 p.144*

Marketing Research and Knowledge Development: An Assessment for Marketing Management. *v.4 p.136*

The Marketing Research Guide. *v.4 p.136*

Marketing the American Creed Abroad: Diasporas in the U. S. and Their Homelands. *v.4 p.571*

Marketing the Menacing Fetus in Japan. *v.6 p.221*

Marketing to American Latinos: A Guide to the In-Culture Approach. *v.4 p.139, v.6 p.526*

Marketing to Leading-Edge Baby Boomers: Perceptions, Principles, Practices, Predictions. *v.4 p.138*

Marketing to Moviegoers: A Handbook of Strategies Used by Major Studios and Independents. *v.6 p.346*

Marketing to the New Super Consumer Mom and Kid. *v.4 p.138, p.139*

▢ MarketResearch.com. *v.4 p.135*

Markets for Clean Air: The U. S. Acid Rain Program. .*v.6 p.299*

▢ MarketWatch. *v.4 p.93, p.101, p.102*

Marking the Sparrow's Fall: Wallace Stegner's American West. *v.2 p.121*

Marks and Monograms of the Modern Movement, 1875-1930: A Guide to the Marks of Artists, Designers, Retailers, and Manufacturers, from the Period of the Aesthetic Movement to Art Deco and Style Moderne. *v.1 p.664*

Mark's Standard Handbook for Mechanical Engineers on CD-ROM. *v.5 p.731*

Marlene Dietrich. *v.6 p.419*

Marlowe and His Circle: A Biographical Survey. . . .*v.2 p.220*

Marmalade Me. *v.1 p.39*

The Maroon Narrative: Caribbean Literature in English Across Boundaries, Ethnicities and Centuries. *v.2 p.767*

Maroon Societies: Rebel Slave Communities in the Americas. *v.4 p.41*

Marpingen: Apparitions of the Virgin Mary in Bismarckian Germany. *v.3 p.163*

Marquetry. *v.1 p.809, p.810*

The Marquis de Sade: A Life. *v.2 p.484*

The Marquis de Sade: A Very Short Introduction. . . .*v.2 p.484*

The Marquise of O--, and other stories. *v.2 p.600*

Marriage, a History: From Obedience to Intimacy, or How Love Conquered Marriage. *v.5 p.638*

Marriage a la Mode. *v.2 p.246*

Marriage and Divorce in Islamic South-East Asia. . . .*v.4 p.733*

Marriage and Kinship Among the Indians in Surinam. .*v.3 p.323*

Marriage and Marital Therapy: Psychoanalytic, Behavioral and Systems Theory Perspectives. *v.5 p.668*

Marriage and Same-Sex Unions: A Debate. *v.6 p.389*

Marriage, Divorce, and Children's Adjustment, Vol. 14. . . . .*v.5 p.639, p.640*

Marriage, Divorce and Children's Adjustment. *v.4 p.735*

Marriage, Divorce, Remarriage. *v.4 p.739*

The Marriage Feast. *v.2 p.630*

Marriage in Maradi: Gender and Culture in a Hausa Society in Niger, 1900-1989. . . . .*v.6 p.70*

Marriage in the Western Church: The Christianization of Marriage During the Patristic Medieval Periods. . .*v.1 p.657*

Marriage in Tribal Societies. *v.4 p.32*

A Marriage of Convenience: Relations Between Mexico and the United States: A Twentieth Century Fund Report. .*v.3 p.296*

The Marriages Between Zones Three, Four and Five. .*v.2 p.365*

The Married Man: A Novel. *v.6 p.380, p.400*

Married to the Brand: Why Consumers Bond with Some Brands for Life. *v.4 p.142*

Married to the Empire: Gender, Politics and Imperialism in India, 1883-1947. . . . .*v.6 p.150*

Marrow of the Nation: A History of Sport and Physical Culture in Republican China. *v.4 p.808, v.6 p.194*

Mars: A Warmer, Wetter Mars. *v.5 p.69*

Marsden Hartley: American Modernist. *v.1 p.742*

The Marsh (Gavkhuni). *v.6 p.672*

Marsha Norman: Collected Plays Works. *v.1 p.121*

Marshall's Evolutionary Economics. *v.4 p.228*

Marsilius of Padua: The Defender of the Peace. . . .*v.4 p.490*

Una Marson and Louise Bennett. *v.2 p.767*

Martereau. *v.2 p.527*

Martha Brae's Two Histories: European Expansion and Caribbean Culture-Building in Jamaica. *v.4 p.40*

Martha Graham: Sixteen Dances in Photographs. . . .*v.1 p.27*

Martha Graham: The Evolution of Her Dance Theory and Training. *v.1 p.28, p.30, p.42*

Martha Graham. *v.1 p.10*

Martha Quest. *v.2 p.365*

Martha: The Life and Work of Martha Graham. *v.1 p.7*

Martial Arts in the Modern World. *v.4 p.863*

Martial Races: The Military, Race, and Masculinity in British Imperial Culture, 1857-1914. . . . .*v.3 p.126*

Martial: Select Epigrams. *v.2 p.438*

The Martial Spirit. *v.3 p.399, p.437*

Martial: The Epigrams. *v.2 p.437*

Martial: The Unexpected Classic. *v.2 p.438*

Martial's Epigrams, Bk. 2. . . . .*v.2 p.438*

The Martian Chronicles. *v.2 p.63*

The Martian Climate Revisited: Atmosphere and Environment of a Desert Planet. *v.5 p.69*

Martin A. Hansen. *v.2 p.627*

Martin Buber: Reforming Church and Community. .*v.1 p.603*

Martin Buber: The Life of Dialogue. *v.1 p.468*

Martin Dies. *v.3 p.458*

Martin Dressler: The Tale of an American Dreamer. .*v.2 p.150*

Martin Du Gard, romancier. *v.2 p.522*

Martin Fierro. *v.2 p.678*

Martin Gardner's Mathematical Games: The Entire Collection of his Scientific American Columns. *v.5 p.469*

Martin Luther: The Preservation of the Church, 1532-1546. . . . .*v.1 p.602*

Martin Luther's Basic Theological Writings. .*v.1 p.603, v.3 p.166*

Martin Puryear. *v.1 p.778*

Martin Van Buren: The Romantic Age of American Politics. *v.3 p.417*

Martina: Autobiography. *v.6 p.384*

Martindale: The Complete Drug Reference. *v.5 p.526*

⬚ Martindale's the. *v.5 p.255*

Martyrdom and Persecution in the Early Church. . .*v.1 p.612*

The Martyred City: Death and Rebirth in the Andes. .*v.3 p.330*

Maru. *v.2 p.756*

Marva Collins' Way: Returning to Excellence in Education. *v.4 p.337*

The Marvel of Maps: Art, Cartography, and Politics in Renaissance Italy. *v.3 p.200*

Marvell and Liberty. *v.2 p.252*

Marvell: Poems. *v.2 p.252*

Marvell: The Writer in Public Life. *v.2 p.252*

Marvelous Journey: A Survey of Four Centuries of Brazilian Writing. *v.2 p.692*

Marx after Marxism: The Philosophy of Karl Marx. *v.1 p.465, v.4 p.236*

Marx and Engels on the Population Bomb. *v.4 p.222*

Marx and the French Revolution. *v.3 p.158*

Marx: Early Political Writings. *v.4 p.492*

Marx for the 21st Century. *v.4 p.237*

Marx@2000: Late Marxist Perspectives. *v.4 p.236*

The Marx-Engels Reader. *v.4 p.507*

Marxism and Anthropology: The History of a Relationship. *v.4 p.23*

Marxism and Democracy in Chile: From 1932 to the Fall of Allende. *v.3 p.353*

Marxism and History. *v.1 p.508*

Marxism and Literature. *v.2 p.571*

Marxism and Modernism: An Historical Study of Lukacs, Brecht, Benjamin, and Adorno. *v.1 p.508*

Marxism and the Call of the Future: Conversations on Ethics, History, and Politics. *v.4 p.507, p.508*

Marxism and the Leap to the Kingdom of Freedom: The Rise and Fall of the Communist Utopia. *v.4 p.509*

Marxism and the Philosophy of Language. *v.1 p.509*

Marxism at Work: Ideology, Class and French Socialism During the Third Republic. *v.3 p.155*

Marxism: For and Against. *v.4 p.235, p.236*

Marxism in the Chinese Revolution. *v.6 p.192*

A Marxist Looks at Jesus. *v.1 p.641*

Marx's Capital. *v.4 p.235*

Marx's Concept of Man. *v.4 p.235*

Marx's Critique of Political Economy: Intellectual Sources and Evolution, Vol. 1. . . . .*v.4 p.236*

Marx's Theory of Money: Modern Appraisals. . . .*v.4 p.236*

Mary Ann Shadd Cary: The Black Press and Protest in the Nineteenth Century. .*v.6 p.431, p.432, p.435, p.448, p.455*

Mary Baker Eddy: An Interpretive Biography of the Founder of Christian Science. *v.1 p.583*

Mary Barton. *v.2 p.288*

Mary Boykin Chestnut: A Confederate Woman's Life. *v.3 p.501*

Mary Cassatt: Modern Woman. *v.1 p.735*

Mary Cassatt: Painter of Modern Women. *v.1 p.745*

Mary Cassat. *v.1 p.739*

Mary Chesnut's Civil War. *v.3 p.394, p.428*

Mary Ellen Mark: American Odyssey,
1963-1999. . . . .*v.1 p.767, p.768*

Mary in the New Testament. *v.1 p.642*

Mary Lincoln: Biography of a Marriage. *v.3 p.426*

Mary McCarthy: Gender, Politics, and the Postwar
Intellectual. *v.2 p.99*

Mary McLeod Bethune and Black Women's Political
Activism. *v.6 p.5, p.17, p.43*

Mary, Mother of the Lord. *v.1 p.642*

Mary Renault: A Biography. *v.6 p.404*

Mary Schafer, American Quilt Maker. *v.1 p.802, p.809*

Mary Shelley: Her Life, Her Fiction, Her Monsters. .*v.2 p.310*

Mary Shelley. *v.2 p.310*

Mary Somerville: Science, Illumination, and the Female
Mind. *v.5 p.397*

Mary Stuart, a Romantic Drama. *v.2 p.792*

Mary Stuart. *v.2 p.601*

Mary Todd Lincoln: Her Life and Letters. *v.3 p.427*

The Mary Wigman Book. *v.1 p.12*

Mary Wollstonecraft: A Revolutionary Life. *v.2 p.318*

Mary Wollstonecraft Shelley: An Introduction. . . .*v.2 p.310*

Maryland: A New Guide to the Old Line State. . . .*v.3 p.493*

Maryland, the History of a Palatinate. *v.3 p.493*

Maryland under the Commonwealth: A Chronicle of the Years,
1649-1658. . . . .*v.3 p.493*

Mascagni: An Autobiography Compiled, Edited and Translated
from Original Sources. *v.1 p.224, p.340*

Mascara: A Novel. *v.2 p.680*

Maschere nude, vol. 1. . . . .*v.2 p.722*

Maschere nude, vol. 2. . . . .*v.2 p.722*

Maschere nude, vol. 3. . . . .*v.2 p.722*

Masculine Domination. *v.4 p.743*

The Masculine Woman in America, 1890-1935. . . . .*v.6 p.366*

Masculinist Impulses: Toomer, Hurston, Black Writing, and
Modernity. *v.2 p.126*

Masculinities and Crime: Critique and Reconceptualization of
Theory. *v.6 p.257*

Masculinities and Violence, Vol. 1. . . . .*v.6 p.257*

Masculinities: Football, Polo and the Tango in
Argentina. *v.3 p.347*

Masculinities, Gender Relations, and Sport, Vol.
11. . . . .*v.4 p.818, p.837*

Masculinities Without Men?: Female Masculinity in
Twentieth-Century Fictions. *v.6 p.429, p.480*

Masculinities. *v.4 p.743, p.745,v.6 p.429*

Masculinity Studies and Feminist Theory. . *v.4 p.745, v.6 p.429*

The Masculinity Studies Reader. . . *v.4 p.745, v.6 p.369, p.428*

Mask or Face: Reflections in an Actor's Mirror. . . .*v.1 p.145*

The Masked Media: Aymara Fiestas and Social Interaction in
the Bolivian Highlands. *v.3 p.323*

Masking and Power: Carnival and Popular Culture in the
Caribbean. *v.3 p.266*

Masking Selves, Making Subjects: Japanese American Women,
Identity, and the Body. *v.6 p.98, p.113, p.133, p.481*

Masks and Mirrors: Generation X and the Chameleon
Personality. *v.4 p.693*

Masks in a Pageant. *v.3 p.379*

Masks, Mimes and Miracles. *v.1 p.91, p.93, p.94, p.97*

Masks of Conquest: Literary Study and British Rule in
India. *v.2 p.763*

The Masks of Mary Renault: A Literary Biography. . .*v.6 p.404*

The Masks of Othello: The Search for the Identity of Othello,
Iago, and Desdemona by Three Centuries of Actors and
Critics. *v.2 p.231*

Masons and Sculptors. *v.1 p.796*

Masquerade: Dancing Around Death in Nazi Occupied
Hungary. *v.3 p.86, p.87, p.187*

Mass and Elite in Democratic Athens: Rhetoric, Ideology, and
the Power of the People. *v.3 p.18*

Mass Communication and American Social Thought: Key Texts,
1919-1968. . . . .*v.4 p.696*

Mass Communication Law and Ethics. *v.4 p.406*

Mass Extinctions: Processes and Evidence. *v.5 p.450*

Mass Hysteria: Critical Psychology and Media Studies. .*v.4 p.714*

Mass Identity Architecture: Architectural Writings of Jean
Baudrillard. *v.1 p.704, p.787*

Mass Media and New Democracies. *v.4 p.424, p.425*

Mass Media and Society in the Middle East. *v.4 p.415*

Mass Media and Society. *v.4 p.416*

Mass Media and the Constitution: An Encyclopedia of Supreme
Court Decisions. *v.4 p.405, p.445*

Mass Media and the Supreme Court. *v.4 p.445*

Mass Media in a Mass Society: Myth and
Reality. *v.4 p.696, v.5 p.621, p.624*

Mass Media in Sub-Saharan Africa. *v.4 p.415*

Mass Media in the New Millennium: Structures, Functions,
Issues and Ethics. *v.4 p.417*

Mass Media Law, 2007/2008 Edition with PowerWeb. .*v.4 p.445*

Mass Politics and Culture in Democratizing Korea. . .*v.4 p.621*

Mass Spec Desk Reference. *v.5 p.272*

Mass Spectrometry: Analytical Chemistry by Open
Learning. *v.5 p.271*

Mass Spectrometry and Genomic Analysis. *v.5 p.88*

Mass Spectrometry of Polymers. *v.5 p.323*

Mass Spectrometry: Principles and Applications. . . .*v.5 p.271*

Mass Uprisings in the U. S. S. R.: Protest and Rebellion in the
Post-Stalin Years. *v.3 p.228*

Massachusetts: A Concise History. *v.3 p.487*

Massacre in Jedwabne, July 10 1941: Before During,
After. *v.3 p.254*

Massacre in Shansi. *v.6 p.188, p.203*

Massenet: A Chronicle of His Life and Times. .*v.1 p.198, p.340*

Masses in Latin America. *v.4 p.703, p.704*

Massine: A Biography. *v.1 p.8*

Mass-Mediated Terrorism: The Central Role of the Media in
Terrorism and Counterterrorism. *v.4 p.558, p.559*

The Master and Margarita: A Critical Companion. . . .*v.2 p.802*

The Master and Margarita. *v.2 p.801, p.802*

Master AP Biology. *v.5 p.244*

Master Class: Lessons from Leading Writers. *v.2 p.574*

Master Harold and the Boys. *v.2 p.755*

Master Harold. *v.1 p.62, p.128, p.130,v.2 p.755*

The Master of Ballantrae and Weir of Hermiston. .*v.2 p.312, p.313*

The Master of Go. *v.6 p.230*

The Master of Petersburg. *v.2 p.754*

The Master of Seventh Avenue: David Dubinsky and American
Labor Movement. *v.4 p.128*

The Master of the Russian Ballet: The Memoirs of Cav. Enrico
Cecchetti. *v.1 p.11*

Master of the Senate: The Years of Lyndon Johnson. .*v.3 p.467*

A Master on the Periphery of Capitalism: Machado de
Assis. *v.2 p.693*

The Master Pipers. *v.2 p.500*

Master Roger Williams, a Biography. *v.3 p.489*

Master Tung's Western Chamber Romance: A Chinese
Chantefable. *v.6 p.209*

Mastering MATLAB 6. . . . .*v.5 p.461*

Mastering Public Administration: From Max Weber to Dwight
Waldo. *v.4 p.545, p.580*

Mastering the Art of Performance: A Primer for
Musicians. *v.1 p.395, p.397, p.398, p.400*

Mastering the Novels of Jane Austen. *v.2 p.267*

Mastering Your Inner Game. *v.5 p.582*

e Masterman Ready. *v.2 p.299*

Masterpieces of African American Literature. . . .*v.6 p.26, p.33*

Masterpieces of American Furniture from the
Munson-Williams-Proctor Institute. *v.1 p.803*

Masterpieces of American Indian Literature. . .*v.6 p.698, p.699*

Masterpieces of Ballet Design. *v.1 p.38*

Masterpieces of Chicago Architecture. *v.1 p.791*

Masterpieces of Classic Greek Drama. *v.1 p.71, p.72*

Masterpieces of Kabuki: Eighteen Plays on
Stage. *v.1 p.129, p.132, p.133,v.6 p.234*

Masterpieces of Modern British and Irish Drama. . .*v.2 p.189*

Masterpieces of Negro Eloquence: African-American Women
Writers, 1910-1940 by Dunbar-Nelson. *v.2 p.19*

Masterpieces of the J. Paul Getty Museum - Drawings.*v.1 p.722*

The Masterpiece. *v.2 p.505, p.506*

Masterplots. *v.2 p.549*

The Masters and the Slaves: A Study in the Development of
Brazilian Civilization. *v.3 p.271, p.340*

Masters of American Comics. *v.1 p.701*

Masters of Animation. *v.6 p.307*

Masters of Illusion: The World Bank and the Poverty of
Nations. *v.4 p.630*

Masters of Light: Dutch Painters in Utrecht During the Golden
Age. *v.1 p.747*

Masters of Movement: Portraits of America's Great
Choreographers. *v.1 p.45*

Masters of Sociological Thought: Ideas in Historical and Social
Context. *v.4 p.682*

Masters of the Dew. *v.2 p.537, p.538*

Masters of the Keyboard: Individual Style Elements in the Piano
Music of Bach, Haydn, Mozart, Beethoven, and
Schubert. *v.1 p.244*

Masters Running: A Guide to Running and Staying Fit After
40. . . . .*v.4 p.791, p.841, p.866*

Masters Track and Field: A History. . . .*v.4 p.841, p.847, p.869*

Masters Without Slaves. *v.3 p.400, p.438*

The Mastersingers of Nuremberg. .*v.1 p.206, p.234, p.366, p.410*

The Master. *v.6 p.399*

The Masterwork in Music: A Yearbook (1925). . . .*v.1 p.373*

Masterworks of 20th-Century Music: The Modern Repertory of
the Symphony Orchestra. *v.1 p.218, p.241*

Mastery and Elegance: Two Centuries of French Drawings from
the Collection of Jeffrey E. Horvitz. *v.1 p.721*

Mastery and Escape: T. S. Eliot and the Dialectic of
Modernism. *v.2 p.71*

Mastery of Movement. *v.1 p.47*

Mastro Don Gesualdo. *v.2 p.713*

Mastro-don Gesualdo : edizione critica. *v.2 p.713*

Masturbation: The History of a Great Terror. *v.4 p.748*

The Match: Althea Gibson and a Portrait of a
Friendship. *v.4 p.809, p.833, p.838, p.864*

Mate Selection: A Study of Complementary Needs. . .*v.4 p.739*

Mate Selection Across Cultures. *v.4 p.738, p.742*

Material Beings. *v.1 p.489*

Material Dreams: Southern California Through the
1920s. *v.3 p.532*

Material Girls: Making Sense of Feminist Cultural
Theory. *v.6 p.428, p.449*

Material Queer: A Lesbigay Cultural Studies Reader. .*v.6 p.357*

Materialism and the Mind-Body Problem. *v.1 p.509*

A Materialist Theory of the Mind. *v.1 p.496*

Materials and Processes, Set, Pt. A. *v.5 p.733*

Materials and Processes, Set, Pt. B. *v.5 p.733, p.734*

Materials and Techniques in the Decorative Arts: An Illustrated
Dictionary. *v.1 p.798, p.799, p.803*

Materials and Techniques of 20th Century Music. . .*v.1 p.371*

Materials for Civil and Construction Engineers. . . .*v.5 p.690*

Materials for Engineering. *v.5 p.732*

Materials for the Study of Variation: Treated with Especial
Regard to Discontinuity in the Origin of Species. .*v.5 p.198*

Materials Handbook: A Concise Desktop Reference. .*v.5 p.688*

Materials Handbook. *v.5 p.691, p.692*

The Materials of Sculpture. *v.1 p.782*

▢ Materials Properties Locator Database. *v.5 p.406*

▢ Materials Safety Data Sheets. *v.5 p.265*

Materials Science and Engineering: An Introduction. .*v.5 p.688*

Materials Science and Engineering Handbook. *v.5 p.691*

Materials Science and Metallurgy. *v.5 p.690*

Materials Science and Technology: A Comprehensive Treatment,
Set. *v.5 p.318*

Materials Science and Technology, Synthesis of
Polymers. *v.5 p.318*

Materials Selection for Corrosion Control. . . .*v.5 p.688, p.734*

Maternal-Fetal Medicine. *v.5 p.524*

Maternity Nursing. *v.5 p.524*

Math and Bio 2010: Linking Undergraduate Disciplines. .*v.5 p.246*

▢ Math and Science Gateway. *v.4 p.367*

▢ Math Archives: Lessons, Tutorials and Lecture Notes. *v.5 p.457, p.460*

Math into LaTeX. *v.5 p.461*

🏵 The Math Life. *v.5 p.458*

Math Matters: Understanding the Math You Teach, Grades K-6. . . . .*v.5 p.462*

Math Talks for Undergraduates. *v.5 p.459*

Math Through the Ages: A Gentle History for Teachers and Others. *v.5 p.465*

The Mathematica Book. *v.5 p.462*

Mathematica Programs for Physical Chemistry. *v.5 p.288*

Mathematical Adventures for Students and Amateurs. .*v.5 p.458*

Mathematical Analysis: An Introduction. *v.5 p.489*

Mathematical Bioeconomics: The Optimal Management of Renewable Resources. *v.5 p.503*

Mathematical Biology: An Introduction. *v.5 p.91, p.502*

Mathematical Biology: Spatial Models and Biomedical Applications. *v.5 p.91, p.94*

The Mathematical Century: The 30 Greatest Problems of the Last 100 Years. *v.5 p.459, p.467*

Mathematical Discovery: On Understanding, Learning, and Teaching Problem Solving. *v.5 p.464*

Mathematical Evolutionary Theory. *v.5 p.91, p.192*

Mathematical Formulas for Economists. *v.4 p.175*

The Mathematical Gardner. *v.5 p.469*

Mathematical Gems from Elementary Combinatorics, Number Theory, and Geometry. . . .*v.5 p.476, p.478, p.479, p.495*

A Mathematical Gift I: The Interplay Between Topology, Functions, Geometry, and Algebra. *v.5 p.460, p.474, p.494, p.496*

A Mathematical Introduction to Linear Programming and Game Theory. *v.5 p.683*

Mathematical Investigations in the Theory of Value and Prices: Appreciation and Interest. *v.4 p.199, p.251*

Mathematical Methods for Physicists: A Concise Introduction. *v.5 p.548*

Mathematical Methods for Physicists. *v.5 p.548*

Mathematical Methods in the Physical Sciences. . . .*v.5 p.548*

Mathematical Methods of Classical Mechanics. .*v.5 p.546, p.548*

Mathematical Modeling: Case Studies from Industry. .*v.5 p.683*

Mathematical Modeling for the Life Sciences. . .*v.5 p.99, p.100*

Mathematical Modeling in the Environment. *v.5 p.502*

Mathematical Modelling: Classroom Notes in Applied Mathematics. *v.5 p.500*

Mathematical Models in Biology: An Introduction. .*v.5 p.91, p.94*

Mathematical Models in Biology. *v.5 p.91*

Mathematical Models in Linguistics. *v.5 p.503*

Mathematical Models in Population Biology and Epidemiology. *v.5 p.91, p.93, p.188, p.189*

Mathematical models of economic growth. *v.4 p.205*

Mathematical Optimization and Economic Theory. .*v.4 p.175*

Mathematical People: Profiles and Interviews. *v.5 p.464*

Mathematical Physiology. *v.5 p.502*

Mathematical Problem Solving. *v.5 p.460, p.464*

Mathematical Psychics: An Essay on the Application of Mathematics to the Moral Sciences. *v.4 p.223*

Mathematical Psychics and Other Essays: Commentaries by Marshall, Jevons and Keynes. *v.4 p.223*

Mathematical Psychology; an Elementary Introduction. .*v.5 p.599*

Mathematical Puzzles: A Connoisseur's Collection. . .*v.5 p.470*

Mathematical Recreations and Essays. *v.5 p.468*

Mathematical Recreations of Lewis Carroll. . .*v.5 p.468, p.469*

Mathematical Recreations. *v.5 p.469*

Mathematical Sorcery: Revealing the Secrets of Numbers. *v.5 p.465*

The Mathematical Theory of Relativity. *v.5 p.556*

Mathematical Thought from Ancient to Modern Times, Vol. 1. . . . .*v.5 p.467*

Mathematical Thought from Ancient to Modern Times, Vol. 2. . . . .*v.5 p.467*

Mathematical Thought from Ancient to Modern Times, Vol. 3. . . . .*v.5 p.467*

The Mathematical Tourist: New and Updated Snapshots of Modern Mathematics. *v.5 p.459, p.467*

Mathematical Treks: From Surreal Numbers to Magic Circles. *v.5 p.459, p.460, p.469*

Mathematical Vistas: From a Room with Many Windows. *v.5 p.458*

Mathematically Speaking: A Dictionary of Quotations. *v.5 p.458, p.461*

A Mathematician's Apology. *v.5 p.458*

The Mathematicians' Apprenticeship: Science, Universities and Society in England, 1560-1640. . . . .*v.3 p.47*

Mathematico-Deductive Theory of Rote Learning: A Study in Scientific Methodology. *v.4 p.357*

Mathematics: A Simple Tool for Geologists. *v.5 p.420*

Mathematics: A Very Short Introduction. *v.5 p.458*

Mathematics Across Cultures: The History of Nonwestern Mathematics. *v.5 p.467, p.468*

Mathematics: An Applied Approach. *v.5 p.500*

Mathematics and 21st Century Biology. *v.5 p.90*

Mathematics and Democracy: The Case for Quantitative Literacy. *v.5 p.464*

Mathematics and Optimal Form. *v.5 p.495*

Mathematics and Sports. *v.4 p.871*

Mathematics Applied to Deterministic Problems in the Natural Sciences. *v.5 p.501*

The Mathematics Dictionary. *v.5 p.458, p.461*

Mathematics Elsewhere: An Exploration of Ideas Across Cultures. *v.5 p.457, p.465*

Mathematics for Economists: Answers Pamphlet. . .*v.4 p.204*

Mathematics for Economists. *v.4 p.203, p.204*

Mathematics for Finance: An Introduction to Financial Engineering. *v.5 p.503*

Mathematics Handbook for Science and Engineering. *v.5 p.461, p.500*

Mathematics in Population Biology. *v.5 p.92, p.189*

Mathematics in Western Culture. *v.5 p.467*

Mathematics into Type. *v.5 p.461*

The Mathematics of Choice. *v.5 p.479*

The Mathematics of Coding Theory. *v.5 p.476*

The Mathematics of Games and Gambling. *v.5 p.484*

Mathematics of Genome Analysis. *v.5 p.136, p.142*

Mathematics of Interest Rates, Insurance, Social Security, and Pensions. *v.4 p.175*

The Mathematics of Projectiles in Sport. *v.4 p.871*

Mathematics: People, Problems, Results. *v.5 p.457*

Mathematics with Applications in Management and Economics. *v.5 p.503, p.504*

The Mathers on Dancing. *v.1 p.22*

Mathers: Three Generations of Puritan Intellectuals, 1596-1728. . . . .*v.3 p.487*

Matheson Gas Data Book. *v.5 p.316*

Mathnawi of Jalalu'ddin Rumi: English Translation. . .*v.6 p.672*

Maths: A Self-Help Workbook for Science and Engineering Students. *v.5 p.459*

Maths for Economics. *v.4 p.204*

MathSciNet/Mathematical Reviews (MR). *v.5 p.460*

Matigari. *v.2 p.759*

The Mating Season. *v.2 p.391*

Matisse the Master: A Life of Henri Matisse, the Conquest of Colour, 1909-1954. . . . .*v.1 p.699, p.747*

Matisse/Picasso. *v.1 p.695*

Matisse's Notes of a Painter: Criticism, Theory, and Context, 1891-1908. . . . .*v.1 p.750*

Matlovich. *v.6 p.389*

Le Matou. *v.2 p.540*

The Matriarch. *v.2 p.746*

The Matrifocal Family: Power, Pluralism and Politics. *v.4 p.33*

Matrilineal Kinship. *v.4 p.32, p.33*

Matrix Algebra for Applied Economics. . . . *v.4 p.175, p.204*

Matrix Analysis of Structural Dynamics: Applications and Earthquake Engineering. *v.5 p.693*

Matrix Computations. *v.5 p.472*

Matrix of Language: Contemporary Linguistic Anthropology. *v.4 p.18*

Matrix Structural Analysis. *v.5 p.693*

Matrona Docta: Educated Women in the Roman Elite from Cornelia to Julia Domna. *v.6 p.451, p.463*

Matter and Interactions I: Modern Mechanics. *v.5 p.539*

Matter and Interactions II: Electric and Magnetic Interactions Version 1.2. . . . .*v.5 p.539*

Matter and Memory. *v.1 p.456*

Matter and Methods at Low Temperatures. *v.5 p.563*

Matter and Method. *v.5 p.402*

A Matter of Choices: Memoirs of a Female Physicist. *v.5 p.542*

A Matter of Definition: Is there truly a shortage of school principals? *v.4 p.282*

Matter of Glory : A New Preface to Paradise Lost. . *v.2 p.366*

A Matter of Law: A Memoir of Struggle in the Cause of Equal Rights. *v.6 p.17, p.22*

A Matter of Life and Death. *v.2 p.622*

A Matter of Principle. *v.4 p.441*

The Matter of Revolution: Science, Poetry, and Politics in the Age of Milton. *v.3 p.48*

A Matter of Trust: Connecting Teachers and Learners in the Early Childhood Classroom. *v.4 p.369*

Matters of Culture: Cultural Sociology in Practice. *v.4 p.699, p.700*

Matters of Life and Death: New Introductory Essays in Moral Philosophy. *v.1 p.485*

Matters of Principle: America's Rejection of the Bork Nomination to the Supreme Court of the United States. *v.4 p.536*

Matthew Arnold: A Life. *v.2 p.265, p.266*

Matthew Arnold: A Literary Life. *v.2 p.266*

Matthew Arnold in His Time and Ours: Centenary Essays. *v.2 p.266*

Matthew Arnold: Prose Writings. *v.2 p.265*

Matthew Arnold: The Poetry. *v.2 p.265*

Matthew Arnold. *v.2 p.265, p.266*

Matthew As Story. *v.1 p.629*

Matthew Prior: Poet and Diplomatist. *v.2 p.256*

Matthias Grunewald. *v.1 p.750*

Matthias Lexers Mittelhochdeutsches Taschenworterbuch. *v.2 p.621*

Matty: Christy Mathewson of the New York Giants. . *v.4 p.859*

The Mature Laurel: Essays on Modern Polish Poetry. *v.2 p.788, p.789*

Mau Mau's Daughter: A Life Story. *v.6 p.18, p.29, p.45*

Maud, and Other Poems, by Alfred Tennyson. . . .*v.2 p.314*

Maugham Plays 2. . . . .*v.2 p.370*

Maugham's Choice of Kipling's Best. *v.2 p.297*

Maupassant: A Lion in the Path. *v.2 p.497*

Maupassant: Short Stories. *v.2 p.497*

Maupassant: The Semiotics of Text: Practical Exercises. *v.2 p.497*

Mauprat. *v.2 p.500*

Maurice Brazil Prendergast - Charles Prendergast: A Catalogue Raisonne. *v.1 p.695, p.696*

Maurice Denis: A Catalogue Raisonné of the Etchings and Lithographs. *v.1 p.755*

Maurice Sceve. *v.2 p.472*

Maurice. *v.2 p.345, v.6 p.396*

Maus: A Survivor's Tale: And Here My Troubles Began. *v.2 p.156*

Maus: A Survivor's Tale: My Father Bleeds History. *v.2 p.156, v.3 p.87*

Le mauvais sang ; suivi de Feu de brousse ; et, A triche-coeur. *v.2 p.546*

Mauve Gloves and Madmen, Clutter and Vine. . . .*v.2 p.159*

Mauve: How One Man Invented a Color That Changed the World. *v.5 p.262*

Mavericks and Other Traditions in American Music. . *v.1 p.277*

Max Beerbohm: Collected Verse. *v.2 p.331*

Max Ernst: A Retrospective. *v.1 p.699*

Max Havelaar: Or, the Coffee Auctions of the Dutch Trading Company. *v.2 p.623*

Max Klinger: The Late Graphic Work 1909-1919, Catalogue Raisonné. *v.1 p.755*

Max Klinger's Graphic Work: Catalogue Raisonné, 1878-1903. . . . .*v.1 p.758*

Max Reinhardt and His Theatre. . . *v.1 p.83, p.85, p.148, p.153*

Max Reinhardt's Grosses Schauspielhaus: Its Artistic Goals, Planning, and Operation, 1910-1933. . . . .*v.1 p.82, p.85, p.109, p.152, p.154, p.155*

Max Steiner's Now, Voyager: A Film Score Guide. . .*v.1 p.255*

Max Weber: An Intellectual Portrait. *v.4 p.684*

Max Weber and the Idea of Economic Sociology. . . .*v.4 p.681*

Max Weber on Law in Economy and Society. *v.4 p.435*

Max Weber's Comparative-Historical Sociology. . . .*v.4 p.681*

Max Weber's Methodologies: Interpretation and Critique. *v.4 p.681*

Max Weber's Methodology: The Unification of the Cultural and Social Sciences. *v.4 p.681*

Max Wertheimer and Gestalt Theory. *v.5 p.597*

Maxfield Parrish: 1870-1966. . . . .*v.1 p.750*

Maxfield Parrish. *v.1 p.720*

Maxima and Minima Without Calculus. *v.5 p.489*

Maximes et Reflexions Diverses. *v.2 p.477*

Maximilian I (1459-1519): An Analytical biography. .*v.3 p.182*

Maximillian I, 1459-1519. . . . .*v.3 p.163*

Maximizing Intelligence. *v.5 p.651*

Maxims. *v.2 p.474*

Maximum Danger: Kennedy, the Missiles, and the Crisis of American Confidence. *v.3 p.481*

Maximum Feasible Misunderstanding. *v.4 p.266*

Maximum Security Ward and Other Poems. *v.2 p.79*

The Maximus Poems. *v.2 p.108*

Maxine Hong Kingston's Broken Book of Life: An Intertextual Study of the Woman Warrior and China Men.*v.6 p.97, p.128*

Maxine Kumin: Selected Poems, 1960-1990. . . . . .*v.2 p.92*

Maxwell's Demon: Why Warmth Disperses and Time Passes. *v.5 p.560*

The May Fourth Movement: Intellectual Revolution in Modern China. *v.6 p.189*

May It Fill Your Soul: Experiencing Bulgarian Music.*v.1 p.298*

May O'Donnell: Modern Dance Pioneer. *v.1 p.9*

May Sarton: A Self Portrait. *v.2 p.119*

May Sarton: Biography. *v.6 p.403*

May Sarton, Revisited. *v.2 p.118*

May the Best Team Win: Baseball Economics and Public Policy, Expanded and Updated. *v.4 p.853, p.890*

The Maya and Teotihuacan: Reinterpreting Early Classic Interaction. *v.3 p.260*

Maya Atlas: Fighting for Land Rights in Southern Belize. *v.3 p.297*

Maya Cosmos. *v.3 p.261, v.4 p.9*

Maya Plisetskaya. *v.1 p.11*

Maya Resistance to Spanish Rule: Time and History on a Colonial Frontier. *v.3 p.297*

Maya Revolt and Revolution in the Eighteenth Century. *v.3 p.287, p.294*

Maya Sculpture of Copan: The Iconography. . .*v.1 p.774, p.775*

The Maya World: Yucatec Culture and Society, 1550-1850. . . . .*v.3 p.287*

Mayakovsky--Plays. *v.2 p.806*

Maya. *v.4 p.9*

Mayday. *v.2 p.74*

Maynard Keynes: An Economists' Biography. *v.4 p.228*

The Mayor of Casterbridge. *v.2 p.292*

The Mayor of Castro Street: The Life and Times of Harvey Milk. *v.6 p.390*

The Mayor of Queensborough, or Hengist King of Kent.*v.2 p.221*

Mayors in the Middle: Politics, Race, and Mayoral Control of Urban Schools. *v.4 p.543, p.544*

The Mayors: The Chicago Political Tradition. *v.3 p.515*

Mazarin: Crisis of Absolutism. *v.3 p.146*

Maze of Justice: Diary of a Country Prosecutor. . . .*v.6 p.656*

Mazurca para Dos Muertos. *v.2 p.657*

Mazurka for Two Dead Men. *v.2 p.657*

Mazzini: A Life for the Religion of Politics. . .*v.3 p.201, p.202*

The MBA Handbook: Skills for Mastering Management. *v.4 p.176*

MBA: The First Century. *v.4 p.176*

The Mbuti Pygmies: Adaptation and Change in Ituri Forest. *v.4 p.39*

McCance and Widdowson's the Composition of Foods.*v.5 p.33*

McCarthyism, the Great American Red Scare: A Documentary History. *v.3 p.447*

McClellan, Sherman, and Grant. *v.3 p.427*

McCloskey's Economic Thought: The Rhetoric of an Economist. *v.4 p.268*

McGowan/Interior Graphic Standards and Interior Graphic Standards, Set. *v.1 p.803*

McGraw-Hill 2006 Yearbook of Science and Technology. *v.5 p.387*

McGraw-Hill Concise Encyclopedia of Bioscience. . .*v.6 p.284*

McGraw-Hill Concise Encyclopedia of Earth Science.*v.5 p.417*

McGraw-Hill Concise Encyclopedia of Science and Technology. *v.5 p.387*

McGraw-Hill Construction. *v.1 p.782, p.784*

McGraw-Hill Dictionary of Chemistry. *v.5 p.257*

McGraw-Hill Dictionary of Environmental Science. . *v.5 p.28*

McGraw-Hill Dictionary of Materials Science. *v.5 p.679*

McGraw-Hill Dictionary of Scientific and Technical Terms. *v.5 p.387, p.388*

The McGraw-Hill Encyclopedia of Economics. *v.4 p.189*

McGraw-Hill Encyclopedia of Science and Technology, Set. *v.5 p.387*

McGraw-Hill Encyclopedia of World Drama, Vol. 99. .*v.1 p.60*

The McGraw-Hill Recycling Handbook. *v.5 p.376, p.377*

McGraw-Hill's Compound Interest and Annuity Tables.*v.4 p.163*

McKinsey's Marvin Bower: Vision, Leadership, and the Creation of Management Consulting. *v.4 p.64, p.147*

McMinn's Color Atlas of Human Anatomy. *v.5 p.158*

MD Consult. *v.5 p.509*

Me Again: Uncollected Writings of Stevie Smith. . .*v.2 p.383*

Mea Cuba. *v.3 p.310*

The Meadows of Gold. *v.6 p.585*

Mean Spirit. *v.2 p.147, v.6 p.698*

Mean Streets: Youth Crime and Homelessness. *v.6 p.255*

Meaning and Action: A Critical History of Pragmatism. .*v.1 p.513*

Meaning and Argument: An Introduction to Logic Through Language. *v.1 p.493*

Meaning and Moral Order: Explorations in Cultural Analysis. *v.4 p.720*

Meaning and Necessity: A Study in Semantics and Modal Logic. *v.1 p.468, p.489*

Meaning and the Structure of Language. *v.2 p.559*

Meaning, Expression and Thought. *v.1 p.490*

Meaning in Film: Relevant Structures in Soundtrack and Narrative. *v.1 p.256*

Meaning in Motion: New Cultural Studies of Dance. .*v.1 p.41*

Meaning, Medicine and the 'Placebo Effect'. *v.4 p.47*

The Meaning of Anxiety. *v.5 p.654, p.655*

The Meaning of Europe. *v.3 p.87*

The Meaning of Heidegger: A Critical Study of an Existentialist Phenomenology. *v.1 p.471*

The Meaning of Ichiro: The New Wave from Japan and the Transformation of Our National Pastime. .*v.4 p.820, p.834, p.852, p.853, p.890, p.898, p.899*

The Meaning of Mallarme: A Bilingual Edition of His Poesie and Un Coup de Des. *v.2 p.496, p.497*

The Meaning of Quantum Chemistry: A Guide for Students of Chemistry and Physics. *v.5 p.279*

The Meaning of Relativity: Including the Relativistic Theory of the Non-Symmetric Field. *v.5 p.556*

The Meaning of Religious Conversion in Africa: The Case of the Igbo of Nigeria. *v.6 p.72*

The Meaning of Revelation: Library of Theological Terms. *v.1 p.639*

The Meaning of Shakespeare, Vol. 1. . . . .*v.2 p.229*

The Meaning of Sports: Why Americans Watch Baseball, Football, and Basketball and What They See When They Do. *v.4 p.817*

The Meaning of the Dead Sea Scrolls: Their Significance for Understanding the Bible, Judaism, Jesus, and Christianity. *v.1 p.546*

The Meaning of the Nuclear Revolution: Statecraft and the Prospect of Armageddon. *v.4 p.656*

The Meaning of Truth. *v.1 p.513*

The Meaning of Wilderness: Essential Articles and Speeches. *v.5 p.80, p.224*

Meaning Reconstruction and the Experience of Loss. .*v.5 p.655*

Meaning, Use and Truth: The Philosophy of Natural Language. *v.1 p.489, p.490*

Meaningful Differences in the Everyday Experience of Young American Children. *v.4 p.356, p.368*

Meanings of Multiethnicity: A Case-Study of Ethnicity and Ethnic Relations in Singapore. *v.6 p.173*

Meaning. *v.1 p.490*

Means and Ends in American Abolitionism: Garrison and His Critics on Strategy and Tactics, 1834-1850. .*v.3 p.398, p.420*

Means Estimating Handbook. *v.5 p.686*

Means of Ascent: The Years of Lyndon Johnson. . . .*v.3 p.467*

Measure and Integral: An Introduction to Real Analysis. .*v.5 p.490*

Measure for Measure, the Law and the Convent. . . .*v.2 p.229*

Measure for Measure. *v.2 p.223*

The Measure of Life: Virginia Woolf's Last Years. . .*v.2 p.393*

The Measure of Reality: Quantification in Western Europe, 1250-1600. . . . .*v.3 p.70*

The Measure of Value Stated and Illuminated. *v.4 p.222*

Measure, Topology and Fractal Geometry. *v.5 p.498*

A Measured Pace: Toward a Philosophical Understanding of the Arts of Dance. *v.1 p.44*

Measurement and Assessment in Teaching. *v.5 p.604*

Measurement and Evaluation in Education and Psychology. *v.5 p.604*

Measurement and Evaluation in Psychology and Education. *v.5 p.602, p.604*

Measurement and Meaning: Combining Quantitative and Qualitative Methods for the Analysis of Poverty and Social Exclusion in Latin America. . . .*v.4 p.687, p.731*

🄴 Measurement Error and Latent Variables in Econometrics. *v.4 p.205*

Measurement Errors and Uncertainties: Theory and Practice. *v.5 p.562, p.563*

Measurement in Pediatric Exercise Science. *v.4 p.874*

Measurement in Psychology: A Critical History of a Methodological Concept. *v.5 p.599*

The Measurement of Intelligence. *v.4 p.359*

The Measurement of Meaning. *v.5 p.604*

The Measurement of Starlight: Two Centuries of Astronomical Photometry. *v.5 p.65*

Measurement Problems in Criminal Justice Research: Workshop Summary. *v.6 p.246*

Measurement, Quantification and Economic Analysis: Numeracy in Economics. *v.4 p.204*

The Measurements of Environmental and Resource Values: Theory and Methods. *v.4 p.61*

Measures of Equality. *v.3 p.307*

Measures of Personality and Social Psychological Attitudes, Vol. 1. . . . .*v.5 p.603*

Measures of Political Attitudes. *v.5 p.644, p.645*

Measuring and Improving Patient Satisfaction. .*v.5 p.513, p.514*

Measuring and Monitoring Biological Diversity: Standard Methods for Mammals. *v.5 p.359*

Measuring Delinquency. *v.6 p.255*

Measuring Excellence: The History of Correctional Standards and Accreditation. *v.6 p.275*

Measuring Mass: From Positive Rays to Proteins. . . .*v.5 p.271*

Measuring Minds: Henry Herbert Goddard and the Origins of American Intelligence Testing. *v.4 p.287, v.5 p.599, p.600, p.609, p.657*

Measuring Sustainable Development: Macroeconomics and the Environment. *v.4 p.267, v.5 p.12, p.28*

Measuring the Benefits of Federal Wetland Programs. *v.5 p.177, p.181*

Measuring the Universe: Our Historic Quest to Chart the horizons of Space and Time. *v.5 p.61*

Measuring the Universe: The Cosmological Distance Ladder. *v.5 p.72*

Measuring Up: Educational Assessment Challenges and Practices for Psychology. *v.4 p.285, p.286,v.5 p.593*

Measuring Up. *v.4 p.289*

Measuring What Counts: A Conceptual Guide for Mathematics
Assessment. *v.5 p.463*

Mecca: A Literary History of the Muslim Holy Land. .*v.6 p.625*

Meccan Trade and the Rise of Islam. *v.6 p.583*

Mechanic Accents: Dime Novels and Working Class Culture of
America. *v.2 p.577*

Mechanical Alloying. *v.5 p.736*

Mechanical Behavior of Materials. *v.5 p.324, p.731*

Mechanical Design and Systems Handbook. *v.5 p.715*

Mechanical Design Handbook. *v.5 p.715*

Mechanical Engineering Design. *v.5 p.708*

Mechanical Estimating Methods: Standards and
Procedures. *v.1 p.784*

The Mechanical Investigations of Leonardo da
Vinci. *v.5 p.396, p.397*

Mechanical Man: John B. Watson and the Beginnings of
Behaviorism. *v.5 p.595*

Mechanical Metallurgy: Principles and Applications. .*v.5 p.690*

Mechanical Metallurgy. *v.5 p.688*

Mechanics and Analysis of Beams, Columns and Cables: A
Modern Introduction to the Classic Theories. . . .*v.5 p.695*

Mechanics and Mechanisms of Fracture: An
Introduction. *v.5 p.732*

Mechanics and Thermodynamics of Propulsion. . . .*v.5 p.719*

Mechanics in Structural Geology. *v.5 p.441*

Mechanics of Fiber-Reinforced Concrete: Material Design for
Structural Applications. *v.5 p.696*

Mechanics of Flight. *v.5 p.718*

Mechanics of Materials 2: The Mechanics of Elastic and Plastic
Deformation of Solids and Structural Materials. . .*v.5 p.689*

Mechanics of Materials: An Introduction to the Mechanics of
Elastic and Plastic Deformation of Solids and Structural
Materials. *v.5 p.689*

Mechanics of Materials with Tront Eureka. *v.5 p.689*

Mechanics of Materials. *v.5 p.687, p.688, p.689*

Mechanics of Soil and Foundations. *v.5 p.698*

Mechanics of Structures: Variational and Computational
Methods. *v.5 p.696*

Mechanics, Vol. 1. . . . .*v.5 p.546*

Mechanics. *v.5 p.547*

Mechanism and Synthesis. *v.5 p.328*

Mechanisms and Mechanical Devices Sourcebook. . .*v.5 p.715*

Mechanisms of Inorganic Reactions: A Study of Metal
Complexes in Solution. *v.5 p.304*

Mechanisms of Molecular Evolution. *v.5 p.201*

The Mechanization of the World Picture: Pythagoras to
Newton. *v.5 p.390*

Mechatronics: An Introduction. *v.5 p.714*

The Mechatronics Handbook Second Edition. *v.5 p.714*

Mechatronics: Principles and Applications. *v.5 p.715*

Medallions. *v.2 p.791*

Medea: Essays on Medea in Myth, Literature, Philosophy, and
Art. *v.2 p.410*

Medea. *v.2 p.411*

Media and Conflict: Framing Issues, Making Policy, Shaping
Opinions. *v.4 p.407*

Media and Crime. *v.6 p.256*

Media and Performance: Along the Border. *v.1 p.40*

Media and Revolution. *v.3 p.37*

The Media and the War on Terrorism. *v.4 p.563*

Media Art Net 2: Topical Highlights. *v.1 p.771*

Media Art Net. *v.1 p.770*

The Media at War: Communication and Conflict in the
Twentieth Century. *v.4 p.406*

Media Ethics: Cases and Moral Reasoning. *v.4 p.405*

Media Freedom and Accountability. *v.4 p.405*

Media Gender and Identity: An Introduction. . .*v.4 p.743, p.744*

The Media Handbook. *v.4 p.427, p.428*

The Media in Europe: The Euromedia Handbook. . . .*v.4 p.415*

Media Organizations and Convergence: Case Studies of Media
Convergence Pioneers. *v.4 p.418*

Media Planning: A Practical Guide. *v.4 p.428*

Media Relations in Sport. *v.4 p.902, p.906*

Media Review Digest. *v.6 p.305*

Media Sport Stars: Masculinities and Moralities. .*v.4 p.820, p.903*

Media Systems in Society: Understanding Industries, Strategies,
and Power. *v.4 p.696*

Media Talk: Language and Interaction on Radio and
Television. *v.4 p.418*

Media Technology and Society: A History from the Telegraph to
the Internet. *v.4 p.419*

Media Writer's Handbook: A Guide to Common Editing and
Writing Problems. *v.4 p.413*

Mediaeval Feudalism. *v.3 p.68*

Mediaeval Netherlands Religious Literature. *v.2 p.622*

Mediamark Reporter. *v.4 p.137, p.139*

The Median and Archaemenian Periods. *v.6 p.629*

Mediasport. *v.4 p.820, p.892, p.903, p.907*

The Mediated Presidency: Television News and Presidential
Governance. *v.4 p.558*

Mediated Women: Representations in Popular Culture. *v.6 p.448*

Mediation in the Yugoslav Wars: The Critical Years,
1990-95. . . . .*v.4 p.650, p.651*

Medical and Healthcare Marketplace Guide. *v.4 p.160*

Medical and Physiological Aspects of Sport Psychology. *v.5 p.582*

Medical and Social Aspects of Alcohol Abuse. .*v.5 p.512, p.522*

Medical Anthropology and African American Health. . *v.4 p.46*

Medical Anthropology and the World System. *v.5 p.536*

Medical Anthropology in Ecological
Perspective. *v.5 p.536, p.537, p.539*

The Medical Biochemistry Page. *v.5 p.111*

Medical Biochemistry. *v.5 p.329*

Medical Dictionary. *v.5 p.509*

Medical Genetics at a Glance. *v.5 p.151*

Medical Genetics. *v.5 p.149*

Medical Malpractice on Trial. *v.4 p.445*

The Medical Management of AIDS. *v.5 p.515, p.516*

Medical Microbiology: With Student Consult Access. .*v.5 p.515*

Medical Physiology: With Student Consult Access. . .*v.5 p.164*

The Medical Profession in Mid-Victorian London. . . .*v.3 p.114*

Medical Response to Terrorism. *v.5 p.532*

Medical Science and Democratic Truth: Doctors and Revolution in Nepal. *v.4 p.46*

Medical Sociology: Major Themes in Health and Social Welfare. *v.4 p.756*

Medical Spanish: A Conversational Approach. *v.2 p.636*

Medical-Surgical Nursing: Health and Illness Perspectives. *v.5 p.522*

Medicinal Plants: Chemistry and Properties. *v.5 p.211*

Medicinal Plants of Asia and the Pacific. *v.5 p.211*

Medicinal Plants of the Asia-Pacific: Drugs for the Future? *v.5 p.211*

Medicinal Plants of the World: Chemical Constituents, Traditional and Modern Medicinal Uses, Vol. 1. . .*v.5 p.211*

Medicinal Plants of the World: Chemical Constituents, Traditional and Modern Medicinal Uses. *v.5 p.211*

Medicinal Resources of the Tropical Forest: Biodiversity and Its Importance to Human Health. *v.5 p.16, p.36, p.353*

Medicine: An Illustrated History. *v.5 p.510*

Medicine and Power in Tunisia, 1780-1900. . . . . .*v.6 p.641*

Medicine and Society in Early Modern Europe. *v.3 p.47, p.50,v.5 p.510*

The Medicine of Memory: A Mexica Clan in California. *v.6 p.490, p.536*

Medicine That Walks: Medicine, Disease and Canadian Plains Aboriginal People, 1880-1945. . . . .*v.6 p.702*

Medicine Ways: Disease, Health, and Survival among Native Americans. *v.6 p.702*

Medieval and Early Modern Science, Vol. 1. . . . .*v.5 p.390*

Medieval and Early Modern Science, Vol. 2. . . . .*v.5 p.390*

Medieval and Early Renaissance Medicine: An Introduction to Knowledge and Practice. *v.3 p.50*

Medieval and Tudor Drama: Twenty-Four Plays. *v.1 p.65, p.69, p.73, p.100*

Medieval Archaeology: An Encyclopedia. *v.6 p.555*

Medieval Archaeology: Understanding Traditions and Contemporary Approaches. *v.6 p.555*

Medieval Architecture in Western Europe: From A.D. 300 to 1500. . . . .*v.1 p.785, p.786*

Medieval Architecture. *v.1 p.786*

Medieval Art: A Topical Dictionary. *v.1 p.666, p.672, p.709, p.710*

Medieval Art: Painting, Sculpture, Architecture, 4th-14th Century. *v.1 p.672*

Medieval Art. *v.1 p.672, p.673,v.6 p.556*

Medieval Chinese Warfare 300-900. . . . .*v.6 p.185*

Medieval Christian Literary Imagery: A Guide to Interpretation. *v.6 p.565, p.571*

The Medieval Church: A Brief History. *v.1 p.600, v.3 p.57, p.68*

Medieval Cities: Their Origins and the Revival of Trade. *v.3 p.67, v.6 p.577*

Medieval Civilization, 400-1500. . . . .*v.6 p.563*

Medieval Cosmology: Theories of Infinity, Place, Time, Void, and the Plurality of Worlds. *v.1 p.432, p.500*

Medieval Culture and Society. *v.6 p.576*

Medieval Culture and the Mexican American Borderlands. *v.6 p.486, p.487, p.534*

Medieval England, an Aerial Survey. *v.3 p.126*

Medieval England. *v.3 p.96*

Medieval Epics: Beowulf, the Song of Roland, the Nibelungenlied, and the Cid. *v.2 p.467, p.468,v.6 p.565, p.566*

Medieval Europe: A Short History. *v.3 p.68*

Medieval European Pilgrimage, C.700 - C.1500. . . .*v.1 p.601*

The Medieval European Stage, 500-1550. . . . .*v.1 p.73, p.74, p.97, p.98, p.155*

The Medieval Expansion of Europe. *v.3 p.69, v.4 p.379*

Medieval Farming and Technology: The Impact of Agricultural Change in Northwest Europe. *v.3 p.42*

Medieval Flanders. *v.6 p.564*

Medieval Folklore: A Guide to Myths, Legends, Tales, Beliefs, and Customs. *v.2 p.585*

Medieval Foundations of the Western Intellectual Tradition, 400-1400. . . . .*v.1 p.600*

Medieval France: An Encyclopedia. *v.3 p.141, p.142*

Medieval French Drama. *v.2 p.461*

Medieval Games: Sports and Recreations in Feudal Society, 30. . . . .*v.4 p.783, p.804*

Medieval German Literature : A Survey. *v.2 p.589, p.590*

Medieval Germany, 1056-1273. . . . .*v.3 p.161*

Medieval Germany: An Encyclopedia. *v.3 p.161*

Medieval Hagiography: An Anthology. *v.1 p.613*

Medieval Heresy: Popular Movements from the Gregorian Reform to the Reformation. *v.1 p.646, v.3 p.57, p.69,v.6 p.572*

The Medieval Hero on Screen: Representations from Beowulf to Buffy. *v.6 p.562*

Medieval Households. *v.6 p.557*

Medieval Iberia: An Encyclopedia. *v.6 p.563*

Medieval Iberia: Readings from Christian, Muslim, and Jewish Sources. *v.3 p.237*

Medieval Imagination: Rhetoric and the Poetry of Courtly Love. *v.2 p.457*

The Medieval Imagination. *v.6 p.563*

Medieval India: Researches in the History of India, 1200-1750. . . . .*v.6 p.155*

Medieval Inquisition. *v.3 p.69*

Medieval Ireland: The Enduring Tradition. *v.3 p.137*

Medieval Islamic Civilization: An Encyclopedia. . . .*v.6 p.574*

Medieval Islamic Philosophical Writings. *v.1 p.431*

Medieval Italy: An Encyclopedia. *v.6 p.563*

The Medieval Kingdoms of Nubia: Pagans, Christians and Muslims on the Middle Nile. *v.6 p.59*

Medieval Latin: An Introduction and Bibliographical Guide. *v.2 p.449*

Medieval Latin. *v.2 p.449*

Medieval Lays and Legends of Marie de France. . . .*v.2 p.467*

Medieval Literature of Poland: An Anthology. *v.2 p.787, p.788, p.791*

Medieval Logic: An Outline of Its Development from 1250 to c. 1400. . . . .*v.6 p.567*

Medieval Lyric: Middle English Lyrics, Ballads, and Carols. *v.2 p.199*

The Medieval Manichee: A Study of the Christian Dualist Heresy. *v.1 p.601, v.3 p.58*

Medieval Marriage: Two Models from Twelfth-Century France. *v.6 p.559*

Medieval Misogyny and the Invention of Western Romantic Love. *v.3 p.51*

Medieval Monasticism: Forms of Religious Life in Western Europe in the Middle Ages. . .*v.1 p.578, v.3 p.66, v.6 p.572*

Medieval Music and the Art of Memory. *v.1 p.176*

Medieval Music: The Sixth Liberal Art. *v.6 p.567*

Medieval Music. *v.1 p.177*

The Medieval Papacy. *v.1 p.572, v.3 p.56*

Medieval Philosophy: A New History of Western Philosophy. *v.1 p.432*

Medieval Philosophy: An Introduction. *v.1 p.431*

Medieval Philosophy and the Classical Tradition: In Islam, Judaism and Christianity. *v.1 p.432, v.6 p.567, p.571*

Medieval Philosophy: From Augustine to Duns Scotus. .*v.1 p.432*

Medieval Philosophy, Vol. 3. . . . .*v.1 p.433*

Medieval Philosophy. *v.1 p.433*

Medieval Popular Culture: Problems of Belief and Perception. *v.6 p.571*

Medieval Reading: Grammar, Rhetoric and the Classical Text. *v.2 p.449*

Medieval Religious Houses in England and Wales. . .*v.1 p.578*

Medieval Religious Women I: Distant Echoes. .*v.6 p.560, p.572*

Medieval Russia, 980-1584. . . . .*v.3 p.215*

Medieval Russian Epics, Chronicles, and Tales. . . .*v.2 p.795*

Medieval Scandinavia: From Conversion to Reformation, Circa 800-1500. . . . .*v.3 p.232, p.233*

Medieval Schools: Roman Britain to Renaissance England. *v.4 p.336, v.6 p.558*

Medieval Science, Technology and Medicine: An Encyclopedia. *v.3 p.44, v.5 p.388*

Medieval Society. *v.3 p.66, p.67,v.6 p.576*

The Medieval Spains. *v.3 p.66, p.238*

The Medieval Stage. *v.1 p.73, p.154*

Medieval Studies: A Bibliographical Guide. *v.6 p.555*

Medieval Studies: An Introduction. *v.6 p.555*

Medieval Technology and Social Change. *v.3 p.68*

The Medieval Theatre. *v.1 p.74*

Medieval Thought: The Western Intellectual Tradition from Antiquity to the Thirteenth Century. . . .*v.1 p.432, v.6 p.567*

Medieval Thought. *v.1 p.433*

The Medieval Town: A Reader in English Urban History, 1200-1540. . . . .*v.6 p.577*

Medieval Trade in the Mediterranean World: Illustrative Documents. *v.3 p.69, p.198,v.6 p.558*

The Medieval Vision: Essays in History and Perception. *v.6 p.562*

Medieval Welsh Society: Selected Essays. *v.4 p.705*

Medieval Women: A Social History of Women in England, 450-1500. . . . .*v.6 p.560*

Medieval Women and the Sources of Medieval History. *v.6 p.561*

Medieval Women Writers. *v.6 p.561, p.566*

Medieval Women. *v.6 p.451, p.560*

Medieval Worlds: A Sourcebook. *v.3 p.62*

The Medieval World. *v.6 p.555*

Medieval Writers and Their Work: Middle English Literature and Its Background, 1100-1500. . . . .*v.6 p.564*

Medio Siglo de Literatura Cubana, 1902-1952. . . .*v.2 p.671*

The Meditations of Marcus Aurelius: A Study. . . .*v.1 p.429*

Meditations on a Hobby Horse and Other Essays on the Theory of Art. *v.1 p.703*

Meditations on Modern Political Thought: Masculine - Feminine Themes from Luther to Arendt. *v.6 p.440, p.464*

Meditations on Quixote: Translated from the Spanish by Evelyn Rugg and Diego Marin Introduction and Notes by Julian Marias. *v.2 p.651*

Meditations on the Sacraments. *v.1 p.577*

Meditations. *v.1 p.428*

The Mediterranean and the Mediterranean World in the Age of Philip II. *v.3 p.38*

Mediterranean Countrymen : Essays in the Social Anthropology of the Mediterranean. *v.4 p.705*

Mediterranean Crossroads: Migration Literature in Italy. *v.2 p.698*

Mediterranean Encounters, Economic, Religious, Political, 1100-1550. . . . .*v.3 p.65*

Mediterranean in the Ancient World. *v.3 p.3*

A Mediterranean Society. *v.6 p.597*

Mediterranean Urbanization 800-600 BC. *v.4 p.12, p.13*

The Mediterranean World in Late Antiquity, AD 395-600. . . . .*v.3 p.30, p.192*

The Medium Is the Message. *v.5 p.625*

☐ MedlinePlus: A Service of the National Library of Medicine and the National Institutes of Health. *v.5 p.509*

Meech Lake: The Inside Story. *v.4 p.587*

Meet Me in the Middle: Becoming an Accomplished Middle-Level Teacher. *v.4 p.366*

Meet Mr. Mulliner. *v.2 p.391*

The Meeting at Telgte. *v.2 p.608*

A Meeting by the River. *v.2 p.356*

The Meeting of Religions and the Trinity. *v.1 p.597*

Meeting the Communist Threat: Truman to Reagan. *v.3 p.453, p.454*

Meeting the Expectations of the Land: Essays in Sustainable Agriculture and Stewardship. *v.5 p.12*

Meetings, Expositions, Events and Conventions: An Introduction to the Industry. *v.4 p.161*

Megaevents and Modernity: Olympics, Expos and the Growth of Global Culture. *v.4 p.846, p.889, p.892*

Megalithic Art of Western Europe. *v.1 p.669*

Mega-Projects: The Changing Politics of Urban Public Investment. *v.6 p.722*

Megawatts and Megatons: A Turning Point in the Nuclear Age? *v.5 p.553*

The Megiddo Modern Dictionary: English-Hebrew, Hebrew-English. *v.6 p.646*

Mehmed the Conqueror and His Time. *v.6 p.589, p.622*

Meinong. *v.1 p.464*

Meister Eckhart: The Essential Sermons, Commentaries, Treatises and Defense. *v.1 p.652, p.653*

Meisterdramen. *v.2 p.616*

El Mejor Alcalde, el Rey Fuenteovejuna. *v.2 p.653*

Melancholia and Depression: From Hippocratic Times to
Modern Times. *v.5 p.659*

Melancholia and Moralism: Essays on AIDS and Queer
Politics. *v.6 p.378*

Melancholy and the Secular Mind in Spanish Golden Age
Literature. *v.2 p.639*

The Melancholy of Rebirth: Essays from Post-Communist
Central Eruope, 1989-1994. . . . *v.2 p.784, p.785,v.3 p.187*

The Melancholy of Resistance. *v.2 p.786*

Melanesian Religion. *v.1 p.544*

Melanges. *v.2 p.485*

Melbourne. *v.3 p.93, p.111*

Melmoth the Wanderer. *v.2 p.299*

ⓔ Melodrama and Modernity: Early Sensational Cinema and Its
Contexts. *v.6 p.327, p.333, p.343*

Melodrama: Plots That Thrilled. *v.1 p.88*

Melodrama: The Cultural Emergence of a
Genre. *v.1 p.88, p.96, p.115,v.2 p.188*

Melodramatic Tactics: Theatricalized Dissent in the English
Marketplace, 1800-1885. . . . . *v.6 p.754, p.758*

▢ Melpomene Institute. *v.4 p.789, p.794, p.834, p.872*

The Melting Pot in Israel: The Commission of Inquiry
Concerning the Education of Immigrant Children During the
Early Years of the State. *v.4 p.337*

Melting the Earth: The History of Ideas on Volcanic
Eruptions. *v.5 p.437, p.438*

A Melville Encyclopedia: The Novels. *v.2 p.48*

Melville: The Critical Heritage. *v.2 p.47*

Melville's Muse: Literary Creation and the Forms of
Philosophical Fiction. *v.2 p.49*

Melville. *v.2 p.48*

Member of Parliament: The Job of a Backbencher. . *v.4 p.606*

A Member of the Family: Gay Men Write about Their Closest
Relations. *v.6 p.375*

The Member of the Wedding: A Play. *v.2 p.100*

Memed, My Hawk. *v.6 p.667*

Memmler's Structure and Function of the Human Body. *v.5 p.164*

A Memoir of Jane Austen: And Other Family
Recollections. *v.2 p.267*

Memoir of the Bobotes. *v.2 p.338*

Memoires D'Outre-Tombe, Tombe 2. . . . . *v.2 p.488*

Memoires D'Outre-Tombe, Tome 1. . . . . *v.2 p.488*

Memoires Improvises. *v.2 p.513*

Memoirs, 1925-1950. . . . . *v.3 p.459*

Memoirs, 1945: Year of Decisions. *v.3 p.481*

Memoirs: A Twentieth Century Journey in Science and
Politics. *v.5 p.544*

Memoirs and Opinions, 1926-1974. . . . . *v.2 p.125*

Memoirs from the Beijing Film Academy: The Genesis of
China's Fifth Generation. *v.6 p.209, p.335*

Memoirs from the Greek War of Independence,
1821-1883. . . . . *v.3 p.195*

Memoirs from the Women's Prison. *v.6 p.657*

Memoirs of a Beatnik. *v.2 p.143*

Memoirs of a Cavalier, or, A Military Journal of the Wars in
Germany and the Wars in England. *v.2 p.245*

Memoirs of a Counter-Revolutionary: Life with the Contras, the
Sandinistas, and the CIA. *v.3 p.301*

Memoirs of a Dutiful Daughter. *v.2 p.508*

Memoirs of a Fox-Hunting Man. *v.2 p.379, p.380*

Memoirs of a Madman. *v.2 p.490*

Memoirs of a Militia Sergeant. *v.2 p.690*

The Memoirs of a Shy Pornographer. *v.2 p.110, p.111*

Memoirs of a Tourist. *v.2 p.502*

Memoirs of a Woman Doctor. *v.6 p.656, p.657*

Memoirs of an Egotist. *v.2 p.502*

Memoirs of an Exile. *v.6 p.667*

Memoirs of an Infantry Officer. *v.2 p.380*

Memoirs of Bernardo Vega: A Contribution to the History of the
Puerto Rican Community in New York. . . *v.6 p.491, p.536*

The Memoirs of Catherine the Great. *v.3 p.217*

The Memoirs of Chief Justice Earl Warren. *v.4 p.469*

The Memoirs of Cordell Hull, Set. *v.3 p.459*

The Memoirs of Emma Courtney and Adeline Mowbray; or the
Mother and the Daughter. *v.2 p.290*

Memoirs of Extraordinary Popular Delusions and the Madness
of Crowds: The Essential Library Edition. . . . *v.4 p.244*

The Memoirs of Gluckel of Hamelin. *v.3 p.180*

Memoirs of Hadrian. *v.6 p.400*

Memoirs of Harry S. Truman: Years of Trial and Hope. *v.3 p.481*

Memoirs of Hecate County. *v.2 p.137*

The Memoirs of Hector Berlioz. *v.1 p.194, p.310*

The Memoirs of Herbert Hoover. *v.3 p.459, p.472*

Memoirs of John Quincy Adams, Comprising Portions of His
Diary from 1795 to 1848, Set. *v.3 p.416*

Memoirs of King Abdullah of Transjordan. *v.6 p.620*

The Memoirs of Lady Hyegyong: The Autobiographical
Writings of a Crown Princess of Eighteenth-Century
Korea. *v.6 p.237*

Memoirs of Lorenzo Da Ponte. . *v.1 p.188, p.189, p.319, p.320*

Memoirs of Montparnasse. *v.2 p.735*

Memoirs of Mr. Laurence Sterne, the Life and Opinions of
Tristram Shandy, a Sentimental Journey, Selected
Sermons and Letters. *v.2 p.262*

Memoirs of Nikita Khrushchev. *v.3 p.224*

Memoirs of Rear-Admiral John Paul Jones. *v.3 p.411*

Memoirs of the Life and Writings of the Late Dr Samuel
Johnson/[by] William Shaw ; [and], Anecdotes of
the Late Samuel Johnson, LL.D. During the Last Twenty
Years of His Life/[by] Hesther [i.e. Hester] Lynch
Piozzi. *v.2 p.251*

Memoirs of the Life of Henriette-Sylvie de Moliere: A
Novel. *v.2 p.478*

Memoirs of the Life of the Right Honorable Richard Brinsley
Sheridan. *v.2 p.260*

Memoirs of the Polish Baroque: The Writings of Jan
Chryzostom Pasek, a Squire of the Commonwealth of Poland
and Lithuania. *v.2 p.791*

Memoirs. *v.2 p.328, p.681,v.3 p.542*

Memorabilia and Oeconomicus, Symposium, and Apologia, Vol.
4. . . . . *v.2 p.422*

Memorabilia. *v.1 p.423*

The Memorial: Portrait of a Family. *v.2 p.356*

Memorials of Alfred Marshall. *v.4 p.224*

Memorias del Nuevo Mundo. *v.2 p.666*

Memories and Commentaries, Vol. 1. . . . . .*v.1 p.225, p.360*

Memories Cast in Stone: The Relevance of the Past in Everyday
Life. *v.3 p.196*

Memories of a Future Home: Diasporic Citizenship of Chinese
in Panama. *v.3 p.306*

The Memories of Ana Calderon. *v.6 p.500, p.501*

Memories of Chicano History: The Life and Narrative of Bert
Corona. *v.6 p.488, p.535, p.536*

Memories of My Life, Being My Personal, Professional, and
Social Recollections As Woman and Artist. *v.1 p.105, p.143*

Memories of My Melancholy Whores. *v.2 p.683*

Memories of Revolt: The 1936-39 Rebellion and the Palestinian
National Past. *v.6 p.612*

Memories of Summer: When Baseball Was an Art and Writing
about It a Game. *v.4 p.811, p.851*

Memories, Thoughts and Emotions: Essays in Honor of George
Mandler. *v.5 p.605*

Memory and Agony: Dutch Stories from Indonesia. .*v.2 p.623*

Memory and American History. *v.3 p.375*

Memory and Cognition. *v.5 p.605*

Memory and Emotion: The Making of Lasting
Memories. *v.5 p.610*

Memory and Emotion. *v.5 p.610*

Memory and Imagination: The Legacy of Maidu Indian Artist
Frank Day. *v.1 p.738, v.6 p.678*

Memory and Learning: The Ebbinghaus Centennial
Conference. *v.5 p.610*

Memory and the Impact of Political Transformation in Public
Space. *v.3 p.300, p.303*

Memory and the Mediterranean. *v.3 p.3*

Memory Babe: A Critical Biography of Jack Kerouac. *v.2 p.93*

Memory Development Between 2 and 20. . . .*v.5 p.629, p.630*

Memory for Forgetfulness: August, Beirut, 1982. *v.6 p.606, p.659*

Memory in the Real World. *v.5 p.610*

Memory Mambo. *v.6 p.398, p.508*

The Memory Palace of Matteo Ricci. *v.6 p.218*

Memory: The Key to Consciousness. *v.5 p.610, p.611*

Memory's Nation: The Place of Plymouth Rock. *v.3 p.488, p.489*

Memory's Orbit: Film and Culture 1999-2000. . . .*v.6 p.332*

Memory. *v.5 p.609, p.610*

🄴 The Memphis Diary of Ida B. Wells. *v.6 p.19*

The Memphis Diary of Ida B. Wells. *v.6 p.17, p.43*

Men Against McCarthy. *v.3 p.458*

Men and Aging: A Selected, Annotated Bibliography. *v.6 p.445*

Men and Destiny. *v.3 p.455*

Men and Masculinities: A Social, Cultural, and Historical
Encyclopedia. *v.6 p.425*

Men and Popular Music in Algeria: The Social Significance of
Raï. *v.6 p.644*

Men and Speed: A Wild Ride Through NASCAR's Breakout
Season. *v.4 p.848*

Men as Women, Women as Men: Changing Gender in Native
American Cultures. *v.6 p.370, p.371*

Men at Midlife. *v.4 p.741, v.6 p.445*

Men at War 1914-1918: National Sentiment and Trench
Journalism in France during the First World War. . *v.3 p.154*

Men Engaging Feminisms: Pro-Feminism, Backlashes and
Schooling. *v.6 p.463*

Men in the Sun and Other Palestinian Stories. *v.6 p.661*

Men in Wonderland: The Lost Girlhood of the Victorian
Gentleman. *v.2 p.277, v.6 p.748*

Men, Makeup and Monsters: Hollywood's Masters of Illusion
and FX. *v.6 p.351*

Men, Masculinities and Social Welfare. . .*v.4 p.755, v.6 p.470*

Men of Blood: Violence, Manliness, and Criminal Justice in
Victorian England. *v.6 p.744*

Men of Property: The Very Wealthy in Britain Since the
Industrial Revolution. *v.3 p.115, p.123*

Men of Science in America: The Story of American Science
Told Through the Lives and Achievements of
Twenty Outstanding Men from Earliest Colonial Times to the
Present Day. *v.5 p.388, p.393*

Men of the West: Life on the American Frontier. . . .*v.3 p.521*

Men Own the Fields, Women Own the Crops: Gender and
Power in the Cameroon Grassfields. *v.4 p.30*

The Men They Will Become: The Nature and Nurture of the
Male Character. *v.5 p.642, v.6 p.446*

Men Who Beat the Men Who Love Them: Battered Gay Men
and Domestic Violence. *v.6 p.377*

Men Who Believe in Feminism: Dismantling the Master's
House? *v.6 p.434*

The Men with the Pink Triangle: The True Life and Death Story
of Homosexuals in the Nazi Death Camps. *v.3 p.84, v.6 p.365*

Men, Women, and Aggression. *v.5 p.651*

Men, Women, and Chain Saws: Gender in the Modern Horror
Film. *v.6 p.317*

Men, Women and Pianos: A Social History. .*v.1 p.377, p.390*

Menander - Heros, Theophoroumene, Karchedonios, Kitharistes,
Kolax, Koneiazomenai, Leukadia, Misoumenos,
Perikeiromene, Perinthia, Vol. 2. . . . .*v.2 p.416*

Menander: Samia, Sikyonioi, Synaristosai, Phasma, Unidentified
Fragments. *v.2 p.416*

Menander, the Plays and Fragments. .*v.1 p.71, p.90,v.2 p.416*

Mencius and Early Chinese Thought. *v.1 p.418*

Mencius. *v.1 p.418*

Mencken's America. *v.3 p.443*

Mende Government and Politics under Colonial Rule: A
Historical Study of Political Change in Sierra Leone,
1890-1937. . . . .*v.6 p.72*

Mendel's Legacy: The Origin of Classical Genetics. . .*v.5 p.131*

Mendelssohn: A Life in Music. *v.1 p.205, p.341*

Mendelssohn and His World by Todd. *v.1 p.205, p.341*

Mendelssohn: The Hebrides and Other
Overtures. *v.1 p.205, p.243, p.341*

Mendelssohn's 'Italian' Symphony. . . .*v.1 p.196, p.238, p.340*

The Mendelssohns: Their Music in
History. *v.1 p.196, p.331, p.340*

⬜ MENIC: The Middle East Information Center - Countries &
Regions. *v.4 p.615, v.6 p.595*

⬜ The Men's Bibliography. *v.6 p.425, p.429*

Men's Studies Modified: The Impact of Feminism on the Academic Disciplines. . . . . *.v.6 p.464*

Der Mensch Erscheint Im Holozan. . . . . *.v.2 p.607*

Mental Acts, 1971. *.v.1 p.496*

Mental and Physical Traits of a Thousand Gifted Children. . . . . *.v.5 p.576*

The Mental Athlete. . . . . *.v.5 p.582, p.583*

Mental Causation. . . . . *.v.1 p.497*

Mental Disability Law: Cases and Materials. . *.v.5 p.592, p.593*

The Mental Game Plan. . . . . *.v.5 p.581*

Mental Health Practice for Children and Youth: A Strengths and Well-Being Model. . . . . *.v.5 p.513*

Mental Health Services: A Public Health Perspective. *.v.5 p.671*

Mental Health. . . . . *.v.5 p.672*

Mental Life of Monkeys and Apes. . . . . *.v.5 p.616*

Mental Measurements Yearbook, Vol. 16. . . . *.v.5 p.601, p.602*

Mental Retardation: An Introduction to Intellectual Disability. . . . . *.v.5 p.517*

Mental Retardation: Definition, Classification, and Systems of Supports. . . . . *.v.5 p.517*

Mental Retardation in the 21st Century. . . . . . *.v.5 p.517*

Mental Retardation. . . . . *.v.5 p.517*

Mental Territories: Mapping the Inland Empire. . . . *.v.3 p.530*

Mental Toughness: A Champion's State of Mind. . . *.v.5 p.582*

The Mentality of Apes. . . . . *.v.5 p.615*

The Mentally Ill in Jail: Planning for Essential Services. *.v.6 p.277*

Mentoring Across Boundaries: Helping Beginning Teachers Succeed in Challenging Situations. . . . . . . *.v.4 p.277*

Mentoring Beginning Teachers: Guiding, Reflecting, Coaching. . . . . *.v.4 p.277*

Mentoring New Special Education Teachers: A Guide for Mentors and Program Developers. . . . . . . *.v.4 p.277*

Mentoring New Teachers. . . . . *.v.4 p.277*

Mephistopheles: The Devil in the Modern World. . . *.v.1 p.529*

Mephisto. . . . . *.v.2 p.618*

Merc: The Emergence of a Global Financial Powerhouse. . . . . *.v.4 p.102, p.163*

Mercantilism, Set. . . . . *.v.4 p.216*

Mercantilism. *.v.4 p.215*

Merce Cunningham: Fifty Forward. . . . . . *.v.1 p.29, p.31*

Merce Cunningham: Fifty Years. . . . . *.v.1 p.13, p.26*

Merce Cunningham: The Modernizing of Modern Dance. . . . . *.v.1 p.28, p.30*

Merce Cunningham. . . . . *.v.1 p.9, p.10*

Merchant Capital and the Roots of State Power in Senegal, 1930-1985. . . . . *.v.6 p.72*

The Merchant of Venice: Texts and Contexts. . . . . *.v.2 p.224*

Merchants and Migrants in Nineteenth Century Beirut. *.v.6 p.605*

Merchants and Shopkeepers: An Historical Anthropology of an Irish Market Town, 1200-1986. . . . . *.v.4 p.42*

Merchants of Buenos Aires, Seventeen Seventy-Eight to Eighteen Hundred and Ten. . . . . *.v.3 p.347*

Merciful Disguises: Published and Unpublished Poems. *.v.2 p.126*

The Merck Index: An Encyclopedia of Chemicals, Drugs, and Biologicals. . . . . *.v.5 p.259, v.6 p.286*

The Merck Index, Internet Edition. . . . . *.v.5 p.259*

The Merck Manual of Diagnosis and Therapy. . . . *.v.5 p.515*

The Merck Veterinary Manual. . . . . *.v.5 p.55, p.57*

Mercosur: The Common Market of the Southern Cone. *.v.4 p.61*

Mercury - Cadmium - Lead: Handbook for Sustainable Heavy Metals Policy and Regulation. . . . . . . *.v.5 p.372, p.374*

The Mercury 13: The Untold Story of Thirteen American Women and the Dream of Space Flight. . . *.v.5 p.718, p.719*

Mercy of a Rude Stream. . . . . *.v.2 p.114*

Mercy on Trial: What It Means to Stop an Execution. *.v.6 p.272*

Mere Christianity. . . . . *.v.1 p.597*

Meredith: A Change of Masks. . . . . *.v.2 p.299, p.300*

Meredith Monk. . . . . . *.v.1 p.9, p.26, p.217, p.342*

Meredith. . . . . *.v.2 p.300*

Merengue: Dominican Music and Dominican Identity. . . . . *.v.1 p.291, v.3 p.266, p.316*

Mergent Online Industry Reports. . . . . *.v.4 p.150*

Mergers and Acquisitions Basics: The Key Steps of Acquisitions, Divestitures, and Investments. . . . . *.v.4 p.84*

Mergers and Acquisitions: Business Strategies for Accountants. . . . . *.v.4 p.84*

Mergers and Acquisitions from A to Z. . . . . . . *.v.4 p.85*

Mergers and Acquisitions. . . . . *.v.4 p.85*

Merging Traffic: The Consolidation of the International Automobile Industry. . . . . *.v.4 p.153, p.664*

Merleau-Ponty. . . . . *.v.1 p.457*

Merlin and the Hibiscus: Contemporary Short Stories from Singapore and Malaysia. . . . . *.v.2 p.760*

Mermaids on Parade: America's Love Affair with Its First Olympic Swimmers. . . . . *.v.4 p.823, p.835, p.845, p.868*

The Merovingian Kingdoms, 450-751. . . . . *.v.3 p.67*

Merriam-Webster's Dictionary of English Usage. *.v.2 p.549, p.557*

Merriam-Webster's Geographical Dictionary. . *.v.4 p.373, p.374*

Merritt's Neurology: Integrating the Physical Exam and Echocardiography. . . . . *.v.5 p.516*

Merry Wheels and Spokes of Steel: A Social History of the Bicycle. . . . . *.v.4 p.819, p.857*

Merry Wives and Others: A History of Domestic Humor Writing. . . . . *.v.2 p.195*

The Merry Wives of Windsor. . . . . *.v.2 p.225*

Merry-Making in Old Russia: And Other Stories. . . *.v.2 p.807*

Meselson, Stahl, and the Replication of DNA: A History of "The Most Beautiful Experiment in Biology". . . *.v.5 p.122*

Mesmer and Animal Magnetism: A Chapter in the History of Medicine. . . . . *.v.5 p.597, p.598*

Mesmerized: Powers of Mind in Victorian Britain. . *.v.6 p.751*

Mesoamerican Archaeology: Theory and Practice. . . *.v.4 p.9*

Mesoamerican Architecture As a Cultural Symbol. . *.v.3 p.261*

The Mesoamerican Ballgame. . . . . *.v.3 p.262*

MesoAmerican Native Spirituality: From the Cult of the Feathered Serpent to the Theology of Liberation. . *.v.3 p.296*

Mesoamerican Writing Systems: Propaganda, Myth, and History in Four Ancient Civilizations. . . . . . . *.v.3 p.261*

Mesopotamia and Persia Under the Mongols in the Fourteenth Century A.D. . . . . *.v.6 p.585*

Mesopotamia and the Bible. . . . . *.v.3 p.4*

Mesopotamia: The Invention of the City. *v.3 p.5, p.6*

Mesopotamia: The Material Foundations. *v.3 p.6*

Mesopotamian Civilization: The Material Foundations. . *v.3 p.6*

Le message : roman. *v.2 p.529*

Message poetique du symbolisme. *v.2 p.461*

Message to Aztlan: Selected Readings. *v.6 p.499, p.540*

The Message to the Planet. *v.2 p.372*

Messages to the World: The Statements of Osama Bin
    Laden. *v.4 p.658*

The Message. *v.1 p.613*

The Messenger's Motives: Ethical Problems of the News
    Media. *v.4 p.405*

The Messiaen Companion. *v.1 p.216, p.341*

Messiaen: Quatuor Pour la Fin du Temps. .*v.1 p.221, p.242, p.341*

Messiaen. *v.1 p.216, p.341*

The Messianic Idea in Judaism: And Other Essays on Jewish
    Spirituality. *v.1 p.552*

Messianic Judaism: A Rabbi's Journey Through Religious
    Change in America. *v.1 p.597*

Mestizaje: Critical Uses of Race in Chicano Culture. .*v.6 p.544*

Mestizaje Upside-Down: Aesthetic Politics in Modern
    Bolivia. *v.3 p.324*

Mestizo Democracy: The Politics of Crossing Borders. .*v.6 p.537*

The Mestizo Mind: The Intellectual Dynamics of Colonization
    and Globalization. *v.3 p.263*

Mestizo Modernism: Race, Nation and Identity in Latin
    American Culture, 1900-1940. . . . .*v.3 p.267*

Meta-Analysis, a Comparison of Approaches. *v.4 p.689*

The Metabolic and Molecular Bases of Inherited
    Disease. *v.5 p.533*

☐ Metabolic Pathways of Biochemistry. *v.5 p.111*

Metabolic Profiling: Its Role in Biomarker Discovery and Gene
    Function Analysis. *v.5 p.127*

Metabolome Analyses: Strategies for Systems
    Biology. *v.5 p.108, p.143, p.147, p.152*

Metacommunities: Spatial Dynamics and Ecological
    Communities. *v.4 p.394*

☐ METADEX. *v.5 p.731*

Meta-Ethnography: Synthesizing Qualitative Studies. . .*v.4 p.24*

Metal Complexes in Organic Chemistry. *v.5 p.299*

Metal Fatigue in Engineering. *v.5 p.691*

Metallic Materials: Physical, Mechanical, and Corrosion
    Properties, Vol. 19. . . . .*v.5 p.691, p.735*

Metallic Materials Specification Handbook. *v.5 p.691*

Metallography: Principles and Practice. *v.5 p.734*

Metallurgical Failure Analysis. *v.5 p.687*

Metallurgical Reminiscences and Dialogue. *v.5 p.735*

Metallurgy for the Non-Metallurgist. *v.5 p.731*

☐ Metallurgy Resources on the Internet. *v.5 p.731*

Metalogic: An Introduction to the Metatheory of Standard First
    Order Logic. *v.1 p.494*

The Metalogicon of John of Salisbury. *v.1 p.432*

Metals and Alloys in the Unified Numbering System. .*v.5 p.686*

Metals and Ligand Reactivity: An Introduction to the Organic
    Chemistry of Metal Complexes. *v.5 p.299*

Metals Handbook: Desk Edition. *v.5 p.688*

Metamorphic Rocks and Their Geodynamic Significance: A
    Petrological Handbook. *v.5 p.440*

Metamorphism and Metamorphic Belts. *v.5 p.440*

Metamorphoses, Bks. 1-6. . . . .*v.2 p.429*

Metamorphoses, Bks. 7-11. . . . .*v.2 p.428*

Metamorphoses, Bks. 9-15. . . . .*v.2 p.439*

The Metamorphoses of Apuleius: On Making An Ass of
    Oneself. *v.2 p.429*

The Metamorphoses of Ovid. *v.2 p.439*

The Metaphorical Brain 2: Neural Networks and
    Beyond. *v.5 p.407*

The Metaphorical Brain: An Introduction to Cybernetics as
    Artificial Intelligence and Brain Theory. *v.5 p.407*

Metaphors of Change in the Language of Nineteenth-Century
    Fiction: Scott, Gaskell, and Kingsley. .*v.2 p.289, p.296, p.308*

Metaphors We Live By. *v.2 p.562, v.4 p.20*

The Metaphysical Club: A Story of Ideas in America. .*v.1 p.439*

Metaphysical Lyrics and Poems of the Seventeenth Century:
    Donne to Butler. *v.2 p.199*

Metaphysical Poetry. *v.2 p.201*

The Metaphysical Poets. *v.2 p.182, p.183, p.199*

Metaphysica. *v.2 p.408*

Metaphysics: An Anthology. *v.1 p.488*

Metaphysics and Oppression: Heidegger's Challenge to Western
    Philosophy. *v.1 p.471*

Metaphysics and the Origin of Species. *v.5 p.192*

Metaphysics As a Guide to Morals: Philosophical
    Reflections. *v.1 p.488*

Metaphysics: Books M and N. *v.1 p.426*

The Metaphysics of Evolution. *v.5 p.193*

The Metaphysics of Free Will: An Essay on Control. .*v.1 p.503*

The Metaphysics of Logical Positivism. *v.1 p.511*

The Metaphysics of Love: Studies in Renaissance Love Poetry
    from Dante to Milton. *v.2 p.182*

Metaphysics. *v.1 p.439, p.489*

Metapopulation Biology: Ecology, Genetics, and
    Evolution. *v.5 p.184, p.188*

Metapopulation Dynamics: Empirical and Theoretical
    Investigations. *v.5 p.91, p.184, p.188*

Metapopulation Ecology. *v.5 p.184, p.188*

Meteorites: A Journey Through Space and Time. .*v.5 p.69, p.434*

Meteorological Measurement Systems. *v.5 p.425*

Meteorology Today. *v.4 p.393*

Meter As Rhythm. *v.1 p.370, p.371*

Method Acting Reconsidered: Theory, Practice,
    Future. *v.1 p.139, p.145*

Method and Appraisal in Economics. *v.4 p.269*

The Method and Theory of Ethnology. *v.4 p.24*

A Method of Lighting the Stage. *v.1 p.148*

Methodism: Empire of the Spirit. *v.1 p.586*

The Methodist Experience in America: Sourcebook. . .*v.1 p.586*

The Methodology of Economic Model Building: Methodology
    after Samuelson. *v.4 p.194*

The Methodology of Economics: Or, How Economists
    Explain. *v.4 p.194*

Title Index

The Methodology of Empirical Macroeconomics. . . .*v.4 p.195*

Methods and Materials for Teaching the Gifted. *v.4 p.317*

The Methods and Materials of Demography: Condensed
Edition. *v.4 p.376*

Methods and Materials of Painting of the Great Schools and
Masters. *v.1 p.751*

Methods for Fish Biology. *v.5 p.216*

Methods for the Oxidation of Organic Compounds: Alkanes,
Alkenes, Alkynes, and Arenes, Vol. 1. . . . . . .*v.5 p.295*

Methods in Cell Biology: Fluorescence Microscopy of Living
Cells in Culture: Fluorescent Analogs, Labeling Cells
and Basic Microscopy. *v.5 p.86, p.87*

Methods in Computational Chemistry: Electron Correlation in
Atoms and Molecules. *v.5 p.280*

Methods in Ecological and Agricultural Entomology. . .*v.5 p.11*

Methods in Enzymology. *v.5 p.326*

Methods in Medical Ethics. *v.5 p.511*

Methods in Modern Biophysics. *v.5 p.125*

Methods in Plant Molecular Biology and
Biotechnology. *v.5 p.133*

Methods in Proteome and Protein Analysis. *v.5 p.116*

Methods in Soil Biology. *v.5 p.89*

Methods of Biochemical Analysis. *v.5 p.326*

Methods of Evaluating Educational Technology. . . .*v.4 p.351*

Methods of Logic. *v.1 p.492*

Methods of Mathematical Physics, Vol. 2. . . . . . .*v.5 p.500*

Methods of Mathematical Physics. *v.5 p.500*

Methods of Meta-Analysis: Correcting Error and Bias in
Research Findings. *v.4 p.689*

Methods of Microarray Data Analysis, Vol. 4.   *v.5 p.101, p.137*

Methods of Microarray Data Analysis. *v.5 p.100, p.110*

Methods of Modifying Habitat to Benefit the Great Lakes
Ecosystem. *v.5 p.174, p.234*

Methods of Multivariate Analysis: Basic Applications. *v.5 p.483*

Methods of Numerical Integration. *v.5 p.492*

Methods of Quantum Field Theory in Statistical
Physics. *v.5 p.558*

Methods of Soil Analysis: Chemical Methods. *v.5 p.51*

Methods of Soil Analysis: Microbiological and Biochemical
Properties. *v.5 p.51, p.52*

Methods of Soil Analysis: Physical and Mineralogical
Methods. *v.5 p.50*

Methods of Soil Analysis: Physical Methods. *v.5 p.48*

Methods of Theoretical Physics, Vol. 2. . . . .*v.5 p.548*

The Methuen Book of Latin American Plays: La Chunga, Paper
Flowers, Medea in the Mirror. *v.2 p.645*

Metre, Rhythm and Verse Form. *v.2 p.181*

Metromarxism: A Marxist Tale of the City. *v.6 p.718*

The Metropolitan Frontier: Cities in the Modern American
West. *v.3 p.519, v.6 p.710*

Metropolitan Government and Governance: Theoretical
Perspectives, Empirical Analysis, and the Future. . *v.4 p.543*

The Metropolitan Opera Book of Mozart
Operas. *v.1 p.191, p.231, p.344, p.409*

Metropolitan Railways: Rapid Transit in America. . . .*v.5 p.700*

Metropolitics: A Regional Agenda for Community and
Stability. *v.6 p.724*

Metternich and His Times. *v.3 p.183*

Metternich: The Autobiography, 1773-1815. . . . . .*v.3 p.184*

Metternich's German Policy: The Congress of Vienna,
1814-1815, Vol. 2. . . . .*v.3 p.184*

Metternich's German Policy: The Contest with Napoleon,
1799-1814. . . . .*v.3 p.183, p.184*

La Mettrie: Medicine, Philosophy, and
Enlightenment. *v.3 p.50, p.148*

The Mexican American Experience: An Encyclopedia. *v.6 p.485*

The Mexican American Family: Tradition and Change. *v.6 p.545*

The Mexican American Orquesta: Music, Culture, and the
Dialectic of Conflict. *v.6 p.519*

Mexican American Theatre: Then and
Now. *v.1 p.124, v.6 p.513, p.517*

Mexican American Women Activists: Identity and Resistance in
Two Los Angeles Communities. . . .*v.6 p.431, p.546, p.550*

Mexican American Women: Changing Images. *v.6 p.546*

🅔 Mexican American Youth Organization: Avant-Garde of the
Chicano Movement in Texas. *v.6 p.541*

Mexican Americans and Health: Sana! Sana!. *v.6 p.551*

Mexican Americans and the Environment: Tierra y
Vida. *v.6 p.522, p.551*

Mexican Americans and the Law: El Pueblo Unido Jamás Ser
Vencido!. *v.4 p.458, v.6 p.541*

Mexican Americans in Texas: A Brief History. *v.3 p.508*

Mexican Americans in the 1990s: Politics, Policies, and
Perceptions. *v.6 p.538*

Mexican Americans: Leadership, Ideology, and Identity,
1930-1960. . . . .*v.6 p.538, p.544*

The Mexican Americans. *v.6 p.521*

Mexican Anarchism after the Revolution. *v.3 p.293*

Mexican Chicano Music. *v.6 p.519*

The Mexican Congress: Old Player, New
Power. *v.3 p.296, v.4 p.594*

Mexican Consuls and Labor Organizing: Imperial Politics in the
American Southwest. *v.6 p.525, p.526*

The Mexican Corrido: A Feminist Analysis. . .*v.6 p.513, p.523*

Mexican Democracy: A Critical View. *v.3 p.293*

The Mexican Economy, 1870-1930: Essays on the Economic
History of Institutions, Revolution, and Growth. . .*v.3 p.290*

The Mexican Frontier, 1821-1846: The American Southwest
under Mexico. *v.3 p.529, v.6 p.686*

Mexican Governance: From Single-Party Rule to Divided
Government. *v.3 p.294, p.295*

The Mexican Government Today. *v.3 p.295*

Mexican Immigrant Workers in the United States. . . .*v.6 p.525*

Mexican Immigrants and Mexican Americans: An Evolving
Relation. *v.6 p.528, p.542*

Mexican Labor and World War II: Braceros in the Pacific
Northwest, 1942-1947. . . . .*v.6 p.525*

Mexican Liberalism in the Age of Mora, 1821-1853.   *v.3 p.289*

Mexican Militarism: The Political Rise and Fall of the
Revolutionary Army, 1910-1940. . . . . . .*v.3 p.275, p.294*

The Mexican Muralists in the United States. . .*v.1 p.732, p.741*

Mexican Murals in Times of Crisis. *v.3 p.266*

The Mexican Outsiders: A Community History of
  Marginalization and Discrimination in California.   *.v.6 p.540*

Mexican Politics in Transition. . . . .*.v.3 p.292*

Mexican Politics: The Containment of Conflict. . . . *.v.4 p.593*

The Mexican Profit-Sharing Decision: Politics and Economic
  Change in an Authoritarian Regime. . . . .*.v.3 p.295*

The Mexican Revolution, 1910-1940. . . . .*.v.3 p.292*

The Mexican Revolution: A New Press People's
  History. . . . .*.v.3 p.292*

The Mexican Revolution and the Catholic Church,
  1910-1929. . . . .*.v.3 p.295*

The Mexican Revolution in Puebla, 1908-1913: The Maderista
  Movement and the Failure of Liberal Reform. . . .*.v.3 p.293*

The Mexican Revolution. . . . .*.v.3 p.293*

Mexican Suite: A History of Photography in Mexico. *.v.1 p.763*

The Mexican Texans. . . . .*.v.6 p.532*

The Mexican Treasury: The Writings of Dr. Francisco
  Hernández. . . . .*.v.5 p.234*

The Mexican War, 1846-1848. . . . .*.v.3 p.418*

The Mexican War. . . . .*.v.3 p.418*

Mexican Workers and American Dreams: Immigration,
  Repatriation, and California Farm Labor,
  1900-1939. . . . . *.v.6 p.525, p.529*

Mexicana Encounters: The Making of Social Identities on the
  Borderlands. . . . . *.v.3 p.527, v.6 p.340, p.486, p.546*

Mexican-Americans in the Southwest. . . . .*.v.6 p.531*

Mexicano Resistance in the Southwest. . . . .*.v.6 p.535*

Mexican-Origin People in the United States: A Topical
  History. . . . .*.v.6 p.532*

Mexicanos: A History of Mexicans in the U. S. . . . *.v.6 p.531*

Mexicans at Arms: Puro Federalists and the Politics of War,
  1845-1848. . . . .*.v.3 p.289*

Mexicans in the Midwest, 1900-1932. . . . .*.v.6 p.535*

ⓔ Mexico: An Encyclopedia of Contemporary Culture and
  History. . . . .*.v.4 p.383*

Mexico and the Hispanic Southwest in American
  Literature. . . . .*.v.6 p.515*

Mexico and the Spanish Conquest: Wars in
  Context. . . . .*.v.3 p.285, p.286*

Mexico and the United States: Ambivalent Vistas. . . *.v.3 p.391*

Mexico and United States, 1821 1973: Conflict and
  Coexistence. . . . .*.v.3 p.392*

Mexico at the World's Fair: Crafting a Modern Nation. *.v.3 p.265*

Mexico Between Hitler and Roosevelt: Mexican Foreign
  Relations in the Age of Lazaro Cardenas, 1934-1940. *.v.3 p.295*

Mexico: Biography of Power. . . . .*.v.3 p.293*

Mexico City Blues: Two Hundred Forty-Two Choruses. *.v.2 p.93*

Mexico: From the Olmecs to the Aztecs. . . . .*.v.4 p.9*

Mexico in Focus: A Guide to the People, Politics, and
  Culture. . . . .*.v.4 p.383*

Mexico in Transition: Neoliberal Globalism, the State and Civil
  Society. . . . .*.v.4 p.383*

Mexico Otherwise: Modern Mexico in the Eyes of Foreign
  Observers. . . . .*.v.3 p.291*

Mexico: Splendors of Thirty Centuries. . . . .*.v.1 p.684*

Mexico, the End of the Revolution. . . . .*.v.4 p.593*

Mexico: The Struggle for Democratic
  Development. . . . .*.v.3 p.293, p.294*

Mexico under Salinas. . . . .*.v.4 p.594*

Mexico's Accion Nacional: A Catholic Alternative to
  Revolution. . . . .*.v.3 p.294*

Mexico's Democracy at Work: Political and Economic
  Dynamics. . . . .*.v.3 p.291*

Mexico's Dilemma: The Political Origins of Economic
  Crisis. . . . .*.v.3 p.294*

Mexico's Hidden Revolution: The Catholic Church in Law and
  Politics since 1929. . . . .*.v.3 p.295*

Mexico's Mandarins: Crafting a Power Elite for the
  Twenty-First Century. . . . .*.v.3 p.291*

Mexico's Merchant Elite, 1590-1660: Silver, State, and
  Society. . . . .*.v.3 p.286*

Mexico's Military on the Democratic Stage. . . . . *.v.3 p.291*

Mexico's New Politics: The PAN and Democratic
  Change. . . . .*.v.3 p.295*

Mexico's Private Sector: Recent History, Future
  Challenges. . . . .*.v.3 p.295*

Mémoires dune jeune fille rangée. . . . .*.v.2 p.508*

Mémoires improvisés : quarante et un entretiens avec Jean
  Amrouche. . . . .*.v.2 p.513*

México en Guerra (1846-1848): Perspectivas
  Regionales. . . . .*.v.3 p.289*

Le mât de cocagne : roman. . . . .*.v.2 p.537*

Música Tejana : The Cultural Economy of Artistic
  Transformation. . . . .*.v.1 p.293, p.294*

Mi Abuela Fumaba Puros. . . . .*.v.6 p.504*

Mi Raza Primero! (My People First!): Nationalism, Identity, and
  Insurgency in the Chicano Movement in Los Angeles,
  1966-1978. . . . .*.v.6 p.540*

Miami Now: Immigration, Ethnicity, and Social
  Change. . . . .*.v.6 p.544, p.549*

Miau. . . . .*.v.2 p.655*

Micah: A New Translation with Introduction and
  Commentary. . . . .*.v.1 p.622*

Michael Collins: The Man Who Made Ireland. . . . *.v.3 p.138*

Michael Dummett. . . . .*.v.1 p.514*

The Michael Eric Dyson Reader. . . . .*.v.4 p.729*

Michael Jordan, Inc.: Corporate Sport, Media Culture, and Late
  Modern America. . . . . *.v.4 p.853, p.882, p.895, p.901*

Michael Oakeshott: An Introduction. . . . .*.v.4 p.491*

Michael Van Valkenburgh Associates: Allegheny Riverfront
  Park. . . . .*.v.1 p.812, p.813*

Michal Rovner: The Space Between. . . . .*.v.1 p.774*

Michel Butor. . . . .*.v.2 p.511*

Michel Fokine and His Ballets. . . . .*.v.1 p.22*

Michel Fokine. . . . .*.v.1 p.9*

Michel Foucault: Beyond Structuralism and
  Hermeneutics. . . . .*.v.1 p.458*

Michel Foucault: Materialism and Education. . . . . *.v.4 p.344*

Michel Foucault. . . . .*.v.1 p.459*

Michel Houellebecq : le plaisir du texte. . . . .*.v.2 p.532*

Michel Tournier. . . . .*.v.2 p.532, p.535*

Michel Tremblay. . . . .*.v.2 p.541*

Michelangelo and His Drawings. . . . .*.v.1 p.723*

Michelangelo and the Pope's Ceiling. *v.1 p.742, v.3 p.200*

Michelangelo and the Reform of Art. *v.1 p.698*

Michelangelo: Architect. *v.1 p.791*

Michelangelo Drawings: Closer to the Master. *v.1 p.723*

Michelangelo: Life, Letters, and Poetry. *v.2 p.708*

Michelangelo's 'Last Judgment'. *v.1 p.740*

Michelangelo's Mountain: The Quest for Perfection in the Marble Quarries of Carrara. *v.1 p.781*

Michelangelo. *v.1 p.698, p.740*

Michigan: A Guide to the Wolverine State. *v.3 p.516*

Michigan: A History of the Wolverine State. *v.3 p.516*

Michigan: Bicentennial and History Guide. *v.3 p.516*

Michigan: History of a Great Lakes State. . .*v.3 p.516, p.517*

Michio Ito: The Dancer and His Dances. *v.1 p.6*

Microarray Analysis: Mining the Human Genome. *v.5 p.110, p.146*

Microarray Bioinformatics. *v.5 p.101*

Microarray Gene Expression Data Analysis: A Beginner's Guide. *v.5 p.110*

Microarray Quality Control. *v.5 p.101, p.102*

Microarray Technology and Its Applications. *v.5 p.110*

Microarrays and Microplates: Applications in Biomedical Sciences. *v.5 p.110, p.121, p.148*

Microarrays for an Integrative Genomics. *v.5 p.100, p.110, p.127, p.135*

Microarrays Methods and Applications. *v.5 p.127*

Microarrays. *v.5 p.110*

Microbial Functional Genomics. *v.5 p.153*

Microbial Genomes. *v.5 p.139*

The Microbial Models of Molecular Biology: From Genes to Genomes. *v.5 p.132*

Microbiology for the Health Sciences. *v.5 p.514*

☐ The Microbiology Network. *v.5 p.205*

Microbiology of Fermented Foods, Vols. 1, 2. . . . .*v.5 p.36*

Microcomputer Engineering. *v.5 p.730*

Microcomputers and Microprocessors: The 8080, 8085, and Z-80 Programming, Interfacing, and Troubleshooting. *v.5 p.344, p.345, p.730*

Microeconomics: Behavior, Institutions, and Evolution. *v.4 p.249, p.251*

Microelectronic Circuit Analysis and Design. *v.5 p.722*

Microelectronic Circuit Design. *v.5 p.722*

Microfabricated Sensors: Application of Optical Technology for DNA Analysis. *v.5 p.100, p.122*

Microfacies of Carbonate Rocks. *v.5 p.439*

Microfossils. *v.5 p.448*

Microfoundations and Macroeconomics: An Austrian Perspective. *v.4 p.234*

Microfoundations of Economic Growth: A Schumpeterian Perspective. *v.4 p.230, p.235, p.243*

Microfoundations of Financial Economics: An Introduction to General Equilibrium Asset Pricing. *v.4 p.263*

Micromegas and Other Short Fictions. *v.2 p.484*

Micrometeorology in Agricultural Systems. . . .*v.5 p.29, p.30*

Micronutrients in Agriculture. *v.5 p.50*

Microorganisms and Bioterrorism. *v.5 p.148, p.149, p.166*

Microprocessors and Microcomputers: Hardware and Software. *v.5 p.344, p.730*

Microscopic and Chemical Parts of Plants. *v.5 p.155*

Microscopic Techniques in Biotechnology. . . .*v.5 p.86, p.218*

Microscopy and Histology for Molecular Biologists: A User's Guide. *v.5 p.86, p.159*

Microsociology: Discourse, Emotion, and Social Structure. *v.4 p.775*

⚫ Microsoft Encarta Africana 2000. . . . .*v.6 p.33*

Microwave Circuit Design Using Linear and Nonlinear Techniques. *v.5 p.729*

Microwave Electronics: Measurement and Materials Characterization. *v.5 p.729*

Microwave Engineering. *v.5 p.729*

Microwave Spectroscopy. *v.5 p.562*

Microwave Techniques and Protocols. *v.5 p.88*

Midaq Alley. *v.6 p.661*

The Mid-Atlantic Region. *v.3 p.490*

Midcentury Quartet: Bishop, Lowell, Jarrell, Berryman and the Making of a Postmodern Aesthetic. *v.2 p.61, p.62, p.91, p.96, p.97*

The Middle Ages: Readings in Medieval History. . . .*v.3 p.68*

The Middle Ages: Sources of Medieval History. . . .*v.3 p.68*

The Middle Ages. *v.2 p.455*

Middle: Class Democracy and the Revolution in Massachusetts 1691. . . . .*v.3 p.487*

Middle Earth: Poems. *v.2 p.143*

The Middle East: A History. *v.6 p.581*

The Middle East and Central Asia: an Anthropological Approach. *v.6 p.581*

The Middle East and North Africa in World Politics: A Documentary Record. *v.6 p.582*

Middle East and North African Immigrants in Europe: Current Impact; Local and National Responses. *v.4 p.765*

The Middle East and the Peace Process: The Impact of the Oslo Accords. *v.6 p.617*

The Middle East Dilemma: The Politics and Economics of Arab Integration. *v.6 p.583*

Middle East Dilemmas: The Background of United States Policy. *v.6 p.593*

The Middle East Enters the Twenty-First Century. . . .*v.6 p.592*

Middle East: From the End of Empire to the End of the Cold War. *v.6 p.595*

The Middle East in the Twentieth Century. *v.6 p.595*

Middle East Monarchies: The Challenge of Modernity. *v.4 p.614, v.6 p.593, p.594*

The Middle East on the Eve of Modernity: Aleppo in the 18th Century. *v.6 p.607*

Middle East Politics Today: Government and Civil Society. *v.4 p.614, v.6 p.593*

The Middle East Today. *v.6 p.594*

Middle Eastern Dance. *v.1 p.16*

Middle English Dictionary, Vol. A. 1. . . . . . .*v.2 p.551*

Middle English Literature: A Critical Study of the Romances, the Religious Lyrics, "Piers Plowman". *v.2 p.168*

Middle English Literature: An Historical Sourcebook. *v.2 p.168*

Middle English Verse Romances. *v.2 p.197, p.206*

The Middle Ground: Indians, Empires, and Republics in the
    Great Lakes Region, 1650-1815. . . .*v.6 p.684, p.686, p.687*

The Middle High German Poem of Willehalm. *v.2 p.595*

The Middle Passage: White Ships/Black Cargo. . *v.6 p.16, p.37*

The Middle Platonists: 80 B.C. to A.D. 220. . . . .*v.1 p.430*

The Middle West: Its Meaning in American Culture. . .*v.3 p.506*

Middle Works of John Dewey, 1899-1924: 1920. . . .*v.4 p.345*

The Middle Works of John Dewey, 1899-1924. . . . .*v.1 p.443*

Middle-Class Blacks in a White Society: Prince Hall Freemason
    in America. *v.4 p.719*

Middlemarch. *v.2 p.286*

Middlesex: A Novel. *v.2 p.145, v.6 p.396*

Middleton's Tragedies. *v.2 p.221*

Middletown: A Study in Modern American Culture. . .*v.4 p.704*

Middletown Families: Fifty Years of Change and
    Continuity. *v.4 p.732*

Middletown in Transition: A Study in Cultural Conflicts. .*v.4 p.704*

MIDI: A Comprehensive Introduction, Vol. 7. . .*v.1 p.387, p.388*

Midlife Lesbian Relationships: Friends, Lovers, Children, and
    Parents. *v.6 p.374*

Midlife Queer: Autobiography of a Decade,
    1971-1991. . . . .*v.6 p.365, p.401*

Midnight at Mabel's: The Mabel Mercer Story. *v.6 p.409*

Midnight Dreary: The Mysterious Death of Edgar Allan
    Poe. *v.2 p.50*

Midnight Eye Guide to New Japanese Film. . .*v.6 p.306, p.336*

Midnight's Children. *v.2 p.766*

Midnight. *v.6 p.213*

Midquest: A Poem. *v.2 p.143*

The Midrash on Psalms. *v.1 p.550*

Midrash Rabbah, Set. *v.1 p.550*

A Midsummer Night's Dream. *v.2 p.223*

Midsummer Snowballs. *v.1 p.697*

Midterm Madness: The Elections of 2002. . . . . .*v.4 p.549*

The Mid-Victorian Generation 1846-1886. . . . . .*v.6 p.735*

Mid-Victorian Imperialists: British Gentlemen and the Empire of
    the Mind. *v.3 p.88, p.124*

The Midwest and the Nation: Rethinking the History of an
    American Region. *v.3 p.512*

The Midwestern Ascendancy in American Writing. . . .*v.2 p.15*

Midwestern Landscape Architecture. *v.1 p.814*

The Midwestern Pastoral: Place and Landscape in Literature of
    the American Heartland. *v.2 p.14*

The Midwest. *v.3 p.513*

Mies in America. *v.1 p.793*

Mies Van der Rohe in Berlin. *v.1 p.794, p.795*

Mightier Than the Sword: How the News Media Have Shaped
    American History. *v.4 p.404*

Mighty Like a River: The Black Church and Social
    Reform. *v.4 p.720*

Mighty Peculiar Elections: The New South Gubernatorial
    Campaigns of 1970 and the Changing Politics of
    Race. *v.4 p.549*

Mighty River: A Portrait of the Fraser. *v.3 p.546*

Mighty Stonewall. *v.3 p.402, p.427*

Migrant Song: Politics and Process in Contemporary Chicano
    Literature. *v.6 p.501, p.514*

Migrants in Modern France. *v.3 p.157*

Migrating to the Movies: Cinema and Black Urban
    Modernity. *v.6 p.8, p.15, p.331*

Migration and Mythmaking in Anglo-Saxon England. .*v.2 p.167*

Migration and Vodou. *v.4 p.41*

The Migration Experience in Africa. *v.4 p.764*

Migration in Colonial Spanish America. .*v.3 p.287, p.303, p.304*

Migration: New and Selected Poems. *v.2 p.101*

Miguel de Unamuno: The Agony of Belief. *v.2 p.662*

Miguel Hernandez. *v.2 p.661*

Miguel Marmol. *v.2 p.675*

Miguel Mendez in Aztlan: Two Decades of Literary
    Production. *v.6 p.500, p.513*

The Mikado: Institution and Person a Study of the Internal
    Political Forces of Japan. *v.6 p.227*

Mike: The Memoirs of the Right Honourable Lester B. Pearson,
    Vol. 1. . . . .*v.3 p.541*

Mike Tyson: Nurture of the Beast. *v.4 p.855*

Mikhail Larionov and the Russian Avant-Garde. . . .*v.1 p.698*

The Milagro Beanfield War: A Novel. *v.2 p.151*

Milagros de Nuetras Sra (Miracles of Our Lady). . .*v.2 p.645*

Milan Kundera and the Art of Fiction: Critical Essays. .*v.2 p.782*

Milan Kundera. *v.2 p.782*

A Miles Davis Reader. *v.1 p.260, p.320*

Miles Davis: The Definitive Biography. .*v.1 p.257, p.258, p.320*

Miles Gloriosus. *v.2 p.440*

Miles of Tiles. *v.5 p.498*

Miles: The Autobiography. *v.1 p.258, p.320*

Miles to Go: A Personal History of Social Policy. . .*v.4 p.769*

Milestones in 150 Years of the Chemical Industry, No.
    96. . . . .*v.5 p.316, p.741*

Milestones in Glasnost and Perestroyka: Politics and
    People. *v.3 p.228*

Milestones in Systematics. *v.5 p.171*

Militant Islam in Southeast Asia: Crucible of Terror. . *v.4 p.657*

A Militant New World, 1607-1640. . . . .*v.3 p.384*

The Militant South, 1800-1861. . . . .*v.3 p.495*

Militarism and Politics in Latin America: Peru from Sanchez
    Cerro to Sendero Luminoso. *v.3 p.275*

Militarism and Social Revolution in the Third World. .*v.4 p.574*

Militarization and Demilitarization in El Salvador's Transition to
    Democracy. *v.3 p.278, v.4 p.593*

Militarization, Democracy and Development: The Perils of
    Praetorianism in Latin America. *v.3 p.273*

The Militarization of Culture in the Dominican Republic, from
    the Captains General to General Trujillo. *v.3 p.317*

The Militarization of the U. S.-Mexico Border, 1978-1992:
    Low-Intensity Conflict Doctrine Comes
    Home. *v.6 p.486, p.529, p.537*

Militarizing the American Criminal Justice System: The
    Changing Roles of the Armed Forces and the Police. .*v.6 p.261*

The Military and American Society. *v.4 p.717*

The Military and Democracy: The Future of Civil-Military Relations in Latin America. *v.3 p.274*

The Military and Politics in Postauthoritarian Chile. *v.3 p.277, p.278, p.356,v.4 p.593*

The Military and Society in Colonial Peru 1750-1810. . . . . *v.3 p.273, p.274*

The Military and Society in Latin America. . *v.3 p.274, v.4 p.717*

The Military and Society in Russia, 1450-1917. . . . .*v.3 p.212*

The Military and the State in Latin America. *v.3 p.277, v.4 p.592, p.593*

The Military and United States Indian Policy, 1865-1903. . . . .*v.6 p.688, p.693*

Military Ascendancy and Political Culture: A Study of Indonesia's Golkar. *v.4 p.623*

The Military Coup d'Etat as a Political Process: Ecuador, 1948-1966. . . . .*v.3 p.274*

▢ Military Family Research Institute, Purdue University. *v.5 p.579*

The Military Foundations of Panamanian Politics. . .*v.3 p.304*

Military Geology in War and Peace. *v.5 p.422*

Military Government and Popular Participation in Panama: The Torrijos Regime, 1968-1975. . . . .*v.3 p.305*

A Military History of Canada: From Champlain to Kosovo. *v.3 p.537*

The Military History of Tsarist Russia. *v.3 p.211*

The Military in Chilean History. *v.3 p.276*

The Military in Greek Politics: The 1909 Coup D'Etat.*v.3 p.196*

The Military in Politics; Changing Patterns in Brazil. *v.3 p.277*

Military Innovation in the Interwar Period. *v.3 p.79*

Military Life: The Psychology of Serving in Peace and Combat [Four Volumes]. *v.5 p.583*

The Military Orders: From the Twelfth to the Early Fourteenth Centuries. *v.6 p.566, p.567, p.571*

Military Politics and Democratization in Indonesia. *v.4 p.622, p.623*

Military Power and Popular Protest: The U. S. Navy in Vieques, Puerto Rico. *v.3 p.320*

Military Rebellion in Argentina: Between Coups and Consolidation. *v.3 p.276, p.348, p.349,v.4 p.592*

Military Reform and Society in New Granada, 1773-1808. . . . . *v.3 p.275, p.356*

The Military Reforms of Nicholas I: The Origins of the Modern Russian Army. *v.3 p.219*

The Military Revolution and Political Change: Origins of Democracy and Autocracy in Early Modern Europe.*v.4 p.501*

The Military Revolution: Military Innovation and the Rise of the West, 1500-1800. . . . .*v.3 p.36*

Military Rule in Latin America. *v.3 p.276, p.277*

Military Situation in the Far East: U. S. Congress, Senate Committee on Armed Services and the Committee on Foreign Relations, Set. *v.6 p.235, p.236*

Military Tribunals and Presidential Power: American Revolution to the War on Terrorism. *v.4 p.464*

The Mill on the Floss. *v.2 p.287*

The Mill on the Po. *v.2 p.713*

Millenarian Vision, Capitalist Reality: Brazil's Contestado Rebellion, 1912-1916. . . . . *v.3 p.339*

Millenarianism and Peasant Politics in Vietnam. *v.6 p.167*

Millennial Keynes: An Introduction to the Origin, Development, and Later Currents of Keynesian Thought. *v.4 p.229*

The Millennials: Americans Born 1977 To 1994. . . . .*v.4 p.138, v.5 p.585*

Millennium Approaches. *v.2 p.148*

A Millennium of Classical Persian Poetry: A Guide to the Reading and Understanding of Persian Poetry from the Tenth to the Twentieth Century. *v.6 p.673*

A Millennium of Family Change: Feudalism to Capitalism in North Western Europe. *v.4 p.738*

Millennium Problems: The Seven Greatest Unsolved Mathematical Puzzles of Our Time. *v.5 p.458, p.465*

Miller Complete GAAP Library 2006, Vol. 2. . . . . .*v.4 p.105*

Miller's Guide to the Dissection of the Dog. *v.5 p.88*

Million Dollar Consulting Toolkit: Step-by-Step Guidance, Checklists, Templates, and Samples from the Million Dollar Consultant. *v.4 p.65*

Million Dollar Directory: America's Leading Public and Private Companies. *v.5 p.397*

Mill's the Subjection of Women: Critical Essays. . . *v.4 p.223*

Mill. *v.1 p.445*

Milton: A Biographical Commentary. *v.2 p.255*

Milton: A Biography. *v.2 p.255*

Milton and Augustine: Patterns of Augustinian Thought in Milton's Paradise Lost. *v.2 p.253*

Milton and His Epic Tradition. *v.2 p.255, p.256*

Milton and the Baroque. *v.2 p.255*

Milton and the Culture of Violence. *v.2 p.254*

Milton and the English Revolution. *v.2 p.254*

Milton and the Grounds of Contention. *v.2 p.254*

Milton Avery: The Late Paintings. *v.1 p.740*

Milton Friedman: Economics in Theory and Practice. *v.4 p.232*

Milton Friedman's Monetary Framework: A Debate with His Critics. *v.4 p.232, p.238*

Milton Friedman. *v.4 p.231*

Milton: Paradise Lost. *v.2 p.255*

Milton: Poet of Exile. *v.2 p.254*

Milton's Contemporary Reputation. *v.2 p.255*

Milton's Epic Voice: The Narrator in Paradise Lost. .*v.2 p.253*

Milton's Eve. *v.2 p.254*

Milton's God. *v.2 p.253*

Milton's Good God: A Study in Literary Theodicy. . *v.2 p.253*

Milton's Grand Style. *v.2 p.255*

Milton's Imagery and the Visual Arts: Iconographic Tradition in the Epic Poems. *v.2 p.254*

Milton's Paradise Lost. *v.2 p.253*

Mimbres Painted Pottery. *v.6 p.678*

Mimesis: The Representation of Reality in Western Literature. *v.2 p.572*

Mimetic Disillusion: Eugene O'Neill, Tennessee Williams and U. S. Dramatic Realism. *v.1 p.79, p.82, p.113*

The Mimic Men: A Novel. *v.2 p.769*

Mimicking Nature's Fire: Restoring Fire-Prone Forests in the West. *v.5 p.31, p.36*

Mind: A Brief Introduction. *v.1 p.497, v.5 p.619*

[e] A Mind Always in Motion: The Autobiography of Emilio
Segre. *v.5 p.544*

The Mind and Art of Calderon: Essays on the Comedias. .*v.2 p.647*

Mind and Brain: A Dialogue on the Mind-Body
Problem. *v.1 p.504*

The Mind and Its Depths. *v.1 p.498*

Mind and Labor on the Farm in Black-Earth
Russia. *v.3 p.217, p.218*

Mind and Maze: Spatial Cognition and Environmental
Behavior. *v.5 p.608*

The Mind and Method of the Economist: A Critical Appraisal of
Major Economists in the 20th Century. . . .*v.4 p.195, p.215*

Mind and Morality: An Examination of Hume's Moral
Psychology. *v.1 p.451*

Mind and Muscle: Psych up, Build Up. *v.5 p.583*

The Mind and Society, Set. *v.4 p.249*

Mind and Society, Vol. 1. . . . .*v.4 p.685*

Mind and Society, Vol. 2. . . . .*v.4 p.685*

Mind and Society, Vol. 3. . . . .*v.4 p.685*

Mind and Society, Vol. 4. . . . .*v.4 p.685*

The Mind Behind the Musical Ear: How Children Develop
Musical Intelligence. *v.1 p.375*

Mind Design II: Philosophy, Psychology, Artificial
Intelligence. *v.5 p.590*

The Mind Has No Sex?: Women in the Origins of Modern
Science. *v.3 p.48*

Mind in a Physical World: An Essay on the Mind-Body Problem
and Mental Causation. *v.1 p.497*

The Mind in Sleep: Psychology and Psychophysiology. .*v.5 p.612*

The Mind in the Cave: Consciousness and the Origins of
Art. *v.1 p.668*

The Mind: Its Nature and Origin. *v.5 p.650*

Mind Matters: A Tribute to Allen Newell. *v.5 p.590*

Mind Models: New Forms of Musical Experience. . .*v.1 p.222*

The Mind of a Mnemomist: A Little Book about a Vast
Memory. *v.5 p.610*

The Mind of Egypt: History and Meaning in the Time of the
Pharaohs. *v.3 p.8*

The Mind of Frederick Douglass. *v.3 p.420*

The Mind of John Locke: A Study of Political Theory in Its
Intellectual Setting. *v.4 p.491*

A Mind of One Piece; Brandeis and American Reform. .*v.3 p.435*

The Mind of the Middle Ages: An Historical
Survey. *v.3 p.67, v.6 p.576*

Mind of the Old South. *v.3 p.495*

The Mind of the Oxford Movement. *v.1 p.582*

The Mind of the Political Terrorist. *v.4 p.661*

The Mind of the Qur'an: Chapters in Reflection. . .*v.1 p.556*

The Mind of the South: Fifty Years Later. *v.3 p.494*

The Mind of the South. *v.3 p.493*

The Mind of Wall Street: A Legendary Financier on the Perils of
Greed and the Mysteries of the Market. . . .*v.4 p.96, p.100*

Mind over Magma: The Story of Igneous Petrology. . .*v.5 p.437*

Mind Regained: How Mind Functions As a Real Cause in the
Material World. *v.1 p.497*

Mind, Self, and Society: From the Standpoint of a Social
Behaviorist. *v.4 p.693*

A Mind So Rare: The Evolution of Human
Consciousness. *v.5 p.608, p.612*

Mind Wide Open: Your Brain and the Neuroscience of Everyday
Life. *v.5 p.617*

The Mind Within the Net: Models of Learning, Thinking and
Acting. *v.5 p.591*

Mind-Body Maturity: Psychological Approaches to Sports,
Exercise, and Fitness. *v.5 p.581*

Mindfield: New and Selected Poems. *v.2 p.65*

Mind-Forg'd Manacles: Slavery and the English Romantic
Poets. *v.2 p.183*

Mindful Learning: Teaching Self-Discipline and Academic
Accomplishment. *v.4 p.358, p.359*

Mindfulness. *v.5 p.611*

Minding American Education: Reclaiming the Tradition of
Active Learning. *v.4 p.346*

Minding the Spirit: The Study of Christian Spirituality. .*v.1 p.650*

Minds and Gods: The Cognitive Foundations of
Religion. *v.1 p.524*

Minds behind the Brain: A History of the Pioneers and Their
Discoveries. *v.5 p.616*

[e] The Minds of the West: Ethnocultural Evolution in the Rural
Middle West, 1830-1917. . . . .*v.3 p.506*

Mindsight: Image, Dream, Meaning. *v.1 p.497*

Mine Eyes Have Seen the Glory: A Biography of Julia Ward
Howe. *v.2 p.39*

Mine Eyes Have Seen the Glory: A Journey into the Evangelical
Subculture in America. *v.4 p.720*

Mine Health and Safety Management. *v.5 p.738*

Mineral Facts and Problems. *v.5 p.733, p.738, p.739*

Mineral Names: What Do They Mean? *v.5 p.435*

Mineral Nutrition of Crops: Fundamental Mechanisms and
Implications. *v.5 p.23*

Mineral Nutrition of Plants. *v.5 p.45*

Mineral Resources, Economics, and the Environment. .*v.5 p.738*

Mineralogy: Concepts and Principles. *v.5 p.435, p.436*

Mineralogy: Concepts, Descriptions, Determinations. .*v.5 p.435*

Minerals: Foundations of Society. *v.5 p.737*

Minerals in Soil Environments. *v.5 p.49*

[□] Minerals Information : U.S.G.S. *v.5 p.737*

Minerals Yearbook, Area Reports: Domestic 2003. . .*v.6 p.285*

[□] Minerals Yearbook. *v.5 p.450*

Miners, Merchants, and Farmers in Colonial
Colombia. *v.3 p.356, p.359*

Miners of the Red Mountain: Indian Labor in Potosi,
1545-1650. . . . .*v.3 p.323*

Miners on Strike: Class Solidarity and Division in
Britain. *v.4 p.128*

Minerva and the Muse: A Life of Margaret Fuller. . .*v.2 p.39*

Mines of Silver and Gold in the Americas. *v.3 p.325*

The Ming Dynasty: 1368-1644. . . . .*v.6 p.186*

The Ming Dynasty, 1368-1644. . . . .*v.6 p.186*

The Mingling of Heaven and Earth. *v.2 p.326*

Miniatures: Dictionary and Guide. *v.1 p.725*

Minimal Art: A Critical Anthology. *v.1 p.677*

A Minimal Future?: Art As Object 1958-1968. . . . .*v.1 p.678*

Minimalism: Art of Circumstance. *v.1 p.677*

Minimalism: Origins. *v.1 p.225*

Minimalism. *v.1 p.680*

Minimum Design Loads for Buildings and Other
  Structures. *v.5 p.685*

Mining America: The Industry and the Environment,
  1800-1980. . . . .*v.6 p.296*

Mining and Agriculture in Highland Bolivia: Ecology, History,
  and Commerce among the Jukumanis. *v.3 p.323*

Mining Frontiers of the Far West, 1848-1880. . . . .*v.3 p.519*

Mining, the Environment, and Indigenous Development
  Conflicts. *v.6 p.680*

Ministers of Reform: The Progressives' Achievement in
  American Civilization, 1889-1920. . . . .*v.3 p.436*

The Ministry of Fear: An Entertainment. *v.2 p.350*

Minnesota, a History of the State. *v.3 p.522*

Minnesota: A State Guide. *v.3 p.522*

Minnesota Bicenntenial and History Guide. *v.3 p.522*

Minnesota Rag: The Dramatic Story of the Landmark Supreme
  Court Case That Gave New Meaning to Freedom of the
  Press. *v.4 p.439*

Minoan and Mycenaean Art. *v.1 p.670, p.687, v.3 p.16*

Minoans. *v.3 p.15, p.16*

Minor Authors of the Corpus Tibullianum. *v.2 p.445*

Minor Characters: A Beat Memoir. *v.2 p.90*

Minor Omissions: Children in Latin American History and
  Society. *v.3 p.286*

Minor Papers on the Currency Question, 1809-1823. .*v.4 p.220*

The Minor Poems, Pt. 1. . . . .*v.2 p.208*

Minor White: The Eye That Shapes. *v.1 p.766*

Minority Education: Anthropological
  Perspectives. *v.4 p.302, p.312*

Minority Party Politics in a Multinational State: The German
  Social Democrats of Czechoslovakia, 1918-1938. .*v.3 p.189*

The Minority Rights Revolution. *v.4 p.495, p.511, p.516*

Minotaur: Sir Arthur Evans and the Archaeology of the Minoan
  Myth. *v.3 p.16*

Minsky's Burlesque. *v.1 p.35, p.36*

Mintel Reports (database). *v.5 p.586*

The Minutemen and Their World. *v.3 p.409, p.488*

Miracle Fair: Selected Poems of Wislawa Szymborska. .*v.2 p.792*

Miracle of the Rose. *v.2 p.519*

The Miracle of Theism: Arguments for and Against the
  Existence of God. *v.1 p.523*

The Miracle Years: A Cultural History of West Germany,
  1949-1968. . . . .*v.3 p.177*

Miracles and Idolatry. *v.2 p.484*

Miracles and Pilgrims: Popular Beliefs in Medieval
  England. *v.6 p.570*

Miracles and the Medieval Mind: Theory, Record, and Event,
  1000 to 1215. . . . .*v.6 p.573*

Miracles of Our Lady. *v.2 p.645, p.646*

Miracles of the Virgin Mary, in Verse: Miracula Sancte Dei
  Genitricis Virginis Marie, Versifice. *v.2 p.449*

Miracles on the Border: Retablos of Mexican Migrants to the
  United States. *v.1 p.684, v.6 p.492, p.523*

The Miraculous Day of Amalia Gómez: A
  Novel. *v.2 p.154, v.6 p.502*

Miraculous Stories from the Japanese Buddhist Tradition: The
  Nihon Ryoiki of the Monk Kyokai. *v.1 p.566*

Mirages of Transition: The Peruvian Altiplano,
  1780-1930. . . . .*v.3 p.327*

Miramar. *v.6 p.662*

The Miranda Debate: Law, Justice, and Policing. . . .*v.4 p.473*

Miranda: The Story of America's Right to Remain
  Silent. *v.6 p.267, p.271*

Miranda's Waning Protections: Police Interrogation Practices
  after Dickerson. *v.4 p.474, v.6 p.267, p.271*

Mircea Eliade: The Mythical Narrative. *v.2 p.817*

Miriam Schapiro: Shaping the Fragments of Art and
  Life. *v.1 p.697*

Le miroir qui revient. *v.2 p.525*

The Mirror and the Lamp: Romantic Theory and the Critical
  Tradition. *v.2 p.171, p.173, p.183, p.567*

Mirror for the Moon. *v.6 p.233*

The Mirror Makers: A History of American Advertising and Its
  Creators. *v.4 p.426*

Mirror of Empire: Dutch Marine Art of the Seventeenth
  Century. *v.1 p.675, p.687, p.688*

The Mirror of Herodotus: The Representation of the Other in
  the Writing of History. *v.2 p.412*

The Mirror of Lida Sal: Tales Based on Mayan Myths and
  Guatemalan Legends. *v.2 p.675*

The Mirror of Salvation; A Moral Play of Everyman C.
  1490. . . . .*v.2 p.622*

The Mirror of Spain, 1500-1700: The Formation of a
  Myth. *v.3 p.239*

Mirror of the Gods. *v.3 p.70*

Mirror of the Indies: A History of Dutch Colonial
  Literature. *v.2 p.623*

Mirror to America: The Autobiography of John Hope
  Franklin. *v.3 p.374*

A Mirror to Kathleen's Face: Education in Independent Ireland,
  1922-1960. . . . .*v.4 p.333*

The Mirrored Window: Focus Groups from a Moderator's Point
  of View. *v.4 p.136, p.137*

Mirrors in Mind. *v.5 p.606*

Mirrors of Destruction: War, Genocide, and Modern
  Identity. *v.4 p.651*

Mirrors of Paradise: The Gardens of Fernando
  Caruncho. *v.1 p.815*

Mirrors. *v.6 p.661*

Mirrorwork: 50 Years of Indian Writing, 1947-1997. .*v.2 p.763*

Mis and Mis: Polish Literature in the Context of Cross-Cultural
  Communication. *v.2 p.789*

The Misanthrope and Other Plays. *v.2 p.475*

The Misanthrope, Tartuffe, and Other Plays. *v.2 p.475*

Miscellaneous Poems. *v.2 p.281*

The Miscellaneous Works of John Bunyan: The Doctrine of the
  Law and Grace Unfolded and I Will Pray with the
  Spirit. *v.1 p.593*

The Miscellaneous Works of John Bunyan: The Poems. .*v.1 p.593*

Miscellaneous Works of Joseph Addison. *v.2 p.236*

Miscellanies by Henry Fielding, Esq.: Jonathan Wild. .*v.2 p.247*

A Miscellany. *v.2 p.166*

Misconceiving Canada: The Struggle for National
  Unity. *v.3 p.541*

La mise en scène. *v.2 p.532*

The Mis-education of the Negro. *v.4 p.310, p.311,v.6 p.21*

The Mise-en-Scene. *v.2 p.532*

The Miser and Other Plays: A New Selection. *v.2 p.475*

Les Miserables. *v.2 p.493, p.494*

The Misfits: An Original Screenplay. *v.2 p.102*

The Misfortunes of Virtue and Other Early Tales. . . .*v.2 p.483*

Mishkat al-Masabih, Set. *v.1 p.556*

The Mishnah: A New Translation. *v.1 p.550*

The Mishnah. *v.1 p.550*

Misleading Evidence and Evidence-Led Policy: Making Social
  Science More Experimental. *v.4 p.680*

The Mismeasure of Crime. *v.6 p.251*

The Mismeasure of Man. *v.5 p.608, p.653*

Miss Herbert. *v.2 p.748*

Miss Leavitt's Stars: The Untold Story of the Forgotten Woman
  Who Discovered How to Measure the Universe. . .*v.5 p.62*

Miss Lulu Bett - Birth. *v.2 p.78*

Miss Marple: The Complete Short Stories. . . .*v.2 p.338, p.339*

Miss Muriel and Other Stories. *v.2 p.109*

Miss Ravenel's Conversion from Secession to Loyalty. .*v.2 p.36*

The Missing Gospels: Unearthing the Truth Behind Alternative
  Christianities. *v.1 p.598*

Missing Links: Evolutionary Concepts and Transistions Through
  Time. *v.5 p.447*

The Missing Middle: Working Families and the Future of
  American Social Policy. *v.4 p.769*

The Missing Peace: The Inside Story of the Fight for Middle
  East Peace. *v.4 p.650*

Missing Persians: Discovering Voices in Iranian Cultural
  History. *v.6 p.672*

Missing Persons and Other Essays. *v.2 p.604*

Missing Stories: An Oral History of Ethnic and Minority Groups
  in Utah. *v.3 p.529*

Mission Furniture: From the American Arts and Crafts
  Movement. *v.1 p.804, p.805*

Mission Statements: A Guide to the Corporate and Nonprofit
  Sectors. *v.4 p.172, p.173*

Mission to Kala. *v.2 p.544*

Mission to Saturn: Cassini and the Huygens Probe. . .*v.5 p.69*

Missionary Capitalist: Nelson Rockefeller in Venezuela.*v.3 p.361*

The Missionary Enterprise in China and America. . . .*v.6 p.218*

The Missionary Movement in Christian History: Studies in the
  Transmission of Faith. *v.1 p.648*

Missions and Empire. *v.3 p.88, p.89, p.124, p.125*

Missions of James,Peter,And Paul: Tensions in Early
  Christianity. *v.1 p.626*

Missions of the College Curriculum: A Contemporary Review
  with Suggestions: a Commentary of the Carnegie
  Foundation for the Advancement of Teaching. . . .*v.4 p.294*

Mississippi: A History. *v.3 p.504*

Mississippi: An American Journey. *v.3 p.506*

The Mississippi Question, 1985 to 1803. . . . .*v.3 p.506, p.507*

Mississippi Solo: A River Quest. *v.3 p.506*

Mississippi: The WPA Guide to the Magnolia State. . .*v.3 p.504*

The Mississippi Valley in British Politics: A Study of the Trade,
  Land Speculation and Experiments in Imperialism
  Culminating in the American Revolution. *v.3 p.505*

Mississippi. *v.3 p.506*

Missouri: A Guide to the "Show Me" State. *v.3 p.512*

Missouri: A History. *v.3 p.512*

The Missouri Controversy, 1819-1821. . . . .*v.3 p.417*

The Missouri River. *v.3 p.522*

Missouri: The Heart of the Nation. *v.3 p.512*

Mist: A Tragicomic Novel. *v.2 p.662*

Mistaken Identification: The Eyewitness, Psychology and the
  Law. *v.4 p.473, v.5 p.592*

Mistakes Worth Making: How to Turn Sports Errors into
  Athletic Excellence. *v.5 p.582*

Misteaching of Academic Discourses: The Politics of Language
  in the Classroom. *v.4 p.349*

Misteaks... and How to Find Them Before the Teacher Does: A
  Calculus Supplement. *v.5 p.457*

Mister Jelly Roll: The Fortunes of Jelly Roll Morton, New
  Orleans Creole and "Inventor of Jazz". . . .*v.1 p.261, p.343*

Mister Johnson. *v.2 p.338*

Mister Roberts. *v.2 p.81*

The Mistress of Spices. *v.6 p.99, p.100*

Mistress of the House, Mistress of Heaven: Women in Ancient
  Egypt. *v.1 p.670, p.690, p.706*

Mistress to an Age: A Life of Madame de Stael. . . .*v.3 p.152*

The Mists of Avalon. *v.2 p.141*

Mists of Regret: Culture and Sensibility in Classic French
  Film. *v.6 p.337*

The Misunderstood Gene. *v.5 p.135*

Misused Statistics. *v.4 p.178*

The MIT Encyclopedia of Communication
  Disorders. *v.5 p.621, p.665, p.673*

The MIT Encyclopedia of the Cognitive Sciences
  (MITECS). *v.5 p.609*

The Mitchell Beazley Family Encyclopedia of Nature. .*v.5 p.224*

Mitchell Leisen, Hollywood Director. *v.6 p.418*

Mitteleuropa and German Politics: 1848 to the Present.*v.3 p.160*

The Mitterrand Experiment: Continuity and Change in Modern
  France. *v.4 p.609*

Mixed Blessings: Gender and Religious Fundamentalism Cross
  Culturally. *v.6 p.458*

Mixed Feelings: Feminism, Mass Culture and Victorian
  Sensationalism. *v.2 p.190, v.6 p.747, p.755*

Mixed Messages: U.S. Human Rights Policy and Latin
  America. *v.4 p.513*

A Mixed Race: Ethnicity in Early America. *v.2 p.9*

Mixed-Member Electoral Systems: The Best of Both
  Worlds?. *v.4 p.576*

Mixing Messages: Graphic Design in Contemporary American
  Culture. *v.1 p.714*

The Mixquiahuala Letters. . . . . *.v.6 p.498*

The Mixtecs of Colonial Oaxaca: Ñudzahui History, Sixteenth Through Eighteenth Centuries. . . . . *.v.3 p.288*

"A Problem from Hell": America and the Age of Genocide. . . . . *.v.4 p.715*

"After Mecca": Women Poets and the Black Arts Movement. . . . . *.v.2 p.15, v.6 p.24, p.42*

"Aryanization" in Hamburg. . . . . *.v.3 p.82, p.171*

"Bold! Daring! Shocking! True!": A History of Exploitation Films, 1919-1959. . . . . *.v.6 p.314*

The "Domostroi": Rules for Russian Households in the Time of Ivan the Terrible. . . . . *.v.3 p.215*

"For Bread with Butter": The Life-Worlds of East Central Europeans in Johnstown, Pennsylvania, 1890-1940. . . . . *.v.3 p.492, p.493*

The "Higher Law" Background of American Constitutional Law. . . . . *.v.4 p.452*

The "Kulturkampf" in Prussian Poland. . . . . *.v.3 p.253*

"Law Never Here": A Social History of African American Responses to Issues of Crime and Justice. . . . . *.v.6 p.257*

"Licentious Liberty" in a Brazilian Gold-Mining Region: Slavery, Gender and Social Control in Eighteenth-Century Sabara, Minas Gerais. . . . . *.v.3 p.334*

"My Heart Is a Large Kingdom": Selected Letters of Margaret Fuller. . . . . *.v.2 p.39*

"No Mentor but Myself": Jack London on Writing and Writers. . . . . *.v.2 p.96*

The "Other Tuscany": Essays in the History of Lucca, Pisa, and Siena During the Thirteenth, Fourteenth and Fifteenth Centuries. . . . . *.v.6 p.561*

"Pariah States" and Sanctions in the Middle East: Iraq, LIbya, Sudan. . . . . *.v.6 p.594*

"Romance of the Rose". . . . . *.v.2 p.467*

"Schools of Tomorrow," Schools of Today: What Happened to Progressive Education. . . . . *.v.4 p.348*

A "Scottsboro" Case in Mississippi: The Supreme Court and Brown vs. Mississippi. . . . . *.v.4 p.535, p.536*

The "Stanze" of Angelo Poliziano. . . . . *.v.2 p.708*

"Surely You're Joking, Mr. Feynman!": Adventures of a Curious Character. . . . . *.v.5 p.542*

ML for the Working Programmer. . . . . *.v.5 p.347*

MLA Handbook for Writers of Research Papers. *.v.2 p.565, p.566*

MLA International Bibliography of Books and Articles on the Modern Languages and Literatures, Set. . . . . . *.v.2 p.566*

Mme. de Stael. . . . . *.v.2 p.501*

Mob Nemesis: How the FBI Crippled Organized Crime. .*.v.6 p.259*

Mobile Robotics: A Practical Introduction. . . . . . *.v.5 p.711*

Mobile Robots: Inspiration to Implementation. *.v.5 p.339, p.341*

Mobile Wireless Communications. . . . . *.v.4 p.422*

Mobile. *.v.2 p.511*

Mobility and Integration in Urban Argentina: Cordoba in the Liberal Era. . . . . *.v.3 p.349*

The Mobility of Workers under Advanced Capitalism: Dominican Migration to the United States. *.v.6 p.524, p.529*

The Mobilizaiton of Muslim Women in Egypt. . . . *.v.6 p.638*

The Mobilization of Intellect: French Scholars and Writers During the Great War. . . . . . . *.v.3 p.79, p.155*

Mobilization, Participation and Democracy in America. .*.v.4 p.547*

Mobilizing an Asian American Community. . .*.v.6 p.108, p.121*

Mobilizing for Peace: Conflict Resolution in Northern Ireland, Israel/Palestine, and South Africa. . . . . .*.v.4 p.640, p.649*

Mobilizing the Community: Local Politics in the Era of the Global City, Vol. 41. . . . . *.v.6 p.723*

Mobilizing the Masses: Building Revolution in Henan. . . . .*.v.6 p.193, p.207*

Mocking Desire. . . . .*.v.2 p.813*

Moctezuma's Children: Aztec Royalty under Spanish Rule, 1520-1700. . . . .*.v.3 p.285*

Modal Logic. . . . .*.v.1 p.491*

Modal Subjectivities: Self-Fashioning in the Italian Madrigal. . . . .*.v.1 p.180*

Model Making for the Stage: A Practical Guide. . . .*.v.1 p.147*

Model Selection and Multi-Model Inference: A Practical Information-Theoretic Approach. . . . . . .*.v.5 p.92, p.93*

Model Theory: An Introduction. . . . .*.v.5 p.470*

Model Theory. . . . .*.v.5 p.470*

Modeling, Analysis and Control of Dynamic Elastic Multi-Link Structures. . . . .*.v.5 p.695*

Modeling and Simulation in Medicine and the Life Sciences. . . . .*.v.5 p.94*

Modeling Biological Systems: Principles and Applications. . . . .*.v.5 p.91, p.93, p.502*

Modeling Differential Equations in Biology. . . .*.v.5 p.92, p.94*

Modeling Dynamic Phenomena in Molecular and Cellular Biology. . . . .*.v.5 p.502*

Modeling Nature: Episodes in the History of Population Ecology. . . . .*.v.5 p.184*

Modeling of Complex Systems. . . . .*.v.5 p.407*

Modeling Plant and Soil Systems. . . . .*.v.5 p.50*

Modelling Biological Populations in Space and Time. . . . .*.v.5 p.170, p.171*

Modelling Frequency and Count Data. . . . .*.v.5 p.481, p.503*

Modelling Geographical Systems: Statistical and Computational Applications. . . . .*.v.4 p.386*

Modelling High-Level Cognitive Processes. . . . . .*.v.5 p.590*

Modelling in Molecular Biology. . . . .*.v.5 p.126*

Modelling Individual Choice: The Econometrics of Corners, Kinks and Holes. . . . .*.v.4 p.204*

Modelling Nonlinear Economic Relationships. . . .*.v.4 p.207*

Modelling the Human Impact on Nature: Systems Analysis of Environmental Problems. . . . .*.v.5 p.358*

Modelling the Middle Ages: The History and Theory of England's Economic Development. . . . . .*.v.3 p.40, p.96*

Models As Mediators: Perspectives on Natural and Social Science. . . . .*.v.4 p.687*

Models for Christian Higher Education: Strategies for Success in the Twenty-First Century. . . . .*.v.4 p.308*

Models, Numbers, and Cases: Methods for Studying International Relations. . . . .*.v.4 p.627*

Models of Business Cycles. . . . .*.v.4 p.233, p.244*

Models of Economic Growth: Proceedings of a Conference Held by the International Economic Association at Jerusalem. . . . .*.v.4 p.244*

Models of Intelligence: International Perspectives. . .*.v.5 p.657*

Models of Sustainable Development. *v.5 p.14*

Models of the Family in Modern Societies: Ideals and
    Realities. *v.4 p.733*

Moderate Puritans and the Elizabethan Church. . . . *v.1 p.588*

Moderating Focus Groups. *v.4 p.136*

Moderato cantabile : suivi de Moderato cantabile et La Presse
    française. *v.2 p.516*

Moderato Cantabile. *v.2 p.516*

Modern Afghanistan: A History of Struggle and
    Survival. *v.6 p.634*

Modern African Drama. *v.1 p.130, v.2 p.752*

Modern Algeria: The Origins and Development of a
    Nation. *v.6 p.642*

Modern American Drama: The Female Canon. *v.1 p.122*

Modern American Literature. *v.2 p.10*

The Modern American Presidency. *v.3 p.378, p.441*

Modern and Past Glacial Environments. *v.5 p.425*

Modern Antenna Design. *v.5 p.728*

Modern Antennas. *v.5 p.728*

The Modern Anthropology of South-East Asia: An
    Introduction. *v.4 p.39*

Modern Arabic Literature: A Bibliography. *v.6 p.662*

Modern Arabic Literature. *v.6 p.658*

Modern Arabic Poetry: An Anthology. *v.6 p.660*

Modern Arabic Poetry. *v.6 p.657*

Modern Arabic Short Stories. *v.6 p.660, p.661*

Modern Architectural Theory: A Historical Survey,
    1673-1968. . . . . *v.1 p.703, p.787*

Modern Architecture and Other Essays. *v.1 p.787*

Modern Architecture. *v.1 p.786*

Modern Armenia: People, Nation, State. *v.6 p.633*

Modern Art, 1851-1929: Capitalism and Representation. *v.1 p.677*

Modern Art in Eastern Europe: From the Baltic to the Balkans,
    ca. 1890-1939. . . . . *v.1 p.680, p.688*

Modern Art. *v.1 p.679*

Modern Austrian Writing: Literature and Society after
    1945. . . . . *v.2 p.590*

Modern Belgium. *v.3 p.205, p.206*

Modern Biology and Visions of Humanity. *v.5 p.250*

Modern Biopharmaceuticals: Design, Development and
    Optimization. *v.4 p.156*

Modern Bodies: Dance and American Modernism from Martha
    Graham to Alvin Ailey. *v.1 p.28, p.30, p.41*

Modern British Drama: The Twentieth Century. . . . *v.2 p.188*

The Modern British Novel of the Left: A Research
    Guide. *v.2 p.194*

The Modern British Novel. *v.2 p.194*

Modern British Poetry, 1900-1939. . . . . *v.2 p.184*

Modern British Poetry. *v.2 p.201*

Modern Cabinetmaking. *v.1 p.805*

Modern China: An Encyclopedia of History, Culture, and
    Nationalism. *v.6 p.191, p.195*

Modern Chinese Poetry: Theory and Practice since
    1917. . . . . *v.6 p.211*

Modern Chinese Stories and Novellas, 1919 to 1949. *v.6 p.213*

Modern Clan Politics: The Power of "Blood" in Kazakhstan and
    Beyond. *v.3 p.231*

Modern Classics Poems. *v.2 p.719*

A Modern Comedy. *v.2 p.347*

Modern Compiler Implementation in Java. *v.5 p.348*

Modern Control Systems. *v.5 p.710*

The Modern Corporation and Private Property. . *v.4 p.85, p.146*

Modern Cosmology. *v.5 p.71*

A Modern Course in Statistical Physics. *v.5 p.559*

Modern Criticism and Theory: A Reader. . *v.2 p.567, p.568, p.569*

Modern Dance Forms: In Relation to the Other Modern
    Arts. *v.1 p.26*

Modern Dance in America: The Bennington Years. . . *v.1 p.26*

Modern Dance, Negro Dance: Race in
    Motion. *v.1 p.18, p.29, p.30*

The Modern Dance: Seven Statements of
    Belief. *v.1 p.26, p.40, p.41*

Modern Dance Terminology: The ABC's of Modern Dance as
    Defined by Its Originators. *v.1 p.4*

The Modern Dance. *v.1 p.27*

Modern Dance. *v.1 p.27, p.29*

Modern Dancing. *v.1 p.34*

A Modern Dictionary of Geography. *v.4 p.374*

Modern Digital and Analog Communication Systems. *v.5 p.726*

Modern Digital Control Systems, Vol. 89. . . . . . . *v.5 p.711*

Modern Digital Electronics. *v.5 p.722*

Modern Diplomacy. *v.4 p.645*

Modern Drama and German Classicism: Renaissance from
    Lessing to Brecht. *v.2 p.591, p.594*

Modern Drama and the Rhetoric of
    Theater. *v.1 p.57, p.70, p.105, p.119, p.138*

Modern Drama in Theory and Practice: Expressionism and Epic
    Theatre, Vol. 3. . . . . *v.1 p.86, p.97*

Modern Drama in Theory and Practice: Realism and Naturalism,
    Vol. 1. . . . . *v.1 p.81, p.97*

Modern Drama in Theory and Practice: Symbolism, Surrealism
    and the Absurd. *v.1 p.83, p.97*

Modern Dramatists: A Casebook of the Major British and
    American Playwrights. . . *v.1 p.101, p.115, p.116, v.2 p.188*

Modern Educational Dance. *v.1 p.47*

Modern Egypt: Orientalism. *v.6 p.637*

Modern Egypt: The Formation of a Nation-State. . . *v.6 p.637*

Modern Egyptian Art 1910-2003. . . . . . . *v.1 p.679, p.690*

The Modern Egyptian Novel. *v.6 p.661*

Modern electric, hybrid electric, and fuel cell vehicles :
    fundamentals, theory, and design. *v.5 p.716*

Modern Electrochemistry 1: Ionics. *v.5 p.285*

Modern Electrochemistry, 3 vols. *v.5 p.284, p.285*

Modern Electrochemistry: Electrodics in Chemistry,
    Engineering, Biology and Environmental Science. *v.5 p.285*

Modern Electrochemistry: Fundamentals of Electrodics. *v.5 p.285*

Modern Electronic Communication. *v.5 p.725*

Modern Engendering: Critical Feminist Readings in Modern
    Western Philosophy. *v.1 p.506*

Modern England: From the Eighteenth Century to the
    Present. *v.3 p.116, p.117*

Modern English Biography: Containing Many Thousand Concise Memoirs of Persons Who Have Died since 1850, with an Index of the Most Interesting Matter. *v.6 p.735*

A Modern English Grammar on Historical Principles. . *v.2 p.557*

Modern Environmentalism: An Introduction. *v.5 p.370*

Modern ESCA: The Principles and Practice of X-ray Photoelectron Spectroscopy. *v.5 p.273*

Modern Essays on Eighteenth-Century Literature. . . *v.2 p.171*

Modern Europe: Place, Culture and Identity. *v.3 p.87*

Modern European Art: Impressionism to Abstract Art. *v.1 p.677, p.685*

Modern French Drama, 1940-1990. . . . . *v.2 p.461*

Modern French Philosophy: From Existentialism to Postmodernism. *v.1 p.458*

Modern French Philosophy. *v.1 p.456*

Modern French Poetry: A Bilingual Anthology. . . . *v.2 p.464*

Modern French Poets on Poetry: An Anthology. *v.2 p.460, p.464*

Modern French Short Fiction: An Anthology. *v.2 p.465*

Modern French Theatre: From Giraudoux to Genet. *v.2 p.461, p.462*

Modern French Theatre: The Avant-Garde, Dada and Surrealism. *v.2 p.461*

Modern Furniture Classics: Postwar to Postmodern. . *v.1 p.804*

The Modern Garden. *v.1 p.818*

Modern Geographers: An Outline of Progress in Geography since 1800 A. D. *v.4 p.377*

Modern Geographic Thought: Richard Peet. *v.4 p.375*

Modern German Drama: A Study in Form. *v.2 p.591*

Modern German Drama. *v.2 p.594*

The Modern German Novel: A Series of Studies and Appreciations. *v.2 p.592*

Modern Germany: Its History and Civilization. . . . *v.3 p.164*

Modern Germany Reconsidered. *v.3 p.164*

Modern Greece: A Short History. *v.3 p.194*

A Modern Guide to Economic Thought: An Introduction to Comparative Schools of Thought in Economics. . *v.4 p.195*

A Modern Guide to Macroeconomics: An Introduction to Competing Schools of Thought. *v.4 p.241*

Modern Hebrew: An Essential Grammar. *v.6 p.646*

Modern Hebrew Fiction. *v.6 p.651*

Modern Hebrew for Beginners: A Multimedia Program for Students at the Beginning and Intermediate Levels. *v.6 p.646*

The Modern Hebrew Poem Itself. *v.6 p.648*

Modern Hebrew Poetry: A Billingual Anthology. . . *v.6 p.650*

A Modern History of Hong Kong: 1841-1998. . . . *v.6 p.206*

The Modern History of Iraq. *v.6 p.603*

The Modern History of Jordan. *v.6 p.620*

The Modern History of Kuwait, 1750-1965. . . . . *v.6 p.627*

The Modern History of Lebanon. *v.6 p.605*

Modern History of Mongolia. *v.6 p.239, p.240*

A Modern History of Oman: Formation of the State since 1920. . . . . *v.6 p.627*

A Modern History of Somalia: Nation and State in the Horn of Africa. *v.6 p.65*

A Modern History of Syria: Including Lebanon and Palestine. *v.6 p.605, p.608, p.611*

A Modern History of the Kurds. *v.6 p.599*

Modern Human Origins: The Other View. *v.4 p.16*

Modern India: The Origins of an Asian Democracy. . *v.6 p.156*

Modern Indian Poetry in English. *v.2 p.763*

Modern Indonesia: A History since 1945. . . . . . *v.6 p.176*

Modern Information Retrieval. *v.5 p.338*

Modern Infrared Spectroscopy. *v.5 p.271*

Modern Inquisitions: Peru and the Colonial Origins of the Civilized World. *v.3 p.326*

The Modern Invention of Medieval Music: Scholarship, Ideology, Performance. *v.1 p.177*

Modern Iran: Roots and Results of Revolution. . . . *v.6 p.631*

Modern Iraqi Arabic: A Textbook. *v.6 p.653*

Modern Ireland, 1600-1972. . . . . *v.3 p.134*

Modern Irish Drama. *v.2 p.202*

Modern Irish Short Stories. *v.2 p.202*

Modern Israeli Drama: An Anthology. *v.6 p.649*

The Modern Italian Novel: From Pea to Moravia. . . *v.2 p.698*

Modern Japan: A Historical Survey. *v.6 p.224*

Modern Japanese Diaries: The Japanese at Home and Abroad as Revealed Through Their Diaries. *v.6 p.227*

Modern Japanese Fiction and Its Traditions: An Introduction. *v.6 p.232*

Modern Japanese Poets and the Nature of Literature. *v.6 p.234*

Modern Jazz Dance. *v.1 p.31*

Modern Kongo Prophets: Religion in a Plural Society. *v.1 p.611*

Modern Korean Fiction: An Anthology. *v.6 p.238*

The Modern Latin American Novel. *v.2 p.665*

The Modern Library Writer's Workshop: A Guide to the Craft of Fiction. *v.2 p.574*

Modern Libya: A Study in Political Development. . . *v.6 p.641*

A Modern Life: Art and Design in British Columbia, 1945-1960. . . . . *v.1 p.678, p.682*

Modern Linear and Nonlinear Econometrics. *v.4 p.203*

Modern Logic: A Text in Elementary Symbolic Logic. *v.1 p.492*

Modern Love. *v.2 p.300*

Modern Machine Shop Guide to Engineering Materials. *v.5 p.731*

Modern Machine Shops Guide to Threads, Threading, and Threaded Fasteners. *v.5 p.731*

Modern Machine Shop's Machinist's Handbook for the Metalworking Industries. *v.5 p.731*

Modern Macroeconomics. *v.4 p.241*

Modern Manufacturing Processes. *v.5 p.684*

Modern Measurement: Theory, Principles, and Applications of Mental Appraisal. *v.5 p.601*

The Modern Mexican Military: A Reassessment. . . *v.3 p.277*

Modern Microwave and Millimeter-Wave Power Electronics. *v.5 p.729*

The Modern Middle East: A History. *v.6 p.592*

The Modern Middle East: A Reader. *v.6 p.593*

Modern Middle East: An Introductory and International History since 1945. . . . . *v.6 p.594*

Modern Mongolia: From Khans to Commissars to Capitalists. *v.6 p.240*

A Modern Multilingual Glossary for Taxonomic
　　Pteridology. *v.5 p.210*

Modern Music and After. *v.1 p.215*

The Modern North: People, Politics and the Rejection of
　　Colonialism. *v.3 p.546*

The Modern Novel: A Short Introduction. *v.2 p.194*

Modern Nuclear Chemistry. *v.5 p.308*

The Modern Olympics: A Struggle for Revival. . . .*v.4 p.847*

Modern Opera Houses and Theatres, Set. *v.1 p.155*

Modern Operating Systems. *v.5 p.348*

Modern Persian Drama: An Anthology. *v.6 p.670*

Modern Persian: Elementary Level. *v.6 p.669*

Modern Persian: Intermeditate Level. *v.6 p.669*

Modern Persian Poetry. *v.6 p.672*

Modern Persian Prose Literature. *v.6 p.671*

Modern Persian Short Stories. *v.6 p.673*

Modern Persian: Spoken and Written. *v.6 p.669*

Modern Philosophy of Science: Selected
　　Essays. *v.5 p.400, p.403, p.404*

Modern Physical Methods in Biochemistry, Pt. A. . . .*v.5 p.326*

Modern Physics. *v.5 p.547, p.548*

A Modern Pilgrimage in New Testament Christology. .*v.1 p.640*

Modern Poetry: A Personal Essay. *v.2 p.368*

Modern Political Culture in the Caribbean. *v.3 p.315*

Modern Power Electronics and AC Drives. *v.5 p.723*

Modern Power System Analysis. *v.5 p.724*

Modern Practice of Gas Chromatography. *v.5 p.269*

The Modern Presidency and Civil Rights: Rhetoric on Race
　　from Roosevelt to Nixon. *v.3 p.378*

The Modern Presidency. *v.4 p.527*

Modern Protein Chemistry: Practical Aspects. *v.5 p.116*

Modern Psychometrics: The Science of Psychological
　　Assessment. *v.5 p.601*

Modern Quantum Mechanics. *v.5 p.550*

A Modern Reader's Guide to Dante's Inferno. *v.2 p.705*

Modern Russian Historiography. *v.3 p.210*

The Modern Schism: Three Paths to the Secular. . . .*v.1 p.545*

The Modern School Movement: Anarchism and Education in the
　　United States. *v.4 p.324*

Modern Science and Human Values. . . .*v.5 p.410, p.412, p.413*

Modern Scientists and Engineers. *v.5 p.395*

Modern Sculpture. *v.1 p.776*

Modern Sons of the Pharaohs. *v.6 p.638*

Modern South Asian Literature in English. *v.2 p.759*

Modern Spain: A Documentary History. *v.3 p.243*

Modern Spanish American Poets. *v.2 p.665*

Modern Spanish Stage: Four Plays. *v.2 p.643*

Modern Spectroscopy. *v.5 p.562*

Modern Sri Lankan Drama. *v.2 p.760*

Modern Standard Arabic: Intermediate Level. *v.6 p.653*

Modern Stories from Holland and Flanders. *v.2 p.622*

Modern Switzerland. *v.3 p.245*

Modern Synthetic Reactions. *v.5 p.294*

Modern Systems of Government: Exploring the Role of
　　Bureaucrats and Politicians. *v.4 p.546*

Modern Techniques in Applied Molecular Spectroscopy. .*v.5 p.273*

Modern Theatre: Seven Plays and an Essay. *v.2 p.630*

Modern Theologians: An Introduction to Christian Theology
　　since 1918. . . . .*v.1 p.633, p.635*

Modern Theories of Drama: A Selection of Writings on Drama
　　and Theatre, 1850-1990. . . . .*v.1 p.55*

Modern Thermodynamics: From Heat Engines to Dissipative
　　Structures. *v.5 p.277, p.278, p.560*

Modern Times: From World War I to the Present. . .*v.1 p.219*

Modern Trends in Geomechanics. *v.5 p.699*

The Modern Trombone: A Definition of Its
　　Idioms. *v.1 p.393, p.397*

Modern Turkish Drama: An Anthology. *v.6 p.666*

Modern Ukrainian Short Stories. *v.2 p.813*

A Modern Utopia. *v.2 p.319, p.320*

The Modern Uzbeks: From the Fourteenth Century to the
　　Present, a Cultural History. *v.3 p.230*

Modern Wales: A Concise History, C. 1485-1979. . .*v.3 p.132*

Modern Welfare States : Politics and Policies in Social
　　Democratic Scandinavia. *v.3 p.232*

Modern Wildlife Painting. *v.1 p.751*

Modern Women Playwrights of Europe. *v.1 p.63, p.94*

The Modern World System: Capitalist Agriculture and the
　　Origins of the European World-Economy in the 16th
　　Century. *v.3 p.42*

The Modern World System: Mercantilism and the Consolidation
　　of the European World-Economy, 1600-1750. . . .*v.3 p.42*

The Modern World-System: The Second Era of Great Expansion
　　of the Capitalist World-Economy, 1730s-1840s. . .*v.3 p.42*

Modern Yemen, 1918-1966. . . . .*v.6 p.628*

The Modernisation of Russia, 1676-1825. . . . . . .*v.3 p.215*

Modernism: A Short Introduction. *v.2 p.177*

Modernism and Music: An Anthology of Sources. . . .*v.1 p.208*

Modernism and Revolution: Russian Literature in
　　Transition. *v.2 p.798*

Modernism and the Decorative Arts in France: Art Nouveau to
　　le Corbusier. *v.1 p.801*

Modernism from Right to Left: Wallace Stevens, the Thirties,
　　and Literary Radicalism. *v.2 p.10, p.123, p.124*

Modernism in American Silver: 20th-Century
　　Design. *v.1 p.713, p.806*

Modernism in European Drama: Ibsen, Strindberg, Pirandello,
　　Beckett: Essays from Modern Drama. *v.1 p.83, p.97*

Modernism in the Second World War: The Later Poetry of Ezra
　　Pound, T. S. Eliot, Basil Bunting and Hugh
　　MacDiarmid. *v.2 p.71*

Modernism, Medicine and William Carlos Williams. .*v.2 p.136*

Modernismo: Architecture and Design in Spain. . . .*v.1 p.789*

Modernismo, Modernity, and the Development of Spanish
　　American Literature. *v.2 p.664*

Modernism. *v.2 p.179*

The Modernist Garden in France. *v.1 p.819*

The Modernist Idea: A Critical Survey of Brazilian Writing in
　　the Twentieth Century. *v.2 p.692*

The Modernist Impulse in American
Protestantism. *v.1 p.580, p.636*

Modernist Islam, 1840-1940: A Sourcebook. . . *v.1 p.557, p.558*

The Modernist Muslim Movement in Indonesia,
1900-1942. . . . .*v.1 p.554*

Modernist Quartet. *v.2 p.72, p.77, p.111, p.112, p.124*

Modernities and Other Writings. *v.2 p.513*

Modernity and Crises of Identity: Culture and Society in
Fin-de-Siecle Vienna. *v.3 p.184*

Modernity and Metropolis: Writing, Film and Urban
Formations. *v.6 p.730*

Modernity and Modernism: French Painting in the Nineteenth
Century. *v.1 p.727*

Modernity and the Architecture of Mexico. *v.3 p.266*

Modernity and the Dilemma of North American Anglican
Identities, 1880-1950. . . . .*v.1 p.582*

Modernity at the Edge of Empire: State, Individual and Nation
in the Northern Peruvian Andes, 1885-1935. . . .*v.3 p.328*

Modernity Disavowed: Haiti and the Cultures of Slavery in the
Age of Revolution. *v.3 p.314, p.316, p.317*

Modernity, Medicine and Health: Medical Sociology Towards
2000. . . . .*v.5 p.511*

Modernization, Dislocation, and Aprismo: Origins of the
Peruvian Aprista Party, 1870-1932. . . . .*v.3 p.330*

Modernization in Colombia: The Laureano Gomez Years,
1889-1965. . . . .*v.3 p.357*

The Modernization of Fatherhood: A Social and Political
History. *v.4 p.739, v.6 p.467*

The Modernization of Inner Asia. *v.4 p.623, v.6 p.239*

The Modernization of Iran, 1921-1941. . . . .*v.6 p.631*

The Modernization of Irish Society. *v.3 p.139*

Modes of Production of Victorian Novels. *v.6 p.756*

Modes of Thinking in Young Children: A Study of the
Creativity-Intelligence Distinction. . .*v.5 p.629, p.630, p.631*

A Modest Defence of Publick Stews: or An Essay upon
Whoring, As It Is Now Practis'd in These
Kingdoms. *v.2 p.251, p.252*

Modigliani: Beyond the Myth. *v.1 p.742*

Modigliani. *v.1 p.743*

Modular Protein Domains. *v.5 p.115*

Mohammad Mosaddeq and the 1953 Coup in Iran. . .*v.6 p.631*

Mohammed: The Man and His Faith. *v.1 p.555*

Moi, Tituba sorcière-- : noire de Salem. *v.2 p.536*

☐ MolChem--Inorganic Chemistry. *v.5 p.309*

☐ MolData--Analytical Chemistry. *v.5 p.274*

☐ MolData--Biochemistry. *v.5 p.324*

☐ MolData--Environmental Chemistry. *v.5 p.309*

☐ MolData--General Chemistry. *v.5 p.255*

☐ MolData--Organic Chemistry. *v.5 p.288*

☐ MolData--Physical Chemistry. *v.5 p.274*

Molding Their Hearts and Minds: Education, Communications
and Social Change in Latin America. *v.4 p.333*

Moldova: Diplomatic History from the Archives of the Great
Powers: a Romanian Province under Russian Rule. *v.3 p.230*

The Moldovans: Romania, Russia and the Politics of
Culture. *v.3 p.230*

The Mole People: Life in the Tunnels Beneath New York
City. *v.4 p.709*

Molecular Activities of Plant Cells. *v.5 p.124, p.125*

Molecular Analysis and Genome Discovery. *v.5 p.128*

Molecular Anatomy of Cellular Systems. *v.5 p.126*

Molecular and Cellular Physiology of Neurons. . . .*v.5 p.154*

Molecular and Genetic Analysis of Human Traits. . . *v.5 p.135*

The Molecular and Supramolecular Chemistry of Carbohydrates:
A Chemical Introduction to the Glycosciences. . . *v.5 p.330*

Molecular Approaches to Crop Improvement. *v.5 p.7, p.20, p.21*

Molecular Approaches to Malaria. *v.5 p.206*

Molecular Basis of Blood Diseases. *v.5 p.521*

The Molecular Basis of Cancer. *v.5 p.520*

Molecular Beams. *v.5 p.554*

Molecular Biology and Biotechnology: A Comprehensive Desk
Reference. *v.5 p.8*

Molecular Biology and Biotechnology of Plant Organelles:
Chloroplasts and Mitochondria. *v.5 p.126, p.163*

Molecular Biology and Pathogenicity of Mycoplasmas. *v.5 p.128*

☐ Molecular Biology Gateway: The Gateway to Web Resources
for Molecular Biology, Genomics, PCR, Protocols,
Microbiology, and Biochemistry. *v.5 p.125*

Molecular Biology of the Cell. *v.5 p.111, p.153, p.154*

Molecular Biology of the Gene. *v.5 p.138*

Molecular Biology Problem Solver: A Laboratory
Guide. *v.5 p.127*

Molecular Biology Techniques: An Intensive Laboratory
Course. *v.5 p.89, p.128*

Molecular Biology: Understanding the Genetic
Revolution. *v.5 p.126*

Molecular Biology. *v.5 p.129*

Molecular Biotechnology: Principles and Applications of
Recombinant DNA. *v.5 p.123, p.133*

Molecular Botany: Signals and the Environment. . . .*v.5 p.124*

Molecular Carcinogenesis and the Molecular Biology of Human
Cancer. *v.5 p.129, p.143*

Molecular Cell Biology. *v.5 p.154*

Molecular Computation Models: Unconventional
Approaches. *v.5 p.93, p.105, p.127*

Molecular Driving Forces: Statistical Thermodynamics in
Chemistry and Biology. *v.5 p.558*

Molecular Dynamics Simulation: Elementary
Methods. *v.5 p.287, p.551*

Molecular Dynamics. *v.5 p.551*

Molecular Embryology of Flowering Plants. *v.5 p.161*

Molecular Evolution: A Phylogenetic Approach. *v.5 p.200*

Molecular Evolution and Adaptive Radiation. *v.5 p.200*

Molecular Evolution and Phylogenetics. *v.5 p.200*

Molecular Evolution: Computer Analysis of Protein and Nucleic
Acid Sequences. *v.5 p.120*

Molecular Evolution, Producing the Biochemical Data, Part
B. *v.5 p.115, p.201*

Molecular Genetics of Bacteria. *v.5 p.132*

Molecular Mechanics Across Chemistry. *v.5 p.276*

Molecular Medicine. *v.5 p.129*

Molecular Modeling of Inorganic Compounds. *v.5 p.303*

Molecular Modelling and Bonding. *v.5 p.293*

☐ Molecular Models for Biochemistry. *v.5 p.111, p.124*

Molecular Models of Life: Philosophical Papers on Molecular
    Biology. *v.5 p.129*

Molecular Motors. *v.5 p.114*

Molecular Nuclear Medicine: The Challenge of Genomics and
    Proteomics to Clinical Practice. *v.5 p.148*

Molecular Oncology of Breast Cancer. *v.5 p.159, p.163*

The Molecular Orbital Theory of Organic Chemistry. .*v.5 p.293*

Molecular Oribital Theory: An Introductory Lecture Note and
    Reprint Volume. *v.5 p.303*

Molecular Plant Pathology. *v.5 p.46*

Molecular Principles of Animal Development. *v.5 p.164*

Molecular Quantum Mechanics. *v.5 p.278, p.279*

Molecular Spectra and Molecular Structure: Electronic Spectra
    and Electronic Structure of Polyatomic Molecules, Vol.
    3. . . . .*v.5 p.270*

Molecular Spectra and Molecular Structure: Infrared and Raman
    of Polyatomic Molecules, Vol. 2. . . . . .*v.5 p.270, p.562*

Molecular Spectra and Molecular Structure: Spectra of Diatomic
    Molecules, Vol. 1. . . . .*v.5 p.270*

Molecular Strategies in Biological Evolution. . *v.5 p.199, p.200*

☐ Molecular Structure Calculations. *v.5 p.280*

Molecular Systematics and Evolution: Theory and
    Practice. *v.5 p.126, p.200*

Molecular Systematics. *v.5 p.127*

Molecular Thermodynamics: A Statistical Approach. .*v.5 p.278*

Molecular Thermodynamics. *v.5 p.278*

The Molecule Hunt: Archaeology and the Search for Ancient
    DNA. *v.5 p.122*

Molecules at an Exhibition: Portraits of Intriguing Materials in
    Everyday Life. *v.5 p.264*

Moliere: A New Criticism. *v.2 p.475, p.476*

Moliere and the Comedy of Intellect. *v.2 p.475*

The Moliere Encyclopedia. *v.2 p.475*

Moliere: The Theory and Practice of
    Comedy. *v.1 p.89, p.105, p.143*

Moliere. *v.2 p.476*

Molière: A Theatrical Life. *v.2 p.476*

Moll Flanders. *v.2 p.245*

La Mollie and the King of Tears. *v.6 p.500*

Mollie's Job: A Story of Life and Work on the Global Assembly
    Line. *v.4 p.759*

Molloy; Malone Dies; The Unnamable: A Triology. . *v.2 p.332*

Molloy. *v.2 p.509*

The Molly Maguire Riots: Industrial Conflict in the
    Pennsylvania Coal Region. *v.4 p.124, p.125*

Moltke and the German Wars, 1864-1871. . . . . .*v.3 p.168*

Moltke, Schlieffen and Prussian War Planning. . . .*v.3 p.160*

Mombasa, the Swahili, and the Making of the Mijikenda. .*v.6 p.65*

The Moment of Explosion: Blake and the Illustration of
    Milton. *v.2 p.238, p.253*

The Moment of Self-Portraiture in German Renaissance
    Art. *v.1 p.675, p.688*

A Moment of True Feeling. *v.2 p.617*

Moments of Being: Unpublished Autobiographical
    Writings. *v.2 p.395, p.397, p.399*

Moments of Truth in Genetic Medicine. *v.5 p.149*

Momentum, Heat and Mass Transfer Fundamentals. . .*v.5 p.743*

Mona and Other Tales. *v.2 p.670*

Mona in the Promised Land: A Novel. *v.6 p.100*

Mona Lisa's Escort: Andre Malraux and the Reinvention of
    French Culture. *v.2 p.522*

Monad to Man: The Concept of Progress in Evolutionary
    Biology. *v.5 p.81, p.196*

Monarchies 1000-2000. . . . .*v.4 p.502*

Monarchs and Ministers: The Grand Council in Mid-Ch'ing
    China, 1723-1820. . . . .*v.4 p.617, p.619*

Monarchy and Lordships in the Latin Kingdom of Jerusalem,
    1099-1291. . . . .*v.3 p.64, p.65*

Monarchy, Aristocracy, and the State in Europe
    1300-1800. . . . .*v.4 p.502*

Monarchy in the Emperor's Eyes: Image and Reality in the
    Chien-Lung Reign. *v.6 p.187, p.200*

The Monastery. *v.2 p.307*

The Monastic Order in England: A History of Its Development
    from the Times of St. Dunstan to the Fourth Lateran Council,
    940-1216. . . . .*v.3 p.57, v.6 p.572*

Monasticism in North-Western Europe,
    800-1200. . . . .*v.3 p.232, p.233*

Le Monde. *v.5 p.399*

Monet and Modernism. *v.1 p.746*

Monet: Art Institute of Chicago. *v.1 p.738*

Monet at Giverny. *v.1 p.746*

Monet. Complete Paintings.: Catalogue Raisonné,
    1858-1885. . . . .*v.1 p.750*

Monet, Complete Paintings.: Catalogue Raisonné,
    1885-1901. . . . .*v.1 p.749, p.750*

Monet in the 20th Century. *v.1 p.748*

Monet in the '90's: The Series Paintings. *v.1 p.748*

Monet, Narcissus, and Self-Reflection: The Modernist Myth of
    the Self. *v.1 p.743*

Monet on the Normandy Coast: Tourism and Painting,
    1867-1886. . . . .*v.1 p.740*

Monetarism and Macroeconomic Policy. *v.4 p.238, p.246, p.247*

The Monetarist Controversy: A Seminar Discussion. . *v.4 p.232*

Monetarist Economics. *v.4 p.231*

Monetary Economics. *v.4 p.237, p.241*

Monetary Equilibrium. *v.4 p.239*

The Monetary Geography of Africa. *v.4 p.398*

Monetary History of the United States, 1867-1960. . *v.4 p.238*

Monetary Policy. *v.4 p.246*

Monetary Statistics of the United States: Estimates, Sources,
    Methods. *v.4 p.238*

Monetary Theory: Inflation, Interest and Growth in the World
    Economy. *v.4 p.238, p.239*

Monetary Trends in the United States and the United Kingdom:
    Their Relation to Income, Prices, and Interest Rates,
    1867-1975. . . . .*v.4 p.238*

Monetary Trends in the United States and the United Kingdom,
    Their Relation to Income, Prices, and Interest Rates,
    1867-1975. . . . .*v.4 p.269*

Monet. *v.1 p.747*

Money and Credit in Capitalist Economies: The Endogenous
Money Approach. *v.4 p.233*

Money and Finance in the Age of Merchant Capitalism. .*v.3 p.39*

Money and Its Use in Medieval Europe. *v.6 p.558*

Money and Power in Provincial Thailand. *v.6 p.171*

Money and the Economy: Issues in Monetary Analysis. .*v.4 p.231*

Money and the Mechanism of Exchange. *v.4 p.231*

The Money and the Power: The Making of Las Vegas and Its
Hold on America, 1947-2000. . . . . . *v.3 p.529, v.6 p.711*

Money, Banking and Credit in Mediaeval Bruges. . . .*v.6 p.557*

Money, Capital and Fluctuations: Early Essays. .*v.4 p.234, 238*

Money, Credit, and Commerce. *v.4 p.224, p.238*

Money Doctors, Foreign Debts and Economic Reforms in Latin
America from the 1890s to the Present. . . .*v.3 p.259, p.260*

Money, Expectations, and Business Cycles: Essays in
Macroeconomics. *v.4 p.242*

Money Has No Smell: The Africanization of New York
City. *v.4 p.759*

Money, History, and International Finance: Essays in Honor of
Anna J. Schwartz. *v.4 p.255*

Money in Congressional Elections. *v.4 p.557, p.558*

Money, Interest and Capital: A Study in the Foundations of
Monetary Theory. *v.4 p.247, p.270*

Money, Labour and Land: Approaches to the Economies of
Ancient Greece. *v.3 p.13*

Money Matters: A Keynesian Approach to Monetary
Economics. *v.4 p.227, p.237*

The Money Men. *v.4 p.558*

Money Mischief: Episodes in Monetary History. . . .*v.4 p.231*

Money, Myths, and Change: The Economic Lives of Lesbians
and Gay Men. *v.6 p.382*

Money, Politics, and Law: A Study of Electoral Campaign
Finance Reform in Canada. *v.4 p.581*

Money, Sex and Power: Toward a Feminist Historical
Materialism. *v.4 p.273*

Money, the Financial System, and the Economy Plus Myeconlab
Student Access Kit. *v.4 p.247, p.263*

The Money-Order with White Genesis. *v.2 p.545*

Mongolia in the Twentieth Century. *v.6 p.240*

Mongolian Music, Dance and Oral Narrative: Performing
Diverse Identities. *v.1 p.43*

The Mongols. *v.6 p.239*

Monica's Story. *v.3 p.476*

Monitored Peril: Asian Americans and the Politics of TV
Representation. *v.6 p.89, p.90*

La Monja: Ixoq rusamajel Ajaw. *v.2 p.676*

Monk and Two Peas: The Story of Gregor Mendel and the
Discovery of Genetics. *v.5 p.230*

Monkey Farm: A History of the Yerkes Laboratories of Primate
Biology, Orange Park, Florida, 1930-1965. . . . . .*v.5 p.614*

Monkey Hunting. *v.2 p.145*

The Monkey in the Mirror: Essays on the Science of What
Makes Us Human. *v.4 p.16*

The Monkey Wrench Gang. *v.2 p.139*

The Monkey's Bridge: Mysteries of Evolution in Central
America. *v.5 p.197*

Monkey. *v.6 p.212*

Monmouth's Rebels. *v.3 p.105*

Monologue of a Dog. *v.2 p.792*

Monopoly Rules: How to Find, Capture, and Control the Most
Lucrative Markets in Any Business. *v.4 p.82*

Monotype: Mediums and Methods for Painterly
Printmaking. *v.1 p.759*

The Monroe Doctrine and American Expansionism
1843-1849. . . . .*v.3 p.420, p.421*

Monsieur de Saint-George: Virtuoso, Swordsman,
Revolutionary: A Legendary Life
Rediscovered. *v.1 p.189, p.281, p.352*

Monsieur Thôgô-gnini : comédie. *v.2 p.542*

Monsieur Toussaint : version scénique. *v.2 p.537*

Monsieur Toussaint. *v.2 p.537*

Monsignor Quixote. *v.2 p.350*

The Monster at Our Door: The Global Threat of Bird
Flu. *v.5 p.365*

The Monster Show: A Cultural History of Horror. . . .*v.6 p.320*

Monster: The Autobiography of an L. A. Gang Member. .*v.4 p.714*

Monsters and Mad Scientists: A Cultural History of the Horror
Movie. *v.6 p.320*

Monsters in the Closet: Homosexuality and the Horror
Film. *v.6 p.317, p.415*

Montaigne: A Biography. *v.2 p.470*

Montaigne in Motion. *v.2 p.471*

Montaigne's Discovery of Man: The Humanization of a
Humanist. *v.2 p.470*

Montaigne. *v.2 p.470, p.471*

Montaillou: The Promised Land of Error. *v.3 p.143*

Montana: A History. *v.3 p.526*

Montana: A State Guide Book. *v.3 p.525*

La Montana de las Mariposas. *v.2 p.666, p.667*

Montana: High, Wide, and Handsome. *v.3 p.525*

Montana: History of 2 Centuries. *v.3 p.525*

Montana: Land of Contrast. *v.3 p.525*

Montana's Fur Trade Era. *v.3 p.525*

Montauk. *v.2 p.607*

Montcalm and Wolfe: The French and Indian War. . .*v.3 p.406*

Monte Carlo Methods in Statistical Physics. . .*v.5 p.551, p.559*

Monte Carlo Methods. *v.5 p.551*

Monte Carlo Simulation in Statistical Physics: An
Introduction. *v.5 p.551, p.558*

Monte Carlo Strategies in Scientific Computing. . . .*v.5 p.551*

Monte Verde: A Late Pleistocene Settlement in Chile: A
Paleoenvironment and Site Context. *v.4 p.11*

Monte Verde: A Late Pleistocene Settlement in Chile: The
Archaeological Context and Interpretation. *v.4 p.11*

The Monterey Bay Shoreline Guide. *v.5 p.83*

Montesquieu and Rousseau: Forerunners of Sociology. .*v.4 p.682*

Montesquieu Revisited. *v.2 p.480*

Montesquieu. *v.2 p.481*

Montessori: A Modern Approach. *v.4 p.343*

The Montessori Method. *v.4 p.344*

Montessori: The Science Behind the Genius. . .*v.4 p.337, p.338*

Monteverdi and the End of the Renaissance. . .*v.1 p.187, p.342*

Monteverdi, Vespers (1610). *v.1 p.187, p.237, p.342*

The Monteverdi Vespers of 1610: Music, Context, and Performance. *v.1 p.185, p.342*

Monteverdi's Musical Theatre. *v.1 p.183, p.229, p.342*

The Montgolfier Brothers and the Invention of Aviation, 1783-1784: With a Word on the Importance of Ballooning for the Science of Heat and the Art of Building Railroads. *v.5 p.717*

Montgomery Clift: A Biography. *v.6 p.417, p.418*

Montreal: A History. *v.3 p.544*

Montreal Stories. *v.2 p.735*

Montreal. *v.3 p.543, p.544*

Monumenta Bulgarica: A Bilingual Anthology of Bulgarian Texts from the 9th to the 19th Centuries. *v.2 p.779*

A Monumental Vision: The Sculpture of Henry Moore.*v.1 p.780*

Monumentality in Early Chinese Art and Architecture.*v.1 p.694*

Mood and Temperament. *v.5 p.657*

Mood Genes: Hunting for Origins of Mania and Depression. *v.5 p.659*

Mood. *v.5 p.660*

Moody's Industrial Manual. *v.5 p.397*

The Moon and Sixpence. *v.2 p.370*

The Moon and the Bonfires. *v.2 p.720, p.721*

The Moon in the Gutter. *v.2 p.80*

Moon, Sun and Witches: Gender Ideologies and Class in Inca and Colonial Peru. *v.3 p.264, p.283, p.326*

Moonchild: The Films of Kenneth Anger. *v.6 p.416*

Moons and Planets. *v.5 p.69, p.434*

The Moons of Jupiter: Stories. *v.2 p.737*

The Moonstone. A novel. by Wilkie Collins. *v.2 p.280*

The Moonstone. *v.2 p.280*

Moore. *v.1 p.445*

Moorings and Metaphors: Figures of Culture and Gender in Black Women's Literature. *v.6 p.479*

Moorish Spain. *v.3 p.237*

The Moor's Last Sigh. *v.2 p.766*

Moo. *v.2 p.155*

▢ Moral and Character Development. *v.4 p.306*

Moral Desperado: A Life of Thomas Carlyle. *v.2 p.276*

Moral Development Theories - Secular and Religious: A Comparative Study. *v.5 p.629*

The Moral Dimension of Marketing: Essays on Business Ethics. *v.4 p.146*

The Moral Dimension: Toward a New Economics. . *v.4 p.185*

The Moral Dimensions of Teaching. *v.4 p.282*

Moral Education: A Study in the Theory and Application of the Sociology of Education. *v.4 p.306*

Moral Education in America: Schools and the Shaping of Character from Colonial Times to the Present. . .*v.4 p.306*

Moral Judgment: Does the Abuse Excuse Threaten Our Legal System? *v.6 p.269*

The Moral Judgment of the Child. *v.4 p.358*

Moral Letters: Epistles 1-65. . . . .*v.1 p.429*

Moral Letters: Epistles 66-92. . . . .*v.1 p.429*

Moral Luck: Philosophical Papers, 1973-1980. . . . .*v.1 p.485*

Moral Man and Immoral Society: A Study in Ethics and Politics. *v.4 p.484, p.770*

Moral Maxims. *v.2 p.477*

The Moral Media: How Journalists Reason about Ethics. *v.4 p.417*

The Moral Obligation to Be Intelligent: Selected Essays. *v.2 p.569*

The Moral Philosophy of Management: From Quesnay to Keynes. *v.4 p.215*

Moral Philosophy. *v.1 p.451*

The Moral Property of Women: A History of Birth Control Politics in America. .*v.4 p.569, p.775, v.6 p.464, p.465, p.469*

Moral Questions in the Classroom: How to Get Kids to Think Deeply about Real Life and Their School Work. . .*v.4 p.306*

Moral Realism and the Foundations of Ethics. .*v.1 p.487, p.514*

Moral Relativism: A Reader. *v.1 p.515*

Moral Relativism and Moral Objectivity, L. . .*v.1 p.514, p.515*

The Moral Status of Persons: Perspectives on Bioethics.*v.5 p.246*

Moral Tales. *v.2 p.495*

The Moral Trollope. *v.2 p.316*

The Moral Vision of Oscar Wilde. *v.2 p.320*

The Morality of Groups: Collective Responsibility, Group-Based Harm and Corporate Rights. *v.4 p.713*

The Morality of Happiness. *v.1 p.483*

The Morality of Law. *v.4 p.434*

The Morality of Nationalism. *v.4 p.494*

Morality Politics in American Cities. *v.6 p.725*

Morality, Reason, and Power: American Diplomacy in the Carter Years. *v.3 p.480*

The Morals and Politics of Psychology: Psychological Discourse and the Status Quo. *v.5 p.675*

Moravagine : roman. *v.2 p.512*

Moravagine. *v.2 p.512*

Moravia Magna : The Great Moravian Empire, its Art and Times. *v.3 p.191*

Moravian Women's Memoirs: Their Related Lives, 1750-1820. . . . .*v.1 p.590*

More 19th-Century Studies: A Group of Honest Doubters. *v.6 p.751, p.753*

More Conversations with Eudora Welty. *v.2 p.130*

More Damned Lies and Statistics: How Numbers Confuse Public Issues. *v.4 p.689*

More Mathematical People: Contemporary Conversations. *v.5 p.464*

More Matter: Essays and Criticism. *v.2 p.157*

More Modern Chemical Techniques. *v.5 p.268*

More Pricks Than Kicks. *v.2 p.332*

More Secure, Less Free?: Antiterrorism Policy and Civil Liberties after September 11. . . . .*v.4 p.565, p.572*

More Speech, Not Less: Communications Law in the Information Age. *v.4 p.406, p.445*

More Stories We Tell: The Best Contemporary Short Stories by American Women. *v.2 p.583*

More Than a Game: An Unauthorized History of Australian Rules Football. *v.4 p.806, p.816, p.843, p.844, p.847*

More than a Game: One Woman's Fight for Gender Equity in Sport. *v.4 p.822, p.837, p.901*

More Than a Game. *v.4 p.832, p.854*

More Than a Method: Trends and Traditions in Contemporary Film Performance. *v.6 p.347*

More Than Black: Afro-Cubans in Tampa. . . *v.6 p.544, p.549*

More Than Human: Embracing the Promise of Biological Enhancement. *v.5 p.152*

More Than Just a Game: Sports in American Life since 1945. . . . . *v.4 p.716, p.816, p.817*

More Than Just Minstrel Shows: The Rise of Black Musical Theatre at the Turn of the Century. *v.1 p.120*

More than Meets the Eye: Studies on Upper Palaeolithic Diversity in the Near East. *v.4 p.16*

More Than One Life. *v.2 p.783*

More Wives Than One: Transformation of the Mormon Marriage System, 1840-1910. . . . . *v.4 p.747*

More Wren Songs. *v.2 p.374*

The More You Watch, the Less You Know: News Wars - (Sub)Merged Hopes - Media Adventures. . . *v.4 p.417, p.418*

Morels. *v.5 p.209*

Morgante: The Epic Adventures of Orlando and His Giant Friend Morgante. *v.2 p.708*

The Morgesons and Other Writings, Published and Unpublished. *v.2 p.51*

Mori Ogai and the Modernization of Japanese Culture. . *v.6 p.226*

Mori Ogai. *v.6 p.228*

Mormon Polygamous Families: Life in the Principle. . *v.4 p.740*

Mormon Polygamy: A History. *v.4 p.740, p.749*

The Mormon Question: Polygamy and Constitutional Conflict in Nineteenth-Century America. *v.1 p.587*

The Mormon Trail: Yesterday and Today. *v.3 p.520*

Mormonism and Music: A History. *v.1 p.277*

Mormons and the Bible: The Place of the Latter-Day Saints in American Religion. *v.1 p.587*

The Morning After: Sexual Politics at the End of the Cold War. *v.6 p.440, p.441*

Morning by Morning: How We Home-Schooled Our African-American Sons to the Ivy League. *v.4 p.296*

Morning in America: How Ronald Reagan Invented the 1980's. *v.3 p.371*

Mornings on Horseback: The Story of an Extraordinary Family, a Vanished Way of Life, and the Unique Child Who Became Theodore Roosevelt. *v.3 p.475*

Morningstar Guide to Mutual Funds: Five-Star Strategies for Success. *v.4 p.93*

▢ Morningstar. *v.4 p.93, p.101, p.103*

Morocco and Tunisia: A Comparative History. *v.6 p.61*

Morocco: From Empire to Independence. *v.6 p.644*

Morocco Since 1830: A History. *v.6 p.61, p.644*

Morocco: The Islamist Awakening and Other Challenges. *v.6 p.643*

Morocco Under King Hassan. *v.6 p.643*

Morphogenesis: The Cellular and Molecular Processes of Developmental Anatomy. *v.5 p.159*

Morphology of Plants and Fungi. *v.5 p.207, p.208*

Morphology, Shape and Phylogeny. *v.5 p.155, p.199*

Morphometric Tools for Landmark Data: Geometry and Biology. *v.5 p.90, p.91, p.93*

Morphometrics for the Life Sciences. *v.5 p.155*

Morphometrics. *v.5 p.204*

Morphosis. *v.1 p.794*

Morris and Co. *v.1 p.802*

Morrissey: Scandal and Passion. *v.6 p.409*

The Morrow Anthology of Younger American Poets. . *v.2 p.24*

Une mort très douce. *v.2 p.508*

Mortal Engines. *v.4 p.802, p.806, p.832, p.873*

Mortal Questions. *v.1 p.486*

Mortal Secrets: Truth and Lies in the Age of AIDS. . *v.6 p.379*

Mortality Immortality?: The Legacy of 20th-Century Art. *v.1 p.822*

Mortality of Hispanic Populations: Mexicans, Puerto Ricans, and Cubans in the United States and in the Home Country. *v.6 p.551*

Le Morte d'Arthur: King Arthur and the Legends of the Round Table. *v.2 p.212*

Le Morte Darthur: The Winchester Manuscript. . . . *v.2 p.212*

Le Morte d'Arthur. *v.2 p.212*

The Mortgaged Heart: Selected Writings. *v.2 p.100*

Mortgaging Women's Lives: Feminist Critiques of Structural Adjustment. *v.6 p.458*

Mosaic of Despair: Human Breakdowns in Prison. . *v.6 p.277*

The Mosaic of Economic Growth. *v.4 p.244*

A Mosaic of Victims: Non-Jews Persecuted and Murdered by the Nazis. *v.6 p.364*

Mosby's Clinical Nursing. *v.5 p.522, p.523*

Mosby's Complementary and Alternative Medicine: A Research-Based Approach. *v.5 p.531*

Mosby's Emergency Nursing Reference. *v.5 p.531*

Mosby's Guide to Physical Examination. *v.5 p.521*

Mosby's Memoirs and Other Stories. *v.2 p.60*

▢ Mosby's Nursing Consult: The Latest Knowledge for the Greatest Care. *v.5 p.526, p.527*

Mosby's Pediatric Nursing Reference. . *v.5 p.524, p.525, p.527*

Mosby's Pharmacology in Nursing. *v.5 p.526*

Moscow 1812: Napoleon's Fatal March. *v.3 p.153*

Moscow and the Middle East: Soviet Policy since the Invasion of Afghanistan. *v.6 p.592*

The Moscow Art Theatre. *v.1 p.81, p.84, p.111, p.138*

Moscow Politics and the Rise of Stalin: The Communist Party in the Capital, 1925-32. . . . . *v.3 p.226*

Moscow to the End of the Line. *v.2 p.803*

Moses and Other Poems. *v.2 p.814*

Moses Maimonides. *v.1 p.432, p.433*

Moses Mendelssohn: A Biographical Study. *v.1 p.460*

Moses Mendelssohn and the Enlightenment. *v.1 p.460*

Moses Mendelssohn: Philosophical Writings. *v.1 p.460*

Moses the Egyptian: The Memory of Egypt in Western Monotheism. *v.3 p.8*

Mosquito and Ant Poems. *v.6 p.103*

Mosquitoes, Malaria, and Man: A History of the Hostilities since 1880. . . . . *v.5 p.356, p.364*

Mosquitoes. *v.2 p.74*

Mosses and Other Bryophytes: An Illustrated Glossary. .*v.5 p.209*

Mosses of Eastern North America. *v.5 p.209*

Mosses with Hand Lens and Microscope. *v.5 p.209*

The Most Activist Supreme Court in History: The Road to
Modern Judicial Conservatism. *v.4 p.470, p.537*

The Most Beautiful Molecule: The Discovery of the
Buckyball. *v.5 p.305*

Most of the Most of S. J. Perelman. *v.2 p.111*

A Most Remarkable Fella: Frank Loesser and the Guys and
Dolls in His Life: A Portrait by His Daughter. .*v.1 p.252, p.337*

Mostly Miniatures: An Introduction to Persian
Painting. *v.1 p.691, p.731*

Moth Smoke: A Novel. *v.2 p.760*

Mother Camp: Female Impersonators in America. . . .*v.6 p.371*

Mother India: Selections from the Controversial 1927 Text,
Edited and with an Introduction by Mrinalini Sinha. *v.6 p.150*

Mother Jones: An American Life. *v.4 p.126*

Mother Love, Mother Earth. *v.2 p.529*

Mother Nature: Maternal Instincts and How They Shape the
Human Species. *v.4 p.744*

Mother Night. *v.2 p.158*

The Mother of Eve: As a First Language Teacher. . . .*v.4 p.358*

Mother of My Heart, Daughter of My Dreams: Kali and Uma in
the Devotional Poetry of Bengal. *v.6 p.152*

Mother Stone: The Vitality of Modern British Sculpture. .*v.1 p.778*

Mother Tongue. *v.6 p.501*

Mother Wit from the Laughing Barrel: Readings in the
Interpretation of Afro-American Folklore. *v.2 p.17*

Mothering Across Cultures: Postcolonial
Representations. *v.6 p.480*

Mothering, Education, and Ethnicity: The Transformation of
Japanese American Culture. . .*v.6 p.108, p.110, p.111, p.131*

Motherloss. *v.5 p.626, p.652,v.6 p.445*

Mothers Alone: Strategies for a Time of Change. .*v.6 p.465, p.467*

Mothers in the Fatherland: Women, Family Life and Nazi
Ideology, 1919-1945. . . . .*v.3 p.53, p.172*

Mothers in the Fatherland: Women, the Family and Nazi
Politics. *v.3 p.172*

Mothers of Heroes and Martyrs: Gender Identity Politics in
Nicaragua, 1979-1999. . . . .*v.3 p.301*

Mothers of Invention: Women of the Slaveholding South in the
American Civil War. *v.4 p.520*

Mothers of the Revolution: The War Experiences of Thirty
Zimbabwean Women. *v.6 p.77, p.78*

Mother. *v.2 p.804*

The Moths and Other Stories. *v.6 p.504*

Motif-Index of Folk-Literature: A Classification of Narrative
Elements in Folk Tales, Ballads, Myths, Fables,
Mediaeval Romances, Exempla, Fabliaux, Jest-Books, and
Local Legends. *v.2 p.585*

Motion: American Sports Poems. *v.4 p.811*

The Motion Picture Guide, Vol. 110. . . . .*v.6 p.306*

Motivate Teams, Maximize Success: Effective Strategies for
Realizing Your Goals. *v.4 p.80, p.81*

Motivating Soldiers: Morale or Mutiny. *v.5 p.584*

Motivation: A Biobehavioural Approach. *v.5 p.658*

Motivation Counts. *v.5 p.463*

Motivation, Emotion, and Cognition: Integrative Perspectives on
Intellectual Functioning and Development. *v.5 p.652*

Motivation in Work Organizations. *v.5 p.579*

The Motivation of Politicians. *v.5 p.644*

The Motivation to Work. *v.5 p.579*

Motor Control Electronics Handbook. *v.5 p.725*

Motor Control: Theory and Practical Applications. . .*v.4 p.910*

Motor Learning and Performance. *v.4 p.910*

Motor Learning: Concepts and Applications. *v.4 p.909*

The Motor Vehicle. *v.5 p.716*

Les mots en liberté futuristes. *v.2 p.718*

Les mots pour le dire. *v.2 p.528*

Les Mots. *v.2 p.527*

Moulds of Understanding: A Pattern of Natural
Philosophy. *v.5 p.403*

Mountain and the Valley. *v.2 p.733*

The Mountain Encyclopedia: An A-Z Compendium of over
2,250 Terms, Concepts, Ideas, and People. *v.6 p.283*

Mountain Geomorphology. *v.4 p.391*

Mountain Islands and Desert Seas: A Natural History of the
U.S.-Mexican Borderlands. *v.3 p.269*

Mountain Lion. *v.2 p.120*

Mountain Men of the American West. *v.3 p.519*

Mountain of Fame: Portraits in Chinese History. . *v.6 p.199*

The Mountain of Green Tea. *v.6 p.655*

Mountain of the Condor: Metaphor and Ritual in an Andean
Ayllu. *v.3 p.323*

The Mountain of the Moon. *v.6 p.150*

Mountain River: Vietnamese Poetry from the Wars,
1948-1993. . . . .*v.6 p.169*

The Mountain States of America: People, Politics and Power in
the Eight Rocky Mountain States. *v.3 p.525*

The Mountainous West: Explorations in Historical
Geography. *v.3 p.525*

Mountains and Rivers Without End. *v.2 p.156*

Mountains of Memory: A Fire Lookout's Life in the River of
No Return Wilderness. *v.6 p.288*

Mountbatten. *v.3 p.91*

Mountolive. *v.2 p.344*

The Mourning Bride, Poems and Miscellanies. *v.2 p.244*

Mouse Genome Resources. . .*v.5 p.103, p.108, p.144, p.212*

The Mousetrap and Other Plays. *v.2 p.339*

Les mousquetaires, Vol. 1. . . . .*v.2 p.489*

Les mousquetaires, Vol. 2. . . . .*v.2 p.488, p.489*

Les mousquetaires, Vol. 3. . . . .*v.2 p.489*

A Mouth Sweeter Than Salt: An African Memoir. . . .*v.4 p.702*

The Mouth That Begs: Hunger, Cannibalism and the Politics of
Eating in Modern China. *v.6 p.209*

The Move to Community Policing: Making Change
Happen. *v.6 p.264*

A Moveable Feast. *v.2 p.84*

The Movement: A History of the American New Left,
1959-1972. . . . .*v.4 p.332*

The Movement Against Teaching English in Schools of Puerto Rico. *v.3 p.319*

Movement and Drama in Therapy. *v.1 p.51*

Movement and Meaning: Creativity and Interpretation in Ballet and Mime. *v.1 p.43*

Movement and Modernism: Yeats, Eliot, Williams and Early Twentieth-Century Dance. *v.1 p.46*

Movement, Body and Awareness: Exploring Somatic Processes. *v.1 p.52*

The Movement for Indian Assimilation, 1860 to 1890. .*v.6 p.688*

Movement Skill Assessment. *v.4 p.873, p.907, p.909*

Movement System Variability. *v.4 p.908, p.909, p.910*

Movements in Art since 1945. . . . .*v.1 p.679, p.680*

Movements in Chicano Poetry: Against Myths, Against Margins. *v.6 p.502, p.510, p.511, p.515*

Movements of Political Protest in Canada, 1640-1840. .*v.3 p.536*

Movements of Thought in the Nineteenth Century. . .*v.1 p.438*

Movie Acting, the Film Reader. *v.6 p.348*

Movie Awards: The Ultimate, Unofficial Guide to the Oscars, Golden Globes, Critica, Guild and Indie Honors. . .*v.6 p.346*

Movie Blockbusters. *v.6 p.331*

Movie Marketing: Opening the Picture and Giving It Legs. *v.6 p.345, p.346*

Movie Money: Understanding Hollywood's Creative Account Practices. *v.6 p.344*

The Moviegoer. *v.2 p.152, p.153*

Movies and Mass Culture. *v.6 p.320*

Movies and Money: Undeclared War Between Europe and America. *v.6 p.345*

Movies Were Always Magical: Interviews with 13 Actors, Directors, and Producers from the Hollywood of the 1950s. *v.6 p.344*

Movie-Struck Girls: Women and Motion Picture Culture after the Nickelodeon. *v.6 p.329, p.475*

Moving and Learning: The Elementary School Physical Education Experience with PowerWeb: Health and Human Performance. *v.4 p.796, p.798*

Moving Away from Silence: Music of the Peruvian Altiplano and the Experience of Urban Migration. *v.1 p.295*

Moving Europeans: Migration in Western Europe since 1650. . . . .*v.4 p.602*

Moving from the Margins: A Chicana Voice on Public Policy. *v.6 p.539*

Moving History: Dancing Cultures: A Dance History Reader. *v.1 p.41*

Moving Horizons: The Landscape Architecture of Kathryn Gustafson and Partners. *v.1 p.815*

Moving House and Other Stories. *v.2 p.790*

▢ Moving Image Archive. *v.6 p.344*

Moving Lessons: Margaret H'Doubler and the Beginning of Dance in American Education. *v.1 p.48*

Moving Mountains: Japanese Education Reform. . . .*v.4 p.336*

Moving Notation: A Handbook of Musical Rhythm and Elementary Labanotation for the Dancer. *v.1 p.38*

Moving Parts. *v.2 p.792*

Moving Stories: Migration and the American West, 1850-2000. . . . .*v.3 p.521*

Moving the Image: Independent Asian Pacific American Media Arts 1970-1990. . . . .*v.6 p.88*

Moving the Mountain: Women Working for Social Change. *v.6 p.433*

Moving Toward Balance: 8 Weeks of Yoga with Rodney Yee. *v.4 p.793*

Moving Words: Re-Writing Dance. *v.1 p.39, p.43*

Le Moyen âge. *v.2 p.457*

Mozambique: Who Calls the Shots? *v.6 p.76*

Mozart: A Documentary Biography. *v.1 p.189, p.343*

Mozart: A Life. *v.1 p.192, p.344*

Mozart: A Musical Biography. *v.1 p.190, p.344*

Mozart and the Pianist: A Guide for Performers and Teachers to Mozart's Major Works for Solo Piano. *v.1 p.189, p.238, p.239, p.343, p.397*

Mozart: Clarinet Concerto. *v.1 p.191, p.241, p.344*

The Mozart Family: Four Lives in a Social Context. *v.1 p.189, p.343*

Mozart: Piano Concertos. *v.1 p.239, p.343*

The Mozart Repertory: A Guide for Musicians, Programmers, and Researchers. *v.1 p.165, p.193, p.345*

Mozart: The 'Haydn' Quartets. *v.1 p.190, p.240, p.344*

Mozart, the "Jupiter" Symphony, No. 41 in C Major, K. 551. . . . .*v.1 p.192, p.243, p.344*

Mozart's Letters, Mozart's Life. *v.1 p.192, p.344, p.345*

Mozart's "Thematic Catalogue". *v.1 p.164, p.344*

Mozart's Operas. *v.1 p.190, p.230, p.343, p.344*

Mozart's Piano Concertos: Text, Context, Interpretation. *v.1 p.193, p.244, p.345*

Mozart's Requiem: Historical and Analytical Studies, Documents, Score. *v.1 p.192, p.237, p.238, p.345*

Mozart's Symphonies: Context, Performance Practice, Reception. *v.1 p.193, p.244, p.345*

Mozart's Women: His Family, His Friends, His Music. *v.1 p.189, p.343, p.379*

▢ MPA = Music Publisher's Association of the United States. *v.1 p.172, p.385*

Mr. Baruch. *v.3 p.457*

Mr. Cibber of Drury Lane. *v.2 p.242*

Mr. Clemens and Mark Twain: A Biography. *v.2 p.33*

Mr. Ives' Christmas. *v.2 p.147*

Mr. Jefferson's Lost Cause: Land, Farmers, Slavery, and the Louisiana Purchase. *v.5 p.5*

Mr. Justice Murphy: A Political Biography. *v.4 p.468*

Mr. Keynes and the Post Keynesians: Principles of Macroeconomics for a Monetary Production Economy. *v.4 p.226, p.227, p.242*

Mr. Lincoln's Army. *v.3 p.430*

Mr. Madison's War: Politics, Diplomacy and Warfare in the Early American Republic, 1783-1830. . . . . . .*v.3 p.418*

Mr. Midshipman Easy. *v.2 p.299*

Mr. Midshipman Hornblower. *v.2 p.345*

Mr. Moody and the Evangelical Tradition. *v.1 p.648*

Mr. Palomar. *v.2 p.714, p.715*

Mr. Polk's War: American Opposition and Dissent, 1846-1848. . . . .*v.3 p.401, p.418*

Mr. Potter. *v.2 p.768*

Mr. Republican; a Biography of Robert A. Taft. *v.3 p.461*

Mr. Sammler's Planet. *v.2 p.60*

Mr. Sampath: The Printer of Malgudi. *v.2 p.765*

Mr. Secretary Peel: The Life of Sir Robert Peel to
1830. . . . .*v.3 p.94, p.111*

Mr. Smith Goes to Tokyo: Japanese Cinema under the American
Occupation, 1945-1952. . . . .*v.6 p.336*

Mr. Tompkins in Paperback: Comprising 'Mr. Tompkins in
Wonderland' and 'Mr. Tompkins Explores the
Atom'. *v.5 p.539, p.540*

☐ Mr. William Shakespeare and the Internet. *v.2 p.222*

MRI for Technologists. *v.5 p.534, p.535*

The Mrozek Reader. *v.2 p.791*

☐ MRQE: Review Query Engine. *v.6 p.307*

Mrs. Beeton's Book of Household Management. .*v.6 p.746, p.761*

Mrs. Craddock. *v.2 p.370*

The Mrs. Dalloway Reader. *v.2 p.395*

Mrs. Dalloway. *v.2 p.394*

Mrs. Spring Fragrance and Other Writings. *v.6 p.101*

Mrs. Stanton's Bible: Elizabeth Cady Stanton and the Woman's
Bible. *v.6 p.431, p.459*

Mrs. Stevens Hears the Mermaids Singing. .*v.2 p.119, v.6 p.399*

Mrs. Vargas and the Dead Naturalist. *v.6 p.497*

☐ MSDS Hyper Glossary. *v.5 p.265*

MTV: The Making of a Revolution. *v.1 p.256, p.272*

Much Ado about Nothing. *v.2 p.225*

A Much Misunderstood Man: Selected Letters of Ambrose
Bierce. *v.2 p.31, p.32*

Much More Than a Game: Players, Owners and American
Baseball since 1921. . . . .*v.4 p.850, p.882, p.895*

Much Obliged Jeeves. *v.2 p.391*

Muckraking and Objectivity: Journalism's Colliding Traditions,
18. . . . .*v.4 p.406*

Muckraking!: The Journalism That Changed America. .*v.4 p.404*

Mud and Mudstone: Introduction and Overview. . . .*v.5 p.438*

Mud, Sweat and Beers: A Cultural History of Sport and
Alcohol. *v.4 p.814*

Muddied Waters: Race, Region, and Local History in Colombia,
1846-1948. . . . .*v.3 p.357*

Muddy Cup: A Dominican Family Comes of Age in a New
America. *v.6 p.488, p.543*

Mudie's Circulating Library and the Victorian
Novel. *v.3 p.119, p.120*

Muenscher's Keys to Woody Plants: An Expanded Guide to
Native and Cultivated Species. *v.5 p.43*

La Muerte de Artemio Cruz. *v.2 p.668*

La Muerte y la Doncella. *v.2 p.680*

Mughal and Rajput Painting. *v.1 p.730*

The Mughal Empire. *v.6 p.156*

Mughal Gardens: Sources, Places, Representations, and
Prospects. *v.1 p.820*

Muhammad Ali Reader. *v.4 p.811, p.831, p.855*

Muhammad Ali: The People's Champ. . .*v.4 p.831, p.832, p.855*

Muhammad Al-Qadiri's Nashr Al-Mathani: The
Chronicles. *v.6 p.643*

Muhammad and the Christian: A Question of Response. .*v.1 p.558*

Muhammad at Mecca. *v.1 p.555*

Muhammad at Medina. *v.1 p.555*

Muhammad: His Life Based on the Earliest Sources. .*v.1 p.555*

Muhammad's Mecca: History in the Qur'an. *v.6 p.625*

Muhammad. *v.1 p.555*

Mulberry and Peach: Two Women of China. . .*v.6 p.101, p.213*

The Mulberry Bush, a Play in Three Acts. *v.2 p.389*

Mules and Men. *v.2 p.17, v.6 p.16, p.26*

Mullas, Sufis and Heretics: The Role of Religion in Kurdish
Society. *v.6 p.600*

Muller Vs. Oregon: A Brief History with Documents. .*v.4 p.439*

The Mulligan Guide to Sports Journalism Careers. . .*v.4 p.907*

Mulliner Nights. *v.2 p.391*

The Multicampus System: Perspectives on Practice and
Prospects. *v.4 p.292*

Multicultural and Diversity Education: A Reference
Handbook. *v.4 p.308*

A Multicultural Approach to Physical Education: Proven
Strategies for Middle and High School. . . .*v.4 p.797, p.799*

Ⓔ Multicultural Citizenship: A Liberal Theory of Minority
Rights. *v.4 p.547, p.551, p.573, p.579*

Multicultural Competencies: A Guidebook of Practices. .*v.5 p.637*

Multicultural Counselling: A Reader. *v.5 p.637*

Multicultural Education: A Source Book. *v.4 p.309*

Multicultural Education in a Pluralistic Society. *v.4 p.363*

Multicultural Geographies: The Changing Racial/Ethnic Patterns
of the United States. *v.4 p.382*

Multicultural Gifted Education. *v.4 p.317*

Multicultural Law Enforcement: Strategies for Peacekeeping in a
Diverse Society. *v.6 p.265*

Multicultural Science Education: Theory, Practice, and
Promise. *v.4 p.367*

Multicultural Teaching: A Handbook of Activities, Information,
and Resources. *v.4 p.309*

Multicultural Theatre II: Contemporary Hispanic, Asian and
African-American Plays. *v.1 p.120*

Multiculturalism and American Democracy. *v.4 p.573*

Multiculturalism and the History of Canadian Diversity. .*v.3 p.542*

Multifetal Pregnancy: A Handbook for Care of the Pregnant
Patient. *v.5 p.524*

A Multilevel Approach to the Study of Motor Control and
Learning. *v.4 p.874, p.908, p.910*

Multimedia Projects in the Classroom: A Guide to Development
and Evaluation. *v.4 p.351*

Multimethod Research: Synthesizing Styles. *v.4 p.686*

Multinational Firms in the World Economy. . .*v.4 p.257, p.261*

Multiparty Democracy and Political Change: Constraints to
Democratization in Africa. *v.4 p.505, p.585, p.612*

Multiple Aspects of DNA and RNA from Biophysics to
Bioinformatics: Lecture Notes of the les Houches Summer
School 2004. . . . .*v.5 p.121, p.123, p.124*

Multiple Cropping Systems. *v.5 p.21*

Multiple Modernities: Cinemas and Popular Media in
Transcultural East Asia. *v.6 p.334*

Title Index

Multiple Paths to Knowledge in International Relations: Methodology in the Study of Conflict Management and Conflict Resolution. *v.4 p.650*

Multiple Perspectives on Play in Early Childhood Education. *v.4 p.369*

Multiple Stressor Effects in Relation to Declining Amphibian Populations. *v.6 p.291*

Multiple Voices in Feminist Film Criticism. *v.6 p.474*

The Multiracial Experience: Racial Borders as the New Frontier. *v.6 p.124*

Multi-Scale Integrated Analysis of Agroecosystems: An Integrated Assessment. *v.5 p.11*

Multitude: War and Democracy in the Age of Empire. *v.4 p.504*

Multivariable Calculus: Concepts and Contexts. *v.4 p.206*

Multivariable Mathematics. *v.5 p.486*

Mum and Mr. Armitage: Selected Stories of Beryl Bainbridge. *v.2 p.330*

Mumbo Jumbo. *v.2 p.154, v.6 p.27*

The Muqaddimah: An Introduction to History. Abridged ed. *v.6 p.585*

The Murals of Bonampak. *v.3 p.261*

The Murals of Revolutionary Nicaragua, 1979-1992. .*v.3 p.302*

Murder at the Sleepy Lagoon: Zoot Suits, Race, and Riot in Wartime L.A. *v.6 p.536, p.541, p.550*

Murder in Byzantium: A Novel. *v.2 p.531*

Murder, Mayhem, Pillage, and Plunder: The History of the Lebanon in the 18th and 19th Centuries by Mikhayil Mishaqa (1800-1873). *v.6 p.605*

Murder Must Advertise. *v.2 p.382*

The Murder of Chile: Eyewitness Accounts of the Coup, The Terror, and the Resistance Today. *v.3 p.352*

The Murder of Roger Ackroyd: A Hercule Poirot Mystery. *v.2 p.339*

Murder on the Nile, the World Trade Center and Global Terror. *v.4 p.657*

Murder Trials. *v.2 p.431*

A Muriel Rukeyser Reader. *v.2 p.113*

Muriel Rukeyser: Selected Poems. *v.2 p.114*

Muriel Spark. *v.2 p.383*

Murky Business. *v.2 p.486*

Murray Louis on Dance. *v.1 p.10, p.43*

Musaddiq and the Struggle for Power in Iran. *v.6 p.631*

Muscat and Oman: The End of an Era. *v.6 p.627, p.628*

Muscles, Reflexes, and Locomotion. *v.4 p.909*

Muscletown USA: Bob Hoffman and the Manly Culture of York Barbell. *v.4 p.715*

Muscovy and Sweden in the Thirty Years' War, 1630-1635. . . . .*v.3 p.216*

A Muse for Heroes: Nine Centuries of the Epic in France. *v.2 p.455*

The Muse's Method: An Introduction to Paradise Lost. *v.2 p.255*

Museum Administration: An Introduction. *v.1 p.828*

The Museum Companion: Understanding Western Art. *v.1 p.665*

Museum Educator's Handbook. *v.1 p.828*

Museum Movies: The Museum of Modern Art and the Birth of Art Cinema. *v.6 p.331, p.332*

The Museum of Broadcast Communications Encyclopedia of Radio. *v.4 p.418*

The Museum of Unconditional Surrender. *v.2 p.818*

Museum Store Management. *v.1 p.828, p.829*

Museums after Modernism: Strategies of Engagement. *v.1 p.829*

Museums and Source Communities: A Routledge Reader. *v.4 p.48*

☐ MUSÉE. *v.1 p.661, p.667, p.827*

Mushrooms of Northeastern North America. *v.5 p.209*

Music: A View from Delft. Selected Essays. *v.1 p.211*

Music Abbreviations: A Reverse Dictionary. *v.1 p.160*

Music Alone: Philosophical Reflections on the Purely Musical Experience. *v.1 p.381*

Music Analyses: An Annotated Guide to the Literature. *v.1 p.166*

Music and Black Ethnicity: The Caribbean and South America. *v.1 p.280*

Music and Ceremony at Notre Dame of Paris, 500-1550. *v.1 p.178*

Music and Color: Conversations with Claude Samuel. *v.1 p.218, p.341*

Music and Copyright. *v.1 p.384*

Music and Cultural Theory. *v.1 p.377*

Music and Culture in Eighteenth-Century Europe: A Source Book. *v.1 p.189*

Music and Dance of the Tewa Pueblos. *v.1 p.49*

The Music and Dance of the World's Religions: A Comprehensive, Annotated Bibliography of Materials in the English Language. *v.1 p.21, p.169, p.284*

Music and Discourse: Toward a Semiology of Music. *v.1 p.372*

Music and Emotion: Theory and Research. *v.1 p.375, p.376, v.5 p.612, p.619*

Music and Gender. *v.1 p.379*

Music and German National Identity. *v.1 p.245, v.3 p.178*

The Music and History of the Baroque Trumpet Before 1721. . . . .*v.1 p.186, p.391*

Music and Holocaust: Confronting Life in the Nazi Ghettos and Camps. *v.1 p.299*

Music and Ideas in the Sixteenth and Seventeenth Centuries. *v.1 p.181*

Music and Ideology in Cold War Europe. *v.1 p.211, p.376*

Music and Mathematics: From Pythagoras to Fractals. *v.1 p.374*

Music and Musical Life in Soviet Russia, 1917-1981. *v.1 p.246*

Music and Musicians in Ancient Egypt. *v.1 p.175*

Music and Musicians in Ancient Greece. *v.1 p.175*

Music and Musicians in Nineteenth Century Italy. *v.1 p.203, p.246*

Music and Performance During the Weimar Republic. *v.1 p.245*

Music and Poetry in a Colombian Village: A Tri-Cultural Heritage. *v.1 p.292*

Music and Poetry: The Nineteenth Century and After. *v.1 p.199*

Music and Silence. *v.2 p.385*

Music and Social Movements: Mobilizing Traditions in the Twentieth Century. *v.1 p.377*

Music and Society: The Politics of Composition, Performance and Reception. *v.1 p.377*

Music and Technoculture. *v.1 p.218, p.387*

Music and Technology in the Twentieth Century. *v.1 p.210, p.244, p.386*

Music and Text: Critical Inquiries. *v.1 p.382*

Music and the Emotions: The Philosophical Theories. .*v.1 p.380*

Music and the Historical Imagination. *v.1 p.383*

Music and the Mind. *v.5 p.619*

Music and the Racial Imagination. *v.1 p.282, p.377*

Music and War: A Research and Information Guide. . .*v.1 p.165*

Music As Cultural Practice,
  1800-1900. . . . .*v.1 p.199, p.200, p.377, p.381*

Music As Heard: A Study in Applied Phenomenology. .*v.1 p.380*

Music as Medicine: The History of Music Therapy Since
  Antiquity. *v.1 p.406*

Music as Propaganda: Art to Persuade, Art to Control. .*v.1 p.376*

Music at the Long Verney: Twenty Stories. *v.2 p.387*

Music Business Handbook and Career Guide. *v.1 p.383*

Music by Black Women Composers: A Bibliography of
  Available Scores. *v.6 p.30, p.35, p.47*

Music by Philip Glass. *v.1 p.214, p.326*

Music, Cognition, and Computerized Sound: An Introduction to
  Psychoacoustics. *v.1 p.374*

Music, Culture, and Experience: Selected Papers of John
  Blacking. *v.1 p.376*

Music, Culture, and Society: A Reader. *v.1 p.377*

Music Cultures in the United States: An
  Introduction. *v.1 p.278, p.296*

Music Cultures of the Pacific, the Near East and
  Asia. *v.1 p.283, p.287, p.288, p.289*

Music, Discipline, and Arms in Early Modern France. .*v.1 p.22*

Music Education, and Multiculturalism. *v.1 p.406*

Music Education: Historical Contexts and Perspectives. .*v.1 p.405*

Music Education: Source Readings from Ancient Greece to
  Today. *v.1 p.405*

Music, Electronic Media and Culture. . .*v.1 p.213, p.244, p.386*

Music for Chameleons. *v.2 p.66*

Music for Piano: A Short History. *v.1 p.240*

Music for Pleasure: Essays in the Sociology of Pop. . .*v.1 p.269*

Music for Sight Singing. *v.1 p.404*

Music from Cuba: Mongo Santamaria, Chocolate Armenteros
  and Other Stateside Cuban Musicians. *v.6 p.518*

Music, Gender, Education. *v.1 p.379*

Music Genres and Corporate Cultures. *v.1 p.385*

Music Grooves: Essays and Dialogues. *v.1 p.377, p.381*

Music, Imagination, and Culture. *v.1 p.380, v.5 p.618*

Music in America: Experiencing Music, Expressing
  Culture. *v.1 p.279, p.297*

Music in American Religious Experience. . .*v.1 p.276, p.277*

Music in Ancient Greece and Rome. *v.1 p.175*

Music in Aztec and Inca Territory. *v.1 p.294, v.3 p.262*

Music in Bali: Experiencing Music, Expressing
  Culture. *v.1 p.288, v.6 p.174, p.176*

Music in Bali. *v.1 p.289*

Music in Bulgaria: Experiencing Music, Expressing
  Culture. *v.1 p.298*

Music in Childhood: From Preschool Through the Elementary
  Grades. *v.1 p.405, v.4 p.362*

Music in Cuba. *v.1 p.291*

Music in Early Christian Literature. *v.1 p.175, p.176*

Music in East Africa: Experiencing Music, Expressing
  Culture. *v.1 p.284*

Music in European Capitals: The Galant Style 1720 to
  1780. . . . .*v.1 p.190*

Music in Everyday Life. *v.1 p.377*

Music in Fascist Italy. *v.1 p.246*

Music in Human Life: Anthropological Perspectives on
  Music. *v.4 p.26*

Music in Imperial Rio de Janeiro: European Culture in a
  Tropical Milieu. *v.3 p.265*

Music in India: The Classical Traditions. *v.1 p.290*

Music in Ireland: Experiencing Music, Expressing
  Culture. *v.1 p.299*

Music in Japan: Experiencing Music, Expressing
  Culture. *v.1 p.290*

Music in Latin America: An Introduction. *v.1 p.291*

Music in Latin America and the Caribbean: Performing Beliefs:
  Indigenous Peoples of South America, Central America, and
  Mexico. *v.1 p.292*

Music in Latin American Culture: Regional
  Traditions. *v.1 p.294, v.3 p.270, p.271*

Music in Medieval Europe. *v.1 p.178, p.179*

Music in North India: Experiencing Music, Expressing
  Culture. *v.1 p.289*

Music in Puerto Rico: A Reader's Anthology. *v.1 p.295*

Music in Shakespearean Tragedy. *v.1 p.181*

Music in South India : Tthe Karnatak Concert Tradition and
  Beyond : Experiencing Music, Expressing Culture. .*v.1 p.290*

Music in Terezin, 1941-1945. . . . .*v.1 p.246, p.300*

Music in the Age of Confucius. *v.1 p.290*

Music in the Age of the Renaissance. *v.1 p.181*

Music in the Air: America's Changing Taste in Popular Music,
  1920-1980. . . . .*v.1 p.268*

Music in the Classic Period. *v.1 p.191*

Music in the French Secular Theater, 1400-1550. . .*v.1 p.179*

Music in the Jewish Community of Palestine 1880-1948: A
  Social History. *v.1 p.300*

Music in the Medieval World. *v.6 p.567*

Music in the Middle Ages. *v.6 p.567*

Music in the Mind: The Concepts of Music and Musician in
  Afghanistan. *v.1 p.287*

Music in the New World. *v.1 p.277*

Music in the Renaissance. *v.1 p.181*

Music in the Romantic Era. *v.1 p.197*

Music in the Third Reich. *v.3 p.172*

Music in the United States: A Historical
  Introduction. *v.1 p.277, p.278*

Music in the Western World. *v.1 p.175*

Music in the World of Islam: A Socio-Cultural Study. .*v.1 p.287*

Music in Transition: A Study of Tonal Expansion and Atonality,
  1900-1920. . . . .*v.1 p.222, p.373*

Music in West Africa: Experiencing Music, Expressing
  Culture. *v.1 p.286*

Music in Western Civilization. *v.1 p.174*

☐ Music Index. *v.1 p.163*

Music Is My Mistress. *v.1 p.258, p.323*

Music Like Dirt. *v.2 p.141*

The Music Machine: Selected Readings from Computer Music Journal. *v.1 p.222, p.245, p.387*

Music Makes the Difference. *v.1 p.405, p.406*

Music Matters: A New Philosophy of Music Education. .*v.1 p.405*

The Music Men: An Illustrated History of Brass Bands in America, 1800-1920. . . . .*v.1 p.277*

Music, Modernity, and the Global Imagination: South Africa and the West. *v.1 p.285*

Music Notation: A Manual of Modern Practice. . . .*v.1 p.393*

Music Notation in the Twentieth Century: A Practical Guidebook. *v.1 p.394*

Music of Afghanistan: Professional Musicians in the City of Herat. *v.1 p.286*

The Music of Africa. *v.1 p.285, p.286*

The Music of Alban Berg. *v.1 p.215, p.216, p.309*

The Music of Alexander Scriabin. *v.1 p.209, p.355*

The Music of American Folk Song and Selected Other Writings on American Folk Music. *v.1 p.297*

The Music of Ancient Greece. *v.1 p.176*

The Music of Anthony Braxton. .*v.1 p.215, p.260, p.313, p.314*

The Music of Bela Bartok: A Study of Tonality and Progression in Twentieth Century Music. *v.1 p.208, p.304*

The Music of Bela Bartok. *v.1 p.227, p.305*

The Music of Benjamin Britten. *v.1 p.213, p.314*

The Music of Berlioz. *v.1 p.203, p.311*

Music of Black America: A History. . . .*v.6 p.30, p.34, p.35*

The Music of Black Americans: A History. *v.1 p.282*

The Music of Brazil. *v.1 p.291*

The Music of Canada. *v.1 p.278, p.279*

The Music of Charles Ives. *v.1 p.217, p.218, p.333*

The Music of Chopin. *v.1 p.203, p.204, p.317*

The Music of Claude Debussy. *v.1 p.220, p.321*

The Music of Conlon Nancarrow. *v.1 p.214, p.345*

The Music of Czechoslovakia. *v.1 p.246*

The Music of Edgard Varese. *v.1 p.209, p.363*

Music of El Dorado: The Ethnomusicology of Ancient South American Cultures. *v.1 p.293*

The Music of Elliott Carter. *v.1 p.223, p.316*

The Music of European Nationalism:Cultural Identity and Modern History. *v.1 p.297, p.298*

The Music of Gershwin. *v.1 p.214, p.250, p.325*

The Music of Harrison Birtwistle. . . .*v.1 p.208, p.311, p.312*

Music of Hindu Trinidad: Songs from the India Diaspora. *v.1 p.293*

Music of Human Flesh. *v.6 p.659*

The Music of Igor Stravinsky. *v.1 p.226, p.361*

The Music of Israel: From the Biblical Era to Modern Times. *v.1 p.299*

The Music of Johann Sebastian Bach: The Sources, the Style, the Significance. *v.1 p.185, p.303*

The Music of John Cage. *v.1 p.221, p.315*

The Music of Louis Andriessen. *v.1 p.226, p.301*

The Music of Luigi Dallapiccola. *v.1 p.213, p.319*

The Music of Lutoslawski. *v.1 p.222, p.338*

The Music of Malaysia: The Classical, Folk and Syncretic Traditions. *v.1 p.289*

The Music of Morton Feldman. *v.1 p.212, p.324*

The Music of Paul Hindemith. *v.1 p.219, p.332*

The Music of Pauline Oliveros. *v.1 p.226, p.346*

The Music of Ruth Crawford Seeger. *v.1 p.225, p.355*

The Music of Sergei Prokofiev. *v.1 p.219, p.348*

The Music of Silence: A Composer's Testament.*v.1 p.226, p.362*

The Music of South Asia. *v.1 p.290*

Music of Spain. *v.1 p.245*

The Music of Stravinsky. *v.1 p.226, p.361*

The Music of the Arabs. *v.1 p.287, p.288*

Music of the Billion: An Introduction to Chinese Musical Culture. *v.1 p.288*

Music of the Civil War Era. *v.1 p.277*

Music of the Counterculture Era. *v.1 p.273, p.279*

The Music of the Jews: An Historical Appreciation. . .*v.1 p.300*

Music of the Middle Ages: Style and Structure. *v.1 p.178*

The Music of the Sumerians and Their Immediate Successors, the Babylonians and Assyrians. *v.1 p.175*

The Music of the Troubadours. *v.1 p.176*

Music of the Twentieth Century: Style and Structure. .*v.1 p.224*

Music of the Twentieth-Century Avant-Garde: A Biocritical Sourcebook. *v.1 p.224*

Music of the Warao of Venezuela: Song People of the Rain Forest. *v.1 p.293*

The Music of Toru Takemitsu. *v.1 p.210, p.362*

Music Printing and Publishing. *v.1 p.168, p.384*

The Music Profession in Britain since the Eighteenth Century: A Social History. *v.6 p.757*

Music, Race, and Nation: Musica Tropical in Colombia. *v.1 p.295*

Music Radio: The Great Performers and Programs of the 1920s Through Early 1960s. *v.1 p.267*

Music Reference and Research Materials: An Annotated Bibliography. *v.1 p.166*

⌨ Music Resources. *v.1 p.173*

Music since 1900. . . . .*v.1 p.224*

Music since 1945: Issues, Materials, and Literature. . .*v.1 p.223*

Music, Society, Education. *v.1 p.377*

Music Subject Headings, Compiled from Library of Congress Subject Headings. *v.1 p.167*

Music, the Arts, and Ideas: Patterns and Predictions in Twentieth-Century Culture. *v.1 p.382*

Music Theory from Zarlino to Schenker: A Bibliography and Guide. *v.1 p.165, p.370*

Music Therapy: An Introduction. *v.1 p.406*

Music Therapy and Medicine: Theoretical and Clinical Approaches. *v.1 p.406*

Music Therapy Research: Second Edition. . . .*v.1 p.406, p.407*

Music Translation Dictionary: An English, Czech, Danish, Dutch, French, German, Hungarian, Italian, Polish, Portuguese, Russian, Spanish, Swedish Vocabulary of Music. *v.1 p.160*

The Music Window (Musica Cercana). *v.2 p.656, p.657*

Music with Words: A Composer's View. . . .*v.1 p.237, p.374*

Musica Brasileira: A History of Popular Music and the People of Brazil. *v.1 p.294*

Musica Cercana. *v.2 p.657*

Musica de la Raza: Mexican and Chicano Music in Minnesota. *v.6 p.518, p.519*

Musica Enchiriadis: And Scolica Enchiriadis. *v.1 p.178*

Musica Tejana: The Cultural Economy of Artistic Transformation. *v.6 p.519*

The Musical: A Concise History. *v.1 p.250*

The Musical: A Research Guide to Musical Theater and Film. *v.1 p.166, p.249*

Musical Acoustics. *v.1 p.374, p.375*

Musical Aesthetics: A Historical Reader - The Twentieth Century. *v.1 p.382*

Musical America Worldwide. *v.1 p.172*

Musical Arts in Africa : Theory, Practice, and Education. *v.1 p.285*

Musical Autographs from Monteverdi to Hindemith. *v.1 p.175*

Musical Beginnings: Origins and Development of Musical Competence. *v.1 p.375*

Musical Comedy in America: From the Black Crook Through Sweeney Todd. *v.1 p.93, p.118*

Musical Communication. *v.1 p.376*

Musical Design in Aeschylean Theater. *v.1 p.176*

Musical Design in Sophoclean Theater. *v.1 p.176*

Musical Form and Musical Performance. *v.1 p.370*

The Musical from the Inside Out. *v.1 p.404*

Musical Gumbo: The Music of New Orleans. *v.1 p.278*

Musical Identities. *v.1 p.376*

Musical Instruments and Their Symbolism in Western Art: Studies in Musical Iconology. *v.1 p.392*

Musical Instruments: History, Technology, and Performance of Instruments of Western Music. *v.1 p.390*

Musical Instruments of the Bible. *v.1 p.176*

The Musical Madhouse: An English Translation of Berlioz's les Grotesques de la Musique. *v.1 p.194, p.310*

Musical Meaning and Expression. *v.1 p.380, p.381*

Musical Meaning: Toward a Critical History. *v.1 p.381*

Musical Networks: Parallel Distributed Perception and Performance. *v.1 p.375*

Musical Perceptions. *v.5 p.618*

Musical Ritual in Mexico City: From the Aztec to NAFTA. *v.1 p.293*

Musical Stages: An Autobiography. *v.1 p.253, p.351*

Musical Structure and Performance. *v.1 p.369*

The Musical Temperament: Psychology and Personality of Musicians. *v.1 p.376, v.5 p.619*

Musical Terminology: A Practical Compendium in Four Languages. *v.1 p.159*

Musical Theater in America. *v.1 p.32*

Musical Thought in Ancient Greece. *v.1 p.175*

Musicals!: Directing School and Community Theatre. *v.1 p.404*

Musician's Guide to Perception and Cognition. *v.1 p.375*

Musician's Guide to Theory and Analysis. *v.1 p.369, p.370*

Musicology and Difference: Gender and Sexuality in Music Scholarship. *v.1 p.380, v.6 p.475*

Musicology: The Key Concepts. *v.1 p.173*

Musics of Multicultural America. *v.1 p.296*

Musings of the Masters: An Anthology of Mathematical Reflections. *v.5 p.470*

Musings: The Musical Worlds of Gunther Schuller. *v.1 p.223, p.263*

The Muslim Brotherhood and the Kings of Jordan, 1945-1993. *v.6 p.621*

The Muslim Creed: Its Genesis and Historical Development. *v.1 p.557, p.558*

The Muslim Diaspora: A Comprehensive Reference to the Spread of Islam in Asia, Africa, Europe and the Americas, 1500-1799. *v.1 p.559*

The Muslim Diaspora: A Comprehensive Reference to the Spread of Islam in Asia, Africa, Europe, and the Americas, V. 1: 570-1500. *v.1 p.559*

The Muslim Diaspora: A Comprehensive Reference to the Spread of Islam in Asia, Africa, Europe and the Americas. *v.1 p.559*

The Muslim Discovery of Europe. *v.6 p.582*

Muslim Extremism in Egypt: The Prophet and Pharaoh. *v.6 p.638*

Muslim Minorities in the West: Visible and Invisible. *v.1 p.554*

Muslim Schools, Education, Children and Family Life. *v.4 p.308*

Muslim Societies in African History. *v.6 p.54*

Muslim Society. *v.1 p.558*

Muslim Spain and Portugal: A Political History of Al-Andalus. *v.3 p.65, p.237, p.238, v.6 p.585*

Muslim Spain, Its History and Culture. *v.3 p.65*

Muslims in Spain, 1500 To 1614. *v.3 p.239*

Muslim Studies, Vol. 2. *v.1 p.554*

Muslim Studies. *v.1 p.554*

A Muslim Theologian's Response to Christianity: A Translation of Ibn Taymiyya's Jawab al-Sahih li-man Baddala din al-Masih. *v.1 p.558*

Muslim Women Throughout the World: A Bibliography with Selected Annotations. *v.6 p.459*

Muslim-Christian Relations and Inter-Christian Rivalries in the Middle East: The Case of the Jacobites in an Age of Transition. *v.6 p.600, p.606, p.607*

Muslims and Christians Face to Face. *v.1 p.559*

The Muslims of Bosnia - Herzegovina: Their Historic Development from the Middle Ages to the Dissolution of Yugoslavia. *v.3 p.249*

Muslims of the Soviet Empire: A Guide. *v.3 p.212, p.213*

Muslims' Place in the American Public Square: Hopes, Fears, and Aspirations. *v.4 p.721*

Muslims: Their Religious Beliefs and Practices. *v.1 p.559*

Musorgsky: His Life and Works. *v.1 p.195, p.345*

Musorgsky: Pictures at an Exhibition. *v.1 p.203, p.242, p.345*

Musorgsky Remembered. *v.1 p.201, p.345*

Musset: Five Plays. *v.2 p.498*

Mussolini and Fascism: The View from America. *v.3 p.203*

Mussolini Unleashed, 1939-1941: Politics and Strategy in Fascist Italy's Last War. *v.3 p.203*

Mussolini's Enemies: The Italian Anti-Fascist Resistance. *v.3 p.203*

Mussolini's Intellectuals: Fascist Social and Political Thought. *v.3 p.203*

Mussolini's Rome: Rebuilding the Eternal City. .*v.3 p.197, p.204*

Mussolini. *v.3 p.203*

Must God Remain Greek? : Afro Cultures and God-talk. .*v.4 p.720*

Musui's Story: The Autobiography of a Tokugawa Samurai. *v.6 p.227*

Mutagenicity, Carcinogenicity, and Teratogenicity of Industrial Pollutants. *v.5 p.364, p.373, p.375*

The Muted Conscience: Moral Silence and the Practice of Ethics in Business. *v.4 p.145, p.146*

Muted Voices: Latinos and the 2000 Election. *v.6 p.537*

Mutiny on the Bounty. *v.2 p.103*

Mutmassungen Uber Jakob. *v.2 p.618*

Mutsu Munemitsu and Identity Formation of the Individual and the State in Modern Japan. *v.6 p.228*

The Mutual Flame: On Shakespeare's Sonnets and The Phoenix and the Turtle. *v.2 p.225*

The Mutual Flame: On Shakespeare's Sonnets and the Phoenix and the Turtle. *v.2 p.225*

The Mutual Friend. *v.2 p.141*

The Mutual-Aid Approach to Working with Groups: Helping People Help One Another. *v.5 p.669*

My American Journey: An Autobiography. . . .*v.3 p.461, p.462*

My Apprenticeship. *v.4 p.271*

My Beautiful Laundrette, Sammy and Rosie Get Laid: Collected Screenplays. *v.2 p.361*

My Beloved Toto: Letters from Juliette Drouet to Victor Hugo, 1833-1882. . . . .*v.2 p.492*

My Body, the Buddhist. *v.1 p.28, p.30*

My Brilliant Career. *v.2 p.745*

My Brother's Keeper: James Joyce's Early Years. . . .*v.2 p.359*

My Century: The Odyssey of a Polish Intellectual. .*v.3 p.254*

My Century. *v.2 p.792*

My Chicago. *v.3 p.515*

My Childhood at the Gate of Unrest: A Romanian Memoir. *v.2 p.817*

My Childhood. *v.2 p.804*

My Country Versus Me: The First Hand Account by the Los Alamos Scientist Who Was. *v.6 p.94, p.117, p.141*

My Country. *v.6 p.613*

My Days. *v.2 p.765*

My Deep Dark Pain Is Love: A Collection of Latin American Gay Fiction. *v.6 p.406*

My Experiences in the First World War. *v.3 p.478*

My Face Is Black Is True: Callie House and the Struggle for Ex-Slave Reparations. *v.6 p.3*

My Family and Other Animals. *v.5 p.227*

My Family's Role in the World Revolution: And Other Prose. *v.2 p.811*

My Father, Bertrand Russell. *v.1 p.447*

My Father Was a Toltec. *v.6 p.498, p.510*

My Father's Friend and Other Stories. *v.6 p.150*

My Father's Son. *v.2 p.374*

My FBI: Bringing down the Mafia, Investigating Bill Clinton, and Fighting the War on Terror. *v.6 p.259*

My Fifty Years in China: The Memoirs of John Leighton Stuart, Missionary and Ambassador. *v.6 p.201, p.218*

My Friend, My Friend: The Story of Thoreau's Relationship with Emerson. *v.2 p.38, p.52*

My Friendship with Oscar Wilde, Being the Autobiography of Lord Alfred Douglas. *v.6 p.401*

My Grandfather's Tale. *v.6 p.660*

My Happy Life. *v.1 p.219, p.341*

My History, Not Yours: The Formation of Mexican American Autobiography. *v.6 p.490, p.532*

My Home, My Prison. *v.6 p.620*

My Husband Betty: Love, Sex, and Life with a Crossdresser. *v.6 p.369*

My Invented Country: A Memoir. *v.3 p.352*

My Invented Country: A Nostalgic Journey Through Chile. *v.2 p.679*

My Job, My Self: Work and Creation of Modern Individual. *v.5 p.579*

My Journey to Lhasa. *v.6 p.240*

My Kind of Geography. *v.4 p.382*

My Land and My People: The Original Autobiography of His Holiness the Dalai Lama of Tibet. . . . *v.1 p.566, v.6 p.240*

My Life and Ethiopia's Progress 1892-1937: The Autobiography of Haile Sellassie. *v.6 p.64*

My Life and Ethiopia's Progress: The Autobiography of Haile Sellaissie, Vol. 2. . . . .*v.6 p.64*

My Life in Art. *v.1 p.138, p.139*

My Life in Ballet. *v.1 p.10*

My Life on the Plains: Or, Personal Experiences with Indians. *v.3 p.519*

My Lifetime in Letters. *v.2 p.119, p.120*

My Life. *v.1 p.7, p.205, p.366,v.2 p.500, v.3 p.468*

My Little Sister and Selected Poems. *v.6 p.650*

My Lord, What a Morning: An Autobiography. .*v.1 p.280, p.301*

My Lost City: Personal Essays, 1920-1940. . . . . .*v.2 p.76*

My Mark Twain: Reminiscences and Criticisms. .*v.2 p.33, p.42*

My Memories Completed: al-Takmilah. *v.6 p.620*

My Michael. *v.6 p.650*

My Mother Who Fathered Me: A Study of the Families in Three Selected Communities of Jamaica. *v.4 p.40*

My Mother's House; and Sido. *v.2 p.515*

My Music: Explorations of Music in Daily Life. .*v.1 p.376, p.377*

My Music Is My Flag: Puerto Rican Musicians and Their New York Communities, 1917-1940. . .*v.6 p.488, p.489, p.518*

My Name Is Red. *v.6 p.667*

My Nine Lives: Chapters of a Possible Past. *v.2 p.355*

My Odyssey: An Autobiography. *v.6 p.71*

My Own Story. *v.4 p.604, p.606*

My Past and Thoughts: The Memoirs of Alexander Herzen. *v.3 p.217*

My Quarter Century of American Politics. *v.3 p.433*

My Several Worlds. *v.2 p.58, p.59*

My Sister--Life. *v.2 p.806*

My Sister's Hand in Mine: The Collected Works of Jane Bowles. *v.2 p.58*

My Son the Fanatic. *v.2 p.361*

My Soul Looks Back in Wonder: Voices of the Civil Rights Experience. *v.6 p.12*

My Soul's High Song: The Collected Writings of Countee Cullen, Voice of the Harlem Renaissance. *.v.2 p.65, v.6 p.24*

My Talks with Arab Leaders. *v.6 p.613*

My Theatre Life. *v.1 p.6*

My Thirty-Three Years' Dream: The Autobiography of Miyazaki Toten. *v.6 p.227, p.228*

My Tibet. *v.6 p.241*

My Turn: The Memoirs of Nancy Reagan. *v.3 p.478*

My Uncle Napoleon. *v.6 p.672*

My Way to Typography. *v.1 p.719, p.720*

My World and Welcome to It. *v.2 p.125, p.126*

My World Line: Fragments of A. *v.5 p.543*

My Year of Meats. *v.6 p.101, p.102*

My Years with General Motors. *v.4 p.154*

My Youth in Vienna. *v.2 p.615*

Mycenae and the Mycenaean Age. *v.3 p.16*

The Mycenaean World. *v.3 p.15*

Mycenaeans. *v.3 p.15*

The Mycenaeans. *v.3 p.16*

The Mycota: A Comprehensive Treatise on Fungi As Experimental Systems for Basic and Applied Research. *v.5 p.209*

Myer Myers: Jewish Silversmith in Colonial New York. *.v.1 p.806*

Myne Owne Ground: Race and Freedom on Virginia's Eastern Shore, 1640-1676. . . . .*v.3 p.499*

Myra Breckinridge and Myron. *v.2 p.127, v.6 p.399*

Myself When I Am Real: The Life and Music of Charles Mingus. *v.1 p.263, p.341, p.342*

Myself When Young: The Shaping of a Writer. *v.2 p.385*

Mysteries of Ancient China: New Discoveries from the Early Dynasties. *v.4 p.9*

Mysteries of Small Houses. *v.2 p.151*

The Mysteries of Terra Firma: The Age and Evolution of the Earth. *v.5 p.446*

Mysteries of the Alphabet. *v.2 p.563*

Mysteries of the Rain Forest. *v.5 p.239*

The Mysteries of Udolpho. *v.2 p.303*

Mysteries. *v.2 p.628*

Mysterious Fayum Portraits: Faces from Ancient Egypt. *.v.1 p.727*

Mysterious Island. *v.2 p.504*

Mysterious Skin. *v.6 p.397*

Mystery and Manners: Occasional Prose. *v.2 p.106*

Mystery and Suspense Writers: The Literature of Crime Detection and Espionage, Set. *v.2 p.580*

Mystery, Detective, and Espionage Magazines. *v.2 p.580*

The Mystery of Edwin Drood, Master Humphrey's clock, and Sketches by Boz. by Charles Dickens. *v.2 p.283*

Mystery of Mysteries: Is Evolution a Social Construction? *v.3 p.49, v.5 p.196*

The Mystery of Orcival. *v.2 p.492*

The Mystery of Samba: Popular Music and National Identity in Brazil. *v.1 p.20, p.295*

The Mystery Train: Images of America in Rock-n-Roll. *v.1 p.271, p.272*

Mystery, Violence, and Popular Culture: Essays. . . .*v.2 p.577*

The Mystic Fable: The Sixteenth and Seventeenth Centuries, Vol. 1. . . . .*v.1 p.530*

The Mystic of Tunja: The Writings of Madre Castillo, 1671-1742. . . . .*v.3 p.263*

Mystic Stories: The Sacred and the Profane. *v.2 p.817*

Mystic Synthesis in Java: A History of Islamization from the Fourteenth to the Early Nineteenth Centuries. . . .*v.6 p.177*

The Mystical Design of 'Paradise Lost'. *v.2 p.253*

Mystical Dimensions of Islam. *v.1 p.559, p.560*

The Mystical Language of Sensation in the Later Middle Ages. *v.6 p.569*

Mystical Poems of Rumi: Second Selection, Poems 201-400, Vol. 34. . . . .*v.6 p.672*

The Mystical Thought of Meister Eckhart: The Man from Whom God Hid Nothing. *v.1 p.653*

The Mystical World of Indonesia: Culture and Economic Development in Conflict. *v.6 p.175, p.178*

Mysticism and Language. *v.1 p.531*

Mysticism and Logic. *v.1 p.494*

Mysticism and Philosophical Analysis. *v.1 p.531*

Mysticism and Religion. *v.1 p.530, p.531*

Mysticism and Religious Traditions. *v.1 p.531*

Mysticism and Sacred Scripture. *v.1 p.531*

Mysticism: Christian and Buddhist. *v.1 p.531*

Mysticism: Holiness East and West. *v.1 p.530*

Mystics and Missionaries: The Jews in Palestine, 1799-1840. . . . .*v.6 p.610*

Mystics, Monarchs and Messiahs: Cultural Landscapes of Early Modern Iran. *v.6 p.630, p.631*

Myth and Archive: A Theory of Latin American Narrative. *v.2 p.664*

Myth and Christianity: An Inquiry into the Possibility of Religion without Myth. *v.1 p.523*

Myth and Mythology in the Theater of Pedro Calderon de la Barca. *v.2 p.647*

Myth and Society in Ancient Greece. *v.3 p.15*

Myth and the History of the Hispanic Southwest: Essays. *v.3 p.528, v.6 p.533*

The Myth of Aunt Jemima: Representations of Race and Religion. *v.6 p.36, p.40, p.45, p.46*

The Myth of Deliverance: Reflections of Shakespeare's Problem Comedies. *v.2 p.233*

The Myth of Democratic Failure: Why Political Institutions Are Efficient. *v.4 p.506*

The Myth of Ethnic War: Serbia and Croatia in the 1990s. *v.3 p.247*

The Myth of Excellence: Why Great Companies Never Try to Be the Best at Everything. *v.4 p.135*

The Myth of Free Trade: The Pooring of America. *v.4 p.256, p.260, p.261, p.264*

The Myth of Greater Albania. *v.3 p.249*

The Myth of Green Marketing: Tending Our Goats at the Edge of Apocalypse. *v.4 p.63*

The Myth of Human Races. *v.4 p.17*

The Myth of José Martí: Conflicting Nationalisms in Early Twentieth-Century Cuba. *v.3 p.309*

The Myth of Judicial Activism: Making Sense of Supreme Court Decisions. *v.4 p.541*

The Myth of Matriarchal Prehistory: Why an Invented Past Will Not Give Women a Future. *v.3 p.51*

The Myth of Monogamy: Fidelity and Infidelity in Animals and People. *v.4 p.731, v.5 p.614*

The Myth of New Orleans in Literature: Dialogues of Race and Gender. *v.2 p.13*

The Myth of Return in Early Greek Epic. *v.2 p.402*

The Myth of Santa Fe: Creating a Modern Regional Tradition. *v.6 p.533, p.551*

The Myth of Scientific Literacy. *v.5 p.407*

The Myth of Shangri-la: Tibet, Travel Writing and the Western Creation of Sacred Landscape. *v.6 p.240*

The Myth of Sisyphus and Other Essays. *v.2 p.512*

The Myth of the American Frontier; Its Relevance to America, Canada and Australia. *v.3 p.382*

The Myth of the First Three Years: A New Understanding of Early Brain Development and Lifelong Learning. . *v.5 p.608*

The Myth of the French Bourgeoisie: An Wssay on the Social Imaginary, 1750-1850. . . . . *v.3 p.149*

The Myth of the Goddess: Evolution of an Image. . . *v.1 p.528*

The Myth of the Judeo-Christian Tradition, and Other Dissenting Essays. *v.1 p.549*

Myth of the Mau Mau: Nationalism in Kenya. *v.6 p.65*

The Myth of the Military-Nation: Militarism, Gender, and Education in Turkey. *v.6 p.623*

The Myth of the Negro Past. *v.6 p.10*

Myth or Reality: Adaptive Strategies of Asian Americans in California. *v.6 p.108*

Myth, Ritual, and Kingship in Buganda. *v.6 p.67*

Mythic Giacometti. *v.1 p.780*

The Mythic Image. *v.1 p.527*

The Mythic West in Twentieth-Century America. . . *v.6 p.323*

The Mythical Man-Month: Essays on Software Engineering. *v.5 p.345, p.346*

Mythography: The Study of Myths and Rituals. . . . *v.1 p.527*

Mythologies. *v.2 p.327, p.575*

The Mythologizing of Mark Twain. *v.2 p.33*

Mythology and Humanism: The Correspondence of Thomas Mann and Karl Kerenyi. *v.2 p.612*

Myths from Mesopotamia: Creation, the Flood, Gilgamesh, and Others. *v.1 p.538, p.539, v.3 p.5*

Myths in Education: Beliefs That Hinder Progress and Their Alternatives. *v.4 p.341*

Myths of Ethnicity and Nation: Immigration, Work, and Identity in the Belize Banana Industry. *v.3 p.297*

Myths of Power: A Marxist Study of the Brontes. . . *v.2 p.270*

Myths of Rome. *v.1 p.533*

Myths of the Greeks and Romans. *v.1 p.532*

Myth. *v.1 p.527*

N

Nabokov and His Fiction: New Perspectives. *v.2 p.104*

Nabokov's Blues: The Scientific Odyssey of a Literary Genius. *v.2 p.104*

Nabokov's Butterflies. *v.2 p.104*

Nabokov's Pale Fire: The Magic of Artistic Discovery. *v.2 p.104*

Nabokov's World: Reading Nabokov. *v.2 p.104*

Nach der Anatur. *v.2 p.618*

Nachahmung und Schöpfung im Barock; Studien um Grimmelshausen. *v.2 p.596*

Nachdenken Uber Christa T. *v.2 p.619, p.620*

Nachricht vom Tag. Erzählungen. *v.2 p.602*

Nada. *v.2 p.661*

Nadia Boulanger: A Life in Music. . *v.1 p.222, p.312, v.6 p.410*

Nadja. *v.2 p.510*

NAFTA's Impact on North America: The First Decade. *v.4 p.61*

Nag Hammadi Library: Definitive Translation of the Gnostic Scriptures. *v.1 p.647*

Nahua Views of Spanish Colonial Mexico. *v.3 p.264*

The Nahuas after the Conquest: A Social and Cultural History of the Indians of Central Mexico, Sixteenth Through Eighteenth Centuries. *v.3 p.286*

Nahum, Habakkuk and Zephaniah: A Commentary. . *v.1 p.623*

Naipaul's Strangers. *v.2 p.768*

Naive Set Theory. *v.5 p.471*

Najib Mahfuz: The Novelist-Philosopher of Cairo. . *v.6 p.662*

The Naked and the Dead: With a New Introduction by the Author. *v.2 p.99*

The Naked and the Undead: Evil and the Appeal of Horror. *v.6 p.318*

Naked Ape: A Zoologist's Study of the Human Animal. *v.5 p.201*

The Naked Civil Servant. *v.6 p.401*

The Naked Face of Genius: Béla Bartók's American Years. *v.1 p.213, p.305*

Naked in the Promised Land: A Memoir. *v.6 p.401*

Naked Lunch: The Restored Text. *v.2 p.64, v.6 p.395*

The Naked Olympics: The True Story of the Ancient Games. *v.4 p.808*

Naked Tropics: Essays on Empire and Other Rogues. *v.3 p.341*

The Name of the Rose. *v.2 p.724*

The Name of War: King Philip's War and the Origins of American Identity. *v.3 p.406, v.6 p.686*

Name Reactions: A Collection of Detailed Reaction Mechanisms. *v.5 p.296*

Name Reactions and Reagents in Organic Synthesis. *v.5 p.296*

Named Organic Reactions. *v.5 p.295, p.296*

☐ Named Reactions in Organic Chemistry. *v.5 p.295*

☐ Named Reagents. *v.5 p.290*

☐ Named Rules and Effects in Organic Chemistry. . *v.5 p.289*

The Names of Plants. *v.5 p.207*

Names, Synonyms, and Structures of Organic Compounds: a CRC Reference Handbook, 3 v. *v.5 p.289*

The Namesake: A Novel. *v.6 p.100*

Naming and Necessity. *v.1 p.490*

Naming Organic Compounds: A Systematic Instruction Manual. *v.5 p.289*

Naming the Enemy: Anti-Corporate Social Movements Confront Globalization. *v.4 p.712*

Namoluk Beyond the Reef: The Transformation of a Micronesian Community. *v.4 p.43*

Nana. *v.2 p.505*

Nancy Clark's Sports Nutrition Guidebook. *v.4 p.801, p.876*

Nancy Hanks: An Intimate Portrait: The Creation of a National Commitment to the Arts. *v.1 p.825*

The Nanny and the Iceberg. *v.2 p.680*

Nanocosm: Nanotechnology and the Big Changes Coming from the Inconceivably Small. *v.5 p.265*

Nanophotonics. *v.5 p.562*

Nanoscale energy transport and conversion: a parallel treatment of electrons, molecules, phonons, and photons. . . .*v.5 p.318*

Nanoscale Science and Technology. *v.5 p.742*

Nanostructured Materials and Nanotechnology: Concise Edition. *v.5 p.690*

Nanosystems: Molecular Machinery, Manufacturing, and Computation. *v.5 p.265, p.684*

Nanotechnology: Basic Science and Emerging Technologies. *v.5 p.265*

Nanotechnology: Environmental Implications and Solutions. *v.5 p.318, p.705*

☐ NanoTechWeb news. *v.5 p.321*

Napoleon and the Awakening of Europe. *v.3 p.152*

Napoleon and Wellington: The Battle of Waterloo - And the Great Comanders Who Fought It. *v.3 p.152*

Napoleon, For and Against. *v.3 p.158*

Napoleon in Egypt: Al-Jabartai's Chronicle of the French Occupation 1798 Expanded Edition for the 250th Anniversary of Al-Jabarti's Birth. *v.6 p.636*

Napoleon in Egypt. *v.6 p.637*

The Napoleon of Notting Hill. *v.2 p.277*

Napoleon, Set. *v.3 p.152*

Napoleon: The Last Phase. *v.3 p.152*

The Napoleonic Empire in Italy, 1796-1814: Cultural Imperialism in a European Context?. *v.3 p.201*

Napoleonic Propaganda. *v.3 p.152*

The Napoleonic Source Book. *v.3 p.74*

Napoleon's Integration of Europe. *v.3 p.75*

Napoleon's Men: The Soldiers of the Revolution and Empire. *v.3 p.152*

Napoleon's Satellite Kingdoms: Managing Conquered Peoples. *v.3 p.75*

Napoleon. *v.3 p.152, p.158*

Nappy: Growing up Black and Female in America. *v.6 p.5, p.17, p.43*

☐ NARA: U.S. Electoral College. *v.4 p.556, p.557*

Narcissus and Goldmund. *v.2 p.610*

Narcodiplomacy: Exporting the U. S. War on Drugs. .*v.3 p.281*

El Narrador Picaro: Guzman de Alfarache. *v.2 p.651*

Narrated Films: Storytelling Situations in Cinema History. *v.6 p.331*

Narrating Nationalisms: Ideology and Form in Asian American Literature. *v.6 p.97*

Narrating Scotland: The Imagination of Robert Louis Stevenson. *v.2 p.312*

Narrating the Past: Fiction and Historiography in Postwar Spain. *v.2 p.641*

Narrative and Dramatic Sources of Shakespeare. . . .*v.2 p.228*

Narrative Discourse: An Essay in Method. *v.2 p.524*

Narrative Intelligence. *v.5 p.589*

Narrative Means to Sober Ends: Treating Addiction and Its Aftermath. *v.5 p.673*

A Narrative of the Life of David Crockett of the State of Tennessee. *v.3 p.510*

Narrative of the Life of Frederick Douglass: An American Slave, Written by Himself. *v.3 p.419*

Narrative of the Life of Frederick Douglass: An American Slave. *v.3 p.395*

Narrative of Travels in Europe, Asia and Africa in the 17th Century. *v.6 p.589, p.622*

Narratives for a New Belonging: Diasporic Cultural Fictions. *v.6 p.320*

Narratives of Desire: 19th-Century Spanish Fiction by Women. *v.2 p.641*

Narratives of Empire: The Fictions of Rudyard Kipling. .*v.2 p.298*

Narratives of Greater Mexico: Essays on Chicano Literary History, Genre, and Borders. *v.6 p.498, p.511*

Narratives of the Coranado Expedition, 1540-1542. . .*v.3 p.403*

The Narrow Corner. *v.2 p.370*

The Narrow Road to the Deep North and Other Travel Sketches. *v.6 p.229*

Narrowing the Nation's Power: The Supreme Court Sides with the States. *v.4 p.443, p.444, p.538*

The Narrows. *v.2 p.109*

☐ The NASA Astrophysics Data System (ADS). *v.5 p.64*

☐ NASA Image Exchange (NIX). *v.5 p.417*

☐ NASA/IPAC Extragalactic Database (NED). *v.5 p.63*

The NASCAR Way: The Business That Drives the Sport. *v.4 p.848, p.888, p.896, p.902*

☐ The NASDAQ Stock Market. *v.4 p.90, p.93, p.101*

Nasir-i Khusraw's Book of Travels. *v.6 p.671, p.672*

Nassau Senior and Classical Economics. *v.4 p.217*

Nasser's Blessed Movement: Egypt's Free Officers and the July Revolution. *v.6 p.639*

Nasser's Egypt, Arab Nationalism and the United Arab Republic. *v.6 p.58*

Natalia Ginzburg: Voice of the Twentieth Century. . . .*v.2 p.718*

Natasha's Dance: A Cultural History of Russia. *v.3 p.210*

Nathalie Sarraute, Fiction and Theory: Questions of Difference. *v.2 p.527*

Nathanael West - Novels and Other Writings: The Dream Life of Balso Snell; Miss Lonelyhearts; A Cool Million; The Day of the Locust; Other Writings; Letters. . .*v.2 p.131*

Nathanael West: The Art of His Life. *v.2 p.131*

Nathanael West: The Ironic Prophet. *v.2 p.131*

Nathanael West's Novels. *v.2 p.131*

Nathaniel Hawthorne and His Wife a Biography, Vol. 1. .*v.2 p.41*

Nathaniel Hawthorne and His Wife a Biography, Vol. 2. .*v.2 p.41*

Nathaniel Hawthorne: Tradition and Revolution. *v.2 p.41*

Nathaniel Hawthorne's the Scarlet Letter: A Critical Resource Guide and Comprehensive Annotated Bibliography of Literary Criticism 1950-2000. . . . .*v.2 p.41*

Nathaniel Hawthorne. *v.2 p.41*

Nathaniel's Nutmeg: Or, the True and Incredible Adventures of the Spice Trader Who Changed the Course of History. *v.6 p.177*

Nation Against Nation: What Happened to the U. N. Dream and What the U. S. Can Do about It. *v.4 p.633*

A Nation among Nations: America's Place in World History. *v.3 p.379*

Nation and Citizen in the Dominican Republic, 1880-1916. *v.3 p.317*

Nation and Identity. *v.4 p.495*

The Nation and Its Fragments: Colonial and Postcolonial Histories. *v.6 p.156*

The Nation and Its New Women: Feminism, Nationalism, Colonialism, and the Palestinian Women's Movement, 1920-1948. . . . . *v.6 p.612*

Nation and Narration. *v.2 p.759*

Nation and Novel: A Study of Persian and Kurdish Narrative Discourse. *v.6 p.668, p.669*

Nation and Novel: The English Novel from Its Origins to the Present Day. *v.2 p.189*

Nation and Religion in the Middle East. *v.6 p.593*

A Nation at Risk: The Full Account. *v.4 p.322, p.323*

☐ A Nation at Risk: the Imperative for Educational Reform: a Report to the Nation and the Secretary of Education, United States Department of Education. *v.4 p.323*

Nation at War. *v.3 p.475*

A Nation Divided: Diversity, Inequality and Community in American Society. *v.4 p.725*

A Nation for All: Race, Inequality, and Politics in Twentieth-Century Cuba. *v.3 p.278, p.308*

Nation in Barracks: Modern Germany, Military Conscription and Civil Society. *v.3 p.160*

A Nation in the Making: The Philippines and the United States, 1899-1921. . . . . *v.6 p.180*

A Nation of Behavers. *v.1 p.605*

Nation of Immigrants: Readings in Canadian History, 1840-1960. . . . . *v.3 p.542*

A Nation Prepared: Teachers for the 21st Century: the Report of the Task Force on Teaching As a Profession, Carnegie Forum on Education and the Economy, May 1986. *v.4 p.278*

A Nation Reformed?: American Education Twenty Years after a Nation at Risk. *v.4 p.326*

A Nation So Conceived: Reflections on the History of America from Its Early Visions to Its Present Power. . . . *v.3 p.376*

Nation, State and Territory: A Political Geography. . *v.4 p.495*

Nation, State, and Territory: Origins, Evolutions, and Relationships. . *v.4 p.383, p.384, p.399, p.400, p.488, p.496*

A Nation under Lawyers: How the Crisis in the Legal System Is Transforming American Society. *v.4 p.440*

National Abjection: The Asian American Body on Stage. *v.6 p.90, p.99*

☐ National Academic Advising Association. . *v.5 p.576, p.577*

☐ The National Academies. *v.5 p.385*

☐ National Adult Literacy Database. *v.4 p.319*

☐ National Aeronautics and Space Administration (NASA). *v.5 p.61*

☐ National Agricultural Library Portal. . . . *v.4 p.152, p.164*

☐ National Alliance for Youth Sports. . *v.4 p.789, p.794, p.839*

The National and Religious Song Reader: Patriotic, Traditional and Sacred Songs from Around the World. *v.1 p.237*

National Asian Pacific American Political Almanac 2005-2006. . . . . *v.6 p.120*

☐ National Association for Gifted Children. *v.5 p.575*

☐ National Association for Rural Mental Health. . . *v.5 p.671*

☐ National Association of Elementary School Principals. *v.4 p.282*

☐ National Association of School Psychologists. . . *v.5 p.577*

☐ National Atals of the United States of America. . *v.4 p.379*

☐ National Athletic Trainers Association. *v.4 p.824, p.828, p.872, p.903*

☐ National Audubon Society Field Guide to Fishes: North America. *v.5 p.216*

The National Bioethics Advisory Commission: Contributing to Public Policy. *v.5 p.247*

☐ The National Biological Information Infrastructure (NBII): Systematics. *v.5 p.204*

The National Black Drama Anthology: Eleven Plays from America's Leading African-American Theaters. *v.1 p.67, p.123*

National Bolshevism: Stalinist Mass Culture and the Formation of Modern Russian National Identity, 1931-1956. . *v.3 p.225*

☐ National Career Development Association. *v.5 p.578*

☐ National Center for Appropriate Technology: Local Solutions for a Sustainable Future. *v.5 p.12*

☐ National Center for Biotechnology Information (NCBI). *v.5 p.217*

☐ National Center for Children in Poverty, Columbia University. *v.5 p.671*

☐ National Center for Education Statistics. *v.4 p.322*

☐ National Center for Post-Traumatic Stress Disorder, U.S. Department of Veterans Affairs. *v.5 p.662*

☐ National Center for the Study of Adult Learning and Literacy (NCSALL). *v.4 p.304, p.319*

☐ National Child Welfare Resource Center, Muskie School of Public Service, University of Southern Maine. . . *v.5 p.671*

National Cleansing: Retribution against Nazi Collaborators in Postwar Czechoslovakia. *v.3 p.189*

☐ National Clearinghouse on Child Abuse and Neglect Information. *v.4 p.756*

☐ National Climatic Data Center Home Page. . . . *v.5 p.426*

☐ National Coal Assessment. *v.5 p.451*

The National Collegiate Athletic Association: A Study in Cartel Behavior. *v.4 p.883, p.887, p.888*

National Construction Estimator. *v.4 p.159*

☐ National Council for Accreditation of Teacher Education. *v.4 p.279*

☐ National Council for Research on Women. *v.6 p.432*

☐ National Council on Measurement in Education. . *v.5 p.604*

A National Crime: The Canadian Government and the Residential School System, 1879-1986. *v.4 p.335, v.6 p.680*

National Cyclopedia of American Biography. *v.3 p.376*

☐ A National Deceived: How Schools Hold Back America's Brightest Students. *v.5 p.575, p.576*

National Differences, Global Similarities: World Culture and the Future of Schooling. *v.4 p.313, p.333*

National Domestic Violence Hotline. *v.6 p.468*

National Economic Policy. *v.4 p.239*

National Educational Technology Standards for Teachers:
   Preparing Teachers to Use Technology. *v.4 p.351*

National Educational Technology Standards. . . . *v.4 p.359*

National Electrical Code 2005. . . . .*v.5 p.682, p.686*

The National Environmental Policy Act: Judicial
   Misconstruciton, Legislative Indifference, and Executive
   Neglect. *v.5 p.29, v.6 p.300*

National Excellence: A Case for Developing America's
   Talent. *v.5 p.576*

National Fire Protection Association (NFPA). . . *v.1 p.785*

National Gallery of Art: Master Paintings from the
   Collection. *v.1 p.726*

National Gay and Lesbian Task Force. *v.6 p.357*

National Geographic Historical Atlas of the United
   States. *v.4 p.382*

National Geographic World Physical/Ocean Floor. . . *v.4 p.392*

National Geography Standards. *v.4 p.360*

National Geologic Maps Database: Geologic Map Image
   Library. *v.5 p.417, p.423*

National Governments and Control of the Internet. . *v.4 p.773*

National Household Survey on Drug Abuse: Population
   Estimates, 1996. . . . .*v.4 p.776*

National Identities and Socio-Political Changes in Latin
   America. *v.4 p.703*

National Ideology under Socialism: Identity and Cultural Politics
   in Ceausescu's Romania. *v.3 p.251*

National Institute for Literacy (NIFL). . . .*v.4 p.304, p.354*

National Institute of Corrosion Engineers NACE: Protecting
   People, Assets, and the Environment from the Effects of
   Corrosion. *v.5 p.734*

National Institute of Mental Health. *v.5 p.671*

The National Integration of Italian Return Migration,
   1870-1929. . . . .*v.3 p.202*

The National Job Bank 2005. . . . .*v.4 p.168*

National Library of Medicine PubMed Tutorial. . .*v.5 p.144*

National Mental Health Association. *v.5 p.671*

National Music and Other Essays. *v.1 p.227, p.363*

National Nuclear Data Center. *v.5 p.545*

National Oceanographic Data Center (NODC). . .*v.5 p.428*

National Outdoor Leadership School's Wilderness Guide: The
   Classic Wilderness Guide. *v.4 p.788, p.884*

National Park Service Environmental Contaminants
   Encyclopedia. *v.5 p.311*

The National Park Service. *v.5 p.18*

National Parks, Conservation, and Development: The Role of
   Protected Areas in Sustaining Society. *v.5 p.17, p.18*

National Parks: The American Experience. . .*v.5 p.18, v.6 p.296*

The National Party Chairmen and Committees: Factionalism at
   the Top. *v.4 p.551*

National Pastime: How Americans Play Baseball and the Rest of
   the World Plays Soccer. *v.4 p.820, p.844, p.845, p.852, p.899*

National Performances: The Politics of Class, Race, and Space
   in Puerto Rican Chicago. *v.6 p.539, p.550*

The National Plant Genome Initiative: Objectives for
   2003-2008. . . . .*v.5 p.136*

National Polity and Local Power: The Transformation of Late
   Imperial China. *v.4 p.620*

The National Question in Yugoslavia: Origins, History,
   Politics. *v.3 p.246, p.247*

National Register of Historic Places, National Park
   Service. *v.1 p.811, p.821*

National Research Center on the Gifted and Talented
   (University of Connecticut). *v.5 p.575*

National Rhythms, African Roots: The Deep History of Latin
   American Popular Dance. *v.3 p.266, p.278*

National Romanticism and Modern Architecture in Germany and
   the Scandinavian Countries. *v.1 p.787*

National Safety Council. *v.5 p.580*

National Schools of Singing: English, French, German and
   Italian Techniques of Singing Revisited. . . .*v.1 p.395, p.401*

National Science Education Standards. *v.4 p.359*

National Security Agency Declassification
   Initiatives. *v.4 p.481*

National Security and Democracy in Israel. *v.6 p.616*

National Security Archive Documents. *v.4 p.561*

National Security in Saudi Arabia: Threats, Responses, and
   Challenges. *v.6 p.626*

National Senior Games Assocation. . *v.4 p.789, p.840, p.847*

National Sexual Violence Resource Center. *v.6 p.468*

National Society for the Study of Education
   (NSSE). *v.4 p.297, p.323, p.354*

National Sports Policies: An International
   Handbook. *v.4 p.843, p.887, p.891, p.898*

National Staff Development Council. *v.4 p.283*

National Standards for Dance Education. *v.1 p.4*

National Standards for Foreign Language Education. .*v.4 p.359*

National Standards for History Basic Edition. . . .*v.4 p.359*

National Statistics Online. *v.4 p.604*

National Strength and Conditioning
   Association. *v.4 p.827, p.828, p.829, p.872, p.878*

National Survey of State Laws. *v.4 p.441*

National Theater in Northern and Eastern Europe,
   1746-1900. . . . .*v.3 p.62*

National Wildlife Federation Book of Family Nature Activities:
   50 Simple Projects and Activities. *v.5 p.228*

National Women's Law Center Athletics
   page. *v.4 p.821, p.882, p.890, p.893, p.900*

National Youth Sport Safety Foundation. . .*v.4 p.827, p.839*

Nationalism and African Intellectuals. *v.6 p.55*

Nationalism and Capitalism in Peru: A Study in
   Neo-Imperialism. *v.3 p.331*

Nationalism and Communism in Romania: The Rise and Fall of
   Ceausescu's Personal Dictatorship. *v.4 p.508, p.600*

Nationalism and Development in Africa: Selected Essays. *v.6 p.55*

Nationalism and Federalism in Australia. *v.4 p.624*

Nationalism and Hybridity in Mongolia. *v.6 p.240*

Nationalism and Language in Kurdistan, 1918-1985: The
   Language Factor in National Development. *v.6 p.668*

Nationalism and Language Reform in China. *v.6 p.207*

Nationalism and Modernism: A Critical Survey of Recent Theories of Nations and Nationalism. *v.4 p.495*

Nationalism and New States in Africa: From about 1935 to the Present. *v.6 p.54*

Nationalism and Revolution in Indonesia. *v.6 p.177*

Nationalism and Social Communication: An Inquiry into the Foundations of Nationality. *v.3 p.61*

Nationalism and Territory: Constructing Group Identity in Southeastern Europe. *v.3 p.246*

Nationalism and the Crowd in Liberal Hungary, 1848-1914. . . . .*v.3 p.186*

Nationalism and the Genealogical Imagination: Oral History and Textual Authority in Tribal Jordan. *v.6 p.620*

Nationalism and the International Labor Movement: The Idea of the Nation in Socialist and Anarchist Theory. . . .*v.4 p.494*

Nationalism and the Politics of Culture in Quebec. *v.3 p.543, v.4 p.581*

Nationalism, Antisemitism, and Fascism in France. . . .*v.3 p.61*

Nationalism: Critical Concepts in Political Science. . . .*v.3 p.61*

Nationalism, Democracy, and Development: State and Politics in India. *v.6 p.158*

Nationalism: Five Roads to Modernity. *v.3 p.61*

Nationalism in a Non-National State: The Dissolution of the Ottoman Empire. *v.6 p.590*

Nationalism in Belgium: Shifting Identities, 1780-1995. .*v.3 p.206*

Nationalism in Indo-Anglican Fiction. *v.2 p.762*

Nationalism in Southeast Asia. *v.6 p.165*

Nationalism Without a Nation in India. . . .*v.4 p.617, v.6 p.156*

Nationalism. *v.4 p.494, p.495*

The Nationalist Era in China, 1927-1949. . . . . . .*v.6 p.190*

Nationalists and Nomads: Essays on Francophone African Literature and Culture. *v.2 p.542*

Nationalists, Cosmopolitans, and Popular Music in Zimbabwe. *v.1 p.286*

ⓔ A Nationality of Her Own: Women, Marriage, and the Law of Citizenship. *v.6 p.468*

The Nationalization of the Masses: Political Symbolism and Mass Movements in Germany, from the Napoleonic Wars Through the Third Reich. *v.3 p.61, p.62*

Nationalizing Blackness: Afrourbanismo and Artistic Revolution in Havana, 1920-1940. . . . .*v.3 p.267, p.279*

Nationalizing the Russian Empire: The Campaign Against Enemy Aliens During World War I. *v.4 p.653*

Nation-Building in the Post-Soviet Borderlands: The Politics of National Identities. *v.3 p.229*

Nationhood and Political Theory. *v.4 p.494*

Nations and Nationalism since 1780: Programme, Myth, Reality. *v.3 p.61, v.4 p.494*

Nations and Nationalism. *v.3 p.61*

Nations and States: An Enquiry into the Origins of Nations and the Politics of Nationalism. *v.3 p.62*

Nations Before Nationalism. *v.4 p.494*

Nations, Language and Citizenship. *v.2 p.559*

The Nation's Report Card: Evolution and Perspectives. .*v.4 p.355*

The Nation's Tortured Body: Violence, Representation and the Formation of a Sikh "Diaspora". *v.6 p.153*

The Nations Within: The Past and Future of American Indian Sovereignty. *v.6 p.695*

Nations Without States. *v.4 p.494*

A Nation-State by Construction: Dynamics of Modern Chinese Nationalism. *v.6 p.191, p.192, p.195*

Native American Art in the Twentieth Century: Makers, Meanings and Histories. *v.1 p.683, v.6 p.679*

Native American Art: The Collections of the Ethnological Museum Berlin. *v.6 p.678*

Native American Dance: Ceremonies and Social Traditions. *v.1 p.15, v.6 p.699, p.700*

Native American in the Land of the Shogun: Ranald MacDonald and the Opening of Japan. *v.6 p.228*

Native American Religions: A Geographical Survey. . .*v.6 p.700*

The Native American Rights Movement. *v.4 p.464, v.6 p.689, p.694*

▢ Native American Sites. *v.6 p.677*

Native American Tradition. *v.6 p.701*

Native American Tribalism: Indian Survivals and Renewals. *v.6 p.692*

Native American Women: A Biographical Dictionary. *v.6 p.425, p.705*

Native American Women's Writing: An Anthology c. 1800-1924. . . . .*v.2 p.19, v.6 p.698*

The Native Americans: An Illustrated History. *v.6 p.683*

Native Americans and Political Participation. . .*v.6 p.692, p.693*

ⓔ Native Americans and the Law: A Dictionary. . . .*v.6 p.692*

Native Americans in Sports. *v.4 p.841*

Native Arts of North America. *v.1 p.682, v.6 p.678*

The Native Brotherhoods: Modern Intertribal Organizations on the Northwest Coast. *v.6 p.702, p.703*

▢ Native Health Databases. *v.6 p.701*

Native Languages of the Southeastern United States. .*v.6 p.690*

Native Literature in Canada from the Oral Tradition to the Present. *v.2 p.731*

Native Modernism: The Art of George Morrison and Allan Houser. *v.6 p.679*

Native North American Art. *v.1 p.681, v.6 p.678*

Native North American Literature : Biographical and Critical Information on Native Writers and Orators from the United States and Canada from Historical Times to the Present. *v.6 p.699*

Native Peoples of the Southwest. *v.6 p.703*

Native Peoples: The Canadian Experience. .*v.6 p.682, p.692, p.703*

The Native Population of the Americas in 1492. . . . .*v.3 p.301, v.6 p.684*

Native Religions and Cultures of North America: Anthropology of the Sacred. *v.6 p.701, p.704*

Native Resistance and the Pax Colonial in New Spain. .*v.3 p.287*

Native Science: Natural Laws of Interdependence. *v.6 p.680, p.681*

Native Speaker. *v.6 p.101*

Native Waters: Contemporary Indian Water Settlements and the Second Treaty Era. *v.6 p.681, p.689, p.696*

Native-American Literature: A Brief Introduction and Anthology. *v.2 p.20*

Natives and Newcomers: Ethnic Southerners and Southern
Ethnics. *v.3 p.498*

Natives and Newcomers: The Making of Irish Colonial Society
1534-1641. . . . .*v.3 p.134, p.136*

The Natives of Hemso. *v.2 p.631*

☐ NativeWeb. *v.6 p.677*

Nativism and Slavery: The Northern Know Nothings and the
Politics of the 1850s. *v.3 p.394*

NATO and the Quest for Post-Cold War Security. . . .*v.4 p.639*

NATO, Britain, France, and the FRG: Nuclear Strategies and
Forces for Europe, 1949-2000. . . . . . .*v.4 p.639, p.654*

ⓔ NATO Enlargement During the Cold War: Strategy and
System in the Western Alliance. *v.4 p.639*

NATO Enters the 21st Century. *v.4 p.639*

NATO in the Post-Cold War Era: Does It Have a
Future? *v.4 p.639*

NATO Transformed: The Alliance's New Roles in International
Security. *v.4 p.639, p.640, p.655*

Natural Agency: An Essay on the Causal Theory of
Action. *v.1 p.503*

☐ Natural Aggregate: Building America's Future (USGS
Circular 1110). *v.5 p.452*

Natural Aggregate: Building America's Future. . . .*v.5 p.452*

☐ Natural Aggregates of the Conterminous United States
(USGS Bulletin 1594). *v.5 p.452*

Natural Aggregates of the Conterminous United States. .*v.5 p.452*

☐ Natural Aggregates. *v.5 p.452*

Natural Born Celebrities: Serial Killers in American
Culture. *v.6 p.256*

Natural Classroom Assessment: Designing Seamless Instruction
and Assessment. *v.4 p.287*

A Natural Curiosity. *v.2 p.343*

Natural Enemies Handbook: The Illustrated Guide to Biological
Pest Control. *v.5 p.9, p.26*

Natural Enemies: The United States and the Soviet Union in the
Cold War, 1917-1991. . . . .*v.3 p.389*

Natural Gas and Electric Power in Nontechnical
Language. *v.5 p.708*

Natural Hazards. *v.5 p.423*

Natural High. *v.5 p.224*

Natural History: A Selection. *v.5 p.223*

Natural History: Bks. 12-16, Vol. 4. . . . .*v.2 p.441*

Natural History: Bks. 17-19, Vol. 5. . . . .*v.2 p.441*

Natural History: Bks. 20-23, Vol. 6. . . . .*v.2 p.441*

Natural History: Bks. 33-35, Vol. 9. . . . .*v.2 p.441*

Natural History: Bks. 36-37, Vol. 10. . . . . .*v.2 p.440, p.441*

Natural History: Bks. 8-11, Vol. 3. . . . .*v.2 p.441*

Natural History Collections: their management and
value. *v.5 p.227*

The Natural History Essays. *v.5 p.227*

Natural History, General and Particular. *v.5 p.220, p.221*

Natural History: Index of Fishes, Vol. 8. . . . . . .*v.2 p.440*

Natural History: Index of Plants, Vol. 7. . . . . . .*v.2 p.441*

A Natural History of Ferns. *v.5 p.210*

The Natural History of H. G. Wells. *v.2 p.319*

A Natural History of Homosexuality. *v.6 p.372, p.420*

A Natural History of Latin. *v.2 p.423*

Natural History of Orkney. *v.5 p.175, p.236, p.237*

The Natural History of Pompeii. *v.5 p.236*

The Natural History of Religion. *v.1 p.523*

A Natural History of the Antarctic: Life in the
Freezer. *v.5 p.175, p.238*

Natural History of the Antarctic Peninsula. *v.5 p.238*

The Natural History of the Soul in Ancient Mexico. . .*v.3 p.261*

Natural History, Vol. 1. . . . .*v.2 p.441*

Natural History, Vol. 2. . . . .*v.2 p.441*

Natural Impressions: Taking an Artistic Path Through
Nature. *v.1 p.759*

A Natural Introduction to Probability Theory. *v.5 p.484*

Natural Kinds and Conceptual Change. *v.5 p.155*

Natural Language and Universal Grammar: Essays in Linguistic
Theory. *v.2 p.562*

Natural Language Processing and Knowledge Representation:
Language for Knowledge and Knowledge for
Language. *v.5 p.339, p.341*

Natural Law and Civil Sovereignty: Moral Right and State
Authority in Early Modern Political Thought. . . .*v.4 p.496*

Natural Law and Moral Philosophy: From Grotius to the
Scottish Enlightenment. *v.1 p.491*

Natural Law: Reflections on Theory and Practice. . . .*v.4 p.513*

Natural Liberty and Civil Government: The Two Treatises on
the Art of Ruling Humanity. *v.4 p.215, p.216*

The Natural Order of Things. *v.2 p.688*

Natural Particulars: Nature and the Disciplines in Renaissance
Europe. *v.5 p.79, p.237*

Natural Products in the New Millennium: Prospects and
Industrial Application. *v.5 p.219*

The Natural Rate of Unemployment: Reflections on 25 Years of
the Hypothesis. *v.4 p.252*

Natural Resources Engineering. *v.5 p.6*

Natural Resources, Growth and Development: Economics,
Ecology and Resource-Scarcity. *v.4 p.62*

Natural Resources Policy and Law: Trends and
Directions. *v.4 p.463*

Natural Rights Republic: Studies in the Foundation of the
American Political Tradition. *v.4 p.513, p.514*

Natural Selection: Domains, Levels, and Challenges. .*v.5 p.198*

Natural Selections: National Parks in Atlantic Canada,
1935-1970. . . . .*v.5 p.18, v.6 p.295*

The Natural Superiority of
Women. *v.4 p.14, p.744, v.6 p.435, p.461*

Natural Supernaturalism: Tradition and Revolution in Romantic
Literature. *v.2 p.183, p.567*

Natural Symbols: Explorations in Cosmology. *v.1 p.521*

The Natural: The Misunderstood Presidency of Bill
Clinton. *v.3 p.473*

A Natural Theology for Our Time. *v.1 p.525*

Naturalism: A Critical Appraisal. *v.1 p.516*

Naturalism and Ontology. *v.1 p.489*

Naturalism Without Foundations. *v.1 p.516*

Naturalistic Decision Making. *v.5 p.589*

Naturalists: A Journal. *v.5 p.232*

Naturalists and Society: The Culture of Natural History in Britain, 1700-1900. . . . . *v.5 p.236*

A Naturalist's Guide to the Arctic. *v.5 p.238*

A Naturalist's Guide to Wetland Plants: An Ecology for Eastern North America. *v.5 p.53, v.6 p.290*

The Naturalist's Path: A Handbook for Beginning the Study of Nature. *v.5 p.227*

Naturalist. *v.5 p.397*

Naturalizing the Mind. *v.1 p.496*

Naturally Dangerous: Surprising Facts about Food, Health and the Environment. *v.6 p.289*

Naturally Speaking: A Dictionary of Quotations on Biology, Botany, Nature and Zoology. *v.5 p.225*

The Naturalness of Religious Ideas: A Cognitive Theory of Religion. *v.5 p.633*

The Natural. *v.2 p.149*

Nature a Day at a Time: An Uncommon Look at Common Wildlife. *v.5 p.222*

Nature and Art: Dutch Garden and Landscape Architecture 1650-1740. . . . . *v.1 p.818*

Nature and Culture in the Andes. *v.3 p.269*

The Nature and Destiny of Man: A Christian Interpretation, Vol. 2. . . . . *v.1 p.643*

Nature and Ideology: Nature and Garden Design in the Twentieth Century. *v.1 p.820*

Nature and Its Symbols. *v.1 p.709*

Nature and Life. *v.5 p.404*

The Nature and Logic of Capitalism. *v.4 p.214*

Nature and Practice of Biological Control of Plant Pathogens. *v.5 p.7*

The Nature and Properties of Engineering Materials. . *v.5 p.689*

The Nature and Properties of Soils. *v.5 p.48*

The Nature and Role of Algebra in the K - 14 Curriculum: Proceedings of a National Symposium. . . . *v.5 p.463*

The Nature and Significance of Economic Science. . *v.4 p.210*

The Nature and Sources of the Law. *v.4 p.441*

Nature and the American: Three Centuries of Changing Attitudes. *v.5 p.79, p.234*

Nature and the English Diaspora: Environment and History in the United States, Canada, Australia, and New Zealand. *v.5 p.221*

Nature and the Victorian Imagination. *v.6 p.737, p.764*

The Nature and Types of Sociological Theory. . . *v.4 p.680*

Nature by Design: People, Natural Process, and Ecological Restoration. *v.6 p.283*

The Nature Encyclopedia: An A-Z Guide to Life on Earth. *v.5 p.225*

Nature Encyclopedia of the Human Genome. . . . *v.5 p.139*

Nature in Ireland: A Scientific and Cultural History. . *v.5 p.237*

Nature Journaling: Learning to Observe and Connect with the World Around You. *v.5 p.232*

Nature, Man and Society in the 12th Century. . . . *v.1 p.633*

Nature, Man, and Society in the Twelfth Century: Essays on New Theological Perspectives in the Latin West. with a Preface by Etienne Gilson. *v.6 p.570*

Nature, Nurture, and the Transition to Early Adolescence. *v.5 p.658*

The Nature of Biological Systems As Revealed by Thermal Methods. *v.5 p.88, p.113*

The Nature of Capital and Income. *v.4 p.199, p.200, p.224, p.225, p.246*

The Nature of Chinese Politics: From Mao to Jiang. . *v.4 p.620*

The Nature of Culture. *v.4 p.24*

The Nature of Doctrine: Religion and Theology in a Postliberal Age. *v.1 p.568, p.636*

The Nature of Emotion: Fundamental Questions. . . *v.5 p.611*

The Nature of Gold: An Environmental History of the Klondike Gold Rush. *v.3 p.533, p.547*

The Nature of Grief: The Evolution and Psychology of Reactions to Loss. *v.5 p.651*

The Nature of History in Ancient Greece and Rome. *v.2 p.402*

The Nature of Hysteria. *v.4 p.714*

The Nature of Insight. *v.5 p.609*

The Nature of Life: Readings in Biology. *v.5 p.232*

The Nature of Managerial Work. *v.4 p.64*

The Nature of Mass Poverty. *v.4 p.265*

The Nature of Mathematical Modeling. *v.5 p.500*

The Nature of Matter. *v.5 p.554*

The Nature of Mediterranean Europe: An Ecological History. *v.5 p.79, p.168, p.176, p.237*

The Nature of Melancholy: From Aristotle to Kristeva. *v.5 p.660*

The Nature of Morality: An Introduction to Ethics. . *v.1 p.487*

The Nature of Natural History. *v.5 p.227*

The Nature of Nature: New Essays from America's Finest Writers on Science. *v.5 p.81, p.226*

The Nature of Necessity. *v.1 p.493*

The Nature of Nursing: Reflections after 25 Years. . *v.5 p.527*

The Nature of Order: An Essay on the Art of Building and the Nature of the Universe, Set. *v.1 p.796*

The Nature of Paleolithic Art. *v.1 p.668, v.4 p.17*

The Nature of Peace. *v.4 p.251*

The Nature of Prejudice. *v.5 p.646*

The Nature of Rationality. *v.1 p.493, p.514*

The Nature of Roman Comedy, A Study in Popular Entertainment. *v.1 p.72, p.90*

The Nature of Roman Comedy: A Study in Popular Entertainment. *v.2 p.425*

The Nature of Social and Educational Inquiry: Empiricism vs. Interpretation. *v.4 p.355*

The Nature of the Chemical Bond and the Structure of Molecules and Crystals: An Introduction to Modern Structural Chemistry. *v.5 p.282*

The Nature of the Child. *v.5 p.627*

The Nature of the Gods. *v.2 p.433*

The Nature of True Virtue. *v.1 p.483*

Nature Out of Place: Biological Invasions in the Global Age. *v.5 p.182*

Nature Printing. *v.1 p.760*

Nature Projects on File. *v.5 p.227*

The Nature Reader. *v.5 p.232*

Nature Religion in America: From the Algonkian Indians to the New Age. *v.1 p.527, v.6 p.700*

Nature: Western Attitudes since Ancient Times. *v.5 p.78, p.221*

Nature Writing: The Tradition in English. *v.5 p.226*

Nature-Based Tourism in Peripheral Areas: Development or
  Disaster? *v.5 p.357, p.358*

Nature-Friendly Communities: Habitat Protection and Land Use
  Planning. *v.1 p.817*

Nature's Building Blocks: An A-Z Guide to the
  Elements. *v.5 p.264*

Nature's Everyday Mysteries: A Field Guide to the World in
  Your Backyard. *v.5 p.227*

Nature's Government: Science, British Imperialism and the
  Improvement of the World. *v.6 p.295*

Nature's Harvest: A Produce Reference Guide to Fruits and
  Vegetables from Around the World. . . .*v.5 p.21, p.22, p.26*

Nature's Justice: Writings of William O. Douglas. . . .*v.4 p.467*

Nature's Magic: Synergy in Evolution and the Fate of
  Humankind. *v.5 p.191, p.201*

Nature's Metropolis: Chicago and the Great
  West. *v.6 p.295, p.711*

Nature's Mind: The Biological Roots of Thinking, Emotions,
  Sexuality, Language, and Intelligence. *v.5 p.617*

Nature's State: Imagining Alaska As the Last Frontier.*v.6 p.286*

The Nautical Chart. *v.2 p.662*

The Navaho. *v.6 p.703*

Navajo Ceremonial Baskets: Sacred Symbols, Sacred
  Space. *v.1 p.683, p.806,v.6 p.679*

Navajo Kinship and Marriage. *v.6 p.704*

Navajo/English Bilingual Dictionary. *v.6 p.690*

Naval Documents of the American Revolution. . . .*v.3 p.414*

A Naval History of the American Revolution, Set. . . .*v.3 p.413*

The Naval History of the Civil War: Illustrated from Original
  Sketches Made by Rear-Admiral Walke and Others..*v.3 p.432*

Naval War of 1812: A Documentary History, 1813, Vol.
  2. . . . .*v.3 p.416*

The Naval War of 1812. . . . .*v.3 p.418*

Naven: A Survey of the Problems Suggested by a Composite
  Picture of the Culture of a New Guinea Tribe
  Drawn from Three Points of View. *v.4 p.42*

Navigating Through Geometry in Grades 6-8. . . . . .*v.5 p.462*

Navigating Through Geometry in Grades 9-12. . . .*v.5 p.462*

Nazarin. *v.2 p.654*

☐ Nazi and East German Propaganda Guide. . .*v.3 p.171, p.176*

The Nazi Dictatorship: Problems and Perspectives of
  Interpretation. *v.3 p.172*

The Nazi Doctors: Medical Killing and the Psychology of
  Genocide. *v.3 p.172, v.4 p.653*

Nazi Family Policy, 1933-1945. . . . .*v.3 p.173*

Nazi Germany and the Jews: The Years of Persecution,
  1933-1939. . . . .*v.3 p.59, p.171*

The Nazi Menace in Argentina, 1931-1947. . . . . .*v.3 p.348*

The Nazi Olympics: Sport, Politics, and Appeasement in the
  1930s. *v.4 p.807, p.846, p.891*

The Nazi Olympics. . .*v.3 p.172, p.173,v.4 p.807, p.808, p.846*

The Nazi Party: A Social Profile of Members and Leaders,
  1919-1945. . . . .*v.4 p.609*

The Nazi Persecution of the Gypsies. *v.3 p.85*

Nazi Policy, Jewish Workers, German Killers. *v.3 p.83*

Nazi Propaganda Films: A History and Filmography. .*v.6 p.338*

The Nazi Seizure of Power: The Experience of a Single German
  Town, 1922-1945. . . . .*v.3 p.169*

The Nazi Voter: The Social Foundations of Fascism in Germany,
  1919-1933. . . . .*v.3 p.170, v.4 p.609*

Nazis in Skokie: Freedom, Community, and the First
  Amendment. *v.4 p.458, p.459*

NBER Macroeconomics Annual 2004. . . . . .*v.4 p.189, p.200*

The NBS Tables of Chemical Thermodynamic Properties:
  Selected Values for Inorganic and Cl and C2
  Organic Substances in SI Units. *v.5 p.302*

☐ NCBI Education. *v.5 p.331*

☐ NCBI: National Center for Biotechnology Information, A
  Science Primer. *v.5 p.130*

☐ NCBI: National Center for Biotechnology
  Information. *v.5 p.130*

☐ NCBI: The NCBI Taxonomy Homepage. *v.5 p.205*

☐ NCJ (National Criminal Justice) Thesaurus. . . .*v.6 p.246*

☐ NCJRS Abstracts Database. *v.6 p.246*

☐ NCLR: National Center for Lesbian Rights. . . .*v.6 p.357*

The Neanderthal Legacy: An Archaeological Perspective of
  Western Europe. *v.4 p.17*

Neanderthals and Modern Humans: An Ecological and
  Evolutionary Perspective. *v.4 p.15*

The Neanderthals: Changing the Image of Mankind. . .*v.4 p.17*

The Neanderthal's Necklace: In Search of the First
  Thinkers. *v.4 p.16*

Near Eastern Archaeology: A Reader. *v.3 p.4*

Near Eastern Culture and Society: A Symposium on the Meeting
  of East and West. *v.6 p.582*

The Near Northwest Side Story: Migration, Displacement, and
  Puerto Rican Families. *v.6 p.530, p.550*

Near to the Wild Heart. *v.2 p.691*

Nearest Star: The Surprising Science of Our Sun. . . .*v.5 p.68*

The Nearsighted Naturalist. *v.5 p.231*

Nebraska: A Guide to the Cornhusker State. *v.3 p.524*

The Nebraska Question, 1852-1854. . . . .*v.3 p.420*

Nebraska Symposium on Motivation 1995: Perspectives on
  Anxiety, Panic, and Fear. *v.5 p.612*

Necessary Theatre: Six Plays about the Chicano
  Experience. *v.6 p.496, p.517*

The Necessary Theatre. *v.1 p.139, p.152*

Nectar Gaze and Poison Breath: An Analysis and Translation of
  the Rajasthani Oral Narrative of Devnarayan. . . .*v.6 p.152*

A Ned Rorem Reader. *v.1 p.247, p.351,v.6 p.410*

Ned Wayburn and the Dance Routine: From Vaudeville to the
  Ziegfeld Follies. *v.1 p.35, p.36*

Nedjma : roman. *v.2 p.545*

Nedjma: Kateb Yacine. *v.2 p.546, p.547, p.549*

Nedjma. *v.2 p.546*

Needed Research in American Dialects. *v.2 p.553*

Needed Research in American English. *v.2 p.552*

The Needs of the Dying: A Guide for Bringing Hope, Comfort,
  and Love to Life's Final Chapter. *v.5 p.532*

Nefertiti: Egypt's Sun Queen. *v.6 p.58*

Negara: The Theatre State in 19th Century Bali. . . .*v.6 p.176*

Negative Dialectics. *v.1 p.502*

Negotiate This!: By Caring, but Not T-H-A-T Much. . .*v.4 p.74*

Negotiate to Win: The 21 Rules for Successful Negotiating. *v.4 p.75*

Negotiating a Complex World: An Introduction to International Negotiation. *v.4 p.646*

Negotiating Competitiveness: Employment Relations and Organizational Innovation in Germany and the United States. *v.4 p.123*

Negotiating Cooperation: The United States and China, 1969-1989. . . . . *v.3 p.391, p.392*

Negotiating Democracy: Politicians and Generals in Uruguay. *v.3 p.274, v.4 p.591, p.592*

Negotiating Development: African Farmers and Colonial Experts at the Office du Niger, 1920-1960. . . . . *v.6 p.71*

Negotiating Globally: How to Negotiate Deals, Resolve Disputes and Make Decisions Across Cultural Boundaries. *v.4 p.74*

Negotiating Identity: Catholic Higher Education since 1960. . . . . *v.4 p.307, p.308*

Negotiating National Identity: Immigrants, Minorities, and the Struggle for Ethnicity in Brazil. *v.3 p.341*

Negotiating on the Edge: North Korean Negotiating Behavior. *v.4 p.644, p.646*

Negotiating Outside the Law: Why Camp David Failed. *v.4 p.649*

Negotiating Parent-Adolescent Conflict: A Behavioral-Family Systems Approach. *v.5 p.668*

Negotiating Peace in El Salvador: Civil-Military Relations and the Conspiracy to End the War. *v.3 p.299*

Negotiating Performance: Gender, Sexuality, and Theatricality in Latin-o America. *v.6 p.516, p.518*

Negotiating Rationally. *v.4 p.74*

Negotiating with the Dead: A Writer on Writing. . . *v.2 p.728*

Negotiation Analysis: The Science and Art of Collaborative Decision Making. *v.4 p.74*

The Negotiation Fieldbook. *v.4 p.74*

Negre a Paris. *v.2 p.542*

The Negritude Poets: An Anthology of Black Poetry Translated from the French. *v.2 p.535*

The Negro Church in America/the Black Church since Frazier. *v.6 p.35, p.36*

A Negro Explorer at the North Pole: The Autobiography of Matthew Henson. *v.6 p.5, p.17*

Negro Family in British Guiana: Family Structure and Social Status in the Villages. *v.4 p.33*

Negro Folk Music U. S. A. *v.1 p.34, p.281, p.295*

The Negro in the American Rebellion: His Heroism and His Fidelity. *v.6 p.4*

The Negro in the American Revolution. *v.3 p.410*

Negro in the Civil War. *v.3 p.400, p.432*

The Negro in the South: His Economic Progress in Relation to His Moral and Religious Development. *v.6 p.9*

Negro League Baseball: The Rise and Ruin of a Black Institution. . . *v.4 p.807, p.832, p.851, p.884, p.888, p.896*

The Negro Leagues, 1869-1960. . . . *v.4 p.806, p.832, p.850*

The Negro Leagues 1869-1960. . . . . *v.6 p.41*

The Negro Leagues Book. . . . *v.4 p.804, p.831, p.850, p.896*

Negro Militia and Reconstruction. *v.3 p.438*

Nehru: A Political Life. *v.6 p.158*

Neighborhood Services: Making Big Cities Work. . . .*v.4 p.544*

Neighborhood Structure, Crime and Fear of Crime: Testing Bursik and Grasmick's Neighborhood Control Theory. *v.6 p.258*

Neighborhood Tokyo. *v.6 p.218*

The Neighbors Respond: The Controversy over the Jedwabne Massacre in Poland. *v.3 p.86, p.254, p.255*

Neighbors: The Destruction of the Jewish Community in Jedwabne, Poland. *v.3 p.84, p.254*

Neighbours, Not Friends: Iraq and Iran after the Gulf Wars. *v.6 p.603, p.631*

Neither Black nor White: Slavery and Race Relations in Brazil and the U.S. *v.3 p.278, p.336*

Neither Man nor Woman: The Hijras of India. *v.4 p.746, v.6 p.374, p.421*

Nelson Algren. *v.2 p.56*

Nelson's Textbook of Pediatrics. *v.5 p.524*

Neo-Bohemia: Art and Commerce in the Post Industrial City. *v.6 p.718*

Neoclassical Finance. *v.4 p.89, p.264*

Neoclassical Microeconomics, Vol. I. *v.4 p.224, p.248*

Neoclassical Theatre: A Historiographical Handbook. *v.1 p.78, p.106*

Neoclassical Theory of International Trade: The Origins of International Economics. *v.4 p.257*

The Neoclassical Theory of Production and Distribution. *v.4 p.223, p.225*

Neo-Colonialism: The Last Stage of Imperialism. . . .*v.2 p.760*

Neoconservatism: The Autobiography of an Idea. .*v.4 p.511, p.516*

Neo-Lamarckism and the Evolution Controversy in France, 1870-1920. . . . .*v.5 p.80, p.195*

Neoliberalism in Crisis, Accumulation, and Rosa Luxemburg's Legacy. *v.4 p.239*

The Neon Wilderness: 24 Short Stories. *v.2 p.56*

Neonatal-Perinatal Medicine: Diseases of the Fetus and Infant. *v.5 p.525*

The Neoplatonists. *v.1 p.430*

Neptune and the Netherlands: State, Economy, and War at Sea in the Renaissance. *v.3 p.205*

[e] Nero: The End of a Dynasty. *v.3 p.28*

Nero. *v.3 p.27, p.28*

Nervous Conditions. *v.2 p.754*

A Nervous Splendor: Vienna, 1888-1889. . . . . . .*v.3 p.184*

The Net Effect. *v.4 p.425*

The Nether World. *v.2 p.290*

Netherlands in Focus: Exemplary Ideas and Concepts for Town and Landscape. *v.1 p.814*

Netherlands India: A Study of Plural Economy. *v.6 p.176*

Netscape Time: The Making of the Billion-Dollar Start-Up That Took on Microsoft. *v.4 p.157*

Network Flows: Theory, Algorithms, and Applications.*v.5 p.478*

The Network Society: Social Aspects of New Media. *v.4 p.419*

Networks and Marginality: Life in a Mexican Shantytown. *v.4 p.704*

Networks and Telecommunications: Design and Operation. *v.4 p.422*

Networks of Champions: Leadership, Access and Advisory in the U. S. House of Representatives. *v.4 p.533*

Networks of Nazi Persecution: Bureaucracy, Business, and the Organization of the Holocaust. *v.3 p.171*

Networks of Power: Electrification in Western Society, 1880-1930. . . . .*v.3 p.49, v.4 p.159*

Networks of Privilege in the Middle East: The Politics of Economic Reform Revisited. *v.4 p.614*

Neue Gesamtausgabe der Werken und Schriften in vier Bänden. *v.2 p.596*

The Neural Control of Sleep and Waking. . . .*v.5 p.617, p.618*

Neural Correlates of Consciousness: Empirical and Conceptual Questions. *v.5 p.613*

Neural Networks: An Introductory Guide for Social Scientists. *v.5 p.591*

Neural Networks and Genome Informatics. .*v.5 p.99, p.143, p.147*

Neural Networks, Vol. 124. . . . .*v.5 p.591*

Neural Theories of Mind: Why the Mind-Brain Problem May Never Be Solved. *v.5 p.618*

Neurobiology of Attention. *v.5 p.611*

Neurobiology of Mental Illness. *v.5 p.617*

The Neuroendocrine Regulation of Behavior. *v.5 p.617*

Neuromechanics of Human Movement. *v.4 p.908, p.909*

Neuronal Signal Transduction and Alzheimer's Disease, Vol. 67. . . . .*v.5 p.165*

Neurophysiological Basis of Movement. *v.4 p.908, p.909*

Neuropsychological Bases of God Beliefs. *v.5 p.635*

Neuropsychology of Art: Neurological, Cognitive and Evolutionary Perspectives. *v.5 p.619*

The Neuropsychology of Lashley: Selected Papers,. . .*v.5 p.617*

Nevada: A Bicentennial History. *v.3 p.529*

Nevada: Magnificent Wilderness. *v.5 p.235*

Never a Soul at Home: New Zealand Literary Nationalism and the 1930's. *v.2 p.741*

Never at Rest: A Biography of Isaac Newton. .*v.3 p.130, v.5 p.544*

Never at War: Why Democracies Will Not Fight One Another. *v.4 p.506, p.627, p.648, p.651*

Never Going Back: A History of Queer Activism in Canada. *v.4 p.712*

Never in Anger: Portrait of an Eskimo Family. *v.6 p.702*

Never Just a Game: Players, Owners and American Baseball to 1920. . . . .*v.4 p.804, p.850, p.887, p.895, p.896*

Never Let Me Go. *v.2 p.355*

Never Mind the Bollocks, Here's the Sex Pistols: The Sex Pistols. *v.1 p.270, p.356*

Neverending Wars: The International Community, Weak States, and the Perpetuation of Civil War. *v.4 p.647*

Nevermind: Nirvana. *v.1 p.266, p.345, p.346*

The New A to Z of Women's Health. *v.5 p.523*

The New African Poetry: An Anthology. . .*v.2 p.752, v.6 p.80*

The New Age of Franklin Roosevelt, 1932-1945. . . .*v.3 p.478*

The New Amateur Astronomer. *v.5 p.63*

The New Ambidextrous Universe: Symmetry and Asymmetry from Mirror Reflections to Superstrings. *v.5 p.540*

The New American Cinema. *v.6 p.345*

The New American Democracy. *v.4 p.503*

The New American Ghetto. *v.6 p.719*

The New American Grandparent: A Place in the Family, a Life Apart. *v.4 p.740, p.741*

The New American History. *v.3 p.374*

The New American Musical: An Anthology from the End of the 20th Century. *v.1 p.250, p.408*

The New American Poetry, 1945-1960. . . . .*v.2 p.22*

New American Poets of the 80's. *v.2 p.24*

The New American Sport History: Recent Approaches and Perspectives. *v.4 p.809, p.813*

New American Standard Bible: Reader's Pew Edition. .*v.1 p.613*

The New American Village. *v.6 p.729*

The New Americans: Seven Families Journey to Another Country. *v.4 p.765*

New and Collected Poems, 1966-2006. . . .*v.2 p.154, v.6 p.27*

New and Collected Poems, 1970-1985. . . . .*v.2 p.89*

New and Complete Concordance of Shakespeare. . . .*v.2 p.226*

New and Emerging Proteomic Techniques. *v.5 p.117*

New and Selected Essays. *v.2 p.7*

New and Selected Poems. *v.2 p.328, p.510*

New and Selected Things Taking Place: Poems. *v.2 p.117*

The New Annotated Sherlock Holmes: A Study in Scarlet; The Sign of the Four; The Hound of the Baskervilles; and the Valley of Fear. *v.2 p.285*

New Annotated Sherlock Holmes, Vol. 1. . . . . . .*v.2 p.285*

The New Annotated Sherlock Holmes, Vols. 1 & 2. . .*v.2 p.285*

A New Anthology of Art Songs by African American Composer. *v.6 p.30*

The New Anti-Catholicism: The Last Acceptable Prejudice. *v.1 p.576*

New Approaches on Energy and the Environment: Policy Advice for the President. *v.4 p.62*

New Approaches to Structural Mechanics, Shells and Biological. *v.5 p.693*

A New Arabic Grammar of the Written Language. . .*v.6 p.654*

New Art City: The Painters and Sculptors of Manhattan, 1950-1965. . . . .*v.1 p.680, p.682*

The New Art History: A Critical Introduction. *v.1 p.703*

New Art of Cuba. *v.1 p.684*

The New Asian Immigration in Los Angeles and Global Restructuring. *v.6 p.116, p.118*

The New Avenues in Bioinformat. *v.5 p.98, p.243*

The New Ayn Rand Companion. *v.2 p.113*

The New Bach Reader: A Life of Johann Sebastian Bach in Letters and Documents. *v.1 p.183, p.303*

The New Ballet: Kurt Jooss and His Work. *v.1 p.7*

The New Battle over Workplace Privacy: Safe Practices to Minimize Conflict, Confusion and Litigation. . . .*v.4 p.446*

The New Berlin: Memory, Politics, Place. *v.3 p.181*

New Bible Dictionary. *v.1 p.614*

The New Big Book of Logos. *v.1 p.717*

New Biology for Engineers and Computer Scientists. . .*v.5 p.98*

The New Biology: Law, Ethics, and Biotechnology. *v.5 p.220, p.249*

The New Black Renaissance: The Souls Anthology of Critical African-American Studies. *v.6 p.14*

The New Blackwell Guide to Recorded Blues. .*v.1 p.170, p.258*

The New Bloomsday Book: A Guide Through Ulysses. .*v.2 p.357*

The New Brain Sciences: Perils and Prospects. *v.5 p.617*

The New British Drama: 14 Playwrights since Osborne and Pinter. *v.2 p.188*

New Brunswick in History. *v.3 p.542*

The New Cambridge History of India: Vijayanagara. .*v.6 p.162*

The New Cambridge Medieval History, Set. *v.3 p.66, v.6 p.562, p.563*

New Caribbean Thought : A Reader. *v.4 p.685*

A New Catechism: Catholic Faith for Adults. *v.1 p.576*

e New Catholic Encyclopedia, Set. *v.1 p.571*

New Challenges for Documentary. *v.6 p.310*

The New Chemistry. *v.5 p.265*

New Chicana - Chicano Writing. *v.6 p.503, p.504, p.516*

New Chicana/Chicano Writing, Set. *v.6 p.496, p.504*

The New Chinatown. *v.6 p.127*

New Chinese Cinema. *v.6 p.335*

The New Citizenship: Origins of Progressivism in Wisconsin, 1885-1900. . . . .*v.3 p.517*

The New Civic Art: Elements of Town Planning. . . .*v.1 p.796*

The New Civil War: The Psychology, Culture and Politics of Abortion. *v.4 p.775*

The New Class Society: Goodbye American Dream? .*v.4 p.725*

The New Classical Macroeconomics, Set. *v.4 p.217*

A New Commentary on the Poems of W. B. Yeats. . .*v.2 p.326*

New Commonwealth, 1877-1890. . . . .*v.3 p.436*

A New Companion to Homer. *v.2 p.415*

New Comparative Grammar of Greek and Latin. . . .*v.2 p.400*

The New Complete Works of Josephus. *v.1 p.546*

New Comprehensive Biochemistry. *v.5 p.326*

New Concise World Atlas. *v.4 p.380*

The New Confessions: A Novel. *v.2 p.335*

The New Conservatism: Cultural Criticism and the Historians' Debate. *v.4 p.511*

New Contexts of Canadian Criticism. *v.2 p.729*

The New Corporate Finance. *v.4 p.88*

The New Corporate Strategy. *v.4 p.81*

New Cosmopolitanisms: South Asians in the US. .*v.6 p.137, p.138*

The New Cosmos: An Introduction to Astronomy and Astrophysics. *v.5 p.65*

New Critical Approaches to the Short Stories of Ernest Hemingway. *v.2 p.83*

A New Critical History of Old English Literature. *v.2 p.167, v.6 p.565*

New Croatian - English Dictionary. *v.2 p.774*

The New Crusades: Constructing the Muslim Enemy. .*v.4 p.661*

The New Czech Poetry. *v.2 p.781*

The New Deal and the Triumph of Liberalism. *v.3 p.443, v.4 p.522*

The New Deal and World Affairs, Vol. 56. . . . . .*v.3 p.453*

The New Deal at Work: Managing the Market-Driven Workforce. *v.4 p.85*

New Deal Modernism: American Literature and the Invention of the Welfare State. *v.2 p.11*

The New Deal: The Depression Years, 1933-1940. . .*v.3 p.439*

New Deal Thought. *v.3 p.482, v.4 p.522*

e The New Dealers' War: Franklin D. Roosevelt and the War Within World War II. *v.3 p.458*

The New Deal. *v.3 p.468*

The New Dialectic and Marx's Capital. *v.4 p.235*

New Diasporas: The Mass Exodus, Dispersal and Regrouping of Migrant Communities. *v.4 p.765*

The New Dickson Baseball Dictionary. *v.4 p.850*

New Dictionary of American History, Vol. 10. . . . .*v.3 p.373*

New Dictionary of American History, Vol. 1. . . . . .*v.3 p.373*

New Dictionary of American History, Vol. 2. . . . . .*v.3 p.373*

New Dictionary of American History, Vol. 3. . . . . .*v.3 p.373*

New Dictionary of American History, Vol. 4. . . . . .*v.3 p.373*

New Dictionary of American History, Vol. 5. . . . . .*v.3 p.373*

New Dictionary of American History, Vol. 6. . . . . .*v.3 p.373*

New Dictionary of American History, Vol. 7. . . . . .*v.3 p.373*

New Dictionary of American History, Vol. 8. . . . . .*v.3 p.373*

New Dictionary of American History, Vol. 9. . . . . .*v.3 p.373*

The New Dictionary of Catholic Social Thought. . . .*v.1 p.571*

New Dictionary of the History of Ideas. *v.1 p.416*

New Directions for Clarinet. *v.1 p.393, p.398*

New Directions for Equity in Mathematics Education. .*v.5 p.464*

New Directions in African Literature, 1970-1990. . . .*v.2 p.752*

New Directions in Anthropological Kinship. *v.4 p.33*

New Directions in Anthropology and Environment: Intersections. *v.4 p.29*

New Directions in Creativity. *v.5 p.576*

New Directions in Dance. *v.1 p.44*

New Directions in Group Communication. *v.5 p.647*

New Directions in Music. *v.1 p.211*

New Directions in the Sociology of Global Development. *v.4 p.375*

New Directions in the Study of Language. *v.4 p.357*

New Directions in Water Resources Planning for the U. S. Army Corps of Engineers. *v.5 p.703*

New Discoveries in Agrochemicals. *v.5 p.9*

The New Division of Labor: How Computers Are Creating the Next Job Market. *v.4 p.253, p.254*

New Documentary: A Critical Introduction. *v.6 p.309*

The New Dollars and Dreams: American Incomes and Economic Change. *v.4 p.244, p.245, p.254, p.265*

A New Economic History of Argentina. *v.3 p.346*

The New Economic Sociology: A Reader. .*v.4 p.195, p.268, p.269*

The New Economics One Decade Older. *v.4 p.239*

New Economy Handbook. *v.4 p.190*

The New Empire: An Interpretation of American Expansion, 1860-1898. . . . .*v.3 p.398*

New Empire: An Interpretation of American Expansion, 1860-1898. . . . .*v.3 p.433*

The New Empire of Diocletian and Constantine. . . .*v.3 p.30*

New Encyclopedia of Southern Culture: Religion. . .*v.3 p.494*

The New Encyclopedia of the American West. *v.3 p.518*

New England: A Bibliography of Its History. *v.3 p.485*

New England: Additions to the 6 State Bibliographies. .*v.3 p.485*

The New England Clergy and the American Revolution. .*v.3 p.407*

New England Dissent, 1630-1833: The Baptists and the Separation of Church and State, Set. *v.1 p.583*

New England Frontier: Puritans and Indians, 1620-1675. . . . .*v.3 p.486, v.6 p.686*

New England Humor: From the Revolutionary War to the Civil War. *v.2 p.12*

New England in the English Nation, 1689-1713. . . .*v.3 p.485*

New England Indian Summer. *v.2 p.12*

New England Life in the 18th Century. *v.3 p.485*

New England Literary Culture: From the Revolution to the Renaissance. *v.2 p.12*

The New England Mind: From Colony to Province. *v.1 p.588, v.3 p.406, p.485*

The New England Mind: The Seventeenth Century. *v.1 p.588, v.3 p.406, p.485*

New England Saints. *v.3 p.486*

The New England Soul: Preaching and Religious Culture in Colonial New England. *v.1 p.588, p.649, p.650*

New England: The Greenwood Encyclopedia of American Regional Cultures. *v.3 p.485, p.486*

ⓔ New England's Moral Legislator: A Life of Timothy Dwight, 1752-1817. . . . .*v.1 p.584*

New English - Croatian Dictionary. *v.2 p.774*

The New English Novel in English: A Study of the 1980s. *v.2 p.760*

New Essays on Billy Budd. *v.2 p.49*

New Essays on Hemingway's Short Fiction. *v.2 p.85*

New Essays on the Country of the Pointed Firs. . . .*v.2 p.46*

New Essays on the Psychology of Art. *v.5 p.618*

New Eusebius. *v.1 p.600*

The New Face of Asian Pacific America: Numbers, Diversity, and Change in the 21st Century. *v.6 p.86*

New Faiths, Old Fears: Muslims and Other Asian Immigrants in American Religious Life. *v.6 p.106*

New Federalism: Intergovernmental Reform from Nixon to Reagan. *v.4 p.523*

New Feminist Art Criticism: Critical Strategies. . . .*v.1 p.706*

New Feminist Criticism: Art, Identity, Action. *v.6 p.472*

The New Financial Capitalists: Kohlberg Kravis Roberts and the Creation of Corporate Value. *v.4 p.90, p.99*

The New Financial Order: Risk in the 21st Century. *v.4 p.90, p.92, p.93, p.100*

The New Foreign Policy: U. S. and Comparative Foreign Policy in the 21st Century. *v.3 p.477*

New Formations, New Questions - Asian American Studies: Positions Special Issue, Vol. 5. . . . .*v.6 p.108*

New Found Lands: Maps in the History of Exploration. *v.4 p.379*

New Foundations: Ireland, 1660-1800. . . . .*v.3 p.137*

The New French Poetry. *v.2 p.464*

New Frontiers in Economics. *v.4 p.197*

New Game Plans for College Sport. *v.4 p.822, p.894*

The New Genetic Medicine: Theological and Ethical Reflections. *v.5 p.151*

New Genetics and New Public Health. *v.5 p.148*

The New German Cinema: Music, History, and the Matter of Style. *v.6 p.338*

New Ghosts, Old Dreams: Chinese Rebel Voices. . . .*v.6 p.196*

The New Girl: Girls' Culture in England, 1880-1915. .*v.6 p.479*

The New Global Mission: The Gospel from Everywhere to Everyone. *v.1 p.647*

The New Golden Rule: Community and Morality in a Democratic Society. *v.4 p.770*

The New Grove Dictionary of American Music. *v.1 p.160, p.278*

The New Grove Dictionary of Jazz. *v.1 p.160, p.260*

The New Grove Dictionary of Music and Musicians. .*v.1 p.162*

The New Grove Dictionary of Musical Instruments. *v.1 p.161, p.162, p.391*

The New Grove Dictionary of Opera, Set. .*v.1 p.162, p.232, p.233*

New Grove Dictionary of Women Composers. .*v.1 p.161, p.380*

New Grub Street. *v.2 p.290*

New Hampshire: A Guide to the Granite State. . . .*v.3 p.486*

A New Handbook of Christian Theology. *v.1 p.633*

New Handbook of Greek Mythology. *v.1 p.533, v.2 p.401*

The New Handbook of Organizational Communication: Advances in Theory, Research, and Methods. . . .*v.4 p.174*

The New Handbook of Research on Music Teaching and Learning: A Project of the Music Educators National Conference. *v.1 p.405*

New Hart's Rules: The Handbook of Style for Writers and Editors. *v.2 p.574*

The New Harvard Guide to Women's Health. *v.5 p.523*

New Historical Anthology of Music by Women. . . .*v.6 p.475*

A New Historical Geography of England. *v.3 p.126*

New Historicism and Cultural Materialism. *v.2 p.570*

New Historicism and Renaissance Drama: Longman Critical Readers. *v.2 p.186*

The New Historicism. *v.2 p.571*

A New History of Classical Rhetoric. *v.2 p.405*

A New History of Documentary Film. *v.6 p.309*

A New History of Early English Drama. .*v.1 p.73, p.99, v.2 p.185*

The New History of Florida. *v.3 p.504*

A New History of French Literature. *v.2 p.456*

A New History of German Literature. *v.3 p.160*

A New History of Identity: A Sociology of Medical Knowledge. *v.5 p.511*

A New History of India. *v.6 p.155*

New History of Ireland: Eighteenth Century Ireland, 1691-1800. . . . .*v.3 p.137*

A New History of Ireland: Medieval Ireland, 1169-1534. . . . .*v.3 p.136, v.6 p.562*

A New History of Japanese Cinema: A Century of Narrative Film. *v.6 p.336, p.337*

New History of Kentucky. *v.3 p.511*

New History of Portugal. *v.3 p.243, p.244*

A New History of Spanish Literature. *v.2 p.638*

A New History of the English Public Library: Social and Intellectual Contexts, 1850-1914. . . . .*v.6 p.738*

The New Hollywood: What the Movies Did with the New Freedoms of the Seventies. *v.6 p.340*

A New Home, Who'll Follow? *v.2 p.43*

New Horizons in Economic Thought: Appraisals of Leading Economists. *v.4 p.186*

New Horizons in the Study of Language and Mind. *v.5 p.620, p.623, p.624*

New Horizons: Yesterday's Portraits of Tomorrow. . . .*v.2 p.18*

The New Illustrated Encyclopedia of Billiards. *v.4 p.855*

New Imperialism. *v.3 p.447*

The New Industrial Economics: Recent Developments in Industrial Organization, Oligopoly and Game Theory. *v.4 p.207, p.252*

The New Industrial State. *v.4 p.213*

The New Institutional Economics of Corruption. .*v.4 p.252, p.263*

The New International Economic Order: The North-South Debate. *v.4 p.255*

The New International Money Game. *v.4 p.57, p.93, p.98, p.99, p.162*

The New Interpreter's Bible, Vol. 11. . . . .*v.1 p.615*

A New Introduction to Bibliography. *v.2 p.576*

A New Introduction to Chaucer: Longman Medieval and Renaissance. *v.2 p.207*

A New Introduction to Modal Logic. *v.1 p.492*

The New Iranian Cinema: Politics, Representation and Identity. *v.6 p.334*

The New Islamic Dynasties: a Chronological and Genealogical Manual. *v.6 p.581*

A New Island Biogeography of the Sea of Cortes. .*v.5 p.167, p.172*

The New Israel: Peacemaking and Liberalization. . . .*v.6 p.615*

The New Italian Poetry, Nineteen Forty-Five to the Present: A Bilingual Anthology. *v.2 p.700*

The New Italian Republic: From the Fall of the Berlin Wall to Berlusconi. *v.4 p.594*

The New Jerome Biblical Commentary. *v.1 p.615*

New Jersey: A Guide to Its Present and Past. *v.3 p.491*

New Jersey: Bicentennial and History Guide. *v.3 p.491*

New Kabuki Encyclopedia: A Revised Adaptation of Kabuki Jiten. *v.6 p.235*

New Keynesian Economics: Coordination Failures and Real Rigidities. *v.4 p.225*

New Keynesian Economics: Imperfect Competition and Sticky Prices. *v.4 p.225*

New Kid in School: Using Literature to Help Children in Transition. *v.4 p.312, p.365*

A New Kind of Science. *v.5 p.501*

The New Knighthood: A History of the Order of the Temple. *v.3 p.63*

The New Kobbe's Opera Book. *v.1 p.232*

New Labour's Pasts: The Labour Party and Its Discontents. *v.4 p.606*

New Lands, New Men: America and the Second Great Age of Discovery. *v.3 p.381*

New Latin Grammar. *v.2 p.423*

A New Latin Syntax. *v.2 p.424*

New Left Diplomatic Histories and Historians: The American Revisionists. *v.3 p.454*

New Life for the College Curriculum: Assessing Achievements and Furthering Progress in the Reform of General Education. *v.4 p.294*

The New Life. *v.6 p.667*

A New Look at Thai AIDS: Perspectives from the Margin. *v.4 p.668*

The New Mamluks: Egyptian Society and Modern Feudalism. *v.6 p.640*

The New Mandarins: How British Foreign Policy Works. *v.4 p.643, 645*

New Media: An Introduction. *v.4 p.419*

New Media and Public Imagination: Launching Radio, Television, and Digital Media in the United States. *v.4 p.418*

New Media in Art. *v.1 p.772*

New Media Technology: Cultural and Commercial Perspectives. *v.4 p.419*

New Men, New Cities, New South: Atlanta, Nashville, Charleston, Mobile, 1860-1910. . . . .*v.3 p.494*

The New Men's Studies: A Selected and Annotated Interdisciplinary Bibliography. *v.6 p.428*

New Methods of Celestial Mechanics, Set. *v.5 p.66*

New Methods of Measuring Marginal Utility. *v.4 p.195*

New Mexican Lives: Profiles and Historical Stories. . *v.3 p.528*

New Mexico: An Interpretive History. *v.3 p.528*

The New Middle Class and the Remaking of the Central City. *v.6 p.724*

The New Middle East. *v.6 p.594*

The New Model Army: In England, Ireland and Scotland, 1645-1653. . . . .*v.3 p.103*

The New Movement in the Theatre. *v.1 p.81, p.95, p.142*

New Mozart Documents: A Supplement to O. E. Deutsch's Documentary Biography. *v.1 p.189, p.343*

New Museum Theory and Practice: An Introduction. .*v.1 p.828*

The New Music, 1900-1960. . . . .*v.1 p.211, p.318*

New Musical Figurations: Anthony Braxton's Cultural Critique. *v.1 p.222, p.263, p.314*

New Musical Resources. *v.1 p.212, p.370*

The New Naked Poetry: Recent American Poetry in Open Forms. *v.2 p.22*

New Native American Drama: Three Plays. *v.1 p.65, p.124, v.6 p.698*

The New Negro. *v.6 p.7, p.39*

New Nukes: India, Pakistan and Global Nuclear Disarmament. *v.4 p.655*

The New Organon, and Related Writings. *v.1 p.447*

New Orleans: A Cultural History. *v.3 p.507*

New Orleans in the Gilded Age: Politics and Urban Progress, 1880-1896. . . . .*v.3 p.507, v.6 p.713*

The New Ourselves, Growing Older. *v.6 p.445*

New Oxford Annotated Bible: New Revised Standard Version with the Apocrypha. *v.1 p.613*

The New Oxford Book of American Verse. *v.2 p.22*

The New Oxford Book of Australian Verse. *v.2 p.743*

The New Oxford Book of Canadian Short Stories in English. *v.2 p.731*

The New Oxford Book of Canadian Verse in English. *v.2 p.731*

The New Oxford Book of Christian Verse. . . .*v.2 p.198, p.199*

The New Oxford Book of Eighteenth Century Verse. *v.2 p.200*

The New Oxford Book of English Light Verse. *v.2 p.198*

The New Oxford Book of English Prose. *v.2 p.202*

🄮 The New Oxford Book of Food Plants. *v.5 p.24*

The New Oxford Book of Romantic Period
   Verse. *v.2 p.197, p.200*

The New Oxford Book of Seventeenth-Century
   Verse. *v.2 p.196, p.199*

The New Oxford Book of Sixteenth-Century
   Verse. *v.2 p.197, p.199, p.200*

The New Oxford Book of Victorian Verse. . . .*v.2 p.197, p.201*

The New Oxford Companion to Literature in French. .*v.2 p.455*

The New Oxford History of Music: Romanticism
   (1830-1890). *v.1 p.193*

The New Oxford History of Music: The Early Middle Ages to
   1300. . . . .*v.1 p.177*

The New Painting: Impressionism 1874-1886. .*v.1 p.732, p.733*

The New Palaces of Medieval
   Venice. . . .*v.1 p.787, v.6 p.555, p.556, p.577, p.579, p.581*

The New Palgrave: A Dictionary of Economics. . . .*v.4 p.192*

The New Palgrave Dictionary of Economics and the
   Law. *v.4 p.191, p.434*

The New Paradigm in Architecture: The Language of
   Post-Modernism. *v.1 p.786*

New Party Politics: From Jefferson and Hamilton to the
   Information Age. *v.4 p.552, p.553*

The New Penguin Atlas of Ancient History. *v.3 p.3*

The New Penguin Dictionary of Biology. *v.5 p.224*

The New Penguin Dictionary of Science. *v.5 p.386*

New Perspectives on the Chinese Revolution. *v.6 p.192*

New Perspectives on the Civil War: Myths and Realities of the
   National Conflict. *v.3 p.401*

New Perspectives on the Cultural Revolution. *v.6 p.195*

The New Physical Anthropology. *v.4 p.15*

New Pioneers in the Heartland: Hmong Life in
   Wisconsin. *v.6 p.139*

The New Pioneers: The Men and Women Who are Transforming
   the Workplace and Market Place. *v.4 p.717*

The New Political Economy of J. S. Mill. *v.4 p.223*

The New Politics of Pornography. *v.6 p.469*

The New Politics of Science. *v.5 p.393, p.411*

The New Politics of the Budgetary Process. *v.6 p.301*

A New Pot of Gold: Hollywood Under the Electric Rainbow,
   1980-1989, Vol. 10. . . . .*v.6 p.343*

New Product Development and Delivery: Ensuring Successful
   Products Through Integrated Process Management. .*v.4 p.118*

New Product Development: Successful Innovation in the
   Marketplace. *v.4 p.144*

The New Public Service: Serving, Not
   Steering. *v.4 p.545, p.546, p.580*

The New Queer Aesthetic on Television: Essays on Recent
   Programming. *v.6 p.419*

New Queer Cinema: A Critical Reader. *v.6 p.415*

The New Quotable Woman. *v.6 p.426*

The New Radicalism in America, 1889-1963: The Intellectual
   As a Social Type. *v.4 p.768*

The New Ranch Handbook: A Guide to Restoring Western
   Rangelands. *v.5 p.42*

The New Rank and File. *v.4 p.127*

A New Reference Grammar of Modern Spanish. . . .*v.2 p.635*

The New Regime: Transformations of the French Civic Order,
   1789-1820s. *v.3 p.153*

The New Regionalism in Africa. *v.4 p.611*

New Relationship: Human Capital in the American
   Corporation. *v.4 p.76*

New Religions: New Religious Movements, Sects and
   Alternative Spiritualities. *v.1 p.658, p.659, p.661*

New Religious Movements in Nigeria. *v.6 p.71*

The New Religious-Political Right in America. . . .*v.3 p.472*

A New Republic: A History of the United States in the
   Twentieth Century. *v.3 p.369*

The New Restaurant Entrepreneur: An Inside Look at Restaurant
   Deal-Making and Other Tales from the Culinary
   Trenches. *v.4 p.165*

The New Right in Chile, 1973-97. . . . .*v.3 p.354*

The New Rolling Stone Album Guide. *v.1 p.170, p.266*

The New Royal Horticultural Society Dictionary of Gardening,
   Set. *v.5 p.43*

The New Rules of Measurement: What Every Psychologist and
   Educator Should Know. *v.5 p.600*

New Rules of Sociological Method. *v.4 p.686*

The New Ruthless Economy: Work and Power in the Digital
   Age. *v.4 p.69*

New Schools for a New Century: The Redesign of Urban
   Education. *v.4 p.315*

The New Science Literacy: Using Language Skills to Help
   Students Learn Science. *v.4 p.366*

New Science, New World. *v.4 p.378*

The New Science of Astrobiology: From Genesis of the Living
   Cell to Evolution of Intelligent Behavior in the
   Universe. *v.5 p.183, p.242*

The New Science of Intimate Relationships. *v.5 p.647*

New Science: Principles of the New Science Concerning the
   Common Nat- ure of Nations. *v.1 p.473*

A New Season: Using Title IX to Reform College
   Sports. *v.4 p.822, p.837, p.894, p.901*

New Selected Poems of Stevie Smith. *v.2 p.383*

A New Selected Poems. *v.2 p.92*

The New Shostakovich. *v.1 p.218, p.356*

New Social Movements: From Ideology to Identity. . .*v.4 p.710*

The New Society: The Anatomy of Industrial
   Order. *v.4 p.112, p.149*

The New Solar System. *v.5 p.68*

New Song and Dance from the Central Pacific: Creating and
   Performing the Fatele of Tokelau in the Islands and in New
   Zealand. *v.1 p.17*

New Sounds for Woodwind. *v.1 p.393, p.397*

The New South Creed: A Study in Southern
   Mythmaking. *v.3 p.494*

A New South Dakota History. *v.3 p.523*

New Soviet Thinking and U. S. Nuclear Policy. . . .*v.4 p.655*

The New Spaniards: A Portrait of the New Spain. . .*v.3 p.243*

A New Species of Trouble: Exploration in Community, Disaster
   and Trauma. *v.4 p.760*

The New Spirit: Modern Architecture in Vancouver,
   1938-1963. . . . .*v.1 p.790*

A New Stoicism. *v.1 p.428*

New subways for New York. *v.5 p.700*

The New Sufferings of Young W. *v.2 p.618*

A New Teacher's Guide: Surviving Your First Year. . *v.4 p.279*

New Technology of Pest Control. *v.5 p.9, p.368, p.380*

The New Testament: A Historical Introduction to the Early
    Christian Writings. *v.1 p.624*

The New Testament and Rabbinic Judaism. *v.1 p.625*

New Testament Apocrypha: Gospels and Related
    Writings. *v.1 p.632*

New Testament Apocrypha: Writings Relating to the Apostles;
    Apocalypses and Related Topics. *v.1 p.632*

New Testament Cities in Western Asia Minor: Light from
    Archaeology on Cities of Paul and the Seven Churches of
    Revelation. *v.1 p.618*

The New Testament Environment. *v.1 p.627*

New Testament Foundations: A Guide for Christian
    Students. *v.1 p.624*

New Testament History. *v.1 p.626*

The New Testament in Its Literary Environment. . . .*v.1 p.624*

New Testament in Modern English. *v.1 p.613, p.614*

New Testament Interpretation and Methods: A Sheffield
    Book. *v.1 p.625*

New Testament Interpretation Through Rhetorical
    Criticism. *v.1 p.625*

New Testament Interpretation. *v.1 p.625*

The New Testament: The History of the Investigation of Its
    Problems. *v.1 p.625*

New Testament Theology. *v.1 p.641*

The New Testament World: Insights from Cultural
    Anthropology. *v.1 p.625*

New Thinking in Economics. *v.4 p.197*

The New Tibetan-English Dictionary of Modern
    Tibetan. *v.6 p.241*

New Towns for Old: Achievements in Civic Improvement in
    Some American Small Towns and Neighborhoods. *v.1 p.814*

The New Transnational Activism. *v.4 p.625*

New Trends in Allergy IV, Together with Environmental Allergy
    and Allergotoxicology III: Joint International
    Symposium, Hamburg, April 29-May 1, 1995. . . .*v.5 p.365*

New Trends in Allergy V. *v.5 p.365*

New Trends in Macroeconomics. *v.4 p.199, p.240*

The New Unionism: Employee Involvement in the Changing
    Corporation. *v.4 p.122*

The New Update on Adult Learning Theory: New Directions for
    Adult and Continuing Education. *v.4 p.321*

The New Urban Frontier: Gentrification and the Revanchist
    City. *v.6 p.729*

The New Urban Reality. *v.6 p.719*

New Urbanism and American Planning: The Conflict of
    Cultures. *v.6 p.715*

A New Variorum Edition of Shakespeare, Set. *v.2 p.223*

New Views of Borderlands History. *v.3 p.527*

New Views of Nineteenth-Century Ireland: A Guide to Recent
    Research. *v.3 p.138*

New Vision for Management Education: Leadership
    Challenges. *v.4 p.176*

The New Vision: Photography Between the World Wars-The
    Ford Motor Company Collection at the Metropolitan
    Museum of Art. *v.1 p.762*

New Visions in Asian American Studies: Diversity, Community,
    Power. *v.6 p.85, p.109*

The New Westminster Dictionary of Christian
    Spirituality. *v.1 p.651*

The New Westminster Dictionary of Liturgy and
    Worship. *v.1 p.654*

New Wineskins: Reimagining Religious Life Today. . *v.1 p.578*

New Woman Strategies: Sarah Grand, Olive Schreiner, and
    Mona Caird. *v.2 p.191*

New Women, New Novels: Feminism and Early
    Modernism. *v.2 p.173, v.6 p.746, p.755*

New Women: Short Stories by Canadian Women,
    1900-1920. . . . .*v.2 p.731*

The New Workplace: A Guide to the Human Impact of Modern
    Working Practices. *v.5 p.580*

New World Avenue and Vicinity. *v.2 p.790*

New World Coming: The 1920s and the Making of Modern
    America. *v.3 p.372*

New World Coming: The 1920's and the Making of Modern
    America. *v.3 p.372*

New World Coming: The 1920s and the Making of Modern
    America. *v.3 p.449*

New World Coming: The 1920's and the Making of Modern
    America. *v.3 p.449*

New World Disorder: The Leninist Extinction. *v.4 p.491, p.492*

The New World Disorder. *v.4 p.629*

The New World Inside a Basque Village: The Oiartzun Valley
    and Its Atlantic Emigrants, 1550-1800. . . . . .*v.3 p.287*

New World Modernisms: T. S. Eliot, Derek Walcott, and Kamau
    Brathwaite. *v.2 p.768*

New World, New Rules: The Changing Role of the American
    Corporation. *v.4 p.271*

The New World of Mr. Tompkins. *v.5 p.540*

The New World Power: American Foreign Policy,
    1898-1917. . . . .*v.3 p.452*

New Worlds, New Animals: From Menagerie to Zoological Park
    in the Nineteenth Century. *v.5 p.83*

New Worlds, New Lives: Globalization and People of Japanese
    Descent in the Americas and from Latin America in
    Japan. *v.6 p.118, p.131*

New Worlds of Dvorak: Searching in America for the
    Composers Inner Life. *v.1 p.193, p.194, p.322*

New Worlds: The Great Voyages of Discovery,
    1400-1600. . . . .*v.4 p.377, p.378*

New Writing in Israel. *v.6 p.652*

New Year in Cuba: Mary Gardner Lowell's Travel Diary,
    1831-1832. . . . .*v.3 p.311*

New York 1880: Architecture and Urbanism in the Gilded
    Age. *v.1 p.791*

New York Before Chinatown: Orientalism and the Shaping of
    American Culture, 1776-1882. . . . *v.6 p.114, p.124, p.128*

The New York Botanical Garden: An Illustrated Chronicle of
    Plants and People. *v.5 p.85*

New York Botanical Garden Illustrated Encyclopaedia of
    Horticulture, Vol. 1. . . . .*v.5 p.44*

New York Botanical Garden Illustrated Encyclopaedia of
Horticulture, Vol. 2. . . . .*v.5 p.44*

New York Botanical Garden Illustrated Encyclopaedia of
Horticulture, Vol. 3. . . . .*v.5 p.44*

New York Botanical Garden Illustrated Encyclopaedia of
Horticulture, Vol. 4. . . . .*v.5 p.44*

New York: Capital of Photography. *v.1 p.764*

New York, Chicago, Los Angeles: America's Global
Cities. *v.6 p.722*

New York City: A Short History. *v.3 p.491, v.6 p.714*

The New York Musicals of Comden and Green: On the Town,
Wonderful Town, Bells Are Ringing. *v.1 p.249, p.311, p.407*

The New York Public Library African American Desk
Reference. *v.6 p.14, p.34*

The New York Public Library American History Desk
Reference. *v.3 p.372*

New York Public Library Desk Reference to the Performing
Arts. *v.1 p.4*

New York Ricans from the Hip Hop Zone. *v.6 p.519*

The New York Schools of Music and Visual Arts : John Cage,
Morton Feldman, Edgard Varèse, Willem De
Kooning, Jasper Johns, Robert Rauschenberg. . .*v.1 p.207*

New York State: A Guide to the Empire State. . . .*v.3 p.490*

New York: State and City. *v.3 p.490*

The New York Times Encyclopedia of Film, Set. . .*v.6 p.305*

The New York Times Guide to the Best Children's
Videos. *v.6 p.311*

The New York Times Theater Reviews,
1870-1990. . . . .*v.1 p.111, p.137, p.139*

The New York Times Theater Reviews,
1995-1996. . . . .*v.1 p.111, p.137, p.139*

The New York Times Theater Reviews
1997-1998. . . . .*v.1 p.118, p.138, p.141*

The New York Times Theatre Reviews,
1991-92. . . . .*v.1 p.117, p.137, p.141*

The New York Times Theatre Reviews,
1999-2000. . . . .*v.1 p.117, p.137, p.141*

New York Trilogy. *v.2 p.140*

New Zealand: Aotearoa — Land of the Long White
Cloud. *v.4 p.385*

☐ New Zealand Electronic Poetry Centre. *v.2 p.743*

☐ New Zealand Electronic Text Centre. *v.2 p.742*

The New Zealand Liberals: The Years of Power,
1891-1912. . . . .*v.4 p.624*

☐ New Zealand Literature File. *v.2 p.740*

New Zealand Multicultural Writing. *v.2 p.740*

The New Zealand Wars Trilogy: House of Strife, Monday's
Warriors, Season of the Jew. *v.2 p.748*

☐ New Zealand Writer Files. *v.2 p.740*

The Newark Teacher Strikes: Hopes on the Line. . .*v.4 p.282*

New-Brutality Film: Race and Affect in Contemporary American
Film. *v.6 p.321*

The Newcomes. *v.2 p.315, p.316*

A Newer World: Kit Carson, John C. Fremont and the Claiming
of the American West. *v.3 p.520*

Newfoundland and Labrador. *v.3 p.547*

Newfoundland in the Nineteenth and Twentieth Centuries:
Essays in Interpretation. *v.3 p.547*

Newfoundland. *v.3 p.547*

Newjack: Guarding Sing Sing. *v.6 p.275, p.276*

The Newly Independent States of Eurasia: Handbook of Former
Soviet Republics. *v.3 p.229*

The News at Any Cost: How Journalists Compromise Their
Ethics to Shape the News. *v.4 p.405*

News, Crime and Culture. *v.4 p.407*

News from Nowhere and Selected Writings and Design. .*v.2 p.302*

News from Nowhere or an Epoch of Rest. *v.2 p.301*

News from Nowhere. *v.4 p.499*

News, Gender and Power. *v.4 p.414*

News in a New Century: Reporting in an Age of Converging
Media. *v.4 p.414*

News of the World: World Cultures Look at Television
News. *v.4 p.414*

News Ombudsmen in North America: Assessing an Experiment
in Social Responsibility. *v.4 p.411*

News Reporting and Writing. *v.4 p.414*

☐ Newsletter for Educational Psychologists. *v.5 p.571*

☐ Newspaper Association of America. *v.4 p.410*

Newspapers and the Making of Modern America: A
History. *v.4 p.411*

News. *v.4 p.412*

Newton D. Baker: America at War. *v.3 p.477*

Newton on the Tee: A Good Walk Through the Science of
Golf. *v.4 p.861, p.871*

Newtonian Mechanics. *v.5 p.546*

The Newtonian Moment: Isaac Newton and the Making of
Modern Culture. *v.3 p.47*

Newton's Principia for the Common
Reader. *v.5 p.61, p.546, p.555, p.556*

The Next America: The Decline and Rise of the United
States. *v.4 p.703*

The Next Attack: The Failure of the War on Terror and a
Strategy for Getting It Right. *v.4 p.562*

The Next Christendom: The Coming of Global
Christianity. *v.1 p.596, p.597, p.647*

Next Generation Wireless Systems and Networks. . . .*v.5 p.726*

Next Week, Swan Lake: Reflections on Dance and
Dances. *v.1 p.23, p.40*

Next Year in Cuba: A Cubano's Coming-Of-Age in
America. *v.6 p.490, p.542*

Next-Day Job Interview: Prepare Tonight and Get the Job
Tomorrow. *v.4 p.169*

Ngugi Wa Thiong'o: An Exploration of His Writings. .*v.2 p.758*

Ngugi Wa Thiong'o Speaks: Interviews with the Kenyan
Writer. *v.2 p.758*

Ngugi Wa Thiong'o: Text and Contexts. *v.2 p.758*

Ngugi wa Thiong'o. *v.2 p.758*

Ngugi Wa Thiongo. *v.2 p.758*

Ngugi's Novels and African History: Narrating the
Nation. *v.2 p.759*

☐ NHERI: National Home Education Resource
Institute. *v.4 p.296*

Nibelungenlied. Mittelhochdeutsch / Neuhochdeutsch. .*v.2 p.594*

The Nibelungenlied: Prose Translation. *v.2 p.595*

Nicaragua Colonial. *v.3 p.302*

Nicaragua's Other Revolution: Religious Faith and Political Struggle. *v.3 p.301*

Niccolo Machiavelli. *v.2 p.709*

Niccolo's Smile: A Biography of Machiavelli.. . . . .*v.3 p.200*

The Nice and the Good. *v.2 p.372*

Nice Girls Don't Get the Corner Office: 101 Unconscious Mistakes Women Make That Sabotage Their Careers. *v.4 p.167*

Nice Work If You Can Get It: My Life in Rhythm and Rhyme. *v.6 p.409*

Nicholas I: Emperor and Autocrat of All the Russias. .*v.3 p.219*

Nicholas II. *v.3 p.220*

Nicholas Kaldor and the Real World. *v.4 p.271*

Nicholas Nickleby. *v.2 p.284*

Nicholas of Cusa: The Catholic Concordance. *v.1 p.576*

Nicholas Rowe and the Beginnings of Feminism on the London Stage. *v.2 p.258*

Nicholas Rowe. *v.2 p.258*

Nicholas the First and the Russian Intervention in Hungary. *v.3 p.186, p.219*

The Nick Adams Stories. *v.2 p.84*

Nickel and Dimed: On (Not) Getting by in America. .*v.6 p.464*

Nickel and Human Health: Current Perspectives. . . .*v.5 p.366*

Nickel, Cobalt, and Their Alloys. *v.5 p.736*

Nicolas Poussin. *v.1 p.744*

Nicolas Slonimsky: The First Hundred Years. *v.1 p.248*

Nicolaus Copernicus: An Essay on His Life and Work. .*v.3 p.47*

The Nicomachean Ethics, Bks. VIII & IX. *v.1 p.426*

The Nicomachean Ethics. *v.2 p.408*

Niels Lyhne. *v.2 p.627*

Nietzsche: A Philosophical Biography. *v.1 p.467*

Nietzsche and Modern Times: A Study of Bacon, Descartes, and Nietzsche.. . . . .*v.1 p.466*

Nietzsche and Music. *v.1 p.200, p.381, p.382*

Nietzsche and Philosophy. *v.1 p.466*

Nietzsche and the Politics of Aristocratic Radicalism. .*v.4 p.491*

Nietzsche As Philosopher. *v.1 p.466*

Nietzsche: Beyond Good and Evil. *v.1 p.467*

Nietzsche, Genealogy, Morality: Essays on Nietzsche's Genealogy of Morals. *v.1 p.467*

Nietzsche: Philosopher, Psychologist, Antichrist.. . . .*v.1 p.466*

Nietzsche: The Anti-Christ, Ecce Homo, Twilight of the Idols: And Other Writings. *v.1 p.466*

Nietzsche: The Anti-Christ, Ecce Homo, Twilight of the Idols:And Other Writings. *v.1 p.467*

Nietzsche: The Birth of Tragedy and Other Writings. .*v.1 p.467*

Nietzsche: The Man and his Philosophy. *v.1 p.466*

Nietzsche: Thus Spoke Zarathustra. *v.1 p.467*

Nietzsche, Vols. 1&2. . . . .*v.1 p.466*

Nietzsche's Revaluation of Values: A Study in Strategies. *v.1 p.467*

Nietzsche. *v.1 p.467*

La Niña y Otros Relatos. *v.2 p.661*

Nigeria, Africa, and the United States: From Kennedy to Reagan. *v.3 p.392*

Nigerian Theatre in English. *v.1 p.58, p.59, p.130*

Nigerian Women Mobilized: Women's Political Activity in Southern Nigeria, 1900-1965. . . . .*v.6 p.71, p.72*

Nigger Heaven. *v.2 p.126*

The Nigger of the Narcissus. *v.2 p.340, p.341*

Night: A Novel. *v.6 p.667*

Night and Day. *v.2 p.394*

Night and Horses and the Desert: An Anthology of Classical Arabic Literature. *v.6 p.660*

The Night Battles: Witchcraft and Agrarian Cults in the Sixteenth and Seventeenth Centuries. *v.3 p.201*

The Night Country. *v.5 p.221*

Night Flight. *v.2 p.526*

Night Kites. *v.6 p.379, p.397*

'Night, Mother. *v.2 p.151*

Night of Denial: Stories and Novellas. *v.2 p.802*

A Night of Terror. *v.2 p.497*

Night of the First Billion. *v.6 p.663*

Night Rider. *v.2 p.129*

Night Thoughts of a Classical Physicist. *v.5 p.543*

The Nightingale's Burden: Women Poets and American Culture Before 1900. . . . .*v.2 p.8, p.9*

A Nightingale's Lament: Selections from the Poems and Fables of Parvin Etesami (1907-41). *v.6 p.671*

Nightly Business Report Presents Lasting Leadership: What You Can Learn from the Top 25 Business People of our Times. *v.4 p.71*

Nightmare Abbey. *v.2 p.302*

Nightmare in Red: The McCarthy Era in Perspective. .*v.3 p.447*

The Nightmare of Reason: A Life of Franz Kafka. . .*v.2 p.611*

The Nightmare: Psychological and Biological Foundations. *v.5 p.613*

Nightmare: The Underside of the Nixon Years. . . .*v.3 p.474*

Nights at the Circus. *v.2 p.336*

Nights in the Gardens of Spain. *v.2 p.746*

Nightsong: Performance, Power, and Practice in South Africa. *v.1 p.285*

Nightwatch: The Politics of Protest in the Peruvian Andes. *v.3 p.331*

Nightwood: The Original Version and Related Drafts. .*v.6 p.394*

Nightwood. *v.2 p.330, p.331*

Nightwork: Sexuality, Pleasure, and Corporate Masculinity in a Tokyo Hostess Club. *v.6 p.218*

Nihilistic Egoist. *v.1 p.504*

Nihongi: Chronicles of Japan from the Earliest Times to A.D. 697. . . . .*v.6 p.223*

Nijinsky, Pavlova, Duncan: Three Lives in Dance.. . .*v.6 p.414*

Nijinsky. *v.1 p.6*

Nike Is a Goddess: The History of Women in Sports. *v.4 p.809, p.810, p.838*

Nikola the Outlaw. *v.2 p.784*

Nikolaus Lenau. *v.2 p.601, p.602*

Nilda. *v.6 p.507*

Nimes at War: Religion, Politics, and Public Opinion in the Gard, 1938-1944. . . . . *v.3 p.156*

Nimrud: An Assyrian Imperial City Revealed. *v.3 p.6*

Nine and Counting: American Politics as Seen by the Most Influential Women Who Make and Shape It. . . . *v.3 p.455*

Nine Classic French Plays. *v.2 p.465*

Nine Indian Women Poets: An Anthology. *v.2 p.763*

Nine Lives?: The Politics of Constitutional Reform in Japan. *v.4 p.621*

Nine, Novena. *v.2 p.691*

Nine Stories. *v.2 p.118*

The Nine Tailors. *v.2 p.382*

Nineteen Eighty-Four. *v.2 p.376*

Nineteen Ways of Looking at Wang Wei: How a Chinese Poem is Translated. *v.6 p.210*

Nineteen Weeks: America, Britain, and the Fateful Summer of 1940. . . . . *v.4 p.647*

The Nineteenth and Twentieth Centuries, 1870-1940. . *v.2 p.455*

The Nineteenth Century, 1789-1870. . . . . *v.2 p.455*

Nineteenth Century Art: A Critical History. *v.1 p.678*

Nineteenth Century French Plays. *v.2 p.461*

Nineteenth Century Ireland: The Search for Stability. *v.3 p.134, p.138*

The Nineteenth Century Novel: A Critical Reader. *v.2 p.176, p.193*

Nineteenth Century Stories by Women: An Anthology. *v.2 p.27*

The Nineteenth Century Symphony. *v.1 p.198, p.240*

The Nineteenth Century. *v.1 p.438*

Nineteenth-Century American Poetry. *v.2 p.24*

Nineteenth-Century American Women Writers: A Bio-Bibliographical Critical Sourcebook. *v.6 p.479*

Nineteenth-Century Britain: Integration and Diversity. *v.3 p.115, v.6 p.735*

Nineteenth-Century Decoration: The Art of the Interior. *v.1 p.799*

Nineteenth-Century European Art: A Topical Dictionary. *v.1 p.666*

Nineteenth-Century European Art. *v.1 p.677, p.686*

Nineteenth-Century French Poetry: Introductions to Close Reading. *v.2 p.461*

Nineteenth-Century Media and the Construction of Identities. *v.6 p.740, p.741*

Nineteenth-Century Music and the German Romantic Ideology. *v.1 p.196, p.245*

Nineteenth-Century Music: The Western Classical Tradition. *v.1 p.197*

A Nineteenth-Century Musical Chronicle: Events, 1800-1899, 21B. *v.1 p.197, p.198*

Nineteenth-Century Music. *v.1 p.196*

The Nineteenth-Century Novel: Identities. . . *v.2 p.177, p.194*

Nineteenth-Century Philosophy. *v.1 p.438*

Nineteenth-Century Russian Literature in English: A Bibliography of Criticism and Translations. . . . *v.2 p.795*

Nineteenth-Century Studies, Coleridge to Matthew Arnold. *v.6 p.751, p.753, p.754*

Nineteenth-Century Watercolors. *v.1 p.734*

Nineteenth-Century Women at the Movies: Adapting Classic Women's Fiction to Film. *v.6 p.326*

Nineteenth-Century Women Poets: An Oxford Anthology. *v.2 p.196, p.198*

Ninety-Nine Poems in Translation: An Anthology. . . *v.2 p.583*

Nineveh and Its Remains: With a New Introduction by Stephanie Dalley. *v.3 p.5*

Ninfale fiesolano. *v.2 p.701*

El Nino Que Buscaba a Ayer. *v.2 p.674*

Ninth Justice: The Fight for Bork. *v.4 p.538*

The Ninth State: New Hampshire's Formative Years. *v.3 p.486, p.487*

☐ NIOSH Manual of Analytical Methods (NMAM). *v.5 p.268*

NIOSH Pocket Guide to Chemical Hazards. *v.5 p.315, v.6 p.285, p.286*

☐ NIOSH Pocket Guide to Chemical Hazards. . . . *v.5 p.315*

☐ NIOSH: The National Institute for Occupational Safety and Health Mining Safety and Health Research. . . . *v.5 p.737*

☐ NIOSHTIC-2 (bibliographic database). *v.5 p.580*

☐ NIRA's World Directory of Think Tanks. *v.4 p.560*

The Nirvana Companion: Two Decades of Commentary. *v.1 p.273, p.274, p.346*

Nisa: The Life and Words of a Kung Woman. *v.4 p.38*

Nisei Daughter. *v.6 p.95*

Nisei/Sansei: Shifting Japanese American Identities and Politics. *v.6 p.132*

☐ NIST Chemistry WebBook. *v.5 p.280*

☐ NIST Chemistry Webbook. *v.5 p.406*

☐ NIST Physical Reference Data. *v.5 p.406, p.545*

☐ NIST Virtual Library--Chemistry. *v.5 p.255*

NIST-JANAF Thermochemical Tables, 2 v. *v.5 p.286*

NIST-JANAF Thermochemical Tables, Pt. 1. . . . . *v.5 p.286*

NIST-JANAF Thermochemical Tables. *v.5 p.286*

The Nitrate Industry and Chile's Crucial Transition. . *v.3 p.351*

Nitric Oxide Protocols. *v.5 p.113*

The Nitro Group in Organic Synthesis. *v.5 p.295*

Nitrogen Cycling in Coastal Marine Environments: Scope 33. . . . . *v.5 p.173*

Nitrogen Fixation at the Millennium. *v.5 p.50*

Nitrogen Fixation. *v.5 p.50*

Nitrogen in Terrestrial Ecosystems: Questions of Productivity, Vegetational Changes and Ecosystem Stability. . . *v.5 p.187*

Nitrogen Management in Irrigated Agriculture. *v.5 p.50*

NIV Ministry/Pew Bible. *v.1 p.614*

Nixon Agonistes: The Crisis of the Self-Made Man. . *v.3 p.482*

Nixon and the Environment. *v.4 p.566, v.6 p.299, p.300*

Nixon in the White House: The Frustration of Power. *v.3 p.470*

Nixon Reconsidered. *v.3 p.472*

Nixon: Ruin and Recovery, 1973-1990. . . . . . . *v.3 p.464*

Nixon: The Education of a Politician, 1913-1962. . . *v.3 p.464*

Nixon: The Triumph of a Politician, 1962-1972. . . . *v.3 p.464*

Nixon-Kissinger Years: The Reshaping of American Foreign Policy. *v.3 p.480*

Nixon's Shadow: The History of an Image. *v.3 p.471*

Nixon. *v.3 p.476*

Njals Saga: A Literary Masterpiece. *v.2 p.625*

Njáls Saga: A Critical Introduction. *v.2 p.624*

Nkrumah and the Chiefs: The Politics of Chieftaincy in Ghana, 1951-1960. . . . .*v.6 p.70*

◻ NMPA = National Music Publishers' Association. *v.1 p.172, p.385*

NMR Data Tables for Organic Compounds, 1. . . . .*v.5 p.290*

NMR, NQR, EPR, and Mossbauer Spectroscopy in Inorganic Chemistry. *v.5 p.305*

NMR of Polymers. *v.5 p.323*

NMR Spectroscopy: Processing Strategies. *v.5 p.272*

No Aging in India: Alzheimer's, Bad Families, and Other Modern Things. *v.6 p.153*

No and Bunraku: Two Forms of Japanese Theatre. *v.1 p.132, p.134*

No Author Better Served: The Correspondence of Samuel Beckett and Alan Schneider. *v.2 p.333*

No Band of Brothers: Problems of the Rebel High Command. *v.4 p.522*

No Bones: A Key to Bugs and Slugs, Worms, and Ticks, Spiders and Centipedes, and Other Creepy Crawlies. *v.5 p.96, p.157*

No Common Power: Understanding International Relations. *v.4 p.625*

No Compromise: Selected Writings of Karl Kraus. .*v.2 p.611*

No Constitutional Right to Be Ladies: Women and the Obligations of Citizenship. *v.6 p.441*

No Distinction of Sex?: Women in British Universities, 1870-1939. . . . .*v.6 p.745, p.747*

No End to War: Terrorism in the 21st Century. *v.4 p.660*

No Excuses!: The True Story of a Congenital Amputee Who Became a Champion in Wrestling and in Life.*v.4 p.842, p.870*

No Exit and Three Other Plays. *v.2 p.527*

No Exit?: The Origin and Evolution of U. S. Policy Toward China, 1945-1950. . . . .*v.3 p.393, v.6 p.205*

No Fire Next Time: Black-Korean Conflicts and the Future of America's Cities. *v.6 p.114, p.123, p.135*

No Fixed Points: Dance in the Twentieth Century. . . .*v.1 p.5*

No Free Lunch: Why Specified Complexity Cannot Be Purchased Without Intelligence. *v.5 p.191*

No Gifts from Chance: A Biography of Edith Wharton.*v.2 p.131*

No Gods and Precious Few Heroes: Scotland, 1914-1980. . . . .*v.3 p.133*

No Holds Barred: Negativity in United States Senate Campaigns. *v.4 p.530*

No Intermissions: The Life of Agnes De Mille. *v.1 p.7*

No Longer Human. *v.6 p.229*

No Longer Invisible: Afro-Latin Americans Today. . .*v.3 p.279*

No Longer Patient: Feminist Ethics and Health Care. *v.6 p.444, p.461, p.462*

No Magic Bullet: A Social History of Venereal Disease in the United States Since 1880. . . . .*v.5 p.516*

No Man Is an Island. *v.1 p.578*

No Man's Garden: Thoreau and a New Vision for Civilization and Nature. *v.5 p.409, v.6 p.288*

No Man's Land, The Place of the Woman Writer in the Twentieth Century: Letters from the Front. *v.2 p.178*

No Man's Land: The Place of the Woman Writer in the Twentieth Century: Sexchanges. *v.2 p.178*

No Man's Land, The Place of the Woman Writer in the Twentieth Century: The War of the Words. *v.2 p.178*

No Man's Land. *v.2 p.351*

No More Kin: Exploring Race, Class, and Gender in Family Networks. *v.4 p.734, p.735*

No More Masks: An Anthology of Twentieth-Century American Women Poets. *v.2 p.23*

No More Rules: Graphic Design and Postmodernism. *v.1 p.713*

No More Secrets: Violence in Lesbian Relationships. *v.6 p.377*

No More. *v.2 p.516*

No Name. *v.2 p.280*

No Neutral Ground: Standing by the Values We Prize in Higher Education. *v.4 p.291*

No One Home: Brazilian Selves Remade in Japan. . . .*v.4 p.39*

No One Writes to the Colonel: And Other Stories. . . .*v.2 p.683*

No Ordinary Genius: The Illustrated Richard Feynman.*v.5 p.540*

No Ordinary Time: Franklin and Eleanor Roosevelt: The Home Front in World War II. *v.3 p.458*

No Other Gods: On Science and American Social Thought. *v.5 p.389, p.394, p.410*

No Other Way Out: States and Revolutionary Movements, 1945-1991. . . . .*v.4 p.497*

No Peace, No War: An Anthropology of Contemporary Armed Conflicts. *v.4 p.34*

No Place for a Woman: A Life of Senator Margaret Chase Smith. *v.3 p.462*

No Place Like Home: Relationships and Family Life among Lesbians and Gay Men. *v.6 p.376*

No Place of Grace: Antimodernism and the Transformation of American Culture, 1880-1920. . . . .*v.3 p.368*

No Room of Their Own: Gender and Nation in Israeli Women's Fiction. *v.6 p.648*

No Safe Haven: Male Violence Against Women at Home, at Work, and in the Community. *v.6 p.446, p.470*

No Shame in My Game: The Working Poor in the Inner City. *v.4 p.771*

No Short Journeys: The Interplay of Cultures in the History and Literature of the Borderlands. *v.6 p.503, p.515*

No Signposts in the Sea. *v.2 p.381*

No Sword to Bury: Japanese Americans in Hawaii During World War II. *v.6 p.116, p.132*

No Thanks. *v.2 p.68*

No Time to be Brief: A Scientific Biography of Wolfgang Pauli. *v.5 p.542*

No Turning Back: The History of Feminism and the Future of Women. *v.6 p.433*

No Way. *v.2 p.717*

◻ NOAA Home Page - Weather Theme Page. *v.5 p.426*

◻ NOAA Paleoclimatology. *v.5 p.445*

◻ NOAA Photo Library. *v.5 p.417*

Noah's Choice: The Future of Endangered Species. . .*v.5 p.180*

Noam Chomsky. *v.2 p.560, p.561*

Nobel Laureates in Chemistry: 1901-1992. . . . . . .*v.5 p.261*

The Nobel Lecture in Literature 2003. . . . .*v.2 p.754*

Nobel Lectures in Chemistry: 1996-2000. . . . .*v.5 p.261*

Nobility and Civility: Asian Ideals of Leadership and the
    Common Good. *v.4 p.616, p.617*

The Nobility of Failure: Tragic Heroes in the History of
    Japan. *v.6 p.228*

The Nobility of Later Medieval England: The Ford Lectures for
    1953 and Related Studies. *v.6 p.576*

Noble Dreams, Wicked Pleasures: Orientalism in America,
    1870-1930. . . . .*v.1 p.678, p.682*

Noble Lives: Biographical Portraits of Three Remarkable Gay
    Men—Glenway Wescott, Aaron Copland, and Dag
    Hammarskjöld. *v.6 p.410*

Noble Nationalists: The Transformation of the Bohemian
    Aristocracy. *v.3 p.188*

Noble Savage Jean Jacques Rousseau. *v.2 p.481*

The Noble Savage: Jean-Jacques Rousseau, 1754-1762..*v.3 p.147*

Nobody's Angels: Middle-Class Women and Domestic Ideology
    in Victorian Culture. . .*v.6 p.744, p.747, p.748, p.756, p.765*

Nobody's Fool. *v.1 p.8*

Nobody's Nation: Reading Derek Walcott. *v.2 p.770*

Nobody's Story: The Vanishing Acts of Women Writers in the
    Marketplace, 1670-1820. . . . .*v.2 p.170*

Nocturnal Butterflies of the Russian Empire: A Novel. *v.2 p.673*

The Nocturnal Naturalist: Exploring the Outdoors at
    Night. *v.5 p.227*

Nocturne and Five Tales of Love and Death. *v.2 p.716*

Nocturnes for the King of Naples. *v.6 p.400*

Noel Coward Collected Plays: Private Lives; Bitter Sweet; The
    Marquise; Post Mortem. *v.2 p.342*

Noel Coward Collected Plays: Semi Monde; Point Valaine;
    South Sea Bubble; Nude with Violin. *v.2 p.342*

Noel Coward Diaries. *v.2 p.342*

Noel Coward: The Complete Illustrated
    Lyrics. *v.1 p.249, p.407, p.411*

Noguchi East and West. *v.1 p.778*

The Noh Drama: Ten Plays from the Japanese Selected and
    Translated by the Special Noh Committee, Japanese
    Classics Translation Committee, Nippon Gakujutsu
    Shinkokai. *v.1 p.129, p.132, p.133*

The Noh Theatre of Japan: With Complete Texts of 15 Classic
    Plays. *v.1 p.129, p.133, p.134,v.6 p.235*

Noise. *v.1 p.376*

Noli Me Tangere. *v.2 p.687*

Nolo's Encyclopedia of Everyday Law: Answers to Your Most
    Frequently Asked Legal Questions. *v.4 p.441*

Nolo's Simple Will Book. *v.4 p.443*

Nom d'une pipe! : dictionnaire français-anglais des expressions
    courantes (2). *v.2 p.453*

Nomads and Ottomans in Medieval Anatolia. *v.6 p.623*

Nomads and Settlers in Syria and Jordan,
    1800-1980. . . . .*v.6 p.607, p.621*

Nomads and the Outside World. *v.4 p.708, p.709*

Nomads of the Nomads: the Al Murrah Bedouin of the Empty
    Quarter. *v.6 p.596*

Nomads of Western Tibet: The Survival of a Way of
    Life. *v.6 p.240*

Nomenclature of Inorganic Chemistry II: Recommendations
    2000. . . . .*v.5 p.302*

Nomenclature of Inorganic Chemistry: Recommendations
    2005. . . . .*v.5 p.301, p.302*

Nomenclature of Organic Chemistry: Sections A, B and
    C. *v.5 p.289*

Nomenclature of Organic Compounds: Principles and
    Practice. *v.5 p.289*

Nomination and Election of the President and Vice President
    of the United States, Including the Manner of
    Selecting Delegates to National Political
    Conventions. *v.4 p.460, p.461*

Nonaqueous Electrochemistry. *v.5 p.285*

Noncommutative Rings. *v.5 p.473*

The Non-Darwinian Revolution: Reinterpreting a Historical
    Myth. *v.5 p.202*

Nondestructive Evaluation: A Tool in Design, Manufacturing
    and Service. *v.5 p.684*

Nondestructive Evaluation and Quality Control. . . .*v.5 p.687*

Nondestructive Testing. *v.5 p.688*

None Is Too Many: Canada and the Jews of Europe,
    1933-1948. . . . .*v.3 p.542*

None of Us Will Return: Auschwitz and After. *v.3 p.83*

The Nonexistent Knight and the Cloven Viscount. . .*v.2 p.714*

Nonfiction Film: A Critical History. *v.6 p.308*

Nonindigenous Freshwater Organisms: Vectors, Biology and
    Impacts. *v.5 p.174, p.204*

Nonlinear Acoustics. *v.5 p.566*

Nonlinear and Optimal Control Systems. *v.5 p.712*

Nonlinear Dynamics of Interacting Populations. *v.5 p.187, p.189*

Nonlinear Econometric Modeling in Time Series: Proceedings of
    the Eleventh International Symposium in Economic
    Theory. *v.4 p.198, p.206, p.207*

Nonlinear Editing Basics: A Primer on Electronic Film and
    Video Editing. *v.6 p.350*

Nonlinear Optics: Basic Concepts. *v.5 p.561*

Nonlinear Programming. *v.5 p.492*

Nonlinear Systems. *v.5 p.488*

Nonlinear Time Series Analysis of Economic and Financial
    Data. *v.4 p.204*

No-No Boy. *v.6 p.101*

The Non-Official British in India to 1920. . . . . .*v.6 p.150*

Nonparametric Statistical Methods. *v.5 p.482*

Non-Places: Introduction to an Anthropology of
    Supermodernity. *v.4 p.22*

Nonprofits Job Finder: Where the Jobs Are in Charities and
    Nonprofits. *v.4 p.170*

The Non-Reality of Free Will. *v.1 p.503*

Nonrequired Reading: Prose Pieces. *v.2 p.792*

Nonsense Novels. *v.2 p.736*

Nonsexist Research Methods: A Practical Guide. . . .*v.4 p.687*

Non-Silicates. *v.5 p.436*

Nonstandard Analysis. *v.5 p.489*

Non-State Actors in World Politics. *v.4 p.640*

Nontechnical Guide to Petroleum Geology, Exploration,
    Drilling, and Production. *v.5 p.451, p.738*

Nonunion Employee Representation: History, Contemporary Practice and Policy. *v.4 p.122*

Nonvascular Plants: An Evolutionary Survey. . .*v.5 p.206, p.207*

Nonverbal Communication Across Disciplines: Culture, Sensory Interaction, Speech, Conversation, Vol. 1. . . . .*v.4 p.424*

Nonverbal Communication in Human Interaction. . .*v.4 p.424*

Nonviolence in America: A Documentary History. . .*v.4 p.766*

Nonviolent Action: A Research Guide. *v.4 p.650*

Nonviolent Insurrection in El Salvador: The Fall of Maximiliano Hernandez Martinez. *v.3 p.299*

Non-Violent Resistance. *v.4 p.766*

Non-Western Educational Traditions: Indigenous Approaches to Educational Thought and Practice. *v.4 p.313*

Noonday Cemetery and Other Stories. *v.2 p.790*

Nootka Sound: And the Surrounding Waters of Maquinna. *v.3 p.547*

Nor Is It over Yet: Florida in the Era of Reconstruction, 1863-1877. . . . .*v.3 p.505*

Nordic Art Music: From the Middle Ages to the Third Millennium. *v.1 p.246*

Nordic Democracy : Ideas, Issues, and Institutions in Politics, Economy, Education, Social and Cultural Affairs of Denmark, Finland, Iceland, Norway, and Sweden. *v.3 p.231, p.232*

The Nordic Parliaments: A Comparative Analysis. *v.3 p.232, p.233*

Nordic States and European Unity. *v.3 p.232, p.233*

Norito: A Translation of the Ancient Japanese Ritual Prayers. *v.6 p.222*

The Norm of Truth: An Introduction to the Philosophy of Logic. *v.1 p.492*

Normal Family Processes: Growing Diversity and Complexity. *v.5 p.639*

The Normal Heart and the Destiny of Me. . . .*v.6 p.379, p.412*

Normal: Transexual CEOs, Crossdressing Cops and Hermaphrodites with Attitude. *v.4 p.746, v.6 p.369*

Normalization of U. S.-China Relations: An International History. *v.3 p.390*

The Norman Conquests: Table Manners, Living Together, Round and Round the Garden. *v.2 p.328*

Norman E. Borlaug: A Bibliography of Papers and Publications. *v.5 p.12*

📕 The Norman Empire. *v.6 p.568*

The Norman Frontier in the Twelfth and Early Thirteenth Centuries. *v.3 p.143*

Norman Mailer. *v.2 p.99*

Norman Rockwell: A Life. *v.1 p.737*

Norman Rockwell: Pictures for the American People. .*v.1 p.740*

Normandy Before 1066. . . . .*v.3 p.97*

The Normans and the Norman Conquest. *v.3 p.97*

The Normans. *v.3 p.235*

Normative Ethics. *v.1 p.484*

The Normative Structure of Sociology : Conservative and Emancipatory Themes in Social Thought. *v.4 p.680*

Norms of Nature: Naturalism and the Nature of Functions. *v.5 p.191*

The Norse Discovery of America, Set. *v.3 p.403, p.405*

The Norse Discovery of America, Vol. 2. . . . . . .*v.3 p.547*

North America Divided; the Mexican War, 1846-1848. . . . .*v.3 p.418, v.6 p.533*

North American Fish. *v.5 p.216*

North American Forest and Conservation History: A Bibliography. *v.4 p.164, v.5 p.37*

North American Geology: Early Writings. . . .*v.5 p.431, p.432*

North American Indian Music: A Guide to Published Sources and Selected Recordings. *v.1 p.167, p.296*

The North American Prairie. *v.5 p.176, p.240*

North American Range Plants. *v.5 p.40, p.42*

📖 North American Society for Psychology of Sport and Physical Activity. *v.4 p.794, p.876*

📖 North American Stratigraphic Code. *v.5 p.446*

📖 The North American Tapestry of Time and Terrain. *v.5 p.431*

North American Terrestrial Vegetation. *v.6 p.290*

The North American Trajectory: Cultural, Economic, and Political Ties among the United States, Canada, and Mexico. *v.3 p.293*

North American Women Artists of the Twentieth Century: A Biographical Dictionary. *v.1 p.664, p.706, v.6 p.472*

North and South. *v.2 p.288*

The North Atlantic Triangle in a Changing World: Anglo-American-Canadian Relations, 1902-1956. . .*v.3 p.537*

North Carolina: A Guide to the Old North State. . . .*v.3 p.502*

North Carolina Planters and Their Children, 1800-1860. .*v.4 p.732*

North Carolina Through Four Centuries. *v.3 p.502*

North Dakota: A Guide to the Northern Prairie State. .*v.3 p.523*

North Dakota. *v.3 p.523*

North from Mexico: The Spanish-Speaking People of the United States. *v.3 p.527, v.6 p.532*

North of Jamaica. *v.2 p.116*

The North Reports the Civil War. *v.3 p.424*

The North the South, and the Powers. *v.3 p.395, p.433*

North to Aztlan: A History of Mexican Americans in the United States. *v.6 p.531*

The North West Company. *v.3 p.545*

North Writers: A Strong Woods Collection. *v.5 p.230*

North Writers: Our Place in the Woods. *v.5 p.230*

Northanger Abbey. *v.2 p.266*

North-Central Section Field Guide. *v.5 p.431*

Northeastern Section Field Guide. *v.5 p.432*

Northern Crusades. *v.3 p.56, p.63*

Northern Editorials on Secession, Set. *v.3 p.365, p.421*

Northern Exposures: Photographing and Filming the Canadian North, 1920-45. . . . .*v.1 p.764*

Northern Governments in Transition: Political and Constitutional Development in the Yukon, Nunavut and the Western Northwest Territories. *v.4 p.589*

Northern Lights. *v.2 p.813*

Northern Naval Superiority and the Economics of the American Civil War. *v.4 p.522*

Northern Protestants: An Unsettled People. . . .*v.3 p.135, p.140*

Northern Renaissance Art: Painting, Sculpture, the Graphic Arts from 1350 to 1575. . . . . . .*v.1 p.675, p.676, p.688, p.689*

Northern Renaissance Art. *v.1 p.675, p.687*

The Northern Renaissance. *v.1 p.675*

Northern Sandlots: A Social History of Maritime
    Baseball. *v.4 p.806, p.807, p.816, p.850, p.851*

Northrop Frye: Anatomy of His Criticism. *v.2 p.729*

Northrop Frye on Shakespeare. *v.2 p.229*

Northrop Frye: The Theoretical Imagination. *v.2 p.729*

North. *v.2 p.515*

Northwest Passage: The Great Columbia River. . . .*v.3 p.530*

Northwest Passage. *v.2 p.113*

Northwest to Fortune: The Search of Western Man for a
    Commercially Practical Route to the Far East. . . .*v.3 p.547*

The Norton Anthology of American Literature: American
    Literature, 1820-1865. . . . .*v.2 p.18*

The Norton Anthology of American Literature: American
    Literature, 1865-1914. . . . .*v.2 p.18*

The Norton Anthology of American Literature: American
    Literature Between the Wars, 1914-1945. . . . . .*v.2 p.18*

The Norton Anthology of American Literature: American
    Literature since 1945. . . . .*v.2 p.18*

The Norton Anthology of American Literature: Literature to
    1820. . . . .*v.2 p.18*

The Norton Anthology of Children's Literature: The Traditions
    in English. *v.2 p.582*

The Norton Anthology of Contemporary Fiction. . . .*v.2 p.26*

The Norton Anthology of English Literature, Eighth Edition,
    Volume 2: the Romantic Period through the Twentieth
    Century. *v.2 p.196*

The Norton Anthology of English Literature: Middle
    Ages. *v.2 p.196*

The Norton Anthology of English Literature: The Middle Ages
    through the Restoration and the Eighteenth Century. .*v.2 p.196*

Norton Anthology of Literature by Women: The Tradition in
    English. *v.2 p.195, p.196*

Norton Anthology of Literature by Women: The Traditions in
    English. *v.2 p.19*

Norton Anthology of Modern and Contemporary Poetry, Vol.
    1. . . . .*v.2 p.582, p.583*

The Norton Anthology of Modern and Contemporary
    Poetry. *v.2 p.200, p.201*

The Norton Anthology of Modern Poetry. *v.2 p.22*

The Norton Anthology of Poetry. *v.2 p.199*

The Norton Anthology of Theory and Criticism. .*v.2 p.567, p.568*

The Norton Book of Nature Writing. *v.5 p.226*

The Norton Dictionary of Modern Thought. *v.2 p.549*

Norton History of Astronomy and Cosmology. *v.5 p.62*

The Norton History of Chemistry. *v.5 p.262*

Norton Manual of Music Notation. *v.1 p.393*

The Norton Shakespeare: Based on the Oxford Edition.*v.2 p.224*

Norton's Star Atlas and Reference Handbook. *v.5 p.64*

Norway: A History from the Vikings to Our Own Times.*v.3 p.234*

Norway: Elites on Trial. *v.4 p.594*

Norway's Foreign Relations : A History. *v.3 p.234*

Nosotros: The Hispanic People of Oregon, Essays and
    Recollections. *v.6 p.521, p.548, p.549*

Nostalgia and Beyond: Eleven Latvian Women
    Writers. *v.2 p.780, p.781*

Nostalgia for Death and Hieroglyphs of Desire: Poetry.*v.2 p.669*

Nostalgia. *v.2 p.816*

The Nostalgic Drum. *v.2 p.757*

Nostromo: A Tale of the Seaboard. *v.2 p.340*

Not a Day Goes By. *v.6 p.397*

Not a Passing Phase: Reclaiming Lesbians in History,
    1840-1985. . . . .*v.6 p.363*

Not All Black and White: Affirmative Action and American
    Values. *v.4 p.456, p.457*

Not by Genes Alone: How Culture Transformed Human
    Evolution. *v.4 p.15, p.16*

Not God: A History of Alcoholics
    Anonymous. *v.4 p.776, v.5 p.673*

Not Guilty. *v.4 p.438*

Not Honour More. *v.2 p.338*

Not in Front of the Audience: Homosexuality on Stage.*v.6 p.411*

Not in Sisterhood: Edith Wharton, Willa Cather, Zona Gale and
    the Politics of Female Authorship. *v.2 p.67, p.132*

Not June Cleaver: Women and Gender in the Postwar America,
    1945-1960. . . . .*v.6 p.455*

Not Just Anywhere: The Story of W.H.A.L.E. and New
    Bedford's Waterfront Historic District. *v.1 p.823*

Not Just Pumping Iron: On the Psychology of Lifting
    Weights. *v.5 p.583*

Not Just Victims: Conversations with Cambodian Community
    Leaders in the United States. *v.6 p.138, p.139*

Not Out of Africa: How Afrocentrism Became an Excuse to
    Teach Myth as History. *v.3 p.12*

Not Out of Africa: How Afrocentrism Became an Excuse to
    Teach Myth As History. *v.6 p.10, p.20*

Not Shakespeare: Bardolatry and Burlesque in the Nineteenth
    Century. *v.2 p.189*

The Not So Big House: A Blueprint for the Way We Really
    Live. *v.1 p.801*

Not the Way It's Supposed to Be: A Breviary of Sin. .*v.1 p.643*

Not Wanted on the Voyage. *v.2 p.735*

Not Without Honor: The History of American
    Anti-Communism. *v.3 p.449*

Not Your Father's Union Movement: Inside the
    AFL-CIO. *v.4 p.127, p.128*

Notable American Women: A Biographical Dictionary:
    Completing the Twentieth Century. *v.6 p.426*

Notable Black American Scientists. *v.5 p.395*

Notable Black American Women. *v.6 p.19, p.34, p.46*

Notable Black Men. *v.6 p.19, p.34*

Notable Caribbeans and Caribbean Americans: A Biographical
    Dictionary. *v.6 p.485, p.490*

Notable Latino Americans: A Biographical
    Dictionary. *v.6 p.485, p.489, p.490*

Notable Twentieth-Century Scientists Supplement. . .*v.5 p.395*

Notable Twentieth-Century Scientists. *v.5 p.395*

Notable Women in Mathematics: A Biographical
    Dictionary. *v.5 p.467*

Notable Women in the American Theatre: A Biographical
    Dictionary. *v.6 p.475*

Notable Women in the Life Sciences: A Biographical
    Dictionary. *v.5 p.224*

Notable Women in the Physical Sciences: A Biographical
Dictionary. *v.5 p.396*

Notable Women in World History: A Guide to Recommended
Biographies and Autobiographies. *v.6 p.425*

Notation of Polyphonic Music, 900-1600. . . . *v.1 p.176, p.179*

The Notation of Western Music: An Introduction. . . . *v.1 p.372*

Notebooks, 1914-1916. . . . .*v.1 p.472*

The Notebooks of Don Rigoberto. *v.2 p.686*

The Notebooks of Malte Laurids Brigge. *v.2 p.614, p.615*

The Note-Books of Samuel Butler. *v.2 p.273*

The Notebooks of Samuel Taylor Coleridge: 1827-1834. .*v.2 p.279*

Notebooks. *v.2 p.279*

Notes and Lectures upon Shakespeare and Some of the Old
Poets and Dramatists: With Other Literary Remains
of S. T. Coleridge, Vol. 2. . . . .*v.2 p.279*

Notes and Tones: Musician-to-Musician Interviews. . .*v.1 p.264*

Notes et contre-notes. *v.2 p.520*

Notes from the Balkans: Locating Marginality and Ambiguity on
the Greek-Albanian Border. *v.4 p.42*

Notes from the Divided Country: Poems. *v.2 p.160*

Notes from the Underground. *v.2 p.803*

Notes of a Pianist. *v.1 p.197, p.327*

Notes of a Provincial Wildfowler. *v.2 p.801*

Notes of a Red Guard. *v.3 p.224*

Notes on Fishing. *v.2 p.801*

☐ Notes on Individual Crystallographyers--History of
Crystallography--People. *v.5 p.283*

Notes on Molecular Orbital Calculations. *v.5 p.293*

Notes on the Methodology of Scientific Research. . . .*v.5 p.409*

Notes on the State of Virginia. *v.3 p.499*

Nothing But Freedom: Emancipation and Its Legacy. .*v.4 p.727*

Nothing Is Lost: Selected Poems. *v.2 p.813*

Nothing Like the Sun: A Story of Shakespeare's
Love-Life. *v.2 p.336*

The Nothing That Is: A Natural History of Zero. . . .*v.5 p.476*

No-Tillage and Surface Tillage Agriculture: The Tillage
Revolution. *v.5 p.51*

No-Tillage Seeding: Science and Practice. *v.5 p.47*

Not-Knowing: The Essays of Donald Barthelme. . . .*v.2 p.140*

Notre-Dame de Paris. *v.2 p.493*

Le nouveau petit Robert : dictionnaire alphabétique et
analogique de la langue française. *v.2 p.454*

Les Nouveaux contes d'Amadou Koumba. *v.2 p.544*

La Nouvelle France: The Making of French Canada - A Cultural
History. *v.3 p.538*

Nouvelles du XVIIe siècle. *v.2 p.465*

Nouvelles du XVIIIe siècle. *v.2 p.465*

Nouvelles et textes pour rien. *v.2 p.509*

A Nova Literatura Brasileira: Critica e Antologia. . .*v.2 p.689*

Nova Scotia and Confederation, 1864-74. . . . . . .*v.3 p.543*

Novalis. *v.2 p.601*

The Novel According to Cervantes. *v.2 p.649*

The Novel and the Police. *v.2 p.193, v.6 p.756*

The Novel in Antiquity. *v.2 p.405*

The Novel in France: Mme. de Lafayette, Laclos, Constant,
Stendhal, Balzac, Flaubert, Proust. *v.2 p.463*

The Novel of the Spanish Civil War (1936-1975). . . .*v.2 p.642*

The Novel of Worldliness: Crebillon, Marivaux, Laclos,
Stendhal. *v.2 p.462*

Novel on Yellow Paper. *v.2 p.383*

Novel Relations: The Transformation of Kinship in English
Literature and Culture, 1748-1818. . . . .*v.2 p.192*

Novel Sensors and Sensing. *v.5 p.742*

Novel to Romance: A Study of Cervantes' Novelas
Ejemplares. *v.2 p.649*

La Novela de la Revolucion Mexicana. *v.2 p.666*

La Novela Del XIX: Estudio Sobre Su Evolucion
Formal. *v.2 p.641*

La Novela Picaresca Espanola. *v.2 p.645*

Novela-Nivola. *v.2 p.662*

Novelas Breves de Escritoras Españolas: 1900-1936. .*v.2 p.642*

Novelas Ejemplares I. *v.2 p.647, p.648*

The Novelist As Philosopher: Studies in French Fiction,
1935-1960. . . . .*v.2 p.463*

Novelle per un anno, vol. 1, bk. 1. . . . .*v.2 p.722*

Novelle per un anno, vol. 1, bk. 2. . . . .*v.2 p.722*

Novelle per un anno, vol. 2, bk. 1. . . . .*v.2 p.722*

Novelle per un anno, vol. 2, bk. 2. . . . .*v.2 p.722*

Novelle per un anno, vol. 3, bk. 1. . . . .*v.2 p.722*

Novelle per un anno, vol. 3, bk. 2. . . . .*v.2 p.722*

The Novellino or One Hundred Ancient Tales: A Edition and
Translation Based on the 1525 Gualteruzzi Editio
Princeps. *v.2 p.700, p.701*

Novels, 1871-1880: Watch and Ward; Roderick Hudson; The
American; The Europeans; Confidence. *v.2 p.45*

Novels, 1875-1886: A Foregone Conclusion; A Modern Instance;
Indian Summer; The Rise of Silas Lapham. *v.2 p.42*

Novels, 1881-1886: Washington Square; The Portrait of a Lady;
The Bostonians. *v.2 p.45*

Novels, 1886-1890: The Princess Casamassima; The
Reverberator; The Tragic Muse. *v.2 p.44*

Novels, 1926-1929. . . . .*v.2 p.74*

Novels, 1936-1940: Absalom, Absalom!; If I Forget Thee,
Jerusalem (The Wild Palms); The Unvanquished; The
Hamlet. *v.2 p.74*

Novels, 1942-1954: Go Down Moses; Intruder in the Dust;
Requiem for a Nun; A Fable. *v.2 p.74*

Novels, 1957-1962: The Town; The Mansion; The
Reivers. *v.2 p.74*

Novels and Essays: Vandover and the Brute; McTeague; The
Octopus; Essays. *v.2 p.49*

The Novels and Related Works of Charles Brockden Brown:
Clara Howard and Jane Talbot. *v.2 p.31*

The Novels and Related Works of Charles Brockden Brown:
Edgar Huntly; or, Memoirs of a Sleep-Walker. . .*v.2 p.31*

Novels and Social Writings: The People of the Abyss, the Road,
the Iron Heel, Martin Eden, John Barleycorn, Essays. .*v.2 p.95*

Novels and Stories: Deephaven; A Country Doctor; The Country
of the Pointed Firs; Dunnet Landing Stories; Selected
Stories and Sketches. *v.2 p.46*

Novels and Stories: Jonah's Gourd Vine; Their Eyes Were Watching God; Moses, Man of the Mountain; Seraph on the Suwanee. *v.2 p.81, v.6 p.26, p.44*

Novels and Stories: The Call of the Wild, White Fang, The Sea-Wolf, Klondike and Other Stories. *v.2 p.95*

The Novels: Not Without Laughter and Tambourines to Glory. *v.2 p.87*

Novels of Anatole France: Penguin Island; the Crime of Sylvestre Bonnard and the Revolt of the Angels. *v.2 p.489, p.490*

The Novels of Anthony Trollope. *v.2 p.316*

The Novels of August Strindberg: A Study in Theme and Structure. *v.2 p.629*

The Novels of Frank Norris. *v.2 p.49, p.50*

Novels of Hermann Hesse: A Study in Theme and Structure. *v.2 p.610*

The Novels of Jane Austen. *v.2 p.267, p.268*

The Novels of John Steinbeck: A Critical Study. . . *v.2 p.123*

The Novels of Kurt Vonnegut: Imagining Being an American. *v.2 p.158*

The Novels of Max Frisch. *v.2 p.607*

The Novels of Samuel Beckett: The Grove Centenary Editions. *v.2 p.333, p.509*

The Novels of Samuel Beckett. *v.2 p.332, p.333, p.509*

Novels of the 1840s. *v.2 p.194, v.6 p.757*

The Novels of the German Romantics. *v.2 p.592*

The Novels of Virginia Woolf. *v.2 p.392*

Novels of William Faulkner: A Critical Interpretation. . *v.2 p.75*

Novels: The House of Mirth; The Reef; The Custom of the Country; The Age of Innocence. *v.2 p.132*

Novels. *v.2 p.601*

November: Fragments in a Nondescript Style. *v.2 p.490*

Novus Ordo Seclorum: The Intellectual Origins of the Constitution. *v.3 p.414*

Now Hiring: The Feminization of Work in the United States, 1900-1995. . . . . *v.6 p.455*

Now My Soul Is Hardened: Abandoned Children in Soviet Russia, 1918-1930. . . . . *v.3 p.224*

Now That I'm Out What Do I Do. *v.6 p.369*

Now That My Father Lies down Beside Me: New and Selected Poems, 1970-2000. . . . . *v.2 p.153*

Now the Volcano: An Anthology of Latin American Gay Literature. *v.6 p.406, p.407*

Now You See It: Studies on Lesbian and Gay Film. . *v.6 p.416*

Le Nozze Di Figaro. *v.1 p.188, p.229, p.343*

NSCA's Essentials of Personal Training. *v.4 p.791, p.903, p.904*

☐ NSDL The National Science Digital Library. . . . *v.5 p.406*

NSTA Guide to School Science Facilities. *v.4 p.288*

NTC's Dictionary of Latin American Spanish. *v.2 p.636, p.637*

NTC's Dictionary of Theatre and Drama Terms. *v.1 p.140, p.141*

Nubia: Corridor to Africa. *v.6 p.59*

The Nubian Past: An Archaeology of the Sudan. . . . *v.6 p.59*

Nubians in Egypt: Peaceful People. *v.6 p.58, p.635*

Nuclear and Particle Physics. *v.5 p.553, p.554*

Nuclear and Radiochemistry: Fundamentals and Applications. *v.5 p.308*

Nuclear and Radiochemistry. *v.5 p.308*

Nuclear Choices: A Citizen's Guide to Nuclear Technology. *v.5 p.360, p.374*

Nuclear Deterrence, Morality and Realism. *v.4 p.656*

☐ Nuclear Energy Institute. *v.5 p.739*

Nuclear Energy Policy: A Reference Handbook. . . . *v.5 p.740*

Nuclear Energy: Principles, Practices, and Prospects. . *v.5 p.739*

☐ Nuclear Engineering Virtual Library. *v.5 p.739*

Nuclear Magnetic Resonance and Nucleic Acids, Vol. 261. . . . . *v.5 p.134*

Nuclear Magnetic Resonance and Relaxation. *v.5 p.272*

Nuclear Magnetic Resonance: Applications to Organic Chemistry. *v.5 p.297*

Nuclear Magnetic Resonance of Biological Macromolecules, Part C: Methods in Enzymology. *v.5 p.88*

Nuclear Physics. *v.5 p.553*

Nuclear Politics in America: A History and Theory of Government Regulation. *v.5 p.360, p.374*

Nuclear Power: A Reference Handbook. . . . *v.5 p.709, p.740*

Nuclear Power and Its Environmental Effects. *v.5 p.360, p.374, p.376*

Nuclear Power and Social Power. *v.4 p.773*

Nuclear Power Plants Worldwide. *v.5 p.739*

Nuclear Reactions: The Politics of Opening a Radioactive Waste Disposal Site. *v.6 p.300*

Nuclear Reactions. *v.5 p.553*

Nuclear Reactor Engineering. *v.5 p.360, p.374*

Nuclear Technology. *v.3 p.49, v.5 p.359, p.739*

The Nuclear Tipping Point: Why States Reconsider Their Nuclear Choices. *v.4 p.655*

The Nucleic Acid Protocols Handbook. *v.5 p.120*

Nucleic Acids in Chemistry and Biology. . . . *v.5 p.131, p.328*

Nucleic Acids Isolation Methods. *v.5 p.120*

Nucleic Acids: Structures, Properties, and Functions. *v.5 p.120*

Nucleic Acids. *v.5 p.120*

The Nucleolus. *v.5 p.113*

The Nude in French Art and Culture, 1870-1910. *v.1 p.677, p.686*

The Nuer: A Description of the Modes of Livelihood and Political Institutions of a Nilotic People. . *v.4 p.38, v.6 p.59*

Nuestro New York: An Anthology of Puerto Rican Plays. *v.6 p.495, p.505, p.516*

La Nueva California: Latinos in the Golden State. *v.6 p.521, p.544*

Nueve Siglos de Literatura Espanola (Nine Centuries of Spanish Literature): Bilingual Edition. *v.2 p.645*

The NUM and British Politics, Vol. 2. . . . . . . *v.4 p.129*

The NUM and British Politics. *v.4 p.129*

Number: From Ahmes to Cantor. *v.5 p.466, p.476*

ⓔ The Number: How the Drive for Quarterly Earnings Corrupted Wall Street and Corporate America. . . . *v.4 p.53, p.93, p.101, p.104, p.105, p.111*

The Number [pi]. *v.5 p.475, p.476*

Number Theory: An Approach Through History. from Hammurapi to Legendre. *v.5 p.468, p.477*

Number Theory for Beginners. *v.5 p.477*

Number Theory. *v.5 p.475*

Numbers 1 to 20: A New Translation with Introduction and Commentary. *v.1 p.620*

Numbers 21-36. . . . .*v.1 p.620*

Numbers and Geometry. *v.5 p.477, p.496*

Numbers and Nationhood: Writing Statistics in Nineteenth-Century Italy. *v.3 p.201*

Numbers Guide: The Essentials of Business Numeracy. .*v.4 p.175*

Numbers in the Dark and Other Stories. *v.2 p.714*

Numerical Analysis: A Mathematical Introduction. . . .*v.5 p.492*

Numerical Analysis: An Introduction. *v.5 p.492*

Numerical Analysis for Applied Science. *v.5 p.491*

Numerical Analysis: Mathematics of Scientific Computing. *v.5 p.492*

Numerical Analysis. *v.5 p.491*

Numerical Approximation of Partial Differential Equations. *v.5 p.488, p.492*

Numerical Heat Transfer and Fluid Flow. *v.5 p.560*

Numerical Issues in Statistical Computing for the Social Scientist. *v.4 p.689*

Numerical Mathematics. *v.5 p.492*

Numerical Methods in Economics. *v.4 p.202*

Numerical Methods That Work. *v.5 p.491*

Numerical Optimization. *v.5 p.492, p.493*

Numerical Recipes in C++: The Art of Scientific Computing. *v.5 p.337, p.347*

Numerical Recipes. *v.5 p.492*

The Numerical Solution of Integral Equations of the Second Kind. *v.5 p.488, p.491*

Numerical Solution of Ordinary Differential Equations. *v.5 p.487, p.492*

Nuns and Soldiers. *v.2 p.372*

The Nun's Priest's Tale. *v.2 p.208*

The Nun. *v.2 p.479*

Nuremberg Case. *v.3 p.176*

The Nuremberg War Crimes Trial, 1945-46: A Documentary History. *v.3 p.85, p.176*

Nureyev: His Life. *v.1 p.12, v.6 p.415*

Nurses and Families: A Guide to Family Assessment and Intervention. *v.5 p.525, p.528*

Nurses at the Front: Writing the Wounds of the Great War. *v.3 p.208*

Nurse's Handbook of Alternative and Complementary Therapies. *v.5 p.531*

Nursing As Caring: A Model for Transforming Practice. .*v.5 p.527*

Nursing Care in the Genomic Era: A Care Based Approach. *v.5 p.533*

Nursing Care of Older Adults: Theory and Practice. . .*v.5 p.519*

Nursing Care Planning Guides: For Adults in Acute, Extended and Home Care Settings. *v.5 p.528*

Nursing Care Plans: Nursing Diagnosis and Intervention. *v.5 p.527*

Nursing: Concepts of Practice. *v.5 p.530*

Nursing Diagnosis Reference Manual. *v.5 p.528*

Nursing Ethics: Holistic Caring Practice. .*v.5 p.511, p.529, p.530*

Nursing: Human Science and Human Care. *v.5 p.528*

Nursing into the 21st Century. *v.5 p.527*

Nursing Support for Families of Dying Patients. *v.5 p.530*

Nursing Theorists and Their Work. *v.5 p.530*

Nursing Theory: Utilization and Application. *v.5 p.530*

The Nurture Assumption: Why Children Turn Out the Way They Do. *v.5 p.513*

Nurturing Doubt: From Mennonite Missionary to Anthropologist in the Argentine Chaco. *v.4 p.37*

Nurturing Native Languages. *v.6 p.691*

Nutcracker Nation: How an Old World Ballet Became a Christmas Tradition in the New World. *v.1 p.23*

Nutrient Cycling in Terrestrial Ecosystems: Field Methods, Application, and Interpretation. *v.5 p.184*

Nutrient Disequilibria in Agroecosystems: Concepts and Case Studies. *v.5 p.11*

Nutrient Requirements of Beef Cattle: Update 2000. . .*v.5 p.55*

Nutrient Requirements of Dairy Cattle, 2001. . . . .*v.5 p.54*

Nutrient Requirements of Dogs, 1985. . . . .*v.5 p.55*

Nutrient Requirements of Dogs and Cats. *v.5 p.55*

🄴 Nutrient Requirements of Goats: Angora, Dairy, and Meat Goats in Temperate and Tropical Countries. *v.5 p.53*

Nutrient Requirements of Horses, Set. *v.5 p.55*

Nutrient Requirements of Poultry. *v.5 p.56*

Nutrient Requirements of Sheep. *v.5 p.55*

Nutrient Requirements of Swine, 1988. . . . .*v.5 p.55*

Nutrient Requirements of Swine. *v.5 p.55*

Nutrition: An Integrated Approach. *v.5 p.329*

Nutrition and Environmental Health, Vol. 1. . . . . .*v.5 p.364*

Nutrition: Chemistry and Biology. *v.5 p.329*

Nutrition for Health, Fitness and Sport. .*v.4 p.791, p.792, p.876*

Nutrition in Sport. *v.4 p.825, p.876*

Nutritional Anthropology: Biocultural Perspectives on Food and Nutrition. *v.4 p.45*

Nutritional Biochemistry and Metabolism, with Clinical Applications. *v.5 p.124, p.125*

Nutritional Biochemistry of the Vitamins. *v.5 p.329*

Nutritional Biochemistry. *v.5 p.329*

Nutritional Health: Strategies for Disease Prevention. .*v.5 p.513*

Nutritional Quality of Cereal Grains: Genetic and Agronomic Improvement. *v.5 p.15, p.23*

🖵 Nutrition.gov. *v.5 p.33*

The Nuyorasian Anthology: Asian American Writings on New York City. *v.6 p.92*

Nuyorican Poetry: An Anthology of Puerto Rican Words and Feelings. *v.6 p.495, p.509*

🖵 NWSA: National Women's Studies Association. . .*v.6 p.462*

The Nymph of Fiesole. *v.2 p.701*

NYPD: A City and Its Police. *v.6 p.261*

NYPD Battles Crime: Innovative Strategies in Policing. .*v.6 p.263*

🖵 NYPL Digital Gallery. *v.1 p.711*

🖵 NYSE, New York Stock Exchange. . . .*v.4 p.90, p.93, p.101*

O

O Beulah Land. *v.2 p.115*

O Canada: It's Geography, History and the People Who Call It Home. *v.3 p.535*

O God of Players: The Story of the Immaculata Mighty Macs. *v.4 p.835, p.853*

O. Henry. *v.2 p.50, p.51*

O Solo Homo: The New Queer Performance. *v.6 p.412*

O the Chimneys: Selected Poems, Including the Verse Play,
　Eli. *v.2 p.615*

Oak Forest Ecosystems: Ecology and Management for
　Wildlife. *v.5 p.185, p.240*

Obadiah: A New Translation with Introduction and
　Commentary. *v.1 p.623*

Obasan. *v.2 p.735, v.6 p.100*

Obedience to Authority: An Experimental View. . . . *v.4 p.695*

Oberammergau: The Troubling Story of the World's Most
　Famous Passion Play. *v.3 p.61*

Oberiu: An Anthology of Russian Absurdism. *v.2 p.794*

The Object of Memory: Arab and Jew Narrate the Palestinian
　Village. *v.6 p.611*

Objective Knowledge: An Evolutionary Approach. . . *v.1 p.482*

Objectivism: The Philosophy of Ayn Rand. *v.1 p.510*

Objectivity, Relativism, and Truth: Philosophical Papers, Vol.
　1. . . . .*v.1 p.442, p.514*

Objectivity: The Obligations of Impersonal
　Reason. *v.1 p.482, p.483*

Object-Oriented Design with Applications. *v.5 p.349*

Objects and Others: Essays on Museums and Material
　Culture. *v.4 p.48, p.49, p.51*

Objects for Use: Handmade by Design. *v.1 p.721*

Objects of Desire: Design and Society, 1750-1980. . *v.1 p.713*

Oblomov. *v.2 p.804*

Oboe Technique. *v.1 p.398*

Oboe Unbound: Contemporary Techniques. . .*v.1 p.394, p.399*

The Oboe. *v.1 p.389*

Obras Completas: Con una Nota Biobibliográfica. . . *v.2 p.656*

Obras Completas, Vol. 1. . . . .*v.2 p.677*

Obras Completas, Vol. 2. . . . .*v.2 p.677*

Obras Completas, Vol. 3. . . . .*v.2 p.677*

Obras Completas, Vol. 4. . . . .*v.2 p.677*

Obras Completas. *v.2 p.653, p.659, p.661, p.662, p.667*

Obras en un Acto. *v.2 p.673*

O'Brien, Stories and Plays. *v.2 p.373*

The Obscene Bird of Night. *v.2 p.680*

Obscenity and Public Morality: Censorship in a Liberal
　Society. *v.4 p.472*

Obscure Scribblers: A History of Parliamentary
　Reporting. *v.3 p.120*

Observational Astrophysics. *v.5 p.65*

Observations on the Fairy Queen of Spenser, Vol. 1. . .*v.2 p.216*

Observations on the Feeling of the Beautiful and
　Sublime. *v.1 p.461, p.480, p.481*

Observations on the Nature of Civil Liberty, the Principles of
　Government, and the Justice and Policy of the War
　with America. to Which Is Added an Appendix, Containing a
　State of the National Debt, an Estimate of the Money
　Drawn from the Public by the T. *v.3 p.410*

Observations upon Liberal Education. *v.4 p.346*

Observers Observed: Essays on Ethnographic Fieldwork. *v.4 p.5*

Observing Variable Stars. *v.5 p.70*

An Obsession with History: Russian Writers Confront the
　Past. *v.2 p.800*

The Obstacle Race: Aborigines in Sport. *v.4 p.830*

An Occasion for War: Ethnic Conflict in Lebanon and Damascus
　in 1860. . . . .*v.6 p.605, p.607*

Occasional Form: Henry Fielding and the Chains of
　Circumstance. *v.2 p.247*

The Occasional Papers on Population and Political Economy
　from Contemporary Journals. *v.4 p.222*

The Occasions. *v.2 p.719*

Occupation and Resistance: The Greek Agony,
　1941-1944. . . . .*v.3 p.195*

The Occupation of Alcatraz Island: Indian Self-Determination
　and the Rise of Indian Activism. *v.6 p.689, p.694*

Occupational and Environmental Health Nursing: Concepts and
　Practice. *v.5 p.535*

Occupational and Environmental Health. *v.5 p.535*

Occupational Choice: An Approach to a General
　Theory. *v.5 p.577*

Occupational Ghettos: The Worldwide Segregation of Women
　and Men. *v.4 p.723*

Occupational Health and Safety. *v.5 p.682*

Occupational Outlook Handbook: 2006-2007
　Edition. *v.5 p.577, p.578*

📖 Occupational Outlook Handbook. *v.4 p.168, p.304*

📖 Occupational Safety and Health Administration, U.S.
　Department of Labor. *v.5 p.580*

Occupational Subcultures in the Workplace. *v.5 p.579*

Occupational Therapy As a Career: An Introduction to the Field
　and a Structured Method for Observation. *v.5 p.535*

Occupied America: A History of Chicanos. *v.6 p.530*

The Ocean Basins and Margins: The Indian Ocean. . *v.5 p.433*

The Ocean Basins and Margins: The Pacific Ocean. . *v.5 p.433*

The Ocean Basins and Margins: The Tethys Ocean. . *v.5 p.433*

Ocean Biogeochemical Dynamics. . .*v.4 p.393, v.5 p.429, p.430*

Ocean Biogeochemistry: A Synthesis of the Joint Global Ocean
　Flux Study (JGOFS). *v.5 p.112, p.113, p.172*

The Ocean Carbon Cycle and Climate: Proceedings of the
　NATO Asi on Ocean Carbon Cycle and Climate,
　Ankara, Turkey, from 5 to 16 August 2002. . . . .*v.4 p.392*

The Ocean Carbon Cycle and Climate: Proceedings of the
　NATO asi on Ocean Carbon Cylce and Climate,
　Ankara, Turkey, from 5 to 16 August 2002. . . . .*v.5 p.429*

Ocean Circulation. *v.5 p.430*

Ocean Life. *v.5 p.173*

Ocean of Sound: Aether Talk, Ambient Sound and Imaginary
　Worlds. *v.1 p.226*

An Ocean of Story. *v.2 p.749*

Ocean Politics and Policy: A Reference Handbook. . .*v.5 p.430*

Ocean Remote Sensing and Imaging, II. *v.4 p.388*

Oceania: The Native Cultures of Australia and the Pacific
　Islands. *v.4 p.43*

Oceanic Art. *v.1 p.694*

Oceanic Homosexualities. *v.6 p.421*

Oceanographic Processes of Coral Reefs: Physical and
　Biological Links in the Great Barrier
　Reef. *v.5 p.173, p.213, p.241*

Oceanography: An Illustrated Text. *v.5 p.429*

Oceanography: An Invitation to Marine Science. . . . *v.5 p.428*

☐ Oceans and Law of the Sea. *v.4 p.478*

The Oceans: Physical-Chemical Dynamics and Human
Impact. *v.4 p.392*

Oceans, Seas, and Reefs. *v.5 p.172*

The Oceans. *v.5 p.429*

Ockham on the Virtues. *v.1 p.651, p.652*

Ockham's Theory of Terms: Summa Logicae. *v.1 p.433, p.510*

O'Connell: The Life of Daniel O'Connell, 1775-1847. *v.3 p.136*

O'Connor: Collected Works: Wise Blood; a Good Man Is Hard
to Find; the Violent Bear It Away; Everything That
Rises Must Converge; Essays and Letters. *v.2 p.106*

The Octavius of Marcus Minucius Felix. *v.1 p.591*

October Cities: The Redevelopment of Urban
Literature. *v.6 p.731*

October Light. *v.6 p.104*

October Surprise: America's Hostages in Iran and the Election
of Ronald Reagan. *v.3 p.480*

Odd Girl Out. *v.6 p.394*

Odd Girls and Twilight Lovers: A History of Lesbian Life in
Twentieth-Century America. *v.6 p.401*

An Odd Kind of Fame: Stories of Phineas Gage. . . *v.5 p.658*

The Odd Women. *v.2 p.289*

Ode to Walt Whitman and Other Poems. *v.2 p.658*

The Odes of Horace: A Critical Study. *v.2 p.434*

The Odes of John Keats. *v.2 p.295, p.296*

Odessa, 1941-1944: A Case Study of Soviet Territory under
Foreign Rule. *v.3 p.226, p.227*

Odets the Playwright. *v.2 p.108*

Odilon Redon: Prince of Dreams. *v.1 p.696*

Odious Commerce: Britain, Spain and the Abolition of the
Cuban Slave Trade. *v.4 p.728*

Odori: Japanese Dance. *v.1 p.16*

Odyssey, Bks. VI-VIII. *v.2 p.414*

Odysseys Home: Mapping African-Canadian Literature. *v.2 p.729*

The Odyssey. *v.2 p.414*

Oeconomicus: A Social and Historical Commentary. . *v.3 p.15*

Oedipus at Colonus. *v.2 p.420*

Oedipus at Thebes: Sophocles' Tragic Hero and His
Time. *v.2 p.419*

Oedipus Rex and the Rake's
Progress. *v.1 p.225, p.233, p.360, p.410*

Oedipus the King. *v.2 p.420*

Oedipus Tyrannus: Tragic Heroism and the Limits of
Knowledge. *v.2 p.420*

OEuvre poétique. *v.2 p.543*

OEuvres : sources et postérité d'Esope à l'Oulipo. . . *v.2 p.474*

OEuvres autobiographiques, Vol. 1. . . . . *v.2 p.499*

OEuvres autobiographiques, Vol. 2. . . . . *v.2 p.499*

Oeuvres Completes, Set. *v.2 p.477, p.483*

Oeuvres Completes, Tome 1. . . . . *v.2 p.487*

Oeuvres completes, Vol. 1. . . . . *v.2 p.471, p.472*

Oeuvres Completes, Vol. 1. . . . . . . *v.2 p.473, p.475, p.496*

Oeuvres Completes, Vol. 2. . . . . *v.2 p.473, p.475*

Oeuvres Completes, Vol. 3. . . . . *v.2 p.473*

Oeuvres Completes. *v.2 p.474, p.478, p.480, p.487, p.495, p.513*

OEuvres Completes. *v.2 p.527*

Oeuvres complètes de Michel Butor, vol. 1. . . . . *v.2 p.511*

Oeuvres complètes de Michel Butor, vol. 2. . . . . . *v.2 p.511*

OEuvres complètes, Vol. 1: Écrits de Jeunesse. Premiers romans.
la tentation de saint Antoine. Madame Bovary.
Salambo. *v.2 p.490*

Oeuvres complètes, vol. 1: La deffence, et illustration de la
langue françoyse. *v.2 p.471*

Oeuvres complètes, Vol. 1: Les confessions. Autres textes
autobiographiques. *v.2 p.482*

Oeuvres complètes, vol. 1: Les débuts, 1858-1865. . *v.2 p.504*

OEuvres complètes, vol. 10. . . . . *v.2 p.493*

OEuvres complètes, vol. 10. . . . . *v.2 p.504*

OEuvres complètes, Vol. 11. . . . . *v.2 p.493*

OEuvres complètes, vol. 12: Souffrance et révolte,
1884-1885. . . . . *v.2 p.504*

OEuvres complètes, Vol. 12. . . . . *v.2 p.493*

OEuvres complètes, Vol. 13. . . . . *v.2 p.493*

OEuvres complètes, Vol. 14. . . . . *v.2 p.493*

OEuvres complètes, Vol. 15. . . . . *v.2 p.493*

OEuvres complètes, vol. 1. . . . . *v.2 p.470*

OEuvres complètes, Vol. 1. . . . . . . *v.2 p.476, p.490*

Oeuvres complètes, Vol. 1. . . . . *v.2 p.493*

OEuvres complètes, Vol. 1. . . . . *v.2 p.498*

Oeuvres complètes, vol. 1. . . . . *v.2 p.511*

OEuvres complètes, vol. 1. . . . . . *v.2 p.511, p.512, p.516*

OEuvres complètes, vol. 1. *v.2 p.518, p.520, p.521, p.522, p.523*

Oeuvres complètes, Vol. 2: Cinquante sonnetz à la louange de
l'Olive. L'anterotique de la vieille, & de la jeune Amye. Vers
lyriques. *v.2 p.471*

Oeuvres complètes, Vol. 2: La nouvelle Héloïse. Théatre.
Poésies. Essais littéraires. *v.2 p.482*

OEuvres complètes, vol. 2: Le feuilletoniste,
1866-1867. . . . . *v.2 p.504, p.505*

OEuvres complètes, Vol. 2: L'éducation sentimentale. Trois
contes. Bouvard et Pécuchet. Théâtre. Voyages. . *v.2 p.490*

OEuvres complètes, vol. 2. . . . . *v.2 p.470*

OEuvres complètes, Vol. 2. . . . . *v.2 p.471*

OEuvres complètes, Vol. 2. . . . . *v.2 p.493*

OEuvres complètes, Vol. 2. . . . . *v.2 p.496*

OEuvres complètes, vol. 2. . . . . *v.2 p.511*

Oeuvres complètes, vol. 2. . . . . . . *v.2 p.511, p.512, p.516*

OEuvres complètes, vol. 2. . . . *v.2 p.518, p.521, p.522, p.523*

Oeuvres complètes, Vol. 3: Du contrat social. Écrits
politiques. *v.2 p.482*

OEuvres complètes, vol. 3: La naissance du naturalisme,
1868-1870. . . . . *v.2 p.505*

OEuvres complètes, vol. 3. . . . . *v.2 p.470*

OEuvres complètes, Vol. 3. . . . . *v.2 p.492*

OEuvres complètes, Vol. 3. . . . . *v.2 p.493*

OEuvres complètes, Vol. 3. . . . . *v.2 p.511*

OEuvres complètes, vol. 3. . . . . *v.2 p.512*

OEuvres complètes, vol. 3. . . . . . . *v.2 p.518, p.521, p.523*

Oeuvres complètes, Vol. 4: Emile. Education-morale-
botanique. *v.2 p.482*

OEuvres complètes, vol. 4: La guerre et la Commune
(1870-1871). *v.2 p.505*

Oeuvres complètes, vol. 4. . . . .*v.2 p.470*

Oeuvres complètes, Vol. 4. . . . .*v.2 p.493*

OEuvres complètes, vol. 4. . . . .*v.2 p.512*

OEuvres complètes, vol. 4. . . . .*v.2 p.518*

Oeuvres complètes, vol. 5: Ecrits sur la musique, la langue et le
théâtre. *v.2 p.482*

OEuvres complètes, vol. 5. . . . .*v.2 p.470*

OEuvres complètes, Vol. 5. . . . .*v.2 p.493*

OEuvres complètes, vol. 5. . . . .*v.2 p.505*

Oeuvres complètes, vol. 5. . . . .*v.2 p.512, p.513*

OEuvres complètes, vol. 5. . . . .*v.2 p.518*

Oeuvres complètes, vol. 6. . . . .*v.2 p.470*

Oeuvres complètes, Vol. 6. . . . .*v.2 p.493*

Oeuvres complètes, vol. 6. . . . .*v.2 p.505*

Oeuvres complètes, vol. 6. . . . .*v.2 p.513*

Oeuvres complètes, vol. 6. . . . .*v.2 p.518*

OEuvres Complètes, Vol. 7: La République en Marche,
1875-1876. . . . .*v.2 p.505*

Oeuvres complètes, Vol. 7. . . . .*v.2 p.493*

OEuvres complètes, vol. 7. . . . .*v.2 p.518*

OEuvres complètes, vol. 8: Le scandale de L'assommoir,
1877-1879. . . . .*v.2 p.505*

Oeuvres complètes, Vol. 8. . . . .*v.2 p.493*

OEuvres complètes, vol. 8. . . . .*v.2 p.513*

OEuvres complètes, vol. 8. . . . .*v.2 p.518*

Oeuvres complètes, Vol. 9. . . . .*v.2 p.493*

OEuvres complètes, vol. 9. . . . .*v.2 p.505*

OEuvres complètes. *v.2 p.466, p.469, p.470*

Oeuvres complètes. *v.2 p.471*

OEuvres complètes. *v.2 p.472, p.476, p.492, p.513*

Oeuvres complètes. *v.2 p.522*

OEuvres complètes. *v.2 p.523*

Oeuvres complètes. *v.2 p.523*

OEuvres complètes. *v.2 p.525*

OEuvres de Leconte de Lisle, Vol. 1: Poèmes antiques. .*v.2 p.495*

OEuvres de Leconte de Lisle, Vol. 2: Poèmes barbares. .*v.2 p.495*

OEuvres de Leconte de Lisle, Vol. 3: Poèmes tragiques.
Derniers poèmes. *v.2 p.495*

OEuvres de Leconte de Lisle, Vol. 4: OEuvres
diverses. *v.2 p.495, p.496*

Oeuvres Diverses, Tome II. *v.2 p.474*

Oeuvres en prose complètes, vol. 1. . . . .*v.2 p.506*

OEuvres en prose complètes, vol. 1. . . . .*v.2 p.523*

Oeuvres en prose complètes, vol. 2. . . . . .*v.2 p.506, p.523*

Oeuvres en prose complètes, vol. 3. . . . .*v.2 p.506*

Oeuvres en prose. *v.2 p.513*

OEuvres intimes, Vol. 1. . . . .*v.2 p.501*

OEuvres intimes, Vol. 2. . . . .*v.2 p.501, p.502*

Oeuvres: Poesies - Lettres. *v.2 p.474*

Oeuvres Poetiques Completes. *v.2 p.495, p.503*

Oeuvres poétiques complètes. *v.2 p.506*

OEuvres poétiques complètes. *v.2 p.523, p.527*

OEuvres poétiques, vol. 1: Petites inventions. Odes d'Anacréon.
OEuvres diverses (1554-1561). *v.2 p.471*

OEuvres poétiques, vol. 2: La Bergerie. *v.2 p.471*

OEuvres poétiques, vol. 3: Ode à Nogent. Dictamen metrificum
de Bello Huguenotico. OEuvres diverses de 1565 à
1572. . . . .*v.2 p.471*

OEuvres poétiques, vol. 4: La Bergerie divisée en une Première
et Seconde Iournée. *v.2 p.471*

OEuvres poétiques, vol. 5: 1573-1577, Odes d'Anacréon
(1573-1574). Amours et nouveaux eschanges des
pierres précieux. Poéies diverses. Tombeau de
Belleau. *v.2 p.471*

OEuvres poétiques, vol. 6: OEuvres posthumes (1578). .*v.2 p.471*

OEuvres poétiques. *v.2 p.488*

Les oeuvres romanesques : Gargantua, Pantagruel, le tiers livre,
le quart livre, le cinquième livre. *v.2 p.472*

OEuvres romanesques ; suivies de, Dialogues des
carmélites. *v.2 p.508*

OEuvres romanesques complètes, Vol. 1. . . . . . .*v.2 p.502*

OEuvres romanesques complètes, vol.
1. . . . .*v.2 p.506, p.507, p.517, p.518*

OEuvres romanesques complètes, vol.
2. . . . .*v.2 p.506, p.507, p.517, p.518*

OEuvres romanesques complètes, vol. 3. .*v.2 p.506, p.507, p.517*

OEuvres romanesques complètes, vol. 4. . . . . . .*v.2 p.517*

OEuvres romanesques complètes, vol. 5. . . . . . .*v.2 p.517*

OEuvres romanesques complètes, vol. 6. . . . . . .*v.2 p.517*

OEuvres romanesques et théâtrales complètes, vol. 1. .*v.2 p.522*

OEuvres romanesques et théâtrales complètes, vol. 2. .*v.2 p.522*

OEuvres romanesques et théâtrales complètes, vol. 3. .*v.2 p.522*

OEuvres romanesques et théâtrales complètes, vol. 4. .*v.2 p.522*

Oeuvres Romanesques. *v.2 p.479, p.527, p.528*

Oeuvres, Vol. 1. . . . .*v.2 p.492*

OEuvres, vol. 1. . . . .*v.2 p.514, p.528*

Oeuvres, Vol. 2. . . . .*v.2 p.492*

OEuvres, vol. 2. . . . .*v.2 p.514, p.528*

OEuvres, vol. 3. . . . .*v.2 p.514*

OEuvres, vol. 4. . . . .*v.2 p.514*

OEuvres. *v.2 p.469, p.473*

Oeuvres. *v.2 p.478, p.479*

OEuvres. *v.2 p.507, p.515*

Oeuvres. *v.2 p.521*

OEuvres. *v.2 p.525*

Of Cigarettes, High Heels and Other Interesting Things: An
Introduction to Semiotics. *v.4 p.424*

Of Critical Theory and Its Theorists. *v.1 p.502*

Of Grammatology. *v.2 p.567, p.570*

Of Human Bondage. *v.2 p.370*

Of Human Freedom. *v.1 p.458*

Of Human Potential. *v.4 p.329*

Of Law and Life and Other Things That Matter: Papers and
Addresses of Felix Frankfurter, 1956-1963. . . .*v.4 p.437*

Of Learned Ignorance. *v.1 p.433*

Of Love and Other Demons. *v.2 p.683*

Of Mice and Magic: A History of American Animated
    Cartoons. *v.6 p.308*

Of Mind and Other Matters. *v.1 p.490*

Of Minds and Molecules: New Philosophical Perspectives on
    Chemistry. *v.5 p.264*

Of Moths and Men: An Evolutionary Tale: The Untold Story of
    Science and the Peppered Moth. *v.5 p.193*

Of One Blood: Abolitionism and the Origins of Racial
    Equality. *v.3 p.397*

Of Orphans and Warriors: Inventing Chinese-American Culture
    and Identity. *v.6 p.113, p.126*

Of Paradise and Power: America and Europe in the New World
    Order. *v.4 p.637, p.641*

Of Plymouth Plantation. *v.3 p.405*

Of Power and Right: Hugo Black, William O. Douglas and
    America's Constitutional Revolution. *v.4 p.467*

Of Revelation and Revolution: Christianity, Colonialism, and
    Consciousness in South Africa. *v.1 p.610, p.611*

Of Revelation and Revolution: The Dialectics of Modernity on a
    South African Frontier. *v.1 p.611*

Of the Conduct of the Understanding. *v.4 p.216*

Of the Presence of the Body: Essays on Dance and Performance
    Theory. *v.1 p.43*

Of the Standard of Taste and Other Essays. *v.1 p.451*

Of Time and Judicial Behavior: United States Supreme Court
    Agenda-Setting and Decision-Making, 1888-1997. *v.4 p.537*

Of Time and Power: Leadership Duration in the Modern
    World. *v.4 p.511, p.512*

Of Time and the River: A Legend of Man's Hunger in His
    Youth. *v.2 p.138*

Of Woman Born: Motherhood as Experience and
    Institution. *v.4 p.737, v.6 p.465, p.466, p.467*

Of Women, Outcastes, Peasants, and Rebels: A Selection of
    Bengali Short Stories. *v.6 p.151*

Of Women, Poetry, and Power: Strategies of Address in
    Dickinson, Miles, Brooks, Lorde, and Angelou. . . .*v.2 p.8*

Of Wonders and Wise Men: Religion and Popular Cultures in
    Southeast Mexico. *v.3 p.265, p.289*

Off Center: The Republican Revolution and the Erosion of
    American Democracy. *v.4 p.553*

Off the Map: Tales of Endurance and Exploration. . .*v.4 p.378*

Off the Road: My Years with Cassady, Kerouac, and
    Ginsberg. *v.2 p.79, p.92*

Offenbach: His Life and Times. *v.1 p.197, p.249, p.346*

The Offender in the Community. *v.6 p.278*

Offender Profiling: An Introduction to the Sociopsychological
    Analysis of Violent Crime. *v.6 p.254, p.267*

Offender Profiling and Crime Analysis. *v.6 p.251*

Offender Rehabilitation: Effective Correctional
    Intervention. *v.6 p.277*

Offender Rehabilitation in Practice: Implementing and
    Evaluating Effective Programs. *v.6 p.277*

Offensive Films. *v.6 p.313*

▢ Offical Documents of the United Nations. *v.4 p.482*

▢ Office of Scientific and Technical Information. . .*v.5 p.406*

Office of the Revels: The Dramatic Records of Sir Henry
    Herbert, Master of the Revels,
    1623-1673. . . . .*v.1 p.57, p.98, p.139*

▢ Office of the United Nations High Commissioner for Human
    Rights Documents. *v.4 p.670*

▢ Office of Travel and Tourism Industries Portal. . .*v.4 p.161*

▢ Office of Violence Against Women. *v.6 p.468*

Official and Standardized Methods of Analysis. . . .*v.5 p.268*

✇ Official Documents of the United Nations. *v.4 p.476*

Official Guide for GMAT Review. *v.4 p.176*

The Official Guide to Country Dance Steps. *v.1 p.34*

Official Methods and Recommended Practices of the
    AOCS. *v.5 p.34*

Official Methods of Analysis of AOAC International. . *v.5 p.34*

Official Methods of Analysis of the AOAC
    International. *v.5 p.33, p.268*

The Official Museum Directory. *v.1 p.667*

Official Papers of Alfred Marshall: A Supplement. . .*v.4 p.224*

Official Papers. *v.4 p.224*

▢ The Official String Theory Web Site. *v.5 p.550*

▢ Official Website of the Olympic Movement. . . .*v.4 p.845*

Officially Gay: The Political Construction of Sexuality in the U.
    S. Military. *v.6 p.390*

Officiating Soccer. *v.4 p.867, p.905*

Officiating Softball. *v.4 p.795, p.839, p.840, p.868*

Officiating Track and Field and Cross Country. *v.4 p.869, p.905*

Offshore. *v.2 p.344*

▢ OFFSTATS: Official Statistics on the Web. *v.4 p.179*

Ogallala: Water for a Dry Land. *v.5 p.11*

Ogden Nash: The Life and Work of America's Laureate of Light
    Verse. *v.2 p.103*

Oglethorpe in America. *v.3 p.503*

Oglethorpe in Perspective: Georgia's Founder after Two
    Hundred Years. *v.3 p.503, p.504*

The Ogre. *v.2 p.534*

The O'Hara Concern: A Biography of John O'Hara. . *v.2 p.106*

Ohio: A History. *v.3 p.513*

Ohio and Its People. *v.3 p.513*

The Ohio Frontier: Crucible of the Old Northwest,
    1720-1830. . . . .*v.3 p.513*

Ohio: The History of a People. *v.3 p.513*

Ohio: The Ohio Guide. *v.3 p.513*

Oil & Gas Journal. *v.4 p.160*

Oil and Development in Venezuela During the 20th
    Century. *v.3 p.361*

Oil and Gas Pipelines in Nontechnical Language. . . *v.5 p.738*

Oil and Gas Production in Nontechnical Language. . *v.5 p.738*

Oil and Politics in the Gulf: Rulers and Merchants in Kuwait
    and Qatar. *v.6 p.627*

Oil and Revolution in Mexico. *v.3 p.290*

Oil Crops of the World. *v.5 p.23*

Oil for the Lamps of China. *v.6 p.215*

The Oil Palm. *v.5 p.20, p.26*

Oil Spills. *v.5 p.363, p.375*

Oil Titans: National Oil Companies in the Middle East. .*v.4 p.398*

Ojibwa Warrior: Dennis Banks and the Rise of the American Indian Movement. *v.6 p.688, p.693*

Ojibwa Woman. *v.6 p.703, p.705*

Ojos de Otro Mirar: Poesia 1960-2001. . . . .*v.2 p.667*

Okinawa: Cold War Island. *v.6 p.235*

Okinawa: The History of an Island People. *v.6 p.235*

Oklahoma: A History of Five Centuries. *v.3 p.523*

Oklahoma: A History. *v.3 p.524*

Oklahoma Politics: A History. *v.3 p.524*

Oklahoma: The History of an American State. *v.3 p.523*

Ol' Strom: An Unauthorized Biography of Strom Thurmond. *v.3 p.455*

Olafur Eliasson. *v.1 p.772*

Old Age in the New Land: The American Experience since 1790. . . . .*v.4 p.741*

Old and Middle English C.890-C.1400: An Anthology. .*v.2 p.197*

Old and Middle English Poetry. *v.2 p.168, p.169, p.201*

The Old and New World Romanticism of Washington Irving. *v.2 p.42*

The Old Brown Dog: Women, Workers and Vivisection in Edwardian England. *v.6 p.748*

Old Bullion Benton, Senator from the New West: Thomas Hart Benton 1782. . . . .*v.3 p.415*

The Old College Try: Balancing Academics and Athletics in Higher Education. *v.4 p.822, p.895*

Old Creole Days. *v.2 p.32*

The Old Curiosity Shop. by Charles Dickens. (Boz.) with ... illustrations. from designs by George Cattermole and H. K. Browne. *v.2 p.283*

Old Czech Legends. *v.2 p.783*

The Old Devils. *v.2 p.328*

The Old Dominion and the New Nation, 1788-1801. .*v.3 p.499*

The Old Dominion in the Seventeenth Century: A Documentary History of Virginia, 1606-1689. . . . .*v.3 p.499*

Old Drury of Philadelphia: A History of the Philadelphia Stage, 1800-1835. . . . .*v.1 p.119, p.155, p.157, p.159*

Old English and Its Closest Relatives: A Survey of the Earliest Germanic Languages. *v.2 p.206, p.550*

Old English and Medieval Literature. *v.2 p.196*

Old English and Middle English Poetry. *v.2 p.181*

The Old English Baron. *v.2 p.258*

Old English: Grammar and Reader. . .*v.2 p.205, p.206, p.550*

Old English Literature: A Short Introduction. *v.2 p.167*

Old English Literature: Selected Essays. *v.2 p.167, p.168*

Old English Pages. *v.2 p.203*

Old Farm Tools and Machinery: An Illustrated History. .*v.5 p.3*

Old French-English Dictionary. *v.2 p.453*

Old Gentlemen's Convention: The Washington Peace Conference Of 1861. . . . .*v.3 p.365, p.420*

The Old Glory: Endecott and the Red Cross; My Kinsman, Major Molineux; and Benito Cereno. *v.2 p.96*

Old High German Literature. *v.2 p.589*

Old Icelandic Poetry: Eddic Lay and Skaldic Verse. .*v.2 p.624*

The Old Jest. *v.2 p.355*

Old Jules: 50th Anniversary Edition. *v.3 p.525*

Old Labour to New: The Dreams That Inspired, the Battles That Divided. *v.2 p.197, p.198, v.4 p.606, p.607*

Old Las Vegas: Hispanic Memories from the New Mexico Meadowlands. *v.6 p.488, p.523*

The Old Life. *v.2 p.82*

The Old Man and the Sea. *v.2 p.85*

The Old Man and the Wolves: A Novel. *v.2 p.531*

Old Man Goya. *v.1 p.695*

The Old Man Who Does As He Pleases. *v.6 p.210*

The Old Manor House. *v.2 p.261*

The Old Marlborough Road: "A Journey into Wonder". .*v.5 p.224*

Old Masters Signatures and Monograms, 1400-Born 1800. . . . .*v.1 p.663*

Old New York. *v.2 p.132*

Old Newfoundland: A History to 1843. . . . . . .*v.3 p.547*

Old Norse - Icelandic Literature: A Critical Guide. . .*v.2 p.624*

The Old Northwest As the Keystone of the Arch of American Federal Union: A Study in Commerce and Politics. *v.3 p.512, p.513*

The Old Northwest: Pioneer Period, 1815-1840. . . .*v.3 p.512*

The Old Northwest. *v.3 p.513*

The Old Oligarch: Pseudo-Xenophon's Constitution of the Athenians. *v.3 p.18*

The Old Order: Stories of the South from the Leaning Tower, Pale Horse, Pale Rider and Flowering Judas. . . .*v.2 p.109*

Old Peking Revisited. *v.6 p.205*

Old People and the Things that Pass. *v.2 p.622, p.623*

Old People, New Lives: Community Creation in a Retirement Residence. *v.4 p.742*

Old Poisons, New Problems: A Museum Resource for Managing Contaminated Cultural Materials. *v.1 p.828*

Old Polish Literature Online. *v.2 p.787*

Old Possum's Book of Practical Cats. *v.2 p.71*

The Old Regime and the Revolution: Notes on the French Revolution and Napolean. *v.3 p.157, p.158*

Old Regime France: 1648-1788. . . . .*v.3 p.147*

Old Rosa: A Novel in Two Stories. *v.2 p.670*

The Old Rus' Kievan and Galician-Volhynian Chronicles: The Ostroz'kyj (Xlebnikov) and akCetvertyns'kyj (Pogodin) Codices. *v.2 p.814*

The Old Social Classes and the Revolutionary Movements of Iraq: A Study of Iraq's Old Landed and Commercial Classes and of Its Communists, Ba'thists and Free Officers. *v.6 p.602*

Old Soldiers Never Die: The Life of Douglas MacArthur. *v.3 p.461*

The Old South. *v.3 p.495*

Old Spookses' Pass. *v.2 p.732*

Old Testament Figures in Art: A Guide to Imagery. . .*v.1 p.709*

Old Testament Interpretation: Past, Present, and Future: Essays in Honor of Gene M. Tucker. *v.1 p.619*

Old Testament Pseudepigrapha: Expansions of the Old Testament and Legends, Wisdom and Philosophical Literature, Prayers, Psalms and Odes, Fragments of Lost Judeo-Hellenistic Words, Vol. 2. . . . .*v.1 p.623*

Old Testament Theology. *v.1 p.620*

Old Textbooks: Spelling, Grammar, Reading, Arithmetic, Geography, American History, Civil Government, Physiology, Penmanship, Art, Music, As Taught in the Common Schools from Colonial Days To 1900. I. .*v.4 p.285*

Old Thad Stevens: A Story of Ambition. .*v.3 p.422, p.423, p.428*

Old Toronto Houses. *v.1 p.789*

Old West, New West. *v.3 p.518*

The Old Wives' Tale. *v.2 p.334*

The Old World and the New: 1492-1650. . . . . .*v.3 p.73*

The Older Sophists. *v.1 p.427*

The Oldest Cuisine in the World: Cooking in Mesopotamia. *v.3 p.5*

The Oldest Old. *v.4 p.742*

The Oldest Revolutionary: Essays on Benjamin Franklin. .*v.2 p.29*

The Oldest Vocation: Christian Motherhood in the Middle Ages. *v.6 p.559*

Old-House Dictionary: An Illustrated Guide to American Domestic Architecture (1600-1940). *v.1 p.821*

Oleanna. *v.1 p.62, p.87, p.116*

Olfaction, Taste, and Cognition. *v.5 p.607*

The Olive in California: History of an Immigrant Tree. .*v.5 p.24*

Oliver Cromwell and the English Revolution. *v.3 p.104*

Oliver Cromwell's Letters and Speeches with Elucidations: The Works of Thomas Carlyle. *v.2 p.276*

Oliver Goldsmith Revisited. *v.2 p.248*

Oliver Goldsmith. *v.2 p.248*

Oliver Twist. *v.2 p.283, p.284*

Oliver Wendell Holmes. *v.4 p.540*

Olivier de Clisson and Political Society in France under Charles V and Charles VI. *v.3 p.144*

Olmec Art and Archaeology in Mesoamerica. *v.3 p.261*

Olmecs. *v.4 p.9*

Olodumare: God in Yoruba Belief. *v.1 p.542*

Olympic Black Women. *v.6 p.41, p.45*

The Olympic Book of Sports Medicine, Vol. 1. . . . .*v.4 p.825*

The Olympic Century. *v.4 p.846*

Olympic Marathon: A Centennial History of the Games' Most Storied Race. *v.4 p.846, p.863*

Olympic Turnaround: How the Olympic Games Stepped Back from the Brink of Extinction to Become the World's Best Known Brand. *v.4 p.142*

The Olympics: A History of the Modern Games. . . .*v.4 p.846*

The Olympics at the Millennium: Power, Politics, and the Games. *v.4 p.846, p.892*

Oman: A History. *v.6 p.627*

Oman and the World: The Emergence of an Independent Foreign Policy. *v.6 p.627*

Oman: Economic, Social and Strategic Developments. .*v.6 p.627*

Omani Traditional Music. *v.1 p.287*

Omar Khayyam's the Rubaiyat: A Literal Translation. .*v.6 p.671*

Ombre sultane : roman. *v.2 p.544*

Omeros. *v.2 p.770*

▭ OMIN--Online Mendelian Inheritance in Man. *v.5 p.130, p.148, p.153*

Omissions Are Not Accidents: Gender in the Art of Marianne Moore. *v.2 p.102*

Omneros. *v.2 p.542*

The Omnibus Idea. *v.1 p.374*

On a Bed of Rice: An Asian American Erotic Feast. . .*v.6 p.100*

On Active Service in Peace and War. *v.3 p.463*

On Adam Smith's Wealth of Nations: A Philosophical Companion. *v.4 p.219*

On African Socialism. *v.6 p.72*

On Apology. *v.5 p.648*

On Aristotle and Greek Tragedy. *v.2 p.402*

On Art, Religion, and the History of Philosophy: Introductory Lectures. *v.1 p.463*

On Beauty. *v.2 p.380*

On Becoming a Biologist. *v.5 p.245*

On Becoming a Leader: The Leadership Classic. . . .*v.4 p.70*

On Becoming Chinese American: A History of Communities and Institutions, Vol. 13. . . . .*v.6 p.127*

On Becoming Cuban: Identity, Nationality and Culture. .*v.3 p.312*

On Becoming Filipino: Selected Writings of Carlos Bulosan. *v.6 p.104, p.105, p.129*

On Becoming Nuyorican. *v.6 p.527*

On Being a Christian. *v.1 p.646*

On Being a Jewish Feminist. *v.1 p.553*

On Being a Muslim: Finding a Religious Path in the World Today. *v.1 p.559*

On Being a Teacher. *v.4 p.327*

On Being and Essence. *v.1 p.434*

On Being Female, Black and Free: Essays by Margaret Walker, 1932-1992. . . . .*v.6 p.47*

On Being Human. *v.4 p.760*

On Boxing. *v.4 p.812, p.856*

On Calderon. *v.2 p.647*

On Camus. *v.1 p.456*

On Certainty. *v.1 p.471, p.483*

On Christian Teaching. *v.1 p.592*

On Christian Theology. *v.1 p.637*

On Classical Economics. *v.4 p.218*

On Competition. *v.4 p.51, p.57, p.58, p.61*

On Concepts and Classifications of Musical Instruments. *v.1 p.390*

On Creativity, Innovation, and Renewal: A Leader to Leader Guide. *v.4 p.66*

On Davidson. *v.1 p.443*

On Death and Dying. *v.4 p.742*

On Deconstruction: Theory and Criticism after Structuralism. *v.2 p.570*

On Directing Film. *v.6 p.350*

On Directing. *v.1 p.152*

On Drama: Boundaries of Genre, Borders of Self. . .*v.1 p.56*

On Durkheim's Rules of Sociological Method. *v.4 p.681*

On Early English Pronunciation, with Especial Reference to Shakespeare and Chaucer, Set. *v.2 p.556*

On Economic Theory and Socialism: Collected Papers. *v.4 p.208, p.209*

On Edge: Performance at the End of the Twentieth Century. *v.1 p.28, p.29, p.30, p.38, p.39*

On Editing Shakespeare and the Elizabethan Dramatists. .*v.2 p.228*

On Every Front: The Making and Unmaking of the Cold War. *v.3 p.454*

On Film-Making: An Introduction to the Craft of the Director. *v.6 p.350*

On Food and Cooking: The Science and Lore of the Kitchen. *v.5 p.35*

On Forsyte 'Change. *v.2 p.347, p.348*

On Free Choice of the Will. *v.1 p.431, p.503, p.592*

On Friendship. *v.2 p.470, p.471*

ⓔ On Germans and Other Greeks: Tragedy and Ethical Life. *v.1 p.57, p.71, p.89*

On Golf: The Game, the Players, and a Personal History of Obsession. *v.4 p.861*

On Great Writing (On the Sublime). *v.2 p.416*

On Gwendolyn Brooks: Reliant Contemplation. . . . *v.2 p.64*

On Her Own Ground: The Life and Times of Madam C. J. Walker. *v.6 p.16, p.17, p.42*

On Heroes, Hero Worship and the Heroic in History. .*v.2 p.276*

On Hollywood: The Place, the Industry. *v.6 p.345*

On Human Conduct. *v.1 p.485*

On Human Memory: Evolution, Progress, and Reflections on the 30th Anniversary of the Atkinson-Shiffrin Model. .*v.5 p.610*

On Human Nature. *v.5 p.619, p.620*

On Husserl. *v.1 p.470*

On Interpreting Keynes: A Study in Reconciliation. . .*v.4 p.228*

On Invention, the Best Kind of Orator, Topics: Rhetorical Treatises. *v.2 p.433*

On James. *v.1 p.440*

On Keynesian Economics and the Economics of Keynes: A Study in Monetary Theory. *v.4 p.225*

On Keynes's Method. *v.4 p.226*

On Killing: The Psychological Cost of Learning to Kill in War and Society. *v.5 p.584*

On Language. *v.2 p.561*

On Leadership. *v.4 p.697*

On Learning to Read: The Child's Fascination with Meaning. *v.4 p.362*

On Liberty and Other Essays. *v.4 p.515*

On Liberty. *v.4 p.223, p.515*

On Lies, Secrets and Silence: Selected Prose, 1966-1978. . . . .*v.2 p.115*

On Literature Today. *v.2 p.6*

On Literature. *v.2 p.164, p.568*

On Losing the Soul: Essays in the Social Psychology of Religion. *v.5 p.633, p.634*

On Lynchings. *v.4 p.752, v.6 p.9*

On Marx. *v.1 p.508*

On Matters Southern: Essays about Literature and Culture, 1964-2000. . . . .*v.2 p.14*

On Measuring and Planning the Quality of Life. . . .*v.4 p.265*

On Modern Origins: Essays in Early Modern Philosophy. *v.1 p.437*

On Money, Method and Keynes: Selected Essays by Victoria Chick. *v.4 p.226*

On Monique Wittig: Theoretical, Political, and Literary Essays. *v.2 p.533*

On Morality and Society: Selected Writings. *v.4 p.684*

On Motion and on Mechanics. *v.5 p.546*

On Murder Considered As One of the Fine Arts and Other Related Texts. *v.2 p.281*

On Music and Musicians. *v.1 p.204, p.355*

On My Own: Korean Businesses and Race Relations in America. *v.6 p.107, p.125, p.137*

On Nationality. *v.4 p.494*

On Native Grounds: An Interrpetation of Modern American Prose Literature. *v.2 p.4*

On New Ground: Contemporary Hispanic-American Plays. *v.6 p.496, p.517*

On Nietzsche. *v.1 p.466*

On Nineteen Eighty-Four: Orwell and Our Future. . .*v.2 p.375*

On Obligations. *v.2 p.433*

On Organizational Learning. *v.4 p.78*

On Other Grounds: Landscape Gardening and Nationalism in Eighteenth-Century England and France. *v.1 p.815*

On Our Minds: How Evolutionary Psychology Is Reshaping the Nature versus Nurture Debate. *v.5 p.653*

On Our Own Terms: Race, Class and Gender in the Lives of African-American Women. *v.6 p.40, p.45, p.470*

On Paul Ricoeur: Narrative and Interpretation. . . .*v.1 p.458*

On Peirce. *v.1 p.440*

On Philosophy in China. *v.1 p.475*

On Playing the Flute. *v.1 p.398, p.402*

On Politics: A Carnival of Buncombe. *v.3 p.449*

On Quaternions and Octonions. *v.5 p.473*

On Racine. *v.2 p.476*

On Reading: A Common-Sense Look at the Nature of Language and the Science of Reading. *v.5 p.574*

On Reading French Verse: A Study of Poetic Form. *v.2 p.460, p.461*

On Reading. *v.2 p.524*

On Religion and Psychology. *v.2 p.279*

On Religion. *v.1 p.545*

On Revolution. *v.4 p.497*

On Rhetoric: A Theory of Civic Discourse. *v.2 p.408*

On Roman Time: The Codex-Calendar of 354 and the Rhythms of Urban Life in Late Antiquity. *v.3 p.32*

On Romanticism in Slavic Literature. *v.2 p.779*

On Same-Sex Marriage, Civil Unions, and the Rule of Law: Constitutional Interpretation at the Crossroads. . .*v.6 p.389*

On Santayana. *v.1 p.439*

On Seeing Forms. *v.5 p.606*

On Semantics. *v.2 p.564*

On Signs. *v.2 p.570*

On Social Facts. *v.4 p.713*

On Stories: And Other Essays on Literature. *v.2 p.164*

On Strike at Hormel: The Struggle for a Democratic Labor Movement. *v.4 p.126*

On Teaching. *v.4 p.348*

On the Aesthetic Education of Man. *v.1 p.460, p.481*

On the Art of Singing. *v.1 p.395*

On the Art of the Theatre. *v.1 p.56, p.81, p.138*

On the Art of Writing Copy: The Best of Print, Broadcast, Internet, Direct Mail. *v.4 p.173*

On the Backroad to Heaven: Old Order Hutterites, Mennonites, Amish and Brethren. *v.1 p.586*

On the Blossoming. *v.6 p.648*

On the Border: Society and Culture Between the United States and Mexico. *v.4 p.765*

On the Corner: Male Social Life in a Paramaribo Creole Neighborhood. *v.3 p.322*

On the Count of One: The Art, Craft, and Science of Teaching Modern Dance. *v.1 p.38*

On the down Low: A Journey into the Lives of "Straight" Black Men Who Sleep with Men. . . . *v.4 p.750, v.6 p.369, p.375*

On the Edge of Anarchy: Locke, Consent, and the Limits of Society. *v.4 p.773*

On the Edge of Reason. *v.2 p.818*

On the Edge of the Auspicious: Gender and Caste in Nepal. *v.6 p.163*

On the Edge: The Clinton Presidency. *v.3 p.469*

On the Edge: Ukrainian-Central European-Russian Security Triangle. *v.4 p.597*

On the Edge: Women Making Hockey History. *v.4 p.835, p.862*

On the Eternal in Man. *v.1 p.523*

On the Freedom of the Will. *v.1 p.465, p.466*

On the Front Lines: Following America's Foreign Correspondents Across the Twentieth Century. . . .*v.4 p.406*

On the Future of Our Educational Institutions. . . .*v.4 p.344*

On the Genealogy of Morality. *v.1 p.467*

On the Historical Novel. *v.2 p.712*

On the History of Economic Thought: British and American Economic Essays, Vol. 1. . . . .*v.4 p.211*

On the Home Front: The Cold War Legacy of the Hanford Nuclear Site. *v.5 p.364, p.374*

On the Human Condition. *v.1 p.507*

On the Kabbalah and Its Symbolism. *v.1 p.551*

On the Lam: Narratives of Flight in J. Edgar Hoover's America. *v.6 p.340*

On the Malice of Herodotus, Causes of Natural Phenomena, Vol. 11. . . . .*v.2 p.418*

On the Marble Cliffs. *v.2 p.610*

On the Medieval Origins of the Modern State. . .*v.3 p.68, p.69*

On the Modes: Part Four of le Istitutioni Armoniche, 1558. . . . .*v.1 p.181, p.182*

On the Move: How and Why Animals Travel in Groups. *v.5 p.614*

On the Musically Beautiful. *v.1 p.381*

On the Nature of Organizations. *v.4 p.718*

On the Nature of Prejudice: Fifty Years after Allport. *v.5 p.653*

On the Nature of Things: Contemporary American Landscape Architecture. *v.1 p.813*

On the Nature of Things. *v.2 p.437*

On the Origins of Classical Economics: Distribution and Value from William Petty to Adam Smith. *v.4 p.218*

On the Outside Looking Out: John Ashbery's Poetry. . *v.2 p.58*

On the Phenomenology of the Consciousness of Internal Time (1893-1917). *v.1 p.469*

On the Philosophy of Higher Education. *v.4 p.289*

On the Poems of Henry Vaughan: Characteristics and Intimations. *v.2 p.263, p.264*

On the Poetry of Allen Ginsberg. *v.2 p.79*

On the Poetry of Keats. *v.2 p.295*

On the Practice of Sociology. *v.4 p.683*

On the Pragmatics of Communication. *v.1 p.490, v.5 p.620, p.621*

On the Prosody of Paradise Regained and Sampson Agonistes. *v.2 p.253*

On the Road Again: Developing and Managing Traveling Exhibitions. *v.1 p.828*

On the Road: Kerouac's Ragged American Journey. . *v.2 p.92*

On the Road of the Winds: An Archaeological History of the Pacific Islands before European Contact. *v.4 p.13*

On the Road to the Wolf's Lair: German Resistance to Hitler. *v.3 p.171, p.172*

On the Road. *v.2 p.93*

On the Sensations of Tone. *v.1 p.375, v.5 p.607*

On the Shoulders of Giants: New Approaches to Numeracy. *v.5 p.463*

On the Silence of the Declaration of Independence. . *v.4 p.518*

On the Social Contract. *v.4 p.492*

On the Sociology of Islam. *v.4 p.721*

On the Study of Greek Poetry. *v.2 p.601*

On the Subject of "Java". *v.6 p.175, p.177*

On the Sublime. *v.2 p.416*

On the theology of death. *v.1 p.645*

On the Theory of Economic Policy. *v.4 p.245*

On the Track: A Guide to Contemporary Film Scoring. *v.1 p.255, v.6 p.351*

On the Track of the New Brunswick Panther: The Story of Bruce Wright and the Eastern Panther. *v.5 p.229*

On the Trail of the Assassins: My Investigation and Prosecution of the Murder of President Kennedy. *v.3 p.471*

On Thrones of Gold: Three Javanese Shadow Plays. *v.1 p.129, p.133*

On Toleration. *v.4 p.513*

On Translating Homer. *v.2 p.265*

On Trying to Teach: The Mind in Correspondence. . *v.4 p.347*

On Tycho's Island: Tycho Brahe and His Assistants, 1570-1601. . . . .*v.3 p.46*

On Understanding Islam. *v.1 p.554*

On Violence. *v.4 p.497*

On War. *v.3 p.36*

On What Is Learned in School. *v.4 p.300*

On William Stafford: The Worth of Local Things. . . *v.2 p.115*

On with the Show!: The First Century of American Show Business. *v.1 p.35, p.36*

On with the Story: Stories. *v.2 p.142*

On Wittgenstein. *v.1 p.472*

On Women and Judaism: A View from Tradition. . . .*v.1 p.553*

On Wounds in the Head, in the Surgery, on Fractures, on Joints, Mochlikon, Vol. 3. . . . .*v.2 p.404, v.5 p.510*

On Writing Well: The Classic Guide to Writing Nonfiction. *v.2 p.574*

Once a Dancer: An Autobiography. *v.1 p.9*

The Once and Future Budapest. *v.3 p.186*

The Once and Future King. *v.2 p.387*

The Once and Future School: Three Hundred and Fifty Years of American Secondary Education. *v.4 p.327*

Once Five Years Pass: And Other Dramatic Works. . .*v.2 p.659*

Once upon a Time. *v.6 p.671*

Once upon Four Robbers. *v.2 p.757*

Once Were Warriors. *v.2 p.744*

The Oncogenomics Handbook: Understanding and Treating Cancer in the 21st Century. *v.5 p.165*

Oncogenomics: Molecular Approaches to Cancer. . . .*v.5 p.148*

Oncology Nursing: Assessment and Clinical Care. *v.5 p.520, p.528*

Oncology Nursing. *v.5 p.520, p.528*

One and Inseparable: Daniel Webster and the Union. .*v.3 p.415*

One Billion Customers: Lessons from the Front Lines of Doing Business in China. *v.6 p.194, p.197*

One Body in Christ: The History and Significance of the Evangelical Alliance. *v.1 p.568*

One Case at a Time: Judicial Minimalism on the Supreme Court. *v.4 p.540*

One Chord Wonders: Power and Meaning in Punk Rock. *v.1 p.271*

One Christmas in Washington: The Secret Meeting Between Roosevelt and Churchill That Changed the World. *v.4 p.628*

One Country or Two? *v.3 p.536*

One Day in China: May 21, 1936. . . . .*v.6 p.189*

One Day in the Life of Ivan Denisovich: A Novel. *v.2 p.808, p.809*

One Day of Life. *v.2 p.674*

One Discipline, Four Ways: British, German, French, and American Anthropology. *v.4 p.4*

One Flew over the Cuckoo's Nest: Text and Criticism.*v.2 p.148*

One Flew over the Cuckoo's Nest. *v.2 p.148*

One for All: The Logic of Group Conflict. *v.4 p.766*

One Greater Man: Justice and Damnation in Paradise Lost. *v.2 p.254*

One Hell of a Gamble: Khruschev, Castro and Kennedy, 1958-1964. . . . .*v.3 p.228, p.309*

One Hundred and One Poems by Paul Verlaine: A Bilingual Edition. *v.2 p.503*

One Hundred Love Sonnets/Cien Sonetos de Amor. . .*v.2 p.681*

One Hundred New Tales: Les Cents Nouvelles Nouvelles. *v.2 p.469*

One Hundred One Classroom Demonstrations and Experiments for Teaching Physics. *v.5 p.563*

One Hundred Years after Tomorrow: Brazilian Women's Fiction in the Twentieth Century. *v.2 p.693*

One Hundred Years' History of the Chinese in Singapore. *v.6 p.173*

One Hundred Years of Homosexuality: And Other Essays on Greek Love. *v.6 p.364*

One Hundred Years of Socialism: The West European Left in the Twentieth Century. *v.4 p.507*

One Hundred Years of Solitude: Essays. *v.2 p.684*

One Hundred Years of Solitude: Modes of Reading. . *v.2 p.683*

One Hundred Years of Solitude. *v.2 p.683*

One Hundred Years of the Negro in Show Business. . *v.1 p.34*

One King, One Faith: The Parlement of Paris and the Religious Reformations of the Sixteenth Century. *v.3 p.146*

One L: The Turbulent True Story of a First Year at Harvard Law School. *v.4 p.441*

One Land, Two Peoples: The Conflict over Palestine. *v.6 p.617*

One Long Argument: Charles Darwin and the Genesis of Modern Evolutionary Thought. *v.3 p.49, v.5 p.203*

One Man's Meat. *v.2 p.133*

One Matchless Time: A Life of William Faulkner. . .*v.2 p.75*

One Million Men: The Civil War Draft in the North. *v.3 p.431*

One Moldavian Summer. *v.2 p.817, p.818*

One More Kiss: The Broadway Musical in the 1970s.*v.1 p.252*

One More River: Over the River. *v.2 p.348*

One More River to Cross: Black and Gay in America.*v.6 p.366*

One Nation, after All: What Middle-Class Americans Really Think about God, Country, Family, Racism, Welfare, Immigration, Homosexuality, Work, the Right, the Left and Each Other. *v.4 p.697*

One Nation under a Groove: Motown and American Culture. *v.1 p.383*

☐ ONE National Gay & Lesbian Archives. *v.6 p.357*

One Night Out Stealing. *v.2 p.744*

One of Us: Richard Nixon and the American Dream. *v.3 p.482*

One Palestine, Complete: Jews and Arabs under the British Mandate. *v.6 p.612*

One Singular Sensation: The Michael Bennett Story. .*v.6 p.414*

One Step Ahead in China: Guangdong under Reform. *v.6 p.197, p.198*

One Teacher in 10. . . . .*v.6 p.383, p.385*

One Teenager in Ten: Writings by Gay and Lesbian Youth. *v.6 p.406*

One Thousand and One Night Stands. *v.1 p.12*

🄮 The One to One Manager: Real-World Lessons in Customer Relationship Management. *v.4 p.143*

One Two Three... Infinity: Facts and Speculations of Science. *v.5 p.399*

One Vast Winter Count: The Native American West Before Lewis and Clark. *v.6 p.686*

One World, Ready or Not: The Manic Logic of Global Capitalism. *v.4 p.664*

One Writer's Beginnings. *v.2 p.130*

One Writer's Imagination: The Fiction of Eudora Welty.*v.2 p.130*

One-Dimensional Man: Studies in the Ideology of Advanced Industrial Society. *v.4 p.700, p.761*

One-Eyed Science: Occupational Health and Women Workers. *v.6 p.444, p.457*

The Oneida Land Claims: A Legal History. *v.6 p.683, p.696, p.697*

O'Neill Complete Plays, 1913-1920, Vol. 1. *v.1 p.117, v.2 p.107*

O'Neill Complete Plays, 1920-1931, Vol. 2. *v.1 p.117, v.2 p.107*

O'Neill Complete Plays, 1933-1943, Vol. 3. . . . .*v.1 p.117, v.2 p.107, p.108*

O'Neill: Son and Artist. *v.2 p.108*

O'Neill: Son and Playwright. *v.2 p.108*

The One-State Solution: A Breakthrough for Peace in the Israeli-Palestinian Deadlock. *v.4 p.650*

O*Net OnLine. *v.5 p.577, p.578*

Onfim Nos...Finally Us...: Escritoras Negras Brasileviras Contemporaneas - Contemporary Black Brazilian Women Writers. *v.2 p.689*

Onitsha : roman. *v.2 p.531*

Onitsha. *v.2 p.531*

Online Assessment and Measurement: Case Studies from Higher Education, K-12 and Corporate. *v.5 p.601*

Online Consumer Psychology. *v.4 p.139, p.140*

Online Psychology Career Center. *v.5 p.676*

Online Searching: A Scientist's Perspective. *v.5 p.256*

Online Social Research: Methods, Issues and Ethics. *v.4 p.691*

Only Connect...: Art and the Spectator in the Italian Renaissance. *v.1 p.675*

Only Connect: Cultural Hist of Broadcasting in U. S. W/Infotrac. *v.4 p.412*

Only in London. *v.6 p.657*

The Only Investment Guide You'll Ever Need. *v.4 p.98*

Only Paradoxes to Offer: French Feminists and the Rights of Man. *v.3 p.54*

Only the Nails Remain: Scenes from the Balkan Wars. *v.3 p.247*

Only the Paranoid Survive: How to Exploit the Crisis Points that Challenge Every Company. *v.4 p.81*

Only the Voice. *v.2 p.676*

Only What We Could Carry: The Japanese American Internment Experience. *v.6 p.134*

Only Woman in the Room: A Memoir. *v.6 p.226*

Only Words. *v.4 p.459*

Only Yesterday: An Informal History of the 1920's. *v.3 p.371, p.445*

Only Yesterday. *v.6 p.647*

Onoto Watanna: The Story of Winnifred Eaton. . *v.6 p.92, p.93*

Ontario Provincial Park Trail Guide. *v.5 p.235*

The Ontogeny of Information: Developmental Systems and Evolution. *v.5 p.160, p.170, p.195*

Ontological Relativity and Other Essays. . . . *v.1 p.444, p.490*

Ontologies for Bioinformatics. *v.5 p.105*

Ontology, Identity, and Modality: Essays in Metaphysics. *v.1 p.489*

Open a New Window: The Broadway Musical in the 1960s. *v.1 p.252*

Open and Distance Learning in Developing World. . *v.4 p.314*

The Open Boat: Poems from Asian America. . *v.6 p.91, p.103*

Open Boundaries: Jain Communities and Cultures in Indian History. *v.1 p.538*

The Open Circle: The Theater Environment of Peter Brook. *v.1 p.148, p.153*

Open City: Seven Writers in Postwar Rome. *v.2 p.700*

Open Closed Open: Poems. *v.6 p.647*

The Open Door. *v.1 p.138, p.152, v.6 p.657*

An Open Economy Macroeconomics Reader. *v.4 p.239*

An Open Elite?: England 1540-1880. . . . . *v.4 p.726*

The Open Heaven: A Study of Apocalyptic in Judaism and Early Christianity. *v.1 p.617*

Open Secret: Gay Hollywood, 1928-2000. . . . . . *v.6 p.416*

Open Secrets: Stories. *v.2 p.737*

Open Sky: Sonny Rollins and His World of Improvisation. *v.1 p.262, p.351*

The Open Society and Its Enemies. *v.1 p.501, v.4 p.488*

The Open Society Paradox: Why the Twenty-First Century Calls for More Openness-Not Less. *v.4 p.773*

The Open Stage and the Modern Theatre in Research and Practice. *v.1 p.155*

Open to all: Ttile IX at Thirty. *v.4 p.821, p.882, p.890, p.893, p.900*

Open Wide: How Hollywood Box Office Became a National Obsession. *v.6 p.344*

Open Your Eyes and Soar: Cuban Women Writing Now. *v.3 p.306*

Opened Ground: Selected Poems, 1966-1996. . . . . *v.2 p.352*

Opening Cybernetic Frontier: Cities of the Prairie. . *v.4 p.543*

Opening NATO's Door: How the Alliance Remade Itself for a New Era. *v.4 p.639*

The Opening of the Field. *v.2 p.69*

Opening Spaces: An Anthology of Contemporary African Women's Writings. *v.2 p.752*

Opening Spaces: Design As Landscape Architecture. . *v.1 p.813*

Opening the Book: New Essays on New Zealand Writing. *v.2 p.742*

Open-Mindedness and Education. *v.4 p.339*

OpenSecrets.org. *v.4 p.557*

opensecrets.org. *v.4 p.559*

Opera: A History in Documents. *v.1 p.234*

Opera: A Research and Information Guide. . . *v.1 p.168, p.231*

Opera and Drama. *v.1 p.206, p.366*

Opera and Its Symbols: The Unity of Words, Music, and Staging. *v.1 p.229*

Opera As Drama. *v.1 p.230*

Opera: Clitopho, Respublica, Timaeus, Critias, Vol. IV. *v.2 p.417*

Opera in America: A Cultural History. *v.1 p.229, p.277*

Opera in Context: Essays on Historical Staging from the Late Renaissance to the Time of Puccini. . . . *v.1 p.232, p.404*

Opera in Seventeenth-Century Venice: The Creation of a Genre. *v.1 p.186, p.232, p.246*

The Opera Industry in Italy from Cimarosa to Verdi: The Role of the Impresario. *v.1 p.232, p.246, p.385*

Opera Minora. *v.2 p.445*

Opera: Minos, Leges, Epinomis, Epistulae, Definitiones, Vol. V. *v.2 p.417*

Opera Muliebria: Women and Work in Medieval Europe. *v.3 p.51*

Opera on Film. *v.6 p.316*

Opera: Parmenides, Philebus, Symposium, Phaedrus, Alcibiades I and II, Hipparchus, Amatores, Vol. II. *v.2 p.417*

Opera: The Art of Dying. *v.1 p.230*

Opera: The Undoing of Women. *v.1 p.378*

Opera: Theages, Charmides, Laches, Lysis, Euthydemus, Protagoras, Gorgias, Meno, Hippias Maior, Hippas Minor, Io, Menexenus, Vol. III. *v.2 p.417*

Opera Workshop. *v.1 p.234, p.404*

The Operas of Alban Berg: Lulu. *v.1 p.221, p.232, p.309*

The Operas of Alban Berg: Wozzeck. . .*v.1 p.221, p.232, p.309*

Operas of Monteverdi: Includes Orfeo, Return of Ulysses, Coronation of Poppea. .*v.1 p.185, p.186, p.231, p.342, p.409*

The Operas of Puccini. *v.1 p.193, p.228, p.349*

The Operas of Verdi: From Don Carlos to Falstaff, Vol. 3. . . . .*v.1 p.195, p.228, p.364*

The Operas of Verdi: From Il Trovatore to la Forza Del Destino, Vol. 2. . . . .*v.1 p.195, p.228, p.364*

The Operas of Verdi: From Oberto to Rigoletto, Vol. 1. . . . .*v.1 p.195, p.228, p.364*

Operation Gatekeeper: The Rise of the 'Illegal Alien' and Remaking of U. S. - Mexico Boundary. . . .*v.6 p.487, p.530*

Operation Just Cause: Lessons for Operations Other Than War. *v.3 p.306*

Operation Just Cause: The Incursion into Panama. . . .*v.3 p.305*

Operation Just Cause. *v.3 p.304*

Operation Shylock: A Confession. *v.2 p.154*

Operations Management: A Supply Chain Approach. . .*v.4 p.118*

Operative Rights. *v.4 p.513*

Operative Trauma Management. *v.5 p.522*

The Operator: David Geffen Builds, Buys, and Sells the New Hollywood. *v.6 p.418*

Operators and Promoters: The Story of Molecular Biology and Its Creators. *v.5 p.126*

Opere : romanzi e racconti, vol. 1. . . . . . .*v.2 p.719*

Opere : romanzi e racconti, vol. 2. . . . . . .*v.2 p.719, p.720*

Opere : romanzi e racconti, vol. 3. . . . . . .*v.2 p.720*

Opere di Giovanni Verga. *v.2 p.713*

Opere italiane, vol. 1. . . . .*v.2 p.706*

Opere italiane, vol. 2. . . . .*v.2 p.706*

Opere scelte di Giosue Carducci, vol. 1. . . . . .*v.2 p.710*

Opere scelte di Giosue Carducci, vol. 2. . . . . .*v.2 p.710*

Opere scelte. *v.2 p.716*

Opere, vol. 1. . . . .*v.2 p.709, p.710, p.712, p.717*

Opere, vol. 2. . . . .*v.2 p.709, p.710, p.712, p.717*

Opere, vol. 3. . . . .*v.2 p.709, p.712*

Operetta: A Theatrical History. *v.1 p.233, p.254*

Operette Morali: Essays and Dialogues. *v.2 p.711*

Opere. *v.2 p.708, p.709, p.711, p.723*

Opinion Polls: History, Theory and Practice. *v.4 p.435*

Opium and Empire: Chinese Society in Colonial Singapore, 1800-1910. . . . .*v.6 p.173*

Opium, empire, and the global political economy : a study of the Asian opium trade, 1750-1950. . . . . . .*v.6 p.145*

Opium Regimes: China, Britain and Japan, 1839-1952. .*v.6 p.180*

Opium to Java: Revenue Farming and Chinese Enterprise in Colonial Indonesia, 1860-1910. . . . . . .*v.6 p.177, p.178*

The Opium War, 1840-1842: Barbarians in the Celestial Empire in the Early Part of the Nineteenth Century and the War by Which They Forced Her Gates Ajar. . . .*v.6 p.187, p.204*

The Opium War Through Chinese Eyes. *v.6 p.188, p.204*

Oppenheimer: Portrait of an Enigma. *v.5 p.542*

Opportunities and Dangers of Soviet-Cuban Expansion: Towards a Pragmatic U. S. Policy. *v.3 p.391*

Opportunities in Biological Science Careers. *v.5 p.251, p.253, p.255*

Opportunities in Environmental Careers. *v.5 p.250*

Opportunities in Landscape Architecture, Botanical Gardens, and Arboreta Careers. *v.5 p.250*

Opportunities in Sports and Fitness Careers. *v.4 p.903*

Opportunities in Zoo Careers. *v.5 p.250*

The Opportunity: America's Moment to Alter History's Course. *v.3 p.483*

Opposing Hate Speech. *v.4 p.422, p.423*

The Opposing Self: Nine Essays in Criticism. *v.2 p.569*

Opposition in South Africa: The Leadership of Z. K. Matthews, Nelson Mandela and Stephen Biko. *v.6 p.79*

Oppressed but Not Defeated. Peasant Struggles among the Aymara and Qechwa in Bolivia. *v.3 p.324*

Optical Crystallography. *v.5 p.436*

Optical Mineralogy: The Nonopaque Minerals. . . .*v.5 p.436*

Optical Signal Processing. *v.5 p.701, p.702*

Opticks: Or Treatise of the Reflections, Inflections, and Colours of Light. *v.5 p.561*

Optics and Lasers: Including Fibers and Optical Waveguides. *v.5 p.561*

Optics and Photonics: An Introduction. *v.5 p.73, p.561*

Optics. *v.5 p.73, p.561*

Optima for Animals. *v.5 p.190*

Optimal Control: Basics and Beyond. *v.5 p.712*

The Optimal International Division of Labour: A WEP Study. *v.4 p.254*

Optimal Set Covering for Biological Classification: Theory of Conditional Clustering and Its Use in Biological Classification and Identification. *v.5 p.100*

Optimality Theory. *v.2 p.561*

Optimism and Pessimism: Implications for Theory, Research and Practice. *v.5 p.651*

Optimum Social Welfare and Productivity: A Comparative View. *v.4 p.266, p.267*

Options, Futures, and Other Derivatives. *v.5 p.503*

Opus Posthumous: Poems, Plays, Prose. *v.2 p.124*

Or Else, the Lightning God and Other Stories. *v.2 p.760*

Oracle Night: A Novel. *v.2 p.139, p.140*

Oral Arguments and Decision Making on the United States Supreme Court. *v.4 p.537*

Oral Embryology and Microscopic Anatomy: A Textbook for Students in Dental Hygiene. *v.5 p.525*

Oral History: A Novel. *v.2 p.155, p.156*

Oral History of the Principalship. *v.4 p.281*

Oral Literature of the Trio Indians of Surinam. . . .*v.3 p.322*

Oral Pathology for the Dental Hygienist. *v.5 p.525*

Oral Storytelling and Teaching Mathematics: Pedagogical and Multicultural Perspectives. *v.4 p.365*

Oral Tradition and Written Record in Classical Athens. .*v.3 p.19*

Orality and Literacy: The Technologizing of the Word. .*v.3 p.37*

Oranges Are Not the Only Fruit. *v.2 p.387, v.6 p.400*

Orator Hunt: Henry Hunt and English Working-Class Radicalism. *v.3 p.110, p.130*

The Orator in Action and Theory in Greece and Rome: Essays in Honor of George A. Kennedy. *v.2 p.427*

The Oratorio in the Baroque Era: Italy, Vienna, Paris. *v.1 p.186, p.237*

The Oratorio in the Baroque Era: Protestant Germany and England. *v.1 p.186, p.237*

The Oratorio in the Classical Era. *v.1 p.192, p.237*

The Oratorio in the Nineteenth and Twentieth Centuries. *v.1 p.204, p.224, p.237*

The Orator's Education: Bks. 11-12, Vol. 5. . . . . . .*v.2 p.442*

The Orator's Education: Bks. 1-2, Vol. 1. . . . . . .*v.2 p.442*

The Orator's Education, Bks. 3-5,Vol. 2. . . . . . .*v.2 p.442*

The Orator's Education: Bks. 6-8, Vol. 3. . . . . . .*v.2 p.442*

The Orator's Education: Bks. 9-10, Vol. 4. . . . . . .*v.2 p.442*

Orazio and Artemisia Gentileschi. *v.1 p.736, p.737*

Orbital Interaction Theory of Organic Chemistry. . . .*v.5 p.293*

Orbital Mechanics: Theory and Applications. *v.5 p.720*

Orbitals in Chemistry: A Modern Guide for Students. .*v.5 p.276*

The Orchard. *v.2 p.148*

Orchesographie. *v.1 p.21*

The Orchestra from Beethoven to Berlioz. *v.1 p.393*

Orchestra: or a Poem of Dancing. *v.1 p.22*

e Orchestra. *v.2 p.213*

Orchestral Combinations: The Science and Art of Instrumental Tone-Color. *v.1 p.393*

Orchestral Music: A Handbook. *v.1 p.165, p.238*

The Orchid Boat. *v.6 p.210*

Ordaining Women: Culture and Conflict in Religious Organizations. *v.1 p.658*

The Ordeal: A Trilogy - Book Three: Bleak Morning, Vol. 3. . . . .*v.2 p.809*

The Ordeal: A Trilogy - Book Two: 1918, Vol. 2. . . .*v.2 p.809*

The Ordeal: A Trilogy: The Sisters, Vol. 1. . . . . .*v.2 p.809*

Ordeal by Fire: The Civil War and Reconstruction. *v.3 p.399, p.431*

Ordeal by Slander. *v.3 p.460*

The Ordeal of Integration: Progress and Resentment in America's "Racial" Crisis. *v.4 p.729*

The Ordeal of Mark Twain. *v.2 p.33*

The Ordeal of Richard Feverel: A History of a Father and Son. *v.2 p.300*

The Ordeal of the African Writer. *v.6 p.80*

Ordeal of the Union: A House Dividing, 1852-1857, Vol. 2. . . . .*v.3 p.423*

Ordeal of the Union: Fruits of Manifest Destiny, 1847-1852. . . . .*v.3 p.423*

Ordeal of the Union, Vol. 2. . . . .*v.3 p.423*

The Ordeal of Thomas Hutchinson. *v.3 p.487*

The Ordeal of Woodrow Wilson. *v.3 p.472*

Order and Justice in International Relations. *v.4 p.626*

Order and Might. *v.4 p.499*

Order and Progress: Brazil from Monarchy to Republic.*v.3 p.336*

Order and Rebellion in Tribal Africa. *v.4 p.34, p.38*

The Order of Terror: The Concentration Camp. *v.3 p.86*

Order Out of Chaos: Man's New Dialogue with Nature.*v.5 p.404*

An Ordered Society: Family and Village in England, 1560-1725. . . . .*v.3 p.130*

Ordering Anarchy: Armies and Leaders in Tacitus' Histories. *v.2 p.444*

The Ordering of Love: The New and Collected Poems of Madeleine L'Engle. *v.2 p.148, p.149*

Ordinal Measurement in the Behavioral Sciences. . . .*v.5 p.599*

Ordinary Differential Equations: A Brief Eclectic Tour.*v.5 p.487*

Ordinary Differential Equations. *v.5 p.487*

Ordinary Families, Special Children: A Systems Approach to Childhood Disability. *v.5 p.668, p.669*

Ordinary Men: Reserve Battalion 101 and the Final Solution in Poland. *v.3 p.83*

Ordinary People in Extraordinary Times: The Citizenry and the Breakdown of Democracy. *v.4 p.503*

Ordinary Prussians: Brandenburg Junkers and Villagers, 1500-1840. . . . .*v.3 p.181*

Ore Microscopy and Ore Petrography. *v.5 p.436*

Oregon: End of the Trail. *v.3 p.532*

The Oregon Question: Essays in Anglo-American Diplomacy and Politics. *v.3 p.532*

The Oregon Trail: An American Saga. *v.3 p.521*

The Oregon Trail: The Missouri River to the Pacific Ocean. *v.3 p.532*

The Oregon Trail. *v.3 p.520*

Oregon's Promise: An Interpretive History. *v.3 p.532*

The Oresteia of Aeschylus. *v.2 p.352*

The Oresteia. *v.2 p.407*

Orfeo. *v.1 p.190, p.230, p.326*

The Organ in Western Culture, 750-1250. . . .*v.1 p.178, p.392*

The Organ: Its Evolution, Principles of Construction and Use. *v.1 p.392*

Organ Literature : A Comprehensive Survey. *v.1 p.238*

The Organ Music of J. S. Bach. *v.1 p.187, p.244, p.304*

Organ Technique: Modern and Early. *v.1 p.398, p.402*

Organic and Inorganic Photochemsitry, Vol. 2. . . .*v.5 p.278*

The Organic Chem Lab Survival Manual: A Student's Guide to Techniques. *v.5 p.301*

Organic Chemical Nomenclature. *v.5 p.289*

Organic Chemistry Info (Hans Reich--UW-Madison). *v.5 p.288*

Organic Chemistry: Methane to Macromolecules. . . .*v.5 p.292*

Organic Chemistry. *v.5 p.301*

The Organic Chemist's Book of Orbitals. *v.5 p.293*

The Organic Codes: An Introduction to Semantic Biology. *v.5 p.97, p.199*

Organic Electrochemistry: An Introduction and a Guide.*v.5 p.293*

Organic Electronic Spectral Data. *v.5 p.297*

Organic Experiments. *v.5 p.301*

Organic Farming. *v.5 p.30, p.31*

Organic Functional Group Preparations, Vol. I. . . .*v.5 p.295*

Organic Geochemistry: Principles and Applications. . .*v.5 p.440*

Organic Molecular Solids: Properties and Applications.*v.5 p.292*

Organic Peroxides. *v.5 p.291, p.292*

Organic Photochemistry: A Visual Approach. *v.5 p.278*

Organic Reactions in Aqueous Media. *v.5 p.296*

Organic Reactions. *v.5 p.295*

Organic Solvents: Physical Properties and Methods of
Purification. *v.5 p.291*

Organic Solvents, Vol. 1: Physical Properties and Methods of
Purification. *v.5 p.291*

Organic Stereochemistry. *v.5 p.298*

Organic Structural Spectroscopy. *v.5 p.297*

Organic Structure Analysis. *v.5 p.300*

Organic Structures from Spectra. *v.5 p.297*

Organic Syntheses Based on Name Reactions. *v.5 p.294*

Organic Syntheses: Reaction Guide. *v.5 p.293*

Organic Syntheses. *v.5 p.293*

Organic Synthesis Highlights II. *v.5 p.294*

Organic Synthesis Highlights. *v.5 p.294*

Organic Synthesis: The Roles of Boron and Silicon. .*v.5 p.296*

Organic Synthesis: The Science Behind the Art. . . .*v.5 p.294*

Organic Synthesis. *v.5 p.294*

The Organisation of Thought, Educational and
Scientific. *v.4 p.340*

Organisms and Artifacts: Design in Nature and
Elsewhere. *v.5 p.222*

Organization and Assembly of Plant and Animal Extracellular
Matrix. *v.5 p.206*

Organization Constraints on the Dynamics of Evolution. .*v.5 p.196*

The Organization of Academic Work. *v.4 p.292*

Organization of African Unity: An Annotated
Bibliography. *v.4 p.630, p.631*

Organization of American States (OAS). *v.3 p.259*

The Organization of American States, Vol. 11. . . .*v.4 p.631*

The Organization of Behavior: A Neuropsychological
Theory. *v.5 p.617*

The Organization of the Future. *v.4 p.73*

The Organization of the Social System and the Compositon of
the Social Forces, Set. *v.4 p.249*

Organizational Analysis: A Sociological View. *v.4 p.717*

Organizational Change and Gender Equity: International
Perspectives on Fathers and Mothers at the
Workplace. *v.6 p.465, p.466*

Organizational Citizenship Behavior: Its Nature, Antecedents,
and Consequences. *v.5 p.579*

Organizational Culture and Leadership. *v.4 p.75*

Organizational Improvement and Accountability. . .*v.4 p.281*

Organizational Learning from Performance Feedback: A
Behavioral Perspective on Innovation and
Change. *v.4 p.78, p.79*

Organizational Learning, Performance and Change: An
Introduction to Strategic Human Resource
Development. *v.4 p.76*

Organizational Learning. *v.4 p.78*

Organizational Literacy for Educators. *v.4 p.280*

Organizational Survival in the New World: The Intelligent
Complex Adaptive System. *v.4 p.78*

Organized Activities As Contexts of Development:
Extracurricular Activities, After-School and Community
Programs. *v.4 p.288*

Organized Crime and Democratic Governability: Mexico and the
U.S.-Mexican Borderlands. *v.3 p.290*

Organized Crime in America. *v.6 p.251*

Organized Labor in Postcommunist States: From Solidarity to
Infirmity. *v.4 p.127*

Organized Labor in Venezuela, 1958-1991: Behavior and
Concerns in a Democratic Setting. *v.3 p.360*

The Organized Labor Movement in Puerto Rico. . . .*v.3 p.319*

Organizing Asian American Labor: The Pacific Coast
Canned-Salmon Industry, 1870-1942. . . . . . .*v.6 p.116*

Organizing Business Knowledge: The MIT Process
Handbook. *v.4 p.77*

Organizing Crime: Essays in Opposition. *v.4 p.751*

Organizing Crime In Chinatown: Race and Racketeering in New
York City, 1890-1910. . . . . . .*v.6 p.119, p.124, p.127*

Organizing Dissent. *v.3 p.291*

Organizing Empire: Individualism, Collective Agency, and
India. *v.6 p.156*

Organizing for Peace: Neutrality, the Test Ban, and the
Freeze. *v.4 p.559, p.560*

Organizing Genius. *v.4 p.65*

Organizing to Win: New Research on Union Strategies. .*v.4 p.124*

Organizing Women: Formal and Informal Women's Groups in
the Middle East. *v.6 p.592*

Organometallic Compounds: Groups IV and V. *v.5 p.299*

Organometallic HyperTextBook (OH). *v.5 p.299*

Organotin Chemistry. *v.5 p.299*

Organotransition Metal Chemistry: Fundamental Concepts and
Applications. *v.5 p.307*

Organotransition Metal Chemistry. *v.5 p.307*

The Orient Express. *v.2 p.350*

The Orient Within: Muslim Minorities and the Negotiation of
Nationhood in Modern Bulgaria. *v.3 p.251*

Oriental Children in American Homes: How Do They
Adjust? *v.6 p.110*

Oriental Despotism: A Comparative Study of Total
Power. *v.6 p.182*

Oriental Enlightenment: The Encounter Between Asian and
Western Thought. *v.1 p.475*

Orientalism and Empire: North Caucasus Mountain Peoples and
the Georgian Frontier, 1845-1917. . . . .*v.3 p.213*

Orientalism and Religion: Postcolonial Theory, India and "the
Mystic East". *v.1 p.540*

Orientalism and Visual Culture: Imagining Mesopotamia in
Nineteenth-Century Europe. *v.1 p.673, p.677*

Orientalism: Western Concepts of the Orient. .*v.2 p.572, v.6 p.595*

Orientalism. *v.6 p.97, p.114, p.124*

The Orientalizing Revolution: Near Eastern Influence on Greek
Culture in the Early Archaic Age. *v.3 p.16*

Orientals: Asian Americans in Popular Culture. . .*v.6 p.88, p.90*

Orientations: Collected Writings. *v.1 p.209, p.210, p.312*

Origami Design Secrets: Mathematical Methods for an Ancient
Art. *v.5 p.469*

Origen, Prayer, Exhortation to Martyrdom. *v.1 p.591*

Origen: Selected Writings. *v.1 p.593*

Origen. *v.1 p.613*

The Origin and Early Diversification of Land Plants: A Cladistic Study. *v.5 p.449*

The Origin and Early Evolution of Life. *v.5 p.192*

The Origin and Evolution of Mammals. *v.5 p.448*

The Origin and Evolution of New Businesses. *v.4 p.67*

The Origin and Evolution of Planetary Nebulae. *v.5 p.69, p.70*

The Origin and Meaning of Courtly Love. *v.2 p.457*

The Origin and Meaning of Hasidism. *v.1 p.546*

The Origin and Prevention of Major Wars. *v.4 p.647*

The Origin of Animal Body Plans: A Study in Evolutionary Developmental Biology. *v.5 p.161*

Origin of Brands: How Product Evolution Creates Endless Possibilities for New Brands. *v.4 p.142*

The Origin of Consciousness in the Breakdown of the Bicameral Mind. *v.5 p.596*

Origin of Intelligence in the Child, Vol. 3. . . . . . *v.5 p.513*

The Origin of Mind: Evolution of Brain, Cognition, and General Intelligence. *v.5 p.653*

The Origin of Philosophy. *v.1 p.474*

The Origin of Species and the Voyage of the Beagle. *v.6 p.291*

The Origin of Species Revisited, Set. *v.5 p.202*

The Origin of Species, Revisited: The Search for a Victorian Who Anticipated Modern Developments in Darwin's Theory. *v.5 p.78, p.203*

Origin of the Family, Private Property, and the State. . *v.4 p.34*

The Origin of the Family, Private Property, and the State. *v.4 p.737*

Origin of the Human Species. *v.5 p.201*

Original Enlightenment and the Transformation of Medieval Japanese Buddhism. *v.1 p.562*

Original Fire: Selected and New Poems. *v.2 p.145*

Original Gay and Lesbian Writing: Science Fiction. . *v.6 p.406*

Original Intent and the Struggle for the Supreme Court: The Politics of Judicial Appointments. *v.4 p.541*

Original Meanings: Politics and Ideas in the Making of the Constitution. *v.4 p.452*

Original Modern Reader's Japanese-English Character Dictionary. *v.6 p.232*

The Original People. *v.6 p.683*

Original Plays. *v.2 p.288*

Original Sin: Clarence Thomas and the Failure of the Constitutional Conservatives. *v.4 p.538*

Original Story by Arthur Laurents: A Memoir of Broadway and Hollywood. *v.6 p.418*

Origination of Organismal Form: Beyond the Gene in Developmental and Evolutionary Biology. *v.5 p.160*

The Origins and Development of Federal Crime Control Policy: Herbert Hoover's Initiatives. *v.4 p.523*

The Origins and Development of Professional Football, 1890-1920. . . . . *v.4 p.807, p.859*

The Origins and Development of Pure Land Buddhism: A Study and Translation of Gyonen's Jodo Homon Genrusho. *v.1 p.567*

The Origins and Development of the English Language. *v.2 p.553*

Origins and Development of the Turkish Novel. . . . *v.6 p.666*

Origins and Species: A Study on the Historical Sources of Darwinism and the Contexts of Some Other Accounts of Organic Diversity from Plato and Aristotle On. *v.5 p.79, p.203*

Origins: Genesis, Evolution and Diversity of Life. . . *v.5 p.196*

Origins, Icons and Illusions. *v.5 p.77*

Origins of a Civilization: The Prehistory and Early Archaeology of South Asia. *v.4 p.8*

The Origins of a Pacific Coast Chiefdom: The Chumash of the Channel Islands. *v.4 p.10, v.6 p.684*

The Origins of Adversary Criminal Trial. *v.6 p.270*

The Origins of Agriculture in the Lowland Neotropics. *v.5 p.16*

The Origins of American Constitutionalism. *v.4 p.452*

Origins of Analytical Philosophy. *v.1 p.502*

The Origins of Anti-Semitism: Attitudes Toward Judaism in Pagan and Christian Antiquity. *v.1 p.549*

The Origins of Arab Nationalism. *v.6 p.583*

The Origins of Argentina's Revolution of the Right. . *v.3 p.349*

The Origins of Chinese Civilization. *v.6 p.184*

The Origins of Chinese Communism. *v.6 p.192*

Origins of Class Struggle in Louisiana: A Social History of White Farmers and Laborers During Slavery and After, 1840-1875. . . . . *v.3 p.507*

The Origins of Courtliness: Civilizing Trends and the Formation of Courtly Ideals, 939-1210. . . . . . . *v.6 p.556, p.565*

The Origins of Criticism: Literary Culture and Poetic Theory in Classical Greece. *v.2 p.400*

Origins of Cyberspace: A Library on the History of Computing and Computer-Related Telecommunications. . . . *v.4 p.420*

The Origins of Democratization in Poland: Workers, Intellectuals, and Oppositional Politics, 1976-1980. *v.3 p.255*

Origins of European Printmaking: Fifteenth-Century Woodcuts and Their Public. *v.1 p.753, p.754*

Origins of Existence: How Life Emerged in the Universe. *v.5 p.190, p.242*

Origins of Icelandic Literature. *v.2 p.625*

Origins of Instability in Early Republican Mexico. . *v.3 p.289*

Origins of Intelligence in Children. *v.5 p.628, p.630*

Origins of Intelligence: The Evolution of Cognitive Development in Monkeys, Apes, and Humans. . . *v.5 p.609*

The Origins of International Economics, Vol. 1. . . . *v.4 p.255*

Origins of Language: What Nonhuman Primates Can Tell Us. *v.4 p.19*

Origins of Leftwing Cinema in China, 1932-37. *v.6 p.334, p.335*

The Origins of Life and the Universe. *v.5 p.194, p.243*

Origins of Life: Biblical and Evolutionary Models Face Off. *v.5 p.195*

The Origins of Life: From the Birth of Life to the Origin of Language. *v.5 p.194*

Origins of Life: On Earth and in the Cosmos. *v.5 p.243, p.244*

The Origins of Malay Nationalism. *v.6 p.173*

The Origins of Modern African Thought. *v.6 p.54*

The Origins of Modern English Society: 1780-1880. . *v.3 p.114*

Origins of Modern English Society. *v.6 p.735, p.742*

The Origins of Modern Germany. . . *v.3 p.67, p.161, v.6 p.568*

The Origins of Modern Russian Education: An Intellectual Biography of Count Sergei Uvarov, 1786-1855. . *v.3 p.218*

The Origins of Modern Science. *v.3 p.46, v.5 p.390*

The Origins of Muhammadan Jurisprudence. *v.1 p.556*

The Origins of Music. *v.1 p.284*

Origins of Nationality in South Asia: Patriotism and Ethical
Government in the Making of Modern India. . . . *v.6 p.146*

The Origins of Nazi Genocide: From Euthanasia to the Final
Solution. *v.3 p.83, v.4 p.652*

Origins of Neuroscience: A History of Explorations into Brain
Function. *v.5 p.616*

The Origins of Nonliberal Capitalism: Germany and Japan in
Comparison. *v.6 p.226*

Origins of Papal Infallibility,1150-1350: A Study on the
Concepts of Infallibility, Sovereignty and
Tradition in the Middle Ages. *v.1 p.576*

The Origins of Peasant Servitude in Medieval
Catalonia. *v.6 p.575*

The Origins of Science: An Inquiry into the Foundations of
Western Thought. *v.5 p.402*

Origins of Terrorism: Psychologies, Ideologies, Theologies,
States of Mind. *v.4 p.661*

The Origins of the American High School. *v.4 p.328*

The Origins of the Arab-Israeli Wars. *v.6 p.611*

The Origins of the Authoritarian Welfare State in Prussia:
Conservatives, Bureaucracy, and the Social Question,
1815-70. . . . .*v.3 p.168*

Origins of the Bill of Rights. *v.4 p.456*

The Origins of the Boxer Uprising. *v.6 p.188*

Origins of the Chinese Revolution, 1915-1949. . . .*v.6 p.192*

The Origins of the Chosfon Dynasty. *v.4 p.621, v.6 p.236*

The Origins of the Cultural Revolution: Contradictions among
the People, 1956-1957. . . . .*v.6 p.195, p.196*

The Origins of the Cultural Revolution: The Great Leap
Forward. *v.6 p.196*

Origins of the Czech National Renascence. *v.3 p.188*

Origins of the Druze People and Religion: With Extracts from
Their Sacred Writings. *v.6 p.600*

The Origins of the English Civil War. *v.3 p.104*

Origins of the English Language: A Social and Linguistic
History. *v.2 p.555*

The Origins of the English Novel, 1600-1740. *v.2 p.192, p.578*

Origins of the European Economy: Communications and
Commerce AD 300-900. . . . .*v.3 p.66*

Origins of the Fifth Amendment: The Right Against
Self-Incrimination. *v.4 p.473*

The Origins of the Final Solution: The Evolution of Nazi Jewish
Policy, September 1939-March 1942. . . . . . .*v.3 p.83*

Origins of the First World War. *v.3 p.79*

Origins of the French Revolution. *v.3 p.150*

The Origins of the Great Schism: A Study in the
Fourteenth-Century Ecclesiastical History. . . .*v.3 p.69, p.70*

The Origins of the Great Schism. *v.1 p.574*

Origins of the Greek Nation: The Byzantine Period
1204-1461. . . . .*v.3 p.191*

The Origins of the Inquisition in Fifteenth Century
Spain. *v.3 p.57, p.240*

Origins of the Islamic State. *v.6 p.584*

Origins of the Israeli Polity: Palestine under the
Mandate. *v.6 p.612*

The Origins of the Keynesian Revolution. *v.4 p.227*

The Origins of the Korean War, 1947-1950: The Roaring of the
Cataract. *v.6 p.236*

The Origins of the Korean War: Liberation and the Emergence
of Separate Regimes. *v.6 p.236*

The Origins of the Korean War. *v.6 p.237*

The Origins of the Modern Jew: Jewish Identity and European
Culture in Germany, 1749-1824. . . . .*v.1 p.547*

Origins of the New South, 1877-1913. . . . .*v.3 p.403, p.497*

Origins of the New South Fifty Years Later: The Continuing
Influence of a Historical Classic. *v.3 p.496*

The Origins of the Ottoman Empire. *v.6 p.590*

Origins of the Peruvian Labor Movement, 1883-1919. *v.3 p.328*

Origins of the Popular Style: The Antecedents of
Twentieth-Century Popular Music. *v.1 p.275*

The Origins of the Republican Party, 1852-1856. . .*v.3 p.397*

Origins of the Russian Intelligensia: The Eighteenth-Century
Nobility. *v.3 p.216*

The Origins of the Second World War: American Foreign Policy
and World Politics, 1917-1941. . . . .*v.3 p.453*

Origins of the Social Mind: Evolutionary Psychology and Child
Development. *v.5 p.626*

The Origins of the University: The Schools of Paris and Their
Critics, 1100-1215. . . . .*v.6 p.558*

The Origins of the Urban Crisis: Race and Inequality in Postwar
Detroit. *v.3 p.517, v.4 p.771, v.6 p.725*

The Origins of the Vietnam War. *v.6 p.169*

The Origins of the War of 1914. . . . .*v.3 p.80*

The Origins of Totalitarianism. *v.4 p.509*

Origins of Value: A Document History of
Finance. *v.4 p.89, p.146, p.147*

The Origins of Virtue: Human Instincts and the Evolution of
Cooperation. *v.5 p.195*

The Origins of World War I. *v.3 p.79*

Origins: The Evolution of Continents, Oceans, and Life. .*v.5 p.445*

The Oriki of a Grasshopper, and Other Plays. *v.2 p.757*

The Orion Nebula: Where Stars Are Born. *v.5 p.70*

Orkneyinga Saga: The History of the Earls of Orkney. *v.2 p.625*

Orlando: A Biography. *v.2 p.394, v.6 p.400*

Orlando Furioso, Pt. 1. . . . .*v.2 p.707*

Orlando Furioso: The Frenzy of Orlando: A Romantic
Epic. *v.2 p.707*

Orlando furioso. *v.2 p.707*

Orlando Furioso. *v.2 p.707*

Orlando Innamorato. *v.2 p.708*

Orley Farm. *v.2 p.318*

The Ornament of the World: How Muslims, Jews, and
Christians Created a Culture of Tolerance in Medieval
Spain. *v.3 p.238*

Ornamentalism: How the British Saw Their
Empire. *v.6 p.745, p.746*

Ornette Coleman: His Life and Music. .*v.1 p.264, p.317, p.318*

Oroonoko: A Tragedy. *v.2 p.260*

Oroonoko. *v.2 p.238*

Orphan Warriors: Three Manchu Generations and the End of the Qing World. *v.6 p.188*

The Orphan. *v.2 p.252*

Orpheus and Greek Religion: A Study of the Orphic Movement. *v.1 p.532*

Orpheus and Power: The Movimento Negro of Rio de Janeiro and Sao Paulo, Brazil 1945-1988. . . . .*v.3 p.279*

Orphic Songs. *v.2 p.713, p.714*

Orthodox Christians in America. *v.1 p.569*

The Orthodox Church in the Byzantine Empire. *v.1 p.569, v.3 p.56, p.57*

The Orthodox Church: Its Past and Its Role in the World Today. *v.1 p.570*

The Orthodox Church. *v.1 p.570*

The Orthodox Liturgy: The Development of the Eucharistic Liturgy in the Byzantine Rite. *v.1 p.570*

Orthodox Russia: Belief and Practice under the Tsars and Beyond. *v.1 p.569*

Orthodoxy and Heresy in Earliest Christianity. . . .*v.1 p.646*

Orthodoxy, Heresy, and Schism in Early Christianity. .*v.1 p.646*

Orthodoxy. *v.1 p.596, v.2 p.277*

Orthosilicates. *v.5 p.436*

Ortlich Betaubt. *v.2 p.608*

Ortografia de la Lengua Española. *v.2 p.637*

Orton Diaries: Including the Correspondence of Edna Welthorpe and Others. *v.2 p.374*

Orwell for Beginners. *v.2 p.376*

The Orwell Mystique: A Study in Male Ideology. . .*v.2 p.376*

Orwell: The Life. *v.2 p.376*

Orwell to the Present: Literature in England, 1945-2000. *v.2 p.178*

Orwell: Wintry Conscience of a Generation. *v.2 p.375*

Orwell's 1984: Text, Sources, Criticism. *v.2 p.375*

Orwell's Politics. *v.2 p.375*

Oryx and Crake. *v.2 p.734*

The Oryx Resource Guide to el Nino and la Nina. . .*v.6 p.285*

Os Lusiadas. *v.2 p.688*

Osama: The Making of a Terrorist. *v.4 p.661*

Oscar and Lucinda. *v.2 p.744*

Oscar Micheaux and His Circle: African-American Filmmaking and Race Cinema of the Silent Era. *v.6 p.329, p.340*

Oscar Wilde - the Major Works: Including The Picture of Dorian Gray. *v.2 p.322*

Oscar Wilde: A Certain Genius. *v.2 p.320*

Oscar Wilde: A Collection of Critical Essays. *v.2 p.321*

Oscar Wilde: A Life in Letters. *v.2 p.322*

Oscar Wilde, a Pictorial Biography. *v.2 p.321*

Oscar Wilde and the Poetics of Ambiguity. *v.2 p.321*

The Oscar Wilde Encyclopedia. *v.2 p.320*

Oscar Wilde, His Life and Confessions. *v.2 p.321*

Oscar Wilde in the 1990s: The Critic As Creator. . .*v.2 p.321*

Oscar Wilde: Myths, Miracles and Imitations. *v.2 p.321*

Oscar Wilde: Recent Research: A Supplement to 'Oscar Wilde Revalued'. *v.2 p.321*

Oscar Wilde: The Man, His Writings, and His World. *v.2 p.321*

Oscar Wilde. *v.2 p.320, p.321, v.6 p.401*

Oscar Zeta Acosta: The Uncollected Works. *v.6 p.491, p.503, p.516*

OSI Reference Model for Telecommunications. . . .*v.4 p.115*

Osip Mandelstam and the Modernist Creation of Tradition. *v.2 p.802*

Osmoregulation and Drinking in Vertebrates. *v.5 p.163*

Ostracism: The Power of Silence. *v.5 p.649*

Ostrogoths. Kinship and Society. *v.3 p.30*

OSU Virtual Finance Library. . *v.4 p.90, p.93, p.101, p.103*

Oswald Mosley. *v.3 p.119*

Othello: A Contextual History. *v.2 p.232*

Othello: Critical Essays. *v.2 p.230*

The Other Bostonians: Poverty and Progress in the American Metropolis, 1880-1970. . . . .*v.4 p.707*

The Other Civil War: American Women in the Nineteenth Century. *v.6 p.453*

Other Dickens: Pickwick to Chuzzlewit. *v.2 p.282*

The Other Elites: Women, Politics, and Power in the Executive Branch. *v.4 p.526*

The Other Founders: Anti-Federalism and the Dissenting Tradition in America, 1788-1828. . . . .*v.4 p.523*

The Other Greeks: The Family Farm and the Agrarian Roots of Western Civilization. *v.3 p.17*

The Other Harmony: The Collected Poetry of Eli Mandel. *v.2 p.736*

The Other Henry James. *v.2 p.45, p.46*

The Other Hollywood: The Uncensored Oral History of the Porn Film Industry. *v.6 p.317*

The Other Israel: Voices of Refusal and Dissent. . .*v.6 p.615*

The Other Kurds: Yazidis in Colonial Iraq. *v.6 p.598, p.602, p.603*

The Other Lover. *v.2 p.155*

The Other Man: Conversations with Graham Greene. *v.2 p.348, p.349*

The Other Modernism: F. T. Marinetti's Futurist Fiction of Power. *v.2 p.718*

The Other Path: The Invisible Revolution in the Third World. *v.3 p.329*

Other People's Children: Cultural Conflict in the Classroom. *v.4 p.309*

Other Planets: The Music of Karlheinz Stockhausen. *v.1 p.218, p.358*

The Other Rebellion: Popular Violence, Ideology, and the Mexican Struggle for Independence, 1810-1821. . .*v.3 p.288*

The Other Reconstruction: Where Violence and Womanhood Meet in the Writings of Ida B. Wells-Barnett, Angelina Weld Grimke, and Nella Larsen. . . .*v.6 p.7, p.18*

Other Septembers, Many Americas: Selected Provocations, 1980-2004. . . . .*v.2 p.680*

The Other Side of Russia: A Slice of Life in Siberia and the Russian Far East. *v.3 p.214*

The Other Side of Silence: Men's Lives and Gay Identities - a Twentieth-Century History. *v.6 p.367, p.375, p.376*

The Other Side of Silence: Voices from the Partition of India. *v.6 p.160*

The Other Side of the '60s: Young Americans for Freedom and the Rise of Conservative Politics. *v.4 p.516*

The Other Side of the Asian American Success
   Story. *v.4 p.311, v.6 p.109*

The Other Side of the Closet: The Coming-Out Crisis for
   Straight Spouses and Families. *v.6 p.368*

The Other Side: The Fault Lines, Guerrilla Saints and True
   Heart of Rock 'n' Roll. *v.6 p.521, p.522*

The Other South: Southern Dissenters in the Nineteenth
   Century. *v.3 p.428*

'Other' Spanish Theatres: Erasure and Inscription on the
   Twentieth-Century Spanish Stage. *v.1 p.108*

Other Traditions. *v.2 p.57*

The Other Victorians: A Study of Sexuality and Pornography in
   Mid-Nineteenth Century England. *v.6 p.759, p.760*

The Other Voice: Essays on Modern Poetry. *v.2 p.577*

The Other Voices: A History of Homosexuality and Popular
   Music. *v.6 p.408*

Other Voices, Other Rooms. *v.2 p.66, v.6 p.395*

The Other World: Spiritualism and Psychical Research in
   England, 1850-1914. . . . .*v.3 p.114, p.129*

Other Worlds: The Comical History of the States and Empires
   of the Moon and Sun. *v.2 p.472, p.473*

Other Worlds: The Search for Life in the Universe. . .*v.5 p.74*

Otherwise: Last and First Poems of Eugenio Montale. .*v.2 p.719*

Otherwise Than Being or Beyond Essence. *v.1 p.456*

The Otis Guernsey-Burns Mantle Theater Yearbook: The Best
   Plays of 1992-1993. . . . .*v.1 p.66, p.115*

The Otis Guernsey-Burns Mantle Theater Yearbook: The Best
   Plays of 1993-1994. . . . .*v.1 p.66, p.115*

The Otis Guernsey-Burns Mantle Theater Yearbook: The Best
   Plays of 1994-1995. . . . .*v.1 p.66, p.115*

The Otis Guernsey-Burns Mantle Theater Yearbook: The Best
   Plays of 1995-1996. . . . .*v.1 p.65, p.66, p.114*

The Otis Guernsey-Burns Mantle Theater Yearbook: The Best
   Plays of 1996-1997. . . . .*v.1 p.65, p.114*

The Otis Guernsey-Burns Mantle Theater Yearbook: The Best
   Plays of 1997-1998. . . . .*v.1 p.65, p.114*

Otto Hahn: A Scientific Autobiography. *v.5 p.261*

Otto III. *v.3 p.162*

Ottoman Art in the Service of Empire. *v.1 p.674, p.801*

Ottoman Borderlands: Issues, Personalities, and Political
   Changes. *v.6 p.590*

Ottoman Civil Officialdom: A Social History. *v.4 p.614*

Ottoman Diplomacy in Hungary. *v.3 p.186*

The Ottoman Empire, 1700-1922. . . . .*v.6 p.591*

The Ottoman Empire and Early Modern Europe. .*v.6 p.589, p.590*

The Ottoman Empire and European Capitalism, 1820-1913:
   Trade, Investment and Production. *v.6 p.624*

Ottoman Empire and Islamic Tradition. . . .*v.3 p.69, v.6 p.590*

The Ottoman Empire and the World Around
   It. *v.4 p.641, v.6 p.589*

The Ottoman Empire and the World Economy: The Nineteenth
   Century. *v.6 p.590*

The Ottoman Empire: The Classical Age, 1300-1600. .*v.6 p.590*

Ottoman Greeks in the Age of Nationalism: Politics, Economy
   and Society in the Nineteenth Century. *v.3 p.195*

Ottoman Lyric Poetry: An Anthology. *v.6 p.666*

Ottoman Manufacturing in the Age of the Industrial
   Revolution. *v.6 p.591*

The Ottoman Peoples and the End of Empire. *v.6 p.590*

Ottoman Statecraft: The Book of Council for Vezirs and
   Governors (Nasaih Ul-Vuzera Ve' Lumera) of
   Sari Mehmed Pasha, the Defterdar. *v.6 p.590*

An Ottoman Tragedy: History and Historiography at
   Play. *v.6 p.591*

The Ottoman Turks: An Introductory History to 1923. .*v.6 p.590*

Ottoman Warfare, 1500-1700. . . . .*v.3 p.36*

Ottonian Germany: The Chronicon of Thietmar of
   Merseburg. *v.3 p.162, p.163*

Otway and Lee: Biography from a Baroque Age. . .*v.2 p.251*

Ouï dire. *v.2 p.529*

Our Affair with el Nino: How We Transformed an Enchanting
   Peruvian Current into a Global Climate Hazard. . .*v.5 p.430*

Our Age: Portrait of a Generation. *v.3 p.118, p.127*

Our Appalachia: An Oral History. *v.3 p.498*

Our Bodies, Ourselves: A New Edition for a New Era. .*v.5 p.523*

Our Bodies, Ourselves for the New Century: A Book by and for
   Women. *v.6 p.443*

Our Children, Their Children: Confronting Racial and Ethnic
   Differences in American Juvenile Justice. *v.6 p.248*

Our Common Lands: Defending the National Parks. . .*v.4 p.463*

Our Common Seas. *v.5 p.241*

Our Dramatic Heritage: Expressing the Inexpressible, Vol.
   6. . . . .*v.1 p.66, p.82*

Our Dramatic Heritage: Reactions to Realism, Vol.
   5. . . . .*v.1 p.66, p.70, p.79, p.80, p.82*

Our Dramatic Heritage: Romanticism and
   Realism. *v.1 p.66, p.69, p.70, p.79*

Our Dramatic Heritage: The 18th Century, Vol. 3. .*v.1 p.66, p.78*

Our Dramatic Heritage: The Golden Age. . .*v.1 p.66, p.74, p.108*

Our Dramatic Heritage, Vol. 1. . .*v.1 p.66, p.70, p.71, p.72, p.73*

Our Earth's Changing Land: An Encyclopedia of Land-Use and
   Land-Cover
   Change. *v.1 p.812, v.4 p.267, p.268,v.5 p.17, v.6 p.285*

Our Feet Walk the Sky: Women of the South Asian
   Diaspora. *v.6 p.92, p.138*

Our Final Hour: A Scientist's Warning: How Terror, Error, and
   Environmental Disaster Threaten Humankind's Future
   in This Century - On Earth and Beyond. . .*v.4 p.661, p.667*

Our Friend Manso. *v.2 p.654*

Our Government: The Supreme Court and the Judicial
   Branch. *v.4 p.534*

Our Guerrillas, Our Sidewalks: A Journey into the Violence of
   Colombia. *v.3 p.357*

Our Kentucky: A Study of the Bluegrass State. *v.3 p.511*

Our Kind of Guys: The United States and the Indonesian
   Military. *v.6 p.175, p.177*

Our Kind: Who We Are, Where We Came from, Where We Are
   Going. *v.4 p.22*

Our Knowledge of the External World: As a Field for Scientific
   Method in Philosophy. *v.1 p.483*

Our Labeled Children: What Every Parent and Teacher Needs to
   Know about Learning Disabilities. *v.4 p.319*

Our Lady of Class Struggle: The Cult of the Virgin Mary in Haiti. *v.3 p.315*

Our Lady of Guadalupe: The Origins and Sources of a Mexican National Symbol, 1531-1797. . . . . *v.3 p.264, p.287*

Our Lady of the Flowers. *v.2 p.519, v.6 p.396*

Our Land Is Made of Courage and Glory: Nationalist Drama of Nicaragua and Guatemala. *v.3 p.303*

Our Lives: Canada since 1945. . . . . *v.3 p.541*

Our Lives for Ourselves: Women Who Have Never Married. *v.4 p.738*

Our Living World: Over 15 Complete Printable Unit Studies with Interactive Links. *v.5 p.228*

Our Man in Havana. *v.2 p.350*

Our Molecular Future: How Nanotechnology, Robotics, Genetics, and Artificial Intelligence Will Transform Our World. *v.5 p.136, p.265*

Our Movie Heritage. *v.6 p.331*

Our Musicals, Ourselves: A Social History of the American Musical Theater. *v.1 p.251*

Our Mutual Friend. by Charles Dickens (Boz.) with forty-one illustrations. from designs by Marcus Stone. . . . *v.2 p.283*

Our Mutual Friend. *v.2 p.284*

Our Naked Frailties: Sensational Art and Meaning in Macbeth. *v.2 p.230*

Our National Parks and the Search for Sustainability. . *v.5 p.18*

Our Nation's Government: Judicial Branch. *v.4 p.535*

Our Nig: Or, Sketches from the Life of a Free Black. *v.2 p.53, v.6 p.28, p.47*

Our Only Star and Compass: Locke and the Struggle for Political Rationality. *v.4 p.492, p.502*

Our Place on Campus: Lesbian, Gay, Bisexual, Transgender Services and Programs in Higher Education. *v.6 p.385, p.386*

Our Plant Home. *v.5 p.221*

Our Posthuman Future: Consequences of the Biotechnology Revolution. *v.5 p.217, p.247*

Our Right to Choose: Toward a New Ethic of Abortion. *v.6 p.465, p.469*

Our Rightful Share: The Afro-Cuban Struggle for Equality, 1886-1912. . . . . *v.3 p.279, p.310*

Our Schools and Our Future: Are We Still at Risk? . *v.4 p.328*

Our Sister Editors: Sarah J. Hale and the Tradition of Nineteenth-Century American Women Editors. *v.4 p.409, p.410*

Our Sister Killjoy: Longman African Writers. *v.2 p.752*

Our Sisters' Promised Land: Women, Politics, and Israeli-Palestinian Coexistence. *v.6 p.617*

Our Studies, Ourselves: Sociologists' Lives and Work. *v.4 p.675*

Our Times: The United States, 1900-1925. . . . . *v.3 p.450*

Our Unfree Press: 100 Years of Radical Media Criticism. *v.4 p.558*

Our Vampires, Ourselves. *v.2 p.174, p.190*

Ourselves Alone: Women's Emigration from Ireland, 1885-1920. . . . . *v.3 p.135*

Out and about Campus: Personal Accounts by Lesbian, Gay, Bisexual and Transgendered College Students. . . *v.6 p.385*

Out Cry. *v.2 p.135*

Out for Good: The Struggle to Build a Gay Rights Movement in America. *v.6 p.365, p.386*

Out Front: Contemporary Gay and Lesbian Plays. . . *v.6 p.413*

Out in All Directions: The Almanac of Gay and Lesbian America. *v.6 p.361*

Out in Force: Sexual Orientation and the Military. *v.6 p.389, p.390*

Out in the Field: Reflections of Lesbian and Gay Anthropologists. *v.4 p.25*

Out in the South. *v.6 p.368*

Out in the World: Gay and Lesbian Life from Buenos Aires to Bangkok. *v.6 p.421*

Out in Theory: The Emergence of Lesbian and Gay Anthropology. *v.4 p.24*

Out of Africa. *v.2 p.626*

Out of Bounds: Inside the NBA's Culture of Rape, Violence, and Crime. *v.4 p.813, p.814, p.853*

Out of Bounds: Sports, Media and the Politics of Identity. *v.4 p.813, p.901*

Out of China's Earth. *v.6 p.184*

Out of Danger: Poems. *v.2 p.344*

Out of Eden: An Odyssey of Ecological Invasion. . . *v.5 p.186*

Out of Exile. *v.6 p.175, p.178*

Out of Gas: The End of the Age of Oil. *v.4 p.160*

Out of It: A Cultural History of Intoxication. *v.4 p.777*

Out of Many, One: A History of the American College of Sports Medicine. *v.4 p.803, p.824*

Out of My Later Years. *v.5 p.542*

Out of Our Lives: A Selection of Contemporary Black Fiction. *v.2 p.27*

Out of Our Minds: Anti-Intellectualism and Talent Development in American Schooling. *v.4 p.317*

Out of Our Past: The Forces That Shaped Modern America. *v.3 p.379, p.440, p.446*

Out of Place: Restoring Identity to the Regional Landscape. *v.1 p.813*

Out of the Ashes: The Impact of American Jews on Post-Holocaust European Jewry. *v.3 p.82*

Out of the Barrio: Toward a New Politics of Hispanic Assimilation. *v.6 p.540*

Out of the Fringe: Contemporary Latina/o Theatre and Performance. *v.6 p.516, p.518*

Out of the Ghetto: The Social Background of Jewish Emancipation, 1770-1870. . . . . *v.3 p.59*

Out of the Jungle: Jimmy Hoffa and the Remaking of the American Working Class. *v.4 p.129*

ⓔ Out of the Margin: Feminist Perspectives on Economics. *v.4 p.274*

Out of the Mouths of Slaves: African American Language and Educational Malpractice. *v.2 p.551*

Out of the Ordinary: Essays on Growing up with Gay, Lesbian and Transgender Parents. *v.6 p.367, p.375*

Out of the Past. *v.6 p.363*

Out of the Red Shadows: Anti-Semitism in Stalin's Russia. *v.3 p.60, p.226*

Out of the Shadow of Antiquity: The Politics of Technological Change in Prussia, 1809-1848. . . . . *v.3 p.167, p.168*

Out of the Shadows: Women and Politics in the French Revolution, 1789-95. *.v.3 p.54, p.151, p.158,v.6 p.453, p.454*

Out of the Silent Planet.. . . . . *.v.2 p.366*

Out of Their Minds: The Lives and Discoveries of 15 Great Computer Scientists.. . . . . *.v.5 p.342, p.344*

Out on Stage: Lesbian and Gay Theater in the Twentieth Century.. *.v.2 p.16*

Out Takes: Essays on Queer Theory and Film. . . . *.v.6 p.416*

Out Visiting and Back Home: Russian Stories on Aging. *.v.2 p.794*

The Outbreak of the Peloponnesian War.. . . . . . . *.v.3 p.18*

Outcast London: A Study in the Relationship Between Classes in Victorian Society.. . . . . *.v.3 p.113, p.131*

☐ Outcome Measurement Resource Network. . . . *.v.5 p.672*

Outcome-Based Evaluation.. . . . . *.v.5 p.672*

Outdoor Action Games for Elementary Children: Active Games and Academic Activities for Fun and Fitness. *.v.4 p.787, p.795*

Outdoor Careers: Exploring Occupations in Outdoor Fields.. . . . . *.v.5 p.251*

Outdoor Guide to Using Your GPS. . . . . *.v.4 p.390*

Outdoor Leadership: Theory and Practice. . . . . . *.v.4 p.787*

Outdoor Recreation in America.. . . . . *.v.4 p.787, p.823*

Outdoor Recreation Policy: Pleasure and Preservation, Vol. 263.. . . . . *.v.4 p.787*

Outdoor Recreation Safety. . . . . *.v.4 p.786, p.788*

Outdoor Recreation: United States National Parks, Forests, and Public Lands.. . . . . *.v.4 p.788*

The Outer Banks.. . . . . *.v.3 p.502*

☐ Outing Age: Public Policy Issues Affecting Gay, Lesbian Bisexual and Transgender Elders.. . . . . *.v.6 p.380*

Outing: Shattering the Conspiracy of Silence.. . . . *.v.6 p.368*

Outing Yourself: How to Come Out to Your Family, Your Friends, and Your Coworkers.. . . . . *.v.6 p.369*

The Outlaw Bible of American Poetry. . . . . *.v.2 p.23*

Outlaw Masters of Japanese Film.. . . . . *.v.6 p.335*

Outlaw: The Lives and Careers of John Rechy.. . . . *.v.6 p.407*

Outlaws of the Marsh. . . . . *.v.6 p.212*

An Outline History of China.. . . . . *.v.6 p.183*

Outline of a Theory of Practice.. . . . . *.v.4 p.23*

An Outline of European Architecture. . . . . . . *.v.1 p.790*

An Outline of International Price Theories.. . . . . *.v.4 p.251*

An Outline of Metallurgy.. . . . . *.v.5 p.733*

An Outline of Middle English Grammar. . . . . . . *.v.2 p.550*

Outlines of Entomology.. . . . . *.v.5 p.212*

Outlines of the History of Ethics.. . . . . *.v.1 p.485*

Outposts of Empire: Korea, Vietnam, and the Origins of the Cold War in Asia, 1949-1954. . . . *.v.6 p.169, p.236, p.237*

Outrageous fortune: the tragedy of Leopold III of the Belgians, 1901-1941.. . . . . *.v.3 p.206*

Outside In: Minorities and the Transformation of American Education. . . . . *.v.4 p.326*

Outside the Lines: African-Americans and the Integration of the National Football League.. . . . . *.v.4 p.833, p.852*

Outsiders in the Clubhouse: The World of Women's Professional Golf.. . . . . *.v.4 p.815, p.835, p.860*

Outsiders Together: Virginia and Leonard Woolf. . . *.v.2 p.393*

Outsiders.. . . . . *.v.4 p.695, p.776*

Outsource: Competing in the Global Productivity Race. *.v.4 p.70*

Outstanding in His Field: Perspectives on American Agricultural History in Honor of Wayne D. Rasmussen. . . .*.v.5 p.3, p.4*

Outstanding Women Athletes: Who They Are and How They Influenced Sports in America. . . . . . . *.v.4 p.838, p.839*

The Outward Bound Canoeing Handbook. . . .*.v.4 p.788, p.789*

Outward Bound Wilderness Survival Handbook.. . . .*.v.4 p.788*

Over and over Again.. . . . . *.v.5 p.457*

Over Here: The First World War and American Society. . . . . *.v.3 p.442, p.473*

Over Prairie Trails.. . . . . *.v.2 p.732*

Over the Edge of the World: Magellan's Terrifying Circumnavigation of the Globe.. . . . . . . *.v.3 p.72, p.73*

The Overburian Characters, to Which Is Added, a Wife. *.v.2 p.215*

Overcoming Heterosexism and Homophobia: Strategies That Work.. *.v.6 p.382*

Overcoming the Five Dysfunctions of a Team: A Field Guide for Leaders, Managers, and Facilitators. . . . . . .*.v.4 p.80*

Overland from Canada to British Columbia: By Mr. Thomas McMicking of Queenston, Canada West.. . . . . .*.v.3 p.545*

The Overlook Film Encyclopedia: Horror. . . . . .*.v.6 p.319*

The Overlook Film Encyclopedia: Science Fiction. . .*.v.6 p.318*

The Overlook Film Encyclopedia: The Western.. . . .*.v.6 p.324*

Overlooking Nazareth: The Ethnography of Exclusion in Galilee, Vol. 105.. . . . .*.v.6 p.615*

Oversold and Underused: Computers in Classrooms, 1980-2000.. . . . .*.v.4 p.351*

Overthrowing Geography: Jaffa, Tel Aviv, and the Struggle for Palestine, 1880-1948.. . . . .*.v.6 p.610*

Overtime: Selected Poems.. . . . .*.v.2 p.128*

Overtones and Undertones: Reading Film Music. . . .*.v.1 p.255*

Overtraining in Sport. . . . . . .*.v.4 p.827, p.828, p.875, p.879*

Overworked American: The Unexpected Decline of Leisure.. . . . .*.v.5 p.581*

Ovid: Amores I. . . . .*.v.2 p.438*

Ovid As an Epic Poet. . . . .*.v.2 p.438*

Ovid: Fasti, Bk. IV.. . . . .*.v.2 p.438*

Ovid: Heroides: Select Epistles.. . . . .*.v.2 p.439*

Ovid Metamorphoses: Books 1-8, Vol. 3.. . . . . .*.v.2 p.439*

Ovid: Metamorphoses.. . . . .*.v.2 p.439*

Ovid Recalled.. . . . .*.v.2 p.439*

Ovid's Fasti: Roman Holidays.. . . . .*.v.2 p.439*

Ovid's Heroides.. . . . .*.v.2 p.438*

Ovid's Metamorphoses, Bks. 1-5.. . . . .*.v.2 p.438*

Ovid's Metamorphoses, Bks. 6-10.. . . . .*.v.2 p.438*

Ovid's Metamorphoses.. . . . .*.v.2 p.438, p.439*

Ovid's Poetics of Illusion.. . . . .*.v.2 p.438*

Ovid.. . . . .*.v.2 p.438*

☐ O.W. Toad: Margaret Atwood Reference Site. . . .*.v.2 p.734*

Owen Lattimore and the "Loss" of China. . . .*.v.6 p.201, p.216*

The Owl and the Nightingale: Musical Life and Ideas in France, 1100-1300.. . . . .*.v.1 p.178*

The Owl and the Nightingale: Text and Translation. .*.v.2 p.203*

Owls Do Cry. . . . .*.v.2 p.745*

The Owner of the House: New Collected Poems 1940-2001. . . . . *v.2 p.116*

The Owner of the House. *v.6 p.657*

Owning the Genome: A Moral Analysis of DNA Patenting. *v.5 p.136*

Ox-Bow Incident. *v.2 p.65*

□ Oxford African American Studies Center. *v.6 p.34*

Oxford Albanian-English Dictionary. *v.2 p.778*

Oxford Anthology of African-American Poetry. *v.6 p.27*

The Oxford Anthology of Australian Literature. . . . *v.2 p.743*

The Oxford Anthology of English Literature: Medieval English Literature. *v.2 p.197*

The Oxford Anthology of English Poetry: Blake to Heaney. *v.2 p.201*

The Oxford Anthology of English Poetry: Spenser to Crabbe, Vol. I. *v.2 p.201*

The Oxford Anthology of Raj Stories. *v.2 p.763*

Oxford Anthology of the Brazilian Short Story. . . . *v.2 p.691*

The Oxford Book of American Poetry. *v.2 p.23*

The Oxford Book of American Short Stories. *v.2 p.26*

Oxford Book of American Verse. *v.2 p.24*

The Oxford Book of Australian Essays. *v.2 p.743*

The Oxford Book of Australian Short Stories. *v.2 p.743*

The Oxford Book of Australian Women's Verse. . . *v.2 p.743*

The Oxford Book of Caribbean Short Stories. *v.2 p.767*

The Oxford Book of Children's Verse in America. . . *v.2 p.23*

The Oxford Book of Comic Verse. *v.2 p.199*

The Oxford Book of English Detective Stories. . . . *v.2 p.202*

The Oxford Book of English Mystical Verse. *v.2 p.200*

The Oxford Book of English Short Stories. *v.2 p.202*

The Oxford Book of English Verse. *v.2 p.201*

The Oxford Book of Essays. *v.2 p.202, p.203*

The Oxford Book of French Short Stories. *v.2 p.465*

Oxford Book of French Verse, Thirteenth Century to Twentieth Century. *v.2 p.464*

Oxford Book of German Verse, Twelfth to Twentieth Century. *v.2 p.594*

The Oxford Book of Late Medieval Verse and Prose. *v.2 p.199*

The Oxford Book of Latin American Essays. *v.2 p.666*

The Oxford Book of Latin American Short Stories. . *v.2 p.666*

The Oxford Book of Letters. *v.2 p.203*

Oxford Book of Medieval Latin Verse. *v.2 p.449*

The Oxford Book of Narrative Verse. *v.2 p.200*

The Oxford Book of Nature Writing. *v.5 p.232*

The Oxford Book of New Zealand Short Stories. . . *v.2 p.743*

The Oxford Book of Scottish Verse. *v.2 p.200*

The Oxford Book of Sonnets. *v.2 p.199*

The Oxford Book of Stories by Canadian Women in English. *v.2 p.732*

The Oxford Book of the American South: Testimony, Memory, and Fiction. *v.2 p.21*

The Oxford Book of War Poetry. *v.2 p.583*

The Oxford Classical Dictionary. *v.2 p.399*

The Oxford Companion to Aboriginal Art and Culture. *v.1 p.668, p.694, p.695, v.4 p.26*

The Oxford Companion to American Literature. *v.2 p.3*

The Oxford Companion to American Military History. *v.3 p.382*

The Oxford Companion to American Theatre. . *v.1 p.58, p.112*

The Oxford Companion to Australian Children's Literature. *v.2 p.741*

The Oxford Companion to Australian Film. *v.6 p.337*

The Oxford Companion to Australian Gardens. *v.1 p.811, p.818*

Oxford Companion to Australian Literature. *v.2 p.742*

The Oxford Companion to Australian Sport. *v.4 p.824*

The Oxford Companion to Bach. . . . *v.1 p.182, p.302, p.303*

The Oxford Companion to Canadian History. *v.3 p.536*

The Oxford Companion to Canadian Literature. . . . *v.2 p.729*

The Oxford Companion to Canadian Theatre. *v.1 p.58, p.126, p.127, v.2 p.728, p.729*

The Oxford Companion to Christian Thought. *v.1 p.594*

The Oxford Companion to Classical Literature. . . . *v.2 p.399*

The Oxford Companion to Crime and Mystery Writing. *v.2 p.580*

The Oxford Companion to English Literature. *v.2 p.163*

The Oxford Companion to Fairy Tales. *v.2 p.585*

Oxford Companion to French Literature. *v.2 p.456*

The Oxford Companion to German Literature. . . . *v.2 p.589*

The Oxford Companion to Indian Archaeology: The Archaeological Foundations of Ancient India. . . . *v.4 p.8*

The Oxford Companion to Indian Theatre. . . . *v.1 p.59, p.131*

The Oxford Companion to J. M. W. Turner. . *v.1 p.741, p.742*

The Oxford Companion to Jazz. *v.1 p.260, p.261*

Oxford Companion to Jazz. *v.6 p.30*

Oxford Companion to Law. *v.4 p.433*

The Oxford Companion to Musical Instruments. . . *v.1 p.388*

The Oxford Companion to Music. *v.1 p.161*

The Oxford Companion to New Zealand Literature. . *v.2 p.741*

The Oxford Companion to Philosophy. *v.1 p.415*

The Oxford Companion to Shakespeare. *v.2 p.222*

The Oxford Companion to the Bible. *v.1 p.614*

The Oxford Companion to the English Language. . . *v.2 p.552*

The Oxford Companion to the History of Modern Science. *v.3 p.45*

e The Oxford Companion to the Mind. *v.1 p.496*

The Oxford Companion to the Photograph. *v.1 p.762*

The Oxford Companion to the Second World War. . . *v.3 p.80*

The Oxford Companion to the Supreme Court of the United States. *v.4 p.466, p.537*

Oxford Companion to the Theatre. . *v.1 p.55, p.59, p.61, p.128*

The Oxford Companion to Twentieth-Century Poetry in English. *v.2 p.178, p.184*

The Oxford Companion to United States History. . . *v.3 p.372*

The Oxford Companion to Western Art. *v.1 p.662*

The Oxford Companion to World Mythology. *v.1 p.527*

Oxford Dictionary of Accounting. *v.4 p.104*

Oxford Dictionary of Biochemistry and Molecular Biology. *v.5 p.114, p.325*

The Oxford Dictionary of Classical Myth and Religion. *v.1 p.533*

The Oxford Dictionary of Dance. *v.1 p.3*

Oxford Dictionary of National Biography. *v.6 p.735*

The Oxford Dictionary of Philosophy. *v.1 p.415*

Oxford Dictionary of Phrase and Fable. *v.2 p.549*

Oxford Dictionary of Political Quotations. *v.4 p.482*

Oxford Dictionary of Pronunciation for Current English. .*v.2 p.558*

The Oxford Dictionary of Saints. *v.1 p.579, p.612*

The Oxford Dictionary of Sports Science and
Medicine. *v.4 p.825, p.873*

The Oxford Dictionary of the Christian Church. *v.1 p.594*

The Oxford Dictionary of World Religions. *v.1 p.522*

☐ Oxford DNB: Oxford Dictionary of National
Biography. *v.3 p.90*

Oxford Duden-English Pictorial Dictionary. *v.2 p.620*

The Oxford Encyclopedia of Ancient Egypt, Set. *v.3 p.10*

The Oxford Encyclopedia of Archaeology in the Near East, Set,
Vols. 1-4. . . . .*v.1 p.617*

The Oxford Encyclopedia of Economic History,
Set. *v.3 p.41, v.4 p.192*

The Oxford Encyclopedia of Mesoamerican Cultures: The
Civilizations of Mexico and Central America. *v.4 p.9*

The Oxford Encyclopedia of Theatre and Performance,
Set. *v.1 p.59, p.140*

The Oxford English Grammar. *v.2 p.556*

The Oxford English Literary History: 1350-1547: Reform and
Cultural Revolution. *v.2 p.168*

The Oxford English Literary History: 1830-1880: the
Victorians. *v.2 p.174, p.175,v.6 p.752*

The Oxford English Literary History, 1948-2000: The
Internationalization of English
Literature. *v.2 p.178, p.179, p.727*

The Oxford English Literary History: 1960-2000: The Last of
England? *v.2 p.179*

The Oxford English Literary History: The Modern Movement
(1910-1940), Vol. 10. . . . .*v.2 p.177, p.178*

Oxford English Literary History. *v.2 p.166*

The Oxford English-Arabic Dictionary of Current
Usage. *v.6 p.653*

The Oxford English-Hebrew Dictionary of Current
Usage. *v.6 p.645, p.646*

Oxford Grammar of Classical Greek. *v.2 p.400*

The Oxford Guide to Literature in English Translation. .*v.2 p.574*

The Oxford Guide to the Book of Common Prayer: A
Worldwide Survey. *v.1 p.582*

The Oxford Guide to United States Supreme Court
Decisions. *v.4 p.454*

The Oxford Guide to Writing. *v.2 p.565*

Oxford Guides to Chaucer: The Canterbury
Tales. *v.2 p.208, p.209*

Oxford Guides to Chaucer: Troilus and Criseyde. . . .*v.2 p.211*

The Oxford Handbook of Contemporary Philosophy. .*v.1 p.417*

The Oxford Handbook of Criminology. *v.6 p.249*

Oxford Handbook of Deaf Studies, Language, and
Education. *v.4 p.318*

The Oxford Handbook of Epistemology. *v.1 p.482*

The Oxford Handbook of Ethical Theory. *v.1 p.483*

The Oxford Handbook of Free Will. *v.1 p.503*

The Oxford Handbook of Innovation. *v.4 p.66*

The Oxford Handbook of Memory. *v.5 p.611*

The Oxford Handbook of Metaphysics. *v.1 p.488*

The Oxford Handbook of New Religious Movements. .*v.1 p.658*

Oxford Handbook of Political Psychology.   *v.4 p.484, v.5 p.645*

The Oxford Handbook of Practical Ethics. *v.1 p.486*

The Oxford History of Ancient Egypt. . . . *v.3 p.10, v.6 p.58*

The Oxford History of Christian Worship. *v.1 p.654*

The Oxford History of Christianity. *v.1 p.598*

The Oxford History of English Music: C. 1715 to the Present
Day, Vol. II. *v.1 p.245*

The Oxford History of English Music: From the Beginnings to
c. 1715. . . . .*v.1 p.245*

The Oxford History of Hungarian Literature from the Earliest
Times to the Present. *v.2 p.785*

The Oxford History of Mexico. *v.3 p.284*

The Oxford History of New Zealand Literature. *v.2 p.742*

The Oxford History of the American West. *v.3 p.518*

The Oxford History of the Biblical World.   .*v.1 p.617, v.3 p.7*

The Oxford History of the British Empire:
Historiography. *v.3 p.35, p.90*

The Oxford History of the British Empire: The Eighteenth
Century. *v.3 p.89, p.125,v.4 p.605*

The Oxford History of the British Empire: The Nineteenth
Century. *v.3 p.89, p.125,v.4 p.605*

The Oxford History of the British Empire: The Origins of
Empire: British Overseas Enterprise to the Close
of the Seventeenth Century. *v.3 p.88, p.124,v.4 p.605*

The Oxford History of the British Empire: The Twentieth
Century. *v.3 p.88, p.124,v.4 p.605*

The Oxford History of the Classical World. *v.3 p.3*

The Oxford History of the French Revolution. *v.3 p.150*

The Oxford History of Western Music, Set. . . *v.1 p.174, p.175*

The Oxford Ibsen. *v.2 p.628*

The Oxford Illustrated History of Opera. *v.1 p.231, p.232*

The Oxford Illustrated History of Prehistoric Europe. . .*v.4 p.12*

The Oxford Illustrated History of the Bible. *v.1 p.614*

The Oxford Illustrated History of Western Philosophy. .*v.1 p.417*

The Oxford Illustrated Jane Austen, Set. *v.2 p.266*

The Oxford Illustrated Literary Guide to the United States. .*v.2 p.7*

The Oxford India Ghalib: Life, Letters, and Ghazals. .*v.6 p.152*

The Oxford India Premchand. *v.6 p.152*

Oxford Latin Dictionary. *v.2 p.423*

The Oxford Literary History of Australia. *v.2 p.740*

The Oxford Picture Dictionary: English/Russian
Edition. *v.2 p.776*

Oxford Reader's Companion to Conrad. *v.2 p.341*

The Oxford Reader's Companion to George Eliot. . .*v.2 p.288*

Oxford Reader's Companion to Trollope. *v.2 p.317*

Oxford Readings in Aristophanes. *v.2 p.423*

Oxford Readings in Euripides. *v.2 p.411, p.412*

Oxford Readings in Greek Tragedy. *v.2 p.402*

Oxford Readings in Homer's Iliad. *v.2 p.413*

Oxford Readings in Menander, Plautus, and Terence. .*v.2 p.425*

Oxford Readings in the Greek Novel. *v.2 p.405, p.406*

Oxford Readings in the Roman Novel. *v.2 p.425*

Oxford Readings in Vergil's Aeneid. *v.2 p.446*

The Oxford Russian Dictionary. *v.2 p.776*

The Oxford Spanish Dictionary. *v.2 p.636*

Oxford Studies in Early Modern Philosophy. *v.1 p.436*

The Oxford Turkish Dictionary: Turkish-English,
English-Turkish. *v.6 p.665*

The Oxford Turkish-English Dictionary. *v.6 p.665*

Oxford World Atlas. *v.4 p.380*

Das Oxforder Buch deutscher Prosa von Luther bis
Rilke. *v.2 p.594*

The Oxford-Hachette French Dictionary. *v.2 p.453*

The Oxidation States of the Elements and Their Potentials in
Aqueous Solutions [Known As Oxidation
Potentials]. *v.5 p.285*

Oxidizing and Reducing Agents. *v.5 p.291*

Oxygen Chemistry. *v.5 p.309*

Ozark Baptizings, Hangings, and Other Diversions: Theatrical
Folkways of Rural Missouri, 1885-1910. . . . .*v.3 p.512*

Ozu's Anti-Cinema. *v.6 p.337*

Ozu's Tokyo Story. *v.6 p.335, p.344*

P

P. A. Stolypin: The Search for Stability in Late Imperial
Russia. *v.3 p.219*

P. G. T. Beauregard: Napoleon in Gray. *v.3 p.427*

P. G. Wodehouse: A Comprehensive Bibliography and
Checklist. *v.2 p.390*

P. G. Wodehouse: An Illustrated Biography: with Complete
Bibliography and Collector's Guide. *v.2 p.389, p.390*

P. G. Wodehouse, in His Own Words. *v.2 p.391*

P. G. Wodehouse. *v.2 p.389*

P. Smith in the City. *v.2 p.391*

Pablo Neruda: Nobel Prize-Winning Poet. *v.2 p.680*

Pablo Neruda. *v.2 p.679*

Pablo Picasso: The Sculptures. *v.1 p.781*

Pablo Picasso. *v.1 p.746*

Pacem in Maribus. *v.4 p.478*

Pachomius: The Making of a Community in Fourth-Century
Egypt. *v.1 p.653, v.3 p.11*

Pacific Asia. *v.4 p.618, p.619, p.622*

Pacific Diaspora: Island Peoples in the United States and Across
the Pacific. *v.6 p.131*

Pacific Island Style. *v.1 p.790*

The Pacific Northwest: An Interpretive History. . . .*v.3 p.530*

Pacific Overtures. *v.1 p.254, p.358, p.411*

Pacific Pioneers: Japanese Journeys to Hawaii and America,
1850-80. . . . .*v.6 p.120, p.133*

The Pacific Region. *v.3 p.530*

Pacific Rim Letters. *v.6 p.94*

Pacific Seaweeds: A Guide to Common Seaweeds of the Pacific
Northwest. *v.5 p.208*

The Pacific Slope: A History of California, Oregon, Washington,
Idaho, Utah, and Nevada. *v.3 p.530*

The Pacific States of America; People, Politics, and Power in
the Five Pacific Basin States. *v.3 p.530*

Pacifism in the Twentieth Century: A Survey from Antiquity to
the Outset of the Twentieth Century. *v.4 p.648*

The Packaging Designer's Book of Patterns. *v.1 p.718*

Paddy and Mr. Punch: Connections in Irish and English
History. *v.3 p.138, v.6 p.746, p.763*

Paddy Clarke Ha Ha Ha. *v.2 p.343*

P-Adic Numbers: An Introduction. *v.5 p.476*

Padres: The National Chicano Priest Movement. . . .*v.6 p.520*

Paganism and Christianity, 100-425 C. E.: A
Sourcebook. *v.1 p.599*

Page and Stage: An Approach to Script Analysis. . . .*v.1 p.139*

The Pages of Day and Night. *v.6 p.655*

Paginas Escogidas. *v.2 p.657*

Le pagne noir : contes africains. *v.2 p.542*

Pagne Noir. *v.2 p.542*

Pahari Masters: Court Painters of Northern India. . .*v.1 p.731*

Paideia Proposal. *v.4 p.324*

Pain and Touch. *v.5 p.606*

The Pain Behind the Mask: Overcoming Masculine
Depression. *v.5 p.660*

Paine, Collected Writings: Common Sense; the Crisis; Rights of
Man; the Age of Reason; Pamphlets, Articles and
Letters. *v.3 p.410*

The Painful Field: The Psychiatric Dimension of Modern War,
75. . . . .*v.5 p.584*

Painful Partings: Divorce and Its Aftermath. *v.5 p.640*

Painful Transition: Bourgeois Democracy in India. . .*v.4 p.618*

Paint by Number: The How-to Craze That Swept the
Nation. *v.1 p.750*

The Painted Bed: Poems. *v.2 p.82*

Painted Bird. *v.2 p.148*

Painted Love: Prostitution in French Art of the Impressionist
Era. *v.1 p.677, p.686*

The Painted Photograph, 1839-1914: Origins, Techniques,
Aspirations. *v.1 p.762, p.763*

Painted Prints: The Revelation of Color in Northern Renaissance
and Baroque Engravings, Etchings, and
Woodcuts. *v.1 p.752, p.753*

The Painted Veil. *v.2 p.370*

Painters and the American West: The Anschutz
Collection. *v.1 p.733*

Painters of the Golden Age: A Biographical Dictionary of
Seventeenth-Century European Painting. *v.1 p.725*

The Painter's Practice: How Artists Lived and Worked in
Traditional China. *v.1 p.731*

Painting a New World: Mexican Art and Life,
1521-1821. . . . .*v.3 p.287*

Painting and Sculpture in Europe: 1780-1880. . . . .*v.1 p.728*

Painting and Sculpture in Europe:
1880-1940. . . . .*v.1 p.678, p.679, p.687*

Painting and Sculpture in France, 1700-1789. . .*v.1 p.679, p.688*

Painting and Sculpture in Germany and the Netherlands,
1500-1600. . . . .*v.1 p.676, p.689*

Painting by Numbers: Komar and Melamid's Scientific Guide to
Art. *v.1 p.703*

Painting Gender, Constructing Theory: The Alfred Stieglitz
Circle and American Formalist Aesthetics. . .*v.1 p.705, p.706*

Painting in Britain: 1530-1790. . . . .*v.1 p.729*

Painting in Italy, 1500-1600. . . . .*v.1 p.727*

Painting in Late Medieval and Renaissance Siena
(1260-1555). *v.6 p.556*

Painting in Spain, 1500-1700. . . . .*v.1 p.726, p.731*

Painting Murals. *v.1 p.751*

Painting on Light: Drawings and Stained Glass in the Age of
Durer and Holbein. *v.1 p.721*

Painting, Psychoanalysis and Spirituality. *v.1 p.708*

Painting the Dark Side: Art and the Gothic Imagination in
Nineteenth-Century America. *v.1 p.731*

Painting the Mughal Experience. *v.1 p.733, p.734*

Painting the Past: The Victorian Painter and British
History. *v.6 p.738*

Painting the Word: Christian Pictures and Their
Meanings. *v.1 p.709*

Painting Women: Victorian Women Artists. *v.6 p.746*

Paintings - Genuine, Fraud, Fake: Modern Methods of
Examining Paintings. *v.1 p.751*

The Paintings and Drawings of William Blake. . . .*v.2 p.239*

Paintings from Books: Art and Literature in Britain,
1760-1900. . . . .*v.6 p.737, p.752*

Paintings in the Musée D'Orsay. *v.1 p.728*

The Paintings of Eugene Delacroix: Fourth Supplement and
Reprint of Third Supplement. *v.1 p.741*

The Paintings of George Caleb Bingham: A Catalogue
Raisonné. *v.1 p.736*

The Paintings of Joan Mitchell. *v.1 p.743*

The Paintings of Lucas van Leyden: A New Appraisal, with
Catalogue Raisonné. *v.1 p.747*

Paintings of Paul Cezanne: A Catalogue Raisonné. .*v.1 p.745*

The Paintings of Thomas Gainsborough. *v.1 p.737*

PAIS International & PAIS Archive. *v.4 p.481*

Paisajes Despues de la Batalla. *v.2 p.658*

Paisajes y Leyendas (Landscapes and Legends). . . .*v.2 p.666*

Los Paisanos: Spanish Settlers on the Northern Frontier of New
Spain. *v.3 p.528*

Pakistan: A Nation in the Making. *v.6 p.162*

Pakistan at the Millennium. *v.6 p.162*

Pakistan: Between Mosque and Military. *v.4 p.617*

Pakistani Short Stories. *v.2 p.760*

Pal Joey. *v.2 p.107*

Palabras para Julia y Otros Poemas. *v.2 p.668*

Palace of Desire. *v.6 p.661, p.662*

The Palace of the White Skunks. *v.2 p.670*

Palace Walk. *v.6 p.662*

Palaces and Gardens of Persia. *v.1 p.819*

Palaces in the Night: Whistler in Venice. *v.1 p.723*

The Palaces of Crete. *v.3 p.16*

Palaces of Minoan Crete. *v.3 p.15*

The Palaeolithic Societies of Europe. *v.4 p.16*

Pale Horse, Pale Rider: Three Short Novels. *v.2 p.109*

Paleoclimate, Global Change and the Future. *v.5 p.425*

Paleoclimatology: Reconstructing Climates of the Quaternary,
Vol. 68. . . . .*v.5 p.445*

Paleoclimatology. *v.5 p.425, p.445*

Paleoethnobotany: A Handbook of Procedures. *v.4 p.7*

Paleolimnology: The History and Evolution of Lake
Systems. *v.5 p.427, p.449*

Paleomagnetism: Continents and Oceans. *v.5 p.443, p.444*

☐ PALEOMAP Project. *v.5 p.445*

☐ The Paleontology Portal. *v.5 p.447*

Paleopalynology. *v.5 p.449*

Paleoseismology. *v.5 p.422*

Palestine - A Twice-Promised Land?: The British, the Arabs, and
Zionism. *v.6 p.617*

Palestine and Israel in the 19th and 20th Centuries. . .*v.6 p.610*

Palestine and the Egyptian National Identity. *v.6 p.620*

Palestine and the Palestinians. *v.6 p.617*

Palestine: Mohammedan Holy Land. *v.6 p.609*

Palestine Reborn. *v.6 p.618*

Palestine's Children: Returning to Haifa and Other
Stories. *v.6 p.661*

Palestinian Arab Music: A Maqam Tradition in Practice. .*v.1 p.286*

The Palestinian Arab National Movement, 1929-1939: From
Riots to Rebellion. *v.6 p.612*

The Palestinian Hamas: Vision, Violence and
Coexistence. *v.6 p.618, p.619*

Palestinian Identity: The Construction of Modern National
Consciousness. *v.6 p.618*

Palestinian Peasants and Ottoman Officials: Rural Administration
Around Sixteenth-Century Jerusalem. *v.6 p.611*

The Palestinian People: A History. *v.6 p.618*

Palestinian Refugees: Mythology, Identity, and the Search for
Peace. *v.6 p.617*

The Palestinian regime: a partial democracy. *v.4 p.614*

Palestinian Religious Terrorism: Hamas and Islamic
Jihad. *v.4 p.614, v.6 p.616*

Palestinian Terrorism and U.S. Foreign Policy, 1969-1977:
Dynamics of Response. *v.3 p.389*

The Palestinian Wedding: A Bilingual Anthology of
Contemporary Palestinian Resistance Poetry. . . .*v.6 p.659*

Palestinian Women of Gaza and the West Bank. . . .*v.6 p.619*

Palestinian Women: Patriarchy and Resistance in the West
Bank. *v.6 p.619*

The Palestinians: In Search of a Just Peace. *v.6 p.619*

Palestinians in the Arab World: Institution Building and the
Search for State. *v.6 p.617*

Palgrave Advances in Charles Dickens Studies. . . .*v.2 p.285*

Palgrave Advances in Oscar Wilde Studies. *v.2 p.321*

The Palgrave Concise Historical Atlas of South East
Asia. *v.6 p.164*

Palgrave Handbook of Econometrics: Econometric
Theory. *v.4 p.203*

Palimpsest: A Memoir. *v.2 p.127, v.6 p.404*

The Palladium of Justice: Origins of Trial by
Jury. *v.4 p.435, v.6 p.271*

Palliative Care Nursing: A Guide to Practice. *v.5 p.528*

The Palliser Expedition: The Dramatic Story of Western
Canadian Exploration, 1857-1860. . . . .*v.3 p.546*

Palmerston and Liberalism, 1855-1865. . . . .*v.3 p.116*

Palmerston, the Early Years, 1784-1841. . . . .*v.3 p.93*

Palmerston: The Early Years 1784-1841. . . . .*v.3 p.108, p.110*

Palmerston, the Early Years, 1784-1841. . . . .*v.3 p.110*

Palm-Wine Drinkard and His Dead Palm-Wine Tapster in the
Dead's Town. *v.2 p.757*

Pamela: Or Virtue Rewarded. *v.2 p.259*

Pamela, Shamela. *v.2 p.258, p.259*

Pamphlets of Protest: An Anthology of Early African-American
Protest Literature, 1790-1860. . . . .*v.4 p.572*

Pamphlets of the American Revolution, 1750-1765, Vol.
1. . . . .*v.3 p.407*

The Pamphlets of Thomas Robert Malthus, 1800-1817. .*v.4 p.222*

Pan African Nationalism in the Americas: The Life and Times
of John Henrik Clarke. *v.6 p.4, p.17*

Pan Africanism in the African Diaspora: An Analysis of Modern
Afrocentric Political Movements. *v.6 p.9, p.32*

The Pan Am Building and the Shattering of the Modernist
Dream. *v.1 p.786*

Pan: From Lieutenant Thomas Glahn's Papers. *v.2 p.628*

Pan Tadeusz. *v.2 p.791*

Pan-African Chronology, 1400-1865: A Comprehensive
Reference to the Black Quest for Freedom in Africa, the
Americas, Europe and Asia, 1400-1865. . . .*v.6 p.10, p.11*

Pan-African Chronology 1865-1915: A Comprehensive
Reference to the Black Quest for Freedom in Africa, the
Americas, Europe and Asia, 1865-1915. . . .*v.6 p.10, p.11*

Pan-African Chronology 1914-1929: Reference to the Black
Quest for Freedom in Africa, the Americas, Europe,
Asia, and Australia, 1914-1929. . . . .*v.6 p.10, p.11*

Pan-African History: Political Figures from Africa and the
Diaspora since 1787. . . . .*v.6 p.13, p.55*

Pan-African Issues in Crime and Justice. *v.6 p.250*

The Pan-African Movement: A History of Pan-Africanism in
America, Europe and Africa. *v.6 p.55*

Pan-Africanism and Nationalism in West Africa, 1900-1945: A
Study in Ideology and Social Classes. *v.6 p.68*

Panama Canal in American National Consciousness,
1870-1990. . . . .*v.3 p.391*

The Panama Canal Negotiations. *v.3 p.304*

The Panama Canal: The Crisis in Historical Perspective. .*v.3 p.305*

Panama Money in Barbados, 1900-1920. . . . . . .*v.3 p.305*

The Panama Route, 1848-1869. . . . .*v.3 p.304, p.305*

Panamanian Militarism: A Historical
Interpretation. *v.3 p.275, p.305*

Panbiogeography: Tracking the History of Life. . . .*v.5 p.168*

Pancatantra: The Book of India's Folk Wisdom. . . .*v.6 p.152*

Pancreatic Cancer Cb. *v.5 p.165*

The Panda's Thumb: More Reflections in Natural
History. *v.5 p.221*

Pandora's Poison: Chlorine, Health, and a New Environmental
Strategy. *v.5 p.315*

Panel Data Econometrics. *v.4 p.198*

Pangs of Love: And Other Stories. *v.6 p.101*

Panico O Peligro. *v.2 p.669*

Panorama de Literatura Brasileira: Introducoes e Notas de
Afranio Peixoto. *v.2 p.692*

A Panorama of Harmonic Analysis. *v.5 p.494*

A Panorama of the World's Legal Systems, Set. *v.4 p.435*

Panoramas: Poems. *v.6 p.506, p.510*

Panslavism and National Identity in Russia and in the Balkans,
1830-1880: Images of the Self and Others. *v.3 p.246*

Pantanal: South America's Wetland Jewel. .*v.5 p.167, p.235, p.241*

Panteleimon Kulish: A Sketch of His Life and Times. .*v.2 p.814*

Panthea's Children: Hellenistic Novels and Medieval Persian
Romances. *v.6 p.670*

The Pantomime. *v.1 p.93*

Papa Jack: Jack Johnson and the Era of White
Hopes. *v.4 p.819, p.856*

The Papacy, 1073-1198: Continuity and
Innovation. *v.3 p.57, v.6 p.572, p.573*

The Papacy and the Levant, 1204-1571: The Fifteenth
Century. *v.3 p.64*

The Papacy and the Levant, 1204-1571: The Sixteenth Century,
Vol. 3. . . . .*v.3 p.63, p.64*

The Papacy and the Levant, 1204-1571: The Thirteenth and
Fourteenth Centuries. *v.3 p.64*

Papageno: Emanuel Schikaneder - Man of the Theater in
Mozart's Time. *v.1 p.190, p.353*

The Papal Encyclicals in Their Historical Context. . .*v.1 p.571*

Paper and Iron: Hamburg Business and German Politics in the
Era of Inflation, 1897-1927. . . . .*v.3 p.169*

Paper Chemistry. *v.5 p.320*

The Paper Men. *v.2 p.347*

Paper Son: One Man's Story. *v.6 p.93, p.126*

Paper Tangos. *v.1 p.21, p.49*

Papercutting: An International Bibliography and Selected Guide
to U. S. Collections. *v.1 p.806*

Papers and Correspondence of William Stanley Jevons: Vol.1,
Biography and Personal Journal. *v.4 p.212*

The Papers and the Papers; an Account of the Legal and
Political Battle over the Pentagon Papers. *v.3 p.481*

The Papers and the Papers: An Account of the Legal and
Political Battle Over the Pentagon Papers. *v.4 p.438*

Papers in Experimental Economics. *v.4 p.272*

The Papers of Frederick Law Olmsted: Creating Central Park,
1857-1861, Vol. 3. . . . .*v.1 p.815*

The Papers of Frederick Law Olmsted: Defending the Union:
the Civil War and the U. S. Sanitary Commission,
1861-1863. . . . .*v.1 p.816*

The Papers of Frederick Law Olmsted: Slavery and the South,
1852-1857. . . . .*v.1 p.816*

The Papers of Frederick Law Olmsted: The California Frontier,
1863-1865. . . . .*v.1 p.816*

The Papers of Frederick Law Olmsted: The Formative Years,
1822-1853. . . . .*v.1 p.816*

The Papers of Frederick Law Olmsted: The Years of Olmsted,
Vaux and Company, 1865-1874. . . . .*v.1 p.816*

The Papers of George Catlett Marshall: The Soldierly Spirit,
December 1880 - June 1939. . . . .*v.3 p.460*

The Papers of Jefferson Davis, Vol. 2. . . . .*v.3 p.424*

The Papers of John C. Calhoun, 1846. . . . .*v.3 p.412*

Papers of John C. Calhoun, 1847-1848. . . . .*v.3 p.413*

The Papers of John C. Calhoun: 1848-1849. . .*v.3 p.412, p.413*

The Papers of Joseph Henry: January 1858-December 1865, the
Smithsonian Years. *v.5 p.386*

The Papers of Joseph Henry: The Princeton Years, January 1836-December 1837. . . . .*v.5 p.385*

The Papers of Joseph Henry: The Princeton Years, January 1838-December 1840. . . . .*v.5 p.385, p.386*

The Papers of Joseph Henry: The Princeton Years, January 1841-December 1843. . . . .*v.5 p.386*

The Papers of Joseph Henry: The Princeton Years, January 1844 - December 1846. . . . .*v.5 p.386*

The Papers of Joseph Henry: The Princeton Years, November 1832-December 1835. . . . .*v.5 p.386*

The Papers of Joseph Henry: The Smithsonian Years, January 1847 - December 1849. . . . .*v.5 p.386*

The Papers of Joseph Henry: The Smithsonian Years, January 1850-December 1853. . . . .*v.5 p.386*

The Papers of Joseph Henry: The Smithsonian Years, January 1854-December 1857. . . . .*v.5 p.386*

Papers of Robert Redfield, Vol. 1. . . . .*v.4 p.24*

The Papers of William Penn, 1701-1718, Vol. IV. . . .*v.3 p.492*

Papers on Playmaking. *v.1 p.56, p.136, p.137*

Papers on Public Credit, Commerce and Finance. . . .*v.4 p.213*

Papers Relating to Political Economy. *v.4 p.223*

Papyri. *v.3 p.10*

Parables and Paradoxes: Parabeln und Paradoxe. . . .*v.2 p.610*

Parables of Jesus. *v.1 p.642*

The Parables of the Kingdom. *v.1 p.642*

Paracas Ritual Attire: Symbols of Authority in Ancient Peru. *v.3 p.261, p.262*

Parade's End. *v.2 p.345*

Paradigms and Exercises in Syriac Grammar. *v.6 p.652*

Paradigms and Revolutions: Appraisals and Applications of Thomas Kuhn's Philosophy of Science. *v.5 p.399, p.400, p.402*

Paradigms in Black Studies: Intellectual History, Cultural Meaning and Political Ideology. *v.6 p.13*

Paradigms of Personality Assessment. *v.5 p.603*

Paradise for Sale: Back to Sustainability. *v.6 p.298*

The Paradise Garden Murals of Malinalco: Utopia and Empire in Sixteenth-Century Mexico. *v.3 p.263, p.264*

Paradise Lost As Myth. *v.2 p.254*

A Paradise Lost: The Imperial Garden Yuanming Yuan. .*v.1 p.820*

Paradise Lost. *v.2 p.254, p.255*

Paradise Remade: The Politics of Culture and History in Hawai'i. *v.3 p.533, v.6 p.130*

Paradise Won. *v.5 p.182*

Paradise. *v.2 p.140*

Paradiso. *v.2 p.672*

The Paradox of American Unionism: Why Americans Like Unions More Than Canadians Do, but Join Much Less. *v.4 p.122*

The Paradox of Choice: Why More Is Less. *v.5 p.650*

The Paradox of Excellence: How Great Performance Can Kill Your Business. *v.4 p.73*

The Paradox of George Orwell. *v.2 p.376*

The Paradox of Loyalty: An African American Response to the War on Terrorism. *v.4 p.564*

Paradox of Plenty: A Social History of Eating in Modern America. *v.5 p.34*

The Paradox of Plenty: Oil Booms and Petro-States. . .*v.3 p.360*

The Paradox of Progressive Thought. *v.3 p.369*

The Paradox of Revolution: Labor, the State, and Authoritarianism in Mexico. *v.3 p.294*

The Paradox of Scottish Culture: The Eighteenth-Century Experience. *v.3 p.133*

The Paradox of Sleep: The Story of Dreaming. *v.5 p.613*

The Paradox of Southern Progressivism, 1880-1930. . . . .*v.3 p.443, p.448, p.497*

Paradoxes of Gender. *v.4 p.746, v.6 p.429*

Paradoxes of Postcolonial Culture: Contemporary Women Writers of the Indian and Afro-Italian Diaspora. . .*v.2 p.761*

Paradoxes of Power: Reflections on the Thatcher Interlude. *v.4 p.607*

Paradoxes of Youth and Sport. *v.4 p.815, p.840*

Paradoxes. *v.1 p.493*

Paragraph 175. . . . .*v.6 p.365, p.388, p.421*

Paraguay and the Triple Alliance: The Postwar Decade, 1869-1878. . . . .*v.3 p.344*

Paraguay: Corruption, Reform, and the Financial System. *v.3 p.344*

Paraguay: The Personalist Legacy. *v.3 p.344, p.345*

Paraguay under Stroessner. *v.3 p.345*

The Paraguayan War: Causes and Early Conduct. . . .*v.3 p.278*

Paraguay's Autonomous Revolution, 1810-1840. . . .*v.3 p.344*

Parallax Visions: Making Sense of American-East Asian Relations at the End of the Century. *v.6 p.180, p.181*

Parallel Computing for Bioinformatics and Computational Biology: Models, Enabling Technologies and Case Studies. *v.5 p.106, p.107, p.108, p.109*

The Parallel Curriculum: A Design to Develop High Potential and Challenge High-Ability Learners. *v.5 p.574*

The Parallel Curriculum in the Classroom: Essays for Application Across the Content Areas K-12. . . .*v.5 p.574*

The Parallel Curriculum in the Classroom: Units for Application Across the Content Areas K-12. . . . .*v.5 p.573*

Parallel Lines: Media Representation of Dance. *v.1 p.37, p.42, p.45*

Parallel Lines: Printmakers, Painters and Photographers in 19th Century France. *v.1 p.677, p.685*

Parallel Lives. *v.2 p.418, p.419*

Parallel Paths to Constructivism: Jean Piaget and Lev Vygotsky. *v.4 p.345*

Parallel Worlds: A Journey Through Creation, Higher Dimensions, and the Future of the Cosmos. *v.5 p.391, p.392, p.403*

Paramedic Field Care: A Complaint Based Approach. .*v.5 p.534*

Paramedic Protocols. *v.5 p.534*

Parameters of Popular Culture. *v.3 p.371*

The Paranoid Style in American Politics: And Other Essays. *v.3 p.441, p.448*

Parasite Genomics Protocols. *v.5 p.141*

Parasitology: The Biology of Animal Parasites. . . .*v.5 p.213*

Parc. *v.2 p.533, p.534*

Pardon and Amnesty under Lincoln and Johnson: The Restoration of the Confederates to Their Rights and Privileges, 1861-1898. . . . .*v.3 p.395, p.436*

Title Index

Parenthood in America: An Encyclopedia. *v.4 p.676*

Parenting and Child Development in Nontraditional
Families. *v.5 p.641*

Parenting in an Unresponsive Society: Managing Work and
Family Life. *v.4 p.732*

Parenting Stress. *v.5 p.639, p.641*

Les Parents Terribles. *v.2 p.514*

Parent-School Collaboration: Feminist Organizational
Structures and School Leadership. *v.6 p.463*

Parerga and Paralipomena: Short Philosophical Essays, Vol.
1. . . . . *v.1 p.466*

Pareto's Italian Letters. *v.4 p.249*

Pariahs, Partners, Predators: German-Soviet Relations,
1922-1941. . . . .*v.3 p.161, p.212*

Paris 1919: Six Months That Changed the World. . . .*v.4 p.630*

Paris after the Liberation, 1944-1949. . . . .*v.4 p.581*

Paris and London in Eighteenth Century. *v.4 p.706*

Paris, Capital of Modernity. *v.3 p.158, p.159,v.6 p.713*

Paris, City of Art. *v.1 p.686*

The Paris Diary and the New York Diary, 1951-1961. .*v.6 p.410*

Paris in the Age of Absolutism. *v.3 p.146*

The Paris Review Book: Of Heartbreak, Madness, Sex, Love,
Betrayal, Outsiders, Intoxication, War, Whimsy,
Horrors, God, Death, Dinner, Baseball, Travels, the Art of
Writing, and Everything Else in the World since
1953. . . . . *v.2 p.584*

Paris: The Biography of a City. *v.3 p.159*

Paris, the Provinces and the French Revolution. . . . *v.3 p.150*

A Parisian Affair and Other Stories. *v.2 p.497*

A Parisian in Brazil: The Travel Account of a Frenchwoman in
Nineteenth-Century Rio de Janiero. *v.3 p.338*

The Parisian Prowler: Le Spleen de Paris, Petits Poemes en
Prose. *v.2 p.487*

Paris. *v.1 p.766*

The Park and the People: A History of Central
Park. *v.1 p.819, v.6 p.715*

Parker on the Iroquois: Iroquois Uses of Maize and Other Food
Plants. *v.6 p.704*

Parks Directory of the United States: A Guide to 4,000 National
and State Parks, Recreational Areas, Historic Sites,
Battlefields, Monuments, Forests, Preserves, Memorials,
Seashores, and Other Designated Recreation Areas in
the United States Administered by National and State Park
Agencies. *v.4 p.783, p.788,v.5 p.19*

Parks: Green Spaces in European Cities. *v.1 p.814, p.815*

The Park. *v.2 p.534*

Parlez-vous franglais? : fol en France, mad in France--la belle
France, label France. *v.2 p.453*

The Parliament of England, 1559-1581. . . . . .*v.3 p.93, p.99*

Parliament, Party, and the Art of Politics in Britain,
1855-1859. . . . .*v.3 p.112*

Parliament under Blair. *v.4 p.606*

Parliamentary Politics in Revolutionary Iran: The
Institutionalization of Factional Politics. *v.4 p.616*

Parliamentary Power in Russia, 1994-2001: A New
Era. *v.3 p.229, v.4 p.599*

Parliaments in the Czech and Slovak Republics: Party
Competition and Parliamentary
Institutionalization. *v.4 p.575, p.596*

Parlor and Kitchen: Housing and Domestic Culture in Budapest,
1870-1940. . . . .*v.3 p.186, p.187*

Parmenides of Elea Fragments. *v.1 p.421*

Parmenides. *v.1 p.421, p.424, p.489*

Parmigianino. *v.1 p.739*

Parody As Film Genre: Never Give a Saga an Even
Break. *v.6 p.312*

Parsifal. *v.1 p.206, p.234, p.366, p.410*

Part of My Soul Went with Him. *v.6 p.29, p.45*

Part of Nature: Self-Knowledge in Spinoza's Ethics. . *v.1 p.477*

A Part, Yet Apart: South Asians in Asian
America. *v.6 p.124, p.138*

The Partha Chatterjee Omnibus: Nationalist Thought and the
Colonial World, the Nation and Its Fragments, a Possible
India. *v.6 p.156, p.157*

The Parthenon and Its Impact in Modern Times. . . .*v.3 p.191*

The Parthenon Frieze. *v.1 p.775, p.776*

Partial Differential Equations: Analytical and Numerical
Methods. *v.5 p.487, p.488, p.492*

Partial Differential Equations. *v.5 p.487*

Participant Observation: A Methodology for Human
Studies. *v.4 p.690*

Participating in Development: Approaches to Indigenous
Knowledge. *v.4 p.45*

Participation and Political Equality: A Seven-Nation
Comparison. *v.4 p.578, p.580*

Participation in America: Political Democracy and Social
Equality. *v.4 p.506, p.555, p.580*

Participation in American Politics: The Dynamics of Agenda
Building. *v.4 p.554*

The Particle Adventure. *v.5 p.552*

The Particle Garden: Our Universe As Understood by Particle
Physicists. *v.5 p.552*

Particle-Induced X-Ray Emission Spectrometry (PIXE). *v.5 p.273*

Particular Voices: Portraits of Gay and Lesbian Writers. *v.6 p.391*

Les particules élémentaires : roman. *v.2 p.530*

Parties and Democracy in the Post-Soviet Republics: The Case
of Estonia. *v.4 p.578, p.584, p.597*

Parties and Elections in Greece: The Search for
Legitimacy. *v.3 p.195, v.4 p.597*

Parties and Parliaments: Political Change in Norway. *v.4 p.594*

Parties and Party Systems: A Framework for Analysis, Vol.
2. . . . . *v.4 p.579*

Parties and Politics in America. *v.3 p.385*

Parties and Politics in Post 1989 Poland. *v.4 p.579, p.580, p.597*

Parties and the Party System in France: A Disconnected
Democracy?. *v.4 p.609*

Parties and Voters in France. *v.4 p.609*

Parties, Policies, and Democracy. *v.4 p.579*

The Parties Respond: Changes in American Parties and
Campaigns. *v.4 p.551*

Parties, Slavery, and the Union in Antebellum Georgia. *v.3 p.503*

A Parting of the Ways: Government and the Educated Public in
Russia, 1801-1855. . . . .*v.3 p.218*

Parting the Cosmic Veil. *v.5 p.68*

Parting the Waters: America in the King Years,
    1954-1963. . . . .*v.3 p.439, v.6 p.12*

The Partisan Imperative: The Dynamics of American Politics
    Before the Civil War. *v.3 p.415*

Partisan Politics, Divided Government, and the
    Economy. *v.4 p.247*

Partisans and Poets: The Political Work of American Poetry in
    the Great War. *v.2 p.11*

The Partition of Palestine: Decision Crossroads in the Zionist
    Movement. *v.6 p.617*

Partitions Poland 1772. . . . .*v.3 p.253*

Partnering Dance and Education: Intelligent Moves for
    Changing Times. *v.1 p.47*

Partnering: The New Face of Leadership. *v.4 p.72*

Partners and Rivals: Representation in U. S. Senate
    Delegations. *v.4 p.534*

Partners in Command: The Relationships Between Leaders in
    the Civil War. *v.4 p.520*

Partners in Conflict: The Politics of Gender, Sexuality and
    Labor in the Chilean Agrarian Reform, 1950-1973. *v.3 p.355*

Partners in Power: The Clintons and Their America. . .*v.3 p.476*

Partners in Prosperity: The Changing Geography of the
    Transatlantic Economy. *v.4 p.60*

Partners in Revolution: The United Irishmen and
    France. *v.3 p.137*

Partnerships in Chemical Research and Education. . . .*v.5 p.264*

Party Competition in Argentina and Chile: Political Recruitment
    and Public Policy, 1890-1930. . . . .*v.3 p.349, p.354*

Party Ideology and Popular Politics at the Accession of George
    Third. *v.3 p.93, p.108*

Party Ideology in Britian. *v.4 p.607*

The Party of Order: The Conservatives, the State, and Slavery in
    the Brazilian Monarchy, 1831-1871. . . . .*v.3 p.337*

Party Politics in Canada. *v.4 p.589*

Party Politics in the Age of Caesar. *v.3 p.26*

Party Systems and Voter Alignments
    Revisited. *v.4 p.554, p.555, p.579*

Party vs. State in Post-1949 China: The Institutional
    Dilemma. *v.4 p.621*

Parzival: Text und Ubersetzung. *v.2 p.595*

Parzival. *v.2 p.595*

Le pas au-delà. *v.2 p.510*

Pas de Deux: A Textbook on Partnering. *v.1 p.25, p.48*

Pascal: The Man and His Two Loves. *v.2 p.476*

Pascal. *v.2 p.476*

The Pasha's Peasants: Society and Economy in Lower Egypt,
    1740-1858. . . . .*v.6 p.637*

El Paso: A Borderlands History. *v.3 p.509*

Paso Por Aqui: Critical Essays on the New Mexican Literary
    Tradition, 1542-1988. . . . .*v.6 p.499, p.512*

Pasoh. *v.5 p.177, p.185*

Pasolini: Forms of Subjectivity. *v.2 p.721*

Pasolini Old and New: Surveys and Studies. *v.2 p.721*

Pasolini Requiem. *v.2 p.722*

Pasolini. *v.2 p.722*

Los Pasos Perdidos. *v.2 p.671*

Pass on, No Pass Back!. *v.6 p.101*

Passage of Arms. *v.6 p.173*

A Passage to India: Nation and Narration. *v.2 p.346*

A Passage to India. *v.2 p.345*

Passage. *v.1 p.779*

Passageways: An Interpretive History of Black America. *v.6 p.8*

Le passé défini : journal. *v.2 p.514*

Passing of the Whigs 1832-1886. . . . . .*v.3 p.95, p.115, p.116*

Passing Performances: Queer Readings of Leading Players in
    American Theater History. . . . *v.1 p.126, p.135, v.6 p.413*

Passing the Buck: Congress, the Budget, and Deficits. *v.4 p.531*

Passing Time & A Change of Heart: Two Novels. . . .*v.2 p.511*

Passing. *v.2 p.94*

Passion and Craft: Economists at Work. *v.4 p.186*

Passion and Paradox: Intellectuals Confront the National
    Question. *v.4 p.494*

Ⓔ Passion Branding: Harnessing the Power of Emotion to Build
    Strong Brands. *v.4 p.141, p.142*

A Passion for Birds: American Ornithology after
    Audubon. *v.5 p.77, p.214*

A Passion for Democracy: American Essays. . *v.4 p.502, p.554*

A Passion for Physics: The Story of a Woman Physicist. *v.5 p.543*

A Passion for Planning: Financials, Operations, Marketing,
    Management and Ethics. *v.4 p.143, p.144*

A passion for the particular : Dorothy Wordsworth : a
    portrait. *v.2 p.322*

A Passion for the Past: Creative Teaching of United States
    History. *v.3 p.375*

Passion Lends Them Power: A Study of Shakespeare's Love
    Tragedies. *v.2 p.235*

Passion, Memory, and Identity: 20th Century Latin American
    Jewish Women Writers. *v.3 p.351*

The Passion of Claude McKay. *v.2 p.97*

Passion of the People: Football in Latin
    America. *v.4 p.817, p.844, p.867*

Passion simple. *v.2 p.530*

A Passion to Know: 20 Profiles in Science. *v.5 p.395*

The Passionate Economist: Finding the Power and Humanity
    Behind the Numbers. *v.4 p.271*

Passionate Liberator: Theodore Dwight Weld and the Dilemma
    of Reform. *v.3 p.419*

Passionate Nation: The Epic History of Texas. *v.3 p.508*

The Passionate Philosopher: A Marquis de Sade Reader. *v.2 p.483*

Passions of the Cut Sleeve: The Male Homosexual Tradition in
    China. *v.6 p.185, p.421*

Passions of the Soul. *v.1 p.453*

The Passions. *v.5 p.656*

Passport Photos. *v.6 p.118, p.138*

Passport to Jewish Music: Its History, Traditions and
    Culture. *v.1 p.300*

Past and Present. *v.2 p.276*

Past Continuous. *v.6 p.651*

Past Imperfect, Future Uncertain: The United Nations at
    Fifty. *v.4 p.635*

Past Imperfect: History According to the Movies. . . .*v.6 p.314*

Past Impersonal: Group Process in Human History. . . .*v.5 p.646*

The Past in Question: Modern Macedonia and the Uncertainties of Nation. *v.3 p.250*

Past Meets Future: Saving America's Historic Environment. *v.1 p.822*

Past Perfect. *v.6 p.651*

Past, Present and Future. *v.1 p.492*

Past, Present and Personal: Teaching Writing in U. S. History. *v.3 p.375*

Past, Present, and Personal: The Family and the Life Course in American History. *v.4 p.731*

The Past Through Tomorrow. *v.2 p.81*

Past Time, Past Place: GIS for History. *v.4 p.387*

Pastimes and Politics: Culture, Community and Identity in Post-Abolition Urban Zanzibar, 1890-1945. . . . .*v.6 p.66*

The Paston Family in the Fifteenth Century: Endings. *v.6 p.576, p.577*

The Paston Family in the Fifteenth Century: Fastolf's Will. *v.6 p.577*

The Paston Family in the Fifteenth Century: The First Phase. *v.6 p.576*

The Paston Letters. *v.3 p.99*

The Pastons and Their England: Studies in an Age of Transition. *v.3 p.99*

Pastoral Care: An Essential Guide. *v.1 p.649*

The Pastoral Epistles. *v.1 p.630*

Pastoral Epistles. *v.1 p.631*

Pastoral Theology in the Classical Tradition. *v.1 p.649*

Pastoralists: Equality, Hierarchy, and the State. *v.4 p.30*

Pastoral. *v.6 p.405*

Los Pastores: History and Performance in the Mexican Shepherd's Play of South Texas. *v.6 p.517, p.523*

Pastures of Plenty: A Self-Portrait. *v.1 p.296, p.328*

Patagonia: Notes from the Field. *v.5 p.175, p.236*

Patai's Guide to the Chemistry of Functional Groups. *v.5 p.296*

Patchwork Nation: Sectionalism and Political Change in American Politics. *v.4 p.551*

A Patchwork Shawl: Chronicles of South Asian Women in America. *v.6 p.93, p.137*

Patent, Copyright and Trademark: An Intellectual Property Desk Reference. *v.4 p.109, p.110, p.180*

Patent Inventions: Intellectual Property and the Victorian Novel. *v.6 p.756*

Paterson. *v.3 p.491*

Path Integrals in Quantum Mechanics, Statistics and Polymer Physics. *v.5 p.549*

The Path of a Genocide: The Rwanda Crisis from Uganda to Zaire. *v.4 p.651*

The Path of God's Bondsmen: From Origin to Return. *v.1 p.559*

The Path of Purification: Visuddhimagga. *v.1 p.563*

The Path of the Buddha: Buddhism Interpreted by Buddhists. *v.1 p.565*

The Path to Christian Democracy: German Catholics and the Party System from Windthorst to Adenauer. . . . *v.4 p.609*

The Path to Dropping Out: Evidence for Intervention. *v.4 p.299*

The Path to Geneva: The Quest for a Permanent Agreement, 1996-2003. . . . .*v.4 p.629*

Path to Investing. *v.4 p.93, p.99*

The Path to Power. *v.3 p.467*

The Path to the Spiders' Nests. *v.2 p.714*

The Path to Victory: The Mediterranean Theater in World War II. *v.3 p.81*

The Path We Tread: Blacks in Nursing Worldwide, 1854-1994. . . . .*v.5 p.528*

Pathelin and Others Farces. *v.2 p.465*

Pather Panchali: Song of the Road. *v.6 p.150*

The Pathfinder; or, the inland sea. by J. Fenimore Cooper. *v.2 p.35*

Pathmarks. *v.1 p.470*

Pathological Gambling: Etiology, Comorbidity, and Treatments. *v.5 p.661*

Pathologies of Power: Health, Human Rights, and the New War on the Poor. *v.4 p.27, p.46*

Pathology for the Health Professions. *v.5 p.514*

Paths in the Rainforests: Toward a History of Political Tradition in Equatorial Africa. *v.6 p.61, p.62*

Paths in Utopia. *v.4 p.499*

Paths of Accommodation: Muslim Societies and French Colonial Authorities in Senegal and Mauritania, 1880-1920. *v.6 p.72*

The Paths of Heidegger's Life and Thought. *v.1 p.471*

Paths of Life: Seven Scenarios. *v.5 p.658*

Paths to a Green World: The Political Economy of the Global Environment. *v.4 p.666*

Paths to Power: The Historiography of American Foreign Relations to 1941. . . . .*v.3 p.385*

A Pathway into Number Theory. *v.5 p.475*

Pathways of Memory and Power: Ethnography and History among an Andean People. *v.3 p.323*

Pathways of Power: Building an Anthropology of the Modern World. *v.4 p.35*

Pathways to Democracy: The Political Economy of Democratic Transitions. *v.4 p.504*

Patience & Sarah. *v.6 p.398*

The Patient Stone. *v.6 p.670*

The Patina of Place: The Cultural Weathering of a New England Industrial Landscape. *v.1 p.822*

The Patriarch Nicephorus of Constantinople: Ecclesiastical Policy and Image Worship in the Byzantine Empire. *v.3 p.56*

Patriarchy and Accumulation on a World Scale: Women in the International Division of Labour. *v.6 p.457*

Patriarchy and Socialist Revolution in China. *v.4 p.734*

Patricia Highsmith. *v.2 p.86*

Patrician and Plebian in Virginia: Or, the Origin and Development of the Social Classes of the Old Dominion. *v.3 p.500, p.501*

Patricians and Parvenus: Wealth and High Society in Wilhelmine Germany. *v.3 p.180*

Patrick J. Hurley and American Foreign Policy. . . . *v.3 p.456*

Patrick Modiano. *v.2 p.532*

Patrick White: A Bibliography. *v.2 p.749, p.750*

Patrick White: A Life. *v.2 p.749*

Patrick White: Fiction and the Unconscious. *v.2 p.750*

Patrick White. *v.2 p.750*

The Patriot Chiefs: A Chronicle of American Indian Resistance. . . . .*.v.6 p.682*

Patriotic Culture in Russia During World War I. . . . .*.v.3 p.220*

Patriotic Games: Sporting Traditions in the American Imagination, 1876-1926. . . . .*.v.4 p.809*

Patriots and Liberators: Revolution in the Netherlands, 1780-1813. . . . .*.v.3 p.205*

Patriots and Paupers: Hamburg, 1712-1830. . . . . .*.v.3 p.167*

Patrolling Chaos: The United States Border Patrol in Deep South Texas. . . . . *.v.6 p.487, p.538*

Patron Saints: Five Rebels Who Opened America to a New Art, 1928-1943. . . . .*.v.1 p.681, p.683*

The Patron State: Culture and Politics in Fascist Italy. .*.v.3 p.203*

Patronage and Politics in Nineteenth-Century Brazil. . .*.v.3 p.336*

Patronage and Politics in the U. S. S. R. . . . . . .*.v.4 p.599*

Patronage and Royal Science in 17th-Century France: The Academie de Physique in Caen. . . . .*.v.3 p.145*

Patrons, Clients, Brokers: Ontario Society and Politics, 1791-1896. . . . .*.v.3 p.544*

Pattern Classification, Part 1. . . . . . .*.v.5 p.340, p.407, p.408*

Pattern in the Material Folk Culture of the Eastern United States. . . . .*.v.2 p.17*

The Pattern of Evolution. . . . .*.v.5 p.191*

Pattern of the Chinese Past. . . . .*.v.6 p.184*

The Pattern of Tragicomedy in Beaumont and Fletcher. .*.v.2 p.217*

Patterns and Processes of Vertebrate Evolution. .*.v.5 p.447, p.448*

Patterns from the Sod. . . . .*.v.3 p.514, p.515*

Patterns in Criminal Homicide. . . . .*.v.6 p.252*

Patterns in Freshwater Fish Ecology. . . . .*.v.5 p.216*

Patterns in History: A Christian Perspective on Historical Thought. . . . .*.v.1 p.595*

Patterns in the Dust: Chinese-American Relations and the Recognition Controversy, 1949-1950. . . . . . .*.v.3 p.393*

Patterns of Ambivalence: The Poetry and Fiction of Stevie Smith. . . . .*.v.2 p.382*

Patterns of Childhood. . . . .*.v.2 p.620*

Patterns of Culture. . . . .*.v.4 p.22*

Patterns of Decay: Shakespeare's Early Histories. . . .*.v.2 p.233*

Patterns of Democracy: Government Forms and Performance in Thirty-Six Countries. . . . .*.v.4 p.504*

Patterns of Discovery: An Enquiry into the Conceptual Foundations of Science. . . . .*.v.5 p.402*

Patterns of Growth and Development in the Genus Homo. . . . .*.v.4 p.15*

Patterns of Language: Structure, Variation, Change. . .*.v.2 p.559*

Patterns of Life: Biogeography of a Changing World. . . . .*.v.5 p.168, p.169*

Patterns of Provocation: Police and Public Disorder. . .*.v.6 p.262*

Patterns of Reformation. . . . .*.v.1 p.603*

Patterns of Relating: An Adult Attachment Perspective. . . . .*.v.5 p.649, p.657, p.658*

Patterns of Time: Mizoguchi and the 1930s. . . . .*.v.6 p.336*

The Patterns of War since the Eighteenth Century. . . . .*.v.4 p.627, p.646*

Patterson's German-English Dictionary for Chemists. .*.v.5 p.258*

Patti Smith: Early Works, 1970-1979. . . . .*.v.2 p.156*

Patton: A Biography. . . . .*.v.3 p.455*

Patton: A Genius for War. . . . .*.v.3 p.457*

Patton Papers, 1885 to 1940, Vol. 1. . . . .*.v.3 p.456*

Patton Papers: 1940-1945. . . . .*.v.3 p.461*

Patton: The Man Behind the Legend, 1885-1945. . . .*.v.3 p.456*

Patty's Industrial Hygiene and Toxicology: General Principles, Vol. 1, Pt. A. . . . .*.v.5 p.314*

Patty's Industrial Hygiene and Toxicology: General Principles, Vol. 1, Pt. B, General Principles. . . . .*.v.5 p.314*

Patty's Industrial Hygiene and Toxicology, Set. . . . .*.v.5 p.364, p.367, p.374*

Patty's Industrial Hygiene, I: Introduction to Industrial Hygiene, II: Recognition and Evaluation of Chemical Agents. .*.v.5 p.314*

Patty's Industrial Hygiene, III: Physical Agents IV: Biohazards V: Engineering Control and Personal Protection. . .*.v.5 p.314*

Patty's Industrial Hygiene, VI: Law, Regulation, and Management. . . . .*.v.5 p.314*

Patty's Industrial Hygiene VII: Specialty Areas and Allied Professions. . . . .*.v.5 p.314*

Patty's Industrial Hygiene, Vol. 4. . . . . . .*.v.5 p.314, p.682*

☐ Patty's Toxicology (vol. 1-8). . . . .*.v.5 p.314*

Paul A. Samuelson: Critical Assessments, Set. . . . .*.v.4 p.197*

Paul A. Samuelson. . . . .*.v.4 p.197*

Les Paul: An American Original. .*.v.1 p.263, p.274, p.347, p.388*

Paul and Palestinian Judaism: A Comparison of Patterns of Religion. . . . .*.v.1 p.548, p.627*

Paul and Rabbinic Judaism: Some Rabbinic Elements in Pauline Theology. . . . .*.v.1 p.626*

Paul: Apostle of the Heart Set Free. . . . .*.v.1 p.626*

Paul Bowles: A Life. . . . .*.v.2 p.62, v.6 p.409*

Paul Bowles: Collected Stories and Later Writings. . . .*.v.2 p.62*

Paul Bowles: The Sheltering Sky/ Let It Come down/ the Spider's House. . . . .*.v.2 p.62*

Paul Bowles. . . . .*.v.2 p.62*

Paul Cadmus: The Male Nude. . . . .*.v.1 p.724*

Paul Celan: Poems. . . . .*.v.2 p.606*

Paul Dirac: The Man and his Work. . . . . .*.v.5 p.543, p.544*

Paul Eluard. . . . .*.v.2 p.517*

Paul Hindemith in the United States. . . . . .*.v.1 p.220, p.332*

Paul Hindemith: The Man Behind the Music. . *.v.1 p.224, p.332*

Paul I of Russia, 1754-1801. . . . .*.v.3 p.216*

Paul in Chains: Roman Imprisonment and the Letters of St. Paul. . . . .*.v.1 p.630*

Paul Kagame and Rwanda: Power, Genocide and the Rwandan Patriotic Front. . . . .*.v.4 p.654*

Paul McCarthy: Piccadilly Circus/Bunker Basement. . *.v.1 p.773*

Paul Revere's Ride. . . . .*.v.3 p.409*

Paul Ricoeur. . . . .*.v.1 p.457*

Paul Robeson: A Biography. . . . .*.v.6 p.4, p.17*

Paul Samuelson and Modern Economic Theory. . . . .*.v.4 p.213*

Paul Samuelson and the Foundations of Modern Economics. . . . .*.v.4 p.197*

Paul Samuelson: On Being an Economist. . . . . .*.v.4 p.186*

Paul Scott: A Life of the Author of the Raj Quartet. . .*.v.2 p.382*

Paul Scott's Philosophy of Place(s): The Fiction of Relationality. . . . .*.v.2 p.382*

The Paul Simon Companion: 4 Decades of Commentary. *v.1 p.271, p.357*

The Paul Street Boys. *v.2 p.786*

Paul, the Law and the Jewish People. *v.1 p.631*

Paul Tillich: His Life and Thought. *v.1 p.581*

Paul Verlaine Revisited. *v.2 p.503*

Paul Whiteman: Pioneer in American Music, Vol. 1. . . . .*v.1 p.263, p.368*

Pauline Writings. *v.1 p.631*

Paul. *v.1 p.631, p.632*

Pausanias' Guide to Ancient Greece. *v.3 p.12*

Pause and Effect: An Introduction to the History of Punctuation in the West. *v.3 p.37*

Pawns or Players?: Studies on Medieval and Early Modern Women. *v.6 p.560*

Pax Americana. *v.3 p.454*

Pay and Organizational Effectiveness: A Psychological View. *v.5 p.579*

Pay Any Price: Lyndon Johnson and the Wars for Vietnam. *v.3 p.440, p.441*

Pay Dirt: The Business of Professional Team Sports. *v.4 p.889, p.897*

Pay up and Play the Game: Professional Sport in Britain, 1875-1914. . . . .*v.4 p.810, p.898, p.899*

Paying the Farm Bill: U. S. Agricultural Policy and the Transition to Sustainable Agriculture. *v.5 p.29*

Paying the Price: Ignacio Ellacuria and the Murdered Jesuits of El Salvador. *v.3 p.300*

Paying the Price of Freedom: Family and Labor among Lima's Slaves, 1800-1854. . . . .*v.3 p.327*

Paying with Plastic: The Digital Revolution in Buying and Borrowing. *v.4 p.95, p.155, p.245, p.263*

PC Hardware in a Nutshell. *v.4 p.114, v.5 p.344*

PCAOB: The Public Company Accounting Oversight Board. *v.4 p.103, p.104, p.105*

PCR Methods Manual. *v.5 p.133*

PCR Protocols: Current Methods and Applications. *v.5 p.90, p.101, p.102*

PCR Technology: Principles and Applications for DNA Amplification. *v.5 p.121*

PCR/RT-PCR in Situ Light and Electron Microscopy. . .*v.5 p.89*

The PDMA Handbook of New Product Development. .*v.4 p.144*

The PDR Family Guide to Prescription Drugs: America's Leading Drug Guide for over 60 Years. *v.5 p.526*

PDR for Nutritional Supplements. *v.5 p.526*

PDR® for Herbal Medicines. *v.5 p.526*

Peace and Its Discontents: Essays on Palestine in the Middle East Peace Process. *v.6 p.620*

Peace and the Peacemakers: The Treaty of 1783. . . .*v.4 p.630*

Peace As a Women's Issue: A History of the U. S. Movement for World Peace and Women's Rights. *v.6 p.439*

Peace Enforcement: The United Nations Experience in Congo, Somalia and Bosnia. *v.4 p.648*

Peace in Tatters: Israel, Palestine, and the Middle East. *v.6 p.618*

Peace in War: A Novel: Selected Works of Miguel de Unamuno, Vol. 1. . . . .*v.2 p.662*

The Peace Negotiations. *v.4 p.631*

The Peace of Nicias and the Sicilian Expedition. . . .*v.3 p.18*

Peace Operations and Global Order. *v.4 p.648*

Peace or War: The American Struggle, 1636-1936. . . . .*v.4 p.647, p.648*

Peace Process: American Diplomacy and the Arab-Israeli Conflict since 1967. . . . .*v.6 p.619*

The Peace Progressives and American Foreign Relations. *v.3 p.452*

The Peace Reform in American History. *v.4 p.649*

Peace Signs: The Anti-War Movement Illustrated. . .*v.1 p.718*

Peace Soldiers: The Sociology of a United Nations Military Force. *v.4 p.634, p.650*

A Peace to End All Peace: The Fall of the Ottoman Empire and the Creation of the Modern Middle East. . . .*v.6 p.592*

Peace, War, and Trade along the Great Wall: Nomadic-Chinese Interaction Through Two Millennia. *v.6 p.204*

The Peaceable Kingdom: A Year in the Life of America's Oldest Zoo. *v.5 p.85*

Peaceable Kingdom: Stability and Change in Modern Britain. *v.3 p.112*

Peacebuilding and Police Reform. *v.6 p.262*

A Peaceful and Working People: Manners, Morals, and Class Formation in Northern Mexico. *v.3 p.264, p.265, p.289, p.292*

The Peaceful Liberators: Jain Art from India. *v.1 p.692*

Peacekeeping and the United Nations. *v.4 p.649*

Peacekeeping in Transition: The United Nations in Cambodia. *v.4 p.649*

The Peach Blossom Fan. *v.6 p.209*

Pearl: An Edition with Verse Translation. *v.2 p.204*

Pearl of Great Price. *v.1 p.587*

Pearl S. Buck: A Cultural Biography. *v.2 p.59, v.6 p.200, p.201, p.214*

Pearls in Graph Theory: A Comprehensive Introduction. *v.5 p.480*

Pearl. *v.2 p.204*

Pearson and Canada's Role in Nuclear Disarmament and Arms Control Negotiations, 1945-1957. . . . . . .*v.4 p.644, p.656*

Pearson, His Life and World. *v.3 p.540, p.541*

Pearson: The Unlikely Gladiator. *v.3 p.541*

Peasant and Nation: The Making of Postcolonial Mexico and Peru. *v.3 p.327*

The Peasant Armed: The Indian Revolt of 1857. . . .*v.6 p.158*

The Peasant Cotton Revolution in West Africa: Cotte D'Ivoire, 1880-1995. . . . .*v.6 p.69*

Peasant Intellectuals: Anthropology and History in Northern Tanzania. *v.6 p.66*

Peasant Life in China: A Field Study of Country Life in the Yangtze Valley. *v.6 p.190*

Peasant Life in the Medieval West. *v.6 p.575*

Peasant Nationalism and Communist Power: The Emergence of Revolutionary China, 1937-1945. . . . .*v.6 p.192*

Peasant Politics: Struggle in a Dominican Village. . .*v.3 p.318*

Peasant Protest and Social Change in Colonial Korea. *v.4 p.711, p.712*

Peasant Russia: Family and Community in the Post-Emancipation Period. *v.3 p.218*

Peasant State and Society in Medieval South India. . .*v.6 p.162*

Peasant Wars of the Twentieth Century. *v.4 p.35*

Peasant Women and Politics in Fascist Italy: The Massaie Rurali Section of the PNF. *v.3 p.203*

The Peasantries of Europe: From the Fourteenth to the Eighteenth Centuries. *v.3 p.43*

Peasants and Resistance in India, 1858-1914. . . . . .*v.6 p.157*

Peasants and Tobacco in the Dominican Republic, 1870-1930. . . . .*v.3 p.316*

Peasants in Socialist Transition: Life in a Collectivized Hungarian Village. *v.4 p.701*

Peasants in the Middle Ages. *v.6 p.575*

Peasants into Frenchmen: The Modernization of Rural France, 1870-1914. . . . .*v.3 p.155*

Peasants, Merchants and Markets: Inland Trade in Medieval England, 1150-1350. . . . .*v.6 p.558*

Peasants on Plantations: Subaltern Strategies of Labor and Resistance in the Pisco Valley, Peru. *v.3 p.331*

Peasants, Politics, and the Formation of Mexico's National State. *v.3 p.289*

Peasants, Rebels, Women, and Outcastes: The Underside of Modern Japan. *v.4 p.703*

Peasants, Traders, and Wives: Shona Women in the History of Zimbabwe, 1870-1939. . . . .*v.6 p.77*

Peasants, Warriors, and Wives: Popular Imagery in the Reformation. *v.1 p.753*

Peasants. *v.4 p.29*

The Peculiar Institution: Slavery in the Ante. *v.6 p.37*

Peculiar Institution. *v.3 p.401*

Peculiar Passages: Black Women Playwrights, 1875 to 2000. . . . . *v.1 p.120, p.122*

The Peculiarities of German History: Bourgeois Society and Politics in Nineteenth-Century Germany. *v.3 p.159*

Pedagogy and the Politics of the Body: A Critical Praxis. .*v.1 p.48*

Pedagogy and the Struggle for Voice: Issues of Language, Power, and Schooling for Puerto Ricans. *v.6 p.494, p.495, p.528*

Pedagogy of Hope: Reliving Pedagogy of the Oppressed. *v.4 p.342*

Pedagogy of Place: Seeing Space As Cultural Education. *v.4 p.300*

Pedagogy of Praxis: A Dialectical Philosophy of Education. *v.4 p.342*

Pedagogy of the Oppressed. . .*v.3 p.340, v.4 p.342, p.761, p.762*

Peder Victorious: A Tale of the Pioneers 20 Years Later. .*v.2 p.629*

Pediatric AIDS: The Challenge of HIV Infection in Infants, Children and Adolescents. *v.5 p.515*

Pediatric Emergencies: A Manual for Prehospital Care Providers. *v.5 p.534*

Pediatric Skills for Occupational Therapy Assistants. .*v.5 p.535*

Un pedigree. *v.2 p.532*

Pedometer Power: 67 Lessons for K-12. . . . *v.4 p.798, p.799*

Pedro Almodovar: Interviews. *v.6 p.417*

Pedro Moya de Contreras: Catholic Reform and Royal Power in New Spain, 1571-1591. . . . .*v.3 p.287, p.288*

Pedro Paramo. *v.2 p.669*

Peer Assisted Learning: A Practical Guide for Teachers. .*v.4 p.350*

Peer Instruction: A User's Manual. *v.5 p.563*

Peer-Assisted Learning. *v.4 p.350*

Peering Behind the Curtain: Cisability, Illness, and the Extraordinary Body in Contemporary Theater. .*v.1 p.86, p.94*

Pegasus in Harness: Victorian Publishing and W. M. Thackeray. *v.2 p.315, v.6 p.742*

Peirce and Pragmatism. *v.1 p.512, p.513*

Peirce's Philosophy of Science: Critical Studies in His Theory of Induction and Scientific Method. *v.5 p.404*

Peking Opera and Politics in Taiwan. *v.1 p.288*

Peking Opera Painted Faces with Notes on 200 Operas. *v.1 p.131, p.132, p.140, p.151*

Peking Opera. *v.1 p.288*

Pelagic Nutrient Cycles: Herbivores As Sources and Sinks. *v.5 p.173*

Pelagie-la-Charrette. *v.2 p.541*

Pelleas and Melisande. *v.1 p.212, p.229, p.407*

Pelléas et Mélisande. *v.2 p.522*

The Peloponnesian War, Bk. II. *v.2 p.422*

The Peloponnesian War. *v.2 p.422, v.3 p.18*

Peltse and Pentameron. *v.2 p.814*

Penal ERA and Golden Age: Essays in Irish History, 1690-1800. . . . .*v.3 p.134, p.137*

The Pendergast Machine. *v.3 p.512*

Pendergast!. *v.3 p.512*

Pendulum: Leon Foucault and the Triumph of Science. .*v.5 p.542*

The Penelopiad: The Myth of Penelope and Odysseus. .*v.2 p.734*

Penguin Atlas of Food: Who Eats What Where and Why. *v.4 p.152, p.165*

The Penguin Atlas of Women in the World. *v.6 p.426*

Penguin Book of 19th Century Australian Literature. .*v.2 p.742*

The Penguin Book of Contemporary American Essays. .*v.2 p.27*

Penguin Book of Contemporary British Verse. *v.2 p.200*

The Penguin Book of First World War Poetry. *v.2 p.201*

Penguin Book of French Verse. *v.2 p.464*

The Penguin Book of Hebrew Verse. *v.6 p.648*

The Penguin Book of Homosexual Verse. *v.6 p.404*

Penguin Book of Irish Verse. *v.2 p.200*

The Penguin Book of Italian Verse. *v.2 p.700*

The Penguin Book of Modern Australian Poetry. . . .*v.2 p.743*

The Penguin Book of New Russian Writing. *v.2 p.794*

The Penguin Book of New Zealand Verse. *v.2 p.743*

The Penguin Book of Romantic Poetry. *v.2 p.201, p.583*

The Penguin Book of the Sonnet: 500 Years of a Classic Tradition in English. *v.2 p.200*

Penguin Book of Victorian Verse. *v.2 p.200*

Penguin Companion to European Union. *v.4 p.636*

The Penguin Dictionary of Architecture and Landscape Architecture. *v.1 p.784, p.812*

The Penguin Dictionary of Biology. *v.5 p.225*

The Penguin Dictionary of Curious and Interesting Geometry. *v.5 p.496*

The Penguin Dictionary of Geography. *v.4 p.373*

The Penguin Dictionary of International Relations. . .*v.4 p.626*

The Penguin Dictionary of Literary Terms and Literary Theory. *v.2 p.549*

The Penguin Dictionary of Physics. *v.5 p.545*

The Penguin Dictionary of Psychology. *v.5 p.594*

The Penguin Dictionary of Religions. *v.1 p.522*

Penguin Dictionary of the Theatre. *v.1 p.59*

The Penguin Gandhi Reader. *v.1 p.540*

The Penguin Historical Atlas of Ancient
  Civilizations. *v.3 p.3, v.4 p.380*

Penguin Historical Atlas of Ancient Greece. . . .*v.3 p.12, p.13*

The Penguin Historical Atlas of the Medieval World. .*v.4 p.380*

Penguin History of NZ Literature. *v.2 p.740*

The Penguin New Literary History of Australia. . . .*v.2 p.741*

The Penguin State of the World Atlas. *v.4 p.381*

Penhally. *v.2 p.78*

The Peninsular War: A New History. . . .*v.3 p.75, p.152, p.240*

The Penland Book of Handmade Books: Master Classes in
  Bookmaking Techniques. *v.1 p.761*

The Penland Book of Jewelry: Master Classes in Jewelry
  Techniques. *v.1 p.715, p.716, p.720, p.721*

Pennies from Heaven: The American Popular Music Business in
  the Twentieth Century. *v.1 p.385*

Pennsylvania: A Guide to the Keystone State. . .*v.3 p.491, p.492*

Pennsylvania: A History of the Commonwealth. . . .*v.3 p.492*

Penny Ante Imperialism: The Mosquito Shore and the Bay of
  Honduras, 1600-1914. . . . .*v.3 p.297*

Pensacola During the Civil War: A Thorn in the Side of the
  Confederacy. *v.4 p.521*

El Pensamiento de Cervantes, Por Americo Castro. . .*v.2 p.647*

Pensees and Other Writings. *v.1 p.595, v.2 p.476*

Pensees. *v.2 p.476*

Pensées. *v.1 p.452*

The Pentagon and the Presidency: Civil-Military Relations from
  FDR to George W. Bush. *v.3 p.447*

The Pentagon Papers: The Defense Department History of
  United States Decisionmaking on Vietnam. *v.3 p.393*

Pentecost in Asia: A New Way of Being Church. . . .*v.1 p.573*

Pentimento. *v.2 p.83*

Penultimate Words, and Other Essays. *v.1 p.474*

Penumbral Visions: Making Polities in Early Modern South
  India. *v.6 p.162*

The Peony Pavilion. *v.1 p.129, p.132,v.6 p.209*

People and Environment in Africa. *v.4 p.384, v.6 p.51*

People and Nature: An Introduction to Human Ecological
  Relations. *v.4 p.30*

People and Places in Colonial Venezuela. *v.3 p.359*

People and Politics in France, 1848-1870. . . . . .*v.3 p.154*

People and Politics in Urban America. *v.6 p.723, p.724*

People and Predators: From Conflict to Coexistence. .*v.6 p.283*

The People and the Court: Judicial Review in a
  Democracy. *v.4 p.454*

The People and the King: The Comunero Revolution in
  Colombia, 1781. . . . .*v.3 p.358*

The People and the Word: Reading Native Nonfiction. .*v.6 p.699*

People and Trees: The Role of Social Forestry in Sustainable
  Development. *v.5 p.37*

People Are Not the Same: Leprosy and Identity in
  Twentieth-Century Mali. *v.6 p.74*

A People in Revolution: The American Revolution and Political
  Society in New York, 1760-1790. . . . . . .*v.3 p.407, p.408*

People in Trouble. *v.6 p.399*

People Managing Forests: The Links between Human
  Well-Being and Sustainability. *v.4 p.164*

A People Numerous and Armed: Reflections on the Military
  Struggle for American Independence. *v.3 p.414*

People of India: National Series: The Scheduled Tribes.*v.6 p.149*

The People of New France. *v.3 p.538*

People of Paradox: An Inquiry Concerning the Origins of
  American Civilization. *v.3 p.365*

People of Paris: An Essay in Popular Culture in the 18th
  Century. *v.3 p.148*

People of Plenty: Economic Abundance and the American
  Character. *v.3 p.369*

People of Prowess: Sport, Leisure, and Labor in Early
  Anglo-America. *v.4 p.810, p.819, p.820*

People of Sunlight and Starlight: Barrenland Archaeology in the
  Northwest Territories. *v.4 p.11, v.6 p.703*

The People of the Plain: Class and Community in Lower
  Andalusia. *v.4 p.703*

The People of the Sea: Environment, Identity, and History in
  Oceania. *v.4 p.384*

People of the Sea: The Search for the Philistines. . . .*v.3 p.7*

The People of the Sierra. *v.4 p.42*

People Places: Design Guidelines for Urban Open
  Space. *v.6 p.728*

People, Plants, and Landscapes: Studies in
  Paleoethnobotany. *v.4 p.7*

People Who Dance. *v.1 p.8*

A People Without a Country: The Kurds and Kurdistan.*v.6 p.598*

Peoples and Cultures of Africa. *v.4 p.384*

Peoples and Empires: A Short History of European Migration,
  Exploration, and Conquest, from Greece to the
  Present. *v.3 p.74*

A People's Contest: The Union and Civil War,
  1861-1865. . . . .*v.3 p.399*

The People's Emperor: Democracy and the Japanese Monarchy,
  1945-1995. . . . .*v.4 p.622, v.6 p.225*

The People's Health, 1830-1910. . . . .*v.3 p.92, p.115*

A People's History of Iraq: The Iraqi Communnist Party,
  Workers Movements, and the Left 1923-2004. . . .*v.6 p.603*

A People's History of Prince Edward Island. *v.3 p.543*

A People's History of the Civil War: Struggles for the Meaning
  of Freedom. *v.3 p.432*

The Peoples of Canada: A Post-Confederation
  History. *v.3 p.535, p.536*

Peoples of the Gambia:. I, The Wolof. *v.6 p.69*

The Peoples of the Middle Niger: The Island of
  Gold. *v.6 p.68, p.69*

Peoples of the Northwest Coast: Their Archaeology and
  Prehistory. *v.4 p.10, v.6 p.702*

Peoples of the World. *v.4 p.399*

The People's Peace: British History, 1945-1990. . . .*v.3 p.119*

The People's Republic of China, 1979-1984: A Documentary
  Survey, Set. *v.6 p.197*

The People's Republic of China, Nineteen Forty-Nine to Nineteen Seventy-Nine: A Documentary Survey. . . *v.6 p.194*

The People's Republic: Revolutions Within the Chinese Revolution, 1966-1982. . . . .*v.6 p.194*

The People's Republic: The Emergence of Revolutionary China, 1949-1965. . . . .*v.6 p.194*

The People's Tycoon: Henry Ford and the American Century. *v.3 p.463, v.4 p.154*

The People's War: Responses to World War II in the Soviet Union. *v.3 p.227*

The People's Welfare: Law and Regulation in Nineteenth-Century America. *v.4 p.440*

People's Witness: The Journalist in Modern Politics. . *v.4 p.403*

The Peppered Moth. *v.2 p.343*

Peptide Biosynthesis and Processing. *v.5 p.328*

Pepys: A Biography. *v.2 p.256*

The Pequot War. *v.3 p.405, v.6 p.685*

Per il cinema. *v.2 p.721*

Perceiving God: The Epistemology of Religious Experience. *v.1 p.522*

Perception and Cognition at Century's End: History, Philosophy, Theory. *v.5 p.605*

Perception and Discovery: An Introduction to Scientific Inquiry. *v.5 p.402*

📧 Perception and Illusion: Historical Perspectives. . *v.5 p.598*

Perception and Passion in Dante's Comedy. *v.2 p.704*

Perception and Reality: A History from Descartes to Kant. *v.1 p.436*

The Perception of Women in Spanish Theater of the Golden Age. *v.2 p.641*

Perceptrons: An Introduction to Computational Geometry. *v.5 p.498*

Perceptual Learning: Advances in Research and Theory, Vol. 36. . . . .*v.5 p.605*

Perceval: The Story of the Grail. *v.2 p.466*

Percussion Instruments and Their History. *v.1 p.389*

Percussion. *v.1 p.390*

Percy Bysshe Shelley: Exile of Unfulfilled Reknown, 1816-1822. . . . .*v.2 p.311*

Percy Bysshe Shelley: Youth's Unextinguished Fire, 1792-1816. . . . .*v.2 p.311*

Percy Bysshe Shelley. *v.2 p.312*

Percy Grainger. *v.1 p.209, p.327*

Le Pere Goriot: A New Translation: Responses, Contemporaries and Other Novelists, 20th Century Criticism. . . . *v.2 p.486*

Pere Goriot. *v.2 p.486*

Peregrinations of a Pariah. *v.3 p.328*

Perelandra. *v.2 p.366*

Perestroika under the Tsars. *v.3 p.218*

Perfect Answers to Interview Questions: The Must-Have Guide to Getting That Job!. *v.4 p.169*

The Perfect Crime. *v.1 p.455, p.456*

The Perfect Hour: The Romance of F. Scott Fitzgerald and Ginevra King, His First Love. *v.2 p.77*

The Perfect House: A Journey with the Renaissance Architect Andrea Palladio. *v.1 p.795*

The Perfect Impossibility of General Equilibrium Theory. *v.4 p.205, p.206*

Perfect Package: How to Add Value Through Graphic Design. *v.1 p.717, p.718*

A Perfect Peace. *v.6 p.651*

Perfect Recall: New Stories. *v.2 p.140, p.141*

A Perfect Silence. *v.6 p.505*

Perfect Symmetry: The Accidental Discovery of Buckminsterfullerene. *v.5 p.305*

A Perfect War of Politics: Parties, Politicians, and Democracy in Louisiana, 1824-1861. . . . .*v.3 p.507*

The Perfection of Wisdom in Eight Thousand Lines and Its Verse Summary. *v.1 p.563*

Perfectly Japanese: Making Families in an Era of Upheaval. *v.6 p.222, p.223*

Perfectly Legal: The Secret Campaign to Rig Our Tax System to Benefit the Super Rich—and Cheat Everybody Else. .*v.4 p.107*

Perfectly Reasonable Deviations from the Beaten Track: The Letters of Richard P. Feynman. *v.5 p.542*

Performance and Literature in the Commedia Dell'Arte. *v.1 p.91, p.135, p.144*

Performance Art: from Futurism to the Present. *v.1 p.28, p.30, p.42*

Performance Art. *v.1 p.40*

Performance: Live Art Since 1960. . . . .*v.1 p.42*

The Performance of Emotion among Paxtun Women: "The Misfortunes Which Have Befallen Me". *v.6 p.634*

The Performance of Gender: An Anthropology of Everyday Life in a South Indian Fishing Village. *v.4 p.30*

The Performance of Healing. *v.4 p.46*

Performance on Lute, Guitar, and Vihuela: Historical Practice and Modern Interpretation. *v.1 p.400*

Performance Practice: A Dictionary Guide for Musicians. *v.1 p.160, p.400, p.401*

Performance Practice: Music after 1600. *v.1 p.182, p.188, p.400*

Performance Practice: Music Before 1600. *v.1 p.176, p.179, p.400*

Performance Practices in Classic Piano Music: Their Principles and Applications. *v.1 p.398, p.402*

Performance Studies: An Introduction. *v.1 p.136*

The Performance Studies Reader. *v.1 p.134, p.135*

Performance Studies. *v.1 p.136*

Performance Theory. *v.1 p.136*

Performance-Based Assessment for Middle and High School Physical Education. *v.4 p.798, p.799*

Performance-Enhancing Substances in Sport and Exercise. *v.4 p.826, p.874*

Performer Training: Developments Across Cultures. *v.1 p.136, p.142, p.143*

A Performer's Guide to Medieval Music. . . . *v.1 p.177, p.400*

A Performer's Guide to Music of the Classical Period. *v.1 p.188, p.400*

A Performer's Guide to Music of the Romantic Period. *v.1 p.195, p.400*

A Performer's Guide to Renaissance Music. . *v.1 p.180, p.401*

A Performer's Guide to Seventeenth-Century Music. *v.1 p.183, p.400*

Performing Africa. *v.1 p.285*

Performing Arts Resources: The Drews and the Barrymores, a Dynasty of Actors. . . . *v.1 p.112, p.137, p.140, p.143, p.144*

Performing Asian America: Race and Ethnicity on the Contemporary Stage. *v.6 p.90, p.96, p.99*

Performing Beethoven. *v.1 p.204, p.205, p.308, p.402*

Performing Blackness: Enactments of African-American Modernism. *v.2 p.3*

Performing Brahms: Early Evidence of Performance Style. *v.1 p.201, p.313, p.401*

Performing Dreams: Discourses of Immortality among the Xavante of Central Brazil. *v.3 p.340*

Performing Glam Rock: Gender and Theatricality in Popular Music. *v.1 p.265, p.378*

Performing Identities on the Restoration Stage. . . . *v.2 p.187*

Performing in Extreme Environments: Training and Working in Intense Heat, Frigid Cold, under Water, High Altitude, Air Pollution. *v.4 p.874, p.878*

Performing Medieval and Renaissance Music: An Introductory Guide. *v.1 p.178, p.181, p.402*

Performing Motherhood: The Sevigne Correspondence. *v.2 p.477*

Performing Music in the Age of Recording. *v.1 p.387, p.401, p.402*

Performing National Identities: International Perspectives on Contemporary Canadian Theatre. *v.1 p.127*

Performing Piety: Musical Cultures in Medieval English Nunneries. *v.1 p.178, p.380*

Performing Rites: On the Value of Popular Music. . . *v.1 p.269*

Performing the Nation: Swahili Music and Cultural Politics in Tanzania. *v.1 p.284*

Performing the Visual: The Practice of Buddhist Wall Painting in China and Central Asia, 618-960. . . . . *v.1 p.727*

Performing Twentieth-Century Music: A Handbook for Conductors and Instrumentalists. *v.1 p.399, p.403*

Perfume Dreams: Reflections on the Vietnamese Diaspora. *v.6 p.94, p.140*

Pericles. *v.2 p.224*

The Perilous Frontier: Nomadic Empires and China. *v.4 p.623, v.6 p.238*

Perilous Performances: Gender and Regency in Early Modern France. *v.3 p.144*

Perilous Prospects: The Peace Process and the Arab-Israeli Military Balance. *v.6 p.613*

Perilous Times: Free Speech in Wartime from the Sedition Act of 1798 to the War on Terrorism. . . *v.4 p.505, p.565, p.567*

The Perils of Prosperity, 1914-1932. . . *v.3 p.442, p.448, p.474*

Period Costume for Stage and Screen: Dominos, Dolmans, Coats, Pelisses, Spencers, Callashes, Hoods and Bonnets. *v.1 p.151*

Period Costume for Stage and Screen: Medieval-1500. *v.1 p.151*

Period Costume for Stage and Screen: Patterns for Outer Garments: Cloaks, Capes, Stoles and Wadded Mantles. *v.1 p.151*

Period Costume for Stage and Screen: Patterns for Women's Dress, 1500-1800. . . . . *v.1 p.151*

Period Costume for Stage and Screen: Patterns for Women's Dress, 1800-1909. . . . . *v.1 p.151*

Period Costume for the Stage: A Practical Guide. . . . *v.1 p.150*

The Period from the Arab Invasion to the Salj. . . . *v.6 p.629*

Period Make-Up for the Stage. *v.1 p.151*

Period Piece: The Victorian Childhood of Charles Darwin's Granddaughter. *v.6 p.762, p.765*

The Periodic Kingdom: A Journey into the Land of the Chemical Elements. *v.5 p.264*

The Periodic Table. *v.2 p.715*

Periodicals of Queen Victoria's Empire: An Exploration. *v.2 p.728*

Periodization Training for Sports. *v.4 p.792, p.878*

Periodontology for the Dental Hygienist. *v.5 p.525*

Peripheral Light: Selected and New Poems. *v.2 p.747*

Peripheral Migrants: Haitians and Dominican Republic Sugar Plantations. *v.4 p.41*

The Perishable Empire: Essays on Indian Writing in English. *v.2 p.762*

Perjury: The Hiss-Chambers Case. *v.3 p.450, p.464*

Perl Programming for Biologists. *v.5 p.109*

Permanence of Yeats. *v.2 p.326*

The Permanent International Criminal Court: Legal and Policy Issues. *v.6 p.268*

Permissible Advantage?: The Moral Consequences of Elite Schooling. *v.4 p.297*

Peronism and Argentina. *v.3 p.347*

Perrault's Complete Fairy Tales. *v.2 p.476*

Perry's Chemical Engineers' Handbook. . . . *v.5 p.316, p.741*

Perry's Chemical Engineers' Handbook. *v.5 p.315*

Persephone. *v.1 p.27*

Perseus Digital Library. *v.2 p.399*

Pershing, General of the Armies. *v.3 p.463*

Pershing: General of the Armies. *v.3 p.480*

Persia and the Bible. *v.1 p.618*

The Persian Album, 1400-1600: From Dispersal to Collection. *v.1 p.674, p.691*

The Persian Book of Kings: An Epitome of the Shahnama of Firdawsi. *v.6 p.672*

The Persian Boy. *v.6 p.398*

Persian Brides: A Novel. *v.6 p.651*

The Persian Empire. *v.3 p.11*

Persian Fiction Reader. *v.6 p.671*

Persian Grammar. *v.6 p.669*

Persian Handwriting: Manual for Persian (Farsi) Handwriting. *v.6 p.669*

The Persian Letters. *v.2 p.481, v.3 p.147*

Persian Literature. *v.6 p.673, p.675*

Persian Myths. *v.6 p.670*

Persian Nights. *v.2 p.147*

The Persian Puzzle: The Conflict Between Iran and America. *v.3 p.391*

A Persian Requiem. *v.6 p.670*

Persian Tales: Fifty-Eight Traditional and Folk Tales from Iran. *v.6 p.672*

Persian Vocabulary. *v.6 p.669*

Persistencias y Cambios: Salta y el Noroeste Argentino, 1770-1840. . . . . *v.3 p.347*

The Persistent Desire: A Femme-Butch Reader. *v.6 p.367*

Persistent Disparity: Race and Economic Inequality in the U. S. since 1945. . . . .*v.4 p.265, v.6 p.20*

Persistent Pollutants in Marine Ecosystems. . .*v.5 p.363, p.380*

Persius and the Programmatic Satire: A Study in Form and Imagery. *v.2 p.439*

The Person As Patient: Psychosocial Perspectives for the Health Care Professional. *v.5 p.533*

Person Environment Psychology: New Directions and Perspectives. *v.5 p.588*

Person to Person: Communicative Speaking and Listening Skills. *v.4 p.423*

Person to Person: Fieldwork, Dialogue, and the Hermeneutic Method. *v.4 p.25*

A Personal Approach to Teaching: Beliefs That Make a Difference. *v.4 p.347*

Personal History. *v.4 p.410*

Personal Identity in Theological Perspective. *v.1 p.643*

Personal Justice Denied: Report of the Commission on Wartime Relocation and Internment of Civilians. *v.6 p.134*

Personal Knowledge: Towards a Post-Critical Philosophy. *v.5 p.400*

A Personal Matter. *v.6 p.232*

Personal Memoirs of U. S. Grant. *v.3 p.437*

A Personal Record: The Labour Government, 1964-1970. . . . .*v.3 p.95, p.119*

Personal Rule in Black Africa: Prince, Autocrat, Prophet, Tyrant. *v.6 p.54*

The Personal Trainer's Handbook. *v.4 p.791, p.904*

Personal Witness. *v.6 p.613*

Personality and Intellectual Competence. *v.5 p.651*

Personality and Interpersonal Behavior. *v.4 p.692*

Personality and Organizations. *v.5 p.656*

Personality and Prediction: Principals of Personality Assessment. *v.5 p.603, p.604*

Personality Assessment: Methods and Practices. . . .*v.5 p.603*

Personality Assessment. *v.5 p.603*

Personality, Character, and Leadership in the White House: Psychologists Assess the Presidents. *v.4 p.698*

Personality Comedians As Genre: Selected Players. . .*v.6 p.312*

Personality in Adulthood: A Five-Factor Theory Perspective. *v.5 p.658*

Personality in Intimate Relationships: Socialization and Psychopathology. *v.5 p.658, p.661, p.668*

Personality in Japanese History. *v.6 p.226*

☐ The Personality Project. *v.5 p.603*

Personalized Instruction: Changing Classroom Practice. .*v.4 p.349*

Personalizing Education: Values Clarification and Beyond. *v.4 p.306*

Personnel Administration in Higher Education: Handbook of Faculty and Staff Personnel Practices. *v.4 p.292*

Person/Planet: The Creative Disintegration of Industrial Society. *v.4 p.761*

The Perspective of the World: Civilization and Capitalism, 15th-18th Century. *v.3 p.38*

Perspective on the Nature of Geography. *v.4 p.375*

Perspectives and Practices in Prison Theatre. *v.1 p.94*

Perspectives in Environmental Chemistry. *v.5 p.310*

Perspectives in Mexican American Studies: Community, Identity and Education. *v.6 p.527, p.544*

Perspectives in Mexican American Studies, Vol. 7. . .*v.6 p.521*

Perspectives in World Food Agriculture, Vol. 2. . . . .*v.5 p.13*

Perspectives of Four Women Writers on the Second World War: Gertrude Stein, Janet Flanner, Kay Boyle, and Rebecca West. *v.2 p.63, p.121, p.122, p.388, p.389*

Perspectives on Adults Learning Mathematics: Research and Practice. *v.4 p.319*

Perspectives on Africa: A Reader in Culture, History and Representation. *v.4 p.38*

Perspectives on Climate Change: Science, Economics, Politics, Ethics. *v.4 p.394*

Perspectives on Contemporary Spanish American Theatre. *v.1 p.127*

Perspectives on Cuban Economic Reforms. *v.3 p.312*

Perspectives on Habermas. *v.1 p.468*

Perspectives on Korean Dance. *v.1 p.16*

Perspectives on Modern China: Four Anniversaries. . .*v.6 p.183*

Perspectives on Pain: Mapping the Territory. *v.5 p.530*

Perspectives on Peter Maxwell Davies. *v.1 p.218, p.320*

Perspectives on Post-Colonial Literature. *v.2 p.727*

Perspectives on Properties of the Human Genome Project, Vol. 50. . . . .*v.5 p.140*

Perspectives on Radio and Television: Telecommunication in the United States. *v.4 p.412*

Perspectives on Safe and Sound Banking: Past, Present, and Future. *v.4 p.88*

Perspectives on Shakespeare in Performance. *v.1 p.77, p.104, p.142*

Perspectives on the T'ang. *v.6 p.185*

Perspectives on Wole Soyinka: Freedom and Complexity. *v.2 p.757*

Persuasion in Advertising. *v.4 p.426*

Persuasion: Psychological Insights and Perspectives. *v.5 p.646, p.647, p.648*

Persuasions of the Witch's Craft: Ritual Magic in Contemporary England. *v.4 p.36*

Persuasion. *v.2 p.266*

Perturbed Spirit: The Life and Personality of Samuel Taylor Coleridge. *v.2 p.280*

Peru 1890-1897. . . . .*v.3 p.332*

Peru and the History of Coca: Divine Plant of the Incas. .*v.3 p.282*

Peru and the United States: The Condor and the Eagle. .*v.3 p.329*

Peru in Crisis: Dictatorship or Democracy? .*v.3 p.277, v.4 p.593*

The Peru Reader: History, Culture, Politics, Vol. 2. . .*v.3 p.331*

Peru: Society and Nationhood in the Andes. *v.3 p.330*

Peru: The Evolution of a Crisis. *v.4 p.593*

Peru: Time of Fear. *v.3 p.331*

Peru Under Fire: Human Rights Since the Return to Democracy. *v.3 p.328*

Peru under Garcia: An Opportunity Lost. *v.3 p.329*

Peru's APRA: Parties, Politics, and the Elusive Quest for Democracy. *v.3 p.330*

Peruvian Democracy under Economic Stress: An Account of the Balaunde Administration, 1963-1968. . . . .*v.3 p.330*

The Peruvian Experiment: Continuity and Change under Military Rule. *v.3 p.330*

The Peruvian Experiment Reconsidered. *v.3 p.330*

The Peruvian Labyrinth. *v.3 p.329*

Peruvian Nationalism: A Corporatist Revolution. . . .*v.3 p.329*

Perverzion. *v.2 p.814*

Pesikta Rabbati: Homiletical Discourses for Festal Days and Special Sabbaths. *v.1 p.550*

Pestalozzi and Education. *v.4 p.343*

Pesticides and Politics: The Life Cycle of a Public Issue. *v.4 p.449*

Pesticides in Agriculture and the Environment. . .*v.5 p.10, p.27*

Pesticides in the Soil Environment: Processes, Impacts, and Modeling. *v.5 p.49*

Pesticides in Urban Environments: Fate and Significance. .*v.5 p.10*

Pesticides Studied in Man. *v.5 p.9, p.354, p.366*

Pests of the Garden and Small Farm: A Grower's Guide to Using Less Pesticide. *v.5 p.9, p.26*

Petals of Blood. *v.2 p.759*

Peter Behrens and a New Architecture for the Twentieth Century. *v.1 p.791*

Peter Camenzind: A Novel. *v.2 p.610*

Peter Handke and the Postmodern Transformation: The Goalie's Journey Home. *v.2 p.617*

Peter in the New Testament: A Collaborative Assessment by Protestant and Roman Catholic Scholars. *v.1 p.626*

Peter Kogler. *v.1 p.773*

Peter Lombard. *v.1 p.580*

The Peter Matthiessen Reader. *v.2 p.149*

Peter Maxwell Davies: A Bio-Bibliography. *v.6 p.410*

Peter Pan and Other Plays: The Admirable Crichton; Peter Pan; When Wendy Grew Up; What Every Woman Knows; Mary Rose. *v.2 p.269*

Peter Pan. *v.2 p.269*

Peter the Great: The Struggle for Power, 1671-1725. .*v.3 p.216*

Peter the Great. *v.3 p.216, p.217*

Peter Walker and Partners: Defining the Craft. *v.1 p.817*

Peter Wilkins. *v.2 p.256*

Petersburg: Crucible of Cultural Revolution. *v.3 p.214*

Peterson First Guide to Fishes. *v.5 p.214, p.215*

☐ Peterson's Education Portal. *v.4 p.289*

Peterson's Internships. *v.4 p.170*

La Petite Patrie. *v.2 p.540*

La Petite Poule d'Eau. *v.2 p.539*

The Petkau Effect: The Devastating Effect of Nuclear Radiation on Human Health and the Environment. *v.6 p.291*

Petra and the Lost Kingdom of the Nabataeans. *v.3 p.7*

Petra Rediscovered: Lost City of the Nabataeans. *v.3 p.7*

Petrarch and His World. *v.2 p.705*

Petrarch: Poet and Humanist. *v.2 p.705, p.706*

Petrarch the Poet: An Introduction to the Rerum Vulgarium Fragmenta. *v.2 p.706*

Petrarch's Songbook: Rerum Vulgarium Fragmenta. A Verse Translation. *v.2 p.705*

Petrarch. *v.2 p.705, p.706*

The Petrified Forest. *v.2 p.116*

The Petrine Revolution in Russian Architecture. .*v.3 p.216, p.217*

The Petrine Revolution in Russian Culture. *v.3 p.216*

The Petrine Revolution in Russian Imagery. *v.3 p.216*

Petrogenesis of Metamorphic Rocks. *v.5 p.440*

Petroleum Geochemistry and Geology. *v.5 p.451*

Petroleum Geoscience. *v.5 p.451, p.738*

The Petroleum Industry: A Nontechnical Guide. *v.5 p.737*

Petroleum Provinces of the Twenty-First Century. . . .*v.5 p.737*

Petrotyranny. *v.6 p.299*

Petty Capitalism in Spanish America: The Pulperos of Puebla, Mexico City, Caracas, and Buenos Aires, Vol. 21. .*v.3 p.347*

Petty Capitalism in Spanish America: The Pulperos of Puebla, Mexico City, Caracas and Buenos Aires. *v.3 p.347*

The Petty Demon. *v.2 p.808*

Pew Bible - NKJV. *v.1 p.613*

☐ Pew Hispanic Center, Chronicling Latinos Diverse Experience in a Changing America. *v.6 p.520*

PGA Tour Complete Book of Golf: Lessons and Advice from the Best Players of the Game. *v.4 p.860*

Phaedo. *v.1 p.424, v.2 p.417*

Phaedra, by Racine. *v.2 p.477*

Phaedra. *v.2 p.477*

The Phaidon Atlas of Contemporary World Architecture. *v.1 p.784*

Phanerozoic reef patterns. *v.5 p.438*

Phantastes. *v.2 p.299*

Phantastica: A Classic Survey on the Use and Abuse of Mind-Altering Plants. *v.4 p.777*

Phantasus. *v.2 p.609*

The Phantom of the Cinema: Character in Modern Film. *v.6 p.331*

Phantoms in the Brain: Probing the Mysteries of the Human Mind. *v.5 p.617*

Pharaoh's People: Scenes from Life in Imperial Egypt. *v.3 p.9, v.6 p.57*

Pharmaceutical Achievers: The Human Face of Pharmaceutical Research. *v.5 p.326*

Pharmaceutical Marketing: Principles, Environment, and Practice. *v.4 p.156*

Pharmacology for Chemists. *v.5 p.329*

Pharmacotherapy: A Pathophysiologic Approach. . . .*v.5 p.526*

Phase Diagrams of the Elements. *v.5 p.282*

Phase Equilibria, Phase Diagrams and Phase Transformations: Their Thermodynamic Basis. *v.5 p.282*

Phedre: A Play. *v.2 p.476*

Phedre: Dual Language Edition. *v.2 p.477*

Phenomenological Interpretation of Kant's Critique of Pure Reason. *v.1 p.461*

The Phenomenological Movement. *v.1 p.511*

Phenomenology and the Foundations of the Sciences. *v.1 p.469*

Phenomenology and the Return to Beginnings. *v.1 p.511*

The Phenomenology of Aesthetic Experience. *v.1 p.479*

The Phenomenology of Dance. *v.1 p.43, p.44*

The Phenomenology of Merleau-ponty: A Search for the Limits of Consciousness. *v.1 p.457*

Phenomenology of Perception: An Introduction. . . .*v.1 p.457*

Phenomenology of Perception. *v.1 p.457, p.511*

Phenomenology of Spirit. *v.1 p.463*

Phenomenology of the Social World. *v.4 p.686*

Phenomenology Reader. *v.1 p.511*

Phenomenology. *v.1 p.511*

The Philadelawareans, and Other Essays Relating to
Delaware. *v.4 p.542*

Philadelphia: A Three Hundred Year History. *v.3 p.492*

Philadelphia Gentlemen: The Making of a National Upper
Class. *v.4 p.725, p.726*

The Philadelphia Negro: A Social Study. *v.4 p.729*

Philadelphia: Neighborhoods, Division, and Conflict in a
Postindustrial City. *v.6 p.716*

The Philadelphia Story: A Comedy in Three Acts. . . .*v.2 p.58*

Philaster: Or, Love Lies A-Bleeding. *v.2 p.217*

The Philebus of Plato. *v.4 p.216*

Philip Freneau: The Poet of the Revolution. *v.2 p.28*

Philip Guston. *v.1 p.735*

Philip Johnson: Life and Work. *v.1 p.795*

Philip Larkin: A Bibliography, 1933-1994. . . . . . .*v.2 p.361*

Philip Larkin. *v.2 p.361*

Philip Massinger, the Man and the Playwright. *v.2 p.221*

Philip of Macedon. *v.3 p.19*

Philip of Spain. *v.3 p.239*

Philip Roth: Novels, 1967-1972. . . . .*v.2 p.154*

Philip Roth: Novels and Stories, 1959-1962. . . . . .*v.2 p.154*

Philip V of Spain: The King Who Reigned Twice. . . .*v.3 p.239*

Philip Vera Cruz: A Personal History of Filipino Immigrants and
the Farmworkers Movement.   .*v.6 p.95, p.117, p.119, p.130*

Philippe Bunau-Varilla: The Man Behind the Panama
Canal. *v.3 p.304*

Philippine Dance: Mainstream and Crosscurrents. . . .*v.1 p.17*

Philippine Social History: Global Trade and Local
Transformations. *v.4 p.705*

The Philippine Temptation: Dialectics of Philippines - U. S.
Literary Relations. *v.6 p.97, p.130*

The Philippine War, 1899-1902. . . . .*v.6 p.180*

Philippine Writing: An Anthology. *v.6 p.179*

The Philippines: A Study in National Development. . .*v.6 p.179*

Philippines: A Treasure and a Problem. *v.6 p.180*

The Philippines in World War II, 1941-1945: A Chronology and
Select Annotated Bibliography of Books and Articles in
English. *v.6 p.179*

The Philippines Reader: A History of Colonialism,
Neocolonialism, Dictatorship, and Resistance. . . .*v.3 p.392*

Philippines to the End of the Commission Government: A Study
in Tropical Democracy. *v.6 p.179*

The Philistines and Their Material Culture. *v.3 p.7*

Phillips Curve and Labor Markets. *v.4 p.253*

Philo: Foundations of Religious Philosophy in Judaism,
Christianity and Islam, Set. *v.1 p.431*

Philoctetes. *v.2 p.420*

Philosopher - Kings: The Argument of Plato's
"Republic". *v.4 p.489*

Philosopher Looks at Science. *v.5 p.403*

The Philosopher's Index. *v.1 p.415*

Philosophers of Nothingness: An Essay on the Kyoto
School. *v.1 p.476, p.509*

Philosophers of Process. *v.1 p.513*

Philosophers on Education. *v.4 p.323, p.324, p.340*

The Philosopher's Pupil. *v.2 p.372*

Philosophic Classics: Asian Philosophy. *v.1 p.474*

Philosophic Inquiry in Sport. *v.4 p.803*

The Philosophic Mind: A Study of Wordsworth's Poetry and
Thought, 1797-1805. . . . .*v.2 p.323*

Philosophical Analysis in the Twentieth Century: The Age of
Meaning. *v.1 p.438*

Philosophical Analysis in the Twentieth Century: The Dawn of
Analysis. *v.1 p.438, p.439*

Philosophical and Theological Writings. *v.1 p.460*

Philosophical Applications of Cognitive Science. . . .*v.1 p.496*

The Philosophical Books of Cicero. *v.2 p.433*

Philosophical Dictionary. *v.2 p.484*

Philosophical Documents in Education. *v.4 p.323, p.340*

Philosophical Essays and Correspondence. *v.1 p.453*

Philosophical Essays on Dance: With Responses from
Choreographers, Critics and Dancers. *v.1 p.41*

Philosophical Essays. *v.1 p.459*

Philosophical Explanations. *v.1 p.417*

Philosophical Foundations of Adult Education. *v.4 p.320*

Philosophical Fragments, or a Fragment of Philosophy/Johannes
Climacus, or de Omnibus Dubitandum Rst. *v.1 p.478, p.523*

Philosophical Grammar. *v.1 p.472*

Philosophical Hermeneutics. *v.1 p.507*

Philosophical Investigations. *v.1 p.472, p.473*

Philosophical Lectures, 1818-19. . . . .*v.2 p.279*

Philosophical Naturalism. *v.1 p.516*

Philosophical Occasions, 1912-1951. . . . .*v.1 p.472*

Philosophical Papers. Philosophy and the Human Sciences, Vol.
2. . . . .*v.1 p.496*

Philosophical Papers, Vol. 1: Human Agency and
Language. *v.1 p.495, p.496*

Philosophical Papers. *v.1 p.445, p.446*

Philosophical Perspectives on Music. *v.1 p.380*

Philosophical Political Profiles. *v.1 p.468*

Philosophical Problems of Quantum Physics. *v.5 p.541*

Philosophical Sketches. *v.1 p.441, p.442*

Philosophical Texts. *v.1 p.459*

Philosophical Thinking in Educational Practice. . . .*v.4 p.343*

Philosophical Writings: A Selection. *v.1 p.433*

The Philosophical Writings of Descartes, Vol. 1. . . .*v.1 p.453*

The Philosophical Writings of Descartes, Vol. 2. . . .*v.1 p.453*

Philosophical Writings. *v.1 p.466*

The Philosophies of Asia. *v.1 p.476*

Philosophies of Mathematics. *v.5 p.470*

Philosophies of Music History: A Study of General Histories of
Music, 1600-1960. . . . .*v.1 p.173*

Philosophy: A Guide to Reference Literature. .*v.1 p.416, v.5 p.405*

The Philosophy and Aesthetics of Music. *v.1 p.382*

The Philosophy and Economics of J. M. Keynes. . . .*v.4 p.227*

Philosophy and Its Place in Our Culture. *v.1 p.417*

The Philosophy and Opinions of Marcus Garvey: Or, Africa for the Africans. *v.6 p.12*

Philosophy and Ordinary Language: The Bent and Genius of Our Tongue. *v.1 p.510*

Philosophy and Post-Structuralist Theory: From Kant to Deleuze. *v.1 p.512*

Philosophy and Practice of Organizational Learning, Performance and Change. *v.4 p.78*

Philosophy and Psychology in the Abhidharma. *v.1 p.565*

Philosophy and Public Policy. *v.1 p.441*

Philosophy and Romantic Nationalism: The Case of Poland. *v.3 p.253*

Philosophy and the Analysis of Music: Bridges to Musical Sound, Form, and Reference. *v.1 p.381*

🄴 Philosophy and the Darwinian Legacy. *v.1 p.516*

Philosophy and the Mirror of Nature. *v.1 p.417*

Philosophy and the Spontaneous Philosophy of the Scientists: And Other Essays. *v.1 p.455*

Philosophy and the World. *v.1 p.468*

Philosophy, Biology and Life. *v.5 p.248*

Philosophy, Crime, and Criminology. *v.6 p.249*

Philosophy Guidebook to Hegel and Phenomenology of Spirit. *v.1 p.464*

Philosophy in a New Key: A Study in the Symbolism of Reason, Rite, and Art. *v.1 p.442*

Philosophy in Classical India: The Proper Work of Reason. *v.1 p.419*

Philosophy in France Today. *v.1 p.457*

Philosophy in Late Antiquity. *v.1 p.431*

Philosophy in Process, Vol. 11. . . . . *v.1 p.513*

Philosophy in the Flesh: The Embodied Mind and Its Challenge to Western Thought. *v.4 p.27*

Philosophy in the Middle Ages: The Christian, Islamic and Jewish Traditions. *v.1 p.432*

Philosophy in the Twentieth Century. *v.1 p.438*

Philosophy of Aikido. *v.4 p.803, p.863*

The Philosophy of Artificial Intelligence. *v.5 p.590*

The Philosophy of Artificial Life. *v.5 p.589*

The Philosophy of As If: A System of the Theoretical, Practical and Religious Fictions of Mankind. *v.1 p.469*

The Philosophy of Benedetto Croce. *v.1 p.473*

The Philosophy of Biology: An Episodic History. . . . *v.5 p.79*

Philosophy of Biology. *v.5 p.196, p.249*

The Philosophy of Color. *v.1 p.710*

The Philosophy of Discourse: The Rhetorical Turn in Twentieth-Century Thought. *v.1 p.438*

The Philosophy of Donald Davidson. *v.1 p.441*

Philosophy of Education: An Encyclopedia. . *v.4 p.323, p.339*

Philosophy of Education: Essays and Commentaries. *v.4 p.323, p.339*

The Philosophy of Education: Major Themes in the Analytic Tradition. *v.4 p.323, p.339*

The Philosophy of Ernst Cassirer. *v.1 p.469*

Philosophy of Existence. *v.1 p.505*

The Philosophy of G. E. Moore. *v.1 p.446*

The Philosophy of Gandhi: A Study of His Basic Ideas. *v.1 p.475*

The Philosophy of Giambattista Vico. *v.1 p.473*

The Philosophy of Grammar. *v.2 p.557, p.561*

The Philosophy of History. *v.1 p.473*

The Philosophy of Horror: Paradoxes of the Heart. . *v.6 p.317*

The Philosophy of Humanism. *v.1 p.507, p.508*

The Philosophy of J. S. Mill. *v.1 p.444*

The Philosophy of Jean-Paul Sartre. *v.1 p.458*

The Philosophy of John Dewey. *v.1 p.443*

The Philosophy of Josiah Royce. *v.1 p.439, p.440*

The Philosophy of Karl Popper. *v.1 p.445, p.446*

The Philosophy of Language. *v.1 p.442, p.490, v.2 p.550, p.562*

The Philosophy of Law: A Very Short Introduction. . *v.1 p.491*

Philosophy of Law: An Introduction. *v.1 p.491*

The Philosophy of Law: The Fundamentals. *v.1 p.491*

The Philosophy of Law. *v.4 p.434*

The Philosophy of Leibniz. *v.1 p.460*

The Philosophy of Lev Shestov, 1866-1938: A Russian Religious Existentialist. *v.1 p.474*

The Philosophy of Literary Form. *v.2 p.575*

Philosophy of Logics. *v.1 p.493*

Philosophy of Logic. *v.1 p.493*

The Philosophy of Mathematics Education. *v.5 p.462*

Philosophy of Mathematics: Selected Readings. . . . *v.5 p.471*

Philosophy of Meaning, Knowledge and Value in the 20th Century. *v.1 p.438*

The Philosophy of Mind: An Introduction. *v.1 p.497*

Philosophy of Mind: Classical and Contemporary Readings. *v.1 p.496*

Philosophy of Mind. *v.1 p.497*

Philosophy of Modern Music. *v.1 p.380*

The Philosophy of Nature: A Guide to the New Essentialism. *v.1 p.505*

The Philosophy of Peter Abelard. *v.3 p.57*

The Philosophy of Physical Science. *v.5 p.541*

Philosophy of Psychology. *v.5 p.619*

Philosophy of Religion: An Anthology. *v.1 p.523*

The Philosophy of Religion. *v.1 p.498, p.499*

Philosophy of Right. *v.1 p.463, p.491*

The Philosophy of Rousseau. *v.2 p.482*

The Philosophy of Rudolph Carnap, Vol. 11. . . . . *v.1 p.469*

The Philosophy of Samuel Beckett. *v.2 p.333*

The Philosophy of Schopenhauer. *v.1 p.465*

Philosophy of Science, Logic and Mathematics in the 20th Century, Vol. 9. . . . . *v.1 p.499, p.500*

Philosophy of Science: The Link Between Science and Philosophy. *v.5 p.401*

Philosophy of Science Today. *v.1 p.499, v.5 p.401*

Philosophy of Science. *v.5 p.401, p.402*

The Philosophy of Science. *v.5 p.404*

Philosophy of Socrates. *v.1 p.423*

The Philosophy of Space and Time. *v.1 p.500*

Philosophy of Sport and Exercise Science: Critical Perspectives on Scientific Method and Enquiry in Sport, Exercise and Health. *v.4 p.802, p.873, p.874*

The Philosophy of St. Bonaventure. *v.6 p.567, p.571*

The Philosophy of Symbolic Forms. *v.1 p.468*

Philosophy of the Arts: An Introduction to Aesthetics. .*v.1 p.479*

The Philosophy of the Church Fathers: Faith, Trinity, Incarnation. *v.1 p.634*

The Philosophy of the Enlightenment. *v.1 p.437, v.3 p.71*

The Philosophy of the Inductive Sciences. *v.5 p.404*

The Philosophy of the Present. *v.1 p.442*

Philosophy of the Sixteenth and Seventeenth Centuries. *v.1 p.435, p.437*

The Philosophy of the Young Kant: The Precritical Project. *v.1 p.462*

The Philosophy of Time. *v.1 p.500*

Philosophy of Time. *v.1 p.500*

The Philosophy of Utopia. *v.4 p.499*

The Philosophy of W. V. Quine: An Expository Essay. .*v.1 p.443*

The Philosophy of W. V. Quine. *v.1 p.443*

The Philosophy of Wealth: Economic Principles Newly Formulated. *v.4 p.208, p.223*

The Philosophy of Wilhelm Dilthey. *v.1 p.464, p.465*

Philosophy Pages. *v.1 p.415*

Phineas Finn: The Irish Member. *v.2 p.317*

Phineas Redux. *v.2 p.317*

Phoenicians. *v.3 p.7*

Phoenix Eyes and Other Stories. *v.6 p.101*

The Phoenix Gone, the Terrace Empty: Poems. . . .*v.6 p.103*

A Phoenix in the Ashes: The Rise and Fall of the Koch Coalition in New York City Politics. *v.6 p.714*

Phoenix Over the Galilee. *v.6 p.649*

Phoenix: The History of a Southwestern Metropolis. . .*v.3 p.528*

Phonemics: A Technique for Reducing Language to Writing. *v.2 p.563*

Phonetic Symbol Guide. *v.2 p.563*

Phonetics: A Critical Analysis of Phonetic Theory and a Technic for the Practical Description of Sounds. *v.2 p.563*

Phonics in Proper Perspective. *v.4 p.363*

Phonological Analysis: Focus on American English. . .*v.2 p.558*

Phonological Theory: The Essential Readings. *v.2 p.560*

Phonology in Generative Grammar. *v.2 p.562*

Phosphorus: Agriculture and the Environment. *v.5 p.11*

Phosphorus Biogeochemistry in Sub-Tropical Ecosystemst. *v.5 p.177*

Photochemistry. *v.5 p.278*

Photographers: A Sourcebook for Historical Research. .*v.1 p.761*

Photographer's Guide to Polaroid Transfer: Step-by-Step. *v.1 p.759*

The Photographic Art of William Henry Fox Talbot. . .*v.1 p.768*

The Photographic Experience, 1839-1914: Images and Attitudes. *v.1 p.763*

Photographic Guide to Sea and Shore Life of Britain and North-West Europe. *v.5 p.172, p.173, p.237*

The Photograph. *v.1 p.762*

Photography: A Cultural History. *v.1 p.764, p.767*

Photography and Its Critics: A Cultural History, 1839-1900. . . . .*v.1 p.764*

The Photography Book. *v.1 p.762*

The Photography Encyclopedia. *v.1 p.762*

Photography from 1839 to Today: George Eastman House, Rochester, NY. *v.1 p.763*

Photography in Print: Writings from 1816 to Present. .*v.1 p.762*

Photography Past and Forward: Aperture at Fifty. . . .*v.1 p.762*

Photography with a Microscope. *v.5 p.86*

Photography's Antiquarian Avant-Garde: The New Wave in Old Processes. *v.1 p.768*

PhotoHistorica, Landmarks in Photography: Rare Images from the Collection of the Royal Photographic Society. .*v.1 p.768*

Photomontage. *v.1 p.762*

Photons and Atoms: Introduction to Quantum Electrodynamics. *v.5 p.566*

Photosynthesis in Algae. *v.5 p.208*

Phrase Rhythm in Tonal Music. *v.1 p.372*

Phrases and Passages of a Salutary Song. *v.2 p.716*

PHTLS Basic and Advanced Prehospital Trauma Life Support. *v.5 p.534*

Phycology. *v.5 p.208*

Phylloxera: How Wine Was Saved for the World. . . .*v.5 p.46*

Phylogenetic Analysis of DNA Sequences. *v.5 p.122, p.123, p.194, p.195*

Phylogenetic Analysis of Morphological Data. *v.5 p.155, p.199, p.201*

The Phylogenetic Handbook: A Practical Approach to DNA and Protein Phylogeny. *v.5 p.137*

Phylogenetics. *v.5 p.205*

Phylogeography: The History and Formation of Species. .*v.5 p.204*

Physical Activity and Obesity. *v.4 p.790, p.876*

Physical Activity, Fitness, and Health Consensus Statement: International Proceedings and Consensus Statement. *v.4 p.790*

Physical Activity for Health and Fitness. *v.4 p.791*

Physical Activity Instruction of Older Adults. . .*v.4 p.795, p.841*

Physical and Non-Physical Methods of Solving Crystal Structures. *v.5 p.284*

Physical and Thermodynamic Properties of Aliphatic Alcohols. *v.5 p.287*

Physical and Thermodynamic Properties of Pure Chemicals: Data Compilation. *v.5 p.281, p.741*

The Physical Basis of Biochemistry: The Foundations of Molecular Biophysics. *v.5 p.111*

The Physical Basis of Chemistry. *v.5 p.277*

Physical Being: A Theory for a Corporeal Psychology. *v.5 p.594*

Physical Ceramics for Engineers. *v.5 p.692*

Physical Chemistry: A Molecular Approach. *v.5 p.278*

Physical Chemistry, an Advanced Treatise. *v.5 p.276*

Physical Chemistry for the Biosciences. . .*v.5 p.82, p.112, p.327*

Physical Chemistry: Interactive Software. *v.5 p.288*

Physical Chemistry Laboratory Experiments. . .*v.5 p.287, p.288*

Physical Chemistry of Biological Interfaces. . .*v.5 p.326, p.327*

Physical Chemistry of Surfaces. *v.5 p.283*

Physical Chemistry: Principles and Applications in Biological Sciences. *v.5 p.114, p.328*

Physical Chemistry Source Book. *v.5 p.274, p.275*

Physical Chemistry. *v.5 p.275, p.276, p.278*

Physical Constants of Hydrocarbons, 5 vols., 1939-. . .*v.5 p.290*

Physical Dimensions of Aging. *v.4 p.875, p.880*

The Physical Education Activity Handbook. *v.4 p.798, p.799, p.800*

Physical Education and Kinesiology in North America: Professional and Scholarly Foundations. *v.4 p.797*

Physical Education Methods for Classroom Teachers. *v.4 p.798, p.799*

Physical Education: Teachers' Lives and Careers. .*v.4 p.795, p.903*

Physical Education Tips from the Trenches. *v.4 p.800*

Physical Education Unit Plans for Preschool-Kindergarten, for Grades 1-2, for Grades 3-4, for Grades 5-6. . . . .*v.4 p.798*

Physical Fluid Dynamics. *v.5 p.547*

Physical Foundations of Materials Science. *v.5 p.732*

Physical Geodesy. *v.4 p.389*

The Physical Geography of Southeast Asia. *v.4 p.384*

The Physical Geography of the Sea and Its Meteorology. *v.4 p.394*

Physical Geography of Western Europe. *v.4 p.383*

Physical Geology. *v.4 p.390, v.5 p.419*

Physical Inorganic Chemistry: A Coordination Chemistry Approach. *v.5 p.303*

Physical Kinetics, Vol. 10. . . . .*v.5 p.566*

Physical Metallurgy Handbook. *v.5 p.733*

The Physical Metallurgy of Microalloyed Steels. . .*v.5 p.736*

Physical Metallurgy. *v.5 p.732*

Physical Methods in Chemistry. *v.5 p.276*

Physical Methods in Determinative Mineralogy. . . .*v.5 p.436*

Physical Methods in Modern Chemical Analysis, 1978-1983, 3 vols. *v.5 p.268*

Physical Methods of Chemistry: Determination of Elastic and Mechanical Properties. *v.5 p.276*

Physical Methods of Chemistry: Determination of Electronic and Optical Properties, Vol. 8. . . . .*v.5 p.276*

Physical Methods of Chemistry: Determination of Structural Features of Crystalline and Amorphous Solids, Vol. 5. . . . .*v.5 p.277*

Physical Methods of Chemistry, Determination of Thermodynamic Properties, Vol. 6. . . . .*v.5 p.277*

Physical Methods of Chemistry, Electrochemical Methods, Vol. 2. . . . .*v.5 p.277*

Physical Methods of Chemistry: Investigations of Surfaces and Interfaces. *v.5 p.276*

Physical Methods of Chemistry: Microscopy, Vol. 4. . .*v.5 p.277*

Physical Methods of Chemistry, Supplement and Cumulative Index, Vol. 10. . . . .*v.5 p.275*

Physical Methods of Chemistry. *v.5 p.277*

Physical Oceanography: Developments Since 1950. . . . .*v.4 p.392, v.5 p.430*

Physical Organic Chemistry. *v.5 p.292, p.293*

Physical Principles of Electron Microscopy: An Introduction to TEM, SEM, and AEM. *v.5 p.88*

Physical Processes in Lakes and Oceans. *v.4 p.392*

Physical Processes in the Interstellar Medium. *v.5 p.70*

Physical Properties of Chemical Compounds; Advances in Chemistry Series, Nos. 15, 22, 29. . . . .*v.5 p.281*

The Physical Properties of Glass. *v.5 p.689*

Physical Properties of Polymers Handbook. . . .*v.5 p.324*

Physical Properties of Polymers Handbook. . . .*v.5 p.324, p.690*

Physical Rehabilitation of the Injured Athlete. *v.5 p.519*

Physical Science in the Middle Ages. *v.5 p.399*

The Physical Universe. *v.5 p.72*

Physicalism and Its Discontents. *v.1 p.509*

Physicalism, or Something near Enough. *v.1 p.509*

Physicalism: The Philosophical Foundations. *v.1 p.509*

A Physicalist Manifesto: Thoroughly Modern Materialism. *v.1 p.509*

Physically Speaking: A Dictionary of Quotations on Physics and Astronomy. *v.5 p.545*

The Physician and Sexuality in Victorian America. .*v.4 p.774*

Physician Assistant: A Guide to Clinical Practice. . .*v.5 p.534*

The Physician's Tale. *v.2 p.208*

The Physicist's Conception of Nature. *v.5 p.402*

Physico Chemical Constants of Pure Organic Compounds, v. 1. . . . .*v.5 p.300, p.301*

The Physico-Chemical Constants of Binary Systems in Concentrated Solutions. *v.5 p.282*

Physicochemical Properties and Environmental Fate Handbook. *v.5 p.286*

Physics 2000. . . . .*v.5 p.548*

The Physics and Chemistry of Color: The Fifteen Causes of Color. *v.5 p.562*

Physics and Chemistry of Lakes. *v.5 p.427*

The Physics and Chemistry of Solids. *v.5 p.305*

Physics and Chemistry of the Solar System. *v.5 p.68*

Physics and Its 5th Dimension: Society. *v.5 p.411*

Physics and Metaphysics: Theories of Space and Time. .*v.1 p.500*

Physics and Philosophy: The Revolution in Modern Science. *v.5 p.541, p.542*

The Physics and Technology of Tennis. *v.4 p.864, p.871*

Physics and the Art of Dance: Understanding Movement. *v.1 p.42, p.43*

Physics, Bks. III and IV. *v.1 p.426*

Physics: Demonstration Experiments. *v.5 p.563, p.564*

Physics for Poets. *v.5 p.540*

The Physics Handbook: Fundamentals and Key Equations. *v.5 p.545, p.546*

Physics in Molecular Biology. *v.5 p.125, p.129*

Physics in the 20th Century. *v.5 p.541*

Physics in the Nineteenth Century. *v.5 p.540*

Physics Internet Resources. *v.5 p.545*

The Physics of Astrophysics: Gas Dynamics. *v.5 p.67*

The Physics of Astrophysics: Radiation Processes. . .*v.5 p.67*

The Physics of Atoms and Molecules. *v.5 p.554*

The Physics of Baseball. *v.5 p.540*

Physics of Climate. *v.5 p.426*

The Physics of Dance. *v.1 p.49*

Physics of Everyday Phenomena: A Conceptual Introduction to
    Physics. *v.5 p.539*

The Physics of Extragalactic Radio Sources. *v.5 p.68*

The Physics of Football: Discover the Science of
    Bone-Crunching Hits, Soaring Field Goals, and Awe-Inspiring
    Passes. *v.4 p.858, p.871*

The Physics of Golf. *v.4 p.861, p.871*

The Physics of Hockey. *v.4 p.862, p.871*

The Physics of Low-Dimensional Semiconductors: An
    Introduction. *v.5 p.555*

The Physics of Particle Detectors. *v.5 p.552*

The Physics of Polymers: Concepts for Understanding Their
    Structures and Behavior. *v.5 p.324*

The Physics of Quantum Fields. *v.5 p.550*

The Physics of Sailing Explained. *v.4 p.866, p.871*

Physics of Semiconductor Devices. *v.5 p.555*

Physics of Semiconductors. *v.5 p.555*

The Physics of Skiing: Skiing at the Triple Point.*v.4 p.867, p.871*

The Physics of Solids. *v.5 p.555*

Physics of Space Plasmas: An Introduction. *v.5 p.444*

The Physics of Star Trek. *v.5 p.541*

The Physics of Superconductors. *v.5 p.565*

Physics of the Space Environment. *v.5 p.73, p.444*

The Physics of Waves. *v.5 p.561*

Physics: Principles with Applications. *v.5 p.539*

Physics. *v.5 p.399, p.539*

Physiological Assessment of Human Fitness. . .*v.4 p.791, p.875*

Physiology and Behavior. *v.5 p.522*

Physiology and Form of Fish Circulation. *v.5 p.216*

The Physiology of Fishes. *v.5 p.214*

The Physiology of Psychological Disorders: Schizophrenia,
    Depression, Anxiety, and Substance Abuse. *v.5 p.659, p.660*

Physiology of Sport and Exercise. *v.4 p.878*

Physiology of Stressed Crops: The Stress of
    Allelochemicals. *v.5 p.21*

Physiology of the Heart. *v.5 p.520*

Physiology of Woody Plants. *v.5 p.38*

Physlets: Teaching Physics with Interactive Curricular
    Material. *v.5 p.563*

Phytophthora Diseases Worldwide. *v.5 p.46*

Pi - Unleashed. *v.5 p.475*

PI and the AGM: A Study in Analytic Number Theory and
    Computational Complexity. *v.5 p.475*

A Piaget Primer: How a Child Thinks. *v.5 p.629*

Piaget's Conception of Evolution: Beyond Darwin and
    Lamarck. *v.5 p.597*

The Pianist: The Extraordinary True Story of One Man's
    Survival in Warsaw, 1939-1945. . . . .*v.3 p.87*

The Pianist's Bookshelf: A Practical Guide to Books, Videos,
    and Other Resources. *v.1 p.167, p.239, p.398*

The Pianist's Dictionary. *v.1 p.160, p.389, p.390*

The Pianist's Guide to Pedaling. *v.1 p.397*

The Pianist. *v.3 p.255*

The Piano: A History. *v.1 p.389, v.3 p.111, p.127, p.128*

The Piano: An Encyclopedia. *v.1 p.161, p.391*

The Piano in America, 1890-1940. . . . .*v.1 p.279, p.391*

The Piano Lesson. *v.1 p.123, v.2 p.159*

The Piano Trio: Its History, Technique, and Repertoire.*v.1 p.243*

The Pianoforte in the Classical Era. *v.1 p.389*

Picadilly Jim. *v.2 p.391*

The Picador Book of Latin American Stories. *v.2 p.666*

The Picaresque: Tradition and Displacement. *v.2 p.641*

Picasso and Printmaking in Paris. *v.1 p.757*

Picasso and the Invention of Cubism. *v.1 p.742*

Picasso and the War Years, 1937-1945. . . . .*v.1 p.744*

Picasso: The Art of the Poster, Catalogue Raisonné. .*v.1 p.718*

Picasso's Guernica: History, Transformations,
    Meanings. *v.1 p.736*

Picasso's Paintings, Watercolors, Drawings and Sculpture - A
    Comprehensive Illustrated Catalogue: Liberation and
    Post-War Years, 1944-1949. . . . .*v.1 p.745*

The Pickup: A Novel. *v.2 p.755*

Pickup Artists: Street Basketball in America. . .*v.4 p.813, p.853*

The Pickwick Papers. *v.2 p.284*

Pictographic Score Notation: A Compendium. *v.1 p.393*

A Pictorial Approach to Molecular Bonding and
    Vibrations. *v.5 p.277*

The Pictorial Arts of the West, 800-1200. . . .*v.1 p.671, p.727*

Pictorial Dictionary of British 18th Century Furniture
    Design. *v.1 p.805*

A Pictorial History of Burlesque. *v.1 p.36*

A Pictorial History of Music. *v.1 p.174*

A Pictorial History of Psychology. *v.5 p.595*

A Pictorial History of Vaudeville. *v.1 p.35, p.90, p.91*

Pictorial Human Embryology. *v.5 p.162*

The Picture Book Comes of Age: Looking at Childhood
    Through the Art of Illustration. *v.1 p.716*

Picture Bride. *v.6 p.104*

Picture Perfect. *v.6 p.347*

Picture Window: Poems. *v.2 p.87*

Pictures and Passions: A History of Homosexuality in the Visual
    Arts. *v.1 p.707*

Pictures from an Institution. *v.2 p.91*

The Picturesque Prison: Evelyn Waugh and His Writing. .*v.2 p.387*

Picturing Chinatown: Art and Orientalism in San
    Francisco. *v.6 p.88, p.90, p.127*

Picturing Empire: Photography and the Visualization of the
    British Empire. *v.1 p.764*

Picturing Faith: Photography and the Great Depression.*v.1 p.764*

Picturing Japaneseness: Monumental Style, National Identity,
    Japanese Film. *v.6 p.335*

Picturing Men: A Century of Male Relationships in Everyday
    American Photography. *v.1 p.708*

Picturing Power in the People's Republic of China: Posters of
    the Cultural Revolution. *v.6 p.195*

Picturing the Passion in Late Medieval Italy: Narrative Painting,
    Franciscan Ideologies, and the Levant. *v.1 p.727*

Piece of My Heart: A Lesbian of Colour Anthology. . .*v.6 p.405*

Pieces of a Song: Selected Poems of Diane DiPrima. .*v.2 p.144*

Pier Paolo Pasolini: Contemporary
    Perspectives. *v.2 p.721, p.722, v.6 p.417*

Pier Paolo Pasolini. *v.2 p.721*

Pierce's Disease. *v.5 p.53*

Pierre Bismuth. *v.1 p.772*

Pierre Boulez. *v.1 p.216, p.312, p.313*

Pierre Bourdieu: Agent Provocateur. *v.4 p.682*

Pierre Corneille Revisited. *v.2 p.473*

Pierre de la Rue and Musical Life at the Habsburg-Burgundian
Court. *v.1 p.180, p.335*

Pierre de Ronsard. *v.2 p.470, p.471*

Pierre et Jean. *v.2 p.497*

Pierre Gassendi: From Aristotelianism to a New Natural
Philosophy. *v.1 p.452*

Pierre, Israel Potter, the Confidence-Man, the Piazza
Tale. *v.2 p.48*

Pierre Simon Laplace, 1749-1827: A Determined
Scientist. *v.5 p.396*

Piers Plowman: A New Translation of the B-Text. . . .*v.2 p.211*

Piers Plowman: An Edition of the C-Text. *v.2 p.211*

Piers Plowman: An Introduction to the B-Text. .*v.2 p.204, p.211*

Piers Plowman and the Problem of Belief. *v.2 p.211*

Piers Plowman As A: Century Apocalypse. *v.2 p.211*

Piers Plowman: The Prologue and Passus I-VII of the B Text As
Found in Bodleian Ms. Laud Misc. 581. . . . . .*v.2 p.211*

Piers Plowman: The Three Versions. *v.2 p.211*

Piers Plowman. *v.2 p.211*

Piet Mondrian: Catalogue Raisonné. *v.1 p.697*

Pietro Belluschi: Modern American Architect. *v.1 p.792*

Pietro Mascagni and His Operas. *v.1 p.218, p.231, p.340*

Piety and Family in Early Modern Europe: Essays in Honour of
Steven Ozment. *v.1 p.601*

Piety and Tolerance: Pennsylvania German Religion,
1700-1850. . . . .*v.1 p.607*

Piety Versus Moralism: Passing of the New England
Theology. *v.1 p.633*

Pièces baroques. *v.2 p.506*

Pièces farceuses. *v.2 p.506*

Pig Earth. *v.6 p.287*

Pig Tales: A Novel of Lust and Transformation. *v.2 p.529*

The Pigeonpea. *v.5 p.22*

Pigments ; Névralgies. *v.2 p.536*

Pigs for the Ancestors: Ritual in the Ecology of a New Guinea
People. *v.4 p.30*

Pigs Have Wings. *v.2 p.391*

The Pilates Program for Everybody: Simple, Effective
Exercises— Amazing Benefits for All Ages. *v.4 p.793*

Pilchuck: A Glass School. *v.1 p.811*

Pilgrim at Sea. *v.2 p.630*

Pilgrim at Tinker Creek. *v.5 p.224*

Pilgrim Colony: A History of New Plymouth,
1620-1691. . . . .*v.3 p.487*

The Pilgrim Hawk: A Love Story. *v.2 p.128*

Pilgrimage and Healing. *v.1 p.530*

Pilgrimage for Peace: A Secretary General's
Memoir. *v.4 p.635, p.650*

Pilgrimage in Indian Civilization. *v.1 p.534*

Pilgrims and Sacred Sites in China. *v.1 p.566*

Pilgrims in Aztlan. *v.6 p.501*

Pilgrims in Their Own Land: 500 Years of Religion in
America. *v.1 p.605*

The Pilgrims of Hope. *v.2 p.301*

The Pilgrim's Progress and Grace Abounding to the Chief of
Sinners. *v.2 p.241*

The Pilgrim's Progress: Critical and Historical Views. *v.2 p.241*

The Pilgrim's Progress. *v.1 p.593, v.2 p.241*

The Pill, Pygmy Chimps, and Degas' Horse: The Remarkable
Autobiography of the Award Winning Scientist Who
Synthesized the Pill. *v.5 p.260*

Pillar of Sand: Can the Irrigation Miracle Last? *v.6 p.289*

Pillars of the Republic: Common Schools and American Society,
1780-1860. . . . .*v.4 p.327*

The Pillow Book of Sei Shonagon. *v.6 p.232*

Pills, Petticoats, and Plows; the Southern Country Store. *v.3 p.496*

Pilot Analysis of Global Ecosystems: Agroecosystems. *v.5 p.11*

The Pilot's Burden: Flight Safety and the Roots of Pilot
Error. *v.5 p.717*

The Piltdown Forgery. *v.4 p.16*

Pina Bausch Wuppertal Dance Theater: On the Art of Training a
Goldfish--Excursions into Dance. *v.1 p.12*

Pinay Power: Peminist Critical Theory. *v.6 p.111, p.129*

Pindar: Nemean Odes, Isthmian Odes, Fragments. . . .*v.2 p.417*

Pindar: Olympian Odes, Pythian Odes. *v.2 p.417*

Pindar: Olympians 2, 7 and 11; Nemean 4; Isthmians 3, 4 and
7. . . . .*v.2 p.417*

Pindar's Homer: The Lyric Possession of an Epic Past. *v.2 p.417*

Pindar. *v.2 p.416, p.417*

Pine River and Lone Peak: An Anthology of 3 Choson Dynasty
Poets. *v.6 p.238*

The Pineapple: Botany, Production and Uses. . . .*v.5 p.20, p.25*

The Pink and the Green with Mina de Vanghel. *v.2 p.502*

The Pink Triangle: The Nazi War Against Homosexuals. *v.6 p.366*

Pinocchio's Progeny: Puppets, Marionettes, Automatons, and
Robots in Modernist and Avant-Garde Drama. *v.1 p.85, p.93*

The Pinochet Case: Origins, Progress, and Implications. *v.3 p.352*

The Pinochet File: A Declassified Dossier on Atrocity and
Accountability. *v.3 p.354*

Pinochet in Piccadilly: Britain and Chile's Secret
History. *v.3 p.352*

Pinochet: The Politics of Power. . . .*v.3 p.273, p.352, v.4 p.591*

Pinochet: The Politics of Torture. *v.3 p.354*

The Pinter Ethic: The Erotic Aesthetic. *v.2 p.377*

Pioneer Days in the Early Southwest. *v.3 p.510*

Pioneer Naturalists: The Discovery and Naming of North
American Plants and Animals. *v.5 p.230*

Pioneer of Tropical Landscape Architecture: William Lyman
Phillips in Florida. *v.1 p.816*

Pioneer Settlements in Early Canada. *v.3 p.544*

Pioneer Women: The Lives of Women on the Frontier. *v.3 p.521*

Pioneers and Homemakers: Jewish Women in Pre-State
Israel. *v.6 p.612*

Pioneers in Criminology. *v.6 p.245, p.250*

Pioneers of Change in Ethiopia: The Reformist Intellectuals of the Early Twentieth Century. *v.6 p.64*

Pioneers of Early Childhood Education: A Bio-Bibliographical Guide. *v.4 p.338*

Pioneers of Financial Economics: Contributions Prior to Irving Fisher. *v.4 p.204, p.264*

Pioneers of France in the New World. *v.3 p.538*

Pioneers of Islamic Revival: With Major New Introduction. *v.1 p.557*

Pioneers of Modern Geography: Translations Pertaining to German Geographers of the Late Nineteenth and Early Twentieth Centuries, 28. . . . .*v.4 p.378*

Pioneers of Modern Typography. *v.1 p.719*

Pioneers of Psychology. *v.5 p.596*

Pioneers of the Hardwood: Indiana and the Birth of Professional Basketball. *v.4 p.806, p.854*

The Pioneers; or, the sources of the Susquehanna. A descriptive tale. by J. Fenimore Cooper. *v.2 p.35*

Pious and Rebellious: Jewish Women in Medieval Europe.   *v.3 p.51, p.58,v.6 p.434, p.459, p.465, p.560, p.571*

Pious and Secular America. *v.3 p.369*

Piracy and Diplomacy in 17th Century North Africa: The Journal of Thomas Baker, English Consul in Tripoli, 1677-1685. . . . .*v.6 p.641*

Pirandello: Six Characters in Search of an Author. . . .*v.2 p.722*

Pirates and Emperors, Old and New: International Terrorism in the Real World. *v.4 p.658*

The Pirate. *v.2 p.308*

The Pirir Papers. *v.3 p.298*

Pisanello: Painter to the Renaissance Court. *v.1 p.739*

Pissing on Demand: Workplace Drug Testing and the Rise of the Detox Industry. *v.4 p.131*

Pitchfork Ben Tillman, South Carolinian. *v.3 p.434*

Pitied but Not Entitled: Single Mothers and the History of Welfare. *v.4 p.754, v.6 p.469*

Pittsburgh, the Story of an American City: The Millennium Edition. *v.3 p.492, v.6 p.714*

The Pity of War: Explaining World War I. *v.3 p.78*

Pity the Nation: Lebanon's Abduction. *v.6 p.606*

Pivotal Decades: The United States, 1900-1920. . . .*v.3 p.440*

☐ PKa Values (Acids, Bases, Alcohols, etc.). . .*v.5 p.290, p.300*

Place: A Short Introduction. *v.4 p.373*

Place and Space in Modern Fiction. *v.2 p.191*

A Place Apart: An Anthropological Study of the Icelandic World. *v.4 p.42*

A Place Called Milagro de la Paz. *v.2 p.674*

A Place for Strangers: Towards a History of Australian Aboriginal Being. *v.4 p.43*

Place for Us: Essay on the Broadway Musical. *v.6 p.412*

A Place for Wayfaring: The Poetry and Prose of Gary Snyder. *v.2 p.155*

A Place in El Paso: A Mexican-American Childhood. *v.6 p.489, p.501*

A Place in History: A Guide to Using GIS in Historical Research. *v.4 p.387*

A Place in History: Modernism, Tel Aviv, and the Creation of Jewish Urban Space. *v.6 p.714*

A Place in History: Social and Monumental Time in a Cretan Town. *v.3 p.196*

A Place in the Rain Forest: Settling the Costa Rican Frontier. *v.3 p.268*

A Place in the Sun: Africa in Italian Colonial Culture from Post-Unification to the Present. *v.3 p.198*

A Place in the Sun: Liberation Theology in the Third World. *v.1 p.638*

Place Matters: Metropolitics for the Twenty-First Century. *v.6 p.722*

The Place of Geography. *v.4 p.373*

The Place of Morality in Foreign Policy. *v.4 p.646*

The Place of Narrative: Mural Decoration in Italian Churches, 431-1600. . . . .*v.1 p.728, p.732*

The Place of Science in Modern Civilization. *v.4 p.251*

A Place on the Corner. *v.4 p.692*

A Place on the Team: The Triumph and Tragedy of Title IX. *v.6 p.438*

The Place Royale and Urban Design in the Ancien Régime. *v.1 p.796*

A Place to Grow Old: The Meaning of Environment in Old Age. *v.4 p.742*

A Place to Live: And Other Selected Essays of Natalia Ginzburg. *v.2 p.718*

A Place to Stand: Essays for Educators in Troubled Times. *v.4 p.341*

Place, Void, and Eternity. *v.1 p.500*

Places and Regions in Global Context: Human Geography. *v.4 p.396*

Places of Performance: The Semiotics of Theatre Architecture. *v.1 p.154*

Places of Their Own: African American Suburbanization in the Twentieth Century. *v.6 p.716*

La Place. *v.2 p.530*

Placing Aesthetics: Reflections on the Philosophic Tradition. *v.1 p.480*

Placing Animals in the Neolithic: Social Zooarchaeology of Prehistoric Farming Communities. *v.4 p.12*

A Plague of Rats and Rubbervines: The Growing Threat of Species Invasions. *v.5 p.182, p.183, p.186, p.187*

A Plague of Sheep: Environmental Consequences of the Conquest of Mexico. *v.3 p.269, p.286, p.287*

The Plague Pamphlets of Thomas Dekker. *v.2 p.218*

The Plague, the Fall, Exile and the Kingdom, and Selected Essays. *v.2 p.512*

Plagues and People. *v.5 p.370, v.6 p.296*

A Plain Account of Christian Perfection. *v.1 p.644, p.645*

A Plain and Easy Introduction to Practical Music. . .*v.1 p.180*

The Plain English Approach to Business Writing. . . .*v.4 p.171*

Plain Folk of the Old South. *v.3 p.495*

Plain Lives in a Golden Age: Popular Culture, Religion and Society in Seventeenth-Century Holland. *v.3 p.205*

Plain People of the Confederacy. *v.3 p.496*

Plain Speaking Biography of H. S. Truman. *v.3 p.476*

Plain Tales from the Hills. *v.2 p.297*

The Plains Across: The Overland Emigrants and the Trans-Mississippi West, 1840-60. . . . .*v.3 p.520*

Plains Folk: A Commomplace of the Great Plains. . . .*v.3 p.520*

Plains Folk: North Dakota's Ethnic History. *v.3 p.523*

The Plains Sioux and U. S. Colonialism from Lewis and Clark
to Wounded Knee. *v.6 p.682*

Plains Song: For Female Voices. *v.2 p.103*

The Plan for Perpetual Peace, on the Government of Poland,
and Other Writings on History and Politics. *v.2 p.482*

Plan of Attack. *v.3 p.484*

The Plan of St. Gall in Brief: An Overview Based on the
3-Volume Work by Walter Horn and Ernest Born. .*v.3 p.245*

Planar Antennas for Wireless Communications. *v.5 p.729*

The Plane Truth for Golfers: Breaking Down the One-Plane
Swing and the Two-Plane Swing and Finding the
One That's Right for You. *v.4 p.860, p.861*

Planet of Slums. *v.6 p.717*

Planet Quest: The Epic Discovery of Alien Solar
Systems. *v.5 p.69, p.74*

Planet U: Sustaining the World, Reinventing the
University. *v.4 p.398*

The Planetarium. *v.2 p.527*

☐ The Planetary Data System (PDS). *v.5 p.63, p.68*

Planetary Politics: Human Rights, Terror, and Global
Society. *v.4 p.624, p.658, p.669*

Planetary Science: The Science of Planets Around
Stars. *v.5 p.69, p.434*

Planetary Sciences. *v.5 p.69, p.434*

The Planetary Scientist's Companion. *v.5 p.69*

The Planetary System. *v.5 p.69*

Planets, Stars, and Orbs: The Medieval Cosmos,
1200-1687. . . . .*v.5 p.61*

Planks of Reason: Essays on the Horror Film. *v.6 p.320*

Planning and Conducting Needs Assessments: A Practical
Guide. *v.4 p.82*

Planning and Developing Open and Distance Learning: A
Framework for Quality. *v.4 p.322*

Planning and Managing a PR Campaign: A Step by Step
Guide. *v.4 p.429*

Planning and Managing School Facilities. *v.4 p.288*

Planning Development with Women: Making a World of
Difference. *v.6 p.458*

Planning Education Reforms in Developing Countries: The
Contingency Approach. *v.4 p.314*

Planning Focus Groups. *v.4 p.137*

Planning for Field Safety. *v.5 p.420*

Planning for Technology: A Guide for Administrtors,
Technology Coordinators and Curriculum Leaders. *v.4 p.352*

Planning Media. *v.4 p.427*

Planning Models for Colleges and Universities. . . .*v.4 p.293*

Planning of Experiments. *v.5 p.409*

Planning World Cities: Globalization, Urban Governance and
Policy Dilemmas. *v.6 p.729*

Plans and the Structure of Behavior. *v.5 p.594*

Plans, Pragmatism and People: The Failure of Soviet City
Planning. *v.6 p.720*

Plant Anatomy. *v.5 p.155*

Plant and Animal Populations: Methods in Demography. *v.5 p.188*

Plant Biochemical Regulators, Vol. 21. . . . .*v.5 p.124*

Plant Biochemistry and Molecular Biology. . . .*v.5 p.124, p.128*

Plant Biochemistry. *v.5 p.124*

Plant Biotechnology: Current and Future Applications of
Genetically Modified Crops. *v.5 p.218*

Plant Biotechnology: The Genetic Manipulation of
Plants. *v.5 p.219, p.220*

Plant Cell Biology: A Practical Approach. *v.5 p.154*

Plant Contamination: Modeling and Simulation of Organic
Chemical Processes. *v.5 p.355*

Plant Development and Biotechnology. *v.5 p.156*

Plant Dormancy: Physiology, Biochemistry and Molecular
Biology. *v.5 p.124*

Plant Engineering Magazine's Fluid Power Handbook, vol. 1:
System Design, Maintenance, and Troubleshooting. *v.5 p.709*

Plant Engineering Magazine's Fluid Power Handbook, vol. 2:
System Applications and Components. *v.5 p.709*

Plant Evolution and the Origin of Crop Species. *v.5 p.21, p.45*

Plant functional Genomics. *v.5 p.133*

Plant Genome:Cryptogams: Lower Groups. *v.5 p.125*

Plant Genome:Phanerogams: Biodiversity and
Evolution. *v.5 p.125*

Plant Genomics and Proteomics. *v.5 p.124, p.139*

Plant Genomics: Emerging Tools. *v.5 p.136*

Plant Hormones: Physiology, Biochemistry and Molecular
Biology. *v.5 p.124*

Plant Identification Terminology: An Illustrated
Glossary. *v.5 p.207*

Plant Invaders: The Threat to Natural
Ecosystems. *v.6 p.290, p.291*

Plant Layout and Materials Handling. *v.4 p.116*

Plant Metabolism. *v.5 p.124*

Plant Pathology. *v.5 p.45*

Plant Resins: Chemistry, Evolution, Ecology, and
Ethnobotany. *v.5 p.16*

Plant Response to Air Pollution. *v.5 p.354*

Plant Stems: Physiology and Functional Morphology. *v.5 p.155*

Plant Structure: Function and Development. *v.5 p.156*

Plantation Agriculture and Social Control in Northern Peru,
1875-1933. . . . .*v.3 p.329, p.330*

Plantation Forestry in the Tropics: The Role, Silviculture, and
Use of Planted Forests for Industrial, Social,
Environmental, and Agroforestry Purposes. *v.5 p.37*

Plantation Slavery in Barbados: An Archaeological and
Historical Investigation. *v.4 p.14, p.728*

The Plantation Tamils of Ceylon. *v.6 p.163*

The Planters of Colonial Virginia. *v.3 p.501*

Planting Corn Belt Culture: The Impress of the Upland
Southerner and Yankee in the Old Northwest. . . .*v.3 p.513*

Planting of Civilization in Western Pennsylvania. . . .*v.3 p.491*

Plants and Their Names: A Concise Dictionary. . . .*v.5 p.207*

Plants and UV-B: Responses to Environmental
Change. *v.5 p.354, p.355, p.356, p.375*

Plants, Genes, and Crop Biotechnology. *v.5 p.7*

Plants of the Gods: Their Sacred, Healing and Hallucinogenic
Powers. *v.5 p.16*

Plants, People and Culture: The Science of Ethnobotany, a Scientific American Library Book. *v.5 p.15, p.16*

The Plants That Shaped Our Gardens. *v.1 p.820*

Plants under Stress. *v.5 p.124*

Plasma: The Fourth State of Matter. *v.5 p.566*

Plastic Deformation of Metals. *v.5 p.689*

Plastic: The Making of a Synthetic Century. *v.5 p.319*

Plasticity and Geomechanics. *v.5 p.698*

The Plastics Age: From Bakelite to Beanbags and Beyond. *v.5 p.319*

Plastics: America's Packaging Dilemma. *v.5 p.320*

Plastics: How Structure Determines Properties. . . .*v.5 p.320*

Plastics Materials. *v.5 p.319, p.320*

Un Plat de porc aux bananes vertes: roman. *v.2 p.538*

Plate Tectonics: An Insider's History of the Modern Theory of the Earth. *v.5 p.418, p.443*

Plate Tectonics and How the Earth Works. *v.5 p.442*

Plateforme : roman. *v.2 p.530*

Platero y Yo. *v.2 p.660*

Platform. *v.2 p.530*

Platicas: Conversations with Hispano Writers of New Mexico. *v.6 p.498, p.512*

Plato: A Collection of Critical Essays, Vol. 1. . . . . .*v.1 p.425*

Plato: Alcibiades. *v.2 p.417, p.418*

Plato and Education. *v.4 p.340*

Plato and Parmenides: Parmenides' Way of Truth and Plato's Parmenides. *v.1 p.423*

Plato and the Socratic Dialogue: The Philosophical Use of a Literary Form. *v.1 p.424*

Plato: Arguments of the Philosophers, Set. . . .*v.1 p.423, p.424*

Plato on Poetry: Ion; Republic 376e-398b9; Republic 595-608b10. . . . .*v.2 p.418*

Plato: Phaedo. *v.2 p.418*

Plato: Symposium. *v.2 p.418*

Plato: The Man and His Work. *v.1 p.425, v.2 p.418*

Plato the Myth Maker. *v.2 p.417*

Platonis Opera: Euthyphro, Apologia Socratis, Crito, Phaedo, Cratylus, Sophista, Politicus, Theaetetus. *v.2 p.418*

Platonis Respublica. *v.2 p.418*

Platonism and the English Imagination. *v.2 p.163*

Platonism. *v.1 p.419*

Plato's Cosmology. *v.1 p.423, p.500*

Plato's Ethics. *v.1 p.424*

Plato's First Interpreters. *v.1 p.425*

🄴 Plato's Invisible Cities: Discourse and Power in the Republic. *v.4 p.489*

Plato's Literary Garden: How to Read a Platonic Dialogue. *v.1 p.425*

Plato's Moral Theory: The Early and Middle Dialogues. .*v.1 p.424*

Plato's Parmenides: Translation and Analysis. *v.1 p.424*

Plato's Parmenides. *v.1 p.424*

Plato's Phaedo. *v.1 p.422*

Plato's Republic: A Study. *v.2 p.418*

Plato's Socrates. *v.1 p.422, v.2 p.417*

Plato's Theory of Knowledge. *v.1 p.424*

Plato's Thought in the Making: A Study of the Development of His Metaphysics. *v.1 p.425*

Plato's Thought. *v.1 p.424*

Plato's Universe. *v.1 p.425*

Plato. *v.1 p.423, v.4 p.489*

The Plausibility of Life: Resolving Darwin's Dilemma. .*v.5 p.203*

Plautus: Amphitruo. *v.2 p.440*

Plautus: Casina. *v.2 p.440*

Plautus' Curculio. *v.2 p.440*

Plautus in Performance: The Theatre of the Mind. .*v.1 p.73, p.90*

Plautus: Menaechmi. *v.2 p.440*

Plautus: The Comedies. *v.1 p.73, p.90*

The Play, a Critical Anthology. *v.1 p.63, p.94, p.95*

Play and Educational Theory and Practice. *v.4 p.357*

Play and Literacy in Early Childhood: Research from Multiple Perspectives. *v.4 p.369*

Play as Exploratory Learning: Studies of Curiosity Behavior. *v.4 p.358*

Play, Dreams and Imitation in Childhood. *v.5 p.628*

Play in Practice: Case Studies in Young Children's Play. .*v.4 p.356*

Play It Safe: An Anthology of Playground Safety. . . .*v.4 p.787*

Play Like a Man, Win Like a Woman: What Men Know about Success That Women Need to Learn. *v.4 p.167*

The Play of Allegory in the Autos Sacramentales of Pedro Calderon de la Barca. *v.2 p.647*

The Play of Character in Plato's Dialogues. *v.1 p.423*

The Play of Power: Mythological Court Dramas of Calderon de la Barca. *v.2 p.647*

Play Therapy. *v.4 p.355*

Play-by-Play: Radio, Television and Big-Time College Sports. *v.4 p.810, p.895, p.902, p.903*

Player Piano. *v.2 p.158*

Players of Shakespeare 6: Essays in the Performance of Shakespeare's History Plays. *v.1 p.77, p.104, p.136*

Playground Safety Is No Accident. *v.4 p.787, p.796*

Playing and Teaching the Strings. *v.1 p.398, p.406*

Playing Bach on the Keyboard: A Practical Guide. *v.1 p.187, p.243, p.244, p.304, p.402*

Playing by the Rules: Sport, Society, and the State. *v.4 p.716, p.820, p.892*

Playing Cowboys: Low Culture and High Art in the Western. *v.6 p.324*

Playing for Dollars: Labor Relations and the Sports Business. *v.4 p.886, p.889, p.897, p.898*

Playing for Keeps: Michael Jordan and the World He Made. *v.4 p.854, p.896*

Playing for Real: Game Theory. *v.4 p.83*

Playing for Their Nation: Baseball and the American Military During World War II. *v.4 p.804, p.849, p.850, p.890*

Playing Hardball: Campaigning for the U. S. Congress. .*v.4 p.549*

Playing in the Zone. *v.4 p.824*

Playing It Safe: How the Supreme Court Sidesteps Hard Cases and Stunts the Development of Law. *v.4 p.537*

Playing Nice and Losing: The Struggle for Control of Women's Intercollegiate Athletics, 1960-2000. .*v.4 p.811, p.839, v.6 p.438*

Playing Nice: Politics and Apologies in Women's
Sports. *v.4 p.821, p.835*

Playing on Words: A Guide to Luciano Berio's
Sinfonia. *v.1 p.220, p.236, p.310*

Playing the Beethoven Piano
Sonatas. *v.1 p.205, p.243, p.308, p.399*

Playing the Field: Why Sports Teams Move and Cities Fight to
Keep Them. *v.4 p.883, p.891, p.896*

Playing the Game: Inside Athletic Recruiting in the Ivy
League. *v.4 p.885, p.888, p.894*

Playing the Game: Sport and British Society,
1914-1945. . . . .*v.4 p.804*

Playing the Game: Sport and the Physical Emancipation of
English Women, 1870-1914. . . . .*v.4 p.808, p.837*

Playing the Game: The Homosexual Novel in
America. *v.6 p.391, p.392*

Playing the Harpsichord Expressively: A Practical and Historical
Guide. *v.1 p.401*

Playing to the Camera: Film Actors Discuss Their Craft. .*v.6 p.348*

Playing to Win: Sports and the American Military,
1898-1945. . . . .*v.4 p.810*

Playing with Anger: Teaching Coping Skills to African
American Boys through Athletics and Culture. . . .*v.4 p.304*

Playing with History: The Historical Approach to Musical
Performance. *v.1 p.400*

Playing with Power in Movies, Television, and Video Games:
From Muppet Babies to Teenage Mutant Ninja
Turtles. *v.6 p.311, p.312*

Playing with Signs. *v.1 p.369*

Plays 1. . . . .*v.1 p.71, p.88, p.107,v.2 p.370, p.724*

Plays 2. . . . .*v.2 p.724*

Plays 3, Vol. 3. . . . .*v.1 p.72, p.89*

The Plays and Novels of Peter Handke. *v.2 p.617*

Plays and Other Dramatic Writings by W. H. Auden, 1928-1938,
Vol. I. *v.2 p.329*

Plays and Pageants from the Life of the Negro. *v.2 p.25*

Plays and Players: Essays on the Theatre. *v.1 p.80, p.103*

Plays and Poems of Philip Massinger. *v.2 p.221*

The Plays and Poems of Robert Greene. *v.2 p.218*

Plays and Poems. *v.2 p.217*

Plays and Stories. *v.2 p.615*

Plays by American Women, 1900-1930. . . . .*v.2 p.24*

Plays by American Women, 1930-1960. . . . .*v.1 p.120*

Plays by Early American Women, 1775-1850..*v.1 p.121, v.2 p.25*

Plays by French and Francophone Women: A Critical
Anthology. *v.2 p.465*

Plays by Susan Glaspell. *v.2 p.78*

Plays: Contains: As You Desire Me; Think It over Giaccomino!;
This Time It Will Be Different; the Imbecile. . . .*v.2 p.723*

Plays: Contains: Henry IV; Right You Are If You Think You
Are; Lazarus; the Man with the Flower in His
Mouth. *v.2 p.722*

Plays: Contains: No One Knows Why; Cap and Bells; the Jar; I
Haven't Yet Chosen. *v.2 p.722, p.723*

Plays: Egmont, Iphigenia in Tauris, Torquato
Tasso. *v.1 p.79, p.108, p.109*

Plays Extravagant: Too True to Be Good; the Simpleton of the
Unexpected Isles; the Millionairess. *v.2 p.310*

Plays Five. *v.1 p.71, p.88*

The Plays for Radio, 1964-1991. . . . .*v.2 p.385*

Plays Four. *v.1 p.71, p.88*

Plays from the Cynical Life. *v.2 p.631*

The Plays of Colley Cibber, Vol. 1. . . . .*v.2 p.243*

Plays of Confession and Therapy: To Damascus I, To Damascus
II and To Damascus III. *v.2 p.630, p.631*

The Plays of Hrotswitha of Gandersheim. *v.2 p.448*

The Plays of John Galsworthy. *v.2 p.348*

The Plays of Juan Ruiz de Alarcón. *v.2 p.646*

The Plays of Max Frisch. *v.2 p.607*

Plays of Protest: The Naturewoman, the Machine, the
Second-Story Man, Prince Hagen. *v.2 p.120*

The Plays of Richard Steele. *v.2 p.262*

Plays of Schiller. *v.2 p.601*

Plays of the New Democratic Spain, 1975-1990. . . . .*v.2 p.644*

The Plays of Thornton Wilder: A Critical Study. . . .*v.2 p.133*

Plays One. *v.1 p.99, v.2 p.331*

Plays: One. *v.2 p.517*

Plays One. *v.2 p.659*

Plays: Pleasant and Pleasant. *v.1 p.80, p.103*

Plays Political. *v.2 p.310*

Plays, Prefaces and Postscripts of Tawfiq Al-Hakim. 2
vols. *v.6 p.656*

Plays: The Black Maskers, the Life of Man, the Sabine
Women. *v.2 p.801*

Plays: The Threepenny Opera, the Measures Taken, Galileo,
Mother Courage and Her Children, Baal. . . .*v.1 p.81, p.108*

Plays Three. *v.1 p.83, p.110*

Plays Two: Hecuba, the Women of Troy, Iphigenia at Aulis,
Cyclops. *v.1 p.71, p.88*

Plays Two, Vol. 2. . . . .*v.1 p.99, v.2 p.337*

Plays Two. *v.1 p.83, p.110,v.2 p.331*

Plays: Two. *v.2 p.517*

Plays Unpleasant: Widowers' Houses; the Philanderer; Mrs
Warren's Professssion. *v.2 p.309*

Plays Well with Others. *v.6 p.378, p.396, p.397*

Plays. *v.1 p.79, p.89, p.99, p.110,v.2 p.36, p.302,
p.337, p.600, p.656, p.806*

The Playwright As Thinker: A Study of Drama in Modern
Times. *v.1 p.55*

Playwrights of Color. *v.1 p.120*

Playwriting Women: Female Voices in English Canada. .*v.2 p.731*

The Plaza Mayor and the Shaping of Baroque
Madrid. *v.1 p.796, p.797*

Plazas and Barrios: Heritage Tourism and Globalization in the
Latin American Centro Historico. *v.1 p.823*

Plea Bargaining's Triumph: A History of Plea Bargaining in
America. *v.4 p.473*

Plea Bargainings Triumph. *v.6 p.270*

A Pleasant Vintage of Till Eulenspiegel. *v.2 p.593*

Please Be Ad-Vised: The Legal Reference Guide for the
Advertising Executive. *v.4 p.427*

Please Kill Me: The Uncensored Oral History of Punk. .*v.1 p.272*

Please, No Police: A Novella. *v.6 p.667*

Pleasure and Danger: Exploring Female
    Sexuality. *v.4 p.749, v.6 p.447*

Pleasure and the Good Life: Concerning the Nature, Varieties,
    and Plausibility of Hedonism. *v.1 p.507*

Pleasure and the Nation: The History, Politics and Consumption
    of Popular Culture in India. *v.6 p.150*

The Pleasure of Eliza Lynch. *v.3 p.343*

The Pleasure of Modernist Music: Listening, Meaning,
    Intention, Ideology. *v.1 p.208*

Pleasures and Pains: Opium and the Orient in
    Nineteenth-Century British Culture. *v.6 p.746, p.754, p.760*

The Pleasures of Counting. *v.5 p.459*

The Plebeian Republic: The Huanta Rebellion and the Making
    of the Peruvian State, 1820-1850. . . . . *v.3 p.328*

Plebs and Politics in the Late Roman Republic. . . .*v.3 p.26*

Pleistocene Mammals of North America. *v.5 p.448*

Plessy vs. Ferguson: A Brief History with Documents. *v.4 p.438*

PLFAG (Parents, Families and Friends of Lesbians and
    Gays). *v.6 p.357*

Pliny: Letters and Panegyricus, Vol. 1. . . . .*v.2 p.441*

Pliny the Elder's Natural History: The Empire in the
    Encyclopedia. *v.2 p.440, v.5 p.225*

The Plot and Its Construction in Eighteenth Century Criticism of
    French Comedy: A Study of the Theory with Relation to
    the Practice of Beaumarchais. *v.1 p.90, p.105*

A Plot of Her Own: The Female Protagonist in Russian
    Literature. *v.2 p.798*

Plotinus: An Introduction to the Enneads. . . .*v.1 p.430, p.431*

Plotinus: The Enneads. *v.1 p.430*

Plotinus: The Road to Reality. *v.1 p.431*

Plotinus. *v.1 p.430*

Plotting the Globe: Stories of Meridians, Parallels, and the
    International Date Line. *v.4 p.389*

Les Plouffe. *v.2 p.539*

The Plough Women: Records of the Pioneer Women of
    Palestine. *v.6 p.612*

Ploughing the Seas: the Nicaraguan Resistance and the CIA in
    the Jungles of Southern Nicaragua, 1984-1987. . . .*v.3 p.302*

The Ploughshare of War: The Origins of the Anglo-Zulu War of
    1879. . . . .*v.6 p.78*

The Ploughshares Reader: New Fiction for the 80's. . .*v.2 p.26*

Plows, Plagues, and Petroleum: How Humans Took Control of
    Climate. . . . *v.5 p.355, p.356, p.358, p.360, p.371, p.373*

Pluie et vent sur Télumée Miracle : roman. *v.2 p.538*

The Plum in the Golden Vase: Chin P'ing Mei The Gathering,
    Vol. 1. . . . .*v.6 p.212*

The Plum in the Golden Vase, or Chin P'ing Mei: The
    Rivals. *v.6 p.212*

The Plum in the Golden Vase, Vol. 3. . . . .*v.6 p.212*

The Plum Plum Pickers. *v.6 p.497*

Plum Sauce. *v.2 p.390*

Plumb. *v.2 p.746*

The Plumed Serpent. *v.2 p.363*

Plunkett Research Online. *v.4 p.150*

Plunkett's Advertising and Branding Industry Almanac
    2006. . . . .*v.4 p.150*

Plunkett's Airline, Hotel and Travel Industry Almanac 2006
    (E-Book). *v.4 p.151*

Plunkett's Airline, Hotel and Travel Industry Almanac
    2006. . . . .*v.4 p.152*

Plunkett's Airline, Hotel and Travel Industry Trends and
    Statistics 2006 (Summary). *v.4 p.152*

Plunkett's Apparel and Textiles Industry Almanac 2006. *v.4 p.153*

Plunkett's Automobile Industry Almanac 2005: The Only
    Complete Guide to the Automobile, Truck and
    Specialty Vehicle Industry. *v.4 p.154*

Plunkett's Biotech and Genetics Industry Almanac 2006: The
    Only Complete Reference to the Business of
    Biotechnology and Genetic Engineering. *v.4 p.156*

Plunkett's E-Commerce and Internet Industry Almanac 2005:
    Your Reference Source to All Facets of the Internet
    Business. *v.4 p.113*

Plunkett's Entertainment and Media Industry Almanac. *v.4 p.157*

Plunkett's Food Industry Almanac 2005: The Only Complete
    Reference to the Business of Creating and Selling
    Food, Beverages and Tobacco. *v.4 p.153*

Plunkett's Infotech Industry Almanac 2005: The Only Complete
    Guide to the Technologies and Companies Changing the
    Way the World Thinks, Works and Shares
    Information. *v.4 p.114*

Plunkett's Renewable, Alternative and Hydrogen Energy
    Industry Almanac 2006: The Only Complete
    Guide to the Business of Renewable, Alternative and
    Hydrogen Energy. *v.5 p.361*

Plunkett's Research Online. *v.4 p.150*

Plunkett's Telecommunications Industry Almanac 2006: Your
    Reference Source to the Telecom Business. *v.4 p.115*

Plunkett's Transportation, Supply Chain and Logistics Industry
    Almanac: Your Complete Guide to All Facets of the
    Business of Transportation, Logistics and Supply
    Chains. *v.4 p.118*

Plupart du temps, 1915-1922. . . . .*v.2 p.525*

Pluralism: Against the Demand for Consensus. *v.1 p.501*

The Pluralist Theory of the State: Selected Writings of G. D. H.
    Cole, J. N. Figgis, and H. J. Laski. *v.4 p.497*

Plutarch and the Historical Tradition. *v.2 p.419*

Plutarch: Life of Antony. *v.2 p.419*

Plutarch: Life of Themistocles. *v.2 p.419*

Plutarch: Lives of Aristides and Cato. *v.2 p.419*

Plutarch's Advice to the Bride and Groom and a Consolation to
    His Wife: English Translations, Commentary,
    Interpretive Essays, and Bibliography. *v.2 p.419*

Plutarch's Lives: Exploring Virtue and Vice. *v.2 p.418*

Plutarch. *v.2 p.418, p.419*

The Plutocratic Cycle in the Economic and Historical Growth of
    Mankind. *v.4 p.249*

Plutonium and the Rio Grande: Environmental Change and
    Contamination in the Nuclear Age. *v.5 p.739*

Pobre Raza!: Violence, Justice, and Mobilization among
    Mexico Lindo Immigrants, 1900-1936. . . .*v.6 p.536, p.541*

Pocahontas's Daughters: Gender and Ethnicity in American
    Culture. *v.2 p.3*

Pocho. *v.6 p.504*

Pocket Book of Technical Writing for Engineers and
  Scientists. *v.5 p.680*

Pocket Companion to Sabiston Textbook of Surgery. . *v.5 p.523*

Pocket Fowler's Modern English Usage. *v.2 p.551*

A Pocket Guide to Technical Writing. *v.5 p.681*

The Pocket Mirror of Heroes. *v.2 p.650, p.651*

The Pocket Mirror. *v.2 p.745*

Pocketbook Power. *v.4 p.139*

Poe Abroad: Influence, Reputation and Affinities. *v.2 p.50*

The Poe Encyclopedia. *v.2 p.50*

Poem and Symbol: A Brief History of French
  Symbolism. *v.2 p.460*

A Poem at the Right Moment: Remembered Verses from
  Premodern South India. *v.6 p.147, p.148*

The Poem of Empedocles, Vol. 39. . . . .*v.1 p.421*

Poem of My Cid/Poema de Mio Cid: A Dual-Language
  Book. *v.2 p.645*

Poem of the Cid: Dual Language Edition. *v.2 p.646*

The Poem of the Cid. *v.2 p.644*

Los Poemas Solares. *v.2 p.666*

Poemes. *v.2 p.539, p.540*

Poems / by Charles Kingsley. *v.2 p.296*

Poems, 1645, Together with Poems from Bodleian MS Don D
  55. . . . .*v.2 p.264*

Poems, 1913-1956. . . . .*v.2 p.605*

The Poems, 1921-1940. . . . .*v.2 p.88*

The Poems, 1941-1950. . . . .*v.2 p.88*

Poems: A New Edition. *v.2 p.265*

Poems and Ballads and Atalanta in Calydon. *v.2 p.313*

Poems and Fables of John Dryden. *v.2 p.246*

Poems and Fragments. *v.2 p.419*

Poems and Letters. *v.2 p.47*

Poems and Plays. *v.2 p.98*

Poems and Prose from the Old English. *v.2 p.197*

The Poems and Prose of Ernest Dowson. *v.2 p.275*

Poems and Prose. *v.2 p.615, p.817*

Poems and Sketches of E. B. White. *v.2 p.133*

Poems and Stories. *v.2 p.40*

Poems and Texts: An Anthology of French Poems. . *v.2 p.464*

Poems and Translations, 1850-1870, Together with the Prose
  Story "Hand and Soul". *v.2 p.304*

Poems and Verse Plays, Vol. 1. . . . .*v.2 p.609*

Poems, Ballads and Sonnets; Selections from the Posthumous
  Poems and from His Translations. *v.2 p.304*

Poems Between Women: Four Centuries of Love, Romantic
  Friendship, and Desire. *v.6 p.404*

Poems, by Alfred Tennyson. *v.2 p.314*

Poems by George Meredith. *v.2 p.300*

Poems by William Ernest Henley. *v.2 p.290*

Poems, English and Latin. *v.2 p.214*

Poems from Captured Documents: A Bilingual Edition: Selected
  and Translated from the Vietnamese. *v.6 p.169*

Poems from Iqbal: Renderings in English Verse with
  Comparative Urdu Text. *v.6 p.151*

Poems from Korea: A Historical Anthology. *v.6 p.238*

Poems in Persons: An Introduction to the Psychoanalysis of
  Literature. *v.2 p.571*

Poems in Two Volumes and Other Poems, 1800-1807. *v.2 p.325*

Poems New and Collected. *v.2 p.792*

The Poems of A. E. Housman. *v.2 p.291*

Poems of Alexander Lawrence Posey, Creek Indian Bard. *v.2 p.49*

The Poems of Alexander Pope: A Reduced Revision of the
  Twickenham Text. *v.2 p.257*

Poems of Ambrose Philips. *v.2 p.256*

Poems of Andre Breton: A Bilingual Anthology. . . . *v.2 p.510*

The Poems of Andrew Marvell: The Complete Works. *v.2 p.252*

The Poems of Archibald Lampman (Including at the Long
  Sault). *v.2 p.732*

The Poems of Archibald Lampman. *v.2 p.732*

The Poems of Arthur Hugh Clough. *v.2 p.278*

The Poems of Bishop Henry King. *v.2 p.245*

Poems of Black Africa. *v.6 p.81*

The Poems of Catullus: A Bilingual Edition. *v.2 p.430*

The Poems of Charles of Orleans. *v.2 p.468*

The Poems of Edward Taylor: A Reference Guide. . .*v.2 p.29*

The Poems of Edward Taylor. *v.2 p.30*

The Poems of Edward Thomas. *v.2 p.385*

The Poems of Emily Dickinson. *v.2 p.37*

The Poems of Exile: Tristia and the Black Sea Letters. *v.2 p.439*

The Poems of Fernando Pessoa. *v.2 p.688*

The Poems of Francois Villon. *v.2 p.469*

Poems of Friedrich Holderlin: The Fire of the Gods Drives Us
  to Set Forth by Day and by Night. *v.2 p.600*

Poems of Gerard Manley Hopkins. *v.2 p.293*

Poems of Jerusalem and Love Poems. *v.6 p.647*

The Poems of John Collop. *v.2 p.243*

The Poems of John Davidson. *v.2 p.275*

The Poems of John Keats. *v.2 p.295*

The Poems of John Oldham. *v.2 p.252*

Poems of Jules Laforgue. *v.2 p.495*

The Poems of Laura Riding: A Newly Revised Edition of the
  1938-1980 Collection. *v.2 p.89*

The Poems of Marianne Moore. *v.2 p.103*

The Poems of Michael Wigglesworth. *v.2 p.28*

Poems of Nazim Hikmet. *v.6 p.666*

The Poems of Patrick Branwell Bronte. *v.2 p.270*

The Poems of Phillis Wheatley. *v.2 p.30*

The Poems of Samuel Johnson. *v.2 p.250*

Poems of Sidney Lanier. *v.2 p.47*

The Poems of Sir Walter Raleigh: An Historical Edition. *v.2 p.215*

Poems of St. John of the Cross. *v.2 p.646*

The Poems of William Cowper, 1748-1782, Vol. I. . *v.2 p.244*

The Poems of William Cowper, 1782-1785, Vol. II. . *v.2 p.244*

The Poems of William Cowper: 1785-1800. . . . .*v.2 p.244*

Poems Retrieved. *v.2 p.105, p.106*

Poems, Set. *v.2 p.251*

The Poems, Short Fiction and Criticism of Samuel Beckett, Vol.
  4. . . . .*v.2 p.332, p.509*

The Poems: The Collected Works of William Butler
    Yeats. *v.2 p.327*

Poems. Translated by Cornelia M. Popescu. *v.2 p.817*

Poems Written Between the Years 1768 and 1794. . . .*v.2 p.29*

ⓔ Poems. *v.2 p.654*

Poems. *v.2 p.40*

The Poems. *v.2 p.88*

Poems. . . .*v.2 p.225, p.237, p.243, p.600, p.610, p.654, p.721*

Poesía Completa. *v.2 p.670, p.685*

Poesía Cubana del Siglo XX: Antología. *v.2 p.671*

Poesia Completa - Manrique. *v.2 p.650*

Poesia del Siglo XVIII. *v.2 p.644*

Poesia Espanola del Siglo XVIII. *v.2 p.645*

Poesia Lirica del Siglo de Oro (Lyric Poetry of the Golden
    Age). *v.2 p.645*

Poesias Castellanas Completas. *v.2 p.645*

Poesias Completas. *v.2 p.671, p.675, p.676*

Poesias Escogidas (Selected Poems) of Juan Ramon
    Jimenez. *v.2 p.660*

Poesias: Jose Asuncion Silva, Edicion Critica de Hector H.
    Orjuela. *v.2 p.684*

Poesias. *v.2 p.654, p.655*

Poesie : 1946-1967. . . . .*v.2 p.531*

Poesie e prose scelte. *v.2 p.720*

Poesie e prose, vol. 1. . . . .*v.2 p.711*

Poesie e prose, vol. 2. . . . .*v.2 p.711*

Poesie volgari, vol. 1: Testi. *v.2 p.708*

Poesie volgari, vol. 2: Commento. *v.2 p.708*

Poesies Completes, 1896-1941. . . . .*v.2 p.539*

Poesie. *v.2 p.708, p.712*

Le poesie. *v.2 p.720*

The Poet and the Mystic: A Study of the Cantico Espiritual of
    San Juan de la Cruz. *v.2 p.646*

The Poet and the Prince: Ovid and Augustan Discourse.*v.2 p.438*

Poet? Criminal? Madman?: Poems. *v.2 p.790, p.791*

Poet in New York/Poeta en Nueva York: A Bilingual
    Edition. *v.2 p.659*

Poet in New York. *v.6 p.396*

The Poet Lucan. *v.2 p.437*

Poetae Melici Graeci. *v.2 p.403*

Poeti del Duecento, vol. 1, bk. 1. . . . .*v.2 p.699*

Poeti del Duecento, vol. 1, bk. 2. . . . .*v.2 p.699*

Poeti del Duecento, vol. 2, bk. 1. . . . .*v.2 p.699*

Poeti del Duecento, vol. 2, bk. 2. . . . .*v.2 p.699*

Poeti Italiani Del Novecento. *v.2 p.700*

Poeti Italiani del Secondo Novecento, 1945-1995. . . .*v.2 p.699*

The Poetic Achievement of Ezra Pound. *v.2 p.111*

ⓔ Poetic Knowledge: The Recovery of Education. . .*v.4 p.340*

Poetic Meaning in the Eighteenth-Century Poems of Mark
    Akenside and William Shenstone. *v.2 p.237, p.260*

Poetic Meter and Poetic Form. *v.2 p.578*

The Poetic Museum: Reviving Historic Collections. . .*v.1 p.828*

The Poetic Vision of Muriel Rukeyser. *v.2 p.113*

Poetic Will: Shakespeare and the Play of Language. . .*v.2 p.233*

Poetic World of William Carlos Williams. *v.2 p.136*

La Poetica de Becquer. *v.2 p.654*

The Poetical and Dramatic works of S. T. Coleridge, with a
    Memoir *v.2 p.279*

Poetical and Dramatic Works. *v.2 p.259*

The Poetical Manuscripts of Mark Akenside. *v.2 p.237*

Poetical Meditations - Meditations Poetiques. *v.2 p.495*

The Poetical works of Alfred Tennyson, Poet Laureate, Etc.
    Complete in one Volume. *v.2 p.314*

The Poetical Works of Alfred Tennyson, Poet Laureate, Etc.
    Two volumes in One. *v.2 p.314, p.315*

The Poetical works of Charles Churchill; with copious notes and
    a life of the author, by W. Tooke, F. R. S. in three
    Volumes. *v.2 p.243*

The Poetical works of Edward Young *v.2 p.264*

The Poetical Works of Gavin Douglas, Bishop of Dunkeld, Vol.
    4. . . . .*v.2 p.213, p.214*

The Poetical Works of Gerard Manley Hopkins. . . .*v.2 p.294*

The Poetical Works of James Russell Lowell. *v.2 p.47*

The Poetical Works of John Keats. with a Life. *v.2 p.295*

The Poetical Works of John Keats. with A Memoir, by James
    Russell Lowell. *v.2 p.295*

The Poetical Works of Leigh Hunt. *v.2 p.291*

The Poetical works of Mark Akenside. Ed. with A Life, by Rev.
    Alexander Dyce. *v.2 p.237*

Poetical Works of Mark Akenside. *v.2 p.237*

The Poetical Works of Mark Akenside. *v.2 p.237*

The Poetical works of Matthew Prior. with a life, by Rev. John
    Mitford. *v.2 p.256*

The Poetical Works of Sir John Denham. *v.2 p.244*

The Poetical Works of Whittier: Cambridge Edition. . .*v.2 p.55*

The Poetical Works of William Cowper. *v.2 p.244*

Poetical Works. *v.2 p.216, p.250, p.259, p.260*

Poetics and Interpretation of Biblical Narrative. . . .*v.1 p.616*

The Poetics of Appalachian Space. *v.2 p.12*

The Poetics of Enclosure: American Women Poets from
    Dickinson to Dove. *v.2 p.9*

The Poetics of Gardens. *v.1 p.819*

The Poetics of Imperialism: Translation and Colonization from
    the Tempest to Tarzan. *v.2 p.727*

Poetics of Loss in the Cantos of Ezra Pound: From Modernism
    to Fascism. *v.2 p.112*

Poetics of Music in the Form of Six
    Lessons. *v.1 p.225, p.360, p.361, p.382*

The Poetics of National and Racial Identity in
    Nineteenth-Century American Literature. *v.2 p.9*

A Poetics of Resistance: Narrative and the Writings of Pier
    Paolo Pasolini. *v.2 p.722*

A Poetics of Resistance: Women Writing in el Salvador, South
    Africa, and the United States. *v.3 p.298, p.299*

The Poetics of Space. *v.1 p.40, p.455*

Poetics of the Holy: A Reading of "Paradise Lost". . .*v.2 p.254*

A Poetics of Transformation: Prudentius and Classical
    Mythology. *v.2 p.442*

Poetics, On the Sublime, and On Style. *v.2 p.566, p.577*

Poetische Werke. *v.2 p.599*

Poetry and Civil War in Lucan's "Bellum Civile". . . .*v.2 p.437*

Poetry and Gender: Statements and Essays on Australian Women Poets. *v.2 p.740*

Poetry and Humanism. *v.2 p.180*

The Poetry and Poetics of Amiri Baraka: The Jazz Aesthetic. *v.2 p.142*

Poetry and Prose in the Sixteenth Century. *v.2 p.169*

Poetry and Prose. *v.2 p.599*

Poetry and Tales. *v.2 p.50*

Poetry and the Cult of the Martyrs: The Liber Peristephanon on Prudentius. *v.2 p.442*

The Poetry Anthology, 1912-1977: 65 Years of America's Most Distinguished Verse Magazine. *v.2 p.23*

The Poetry Archive. *v.2 p.200, p.577, p.583*

Poetry, Enclosure, and the Vernacular Landscape, 1700-1830. . . . .*v.6 p.287*

Poetry from 1660 to 1780: Civil War, Restoration, Revolution. *v.2 p.201*

Poetry from Chaucer to Spenser. . . .*v.2 p.181, p.182, p.210*

The Poetry Handbook. *v.2 p.577*

Poetry in East Germany: Adjustments, Visions and Provocations 1945-1970. . . . .*v.2 p.591*

Poetry in Motion: Studies in Tongan Dance. *v.1 p.17*

Poetry in Motion: Studies of Tongan Dance. . . .*v.1 p.48, p.49*

Poetry in the Age of Democracy: The Literary Criticism of Matthew Arnold. *v.2 p.266*

Poetry in the Museums of Modernism: Yeats, Pound, Moore, Stein. *v.2 p.103, p.112, p.122*

Poetry into Song: Performance and Analysis of Lieder. *v.1 p.396*

The Poetry of Arab Women: A Contemporary Anthology. *v.6 p.659*

The Poetry of Black America: Anthology of the Twentieth Century. *v.2 p.22*

The Poetry of Chaucer: A Guide to Its Study and Appreciation. *v.2 p.210*

The Poetry of Dada and Sur-Realism: Aragon, Breton, Tzara, Eluard and Desnos. *v.2 p.460*

The Poetry of Dannie Abse: Critical Essays and Reminiscences. *v.2 p.328*

The Poetry of Dante 1922. . . . .*v.2 p.704*

The Poetry of Everyday Life. *v.2 p.87*

The Poetry of Experience: The Dramatic Monologue in Modern Literary Tradition. *v.2 p.181*

The Poetry of Ezra Pound. *v.2 p.111*

Poetry of George Wither. *v.2 p.216, p.217*

The Poetry of Greek Tragedy. *v.2 p.402*

The Poetry of Jaroslav Seifert. *v.2 p.784*

The Poetry of John Dryden. *v.2 p.247*

The Poetry of Julian Del Casal: A Critical Edition, Vol. 1. . . . .*v.2 p.671*

The Poetry of Julian Del Casal: A Critical Edition, Vol. 2. . . . .*v.2 p.671*

The Poetry of Leopold Senghor. *v.2 p.543*

The Poetry of Louis Dudek: Definitive Edition. . . .*v.2 p.735*

The Poetry of Michelangelo: An Annotated Translation. *v.2 p.709, v.6 p.405*

The Poetry of Michelangelo: An Introduction. .*v.2 p.708, p.709*

Poetry of Nizami Ganjavi: Knowledge, Love and Rhetoric. *v.6 p.671*

The Poetry of Pablo Neruda. *v.2 p.681*

The Poetry of Petrarch. *v.2 p.706*

The Poetry of Relationship: The Wordsworths and Coleridge, 1797-1800. . . . .*v.2 p.280*

The Poetry of Rimbaud. *v.2 p.498*

Poetry of Robert Frost: Constellations of Intention. . . .*v.2 p.77*

Poetry of Robert Graves. *v.2 p.348*

The Poetry of Seamus Heaney. *v.2 p.352*

Poetry of the Carolingian Renaissance. *v.2 p.449*

The Poetry of the Early T'ang. *v.6 p.210*

Poetry of the Negro, 1746-1970. . . . .*v.6 p.23*

Poetry of the Netherlands in Its European Context, 1170-1930. . . . .*v.2 p.622*

The Poetry of the Sicilian School. *v.2 p.698*

Poetry of the Silver Age: The Various Voices of Russian Modernism. *v.2 p.793, p.800*

The Poetry of Vasko Popa. *v.2 p.818*

The Poetry of W. B. Yeats. *v.2 p.326*

The Poetry of Wang Wei. *v.6 p.210*

Poetry of Wole Soyinka. *v.2 p.758*

Poetry, Symbol, and Allegory: Interpreting Metaphorical Language from Plato to the Present. *v.2 p.181*

Poetry to Heal Your Blues. *v.2 p.146*

Poets and Critics Read Vergil. *v.2 p.446*

The Poets' Dante: Essays on Dante by Twentieth-Century Poets. *v.2 p.704*

Poets in the Public Sphere: The Emancipatory Project of American Women's Poetry, 1800-1900. . . . .*v.2 p.9, p.15*

Poets Laureate in England: Being a History of the Office. *v.2 p.180*

Poets of Bulgaria. *v.2 p.780*

The Poets of Prague: Czech Poetry Between the Wars. *v.2 p.782*

Poets of Reality: Six Twentieth-Century Writers. . . .*v.2 p.179*

Poets of the Civil War. *v.2 p.24*

Poèmes de la nuit et du brouillard ; suivis de Larmes publiques. *v.2 p.512*

Poèmes II, 1970-1980. . . . .*v.2 p.529*

Poèmes. *v.2 p.510*

La poésie québecoise des origines à nos jours. . . .*v.2 p.538*

Poésies d'amour : Poèmes. *v.2 p.469*

Poésies. *v.2 p.513*

La poésie. *v.2 p.536*

Pogroms: Anti-Jewish Violence in Modern Russian History. *v.3 p.60*

Point, Click and Wow!: A Quick Guide to Brilliant Laptop Presentations. *v.4 p.174*

Point Counter Point. *v.2 p.354*

The Point of Christology. *v.1 p.641*

Point of Purchase: How Shopping Changed American Culture. *v.6 p.720*

The Point of View. *v.1 p.478*

The Pointe Book: Shoes, Training and Technique. . . .*v.1 p.22*

Points of the Compass: Stories by Sahar Tawfiq. . . .*v.6 p.664*

Points of View: Five Essays. *v.2 p.370, p.371*

Poirot in the Orient: Murder in Mesopotamia; Death on the Nile; Appointment with Death. *v.2 p.339*

Poison and Medicine: Ethnicity, Power, and Violence in a Nigerian City, 1966 To 1986. . . . .*v.6 p.71*

The Poison in the Gift: Ritual, Prestation, and the Dominant Caste in a North Indian Village. *v.6 p.154*

Poison in the Pot: The Legacy of Lead. *v.5 p.366, p.372*

Poisoned Ivy: Lesbian and Gay Academics Confronting Homophobia. *v.6 p.385*

Poisons of the Past: Molds, Epidemics, and History. . .*v.4 p.778*

The Poisonwood Bible: A Novel. *v.2 p.148*

Poker. *v.2 p.813*

Pol Pot: Anatomy of a Nightmare. *v.6 p.170, p.171*

The Pol Pot Regime: Race, Power, and Genocide in Cambodia under the Khmer Rouge, 1975-79. *v.4 p.652, p.653,v.6 p.170*

Poland, 1918-1945: An Interpretive and Documentary History of the Second Republic. *v.3 p.253*

Poland and the European Union. *v.4 p.596, p.602*

Poland, the United States, and the Stabilization of Europe, 1919-1933. . . . .*v.3 p.391*

Poland's Last King and English Culture: Stanislaw August Poniatowski, 1732-1798. . . . .*v.3 p.253*

Polar Ecology. *v.5 p.186*

Polar Pioneers: John Ross and James Clark Ross. . . .*v.4 p.379*

Polar Rearrangements. *v.5 p.292*

Polaroid Transfers: A Complete Visual Guide to Creating Image and Emulsion Transfers. *v.1 p.759*

Poles Apart: The Natural Worlds of the Arctic and Antarctic. *v.5 p.176, p.238*

Poles Together?: The Emergence and Development of Political Parties in Post-Communist Poland. *v.4 p.579, p.597*

Police and the People: French Popular Protest, 1789-1820. . . . .*v.3 p.149*

Police Brutality: Opposing Viewpoints. *v.6 p.261*

Police Coercion: Application of the Force Continuum. .*v.6 p.261*

Police in a Multicultural Society: An American Story. .*v.6 p.265*

The Police in America: Classic and Contemporary Readings. *v.6 p.261*

Police Misconduct: A Reader for the 21st Century. . .*v.6 p.260*

ⓔ Police Misconduct in America: A Reference Handbook. *v.6 p.260*

Police, Politics and Corruption: The Mixture Dangerous to Freedom and Justice. *v.6 p.260*

Police Traffic Stops and Racial Profiling: Resolving Management, Labor and Civil Rights Conflicts. *v.6 p.264, p.265*

Police Unbound: Corruption, Abuse and Heroism by the Boys in Blue. *v.6 p.260*

Police Violence: Understanding and Controlling Police Abuse of Force. *v.6 p.261*

Police Women: Life with the Badge. *v.6 p.260*

Police Work: A Career Survival Guide. *v.6 p.263*

Policies for Prosperity: Essays in a Keynesian Mode. *v.4 p.239*

Policing Africa: Internal Security and the Limits of Liberalization. *v.6 p.262*

Policing and Community Partnerships. *v.6 p.264*

Policing Cinema: Movies and Censorship in Early-Twentieth-Century America. *v.6 p.341*

Policing Citizens: Authority and Rights. *v.6 p.263*

Policing Gangs and Youth Violence. *v.6 p.264*

Policing, Race and Racism. *v.4 p.774, v.6 p.265*

Policing Rio de Janeiro: Repression and Resistance in a Nineteenth-Century City. *v.3 p.341*

Policing Shanghai, 1927-1937. . . . .*v.6 p.191*

Policing Urban Poverty. *v.6 p.255, p.256*

Policy and Law in Heritage Conservation. *v.1 p.823*

Policy and Politics in Nursing and Health Care. . . .*v.5 p.530*

Policy and Politics in West Germany: A Semisovereign State. *v.4 p.609*

Policy and Practices for Biodiversity in Managed Forests: The Living Dance. *v.5 p.37*

Policy Development in Sport Management. *v.4 p.886*

Policy Indicators: Links Between Social Science and Public Debate. *v.4 p.769*

Policy Issues in Modern Cartography. *v.4 p.375*

Policy Makers and Critics: Conflicting Theories of American Foreign Poilicy. *v.3 p.385*

Policy Making in Israel: Routines for Simple Problems and Coping with the Complex. *v.4 p.615, p.616*

A Policy of Discontent: The Making of a National Energy Strategy. *v.4 p.62, p.63*

Polin: Studies in Polish Jewry: Focusing on Jewish Popular Culture and Its Afterlife. *v.3 p.255*

Polio: An American Story. *v.5 p.533*

Polish: An Essential Grammar. *v.2 p.775*

Polish Baroque and Enlightenment Literature: An Anthology. *v.2 p.789*

The Polish Complex. *v.2 p.790*

Polish Fables: Bilingual Edition. *v.2 p.790*

Polish Film: A Twentieth Century History. *v.6 p.337*

Polish Folk Music: Slavonic Heritage - Polish Tradition - Contemporary Trends. *v.1 p.298*

The Polish Formalist School and Russian Formalism. *v.2 p.779, p.789, p.798*

Polish Paradoxes. *v.3 p.255*

Polish Poetry of the Last Two Decades of Communist Rule: Spoiling Cannibals' Fun. *v.2 p.787*

Polish Politics and Society. *v.4 p.596*

Polish Renaissance Literature: An Anthology. *v.2 p.788*

The Polish Revolution: Solidarity. *v.3 p.255*

Polish Romantic Drama: Three Plays in English Translation. *v.1 p.68, p.69, p.110,v.2 p.788*

Polish Romantic Literature: An Anthology. *v.2 p.788*

Polish Short Story in English: A Guide and Critical Bibliography. *v.2 p.788*

Polish Underground State. *v.3 p.254*

The Polish Way: A Thousand Year History of the Poles and Their Culture. *v.3 p.252*

Polish-American Politics in Chicago, 1888-1940. . . .*v.3 p.515*

Polish-Jewish Literature in the Interwar Years. *v.2 p.789*

The Polish-Lithuanian Monarchy in European Context, C. 1500-1795. *v.3 p.252*

The Polish-Lithuanian State, 1386-1795. . . . *v.3 p.252, p.253*

A Polite and Commercial People: England, 1727-1783. . . . . *v.3 p.107, p.109, p.128, p.129*

A Political and Diplomatic History of Afghanistan, 1863-1901. *v.6 p.634*

A Political and Economic Dictionary of Africa. .*v.4 p.191, p.192*

A Political and Economic Dictionary of East Asia. *v.4 p.189, p.190*

A Political and Economic Dictionary of Eastern Europe. .*v.4 p.188*

A Political and Economic Dictionary of Latin America. .*v.4 p.591*

A Political and Economic Dictionary of South Asia. . .*v.4 p.191*

A Political and Economic Dictionary of Western Europe. *v.4 p.186*

Political and Economic Migrants in America: Cubans and Mexicans. *v.6 p.530*

The Political and Historical Theory of the Elites. . . .*v.4 p.249*

Political and Social Issues in Poland, as Reflected in the Polish Novel. *v.2 p.789*

Political Anthropology: Power and Paradigms. *v.4 p.34*

Political Background on Aeschylean Tragedy. *v.2 p.407*

Political Behavior. *v.4 p.483, v.5 p.642*

Political Business Cycles: The Political Economy of Money, Inflation, and Unemployment. *v.4 p.245*

Political Campaign Communication: Philosophy and Practice. *v.4 p.578*

The Political Career of Floyd B. Olson. *v.3 p.522*

Political Change in Britain, 1963-1970. . . . .*v.4 p.606*

Political Change in Thailand: Democracy and Participation. *v.6 p.171*

Political Change on Taiwan: A Study of Ruling Party Adaptability. *v.4 p.618*

Political Christianity - P. *v.1 p.596*

The Political Collapse of Europe. *v.3 p.178*

Political Communication Ethics: An Oxymoron? . . .*v.4 p.417*

The Political Companion to American Film. . .*v.6 p.328, p.340*

Political Conflict and Constitutional Change in Puerto Rico, 1898-1952. *v.3 p.320*

Political Construction Sites: Nation Building in Russia and the Post-Soviet States. *v.4 p.598*

Political Corruption in America: An Encyclopedia of Scandals, Power, and Greed. *v.4 p.516, p.557, p.558*

Political Corruption. *v.4 p.580*

Political Crisis - Fiscal Crisis: The Collapse and Revival of New York City. *v.6 p.725*

Political Crisis of the 1850's. *v.3 p.398*

Political Culture and Institutional Development in Costa Rica and Nicaragua: World Making in the Tropics. .*v.3 p.301, p.303*

Political Culture and Post-Communism. *v.4 p.599*

Political Culture in Nineteenth-Century Peru: The Rise of the Partido Civil. *v.3 p.328*

Political Culture in the 19th-Century South: Mississippi, 1830-1900. *v.3 p.504*

The Political Culture of Planning: American Land Use Planning in Comparative Perspective. *v.6 p.727*

Political Cultures in the Andes, 1750-1950. . . . . .*v.3 p.327*

Political Cycles and the Macroeconomy. *v.4 p.242*

Political Database of the Americas. . . .*v.3 p.259, v.4 p.591*

Political Deliverance: The Mormon Quest for Utah Statehood. *v.3 p.529*

Political Development and the New Realism in Sub-Saharan Africa. *v.4 p.610*

The Political Development of the Kurds in Iran: Pastoral Nationalism. *v.6 p.599, p.631*

Political Dictionary of Israel. *v.6 p.615*

Political Dissent in Democratic Athens: Intellectual Critics of Popular Rule. *v.3 p.18*

The Political Dynamics of American Education. *v.4 p.298*

Political Economy for Beginners. *v.4 p.209, p.269*

The Political Economy of Agricultural, Natural Resource, and Environmental Policy Analysis. *v.5 p.15*

The Political Economy of Argentina: Power and Class since 1930. . . . .*v.3 p.349*

The Political Economy of Colonialism: The State and Industrialization in Puerto Rico. *v.3 p.318*

The Political Economy of Democratic Transitions. *v.4 p.487, p.504*

The Political Economy of Development: Theoretical and Empirical Contributions. *v.4 p.574*

The Political Economy of Education: Implications for Growth and Inequality. *v.4 p.297*

The Political Economy of Ethiopia. *v.4 p.612*

The Political Economy of Financial Crises. *v.4 p.242, p.246, p.260*

Political Economy of Germany in the 20th Century. . .*v.3 p.172*

The Political Economy of Global Restructuring: Economic Organization and Production, Vol. 1. . . . .*v.4 p.257, p.264*

The Political Economy of Imperialism: Critical Appraisals. *v.4 p.502*

Political Economy of Indian Federalism. *v.4 p.618*

The Political Economy of Integration in the European Community. *v.4 p.211, p.240, p.255, p.256*

The Political Economy of Mexico, Two Studies. . . .*v.3 p.292*

The Political Economy of Nigeria. *v.6 p.72*

The Political Economy of Protection: Theory and the Chilean Experience. *v.3 p.350*

The Political Economy of Spanish America in the Age of Revolution, 1750-1850. . . . .*v.3 p.284*

The Political Economy of the Brazilian State, 1889-1930. . . . .*v.3 p.343*

The Political Economy of Trade Policy: Papers in Honor of Jagdish Bhagwati. *v.4 p.257*

The Political Element in the Development of Economic Theory, Vol. 29. . . . .*v.4 p.210*

The Political Element in the Development of Economic Theory. *v.4 p.210, p.233*

Political Elites in Arab North Africa. *v.6 p.60*

Political Empiricism: Communication Strategies in State and Regional Elections. *v.4 p.550, p.558, p.559*

Political Geography: A Comprehensive Systematic Bibliography. *v.4 p.496*

Political Handbook of the World 2005. . . . .*v.4 p.574*

The Political History of Canada Between 1840 and 1855. . . . . *v.3 p.539*

The Political History of Finland, 1809-1966. . . . . *v.3 p.236*

A Political History of the Civil War in Angola, 1974-1990. . . . . *v.6 p.75*

Political History of Wisconsin. *v.3 p.517*

Political Ideas of the American Revolution. *v.3 p.407*

Political Identity and Social Change: The Remaking of the South African Social Order. *v.6 p.78*

Political Identity. *v.5 p.643*

Political Ideology and Educational Reform in Chile, 1964-1976. . . . . *v.3 p.353*

The Political Integration of Women: Roles, Socialization, and Politics. *v.6 p.442*

Political Islam: Religion and Politics in the Arab World. *v.4 p.500*

Political Islam: Revolution, Radicalism, or Reform? . *v.1 p.554*

Political Judgment: Structure and Process. *v.5 p.643*

The Political Kingdom in Uganda: A Study in Bureaucratic Nationalism. *v.4 p.494, p.610*

Political Leaders and Democracy in Turkey. . . *v.6 p.623*

Political Leaders of Modern China, 1840-2001: A Biographical Dictionary. *v.6 p.199*

Political Leadership among Swat Pathans. *v.4 p.34*

Political Leadership for the New Century: Personality and Behavior among American Leaders. *v.5 p.645*

The Political Legacy of Kwame Nkrumah of Ghana. . *v.6 p.69*

[e] Political Legitimacy in Middle Africa: Father, Family, Food. *v.4 p.613, v.6 p.442*

Political Liberalism. *v.4 p.511, p.514*

Political Liberalization and Democratization in Africa: Lessons from Country Experiences. *v.4 p.585, p.611*

Political Life. *v.5 p.643*

Political Marketing: A Comparative Perspective. *v.4 p.545, p.577*

Political Marketing: An Approach to Campaign Strategy. *v.4 p.558*

Political Nature: Environmentalism and the Interpretation of Western Thought. *v.6 p.288, p.289*

Political Non-Logical Conduct and Theories Transcending Experience. *v.4 p.249*

Political Obligations. *v.4 p.498*

Political Opposition in the Early Turkish Republic: The Progressive Republican Party, 1924-1925. . . . . *v.6 p.625*

Political Order in Changing Societies. *v.4 p.482*

The Political Organization of Space. *v.6 p.721*

Political Paranoia: The Psychopolitics of Hatred. . . *v.5 p.644*

Political Participation in Beijing. *v.4 p.620*

Political Parties and American Political Development from the Age of Jackson to the Age of Lincoln. *v.3 p.398*

Political Parties and Elections in the United States: An Encyclopedia, Set. *v.4 p.548, p.551*

Political Parties and Generations in Paraguay's Liberal Era, 1869-1940. *v.3 p.344*

Political Parties, Growth and Equality: Conservative and Social Democratic Economic Strategies in the World Economy. *v.4 p.550, p.578*

Political Parties in the European Union. *v.4 p.603*

Political Parties in Turkey. *v.4 p.616, v.6 p.624*

Political Parties Matter: Realignment and the Return of Partisan Voting. *v.4 p.552, p.555*

Political Parties of Eastern Europe: A Guide to Politics in the Post-Communist Era. *v.4 p.595, p.596, p.597, p.600*

Political Parties of the Americas, 1980s to 1990s: Canada, Latin America, and the West Indies. *v.4 p.588*

Political Parties of the Americas: Canada, Latin America, and the West Indies. *v.4 p.588*

Political Parties: Their Organization and Activity in the Modern State. *v.4 p.579*

Political Parties. *v.4 p.588*

The Political Persuaders: The Techniques of Modern Election Campaigns. *v.4 p.549*

The Political Philosophies of Plato and Hegel. . . . *v.4 p.489*

The Political Philosophy of Hobbes, Its Basis and Its Genesis. *v.4 p.502*

The Political Philosophy of James Madison. . *v.4 p.492, p.493*

Political Policing: The United States and Latin America. *v.6 p.262*

Political Posters in Central and Eastern Europe 1945-1995: Signs of the Times. *v.1 p.718*

Political Power and Corporate Control: The New Global Politics of Corporate Governance. *v.4 p.86*

Political Power in Pre-Colonial Buganda: Economy, Society and Welfare in the Nineteenth Century. *v.4 p.582, p.612,v.6 p.67*

The Political Prisoner. *v.2 p.720*

The Political Psyche. *v.5 p.645*

Political Psychology: Cultural and Cross-Cultural Foundations. *v.5 p.644*

Political Psychology: Essential Readings. . *v.4 p.483, v.5 p.643*

Political Psychology in International Relations. *v.4 p.484, v.5 p.644*

Political Psychology. *v.5 p.643, p.644*

Political Radicalism in Late Imperial Vienna: Origins of the Christian Social Movement, 1848-1897. . . . . . *v.3 p.183*

Political Reasoning and Cognition: A Piagetian View. *v.5 p.645*

Political Science Research Methods. *v.4 p.483*

Political Shakespeare: Essays in Cultural Materialism. *v.2 p.229*

Political Stability in Federal Governments. *v.4 p.524*

Political Support in Canada: The Crisis Years. . . . *v.4 p.586*

The Political System of the European Union. . *v.4 p.603, p.637*

Political Systems of Highland Burma: A Study of Kachin Social Structure. *v.4 p.34*

Political Terrorism: A New Guide to Actors, Authors, Concepts, Data Bases, Theories, and Literature. *v.4 p.661*

Political Terrorism: Theory, Tactics and Counter-Measures. *v.4 p.662*

Political Theory and the Psychology of the Unconscious: Freud, J. S. Mill, Nietzsche, Dostoevsky, Fromm, Bettelheim, and Erikson. *v.5 p.644*

Political Thought in Europe, 1250-1450. . . . . . . *v.4 p.490*

Political Thought in Medieval Times. . . . *v.4 p.490, v.6 p.568*

Political Thought in Renaissance Poland: An Anthology in English. *v.3 p.252*

Political Thought of Plato and Aristotle. . . . *v.4 p.488, p.489*

The Political Thought of Sallust. *v.2 p.442*

The Political Thought of Samuel Taylor Coleridge. . *v.2 p.279*

The Political Thought of Thomas Aquinas. *v.4 p.490*

The Political Thought of William Ockham. *v.4 p.490*

Political Tolerance and American Democracy. *v.5 p.645*

Political Traditions in Modern France. *v.3 p.140*

The Political Unconscious: Narrative As a Socially Symbolic
Act. *v.2 p.568*

Political Unification Revisited: On Building Supranational
Communities. *v.4 p.629*

The Political University: Policy, Politics, and Presidential
Leadership in the American Research University. . .*v.4 p.295*

Political Violence and Terrorism in Modern America: A
Chronology. *v.4 p.563*

Political Violence under the Swastika: 581 Early Nazis. .*v.3 p.170*

Political Worship: Ethics for Christian Citizens. .*v.1 p.654, p.655*

Politica. *v.2 p.408*

The Politician: The Life and Times of Lyndon Johnson. .*v.3 p.470*

Politicians and Policymaking in Japan. *v.4 p.621*

Politicide: Ariel Sharon's War Against the Palestinians. .*v.6 p.618*

Politicisation of Islam: A Case Study of Tunisia. . . .*v.6 p.641*

The Politicization of Islam: Reconstructing Identity, State, Faith,
and Community in the Late Ottoman State. *v.6 p.590*

Politicized Economies: Monarchy, Monopoly, and
Mercantilism. *v.4 p.215*

Politicizing Magic: An Anthology of Russian and Soviet Fairy
Tales. *v.2 p.794*

The Politicos. *v.3 p.437*

Politics Aesthetics and Culture: A Study of Indo-Anglian
Political Novel. *v.2 p.762*

Politics after Hitler: The Western Allies and the German Party
System. *v.4 p.610*

Politics among Nations: The Struggle for Power and
Peace. *v.3 p.453, v.4 p.626*

Politics among Nations. *v.4 p.626*

Politics and Change in a Traditional Society: Lebanon,
1711-1845. *v.6 p.605*

Politics and Education in Argentina, 1946-1962. . . . *v.3 p.349*

Politics and Empire in Victorian Britain: A Reader. . *v.6 p.745*

The Politics and Ethics of Fieldwork. *v.4 p.690, p.691*

Politics and History in William Golding: The World Turned
Upside Down. *v.2 p.347*

Politics and Ideology in Allende's Chile. *v.3 p.356*

Politics and Ideology in England 1603-1640. . .*v.3 p.95, p.102*

Politics and Language in Dryden's Poetry. *v.2 p.247*

Politics and Parentela in Paraiba: A Case Study of Family-Based
Oligarchy in Brazil. *v.3 p.337*

Politics and Passion: Toward a More Egalitarian
Liberalism. *v.4 p.511, p.514*

Politics and Power in Early Medieval Europe: Alsace and the
Frankish Realm, 600-1000. . . . . *v.3 p.143*

Politics and Practice in Economic Geography. *v.4 p.398*

Politics and Privilege in a Mexican City. *v.3 p.292*

Politics and Property Rights: The Closing of the Open Range in
the Postbellum South. *v.5 p.42, v.6 p.298*

Politics and Psychology: Contemporary Psychodynamic
Perspectives. *v.5 p.644*

Politics and Reform in Spain and Viceregal Mexico: The Life
and Thought of Juan de Palafox 1600-1659. . . . .*v.3 p.284*

Politics and Society in Early Modern Iraq. *v.6 p.603*

Politics and Society in Scotland. *v.4 p.607*

Politics and Society in Ukraine. *v.4 p.597*

Politics and Statecraft in the Kingdom of Greece,
1833-1843. *v.3 p.195*

Politics and Symbols: The Italian Communist Party and the Fall
of Communism. *v.4 p.594*

Politics and Territory: The Sociology of Regional Persistence in
Canada. *v.4 p.587*

Politics and the Arts: Letter to M. D'Alembert on the
Theatre. *v.1 p.139*

Politics and the Churches in Great Britain,
1832-1868. . . . .*v.3 p.113, p.121*

Politics and the Churches in Great Britain,
1869-1921. . . . .*v.3 p.113, p.121*

Politics and the Class Divide: Working People and the Middle
Class Left. *v.4 p.547*

Politics and the Constitution in the History of the United
States. *v.4 p.452*

Politics and the Economy in Jordan. *v.6 p.621*

Politics and the Ends of Identity. *v.5 p.642*

Politics and the Migrant Poor in Mexico City. .*v.3 p.291, v.6 p.717*

Politics and the Parlement of Paris under Louis XV,
1754-1774. *v.3 p.148*

Politics and the Restraint of Science. *v.5 p.410, p.411*

Politics and the Russian Army: Civil-Military Relations,
1689-2000. *v.4 p.599*

Politics and Theater: The Crisis of Legitimacy in Restoration
France, 1815-1830. . . . . *v.3 p.153*

Politics and Urban Growth in Santiago, Chile,
1891-1941. *v.3 p.356*

Politics as a Christian Vocation: Faith and Democracy
Today. *v.1 p.595*

Politics As Development: The Emergence of Political Parties in
Nineteenth-Century Serbia. . . . *v.3 p.248, v.4 p.579, p.600*

Politics, Bks. I & II. *v.4 p.488*

Politics, Bks. III and IV. *v.4 p.488*

Politics, Death, and the Devil: Self and Power in Max Weber
and Thomas Mann. *v.4 p.502*

Politics in a Museum: Governing Post-War Florence. .*v.3 p.204*

Politics in France. *v.4 p.608*

Politics in Francophone Africa. *v.4 p.612, v.6 p.54*

Politics in New Brunswick. *v.4 p.590*

Politics in New Zealand. *v.4 p.624*

Politics in Northern Ireland. *v.4 p.607*

Politics in Russia. *v.4 p.598*

Politics in Southern Africa: State and Society in
Transition. *v.4 p.610, p.613,v.6 p.74*

Politics in Taiwan: Voting for Democracy. *v.6 p.214*

Politics in the Age of Peel: A Study in the Technique of
Parliamentary representation, 1830-1850. . . . . . *v.3 p.111*

Politics in the Ancient World. *v.4 p.489*

Politics in the Andes: Identity, Conflict, Reform. . . *v.3 p.332*

Politics in the New South: Representation of African Americans
in Southern State Legislatures. *v.4 p.530*

Politics in the New South: Republicanism, Race, and Leadership
in the Twentieth Century. *v.3 p.497*

Politics in the Republic of Ireland. *v.4 p.608*

Politics in the Third Turkish Republic. *v.6 p.623*

Politics in the Tokugawa Bakufu, 1600-1843. . . . . .*v.6 p.226*

Politics in the United Nations: A Study of United States
   Influence in the General Assembly. *v.4 p.635*

Politics, Language, and Culture: A Critical Look at Urban
   School Reform. *v.4 p.314*

Politics, Law and Morality: Essays by V. S. Soloviev. *v.1 p.474*

Politics, Law and Ritual in Tribal Society. *v.4 p.433*

Politics, Literature and National
   Character. *v.2 p.501, v.3 p.152, p.153*

e The Politics of Agriculture in Japan. *v.6 p.220*

The Politics of American Individualism: Herbert Hoover in
   Transition, 1918-1921. . . . .*v.3 p.466*

The Politics of American Religious Identity: The Seating of
   Senator Reed Smoot, Mormon Apostle. *v.1 p.587*

The Politics of Antipolitics: The Military in Latin
   America. *v.3 p.275*

The Politics of Arms Control Treaty Ratification. .*v.4 p.562, p.630*

The Politics of Asian Americans: Diversity and
   Community. *v.6 p.120*

The Politics of Assimilation: The French Jewish Community at
   the Time of the Dreyfus Affair. *v.3 p.60*

The Politics of Backwardness in Hungary, 1825-1945. *v.3 p.186*

The Politics of Belgium: A Unique Federalism. *v.4 p.600, p.601*

The Politics of Broadcast Regulation. *v.4 p.445*

The Politics of Canadian Public Policy. *v.4 p.586*

The Politics of Child Support in America. *v.4 p.739*

The Politics of Color in the Fiction of Jessie Fauset and Nella
   Larsen. *v.2 p.4*

The Politics of Command: Factions and Ideas in Confederate
   Strategy. *v.3 p.395*

The Politics of Command. *v.3 p.428*

The Politics of Congo-Brazzaville. *v.6 p.62*

The Politics of Congressional Elections. *v.4 p.530, p.549*

Politics of Conscience: A Biography of Margaret Chase
   Smith. *v.3 p.463*

The Politics of Coronelismo in Brazil: The Case of Bahia,
   1889-1930. . . . .*v.3 p.341, p.342*

The Politics of Cultural Despair: A Study in the Rise of the
   Germanic Ideology. *v.3 p.165, p.179*

The Politics of Cultural Mobilization in India. . . .*v.6 p.158*

The Politics of Cultural Pluralism. *v.4 p.574, p.576, p.577*

The Politics of Deference: A Study of the Mid-Nineteenth
   Century English Political System. *v.3 p.114*

The Politics of Democratization in Korea: The Role of Civil
   Society. *v.4 p.621*

The Politics of Denial: Israel and the Palestinian Refugee
   Problem. *v.6 p.618*

The Politics of Denial. *v.5 p.644*

The Politics of Deviance. *v.4 p.696*

The Politics of Diplomacy: Revolution, War and Peace,
   1989-1992. . . . .*v.3 p.465*

Politics of Disillusionment: The Chinese Communist Party under
   Deng Xiaoping, 1978-1989. . . . .*v.4 p.619*

The Politics of Dissatisfaction: Citizens, Services and Urban
   Institutions. *v.4 p.542, v.6 p.724*

The Politics of Economic Restructuring in Mexico: State-Society
   Relations and Regime Change in Mexico. *v.3 p.294*

The Politics of Electoral Systems: A Handbook. . . .*v.4 p.576*

The Politics of Ethnic Survival : Germans in Prague,
   1861-1914. . . . .*v.3 p.188*

The Politics of EU Police Cooperation: Toward a European
   FBI? *v.6 p.262*

The Politics of European Union Enlargement: Theoretical
   Approaches. *v.4 p.400, p.603*

The Politics of Everyday Life: Making Choices, Changing
   Lives. *v.4 p.577*

The Politics of External Influence in the Dominican
   Republic. *v.4 p.592*

The Politics of Fear: Joseph R. McCarthy and the
   Senate. *v.3 p.458*

The Politics of Fortune: A New Agenda for Business
   Leaders. *v.4 p.54*

The Politics of Freeing Markets in Latin America: Chile,
   Argentina and Mexico. *v.3 p.295, p.349, p.355*

The Politics of Garbage: A Community Perspective on Solid
   Waste Policy Making. *v.4 p.542*

The Politics of Genocide: The Holocaust in
   Hungary. *v.3 p.82, p.83*

The Politics of Globalization: Gaining Perspective, Assessing
   Consequences. *v.4 p.662*

The Politics of God: Christian Theologies and Social
   Justice. *v.1 p.596*

The Politics of Heroin: CIA Complicity in the Global Drug
   Trade. *v.6 p.164, p.165*

The Politics of Hispanic Education: Un Paso Pa'lante y Dos
   Pa'tras. *v.6 p.527*

The Politics of History: Writing the History of the American
   Revolution, 1783-1815. . . . .*v.3 p.410*

The Politics of Homosexuality. *v.6 p.366, p.388*

The Politics of Human Rights in Southeast Asia. . . .*v.4 p.512*

The Politics of Identity: Class, Culture, Social
   Movements. *v.4 p.693*

The Politics of Identity. *v.5 p.633*

Politics of Illusion: The Bay of Pigs Invasion
   Reexamined. *v.3 p.307*

The Politics of Inclusion and Exclusion: Jews and Nationalism
   in Hungary. *v.3 p.60, p.86, p.186, p.187*

The Politics of Indian Removal: Creek Government and Society
   in Crisis. *v.6 p.687, p.691*

The Politics of Individualism: Parties and the American
   Character in the Jacksonian Era. *v.4 p.551, p.552*

The Politics of Indonesia. *v.6 p.175, p.177*

The Politics of Inequality: South Africa Since 1948. . *v.6 p.78*

The Politics of Inertia: The Election of 1876 and the End of
   Reconstruction. *v.3 p.437, p.438*

The Politics of Judicial Interpretation: The Federal Courts,
   Department of Justice and Civil Rights, 1866-1876. .*v.4 p.525*

Politics of Language in the Ex-Soviet Muslim States:
   Azerbaijan, Uzbekistan, Kazakhstan,
   Kyrgyzstan, Turkmenistan, Tajikistan. . . .*v.3 p.230, p.231*

Politics of Latin America: The Power Game. *v.3 p.260*

The Politics of Latin Literature: Writing, Identity and Empire in
   Ancient Rome. *v.2 p.424*

The Politics of Law: A Progressive Critique. *v.4 p.465*

The Politics of Life: Four Plays by Asian American Women. *v.1 p.67, p.125,v.6 p.98*

The Politics of Manpower, 1914-18. . . . . . .*v.3 p.78, p.79*

The Politics of Market Reform in Fragile Democracies: Argentina, Brazil, Peru, and Venezuela. *v.3 p.332, p.343, p.349, p.361*

The Politics of Memory: Native Historical Interpretation in the Colombian Andes. *v.3 p.358*

Politics of Mercantilism. *v.4 p.255*

The Politics of Mexican Development. *v.3 p.292, p.293*

The Politics of Military Rule and Transition in Ecuador, 1972-92: Dancing with the People. *v.3 p.274, p.333*

The Politics of Military Rule in Brazil, 1964-1985. . .*v.3 p.342*

The Politics of Milton's Prose Style. *v.2 p.255*

The Politics of Miscalculation in the Middle East. . .*v.6 p.594*

The Politics of Modernism: Against the New Conformists. *v.2 p.179, p.184, p.185, p.195*

The Politics of Motherhood: British Writing and Culture, 1680-1760. . . . .*v.6 p.477*

The Politics of Nationalism in Canada: Cultural Conflict since 1760. . . . .*v.3 p.536*

The Politics of Normalcy: Governmental Theory and Practice in the Harding-Coolidge Era. *v.3 p.476*

The Politics of Partition: King Abdullah, the Zionists, and Palestine, 1921-1951. . . . .*v.6 p.616, p.621*

The Politics of Penury: Debts and Taxes in Mexico, 1821-1856. . . . .*v.3 p.289*

The Politics of Philosophy: A Commentary on Aristotle's Politics. *v.4 p.489*

The Politics of Pictures: The Creation of the Public in the Age of Popular Media. *v.4 p.416*

The Politics of Prejudice: The Anti-Japanese Movement in California and the Struggle for Japanese Exclusion. *v.3 p.531, v.4 p.570*

The Politics of Pressure: American Arms and Israeli Policy Since the Six Day War. *v.3 p.391*

The Politics of Provincialism: The Democratic Party in Transition, 1918-1932. . . . .*v.3 p.439*

The Politics of Public Space. *v.6 p.724*

The Politics of Rage: George Wallace, the Origins of the New Conservatism and the Transformation of American Politics. *v.3 p.504*

The Politics of Recovery: Roosevelt's New Deal. . . .*v.3 p.444*

The Politics of Reform, 1884. . . . .*v.3 p.113*

The Politics of Reform in Thailand. *v.6 p.172*

The Politics of Regulatory Change: A Tale of Two Agencies. *v.4 p.463*

The Politics of Resentment: British Columbia Regionalism and Canadian Unity. *v.3 p.547*

The Politics of Retribution in Europe: World War II and Its Aftermath. *v.3 p.207*

The Politics of Rights: Lawyers, Public Policy and Political Change. *v.4 p.442*

The Politics of River Trade: Tradition and Development in the Upper Plata, 1780-1870. . . . .*v.3 p.345*

The Politics of Samuel Johnson. *v.2 p.250*

The Politics of School Reform, 1870-1940. . . . . .*v.4 p.328*

The Politics of Sentencing Reform. *v.6 p.269*

The Politics of Serbia in the 1990s. *v.3 p.248*

The Politics of Social Policy in the United States. *v.4 p.526, p.571, p.572*

The Politics of Southern Europe: Integration into the European Union. *v.4 p.603, p.638*

The Politics of Story in Victorian Social Fiction. *v.2 p.174, v.6 p.752, p.755*

Politics of Survival: The Conservative Party of Canada 1939-1945. . . . .*v.4 p.588, p.589*

The Politics of Terror: The Macedonian Revolutionary Movements, 1893-1903. . . . .*v.3 p.251*

The Politics of Terror: The U. S. Response to 9/11. . . . .*v.3 p.483, v.4 p.563*

The Politics of Terrorism. *v.4 p.662*

The Politics of the Environment: Ideas, Activism, Policy. *v.5 p.29, v.6 p.299*

The Politics of the Independence of Kenya. *v.6 p.65*

Politics of the Irish Civil War. *v.3 p.139*

Politics of the Meiji Press: The Life of Fukuchi Gen'ichiro. *v.6 p.227*

Politics of the Middle East. *v.6 p.594*

The Politics of the Miraculous in Peru: Haya de la Torre and the Spiritualist Tradition. *v.3 p.331*

The Politics of the Past in an Argentine Working-Class Neighbourhood. *v.3 p.348*

The Politics of the Prussian Army: 1640-1945. . . .*v.3 p.160*

The Politics of the Prussian Nobility: The Development of a Conservative Ideology, 1770-1848. . . . .*v.3 p.167*

The Politics of the Reformation in Germany: Jacob Sturm (1489-1553) of Strasbourg. *v.3 p.165*

The Politics of the U. S. Cabinet: Representation in the Executive Branch, 1789-1984. . . . .*v.4 p.529*

The Politics of Truth and Reconciliation in South Africa: Legitimizing the Post-Apartheid State. *v.6 p.78*

The Politics of Truth: Inside the Lies That Led to War and Betrayed My Wife's CIA Identity, A Diplomat's Memoir. *v.4 p.562, p.648*

The Politics of Turkish Democracy: Ismet Inonu and the Formation of the Multi-Party System, 1938-1950. *v.6 p.625*

The Politics of Two Sudans: The South and the North, 1821-1969. . . . .*v.6 p.59*

The Politics of Union: Northern Politics During the Civil War. *v.3 p.400*

The Politics of Upheaval: 1935-1936, the Age of Roosevelt. *v.3 p.479*

The Politics of Upheaval, 1935-1936. . . . . .*v.3 p.444, p.450*

The Politics of Urban Development. *v.6 p.725*

The Politics of Utopia: A Study in Theory and Practice. *v.4 p.499*

Politics of War: The World. *v.3 p.453*

The Politics of Women's Bodies: Sexuality, Appearance, and Behavior. *v.6 p.437*

The Politics of Women's Studies: Testimony from Thirty Founding Mothers. *v.6 p.463*

The Politics of Workers' Participation: The Peruvian Approach in Comparative Perspective. *v.3 p.332*

Politics of Writing in Iran: A History of Modern Persian Literature. *v.6 p.673*

Politics or Principle?: Filibustering in the United States Senate. . . . .*.v.4 p.533*

Politics, Parties and Elections in Turkey. . . . .*.v.4 p.616*

Politics, Policy, and Government in British Columbia. . . . .*.v.3 p.546, v.4 p.589*

Politics, Punishment and Populism. . . . .*.v.4 p.567*

Politics, Reform and Expansion: 1890-1900. . . . . .*.v.3 p.436*

Politics, the Constitution and the Warren Court. . . .*.v.4 p.470*

Politics, Vol. 5-6, Bks. VII and VIII. . . . .*.v.4 p.488*

Politique. . . . .*.v.2 p.168, p.169*

Polk: The Diary of a Presidency, 1845-1849, Covering the Mexican War, the Acquisition of Oregon, and the Conquest of California and the Southwest. . . . .*.v.3 p.421*

Polka Happiness. . . . .*.v.1 p.296*

The Pollaiuolo Brothers: The Arts of Florence and Rome. . . . .*.v.1 p.700*

Pollination Ecology and the Rain Forest: Sarawak Studies. . . . .*.v.5 p.185, p.239*

Polling, Policy, and Public Opinion: The Case Against Heeding the Voice of the People. . . . .*.v.4 p.559*

Polling the Nations. . . . .*.v.4 p.697*

PollingReport.com. . . . .*.v.4 p.425, p.559*

Polluted Sites: Remediation of Soils and Groundwater. . . . .*.v.5 p.50, v.6 p.289*

Pollution Abstracts. . . . .*.v.5 p.309*

Pollution Abstracts. . . . .*.v.5 p.309*

Pollution and the Struggle for the World Product: Multinational Corporations, Environment, and International Comparative Advantage. . . . .*.v.4 p.63*

Pollution: Causes, Effects and Control. . . . . .*.v.5 p.310, p.375*

Pollution Control in the United States: Evaluating the System. . . . .*.v.4 p.63*

The Polo Encyclopedia. . . . .*.v.4 p.844, p.863*

Polpop 2: Politics and Popular Culture in America Today. . . . .*.v.3 p.370, p.371*

Polpop: Politics and Popular Culture in America. . .*.v.3 p.370*

Polyarchy: Participation and Opposition. . . . . . .*.v.4 p.575*

Polybius, Rome and the Hellenistic World: Essays and Reflections. . . . .*.v.3 p.25*

Polybius. . . . .*.v.2 p.406*

Polycyclic Aromatic Hydrocarbons. . . . .*.v.5 p.292*

Polyeuctus, the Liar, Nicomedes. . . . .*.v.2 p.473*

Polyhedra. . . . .*.v.5 p.498*

Polymath. . . . .*.v.6 p.659*

Polymer Characterization: Physical Techniques. . . .*.v.5 p.323*

Polymer Characterization. . . . .*.v.5 p.323*

Polymer Chemistry: An Introduction. . . . .*.v.5 p.322*

Polymer Chemistry--Subject Guide (Stanford University). . . . .*.v.5 p.321*

Polymer Handbook. . . . .*.v.5 p.322*

Polymer Materials: An Introduction for Technologists and Scientists. . . . .*.v.5 p.322*

Polymer Nanocomposites: Synthesis, Characterization, and Modeling. . . . .*.v.5 p.689*

Polymer Physics. . . . .*.v.5 p.564*

Polymer Science Dictionary. . . . .*.v.5 p.322*

Polymer Search on the Internet (RAPRA). . . . . .*.v.5 p.321*

Polymer Syntheses, Vol. 1. . . . .*.v.5 p.323*

The Polymerase Chain Reaction: A Textbook. . . . .*.v.5 p.154*

Polymeric Materials Encyclopedia (Set). . . . . . .*.v.5 p.322*

Polymeric Materials Encyclopedia. . . . .*.v.5 p.321, p.322*

Polymeric Multicomponent Materials: An Introduction. *.v.5 p.324*

Polymers from the Inside Out: An Introduction to Macromolecules. . . . .*.v.5 p.321*

Polynesia in Early Historic Times. . . . .*.v.4 p.43*

The Polynesians: Prehistory of an Island People. . . .*.v.4 p.13*

Polyominoes: Puzzles, Patterns, Problems, and Packings. . . . .*.v.5 p.469*

The Polyphony of Saint Martial and Santiago de Compostela. . . . .*.v.1 p.177*

PoMoSexuals: Challenging Assumptions about Gender and Sexuality. . . . .*.v.4 p.746, v.6 p.367*

Pompeii: Public and Private Life. . . . .*.v.3 p.24*

Pompey the Great. . . . .*.v.3 p.26*

Pons Worterbuch der Deutschen Umgangssprache. . .*.v.2 p.620*

Pontormo: Paintings. . . . .*.v.1 p.744*

The Poor Christ of Bomba. . . . .*.v.2 p.544*

Poor Dancer's Almanac: Managing Life and Work in the Performing Arts. . . . .*.v.1 p.38*

The Poor in the Middle Ages: An Essay in Social History. . . . .*.v.6 p.576*

The Poor Indians: British Missionaries, Native Americans, and Colonial Sensibility. . . . .*.v.6 p.686*

Poor Kids in a Rich Country: America's Children in Comparative Perspective. . . . .*.v.4 p.756*

Poor Murderer: A Play. . . . .*.v.2 p.783*

Poor Things. . . . .*.v.2 p.347*

Poor White. . . . .*.v.2 p.57*

Pop. 1280. . . . .*.v.2 p.125*

Pop Art: A Continuing History. . . . .*.v.1 p.679*

Pop Culture Latin America!: Media, Arts, and Lifestyle. . . . .*.v.4 p.712*

The Pop Image: Prints and Multiples. . . . .*.v.1 p.753*

Pop Music - Technology and Creativity: Trevor Horn and the Digital Revolution. . . . .*.v.1 p.275, p.276*

The Pop, Rock, and Soul Reader: Histories and Debates. *.v.1 p.266*

The Pop World of Henry James: From Fairy Tales to Science Fiction. . . . .*.v.2 p.46*

Pope Pius XII and the Holocaust. . . . .*.v.3 p.86*

Pope: Selected Poetry. . . . .*.v.2 p.257*

Popery and Politics in England, 1660-1688. *.v.3 p.94, p.105, p.121*

The Popes Against the Jews: The Vatican's Role in the Rise of Modern Anti-Semitism. . . . .*.v.3 p.59, p.60*

The Popes and European Revolution. . . . .*.v.1 p.572*

Popes and Politics: Reform, Resentment, and the Holocaust. . . . .*.v.1 p.573*

The Popes and the Papacy in the Early Middle Ages, 476-752. . . . .*.v.1 p.574*

Pope. . . . .*.v.2 p.257*

The Popish Plot. . . . .*.v.3 p.105, p.121*

Popol Vuh: Las Antiguas Historias Del Quiche (Indigenous Legends). . . . .*.v.2 p.676*

Title Index

Popol Vuh: The Sacred Book of the Ancient Quiche Maya: Spanish Version of the Original Maya. *v.2 p.676*

Poppa Psychology: The Role of Fathers in Children's Mental Well Being. *v.5 p.642*

Popper Selections. *v.1 p.446*

Popper. *v.1 p.446*

Pop. *v.1 p.678*

Popular American Literature of the 19th Century. *v.2 p.20*

Popular Arts of Mexico: 1850-1950. . . . .*v.1 p.684*

Popular Autocracy in Greece, 1936-41: A Political Biography of General Loannis Metaxas. *v.3 p.196*

Popular Bohemia: Modernism and Urban Culture in Nineteenth-Century Paris. *v.3 p.158*

Popular Cinema in Brazil: 1930-2001. . . . .*v.3 p.266*

Popular Culture: An Introduction. *v.3 p.367*

Popular Culture and Elite Culture in France, 1400-1750. .*v.3 p.146*

Popular Culture and High Culture: An Analysis and Evaluation of Taste. *v.3 p.371*

Popular Culture and Performance in the Victorian City. .*v.6 p.763*

Popular Culture and Political Change in Modern America. *v.3 p.367*

Popular Culture in Medieval Cairo. *v.6 p.635, p.636*

Popular Culture in Seventeenth Century England. *v.3 p.102, p.104, p.105, p.129*

Popular Culture in the Age of White Flight: Fear and Fantasy in Suburban Los Angeles. *v.6 p.535, p.548*

Popular Film and Television Comedy. *v.6 p.313*

The Popular Front and Central Europe: The Dilemmas of French Impotence 1918-1940. . . . .*v.3 p.155*

A Popular History of Minnesota. *v.3 p.522*

Popular Justice: A History of American Criminal Justice. *v.6 p.245*

Popular Justice: Presidential Prestige and Executive Success in the Supreme Court. *v.4 p.540, p.541*

Popular Literatures in Africa. *v.2 p.751*

Popular Movements and Political Change in Mexico. *v.3 p.292, v.4 p.711*

Popular Music and National Culture in Israel. *v.1 p.300*

Popular Music in America: And the Beat Goes On. . .*v.1 p.267*

Popular Music in France from Chanson to Techno: Culture, Identity and Society. *v.1 p.267*

Popular Music in Theory: An Introduction. *v.1 p.273*

Popular Music on Screen: From Hollywood Musical to Music Video. *v.1 p.256*

Popular Music: The Key Concepts. *v.1 p.162, p.274*

Popular Musics of the Non-Western World: An Introductory Survey. *v.1 p.271, p.283*

Popular Music. *v.1 p.269*

Popular Piety in Late Medieval England: The Diocese of Salisbury, 1250-1550. . . . .*v.1 p.608*

Popular Political Support in Urban China. *v.4 p.619*

Popular Politics and Political Culture in Upper Canada, 1800-1850. . . . .*v.3 p.544, p.545*

Popular Puppet Theatre in Europe, 1800-1914. . .*v.1 p.93, p.97*

Popular Recreations English Society. . . .*v.3 p.92, p.107, p.109*

Popular Religion in China: The Imperial Metaphor. . .*v.1 p.539*

Popular Religion in the Middle Ages. *v.6 p.570*

Popular Songs and Ballads of Han China. *v.6 p.209*

Popular Titles and Subtitles of Musical Compositions. .*v.1 p.159*

Popular Uprisings in the Philippines, 1840-1940. . . .*v.6 p.180*

Popular Victorian Women Writers. *v.2 p.174*

Popular Voices in Latin American Catholicism. *v.3 p.360*

Popularizing Pennsylvania: Henry W. Shoemaker and the Progressive Uses of Folklore and History. *v.2 p.16*

Population and Economy: From the Traditional to the Modern World. *v.3 p.43*

Population and Technological Change: A Study of Long-Term Trends. *v.3 p.42*

Population Biology: Concepts and Models.*v.5 p.94, p.189, p.502*

Population Biology. *v.5 p.189*

Population Dynamics in Ecological Space and Time. .*v.5 p.188*

Population Dynamics: New Approaches and Synthesis. *v.5 p.143, p.183, p.188*

Population Dynamics of a Philippine Rain Forest People: The San Ildefonso Agta. *v.4 p.39*

Population Ecology: A Unified Study of Animals and Plants. *v.5 p.183, p.187,v.6 p.290*

Population Ecology: An Introduction to Computer Simulations. *v.5 p.93, p.183, p.187*

Population Ecology: First Principles. *v.5 p.171*

Population Ecology of Individuals. *v.5 p.184, p.189*

Population Harvesting: Demographic Models of Fish, Forest, and Animal Resources. *v.5 p.184, p.188, p.212, p.215*

The Population History of Britain and Ireland 1500-1750. . . . .*v.3 p.43, p.99, p.134*

The Population History of England, 1541-1871: A Reconstruction. *v.3 p.90*

The Population History of England, 1541-1871. . . . .*v.3 p.43*

Population in History: Essays in Historical Demography. .*v.3 p.40*

Population Malthus: His Life and Times. *v.4 p.221*

The Population of Palestine: Population Statistics of the Late Ottoman Period and the Mandate. *v.6 p.610, p.611*

Population Parameters: Estimation for Ecological Models. *v.5 p.100*

Population, Poverty, and Politics in Middle East Cities. .*v.6 p.716*

Population Research Center, RAND Corporation. *v.5 p.580, p.581*

Population: The First Essay. *v.4 p.222*

Populism, Progressivism, and the Transformation of Nebraska Politics, 1885-1915. . . . .*v.3 p.524*

Populist Seduction in Latin America: The Ecuadorian Experience. *v.3 p.333*

Porgy. *v.2 p.81*

Porn Studies. *v.4 p.749, v.6 p.317*

Pornocopia: Porn, Sex, Technology and Desire. *v.6 p.317*

Pornography and Sexual Aggression. *v.4 p.748*

Pornography: Men Possessing Women.*v.4 p.747, v.6 p.447, p.469*

The Pornography of Meat. *v.6 p.447*

Pornography, Sex and Feminism. *v.6 p.436, p.462*

Port Cities and Intruders: The Swahili Coast, India, and Portugal in the Early Modern Era. *v.6 p.156*

The Port Jews of Habsburg Trieste: Absolutist Politics and Enlightenment Culture. *v.3 p.58, p.183*

The Portable Beat Reader. *v.2 p.20*

The Portable Charles Lamb. *v.2 p.298*

Portable Conrad. *v.2 p.341*

Portable D. H. Lawrence. *v.2 p.363, p.364*

The Portable Dorothy Parker. *v.2 p.110*

The Portable Enlightenment Reader. *v.3 p.72*

The Portable Graham Greene. *v.2 p.351*

The Portable Hawthorne. *v.2 p.41*

The Portable Henry James. *v.2 p.44*

The Portable Jack Kerouac. *v.2 p.93*

The Portable James Joyce. *v.2 p.359*

The Portable Mark Twain. *v.2 p.35*

The Portable Matthew Arnold. *v.2 p.265*

Portable Medieval Reader. *v.6 p.555*

The Portable Mentor: Expert Guide to a Successful Career in Psychology. *v.5 p.676*

The Portable Milton. *v.2 p.254, p.255*

The Portable Oscar Wilde. *v.2 p.322*

The Portable Petrarch. *v.2 p.706*

The Portable Twentieth-Century Russian Reader. . . .*v.2 p.794*

Portable Veblen. *v.4 p.210, p.211*

The Portable Victorian and Edwardian Poets. *v.2 p.198*

The Portable Voltaire. *v.2 p.485*

The Portrait in Britain and America with a Dictionary of Portrait Painters, 1680-1914. . . . .*v.1 p.666*

Portrait in Brownstone. *v.2 p.55*

Portrait in Sepia: A Novel. *v.2 p.679*

Portrait of a Greek Mountain Village. *v.4 p.702*

The Portrait of a Lady: An Authoritative Text, Henry James and the Novel, Reviews and Criticism. *v.2 p.44*

Portrait of a Marriage: Vita Sackville-West and Harold Nicolson. *v.2 p.380*

Portrait of America: A Cultural History of the Federal Writers' Project. *v.3 p.374*

Portrait of America, Vol. I. *v.3 p.380*

Portrait of American Jews: The Last Half of the Twentieth Century. *v.4 p.764*

Portrait of an Age: Victorian England. *v.3 p.117, p.130,v.6 p.736, p.751*

Portrait of an Unknown Man: Manuel Azana and Modern Spain. *v.3 p.241*

Portrait of Liszt: By Himself and His Contemporaries. *v.1 p.207, p.337*

A Portrait of Mendelssohn. *v.1 p.195, p.340*

Portrait of Mr. B: Photographs of George Balanchine with an Essay. *v.1 p.9*

Portrait of Percy Grainger. *v.1 p.214, p.327*

Portrait of the Artist as a Young Ape. *v.2 p.511*

Portrait of the Artist As a Young Dog. *v.2 p.386*

A Portrait of the Artist As a Young Man: Text, Criticism, and Notes. *v.2 p.359*

A Portrait of the Artist as a Young Man. *v.2 p.359*

Portraits by Ingres: Image of an Epoch. *v.1 p.748*

Portraits of African American Life since 1865. . . .*v.6 p.7, p.8*

Portraits of Palestinian Women. *v.6 p.619*

Portraits of Pioneers in Psychology, Vol. 4. . . . . .*v.5 p.597*

Portraits of the Earth: A Mathematician Looks at Maps. *v.5 p.500, p.501*

Portraits of the Japanese Workplace: Labor Movements, Workers, and Managers. *v.4 p.122*

Portraits of the Whiteman: Linguistic Play and Cultural Symbols among the Western Apache. *v.4 p.20, v.6 p.690*

Portraiture. *v.1 p.708*

Portugal and Africa. *v.6 p.55, p.56*

Portugal in Africa: The Last Hundred Years. *v.6 p.56*

[e] Portuguese: An Essential Grammar. *v.2 p.637, p.638*

Portuguese: An Essential Grammar. *v.2 p.637*

The Portuguese Empire in Asia, 1500-1700: A Political and Economic History. *v.3 p.73*

The Portuguese in India. *v.6 p.155*

The Portuguese Princess and Other Stories. *v.2 p.785*

A Portuguese Rural Society. *v.4 p.701*

Portuguese Seaborne Empire. *v.3 p.73*

Portuguese Verbs and Essentials of Grammar. *v.2 p.638*

A Portuguese-English Dictionary. *v.2 p.638*

The Position of the Chief in the Modern Political System of Ashanti: A Study of the Influence of Contemporary Social Changes on Ashanti Political Institutions. .*v.6 p.69, p.70*

Positioning Yoga. *v.4 p.793*

The Positive Hero in Russian Literature. *v.2 p.799*

Positive Impact Forestry: A Sustainable Approach to Managing Woodlands. *v.5 p.39*

Positive Pleasures: Early Photography and Humor. . .*v.1 p.701*

The Positive Theory of Capital. *v.4 p.234*

Positivism and Sociology: Explaining Social Life. . . .*v.4 p.680*

Positivism in Mexico. *v.1 p.444*

Possessing Culture: Museums, Anthropology and German New Guinea. *v.4 p.47*

Possessing the Past: Treasures from the National Palace Museum, Taipei. *v.1 p.693*

Possession: A Romance. *v.2 p.332*

Possessions : roman. *v.2 p.531*

Possessions: A Novel. *v.2 p.531*

Possibilities: Essays on the State of the Novel. . . .*v.2 p.189*

The Possibility of Altruism. *v.1 p.501*

A Possible India: Essays in Political Criticism. .*v.6 p.158, p.159*

Possible Lives. *v.6 p.570*

Possible Scotlands: Walter Scott and the Story of Tomorrow. *v.2 p.307*

Post Industrial Lives: Roles and Relationships in the 21st Century. *v.4 p.733*

Post Keynesian Econometrics, Microeconomics and the Theory of the Firm: Beyond Keynes, Vol. 1. . . . .*v.4 p.199, p.232*

[e] Post Keynesian Price Theory. *v.4 p.242*

Post Keynesian Price Theory. *v.4 p.233*

Post War Reconstruction in Central America: Lessons from El Salvador, Guatemala and Nicaragua. *v.3 p.301*

The Post-Boom in Spanish American Fiction. *v.2 p.665*

Postcolonial Biblical Criticism: Interdisciplinary
    Intersections. *v.1 p.617, p.618*

The Post-Colonial Condition of African Literature. . .*v.2 p.751*

Postcolonial Discourse and Changing Cultural Contexts: Theory
    and Criticism. *v.2 p.728*

Postcolonial Identities in Africa. *v.4 p.582, p.613*

Postcolonial Images: Studies in North African Film. . *v.6 p.333*

Postcolonial Jane Austen. *v.2 p.269*

The Post-Colonial Literature of Lusophone Africa. . .*v.2 p.693*

Postcolonial Literatures: Achebe, Ngugi, Desai,
    Walcott. *v.2 p.752*

Post-Colonial Literatures in English: Australia,
    1970-1992. . . . .*v.2 p.741*

Post-Colonial Literatures in English: General Theoretical
    Comparative, 1970-1993. . . . .*v.2 p.727*

Post-Colonial Literatures in English: Southeast Asia, New
    Zealand, and the Pacific, 1970-1992. . . . .*v.2 p.742, p.761*

Postcolonial Passages: Handbook of Contemporary
    History-Writing on India. *v.6 p.146*

Post-Colonial Plays: An Anthology. *v.2 p.727*

Postcolonial Studies: A Materialist Critique. *v.2 p.571*

The Post-Colonial Studies Reader. . . . *v.2 p.571, p.572, p.727*

Postcolonial Theory: A Critical Introduction. *v.2 p.727*

Post-Colonial Theory and English Literature: A Reader.*v.2 p.727*

Postcolonial Theory: Contexts, Practices, Politics. . .*v.2 p.728*

Postcolonial Vietnam: New Histories of the National
    Past. *v.6 p.166*

Postcolonialism Meets Economics. *v.4 p.211, p.271*

Postcommunism and the Theory of Democracy. . . .*v.4 p.597*

Postcommunist Belarus. *v.4 p.599*

Post-Communist Transition: Emerging Pluralism in
    Hungary. *v.4 p.595*

The Postdivorce Family: Children, Parenting, and
    Society. *v.5 p.640*

Posterior Analytics. *v.1 p.426*

Posters American Style. *v.1 p.718*

Post-Genome Informatics. *v.5 p.145, p.146*

Postgraduate Studies in the Biological Sciences: A Researcher's
    Companion. *v.5 p.244*

Posthumous Diary: Diario Postumo. *v.2 p.719*

The Posthumous Memoirs of Bras Cubas. *v.2 p.692*

The Posthumous Papers of the Pickwick Club. by Charles
    Dickens. *v.2 p.283*

Post-Keynesian Economics. *v.4 p.232*

The Postman Always Rings Twice. *v.2 p.64*

Postmetropolis: Studies of Cities and Regions. . . .*v.6 p.721*

Post-Modern Algebra. *v.5 p.474*

Postmodern Currents: Art and Artists in the Age of Electronic
    Media. *v.1 p.771*

Postmodern Geographies: The Reassertion of Space in Critical
    Social Theory. *v.6 p.721*

Postmodern Journeys: Film and Culture 1996-1998. . *v.6 p.332*

Postmodern Moments in Modern Economics. *v.4 p.196*

Postmodern Music/Postmodern Thought. . . . *v.1 p.208, p.209*

Postmodern Paletos: Immigration, Democracy and Globalization
    in Spanish Narrative and Film, 1950-2000. *v.2 p.641, v.6 p.339*

The Postmodern Presence: Readings on Postmodernism in
    American Culture and Society. *v.3 p.370*

The Postmodern Presidency: Bill Clinton's Legacy in U. S.
    Politics. *v.3 p.479*

A Postmodern Psychology of Asian Americans: Creating
    Knowledge of a Racial Minority. *v.6 p.122*

Postmodern Semiotics: Material Culture and the Forms of
    Postmodern Life. *v.6 p.709*

The Postmodern Urban Condition. *v.6 p.709*

Postmodern Wetlands: Culture, History, Ecology. . . .*v.5 p.53*

Postmodernism and Performance. *v.1 p.86, p.135*

Post-Modernism and the Social Sciences: Insights, Inroads, and
    Intrusions. *v.4 p.682*

The Postnational Constellation: Political Essays. . . .*v.4 p.494*

Post-Olympism?: Questioning Sport in the Twenty-First
    Century. *v.4 p.818, p.846, p.888, p.892*

Post-Prairie: An Anthology of New Poetry. *v.2 p.731*

The Post-Revolutionary Self: Politics and Psyche in France,
    1750-1850. . . . .*v.3 p.148, p.149*

Postsocialist Cinema in Post-Mao China: The Cultural
    Revolution after the Cultural
    Revolution. *v.6 p.207, p.328, p.334*

Post-Soul Black Cinema: Discontinuities, Innovations and
    Breakpoints, 1970-1995. . . . .*v.6 p.15, p.38*

Post-Soul Nation: The Explosive, Contradictory, Triumphant,
    and Tragic 1980s As Experienced by African
    Americans (Previously Known As Blacks and Before That
    Negroes). *v.6 p.5, p.38*

Post-Soviet Women: From the Baltic to Central Asia. .*v.3 p.229*

Poststructuralism: A Very Short Introduction. *v.1 p.512*

Postsuburban California: The Transformation of Orange County
    since World War II. *v.6 p.713*

Post-Suburbia: Government and Politics in the Edge
    Cities. *v.4 p.544*

Post-Totalitarian Spanish Fiction. *v.2 p.642*

Post-Translational Modification of Proteins: Tools for Functional
    Proteomics. *v.5 p.116*

Posttraumatic Stress Disorder: Acute and Long-Term Responses
    to Trauma and Disaster. *v.4 p.699*

Postwar German Literature: A Critical Introduction. .*v.2 p.590*

Post-War Protection of Human Rights in Bosnia and
    Herzegovina. *v.4 p.513*

Pot Luck. *v.2 p.505*

Potiki. *v.2 p.746*

The Potosi Mita, 1573-1700: Compulsory Indian Labor in the
    Andes. *v.3 p.323*

A Potpourri of Physics Teaching Ideas. *v.5 p.563*

Pots of Promise: Mexicans and Pottery at Hull-House,
    1920-40. . . . .*v.1 p.808*

The Potter's Art. *v.1 p.807*

The Potter's Brush: The Kenzan Style in Japanese
    Ceramics. *v.1 p.808, p.809*

The Potter's Complete Book of Clay and Glazes: A
    Comprehensive Guide to Formulating, Mixing, Applying and
    Firing Clay Bodies and Glazes. *v.1 p.807*

Pottery Analysis: A Sourcebook. *v.1 p.808*

Pottery by American Indian Women: The Legacy of
    Generations. *v.1 p.808, v.6 p.679*

Pottery in Archaeology. *v.4 p.7*

The Pottery of Zia Pueblo. *v.1 p.808*

Pottery, Politics, Art: George Ohr and the Brothers Kirkpatrick. *v.1 p.808*

Pounamu Pounamu. *v.2 p.746*

The Pound Era. *v.2 p.111*

Pound, Yeats, Eliot and the Modernist Movement. *v.2 p.72, p.112, p.327*

Pounders of Grain: A History of Women, Work, and Politics in Mozambique. *v.6 p.76*

Pound's Cantos Declassified. *v.2 p.111*

Pound's Cavalcanti: An Edition of the Translations, Notes and Essays. *v.2 p.702*

Poussiere Sur la Ville. *v.2 p.541*

Poverty and Charity in Medieval Islam: Mamluk Egypt, 1250-1517. . . . .*v.6 p.636*

Poverty and Charity in the Jewish Community of Medieval Egypt. *v.6 p.596, p.635*

Poverty and Compassion: The Moral Imagination of the Late Victorians. *v.6 p.745, p.766*

Poverty and Democracy: Self-Help and Political Participation in Third World Cities. *v.6 p.716*

Poverty and Discrimination. *v.4 p.266*

Poverty and Famines: An Essay on Entitlement and Deprivation. *v.4 p.266*

Poverty and Place: Ghettos, Barrios, and the American City. *v.4 p.771*

Poverty in Eighteenth-Century Spain: The Women and Children of the Inclusa. *v.3 p.241*

The Poverty of Affluence: A Psychological Analysis of Life in the Consumer Society. *v.5 p.585*

The Poverty of Philosophy. *v.4 p.218*

The Poverty of the Linnaean Hierarchy: A Philosophical Study of Biological Taxonomy. *v.5 p.204*

Powder Metallurgy of Iron and Steel. *v.5 p.736*

Power and Civil Society in Pakistan. *v.6 p.162*

Power and Communication Cables: Theory and Applications. *v.5 p.723*

Power and Community: Organizational and Cultural Responses to AIDS. *v.6 p.378*

Power and Democracy in America. *v.4 p.767*

Power and Everyday Life: The Lives of Working Women in Nineteenth-Century Brazil. *v.3 p.336*

Power and Governance in a Partially Globalized World. *v.4 p.663*

Power and Imagination: City-States in Renaissance Italy. *v.3 p.200*

Power and Interdependence. *v.4 p.626*

Power and Its Disguises: Anthropological Perspectives on Politics. *v.4 p.34*

Power and Morality. *v.4 p.484, p.770*

Power and Negotiation. *v.4 p.646*

Power and Peace: The Diplomacy of John Foster Dulles. *v.3 p.475*

Power and Penury: Government, Technology and Science in Philip II's Spain. *v.3 p.239*

Power and Persuasion: Fiestas and Social Control in Rural Mexico. *v.3 p.266, v.4 p.773*

Power and Persuasion: Ideology and Rhetoric in Communist Yugoslavia, 1944-1953. . . . .*v.3 p.247*

Power and Pluralism in American Cities: Researching the Urban Laboratory. *v.4 p.544*

Power and Prejudice: The Politics and Diplomacy of Racial Discrimination. *v.3 p.78*

Power and Privilege: A Theory of Social Stratification. .*v.4 p.722*

Power and Profit: The Merchant in Medieval Europe. .*v.6 p.558*

Power and Prudence: The Presidency of George H. W. Bush. *v.3 p.479, p.484*

Power and Punishment in Scott's Novels. *v.2 p.306*

Power and Purity: Cathar Heresy in Medieval Italy. . .*v.3 p.199*

Power and Purpose: U. S. Policy Toward Russia after the Cold War. *v.3 p.388*

Power and Responsibility: The Life and Times of Theodore Roosevelt. *v.3 p.472*

Power and Society: Greater New York at the Turn of the Century. *v.3 p.490, p.491,v.6 p.712*

Power and Society in Contemporary Peru. . . .*v.3 p.328, p.329*

The Power and the Glory. *v.2 p.350*

Power and the Pursuit of Peace: Theory and Practice in the History of Relations Between States. *v.4 p.649*

Power and Violence in the Colonial City: Oruro from the Mining Renaissance to the Rebellion of Tupac Amaru (1740-1782). *v.3 p.325*

Power at Play: Sports and the Problem of Masculinity. .*v.4 p.745*

The Power Broker: Robert Moses and the Fall of New York. *v.6 p.711*

Power by Design: Constitution-Making in Nationalist China. *v.4 p.621*

Power Control Circuits Manual. *v.5 p.709*

Power Electronic Systems: Theory and Design. *v.5 p.723*

Power Electronics: Circuits, Devices and Applications. *v.5 p.724*

Power Electronics Handbook. *v.5 p.709*

The Power Electronics Handbook. *v.5 p.709*

Power Elite. *v.4 p.724, p.725*

Power from Margins: Incorporation of Dominicans in New York City. *v.6 p.544, p.545, p.550*

Power from Wind: A History of Windmill Technology. .*v.5 p.709*

Power, Gender and Christian Mysticism. .*v.6 p.459, p.560, p.571*

Power Generation and the Environment. *v.5 p.704, p.709*

Power Golf for Women: How to Hit Longer and Straighter from Tee to Green. *v.4 p.836, p.861*

Power in Africa: An Essay in Political Interpretation. *v.4 p.498, p.611*

Power in Movement: Social Movements, Collective Action and Politics. *v.4 p.713*

[e] Power in Practice: Adult Education and the Struggle for Knowledge and Power in Society. *v.4 p.319*

Power in the Party: The Organization of Power and Central-Republican Relations in the CPSU. *v.4 p.508, p.579, p.597, p.598, p.599*

Power Laws, Scale-Free Networks and Genome Biology. *v.5 p.127, p.128*

The Power of Ethical Persuasion: Winning Through Understanding at Work and at Home. *v.4 p.74*

Power of Feminist Art: The American Movement of the 1970s, History and Impact. *v.6 p.472*

The Power of God Against the Guns of Government: Religious Upheaval in Mexico at the Turn of the Nineteenth Century. *v.3 p.289*

The Power of Gold: The History of an Obsession. .*v.4 p.94, p.99*

The Power of Identity: Politics in a New Key. *v.5 p.643*

The Power of Images in the Age of Augustus. *v.3 p.29*

The Power of Images: Studies in the History and Theory of Response. *v.1 p.702*

The Power of Large Numbers: Population, Politics and Gender in Nineteenth-Century France. *v.3 p.53, p.148*

The Power of Legitimacy: Assessing the Role of Norms in Crisis Bargaining. *v.4 p.649*

The Power of Many: How the Living Web Is Transforming Politics, Business and Everyday Life. *v.4 p.425*

The Power of Minds at Work: Leveraging the Power of Organizational Intelligence. *v.4 p.78*

The Power of News: The History of Reuters. *v.4 p.403*

The Power of Persuasion: How We're Bought and Sold. *v.5 p.587, p.648*

The Power of Place: Urban Landscapes As Public History. *v.6 p.713*

The Power of Portfolios: What Children Can Teach Us about Learning and Assessment. *v.4 p.286, p.347, p.363*

The Power of Projections: How Maps Reflect Global Politics and History. *v.4 p.385*

The Power of Reinforcement. *v.5 p.610*

The Power of Steam: An Illustrated History of the World's Steam Age. *v.5 p.391*

The Power of the American Presidency, 1789-2000. . .*v.4 p.526*

📱 The Power of the Gun: The Emergence of Modern Chinese Warlordism. *v.6 p.190*

The Power of the Powerless: Citizens Against the State in Central Eastern Europe. *v.3 p.189*

The Power of the Press: The Birth of American Political Reporting. *v.4 p.404*

The Power of Their Ideas: Lessons from America from a Small School in Harlem. *v.4 p.328*

Power, Patronage and Political Violence: State Building on a Brazilian Frontier, 1822-1889. . . . .*v.3 p.335*

Power Play: Sport, the Media and Popular Culture. *v.4 p.814, p.898, p.901*

Power, Politics and People: The Collected Essays of C. Wright Mills. *v.4 p.769*

Power, Politics and the Olympic Games. *v.4 p.846, p.892*

The Power Press: Its Impact on America and What You Can Do about It. *v.4 p.404*

Power, Profit and Protest: Australian Social Movements and Globalisation. *v.4 p.710*

Power, Racism and Privilege: Race Relations in Theoretical and Sociohistorical Perspectives. *v.4 p.729*

Power Rules: The Evolution of NATO's Conventional Force Posture. *v.4 p.639, p.654*

Power Sharing: Language, Rank, Gender and Social Space in Pohnpei, Micronesia. *v.4 p.21*

Power System Analysis and Design. *v.5 p.723*

Power System Operations and Electricity Markets. *v.5 p.360, p.723*

Power System Stability and Control. *v.5 p.724*

Power Systems Analysis. *v.5 p.724*

Power Tennis Training. *v.4 p.864*

Power, Terror, Peace, and War: America's Grand Strategy in a World at Risk. *v.4 p.560, p.564, p.642*

Power to the People: How the Coming Energy Revolution Will Transform an Industry, Change Our Lives, and Maybe Even Save the Planet. *v.5 p.362, p.369, p.709*

Power to the People: Sunlight to Electriciy Using Solar Cells. *v.5 p.723*

Power, Trust, and Meaning: Essays in Sociological Theory and Analysis. *v.4 p.681*

Power, Vol. 3. . . . .*v.1 p.458*

Power Without Force: The Political Capacity of Nation States. *v.4 p.498*

Power Without Responsibility: How Congress Abuses the People Through Delegation. *v.4 p.532*

The Power-Conflict Story: A Dynamic Model of Interstate Rivalry. *v.4 p.626, p.647*

Powerdown: Options and Actions for a Post-Carbon World. *v.4 p.62*

Powerful Classroom Management Strategies: Motivating Students to Learn. *v.4 p.283*

Powerful Classroom Stories from Accomplished Teachers: Stories from the Classrooms of Accomplished Teachers. *v.4 p.338, p.348*

Powerful Principles of Instruction. *v.4 p.349*

Powerful Proposals: How to Give Your Business the Winning Edge. *v.4 p.174*

Powerful Reforms with Shallow Roots: Improving America's Urban Schools. *v.4 p.314, p.315*

Powerhouse Marketing Plans: 14 Outstanding Real-Life Plans and What You Can Learn from Them to Supercharge Your Own Campaigns. *v.4 p.134*

Powering Up: Learning to Teach Well with Technology. *v.4 p.347, p.351*

PowerPoint Advanced Presentation Techniques. . . .*v.4 p.174*

The Powers of Heaven and Earth: New and Selected Poems. *v.2 p.103*

Powers of Horror: An Essay on Abjection. *v.2 p.571*

Powers of the Press: Newspapers, Power and the Public in Nineteenth-Century England. *v.6 p.738*

The Powers That Be. *v.4 p.410*

Powersharing: White House-Cabinet Relations in the Modern Presidency. *v.4 p.528*

Pox Americana: The Great Smallpox Epidemic of 1775-1782. . . . .*v.5 p.510, p.532*

PR!: A Social History of Spin. *v.4 p.428, p.429*

Practical Applications of Radioactivity and Nuclear Radiations. *v.5 p.740*

A Practical Approach to Microarray Data Analysis. *v.5 p.103, p.110*

A Practical Approach to Occupational and Environmental Medicine. *v.5 p.535*

Practical Aspects of Interview and Interrogation. . . .*v.6 p.267*

📱 The Practical Bioinformatician. *v.5 p.99*

Practical Cinematography. *v.6 p.349*

A Practical Companion to the Constitution: How the Supreme Court Has Ruled on Issues from Abortion to Zoning. *v.4 p.454*

Practical Digital Electronics. *v.5 p.722*

Practical Ecology for Planners, Developers, and Citizens. *v.1 p.797*

A Practical Guide for the Law Enforcement and Security Manager: A Theoretical and Experiential Approach. *v.6 p.265, p.266*

Practical Guide to Etching and Other Intaglio Printmaking Techniques. *v.1 p.759*

Practical Guide to Experimental Design. *v.5 p.683*

Practical Guide to Foreign Direct Investment in the European Union. *v.4 p.60*

A Practical Guide to Graduate Research. *v.5 p.409*

A Practical Guide to Linux Commands, Editors, and Shell Programming. *v.5 p.348, p.349*

A Practical Guide to Vertebrate Mechanics. *v.5 p.157*

Practical HPLC Method Development. *v.5 p.269*

Practical Hydraulic Systems: Operation and Troubleshooting for Engineers and Technicians. *v.5 p.702*

A Practical Introduction to the Simulation of Molecular Systems. *v.5 p.288*

Practical Kinetography Laban. *v.1 p.48*

Practical Manual of Harmony. *v.1 p.372*

Practical Manual of Land Development. *v.5 p.685*

Practical Meta-Analysis. *v.4 p.687*

Practical Numerical Integration. *v.5 p.492*

Practical Philosophy of Sport and Physical Activity. . *v.4 p.796*

Practical Quantum Mechanics. *v.5 p.549*

Practical Research: Planning and Design. *v.5 p.409*

Practical Skills in Biomolecular Sciences. *v.5 p.127*

Practical Statistics for Experimental Biologists. *v.5 p.93*

Practical Taxonomic Computing. *v.5 p.170*

Practical UNIX and Internet Security. . *v.5 p.335, p.345, p.348*

The Practice of Behavior Therapy. *v.5 p.667*

Practice of Chinese Buddhism, 1900-1950. . . . . .*v.1 p.563*

The Practice of Cultural Studies: A Guide to the Practice and Politics of Cultural Studies. *v.4 p.699*

The Practice of Liberal Pluralism. *v.4 p.510, p.511*

The Practice of Management. *v.4 p.64*

The Practice of Poetry: Writing Exercises from Poets Who Teach. *v.2 p.577, p.578*

The Practice of Reading. *v.2 p.163*

The Practice of Research in Criminology and Criminal Justice. *v.6 p.246*

The Practice of Reservoir Engineering. *v.5 p.451*

The Practice of Sport Psychology. *v.4 p.878, v.5 p.583*

Practices of Reason: Aristotle's Nicomachean Ethics. *v.1 p.427*

Practicing Democracy: Elections and Political Culture in Imperial Germany. *v.3 p.163*

Practicing Ethnography in Law: New Dialogues, Enduring Methods. *v.4 p.25*

Practicing Multiculturalism: Affirming Diversity in Counseling and Psychology. *v.5 p.638*

Practicing New Historicism. *v.2 p.570, p.571*

Practicing Sociology in the Community: A Student's Guide. *v.4 p.675*

Praeterita. *v.2 p.305, p.306*

Pragmatic Idealism: Canadian Foreign Policy, 1945-1995. . . . .*v.3 p.541*

Pragmatic Illusions: The Presidential Politics of John F. Kennedy. *v.3 p.476*

The Pragmatic Revolt in American History: Carl Becker and Charles Beard. *v.3 p.376*

Pragmatic Women and Body Politics. *v.4 p.47*

Pragmatism: A Reader. *v.1 p.513*

Pragmatism: An Open Question. *v.1 p.513*

Pragmatism As a Principle and Method of Right Thinking: The 1903 Harvard Lectures on Pragmatism. *v.1 p.513*

Pragmatism, Old and New: Selected Writings. *v.1 p.513*

Pragmatism. *v.1 p.513*

The Prague Slav Congress of 1848. . . . .*v.3 p.188*

Prague Tales. *v.2 p.784*

Prague, the Crown of Bohemia, 1347-1437. .*v.1 p.685, v.3 p.190*

Prairie: A Natural History. *v.5 p.241*

Prairie Directory of North America: The United States and Canada. *v.5 p.233, p.240*

Prairie Liberalism: The Liberal Party in Saskatchewan, 1905-1971. . . . .*v.4 p.590*

Prairie People: A Celebration of My Homeland. . . .*v.3 p.545*

Prairie Populism: The Fate of Agrarian Radicalism in Kansas, Nebraska, and Iowa, 1880-1892. . . . .*v.3 p.522*

Prairie Voices: Iowa's Pioneering Women. *v.3 p.522*

The Prairie West to 1905: A Canadian Sourcebook. . *v.3 p.545*

Prairie. *v.2 p.35*

PrairyErth: A Deep Map. *v.6 p.698*

The Praise of Folly. *v.2 p.623*

Praise of Theory: Speeches and Essays. *v.1 p.507*

Praises to a Formless God: Nirguni Texts from North India. *v.6 p.151, p.152*

Praisesong for the Widow. *v.2 p.768*

Prater Violet. *v.2 p.356*

Praxis and Method: A Sociological Dialogue with Lukacs, Gramsci and the Early Frankfurt School. *v.4 p.685*

Prayer: A Study in the History and Psychology of Religion. *v.1 p.654*

Prayers in Stone: Greek Architectural Sculpture 600-100 BC. *v.1 p.776*

Prayers in the Precincts: The Christian Right in the 1998 Elections. *v.4 p.511*

Praying for Power: Buddhism and the Formation of Gentry Society in Late-Ming China. *v.6 p.186*

Praying Mantis. *v.2 p.623*

Preacher: Billy Sunday and Big-Time American Evangelism. *v.1 p.648*

The Preacher King: Martin Luther King, Jr. and the Word That Moved America. *v.1 p.649*

Preacher Woman Sings the Blues: The Autobiographies of Nineteenth-Century African American Evangelists. *v.1 p.648*

Preachers, Peasants and Politics in South East Africa, 1835-1880: African Communities in Natal, Pondoland and Zululand. *v.1 p.611*

Precalculus Mathematics: A Graphing Approach. . . .*v.5 p.485*

Precalculus. *v.5 p.485, p.486*

Pre-capitalist economic formations. *v.4 p.236*

The Precarious Balance: English Government and Society, 1450-1640. . . . .*v.3 p.101*

Precarious Balance: Hong Kong Between China and Britain, 1842-1992. . . . .*v.6 p.205*

Precarious Dependencies: Gender, Class and Domestic Service in Bolivia. *v.3 p.323*

The Precarious Republic: Political Modernization in Lebanon. *v.6 p.605*

Pre-Christian Gnosticism: A Survey of the Proposed Evidences. *v.1 p.647*

Pre-Christian Ireland: From the First Settlers to the Early Celts. *v.3 p.136*

Precios Del Maíz y Crisis Agrícolas en México (1708-1810). *v.3 p.271*

Los Precios del Trigo en La Historia Colonial de México. *v.3 p.271*

Precious Bane. *v.2 p.386*

The Precious Garland and the Song of the Four Mindfulnesses. *v.1 p.564*

Precious Heritage: The Status of Biodiversity in the United States. *v.6 p.286, p.292*

The Precious Pearl. *v.1 p.557*

The Precise Parallel New Testament. *v.1 p.613*

Preclassic Maya Architecture at Cuello, Belize. *v.3 p.297*

Precolonial and Postcolonial Drama and Theatre in Africa. *v.1 p.130*

Precolonial India in Practice: Society, Region, and Identity in Medieval Andhra. *v.6 p.162*

The Preconceptions of Economic Science. *v.4 p.250*

The Pre-Confederation Premiers: Ontario Government Leaders, 1841-1867. . . . .*v.3 p.544*

The Pre-Conquest Church in England. *v.1 p.609*

The Predator's Ball: How the Junk Bond Machine Staked the Corporate Raiders. *v.4 p.99*

Predatory States: Operation Condor and Covert War in Latin America. *v.4 p.660*

Predecessors of Adam Smith: The Growth of British Economic Thought. *v.4 p.212*

A Preface to Chaucer: Studies in Medieval Perspectives. .*v.2 p.210*

A Preface to D. H. Lawrence. *v.2 p.364*

A Preface to Dryden. *v.2 p.247*

A Preface to Greene. *v.2 p.351*

A Preface to H. G. Wells. *v.2 p.319*

Preface to Hopkins. *v.2 p.294*

A Preface to Morals. *v.1 p.484*

A Preface to Paradise Lost: Being the Ballard Matthews Lectures Delivered at University College, North Wales 1941. . . . .*v.2 p.254*

Preface to Plato. *v.1 p.424*

A Preface to Pope. *v.2 p.257*

A Preface to Spenser. *v.2 p.215*

A Preface to the Faerie Queene. *v.2 p.214*

A Preface to Yeats. *v.2 p.326*

Prefaces to Shakespeare, Set. *v.2 p.228*

The Preference for the Primitive: Episodes in the History of Western Taste and Art. *v.1 p.703*

Pregnant Men: Practice, Theory, and Law. . . .*v.6 p.468, p.469*

Prehistoric Art in Europe. *v.1 p.669*

Prehistoric Art: The Symbolic Journey of Humankind. .*v.1 p.669*

The Prehistoric Exploration and Colonisation of the Pacific. *v.4 p.379*

Prehistoric Hunters of the High Plains. *v.4 p.10, p.11*

Prehistoric Mesoamerica: Third Edition. *v.4 p.9*

Prehistory of the Eastern Arctic. *v.4 p.11*

Prehistory of the Indo-Malaysian Archipelago. *v.4 p.13*

PreHospital Providers' Guide to Medication. *v.5 p.534*

The Pre-Islamic Middle East. *v.6 p.584*

Prejudice Across America. *v.4 p.698*

Prejudice and Your Child. *v.5 p.625, p.631*

Prejudice: Its Social Psychology. *v.5 p.649*

Prejudiced Communication: A Social Psychological Perspective. *v.4 p.698, v.5 p.621, p.622*

The Prelude, 1798-1799. . . . .*v.2 p.325*

The Prelude, 1799, 1805 and 1815. . . . .*v.2 p.325*

Prelude to Calculus. *v.5 p.485*

Prelude to Greatness: Lincoln in the 1850's. *v.3 p.425*

Prelude to Protectorate in Morocco: Precolonial Protest and Resistance, 1860-1912. . . . .*v.6 p.643*

Prelude to the Civil War: The Nullification Controversy in South Carolina 1816-1836. . . . .*v.3 p.416*

A Prelude. *v.2 p.137*

Premarital Sexuality: Attitudes, Relationships, Behavior. *v.4 p.737*

Premonitions: The Kaya Anthology of New Asian American Poetry. *v.6 p.92, p.104*

The Prentice Hall Atlas of Western Civilization. *v.4 p.399*

The Prentice Hall Encyclopedia of Model Business Plans. *v.4 p.172*

Prentice Hall Guide to English Literature. . . .*v.2 p.165, p.166*

Preoccupations: Selected Prose, 1968-1978. . . . . .*v.2 p.352*

Pre-Ottoman Turkey: A General Survey of the Material and Spiritual Culture and History, 1071-1330. . . . .*v.6 p.622*

Preparation of Alkenes: A Practical Approach. *v.5 p.294*

The Preparation of Dispersions in Liquids, Vol. 58. . .*v.5 p.283*

Preparative Chromatography Techniques: Applications in Natural Product Isolation. *v.5 p.299*

Preparative Methods of Polymer Chemistry. *v.5 p.323*

Preparing Adolescents for Life After Foster Care: The Central Role of Foster Parents. *v.4 p.758*

Preparing for Inclusive Teaching: Meeting the Challenges of Teacher Education Reform. *v.4 p.279*

Preparing for the Behavior-Based Interview: Getting the Job You Want. *v.4 p.169*

Preparing Herbarium Specimens. *v.5 p.85*

Preparing Teachers to Teach with Technology. *v.4 p.352*

Prepositions + the Collected Critical Essays: The Wesleyan Cenntenial Edition of the Complete Critical Writings of Louis Zukofsky. *v.2 p.139*

The Pre-Raphaelite Art of the Victorian Novel: Narrative
   Challenges to Visual Gendered Boundaries. *v.2 p.173, p.192*

Pre-Raphaelite Sculpture: Nature and Imagination in British
   Sculpture 1848-1914. . . . . *v.1 p.781*

The Pre-Romantic Ballet. *v.1 p.22*

The Presbyterian Controversy: Fundamentalists, Modernists, and
   Moderates. *v.1 p.588*

Presbyterian Creeds: A Guide to the Book of
   Confessions. *v.1 p.588*

Presbyterians, Their History and Beliefs. *v.1 p.588*

Preschool Education in America: The Culture of Young Children
   from the Colonial Era to the Present. *v.4 p.370*

Preschool in Three Cultures: Japan, China and the United
   States. *v.4 p.370, p.371, p.373*

Preschool Inclusion. *v.4 p.315*

Presence and Desire: Essays on Gender, Sexuality,
   Performance. *v.1 p.125, p.126, p.135*

Presence and Resistance: Postmodernism and Cultural Politics in
   Contemporary American Performance. . . . *v.1 p.86, p.112*

Presence of Mies. *v.1 p.794*

The Presence of the Present: Topics of the Day in the Victorian
   Novel. *v.2 p.173, v.6 p.755*

Present Age in British Literature. *v.2 p.178*

Present at the Creation: My Years in the State
   Department. *v.3 p.450, p.451*

Present at the Flood: How Structural Molecular Biology Came
   About. *v.5 p.126*

The Present History of West Bengal: Essays in Political
   Criticism. *v.6 p.160*

Present Indicative, Vol. 1. . . . . *v.2 p.342*

Present Knowledge in Nutrition. *v.5 p.33*

The Present State of Music in France and Italy. . . . *v.1 p.188*

The Present State of Music in Germany, The Netherlands and
   United Provinces. *v.1 p.188*

The Presentation of Self in Everyday Life. *v.4 p.694*

Presenting to Win: The Art of Telling Your Story. . . *v.4 p.174*

The Preservation of the Village: New Mexico's Hispanics and
   the New Deal. *v.6 p.535*

Preserving Cultural Landscapes in
   America. *v.1 p.812, p.821, p.822*

Preserving Eden: The Nature Conservancy. *v.5 p.82, p.179, p.221*

Preserving Intellectual Freedom: Fighting Censorship in Our
   Schools. *v.4 p.298*

Preserving Nature in the National Parks: A
   History. *v.5 p.18, p.19, v.6 p.296*

Preserving the Living Past: John C. Merriam's Legacy in the
   State and National Parks. *v.5 p.370*

Preserving the World's Great Cities: The Destruction and
   Renewal of the Historic Metropolis. *v.1 p.824*

The Presidencies of Grover Cleveland. *v.3 p.438*

The Presidencies of James A. Garfield and Chester A.
   Arthur. *v.3 p.395, p.436*

The Presidencies of William Henry Harrison and John
   Tyler. *v.3 p.417*

The Presidencies of Zachary Taylor and Millard
   Fillmore. *v.3 p.418*

The Presidency of Abraham Lincoln. *v.3 p.399*

The Presidency of Andrew Jackson. *v.3 p.416*

The Presidency of Andrew Johnson. *v.3 p.394, p.435*

The Presidency of Benjamin Harrison. *v.3 p.438*

The Presidency of Calvin Coolidge. . . *v.3 p.440, p.447, p.470*

The Presidency of Dwight D. Eisenhower. *v.3 p.477*

The Presidency of Franklin Delano Roosevelt. *v.3 p.443, p.475*

The Presidency of Franklin Pierce. *v.3 p.416, p.417*

The Presidency of George Bush. *v.3 p.471, p.472*

The Presidency of George Washington. . . . *v.3 p.414, p.417*

The Presidency of Gerald R. Ford. *v.3 p.471*

The Presidency of Harry S. Truman. *v.3 p.475*

The Presidency of Herbert C. Hoover. . *v.3 p.446, p.447, p.470*

The Presidency of James Buchanan. *v.3 p.418*

The Presidency of James Earl Carter, Jr. *v.3 p.473*

The Presidency of James K. Polk. *v.3 p.416*

The Presidency of James Madison. *v.3 p.418*

The Presidency of James Monroe. *v.3 p.416*

The Presidency of John Adams. *v.3 p.416*

The Presidency of John F. Kennedy. *v.3 p.441, p.471*

The Presidency of John Quincy Adams. *v.3 p.417*

The Presidency of Lyndon B. Johnson. *v.3 p.466*

The Presidency of Martin Van Buren. *v.3 p.418*

The Presidency of Richard Nixon. *v.3 p.444, p.480*

The Presidency of Rutherford B. Hayes. . . . *v.3 p.398, p.436*

The Presidency of Theodore Roosevelt. *v.3 p.471*

The Presidency of Thomas Jefferson. *v.3 p.412*

The Presidency of Warren G. Harding. . *v.3 p.445, p.450, p.481*

The Presidency of William Howard Taft. *v.3 p.468*

The Presidency of William McKinley. . . . *v.3 p.397, p.436*

The Presidency of Woodrow Wilson. *v.3 p.468*

The Presidency of Yuan Shih-K'ai: Liberalism and Dictatorship
   in Early Republican China. *v.6 p.191, p.203*

The President and Congress: Executive Hegemony at the
   Crossroads of American Government. . . . *v.4 p.528, p.532*

The President and Congress in Post-Authoritarian Chile:
   Institutional Constraints to Democratic
   Consolidation. *v.3 p.355*

The President and the Parties: The Transformation of the
   American Party System since the New Deal. . . . *v.4 p.527*

The President As Statesman: Woodrow Wilson and the
   Constitution. *v.4 p.528*

The President As World Leader. *v.4 p.527*

President Edvard Benes, Between East and West,
   1938-1948. . . . . *v.3 p.189*

President James Buchanan: A President. . . . *v.3 p.420, p.437*

President Lyndon Johnson and Soviet Communism. . *v.3 p.388*

President Makers, Eighteen Ninety-Six to Nineteen
   Nineteen. *v.3 p.442*

President Nixon: Alone in the White House. . . *v.3 p.478*

The President: Office and Powers. *v.4 p.461, p.462*

President Reagan: The Role of a Lifetime. *v.3 p.467*

President Roosevelt and the Coming of the War, 1941:
   Appearances and Realities. *v.3 p.465*

Presidential Ballots, 1836-1892. . . . . *v.4 p.556*

The Presidential Branch. *v.4 p.524*

The Presidential Campaign Film: A Critical
   History. *v.4 p.551, v.6 p.342, p.343*

Presidential Campaigns: From George Washington to George W.
   Bush. *v.3 p.377*

Presidential Candidate Images. *v.4 p.696*

Presidential Debates: Forty Years of High-Risk TV. . *v.4 p.556*

Presidential Elections 1789-2004. . . . . *v.4 p.556*

Presidential Greatness: The Image and the Man from George
   Washington to the Present. *v.3 p.377*

Presidential Impeachment. *v.4 p.462*

Presidential Leadership: From Woodrow Wilson to Harry S.
   Truman. *v.3 p.378, p.440*

Presidential Leadership: Rating the Best and the Worst in the
   White House. *v.3 p.378, p.379*

Presidential Management of Science and Technology: The
   Johnson Presidency. *v.5 p.394, p.412*

Presidential Musings from the Meridian: Reflections on the
   Nature of Geography. *v.4 p.374*

Presidential Politics and Science Policy. *v.5 p.388, p.393, p.412*

Presidential Power and the Modern Presidents: The Politics of
   Leadership from Roosevelt to Reagan. *v.3 p.378*

Presidential Power from the New Deal to the New
   Right. *v.3 p.378*

Presidential Primaries and the Dynamics of Public
   Choice. *v.4 p.556*

Presidential Saints and Sinners. *v.3 p.377*

The Presidential Veto. *v.4 p.527, p.528*

Presidential War Power. *v.4 p.462*

The Presidents: A Reference History. *v.3 p.378*

Presidents and Foreign Policy Making: From FDR to
   Reagan. *v.3 p.451*

Presidents and Prime Mininsters. *v.4 p.575*

The President's Cabinet: Gender, Power, and
   Representation. *v.4 p.526*

▢ President's Council on Physical Fitness and
   Sports. *v.4 p.783, p.789, p.794, p.890*

Presidents, First Ladies and Vice Presidents: White House
   Biographies, 1789-2001. . . . . *v.3 p.378*

The Presidents, First Ladies, and Vice Presidents: White House
   Biographies, 1789-2005. . . . . *v.3 p.378*

Presidents, Parties, and the State: A Party System Perspective on
   Democratic Regulatory Choice,
   1884-1936. . . . . *v.4 p.551, p.552, p.579*

Presidents, Prime Ministers and Governors of the
   English-Speaking Caribbean and Puerto Rico: Conversations
   and Correspondence. *v.3 p.318*

Presidents Without Parties: The Politics of Economic Reform in
   Argentina and Venezuela in the 1990s. . . *v.3 p.347, p.360*

The Presocratic Philosophers: A Critical History with a
   Selections of Texts. *v.1 p.422*

The Presocratic Philosophers. *v.1 p.421*

A Presocratics Reader: Selected Fragments and
   Testimonia. *v.1 p.421*

The Press and America: An Interpretive History of the Mass
   Media. *v.4 p.409*

ℯ The Press Effect: Politicians, Journalists, and the Stories That
   Shape the Political World. *v.4 p.404*

The Press in the Arab Middle East: A History. . . . *v.4 p.403*

Press, Revolution and Social Identities in France,
   1830-1835. . . . . *v.3 p.153*

Pressure Volume Temperature Relationship of Organic
   Compounds; a Reference Volume for Reading Directly the
   Variation of Vapor Pressure with Temperature of a
   Compound Belonging to one of the Twenty Three Cox Chart
   Families *v.5 p.286*

Prestel Dictionary of Art and Artists. *v.1 p.666*

Prester John. *v.2 p.331*

Preston's North American Trees. *v.5 p.39*

Prestressed Concrete: A Fundamental Approach. . . . *v.5 p.695*

The Pretend Indians: Images of Native Americans in the
   Movies. *v.6 p.700*

Pretty Pictures: Production Design and the History
   Film. *v.6 p.349*

Preventing Biological Warfare: The Failure of American
   Leadership. *v.4 p.563*

Preventing Early Learning Failure. *v.4 p.361*

Preventing Early School Failure: Research, Policy, and
   Practice. *v.4 p.361*

Preventing Industrial Toxic Hazards: A Guide for
   Communities. *v.5 p.366, p.373, p.376*

Preventing Violence: Research and Evidence-Based Intervention
   Strategies. *v.6 p.259*

Prevention of Alcohol Abuse. *v.5 p.673*

Prevention's Complete Book of Walking: Everything You Need
   to Know to Walk Your Way to Better Health. *v.4 p.788, p.791*

Preventive Psychology. *v.5 p.671*

Preventive Stress Management in Organizations. . . *v.5 p.581*

Prevost: Manon Lescaut. *v.2 p.481*

Présent : poèmes, 1987-1997. . . . . *v.2 p.518*

Présent passé, passé présent. *v.2 p.520*

The Price of Federalism. *v.4 p.525*

The Price of Freedom: A History of East Central Europe from
   the Middle Ages to the Present. *v.3 p.207*

The Price of Greatness: Resolving the Creativity and Madness
   Controversy. *v.5 p.654*

The Price of Indifference: Refugees and Humanitarian Action in
   the New Century. *v.4 p.667, p.670, p.671*

The Price of Loyalty: Tory Writings from the Revolutionary
   Era. *v.3 p.408*

The Price of Poverty: Money, Work, and Culture in the
   Mexican-American Barrio. *v.6 p.524, p.548*

The Price of Power: America Since 1945. . . . . . . *v.3 p.451*

The Price of Salt. *v.2 p.86, v.6 p.397*

Price Theory: A Provisional Text. *v.4 p.237*

Prices and Production. *v.4 p.234, p.238*

Prices and Quantities: A Macroeconomic Analysis. . *v.4 p.239*

Pricing Decisions and Marketing Policy. *v.4 p.144*

Pricing the Priceless Child: The Changing Social Value of
   Children. *v.4 p.735*

Pricing Theory in Post-Keynesian Economics: A Realist
   Approach. *v.4 p.232*

Prick Up Your Ears: The Biography of Joe
   Orton. *v.2 p.374, v.6 p.413*

Pride and Prejudice: A Sourcebook. *v.2 p.268*

Pride and Prejudice: A Study in Artistic Economy. . . .*v.2 p.268*

Pride and Prejudice. *v.2 p.266*

Pride Before the Fall: The Trials of Bill Gates and the End of the Microsoft Era. *v.4 p.158*

The Pride of Havana: A History of Cuban Baseball. *v.3 p.267, p.308*

Pride, Prejudice, and Politics: Roosevelt Versus Recovery, 1933-1938. . . . .*v.3 p.466*

Pride's Purge: Politics in the Puritan Revolution. *v.3 p.95, p.104, p.122*

Priest of Music: The Life of Dimitri Mitropoulos. . . .*v.6 p.410*

Priestess, Mother, Sacred Sister: Religions Dominated by Women. *v.1 p.528*

The Priestly Tribe: The Supreme Court's Image in the American Mind. *v.4 p.466*

Priests and People in Pre-Famine Ireland, 1780-1845. .*v.3 p.137*

The Primacy of the Subjective: Foundations for a Unified Theory of Mind and Language. *v.1 p.515*

Primary Care for Physician Assistants. *v.5 p.534*

Primary Care of the Child with a Chronic Condition. .*v.5 p.525*

Primate and Human Evolution. *v.4 p.15*

Primate Psychology. *v.5 p.615*

Primate Visions: Gender, Race and Nature in the World of Modern Science. *v.4 p.30, p.31*

Prime Ministers of Canada: Selected Speeches 1867-2002, Profiles, Bibliography with Editorial Commentary. .*v.3 p.540*

The Prime Minister. *v.2 p.318*

The Prime Numbers and Their Distribution. *v.5 p.477*

Prime Obsession: Bernhard Riemann and the Greatest Unsolved Problem in Mathematics. *v.5 p.475*

The Prime of Life. *v.2 p.508*

The Prime of Miss Jean Brodie; The Girls of Slender Means; The Driver's Seat; The Only Problem. *v.2 p.384*

The Prime of Miss Jean Brodie. *v.2 p.384*

The Prime Time Closet: A History of Gays and Lesbians on TV. *v.6 p.419*

Primer for Movement Description Using Effort/Shape. .*v.1 p.38*

A Primer for the Gradual Understanding of Gertrude Stein. *v.2 p.122*

Primer for the Monte Carlo Method. *v.5 p.483*

A Primer of Analytic Number Theory: From Pythagoras to Riemann. *v.5 p.468, p.477*

A Primer of Biomechanics. *v.4 p.908*

Primer of Biostatistics. *v.5 p.515*

A Primer of Conservation Biology. *v.5 p.17, p.357*

A Primer of Conservation Genetics. *v.5 p.132, p.133*

A Primer of Ecological Genetics. *v.5 p.131*

A Primer of Ecology. *v.5 p.169, p.170*

A Primer of Freudian Psychology. *v.5 p.659*

A Primer of Genome Science. . .*v.5 p.133, p.139, p.140, p.502*

A Primer of Invertebrate Learning: The Behavioral Perspective. *v.5 p.614*

A Primer of Mathematical Writing: Being a Disquisition on Having Your Ideas Recorded, Typeset, Published, Read and Appreciated. *v.5 p.459, p.461*

A Primer of Medieval Latin: An Anthology of Prose and Poetry. *v.2 p.448*

Primer of Modern Analysis. *v.5 p.489*

A Primer of Real Functions. *v.5 p.490*

A Primer on American Labor Law. *v.4 p.109, p.111, p.112, p.121, p.126, p.446*

A Primer on Business Ethics. *v.1 p.486*

A Primer on Integral Equations of the First Kind. . . .*v.5 p.488*

A Primer on Riemann Surfaces. *v.5 p.490*

A Primer on U. S. Housing Markets and Housing Policy. *v.4 p.166*

Prime-Time Feminism: Television, Media Culture, and the Women's Movement Since 1970. . . . .*v.6 p.448*

Primitive, Archaic and Modern Economies: Essays of Karl Polanyi. *v.4 p.210, p.270*

Primitive Art in Civilized Places. *v.4 p.48*

Primitivism and Identity in Latin America: Essays on Art, Literature and Culture. *v.3 p.316*

Prince Henry "The Navigator": A Life. *v.3 p.73, p.244*

The Prince of Darkness: Radical Evil and the Power of Good in History. *v.1 p.645*

The Prince of Fire: An Anthology of Contemporary Serbian Short Stories. *v.2 p.810*

Prince of Players: Edwin Booth. *v.1 p.118, p.145*

The Prince of Princes: The Life of Potemkin. *v.3 p.216*

A Prince of the Church: Schleiermacher and the Beginnings of Modern Theology. *v.1 p.581*

The Princes of Orange: The Stadholders in the Dutch Republic. *v.3 p.205*

The Princess and the Goblin. *v.2 p.299*

Princess Isabel of Brazil: Gender and Power in the Nineteenth Century. *v.3 p.335*

The Princess of Cleves. *v.2 p.474*

A Princess of Mars. *v.2 p.59*

The Princesse de Cleves: The Princesse de Montpensier, The Comtesse de Tende. *v.2 p.474*

Princesses' Street: Baghdad Memories. *v.6 p.660*

The Princeton Companion to Classical Japanese Literature. *v.6 p.231*

The Princeton Companion to Jonathan Edwards. . . .*v.1 p.584*

☐ The Princeton Dante Project. *v.2 p.703*

The Prince. *v.2 p.709, v.4 p.492*

The Principalship. *v.4 p.282*

Principia Ethica. *v.1 p.446, p.487*

The Principia: Mathematical Principles of Natural Philosophy. *v.5 p.467, p.556, p.557*

Principium Sapientiae: The Origins of Greek Philosophical Thought. *v.1 p.419*

Principled Sentencing: Reading on Theory and Policy. *v.6 p.272*

Principled World Politics: The Challenge of Normative International Relations at the Millennium. *v.4 p.484, p.485, p.627*

☐ Principles & Standards for School Mathematics. . *v.4 p.360*

Principles and a Philosophy for Vocational Education. *v.4 p.305, p.353*

Principles and Agents, Set. *v.5 p.9, p.10, p.312, p.354*

Principles and Applications of Electrochemistry. . . .*v.5 p.285*

Principles and Methods in Plant Molecular Biology, Biochemistry and Genetics. *v.5 p.124*

Principles and Methods of Adapted Physical Education and Recreation: With Activities Booklet and PowerWeb Bind-in Card. *v.4 p.800*

Principles and Practice of Infectious Diseases: Text with Continually Updated Online Reference. *v.5 p.533*

Principles and Practice of Laser-Doppler Anemometry. .*v.5 p.708*

Principles and Practice of Medical Genetics, Set. . . .*v.5 p.151*

The Principles and Practice of Medicine. *v.5 p.510*

Principles and Practice of Orthopaedic Sports Medicine..*v.5 p.519*

Principles and Practice of Pediatric Oncology. .*v.5 p.520, p.525*

Principles and Practice of Psychopharmacotherapy. . .*v.5 p.517*

Principles and Practice of Sport Management. *v.4 p.882*

Principles and Practices in Interscholastic Athletics: Guidelines for Administrators. *v.4 p.799*

Principles and Practices of Aviation Psychology. . . .*v.5 p.588*

Principles and Practices of Interconnection Networks. .*v.5 p.727*

Principles and Practices of Rice Production. . . .*v.5 p.20, p.25*

Principles and Practices of Teaching Reading. *v.4 p.363*

Principles and Standards for School Mathematics. . . .*v.5 p.463*

Principles and Techniques of Contemporary Taxonomy. *v.5 p.170, p.195*

Principles and Types of Public Speaking. *v.4 p.423*

The Principles of Aesthetics. *v.1 p.480*

Principles of Agribusiness Management. *v.4 p.151*

Principles of Algebraic Geometry. *v.5 p.497*

Principles of Analytical Chemistry: A Textbook. . . .*v.5 p.273*

Principles of Applied Civil Engineering Design. . . .*v.5 p.685*

Principles of Athletic Training: A Competency-Based Approach. *v.4 p.828*

Principles of Behavior Modification. *v.5 p.666*

Principles of Biochemisrty. *v.5 p.111*

Principles of Biochemistry. *v.5 p.327*

Principles of Biomedical Ethics. . . *v.1 p.485, v.5 p.511, p.674*

Principles of Biostatistics. *v.5 p.93*

Principles of Cartesian Philosophy: With Metaphysical Thoughts and Lodewijk Meyer's Inaugural Dissertation. . .*v.1 p.477*

Principles of Christian Theology. *v.1 p.636*

Principles of Coaching Football. *v.4 p.858, p.904*

Principles of Colloid and Surface Chemistry. *v.5 p.283*

Principles of Communication Systems Simulation with Wireless Applications. *v.5 p.726*

Principles of Community Psychology: Perspectives and Applications. *v.5 p.650, p.671*

Principles of Computer Integrated Manufacturing. . . .*v.5 p.684*

Principles of Computer Organization and Assembly Language. *v.5 p.730*

Principles of Computer Security: Security and Beyond. .*v.4 p.113*

Principles of Condensed Matter Physics. *v.5 p.554*

Principles of Crop Improvement. *v.5 p.15, p.23*

The Principles of Descartes' Philosophy. *v.1 p.454*

The Principles of Economic Analysis, Set. *v.4 p.220*

Principles of Economics. *v.4 p.224, p.234*

Principles of Electronics: Analog and Digital. *v.5 p.722*

Principles of Emendation in Shakespeare. *v.2 p.229*

Principles of Engineering Geology. *v.5 p.421*

Principles of Enhanced Heat Transfer. *v.5 p.713, p.714*

Principles of Environmental and Resource Economics: A Guide for Students and Decision-Makers. *v.4 p.62*

Principles of Environmental Geochemistry. . . .*v.5 p.423, p.441*

Principles of Feedback Control: Feedback System Design, Vol. 1. . . . .*v.5 p.710*

Principles of Forecasting: A Handbook for Researchers and Practitioners. *v.4 p.118*

Principles of Forensic Mental Health Assessment. . . .*v.5 p.592*

Principles of Foundation and Geotechnical Engineering. .*v.5 p.698*

Principles of Foundation Engineering. *v.5 p.421*

Principles of Fracture Mechanics. *v.5 p.691*

Principles of Fuel Cells. *v.5 p.742*

Principles of Gene Manipulation and Genomics. . . .*v.5 p.142*

Principles of Genetics. *v.5 p.137*

Principles of Genome Analysis and Genomics. . . .*v.5 p.146*

Principles of Geomorphology. *v.4 p.391, v.5 p.424*

Principles of Geotechnical Engineering.Txt. .*v.5 p.422, p.699*

Principles of Geriatric Medicine and Gerontology. . .*v.5 p.519*

Principles of Holography. *v.5 p.561*

Principles of Instructional Design. . .*v.4 p.342, p.343, v.5 p.573*

Principles of Internal Medicine: Digital Edition. . . .*v.5 p.515*

Principles of International Law [1952]. *v.4 p.477*

Principles of International Politics: People's Powers, Preferences, and Perceptions. *v.4 p.625*

Principles of Inventory and Materials Management. . .*v.4 p.116*

The Principles of Life. *v.5 p.95*

Principles of Literary Criticism. *v.2 p.569*

Principles of Mathematical Analysis. *v.5 p.489*

Principles of Mineral Processing. *v.5 p.737*

The Principles of Nonlinear Optics. *v.5 p.561*

Principles of Nuclear Magnetism. *v.5 p.553*

Principles of Operations Research with Applications to Managerial Decisions. *v.5 p.504*

Principles of Optics: Electromagnetic Theory of Propagation, Interference and Diffraction of Light. *v.5 p.73, p.561*

Principles of Orchestration : With Musical Examples Drawn from His Own Works. *v.1 p.393, p.394*

Principles of Physical and Chemical Metallurgy. . . .*v.5 p.731*

Principles of Physical Cosmology. *v.5 p.72*

Principles of Physical Sedimentology. *v.5 p.438*

Principles of Plant Nutrition. *v.5 p.22, p.45*

Principles of Plant Pathology. *v.5 p.47*

Principles of Political Economy: And Chapters on Socialism. *v.4 p.222, p.223*

The Principles of Political Economy and Taxation. . .*v.4 p.220*

Principles of Political Economy, Set. *v.4 p.222*

Principles of Political Economy with Some of Their Applications to Social Philosophy. *v.4 p.222*

Principles of Polymer Chemistry. *v.5 p.322*

Principles of Population Dynamics and Their Application. *v.5 p.183, p.187, p.188*

Principles of Process Research and Chemical Development in the Pharmaceutical Industry. *v.5 p.330*

Principles of Proteomics. *v.5 p.118*

The Principles of Psychology. *v.5 p.594*

Principles of Public International Law. *v.4 p.477*

Principles of Quantum Mechanics: As Applied to Chemistry and Chemical Physics. *v.5 p.279*

The Principles of Quantum Mechanics. *v.5 p.549*

Principles of Quantum Mechanics. *v.5 p.550*

Principles of Research Design in Social Sciences. . . *v.4 p.686*

Principles of Risk Management and Insurance. . . . *v.4 p.163*

Principles of Robot Motion: Theory, Algorithms, and Implementations. *v.5 p.711*

Principles of Science. *v.5 p.402*

The Principles of Scientific Management. *v.4 p.64*

Principles of Sedimentary Basin Analysis. *v.5 p.438*

Principles of Sedimentology and Stratigraphy. *v.5 p.438, p.446*

Principles of Silviculture. *v.5 p.41*

The Principles of Sociology, Vol. 1. . . . . . *v.4 p.683, p.684*

The Principles of Sociology, Vol. 2. . . . . *v.4 p.684*

The Principles of Sociology, Vol. 3. . . . . *v.4 p.684*

The Principles of Sociology, Vol. 4. . . . . *v.4 p.684*

Principles of Soil Chemistry, Vol. 65. . . . . *v.5 p.51*

Principles of Soldering and Brazing. *v.5 p.737*

The Principles of Statistical Mechanics. *v.5 p.559*

Principles of Systematic Zoology. *v.5 p.212*

The Principles of Teaching Based on Psychology. . . *v.4 p.359*

Principles of Textual Criticism. *v.2 p.165*

Principles of the Business Rule Approach. *v.4 p.114*

Principles of the Philosophy of the Future. *v.1 p.464*

Principles of the Surface Treatment of Steels. . . . *v.5 p.736*

Principles of the Theory of Solids. *v.5 p.555*

Principles of Vibration and Sound. *v.5 p.567*

Principles of Violin Playing and Teaching. *v.1 p.397*

Principles of Virology: Molecular Biology, Pathogenesis, and Control of Animal Viruses. *v.5 p.206, p.212*

Principles of Visual Anthropology. *v.6 p.310*

Principles of Voice and Data Communications. . . . *v.5 p.723*

Principles Science, Set. *v.4 p.231*

The Print in the Western World: An Introductory History. *v.1 p.753*

Print Literacy Development: Uniting Cognitive and Social Practice Theories. *v.4 p.304, p.354*

Print Making Without a Press. *v.1 p.759*

Print, Manuscript and the Search for Order, 1450-1830. *v.3 p.37*

Print Matters: The Kenneth E. Tyler Gift. *v.1 p.760*

Print the Legend: Photography and the American West. *v.1 p.764*

The Printed Image and the Transformation of Popular Culture, 1790-1860. . . . . *v.6 p.737, p.738, p.743, p.763*

Printed Stuff: Prints, Posters, and Ephemera by Claes Oldenburg: A Catalogue Raisonné 1958-1996. . . *v.1 p.755*

Printed Writings 1641-1700: Miscellaneous Plays, Vol. 7. . . . . *v.2 p.242, p.243*

The Printing Revolution in Early Modern Europe. *v.2 p.576, v.3 p.37*

Printmaking for Art Therapists. *v.1 p.761*

Printmaking: History and Process. *v.1 p.760*

Printmaking in Britain: A General History from Its Beginnings to the Present Day. *v.1 p.754*

Printmaking in the Sun. *v.1 p.760*

Prints and People: A Social History of Printed Pictures. *v.1 p.760*

Prints and Printmakers of Texas: Proceedings of the Twentieth Annual North American Print Conference. *v.1 p.760*

Prints and Printmaking: A Dictionary and Handbook of the Art in Nineteenth-Century Britaiin. *v.1 p.752*

Prints and Printmaking: An Introduction to the History and Techniques. *v.1 p.753, p.759*

Prints: Art and Techniques. *v.1 p.759*

The Prints of Rockwell Kent: Catalogue Raisonné. . *v.1 p.757*

The Prints of Stanley William Hayter. *v.1 p.755*

Prints of the 20th Century: A History. *v.1 p.752*

The Prints of Theodore Roussel: A Catalogue Raisonné. *v.1 p.759*

Prior Analytics. *v.1 p.426, p.494*

The Prioress's Tale. *v.2 p.208*

The Priority of Love: Christian Charity and Social Justice. *v.1 p.651*

Prison Nation: The Warehousing of America's Poor. . *v.6 p.274*

The Prison of Life: An Autobiography. *v.6 p.656*

Prison of Women: Testimonies of War and Resistance in Spain, 1939-1975. . . . . *v.3 p.242*

Prison Writings: My Life Is My Sun Dance. *v.6 p.694*

Prisoner Litigation: The Paradox of the Jailhouse Lawyer. *v.6 p.276*

Prisoner of Grace. *v.2 p.338*

Prisoner of Love. *v.2 p.518*

Prisoner of the Vatican: The Popes, the Kings, and Garibaldi's Rebels in the Struggle to Rule Modern Italy. . . . *v.3 p.201*

Prisoner Reentry and Crime in America. *v.6 p.279*

Prisoner Without a Name, Cell Without a Number. . *v.3 p.349*

Prisoners of Culture: Representing the Vietnam POW. *v.6 p.322*

Prisoners of Shangri-La: Tibetan Buddhism and the West. *v.6 p.241*

Prisoners Once Removed: The Impact of Incarceration and Reentry on Children, Families, and Communities. *v.6 p.279, p.281, p.283*

Prisoners' Rights: The Supreme Court and Evolving Standards of Decency, 96. . . . . *v.6 p.273, p.274*

The Prison-House of Language: A Critical Account of Structuralism and Russian Formalism. *v.2 p.561*

Prisons and the American Conscience: A History of U. S. Federal Corrections. *v.6 p.273*

Prisons: Crime and Justice. *v.6 p.275*

Prisons of Light - Black Holes. *v.5 p.72*

The Pristine Dao: Metaphysics in Early Daoist Discourse. *v.1 p.418*

The Pritchett Century. *v.2 p.378*

Privacy: Concealing the Eighteenth-Century Self. . . *v.2 p.172*

Privacy, Law, and Public Policy. *v.4 p.443*

Privacy on the Line: The Politics of Wiretapping and Encryption. *v.4 p.473*

Private and Fictional Words: Canadian Women Novelists of the 1970's and 1980's. *v.2 p.729*

Private City: Philadelphia in Three Periods of Its Growth. *v.3 p.492*

Private Domain: An Autobiography. *v.1 p.13*

Private Guns, Public Health. *v.6 p.266*

Private Interests, Public Policy, and American Agriculture. *v.5 p.13, p.14*

Private Life in New Kingdom Egypt. *v.6 p.57*

The Private Life of Chairman Mao: The Memoirs of Mao's Personal Physician. *v.6 p.201, p.202*

Private Life under Changing Socialism: Love, Intimacy, and Family Change in a Chinese Village, 1949-1999. . .*v.4 p.734*

Private Life under Socialism: Love, Intimacy, and Family Change in a Chinese Village, 1949-1999. . . . .*v.4 p.772*

Private Lives: Families, Individuals, and the Law. . .*v.4 p.442*

Private Lives in Renaissance Venice: Art, Architecture, and the Family. *v.1 p.674, p.685*

Private Lives, Public Conflicts: Battles over Gay Rights in American Communities. *v.6 p.387*

The Private Mary Chesnut: The Unpublished Civil War Diaries. *v.3 p.429*

The Private Papers of Henry Ryecroft. *v.2 p.289*

Private Pressure on Public Law: The Legal Career of Justice Thurgood Marshall, 1934-1991. . . . .*v.4 p.467*

Private Prisons: Cons and Pros. *v.6 p.276*

Private Prisons in America: A Critical Race Perspective. .*v.6 p.276*

The Private Roots of Public Action: Gender, Equality, and Political Participation. *v.4 p.503, p.550, v.6 p.440*

Private Science: Biotechnology and the Rise of the Molecular Sciences. *v.5 p.220*

The Private Science of Louis Pasteur. *v.5 p.396*

The Private Self: Theory and Practice of Women's Autobiographical Writings. *v.2 p.8*

The Private Self. *v.4 p.693, v.5 p.655*

Private vs. Public Operation of Juvenile Correctional Facilities. *v.6 p.276*

Privately Owned Public Space: The New York City Experience. *v.6 p.726*

Privatization and Political Change in Mexico. *v.3 p.295*

Privatization in Criminal Justice: Past, Present and Future. *v.6 p.247*

The Privatization of Policing: Two Views. *v.6 p.262*

Privatizing Education: Can the School Marketplace Deliver Freedom of Choice, Efficiency, Equity, and Social Cohesion? *v.4 p.299*

Privilege: A Reader. *v.4 p.724*

Privilege in the Soviet Union. *v.4 p.705*

Privileging Positions: The Sites of Asian American Studies. *v.6 p.109*

Prize Possession: The United States Government and the Panama Canal 1903-1979. . . . .*v.3 p.390*

The Prize: The Epic Quest for Oil, Money and Power. *v.4 p.160*

Pro M. Caelio Oratio. *v.2 p.431*

Probabilistic Methods in Combinatorial Analysis. *v.5 p.479, p.484*

Probabilistic Modeling in Bioinformatics and Medical Informatics. *v.5 p.97*

Probabilistic Modelling. *v.5 p.484*

Probability and Evidence. *v.5 p.402*

Probability and Measure Theory. *v.5 p.480*

Probability and Statistics for Engineering and the Sciences. *v.5 p.480, p.481, p.500, p.683*

Probability and Statistics for Engineers and Scientists. *v.5 p.481, p.501, p.683*

Probability and the Art of Judgment. *v.1 p.495*

Probability and Theistic Explanation. *v.1 p.499*

Probability Distributions. *v.5 p.484*

Probability, Econometrics and Truth: The Methodology of Econometrics. *v.4 p.202*

Probability, Statistics and Truth. *v.5 p.481*

Probability: Theory and Examples. *v.5 p.481*

Probation, Parole and Community Corrections. . . .*v.6 p.278*

Probationary Americans: Contemporary Immigration Policies and the Shaping of Asian American Communities. *v.6 p.117, p.121*

Probing the Depths of German Antisemitism: German Society and the Persecution of the Jews, 1933-1941. . . .*v.3 p.82*

A Problem Like Maria: Gender and Sexuality in the American Musical. *v.1 p.380, v.6 p.413*

The Problem of John Ford. *v.2 p.218*

Problem of Knowledge: Philosophy, Science, and History since Hegel. *v.1 p.481*

The Problem of Leadership and the Conflict Between the Rational and the Irrational Forces in the Stream of History, Set. *v.4 p.249*

The Problem of Order in Changing Societies: Essay on Crime and Policing in Argentina and Uruguay. *v.3 p.345*

The Problem of Pain. *v.1 p.652*

The Problem of Perception. *v.1 p.483*

The Problem of the Media: U. S. Communication Politics in the Twenty-First Century. *v.4 p.425*

The Problem of the Soul: Two Visions of Mind and How to Reconcile Them. *v.5 p.619*

The Problem of Unbelief in the Sixteenth Century: The Religion of Rabelais. *v.2 p.472*

The Problem of Values in Educational Thought. . . .*v.4 p.345*

The Problem Plays of Shakespeare: A Study of Julius Caesar, Measure for Measure, Antony and Cleopatra. . . .*v.2 p.231*

Problem Solving in Analytical Chemistry. *v.5 p.274*

Problem Solving in Recreation and Parks. *v.4 p.785*

Problem-Oriented Policing and Crime Prevention. . .*v.6 p.264*

Problem-Oriented Policing: From Innovation to Mainstream. *v.6 p.264*

Problem-Oriented Policing. *v.6 p.264*

Problems and Theorems in Analysis: Integral Calculus. Theory of Functions. *v.5 p.489*

Problems As Possibilities: Problem-Based Learning for K-16 Education. *v.4 p.349*

Problems at the Roots of Law: Essays in Legal and Political Theory. *v.1 p.491*

Problems in African History: The Precolonial Centuries. *v.6 p.52*

Problems in Algebraic Number Theory. *v.5 p.475*

Problems in Mathematical Analysis: Continuity and Differentiation. *v.5 p.489*

Problems in Mathematical Analysis I: Real Numbers, Sequences
    and Series. *v.5 p.489*

Problems in Probability. *v.5 p.484*

Problems in the History of Modern Africa. *v.6 p.52*

Problems of Analysis: Philosophical Essays. *v.1 p.502*

Problems of Democratic Transition and Consolidation: Southern
    Europe, South America and Post-Communist
    Europe. *v.4 p.505*

Problems of Dostoevsky's Poetics. *v.2 p.797, p.801*

Problems of Empiricism: Philosophical Papers. *v.1 p.499*

The Problems of Physics. *v.5 p.541*

Problems of Plenty: The American Farmer in the Twentieth
    Century. *v.5 p.30*

Problems of Rationality, Vo. 4. . . . .*v.1 p.441, p.514*

Problems of Stability and Progress in International
    Relations. *v.4 p.628*

Problems of the Chinese Revolution. *v.6 p.193, p.216*

Proceedings and Debates of the British Parliaments Respecting
    North America [1924]. *v.3 p.406, p.407*

Process and Pattern in Evolution. *v.5 p.190*

Process and Reality: An Essay in Cosmology. .*v.1 p.447, p.489*

Process Dynamics in Environmental Systems. .*v.5 p.369, p.705*

Process Geomorphology. *v.5 p.424*

The Process of Change. *v.5 p.668*

The Process of Economic Development. *v.4 p.258*

Process of Education. *v.4 p.341*

The Process of Government: A Study of Social
    Pressures. *v.4 p.482*

The Process of Stratification. *v.4 p.724*

Process Philosophy: A Survey of Basic Issues. . . .*v.1 p.513*

Process Selection: From Design to Manufacture. . .*v.4 p.117*

Process Theology: An Introductory Exposition. . . .*v.1 p.637*

The Processes of Fossilization. *v.5 p.446, p.447*

Process/Industrial Instruments and Controls Handbook.*v.4 p.116*

Processing of Polymers. *v.5 p.318*

Le procès-verbal. *v.2 p.531*

Prochain Épisode. *v.2 p.540, p.733*

Proclaiming Revolution: Bolivia in Comparative
    Perspective. *v.3 p.324*

Proclus: Neo-Platonic Philosophy and Science. . . .*v.1 p.431*

The Prodigal: A Poem. *v.2 p.770*

Prodigal Son: Dancing for Balanchine in a World of Pain and
    Magic. *v.1 p.13*

Prodigal Son: Vasilii Shukshin in Soviet Russia Culture.*v.2 p.803*

The Producer as Composer: Shaping the Sounds of Popular
    Music. *v.1 p.272, p.387*

The Producer: John Hammond and the Soul of American
    Music. *v.1 p.385*

Producible Interpretation: Eight English Plays,
    1675-1707. . . . .*v.2 p.187*

Producing India: From Colonial Economy to National
    Space. *v.6 p.157*

Producing Power: Ethnicity, Gender, and Class in a Caribbean
    Workplace. *v.4 p.41*

Product Development Performance: Strategy, Organization, and
    Management in the World Auto Industry. *v.4 p.144*

Product Life Cycles and Product Management. . . .*v.4 p.144*

Product Planning Essentials. *v.4 p.144*

Production and Distribution Theories. *v.4 p.210, p.249*

Production and Inventory Control Handbook. *v.4 p.116*

Production and Reproduction: A Comparative Study of the
    Domestic Domain. *v.4 p.32*

Production Design and Art Direction. *v.6 p.348*

Production Design: Architects of the Screen. *v.6 p.348*

Production Design in the Contemporary American Film: A
    Critical Study of 23 Movies and Their Designers.*v.6 p.348*

Production Economics: A Dual Approach to Theory and
    Applications. *v.4 p.248*

Production, Income and Welfare: The Search for an Optimal
    Social Order. *v.4 p.266*

Production Management: Making Shows Happen. . . .*v.1 p.149*

The Production of Hindu-Muslim Violence in Contemporary
    India. *v.6 p.149*

The Production of Space. *v.6 p.710*

Production Planning and Scheduling in Flexible Assembly
    Systems. *v.4 p.116*

Productive Men and Reproductive Women: The Agrarian
    Household and the Emergence of Separate
    Spheres during the German Enlightenment. . . .*v.3 p.167*

▢ Productscan. *v.4 p.140, p.141, p.150*

Professing in the Contact Zone: Bringing Theory and Practice
    Together. *v.2 p.565, p.566*

Profession of Conscience: The Making and Meaning of
    Life-Sciences Liberalism. *v.5 p.249*

Profession of Government Minister in Western Europe.*v.4 p.601*

The Profession of the Playwright: British Theatre,
    1800-1900. . . . .*v.6 p.740*

Professional and Technical Writing: Communicating in
    Technology and Science. *v.5 p.681*

Professional and Technical Writing: Solving Problems at
    Work. *v.5 p.680*

The Professional Cameraman's Handbook. *v.6 p.349*

Professional Careers Sourcebook. *v.4 p.169*

Professional Development Schools: Schools for Developing a
    Profession. *v.4 p.277, p.278*

Professional Football: The Official Pro Footbal of Fame
    Bibliography. *v.4 p.844, p.859*

Professional Forestry in the United States. *v.5 p.37*

The Professional Golfers' Association Tour: A History.*v.4 p.860*

Professional Guide to Diseases. *v.5 p.528*

Professional Men: The Rise of the Professional Classes in
    Nineteenth-Century England. . .*v.3 p.115, p.131,v.6 p.744*

The Professional Musician's Legal Companion. . . .*v.1 p.383*

The Professional Practice for Interior Designers. . .*v.1 p.801*

Professional Standards for Teaching
    Mathematics. *v.5 p.463, p.464*

The Professional Stranger: An Informal Introduction to
    Ethnography. *v.4 p.25*

The Professionalization of Psychology in Nazi
    Germany. *v.5 p.596*

The Professions: Roles and Rules. *v.4 p.725*

The Professor and the Madman: A Tale of Murder, Insanity, and
    the Making of the Oxford English Dictionary. . . .*v.2 p.553*

The Professor. *v.2 p.270*

A Profile of Correctional Effectiveness and New Directions for
    Research. *v.6 p.274*

Profile of Horace. *v.2 p.435*

Profilers: Leading Investigators Take You Inside the Criminal
    Mind. *v.6 p.254*

Profiles in Canadian Literature. *v.2 p.729*

Profiles in Courage. *v.3 p.376*

Profiles in Injustice: Why Racial Profiling Cannot Work. *v.6 p.264*

Profiles in Landscape Architecture. *v.1 p.815*

Profiles in Terror: The Guide to Middle East Terrorist
    Organizations. *v.4 p.660*

Profiles of African American Stage Performers and Theatre
    People, 1816-1960. . . . .*v.1 p.123, p.141, p.142*

Profiles of American Labor Unions. *v.4 p.125*

Profiles of Nurse Healers. *v.5 p.529*

Profiles of Sport Industry Professionals: The People Who Make
    the Games Happen. *v.4 p.905, p.906*

Profiling and Criminal Justice in America: A Reference
    Handbook. *v.6 p.264*

Profiling Political Leaders: Cross-Cultural Studies of Personality
    and Behavior. *v.4 p.483, v.5 p.643*

Profiting from Multiple Intelligences in the Workplace. *v.4 p.66*

The Profits of Religion: An Essay in Economic
    Interpretation. *v.1 p.545*

Profits Pending: How Life Patents Represent the Biggest
    Swindle of the Twenty-First Century. *v.5 p.130, p.217*

Profits, Priests, and Princes: Adam Smith's Emancipation of
    Economics from Politics and Religion. *v.4 p.219*

Prognostic, Regimen in Acute Diseases, the Sacred Disease, the
    Art, Breaths, Law, Decorum, Physician (Ch. 1),
    Dentition, Vol. 2. . . . .*v.2 p.404, v.5 p.510*

Program Notes for the Singer's
    Repertoire. *v.1 p.165, p.394, p.395*

▢ Program Standards and Report Forms. *v.4 p.359*

Programming for Parks, Recreation, and Leisure
    Services. *v.4 p.783, p.787*

Programming in Prolog: Using the ISO Standard. . . .*v.5 p.346*

Programming Language Pragmatics. *v.5 p.347*

Programming Languages: Concepts and Constructs. . .*v.5 p.347*

Programming on Purpose: Essays on Programming
    Design. *v.5 p.346, p.348*

Programming Pearls. *v.5 p.346, p.349*

Progress and Its Problems: Towards a Theory of Scientific
    Growth. *v.5 p.389, p.394, p.403*

Progress in Behavior Modification, Vol. 30. . . . . .*v.5 p.667*

Progress in Motor Control: Structure-Function Relations in
    Voluntary Movements, Vol. 2. . . . .*v.4 p.909*

Progress in Physical Organic Chemistry. *v.5 p.292*

Progress in Structural Engineering. *v.5 p.694*

The Progress of an Image: The East in English
    Literature. *v.2 p.164*

The Progress of Love. *v.2 p.737*

A Progress of Sentiments: Reflections on Hume's
    Treatise. *v.1 p.451*

Progress of the World's Women: Gender Equality and the
    Millennium Development Goals. *v.6 p.456*

Progressive Education at the Crossroads. *v.4 p.340, p.341*

The Progressive Era in Minnesota, 1899-1918. . . . .*v.3 p.522*

Progressive Intellectuals and the Dilemmas of Democratic
    Commitment. *v.3 p.367*

The Progressive Movement, 1900-1915. . . . . . .*v.3 p.448*

Progressive Oklahoma: The Making of a New Kind of
    State. *v.3 p.523, p.524*

Progressive Presidents: Theodore Roosevelt, Woodrow Wilson,
    Franklin D. Roosevelt, Lyndon B.
    Johnson. *v.3 p.439, p.445, p.446, p.466*

Progressivism and the New Democracy. *v.3 p.476*

Progressivism. *v.3 p.448*

▢ Project 2061 Textbook Evaluations. *v.4 p.284*

Project Apollo: The Way to the Moon. *v.5 p.719*

Project Appraisal and Planning for Developing
    Countries. *v.4 p.259*

▢ Project Gutenberg of Australia. *v.2 p.742*

Project Management for Information Systems. *v.4 p.114*

Projected Cities: Cinema and Urban Space. *v.6 p.730*

Projected Fears: Horror Films and American Culture. *v.6 p.319*

Projecting History: German Nonfiction Cinema,
    1967-2000. . . . .*v.6 p.338*

Projecting the Past: Ancient Rome, Cinema and History. *v.6 p.315*

Projective Geometry. *v.5 p.495*

Prokaryotic Genomics. *v.5 p.145*

Prokofiev: A Biography: From Russia to the West,
    1891-1935. . . . .*v.1 p.219, p.348*

Prokofiev by Prokofiev: A Composer's Memoir. *v.1 p.221, p.348*

Prokofiev's Ballets for Diaghilev. *v.1 p.24*

Prolegomena for the Oxford Shakespeare. *v.2 p.231*

Prolegomena to Any Future Metaphysics That Will Be Able to
    Present Itself As Science: With Two Early Reviews of
    the Critique of Reason. *v.1 p.462, p.463*

Prolegomena to Homer, 1795. . . . .*v.2 p.416*

Proletarian Power: Shanghai in the Cultural
    Revolution. *v.6 p.196, p.206*

Prologue to Conflict: The Crisis and Compromise of
    1850. . . . .*v.3 p.420*

Prologue to Democracy: The Federalists in the South,
    1789-1800. . . . .*v.3 p.495*

Prologue to Nuremberg: The Politics and Diplomacy of
    Punishing War Criminals of the First World War. . *v.4 p.477*

Prologue to Revolution: Cuba, 1898-1958. . . . . .*v.3 p.310*

Prologue to War: England and the United States 1805. *v.3 p.417*

The Prologues and Epilogues of John Dryden. *v.2 p.246*

La Promesa and Other Stories. *v.6 p.502*

Promesas: Geography of the Impossible. *v.6 p.509, p.511*

Prometheans in the Lab: Chemistry and the Making of the
    Modern World. *v.5 p.261*

Prometheus: The Life of Balzac. *v.2 p.487*

Prometheus Wired: The Hope for Democracy in the Age of
    Network Technology. *v.4 p.503*

Prominent Scientists: An Index to Collective
    Biographies. *v.5 p.395*

The Promise and the Performance: The Leadership of John
    F. *v.3 p.477*

The Promise of Cultural Institutions. *v.3 p.370*

Promise of Eden: The Canadian Expansionist Movement and the
Idea of the West, 1856-1900. . . . .*v.3 p.545*

The Promise of Politics: From Theory to Practice. . . .*v.4 p.491*

The Promise of Pragmatism: Modernism and the Crisis of
Knowledge and Authority. *v.3 p.367*

The Promise of Rest. *v.6 p.379, p.398*

The Promise of Schooling: Education in Canada,
1800-1914. . . . .*v.4 p.333*

The Promise of the City: Space, Identity and Politics in
Contemporary Social Thought. *v.6 p.719*

The Promise of the Foreign: Nationalism and the Technics of
Translation in the Spanish Philippines. *v.6 p.180*

The Promise of the New South: Life after
Reconstruction. *v.3 p.394, p.496*

The Promise of Youth: Follow-up Studies of a Thousand Gifted
Children. *v.5 p.575*

Promised Land: Adventures and Encounters in Wild
America. *v.5 p.234*

Promises Broken: Courtship, Class, and Gender in Victorian
England. *v.6 p.747, p.765*

Promises I Can Keep: Why Poor Women Put Motherhood
Before Marriage. *v.4 p.724*

Promises to Keep: Public Health Policy for American Indians
and Alaska Natives in the 21st Century. . . .*v.6 p.701, p.702*

Promoting Active Learning: Strategies for the College
Classroom. *v.4 p.348*

Promotional Strategy. *v.4 p.134*

Pronouncing Arabic. *v.6 p.654*

Pronouncing Shakespeare's Words: A Guide from A to
Zounds. *v.2 p.222, p.226, p.556*

Pronunciation Guide for Choral Literature: French, German,
Hebrew, Italian, Latin, Spanish. *v.1 p.395*

The Pronunciation of English. *v.2 p.557*

Proof in Print: A Community of Printmaking
Studios. *v.1 p.758, p.759*

Proof, Logic, and Conjecture: The Mathematician's
Toolbox. *v.5 p.471*

The Proof. *v.5 p.471, p.472*

Proofs and Confirmations: The Story of the Alternating-Sign
Matrix Conjecture. *v.5 p.478*

Proofs and Refutations: The Logic of Mathematical
Discovery. *v.5 p.470*

Proofs from the Book. *v.5 p.457*

Proofs That Really Count: The Art of Combinatorial
Proof. *v.5 p.478*

Proofs Without Words: Exercises in Visual Thinking. .*v.5 p.459*

Proofs Without Words II: More Exercises in Visual
Thinking. *v.5 p.459*

Proof. *v.2 p.139*

Propaganda and Communication in World History: A Pluralizing
World in Formation, Vol. 3. . . . .*v.4 p.696, p.697*

Propaganda and Communication in World History: Emergence
of Public Opinion in the West, Vol. 2. . . . . .*v.4 p.696*

Propaganda and Communication in World History: The
Symbolic Instrument in Early Times, Vol. 1. . . .*v.4 p.696*

Propaganda and Democracy: The American Experience of
Media and Mass Persuasion. *v.4 p.418*

Propaganda and Mass Persuasion: A Historical Encyclopedia,
1500 to the Present. *v.4 p.425*

Propaganda: The Formation of Men's Attitudes. .*v.4 p.425, p.696*

Proper English: Myths and Misunderstandings about
Language. *v.2 p.553*

The Proper Lady and the Woman Writer: Ideology as Style in
the Works of Mary Wollstonecraft, Mary Shelley, and Jane
Austen. *v.2 p.268, p.310*

A Proper Marriage. *v.2 p.365*

The Properties of Gases and Liquids. *v.5 p.282*

Properties of Liquids and Solutions. *v.5 p.282*

The Properties of Solvents. *v.5 p.282*

Propertius: A Critical Introduction. *v.2 p.442*

Propertius: Elegies, Bk. II. *v.2 p.441*

Propertius: Elegies, Bk. IV. *v.2 p.441*

Propertius: Elegies III, Bk. III. *v.2 p.441*

Propertius: Elegies. *v.2 p.441*

Propertius. *v.2 p.441*

Property and Permissiveness in Bourbon Mexico. . . .*v.3 p.288*

Prophecy and Politics: Socialism, Nationalism, and the Russian
Jews, 1862-1917. . . . .*v.3 p.59*

Prophecy in Islam: Philosophy and Orthodoxy. *v.1 p.558*

The Prophet and the Age of the Caliphates: The Islamic Near
East from the 6th to the 11th Century. *v.6 p.585*

Prophet Harris, the "Black Elijah" of West
Africa. *v.1 p.648, p.649, v.6 p.69*

The Prophet of the Great Smoky Mountains. .*v.2 p.32, p.46, p.47*

Prophet with Honor: The Career of Andrew Jackson Downing,
1815-1852. . . . .*v.1 p.817*

The Prophetic Literature: An Introduction. *v.1 p.623*

Prophetic Pentecostalism in Chile: A Case Study on Religion
and Development Policy. *v.3 p.354*

The Prophetic Sense of History in Medieval and Renaissance
Europe: From Jerusalem to Cyprus. *v.3 p.62*

Prophetic Worlds: Indians and Whites on the Columbia
Plateau. *v.6 p.682, p.701*

Prophets in Their Own Country: Living Saints and the Making
of Sainthood in the Later Middle Ages. *v.6 p.571*

Prophets on the Right: Profiles of Conservative Critics of
American Globalism. *v.3 p.454*

Propriety and Permissiveness in Bourbon Mexico. . . .*v.3 p.262*

Prosa, Dramen, Verse. *v.2 p.616*

Prosas Recobradas (Collected Prose Works). . .*v.2 p.655, p.656*

Prose & poésie : oeuvre complète. *v.2 p.532*

Prose by Victorian Women: An
Anthology. *v.2 p.196, p.202, v.6 p.739, p.746, p.754*

Prose di ricerca, vol. 1. . . . .*v.2 p.716*

Prose di Ricerca, Vol. 2. . . . .*v.2 p.716*

Prose di ricerca. *v.2 p.710*

Prose Edda: Tales from Norse Mythology. *v.1 p.534*

Prose, Essays, Poems. *v.2 p.603*

Prose Observations. *v.2 p.273*

The Prose of Aleksandr Vampilov. *v.2 p.803*

The Prose of John Clare. *v.2 p.278*

The Prose Poem in France: Theory and Practice. . . .*v.2 p.461*

The Prose Poems and La Fanfarlo. *v.2 p.487*

The Prose Works of Andrew Marvell, 1672-1673, Vol. 1. . . . .*v.2 p.252*

The Prose Works of William Wordsworth. . . .*v.2 p.324, p.325*

Prose. *v.2 p.514*

A Proslavery Foreign Policy: Haitian-American Relations During the Early Republic. *v.3 p.315*

The Prospect Before Her, Vol. 2. . . . .*v.3 p.52*

The Prospector. *v.2 p.531*

Prospects in Systematics. *v.5 p.205*

Prosperity and Parenthood. *v.6 p.764*

Prostitution and Victorian Society: Women, Class, and the State. *v.4 p.749, v.6 p.471*

The Prostitution of Sexuality. *v.6 p.468*

Protagoras. *v.1 p.425, p.427*

The Protean Self: Human Resilience in an Age of Fragmentation. *v.5 p.654*

Protecting Abused and Neglected Children. *v.4 p.756*

Protecting Canada's Endangered Spaces: An Owner's Manual. *v.5 p.179, p.234*

Protecting Endangered Species in the United States: Biological Needs, Political Realities, Economic Choices. . . .*v.6 p.301*

Protecting Human Rights in Africa: Roles and Strategies of Non-Governmental Organizations. *v.4 p.640, p.670*

Protecting Motherhood: Women and the Family in the Politics of Postwar West Germany. *v.3 p.177*

Protecting Soldiers and Mothers: The Political Origins of Social Policy in the United States. *v.4 p.769*

Protecting the Ozone Layer: The United Nations History. *v.4 p.666*

The Protection Racket State: Elite Politics, Military Extortion, and Civil War in El Salvador. *v.3 p.299*

Protective Groups in Organic Synthesis. *v.5 p.294*

Protectors of Privilege: Red Squads and Police Repression in Urban America. *v.6 p.260*

Protectors or Praetorians?: The Last Mamluk Sultans and Egypt's Waning as a Great Power. *v.6 p.636*

Protein Arrays, Biochips, and Proteomics: The Next Phase of Genomics Discovery. *v.5 p.102, p.104, p.109, p.138*

Protein Biochemistry and Proteomics. *v.5 p.118*

Protein Biosynthesis: In Focus. *v.5 p.115*

⬜ Protein Data Bank. *v.5 p.328*

Protein Engineering: In Focus. *v.5 p.329*

Protein Engineering, Vol. 388. . . . .*v.5 p.117*

Protein Folding Kinetics: Biophysical Methods. . . .*v.5 p.117*

Protein Nanotechnology: Protocols, Instrumentation, and Applications. *v.5 p.118, p.220*

Protein Purification: Principles, High-Resolution Methods, and Applications. *v.5 p.328*

Protein Sequencing Protocols. *v.5 p.103*

Protein Structure and Function. *v.5 p.117*

Protein Structure and Protein Function: A Practical Appraoch, Set. *v.5 p.115*

Protein-Lipid Interactions: New Approaches and Emerging Concepts. *v.5 p.118*

Proteins, Enzymes and Genes: The Interplay of Chemistry and Biology. *v.5 p.116, p.119*

Proteome Analysis: Interpreting the Genome. . .*v.5 p.105, p.118*

Proteome Characterization and Proteomics, Vol. 65. . .*v.5 p.118*

Proteome Research: Mass Spectrometry. *v.5 p.116*

Proteome Research: New Frontiers in Functional Genomics. *v.5 p.105, p.147*

Proteome Research: Two-Dimensional Gel Electrophoresis and Identification Methods. *v.5 p.89, p.117*

The Proteome Revisited: Theory and Practice of All Relevant Electrophoretic Steps. *v.5 p.89, p.118*

Proteomic and Genomic Analysis of Cardiovascular Disease. *v.5 p.116, p.148*

Proteomics and Nanocrystallography. *v.5 p.114, p.117*

Proteomics and Protein-Protein Interactions: Biology, Chemistry, Bionformatics, and Drug Design. *v.5 p.118, p.220*

Proteomics: Biomedical and Pharmaceutical Applications. *v.5 p.116*

Proteomics: From Protein Sequence to Function. . . .*v.5 p.117*

Proteomics in Cancer Research. *v.5 p.117*

Proteomics in functional Genomics: Protein Structure Analysis. *v.5 p.116*

Proteomics in Practice: A Laboratory Manual of Proteome Analysis. *v.5 p.119*

Proteomics of Microorganisms: Fundamental Aspects and Application. *v.5 p.117, p.205, p.206*

Proteomics of Spermatogenesis. *v.5 p.116, p.153*

🄴 Proteomics Protocols Handbook. *v.5 p.118*

Proteomics Today: Protein Assessment and Biomarkers Using Mass Spectrometry, 2D Electrophoresis, and Microarray Technology. *v.5 p.88, p.110, p.116*

Proteomics. *v.5 p.117*

Protest and Punishment: The Story of the Social and Political Protesters Transported to Australia, 1788-1868. . .*v.4 p.753*

Protest Movements in 1960s West Germany: A Social History of Dissent and Democracy. *v.3 p.177, v.4 p.610, p.712*

Protestant Church Music in America: A Short Survey of Men and Movements from 1564 to the Present. *v.1 p.280*

Protestant Church Music. *v.1 p.235*

The Protestant Crusade, 1800-1860. . . . .*v.3 p.394*

The Protestant Establishment: Aristocracy and Caste in America. *v.4 p.726*

🄴 The Protestant Ethic and the Spirit of Capitalism. .*v.4 p.725*

The Protestant Ethic and the Spirit of Capitalism. *v.1 p.596, v.4 p.721*

The Protestant Evangelical Awakening. *v.1 p.590, p.649*

Protestant Pentecostalism in Latin America: A Study in the Dynamics of Change. *v.1 p.587*

Protestant Theology in the Nineteenth Century: Its Background and History. *v.1 p.633*

Protestant Thought in the Nineteenth Century: 1799-1870. . . . .*v.1 p.634*

Protestant Thought in the Nineteenth Century: 1870-1914. . . . .*v.1 p.634*

The Protestant Voice in American Pluralism. *v.1 p.605*

Protestant--Catholic--Jew: An Essay in American Religious Sociology. *v.1 p.543*

Protestantism and Latinos in the United States: An Original Anthology. *v.6 p.519*

Protestantism and the Rise of Capitalism. *v.4 p.681*

Protestantism in the United States: Righteous Empire. .*v.1 p.605*

Protestants and the Mexican Revolution: Missionaries, Ministers and Social Change. *v.3 p.290*

Protestants in America. *v.1 p.606*

Protestants: The Birth of a Revolution. *v.1 p.602*

Protocol for Profit: A Manager's Guide to Competing Worldwide. *v.4 p.56, p.57*

Proto-Industrialization: The First Phase of Industrialization? *v.3 p.90, p.122*

Proudhon and His Age. *v.3 p.148*

Proust: A Collection of Critical Essays. *v.2 p.524*

The Proust Screenplay. *v.2 p.377*

Proust's Way: A Field Guide to 'In Search of Lost Time'. *v.2 p.524, p.525*

Prove It with Figures: Empirical Methods in Law and Litigation. *v.4 p.179*

Proverbs 1-9. . . . .*v.1 p.621*

Proverbs: A Commentary. *v.1 p.621*

The Province of Piety: Moral History in Hawthorne's Early Tales. *v.2 p.40*

Provinces: Canadian Provincial Politics. *v.4 p.589*

Provinces of the Revolution: Essays on Regional Mexican History, 1910-1929. . . . .*v.3 p.290*

Provincetown as a Stage: Provincetown, the Provincetown Players, and the Discovery of Eugene O'Neill. *v.1 p.79, p.82, p.113, p.144, p.149, p.150*

Provincetown Players and the Culture of Modernity. *v.1 p.80, p.83, p.117*

The Provincial Letters. *v.1 p.452, v.2 p.476*

Provincial Patriarchs: Land Tenure and the Economics of Power in Colonial Peru. *v.3 p.326*

Provincial Politics in Canada: Towards the Turn of the Century. *v.4 p.589*

Provincial Russia in the Age of Enlightenment: The Memoir of a Priest's Son. *v.3 p.216*

Provincial Society, 1690-1763. . . . .*v.3 p.405*

The Provincial State: Politics in Canada's Provinces and Territories. *v.4 p.589*

Provincializing Europe: Postcolonial Thought and Historical Difference. *v.3 p.35*

The Provincials: A Personal History of Jews in the South. *v.3 p.498*

Proving Doctrine: The Uses of Scripture in Modern Theology. *v.1 p.638*

Provisions: A Reader from Nineteenth-Century American Women. *v.2 p.20*

Provocateur: Images of Women and Minorities in Advertising. *v.4 p.426, p.427,v.6 p.448*

Provocations: Spiritual Writings of Kierkegaard. . . .*v.1 p.650*

☐ PROWL - a resource for protein chemistry and mass spectrometry - Amino Acid Information. *v.5 p.111*

Proximity, Distance, and Diversity: Issues on Economic Interaction and Local Development. *v.4 p.397, p.398*

Der Prozess. *v.2 p.611*

Prudent Practices in the Laboratory: Handling and Disposal of Chemicals. *v.5 p.266*

Prudentius: Against Symmachus 2, Crowns of Martyrdom, Scenes from History, Epilogue, Vol. 2. . . . . . .*v.2 p.442*

Psalms I, 1-50. . . . .*v.1 p.621*

Psalms III. *v.1 p.621*

Psalms II. *v.1 p.621*

Pseudoscience and the Paranormal. *v.5 p.613*

☐ Psi Chi. *v.5 p.676*

The Psyche and Schizophrenia: The Bond Between Affect and Logic. *v.5 p.660*

Psyche and Sports: Baseball, Hockey, Martial Arts, Running, Swimming, Tennis and Others. *v.5 p.583*

Psychiatric Justice. *v.4 p.471*

Psychiatry, Psychoanalysis, and the New Biology of Mind. *v.5 p.617*

Psychoanalysis and Infant Research. *v.5 p.627*

Psychoanalysis and the Unconscious and Fantasia of the Unconscious. *v.2 p.363*

Psychoanalysis, Behavior Therapy, and the Relational World. *v.5 p.667*

Psychoanalytic Explorations in Art. *v.5 p.619*

Psychoanalytic Studies of Religion: A Critical Assessment and Annotated Bibliography. *v.5 p.633*

The Psychodynamics of Culture: Abram Kardiner and Neo-Freudian Anthropology. *v.4 p.35*

The Psychoeducational Assessment of Preschool Children. *v.4 p.356, v.5 p.602*

Psychogical Problems, Social Issues and Law. *v.5 p.592*

Psychological Anthropology Reconsidered. *v.4 p.35*

Psychological Anthropology. *v.4 p.35*

The Psychological Assessment of Political Leaders: With Profiles of Saddam Hussein and Bill Clinton. *v.4 p.512, v.5 p.644*

Psychological Birth of the Human Infant: Symbiosis and Individuation. *v.5 p.627, p.628*

Psychological Dimensions of War. *v.5 p.584*

Psychological Dynamics of Sport and Exercise. *v.4 p.877, p.879,v.5 p.582*

Psychological Effects of War and Violence on Children. .*v.5 p.584*

Psychological Factors in Poverty. *v.4 p.264*

The Psychological Foundations of Culture. *v.5 p.637*

Psychological Foundations of Sport. *v.4 p.877, v.5 p.583*

Psychological Issues in Adoption: Research and Practice. *v.5 p.641*

Psychological Issues in Biblical Lore: Explorations in the Old Testament. *v.5 p.635*

Psychological Methods in Criminal Investigation and Evidence. *v.5 p.593*

Psychological Needs and Political Behavior: A Theory of Personality and Political Efficacy. *v.5 p.644*

Psychological Perspectives on Lesbian, Gay, and Bisexual Experiences. *v.6 p.381*

Psychological Perspectives on Politics. . . .*v.4 p.483, v.5 p.642*

Psychological Perspectives on Self and Identity. .*v.5 p.646, p.657*

Psychological Perspectives on Traditional Jewish Practices. *v.5 p.635*

The Psychological Roots of Religious Belief: Searching for Angels and the Parent-God. *v.5 p.633*

Psychological Sense of Community: Research, Applications, and Implications. *v.5 p.649*

The Psychological Significance of Art and Literature. *v.1 p.465*

Psychological Testing: A Practical Approach to Design and Evaluation. *v.5 p.601*

Psychological Testing and Assessment. *v.5 p.600*

Psychological Testing: History Principals and Applications. *v.5 p.601*

Psychological Testing: History, Principles, and Applications. *v.5 p.600*

Psychological Testing: Principles and Applications. . .*v.5 p.601*

Psychological Testing: Theory and Applications. . . .*v.5 p.601*

Psychological Testing. *v.5 p.599*

Psychological Theories of Drinking and Alcoholism. . .*v.5 p.664*

The Psychological World of Natsume Soseki. *v.6 p.229*

The Psychologist as Expert Witness. *v.5 p.591*

Psychology and Christianity: Four Views. *v.5 p.634*

Psychology and Consumer Culture: The Struggle for a Good Life in a Materialistic World. *v.5 p.586*

Psychology and Law: A Critical Introduction. *v.5 p.592*

Psychology and Law: Inside and Outside the Courtroom. *v.5 p.593*

Psychology and Law: Research and Application. . . .*v.5 p.591*

Psychology and Law: Theory, Research, and Application. *v.5 p.591*

Psychology and Law: Truthfulness, Accuracy and Credibility. *v.5 p.592*

The Psychology and Management of Workplace Diversity. *v.4 p.132*

Psychology and Myth. *v.5 p.636*

Psychology and Policing. *v.5 p.591*

Psychology and Public Policy: Balancing Public Service and Professional Need. *v.5 p.643*

Psychology and Religion: Introduction. *v.5 p.632*

Psychology and Religion. *v.1 p.524, v.5 p.634*

Psychology and the Bible: A New Way to Read the Scriptures. *v.5 p.633*

Psychology and the Economic Mind: Cognitive Processes Conceptualization. *v.4 p.272*

Psychology and the Internet: Intrapersonal, Interpersonal, and Transpersonal Implications. *v.5 p.653*

Psychology and the Legal System. *v.5 p.593*

Psychology and the Political Experience. *v.5 p.643*

Psychology and the Soul: A Study of Origin, Conceptual Evolution and Nature of the Soul. *v.5 p.635*

Psychology for Health Fitness Professionals. *v.4 p.790, p.905, p.906*

Psychology for Physical Educators. *v.4 p.797*

Psychology, in Modules, Critical Thinking Companion and PsychInquiry. *v.4 p.692*

Psychology in Prisons. *v.5 p.592*

Psychology in Sport. *v.4 p.877, v.5 p.582*

The Psychology Major's Handbook. *v.5 p.675*

The Psychology of Anomalous Experience. *v.5 p.605*

The Psychology of Art and the Evolution of the Conscious Brain. *v.1 p.704, v.5 p.619*

The Psychology of Attention. *v.5 p.611*

The Psychology of Attitudes. *v.5 p.652*

The Psychology of Conflict and Combat. *v.5 p.584, p.585*

Psychology of Emotions. *v.5 p.612*

The Psychology of Exercise: Integrating Theory and Practice. *v.4 p.875, p.877, v.5 p.582*

The Psychology of Facial Expression. *v.5 p.648*

The Psychology of Graphic Images: Seeing, Drawing, Communicating. *v.5 p.594, p.607*

The Psychology of Gratitude. *v.5 p.652*

The Psychology of Happiness. *v.5 p.611*

The Psychology of Hate. *v.5 p.656*

A Psychology of Human Strengths: Fundamental Questions and Future Directions for a Positive Psychology. .*v.5 p.593, p.670*

The Psychology of Interpersonal Relations. *v.5 p.646*

The Psychology of Investing. *v.4 p.97*

The Psychology of Jealousy and Envy. *v.5 p.656*

The Psychology of Judgment and Decision Making. . *v.5 p.609*

Psychology of Language and Learning. *v.5 p.572*

Psychology of Language: From Data to Theory. .*v.5 p.622, p.624*

The Psychology of Law: Integrations and Applications. *v.5 p.592*

The Psychology of Leadership: New Perspectives and Research. *v.5 p.648*

Psychology of Learning and Motivation: Advances in Research and Theory, Vol. 31. . . . .*v.5 p.574*

Psychology of Learning Mathematics. *v.5 p.464*

The Psychology of Learning. *v.5 p.571*

The Psychology of Love. *v.5 p.657*

The Psychology of Marriage: Basic Issues and Applications. *v.5 p.638*

The Psychology of Mature Spirituality: Integrity, Wisdom, Transcendence. *v.5 p.635*

The Psychology of Music. *v.1 p.375*

Psychology of Music. *v.1 p.376*

The Psychology of Music. *v.5 p.607, p.618*

The Psychology of Myth, Folklore and Religion. . . .*v.5 p.636*

Psychology of Officiating. *v.4 p.878, p.905*

The Psychology of Physical Activity and Exercise. . .*v.5 p.581*

Psychology of Physical Activity: Determinants, Well-Being and Interventions. *v.4 p.876*

The Psychology of Politics. *v.5 p.645*

The Psychology of Prejudice and Discrimination. *v.4 p.698, v.5 p.632, p.650*

The Psychology of Reading: An Introduction. *v.5 p.574*

The Psychology of Religion: An Empirical Approach. *v.5 p.636*

The Psychology of Religion and Coping: Theory, Research, Practice. *v.5 p.635*

Psychology of Religion: Classic and Contemporary. . *v.5 p.636*

The Psychology of Religious Fundamentalism. *v.5 p.634*

The Psychology of Resolving Global Conflicts: From War to Peace. *v.5 p.584*

The Psychology of Saving: A Study on Economic Psychology. *v.4 p.246, p.251*

Psychology of Science: Contributions to Metascience. *v.5 p.594*

The Psychology of Secrets. *v.5 p.646*

The Psychology of Sex, Gender and Jobs: Issues and
Solutions. *v.4 p.133*

The Psychology of Social Movements. *v.4 p.710*

Psychology of Social Norms. *v.4 p.692*

Psychology of Sports, Exercise and Fitness: Social and
Adjustmental Issues. *v.5 p.581, p.582*

The Psychology of Stereotyping. . . .*v.4 p.694, v.5 p.605, p.650*

Psychology of Team Sports. *v.4 p.877, v.5 p.582*

[e] The Psychology of Terrorism. *v.4 p.662*

Psychology of the Child. *v.5 p.628*

The Psychology of the Internet. *v.5 p.588*

The Psychology of Touch. *v.5 p.606*

The Psychology of Transcendence. *v.5 p.613*

The Psychology of Ultimate Concerns: Motivation and
Spirituality in Personality. *v.5 p.652*

The Psychology of War and Peace: The Image of the
Enemy. *v.5 p.584*

The Psychology of War: Comprehending Its Mystique and Its
Madness. *v.5 p.584*

Psychology of Women: A Handbook of Issues and
Theories. *v.6 p.445*

Psychology of Women: Behavior in a Biosocial
Context. *v.6 p.446, p.447*

Psychology, Psychotherapy, Psychoanalysis, and the Politics of
Human Relationships. *v.5 p.645*

Psychology, Religion and Spirituality. . . .*v.1 p.524, v.5 p.634*

Psychology's Grand Theorists: How Personal Experiences
Shaped Professional Ideas. *v.5 p.595, p.596*

Psychometric Methods: Item Response Theory for
Psychologists. *v.5 p.600*

Psychometric Methods. *v.5 p.599*

Psychometric Tests, Vol. 1. . . . .*v.5 p.600*

Psychometric Theory. *v.5 p.599*

Psychomythics: Sources of Artifacts and Misconceptualizations
in Scientific Psychology. *v.5 p.594*

Psychopathia Sexualis: A Clinical-Forensic
Study. *v.4 p.749, v.6 p.420*

Psychopathy: Antisocial, Criminal, and Violent
Behavior. *v.5 p.661*

Psychopharmacology: The Fourth Generation of
Progress. *v.5 p.517*

Psychophysics: The Fundamentals. *v.5 p.605*

Psychosocial Aspects of the Asian-American Experience:
Diversity Within Diversity. *v.6 p.121, p.122*

Psychosocial Issues near the End of Life: A Resource for
Professional Care Providers. *v.5 p.532*

Psychotic Reactions and Carburetor Dung: The Work of a
Legendary Critic: Rock 'N' Roll As Literature
and Literature As Rock 'N' Roll. *v.1 p.265*

[] PsycINFO: Your Source for Psychological Abstracts. .*v.5 p.516*

Pteridology in the New Millennium: NBRI Golden Jubilee
Volume (in Honor of Prof. B.K. Nayar). *v.5 p.210*

Ptolemaic Alexandria. *v.3 p.10, v.6 p.57*

Ptolemy's Geography: An Annotated Translation of the
Theoretical Chapters. *v.4 p.377*

Public Administration and Public Management: The
Principal-Agent Perspective. *v.4 p.75*

Public Administration Theory Primer. *v.4 p.545, p.580*

[] Public Agenda. *v.4 p.559*

Public and Community Health Nursing Practice: A
Population-Based Approach. *v.5 p.531*

Public and Its Problems. *v.4 p.491*

Public and Performance in the Greek
Theatre. *v.1 p.70, p.137, v.2 p.401*

Public and Private Financing of Higher Education: Shaping
Public Policy for the Future. *v.4 p.295*

Public and Private Life of the Soviet People: Changing Values
in Post-Stalin Russia. *v.3 p.223*

Public and Private Roles in Health Care Systems: Experiences
from Seven Countries. *v.5 p.511*

Public Archaeology. *v.4 p.5*

Public Benefits of Archaeology. *v.1 p.823, v.4 p.7*

Public Choice III. *v.4 p.576*

Public Culture of Victorian Middle Class: Ritual and Authority
in the English Industrial City, 1840-1914. . .*v.6 p.743, p.744*

Public Dollars, Private Stadiums. *v.4 p.880, p.883, p.887*

Public Economics: Selected Papers by William
Vickrey. *v.4 p.247, p.248*

Public Education in America: A New Interpretation of Purpose
and Practice. *v.4 p.324*

Public Education in the United States. *v.4 p.325*

Public Finance in a Democratic Society: Collected Papers of
Richard A. Musgrave, Vol. 1. . . . .*v.4 p.247*

The Public Image. *v.2 p.384*

Public Interest Group Profiles 2004-2005. . . . . .*v.4 p.559*

The Public Lands: Studies in the History of the Public
Domain. *v.6 p.294*

Public Lives, Private Secrets: Gender, Honor, Sexuality and
Illegitimacy in Colonial Spanish America. *v.3 p.359*

Public Lives: Women, Family, and Society in Victorian
Britain. *v.6 p.743, p.747*

Public Man, Private Woman: Women in Social and Political
Thought. *v.6 p.440, p.464*

Public Management As Art, Science, and
Profession. *v.4 p.545, p.580*

Public Markets and Civic Culture in Nineteenth-Century
America. *v.6 p.725*

Public Money and the Muse: Essays on Government Funding
for the Arts. *v.4 p.523*

Public Moralists: Political Thought and Intellectual Life in
Britain, 1850-1930. .*v.3 p.111, p.127, v.6 p.750, p.757, p.758*

Public Opinion and Democratic Accountability: How Citizens
Learn about Politics. *v.4 p.559*

Public Opinion and Foreign Policy: America's China Policy,
1949-1979. . . . .*v.3 p.390*

Public Opinion, Polling, and Democracy Around the World: A
Historical Encyclopedia. *v.4 p.425*

Public Opinion. *v.4 p.425, p.697*

The Public Order of the Oceans: A Contemporary International
Law of the Sea,. *v.4 p.478*

[] Public Papers of the Presidents of the United States. .*v.4 p.481*

Public Piers Plowman: Modern Scholarship and Late Medieval
English Culture. *v.2 p.211, v.6 p.564*

Public Policies and the Misuse of Forest Resources. . .*v.5 p.39*

Title Index

Public Policing in the 21st Century: Issues and Dilemmas in the
U. S. and Canada. *v.6 p.262, p.267*

The Public Realm: Exploring the City's Quintessential Social
Territory. *v.4 p.771, v.6 p.718*

Public Relations History: From the 17th to the 20th
Century. *v.4 p.428*

Public Relations on the Net: Winning Strategies to Inform and
Influence the Media, the Investment Community, the
Government, the Public, and More!. *v.4 p.144*

Public Religion and Urban Transformation. *v.6 p.718*

Public School Reform in Puerto Rico: Sustaining Colonial
Models of Development, 60. . . . . *v.4 p.337*

Public Services Delivery. *v.4 p.755*

Public Sex: The Culture of Radical Sex. *v.6 p.368*

Public Speech and the Culture of Public Life in the Age of
Gladstone. *v.6 p.758*

The Public Trust Doctrine and the Management of America's
Coasts. *v.4 p.463*

Public Values, Private Lands: Farmland Preservation Policy,
1933-1985. . . . . *v.5 p.30*

Public Vows: A History of Marriage and the
Nation. *v.4 p.739, v.6 p.466*

Publicans and Sinners: Private Enterprise in the Service of the
Roman Republic. *v.3 p.25, p.26*

Publication Design. *v.1 p.719*

The Public's Right to Know: The Supreme Court and the First
Amendment. *v.4 p.464*

PubMed. *v.5 p.325*

Puccini: A Biography. *v.1 p.201, p.349*

The Puccini Companion. *v.1 p.207, p.349*

Puccini: His Life and Works. *v.1 p.195, p.349*

Puebla de Los Angeles: Industry and Society in a Mexican City,
1700-1850. . . . . *v.3 p.288*

Pueblo Indian Painting: Tradition and Modernism in New
Mexico, 1900-1930. . . . . . *v.1 p.730, p.731,v.6 p.678*

El Pueblo Maya. *v.2 p.676*

Pueblos Indios en la Política. *v.3 p.323*

Puerto Rican Americans: The Meaning of Migration to the
Mainland. *v.6 p.529*

Puerto Rican Arrival in New York: Narrative of the Migration,
1920-150. . . . . *v.3 p.319, v.6 p.529*

Puerto Rican: Born in the USA. *v.6 p.545*

Puerto Rican Chicago. *v.6 p.532, p.550*

Puerto Rican Children on the Mainland: Interdisciplinary
Perspectives. *v.6 p.526*

The Puerto Rican Community and Its Children on the Mainland:
A Source Book for Teachers, Social Workers and Other
Professionals. *v.4 p.311, v.6 p.526*

The Puerto Rican Diaspora: Historical
Perspectives. *v.6 p.530, p.533*

Puerto Rican Food Habits: A Socio-Cultural Approach. *v.3 p.272*

A Puerto Rican in New York and Other Sketches. *v.6 p.535, p.543*

Puerto Rican Jam: Rethinking Colonialism and
Nationalism. *v.3 p.320*

The Puerto Rican Movement: Voices from the Diaspora. *v.6 p.539*

The Puerto Rican Nation on the Move: Identities on the Island
and in the United States. *v.3 p.319, v.6 p.543*

The Puerto Rican Struggle: Essays on Survival in the U.
S. *v.6 p.542*

Puerto Rican Students in U. S. Schools. . . *v.4 p.311, v.6 p.527*

Puerto Rican Voices in English: Interviews with
Writers. *v.6 p.506, p.512*

Puerto Rican Women and Work: Bridges in Transnational
Labor. *v.3 p.320*

Puerto Rican Women's History: New Perspectives. . *v.3 p.320*

Puerto Rican Writers at Home in the U.S.A.: An
Anthology. *v.6 p.496, p.497, p.509*

Puerto Ricans: A Documentary History. *v.6 p.533*

Puerto Ricans and Higher Education Policies: Issues of
Scholarship, Fiscal Policies and Admissions. . . . *v.6 p.527*

Puerto Ricans in the United States: A Contemporary
Portrait. *v.6 p.520, p.521*

Puerto Ricans in the United States. *v.6 p.532*

The Puerto Ricans: Their History, Culture and
Society. *v.6 p.531, p.532*

Puerto Rico 1898: The War after the War. . . *v.3 p.320, p.321*

Puerto Rico 1900: Turn-of-the-Century Architecture in the
Hispanic Caribbean, 1890-1930. . . . . *v.1 p.790*

Puerto Rico: An Interpretive History from Precolumbian Times
To 1900. . . . . *v.3 p.319*

Puerto Rico under Colonial Rule: Political Persecution and the
Quest for Human Rights. *v.3 p.318*

Puerto Rico's Commerce, 1765-1865: From Regional to
Worldwide Market Relations. *v.3 p.321*

Puerto Rico's Revolt for Independence: El Grito de
Lares. *v.3 p.319*

Puerto Rico's Statehood Movement. *v.6 p.538*

El Puertorriqueño y Su Alimentación a Través de Su Historia
(Siglos xvi al xix). *v.3 p.271*

Pugin: A Gothic Passion. *v.6 p.736, p.737*

Pulitzer Prize Feature Stories: America's Best Writing,
1979-2003. . . . . *v.4 p.412*

Pull: Networking and Success since Benjamin
Franklin. *v.4 p.53, p.132, p.147*

The Pullman Strike: The Story of a Unique Experiment and of a
Great Labor Upheaval. *v.4 p.127*

Pulp Fictions of Medieval England: Essays in Popular
Romance. *v.6 p.565*

Pulp Politics: How Political Advertising Tells the Stories of
American Politics. *v.4 p.548*

Pulsars. *v.5 p.70*

Pump Handbook. *v.5 p.713*

Pumped: Straight Facts for Athletes about Drugs, Supplements
and Training. *v.4 p.826*

Punch's Prize Novelists, The Fat Contributor, and Travels in
London. by W. M. Thackeray. *v.2 p.316*

P'ungmul: South Korean Drumming and Dance. *v.1 p.15*

The Punic Wars. *v.3 p.25*

Punished by Rewards: The Trouble with Gold Stars, Incentive
Plans. *v.4 p.284*

Punishing Hate: Bias Crimes under American Law. . *v.4 p.568*

Punishment and Democracy: Three Strikes and You're Out in
California. *v.6 p.275*

Punishment in the Community: Managing Offenders, Making Choices. *v.6 p.278*

Punishment: Theory and Practice. *v.6 p.275*

Puppet: A Chicano Novella. *v.6 p.498*

Puppet Theater in Contemporary Indonesia: New Approaches to Performance-Events. *v.1 p.133, p.134*

Puppetry: A World History. *v.1 p.93, p.133*

Puppets and Puppet Theatre. *v.1 p.93*

Puranic Encyclopaedia. *v.1 p.537*

The Purcell Companion. *v.1 p.182, p.349*

The Purchase of Intimacy. *v.4 p.738*

Pure and Simple Politics: The American Federation of Labor and Political Activism, 1881-1917. . . . . *v.4 p.126*

The Pure and the Impure. *v.6 p.395*

Pure Metals Properties: A Scientific and Technical Handbook. *v.5 p.687*

The Pure Theory of Foreign Trade and the Pure Theory of Domestic Values. *v.4 p.224*

A Purer Taste: The Reading and Writing of Fiction in English in Nineteenth-Century Canada. *v.2 p.731, p.732*

Purgatory. *v.2 p.703*

Purification of Laboratory Chemicals. *v.5 p.301*

Purifying Proteins for Proteomics: A Laboratory Manual. *v.5 p.89, p.118*

The Puritan As Yankee: A Life of Horace Bushnell. . *v.1 p.584*

The Puritan Dilemma. *v.3 p.487*

The Puritan Experiment: New England Society from Bradford to Edwards. *v.3 p.484*

Puritan Family Life: The Diary of Samuel Sewall. . . *v.3 p.487*

The Puritan Family: Religion and Domestic Relations in Seventeenth-Century New England. *v.3 p.485*

A Puritan in Babylon: The Story of Calvin Coolidge. *v.3 p.481*

The Puritan Moment: The Coming of Revolution in an English County. *v.3 p.103, p.121*

The Puritan Origins of the American Self. *v.3 p.366*

The Puritan Tradition in America, 1620-1730. . . . . *v.3 p.486*

Puritan Village: The Formation of a New England Town. *v.3 p.488*

The Puritan Way of Death: A Study in Religion, Culture, and Social Change. *v.1 p.645*

Puritanism and Democracy. *v.3 p.369*

Puritanism and Revolution: Studies in Interpretation of the English Revolution of the 17th Century. . . *v.3 p.103, p.120*

Puritanism and Theatre: Thomas Middleton and Opposition Drama Under the Early Stuarts. *v.2 p.221*

Puritans and Yankees: The Winthrop Dynasty of New England 1630. . . . . *v.3 p.487*

Purity and Danger: An Analysis of Concepts of Pollution and Taboo. *v.4 p.36*

Purity in Print: Book Censorship in America from the Gilded Age to the Computer Age. *v.4 p.458*

The Purity of Blood. *v.2 p.662*

Puro Teatro, a Latina Anthology: A Latina Anthology. *v.1 p.68, p.125,v.2 p.25*

The Purpose of American Politics. *v.3 p.453*

The Purposes of Higher Education. *v.4 p.291*

Pursued by Furies: A Life of Malcolm Lowry. *v.2 p.367*

Pursuing Excellence in Higher Education: Eight Fundamental Challenges. *v.4 p.332*

Pursuing Happiness: American Consumers in the Twentieth Century. *v.5 p.586*

Pursuing Justice for the Child. *v.4 p.473*

Pursuing Power: Latinos and the Political System. *v.6 p.537, p.538*

Pursuing the American Dream: Opportunity and Exclusion over Four Centuries. *v.3 p.385*

Pursuit of a Wound: Poems. *v.2 p.148*

The Pursuit of Equality in American History. *v.4 p.458*

The Pursuit of Fairness: A History of Affirmative Action. *v.4 p.57, p.108, p.133*

The Pursuit of Loneliness; American Culture at the Breaking Point. *v.3 p.371*

The Pursuit of Love and Love in a Cold Climate: Two Novels. *v.2 p.371*

The Pursuit of Perfection: Aspects of Biochemical Evolution. *v.5 p.112*

The Pursuit of Power: Technology, Armed Force, and Society since A. D. 1000. . . . . *v.3 p.36*

The Pursuit of Salvation: A Critical Guide to the Novels of Graham Greene. *v.2 p.349*

The Pursuit of Significance: Strategies for Managerial Success in Public Organizations. *v.4 p.545, p.580*

The Pursuit of Sodomy: Male Homosexuality in Renaissance and Enlightenment Europe. *v.6 p.364, p.375, p.421*

The Pursuit of the Millennium: Revolutionary Millenarians and Mystical Anarchists of the Middle Ages. *v.1 p.600*

The Pursuit of the White House: A Handbook of Presidential Election Statistics and History. *v.4 p.556*

Pursuit of Truth. *v.1 p.444*

Pursuits Amateur and Academic: The Selected Prose of E. J. Pratt. *v.2 p.738*

Pursuits of Happiness: The Hollywood Comedy of Remarriage. *v.6 p.312*

Push Comes to Shove: An Autobiography. *v.1 p.13*

The Pushcart Book of Essays. *v.2 p.27*

Pushing the Bear: A Novel of the Trail of Tears. . . *v.6 p.698*

Pushing the Limits: The Female Administrative Aspirant. *v.4 p.281*

Pushkin House. *v.2 p.801*

Pushkin, Plus . . .: Lyric Poems of Eight Russian Poets. *v.2 p.807*

Pushkin's Children: Writing on Russia and Russians. *v.2 p.809*

Puss in Boots. *v.2 p.602*

Put Out More Flags. *v.2 p.388*

Put to the Test: An Educator's and Consumer's Guide to Standardized Testing. *v.4 p.285*

Put Your Bodies upon the Wheels: Student Revolt in the 1960s. *v.4 p.331*

Putting Asunder: A History of Divorce in Western Society. *v.4 p.740*

Putting History to the Question: Power, Politics and Society in English Renaissance Drama. *v.2 p.186*

Putting Your Daughters on the Stage: British Lesbian Theatre from the 1960s to the Present. *v.6 p.411*

Puzzles and Paradoxes in Economics. *v.4 p.186*

Puzzles, Problems and Enigmas: Occasional Pieces on the Human Aspects of Science. *v.5 p.411, p.413*

The Puzzling Adventures of Dr. Ecco. *v.5 p.469*

Pygmalion and My Fair Lady. . .*v.1 p.253, p.254, p.336, p.409*

Pygmalion in the Classroom: Teacher Expectation and Pupils' Intellectual Development. *v.4 p.358*

The Pyramid Builders of Ancient Egypt: A Modern Investigation of Pharaoh's Workforce. *v.3 p.8*

The Pyramids of Egypt. *v.3 p.8*

The Pyramids: The Mystery, Culture, and Science of Egypt's Greatest Monuments. *v.6 p.57*

Pythagoras and the Pythagoreans. *v.1 p.421*

Q

Q and A: Queer in Asian America. *v.6 p.111*

Q Is for Quantum: An Encyclopedia of Particle Physics. .*v.5 p.552*

Q: The Autobiography of Quincy Jones. *v.1 p.270, p.334*

QED and the Men Who Made It: Dyson, Feynman, Schwinger, and Tomonaga. *v.5 p.544, p.566*

QED: The Strange Theory of Light and Matter. *v.5 p.566*

Quadrille, Vol. 7. . . . .*v.2 p.342*

Quaid-i-Azam Mohammad Ali Jinnah: His Personality and His Politics. *v.6 p.162*

Quaker Spirituality: Selected Writings. *v.1 p.585*

Quakers and Politics: Pennsylvania, 1681-1726. . . . .*v.3 p.492*

The Quakers and the English Revolution. . . .*v.3 p.104, p.121*

The Quakers in America. *v.1 p.585*

Qualitative Analysis of Human Movement. . . .*v.4 p.873, p.909*

Qualitative Interviewing: The Art of Hearing Data. . .*v.4 p.691*

Qualitative Market Research: Principle and Practice. . .*v.4 p.135*

Qualitative Methods for Marketplace Research. *v.4 p.136*

Qualitative Methods in Sports Studies. *v.4 p.812*

Qualitative Research in Early Childhood Settings. *v.4 p.356, p.357*

Qualitative Research Methods in Human Geography. *v.4 p.376, p.396*

Qualitative Research Practice: A Guide for Social Science Students and Researchers. *v.4 p.136, p.137*

Qualitative Research Through Case Studies. *v.4 p.179*

The Qualitative Researcher's Companion. *v.4 p.690*

Qualities of Effective Teachers. *v.4 p.349*

Quality Control and Industrial Statistics. *v.4 p.116*

Quality Lesson Plans for Secondary Physical Education. .*v.4 p.800*

Quality Management Demystified. *v.4 p.73*

Quality Measurement in Economics: New Perspectives on the Evolution of Goods and Services. *v.4 p.196, p.263*

The Quality of Life. *v.4 p.266*

Quality Teaching: Reflection as the Heart of Practice. .*v.4 p.348*

Quality with Soul: How Six Premier Colleges and Universities Keep Faith with Their Religious Traditions. *v.4 p.307*

Quand on refuse on dit non : roman. *v.2 p.545*

Quantifying Archaeology. *v.4 p.7*

Quantifying the World: United Nations Ideas and Statistics. *v.4 p.636*

Quantitative Analysis for Management. *v.4 p.119*

Quantitative Geography: Perspectives on Spatial Data Analysis. *v.4 p.376*

Quantitative Investigations in the Biosciences Using Minitab. *v.5 p.88*

Quantitative Methods for Business: The A to Z of QM. .*v.4 p.178*

Quantitative Methods in Psychology. *v.5 p.599*

Quantitative Seismology: Theory and Methods. .*v.5 p.442, p.444*

Quantities, Units, and Symbols in Physical Chemistry. .*v.5 p.280*

The Quantity Theory of Money: From Locke to Keynes and Friedman. *v.4 p.237*

A Quantum Approach to Condensed Matter Physics. . .*v.5 p.555*

Quantum Chaos: An Introduction. *v.5 p.550*

Quantum Chemistry and Molecular Spectroscopy. . . .*v.5 p.279*

Quantum Chemistry. *v.5 p.279*

Quantum Electrodynamics, Vol. 4. . . . .*v.5 p.566*

Quantum Evolution: The New Science of Life. *v.5 p.194*

Quantum Field Theory in a Nutshell. *v.5 p.550*

Quantum Field Theory. *v.5 p.550, p.551*

Quantum Fields. *v.5 p.550*

Quantum Generations: A History of Physics in the Twentieth Century. *v.5 p.540*

The Quantum Hall Effect. *v.5 p.565, p.566*

Quantum Mechanics: An Introduction. *v.5 p.549*

Quantum Mechanics: Fundamentals. *v.5 p.549*

Quantum Mechanics in Chemistry. *v.5 p.279, p.280*

Quantum Mechanics Non-Relativistic Theory, Vol. 3. . . . .*v.5 p.549, p.550*

Quantum Mechanics of One- and Two-Electron Atoms. .*v.5 p.549*

Quantum Mechanics, Vol. 1. . . . .*v.5 p.549*

Quantum Mechanics, Vol. 2. . . . .*v.5 p.549*

Quantum Mechanics. *v.5 p.548, p.549, p.550*

Quantum Optics. *v.5 p.562*

Quantum Philosophy: Understanding and Interpreting Contemporary Science. *v.5 p.542*

Quantum Physics of Atoms, Molecules, Solids, Nuclei, and Particles. *v.5 p.549*

Quantum Physics. *v.5 p.549*

Quantum Reality: Beyond the New Physics. *v.5 p.541*

Quantum Theory: Aggregates of Particles. *v.5 p.279*

Quantum Theory: Elements. *v.5 p.279*

The Quantum Theory of Light. *v.5 p.562*

Quantum Theory of Many-Particle Systems. *v.5 p.549*

Quantum Theory of Molecules and Solids, Vol. 1, 3 & 4. .*v.5 p.550*

Quantum Theory of Solids. *v.5 p.555*

Quantum Theory: Radiation and High Energy Physics. .*v.5 p.279*

Quantum Theory. *v.5 p.279, p.549*

The Quantum World: Quantum Physics for Everyone. .*v.5 p.539*

Quarantine: A Novel, Set. *v.2 p.337*

Quarantine. *v.2 p.658*

The Quark and the Jaguar: Adventures in the Simple and the Complex. *v.5 p.543*

The Quark Machines: How Europe Fought the Particle Physics War. *v.5 p.540*

Quarks and Leptones: An Introductory Course in Modern Particle Physics. *v.5 p.552*

Quarks, Lepton and Gauge Fields. *v.5 p.552*

Quarrels That Have Shaped the Constitution. *v.4 p.466*

Quarry: A Collection in Lieu of Memoirs by Lincoln
Kirstein. *v.1 p.45*

Quarter Notes and Bank Notes: The Economics of Music
Composition in the Eighteenth and Nineteenth
Centuries. *v.1 p.385*

Quartet in Autumn. *v.2 p.379*

Quartet of Joy. *v.6 p.662*

Quartet. *v.2 p.766, p.769*

Quasars and Active Galactic Nuclei: An Introduction. . *v.5 p.71*

Quasi una Fantasia: Essays on Modern Music. . . . *v.1 p.208*

Quaternary and Glacial Geology. *v.5 p.425*

Quaternary Environmental
Micropalaeontology. . *v.5 p.366, p.367, p.371, p.448, p.449*

Quaternary Glaciations - Extent and Chronology:
Europe. *v.5 p.425, p.432*

Quaternary Glaciations - Extent and Chronology: North
America. *v.5 p.425, p.431*

Quaternary Glaciations - Extent and Chronology: South
America, Asia, Africa, Australia, Antarctica. . . . *v.5 p.425*

Quatrefoil. *v.6 p.394*

Que Vivan los Tamales!: Food and the Making of Mexican
Identity. *v.3 p.267, p.272*

Quebec 70: A Documentary Narrative. *v.3 p.544*

Quebec: A History: 1867-1929. . . . . *v.3 p.544*

The Quebec Act: A Study in Statesmanship. *v.3 p.539*

Quebec and the Constitution: Nineteen Sixty to Nineteen
Seventy-Eight. *v.4 p.590*

Quebec Before Duplessis: The Political Career of
Louis-Alexandre Taschereau. *v.4 p.581*

The Quebec Democracy: Structures, Processes and
Policies. *v.4 p.589, p.590*

Quebec Nationalism in Crisis. *v.3 p.543*

Quebec Society: Tradition, Modernity and Nationhood. .*v.3 p.543*

La Quebecoite. *v.2 p.541*

Queen Anne. *v.3 p.106, p.108*

Queen Christina of Sweden and Her Circle: The Transformation
of a Seventeenth-Century Philosophical Libertine. .*v.3 p.234*

Queen Elizabeth and the Making of Policy, 1572-1588. .*v.3 p.100*

Queen Elizabeth the First. *v.3 p.100*

The Queen of Spades. *v.2 p.807*

The Queen of the Prisons of Greece. *v.2 p.691*

The Queen: The Life of Elizabeth II. *v.3 p.119*

Queen Victoria: Born to Succeed. *v.3 p.113*

Queen Victoria: The Woman, the Monarchy, and the
People. *v.6 p.749, p.758*

Queen Victoria's Secrets. *v.6 p.764*

Queen Victoria. *v.3 p.116*

The Queen's Throat: Opera, Homosexuality, and the Mystery of
Desire. *v.1 p.379, v.6 p.408*

Queer Airwaves: The Story of Gay and Lesbian
Broadcasting. *v.6 p.419*

Queer and Loathing: Rants and Raves of a Raging AIDS
Clone. *v.6 p.378, p.401*

Queer Asian Cinema: Shadows in the Shade. *v.6 p.416*

Queer Blues: The Lesbian and Gay Guide to Overcoming
Depression. *v.6 p.381*

Queer Cinema: The Film Reader. *v.6 p.415*

The Queer Composition of America's Sound: Gay Modernists,
American Music, and National Identity. *v.1 p.379, v.6 p.408*

Queer Cowboys: And Other Erotic Male Friendships in
Nineteenth-Century American Literature. *v.2 p.9*

Queer Dharma: Voices of Gay Buddhists. *v.6 p.374*

The Queer Encyclopedia of Film and Television. .*v.6 p.417, p.419*

The Queer Encyclopedia of the Visual Arts. . .*v.1 p.666, p.707*

Queer Episodes in Music and Modern
Identity. *v.1 p.378, v.6 p.408*

Queer Family Values: Debunking the Myth of the Nuclear
Family. *v.6 p.376*

The Queer German Cinema. *v.6 p.416*

Queer Images: A History of Gay and Lesbian Film in
America. *v.6 p.415*

Queer in America: Sex, the Media and the Closets of
Power. *v.6 p.390*

Queer Italia: Same-Sex Desire in Italian Literature and
Film. *v.6 p.415, p.416*

Queer Jews. *v.6 p.374*

Queer Latinidad: Identity Practices, Discursive Spaces. .*v.6 p.545*

Queer Man on Campus: A History of Non-Heterosexual College
Men 1945-2000. . . . .*v.4 p.749, v.6 p.385*

A Queer Mother for the Nation: The State and Gabriela
Mistral. *v.3 p.353*

Queer Noises: Male and Female Homosexuality in
Twentieth-Century Music. *v.1 p.378, v.6 p.408*

Queer Poetics: Five Modernist Women Writers,
161. . . . .*v.6 p.392, p.393*

Queer Quotes: On Coming Out and Culture, Love and Lust,
Politics and Pride, and Much More. *v.6 p.360*

A Queer Reader: 2500 Years of Male Homosexuality. *v.6 p.406*

The Queer Renaissance: Contemporary American Literature and
the Reinvention of Lesbian and Gay Identities. . . .*v.6 p.393*

Queer Representations: Reading Lives, Reading
Cultures. *v.6 p.392*

Queer Science: The Use and Abuse of Research into
Homosexuality. *v.6 p.420*

A Queer Sort of Materialism: Recontextualizing American
Theater. *v.6 p.413*

Queer Studies: A Lesbian, Gay, Bisexual, and Transgender
Anthology. *v.6 p.366*

Queer Studies: An Interdisciplinary Reader. *v.6 p.357*

Queer Theory: A Bibliography. *v.6 p.359*

Queer Theory and the Jewish Question. *v.6 p.373, p.374*

Queer (Un)Friendly Film and Television. *v.6 p.419*

Queer Wars: The New Gay Right and Its
Critics. *v.4 p.570, v.6 p.387*

A Queer World: The Center for Lesbian and Gay Studies
Reader. *v.6 p.357*

Queering Creole Spiritual Traditions: Lesbian, Gay, Bisexual,
and Transgender Participation in African-Inspired
Traditions in the Americas. *v.6 p.374*

Queering Elementary Education: Advancing the Dialogue about
Sexualities and Schooling. *v.4 p.309, v.6 p.385*

Title Index

Queering India: Same-Sex Love and Eroticism in Indian Culture and Society. *v.2 p.763, v.6 p.422*

Queering the Pitch: The New Gay and Lesbian Musicology. *v.1 p.378, v.6 p.408*

Queerly Phrased: Language, Gender, and Sexuality. . . *v.4 p.21*

Quelling the People: The Military Supression of the Beijing Democracy Movement. *v.6 p.196*

Quentin Durward. *v.2 p.307*

Querelle. *v.6 p.396*

Quesnay's "Tableau Economique": A Critique and Reassessment. *v.4 p.216, p.217*

Quesnay's Tableau Economique. *v.4 p.217*

Quest: An Autobiography. *v.5 p.543*

The Quest for an American Sociology: Robert E. Park and the Chicago School. *v.4 p.685*

The Quest for Being. *v.1 p.441*

The Quest for Certainty: A Study of the Relation of Knowledge and Action. *v.1 p.482*

The Quest for Christa T. *v.2 p.619*

The Quest for Drug Control: Politics and Federal Policy in a Period of Increasing Substance Abuse, 1963-1981. . . . . *v.4 p.568, v.5 p.664*

The Quest for El Cid. *v.6 p.565*

The Quest for Excellence. *v.4 p.345*

The Quest for Excitement: Sport and Leisure in the Civilizing Process. *v.4 p.783, p.815*

The Quest for Global Dominance: Transforming Global Presence into Global Competitive Advantage. . . . *v.4 p.69*

The Quest for Identity: From Minority Groups to Generation Xers. *v.5 p.632*

The Quest for Immortality: Hidden Treasures of Egypt. *v.3 p.9*

The Quest for Postcolonial Utopia: A Comparative Introduction to the Utopian Novel in the New English Literatures. *v.4 p.485*

The Quest for Shakespeare's Globe. *v.2 p.227, p.228*

The Quest for the Quantum Computer. *v.5 p.552*

The Quest for the True Figure of the Earth: Ideas and Expeditions in Four Centuries of Geodesy. *v.4 p.389*

The Quest for Utopia in Twentieth Century America. *v.4 p.499*

The Quest of the Historical Jesus. *v.1 p.627*

Quest: The Essence of Humanity. *v.5 p.80*

The Question Concerning Technology, and Other Essays. *v.1 p.470*

The Question of Being. *v.1 p.470, p.489*

The Question of Discrimination: Racial Inequality in the U. S. Labor Market. *v.4 p.134*

The Question of German Guilt. *v.3 p.178*

Question of Hamlet. *v.2 p.230*

Question of Intent: A Great American Battle with a Deadly Industry. *v.4 p.449*

The Question of Palestine: British-Jewish-Arab Relations, 1914-1918. . . . . *v.6 p.612*

The Question of Reality. *v.1 p.488*

A Question of Torture: CIA Interrogation, from the Cold War to the War on Terror. *v.4 p.562*

Questioning Geography: Fundamental Debates. . . . *v.4 p.375*

The Questioning Presence: Wordsworth, Keats and the Interrogative Mode in Romantic Poetry. *v.2 p.324*

Questioning Romanticism. *v.2 p.278, p.279*

Questioning the Media: A Critical Introduction. . . . *v.4 p.416*

Questionnaire Design: How to Plan, Structure and Write Survey Material for Effective Market Research. *v.4 p.137*

Questionnaires and Inventories: Surveying Opinions and Assessing Personality. *v.5 p.603*

The Questionnaire. *v.2 p.783*

Questions and Answers about Block Scheduling: An Implementation Guide. *v.4 p.287*

Questions and Answers in Attitude Surveys: Experiments on Question Form, Wording, and Context. *v.4 p.691*

Questions and Their Retinue. *v.6 p.660*

Questions of Cultural Identity. *v.2 p.571*

The Questions of King Milinda. *v.1 p.564*

Questions of Possibility: Contemporary Poetry and Poetic Form. *v.2 p.178, p.179*

Questions That Sell: The Powerful Process for Discovering What Your Customer Really Wants. *v.4 p.142*

Quests for a Promised Land: The Works of Martin Andersen Nexo. *v.2 p.627*

The Quetzal and the Macaw: The Story of Costa Rica's National Parks. *v.3 p.270*

Quick and Easy Ways to Connect with Students and Their Parents, Grades K-8: Improving Student Achievement Through Parent Involvement. . . . *v.4 p.353*

The Quick and the Dead. *v.2 p.159*

Quick Reference Dictionary for Athletic Training. . . *v.4 p.828*

Quick Teambuilding Activities for Busy Managers: 50 Exercises That Get Results in Just 15 Minutes. *v.4 p.80*

Quicksand. *v.2 p.94*

Quicksilver: The Autobiography of Marie Rambert. . . *v.1 p.11*

The Quiet American. *v.2 p.350*

Quiet Fire: Asian American Poetry, 1892-1970. *v.6 p.102, p.103*

Quiet Fire: Memoirs of Older Gay Men. *v.6 p.380*

Quiet Flows the Don. *v.2 p.808*

Quiet Odyssey: A Pioneer Korean Woman in America. *v.6 p.94, p.114, p.136*

The Quiet Revolution: Central Banking Goes Modern. *v.4 p.88, p.154*

Quiet Revolution in the South: The Impact of the Voting Rights Act, 1965-1990. . . . . *v.4 p.554, p.573*

The Quilts of Gee's Bend: Masterpieces from a Lost Place. *v.1 p.704, p.809*

Quincas Borba: A Novel. *v.2 p.691*

Quincas Borba. *v.2 p.691*

Quincy's Market: A Boston Landmark. *v.1 p.823*

Quine. *v.1 p.443*

Quintessential Careers: a Career and Job-Hunting Resources Guide. *v.4 p.167, p.170*

A Quire of Seven. *v.2 p.625*

Quisling : A Study in Treason. *v.3 p.234*

Quisqueya on the Hudson: The Transnational Identity of Domincans in Washington. *v.6 p.543, p.548*

Quite Early One Morning. *v.2 p.386*

Quito 1599: City and Colony in Transition. *v.3 p.332*

Quixotic Desire: Psychoanalytic Perspectives on
Cervantes. *v.2 p.649*

Quo Vadis? *v.2 p.792*

Quonset Hut: Metal Living for a Modern Age. *v.1 p.789*

The Quotable Artist. *v.1 p.664*

Quotation and Cultural Meaning in Twentieth-Century
Music. *v.1 p.218, p.219*

Quoting God: How Media Shape Ideas about Religion and
Culture. *v.4 p.719*

The Qur'an and Its Interpreters: Surah Baqarah. . . .*v.1 p.556*

The Qur'an and Its Interpreters: The House of 'Imran. .*v.1 p.556*

Qur'an, Liberation and Pluralism: An Islamic Perspective of
Interreligious Solidarity Against Oppression. *v.1 p.558*

Qwert and the Wedding Gown: A Novel. *v.2 p.672*

R

R. E. Lee: A Biography. *v.3 p.425*

R. E. M.: Behind the Mask. *v.6 p.409*

R. K. Narayan: A Critical Appreciation. *v.2 p.765*

R. K. Narayan: Contemporary Critical Perspectives. . .*v.2 p.765*

A Rabbinic Anthology. *v.1 p.550*

Rabbinic Fantasies: Imaginative Narratives from Classical
Hebrew Literature. *v.6 p.652*

Rabbinic Mind. *v.1 p.552*

Rabbit Novels, Vol. 1. . . . .*v.2 p.157*

Rabbit Novels, Vol. 2. . . . .*v.2 p.157*

Rabelais and His World. *v.2 p.472*

Rabelais and Music. *v.1 p.179*

The Rabelais Encyclopedia. *v.2 p.472*

Rabelais Revisited. *v.2 p.472*

Rabi'a the Mystic and Her Fellow-Saints in Islam. . .*v.1 p.555*

Rabin and Israel's National Security. *v.6 p.614*

The Rabin Memoirs: With Recent Speeches, New Photographs,
and an Afterword. *v.6 p.615*

Rabinal Achi: A Mayan Drama of Sacrifice. *v.2 p.677*

Race after Hitler: Black Occupation Children in Postwar
Germany and America. *v.3 p.176*

Race Against the Court: The Supreme Court and Minorities in
Contemporary America. *v.4 p.457, p.540*

Race and Affluence: An Archaeology of African America and
Consumer Culture. *v.6 p.20*

Race and Class in the Southwest: A Theory of Racial
Inequality. *v.4 p.729*

Race and Color in Brazilian Literature. *v.2 p.689, p.690*

Race and Crime: A Biosocial Analysis. *v.6 p.257*

Race and Culture in the Classroom: Teaching and Learning
Through Multicultural Education. *v.4 p.309*

Race and Culture. *v.4 p.729*

Race and Ethnic Relations in Canada. *v.3 p.542*

Race and Ethnicity in America: A Concise
History. *v.6 p.118, p.122*

Race and Ethnicity in Latin America. *v.3 p.281, v.4 p.731*

Race and Ethnicity in Research Methods. *v.4 p.687*

Race and Ethnicity, Set. *v.4 p.3*

Race and Intelligence: Separating Science from
Myth. *v.5 p.608, p.652*

Race and Labor in the Hispanic Caribbean: The West Indian
Immigrant Worker Experience in Puerto Rico,
1800-1850. . . . .*v.3 p.319*

Race and Nation in Modern Latin America. . .*v.3 p.278, p.296*

Race and Party Competition in Britain. *v.4 p.606*

Race and Place: Race Relations in an American
City. *v.3 p.517, v.6 p.720*

Race and Politics in the Dominican Republic. *v.3 p.317*

Race and Politics: "Bleeding Kansas" and the Coming of the
Civil War. *v.3 p.421*

Race and Racism: Canada's Challenge. *v.3 p.542*

Race and Resistance: Literature and Politics in Asian
America. *v.6 p.97*

Race and Reunion: The Civil War in American Memory. .*v.3 p.394*

Race and Schooling in the City. *v.4 p.301*

Race and Slavery in the Middle East: An Historical
Enquiry. *v.6 p.582*

Race and the Shaping of Twentieth-Century
Atlanta. *v.3 p.503, v.6 p.710*

Race and Time: American Women's Poetics from Antislavery to
Racial Modernity. *v.2 p.15*

Race and U. S. Foreign Policy from 1900 Through World War
II. *v.3 p.315*

Race and Urban Space in American Culture. *v.6 p.718*

Race, Class and Gender in the United States: An Integrated
Study. *v.6 p.471*

Race Consciousness: African-American Studies for the New
Century. *v.6 p.14*

Race, Crime and the Law. *v.4 p.471*

Race, Culture, and Evolution: Essays in the History of
Anthropology. *v.4 p.5*

Race, Gender and Rhetoric: The True State of Race and Gender
Relations in Corporate America. *v.4 p.133*

Race: How Blacks and Whites Think and Feel about the
American Obsession. *v.4 p.730*

Race in Another America: The Significance of Skin Color in
Brazil. *v.3 p.280, p.343*

Race in Contemporary Brazil: From Indifference to
Inequality. *v.3 p.342*

Race in Mind: Race, IQ, and Other Racisms. *v.4 p.17*

Race in the Jury Box: Affirmative Action in Jury
Selection. *v.6 p.270*

Race, Law, and Culture: Reflections on Brown vs. Board of
Education. *v.4 p.451*

Race Matters. *v.4 p.730, v.6 p.41*

Race Music: Black Cultures from Bebop to Hip-Hop. .*v.1 p.282*

Race, Nation, and Religion in the Americas. *v.3 p.315*

Race of the Century: The Heroic True Story of the 1908 New
York-to-Paris Auto Race. *v.4 p.805, p.848*

Race, Place, and Medicine: The Idea of the Tropics in
Nineteenth-Century Brazil. *v.3 p.342*

Race, Police, and the Making of a Political Identity: Mexican
Americans and the Los Angeles Police Department,
1900-1945. . . . . . .*v.4 p.774, v.6 p.265, p.537, p.548*

Race, Racism, and Multiraciality in American
Education. *v.4 p.301*

Race, Racism, and Reparations. *v.6 p.20, p.36*

Race, Rhetoric, and Composition. *v.2 p.565*

Race, Rights and the Asian American
Experience. *v.4 p.456, v.6 p.107, p.117, p.120*

Race Riot: Chicago in the Red Summer of 1919. . . .*v.3 p.516*

Race, Rock and Elvis. *v.1 p.266, p.348*

Race, State, and Armed Forces in Independence-Era Brazil:
Bahia, 1790s-1840s. *v.3 p.274, p.337*

Race to Incarcerate. *v.4 p.753, p.773*

Race to the Finish: Identity and Governance in an Age of
Genomics. *v.5 p.136, p.146*

Race to the Pole: Tragedy, Heroism, and Scott's Antarctic
Quest. *v.4 p.378*

Race-Ing Justice, En-Gendering Power: Essays on Anita Hill,
Clarence Thomas and the Construction of Social
Reality. *v.6 p.470*

Race-Ing Moral Formation: African American Perspectives on
Care and Justice. *v.6 p.33*

The Rachel Papers. *v.2 p.329*

Rachel Ray. *v.2 p.317*

Rachel's Song: A Novel. *v.2 p.670*

Rachmaninoff. *v.1 p.220, p.350*

Racial Castration: Managing Masculinity in Asian
America. *v.6 p.96, p.111*

The Racial Economy of Science: Toward a Democratic
Future. *v.5 p.388*

Racial Formation in the United States: 1960-1990. . .*v.6 p.124*

Racial Formations/Critical Transformations: Articulations of
Power in Ethnic and Racial Studies in the United
States. *v.6 p.97, p.124*

Racial Oppression in America. *v.4 p.728*

Racial Politics in American Cities. *v.6 p.716*

Racial Revolutions: Antiracism and Indigenous Resurgence in
Brazil. *v.3 p.343*

The Racial State: Germany 1933-1945. . . . .*v.3 p.171*

Racing in the Street: The Bruce Springsteen
Reader. *v.1 p.274, p.358*

Racing the Enemy: Stalin, Truman, and the Surrender of
Japan. *v.3 p.81, p.87, p.227,v.4 p.647*

Racism 101. . . . .*v.6 p.25, p.43*

Racism and Social Inequality in Canada: Concepts,
Controversies and Strategies of Resistance. . . .*v.3 p.542*

Racism: From Slavery to Advanced Capitalism. . . .*v.4 p.727*

Racism in a Racial Democracy: The Maintenance of White
Supremacy in Brazil. *v.3 p.280, p.281, p.343*

Racism in College Athletics: The African-American Athlete's
Experience. *v.4 p.814, p.831*

Racism, Modernity, and Identity on the Western Front. *v.4 p.44*

Racism on Trial: The Chicano Fight for Justice. . . .*v.6 p.540*

Racism Without Racists: Color-Blind Racism and the
Persistence of Racial Inequality in the United States. *v.4 p.729*

Racist Culture: Philosophy and the Politics of Meaning. *v.4 p.730*

The Racist Murder of Stephen Lawrence: Media Performance
and Public Transformation. *v.6 p.256*

Radclyffe Hall: A Woman Called John. *v.6 p.401*

The Radetzky March. *v.2 p.614, v.3 p.184*

Radetzkymarsch. *v.2 p.614*

Radiant Textuality: Literature after the World Wide
Web. *v.2 p.191, p.567*

The Radiant Way. *v.2 p.343, p.344*

Radiation and Human Health: A Comprehensive Investigation of
the Evidence Relating Low-Level Radiation to Cancer
and Other Diseases. *v.5 p.364, p.374, p.375, p.376*

Radiation Detection and Measurement. *v.5 p.563*

Radiative Processes in Astrophysics. *v.5 p.67*

A Radical Approach to Real Analysis. *v.5 p.490*

Radical Ecology: The Search for a Livable World. . .*v.6 p.284*

Radical Ecopsychology: Psychology in the Service of
Life. *v.6 p.297*

Radical Enlightenment: Philosophy and the Making of
Modernity 1650-1750. . . . .*v.3 p.72*

Radical Expression: Political Language, Ritual, and Symbol in
England, 1790-1850. . . . .*v.6 p.751, p.758*

Radical Heroes: Gramsci, Freire and the Politics of
Adult. *v.4 p.762*

Radical Interpretation in Religion. *v.1 p.521*

The Radical Kingdom: The Western Experience of Messianic
Hope. *v.1 p.644*

Radical Nationalism in Cameroon: Social Origins of the U. P. C.
Rebellion. *v.6 p.62*

Radical Nationalist in Japan: Kita Ikki,
1883-1937. . . . .*v.6 p.228, p.229*

The Radical Novel in the U. S., 1900-1954: Some Interrelations
of Literature and Society. *v.2 p.11*

Radical Presence: Teaching as Contemplative Practice. *v.4 p.348*

The Radical Reformation. *v.1 p.601, p.602*

Radical Religion in the English Revolution. . .*v.3 p.104, p.121*

Radical Representations: Politics and Form in U. S. Proletarian
Fiction, 1929-1941. . . . .*v.2 p.10*

The Radical Republicans: Lincoln's Vanguard for Racial
Justice. *v.3 p.401, p.421*

The Radical Right in Interwar Estonia. *v.3 p.256*

The Radical Right. *v.3 p.445, p.465*

Radical Right-Wing Populism in Western Europe. . . .*v.4 p.601*

Radical Underworld: Prophets, Revolutionaries and
Pornographers in London,
1795-1840. . . . . .*v.3 p.113, p.131,v.6 p.739, p.760, p.766*

Radical Visions and American Dreams: Culture and Social
Thought in the Depression Years. *v.3 p.369*

Radicalism and Education Reform in 20th-Century China: The
Search for an Ideal Development
Model. *v.4 p.336, v.6 p.191, p.194*

Radicalism and the Origins of the Vietnamese
Revolution. *v.6 p.168*

Radicalism in American Silent Films, 1909-1929: A
Filmography and History. *v.6 p.333*

Radicalism in the States: The Minnesota Farmer-Labor Party
and the American Political Economy. *v.3 p.522*

Radically Gay: Gay Liberation in the Words of Its Founder
Harry Hay. *v.6 p.365, p.390*

Radicals in Organic Synthesis. *v.5 p.294*

Radicals. *v.5 p.276*

The Radif of Persian Music : Studies of Structure and Cultural
Context in the Classical Music of Iran. *v.1 p.287*

Radio and Television Broadcasting in Eastern Europe. *.v.4 p.412*

Radio Drama: A Comprehensive Chronicle of American Network Programs, 1932-1962. . . . . . . *.v.1 p.94, p.114*

Radio Drama. . . . . *.v.1 p.94*

Radio Free Dixie: Robert F. Williams and the Roots of Black Power. . . . . *.v.6 p.13*

Radio Frequency Radiation Dosimetry and Its Relationship to the Biological Effects of Elecromagnetic Fields. . *.v.5 p.376*

Radio Nation: Communication, Popular Culture and Nationalism in Mexico, 1920-1950. . . . . *.v.3 p.267*

Radio, TV and Modern Life: A Phenomenology of Broadcasting. . . . . *.v.4 p.412*

Radioactive Waste Disposal at Sea: Public Ideas, Transnational Policy Entrepreneurs, and Environmental Regimes. . . . . *.v.5 p.376, p.379, p.706,v.6 p.301*

Radiochemistry and Nuclear Chemistry. . . . . . *.v.5 p.307*

Radiogenic Isotope Geology. . . . . *.v.5 p.440, p.444*

Radiologic Science for Technologists: Physics, Biology and Protection. . . . . *.v.5 p.534*

Radiology for the Dental Professional. . . . . . *.v.5 p.525*

Raffles: The Amateur Cracksman. . . . . *.v.2 p.352*

The Raft Fishermen: Tradition and Change in the Brazilian Peasant Economy. . . . . *.v.4 p.28*

The Rag Doll Plagues. . . . . . . *.v.2 p.150, p.151,v.6 p.502*

Raga Mala: The Autobiography of Ravi Shankar. *.v.1 p.289, p.356*

Ragas of Longing: The Poetry of Michael Ondaatje. . . . . *.v.2 p.737, p.738*

Rage for Order: Essays in Criticism. . . . . *.v.2 p.569*

A Rage in Harlem. . . . . *.v.2 p.86*

The Rage of a Privileged Class: Why Do Prosperous Blacks Still Have the Blues? . . . . *.v.4 p.723*

A Rage to Punish: The Unintended Consequences of Mandatory Sentencing. . . . . *.v.6 p.271*

The Ragionamenti: The Lives of Nuns, the Lives of Married Women, the Lives of Courtesans. . . . . *.v.2 p.707*

Ragnar Frisch: Economic Planning Studies. . . *.v.4 p.202, p.203*

Rag-Tags, Scum, Riff-Raff and Commies: The U. S. Intervention in the Dominican Republic, 1965-1966. . . . . . *.v.3 p.316*

Ragtime: A Musical and Cultural History. . . . . . *.v.1 p.257*

Ragtime. . . . . *.v.2 p.144*

Rahel Varnhagen: The Life of a Jewish Woman. . . . *.v.2 p.598*

A Rahner Reader. . . . . *.v.1 p.572*

Rail, Steam, and Speed: The Rocket and the Birth of Steam Locomotion. . . . . *.v.3 p.49, p.50*

Railroads and the Granger Laws. . . . . *.v.4 p.445*

Railroads in the Civil War: The Impact of Management on Victory and Defeat. . . . . *.v.4 p.519*

The Railway Journey: The Industrialization and Perception of Time and Space. . . . . *.v.6 p.766*

Railways and the Victorian Imagination. . . . . . *.v.6 p.765*

Rain Charm for the Duchy and Other Laureate Poems. *.v.2 p.353*

Rain Forest: Ancient Realm of the Pacific Northwest. . . . . *.v.5 p.177, p.235, p.239*

Rain Forest Bibliography: An Annotated Guide to over 1600 Nonfiction Books about Central and South American Jungles. . . . . . . *.v.5 p.177, p.181, p.224, p.239*

Rain Forest Exchanges: Industry and Community on an Amazonian Frontier. . . . . *.v.5 p.41, v.6 p.297*

Rain Forests of the World, Set. . . . . *.v.5 p.176, p.239*

Rain God. . . . . *.v.6 p.500*

Rain of Gold. . . . . *.v.6 p.504*

Rain of Scorpions and Other Stories. . . . . *.v.6 p.504*

Rainbow Boys. . . . . *.v.6 p.399*

A Rainbow for the Christian West. . . . . *.v.2 p.536*

A Rainbow of Gangs: Street Cultures in the Mega-City. . . . . *.v.4 p.714, p.715,v.6 p.125, p.547, p.551*

Rainbow of Mathematics: A History of the Mathematical Sciences. . . . . *.v.5 p.466*

The Rainbow. . . . . *.v.2 p.362*

Rainforests of the World: Water, Fire, Earth and Air. . . . . *.v.5 p.177, p.239*

Rainforests: Overview, Current Abstracts with Indexes. *.v.5 p.178*

Rainforest. . . . . *.v.5 p.239*

Raining Backwards. . . . . *.v.6 p.506*

Raise High the Roof Beam, Carpenters, and Seymour: An Introduction. . . . . *.v.2 p.118*

A Raisin in the Sun and the Sign in Sidney Brustein's Window. . . . . *.v.2 p.80*

Raising Cain: Protecting the Emotional Life of Boys. *.v.5 p.641*

Raising Cane: The World of Plantation Hawaii. *.v.6 p.114, p.117*

Raising the Bar: New Horizons in Disability Sport. . *.v.4 p.830*

The Raj Quartet: A Division of Spoils. . . . . . . *.v.2 p.382*

The Raj Quartet: The Day of the Scorpion. . . . . *.v.2 p.382*

The Raj Quartet: The Jewel in the Crown. . . . . . *.v.2 p.382*

The Rakish Stage: Studies in English Drama, 1660-1800. . . . . *.v.2 p.187*

Raleigh and the British Empire. . . . . *.v.3 p.404*

Rally 'Round the Flag: Chicago and the Civil War. . *.v.3 p.515*

Ralph Waldo Emerson: Essays and Poetry. . . . . . *.v.2 p.38*

Ralph Waldo Emerson. . . . . *.v.2 p.38*

Rama and the Dragon. . . . . *.v.6 p.656*

La Rama. . . . . *.v.2 p.668*

The Ramayana of Valmiki: An Epic of Ancient India, Aranyakanda. . . . . *.v.1 p.536*

The Ramayana of Valmiki: An Epic of Ancient India: Kiskindhakanda. . . . . *.v.1 p.535*

The Ramayana of Valmiki: An Epic of Ancient India. . . . . *.v.1 p.535, p.536*

The Ramayana of Valmiki Balakanda. . . . . *.v.1 p.536*

The Ramayana of Valmiki: Sundarakanda. . . . . . *.v.1 p.535*

RAMBI/Index of Articles on Jewish Studies. . . . *.v.1 p.545*

Ramblin Man: The Life and Times of Woody Guthrie. . . . . *.v.1 p.295, p.328*

Rameau's Nephew and D'Alembert's Dream. *.v.2 p.480, v.3 p.147*

Rameau's Nephew and Other Works. . . . . *.v.2 p.479*

Rampage: The Social Roots of School Shootings. . . *.v.6 p.265*

Rampant Women: Suffragists and the Right of Assembly. . . . . *.v.4 p.519, v.6 p.431*

Ramsey Theory on the Integers. . . . . *.v.5 p.476*

Ranchers, Homesteaders and Traders: Frontiersmen of the South-Central States. . . . . *.v.3 p.510*

Randall Jarrell and His Age. *v.2 p.90*

Random Grim Forge: A Study of Social Ideas in the Work of Gerard Manley Hopkins. *v.2 p.294*

Random Harvest and Other Novellas. *v.6 p.648*

The Random House Book of Twentieth-Century French Poetry: With Translations by American and British Poets. .*v.2 p.463*

Random Violence: Worrying about New Crimes and New Victims. *v.4 p.754, v.6 p.256, p.258*

A Random Walk down Wall Street: The Time Tested Strategy for Successful Investing Completely. *v.4 p.96*

Random Walks in Biology. *v.5 p.564*

Randomized Response: A Method for Sensitive Surveys. *v.4 p.691*

Randomness. *v.5 p.480*

Range Management. *v.5 p.42*

Range Wars: Heated Debates, Sober Reflections, and Other Assessments of Texas Writing. *v.2 p.13*

Rangeland Ecology and Management. *v.5 p.42*

Rangeland Health: New Methods to Classify, Inventory, and Monitor Rangelands. *v.5 p.42*

Rangeland Wildlife. *v.5 p.42*

☐ Rangelands West. *v.5 p.36, p.41, p.42*

Rank and Privilege: The Military and Society in Latin America. *v.3 p.277*

Rap - The Lyrics: The Words to Rap's 175 Greatest Hits. *v.1 p.274, p.412*

Rap Attack 3: From African Jive to Global Hip-hop. .*v.1 p.275*

Rap Music and Street Consciousness. *v.1 p.270*

Rap Music in the 1980s: A Reference Guide. *v.1 p.168, p.272, p.281*

Rape: A Love Story. *v.2 p.152*

The Rape of Belgium: The Untold Story of World War I. .*v.3 p.206*

The Rape of Clarissa: Writing, Sexuality and Class Struggle in Samuel Richardson. *v.2 p.258*

The Rape of Europa: The Fate of Europe's Treasures in the Third Reich and the Second World War. *v.1 p.823*

The Rape of the Lock and Its Illustrations, 1714-1896. .*v.2 p.257*

The Rape of the Lock and Other Poems. *v.2 p.257*

Rape on the Public Agenda: Feminism and the Politics of Sexual Assault. *v.6 p.468*

Rape Warfare: The Hidden Genocide in Bosnia-Herzegovina and Croatia. *v.4 p.651*

A Rapid Biological Assessment of the Northern Cordillera Vilcabamba, Peru. *v.5 p.176, p.236*

Rapid Guide to Hazardous Chemicals in the Workplace. .*v.5 p.313*

Rapid Transit Systems: And the Decline of Steam. . .*v.5 p.700*

Rara!: Vodou, Power, and Performance in Haiti and Its Diaspora. *v.1 p.293*

Rare and Commonplace Flowers: The Story of Elizabeth Bishop and Lota de Macedo Soares. *v.6 p.403*

Rare Earth: Why Complex Life Is Uncommon in the Universe. *v.5 p.74, p.75, p.77*

Rarity. *v.5 p.205*

Rasa: Performing the Divine in India. *v.1 p.16*

Rasem Badran. *v.1 p.795*

Rashomon and Other Stories. *v.6 p.229*

Rastafari: From Outcasts to Culture Bearers. *v.4 p.711*

Rat Bohemia. *v.6 p.399*

Rat Dissection Manual. *v.5 p.90*

The Rat Nervous System: An Introduction to Preparatory Techniques. *v.5 p.87*

The Rate of Interest and Other Essays. *v.4 p.270*

The Rate of Interest: Its Nature, Determination and Relation to Economic Phenomena. *v.4 p.200*

Rates of Exchange. *v.2 p.331*

Ratifying the Constitution. *v.4 p.452*

Rating Scales and Checklists: Evaluating Behavior, Personality, and Attitudes. *v.5 p.603*

Rational Choice and Judgment: Decision Analysis for the Decider. *v.4 p.83*

The Rational Choice Controversy in Historical Sociology. *v.4 p.688*

Rational Choice Theory: Resisting Colonisation. . . .*v.4 p.688*

Rational Choice Theory. *v.4 p.194*

Rational Emotive Behavior Therapy: It Works for Me--It Can Work for You. *v.5 p.665*

Rational Expectations and Econometric Practice, 2. . .*v.4 p.203*

Rational Expectations and Econometric Practice. .*v.4 p.233, p.238*

The Rational Expectations Revolution in Macroeconomics: Theories and Evidence. *v.4 p.237*

Rational Points on Elliptic Curves. *v.5 p.497*

Rational Woman: A Feminist Critique of Dualism. *v.1 p.506, v.6 p.461*

The Rationalists. *v.1 p.513, p.514*

Rationality and Religion: Does Faith Need Reason? .*v.1 p.523*

Rationality and Religious Belief. *v.1 p.522*

The Rationality of Belief and the Plurality of Faith. .*v.1 p.523*

The Rationality of Theism. *v.1 p.499, p.595*

Rationality, Religious Belief, and Moral Commitment: New Essays in the Philosophy of Religion. *v.1 p.522*

Rationalizing Culture: IRCAM, Boulez, and the Institutionalisation of the Avant-Garde. *v.1 p.209*

Rats, Lice and History: A Chronicle of Disease, Plagues, and Pestilence. *v.5 p.366*

The Rattlesnake: A voyage of discovery to the Coral Sea. *v.5 p.241*

Rattlesnake. *v.2 p.674*

The Rat. *v.2 p.608*

Rauschenberg: Art and Life. *v.1 p.697*

Ravel: Man and Musician. *v.1 p.220, p.350*

A Ravel Reader: Correspondence, Articles, Interviews. *v.1 p.222, p.350*

Raven and the Rock: Storytelling in Chukotka. . . .*v.2 p.793*

The Raven and the Whale: The War of Words and Wits in the Era of Poe and Melville. *v.2 p.4*

Ravenswood: The Steelworkers' Victory and the Revival of American Labor. *v.4 p.126*

Raw Judicial Power?: The Supreme Court and American Society. *v.4 p.538*

Raw Silk. *v.6 p.102*

Rawls and Religion: The Case for Political Liberalism. .*v.4 p.510*

Ray Bradbury: A Critical Companion. *v.2 p.63*

Ray Charles: Man and Music. *v.1 p.271, p.317*

Ray K. Metzker: Landscapes. *v.1 p.769*

Rayburn: A Biography. *v.3 p.458*

The Raymond and Frances Bushell Collection of Netsuke: A
   Legacy at the Los Angeles County Museum of Art.*v.1 p.715*

Raymond Chandler: A Biography. *v.2 p.65*

Rayuela. *v.2 p.678*

La Raza Unida Party: A Chicano Challenge to the U. S.
   Two-Party Dictatorship. *v.6 p.539*

Raza y Tierra: La Guerra de Castas y el Heneqén. . . .*v.3 p.289*

The Razor's Edge. *v.2 p.371*

Razzle Dazzle: The Life and Work of Bob Fosse. *v.1 p.8*

Re Joyce. *v.2 p.336, p.357*

The Reach of the State: Sketches of the Chinese Body
   Politic. *v.4 p.620*

Reaching Higher: The Power of Expectations in
   Schooling. *v.5 p.573*

Reaction and Reconstruction in English Politics, 1832 to
   1852. . . . .*v.3 p.94, p.111*

Reaction Index of Organic Syntheses. *v.5 p.293*

Reaction Kinetics. *v.5 p.276*

Reaction Mechanisms of Inorganic and Organometallic
   Systems. *v.5 p.304*

Reactionary Modernism: Technology, Culture, and Politics in
   Weimar and the Third Reich. *v.3 p.159*

Reactions and Characterization of Solids. *v.5 p.305*

Reactions to the English Civil War, 1642-1649. . . .*v.3 p.104*

Reactive Intermediates. *v.5 p.296*

Reactivity and Structure: Concepts in Organic
   Chemistry. *v.5 p.295*

Read All about It!: The Corporate Takeover of America's
   Newspapers. *v.4 p.411*

Read Aloud Handbook. *v.4 p.366*

Read Me: Software Art and Cultures. *v.1 p.771*

Read My Lips: Sexual Subversion and the End of
   Gender. *v.6 p.367*

A Readable "Beowulf": The Old English Epic Newly
   Translated. *v.2 p.204*

Readable Relativity. *v.5 p.556*

The Reader and the Writer. *v.2 p.619*

A Reader in the Anthropology of Religion. *v.4 p.36*

Reader's Companion to F. Scott Fitzgerald's Tender Is the
   Night. *v.2 p.76*

The Reader's Companion to the American Presidency.*v.3 p.377*

The Reader's Companion to U. S. Women's History. .*v.6 p.450*

The Readers Encyclopedia of World Drama. *v.1 p.55*

A Reader's Guide to Australian Fiction. *v.2 p.740*

A Reader's Guide to Canadian History: Beginnings to
   Confederation. *v.6 p.682*

A Reader's Guide to Dylan Thomas. *v.2 p.386*

A Reader's Guide to Ernest Hemingway. *v.2 p.86*

A Reader's Guide to Geoffrey Chaucer. *v.2 p.207*

A Reader's Guide to Gerard Manley Hopkins. *v.2 p.294*

A Reader's Guide to J. D. Salinger. *v.2 p.117*

A Reader's Guide to James Joyce. *v.2 p.360*

Reader's Guide to Lesbian and Gay Studies. . .*v.6 p.357, p.358*

A Reader's Guide to Marcel Proust. *v.2 p.524*

A Reader's Guide to Modern British Drama. *v.2 p.189*

A Reader's Guide to T. S. Eliot: A Poem-by-Poem
   Analysis. *v.2 p.72*

A Reader's Guide to the Contemporary English Novel.*v.2 p.194*

Reader's Guide to the History of Science. . .*v.3 p.45, v.5 p.388*

A Reader's Guide to the Poetry of Richard Wilbur. . .*v.2 p.128*

A Reader's Guide to the Roman de la Rose. *v.2 p.467*

A Reader's Guide to the Short Stories of Willa Cather.*v.2 p.67*

A Reader's Guide to Twentieth-Century Writers. . . .*v.2 p.179*

A Reader's Guide to William Butler Yeats. *v.2 p.327*

A Reader's Guide to William Faulkner: The Novels. . .*v.2 p.75*

A Reader's Guide to William Faulkner: The Short
   Stories. *v.2 p.75*

Reader's Guide to Women's Studies. *v.6 p.425*

Readers of the Book of Life: Contextualizing Developmental
   Evolutionary Biology. *v.5 p.194*

Reading a Japanese Film: Cinema in Context. *v.6 p.336*

Reading American Art. *v.1 p.682*

Reading and Fiction in Golden Age Spain: A Platonist Critique
   and Some Picaresque Replies. *v.2 p.641*

Reading and Learning to Read. *v.4 p.361*

Reading and Writing Nature: The Poetry of Robert Frost,
   Wallace Stevens, Marianne Moore, and Elizabeth
   Bishop. *v.2 p.62, p.78, p.103, p.124*

Reading Asian American Literature: From Necessity to
   Extravagance. *v.6 p.98*

Reading Australian Poetry. *v.2 p.742*

Reading Between the Lines. *v.2 p.170*

Reading Billy Budd. *v.2 p.48*

Reading Blake's Designs. *v.2 p.239, p.240*

Reading Buchi Emecheta: Cross-Cultural
   Conversations. *v.2 p.754*

Reading Chinua Achebe: Language and Ideology in
   Fiction. *v.2 p.753*

Reading Clarissa: The Struggles of Interpretation. . .*v.2 p.259*

Reading Coleridge: Approaches and Applications. . .*v.2 p.280*

Reading Contemporary Fiction. *v.2 p.194, p.578, p.579*

Reading Dance: the Birth of Choreology. *v.1 p.38*

Reading Dancing: Bodies and Subjects in Contemporary
   American Dance. *v.1 p.39*

Reading Dante's Stars. *v.6 p.564, p.575*

Reading Development and the Teaching of Reading: A
   Psychological Perspective. *v.4 p.354*

Reading Dostoevsky. *v.2 p.800, p.809*

Reading Football: How the Popular Press Created an American
   Spectacle. *v.4 p.812, p.818, p.859, p.902*

Reading for Meaning: Fostering Comprehension in the Middle
   Grades. *v.4 p.366*

Reading for the Plot: Design and Intention in
   Narrative. *v.2 p.455, p.570*

Reading Freire and Habermas: Critical Pedagogy and
   Transformative Social Change. *v.4 p.762*

Reading Greek Tragedy. *v.2 p.401*

Reading Hebrew Literature: Critical Discussions of Six Modern Texts. *v.6 p.650*

Reading Hume's Dialogues: A Veneration for True Religion. *v.1 p.452*

Reading Images: The Grammar of Visual Design. . . . *v.1 p.703*

Reading in America: Literature and Social History. . . . *v.2 p.6*

Reading Instruction That Works, Third Edition: The Case for Balanced Teaching. *v.4 p.365, v.5 p.573*

Reading Jazz: A Gathering of Autobiography, Reportage, and Criticism from 1919 to Now. *v.1 p.259*

The Reading Lesson: The Threat of Mass Literacy in Nineteenth-Century British Fiction. *v.2 p.174, v.6 p.738, p.755*

Reading Lolita in Tehran: A Memoir in Books. *v.6 p.632*

Reading Lyrics: More Than 1,000 of the Century's Finest--A Celebration of Our Greatest Songwriters, A Rediscovery of Forgotten Masters, and an Appreciation. *v.1 p.411*

Reading Matters: Narrative in the New Media Ecology. *v.4 p.419*

Reading Medieval Latin. *v.2 p.450*

Reading Mill: Studies in Political Theory. *v.4 p.491*

Reading "Beowulf": An Introduction to the Poem, Its Background, and Its Style. *v.2 p.205*

The Reading Nation in the Romantic Period. *v.6 p.739*

Reading Nietzsche. *v.1 p.467*

A Reading of Beowulf. *v.2 p.205*

A Reading of Hegel's "Phenomenology of Spirit". . . *v.1 p.464*

A Reading of Jane Austen. *v.2 p.267*

Reading Opera. *v.1 p.230*

Reading Paradise Lost. *v.2 p.253*

Reading Petronius. *v.2 p.440*

Reading Pop: Approaches to Textual Analysis in Popular Music. *v.1 p.272*

Reading Popular Prints 1790-1870. . . . . . *v.1 p.753, v.6 p.737*

Reading Rock and Roll: Authenticity, Appropriation and Aesthetics. *v.1 p.267, p.268*

Reading Rodney King - Reading Urban Uprising. *v.6 p.123, p.135*

Reading Roman Women: Sources, Genres, and Real Life. *v.3 p.23*

Reading Sappho: Contemporary Approaches. *v.2 p.419*

Reading Scripture with the Church Fathers. *v.1 p.616*

Reading Seneca. *v.1 p.429*

Reading Sport: Critical Essays on Power and Representation. *v.4 p.814*

Reading the African Novel. *v.2 p.751*

Reading the Apocalypse in Bed: Selected Works. . . *v.2 p.791*

Reading the Body Politic: Feminist Criticism and Latin American Women Writers. *v.6 p.479*

Reading the Literatures of Asian America. *v.6 p.96*

Reading the Novel in English 1950-2000. . . . . . . *v.2 p.194*

Reading the Old Testament: Method in Biblical Study. *v.1 p.618*

Reading the Principia: The Debate on Newton's Mathematical Methods for Natural Philosophy from 1687 to 1736. *v.5 p.466*

Reading the Right Text: An Anthology of Contemporary Chinese Drama. . . *v.1 p.129, p.131, p.133, p.134, v.6 p.209*

Reading the Romance: Women, Patriarchy and Popular Literature. *v.2 p.572, p.577*

Reading the Roots: American Nature Writing Before Walden. *v.5 p.77, p.78*

Reading the Shape of Nature: Comparative Zoology at the Agassiz Museum. *v.5 p.85*

Reading the 'Song of Roland'. *v.2 p.468*

Reading the Splendid Body: Gender and Consumerism in Eighteenth-Century British Writing on India. . . . *v.2 p.171*

Reading the Vampire. *v.6 p.318*

Reading the Virginian in the New West. *v.2 p.128*

Reading to Learn: Lessons from Exemplary Fourth-Grade Classrooms. *v.4 p.361*

Reading Topographic Maps. *v.4 p.390*

Reading U. S. Latina Writers: Remapping American Literature. *v.6 p.502, p.508, p.515*

Reading Vergil's Aeneid: An Interpretive Guide. . . . *v.2 p.446*

Reading Virgil and His Texts: Studies in Intertextuality. *v.2 p.446, p.447*

Reading Virginia Woolf's Essays and Journalism. . . *v.2 p.392*

Reading with Clarice Lispector. *v.2 p.690*

Reading Women Writers and African Literature. . . *v.6 p.476*

Reading, Writing, and Proving: A Closer Look at Mathematics. *v.5 p.458*

Reading Zoos: Representations of Animals and Captivity. *v.5 p.84*

Readings for a History of Anthropological Theory. . . *v.4 p.23*

Readings in African Popular Culture. *v.2 p.750, p.751*

Readings in Black American Music. *v.1 p.282*

Readings in Delaware History. *v.3 p.493*

Readings in Early Anthropology. *v.4 p.4, p.5*

Readings in English Prose of the Nineteenth Century. *v.2 p.202*

Readings in Ethnic Psychology. *v.6 p.121*

Readings in Gender in Africa. *v.6 p.51*

Readings in Han Chinese Thought. *v.1 p.418*

Readings in Judaism, Christianity and Islam. *v.1 p.525*

Readings in Latin American Modern Art. *v.1 p.684*

Readings in Planning Theory. *v.6 p.727*

Readings in Public Education in the United States: A Collection of Sources and Readings to Illustrate the History of Educational Practice and Progress in the United States. *v.4 p.325*

Readings in Renaissance Women's Drama: Criticism, History, and Performance, 1594-1998. . . . . *v.1 p.74, p.99*

Readings in Russian Civilization: Imperial Russia, 1700-1917. *v.3 p.209*

Readings in Russian Civilization: Russia Before Peter the Great, 900-1700. . . . . *v.3 p.209, p.210*

Readings in Russian Civilization: Soviet Russia, 1917 - Present, Vol. 3. . . . . *v.3 p.210*

Readings in Spanish Literature. *v.2 p.644*

Ready-to-Use Motor Skills and Movement Station Lesson Plans for Young Children: Teaching, Remediation and Assessment. *v.4 p.798*

Ready-to-Use Pre-Sport Skills Activities Program: 100 Month-by-Month Lessons with Activities, Games and Assessments for the Elementary Grades. *v.4 p.797, p.799*

Reagan and the Iran-Contra Affair: The Politics of Presidential Recovery. *v.3 p.467*

Reagan and the World: Imperial Policy in the New Cold
War. *v.3 p.475*

Reagan As President: Contemporary Views of the Man, His
Politics and His Policies. *v.3 p.466*

The Reagan Paradox: U. S. Foreign Policy in the 1980s. .*v.3 p.465*

The Reagan Presidency: An Oral History of the ERA. *v.3 p.480*

The Reagan Presidency: Assessing the Man and His
Legacy. *v.3 p.473*

The Reagan Presidency: Pragmatic Conservatism and Its
Legacies. *v.3 p.439*

The Reagan Revolution: An Inside Look at the Transformation
of the U. S. Government. *v.3 p.470*

Reagan's Federalism: His Efforts to Decentralize
Government. *v.4 p.526*

Reagan's Victory: The Presidential Election of 1980 and the
Rise of the Right. *v.3 p.446*

Reagan's War: The Epic Story of His Forty Year Struggle and
Final Triumph over Communism. *v.3 p.479*

Reagent Chemicals: American Chemical Society Specifications,
Official from January 1, 2006. . . . . *v.5 p.267*

Reagents, Auxiliaries and Catalysts for C-C Bond
Formation. *v.5 p.290*

Reagents for Organic Synthesis (Fieser and Fieser's Reagents
for Organic Synthesis). *v.5 p.290*

Real Analysis: Modern Techniques and Their
Applications. *v.5 p.490*

Real and Complex Analysis. *v.5 p.489*

Real Boys: Rescuing Our Sons from the Myths of
Boyhood. *v.5 p.642*

ⓔ Real Choices/new Voices: How Proportional Representation
Elections Could Revitalize American Democracy. *v.4 p.576*

The Real Estate Game: The Intelligent Guide to Successful
Investing and Decision-Making. *v.4 p.97, p.166*

Real Estate Handbook. *v.4 p.95, p.166*

The Real Estate Investment Handbook. *v.4 p.95, p.166*

Real Frank Zappa Book. *v.1 p.276, p.369*

Real Kids: Creating Meaning in Everyday Life. . . . *v.5 p.626*

Real Life in Castro's Cuba. *v.3 p.311, p.312*

The Real Life of Mary Ann Evans: George Eliot, Her Letters
and Fiction. *v.2 p.286*

Real Mathematical Analysis. *v.5 p.490*

Real Men or Real Teachers?: Contradictions in the Lives of
Men Elementary School Teachers. *v.4 p.279*

Real Options: Managing Strategic Investment in an Uncertain
World. *v.4 p.90, p.101*

The Real Price of War: How You Pay for the War on
Terror. *v.4 p.563*

Real Reading, Real Writing: Content-Area Strategies. *v.4 p.366*

Real Research: Conducting and Evaluating Research in the
Social Sciences. *v.4 p.376*

The Real Science Behind the X-Files: Microbes, Meteorites, and
Mutants. *v.5 p.243*

The Real Thing: Stories and Sketches. *v.2 p.365*

Real Time: Stories and a Reminiscence. *v.2 p.764*

Real Tripitaka and Other Pieces V34. . . . . *v.1 p.565*

The Real Worlds of Welfare Capitalism. *v.4 p.500*

Realer Than Reel: Global Directions in Documentary. *v.6 p.309*

Realignment: The Theory That Changed the Way We Think
about American Politics. *v.4 p.549*

Realism and Antirealism. *v.1 p.514*

Realism and Reality: Studies in the German Novelle of Poetic
Realism. *v.2 p.592*

Realism and the Aim of Science. *v.5 p.403*

Realism and the American Dramatic Tradition. . .*v.1 p.79, p.113*

Realism and the Background of Phenomenology. . . *v.1 p.514*

Realism, Rationalism and Scientific Method: Philosophical
Papers, Vol. 1. . . . . *v.1 p.499*

Realism Rescued: How Scientific Progress Is Possible. .*v.5 p.400*

Realism with a Human Face. *v.1 p.514*

Realisms: A Nineteenth-Century Novel. *v.2 p.193*

A Realist Conception of Truth. *v.1 p.514*

Realist Thought from Weber to Kissinger. *v.4 p.627*

Realist Vision. *v.2 p.455*

Realistic Ray Tracing. *v.5 p.340*

The Realities Behind Diplomacy: Background Influences on
British External Policy, 1865-1980. . . . . *v.3 p.91*

Realities of American Foreign Policy. *v.3 p.473*

Reality and Dreams. *v.2 p.384*

Reality and Rhetoric: Studies in the Economics of
Development. *v.4 p.242*

Reality by Design: The Rhetoric and Technology of Authenticity
in Education. *v.4 p.358*

Reality of Faith, the Problem of Subjectivism in
Theology. *v.1 p.644*

The Reality of God and Other Essays. *v.1 p.636*

Realizations: Narrative, Pictorial, and Theatrical Arts of the
Nineteenth Century. *v.6 p.737*

Reallexikon der deutschen Literaturgeschichte. Begründet von
Paul Merker und Wolfgang Stammler. Neu bearb. und
unter redaktioneller Mitarbeit von Klaus Kanzog, sowie
Mitwirkung zahlreicher Fachgelehrter. Hrsg. von
Werner Kohlschmidt und Wolfgang Mohr. *v.2 p.589*

Realm of St. Stephen: A History of Medieval Hungary,
895-1526. . . . . *v.3 p.186, v.6 p.562*

Realms of Freedom in Modern China. *v.4 p.515*

The Realms of Gold. *v.2 p.344*

Realms of Memory: The Construction of the French
Past. *v.3 p.140, p.141*

The Reappearing Characters in Balzac's Comedie
Humaine. *v.2 p.486*

Reason and Democracy. *v.4 p.505*

Reason and Hope: Selections from the Jewish Writings of
Hermann Cohen. *v.1 p.551*

Reason and Human Good in Aristotle. *v.1 p.426*

Reason and Morality. *v.1 p.487*

Reason and Passion: Justice Brennan's Enduring
Influence. *v.4 p.469*

Reason and Revolution. *v.4 p.685*

Reason and Teaching. *v.4 p.329*

Reason and Tradition in Indian Thought: An Essay on the
Nature of Indian Philosophical Thinking. *v.1 p.419*

Reason the Only Oracle of Man or A Compendious System of
Natural Religion. *v.1 p.545*

The Reason Why. *v.3 p.91, p.117*

The Reasonableness of Christianity, with A Discourse of Miracles, and Part of a Third Letter Concerning Toleration. *v.1 p.597, v.4 p.216*

Reasoned Freedom: John Locke and Enlightenment. . .*v.1 p.448*

Reasoning and Choice: Explorations in Political Psychology. *v.5 p.645*

Reasoning and the Logic of Things. *v.1 p.440*

Reasoning with the Infinite: From the Closed World to the Mathematical Universe. *v.5 p.400*

Reasons and Persons. *v.1 p.514*

Reasons for Belonging: Fourteen Contemporary Indian Poets. *v.2 p.763*

Rebecca West: A Celebration. *v.2 p.389*

Rebecca West: A Saga of the Century. *v.2 p.389*

Rebecca West: Heroism, Rebellion, and the Female Epic. *v.2 p.389*

Rebecca's Revival: Creating Black Christianity in the Atlantic World. *v.1 p.648*

Rebecca. *v.2 p.343*

Rebel and Saint: Muslim Notables, Populist Protest, and Colonial Encounters - Algeria and Tunisia, 1800-1904. . . . .*v.6 p.641, p.642*

Rebel at Large, Recollections of Fifty Crowded Years. .*v.3 p.457*

Rebel Brass: The Confederate Command System. .*v.3 p.402, p.432*

Rebel Yell: Stories by Contemporary Southern Gay Authors. *v.2 p.27, v.6 p.407*

Rebellion and Democracy in Meiji Japan: A Study of Commoners in the Popular Rights Movement. . . .*v.6 p.223*

Rebellion and Its Enemies in Late Imperial China, Militarization and Social Structure, 1796-1864. . . . .*v.6 p.187*

Rebellion in Chiapas: An Historical Reader. . .*v.3 p.291, p.292*

Rebellion in the Backlands. *v.3 p.339*

Rebellion in the Borderlands: Anarchism and the Plan of San Diego, 1904-1923. . . . .*v.3 p.295*

The Rebellious Century: 1830-1930. . . . .*v.4 p.707*

Rebellious Fraser's: Nol Yorke's Magazine in the Days of Maginn, Thackeray and Carlyle. *v.6 p.742, p.753*

Rebellious Hearts: British Women Writers and the French Revolution. *v.2 p.171*

Rebels Against War: The American Peace Movement, 1933-1983. . . . .*v.4 p.572, p.651*

Rebels and Gentlemen: Philadelphia in the Age of Franklin. *v.3 p.492*

Rebels in Law: Voices in History of Black Women Lawyers. *v.6 p.442*

The Rebel's Silhouette: Selected Poems. *v.6 p.151, p.162*

Rebels under Sail: The American Navy During the Revolution. *v.3 p.413*

The Rebel. *v.6 p.503*

Rebirth and Destiny of Israel. *v.6 p.613*

Rebirth: Mexican Los Angeles from the Great Migration to the Great Depression. *v.6 p.536, p.549*

Rebirth of a Nation: Wales, 1880-1980. . . . . .*v.3 p.132*

Rebirth of a Nation: Wales 1880-1980. . . . . .*v.3 p.132*

The Rebirth of Russian Democracy: An Interpretation of Political Culture. *v.4 p.585, p.598*

The Rebirth of the Habsburg Army: Friedrich Beck and the Rise of the General Staff. *v.3 p.182*

Rebuilding Labor: Organizing and Organizers in the New Union Movement. *v.4 p.122*

The Rebuke of History: The Southern Agrarians and American Conservative Thought. *v.4 p.516*

Recasting America: Culture and Politics in the Age of Cold War. *v.3 p.371, p.443*

Recasting Bourgeois Europe: Stabilization in France, Germany and Italy in the Decade after World War I. *v.3 p.170*

Recasting: "Gone with the Wind" in American Culture. .*v.2 p.98*

Recent Advances in Game Theory. *v.4 p.207*

Recent Criticism of James Joyce's Ulysses: An Analytical Review. *v.2 p.358*

Recent Developments in Growth Theory. *v.4 p.242*

Recent Developments in Post Keynesian Economics. .*v.4 p.241*

Recent Poetry of Spain: A Bilingual Anthology. . . .*v.2 p.643*

Recent Puerto Rican Theatre: Five Plays from New York. *v.6 p.495, p.516*

Reception and Poetics in Keats: My Ended Poet. . .*v.2 p.295*

The Reception of Darwinism in the Iberian World: Spain, Spanish America and Brazil. *v.5 p.79, p.203*

Reception Studies: New Surveys in the Classics. . .*v.2 p.399*

Reception Theory: A Critical Introduction. *v.2 p.589*

Recess Is Over: A Handbook for Managing Youthful Offenders in Adult Systems. *v.6 p.278*

Recharting the Caribbean: Land, Law, and Citizenship in the British Virgin Islands. *v.4 p.41*

La recherche du temps perdu, vol. 1. . . . .*v.2 p.524*

La recherche du temps perdu, vol. 2. . . . .*v.2 p.524*

La recherche du temps perdu, vol. 3. . . . .*v.2 p.524*

La recherche du temps perdu, vol. 4. . . . .*v.2 p.524*

Reciprocal Net: Common Molecules. *v.5 p.284*

Reckoning with Reagan: America and Its President in the 1980s. *v.3 p.479*

Reckoning with Slavery: Critical Essays in the Quantitative History of American Negro Slavery. *v.3 p.419*

Reclaiming a Scientific Anthropology. *v.4 p.24*

Reclaiming the City. *v.6 p.727*

Reclaiming the Commons: Community Farms and Forests in a New England Town. *v.4 p.771, v.5 p.37*

Reclaiming the Game: College Sports and Educational Values. *v.4 p.821, p.893*

Reclaiming the Last Wild Places: A New Agenda for Biodiversity. *v.5 p.179*

Reclaiming the Sacred: Lay Religion and Popular Politics in Revolutionary France. *v.3 p.150*

Recognition of Health Hazards in Industry: A Review of Materials Processes. *v.5 p.313*

Recognition of Israel: An End and a New Beginning. .*v.6 p.618*

The Recognition of Sakuntala: A Play in Seven Acts. .*v.6 p.151*

The Recognition of Shakuntala. *v.1 p.129, p.131*

Recognizing the Latino Resurgence in U. S. Religion: The Emmaus Paradigm. *v.6 p.520*

Recollected Words of Abraham Lincoln. *v.3 p.396*

Re/Collecting Early Asian America: Essays in Cultural History. *v.6 p.114*

Recollections and Experiences of an Abolitionist, from 1855 to 1865. . . . . *v.3 p.432*

Recollections and Reflections. *v.5 p.544*

Recollections of a Life. *v.3 p.459*

Recollections of My Life as a Woman: The New York Years: A Memoir. *v.2 p.143*

Recollections of the Golden Triangle. *v.2 p.526*

Recollections: The French Revolution of 1848. . . .*v.3 p.153*

Recombinant DNA: Genes and Genomes:A Short Course. *v.5 p.123*

Reconceiving the Renaissance: A Critical Reader. . . *v.2 p.169*

Reconceptualizing the Strengths and Common Heritage of Black Families: Practice, Research, and Policy Issues. . . .*v.6 p.38*

Reconciling Conflicts under the Endangered Species Act: The Habitat Conservation Planning Experience. . . .*v.5 p.178*

Reconciling the Solitudes: Essays on Canadian Federalism and Nationalism. *v.4 p.587*

Reconquest and Crusade in Medieval Spain. . . .*v.3 p.65, p.238*

The Reconquest of Spain. *v.3 p.65*

Reconsiderations on the Revolutionary War: Selected Essays, 14. . . . .*v.3 p.409*

Reconstructed Lives: Women and Iran's Islamic Revolution. *v.6 p.632*

Reconstructing a Chicano/a Literary Heritage: Hispanic Colonial Literature of the Southwest. *v.6 p.499, p.513*

Reconstructing America: The Symbol of America in Modern Thought. *v.3 p.370*

Reconstructing American Literary History. *v.2 p.5, p.6*

Reconstructing Aphra: A Social Biography of Aphra Behn. *v.2 p.238*

Reconstructing Biology: Genetics and Ecology in the New World Order. *v.5 p.137*

Reconstructing City Politics: Alternative Economic Development and Urban Regimes. *v.4 p.544*

Reconstructing Gender in the Middle East: Tradition, Identity, and Power. *v.6 p.592*

Reconstructing OT Theology: After the Collapse of History. *v.1 p.619*

Reconstructing Religious, Spiritual and Moral Education. *v.4 p.307*

Reconstructing Schizophrenia. *v.5 p.660*

Reconstructing the Canon: Russian Writing in the 1980's. *v.2 p.799*

Reconstructing the Common Good in Education: Coping with Intractable American Dilemmas. *v.4 p.325*

Reconstructing the Criminal: Culture, Law, and Policy in England, 1830-1914. . . . . . .*v.3 p.117, p.124,v.6 p.744*

Reconstructing the Dreamland: The Tulsa Riot of 1921: Race, Reparations, and Reconcilation. *v.6 p.20, p.36*

Reconstructing the Dreamland: The Tulsa Riot of 1921: Race, Reparations, and Reconciliation. *v.3 p.523, v.6 p.3*

Reconstructing the Past: Parsimony, Evolution, and Inference. *v.5 p.196*

Reconstructing the Rhythm of Beowulf. . . . *v.2 p.204, p.205*

Reconstructing the Union: Theory and Policy During the Civil War. *v.3 p.394, p.427*

Reconstructing Times Square: Politics and Culture in Urban Development. *v.6 p.726*

Reconstructing Womanhood: The Emergence of the Afro-American Woman Novelist. *v.2 p.8*

Reconstruction after the Civil War. *v.3 p.436*

Reconstruction and Regional Diplomacy in the Persian Gulf. *v.6 p.591*

The Reconstruction of American History. *v.3 p.374*

The Reconstruction of Economics: An Analysis of the Fundamentals of Institutional Economics. *v.4 p.247*

The Reconstruction of Nations: Poland, Ukraine, Lithuania, Belarus, 1569-1999. . . . .*v.3 p.207, p.252*

Reconstruction, Political And Economic, 1865-1877. . *v.3 p.396*

Reconstruction to Reform: Texas Politics, 1876-1906. *v.3 p.508*

The Record of Singing. *v.1 p.236, p.396*

A Record of the Boston Stage. *v.1 p.112, p.140*

Recorded Music in American Life: The Phonograph and Popular Memory, 1890-1945. . . . .*v.4 p.712*

Recording a Vanishing Legacy: The Historic American Buildings Survey in New Mexico, 1933-today. . . .*v.1 p.823*

The Recording Angel: Music, Records and Culture from Aristotle to Zappa. *v.1 p.377, p.386*

Recording Historic Structures. *v.1 p.824*

Recording Industry Sourcebook. *v.1 p.172, p.383*

The Recording Industry. *v.1 p.384*

Records Management Handbook. *v.4 p.115*

Records of the Dawn of Photography: Talbot's Notebooks P and Q. *v.1 p.763*

Records of the Historian: Chapters from the Shih Chi of Ssu-ma Ch'ien. *v.6 p.184, p.209*

Recounting the Seasons: Poems, 1958-2005. . . . .*v.2 p.144*

Recovered Legacies: Authority and Identity in Early Asian American Literature. *v.6 p.96*

Recovering Christina Rossetti: Female Community and Incarnational Poetics. *v.2 p.303*

Recovering History, Constructing Race: The Indian, Black, and White Roots of Mexican Americans. . . .*v.6 p.532, p.544*

Recovering the Sacred: The Power of Naming and Claiming. *v.6 p.681*

Recreating Africa: Kinship, Culture, and Religion in the African-Portuguese World, 1441-1770. *v.3 p.264, p.280, p.335*

Recreating Jane Austen. *v.2 p.269*

Recreation and Sport Planning and Design. *v.4 p.786, p.880, p.883*

Recreational Sport Management. *v.4 p.786*

Recreational Terror: Women and the Pleasures of Horror Film Viewing. *v.6 p.319*

The Recruiting Officer and Other Plays: The Constant Couple; The Twin Rivals; The Recruiting Officer; The Beaux' Stratagem. *v.2 p.244, p.245*

The Rector of Justin: A Novel. *v.2 p.55*

Recumbents: With How to Name by Jacques Derrida. .*v.2 p.529*

The Recurrent Crisis in Corporate Governance. *v.4 p.52, p.54, p.86, p.111*

Recursive Methods in Economic Dynamics. . .*v.4 p.205, p.239*

The Recycler's Manual for Business, Government, and Environmentalists. *v.5 p.377, p.704*

The Recycler's Manual for Business, Government, and the Environmental Community. *v.5 p.377, p.378*

Recycling and Resource Recovery Engineering: Principles of Waste Processing. *v.5 p.377, p.378*

Recycling and Waste Management Guide to the Internet. *v.4 p.159*

Red Against Blue: The Liberal Party in Colombian Politics, 1863-1899. . . . .*v.3 p.357*

The Red and the Black: A Chronicle of 1830. . . . . .*v.2 p.502*

The Red and the Black. *v.2 p.502*

The Red and the Green. *v.2 p.372*

Red Arctic: Polar Exploration and the Myth of the North in the Soviet Union, 1932-1939. . . . .*v.3 p.223*

The Red Army in Romania. *v.3 p.250*

The Red Atlantis: Communist Culture in the Absence of Communism. *v.4 p.508*

The Red Azalea: Chinese Poetry since the Cultural Revolution. *v.6 p.211*

The Red Badge of Courage. *v.2 p.36*

Red Beans. *v.6 p.506, p.510*

Red Capitalists in China: The Party, Private Entrepreneurs, and Prospects for Political Change. *v.4 p.619*

Red Cavalry. *v.3 p.224*

☐ Red de revistas Científicas de América Latina y el Caribe, España y Portugal (Red ALyC). *v.3 p.259*

Red Earth and Pouring Rain. *v.2 p.764*

Red Grange and the Rise of Modern Football. *v.4 p.804, p.858, p.893*

Red Grooms: A Retrospective. *v.1 p.698*

Red Grooms: The Graphic Work. *v.1 p.757*

Red Guard: The Political Biography of Dai Hsiao-Ai. *v.6 p.195, p.199*

The Red Hand: Protestant Paramilitaries in Northern Ireland. *v.4 p.607*

The Red King's Rebellion: Racial Politics in New England, 1675-1677. . . . .*v.6 p.685*

Red Land, Black Land: Daily Life in Ancient Egypt. . .*v.6 p.57*

The Red Limit: The Search for the Edge of the Universe. .*v.5 p.71*

Red Man's Land/White Man's Law: The Past and Present Status of the American Indian. *v.4 p.465, v.6 p.693*

Red Man's Religion: Beliefs and Practices of the Indians North of Mexico. *v.6 p.701*

🄴 Red Priests: Renovationism, Russian Orthodoxy, and Revolution, 1905-1946. . . . .*v.3 p.223*

Red River to Appomattox. *v.3 p.396, p.397*

The Red Rose Crew: A True Story of Women, Winning, and the Water. *v.4 p.835, p.865*

Red Scare: A Study in National Hysteria, 1919-1920. . . . .*v.3 p.443, p.449,v.4 p.714*

Red Scare: A Study in National Hysteria 1919. . . . .*v.3 p.449*

The Red Scare in the Midwest, 1945-1955. . . . . . .*v.3 p.506*

Red Sky at Morning: America and the Crisis of the Global Environment. *v.5 p.358, p.378*

Red Sorghum: A Novel of China. *v.6 p.213*

Red Star over China. *v.6 p.192, p.193*

Red Stars: Personality and the Soviet Popular Song, 1955-1991. . . . .*v.1 p.298*

The Red Tram. *v.2 p.748, p.749*

Red Victory: A History of the Russian Civil War, 1918-1921. . . . .*v.3 p.225*

Red Vienna: Experiment in Working-Class Culture, 1919-1934. . . . .*v.3 p.184*

Red, White, and Black: The Peoples of Early America. .*v.3 p.406*

Red Woman with Backward Eyes and Other Stories. . .*v.6 p.698*

Redating the New Testament. *v.1 p.624*

Redburn, White-Jacket, Moby-Dick. *v.2 p.48*

Redeeming the Communist Past: The Regeneration of Communist Parties in East Central Europe. *v.4 p.601*

Redeeming the South: Religious Cultures and Racial Identities among Southern Baptists, 1865-1925. . . . . . .*v.1 p.583*

Redeeming the Wasteland: Television Documentary and Cold War Politics. *v.4 p.413*

Redefining Efficiency: Pollution Concerns, Regulatory Mechanisms and Technological Change in the U. S. Petroleum Industry. *v.6 p.300*

Redefining Mexican "Security": Society, State, and Region under NAFTA. *v.4 p.593, p.594*

Redefining Self-Help in the Human Services: Policy and Practice. *v.5 p.669*

Redefining the Color Line: Black Activism in Little Rock, Arkansas, 1940-1970. . . . .*v.3 p.510*

Redefining the Self: Coming Out As Lesbian. *v.6 p.369*

Redemption: The Life of Henry Roth. *v.2 p.113*

Redemption. *v.2 p.529*

Redesigning the American Dream: Gender Housing and Family Life. *v.6 p.718*

Redewendungen und Sprichwoertliche Redensarten. *v.2 p.620, p.621*

Redgauntlet. *v.2 p.308*

Red-Hot and Righteous: The Urban Religion of the Salvation Army. *v.1 p.589*

Rediscoveries in American Sculpture: Studio Works, 1893-1939. . . . .*v.1 p.776*

Rediscovering Oscar Wilde. *v.2 p.321*

Rediscovering Palestine: Merchants and Peasants of Jabal Nablus, 1700-1900. . . . .*v.6 p.610*

Rediscovering Russia in Asia: Siberia and the Russian Far East. *v.3 p.214*

Rediscovering the Teachings of Jesus. *v.1 p.627*

The Re-Discovery of America: An Introduction to the Philosophy of American Life. *v.3 p.367*

The Rediscovery of the Holy Land in the Nineteenth Century. *v.6 p.609*

Redon's Etchings and Lithographs: A Catalogue Raisonné. *v.1 p.757*

Redox Mechanisms in Inorganic Chemistry. . .*v.5 p.304, p.305*

The Redress of Poetry. *v.2 p.326, p.352*

Reds: McCarthyism in Twentieth-Century America. . .*v.3 p.449*

Reducing Suicide: A National Imperative. *v.5 p.662*

Reed Reader. *v.2 p.154, v.6 p.27*

Re-Editing Shakespeare for the Modern Reader: Based on Lectures Given at the Folger Shakespeare Library, Washington, D. C. *v.2 p.232*

Reeds in the Wind. *v.2 p.717*

Reefs at Risk: A Map-Based Indicator of Threats to the World's Coral Reefs. *v.4 p.393, v.5 p.359*

Reefscape: Reflections on the Great Barrier Reef. *v.5 p.173, p.241,v.6 p.293, p.294*

Reel Bad Arabs: How Hollywood Vilifies a People. . .*v.6 p.330*

Reel History: In Defense of Hollywood. *v.6 p.315*

Reel Knockouts: Violent Women in the Movies. *v.6 p.321*

The Reel Middle Ages: American, Western and Eastern European, Middle Eastern and Asian Films about Medieval Europe. *v.6 p.314*

Reel Patriotism: The Movies and World War I. *v.6 p.322*

Reel to Real: Race, Sex and Class at the Movies. .*v.6 p.44, p.330*

The Reel World: Scoring for Pictures. . . .*v.1 p.256, v.6 p.351*

Reelpolitik II: Political Idelogies in '50s and '60s Films. .*v.6 p.342*

Reemergence of Established Pathogens in the 21st Century. *v.5 p.526*

The Reenchantment of Nineteenth-Century Fiction: Dickens, Thackeray, George Eliot and Serialization. *v.2 p.285, p.287, p.288, p.315*

Reengineering the Corporation: A Manifesto for Business Revolution. *v.4 p.86*

☐ REENIC: Russian and East European Network Information Center. *v.4 p.595, p.596, p.597, p.600*

Re-Envisioning Egypt, 1919-1952. . . . .*v.6 p.637*

Re-Envisioning Past Musical Cultures: Ethnomusicology in the Study of Gregorian Chant. *v.1 p.177*

A Reevaluation of the Works of American Writer Delmore Schwartz, 1913-1966. . . . .*v.2 p.119*

Re-Examining the Cold War: U. S.-China Diplomacy, 1954-1973. . . . .*v.3 p.392*

Reference and Essence. *v.1 p.505*

The Reference and Research Guide to Mystery and Detective Fiction. *v.2 p.580*

A Reference Grammar of Modern Bulgarian. *v.2 p.774*

A Reference Grammar of Modern French. *v.2 p.453*

A Reference Grammar of Modern Hebrew. *v.6 p.645*

Reference Grammar of Modern Italian. *v.2 p.699*

A Reference Grammar of Modern Standard Arabic. . .*v.6 p.654*

A Reference Grammar of Syrian Arabic. *v.6 p.653*

Reference Grammar of the German Language. *v.2 p.621*

Reference Guide to Famous Engineering Landmarks of the World: Bridges, Tunnels, Dams, Roads and Other Structures. *v.5 p.679*

Reference Guide to Modern Armenian Literature, 1500-1920: With an Introductory History. *v.6 p.665*

Reference Guide to Russian Literature. *v.2 p.796*

Reference Guide to Science Fiction, Fantasy, and Horror. *v.2 p.581*

☐ Reference Sources: Nuclear Engineering: Subject Guides: MIT Libraries. *v.5 p.739*

☐ Reference Style Guidelines. *v.5 p.260*

Referendum: Direct Democracy in Switzerland. . . .*v.4 p.595*

Referendums Around the World: The Growing Use of Direct Democracy. *v.4 p.575*

Refiguring American Film Genres: History and Theory. .*v.6 p.311*

Refiguring Authority: Reading, Writing and Rewriting in Cervantes. *v.2 p.649*

Refiguring the Map of Sorrow: Nature Writing and Autobiography. *v.6 p.287*

Refining Russia: Advice Literature, Polite Culture, and Gender from Catherine to Yeltsin. *v.3 p.210*

Reflections: Essays, Aphorisms, Autobiographical Writings. *v.2 p.575*

Reflections from the Heart of Educational Inquiry: Understanding Curriculum and Teaching through the Arts. *v.4 p.365*

Reflections from the Wrong Side of the Tracks: Class, Identity, and the Working Class Experience in Academe. . .*v.4 p.302*

Reflections in Black: A History of Black Photographers, 1840 to the Present. *v.1 p.705, p.769,v.6 p.9, p.16*

Reflections of a Culture Broker: A View from the Smithsonian. *v.1 p.826*

Reflections of a Nonpolitical Man. *v.2 p.613*

Reflections of a Rock Lobster: A Story about Growing up Gay. *v.6 p.401*

Reflections of Women in Antiquity. *v.6 p.450, p.451*

Reflections on Espionage: The Question of Cupcake. . .*v.2 p.87*

Reflections on Gender and Science. *v.5 p.403*

Reflections on Jesus and Socrates: Word and Silence. .*v.1 p.498*

Reflections on Learning. *v.4 p.343*

Reflections on Liszt. *v.1 p.206, p.336, p.337*

Reflections on Political Identity. *v.5 p.644*

Reflections on Statistics: Agendas for Learning, Teaching, and Assessment in K-12. . . . .*v.5 p.463*

Reflections on the Classical Canon in Economics: Essays in Honor of Samuel Hollander. *v.4 p.217*

Reflections on the Development of Modern Macroeconomics. *v.4 p.241*

Reflections on the Moral and Spiritual Crisis in Education. *v.4 p.306, p.307*

Reflections on the Principles of Psychology: William James after a Century. *v.5 p.596*

Reflections on the Theatre. *v.1 p.105, p.143, p.151*

Reflections on Way to Gallows. *v.6 p.227*

Reflective Faith: Essays in Philosophical Theology. . .*v.1 p.634*

Reflective Thinking: The Method of Education. *v.4 p.357*

Reflexivity in Tristram Shandy: An Essay in Phenomenological Criticism. *v.2 p.262*

Reform and Reaction in Twentieth Century American Politics. *v.3 p.446*

Reform and Reformation: England, 1509-1558. .*v.3 p.99, p.100*

ℯ Reform and Regicide: The Reign of Peter III of Russia. *v.3 p.216*

Reform and Regulation: American Politics from Roosevelt to Wilson. *v.3 p.471*

Reform in the Ottoman Empire, 1856-1876. . . . .*v.6 p.589*

Reform in the Provinces: The Government of Stuart England. *v.4 p.582*

The Reform Judaism Reader: North American Documents. *v.1 p.552*

Reform of the Papacy. *v.1 p.576*

Reform of Undergraduate Education. *v.4 p.294, p.295*

Reform Without Liberalization: China's National People's Congress and the Politics of Institutional Change. .*v.4 p.620*

The Reformation: A History. *v.1 p.601*

The Reformation in Germany. *v.3 p.165, p.166*

The Reformation Theologians: An Introduction to Theology in the Early Modern Period. *v.1 p.602*

Reformation Thought: An Introduction. *v.1 p.602*

The Reformation to the Present Day. *v.1 p.598*

The Reformation World. *v.1 p.602*

The Reformation. *v.3 p.57*

The Reformed Pastor. *v.1 p.649*

The Reformers: An Historical Survey of Pioneer Experiments in the Treatment of Criminals. *v.6 p.274*

Reformers and Activists. *v.6 p.694*

Reformers and Visionaries: The Americanization of the Art of Dance. *v.1 p.27*

Reformers, Critics, and the Paths of German Modernity: Anti-Politics and the Search for Alternatives, 1890-1914. . . . .*v.3 p.169*

Reforming Chile: Cultural Politics, Nationalism, and the Rise of the Middle Class. *v.3 p.352*

Reforming Corrections for Juvenile Offenders: Alternatives and Strategies. *v.6 p.274*

Reforming Federal Regulation. *v.4 p.444*

Reforming Probation and Parole in the 21st Century. *v.6 p.278*

Reforming Rural Russia: State, Local Society, and National Politics, 1855-1914. . . . .*v.3 p.219*

Re-Forming the Center: American Protestantism, 1900 to the Present. *v.1 p.606*

Reforming the US Corporate Tax. *v.4 p.107*

The Reforms of the Council of Constance (1414-1418). *v.1 p.571*

Reframing Japanese Cinema: Authorship, Genre, History. *v.6 p.327, p.328, p.336*

The Reframing of Realism: Galdos and the Discourses of the Nineteenth-Century Spanish Novel. *v.2 p.654*

Reframing Pilgrimage: Cultures in Motion. *v.1 p.530*

Refried Elvis: The Rise of the Mexican Counterculture. *v.3 p.268*

A Refuge in Thunder: Candomble and Alternative Spaces of Blackness. *v.3 p.340*

Refuge of a Scoundrel: The Patriot Act in Libraries. . *v.4 p.451*

Refugee and Immigrant Health: A Handbook for Health Professionals. *v.4 p.668*

Refugees As Immigrants: Cambodians, Laotians and Vietnamese in America. *v.6 p.139, p.140*

Refugees in a Global Era. *v.4 p.400*

Refugees in America in the 1990s: A Reference Handbook. *v.4 p.570*

Refugees in an Age of Genocide: Global, National and Local Perspectives During the Twentieth Century. . . .*v.4 p.668*

Refuges. *v.2 p.816*

Refuge. *v.6 p.650*

Refusal and Transgression in Joyce Carol Oates' Fiction, 135. . . . .*v.2 p.152*

Refusing Heaven: Poems. *v.2 p.145*

Refusing the Favor: The Spanish-Mexican Women of Santa Fe, 1820-1880. . . . .*v.6 p.531, p.546*

The Regal Theater and Black Culture. *v.1 p.18, p.19*

Regarding Children's Words: Teacher Research on Language and Literacy. *v.4 p.361, p.362*

Regarding Ellen Glasgow: Essays for Contemporary Readers. *v.2 p.80*

Regarding the Pain of Others. *v.1 p.704*

Regards et Jeux Dans l'Espace. *v.2 p.538, p.539*

Regency Design, 1790-1840: Gardens, Buildings, Interiors, Furniture. *v.1 p.800*

Regeneration Through Violence: The Mythology of the American Frontier, 1600-1860. . . . .*v.2 p.9*

Regeneration. *v.2 p.330*

Regenerative Design Techniques: Practical Applications in Landscape Design. *v.1 p.817*

La Regenta. *v.2 p.653*

Reggae, Rasta Revolution: Jamaican Music from Ska to Dub. *v.1 p.294*

Reggae, Rastafari, and the Rhetoric of Social Control. *v.1 p.292*

Reggae Routes: The Story of Jamaican Music. . . .*v.1 p.291*

Regime Shift: Comparative Dynamics of the Japanese Political Economy. *v.6 p.220*

Regimes and Oppositions. *v.4 p.575*

Reginald and Reginald in Russia. *v.2 p.381*

Regional Garden Design in the United States. *v.1 p.819*

The Regional Geography of Canada. *v.3 p.535*

Regional Geography of the United States and Canada. *v.4 p.382, p.397*

Regional Geology of Africa. *v.5 p.433*

The Regional Imagination: The South and Recent American History. *v.3 p.496*

Regional Landscapes of the United States and Canada. *v.3 p.365*

Regional Markets and Agrarian Transformation in Bolivia: Cochabamba, 1539-1960. . . . .*v.3 p.324*

Regional Oceanography: An Introduction. *v.5 p.429, p.433, p.434*

Regional Powers and Small State Security: India and Sri Lanka, 1977-1990. . . . .*v.6 p.159*

Regional Silviculture of the United States. *v.5 p.36*

Regional Strategraphy of North America. *v.5 p.431*

Regional Studies: The Interplay of Land and People. *v.3 p.509*

Regional Surveys of the World 2006. . . . .*v.4 p.396*

Regionalism and Realism: A Study of Government in the New York Metropolitan Area. *v.4 p.542, v.6 p.722*

Regionalism, Multilateralism, and Economic Integration: The Recent Experience. *v.4 p.630, p.665*

The Regionalization of Internationalized Innovation: Locations for Advanced Industrial Development and Disparities in Participation. *v.4 p.397*

Regions and Regionalism in the United States. . . .*v.3 p.380*

Regions, Institutions, and Agrarian Change in European History. *v.3 p.43*

Registry of Toxic Effects of Chemical Substances, 1985-1986 Edition: Addendum and User's Guide. *v.5 p.315*

Registry of Toxic Effects of Chemical Substances, RTECS: A Comprehensive Guide. *v.5 p.315*

Regreening the National Parks. *v.5 p.18*

Regression Analysis by Example. *v.5 p.483*

Regression and Anova: An Integrated Approach Using SAS Software. *v.5 p.483*

The Regrets. *v.2 p.471*

Regular and Related Solutions: The Solubility of Gases, Liquids and Solids. *v.5 p.282*

Regular Polytopes. *v.5 p.497, p.498*

Regulating Bodies: Essays in Medical Sociology. .*v.5 p.511, p.512*

Regulating Intimacy: A New Legal Paradigm.   .*v.4 p.471, p.472*

Regulation and the Revolution in United States Farm Productivity. *v.5 p.29*

The Regulation of Agricultural Biotechnology. *v.5 p.8*

Regulation of Alternative Splicing. *v.5 p.152*

The Regulation of Emotion. *v.5 p.655*

Regulation Through Litigation. *v.4 p.110, p.112*

Rehabilitation of Sports Injuries: Scientific Basis. *v.4 p.827, p.828, p.829*

☐ Rehabilitation Research and Training Center, University of South Florida. *v.5 p.667*

Rehabilitation Research: Principles and Applications. .*v.5 p.535*

Rehabilitations and Other Essays. *v.2 p.164*

Rehearsal for Destruction: A Study of Political Anti-Semitism in Imperial Germany. *v.3 p.60*

Rehearsal for Reconstruction: The Port Royal Experiment. *v.3 p.502, v.6 p.8*

Rehearsals for Fascism: Populism and Political Mobilization in Weimar Germany. *v.3 p.170*

Rehearsing New Roles: How College Students Develop As Writers. *v.2 p.564, p.565*

The Rehnquist Court and Civil Rights. *v.4 p.540*

The Rehnquist Court and Criminal Punishment. *v.4 p.540, v.6 p.274*

The Rehnquist Court and the Constitution. . . .*v.4 p.467, p.540*

The Rehnquist Court: In Pursuit of Judicial Conservatism, 76. . . . .*v.4 p.536*

The Rehnquist Court: Judicial Activism on the Right. *v.4 p.539, p.541*

The Rehnquist Legacy. *v.4 p.467*

The Reign of Henry III. *v.3 p.97, p.98*

The Reign of King Pym. *v.3 p.102, p.103*

The Reign of Mary Tudor: Politics, Government and Religion in England, 1553-58. . . . .*v.3 p.100, p.121*

The Reign of Richard Lionheart. *v.3 p.99*

The Reign of the Ayatollash: Iran and the Islamic Revolution. *v.6 p.632*

The Reign of the Phallus: Sexual Politics in Ancient Athens. *v.3 p.14*

The Reign of the Theatrical Director: French Theatre: 1887-1924. . . . .*v.1 p.106, p.152, p.153*

Re-imagining Policing in Canada. *v.6 p.262*

Reimagining the American Pacific: From South Pacific to Bamboo Ridge. *v.6 p.115, p.131*

Reinaldo Arenas. *v.2 p.673*

Reindeer People, Living with Animals and Spirits in Siberia. *v.4 p.772*

La Reine Margot. *v.2 p.489*

Reinforced Concrete, ACI 2005: A Fundamental Approach. *v.5 p.690*

Reinforced Concrete Design for Engineering Technology. *v.5 p.696*

Reinforced Masonry Engineering Handbook Clay and Concrete Masonry. *v.5 p.692*

Reinhold Niebuhr: His Religious, Social, and Political Thought,. *v.1 p.581*

Reinterpreting Russian History: Readings, 860-1860s. .*v.3 p.209*

Reinterpreting the Banana Republic: Region and State in Honduras, 1870-1972. . . . .*v.3 p.300*

Reinterpreting the French Revolution: A Global-Historical Perspective. *v.3 p.75*

Reinventing Anthropology. *v.4 p.24*

Reinventing China: A Generation and Its Films. . . .*v.6 p.207*

Reinventing Dance in the 1960s: Everything Was Possible. *v.1 p.27, p.29*

Reinventing Darwin: The Great Debate at the High Table of Evolutionary Theory. *v.5 p.203*

Reinventing Electric Utilities: Competition, Citizen Action and Clean Power. *v.5 p.724*

Reinventing India: Liberalization, Hindu Nationalism and Popular Democracy. *v.6 p.159*

Reinventing Justice: The American Drug Court Movement. *v.4 p.449*

Reinventing Politics: Eastern Europe from Stalin to Havel. *v.3 p.208*

Reinventing Shakespeare: A Cultural History from the Restoration to the Present. *v.2 p.232*

Reinventing Strategy: Using Strategic Learning to Create and Sustain Breakthrough Performance. *v.4 p.79*

Reinventing the Enemy's Language: Contemporary Native Women's Writing of North America. *v.2 p.19*

Reinventing the Enemy's Language: Contemporary Native Women's Writings of North America. *v.6 p.705*

Reinventing the Melting Pot: The New Immigrants and What It Means to Be American. *v.4 p.571*

Reinventing the Wheel. *v.1 p.717*

The Reinvention of Ignazio Silone. *v.2 p.723*

The Reinvention of Love: Poetry, Politics and Culture from Sidney to Milton. *v.2 p.182*

The Rejected Body: Feminist Philosophical Reflections on Disability. *v.6 p.444*

Rekindling the Movement: Labor's Quest for Relevance in the 21st Century. *v.4 p.129*

The Relapse and Other Plays. *v.2 p.263*

Relapse and Recovery in Addictions. *v.5 p.673*

Relating Religion: Essays in the Study of Religion. *v.1 p.521, p.522*

Relational Discipline: Strategies for in-Your-Face Kids. .*v.4 p.283*

Relational Models Theory: A Contemporary Overview. .*v.5 p.647*

Relational Remembering: Rethinking the Memory Wars. *v.5 p.609*

Relations Between the Sexes in the Plays of George Bernard Shaw. *v.2 p.309*

Relationship Marketing: Strategy and Implementation. .*v.4 p.143*

A Relationship of Reform: Immigrants and Progressives in the Far West. *v.3 p.530*

Relationships Between Score and Choreography in Twentieth-Century Dance: Music, Movement and Metaphor. *v.1 p.42*

Relations. *v.2 p.786*

Relative Values: Reconfiguring Kinship Studies. *v.4 p.32*

Relative/Outsider: The Art and Politics of Identity among Mixed Heritage Students. *v.6 p.109, p.125*

Relativism and the Social Sciences. *v.4 p.679*

Relativism. *v.1 p.514*

Relativistic Quantum Mechanics. *v.5 p.549*

Relativistic Quantum Theory, Vol. 4, Pts. 1-2. . . . . .*v.5 p.550*

Relativity, Gravitation and Cosmology: A Basic Introduction. *v.5 p.72*

Relativity: The Special and General Theory. *v.5 p.556*

Relativity Visualized. *v.5 p.556*

Relevance Lost: The Rise and Fall of Management Accounting. *v.4 p.106*

The Relevance of Canadian History: U. S. and Imperial Perspectives. *v.3 p.536*

The Relevance of Education. *v.5 p.571*

Relevance of Whitehead: Philosophical Essays in Commemoration of the Centenary of the Birth of Alfred North Whitehead. *v.1 p.446*

The Reliability of Sense Perception. *v.1 p.481*

Reliable Knowledge. *v.5 p.405*

Relicarios: Devotional Miniatures from the Americas. .*v.1 p.709*

Relics of the Buddha. *v.1 p.566*

The Relic. *v.2 p.688*

Relief Printmaking. *v.1 p.760, p.761*

☐ Relief Web: Policy and Issues. *v.4 p.668, p.669, p.670, p.671*

Religio Medici, Hydriotaphia, and the Garden of Cyrus. .*v.2 p.241*

☐ Religion & Public Schools. *v.4 p.299*

Religion: A Dialogue, and Other Essays. *v.1 p.466*

Religion: A Humanist Interpretation. *v.4 p.36*

Religion and American Education: Rethinking a National Dilemma. *v.4 p.307*

Religion and American Law: An Encyclopedia. *v.1 p.656, v.4 p.459*

Religion and Culture in Early Modern Russia. . . .*v.3 p.210*

Religion and Culture in Germany, 1400-1800. . . . .*v.3 p.165*

Religion and Custom in a Muslim Society: The Berti of Sudan. *v.4 p.36*

Religion and Dalit Liberation: An Examination of Perspectives. *v.1 p.541*

Religion and Emotion: Approaches and Interpretations. .*v.5 p.633*

Religion and Everyday Life. *v.1 p.524*

Religion and Family in a Changing Society. *v.1 p.650*

Religion and Healing in America. *v.1 p.524*

Religion and Humane Global Governance. *v.4 p.626*

Religion and Legitimation of Power in Sri Lanka. . .*v.1 p.562*

Religion and Literature: A Reader. *v.2 p.572*

Religion and Nation: Iranian Local and Transnational Networks in Britain. *v.4 p.44*

Religion and National Integration in Africa: Islam, Christianity and Politics in the Sudan and Nigeria. *v.6 p.640*

Religion and Philosophy in Germany. *v.3 p.168*

The Religion and Philosophy of the Veda and Upanishads, Set. *v.1 p.536*

Religion and Politics in America. *v.1 p.604*

Religion and Politics in Latin America: The Catholic Church in Venezuela and Columbia. *v.1 p.573*

Religion and Politics in the United States. *v.1 p.606*

Religion and Popular Culture in America. *v.4 p.720*

Religion and Power in Morocco. *v.6 p.61*

Religion and Psychology: A Dialogical Approach. . . .*v.5 p.634*

Religion and Psychology in Transition: Psychoanalysis, Feminism and Theology. *v.5 p.634*

Religion and Rajput Women: The Ethic of Protection in Contemporary Narratives. *v.6 p.154*

Religion and Rational Theology. *v.1 p.461, p.498, p.523*

Religion and Rationality: Essays on Reason, God and Modernity. *v.1 p.522*

Religion and Respectability: Sunday Schools and English Working Class Culture, 1780-1850. . . . . .*v.3 p.113, p.121*

Religion and Revolution in Peru, 1824-1976. . . . .*v.3 p.330*

Religion and Sexuality: The Shakers, the Mormons and the Oneida Community. *v.4 p.721*

Religion and Society in England, 1850-1914. . . . . .*v.1 p.609*

Religion and Society in England and Wales, 1689-1800. .*v.1 p.609*

Religion and Society in Frontier California. *v.1 p.607*

Religion and Sport: The Meeting of Sacred and Profane. *v.4 p.824*

Religion and State in Iran, 1785-1906: The Role of the 'Ulama in the Qajar Period. *v.6 p.630*

Religion and the American Constitutional Experiment: Essential Rights and Liberties. *v.4 p.459, p.460*

Religion and the Body. *v.1 p.530*

Religion and the Decline of Magic: Studies in Popular Beliefs in Sixteenth and Seventeenth Century England. . . .*v.3 p.122*

Religion and the Human Sciences: An Approach via Spirituality. *v.5 p.634*

Religion and the Individual: A Social-Psychological Perspective. *v.1 p.524, v.5 p.632, p.633*

Religion and the Law: A Dictionary. *v.4 p.460*

Religion and the Legitimation of Power in South Asia. *v.1 p.562*

Religion and the People of Western Europe, 1789-1990. .*v.1 p.531*

Religion and the Rise of Capitalism. *v.3 p.122*

Religion and the Rise of Democracy. *v.1 p.596*

Religion and the Unconscious. *v.5 p.636*

Religion, Belief and Unbelief: A Psychological Study. .*v.5 p.636*

Religion, Culture, and Psychology in Arab-Israeli Relations. *v.6 p.594, p.661*

Religion, Education, and Academic Success. *v.4 p.307*

Religion, Education and the American Experience: Reflections on Religion and American Public Life. *v.4 p.307*

Religion Explained: The Evolutionary Origins of Religious Thought. *v.5 p.633*

Religion Explained. *v.4 p.36*

Religion in America since 1945: A History. *v.1 p.543*

Religion in American History: A Reader. . . . *v.1 p.543, p.604*

Religion in America. *v.1 p.604*

Religion in Ancient Etruria. *v.1 p.532*

Religion in Ancient Mesopotamia. *v.1 p.538*

Religion in China Today. *v.1 p.539*

Religion in Contemporary Japan. *v.1 p.541, p.542*

Religion in England, 1688-1791. . . . .*v.1 p.609*

Religion in Hellenistic Athens. *v.3 p.14*

Religion in Mind: Cognitive Perspectives on Religious Belief, Ritual, and Experience. *v.5 p.632*

Religion in Roman Egypt: Assimilation and Resistance. *v.1 p.542*

Religion in the Andes: Vision and Imagination in Early Colonial Peru. *v.3 p.263*

Religion in the Contemporary World: A Sociological Introduction. *v.1 p.524*

Religion in the History of the Medieval West. *v.1 p.601*

Religion in the Making. *v.1 p.522*

Religion in the Modern World: From Cathedrals to Cults. *v.4 p.719, p.720*

Religion in the Old South. *v.1 p.607*

▢ Religion in the Public Schools: A Joint Statement of Current Law. *v.4 p.299*

Religion Is Not about God: How Spiritual Traditions Nurture Our Biological Nature and What to Expect When They Fail. *v.5 p.635, p.636*

Religion, Law and the Land: Native Americans and the Judicial Interpretation of Sacred Land. *v.6 p.691, p.700*

Religion, Learning and Science in the 'Abbasid Period. *v.6 p.664*

Religion: North American Style. *v.1 p.524*

Religion of China. *v.1 p.539*

Religion of India: The Sociology of Hinduism and Buddhism. *v.4 p.722*

The Religion of Israel: From Its Beginnings to the Babylonian Exile. *v.1 p.547, p.548*

The Religion of Java. *v.1 p.540, v.6 p.174, p.176*

The Religion of Socrates. *v.1 p.422*

The Religion of the Heart: A Study of European Religious Life in the Seventeenth and Eighteenth Centuries. *v.1 p.590*

Religion on Trial: How Supreme Court Trends Threaten Freedom of Conscience in America. *v.4 p.537*

Religion, Society, and Culture in Colombia: Antioquia and Medellin 1850-1930. . . . .*v.3 p.357*

Religion, Society, and Psychoanalysis: Readings in Contemporary Theory. *v.5 p.634*

The Religion, Spirituality, and Thought of Traditional Africa. *v.1 p.543*

Religion Within the Limits of Reason Alone. . *v.1 p.461, p.498*

Religions in Asian America: Building Faith Communities. *v.6 p.106, p.136*

Religions in Conflict: Ideology, Cultural Contact and Conversion in Late-Colonial India. *v.1 p.539*

Religions of Asia in Practice: An Anthology. *v.1 p.534*

Religions of China in Practice. *v.1 p.539*

Religions of India in Practice. *v.1 p.540*

Religions of Japan in Practice. *v.1 p.542*

Religions of Late Antiquity in Practice. *v.1 p.531*

The Religions of Mongolia. *v.6 p.240*

The Religions of Oceania. *v.1 p.544*

Religions of Rome: A History, Vol. 1. . . . .*v.1 p.531*

Religions of Rome: A History. *v.3 p.23*

Religions of Rome: A Sourcebook. . . .*v.1 p.531, v.3 p.22, p.23*

Religions of South Asia: An Introduction. *v.1 p.541*

Religions of the Ancient Greeks. *v.1 p.533*

Religions of Tibet in Practice. *v.1 p.566, v.6 p.241*

The Religions of Tibet. *v.1 p.566, p.567*

Religions, Values and Peak Experiences. *v.5 p.635*

Religion. *v.1 p.521*

Religious Art in France of the 13th Century. *v.1 p.688*

Religious Authority in the Spanish Renaissance. .*v.3 p.59, p.239*

The Religious Beliefs of Our Presidents: From Washington to F. D. R. *v.3 p.378*

Religious Conscience, the State, and the Law: Historical Contexts and Contemporary Significance. . .*v.1 p.656, p.657*

The Religious Culture of India: Power, Love and Wisdom. *v.1 p.540*

Religious Encounter and the Making of the Yoruba. . .*v.6 p.72*

Religious Experience, Justification, and History. *v.1 p.524*

Religious Expression and the American Constitution. .*v.4 p.459*

Religious Freedom and Indian Rights: The Case of Oregon vs. Smith. *v.4 p.439, v.6 p.696, p.701*

The Religious Function of the Psyche. *v.5 p.633*

Religious Fundamentalism and American Education: The Battle for the Public Schools. *v.4 p.307*

The Religious History of America: The Heart of the American Story from Colonial Times to Today. *v.1 p.604*

A Religious History of the American People. *v.1 p.604*

Religious Leaders of America: A Biographical Guide to Founders and Leaders of Religious Bodies, Churches and Spiritual Groups in North America. *v.1 p.544, p.605*

Religious Liberty in America: Political Safeguards. . .*v.4 p.459*

Religious Liberty in the Supreme Court: Cases That Define the Debate over Church and State. *v.4 p.536*

▢ Religious Liberty: Religious Liberty in Public Schools. *v.4 p.299*

Religious Minorities in Iran. *v.6 p.630*

The Religious Orders in England: The Old Orders, Vol. 1. . . . .*v.1 p.577, p.578*

The Religious Orders in England, Vol. 3. . . . . . .*v.1 p.578*

Religious Orders, Vol. 1. . . . .*v.6 p.571, p.572*

Religious Orders, Vol. 2. . . . .*v.6 p.571*

The Religious Origins of the French Revolution: From Calvin to the Civil Constitution, 1560-1791. . . . .*v.3 p.151*

The Religious Paintings of Giambattista Tiepolo: Piety and Tradition in Eighteenth-Century Venice. *v.1 p.735*

Religious Pluralism In The Academy: Opening The Dialogue. *v.4 p.307*

Religious Poverty and the Profit Economy in Medieval Europe. *v.1 p.651*

Religious Radicalism and Politics in the Middle East. .*v.6 p.595*

The Religious Right and the Christian Faith. *v.1 p.633*

Religious Thought and the Modern Psychologies. . . .*v.5 p.633*

The Religious Traditions of Africa: A History. *v.1 p.542*

The Religious Traditions of Japan, 500-1600. . . . . .*v.1 p.541*

Religious Violence and Abortion: The Gideon Project. *v.4 p.569*

Reliving Golgotha: The Passion Play of Iztapalapa. . .*v.3 p.268*

Reload: Rethinking Women + Cyberculture. *v.6 p.438*

The Reluctant Belligerent: American Entry into World War II. *v.3 p.469*

Reluctant Partners: Implementing Federal Policy. .*v.4 p.525, p.526*

Reluctant Reformers: The Impact of Racism on American Social Reform Movements. *v.4 p.700*

Reluctant Revolutionaries: New York City and the Road to Independence, 1763-1776. . . . .*v.3 p.491*

Remains in Verse and Prose of Arthur Henry Hallam, with a Preface and Memoir *v.2 p.290*

Remains of Old Latin. *v.2 p.425*

The Remains of the Day. *v.2 p.355*

Remains of the Jews: The Holy Land and Christian Empire in Late Antiquity. *v.1 p.549*

Remaking Chinese America: Immigration, Family and Community, 1940-1965. . . . .*v.6 p.120, p.128, p.129*

Remaking France: Americanization, Public Diplomacy, and the Marshall Plan. *v.3 p.390*

Remaking Social Networks: the Emergence of Embeddedness in Vocational Training. *v.4 p.305, p.306*

Remaking the American Mainstream: Assimilation and Contemporary Immigration. *v.6 p.117, p.122, p.125*

Remaking the Concept of Aptitude: Extending the Legacy of Richard E. Snow. *v.5 p.572*

Remaking the Frankenstein Myth on Film: Between Laughter and Horror. *v.6 p.331*

Remaking the Modern: Space, Relocation, and the Politics of Identity in a Global Cairo. *v.6 p.637*

Remaking the Past: Musical Modernism and the Influence of the Tonal Tradition. *v.1 p.224*

Remaking Women: Feminism and Modernity in the Middle East. *v.6 p.591*

Remapping Asian American History. *v.6 p.85, p.113*

Remapping East Asia. *v.4 p.618*

Remarkable Mathematicians: From Euler to Von Neumann. *v.5 p.466*

Remarkable Survivors: Insights into Successful Aging among Women. *v.6 p.445*

Remarriage, a Study of Marriage. *v.4 p.738, p.739*

The Remasculinization of Korean Cinema. *v.6 p.334*

Rembrandt: Portraits in Print. *v.1 p.756*

Rembrandt the Printmaker. *v.1 p.756*

Rembrandt's Jews. *v.1 p.698*

Remediation: Understanding New Media. *v.4 p.419*

Remember Ruben. *v.2 p.544*

Remember This Titan: Lessons Learned from a Celebrated Coach's Journey. *v.4 p.860*

The Remembered Earth: An Anthology of Contemporary Native American Literature. *v.2 p.19, v.6 p.698*

Remembering Babylon. *v.2 p.747*

Remembering Childhood in the Middle East: Memoirs from a Century of Change. *v.6 p.592*

ReMembering Cuba: Legacy of a Diaspora. . .*v.6 p.489, p.542*

Remembering Defeat: Civil War and Civic Memory in Ancient Athens. *v.3 p.20*

Remembering Elizabeth Bishop: An Oral Biography. . .*v.2 p.61*

Remembering Our Past: Studies in Autobiographical Memory. *v.5 p.610*

Remembering Partition: Violence, Nationalism and History in India. *v.6 p.159*

Remembering Pinochet's Chile: On the Eve of London, 1998. . . . .*v.3 p.355*

Remembering Sepharad: Jewish Culture in Medieval Spain. *v.3 p.236, v.6 p.573*

Remembering the 'Forgotten War': The Korean War Through Literature and Art. *v.6 p.237*

Remembering Woodstock. *v.1 p.265*

Remembrance and Denial: The Case of the Armenian Genocide. *v.3 p.231, v.6 p.624*

Remembrance of Repasts: An Anthropology of Food and Memory. *v.4 p.46*

Remembrance Rock. *v.2 p.115*

Reminiscences: Nineteenth-Century British Literature. .*v.2 p.276*

Reminiscences of a Stock Operator: The Wall Street Classic about the Life and Times of Jesse Livermore. *v.4 p.95, p.96, p.102*

Reminiscences of Rimsky-Korsakov. *v.1 p.207, p.350*

Reminiscences. *v.3 p.460*

Reminiscing in Tempo: A Portrait of Duke Ellington. *v.1 p.262, p.323*

Remote Sensing and Geographic Information System. *v.4 p.386, p.388*

Remote Sensing and Image Interpretation. . .*v.4 p.388, p.389*

Remote Sensing Digital Image Analysis: An Introduction. *v.4 p.389*

Remote Sensing for Environmental Monitoring, GIS Applications, and Geology III. *v.4 p.388, v.5 p.366*

Remote Sensing for Environmental Monitoring, GIS Applications, and Geology II. *v.5 p.366, p.368*

Remote Sensing for Environmental Monitoring, Gis Applications, and Geology, IV. . . . *v.5 p.367, p.368, p.369*

Remote Sensing for Geologists: A Guide to Image Interpretation A. *v.5 p.421*

Remote Sensing for Natural Resource Management and Environmental Monitoring, Vol. 4. . . . .*v.4 p.389*

Remote Sensing Geology. *v.4 p.388, v.5 p.420*

Remote Sensing Image Analysis: Including the Spatial Domain. *v.4 p.388*

Remotely Global: Village Modernity in West Africa. . .*v.6 p.74*

Removal Aftershock: The Seminoles' Struggles to Survive in the West, 1836-1866. . . . .*v.6 p.687*

Remus: A Roman Myth. *v.3 p.24*

The Renaissance, 1493-1520. . . . .*v.3 p.71*

The Renaissance and 17th Century Rationalism. *v.1 p.435*

Renaissance and Enlightenment Paradoxes. *v.3 p.52*

Renaissance and Reformation and the Rise of Science. *v.3 p.47, p.48*

Renaissance and Renewal in the Twelfth Century. . . .*v.6 p.561*

The Renaissance and the Reformation. *v.3 p.69*

Renaissance Art: A Topical Dictionary. .*v.1 p.664, p.674, p.675*

Renaissance Art and Architecture. *v.1 p.674*

Renaissance Artists and Antique Sculpture: A Handbook of Sources. *v.1 p.750*

The Renaissance Bazaar: From the Silk Road to Michelangelo. *v.3 p.70*

Renaissance Diplomacy. *v.3 p.71*

Renaissance Drama: An Anthology of Plays and
Entertainments. *v.1 p.67, p.75*

Renaissance Drama and Contemporary Literary Theory. .*v.2 p.186*

Renaissance Drama, Vol. 34. . . . .*v.1 p.75, p.136*

Renaissance Drama. *v.1 p.75, p.101, p.102*

Renaissance France, 1470-1589. . . . .*v.2 p.456*

The Renaissance: From the 1470's to the End of the 16th
Century. *v.1 p.179*

The Renaissance Hamlet: Issues and Responses in 1600. .*v.2 p.229*

The Renaissance in National Context. *v.3 p.71*

The Renaissance in Rome. *v.3 p.200*

Renaissance Man and Creative Thinking: A History of Concepts
of Harmony, 1400-1700. . . . .*v.1 p.435*

Renaissance Man from Louisiana: A Biography of Arna Wendell
Bontemps, 151. . . . .*v.6 p.18*

Renaissance Music. *v.1 p.179*

The Renaissance of Jewish Culture in Weimar
Germany. *v.3 p.169, p.179*

The Renaissance of Modern Hebrew and Modern Standard
Arabic: Parallels and Differences in the Revival of
Two Semitic Languages. *v.6 p.645, p.653*

The Renaissance of the Twelfth Century. .*v.3 p.67, p.68,v.6 p.563*

Renaissance Philosophy. *v.1 p.435*

Renaissance Poetry. *v.2 p.201*

The Renaissance Print, 1470-1550. . . . .*v.1 p.753*

Renaissance Rome: A Portrait of a Society, 1500-1559. .*v.3 p.200*

Renaissance Self-Fashioning: From More to
Shakespeare. *v.3 p.128*

The Renaissance Sense of the Past. *v.3 p.70*

The Renaissance Stage: Documents of Serlio, Sabbattini and
Furttenbach. *v.1 p.75, p.138, p.148, p.155*

The Renaissance: Studies in Art and Poetry. *v.2 p.303*

The Renaissance Theatre - Texts, Performance and Design:
English and Italian Theatre. *v.1 p.74, p.95, p.146*

Renaissance Theatre: Texts, Performance and Design, Vol.
2. . . . .*v.1 p.74, p.95, p.146*

Renaissance Thought and Its Sources. *v.3 p.71*

Renaissance Transactions: Ariosto and Tasso. . .*v.2 p.707, p.709*

Renaissance Utopias and the Problem of History. . . .*v.4 p.499*

Renaissance Warrior and Patron: The Reign of Francis I. .*v.3 p.145*

Renard the Fox. *v.2 p.468*

▢ Renderosity. *v.1 p.770*

Rendezvous with Destiny: A History of Modern American
Reform. *v.3 p.436, p.447*

Rendezvous with the Wild: The Boreal Forest. *v.5 p.240*

The Rending of Virginia: A History. *v.3 p.499*

Rene Char. *v.2 p.512*

Rene Descartes: Principles of Philosophy. *v.1 p.453*

Rene Herbst: Pioneer of Modernism. *v.1 p.802*

Renewable and Efficient Electric Power
Systems. *v.5 p.361, p.377, p.378, p.724*

Renewable Energy Resources. *v.5 p.361*

Renewable Energy. *v.5 p.361, p.708*

The Renewal of Pagan Antiquity. *v.1 p.676*

The Renewal of the Priesthood: Modernity and Traditionalism in
a South Indian Temple. *v.1 p.535*

Renewing Hope Within Neighborhoods of Despair: The
Community-Based Development Model. *v.4 p.719*

Renewing the Atlantic Partnership: Independent Task Force
Report. *v.4 p.560, p.562*

Renewing the Covenant: A Theology for the Postmodern
Jew. *v.1 p.551*

René Herbst: Pioneer of Modernism. *v.1 p.802*

Renoir Art Institute of Chicago. *v.1 p.738*

Renoir's Portraits: Impressions of an Age. *v.1 p.735*

Renoir. *v.1 p.745*

Renormalization Methods: A Guide for Beginners. . .*v.5 p.559*

Renovating Politics in Contemporary Vietnam. *v.4 p.622*

Renters' Rights: Legal Basics. *v.4 p.442, p.443*

Reordering Marriage and Society in Reformation
Germany. *v.3 p.166*

Repair or Revenge?: Victims and Restorative
Justice. *v.4 p.754, v.6 p.258, p.279*

Reparations in the Time of Globalization. . .*v.6 p.20, p.36, p.37*

Reparations: The Cure for America's Race
Problem. *v.6 p.36, p.38, p.39*

Repentance and Confession in the Orthodox Church. .*v.1 p.569*

The Repertoire of Iraqi Maqam. *v.1 p.287*

Repertory in Review: 40 Years of the New York City
Ballet. *v.1 p.24*

The Repertory Movement: A History of Regional Theatre in
Britain. *v.1 p.103*

Repetition: A Novel. *v.2 p.525*

Replications: A Robotic History of the Science Fiction
Film. *v.6 p.320*

Report from Part One: An Autobiography. *v.2 p.63*

Report from Part Two, Vol. 2. . . . .*v.2 p.63*

Report of the President's Commission on Campus Unrest:
Including the Killings at Jackson State and Kent State
Tragedy. *v.4 p.332, p.333*

Report on the global AIDS epidemic : 4th global report. .*v.4 p.668*

The Reporter and the Law: Techniques of Covering the
Courts. *v.4 p.444, p.445*

The Reporter's Environmental Handbook. *v.4 p.407*

Reporting from the Front: The Media and the Military. .*v.4 p.407*

Reporting Sexual Assault: A Social Ecology
Perspective. *v.6 p.251*

Reporting the News about Religion: An Introduction for
Journalists. *v.4 p.406*

Reports from the Holocaust: The Making of an AIDS
Activist. *v.6 p.379, p.402*

Represent Yourself in Court: How to Prepare and Try a Winning
Case. *v.4 p.470, p.471*

Representations of Empire: Rome and the Mediterranean
World. *v.3 p.22*

Representations of Slavery: Race and Ideology in Southern
Plantation Museums. *v.1 p.828*

Representative Democracy in the Canadian Provinces. .*v.4 p.589*

Representative Government in Early Modern
France. *v.3 p.145, p.146*

Representative Government in Greek and Roman
History. *v.3 p.12*

Representative Man: Ralph Waldo Emerson in His Time. .*v.2 p.38*

Title Index

Representative Medieval and Tudor
   Plays. *v.1 p.67, p.70, p.73, p.101*

Representative Plays by American Dramatists, Vol. 1. . .*v.2 p.25*

The Representative Plays. *v.2 p.269*

Representative Plays. *v.2 p.348*

Representative Spanish Authors: From the Middle Ages Through
   the Eighteenth Century. *v.2 p.644*

Representative Spanish Authors, Vol. II. *v.2 p.644*

A Representative Supreme Court?: The Impact of Race,
   Religion, and Gender on Appointments. *v.4 p.538*

Representing African Music: Postcolonial Notes, Queries,
   Positions. *v.1 p.284*

Representing and Intervening: Introductory Topics in the
   Philosophy of Natural Science. *v.5 p.402*

Representing Blackness: Issues in Film and
   Video. *v.6 p.330, p.331*

Representing: Hip Hop Culture and the Production of Black
   Cinema. *v.6 p.331*

Representing Interests in the European Union. *v.4 p.603*

Representing Ireland: Literature and the Origins of Conflict
   1534-1660. . . . .*v.3 p.136*

Representing Men: Maleness and Masculinity in the
   Media. *v.4 p.416*

Representing Reality: Issues and Concepts in
   Documentary. *v.6 p.309*

Representing Shakespeare: New Psychoanalytic Essays. .*v.2 p.231*

Representing
   Sport.   .*v.4 p.814, p.823, p.831, p.858, p.882, p.887, p.901*

The Repressible Conflict, 1830-1861. . . . . .*v.3 p.395, p.424*

Repression and Dissociation: Implications for Personality
   Theory, Psychopathology and Health. *v.5 p.656*

Repression and Recovery: Modern American Poetry and the
   Politics of Cultural Memory, 1910-1945. . . . . .*v.2 p.15*

Reproducing Empire: Race, Sex, Science and U.S. Imperialism
   in Puerto Rico. *v.3 p.318*

Reproducing Jews: A Cultural Account of Assisted Conception
   in Israel. *v.4 p.32*

Reproducing Persons: Issues in Feminist
   Bioethics. *v.6 p.444, p.461*

Reproducing Reproduction: Kinship, Power, and Technological
   Innovation. *v.4 p.32*

The Reproduction of Mothering: Psychoanalysis and the
   Sociology of Gender. *v.4 p.736, v.6 p.427, p.445*

Reproductive Laws for the 1990s. *v.4 p.447*

Reproductive Rights and Wrongs: The Global Politics of
   Population Control. *v.6 p.447*

The Republic and the School: Horace Mann on the Education of
   Free Men. *v.4 p.344*

Republic. Com. *v.4 p.761*

The Republic in Peril, 1812. . . . .*v.3 p.416*

The Republic in the Village: The People of the War from the
   French Revolution to the Second Republic. . . .*v.3 p.148*

The Republic of Armenia: Between Crescent and Sickle:
   Partition and Sovietization. *v.6 p.633*

The Republic of Armenia: From London to Sevres, February -
   August 1920. . . . .*v.6 p.633*

The Republic of Armenia: The First Year, 1918-1919. .*v.6 p.633*

The Republic of Dreams. *v.2 p.692*

Republic of Egos: A Social History of the Spanish Civil
   War. *v.3 p.242*

The Republic of Letters: A Cultural History of the French
   Enlightenment. *v.3 p.147*

Republic of Love: Selected Poems. *v.6 p.661*

The Republic of Mass Culture: Journalism, Filmmaking, and
   Broadcasting in America since 1941. . . . . . .*v.4 p.417*

Republic of Plato. *v.4 p.489*

The Republic of St. Peter: The Birth of the Papal State,
   680-825. . . . .*v.3 p.199*

The Republic of Whores: A Fagment from the Time of the
   Cults. *v.2 p.784*

Republican China, 1912-1949. . . . .*v.6 p.190*

Republican Empire: Alexander Hamilton on War and Free
   Government. *v.4 p.493*

The Republican Experiment, 1848-1852. . . . .*v.3 p.153*

Republican France: Divided Loyalties. *v.3 p.157*

Republican Iraq: A Study in Iraqi Politics Since the Revolution
   of 1958. . . . .*v.6 p.603*

The Republican Moment: Struggles for Democracy in
   Nineteenth-Century France. *v.3 p.149*

☐ Republican National Committee. *v.4 p.553*

The Republican Option in Canada: Past and Present.   *v.4 p.588*

Republican Rome, the Army and the Allies. *v.3 p.26*

The Republican Roosevelt. *v.3 p.439*

The Republican South: Democratization and Partisan
   Change. *v.4 p.551, p.553*

The Republican War on Science. *v.4 p.566*

Republic.com. *v.4 p.425, p.426*

Republic. *v.2 p.418, v.4 p.489*

Requiem for a Dream. *v.2 p.139*

Requiem for a Nun. *v.2 p.74*

Requiem for Fools and Beasts. *v.2 p.816*

Requiem for Revolution: The United States and Brazil,
   1961-1969. . . . .*v.3 p.341*

A Requiem for the Renascence: The State of Fiction in the
   Modern South. *v.2 p.14*

Required Writing: Miscellaneous Pieces, 1955-1982. . .*v.2 p.361*

Rereading Frederick Jackson Turner: "The Significance of the
   Frontier in American History" and Other
   Essays. *v.3 p.381, p.382*

Rereading George Eliot: Changing Responses to Her
   Experiments in Life. *v.2 p.287*

A Rereading of Romans: Justice, Jews, and Gentiles. *v.1 p.631*

Rereading Russian Poetry. *v.2 p.800*

Rereading the Harlem Renaissance: Race, Class, and Gender in
   the Fiction of Jessie Fauset, Zora Neale Hurston, and
   Dorothy West. *v.2 p.81, p.82*

Rereading the Rabbis: A Woman's Voice. *v.1 p.553*

Rereading Victorian Fiction. *v.2 p.175, p.193*

Res Gestae Divi Augusti. *v.3 p.28, p.29*

Re-Scripting Walt Whitman: An Introduction to His Life and
   Work. *v.2 p.53*

Rescue as Resistance: How Jewish Organizations Fought the
   Holocaust in France. *v.3 p.85*

The Rescue of Romanticism: Walter Pater and John Ruskin. *v.2 p.305*

Rescuing History from the Nation: Questioning Narratives of Modern China. *v.6 p.190*

Research about Leisure: Past, Present and Future. .*v.4 p.784, p.813*

A Research Companion to "Principles and Standards for School Mathematics". *v.5 p.463*

Research for Social Workers: An Introduction to Methods. *v.4 p.757*

Research Guide to Andean History: Bolivia, Chile, Ecuador, and Peru. *v.3 p.332*

A Research Guide to Central Party and Government Meetings in China, 1949-1986. . . . .*v.4 p.620*

Research Guide to Philosophy. *v.1 p.417*

Research in Dance: A Guide to Resources. *v.1 p.3*

Research in Experimental Economics, Vol. 1. . . . . .*v.4 p.271*

Research in Experimental Economics, Vol. 2. . . . . .*v.4 p.271*

Research in Experimental Economics, Vol. 3. . . . . .*v.4 p.271*

Research in the History of Economic Thought and Methodology, Vol. 23, Set. *v.4 p.194, p.208*

Research Interviewing: Context and Narrative. *v.4 p.691*

Research Methods for Organizational Studies. *v.4 p.179*

Research Methods for Sports Studies. *v.4 p.812, p.813*

Research Methods in Anthropology: Qualitative and Quantitative Approaches. *v.4 p.25*

Research Methods in Athletic Training. *v.4 p.828*

Research on Alternative and Non-Traditional Education: Teacher Education Yearbook XIII. *v.4 p.277*

Research-Doctorate Programs in the United States: Continuity and Change. *v.4 p.295*

Researches into the Mathematical Principles of the Theory of Wealth. *v.4 p.198, p.199*

Researching Dance: Evolving Modes of Inquiry. *v.1 p.41*

Researching Human Geography. *v.4 p.396*

Resemblance Nominalism: A Solution to the Problem of Universals. *v.1 p.510*

Reservation and Affirmative Action: Models of Social Integration in India and the United States. *v.4 p.723*

Reservoir Engineering Handbook. *v.5 p.451*

The Reservoir: Stories and Sketches. *v.2 p.745*

Reshaping Palestine: From Muhammad Ali to the British Mandate, 1831-1922. . . . .*v.6 p.612*

Reshaping Rural England: Social History, 1850-1925. .*v.6 p.759*

Reshaping the Asia Pacific Economic Order. *v.4 p.398*

Reshaping the Female Body: The Dilemma of Cosmetic Surgery. *v.6 p.443*

Reshaping the International Order: A Report to the Club of Rome. *v.4 p.262*

Residence on Earth. *v.2 p.681*

Residential Lighting: A Practical Guide. *v.1 p.803*

The Residual Years: Poems, 1934-1948. . . . .*v.2 p.71*

Resilience for Today: Gaining Strength from Adversity. .*v.5 p.653*

Resilience: Learning from People with Disabilities and the Turning Points in Their Lives. *v.5 p.653, p.654*

The Resilient City: How Modern Cities Recover from Disaster. *v.4 p.760, v.6 p.729*

Resistance and Contradiction: Miskitu Indians and the Nicaraguan State, 1894-1987. . . . .*v.3 p.302*

Resistance and Reform in Tibet. *v.6 p.240*

Resistance at Christiana; the Fugitive Slave Rebellion, Christiana, Pennsylvania, September 11, 1851: A Documentary Account. *v.3 p.431*

Resistance in Vichy France: A Study of Ideas and Motivation in the Southern Zone, 1940-42. . . . .*v.3 p.156*

Resistance of the Heart. *v.3 p.87*

Resistance, Parody and Double Consciousness in African American Theatre, 1895-1910. . . . .*v.1 p.123*

Resistance, Rebellion, and Consciousness in the Andean Peasant World, 18th to 20th Centuries. *v.3 p.325*

Resistance, Rebellion, and Death: Essays. *v.2 p.512*

Resistance Rebellion Revolution: Popular Movements in Vietnamese History. *v.6 p.167*

Resistance: The Warsaw Ghetto Uprising. *v.3 p.84*

Resisting Dictatorship: Repression and Protest in Southeast Asia. *v.6 p.179*

Resisting the Third Reich: The Catholic Clergy in Hitler's Berlin. *v.3 p.173, p.174*

Resolving Social Conflicts: Selected Papers on Group Dynamics. *v.4 p.695*

Resort to Arms: International and Civil Wars, 1816-1980. .*v.3 p.36*

The Resource Book of Jewish Music: A Bibliographical and Topical Guide to the Book and Journal Literature and Program Materials. *v.1 p.167, p.300*

Resource Guide to Asian American Literature. . .*v.6 p.87, p.91*

Resource Rebels: Native Challenges to Mining and Oil Corporations. *v.6 p.298, p.681*

Resources for Teaching Linear Algebra. *v.5 p.472*

Resources for the Study of Real Analysis. *v.5 p.490*

Resources in Ancient Philosophy: An Annotated Bibliography of Scholarship in English, 1965-1989. . . . .*v.1 p.419*

Resources in Sacred Dance, 1991: Annotated Bibliography from Christian and Jewish Traditions. *v.1 p.21*

Resources of American Music History: A Directory of Source Materials from Colonial Times to World War II. *v.1 p.167, p.168, p.278*

Respect for Acting. *v.1 p.144*

Respiratory Care Anatomy and Physiology: Foundations for Clinical Practice. *v.5 p.536*

Respiratory Physiology: The Essentials. *v.5 p.536*

Resplendent Synagogue: Architecture and Worship in an Eighteenth-Century Polish Community. *v.1 p.789*

Responding to Crisis: A Rehetorical Approach to Crisis Communication. *v.4 p.173*

The Responsa Literature and a Treasury of Responsa. .*v.1 p.550*

Response to Imperialism: The United States and the Philippine-American War, 1899-1902. . . . .*v.3 p.438*

The Response to Industrialism, 1885-1914. . . . . . .*v.3 p.436*

Response to Modernity: A History of the Reform Movement in Judaism. *v.1 p.548*

Response to Revolution: The United States and the Cuban Revolution, 1959-1961. . . . .*v.3 p.393*

Responses: Prose Pieces, 1953-1976. . . . .*v.2 p.128*

Responsibility and Atonement. *v.1 p.499*

Responsibility and the Moral Sentiments. *v.1 p.503*

Responsible Government in Ontario. *v.4 p.590*

Responsible Partisanship?: The Evolution of American Political Parties since 1950. . . . .*v.4 p.551, p.552*

The Responsive University: Restructuring for High Performance. *v.4 p.332*

The Restaurant: From Concept to Operation. *v.4 p.165*

Restaurant Industry Forecast. *v.4 p.165*

Restaurant Operations Management: Principles and Practices. *v.4 p.165*

Restaurant Start-up Guide. *v.4 p.165*

A Restless Past: History and the American Public. . . .*v.3 p.373*

The Restless Universe: Understanding X-Ray Astronomy in the Age of Chandra and Newton. *v.5 p.67, p.541*

The Restoration, 1660-1688: British History in Perspective. *v.3 p.105, p.106*

The Restoration: A Political and Religious History of England and Wales, 1658-1667. . . . .*v.3 p.94, p.105, p.121*

Restoration Comedy, 1660-1720. . . . .*v.2 p.186*

Restoration Comedy. *v.1 p.65, p.77, p.90, p.100,v.2 p.202*

The Restoration of Engravings, Drawings, Books, and Other Works on Paper. *v.1 p.824*

Restoration of the Great Lakes: Promises, Practices, and Performances. *v.6 p.301*

Restoration Prose Fiction, 1666-1700: An Anthology of Representative Pieces. *v.2 p.203*

Restoration, Revolution, Reaction: Economics and Politics in Germany, 1815-1871. . . . .*v.3 p.168*

Restorative Justice and Criminal Justice: Competing or Reconcilable Paradigms?. *v.6 p.278, p.279*

Restorative Justice and Responsive Regulation. . . .*v.6 p.278*

A Restorative Justice Reader. *v.6 p.279*

Restorative Justice. *v.6 p.279*

Restoried Selves: Autobiographies of Queer Asian-Pacific-American Activists. . . .*v.6 p.94, p.107, p.112*

Restoring American Gardens: An Encyclopedia of Heirloom Ornamental Plants, 1640-1940. . . . . . .*v.1 p.811, p.821*

Restoring the Balance: Women Physicians and the Profession of Medicine, 1850-1995. . . . .*v.6 p.439*

Restoring Trust in American Business. . . .*v.4 p.54, p.86, p.109*

Restoring Women's History Through Historic Preservation. *v.1 p.822*

Restraints on War: Studies in the Limitation of Armed Conflict. *v.4 p.478*

A Restricted Country. *v.6 p.403*

Restructing Political Power in China: Alliances and Opposition, 1978-1998. . . . .*v.4 p.619*

Restructuring Europe: Centre Formation, System Building, and Political Structuring between the Nation State and the European Union. *v.4 p.601*

Restructuring Patriarchy: The Modernization of Gender Inequality in Brazil, 1914-1940. . . . .*v.3 p.338*

Restructuring the Welfare State: Globalisation and Social Policy Reform in Finland and Sweden. *v.4 p.594, p.595*

Resumes for Business Management Careers. *v.4 p.170*

Resumes for College Students and Recent Graduates. *v.4 p.171*

Resumes for Environmental Careers. *v.5 p.251*

Resurgent Voice in Latin America: Indigenous Peoples, Political Mobilization, and Religious Change. *v.4 p.591*

Resurrecting Empire: Western Footprints and America's Perilous Path in the Middle East. *v.4 p.641*

Resurrection: Interpreting the Easter Gospel. *v.1 p.637*

The Resurrection of Ireland: The Sinn Féin Party, 1916-1923. . . . .*v.3 p.139*

The Resurrection of Philip Clairmont. *v.1 p.738*

Resurrection of the Body in Western Christianity, 200-1336. . . . .*v.3 p.56*

Resurrection. *v.2 p.809*

Retable; (la Reverie). *v.2 p.528*

Retailing in the 21st Century: Current and Future Trends. *v.4 p.164, p.165*

Retained by the People: A History of American Indians and the Bill of Rights. *v.4 p.465, v.6 p.693*

Rethinking Aggression and Violence in Sport. *v.4 p.802, p.817*

Rethinking Architecture: A Reader in Cultural Theory. *v.1 p.703*

Rethinking Art History: Meditations on a Coy Science. *v.1 p.709*

Rethinking Bank Regulation: Till Angels Govern. . . .*v.4 p.90*

Rethinking Camelot: JFK, the Vietnam War, and U. S. Political Culture. *v.3 p.440*

Rethinking College Athletics. *v.4 p.802, p.821*

Rethinking Development Geographies. *v.4 p.260, p.268*

Rethinking France: Les Lieux de Memoire: Space. . .*v.3 p.141*

Rethinking Gifted Education. *v.4 p.317*

Rethinking Implicit Memory. *v.5 p.609*

Rethinking Indonesia: Postcolonial Theory, Authoritarianism and Identity. *v.6 p.175, p.177*

Rethinking Linguistic Relativity. *v.4 p.20*

Rethinking Military Politics: Brazil and the Southern Cone. *v.3 p.277, v.4 p.593*

Rethinking Multiculturalism: Cultural Diversity and Political Theory. *v.4 p.484, p.768*

Rethinking Nasserism: Revolution and Historical Memory in Modern Egypt. *v.6 p.640*

Rethinking Northern Ireland: Culture, Ideology and Colonialism. *v.3 p.140*

Rethinking Performance Measurement: Beyond the Balanced Scorecard. *v.4 p.82*

Rethinking Peter Weiss, 32. . . . .*v.2 p.617*

Rethinking Psychological Anthropology: Continuity and Change in the Study of Human Action. *v.4 p.35*

Rethinking Rehabilitation: Why Can't We Reform Our Criminals? *v.6 p.277*

Rethinking Religion: Connecting Cognition and Culture. *v.5 p.634, p.635*

Rethinking Rights and Regulations: Institutional Responses to New Communications Technologies. *v.4 p.761*

Rethinking School Choice: Limits of the Market Metaphor. *v.4 p.347*

Rethinking Sexual Identity in Education. *v.6 p.384*

Rethinking Social Policy: Race, Poverty, and the Underclass. *v.4 p.722*

Rethinking Standards Through Teacher Preparation Partnerships. *v.4 p.279*

Rethinking Substance Abuse: What the Science Shows, and What We Should Do about It. *v.5 p.512, p.522*

Rethinking the Center: Party Politics in Nineteenth- and Twentieth-Century Chile. *v.3 p.351, p.355*

Rethinking the Family: Some Feminist Questions. *v.6 p.466, p.467, p.468*

Rethinking the Korean War: A New Diplomatic and Strategic History. *v.6 p.237*

Rethinking the Mathematics Curriculum. *v.5 p.463*

Rethinking the Novel/Film Debate. *v.6 p.325*

Rethinking the Soviet Experience: Politics and History since 1917. . . . .*v.3 p.222*

Rethinking the Sylph: New Perspectives on the Romantic Ballet. *v.1 p.23*

Rethinking the Synoptic Problem. *v.1 p.628*

Rethinking Urban Parks: Public Space and Cultural Diversity. *v.6 p.297*

Rethinking Victorian Culture. *v.2 p.175*

Rethinking Welfare: A Critical Perspective. *v.4 p.768*

Retorno de lo Vivo Lejano Obra Martiana (Return from the Life Distant). *v.2 p.655*

Retracing a Winter's Journey: Schubert's Winterreise. *v.1 p.207, p.238, p.354*

The Retreat from Race: Asian Admissions and Racial Politics. *v.6 p.109, p.121, p.124*

Retreat from Reconstruction: 1869-1879. . . . . . .*v.3 p.436*

The Retreat of American Power. *v.3 p.466*

Retreat of the Elephants: An Environmental History of China. *v.6 p.184*

Retrospect and Prospect in the Psychological Study of Families. *v.5 p.639*

A Retrospective on the Classical Gold Standard, 1821-1931. . . . .*v.4 p.237*

Retuning Culture: Musical Changes in Central and Eastern Europe. *v.1 p.246, p.299*

Return from Exile: Alternative Sciences, Illegitimacy of Nationalism, the Savage Freud. *v.6 p.157*

The Return of Consciousness. *v.6 p.591*

The Return of Depression Economics. *v.4 p.244*

The Return of King Arthur and the Nibelungen: National Myth in Nineteenth-Century English and German Literature. *v.2 p.176*

The Return of the Armadas: The Last Years of the Elizabethan War Against Spain, 1595-1603. . . . .*v.3 p.101*

Return of the B Science Fiction and Horror Heroes: The Mutant Melding of Two Volumes of Classic Interviews. . .*v.6 p.320*

Return of the Buddha: The Qingzhou Discoveries. . . .*v.1 p.776*

The Return of the King: Being the Third Part of the Lord of the Rings. *v.2 p.386*

The Return of the Native. *v.2 p.291*

The Return of the Soldier. *v.2 p.389*

The Return of the Spirit. *v.6 p.656*

Return the Innocent Earth. *v.2 p.144*

Return to Aztlan: The Social Process of International Migration from Western Mexico. *v.6 p.529, p.530*

Return to Childhood: The Memoir of a Modern Moroccan Woman. *v.6 p.655*

Return to Diversity: A Political History of East Central Europe since World War II. *v.3 p.207, p.208*

Return to Havana: The Decline of Cuban Society under Castro. *v.3 p.310*

Return to Ithaca, the Odyssey Retold as A Modern Novel. *v.2 p.629, p.630*

A Return to the Roots: Conrad, Poland and East- Central Europe. *v.2 p.341*

Return to the Source: Selected Speeches. *v.6 p.73*

Return to Wild America: A Yearlong Search for the Continent's Natural Soul. *v.5 p.182*

Returning Lost Loves: A Novel. *v.6 p.649*

Returning the Gaze: A Genealogy of Black Film Criticism, 1909-1949. . . . .*v.6 p.329, p.341*

Returning to Tradition: The Contemporary Revival of Orthodox Judaism. *v.1 p.551*

Reunion and Reaction: The Compromise of 1877 and the End of Reconstruction. *v.3 p.403, p.439*

Reunion Without Compromise: The South and Reconstruction, 1865-1868. . . . .*v.3 p.437*

Revaluation: Tradition and Development in English Poetry. *v.2 p.181*

Re-Valuing Cummings: Further Essays on the Poet. . .*v.2 p.68*

Revaluing French Feminism: Critical Essays on Difference, Agency, and Culture. *v.6 p.427*

ⓔ Revealing Male Bodies. *v.6 p.437*

Revealing Male Bodies. *v.4 p.745*

Revealing Reveiling: Islamist Gender Ideology in Contemporary Egypt. *v.6 p.640*

Revealing the Buried Past: Geophysics for Archaeologists. *v.4 p.7*

Revealing the Sacred in Asian and Pacific America. . *v.6 p.105*

Revealing the Universe: The Making of the Chandra X-Ray Observatory. *v.5 p.67, p.68*

Reveille in Washington, 1860-1865. . . . .*v.3 p.431*

Revel, Riot, and Rebellion: Popular Politics and Culture in England 1603-1660. . . . .*v.3 p.95, p.104*

Revelation and Theology. *v.1 p.639*

Revelation: Representations of Christ in Photography. *v.1 p.768*

Revelations of Divine Love. *v.1 p.652, p.653*

Revelations: The Autobiography of Alvin Ailey. *v.1 p.5, v.6 p.414*

The Revels History of Drama. *v.2 p.185*

Revenge in Attic and Later Tragedy. *v.2 p.401*

Revenge of the Lawn; The Abortion; So the Wind Won't Blow It All Away. *v.2 p.141*

Revenge of the Microbes: How Bacterial Resistance Is Undermining the Antibiotic Miracle. *v.6 p.284*

The Reveries of the Solitary Walker, Botanical Writings and Letter to Franquieres. *v.2 p.482*

Reverse Discrimination: Dismantling a Myth. *v.4 p.516, v.6 p.470*

Reversible Destiny: Mafia, Antimafia, and the Struggle for Palermo. *v.3 p.204*

Reversing Course: Carter's Foreign Policy, Domestic Politics, and the Failure of Reform. *v.3 p.480*

Reversing Sail: A History of the African Diaspora. . . .*v.6 p.11*

Reversing the Gaze: Amar Singh's Diary, a Colonial Subject's Narrative of Imperial India. *v.6 p.161, p.162*

Reversing the Lens: Ethnicity, Race, Gender, and Sexuality Through Film. . . . . *.v.6 p.475*

Reversing Underachievement among Gifted Black Students: Promising Practices and Programs. . . . . *.v.4 p.317*

Review of Medical Physiology. . . . . *.v.5 p.164*

▢ Review of Particle Physics. . . . . *.v.5 p.545*

Review of Research in Education. . . . . *.v.4 p.354*

Review of the Research Program of the Partnership for a New Generation of Vehicles: Seventh Report. . . . . . *.v.5 p.716*

A Reviewer's Abc: Collected Criticism of Conrad Aiken from 1916 to the Present. . . . . *.v.2 p.56*

Reviewing Asian America: Locating Diversity. . *.v.6 p.85, p.108*

Re-Viewing James Baldwin: Things Not Seen. . . . . *.v.2 p.59*

Revised Medieval Latin Word-List from British and Irish Sources. . . . . *.v.2 p.423, p.424*

Revising Business Prose. . . . . *.v.4 p.173*

Revising Mythologies: The Composition of Thoreau's Major Works. *.v.2 p.52*

Revision and Authority in Wordsworth: The Interpretation of a Career. . . . . *.v.2 p.323*

A Revision of Demand Theory. . . . . *.v.4 p.238*

Revisioning Gender. . . . . *.v.4 p.743, p.744*

Revisioning History: Film and the Construction of a New Past. *.v.6 p.331*

Re-Visioning "Kamakura" Buddhism. . . . . *.v.1 p.562*

Re-Visioning Romanticism: British Women Writers, 1776-1837. . . . . *.v.6 p.480*

Revisiting "The Culture of the School and the Problem of Change". . . . . *.v.4 p.329*

Revisiting the Legacy of Edward Bellamy (1850-1898), American Author and Social Reformer: Uncollected and Unpublished Writings, Scholarly Perspectives for a New Millennium. . . . . *.v.2 p.31*

Revitalization Movements: Some Theoretical Considerations for Their Comparative Study. . . . . *.v.4 p.25*

Revitalizing Political Psychology: The Legacy of Harold D. Lasswell. . . . . *.v.5 p.642*

Revival and Rebellion in Colonial Africa. . . . . . *.v.1 p.611*

Revival and Reform in Islam: A Study of Islamic Fundamentalism. . . . . *.v.1 p.558*

The Revival of Laissez-Faire in American Macroeconomic Theory: A Case Study of Its Pioneers. . . . . . . *.v.4 p.240*

Revive Us Again: The Reawakening of American Fundamentalism. . . . . *.v.1 p.606*

Reviving Ophelia: Saving the Selves of Adolescent Girls. . . . . *.v.5 p.642*

Reviving the American Dream: The Economy, the States, and the Federal Government. . . . . *.v.4 p.266, p.525*

Revolt Against Destiny: An Intellectual History of the United States. . . . . *.v.3 p.366*

The Revolt Against Dualism: An Inquiry Concerning the Existence of Ideas. . . . . *.v.1 p.504*

Revolt Against Regulation: The Rise and Pause of the Consumer Movement. . . . . *.v.4 p.52, p.53*

Revolt in Japan: The Young Officers and the February 26, 1936 Incident. . . . . *.v.6 p.225*

Revolt in the Netherlands: Brussels, 1830. . . . . . *.v.3 p.206*

The Revolt of Owain Glyn Dwr. . . . . *.v.6 p.562*

The Revolt of the Cockroach People. . . . . *.v.6 p.488, p.497*

The Revolt of the Netherlands, 1555 to 1609. . . . . *.v.3 p.204*

Revolt of the Rednecks: Mississippi Politics. . . . . *.v.3 p.505*

The Revolt. . . . . *.v.6 p.609*

Revolución: Cuban Poster Art. . . . . . . *.v.1 p.761, v.3 p.308*

La Revolucion: Mexico's Great Revolution As Memory, Myth and History. . . . . *.v.3 p.266, p.290*

Revolution and Foreign Policy: The Case of South Yemen, 1967-1987. . . . . *.v.6 p.628*

Revolution and Genocide: On the Origins of the Armenian Genocide and the Holocaust. . . . . . . *.v.3 p.85, v.4 p.653*

Revolution and Ideology: Images of the Mexican Revolution in the United States. . . . . *.v.3 p.284*

Revolution and Religion in Ethiopia: Growth and Persecution of the Mekane Yesus Church, 1974-85. . . . . . . *.v.1 p.611*

Revolution and the Transformation of Societies: A Comparative Study of Civilizations. . . . . *.v.4 p.760*

Revolution and the Word: The Rise of the Novel in America. . . . . *.v.2 p.6*

Revolution at the Table: The Transformation of the American Diet. . . . . *.v.5 p.34*

Revolution by Decree: Peru, 1968-1975. . . . . . . *.v.3 p.275*

Revolution by Judiciary: The Structure of American Constitutional Law. . . . . *.v.4 p.454*

Revolution Downeast: The War for American Independence in Maine. . . . . *.v.3 p.486*

Revolution from Abroad: The Soviet Conquest of Poland's Western Ukraine and Western Belorussia. . *.v.3 p.229, p.255*

Revolution from Within: The Hungarian Socialist Workers' Party and the Collapse of Communism. . . *.v.4 p.509, p.595*

Revolution from Without: Yucatán, Mexico, and the United States, 1880-1924. . . . . *.v.3 p.293*

Revolution in America: Confidential Letters and Journals 1776. . . . . *.v.3 p.413*

The Revolution in Corporate Finance. . . . . *.v.4 p.91*

A Revolution in Favor of Government: Origins of the U. S. Constitution and the Making of the American State. . . . . *.v.4 p.523, p.524*

Revolution in Guinea. . . . . *.v.6 p.73*

Revolution in Hungary and the Dissolution of the Multinational State 1918. . . . . *.v.3 p.187*

Revolution in Mexico's Heartland: Politics, War, and State Building in Puebla, 1913-1920. . . . . *.v.3 p.293*

The Revolution in Military Affairs: Implications for Canada and NATO. . . . . *.v.4 p.631, p.655*

The Revolution in Popular Literature: Print, Politics and the People, 1790-1860. . . . . . . *.v.6 p.738, p.758, p.763*

The Revolution in Provincial France: Aquitaine, 1789-1799. . . . . *.v.3 p.150*

The Revolution in Science, 1500-1750. . . *.v.3 p.47, v.5 p.391*

Revolution in Science. . . . . *.v.5 p.390*

Revolution in Texas: How a Forgotten Rebellion and Its Bloody Suppression Turned Mexicans into Americans. . . *.v.6 p.534*

Revolution in the Street: Women, Workers and Urban Protest in Veracruz, 1870-1927. . . . . *.v.3 p.296*

Revolution in the Village: Tradition and Transformation in North Vietnam, 1925-1988. . . . . *.v.6 p.169*

The Revolution of 1525: The German Peasants' War from a New Perspective. *v.3 p.165*

The Revolution of 1688 in England. *v.3 p.107*

The Revolution Of 1905: Authority Restored. . *v.3 p.219, p.220*

The Revolution of 1905 in Odessa: Blood on the Steppes. *v.3 p.221*

The Revolution of 1905: Russia in Disarray. *v.3 p.220*

The Revolution of American Conservatism. *v.3 p.411*

The Revolution of Little Girls. *v.6 p.394*

The Revolution of Peter the Great. *v.3 p.216*

The Revolution of the Dons: Cambridge and Society in Victorian England. *v.3 p.115, p.129,v.6 p.745*

A Revolution of Their Own: Voices of Women in Soviet History. *v.3 p.222*

Revolution on the Border: The United States and Mexico, 1910-1920. . . . .*v.3 p.292*

The Revolution Question: Feminisms in el Salvador, Chile, and Cuba Compared. *v.3 p.283, p.299*

A Revolution Remembered: The Memoirs and Selected Correspondence of Juan N. Seguin. *v.6 p.534*

Revolution, Resistance, and Reform in Village China. .*v.6 p.194*

Revolution: The International Dimensions. *v.4 p.497*

Revolution until Victory?: The Politics and History of the PLO. *v.6 p.619*

Revolutionaries and Reformers: Contemporary Islamist Movements in the Middle East. *v.6 p.595*

Revolutionaries of the Cosmos: The Astro-Physicists. . .*v.5 p.62*

Revolutionary Anglicanism: The Colonial Church of England During the American Revolution. *v.1 p.582*

Revolutionary Apocalypse: Ideological Roots of Terrorism. *v.4 p.661*

The Revolutionary Art of the Future: Rediscovered Poems. *v.2 p.368*

Revolutionary Biology: The New, Gene-Centered View of Life. *v.5 p.138*

The Revolutionary Career of Maximilien Robespierre. *v.3 p.150*

Revolutionary Change. *v.4 p.760*

Revolutionary Cuba and the End of the Cold War. . . .*v.3 p.310*

Revolutionary Dreams: Utopian Vision and Experimental Life in the Russian Revolution. *v.3 p.223*

The Revolutionary Era: Primary Documents on Events from 1776 To 1800. . . . .*v.3 p.315*

Revolutionary France, 1770-1880. . . . .*v.3 p.150*

Revolutionary Grenada: A Study in Political Economy. *v.3 p.321*

The Revolutionary Histories: Contemporary Narratives of the American Revolution. *v.3 p.407*

Revolutionary Iran: Challenge and Response in the Middle East. *v.6 p.632, p.633*

The Revolutionary Left and Terrorist Violence in Chile. *v.3 p.355*

Revolutionary Mexico: The Coming and Process of the Mexican Revolution. *v.3 p.293*

Revolutionary Mothers: Women in the Struggle for America's Independence. *v.6 p.451*

Revolutionary News: The Press in France, 1789-1799. *v.3 p.151*

The Revolutionary Origins of Modern Japan. *v.6 p.224*

Revolutionary Outlaws: Ethan Allen and the Struggle for Independence on the Early American Frontier. . . *v.3 p.411*

A Revolutionary People at War: The Continental Army and American Character, 1775-1783. . . .*v.3 p.410, p.413, p.414*

Revolutionary Politics in Massachusetts: The Boston Committee of Correspondence and the Towns, 1772-1774. . . .*v.3 p.488*

The Revolutionary Reign of Terror: The Role of Violence in Political Change. *v.4 p.497*

Revolutionary Tides: The Art of the Political Poster, 1914-1989. . . . .*v.1 p.718*

Revolutionary Women in Postrevolutionary Mexico. . *v.3 p.294*

Revolutionizing Motherhood: The Mothers of the Plaza De Mayo. *v.6 p.430*

Revolutionizing the Sciences: European Knowledge and Its Ambitions, 1500-1700. . . . .*v.3 p.46*

Revolutions and Reconstructions in the Philosophy of Science. *v.5 p.402*

The Revolutions in Europe, 1848-1849: From Reform to Reaction. *v.3 p.76*

Revolutions in Knowledge: Feminism in the Social Sciences. *v.4 p.255, p.267, p.274, p.275, p.277*

Revolutions of 1848: A Social History. *v.3 p.76*

Revolutions of the Heart: Gender, Power and the Delusions of Love. *v.5 p.654, v.6 p.465, p.467*

Revolutions: Worldwide Introduction to Political and Social Change. *v.4 p.760*

Revue. *v.1 p.26*

Reworking the Past: Hitler, the Holocaust, and the Historians' Debate. *v.3 p.82*

Ⓔ Rewriting Capitalism: Literature and the Market in Late Tsarist Russia and the Kingdom of Poland. *v.2 p.798*

Rewriting North American Borders in Chicano and Chicana Narrative. *v.6 p.486, p.500, p.513*

Re-Writing the French Revolutionary Tradition: Liberal Opposition and the Fall of the Bourbon Monarchy. *v.3 p.153*

Rexford Tugwell and the New Deal. *v.3 p.463*

Reyita: The Life of a Black Cuban Woman in the Twentieth Century. *v.3 p.278, p.307,v.4 p.40*

Reykjavik and Beyond: Deep Reductions in Strategic Nuclear Arsenals and the Future Direction of Arms Control. *v.4 p.656*

Reykjavik: Results and Lessons. *v.3 p.388, p.389*

Reynard the Fox and Other Mediaeval Netherlands Secular Literature. *v.2 p.622*

The Rez Road Follies: Canoes, Casinos, Computers, and Birch Bark Baskets. *v.6 p.698*

La règle du jeu. *v.2 p.521*

Récits et essais. *v.2 p.517*

Rédemption. *v.2 p.528, p.529*

Rhapsody in Plain Yellow. *v.6 p.103*

The Rhetoric and Reality of Mass Education in Mao's China. *v.4 p.336*

Rhetoric and Reform in the Progressive Era: Rhetorical History of the United States. *v.3 p.448*

Rhetoric and Representation in Nonfiction Film. . . .*v.6 p.309*

Rhetoric and Style. *v.2 p.281, p.282*

Rhetoric at Rome: A Historical Survey. *v.2 p.427*

A Rhetoric for Writing Teachers. *v.2 p.565*

Ⓔ Rhetoric in Classical Historiography: Four Studies. *v.2 p.426*

Rhetoric in the Middle Ages: A History of Rhetorical Theory from Saint Augustine to the Renaissance. . . .*v.6 p.558, p.569*

Rhetoric of American Politics: A Study of Documents, 1. . . . .*v.3 p.385*

The Rhetoric of Church and State: A Critical Analysis of Religion Clause Jurisprudence. *v.4 p.460*

The Rhetoric of Economics. *v.4 p.185*

The Rhetoric of English India. *v.2 p.763*

The Rhetoric of Fiction. *v.2 p.578*

The Rhetoric of Terrorism and Counterterrorism. . . .*v.4 p.660*

Rhetorical Analyses of Literary Works. *v.2 p.163*

The Rhetorical Career of Cesar Chavez. *v.6 p.489, p.526*

Rhetorical Deception in the Short Fiction of Hawthorne, Poe and Melville. *v.2 p.41, p.48, p.50*

The Rhetorical Uses of the Authorizing Figure: Fidel Castro and Jose Marti. *v.3 p.312*

Rheumatology, Set. *v.5 p.519, p.520*

The Rhine: An Eco-Biography, 1815-2000. . . . . . .*v.3 p.159*

Rhineland Radicals: The Democratic Movement and the Revolution of 1848-1849. . . . .*v.3 p.168*

The Rhino Man and Other Uncommon Environmentalists: Portraits of Global 500. . . . .*v.5 p.230*

Rhinoceros. *v.2 p.160*

☐ Rhizome.org. *v.1 p.770*

Rhode Island: A Guide to the Smallest State. *v.3 p.489*

Rhode Island: Bicentennial and History Guide. . . .*v.3 p.489*

Rhode Island, the Ocean State: An Illustrated History. *v.3 p.489*

Rhumb Lines and Map Wars: A Social History of the Mercator Projection. *v.4 p.386*

Rhymes and Legends (Selection) / Rimas y Leyendas (seleccion): A Dual-Language Book. *v.2 p.653*

The Rhymes of Robyn Hood: An Introduction to the English Outlaw. *v.2 p.196*

Rhythm and Life: The Work of Emile Jaques-Dalcroze. *v.1 p.12*

Rhythm and Noise: An Aesthetics of Rock. *v.1 p.270*

Rhythm and Resistance: Explorations in the Political Uses of Popular Music. *v.1 p.273*

Rhythm and the Blues: A Life in American Music. . .*v.1 p.386*

Rhythm and Will in Victorian Poetry. . .*v.2 p.174, p.184, p.313*

Rhythm, Music and Education. *v.1 p.47*

Rhythm-a-Ning: Jazz Tradition and Innovation. *v.1 p.259*

Rhythmic Gesture in Mozart: "Le Nozze Di Figaro" and "Don Giovanni". *v.1 p.188, p.227, p.228, p.338*

Rhythmic Gymnastics. *v.4 p.795, p.861, p.862*

The Rhythmic Structure of Music. *v.1 p.370*

Rhythms of Resistance: African Musical Heritage in Brazil. *v.1 p.292, v.3 p.279*

The Rhythms of Tonal Music. *v.1 p.371*

☐ RIAA = Recording Industry Association of America. *v.1 p.173, p.385*

The Ribosome. *v.5 p.129*

Ricardian Economics: A Historical Study, 8—8. . . .*v.4 p.211*

Ricardo, the New View. *v.4 p.220*

Rice As Self: Japanese Identities Through Time. . .*v.6 p.222*

Rice Diseases. *v.5 p.46*

Rice: Origin, History, Technology, and Production. *v.5 p.23, p.24, p.25*

Rice Science and Technology, Vol. 59. . . . .*v.5 p.34*

Rice, Vol. 14. . . . .*v.5 p.19, p.24*

A Ricepaper Airplane. *v.6 p.102*

Rich and Strange: Gender, History, Modernism. . . .*v.2 p.190*

Rich Forests, Poor People: Resource Control and Resistance in Java. *v.5 p.39*

A Rich Land, a Poor People: Politics and Society in Modern Chiapas. *v.3 p.290*

Rich Media, Poor Democracy: Communication Politics in Dubious Times. *v.4 p.416*

Richard B. Russell, Jr., Senator from Georgia. . . .*v.3 p.458*

Richard Barnfield: The Complete Poems. *v.6 p.405*

Richard Beer-Hofmann: His Life and Work. *v.2 p.603*

Richard Boleslavsky: His Life and Work in the Theatre. *v.1 p.110, p.153*

Richard Diebenkorn. *v.1 p.744*

Richard Haag: Bloedel Reserve and Gasworks Park. . *v.1 p.814*

Richard Hofstadter: An Intellectual Biography. . . .*v.3 p.373*

Richard J. Daley: Politics, Race, and the Governing of Chicago. *v.3 p.515*

Richard King: Texas Cattle Rancher. *v.3 p.509*

Richard Meier Architect. *v.1 p.794*

Richard Milhous Nixon: The Rise of an American Politician. *v.3 p.476*

Richard Nixon and His America. *v.3 p.478*

Richard Nixon, Watergate, and the Press: A Historical Retrospective. *v.3 p.474*

The Richard Rodgers Reader. *v.1 p.248, p.351*

Richard Rodgers. *v.1 p.248, p.351*

Richard Rolle: The Fire of Love and the Mending of Life. *v.1 p.577*

Richard Rorty. *v.1 p.441, p.442*

Richard S. Ewell: A Soldier's Life. *v.4 p.521*

Richard Strauss and His World. *v.1 p.214, p.359*

Richard Strauss, Der Rosenkavalier. *v.1 p.216, p.217, p.230, p.359*

Richard Strauss: Man, Musician, Enigma. . . .*v.1 p.217, p.359*

Richard Strauss: "Elektra". *v.1 p.221, p.222, p.232, p.359*

Richard Strauss: Salome. *v.1 p.222, p.232, p.359*

Richard Strauss's Elektra. *v.1 p.214, p.229, p.359*

Richard Tuttle: A Retrospective. *v.1 p.700*

Richard Wagner: A Biography. *v.1 p.206, p.207, p.367*

Richard Wagner: A Guide to Research. . .*v.1 p.164, p.203, p.366*

Richard Wagner and the Anti-Semetic Imagination. *v.1 p.207, p.301, p.367*

Richard Wagner: Der Fliegende Holländer. *v.1 p.197, p.229, p.365*

Richard Wagner: Die Meistersinger von Nürnberg. *v.1 p.206, p.234, p.367*

Richard Wagner: His Life, His Work, His Century. *v.1 p.197, p.365*

Richard Wagner: "Parsifal". *v.1 p.194, p.228, p.365*

Richard Wagner: The Last of the Titans. *v.1 p.199, p.365*

Richard Wagner's Music Dramas. *v.1 p.196, p.229, p.365*

Richard Wollheim on the Art of Painting: Art as Representation and Expression. *v.1 p.701*

Richard Wright: A Collection of Critical Essays. . . *v.2 p.138*

Richard Wright: Ordeal of a Native Son. *v.2 p.138*

The Richard Wright Reader. *v.2 p.138*

Richard Wright: The Critical Reception. *v.2 p.138*

Richard Wright's Hero: The Faces of a Rebel-Victim. *v.2 p.138*

Richelieu and Olivares. *v.3 p.145*

Richmond During the Revolution, 1775-83: Harry M. Ward and Harold E. Greer, Jr. *v.3 p.500*

Richtiges und Gutes Deutsch. *v.2 p.621*

Rickettsioses: From Genome to Proteome, Pathobiology, and Rickettsiae As an International Threat. *v.5 p.206*

e Rickshaw Beijing: City People and Politics in the 1920s. *v.6 p.191, p.206*

Rickshaw: The Novel Lo-t'o Hsiang Tzu. *v.6 p.212*

A Ricoeur Reader: Reflection and Imagination. . . . *v.1 p.457*

The Riddle of Gender: Science, Activism, and Transgender Rights. *v.4 p.744*

The Riddle of the Sands: A Record of Secret Service. *v.2 p.336, p.337*

Riddles of Existence: A Guided Tour of Metaphysics. *v.1 p.488*

Ride to Modernity: The Bicycle in Canada, 1869-1900. . . . . *v.4 p.808, p.857*

Rider Haggard. *v.2 p.290*

Riders in the Chariot. *v.2 p.750*

Riders of the Purple Sage. *v.2 p.78*

Ridiculous!: The Theatrical Life and Times of Charles Ludlam. *v.6 p.413*

Riding on a Blue Note: Jazz and American Pop. . . *v.1 p.259*

Riding the Roller Coaster: A History of the Chrysler Corporation. *v.4 p.154*

Riding the Waves of Culture: Understanding Diversity in Global Business. *v.4 p.59, p.132*

Riding the Windhorse: Spiritual Intelligence and the Growth of the Self. *v.5 p.635*

Riegel's handbook of industrial chemistry. *v.5 p.316*

Riegel's Handbook of Industrial Chemistry. . *v.5 p.316, p.741*

☐ Riegel's Handbook of Industrial Chemistry. . . . *v.5 p.316*

Riel and the Rebellion: 1885 Reconsidered. *v.3 p.545*

Riemannian Geometry: A Beginner's Guide. *v.5 p.496*

Riemannian Geometry and Geometric Analysis. . . . *v.5 p.496*

Riemannian Geometry. *v.5 p.496*

The Rig Veda: An Anthology of One Hundred Eight Hymns. *v.1 p.538*

The Right and the Good. *v.1 p.487*

The Right and the Power. *v.4 p.439*

Right Face: Organizing the American Conservative Movement 1945-65. . . . . *v.4 p.516*

Right Hand, Left Hand: The Origins of Asymmetry in Brains, Bodies, Atoms and Cultures. *v.5 p.594*

Right Ho, Jeeves. *v.2 p.391*

The Right in France: Nationalism and the State, 1789-1996. . . . . *v.3 p.140*

The Right Man: An Inside Account of the Bush White House. *v.3 p.483*

The Right of the People. *v.4 p.455*

The Right Stuff. *v.5 p.720*

Right to Counsel and Privilege Against Self-Incrimination: Rights and Liberties under the Law. *v.6 p.271*

The Right to Die: Policy Innovation and Its Consequences. *v.4 p.448*

The Right to Home School: A Guide to the Law on Parents' Rights in Education. *v.4 p.296, p.450*

The Right to Vote: Politics and the Passage of the 15th Amendment. *v.4 p.461*

Right to Vote: The Contested History of Democracy in the United States. *v.4 p.519*

A Righteous Cause. *v.3 p.433*

Righteous Pilgrim: The Life and Times of Harold L. Ickes, 1874-1952. . . . . *v.3 p.463*

Righting a Wrong: Japanese Americans and the Passage of the Civil Liberties Act of 1988. . . . . . . *v.4 p.571, v.6 p.133*

Rights and Wrongs of Abortion: A Philosophy and Public Affairs Reader. *v.1 p.486*

Rights Beyond Borders: The Global Community and the Struggle over Human Rights in China. *v.4 p.669*

Rights, Not Roses: Unions and the Rise of Working-Class Feminism, 1945-80. . . . . *v.4 p.121*

The Rights of Aliens and Refugees: The Basic ACLU Guide to Alien and Refugee Rights. *v.4 p.460*

The Rights of Authors, Artists, and Other Creative People: The Basic ACLU Guide to Author and Artist Rights. *v.4 p.441, p.442*

The Rights of Employees and Union Members: The Basic ACLU Guide to the Rights of Employees and Union Members. *v.4 p.447*

The Rights of Indians and Tribes: The Authoritative ACLU Guide to Indian and Tribal Rights, Third Edition. *v.4 p.465, v.6 p.696*

The Rights of Lesbians, Gay Men, Bisexuals, and Transgender People: The Authoritative ACLU Guide to the Rights of Lesbians, Gay Men, Bisexuals, and Transgender People. *v.4 p.457*

The Rights of Nature: A History of Environmental Ethics. *v.6 p.289*

The Rights of Others: Aliens, Residents and Citizens. *v.4 p.576, p.669*

The Rights of Patients: The Authoritative ACLU Guide to the Rights of Patients. *v.4 p.448*

The Rights of People Who Are HIV Positive: The Basic ACLU Guide to the Rights of People Living with HIV Disease and AIDS. *v.4 p.448*

The Rights of People with Mental Disabilities: The Authoritative ACLU Guide to the Rights of People with Mental Illness and Mental Retardation. *v.4 p.442*

The Rights of War and Peace: Political Thought and the International Order from Grotius to Kant. *v.4 p.477*

The Rights of Youth: American Colleges and Student Revolt, 1798-1815. . . . . *v.4 p.332*

Rights Talk: The Impoverishment of American Political Discourse. *v.4 p.455*

Rights vs. Public Safety after 9/11: America in the Age of Terrorism. *v.4 p.563, p.572*

Rights vs. Responsibilities: The Supreme Court and the Media, 50. . . . .*v.4 p.405*

Rights, Welfare, and Mill's Moral Theory. *v.1 p.516*

Right-Wing Women in Chile: Feminine Power and the Struggle Against Allende, 1964-1973. . . . .*v.3 p.354*

Rigoberta: La Nieta de Los Mayas. *v.2 p.676*

Rigoberta Menchu and the Story of All Poor Guatemalans. *v.3 p.283, p.284, p.298*

Rilke: A Life. *v.2 p.614*

Rilke: Poems. *v.2 p.614*

☐ RILM Abstracts of Music Literature = International Repertory of Music Literature. *v.1 p.163*

Rimas ; Leyendas ; Cartas Desde Mi Celda. *v.2 p.653*

Rimas y Leyendas. *v.2 p.653, p.654*

Rimbaud: A Biography. *v.2 p.499*

Rimbaud: Complete Works, Selected Letters. *v.2 p.498*

Rimbaud Complete. *v.2 p.499*

Rimbaud. *v.2 p.498*

Rime e trionfi. *v.2 p.706*

The Rime of the Ancient Mariner. *v.2 p.279*

Rime. *v.2 p.702*

Le Rime. *v.2 p.707*

Rimsky-Korsakov. *v.1 p.193, p.350*

Ring Around the Bases: The Complete Baseball Stories of Ring Lardner. *v.2 p.94*

Ring for Jeeves. *v.2 p.391*

The Ring Index. *v.5 p.288*

Ring Lardner. *v.2 p.94*

Ring of Bone: Collected Poems, 1950-1971. . . . .*v.2 p.158*

A Ring of Conspirators: Henry James and His Literary Circle, 1895-1915. . . . .*v.2 p.46*

Ring of Fire: The Johnny Cash Reader. *v.1 p.275, p.316*

Ring of Liberation: Deceptive Discourse in Brazilian Capoeira. *v.1 p.20*

The Ring of the Nibelung. *v.1 p.206, p.234, p.367, p.410*

The Ring of Words: An Anthology of Song Texts. .*v.1 p.236, p.412*

Rings and Ideals. *v.5 p.474*

Rings of Burnished Brass and Other Stories. *v.6 p.660*

Rings of Continuous Functions. *v.5 p.493*

Ringside Seat to a Revolution: An Underground Cultural History of el Paso and Juarez: 1893-1923. . . . .*v.3 p.295*

Rio Claro: A Brazilian Plantation System, 1820-1920. .*v.3 p.336*

El Rio: Novelas de Caballeria. *v.2 p.675*

The Rio Report: Reshaping the International Order: a Report to the Club of Rome Coordinator. *v.4 p.256*

Riot: A Love Story. *v.2 p.767*

Riot and Revelry in Early America. *v.4 p.713*

Riparian Areas: Functions and Strategies for Management. *v.5 p.173, p.174*

Riparian Vegetation and Fluvial Geomorphology. . .*v.4 p.391*

The Ripening Seed. *v.2 p.515*

The Ripening. *v.2 p.537*

A Ripple from the Storm. *v.2 p.365*

The Rise and Demise of German Statism: Loyalty and Political Membership. *v.4 p.609*

The Rise and Fall and Rise of Modern Dance. *v.1 p.27*

The Rise and Fall of American Public Schools: The Political Economy of Public Education in the 20th Century. .*v.4 p.326*

The Rise and Fall of California's Radical Prison Movement. *v.6 p.273*

The Rise and Fall of Class in Britain. *v.6 p.736, p.742*

The Rise and Fall of Gay Culture. . .*v.4 p.712, v.6 p.365, p.387*

The Rise and Fall of HMOs: An American Health Care Revolution. *v.4 p.163*

The Rise and Fall of Palestine: A Personal Account of the Intifada Years. *v.6 p.617*

The Rise and Fall of Peruvian Military Radicals. . . .*v.3 p.331*

The Rise and Fall of States According to Greek Authors. .*v.4 p.500*

The Rise and Fall of Synanon: A California Utopia. . .*v.4 p.720*

The Rise and Fall of the Brezhnev Doctrine in Soviet Foreign Policy. *v.3 p.212*

The Rise and Fall of the British Empire. .*v.3 p.89, p.125, p.126*

The Rise and Fall of the Confederate Government. . .*v.3 p.428*

Rise and Fall of the Cosmic Race: The Cult of Mestizaje in Latin America. *v.3 p.267*

The Rise and Fall of the Elites: An Application of Theoretical Sociology. *v.4 p.249*

The Rise and Fall of the European Defence Community: Anglo-American Relations and the Crises of European Defence, 1950-55. . . . .*v.4 p.638, p.655*

Rise and Fall of the German Democratic Republic 1945-1990. . . . .*v.4 p.609*

The Rise and Fall of the Great Powers: Economic Change and Military Conflict from 1500 to 2000. . . . . . .*v.3 p.36*

The Rise and Fall of the Habsburg Monarchy. . . .*v.3 p.182*

The Rise and Fall of the Hashemite Kingdom of the Hijaz. *v.6 p.626*

The Rise and Fall of the Man of Letters: English Literary Life since 1800. . .*v.2 p.175, v.3 p.112, p.120, p.128,v.6 p.740*

The Rise and Fall of the New Deal Order, 1930-1980. .*v.3 p.471*

The Rise and Fall of the Paraguayan Republic, 1800-1870. . . . .*v.3 p.344*

Rise and Fall of the Peruvian Military Radicals, 1968-1976. . . . .*v.3 p.276*

The Rise and Fall of the Press Box. *v.4 p.902, p.907*

The Rise and Fall of the Second Empire, 1852-1871. .*v.3 p.154*

The Rise and Fall of the Soviet Politburo. . . .*v.4 p.598, p.600*

Rise and Fall of the Zulu Nation. *v.6 p.79*

The Rise and Fall of Weimar Democracy. *v.3 p.170*

The Rise of Afrikanerdom: Power, Apartheid, and the Afrikaner Civil Religion. *v.6 p.79*

The Rise of American Civilization. *v.3 p.379*

The Rise of American Democracy: Jefferson to Lincoln. .*v.3 p.415*

The Rise of American Naval Power, 1776-1918. . . .*v.3 p.384*

The Rise of American Research Universities: Elites and Challengers in the Postwar Era. *v.4 p.331*

Rise of Anthropological Theory: A History of Theories of Culture. *v.4 p.23, p.24*

The Rise of Cable Programming in the United States: Revolution or Evolution?. *v.4 p.421*

The Rise of Candidate-Centered Politics: Presidential Elections of the 1980s. *v.4 p.550, p.556*

The Rise of Christian Democracy in Europe. . . .*v.4 p.601, p.602*

The Rise of Christianity. *v.1 p.599*

The Rise of Commercial Empires: England and the Netherlands
  in the Age of Mercantilism, 1650-1770. . . . . . .*v.4 p.212*

The Rise of East Asia: Critical Visions of the Pacific
  Century. *v.6 p.180*

The Rise of European Liberalism. *v.4 p.767*

The Rise of Evangelicalism: The Age of Edwards, Whitefield
  and the Wesleys. *v.1 p.590*

The Rise of Fishes: 500 Million Years of Evolution. . .*v.5 p.215*

The Rise of Guardian Democracy: The Supreme Court's Role in
  Voting Rights Disputes, 1845-1969. . . . .*v.4 p.461*

The Rise of Hispanic Power. *v.6 p.537*

The Rise of Islam and the Bengal Frontier, 1204-1760. .*v.6 p.160*

Rise of Literary Journalism in the Eighteenth-Century: Anxious
  Employment. *v.4 p.405*

The Rise of Magic in Early Medieval Europe. *v.6 p.569*

The Rise of Mass Literacy: Reading and Writing in Modern
  Europe. *v.3 p.37, p.38, p.120*

The Rise of Modern China. *v.6 p.183*

Rise of Music in the Ancient World. *v.1 p.176*

The Rise of Nationalism in Vietnam, 1900-1941. . . .*v.6 p.167*

The Rise of Neoconservatism: Intellectuals and Foreign Affairs,
  1945-1994. . . . .*v.3 p.451*

The Rise of Political Anti-Semitism in Germany and
  Austria. *v.3 p.60*

The Rise of Political Consultants. *v.4 p.558*

The Rise of Professional Society: England since 1880. *v.3 p.114*

The Rise of Protestant Evangelism in Ecuador,
  1895-1990. . . . .*v.3 p.333*

The Rise of Respectable Society: A Social History of Victorian
  Britain, 1830-1900. . . . . .*v.3 p.116, p.132,v.6 p.736, p.743*

The Rise of Richelieu. *v.3 p.144*

The Rise of Rome, Bks. 1-5. . . . .*v.2 p.436*

The Rise of Rome. *v.3 p.25*

The Rise of Scientific Philosophy. *v.1 p.417*

The Rise of the Anglo-German Antagonism, 1860-1914. .*v.3 p.91*

The Rise of the Atlantic Economies. *v.3 p.39*

The Rise of the Barristers: A Social History of the English Bar,
  1590-1640. . . . .*v.3 p.124*

Rise of the Bourgeoisie, Demise of Empire: Ottoman
  Westernization and Social Change. *v.6 p.589*

The Rise of the European Economy: An Economic History of
  Continental Europe from Fifteenth Hundred to Seventeen
  Fifty. *v.3 p.40*

The Rise of the Fiscal State in Europe, c. 1200-1815. . .*v.3 p.38*

The Rise of the French Novel: Marivaux, Crebillon Fils,
  Rousseau, Stendhal, Flaubert, Alain-Fournier, Raymond
  Radiguet. *v.2 p.463*

The Rise of the Hispanic Market in the United States:
  Challenges, Dilemmas, and Opportunities for Corporate
  Management. *v.6 p.526*

Rise of the Indian Novel in English. *v.2 p.762*

Rise of the Mexican American Middle Class: San Antonio,
  1929-1941. . . . .*v.6 p.535, p.549*

Rise of the Modern German Novel: Crisis and
  Charisma. *v.2 p.592*

The Rise of the Monophysite Movement: Chapters in the
  History of the Church in the Fifth and Sixth
  Centuries. *v.1 p.646*

Rise of the Network Society. *v.6 p.729*

Rise of the New West 1819 To 1829. . . . .*v.3 p.520*

The Rise of the Novel. *v.2 p.190, p.579,v.3 p.130*

The Rise of the Ottoman Empire: Studies on the History of
  Turkey, 13th-15th Centuries. *v.6 p.591*

The Rise of the Parti Quebecois 1967-76. . . . . . .*v.4 p.590*

The Rise of the Public in Enlightenment Europe. *v.3 p.72*

The Rise of the Rogue Executive: How Good Companies Go
  Bad and How to Stop the Destruction. *v.4 p.54, p.72, p.110*

The Rise of the States: Evolution of American State
  Government. *v.4 p.526*

The Rise of the Virtual State: Wealth and Power in the Coming
  Century. *v.4 p.498, p.499*

Rise of the Vulcans: The History of Bush's War
  Cabinet. *v.3 p.483, p.484*

The Rise of the Western World: A New Economic
  History. *v.3 p.41*

Rise of the Young Turks: Politics, the Military, and Ottoman
  Collapse. *v.6 p.622*

The Rise of Theodore Roosevelt. *v.3 p.443*

The Rise of Universities. *v.6 p.558*

The Rise of Western Christendom: Triumph and Diversity
  200-1000 AD. *v.3 p.56*

Rise to Globalism: American Foreign Policy since 1938. .*v.3 p.451*

The Rise to Power, 1919-1934: A Documentary Reader. .*v.3 p.173*

The Rise to Power of the Chinese Communist Party: Documents
  and Analysis. *v.6 p.192*

Rise up, Women!: The Militant Campaign of the Women's
  Social and Political Union, 1903-1914. . . . . . .*v.3 p.117*

Rising '44: The Battle for Warsaw. *v.3 p.254*

Rising above Sweatshops: Innovative Approaches to Global
  Labor Challenges. *v.4 p.69, p.664*

The Rising American Empire. *v.3 p.382*

The Rising in Western Upper Canada, 1837-38: The Duncombe
  Revolt and After. *v.3 p.540*

Rising Tide: Gender Equality and Cultural Change Around the
  World. *v.6 p.441*

Rising Tide: The Great Mississippi Flood of 1927 and How It
  Changed America. *v.3 p.505, p.506*

Rising Up and Rising Down: Some Thoughts on Violence,
  Freedom, and Urgent Means. *v.4 p.751*

Risk and Failure in English Business,
  1700-1800. . . . .*v.3 p.106, p.107, p.108*

Risk and Insurance. *v.4 p.163*

Risk and Reason: Safety, Law, and the
  Environment. *v.4 p.110, p.111, p.112*

Risk Assessment and Management Handbook: For
  Environmental, Health, and Safety Professionals. . .*v.5 p.682*

☐ Risk Management - Wikipedia, the free encyclopedia. .*v.4 p.92*

Risk Regulation at Risk: Restoring a Pragmatic
  Approach. *v.4 p.92, p.110, p.111*

Risk Taking in International Politics: Prospect Theory in
  American Foreign Policy. *v.4 p.642*

Risks of Faith: The Emergence of a Black Theology of Liberation, 1968-1998. . . . . *.v.1 p.635*

Risky Sex?: Gay Men and HIV Prevention. . . *.v.6 p.379, p.380*

Risky Writing: Self-Disclosure and Self-Transformation in the Classroom. . . . . *.v.2 p.564*

Rite and Man: Natural Sacredness and Christian Liturgy. *.v.1 p.576*

Rites and Symbols of Initiation: The Mysteries of Birth and Rebirth. *.v.1 p.530*

The Rites of Christian Initiation: Their Evolution and Interpretation. . . . . *.v.1 p.657*

The Rites of Identity: The Religious Naturalism and Cultural Criticism of Kenneth Burke and Ralph Ellison. . . . *.v.2 p.3*

Rites of Passage. . . . . *.v.2 p.347*

The Rites of Passage. . . . . *.v.4 p.37*

Ritual and Experiment in Modern Poetry. . . . . . . *.v.2 p.326*

Ritual and Religion among Muslims in India. . . . . *.v.1 p.553*

Ritual and Religion in the Making of Humanity. . . . . *.v.1 p.530, v.4 p.37*

Ritual and the Art of Tobi Kahn: Objects of the Spirit. *.v.1 p.778*

Ritual in Early Modern Europe. . . . . *.v.1 p.530*

Ritual, Play, and Performance: Readings in the Social Sciences/Theatre. . . . . *.v.1 p.136*

Ritual, Politics and Power. . . . . *.v.4 p.765, p.766*

Ritual, Politics, and the City in Fatimid Cairo. . . . . *.v.6 p.568, p.575, p.636*

Ritual Theory, Ritual Practice. . . . . *.v.1 p.530*

Rituals of Blood: Consequences of Slavery in Two American Centuries. . . . . *.v.4 p.727*

Rituals of Respect: The Secret of Survival in the High Peruvian Andes. *.v.3 p.328*

Rituals of Rule, Rituals of Resistance: Public Celebrations and Popular Culture in Mexico. . . . . . *.v.3 p.264, p.290*

The Ritz and Other Plays. . . . . *.v.6 p.412*

Rival Enlightenments: Civil and Metaphysical Philosophy in Early Modern Germany. . . . . *.v.1 p.459*

Rival Jerusalems: The Geography of Victorian Religion. *.v.6 p.759*

The Rivalry: Bill Russell, Wilt Chamberlain, and the Golden Age of Basketball. . . . . *.v.4 p.854*

The River and the Gauntlet. . . . . *.v.6 p.237*

River of Blood: The Genesis of a Martyr Cult in Southern Malawi, C. A. D. 1600. . . . . *.v.6 p.76*

River of Earth. . . . . *.v.2 p.156*

The River of Heaven. . . . . *.v.2 p.147, v.6 p.103*

River of Red Wine. . . . . *.v.2 p.98*

River of Song: A Musical Journey down the Mississippi. *.v.1 p.279*

River of the Brokenhearted. . . . . *.v.2 p.738*

The River of the Mother of God: And Other Essays by Aldo Leopold. . . . . *.v.5 p.226*

River Processes: An Introduction to Fluvial Dynamics. *.v.5 p.427*

The River Runs Black: The Environmental Challenge to China's Future. *.v.6 p.196*

River Town: Two Years on the Yangtze. . . . *.v.6 p.214, p.215*

Riverbed of Memory. . . . . *.v.2 p.677*

Rivers and Floodplains: Forms, Processes and Sedmentary Record. *.v.5 p.427*

Rivers for Life: Managing Water for People and Nature. . . . . *.v.5 p.356, p.380*

Rivers: Form and Process in Alluvial Channels. . . . *.v.5 p.427*

Rivers: Forms and Process in Alluvial Channels. . . *.v.5 p.427*

Rivers in Time: The Search for Clues to Earth's Mass Extinctions. . . . . *.v.5 p.450, v.6 p.294*

The Rivers of Canada. . . . . *.v.3 p.535*

Rivers of Gold. . . . . *.v.6 p.77*

Rivers of North America. . . . . . . *.v.5 p.173, p.233, p.241*

Rivers, Streams, Lakes, and Ponds. . . . . *.v.4 p.393*

The Riverside Chaucer. . . . . *.v.2 p.207*

The Riverside Shakespeare. . . . . *.v.2 p.224*

Rivers. *.v.5 p.427*

Riverwalking: Reflections on Moving Water. . . . . *.v.5 p.242*

RN: The Memoirs of Richard Nixon. . . . . *.v.3 p.477*

RNA Interference in Practice: Principles, Basics, and Methods for Gene Silencing in C. elegans, Drosophila, and Mammals. . . . . *.v.5 p.137*

RNA Polymerase and Associated Factors, Vol. 370, Pt. C. . . . . *.v.5 p.130*

RNA Silencing. . . . . *.v.5 p.131, p.133*

RNA Trafficking and Nuclear Structure Dynamics. . *.v.5 p.124*

☐ RNA World Website. . . . . *.v.5 p.328*

The RNA World. . . . . *.v.5 p.121*

The Road Ahead: Middle East Policy in the Bush Administration's Second Term. . . . . *.v.4 p.564*

The Road Back. . . . . *.v.2 p.618*

The Road Before Us (One Hundred Gay Black Poets). *.v.6 p.405*

The Road from Decadence: From Brothel to Cloister - Selected Letters of J. K. Huysmans. . . . . *.v.2 p.494*

The Road from Serfdom: The Economic and Political Consequences of the End of Communism. . . . . *.v.4 p.507*

Road Not Taken: A History of Radical Social Work in the United States. . . . . *.v.4 p.758*

Road to Appomattox. . . . . *.v.3 p.402, p.403*

The Road to Aztlan: Art from a Mythic Homeland. . *.v.6 p.492*

The Road to Berlin: Stalin's War with Germany. . . *.v.3 p.227*

The Road to Confederation: The Emergence of Canada, 1863-1867. . . . . *.v.3 p.539*

The Road to Confrontation: American Policy Toward China and Korea, 1947-1950. . . . . *.v.3 p.392*

The Road to Danger, Guilt and Shame: The Lonely Way of A. E. Housman. . . . . *.v.2 p.290*

The Road to Disunion: Bleeding Kansas to Fort Sumter, Vol. II. . . . . *.v.3 p.397*

The Road to el Cielo: Mexico's Forest in the Clouds. *.v.3 p.270*

Road to Europe. . . . . *.v.2 p.543*

Road to Freedom: On the Canadian-East European Relations, 1963-1991. . . . . *.v.3 p.537*

The Road to Jerusalem: Glubb Pasha, Palestine and the Jews. *.v.6 p.619*

The Road to Khartoum: A Life of General Charles Gordon. . . . . *.v.3 p.90, p.116*

The Road to Maastricht: Negotiating Economic and Monetary Union. . . . . *.v.4 p.629, p.637*

The Road to Martyrs' Square: A Journey into the World of the Suicide Bomber. *v.4 p.661*

The Road to Medical Statistis. *v.5 p.100*

The Road to Ramadan. *v.6 p.58, p.639*

The Road to Reality: A Complete Guide to the Laws of the Universe. *v.5 p.541*

The Road to Redemption: Southern Politics, 1869-1879. . . . . *v.3 p.399, p.497*

Road to Rembetika. *v.1 p.298*

The Road to Romanian Independence. *v.3 p.250*

The Road to San Giovanni. *v.2 p.714*

The Road to Serfdom. *v.4 p.243*

Road to Stonewall. *v.2 p.10, v.6 p.392*

The Road to Tamazunchale. *v.6 p.497*

The Road to the City: Two Novellas. *v.2 p.718*

The Road to the White House: Electing the American President. *v.4 p.526*

The Road to Whatever: Middle-Class Culture and the Crisis of Adolescence. *v.4 p.723, p.724*

The Road to Wigan Pier. *v.2 p.375*

The Road to Xanadu: A Study in the Ways of the Imagination. *v.2 p.280*

Roads Not Taken: Rereading Robert Frost. *v.2 p.78*

The Roads of Chinese Childhood: Learning and Identification in Angang. *v.4 p.40*

The Roads to Congress 2000. . . . . *v.4 p.529*

The Roads to Modernity: The British, French and American Enlightenments. *v.1 p.437*

Roadside Safety Analysis Program (RSAP): Engineer's Manual. *v.5 p.695*

Roanoke Island: The Beginnings of English America. *v.3 p.500, p.502*

Roanoke: The Abandoned Colony. *v.3 p.500*

The Roar of the Twenties. *v.3 p.545*

The Roaring 90s: A New History of the World's Most Prosperous Decade. *v.4 p.256*

Roaring Camp: The Social World of the California Gold Rush. *v.3 p.531*

The Roaring Girl and Other City Comedies. *v.2 p.218*

The Roaring Twenties. *v.3 p.372, p.448*

Rob Roy. *v.2 p.307*

Robbins and Cotran Pathological Basis of Disease: With Student Consult Access. *v.5 p.514*

Robert A. Taft: Ideas, Tradition, and Party in U.S. Foreign Policy. *v.3 p.464*

Robert Browning Revisited. *v.2 p.272*

Robert Browning's Poetry. *v.2 p.271*

Robert Browning. *v.2 p.271, p.272*

Robert Burns: The Man and His Work. *v.2 p.273*

Robert Burns Woodward: Architect and Artist in the World of Molecules. *v.5 p.261*

Robert D. Fitzgerald. *v.2 p.744, p.745*

Robert Drew and the Development of Cinema Verite in America. *v.6 p.309*

Robert E. Lee: A Biography. *v.3 p.401, v.4 p.522*

Robert Frost: A Biography. *v.2 p.77*

The Robert Frost Encyclopedia. *v.2 p.78*

Robert Frost: The Ethics of Ambiguity. *v.2 p.78*

Robert Frost: The People, Places and Stories Behind His New England Poetry. *v.2 p.77*

Robert Frost: The Work of Knowing. *v.2 p.77, p.78*

Robert Graves and Siegfried Sassoon. *v.2 p.348*

Robert Graves and the White Goddess, 1940-1985. . . *v.2 p.348*

Robert Graves: The Lasting Poetic Achievement. . . *v.2 p.348*

Robert Greene. *v.2 p.218*

Robert Grosseteste. *v.1 p.433*

Robert Gwathmey: The Life and Art of a Passionate Observer. *v.1 p.742*

Robert Herrick, a Biographical and Critical Study. . . *v.2 p.250*

Robert Herrick's Hesperides and the Epigram Book Tradition. *v.2 p.249, p.250*

Robert Herrick. *v.2 p.250*

Robert Johnson: Lost and Found. *v.1 p.262, p.334*

Robert Johnson, Mythmaking, and Contemporary American Culture. *v.1 p.263, p.282, p.334*

Robert Lansing and American Neutrality, 1914-1917. *v.3 p.480*

Robert Louis Stevenson: A Literary Life. *v.2 p.312*

Robert Louis Stevenson and the Colonial Imagination. *v.2 p.312*

Robert Lowell: A Biography. *v.2 p.96*

Robert Lowell and the Sublime. *v.2 p.96*

Robert Lowell: Interviews and Memoirs. *v.2 p.96*

Robert Lowell: Life of Art. *v.2 p.96*

Robert Lowell: The Poet and His Critics. *v.2 p.96*

Robert Lowell's Life and Work: Damaged Grandeur. . . *v.2 p.96*

Robert Lowell's Shifting Colors: The Poetics of the Public and the Personal. *v.2 p.96*

Robert Motherwell: The Complete Prints 1940-1991: A Catalogue Raisonné. *v.1 p.756*

Robert Mugabe: A Life of Power and Violence. . . . *v.6 p.77*

Robert Musil and the Crisis of European Culture, 1880-1942. . . . . *v.2 p.614*

Robert Nozick. *v.1 p.442*

Robert Oppenheimer: Letters and Recollections. . . . *v.5 p.543*

Robert Penn Warren and American Idealism. *v.2 p.129*

Robert Penn Warren's Circus Aesthetic and the Southern Renaissance. *v.2 p.129*

Robert Penn Warren. *v.2 p.129*

Robert Redfield and the Development of American Anthropology. *v.4 p.5*

Robert Schumann: Herald of a New Poetic Age. *v.1 p.196, p.354*

Robert Smithson Unearthed: Drawings, Collages, Writings. *v.1 p.724*

Robert the Bruce's Irish Wars: The Invasion of Ireland 1306-1329. . . . . *v.3 p.136*

Roberta's Rules of Order: Sail Through Meetings for Stellar Results Without the Gavel. *v.4 p.80*

Roberto Burle Marx in Caracas: Parque Del Este, 1956-1961. . . . . *v.1 p.815*

Roberto Burle Marx: Landscape Architecture. *v.1 p.816*

Roberto Burle Marx: The Lyrical Landscape. *v.1 p.816*

Robert's Dictionary of Industrial Relations. *v.4 p.123*

Robert's Rules of Order. *v.4 p.575*

Robespierre and the French Revolution. *v.3 p.151*

Robin and Lucienne Day: Pioneers of Modern
Design. *v.1 p.720, p.802*

Robin Hood: A Cinematic History of the English Outlaw and
His Scottish Counterparts. *v.6 p.331*

Robin Hood and Other Outlaw Tales. *v.2 p.197*

Robin Hood. *v.6 p.565*

Robin Williams Design Workshop. *v.4 p.428*

Robinson Crusoe: An Authoritative Text, Backgrounds and
Sources, Criticism. *v.2 p.245*

Robinson Crusoe: Island Myths and the Novel. . . .*v.2 p.246*

The Robinson Crusoe Story. *v.2 p.245, 246*

Robinson Jeffers: The Dimensions of a Poet. *v.2 p.91*

Robinson Jeffers. *v.2 p.91*

Robinson: Selected Poems. *v.2 p.114*

Robinson. *v.2 p.384*

Robo Sapiens: Evolution of a New Species. *v.5 p.711*

Robot Dynamics and Control. *v.5 p.712*

Robot: Mere Machine to Transcendent Mind. . .*v.5 p.339, p.343*

Robot Modeling and Control. *v.5 p.712*

Robot Motion Planning. *v.5 p.711*

Robot Stories: And More Screenplays. *v.6 p.88*

Robot Vision. *v.5 p.710, p.711*

Robotics Demystified. *v.5 p.715*

Robotics: Designing the Mechanisms for Automated
Machinery. *v.5 p.715*

Robotics for Engineers. *v.5 p.711*

Robotics: Introduction, Programming and Projects. . .*v.5 p.710*

Robotics Technology. *v.5 p.714*

Robotnik: A Short History of the Struggle for Worker Self
Management and Free Trade Unions in Poland,
1944-1981. . . . .*v.4 p.129*

🄴 Robust Control System Design: Advanced State Space
Techniques. *v.5 p.712*

Robustness and Evolvability in Living Systems. . . .*v.5 p.201*

La Rochefoucauld: His Mind and Art. *v.2 p.477*

La Rochefoucauld Maximes et Reflexions Diverses. . .*v.2 p.478*

Le rocher de Tanios : roman. *v.2 p.545*

Rochester: The Poems in Context. *v.2 p.259*

Rochester's Poetry. *v.2 p.259*

Rock and Roll: An Introduction. *v.1 p.266*

Rock and Roll Is Here to Stay: An Anthology. *v.1 p.272*

Rock 'n Roll: The Famous Lyrics. . . .*v.1 p.266, p.267, p.411*

Rock, the Primary Text: Developing a Musicology of
Rock. *v.1 p.272*

Rock Weathering and Landform Evolution. *v.5 p.439*

The Rockefellers. *v.3 p.455*

Rocket Propulsion Elements. *v.5 p.720*

The Rockies. *v.3 p.525*

Rockin' in Time: A Social History of Rock and Roll. .*v.1 p.275*

Rockinghorse. *v.6 p.649*

Rocky Mountain Futures: An Ecological Perspective. .*v.6 p.299*

Rocky Mountain Section Field Guide. *v.5 p.431*

Rocky Mountain West: Colorado, Wyoming, and Montana,
1859-1915. . . . .*v.3 p.525*

The Rocky Mountains Region. *v.3 p.525*

Rocky Road: The Irish Economy since the 1920s. . . .*v.3 p.139*

Rococo to Revolution. *v.1 p.728*

Rodale's Encyclopedia of Indoor Gardening. *v.5 p.43*

Rodd's Chemistry of Carbon Compounds; A Modern
Comprehensive Treatise. *v.5 p.292*

Rodd's Chemistry of Carbon Compounds: Heterocyclic
Compounds, Fused-Ring Heterocycles with Three or More N
Atoms, Vol. 4. . . . .*v.5 p.292*

Rodeo Cowboys in the North American Imagination. .*v.4 p.865*

Rodeo in America: Wranglers, Roughstock, and
Paydirt. *v.4 p.865, p.881*

Rodin: Eros and Creativity. *v.1 p.779*

Rodin: The Shape of Genius. *v.1 p.778, p.779*

Rodin. *v.1 p.780*

Roe vs. Wade: The Abortion Rights Controversy in American
History. *v.4 p.439*

Roger Caras' Treasury of Classic Nature Tales. .*v.5 p.78, p.226*

Roger Sessions on Music: Collected Essays. *v.1 p.223*

Rogers Hornsby: A Biography. *v.4 p.849*

Roger's Version. *v.2 p.157*

Rogue State: America at War with the World. *v.3 p.482*

Rogues: Two Essays on Reason. *v.4 p.496, p.509, p.510*

Le roi des Aulnes : roman. *v.2 p.534*

Rolando Hinojosa: A Reader's Guide. *v.6 p.504, p.516*

Rolando Hinojosa and the American Dream. .*v.6 p.500, p.514*

The Rolando Hinojosa Reader. *v.6 p.500, p.513*

The Role of Behavior in Evolution. *v.5 p.195*

The Role of Constructs in Psychological and Educational
Measurement. *v.5 p.601*

Role of Fats in Food and Nutrition. *v.5 p.34*

The Role of Foreign Direct Investment in East Asian Economic
Development. *v.4 p.60*

The Role of History in Latin American Philosophy:
Contemporary Perspectives. *v.1 p.444*

The Role of Legumes in Conservation Tillage Systems. .*v.5 p.50*

The Role of Scientific Societies in the Seventeenth
Century. *v.5 p.392*

The Role of Self in Teacher Development. *v.4 p.279*

Role of the Legislature in Western Democracies. . . .*v.4 p.575*

🄴 The Role of the Reader: Explorations in the Semiotics of
Texts (Advances in Semiotics Ser.). *v.4 p.424*

Role of the Supreme Court in American Politics: The Least
Dangerous Branch? *v.4 p.470*

The Roles of Evaluation for Vocational Education and Training:
Plain Talk in the Field of Dreams. *v.4 p.305*

Roll, Jordan, Roll: The World the Slaves
Made. *v.3 p.397, v.4 p.729*

Roller Skating for Gold. *v.4 p.844, p.866*

Roller-Compacted Concrete. *v.5 p.692*

The Rolling Stone Encyclopedia of Rock and Roll: Revised and
Updated for the 21st Century. *v.1 p.161, p.274*

The Rolling Stone Illustrated History of Rock and Roll: The Definitive History of the Most Important Artists and Their Music. *v.1 p.267*

Rolling Stone Interviews: Talking with the Legends of Rock & Roll, 1967-1980. . . . . *v.1 p.270*

Rolling the R's. *v.6 p.101, p.112*

Rolvaag: His Life and Art. *v.2 p.629*

Romain Rolland. *v.2 p.525*

Romaji Diary and Sad Toys. *v.6 p.230*

Roman Arabia. *v.3 p.27*

The Roman Army: A Social and Institutional History. *v.4 p.718*

The Roman Army at War 100 BC - AD 200. . . . . . *v.3 p.26*

Roman Art: Romulus to Constantine. *v.1 p.670*

Roman Art. *v.1 p.669, p.671, p.686*

Roman Baroque Sculpture: The Industry of Art. . . . *v.1 p.775*

Roman Britain: Outpost of the Empire. *v.3 p.29*

Roman Builders: A Study in Architectural Process. . *v.1 p.796*

The Roman Catholic Church and the Home Rule Movement in Ireland, 1870-1874. . . . . *v.3 p.139*

The Roman Catholic Church in Colonial Latin America. *v.1 p.573*

The Roman Catholic Church in Latin America. . . . *v.1 p.573*

Roman Catholicism in America. *v.1 p.573, p.604, p.605*

The Roman Citizenship. *v.4 p.501*

Roman Civilization, Vols. I & II. *v.3 p.22*

Roman Colonization under the Republic. *v.3 p.25*

Roman Constructions: Readings in Postmodern Latin. *v.2 p.424*

Roman Corinth: An Alternative Model for the Classical City. *v.3 p.21*

Roman Cult of Mithras: The God and His Mysteries. *v.1 p.538*

Le Roman de la Rose. *v.2 p.467*

The Roman Eastern Frontier and Persian Wars: 368-628 A. D. Narrative Sourcebook. *v.3 p.12*

The Roman Eastern Frontier and the Persian Wars, A. D. 226-363: A Documentary History. *v.3 p.11, p.12*

Roman Eloquence: Rhetoric in Society and Literature. *v.2 p.427*

The Roman Empire at Bay: AD 180-395. . . . . . . *v.3 p.29*

The Roman Empire from Severus to Constantine. . . *v.3 p.29*

The Roman Empire of Ammianus. *v.2 p.428*

The Roman Empire. *v.3 p.29*

Roman Epic. *v.2 p.425*

The Roman Family. *v.3 p.23*

Le Roman français depuis la guerre. *v.2 p.463*

Roman Gaul and Germany. *v.3 p.142, p.161*

Roman Gaul. *v.3 p.142*

Roman Government's Response to Crisis, A.D. 235-337. . . . . *v.3 p.28, p.31*

The Roman Historians. *v.2 p.426*

Roman History. *v.2 p.428*

Roman House - Renaissance Palaces: Inventing Antiquity in Fifteenth-Century Italy. *v.1 p.786*

The Roman Household: A Sourcebook. *v.3 p.23*

Roman Imperial Architecture. *v.1 p.671*

The Roman Imperial Army of the First and Second Centuries A. D. *v.3 p.29*

Roman Imperialism in the Late Republic. *v.3 p.26*

Le roman jusqu'à la Révolution. *v.2 p.462*

Roman Laughter: The Comedy of Plautus. *v.2 p.440*

Roman Law in Medieval Europe. *v.4 p.433, p.501*

Roman Literary Culture: From Cicero to Apuleius. . *v.2 p.424*

Roman Nature: The Thought of Pliny the Elder. . . *v.2 p.440*

The Roman Near East, 31 B. C. - A. D. 337. . . . . *v.3 p.28*

Roman Novel. *v.2 p.425*

The Roman Nude: Heroic Portrait Statuary 200 BC-AD 300. . . . . *v.1 p.775*

Roman Painting. *v.1 p.728*

Roman Philosophers. *v.1 p.428*

Roman Poems. *v.2 p.721*

Roman Politics, 220-150 B. C. *v.3 p.25*

Roman Politics and the Criminal Courts, 149-78 B. C. *v.3 p.26*

The Roman Republic in Political Thought. *v.4 p.489*

The Roman Republic. *v.3 p.24*

The Roman Revolution. *v.3 p.26*

Roman Satire: Horace, Juvenal, Persius, Petronius, and Seneca. *v.2 p.427*

Roman Satire. *v.2 p.427*

Roman Sculpture. *v.1 p.775*

Roman Social History. *v.3 p.24*

Roman Social Relations, 50 B. C to A. D. 284. . . . *v.3 p.23*

The Roman Sonnets. *v.2 p.710*

Roman Spain: Conquest and Assimilation. *v.3 p.237*

Roman Spain. *v.3 p.237*

The Roman Spring of Mrs. Stone. *v.2 p.135*

The Roman Stage. *v.2 p.425*

The Roman Succession Crisis of AD 96-99 and the Reign of Nerva. *v.3 p.27*

Roman Syria and the Near East. *v.3 p.27*

The Roman Theatre and Its Audience. *v.1 p.72*

Roman Theatre and Its Audience. *v.1 p.72, v.2 p.425*

Roman Theatres: An Architectural Study. . *v.1 p.72, p.73, p.155*

Roman Tragedy. *v.2 p.425*

Roman Verse Satire. *v.2 p.427*

Roman Verse Satirists Lucilius to Juvenal: A Selection. *v.2 p.427*

Roman Voting Assemblies: From the Hannibalic War to the Dictatorship of Caesar. *v.3 p.25*

Roman Warfare. *v.3 p.22*

Romance and the "Yellow Peril": Race, Sex, and Discursive Strategies in Hollywood Fiction. *v.6 p.89, p.112, p.328, p.330, p.342*

The Romance Epics of Boiardo, Ariosto, and Tasso: From Public Duty to Private Pleasure. *v.2 p.707, p.709*

The Romance Languages. *v.2 p.635*

Romance Linguistics: The Portuguese Context. . . . *v.2 p.638*

The Romance of American Psychology: Political Culture in the Age of Experts. *v.5 p.596*

The Romance of Reynard the Fox. *v.2 p.468*

The Romance of the New World: Gender and the Literary Formations of English Colonialism. *v.2 p.170*

The Romance of the Rose. *v.2 p.466*

The Romance of Tristan and Iseult. *v.2 p.466*

The Romance of Tristan: The Tale of Tristan's Madness. *v.2 p.466*

The Romance of William Morris. *v.2 p.302*

Romance Writings. *v.2 p.256*

Romancero Gitano. *v.2 p.659, p.660*

The Romances of Chretien de Troyes. *v.2 p.467*

Romances with Schools: A Life of Education. *v.4 p.337*

Romances. *v.2 p.655*

Romance. *v.2 p.579*

Romanciers du XVIIe siècle: Sorel, Scarron, Furetière, Mme de
La Fayette. *v.2 p.462*

Romanciers libertins du XVIIIe siècle. *v.2 p.464*

Romancing the Shadow: Poe and Race. *v.2 p.50*

Romania: Borderland of Europe. *v.3 p.250*

Romania in Transition. *v.4 p.600*

Romania since 1989: Politics, Economics, and Society..*v.4 p.600*

Romania under Communist Rule. *v.3 p.250*

The Romanian Novel. *v.2 p.816*

Romanian/Limba Romana: A Course in Modern
Romanian. *v.2 p.778*

Romania. *v.4 p.581*

Romanization in the Time of Augustus. *v.3 p.28*

Romans : et oeuvres de fiction non théâtrales, vol. 1. .*v.2 p.523*

Romans : et oeuvres de fiction non théâtrales, vol. 2. .*v.2 p.523*

Romans 1830. . . . .*v.2 p.499*

Romans 1-8. . . . .*v.1 p.630*

Romans 9-16. . . . .*v.1 p.630, p.631*

Romans, cinéma, théâtre : un parcours, 1943-1993. . .*v.2 p.516*

Les romans de la terre. *v.2 p.503*

Les romans de l'air. *v.2 p.503*

Les romans de l'eau. *v.2 p.503*

Les romans du feu. *v.2 p.504*

Romans et Contes. *v.2 p.484*

Romans et nouvelles. *v.2 p.474*

Romans et voyages, vol. 1. . . . .*v.2 p.508*

Romans et voyages, vol. 2. . . . .*v.2 p.508*

The Romans: From Village to Empire. *v.3 p.22*

Romans, récits et soties, oeuvres lyriques. *v.2 p.520*

[romans], Vol. 1: Le pied de Fanchette ; Le paysan perverti ;
Les contemporaines du commun, choix. *v.2 p.478*

Romans, vol. 1. . . . .*v.2 p.515*

[romans], Vol. 2: La vie de mon père ; La La vie de mon père ;
La femme de laboureur ; La femme infidèle ; Ingénue
Saxancour ; L'épouse d'homme veuf ; La dernière aventure
d'un homme de quarante-cinq ans ; La fille de mon
hôtesse. *v.2 p.478*

Romans, vol. 2. . . . .*v.2 p.515*

Romans, vol. 3. . . . .*v.2 p.515*

Romans, vol. 4. . . . .*v.2 p.515*

Romans. *v.2 p.495, p.529*

The Romantic Ballet in England: Its Development, Fulfillment
and Decline. *v.1 p.24*

The Romantic Ballet in Paris. *v.1 p.8, p.24*

Romantic Complexity: Keats, Coleridge, and
Wordsworth. *v.2 p.324*

Romantic Drama. *v.1 p.78, p.96*

Romantic Ecology: Wordsworth and the Environmental
Tradition. *v.2 p.322, p.323*

The Romantic Generation of Modern Chinese Writers. .*v.6 p.208*

The Romantic Generation. *v.1 p.203*

The Romantic Hero and His Heirs in French
Literature. *v.2 p.454, p.455*

The Romantic Ideology: A Critical Investigation..*v.2 p.172, p.183*

Romantic Interior: The British Collector at Home,
1750-1850. . . . .*v.1 p.801*

Romantic Irony in French Literature: From Diderot to
Beckett. *v.2 p.457*

Romantic Motives: Essays on Anthropological Sensibility. .*v.4 p.5*

The Romantic Movement. *v.2 p.458*

Romantic Music: Sound and Syntax. *v.1 p.202*

Romantic Music. *v.1 p.202*

Romantic Passion: A Universal Experience? *v.5 p.653*

The Romantic Period: The Intellectual and Cultural Context of
English Literature, 1789-1830. . . . .*v.2 p.172*

Romantic Poetry: Recent Revisionary Criticism. . . .*v.2 p.324*

Romantic Poetry. *v.2 p.201*

Romantic Stages: Set and Costume Design in Victorian
England. .*v.1 p.78, p.99, p.100, p.146, p.147, p.148, p.151*

Romantic vs. Screwball Comedy: Charting the
Difference. *v.6 p.312*

Romantic Women Writers: Voices and Countervoices. .*v.2 p.171*

Romanticism: An Oxford Guide. *v.2 p.172, p.183, p.569*

Romanticism and Gender. *v.2 p.172*

Romanticism and Nationalism in the Old South. . . .*v.3 p.495*

▢ Romanticism on the Net. *v.2 p.568*

Romanticism, Writing, and Sexual Difference: Essays on The
Prelude. *v.2 p.323*

Romanticism. *v.2 p.171, p.172, p.173, p.183, p.569*

The Romantics: A Novel. *v.2 p.764, p.765*

Romantics, Rebels and Reactionaries: English Literature and Its
Background,
1760-1830. . . . . .*v.2 p.171, p.174, p.183, p.184, v.3 p.127*

The Romantics: The Context of English Literature. . .*v.2 p.172*

Romantismes français, vol. 1. . . . .*v.2 p.458*

Romantismes français, vol. 2. . . . .*v.2 p.458*

Romanzi e novell. *v.2 p.717*

Romanzi e racconti, vol. 1. . . . .*v.2 p.721*

Romanzi e racconti, vol. 2. . . . .*v.2 p.721*

Romanzi E Racconti. *v.2 p.714*

Romanzi e saggi, vol. 1. . . . .*v.2 p.723*

Romanzi e saggi, vol. 2. . . . .*v.2 p.723*

The Romaunt of the Rose and Le Roman de la Rose. .*v.2 p.208*

Rome and the Barbarians, 100 B. C. - A. D. 400. . . .*v.3 p.22*

Rome and the Enemy: Imperial Strategy in the
Principate. *v.3 p.28*

Rome and the Unification of Italy. *v.3 p.26*

Rome at War: Farms, Families, and Death in the Middle
Republic. *v.3 p.26*

Rome Before Avignon: A Social History of Thirteenth-Century
Rome. *v.3 p.198, v.6 p.577*

Rome in the Age of Enlightenment: The Post-Tridentine
Syndrome and the Ancien Régime. *v.3 p.201*

Rome or Death: The Diversion of General Garibaldi.   *.v.3 p.201*

Rome: Profile of a City, 312-1308.   . *.v.3 p.197, p.204,v.6 p.577*

Rome the Cosmopolis. . . . .*.v.3 p.22*

Romeo and Juliet and West Side Story.   *.v.1 p.251, p.311, p.408*

Romeo and Juliet Before Shakespeare: Four Early Stories of
   Star-Crossed Love. . . . .*.v.2 p.700*

Romeo and Juliet. . . . .*.v.2 p.223*

Rome. . . . .*.v.1 p.675, p.687*

Romola. . . . .*.v.2 p.286, p.287*

Romulo Betancourt and the Transformation of
   Venezuela. . . . .*.v.3 p.360*

Ronald Reagan: How an Ordinary Man Became an
   Extraordinary Leader. . . . .*.v.3 p.470*

Ronald Reagan: The Politics of Symbolism. . . . .*.v.3 p.469*

Ronsard the Poet. . . . .*.v.2 p.471*

Roofed Theaters of Classical Antiquity.   . *.v.1 p.71, p.72, p.155*

Rookwood and the Industry of Art: Women, Culture and
   Commerce, 1880-1913. . . . . . .*.v.1 p.707, p.808, p.826*

Room 4.1.3: Innovations in Landscape Architecture. . *.v.1 p.817*

A Room of His Own: In Search of the Feminine in the Novels
   of Saul Bellow. . . . .*.v.2 p.60*

A Room of One's Own and Three Guineas. . . . . . .*.v.2 p.394*

A Room of One's Own. . . . . . .*.v.2 p.570, v.6 p.480, p.481*

A Room with a View. . . . .*.v.2 p.346*

Roosevelt and Hopkins: An Intimate History. . . . .*.v.3 p.462*

Roosevelt and the Isolationists, 1932-1945. . . . . .*.v.3 p.468*

Roosevelt the Reformer: Theodore Roosevelt As Civil Service
   Commissioner, 1889-1895. . . . .*.v.4 p.546*

Roosevelt: The Soldier of Freedom, 1940-1945. . . .*.v.3 p.456*

The Roosevelts: An American Saga. . . . .*.v.3 p.455*

Roosevelt's Warrior: Harold L. Ickes and the New Deal. *.v.3 p.457*

The Root and the Branch, Judaism and the Free Society. *.v.4 p.722*

The Root Causes of Sudan's Civil Wars. . . . .*.v.6 p.59*

Root of Bitterness: Documents of the Social History of
   American Women. . . . .*.v.6 p.453*

Root of Bitterness: Documents on the Social History of
   American Women. . . . .*.v.6 p.449*

Roots and Wings: Poetry from Spain 1900-1975. . . .*.v.2 p.645*

Roots of African American Drama: An Anthology of Early
   Plays, 1858-1938. . . . .*.v.1 p.66, p.122, p.123*

The Roots of American Industrialization. . . . . . .*.v.6 p.714*

The Roots of Anti-Semitism: In the Age of Renaissance and
   Reformation. . . . .*.v.1 p.549, p.550*

The Roots of Blitzkrieg: Hans von Seeckt and German Military
   Reform. . . . .*.v.3 p.160*

Roots of Chicano Politics, 1600-1940.   . *.v.3 p.527, v.6 p.538*

The Roots of Evil: The Origins of Genocide and Other Group
   Violence. . . . .*.v.4 p.715*

The Roots of Fundamentalism: British and American
   Millenarianism, 1800-1930. . . . .*.v.1 p.636*

Roots of Insurgency: Mexican Regions, 1750-1824. . *.v.3 p.285*

Roots of Miró. . . . .*.v.1 p.696, p.697*

The Roots of Phonics: A Historical Introduction. *.v.2 p.555, p.556*

Roots of Rebellion: Workers' Politics and Organizations in St.
   Petersburg and Moscow, 1900-1914. . . . . . .*.v.3 p.220*

Roots of Reform: Challenging the Assumptions That Control
   Change in Education. . . . .*.v.4 p.324*

The Roots of Southern Writing; Essays on the Literature of the
   American South. . . . .*.v.2 p.13*

The Roots of Tantra. . . . .*.v.1 p.536*

Roots of the Bill of Rights: An Illustrated Source Book of
   American Freedom. . . . .*.v.4 p.456*

The Roots of the Blues: An African Search. . . . . .*.v.1 p.258*

Roots of the Classical: The Popular Origins of Western
   Music. . . . .*.v.1 p.175*

The Roots of the Mountain Wherein is Told Somewhat of the
   Lives of the Men of Burgdale, Their Friends, Their
   Neighbours, Their Foemen and Their Fellows in
   Arms. . . . .*.v.2 p.301*

The Roots of the Radical Theology. . . . .*.v.1 p.633*

The Roots of War and Terror. . . . .*.v.5 p.585*

Roots: The Saga of an American Family. . . . .*.v.6 p.5*

Rope of Gold. . . . .*.v.2 p.81*

A Rope of Sand: The Colonial Agents, British Politics, and the
   American Revolution. . . . .*.v.3 p.406, v.4 p.518*

The Rope, the Chair and the Needle: Capital Punishment in
   Texas, 1923-1990. . . . .*.v.4 p.567*

Rosa Bonheur: A Life and a Legend. . . . .*.v.6 p.407*

Rosa Luxemburg: Her Life and Work. . . . .*.v.4 p.193*

The Rosa Luxemburg Reader. . . . .*.v.4 p.236*

Rosa Luxemburg. . . . .*.v.4 p.193, p.194*

Rosa Parks. . . . .*.v.3 p.456*

Rosalind Franklin: The Dark Lady of DNA. . . . . .*.v.5 p.122*

Rosalind Franklin. . . . .*.v.5 p.81*

Roscoe Conkling of New York: Voice in the Senate. . *.v.3 p.434*

Rose Mellie Rose. . . . .*.v.2 p.533*

Rose Mélie Rose : roman. . . . .*.v.2 p.533*

Rose of Dutcher's Coolly. . . . .*.v.2 p.39*

Rosebery, a Biography of Archibald Philip, Fifth Earl of
   Rosebery. . . . .*.v.3 p.94, p.113*

The Rosenberg File: A Search for the Truth. . . . .*.v.4 p.438*

The Rosendorf Quartet: A Novel. . . . .*.v.6 p.651*

Der Rosenkavalier.   . . . .*.v.1 p.225, p.233, p.359, p.410*

Roses and Thorns: The Second Blooming of the Hundred
   Flowers in Chinese Fiction, 1979-80. . . . . . .*.v.6 p.208*

Rosetta Stone. . . . .*.v.3 p.9*

Rose. . . . .*.v.6 p.103, p.104*

Ross, Histology a Text and Atlas: With Correlated Cell and
   Molecular Biology. . . . . . .*.v.5 p.128, p.129, p.153, p.159*

◻ The Rossetti Archive. . . . .*.v.6 p.737, p.755*

Rossini. . . . .*.v.1 p.201, p.351, p.352*

The Rosy Crucifixion. . . . .*.v.2 p.102*

The Rosy Future of War. . . . .*.v.4 p.498*

Rotating Electrical Machines and Power Systems. . . *.v.5 p.725*

The Rothko Chapel Paintings: Origins, Structure,
   Meaning. . . . .*.v.1 p.744*

Rouen During the Wars of Religion. . . . .*.v.3 p.144*

The Rough Guide to China. . . . .*.v.6 p.182, p.197*

The Rough Guide to Hong Kong and Macau. . . . . .*.v.6 p.206*

The Rough Guide to Irish Music. . . . .*.v.1 p.171, p.299*

The Rough Guide to Reggae. *v.1 p.169, p.291*

Rough Guide to World Music, Vol. 1: Africa, Europe, and the
Middle East. *v.1 p.170, p.285, p.286, p.298*

Rough Guide to World Music, Vol. 2: Latin and North America,
the Caribbean, Asia, and the
Pacific. *v.1 p.170, p.288, p.291, p.295*

Rough Justice: Lynching and American Society,
1874-1947. . . . .*v.4 p.753*

The Rough Road to Renaissance: Urban Revitalization in
America, 1940-1985. . . . .*v.6 p.715*

Roughing It in the Bush; or, Life in Canada, Pt. 1. .*v.2 p.732, p.733*

Roughing It in the Bush; or, Life in Canada, Pt. 2. . .*v.2 p.732*

Round Up: The Stories of Ring W. Lardner. *v.2 p.94*

The Roundtable Talks of 1989: The Genesis of Hungarian
Democracy. *v.4 p.595*

Rousing Minds to Life: Teaching, Learning, and Schooling in
Social Context. *v.4 p.349*

Rousing the Nation: Radical Culture in Depression
America. *v.2 p.69*

A Rousseau Dictionary. *v.2 p.482*

Rousseau, Judge of Jean-Jacques: Dialogues. *v.2 p.482*

Rousseau: Selections: The Great Philosophers. . . .*v.2 p.482*

Rousseau. *v.1 p.454*

La Route d'Altamont. *v.2 p.540*

Routine Activity and Rational Choice. *v.6 p.249, p.250*

Routing, Flow, and Capacity Design in Communication and
Computer Networks. *v.5 p.727*

The Routledge Anthology of Poets on Poets. *v.2 p.181*

Routledge Anthology of Renaissance
Drama. *v.1 p.63, p.74, p.94, v.2 p.201, p.202*

The Routledge Atlas of American History. .*v.3 p.381, v.4 p.380*

The Routledge Atlas of the Arab-Israeli
Conflict. *v.4 p.380, v.6 p.617*

The Routledge Companion to Aesthetics. *v.1 p.479*

Routledge Companion to Linguistics and
Semiotics. *v.5 p.620, p.623*

The Routledge Companion to Postmodernism. . . .*v.1 p.512*

Routledge Companion to Russian
Literature. *v.2 p.793, p.795, p.796*

The Routledge Dictionary of Anthropologists. *v.4 p.3*

🅮 Routledge Encyclopedia of International Political
Economy. *v.4 p.192*

Routledge Encyclopedia of Philosophy, Set. *v.1 p.416*

Routledge Encyclopedia of Translation Studies. . . .*v.2 p.574*

The Routledge Historical Atlas of Women in America. *v.6 p.426*

The Routledge History of Literature in English: Britain and
Ireland. *v.2 p.166*

Routledge History of Philosophy, Set. *v.1 p.417*

Routledge International Encyclopedia of Women: Global
Women's Issues and Knowledge, Set. . . .*v.6 p.425, p.426*

Routledge Library Editions: Anthropology and Ethnology. *v.4 p.3*

A Routledge Literary Sourcebook on Harriet Beecher Stowe's
Uncle Tom's Cabin. *v.2 p.51*

Routledge Philosophy Guidebook to Aristotle on Ethics. *v.1 p.426*

Routledge Philosophy Guidebook to Berkeley and the Principles
of Human Knowledge. *v.1 p.450*

Routledge Philosophy Guidebook to Derrida on
Deconstruction. *v.1 p.457*

Routledge Philosophy GuideBook to Descartes and
Meditations. *v.1 p.454*

Routledge Philosophy Guidebook to Heidegger and Being and
Time. *v.1 p.471*

Routledge Philosophy Guidebook to Hobbes and
Leviathan. *v.1 p.448*

Routledge Philosophy Guidebook to Hume on
Knowledge. *v.1 p.451*

Routledge Philosophy Guidebook to Hume on Religion. .*v.1 p.452*

Routledge Philosophy Guidebook to Kant and "The Critique of
Pure Reason". *v.1 p.461*

Routledge Philosophy Guidebook to Kierkegaard and Fear and
Trembling. *v.1 p.478, p.479*

Routledge Philosophy Guidebook to Leibniz and the
Monadology. *v.1 p.460*

Routledge Philosophy Guidebook to Mill on
Utilitarianism. *v.1 p.445, p.516*

Routledge Philosophy Guidebook to Nietzsche on
Morality. *v.1 p.466*

Routledge Philosophy Guidebook to Plato and the
Republic. *v.1 p.424*

Routledge Philosophy Guidebook to Plato and the Trial of
Socrates. *v.1 p.422*

Routledge Philosophy Guidebook to Rousseau and the Social
Contract. *v.1 p.454*

Routledge Philosophy Guidebook to Spinoza and The
Ethics. *v.1 p.477*

Routledge Philosophy Guidebook to the Later
Heidegger. *v.1 p.471*

Routledge Philosophy Guidebook to Wittgenstein and the
Philosophical Investigations. *v.1 p.472*

The Routledge Reader in Caribbean Literature. . . .*v.2 p.767*

Routledgefalmer Reader in the Philosophy of
Education. *v.4 p.323*

The Rover and Other Plays: The Rover; The Feigned
Courtesans; The Lucky Chance; The Emperor of the
Moon. *v.2 p.238*

Rowing and Sculling. *v.4 p.788, p.865*

Rowing in England: A Social History: The Amateur
Debate. *v.4 p.816, p.865*

🅮 Roxana: The Fortunate Mistress. *v.2 p.245*

Roy Arden: Selected Works 1985-2000. . . . . . .*v.1 p.772*

Royal Arts of Africa: The Majesty of Form. *v.1 p.689*

The Royal Ballet. *v.1 p.23*

Royal Government in Colonial Brazil: With Special Reference
to the Administration of the Marquis of Lavradio, Viceroy,
1769-1779. . . . .*v.3 p.334*

The Royal Guest and Other Classical Danish Narrative. *v.2 p.626*

▢ Royal Historical Society
Bibliography. *v.3 p.88, p.133, v.6 p.736*

Royal Institution: Informan. *v.5 p.385*

The Royal Navy in America, 1760-1775: A Study of the
Enforcement of British Colonial Policy in the Era
of the American Revolution. *v.3 p.414*

The Royal Navy in the River Plate, 1806-1807. . . .*v.3 p.345*

A Royal Passion: Louis XIV as Patron of Architecture. *v.3 p.144*

Royal Representations: Queen Victoria and British Culture, 1837-1876. . . . .*v.6 p.763, p.764*

Royal Society and Its Fellows, 1660-1700: The Morphology of an Early Scientific Institution. *v.5 p.385*

The Royal Society: Concept and Creation. *v.5 p.385*

Royal Society of Chemistry--Historical Chemistry Information Service. *v.5 p.262*

Royal Society of Chemistry. *v.5 p.260*

A Royal Waste of Time: The Splendor of Worshiping God and Being Church for the World. *v.1 p.654*

The Royalty of Negro Vaudeville: The Whitman Sisters and the Negotiation of Race, Gender and Class in African American Theater 1900-1940. . . . .*v.1 p.18, p.35*

Royce's Metaphysics. *v.1 p.439*

RSC Publishing--Journals. *v.5 p.256*

RSVP.01 - The Directory of Illustration and Design. . .*v.1 p.712*

RU 486: The Pill That Could End the Abortion Wars and Why American Women Don't Have It. *v.6 p.470*

Ruanda-Urundi, 1884-1919. . . . .*v.6 p.63, p.64*

Rubaiyat of Omar Khayyam: A Critical Edition. . . .*v.6 p.671*

Rubaiyat. *v.6 p.666*

Rubber Processing: Technology, Materials, Principles. .*v.5 p.320*

Rubbish!: The Archaeology of Garbage. *v.5 p.377, p.378*

The rubble years: the cultural roots of postwar Germany. *v.3 p.176*

Rubens, Jordaens, Van Dyck: 17th Century Flemish Drawings. *v.1 p.722*

Rubyfruit Jungle. *v.6 p.368, p.395*

Rude and Barbarous Kingdom: Russia in the Accounts of Sixteenth-Century English Voyagers. *v.3 p.214*

Rudolph's Pediatrics. *v.5 p.525*

Rudy Giuliani: Emperor of the City. *v.3 p.491*

Rudyard Kipling: A Life. *v.2 p.297, p.298*

Rudyard Kipling: A Literary Life. *v.2 p.297*

Rudyard Kipling. *v.2 p.296*

Rue des Boutiques Obscures. *v.2 p.532*

Rue Deschambault. *v.2 p.539*

Rufinus: A Commentary of the Apostles' Creed. . . .*v.1 p.590*

Rugby Skills, Tactics and Rules. *v.4 p.865, p.866*

Rugby Tough. *v.4 p.865*

Rugby's Great Split: Class, Culture and the Origins of Rugby League Football. *v.4 p.804, p.814, p.865*

The Ruined Cottage and the Pedlar. *v.2 p.325*

Ruins of Identity: Ethnogenesis in the Japanese Islands.*v.6 p.221*

Ruin. *v.2 p.715*

Rule Britannia: Women, Empire and Victorian Writing.*v.6 p.478*

Rule of Darkness: British Literature and Imperialism, 1830-1914. . . . .*v.2 p.174, p.190,v.6 p.745*

Rule of Experts: Egypt, Techno-Politics, Modernity. *v.6 p.639, p.640*

The Rule of St. Benedict: The Abingdon Copy.*v.2 p.448, v.3 p.56*

Rulemaking: How Government Agencies Write Law and Make Policy. *v.4 p.463*

Rules and Procedure. *v.4 p.532, p.534*

Rules and Representations. *v.2 p.559, v.5 p.622, p.623*

The Rules of Art: Genesis and Structure of the Literary Field. *v.2 p.455, p.566*

The Rules of Federalism: Institutions and Regulatory Politics in the EU and Beyond. *v.4 p.637*

The Rules of Play: National Identity and the Shaping of Japanese Leisure. *v.4 p.784, p.834, p.898*

The Rules of Sociological Method. *v.4 p.686*

Rules of the Game: Global Business Protocol. *v.4 p.56*

Rules of Thumb for Chemical Engineers. *v.5 p.740*

The Ruling Caste: Imperial Lives in the Victorian Raj. *v.3 p.89*

Ruling Russia: Law, Crime, and Justice in a Changing Society. *v.6 p.250*

Ruling the Later Roman Empire. *v.3 p.31*

Rumania, 1866-1947. . . . .*v.3 p.250*

Rumba: Dance and Social Change in Contemporary Cuba. *v.1 p.19, v.3 p.308*

Rumba on the River: A History of the Popular Music of Two Congos. *v.1 p.286*

Rumbo al Sur, Deseando el Norte: Un Romance en Dos Lenguas. *v.2 p.680*

Run with the Hunted: A Charles Bukowski Reader. . .*v.2 p.141*

The Runaway Bride: Hollywood Romantic Comedy of the 1930s. *v.6 p.313*

Runaway: Diary of a Street Kid. *v.2 p.736*

Runaway Horses. *v.6 p.231*

Runaway Kids and Teenage Prostitution: America's Lost, Abandoned, and Sexually Exploited Children. . . .*v.4 p.747*

Runaway Slave Settlements in Cuba: Resistance and Repression. *v.3 p.311*

Runaway: Stories. *v.2 p.737*

Runner's World Complete Book of Running: Everything You Need to Know to Run for Fun, Fitness and Competition. *v.4 p.790, p.863, p.866*

Running a 21st-Century Small Business: The Owner's Guide to Starting and Growing Your Company. *v.4 p.87*

Running: Biomechanics and Exercise Physiology in Practice. *v.4 p.878, p.907*

Running in the Family. *v.2 p.730, p.731*

Running Past 50. . . . .*v.4 p.840, p.841, p.847, p.866*

Running Theaters: Best Practices for Leaders and Managers. *v.1 p.150*

Running Wild: New Chinese Writers. *v.6 p.213*

Running with the Devil: Power, Gender, and Madness in Heavy Metal Music. *v.1 p.275*

Rupert Brooke: A Biography. *v.2 p.335*

Rupert Brooke: Life, Death and Myth. *v.2 p.335*

Rural Athens under the Democracy. *v.3 p.18*

Rural China: Imperial Control in the Nineteenth Century. *v.6 p.187*

Rural China. *v.4 p.771, p.772*

Rural Communities in the Medieval West. *v.6 p.575*

The Rural Communities of Hong Kong: Studies and Themes. *v.6 p.205*

Rural Dimensions of Welfare Reform: Welfare, Food Assistance, and Poverty in Rural America. *v.4 p.755*

Rural Economy and Country Life in the Medieval West. *v.6 p.557, p.575*

Rural Geography: Processes, Responses and Experiences in Rural Restructuring. *v.4 p.396*

Rural Hours. . . . .*.v.5 p.78, p.221*

The Rural Landscape. . . . . *.v.4 p.395*

The Rural Life. . . . . *.v.5 p.233*

Rural Mexico. . . . . *.v.4 p.772*

The Rural Poor: Agrarian Changes and Survival Strategies in Chile 1973-1989. . . . .*.v.3 p.352, p.353*

Rural Problems in the Alpine Region: An International Study. . . . .*.v.4 p.701*

Rural Reform in Post-Soviet Russia. . . . . . . *.v.5 p.14, p.15*

Rural Rides. . . . . *.v.3 p.108, p.126*

Rural Society and the Search for Order in Early Modern Germany. . . . .*.v.3 p.166*

Rural Studio: Samuel Mockbee and the Architecture of Decency. . . . .*.v.1 p.792*

Rural Women Battering and the Justice System: An Ethnography. . . . .*.v.4 p.743*

Rus': A Comprehensive Course in Russian. . . . . . *.v.2 p.776*

The Rush to German Unity. . . . . *.v.4 p.609*

The Rushdie File. . . . . *.v.2 p.766*

Ruskin on Architecture: His Thought and Influence. . . . .*.v.6 p.737, p.750*

Ruskin Today. . . . . *.v.2 p.306*

Ruskin's Culture Wars: Fors Clarigera and the Crisis of Victorian Liberalism. . . . .*.v.2 p.306*

Ruskin's Letters from Venice 1851: 1852. . . . . . *.v.2 p.306*

Ruskin's Mythic Queen: Gender Subversion in Victorian Culture. . . . .*.v.2 p.306*

Russell: A Very Short Introduction. . . . . *.v.1 p.447*

Russell, Idealism, and the Emergence of Analytic Philosophy. . . . .*.v.1 p.502*

The Russellian Origins Of Analytical Philosophy. . . *.v.1 p.502*

Russell. . . . . *.v.1 p.447*

Russia after the War: Hopes, Illusions and Disappointments, 1945-1957. . . . .*.v.3 p.228*

Russia and the Golden Horde: The Mongol Impact on Medieval Russian History. . . . .*.v.3 p.215*

Russia and the Mongol Yoke: The History of Russian Principalities and the Golden Horde, 1221-. . . . *.v.3 p.214*

Russia and the Origins of the First World War. . . . *.v.3 p.220*

Russia and the Russians: A History. . . . . *.v.3 p.209*

Russia at War, 1941-1945. . . . . *.v.3 p.228*

Russia; Being a Complete Picture of That Empire; Including a Full Description of Their Government, Laws, Religion, Commerce, Manners, Customs. . . . . *.v.3 p.217*

Russia Confronts Chechnya: Roots of a Separatist Conflict. . . . .*.v.3 p.229*

Russia Enters the Railway Age, 1842-1855. . *.v.3 p.218, p.219*

Russia, Friend or Foe: A Critical Analysis of U. S. Foreign Policy Toward Russia. . . . .*.v.3 p.387*

Russia Gathers Her Jews: The Origins of the "Jewish Question" in Russia, 1772-1825. . . . .*.v.3 p.216*

Russia Goes Dry: Alcohol, State and Society. . . . . *.v.3 p.229*

The Russia Hand: A Memoir of Presidential Diplomacy. *.v.4 p.646*

Russia in Space: The Failed Frontier? . . . . . . *.v.5 p.719*

Russia in the Age of Catherine the Great. . . . . . *.v.3 p.217*

Russia in the Age of Modernisation and Revolution, 1881-1917. . . . .*.v.3 p.220*

Russia in the Age of Peter the Great. . . . . *.v.3 p.217*

Russia in the Nineteenth Century: Autocracy, Reform, and Social Change, 1814-1914. . . . . *.v.3 p.218*

Russia in War and Revolution: General William V. Judson's Accounts from Petrograd, 1917-1918. . . . . . .*.v.3 p.221*

Russia in World History; Selected Essays. . . . . . *.v.3 p.209*

Russia: People and Empire, 1552-1917. . . . . . . *.v.3 p.213*

Russia, Poland, and Universal Regeneration: Studies in Russian and Polish Thought of the Romantic Epoch. . . .*.v.3 p.253*

Russia, the Soviet Union, and the United States: An Interpretive History. . . . .*.v.3 p.388*

Russia, Ukraine and the Breakup of the Soviet Union. *.v.3 p.230*

Russia under Western Eyes: From the Bronze Horseman to the Lenin Mausoleum. . . . .*.v.3 p.209*

Russian: An Essential Grammar. . . . . *.v.2 p.776*

Russian and Polish Women's Fiction. . . . . *.v.2 p.787*

Russian and Slavic Literature. . . . . *.v.2 p.794*

Russian and Soviet Theatre: Tradition and the Avant-Garde. . . . . *.v.1 p.85, p.110*

Russian Animal Tales. . . . . *.v.2 p.793*

Russian Art from Neoclassicism to the Avant-Garde, 1800-1917: Painting, Sculpture, Architecture. . . . .*.v.1 p.688*

Russian Ballet Master: the Memories of Marius Petipa. *.v.1 p.11*

Russian Beauty. . . . . *.v.2 p.803*

The Russian Church under the Soviet Regime. . . . *.v.1 p.570*

The Russian Civil War. . . . . *.v.3 p.225*

The Russian Context: The Context Behind the Language. . . . .*.v.2 p.775, p.776*

Russian Crossroads: Toward the New Millennium. . *.v.4 p.598*

Russian Education: Tradition and Transition. . . . . *.v.4 p.335*

The Russian Empire, 1801-1917. . . . . *.v.3 p.218*

Russian Fairy Tales. . . . .*.v.2 p.793, p.794*

Russian Fascism: Traditions, Tendencies, Movements. *.v.4 p.510*

Russian Folk Belief. . . . . *.v.2 p.793*

Russian Folk Songs: Musical Genres and History. . . *.v.1 p.298*

A Russian Gentleman. . . . . *.v.3 p.215*

The Russian Girl. . . . . *.v.2 p.328*

Russian Gypsy Tales. . . . .*.v.2 p.794, p.795*

The Russian Idea. . . . . *.v.3 p.210*

Russian Intellectual History: An Anthology. . . . . *.v.3 p.210*

The Russian Landed Gentry and the Peasant Emancipation of 1861. . . . .*.v.4 p.726*

Russian Legends. . . . . *.v.2 p.793*

Russian Literature, 1988-1994: The End of an Era. . *.v.2 p.800*

Russian Literature, 1995-2002: On the Threshold of the New Millennium. . . . .*.v.2 p.808*

Russian Literature: A Very Short Introduction. . . . *.v.2 p.798*

Russian Literature and Empire: Conquest of the Caucasus from Pushkin to Tolstoy. . . . .*.v.2 p.799*

Russian Literature and Its Demons. . . . . . .*.v.2 p.797, p.798*

Russian Literature in the Age of Pushkin and Gogol. *.v.2 p.796*

Russian Literature in the Age of Realism. . . . . . *.v.2 p.796*

Russian Literature, Modernism and the Visual Arts. . . .*v.2 p.798*

Russian Literature--Overview and Bibliography. *v.2 p.795*

Russian Marxists and the Origins of Bolshevism. . . .*v.3 p.220*

The Russian Memoir: History and Literature. *v.2 p.798*

The Russian Mirror: Three Plays by Russian Women. .*v.2 p.795*

Russian Modernism: The Transfiguration of the
    Everyday. *v.2 p.798*

The Russian Moment in World History: An Essay in
    Historical. *v.3 p.209*

Russian Monarchy: Eighteenth-Century Rulers and Writers in
    Political Dialogue. *v.4 p.599*

Russian Motion Verbs for Intermediate Students. . . .*v.2 p.776*

Russian Myths. *v.1 p.534*

Russian Narrative and Visual Art: Varieties of Seeing. .*v.2 p.797*

Russian Nationalism and Ukraine: The Nationality Policy of the
    Volunteer Army During the Civil War. . . .*v.3 p.229, p.230*

Russian Nights. *v.2 p.806*

Russian Novelists in the Age of Tolstoy and
    Dostoevsky. *v.2 p.793, p.796*

Russian Overseas Commerce with Great Britain During the
    Reign of Catherine II. *v.3 p.217*

Russian Philosophy: Pre-Revolutionary Philosophy and
    Theology: Philosiphers in Exile: Marxists and Communists,
    Vol. 3. . . . .*v.1 p.473, p.474*

Russian Philosophy: The Beginning of Russian Philosophy: the
    Slavophiles: the Weternizers. *v.1 p.473*

Russian Philosophy: The Nihilists: the Populists: the Critics of
    Religion and Culture, Vol. 2. . . . .*v.1 p.474*

Russian Philosophy, Vol. 10. . . . .*v.1 p.473*

Russian Popular Culture: Entertainment and Society Since
    1900. . . . .*v.3 p.210*

Russian Prose Writers Between the World Wars. . . .*v.2 p.796*

Russian Pulp: The Detektiv and the Russian Way of
    Crime. *v.2 p.799*

Russian Rebels, 1600-1800. . . . .*v.3 p.215*

The Russian Revolution 1917. . . . .*v.3 p.221*

The Russian Revolution, Nineteen Seventeen to Nineteen
    Twenty-One, Vol. 1: 1917-1918: From the
    Overthrow of the Tsar to the Assumption of Power by the
    Bolsheviks. *v.3 p.221*

The Russian Revolution, Nineteen Seventeen to Nineteen
    Twenty-One, Vol. II: 1918-1921: From the Civil
    War to the Consolidation of Power. *v.3 p.221*

The Russian Revolution, Nineteen Seventeen. *v.3 p.221*

The Russian Revolutionary Intelligentsia. *v.3 p.218*

The Russian Revolutionary Novel: Turgenev to
    Pasternak. *v.2 p.798*

The Russian Roots of Nazism: White Émigrés and the Making
    of National Socialism, 1917-1945. . . . .*v.4 p.711*

Russian Short Stories. *v.2 p.795*

Russian Theater, from the Empire to the Soviets. . .*v.1 p.110*

The Russian Theatre after Stalin. *v.2 p.800*

The Russian Theatre. *v.1 p.110*

Russian Thinkers. *v.1 p.473, v.3 p.210*

Russian Trade Unions and Industrial Relations in
    Transition. *v.4 p.124*

The Russian Tradition in Education. *v.4 p.334*

Russian Village Prose: The Radiant Past. *v.2 p.799*

The Russian Way of War: Operational Art, 1904-1940. .*v.3 p.211*

Russian Women Writers. *v.2 p.796, p.800*

The Russian Worker: Life and Labor under the Tsarist
    Regime. *v.3 p.220*

Russian Writers since 1980. . . . .*v.2 p.796*

Russian-English Dictionary of Proverbs and Sayings. .*v.2 p.776*

Russian-English Dictionary of Scientific and Engineering Terms:
    A Guide to Usage. *v.5 p.387*

The Russians and Their Church. *v.1 p.610*

Russians in Alaska: 1732-1867. . . . .*v.3 p.533*

The Russians in Germany: A History of the Soviet Zone of
    Occupation, 1945-1949. . . . .*v.3 p.176*

Russians on Russian Music, 1830-1880: An Anthology in
    Translation. *v.1 p.195, p.245*

The Russian's World. *v.2 p.776*

The Russians. *v.3 p.209*

Russia's Balkan Entanglements, 1806-1914. . .*v.3 p.211, p.246*

Russia's Communists at the Crossroads. *v.4 p.599, p.600*

Russia's Dangerous Texts: Politics Between the Lines. .*v.2 p.799*

Russia's Engagement with the West. *v.4 p.644*

Russia's First World War: A Social and Economic
    History. *v.3 p.220*

Russia's Missing Middle Class: The Professions in Russian
    History. *v.3 p.211*

Russia's Orient: Imperial Borderlands and Peoples,
    1700-1917. . . . .*v.3 p.213*

Russia's Rulers Before the Old Regime. *v.3 p.220*

Russia's Steppe Frontier: The Making of a Colonial Empire,
    1500-1800. . . . .*v.3 p.213*

Russia's War: Blood upon the Snow. *v.3 p.227*

Russnet. *v.2 p.775*

A Rusty Needle. *v.2 p.811*

Ruth Benedict: Beyond Relativity, Beyond Pattern. . . .*v.4 p.5*

Ruth Crawford Seeger: A Composer's Search for American
    Music. *v.1 p.226, p.355, p.356*

Ruth Hall: A Domestic Tale of the Present Time. *v.2 p.37*

Ruth Page: An Intimate Biography. *v.1 p.10*

Rutherford B. Hayes: And His America. *v.3 p.435*

Rutherford's Dreams: A New Zealand Science Fiction
    Collection. *v.2 p.742*

Ruth. *v.1 p.620, v.2 p.288, p.289*

The Rwala Bedouin Today. *v.6 p.596*

Rwanda and Genocide in the Twentieth Century. . . .*v.4 p.652*

The Rwanda Crisis: History of a Genocide. *v.4 p.653*

Ryokan: Zen Monk-Poet of Japan. *v.6 p.234*

Rythmes : poèmes. *v.2 p.529*

S

S.: A Novel about the Balkans. *v.2 p.818*

S. J. Perelman: Critical Essays. *v.2 p.111*

S, M, L, XL: Small, Medium, Large, Extra Large. . . .*v.1 p.797*

Sabbatai Sevi: The Mystical Messiah, 1626-1676. . .*v.1 p.547*

The Sable Arm: Black Troops in the Union Army,
    1861-1865. . . . .*v.3 p.395, p.430*

Sabriya: Damascus Bitter Sweet. *v.6 p.660*

Sacagawea of the Lewis and Clark Expedition. *v.3 p.519*

Sacajawea. *v.3 p.520*

The Sack of Panama. *v.3 p.304*

The Sacralization of Politics in Fascist Italy. *v.3 p.203*

The Sacraments in Protestant Practice and Faith. . . .*v.1 p.657*

Sacraments. *v.1 p.657*

The Sacred and Profane Love Machine. *v.2 p.372*

The Sacred Bridge; The Interdependence of Liturgy and Music in Synagogue and Church During the First Millennium. *v.1 p.301*

Sacred Canopy: Elements of a Sociological Theory of Religion. *v.4 p.719*

Sacred Dance in the Ancient World. *v.1 p.21*

The Sacred Depths of Nature. *v.5 p.221*

The Sacred Desert: Religion, Literature, Art, and Culture. *v.2 p.572*

Sacred Dreams: Women and the Superintendency. . . .*v.4 p.281*

The Sacred Earth: Writers on Nature and Spirit. *v.5 p.232*

Sacred Games: A History of Christian Worship. *v.1 p.654*

The Sacred Hoop: Recovering the Feminine in American Indian Traditions. *v.2 p.3, v.6 p.477*

Sacred Hoops: Spiritual Lessons of a Hardwood Warrior. *v.4 p.802, p.854*

Sacred Hula: The Hula Ala Apapa. *v.1 p.17*

The Sacred Landscape of the Inca: The Cusco Ceque System. *v.3 p.260*

Sacred Landscape: The Buried History of the Holy Land Since 1948. . . . .*v.6 p.613*

Sacred Language, Ordinary People: Dilemmas of Culture and Politics in Egypt. *v.6 p.637*

Sacred Languages and Sacred Texts. *v.1 p.525*

Sacred Latin Texts and English Translations for the Choral Conductor and Church Musician: Propers of the Mass, 68. . . . .*v.1 p.411*

Sacred Luxuries: Fragrance, Aromatherapy, and Cosmetics in Ancient Egypt. *v.3 p.9*

Sacred Mask, Sacred Dance: Evan John Jones and Chas Clifton. *v.1 p.21*

The Sacred Neuron: The Extraordinary New Discoveries Linking Science and Religion. *v.1 p.526*

The Sacred Night. *v.2 p.544*

Sacred Objects and Sacred Places: Preserving Tribal Traditions. *v.1 p.822, v.6 p.701*

Sacred Passions: The Life and Music of Manuel de Falla. *v.1 p.215, p.324*

The Sacred Scriptures of the Japanese: With All Authoritative Variants, Chronologically Arranged. *v.1 p.542*

Sacred Song in America: Religion, Music, and Public Culture. *v.1 p.278*

A Sacred Trust: The League of Nations and Africa, 1929-1946. . . . .*v.4 p.631*

Sacred Visions: Early Paintings from Central Tibet. . .*v.1 p.732*

The Sacred Void: Spatial Images of Work and Ritual among the Giriama of Kenya. *v.4 p.38*

The Sacred: Ways of Knowledge, Sources of Life. . .*v.6 p.700*

The Sacrifice. *v.2 p.739, p.740*

Sad and Luminous Days: Cuba's Struggle with the Superpowers after the Missile Crisis. *v.3 p.307*

The Sad Geraniums, and Other Stories. *v.2 p.603*

A Sad State of Freedom. *v.6 p.666*

Sadaharu Oh: A Zen Way of Baseball. *v.6 p.228*

The Saddharma-Pundaraka or the Lotus of the True Law. *v.1 p.564*

Saddling la Gringa: Gatekeeping in Literature by Contemporary Latina Writers. *v.6 p.500, p.507, p.513*

Sade: A Biography. *v.2 p.484*

Sade, Fourier, Loyola. *v.2 p.454*

Sadeq Chubak: An Anthology. *v.6 p.670*

Sadeq Hedayat: An Anthology. *v.6 p.671*

The Sadler's Wells Royal Ballet: Now the Birmingham Royal Ballet. *v.1 p.25*

Sadtler Guide to Carbon-13 NMR Spectra of Polymers and Resins. *v.5 p.323*

Sadtler Guide to Carbon-13 NMR Spectra. *v.5 p.272*

Sadtler Guide to NMR Spectra. *v.5 p.272*

Sadtler Guide to the NMR Spectra of Polymers. . . .*v.5 p.323*

The Sadtler Handbook of Infrared Spectra. *v.5 p.270*

The Sadtler Handbook of Proton NMR Spectra. . . .*v.5 p.272*

The Sadtler Handbook of Ultraviolet Spectra. . *v.5 p.272, p.273*

Safavid Persia: The History and Politics of an Islamic Society. *v.6 p.630*

Safe Food: Bacteria, Biotechnology, and Bioterrorism. .*v.5 p.35*

Safe Passage into the Twenty-First Century: The United Nations' Quest for Peace, Equality, Justice and Development. *v.4 p.634*

The Safe Sea of Women: Lesbian Fiction, 1969-1989. *v.6 p.394*

Safe Sex. *v.6 p.411*

Safe: The Race to Protect Ourselves in a Newly Dangerous World. *v.4 p.561*

Safed Spirituality: Rules of Mystical Piety, the Beginning of Wisdom. *v.1 p.550*

Safeguarding the Ozone Layer and the Global Climate System: Special Report of the Intergovernmental Panel on Climate Change. *v.4 p.394*

Safety Engineering. *v.5 p.681*

Safety in Academic Chemistry Laboratories. *v.5 p.265*

Safety in Ice Hockey. *v.4 p.862, p.870, p.871*

Safety in the Chemistry and Biochemistry Laboratory. *v.5 p.330, p.331*

Safety Management Practices for Hazardous Materials. .*v.5 p.681*

Safety of Irradiated Foods, Vol. 68. . . . .*v.5 p.33*

The Saffron Wave: Democracy and Hindu Nationalism in Modern India. *v.1 p.540*

La Saga des Poules Mouillees. *v.2 p.541*

The Saga of Dazai Osamu: A Critical Study with Translations. *v.6 p.227, p.231*

The Saga of the Volsungs, the Saga of Ragnar Lodbrook, Together with the Lay of Kraka. *v.2 p.625*

The Saga of the Volsungs. *v.2 p.624*

The SAGE Dictionary of Criminology. *v.6 p.246*

The SAGE Dictionary of Cultural Studies. *v.4 p.676*

The SAGE Encyclopedia of Social Science Research Methods. *v.4 p.686*

The SAGE Handbook of Nonverbal Communication. .*v.4 p.424*

The SAGE Handbook of Social Psychology. *v.5 p.646*

The Sagebrush State: Nevada's History, Government and
Politics.. . . . .*v.3 p.529*

Saggi : 1945-1985.. . . . .*v.2 p.714*

Saggi sulla letteratura e sull'arte.. . . . .*v.2 p.721*

Saggi sulla politica e sulla società. *v.2 p.721*

La Sagouine.. . . . .*v.2 p.541*

Sahara: A Natural History. *v.5 p.175, p.240,v.6 p.61*

☐ Sahitya Akademi.. . . . .*v.6 p.147*

Sailing with Noah: Stories from the World of Zoos. . .*v.5 p.83*

Sailor-Diplomat: A Biography of Commodore James Biddle,
1783-1848.. . . . .*v.3 p.417*

Saint Benedict's Rule. *v.1 p.577*

Saint Exupery.. . . . .*v.2 p.527*

Saint Genet: Actor and Martyr. *v.2 p.519*

Saint Joan.. . . . .*v.2 p.310*

Saint Louis: Crusader King of France. *v.3 p.143*

Saint Patrick's World: The Christian Culture of Ireland's
Apostolic Age.. . . . .*v.1 p.609*

Sainthood: Its Manifestations in World Religions. . .*v.1 p.527*

The Saint-Napoleon: Celebrations of Sovereignty in
Nineteenth-Century France.. . . . .*v.3 p.149*

Saints and Postmodernism: Revisioning Moral
Philosophy.. . . . .*v.1 p.501*

Saints and Revolutionaries: The Ascetic Hero in Russian
Fiction.. . . . .*v.2 p.799*

Saints and Saint Makers of New
Mexico.. . . . .*v.6 p.491, p.492, p.522, p.523*

Saints and Scholars. *v.1 p.609*

Saints and Society: The Two Worlds of Western Christendom,
1000-1700. . . . .*v.6 p.573*

Saints, Goddesses and Kings: Muslims and Christians in South
Indian Society, 1700-1900. . . . .*v.6 p.160*

Saints in Arms; Puritanism and Democracy in Cromwell's
Army. *v.3 p.104, p.122*

Saints, Sinners, Saviors: Strong Black Women in
African-American Literature.. . . . .*v.6 p.26, p.44*

Saint-Saens: A Critical Biography. *v.6 p.410*

Saint-Simon and the Court of Louis XIV.. . . . . .*v.3 p.145*

Une saison au Congo : théâtre. *v.2 p.536*

Une Saison dans la Vie d'Emmanuel. *v.2 p.538*

Saivism in Philosophical Perspective: A Study of the Formative
Concepts, Problems and Methods of Saiva
Siddhanta. *v.1 p.534, p.535*

Sakamoto Ryoma and the Meiji Restoration. *v.6 p.227*

Sakharov: A Biography. *v.3 p.223*

Sal Mineo: His Life, Murder, and Mystery. *v.6 p.418*

Sal Si Puedes (Escape If You Can): Cesar Chavez and the New
American Revolution. *v.6 p.489, p.526*

Saladin and the Crusaders: Selected Annals from Masalik
Al-absar Fi Mamalik Al Amsar.. . . . .*v.6 p.609*

Saladin: The Politics of the Holy War. *v.6 p.585*

Saladin.. . . . .*v.6 p.609*

The Salamander and Other Gothic Tales. *v.2 p.806*

Salammbo.. . . . .*v.2 p.491*

Salamone Rossi: Jewish Musician in Late Renaissance
Mantua.. . . . .*v.1 p.180, p.184, p.299, p.300, p.351*

Salazar's Dictatorship and European Fascism: Problems and
Perspectives of Interpretation.. . . . .*v.3 p.243*

Salem Is My Dwelling Place: A Life of Nathaniel
Hawthorne.. . . . .*v.2 p.41*

Salem: Place, Myth and Memory. *v.3 p.488*

Salem Possessed: The Social Origins of Witchcraft. . .*v.3 p.405*

The Salem Witch Trials.. . . . .*v.3 p.489*

Salem's Lot.. . . . .*v.2 p.148*

Sales and Marketing Management: Survey of Buying
Power.. . . . .*v.4 p.138, p.142*

Sales Forecasting Management: A Demand Management
Approach.. . . . .*v.4 p.137*

Salesman in Beijing. *v.2 p.102, v.6 p.216*

The Salian Century: Main Currents in an Age of
Transition.. . . . .*v.3 p.163*

The Salisbury Plain Poems of William Wordsworth. . .*v.2 p.325*

The Saljuq and Mongol Periods. *v.6 p.629*

La Salle: A Perilous Odyssey from Canada to the Gulf of
Mexico.. . . . .*v.3 p.538*

La Salle and the Discovery of the Great West. *v.3 p.538*

La Salle: Explorer of the North American Frontier. . .*v.3 p.538*

Sallust's Bellum Catilinae. *v.2 p.443*

Sallust. *v.2 p.443*

Sally Hemings.. . . . .*v.6 p.23, p.42*

Salman Rushdie: A Postmodern Reading of His Major
Works.. . . . .*v.2 p.766*

Salman Rushdie. *v.2 p.766*

Salome and Elektra. *v.1 p.225, p.233, p.359, p.410*

The Salome Dancer: The Life and Times of Maud Allan. .*v.1 p.7*

Salome.. . . . .*v.2 p.320*

Salon de Belleza. *v.2 p.667*

The Salon of 1767, Vol. 2. . . . .*v.2 p.479*

Salonica, City of Ghosts: Christians, Muslims, and Jews,
1430-1950. . . . .*v.3 p.194*

Saloon: Public Drinking in Chicago and Boston,
1880-1920. . . . .*v.4 p.699, v.5 p.663*

Salsa and Related Genres: A Bibliographical
Guide. *v.1 p.166, p.292*

The Salsa Guidebook for Piano and Ensemble. *v.1 p.403*

Salsa!: The Rhythm of Latin Music. *v.6 p.518*

Salt: A World History.. . . . .*v.5 p.319*

The Salt Eaters. *v.6 p.22, p.41*

Salt: Grain of Life. *v.5 p.319, p.451*

Salt Is Leaving. *v.2 p.378*

Salt of the Desert Sun: A History of Salt Production and Trade
in the Central Sudan. *v.6 p.68*

Salt of the Earth, Conscience of the Court: The Story of Justice
Wiley Rutledge.. . . . .*v.4 p.536*

The Salterton Trilogy: Tempest-Tost; Leaven of Malice; A
Mixture of Frailties.. . . . .*v.2 p.735*

The Saltwater Wilderness.. . . . .*v.5 p.241*

Salut Galarneau!: Suivi de, le Temps des Galarneau. .*v.2 p.540*

El Salvador at War: An Oral History of Conflict from the 1979
Insurrection to the Present.. . . . .*v.3 p.299*

El Salvador: Central America in the New Cold War. . .*v.3 p.299*

Salvador Dalí's Art and Writing, 1927-1942: The
Metamorphosis of Narcissus. *v.1 p.696*

El Salvador: Military Assistance has Helped Counter but not
Overcome the Insurgency: Report to the Honorable
Edward M. Kennedy. *v.3 p.300*

The Salvadoran Americans. *v.6 p.529, p.542*

Salvadoran Migration to Southern California: Redefining el
Hermano Lejano. *v.6 p.528, p.543*

Salvador. *v.2 p.143*

Salvation and Liberation: In Search of a Balance Between Faith
and Politics. *v.1 p.637*

Salvation and Suicide: Jim Jones, the Peoples Temple, and
Jonestown. *v.1 p.543*

Salvation and the Savage: An Analysis of Protestant Missions
and American Indian Response,
1787-1862. . . . .*v.6 p.681, p.686, p.700*

Salvation at Stake: Christian Martyrdom in Early Modern
Europe. *v.1 p.601*

The Salzburg Tales. *v.2 p.749*

Sam Houston: A Biography of the Father of Texas. .*v.3 p.509*

Sam Houston. *v.3 p.508*

Sam Shepard: Seven Plays. *v.1 p.118*

ⓔ Samba: Resistance in Motion. *v.1 p.19, p.20*

The Same and Not the Same. *v.5 p.264*

The Same Ax, Twice: Restoration and Renewal in a Throwaway
Age. *v.1 p.823*

The Same River Twice: Honoring the Difficult: A Meditation on
Life, Spirit, Art, and the Making of the Film The Color
Purple, Ten Years Later. *v.6 p.28, p.47*

Same Sex: Debating the Ethics, Science, and Culture of
Homosexuality. *v.6 p.420*

Sameness and Substance Renewed. *v.1 p.505*

☐ Same-Sex Couples and Same-Sex Couples Raising Children
in the United States. *v.6 p.376, p.377*

Same-Sex Cultures and Sexualities: An Anthropological
Reader. *v.6 p.357*

Same-Sex Marriage in the United States: Focus on the
Facts. *v.6 p.388*

Same-Sex Marriage: Pro and Con. *v.6 p.389*

Same-Sex Marriage: The Moral and Legal Debate. .*v.6 p.388*

Same-Sex Unions in Premodern
Europe. *v.4 p.739, v.6 p.373, p.420, p.421*

The Sami, an Indigenous People of the Arctic. . . .*v.3 p.232*

Samnium and the Samnites. *v.3 p.25*

Samoan Art and Artists. *v.1 p.695*

Les samouraïs : roman. *v.2 p.531*

Sampling in Archaeology. *v.4 p.7*

La sampogna : con le Egloghe boscarecce. *v.2 p.708*

Samson Agonistes. *v.2 p.255*

Samtliche Werke: Frankfurter Ausg. *v.2 p.600*

Samtliche Werke. *v.2 p.610*

Samuel Barber: The Composer and His
Music. *v.1 p.215, p.304,v.6 p.409*

Samuel Beckett: The Last Modernist. *v.2 p.333*

Samuel Beckett: Waiting for
Godot-Endgame. *v.1 p.81, p.94,v.2 p.333*

Samuel Beckett. *v.2 p.332, p.333*

Samuel Daniel: A Critical and Biographical Study. . .*v.2 p.218*

Samuel Daniel: Selected Poetry and a Defense of
Rhyme. *v.2 p.213*

Samuel Eliot Morison's Historical World: In Quest of a New
Parkman. *v.3 p.374*

Samuel F. B. Morse. *v.1 p.699, p.700*

Samuel Gompers, American Statesman. *v.4 p.129*

Samuel Gompers and Organized Labor in America. . .*v.4 p.127*

Samuel 'Hudibras' Butler. *v.2 p.242*

Samuel I: A New Translation with Introduction and
Commentary. *v.1 p.620*

Samuel II. *v.1 p.620*

Samuel Johnson and Neoclassical Dramatic Theory: The
Intellectual Context of the "Preface to Shakespeare".*v.2 p.232*

Samuel Johnson and the Impact of Print. . .*v.2 p.250, v.3 p.120*

Samuel Johnson, Biographer. *v.2 p.250*

The Samuel Johnson Encyclopedia. *v.2 p.251*

Samuel Johnson: The Life of an Author. *v.2 p.250, p.251*

Samuel Johnson: The Major Works. *v.2 p.250*

Samuel Johnson: the Yale Anthology of His Prose and
Poetry. *v.2 p.250*

Samuel Johnson's Critical Opinions: A Reexamination.*v.2 p.251*

Samuel Johnson's Lives of the Poets: Boxed Set. . .*v.2 p.180*

Samuel Johnson. *v.2 p.250*

Samuel Jones Tilden: A Study in Political
Sagacity. *v.3 p.422, p.423, p.428*

Samuel Richardson: A Biography. *v.2 p.258*

Samuel Richardson, Dramatic Novelist. *v.2 p.258*

Samuelson and Neo-Classical Economics. *v.4 p.213*

The Samurai: A Novel. *v.2 p.531*

Samurai and Silk: A Japanese and American Heritage.*v.6 p.228*

The Samurai Film. *v.6 p.311, p.336*

The San and the Colonization of the Cape 1770-1879: Conflict,
Incorporation, Acculturation. *v.6 p.79*

San Francisco Noir. *v.6 p.730*

San Manuel Bueno Martir and la Novela de Don
Sandalio. *v.2 p.663*

Sanctions for Evil: Sources of Social Destructiveness. *v.4 p.683*

The Sanctity of Rural Life: Nobility, Protestantism, and Nazism
in Weimar Prussia. *v.3 p.169*

Sand and Sandstone. *v.5 p.438*

The Sand Child. *v.2 p.544*

A Sand County Almanac: And Sketches Here and There. *v.5 p.224*

A Sand County Almanac. *v.5 p.17, v.6 p.288*

The Sand Dollar and the Slide Rule: Drawing Blueprints from
Nature. *v.5 p.99*

The Sand Pebbles. *v.6 p.190, p.216*

The Sandcastle. *v.2 p.372*

The Sandglass. *v.2 p.760*

Sandinistas: The Party and the Revolution. *v.3 p.301*

The Sandino Affair. *v.3 p.302*

Sandro Botticelli: The Drawings for Dante's Divine Comedy. *v.1 p.722*

Sands of Time: The History of Beach Volleyball: 1895-1969. . . . . *v.4 p.869*

Sands of Time: The History of Beach Volleyball: 1970-1989, 2. . . . . *v.4 p.869*

Sands of Time: The History of Beach Volleyball: 1990-2004, Vol. 3. . . . . *v.4 p.869*

The Sane Society. *v.4 p.775, v.5 p.645*

Le sang des autres : roman. *v.2 p.508, p.509*

Sangha, State, and Society: Thai Buddhism in History. *v.6 p.171*

Sanitary City: Urban Infrastructure in America from Colonial Times to the Present. *v.6 p.728*

Sanity and Survival in the Nuclear Age: Psychological Aspects of War and Peace. *v.4 p.647, p.649*

Sanity in Bedlam: A Study of Robert Burton's Anatomy of Melancholy. *v.2 p.213*

The Sans-Culottes: The Popular Movement and Revolutionary Government, 1793-1794. . . . . *v.3 p.151*

Sanskrit Play Production in Ancient India. . . *v.1 p.131, p.134*

Santa Barraza, Artist of the Borderlands. . . . *v.6 p.486, p.491*

Santa Evita. *v.3 p.348*

Santa Fe Hispanic Culture: Preserving Identity in a Tourist Town. *v.6 p.534*

The Santa Fe Trail: Its History, Legends, and Lore. . *v.3 p.527*

The Santa Fe Trail. *v.3 p.527*

Santayana. *v.1 p.440*

Santería: The Beliefs and Rituals of a Growing Religion in America. *v.6 p.520*

Santeria Enthroned: Art, Ritual, and Innovation in an Afro-Cuban Religion. *v.1 p.543, v.3 p.278*

Santeria: The Religion. *v.4 p.722*

Santiago de Guatemala, 1541-1773: City, Caste, and the Colonial Experience. *v.3 p.298*

Los Santos, Guia de Calles Y. *v.2 p.689*

San'ya Blues: Laboring Life in Contemporary Tokyo. *v.6 p.219*

Sanyu: Catalogue Raisonné Oil Paintings. *v.1 p.750*

Sapphic Primitivism: Productions of Race, Class, and Sexuality in Key Works of Modern Fiction. *v.2 p.190, p.191*

Sappho and Alcaeus: An Introduction to the Study of Ancient Lesbian Poetry. *v.2 p.419*

Sappho in Early Modern England: Female Same-Sex Literary Erotics, 1550-1714. . . . . *v.6 p.391*

Sappho's Immortal Daughters. *v.6 p.480*

Sappho's Lyre: Archaic Lyric and Women Poets of Ancient Greece. *v.2 p.419*

Saracens: Islam in the Medieval European Imagination. *v.6 p.573, p.575*

Sarah Fielding. *v.2 p.248*

Sarah Orne Jewett: A Writer's Life. *v.2 p.46*

Sarah Orne Jewett, an American Persephone. *v.2 p.46*

A Sarah Orne Jewett Companion. *v.2 p.46*

Sarah Orne Jewett: Her World and Her Work. *v.2 p.46*

Sarajevo Marlboro. *v.2 p.811*

The Sarbanes-Oxley Act: Implications for Records Management. *v.4 p.115*

Sarbanes-Oxley and the Board of Directors: Techniques and Best Practices for Corporate Governance. *v.4 p.86*

Sarmiento and His Argentina. *v.3 p.347*

Sarte. *v.1 p.458*

Sartor Resartus: The Life and Opinions of Herr Teufelsdröckh. *v.2 p.276*

Sartre: A Collection of Critical Essays. *v.2 p.527*

Sartre: A Life. *v.2 p.527*

Sartre on Theater. *v.2 p.528*

SAT II Success Biology E/M. *v.5 p.245*

The Satanic Verses: A Novel. *v.2 p.766*

The Satapatha Brahmana. *v.1 p.537*

Satchmo. *v.1 p.259, p.302*

Satellite Communications for the Nonspecialist. . . . *v.4 p.421*

Satellite Communications: The First Quarter Century of Service. *v.4 p.421*

Satellite Communications. *v.4 p.421, p.422*

Satellite Meteorology: An Introduction. . . . *v.5 p.367, p.371*

Satellite Observations of the Earth's Environment: Accelerating the Transition of Research to Operations. *v.5 p.720*

Satellite Technology: An Introduction. *v.4 p.421*

Satie Remembered. *v.1 p.220, p.352*

Satie the Composer. *v.1 p.220, p.352*

Satire: A Critical Reintroduction. *v.2 p.195*

Satire in Colonial Spanish America: Turning the New World Upside Down. *v.3 p.263*

The Satire of Jonathan Swift. *v.2 p.262*

Satires Against Man: The Poems of Rochester. . . . *v.2 p.259*

Satires and Miscellaneous Poetry and Prose. *v.2 p.242*

Satires, Epigrams and Verse Letters. *v.2 p.213*

Satires, Epistles, the Art of Poetry. *v.2 p.434*

The Satires of Horace: A Study. *v.2 p.435*

The Satires of Persius. *v.2 p.439*

The Satires of Rome: Threatening Poses from Lucilius to Juvenal. *v.2 p.427*

The Satires. *v.2 p.435*

Satire. *v.2 p.195*

Satisfaction Guaranteed: The Making of the American Mass Market. *v.4 p.140*

Satura. *v.2 p.719*

Saturday: A Novel. *v.2 p.368*

Saturday Night and Sunday Morning. *v.2 p.380*

Saturday Night at the Pahala Theatre. *v.6 p.104*

Saturday Review, 1855-1868: Representative Educated Opinion in Victorian England. *v.6 p.739, p.750*

The Satyrica. *v.2 p.440*

The Satyricon. *v.2 p.440*

Saudi Arabia and the United States: Birth of a Security Partnership. *v.3 p.389*

Saudi Arabia Enters the Twenty-First Century: The Political, Foreign Policy, Economic, and Energy Dimensions. *v.6 p.626*

Saudi Arabia in the 1980's: Foreign Policy, Security, and Oil. *v.6 p.626*

Saudi Arabia in the Nineteenth Century. *v.6 p.626*

Saudi Arabia: Power, Legitimacy and Survival. . . . *v.6 p.626*

Saul and Selected Poems. *v.2 p.732*

Saul Bellow Against the Grain. *v.2 p.60*

Saul Bellow: Novels, 1944-1953. . . . .*v.2 p.60*

Saul Bellow. *v.2 p.60*

Savage Art: A Biography of Jim Thompson. *v.2 p.124*

Savage Beauty: The Life of Edna St. Vincent Millay. . *v.2 p.98*

The Savage Father. *v.2 p.721*

Savage Inequalities: Children in America's
Schools. *v.4 p.302, p.315*

The Savage Night. *v.2 p.542*

Savage Reprisals: Bleak House, Madame Bovary,
Buddenbrooks. *v.2 p.284*

A Savage War of Peace: Algeria
1954-1962. . . . .*v.3 p.157, v.4 p.584, v.6 p.643*

The Savage Within: The Social History of British Anthropology,
1885-1945. . . . .*v.4 p.4*

Savages and Beasts: The Birth of the Modern Zoo. . . *v.5 p.85*

Savannah Lives: Animal Life and the Human Evolution of
Africa. *v.5 p.181*

Saving America?: Faith-Based Services and the Future of Civil
Society. *v.4 p.755*

Saving America's Beaches: The Causes of and Solutions to
Beach Erosion. *v.6 p.289*

Saving Graces: Sojourns of a Backyard Biologist. . . *v.5 p.228*

Saving Monticello: The Levy Family's Epic Quest to Rescue the
House That Jefferson Built. *v.1 p.822, p.823*

Saving Nature's Legacy: Protecting and Restoring
Biodiversity. *v.5 p.180*

Saving Strangers: Humanitarian Intervention in International
Society. *v.4 p.671, p.673*

Saving the Planet: The American Response to the Environment
in the Twentieth Century. *v.4 p.62*

Saving the Text: Literature-Derrida-Philosophy. *v.2 p.567, p.571*

Savion!: My Life in Tap. *v.1 p.8, p.32*

Savoring Southeast Asia: Recipes and Reflections on Southeast
Asian Cooking. *v.6 p.164*

Savushun: A Novel about Modern Iran. *v.6 p.670*

The Savvy Negotiator: Building Win/Win Relationships. *v.4 p.74*

Saxo Grammaticus : The History of the Danes, Books I - IX: I.
English text; II. Commentary. *v.3 p.233*

Saxo Grammaticus and the Life of Hamlet: A Translation,
History, and Commentary. *v.2 p.229*

Sax's Dangerous Properties of Industrial
Materials. *v.5 p.311, p.312*

Sax's dangerous properties of industrial materials. . . *v.5 p.312*

Sax's Dangerous Properties of Industrial Materials. . *v.5 p.682*

Sax's Dangerous Properties of Industrial Materials. *v.5 p.311*

Say It with Charts: The Executive's Guide to Visual
Communication. *v.4 p.174*

Saying Something: Jazz Improvisation and Interaction. *v.1 p.262*

The Sayings and Doings of Samuel Slick Together with His
Opinion on Matrimony. *v.2 p.732*

Sayyid Ahmad Khan: A Reinterpretation of Muslim
Theology. *v.1 p.555*

Sayyid Jamal Ad-Din "Al-Afghani": A Political
Biography. *v.1 p.555*

The Scalawag in Alabama Politics, 1865-1881. . . . .*v.3 p.505*

The Scalawags: Southern Dissenters in the Civil War and
Reconstruction. *v.4 p.519*

Scaldic Poetry. *v.2 p.625*

Scale and Scope: The Dynamics of Industrial
Capitalism. *v.3 p.38, p.39*

The Scale of Imprisonment. *v.6 p.272, p.273*

Scaling in Soil Physics: Principles and Applications. . *v.5 p.49*

The Scalpel and the Silver Bear: The First Navajo Woman
Surgeon Combines Western Medicine and Traditional
Healing. *v.6 p.701*

Scandal in a Small Town: Understanding Modern Hungary
Though the Stories of Three Families. *v.3 p.185*

Scandalous Bodies: Diasporic Literature in English
Canada. *v.2 p.729*

The Scandals of Translation: Towards an Ethics of
Difference. *v.4 p.709*

Scandinavia and the Great Powers 1890-1940. .*v.3 p.235, 236*

Scandinavia During the Second World War. . .*v.3 p.232, p.233*

Scandinavia in the Revolutionary Era,
1760-1815. . . . .*v.3 p.232, p.233*

Scandinavia since 1500. . . . .*v.3 p.232, p.233*

Scandinavian Modern Furnishing, 1930-1970: Designed for
Life. *v.1 p.804*

Scandinavian Plays of the Twentieth Century. *v.2 p.624*

The Scandinavian Theatre. *v.2 p.624*

Scandinavia. *v.3 p.232, p.233*

Scanning Electron Microscopy in Taxonomy and Functional
Morphology. *v.5 p.87, 204*

The Scarlet Letter: An Authoritative Text. *v.2 p.41*

The Scarlet Professor: Newton Arvin: A Literary Life Shattered
by Scandal. *v.6 p.404*

Scarlet Song. *v.2 p.543*

Scarred Minds: The Psychological Impact of War on Sri Lankan
Tamils. *v.6 p.163*

Scars of Conquest/Masks of Resistance: The Invention of
Cultural Identities in African, African-American,
and Caribbean Drama. *v.2 p.768*

Scars of War, Wounds of Peace: The Israeli-Arab
Tragedy. *v.4 p.646, p.648*

Scars. *v.2 p.780*

Scattered Be-Longings: Cultural Paradoxes of Race, Nation and
Gender. *v.4 p.31, p.709*

Scenario Planning: The Link Between Future and
Strategy. *v.4 p.82*

Scenarios of Power: Myth and Ceremony in Russian Monarchy
from Peter the Great to the Abdication of Nicholas II. *v.3 p.211*

Scene Design and Stage Lighting. *v.1 p.147, p.148, p.149*

Scene Design for Stage and Screen: Readings on the Aesthetics
and Methodology of Scene Design for Drama, Opera,
Musical Comedy, Ballet, Motion Pictures, Television and
Arena Theatre. *v.1 p.147*

Scenery: Design and Fabrication. *v.1 p.148*

Scenery, Set and Staging in the Italian Renaissance: Studies in
the Practice of Theatre. *v.1 p.74, p.91, p.106, p.146*

Scenes from the High Desert: Julian Steward's Life and
Theory. *v.4 p.4*

Scenes of Clerical Life. *v.2 p.287*

The Scenic Art: Notes and Acting and the Drama. .*v.1 p.56, p.136*

The Scenic Daguerreotype: Romanticism and Early
Photography. *v.1 p.763*

Scenic Design on Broadway: Designers and Their Credits,
1915-1990. . . . . *v.1 p.117, p.147*

Scent of Apples: A Collection of Stories. *v.6 p.102*

Scented Gardens for the Blind. *v.2 p.745*

Scepticism and Literature: An Essay on Pope, Hume, Sterne,
and Johnson. *v.2 p.251, p.257, p.262*

Sceptics. *v.1 p.517*

Schaum's Easy Outline Molecular and Cell Biology. . .*v.5 p.129*

Schaum's Outline of Biochemistry. . . .*v.5 p.331, p.333, p.335*

Schaum's Outline of Calculus. *v.5 p.485*

Schaum's Outline of Differential Geometry. *v.5 p.496*

Schaum's Outline of Feedback and Control Systems. .*v.5 p.710*

Schaum's Outline of Mathematical Methods for Business and
Economics. *v.4 p.175*

Schaum's Outline of Organic Chemistry. *v.5 p.301*

Schaum's Outline of Physical Chemistry. *v.5 p.288*

Schaum's Outline of Theory and Problems of
Combinatorics. *v.5 p.478*

Schaum's Outline of Theory and Problems of Discrete
Mathematics. *v.5 p.478*

Schaum's Outline of Theory and Problems of Graph
Theory. *v.5 p.479, p.480*

Schaum's Outline of Theory and Problems of Linear
Algebra. *v.5 p.472, p.473*

Schaum's Outline of Theory and Problems of Modern Abstract
Algebra. *v.5 p.473*

Schaum's Outline of Theory and Problems of Numerical
Analysis. *v.5 p.492*

Schaum's Outline of Theory and Problems of Partial Differential
Equations. *v.5 p.487*

The Scheduled Castes. *v.4 p.707, v.6 p.149*

Scheduling Strategies for Middle Schools. *v.4 p.288*

Scheherazade Goes West: Different Cultures, Different
Harems. *v.6 p.594*

The Scheme Programming Language. *v.5 p.346*

Schemers and Dreamers: Filibustering in Mexico,
1848-1921. . . . .*v.3 p.295*

Schenker: The Masterwork in Music, Vol. 2. . . . .*v.1 p.373*

Schenker: The Masterwork in Music:1930. . . . . .*v.1 p.373*

Schiller: Five Plays. *v.2 p.601*

Schiller. *v.2 p.599, p.601*

The Schillinger System of Musical Compsition. . . .*v.1 p.373*

Schindler's List. *v.2 p.746, p.747*

Schizophrenia. *v.5 p.660*

Schizophrenic Speech: Making Sense of Bathroots and Ponds
that Fall in Doorways. *v.5 p.661*

Schleiermacher: on Religion: Speeches to Its Cultured
Despisers. *v.1 p.521*

Schliemann of Troy: Treasure and Deceit. *v.3 p.16*

Das Schloss. *v.2 p.611*

Schmelzpunkt Tabellen Organischer Verbindungen/Melting Point
Tables of Organic Compounds. *v.5 p.291*

[e] A Schnittke Reader. *v.1 p.223, p.353*

Schoenberg and His World. *v.1 p.213, p.353*

Schoenberg: His Life, World, and Work. . . . *v.1 p.225, p.353*

Schoenberg: Pierrot Lunaire. *v.1 p.213, p.235, p.353*

A Schoenberg Reader: Documents of a Life. . *v.1 p.208, p.353*

Schoenberg's Serial Odyssey: The Evolution of His
Twelve-Tone Method, 1914-1928. . . . . .*v.1 p.215, p.353*

The Scholar Adventurers. *v.2 p.163*

[☐] Scholarly Sport Sites: A Subject
Directory. *v.4 p.790, p.794, p.823, p.824,
                            p.830, p.843, p.870, p.872, p.881, p.903*

Scholars and the Indian Experience: Critical Reviews of Recent
Writings in the Social Sciences. *v.6 p.678*

Scholarship and Christian Faith: Enlarging the
Conversation. *v.4 p.307*

Scholarship Assessed and Reconsidered Set. . *v.4 p.292, p.330*

The Scholars. *v.6 p.211*

[e] The School and Society. *v.4 p.342*

School Choice and Diversity: What the Evidence Says. *v.4 p.367*

School Choice and Social Justice. *v.4 p.346, p.347*

School Choice in Urban America: Magnet Schools and the
Pursuit of Equity. *v.4 p.367*

School Choice Tradeoffs: Liberty, Equity, and Diversity. *v.4 p.298*

School Community Relations,Under Reform. *v.4 p.303*

School Desegregation in the Twenty-First Century: The Focus
Must Change. *v.4 p.300*

School Discipline and School Violence: The Teacher Variance
Approach. *v.4 p.284*

School Experiences of Gay and Lesbian Youth: The Invisible
Minority. *v.4 p.309*

The School for Husbands and Sganarelle: Or the Imaginary
Cuckold. *v.2 p.475*

The School for Scandal and Other Plays. *v.2 p.260*

The School for Widows. *v.2 p.258*

The School for Wives and The Learned Ladies by Moliere: Two
Comedies in an Acclaimed Translation. *v.2 p.475*

The School in the Service of Evangelization: The Catholic
Educational Impact in Eastern Nigeria 1886-1950. .*v.1 p.574*

School Kids/Street Kids: Identity Development in Latino
Students. *v.6 p.526, p.527, p.543*

School of Classical Dance. *v.1 p.24*

School of Clavier Playing, or, Instructions in Playing the Clavier
for Teachers and Students. *v.1 p.399, p.402*

The School of History: Athens in the Age of
Socrates. *v.3 p.18, p.20*

School Prayer and Discrimination: The Civil Rights of Religious
Minorities and Dissenters. *v.4 p.450*

The School Principal: A Novel. *v.6 p.669*

School Principals and Change. *v.4 p.280, p.281, p.282*

The School Promoters: Education and Social Class in
Mid-Nineteenth Century Upper Canada. *v.4 p.336*

School Psychology at a Turning Point: Ensuring a Bright Future
for the Profession. *v.4 p.353*

School Psychology: Essentials of Theory and Practice. *v.4 p.356*

School Shootings. *v.6 p.265*

School Social Work Worldwide. *v.4 p.757*

School Songs of America's Colleges and Universities: A
Directory. *v.1 p.169*

☐ School Spending: The Business of Education. . . .*v.4 p.280*

School Strikes in Prussian Poland, 1901 to 1907: The Struggle over Bilingual Education. *v.3 p.253*

School: The Story of American Public Education Series. *v.4 p.324*

School: The Story of American Public Education. . . *v.4 p.328*

School Violence: From Discipline to Due Process. . . *v.4 p.283*

School Violence Intervention: A Practical Handbook. *v.4 p.284*

School Violence. *v.6 p.265*

School Vouchers and Privatization: A Reference Handbook. *v.4 p.299*

School-Based Mental Health Services: Creating Comprehensive and Culturally Specific Programs. *v.5 p.576*

Schoolbook Nation: Conflicts over American History Textbooks from the Civil War to the Present. *v.4 p.285*

Schoolbooks and Krags: The United States Army in the Philippines, 1898-1902. . . . .*v.6 p.179*

Schooled to Order: A Social History of Public Schooling in the United States. *v.4 p.328*

Schooled to Work: Vocationalism and the American Curriculum, 1876-1946. . . . .*v.4 p.305*

Schooling America: How the Public Schools Meet the Nation's Changing Needs. *v.4 p.326*

Schooling Disadvantaged Children: Racing Against Catastrophe. *v.4 p.299*

Schooling in Capitalist America : Educational Reform and the Contradictions of Economic life. *v.4 p.762*

Schooling the Symbolic Animal: Social and Cultural Dimensions of Education. *v.4 p.302, p.303*

Schools for Our Time: The Local Classroom in an Uncertain World. *v.4 p.303*

School's Out: The Impact of Gay and Lesbian Issues on America's Schools. *v.6 p.386*

The Schools, the Courts, and the Public Interest. . . *v.4 p.450*

The Schools We Deserve: Reflections on the Educational Crisis of Our Time. *v.4 p.328*

The Schools We Need: And Why We Don't Have Them. *v.4 p.327*

The Schoolwide Enrichment Model: A How-To Guide for Educational Excellence. *v.5 p.573, p.574*

Schopenhauer on the Character of the World: The Metaphysics of Will. *v.1 p.465*

Schopenhauer. *v.1 p.465*

Schriften: die Werke Friedrich von Hardenbergs. . . *v.2 p.601*

Schrifttanz: German Moden Dance Writings of the 1920s and 1930s. *v.1 p.27*

Schubert: Die Schone Mullerin. *v.1 p.207, p.238, p.354*

The Schubert Reader. *v.1 p.196, p.354*

The Schubert Song Companion. *v.1 p.202, p.236, p.354*

Schubert: The Complete Song Texts. *v.1 p.207, p.237, p.354, p.412, p.413, p.415*

Schubert: The Music and the Man. *v.1 p.201, p.354*

Schubert's Song Sets. *v.1 p.198, p.235, p.354*

Schubert's Vienna. *v.1 p.197, p.354*

Schumann and His World. *v.1 p.205, p.355*

Schumann: Fantasie, Op. 17. . . . . . .*v.1 p.200, p.241, p.355*

Schumann: The Inner Voices of a Musical Genius. *v.1 p.201, p.355*

Schumann. *v.1 p.198, p.354*

Schumpeter, Social Scientist. *v.4 p.211, p.230, p.235*

Schumpeterian Dynamics and Metropolitan-Scale Productivity. *v.4 p.230, p.235*

Schumpeterian Economics. *v.4 p.230, p.235*

Schumpeterian Puzzles: Technological Competition and Economic Evolution. *v.4 p.230, p.234*

The Schumpeterian System. *v.4 p.230, p.235*

Schumpeter's Theory of Capitalist Motion: A Critical Exposition and Reassessment. *v.4 p.230*

Schumpeter's Vision: Capitalism, Socialism, and Democracy after 40 Years. *v.4 p.230, p.234*

Schutz. *v.1 p.186, p.355*

Das Schwanenhaus: Roman. *v.2 p.619*

Schwartz's Manual of Surgery. *v.5 p.522*

Science and Anti-Science. *v.5 p.400, p.402*

Science and Christianity: An Introduction. *v.1 p.526*

Science and Citizens: Globalization and the Challenge of Engagement. *v.5 p.167, p.218, p.248*

Science and Civil Society, Vol. 17. . . . .*v.3 p.45*

Science and Civilisation in China: The Social Background General Conclusions and Reflections. . . .*v.6 p.182, p.198*

Science and Common Sense. *v.5 p.408, p.409*

Science and Creation in the Middle Ages: Henry of Langenstein (D. 1397) on Genesis. *v.6 p.568, p.576*

Science and Creationism: A View from the National Academy of Sciences. *v.5 p.195*

Science and Engineering of Materials. *v.5 p.687*

Science and Ethical Values. *v.5 p.401*

Science and Ethics (La Science et I'Ethique), Vol. 11. *v.5 p.247*

Science and Health with Key to the Scriptures: Authorized Edition. *v.1 p.583*

Science and Hypothesis: Historical Essays on Scientific Methodology. *v.5 p.400, p.409*

Science and Information Theory. *v.5 p.408*

Science and Mathematics in Ancient Greek Culture. . *v.2 p.405*

Science and Politics in Canada. *v.5 p.392*

The Science and Politics of Global Climate Change: A Guide to the Debate. *v.6 p.283*

Science and Polity in France at the End of the Old Regime. *v.5 p.392*

Science and Polity in France: The Revolutionary and Napoleonic Years. *v.5 p.392*

Science and Practice of Strength Training. *v.4 p.880, p.908, p.909*

The Science and Psychology of Music Performance: Creative Strategies for Teaching and Learning. . . . *v.1 p.376, p.406*

Science and Racket Sports. *v.4 p.864, p.870*

Science and Religion, 400 B. C. to A. D. 1550: From Aristotle to Copernicus. *v.1 p.526*

Science and Religion: Some Historical Perspectives. . *v.6 p.288*

Science and Salvation: Evangelical Popular Science Publishing in Victorian Britain. *v.6 p.741, p.758, p.759*

Science and Selection: Essays on Biological Evolution and the Philosophy of Science. *v.5 p.193, p.226*

Science and Sensibility. *v.5 p.395, p.401*

Science and Soccer. *v.4 p.868, p.872, p.880*

Science and Society in Restoration England. *v.5 p.392*

Science and Supernature: A Critical Appraisal of
Parapsychology. *v.5 p.613*

Science and Technical Writing: A Manual of Style. . .*v.5 p.681*

Science and Technology; an Introduction to the
Literature. *v.5 p.405*

Science and Technology in China. *v.5 p.393*

Science and Technology in Post-Mao China. *v.5 p.393*

Science and Technology in the Middle East: A Guide to Issues,
Organizations and Institutions. *v.5 p.393*

Science and the Course of History. *v.5 p.402, p.403*

Science and the Endangered Species Act. *v.5 p.178*

Science and the Enlightenment. *v.5 p.390*

Science, Art and Nature in Medieval and Modern
Thought. *v.5 p.390*

Science As Intellectual Property. *v.5 p.410, p.412*

Science at the Frontier. *v.5 p.399*

Science Books & Films. *v.5 p.405*

Science Education of American Girls: A Historical
Perspective. *v.4 p.367*

Science Fiction Cinema: From Outerspace to
Cyberspace. *v.6 p.318*

Science Fiction Directors, 1895-1998. . . . .*v.6 p.318*

Science Fiction, Fantasy, and Weird Fiction Magazine Index
(1890-2003). *v.2 p.581*

Science Fiction, Fantasy, and Weird Fiction Magazines. .*v.2 p.581*

The Science Fiction Film Reader. *v.6 p.319*

Science Fiction, Horror and Fantasy Film and Television
Credits, Vol. 1. . . . .*v.6 p.319*

The Science Fiction of H. G. Wells. *v.2 p.319*

Science for Agriculture: A Long Term Perspective. . .*v.5 p.30*

Science for Exercise and Sport. *v.4 p.874*

Science for the Millennium. *v.5 p.385*

Science Funding: Politics and Porkbarrel. *v.5 p.412*

Science: Growth and Change. *v.5 p.391*

Science in America: A Documentary History,
1900-1939. . . . .*v.5 p.394*

Science in American Society; a Social History. . . .*v.5 p.393*

Science in Contemporary China. *v.5 p.393*

Science in Nineteenth-Century America: A Documentary
History. *v.5 p.389, p.394*

Science in Russia and the Soviet Union: A Short
History. *v.3 p.44, p.45, p.210,v.5 p.392*

Science in Russian Culture, 1861-1917. . . . .*v.5 p.393*

Science in Russian Culture: A History to 1860. . . .*v.5 p.393*

Science in the Enlightenment: An Encyclopedia. . . .*v.3 p.71*

Science in the Middle Ages. *v.5 p.389, v.6 p.576*

Science in the Nineteenth Century Periodical: An Electronic
Index. *v.6 p.759*

Science in Traditional China. *v.5 p.392, p.393*

Science in Translation: Movements of Knowledge Through
Cultures and Time. *v.5 p.389*

Science Instruction in the Middle and Secondary
Schools. *v.5 p.406, p.407*

Science: Its History and Development among the World's
Cultures. *v.5 p.389*

Science K-8: An Integrated Approach. *v.4 p.366*

Science, Magic, and Religion: The Ritual Process of Museum
Magic. *v.4 p.47*

Science Observed: Science As a Social and Intellectual
Activity. *v.5 p.410, p.412*

The Science of Chocolate. *v.5 p.329*

The Science of Color. *v.1 p.710, v.5 p.562, p.606*

The Science of Conservation Planning: Habitat Conservation
under the Endangered Species Act. *v.5 p.180*

The Science of Cooking. *v.5 p.329*

Science of Dance Training. *v.1 p.49*

Science of Desire: The Gay Gene and the Biology of
Behavior. *v.6 p.420*

Science of Education and the Psychology of the Child. .*v.4 p.345*

The Science of Empire: Scientific Knowledge, Civilization, and
Colonial Rule in India. *v.3 p.73*

The Science of Environmental Pollution. *v.5 p.706*

Science of Flexibility. *v.4 p.827, p.828, p.872*

The Science of Musical Sound. *v.1 p.375*

The Science of Music. *v.1 p.375*

The Science of Political Economy. *v.4 p.209*

The Science of Polymer Molecules. *v.5 p.322*

The Science of Self-Control. *v.5 p.612*

The Science of Soccer. *v.4 p.868, p.871*

The Science of Sound. *v.5 p.567*

The Science of Spectroscopy. *v.5 p.287*

The Science of Structures and Materials. *v.5 p.697*

Science of Synthesis - Houben-Weyl Methods of Molecular
Transformations: Category One - Organometallics. .*v.5 p.290*

Science of Synthesis: Houben-Weyl Methods of Molecular
Transformations. *v.5 p.290*

Science on Trial: The Case for Evolution. *v.5 p.192*

Science, Perception and Reality. *v.1 p.499*

Science, Philosophy, and Human Behavior in the Soviet
Union. *v.5 p.392*

Science, Philosophy and Physical Geography. *v.4 p.375*

Science Reorganized. *v.5 p.385*

Science, Revolution and Discontinuity. *v.5 p.403*

Science, Seeds, and Cyborgs: Biotechnology and the
Appropriation of Life. *v.5 p.217*

Science since Babylon. *v.5 p.389*

Science, Technology, and American Foreign Policy. . .*v.3 p.454*

Science, Technology, and Ecopolitics in the U. S. S.
R. *v.3 p.45, p.208, p.209*

Science, Technology, and Reparations: Exploitation and Plunder
in Postwar Germany. *v.3 p.175, p.176*

Science, Technology and Society: A Cross-Disciplinary
Perspective. *v.5 p.411, p.412*

Science, Technology, and Society: An Encyclopedia. . .*v.4 p.678*

Science Textbook Controversies and the Politics of Equal
Time. *v.5 p.392, p.407, p.412*

The Science Times Book of Fish. *v.5 p.216*

Science under Siege: The Politicians' War on Nature and
Truth. *v.4 p.566*

Science-Fiction: The Early Years. *v.2 p.581*

Science-Fiction: The Gernsback Years. *v.2 p.581*

Science.Gov. *v.5 p.385, p.393*

science.gov. *v.5 p.394*

The Sciences of the Artificial. *v.5 p.404*

Scientific American Archive. *v.5 p.385*

Scientific American Science Desk Reference. *v.5 p.388*

Scientific and Common Names of 7,000 Vascular Plants in the United States. *v.5 p.207*

Scientific and Technical Acronyms, Symbols, and Abbreviations. *v.5 p.387*

Scientific and Technical Acronyms, Symbols and Abbreviations. *v.5 p.386*

Scientific and Technical Organizations and Agencies Directory. *v.5 p.386*

Scientific Basis for Nuclear Waste Management XXVII: Proceedings of 27th International Symposium on Scientific Basis for Nuclear Waste Management, Vol. 807. . . . .*v.5 p.372, p.375, p.376*

Scientific Basis for Nuclear Waste Management XXVIII: 2004 MRS Spring Meeting Symposium Proceedings, Vol. 824. . . . .*v.5 p.375*

The Scientific Basis of the Art of Teaching. .*v.4 p.347, v.5 p.573*

Scientific Computing: An Introductory Survey. *v.5 p.337*

The Scientific Credibility of Folk Psychology. *v.5 p.596*

Scientific Electronic Library Online (Scielo). *v.3 p.259*

Scientific Elite: Nobel Laureates in the United States. .*v.5 p.399*

Scientific Explanation and the Causal Structure of the World. *v.5 p.404*

Scientific Inference. *v.5 p.402*

Scientific Information in Wartime: An Allied-German Rivalry, 1939-1945. . . . .*v.3 p.81*

Scientific Method: Optimizing Applied Research Decisions. *v.5 p.408*

Scientific Papers and Presentations. *v.5 p.680*

Scientific Papers of J. Willard Gibbs: Dynamics, Vector Analysis, Multiple Algebra, Electromagnetic Theory of Light, Vol. 2. . . . .*v.5 p.385*

The Scientific Papers of J. Willard Gibbs: Thermodynamics, Vol. 1. . . . .*v.5 p.385*

Scientific Renaissance, 1450-1630. . . . .*v.5 p.391*

The Scientific Revolution: A Historiographical Inquiry. *v.3 p.46, v.5 p.390*

The Scientific Revolution. *v.3 p.48*

Scientific Romance in Britain, 1890-1950. . . . . .*v.2 p.192*

Scientific Thought 1900-1960: A Selective Survey. .*v.5 p.402*

Scientific Visualization: Techniques and Applications. *v.5 p.337, p.339, p.340*

Scientists against Time. *v.5 p.393*

Scientists and World Order: The Uses of Technical Knowledge in International Organizations. *v.5 p.410, p.412*

Scientists at Work. *v.5 p.80, p.230*

Scientists, Business and the State, 1890-1960. .*v.5 p.394, p.412*

Scientists Debate Gaia: The Next Century. *v.5 p.249*

Scientists, Engineers and Organizations. *v.5 p.398*

Scientists Must Write: A Guide to Better Writing for Scientists, Engineers and Students. *v.5 p.680*

The Scientist's Role in Society: A Comparative Study with a New Introduction. *v.5 p.398*

Scientist's Role in Society: A Comparative Study with a New Introduction. *v.5 p.398*

Scientists since 1660: A Bibliography of Biographies. .*v.5 p.395*

SciFinder Scholar. *v.5 p.256*

Scipio Aemilianus. *v.3 p.24*

SCIRUS. *v.5 p.385*

Scoop: A Novel about Journalists. *v.2 p.388*

The Scope and Authority of the Bible. *v.1 p.616*

The Scopes Trial: A Brief History with Documents. . .*v.4 p.438*

Scorched Earth: How the Fires of Yellowstone Changed America. *v.6 p.283*

Score Reliability: Contemporary Thinking on Reliability Issues. *v.5 p.602*

Scoring Points: Politicians, Activists, and the Lower Federal Court Appointment Process. *v.4 p.525*

Scoring Rubrics in the Classroom: Using Performance Criteria for Assessing and Improving Student Performance. .*v.4 p.285*

Scotland and Nationalism: Scottish Society and Politics, 1707-1977. . . . .*v.3 p.133*

Scott Fitzgerald. *v.2 p.77*

Scott Joplin: A Guide to Research. .*v.1 p.164, p.281, p.282, p.334*

Scottish Education in the Twentieth Century. *v.4 p.336*

Scottish Literacy and the Scottish Identity: Illiteracy and Society in Scotland and Northern England, 1600-1800. . . . .*v.3 p.128, p.132*

The Scottish Novel: From Smollett to Spark. *v.2 p.189*

The Scottish Reformation. *v.1 p.603, p.604, p.609*

The Scottish Tradition in Literature. *v.2 p.165*

Scottsboro: A Tragedy of the American South. *v.4 p.438*

Scoundrel Time. *v.2 p.83*

The Scramble for Africa: White Man's Conquest of the Dark Continent from 1876 to 1912. . . . .*v.3 p.77*

Scramble for Africa... . . . .*v.4 p.583*

The Scramble for Southern Africa: Eighteen Seventy-Seven to Eighteen Ninety-Five. *v.6 p.75*

The Scrapbook in American Life. *v.1 p.765*

Scratches on Our Minds: American Views of China and India. *v.6 p.215*

Scratching the Beat Surface: Essays on New Vision from Blake to Kerouac. *v.2 p.4*

Scratch. *v.2 p.98*

Screaming Monkeys: Critiques of Asian American Images. *v.6 p.89, p.96*

Screams. *v.2 p.532*

Screen Traffic: Movies, Multiplexes, and Global Culture. *v.6 p.345*

Screened Out: Playing Gay in Hollywood from Edison to Stonewall. *v.6 p.415*

Screening Asian Americans. *v.6 p.88, p.89*

Screening Culture, Viewing Politics: An Ethnography of Television, Womanhood, and Nation in Post-Colonial India. *v.6 p.448*

Screening Science: Contexts, Texts and Science in Fifties Science Fiction Film. *v.6 p.320*

Screening Space: The American Science Fiction Film. .*v.6 p.320*

Screening the City. *v.6 p.730*

Screening the Gothic. *v.6 p.326*

Screening the Past: Film and the Representation of History. *v.6 p.314*

Screening the Sexes. *v.6 p.417*

Screeno: Stories and Poems. *v.2 p.119*

The Screenplay: A Blend of Film Form and Content. .*v.6 p.353*

Screenplay: The Foundations of Screenwriting. *v.6 p.352*

Screenplays of the African American Experience. .*v.6 p.330, p.342*

Screenprinting. *v.1 p.760*

The Screens. *v.2 p.519*

The Screenwriter's Bible: A Complete Guide to Writing, Formatting, and Selling Your Script. .*v.6 p.353, p.355, p.357*

The Screenwriter's Sourcebook: A Comprehensive Marketing Guide for Screen and Television Writers. *v.6 p.352*

Screenwriting. *v.6 p.353*

Screwball Comedy: A Genre of Madcap Romance. . .*v.6 p.312*

The Screwball Comedy Films: A History and Filmography, 1934-1942. . . . .*v.6 p.312*

The Screwtape Letters. *v.1 p.597*

Scriabin: Artist and Mystic. *v.1 p.223, p.355*

Scribble Scrabble, Learning to Read and Write: Success with Diverse Teachers, Children and Families. *v.4 p.361*

Scribbling Women: Short Stories by 19th Century American Women. *v.2 p.27*

Scribes and Scholars: A Guide to the Transmission of Greek and Latin Literature. *v.2 p.399*

Scriblerus. *v.2 p.257*

Scripta Minora: Hiero, Agesilaus, Constitution of the Lacedaemonians, Ways and Means, Cavalry Commander, Art of Horsemanship, on Hunting, Constitution of the Athenians. *v.2 p.422*

Scriptores Historiae Augustae: Caracalla. Geta. Opellius Macrinus. Diadumenianus. Elagabalus. Severus Alexander. The Two Maximini. The Three Gordians. Maximus and Balbinus, Vol. 2. . . . .*v.3 p.32, p.33, p.35*

Scriptores Historiae Augustae: Hadrian, Aelius, Antoninus Pius, Marcus Aurelius, L. Verus, Avidius Cassius, Commodus, Pertinax, Didius Julianus, Septimius Severus, Pescennius Niger, Clodius Albinus. *v.3 p.32*

Scriptores Historiae Augustae: The Two Valerians, the Two Gallieni, the Thirty Pretenders, the Deified Claudius, the Deified Aurelian, Tacitus, Probus, Firmus, Saturninus, Proculus and Bonosus, Carus, Carinus and Numerian. *v.3 p.29*

Scripts and Scenarios: The Performance of Comedy in Renaissance Italy. *v.1 p.91, p.106*

Scripture of the Lotus Blossom of the Fine Dharma: The Lotus Sutra. *v.1 p.563*

Scritti francesi. *v.2 p.718*

A Scrupulous Meanness: A Study of Joyce's Early Work. *v.2 p.357*

Scuba Diving. *v.4 p.787, p.847*

Sculptors of the West Portals of Chartres Cathedral. .*v.1 p.781*

Sculpture 1900-1945. . . . .*v.1 p.775*

Sculpture, Glass, and American Museums. *v.1 p.775*

Sculpture in Britain: 1530-1830. . . . .*v.1 p.778*

Sculpture in the Netherlands, Germany, France, and Spain: 1400-1500. . . . .*v.1 p.777*

The Sculpture of Austin Wright. *v.1 p.779, p.780*

Sculpture of Charles Sargeant Jagger. *v.1 p.779*

The Sculpture of David Nash. *v.1 p.778*

The Sculpture of David Wynne, 1974-1992. . . . . .*v.1 p.781*

The Sculpture of Frank Dobson. *v.1 p.780*

The Sculpture of Gilbert Ledward. *v.1 p.780, p.781*

The Sculpture of Hubert Dalwood. *v.1 p.781*

The Sculpture of Indonesia. *v.1 p.777*

The Sculpture of Kenneth Armitage. *v.1 p.782*

The Sculpture of Leon Underwood. *v.1 p.782*

The Sculpture of Maurice Lambert. *v.1 p.781*

The Sculpture of Michael Sandle. *v.1 p.780*

The Sculpture of Nanni di Banco. *v.1 p.778*

The Sculpture of Phillip King. *v.1 p.780*

The Sculpture of Robert Adams. *v.1 p.779*

The Sculpture of Stephen Cox. *v.1 p.778*

The Sculpture of William Turnbull. *v.1 p.779*

Sculpture since 1945. . . . .*v.1 p.775*

SDP: The Birth, Life, and Death of the Social Democratic Party. *v.4 p.606*

The Sea Floor: An Introduction to Marine Geology. . .*v.5 p.429*

Sea Ice: An Introduction to its Physics, Chemistry, Biology and Geology. *v.5 p.430*

Sea of Death. *v.2 p.689*

The Sea of Grass. *v.2 p.113*

Sea of Lentils. *v.2 p.670, p.671*

The Sea of Precious Virtues: A Medieval Islamic Mirror for Princes. *v.6 p.630*

The Sea Peoples: Warriors of the Ancient Mediterranean, 1250-1150 BC. *v.3 p.7*

Sea Power in Medieval Mediterranean: The Catalan-Aragonese Fleet in the War of the Sicilian Vespers. *v.6 p.567*

The Sea, the Sea. *v.2 p.372*

The Sea-Crossed Fisherman. *v.6 p.667*

A Seahorse Year: A Novel. *v.6 p.395*

A Sealed and Secret Kinship: The Culture of Policies and Practices in American Adoption. *v.4 p.32*

Seamus Heaney and the Place of Writing. *v.2 p.352*

Search and Destroy: African-American Males in the Criminal Justice System. *v.4 p.730*

The Search for Arab Democracy: Discourses and Counter-Discourses. *v.4 p.615*

The Search for Beulah Land: The Welsh and the Atlantic Revolution. *v.3 p.132*

The Search for Christian America. *v.1 p.606*

The Search for Data in the Physical and Chemical Sciences. *v.5 p.274*

The Search for English-Canadian Literature: An Anthology of Critical Articles from the Nineteenth and Early Twentieth Centuries. *v.2 p.728*

The Search for Enlightenment: An Introduction to Eighteenth-Century French Writing. *v.2 p.459*

The Search for God in Ancient Egypt. *v.3 p.8*

The Search for Isadora Duncan: The Legend and Legacy of Isadora Duncan. *v.1 p.10*

The Search for JFK. *v.3 p.466*

The Search for Life in the Universe. *v.5 p.74*

The Search for Modern China. *v.6 p.183*

The Search for Non-Newtonian Gravity. *v.5 p.557, p.558*

The Search for Order, 1877-1920. . . . .*v.3 p.402, p.438, p.445*

The Search for Psychic Power: ESP and Parapsychology Revisited. *v.5 p.613*

The Search for Public Policy: Regional Politics and Government Finances in Ecuador, 1830-1940. . . . .*v.3 p.333*

The Search for the Perfect Language. *v.2 p.560*

The Search for the Ultimate Sink: Urban Pollution in Historical Perspective. *v.5 p.358, v.6 p.715*

The Search: How Google and Its Rivals Rewrote the Rules of Business and Transformed Our Culture. *v.4 p.157*

⬜ Search Institute. *v.5 p.672*

Search Party: Collected Poems. *v.2 p.149*

Searching for a Better Society: The Peruvian Economy from 1950. . . . .*v.3 p.331*

Searching for Alternatives: Drug-Control Policy in the United States. *v.5 p.664*

Searching for Emma: Gustave Flaubert and Madame Bovary. *v.2 p.491*

Searching for Jane Austen. *v.2 p.266*

Searching for Memory: The Brain, the Mind, and the Past. *v.5 p.610*

Searching for Peace in Central and South Asia: An Overview of Conflict Prevention and Peacebuilding Activities. *v.4 p.623, p.650*

Searching for Robert Johnson. *v.1 p.259, p.334*

Searching for Safe Spaces: Afro-Caribbean Women Writers in Exile. *v.6 p.478*

Searching for Sustainability: Interdisciplinary Essays in the Philosophy of Conservation Biology. . . .*v.5 p.357, p.378*

Searching the Chemical Literature. *v.5 p.256*

Seascape. *v.2 p.139*

A Season for Justice: The Life and Times of Civil Rights Lawyer Morris Dees. *v.4 p.441*

A Season in Granada: Uncollected Poems and Prose. .*v.2 p.659*

Season of High Adventure: Edgar Snow in China. . .*v.6 p.201*

Season of Migration to the North. *v.6 p.663*

Seasonal Feasts and Festivals. *v.6 p.576*

Seasoned Judgments: Constitutional Rights and American History. *v.4 p.452*

Seasons in the Desert: A Naturalist's Notebook. .*v.5 p.178, p.233*

Seasons Observed. *v.5 p.222*

The Seasons of a Man's Life. *v.4 p.741*

The Seasons of a Woman's Life. *v.4 p.741*

Seasons of Harvest: Essays on the Literature of Lusophone Africa. *v.2 p.693*

The Seasons. *v.2 p.263*

Seat of Empire: The Political Role of Eighteenth. . .*v.3 p.499*

The Seats and Causes of Diseases. *v.5 p.510*

Seats and Votes: The Effects and Determinants of Electoral Systems. *v.4 p.578*

The Sea. *v.2 p.330*

Seawater: Its Composition, Properties and Behaviour. .*v.5 p.429*

Seaweed Ecology and Physiology. *v.5 p.208*

The Secession Conventions of the South. .*v.3 p.365, p.421, p.422*

The Secessionist Impulse: Alabama and Mississippi in 1860. . . . .*v.3 p.504*

The Second Amendment in Law and History: Historians and Constitutional Scholars on the Right to Bear Arms. *v.4 p.449*

The Second Book. *v.2 p.811*

A Second Census of Finnegans Wake: An Index of the Characters and Their Roles. Rev. and Expanded from the First Census. *v.2 p.358*

Second Chambers. *v.4 p.574*

A Second Chicago School?: The Development of a Postwar American Sociology. *v.4 p.682*

The Second Common Reader. *v.2 p.394*

A Second Edition of the General Theory, Vol. 1. . .*v.4 p.227*

The Second Generation: Ethnic Identity among Asian Americans. *v.6 p.122, p.124*

Second Home: Life in a Boarding School. *v.4 p.297*

The Second Information Revolution. *v.4 p.420*

Second International Handbook of Mathematics Education. *v.5 p.462*

The Second Maiden's Tragedy. *v.2 p.221*

Second Nature: Environmental Enrichment for Captive Animals. *v.5 p.85*

The Second Nature of Things. *v.5 p.221*

Second Nature: Poems. *v.2 p.806*

Second Nature: The History and Implications of Australia as Aboriginal Landscape. *v.6 p.297*

The Second Practice of Nineteenth Century Tonality. *v.1 p.199, p.371*

The Second Republic. *v.3 p.189*

The Second Sex. *v.4 p.743, v.6 p.366, p.427*

The Second Shift. *v.6 p.467*

Second Skin. *v.2 p.83*

The Second Tree from the Corner. *v.2 p.133*

Secondary Schools at the Turn of the Century. .*v.4 p.329, p.367*

Second-Class Citizen. *v.2 p.754*

La seconde semaison : carnets, 1980-1994. . . . .*v.2 p.531*

Second-Hand Souls: Selected Writing. *v.2 p.816*

Secrecy and Power: The Life of J. Edgar Hoover. . .*v.6 p.259*

The Secret Adversary. *v.2 p.339*

The Secret Agent: A Simple Tale. *v.2 p.340*

Secret Dialogues: Church-State Relations, Torture and Social Justice in Authoritarian Brazil. *v.3 p.277*

The Secret Diary of William Byrd of Westover, 1709-1712. . . . .*v.3 p.499*

The Secret File of Joseph Stalin: A Hidden Life. . .*v.3 p.223*

Secret Gardens, Satanic Mills: Placing Girls in European History, 1750-1960. . . . .*v.3 p.54*

The Secret History of Gender: Women, Men, and Power in Late Colonial Mexico. *v.3 p.288, v.6 p.452*

The Secret History of the Mongols: The Origin of Chingis Khan. *v.6 p.239*

Secret Judgments of God: Old World Disease in Colonial Spanish America. *v.3 p.350*

Secret Knowledge: Rediscovering the Lost Techniques of the Old Masters. *v.1 p.751*

Secret Leaves: The Novels of Walter Scott. *v.2 p.308*

The Secret Life of Bees. *v.2 p.160*

The Secret Life of Oscar Wilde: An Intimate Biography. *v.6 p.402, p.403*

The Secret Life of Saeed: The Pessoptimist. *v.6 p.659*

Secret Lives: And Other Stories. *v.2 p.759*

The Secret Lives of Girls: What Good Girls Really Do--Sex Play, Aggression, and Their Guilt. *v.5 p.641*

The Secret Lore of Egypt: Its Impact on the West. *v.3 p.9*

The Secret Middle Ages: Discovering the Real Medieval World. *v.6 p.555*

Secret Muses: The Life of Frederick Ashton. *v.6 p.414*

The Secret of Childhood. *v.4 p.344*

The Secret of Life: Redesigning the Living World. . .*v.5 p.154*

The Secret of Natural Readers: How Preschool Children Learn to Read. *v.4 p.370*

The Secret of the Hittites: The Discovery of an Ancient Empire. *v.3 p.6*

Secret Service: Untold Stories of Lesbians in the Military. *v.6 p.389*

Secret Sharers in Italian Comedy: From Machiavelli to Goldoni. *v.2 p.698*

The Secret Societies of All Ages and Countries. *v.4 p.719*

The Secret Treachery of Words: Feminism and Modernism in America. *v.2 p.11*

The Secret War in Central America: Sandinista Assault on World Order. *v.3 p.302*

Secret Worlds. *v.5 p.221*

The Secretariat of the United Nations. *v.4 p.632*

Los Secretos de la Olla. Entre el Gusto y La Necesidad: La Alimentación en la Córdoba de Principios del Siglo XX. *v.3 p.272*

Secrets and Lies: Digital Security in a Networked World. *v.5 p.335, p.342, p.343, p.344*

Secrets of Customer Relationship Management: It's All about How You Make Them Feel. *v.4 p.143*

The Secrets of Great Sales Management: Advanced Strategies for Maximizing Performance. *v.4 p.143*

Secrets of Screen Acting. *v.6 p.348*

Secrets of Special Ops Leadership: Dare the Impossible—Achieve the Extraordinary. *v.4 p.70*

Secrets of the Chinese Drama: A Complete Explanatory Guide to Actions and Symbols as Seen in the Performance of Chinese Dramas. *v.1 p.61, p.132*

Secrets of the Lotus: Studies in Buddhist Meditation. .*v.1 p.565*

Secrets of the Soul: A Social and Cultural History of Psychoanalysis. *v.4 p.692*

Secrets of the Temple: How the Federal Reserve Runs the Country. *v.4 p.246*

Secular Furniture of E. W. Godwin: With Catalogue Raisonné. *v.1 p.802, p.805*

The Secular Mind. *v.5 p.633*

Secularism and Revivalism in Turkey: A Hermeneutic Reconsideration. *v.6 p.623*

Secularism, Gender and the State in the Middle East: The Egyptian Women's Movement. *v.6 p.636*

The Secularization of the European Mind in the Nineteenth Century. *v.1 p.545*

Secure Base: Parent-Child Attachment and Healthy Human Development. *v.4 p.735*

Secure from Rash Assault: Sustaining the Victorian Environment. *v.6 p.296, p.297, p.759, p.766*

Securing Our Children's Future: New Approaches to Juvenile Justice and Youth Violence. *v.6 p.248*

Securing Our Dance Heritage: Issues in the Documentation and Preservation of Dance. *v.1 p.52*

Security Analysis. *v.4 p.94*

The Security Dilemmas of Southeast Asia. *v.4 p.643*

Sediment Transport and Depositional Processes. . . .*v.5 p.439*

Sedimentary Basins: Evolution, Facies and Sediment Budget. *v.5 p.438*

Sedimentary Environments: Processes, Facies and Stratigraphy. *v.5 p.438*

Sedimentary Petrology. *v.5 p.439*

Sedimentary Rocks in the Field. *v.5 p.420*

Sedimentary Structures, 1 Vol. *v.5 p.439*

Sedimentary Structures, Vol. 2. . . . .*v.5 p.439*

Sedimentology and Geochemistry of Modern and Ancient Saline Lakes. *v.5 p.438, p.439*

Sedimentology and Sedimentary Basins: From Turbulence to Tectonics. *v.5 p.438*

Sedimentology and Stratigraphy. *v.5 p.446*

Sediments of Time: Environment and Society in Chinese History. *v.6 p.184, p.185, p.198*

Seduced and Abandoned: Essays on Gay Men and Popular Music. *v.6 p.408*

Seduction and Betrayal: Women and Literature. . . .*v.2 p.575*

The Seduction of Culture in German History. *v.3 p.178*

The Seduction of the Mediterranean: Writing, Art and Homosexual Fantasy. *v.6 p.391*

The Seduction of Unreason: The Intellectual Romance with Fascism from Nietzsche to Postmodernism. *v.4 p.510*

See Under. *v.6 p.648*

The Seed and the Soil: Gender and Cosmology in Turkish Village Society. *v.6 p.621*

The Seed Is Mine: The Life of Kas Maine, a South African Sharecropper, 1894-1985. . . . .*v.6 p.79*

Seed Production of Agricultural Crops. *v.5 p.47*

Seed Production: Principles and Practices. *v.5 p.48*

Seed to Civilization: The Story of Food. *v.5 p.4*

The Seed Was Planted: The Sao Paulo Roots of Brazil's Rural Labor Movement, 1888-1988. . . . .*v.3 p.343*

Seeds Handbook: Biology, Production, Processing, and Storage, Vol. 103. . . . .*v.5 p.21, p.47*

Seeds of Change: A Quincentennial Commemoration. .*v.3 p.273*

Seeds of Contention: World Hunger and the Global Controversy over Genetically Modified Crops. *v.5 p.8, p.33*

Seeds of Corruption. *v.6 p.662*

Seeds of Destruction: Nationalist China in War and Revolution, 1937-1949. . . . . *v.6 p.190*

Seeds of Destruction. *v.1 p.643*

Seeds of Extinction: Jeffersonian Philanthropy and the American Indian. *v.6 p.686*

Seeds of Fire: Chinese Voices of Conscience. . *v.6 p.196, p.212*

Seeds of Hope: A Henri Nouwen Reader. *v.1 p.577*

Seeds of Liberty: The Genesis of the American Mind. .*v.3 p.369*

Seeds of Repression: Harry S. Truman and the Orgins of McCarthyism. *v.3 p.480*

The Seeds of Speech: Language Origin and Evolution. *v.5 p.620, p.622*

Seeds: Physiology of Development and Germination. *v.5 p.20, p.47*

Seedtime for Fascism: The Disintegration of Austrian Political Culture, 1867-1918. . . . .*v.4 p.510, p.595*

Seedtime. *v.2 p.531*

Seeing America: Women Photographers Between the Wars. *v.1 p.706, p.764*

Seeing Hardy: Film and Television Adaptations of the Fiction of Thomas Hardy. *v.6 p.326*

Seeing High and Low: Representing Social Conflict in American Visual Culture. *v.1 p.708*

Seeing Indians: A Study of Race, Nation, and Power in el Salvador. *v.3 p.299, p.300*

Seeing Mary Plain: A Life of Mary McCarthy. *v.2 p.99*

Seeing the Newspaper. *v.4 p.409*

Seeing Through Paintings: Physical Examination in Art Historical Studies. *v.1 p.751*

Seeing Through Zen: Encounter, Transformation, and Genealogy in Chinese Chan Buddhism. *v.1 p.568*

Seeing What's Next: Using the Theories of Innovation to Predict Industry Change. *v.4 p.65, p.81*

Seeing with Their Hearts: Chicago Women and the Vision of the Good City, 1871-1933. . . . .*v.6 p.454*

The Seeker and Other Poems. *v.2 p.615*

Seeking Common Ground: Public Schools in a Diverse Society. *v.4 p.298*

Seeking Community in a Global City: Guatemalans and Salvadorans in Los Angeles. *v.6 p.542, p.549*

Seeking Justices: The Judging of Supreme Court Nominees. *v.4 p.535*

Seeking Security: Pathogens, Open Access, and Genome Databases. *v.5 p.139*

Seeking St. Louis: Voices from a River City, 1670-2000. .*v.3 p.512*

Seeking the Centre: The Australian Desert in Literature, Art and Film. *v.2 p.740*

Seelenarbeit: Roman. *v.2 p.619*

Seen and Heard: A Century of Arab Women in Literature and Culture. *v.6 p.479, p.662*

The Seen and Unseen Worlds in Java, 1726-1749: History, Literature and Islam in the Court of Pakubuwana II..*v.6 p.177*

Segu. *v.2 p.536*

Seismic Design Criteria for Structures, Systems, and Components in Nuclear Facilities. *v.5 p.686*

Seismology and Plate Tectonics. *v.5 p.442, p.444*

Seize the Day. *v.2 p.60*

Seize the Time: The Story of the Black Panther Party and Huey P. Newton. *v.6 p.13*

Seizing the Word: History, Art, and Self in the Work of W. E. B. Du Bois. *v.2 p.36*

The Seizure of Power: Fascism in Italy, 1919-1929. . *v.3 p.202*

Sekou Toure's Guinea: An Experiment in National Building. *v.6 p.73*

Le sel noir ; Le sang rivé ; Boises. *v.2 p.537*

A Select Body: The Gay Dance Party Subculture and the HIV/AIDS Pandemic. *v.6 p.414*

Select British Eloquence: Embracing the Best Speeches. . . for the Last Two Centuries. *v.2 p.197*

Select Letters. *v.2 p.429*

Select Translations from Old English Poetry: The Literature Which Inspired Tolkien's Lord of the Rings. *v.2 p.196*

Selected and Last Poems. *v.2 p.160*

Selected Classic Papers from the History of Chemistry. *v.5 p.262*

Selected Critical Writings. *v.2 p.363*

Selected Criticism: Prose, Poetry. *v.2 p.567, p.568*

Selected Cronicas. *v.2 p.691*

Selected Essays of William Carlos Williams. *v.2 p.136*

Selected Essays on the Plays and Fiction of Luigi Pirandello. *v.2 p.722*

Selected Essays: Viacheslav Ivanov. *v.2 p.804, p.805*

Selected Film Criticism, 1896-1911. . . . .*v.6 p.306*

Selected Film Criticism, 1912-1920, Vol. 2. . . . . .*v.6 p.306*

Selected Film Criticism, 1921-1930. . . . .*v.6 p.306*

Selected Film Criticism, 1931-1940. . . . .*v.6 p.306*

Selected Film Criticism, 1941-1950. . . . .*v.6 p.306*

Selected Film Criticism, 1951-1960, Vol. 7. . . . . .*v.6 p.306*

Selected Film Criticism: Foreign Films, 1930-1950. . *v.6 p.306*

Selected Letters and Journals. *v.2 p.242*

Selected Letters of Berlioz. *v.1 p.200, p.310, p.311*

Selected Letters of Bret Harte. *v.2 p.40*

Selected Letters of Charles Baudelaire: The Conquest of Solitude. *v.2 p.487*

Selected Letters of Ezra Pound and William Carlos Williams. *v.2 p.112, p.136*

Selected Letters of Hamlin Garland. *v.2 p.39*

Selected Letters of Horace Walpole. . . .*v.3 p.108, p.110, p.130*

Selected Letters of James Joyce. *v.2 p.358*

Selected Letters of Marquis de Sade. *v.2 p.483*

Selected Letters of Philip Larkin, 1940-1985. . . . .*v.2 p.361*

The Selected Letters of Rebecca West. *v.2 p.389*

Selected Letters of Robert Louis Stevenson. *v.2 p.312*

The Selected Letters of Robinson Jeffers, 1897-1962. . *v.2 p.91*

Selected Letters of Stephane Mallarme. *v.2 p.496*

Selected Letters. *v.2 p.299, p.449, p.491*

Selected Literary Criticism. *v.2 p.575*

Selected Non-Fictions. *v.2 p.678*

Selected Operas and Plays of Gertrude Stein. *v.2 p.122*

Selected Papers in Anthropology. *v.4 p.3*

Selected Papers on Calculus. *v.5 p.485*

Selected Papers on Economic Theory. *v.4 p.241*

Selected Papers on Geometry. *v.5 p.495*

Selected Papers on Precalculus. *v.5 p.485*

Selected Papers. *v.4 p.197*

Selected Philosophical Writings. *v.1 p.434, v.2 p.480*

Selected Plays and Libretti, Vol. 3. . . . .*v.2 p.609*

Selected Plays of Louis MacNeice. *v.2 p.369*

Selected Plays: The Duke of Milan, the Roman Actor, A New
    Way to Pay Old Debts, the City Madam. *v.2 p.221*

Selected Plays. *v.2 p.264, p.265*

Selected Poems, 1957-1987. . . . .*v.2 p.116*

Selected Poems 1957-1994. . . . .*v.2 p.353*

Selected Poems, 1958-1984. . . . .*v.2 p.159*

Selected Poems: 1965-1975. . . . .*v.2 p.734*

Selected Poems: A Bilingual Edition. *v.2 p.723*

Selected Poems and Letters of Arthur Rimbaud: Parallel Text
    Edition with Plain Prose Translations of Each
    Poem. *v.2 p.498, p.499*

Selected Poems and Related Prose. *v.2 p.718*

Selected Poems: Bilingual Edition. *v.2 p.517*

Selected Poems: Dryden. *v.2 p.246*

Selected Poems: E. J. Pratt. *v.2 p.738*

Selected Poems: Henry Howard, Earl of Surrey. .*v.2 p.214, p.215*

Selected Poems II: 1976 - 1986. . . . .*v.2 p.734*

Selected Poems of Antonio Machado. *v.2 p.661*

The Selected Poems of Buddhadeva Bose. *v.6 p.151*

Selected Poems of C. N. Bialik. *v.6 p.648*

Selected Poems of Cyprian Norwid. *v.2 p.791*

The Selected Poems of Denise Levertov. *v.2 p.149*

Selected Poems of Eugenio Montale. *v.2 p.718, p.719*

The Selected Poems of Federico Garcia Lorca. . . .*v.2 p.659*

Selected Poems of Fulke Greville. *v.2 p.214*

Selected Poems of Luis Cernuda. *v.2 p.657*

Selected Poems of Marilyn Hacker,
    1965-1990. . . . .*v.2 p.146, v.6 p.405*

Selected Poems of Padraic Colum. *v.2 p.337*

Selected Poems of Rene Char. *v.2 p.513*

Selected Poems of Robert Duncan. *v.2 p.69*

The Selected Poems of Ronsard. *v.2 p.472*

Selected Poems of Ruben Dario: A Bilingual Anthology. *v.2 p.675*

Selected Poems of Rumi. *v.6 p.672*

Selected Poems of Tudor Arghezi. *v.2 p.816*

Selected Poems of Victor Hugo: A Bilingual Edition. *v.2 p.493*

Selected Poems of Wendell Berry. *v.2 p.141*

Selected Poems: Pascoli. *v.2 p.720*

Selected Poems: Sir Walter Scott. *v.2 p.307*

Selected Poems: Swift. *v.2 p.263*

Selected Poems: The Vision Tree. *v.2 p.739*

Selected Poems: Victor Hugo. *v.2 p.494*

Selected Poems. *v.2 p.63, p.69, p.150, p.156, p.313, p.345, p.367,*
    p.380, p.494, p.503, p.531, p.606, p.607, p.615, p.677, p.735,
    p.747, p.748, p.801, v.6 p.153, p.663

Selected Poetry, 1937-1990. . . . .*v.2 p.690*

Selected Poetry and Drama. *v.6 p.648*

Selected Poetry and Prose. *v.2 p.602, p.791*

Selected Poetry of Archibald Lampman. *v.2 p.732*

The Selected Poetry of Dan Pagis. *v.6 p.651*

The Selected Poetry of Robinson Jeffers. *v.2 p.91*

The Selected Poetry of Vicente Huidobro. *v.2 p.680*

The Selected Poetry of Yehuda Amichai. *v.6 p.647*

Selected Poetry. *v.2 p.379, p.815*

Selected Political Writings [of] Rosa Luxemburg. . . .*v.4 p.236*

Selected Problems in Real Analysis. *v.5 p.490*

Selected Prose and Prose-Poems. *v.2 p.681*

Selected Prose of Christina Rossetti. *v.2 p.304*

Selected Prose of Ezra Pound, 1909-1965. . . . . .*v.2 p.112*

The Selected Prose of Fernando Pessoa. *v.2 p.689*

Selected Prose of Louis MacNeice. *v.2 p.368, p.369*

Selected Prose of Robert Duncan. *v.2 p.69*

Selected Prose, Vol. 1. . . . .*v.2 p.609*

Selected Prose. *v.2 p.57*

Selected Sermons, Prayers and Devotions. *v.1 p.575*

Selected Sermons. *v.2 p.449*

Selected Short Stories of John O'Hara. *v.2 p.107*

Selected Short Stories of Padraic Colum. *v.2 p.337*

A Selected Socio-Legal Bibliography on Ethnic Cleansing,
    Wartime Rape, and Genocide in the Former Yugoslavia and
    Rwanda. *v.4 p.654*

Selected Sonnets: A Bilingual Edition. *v.2 p.688*

Selected Stories from the Southern Review, 1965-1985. *v.2 p.27*

Selected Stories of E. M. Forster. *v.2 p.346*

The Selected Stories of Guy de Maupassant. *v.2 p.497*

Selected Stories of Lu Xun. *v.6 p.213*

Selected Stories of Mary E. Wilkins Freeman. *v.2 p.37*

The Selected Stories of Mavis Gallant. *v.2 p.735*

The Selected Stories of Patricia Highsmith. *v.2 p.86*

Selected Stories of Sylvia Townsend Warner. *v.2 p.387*

Selected Stories. *v.2 p.737*

Selected Subaltern Studies. *v.6 p.146*

Selected Takes: Film Editors on Editing. *v.6 p.350*

Selected Tales. *v.2 p.791*

Selected Values of Chemical Thermodynamic
    Properties. *v.5 p.286, p.287*

Selected Values of Physical and Thermodynamic Properties of
    Hydrocarbons and Related Compounds. *v.5 p.286*

Selected Values of the Thermodynamic Properties of the
    Elements. *v.5 p.286*

Selected Values of Thermodynamic Properties of Binary
    Alloys. *v.5 p.286*

Selected Verse. *v.2 p.659*

Selected Works of Djuna Barnes. *v.2 p.58*

Selected Works of Frances Yates, Set. *v.1 p.473*

Selected Works of Ion Creanga and Mihai
    Eminescu. *v.2 p.815, p.816*

☐ Selected Works of Mao Tse-Tung. *v.6 p.202*

Selected Works of Stephen Vincent Benet. *v.2 p.61*

Selected Works of Zinaida Hippius. *v.2 p.804*

Selected Works. *v.2 p.720*

Selected Writings and Speeches of Marcus Garvey. . .*v.6 p.12*

Selected Writings (Dario, Ruben). *v.2 p.675*

Selected Writings of Andres Bello. *v.2 p.687*

Selected Writings of Apollinaire. *v.2 p.507*

Selected Writings of Artaud. *v.2 p.507*

Selected Writings of Charles Olson. *v.2 p.108*

The Selected Writings of Christine de Pizan: New Translations, Criticism. *v.2 p.468, p.469*

Selected Writings of Edward Sapir in Language, Culture, and Personality. *v.4 p.20, v.5 p.624*

Selected writings of E.T.A. Hoffmann. *v.2 p.599*

Selected Writings of Gertrude Stein. *v.2 p.122*

The Selected Writings of James Weldon Johnson: Social, Political, and Literary Essays, Vol. II. *v.2 p.90*

Selected Writings of Jean Genet. *v.2 p.519*

Selected Writings of Nichiren. *v.1 p.567, v.6 p.221*

Selected Writings of Walter Pater. *v.2 p.302*

The Selected Writings of William Hazlitt. . . .*v.2 p.292, p.293*

Selected Writings. .*v.1 p.431, p.442,v.2 p.39, p.40, p.516, p.517, p.672*

Selecting the President: From 1789 to 1996. . . . . .*v.4 p.526*

Selection in Natural Populations. *v.5 p.189, p.194*

A Selection of English Carols. *v.2 p.199*

A Selection of Greek Historical Inscriptions to the End of the Fifth Century B. C. *v.3 p.18*

Selection: The Mechanism of Evolution. *v.5 p.190*

Selections from Cotton Mather. *v.1 p.584*

Selections from Cultural Writings. *v.2 p.568*

Selections from Don Quixote: A Dual-Language Book. .*v.2 p.648*

Selections from the Attic Orators: Antiphon, Andocides, Lysias, Isocrates and Isaeus. *v.2 p.405*

Selections from the Canzoniere and Other Works. . . .*v.2 p.706*

Selections: Poetry, Prose. *v.2 p.815*

A Selective Guide to Chinese Literature, 1900-1949: The Poem. *v.6 p.211*

Selena: Como la Flor. *v.6 p.490, p.519*

The Self and Its Brain. *v.5 p.619*

Self and Social Identity. *v.4 p.693, v.5 p.653*

The Self and the Dramas of History. *v.1 p.643*

Self Expressions: Mind, Morals, and the Meaning of Life. *v.5 p.652*

Self Help Graphics and Art: Chicano Art in the Heart of East Los Angeles. *v.6 p.492*

The Self We Live By: Narrative Identity in a Postmodern World. *v.5 p.653*

Self-Awareness in Animals and Humans: Developmental Perspectives. *v.5 p.615*

Self-Determination and the Social Education of Native Americans. *v.4 p.312, v.6 p.680, p.692*

Self-Directed Behavior: Self-Modification for Personal Adjustment. *v.5 p.669*

The Self-Dismembered Man: Selected Later Poems of Guillaume Apollinaire. *v.2 p.506, p.507*

Self-Esteem: The Puzzle of Low Self-Regard. *v.5 p.651*

Self-Help: Concepts and Applications. *v.5 p.669*

Self-Help Group Sourcebook: Your Guide to Community and Online Support Groups. *v.5 p.669, p.670*

Self-Help, Inc: Makeover Culture in American Life. .*v.5 p.669*

The Self-Help Movement. *v.5 p.669*

Self-Organisation and Evolution of Biological and Social Systems. *v.5 p.193*

Self-Organization in Biological Systems. *v.5 p.155*

Self-Organizing Maps. *v.5 p.340, p.341*

The Self-Overcoming of Nihilism. *v.1 p.509*

Self-Portrait in a Convex Mirror: Poems. *v.2 p.57*

Self-Portrait of the Other. *v.3 p.312*

Self-Portraits, the Gide-Valery Letters, 1890-1942. . .*v.2 p.520*

Self-Taught: African American Education in Slavery and Freedom. *v.6 p.21, p.37*

A Selftold Life. *v.2 p.603*

Selling Destinations: Geography for the Travel Professional. *v.4 p.161*

Selling It!: The Incredible Shrinking Package and Other Marvels of Modern Marketing. *v.4 p.144*

The Selling of Supreme Court Nominees. *v.4 p.537*

The Selling of the President. *v.3 p.449*

Selling Places: The Marketing and Promotion of Towns and Cities, 1850-2000. . . . .*v.6 p.715, p.716*

Selling Seattle: Representing Contemporary Urban America. *v.3 p.443*

Selling the Five Rings: The IOC and the Rise of Olympic Commercialism. . . .*v.4 p.845, p.886, p.887, p.890, p.901*

Selling the Sea: An Inside Look at the Cruise Industry. .*v.4 p.161*

Selling War: The British Propaganda Campaign Against American Neutrality in World War II. .*v.4 p.643, p.646, p.647*

Selling Water by the River: A Manual of Zen Training. .*v.1 p.568*

Selling Without Selling: 4 1/2 Steps to Success. *v.4 p.143*

Selling Yellowstone: Capitalism and the Construction of Nature. *v.6 p.297, p.298*

Selu: Seeking the Corn-Mother's Widsom. .*v.6 p.680, p.704, p.705*

Semantic Approach to English Grammar. *v.2 p.556*

Semiconductor Physics: An Introduction. *v.5 p.555*

Semiotics and Interpretation. *v.2 p.571*

Semiotics and the Analysis of Film. *v.6 p.327*

Semiotics of Deceit: Language, Drama, and Culture in Maistre Pierre Pathelin. *v.2 p.467*

Semiparametric Regression for the Applied Econometrician. *v.4 p.205*

The Semitic Background of the New Testament. . . .*v.6 p.664*

The Semitic Languages. *v.6 p.665*

Semitic Writing: From Pictograph to Alphabet. . . .*v.6 p.664*

Semper Fidelis: The History of the United States Marine Corps. *v.3 p.383*

Senate Elections and Campaign Intensity. . . .*v.4 p.550, p.557*

The Senate of Imperial Rome. *v.4 p.501*

Senator Gerald P. Nye and American Foreign Relations. .*v.3 p.457*

Senator Joe McCarthy. *v.3 p.462*

Senators on the Campaign Trail: The Politics of Representation. *v.4 p.550, p.557*

Seneca: A Philosopher in Politics. *v.4 p.489*

Seneca: De Otio; de Brevitate Vitae. *v.2 p.443*

Seneca: Phaedra. *v.2 p.443*

Seneca: Select Letters. *v.2 p.443*

Seneca the Elder Declamations, Vol. 1. . . . .*v.2 p.443*

Seneca: The Tragedies. *v.1 p.73, p.89*

Seneca's Thyestes. *v.2 p.443*

Senior Fitness Test Manual. *v.4 p.841, p.880*

El Senor Presidente (The Honorable Mister President). .*v.2 p.675*

El Senor Presidente. *v.2 p.674, p.675*

Sensational Designs: The Cultural Work of American Fiction,
 1790-1860. . . . .*v.2 p.10*

Sensational Victorian: The Life and Fiction of Mary Elizabeth
 Braddon. *v.2 p.265*

Sense and Nonsense about Crime and Drugs: A Policy
 Guide. *v.4 p.568, v.6 p.247*

Sense and Non-Sense. *v.1 p.457*

Sense and Sensibilia. *v.1 p.481*

Sense and Sensibility. *v.2 p.267, p.268*

The Sense of an Ending: Studies in the Theory of
 Fiction. *v.1 p.632, v.2 p.568*

The Sense of Beauty. *v.1 p.440*

The Sense of Hearing. *v.5 p.607*

Sense of History: The Place of the Past in American
 Life. *v.3 p.374, p.376*

The Sense of Shakespeare's Sonnets. *v.2 p.225*

Sense of Siege: The Geopolitics of Islam and the
 West. *v.4 p.488, p.495*

A Sense of the Morning. *v.5 p.222*

Senseless Acts of Beauty: Cultures of Resistance since the
 Sixties. *v.4 p.709*

The Senses Considered As Perceptual Systems. . . .*v.5 p.606*

Sensing Feeling and Action: The Experiential Anatomy of
 Body-Mind Centering. *v.1 p.51, p.52*

Sensing the Self: Women's Recovery from Bulimia. . .*v.5 p.524*

Sensory Exotica: A World Beyond Human
 Experience. *v.5 p.614, p.615*

Sensuous Scholarship: Contemporary Ethnography. . . .*v.4 p.25*

Sent for You Yesterday. *v.2 p.159*

Sentencing Matters. *v.6 p.272*

Sentimental Education. *v.2 p.490*

A Sentimental Journey Through France and Italy by Mr. Yorick:
 With the Journal to Eliza and a Political Romance. .*v.2 p.262*

The Sentimental Novel in America, 1789-1860. . . . .*v.2 p.9*

Separate and Unequal: Black Americans and the U. S. Federal
 Government. *v.4 p.524*

Separate but Unequal: Homer Plessy and the Supreme Court
 Decision that Legalized Racism. *v.4 p.536*

A Separate Creation: The Search for the Biological Origins of
 Sexual Orientation. *v.6 p.420*

A Separate Peace. *v.2 p.92*

The Separate Rose/la Rosa Separada. *v.2 p.681*

Separating Together: How Divorce Transforms
 Families. *v.5 p.640*

Separation, Assimilation, or Accommodation: Contrasting Ethnic
 Minority Policies. *v.4 p.764*

Separation Methods in Proteomics. *v.5 p.118*

The Separation of Church and State: Writings on a Fundamental
 Freedom by America's Founders. *v.1 p.656*

The Separation of Commercial and Investment Banking: The
 Glass-Steagall Act Revisited and Reconsidered. .*v.4 p.90, p.91*

Separation Processes in the Food and Biotechnology Industries :
 PrInciples and Applicaitons. *v.5 p.741*

Separation, Purification and Identification. *v.5 p.268*

Sepharad. *v.2 p.661*

Sephardi and Middle Eastern Jewries: History and
 Culture. *v.6 p.597*

Les sept couleurs. *v.2 p.508*

Les Sept solitudes de Lorsa Lopez : roman. *v.2 p.546*

Septem Quae Supersunt Tragoediae. *v.2 p.407*

September 11: Consequences for Canada. *v.4 p.661*

September 11 in History: A Watershed Moment? . . .*v.4 p.563*

September 11, Terrorist Attacks, and U. S. Foreign
 Policy. *v.3 p.483*

Septimus Severus: The African Emperor. *v.3 p.27*

Sepulchre of Christ and the Medieval West: From the Beginning
 to 1600. . . . .*v.3 p.57*

Sequence - Evolution - Function: Computational Approaches in
 Comparative Genomics. *v.5 p.102, p.140*

Sequence Analysis in a Nutshell: A Guide to Tools and
 Databases. *v.5 p.102*

Sequence Stratigraphy. *v.5 p.446*

Serbia since 1989: Politics and Society under Milosevic and
 After. *v.3 p.248*

Serbia: The Rise and Fall of a Medieval Empire. . .*v.6 p.562*

Serbia Through the Ages. *v.3 p.248*

Serbian: An Essential Grammar. *v.2 p.777*

Serbian Poetry from the Beginnings to the Present: An
 Historical Anthology. *v.2 p.810, p.811*

Serbian-English/English-Serbian Dictionary and Phrasebook:
 Romanized. *v.2 p.776*

The Serbs: Guardians of the Gate. *v.3 p.248*

Serenade of Suffering: A Portrait of Middle East Terrorism,
 1968-1993. . . . .*v.4 p.658*

Serenading the Reluctant Eagle: American Musical Life During
 Crisis, 1925-1945. . . . .*v.1 p.280*

Serengeti II: Dynamics, Management, and Conservation of an
 Ecosystem. *v.5 p.358*

Serfdom and Social Control in Russia: Petrovskoe, a Village in
 Tambov. *v.3 p.217*

Serfs, Peasants, and Socialists: A Former Serf Village in the
 Republic of Guinea. *v.6 p.73*

Serge Diaghilev: His Life, His Work, His
 Legend. *v.6 p.414, p.415*

Sergei Diaghilev. *v.6 p.415*

Sergei Prokofiev: A Biography. *v.1 p.222, p.349*

Sergei Rachmaninoff: A Lifetime in Music. . . .*v.1 p.209, p.350*

Sergei Witte and the Industrialization of Russia. . . .*v.3 p.221*

Sergey Prokofiev. *v.1 p.216, p.348*

Serial Composition and Atonality: An Introduction to the Music
 of Schoenberg, Berg, and Webern. *v.1 p.372*

Serial Music and Serialism: A Research and Information
 Guide. *v.1 p.169, p.374*

Serializing Fiction in the Victorian Press. . . .*v.6 p.741, p.756*

Serious Accidents and Human Factors: Breaking the Chain of
 Events Leading to an Accident. *v.5 p.718*

Serious Cycling. *v.4 p.856*

Serious Fun: A History of Spectator Sport in the U. S. S.
R. *v.4 p.805*

A Serious Occupation: Literary Criticism by Victorian Women
Writers. *v.2 p.176, p.177, p.203*

Serious Play: How the World's Best Companies Simulate to
Innovate. *v.4 p.67*

A Serious Proposal to the Ladies, Pts. I-II. *v.2 p.237*

Serious Strength Training. *v.4 p.792, p.878*

Serious Tennis. *v.4 p.864*

Sermons and Rhetoric of Kievan Rus'. *v.2 p.813*

The Sermons of Charles Wesley: A Critical Edition with
Introduction and Notes. *v.2 p.264*

The Servant of Two Masters: And Other Italian Classics. .*v.2 p.699*

Servants of Globalization: Women, Migration, and Domestic
Work. *v.6 p.116, p.119, p.130*

Servants of the Map: Stories. *v.2 p.140*

Servants of the State: Managing Diversity and Democracy in the
Federal Workforce, 1933-1953. . . . .*v.4 p.546*

Service-Learning: From Classroom to Community to
Career. *v.4 p.168*

Servicemembers Legal Defense Network (SLDN). .*v.6 p.389*

Serving in Silence. *v.6 p.389*

Serving Proudly: A History of Women in the U. S. Navy. .*v.6 p.454*

Servitude and Grandeur of Arms. *v.2 p.502*

Servitude and Greatness. *v.1 p.195, p.310*

SESAC = Society of European Stage Authors and
Composers. *v.1 p.173, p.385*

Set Fair for Roanoke: Voyages and Colonies,
1584-1606. . . . .*v.3 p.404*

Set Lighting Technician's Handbook: Film Lighting Equipment,
Practice, and Electrical Distribution. *v.6 p.349*

Set This House on Fire. *v.2 p.156*

Sets for Mathematics. *v.5 p.471*

Sets in Motion: Art Direction and Film Narrative. . . .*v.6 p.348*

The Setting of the Sermon on the Mount. *v.1 p.642*

The Setting Sun. *v.6 p.229*

Setting the Agenda: The Mass Media and Public
Opinion. *v.4 p.697*

Setting the Moral Compass: Essays by Women
Philosophers. *v.1 p.506*

Setting the Record Straight: A Material History of Classical
Recording. *v.1 p.385, p.386*

Setting the Record Straight: Responses to Misconceptions about
Public Education in the United States. *v.4 p.325*

Setting the Virgin on Fire: Lázaro Cárdenas, Michoacán
Peasants, and the Redemption of the Mexican
Revolution. *v.3 p.290*

Settlement Ecology: The Social and Spatial Organization of
Kofyar Agriculture. *v.4 p.38, p.39*

The Settlement of the Americas: A New Prehistory. . . .*v.4 p.11*

Settling the Score: Music and the Classical Hollywood
Film. *v.1 p.255, v.6 p.341, p.342*

The Set-up-to-Fail Syndrome: How Good Managers Cause Great
People to Fail. *v.4 p.131*

Seurat: A Biography. *v.1 p.745*

Sevasadan. *v.6 p.152*

The Seven Ages. *v.2 p.146*

Seven Comedies by Marivaux. *v.2 p.481*

Seven Commentaries on the Gallic War. *v.2 p.428*

The Seven Concertos of
Beethoven. *v.1 p.198, p.240, p.306, p.307*

The Seven Dials Mystery. *v.2 p.339*

Seven Faces: Brazilian Poetry since Modernism. . . .*v.2 p.692*

Seven Gothic Tales. *v.2 p.626*

Seven Interpretive Essays on Peruvian Reality. *v.3 p.332*

Seven Men and Two Others. *v.2 p.331*

Seven Metaphysical Poets: A Structural Study of the
Unchanging Self. *v.2 p.182*

Seven Military Classics of Ancient China. *v.6 p.184*

Seven Minutes: The Life and Death of the American Animated
Cartoon. *v.6 p.307*

The Seven Myths of Customer Management: How to be
Customer-Driven Without Being Customer-Led. . .*v.4 p.143*

Seven Myths of the Spanish Conquest. *v.3 p.287*

Seven Plays: Marianne, Fantasio, Don't Trifle with Love, the
Candlestick, a Diversion, a Door Must Open or
Shut, You Can't Think of Everything. *v.2 p.498*

Seven Poor Men of Sydney. *v.2 p.749*

Seven Psychologies. *v.5 p.596*

Seven Puccini Librettos. *v.1 p.202, p.232, p.349, p.409*

The Seven Samurai: And Other Screenplays. *v.6 p.344*

Seven Samurai. *v.6 p.336, p.344*

Seven Schools of Macroeconomic Thought: The Arne Ryde
Memorial Lectures. *v.4 p.240*

Seven Short Plays. *v.2 p.288*

The Seven Sins of Memory: How the Mind Forgets and
Remembers. *v.5 p.610*

The Seven Solitudes of Lorsa Lopez. *v.2 p.546*

Seven Troubadours: The Creators of Modern Verse. .*v.2 p.457*

Seven Types of Ambiguity. *v.2 p.568*

Seven Verdi Librettos. *v.1 p.205, p.234, p.364, p.410*

Seven Years in Tibet. *v.6 p.241*

Seventeen Danish Poets: A Bilingual Anthology of
Contemporary Danish Poetry. *v.2 p.626*

Seventeen Modern German Poets. *v.2 p.593*

Seventeen Syllables and Other Stories. *v.6 p.102*

The Seventeenth Century, 1600-1715. . . . .*v.2 p.456, p.457*

The Seventeenth Century French Paintings: National Gallery
Catalogues. *v.1 p.730*

Seventeenth Century Prose and Poetry. *v.2 p.197*

Seventeenth Century Songs and Lyrics. *v.2 p.198*

Seventeenth-Century Poetry: An Annotated Anthology. *v.2 p.198*

Seventeenth-Century Spanish Poetry. *v.2 p.640*

The Seventh Door and Other Stories. *v.6 p.151*

Seventh Generation: An Anthology of Native American
Plays. *v.1 p.124, v.6 p.697*

The Seventh Million: Israel Confronts the Holocaust. .*v.6 p.615*

The Seventh Stream: The Emergence of Rock N Roll in
American Popular Music. *v.1 p.268*

Seventy Great Mysteries of Ancient Egypt. *v.3 p.9*

Several Papers Relating to Money, Interest and Trade, Etc. . . . . *.v.4 p.216*

The Severans: The Changed Roman Empire. . . . . . .*.v.3 p.28*

A Severed Head. . . . .*.v.2 p.372*

Sevigne: Selected Letters. . . . .*.v.2 p.478*

The Seville Communion. . . . .*.v.2 p.662*

Sewage Processing Guidebook: Production, Energy Recovery, Recycling and Technology Developments for Biosolids and Organic Residuals. . . .*.v.5 p.376, p.378, p.379*

The Sewing Circle: Sappho's Leading Ladies. .*.v.6 p.416, p.417*

🄴 Sewing Women: Immigrants and the New York City Garment Industry. . . . .*.v.6 p.106, p.111, p.113*

Sex, Age, and Work: The Changing Composition of the Labor Force. . . . .*.v.4 p.254, p.269*

Sex among Allies: Military Prostitution in U. S.-Korea Relations. . . . .*.v.6 p.237*

Sex and Advantage: A Comparative, Macro-Structural Theory of Sex Stratification. . . . .*.v.4 p.747*

Sex and Cognition. . . . .*.v.5 p.608*

Sex and Enlightenment: Women in Richardson and Diderot. . . . .*.v.2 p.258*

Sex and Gender. . . . .*.v.4 p.746*

Sex and Germs: The Politics of AIDS. . . . .*.v.6 p.379, p.387*

Sex and Manners: Female Emancipation in the West 1890 - 2000. . . . .*.v.4 p.738*

Sex and Marriage in Utopian Communities : 19th Century America. . . . .*.v.4 p.733*

Sex and Psyche: Gender and Self Viewed Cross-Culturally. . . . .*.v.4 p.693*

Sex and Repression in Savage Society. . . . .*.v.4 p.737*

Sex and Society in the World of the Orthodox Slavs, 900-1700. . . . .*.v.3 p.211*

Sex and Society. . . . .*.v.4 p.749*

Sex and Suffrage in Britain, 1860-1914. . . . .*.v.3 p.53, p.92*

Sex and Temperament: In Three Primitive Societies. . .*.v.4 p.23*

Sex and the Empire That Is No More: Gender and the Politics of Metaphor in Oyo Yoruba Religion. . . .*.v.6 p.71, p.459*

Sex and the Gender Revolution: Heterosexuality and the Third Gender in Enlightenment London. . . . .*.v.3 p.55*

Sex and the Workplace: The Impact of Sexual Behavior and Harassment on Women, Men, and Organizations. . . . .*.v.4 p.253, p.254*

Sex Appeal: The Art of Allure in Graphic and Advertising Design. . . . .*.v.1 p.714*

Sex As a Political Variable: Women As Candidates and Voters in U. S. Elections. . . . .*.v.6 p.442*

Sex Bias in the Schools: The Research Evidence. . . .*.v.4 p.301*

Sex, Botany and Empire: The Story of Carl Linnaeus and Joseph Banks. . . . .*.v.5 p.231*

Sex, Cells, and Same-Sex Desire: The Biology of Sexual Preference. . . . .*.v.6 p.420*

Sex Changes: Transgender Politics. . . . .*.v.4 p.746, v.6 p.370*

Sex, Culture and Modernity in China. . . . .*.v.6 p.190*

Sex Differences and Similarities in Communication. . .*.v.5 p.620*

Sex Differences in Antisocial Behaviour: Conduct Disorder, Delinquency, and Violence in the Dunedin Longitudinal Study. . . . .*.v.5 p.662*

Sex Differences in Depression. . . . .*.v.5 p.660*

Sex Exposed: Sexuality and the Pornography Debate. . . . .*.v.6 p.435, p.447, p.471*

Sex in the Marketplace. . . . .*.v.4 p.273, p.274*

Sex, Longing and Not Belonging: A Gay Muslim's Quest for Love and Meaning. . . . .*.v.6 p.367*

Sex, Politics and Society: The Regulation of Sexuality since 1800. . . . .*.v.4 p.570, p.749, v.6 p.363, p.388*

The Sex Revolts: Gender, Rebellion, and Rock 'n' Roll. *.v.6 p.475*

Sex Roles, Life Styles and Childbearing: Changing Patterns in Marriage and the Family. . . . .*.v.4 p.734*

Sex, Sin, and Grace: Women's Experience and the Theologies of Reinhold Niebuhr and Paul Tillich. . . . .*.v.1 p.643*

Sex Variant Women in Literature. . . . .*.v.6 p.392*

Sex, Violence, and Power in Sports: Rethinking Masculinity. . . . .*.v.4 p.818*

Sex Work: Writings by Women in the Sex Industry. . . . .*.v.6 p.456, p.469*

▢ SEXBIBLIO: Bibliography of the History of Western Sexuality. . . . .*.v.6 p.447*

Sex-Crime Panic: A Journey to the Paranoid Heart of the 1950s. . . . .*.v.6 p.366*

Sexing the Body: Gender Politics and the Construction of Sexuality. . . . .*.v.4 p.747, v.6 p.447*

Sexing the Brain. . . . .*.v.6 p.420*

Sexing the Groove: Popular Music and Gender. . . .*.v.6 p.475*

Sexism and God-Talk: Toward a Feminist Theology. . *.v.1 p.644*

Sextus Empiricus: Against the Logicians. . . . . . .*.v.1 p.517*

Sextus Empiricus: Outlines of Scepticism. . . . . .*.v.1 p.517*

Sexual Anarchy: Gender and Culture at the Fin de Siecle. . . . .*.v.2 p.177*

Sexual Anomalies: The Origin, Nature, and Treatment of Sexual Disorders. . . . .*.v.6 p.381, p.420*

Sexual Assault: The Victims, the Perpetrators, and the Criminal Justice System. . . . .*.v.6 p.252, p.259*

Sexual Behavior in the Human Female. . . .*.v.4 p.748, v.6 p.420*

Sexual Behavior in the Human Male. . . . .*.v.4 p.748, v.6 p.420*

The Sexual Brain. . . . .*.v.6 p.420*

Sexual Conversion Therapy: Ethical, Clincial, and Research Perspectives. . . . .*.v.6 p.382*

Sexual Development in Childhood. . . . .*.v.4 p.746*

Sexual (Dis)Orientation: Gender, Sex, Desire and Self-Fashioning. . . . .*.v.4 p.750, v.6 p.371*

▢ Sexual Diversity Studies: Gay, Lesbian, Bisexual & Transgender Abstracts. . . . .*.v.6 p.361*

The Sexual Education of Edith Wharton. . . . . . .*.v.2 p.131*

Sexual Harassment in American Secondary Schools: A Legal Guide for Administrators, Teachers, and Students. *.v.4 p.450*

Sexual Harassment in Higher Education: Reflections and New Perspectives. . . . .*.v.4 p.301*

Sexual Harassment in Workplace. . . . .*.v.4 p.130*

The Sexual Harassment of Women in the Workplace, 1600-1993. . . . .*.v.4 p.131*

Sexual Harassment of Working Women: A Case of Sex Discrimination. . . . .*.v.4 p.446, p.447*

Sexual Harassment. . . . .*.v.4 p.458*

Sexual Identity on the Job: Issues and Services. . . .*.v.4 p.133*

Sexual Inversion. *v.6 p.381*

Sexual Naturalization: Asian Americans and
    Miscegenation. *v.6 p.96, p.123*

The Sexual Organization of the City. *v.4 p.748*

Sexual Orientation and Gender Expression in Social Work
    Practice: Working with Gay, Lesbian, Bisexual, and
    Transgender People. *v.6 p.381*

Sexual Orientation and Mental Health: Examining Identity and
    Development in Lesbian, Gay, and Bisexual People. .*v.6 p.382*

Sexual Orientation and School Policy: A Practical Guide for
    Teachers, Administrators, and Community Activists. .*v.6 p.385*

Sexual Personae: Art and Decadence from Nefertiti to Emily
    Dickinson. *v.5 p.618*

The Sexual Perspective: Homosexuality and Art in the Last 100
    Years in the West. *v.6 p.407*

Sexual Perversity in Chicago and the Duck
    Variations. *v.1 p.87, p.116*

Sexual Politics, Sexual Communities. . . . *v.4 p.749, v.6 p.365*

Sexual Politics. *v.6 p.479*

Sexual Power in British Romantic Poetry. *v.2 p.280*

Sexual Practices and the Medieval Church. . . *v.4 p.746, p.747*

Sexual Preference: Its Development in Men and
    Women. *v.6 p.371*

Sexual Science: The Victorian Construction of
    Womanhood. *v.6 p.748*

Sexual Variance in Society and History. . . *v.4 p.746, v.6 p.362*

Sexuality: A Glossary. *v.4 p.677*

Sexuality and Eroticism among Males in Moslem
    Societies. *v.6 p.374*

Sexuality and Human Rights: A Global Overview. . . *v.6 p.421*

Sexuality and Medicine in the Middle Ages. *v.3 p.50*

Sexuality and War: Literary Masks of the Middle East. *v.6 p.605*

Sexuality in Islam. *v.1 p.559*

Sexuality in Medieval Europe. *v.3 p.55*

Sexuality in the Confessional: A Sacrament
    Profaned. *v.3 p.55, p.59, p.239*

Sexuality in Western Art. *v.1 p.706*

Sexuality in World Cinema, Set. *v.6 p.317*

The Sexuality of Latinas. *v.6 p.515, p.546*

Sexuality, State, and Civil Society in Germany,
    1700-1815. . . . . *v.3 p.55, p.167*

Sexualized Violence Against Women and Children: A
    Psychology and Law Perspective. *v.6 p.252*

Sexually Transmitted Diseasees in Obstetrics and
    Gynecology. *v.5 p.516*

Sexually Transmitted Diseases. *v.5 p.516*

Sexual/Textual Politics: Feminist Literary Theory. . . *v.6 p.479*

Seymour Lipton: An American Sculptor. *v.1 p.781, p.782*

Seymour/Carraher's Polymer Chemistry, Vol. 16. . . *v.5 p.321*

Sämtliche Romane und Erzählungen. *v.2 p.596*

Sämtliche Werke: ausgewählte Briefe, Gespräche,
    Berichte. *v.2 p.597*

Sämtliche Werke: Briefe, Tagebücher und Gespräche. *v.2 p.597*

Sämtliche Werke in fünf Bänden. *v.2 p.600*

Sämtliche Werke in fünf Einzelbänden. [Mit einem Nachwort
    von Fritz Krökel und Anmerkungen von Karl
    Pörnbacher.]. *v.2 p.602*

Sämtliche Werke in sechs Bänden. *v.2 p.599, p.600*

Sämtliche Werke in zwei Bänden. *v.2 p.596*

Sämtliche Werke in Zwei Bänden. *v.2 p.596*

Sämtliche Werke: krit. Ausg. *v.2 p.609*

Sämtliche Werke und Briefe: historisch-kritische Ausgabe mit
    Kommentar. *v.2 p.596*

Sämtliche Werke und Briefe. *v.2 p.600*

Sämtliche Werke. . .*v.2 p.596, p.600, p.601, p.606, p.609, p.614*

Ségou, les murailles de terre : roman. *v.2 p.536*

A Shabby Genteel Story, and Other Tales. by William M.
    Thackeray. *v.2 p.316*

Shace and Epstein's Business Structures in a Nutshell. *v.4 p.110*

The Shade of Swords: Jihad and the Conflict Between Islam and
    Christianity. *v.1 p.560*

Shaded Lives: African American Women and
    Television. *v.6 p.15, p.46, p.448*

Shades of Blue and Gray: An Introductory Military History of
    the Civil War. *v.3 p.397, p.398*

Shades of Citizenship: Race and the Census in Modern
    Politics. *v.3 p.279*

Shades of Freedom: Racial Politics and Presumptions of the
    American Legal Process Race. *v.4 p.457*

Shades of Hiawatha: Staging Indians, Making Americans,
    1880-1930. . . . . *v.3 p.445*

Shades of Loneliness: Pathologies of a Technological
    Society. *v.4 p.695*

Shades of Mao: The Posthumous Cult of the Great
    Leader. *v.6 p.201*

Shadow Culture: Psychology and Spirituality in
    America. *v.5 p.636*

The Shadow Lines: A Novel. *v.2 p.764*

The Shadow of God and the Hidden Inam: Religion, Political
    Order, and Societal Change in Shi'ite Iran from the
    Beginning to 1890. . . . . *v.6 p.629*

Shadow of Heaven: The Life of Lester Pearson. . . *v.3 p.541*

The Shadow of Keynes: Understanding Keynes, Cambridge, and
    Keynesian Economics. *v.4 p.228*

Shadow of Paradise: Sombra Del Paraiso. *v.2 p.656*

The Shadow of the Wind: A Novel. *v.2 p.662*

The Shadow World: Life Between the News Media and
    Reality. *v.4 p.412, p.413*

Shadowboxing: Representations of Black Feminist
    Politics. *v.6 p.434, p.441*

The Shadow-Line: A Confession. *v.2 p.340*

Shadowplay: The Life of Antony Tudor. *v.1 p.11*

Shadows and Wind: A View of Modern Vietnam. *v.6 p.166, p.167*

Shadows of Blue and Gray: The Civil War Writings of Ambrose
    Bierce. *v.2 p.32*

Shadows of Empire: Colonial Discourse and Javanese
    Tales. *v.6 p.178*

Shadows of Empire: The Indian Nobility of Cusco,
    1750-1825. . . . . *v.3 p.265*

The Shadows of Poetry: Vergil in the Mind of
    Augustine. *v.2 p.430*

Shadows of the Future: H. G. Wells, Science Fiction, and
    Prophecy. *v.2 p.319*

Shadows of the Storm: The Image of War, 1861-1865. *v.3 p.431*

Shadows of Vietnam: Lyndon Johnson's Wars. . . . *v.3 p.445*

Shadows on Our Skin. *v.2 p.355*

Shadows on the Past: Studies in the Historical Fiction
    Film. *v.6 p.314*

The Shadow. *v.2 p.109*

Shaftesbury: Characteristics of Men, Manners, Opinions,
    Times. *v.1 p.437*

Shahnameh: The Persian Book of Kings. *v.6 p.671*

Shake Hands with the Devil: The Failure of Humanity in
    Rwanda. *v.4 p.715*

Shaker Design. *v.1 p.714*

The Shaker Experience in America: A History of the United
    Society of Believers. *v.1 p.589*

The Shaker Legacy: Perspectives on an Enduring Furniture
    Style. *v.1 p.803*

The Shaker Spiritual. *v.1 p.297*

The Shakers and the World's People. *v.1 p.589*

Shakespeare: A Biographical Handbook. *v.2 p.226*

Shakespeare: A Life. *v.2 p.227*

Shakespeare after All. *v.2 p.229*

Shakespeare: An Anthology of Criticism and Theory,
    1945-2000. . . . . *v.1 p.76, p.101,v.2 p.231*

Shakespeare: An Introduction. *v.1 p.76, p.102,v.2 p.228*

Shakespeare and Feminist Performance: Ideology on
    Stage. *v.1 p.77, p.87, p.105*

Shakespeare and Modern Theatre: The Performance of
    Modernity. *v.1 p.75, p.81, p.86, p.99*

Shakespeare and the Authority of
    Performance. *v.1 p.77, p.105, p.136*

Shakespeare and the Dance. *v.1 p.44*

Shakespeare and the Editorial Tradition. *v.2 p.231*

Shakespeare and the Force of Modern
    Performance. *v.1 p.77, p.105, p.136*

Shakespeare and the French Poet. *v.2 p.460*

Shakespeare and the Jews. *v.2 p.231, p.232*

Shakespeare and the Moving Image: The Plays on Film and
    Television. *v.6 p.325*

Shakespeare and the Nature of Women. *v.2 p.229*

Shakespeare and the Popular Tradition in the Theater: Studies in
    the Social Dimension of Dramatic Form and
    Function. *v.2 p.232*

Shakespeare and the Romance Tradition. *v.2 p.233*

Shakespeare and Young Learner. *v.4 p.365*

Shakespeare at Work 1592: 1603. . . . . *v.2 p.227*

The Shakespeare Claimants: A Critical Survey of the Four
    Principal Theories Concerning the Authorship of
    the Shakespearean Plays. *v.1 p.76, p.100*

The Shakespeare Company,
    1594-1642. . . . . . *v.1 p.76, p.100, p.144,v.2 p.227, p.229*

Shakespeare Dictionary. *v.2 p.226*

Shakespeare: For All Time. *v.2 p.227*

Shakespeare for Beginners. *v.2 p.222, p.223*

Shakespeare: From 'Richard II' to 'Henry V'. *v.2 p.234*

Shakespeare, from Stage to Screen. *v.6 p.326*

A Shakespeare Glossary. *v.2 p.226*

Shakespeare in Performance: A Collection of
    Essays. *v.1 p.76, p.102, p.135*

Shakespeare in Performance. . . . *v.1 p.77, p.87, p.103, p.136*

Shakespeare Is Hard, but So Is Life: A Radical Guide to
    Shakespearean Tragedy. *v.2 p.235*

Shakespeare Made Easy. *v.2 p.223*

A Shakespeare Music Catalogue: Bibliography. *v.1 p.166, p.179*

A Shakespeare Music Catalogue: Indices. *v.1 p.166, p.179, p.180*

A Shakespeare Music Catalogue: The Catalogue of Music: All's
    Well That Ends Well--Love's Labour's Lost. *v.1 p.166, p.180*

A Shakespeare Music Catalogue: The Catalogue of Music:
    Macbeth--The Taming of the Shrew. . . . *v.1 p.166, p.180*

A Shakespeare Music Catalogue: The Tempest--The Two Noble
    Kinsmen, the Sonnets, the Poems, Commemorative
    Pieces. *v.1 p.166, p.180*

Shakespeare Reshaped, 1606-1623. . . . . *v.2 p.232*

Shakespeare: Seven Tragedies Revisited: The Dramatist's
    Manipulation of Response. *v.2 p.234*

Shakespeare: The Critical Heritage. *v.2 p.232*

Shakespeare the Dramatist: And Other Papers. . . . *v.2 p.227*

Shakespeare, the Globe, and the World. *v.2 p.228*

Shakespeare: The Last Phase. *v.2 p.233*

Shakespeare: The Later Years. *v.2 p.227*

Shakespeare: The Man and His Achievement. *v.2 p.227*

Shakespeare, the Movie II: Popularizing the Plays on Film, TV,
    Video and DVD. *v.6 p.325*

Shakespeare: The Poet in His World. *v.2 p.226*

Shakespeare: The Roman Plays. *v.2 p.234*

Shakespeare to Sheridan. *v.1 p.77, p.104*

Shakespearean Criticism. *v.1 p.76, p.100*

Shakespearean Meanings. *v.2 p.228*

Shakespearean Playhouses: A History of English Theatres from
    the Beginnings to the Restoration. . . *v.1 p.75, p.98, p.154*

Shakespearean Tragedy: Genre, Tradition, and Change in Antony
    and Cleopatra. *v.2 p.234*

Shakespearean Tragedy: Lectures on Hamlet, Othello, King Lear
    and MacBeth. *v.2 p.234*

Shakespeare's Arguments with History. *v.2 p.234*

Shakespeare's Bawdy. *v.2 p.231*

Shakespeare's Caliban: A Cultural History. *v.2 p.232*

Shakespeare's Comedies: A Guide to Criticism. . . . *v.2 p.233*

Shakespeare's Cross-Cultural Encounters. *v.2 p.229*

Shakespeare's Dramatic Challenge: On the Rise of
    Shakespeare's Tragic Heroes. *v.2 p.235*

Shakespeare's Drama. *v.2 p.229*

Shakespeare's English Kings: History, Chronicle, and
    Drama. *v.2 p.234*

Shakespeare's Festive Comedy. *v.2 p.233*

Shakespeare's Globe Rebuilt. *v.1 p.155, v.2 p.227*

Shakespeare's Happy Comedies. *v.2 p.233*

Shakespeare's Histories: A Guide to Criticism. . . . *v.2 p.234*

Shakespeare's Histories: Mirrors of Elizabethan Policy. *v.2 p.233*

Shakespeare's History Plays: Performance, Translation and
    Adaptation in Britain and Abroad. . . *v.1 p.76, p.100, p.135*

Shakespeare's History. *v.2 p.234*

Shakespeare's Imitations. *v.2 p.232*

Shakespeare's Language. *v.2 p.230*

Shakespeare's Last Plays. *v.2 p.232*

Shakespeare's Military World. *v.2 p.230*

Shakespeare's Philosophical Patterns. *v.2 p.228*

Shakespeare's Problem Plays. *v.2 p.232*

Shakespeare's Rhetoric of Comic Character: Dramatic Convention in Classical and Renaissance Comedy. *v.2 p.233*

Shakespeare's Songbook. *v.1 p.179*

Shakespeare's Sonnets. *v.2 p.225, p.226*

Shakespeare's Theatre. . .*v.1 p.60, p.61, p.76, p.77, p.103, p.137*

Shakespeare's Tragedies: Violation and Identity. *v.2 p.235*

Shakespeare's Tragedies. *v.2 p.234, p.235*

Shakespeare's Tragic Frontier: The World of His Final Tragedies. *v.2 p.234*

Shakespeare's Tragic Heroes: Slaves of Passion. . . .*v.2 p.234*

Shakespeare's Tragic Skepticism. *v.2 p.228*

Shakespeare's Tribe: Church, Nation, and Theater in Renaissance England. *v.2 p.186*

Shakespeare's Wooden O. *v.2 p.227*

Shakespeares Words: A Glossary and Language Companion. *v.2 p.226*

Shakespeare's Young Lovers. *v.2 p.232*

Shakespeare. *v.2 p.232*

Shakespearian Comedy. *v.2 p.233*

The Shakespearian Tempest: With a Chart of Shakespeare's Dramatic Universe. *v.2 p.230*

Shaking a Leg: Journalism and Writings. *v.2 p.336*

Shaking the World for Jesus: Media and Conservative Evangelical Culture. *v.1 p.655*

Shakti and Shakta. *v.1 p.534*

Shamanism: An Encyclopedia of World Beliefs, Practices, and Culture. *v.4 p.37*

Shamanism: Archaic Techniques of Ecstasy. *v.1 p.542*

Shamanism, Colonialism, and the Wild Man: A Study in Terror and Healing. *v.3 p.356*

Shamans and Religion: An Anthropological Exploration in Critical Thinking. *v.1 p.542, v.4 p.36*

Shamara and Other Writings. *v.2 p.810*

Shame and Guilt. *v.5 p.649, p.657*

The Shame of the Nation: The Restoration of Apartheid Schooling in America. *v.4 p.315*

The Shameful Life of Salvador Dali. *v.1 p.696*

Shame. *v.2 p.766*

Shanghai Baby: A Novel. *v.6 p.212*

The Shanghai Capitalists and the Nationalist Government, 1927-1937. . . . .*v.6 p.189*

Shanghai: From Market Town to Treaty Port, 1074-1858. . . . .*v.6 p.205*

Shanghai: Global City. *v.6 p.206*

Shanghai Modern: The Flowering of a New Urban Culture in China, 1930-1945. . . . . .*v.6 p.190, p.205, p.206, p.213*

Shank's Mare or Hizakurige: Japan's Great Comic Novel. *v.6 p.230*

Shantytown Protest in Pinochet's Chile. *v.3 p.355*

Shape and Structure, from Engineering to Nature. .*v.5 p.692, p.693*

Shape in Chemistry: An Introduction to Molecular Shape and Topology. *v.5 p.298*

The Shape of Culture: A Study of Contemporary Cultural Patterns in the United States. *v.4 p.712*

The Shape of Death: Life, Death, and Immortality in the Early Fathers. *v.1 p.645*

The Shape of Inca History: Narrative and Architecture in an Andean Empire. *v.3 p.261*

The Shape of Life: Genes, Development, and the Evolution of Animal Form. *v.5 p.200*

The Shape of Space. *v.1 p.500*

The Shape of the Holy: Early Islamic Jerusalem. . . .*v.6 p.574*

Shape of the Liturgy. *v.1 p.654*

The Shape of the River: Long-Term Consequences of Considering Race in College and University Admissions. *v.4 p.294*

The Shape of Things to Come. *v.2 p.320*

Shaped by Wind and Water: Reflections of a Naturalist. .*v.5 p.231*

Shapers of Japanese Buddhism. *v.6 p.221*

The Shapes of Change: Images of American Dance. . .*v.1 p.27*

Shapes of Time: The Evolution of Growth and Development. *v.5 p.194*

Shape-Shifter. *v.2 p.749*

Shaping American Telecommunications: A History of Technology, Policy, and Economics. *v.4 p.166, p.421*

Shaping Biology: The National Science Foundation and American Biological Research, 1945-1975. . . . .*v.5 p.244*

Shaping Constitutional Values: Elected Government, the Supreme Court, and the Abortion Debate. *v.4 p.447*

Shaping Information: The Rhetoric of Visual Conventions. *v.4 p.423*

Shaping Life: Genes, Embryos and Evolution. *v.5 p.160*

The Shaping of America: A Geographical Perspective on 500 Years of History. *v.3 p.380*

The Shaping of America: A Geographical Prespective on 500 Years of History. *v.3 p.380*

The Shaping of American Congregationalism. *v.1 p.584*

The Shaping of American Higher Education: Emergence and Growth of the Contemporary System. *v.4 p.331*

The Shaping of Somali Society: Reconstructing the History of a Pastoral People, 1600 to 1900. . . . .*v.6 p.65*

The Shaping of Southern Culture: Honor, Grace, and War, 1760s-1880s. *v.3 p.496*

The Shaping of the American High School, 1880-1920, Vol. 1. . . . .*v.4 p.327*

The Shaping of the American High School, 1920-1941, Vol. 2. . . . .*v.4 p.327*

Shaping of the Elizabethan Regime. *v.3 p.100*

The Shaping of the Modern Middle East. *v.6 p.594*

The Shaping of Vermont: From the Wilderness to the Centennial 1749-1877. . . . .*v.3 p.486*

Shaping Structures: Statics. *v.5 p.692*

Shaping Suburbia: How Political Institutions Organize Urban Development. *v.6 p.724*

Shaping the Adaptive Organization: Landscapes, Learning and Leadership in Volatile Times. *v.4 p.78*

Shaping the City: Studies in History, Theory and Urban Design. *v.6 p.726*

Shaping the College Curriculum: Academic Plans in Action. *v.4 p.295*

Shaping the Eighteenth Amendment: Temperance Reform, Legal Culture, and the Polity, 1880-1920. . . . .*v.4 p.449*

Shaping the Industrial Century: The Remarkable Story of the Evolution of the Modern Chemical and Pharmaceutical Industries. *v.4 p.146, p.157*

Shaping the World Economy: Suggestions for an International Economy Policy. *v.4 p.256*

Shaping Tomorrow's Family: Theory and Policy for the 21st Century. *v.4 p.734*

Shaping Women's Work: Gender, Employment and Information Technology. *v.4 p.761, v.6 p.458*

Shaping Your HR Role: Succeeding in Today's Organizations. *v.4 p.76*

Shared Beginnings, Divergent Lives: Delinquent Boys to Age 70. . . . .*v.4 p.753, v.6 p.255*

The Shared Heart: Portraits and Stories Celebrating Lesbian, Gay, and Bisexual Young People. *v.6 p.369*

Shared Leadership: Reframing the How's and Why's of Leadership. *v.4 p.80*

A Shared Space: Folklife in the Arizona-Sonora Borderlands. *v.6 p.486, p.523*

Shared Visions, Shared Lives: Communal Living Around the Globe. *v.4 p.740*

A Shared World: Christians and Muslims in the Early Modern Mediterranean. *v.3 p.192, p.193*

Sharing Nature with Children. *v.5 p.227*

Sharing the Dance: Contact Improvisation and American Culture. *v.1 p.43*

Sharing the Dream: White Men in Multicultural America. *v.6 p.470, p.471*

Sharing the Journey: Support Groups and America's New Quest for Community. *v.5 p.670*

The Shattered Dream: Herbert Hoover and the Great Depression. *v.3 p.480*

Shattered Dreams: The Failure of the Peace Process in the Middle East, 1995-2002. . . . .*v.4 p.649*

A Shattered Nation: The Rise and Fall of the Confederacy, 1861-1868. . . . .*v.4 p.522*

Shattered Nerves: Doctors, Patients and Depression in Victorian England. *v.6 p.760*

Shattered Past: Reconstructing German Histories. . . .*v.3 p.178*

The Shattered Self: E. T. A. Hoffmann's Tragic Vision. *v.2 p.598, p.599*

The Shattered Synthesis: New England Puritanism Before the Great Awakening. *v.3 p.485*

Shattering the Myth: Plays by Hispanic Women. *v.1 p.120, p.124, v.6 p.517*

Shattering the Myths of Darwinism. *v.5 p.203*

Shattering the Myths: Women in Academe. *v.4 p.293*

Shaw and Ibsen: Bernard Shaw's The Quintessence of Ibsenism and Related Writings. *v.2 p.628*

Shaw: Interviews and Recollections. *v.2 p.309*

Shaw on Education. *v.4 p.345*

Shaw on Music. *v.1 p.248*

Shaw on Shakespeare. *v.2 p.232*

Shaw on Theatre: A Half Century of Advices. *v.1 p.56, p.103, p.104*

Shaw Shadows. *v.2 p.309*

Shaw's Daughters: Dramatic and Narrative Constructions of Gender. *v.2 p.309*

Shaw's People: Victoria to Churchill. *v.2 p.310*

Shaw's Theater. *v.2 p.309*

Shay's Rebellion: The American Revolution's Final Battle. *v.3 p.488*

She and He. *v.2 p.500*

She Came to Stay. *v.2 p.509*

She Does Math!: Real-Life Problems from Women on the Job. *v.5 p.459*

She Plays with the Darkness: A Novel. *v.2 p.756*

She Stoops to Conquer. *v.2 p.248*

She Who Is: The Mystery of God in Feminist Theological Discourse. *v.1 p.639*

Sheathing the Sword: The U. N. Secretary-General and the Prevention of Internation Conflict. *v.4 p.633, p.648*

Shedding Silence. *v.6 p.104*

Sheehy's Emergency Nursing: Principles and Practice. .*v.5 p.531*

Sheep Housing and Equipment Handbook. *v.5 p.55*

The Sheer Joy of Celestial Mechanics. *v.5 p.66*

⬜ The Sheffield Chemdex: The Directory of Chemistry on the WWW since 1993. . . . .*v.5 p.257*

Shelf Space: Modern Package Design 1945-1965. . . .*v.1 p.718*

The Shell Game: Reflections on Rowing and the Pursuit of Excellence. *v.4 p.865*

Shelley: A Critical Reading. *v.2 p.312*

Shelley: A Life Story. *v.2 p.311*

Shelley and His Circle, 1773-1822, Vols. 1 & 2. . . .*v.2 p.311*

Shelley and His Readers: Beyond Paranoid Politics. . .*v.2 p.312*

Shelley: His Thought and Work. *v.2 p.311*

Shelley in England: New Facts and Letter. *v.2 p.311*

Shelley: The Golden Years. *v.2 p.311*

Shelley's Annus Mirabilis: The Maturing of an Epic Vision. *v.2 p.311*

Shelley's Major Poetry: The Fabric of a Vision. . . .*v.2 p.311*

Shelley's Mythmaking. *v.2 p.311*

Shelley's Poetry and Prose. *v.2 p.311*

The Sheltered Life. *v.2 p.79*

Sherazade. *v.2 p.545*

Sheridan and Goldsmith. *v.2 p.249, p.260*

Sheridan and the Drama of Georgian England. *v.2 p.260*

Sheridan to Robertson: A Study of the Nineteenth-Century London Stage. *v.1 p.104, p.142, p.143*

Sheridan's Plays. *v.2 p.260*

Sherlock Holmes in Babylon and Other Tales of Mathematical History. *v.5 p.464, p.465*

Sherman: Fighting Prophet. *v.3 p.425*

Sherpas Through Their Rituals. *v.1 p.541*

Sherwood Anderson: An American Career. *v.2 p.57*

She's a Rebel: The History of Women in Rock and Roll. *v.1 p.269, p.378, v.6 p.474*

S/He. . . . .*.v.6 p.403*

Shield of the Weak: Feminism and the State in Uruguay, 1900-1932. . . . .*.v.3 p.345, p.346*

Shielded from Justice: Police Brutality and Accountability in United States. . . . .*.v.6 p.260, p.261*

Shifting Contexts: Reinterpreting Samson Agonistes. . .*.v.2 p.256*

Shifting Fortunes: The Rise and Decline of American Labor, from the 1820s to the Present. . . . .*.v.4 p.128*

Shifting Languages: Interaction and Identity in Javanese Indonesia. . . . .*.v.4 p.21*

Shifting Lines in the Sand: Kuwait's Elusive Frontier with Iraq. . . . .*.v.6 p.627*

Shifting Priorities: Gender and Genre in Seventeenth-Century Dutch Painting. . . . .*.v.1 p.688, p.707*

Shifting Sands: The Rise and Fall of Biblical Archaeology. . . . .*.v.1 p.617*

Shifting the Blame: How Victimization Became a Criminal Defense. . . . .*.v.4 p.754*

Shifting: The Double Lives of Black Women in America. . . . .*.v.6 p.434*

The Shiga Hero. . . . .*.v.6 p.233*

The Shiis of Iraq. . . . .*.v.6 p.602*

The Shi'is of Jabal 'Amal and the New Lebanon: Community and Nation State, 1918-1943. . . . .*.v.6 p.604, p.605*

Shi'ism and Social Protest. . . . .*.v.1 p.560*

Shi'ism: Doctrines, Thought, and Spirituality. . . . .*.v.1 p.560*

A Shi'ite Creed: A Translation of Risalatu'l-itiqadat of Muhammad b. 'Ali Ibn Babawayhi al-Qummi, known as Shaykh Saduq. . . . .*.v.1 p.560*

Shi'ite Islam. . . . .*.v.1 p.560*

Shiloh: A Novel. . . . .*.v.2 p.73*

Shingle Styles: Innovation and Tradition in American Architecture, 1874-1984. . . . .*.v.1 p.787*

Shining and Other Paths: War and Society in Peru, 1980-1995. . . . .*.v.3 p.332*

The Shining Path: A History of the Millenarian War in Peru. . . . .*.v.3 p.330*

The Shining Path of Peru. . . . .*.v.3 p.330, p.331*

Shining Path. . . . .*.v.3 p.332*

A Shining Thread of Hope: The History of Black Women in America. . . . .*.v.6 p.6, p.44*

The Shining. . . . .*.v.2 p.148*

Shinohata: A Portrait of a Japanese Village. . . . . .*.v.6 p.221*

Shinto and the State, 1868-1988. . . . .*.v.1 p.541*

Shinto-Bibliography in Western Languages: Bibliography on Shinto and Religious Sects, Intellectual Schools and Movements Influenced by Shintoism. . . . . .*.v.6 p.222*

Ship Channel Design and Operation: (ASCE Manuals and Reports on Engineering Practice No. 107 (revision of MOP 80)). . . . .*.v.5 p.703*

Ship of Fools. . . . .*.v.2 p.109, p.594*

The Ship of Widows. . . . .*.v.2 p.804*

The Shipping News: A Novel. . . . .*.v.2 p.153*

Ships, Money and Politics: Seafaring and Naval Enterprise in the Reign of Charles I. . . . .*.v.3 p.88, p.93, p.101*

Shirin Neshat. . . . .*.v.1 p.773*

Shirley Jackson's American Gothic. . . . .*.v.2 p.90*

Shirley Jackson. . . . .*.v.2 p.90*

Shirley. . . . .*.v.2 p.270*

Shivaji: Hindu King in Islamic India. . . . .*.v.6 p.156*

Shoah: The Complete Text of the Acclaimed Holocaust Film. . . . .*.v.3 p.85*

Shock Cities: The Environmental Transformation and Reform of Manchester and Chicago. . . . .*.v.6 p.714, p.715*

The Shock of Arrival: Reflections on Postcolonial Experience. . . . . . *.v.6 p.104, p.111, p.117, p.118, p.138*

Shock Value: A Tasteful Book about Bad Taste. . . . .*.v.6 p.417*

The Shoemaker's Holiday. . . . .*.v.2 p.218*

Shoji Hamada: A Potter's Way and Work. . . . . . .*.v.6 p.228*

The Shona and Their Neighbors. . . . .*.v.6 p.77*

The Shoot Apical Meristem: Its Growth and Development. . . . .*.v.5 p.161*

Shoot Me: Independent Filmmaking from Creative Concept to Rousing Release. . . . .*.v.6 p.347*

Shoot the Piano Player. . . . .*.v.2 p.80*

Shooting Cowboys and Indians: Silent Western Films, American Culture, and the Birth of Hollywood. . . . . .*.v.6 p.325*

Shooting from the Hip: Photography, Masculinity, and Postwar America. . . . .*.v.1 p.765*

Shooting Stars: Heroes and Heroines of Western Film. *.v.6 p.324*

Shopfloor Matters: Labor-Management Relations in 20th Century American Manufacturing. . . . .*.v.4 p.121*

Shoppers: Two Plays by Denis Johnson. . . . . . .*.v.2 p.355*

A Short Course in International Intellectual Property Rights: Protecting Your Brands, Marks, Copyrights, Patents, Designs, and Related Rights Worldwide. . . .*.v.4 p.58, p.110*

Short Eyes. . . . .*.v.6 p.508, p.517, p.518*

Short Fiction by Hispanic Writers of the United States. .*.v.6 p.496*

The Short Fiction of Charles W. Chesnutt. . . . . . .*.v.2 p.32*

A Short Grammar of Biblical Aramaic. . . . .*.v.6 p.652*

A Short Grammar of Contemporary Bulgarian. . . . .*.v.2 p.774*

A Short Grammar of Latvian. . . . .*.v.2 p.773*

A Short Grammar of Lithuanian. . . . .*.v.2 p.773*

A Short Guide to Writing about Art. . . . .*.v.1 p.662*

A Short Guide to Writing about Biology. . . . . . .*.v.5 p.246*

A Short Guide to Writing about Film. . . . .*.v.6 p.305*

A Short Guide to Writing about Music. . . . .*.v.1 p.173*

A Short Historical English Grammar. . . . .*.v.2 p.555, p.558*

A Short History of African Philosophy. . . . .*.v.1 p.476*

A Short History of Ancient Egypt. . . . .*.v.3 p.9*

A Short History of Canada. . . . .*.v.3 p.536*

A Short History of Chemistry. . . . .*.v.5 p.263*

A Short History of Christian Doctrine: From the First Century to the Present. . . . .*.v.1 p.633*

A Short History of Denmark. . . . .*.v.3 p.234*

Short History of Electoral Systems in Western Europe. *.v.4 p.601*

A Short History of English Drama. . . . .*.v.2 p.185*

A Short History of English Literature. . . . .*.v.2 p.166*

A Short History of Ethics. . . . .*.v.1 p.484*

A Short History of Finland. . . . .*.v.3 p.236*

A Short History of French Literature. . . . .*.v.2 p.455*

Short History of Greek Literature. . . . .*.v.2 p.401*

A Short History of Islamic Spain. . . . .*.v.6 p.564*

A Short History of Laos: The Land in Between. *v.6 p.171*

A Short History of Las Vegas. *v.3 p.529, v.6 p.713, p.714*

A Short History of Malaysia: Linking East and West. *.v.6 p.172*

A Short History of Medieval Philosophy. . .*.v.1 p.433, v.6 p.568*

A Short History of Modern Arabic Literature. . . . . *.v.6 p.658*

A Short History of Modern Bulgaria. . . . . *.v.3 p.251*

A Short History of Modern Philosophy: From Descartes to
  Wittgenstein. . . . . *.v.1 p.436*

A Short History of Nearly Everything. . . . . *.v.5 p.399*

A Short History of Norway. . . . . *.v.3 p.234*

A Short History of Opera. . . . . *.v.1 p.230*

A Short History of Planet Earth: Mountains, Mammals, Fire,
  and Ice. . . . . *.v.5 p.445*

A Short History of Quebec. . . . .*.v.3 p.543, v.4 p.589*

A Short History of Reconstruction. . . . . *.v.3 p.396*

A Short History of Reno. . . . . *.v.3 p.529*

Short History of Scientific Ideas to 1900. . . . . . *.v.5 p.389*

A Short History of Structural Linguistics. . *.v.2 p.562, v.4 p.18*

A Short History of Syriac Literature. . . . . *.v.6 p.653*

A Short History of the Ismailis. . . . . *.v.1 p.560*

A Short History of the Labour Party. . . . . *.v.4 p.606*

A Short History of the Middle Ages. *.v.1 p.600, v.3 p.62, v.6 p.564*

A Short History of the Movies. . . . . *.v.6 p.331*

A Short History of the Netherlands Antilles and
  Surinam. *v.3 p.322*

A Short History of the Papacy in the Middle Ages. . *.v.1 p.574*

A Short History of the Printed Word. . . .*.v.2 p.576, v.3 p.37*

A Short History of Western Legal Theory. . . . . . *.v.4 p.434*

A Short History of Writing Instruction: From Ancient Greece to
  Twentieth-Century America. . . . . *.v.2 p.565*

A Short Introduction to English Grammar. . . . . . *.v.2 p.558*

Short Letter, Long Farewell. . . . . *.v.2 p.617*

Short Novels and Other Writings. . . . . .*.v.2 p.596, p.597*

The Short Novels of John Steinbeck: Critical Essays. *.v.2 p.122*

Short Oxford History of English Literature. . . . . . *.v.2 p.167*

Short Protocols in Cell Biology. *v.5 p.87*

Short Protocols in Human Genetics. *v.5 p.88*

Short Protocols in Immunology. *v.5 p.87, p.88, p.165*

Short Protocols in Molecular Biology. *v.5 p.87, p.125*

Short Protocols in Protein Science. *v.5 p.88*

A Short Reference Grammar of Iraqi Arabic. . . . . *.v.6 p.653*

A Short Reference Grammar of Moroccan
  Arabic. . . . .*.v.6 p.653, p.654*

The Short Reign of Pippin IV: A Fabrication. . . . . *.v.2 p.123*

The Short Season Between Two Silences. . . . . . . *.v.2 p.393*

Short Stories, 1921-1946. . . . . *.v.2 p.605*

Short Stories by the Generation of 1898/Cuentos de la
  Generacion de 1898: A Dual-Language Book. . . *.v.2 p.645*

Short Stories from Pakistan: Fifty Years of Pakistani Short
  Stories. . . . . *.v.6 p.151*

Short Stories in German, Erzahlungen auf Deutsch. . *.v.2 p.594*

Short Stories in Italian. . . . . *.v.2 p.700*

Short Stories in Spanish. . . . . *.v.2 p.644*

Short Stories of John Galsworthy. . . . . *.v.2 p.348*

Short Stories. . . . .*.v.2 p.56*

The Short Stories. . . . .*.v.2 p.84, p.88*

Short Stories. . . . .*.v.6 p.151, p.153*

The Short Works of Mark Twain: A Critical Study. . .*.v.2 p.33*

Shorter Classics. . . . .*.v.4 p.234*

The Shorter Columbia Anthology of Traditional Chinese
  Literature. . . . .*.v.6 p.208, p.211, p.212*

Shorter Finnegans Wake. . . . .*.v.2 p.358*

The Shorter Pepys. . . . .*.v.3 p.105*

Shorter Poems, 1807-1820. . . . .*.v.2 p.325*

The Shorter Science and Civilisation in China, Vol. 1. *.v.6 p.198*

The Shorter Science and Civilisation in China, Vol. 2. *.v.6 p.198*

The Shorter Science and Civilisation in China, Vol. 3. *.v.6 p.198*

The Shorter Science and Civilisation in China, Vol. 4. *.v.6 p.198*

The Shorter Science and Civilisation in China, Vol. 5. *.v.6 p.198*

Shoshone Ghost Dance Religion: Poetry Songs and Great Basin
  Context. . . . . *.v.1 p.297, v.6 p.699*

Shostakovich: A Life. . . . .*.v.1 p.213, p.356*

Shostakovich and His World. . . . .*.v.1 p.213, p.356*

A Shostakovich Casebook. . . . .*.v.1 p.210, p.356*

Shostakovich Reconsidered. . . . .*.v.1 p.216, p.356*

Shot in America: Television, the State and the Rise of Chicano
  Cinema. *v.6 p.493*

Should America Pay? Slavery and Raging Rebate over
  Reparations. . . . .*.v.6 p.20, p.37*

Should Trees Have Standing?: And Other Essays on Law,
  Morals and the Environment. *v.4 p.435*

Should We Risk It?: Exploring Environmental, Health, and
  Technological Problem Solving. *v.5 p.504*

Shoulder to Shoulder?: The American Federation of Labor, the
  United States, and the Mexican Revolution,
  1910-1924. . . . .*.v.3 p.290*

A Shovel of Stars: The Settling of the North American
  Continent 1850-1994. . . . .*.v.3 p.518*

Show Boat. . . . .*.v.2 p.73*

The Show Makers: Great Directors of American Musical
  Theatre. . . . . *.v.1 p.93, p.118, p.153*

Show Me the Numbers: Designing Tables and Graphs to
  Enlighten. . . . .*.v.4 p.172, p.175*

Show Music on Record: The First One Hundred
  Years. . . . .*.v.1 p.171, p.253*

Showboats: The History of an American Institution. . .*.v.1 p.114*

Showdown at Gucci Gulch: Lawmakers, Lobbyists, and the
  Unlikely Triumph of Tax Reform. . . . .*.v.4 p.107*

Showdown: Confronting Modern America in the Western
  Film. . . . .*.v.6 p.324*

Showdown: The Struggle Between the Gingrich Congress and
  the Clinton White House. . . . .*.v.3 p.469*

The Shows of London. . . . . . .*.v.6 p.754, p.760, p.762, p.763*

Showstoppers: Busby Berkeley and the Tradition of
  Spectacle. . . . .*.v.6 p.316*

Showtune: A Memoir by Jerry Herman. *.v.1 p.250, p.331, p.332*

Shreve's Chemical Process Industries. . . . . *.v.5 p.315*

Shrewd Sanctions: Economic Statecraft in An Age of Global
  Terrorism. . . . .*.v.4 p.565*

Shtetl: The Life and Death of a Small Town and the World of Polish Jews. *v.3 p.254, p.255*

The Shunra and the Schmetterling. *v.6 p.649*

Shut Out: A Story of Race and Baseball in Boston. *v.4 p.804, p.831, p.849, p.882, p.890, p.895*

Shut Out: Low Income Mothers and Higher Education in Post-Welfare America. *v.6 p.463*

🄴 Shutterbabe: Adventures in Love and War. *v.1 p.767*

Une Si Longue Lettre. *v.2 p.543*

Siam Becomes Thailand. *v.6 p.172*

Siam Mapped: A History of the Geo-Body of a Nation. .*v.6 p.172*

Siam under Rama III 1824: 1851. . . . .*v.6 p.172*

Sibelius: Symphony No. 5. . . . . . .*v.1 p.215, p.239, p.356*

Siberia on Fire: Stories and Essays by Valentin Rasputin. *v.2 p.807, p.808*

Siberia, Siberia. *v.2 p.808, v.3 p.214*

Siberia: Worlds Apart. *v.3 p.214*

Siberian Village: Land and Life in the Sakha Republic. .*v.3 p.214*

Sibling Abuse Trauma: Assessment and Intervention Strategies for Children, Families and Adults. *v.5 p.667*

Sibling Bond. *v.5 p.625, p.631*

Sibling Relationships: Theory and Issues for Practice. *v.5 p.628, p.629, p.631, p.668*

SIBMAS International Directory of Performing Arts Collections. *v.1 p.4, p.5*

The Sibyl. *v.2 p.630*

Sicilian Stories (Novelle Siciliane): A Dual-Language Book. *v.2 p.713*

Sick and Tired of Being Sick and Tired: Black Women's Health Activism in America, 1890-1950. . . .*v.6 p.22, p.46, p.444*

Sick of Nature. *v.5 p.221*

The Sickness unto Death: A Christian Psychological Exposition for Upbuilding and Awakening. *v.1 p.478*

SID sheep production handbook. *v.5 p.53, p.54*

Siddhartha: An Indian Tale. *v.2 p.610*

Siddur. The Authorised Daily Prayer Book. *v.1 p.552*

Sideshow: Kissinger, Nixon, and the Destruction of Cambodia. *v.6 p.170*

Sidney Lanier, Henry Timrod and Paul Hamilton Hayne: A Reference Guide. *v.2 p.47*

Sidney Lanier. *v.2 p.47*

Sidney Nolan. *v.1 p.699*

The Siege of Budapest: One Hundred Days in World War II. *v.3 p.187*

Siege of Charleston. *v.3 p.414*

Siegfried Sassoon: The Making of a War Poet, a Biography, 1886-1918. . . . .*v.2 p.380*

The Sierra Club Guide to the Ancient Forests of the Northeast. *v.5 p.38*

The Sierra Club Nature Writing Handbook: A Creative Guide. *v.5 p.232*

Sierra Club: One Hundred Years of Protecting Nature. .*v.5 p.81*

The Sierra Club Summer Book. *v.5 p.225*

The Sierra Club Wetlands Reader: A Literary Companion. *v.5 p.242*

Los Siete Libros de la Diana. *v.2 p.651*

Sight Lines. *v.1 p.39*

The Sight of Sound: Music, Representation, and the History of the Body. *v.1 p.377*

Sight Sound Motion: Applied Media Aesthetics. . . .*v.6 p.347*

Sight Unseen: An Exploration of Conscious and Unconscious Vision. *v.5 p.606*

El Siglo de las Drogas: Usos, Percepciones, y Personajes. *v.3 p.281*

🖵 Sigma-Aldrich. *v.5 p.259*

Signal Detection: Mechanisms, Models, and Applications. *v.5 p.606*

Signal Detection Theory and Psychophysics. *v.5 p.606*

Signals, Sound, and Sensation. *v.5 p.606*

Signals, Switches, Regulons, and Cascades: Control of Bacterial Gene Expression. *v.5 p.153, p.206*

Significance of Monuments: On the Shaping of Human Experience in Neolithic and Bronze Age Europe. . .*v.4 p.12*

The Significance of Philosophical Scepticism. *v.1 p.517*

🄴 The Significance of Territory. *v.4 p.495*

The Significance of the Frontier in American History. .*v.3 p.402*

Significant Contemporary American Feminists: A Biographical Sourcebook. *v.6 p.435*

Signifying Art: Essays on Art after 1960. . . . . .*v.1 p.681*

The Signifying Monkey: A Theory of African-American Literary Criticism. *v.2 p.3, p.4*

Signs and Wonders upon Pharaoh: A History of American Egyptology. *v.3 p.11*

Signs and Wonders Upon Pharaoh. *v.6 p.57*

Signs in America's Auto Age: Signatures of Landscape and Place. *v.1 p.715*

Signs in Contemporary Culture: An Introduction to Semiotics. *v.5 p.620*

Signs of Change. *v.2 p.301*

Signs of Life: The Language and Meanings of DNA. .*v.5 p.123*

Signs of Resistance: American Deaf Cultural History, 1900 to 1942. . . . .*v.4 p.699*

Signs of the Inka Khipu: Binary Coding in the Andean Knotted-String Records. *v.3 p.262*

Sihanouk: Prince of Light, Prince of Darkness. . . .*v.6 p.170*

Sikhism. *v.1 p.540*

The Sikhs of the Punjab. *v.1 p.540, v.6 p.161*

Silage Science and Technology. *v.5 p.20*

Silas Marner. *v.2 p.287*

Silence and Power: A Reevaluation of Djuna Barnes. .*v.2 p.58*

Silence: Lectures and Writings. *v.1 p.44, p.210, p.315*

The Silence of Bartleby. *v.2 p.48*

The Silenced Theatre: Czech Playwrights Without a Stage. *v.2 p.782*

Silence. *v.6 p.229*

Silent Bodies: Rediscovering the Women of Romanian Short Fiction. *v.2 p.816*

Silent Covenants: Brown v. Board of Education and the Unfulfilled Hopes for Racial Reform. *v.4 p.449*

Silent Dancing: A Partial Remembrance of a Puerto Rican Childhood. *v.6 p.488, p.505*

Silent Film Necrology. *v.6 p.332*

Silent Films, 1877-1996: A Critical Guide to 646
    Movies. . . . .*.v.6 p.332*

Silent Images: Women in Pharaonic Egypt. *v.1 p.706*

Silent Justice: The Clarence Thomas Story. . . *.v.4 p.536, p.537*

Silent Pioneers: Gay and Lesbian Elders. *v.6 p.380*

The Silent Revolution and the Making of Victorian
    England. *v.6 p.759*

Silent Skies: The Air Traffic Controllers' Strike. *v.4 p.128*

Silent Spring. . . .*v.5 p.17, p.27, p.354, p.369, p.514, v.6 p.290*

Silent Thunder: Breaking Through Cultural, Racial, and Class
    Barriers in Motorsports. *v.4 p.832, p.848*

Silent Voices: Public Opinion and Political Participation in
    America. *v.4 p.559*

The Silent World. *v.6 p.293*

Silicon Alley: The Rise and Fall of a New Media
    District. *v.6 p.723*

Silicon Biomineralization: Biology, Biochemistry, Molecular
    Biology, Biotechnology. *v.5 p.113*

Silicon in Organic, Organometallic, and Polymer
    Chemistry. *v.5 p.296*

Silicon Reagents. *v.5 p.296*

Silicon Snake Oil: Second Thoughts on the Information
    Highway. *v.5 p.408*

Silk and Bamboo Music in Shanghai: The Jiangnan Sizhu
    Instrumental Ensemble Tradition. *v.1 p.290, p.291*

Silk Glove Hegemony - Finnish Soviet Relations,
    1944-1974. . . . .*v.3 p.236*

The Silk Road: Two Thousand Years in the Heart of
    Asia. *v.6 p.239*

The Silk, the Shears and Marina. *v.2 p.818*

Silken Threads: A History of Embroidery in China, Korea,
    Japan, and Vietnam. *v.1 p.715, p.809*

La Silla del Águila. *v.2 p.668*

The Silvae of Statius. *v.2 p.443*

Silvae. *v.2 p.708*

Silver King: The Remarkable Life of the Count of Regla in
    Colonial Mexico. *v.3 p.285*

The Silver Men: West Indian Labour Migration to Panama,
    1850-1914. . . . .*v.3 p.305*

Silver Poets of the Sixteenth Century. *v.2 p.198*

The Silver State. *v.3 p.529*

The SIMBAD Astronomical Database. *v.5 p.63*

Simians, Cyborgs, and Women: The Reinvention of
    Nature. *v.6 p.439*

Simon and Schuster's Guide to Rocks and Minerals. .*v.5 p.435*

Simon Bolivar. *v.3 p.260*

Simon de Montfort. *v.3 p.143*

Simple Animals. *v.5 p.156*

Simple Cobler of Aggawam in America. . . . . . .*.v.2 p.30*

The Simple Flute: From A to Z. *v.1 p.397*

Simple Heuristics That Make Us Smart. *v.5 p.590*

Simple Justice: The History of Brown vs Board of Education
    and Black America's Struggle For Equality. . . .*v.4 p.450*

The Simple Life: Plain Living and High Thinking in American
    Culture. *v.3 p.370*

Simple Passion. *v.2 p.530*

The Simple Science of Flight: From Insects to Jumbo
    Jets. . . . .*.v.5 p.718*

Simple Screenprinting: Basic Techniques and Creative
    Projects. *v.1 p.760*

A Simple Story. *v.6 p.647*

Simple Theory, Hard Reality: The Impact of Sentencing
    Reforms on Courts, Prisons, and Crime. *v.6 p.269*

Simplicissimus. . . . .*.v.2 p.595*

Simulation and Social Theory. *v.4 p.690*

The Simulation of Human Intelligence. *v.5 p.590*

Simulation: The Practice of Model Development and
    Use. *v.5 p.341*

Sin and Confession on the Eve of the Reformation. . .*v.1 p.657*

Sin and Fear: The Emergence of a Western Guilt Culture
    13th-18th Centuries. *v.1 p.600*

Sin in Soft Focus: Pre-Code Hollywood. . . . . .*.v.6 p.314*

Sinai and Zion: An Entry into the Jewish Bible. . . .*v.1 p.619*

Sinatra! The Song Is You: A Singer's Art. . .*v.1 p.269, p.357*

Sinbad the Sailor. *v.2 p.790*

Since 1865: Discovering the American Past: A Look at the
    Evidence. *v.3 p.375, p.376*

Since Records Began: EMI: the First Hundred Years. .*v.1 p.384*

Since Yesterday: The 1930's in America, September 3, 1929 to
    September 3, 1939. . . . .*v.3 p.445*

Since Yesterday: The Nineteen-Thirties in America, September
    3, 1929-September 3 1939. . . . .*v.3 p.445*

Sinclair Lewis as Reader and Critic. . . . .*.v.2 p.95*

Sinclair Lewis: New Essays in Criticism. . . . . . .*.v.2 p.95*

Sinclair Ross' As for Me and My House: Five Decades of
    Criticism. . . . .*.v.2 p.731*

Sinema: American Pornographic Films and the People Who
    Make Them. . . . .*.v.6 p.317*

The Sinews of Power: War, Money and the English State,
    1688-1783. . . . .*v.3 p.93, p.106, p.122*

Sinful Tunes and Spirituals: Black Folk Music to the Civil
    War. . . . .*.v.1 p.281*

Sing for Your Supper: The Broadway Musical in the
    1930s. . . . .*.v.1 p.252, p.253*

Sing Out!: Gays and Lesbians in the Music World. . .*v.6 p.408*

Sing Them Over Again to Me: Hymns and Hymnbooks in
    America. . . . .*.v.1 p.606*

Sing, Whisper, Shout, Pray!: Feminist Visions for a Just
    World. *v.6 p.432, p.433*

Singapore, 1941-1942. . . . .*.v.6 p.173*

Singapore Changes Guard. . . . .*.v.4 p.623*

The Singapore Story: Memoirs of Lee Kuan Yew. . . .*v.6 p.173*

Singapore: The Legacy of Lee Kuan Yew. . . . . .*.v.6 p.173*

Singapore Wealth Power and Culture. . . . .*.v.6 p.173*

The Singer and the Moon. . . . .*.v.6 p.658*

The Singer of Tales. *v.2 p.415, p.819*

Singer's Companion. . . . .*.v.1 p.396*

Singers of Italian Opera: The History of a Profession. .*v.1 p.232*

Singers of the Century. . . . .*.v.1 p.233, p.237, p.396*

Singer's Repertoire: Coloratura Soprano, Lyric Soprano, and
    Dramatic Soprano. . . . .*.v.1 p.165, p.394*

Singer's Repertoire: Mezzo Soprano and Contralto. *v.1 p.165, p.394*

The Singer's Schumann. *v.1 p.202, p.236, p.355, p.412*

The Singing Book. *v.1 p.394*

Singing for Life: HIV/AIDS and Music in Uganda. . .*v.4 p.701*

Singing from the Well. *v.2 p.670*

Singing in Latin: Or Pronunciation Explor'd. *v.1 p.395*

Singing in My Soul. *v.1 p.270*

Singing in Style: A Guide to Vocal Performance Practices. *v.1 p.395, p.400*

Singing in the Saddle: The History of the Singing Cowboy. *v.1 p.270*

Singing Schumann: An Interpretive Guide for Performers. *v.1 p.200, p.236, p.355, p.395*

Singing the French Revolution: Popular Culture and Politics, 1787-1799. . . . .*v.1 p.246*

Singing to Cuba. *v.6 p.506*

The Singing Whakapapa. *v.2 p.748*

A Single Man. *v.2 p.356, v.6 p.397*

A Single Square Picture: A Korean Adoptee's Search for Her Roots. *v.6 p.95, p.110, p.136*

Single-Chain Silicates. *v.5 p.436*

Singular and Different: Business in China Past, Present and Future. *v.4 p.60*

The Singular Mark Twain: A Biography. *v.2 p.33*

Singular Stories, Vol. One: Tales from Singapore. . .*v.2 p.761*

Singularities: Landmarks on the Pathways of Life. .*v.5 p.78, p.126*

The Singularity of Shakespeare and Other Essays. . . .*v.2 p.231*

A Sinhala Village in a Time of Trouble: Politics and Change in Rural Sri Lanka. *v.6 p.163*

Sinister Twilight: The Fall of Singapore. *v.6 p.173*

Sinkholes and Subsidence: Karst and Cavernous Rocks in Engineering and Construction. *v.5 p.421*

Sinners and Saints: The Successors of Vasco Da Gama. .*v.6 p.156*

The Sins of Childhood and Other Stories. *v.2 p.791*

The Sins of the Fathers: Hawthorne's Psychological Themes. *v.2 p.40, p.41*

Sins of the Fathers. *v.2 p.379*

Sins. *v.6 p.179*

Sioux: Life and Customs of a Warrior Society. .*v.6 p.687, p.703*

Sir Charles Grandison. *v.2 p.259*

Sir Gardner Wilkinson and His Circle. *v.3 p.11*

Sir Gawain and the Green Knight: A New Verse Translation. *v.2 p.206*

Sir Gawain and the Green Knight: A Stylistic and Metrical Study. *v.2 p.206*

Sir Gawain and the Green Knight: Patience, and Pearl: Verse Translations. *v.2 p.203*

Sir Gawain and the Green Knight. *v.2 p.206*

Sir John Gielgud: A Life in Letters. *v.6 p.418*

Sir John Harington's Translation of Orlando Furioso. .*v.2 p.707*

Sir John Soane: The Royal Academy Lectures. *v.1 p.795*

Sir John Suckling. *v.2 p.260*

Sir Joshua Reynolds: A Complete Catalogue of His Paintings. *v.1 p.743, p.744*

Sir Philip Sidney As a Literary Craftsman. *v.2 p.215*

Sir Philip Sidney: The Major Works. *v.2 p.216*

Sir Robert Peel: The Life of Sir Robert Peel After 1830. . . . .*v.3 p.94, p.111*

Sir Robert Walpole. *v.3 p.107*

Sir Thomas Browne, a Man of Achievement in Literature. *v.2 p.241*

Sir Thomas Browne. *v.2 p.241*

Sir Thomas Overbury's Vision, and Other English Sources of Nathaniel Hawthorne's The Scarlet Letter Facsimile Reproductions, with an Introd. *v.2 p.215*

Sir Thomas Wyatt and His Background. *v.2 p.216*

Sir Walter and Mr. Jones: Walter Hagen, Bobby Jones and the Rise of American Golf. *v.4 p.861*

Sir Walter Scott. *v.2 p.308*

Sir Walter: Walter Hagen and the Invention of Professional Golf. *v.4 p.860*

Sir William Davenant, Poet Venturer, 1606-1668. . .*v.2 p.218*

☐ SIRCh: Analytical Chemistry--Spectral Sources. . .*v.5 p.270*

☐ SIRCh: Analytical Chemistry. *v.5 p.274*

☐ SIRCh (Selected Internet Resources for Chemistry). .*v.5 p.255*

Siren Songs: Representations of Gender and Sexuality in Opera. *v.1 p.380*

The Sirens of Titan. *v.2 p.158*

The Sirian Experiments. *v.2 p.365*

☐ SIRIUS (Smithsonian Institution Research Information System): Archives, Manuscripts, Photographs Catalog. *v.1 p.661, p.724, p.725, p.774*

☐ SIRIUS (Smithsonian Institution Research Information System): Art Inventories Catalog. *v.1 p.661*

☐ SIRIUS (Smithsonian Institution Research Information System): Pre-1877 Art Exhibition Catalogue Index. .*v.1 p.661*

Sisson and Grossman's The Anatomy of the Domestic Animal, Vol. 2. . . . .*v.5 p.54, p.55*

Sister and Brother: Lesbians and Gay Men Write about Their Lives Together. *v.6 p.375*

Sister Carrie: An Authoritative Text, Backgrounds and Sources Criticism. *v.2 p.70*

Sister Circle: Black Women and Work. *v.6 p.39, p.43*

Sister Gin. *v.6 p.394*

Sister Jamaica: A Study of Women, Work and Households in Kingston. *v.4 p.40*

Sister of My Heart. *v.2 p.764*

Sister Outsider: Essays and Speeches. .*v.4 p.744, v.6 p.372, p.434*

Sister Stew, Fiction and Poetry by Women. *v.6 p.92*

A Sister to Scheherazade. *v.2 p.544*

Sisterhood Is Forever: The Women's Anthology for a New Millennium. *v.6 p.431*

Sisterhood Is Global: The International Women's Movement Anthology. *v.6 p.431*

Sistering: Power and Change in Female Relationships. *v.5 p.628, p.631*

Sisters in the Struggle: African-American Women in the Civil Rights and Black Power Movements. . .*v.6 p.12, p.42, p.430*

Sisters of Salome. *v.1 p.27, p.28, p.29*

The Sisters: The Saga of the Mitford Family. *v.2 p.371*

Sistine Chapel: A Glorious Restoration. *v.1 p.740*

Sita. *v.6 p.403*

Sit-Down: The General Motors Strike of 1936-1937.   *v.4 p.125*

Site Engineering for Landscape Architects. *v.1 p.817*

Sites of Memory, Sites of Mourning: The Great War in
European Cultural History. *v.3 p.80*

Sites of Power: A Concise History of Ontario. . . . *v.3 p.544*

Sites of Sport: Space, Place, Experience. *v.4 p.813*

Sites of Violence: Gender and Conflict Zones. . . . *v.6 p.257*

Situating Salsa: Global Markets and Local Meanings in Latin
American Popular Music. *v.3 p.268*

Six Contemporary French Women Poets: Theory, Practice and
Pleasures. *v.2 p.464*

Six Days. *v.6 p.658*

Six Easy Pieces: Essentials of Physics Explained by Its Most
Brilliant Teacher. *v.5 p.539*

Six Fools and a Dancer: The Timeless Way of the Morris. .*v.1 p.33*

Six French Poets of Our Time: A Critical and Historical
Study. *v.2 p.460*

Six French Poets: Studies in Contemporary Literature. *v.2 p.461*

Six Greek Tragedies: Aeschylus: Persians, Prometheus Bound;
Sophocles: Women of Trachi, Philoctetes; Euripides:
Trojan Women, Bacchae. *v.1 p.63, p.70, p.88*

Six Hidden Views of Japanese Music. *v.1 p.289*

Six Masters of the Spanish Sonnet: Francisco de Quevedo, Sor
Juana Ines de la Cruz, Antonia Machado, Federico
Garcia Lorca, Jorge Luis Borges, Miguel Hernandez. *v.2 p.642*

Six Memos for the Next Millennium. *v.2 p.697*

Six Metaphysical Poets: A Reader's Guide. *v.2 p.183*

Six Modern American Plays. *v.2 p.25*

Six Nineteenth Century French Poets: With Parallel French
Text. *v.2 p.463*

Six Not-So-Easy Pieces: Einstein's Relativity, Symmetry and
Space-Time. *v.5 p.556, p.557*

Six Novels. *v.2 p.514*

Six Plays by Lillian Hellman: The Children's Hour, Days to
Come, The Little Foxes, Watch on the Rhine,
Another Part of the Forest, The Autumn
Garden. *v.1 p.121, v.2 p.83*

Six Plays in Translation from Mexican Contemporary Theatre: A
New Golden Age. *v.1 p.127*

Six Plays. *v.1 p.253, p.328, p.351, p.409*

The Six Questions: Acting Techniques for Dance
Performance. *v.1 p.37*

The Six-Gun Mystique Sequel. *v.6 p.323*

Sixguns and Society: A Structural Study of the Western. *v.6 p.325*

Sixteen Acres: Architecture and the Outrageous Struggle for the
Future of Ground Zero. *v.1 p.797, v.6 p.729*

Sixteenth Century Ireland: The Incomplete
Conquest. *v.3 p.135, p.136*

Sixteenth Century North America; The Land and the People as
Seen by the Europeans. *v.3 p.404*

The Sixteenth-Century Italian Paintings: Brescia, Bergamo and
Cremona. *v.1 p.729, p.733*

Sixties Chicano Movement: Youth, Identity,
Power. *v.6 p.538, p.539, p.541*

Sixty poems. *v.2 p.786*

Sixty-Seven Poems for Downtrodden Saints. *v.2 p.22*

The Size of Nations. *v.4 p.247*

Size, Structure, and the Changing Face of American
Agriculture. *v.5 p.4*

Size-Structured Populations: Ecology and
Evolution. *v.5 p.183, p.187, p.198*

Skelton and Satire. *v.2 p.214*

Skelton, the Life and Times of an Early Tudor Poet. . *v.2 p.214*

A Skeptical Biochemist. *v.5 p.326*

The Skeptical Business Searcher: The Information Advisor's
Guide to Evaluating Web Data, Sites, and Sources. *v.4 p.180*

The Skeptical Environmentalist: Measuring the Real State of the
World. *v.6 p.291, p.292*

Skeptical Philosophy for Everyone. *v.1 p.517*

Skepticism: A Contemporary Reader. *v.1 p.517*

Skepticism and Animal Faith: Introduction to a System of
Philosophy. *v.1 p.440*

Sketches by Boz, illustrative of every-day life and every-day
people. by the author of the Pickwick Papers. . . *v.2 p.283*

Sketches from a Hunter's Album: The Complete
Edition. *v.2 p.810*

Sketches from a Life. *v.3 p.459*

Skill Acquisition in Sport: Research, Theory and
Practice. *v.4 p.874, p.908, p.910*

The Skilled Facilitator: A Comprehensive Resource for
Consultants, Facilitators, Managers, Trainers, and
Coaches. *v.4 p.174*

Skin Deep, Spirit Strong: The Black Female Body in American
Culture. *v.6 p.437, p.449*

Skin Shows: Gothic Horror and the Technology of
Monsters. *v.6 p.318*

Skinny Dipping: And Other Immersions in Water, Myth and
Being Human. *v.5 p.222*

Skinswaps. *v.2 p.812, p.813*

The Skull Mantra. *v.6 p.241*

Skulls and Skeletons: Human Bone Collections and
Accumulations. *v.4 p.15*

☐ Sky & Telescope Astronomy Web Sites. *v.5 p.61*

The Sky Clears: Poetry of the American
Indians. *v.2 p.22, v.6 p.697*

Sky Static: The Space Debris Crisis. *v.5 p.720*

Skylark. *v.2 p.786*

Slang to-Day and Yesterday, with a Short Historical Sketch and
Vocabularies of English, American, and Australian
Slang. *v.2 p.552, p.553*

Slapstick: Or Lonesome No More!. *v.2 p.158*

☐ Slashdot: News for Nerds, Stuff That
Matters. *v.5 p.342, p.343, p.348*

Slash. *v.2 p.733*

Slaughter among Neighbors: Political Origins of Communal
Violence. *v.4 p.512, p.613*

Slaughterhouse: The Handbook of the Eastern Front. . *v.3 p.80*

Slaughterhouse-Five: Or the Children's Crusade. . . *v.2 p.158*

Slave and Citizen: The Classic Comparative Study of Race
Relations in the Americas. *v.3 p.280*

Slave and Citizen: The Life of Frederick Douglass. . *v.3 p.420*

The Slave Coast of West Africa, 1550-1750: The Impact of the
Atlantic Slave Trade on an African Society. . . . *v.6 p.73*

The Slave Community: Plantation Life in the Antebellum South. *v.3 p.394, v.6 p.3, p.37*

Slave Emancipation in Cuba: The Transition to Free Labor, 1860-1899. . . . .*v.3 p.280*

Slave in a Box: The Strange Career of Aunt Jemima. *v.6 p.39, p.40*

Slave Laws in Virginia. *v.4 p.474*

Slave Life in Rio De Janerio, 1808-1850. .*v.3 p.279, p.336, p.337*

Slave Rebellion in Brazil: The Muslim Uprising of 1835 in Bahia. *v.3 p.280, p.337*

Slave Religion: The Invisible Institution in the Antebellum South. *v.1 p.608*

Slave Revolution in the Caribbean, 1789-1804: A Brief History with Documents. *v.3 p.314, v.6 p.11*

Slave Systems of Greek and Roman Antiquity. *v.4 p.727*

Slave Traffic in the Age of Abolition: Puerto Rico, West Africa and the Non-Hispanic Caribbean, 1815-1859. . .*v.3 p.319*

Slave Women in Caribbean Society, 1650-1832. . . . .*v.4 p.727*

Slave Women in the New World: Gender Stratification in the Caribbean. *v.4 p.728*

The Slaveholding Republic: An Account of the United States Government's Relations to Slavery. *v.3 p.396*

Slavery and Abolition in Early Republican Peru. . . .*v.3 p.327*

Slavery and Beyond: The Making of Men and Chikunda Ethnic Identities in the Unstable World of South-Central Africa, 1750-1920. . . . .*v.6 p.76*

Slavery and Colonial Rule in French West Africa. . . .*v.6 p.68*

Slavery and Human Progress. *v.4 p.727*

Slavery and Identity: Ethnicity, Gender, and Race in Salvador, Brazil, 1808-1888. . . . .*v.3 p.265, p.337*

Slavery and Race in American Popular Culture. *v.3 p.402*

Slavery and Rebellion in the Roman World, 140 B.C.-70 B.C. *v.3 p.26*

Slavery and Salvation in Colonial Cartagena de Indias. .*v.3 p.356*

Slavery and Social Death: A Comparative Study. . . .*v.4 p.727*

Slavery and Society at Rome. *v.3 p.23*

Slavery and the Demographic and Economic History of Minas Gerais, Brazil, 1720-1888. . . . .*v.3 p.335*

Slavery and the Law. *v.4 p.453*

Slavery, Colonialism and Economic Growth in Dahomey, 1640-1960. . . . .*v.6 p.74*

Slavery Defended: The Views of the Old South. *v.3 p.420*

Slavery in Russia, 1450-1725. . . . .*v.4 p.728*

Slavery in the American Mountain South. . . .*v.4 p.727, p.728*

Slavery on the Spanish Frontier: The Colombian Choco, 1680-1810. . . . .*v.3 p.358*

Slavery, Propaganda, and the American Revolution. . .*v.3 p.407*

Slavery, Secession and Southern History. *v.4 p.521*

Slavery. *v.3 p.15, p.24*

Slaves and Masters in the Roman Empire: A Study in Social Control. *v.3 p.23*

Slaves and Missionaries: The Disintegration of Jamaican Slave Society, 1787-1834. . . . .*v.4 p.728*

Slaves and Slavery in Muslim Africa, Vol. 1. . . .*v.4 p.728*

Slaves and Slavery in Muslim Africa, Vol. 2. . . . .*v.4 p.728*

Slaves and the courts, 1740-1860. . . . .*v.4 p.437*

The Slave's Narrative. *v.2 p.3*

Slaves of Love and Other Norwegian Short Stories. . .*v.2 p.627*

Slaves of the White God: Blacks in Mexico, 1570-1650. .*v.4 p.728*

Slaves on Horses: The Evolution of the Islamic Polity. .*v.6 p.584*

Slaves on Screen: Film and Historical Vision. . . .*v.6 p.30, p.37*

A Slave's Place, a Master's World: Fashioning Dependency in Rural Brazil. *v.3 p.337*

Slavic & Baltic Languages. *v.2 p.773*

Slavic and East European Language Resource Center. *v.2 p.773*

The Slavic Epic: Gundulic's Osman. *v.2 p.779*

The Slavs in European History and Civilization. .*v.3 p.214, p.215*

Slayer Slang: A Buffy the Vampire Slayer Lexicon. . .*v.2 p.551*

Slaying the Financial Dragon: Strategies for Museums. *v.1 p.827, p.828*

Sleep It off Lady: Stories. *v.2 p.769*

The Sleeper Awakes. *v.2 p.320*

Sleeping Beauty: A Legend in Progress. *v.1 p.25*

Sleeping Fires. *v.2 p.289*

Sleeping in the Forest: Stories and Poems. *v.6 p.666*

Sleeping on a Wire. *v.6 p.614*

Sleeping with Cats: A Memoir. *v.2 p.153*

Sleepwalker in a Fog. *v.2 p.809*

The Sleepwalkers: A History of Man's Changing Vision of the Universe. *v.3 p.47*

The Sleepwalkers: A Trilogy. *v.2 p.603*

Sleepwalking Through History: America in the Reagan Years. *v.3 p.473*

Sleisenger and Fordtran's Gastrointenstinal and Liver Disease: Pathophysiology, Diagnosis, Management. *v.5 p.519*

Sleuthing the Alamo: Davy Crockett's Last Stand and Other Mysteries of the Texas Revolution. *v.3 p.508*

Sliding Piece Puzzles. *v.5 p.469*

The Slippery Earth: Nahua-Christian Moral Dialogue in Sixteenth-Century Mexico. *v.3 p.262*

Slippery Slope Arguments. *v.1 p.493*

Sloan Digital Sky Survey. *v.5 p.63*

Sloan Kettering: Poems. *v.6 p.649, p.650*

Sloan Rules: Alfred P. Sloan and the Triumph of General Motors. *v.4 p.153, p.154*

Sloane's Complete Book of Bicycling: The Cyclist's Bible. *v.4 p.857*

The Slopes of Lebanon. *v.6 p.606*

Slouching Towards Bethlehem: Essays. *v.2 p.143*

Slovene: A Comprehensive Grammar. *v.2 p.777*

Slovene-English/English-Slovene Dictionary and Phrasebook. *v.2 p.777*

Slovenia 1945: Memories of Death and Survival after World War II. *v.3 p.249, p.250*

Slovenia and the Slovenes: A Small State and the New Europe. *v.3 p.250*

Slovensko-Anglicky Slovnik. *v.2 p.777*

Slow Death for Slavery: The Course of Abolition in Northern Nigeria, 1897-1936. . . . .*v.6 p.71*

Slow Homecoming. *v.2 p.617*

Slow Man. *v.2 p.754*

Slow Motion: Changing Masculinities, Changing
   Men. *v.6 p.430, p.446*

The Slow Natives. *v.2 p.744*

The Slum and the Ghetto. *v.3 p.516*

Slumming: Sexual and Social Politics in Victorian
   London. *v.3 p.53, p.54*

Sly and Able: A Political Biography of James F. Byrnes. .*v.3 p.462*

Small Antenna Design. *v.5 p.728*

Small Books and Pleasant Histories: Popular Fiction and Its
   Readership in Seventeenth-Century England. *v.3 p.129*

The Small Business Start-up Kit. *v.4 p.87*

Small Business Start-Up Workbook: A Step-by-Step Guide to
   Starting the Business You've Dreamed Of. *v.4 p.88*

Small Ceremonies. *v.2 p.739*

Small Change. *v.6 p.649*

Small Deaths: Photographs. *v.1 p.765*

The Small Giant : Sweden Enters the Industrial
   Era. *v.3 p.234, p.235*

Small Group Research: A Handbook. *v.5 p.647*

Small Groups: An Introduction. *v.5 p.647*

Small Hours of the Night: Selected Poems of Roque
   Dalton. *v.2 p.675*

Small Islands, Large Questions: Society, Culture and Resistance
   in the Post-Emancipation Caribbean. *v.4 p.40*

A Small Personal Voice: Essays, Reviews, Interviews. .*v.2 p.365*

Small Planets: Saul Bellow and the Art of Short Fiction. .*v.2 p.60*

The Small Room. *v.2 p.119*

Small Towns in Early Modern Europe. *v.3 p.43*

Small Worlds: The Dynamics of Networks Between Order and
   Randomness. *v.5 p.336, p.345*

Smart and Simple Financial Strategies for Busy People. .*v.4 p.97*

Smart Antennas. *v.5 p.728*

Smart Business: How Knowledge Communities Can
   Revolutionize Your Company. *v.4 p.77*

Smart Machines in Education. *v.5 p.590*

Smart Mobs: The Next Social Revolution: Transforming
   Cultures and Communities in the Age of Instant
   Access. *v.4 p.712*

Smartest Guys in the Room: The Amazing Rise and Scandalous
   Fall of Enron. . . .*v.4 p.91, p.92, p.105, p.106, p.109, p.148*

SME Mining Engineering Handbook, Set. *v.5 p.738*

◻ SME: The Society for Mining, Metallurgy and
   Exploration. *v.5 p.731*

Smearing the Queer: Medical Bias in the Health Care of Gay
   Men. *v.6 p.378*

The Smell of Hay. *v.2 p.713*

The Smell of Sweat: Greek Athletics and Greek Culture. .*v.4 p.810*

The Smile of the Lamb. *v.6 p.648*

Smiley's People: A Novel. *v.2 p.361*

Smithells Metals Reference Book. *v.5 p.319, p.732*

Smith's Copius and Critical English-Latin Dictionary. .*v.2 p.424*

The Smithsonian and the American Indian: Making a Moral
   Anthropology in Victorian America. *v.4 p.47*

The Smithsonian Book of Mars. *v.5 p.434*

Smithsonian Book of National Wildlife Refuges. . . .*v.5 p.83*

The Smithsonian Institution. *v.5 p.385*

Smithsonian Physical Tables. *v.5 p.281*

◻ Smithsonian Physical Tables. *v.5 p.741*

Smithsonian Timelines of the Ancient World: A Visual
   Chronology from the Origins of Life to A. D. 1500. .*v.3 p.3*

Smithsonian's New Zoo. *v.5 p.84*

The Smoke That Carried Us: Selected Poems of Rene
   Char. *v.2 p.513*

Smokechasing. *v.5 p.31*

Smoke's Way: Poems from Limited Editions,
   1968-1981. . . . .*v.2 p.117*

Smokestack Diplomacy: Cooperation and Conflict in East-West
   Environmental Politics. *v.6 p.299*

Smoking and Pregnancy: The Politics of Fetal
   Protection. *v.5 p.524*

Smoldering Ashes: Cuzco and the Creation of Republican Peru,
   1780-1840. . . . .*v.3 p.265, p.326, p.327, p.328*

Smollet's Women: A Study in an Eighteenth-Century Masculine
   Sensibility. *v.2 p.261*

Smollett: Author of the First Distinction. *v.2 p.261*

Smollett Studies. *v.2 p.261*

A Smoother Pebble: Mathematical Explorations. .*v.5 p.457, p.465*

Smuggled Chinese: Clandestine Immigration to the United
   States. *v.6 p.118, p.126*

Smugglers, Secessionists and Loyal Citizens on the Ghana-Toga
   Frontier: The Life of the Borderlands since 1914. . .*v.6 p.74*

Snack Food Technology. *v.5 p.34*

The Snake Pit. *v.2 p.128*

Snap Shots of the Century Utopias: Russian Modernist Texts,
   1905-1940. . . . .*v.2 p.794*

Snap to Grid: A User's Guide to Digital Arts, Media, and
   Cultures. *v.1 p.771*

The Sneaker Book: Anatomy of an Industry and an
   Icon. *v.4 p.870, p.881*

Snorri Sturluson-Edda: Prologue and Gylfaginning. .*v.2 p.625*

Snow Country. *v.6 p.230*

The Snow Lion and the Dragon: China, Tibet, and the Dalai
   Lama. *v.6 p.240*

Snow White and Russian Red. *v.2 p.791*

Snow White. *v.2 p.140*

Snowball Earth: The Story of a Maverick Scientist and His
   Theory of the Global Catastrophe That Spawned
   Life as We Know It. *v.5 p.450*

Snow. *v.6 p.667*

So Big. *v.2 p.73*

So Far from God: The U. S. War with Mexico,
   1846-1848. . . . .*v.6 p.534*

So Human an Animal: How We Are Shaped by Surroundings
   and Events. *v.4 p.760*

So Long a Letter. *v.2 p.543*

So Vast the Prison. *v.2 p.545, v.6 p.642*

Soap, Sex, and Cigarettes: A Cultural History of American
   Advertising. *v.4 p.426*

Soaring: The Diary and Letters of a Denishawn Dancer in the
   Far East, 1925-1926. . . . .*v.1 p.12*

Sober as a Judge: The Supreme Court and Republican
   Liberty. *v.4 p.540*

The Soccer Coaching Bible. *v.4 p.867, p.868, p.905*

Soccer, Women, Sexual Liberation: Kicking off a New
Era.. . . . .*v.4 p.836, p.844, p.867,v.6 p.437*

Soccer. *v.4 p.867*

Social Aggression among Girls. *v.5 p.629*

A Social Analysis of the History of Surinam. *v.3 p.322*

Social and Cognitive Approaches to Interpersonal
Communication. *v.5 p.620*

Social and Cultural Anthropology: The Key Concepts. .*v.4 p.23*

Social and Cultural Dynamics. *v.4 p.700*

Social and Cultural Mobility. *v.4 p.700*

Social and Cultural Perspectives in Nutrition. *v.5 p.35*

Social and Economic History of the Hellenistic
World. *v.3 p.14, p.15*

Social and Economic History of the Roman Empire. . .*v.3 p.24*

Social and Economic Modernization in Eastern Germany: From
Honecker to Kohl. *v.3 p.176*

The Social and Educational Thought of Harold Rugg. .*v.4 p.341*

The Social and Emotional Development of Gifted Children:
What Do We Know? *v.4 p.317*

The Social and Political Conflict in Prussia,
1858-1864. . . . .*v.4 p.609, p.610*

Social and Political Ideas of the
Muckrakers. *v.3 p.439, p.440, p.446*

The Social and Political Philosophy of Jacques
Maritain. *v.1 p.457*

The Social and Political Thought of Herbert Spencer. .*v.4 p.686*

Social Anxiety. *v.5 p.654*

The Social Art: Language and Its Uses. *v.2 p.562*

Social Aspects of Alcoholism. *v.5 p.521*

Social Assistance and Bureaucratic Politics: The Montepios of
Colonial Mexico, 1767-1821. . . . .*v.3 p.285*

Social Authorship and the Advent of Print. *v.2 p.169*

The Social Basis of European Fascist Movements. . .*v.4 p.768*

The Social Basis of Scientific Discoveries. *v.5 p.409, p.410, p.411*

Social Behavior and Personality: Contributions of W. I. Thomas
to Theory and Social Research. *v.4 p.688*

Social Capital: A Theory of Social Structure and Action. *v.4 p.269*

Social Casework: A Behavioral Approach. *v.4 p.758*

The Social Causes of Environmental Destruction in Latin
America. *v.3 p.269*

Social Causes of Psychological Distress. *v.4 p.699*

Social Change and Stratification in Eastern Europe: An
Interpretive Analysis of Poland and Her Neighbors. *v.4 p.705*

Social Change and the Individual: Japan Before and After
Defeat in World War II. *v.4 p.707*

Social Change in a Yemeni Highlands Town. *v.4 p.707*

Social Change in Modern France: Towards a Cultural
Anthropology of the Fifth Republic. . . .*v.3 p.141, v.4 p.42*

Social Chaucer. *v.2 p.210*

Social Choice and Individual Values. *v.4 p.206, p.272*

Social Choreography: Ideology As Performance in Dance and
Everyday Movement. *v.1 p.37, p.42*

Social Class and Social Change in Puerto Rico. . . .*v.4 p.707*

Social Class in America: A Manual of Procedure for the
Measurement of Social Status. *v.4 p.725*

Social Classes and Social Relations in Britain,
1850-1914. . . . .*v.3 p.115, p.131*

Social Cognition: Making Sense of People. *v.5 p.649*

Social Cognition: Understanding Self and Others. . . .*v.5 p.650*

Social Communication in Advertising: Persons, Products and
Images of Well-being. *v.4 p.140*

Social Conflict and the City. *v.4 p.771*

The Social Consequences of Long Life. *v.4 p.741*

The Social Consequences of Methamphetamine
Use. *v.6 p.253, p.254*

Social Conservatism and the Middle Classes in Germany,
1914-1933. . . . .*v.3 p.180, p.181*

The Social Construction of International News: We're Talking
about Them, They're Talking about Us. *v.4 p.408*

The Social Construction of
Lesbianism. *v.4 p.750, v.6 p.372, p.381*

The Social Context of Cognitive Development. .*v.5 p.626, p.630*

The Social Contract and Discourses. *v.4 p.492*

The Social Contract: And, the First and Second
Discourses. *v.1 p.454*

The Social Contract, Discourse on the Virtue Most Necessary
for a Hero, Political Fragments and Geneva
Manuscript. *v.2 p.482, p.483*

Social Contracts under Stress: The Middle Classes of America,
Europe, and Japan at the Turn of the Century. . . .*v.4 p.725*

Social Control in Europe. *v.4 p.773*

Social Control in Slave Plantation Societies: A Comparison of
St. Domingue and Cuba. *v.4 p.728*

The Social Control of Cities? *v.6 p.716*

Social Dance: Steps to Success. *v.1 p.34*

Social Darwinism : Selected Essays. *v.4 p.686*

Social Darwinism in American
Thought. *v.3 p.368, p.441,v.4 p.683, p.685*

Social Darwinism in European and American Thought,
1860-1945: Nature as Model and Nature as
Threat. *v.3 p.49, p.77, p.78*

Social Death and Resurrection: Slavery and Emancipation in
South Africa. *v.4 p.727*

Social Diagnosis. *v.4 p.758*

The Social Dimensions of Science. *v.5 p.410*

Social Discipline in the Reformation: Central Europe,
1550-1750. . . . .*v.3 p.166*

Social Dominance: An Intergroup Theory of Social Hierarchy
and Oppression. *v.5 p.656*

The Social Economics of Health Care. *v.5 p.511*

Social Engineering in the Philippines: The Aims, Execution and
Impact of American Colonial Policy, 1900-1913. . .*v.6 p.180*

Social Ethics: Morality and Social Policy. . . .*v.4 p.484, p.770*

Social Ethics: Sociology and the Future of Society. . .*v.4 p.681*

Social Exchange Theory: The Two Traditions. *v.4 p.679*

Social Experience and Anthropological Knowledge. . .*v.4 p.25*

The Social Fabric of Health: An Introduction to Medical
Anthropology. *v.5 p.536*

Social Factors. *v.2 p.562*

Social Foundations of Judiasm. *v.4 p.721, p.722*

Social Geography of the United States. *v.4 p.708*

The Social Gospel: Religion and Reform in Changing
   America. *v.1 p.644*

A Social History of American Technology. *v.3 p.367*

The Social History of an Indonesian Town. *v.4 p.703*

A Social History of Anthropology in the United States. *v.4 p.4*

The Social History of Art. *v.1 p.708*

A Social History of British Broadcasting, 1922-1939: Serving
   the Nation. *v.4 p.413*

A Social History of England. *v.3 p.91*

A Social History of English Rowing. *v.4 p.811, p.865*

A Social History of English. *v.2 p.554, p.555*

A Social History of French Catholicism, 1789-1914. . .*v.3 p.148*

A Social History of Germany 1648-1914. . . . . .*v.4 p.706*

A Social History of Imperial Russia, 1700-1917, Vol. 1. .*v.3 p.211*

Social History of Imperial Russia, 1700-1917, Vol. 2. .*v.3 p.211*

A Social History of Knowledge: From Gutenberg to
   Diderot. *v.1 p.481*

A Social History of Leisure Since 1600. . . . . . .*v.4 p.716*

A Social History of Madness: The World Through the Eyes of
   the Insane. *v.4 p.706*

A Social History of Medicines in the Twentieth Century: To Be
   Taken Three Times a Day. *v.4 p.778*

A Social History of Soviet Trade: Trade Policy, Retail Practices,
   and Consumption, 1917-1953. . . . .*v.4 p.257*

A Social History of the American Family from Colonial Times
   to the Present. *v.4 p.732*

The Social History of the Brazilian Samba. *v.1 p.294, v.3 p.268*

A Social History of the Media: From Gutenberg to the
   Internet. *v.3 p.37*

Social History of the Media: From Gutenburg to the
   Internet. *v.4 p.415*

Social History of Western Europe, 1450-1720: Tensions and
   Solidarities Amongst the Rural People. *v.4 p.708*

Social History Of Women and the Family in the Middle
   East. *v.6 p.594*

A Social History of Women in Ireland
   1870-1970. . . . .*v.3 p.135, p.139*

Social Identifications: A Social Psychology of Intergroup
   Relations and Group Processes. *v.4 p.713*

Social Identity and Social Cognition. *v.5 p.649*

Social Implications of the Scientific and Technological
   Revolution: UNESCO. *v.5 p.409, p.411*

Social Indicators and Social Theory: Elements of an Operational
   System. *v.4 p.769*

Social Inequalities and Cancer. *v.4 p.778*

Social Intelligence: The New Science of Success. .*v.4 p.119, p.166*

Social Interaction: Process and Products. *v.4 p.692*

Social Issues in Contemporary Sport: A Resource
   Guide. *v.4 p.820*

Social Judgments: Implicit and Explicit Processes. . .*v.5 p.649*

Social Justice and Third World Education, Vol. 37. . .*v.4 p.314*

Social Learning and Imitation. *v.4 p.357, p.358*

Social Learning from Broadcast Television. *v.4 p.418*

Social Learning Theory and the Explanation of Crime: A Guide
   for the New Century. *v.6 p.250*

Social Learning Theory. *v.4 p.355, p.356*

Social Life, Local Politics, and Nazism: Marburg,
   1880-1935. . . . .*v.3 p.159, p.160*

The Social Life of a Modern Community. *v.4 p.725*

The Social Life of Painting in Ancient Rome and on the Bay of
   Naples. *v.1 p.728*

Social Marketing: Improving the Quality of
   Life. *v.4 p.51, p.134, p.135*

Social Marketing in the 21st Century. *v.4 p.51, p.134*

The Social Meaning of Money: Pin Money, Paychecks, Poor
   Relief, and Other Currencies. *v.4 p.718, p.719*

The Social Meanings of Suicide. *v.4 p.693*

Social Mindscapes: An Invitation to Cognitive
   Sociology. *v.5 p.650, p.651*

Social Mobility in Britain. *v.4 p.703*

Social Mobility in Industrial Society. *v.4 p.722, p.726*

Social Movements, 1768-2004. . . . .*v.4 p.712*

☐ Social Movements and Culture : A Resource Site. .*v.4 p.710*

Social Movements and Free-Market Capitalism in Latin
   America: Telecommunications Privatization and
   the Rise of Consumer Protest. *v.3 p.355*

Social Movements and Organization Theory. *v.4 p.718*

Social Movements in India: A Review of the Literature. *v.4 p.711*

Social Neuroscience: People Thinking about Thinking
   People. *v.5 p.616*

The Social Order of the Slum: Ethnicity and Territory in the
   Inner City. *v.4 p.707*

Social Organization: A Study of the Larger Mind. .*v.4 p.693, p.694*

The Social Organization of Gay Males. *v.4 p.749, p.750, v.6 p.375*

The Social Organization of Mental Illness, Vol. 1. . . .*v.4 p.775*

The Social Organization of Sexuality: Sexual Practices in the
   United States. *v.4 p.748*

Social Origins of Dictatorship and Democracy: Lord and
   Peasant in the Making of the Modern World. . . .*v.4 p.767*

Social Origins of Mental Ability. *v.5 p.651, p.652*

The Social Origins of Private Life: A History of American
   Families, 1600-1900. . . . .*v.4 p.732, p.733*

The Social Origins of the Modern Middle East. . . .*v.4 p.703*

Social Outsiders in Nazi Germany. *v.3 p.84*

Social Policy and Practice in Canada: A History. . .*v.3 p.536*

The Social Politics of Medieval Diplomacy: Anglo-German
   Relations, 1066-1307. . . . .*v.3 p.161*

Social Preconditions of National Revival in Europe: A
   Comparative Analysis of the Social Composition of Patriotic
   Groups among the Smaller European Nations. . . .*v.3 p.61*

Social Pressures in Informal Groups: A Study of Human Factors
   in Housing. *v.4 p.718*

The Social Problems of an Industrial Civilization. . .*v.5 p.579*

Social Problems. *v.4 p.209, p.750*

The Social Production of Indifference: Exploring the Symbolic
   Roots of Western Bureaucracy. *v.4 p.718*

The Social Production of Urban Space. *v.6 p.723*

Social Psychology: Handbook of Basic Principles. . .*v.5 p.646*

The Social Psychology of Collective Action: Identity, Injustice
   and Gender. *v.5 p.648*

Social Psychology of Exercise and Sport. *v.5 p.582*

The Social Psychology of Good and Evil. .*v.4 p.698, v.5 p.655*

The Social Psychology of Intergroup and International Conflict Resolution. *v.4 p.698*

The Social Psychology of Interpersonal Discrimination. .*v.4 p.698*

Social Psychology of Leisure. *v.5 p.581*

A Social Psychology of Leisure. *v.5 p.582*

Social Psychology of Music. *v.1 p.375*

The Social Psychology of Music. . .*v.1 p.375, v.5 p.618, p.619*

The Social Psychology of Organizations. *v.4 p.716*

The Social Psychology of Politics. *v.5 p.644*

The Social Psychology of Sport. *v.5 p.583*

Social Reality. *v.1 p.500, p.501*

Social Research Methods, Feminist Perspectives. . . .*v.4 p.688*

Social Responsibility in Marketing: A Proactive and Profitable Marketing Management Strategy. *v.4 p.145*

☐ Social Science Electronic Data Library. *v.4 p.689*

Social Security and the Golden Age: An Essay on the New American Demographic. *v.4 p.247*

Social Security, Medicare and Government Pensions: Get the Most Out of Your Retirement and Medical Benefits. *v.4 p.96, p.98*

Social Services Abstracts (bibliographic database). . . .*v.5 p.670*

Social Services for Senior Gay Men and Lesbians. . .*v.6 p.382*

Social statics; or, the conditions essential to human happiness specified, and the first of them developed. by Herbert Spencer ... with a notice of the author and a steel Portrait. *v.4 p.684*

Social Stratification, Class, Race, and Gender in Sociological Perspective. *v.4 p.722*

Social Stratification in Africa. *v.4 p.707*

Social Stratification in India: Issues and Themes. .*v.4 p.706, p.707*

Social Stratification in Science. *v.5 p.410, p.411*

The Social Structures of the Economy. *v.4 p.208*

Social Struggles in Archaic Rome: New Perspectives on the Conflict of the Orders. *v.3 p.25*

Social Studies for Children: A Guide to Basic Instruction. *v.4 p.363*

Social Studies in Elementary Education. *v.4 p.365*

The Social Studies Wars: What Should We Teach the Children? *v.4 p.362, p.363*

Social Theories in the Middle Ages, 1200-1500. . . .*v.6 p.563*

Social Theories of Jacksonian Democracy. *v.3 p.414*

Social Theory and Social Structure. *v.4 p.699*

e Social Theory and the Urban Question. *v.6 p.719*

Social Theory in Archaeology. *v.4 p.6*

Social Theory of International Politics. *v.4 p.627*

Social Theory: The Multicultural and Classic Readings.*v.4 p.675*

Social Things: An Introduction to the Sociological Life.*v.4 p.683*

Social Transformation of American Medicine: The Rise of a Sovereign Profession and the Making of a Vast Industry. *v.5 p.510*

The Social Transformation of Eighteenth-Century Cuba.*v.3 p.310*

The Social Vision of William Blake. *v.2 p.239*

☐ Social Work Abstracts. *v.4 p.757*

The Social Work Dictionary. *v.5 p.670*

The Social Work Interview: A Guide for Human Service Professionals. *v.4 p.757, p.758*

The Social World of the First Christians: Essays in Honor of Wayne A. Meeks. *v.1 p.628*

Social Worlds of Children Learning to Write in an Urban Primary School. *v.4 p.360*

Socialism and Abundance: Radical Socialism in the Danish Welfare State. *v.3 p.234*

Socialism and Populism in Chile, 1932-52. . . . . .*v.3 p.353*

Socialism and Superior Brains: The Political Thought of George Bernard Shaw. *v.2 p.309*

Socialism and the Literary Artistry of William Morris. .*v.2 p.301*

The Socialism of Fools: Georg Ritter Von Schonerer and Austrian Pan-Germanism. *v.3 p.184*

Socialism: Past and Future. *v.4 p.506*

Socialism Unbound. *v.4 p.506*

Socialism: What Went Wrong?: An Inquiry into the Theoretical and Historical Sources of the Socialist Crisis. . . .*v.4 p.507*

Socialism. *v.4 p.506*

Socialist Darwinism: Evolution in German Socialist Thought from Marx to Bernstein. *v.3 p.49*

Socialist Ensembles: Theater and State in Cuba and Nicaragua. *v.3 p.302*

Socialist Ideology and the Struggle for Southern Africa. *v.6 p.74, p.75*

Socialist Iraq: A Study in Iraqi Politics since 1968. . .*v.6 p.603*

Socialist Women: European Socialist Feminism in the Nineteenth and Early Twentieth-Centuries. *v.3 p.52*

Socialization for Achievement: Essays on the Cultural Psychology of the Japanese. *v.4 p.702*

Society and Culture in Early Modern France: Eight Essays by Natalie Zemon Davis. *v.1 p.601, v.3 p.145*

Society and Democracy in Germany. *v.4 p.701*

Society and Drugs; Social and Cultural Observations. .*v.5 p.663*

Society and Economy in Germany, 1300-1600. . . . .*v.3 p.163*

Society and Health in Guyana: The Sociology of Health Care in a Developing Nation. *v.4 p.702*

Society and Politics in Medieval Italy. *v.3 p.198*

Society and Puritanism in Pre-Revolutionary England. *v.3 p.120, p.121*

Society and the Dance: The Social Anthropology of Process and Performance. *v.1 p.49*

Society and the Holy in Late Antiquity. *v.3 p.30*

Society, Culture and Personality: Their Structure and Dynamics. *v.4 p.683*

☐ Society for Community Research and Action (APA Division 27). *v.5 p.672*

☐ Society for Consumer Psychology (APA Division 23). *v.5 p.585*

☐ Society for the Psychological Study of Social Issues (APA Division 9). *v.5 p.672*

☐ Society for the Teaching of Psychology (APA Division 2). *v.5 p.676*

Society in Crisis: France in the Sixteenth Century. . .*v.3 p.146*

Society in Prehistory: The Origins of Human Culture. .*v.4 p.17*

☐ Society of American Foresters: Gorwing better all the time. *v.5 p.36*

The Society of Nations: Its Past, Present, and Possible Future. *v.4 p.631*

The Society of Norman Italy. *v.3 p.198, p.199*

The Society of Six: California Colorists. *v.1 p.750*

A Society on Stage: Essays on Spanish Golden
Age. *v.1 p.74, p.107*

Society Online: The Internet in Context. *v.4 p.425*

Society, Politics, and Economic Development: A Quantitative
Approach. *v.4 p.258*

A Society Without Fathers or Husbands: The Na of
China. *v.4 p.32*

☐ SOCindex. *v.4 p.675*

The Socioeconomics of Sustainable Agriculture: An Annotated
Bibliography. *v.5 p.12*

Socio-Economics: Toward a New Synthesis. *v.4 p.269*

Sociolinguistics of the Spanish-Speaking World: Iberia, Latin
America, United States. *v.2 p.636*

☐ SocioLog : Julian Dierkes' Comprehensive Guide to
Sociology On-line. *v.4 p.675*

☐ Sociological Abstracts. *v.4 p.675*

Sociological Ambivalence and Other Essays. *v.4 p.680*

Sociological Analysis of Aging: The Gay Male
Perspective. *v.6 p.380, p.381*

A Sociological History of Christian Worship. *v.1 p.654*

The Sociological Imagination. *v.4 p.681, p.682*

A Sociological Perspective of Sport. *v.4 p.817*

Sociological Theories of Today. *v.4 p.680*

Sociological Theory: A Book of Readings. *v.4 p.679*

Sociological Theory and Modern Society. *v.4 p.680*

Sociological Theory: Contemporary Debates. *v.4 p.682*

Sociological Theory: What Went Wrong?: Diagnosis and
Remedies. *v.4 p.680*

The Sociological Tradition. *v.4 p.683*

A Sociological View of Sovereignty: A Series of Articles in the
American Journal of Sociology, 1899-1900. . . . .*v.4 p.249*

Sociological Writings. *v.4 p.685*

Sociology : A Mulitple Paradigm Science. *v.4 p.683*

Sociology and Development. *v.4 p.258*

Sociology and Nature: Social Action in Context. . .*v.4 p.680*

Sociology and Philosophy. *v.4 p.685*

Sociology and Pragmatism: The Higher Learning in
America. *v.4 p.762, p.763*

The Sociology and Professionalization of Economics: British
and American Economic Essays. *v.4 p.268*

The Sociology and Psychology of Terrorism: Who Becomes a
Terrorist and Why? *v.4 p.767*

Sociology and the Twilight of Man: Homocentrism and
Discourse in Sociological Theory. *v.4 p.685*

Sociology as an Art Form. *v.4 p.680*

Sociology, Ethnomethodology, and Experience : A
Phenomenological Critique. *v.4 p.688*

Sociology for the South: Or the Failure of Free Society. .*v.3 p.396*

☐ Sociology in Latin America. *v.4 p.704*

Sociology in the Soviet Union and Beyond: Social Enquiry and
Social Change. *v.4 p.684*

The Sociology of Andrew M. Greeley. *v.4 p.720*

Sociology of Deviant Behavior. *v.4 p.695, p.696*

The Sociology of Economic Life. *v.4 p.185*

Sociology of Education and Work. *v.4 p.304, p.761*

The Sociology of Food: Eating, Diet and Culture. . . .*v.4 p.778*

The Sociology of Gambling. *v.4 p.777*

The Sociology of Georg Simmel. *v.4 p.686*

The Sociology of Health, Illness, and Health Care: A Critical
Approach. *v.4 p.774*

The Sociology of HIV Transmission. *v.4 p.779*

Sociology of Leisure. *v.4 p.716*

The Sociology of Marx. *v.4 p.680, p.681*

The Sociology of Medicine. *v.4 p.778*

The Sociology of Religion: An Historical Introduction. .*v.1 p.524*

The Sociology of Religion. *v.4 p.720*

The Sociology of Revolution. *v.4 p.760*

The Sociology of Risk and Gambling Reader. *v.4 p.715*

The Sociology of Secret Societies: Chinese Secret Societies in
Singapore and Peninsular Malaysia. *v.4 p.719*

Sociology of Slavery. *v.4 p.727*

The Sociology of Sport and Physical Education: An Introductory
Reader. *v.4 p.796, p.817*

Sociology of the Arts: Exploring Fine and Popular
Forms. *v.1 p.707*

The Sociology of the Palestinians. *v.4 p.708*

The Sociology of the Third World: Disparity and
Development. *v.4 p.759*

The Sociology of War and Peace. *v.4 p.766*

The Sociology of Work. *v.4 p.717*

Sociology: The Core, with PowerWeb. *v.4 p.675*

Sociology. *v.4 p.675*

Socrates: A Very Short Introduction. *v.1 p.423*

Socrates and the State. *v.4 p.489*

Socrates in the Apology: An Essay on Plato's Apology of
Socrates. *v.1 p.423*

Socrates, Ironist and Moral Philosopher. *v.1 p.423*

Socrates' Muse: Reflections on Effective Case Discussion
Leadership. *v.4 p.177*

Socrates on Trial. *v.1 p.422*

Socrates, Pleasure, and Value. *v.1 p.423*

Socrates, Sport, and Students: A Philosophical Inquiry into
Physical Education and Sport. *v.4 p.794*

Socrates. *v.1 p.423*

Socratic Studies. *v.1 p.423*

Socratic Testimonies. *v.1 p.422*

Sod and Stubble: The Unabridged and Annotated
Edition. *v.3 p.524*

Sod-House Frontier. *v.3 p.518*

Sodom and Gomorrah: In Search of Lost Time. . . .*v.2 p.524*

Soft Condensed Matter. *v.5 p.554*

Soft News Goes to War: Public Opinion and American Foreign
Policy in the New Media Age. *v.4 p.414, p.559*

Software Engineering for Internet Applications. .*v.5 p.338, p.349*

Software Engineering. *v.5 p.346, p.348, p.349*

Software for People. *v.1 p.220, p.346*

Soil and Environmental Science Dictionary. *v.5 p.311*

Soil and Water Conservation Engineering. *v.5 p.703*

Soil Biology: Effects on Soil Quality. *v.5 p.87, p.176*

Soil Biology Guide. v.5 p.87

Soil Biology. v.5 p.90

Soil Chemistry. .v.5 p.48

Soil Constitutive Models: Evaluation, Selection, and Calibration: January 24-26, 2005, Austin, Texas. v.5 p.699

Soil Degradation. v.5 p.51

Soil Ecology in Sustainable Agricultural Systems. . .v.5 p.11

Soil Engineering: Testing, Design, and Remediation. . .v.5 p.421

Soil Fertility and Fertilizers: An Introduction to Nutrient Management. v.5 p.51

Soil Fertility. .v.5 p.49

Soil Genesis and Classification. v.5 p.48

Soil Geography and Land Use. v.5 p.366, p.373

Soil Mechanics and Foundations. v.5 p.698

Soil Mechanics: Concepts and Applications. . .v.5 p.422, p.699

Soil Mechanics for Environmental Engineers. v.5 p.699

Soil Mechanics in Engineering Practice. v.5 p.422

Soil Microbiology and Biochemistry. . . .v.5 p.50, p.113, p.114

Soil Microbiology. v.5 p.51

Soil Mineralogy with Environmental Applications. . .v.5 p.49

Soil Nutrient Bioavailability: A Mechanistic Approach. v.5 p.52, p.356

Soil Physics. v.5 p.49, p.50

Soil Quality and Soil Erosion. v.5 p.359, p.367

Soil Respiration and the Environment. v.5 p.699

Soil Sampling and Methods of Analysis. v.5 p.312

Soil Sampling, Preparation, and Analysis. v.5 p.51

Soil Science: Methods and Applications. v.5 p.50, p.51

Soil Science Society of America. v.5 p.48

Soil Solution Chemistry: Applications to Environmental Science and Agriculture. v.5 p.52

Soil Strength and Slope Stability. v.5 p.699

Soil Testing and Plant Analysis. v.5 p.52

Soils: An Introduction to Soils and Plant Growth. . .v.5 p.50

Soils and Geomorphology. v.5 p.48

Soils and Soil Fertility. v.5 p.51

Soils in Construction. v.5 p.422

Soils in Our Environment. v.6 p.294

The Soils of China. v.5 p.52

Sojourner Black Gay Voice. v.6 p.367, p.406

Sojourners of the Caribbean: Ethnogenesis and Ethnohistory of the Garifuna. v.3 p.271

Sol White's History of Colored Base Ball, with Other Documents on the Early Black Game, 1886-1936. . . . . .v.4 p.810, p.811, p.833, p.852

Solar Electricity. v.5 p.362

Solar Power Plants: Fundamentals, Technology, Systems, Economics. v.5 p.708

Solar System Dynamics. v.5 p.68

Solar System Evolution: A New Perspective. v.5 p.68

Solaris. v.2 p.790

The Soldier and the State in South America: Essays in Civil-Military Relations. v.3 p.277, v.4 p.593

The Soldier and the State: The Theory and Politics of Civil-Military Relations. v.3 p.36

Soldiers and Civilians: The Civil-Military Gap and American National Security. v.4 p.561

Soldiers and Politics in Eastern Europe, 1945-1990: The Case of Hungary. v.3 p.187

Soldiers and Society: The Effects of Military Service and War on American Life. v.4 p.717

Soldiers As Police: The French and Prussian Armies and the Policing of Popular Protest, 1889-1914. . . .v.3 p.155, p.169

Soldiers, Guerrillas, and Politics in Colombia. . . .v.3 p.275

Soldiers in a Narrow Land: The Pinochet Regime in Chile, Updated Edition. v.3 p.355

Soldiers of Christ: Preaching in Late Medieval and Reformation France. .v.3 p.146

Soldiers of Diplomacy (Les Casques Bleus): The United Nations, Peacekeeping and the New World Order. v.4 p.633, p.648

Soldiers of the French Revolution. v.3 p.150

Soldiers of the Patria: A History of the Brazilian Army, 1889-1937. . . . . .v.3 p.275, p.337

Soldiers of the Virgin: The Moral Economy of a Colonial Maya Rebellion. v.3 p.285

Soldier's Pay. v.2 p.73, p.74

A Soldier's Play. v.2 p.145

The Sole Spokesman: Jinnah, the Muslim League and the Demand for Pakistan. v.6 p.157

Soledad Brother: The Prison Letters of George Jackson. v.6 p.6, p.26

Solfege, Ear Training, Rhythm, Dictation, and Music Theory: A Comprehensive Course. v.1 p.404

The Solid Earth: An Introduction to Global Geophysics. .v.5 p.443

Solid Foundation: An Oral History of Reggae. . . .v.1 p.292

The Solid Mandala. v.2 p.750

Solid State Chemistry: Compounds, Vol. 2. . . . . .v.5 p.305

Solid State Electronic Devices. v.5 p.723

Solid State Physics. v.5 p.554

Solid Waste: Assessment, Monitoring and Remediation. v.5 p.369, p.377, p.378

Solidarity: Poland's Independent Trade Union. . . .v.4 p.127

Solid-Phase Extraction: Principles and Practice. . . .v.5 p.268

Solid-Phase Synthesis and Combinatorial Technologies. .v.5 p.295

Solid-State Chemistry: Techniques. v.5 p.305

Solid-State Physics: An Introduction to Principles of Materials Science. .v.5 p.554

Solid-State Power Conversion Handbook. v.5 p.709

Solitary Raven: The Selected Writings of Bill Reid. . .v.6 p.679

The Solitary Self: Jean-Jacques Rousseau in Exile and Adversity. v.2 p.482, v.3 p.147

Solitary Song: An Autobiography. v.1 p.10

Solitudes Crowded with Loneliness. v.2 p.147

Solitudes, Galleries, and Other Poems. v.2 p.661

The Solitudes of Luis de Gongora. the Spanish Text, with an English Translation by Gilbert F. Cunningham. Pref. by A. A. Parker. Introd. by Elias L. Rivers. . . .v.2 p.650

Solo Jazz Piano: The Linear Approach. v.1 p.403

Soltando Amarras: Casting Off. v.2 p.674

Solubilities, Inorganic and Metal Organic Compounds; A Compilation of Solubility Data from the Periodical Literature, 2 volumes. *v.5 p.282*

Solubilities of Inorganic and Metal Organic Compounds; A Compilation of Quantitative Solubility Data from the Periodical Literature, 2 vols. *v.5 p.282*

Solubilities of Inorganic and Organic Compounds, Set. .*v.5 p.282*

Solubility Data Series. *v.5 p.281*

Solubility of Gases in Liquids: A Critical Evaluation of Gas-Liquid Systems in Theory and Practice. *v.5 p.281*

Solution Equilibria. *v.5 p.282*

Solution Techniques for Elementary Partial Differential Equations. *v.5 p.487*

Solutions for Singers: Tools for Performers and Teachers. *v.1 p.395, p.396*

SOLV-DB (Solvents Database). *v.5 p.281*

Solve This: Math Activities for Students and Clubs. *v.5 p.460, p.469*

Solvents Safety Handbook. *v.5 p.311*

Solving Discipline and Classroom Management Problems: Methods and Models for Today's Teachers. *v.4 p.284*

Solving Problems in Couples and Family Therapy: Techniques and Tactics. *v.5 p.669*

Somalia—The Untold Story: The War Through the Eyes of Somali Women. *v.4 p.652*

La Sombra del Caudillo. *v.2 p.668*

Some Aspects of the Tariff Question: An Examination of the Development of American Industries Under Protection. *v.4 p.258*

Some Mathematical Questions in Biology - Models in Population Biology. *v.5 p.91, p.93, p.94, p.188, p.189*

Some Modern Methods of Organic Synthesis. .*v.5 p.293, p.294*

Some of Us: Chinese Women Growing up in the Mao Era. *v.6 p.195, p.217*

Some Other World to Find: Quest and Negation in the Works of Herman Melville. *v.2 p.48*

Some Patterns and Trends in British Publishing, 1800-1919. . . . .*v.6 p.741*

Some Prefer Nettles. *v.6 p.233*

Some Principles of Regional Planning. *v.4 p.260*

Some Reminiscences. *v.2 p.305*

Some Shakespearean Themes and an Approach to "Hamlet". *v.2 p.230*

Some Sort of Epic Grandeur: The Life of F. Scott Fitzgerald. *v.2 p.76*

Some Tame Gazelle. *v.2 p.379*

Some Thoughts Concerning Education. *v.4 p.216, p.343*

Some Time in the Sun: The Hollywood Years of F. Scott Fitzgerald, William Faulkner, Nathanael West, Aldous Huxley, and James Agee. *v.2 p.56, p.73, p.76*

Somebody Else: Arthur Rimbaud in Africa 1880-1891. .*v.2 p.498*

Someone to Run With: A Novel. *v.6 p.648*

Somerset Maugham: A Life. *v.2 p.371*

Something for the Boys: Musical Theater and Gay Culture. *v.6 p.411*

Something in the Soil: Field-Testing the New Western History. *v.3 p.518*

Something in the Way She Moves: Dancing Women from Salome to Madonna. *v.1 p.28, p.29, p.40*

Something Left to Lose: Personal Relations and Survival Among New York's Homeless. *v.4 p.737, p.750*

Something New under the Sun: An Environmental History of the 20th-Century World. *v.6 p.296*

Something New under the Sun: An Environmental History of the Twentieth-Century World. *v.5 p.28, p.356, p.358*

Something to Live For: The Music of Billy Strayhorn. *v.1 p.264, p.361*

Something Wicked This Way Comes. *v.2 p.63*

The Sometime Connection: Public Opinion and Social Policy. *v.4 p.567*

Sometimes a Great Notion. *v.2 p.148*

Sometimes There Is No Other Side: Chicanos and the Myth of Equality. *v.6 p.539*

Son of a Servant: The Story of the Evolution of a Human Being, 1849-1867. . . . .*v.2 p.631*

Son of a Smaller Hero. *v.2 p.738*

The Son of God: The Origin of Christology and the History of Jewish-Hellenistic Religion. *v.1 p.640*

Son of Oscar Wilde. *v.2 p.321*

A Son of the Middle Border. *v.2 p.39*

Son of the Revolution. *v.6 p.195, p.200*

The Sonata Forms. *v.1 p.242*

The Sonata in the Baroque Era. *v.1 p.186*

The Sonata in the Classic Era. *v.1 p.191*

The Sonata since Beethoven. *v.1 p.201, p.219, p.241*

Sondheim on Music: Minor Details and Major Decisions. *v.1 p.254, p.357*

Sonechka: A Novella and Stories. *v.2 p.810*

Song at the Scaffold: A Novel of Horror and Holiness in the Reign of Terror. *v.2 p.612*

Song from the Land of Fire: Continuity and Change in Azerbaijanian Mugham. *v.1 p.287*

A Song in the Dark: The Birth of the Musical Film. . .*v.6 p.315*

The Song of Bernadette. *v.2 p.616*

The Song of Igor's Campaign. *v.2 p.793, p.806*

Song of Lawino and Song of Ocol. *v.2 p.757*

The Song of Names. *v.2 p.361*

The Song of Roland: An Analytical Edition - Introduction and Commentary, Vol. 1. . . . .*v.2 p.466*

The Song of Roland. *v.2 p.467*

Song of Solomon. *v.2 p.151*

Song of Songs. *v.1 p.621, p.622*

The Song of the Dodo: Island Biogeography in an Age of Extinctions. *v.5 p.358, p.359, p.370*

The Song of the Hawk: The Life and Recordings of Coleman Hawkins. *v.1 p.258, p.329*

Song of the Hummingbird. *v.6 p.501*

Song of the Nibelungs: A Verse Translation from the Middle High German Nibelungenlied. *v.2 p.595*

Song of the Outcasts: An Introduction to Flamenco. . .*v.1 p.299*

Song of the Simple Truth: The Complete Poems of Julia de Burgos, Obra Completa Poetica. *v.6 p.505, p.510*

Song of the Turtle: American Indian Literature, 1974-1994. . . . . *v.2 p.18, v.6 p.697*

Song of the Water Saints. . . . . *.v.6 p.508*

Song Sheets to Software: A Guide to Print Music, Software, and Web Sites for Musicians. *v.1 p.172, p.386*

Songoro Cosongo Y Othros Poemas. . . . . . . *.v.2 p.672*

Songs, Dreaming, and Ghosts: The Wangga of North Australia. . . . . *.v.1 p.289*

Songs for Fat People: Affect, Emotion, and Celebrity in the Russian Popular Song, 1900-1955. . . . . . . *.v.1 p.298*

Songs from This Earth on Turtle's Back: An Anthology of Poetry by American Indian Writers. . . . *.v.2 p.22, v.6 p.697*

Songs My Mother Sang to Me: An Oral History of Mexican American Women. . . . . *.v.3 p.271*

Songs My Mother Taught Me: Stories, Plays and Memoir. . . . . *.v.6 p.95, p.99, p.105*

Songs of Flying Dragons: A Critical Reading. . . . . *.v.6 p.238*

Songs of Gold Mountain: Cantonese Rhymes from San Francisco Chinatown. . . . . *.v.6 p.211*

The Songs of Homer. . . . . *.v.2 p.414*

Songs of Mortals, Dialogues of the Gods: Music and Theatre in Seventeenth-Century Spain. . . . . *.v.1 p.187*

The Songs of Robert Schumann. . . . *.v.1 p.203, p.236, p.355*

Songs of the Caged, Songs of the Free: Music and the Vietnamese Refugee Experience. . *.v.1 p.297, v.6 p.89, p.141*

Songs of the Serbian People: From the Collection of Vuk Karadzic. . . . . *.v.2 p.811*

The Songs of the South: An Anthology of Ancient Chinese Poems by Qu Yuan and Other Poets. . . . *.v.6 p.210, p.211*

Songs of the Sun, Love and Death: Selected Poems. . *.v.2 p.811*

Songs of the Theater. . . . . *.v.1 p.168, p.252*

Songs of the Women Troubadours. . . . . . . *.v.2 p.463, p.464*

Songsters and Saints: Vocal Traditions on Race Records. *.v.1 p.281*

Sonic Boom: Napster, MP3, and the New Pioneers of Music. . . . . *.v.1 p.383*

Sonic Design: The Nature of Sound and Music. . . . *.v.1 p.370*

The Sonnet: An Anthology. . . . . *.v.2 p.198*

Sonnet Series and Itinerary Poems, 1820-1845. . . . *.v.2 p.324*

Sonnets from the Portuguese. . . . . *.v.2 p.271*

Sonnets of Giuseppe Belli. . . . . *.v.2 p.710*

Sonnets of Love and Death. . . . . *.v.2 p.472*

The Sonnets. . . . . *.v.2 p.225, p.226*

Sons and Lovers. . . . . *.v.2 p.363*

Sons of Abraham: Jews, Christians, and Moslems. . . *.v.1 p.558*

Sons of Science: The Story of the Smithsonian Institution and Its Leaders. . . . . *.v.5 p.385*

Sons of the Fathers: The Civil Religion of the American Revolution. . . . . *.v.3 p.407*

Sooner or Later: The Timing of Parenthood in Adult Lives. . . . . *.v.4 p.736*

Sopa de Caracol. . . . . *.v.2 p.674*

Sophia, Regent of Russia, Sixteen Fifty-Seven to Seventeen Hundred Four. . . . . *.v.3 p.216*

Sophie's Choice. . . . . *.v.2 p.156*

The Sophistic Movement. . . . . *.v.1 p.427*

The Sophist. . . . . *.v.1 p.425, p.489*

Sophocles - Fragments, Vol. 3. . . . . *.v.2 p.420*

Sophocles: Ajax, Electra, Oedipus Tyrannus. . . . . *.v.2 p.420*

Sophocles: Ajax. . . . . *.v.2 p.420, p.421*

Sophocles: An Interpretation. . . . . *.v.2 p.421*

Sophocles: Antigone, the Women of Trachis, Philoctetes, Oedipus at Colonus. . . . . *.v.2 p.420*

Sophocles: Dramatist and Philosopher. . . . . *.v.2 p.419*

Sophocles: Electra. . . . . *.v.2 p.420*

Sophocles: Oedipus Rex. . . . . *.v.2 p.420*

Sophocles the Seven Plays in English Ver. . . . *.v.1 p.72, p.89*

Sophocles' Tragic World: Divinity, Nature, Society. . *.v.2 p.420*

Sophocles, Vol. 2. . . . . *.v.2 p.420*

Sophocles. . . . . *.v.2 p.419, p.420*

Soranus' Gynecology. . . . . *.v.2 p.405*

Soren Kierkegaard: A Biography. . . . . *.v.1 p.478*

Sorghum: Origin, History, Technology, and Production. *.v.5 p.24*

Sorghum. . . . . *.v.5 p.21*

Sorrow. . . . . *.v.2 p.674*

The Sorting Machine: National Educational Policy since 1945. . . . . *.v.4 p.329*

SOS! Save Outdoor Sculpture. . . . . . . *.v.1 p.774, p.821*

SOSIG : Sociology. . . . . *.v.4 p.675*

Sotheby's Concise Encyclopedia of Furniture. . . . . *.v.1 p.805*

The Sotheby's Wine Encyclopedia. . . . . *.v.5 p.53*

The Sot-Weed Factor. . . . . *.v.2 p.142*

Soul Babies: Black Culture and the Post-Soul Aesthetic. . . . . *.v.6 p.8, p.40*

The Soul Beneath the Skin: The Unseen Hearts and Habits of Gay Men. . . . . *.v.6 p.381, p.382*

The Soul of Education: Helping Students Find Connection, Compassion and Character at School. . . . *.v.4 p.357, p.364*

The Soul of Mbira: Music and Traditions of the Shona People of Zimbabwe. . . . . *.v.1 p.285*

The Soul of the American University: From Protestant Establishment to Established Non-Belief. . *.v.4 p.331, p.332*

Soul on Soul: The Life and Music of Mary Lou Williams. . . . . *.v.1 p.260, p.368*

The Souls of Black Folk. . . . . *.v.6 p.4, p.38*

Soulstealers: The Chinese Sorcery Scare of 1768. . . *.v.6 p.187*

Soulstepping: African American Step Shows. . . . . . *.v.1 p.18*

Soul. *.v.2 p.807*

Soumchi. . . . . *.v.6 p.650*

Sound and Light: La Monte Young Marian Zazeela. . . . . *.v.1 p.212, p.368, p.369*

Sound and Sources of Sound. . . . . *.v.5 p.566, p.567*

Sound and Vision: The Music Video Reader. . . . . *.v.1 p.255*

Sound Design: The Expressive Power of Music, Voice and Sound Effects in Cinema. . . . . *.v.6 p.352*

Sound for Film and Television. . . . . *.v.6 p.351*

Sound of Africa!: Making Music Zulu in a South African Studio. . . . . *.v.1 p.285*

The Sound of Light: A History of Gospel Music. . . *.v.1 p.267*

The Sound of Medieval Song: Ornamentation and Vocal Style According to the Treatises. . . . . *.v.1 p.177, p.178*

The Sound of One Hand Clapping. . . . . *.v.2 p.745*

The Sound of the Kiss, or the Story That Must Never Be
Told. *v.6 p.153*

The Sound of the Mountain. *v.6 p.230*

The Sound of Virtue: Philip Sidney's Arcadia and Elizabethan
Politics. *v.2 p.170, p.217*

The Sound of Waves. *v.6 p.231*

The Sound Pattern of English. *v.2 p.556*

Sound Recording: The Life Story of a Technology. . .*v.1 p.387*

Sound Sentiment: An Essay on the Musical Emotions. .*v.1 p.381*

The Sound Shape of Language. *v.2 p.561*

Sound, Speech, and Music. *v.1 p.380*

Sound Theory - Sound Practice. *v.6 p.351*

Sounding the Center: History and Aesthetics in Thai Buddhist
Performance. *v.1 p.16*

Soundings in French Caribbean Writing, 1950-2000: The Shock
of Space and Time. *v.2 p.537*

Soundpieces: Interviews with American
Composers. *v.1 p.213, p.214*

Soundpieces Two: Interviews with American
Composers. *v.1 p.213*

The Sounds and Spelling Patterns of English: Phonics for
Teachers and Parents. *v.2 p.556*

Sounds, Forms and Uses of Italian: An Introduction to Italian
Linguistics. *v.2 p.698*

The Sounds of Commerce: Marketing Popular Film
Music. *v.1 p.256, p.385*

Sounds of Our Times: Two Hundred Years of Acoustics. .*v.5 p.566*

The Sounds of Slavery: Discovering African American History
Through Songs, Sermons, and Speech. *v.6 p.9, p.37*

The Sounds of the World's Languages. *v.2 p.562*

The Soundscape: Our Sonic Environment and the Tuning of the
World. *v.1 p.375, p.382*

Soundscapes: Exploring Music in a Changing World. .*v.1 p.284*

Soundtracks: An International Dictionary of Film Music
Composers. *v.1 p.159, v.6 p.316*

Source and Meaning in Spenser's Allegory: A Study of the
Faerie Queene. *v.2 p.214*

A Source Book for Russian History from Early Times to
1917. . . . .*v.3 p.210*

Source Book in Astronomy and Astrophysics, 1900-1975. .*v.5 p.61*

A Source Book in Chinese Philosophy. *v.1 p.474, p.475*

A Source Book in Geology, 1400-1900. . . . .*v.5 p.418*

Source Book in Geology, 1900-1950. . . . .*v.5 p.418*

A Source Book in Indian Philosophy. *v.1 p.419*

A Source Book in the History of Psychology. *v.5 p.596*

Source Book of American Architecture: 500 Notable Buildings
from the 10th Century to the Present. *v.1 p.791*

A Source Book of Gestalt Psychology. *v.5 p.606*

Source: Poems. *v.6 p.404*

Source Readings in American Choral Music: Composers'
Writings, Interviews, and Reviews. *v.1 p.277*

Source Readings in Music History. *v.1 p.174*

A Sourcebook for Hispanic Literature and Language: A Selected
Annotated Guide to Spanish, Spanish-American and
United States Hispanic Bibliography, Literature, Linguistics,
Journals, and Other Source Materials. *v.2 p.638*

Sourcebook for Modern Japanese Philosophy: Selected
Documents. *v.1 p.476*

Sourcebook for Research in Music. *v.1 p.173*

Sourcebook of Advanced Organic Laboratory
Preparations. *v.5 p.323*

Sourcebook of African-American Performance. . *v.6 p.15, p.30*

Sourcebook of County Demographics. *v.4 p.138*

☐ Sourcebook of Criminal Justice Statistics. *v.6 p.246*

Sourcebook of Family Theories and Methods: A Contextual
Approach. *v.5 p.638*

Sourcebook of Modern Furniture. *v.1 p.805*

The Sourcebook of Nonverbal Measures: Going Beyond
Words. *v.4 p.424*

The Sourcebook of Parallel Computing. *v.5 p.349*

Sourcebook of Social Support and Personality. . . .*v.5 p.650*

A Sourcebook on Naturalist Theatre. *v.2 p.188*

Sourcebook on Substance Abuse: Etiology, Epidemiology,
Assessment, and Treatment. *v.5 p.512, p.522*

Sourcebook on Violence Against Women. *v.6 p.468*

Sources and Analogues of the Canterbury Tales, Vol. II. .*v.2 p.209*

Sources and Analogues of the Canterbury Tales. . . .*v.2 p.209*

Sources and Methods in African History: Spoken, Written,
Unearthed. *v.6 p.53*

Sources for a Biography of Shakespeare. *v.2 p.226*

Sources for Ancient History. *v.3 p.13*

Sources for the Study of Greek Religion. *v.1 p.533*

Sources: Notable Selections in Environmental Studies. .*v.6 p.285*

Sources: Notable Selections in Race and Ethnicity. . .*v.4 p.17*

Sources of Chinese Tradition: From 1600 Through the Twentieth
Century. *v.6 p.182*

Sources of Chinese Tradition: From Earliest Times to
1600. . . . .*v.6 p.182*

Sources of Culture in the Middle West: Backgrounds Versus
Frontier. *v.3 p.376*

☐ Sources of Information in Transportation. *v.4 p.166*

Sources of Korean Tradition: From the Sixteenth to the
Twentieth Centuries. *v.6 p.235*

The Sources of Normativity. *v.1 p.484*

The Sources of Shakespeare's Plays. *v.2 p.231*

Sources of Shang History: The Oracle-Bone Inscriptions of
Bronze Age China. *v.6 p.184*

Sources of the African American Past: Primary Sources in
American History. *v.6 p.4*

Sources of Twentieth-Century Europe. *v.3 p.75*

Le Sourd dans la Ville. *v.2 p.538*

South Africa: A Country Study. *v.6 p.78*

South Africa: A Modern History. *v.6 p.79*

South Africa and the United States: The Erosion of an Influence
Relationship. *v.3 p.387*

South Africa Belongs to Us: A History of the
ANC. *v.4 p.614, v.6 p.79*

A South African Kingdom: The Pursuit of Security in
Nineteenth-Century Lesotho. *v.6 p.75*

South African Music: A Century of Traditions in
Transformation. *v.1 p.285*

The South African War Reappraised. *v.6 p.79*

South African Writers. *v.2 p.752*

South Africa's Alternative Press: Voices of Protest and
Resistance, 1880-1960. . . . . *v.6 p.79*

The South and the Concurrent Majority. *v.3 p.497*

The South and the New Deal. *v.3 p.496*

The South and the Politics of Slavery, 1828-1856. . . *v.3 p.495*

The South and the Sectional Conflict. *v.3 p.495*

The South and the Southerner. *v.3 p.497*

The South Asian Americans. *v.6 p.137*

South Asian Folklore: An Encyclopedia. . . . *v.6 p.146, p.147*

◻ The South Asian Literary Recordings Project. . . *v.6 p.148*

South Asian Religions in the Americas: An Annotated
Bibliography of Immigrant Religious
Traditions. *v.6 p.86, p.105, p.137*

The South Asian Religious Diaspora in Britain, Canada, and the
United States. *v.6 p.105, p.137*

South Asians in North America: An Annotated and Selected
Bibliography. *v.6 p.87, p.138*

South Asians in the Diaspora: Histories and Religious
Traditions. *v.4 p.764*

South Asians Overseas: Migration and Ethnicity. . . *v.6 p.146*

The South Besieged: The Image of War, 1861-1865. . *v.3 p.431*

South Carolina: A Guide to the Palmetto State. . . . *v.3 p.502*

South Carolina: A History. *v.3 p.501*

South Carolina at the Brink. *v.4 p.541*

South Carolina Begins: The Records of a Proprietary Colony,
1663-1721. . . . . *v.3 p.502*

South Carolina Loyalists in the American Revolution. *v.3 p.409*

South Dakota: A Guide to the State. *v.3 p.522, p.523*

South Dakota: A History. *v.3 p.523*

South East Asian Food: Classic and Modern Dishes from
Thailand, Indonesia, Malaysia, Singapore, Laos,
Cambodia and Vietnam. *v.6 p.164*

The South in Modern America: A Region at Odds. . *v.3 p.496*

The South in the New Nation 1789-1819. . . . . . *v.3 p.494*

The South in the Revolution: 1763. . . . . *v.3 p.494*

South: Modern Southern Literature in Its Cultural
Setting. *v.2 p.14*

South Pacific. *v.4 p.385*

South Reports the Civil War. *v.3 p.424*

South Sea Islands: A Natural History. *v.5 p.241*

South Slavic Writers since World War II. . . . *v.2 p.778, p.779*

The South Through Time: A History of an American
Region. *v.3 p.493*

The South vs. the South: How Anti-Confederate Southerners
Shaped the Course of the Civil War. *v.4 p.520*

South-Central Section Field Guide. *v.5 p.431*

South-East Asia: A Modern History. *v.6 p.165*

South-East Asia: A Political Profile. *v.4 p.622*

Southeast Asia: From Prehistory to History. *v.4 p.13*

Southeast Asia in the Age of Commerce, 1450-1680: Expansion
and Crisis. *v.6 p.165*

Southeast Asia in the Age of Commerce, 1450-1680: The Lands
Below the Winds, Vol. 1. . . . . *v.6 p.165*

Southeast Asia: People, Land and Economy. *v.4 p.384*

Southeast Asia: The Human Landscape of Modernization and
Development. *v.4 p.384*

South-East Asian Ceramics: Thai, Khmer, and Vietnamese from
the Collection of the Art Gallery of South Australia,
Adelaide. *v.1 p.808*

The Southeast Frontier of New Spain. *v.3 p.285*

Southeastern Europe Under Ottoman Rule, 1354-1804. *v.3 p.246*

Southeastern Section Field Guide. *v.5 p.432*

Southern Aberrations: Writers of the American South and the
Problems of Regionalism. *v.2 p.13*

The Southern Appalachians: A History of the
Landscape. *v.3 p.498*

The Southern Colonies in the Seventeenth Century,
1607-1689. . . . . *v.3 p.495*

The Southern Critics: An Introduction to the Criticism of John
Crow Ransom, Allen Tate, Donald Davidson, Robert
Penn Warren, Cleanth Brooks, and Andrew Lytle. . *v.2 p.13*

Southern Cross: The Beginnings of the Bible
Belt. *v.1 p.583, p.607*

Southern Crossing: A History of the American South,
1877-1906. . . . . *v.3 p.496*

Southern Editorials on Secession. *v.3 p.365, p.419*

Southern Exposure: Modern Japanese Literature from
Okinawa. *v.6 p.235*

The Southern Frontier, 1670-1732. . . . . *v.3 p.501*

Southern Furniture 1680-1830: The Colonial Williamsburg
Collection. *v.1 p.804*

Southern Honor: Ethics and Behavior in the Old South. *v.3 p.494*

Southern Justice. *v.4 p.457*

The Southern Movie Place: Rise, Fall, and Resurrection. *v.1 p.822*

Southern Music/American Music. *v.1 p.271*

The Southern Nation: The New Rise of the Old South. *v.3 p.497*

Southern Parties and Elections: Studies in Regional Political
Change. *v.4 p.551, p.552, p.554*

Southern Politics in State and Nation. *v.3 p.496*

Southern Politics in the 1990s. *v.3 p.496, p.497*

A Southern Renaissance: The Cultural Awakening of the
American South, 1930-1955. . . . . *v.2 p.14*

Southern Rights: Political Prisoners and the Myth of
Confederate Constitutionalism. *v.3 p.399, v.4 p.521*

Southern Slavery and the Law, 1619-1860. . . . . *v.4 p.442*

Southern Stories: Slaveholders in Peace and War. . . *v.4 p.520*

Southern Strategies: Southern Women and the Woman Suffrage
Question. *v.4 p.519, p.568, p.569, v.6 p.431, p.454*

The Southern Sudan in Historical Perspective. . . . *v.6 p.59*

The Southern Tradition: The Achievement and Limitations of an
American Conservatism. *v.3 p.494*

The Southern Woman: New and Selected Fiction. . . *v.2 p.116*

Southern Women Writers: The New Generation. . . . *v.2 p.13*

Southern Writers: A New Biographical Dictionary. *v.2 p.7, p.13*

The Southerner As American. *v.3 p.494*

A Southerner Discovers the South. *v.3 p.496*

Southerners, Too?: Essays on the Black South, 1733-1990. *v.6 p.6*

The Southpaw. *v.2 p.81*

The South. *v.3 p.494*

Southwest: A Contemporary Anthology. *v.2 p.21*

Southwest Heritage; a Literary History with
    Bibliographies. *v.2 p.14*

Southwest Heritage: Literary History with Bibliography. .*v.2 p.15*

Southwest Tales: A Contemporary Collection. *v.2 p.21*

Southwest: Three Peoples in Geographical Change,
    1600-1970. . . . .*v.3 p.527*

The Southwest. *v.3 p.526*

Souvenirs du triangle d'or : roman. *v.2 p.525*

Souvenirs et voyages. *v.2 p.520*

Sovereign Bodies: Citizens, Migrants, and States in the
    Postcolonial World. *v.4 p.34*

The Sovereign Flower: On Shakespeare as the Poet of
    Royalism. *v.2 p.230*

The Sovereign Map: Theoretical Approaches in Cartography
    throughout History. *v.4 p.385*

The Sovereign Prerogative: The Supreme Court and the Quest
    for Law. *v.4 p.470*

The Sovereign State and Its Competitors: An Analysis of
    Systems Change. *v.4 p.496, p.497*

The Sovereign States, 1775-1783. . . . .*v.3 p.409*

Sovereign Virtue: The Theory and Practice of Equality. .*v.4 p.514*

Sovereigns and Surrogates: Constitutional Heads of State in the
    Commonwealth. *v.4 p.605*

Sovereignty and Authenticity: Manchukuo and the East Asian
    Modern. *v.4 p.496, v.6 p.205*

Sovereignty and Society in Colonial Brazil: The High Court of
    Bahia and Its Judges, 1609-1751. . . . .*v.3 p.335*

Sovereignty, Colonialism, and the Future of Indigenous
    Nations. *v.6 p.696*

Sovereignty for Sale. *v.3 p.304*

The Sovereignty of Good. *v.1 p.487*

Soviet Century. *v.3 p.222*

Soviet Choreographers in the 1920s. *v.1 p.12*

Soviet Diary, 1927 and Other Writings. .*v.1 p.221, p.348, p.349*

Soviet Disunion: A History of the Nationalities Problem in the
    U. S. S. R. *v.3 p.213*

The Soviet Elite from Lenin to Gorbachev: The Central
    Committee and Its Members,
    1917-1991. . . . .*v.3 p.222, p.223,v.4 p.598*

The Soviet Experiment: Russia, the U. S. S. R., and the
    Successor States. *v.3 p.223*

Soviet Foreign Policy, 1917-1941. . . . .*v.3 p.211, p.212, p.389*

Soviet Foreign Policy, the League of Nations and Europe,
    1917-1939. . . . .*v.4 p.631, p.645*

Soviet Grotesque. *v.2 p.794*

Soviet History in the Yeltsin Era. *v.3 p.229*

Soviet Images of America. *v.3 p.452*

The Soviet Legacy in Central Asia. *v.3 p.230*

Soviet Literature in the 1980s: Decade of Transition. .*v.2 p.800*

Soviet Marxism: A Critical Analysis. *v.4 p.508*

Soviet Marxism and Natural Science, 1917-1932. . . .*v.5 p.402*

The Soviet Novel: History As Ritual. *v.2 p.797*

Soviet Political Indoctrination: Developments in Mass Media
    and Propaganda Since Stalin. *v.4 p.703*

The Soviet Study of International Relations. *v.3 p.212*

The Soviet Tragedy: A History of Socialism in Russia
    1917-1991. . . . .*v.4 p.508, p.598*

Soviet-American Relations, 1917-1920: Russia Leaves the
    War. *v.3 p.389*

Soviet-American Relations, 1917-1920: The Decision to
    Intervene. *v.3 p.389*

Soviet-Polish Relations, 1917-1921. . . . . . .*v.3 p.253, p.254*

Soviets: Pictures from the End of the U.S.S.R. *v.1 p.768*

Sowing the Seeds of Democracy in China: Political Reform in
    the Deng Xiaoping Era. *v.6 p.197*

Soybean Physiology, Agronomy, and Utilization. .*v.5 p.22, p.25*

Soybeans: Improvement, Production, and Uses. *v.5 p.20*

Soyuz: A Universal Spacecraft. *v.5 p.719*

Space and Life. *v.5 p.243*

Space and Place in the Works of D. H. Lawrence. . .*v.2 p.364*

Space and Place: The Perspective of Experience. . .*v.4 p.375*

Space and Place. *v.6 p.721*

Space and Social Theory: Interpreting Modernity and
    Postmodernity. *v.4 p.377*

Space Between Words: The Origins of Silent Reading. .*v.6 p.569*

Space Calculated in Seconds: The Philips Pavilion, le Corbusier,
    Edgard Varese. *v.1 p.226, p.363*

Space, City and Social Theory. *v.6 p.710*

Space, Geography, and Politics in the Early Roman
    Empire. *v.4 p.377*

Space in Motion. *v.2 p.658*

Space Is the Place: The Lives and Times of Sun
    Ra. *v.1 p.264, p.361, p.362*

Space Policy in the Twenty-First Century. *v.5 p.719*

Space Shuttle: The History of the National Space Transportation
    System. *v.5 p.719*

The Space Telescope: A Study of NASA, Science, Technology
    and Politics. *v.5 p.62*

Space, Time, and Freedom: The Quest for Nationality and the
    Irrepressible Conflict, 1815-1861, 35. . . . . .*v.3 p.415*

Space, Time and Gravitation: An Outline of the General
    Relativity Theory. *v.5 p.556, p.558*

Spacecraft Attitude Dynamics. *v.5 p.719*

Spacecraft Systems Engineering. *v.5 p.719*

Spaces of Capital: Towards a Critical Geography. . .*v.6 p.721*

Spaces of Global Capitalism: A Theory of Uneven Geographical
    Development. *v.6 p.721*

Spaces, Worlds, and Grammar. *v.2 p.560*

Spacetime Physics. *v.5 p.73, p.557*

SpaceWeather.com -- News and Information about the
    Sun-Earth Environment. *v.5 p.444*

Spaghetti Westerns: Cowboys and Europeans from Karl May to
    Sergio Leone, Vol. 1. . . . .*v.6 p.324*

Spaghetti Westerns the Good, the Bad and the Violent: A
    Comprehensive, Illustrated Filmography of 558
    Eurowesterns and Their Personnel, 1961-1977. . .*v.6 p.325*

Spain, 1469-1714: A Society of Conflict. *v.3 p.65, p.239*

Spain: A History. *v.3 p.243*

Spain after Franco: The Making of a Competitive Party
    System. *v.4 p.608*

Spain and Portugal in the New World, 1492-1700. . .*v.3 p.404*

Spain and Portugal Today. *v.3 p.242*

Spain and the Independence of Colombia, 1808-1825. .*v.3 p.357*

Spain and the Loss of America. *v.3 p.273*

Spain and the Plains: Myths and Realities of Spanish
    Exploration and Settlement on the Great Plains. . .*v.3 p.529*

Spain: Between War and Revolution. *v.3 p.241*

Spain, Europe, and the 'Spanish Miracle', 1700-1900. .*v.3 p.241*

Spain in Our Hearts/Espana en el Corazon: Hymn to the Glories
    of the People at War/Himno a Las Glorias del Pueblo en la
    Guerra. *v.2 p.681*

Spain in the Age of Exploration, 1492-1819. . . .*v.3 p.73, p.239*

Spain in the Middle Ages: From Frontier to Empire,
    1000-1500. . . . .*v.3 p.238, v.6 p.563, p.564*

The Spain of Fernando de Rojas; the Intellectual and Social
    Landscape of la Celestina. *v.2 p.651*

The Spain of the Catholic Monarchs, 1474-1520. . . .*v.3 p.238*

Spain's First Democracy: The Second Republic,
    1931-1936. . . . .*v.3 p.241*

Spain's Golden Fleece: Wool Production and the Wool Trade
    from the Middle Ages to the Nineteenth Century. . *v.3 p.243*

Spanish American Saints and the Rhetoric of Identity,
    1600-1810. . . . .*v.3 p.263, p.326*

Spanish and Latin American Transitions to Democracy. *v.3 p.345*

Spanish Artists from the Fourth to the Twentieth Century: A
    Critical Dictionary, Set. *v.1 p.664*

The Spanish Avantgarde. *v.2 p.639*

Spanish Ballads. *v.2 p.645*

Spanish, Catalan and Spanish-American Poetry from
    "Modernismo" to the Spanish Civil War: The Hispanic
    Connection. *v.2 p.639, p.640*

Spanish Cathedral Music in the Golden Age. *v.1 p.181*

Spanish Catholicism: An Historical Overview. *v.1 p.574*

The Spanish Civil War, 1936-1939: American Hemispheric
    Perspectives. *v.3 p.241, p.260*

The Spanish Civil War: Revolution and
    Counterrevolution. *v.3 p.241*

The Spanish Civil War. *v.3 p.242*

Spanish Colonial Administration, 1782-1810: The Intendant
    System in the Viceroyalty of the Rio De la Plata,
    5. . . . .*v.3 p.347, v.4 p.592*

Spanish Dancing. *v.1 p.20*

Spanish Drama of the Golden Age: Twelve Plays. . . .*v.2 p.644*

Spanish Drama of the Golden Age. *v.2 p.641*

Spanish Englishwoman: The Glass Graduate and the Power of
    Blood. *v.2 p.648*

Spanish Exploration in the Southwest, 1542-1706. . .*v.3 p.528*

The Spanish Inquisition: A Historical Revision. . . .*v.3 p.239*

The Spanish Inquisition: A History. *v.3 p.240*

The Spanish Kingdoms, 1250-1516: 250-1410 Precarious
    Balance. *v.3 p.237*

The Spanish Kingdoms, 1250-1560: Castilian Hegemony,
    1410-1516. . . . .*v.3 p.237*

The Spanish Labyrinth: An Account of the Social and Political
    Background of the Spanish Civil War. *v.3 p.241*

The Spanish Language Today. *v.2 p.637*

The Spanish Language, Together with Portuguese, Catalan and
    Basque. *v.2 p.635*

Spanish Music in the Age of Columbus. *v.1 p.181*

Spanish Naval Power, 1589-1665: Reconstruction and
    Defeat. *v.3 p.239*

Spanish Peru, 1532-1560: A Social History. *v.3 p.326*

Spanish Picaresque Fiction: A New Literary History. . *v.2 p.641*

The Spanish Picaresque Novel and the Point of
    View. *v.2 p.641, p.642*

The Spanish Pioneers in United States History the Melungeons:
    The Pioneers of the Interior Southeastern U. S.,
    1526-1997. . . . .*v.3 p.498*

Spanish Poetry of the Golden Age. *v.2 p.642*

Spanish Poetry of the Grupo Poetico de 1927. .*v.2 p.642, p.643*

Spanish Poetry of the Twentieth Century: Modernity and
    Beyond. *v.2 p.639*

Spanish Poetry: Poesia Espanola: A Dual-Language
    Anthology. *v.2 p.643*

Spanish Policy in Colonial Chile: The Struggle for Social
    Justice, 1535-1700. . . . .*v.3 p.350*

The Spanish Redemption: Heritage, Power, and Loss on New
    Mexico's Upper Rio Grande. *v.6 p.534*

The Spanish Republic at War 1936-1939. . . . . . .*v.3 p.241*

The Spanish Seaborne Empire. *v.3 p.74*

The Spanish Speakers in the United States: A History. *v.6 p.531*

Spanish Speaking Radio and TV: Emisoras de Radio y
    Television en Español. *v.6 p.493*

Spanish Stories of the Late Nineteenth Century: A
    Dual-Language Book. *v.2 p.642*

Spanish Texas, 1519-1821. . . . .*v.3 p.508*

Spanish Theatre, 1920-1995: Strategies in Protest and
    Imagination 3. . . . .*v.1 p.107*

The Spanish Theory of Empire in the Sixteenth Century. *v.3 p.404*

Spanish Traditional Ballads: Romances Viejos
    Espanoles. *v.2 p.642*

The Spanish Traditional Lyric. *v.2 p.643*

The Spanish Tragedy. *v.2 p.218, p.219*

Spanish Unabridged Dictionary. *v.2 p.636*

Spanish Writers in Exile. *v.2 p.643*

Spanish-American Homeland: Four Centuries in New Mexico's
    Rio Arriba. *v.6 p.530, p.531*

Spanish-American Short Stories / Cuentos Hispanoamericanos:
    A Dual-Language Book. *v.2 p.665*

Spanish-Americans of New Mexico: A Heritage of
    Pride. *v.6 p.531*

Spanish-English Contrasts: An Introduction to Spanish
    Linguistics. *v.2 p.637*

Spanish-Language Radio in the Southwestern United
    States. *v.6 p.493*

The Spanish-Speaking World: A Practical Introduction to
    Sociolinguistic Issues. *v.2 p.636*

Spanning the Century: The Life of W. Averell Harriman,
    1891-1986. . . . .*v.3 p.455*

The Spark: Igniting the Creative Fire That Lives Within Us
    All. *v.4 p.65, p.66*

Spark of Life: Darwin and the Primeval Soup. *v.5 p.204*

Sparks of Life: Darwinism and the Victorian Debates over
    Spontaneous Generation. *v.5 p.81*

Sparta and Lakonia: A Regional History, 1300-362 BC. *v.3 p.17*

Spartan Reflections. *v.3 p.17*

The Spartan Tradition in European Thought. *v.3 p.191*

Spartan Women. *v.3 p.14*

Spatial Databases: A Tour. *v.5 p.335, p.337*

Spatial Disparities in Human Development: Perspectives from
Asia. *v.4 p.397*

The Spatial Factor in African History: The Relationship of the
Social, Material, and Perceptual. *v.4 p.384*

Spatial Interaction Theory and Planning Models. . . .*v.4 p.202*

Spatial Statistics for Remote Sensing. *v.4 p.389*

Spatially Integrated Social Science. *v.4 p.375*

Speak It Louder: Asian Americans Making Music. . . .*v.1 p.297*

Speak Like a CEO: Secrets for Commanding Attention and
Getting Results. *v.4 p.171, p.172*

Speak, Memory: An Autobiography Revisited. . . .*v.2 p.104*

Speak, So You Can Speak Again: The Life of Zora Neale
Hurston. *v.2 p.81*

Speak Truth to Power: Black Professional Class in United States
History. *v.6 p.6, p.39*

The Speaker and the Budget: Leadership in the Post-Reform
House of Representatives. *v.4 p.533*

The Speaker: Leadership in the U. S. House of
Representatives. *v.4 p.533*

The Speakers of the U. S. House of Representatives: A
Bibliography, Seventeen Eighty-Nine to Nineteen
Eighty-Four. *v.4 p.533*

Speaking Back: The Free Speech Versus Hate Speech
Debate. *v.4 p.423*

Speaking for Our Lives: Historic Speeches and Rhetoric for Gay
and Lesbian Rights/1892-2000. . . . . . .*v.6 p.363, p.388*

Speaking Frankly. *v.3 p.456*

Speaking Havoc: Social Suffering and South Asian
Narratives. *v.6 p.334*

Speaking into the Air: A History of the Idea of
Communication. *v.4 p.416, v.5 p.621*

Speaking of Crime: The Language of Criminal Justice. .*v.6 p.245*

Speaking of Diaghiley. *v.1 p.7*

Speaking of Ethnography. *v.4 p.25*

Speaking the Unspeakable: Marital Violence among South Asian
Immigrants in the United States. *v.6 p.111, p.137*

Speaking Truth to Power. *v.4 p.441*

The Spearless Leader. *v.3 p.455*

□ Specarb: Raman Spectra of Carbohydrates. . . .*v.5 p.330*

A Special Agent: Gay and Inside the FBI. *v.6 p.383*

Special Education in the 21st Century: Issues of Inclusion and
Reform. *v.4 p.316*

Special Education Law. *v.4 p.450, p.451*

The Special Educator's Book of Lists. *v.4 p.316*

Special Educator's Complete Guide to 109 Diagnostic Tests:
How to Select and Interpret Tests, Use Results in
IEPs and Remediate Specific Difficulties. *v.4 p.316*

Special Effects: An Oral History. *v.6 p.352*

Special Effects Make-Up. *v.6 p.351*

Special Effects: Still in Search of Wonder. . .*v.6 p.319, p.352*

Special Effects: The History and the Technique. . . .*v.6 p.352*

Special Functions. *v.5 p.493*

Special Make-up Effects. *v.6 p.351*

A Special Relationship: Anglo-American Relations in the Cold
War and After. *v.3 p.388*

A Special Relationship: The United States and Military
Government in Thailand, 1947-1958. . . . .*v.6 p.171*

Special Relativity. *v.5 p.557, p.558*

Special Trust: Pride, Principle and Politics Inside the White
House. *v.3 p.475*

Specialty Chemicals Source Book, Vol. 2. . . . . .*v.5 p.317*

Specialty Cut Flowers: The Production of Annuals, Perennials,
Bulbs, and Woody Plants for Fresh and Dried Cut
Flowers. *v.5 p.43*

Speciation and Its Consequences. *v.5 p.199*

Speciation and the Recognition Concept: Theory and
Application. *v.5 p.199*

Speciation. *v.5 p.198*

Species Concepts and Phylogenetic Theory: A Debate. .*v.5 p.199*

Species Conservation: A Population-Biological
Approach. *v.5 p.171, p.181*

Species Dispersal in Agricultural Habitats. . .*v.5 p.167, p.198*

Species Invasions: Insights into Ecology, Evolution, and
Biogeography. *v.4 p.394, v.5 p.169, p.181*

Species: New Interdisciplinary Essays. *v.5 p.205*

The Species Problem: Biological Species, Ontology, and the
Metaphysics of Biology. *v.5 p.249*

Species: The Units of Biodiversity. *v.5 p.198*

Specimens of Slavonic Literature: Croatian, Serbian, Slovak,
Little Russian, Bohemian, Slovene. *v.2 p.818*

The Spectacle of Intimacy: A Public Life for the Victorian
Family. *v.6 p.764, p.765*

The Spectacle of the Races: Scientists, Institutions and the Race
Question in Brazil, 1870-1930. . . . .*v.3 p.342*

The Spectacle of U. S. Senate Campaigns. .*v.4 p.530, p.551, p.557*

Spectacles of Strangeness: Imperialism, Alienation, and
Marlowe. *v.2 p.220*

The Spectacular City: Violence and Performance in Urban
Bolivia. *v.3 p.323, p.324*

The Specter of Communism: The United States and the Origins
of the Cold War, 1917-1953. . . . .*v.3 p.453*

The Specter of Dido: Spenser and Virgilian Epic. . . .*v.2 p.216*

The Specter of Genocide: Mass Murder in Historical
Perspective. *v.4 p.652*

Spectra of Atoms and Molecules. *v.5 p.561, p.562*

Spectral Analysis of Economic Time Series. *v.4 p.206*

□ Spectral Database for Organic Compounds, SDBS. .*v.5 p.297*

□ Spectral Database for Organic Compunds, SDBS. .*v.5 p.297*

Spectral Emanations: New and Selected Poems. . . .*v.2 p.87*

□ Spectral Information Resources (Stanford
University). *v.5 p.270*

Spectrometric Identification of Organic Compounds. . .*v.5 p.297*

Spectroscopic Techniques for Organic Chemists. . . .*v.5 p.297*

Spectroscopy of Polymers. *v.5 p.323*

Specular City: The Transformation of Culture, Consumption,
and Space after Peron. *v.3 p.349*

Speculations about Jakob. *v.2 p.618*

Speculative Management: Stock Market Power and Corporate Change. *v.4 p.86*

Speculum Mentis: The Map of Knowledge. . . *v.1 p.481, p.482*

Speculum of the Other Woman. . *v.6 p.434, p.445, p.446, p.461*

Speech Acts: An Essay in the Philosophy of Language. *v.1 p.442, p.490*

Speech and Law in a Free Society. *v.4 p.459*

Speech Correction: An Introduction to Speech Pathology and Audiology. *v.5 p.674*

Speech Genres and Other Late Essays. *v.2 p.797*

Speech Physiology, Speech Perception, and Acoustic Phonetics. *v.2 p.562*

Speech Play and Verbal Art. *v.4 p.19*

□ Speeches and Speechmakers. *v.4 p.422*

Speeches by the Rt. Hon. Thomas Babington Macaulay.*v.2 p.299*

Speeches: Literary and Social. *v.2 p.283*

Speed-the-Plow. *v.1 p.62, p.116*

Speleology: Caves and the Cave Environment. . . . *v.5 p.424*

Spelling the Word: George Herbert and the Bible. . . *v.2 p.249*

Spenser Handbook. *v.2 p.215*

Spenser: The Faerie Queene. *v.2 p.214*

Spenser's Allegory: The Anatomy of Imagination. . . *v.2 p.215*

Spenser's Art: A Companion to Book One of the Faerie Queen. *v.2 p.215*

Spenser's Life and the Subject of Biography. *v.2 p.212*

Spenser's Supreme Fiction: Platonic Natural Philosophy and the Faerie Queene. *v.2 p.215*

Spenser's World of Glass: A Reading of The Faerie Queen. *v.2 p.216*

Spheres of Justice: A Defense of Pluralism and Equality.*v.4 p.514*

The Spheres of Music: A Gathering of Essays. . . . *v.1 p.382*

Spices. *v.5 p.23, p.33*

Spider Eaters: A Memoir. *v.6 p.196*

Spiders in the House and Workers in the Field. . . . *v.6 p.540*

Spies: A Novel. *v.2 p.345*

Spike Lee: That's My Story and I'm Sticking to It. *v.6 p.330, p.342*

Spiks. *v.6 p.509*

Spin Choreography: Basic Steps in High Resolution NMR. *v.5 p.272*

Spin Electronics. *v.5 p.566*

Spin Sisters: How the Women of the Media Sell Unhappiness —- and Liberalism — to the Women of America. *v.6 p.447*

Spineless Wonders: Strange Tales from the Invertabrate World. *v.5 p.156*

Spinning Blues into Gold: The Chess Brothers and the Legendary Chess Records. *v.1 p.383*

Spinning Wheels: The Politics of Urban School Reform.*v.4 p.315*

Spinoza: A Life. *v.1 p.477*

Spinoza: A Very Short Introduction. *v.1 p.477*

Spinoza and Spinozism. *v.1 p.477*

Spinoza: Complete Works. *v.1 p.477*

A Spinoza Reader: The Ethics and Other Works. .*v.1 p.477, p.478*

Spinoza's Modernity: Mendelssohn, Lessing, and Heine. *v.1 p.477*

Spinoza. *v.1 p.477*

Spinster, a Novel. *v.2 p.743*

Spiral Road: Change in a Chinese Village Through the Eyes of a Communist Party Leader. *v.6 p.197*

Spirit and Reason: The Vine Deloria, Jr. Reader. . . *v.6 p.701*

The Spirit and the Flesh: Sexual Diversity in American Indian Culture. *v.6 p.367, p.368*

Spirit Capture: Photographs from the National Museum of the American Indian. *v.1 p.764, v.6 p.678, p.679*

The Spirit Catches You and You Fall Down: A Hmong Child, Her American Doctors, and the Collision of Two Cultures. *v.4 p.778, v.6 p.139, p.141*

Spirit Fruit: A Gentle Utopia. *v.4 p.499*

The Spirit Level: Poems. *v.2 p.352*

The Spirit of American Philosophy. *v.1 p.439*

The Spirit of Catholicism. *v.1 p.575*

Spirit of Chinese Philosophy. *v.1 p.475*

The Spirit of Community: Rights, Responsibilities, and the Communitarian Agenda. *v.4 p.768*

The Spirit of Eastern Christendom (600-1700), Vol. 2. *v.1 p.634*

The Spirit of Eastern Christendom, 600-1700. . . . . *v.3 p.57*

The Spirit of Hidalgo: The Mexican Revolution in Coahuila. *v.3 p.294*

The Spirit of Islamic Law. *v.1 p.556*

The Spirit of Liberty. *v.4 p.437*

The Spirit of Medieval Philosophy. *v.1 p.432*

The Spirit of Modern Philosophy. *v.1 p.436*

The Spirit of Montmartre: Cabarets, Humor, and the Avant-Garde, 1875-1905. . . . . *v.1 p.84, p.95*

The Spirit of Reform: British Literature and Politics, 1832-1867. . . . . *v.2 p.174, v.6 p.752, p.757, p.766*

The Spirit of Romance. *v.2 p.457*

The Spirit of Russia: Studies in History, Literature and Philosophy. *v.3 p.210*

The Spirit of Seventy-Six. *v.3 p.407*

The Spirit of the Common Law. *v.4 p.434*

The Spirit of the Laws. *v.2 p.480*

Spirit of the Mountains. *v.2 p.46*

Spirit of Wit: Reconsiderations of Rochester. *v.2 p.259*

The Spirited Earth. *v.1 p.15*

The Spirits of America: A Social History of Alcohol. *v.4 p.709, p.710*

Spiritual and Anabaptist Writers. *v.1 p.602*

A Spiritual Audit of Corporate America: A Hard Look at Spirituality, Religion, and Values in the Workplace. *v.4 p.52, p.54*

Spiritual Care. *v.1 p.649*

The Spiritual Conquest of Mexico: An Essay on the Apostolate and the Evangelizing Methods of the Mendicant Orders in New Spain, 1523-1572. . . . . *v.1 p.574*

Spiritual Crisis of the Gilded Age. *v.1 p.606*

Spiritual Development in the State School: A Perspective on Worship and Spirituality in the Education System of England and Wales. *v.4 p.333*

Spiritual Exercises of St. Ignatius. *v.1 p.577, p.612*

The Spiritual Quixote: A Comic Romance. *v.2 p.245*

Spiritual Sonnets: Sonetos Espirituales. *v.2 p.660*

Spirituality in Nursing: From Traditional to New Age. *v.5 p.529*

Spirituality in Nursing: Standing on Holy
 Ground. *v.5 p.528, p.530*

Spirituality of Sport: Balancing Body and Soul. *v.4 p.803, p.865*

The Spirituals and the Blues. *v.6 p.29, p.35*

The Splendid Century: Life in the France of Louis XIV. *v.3 p.145*

The Splendid Feast of Reason. *v.5 p.249*

Splendid Hôtel : roman. *v.2 p.533*

Splendid Monarchy: Power and Pageantry in Modern
 Japan. *v.6 p.226*

Splendor in the Grass. *v.2 p.89*

Splendors of China's Forbidden City: The Glorious Reign of
 Emperor Qianlong. *v.1 p.693*

Splendors of Imperial Japan: Arts of the Meiji Period from the
 Khalili Collection. *v.1 p.693*

Splintering Urbanism: Networked Infrastructures, Technological
 Mobilities and the Urban Condition. *v.6 p.718, p.720, p.721*

Split Britches: Lesbian Practice - Feminist
 Performance. *v.1 p.120, p.125, p.135*

Split Image: African Americans in the Mass
 Media. *v.4 p.416, v.5 p.620, p.624*

Split Image: The Life of Anthony Perkins. *v.6 p.419*

Split Seconds; a Remembrance. *v.1 p.8*

Split-Gut Song: Jean Toomer and the Poetics of
 Modernity. *v.2 p.126*

Splitting Up: Enmeshment and Estrangement in the Process of
 Divorce. *v.5 p.640*

Spoilsports: Understanding and Preventing Sexual Exploitation
 in Sport. *v.4 p.814, p.840*

Spoilt Children of Empire: Westerners in Shanghai and the
 Chinese Revolution of the 1920s. *v.6 p.203*

Spoken Discourse and Social Interaction. *v.4 p.423*

Sponsored Identities: Cultural Politics in Puerto Rico. *v.3 p.319*

Spontaneous Activity in Education. *v.4 p.344*

Spontaneous Apprentices: Children and Language. . . *v.4 p.357*

Spontaneous Mind: Selected Interviews, 1958-1996. . .*v.2 p.79*

The Spook Who Sat by the Door. *v.6 p.25*

Spoon River Anthology. *v.2 p.97*

Sport: A Critical Sociology. *v.4 p.815*

Sport; a Philosophic Inquiry. *v.4 p.803*

Sport and American Mentality, 1880-1910. . . *v.4 p.808, p.818*

Sport and American Society. *v.4 p.819*

Sport and Broadcasting: Economic, Legal, and Technological
 Developments in the Digital Age. *v.4 p.882, p.887, p.901*

Sport and Canadian Diplomacy. *v.4 p.891, p.898*

Sport and Exercise Psychology. *v.4 p.877, v.5 p.582*

Sport and Exercise Science: Essays in the History of Sports
 Medicine. *v.4 p.803, p.825, p.873*

Sport and Gender in Canada. *v.4 p.820*

Sport and Information Technology, Vol. 4. . . . . .*v.4 p.812*

Sport and International Politics. *v.4 p.844, p.892, p.899*

Sport and Memory in North America. *v.4 p.811, p.820*

Sport and Modern Social Theorists: Theorizing Homo
 Ludens. *v.4 p.715, p.815*

Sport and Physical Education in China. *v.4 p.796, p.797, v.6 p.194*

Sport and Politics in Canada: Federal Government Involvement
 since 1961. . . . .*v.4 p.588*

Sport and Recreation in Ancient Greece: A Sourcebook With
 Translations. *v.4 p.810, p.813*

Sport and Society: A Student Introduction. *v.4 p.816*

Sport and Society in Ancient Greece. *v.3 p.14*

Sport and the British: A Modern History. *v.4 p.806*

Sport and the Color Line: Black Athletes and Race Relations in
 Twentieth Century America. *v.4 p.818, p.832*

Sport and the Spirit of Play in Contemporary American
 Fiction. *v.4 p.812*

Sport and Women: Social Issues in International
 Perspective. *v.4 p.716, p.816, p.836, v.6 p.437*

Sport as Symbol: Images of the Athlete in Art, Literature and
 Song. *v.1 p.710*

Sport Business in the Global Marketplace: A Study of Strategic
 Cognition. *v.4 p.845, p.886, p.892, p.899*

Sport, Culture and the Media: The Unruly
 Trinity. *v.4 p.819, p.902*

Sport, Economy and Society in Britain
 1750-1914. . . . .*v.4 p.810, p.889, p.892*

Sport Ethics: Applications for Fair Play with PowerWeb Bind-In
 Passcard. *v.4 p.802*

Sport Facility Management: Organizing Events and Mitigating
 Risks. *v.4 p.880, p.882*

Sport Facility Planning and Management. *v.4 p.880, p.881, p.883*

Sport Finance. *v.4 p.884, p.888, p.891*

Sport Governance. *v.4 p.884, p.891*

Sport, Health and Drugs: A Critical Sociological
 Perspective. *v.4 p.820, p.826*

Sport in America: From Wicked Amusement to National
 Obsession. *v.4 p.811*

Sport in Canada: A History. *v.4 p.808*

Sport in Contemporary Society (P): An Anthology. . .*v.4 p.815*

Sport in Cuba: The Diamond in the
 Rough. *v.4 p.885, p.892, p.899*

Sport in Greece and Rome. *v.4 p.806*

Sport in Industrial America, 1850-1920. . . . . . .*v.4 p.809*

Sport in Latin America and the Caribbean. *v.3 p.266*

Sport in Latin American Society: Past and Present. . .*v.4 p.716*

Sport in Social Development: Traditions, Transitions, and
 Transformations. *v.4 p.816*

Sport in the Global Village. *v.4 p.845, p.899*

Sport Inside Out: Readings in Literature and
 Philosophy. *v.4 p.803, p.812*

Sport, Leisure and Tourism Information Sources: A Guide for
 Researchers. *v.4 p.161, p.785, p.813*

Sport Management Field Experiences. *v.4 p.905*

Sport Marketing. *v.4 p.885*

Sport Matters: Sociological Studies of Sport, Violence, and
 Civilisation. *v.4 p.815*

Sport, Media, Culture: Global and Local
 Dimensions. *v.4 p.817, p.844, p.902*

Sport Nutrition: An Introduction to Energy Production and
 Performance. *v.4 p.876*

Sport, Physical Activity and the Law. . *v.4 p.795, p.883, p.900*

Sport, Play, and Ethical Reflection. *v.4 p.715*

Sport, Power and Culture: A Social and Historical Analysis of Popular Sports in Britain. *v.4 p.816*

Sport Progressions. *v.4 p.797*

Sport Promotion and Sales Management. *v.4 p.906*

Sport Psychology: Concepts and Applications. . . . *v.4 p.877*

Sport Psychology: Contemporary Themes. .*v.4 p.877, v.5 p.582*

Sport Psychology in Practice. *v.4 p.876, v.5 p.581*

Sport Psychology: The Key Concepts. *v.4 p.877*

Sport Psychology: The Psychological Health of the Athlete. *v.5 p.582*

Sport Psychology. *v.4 p.877*

Sport Public Relations: Managing Organizational Communication. *v.4 p.886, p.903, p.907*

Sport Science. *v.4 p.870*

Sport Technology: History, Philosophy and Policy. . .*v.4 p.870*

Sportcult. *v.4 p.817*

Sporting Equality: Title IX Thirty Years Later. *v.4 p.809, p.822, p.838, p.901*

Sporting Females: Critical Issues in the History and Sociology of Women's Sports. *v.4 p.806, p.816, p.836, v.6 p.437*

Sporting Muse: A Critical Study of Poetry About Athletes and Athletics. *v.4 p.811*

Sporting with the Gods: The Rhetoric of Play and Game in American Literature. *v.4 p.812*

The Sporting World of the Modern South. *v.4 p.818*

SPORTQuest. *v.4 p.790, p.802, p.824, p.872*

Sports: A Reference Guide and Critical Commentary, 1980-1999. . . . .*v.4 p.812*

Sports: A Reference Guide. *v.4 p.823*

Sports and Education: A Reference Handbook. .*v.4 p.821, p.823*

Sports and Exercise Nutrition. *v.4 p.801, p.876*

Sports and Fitness Equipment Design. *v.4 p.870, p.872*

Sports and Freedom: The Rise of Big-Time College Athletics. *v.4 p.810, p.822, p.895*

Sports and Games of Ancient Egypt. *v.4 p.805*

Sports and Recreational Activities with PowerWeb Bind-In Passcard. *v.4 p.784, p.796*

Sports and the American Jew. *v.4 p.809, p.842*

Sports and the Law: Major Legal Cases. *v.4 p.786, p.885, p.901*

Sports Biomechanics: Preventing Injury and Improving Performance. *v.4 p.907*

Sports, Body and Health. *v.4 p.876, p.879*

Sports Culture: An A-Z Guide. *v.4 p.823*

Sports Economics: Current Research. *v.4 p.887*

Sports Ethics: An Anthology. *v.4 p.802*

Sports Ethics in America: A Bibliography, 1970-1990. . . . .*v.4 p.802, p.813*

Sports, Everyone!: Recreation and Sports for the Physically Challenged of All Ages. *v.4 p.795*

Sports, Exercises, and Fitness: A Guide to Reference and Information Sources. *v.4 p.823*

Sports Fields: A Manual for Design, Construction and Maintenance. *v.4 p.872, p.881, p.906*

Sports, Games, and Play: Social and Psychological Viewpoints. *v.5 p.582*

Sports Geography. *v.4 p.813*

Sports Gynecology: Problems and Care of the Athletic Female. *v.4 p.826, p.878*

The Sports Immortals: Deifying the American Athlete. .*v.4 p.716*

Sports in American Life. *v.4 p.814, p.815*

Sports in School: The Future of an Institution. *v.4 p.805*

Sports in the Lives of Children and Adolescents: Success on the Field and in Life. *v.4 p.840*

Sports in the Western World. *v.4 p.813*

Sports in Zion: Mormon Recreation, 1890-1940. *v.4 p.807, p.824*

Sports Injuries: A Unique Guide to Self-Diagnosis and Rehabilitation. *v.4 p.825, p.826*

Sports Injuries and Illnesses: Their Prevention and Treatment. *v.4 p.827, p.828, p.829*

Sports Injuries: Basic Principles of Prevention and Care. .*v.4 p.827*

Sports Injuries Sourcebook. *v.4 p.826*

Sports Injuries: Their Prevention and Treatment. . . .*v.4 p.827*

Sports, Jobs and Taxes: The Economic Impact of Sports Teams and Facilities. *v.4 p.888, p.889, p.897*

Sports Journalism: A Practical Introduction. . .*v.4 p.408, p.906*

Sports Law: Cases, Documents and Materials. *v.4 p.900*

Sports Law for Paralegals. *v.4 p.883, p.900*

Sports Law in a Nutshell. *v.4 p.883, p.900*

Sports Law. *v.4 p.884, p.900*

Sports Market Place Directory 2005. . . . .*v.4 p.881*

Sports Marketing: A Strategic Perspective. *v.4 p.886*

Sports Massage. *v.4 p.826*

Sports Matters: Race, Recreation, and Culture. *v.4 p.814, p.830*

Sports Mechanics for Coaches. *v.4 p.873, p.907*

Sports Media: Reporting, Producing, and Planning. *v.4 p.408, p.409, p.902, p.907*

Sports Medicine Bible: Prevent, Detect, and Treat Your Sports Injuries Through the Latest Medical Techniques. . .*v.4 p.825*

Sports Medicine: Ethics and the Law. . .*v.4 p.825, p.884, p.901*

Sports Nutrition: Vitamins and Trace Elements. *v.4 p.825, p.876*

Sports on New York Radio: A Play-by-Play History. *v.4 p.408, p.806, p.823, p.902, p.906*

The Sports Process: A Comparative and Developmental Approach. *v.4 p.815*

The Sports Psych Handbook. *v.4 p.877, v.5 p.582*

Sports Psychiatry. *v.5 p.581*

Sports Psychology in Performance: Applying Principles to Practice. *v.4 p.877, v.5 p.581*

Sports Science Handbook: The Essential Guide to Kinesiology, Sport and Exercise Science. *v.4 p.873*

Sports Speed. *v.4 p.874, p.879*

Sports Talk: A Journey Inside the World of Sports Talk Radio. *v.4 p.406*

Sports: The All-American Addiction. *v.4 p.815*

Sports: The First Five Millenia. *v.4 p.715, p.716*

Sports Writing Handbook. *v.4 p.407, p.903, p.907*

SPORTSCIENCE a peer-reviewed site for Sport Research. *v.4 p.824, p.872, p.907, p.909*

Sportsdykes: Stories from on and off the Field. *v.4 p.839*

Sportsex. *v.6 p.384, p.437, p.438, p.448*

SportsWars: Athletes in the Age of Aquarius. . .*v.4 p.811, p.820*

Sportswriter: The Life and Times of Grantland Rice. *v.4 p.811, p.906*

Sportswriting: The Lively Game. *v.4 p.407*

Spot Tests in Inorganic Analysis. *v.5 p.309*

Spot Tests in Organic Analysis. *v.5 p.300*

Sprawl: A Compact History. . . .*v.1 p.796, v.4 p.771, v.6 p.727*

Spraycan Art. *v.1 p.750*

Spreading the American Dream: American Economic and Cultural Expansion, 1890-1945. . . . .*v.3 p.454*

Spreading Time: Remarks on Canadian Writing and Writers, 1904-1949. . . . .*v.2 p.729*

Spreadsheet Applications in Chemistry Using Microsoft Excel. *v.5 p.267*

Spreadsheet Modeling and Decision Analysis. *v.4 p.179*

Spring Fever. *v.2 p.391*

Spring Snow. *v.6 p.231*

The Spring Will Be Ours: Poland and the Poles from Occupation to Freedom. *v.3 p.255, v.4 p.596*

Springboard and Platform Diving. *v.4 p.860*

Spruce Root Basketry of the Haida and Tlingit. . . .*v.1 p.806*

Sputnik, Scientists, and Eisenhower: A Memoir of the First Special Assistant to the President for Science and Technology. *v.5 p.397*

The Spy Story. *v.2 p.190*

The Spy Who Came in from the Cold. *v.2 p.361*

Spying with Maps: Surveillance Technologies and the Future of Privacy. *v.4 p.386*

Squandered Victory: The American Occupation and Bungled Effort to Bring Democracy to Iraq. *v.4 p.647*

Square and Folk Dancing. *v.1 p.33*

The Square Egg and Other Sketches with Three Plays. *v.2 p.381*

Square Foot Costs. *v.5 p.684*

The Square Moon: Supernatural Tales. *v.6 p.663*

The Square Root of Wonderful. *v.2 p.100*

Squash: A History of the Game. *v.4 p.864, p.865*

The Squatter and the Don. *v.6 p.503*

Squatters and Oligarchs: Authoritarian Rule and Policy Change in Peru. *v.3 p.329*

The Squire's Tale. *v.2 p.208*

▢ SRA International Grants Web. *v.4 p.293*

Sri Lanka: Ethnic Fratricide and the Dismantling of Democracy. *v.6 p.163*

St. Anselm: A Portrait in a Landscape. *v.1 p.580*

St. Benedict and the Sixth Century. *v.1 p.578, p.579*

St. Cyprian, the Lapsed, the Unity of the Catholic Church. *v.1 p.592*

St. Gregory the Great: Pastoral Care. *v.1 p.592*

St. Irenaeus: Proof of the Apostolic Preaching. . . .*v.1 p.592*

St. James Encyclopedia of Labor History Worldwide: Major Events in Labor History and Their Impact, Set. . .*v.4 p.129*

St. James Encyclopedia of Popular Culture, Set. . . .*v.3 p.443*

St. James Guide to Black Artists. . . .*v.1 p.665, p.666, p.705*

St. James Guide to Hispanic Artists: Profiles of Latino and Latin American Artists. *v.6 p.490, p.493*

St. James Guide to Native North American Artists. *v.1 p.665, v.6 p.679*

St. James Press Gay and Lesbian Almanac. *v.6 p.360*

St. John de Crevecoeur. *v.2 p.29*

St John of the Cross. *v.1 p.578*

St. Justin Martyr: The First and Second Apologies. . .*v.1 p.590*

The St. Lawrence and the Saguenay and Other Poems. *v.2 p.733*

St. Paul: A Study in Social and Religious History. . . .*v.1 p.626*

St. Petersburg: Architecture of the Tsars. *v.3 p.214*

St. Petersburg: Russia's Window to the Future—The First Three Centuries. *v.3 p.214*

St. Ronan's Well. *v.2 p.308*

St. Thomas and Philosophy. *v.1 p.434, p.435*

Stability Analysis and Design of Structures. *v.5 p.694*

Stability and Inflation: A Volume of Essays to Honour the Memory of A. W. H. Phillips. *v.4 p.239, p.240*

Stability and Optimization of Flexible Space Structures. *v.5 p.693*

Stability and Strife: England 1714-1760. . . .*v.3 p.91, p.109*

Stability Constants of Metal Ion Complexes. *v.5 p.282*

Stability in Model Populations. *v.5 p.170*

Stabilization of the Domestic and International Economy. *v.4 p.240, p.255*

Stable Isotope Geochemistry. *v.5 p.440*

Stable Isotopes and Biosphere - Atmosphere Interactions: Processes and Biological Controls. *v.5 p.113*

Stack and Sway: The New Science of Jury Consulting. *v.6 p.270, p.271*

Stage Directions. *v.1 p.144*

Stage Fright: Modernism, Anti-Theatricality, and Drama. *v.2 p.189*

The Stage Is Set. *v.1 p.139, p.148, p.149*

Stage It with Music: An Encyclopedic Guide to the American Musical Theatre. *v.1 p.59, p.92, p.115*

The Stage Life of Props. *v.1 p.148*

Stage Lighting Design: The Art - The Craft - The Life. *v.1 p.149*

Stage Makeup: Special Edition. *v.1 p.150*

Stage Makeup: The Actor's Complete Guide to Today's Techniques and Materials. *v.1 p.151*

Stage Makeup. *v.1 p.150*

Stage Management and Theatrecraft: A Stage Manager's Handbook. *v.1 p.146, p.149*

Stage Management. *v.1 p.150*

Stage Presence from Head to Toe: A Manual for Musicians. *v.1 p.395, p.398*

The Stage Producer's Business and Legal Guide. . . .*v.1 p.150*

Stage to Studio: Musicians and the Sound Revolution, 1890-1950. . . . .*v.1 p.384*

The Stagecraft of Aeschylus: The Dramatic Use of Exits and Entrances in Greek Tragedy. *v.2 p.407*

Stages of Desire: Male and Female Homosexuality in British and American Theatre. *v.6 p.412*

Stages of History: Shakespeare's English Chronicles. *v.2 p.234*

Stages of Reading Development. *v.5 p.574*

Stagestruck: Theater, AIDS and Marketing of Gay America. *v.1 p.253, p.380, v.6 p.413*

Stage-Structured Populations: Sampling, Analysis and Simulation. *v.5 p.100*

Stagg's University: The Rise, Decline and Fall of Big-Time Football at the University of Chicago. *v.4 p.807, p.858, p.859, p.894*

Staging a Revolution: The Art of Persuasion in the Islamic Republic of Iran. *v.6 p.632*

Staging and Stagers in Modern Jewish Palestine: The Creation of Festive Lore in a New Culture, 1882-1948. . . .*v.6 p.611*

Staging Consciousness: Theater and the Materialization of Mind. *v.1 p.138*

Staging Dance. *v.1 p.37*

Staging Desire: Queer Readings of American Theater History. *v.1 p.126, p.135, v.2 p.16, v.6 p.413*

Staging Difference: Cultural Pluralism in American Theatre and Drama. *v.1 p.87, p.120*

Staging Gay Lives: An Anthology of Contemporary Gay Theater. *v.2 p.24, v.6 p.411*

The Staging Handbook. *v.1 p.139, p.147, p.148*

Staging Japanese Theatre: Noh and Kabuki. *v.1 p.132, p.133, p.135*

Staging Modern Playwrights. *v.1 p.139*

Staging Resistance: Essays on Political Theater. . . .*v.6 p.147*

Staging the Olympics: The Event and Its Impact. *v.4 p.845, p.887, p.890, p.898*

Staging the Past: The Politics of Commemoration in Habsburg Central Europe, 1848 to the Present. . . .*v.3 p.181, p.183*

Staging the Pastoral: Tasso's Aminta and the Emergence of Modern Western Theater. *v.2 p.709*

Staging the World: Chinese Nationalism at the Turn of the 20th Century. *v.4 p.494*

Stained Glass and the Victorian Gothic Revival. . . .*v.1 p.810*

Stained Glass in Catholic Philadelphia. *v.1 p.810*

Stainless Steels. *v.5 p.736*

Staircases: Structural Analysis and Design. *v.5 p.692*

Stakeholder Theory and Organizational Ethics. *v.4 p.87*

The Stakes of Power: 1845-1877. . . . .*v.3 p.399*

Stalin: A Biography. *v.3 p.223, p.224*

Stalin and the Bomb: The Soviet Union and Atomic Energy, 1939-1956. . . . .*v.3 p.225, p.226*

Stalin and the Bomb: The Soviet Union and Atomic Energy, 1939-56. . . . .*v.3 p.49, p.208*

Stalin in Power: An Interpretive History. *v.3 p.224*

Stalin: The Court of the Red Tsar. *v.3 p.223*

The Stalin Years: A Reader. *v.3 p.226*

Stalingrad: The Fateful Siege, 1942-1943. . . .*v.3 p.174, p.226*

Stalinism as a Way of Life: A Narrative in Documents. .*v.3 p.226*

Stalinism for All Seasons: A Political History of Romanian Communism. *v.3 p.250, p.251, v.4 p.509, p.600*

Stalinism in Ukraine in the 1940s. *v.3 p.229*

Stalinist Values: The Cultural Norms of Soviet Modernity, 1917-1941. . . . .*v.3 p.225*

Stalin's Folly: The Tragic First Ten Days of World War Two on the Eastern Front. *v.3 p.227*

Stalin's Ocean-Going Fleet: Soviet Naval Strategy and Shipbuilding Programs 1935-1953. . . . .*v.3 p.212*

Stalin's Other War: Soviet Grand Strategy, 1939-1941. . . . .*v.3 p.227, p.228*

Stalin's Peasants: Collectiveness and Popular Resistance in Russia. *v.3 p.225*

Stalin's Railroad: Turksib and the Building of Socialism. *v.3 p.231*

Stalin's War with Germany. *v.3 p.227*

Stalking and Domestic Violence: Current Issues. . . .*v.6 p.259*

Stalking Sociologists: J. Edgar Hoover's FBI Surveillance of American Sociology. *v.4 p.683*

The Stamp Act Crisis: Prologue to Revolution. *v.3 p.410*

Stan Getz: A Life in Jazz. *v.1 p.261, p.326*

Stand and Prosper: Private Black Colleges and Their Students. *v.4 p.291*

🖥 Standard & Poor's Industry Surveys Online. *v.4 p.150*

The Standard and Poor's Guide to Personal Finance. . .*v.4 p.94*

Standard and Poor's Register of Corporations, Directors, and Executives, United States and Canada. *v.5 p.397*

Standard English - Macedonian, Macedonian - English Dictionary. *v.2 p.775*

Standard English and the Politics of Language. . . .*v.2 p.551*

Standard English: The Widening Debate. *v.2 p.551*

Standard English-SerboCroatian, SerboCroatian-English Dictionary: A Dictionary of Bosnian, Croatian, and Serbian Standards. *v.2 p.774*

The Standard Handbook for Aeronautical and Astronautical Engineers. *v.5 p.717*

Standard Handbook for Civil Engineers. *v.5 p.686*

Standard Handbook of Environmental Engineering. *v.5 p.367, p.706*

Standard Handbook of Lubrication Engineering. *v.5 p.714*

Standard Handbook of Machine Design. *v.5 p.715*

Standard Handbook of Petroleum and Natural Gas Engineering. *v.5 p.451, p.738*

Standard Methods for the Examination of Dairy Products. *v.5 p.35*

🖥 Standard methods for the examination of water and wastewater [computer file]. *v.5 p.312*

Standard Methods for the Examination of Water and Wastewater. *v.5 p.312*

Standard Methods of Chemical Analysis, Set. *v.5 p.268*

Standard Music Notation Practice. *v.1 p.392*

The Standard of Living in Britain in the Industrial Revolution. *v.3 p.88, p.116*

The Standard of Living. *v.4 p.266*

Standard Pressure-Volume-Temperature Data for Polymers. *v.5 p.324*

Standardized Survey Interviewing: Minimizing Interviewer-Related Error. *v.4 p.691*

🖥 Standards and National Board Certification. *v.4 p.278*

🖥 Standards (Art Education). *v.4 p.359*

Standards for Educational and Psychological Testing. *v.4 p.285, v.5 p.604*

Standards for Educational and Psychological Tests Prepared by a Joint Committee of the American Psychological Association, American Educational Research Association and National Council on Measurement in Education. . .*v.5 p.600*

Standards-Based Activities with Scoring Rubrics: Middle and High School English Performance-Based Portfolios. *v.4 p.286*

Standards-Based Activities with Scoring Rubrics: Middle and High School English Performance-Based Projects. *v.4 p.286*

Standards-Based Lessons for Tech-Savvy Students: A Multiple Intelligences Approach. *v.4 p.351*

Standing Against the Whirlwind: Evangelical Episcopalians in Nineteenth-Century America. *v.1 p.582*

Standing Out, Standing Together: The Political and Social Impact of Gay-Straight Alliances. *v.6 p.385*

The Stand. *v.2 p.148*

The Stanford Companion to Victorian Fiction. *v.2 p.193, v.6 p.736, p.740, p.753, p.757*

Stanford Encyclopedia of Philosophy. *v.1 p.415, p.416*

Stanley: An Adventurer Explored. *v.6 p.51*

Stanley and the Women. *v.2 p.328*

Stanley K. Hornbeck and the Open Door Policy, 1919-1937. *v.3 p.459*

Stanley Kunitz: An Introduction to the Poetry. *v.2 p.92*

Stanton: The Life and Times of Lincoln's Secretary of War. *v.3 p.426, p.427*

Stanwyck. *v.6 p.418*

A Star Called Henry. *v.2 p.343*

Star Eternal. *v.6 p.649*

Star Names and Their Meanings. *v.5 p.70*

The Star Raft: China's Encounters with Africa. *v.6 p.56*

Star Struck: One Thousand Years of the Art and Science of Astronomy. *v.5 p.61*

Starched Blue Sky of Spain and Other Memoirs, Reissued Ed. *v.2 p.81*

A Star-Crossed Golden Age: Myth and the Spanish Comedia. *v.2 p.640*

Stardom: Industry of Desire. *v.6 p.331*

The Star-Entangled Banner: One Hundred Years of America in the Philippines. *v.3 p.388*

Stargazer: The Life and Times of the Telescope. *v.5 p.66*

Stargazing with a Telescope. *v.5 p.66*

Starr Report: The Findings of Independent Counsel Kenneth Starr on President Clinton and the Lewinsky Affair. *v.3 p.480*

The Stars: A New Way to See Them. *v.5 p.70*

The Stars Above, the Earth Below: American Indians and Nature. *v.6 p.680*

Stars in My Pocket Like Grains of Sand. *v.6 p.395*

Stars, Minds and Fate: Essays on Ancient and Medieval Cosmology. *v.6 p.576*

The Star-Spangled Screen: The American World War II Film. *v.6 p.322*

Start and Run Your Own Business: The Complete Guide to Setting up and Managing a Small Business. *v.4 p.87*

Start Your Own Information Consultant Business: Your Step by Step Guide to Success. *v.4 p.65*

The Starter Marriage and the Future of Matrimony. *v.4 p.739*

Starting from Scratch: Secrets from 21 Ordinary People Who Made the Entrepreneurial Leap. *v.4 p.68*

Starting Out Right: A Guide to Promoting Children's Reading Success. *v.4 p.361*

StartupNation: America's Leading Entrepreneurial Experts Reveal the Secrets to Building a Blockbuster Business. *v.4 p.68*

State and Countryside: Development Policy and Agrarian Politics in Latin America. *v.4 p.772*

The State and Economic Development: Peru since 1968. *v.3 p.329*

The State and Labor in Modern America. *v.4 p.125*

The State and Labor in Modern Japan. *v.6 p.224*

State and Opposition in Military Brazil. *v.3 p.273, v.4 p.591*

State and Reservation: New Perspectives on Federal Indian Policy. *v.6 p.695*

State and Revolution in Cuba: Mass Mobilization and Political Change, 1920-1940. *v.3 p.314*

The State and Revolution: Marxist Teaching about the Theory of the State and the Tasks of the Proletariat in the Revolution. *v.4 p.508*

The State and Revolution. *v.4 p.237*

State and Society in Early Modern Austria. *v.3 p.181*

State and Society in Pre-Colonial Asante. *v.6 p.70*

State and Society in Spanish America During the Age of Revolution. *v.3 p.359*

State and Society in the Taiwan Miracle. *v.6 p.214*

The State and Society: Peru in Comparative Perspective. *v.3 p.331, p.332*

The State and the Family: A Comparative Analysis of Family Policies in Industrialized Countries. *v.4 p.731*

The State at War in South Asia. *v.6 p.145, p.146*

State Building in Ukraine: The Ukrainian Parliament, 1990-2003. *v.4 p.576, p.586, p.599*

The State, Bureaucracy, and Revolution in Modern Iran: Agrarian Reforms and Regime Politics. *v.4 p.616*

State, Conflict and Democracy in Africa. *v.4 p.611*

State, Conflict, and Democracy in Africa. *v.4 p.611*

State Constitutions and Criminal Justice, Vol. 65. *v.6 p.268, p.269*

State Contacts for Alternative Teacher Education. *v.4 p.278*

State Crime: Governments, Violence and Corruption. *v.6 p.253*

State Crime, the Media, and the Invasion of Panama. *v.3 p.304*

State, Economy and Society 1933-39: A Documentary Reader. *v.3 p.173*

State Election Laws & Administration Issues. *v.4 p.549*

The State in Africa: The Politics of the Belly. *v.4 p.611*

The State in Burma. *v.6 p.165, p.166*

The State in Relation to Labour. *v.4 p.231*

State in Society: Studying How States and Societies Transform and Constitute One Another. *v.4 p.773*

A State in the Making: Myth, History, and Social Transformation in Pre-Colonial Ufipa. *v.6 p.66*

State, Markets, and Just Growth: Development in the Twenty-First Century. *v.4 p.665*

State of a Union: Inside the Complex Marriage of Bill and Hillary Clinton. *v.3 p.477*

The State of Asian America: Activism and Resistance in the 1990s. *v.6 p.107, p.108*

The State of Asian America: Reframing the Immigration Debate. *v.6 p.118*

The State of Asian Pacific America: Transforming Race Relations. *v.6 p.85, p.109*

The State of China Atlas: Mapping the World's Fastest Growing Economy. *v.6 p.182*

The State of Food and Agriculture, 2003-04. . .*v.4 p.151, p.152*

The State of Latino Theater in the U. S.: Hybridity, Transculturation and Identity. *v.6 p.515, p.518*

The State of Martial Rule: The Origins of Pakistan's Political Economy of Defence. *v.6 p.162*

A State of Nations: Empire and Nation-Making in the Age of Lenin and Stalin. *v.3 p.213*

State of Rebellion: Reconstruction in South Carolina. .*v.3 p.502*

State of Siege. *v.2 p.658*

The State of the Animals, 2001. . . . .*v.5 p.85*

The State of the Nation: Ernest Gellner and the Theory of Nationalism. *v.4 p.494*

The State of the Nation's Ecosystems: Measuring the Lands, Waters, and Living Resources of the United States. *v.5 p.17, p.170, p.356,v.6 p.291*

☐ State of the Nation's Housing 2005. . . . .*v.4 p.158*

State of the Space Industry — 2005. . . . .*v.4 p.151*

State of the Union: A Century of American Labor. . .*v.4 p.127*

State of the Union: America in the 1990s: Economic Trends. *v.4 p.763*

State of the Union: America in the 1990s: Social Trends. .*v.4 p.763*

State of the World 2001: A Worldwatch Institute Report on Progress Toward a Sustainable Society. *v.4 p.267*

The State of the World's Children 2004: Girls, Education and Development. *v.4 p.668*

State of the World's Children 2005: Childhood under Threat. *v.4 p.670*

The State of the World's Children 2006: Excluded and Invisible. *v.4 p.670*

The State of the World's Cities 2004/2005: Globalization and Urban Culture. *v.4 p.663, v.6 p.725, p.726*

The State of the World's Refugees 2000: Fifty Years of Humanitarian Action. *v.4 p.765*

The State of World Population (2000): Lives Together, Worlds Apart - Men and Women in a Time of Change. . .*v.6 p.426*

State of World Population 2004: The Cairo Consensus at Ten; Population, Reproductive Health and the Global Effort to End Poverty. *v.4 p.669*

State of World Population 2005: The Promise of Equality, Gender Equity, Reproductive Health and the Millennium Development Goals. *v.4 p.663*

☐ State Policy Inventory Database Online. *v.4 p.295*

State Power and World Markets: The International Political Economy. *v.4 p.626*

State Resistance to Globalisation in Cuba. *v.3 p.306*

State Rights in the Confederacy. *v.3 p.399*

State, Society and University in Germany, Seventeen Hundred to Nineteen Fourteen. *v.3 p.179*

State Terrorism and Political Identity in Indonesia: Fatally Belonging. *v.6 p.174, p.176, p.177*

Statecraft and Political Economy on the Taiwan Frontier, 1600-1800. . . . .*v.6 p.214*

Stateliest Measures: Tennyson and the Literature of Greece and Rome. *v.2 p.313*

State-Local Relations: A Partnership Approach. .*v.4 p.462, p.463*

Statements: Three Plays. *v.2 p.755*

Statements Two: New Fiction. *v.2 p.26*

States and Power in Africa: Comparative Lessons in Authority and Control. *v.4 p.611*

States and Social Revolutions: A Comparative Analysis of France, Russia and China. *v.4 p.760*

States and Women's Rights: The Making of Postcolonial Tunisia, Algeria, and Morocco. *v.6 p.440, p.453, p.641*

States, Ideologies and Social Revolutions: A Comparative Analysis of Iran, Nicaragua and the Philippines. *v.3 p.303, v.4 p.500*

States of Desire: Travels in Gay America. *v.6 p.366*

States of Injury: Power and Freedom in Late Modernity. .*v.6 p.440*

States of Mind: Two cCnturies of Anglo-Irish Conflict, 1780-1980. . . . .*v.3 p.136*

States of Nature: Science, Agriculture, and Environment in the Spanish Caribbean, 1760-1940. . . . .*v.3 p.269*

States, Parties, and Social Movements. *v.4 p.579, p.711*

States' Rights and American Federalism: A Documentary History. *v.4 p.523*

The State's Servants: The Civil Service of the English Republic, 1649-1660. . . . .*v.3 p.102*

Statesman and Saint: Wolsey and More, a Study in Contrast. *v.3 p.101*

The Statesman's Book of John of Salisbury, Being the Fourth, Fifth, and Sixth Books, and Selections from the Seventh and Eighth Books, of the Policraticus. . . .*v.4 p.490*

The Statesman's Yearbook: The Politics, Cultures and Economies of the World. . . .*v.4 p.374, p.575, p.576, p.625*

State-Society Relations in Mexico: Clientelism, Neoliberal State Reform and the Case of Conasupo. *v.3 p.272*

Stateville: The Penitentiary in Mass Society. *v.6 p.273*

Statewide Wetlands Strategies: A Guide to Protecting and Managing the Resource. *v.5 p.178, p.182*

The Station Hill Blanchot Reader: Essays and Fiction. .*v.2 p.510*

Statistical Abstract of the United States: The National Data Book, 2004-2005. . . . .*v.6 p.284, p.285*

☐ Statistical Abstract of the United States. . . .*v.4 p.482, p.679*

☐ Statistical Agencies (International). *v.4 p.179*

Statistical Analysis of Gene Expression Microarray Data. *v.5 p.101, p.102*

Statistical Analysis of Geographic Information with ArcView GIS and ArcGIS. *v.4 p.387*

Statistical and Inductive Probabilities. *v.1 p.495*

Statistical Concepts: A Second Course for Education and the Behavioral Sciences. *v.5 p.482, p.503*

Statistical Concepts for Education and the Behavioral Sciences. *v.4 p.355*

Statistical Distributions. *v.5 p.481*

Statistical Dynamics and Reliability Theory for Mechanical Structures. *v.5 p.696*

Statistical Dynamics. *v.5 p.558*

Statistical Handbook on the Social Safety Net. *v.4 p.758*

Statistical Handbook on Women in America. *v.6 p.426*

A Statistical History of the American Electorate. *v.4 p.548, p.549, p.555*

Statistical Mechanics: A Set of Lectures. *v.5 p.558*

Statistical Mechanics: Kinetic, Theory and Stochastic Process. *v.5 p.558*

The Statistical Mechanics of Fianancial Markets. . . .*v.5 p.559*

Statistical Mechanics of Learning. *v.5 p.558*

Statistical Mechanics of Phase Transitions. *v.5 p.559*

Statistical Mechanics. *v.5 p.558, p.559*

Statistical Methods, Experimental Design, and Scientific Inference: A Re-issue of Statistical Methods for Research Workers, the Design of Experiments, and Statistical Methods and Scientific Inference. *v.5 p.482*

Statistical Methods for Geography: A Student's Guide. *v.4 p.376*

Statistical Methods for Geography. *v.4 p.376*

Statistical Methods for the Social Sciences. *v.4 p.483*

Statistical Methods in Bioinformatics: An Introduction. *v.5 p.107, p.482, p.502*

Statistical Methods in Education and Psychology. . . .*v.5 p.599*

Statistical Methods in Genetic Epidemiology. *v.5 p.93, p.144, p.152*

Statistical Methods in Soil and Land Resource Survey. *v.5 p.52*

Statistical Methods. *v.5 p.483*

Statistical Physics, Vol. 9, Pt. 2. . . . .*v.5 p.559*

Statistical Physics. *v.5 p.559*

Statistical Record of Women Worldwide 3. . . . . . .*v.6 p.425*

Statistical Techniques in Bioassay. *v.5 p.92*

Statistical Testing of Business-Cycle Theories. *v.4 p.245*

Statistical Theory. *v.5 p.482*

Statistical Yearbook, No. 44. . . . .*v.4 p.763*

Statistical Yearbook of the Electric Power Industry. . .*v.4 p.159*

Statisticians of the Centuries. *v.5 p.466, p.481*

Statistics: A Guide to Business and Economics. *v.5 p.483, p.504*

Statistics: A Guide to Political and Social Issues. *v.5 p.483, p.504*

Statistics: A Guide to the Unknown. *v.5 p.483*

Statistics and Data Analysis in Geology. . . . *v.5 p.419, p.420*

☐ Statistics and Research Sources. *v.6 p.246*

Statistics: Concepts and Controversies. *v.5 p.481*

Statistics for Environmental Investigations. . . *v.5 p.483, p.502*

Statistics for Experimenters: An Introduction to Design, Data Analysis, and Model Building. *v.5 p.481, p.482*

Statistics for Management and Economics (Ise). *v.4 p.178, p.179*

Statistics for Microarrays: Design, Analysis and Inference. *v.5 p.101*

Statistics for the Life Sciences. *v.5 p.93*

☐ Statistics in Sports a section of the American Statistical Association. *v.4 p.871*

Statistics in Theory and Practice. *v.5 p.64*

Statistics on the Table: The History of Statistical Concepts and Methods. *v.5 p.468, p.481*

Statistics with Applications to the Biological and Health Sciences. *v.5 p.93*

Statistics with Mathematica. *v.5 p.482*

Statistics. *v.5 p.481*

☐ Stat!Ref Electronic Resources for Healthcare Professionals. *v.5 p.509*

☐ Status of the American Public School Teacher 2000-2002. . . . .*v.4 p.283*

ⓔ Stay Tuned: A History of American Broadcasting. *v.4 p.412*

Stücke, Erzählungen, Aufsätze, Gedichte. *v.2 p.611*

Steal This Idea: Intellectual Property Rights and the Corporate Confiscation of Creativity. *v.4 p.67*

Stealing Glances: Three Interviews with Wallace Stegner. *v.2 p.121*

Stealing History: Tomb Raiders, Smugglers, and the Looting of the Ancient World. *v.1 p.826, p.827*

Stealing the Language: The Emergence of Women's Poetry in America. *v.2 p.8*

Stealing Time: Steve Case, Jerry Levin, and the Collapse of AOL Time Warner. *v.4 p.157*

ⓔ Stealth Democracy: Americans' Beliefs about How Government Should Work. *v.4 p.554*

Stedman's Medical Dictionary, 1995. . . . . . .*v.5 p.325*

Stedman's Surinam: Life in an Eighteenth-Century Slave Society. An Abridged, Modernized Edition of Narrative of a Five Years Expedition against the Revolted Negroes of Surinam. *v.3 p.323*

Steel & Silk: Men & Women Who Shaped Syria, 1900-2000. . . . .*v.6 p.607, p.608*

Steel and Steelworkers: Race and Class Struggle in Twentieth-Century Pittsburgh. *v.4 p.126*

Steel Chair to the Head: The Pleasure and Pain of Professional Wrestling. *v.4 p.819, p.863*

Steel City: Urban and Ethnic Patterns in Gary, Indiana, 1906-1950. . . . .*v.3 p.514*

Steel Corrosion in Concrete: Fundamentals and Civil Engineering Practice. *v.5 p.693*

The Steelband Movement: The Forging of a National Art in Trinidad and Tobago. *v.1 p.294, p.295*

Steeltown U. S. A.: Work and Memory in Youngstown. *v.3 p.513*

Stefansson and the Canadian Arctic. *v.3 p.546, p.547*

Steichen's Legacy: Photographs, 1895-1973. . . . . *v.1 p.769*

Stein, 1903-1932: Q. E. D. ; Three Lives; Autobiography of Alice B. Toklas; Portraits. *v.2 p.122*

Stein, 1903-1932: Q. E. D.; Three Lives; Autobiography of Alice B. Toklas; Portraits. *v.6 p.404*

Stein, 1932-1946: Stanzas in Meditation; Lectures in America; the Geographical History of America; Ida, Brewsie and Willie and Other Works. *v.2 p.122*

Steinbeck, 1932-1937: The Pastures of Heaven; To a God Unknown; Tortilla Flat; In Dubious Battle; Of Mice and Men. *v.2 p.123*

Steinberg at the New Yorker. *v.1 p.702*

Stelarc: The Monograph. *v.1 p.773*

Stella Manhattan. *v.2 p.693*

Stellar Structure and Evolution. *v.5 p.70*

Stem Cell Biology and Gene Therapy. *v.5 p.151, p.152*

Stendhal: A Collection of Critical Essays. *v.2 p.501*

Stendhal Revisited. *v.2 p.502*

Stendhal, the Red and the Black and the Charterhouse of Parma. *v.2 p.501*

Stendhal: The Red and the Black. *v.2 p.501*

Stendhal's The Red and the Black. *v.2 p.501*

Stendhal. *v.2 p.501*

Stengel: His Life and Times. *v.4 p.850*

Step-by-Step: Nature Craft Projects for Kids. *v.5 p.229*

The Stepchild: Angaliyat. *v.6 p.152*

Title Index

Stepchildren of Nature: Krafft-Ebing, Psychiatry, and the Making of Sexual Identity. *v.4 p.748*

Stepfamilies: A Guide to Working with Stepparents and Stepchildren. *v.4 p.732*

Stepfamilies: Who Benefits? Who Does Not? *v.5 p.639*

Stepfamily Relationships: Development, Dynamics, and Interventions. *v.4 p.740, v.5 p.640, p.668*

Stephane Mallarme. *v.2 p.496*

Stephane Millarme. *v.2 p.497*

Stephen A. Douglas, Defender of the Union. *v.3 p.422, p.423, p.427*

Stephen A. Douglas. *v.3 p.398, p.422, p.423, p.428*

Stephen Crane: A Collection of Critical Essays. . .*v.2 p.35, p.36*

Stephen Crane: A Critical Biography. *v.2 p.36*

Stephen Crane and Literary Impressionism. *v.2 p.36*

Stephen Crane: From Parody to Realism. *v.2 p.36*

Stephen Crane. *v.2 p.36*

Stephen F. Austin: Empresario of Texas. *v.3 p.508*

Stephen Hawking: A Life in Science. *v.5 p.544*

Stephen Hero. *v.2 p.359*

Stephen J. Field: Craftsman of the Law. *v.4 p.469*

Stephen Sondheim: A Life. *v.1 p.253, p.357,v.6 p.410*

Stephen Sondheim and Andrew Lloyd Webber: The New Musical. *v.1 p.249, p.337, p.357*

Stephen Spender: A Life in Modernism. *v.2 p.384*

Stephen Spender: A Literary Life. *v.2 p.384*

Stephen Széchenyi and the awakening of Hungarian nationalism, 1791-1841. . . . .*v.3 p.186*

Stephen Vincent Benet: The Life and Times of an American Man of Letters, 1898-1943. . . . .*v.2 p.61*

Stephen Vincent Benét: Essays on His Life and Work. .*v.2 p.61*

Stepparenting: Creating and Recreating Families in America Today. *v.5 p.639*

Steppenwolf. *v.2 p.609*

Steppin' on the Blues: The Visible Rhythms of African American Dance. *v.1 p.32*

Steppin' Out: New York Nightlife and the Transformation of American Culture. *v.3 p.490*

Stepping Left: Dance and Politics in New York City, 1928-1942. . . . .*v.1 p.26*

Stepping over the Color Line: African-American Students in White Suburban Schools. *v.4 p.301*

Steps in Time. *v.1 p.6*

Steps to an Ecology of Mind: Collected Essays in Anthropology, Psychiatry, Evolution, and Epistemology. *v.4 p.23*

Steps to Small Business Start-Up. *v.4 p.87, p.88*

☐ Stereochemical Glossary. *v.5 p.257*

Stereochemistry of Coordination Compounds. *v.5 p.304*

Stereochemistry of Organic Compounds. *v.5 p.298*

Stereochemistry. *v.5 p.298*

Stereoselective Synthesis: A Practical Approach. . . .*v.5 p.295*

Stereotypes and Social Cognition. *v.4 p.694*

Stereotyping and Prejudice. *v.4 p.694*

Stern's Performing Arts Directory 2000. . . . .*v.1 p.4*

The Steroids Game. *v.4 p.826, p.827*

Steuben Glass: An American Tradition in Crystal. . . .*v.1 p.810*

Stevenage: A Sociological Study of a New Town. . . .*v.4 p.705*

Stevens: Collected Poetry and Prose. *v.2 p.124*

Stevie Smith: A Selection. *v.2 p.383*

Stevie Smith: Between the Lines. *v.2 p.382*

Stéphane Grappelli: With and Without Django. .*v.1 p.257, p.327*

Sticks and Stones: The Troublesome Success of Children's Literature from Slovenly Peter to Harry Potter. . . .*v.2 p.582*

Sticky Knowledge: Barriers to Knowing in the Firm. . .*v.4 p.79*

Stieglitz: A Beginning Light. *v.1 p.767*

Stiffed: The Betrayal of the American Man. . .*v.6 p.429, p.469*

Stiff-Necked People, Bottle-Necked System: The Evolution and Roots of Israeli Public Protest, 1949-1986. . . . .*v.4 p.615*

Still Acting Gay: Male Homosexuality in Modern Drama. *v.6 p.411*

Still Alive: A Holocaust Girlhood Remembered. . . .*v.3 p.85*

Still Another Day/aun. *v.2 p.681*

Still Black, Still Strong: Survivors of the War Against Black Revolutionaries. *v.6 p.3, p.31*

Still Life with Bombers: Israel in the Age of Terrorism. .*v.6 p.614*

Still Life. *v.1 p.727, v.2 p.332*

Still Lifting, Still Climbing: African American Women's Contemporary Activism. *v.6 p.31, p.32, p.46*

Still Looking: Essays on American Art. *v.1 p.683*

Still Seeing Red: How the Cold War Shapes the New American Politics. *v.3 p.481*

Still the Promised City?: African-Americans and New Immigrants in Postindustrial New York. *v.4 p.730, v.6 p.719, p.720*

Stiller. *v.2 p.607*

A Stillness at Appomattox. *v.3 p.430*

Stilwell and the American Experience in China, 1911-45. . . . .*v.3 p.463, v.6 p.193, p.201*

The Stilwell Papers. *v.6 p.193, p.201, p.216*

Das Stilworterbuch. *v.2 p.621*

Stimulating Concepts in Chemistry. *v.5 p.265*

Stinging Trees and Wait-a-Whiles: Confessions of a Rainforest Biologist. *v.5 p.239*

Stiquito Controlled!: Making a Truly Autonomous Robot. *v.5 p.714*

Stirring the Head, Heart, and Soul: Redefining Curriculum and Instruction, Vol. 6. . . . .*v.4 p.362*

Stitches on Time: Colonial Textures and Postcolonial Tangles. *v.6 p.155*

Stitching a Revolution: The Making of an AIDS Activist. *v.6 p.379, p.402*

Stochastic Dynamic Macroeconomics: Theory, Numerics, and Empirical Evidence. *v.4 p.200*

Stochastic Integration and Differential Equations. .*v.5 p.484, p.487*

Stochastic Models in Operations Research: Stochastic Optimization. *v.5 p.484, p.493*

Stochastic Models in Operations Research: Stochastic Processes and Operating Characteristics. *v.5 p.484, p.493*

Stochastic Population Dynamics in Ecology and Conservation. *v.5 p.180, p.189*

Stochastic Population Models: A Compartmental Perspective. *v.5 p.100*

Stochastic Processes and Their Applications. *v.5 p.483*

Stochastic Processes. *v.5 p.483*

Stock Market Capitalism: Japan and Germany versus the Anglo-Saxons. *v.6 p.219*

The Stock Market. *v.4 p.97, p.98, p.102, p.163*

Stockhausen: A Biography. *v.1 p.217, p.358*

Stockhausen on Music: Lectures and Interviews. .*v.1 p.224, p.358*

Stocks for the Long Run: The Definitive Guide to Financial Market Returns and Long-Term Investment Strategies. *v.4 p.97, p.102*

Stocktakings from an Apprenticeship. *v.1 p.210, p.312*

Stoic Logic. *v.1 p.494*

Stoic Studies. *v.1 p.429*

Stoicism: Traditions and Transformations. *v.1 p.429*

Stoicism. *v.1 p.429*

Stoics, Epicureans and Sceptics: Introduction to Hellenistic Philosophy. *v.1 p.428*

The Stoics, Epicureans and Skeptics. *v.1 p.428*

The Stoics. *v.1 p.429*

Stolen Legacy. *v.6 p.10*

Stolen Time: The History of Tempo Rubato. *v.1 p.400*

Stone Age Economics. *v.4 p.28, p.29*

The Stone Angel. *v.2 p.736*

Stone Butch Blues. *v.6 p.370, p.396*

The Stone Diaries. *v.2 p.739*

Stone in Architecture: Properties, Durability. *v.5 p.452*

The Stone of Laughter: A Novel. *v.6 p.658*

The Stone Skeleton: Structural Engineering of Masonry Architecture. *v.1 p.796, v.5 p.697*

The Stone Trumpet: A Story of Practical School Reform, 1960-1990. . . . .*v.4 p.326*

The Stone Virgins: A Novel. *v.2 p.759*

Stonefish. *v.2 p.746*

Stonehenge Complete. *v.4 p.12*

The Stones of Athens. *v.3 p.19*

Stonewall: The Riots That Sparked the Gay Revolution. *v.4 p.710, p.711*

▢ Stonewalled: Police Abuse and Misconduct Against Lesbian, Gay, Bisexual and Transgender People in the U.S. .*v.6 p.387*

Stonewall. *v.6 p.365, p.387, p.388*

The Stop Motion Filmography: A Critical Guide to over 325 Features Using Puppet Animation. *v.6 p.308*

Stoppard's Theatre: Finding Order amid Chaos. . . .*v.2 p.384*

Stopped Rocking and Other Screenplays. *v.2 p.135*

Stopping Rape: Successful Survival Strategies. . . .*v.4 p.757*

Storage of Cereal Grains and Their Products. *v.5 p.23*

Storage of Natural History Collections: A Preventive Conservation Approach, Vol. 1. . . . .*v.5 p.228*

Storia dell'età barocca in Italia : pensiero, poesia e letteratura, vita morale. *v.2 p.698*

Storied Lives: Japanese American Students and World War II. *v.6 p.114, p.132*

Stories and Prose Poems. *v.2 p.808*

Stories by Egyptian Women: My Grandmother's Cactus. *v.6 p.658*

Stories Employers Tell: Race, Skill and Hiring in America. *v.4 p.133*

Stories, Essays and Memoir: A Curtain of Green; The Wide Net; The Golden Apples; The Bride of the Innisfallen; Selected Essays One Writer's Beginnings. *v.2 p.130*

Stories, Fables and Other Diversions. *v.2 p.105*

Stories from a Ming Collection. *v.6 p.211*

Stories from a Siberian Village. *v.2 p.808*

Stories from Iran, 1921-1991: A Chicago Anthology. *v.6 p.669, p.670*

Stories from the City of God: Roman Stories and Chronicles, 1950-1966. . . . .*v.2 p.721*

Stories from the Nerve Bible: A Twenty-Year Retrospective. *v.1 p.208, p.301*

Stories from Washington Heights and Other Corners of the World - Historias de Washington Heights y Otros Rincones del Mundo. *v.6 p.495, p.505*

Stories in Red and Black: Pictorial Histories of the Aztec and Mixtec. *v.1 p.683, v.3 p.260*

Stories in the Time of Cholera: Racial Profiling During a Medical Nightmare. *v.3 p.360*

Stories of a Lifetime. *v.2 p.613*

Stories of Art. *v.1 p.701*

Stories of Beginning Teachers: First Year Challenges and Beyond. *v.4 p.279*

Stories of Chicago. *v.2 p.30*

Stories of Democracy: Politics and Society in Contemporary Kuwait. *v.6 p.627*

The Stories of English. *v.2 p.554*

The Stories of Eva Luna. *v.2 p.679*

Stories of Frank Sargeson. *v.2 p.748*

The Stories of Heinrich Boll. *v.2 p.604*

The Stories of John Cheever. *v.2 p.67*

Stories of Our Way: An Anthology of American Indian Plays. *v.1 p.124, v.6 p.697, p.698*

The Stories of Ray Bradbury. *v.2 p.63*

Stories of Scottsboro. *v.3 p.441*

Stories of Teaching: A Foundation for Educational Renewal. *v.4 p.348*

Stories of the Invisible: A Guided Tour of Molecules. .*v.5 p.264*

Stories of the Steppe. *v.2 p.804*

Stories of Three Decades. *v.2 p.613*

The Stories of Vladimir Nabokov. *v.2 p.104*

Stories of Women: Gender and Narrative in the Postcolonial Nation. *v.2 p.727*

Stories Out of School: Memories and Reflections on Care and Cruelty in the Classroom. *v.4 p.338*

Stories That Could Be True: New and Collected Poems. .*v.2 p.117*

Stories to Live By: Continuity and Change in Three Generations of Puerto Rican Women. *v.6 p.488*

The Stories We Live By: Personal Myths and the Making of the Self. *v.5 p.655*

Stories. *v.2 p.365, p.369, p.600*

The Storm and Other Things. *v.2 p.719*

Storm Center: The Supreme Court in American Politics. *v.4 p.466, p.538*

Storm over Texas: The Annexation Controversy and the Road to Civil War. *v.3 p.509, v.4 p.542*

Storms Brewed in Other Men's Worlds: The Confrontation of Indians, Spanish, and French in the Southwest, 1540-1795. . . . .*v.6 p.684, p.685*

Storms from the Sun: The Emerging Science of Space Weather. *v.5 p.73, p.444*

Storm. *v.2 p.117*

The Storm. *v.2 p.245*

Stormwater Management for Land Development: Methods and Calculations for Quantity Control. *v.5 p.703*

Stormy Ben Butler. *v.3 p.425*

Stormy Weather: The Music and Lives of a Century of Jazzwomen. *v.6 p.474*

Stormy Weather: The New Hampshire Primary and Presidential Politics. *v.4 p.549*

Story of a City: A Childhood in Amman. *v.6 p.620, p.621, p.656*

The Story of a Life: A Memoir. *v.6 p.647*

The Story of a New Zealand River. *v.2 p.747*

Story of a Soul: The Autobiography of Saint Thérèse of Lisieux. *v.1 p.580*

The Story of a Wonder Man Being the Autobiography of Ring Lardner. *v.2 p.94*

Story of Alchemy and Early Chemistry. *v.5 p.263, p.264*

The Story of American Methodism. *v.1 p.586*

The Story of an African Farm. *v.2 p.757*

The Story of Art. *v.1 p.668*

The Story of Bioethics: From Seminal Works to Contemporary Explorations. *v.5 p.250*

The Story of Christian Theology: Twenty Centuries of Tradition and Reform. *v.1 p.598*

The Story of English. *v.2 p.555*

The Story of Great Aunt Shlomzion. *v.6 p.649*

The Story of Ireland's National Theatre: The Abbey Theatre Dublin. *v.1 p.108*

Story of Labrador. *v.3 p.547*

Story of Layla and Majnun. *v.6 p.672*

The Story of Leisure: Context, Concepts, and Current Controversy. *v.4 p.785*

The Story of Life. *v.5 p.249*

The Story of Lucy Gault. *v.2 p.385*

The Story of Modern Art. *v.1 p.680*

Story of My Life: The Autobiography of George Sand. *v.2 p.500*

Story of O. *v.2 p.533*

The Story of Psychology: A Thematic History. . . .*v.5 p.595*

Story of Punishment: A Record of Man's Inhumanity to Man. *v.4 p.752*

The Story of Sadler's Wells, 1683-1977. . . . .*v.1 p.98, p.143, p.149, p.154*

The Story of Sapho. *v.2 p.477*

The Story of Telecommunications: From the Deep South to the Top of the Big Apple. *v.4 p.420, p.421*

The Story of the Blues. *v.1 p.262*

Story of the CIO. *v.4 p.129*

The Story of the Daughters of Quchan: Gender and National Memory in Iranian History. *v.6 p.629, p.630*

The Story of the Glittering Plain. *v.2 p.301*

The Story of the Iliad. *v.2 p.415*

The Story of the Landless Movement in Brazil. . . .*v.3 p.338*

The Story of the Night: A Novel. *v.6 p.399*

The Story of the Night: Studies in Shakespeare's Major Tragedies. *v.2 p.234*

The Story of the Odyssey. *v.2 p.415*

The Story of the Space Shuttle. *v.5 p.719*

The Story of the Stone: The Crab-Flower Club. . . .*v.6 p.211*

The Story of the Stone: The Debt of Tears. *v.6 p.211*

The Story of the Stone: The Dreamer Awakes. . . .*v.6 p.211*

The Story of the Stone: The Golden Days. *v.6 p.211*

The Story of the Stone: The Warning Voice. *v.6 p.211*

The Story of Thomas Ashe. *v.2 p.374*

The Story of Toronto. *v.3 p.544*

The Story of Vermont: A Natural and Cultural History. *v.3 p.486*

The Story of Worker Sport. *v.4 p.807, p.888*

The Story of World Rowing. *v.4 p.843, p.865*

The Story of Zahra: A Novel. *v.6 p.657*

The Story Performance Handbook. *v.4 p.365*

Story: Style, Structure, Substance, and the Principles of Screenwriting. *v.6 p.353*

A Story Teller's Story. *v.2 p.57*

The Storyteller: A Novel. *v.2 p.686*

Storyteller. *v.2 p.155, v.4 p.365, v.6 p.699*

Storytelling in the New Hollywood: Understanding Classical Narrative Technique. *v.6 p.353*

Story-Telling Techniques in the Arabian Nights. . . .*v.6 p.663*

Storytelling Through Animation. *v.6 p.348*

Story-Wallah: Short Fiction from South Asian Writers. *v.2 p.584*

The Stowe Debate: Rhetorical Strategies in Uncle Tom's Cabin. *v.2 p.51*

Stowe: Three Novels: Uncle Tom's Cabin; the Minister's Wooing; Oldtown Folks. *v.2 p.52*

Strafford, 1593-1641. . . . .*v.3 p.104*

Straight Lick: The Cinema of Oscar Micheaux. *v.6 p.329, p.341*

The Straight Mind and Other Essays. . . . *v.4 p.749, v.6 p.368*

Straight News: Gays, Lesbians, and the News Media. *v.6 p.390*

Straight, No Chaser: The Life and Genius of Thelonious Monk. *v.1 p.259, p.342*

Straight Talk about Gays in the Workplace. *v.4 p.132, p.168, v.6 p.382*

Straight-Acting: Popular Gay Drama from Wilde to Rattigan. *v.6 p.412*

A Strand of a Thousand Pears: A Novel. *v.6 p.651*

Strands. *v.2 p.746*

Strange and Lurid Bloom: A Study of the Fiction of Caroline Gordon. *v.2 p.78*

The Strange Attractor: New and Selected Poems. . .*v.2 p.151*

Strange Beauty: Murray Gell-Mann and the Revolution in Twentieth-Century Physics. *v.5 p.543*

Strange Bodies: Gender and Identity in the Novels of Carson McCullers. *v.2 p.100*

The Strange Career of Bilingual Education in Texas, 1836-1981. . . . .*v.6 p.526*

The Strange Career of Jim Crow. *v.3 p.403, v.6 p.9, p.41*

The Strange Career of Marihuana: Politics and Ideology of Drug Control in America, 94. . . . .*v.5 p.663, p.664*

Strange Case of Dr. Jekyll and Mr. Hyde. *v.2 p.312*

The Strange Children. *v.2 p.78*

Strange Constellations: A History of Australian Science Fiction. *v.2 p.740*

The Strange Death of American Liberalism. *v.3 p.446*

The Strange Death of Liberal England. *v.3 p.117, p.118*

Strange Defeat: A Statement of Evidence Written in 1940. . . . .*v.3 p.156*

Strange Empire, a Narrative of the Northwest. *v.3 p.545*

Strange Fruit. *v.2 p.116*

Strange Future: Pessimism and the 1992 Los Angeles Riots. *v.6 p.97, p.105*

A Strange Manuscript Found in a Copper Cylinder. . .*v.2 p.732*

Strange Multiplicity: Constitutionalism in an Age of Diversity. *v.4 p.526*

Strange Nation of Rafael Mende. *v.2 p.693*

Strange Parallels: Southeast Asia in Global Context, C. 800-1830. . . . .*v.6 p.164*

Strange Pilgrims. *v.2 p.683*

Strange Red Cow: And Other Curious Classified Ads from the Past. *v.4 p.141*

Strange Things: The Malevolent North in Canadian Literature. *v.2 p.728*

Strange Times, My Dear: The PEN Anthology of Contemporary Iranian Literature. *v.6 p.672*

Stranger and Friend. *v.4 p.25*

Stranger at the Gate: To Be Gay and Christian in America. *v.6 p.373*

The Stranger from Paradise: A Biography of William Blake. *v.1 p.695, v.2 p.238*

Stranger in a Strange Land. *v.2 p.81*

Stranger in Our Midst: Images of the Jew in Polish Literature. *v.2 p.789*

Stranger Music: Selected Poems and Songs. *v.2 p.734*

The Stranger Next Door: The Story of a Small Community's Battle over Sex, Faith, and Civil Rights. *v.4 p.570, v.6 p.387*

Stranger Shores: Literary Essays, 1986-1999. . . . .*v.2 p.754*

A Stranger to Myself: The Inhumanity of War: Russia, 1941-44. . . . .*v.3 p.175*

Strangers among Us: How Latino Immigration Is Transforming America. *v.6 p.530*

Strangers at Home: Amish and Mennonite Women in History. *v.3 p.344*

Strangers from a Different Shore: A History of Asian Americans. *v.6 p.85, p.114*

Strangers: Homosexual Love in the Nineteenth Century. *v.6 p.364, p.421*

Strangers in the Ethnic Homeland: Japanese Brazilian Return Migration in Transnational Perspective. . . .*v.6 p.115, p.133*

Strangers in the House: Coming of Age in Occupied Palestine. *v.6 p.620*

Strangers in the South Seas: The Idea of the Pacific in Western Thought. *v.4 p.385*

Strangers on a Train. *v.2 p.86*

Strangers to Ourselves: Discovering the Adaptive Unconscious. *v.5 p.657*

The Stranger. *v.2 p.512*

The Strangled Traveler: Colonial Imaginings and the Thugs of India. *v.6 p.149*

Strategic Advertising Campaigns. *v.4 p.427*

Strategic Advertising Management. *v.4 p.427*

The Strategic Bombing of Germany, 1940-1945. .*v.3 p.81, p.175*

Strategic Business Forecasting: The Complete Guide to Forecasting Real World Company Performance. . .*v.4 p.137*

Strategic Choice and International Relations. *v.4 p.625*

The Strategic Defence Initiative: US Policy and the Soviet Union. *v.3 p.388*

The Strategic Dynamics of Latin American Trade. . .*v.4 p.256*

Strategic Human Resource Management: Theory and Practice. *v.4 p.76, p.77*

Strategic Human Resource Management. *v.4 p.75*

Strategic Interpersonal Communication. *v.5 p.647*

Strategic Management of Built Facilities. *v.4 p.113*

Strategic Management of E-Business. *v.4 p.113*

The Strategic Management of Intellectual Capital. . . .*v.4 p.79*

Strategic Management Theory: An Integrated Approach. *v.4 p.81*

Strategic Media Decisions: Understanding the Business End of the Advertising Business. *v.4 p.427*

Strategic Negotiations: A Theory of Change in Labor-Management Relations. *v.4 p.123*

Strategic Operations Management. *v.4 p.119*

Strategic Partnerships: An Entrepreneur's Guide to Joint Ventures and Alliances. *v.4 p.69*

Strategic Planning for Information Systems. *v.4 p.115*

Strategic Renaissance: New Thinking and Innovative Tools to Create Great Corporate Strategies. . . Using Insights from History and Science. *v.4 p.66*

The Strategic Use of Stories in Organizational Communication and Learning. *v.4 p.78*

Strategic Writing: Multimedia Writing for Public Relations, Advertising, Sales and Marketing, and Business Communication. *v.4 p.173*

Strategies for Addressing Behavior Problems in the Classrooms. *v.4 p.284*

Strategies for Competitive Volleyball. *v.4 p.869*

Strategies of British India: Britain, Iran, and Afghanistan, 1798-1850. . . . .*v.3 p.77*

Strategies of Containment. *v.3 p.452*

Strategies of Slaves and Women. *v.6 p.62*

Strategy and Market Structure: Competition, Oligopoly and the Theory of Games. *v.4 p.252*

Strategy and Organization of Corporate Banking. . . .*v.4 p.155*

Strategy and Tactics of the Salvadoran FMLN Guerrillas: Last Battle of the Cold War, Blueprint for Future Conflicts. *v.3 p.298*

Strategy Maps: Converting Intangible Assets into Tangible Outcomes. *v.4 p.82*

The Strategy of Social Protest. *v.4 p.710*

The Strategy-Focused Organization: How Balanced Scorecard Companies Thrive in the New Business Environment. *v.4 p.73, p.82*

Strategy. *v.3 p.36*

Stratospheric Ozone and Man: Stratospheric Ozone. . .*v.5 p.375*

Strauss: Also Sprach Zarathustra. *v.1 p.207, p.244, p.359*

Strauss's Handbook of Business Information: A Guide for Librarians, Students, and Researchers. *v.4 p.96, p.180*

Stravinsky: A Creative Spring: Russia and France, 1882-1934. . . . .*v.1 p.226, p.227, p.361*

Stravinsky: An Autobiography. *v.1 p.225, p.360*

Stravinsky and Balanchine: A Journey of Invention. *v.1 p.24, p.217, p.360*

Stravinsky and the "Rite of Spring": The Beginnings of a Musical Language. *v.1 p.226, p.233, p.234, p.361*

Stravinsky and the Russian Traditions: A Biography of the Works Through "Mavra". *v.1 p.226, p.361*

Stravinsky: Chronicle of a Friendship. *v.1 p.212, p.360*

Stravinsky: In Pictures and Documents. . . .*v.1 p.225, p.361*

Stravinsky Inside Out. *v.1 p.217, p.360*

The Stravinsky Legacy. *v.1 p.212, p.360*

Stravinsky: Oedipus Rex. *v.1 p.227, p.237, p.361*

Stravinsky: Selected Correspondence, Vol. II. *v.1 p.212, p.359, p.360*

Stravinsky: Selected Correspondence, Vol. I. . .*v.1 p.212, p.360*

Stravinsky: Selected Correspondence. *v.1 p.212, p.360*

Stravinsky: The Composer and His Works. . . .*v.1 p.227, p.361*

Stravinsky: The Rite of Spring. *v.1 p.216, p.239, p.360*

Stravinsky: The Second Exile: France and America, 1934-1971. . . . .*v.1 p.227, p.361*

Stravinsky's Late Music. *v.1 p.224, p.225, p.360*

Stray Dog of Anime: The Films of Mamoru Oshii. . .*v.6 p.336*

A Stream of Light: A Short History of American Unitarianism. *v.1 p.590*

A Stream of Windows: Unsettling Reflections on Trade, Immigration and Democracy. *v.4 p.255*

The Street Addict Role: A Theory of Heroin Addiction. .*v.5 p.664*

Street Corner Society: The Social Structure of an Italian Slum. *v.4 p.752, v.6 p.720*

Street Gangs Throughout the World. *v.4 p.714*

Street Justice: A History of Police Violence in New York City. *v.6 p.261*

Street of Crocodiles. *v.2 p.791*

Street People and the Contested Realms of Public Space. *v.6 p.716*

Street Where I Live. *v.1 p.252, p.336*

Streetcar Suburbs: The Process of Growth in Boston, 1870-1900. . . . .*v.6 p.296*

Streetlife China. *v.6 p.196*

Streets: Critical Perspectives on Public Space. *v.6 p.711*

The Street. *v.2 p.109*

Streetwise. *v.6 p.659*

Strength and Fracture of Engineering Solids. *v.5 p.688*

Strength and Power in Sport, Vol. III. *v.4 p.825, p.874, p.875, p.879*

Strength of Materials, Pt. 2: Advanced Theory and Problems, Set. *v.5 p.691*

Strength of Materials. *v.5 p.691*

The Strength of Poetry: The Oxford Lecturers on Poetry, 1994-1999. . . . .*v.2 p.180*

Strength Training for Sport. *v.4 p.875, p.879*

Strength Training for Women. *v.4 p.791, p.879*

Strengthening Research Methodology: Psychological Measurement and Evaluation. *v.5 p.599*

Strengths of Their Own - Home Schoolers Across America: Academic Achievement, Family Characteristics, and Longitudinal Traits. *v.4 p.296*

Stress: A Brief History. . . .*v.4 p.698, p.699, v.5 p.580, p.652*

Stress Analysis of Polymers. *v.5 p.692*

Stress, Culture, and Aggression. *v.4 p.699*

Stress, Strain, and Structural Dynamics: An Interactive Handbook of Formulas, Solutions, and MATLAB Toolboxes. *v.5 p.697*

Stress-Corrosion Cracking: Materials Performance and Evaluation. *v.5 p.734*

Stretching the Federation: The Art of the State in Canada. *v.4 p.581*

Striding Out: Aspects of Contemporary and New Dance in Britain. *v.1 p.42*

The Strike That Changed New York: Blacks, Whites, and the Ocean Hill-Brownsville Crisis. *v.4 p.283*

Strikes in the United States, 1880-1936. . . . .*v.4 p.128*

Striking a Balance: Dancers Talk About Dancing. *v.1 p.11*

Striking First: The Preventive War Doctrine and the Reshaping of U. S. Foreign Policy. *v.3 p.483*

Striking Terror: America's New War. *v.4 p.564*

Strindberg As Dramatist. *v.2 p.630*

Strindberg in Inferno. *v.2 p.629*

Strindberg: Other Sides: Seven Plays. *v.1 p.83, p.110*

Strindberg: Plays One. *v.1 p.83, p.110*

Strindberg's Dramaturgy. *v.2 p.630*

Strindberg's One-Act Plays. *v.2 p.631*

The String Quartet, 1750-1797: Four Types of Musical Conversation. *v.1 p.191, p.241*

String Quartets: A Research and Information Guide. *v.1 p.169, p.241*

The String Quartets of Joseph Haydn. . .*v.1 p.189, p.239, p.330*

Stringed Instruments of Ancient Greece. *v.1 p.175*

Stringing Together a Nation: Dido Mariano Da Silva Rondon and the Construction of a Modern Brazil, 1906-1930. .*v.3 p.339*

The Stripping of the Altars: Traditional Religion in England, 1400-1580. . . . .*v.1 p.604, p.609*

Striptease: The Untold History of the Girlie Show. . . .*v.1 p.36*

The Stroessner Era: Authoritarian Rule in Paraguay. . *v.3 p.345*

Strokes of Genius: Contemporary Iraqi Art. *v.1 p.691*

Strom Thurmond: And the Politics of Southern Change. *v.3 p.457*

Strong Democracy: Participatory Politics for a New Age. *v.4 p.502, p.503*

Strong of Body, Brave and Noble: Chivalry and Society in Medieval France. *v.3 p.142*

Strong on Music: Repercussions, 1857-1862. . . . . .*v.1 p.278*

Strong on Music: Resonances, 1836-1849. . . . . . .*v.1 p.278*

Strong on Music: Reverberations, 1850-1856, Vol. 2. .*v.1 p.278*

Strong Opinions. *v.2 p.104*

Strong Presidents: A Theory of Leadership. *v.3 p.377*

Strong Women, Deep Closets: Lesbians and Homophobia in Sport. *v.4 p.815, p.839,v.6 p.384*

The Stronger Women Get, the More Men Love Football: Sex and Sports in America. *v.4 p.818, p.837,v.6 p.438*

The Strongest Strong's Exhaustive Concordance. . . .*v.1 p.614*

Structronic Systems: Active Structures, Devices and Systems. *v.5 p.694*

Structurae; International Database and Gallery of Structures. *v.1 p.711, p.783*

Structural Analysis: A Classical and Matrix Approach. .*v.5 p.695*

Structural Analysis: A Historical Approach. *v.5 p.694*

Structural Analysis and Synthesis: A Laboratory Course in Structural Geology. *v.5 p.441, p.442*

Structural Analysis of Historic Buildings: Restoration, Preservation, and Adaptive Reuse Applications for Architects and Engineers. *v.1 p.824*

Structural Analysis with Finite Elements. *v.5 p.694*

Structural Analysis. *v.5 p.694*

Structural Anthropology. *v.4 p.24*

Structural Bioinformatics. *v.5 p.103, p.104, p.105*

Structural Chemistry of Silicates: Structure, Bonding and Classification. *v.5 p.307*

Structural Earthquake Engineering. *v.5 p.695*

Structural Engineering and Applied Mechanics Data Handbook: Frames, Vol. 2. . . . .*v.5 p.694*

Structural Engineering and Applied Mechanics Data Handbook: Plates. *v.5 p.694*

Structural Engineering and Applied Mechanics Data Handbook, Vol. 4. . . . .*v.5 p.694*

Structural Engineering Formulas. *v.5 p.695*

Structural Engineering: History and Development. . .*v.5 p.695*

Structural Engineering: The Nature of Theory and Design. *v.5 p.692*

Structural Engineering, Vol. 2. . . . .*v.5 p.692*

Structural Function of Harmony. *v.1 p.373*

Structural Functions in Music. *v.1 p.369*

Structural Geology of Fold and Thrust Belts. *v.5 p.441*

Structural Geology of Rocks and Regions. *v.5 p.441*

Structural Geology on the Web. *v.5 p.441*

Structural Geology. *v.5 p.442*

Structural Hearing: Tonal Coherence in Music. .*v.1 p.372, p.373*

Structural Impact. *v.5 p.697*

Structural Mechanics: Graph and Matrix Methods. . .*v.5 p.695*

Structural Methods in Inorganic Chemistry. *v.5 p.303*

Structural Modeling and Analysis. *v.5 p.693*

Structural Package Designs. *v.1 p.718*

Structural Plastics: Composition - Properties - Processing. *v.5 p.320*

Structural Proteomics. *v.5 p.118*

Structural Safety and Its Quality Assurance. *v.5 p.685*

Structural Steel Design: LRFD Approach. *v.5 p.697*

The Structural Transformation of the Public Sphere: An Inquiry into a Category of Bourgois Society. *v.4 p.765*

Structuralism: A Philosophy for the Human Science. . .*v.1 p.515*

Structuralism and Semiotics. *v.2 p.561*

Structuralism in Literature: An Introduction. . .*v.2 p.567, p.571*

Structuralism. *v.1 p.515, v.2 p.567, p.571*

Structuralist Poetics: Structuralism, Linguistics and the Study of Literature. *v.2 p.570*

The Structuralists. *v.1 p.515*

Structure and Bonding in Crystals, Vol. 1. . . . . .*v.5 p.284*

Structure and Bonding in Crystals, Vol. 2. . . . . .*v.5 p.284*

Structure and Bonding in Solid State Chemistry. . .*v.5 p.306*

Structure and Bonding. *v.5 p.303*

Structure and Change in Economic History. *v.3 p.41*

The Structure and Composition of Foods, Vol. 4. . . .*v.5 p.33*

The Structure and Dynamics of Geographic Ranges. .*v.5 p.168*

The Structure and Dynamics of Networks. *v.4 p.422*

Structure and Evolution of the Stars. *v.5 p.70, p.71*

Structure and Function in Primitive Society, Essays and Addresses. *v.4 p.24*

Structure and Function of the Body. *v.5 p.164*

Structure and Interpretation of Computer Programs. *v.5 p.346, p.349*

Structure and Mechanism in Protein Science: A Guide to Enzyme Catalysis and Protein Folding. *v.5 p.119*

Structure and Mobility: The Men and Women of Marseille, 1820-1870. . . . .*v.4 p.706*

Structure and Process in Modern Societies. *v.4 p.716*

Structure and Processes in the Mediterranean Ecosystem. *v.5 p.173, p.237*

Structure and Properties of Engineering Alloys. . . .*v.5 p.691*

Structure and Scale in the Roman Economy. *v.3 p.23*

Structure Determination of Organic Compounds: Tables of Spectral Data. *v.5 p.291*

Structure Formation in the Universe. *v.5 p.72*

Structure in Protein Chemistry, Vol. 1. . . . . .*v.5 p.116, p.117*

The Structure of American Industry. *v.4 p.148*

The Structure of an African Pastoralist Community: Demography, History, and Ecology of the Ngamiland Herero. *v.6 p.75*

The Structure of Atonal Music. *v.1 p.370*

The Structure of Biological Theories. *v.5 p.197*

The Structure of Byron's Major Poems. *v.2 p.274*

The Structure of Evolutionary Theory. *v.5 p.192*

The Structure of Freedom. *v.4 p.515*

The Structure of Nations and Empires: A Study of the Recurring Patterns and Problems of the Political Order in Relation to the Unique Problems of the Nuclear Age. *v.4 p.496*

The Structure of Politics at the Accession of George III. .*v.3 p.114*

Structure of Science: Problems in the Logic of Scientific Explanation. *v.5 p.403*

The Structure of Scientific Revolutions. *v.1 p.499, v.3 p.47, v.5 p.403*

The Structure of Sociological Theory. *v.4 p.684*

The Structure of the American Economy 1919-1939: An Empirical Application of Equilibrium Analysis. *v.4 p.213, p.214*

The Structure of the Canterbury Tales. *v.2 p.209*

Structure of the Human Brain: A Photographic Atlas. .*v.5 p.616*

The Structure of the Terror. *v.3 p.150, p.151*

The Structure of Thucydides' History. *v.2 p.421*

The Structure of Verse. *v.2 p.578*

Structured Computer Organization. *v.5 p.730*

Structured Fluids: Polymers, Colloids, Surfactants. . .*v.5 p.555*

Structured-Population Models in Marine, Terrestrial, and
Freshwater Systems. *v.5 p.172*

Structure-Function Relations of Warm Desert
Plants. *v.5 p.155, p.240*

Structure-Property Relations in Nonferrous
Metals. *v.5 p.697, p.733*

Structures: From Theory to Practice. *v.5 p.694*

Structures in the New Millenium: Proceedings of the 4th
International Kerensky Conference, Hong Kong,
3-5 September 1997. . . . .*v.5 p.695*

Structures of Desire: British Cinema, 1939-1955. . .*v.6 p.339*

The Structures of Everyday Life - The Limits of the
Possible. *v.3 p.38*

Structuring Conflict in the Arab World: Incumbents, Opponents
and Institutions. *v.4 p.615*

Structuring the State: The Formation of Italy and Germany and
the Puzzle of Federalism. *v.3 p.168, p.169, p.202*

The Struggle: A History of the African National
Congress. *v.4 p.613*

The Struggle Against the Bomb: One World or None: A History
of the World Nuclear Disarmament Movement Through
1953. . . . .*v.4 p.657*

The Struggle Against the Bomb: Resisting the Bomb: A History
of the World Nuclear Disarmament Movement,
1954-1970. . . . .*v.4 p.657*

The Struggle and the Triumph: An
Autobiography. *v.4 p.129, p.130*

The Struggle for Aboriginal Rights: A Documentary
History. *v.4 p.624*

The Struggle for Canadian Sport. *v.4 p.807, p.817*

The Struggle for Control of Public Education: Market Ideology
vs. Democratic Values. *v.4 p.326*

The Struggle for Democracy in Chile, 1982-1990. . .*v.3 p.353*

The Struggle for Democratic Politics in the Dominican
Republic, 1961-1996. . . . .*v.3 p.317*

Struggle for Equality: Abolitionists and the Negro in the Civil
War and Reconstruction. *v.3 p.399*

The Struggle for Equality: Abolitionists and the Negro in the
Civil War and Reconstruction. *v.3 p.420*

Struggle for Ethnic Identity: Narratives by Asian American
Professionals. *v.6 p.106, p.116, p.136*

The Struggle for Greek Independence: Essays to Mark the 150th
Anniversary of the Greek War of Independence. . .*v.3 p.194*

The Struggle for Land: A Political Economy of the Pioneer
Frontier in Brazil from 1930 to the Present Day. . .*v.3 p.340*

Struggle for Mastery: Disfranchisement in the South,
1888-1908. . . . .*v.4 p.519, p.573*

The Struggle for Modern Tibet: The Autobiography of Tashi
Tsering. *v.6 p.242, p.243, p.245*

The Struggle for Palestine. *v.6 p.617, p.618*

The Struggle for Power in Medieval Italy: Structures of Political
Rule, 400-1400. . . . .*v.3 p.200*

The Struggle for Power in Syria: Politics and Society under
Asad and the Ba'th Party. *v.6 p.608*

The Struggle for Quebec. *v.3 p.544*

The Struggle for Responsible Government in the North-West
Territories 1870-97. . . . .*v.4 p.590*

The Struggle for Swazi Labour, 1890-1920. . . . . .*v.6 p.78*

The Struggle for Syria: A Study of Post-War Arab Politics,
1945-1958. . . . .*v.6 p.608*

Struggle for the Breeches: Gender and the Making of the British
Working Class. .*v.3 p.52, p.53,v.6 p.456, p.743, p.746, p.765*

The Struggle for the Gulf Borderlands: The Creek War and the
Battle of New Orleans, 1812-1815. . . . .*v.3 p.417*

The Struggle for the Soul of the Nation: Czech Culture and the
Rise of Communism. . . .*v.3 p.189, v.4 p.506, p.507, p.508*

Struggle in the Andes: Peasant Political Mobilization in
Peru. *v.3 p.330*

The Struggle over Eritrea, 1962-1978: War and Revolution in
the Horn of Africa. *v.6 p.67*

The Struggle over Lebanon. *v.6 p.606*

Struggles for Freedom: Essays on Slavery, Colonialism, and
Culture in the Caribbean and Central America. . . .*v.3 p.296*

Struggles for Representation: African American Documentary
Film and Video. *v.6 p.330, p.342*

Struggles over the Word: Race and Religion in O'Connor,
Faulkner, Hurston and Wright. *v.2 p.73, p.138*

Struggling for the Soul: The Politics of Schooling and the
Construction of the Teacher. *v.4 p.315*

Struggling to Be Heard: The Unmet Needs of Asian Pacific
American Children. *v.6 p.109*

Struggling with Destiny in Karimpur, 1925-1984. . .*v.6 p.155*

The Strumpet Muse: Art and Morals in Chaucer's
Poetry. *v.2 p.209*

The Stuart Age. *v.3 p.101, p.102*

Stuart Symington: A Life. *v.3 p.461*

Stubborn Twig: Three Generations in the Life of a Japanese
American Family. *v.6 p.134*

Stubborn Weeds: Popular and Controversial Chinese Literature
after the Cultural Revolution. *v.6 p.213*

Stuck Rubber Baby. *v.6 p.395*

Stucke II. *v.2 p.607*

Stucke I. *v.2 p.607*

Student Activities in Today's Schools: Essential Learning for All
Youth. *v.4 p.288*

The Student Aid Game: Meeting Need and Rewarding Talent in
American Higher Education. *v.4 p.293*

Student Companion to Accompany Biochemistry. . . .*v.5 p.114*

The Student Evaluation Standards: How to Improve Evaluations
of Students. *v.5 p.604*

A Student Grammar of Modern Standard Arabic. . . .*v.6 p.654*

A Student Handbook for Writing in Biology. *v.5 p.245*

Student Learning in Physical Education: Applying Research to
Enhance Instruction. *v.4 p.798, p.799, p.800*

Student Life and Customs. *v.4 p.289*

Student Politics in America: A Historical Analysis. . .*v.4 p.330*

Student Protests in Twentieth-Century China: The View from
Shanghai. *v.6 p.191, p.206*

Student Services: A Handbook for the Profession. . . .*v.4 p.293*

The Student Teacher's Handbook. *v.4 p.277*

The Student Voice, 1960-1965: Periodical of the Student
Nonviolent Coordinating Committee. *v.6 p.12*

Student Workbook to Accompany Torres and Ehrlich Modern
Dental Assisting. *v.5 p.525*

Students Abroad: Strangers at Home: Education for a Global
Society. *v.4 p.313*

ⓔ Students and University in 20th Century Egyptian
Politics. *v.6 p.637*

The Student's Catullus. *v.2 p.430*

A Student's Introduction to English Grammar. . . .*v.2 p.556*

Students, Professors, and the State in Tsarist Russia. . .*v.3 p.220*

The Studhorse Man. *v.2 p.735, p.736*

Studies in American Indian Languages: Description and
Theory. *v.6 p.690*

Studies in Applied Economics: Theory of the Production of
Social Wealth. *v.4 p.197*

Studies in Business-Cycle Theory. *v.4 p.244*

Studies in Classic American Literature. *v.2 p.7*

Studies in Classic Australian Fiction. *v.2 p.742*

Studies in Combinatorics. *v.5 p.479*

Studies in Contemporary Indian-English Short Story: A
Collection of Critical Essays. *v.2 p.762*

Studies in Early Christology. *v.1 p.640*

Studies in Econometrics, Time Series and Multivariate Statistics:
Monograph. *v.4 p.206*

Studies in Ethnomethodology. *v.4 p.688*

Studies in European Realism: A Sociological Survey of the
Writings of Balzac, Stendhal, Zola, Tolstoy, Gorki and
Others. *v.2 p.487, p.501, p.504*

Studies in Fifteenth-Century Stagecraft. *v.2 p.185*

Studies in Greek Philosophy, Set. *v.1 p.421*

Studies in Human Time. *v.2 p.456*

Studies in Japanese Buddhism. *v.1 p.562*

Studies in Judaism, Vol. 1. . . . .*v.1 p.547*

Studies in Judaism, Vol. 2. . . . .*v.1 p.547*

Studies in Judaism, Vol. 3. . . . .*v.1 p.547*

Studies in Keats. *v.2 p.295*

Studies in Leadership. *v.4 p.695*

Studies in Literature from the Ancient Near East: Dedicated to
Samuel Noah Kramer. *v.6 p.651, p.665*

Studies in Literature: Second Series. *v.2 p.575*

Studies in Medieval and Renaissance
Literature. *v.2 p.168, p.169, p.170*

Studies in Medieval Legal Thought: Public Law and the State,
1100-1322. . . . .*v.6 p.568*

Studies in Modern Albanian Literature and Culture. . .*v.2 p.815*

▯ Studies in Moral Development and Education: Developing
Fairness and Concern for Others. *v.4 p.306*

Studies in Number Theory. *v.5 p.476*

Studies in Outdoor Recreation: Search and Research for
Satisfaction. *v.4 p.786, p.787*

Studies in Pessimism. *v.1 p.465*

Studies in Power and Class in Africa. *v.6 p.55*

Studies in Self-Interest: From Descartes to La Bruyère. *v.2 p.459*

Studies in the Development of Capitalism. *v.4 p.208*

Studies in the Economic and Social History of Palestine in the
19th and 20th Centuries. *v.6 p.611*

Studies in the Elizabethan Theatre. *v.1 p.75, p.103*

Studies in the History of Transjordan. *v.6 p.621*

Studies in the New Experimental Aesthetics. *v.5 p.618*

Studies in the Origins of Buddhism. *v.1 p.562*

Studies in the Prose Style of Joseph Addison. *v.2 p.237*

Studies in the Psychology of Sex: Analysis of the Sexual
Impulse - Love and Pain - the Sexual Impulse in
Women. *v.4 p.747*

Studies in the Psychology of Sex: Erotic Symbolism - the
Mechanism of Detumescence - the Psychic State in
Pregnancy. *v.4 p.747*

Studies in the Psychology of Sex: Sexual Inversion. . .*v.4 p.747*

Studies in the Psychology of Sex: Sexual Selection in
Man. *v.4 p.747*

Studies in the Psychology of Sex: The Evolution of Modesty -
the Phenomena of Sexual Periodicity -
Auto-Erotism. *v.4 p.747*

Studies in the Quantity Theory of Money. *v.4 p.231, p.237, p.238*

Studies in the Religious Life of Ancient and Medieval
India. *v.1 p.541*

Studies in the Structure of the Urban Economy. . . .*v.6 p.724*

Studies in the Theory of Business Cycles, 1933-39. . .*v.4 p.244*

Studies in the Way of Words. *v.1 p.490*

Studies in U. S. Supreme Court Behavior. *v.4 p.535*

Studies in World Literature. *v.2 p.760*

Studies on Canadian Literature: Introductory and Critical
Essays. *v.2 p.729*

Studio A: The Bob Dylan Reader. *v.1 p.270, p.322, p.323*

The Studio System. *v.6 p.343*

Study Guide to Accompany Economics. *v.4 p.210*

The Study of Agricultural Geography: A Scholarly Guide and
Bibliography. *v.4 p.396*

The Study of American Folklore: An Introduction. . . .*v.2 p.17*

The Study of Ancient Judaism: Mishnah, Midrash,
Siddur. *v.1 p.548*

The Study of Ancient Judaism: The Palestinian and Babylonian
Talmuds, Vol. II. *v.1 p.548*

▢ A Study of Charter School Accountability. *v.4 p.280*

Study of Counterpoint. *v.1 p.370*

The Study of Ethnomusicology: Thirty-One Issues and
Concepts. *v.1 p.173, v.4 p.26*

The Study of Folk Music in the Modern World. *v.1 p.173, p.283*

The Study of Folklore. *v.2 p.584*

The Study of Fugue. *v.1 p.371, p.372*

A Study of Gawain and the Green Knight. *v.2 p.206*

A Study of Goethe. *v.2 p.597*

ⓔ The Study of Greek Inscriptions. *v.3 p.13*

The Study of Indian Music in the Nineteenth Century. *v.1 p.295*

The Study of Instinct. *v.5 p.615*

The Study of Liturgy. *v.1 p.654*

The Study of Orchestration. *v.1 p.392, p.393*

The Study of Sociology. *v.4 p.684*

A Study of Sophoclean Drama. *v.2 p.419*

A Study of Spinoza's Ethics. *v.1 p.477*

The Study of Spirituality. *v.1 p.650*

A Study of the Chinese in Cuba, 1847-1947. . . . . *v.3 p.308*

A Study of the History of Nestorian Christianity in China and Its Literature in Chinese: Together with a New English Translation of the Dunhuang Nestorian Documents, Vol. 87. . . . .*v.1 p.570*

A Study of War. *v.3 p.36*

Study Skills for Geography Students: A Practical Guide. .*v.4 p.377*

☐ studyfinance.com. *v.4 p.88, p.93*

Studying a Study and Testing a Test: How to Read the Medical Evidence. *v.5 p.515*

Studying Law: Selections from the Writings of Albert J. Beveridge, John Maxcy Zane, Munroe Smith and Others *v.4 p.440*

Studying Music History: Learning, Reasoning, and Writing about Music History and Literature. *v.1 p.174*

Studying Personality Cross: Culturally. *v.4 p.35*

Studying Popular Music. *v.1 p.272*

Studying Teacher Education: The Report of the AERA Panel on Research and Teacher Education. *v.4 p.279, p.355*

Studying the Jew: Scholarly Antisemitism in Nazi Germany. *v.3 p.174*

Studying the Synoptic Gospels. *v.1 p.629*

Studying Those Who Study Us: An Anthropologist in the World of Artificial Intelligence. *v.4 p.44*

Stuffed Animals and Pickled Heads: The Culture and Evolution of Natural History Museums. *v.3 p.44*

The Stuffed Owl: An Anthology of Bad Verse. *v.2 p.586, p.587, p.589*

Stupidity and Tears: Teaching and Learning in Troubled Times. *v.5 p.573*

Sturdy Econometrics. *v.4 p.202*

Sturm und Drang; dramatische Schriften. *v.2 p.590*

Stuttering: The Search for a Cause and Cure. *v.5 p.665*

Stuttering. *v.5 p.665, p.673, p.674*

Style and Idea in the Lyric Suite of Alban Berg. *v.1 p.221, p.241, p.309*

Style and Idea: Selected Writings of Arnold Schoenberg. *v.1 p.223, p.353*

Style and Music: Theory, History, and Ideology. . . .*v.1 p.382*

Style and Temper: Studies in French Fiction, 1925-1960. . . . .*v.2 p.463*

Style and Tradition in Catullus. *v.2 p.430, p.431*

Style Apollinaire: The Writing of Guillaume Apollinaire. *v.2 p.507*

Style Guide. *v.4 p.172*

The Style Hongrois in the Music of Western Europe. .*v.1 p.245*

Style in the French Novel. *v.2 p.463*

Style Manual for Political Science. *v.4 p.482*

The Style of Palestrina and the Dissonance. *v.1 p.180, p.346, p.371*

Style: The Basics of Clarity and Grace. *v.2 p.565*

Styles and Types of North American Architecture: Social Function and Cultural Expression. *v.1 p.789*

The Styles of Eighteenth Century Ballet. *v.1 p.23*

Styles, Schools and Movements: The Essential Encyclopaedic Guide to Modern Art. *v.1 p.663, p.678*

Stylin': African American Expressive Culture from Its Beginnings to the Zoot Suit. *v.1 p.19*

The Stylistic Development of Keats. *v.2 294*

A Su Salud!: Spanish for Health Professionals. . . . *v.2 p.635*

Su Tung-P'o: Selections from a Sung Dynasty Poet. . *v.6 p.210*

Su Unico Hijo. *v.2 p.653*

A Subaltern Studies Reader, 1986-1995. . . . . . .*v.6 p.157*

Subaltern Studies: Writings on South Asian History and Society, Vol. 1. . . . .*v.6 p.146*

Subaltern Studies: Writings on South Asian History and Society, Vol. 2. . . . .*v.6 p.146*

Subaltern Studies: Writings on South Asian History and Society, Vol. 3. . . . .*v.6 p.146*

Subaltern Studies: Writings on South Asian History and Society, Vol. 4. . . . .*v.6 p.146*

Subaltern Studies: Writings on South Asian History and Society, Vol. 5. . . . .*v.6 p.146*

Subaltern Studies: Writings on South Asian History and Society, Vol. 6. . . . .*v.6 p.146*

Subaltern Studies: Writings on South Asian History and Society. *v.2 p.759*

Subcultural Sounds: Micromusics of the West. *v.1 p.284*

The Subject and Other Subjects: On Ethical, Aesthetic, and Political Identity. *v.1 p.515*

Subject Headings for African American Materials. *v.6 p.13, p.14, p.33*

The Subject of Documentary. *v.6 p.310*

The Subject of Semiotics. *v.2 p.567, p.571*

Subject to Change: Guerrilla Television Revisited. . . *v.4 p.413*

Subject to Debate: Sense and Dissents on Women, Politics, and Culture. *v.6 p.442*

Subject to Solution: Problems in U. S. - Cuban Relations. *v.3 p.313*

The Subjection of Women. *v.4 p.222*

Subjects Matter: Every Teacher's Guide to Content-Area Reading. *v.4 p.284, p.285*

Subjects of the Sultan: Culture and Daily Life in the Ottoman Empire. *v.6 p.589*

Subjugated Knowledges: Journalism, Gender, and Literature in the Nineteenth Century. *v.6 p.740*

The Sublime: A Reader in British Eighteenth-Century Aesthetic Theory. *v.1 p.479*

The Sublime Object of Ideology. *v.1 p.501*

Sublime Thoughts - Penny Wisdom: Situating Emerson and Thoreau in the American Market. . . .*v.2 p.38, p.52, p.53*

Submerged Cultural Resource Management: Preserving and Interpreting Our Maritime Heritage: Proceedings of the Society for Historical Archaeology Conference on Historical and Underwater Archaeology (33rd: 2000: Quebec). *v.4 p.14*

Subnational Politics and Democratization in Mexico. *v.3 p.291*

Subordination or Empowerment?: African-American Leadership and the Struggle for Urban Political Power. *v.4 p.555, p.573*

Sub-Saharan African Films and Filmmakers: An Annotated Bibliography, 1987-1992. . . . .*v.6 p.334*

Substance Abuse: A Comprehensive Textbook. *v.5 p.512, p.522*

▢ Substance Abuse and Mental Health Data Archive (SAMHDA). *v.4 p.777*

▢ Substance Abuse and Mental Health Services Administration. *v.5 p.672*

Substance among Other Categories. *v.1 p.488*

Substance and Attribute: A Study in Ontology. *v.1 p.510*

Substance and Essence in Aristotle: An Interpretation of Metaphysics, VII-IX. *v.1 p.427, p.505*

Substance Use and Abuse: Sociological Perspectives. *v.4 p.777, v.5 p.664*

A Substitute for Victory: The Politics of Peacemaking at the Korean Armistice Talks. *v.6 p.236*

Substitutes for Hazardous Chemicals in the Workplace. .*v.5 p.682*

The Subterraneans. *v.2 p.93*

Subtle Is the Lord: The Science and the Life of Albert Einstein. *v.3 p.46, v.5 p.544*

The Subtle Knife. *v.2 p.373*

Suburban Landscapes: Culture and Politics in a New York Metropolitan Community. *v.6 p.718*

Suburban Nation: The Rise of Sprawl and the Decline of the American Dream. *v.4 p.770, v.6 p.726*

The Suburban Wild. *v.5 p.233*

SuburbiaNation: Reading Suburban Landscape in Twentieth-Century American Fiction and Film. *v.6 p.340, p.730*

Subversive Expectations: Performance Art and Paratheater in New York, 1976-85. . . . .*v.1 p.27, p.29, p.38*

The Subversive Family: An Alternative History of Love and Marriage. *v.4 p.733*

The Subversive Voice of Carmen Lyra: Selected Works. .*v.2 p.676*

Subverting Colonial Authority: Challenges to Spanish Rule in Eighteenth-Century Southern Andes. *v.3 p.324, p.325*

Success for All: Research and Reform in Elementary Education. *v.4 p.281, p.365*

Success in Early Intervention: The Chicago Child-Parent Centers. *v.4 p.316*

Successful Coaching. *v.4 p.904*

The Successful College Athletic Program: The New Standard. *v.4 p.821, p.894*

Successful Fitness Motivation Strategies. .*v.4 p.790, p.878, p.879*

The Successful Interview and Beyond. *v.4 p.170*

Successful Schools for Young Adolescents. *v.4 p.367*

Successful Sport Management: A Guide to Legal Issues. *v.4 p.882, p.900, p.905*

Successful Sports Officiating. *v.4 p.905*

Succession in Saudi Arabia. *v.6 p.626*

The Successors of Genghis Khan. *v.6 p.238*

Sucesion Presidencial: The Nineteen Eighty-Eight Mexican Presidential Election. *v.3 p.291*

Such a Long Journey. *v.2 p.765*

ⓔ Such Is Life: Being Certain Extracts from the Diary of Tom Collins. *v.2 p.745*

Sudan, 1898-1989: The Unstable State. *v.6 p.59*

Sudan: Islam, Sectarianism, and Politics since the Mahdiyya. *v.6 p.640*

Sudan's Blood Memory: The Legacy of War, Ethnicity, and Slavery in South Sudan. *v.6 p.59*

Sudden Origins: Fossils, Genes, and the Emergence of Species. *v.5 p.199*

The Sudeten Problem, 1933-1938: "Volkstumpolitik" and the Formulation of Nazi Foreign Policy. *v.3 p.189*

Sueños y discursos. *v.2 p.650*

Suetonius: Diuus Claudius. *v.2 p.444*

Suetonius: Lives of Galba, Otho and Vitellius. . . .*v.2 p.444*

Suetonius: The Flavian Emperors. *v.2 p.444*

Suetonius. *v.2 p.444*

Suffer and Be Still: Women in the Victorian Age. *v.3 p.116, v.6 p.749*

The Sufferers. *v.6 p.660*

The Sufferings of Young Werther. *v.2 p.598*

The Suffragette; the History of the Women's Militant Suffrage Movement, 1905-1910. . . . .*v.4 p.604*

Sufi Music of India and Pakistan: Sound, Context and Meaning in Qawwali. *v.1 p.289*

Sufi Saints and State Power: The Pirs of Sind, 1843-1947. . . . .*v.6 p.148*

Sufism: An Account of the Mystics of Islam. *v.1 p.559*

Sugar and Power in the Dominican Republic: Eisenhower, Kennedy and the Trujillos. *v.3 p.317*

Sugar and Slavery in Puerto Rico: The Plantation Economy of Ponce, 1800-1850. . . . .*v.3 p.321*

Sugar and the Origins of Modern Philippine Society. .*v.6 p.180*

Sugar Beet. *v.5 p.21*

Sugar Cane Cultivation and Management. *v.5 p.20, p.25*

The Sugar Cane Industry: An Historical Geography from its Origins To 1914. . . . .*v.4 p.399*

The Sugar Industry in Pernambuco, 1840-1910: Modernization Without Change. *v.3 p.336*

Sugar Is Made with Blood: The Conspiracy of la Escalera and the Conflict Between Empires over Slavery in Cuba. .*v.3 p.312*

Sugar Plantations in the Formation of Brazilian Society: Bahia, 1550-1835. . . . .*v.3 p.280, p.335*

Sugar, Slavery, and Freedom in Nineteenth-Century Puerto Rico. *v.3 p.319*

Sugar Street. *v.6 p.662*

Sugar's Secrets: Race and the Erotics of Cuban Nationalism. *v.2 p.672*

Suharto: A Political Biography. *v.6 p.174, p.176*

Suharto's Indonesia. *v.6 p.177*

Sui and T'ang China, 589-906 AD. *v.6 p.185*

The Sui Dynasty. *v.6 p.185*

Sui Sin Far - Edith Maude Eaton: A Literary Biography. .*v.6 p.95*

Suicide: A Study in Sociology. *v.4 p.693*

Suicide in Victorian and Edwardian England. . .*v.3 p.110, p.123*

Suing the Gun Industry: A Battle at the Crossroads of Gun Control and Mass Torts. *v.6 p.266*

A Suitable Boy: A Novel. *v.2 p.766*

Suits Me: The Double Life of Billy Tipton. . . .*v.6 p.371, p.409*

Suki Schorer on Balanchine Technique. *v.1 p.25*

Sula. *v.2 p.151*

Sulcando o Mar: Poemas de Os LusíAdas. *v.2 p.688*

Suleiman the Magnificent, 1520-1566. . . . . .*v.6 p.590, p.591*

Suleiman the Magnificent: The Man, His Life, His Epoch. *v.6 p.589*

Sulla, the Last Republican. *v.3 p.26*

Sulphur Cycling on the Continents: Wetlands, Terrestrial Ecosystems and Associated Water Bodies. *v.5 p.173*

Sultana's Dream: And Selections from the Secluded Ones. *v.2 p.764*

The Sultan's Jew: Morocco and the Sephardi World. *v.6 p.598, p.644*

A Sum of Destructions: Picasso's Cultures and the Creation of Cubism. *v.1 p.700*

The Sum of Our Parts: Mixed-Heritage Asian Americans. *v.6 p.125*

Sumerian Mythology: A Study of Spiritual and Literary Achievement in the Third Millenium B.C. *v.3 p.5*

The Sumerians: Their History, Culture, and Character. . .*v.3 p.5*

The Summer Before the Dark. *v.2 p.365*

Summer Brave. *v.2 p.89*

Summer for the Gods: The Scopes Trial and America's Continuing Debate over Science and Religion. *v.3 p.442, v.4 p.438*

A Summer Full of Love. *v.6 p.666*

Summer Jobs Abroad 2006. . . . .*v.4 p.171*

Summer Jobs in Britain 2005. . . . .*v.4 p.171*

Summer Lightning. *v.2 p.391*

Summer Madness: The Wild, Wacky, Wonderful World of the WNBA. *v.4 p.836, p.854, p.896*

Summer Moonshine. *v.2 p.391*

A Summer of Faulkner: Three Novels: As I Lay Dying, the Sound and the Fury, Light in August, Set. *v.2 p.74*

Summer Snow: Reflections from a Black Daughter of the South. *v.6 p.26, p.44*

Summerfolk: A History of the Dacha, 1710-2000. . . .*v.3 p.210*

Summing Up: An Autobiography. *v.6 p.616*

The Summoner's Tale. *v.2 p.208*

Sumner Welles: FDR's Global Strategist: A Biography. *v.3 p.445, p.464*

The Sun Also Rises. *v.2 p.84*

The Sun Always Shines for the Cool/Midnight Moon at the Greasy Spoon: Eulogy for a Small Time Thief. *v.6 p.508, p.518*

The Sun from Space. *v.5 p.68*

The Sun in the Church: Cathedrals as Solar Observatories. *v.3 p.47*

The Sun Maiden and the Crescent Moon: Siberian Folk Tales. *v.2 p.793*

Sun on a Cloudy Day. *v.6 p.662*

Sun Power: The Global Solution for the Coming Energy Crisis. *v.5 p.709*

The Sun, the Genome and the Internet: Tools of Scientific Revolutions. *v.5 p.132*

Sun under Wood. *v.2 p.146*

Sun Yat-Sen. *v.6 p.189, p.202*

Sundance to Sarajevo: Film Festivals and the World They Made. *v.6 p.346*

Sunday Baseball: The Major Leagues' Struggle to Play Baseball on the Lord's Day, 1876-1934. . . . . . .*v.4 p.803, p.804, p.824, p.849, p.890*

The Sunday Game: At the Dawn of Professional Football. *v.4 p.859, p.897, p.902*

Sunday, Monday and Always: Stories by Dawn Powell. *v.2 p.113*

Sundiata: An Epic of Old Mali. *v.6 p.69*

The Sunflower Forest: Ecological Restoration and the New Communion with Nature. *v.6 p.283*

Sunflower Splendor: Three Thousand Years of Chinese Poetry. *v.6 p.210, p.211*

Sunflower. *v.2 p.389, p.786*

Sunlight at Midnight: St. Petersburg and the Rise of Modern Russia. *v.3 p.214*

Sunset Boulevard. *v.1 p.248, p.337, p.407*

Sunshine Sketches of a Little Town. *v.2 p.736*

Suntanning in 20th Century America. *v.4 p.774*

Sun-Tzu: The Art of War: New Translation Incorporating the Recently Discovered Yin-Ch Ueh-Shan Texts. . . .*v.6 p.183*

Super Chief: Earl Warren and His Supreme Court, A Judicial Biography. *v.4 p.469*

El Super: (Tragi-Comdeia). *v.6 p.516*

Superconductivity: Fundamentals and Applications. . .*v.5 p.565*

Superconductivity. *v.5 p.540, p.565*

Superfluidity and Superconductivity. *v.5 p.565*

The Superfluous Men: Conservative Critics of Modern Culture, 1900-1945. . . . .*v.3 p.367*

Superfluous Things: Material Culture and Social Status in Early Modern China. *v.6 p.186*

Superhighway Robbery: Preventing E-Commerce Crime. *v.6 p.253*

Superintending Democracy: The Courts and the Political Process. *v.4 p.535*

Superman on the Couch: What Superheros Really Tell Us about Ourselves and Our Society. *v.2 p.581*

Supernatural Fiction Writers, Set. *v.2 p.581*

The Supernatural Index: A Listing of Fantasy, Supernatural, Occult, Weird, and Horror Anthologies. *v.2 p.580*

Supernatural Literature of the World: An Encyclopedia. *v.2 p.581*

Supernovae and Nucleosynthesis: An Investigation of the History of Matter, from the Big Bang to the Present. *v.5 p.70*

Superpatriotism. *v.4 p.498*

The Superpower Myth: The Use and Misuse of American Might. *v.4 p.562*

Superstructuralism: The Philosophy of Structuralism and Post-Structuralism. *v.1 p.512*

Supersymmetry and Supergravity. *v.5 p.553*

Supersymmetry: Unveiling the Ultimate Laws of Nature. *v.5 p.552*

Supervision in Social Work. *v.4 p.757*

Supervision Strategies for the First Practicum. *v.5 p.676*

A Supplement to the Bright Star Catalogue. *v.5 p.64*

Supplement to the Heritage Encyclopedia of Band Music. *v.1 p.161*

Supplemental Tables of Molecular Orbital Calculations. With a Dictionary of Pi Electron Calculations, 2 v. *v.5 p.287*

Supplemental Tables of Molecular Orbital Calculations. *v.5 p.287*

Supplementum Lyricum: Poetarum Lyricorum Graecorum Fragmenta Qua Recens Innotuerunt. *v.2 p.403*

Supplying the Nuclear Arsenal: American Production Reactors, 1942-1992. . . . . *v.5 p.739*

Support Systems and Community Mental Health. *v.5 p.670, p.671*

Supporting Lifelong Learning: Making Policy Work. . *v.4 p.320*

Supporting Lifelong Learning: Organising Learning. *v.4 p.320, p.321*

Supporting Lifelong Learning: Perspective on Learning, Vol. 1. *v.4 p.320*

Supportive Supervision in Schools: A Guide for Teachers and Administrators. *v.4 p.282*

Supreme Chaos: The Politics of Judicial Confirmation and the Culture War. *v.4 p.541*

Supreme Command: Soldiers, Statesmen, and Leadership in Wartime. *v.4 p.575*

The Supreme Commander: The War Years of Dwight D. Eisenhower. *v.3 p.464*

The Supreme Court: A New Edition of the Chief Justice's Classic History. *v.4 p.466*

The Supreme Court A to Z. *v.4 p.537*

The Supreme Court and Constitutional Democracy. . . *v.4 p.462*

The Supreme Court and Constitutional Theory, 1953-1993. . . . . *v.4 p.470*

Supreme Court and Education. *v.4 p.450*

The Supreme Court and Individual Rights. *v.4 p.456*

The Supreme Court and Libel. *v.4 p.443*

The Supreme Court and Puerto Rico: The Doctrine of Separate and Unequal. *v.3 p.321*

The Supreme Court and Religion in American Life: From Higher Law to Sectarian Scruples. *v.4 p.460*

The Supreme Court and Religion in American Life: The Odyssey of the Religion Clauses. *v.4 p.460*

The Supreme Court and the Attitudinal Model Revisited. *v.4 p.466*

The Supreme Court and the Commander in Chief. . . *v.4 p.464*

The Supreme Court and the Constitution. *v.4 p.454*

Supreme Court and the Intimate Lives of Americans: Birth, Sex, Marriage, Childrearing, and Death. *v.4 p.447*

The Supreme Court and the Judicial Branch. *v.4 p.534*

The Supreme Court and the Mass Media: Selected Cases, Summaries, and Analyses. *v.4 p.444*

The Supreme Court, Crime, and the Ideal of Equal Justice. *v.6 p.249, p.268*

Supreme Court Decisions and Women's Rights: Milestones to Equality. *v.4 p.458*

The Supreme Court from Taft to Burger. *v.4 p.470*

Supreme Court Justice Joseph Story: Statesman of the Old Republic. *v.4 p.468, p.469*

The Supreme Court Justices: Illustrated Biographies, 1789-1995. . . . . *v.4 p.467*

Supreme Court of the United States, 1789-1980: An Index to Opinions Arranged by Justice. *v.4 p.436*

The Supreme Court Reborn: Constitutional Revolution in the Age of Roosevelt. *v.4 p.466*

The Supreme Court under Chief Justice Edward Douglass White, 1910-1921. . . . . *v.4 p.469*

Supremely American: Popular Song in the 20th Century: Styles, Singers, and Milieus, and How They Reflected American Society. *v.1 p.275*

Surface and Colloid Chemistry Handbook. *v.5 p.283*

Surface and Symbol: The Consistancy of James Joyce's Ulysses. *v.2 p.356, p.357*

Surface Chemistry. *v.5 p.283*

Surface Mining, 2e. *v.5 p.738*

Surface Science: An Introduction. *v.5 p.554, p.555*

Surface Water Quality Modeling. *v.5 p.702, p.704*

Surfaces, Interfaces, and Colloids: Principles and Applications. *v.5 p.283*

Surinam: Politics, Economics and Society. *v.3 p.322*

Surpassing the Love of Men: Romantic Friendship and Love Between Women from the Renaissance to the Present. *v.4 p.750, v.6 p.364*

Surprise Heirs I: Illegitimacy, Patrimonial Rights, and Legal Nationalism in Luso-Brazilian Inheritance, 1750-1821. . . . . *v.3 p.334*

Surprise Heirs II: Illegitimacy, Inheritance Rights, and Public Power in the Formation of Imperial Brazil, 1822-1889. . . . . *v.3 p.334*

Surprise, Uncertainty, and Mental Structures. . . . *v.5 p.649*

Surprised by Joy: The Shape of My Early Life. . . . *v.2 p.366*

Surprised by Shame: Dostoevsky's Liars and Narrative Exposure. *v.2 p.806*

Surprised by Sin: The Reader in Paradise Lost. . . . *v.2 p.253*

Surrealism and the Visual Arts: Theory and Reception. *v.1 p.678*

Surrealism; the Road to the Absolute. *v.2 p.460*

Surrealist Art and Writing, 1919-1939: The Gold of Time. *v.1 p.681*

Surrealist Painters and Poets: An Anthology. . . . *v.1 p.677*

Surrealist Prints. *v.1 p.753*

Surrealist Women: An International Anthology. . . . *v.1 p.680*

Surrogate Motherhood: Politics and Privacy. . . . *v.4 p.442*

Surrogate Tissue Analysis: Genomic, Proteomic and Metabolomic Approaches. *v.5 p.104, p.145*

The Surrounded. *v.2 p.97*

Surveillance after September 11. . . . . . . *v.4 p.562, p.572*

Le Survenant. *v.2 p.539*

Survey of American Poetry: Civil War and Aftermath (1861-1889)., Vol. V+. *v.2 p.23*

Survey of American Poetry: Colonial Period (1607-1765). *v.2 p.22, p.23*

Survey of American Poetry: Early Nineteenth Century, 1800-1829. . . . . *v.2 p.23*

Survey of American Poetry: First Great Period, 1830-1860. . . . . *v.2 p.22*

Survey of American Poetry: Interval Between World Wars (1920-1939). *v.2 p.24*

Survey of American Poetry: Midcentury to 1984. . . *v.2 p.24*

Survey of American Poetry: Poetic Renaissance (1913-1919). *v.2 p.24*

Survey of American Poetry: Revolutionary Era, 1766-1799, Vol. II. *v.2 p.22*

Survey of American Poetry: Twilight Interval, 1890-1912, Vol. VI. *v.2 p.22*

Survey of American Poetry: World War II and Aftermath (1940-1950). *v.2 p.24*

Survey of British Commonwealth Affairs: Problems of Wartime Cooperation and Post-War Change, 1939-1952. . . .*v.3 p.89*

Survey of Buying Power and Media Markets. *v.4 p.143*

▢ Survey of Current Business. *v.4 p.51*

Survey of Geometry. *v.5 p.495*

A Survey of Hinduism. *v.1 p.537*

Survey of London. *v.3 p.127*

A Survey of Metaphysics. *v.1 p.488*

A Survey of Modern Algebra. *v.5 p.473*

Survey of Organic Syntheses. *v.5 p.293*

▢ Survey of Real Estate Trends. *v.4 p.158*

Survey of Text Mining: Clustering, Classification, and Retrieval. *v.5 p.337, p.338, p.341*

Survey Research Handbook. *v.4 p.137*

Survey Research: In-Person, Mail, Telephone and Web Methods. *v.4 p.691*

Survey Research. *v.4 p.697*

Surveying Natural Populations. *v.5 p.189*

Surveying: Principles and Applications. *v.4 p.389*

Surveying. *v.4 p.389*

Survival: A Thematic Guide to Canadian Literature. .*v.2 p.728*

The Survival Game: How Game Theory Explains the Biology of Cooperation and Competition. *v.4 p.83*

Survival Guide for Physical Chemistry. *v.5 p.288*

Survival in Auschwitz. *v.3 p.85*

The Survival League. *v.2 p.818*

Survival Math for Marketers. *v.4 p.176*

The Survival of a Counterculture: Ideological Work and Everyday Life among Rural Communards. *v.4 p.740*

Survival of the African American Family: The Institutional Impact of U. S. Social Policy. *v.6 p.39*

The Survival of the Pagan Gods: The Mythological Tradition and Its Place in Renaissance Humanism and Art. .*v.1 p.533*

Surviving Globalization in Three Latin American Communities. *v.3 p.269*

Surviving Poverty in Medieval Paris: Gender, Ideology, and the Daily Lives of the Poor. *v.3 p.142*

Surviving the Swastika: Scientific Research in Nazi Germany. *v.5 p.392, p.412*

The Survivor: Bill Clinton in the White House. *v.3 p.472*

Survivors: Cambodian Refugees in the United States. .*v.6 p.138*

Susan Glaspell: A Critical Biography. *v.2 p.79*

Susan Glaspell: Her Life and Times. *v.2 p.78*

Susan Glaspell in Context: American Theater, Culture, and Politics, 1915-48. . . . .*v.2 p.78*

Susan Rothenberg. *v.1 p.747*

A Susan Sontag Reader. *v.2 p.567*

Susanna Centlivre. *v.2 p.243*

Susanna, "Jeanie," and "The Old Folks at Home": The Songs of Stephen C. Foster from His Time to Ours. .*v.1 p.276, p.324*

Suspended License: Censorship and the Visual Arts. .*v.1 p.827*

Suspicion and Faith: The Religious Uses of Modern Atheism. *v.1 p.595*

Sustainability Civil Society and International Governance: Local North American and Global Perspectives. *v.4 p.663*

Sustainability in Agricultural and Rural Development. .*v.5 p.12*

The Sustainability of Rural Systems: Geographical Interpretations: A Study Initiated by the International Geographical Union's Commission on the Sustainability of Rural Systems. *v.5 p.12*

Sustainable Agriculture and the Environment in the Humid Tropics. *v.5 p.13*

Sustainable Agriculture and the Environment: Perspectives on Growth and Constraints. *v.5 p.13*

Sustainable Aquaculture. *v.5 p.32*

Sustainable Construction: Green Building Design and Delivery. *v.1 p.796, v.4 p.158, p.159*

Sustainable Energy: Choosing among Options. .*v.5 p.452, p.453*

Sustainable Golf Courses: A Guide to Environmental Stewardship. *v.4 p.880, p.883, p.887*

Sustainable Growth and Performance in East Asia, Bk.. III. *v.4 p.243, p.259*

Sustainable Horticulture: Today and Tomorrow. . . .*v.5 p.44*

ⓔ Sustainable Management of Soil Resources in the Humid Tropics. *v.5 p.50*

Sustainable Nuclear Power. *v.5 p.360, p.374, p.378*

Sustainable Ocean Governance: A Geographical Perspective. *v.5 p.430*

Sustainable Practices for Plant Disease Management in Traditional Farming Systems. *v.5 p.47*

The Sustainable Urban Development Reader. *v.4 p.268*

Sustaining Abundance: Environmental Performance in Industrial Democracies. *v.4 p.63*

Sustaining America's Dance Legacy: How the Field of Dance Heritage Can Build Capacity and Broaden Awareness to Dance in the Next Ten Years. *v.1 p.52*

Sustaining Soil Fertility in West Africa. . . .*v.5 p.49, v.6 p.289*

Sutra and Other Stories. *v.6 p.670*

Sutton Hoo: Burial Ground of Kings. *v.6 p.555*

Swahili Modernities: Culture, Politics, and Identity on the East Coast of Africa. *v.4 p.38*

The Swahili. *v.4 p.724, v.6 p.63*

Swallow barn, or A sojourn in the Old Dominion. . . .*v.2 p.43*

Swamp Angel. *v.2 p.739*

The Swamp: The Everglades, Florida, and the Politics of Paradise. *v.4 p.541, p.542*

Swan and the Eagle: Essays on Indian English Literature. *v.2 p.762*

The Swan Villa. *v.2 p.619*

Swann's Way: In Search of Lost Time. *v.2 p.524*

Sweatshop Warriors: Immigrant Women Workers Take on the Global Factory. *v.6 p.457*

Sweaty Palms: The Neglected Art of Being Interviewed. *v.4 p.170*

Sweden ; The Middle Way. *v.3 p.234*

Sweden and Visions of Norway: Politics and Culture, 1814-1905. . . . .*v.3 p.234*

Sweden in the Seventeenth Century. *v.3 p.235*

Sweden: Social Democracy in Practice. *v.3 p.235*

Sweden, the Nation's History. *v.3 p.235*

Sweden's Right to Be Human : Sex-Role Equality: The Goal and the Reality. *v.4 p.706*

Swedish Politics During the 20th Century. *v.3 p.235*

The Sweet Hereafter. *v.2 p.140*

Sweet Mother: Modern African Music. *v.1 p.285*

Sweet Thursday. *v.2 p.123*

Sweetness and Power: The Place of Sugar in Modern History. *v.4 p.46*

☐ Sweets Product Marketplace. *v.1 p.784, p.785, p.796*

A Swell-Looking Babe. *v.2 p.125*

Swept under the Rug: A Hidden History of Navajo Weaving. *v.1 p.716, p.809, v.6 p.679*

Swift as Desire. *v.2 p.667*

Swift: The Man, His Works, and the Age: Dr. Swift, Vol. II. *v.2 p.262, p.263*

A Swiftly Tilting Planet. *v.2 p.149*

Swift's Landscape. *v.2 p.263*

Swift's Poetic Worlds. *v.2 p.262*

The Swim Coaching Bible. *v.4 p.794, p.868, p.904*

Swimming Fastest. *v.4 p.868, p.879*

Swimming Past 50. . . . . *v.4 p.792, p.841, p.868*

The Swimming-Pool Library. *v.6 p.397*

Swimming. *v.4 p.825, p.868, p.879*

Swinburne - The Major Poems and Selected Prose. . . *v.2 p.313*

Swinburne: An Experiment in Criticism. *v.2 p.306*

Swine Breeding and Gestation Facilities Handbook. . *v.5 p.55*

Swine Science. *v.5 p.55*

The Swing Book. *v.1 p.34*

The Swing Era: The Development of Jazz, 1930-1945. *v.1 p.263*

Swing, Swing, Swing: The Life and Times of Benny Goodman. *v.1 p.258, p.326, p.327*

Swingin' at the Savoy: The Memoir of a Jazz Dancer. *v.1 p.10, p.11*

Swings and Misses: Moribund Labor Relations in Professional Baseball. *v.4 p.122*

Swiss Foreign Policy, 1945-2002. . . . . *v.3 p.244*

Swiss Foreign Policy: Foundations and Possibilities. . *v.3 p.244*

The Swiss Reformation. *v.1 p.604*

Switching to Renewable Power: A Framework for the 21st Century. *v.5 p.709*

Switzerland: A Village History. *v.3 p.244*

Switzerland, from Earliest Times to the Roman Conquest. *v.3 p.245*

Switzerland: From Roman Times to the Present. . . . *v.3 p.245*

Switzerland Under Siege 1939-1945: A Neutral Nation's Struggle for Survival. *v.3 p.245*

Switzerland. *v.3 p.244, p.245*

The Sword and the Dollar. *v.3 p.477*

Sword and the Flute; Kali and Krsna: Dark Visions of the Terrible and Sublime in Hindu Mythology. . . . *v.1 p.536*

Sword Dances of Northern England Together with the Horn Dance of Abbots Bromley. *v.1 p.16*

Sword Dancing: A History. *v.1 p.33*

The Sword of Damocles: U.S. Financial Hegemony in Columbia and Chile, 1950-1970. . . . . *v.3 p.354*

The Sword of Honour Trilogy. *v.2 p.388*

The Sword of the Republic: The United States Army on the Frontier, 1783-1846. . . . . *v.3 p.384*

Swords and Plowshares. *v.3 p.463*

Swords into Plowshares: The Problems and Progress of International Organization. *v.4 p.628*

Sybil: Or, the Two Nations. *v.2 p.275*

Symbol and Truth in Blake's Myth. *v.2 p.239*

Symbolic Crusade: Status Politics and the American Temperance Movement. *v.4 p.776, v.5 p.663*

Symbolic Domination: Cultural Symbols and Historical Change in Morocco. *v.6 p.643*

Symbolic Interaction and Ethnographic Research: Intersubjectivity and the Study of Human Lived Experience. *v.4 p.687, p.688*

Symbolic Interactionism: Perspective and Method. . . *v.4 p.695*

Symbolic Meaning, Uncollected Versions of 'Studies in Classic American Literature'. *v.2 p.7*

The Symbolic Uses of Politics: With a New Afterward. *v.5 p.642*

Symbolism and Interpretation. *v.1 p.507*

Symbolism and Modern Urban Society. *v.1 p.709*

Symbolism and Some Implications of the Symbolic Approach: W. B. Yeats During the Eighteen Nineties. . . . *v.2 p.327*

The Symbolism of Evil. *v.1 p.644*

Symbolist Art. *v.1 p.680*

The Symbolists. *v.1 p.678, p.709*

Symbols and Allegories in Art. *v.1 p.709*

Symbols of Church and Kingdom: A Study in Early Syriac Tradition. *v.1 p.656*

Symbols: Public and Private. *v.1 p.530*

Symeon, the New Theologian: The Discourses. . . . *v.1 p.653*

Symmetries of Culture: Theory and Practice of Plane Pattern Analysis. *v.1 p.721*

Symmetry and Sense: The Poetry of Sir Philip Sidney. *v.2 p.215*

Symmetry and Structure. *v.5 p.276*

Symmetry Comes of Age: The Role of Pattern in Culture. *v.1 p.704, p.714*

Symmetry in Mechanics: A Gentle, Modern Introduction. *v.5 p.548*

Symmetry Through the Eyes of a Chemist. *v.5 p.276*

Symmetry. *v.5 p.496*

The Symphonic Repertoire: The Second Golden Age of the Viennese Symphony. *v.1 p.194, p.238*

The Symphonies of Joseph Haydn. *v.1 p.190, p.191, p.241, p.330*

The Symphony: A Listener's Guide. *v.1 p.243*

Symposium of Plato. *v.4 p.215*

The Symposium. *v.1 p.423, p.425*

Synchronized Swimming: An American History. . . . *v.4 p.868*

Synesthesia: A Union of the Senses. *v.5 p.616*

Synopsis of the Four Gospels. *v.1 p.628*

The Syntactic Phenomena of English. *v.2 p.557*

Syntactic Structures. *v.2 p.559*

Syntactic Theory: The Essential Readings. . . *v.2 p.561, p.562*

Syntax of Plautus. *v.2 p.440*

The Syntax of Spanish. *v.2 p.637*

Syntax of the Moods and Tenses of the Greek Verb. . .*v.2 p.400*

Synthetic Methods of Organometallic and Inorganic Chemistry:
    Groups 1, 2, 13, and 14. . . . . *v.5 p.306*

Synthetic Methods of Organometallic and Inorganic Chemistry:
    (Herman/Brauer). *v.5 p.306*

Synthetic Methods of Organometallic and Inorganic Chemistry:
    Lanthanides and Actinides. *v.5 p.306*

Synthetic Methods of Organometallic and Inorganic Chemistry:
    Literature, Laboratory Techniques, and COmmon Starting
    Materials. *v.5 p.307*

Synthetic Methods of Organometallic and Inorganic Chemistry:
    Phosphorus, Arsenic, Antimony, and Bismuth. . . .*v.5 p.306*

Synthetic Methods of Organometallic and Inorganic Chemistry:
    Sulfur, Selenium, and Tellurium, Vol. 4. . . . . . *v.5 p.306*

Synthetic Methods of Organometallic and Inorganic Chemistry:
    Transition Metals, Pt. 1. . . . . *v.5 p.306*

Synthetic Methods of Organometallic and Inorganic Chemistry:
    Transition Metals, Vol. 2. . . . . *v.5 p.306*

Synthetic Methods of Organometallic and Inorganic Chemistry,
    Vol. 2. . . . . *v.5 p.306*

Synthetic Methods of Organometallic and Inorganic Chemistry,
    Vol. 3. . . . . *v.5 p.306, p.307*

Synthetic Methods of Organometallic and Inorganic Chemistry,
    Vol. 5. . . . . *v.5 p.307*

Synthetic Methods of Organometallic and Inorganic Chemistry,
    Vol. 6. . . . . *v.5 p.306, p.307*

Synthetic Methods of Organometallic and Inorganic Chemistry,
    Vol. 7. . . . . *v.5 p.307*

Synthetic Methods of Organometallic and Inorganic
    Chemistry. *v.5 p.307*

Syria, 1945-1986: Politics and Society. *v.6 p.607*

Syria and Lebanon under French Mandate, 1968. *v.6 p.605, p.607*

Syria and the French Mandate: The Politics of Arab
    Nationalism, 1920-1945. . . . . *v.6 p.607*

Syria: Neither Bread nor Freedom. *v.4 p.616*

Syria: Revolution from Above. *v.6 p.607*

Syrian Christians in Muslim Society: An
    Interpretation. *v.6 p.600, p.606*

Syrian Intervention in Lebanon. *v.6 p.606, p.608*

The Syrian Involvement in Lebanon since 1975. *v.6 p.605, p.606*

Syria's Peasantry, the Descendants of Its Lesser Rural Notables,
    and Their Politics. *v.6 p.607*

Syria's Terrorist War on Lebanon and the Peace
    Process. *v.6 p.606, p.607*

A System in Crisis: The Dynamics of Free Market
    Capitalism. *v.3 p.333*

System of Logic Ratiocinative and Induct. *v.1 p.494*

A System of Moral Philosophy. *v.1 p.450, p.484*

System of Positive Polity 1875-1877, Set. *v.4 p.684*

A System of Social Science: Papers Relating to Adam
    Smith. *v.4 p.212*

System of Transcendental Idealism. *v.1 p.465*

The Systematic Identification of Organic Compounds. *v.5 p.300*

Systematic Nomenclature in Organic Chemistry: A Directory to
    Comprehension and Application of It's Basic
    Principles. *v.5 p.289*

Systematic Theology, Set. *v.1 p.636*

Systematic Theology. *v.1 p.637*

Systematics and the Origin of Species: On Ernst Mayr's 100th
    Anniversary. *v.5 p.198*

Systems Approach to Computer-Integrated Design and
    Manufacturing. *v.5 p.684*

Systems Biology: Properties of Reconstructed
    Networks. *v.5 p.128, p.142, p.151*

Systems Biology: Volume 1:
    Genomics. *v.5 p.114, p.128, p.142, p.146*

Systems Biology. *v.5 p.106, p.114, p.142, p.151*

Systems of Rehearsal: Stanislavsky, Brecht, Grotowski and Peter
    Brook. *v.1 p.109, p.145*

S/Z: An Essay. *v.2 p.486*

T

T. C. Boyle Stories: The Collected Stories of T. Coraghessan
    Boyle. *v.2 p.141*

T. E. Lawrence in War and Peace: An Anthology of the Military
    Writings of Lawrence of Arabia. *v.3 p.78*

T. G. Masaryk: Against the Current, 1882-1914. . . .*v.3 p.188*

T. Rex and the Crater of Doom. *v.5 p.449*

T. S. Eliot: A Collection of Critical Essays. *v.2 p.72*

T. S. Eliot: An Imperfect Life. *v.2 p.71, p.72*

T. S. Eliot: An Introduction. *v.2 p.71*

T. S. Eliot and American Philosophy: The Harvard Years. *v.2 p.72*

T. S. Eliot and Ideology. *v.2 p.71*

T. S. Eliot and the Cultural Divide. *v.2 p.71*

T. S. Eliot: The Making of an American Poet, 1888-1922. *v.2 p.72*

T. S. Eliot's Intellectual and Poetic Development
    1909-1922. *v.2 p.72*

Tab Hunter Confidential: The Making of a Movie Star. *v.6 p.418*

Taber's Cyclopedic Medical Dictionary. *v.5 p.509*

Table of Integrals, Series, and Products. . .*v.5 p.63, p.461, p.486*

Table of Isotopes: 1999. . . . . *v.5 p.281*

Table of Isotopes, Vol. 1. . . . . *v.5 p.545*

☐ Table of Isotopes. *v.5 p.307*

☐ Table of Nuclides. *v.5 p.545*

☐ Table of the Properties of 200 Linear Macromolecules and
    Small Molecules. *v.5 p.324*

Table Talk. *v.2 p.292*

Tables of Chemical Kinetics, Homogeneous Reactions. *v.5 p.287*

Tables of Experimental Dipole Moments. *v.5 p.287*

Tables of Physical and Chemical Constants. *v.5 p.281*

Tabloid Television: Popular Journalism and the "Other
    News". *v.4 p.414, p.415*

Taboo: Why Black Athletes Dominate Sports and Why We're
    Afraid to Talk about It. *v.4 p.815, p.831*

Tacitus: Annals I. *v.2 p.445*

Tacitus: Annals XIV. *v.2 p.445*

Tacitus: Dialogus de Oratoribus. *v.2 p.444, p.445*

Tacitus: Histories, Vol. 1. . . . . *v.2 p.444*

Tacitus IV: Annals. *v.2 p.444*

Tacitus Reviewed. *v.2 p.445*

Tacitus. *v.2 p.444*

Tackling Gay Issues in School. *v.6 p.385*

Tackling Jim Crow: Racial Segregation in Professional
    Football. *v.4 p.817, p.832, p.859, p.896, p.897*

Tactical Exercise. . . . . *.v.2 p.388*

Tactical Missile Propulsion. . . . . *.v.5 p.719*

Taft and Roosevelt. . . . . *.v.3 p.456*

Taft, Roosevelt, and the Limits of Friendship. . . . . *.v.3 p.439*

Taft, Wilson, and World Order. . . . . . . *.v.3 p.467, v.4 p.631*

Taguchi's Quality Engineering Handbook. . . . . . . *.v.5 p.686*

Tahiti and French Polynesia. . . . . *.v.4 p.385*

Tahitians: Mind and Experience in the Society Islands. *.v.4 p.43*

Tai Chi: An Introductory Guide to the Chinese Art of
Movement. *.v.4 p.793*

Taiheiki: A Chronicle of Medieval Japan. . . . . . . *.v.6 p.225*

The Tail of the Dragon: New Dance, 1976-1982. *.v.1 p.39, p.44*

The Taiping Rebellion: Documents and Comments. . *.v.6 p.188*

Taiwan: A New History. . . . . *.v.6 p.214*

Taiwan: A Political History. . . . . *.v.6 p.214*

Taiwan: National Identity and Democratization. . . . *.v.6 p.214*

Taiwan's Presidential Politics: Democratization and Cross-Strait
Relations in the Twenty- First Century. . . . . . *.v.4 p.618*

Takarazuka: Sexual Politics and Popular Culture in Modern
Japan. . . . . *.v.6 p.222, p.448*

Take Back the Night: Women on Pornography. . . . *.v.4 p.748*

Take Back the Word: A Queer Reading of the Bible. . *.v.6 p.373*

Take Me Out: A Play. . . . . *.v.6 p.411*

Take Me Out to the Ballgame: Communicating
Baseball. . . . . *.v.4 p.408, p.906*

Take on the Street: What Wall Street and Corporate America
Don't Want You to Know: What You Can Do to Fight
Back. . . . . *.v.4 p.96*

Take Out: Queer Writing from Asian Pacific
America. . . . . *.v.6 p.91, p.111, p.405, p.406*

Take Stage!: How to Direct and Produce a Lesbian Play. *.v.6 p.411*

Take the Young Stranger by the Hand: Same-Sex Relations and
the YMCA. . . . . *.v.4 p.719, v.6 p.365, p.384*

Taken by Surprise: A Dance Improvisation Reader. *.v.1 p.27, p.29*

Taking Care of Men: Sexual Politics in the Public
Mind. . . . . *.v.4 p.745, v.6 p.446*

Taking Chances: Abortion and the Decision Not to
Contracept. . . . . *.v.4 p.775, v.6 p.465, p.470*

Taking Chances: Winning with Probability. . . . . . *.v.5 p.481*

Taking Darwin Seriously: A Naturalistic Approach to
Philosophy. . . . . *.v.5 p.204*

Taking Faith Seriously. . . . . *.v.4 p.720*

Taking Haiti: Military Occupation and the Culture of U. S.
Imperialism, 1915-1940. . . . . *.v.3 p.315*

Taking in a Game: A History of Baseball in
Asia. . . . . *.v.4 p.819, p.834, p.844, p.851, p.899*

Taking It to the Streets: The Social Protest Theater of Luis
Valdez and Amiri Baraka. . . . . *.v.6 p.512, p.517*

Taking Journalism Seriously: News and the Academy. *.v.4 p.403*

Taking Life and Death Seriously - Bioethics from Japan. *.v.5 p.249*

Taking on Goliath: Party Formation, Party System Change, and
Democratization in Mexico. . . . *.v.3 p.290, p.291,v.4 p.593*

Taking Root to Fly. . . . . *.v.1 p.49*

Taking Sides: Clashing Views on Controversial Bioethical
Issues. . . . . *.v.5 p.135, p.248*

Taking the Field: Women, Men and
Sports. . . . . *.v.4 p.745, p.818,v.6 p.437*

Taking Their Place: A Documentary of Women in
Journalism. . . . . *.v.6 p.447*

Taking Trade to the Streets: The Lost History of Public Efforts
to Shape Globalization. . . . . *.v.4 p.663*

The Takings Issue: Constitutional Limits on Land Use Control
and Environmental Regulation. . . . . . . *.v.4 p.463, p.464*

The Talcott Parsons Reader. . . . . *.v.4 p.675*

Talcott Parsons Today: His Theory and Legacy in Contemporary
Sociology. . . . . *.v.4 p.687*

A Tale of Eleventh Century Japan: Hamamatsu Chunagon
Monogatari. . . . . *.v.6 p.233*

Tale of Genji: A Reader's Guide. . . . . *.v.6 p.232*

The Tale of Genji: Legends and Paintings. . . . . . *.v.1 p.733*

The Tale of Genji. . . . . *.v.6 p.232, p.233*

The Tale of Healer Miguel Perdomo Neira: Medicine, Ideologies
and Power in the Nineteenth-Century Andes. . . . *.v.3 p.333*

The Tale of Kieu: A Bilingual Edition of Nguyen Du's Truyen
Kieu. . . . . *.v.6 p.169*

A Tale of Love and Darkness. . . . . *.v.6 p.650*

The Tale of Old Mortality. . . . . *.v.2 p.308*

The Tale of Sinuhe: And Other Ancient Egyptian Poems,
1940-1640 B. C. . . . . *.v.6 p.644*

The Tale of the Heike. . . . . *.v.6 p.229*

A Tale of Two Cities ... . *.v.2 p.283*

A Tale of Two Cities. . . . . *.v.2 p.283*

A Tale of Two Factions: Myth, Memory, and Identity in
Ottoman Egypt and Yemen. . . . . *.v.6 p.628, p.638*

A Tale of Two Leagues: How Baseball Changed as the Rules,
Balls, Franchises, Stadiums and Players Changed,
1900-1998. *.v.4 p.811, p.853, p.886, p.890, p.892, p.893, p.898*

Talent Flow: A Strategic Approach to Keeping Good Employees,
Helping Them Grow, and Letting Them Go. . . . *.v.4 p.76*

Talent to Annoy: Selected Journalism. . . . . *.v.2 p.371*

The Talented Mr. Ripley; Ripley under Ground; and Ripley's
Game. . . . . *.v.2 p.86*

Tales and Stories. . . . . *.v.2 p.626*

Tales from a Forgotten Place. . . . . *.v.3 p.297*

Tales from Shakespeare. . . . . *.v.2 p.298*

Tales from the Underground: A Natural History of Subterranean
Life. . . . . *.v.6 p.292, p.293*

Tales in Political Economy. . . . . *.v.4 p.209, p.269*

Tales My Father Taught Me: An Evocation of Extravagant
Episodes. *.v.2 p.382*

Tales of Fantasy and Magic. . . . . *.v.2 p.818*

Tales of Galicia. . . . . *.v.2 p.792*

Tales of Ise: Lyrical Episodes from Tenth-Century
Japan. . . . . *.v.6 p.231*

Tales of Moonlight and Rain: Japanese Gothic Tales. *.v.6 p.234*

Tales of Nasrettin Hoca. . . . . *.v.6 p.667*

Tales of the City. . . . . *.v.6 p.397*

Tales of the Early Days. . . . . *.v.2 p.749*

Tales of the Earth: Paroxysms and Perturbations of the Blue
Planet. . . . . *.v.6 p.294*

Tales of the Hasidim. . . . . *.v.1 p.546*

Tales of the Lavender Menace: A Memoir of
Liberation. *v.6 p.365, p.390*

Tales of the South Pacific. *v.2 p.98*

Tales of the Wilderness. *v.2 p.807*

Tales of the Working Girl: Wage-Earning Women in American
Literature, 1890-1925. . . . .*v.2 p.4*

Tales of Two Cities: Race and Economic Culture in Early
Republican North and South America. *v.3 p.333*

Tales of Wayward Girls and Immoral Women: Case Records and
the Professionalization of Social Work. . . .*v.4 p.755, p.758*

Tales of Yamato: A Tenth-Century Poem - Tale. *v.6 p.233*

Tales. *v.2 p.281*

Taliban: Militant Islam, Oil and Fundamentalism in Central
Asia. *v.6 p.634*

The Talisman. *v.2 p.307*

Talk about Sex: The Battle over Sex Education in the United
States. *v.4 p.569*

Talk of Love: How Culture Matters. *v.4 p.738*

Talk, Talk, Talk: The Cultural Life of Everyday
Conversation. *v.5 p.648*

Talkin' to Myself: Blues Lyrics, 1921-1942. . .*v.1 p.264, p.412*

Talking Ape: How Language Evolved. *v.4 p.19*

Talking Back: Thinking Feminist, Thinking Black. .*v.6 p.44, p.427*

Talking Culture: Ethnography and Conversation
Analysis. *v.4 p.19*

Talking from 9 to 5: Women and Men at Work. *v.5 p.581*

Talking, Listening and Learning. *v.4 p.423*

Talking Music: Conversations with John Cage, Philip Glass,
Laurie Anderson and Five Generations of American
Experimental Composers. *v.1 p.213*

Talking Proper: The Rise of Accent As Social Symbol. .*v.6 p.751*

Talking Sense in Science: Helping Children Understand Through
Talk. *v.4 p.364, p.365*

Talking Terrorism: A Dictionary of the Loaded Language of
Political Violence. *v.4 p.659*

Talking to Fireflies, Shrinking the Moon: A Parent's Guide to
Nature Activities. *v.5 p.228, p.229, p.245*

Talking to Fireflies, Shrinking the Moon: Nature Activities for
All Ages. *v.5 p.228, p.245*

Talking to Strangers: Improving American Diplomacy at Home
and Abroad. *v.4 p.560, p.566*

Talking with Computers: Explorations in the Science and
Technology of Computing. *v.5 p.343*

Talks of Napoleon at St. Helena with General Baron
Gourgaud. *v.3 p.152*

Talks to Teachers on Psychology and to Students on Some of
Life's Ideals. *v.4 p.357*

Talks with T. G. Masaryk. *v.3 p.189*

Tall Tales of the Southwest: An Anthology of Southern and
Southwestern Humor, 1830-1860. . . . .*v.2 p.21*

The Tall Woman. *v.2 p.144*

Talley's Folly. *v.2 p.159*

Tallulah!: The Life and Times of a Leading Lady. . . .*v.6 p.418*

Tally's Corner: A Study of Negro Streetcorner Men. . .*v.4 p.704*

Tamarind Lithography Workshop Inc. Catalog Raisonné,
1960-1970. . . . .*v.1 p.759*

Tambo and Bones: A History of the American Minstrel
Stage. *v.1 p.35, p.120*

Tambo: Life in an Andean Village. *v.3 p.330*

Tamil Temple Myths: Sacrifice and Divine Marriage in the
South Indian Saiva Tradition. *v.1 p.537*

Taming Intractable Conflicts: Mediation in the Hardest
Cases. *v.4 p.645*

The Taming of the Samurai: Honorific Individualism and the
Making of Modern Japan. *v.6 p.224*

The Taming of the Shrew. *v.2 p.224*

Taming Regulation: Superfund and the Challenge of Regulatory
Reform. *v.4 p.109, p.110, p.111,v.6 p.301*

Taming the Sovereigns: Institutional Change in International
Politics. *v.4 p.624*

Taming the Wild Field: Colonization and Empire on the Russian
Steppe. *v.3 p.213*

Tan Veloz Como el Deseo. *v.2 p.667*

Tana Toraja: A Social History of an Indonesian People. .*v.4 p.701*

Tanakh, the Holy Scriptures: The New Translation According to
the Traditional Hebrew Text. *v.1 p.618*

Tangible Visions: Northwest Coast Indian Shamanism and Its
Art. *v.1 p.683, v.6 p.679, p.680, p.701*

The Tangled Chain: The Structure of Disorder in the Anatomy
of Melancholy. *v.2 p.214*

The Tangled Field: Barbara McClintock's Search for the
Patterns of Genetic Control. *v.5 p.131*

Tangled Hierarchies: Teachers As Professionals and the
Management of Schools. *v.4 p.283*

The Tangled Roots of Feminism, Environmentalism, and
Appalachian Literature. *v.2 p.8, p.12*

Tangled up in Red, White and Blue: New Social Movements in
America. *v.4 p.711*

A Tangled Web: The Making of Foreign Policy in the Nixon
Presidency. *v.3 p.439, p.467*

Tango and the Political Economy of Passion. .*v.1 p.15, p.19, p.20*

The Tango in the United States: A History. *v.1 p.15, p.34*

Tango!: The Dance, the Song, the Story. *v.1 p.20*

Tangsir: A Persian Novel. *v.6 p.670*

Tanker Spills: Prevention by Design. *v.5 p.368, p.380*

Tannhauser. *v.1 p.206, p.234, p.366, p.410*

Tannir. English / Water. *v.6 p.150*

Tantra in Practice. *v.1 p.567*

The Tantric Body: The Secret Tradition of Hindu
Religion. *v.1 p.535, p.567*

The Tantric Tradition. *v.1 p.567*

Tanu Women: Gender and Culture in the Making of
Tanganyikan Nationalism, 1955-1965. . . . . . .*v.6 p.66*

Tanzania: An African Experiment. *v.6 p.66*

Tanzania: The Story of Julius Nyerere through the Pages of
Drum. *v.6 p.66*

The Tao of Physics: An Exploration of the Parallels Between
Modern Physics and Easter Mysticism. *v.5 p.540*

Tao Te Ching: Lac Tzu. *v.1 p.418*

Taoism and the Arts of China. *v.1 p.693*

The Tap Dance Dictionary. *v.1 p.3, p.4, p.32, p.33*

Tap!: The Greatest Tap Dance Stars and Their Stories,
1900-1955. . . . .*v.1 p.32*

The Tape-Recorded Interview: A Manual for Field Workers in
   Folklore and Oral History. *v.2 p.585*

A Tapestry of Orbits. *v.5 p.719*

Tapestry of Terror: A Portrait of Middle East Terrorism,
   1994-1999. . . . .*v.4 p.658*

Taphonomy: A Process Approach. *v.5 p.447*

Taps for Private Tussie. *v.2 p.117*

The Tar Heel State: A History of North Carolina. . . .*v.3 p.502*

Tara Revisited: Women, War, and the Plantation
   Legend. *v.4 p.519, p.520*

☐ Taras Shevchenko Museum. *v.2 p.814, p.815*

Target Switzerland: Swiss Armed Neutrality in World War
   II. *v.3 p.244*

Targeting Development. *v.4 p.258*

Targeting Terror: U.S. Policy Toward Middle Eastern State
   Sponsors and Terrorist Organizations, Post-September
   11. . . . .*v.4 p.564*

Tartarin of Tarascon. *v.2 p.488*

Tartuffe and Other Plays. *v.2 p.475*

Tartuffe. *v.2 p.475*

Tarzan Forever: The Life of Edgar Rice Burroughs Creator of
   Tarzan. *v.2 p.59*

Tarzan of the Apes. *v.2 p.59*

Tasso's Dialogues: A Selection, with the "Discourse on the Art
   of the Dialogue". *v.2 p.710*

A Taste for Diversions: Sport in Georgian England. . .*v.4 p.804*

A Taste of Indochina. *v.6 p.166*

The Taste of Power. *v.2 p.812*

The Tastemakers. *v.3 p.369*

Tastes of Paradise: A Social History of Spices, Stimulants, and
   Intoxicants. *v.3 p.282, v.4 p.710*

Tasting and Smelling. *v.5 p.606*

Tasting Food, Tasting Freedom: Excursions into Eating, Power,
   and the Past. *v.3 p.272, p.282,v.4 p.46*

The Tatars of Crimea: Their Struggle for Survival. . .*v.3 p.212*

Tatian's Diatessaron: Its Creation, Dissemination, Significance,
   and History in Scholarship. *v.1 p.591*

Tattooed Soldier. *v.6 p.509*

A Tawdry Place of Salvation: The Art of Jane Bowles. .*v.2 p.59*

☐ Tax - Wikipedia, the free encyclopedia. *v.4 p.106*

☐ Tax and Accounting Sites Directory. *v.4 p.104, p.106*

The Tax Decade, 1981-1990. . . . .*v.4 p.108*

☐ The Tax Foundation. *v.4 p.106*

☐ Tax History Project. *v.4 p.108, p.146*

Tax Justice: The Ongoing Debate. *v.4 p.108*

☐ Tax Policy Center. *v.4 p.108*

Tax Policy in the Real World. *v.4 p.108*

Tax Reform: A Reference Handbook. *v.4 p.464*

Tax Research Techniques. *v.4 p.107*

Taxation: An Interdisciplinary Approach to Research. .*v.4 p.107*

Taxes and Business Strategy: A Planning Approach. . .*v.4 p.248*

The Taxi-Dance Hall: A Sociological Study in Commercialized
   Recreation and City Life. *v.6 p.717*

Taxing Choices. *v.4 p.464*

Taxing Ourselves: A Citizen's Guide to the Debate over
   Taxes. *v.4 p.108*

Taxing the Future: Fiscal Policy in the Bush
   Administration. *v.4 p.107*

☐ Taxonomy Browser. . .*v.5 p.107, p.204, p.205, p.206, p.211*

A Taxonomy for Learning, Teaching and Assessing: A Revision
   of Bloom's Taxonomy of Educational
   Objectives. *v.4 p.338, v.5 p.573*

Taxonomy for the Technology Domain. *v.4 p.352*

Tay John. *v.2 p.733*

The Tay Son Uprising: Society and Rebellion in
   Eighteenth-Cenury Vietnam. *v.6 p.167*

Taylor's Encyclopedia of Garden Plants: The Most Authoritative
   Guide to the Best Flowers, Trees, and Shrubs for North
   American Gardens. *v.1 p.812*

Tchaikovsky: A Biography. *v.6 p.409*

Tchaikovsky: A Self-Portrait. *v.1 p.201, p.362*

Tchaikovsky and His World. *v.1 p.199, p.362*

The Tchaikovsky Handbook: Catalogue of Letters,
   Bibliography. *v.1 p.164, p.202, p.362*

The Tchaikovsky Handbook: Thematic Catalogue of Works,
   Catalogue of Photographs,
   Autobiography. *v.1 p.164, p.202, p.362, p.363*

Tchaikovsky Remembered. *v.1 p.195, p.362*

Tchaikovsky: Symphony No. 6
   (Pathétique). *v.1 p.198, p.240, p.362*

Tchaikovsky: The Quest for the Inner Man. *v.6 p.410*

Tchaikovsky's Ballets: Swan Lake, Sleeping Beauty,
   Nutcracker. *v.1 p.25*

Tchaikovsky's Last Days: A Documentary Study. .*v.1 p.202, p.362*

Te Dejo el Mar. *v.2 p.663*

Te Kaihau: The Windeater. *v.2 p.746*

Teach the Nation: Public School, Racial Uplift, and Women's
   Writing in the 1890's. *v.6 p.8, p.21, p.45*

Teach Them ALL to Read: Catching the Kids Who Fall Through
   the Cracks. *v.4 p.360*

Teach Us to Outgrow Our Madness: Four Short Novels. .*v.6 p.232*

Teach Your Own: The John Holt Book of Home
   Schooling. *v.4 p.296*

Teach Yourself 101 Key Ideas: Genetics. *v.5 p.134*

Teach Yourself Romanian Complete Course. *v.2 p.778*

Teach Yourself Ukrainian: A Complete Course for
   Beginners. *v.2 p.777*

Teacher - Mentor: A Dialogue for Collaborative
   Learning. *v.4 p.279*

Teacher: Anne Sullivan Macy. *v.4 p.337*

Teacher As Stranger: Educational Psychology for the Modern
   Age. *v.4 p.343*

Teacher Education Programs in the United States: A
   Guide. *v.4 p.279, p.280*

Teacher in America. *v.4 p.292*

Teacher Man: A Memoir. *v.4 p.338*

☐ Teacher Preparation and Professional Development:
   2000. . . . .*v.4 p.277*

The Teacher Rebellion. *v.4 p.283*

Teacher Thinking in Cultural Contexts. *v.4 p.350*

Teachers and Educational Change: The Lived Experience of Secondary School Restructuring. *v.4 p.283*

Teachers and Machines: The Classroom Use of Technology since 1920. . . . .*v.4 p.351*

Teachers and the Law. *v.4 p.450*

Teachers As Cultural Workers: Letters to Those Who Dare Teach with New Essays by Shirley Steinberg, Joe Kincheloe, and Peter McClaren. *v.4 p.342*

Teachers As Researchers: Qualitative Inquiry As a Path to Empowerment. *v.4 p.355*

Teachers at Work: Achieving Success in Our Schools. .*v.4 p.278*

A Teacher's Guide to Including Students with Disabilities in General Physical Education. *v.4 p.800*

The Teacher's Guide to National Board Certification: Unpacking the Standards. *v.4 p.278*

A Teacher's Guide to Using Technology in the Classroom. *v.4 p.351*

Teachers of the Inner Chambers: Women and Culture in Seventeenth-Century China. *v.6 p.452*

The Teacher's Sourcebook for Cooperative Learning: Practical Techniques, Basic Principles, and Frequently Asked Questions. *v.4 p.349*

Teacher-Student Relationships: Causes and Consequences. *v.4 p.349*

Teacher. *v.4 p.337*

Teaching a Stone to Talk: Expeditions and Encounters. .*v.5 p.227*

Teaching about Evolution and the Nature of Science. *v.5 p.195, p.246*

□ Teaching About Religion: Worldview Education. . .*v.4 p.299*

Teaching Academic Subjects to Diverse Learners: What Teachers Need to Know. *v.4 p.348*

Teaching and Learning in Japan. *v.4 p.336, v.6 p.222*

Teaching and Learning in Two Languages: Bilingualism and Schooling in the United States. *v.4 p.312*

Teaching and Learning: Lessons from Psychology. . .*v.5 p.571*

Teaching and Learning Middle Grades Mathematics. . .*v.5 p.464*

Teaching and Learning Secondary Science: Contemporary Issues and Practical Approaches. *v.4 p.367, p.368*

Teaching and Learning with Cases: A Guidebook. . .*v.4 p.178*

Teaching and the Case Method. *v.4 p.177*

Teaching and Writing Case Studies. *v.4 p.177*

Teaching as a Performing Art. *v.4 p.348*

Teaching As a Subversive Activity. *v.4 p.323*

Teaching Asian America: Diversity and the Problem of Community. *v.6 p.108*

Teaching Asian American History. *v.6 p.109*

Teaching Children Gymnastics: A Developmentally Appropriate Approach. *v.4 p.799, p.862*

Teaching Children Physical Education: Becoming a Master Teacher. *v.4 p.798*

Teaching Children with Autism: Strategies for Initiating Positive Interactions and Improving Learning Opportunities. .*v.4 p.318*

Teaching Cooperative Learning: The Challenge for Teacher Education. *v.4 p.349*

Teaching Criminal Justice Ethics: Strategic Issues. . .*v.6 p.245*

Teaching Critical Thinking. *v.4 p.344*

Teaching Cues for Sport Skills for Secondary School Students. *v.4 p.798*

Teaching Dance Studies. *v.1 p.46*

Teaching Dance to Senior Adults. *v.1 p.47*

Teaching Developmental Gymnastics: Skills to Take Through Life. *v.4 p.798*

Teaching Early Literacy: Development, Assessment, and Instruction. *v.4 p.360*

Teaching Economics to Undergraduates: Alternatives to Chalk and Talk. *v.4 p.185*

Teaching English Today: Advocating Change in the Secondary Curriculum. *v.4 p.366, p.367*

Teaching Ethnic Diversity with Film: Essays and Resources for Educators in History, Social Studies, Literature and Film Studies. *v.6 p.321*

Teaching Evolution in Higher Education: Methodological, Religious, and Nonreligious Issues. *v.5 p.202, p.244*

Teaching for Lifetime Physical Activity Through Quality High School Physical Education. *v.4 p.799, p.800*

Teaching for Understanding: What It Is and How to Do It. *v.4 p.348*

Teaching from the Deep End: Succeeding with Today's Classroom Challenges. *v.4 p.346*

Teaching Fundamental Gymnastic Skills. *v.4 p.796, p.862*

Teaching Hearts and Minds: College Students Reflect on the Vietnam War in Literature. *v.6 p.169*

Teaching Immigrant and Second-Language Students: Strategies for Success. *v.4 p.312*

Teaching in the Knowledge Society: Education in the Age of Insecurity. *v.4 p.347*

Teaching Introductory Physics. *v.5 p.563*

Teaching Is an Art: An A-Z Handbook for Successful Teaching in Middle Schools and High Schools. . . .*v.4 p.348, p.349*

Teaching Lifetime Sports. *v.4 p.790, p.795*

Teaching Literacy to Students with Significant Disabilities: Strategies for the K-12 Inclusive Classroom. . . .*v.4 p.318*

Teaching Literature As Reflective Practice. *v.2 p.566*

Teaching Literature. *v.2 p.566*

Teaching Models in Education of the Gifted. *v.5 p.575*

Teaching, Multimedia and Mathematics: Investigations of Real Practice. *v.5 p.463*

Teaching Music Globally. *v.1 p.283, p.405*

Teaching Music History. *v.1 p.406*

Teaching Music in the Twenty-First Century. *v.1 p.405*

The Teaching of Instrumental Music. *v.1 p.397, p.405*

Teaching Percussion, Set. *v.1 p.397*

Teaching Performance Studies. *v.1 p.136*

Teaching Physical Education. *v.4 p.798, p.799*

Teaching Physics: With the Physics Suite. *v.5 p.564*

Teaching Problems and the Problems of Teaching. . .*v.5 p.463*

Teaching Psychology: A Step by Step Guide. *v.5 p.675*

Teaching Psychology in America: A History. *v.5 p.676*

□ Teaching Resources Depository (TRD). *v.4 p.676*

Teaching Rhythmic Gymnastics: A Developmentally Appropriate Approach. *v.4 p.796, p.862*

Teaching Science Through Discovery. *v.4 p.362*

Teaching Science to Children: An Inquiry Approach.   .*v.4 p.363*

Teaching Secondary School Science: Strategies for Developing Scientific Literacy. *v.4 p.367*

Teaching Secondary Science with ICT. *v.4 p.367*

Teaching Sex: The Shaping of Adolescence in the 20th Century. *v.4 p.736*

Teaching Social Studies That Matters: Curriculum for Active Learning. *v.4 p.366*

Teaching Sociology: The Quest for Excellence. *v.4 p.675*

Teaching Sport and Physical Activity: Insights on the Road to Mastery. *v.4 p.797*

Teaching Statistics: Resources for Undergraduate Instructors. *v.5 p.482*

Teaching Statistics Using Baseball. *v.5 p.482*

Teaching Strategies for Nurse Educators. *v.5 p.529*

Teaching Students with Learning and Behavior Problems: Managing Mild-To-Moderate Difficulties in Resource and Inclusive Settings. *v.4 p.318*

Teaching Students with Mental Retardation: Providing Access to the General Curriculum. *v.4 p.319*

Teaching the Gifted Child. *v.4 p.317*

Teaching the Nuts and Bolts of Physical Activity: Building Basic Movement Skills. *v.4 p.797*

Teaching U. S. Puerto Rican History. *v.6 p.532, p.533*

Teaching with Authority: A Theology of the Magisterium in the Church. *v.1 p.575*

Teaching with Cases. *v.4 p.177*

Teaching with Documents, Vol. 1. . . . .*v.3 p.375*

Teaching with Love: A Feminist Approach to Early Childhood Education. *v.4 p.368*

Teaching Working Class. *v.4 p.302*

Teachings from the Worldly Philosophy. *v.4 p.195*

Team Cognition: Understanding the Factors That Drive Process and Performance. *v.4 p.80*

Team Handball: Steps to Success. *v.4 p.847*

Team Players and Teamwork. *v.4 p.80*

Team Spirits: The Native American Mascots Controversy. *v.4 p.817, p.841*

Team Troubleshooter: How to Find and Fix Team Problems. *v.4 p.79*

Team-Based Learning: A Transformative Use of Small Groups. *v.4 p.350*

Teasing Secrets from the Dead: My Investigations at America's Most Infamous Crime Scenes. *v.6 p.266*

Teatro Argentino Contemporaneo: Antologia. *v.2 p.678*

El Teatro Campesino: Theater in the Chicano Movement. *v.1 p.124, v.6 p.517*

Teatro Completo. *v.2 p.648*

Teatro Hispano!: Three Major New York Companies. .*v.6 p.517*

Teatro. *v.2 p.678, p.721, p.724*

Technical Communication: A Practical Approach. . . .*v.5 p.681*

Technical Communication and the World Wide Web. .*v.5 p.589*

Technical Communication for Readers and Writers. . .*v.5 p.681*

Technical Communication. *v.5 p.680, p.681*

Technical Writing Basics: A Guide to Style and Form. .*v.5 p.680*

A Technique for Producing Ideas. *v.4 p.428*

The Technique of Film and Video Editing: History, Theory, and Practice. *v.6 p.350*

Technique of Film Editing. *v.6 p.350, p.351*

The Technique of Martha Graham. *v.1 p.26*

The Technique of My Musical Language. .*v.1 p.218, p.341, p.372*

Techniques in Bioinformatics and Medical Informatics. .*v.5 p.98*

Techniques in Underground Mining: Selections from Underground Mining Methods Handbook. . .*v.5 p.737, p.738*

Techniques of Chemistry: Solutions and Solubilities, Vol. 8. . . . .*v.5 p.276*

Techniques of Chemistry. *v.5 p.277*

Techniques of Family Therapy. *v.5 p.668*

The Techniques of Modern Structural Geology: Applications of Continuum Mechanics in Structural Geology. . . .*v.5 p.441*

The Techniques of Modern Structural Geology: Folds and Fractures. *v.5 p.441*

The Techniques of Modern Structural Geology: Strain Analyses. *v.5 p.441*

Techniques of Printmaking. *v.1 p.760*

Techniques of Problem Solving. *v.5 p.459*

Techniques of the Contemporary Composer. *v.1 p.370*

Techniques of the Impressionists. *v.1 p.750*

Technologies of Procreation: Kinship in the Age of Assisted Conception. *v.4 p.31, p.32*

Technologies of the Gendered Body: Reading Cyborg Women. *v.6 p.438*

Technology and Science, Peoples Republic of China: Introduction. *v.5 p.393*

Technology and Teacher Education: A Guide for Educators and Policy Makers. *v.4 p.352*

Technology and the Dream: Reflections on the Black Experience at MIT, 1941-1999. . . . .*v.6 p.21*

Technology, Development, and Democracy: International Conflict and Cooperation in the Information Age. .*v.4 p.425*

Technology for Teachers: Mastering New Media and Portfolio Development. *v.4 p.351*

Technology, Guilds, and Early English Drama. . .*v.1 p.73, p.99*

Technology of Wine Making. *v.5 p.52*

Technology Planning for Effective Teaching and Learning. *v.4 p.350*

Technology Transfer: An International Good Practice Guide for Pharmaceuticals and Allied Industries. *v.4 p.156*

The Tectonic Evolution of Asia. *v.5 p.433*

Tectonic Evolution of Southeast Asia. *v.5 p.432*

Tectonic Geomorphology. *v.5 p.424*

Tectonics of Sedimentary Basis. *v.5 p.438*

Tecumseh, A Drama and Canadian Poems. *v.2 p.732*

Ted Hughes at 70. . . . .*v.2 p.353*

Ted Hughes: The Life of a Poet. *v.2 p.352, p.353*

Ted Shawn, Father of American Dance: A Biography. .*v.6 p.415*

Ted Williams: A Baseball Life. *v.4 p.852*

Teen Mothers and the Revolving Welfare Door. *v.4 p.756*

Teenage Fathers. *v.4 p.737*

Teenage Wasteland: Suburbia's Dead End Kids. *v.4 p.736*

The Teenage World: Adolescents' Self-Image in Ten Countries. *v.4 p.693*

Teetering on the Rim: Global Restructuring, Daily Life and the Armed Retreat of the Bolivian State. *v.3 p.323*

Teewinot: Climbing and Contemplating the Teton Range. *v.6 p.284*

The Tejano Community, 1836-1900. . . . .*v.6 p.534*

Tejano Origins in Eighteenth-Century San Antonio. *v.6 p.534, p.550*

Tejano Religion and Ethnicity: San Antonio, 1821-1860. . . . .*v.6 p.520, p.532, p.549*

Tejano South Texas: A Mexican American Cultural Province. *v.6 p.530, p.543*

Tektites. *v.5 p.436*

Telebomb: The Truth Behind the $500-Billion Telecom Bust and What the Industry Must Do to Recover. . . .*v.4 p.111, p.166*

Telecommunication Policy for the Information Age: From Monopoly to Competition. *v.4 p.420*

Telecommunication System Engineering. *v.5 p.725*

Telecommunication Transmission Systems: Microwave, Fiber Optic, Mobile Cellular Radio, Data, and Digital Multiplexing. *v.5 p.702*

Telecommunications in Europe. *v.4 p.420*

The Telecommunications Industry. *v.4 p.166*

Telecommunications Network Design and Management. .*v.5 p.725*

Telecommunications Policy and Economic Development: The New State Role. *v.4 p.420*

Telecommunications Politics: Ownership and Control of the Information Highway in Developing Countries. . .*v.4 p.420*

Telecommunications Research Resources: An Annotated Guide. *v.4 p.419*

Telecommunications: Restructuring Work and Employment Relations Worldwide. *v.4 p.419, p.420*

Telecosmos: The Next Great Telecom Revolution. . .*v.4 p.115*

The Telegraph: A History of Morse's Invention and Its Predecessors in the United States. *v.4 p.421*

The Telegraph: How Technology Innovation Caused Social Change. *v.4 p.421*

Telegraph Messenger Boys: Labor Communication and Technology, 1850-1950. . . . .*v.4 p.421*

Telephone Survey Methodology. *v.4 p.691*

Televangelism: The Marketing of Popular Religion. . .*v.1 p.655*

The Television Plays of Paddy Chayefsky. *v.2 p.65*

Television: The Critical View. *v.4 p.418*

Television Week. *v.4 p.157*

Tell about the South: The Southern Rage to Explain. . .*v.2 p.13*

Tell This Silence: Asian American Women Writers and the Politics of Speech. *v.6 p.96, p.111*

Tell Your Story: A Dictionary of Jazz and Blues Recordings 1917-1950, Vol. 1. . . . .*v.1 p.163, p.171, p.264*

Tell Your Story: A Dictionary of Jazz and Blues Recordings 1951-1975, Vol. 2. . . . .*v.1 p.163, p.171, p.264*

Telling Lives in India: Biography, Autobiography, and Life History. *v.6 p.155*

Telling Lives, Telling Histories: Autobiography and Historical Imagination in Modern Indonesia. *v.6 p.175, p.177*

Telling Lives: Women's Self-Writing in Modern Japan. .*v.6 p.477*

Telling Moments: Fifteen Gay Monologues. *v.6 p.412*

Telling Our Own Stories: Local Histories from South Mara, Tanzania. *v.6 p.66*

Telling Tales. *v.2 p.583*

Telling the Story: The Convergence of Print, Broadcast, and Online Media. *v.4 p.416*

Temperate Agroforestry Systems. *v.5 p.37*

Temperate Forests. *v.5 p.36*

Temperature, Its Measurement and Control in Science and Industry; Papers Presented at a Symposium Held in New York City, November 1939. . . . .*v.5 p.280*

Temperatures Very Low and Very High. *v.5 p.560*

Temperature. *v.5 p.560*

Tempered Strength: Studies in the Nature and Scope of Prudential Leadership. *v.5 p.652*

Tempest over Teapot Dome: The Story of Albert B. Fall. .*v.3 p.463*

The Tempest. *v.2 p.225*

Une Tempête : Théâtre. *v.2 p.536*

Templars, Hospitallers and Teutonic Knights: The Image of the Military Orders, 1128-1291. . . . .*v.3 p.63*

The Temple of Dawn. *v.6 p.231*

The Temple of Memories: History, Power, and Morality in a Chinese Village. *v.6 p.197*

The Temple of the Golden Pavilion. *v.6 p.231*

Temples of Gold: Seven Centuries of Thai Buddhist Painting. *v.1 p.732*

Temples, Tombs and Hieroglyphs: A Popular History of Ancient Egypt. *v.3 p.9*

The Temple. *v.2 p.384*

Templum Dei: Edited from MS 27 of Emmanuel College, Cambridge. *v.2 p.449*

Temporal Stay: Poems. *v.2 p.787*

The Temptation of St. Anthony. *v.2 p.491*

The Temptation of the West. *v.2 p.522*

Temptation of the Word: The Novels of Mario Vargas Llosa. *v.2 p.685*

The Temptations of Big Bear. *v.2 p.739*

The Tempting of America: The Political Seduction of the Law. *v.4 p.462*

The Ten Cents War: Chile, Peru and Bolivia in the War of the Pacific, 1879-1884. . . . .*v.3 p.274*

Ten Centuries of Spanish Poetry: An Anthology in English Verse with Original Texts, From the Eleventh Century to the Generation of 1898. . . . .*v.2 p.645*

The Ten Commandments of Quality Management: Best Practices to Develop New Leaders and Create a Quality Environment. *v.4 p.73, p.74*

Ten Days That Shook the World. *v.3 p.221*

Ten Great Economists: From Marx to Keynes. .*v.4 p.210, p.229*

Ten Lectures on Wavelets. *v.5 p.493*

Ten Little Indians: Stories. *v.2 p.139*

Ten Lost Plays. *v.2 p.107*

Ten North Frederick. *v.2 p.107*

Ten Novels and Their Authors. *v.2 p.578*

Ten Questions about Human Error: A New View of Human Factors and System Safety. *v.5 p.587*

Ten Rules for Strategic Innovators: From Idea to Execution. *v.4 p.68*

Ten Thousand Years of Pottery. *v.1 p.807*

Ten Years in Japan: A Contemporary Record Drawn from the Diaries and Private and Official Papers of Joseph C. Grew, United States Ambassador to Japan, 1932-1942. . . . . *v.6 p.226, p.227*

Ten Years of Exile. *v.2 p.501, v.3 p.153*

Tenacious of Their Liberties: The Congregationalists in Colonial Massachusetts. *v.1 p.584*

The Tenant of Wildfell Hall. *v.2 p.270*

Tender Buttons: Objects, Food, Rooms. *v.2 p.122*

Tender Is the Night. *v.2 p.76*

Tender Violence: Domestic Visions in an Age of U.S. Imperialism. *v.1 p.765*

Tending Fire: Coping with America's Wildland Fires. . .*v.5 p.31*

Tenement Songs: The Popular Music of the Jewish Immigrants. *v.1 p.301*

Tengu Child. *v.6 p.230*

Tennessee: A Guide to the State. *v.3 p.510*

Tennessee: A Political History. *v.3 p.510, p.511*

Tennessee: A Short History. *v.3 p.510*

Tennessee History: The Land, the People, and the Culture. *v.3 p.511*

Tennessee Williams: A Guide to Research and Performance. *v.1 p.116*

Tennessee Williams: A Study of Short Fiction. . . . *v.2 p.135*

Tennessee Williams A to Z: The Essential Reference to His Life and Work. *v.2 p.134*

Tennessee Williams and Elia Kazan: A Collaboration in the Theatre. *v.2 p.134*

Tennessee Williams and the South. *v.2 p.134*

The Tennessee Williams Encyclopedia. *v.2 p.134*

Tennessee Williams: Memoirs. *v.2 p.135*

Tennessee Williams: Plays 1937-1955. . . .*v.1 p.119, v.2 p.135*

Tennessee Williams: Plays 1957-1980. . . .*v.1 p.119, v.2 p.135*

Tennessee Williams. *v.2 p.134*

Tennessee. *v.3 p.510*

Tennis: A Cultural History. *v.4 p.815, p.864*

The Tennis Court Oath: A Book of Poems. *v.2 p.57*

The Tennis Drill Book. *v.4 p.864*

Tennis Skills: The Player's Guide. *v.4 p.864*

Tennozan: The Battle of Okinawa and the Dropping of the Atom Bomb. *v.6 p.235*

Tennyson: An Illustrated Life. *v.2 p.313*

A Tennyson Chronology. *v.2 p.313*

A Tennyson Dictionary. *v.2 p.313*

Tennyson's Epic Drama. *v.2 p.313*

Tennyson's Language. *v.2 p.313*

Tennyson's Maud: A Definitive Edition. *v.2 p.314*

Tennyson's Poetry. *v.2 p.314*

Tennyson's Suppressed Poems. *v.2 p.314*

Tennyson. *v.2 p.313*

Tenochtitlán. *v.4 p.10*

The Tent Peg: A Novel. *v.2 p.739*

The Tented Field: A History of Cricket in America. *v.4 p.808, p.856*

The Tenth Amendment and State Sovereignty: Constitutional History and Contemporary Issues. *v.4 p.524*

The Tenth Man. *v.2 p.350*

Teoria e invenzione futurista. *v.2 p.718*

Teotihuacan: An Experiment in Living. *v.3 p.261*

Terapia. *v.2 p.680*

Terence: Adelphoe. *v.2 p.445*

Terence: Eunuchus. *v.2 p.445*

Terence Rattigan: The Man and His Work. *v.2 p.379*

Terence: The Comedies. *v.2 p.445*

Term Limits and the Dismantling of State Legislative Professionalism. *v.4 p.530*

Termination Revisited: American Indians on the Trail to Self-Determination, 1933-1953. . . .*v.6 p.689, p.690, p.696*

Terminological Dictionary of Ecology, Geobotany and Pedology. *v.6 p.285*

Terms of Survival. *v.6 p.505, p.510*

Terra Cotta Skyline: New York's Architectural Ornament. *v.1 p.778*

Terra Nostra. *v.2 p.668*

The Terragni Atlas: Built Architecture. *v.1 p.793, p.794*

Terraqué, suivi de Exécutoire. *v.2 p.518*

Terrarium Habitats, Grades K-6. . . . . *v.5 p.229*

Terrarium Habitats. *v.5 p.229*

Terrariums: An easy guide to growing a host of miniature gardens, using traditional terrariums, glass bottles and decorative dishes. *v.5 p.229*

Terrariums for Your New Pet. *v.5 p.228*

Terrestrial Carbon Observation: The Rio de Janeiro Recommendations for Terrestrial and Atmospheric Measurements. *v.5 p.113*

Terrestrial Ecoregions of North America: A Conservation Assessment. *v.5 p.169, p.185, p.235*

Terrestrial Ecosystems Through Time: Evolutionary Paleoecology of Terrestrial Plants and Animals. . .*v.5 p.449*

The Terrestrial Invasion: An Ecophysiological Approach to the Origins of Land Animals. *v.5 p.182, p.193*

Terrestrial Vertebrates. *v.5 p.56*

Terrible Gift: The Brave New World of Genetic Medicine. *v.5 p.148*

A Terrible Love of War. *v.5 p.584*

The Terrible Power of a Minor Guilt: Literary Essays. .*v.6 p.652*

Territoires du souffle : poèmes. *v.2 p.529*

Territorial Games: Understanding and Ending Turf Wars at Work. *v.4 p.74*

Territorial Government in Canada: The Autonomy Question in the Old North-West Territories. *v.4 p.590*

Territorial Politics and Government in Montana, 1864-89. . . . . *v.3 p.526*

Territories of the Psyche: The Fiction of Jean Rhys. . .*v.2 p.770*

Territory and State Power in Latin America: The Peruvian Case. *v.3 p.331*

Territory, Democracy, and Justice: Regionalism and Federalism in Western Democracies. *v.4 p.400*

Terror and Civilization: Christianity, Politics, and the Western Psyche. *v.4 p.658*

Terror and Decorum: Poems, 1940-1948. . . . . . .*v.2 p.126*

Terror and Everyday Life: Singular Moments in the History of the Horror Film. *v.6 p.317*

Terror and Liberalism. *v.4 p.562, p.657, p.658*

Terror and Violence: Imagination and the Unimaginable. *v.6 p.252*

Terror in the Mind of God: The Global Rise of Religious Violence. *v.1 p.524*

Terror in the Name of God: Why Religious Militants Kill. *v.4 p.662*

Terror Incorporated: Tracing the Dollars Behind the Terror Networks. *v.4 p.660*

ⓔ The Terror of the Machine: Technology, Work, Gender, and Ecology on the U.S.-Mexico Border. *v.6 p.487, p.525*

Terror Out of Zion: The Fight for Israeli Independence. .*v.6 p.609*

Terror, Terrorism, and the Human Condition. *v.4 p.662*

Terrorism: A Documentary and Reference Guide. .*v.4 p.565, p.661*

Terrorism: A Documentary History. *v.4 p.660*

Terrorism: A Guide to Events and Documents. .*v.4 p.659, p.660*

Terrorism and Counter-Terrorism: Criminological Perspectives. *v.6 p.251*

Terrorism and Counter-Terrorism: Understanding the New Security Environment, Readings and Interpretations. .*v.4 p.564*

Terrorism and the Constitution: Sacrificing Civil Liberties in the Name of National Security. *v.4 p.460, p.563, p.572*

Terrorism and the Liberal State. *v.4 p.498*

Terrorism and the Media. *v.4 p.559, p.661*

Terrorism and the UN: Before and after September 11. . . . .*v.4 p.633, p.658*

Terrorism and U. S. Foreign Policy. *v.4 p.565*

Terrorism and Violence in Southeast Asia: Transnational Challenges to States and Regional Stability. *v.4 p.662*

Terrorism, Freedom, and Security: Winning Without War. *v.4 p.563, p.564, p.659*

Terrorism in America: Pipe Bombs and Pipe Dreams. .*v.4 p.565*

Terrorism in Perspective. *v.6 p.251, p.252*

Terrorism: Origins and Evolution. *v.4 p.660*

Terrorism, Radicalism, and Populism in Agriculture. . .*v.5 p.15*

Terrorism: The Philosophical Issues. *v.4 p.661*

Terrorism vs. Democracy: The Liberal State Response. *v.4 p.498, p.662*

Terrorism's War with America: A History. *v.4 p.565*

▢ Terrorism. *v.4 p.565*

Terrorist Challenge to America. *v.4 p.563*

A Terry Teachout Reader. *v.1 p.46*

Tertiary Education in Colombia: Paving the Way for Reform. *v.4 p.337*

Tertullian, Treatise on Marriage and Remarriage: To His Wife, an Exhortation to Chastity Monogamy. *v.1 p.591*

Tertullian. *v.1 p.593*

Tess of the D'Urbervilles. *v.2 p.292*

Test Better, Teach Better: The Instructional Role of Assessment. *v.4 p.286*

Test Critiques, Vol. X. *v.5 p.601*

Test Equating, Scaling, and Linking: Methods and Practices. *v.5 p.601*

Test Interpretation and Diversity: Achieving Equity in Assessment. *v.4 p.286*

Test Theory: A Unified Treatment. *v.4 p.689*

Testament from a Prison Cell. *v.6 p.179*

Testimonio: On the Politics of Truth. *v.2 p.663*

Testimony: The Memoirs of Dmitri Shostakovich. *v.1 p.223, p.224, p.356*

▢ Testing and Accountability. *v.4 p.287*

Testing and Measurement: A User-Friendly Guide. . .*v.5 p.602*

Testing and Standards: A Brief Encyclopedia. *v.4 p.287*

Testing Statistical Hypotheses. *v.5 p.482*

Testing the Roosevelt Coalition: Connecticut Society and Politics in the Era of World War II. *v.3 p.489*

Testing Women, Testing the Fetus: The Social Impact of Amniocentesis in America. *v.4 p.47*

Testing Your Mettle: Tough Problems and Real-World Solutions for Middle and High School Teachers. *v.4 p.283*

Tests in Print, No. IV. *v.5 p.601*

Tests in Print VII. *v.5 p.600*

Texaco : roman. *v.2 p.536*

Texaco: A Novel. *v.2 p.536*

Texas; a Guide to the Lone Star State. *v.3 p.509, p.510*

▢ Texas Advertising. *v.4 p.426*

Texas after the Civil War: The Struggle of Reconstruction. *v.3 p.509*

Texas and the Mexican Revolution: A Study in State and National Border Policy, 1910-1920. . . . .*v.3 p.291*

Texas Panhandle Frontier. *v.3 p.509*

The Texas Rangers and the Mexican Revolution: The Bloodiest Decade, 1910-1920. . . . .*v.3 p.293, v.6 p.536*

Texas Rangers. *v.3 p.509*

Texas: The Lone Star State. *v.3 p.509*

A Texas-Mexican Cancionero: Folksongs of the Lower Border. *v.6 p.487, p.519, p.524*

The Texas-Mexican Conjunto: History of a Working-Class Music. *v.6 p.519*

Texas. *v.3 p.508*

The Texbook, Vol. A. *v.5 p.461*

Text and Act: Essays on Music and Performance. . . .*v.1 p.402*

The Text of the New Testament: An Introduction to the Critical Editions and to the Theory and Practice of Modern Textual Criticism. *v.1 p.624*

The Text of the New Testament: Its Transmission, Corruption, and Restoration. *v.1 p.626*

Textbook of Clinical Occupational and Environmental Medicine. *v.5 p.535*

Textbook of Medical Physiology: With Student Consult Access. *v.5 p.164*

A Textbook of Oarmanship. *v.4 p.865*

Textbook of Performing Arts Medicine. *v.1 p.50*

Textbook of Physical Chemistry. *v.5 p.276*

Textbook of Physical Diagnosis: History and Examination with Student Consult Access. *v.5 p.521*

Textbook of Polymer Science. *v.5 p.322*

Textbook of Pulmonary Diseases. *v.5 p.518*

Textbook of the Autoimmune Diseases. *v.5 p.517*

Textbook of Veterinary Internal Medicine: Diseases of the Dog and Cat. *v.5 p.54, p.57*

Textes pour un poème, 1949-1970. . . . . *v.2 p.529*

Textile Designs: Two Hundred Years of European and American Patterns for Printed Fabrics. *v.1 p.809*

Textiles: 5000 Years. *v.1 p.809*

Textiles and Capitalism in Mexico: An Economic History of the Obrajes, 1539-1840. . . . . *v.3 p.287*

Texts and Traditions: A Source Reader for the Study of Second Temple and Rabbinic Judaism. *v.1 p.548*

Texts and Transmission: A Survey of the Latin Classics. *v.2 p.425*

The Texts of Keats' Poems. *v.2 p.295*

Texts of Terror. *v.1 p.619*

Text--Sound Texts. *v.2 p.17*

Textual Criticism and Literary Interpretation. *v.2 p.164*

Textual Sources for the Study of Zoroastrianism. . . . *v.1 p.538*

e̲ The Texture of the Divine: Imagination in Medieval Islamic and Jewish Thought. *v.6 p.573, p.574*

Tönnies: Community and Civil Society. *v.6 p.719*

Thackeray and Slavery. *v.2 p.316*

Thackeray and Women. *v.2 p.315, v.6 p.746, p.747, p.755*

Thackeray: The Life of a Literary Man. *v.2 p.315*

Thackeray the Writer: From Pendennis to Denis Duval. *v.2 p.315*

Thaddeus Stevens: Nineteenth-Century Egalitarian. . *v.3 p.401*

Thai Radical Discourse: The Real Face of Thai Feudalism Today. *v.6 p.171*

Thailand: A Handbook of Historical Statistics. . . . *v.6 p.172*

Thailand: A Short History. *v.6 p.172*

Thailand and Japan's Southern Advance, 1940-1945. . . . . *v.6 p.171, p.172, p.181*

Thailand's Secret War: OSS, SOE and the Free Thai Underground During World War II. *v.6 p.172*

Thais. *v.2 p.490*

The Thames and Hudson Dictionary of Art and Artists. *v.1 p.665*

Thames and Hudson Dictionary of Art Terms. . . . *v.1 p.665*

The Thames and Hudson Dictionary of Graphic Design. *v.1 p.712*

Thank You, Comrade Stalin!: Soviet Public Culture from Revolution to Cold War. *v.3 p.225*

Thank You, Jeeves. *v.2 p.391*

The Thanks of the Fatherland: German Veterans after the Second World War. *v.3 p.176*

Thanks to God and the Revolution: The Oral History of a Nicaraguan Family. *v.3 p.302*

That American Rag: The Story of Ragtime in the United States. *v.1 p.260*

That Awful Mess on Via Merulana. *v.2 p.715*

That Championship Season. *v.2 p.150*

That Furious Lesbian: The Story of Mercedes de Acosta. *v.6 p.403*

That Greece Might Still Be Free: the Philhellenes in the War of Independence. *v.3 p.195*

That Half-Barbaric Twang: The Banjo in American Popular Culture. *v.1 p.278, p.390*

That Hideous Strength. *v.2 p.366*

That Night. *v.2 p.150*

That Noble Dream: The "Objectivity Question" and the American Historical Profession. *v.3 p.376*

That Noble Science of Politics: A Study in Nineteenth-Century Intellectual History. *v.3 p.111, p.127*

That Shining Band. *v.2 p.743*

That Was the Wild East: Film Culture, Unification, and the New Germany. *v.6 p.338*

The Thatcher Decade: Britain in the 1980s. *v.4 p.605*

That's Enough Folks: Black Images in Animated Cartoons, 1900-1960. . . . . *v.6 p.308*

The Thaw in Bulgarian Literature. *v.2 p.780*

Thayer's Life of Beethoven, Vol. 1. . . . . . *v.1 p.205, p.308*

Thayer's Life of Beethoven, Vol. 2. . . . . . *v.1 p.205, p.308*

Theaetetus. *v.1 p.424, p.425, p.482*

Theater and the Politics of Culture in Contemporary Singapore. *v.6 p.173*

The Theater Dictionary: British and American Terms in the Drama, Opera, and Ballet. *v.1 p.59*

Theater Essays of Arthur Miller. *v.2 p.102*

Theater in the Planned Society: Contemporary Drama in the German Democratic Republic in its Historical, Political and Cultural Context. *v.2 p.591*

Theater Management Handbook. *v.1 p.150*

Theater Neapolitan Style: Five One-Act Plays. . . . *v.2 p.715*

The Theater of Devotion: East Anglican Drama and Society in the Late Middle Ages. *v.2 p.185*

Theater of the Avant-Garde, 1890-1950: A Critical Anthology. *v.1 p.63, p.84, p.95*

The Theater of the Bauhaus. *v.1 p.148*

The Theater of Transformation: Postmodernism in American Drama. *v.1 p.87, p.118*

Theaters of Conversion: Religious Architecture and Indian Artisans in Colonial Mexico. *v.3 p.263*

Theaters. *v.1 p.155*

Theatre, 1. . . . . *v.2 p.514*

Theatre, 2. . . . . *v.2 p.513, p.514*

Theatre and Drama in Francophone Africa: A Critical Introduction. *v.1 p.130*

Theatre and Its Double. *v.1 p.55, p.138*

Theatre and Religion: Lancastrian Shakespeare. . . *v.2 p.229*

Theatre Architecture and Stage Machines: Engravings from the Encyclopedie, ou Dictionnaire Raisonne des Sciences, des Arts, et des Metiers. *v.1 p.154*

Theatre As Action: Soviet Russian Avant-Garde Aesthetics. *v.1 p.85, p.109*

Theatre Audiences: A Theory of Production and Reception. *v.1 p.138*

Theatre Australia (Un)limited: Australian Theatre since the 1950s. *v.2 p.741*

Theatre Backstage from A to Z. *v.1 p.140*

Theatre Companies of the World: Africa, Asia, Australia, and New Zealand, Canada, Eastern Europe, Latin America, the Middle East, Scandinavia, Vol. 1. . . . . *v.1 p.96, p.127, p.128, p.130, p.136*

Theatre, Court and City, 1595-1610: Drama and Social Space in London. *v.2 p.185*

A Theatre for Everybody: The Story of the Old Vic and Sadler's Wells. *v.1 p.99, p.144, p.149, p.154*

Theatre Guild, the First Ten Years, with Articles by the Directors. *v.1 p.113, p.144, p.149, p.152*

Theatre in Ancient India. *v.1 p.131, p.133*

Theatre in India. *v.1 p.131*

Theatre in Spain, 1490-1700. . . . . *v.2 p.640*

The Theatre in the Middle Ages: Western European Stage Conditions, C. 800-1576. . . . . . . *v.1 p.73, p.97, p.155*

Theatre in the Victorian Age. *v.2 p.188, v.6 p.754*

Theatre Language: A Dictionary of Terms in English of the Drama and Stage from Medieval to Modern Times,. *v.1 p.58*

Theatre Lighting from A to Z. *v.1 p.148*

Theatre Management: A Successful Guide to Producing Plays on Commercial and Non-Profit Stages. *v.1 p.149*

Theatre Management and Production in America: Commercial, Stock, Resident, College, Community, Theatre, and Presenting Organizations. *v.1 p.116, p.137*

Theatre Matters: Performance and Culture on the World Stage. *v.1 p.127, p.128*

Theatre of Dionysys in Athens. *v.2 p.402*

The Theatre of Erwin Piscator: Half a Century of Politics in the Theatre. *v.1 p.139, p.153*

The Theatre of García Lorca: Text, Performance, Psychoanalysis. *v.2 p.660*

The Theatre of Joseph Conrad: Reconstructed Fictions. *v.2 p.341*

The Theatre of Max Reinhardt. *v.1 p.81, p.84, p.108, p.146, p.148, p.152*

The Theatre of Mixed Means. *v.1 p.86*

The Theatre of Revolt: Studies in Modern Drama from Ibsen to Genet. *v.1 p.81, p.95*

The Theatre of Robert Wilson. *v.1 p.45*

The Theatre of Tennessee Williams: Twenty-Seven Wagons Full of Cotton and Other Short Plays, Vol. 6. . . . . . *v.2 p.135*

The Theatre of the Absurd. *v.1 p.92, p.96*

The Theatre of the London Fairs in the 18th Century. *v.1 p.103*

The Theatre of Yesterday and Tomorrow: Commedia Dell'Arte on the Modern Stage. *v.1 p.91, p.107*

Theatre, Performance and Technology: The Development of Scenography in the Twentieth Century. *v.1 p.146*

Theatre Performance and Technology: The Development of Scenography in the Twentieth Century. *v.1 p.146*

Theatre, Performance, and the Historical Avant-Garde. *v.1 p.84, p.95*

The Theatre Props Handbook. *v.1 p.147*

Theatre Street. *v.1 p.9*

Theatre, the Rediscovery of Style. *v.1 p.153*

Theatre, Theory, Postmodernism. *v.1 p.40, p.55, p.86*

Theatre USA, 1668 to 1957. . . . . *v.1 p.115*

Theatres and Opera Houses. *v.1 p.154*

Theatres of Independence: Drama, Theory, and Urban Performance in India since 1947. . . . . . *v.1 p.131, p.134*

The Theatres of London. *v.1 p.101, p.155*

The Theatres Trust Guide to British Theatres, 1750-1950. . . . . *v.1 p.61, p.103*

Theatre. *v.2 p.371, p.541*

Theatrical Costume, Masks, Make-Up and Wigs: A Bibliography and Iconography. *v.1 p.140, p.151*

Theatrical Design and Production: An Introduction to Scene Design and Construction, Lighting, Sound, Costume, and Makeup. *v.1 p.134, p.142*

Theatrical Designers: An International Biographical Dictionary. *v.1 p.140, p.147*

Theatrical Gestures of Belgian Modernism: Dada, Surrealism, Futurism, and Pure Plastic in the Twentieth Century Belgian Theatre. *v.1 p.84, p.86, p.111*

Theatrical Space: A Guide for Directors and Designers. *v.1 p.142, p.146, p.152, p.154*

Thebaid: Achilleid, Books 8-12. . . . . *v.2 p.443*

Thebaid: Bks. 1-7. . . . . *v.2 p.443*

The Thebaid: Seven Against Thebes. *v.2 p.443*

The Theban Hegemony, 371-362 B. C. *v.3 p.19*

Thebes in the Fifth Century. *v.3 p.17, v.6 p.711*

Their Day in the Sun: Women of the 1932 Olympics. . . . *v.4 p.808, p.837, p.846, p.860, p.868, p.869*

Their Fathers' God. *v.2 p.629*

Their Majesties' Servants or Annals of the English Stage from Thomas Betterton to Edmund Kean; Actors, Authors, Audiences. *v.1 p.99, p.140, p.144*

Their Tattered Flags: The Epic of the Confederacy. *v.3 p.402, p.429*

The Thelonious Monk Reader. *v.1 p.264, p.342*

Them: Stalin's Polish Puppets. *v.3 p.255*

Thematic Cartography and Geographic Visualization. *v.4 p.376*

Thematic Catalogues in Music: An Annotated Bibliography. *v.1 p.165*

Thematic Origins of Scientific Thought: Kepler to Einstein. *v.5 p.390, p.391*

The Thematic Process in Music. *v.1 p.372*

Thematisch-systematisches Verzeichnis der musikalischen Werke von Johann Sebastian Bach: Bach-Werke-Verzeichnis (BWV). *v.1 p.164, p.186, p.304*

Theme Park Landscapes: Antecedents and Variations. *v.1 p.820*

Themes and Conventions of Elizabethan Tragedy. . . *v.2 p.185*

Themes and Episodes. *v.1 p.225, p.360*

Themes and Variations in Shakespeare's Sonnets. . . *v.2 p.225*

Themes in Economic Anthropology. *v.4 p.28*

Themes in the History of Japanese Garden Art. *v.1 p.819*

Themes of Islamic Civilization. *v.1 p.554, p.555*

The Theming of America: American Dreams, Media Fantasies, and Themed Environments. *v.6 p.712*

Themis, a Study of the Social Origins of Greek Religion. *v.1 p.532*

Then and Now. *v.2 p.371*

Then I Was Black: South African Political Identitites in Transition. *v.4 p.614*

Then to the Rock Let Me Fly: Luther Bohanon and Judicial Activism. *v.4 p.541*

The Theocrat. *v.6 p.659*

Theocritus: Idylls 1, 3, 4, 6, 7, 10, 11 and 13. . . . . *v.2 p.421*

Theocritus' Pastoral Analogies: The Formation of a Genre. *v.2 p.421*

Theocritus: Select Poems. *v.2 p.421*

Theodicy. *v.1 p.459*

Theodor Storm's Craft of Fiction. *v.2 p.598*

Theodor Storm.. . . . .*v.2 p.598*

Theodore Dreiser: An American Journey. *v.2 p.70*

Theodore Dreiser, Apostle of Nature. *v.2 p.70*

Theodore Dreiser: Beyond Naturalism. *v.2 p.70*

A Theodore Dreiser Encyclopedia. *v.2 p.70*

Theodore Dreiser Revisited. *v.2 p.70*

Theodore Roethke: Selected Poems. *v.2 p.114*

Theodore Roethke's Far Fields: The Evolution of His
    Poetry. *v.2 p.113*

Theodore Roosevelt: A Strenuous Life. *v.3 p.469*

Theodore Roosevelt, American Politician: An
    Assessment. *v.3 p.439*

Theodore Roosevelt: An Autobiography. *v.3 p.478, p.479*

Theodore Roosevelt and the Rise of the Modern Navy. .*v.3 p.384*

Theodore Roosevelt and World Order: Police Power in
    International Relations. *v.3 p.304*

Theodore Roosevelt: Letters and Speeches. *v.3 p.478*

The Theodosian Code. *v.3 p.192*

Theodosian Empresses: Women and Imperial Dominion in Late
    Antiquity. *v.3 p.31*

Theogony and Works and Days. *v.1 p.532, v.2 p.413*

Theologians of the Baptist Tradition. *v.1 p.583*

Theological Aesthetics: A Reader. *v.1 p.596*

Theological Tractates and the Consolation of
    Philosophy. *v.2 p.448*

A Theologico-Political Treatise and a Political Treatise. .*v.1 p.477*

Theology and the Kingdom of God. *v.1 p.638*

Theology and the Scientific Imagination from the Middle Ages
    to the Seventeenth Century. *v.3 p.47*

Theology in America: Christian Thought from the Age of the
    Puritans to the Civil War.. . . . .*v.1 p.605*

Theology in America: The Major Protestant Voices from
    Puritanism to Neo-Orthodoxy. *v.1 p.633*

The Theology of al-Ash'ari : The Arabic Texts of al-Ash'ari's
    Kitab al-luma' and Risalat istihsan al-khawd fi 'ilm
    al-kalam : with Briefly Annotated Translations, and Appendices
    Containing Material Pertinent to the Study of
    al-Ash'ari. *v.1 p.556*

Theology of Culture. *v.1 p.634*

Theology of Discontent: The Ideological Foundation of the
    Islamic Revolution in Iran. *v.6 p.632*

Theology of Hope: On the Ground and the Implications of a
    Christian Eschatology. *v.1 p.645*

Theology of Jewish Christian Reality: Discerning the Way, Pt.
    1. . . . .*v.1 p.637*

The Theology of John Calvin. *v.1 p.588*

Theology of Liberation. *v.1 p.643*

The Theology of Paul the Apostle. *v.1 p.631*

The Theology of the Book of Revelation. *v.1 p.632*

The Theology of the Gospel of Matthew. *v.1 p.629*

Theology of the New Testament. *v.1 p.625*

A Theology of the New Testament. *v.1 p.625*

Theology of the Old Testament: Testimony, Dispute,
    Advocacy. *v.1 p.618*

The Theology of Unity. *v.1 p.557*

Theophile Gautier. *v.2 p.492*

Theophrastus - Characters: Herodas - Mimes: Sophron and
    Other Mime Fragments. *v.2 p.421*

Theophrastus: Characters. *v.2 p.421*

Theorems and Counterexamples in Mathematics. . . .*v.5 p.489*

Theoretical Acoustics.. . . . .*v.5 p.567*

Theoretical and Physical Principles of Organic
    Reactivity. *v.5 p.296*

Theoretical Anthropology. *v.4 p.23*

Theoretical Concepts in Physics: An Alternative View of
    Theoretical Reasoning in Physics. *v.5 p.548*

Theoretical Criminology. *v.6 p.249*

Theoretical Debates in Spanish American Literature. . .*v.2 p.664*

Theoretical Ecosystem Ecology: Understanding Nutrient
    Cycles. *v.5 p.182, p.189*

Theoretical Foundations of Behavior Therapy. *v.5 p.666*

Theoretical Logic in Sociology. *v.4 p.679*

Theoretical Mechanics. *v.5 p.547*

Theoretical Morphology: The Concept and Its
    Applications. *v.5 p.155*

Theoretical Nuclear and Subnuclear Physics. *v.5 p.553*

Theoretical Numerical Analysis: A Functional Analysis
    Framework. *v.5 p.491*

Theoretical Perspectives on Cognitive Aging. . .*v.5 p.628, p.632*

Theoretical Writings. *v.1 p.455*

Theories and Documents of Contemporary Art: A Sourcebook of
    Artists' Writings. *v.1 p.681*

Theories of Consciousness: An Introduction. *v.1 p.497*

Theories of Culture: A New Agenda for Theology. . .*v.1 p.637*

Theories of Culture in Postmodern Times. *v.4 p.22*

Theories of Democracy: A Reader. *v.4 p.506*

Theories of Economic Growth and Development. . . .*v.4 p.242*

Theories of Ethics. *v.1 p.487*

Theories of International Relations: Transition vs.
    Persistence. *v.4 p.627*

Theories of Learning. *v.4 p.356*

Theories of Mathematics Learning. *v.5 p.464*

Theories of Memory. *v.5 p.610*

Theories of Mood and Cognition: A Users Handbook. .*v.5 p.657*

Theories of Nationalism: A Critical Introduction. . . .*v.4 p.495*

Theories of Perception and the Concept of Structure: A Review
    and Critical Analysis with an Introduction to a
    Dynamic. *v.5 p.605, p.606*

Theories of Scientific Method: The Renaissance Through the
    Nineteenth Century. *v.5 p.399, p.400*

Theories of Society, Vol. 1. . . . .*v.4 p.683*

Theories of Surplus Value. *v.4 p.238*

Theories of the Symbol.. . . . .*v.5 p.622*

Theories of the Theatre: A Historical and Critical Survey from
    the Greeks to the Present. *v.1 p.56, p.138*

Theories of Translation: An Anthology of Essays from Dryden
    to Derrida. *v.2 p.574*

Theories of Truth: A Critical Introduction. . . .*v.1 p.482, p.493*

Theories of Value and Distribution since Adam Smith: Ideology
    and Economic Theory. *v.4 p.217*

Title Index

Theories of Women's Studies. *v.6 p.462*

Theories on the Scrap Heap: Scientists and Philosophers on the Falsification, Rejection, and Replacement of Theories. *v.3 p.45*

Theorizing Black Feminisms: The Visionary Pragmatism of Black Women. *v.6 p.6, p.44, p.428*

Theorizing Composition: A Critical Sourcebook of Theory and Scholarship in Contemporary Composition Studies. *v.2 p.565*

Theorizing Documentary. *v.6 p.310*

Theorizing Nationalism: Debates and Issues in Social Theory. *v.4 p.494*

Theorizing Satire: Essays in Literary Criticism. *v.2 p.195*

Theorizing the City: The New Urban Anthropology Reader. *v.6 p.710*

Theory and Applications in Inorganic Chemistry. . . .*v.5 p.305*

The Theory and Design of Economic Development. . *v.4 p.258*

Theory and Measurement: Causality Issues in Milton Friedman's Monetary Economics. *v.4 p.232*

Theory and Methods of Scaling. *v.5 p.599*

Theory and Practice in Archaeology. *v.4 p.6*

Theory and Practice in the Organic Laboratory: With Microscale and Standard Scale Experiments. *v.5 p.301*

Theory and Practice of Community Social Work. . . .*v.4 p.758*

The Theory and Practice of Group Psychotherapy. . .*v.5 p.669*

Theory and Practice of Lubrication for Engineers. . . .*v.5 p.708*

Theory and Practice of Modern Government. *v.4 p.574*

Theory and Research on Small Groups. *v.4 p.688*

Theory and Resistance in Education: Towards a Pedagogy for the Opposition. *v.4 p.343*

A Theory for All Music: Problems and Solutions in the Analysis of Non-Western Forms. *v.1 p.382*

Theory for Art History. *v.1 p.702*

Theory in Archaeology: A World Perspective. *v.4 p.6*

Theory in Landscape Architecture: A Reader. *v.1 p.814*

The Theory of Atomic Spectra. *v.5 p.562*

The Theory of Business Enterprise. *v.4 p.251*

Theory of Capitalist Development. *v.4 p.236, p.237*

Theory of Collective Behavior. *v.4 p.692*

A Theory of Content and Other Essays. *v.1 p.482*

The Theory of Drama. *v.1 p.56, p.87*

The Theory of Economic Development: An Inquiry into Profits, Capital, Credit, Interest and the Business Cycle. *v.4 p.212, p.230, p.235, p.245*

Theory of Economic Dynamics. *v.4 p.202*

A Theory of Economic History. *v.4 p.209*

Theory of Elasticity, Vol. 7. . . . .*v.5 p.546*

The Theory of Equilibrium Growth. *v.4 p.243*

The Theory of Evolution: What It Is, Where It Came from, and Why It Works. *v.5 p.194*

Theory of Evolving Tonality. *v.1 p.374*

The Theory of Finite Groups: An Introduction. . . .*v.5 p.474*

A Theory of Freedom. *v.4 p.515*

Theory of Functions of a Real Variable, Vol.1. . . .*v.5 p.490*

Theory of Games and Economic Behavior. *v.5 p.505*

Theory of Garden Art. *v.1 p.818*

A Theory of Goal Setting and Task Performance. . .*v.5 p.579*

Theory of Ground Vehicles. *v.5 p.716, p.717*

The Theory of Groups. *v.5 p.474*

Theory of Harmony. *v.1 p.373*

Theory of Information and Coding. *v.5 p.408*

The Theory of Interest: As Determined by Impatience to Spend and Opportunity to Invest It. *v.4 p.200*

The Theory of Interest. *v.4 p.225, p.246*

Theory of Interest. *v.5 p.504*

Theory of International Law. *v.4 p.627*

Theory of International Politics. *v.4 p.625, p.627*

The Theory of Intuition in Husserl's Phenomenology. *v.1 p.469, p.470*

The Theory of Island Biogeography. *v.5 p.168*

A Theory of Justice. *v.1 p.501, v.4 p.514*

The Theory of Knowledge: A Thematic Introduction. *v.1 p.482*

Theory of Knowledge. *v.1 p.482*

Theory of Literature. *v.2 p.567*

Theory of Matrices, 2 v. *v.5 p.472*

The Theory of Money, Price and Exchange. *v.4 p.234*

The Theory of Moral Sentiments. *v.4 p.219, p.220*

The Theory of Morality. *v.1 p.487*

Theory of Ordinary Differential Equations. *v.5 p.487*

A Theory of Parties and Electoral Systems. *v.4 p.579*

The Theory of Play and Recreation. *v.4 p.358*

The Theory of Political Economy. *v.4 p.231*

Theory of Population Genetics and Evolutionary Ecology: An Introduction. *v.5 p.502*

The Theory of Precious Metals and of Money. *v.4 p.220*

A Theory of Psychological Scaling. *v.5 p.599*

The Theory of Public Finance: A Study in Public Economy. *v.4 p.247*

Theory of Recursive Functions and Effective Computability. *v.5 p.471*

A Theory of Semiotics. *v.2 p.570, v.4 p.424*

Theory of Sets. *v.5 p.471*

The Theory of Social and Economic Organization. . .*v.4 p.213*

Theory of Sound, 1. . . . .*v.5 p.567*

Theory of Superconductivity. *v.5 p.565*

Theory of the Consumption Function. *v.4 p.231, p.250*

A Theory of the Evolution of Development. *v.5 p.190*

A Theory of the Good and the Right. *v.1 p.486, p.487*

The Theory of the Leisure Class. *v.4 p.251, p.725*

The Theory of the Mixed Constitution in Antiquity: A Critical Analysis of Polybuis Political Ideas. *v.4 p.490*

Theory of the Novel: A Historical Approach. *v.2 p.578*

The Theory of the Novel: A Historico-Philosophical Essay on the Forms of Great Epic Literature. *v.2 p.462*

Theory of Unemployment. *v.4 p.254*

The Theory of Value. *v.4 p.234*

The Theory of Wages in Classical Economics: A Study of Adam Smith, David Ricardo and Their Contemporaries. . *v.4 p.220*

The Theory of Wages. *v.4 p.254*

Theory of Wing Sections: Including a Summary of Airfoil Data. *v.5 p.717*

Theory on Gender: Feminism on Theory. *v.6 p.427*

Theory/Theatre: An Introduction. *v.1 p.56*

Thera, Pompeii of the Ancient Aegean: Excavations at Akrotiri, 1967-1979. . . . .*v.3 p.15*

Therapeutic Immunology. *v.5 p.518*

Therapeutic Modalities in Rehabilitation. *v.5 p.535*

Therapeutic Recreation and the Nature of Disabilities. *v.4 p.786, p.801, p.830*

Therapeutic Recreation: Cases and Exercises. *v.4 p.786, p.787, p.830*

Therapeutic Recreation for Exceptional Children: Let Me in, I Want to Play. *v.4 p.783, p.800, p.829, p.830*

Therapeutic Recreation Programs in the Community: An Inclusive Approach. *v.4 p.783, p.785, p.829*

Therapeutic Riding II Strategies for Rehabilitation. *v.4 p.829, p.879*

The Therapy of Desire: Theory and Practice in Hellenistic Ethics. *v.1 p.428*

There Are No Slaves in France: The Political Culture of Race and Slavery in the Ancien Regime. *v.3 p.147*

There Are Two Errors in the the Title of This Book: A Sourcebook of Philosophical Puzzles, Problems and Paradoxes. *v.1 p.492*

There Is a River: The Black Struggle for Freedom in America. *v.6 p.5*

There Never Was a Once upon a Time. *v.2 p.676*

There She Is, Miss America: The Politics of Sex, Beauty, and Race in America's Most Famous Pageant. *v.6 p.449*

Theremin: Ether Music and Espionage. .*v.1 p.214, p.244, p.363*

There's Still Time: The Success of the Endangered Species Act. *v.5 p.179*

Therese et Peirrette a l'Ecole des Saints-Anges: Roman. .*v.2 p.541*

Therese Raquin. *v.2 p.505*

Thermal Analysis: Fundamentals and Applications to Polymer Science. *v.5 p.323*

Thermal Conductivity of the Elements: A Comprehensive Review. *v.5 p.286*

Thermal Constants of Substances, Set. *v.5 p.287*

Thermal Physics. *v.5 p.559, p.560*

Thermochemical Data of Elements and Compounds. . .*v.5 p.286*

Thermochemical Data of Organic Compounds. . . .*v.5 p.300*

Thermochemical Data of Pure Substances. *v.5 p.285*

Thermochemical Properties of Inorganic Substances, Set. *v.5 p.302*

Thermochemical Properties of Inorganic Substances, v. 1. . . . .*v.5 p.302*

Thermochemical Properties of Inorganic Substances. .*v.5 p.302*

Thermodex: An Index of Selected Thermodynamic and Physical Property Resources. *v.5 p.285*

Thermodynamic and Physical Property Data. *v.5 p.287*

Thermodynamic Properties of Individual Substances, Various Volumes. *v.5 p.286*

Thermodynamics and an Introduction to Thermostatistics, Level 4. . . . .*v.5 p.559, p.560*

Thermodynamics and Kinetics for the Biological Sciences. *v.5 p.327*

Thermodynamics and Statistical Mechanics. . .*v.5 p.277, p.560*

Thermodynamics in Geochemistry: The Equilibrium Model. *v.5 p.440*

Thermodynamics of Biochemical Reactions. *v.5 p.111*

Thermodynamics of Complex Systems. *v.5 p.564*

Thermodynamics of Materials, Vol. 1. . . . .*v.5 p.324, p.712*

Thermodynamics of Materials, Vol. 2. . . . .*v.5 p.324, p.712*

Thermodynamics of Molecular Species. *v.5 p.279*

Thermodynamics of Natural Systems. *v.5 p.277*

Thermodynamics: Principles Characterizing Physical and Chemical Processes. *v.5 p.277*

Thermodynamics. *v.5 p.560*

Thermofluids: An Integrated Approach to Thermodynamics and Fluid Mechanics Principles. *v.5 p.712*

Thesaurus of Metallurgical Terms : The Vocabulary That Controls Storage and Retrieval of Technical Information in Metallurgy. *v.5 p.731*

Thesaurus of Orchestral Devices. *v.1 p.393*

Thesaurus of Scales and Melodic Patterns. . . .*v.1 p.373, p.374*

These Are My Rivers: New and Selected Poems, 1955-1993. . . . .*v.2 p.75*

These Days. *v.2 p.344, p.345*

They Burn the Thistles: Memed My Hawk, Part II. . .*v.6 p.667*

They Called Me King Tiger: My Struggle for the Land and Our Rights. *v.6 p.536, p.540*

They Called Them Greasers: Anglo Attitudes Toward Mexicans in Texas, 1821-1900. . . . .*v.3 p.508*

They Called Them Greasers: Anglo Attitudes toward Mexicans in Texas, 1821-1900. . . . .*v.6 p.534*

They Came Before Columbus: The African Presence in Ancient America. *v.6 p.9*

They Came Like Swallows. *v.2 p.97*

They Came to Japan: An Anthology of European Reports on Japan, 1543-1640. . . . .*v.6 p.223*

They Cleared the Lane: The NBA's Black Pioneers. *v.4 p.833, p.854, p.855, p.898*

They Don't Teach Corporate in College: A Twenty-Something's Guide to the Business World. *v.4 p.167*

They Eat from Their Labor: Work and Social Change in Colonial Bolivia. *v.3 p.325*

They Saw It Happen: An Anthology of Eye-Witnesses' Accounts of Events in British History, 1465-1688. . . . . .*v.3 p.90*

They Shoot Horses, Don't They? *v.2 p.97*

They Would Never Hurt a Fly: War Criminals on Trial in the Hague. *v.2 p.818*

They're All My Children: Foster Mothering in America. .*v.4 p.759*

They're Not Dumb, They're Different: Stalking the Second Tier. *v.5 p.464*

Théâtre complet, Vol. 1. . . . .*v.2 p.481*

Théâtre complet, Vol. 2. . . . .*v.2 p.481*

Théâtre complet. *v.2 p.506, p.514, p.518*

Théâtre Complet. *v.2 p.518*

Théâtre complet. *v.2 p.520, p.523*

Théâtre Complet. *v.2 p.528*

Théâtre de Clara Gazul ; Romans et nouvelles. . . .*v.2 p.498*

Théâtre, Vol. 1. . . . .*v.2 p.495*

Théâtre, vol. 1. . . . .*v.2 p.513, p.516, p.517, p.526*

Théâtre, Vol. 2. . . . . *v.2 p.495*

Théâtre, vol. 2. . . . . *v.2 p.513, p.516, p.517, p.526*

Théâtre, vol. 3. . . . . *v.2 p.516, p.517*

Théâtre, vol. 4. . . . . *v.2 p.516, p.517*

Théâtre, vol. 5. . . . . *v.2 p.517*

Théâtre, vol. 6. . . . . *v.2 p.517*

Théâtre. *v.2 p.507, p.509, p.520, p.523, p.529*

Thérèse et Isabelle : texte intégral. *v.2 p.521*

The Thief's Journal. *v.2 p.519, v.6 p.396*

A Thin Cosmic Rain: Particles from Outer Space. . . *v.5 p.73*

Thin Ice: Unlocking the Secrets of Climate in the World's
Highest Mountains. *v.6 p.293*

The Thin Red Line. *v.2 p.90*

Thin-Film Solar Cells: Next Generation Photovoltaics and Its
Applications. *v.5 p.362*

Things: A Story of the Sixties. *v.2 p.533*

Things Come to Life: Spontaneous Generation
Revisited. *v.5 p.79, p.113*

Things Fall Apart. *v.2 p.753*

Things from the Bush: A Contemporary History of the Omaheke
Bushmen. *v.6 p.76, p.77*

Things of Darkness: Economies of Race and Gender in Early
Modern England. *v.6 p.478*

Things Seen and Unseen: Discourse and Ideology in Tokugawa
Nativism. *v.6 p.224*

Things That Happen Because They Should: A Teleological
Approach to Action. *v.1 p.514*

The Things They Carried. *v.2 p.151*

The Things They Say Behind Your Back: Stereotypes and the
Myths Behind Them. *v.4 p.694*

The Things We Used to Say. *v.2 p.718*

Think: A Compelling Introduction to Philosophy. . . *v.1 p.416*

Thinking about Consciousness. *v.1 p.497*

Thinking about Crime: Sense and Sensibility in American Penal
Culture. *v.6 p.274*

Thinking about Crime. *v.6 p.250, p.251*

Thinking about Growth: And Other Essays on Economic Growth
and Welfare. *v.4 p.242*

Thinking about International Ethics: Moral Theory and Cases
from American Foreign Policy. *v.4 p.641, p.644*

Thinking about Logic: An Introduction to the Philosophy of
Logic. *v.1 p.493, p.494*

Thinking about "Beowulf". *v.2 p.205*

Thinking about Ordinary Differential Equations. . . . *v.5 p.487*

Thinking about Political Psychology. . . . *v.4 p.483, v.5 p.643*

Thinking about the Earth: A History of Ideas in
Geology. *v.5 p.418*

Thinking about Urban Form: Papers on Urban Morphology,
1932-1998. . . . . *v.4 p.395, v.6 p.720*

Thinking about Women: Sociological Perspectives on Sex and
Gender. *v.4 p.743, v.6 p.433*

Thinking Again: Education after Postmodernism. *v.4 p.338, p.339*

Thinking: An Experimental and Social Study. . . . *v.5 p.608*

Thinking and Deciding. *v.4 p.82*

Thinking and Writing about Art History. *v.1 p.701*

The Thinking Body: A Study of the Balancing Forces of
Dynamic Man. *v.1 p.52*

Thinking Globally, Acting Regionally: GIS and Data
Visualization for Social Science and Public Policy
Research. *v.4 p.387*

Thinking in Jazz: The Infinite Art of Improvisation. . *v.1 p.257*

e Thinking in the Spirit: Theologies of the Early Pentecostal
Movement. *v.1 p.587*

Thinking Inside the Block Schedule: Strategies for Teaching in
Extended Periods of Time. *v.4 p.288*

Thinking It Through: An Introduction to Contemporary
Philosophy. *v.1 p.416*

Thinking Medieval: An Introduction to the Study of the Middle
Ages. *v.3 p.62*

Thinking Musically: Experiencing Music, Expressing
Culture. *v.1 p.284*

Thinking Orientals: Migration, Contact, and Exoticism in
Modern America. *v.6 p.115, p.120, p.125*

Thinking Physics: Practical Lessons in Critical Thinking,
Gedanken Physics. *v.5 p.563*

Thinking Queer: Sexuality, Culture and Education. . *v.6 p.386*

Thinking Styles. *v.5 p.609*

The Third Current of Revolution: Inside the North American
Front of el Salvador's Guerrilla War. *v.3 p.300*

The Third Dimension. *v.5 p.293*

The Third Eye: Race, Cinema, and Ethnographic
Spectacle. *v.6 p.310, p.311*

The Third Man and the Fallen Idol. *v.2 p.350*

The Third Policeman. *v.2 p.373*

The Third Reich: A New History. *v.3 p.171*

The Third Rose: Gertrude Stein and Her World. . . . *v.2 p.121*

The Third Way and Its Critics. *v.4 p.493*

Third World Debt: The Search for a Solution. *v.4 p.258*

A Third World Novel of Expatriation: A Study of Emigre
Fiction by Indian, West African and Caribbean
Writers. *v.2 p.762*

Third World Women and the Politics of Feminism. . *v.6 p.457*

The Thirst of the Salt Mountain: A Trilogy of Plays. . *v.2 p.817*

Thirsty for God. *v.1 p.650*

The Thirteen Books of Euclid's Elements, Vol. 1. *v.5 p.465, p.495*

The Thirteen Books of Euclid's Elements, Vol. 2. *v.5 p.465, p.495*

The Thirteen Books of Euclid's Elements, Vol. 3. *v.5 p.465, p.495*

Thirteen Days: A Memoir of the Cuban Missile
Crisis. *v.3 p.389, p.390, p.473*

Thirteen Ways of Looking at the Novel. *v.2 p.579*

The Thirties and After: Essays. *v.2 p.384*

The Thirties: From Notebooks and Diaries of the
Period. *v.2 p.137*

Thirty an' Seen a Lot. *v.6 p.504, p.511*

Thirty Poems from the Carmina Burana. *v.2 p.450*

e Thirty Years a Slave: From Bondage to Freedom. *v.6 p.6, p.17*

Thirty Years of Treason. *v.3 p.445*

The Thirty Years War: The Holy Roman Empire and Europe,
1618 to 1648. . . . . *v.3 p.165*

The Thirty Years War. *v.3 p.166*

This Affair of Louisiana. *v.3 p.411*

This Bittersweet Soil: The Chinese in California Agriculture, 1860-1910. . . . .*v.6 p.116, p.126*

This Blinding Absence of Light. *v.2 p.544*

This Bloody Mary Is the Last Thing I Own. *v.4 p.856*

This Book of Starres: Learning to Read George Herbert. *v.2 p.249*

This Bridge Called My Back: Writings by Radical Women of Color. *v.6 p.97, p.113, p.479*

This Bridge We Call Home: Radical Visions for Transformation. *v.6 p.479*

This Business of Music: The Definitive Guide to the Music Industry. *v.1 p.384*

This Changes Everything: The Relational Revolution in Psychology. *v.5 p.648*

This Culture of Ours: Intellectual Transitions in T'ang and Sung China. *v.6 p.185*

This Day in American History. *v.3 p.372, p.373*

This Dynamic Earth. *v.5 p.418*

This Far by Faith: Stories from the African American Religious Experience. *v.6 p.36*

This Fine Piece of Water: An Environmental History of Long Island Sound. *v.6 p.294*

This Fragile Land: A Natural History of the Nebraska Sandhills. *v.3 p.524*

This Great Calamity: The Irish Famine 1845-52. .*v.3 p.138, p.139*

This Great Stage: Image and Structure in King Lear. . *v.2 p.230*

This Hallowed Ground. *v.3 p.430*

This Incomparable Land: A Book of American Nature Writing. *v.5 p.232*

This Is Detroit, 1701-2001. . . . .*v.3 p.517*

This Is My Best: Great Writers Share Their Favorite Work. *v.2 p.19*

This Is No Place for a Woman: Nadine Gordimer, Nayantara Sahgal, Buchi Emecheta, and the Politics of Gender. *v.2 p.755, p.756*

This Is Not a Story and Other Stories. *v.2 p.479*

This Is Not a Weasel: A Close Look at Nature's Most Confusing Terms. *v.5 p.80, p.246*

This Is the Beat Generation: New York, San Francisco, Paris. *v.2 p.10, v.6 p.730, p.731*

This Is Where I Came In: Black America in the 1960s. *v.6 p.4, p.15*

This Kind of War: The Classic Korean War History. . *v.6 p.236*

This Land Is Our Land: Immigrants and Power in Miami. *v.6 p.539, p.550*

This Real Night. *v.2 p.389*

This Sacred Trust: American Nationality, 1778-1898. .*v.3 p.369*

This Side of Peace: A Personal Account. *v.6 p.616*

This Side of Reality: Modern Czech Writing. *v.2 p.781*

This Side Up: Spatial Determination in the Early Development of Animals. *v.5 p.162*

This Sovereign Land: A New Vision for Governing the West. *v.6 p.300*

This Strange Illness: Alcoholism and Bill W. *v.5 p.664*

This Thing of Darkness: A Sociology of the Enemy. . *v.4 p.766*

This Time: New and Selected Poems. *v.2 p.156*

This Time We Knew: Western Responses to Genocide in Bosnia. *v.4 p.652*

This Way for the Gas, Ladies and Gentlemen. *v.2 p.789*

This We Believe: Successful Schools for Young Adolescents: A Position Paper of the National Middle School Association. *v.4 p.367*

This Well-Wooded Land: Americans and Their Forests from Colonial Times to the Present. *v.5 p.37*

Thomas - Treaties. *v.4 p.437, p.476*

Thomas and Jane Carlyle: The Portrait of a Marriage. .*v.2 p.275*

Thomas and Joseph Warton. *v.2 p.264*

Thomas B. Reed, Parliamentarian. *v.3 p.434*

Thomas Carlyle: A Biography. *v.2 p.277*

Thomas Carlyle: A History of His Life in London. . .*v.2 p.276*

Thomas Carlyle: A History of the First Forty Years of His Life. *v.2 p.276*

Thomas Carlyle. *v.2 p.277*

Thomas Cranmer. *v.3 p.101, p.122*

Thomas Dekker. *v.2 p.218*

Thomas E. Dewey and His Times. *v.3 p.461*

Thomas Eakins: His Life and Art. *v.1 p.740, p.741*

Thomas Eakins. *v.1 p.699*

Thomas Food and Beverage Market Place, 2002/2003. .*v.4 p.160*

Thomas Food and Beverage Market Place 2006. . . .*v.4 p.160*

Thomas Gainsborough. *v.1 p.746*

Thomas Gray: A Life. *v.2 p.249*

Thomas Hardy A to Z: The Essential Reference to His Life and Work. *v.2 p.292*

Thomas Hardy: His Life and Work. *v.2 p.291*

Thomas Hardy's 'Facts' Notebook: A Critical Edition. *v.2 p.291*

Thomas Harriot: A Biography. *v.5 p.397*

Thomas Harriot: An Elizabethan Man of Science. . .*v.5 p.396*

Thomas Heywood. *v.2 p.219*

Thomas Hood: His Life and Times. *v.2 p.291*

Thomas Hutchinson and the Origins of the American Revolution. *v.3 p.488*

Thomas Jefferson: An Intimate History. *v.3 p.411*

Thomas Jefferson and the Development of American Public Education. *v.4 p.341*

Thomas Jefferson: And the New Nation - Return to Monticello, Vol. 2. . . . .*v.3 p.412*

Thomas Jefferson: And the New Nation - to the Vice Presidency, Set. *v.3 p.412*

Thomas Jefferson and the Stony Mountains: Exploring the West from Monticello. *v.3 p.411*

Thomas Jefferson's Views on Public Education. *v.4 p.298*

Thomas l'imposteur : histoire. *v.2 p.514*

Thomas l'obscur : Première version, 1941 : roman. . .*v.2 p.510*

Thomas Lodge and Other Elizabethans. *v.2 p.216*

Thomas Love Peacock. *v.2 p.302*

Thomas Mann: A Life. *v.2 p.613*

Thomas Mann Diaries, 1918-1939. . . . .*v.2 p.613*

Thomas Mann: Eros and Literature. *v.6 p.402*

Thomas Mann: The Uses of Tradition. *v.2 p.613*

Thomas McKnight: Windows on Paradise. *v.1 p.760*

A Thomas Merton Reader. *v.2 p.98*

Thomas Middleton and the New Comedy Tradition. . .*v.2 p.221*

Thomas' "Tristan" and the "Folie Tristan d'Oxford". . *v.2 p.466*

Thomas More: A Biography. *v.3 p.100*

Thomas More: History and Providence. *v.3 p.100, p.120*

Thomas More. *v.1 p.579, v.3 p.100*

Thomas Muentzer, a Destroyer of the Godless: The Making of a
    Sixteenth-Century Religious Revolutionary. *v.1 p.603*

Thomas Muntzer: Apocalyptic Mystic and
    Revolutionary. *v.1 p.603*

Thomas Muntzer: Theology and Revolution in the German
    Reformation. *v.3 p.166*

Thomas Paine: Social and Political Thought. *v.4 p.491*

Thomas R. R. Cobb: The Making of a Southern
    Nationalist. *v.3 p.503*

Thomas Register of American Manufacturers. *v.5 p.397*

Thomas Reid on the Animate Creation: Papers Relating to the
    Life Sciences. *v.5 p.227*

Thomas Reid. *v.1 p.450*

Thomas the Obscure. *v.2 p.510*

Thomas Traherne: Poetry and Prose. *v.1 p.652*

□ THOMAS. *v.4 p.481*

Thompson and Thompson Genetics in Medicine. .*v.5 p.150, p.151*

Thomson Delmar Learning's Comprehensive Medical Assisting:
    Administrative and Clinical Competencies. *v.5 p.534*

Thoreau's Ecstatic Witness. *v.2 p.52*

Thoreau's Morning Work: Memory and Perception in a Week on
    the Concord and Merrimack Rivers, the Journal and
    Walden. *v.2 p.52*

Thoreau's Sense of Place: Essays in American Environmental
    Writing. *v.2 p.52, v.6 p.288*

The Thorn Birds. *v.2 p.747*

Thorndike Encyclopedia of Banking and Financial
    Tables. *v.4 p.175, p.176, p.181*

Thorns and Thistles: Juvenile Delinquents in the United States,
    1825-1940. . . . . *v.6 p.255*

Thornton Wilder. *v.2 p.133*

Thoroughbass Method. *v.1 p.184, p.401*

Thorstein Veblen. *v.4 p.212*

Those Terrible Carpetbaggers: A Reinterpretation. . .*v.3 p.395*

Those Who Perish. *v.2 p.69*

Those Who Play with Fire: Gender, Fertility and Transformation
    in East and Southern Africa. *v.4 p.31*

Thought and Behavior in Modern Japanese Politics. . .*v.6 p.225*

The Thought and Character of William James. . . . *v.1 p.439*

Thought and Knowledge: An Introduction to Critical
    Thinking. *v.5 p.608*

Thought and Letters in Western Europe, A. D.
    500-900. . . . .*v.2 p.449, v.6 p.567, p.568*

The Thought of Gregory the Great. *v.3 p.56*

Thoughts on Death and Immortality: From the Papers of a
    Thinker, along with an Appendix of Theological
    Satirical Epigrams, Edited by One of His Friends. .*v.1 p.464*

Thoughts on the Interpretation of Nature and Other
    Philosophical Works. *v.2 p.480*

Thoughts. *v.2 p.711*

A Thousand Acres: A Novel. *v.2 p.155*

The Thousand and One Nights in Arabic Literature and
    Society. *v.6 p.659*

Thousand Cranes. *v.6 p.230*

A Thousand Days: John F. Kennedy in the White House. *v.3 p.479*

A Thousand Miles up the Nile. *v.3 p.11*

Thousand Pieces of Gold: A Biographical Novel. . . . *v.6 p.94*

The Thrales of Streatham Park. *v.2 p.263*

Thread of Blood (H&E): Colonialism, Revolution, and Gender
    on Mexico's Northern Frontier. *v.3 p.290*

Threats and Promises: The Pursuit of International
    Influence. *v.4 p.625, p.626*

Threats to Democracy: The Radical Right in Italy after the
    War. *v.4 p.594*

Three American Plays. *v.2 p.55*

Three Asian American Writers Speak Out on
    Feminism. *v.6 p.105, p.113*

Three Behaim Boys: Growing Up in Early Modern Germany -
    A Chronicle of Their Lives. *v.3 p.166*

The Three Bells of Civilization. *v.4 p.42*

Three Billion New Capitalists: The Great Shift of Wealth and
    Power to the East. *v.4 p.51*

Three Centuries and the Island: A Historical Geography of
    Settlement and Agriculture in Prince Edward Island,
    Canada. *v.3 p.543*

Three Chilean Thinkers. *v.3 p.350*

Three Classics in the Aesthetic of
    Music. *v.1 p.212, p.320, p.333, p.381*

Three Comedies: Mine Hostess, the Boors, and the Fan. *v.2 p.711*

Three Comedies: The Birds, the Clouds, the Wasps. . *v.2 p.423*

Three Comedies. *v.2 p.647*

Three Continents. *v.2 p.355*

Three Dialogues Between Hylas and Philonous. . . . *v.1 p.449*

Three Dublin Plays: The Shadow of a Gunman; Juno and the
    Paycock, and the Plough and the Stars. *v.2 p.374*

The Three Edwards: War and State in England,
    1272-1377. . . . . *v.3 p.98*

Three Essays on Religion: Nature, the Utility of Religion, and
    Theism. *v.1 p.523*

Three Essays on the Theory of Sexuality. *v.4 p.748*

The Three Estates: A Pleasant Satire in Commendation of Virtue
    and in Vituperation of Vice. *v.2 p.219*

The Three Estates in Medieval and Renaissance
    Literature. *v.2 p.569, v.6 p.566*

Three Exemplary Novels. *v.2 p.648*

Three Faces of Imperialism: British and American Approaches
    to Asia and Africa, 1870-1970. . . . . *v.3 p.76*

Three French Comedies: Turcaret, the Triumph of Love, and
    Eating Crow. *v.2 p.465*

Three French Farces. *v.2 p.465*

Three Frontiers: Family, Land, and Society in the American
    West, 1850-1900. . . . . *v.3 p.532*

Three Great Economists: Smith, Malthus,
    Keynes. *v.4 p.228, p.229*

Three Guineas. *v.2 p.394*

Three Imperial Mathematicians. *v.3 p.48*

Three Italian Chronicles. *v.2 p.502*

Three Italian Renaissance Comedies: Ariosto's The Supposes; Machiavelli's The Mandrake; Intronati's The Deceived. *v.1 p.67, p.68, p.75, p.107*

The Three Jewels: A Study and Translation of Minamoto Tamenori's Sanboe. *v.6 p.230*

Three Kingdoms: A Historical Novel. *v.6 p.211*

Three Latin Comedies. *v.2 p.448*

Three Lives of English Saints. *v.2 p.450, p.451, p.453*

Three Major Plays. *v.2 p.653*

Three Marchen of E.T.A. Hoffman. *v.2 p.599*

The Three Marias: New Portuguese Letters. *v.2 p.688*

Three Melodramas. *v.2 p.712*

Three Mile Island: A Nuclear Crisis in Historical Perspective. *v.5 p.364, p.412*

Three Mile Island Clean-Up: Experiences, Waste Disposal and Environmental Impact. *v.5 p.744*

Three Modern Italian Poets: Saba, Ungaretti, Montale. *v.2 p.697*

The Three Musketeers. *v.2 p.489*

Three Novels by Mariano Azuela: The Trials of a Respectable Family; The Underdogs; The Firefly. *v.2 p.667*

Three novels: Soft Soap; The Leg; Will-o'-the-Wisp. *v.2 p.623*

The Three Orders: Feudal Society Imagined. *v.6 p.562*

The Three Pillars of Zen. *v.1 p.567, p.568*

Three Plays: Andromache, Britannicus [and] Phaedra. *v.1 p.78, p.106*

Three Plays by Luigi Pirandello: Six Characters in Search of an Author; Henry IV and Right You Are. . . . *v.1 p.83, p.107*

Three Plays for Puritans by Bernard Shaw Being the Third Volume of His Collected Plays. . . . *v.1 p.80, p.81, p.103*

Three Plays for Puritans. *v.2 p.310*

Three Plays: My Heart's in the Highlands, The Time of Your Life, Love's Old Sweet Song. *v.2 p.118*

Three Plays: Naga-Mandala; Hayavadana; Tughlaq. . *v.6 p.151*

Three Plays: Our Town/The Skin of Our Teeth/The Matchmaker. *v.2 p.134*

Three Plays: Tamerlane, the Fair Penitent, Jane Shore. *v.2 p.258*

Three Plays: The Marriage; The Gamblers; The Government Inspector. *v.2 p.803, p.804*

Three Plays: The Sleep of Reason, The Foundation, and In the Burning Darkness. *v.2 p.657*

Three Plays. *v.1 p.123*

Three plays. *v.2 p.599*

Three Plays. *v.2 p.607*

Three plays. *v.2 p.713*

Three Premiers of Nova Scotia: The Honorable J.W. Johnstone, the Hon. Joseph Howe, the Hon. Charles Tupper. . *v.3 p.540*

Three Pre-Surrealist Plays. *v.1 p.85, p.109*

Three Radical Women Writers: Class and Gender in Meridel le Sueur, Tillie Olsen, and Josephine Herbst. . . . *v.4 p.485*

Three Roads to Quantum Gravity. *v.5 p.556, p.557*

Three Sad Races: Racial Identity and National Consciousness in Brazilian Literature. *v.2 p.691*

The Three Sarahs: Documents of Antebellum Black College Women. *v.6 p.21, p.45*

Three Short Novels. *v.2 p.141*

Three Spanish Golden Age Plays: The Duchess of Amalfi's Steward/The Capulets and Montagues/Cleopatra. *v.1 p.69, p.75, p.108, v.2 p.653*

Three Spanish Philosophers: Unamuno, Ortega, Ferrater Mora. *v.1 p.474*

Three Strikes and You're Out: Vengeance as Social Policy. *v.6 p.271*

Three Studies in Medieval Religious and Social Thought: The Interpretation of Mary and Martha, the Ideal of the Imitation of Christ, the Orders of Society. . *v.1 p.650, v.6 p.570*

Three Studies in the Renaissance: Sidney, Jonson, Milton. *v.2 p.217*

Three Tales. *v.2 p.491*

Three Tall Women: A Play in Two Acts. *v.2 p.139*

Three Theories of Child Development. *v.5 p.628*

Three Thousand Years of Chinese Painting. *v.1 p.692, p.730, p.734*

Three Thousand Years of Educational Wisdom: Selections from Great Documents. *v.4 p.323, p.329*

Three Times a Woman: Chicana Poetry. *v.6 p.495, p.498, p.499, p.510*

Three Trapped Tigers. *v.2 p.672*

Three Ways of Thought in Ancient China. *v.1 p.418*

Three Women. *v.2 p.153*

The Three-Cornered Hat and Captain Poison: A Dual Language Book. *v.2 p.653*

Three-Dimensional Geometry and Topology. *v.5 p.496*

Three-Language List of Botanical Name Components. *v.5 p.207*

The Threepenny Opera. *v.1 p.248, p.367, p.368, p.407*

Thresholds (Umbrales): Poems. *v.2 p.674*

Through a Speculum That Shines: Vision and Imagination in Medieval Jewish Mysticism. *v.6 p.574*

Through African Eyes: Culture and Society: Continuity and Change. *v.6 p.51*

Through Corridors of Power: Institutions and Civil-Military Relations in Argentina. *v.3 p.276, v.4 p.592*

Through Ebony Eyes: What Teachers Need to Know but Are Afraid to Ask about African American Students. . *v.4 p.310*

Through the Arc of the Rain Forest. *v.6 p.102*

Through the Earth Darkly: Female Spirituality in Comparative Perspective. *v.1 p.528*

Through the Lens: National Geographic Greatest Photographs. *v.1 p.763*

Through the Lens of Israel: Explorations in State and Society. *v.6 p.614*

Through the Looking Glass: Further Adventures and Misadventures in the Realm of Children's Literature. *v.2 p.582*

Through the Looking Glass: Issues of Psychological Well-Being in Captive Nonhuman Primates. *v.5 p.615*

Through the Looking-Glass: Personality in Culture. . *v.5 p.637*

Through the Rearview Mirror: Historical Reflections on Psychology. *v.5 p.597*

Through the Screen Door: What Happened to the Broadway Musical When it Went to Hollywood. *v.6 p.316*

Through the Woods: The English Woodland - April to April. *v.5 p.174, p.228*

Throwaways: Work Culture and Consumer Education. *v.4 p.759*

Throwing the Scabbard Away: Byron's Battle Against the Censors of Don Juan. *v.2 p.273*

Thrown among Strangers: The Making of Mexican Culture in Frontier California. *v.6 p.534, p.535*

Thucydides: An Introduction for the Common Reader. .*v.2 p.422*

Thucydides and the Ancient Simplicity: The Limits of Political Realism. *v.2 p.421*

Thucydides, Bk. 7. . . . .*v.2 p.422*

Thucydides Book I: A Students' Grammatical Commentary. *v.2 p.421*

Thucydides Book VI, Vol. 6. . . . .*v.2 p.422*

Thucydides: Man's Place in History. *v.2 p.421, p.422*

Thucydides: Mythistoricus. *v.2 p.421*

Thunder at Hampton Roads. *v.3 p.431*

Thunder at Twilight: Vienna, 1913-1914. . . . . . .*v.3 p.184*

Thunder from the East: Portrait of a Rising Asia. . .*v.6 p.145*

Thunder Out of China. *v.6 p.191, p.216, p.217*

Thurber Carnival. *v.2 p.126*

The Thurber Letters: The Wit, Wisdom, and Surprising Life of James Thurber. *v.2 p.125*

Thurgood Marshall: American Revolutionary. . .*v.4 p.469, p.470*

Thus Spoke Zarathustra: A Book for Everyone and Nobody. *v.1 p.466, p.467*

Ti Jean L'horizon : roman. *v.2 p.538*

La Tia Julia y el Escribidor. *v.2 p.686*

The Tiananmen Papers. *v.6 p.197*

Tiberius the Politician. *v.3 p.28*

The Tibetan Book of the Dead: Or, the After-Death Experiences on the Bardo Plane, According to Lama Kazi Dawa-Samdup's English Rendering. *v.1 p.563*

The Tibetan Book of the Dead: The Great Book of Natural Liberation Through Understanding in the Between. *v.6 p.241, p.242*

Tibetan Book of the Dead. *v.1 p.565*

The Tibetan Book of the Great Liberation: Or, the Method of Realizing Nirvana Through Knowing the Mind. . .*v.1 p.561*

Tibullus: A Commentary. *v.2 p.445*

Ticket to Minto: Stories of India and America. . . .*v.2 p.160*

Tidal Energy. *v.5 p.361*

Tidal Power. *v.5 p.362, p.363*

The Tide of Empire: America's March to the Pacific. .*v.3 p.532*

The Tides of Reform: Making Government Work, 1945-1995. . . . .*v.4 p.546*

A Tidewater Morning: Three Tales from Youth. . . .*v.2 p.156*

Tierra Amarilla: Stories of New Mexico/Cuentos de Nuevo Mexico. *v.6 p.504*

Ties That Stress: The New Family Imbalance. *v.5 p.626*

A Tiger by the Tail: The Keynesian Legacy of Inflation. .*v.4 p.227*

Tigers are Better-Looking: With a selection from the Left Bank. *v.2 p.769*

Tigers of the Snow and Other Virtual Sherpas: An Ethnography of Himalayan Encounters. *v.6 p.163*

Tigers on the Tenth Day and Other Stories. *v.6 p.664*

Tigers, Rice, Silk, and Silt: Environment and Economy in Late Imperial South China. *v.6 p.186, p.206*

Tilings and Patterns. *v.5 p.498*

Till We Have Faces: A Myth Retold. *v.2 p.366*

Tiller's Guide to Indian Country: Economic Profiles of American Indian Reservations. *v.6 p.678*

Tilman Riemenschneider: Master Sculptor of the Late Middle Ages. *v.1 p.779*

Tilting the Continent: Southeast Asian American Literature. *v.6 p.91*

Tilting the Playing Field: Schools, Sports, Sex and Title IX. *v.4 p.821, p.836, p.894, p.900, p.901, v.6 p.437*

Tim Hawkinson. *v.1 p.699*

Tim Page on Music: Views and Reviews. *v.1 p.247*

Timber Committee Forest Products Statistics. .*v.4 p.152, p.164*

Timber Construction Manual. *v.5 p.684, p.685, p.687*

The Time . . . Night. *v.2 p.807*

Time and Money: The Macroeconomics of Capital Structure. *v.4 p.245*

Time and Narrative. *v.1 p.457, p.507*

Time and the Riddle: Thirty-One Zen Stories. *v.2 p.73*

Time Between Ashes and Roses. *v.6 p.655*

The Time Bind: When Work Becomes Home and Home Becomes Work. *v.4 p.731, p.732, v.5 p.580, v.6 p.467*

Time Bites: Views and Reviews. *v.2 p.365*

Time, Change and the American Newspaper. *v.4 p.149*

Time for a Model Change: Re-Engineering the Global Automotive Industry. *v.4 p.154*

Time, Forward!. *v.2 p.805*

A Time Full of Trial: The Roanoke Island Freedmen's Colony, 1862-1867. . . . .*v.3 p.501*

Time Gifts. *v.2 p.812*

Time, History, and Belief in Aztec and Colonial Mexico. *v.3 p.261, p.286*

The Time Machines: The Story of the Science-Fiction Pulp Magazines from the Beginning to 1950. . . . . . .*v.2 p.580*

The Time Machine. *v.2 p.320*

Time Must Have a Stop. *v.2 p.354*

Time of Apprenticeship: The Fiction of Young James Joyce. *v.2 p.360*

A Time of Coalitions: Divided We Stand. *v.4 p.618*

The Time of Illusion. *v.3 p.479*

The Time of Indifference: A Novel. *v.2 p.720*

Time of Liberty: Popular Political Culture in Oaxaca, 1750-1850. . . . .*v.3 p.285*

The Time of Miracles: A Legend. *v.2 p.811*

The Time of Music: New Meanings, New Temporalities, New Listening Strategies. *v.1 p.371*

The Time of My Life: An Autobiography. *v.1 p.444*

Time of Parting: A Novel. *v.2 p.780*

A Time of Silence: Civil War and the Culture of Repression in Franco's Spain, 1936-1945. . . . .*v.3 p.242*

The Time of the Generals: Latin American Professional Militarism in World Perspective. *v.3 p.276*

The Time of the Gypsies. *v.4 p.42*

Time of Transition: The Growth of Families Headed by Women. *v.4 p.266*

Time of Troubles: A Historical Study of the Internal Crisis and Social Struggles in Sixteenth and Seventeenth-Century Muscovy. *v.3 p.215*

Time on the Cross: The Economics of American Negro Slavery. *v.3 p.419, p.420*

The Time Regulation Institute. *v.6 p.668*

Time Series Analysis and Inverse Theory for Geophysicists. *v.5 p.443*

Time Series with Long Memory. *v.4 p.204*

Time to Choose: America at the Crossroads of School Choice Policy. *v.4 p.299*

A Time to Every Purpose: The Four Seasons in American Culture. *v.3 p.368*

A Time to Speak Out: The Leipzig Citizen Protests and the Fall of East Germany. *v.3 p.176*

Time Travel in Einstein's Universe: The Physical Possibilities of Travel Through Time. *v.5 p.72*

Time Warps: Silent and Evasive Pasts in Indian Politics and Religion. *v.6 p.150*

Time Warps, String Edits, and Macromolecules: The Theory and Practice of Sequence Comparision. *v.5 p.336, p.341*

Time, Work, and Culture in the Middle Ages. *v.6 p.576*

Time Zones: Recent Film and Video. *v.1 p.771, p.772*

Time-Based Competition: The Next Battle Ground in American Manufacturing. *v.4 p.119*

The Timeless Land. *v.2 p.744*

The Times Are Never So Bad: A Novella and Eight Short Stories. *v.2 p.144*

Time's Arrow: Or the Nature of the Offense. *v.2 p.329*

Time's Arrow, Time's Cycle: Myth and Metaphor in the Discovery of Geological Time. *v.5 p.446*

The Times Atlas of the World: Comprehensive Edition. *v.4 p.379, p.380*

The Times Comprehensive Atlas of the World. *v.4 p.379*

Times Digital Archive, 1785-1985. . . . .*v.6 p.735*

Times Gone By: Memoirs of a Man of Action. *v.3 p.351*

Times Square: Graphics from the Great White Way. . .*v.1 p.714*

Time-Saver Standards for Architectural Design. *v.1 p.785*

Time-Saver Standards for Building Materials and Systems: Design Criteria and Selection Data. *v.1 p.796*

Time-Saver Standards for Building Types. *v.1 p.785*

Time-Saver Standards for Interior Design and Space Planning. *v.1 p.803*

Time-Saver Standards for Landscape Architecture. *v.1 p.785, p.817*

Time-Saver Standards for Urban Design. *v.1 p.798*

The Timetables of African-American History: A Chronology of the Most Important People and Events in African-American History. *v.6 p.5, p.17*

Timon of Athens. *v.2 p.223, p.224*

Timothy Asch and Ethnographic Film. *v.6 p.310*

Timpani and Percussion. *v.1 p.390*

The Timurid and Safavid Periods. *v.6 p.629*

The Tin Drum. *v.2 p.608*

Tin Pan Alley: An Encyclopedia of the Golden Age of American Song. *v.1 p.160, p.270*

Tina. *v.2 p.626*

Tinderbox: U. S. Foreign Policy and the Roots of Terrorism. *v.4 p.565*

Tinker, Tailor, Soldier, Spy. *v.2 p.361*

Tinkering Toward Utopia: A Century of Public School Reform. *v.4 p.297, p.298, p.325*

Tinkering with Eden: A Natural History of Exotics in America. *v.6 p.292*

Tip O'Neill and the Democratic Century: A Biography. *v.3 p.457, p.458*

The Tipping Point: How Little Things Can Make a Big Difference. *v.4 p.51, p.139,v.5 p.586*

Tipping the Velvet: A Novel. *v.6 p.399*

Tirano Banderas. *v.2 p.662*

Tirso de Molina: Damned for Despair. *v.2 p.650*

Tirso de Molina: The Trickster of Seville and the Stone Guest. *v.2 p.650*

Tis Pity She's a Whore. *v.2 p.218*

Titans: A Three-Generation Biography of the Dumas. .*v.2 p.489*

The Titan. *v.2 p.70*

Title IX. *v.4 p.449, p.835, p.882, p.883, p.893, p.900*

Tito: And the Rise and Fall of Yugoslavia. . . .*v.3 p.247, p.248*

Tito, Mihailovic, and the Allies. *v.3 p.247*

Tito Puente and the Making of Latin Music. *v.1 p.293, p.349,v.6 p.489, p.518*

Titus Andronicus. *v.2 p.224*

Tivolem. *v.2 p.765*

The Tiwanaku: Portrait of an Andean Civilization. . .*v.3 p.261*

Tiwi Wives: A Study of the Women of Melville Island, North Australia. *v.4 p.43*

TM: Trademarks Designed by Chermayeff and Geismar Inc. *v.1 p.717*

TMI 25 Years Later: The Three Mile Island Nuclear Power Plant Accident and Its Impact. *v.5 p.364, p.740*

TMS OnLine: Home of The Minerals, Metals & Materials Society. *v.5 p.731*

To a Rocky Moon: A Geologist's History of Lunar Exploration. *v.5 p.418, p.435*

To a Widow with Children. *v.6 p.498*

To Advance Knowledge: The Growth of American Research Universities, 1900-1940. . . . .*v.5 p.393*

To Assure Pride and Confidence in the Electoral Process: Report of the National Commission on Federal Election Reform. *v.4 p.548, p.549*

To Be a Jew: A Guide to Jewish Observance in Contemporary Life. *v.1 p.552*

To Be a Pilgrim, Vol. 2. . . . .*v.2 p.338*

To Be a Slave in Brazil: 1550-1888. . . . .*v.3 p.334*

To Be a Worker: Identity and Politics in Peru. *v.3 p.331*

To Be an American: Cultural Pluralism and the Rhetoric of Assimilation. *v.4 p.763*

To Be Loved: The Music, the Magic, the Memories of Motown an Autobiography. *v.1 p.269, p.270, p.384*

To Be or Not to Bop: Memoirs. *v.1 p.259, p.326*

To Be Real: Telling the Truth and Changing the Face of Feminism. *v.6 p.428, p.436*

To Be Useful to the World: Women in Revolutionary America, 1740-1790. . . . .*v.6 p.452*

To Be Young, Gifted and Black: A Portrait of Lorraine Hansberry in Her Own Words. *v.6 p.27, p.45*

To Better Our World: Black Women in Organized Reform, 1890-1920. . . . . *v.6 p.40, p.46*

To Chain the Dog of War: The War Power of Congress in History and Law. *v.4 p.461, p.532*

To Change China: Western Advisors in China, 1620-1960. . . . . *v.6 p.187, p.191, p.201, p.216*

To Come to the Land: Immigration and Settlement in Sixteenth-Century Eretz-Israel. *v.6 p.610*

To Conserve a Legacy: American Art from Historically Black Colleges and Universities. *v.1 p.705*

To Create a New World? American Presidents and the United Nations. *v.4 p.634*

To Criticize the Critic and Other Writings. *v.2 p.71*

To Dance Is Human: A Theory of Nonverbal Communication. *v.1 p.48*

To Die for Germany: Heroes in the Nazi Pantheon. . .*v.3 p.171*

To Die for the People: The Writings of Huey P. Newton. *v.6 p.13, p.27*

To Dwell among Friends: Personal Networks in Town and City. *v.4 p.770, v.6 p.717*

To End All Wars: Woodrow Wilson and the Quest for a New World Order. *v.3 p.473, v.4 p.631*

To Enforce Education: A History of the Founding Years of the United States Office of Education. *v.4 p.281, p.324*

To Grasp the Essence of Life: A History of Molecular Biology. *v.5 p.127*

To Have and Have Not. *v.2 p.84*

To Have or to Be? *v.5 p.585*

To Hell and Back: Race and Betrayal in the Southern Novel. *v.2 p.12*

To Hell with Culture: And Other Essays on Art and Society. *v.2 p.379, p.575, p.576*

To Inherit the Earth: Brazil's Landless People and the Struggle to Transform a Nation. *v.3 p.270, p.343*

To Joy My Freedom: Southern Black Women's Lives and Labors after the Civil War. *v.6 p.6, p.44*

To Keep the Ball Rolling: The Memoirs of Anthony Powell. *v.2 p.378*

To Kill a Mockingbird. *v.2 p.94*

To Know a Woman. *v.6 p.650*

To Lead As Equals: Rural Protest and Political Consciousness in Chinandega, Nicaragua, 1912-1979. . . . . .*v.3 p.301, p.302*

To Lhasa in Disguise: an Account of a Secret Expedition Through Mysterious Tibet. *v.6 p.241*

To Love, Honor, and Obey in Colonial Mexico: Conflicts over Marriage Choice, 1574-1821. . . . .*v.3 p.264, p.287*

To Make a Nation: The Rediscovery of American Federalsim. *v.4 p.523*

To Make a Spotless Orange: Biological Control in California. *v.5 p.27*

To Make a World Safe for Revolution: Cuba's Foreign Policy. *v.3 p.308*

To Moscow, Not Mecca: The Soviet Campaign Against Islam in Central Asia, 1917-1941. . . . .*v.3 p.230*

To Painting: A Bilingual Collection. *v.2 p.655*

To Perpetual Peace. *v.1 p.462, v.4 p.649*

To Provide for the General Welfare: A History of the Federal Spending Power. *v.4 p.525*

To Purge This Land with Blood: A Biography of John Brown. *v.3 p.399, p.431, p.432*

To Reach the High Frontier: A History of U.S. Launch Vehicles. *v.5 p.719, p.720*

To Save China, to Save Ourselves: The Chinese Hand Laundry Alliance of New York. *v.6 p.107, p.128*

To Serve and Protect: Privatization and Community in Criminal Justice. *v.6 p.246*

To Set the Record Straight: The Break-in, the Tapes, the Conspirators, the Pardon. *v.4 p.438*

To Show Heart: Native American Self-Determination and Federal Indian Policy, 1960-1975. . . . .*v.6 p.695*

To Show What an Indian Can Do: Sports at Native American Boarding Schools. *v.4 p.841, v.6 p.680*

To Skin a Cat: Stories. *v.2 p.150*

To Steal a Book Is an Elegant Offense: Intellectual Property Law in Chinese Civilization. *v.4 p.475*

To Stretch Our Ears: A Documentary History of America's Music. *v.1 p.276*

To the Actor: On Technique of Acting. *v.1 p.143*

To the Arctic: An Introduction to the Far Northern World. *v.5 p.238*

To the Bitter End: Paraguay and the War of the Triple Alliance. *v.3 p.344, p.345*

To the Desert and Back: The Story of One of the Most Dramatic Business Transformations on Record. . . .*v.4 p.84*

To the Director and Playwright. *v.1 p.152*

To the Distant Observer: Form and Meaning in Japanese Cinema. *v.6 p.335*

To the End of the Solar System: The Story of the Nuclear Rocket. *v.5 p.719*

To the Extreme: Alternative Sports, Inside and Out. . .*v.4 p.857*

To the Flag: The History of the Pledge of Allegiance. .*v.4 p.547*

To the Glory of Her Sex: Women's Roles in the Composition of Medieval Texts. *v.6 p.559, p.560*

To the Halls of the Montezumas: The Mexican War in the American Imagination. *v.3 p.418, v.6 p.534*

To the Happy Few: Selected Letters of Stendhal. . . .*v.2 p.502*

To the Is-Land: An Autobiography, Vol. 1. . . . . .*v.2 p.745*

To the Land of the Cattails. *v.6 p.647*

To the Last Man: Spring 1918. . . . .*v.3 p.79*

To the Lighthouse. *v.2 p.394*

To the North. *v.2 p.334, p.335*

To the People: James Yen and Village China. . .*v.6 p.190, p.202*

To the Webster-Ashburton Treaty: A Study in Anglo-American Relations, 1783-1843. . . . .*v.3 p.417*

To Wake the Nations: Race in the Making of American Literature. *v.2 p.5*

To Walt Whitman, America. *v.2 p.54*

A to Z of American Women in Sports. *v.6 p.437*

A to Z of Women in Science and Math. *v.5 p.396*

The Tobacco Book: A Reference Guide of Facts, Figures, and Quotations about Tobacco. *v.4 p.153*

Tobacco Culture: The Mentality of the Great Tidewater Planters on the Eve of Revolution. *v.3 p.499*

Tobacco Industry and Smoking. *v.4 p.153*

Tobacco Road. *v.2 p.66*

Tobias Smollett. *v.2 p.261*

Tobit: A New Translation with Introduction and
    Commentary. *v.1 p.624*

Tocqueville and the Nature of Democracy. *v.4 p.492*

Tocqueville and the Two Democracies. *v.4 p.492*

Tocqueville Between Two Worlds: The Making of a Political
    and Theoretical Life. *v.4 p.493*

The Tocqueville Reader: A Life in Letters and Politics. .*v.4 p.491*

Todd Haynes: A Magnificent Obsession. *v.6 p.418*

Todos Los Cuentos de Gabriel Garcia Marquez
    (1947-1972). *v.2 p.683*

Together at the Table: Sustainability and Sustenance in the
    American Agrifood System. *v.5 p.12*

Togo under Imperial Germany, 1884-1914: A Case Study in
    Colonial Rule. *v.6 p.73*

The Toilers of the Sea: A Novel. with Two Engravings from
    Original Pictures by Gustave Doré. *v.2 p.493*

The Toilers of the Sea. *v.2 p.494*

The Toils of Scepticism. *v.1 p.516, p.517*

Tojo and the Coming of the War. *v.6 p.223*

Tokugawa Ieyasu: Shogun. *v.6 p.228*

Tokugawa Japan: The Social and Economic Antecedents of
    Modern Japan. *v.6 p.225*

Tokugawa Religion. *v.1 p.541*

Tokyo City Atlas: A Bilingual Guide. *v.6 p.219*

Told Round a Brushwood Fire: The Autobiography of Arai
    Hakuseki. *v.6 p.227*

Tolstoy: Anna Karenina. *v.2 p.809*

Tolstoy As Teacher: Leo Tolstoy's Writings on
    Education. *v.4 p.346*

Tom Brown's Schooldays. *v.2 p.291*

Tom Brown's Universe: The Development of the English Public
    School of the 19th Century. *v.3 p.112, p.128, v.6 p.745, p.747*

Tom Jones a Foundling. *v.2 p.247*

Tom MBoya: The Man Who Kenya Wanted to
    Forget. *v.6 p.64, p.65*

Tom Patti: Illuminating the Invisible. *v.1 p.782*

Tom Sawyer Abroad and Tom Sawyer, Detective. . . .*v.2 p.35*

Tom Stoppard: A Life. *v.2 p.385*

Tom Stoppard: A Separate Peace, Teeth, Another Moon Called
    Earth, Neutral Ground, Professional Foul, Squaring the
    Circle. *v.2 p.385*

Tom Stoppard: Arcadia, The Real Thing, Night and Day, Indian
    Ink, Hapgood. *v.1 p.87, p.104, v.2 p.385*

Tom Stoppard: Dalliance, Undiscovered Country, Rough
    Crossing, on the Razzle, The Seagull. *v.2 p.385*

Tom Stoppard in Conversation. *v.2 p.385*

Tom Stoppard: The Dissolution of Dominic Boot; 'M' Is for
    Moon among Other Things; If You're Glad I'll Be
    Frank; Albert's Bridge; Where Are They Now?; Artist
    Descending a Staircase; The Dog It Was That Died; In the
    Native State. *v.2 p.385*

Tom Stoppard: The Real Inspector Hound; Dirty Linen; Dogg's
    Hamlet; Cahoot's MacBeth... . . . .*v.1 p.87, p.104*

Tom: The Unknown Tennessee Williams. . .*v.2 p.134, v.6 p.402*

Tom Watson: Agrarian Rebel. *v.3 p.403, p.435*

Tomas Rivera, 1935-1984: The Man and His
    Work. *v.6 p.500, p.513, p.514*

Tomaso Albinoni: The Venetian Composer and His
    World. *v.1 p.187, p.301*

Tomb for 500,000 Soldiers. *v.2 p.530*

A Tomb for Anatole. *v.2 p.496*

The Tomb of Tut Ankh Amen: Search, Discovery and the
    Clearance of the Antechamber. *v.3 p.8*

The Tomb of TutAnkhAmen: The Annexe and Treasury. .*v.3 p.8*

The Tomb of TutAnkhAmen: The Burial Chamber. . . .*v.3 p.8*

Tombeau pour cinq cent mille soldats : sept chants. . .*v.2 p.530*

Tomorrow, God Willing: Self-Made Destinies in Cairo. .*v.4 p.39*

Tomorrow's Energy: Hydrogen, Fuel Cells, and the Prospects
    for a Cleaner Planet. *v.5 p.742*

Toms, Coons, Mulattoes, Mammies, and Bucks: An Interpretive
    History of Blacks in American Films. *v.6 p.3, p.15*

Tonal Harmony at the Keyboard. *v.1 p.374*

Tonal Harmony. *v.1 p.370, p.371*

The Tongue Set Free: Remembrance of a European
    Childhood. *v.2 p.606*

The Tongue Snatchers. *v.6 p.434*

Tongue Tied: The Lives of Multilingual Children in Public
    Education. *v.4 p.312*

Tongues of Fire: The Explosion of Protestantism in Latin
    America. *v.1 p.580*

Tono-Bungay. *v.2 p.320*

Der Tonwille: Pamphlets in Witness of the Immutable Laws of
    Music: Issues 1-5 (1921-1923). *v.1 p.373*

Der Tonwille: Pamphlets in Witness of the Immutable Laws of
    Music. *v.1 p.373*

Tony Richardson: A Bio-Bibliography. *v.6 p.419*

Tony Soprano's America: The Criminal Side of the American
    Dream. *v.6 p.256*

Too Close to Call: The Thirty-Six-Day Battle to Decide the
    2000 Election. *v.3 p.480*

Too Good to Be True: The Colossal Book of Urban
    Legends. *v.2 p.17*

Too Heavy a Load: Black Women in Defense of Themselves,
    1894-1994. . . . .*v.6 p.12, p.47*

Too Marvelous for Words: The Life and Genius of Art
    Tatum. *v.1 p.261, p.362*

Too Much of a Good Thing...: Quotes You Can't Get Enough
    Of. *v.6 p.360*

Too Queer: Essays from a Radical Life. *v.6 p.401*

Tool and Manufacturing Engineers Handbook: Continuous
    Improvement. *v.5 p.733*

Tool and Manufacturing Engineers Handbook: Design for
    Manufacturability, Vol. 6. . . . .*v.5 p.733*

Tool and Manufacturing Engineers Handbook: Forming. .*v.5 p.733*

Tool and Manufacturing Engineers Handbook:
    Machining. *v.5 p.733*

Tool and Manufacturing Engineers Handbook: Manufacturing
    Management. *v.5 p.733*

Tool and Manufacturing Engineers Handbook: Material and Part
    Handling in Manufacturing. *v.5 p.733*

Tool and Manufacturing Engineers Handbook: Materials, Finishing and Coating. *v.5 p.733*

Tool and Manufacturing Engineers Handbook: Plastic Part Manufacturing. *v.5 p.733*

Tool and Manufacturing Engineers Handbook: Quality Control and Assembly. *v.5 p.733*

Tools and Applications of Biochemical Engineering Science. *v.5 p.742*

ⓔ Tools in Fluvial Geomorphology. *v.4 p.391*

The Tools of Empire: Technology and European Imperialism in the Nineteenth Century. *v.3 p.76*

Tools of Radio Astronomy. *v.5 p.67*

Toothpicks and Logos: Design in Everyday Life. . . .*v.1 p.717*

The Top 1,000 Words for Understanding Media Arabic. .*v.6 p.654*

▢ The Top American Research Universities. *v.4 p.289*

Top Country Singles, 1944 to 2001: Chart Data Compiled from Billboard's Country Singles Charts, 1944-2001. . . . .*v.1 p.172, p.276*

Top Pop Singles 1955-2002. . . . .*v.1 p.172, p.276*

Topaz Moon: Chiura Obata's Art of the Internment. *v.6 p.88, p.134*

Topdog-Underdog. *v.2 p.152*

Topics for Mathematics Clubs. *v.5 p.462*

Topics in Algebra. *v.5 p.473*

Topics in Complex Function Theory. *v.5 p.491, p.494*

Topics in Environmental Epidemiology. *v.5 p.365*

Topics in Stereochemistry. *v.5 p.298*

Topobiology: An Introduction to Molecular Embryology. *v.5 p.160*

Topographic Surveying. *v.4 p.390*

Topographical Stories: Studies in Landscape and Architecture. *v.1 p.813*

A Topological Aperitif. *v.5 p.499*

Topological Graph Theory. *v.5 p.480, p.499*

Topology from the Differentiable Viewpoint. *v.5 p.499*

Topology Now!. *v.5 p.499*

The Topology of Chaos: Alice in Stretch and Squeezeland. *v.5 p.499*

Topology Optimization: Theory, Methods, and Applications. *v.5 p.693*

Topology. *v.5 p.499*

Topper. *v.2 p.116*

Torah (New Translation). *v.1 p.621*

The Torch in My Ear. *v.2 p.606*

Torch Song Trilogy: Three Plays. *v.6 p.411*

Tories and Democrats: British Diplomats in Pre-Jacksonian America. *v.4 p.644, p.645*

Torn Between Empires: Economy, Society, and Patterns of Political Thought in the Hispanic Caribbean, 1840-1878. . . . .*v.3 p.317, p.320*

The Tornado: Nature's Ultimate Windstorm. *v.5 p.426*

▢ Tornadoes. *v.5 p.426*

Toronto: The World Within a City. *v.3 p.544*

Torquato Tasso: A Study of the Poet and of his Contribution to English Literature. *v.2 p.709*

Torquemada. *v.2 p.654*

The Torre-Bueno Glossary of Entomology. *v.5 p.10*

The Torrent: Novellas and Short Stories. *v.2 p.539*

Tort Law in America: An Intellectual History. *v.4 p.443*

Tortilleras: Hispanic and U. S. Latina Lesbian Expression. *v.6 p.393*

Torts in a Nutshell. *v.4 p.443*

The Torture Debate in America. *v.4 p.562*

Torture in Brazil: A Shocking Report on the Pervasive Use of Torture by Brazilian Military Governments, 1964-1979, Secretly Prepared by the Archiodese of São Paulo. *v.3 p.338*

Torture: The Role of Ideology in the French-Algerian War. *v.3 p.157*

The Tory Syndrome: Leadership Politics in the Progressive Conservative Party. *v.4 p.589*

Toscanini's Fumble and Other Tales of Clinical Neurology. *v.5 p.516*

Total Baseball: The Ultimate Baseball Encyclopedia. .*v.4 p.852*

Total Basketball: The Ultimate Basketball Encyclopedia. *v.4 p.854*

Total Facilities Management. *v.4 p.112*

Total Football: The Official Encyclopedia of the National Football. *v.4 p.858*

Total Hockey: The Official Encyclopedia of the National Hockey League. *v.4 p.862*

Total Productive Maintenance: A Collection of Applications and Thoughts. *v.4 p.117*

The Total Synthesis of Natural Products, Vol. 1. . . .*v.5 p.299*

Total Tennis: The Ultimate Tennis Encyclopedia. .*v.4 p.843, p.864*

Total War: Causes and Courses of the Second World War. .*v.3 p.80*

Totalitarianism in Burma: prospects for economic development. *v.4 p.617*

Totem Pole Carving: Bringing a Log to Life. *v.1 p.782*

Totems and Teachers: Perspectives on the History of Anthropology. *v.4 p.4*

Totto-Chan: The Little Girl at the Window. *v.6 p.227*

Touch the Water, Touch the Wind. *v.6 p.650*

Touched with Fire: Civil War Letters and Diary of Oliver Wendell Holmes, Jr., 1861-1864. . . . .*v.3 p.425*

Touched with Fire: Manic-Depressive Illness and the Artistic Temperament. *v.5 p.659, p.660*

Touching Base: Professional Baseball and American Culture in the Progressive Era. *v.4 p.819, p.852, p.897*

Touching the Web of Southern Novelists. *v.2 p.14*

Touchstone for Ethics, 1893-1943. . . . .*v.1 p.484*

The Touchstone of Life: Molecular Information, Cell Communication, and the Foundations of Life. . . .*v.5 p.154*

Tough Acts to Follow: One-Act Plays on the Gay-Lesbian Experience. *v.6 p.410*

The Toughest Indian in the World. *v.2 p.139*

Toulouse-Lautrec and Montmartre. *v.1 p.700*

Toulouse-Lautrec. *v.1 p.737*

Le Tour: A History of the Tour de France, 1903-2003. . . . .*v.4 p.845, p.857*

The Tour de France, 1903-2003: A Century of Sporting Structures, Meanings and Values - Sport in the Global Society. *v.4 p.804, p.805, p.843, p.856, p.857*

A Tour of the Calculus. *v.5 p.485*

A Tour of the Subatomic Zoo: A Guide to Particle
Physics. *v.5 p.552, p.553*

A Tour Through England and Wales; Divided into Circuits or
Journies. *v.3 p.105, p.126*

Tourism and Politics: Policy, Power and Place. *v.5 p.371*

Tourism and Transition: Governance, Transformation and
Development. *v.4 p.259*

Tournament of Shadows: The Great Game and the Race for
Empire in Central Asia. *v.4 p.623, v.6 p.239*

Tous les hommes sont mortels. *v.2 p.509*

Toussaint's Clause: The Founding Fathers and the Haitian
Revolution. *v.3 p.314*

Tout compte fait. *v.2 p.509*

Toward a Better Understanding of Physical Fitness and Activity:
Selected Topics. *v.4 p.790*

Toward a Discourse of Consent: Mass Mobilization and
Colonial Politics in Puerto Rico, 1932-1948. . . . .*v.3 p.321*

Toward a European Army: Military Power in the
Making? *v.4 p.638*

Toward a Feminist Theory of the State. *v.6 p.441*

Toward a General Science of Viable Systems. *v.5 p.407*

Toward a General Theory of Action. *v.4 p.692*

Toward a Modern Japanese Theatre: Kishida
Kunio. *v.6 p.232, p.233*

Toward a New Christianity: Readings in the Death of God
Theology. *v.1 p.637*

Toward a New Cuba?: Legacies of a Revolution. . . .*v.3 p.307*

Toward a New Order of Sea Power. *v.3 p.384*

Toward a New Poetics: Contemporary Writing in
France. *v.2 p.459*

Toward a New World Outlook: A Documentary History of
Education in the People's Republic of China,
1949-1976. . . . .*v.4 p.335*

Toward a Patriarchal Republic: The Secession of
Georgia. *v.3 p.503*

Toward a Renaissance of Puerto Rican Studies in University
Education. *v.6 p.487*

Toward a Science of Consciousness: The First Tucson
Discussions and Debates. *v.5 p.613*

Toward a Science of Human Nature: Aspirations of Nineteenth
Century Psychology. *v.5 p.598*

Toward a Social History of American English. *v.2 p.554*

Toward a Social History of the American Civil War: Exploratory
Essays. *v.3 p.402*

Toward a Theory of Instruction. *v.4 p.341, v.5 p.573*

Toward a Theory on Biological-Physical Interactions in the
World Ocean. *v.4 p.392, p.393*

Toward an Aesthetics of the Puppet: Puppetry As a Theatrical
Art. *v.1 p.93*

Toward an Evolutionary Biology of Language. *v.4 p.19*

Toward an Intellectual History of Women: Essays by Linda K.
Kerber. *v.6 p.450*

Toward an Islamic Reformation: Civil Liberties, Human Rights
and International Law. *v.1 p.553*

Toward Civil Society in the Middle East?: A Primer. *v.6 p.595*

Toward Effective Public School Programs for Deaf Students:
Context, Process and Outcomes. *v.4 p.312*

Toward Lexington: The Role of the British Army in the Coming
of the American Revolution. *v.3 p.414*

Toward Mexico's Democratization: Parties, Campaigns,
Elections and Public Opinion. *v.3 p.292*

Toward Modern Art: From Puvis de Chavennes to Matisse and
Picasso. *v.1 p.728*

Toward New Perspectives in Folklore. *v.2 p.585*

Toward Nuclear Abolition: A History of the World Nuclear
Disarmament Movement, 1971-Present. *v.4 p.657*

Toward Restoration: The Growth of Political Consciousness in
Tokugawa Japan. *v.6 p.224*

Toward Samson Agonistes: The Growth of Milton's
Mind. *v.2 p.255*

Toward Standards: A Study of the Present. *v.2 p.3*

Toward Stonewall: Homosexuality and Society in the Modern
Western World. *v.6 p.362*

Toward the Decolonization of African Literature: African Fiction
and Poetry and Their Critics. *v.2 p.751, v.6 p.80*

Toward the Final Solution: A History of European
Racism. *v.3 p.60, p.78*

Toward the Livable City. *v.6 p.727*

Toward the Radical Cente: A Karel Capek Rader. . . .*v.2 p.783*

Toward the Splendid City: Poems. *v.2 p.679*

Toward Wholeness in Paule Marshall's Fiction. *v.2 p.768*

Towards a Critical Theory of Society. *v.1 p.502*

Towards a Democratic Nepal: Inclusive Political Institutions for
a Multicultural Society. *v.4 p.617*

Towards a European Habitat Classification: Background Review
1989-1995. . . . .*v.5 p.180*

Towards a Just Social Order. *v.4 p.770*

Towards a Mythology: Studies in the Poetry of W. B.
Yeats. *v.2 p.327*

Towards a New Cold War: U. S. Foreign Policy from Vietnam
to Reagan. *v.3 p.451*

Towards a New Museum. *v.1 p.790*

Towards a New Past: Dissenting Essays in American
History. *v.3 p.373*

Towards a Society That Serves Its People: The Intellectual
Contribution of El Salvador's Murdered Jesuits. . .*v.3 p.299*

Towards a World of Plenty? *v.4 p.267, p.271*

Towards an Intellectual History of Ukraine: An Anthology of
Ukrainian Thought, 1710-1993. . . . .*v.2 p.814*

Towards Poor Theatre. *v.1 p.85, p.109, p.138, p.139*

Towards Standards of Criticism: Selections from the Calendar of
Modern Letters, 1925-1927. . . . .*v.2 p.164, p.568*

Towards Sustainable Aviation. *v.5 p.718*

Towards Sustainable Cities: East Asian, North American and
European Perspectives on Managing Urban Regions. *v.6 p.729*

Towards the Edge of the Universe: A Review of Modern
Cosmology. *v.5 p.71*

Towards Union in Palestine: Essays on Zionism and
Jewish-Arab Cooperation. *v.6 p.610*

Tower of Babel: The Evidence Against the New
Creationism. *v.5 p.195*

The Tower Struck by Lightning. *v.2 p.507*

The Towers of Silence, Vol. 3. . . . .*v.2 p.382*

Town and Region in the Mexican North: Saltillo,
1770-1810. . . . .*v.3 p.287*

The Town and the City. *v.2 p.93*

Town, Country, and Regions in Reformation Germany. .*v.3 p.166*

Town Houses: Urban Houses from 1200 to the Present
Day. *v.1 p.785*

Town into City: Springfield, Massachusetts, and the Meaning of
Community, 1840-1880. . . . .*v.3 p.488*

The Town of San Felipe and Colonial Cacao
Economics. *v.3 p.359*

Townlife in Fourteenth Century Scotland. *v.6 p.577*

Township: Diffusion and Persistence of Grassroots Government
in Illinois, 1850-2000. . . . .*v.4 p.542*

Toxic and Hazardous Materials: A Sourcebook and Guide to
Information Sources. *v.5 p.309*

Toxic Drift: Pesticides and Health in the Post-World War II
South. *v.6 p.283*

Toxic Waste and Environmental Policy in the 21st Century
United States. *v.4 p.63, v.6 p.301*

Toxicogenomics: Principles and Applications. *v.5 p.149*

Toxicologic Emergencies. *v.5 p.514, p.534*

Toxicological Chemistry and Biochemistry. *v.5 p.314*

Toxicology: A Case-Oriented Approach. *v.5 p.314*

Toxicology for the Next Millennium. *v.5 p.163*

TOXLINE on SilverPlatter. *v.5 p.315*

TOXLINE. *v.5 p.310*

TOXNET. National Library of Medicine. *v.5 p.310*

TOXNET. *v.5 p.314*

The Toys of Peace and Other Papers. *v.2 p.381*

Trace Elements in Terrestrial Environments: Biogeochemistry,
Bioavailability and Risks of Metals. *v.5 p.364, p.377*

Trace Elements in the Environment: Biogeochemistry,
Biotechnology, and Bioremediation. *v.5 p.170, p.219*

Trace Fossils: Biology, Taphonomy and Applications. .*v.5 p.450*

Trace Gas Exchange in a Global Perspective. *v.5 p.114*

Tracers in the Sea. *v.5 p.429*

Traces of Another Time: History and Politics in Postwar British
Fiction. *v.2 p.191, p.192*

Traces of the Past: Unraveling the Secrets of Archaeology
Through Chemistry. *v.5 p.263*

Tracing the History of Eukaryotic Cells: The Enigmatic
Smile. *v.5 p.153, p.191*

Tracings of Light: Sir John Herschel and the Camera
Lucida. *v.1 p.724*

Trackings: Composers Speak with Richard Dufallo. . .*v.1 p.213*

Tracks. *v.6 p.697*

Tractates and Sermons. *v.1 p.582*

Tractatus Logico-Philosophicus. *v.1 p.472*

Tracts and Other Papers: Relating Principally to the Origin,
Settlement, and Progress of the Colonies in North
America, from the Discovery of the Country to the Year
1776, Set. *v.3 p.405*

Tracts and Pamphlets of Richard Steele. *v.2 p.262*

Trade and Conflict in Angola: The Mbundu and Their Neighbors
under the Influence of the Portuguese, 1483-1790. . .*v.6 p.75*

Trade and Development Report 2005: New Features of Global
Interdependence. *v.4 p.666*

Trade and Empire in the Atlantic, 1400-1600. . . . .*v.4 p.582*

Trade and Gunboats: The United States and Brazil in the Age of
Empire. *v.3 p.338*

Trade and Market in the Early Empires: Economies in History
and Theory. *v.4 p.210*

Trade and Politics in the Niger Delta, 1830-1885: An
Introduction to the Economic and Political History of
Nigeria. *v.6 p.71*

Trade and Politics on the Gold Coast, 1600-1720: a Study of the
African Reaction to European Trade. *v.6 p.70*

Trade and Traders in Muslim Spain: The Commercial
Realignment of the Iberian Peninsula,
900-1500. . . . .*v.3 p.65, p.237*

Trade, Environment and the Millennium. *v.6 p.298*

Trade Policy at the Crossroads: The Recent Experience of
Developing Countries. *v.4 p.60*

Trade, Stability, and Macroeconomics: Essays in Honor of Lloyd
A. Metzler. *v.4 p.257*

Trade, Transport and Society in the Ancient World: A
Sourcebook. *v.3 p.23*

Trade Unions and Sustainable Democracy in Africa. . .*v.4 p.122*

Trade Unions: Resurgence or Decline? *v.4 p.253*

Trademark: Legal Care for Your Business and Product
Name. *v.4 p.446*

Tradiciones Nuevomexicanas: Hispano Arts and Culture of New
Mexico. *v.6 p.492, p.493, p.523*

Trading Beyond the Mountains: The British Fur Trade on the
Pacific, 1793-1843. . . . .*v.3 p.545*

Trading Blocs: Alternative Approaches to Analyzing Preferential
Trade Agreements. *v.4 p.256*

Trading Blocs: States, Firms, and Regions in the World
Economy. *v.4 p.60*

Trading Gazes: Euro-American Women Photographers and
Native North Americans, 1880-1940. . . . .*v.1 p.705, p.763*

Tradition Alive: On the Church and the Christian Life in Our
Time. *v.4 p.721*

Tradition and Avante-Garde: Literature and Arts in Serbian
Culture, 1900-1918. . . . .*v.2 p.811*

Tradition and Change in the Nicaraguan Press: Newspapers and
Journalists in a New Democratic Era. *v.3 p.302*

Tradition and Folk Life. *v.3 p.132*

Tradition and Innovation: A Basket History of the Indians of the
Yosemite- Mono Lake Area. . . . *v.1 p.805, p.806,v.6 p.678*

Tradition and Innovation in French Garden Art: Chapters of a
New History. *v.1 p.813*

Tradition and Modernity in Arabic Literature. *v.6 p.658*

Tradition and Originality in Roman Poetry. *v.2 p.425*

Tradition and Style in the Works of Darius Milhaud
1912-1939. . . . .*v.1 p.217, p.341*

Tradition and Transition: Historical Perspectives on Vatican
II. *v.1 p.570*

Tradition as Truth and Communication: A Cognitive Description
of Traditional Discourse. *v.4 p.27*

The Tradition of the Trojan War in Homer and the Epic
Cycle. *v.2 p.402*

Tradition Transformed: The Jewish Experience in America. *v.1 p.549*

Tradition versus Democracy in the South Pacific: Fiji, Tonga and Western Samoa. *v.4 p.624*

Traditional Aerobics. *v.4 p.793*

Traditional Archery. *v.4 p.795, p.847*

Traditional Balinese Culture: Essays. *v.6 p.173, p.176*

Traditional Dancing in Scotland. *v.1 p.33*

The Traditional Dietary Culture of Southeast Asia: A Culinary History. *v.6 p.164*

Traditional Japanese Music and Musical Instruments. .*v.1 p.289*

Traditional Japanese Theater: An Anthology of Plays. *v.1 p.129, p.132, p.133*

Traditional Jewish Papercuts: An Inner World of Art and Symbol. *v.1 p.807*

The Traditional Music of Thailand. *v.1 p.289*

Traditional Music of the Lao: Kaen Playing and Mawlum Singing in Northeast Thailand, 13. . . . .*v.1 p.289*

Traditional Politics and Regime Change in Brazil. . .*v.3 p.340*

Traditional Storytelling Today: An International Sourcebook. *v.2 p.585*

Traditional Techniques in Contemporary Chinese Printmaking. *v.1 p.759*

☐ Traditional Tree Initiative. *v.5 p.26, p.40, p.41*

The Traditional Tunes of the Child Ballads: With Their Texts, According to the Extant Records of Great Britain and America. *v.1 p.298*

Traditions and Values in Politics and Diplomacy: Theory and Practice. *v.3 p.386*

Traditions of Gamelan Music in Java: Musical Pluralism and Regional Identity. *v.1 p.290*

Traditions of Islam: An Introduction to the Study of the Hadith Literature. *v.1 p.556*

Traditions of Victorian Women's Autobiography: The Poetics and Politics of Life Writing. . *v.6 p.480, p.740, p.748, p.754*

Trafalgar. *v.3 p.91*

Traffic and Environment. *v.5 p.354, p.368*

Traffic Engineering. *v.5 p.701*

The Traffic in Praise: Pindar and the Poetics of Social Economy. *v.2 p.417*

Traffic Safety. *v.5 p.682*

The Tragedies of Ennius: The Fragments. *v.2 p.434*

The Tragedies of George Chapman. *v.2 p.217*

Tragedies. *v.2 p.217*

Tragedy and Civilization: An Interpretation of Sophocles. *v.2 p.420*

The Tragedy and Comedy of Resistance: Reading Modernity Through Black Women's Fiction. *v.2 p.5*

Tragedy and Scepticism in Shakespeare's England. . .*v.2 p.186*

Tragedy and Tragic Theory: An Analytical Guide. .*v.1 p.57, p.89*

Tragedy in Athens: Performance Space and Theatrical Meaning. *v.2 p.402*

Tragedy in Dedham; the Story of the Sacco-Vanzetti Case. *v.4 p.438*

Tragedy in Havana: November 27, 1871. . . . .*v.3 p.313, p.314*

The Tragedy of American Diplomacy. *v.3 p.454*

The Tragedy of Arthur: A Study of the Alliterative Morte Arthure. *v.2 p.206*

The Tragedy of Cambodian History: Politics, War, and Revolution Since 1945. . . . .*v.6 p.170*

The Tragedy of Sohrab and Rostam: From the Persian National Epic, the Shahname of Abu'l-Qasem Ferdowsi. *v.6 p.670, p.671*

The Tragedy of the Chinese Revolution. . . . *v.6 p.192, p.215*

The Tragedy of the Middle East. *v.6 p.595*

The Tragedy of the Tragedies for the Life and Death of Tom Thumb the Great. *v.2 p.247*

La tragédie du roi Christophe : théâtre. *v.2 p.536*

The Tragic Actor. *v.1 p.101, p.145*

The Tragic Conflict. *v.3 p.398, p.428*

The Tragic Satire of John Webster. *v.2 p.235*

Tragic Sense of Life. *v.1 p.474*

The Tragic Vision of Politics: Ethics, Interests and Orders. *v.4 p.484, p.626*

The Tragicall History of Christopher Marlowe. *v.2 p.220*

Tragicomedy and Contemporary Culture: Play and Performance from Beckett to Shepard. *v.1 p.57, p.87, p.89, p.92*

Tragicomedy and Novelistic Discourse in Celestina. . .*v.2 p.652*

The Trail Home: Essays. *v.5 p.226*

A Trail Through Leaves: The Journal As a Path to Place. .*v.5 p.232*

Trailblazing: The True Story of America's First Openly Gay Track Coach. *v.6 p.383*

Trails: Toward a New Western History. *v.3 p.518*

Train to Pakistan. *v.2 p.766*

Trained to Kill: Soldiers at War. *v.5 p.584*

Training for Professionals Who Work with Gay and Lesbian Youth. *v.6 p.384*

Traité de versification française des origines à nos jours. .*v.2 p.453*

A Traitor's Kiss: The Life of Richard Brinsley Sheridan. .*v.2 p.260*

Traits and Stories of the Irish Peasantry, Vol. 1. .*v.2 p.274, p.275*

Traits and Stories of the Irish Peasantry, Vol. 2. . . . .*v.2 p.274*

Trammell Crow: A Legacy of Real Estate Business Innovation. *v.4 p.148, p.166*

Tramp Art: A Folk Art Phenomenon. *v.1 p.809*

La Trampa. *v.2 p.661*

Trance and Transformation of the Actor in Japanese Noh and Balinese Masked Dance-Drama. *v.1 p.132, p.144*

Trance Formation: The Spiritual and Religious Dimensions of Global Rave Culture. *v.1 p.275*

Tranquil Power: The Art and Life of Perle Fine. *v.1 p.741*

Trans Liberation: Beyond Pink or Blue. *v.6 p.366*

Transaction Processing: Concepts and Techniques. *v.5 p.337, p.338, p.339*

Transactions on Computational Systems Biology I. *v.5 p.128, p.142, p.151*

The Trans-Appalachian Frontier: People, Societies, and Institutions, 1775-1850. . . . .*v.3 p.513*

Trans-Atlantic Dimensions of Ethnicity in the African Diaspora. *v.6 p.11, p.39*

Transatlantic Encounters: Europeans and Andeans in the Sixteenth Century. *v.3 p.325*

Transatlantic Images and Perceptions: Germany and America since 1776. . . . . *v.3 p.386, p.387*

The Transatlantic Slave Trade: A History. *v.4 p.727*

Transatlantic Sport: The Comparative Economics of North American and European Sports. . . . *v.4 p.843, p.882, p.887*

Transatlantic Ties in the Spanish Empire: Brihuega, Spain, and Puebla, Mexico, 1560-1620. . . . . *v.3 p.284*

Trans-Atlantyk. *v.2 p.787*

Transbluesency: The Selected Poems of Amiri Baraka/Leroi Jones. *v.2 p.140*

The Transcendentalists: An Anthology. *v.1 p.515*

Transcending Conquest: Nahua Views of Spanish Colonial Mexico. *v.3 p.288*

Transcultural Cinema. *v.6 p.310*

Transcultural Nursing. *v.5 p.530*

Transducing the Genome: Information, Anarchy, and Revolution in the Biomedical Sciences. *v.5 p.130*

The Transfer in Power of Africa: Decolonization, 1940-1960. . . . . *v.4 p.583, v.6 p.54*

The Transfer of Cognitive Skill. *v.4 p.358*

The Transfer of the Sudeten Germans. *v.3 p.190*

Transference and Empathy in Asian American Psychotherapy: Cultural Values and Treatment Needs. *v.6 p.121*

Transferring Learning to Behavior: Using the Four Levels to Improve Performance. *v.4 p.79*

The Transfiguration of the Commonplace: A Philosophy of Art. *v.1 p.479*

Transfigurations of the Maghreb: Feminism, Decolonization, and Literatures. *v.2 p.542*

The Transfigured Kingdom: Sacred Parody and Charismatic Authority at the Court of Peter the Great. *v.3 p.217*

The Transforamtion of Nomadic Society in the Arab East. *v.6 p.596*

Transform Circuit Analysis for Engineering and Technology. *v.5 p.721*

Transformation and Struggle: Cuba Faces the 1990s. *v.3 p.309, p.310*

The Transformation of Agriculture in the West. *v.3 p.43*

The Transformation of American Foreign Relations, 1865-1900. . . . . *v.3 p.432, p.433*

The Transformation of American Law, 1780-1860. . . *v.4 p.440*

The Transformation of American Law, 1870-1960: The Crisis of Legal Orthodoxy. *v.4 p.441*

The Transformation of American Quakerism: Orthodox Friends, 1800-1907. . . . . *v.1 p.585*

The Transformation of Central Asia: States and Societies from Soviet Rule to Independence. *v.3 p.230, v.4 p.623*

The Transformation of Democracy. *v.4 p.249*

The Transformation of Europe 1300-1600. . . . . . . *v.3 p.41*

The Transformation of European Politics 1763-1848. . *v.3 p.75*

The Transformation of Hera: A Study of Ritual, Hero, and the Goddess in the Iliad. *v.1 p.533*

The Transformation of Intellectual Life in Victorian England. *v.3 p.112, p.128, v.6 p.750*

The Transformation of Ireland. *v.3 p.138*

The Transformation of Liberalism in Late Nineteenth-Century Mexico. *v.3 p.292*

The Transformation of Mexican Agriculture: International Structure and the Politics of Rural Change. . . . *v.3 p.272*

The Transformation of Palestine: Essays on the Origin and Development of the Arab-Israeli Conflict. *v.6 p.616*

The Transformation of Psychology: Influences of 19th Century Philosophy, Technology and Nature Science. . . . *v.5 p.596*

The Transformation of Rural Life: Southern Illinois, 1890-1990. . . . . *v.3 p.514*

The Transformation of South Korea: Reform and Reconstitution in the Sixth Republic under Roe Tae Woo, 1987-1992. . . . . *v.4 p.621*

The Transformation of the North Atlantic World, 1492-1763: An Introduction. *v.4 p.379*

The Transformation of U. S. Unions: Voices, Visions, and Strategies from the Grassroots. *v.4 p.129*

The Transformation of Virginia, 1740-1790. . . . . . *v.3 p.499*

The Transformation of Wall Street: A History of the Securities and Exchange Commission and Modern Corporate Finance. *v.4 p.92, p.100, p.147, p.155, p.156, p.162*

Transformations in Slavery: A History of Slavery in Africa. *v.4 p.728, v.6 p.53*

Transformations: Migration, Family Life, and Achievement Motivation among Latino Adolescents. *v.6 p.530*

Transformations: The History of the Science Fiction Magazine 1950 to 1970. . . . . *v.2 p.580*

Transformed by Crisis: The Presidency of George W. Bush and American Politics. *v.3 p.484*

Transformed Cladistics, Taxonomy and Evolution. *v.5 p.171, p.201, p.202*

Transforming Brazil: A Reform Era in Perspective. . *v.3 p.340*

Transforming Democracy: Legislative Campaign Committees and Political Parties. *v.4 p.531*

Transforming Economics: Perspectives on the Critical Realist Project. *v.4 p.259*

Transforming HR: Creating Value Through People. . . *v.4 p.76*

Transforming Images: How Photography Complicates the Picture. *v.1 p.764, p.765*

Transforming Learning with Block Scheduling: A Guide for Principals. *v.4 p.287*

Transforming Masculinities. *v.6 p.430*

Transforming Matter: A History of Chemistry from Alchemy to the Buckyball. *v.5 p.263*

Transforming Mission: Paradigm Shifts in Theology of Mission. *v.1 p.647*

Transforming Modernity: Popular Culture in Mexico. *v.3 p.267*

Transforming Paris: The Life and Labors of Baron Haussmann. *v.3 p.154, p.159*

Transforming Public Education: A New Course for America's Future. *v.4 p.325*

Transforming Rural Life: Dairying Families and Agricultural Change, 1820-1885. . . . . *v.5 p.30*

Transforming Shakespeare: Contemporary Women's Re-Visions in Literature and Performance. . . . *v.1 p.76, p.102, p.135*

Transforming the Appalachian Countryside: Railroads, Deforestation, and Social Change in West Virginia, 1880-1920. . . . . *v.5 p.40, p.354, p.356, p.373*

Transforming the Common-Place: Selections from Laurie Olin's Sketchbooks. *v.1 p.816*

Transforming the Disciplines: A Women's Studies
Primer. *v.6 p.463*

Transforming the Legacy: Couple Therapy with Survivors of
Childhood Trauma. *v.5 p.667*

Transforming the Multicultural Education of Teachers: Theory,
Research, and Practice. *v.4 p.280*

Transforming the Past: Tradition and Kinship among Japanese
Americans. *v.6 p.133*

Transgender Emergence: Therapeutic Guidelines for Working
with Gender-Variant People and Their Families. . .*v.6 p.381*

Transgender Warriors: Making History from Joan of Arc to
Dennis Rodman. *v.6 p.362, p.370*

Transgenic Crop Protection: Concepts and
Strategies. *v.5 p.8, p.22*

Transgenic Crops: An Environmental Assessment. *v.5 p.7, p.21*

☐ Transgenic Crops: An Introduction and Resource
Guide. *v.5 p.7, p.19*

Transgression and Conformity: Cuban Writers and Artists after
the Revolution. *v.3 p.310*

Transit truths, by Gerhard M. Dahl. *v.5 p.700*

Transition Demo in Paraguay. *v.3 p.344*

The Transition from Infancy to Language: Acquiring the Power
of Expression. *v.4 p.368*

Transition Metal Oxides. *v.5 p.309*

Transition Metal Reagents and Catalysts: Innovations in Organic
Synthesis. *v.5 p.295*

Transition Metals in the Synthesis of Complex Organic
Molecules. *v.5 p.299*

Transition Metals, Vol. 3. . . . .*v.5 p.306*

Transition of Power: Britain's Loss of Global Pre-Eminence to
the United States, 1930-1945. . . . . . .*v.3 p.390, p.391*

The Transition to Democracy in Latin America: The Role of the
Military. *v.3 p.274, v.4 p.591*

Transition to Democracy in Poland. . . .*v.4 p.585, p.596, p.597*

The Transition to Democratic Governance in Africa: The
Continuing Struggle. *v.4 p.585, p.612*

Transitions from Authoritarianism: The Role of the
Bureaucracy. *v.4 p.545*

Transitions in Consciousness from an African American
Perspective. *v.6 p.32, p.38*

Transitions Through Adolescence: Interpersonal Domains and
Context. *v.5 p.626, p.627*

Translating America: An Immigrant Press Visualizes American
Popular Culture, 1895-1918. . . . .*v.4 p.410*

Translating Israel: Contemporary Hebrew Literature and Its
Reception in America. *v.6 p.650*

Translating the Message: The Missionary Impact on
Culture. *v.1 p.647*

Translation Nation: Defining a New American Identity in the
Spanish-Speaking United States. *v.6 p.545*

A Translation of Jose Zorrilla's Don Juan Tenorio. .*v.2 p.655*

A Translation of the Orpheus of Angelo Politian and the Aminta
of Torquato Tasso. *v.2 p.708, p.709*

The Translation Studies Reader. *v.2 p.574*

Translation Studies. *v.2 p.574*

Translations from the Chinese. *v.6 p.208*

Translations from the Night. *v.2 p.543*

Translations from the Philosophical Writings of Gottlob
Frege. *v.1 p.493*

Translations of Ancient Arabian Poetry. *v.6 p.661*

Translations of Eastern Poetry and Prose. *v.6 p.663*

Translingual Practice: Literature, National Culture, and
Modernity - China, 1900-1937. . . . .*v.6 p.204*

Transmembrane Signaling Protocols. *v.5 p.158*

Transmen and FTMs: Identities, Bodies, Genders, and
Sexualities. *v.6 p.370*

The Transmission of Chinese Medicine. *v.4 p.46*

Transmutation: Natural and Artificial. *v.5 p.308*

Transnational Adoption: A Cultural Economy of Race, Gender,
and Kinship. *v.6 p.110, p.125*

Transnational Asian American Literature: Sites and
Transits. *v.6 p.97, p.119*

Transnational Aspects of Iu-Mien Refugee Identity. . .*v.6 p.140*

The Transnational Villagers. *v.4 p.44*

☐ Trans-NIH Mouse
Initiatives. *v.5 p.93, p.102, p.103, p.109, p.144*

Transparent Designs: Reading, Performance, and Form in the
Spectator Papers. *v.2 p.258, p.261*

Transparent Simulacra: Spanish Fiction, 1902-1926. . .*v.2 p.642*

Transplantation Immunology. *v.5 p.165*

The Transplanted: A History of Immigrants in Urban
America. *v.6 p.710*

The Transplanted Executive: Why You Need to Understand How
Workers in Other Countries See the World Differently. *v.4 p.56*

Transport for a sustainable future: the case for Europe. *v.5 p.701*

Transport Properties and Related Thermodynamic Data of
Binary Mixtures, Vol. 1. . . . .*v.5 p.286*

Transport Properties and Related Thermodynamic Data of
Binary Mixtures, Vol. 2. . . . .*v.5 p.286*

Transportation and Global Climate Change. *v.5 p.700*

Transportation and Public Utilities USA. *v.4 p.166*

Transportation Engineering: An Introduction. *v.5 p.700*

Transportation Engineering Basics. *v.5 p.700*

Transportation Engineering: Planning and Design. . . .*v.5 p.701*

Transportation for Livable Cities. *v.6 p.729*

Transportation Planning Handbook. *v.5 p.700*

Transportation Planning on Trial: The Clean Air Act and Travel
Forecasting. *v.5 p.700*

Transportation, Storage, and Disposal of Radioactive
Materials. *v.6 p.289*

Transsexualism: Illusion and Reality. *v.6 p.370*

Transuranium Elements: A Half Century. *v.5 p.308*

The Transuranium People: The Inside Story. *v.5 p.308*

Transvestites: The Erotic Drive to
Cross-Dress. *v.4 p.743, v.6 p.370, p.381, p.420*

Transylvanian Villagers: Three Centuries of Political, Economic
and Ethnic Change. *v.3 p.185, p.251*

Trapped Between the Map and Reality: Geography and
Perceptions of Kurdistan. *v.6 p.599*

Trapped: Modern-Day Slavery in the Brazilian Amazon. *v.4 p.728*

The Trap. *v.2 p.791*

Trash: Stories and Poems. *v.6 p.394*

Trauma Culture: The Politics of Terror and Loss in Media and Literature. *v.4 p.558*

The Trauma of Gender: A Feminist Theory of the English Novel. *v.2 p.571*

Travel and Ethnology in the Renaissance: South India Through European Eyes, 1250-1625. . . . .*v.6 p.154*

Travel by Train: The American Railroad Poster, 1870-1950. . . . .*v.1 p.719*

The Travel Diaries of Peter Pears, 1936-1978. . . . .*v.6 p.410*

Travel Industry World Yearbook: The Big Picture. .*v.4 p.161*

Travelers of a Hundred Ages: The Japanese As Revealed Through 1,000 Years of Diaries. *v.6 p.227*

Traveling in Family. *v.2 p.690*

Traveling Light: Collected and New Poems. *v.2 p.128*

The Traveling Salesman Problem: A Guided Tour of Combinatorial Optimization. *v.4 p.119*

Traveling the Trans-Canada: From Newfoundland to British Columbia. *v.3 p.535*

Traveling Through Text: Message and Method in Late Medieval Pilgrimage Accounts. *v.6 p.573, p.574, p.575*

A Traveller's History of Athens. *v.3 p.196*

Travels and Archaeology in South Chile. *v.4 p.11*

Travels in Alaska. *v.3 p.533*

Travels in Four Dimensions: The Enigmas of Space and Time. *v.1 p.500*

Travels in Greeneland: The Complete Guide to the Cinema of Graham Greene. *v.2 p.349*

Travels in Hyper Reality: Essays. *v.2 p.724*

Travels in Tartary, Thibet and China, 1844-1846. . . .*v.6 p.215*

The Travels of a T-Shirt in the Global Economy: An Economist Examines the Markets, Power and Politics of World Trade. *v.4 p.55, p.58*

Travels of Ibn Battuta. *v.6 p.584*

The Travels of Ibn Jubayr: Arabic Text of the Rihla. .*v.6 p.585*

The Travels of Marco Polo: The Complete Yule-Cordier Edition. *v.6 p.186, p.216, p.239*

The Travels of Marco Polo. *v.6 p.186, p.216*

Travels Through France and Italy. *v.2 p.261*

Travels with My Aunt. *v.2 p.350*

A travers un verger ; suivi de, Les cormorans ; et de, Beauregard. *v.2 p.531*

Travesti: Sex, Gender, and Culture among Brazilian Transgendered Prostitutes. *v.4 p.746*

Treadwinds: Poems and Intermedia Works. *v.6 p.104*

Treason by the Book. *v.6 p.188*

Treasure Island. *v.2 p.312*

The Treasure of the City of Ladies. *v.2 p.469*

Treasures of a Lost Art: Italian Manuscript Painting of the Middle Ages and Renaissance. *v.1 p.728, p.729*

Treasures of Art Nouveau: Through the Collections of Anne-Marie Gillion Crowet. *v.1 p.678*

A Treasury of African Folklore: The Oral Literature, Traditions, Myths, Legends, Epics, Tales, Recollections, Wisdom, Sayings, and Humor of Africa. *v.2 p.752*

A Treasury of American Poetry. *v.2 p.24*

Treasury of Damon Runyon. *v.2 p.114*

A Treasury of Flowers: Rare Illustrations from the Collection of the New York Botanical Garden. *v.5 p.82*

A Treasury of Great American Speeches, Our Country's Life and History in the Words of Its Great Men. . .*v.2 p.27, p.28*

Treasury of the World: Jeweled Arts of India in the Age of the Mughals. *v.1 p.715*

Treat It Gentle: An Autobiography. *v.1 p.257, p.306*

Treaties and Agreements OAS. *v.4 p.437, p.474, p.476*

Treaties In Force. *v.4 p.437, p.476, p.477*

Treaties. *v.4 p.636*

Treating Lesbians and Bisexual Women: Challenges and Strategies for Health Professionals. *v.6 p.377*

Treating Substance Abuse: Theory and Technique. . .*v.5 p.673*

A Treatise Concerning the Principles of Human Knowledge. *v.1 p.449, p.481*

Treatise of Civil Government and a Letter Concerning Toleration. *v.4 p.216*

A Treatise of Human Nature. *v.1 p.451*

Treatise on Analytical Chemistry: Theory and Practice, Vol. 8, Pt. 1. . . . .*v.5 p.273*

Treatise on Analytical Chemistry. *v.5 p.273*

A Treatise on Electricity and Magnetism, Vol. 2. . . .*v.5 p.565*

Treatise on Geochemistry, Set. *v.5 p.363, p.367*

A Treatise on Harmony. *v.1 p.372*

Treatise on Inorganic Chemistry. *v.5 p.303*

A Treatise on Probability. *v.1 p.495*

Treatise on Solid State Chemistry, 6 vols..in 7. .*v.5 p.305, p.306*

A Treatise on the Astrolabe. *v.2 p.208*

A Treatise on the Constitutional Limitations Which Rest upon the Legislative Power of the States of the American Union 1868. . . . .*v.4 p.455*

Treatise on the Fugue. *v.1 p.370*

A Treatise on the Fundamental Principles of Violin Playing. *v.1 p.398, p.401*

The Treatise on the Laws and Customs of the Realm of England Commonly Called Glanvill. *v.3 p.98*

Treatise on the Love of God: Also Known Simply As: on the Love of God. *v.1 p.576, p.577*

Treatises and Essays on Subjects Connected with Economical Policy: With Biographical Sketches of Quesnay, Adam Smith and Ricardo. *v.4 p.216, p.240*

Treatment and Rehabilitation of the Chronic Alcoholic. .*v.5 p.521*

Treatment for Chronic Depression: Cognitive Behavioral Analysis System of Psychotherapy (CBASP). .*v.5 p.660, p.665*

Treatment Matching in Alcoholism. *v.5 p.516, p.517*

The Treatment of Shakespeare's Text by His Earlier Editors, 1709-1768. . . . .*v.2 p.231*

The Treaty of Guadalupe Hidalgo: A Legacy of Conflict. *v.6 p.533, p.534*

Tree Anatomy. *v.5 p.156*

Tree: Belief/Culture/Balance. *v.1 p.28, p.29, p.30*

A Tree Grows in Brooklyn. *v.2 p.116*

Tree Growth. *v.5 p.38*

Tree of Life. *v.2 p.536*

The Tree of Man. *v.2 p.750*

Trees and Woodland in the British Landscape: The Complete History of Britain's Trees, Woods and Hedgerows. *.v.6 p.575*

Trees in the Urban Landscape: Site Assessment, Design, and Installation. . . . .*.v.1 p.817, p.818*

Trekking Through History: The Huaorani of Amazonian Ecuador. . . . .*.v.3 p.269, p.270*

Tremble Purple: Seven Poems. . . . .*.v.2 p.139*

The Trench. . . . .*.v.6 p.662*

Trends in Bioinformatics Research. . . . .*.v.5 p.99*

Trent and All That: Renaming Catholicism in the Early Modern Era. . . . .*.v.1 p.612*

Trent Intervenes and Other Stories. . . . .*.v.2 p.331*

Trente Arpents. . . . .*.v.2 p.539*

Trent's Last Case. . . . .*.v.2 p.331*

Treny: The Laments of Kochanowski. . . . .*.v.2 p.789*

Tres Novelas de Mariano Azuela: La Malhora/El Desquite/La Luciernaga. . . . .*.v.2 p.667*

Trespassers on the Roof of the World: The Secret Exploration of Tibet. . . . .*.v.6 p.239*

The Trial: A New Translation Based on the Restored Text. . . . .*.v.2 p.611*

The Trial and Death of Socrates: Euthyphro, Apology, Crito, Death Scene from Phaedo. . . . .*.v.1 p.422*

Trial and Error: the Autobiography of Chaim Weizmann. . . . .*.v.6 p.616*

The Trial and Execution of Socrates: Sources and Controversies. . . . .*.v.2 p.417*

Trial Balance: The Collected Short Stories of William March. . . . .*.v.2 p.97*

Trial by Battle. . . . .*.v.6 p.567*

Trial by Fire. . . . .*.v.6 p.567*

Trial Consulting. . . . .*.v.6 p.271*

The Trial of Christopher Okigbo. . . . .*.v.2 p.756*

The Trial of Peter Zenger. . . . .*.v.4 p.438*

Trials of Nation Making: Liberalism, Race, and Ethnicity in the Andes, 1810-1910. . . . .*.v.3 p.324, p.327*

The Trials of Persiles and Sigismunda: A Northern Story. . . . .*.v.2 p.648*

The Trials of Phillis Wheatley: America's First Black Poet and Her Encounters with the Founding Fathers. . . . .*.v.2 p.29, v.6 p.25, p.43*

The Trials of Socrates: Six Classic Texts. . . . . . .*.v.2 p.417*

Trials Without Truth: Why Our System of Criminal Trials Has Become an Expensive Failure and What We Need to Do to Rebuild It. . . . .*.v.6 p.269*

Le Triangle Noir: Laclos, Goysa, Saint-Just. . .*.v.2 p.480, p.481*

Triangle: The Fire That Changed America. . . . . .*.v.4 p.129*

The Triarchic Mind: A New Theory of Human Intelligence. . . . .*.v.5 p.572*

Triathlon: Achieving Your Personal Best. . . . .*.v.4 p.863, p.866*

Tribal Art: Africa, Oceania, Southeast Asia. . . . .*.v.1 p.690, p.692, p.694*

The Tribal Arts of Africa. . . . .*.v.1 p.689*

Tribal Identity and the Modern World. . . . .*.v.6 p.154, p.155*

Tribal Nation: The Making of Soviet Turkmenistan. . .*.v.3 p.231*

Tribal Wars of the Southern Plains. . . . . . .*.v.6 p.684, p.685, p.686, p.687, p.688*

The Tribe of John: Ashbery and Contemporary Poetry. *.v.2 p.58*

Tribes and State Formation in the Middle East. . . . .*.v.6 p.593*

Tribes, Government, and History in Yemen. . . . . .*.v.6 p.628*

Tribes, Treaties, and Constitutional Tribulations. *.v.6 p.695, p.696*

Tribes, Treaties and Constitutional Tribulations. . . .*.v.6 p.696*

The Tribulations of a Chinese Gentleman. . . *.v.2 p.503, p.504*

The Tribute of Blood: Army, Honor, Race, and Nation in Brazil, 1864-1945. . . . .*.v.3 p.273, p.338*

Tributes: Celebrating 50 Years of New York City Ballet. *.v.1 p.24*

The Trick of It: A Novel. . . . .*.v.2 p.345*

Tricks of the Trade: How to Think about Your Research While You're Doing It. . . . .*.v.4 p.687*

The Tricks of the Trade. . . . .*.v.2 p.724, p.725, p.727*

The Trickster Shift: Humour and Irony in Contemporary Native Art. . . . .*.v.1 p.701, p.702,v.6 p.679*

Tricksterism in Turn-of-the-Century American Literature: A Multicultural Perspective. . . . .*.v.2 p.5*

The Triggering Town: Lectures and Essays on Poetry and Writing. . . . .*.v.2 p.578*

Trigonometric Delights. . . . .*.v.5 p.485*

Trigonometric Series. . . . .*.v.5 p.494*

Trigonometry. . . . .*.v.5 p.485*

Trilby. . . . .*.v.2 p.275*

Trilce. . . . .*.v.2 p.685*

Trilogia: Gens du Silence, Addolorata, Deja l'Agonie. *.v.2 p.541*

Trilogy: The Square, 10:30 on a Summer Night, the Afternoon of M. Andesmas. . . . .*.v.2 p.516*

Trilogy: The Walls Do Not Fall; Tribute to the Angels; The Flowering of the Rod. . . . .*.v.2 p.88*

The Trinitarian Controversy. . . . .*.v.1 p.639*

The Trinity and the Kingdom: The Doctrine of God. . *.v.1 p.639*

Trinity, Incarnation, and Atonement: Philosophical and Theological Essays. . . . .*.v.1 p.594*

The Trinity. . . . .*.v.1 p.592*

Triple Bottom Line: Why the Smartest Companies Are Adopting Sustainability As the New Business Model and What You Need to Know about It. . . . . . .*.v.4 p.61, p.62, p.64*

The Triple Helix: Gene, Organism, and Environment. . . . .*.v.5 p.80, p.128, p.135, p.200*

The Triplet Genetic Code: Key to Living Organisms. *.v.5 p.137*

Tripmaster Monkey: His Fake Book. . . . .*.v.6 p.100*

Trisha Brown: Dance and Art in Dialogue, 1961-2001. . . . .*.v.1 p.29, p.31*

Tristan and Isolde. . . . *.v.1 p.206, p.234, p.366, p.367, p.410*

The Tristan Chord: Wagner and Philosophy. . *.v.1 p.200, p.365*

Tristan et Yseut : les premières versions européennes. *.v.2 p.467*

Tristan und Isold. . . . .*.v.2 p.594, p.595*

Tristia, Ex Ponto, Vol. VI. . . . .*.v.2 p.439*

Tristia. . . . .*.v.2 p.806*

The Triumph and Tragedy of Lyndon Johnson: The White House Years. . . . .*.v.3 p.467*

The Triumph of Death. . . . .*.v.2 p.716*

The Triumph of Ethnic Progressivism: Urban Political Culture in Boston, 1900-1925. . . . .*.v.3 p.488, v.6 p.711*

Triumph of Good Will: How Terry Sanford Beat a Champion of Segregation and Reshaped the South. . . . .*.v.3 p.501*

The Triumph of Light and Nature: Nordic Art 1740-1940. . . . .*v.1 p.687*

The Triumph of Sectionalism: The Transformation of Ohio Politics, 1844-1856. . . . .*v.3 p.513*

The Triumph of the Embryo. *v.5 p.162*

Triumph of the Fatherland: German Unification and the Marginalization of Women. *v.3 p.177, p.178,v.4 p.610*

Triumph of the Right: The Rise of the California Conservative Movement, 1945-1966. . . . .*v.3 p.531*

The Triumph of Time: A Study of the Victorian Concepts of Time, History, Progress, and Decadence. *v.6 p.750, p.752, p.763*

Triumphs. *v.2 p.706*

The Triune Creator: A Historical and Systematic Study. .*v.1 p.635*

The Triune Identity: God According to the Gospel. . .*v.1 p.639*

The Trobrianders of Papua New Guinea: Case Studies in Cultural Anthropology. *v.4 p.43, p.44*

Troilus and Cressida. *v.2 p.224*

The Trojan Women: Iphigenia among the Taurians, Ion. .*v.2 p.411*

Trojans and Their Neighbours. *v.3 p.15*

Trollope: A Biography. *v.2 p.316*

Trollope: A Commentary. *v.2 p.317*

Trollope and Comic Pleasure. *v.2 p.316*

Trollope and Vicorian Moral Philosophy. *v.2 p.317*

Trollope and Women. *v.2 p.316, p.317*

Trollope Companion. *v.2 p.317*

Trollope: His Life and Art. *v.2 p.317*

Trombone Technique. *v.1 p.399*

The Trombone: The Instrument and Its Music. *v.1 p.389*

The Trombone. *v.1 p.389*

Tropes, Parables, Performatives: Essays on Twentieth-Century Literature. *v.2 p.179*

Trophic Organization in Coastal Systems. *v.5 p.173*

The Tropic of Baseball: Baseball in the Dominican Republic. *v.3 p.267, p.268, p.317*

Tropic of Cancer. *v.2 p.102*

Tropic of Capricorn. *v.2 p.102*

A Tropical Belle Epoque: Elite Culture and Society in Turn-of-the-Century Rio de Janeiro. *v.3 p.337*

Tropical Capitalism: The Industrialization of Belo Horizonte, Brazil. *v.3 p.340*

The Tropical Deciduous Forest of Alamos: Biodiversity of a Threatened Ecosystem in Mexico. *v.5 p.177, p.185*

Tropical Deforestation and Species Extinction. *v.5 p.182*

Tropical Deforestation: The Human Dimension. *v.5 p.39*

Tropical Forest Remnants: Ecology, Management, and Conservation of Fragmented Communities. *v.5 p.41, p.353, p.354, p.373*

Tropical Fruits. *v.5 p.22, p.26*

A Tropical Garden Flora: Plants Cultivated in the Hawaiian Islands and Other Tropical Places. *v.5 p.44*

Tropical Rain Forest: A Wider Perspective. . . .*v.5 p.175, p.239*

Tropical Rain Forest Ecosystems: Structure and Function. *v.5 p.41, p.353, p.357*

Tropical Rain Forests: An Ecological and Biogeographical Comparison. *v.5 p.169, p.177, p.181*

Tropical Rainforests: A Golden Guide from St. Martin's Press. *v.5 p.177, p.239*

Tropical Rainforests: Latin American Nature and Society in Transition. *v.3 p.269*

Tropical Rainforests of the Guianan Shield. *v.5 p.168, p.176, p.236, p.239*

Tropical Rainforests: Past, Present, and Future. *v.5 p.174, p.175, p.238, p.239*

Tropical Savannas. *v.5 p.357*

Tropical Soil Biology and Fertility: A Handbook of Methods. *v.5 p.48*

Tropical Truth: A Story of Music and Revolution in Brazil. *v.1 p.295*

Tropical Versailles: Empire, Monarchy, and the Portuguese Royal Court in Rio de Janeiro, 1808-1821. . . . .*v.3 p.77, p.244, p.337*

Tropics of History: Cuba Imagined. *v.3 p.314*

Tropisms. *v.2 p.527*

Trotsky: The Eternal Revolutionary. *v.3 p.224*

Trotsky. *v.3 p.224*

The Troubadours: An Introduction. *v.2 p.457*

Trouble at Willow Gables: And Other Fiction 1943-1953. . . . .*v.2 p.361*

Trouble in Paradise: Globalization and Environmental Crises in Latin America. *v.3 p.270*

Trouble in Utopia: The Overburdened Polity of Israel. .*v.4 p.615*

⊠ Trouble Showed the Way: Women, Men, and Trade in the Nairobi Area, 1890-1990. . . . .*v.6 p.65*

The Trouble with Harry Hay: Founder of the Modern Gay Movement. *v.6 p.404*

The Trouble with Normal: Sex, Politics, and the Ethics of Queer Life. *v.6 p.389*

Trouble with Passion: Political Theory Beyond the Reign of Reason. *v.5 p.643*

Troubled Crusade: American Education, 1945-1980. . .*v.4 p.328*

Troubled Harvest: Agronomy and Revolution in Mexico, 1880-2002. . . . .*v.3 p.291*

The Troubled Heart of Africa: A History of the Congo. .*v.6 p.62*

Troubled Lands: The Legacy of Soviet Environmental Destruction. *v.3 p.223*

Troubled Sleep: A Novel. *v.2 p.528*

Troubled Waters: The Origins of the 1881 Anti-Jewish Pogroms in Russia. *v.3 p.59, p.219*

Troubles of Journalism: A Critical Look at What's Right and Wrong with the Press. *v.4 p.403*

Troublesome Border. *v.3 p.527, v.6 p.487, p.532*

Troubling the Angels: Women Living with HIV/AIDS. .*v.6 p.443*

Trout Fishing in America; The Pill Versus the Springhill Mine Disaster; In Watermelon Sugar. *v.2 p.141*

Trout Fishing in America. *v.2 p.58*

Troy and Homer: Towards a Solution of an Old Mystery. *v.2 p.414, p.415*

Troy and Its Remains. *v.3 p.16*

□ TRPI: Tomás Rivera Policy Institute. *v.6 p.520*

Trudeau and the End of a Canadian Dream. *v.3 p.541*

Trudeau's Shadow: The Life and Legacy of Pierre Elliott Trudeau. *v.3 p.541*

Trudeau. *v.3 p.541*

The True Believer: Thoughts on the Nature of Mass
Movements. *v.4 p.710*

True Catholic Womanhood: Gender Ideology in Franco's
Spain. *v.3 p.242*

The True Confessions of an Albino Terrorist. *v.2 p.623*

True France: The Wars over Cultural Identity,
1900-1945. . . . .*v.3 p.140*

True Genius: The Life and Science of John Bardeen; the Only
Winner of Two Nobel Prizes in Physics. *v.5 p.543*

True History of the Kelly Gang: A Novel. *v.2 p.744*

True North: The Yukon and Northwest Territories. . .*v.3 p.547*

True Security: Rethinking American Social Insurance. *v.4 p.722*

True Selves: Understanding Transsexualism—for Families,
Friends, Coworkers, and Helping
Professionals. *v.6 p.369, p.370, p.374*

The True Subject: Selected Poems of Faiz Ahmed
Faiz. *v.6 p.151, p.162*

True to Our Feelings: What Our Emotions Are Really Telling
Us. *v.1 p.497, p.498*

Truisms. *v.2 p.529*

The Truly Disadvantaged: The Inner City, the Underclass, and
Public Policy. *v.4 p.771, v.6 p.720*

The Truman Administration, Its Principles and Practice. *v.3 p.481*

Truman and Pendergast. *v.3 p.512*

Truman Capote: A Study of the Short Fiction. *v.2 p.66*

Truman Capote: Conversations. *v.2 p.66*

Truman Capote: In Which Various Friends, Enemies,
Acquaintances, and Detractors Recall His Turbulent
Career. *v.2 p.66*

The Truman Doctrine and the Origins of McCarthyism: Foreign
Policy, Domestic Policy, and Internal Security,
1946-48. . . . .*v.3 p.471*

[e] The Truman Scandals and the Politics of Morality. *v.3 p.470*

Truman. *v.3 p.475*

A Trumpet in the Wadi: A Novel. *v.6 p.650*

The Trumpet Shall Sound: A Study of Cargo Cults in
Melanesia. *v.1 p.544, p.545,v.4 p.37*

Trumpet Soundeth: William Jennings Bryan and His Democracy,
1896-1912. . . . .*v.3 p.397*

The Trumpet Soundeth: William Jennings Bryan and His
Democracy 1896. . . . .*v.3 p.433, p.434*

Trumpet Technique. *v.1 p.397*

Trumpets from the Islands of Their Eviction. . *v.6 p.506, p.512*

Trumpet. *v.1 p.391, p.392*

Trust: A Sociological Theory. *v.4 p.695*

Trust and Mistrust in International Relations. . *v.4 p.624, p.625*

The Trust: The Private and Powerful Family Behind the New
York Times. *v.4 p.149, p.150*

The Trust: The Private and Powerful Family behind the New
York Times. *v.4 p.411*

Trust-Based Selling. *v.4 p.142*

Trusteeship in Change: Toward Tribal Autonomy in Resource
Management. *v.6 p.681, p.693*

Truth, 3 vols. *v.1 p.434*

The Truth about Burnout: How Organizations Cause Personal
Stress and What to Do about It. *v.5 p.580*

Truth and Consequence in Medieval Logic. . . .*v.1 p.494, p.495*

Truth and Justification. *v.1 p.482*

Truth and Method. *v.1 p.468, p.507*

Truth and Other Enigmas. *v.1 p.494*

Truth and Reconciliation: Commission of South Africa
Report. *v.4 p.731*

Truth and Symbol: The Apprehension and Consciousness of
Being. *v.1 p.468*

Truth and the End of Inquiry: A Peircean Account of
Truth. *v.1 p.482*

Truth, Freedom, and Evil: Three Philosophical
Dialogues. *v.1 p.431*

Truth in Memory. *v.5 p.610*

The Truth in Painting. *v.1 p.479*

Truth Needs No Ally: Inside Photojournalism. *v.4 p.409*

The Truth of Authority: Ideology and Communication in the
Soviet Union. *v.4 p.598, p.599*

The Truth of Ecology: Nature, Culture, and Literature in
America. *v.2 p.5*

Truth, Probability, and Paradox: Studies in Philosophical
Logic. *v.1 p.494*

The Truth That Killed. *v.2 p.780*

The Truth That Never Hurts: Writings on Race, Gender and
Freedom. *v.6 p.432, p.480*

Truth Versus Precision in Economics. *v.4 p.195, p.196*

Trying Hard to Hear You. *v.6 p.399*

Tsar Nicholas I and the Jews: The Transformation of Jewish
Society in Russia, 1825-1855. . . . .*v.3 p.219*

The Tsarist Secret Police and Russian Society,
1880-1917. . . . .*v.3 p.221*

The Tsar's Colonels: Professionalism, Strategy, and Subversion
in Late Imperial Russia. *v.3 p.212*

The Tso Chuan: Selections from China's Oldest Narrative
History. *v.6 p.184, p.209*

Tsukiji: The Fish Market at the Center of the World. *v.6 p.221*

Tu Fu, China's Greatest Poet. *v.6 p.185, p.200, p.209*

The Tuareg: People of Ahaggar. *v.6 p.60*

The Tuba Family. *v.1 p.389*

Tuberculosis and Nontuberculosis Mycobacterial
Infections. *v.5 p.533*

Tuberculosis and the Tubercle Bacillus. *v.5 p.153, p.158, p.159*

Tucson: The Life and Times of an American
City. *v.3 p.528, p.529,v.6 p.715*

Los Tucsonenses: The Mexican Community in Tucson,
1854-1941. . . . .*v.6 p.533, p.550*

The Tudor and Stuart Town: A Reader in English Urban History,
1530-1688. . . . .*v.3 p.99, p.101, p.102*

The Tudor Constitution: Documents and
Commentary. *v.3 p.93, p.100*

Tudor Cornwall. *v.3 p.92, p.101, p.126*

Tudor England. *v.3 p.100*

The Tudor House and Garden: Architecture and Landscape in
the Sixteenth and Early Seventeenth Centuries. . .*v.1 p.786*

The Tudor Interlude: Stage, Costume, and
Acting. *v.1 p.99, p.144, p.150, p.151, p.154*

Tuition Rising: Why College Costs So Much. *v.4 p.293*

Tumor Progression and Therapeutic Resistance. *v.5 p.165*

Tumultuous Years: The Presidency of Harry S. Truman, 1949-1953. . . . .*v.3 p.469*

Tuned Out: Why Americans under 40 Don't Follow the News. *v.4 p.417*

Tuning and Temperament: A Historical Survey. *v.1 p.374*

Tuning Out Blackness: Race and Nation in the History of Puerto Rican Television. *v.3 p.321*

Tuning the Historical Temperaments by Ear. . . *v.1 p.375, p.401*

Tunisia: Crossroads of the Islamic and European Worlds. .*v.6 p.60*

The Tunisia of Ahmad Bey, 1837 to 1855. . . . . . .*v.6 p.641*

Tunisian Peasants in the Eighteenth and Nineteenth Centuries. *v.6 p.642*

The Tunnel: The Underground Homeless of New York City. *v.4 p.751, v.6 p.718*

Turbulence: A Novel. *v.2 p.690*

Turbulence: The Legacy of A. N. Kolmogorov. *v.5 p.547*

Turbulent Era: A Diplomatic Record of Forty Years, 1904-1945, Set. *v.3 p.458*

Turbulent Flows. *v.5 p.547*

Turf Managers' Handbook for Golf Course Construction, Renovation, and Grow-In. *v.4 p.881, p.886, p.906*

Turf Wars: How Congressional Committees Claim Jurisdiction. *v.4 p.524*

Turkestan and the Fate of the Russian Empire. . . . *v.3 p.213*

Turkey: A Modern History. *v.6 p.625*

Turkey: A Short History. *v.6 p.621*

Turkey and the European Union: Domestic Politics, Economic Integration and International Dynamics. *v.4 p.602, p.636, p.637*

Turkey and the West: Changing Political and Cultural Identities. *v.6 p.623*

Turkey Faces West. *v.6 p.623*

Turkey: From Empire to Nation. *v.6 p.666*

Turkey in World Politics: An Emerging Multiregional Power. *v.6 p.624, p.625*

The Turkey of Ataturk: Social Process in the Turkish Reformation. *v.6 p.625*

Turkey: Political, Social and Economic Challenges in the 1990s. *v.4 p.616*

Turkey Today. *v.6 p.624*

Turkey-Iran Relations, 1979-2004: Revolution, War, Ideology, Coups, and Geopolitics. *v.6 p.624*

Turkey's Relations with a Changing Europe. *v.4 p.638*

Turkey's Relations with Iran, Syria, Israel and Russia, 1991-2000: The Kurdish and Islamist Question. *v.6 p.599, p.624*

Turkish Embassy Letters. *v.2 p.256*

Turkish Foreign Policy, 1774-2000. . . . .*v.6 p.621*

Turkish Foreign Policy During the Gulf War of 1990-91. .*v.6 p.623*

Turkish Grammar. *v.6 p.665*

Turkish Islam and the Secular State: The Gulen Movement. *v.6 p.625*

The Turkish Lover: A Memoir. *v.2 p.155*

Turkish Nationalism and Western Civilization: Selected Essays. *v.6 p.623*

The Turkish Ordeal. *v.6 p.623*

Turkish Phrase Book. *v.6 p.665, p.666*

Turkish Reader. *v.6 p.666*

The Turkish State and History: Clio Meets the Gray Wolf. *v.6 p.622*

Turkish-English, English-Turkish Dictionary: New Red House. *v.6 p.666*

The Turks Today. *v.6 p.624*

Turmoil in the Peacable Kingdom: The Quebec Sovereignty Movement and Its Implications for Canada and the U. S. *v.4 p.581, p.590*

The Turn of the Mind: Constituting Consciousness in Henry James. *v.2 p.45*

The Turn of the Screw: Bewildered Vision. *v.2 p.43*

The Turn of the Screw. *v.2 p.45*

Turn the Beat Around: The Secret History of Disco. . .*v.6 p.408*

Turn the Pulpit Loose: Two Centuries of American Women Evangelists. *v.1 p.648*

The Turnaround: How America's Top Cop Reversed the Crime Epidemic. *v.6 p.259*

Turnaround: How Carlos Ghosn Rescued Nissan. *v.4 p.69*

Turning Japanese: Memoirs of a Sansei. *v.6 p.94*

Turning off the Heat: Why America Must Double Energy Efficiency to Save Money and Reduce Global Warming. *v.5 p.713*

Turning Passions into Profits: Three Steps to Wealth and Power. *v.4 p.66*

The Turning Point: Science, Society and the Rising Culture. *v.5 p.410*

Turning Points: Decisive Moments in the History of Christianity. *v.1 p.598*

Turning Points of the Civil War (New Edition). .*v.3 p.400, p.426*

Turns in the Road: Narrative Studies of Lives in Transition. *v.5 p.655*

Turtle Island. *v.2 p.156*

Tuscan Poetry of the Duecento: An Anthology. .*v.2 p.699, p.700*

The Tuskegee Syphilis Study: The Real Story and Beyond. .*v.6 p.5*

Tuskegee's Truths: Rethinking the Tuskegee Syphilis Study. *v.6 p.8*

Tutte le novelle. *v.2 p.713*

Tutte le opere, vol. 1. . . . .*v.2 p.723*

Tutte le opere, vol. 2. . . . .*v.2 p.723*

Tutte le opere, vol. 3. . . . .*v.2 p.723*

Tutte le opere, Volume primo. *v.2 p.712*

Tutte le opere, Volume secondo. *v.2 p.712*

Tutte le opere. *v.2 p.702*

Tutte le poesie. *v.2 p.716, p.719, p.721*

Tutte le prose. *v.2 p.723*

Tutti i racconti, vol. 1. . . . .*v.2 p.720*

Tutti i racconti, vol. 2. . . . .*v.2 p.720*

Tutti i romanzi, vol. 1. . . . .*v.2 p.722*

Tutti i romanzi, vol. 2. . . . .*v.2 p.722*

Tutti i romanzi. *v.2 p.720*

Tuxedo Park: A Wall Street Tycoon and the Secret Palace of Science That Changed the Course of World War II. .*v.5 p.542*

TV or Not TV: Television, Justice, and the Courts. *v.4 p.465, v.6 p.270*

Twain: Collected Tales, Sketches, Speeches and Essays, 1891-1910, Vol. 2. . . . .*v.2 p.34*

Twelfth Night: Or, What You Will. *v.2 p.224*

Twelve African Writers. *v.6 p.80*

Twelve Against the Empire: The Anti-Imperialists, 1898-1900. . . . .*v.3 p.394, p.435*

Twelve and a Tilly: Essays on the Occasion of the 25th Anniversary of Finnegans Wake. *v.2 p.357, p.358*

Twelve Bar Blues. *v.2 p.368*

The Twelve Caesars. *v.2 p.444*

Twelve Centuries of Japanese Art from the Imperial Collections. *v.1 p.694*

The Twelve Chairs. *v.2 p.807*

Twelve Million Black Voices: A Folk History of the Negro in the U. S. *v.6 p.9, p.41*

Twelve Steps and Twelve Traditions. *v.5 p.672*

Twelve Thousand Years: American Indians in Maine. *v.4 p.10, v.6 p.702*

Twelve Who Ruled: The Year of the Terror in the French Revolution. *v.3 p.151*

The Twelve-Note Music of Anton Webern: Old Forms in a New Language. *v.1 p.209, p.367*

The Twenties in America. *v.3 p.366*

Twentieth Century Artists on Art: An Index to Artists' Writings, Statements, and Interviews. *v.1 p.662*

Twentieth Century Caribbean Literature. *v.2 p.767*

Twentieth Century Europe. *v.3 p.50*

Twentieth Century Interpretations of Moby Dick. . . .*v.2 p.48*

Twentieth Century Interpretations of The Scarlet Letter. .*v.2 p.41*

Twentieth Century Korean Literature. *v.6 p.238*

Twentieth Century Music: An Introduction. *v.1 p.222*

Twentieth Century Music. *v.1 p.208*

Twentieth Century Opera: A Guide. *v.1 p.218, p.231*

The Twentieth Century Performance Reader. *v.1 p.42*

Twentieth Century Physics. *v.5 p.545*

Twentieth Century Piano Music, Vol. 132. . . . . . .*v.1 p.210*

Twentieth-Century American Art. *v.1 p.678, p.682*

Twentieth-Century American Historians. *v.3 p.375*

Twentieth-Century Analytic Philosophy. *v.1 p.502*

Twentieth-Century Art of Latin America. *v.1 p.683*

Twentieth-Century Attitudes: Literary Powers in Uncertain Times. *v.2 p.177*

Twentieth-Century Caribbean and Black African Writers. *v.2 p.751*

Twentieth-Century Chamber Music. *v.1 p.218, p.241*

Twentieth-Century Design. *v.1 p.713*

Twentieth-Century Eastern European Writers. *v.2 p.779, p.782, p.785, p.788*

Twentieth-Century French Literature, 1920-1970. . . .*v.2 p.459*

Twentieth-Century Furniture: Materials, Manufacture, and Markets. *v.1 p.803, p.804*

Twentieth-century German Verse. *v.2 p.593*

Twentieth-Century Harmony: Creative Aspects and Practice. *v.1 p.372*

Twentieth-Century Italian Drama: An Anthology, the First Fifty Years. *v.1 p.67, p.107,v.2 p.699*

Twentieth-Century Italian Poetry; a Bilingual Anthology. *v.2 p.700*

Twentieth-Century Italian Poetry: An Anthology. . . .*v.2 p.700*

Twentieth-Century Microtonal Notation. *v.1 p.393*

🔲 Twentieth-Century Montana: A State of Extremes. .*v.3 p.526*

Twentieth-Century Music : A History of Musical Style in Modern Europe and America. *v.1 p.219*

A Twentieth-Century Musical Chronicle: Events, 1900-1988, 20. . . . .*v.1 p.215*

Twentieth-Century Russian Drama: From Gorky to the Present. *v.2 p.795*

Twentieth-Century Spanish American Literature since 1960, Pt. 2. . . . .*v.2 p.664*

Twentieth-Century Spanish American Literature to 1960, Pt. 1. . . . .*v.2 p.664*

The Twentieth-Century Spanish American Novel. . . .*v.2 p.665*

Twentieth-Century Spanish Poets. *v.2 p.640*

Twentieth-Century Suspense: The Thriller Comes of Age. *v.2 p.190*

Twentieth-Century Textbook Wars: A History of Advocacy and Opposition. *v.4 p.285*

Twentieth-Century Women Novelists: Feminist Theory into Practice. *v.2 p.569, p.570*

Twenty Ads That Shook the World: The Century's Most Groundbreaking Advertising and How It Changed Us All. *v.4 p.427*

Twenty Against the Underworld. *v.3 p.457*

Twenty Contemporary Norwegian Poets: A Bilingual Anthology. *v.2 p.627*

Twenty Million New Customers!: Understanding Gay Men's Consumer Behavior. *v.6 p.382*

Twenty Stories from South Asia. *v.6 p.147*

Twenty Studies That Revolutionized Child Psychology.*v.5 p.641*

Twenty Years After. *v.2 p.489*

Twenty Years at Hull House. *v.4 p.757*

Twenty-First-Century Feminist Classrooms: Pedagogies of Identity and Difference. *v.6 p.464*

Twenty-Five Black African Filmmakers: A Critical Study, with Filmography and Bio-Bibliography. *v.6 p.334*

Twenty-Four Ways of Looking at Mary McCarthy: The Writer and Her Work. *v.2 p.99, p.100*

The Twenty-Three Days of the City of Alba: Stories. .*v.2 p.715*

Twenty-Three New Poems. *v.2 p.739*

Twice Blessed: On Being Lesbian or Gay and Jewish. .*v.6 p.373*

🔲 Twice Dead: Organ Transplants and the Reinvention of Death. *v.6 p.222*

Twice Round the Black Church: Early Memories of Ireland and England. *v.2 p.337*

Twilight at the Equator: A Novel. *v.6 p.507*

Twilight in the Desert: The Coming Saudi Oil Shock and the World Economy. *v.4 p.268*

The Twilight of Atheism: The Rise and Fall of Disbelief in the Modern World. *v.1 p.545*

The Twilight of British Ascendancy in the Middle East: A Case Study of Iraq, 1941-1950. . . . .*v.6 p.603*

Twilight of Federalism: The Disintegration of the Federalist Party - 1815-1830. . . . .*v.3 p.414*

The Twilight of French Eastern Alliances, 1926-1936: French-Czechoslovak-Polish Relations from Locarno to the Remilitarization of the Rhineland. *v.3 p.254*

Twilight of the Idols. *v.1 p.467*

The Twilight Years. *v.6 p.229*

Twilight--Los Angeles, 1992: On the Road: A Search for American Character. *v.1 p.122*

Twin Towers: The Life of New York City's World Trade Center. *v.1 p.797, v.6 p.728*

Twisted Cross: The German Christian Movement in the Third Reich. *v.3 p.82*

The Twisted Muse: Musicians and Their Music in the Third Reich. *v.1 p.246*

The Twisted Road to Auschwitz: Nazi Policy Toward German Jews, 1933-1939. . . . .*v.3 p.86, p.173*

Two Ages: The Age of Revolution and the Present Age: A Literary Review. *v.2 p.627*

Two Blades of Grass: A History of Scientific Development in the U. S. Department of Agriculture. *v.5 p.4*

Two Centuries of American Medicine, 1776-1976. . . . .*v.5 p.509, p.510*

Two Cheers for Democracy. *v.2 p.345, p.346*

Two Cities: Medieval Europe, 1050-1320. . . . . . .*v.3 p.67*

Two Comedies by Thomas D'Urfey. *v.2 p.245*

The Two Cultures. *v.4 p.291*

Two Families in Colonial Chile. *v.3 p.350*

Two French Moralists. *v.2 p.477*

The Two Gentlemen of Verona. *v.2 p.224*

Two Hundred Fifty Years of Afro-American Art: An Annotated Bibliography. *v.1 p.662, p.704*

Two Hundred Years of American Communes. *v.4 p.740*

Two Hundred Years of American Educational Thought. *v.4 p.323, p.328*

The Two Intellectual Worlds of John Locke: Man, Person, and Spirits in the Essay. *v.1 p.449*

The Two Italies: Economic Relations Between the Norman Kingdom of Sicily and the Northern Communes. *v.3 p.163, p.198*

Two Japanese Novelists. *v.6 p.231*

The Two Koreas: A Contemporary History. *v.6 p.237*

Two Lives of Charlemagne. *v.3 p.142, p.162*

Two Lucky People: Memoirs. *v.4 p.232*

Two Millennia of Mathematics: From Archimedes to Gauss. *v.5 p.467*

Two Minutes of Silence: Selected Short Stories. . . .*v.2 p.626*

Two Nations: Black and White, Separate, Hostile, Unequal. *v.4 p.730*

Two Nations, Many Cultures: Ethnic Groups in Canada. *v.3 p.542*

Two Nations over Time: Spain and the United States, 1776-1977. . . . .*v.3 p.387*

The Two Noble Kinsmen. *v.2 p.224*

Two Novels: You Didn't Even Try and Imaginary Speeches for a Brazen Head. *v.2 p.158*

Two or Three Things I Know for Sure. *v.6 p.394*

Two Paychecks: Life in Dual Earner Families. *v.6 p.466*

The Two Reconstructions: The Struggle for Black Enfranchisement. *v.6 p.8, p.9, p.32*

Two Roads to Sumter. *v.3 p.427*

Two Serious Ladies. *v.6 p.394*

The Two Sexes: Growing up Apart, Coming Together. *v.4 p.737*

Two Sisters for Social Justice: A Biography of Grace and Edith Abbott. *v.4 p.273*

Two Spanish Masterpieces: The Book of Good Love, and the Celestina. *v.2 p.651, p.652*

Two Spanish Picaresque Novels. *v.2 p.643*

Two Strange Tales. *v.2 p.816, p.817*

Two Strategies for Europe: De Gaulle, the United States and the Atlantic Alliance. *v.4 p.643*

Two Thousand Years of Coptic Christianity. *v.1 p.569*

Two Thousand Years of Jewish Life in Morocco. *v.6 p.598, p.643*

The Two Towers: Being the Second Part of the Lord of the Rings. *v.2 p.386*

Two Treatises of Government and a Letter Concerning Toleration. *v.4 p.216*

Two Treatises of Government: In the Former, the False Principles and Foundation of Sir Robert Filmer, and His Followers Are Detected and Overthrown: The Latter Is an Essay Concerning the True Original, Extent, and End of Civil-Government. *v.4 p.216*

Two Views on Women in Ministry. *v.1 p.657, p.658*

Two Villages on Stilts; Economic and Family Change in Nigeria. *v.4 p.701*

Two Worlds and Their Ways. *v.2 p.339*

A Two-Colored Brocade: The Imagery of Persian Poetry. *v.6 p.673*

The Twyborn Affair. *v.2 p.750, v.6 p.400*

Ty Cobb. *v.4 p.849*

Tycho and Kepler: The Unlikely Partnership That Forever Changed Our Understanding of the Heavens. *v.5 p.62*

Type Talk at Work: How the 16 Personality Types Determine Your Success on the Job. *v.4 p.173*

Typee, Omoo, Mardi. *v.2 p.48*

Types of Christian Theology. *v.1 p.635*

Typhoon and Other Tales. *v.2 p.341*

Typical American. *v.6 p.100*

Tyranny and Political Culture in Ancient Greece. *v.4 p.500, p.501*

The Tyranny of Taste: The Politics of Architecture and Design in Britain, 1550-1960. . . . .*v.1 p.800*

Tyrone's Rebellion: The Outbreak of the Nine Years War in Tudor Ireland. *v.3 p.135, p.137*

Tzintzuntzan: Mexican Peasants in a Changing World. *v.4 p.702*

U

U. S. - Cuban Relations in the 1990s. *v.3 p.308*

U. S. - Mexico Borderlands: Historical and Contemporary Perspectives. *v.3 p.527*

U. S. - Soviet Relations During the Detente. *v.3 p.388*

U. S. - Soviet Summits: An Account of East-West Diplomacy at the Top, 1955-1985. . . . .*v.3 p.393*

U. S. A.: The 42nd Parallel; 1919; The Big Money. . .*v.2 p.69*

The U. S. Acquires the Philippines: Consensus vs. Reality. *v.3 p.389*

The U. S. and Pakistan, 1947-2000: Disenchanted Allies. *v.4 p.644*

U. S. Bank Deregulation in Historical Perspective. *v.4 p.111, p.154*

⊡ U. S. Bureau of Indian Affairs. *v.6 p.677*

The U. S. Constitution and the Power to Go to War: Historical
    and Current Perspectives. *v.4 p.462, p.532*

U. S. Defense Policy Handbook. *v.4 p.151*

U. S. Department of Defense Handbook. *v.4 p.151*

U. S. Diplomacy since 1900. . . . .*v.3 p.454*

The U. S. Environmental Industry: Meeting the Challenge: U. S.
    Industry Faces the 21st Century. *v.4 p.159*

The U. S. EPA Manual of Chemical Methods for Pesticides and
    Devices. *v.5 p.312*

U. S. Foreign Policy and International Politics: George W. Bush,
    9/11, and the the Global Terrorist Hydra. *v.3 p.482*

U. S. Foreign Policy and the Horn of Africa. *v.3 p.393*

U. S. Foreign Policy and the Iran Hostage
    Crisis. *v.3 p.389, p.441, p.442*

The U. S. Forest Service: A
    History. *v.4 p.152, p.164,v.5 p.39, p.40*

U. S. Grant and the American Military Tradition. . . .*v.3 p.435*

U. S. History As Women's History: Knowledge, Power, and
    State Formation. *v.6 p.450*

U. S. Homeland Security: A Reference
    Handbook. *v.4 p.150, p.151*

The U. S. House of Representatives: Reform or
    Rebuild? *v.4 p.533*

U. S. Intelligence and the Nazis. *v.3 p.83*

U. S. Latino Issues. *v.6 p.521*

U. S. Latino Literature: A Critical Guide for Students and
    Teachers. *v.6 p.511*

The U. S. Naval Mission to Haiti, 1959-1963. . . . .*v.3 p.316*

U. S. News Ultimate Guide to Becoming a Teacher. . .*v.4 p.278*

U. S. Policy Toward Israel: The Role of Political Culture in
    Defining the "Special Relationship". *v.3 p.392*

U. S. Protestant Missions in Cuba: From Independence to
    Castro. *v.3 p.314*

The U. S. Supreme Court and the Electoral Process. . .*v.4 p.461*

U. S. Tax Aspects of Doing Business Abroad. . .*v.4 p.92, p.108*

The U. S.-Mexico Border. *v.3 p.527*

The UAW and the Heyday of American Liberalism,
    1945-1968. . . . .*v.4 p.124*

UAW Politics in the Cold War Era. *v.4 p.126*

Uber die Pflicht: Eine Analyse des Werkes von Siegfried
    Lenz. *v.2 p.612*

The Ubu Plays: Ubu Rex; Ubu Cuckolded; Ubu
    Enchained. *v.2 p.521*

The UFA Story: A History of Germany's Greatest Film
    Company, 1918-1945. . . . .*v.3 p.178*

Uganda since Independence. *v.6 p.66, p.67*

Ugetsu Monogatari: Tales of Moonlight and Rain : A Complete
    English Version Of The Eighteenth-century Japanese
    Collection Of Tales of the Supernatural. . .*v.6 p.233, p.234*

Ugetsu. *v.6 p.344*

The Ugly American. *v.2 p.94*

The Ugly Duchess. *v.2 p.607*

Ugo Foscolo: Poet of Exile. *v.2 p.710*

Ugo Foscolo. *v.2 p.711*

Uhlig's Corrosion Handbook. *v.5 p.690*

UICC Manual of Clinical Oncology. *v.5 p.164*

Ukiyo-E. *v.1 p.692*

Ukraine: A History. *v.3 p.230*

Ukraine under Kuchma: Political Reform, Economic
    Transformation, and Security in Independent
    Ukraine. *v.4 p.598*

Ukrainian: A Comprehensive Grammar. *v.2 p.777, p.778*

Ukrainian Futurism: 1914-1930: A Historical and Critical
    Study. *v.2 p.814*

Ukrainian Literature in the Twentieth Century: A Reader's
    Guide. *v.2 p.813, p.814*

Ukrainian Prose Manual: A Text for Intermediate Language
    Studies. *v.2 p.778*

Ukrainian-English - English-Ukrainian Standard
    Dictionary. *v.2 p.777*

Ukrainian-English - English-Ukrainian. *v.2 p.777*

Ukridge. *v.2 p.391*

Ullmann's Encyclopedia of Industrial Chemistry: A1-A28,
    B1-B8. . . . .*v.5 p.316*

Ullmann's Encyclopedia of Industrial
    Chemistry. *v.5 p.315, p.316, p.740*

⊡ Ullmann's Encyclopedia of Industrial Chemistry. . .*v.5 p.316*

Ulrichs: The Life and Works of Karl Heinrich Ulrichs, Pioneer
    of the Modern Gay Movement. *v.6 p.402*

🄮 The Ultimate Accountants' Reference Including GAAP, IRS
    and SEC Regulations, Leases, and More. *v.4 p.104*

The Ultimate Assist: The Relationship and Broadcast Strategies
    of the NBA and Television
    Networks. *v.4 p.853, p.854, p.896, p.902*

Ultimate Book of the World Cup: A Complete
    History. *v.4 p.847, p.867*

The Ultimate Business Dictionary: Defining the World of
    Work. *v.4 p.174*

The Ultimate Field Guide to the U. S. Economy: A Compact
    and Irreverent Guide to Economic Life in America. .*v.4 p.269*

The Ultimate Film Festival Survival Guide. *v.6 p.346*

Ultimate Fitness: The Quest for Truth about Health and
    Exercise. *v.4 p.791*

Ultimate Foundation of Economic Science: An Essay on
    Method. *v.4 p.197*

The Ultimate Guide to Sports Marketing. *v.4 p.884*

The Ultimate Intimacy. *v.2 p.783*

Ultimate Journey: Retracing the Path of an Ancient Buddhist
    Monk Who Crossed Asia in Search of
    Enlightenment. *v.6 p.202*

The Ultimate Movie Thesaurus: The Only Book You'll Ever
    Need to Find the Movie You Want. *v.6 p.311*

The Ultimate Question: Driving Good Profits and True
    Growth. *v.4 p.143*

Ultra in the West: The Normandy Campaign, 1944-45. .*v.3 p.80*

Ultra Violet Spectrometry: Practical Techniques, Instrumentation
    and Data Handling. *v.5 p.272*

Ultramarine. *v.2 p.367*

Ultraviolent Movies: From Sam Peckinpah to Quentin
    Tarantino. *v.6 p.320*

Ultraviolet and Visible Absorption Spectra: Index for
    1930-1954. . . . .*v.5 p.272*

Ultraviolet Radiation in Antarctica: Measurements and
Biological Effects. *v.5 p.90*

Ultraviolet Spectra of Aromatic Compounds. *v.5 p.297*

Ultra-Wideband Communications: Fundamentals and
Applications. *v.5 p.727*

Ultra-Wideband Radio Technology. *v.5 p.727*

Ulysses: A Reader's Edition. *v.2 p.359*

Ulysses: Fifty Years. *v.2 p.360*

Ulysses (Gabler Edition). *v.2 p.359*

Ulysses in Progress. *v.2 p.358*

Ulysses on the Liffey. *v.2 p.358*

Ulysses: The Mechanics of Meaning. *v.2 p.358*

Ulysses. *v.2 p.359*

▢ UMIST Corrosion and Protection Centre. *v.5 p.734*

The UN and Global Political Economy: Trade, Finance, and
Development. *v.4 p.665, p.666*

🄴 UN Contributions to Development Thinking and
Practice. *v.4 p.634, p.664*

▢ UN Documentation Centre. *v.4 p.635*

▢ UN Millennium Development Goals. *v.4 p.635*

The UN Secretary General and Secretariat. *v.4 p.633*

The UN Security Council: From the Cold War to the 21st
Century. *v.4 p.634*

UN Voices: The Struggle for Development and Social
Justice. *v.4 p.636*

An Unabridged Translation of Simplicius
Simplicissimus. *v.2 p.595*

The Unaccommodated Calvin: Studies in the Foundation of a
Theological Tradition. *v.1 p.603*

Unadjusted Girl, with Cases and Standpoint for Behavior
Analysis. *v.4 p.752*

Unamuno, a Philosophy of Tragedy. *v.1 p.474*

Unapologetic Theology: A Christian Voice in a Pluralistic
Conversation. *v.1 p.636*

Unarmed Forces: The Transnational Movement to End the Cold
War. *v.4 p.656*

Unarmed Insurrections. *v.4 p.766, p.767*

Unbank the Fire: Visions for the Education of African American
Children. *v.4 p.310*

The Unbearable Bassington. *v.2 p.381*

The Unbearable Lightness of Being. *v.2 p.784*

Unbearable Weight: Feminism, Western Culture, and the
Body. *v.6 p.436*

The Unbound Prometheus: Technological Change and Industrial
Development in Western Europe from 1750 to
Present. *v.3 p.40*

Unbound Voices: A Documentary History of Chinese Women in
San Francisco. *v.6 p.113, p.128*

Unbounding the Future: The Nanotechnology
Revolution. *v.5 p.265*

🄴 Unbroken Thread: An Anthology of Plays by Asian American
Women. *v.6 p.99*

Unbroken Thread: An Anthology of Plays by Asian American
Women. *v.1 p.69, p.122, p.125*

The Uncensored War: The Media and Vietnam. *v.4 p.407*

An Uncertain Grace. *v.1 p.768*

Uncertain Greatness: Henry Kissinger and American Foreign
Policy. *v.3 p.476*

An Uncertain Hour: The French, the Germans, the Jews, and the
City of Lyon, 1940-1945. . . . .*v.3 p.156*

Uncertain Legacies: Federal Budget Policy from Roosevelt
Through Reagan. *v.4 p.524*

An Uncertain Tradition: American Secretaries of State in the
Twentieth Century. *v.3 p.452*

Uncertain Years: Chinese-American Relations,
1947-1950. . . . .*v.3 p.387*

The Uncertainties of Knowledge. *v.4 p.762*

Uncertainty and Optimality: Probability, Statistics and
Operations Research. *v.5 p.100, p.101*

Uncertainty and Structure As Psychological Concepts. .*v.5 p.594*

Uncharted Journey: Promoting Democracy in the Middle
East. *v.4 p.615*

The Uncivil War: Irregular Warfare in the Upper South,
1861-1865. . . . .*v.4 p.521*

The Unclassed. *v.2 p.289*

Uncle Fred in the Springtime. *v.2 p.391*

Uncle Peretz Takes Off. *v.6 p.651*

Uncle Sam's War of 1898 and the Origins of
Globalization. *v.3 p.400, p.401*

Uncle Tom's Cabin and American Culture. *v.2 p.51*

Uncle Tom's Cabin: Evil, Affliction, and Redemptive
Love. *v.2 p.51*

Uncle Tom's Cabin. *v.2 p.51, p.52,v.3 p.421*

Uncle Tungsten: Memories of a Chemical Boyhood. . .*v.5 p.326*

Uncollected Prose: Early Reviews and Articles, 1897-1939, Vol.
1. . . . .*v.2 p.327, p.328*

Uncollected Prose: Later Reviews, Articles and Other
Miscellaneous Prose, 1897-1939, Vol. 2. . . . . . .*v.2 p.328*

An Uncomfortable Authority: Maria Edgeworth and Her
Contexts. *v.2 p.286*

Uncommon Caring: Learning from Men Who Teach in the
Primary Grades. *v.4 p.278, p.279*

An Uncommon Man: The Triumph of Herbert Hoover. .*v.3 p.480*

Uncommon Places: The Complete Works. . . .*v.1 p.768, p.769*

The Uncommon Vision of Sergei Konenkov, 1874-1971: A
Russian Sculptor and His Times. *v.1 p.780*

The Uncompleted Past: Postwar German Novels and the Third
Reich. *v.2 p.592*

The Unconscious Civilization. *v.4 p.510*

Uncontained: Urban Fiction in Postwar America. *v.2 p.11*

Uncovering Our History: Teaching with Primary
Sources. *v.3 p.375*

The Uncrowned King of Swing: Fletcher Henderson and Big
Band Jazz. *v.1 p.261, p.331*

Undaunted Courage: Meriwether Lewis, Thomas Jefferson and
the Opening of the American West. *v.3 p.519*

Under a Cruel Star : A Life in Prague, 1941-1968. . .*v.3 p.190*

Under a Glass Bell. *v.2 p.105*

Under African Skies: Modern African Stories. .*v.2 p.752, v.6 p.80*

Under Clouded Skies/Beauregard. *v.2 p.531*

Under Crescent and Cross: The Jews in the Middle
Ages. *v.1 p.548, v.3 p.67, v.6 p.573*

Under Flag. *v.6 p.103*

Under His Very Windows: The Vatican and the Holocaust in Italy. *v.4 p.654*

Under Human Species. *v.2 p.716*

Under Kilimanjaro. *v.2 p.84*

Under Milk Wood, a Play for Voices. *v.2 p.386*

Under My Skin: My Autobiography, to 1949. . . . . *v.2 p.365*

Under Satan's Sun. *v.2 p.508*

Under Southern Seas: The Ecology of Australia's Rocky Reefs. *v.5 p.173*

Under the Big Stick: Nicaragua and the United States since 1848. . . . . *v.3 p.387*

Under the Cope of Heaven: Religion, Society, and Politics in Colonial America. *v.1 p.543, v.3 p.405*

Under the Cover of Kindness: The Invention of Social Work. *v.4 p.737, p.758*

Under the Guardianship of the Nation: The Freedmen's Bureau and the Reconstruction of Georgia, 1865-1870. . . *v.3 p.503*

Under the Jaguar Sun. *v.2 p.715*

Under the Krishnachura: Fifty Years of Bangladeshi Writing. *v.6 p.148, p.149*

Under the Naked Sky: Short Stories from the Arab World. *v.2 p.583*

Under the Radiant Sun and Crescent Moon. *v.2 p.715*

Under the Volcano: A Novel. *v.2 p.367*

Under the Yoke. *v.2 p.780*

Under This Blazing Light. *v.6 p.611*

Under Two Flags: The American Navy in the Civil War. *v.4 p.520*

Under Western Eyes: India from Milton to Macaulay. *v.2 p.165*

Under Western Eyes. *v.2 p.340*

The Underachieving School. *v.4 p.327*

Underclass. *v.4 p.726*

Undercover-Police Surveillance in Comparative Perspective. *v.6 p.267*

Undergraduate Algebraic Geometry. *v.5 p.497*

Undergraduate Commutative Algebra. *v.5 p.474*

Undergraduate Econometrics. *v.4 p.201, p.202*

The Undergraduate's Companion to Arab Writers and Their Web Sites. *v.6 p.664*

Underground Codes: Race, Crime and Related Fires. *v.6 p.257*

Underground: The Tokyo Gas Attack and the Japanese Psyche. *v.6 p.232*

The Underground Woman. *v.2 p.63*

The Undermining of Austria-Hungary: The Battle for Hearts and Minds. *v.3 p.78, p.184*

Understanding African-American Rhetoric: Classical Origins to Contemporary Innovations. *v.6 p.20*

Understanding Agriculture: New Directions for Education. *v.5 p.11, p.12*

Understanding Analysis. *v.5 p.489*

Understanding and Applying Medical Anthropology. . *v.5 p.536*

Understanding and Helping Families: A Cognitive-Behavioral Approach. *v.5 p.666, p.668*

Understanding and Treating Schizophrenia: Contemporary Research, Theory, and Practice. *v.5 p.661*

Understanding Anthony Powell. *v.2 p.377*

Understanding Arbitrage: An Intuitive Approach to Financial Analysis. *v.4 p.91, p.92, p.94, p.98, p.101, p.103*

Understanding Arguments: An Introduction to Informal Logic. *v.1 p.492*

Understanding Arthur Miller. *v.2 p.101*

Understanding Attitudes and Predicting Social Behavior. *v.5 p.585, p.604*

Understanding Batteries. *v.5 p.285*

Understanding Camilo Jose Cela. *v.2 p.657*

Understanding Capitalism: Competition, Command, and Change. *v.4 p.214, p.251, p.252*

Understanding Carson Mccullers. *v.2 p.100*

Understanding Central America: Global Forces, Rebellion, and Change. *v.3 p.300, p.303*

Understanding Chekhov: A Critical Study of Chekhov's Prose and Drama. *v.2 p.808*

Understanding Children's Literature. *v.2 p.582*

Understanding Church Growth. *v.1 p.647*

Understanding Classical Sociology: Marx, Weber, Durkheim. *v.4 p.683*

Understanding Comics. *v.2 p.582*

Understanding Commodity Cultures: Explorations in Economic Anthropology with Case Studies from Mexico. . . *v.4 p.28*

Understanding Consumer Choice. *v.4 p.139*

Understanding Contemporary Chicana Literature. *v.6 p.479, p.501, p.514*

Understanding Curriculum: An Introduction to the Study of Historical and Contemporary Curriculum Discourses. *v.4 p.365*

Understanding Dance. *v.1 p.43*

Understanding Dante. *v.2 p.705*

Understanding Depression. *v.5 p.659*

Understanding Digital Color. *v.1 p.759*

Understanding DNA and Gene Cloning: A Guide for the Curious. *v.5 p.121*

Understanding DNA: The Molecule and How it Works. *v.5 p.120, p.121*

Understanding Earth. *v.5 p.419*

Understanding Educational Reform in Global Context: Economy, Ideology and the State. *v.4 p.313*

Understanding Electric Power Systems: An Overview of the Technology and the Marketplace. *v.5 p.723*

Understanding Energy: Energy, Entropy and Thermodynamics for Every Man. *v.5 p.559*

Understanding English Grammar: A Linguistic Approach. *v.2 p.558*

Understanding Environmental Pollution: A Primer. *v.5 p.705*

Understanding Ethnic Violence: Fear, Hatred, and Resentment in Twentieth-Century Eastern Europe. *v.3 p.207*

Understanding Eudora Welty. *v.2 p.130*

Understanding European Trade Unionism: Between Market, Class and Society. *v.4 p.126*

Understanding Explosions. *v.5 p.743*

Understanding Federico Garcia Lorca. *v.2 p.660*

Understanding Fiction. *v.2 p.579*

Understanding Fossils: An Introduction to Invertebrate Palaeontology. *v.5 p.447*

Understanding Franz Werfel. *v.2 p.616*

Understanding Gabriel Garcia Marquez. *v.2 p.684*

Understanding Gary Snyder. *v.2 p.155*

Understanding Gay and Lesbian Youth: Lessons for Straight School Teachers, Counselors, and Administrators. .*v.6 p.385*

Understanding Genetics: A Primer for Couples and Families. *v.5 p.151*

Understanding Gliding. *v.4 p.788, p.848*

Understanding Global Environmental Politics: Domination, Accumulation, Resistance. *v.6 p.301*

Understanding Global News: A Critical Introduction. .*v.4 p.408*

Understanding GPS: Principles and Applications. . . .*v.4 p.390*

Understanding Greek Vases: A Guide to Terms, Styles, and Techniques. *v.1 p.663, p.669, p.807*

Understanding Harold Pinter. *v.2 p.376, p.377*

Understanding Homicide. *v.6 p.252*

Understanding Human Motivation: What Makes People Tick? *v.5 p.658*

Understanding Hume. *v.1 p.451*

Understanding Installation Art: From Duchamp to Holzer. *v.1 p.772*

Understanding International Conflicts: An Introduction to Theory and History. *v.4 p.626, p.627*

Understanding Iraq: The Whole Sweep of Iraqi History, from Genghis Khan's Mongols to the Ottoman Turks to the British Mandate to the American Occupation. . .*v.6 p.602*

Understanding Italo Calvino. *v.2 p.715*

Understanding Jack Kerouac. *v.2 p.93, p.94*

ⓔ Understanding Jamaica Kincaid's Annie John: A Student Casebook to Issues, Sources, and Historical Documents. *v.2 p.768*

Understanding Japanese Society. *v.6 p.221*

Understanding Jihad. *v.1 p.560*

Understanding John Fowles. *v.2 p.346*

Understanding Juan Goytisolo. *v.2 p.658*

Understanding Julio Cortazar. *v.2 p.679*

Understanding Karl Rahner: An Introduction to His Life and Thought. *v.1 p.580*

Understanding Keynes: An Analysis of the General Theory. *v.4 p.227*

Understanding Korean Literature. *v.6 p.238*

Understanding Language Change. *v.2 p.563*

Understanding Lillian Hellman. *v.2 p.83*

Understanding Locke. *v.1 p.448*

Understanding Luigi Pirandello. *v.2 p.722*

Understanding Mainland Puerto Rican Poverty. . . .*v.6 p.524*

Understanding Mario Vargas Llosa. *v.2 p.685*

Understanding Marriage: Developments in the Study of Couple Interaction. *v.5 p.639*

Understanding Marx: A Reconstructive and Critique of Capital. *v.4 p.237*

Understanding Mass Spectra: A Basic Approach. .*v.5 p.271, p.272*

Understanding Materials Science: History, Properties, Applications. *v.5 p.732*

Understanding May Sarton. *v.2 p.118, p.119*

Understanding Media: The Extensions of Man (Critical Edition). *v.4 p.416, p.417, v.5 p.625*

Understanding Medicinal Plants: Their Chemistry and Therapeutic Action. *v.5 p.211*

Understanding "Les Fleurs du Mal" Critical Readings. .*v.2 p.488*

Understanding Molecular Simulation: From Algorithms to Applications. *v.5 p.551*

Understanding Mysticism. *v.1 p.531*

Understanding Nelson Algren. *v.2 p.56*

Understanding Nonlinear Dynamics. *v.5 p.488, p.501*

Understanding Optical Fiber Communications. . . .*v.5 p.701*

Understanding Owls. *v.5 p.157*

Understanding Paranoia: A Guide for Professionals, Families, and Sufferers. *v.5 p.660*

Understanding Pathophysiology. *v.5 p.514*

Understanding Phenomenal Consciousness. *v.1 p.497*

Understanding Police Culture. *v.6 p.263*

Understanding Police Use of Force: Officers, Suspects, and Reciprocity. *v.6 p.260*

Understanding Police Use of Force. *v.6 p.261*

Understanding Political Change: The British Voter 1964-1987. . . . .*v.4 p.606*

Understanding Polymer Morphology. *v.5 p.323, p.324*

Understanding Power Quality Problems: Voltage Sags and Interruptions. *v.5 p.723*

Understanding Psychological Preparation for Sport: Theory and Practice of Elite Performers. *v.5 p.582*

Understanding Regression Analysis. *v.5 p.483*

Understanding Relativity: A Simplified Approach to Einstein's Theories. *v.5 p.557*

Understanding Renewable Energy Systems. *v.5 p.361*

Understanding Research Methods and Statistics: An Integrated Introduction for Psychology. *v.5 p.600, p.601*

Understanding Robust and Exploratory Data Analysis. *v.5 p.482*

Understanding Rock: Essays in Musical Analysis. . .*v.1 p.267*

Understanding Roman Inscriptions. *v.3 p.22*

Understanding Search Engines: Mathematical Modeling and Text Retrieval. *v.5 p.338*

Understanding Self-Help/Mutual-Aid: Experiential Learning in the Commons. *v.5 p.669*

Understanding Shyness: Psychological Perspectives. .*v.5 p.652*

Understanding Sleep and Dreaming. *v.5 p.613*

Understanding Sport Organizations: The Application of Organization Theory. *v.4 p.886, p.889*

Understanding Sport Organizations: The Application of Organizational Theory. *v.4 p.819, p.886*

Understanding Sports Coaching: The Social, Cultural and Pedagogical Foundations of Coaching Practice. . .*v.4 p.904*

Understanding Sports Massage. . .*v.4 p.790, p.825, p.828, p.873*

Understanding State Constitutions. *v.4 p.454*

Understanding Student Learning. *v.5 p.574*

Understanding Tennessee Williams. *v.2 p.134*

Understanding Terence. *v.2 p.445*

Understanding Terrorism: Psychosocial Roots, Consequences, and Interventions. *v.4 p.660, p.767*

Understanding the Beats. *v.2 p.10, p.11*

Understanding the Black Mountain Poets. *v.2 p.13*

Understanding the Census: A Guide for Marketers, Planners, Grant-Writers and Other Data Users. *v.4 p.180*

Understanding the City: Contemporary and Future Perspectives. *v.6 p.717*

Understanding the Corporate Annual Report: Nuts, Bolts and a Few Loose Screws. *v.4 p.91, p.95, p.105, p.106*

Understanding the Cultural Landscape. *v.4 p.399*

Understanding the European Union: A Concise Introduction. *v.3 p.87*

Understanding the Family. *v.5 p.639*

Understanding the Fourth Gospel. *v.1 p.628*

Understanding the Gender Gap: An Economic History of American Women. *v.4 p.133*

Understanding the Genome. *v.5 p.146, p.147*

Understanding the Greek Orthodox Church Its Faith, History and Life. *v.1 p.569*

Understanding the Human Genome Project. *v.5 p.136*

Understanding the I Ching: The Wilhelm Lectures on the Book of Changes. *v.6 p.184*

Understanding the Language of Science. *v.5 p.401, p.406*

Understanding the North American Free Trade Agreement: Legal and Business Consequences of NAFTA. *v.4 p.436*

Understanding the Philosophy of Science. *v.5 p.403*

Understanding the Present: Science and the Soul of Modern Man. *v.5 p.400*

Understanding the Principalship: Metaphorical Themes, 1920s-1990s. *v.4 p.281*

Understanding the Process of Economic Change. .*v.4 p.196, p.210*

Understanding the Self-Help Organization: Frameworks and Findings. *v.5 p.669*

Understanding the Visual. *v.4 p.424*

Understanding the Windsor Report. *v.1 p.582*

Understanding Theology and Popular Culture. .*v.1 p.595, p.596*

Understanding Things Fall Apart: A Student Casebook to Issues, Sources and Historical Documents. *v.2 p.753*

Understanding Ultra Wide Band Radio Fundamentals. .*v.5 p.726*

Understanding Urban Policy: A Critical Introduction. .*v.6 p.722*

Understanding Victims and Restorative Justice. . . .*v.6 p.258*

Understanding W. S. Merwin. *v.2 p.101*

Understanding Waiting for Godot by Samuel Beckett: Text and Critical Commentary. *v.2 p.333*

Understanding Wall Street. *v.4 p.96, p.100*

|e| Understanding Wetlands: Fen, Bog, and Marsh. . .*v.4 p.392*

Underworld: A Novel. *v.2 p.143*

The Undivine Comedy: Detheologizing Dante. . . .*v.2 p.703*

The Un-Divine Comedy. *v.2 p.790*

Undocumented in L. A.: An Immigrant's Story. .*v.6 p.489, p.529*

Undocumented Mexicans in the U. S. A. *v.6 p.529*

Undoing the Social: Towards a Deconstructive Sociology. *v.4 p.679*

The Undressed Art: Why We Draw. *v.1 p.724*

Undressing Cinema: Clothing and Identity in the Movies. *v.6 p.349*

Undue Process: The NCAA's Injustice for All. *v.4 p.822, p.823, p.895, p.901*

Uneasy Asylum: France and the Jewish Refugee Crisis, 1933-1942. . . . .*v.3 p.154*

Uneasy Dreams: The Golden Age of British Horror Films, 1956-1976. . . . .*v.6 p.339*

Uneasy Lies the Head: The Autobiography of King Hussein I of Jordan. *v.6 p.621*

Uneasy Money. *v.2 p.391*

The Uneasy State: The United States from 1915 to 1945. . . . .*v.3 p.448*

The Unedited Diaries of Carolina Maria De Jesus. . .*v.3 p.336*

Unemployment and the Multinationals: A Strategy for Technological Change in Latin America. . .*v.4 p.253, p.263*

Unending Blues: Poems. *v.2 p.155*

Unequal Allies?: United States Security and Alliance Policy Toward Japan, 1945-1960. . . . .*v.3 p.392*

Unequal Chances: Family Background and Economic Success. *v.4 p.264*

Unequal Childhood: The Importance of Social Class in Family Life. *v.4 p.728, p.729*

Unequal Childhoods: Young Children's Lives in Poor Countries. *v.4 p.756*

Unequal Giants: Diplomatic Relations Between the United States and Brazil, 1889-1930. . . . .*v.3 p.342, p.343*

Unequal Partners: Charles Dickens, Wilkie Collins, and Victorian Authorship. *v.2 p.281, p.285,v.6 p.740*

Unequal Sisters: A Multicultural Reader in U. S. Women's History. *v.6 p.40, p.46, p.450*

Uneven Developments: The Ideological Work of Gender in Mid-Victorian England. *v.2 p.176, v.6 p.748*

Uneven Ground: American Indian Sovereignty and Federal Law. *v.6 p.697*

Uneven Grounds: American Indian Sovereignty and Federal Law. *v.4 p.526*

The Unexpected Legacy of Divorce: The 25 Year Landmark Study. *v.5 p.640*

Unfair Arguments with Existence. *v.2 p.75*

Unfair Housing: How National Policy Shapes Community Action. *v.4 p.567, v.6 p.725*

Unfinished Business: America and Cuba after the Cold War, 1989-2001. . . . .*v.3 p.311*

Unfinished Dreams: Contemporary Poetry of Acadie. .*v.2 p.538*

The Unfinished Liberation of Chinese Women, 1949-1980. . . . .*v.6 p.433, p.453*

An Unfinished Life: An Autobiography. *v.1 p.12, p.13*

An Unfinished Life: John F. Kennedy, 1917-1963. . .*v.3 p.469*

The Unfinished Print. *v.1 p.754*

The Unfinished Quest of Richard Wright. *v.2 p.138*

An Unfinished Season: A Novel. *v.2 p.147*

The Unfinished System of Nonknowledge. *v.1 p.455*

Unfinished Transitions: Gendered Political Opportunities and Women's Organizing in Latin American Democratization. *v.3 p.360*

Unfinished Twentieth Century: The Crisis of Arms Control. *v.4 p.657*

An Unfinished Woman: A Memoir. *v.2 p.83*

Unfocused Kids: Helping Students to Focus on Their Education and Career Plans: A Resource for Educators. *v.4 p.306, p.353, p.354*

Unforeseen History. *v.1 p.456*

Unforgettable: The Life and Mystique of Nat King Cole. *v.1 p.259, p.281, p.317*

Unforgivable Blackness: The Rise and Fall of Jack Johnson. *v.6 p.41*

The Unfortunate Traveller: Or, the Life of Jack Wilton. *v.2 p.222*

Unfortunately, It Was Paradise: Selected Poems. *v.6 p.659*

The Unfree Professions: German Lawyers, Teachers, and Engineers, 1900-1950. . . . .*v.3 p.180*

Unfulfilled Union: Canadian Federalism and National Unity. *v.4 p.587*

Das Ungezwungne Leben Kasts; Drei Berichte. *v.2 p.616*

Das ungezwungne Leben Kasts; drei Berichte. *v.2 p.616*

The Ungovernable City: John Lindsay and His Struggle to Save New York. *v.3 p.490, v.6 p.711*

An Ungovernable People: The English and Their Law in the Seventeenth and Eighteenth Centuries. *v.3 p.103, p.106, p.108, p.123*

Ungrounded Empires: The Cultural Politics of Modern Chinese Transnationalism. *v.6 p.204*

□ UNHCR : The UN Refugee Agency. *v.4 p.765*

The UNHCR and World Politics: A Perilous Path. .*v.4 p.634, p.670*

Unheard Melodies: Narrative Film Music. *v.1 p.255*

Unheard Voices: The Effects of Silence on Lesbian and Gay Educators. *v.6 p.383, p.386*

An Unholy Alliance: The Sacred and Modern Sports. .*v.4 p.824*

Unholy War: Terror in the Name of Islam. *v.4 p.658*

The Unicorn Tapestries at the Metropolitan Museum of Art. *v.1 p.709*

The Unicorn. *v.2 p.619*

The Unification of Greece. *v.3 p.194*

The Unified Modeling Language Reference Manual. *v.5 p.347, p.348*

The Unified Modeling Language User Guide. . *v.5 p.345, p.349*

Uniform Central Limit Theorems. *v.5 p.483*

□ Uniform Crime Reports. *v.6 p.246*

Unifying Biology: The Evolutionary Synthesis and Evolutionary Biology. *v.5 p.81, p.196*

Unilateralism and U. S. Foreign Policy: International Perspectives. *v.4 p.642*

The Unintended Consequences of High-Stakes Testing. .*v.4 p.286*

Uninvited: Classical Hollywood Cinema and Lesbian Representation. *v.6 p.417*

Union Cavalry in the Civil War: From Fort Sumter to Gettysburg. *v.3 p.432*

Union Cavalry in the Civil War: The War in the East, from Gettysburg to Appomattox, 1863-1865. . . . . .*v.3 p.432*

Union Cavalry in the Civil War: The War in the West, 1861-1865. . . . .*v.3 p.432*

The Union Divided: Party Conflict in the Civil War North. *v.3 p.399*

Union in Peril: The Crisis over British Intervention in the Civil War. *v.4 p.521*

□ Union List of Artist Names Online. *v.1 p.661*

Union Management Relations in Canada. *v.4 p.120*

The Union Nationale: Quebec Nationalism from Duplessis to Levesque. *v.4 p.590*

Union Street. *v.2 p.330*

Union Violence: The Record and the Response of the Courts, Legislators and NLBR. *v.4 p.446*

Unions and Public Policy: The New Economy, Law, and Democratic Politics, 364. . . . .*v.4 p.121*

Unions and Workplace Reorganization. *v.4 p.128*

Unions in a Globalized Environment: Changing Borders, Organizational Boundaries, and Social Roles. .*v.4 p.572, p.665*

Unions in America. *v.4 p.124*

Unions, Radicals, and Democratic Presidents: Seeking Social Change in the Twentieth Century. *v.4 p.122*

Unipress: United Press International: Covering the 20th Century. *v.4 p.404*

Unit Operations of Chemical Engineering. *v.5 p.744*

The Unitarian Conscience. *v.1 p.589, p.590*

United Apart: Gender and the Rise of Craft Unionism. *v.4 p.125*

The United Brotherhood of Carpenters: The First Hundred Years. *v.4 p.126*

United Methodism in America: A Compact History. . .*v.1 p.586*

The United Mine Workers of America: A Model of Industrial Solidarity? *v.4 p.127*

The United Nations and Apartheid, 1948-1994. . . .*v.4 p.635*

The United Nations and Cambodia, 1991-1995. .*v.4 p.586, p.636*

The United Nations and Changing World Politics. . .*v.4 p.633*

The United Nations and El Salvador, 1990-1995. .*v.4 p.636, p.651*

The United Nations and Electoral Assistance. *v.4 p.632*

The United Nations and Haiti. *v.4 p.632, p.648*

The United Nations and International Law. *v.4 p.477, p.478, p.634*

The United Nations and Iraq: Defanging the Viper. *v.4 p.656, v.6 p.603*

The United Nations and Mozambique, 1992-1995. . . . .*v.4 p.633, p.646, p.648*

The United Nations and Nuclear Non-Proliferation. *v.4 p.635, p.657*

The United Nations and the Advancement of Women, 1945-1995. . . . .*v.4 p.632*

The United Nations and the Quest for Nuclear Disarmament. *v.4 p.655*

The United Nations and the Superpowers: China, Russia and America. *v.4 p.635*

The United Nations As a Political Institution. *v.4 p.635*

The United Nations at the End of the 1990's. *v.4 p.632*

The United Nations at the Millennium. *v.4 p.633, p.634*

□ United Nations Bibliographic Information System UNBisNet. *v.4 p.476*

□ United Nations Common Database. *v.4 p.574, p.625*

United Nations Disarmament Yearbook 2004. . . . . .*v.4 p.657*

United Nations, Divided World: The U. N.'s Roles in International Relations. *v.4 p.635*

□ United Nations Documentation: Research Guide. . *v.4 p.476*

United Nations Handbook. *v.4 p.634, p.635*

The United Nations in the New World Order: The World Organization at Fifty. *v.4 p.633*

The United Nations in the Post-Cold War Era. . . .*v.4 p.634*

The United Nations: International Organization and World
Politics. *v.4 p.636*

The United Nations, Iran and Iraq: How Peacemaking
Changed. *v.4 p.649*

The United Nations Peacekeeper of American Policies and
Uncivilizations. *v.4 p.633*

United Nations Peacekeeping in Africa Since
1960. . . . .*v.4 p.649, p.650*

The United Nations: Reality and Ideal. *v.4 p.632*

United Nations System: An Annotated Bibliography. . .*v.4 p.632*

United Nations: The First Fifty Years. *v.4 p.634*

☐ United Nations Treaty Collection. *v.4 p.476*

The United Nations under Boutros Boutros-Ghali,
1992-1997. . . . .*v.4 p.633*

The United Nations under Dag Hammarskjold,
1953-1961. . . . .*v.4 p.634*

United States, 1830-1850: The Nation and Its Sections. .*v.3 p.415*

The United States and Brazil: A Long Road of Unmet
Expectations. *v.3 p.389*

The United States and Cambodia, 1969-2000: A Troubled
Relationship. *v.6 p.170*

The United States and Coercive Diplomacy. . .*v.4 p.644, p.645*

The United States and Germany: A Diplomatic History. .*v.3 p.389*

The United States and Germany in the Era of the Cold War,
1945-1990: A Handbook. *v.3 p.389*

The United States and Poland. *v.3 p.393*

The United States and the Andean Republics: Peru, Bolivia, and
Ecuador. *v.3 p.331*

The United States and the Hawaiian Kingdom: A Political
History. *v.3 p.393*

The United States and the Middle East, 1900 to 9/11, Parts
I-II. *v.6 p.595*

The United States and the Origins of the Cold War,
1941-1947. . . . .*v.3 p.452*

The United States and the Origins of the Cuban Revolution: An
Empire of Liberty in an Age of National Liberation. .*v.3 p.306*

The United States and the Rule of Law in International
Affairs. *v.4 p.477*

The United States and the Second Hague Peace Conference:
American Diplomacy and International Organization,
1899-1914. . . . .*v.4 p.645, p.648, p.649*

The United States and the Southern Cone: Argentina, Chile, and
Uruguay. *v.3 p.346, p.356*

United States and World Organization, 1920-1933. . .*v.4 p.631*

The United States Army and Reconstruction,
1865-1877. . . . .*v.3 p.438*

☐ United States Census 2000. . . . .*v.4 p.482*

☐ United States Code. *v.4 p.481, p.482*

United States Congressional Elections, 1788-1997: The Official
Results of the Elections of the 1st Through 105th
Congresses. *v.4 p.557*

United States Counties. *v.4 p.542*

The United States Crusade in China, 1938-1945. . . .*v.3 p.392*

☐ United States Department of Agriculture National
Agricultural Library Catalog (AGRICOLA). *v.5 p.3*

☐ United States Department of Agriculture National
Agricultural Statistics Service 2002 Census of
Agriculture. *v.5 p.3*

☐ United States Department of Agriculture Natural Resources
Conservation Service PLANTS Database. . .*v.5 p.16, p.45*

☐ United States Department of Agriculture NCRS Natural
Resources Conservation Service Web Soil Survey. . *v.5 p.48*

☐ United States Department of Agriculture NRCS National
Resources Conservation Service Soils. *v.5 p.48*

The United States Discovers Panama: The Writings of Soldiers,
Scholars, Scientists, and Scoundrels, 1850-1905. . *v.3 p.305*

United States: Essays, 1952-1992. . . . .*v.2 p.127*

The United States Executive Branch: A Biographical Directory
of Heads of State and Cabinet Officials. *v.4 p.529*

United States Government Documents on Women, 1800-1990: A
Comprehensive Bibliography - Social Issues, Vol. 1. .*v.6 p.425*

United States Government Documents on Women, 1800-1990: A
Comprehensive Bibliography, Labor. *v.6 p.425*

☐ The United States Government Manual. *v.4 p.481*

United States Industry and Trade Outlook 1998: Business
Forecasts for 350 Industries. *v.4 p.150*

☐ United States National Library of Medicine National
Institutes of Health: The Visible Human
Project®. *v.5 p.158, p.164*

United States Navy in the Pacific, 1897-1909. . . . .*v.3 p.382*

The United States Navy in the Pacific, 1909-1922. . .*v.3 p.382*

United States of Ambition: Politicians, Power, and the Pursuit of
Office. *v.4 p.516, p.554*

The United States of America V. *v.4 p.437, p.438*

The United States of Europe: The New Superpower and the End
of American Supremacy. *v.4 p.638*

United States Relations with Belgium and the Congo,
1940-1960. . . . .*v.3 p.389*

☐ United States reports. vol. 150- , 1893-. *v.4 p.437*

The United States, Revolutionary Russia,and the Rise of
Czechoslovakia. *v.3 p.188, p.189*

The United States: The History of a Republic. *v.3 p.380*

The United States, the United Nations, and Human Rights: The
Eleanor Roosevelt and Jimmy Carter Eras, 4. . . .*v.4 p.435*

United States vs. Nixon: The President Before the Supreme
Court. *v.4 p.454*

United States-Canadian Tables of Feed Composition: Nutritional
Data for United States and Canadian Feeds. . *v.5 p.55, p.56*

United We Stand: A History of Britain's Trade Unions. .*v.4 p.128*

Uniting Germany: Documents and Debates, 1944-1993. .*v.3 p.177*

Uniting North American Business: NAFTA Best
Practices. *v.4 p.61*

The Uniting of Europe: Political, Social, and Economical
Forces, 1950-1957. . . . .*v.4 p.637*

The Units of Evolution: Essays on the Nature of the
Species. *v.5 p.198, p.226*

Unity and Diversity in Development Ideas: Perspectives from
the U. N. Regional Commissions. *v.4 p.633, p.663*

Unity and Struggle: Speeches and Writings. *v.6 p.73*

Unity in Psychology: Possibility or Pipedream? *v.5 p.594*

The Universal Book of Astronomy: From the Andromeda
Galaxy to the Zone of Avoidance. *v.5 p.62*

The Universal Computer: The Road from Leibniz to Turing. *v.5 p.335, p.336, p.337, p.342*

The Universal Declaration of Human Rights: Origins and Intent. *v.4 p.435*

Universal History of Iniquity. *v.2 p.678*

Universals: An Opinionated Introduction. . . . *v.1 p.509, p.510*

Universals and Scientific Realism: Nominalism and Realism. *v.1 p.510*

The Universe and the Teacup: The Mathematics of Truth and Beauty. *v.5 p.457, p.458, p.470*

The Universe at Midnight: Observations Illuminating the Cosmos. *v.5 p.68*

The Universe: Encyclopaedia of Natural History. . . .*v.5 p.225*

The Universe in a Nutshell. . . .*v.5 p.540, p.541, p.556, p.557*

The Universe in Gamma Rays. *v.5 p.67*

The Universe Unveiled: Instruments and Images Through History. *v.5 p.66*

Universe. *v.5 p.65*

Universities: American, English, German. *v.4 p.326*

Universities and Science in the Early Modern Period. *v.4 p.334*

Universities in the Business of Repression: The Academic-Military-Industrial Complex in Central America. *v.4 p.334*

The Universities of Europe in the Middle Ages, Vol. I: Salerno-Bologna-Paris. *v.6 p.558, p.559*

The Universities of Europe in the Middle Ages, Vol. II: Italy-Spain-France-Germany-Scotland, etc. *v.6 p.559*

The Universities of Europe in the Middle Ages, Vol. III: English Universities - Student Life. *v.6 p.559*

The Universities of the Italian Renaissance. *v.3 p.199, v.4 p.334*

University: An Owner's Manual. *v.4 p.290*

The University and the City: From Medieval Origins to the Present. *v.4 p.762*

University Hospitals and School Managers Guide to Environment: A Guide for University, Hospital, and School Managers. *v.5 p.682*

The University in a Corporate Culture. *v.4 p.297*

□ University of California Berkeley: Museum of Paleontology History of Biology. *v.5 p.77*

University of California Sotheby Book of California Wine. *v.5 p.52*

The University of Chicago Spanish Dictionary: Spanish-English, English-Spanish. *v.2 p.637*

□ University of Illinois Ad Collections Index. *v.4 p.141*

□ University of Minnesota Human Rights Library. *v.4 p.477, p.670*

The University of Utopia. *v.4 p.327*

□ University of Washington HealthLinks BioResearcher Toolkit. *v.5 p.96*

The University System and Economic Development in Mexico since 1929. . . . .*v.4 p.335*

The University Teacher As Artist. *v.4 p.292*

The University, the State, and the Market: The Political Economy of Globalization in the Americas. *v.4 p.398*

UNIX Power Tools. *v.5 p.348, p.349*

Unkenrufe. *v.2 p.608*

Unknowing: The Work of Modernist Fiction. *v.2 p.573*

Unknown Amazon: Culture in Nature in Ancient Brazil. .*v.4 p.12*

The Unknown Country: Canada and Her People. . . .*v.3 p.535*

The Unknown Light. *v.2 p.650*

The Unknown Matisse: A Life of Henri Matisse: the Early Years, 1869-1908. . . . .*v.1 p.699*

The Unknown Max Weber. *v.4 p.681*

Unknown Orwell and Orwell: The Transformation. . .*v.2 p.376*

Unknown Tongues: Black Women's Political Activism in the Antebellum Era, 1830-1860. . . . . . .*v.6 p.8, p.32, p.46*

Unleashing the Killer App.: Digital Strategies for Market Dominance. *v.4 p.51*

Unlikely Heroes. *v.4 p.470*

Unlimited Embrace: A Canon of Gay Fiction, 1945-1995. . . . .*v.6 p.394*

The Unlit Lamp: A Novel. *v.6 p.397*

Unlocking the Air: Stories. *v.2 p.148*

Unlocking the Bureaucrat's Kingdom: Deregulation and the Japanese Economy. *v.6 p.219*

Unlocking the Groove: Rhythm, Meter, and Musical Design in Electronic Dance Music. *v.1 p.267*

Unlocking the Past: Celebrating Historical Archaeology in North America. *v.4 p.13*

Unlocking Your Genetic History: A Step-by-Step Guide to Discovering Your Family's Medical and Genetic Heritage. *v.5 p.137*

Unmaking Imperial Russia: Mykhailo Hrushevsky and the Writing of Ukrainian History. *v.3 p.229*

Unmanageable Revolutionaries: Women and Irish Nationalism. *v.3 p.135, p.139*

Unmanning Modernism: Gendered Re-Readings. *v.1 p.82, p.85, p.96, p.115*

The Unmasterable Past: History, Holocaust, and German National Identity. *v.3 p.178*

The Unmentionable Vice. *v.6 p.362*

Unnatural Doubts: Epistemological Realism and the Basis of Skepticism. *v.1 p.517, p.519*

Unnatural Lives: Studies in Australian Convict Fiction. *v.2 p.741*

The Unnatural Scene: A Study in Shakespearean Tragedy. *v.2 p.235*

Unnatural Selections. *v.2 p.10*

Unpaid Professionals: Commercialism and Conflict in Big-Time College Sports. *v.4 p.895*

Unplanned Parenthood: The Social Consequences of Teenage Childbearing. *v.4 p.736*

Unplanned Suburbs: Toronto's American Tragedy, 1900 - 1950. . . . .*v.6 p.713*

Unpublished Opinions of Mr. Justice Brandeis: The Supreme Court at Work. *v.4 p.437*

An Unquiet Mind: A Memoir of Moods and Madness. *v.5 p.660*

Unquiet Soul: A Biography of Charlotte Bronte. . . .*v.2 p.271*

The Unraveling of America: A History of Liberalism in the 1960s. *v.3 p.475*

The Unraveling of Representative Democracy in Venezuela. *v.3 p.361*

Unraveling Somalia: Race, Violence and the Legacy of Slavery. *v.6 p.65, p.66*

Unraveling the "Model Minority" Stereotype: Listening to Asian American Youth. *v.6 p.108, p.109, p.122*

Unruly Eloquence: Lucian and the Comedy of Traditions. *v.2 p.416*

Unruly Practices: Power, Discourse and Gender in Contemporary Social Theory. *v.6 p.427*

Unruly Women: The Politics of Social and Sexual Control in the Old South. *v.6 p.451, p.452*

The UN's Role in Nation-Building: From the Congo to Iraq. *v.4 p.633*

Unsafe at Any Margin: Interpreting Congressional Elections. *v.4 p.549*

Unsafe at Any Speed; the Designed-in Dangers of the American Automobile. *v.5 p.716*

Unsaturated Soils 2006: Geotechnical Special Publication No. 147. . . . .*v.5 p.699*

Unsaturated Soils. *v.5 p.699*

The Unschooled Mind: How Children Think and How Schools Should Teach. *v.5 p.571*

Unseasonal Migrations: The Effects of Rural Labor Scarcity in Peru. *v.3 p.329*

Unseen Genders: Beyond the Binaries. *v.6 p.370*

Unselfishness: The Role of the Vicarious Affects in Moral Philosophy and Social Theory. *v.1 p.501*

Unsettled Boundaries: Fraser Gold and the British-American Northwest. *v.3 p.547*

Unsettling Memories: Narratives of the Emergency in Delhi. *v.6 p.160*

Unsilent Revolution: Television News and American Public Life, 1948-1991. . . . .*v.4 p.414*

Unspeakable Images: Ethnicity and the American Cinema. *v.6 p.329, p.341*

Unspoken Worlds: Women's Religious Lives. .*v.1 p.528, v.6 p.459*

Unsportsmanlike Conduct: Exploiting College Athletes. *v.4 p.821, p.893*

Unsubmissive Women: Chinese Prostitutes in Nineteenth-Century San Francisco. *v.6 p.113, p.128*

Unsung: A History of Women in American Music. *v.1 p.378, v.6 p.473*

Unsung Genius: The Passion of Dancer-Choreographer Jack Cole. *v.1 p.10, p.32,v.6 p.415*

Unsung Heroes: A History of American Immigrants. . .*v.3 p.506*

Unsung Heroes: Federal Execucrats Making a Difference. *v.4 p.525, p.546*

Unsung Voices: Opera and Musical Narrative in the Nineteenth Century. *v.1 p.193, p.227*

Unsuspected Eloquence: A History of the Relations Between Poetry and Music. *v.1 p.248*

The Untameables. *v.2 p.718*

Untamed and Unabashed: Essays on Women and Humor in British Literature. *v.2 p.195*

Der Untertan: Roman. *v.2 p.614*

The Unthinkable Revolution in Iran. *v.6 p.632*

Unthinking Social Science: The Limits of Nineteenth-Century Paradigms. *v.4 p.680*

Untidy Gender: Domestic Service in Turkey. *v.6 p.624*

Until the Last Trumpet Sounds: The Life of General of the Armies John J. Pershing. *v.3 p.462*

Unto a Good Land. *v.2 p.630*

Unto Death: Crusade and Late Love. *v.6 p.651*

Unto Others: The Evolution and Psychology of Unselfish Behavior. *v.5 p.650*

Unto the Soul. *v.6 p.647*

Untold Decades. *v.6 p.405*

Untold Lives: The First Generation of American Women Psychologists. *v.5 p.598*

Untold Millions: The Truth about Gay and Lesbian Consumers. *v.6 p.382, p.383*

The Untold Story: The Life of Isadora Duncan 1921 To 1927. . . . .*v.6 p.414*

Untouchable Freedom: A Social History of a Dalit Community. *v.4 p.723, v.6 p.149*

Untouchables: My Family's Triumphant Journey Out of the Caste System in Modern India. *v.4 p.733*

The Untouchables of India. *v.4 p.702*

The Untouchables: Subordination, Poverty and the State in Modern India. *v.6 p.149*

Untouchable. *v.2 p.764*

The Untuning of the Sky: Ideas of Music in English Poetry, 1500-1700. . . . .*v.1 p.247*

Unveiling Eve: Reading Gender in Medieval Hebrew Literature. *v.6 p.560, p.561, p.566, p.574*

Unvollendete Geschichte. *v.2 p.616*

The Unwanted: A Memoir. *v.6 p.94, p.141*

The Unwanted Gaze: The Destruction of Privacy in America. *v.4 p.443*

Unwanted Sex: The Culture of Intimidation and the Failure of Law. *v.4 p.472*

Unwelcome and Unlawful: Sexual Harassment in the American Workplace. *v.4 p.446*

Unwelcome Voices: Subversive Fiction in the Antebellum South. *v.2 p.13, p.14*

Unwinding Threads: Writing by Women in Africa. . . .*v.2 p.752*

The Unwritten Alliance: Riobanco and Brazilian-American Relations. *v.3 p.339*

The Unwritten War: American Writers and the Civil War. .*v.2 p.5*

Up at the Villa. *v.2 p.371*

Up Before Daylight: Life Histories from the Alabama Writers' Project, 1938-1939. . . . .*v.3 p.504*

Up from Dragons: The Evolution of Human Intelligence. *v.5 p.656*

Up from Invisibility: Lesbians, Gay Men, and the Media in America. *v.4 p.416, v.6 p.390*

Up from Serfdom: My Childhood and Youth in Russia, 1804-1824. . . . .*v.3 p.218*

Up from Slavery: An Authoritative Text, Contexts and Composition History, Criticism. *v.2 p.53*

Up from Slavery. *v.6 p.19, p.32*

Up from the Country: Infidelities - The Games of Love and Chance. *v.2 p.481*

Up from Zero: Politics, Architecture, and the Rebuilding of New York. *v.1 p.789, p.797,v.6 p.712*

Up in the Old Hotel. *v.2 p.98*

Up to Now: An Autobiography. *v.3 p.462*

Up to the Star: The Life and Work of the Romanina Poet Mihai Eminescu. *v.2 p.817*

Upanisads. *v.1 p.537, v.6 p.152*

Updating the Literary West: Western Literature Association. *v.2 p.15*

Upgrading Evolution: Documents of the Committee on Common Problems of Genetics, Paleontology, and Systematics. *v.5 p.131, p.191*

Upheaval from the Abyss: Ocean Floor Mapping and the Earth Science Revolution. *v.5 p.428*

Upheavals of Thought: The Intelligence of Emotions. *v.1 p.497, v.5 p.655*

Upon Further Review: Controversy in Sports Officiating. *v.4 p.905*

Upon Further Review: Sports in American Literature. *v.4 p.811*

Upon the Altar of the Nation: A Moral History of the Civil War. *v.1 p.607*

Uprising in East Germany 1953: The Cold War, the German Question and the First Major Upheavel Behind the Iron Curtain. *v.4 p.641*

The Uprising. *v.2 p.817*

Uprooted Children: The Early Life of Migrant Farm Workers. *v.4 p.755*

The Uprooted of the Western Sahel: Migrants' Quest for Cash in the Senegambia. *v.6 p.72*

The Uprooted: The Epic Story of the Great Migrations That Made the American People. *v.3 p.367, p.441, p.447,v.4 p.571*

The Upstart Crow: An Introduction to Shakespeare's Plays. *v.2 p.230, p.231*

UpToDate. *v.5 p.509*

Upton Sinclair A Study in Social Protest. *v.2 p.119*

Upton Sinclair, the Forgotten Socialist. *v.2 p.119*

Ur 'of the Chaldees': A Revised and Updated Edition of Sir Leonard Woolley's Excavations at Ur by P. R. S. Moorey. *v.3 p.6*

Urban Agriculture: Food, Jobs and Sustainable Cities. *v.3 p.306*

Urban and Regional Planning. *v.6 p.728*

Urban and Rural Communities in Medieval France: Provence and Languedoc, 1000-1500. . . . . *v.3 p.142*

Urban Blues. *v.1 p.260*

Urban Centers and Rural Contexts in Late Antiquity. *v.3 p.30, v.6 p.711*

Urban Civilization in Pre-Crusade Europe: A Study of Organized Town-Life in Northwestern Europe During the Tenth and Eleventh Centuries Based on the Responsa Literature. *v.6 p.577*

The Urban Crucible: Social Change, Political Consciousness, and the Origins of the American Revolution. . . . *v.3 p.406*

The Urban Development of Rome in the Age of Alexander VII. *v.1 p.797*

Urban Dynamics and Growth: Advances in Urban Economics. *v.6 p.722*

Urban Economics and Land Use in America: The Transformation of Cities in the Twentieth Century. *v.6 p.725*

Urban Entomology: Insect and Mite Pests. *v.5 p.213*

Urban entomology. *v.5 p.26*

Urban Europe, 1100-1700. . . . . *v.3 p.44*

Urban Europe, 1500-1700. . . . . *v.3 p.43*

The Urban Forest: Comprehensive Management. *v.5 p.37*

Urban Fortunes: The Political Economy of Place. . . *v.6 p.724*

The Urban Frontier: The Rise of Western Cities, 1790-1830. . . . . *v.3 p.514*

Urban Geography in America, 1950-2000: Paradigms and Personalities. *v.4 p.381, v.6 p.720*

The Urban Geography Reader. *v.4 p.395, v.6 p.721*

Urban Geography. *v.4 p.395, v.6 p.721*

Urban Geoscience. *v.5 p.420*

Urban Hydrology, Hydraulics, and Stormwater Quality: Engineering Applications and Computer Modeling. *v.5 p.702*

Urban Inequality: Evidence from Four Cities. . . . *v.6 p.724*

Urban Life in Transition. *v.6 p.717, p.718*

Urban Life: Readings in the Anthropology of the City. *v.4 p.37, v.6 p.722*

The Urban Nation: 1920-1980. . . . . *v.3 p.443, p.449*

The Urban Order: An Introduction to Urban Geography. *v.4 p.395, v.6 p.721*

The Urban Origins of Suburban Autonomy. *v.4 p.542, v.6 p.722*

Urban Patterns: Studies in Human Ecology. *v.6 p.719*

Urban Planning and Civic Order in Germany, 1860-1914. . . . . *v.3 p.169*

Urban Planning and Cultural Identity. *v.4 p.395, v.6 p.728, p.729*

Urban Planning in a Changing World: The Twentieth Century Experience. *v.6 p.727*

Urban Policy Problems: Federal Policy and Institutional Change. *v.4 p.525*

Urban Policy Reconsidered: Dialogues on the Problems and Prospects of American Cities. *v.6 p.723*

Urban Politics: Power in Metropolitan America. . . . *v.6 p.724*

Urban Poverty, Political Participation, and the State: Lima, 1970-1990. . . . . *v.3 p.329*

Urban Public Debts, Urban Governments and the Market for Annuities in Western Europe. *v.3 p.43*

Urban Recycling and the Search for Sustainable Community Development. *v.6 p.299, p.727*

Urban Revitalization: Policies and Programs. . *v.6 p.726, p.727*

The Urban Revolution. *v.6 p.710*

The Urban School: A Factory for Failure. . . *v.4 p.301, p.310*

Urban Sociology. *v.6 p.716, p.717*

Urban Sprawl: A Comprehensive Reference Guide. . *v.6 p.284*

Urban Sprawl and Public Health: Designing, Planning, and Building for Healthy Communities. *v.6 p.727*

Urban Sprawl: European patterns and Policy. *v.6 p.727*

Urban Studies & Planning: A SAGE Full-Text Collection. *v.6 p.709*

Urban Theory: A Critical Assessment. *v.6 p.710*

The Urban Transformation of the Developing World. *v.6 p.718*

Urban Transportation Planning in the United States: An Historical Overview. *v.4 p.166, v.6 p.716*

Urban Travel Demand. *v.4 p.268*

Urban Village: Population, Community, and Family Structure in Germantown, Pennsylvania, 1683-1800. . . . . *v.4 p.708*

The Urban Villagers. *v.4 p.702, p.703,v.6 p.717*

Urban Voices: Contemporary Short Stories from Brazil. *v.2 p.690*

The Urban Voter: Group Conflict and Mayoral Voting Behavior in American Cities. *v.4 p.544*

Urban Workers and Labor Unions in Chile, 1902-1927. . *v.3 p.353*

Urbanization and Migration in West Africa. *v.6 p.68*

Urbanization and the New Agriculture. *v.5 p.13*

Urbanization in History: A Process of Dynamic Interactions. *v.3 p.44*

The Urgings of Conscience: A Theory of Punishment. *v.6 p.274, p.275*

Urinetown: The Musical. *v.1 p.251, p.408*

Ursule Mirouet. *v.2 p.486*

Das Urteil und andere Erzaehlungen. *v.2 p.610*

Uruguay: Democracy at the Crossroads. *v.3 p.346*

Uruguay's Tupamaros: The Urban Guerilla. *v.3 p.346*

The Uruk World System: The Dynamics of Expansion of Early Mesopotamian Civilization. *v.4 p.8*

☐ U.S. Department of Agriculture's Home and Garden Bulletin Archive. *v.5 p.19, p.32, p.43*

☐ U.S. Department of Education. *v.4 p.322*

☐ U.S. Dept. of Agriculture NRCS National Resources Conservation Service: Keys to Soil Taxonomy. . . *v.5 p.48*

☐ U.S. Food and Drug Administration. Library of Chemistry Information. *v.5 p.255*

☐ U.S. Geological Survey World Petroleum Assessment 2000: Description and Results. *v.5 p.451*

U.S. Hegemony and International Organizations. . . *v.4 p.630*

☐ The U.S. Homebuilding Industry: A Half Century of Building the American Dream. *v.4 p.158*

U.S. Involvement in Central America: Three Views from Honduras. *v.3 p.300*

U.S. Latino Literature Today. *v.6 p.497*

US Laws, Acts, and Treaties, Volume 1: 1776-1928. . *v.4 p.629*

US Laws, Acts, and Treaties, Volume 2: 1929-1970. . *v.4 p.629*

US Laws, Acts, and Treaties, Volume 3: 1970-2002. . . . . *v.4 p.629, p.630*

US National Security: A Reference Handbook. . . . *v.4 p.562*

☐ U.S. Nuclear Regulatory Commission. *v.5 p.739*

☐ US Presidential Election Maps: 1860-1996. . . . *v.4 p.556*

☐ U.S. Securities and Exchange Commission. *v.4 p.93, p.99, p.104, p.105, p.111*

☐ U.S. State Constitutions and Web Sites. *v.4 p.451*

The USA in the Making of the USSR: The Washington Conference, 1921-1922, and "Uninvited Russia". *v.4 p.641, p.656*

The USA Patriot Act: A Reference Handbook. . . . *v.4 p.460*

☐ USDA National Nutrient Database for Standard Reference, Release 18. Nutrient Data Laboratory Home Page. . *v.5 p.32*

The Use of Force: Military Power and International Politics. *v.4 p.654*

Use of Force: The Practice of States, 1945-1991. *v.4 p.648, p.651*

The Use of Plant Genetic Resources. *v.5 p.15*

The Use of Poetry and the Use of Criticism: Studies in the Relation of Criticism to Poetry in England. . . . *v.2 p.180*

The Use of the Bible in Milton's Prose, with an Index of the Biblical Quotations and Citations Arranged in the Chronological Order of the Prose Works. *v.2 p.253*

Useful Knowledge: The Victorians, Morality and the March of Intellect. *v.6 p.751*

User Interface Design for Programmers. *v.5 p.339, p.346, p.349*

The User Manual Manual: How to Research, Write, Test, Edit and Produce a Software. *v.5 p.680*

The Uses of Argument. *v.1 p.493*

The Uses of Enchantment: The Meaning and Importance of Fairy Tales. *v.2 p.582*

The Uses of Life: A History of Biotechnology. . *v.5 p.78, p.217*

The Uses of Literacy in Early Medieval Europe. . . *v.6 p.569*

The Uses of Literacy. *v.3 p.112, p.128*

The Uses of Literature: Essays. *v.2 p.697*

The Uses of Schooling. *v.4 p.341*

Uses of the Past in the Novels of William Faulkner. . *v.2 p.75*

The Uses of the University. *v.4 p.290*

☐ USGS Earth Science Photographic Library Archive. *v.5 p.417*

☐ USGS Earthquake Hazards Program. *v.5 p.442*

☐ USGS Geology in the Parks. *v.5 p.418*

☐ USGS National Geomagnetism Program. *v.5 p.443*

Using Computers in Archaeology: Towards Virtual Pasts. *v.4 p.7*

Using Computers in Chemistry and Chemical Education. *v.5 p.267*

Using Documents in Social Research. *v.4 p.687*

Using Econometrics: A Practical Guide. *v.4 p.205*

Using French: A Guide to Contemporary Usage. . . *v.2 p.453*

Using Literature to Support Skills and Critical Discussion for Struggling Readers: Grades 3-9. . . . . *v.4 p.366*

Using Mathematics in Economic Analysis. *v.4 p.201*

Using Picture Storybooks to Teach Character Education. *v.4 p.360*

Using Qualitative Methods in Organizational Research. *v.4 p.689*

Using Spanish: A Guide to Contemporary Usage. . . *v.2 p.635*

Using Technology to Increase Student Learning. . . *v.4 p.352*

Using Technology Wisely: The Keys to Success in Schools. *v.4 p.352*

Using the Agricultural, Environmental, and Food Literature, Vol. 61. . . . . *v.5 p.309*

Using the Biological Literature: A Practical Guide, Vol. 60. . . . . *v.5 p.324, p.325*

Using the Law for Competitive Advantage. . . *v.4 p.82, p.110*

Using the Mathematics Literature, Vol. 66. . . *v.5 p.458, p.461*

Using USGS Topographic Maps, Vol. 20. . . . . . *v.4 p.390*

The U.S.-Mexico Border: Transcending Divisions, Contesting Identities. *v.3 p.527, v.6 p.487, p.522*

Usp Di: Advice for the Patient, Drug Information in Lay Language, Vol. 2. . . . . *v.5 p.526*

Usp Di: Approved Drug Products and Legal Requirements, Vol. 3. . . . . *v.5 p.526*

Usp Di: Drug Information for the Healthcare Professional. *v.5 p.526*

Usurpers. *v.2 p.656*

Utah: A Guide to the State. *v.3 p.529*

Utah: A People's History. *v.3 p.529*

Utah: A Portrait. *v.3 p.530*

Utah Bicentennial and History. *v.3 p.530*

Utah, the Right Place: The Official Centennial History. *v.3 p.529*

Utilisation of Space: Basics, Fields of Usage, Future Developments. *v.5 p.720*

Utilitarianism. *v.1 p.445, p.516,v.4 p.222*

The Utilization of Classroom Peers As Behavior Change Agents. *v.4 p.353*

Utopia: An Elusive Vision. *v.4 p.499*

Utopia Lost: The United Nations and World Order. . .*v.4 p.635*

Utopia Parkway: The Life and Work of Joseph Cornell. *v.1 p.46*

Utopian Communities. *v.4 p.733*

Utopian Entrepreneur. *v.4 p.55, p.57, p.63*

Utopian Episodes: Daily Life in Experimental Colonies Dedicated to Changing the World. *v.4 p.499*

Utopia's Garden: French Natural History from Old Regime to Revolution. *v.5 p.81*

Utopia. *v.2 p.215, v.4 p.499*

UV-VIS-Spektroskopie und Ihre Anwendungen. *v.5 p.297*

UWB: Theory and Applications. *v.5 p.727*

Uwe Johnson. *v.2 p.617*

V

V. S. Pritchett: A Working Life. *v.2 p.378, p.379*

V Was for Victory: Politics and American Culture During World War 2. . . . .*v.3 p.466*

Vaclav Havel: Civic Responsibility in the Postmodern Age. *v.4 p.492*

Vagabond Stars: A World History of Yiddish Theater. *v.1 p.97, p.126*

The Vagabond. *v.2 p.514*

The Vagrant Mood. *v.2 p.371*

Vagrants and Citizens: Politics and the Masses in Mexico City from Colony to Republic. *v.3 p.288*

Vale of Tears: Revisiting the Canudos Massacre in Northeastern Brazil, 1893-1897. . . . .*v.3 p.337*

Valentino's Hair. *v.6 p.509*

Valle-Inclan: Plays One. *v.2 p.663*

The Valley. *v.6 p.499*

Valuable Disconnects in Organizational Learning Systems: Integrating Bold Visions and Harsh Realities. *v.4 p.78*

Valuation: Measuring and Managing the Value of Companies. *v.4 p.89, p.91, p.95*

Value and Capital: An Inquiry into Some Fundamental Principles of Economic Theory. *v.4 p.209*

Value and Justification: The Foundations of Liberal Theory. *v.1 p.501*

Value and Valuation of Natural Science Collections. *v.5 p.227, p.228*

Value Based Management: The Corporate Response to the Shareholder Revolution. *v.4 p.64, p.91*

Value, Capital and Growth. *v.4 p.260*

Value, Capital and Rent. *v.4 p.241*

The Value of a Dollar: 1600-1865. . . . .*v.4 p.188*

The Value of a Dollar: 1860-2004. . . . .*v.4 p.188*

The Value of Recreational Sports in Higher Education: Impact on Student Enrollment, Success, and Buying Power. *v.4 p.800*

Value Shift: Why Companies Must Merge Social and Financial Imperatives to Achieve Superior Performance. *v.4 p.54*

Value-Added Public Relations: The Secret Weapon of Integrated Marketing. *v.4 p.144*

Value-Added Records Management: Protecting Corporate Assets, Reducing Business Risks. *v.4 p.115, p.116*

Values and Ideals of American Youth. *v.4 p.735*

Values and Teaching: Working with Values in the Classroom. *v.4 p.350*

Values, Nature, and Culture in the American Corporation. *v.4 p.53*

Valuing Crop Biodiversity: On-Farm Genetic Resources and Economic Change. *v.5 p.9, p.16, p.23*

The Vampire Film: From Nosferatu to Interview with a Vampire. *v.6 p.320*

Vampires and Violets: Lesbians in Film. *v.6 p.417*

Vamps, Virgins and Victims: How Can Women Fight AIDS? *v.6 p.443*

Van Dale Groot Woordenboek Engels-Nederlands. . . *v.2 p.621*

Van Dale'Woordenboek Dutch - Englis. *v.2 p.622*

Van Dyck: A Complete Catalogue of the Paintings. .*v.1 p.735*

Van Gogh and Gauguin: The Studio of the South. . .*v.1 p.738*

Van Gogh's Van Goghs. *v.1 p.742*

Van Gogh. *v.1 p.746*

Van Nostrand Rheinhold Encyclopedia of Chemistry. *v.5 p.257*

Van Nostrand's Scientific Encyclopedia, Set. . .*v.5 p.386, p.387*

Vanbrugh and Farquhar. *v.2 p.264*

Vancouver and Its Region. *v.3 p.547*

Vancouver's Chinatown: Racial Discourse in Canada, 1875-1980. . . . .*v.6 p.710*

Vandals, Romans and Berbers: New Perspectives on Late Antique North Africa. *v.6 p.60*

The Vanek Plays: Four Authors, One Character. . . .*v.2 p.781*

Vanessa Beecroft: Performances 1993-2003. . . . .*v.1 p.695*

Vanguard Landscapes and Gardens. *v.1 p.816*

Vanguard of Empire: Ships of Exploration in the Age of Columbus. *v.3 p.73*

The Vanguard of Islamic Revolution: The Jamaat-I Islami of Pakistan. *v.4 p.615, p.617*

Vanguard Revolutionaries in Latin America: Peru, Colombia, Mexico. *v.4 p.592*

A Vanished World: Medieval Spain's Golden Age of Enlightenment. *v.3 p.238*

The Vanishing Adolescent. *v.4 p.736*

Vanishing Borders: Protecting the Planet in the Age of Globalization. *v.6 p.300*

Vanishing Georgia: Photographs from the Vanishing Georgia Collection, Georgia Department of Archives and History. *v.3 p.503*

The Vanishing Hectare: Property and Value in Postsocialist Transylvania. *v.3 p.251, v.4 p.42*

Vanishing Histories: 100 Endangered Sites from the World Monuments Watch. *v.1 p.821*

Vanishing Lives: Style and Self in Tennyson, D. G. Rossetti, Swinburne, and Yeats. *v.2 p.304, p.313, p.327*

The Vanishing Newspaper: Saving Journalism in the Information Age. *v.4 p.149, p.411*

The Vanishing Peasant: Innovation and Change in French Agriculture. *v.4 p.705*

Vanishing Points. *v.2 p.744*

Vanishing Rooms. *v.6 p.395*

Vanishing Species?: Saving the Fish, Sacrificing the Fisherman. *v.5 p.216*

Vanishing Voices: The Extinction of the World's Languages. *v.2 p.563, v.4 p.19*

The Vanishing Voter: Public Involvement in an Age of Uncertainty. *v.4 p.549, p.555*

Vanity fair. A novel without a hero. by William Makepeace Thackeray; with illustrations by the Author. *v.2 p.316*

Vanity Fair. *v.2 p.315, p.316*

Vanity of Duluoz: An Adventurous Education, 1935-1946. . . . .*v.2 p.93*

The Vanity of Power: American Isolationism and the First World War, 1914-1917, 3. . . . .*v.3 p.468*

The Vantage Point; Perspectives of the Presidency, 1963-1969. . . . .*v.3 p.473*

Vapor Pressure of Organic Compounds. *v.5 p.281*

Vapor-Liquid Equilibrium Data Collection: Aqueous-Organic Systems. *v.5 p.290, p.741*

Vapor-Liquid Equilibrium Data Collection Tables and Diagrams of Data for Binary and Multicomponent Mixtures up to Moderate Pressures: Constants of Correlation Equations for Computer Use: Part 2a: Organic Hydroxy Compounds: Alcohols, Vol. 1. . . . .*v.5 p.281, p.282*

Vaqueros, Cowboys, and Buckaroos: The Genesis and Life of the Mounted North American Herders. *v.3 p.521*

Varese: A Looking-Glass Diary. *v.1 p.226, p.363*

Varese: Astronomer in Sound. *v.1 p.218, p.363*

Vargas of Brazil: A Political Biography. *v.3 p.340*

The Vargas Regime. *v.3 p.341*

Variation: A Central Concept in Biology. *v.5 p.192*

Variation and Change in Spanish. *v.2 p.637*

The Variational Principles of Mechanics. *v.5 p.548*

Variations in Time: Nathan Oliveira, Monotypes and Monoprints. *v.1 p.757*

Variations on a Theme Park: The New American City and the End of Public Space. *v.6 p.719, p.726*

Variations on Night and Day. *v.6 p.656*

The Varied Sociology of Paul F. Lazarsfeld. *v.4 p.685*

Varieties of African-American Religious Experience. . .*v.6 p.36*

Varieties of Anomalous Experience: Examining the Scientific Evidence. *v.5 p.613*

Varieties of Contemporary French. *v.2 p.454*

Varieties of Religion Today: William James Revisited. *v.5 p.636*

The Varieties of Religious Experience: A Study in Human Nature. *v.5 p.634*

The Varieties of Religious Experience. *v.1 p.521, p.524*

Variety Music Cavalcade, 1620-1969; A Chronology of Vocal and Instrumental Music Popular in the United States. *v.1 p.168, p.278*

The Variety of Life: A Survey and a Celebration of All the Creatures that Have Ever Lived. *v.5 p.223*

The Variorum Commentary on the Poems of John Milton, Vol. 4. . . . .*v.2 p.254*

The Variorum Edition of the Poems of W. B. Yeats. . *v.2 p.327*

Various Voices: Prose, Poetry, Politics, 1948-1998. . .*v.2 p.377*

The Vasa Trilogy. *v.2 p.631*

Vasari's Florence: Artists and Literati at the Medicean Court. *v.1 p.676, p.689*

Vascular Nursing. *v.5 p.527*

Vaslav Nijinsky: A Leap into Madness. *v.6 p.415*

Vassouras: A Brazilian Coffee County, 1850-1900: The Roles of Planter and Slave in a Plantation Society. *v.3 p.280, p.337, p.338*

A Vast Conspiracy: The Real Story of the Sex Scandal That Nearly Brought down a President. *v.3 p.480, p.481*

Vast Encyclopedia: The Theatre of Thornton Wilder. . *v.2 p.133*

Vaste est la prison : roman. *v.2 p.544*

Vathek. *v.2 p.264*

Vatican and Italian Fascism, 1929-32: A Study in Conflict. *v.3 p.203*

Vatican Council II: More Post-Conciliar Documents. . *v.1 p.570*

Vatican Council II. *v.1 p.570*

Vaudeville: From the Honky-Tonks to the Palace. . . .*v.1 p.35*

Vaudeville, Old and New: An Encyclopedia of Variety Performers. *v.1 p.58, p.90*

Vaudeville U.S.A. *v.1 p.35*

The Vaudevillians. *v.1 p.35*

Vaughan Williams and the Symphony. . *v.1 p.221, p.242, p.363*

Vault Career Guide to Biotech. *v.5 p.251*

Vault Career Guide to Book Publishing. *v.4 p.149*

Vault Guide to Corporate America for Women and Minorities. *v.4 p.167*

Vault Guide to the Top Pharmaceuticals and Biotech Employers. *v.4 p.156*

Vector and Tensor Analysis. *v.5 p.486*

Vector Calculus. *v.5 p.486*

The Vedanta Sutras: The Sacred Books of the East Part Thirty-Eight. *v.1 p.537*

The Vedanta Sutras: The Sacred Books of the East Part Thirty-Four. *v.1 p.537*

Vegetable Growing Handbook: Organic and Traditional Methods. *v.5 p.24, p.26, p.31*

The Vegetarian Sports Nutrition Guide: Peak Performance for Everyone from Beginners to Gold Medalists. *v.4 p.801, p.876*

Vegetation and the Terrestrial Carbon Cycle: The First 400 Million Years. *v.5 p.167, p.190*

Vehi-Ciosane, ou, Blanche-Genèse : suivi du Mandat. *v.2 p.545*

Vehicle dynamics. *v.5 p.716*

Vehicular Electric Power Systems: Land, Sea, Air, and Space Vehicles, Vol. 22. . . . .*v.5 p.716*

The Veil and the Male Elite: A Feminist Interpretation of Women's Rights in Islam. *v.1 p.557*

Veiled Empire: Gender and Power in Stalinist Central Asia. *v.3 p.213*

Veiled Sentiments: Honor and Poetry in a Bedouin Society. *v.4 p.30, v.6 p.596*

Veils and Words: The Emerging Voices of Iranian Women Writers. *v.6 p.672*

Vein of Iron. *v.2 p.79, p.80*

Velazquez in Seville. *v.1 p.737*

Velky Anglicko-Cesky Slovnik. *v.2 p.774*

Velky Cesko-Anglicky Slovnik. *v.2 p.774*

Velvet Horn. *v.2 p.95*

Velvet Mites and Silken Webs: The Wonderful Details of Nature in Photographs and Essays. *v.5 p.226*

Velvet on Iron: The Diplomacy of Theodore Roosevelt. .*v.3 p.475*

The Velvet Rage: Overcoming the Pain of Growing up Gay in a Straight Man's World. *v.4 p.749, v.6 p.371, p.376*

The Velvet Underground Companion: 4 Decades of Commentary. *v.1 p.276, p.363, p.364*

The Velveteen Father: An Unexpected Journey to Parenthood. *v.6 p.376*

Venda Children's Songs: A Study in Ethnomusicological Analysis. *v.1 p.285*

The Vendee: A Sociological Analysis of the Counter-Revolution of 1793. . . . .*v.3 p.151*

Vendredi ; ou, Les limbes du Pacifique : roman. *v.2 p.534*

Venedikt Erofeev's Moscow - Petushki: Critical Perspectives. *v.2 p.808*

Venetian Colour: Marble, Mosaic and Glass, 1250-1550. .*v.1 p.710*

The Venetian Glass Nephew. *v.2 p.129*

Venezuela: A Century of Change. *v.3 p.360*

Venezuela and the United States: From Monroe's Hemisphere to Petroleum's Empire. *v.3 p.360, p.388*

Venezuela: The Political Economy of Oil. *v.3 p.360*

Venezuela: The Search for Order, the Dream of Progress. *v.3 p.360*

The Venezuela-Guyana Border Dispute: Britain's Colonial Legacy in Latin America. *v.3 p.359*

The Venezuelan Armed Forces in Politics, 1935-1959. .*v.3 p.273*

Venezuelan Politics in the Chavez Era: Class, Polarization, and Conflict. *v.3 p.360*

Venice: A Maritime Republic. *v.3 p.198*

Venice Reconsidered: The History and Civilization of an Italian City-State, 1297-1797. . . . . *v.3 p.197, p.204*

Venice, the Tourist Maze: A Cultural Critique of the World's Most Touristed City. *v.3 p.197, p.204*

Venice Triumphant: The Horizons of a Myth. . .*v.3 p.197, p.204*

Un Vent Se le Qui Iparpille. *v.2 p.540*

The Ventriloquist's Tale. *v.2 p.368*

The Venture of Islam: The Classical Age of Islam. *v.1 p.555, p.556*

The Venture of Islam. *v.6 p.581*

Venus Envy: A History of Cosmetic Surgery. .*v.4 p.774, v.6 p.443*

Venus: The Geological Story. *v.5 p.434*

Vera: Mrs. Vladimir Nabokov. *v.2 p.105*

Verbal Behavior. *v.5 p.622, p.624*

La Verdad Sospechosa. *v.2 p.652*

Verdi: A Biography. *v.1 p.201, p.202, p.364*

The Verdi Companion. *v.1 p.207, p.364*

Verdi: Requiem. *v.1 p.203, p.236, p.364*

Verdict: Assessing the Civil Jury System. *v.4 p.471*

Verdict on Vichy: Power and Prejudice in the Vichy France Regime. *v.3 p.83*

Verdi. *v.1 p.195, p.364*

Vergil in the Middle Ages. *v.2 p.446*

Verificationism: Its History and Prospects. *v.1 p.504*

The Veritable Years: Poems, 1949-1966. . . . . . .*v.2 p.71*

Veritatis Splendor: American Responses. *v.1 p.575*

Vermeer and the Art of Painting. *v.1 p.749*

Vermeer and the Delft School. *v.1 p.697, p.698*

Vermeer. *v.1 p.739, p.749*

The Vermilion Bird: T'ang Images of the South. . . .*v.6 p.185*

Vermont: An Illustrated History. *v.3 p.486*

Vermont: Bicentennial and History Guide. *v.3 p.486*

The Vermont Encyclopedia. *v.3 p.486*

Vernon God Little. *v.2 p.373*

Vers Libre: The Emergence of Free Verse in France 1886-1914. . . . .*v.2 p.461*

Versailles and After, 1919-1933. . . . .*v.4 p.631*

The Versailles Settlement: Peacemaking in Paris, 1919. .*v.4 p.650*

Verschenkter Rat: Gedichte. *v.2 p.602*

Versos Sencillos. *v.2 p.672*

Vertebrate Dissection. *v.5 p.89, p.157*

Vertebrate Functional Morphology: Horizon of Research in the 21st Century. *v.5 p.157*

Vertebrate Palaeontology. *v.5 p.447*

Vertebrate Paleontology and Evolution. *v.5 p.447*

Vertebrate Taphonomy. *v.5 p.448*

Vertebrates: Comparative Anatomy, Function, Evolution. *v.5 p.157, p.193*

The Vertical Mosaic: An Analysis of Social Class and Power in Canada. *v.4 p.706*

A Very Civil War: The Swiss Sonderbund War of 1847. .*v.3 p.245*

A Very Double Life: The Private World of Mackenzie King. *v.3 p.540*

The Very Inside: An Anthology of Writings by Asian and Pacific Islander Lesbians. *v.6 p.92, p.112*

A Very Pleasant Evening with Stevie Smith: Selected Shorter Prose. *v.2 p.383*

Very Private Eye: An Autobiography in Diaries and Letters. *v.2 p.379*

The Very Quick Job Search. *v.4 p.169*

Vespasian. *v.3 p.28*

Vestal Fire: An Environmental History, Told Through Fire, of Europe and Europe's Encounter with the World. . . .*v.5 p.31*

The Vested Interests and the Common Man. *v.4 p.250*

Vested Interests: Cross-Dressing and Cultural Anxiety. .*v.6 p.370*

Veterinary Medicine: A Textbook of the Diseases of Cattle, Sheep, Pigs, Goats and Horses. *v.5 p.56, p.57*

Veterinary Medicine: An Illustrated History. .*v.5 p.54, p.56, p.57*

Veto Players: How Political Institutions Work. *v.4 p.575*

Vettriano: A Life. *v.1 p.749*

Vexed and Troubled Englishmen, 1590-1642. . . . .*v.3 p.101*

A Via Crucis Do Corpo. *v.2 p.691*

Viable Utopian Ideas: Shaping a Better World. . . .*v.4 p.500*

The Vibrational Spectroscopy of Polymers. *v.5 p.323*

The Vicar of Wakefield. *v.2 p.248, p.249*

Vice Chamberlain Coke's Theatrical Papers, 1706-1715. .*v.1 p.102*

Vice Versa: Bisexuality and the Eroticism of Everyday Life. *v.6 p.367*

The Vices of Economists: The Virtues of the Bourgeoisie. *v.4 p.185*

Vichy France and the Jews. *v.3 p.60, p.156*

Vichy France: Old Guard and New Order. *v.3 p.156*

The Vichy Syndrome: History and Memory in France since
    1944. . . . .*v.3 p.157*

Vico: Selected Writings. *v.2 p.709*

Vico: The First New Science. *v.1 p.473*

Vico's Science of Imagination. *v.1 p.473*

The Victim of Prejudice. *v.2 p.290*

Victimizing Vulnerable Groups: Images of Uniquely High-Risk
    Crime Targets. *v.6 p.258*

Victims: A True Story of the Civil War. *v.3 p.502*

Victims at Sarajevo: the romance and tragedy of Franz
    Ferdinand and Sophie. *v.3 p.184*

Victims in the War on Crime: The Use and Abuse of Victims'
    Rights. *v.6 p.258*

Victims of a Map: A Bilingual Anthology of Arabic
    Poetry. *v.6 p.655*

Victims of Progress. *v.4 p.27*

Victims of the Chilean Miracle: Workers and Neoliberalism in
    the Pinochet Era, 1973-2002. . . . .*v.3 p.353*

Victims of the Miracle. *v.3 p.339*

Victims of the System: Crime Victims and Compensation in
    American Politics and Criminal Justice. *v.4 p.752*

Victor Hugo and the Romantic Drama. *v.2 p.492, p.493*

Victor Hugo and the Visionary Novel. *v.2 p.492*

Victor Hugo: Hernani, Marion de Lorme, Lucrece Borgia and
    Ruy Blas. *v.2 p.493*

Victor Hugo. *v.2 p.492, p.494*

Victoria Research Web. *v.6 p.735, p.749*

The Victoria Woodhull Reader. *v.4 p.708*

Victorian Afterlife: Postmodern Culture Rewrites the Nineteenth
    Century. *v.2 p.175*

The Victorian Age. *v.2 p.175*

Victorian America and the Civil War. *v.3 p.400*

Victorian Anthropology. *v.6 p.751*

The Victorian Artist: Artists' Lifewritings in Britain, c.
    1870-1910. . . . .*v.1 p.677, p.686*

Victorian Babylon: People, Streets and Images in
    Nineteenth-Century London. *v.6 p.731, p.763*

Victorian Britain: An Encyclopedia. *v.6 p.735*

Victorian Church, Pt.1. . . . .*v.6 p.758*

The Victorian Church. *v.3 p.111, p.120*

Victorian Cities. *v.3 p.91, p.110,v.6 p.710, p.762*

The Victorian City: Images and Realities, Vol.
    2. . . . .*v.6 p.711, p.762, p.763*

The Victorian City: Images and Realities. *v.3 p.111*

The Victorian Clergy. *v.3 p.112, p.120*

Victorian Conventions. . . .*v.2 p.176, p.193,v.6 p.753, p.762*

The Victorian Country
    House. *v.3 p.111, p.112, p.130,v.6 p.737, p.744*

Victorian Countrywomen. *v.3 p.53*

Victorian Culture and Society: The Essential Glossary. .*v.2 p.176*

Victorian Demons: Medicine, Masculinity and the Gothic at the
    Fin-de-Siecle. *v.2 p.177, p.192*

Victorian Detective Fiction and the Nature of Evidence: The
    Scientific Investigations of Poe, Dickens and
    Doyle. *v.2 p.284, p.285, p.286*

The Victorian Economy. *v.3 p.111*

Victorian Families in Fact and Fiction. *v.6 p.756, p.765*

Victorian Fantasy. *v.2 p.176, p.191*

Victorian Fiction: Writers, Publishers,
    Readers. *v.2 p.177, v.6 p.738, p.757*

The Victorian Frame of Mind 1830-1870. . . . . . .*v.3 p.112*

The Victorian Frame of Mind, 1830-1870. . . . . .*v.3 p.112*

The Victorian Frame of Mind 1830-1870. . . . . . .*v.3 p.128*

The Victorian Frame of Mind, 1830-1870. . . . . .*v.3 p.128*

Victorian Frame of Mind, 1830-1870. . . . .*v.6 p.750*

The Victorian Illustrated Book. *v.6 p.737, p.740*

The Victorian Internet: The Remarkable Story of the Telegraph
    and the Nineteenth Century's On-Line
    Pioneers. *v.3 p.37, v.4 p.421*

Victorian Knight-Errant: A Study of the Early Literary Career of
    James Russell Lowell. *v.2 p.47*

Victorian Literature: 1830-1900. . . . .*v.2 p.197*

Victorian Literature and the Victorian State: Character and
    Governance in a Liberal
    Society. *v.2 p.175, v.6 p.752, p.758, p.763*

The Victorian Marionette Theatre. *v.1 p.93, p.101*

Victorian Masculinities: Manhood and Masculine Poetics in
    Early Victorian Literature and Art. *v.6 p.749*

Victorian Minds. *v.3 p.112, p.128*

The Victorian Mirror of History. *v.6 p.736, p.750*

Victorian News and Newspapers. . .*v.3 p.127, v.6 p.738, p.741*

The Victorian Novel: A Guide to Criticism. . . .*v.2 p.176, p.193*

Victorian Novel: Modern Essays in Criticism. *v.2 p.194*

Victorian Novelists and Publishers. . .*v.6 p.740, p.742, p.757*

Victorian Novel. *v.2 p.175, p.193*

Victorian Painters' Monograms: Identify Almost 2000
    Signatures. *v.1 p.726*

Victorian Painting. *v.1 p.728*

The Victorian Parlour: A Cultural Study. *v.6 p.761*

Victorian Parlour Poetry: An Annotated Anthology. . *v.2 p.201*

Victorian People: A Reassessment of Persons and Themes,
    1851-67. . . . .*v.3 p.91, p.110,v.6 p.735, p.757*

Victorian People and Ideas. . *v.3 p.110, v.6 p.735, p.749, p.760*

The Victorian Period: The Intellectual and Cultural Context of
    English Literature 1830-1890. . . . .*v.6 p.750*

The Victorian Periodical Press: Samplings and
    Soundings. *v.6 p.753*

Victorian Periodicals and Victorian Society. . . .*v.6 p.742, p.753*

The Victorian Poet: Poetics and Persona. *v.2 p.174, p.184*

Victorian Poetry: An Annotated Anthology. *v.2 p.200*

Victorian Poetry, Drama, and Miscellaneous Prose,
    1832-1890. . . . .*v.2 p.203*

Victorian Poetry: Poetry, Poetics,
    Politics. *v.2 p.173, p.183, p.184,v.6 p.755*

Victorian Poetry. *v.2 p.198*

Victorian Poets and the Politics of Culture: Discourse and
    Ideology. *v.2 p.175, p.184*

Victorian Popular Fiction, 1860-80. . . . . . .*v.6 p.739, p.757*

Victorian Prose: An Anthology. *v.2 p.203*

Victorian Publisher. *v.6 p.741, p.756*

Victorian Publishing: The Economics of Book Production for a
    Mass Market 1836-1916. . . . .*v.6 p.742*

The Victorian Railway. *v.3 p.115, v.6 p.766*

A Victorian Romantic, Dante Gabriel Rossetti. *v.2 p.303*

Victorian Sage: Studies in Argument. *v.6 p.750, p.752*

Victorian Sages and Cultural Discourse: Renegotiating Gender
    and Power. *v.6 p.748, p.764*

Victorian Sappho. *v.2 p.176*

Victorian Science and Victorian Values: Literary
    Perspectives. *v.5 p.410, p.412*

Victorian Science Fiction in the U. K.: The Discourses of
    Knowledge and of Power. *v.2 p.192*

Victorian Sensation, or, the Spectacular, the Shocking, and the
    Scandalous in Nineteenth-Century Britain. *v.6 p.759*

Victorian Sensation: The Extraordinary Publication, Reception,
    and Secret Authorship of Vestiges of the Natural History of
    Creation. *v.6 p.739, p.751, p.760*

The Victorian Serial. *v.6 p.741, p.756*

Victorian Soundscapes. *v.6 p.754, p.755, p.762, p.764*

Victorian Subjects. *v.2 p.176*

The Victorian Temper: A Study in Literary Culture. . .*v.2 p.174*

Victorian Temper: A Study in Literary Culture. .*v.3 p.110, p.127*

The Victorian Temper: A Study in Literary Culture. . .*v.6 p.752*

Victorian Things. *v.3 p.91, p.110, v.6 p.761*

Victorian Thinkers: Carlyle, Ruskin, Arnold, Morris. . *v.2 p.277*

Victorian Types, Victorian Shadows: Biblical Typology in
    Victorian Literature, Art and Thought. . . . *v.6 p.750, p.752*

Victorian Values: Personalties and Perspectives in
    Nineteenth-Century Society. *v.6 p.735, p.764*

☐ The Victorian Web. *v.6 p.749, p.750, p.752*

Victorian Women Poets: A New Anthology. *v.2 p.198*

Victorian Women Poets: An Anthology. . . .*v.2 p.197, p.200*

Victorian Women Writers and the Woman
    Question. *v.2 p.177, p.193, p.194*

☐ Victorian Women Writers Project. *v.6 p.476*

The Victorian World Picture: Perceptions and Introspections in
    an Age of Change. *v.6 p.749, p.764*

The Victorians: An Age in Retrospect. *v.6 p.735*

The Victorians and Ancient
    Greece. *v.3 p.113, p.128, v.6 p.750, p.764*

Victorians and the Machine: Literary Response to
    Technology. *v.6 p.757, p.762*

The Victorians and Their Reading. *v.6 p.738*

The Victorians since 1901: Histories, Representations and
    Revisions. *v.6 p.736, p.751*

Victoria's Year: English Literature and Culture,
    1837-1838. . . . .*v.6 p.753, p.758, p.762*

Victors and Vanquished: Spanish and Nahua Views of the
    Conquest of Mexico. *v.3 p.287*

Victors' Justice: The Tokyo War Crimes Trial. . . .*v.4 p.477*

Victory: An Island Tale. *v.2 p.340*

Victory and Vexation in Science: Einstein, Bohr, Heisenberg,
    and Others. *v.3 p.46, p.49, v.5 p.391, p.392*

Victory Dances: The Story of Fred Berk, a Modern Day Jewish
    Dancing Master. *v.1 p.9*

Victory Deferred: How AIDS Changed Gay Life in
    America. *v.6 p.378*

Victory in Europe, 1945: From World War to Cold War. .*v.3 p.391*

Victory Over Violence and Was Jesus a Revolutionist? *v.1 p.643*

Vida Clandestina: My Life in the Cuban Revolution. .*v.3 p.312*

Vida de Lazarillo de Tormes (Life of Lazarillo of
    Tormes). *v.2 p.662*

La Vida Es Sueno y El Alcalde de Zalamea. *v.2 p.647*

Vida Perdida. *v.2 p.675*

Vidas Sombrías. *v.2 p.656*

Vida. *v.2 p.654*

Video Art: A Guided Tour. *v.1 p.771*

Video Source Book. *v.6 p.305*

VideoHound's War Movies: Classic Conflict on Film. *v.6 p.323*

Une vie de boy. *v.2 p.543*

La vie de Marianne, ou, Les aventures de madame la comtesse
    de ***. *v.2 p.481*

La vie et demie : roman. *v.2 p.546*

La vie mode d'emploi : roman. *v.2 p.533*

La vie scélérate : roman. *v.2 p.536*

Le vieil homme et les loups : roman. *v.2 p.531*

Vienna, 1900. . . . .*v.1 p.685*

Vienna and the Jews, 1867-1938: A Cultural
    History. *v.3 p.58, p.59, p.183*

Vietnam, 1945: The Quest for Power. *v.6 p.167*

Vietnam: A Global Studies Handbook. *v.6 p.166*

Vietnam: A History. *v.6 p.168*

Vietnam and the American Political Tradition: The Politics of
    Dissent. *v.3 p.445*

Vietnam and the Chinese Model: A Comparative Study of
    Vietnamese and Chinese Government in the First
    Half of the Nineteenth Century. *v.6 p.167*

Vietnam and the Third Indochina War. *v.6 p.168*

Vietnam at 24 Frames a Second: A Critical and Thematic
    Analysis of over 400 Films about the Vietnam War. *v.6 p.322*

Vietnam Joins the World. *v.6 p.168*

The Vietnam Plays: The Basic Training at Paulo Hummel and
    Sticks and Bones. *v.2 p.153, p.154*

Vietnam: Revolution in Transit. *v.6 p.167*

The Vietnam Trauma in American Foreign Policy,
    1945-1975. . . . .*v.3 p.389*

Vietnam Veteran Films. *v.6 p.323*

The Vietnam War - the American War: Images and
    Representations in Euro-American and Vietnamese Exile
    Narratives. *v.6 p.96, p.115, p.140*

Vietnam War Films: Over 600 Feature, Made-for-TV, Pilot and
    Short Movies, 1939-1992, from the United States,
    Vietnam, France, Belgium, Australia, Hong Kong, South
    Africa, Great Britain and Other Countries. *v.6 p.323*

The Vietnam War in History, Literature and Film. . . .*v.6 p.169*

The Vietnam War: Its History, Literature, and Music. *v.6 p.168*

The Vietnam War on Campus: Other Voices, More Distant
    Drums. *v.4 p.331*

The Vietnam Wars, 1945-1990. . . . .*v.6 p.169*

Vietnamerica: The War Comes Home. *v.6 p.140*

The Vietnamese American 1.5 Generation: Stories of War, Revolution, Flight and New Beginnings. *v.6 p.93, p.115, p.140*

The Vietnamese Americans. *v.6 p.140*

Vietnamese Anticolonialism, 1885-1925. . . . . . .*v.6 p.167*

Vietnamese Tradition on Trial, 1920-1945. . . . . .*v.6 p.167*

Le vieux nègre et la médaille : roman. *v.2 p.543*

View from the Fazenda: A Tale of the Brazilian Heartlands. *v.3 p.334*

⋐ A View from the Mangrove. *v.2 p.670*

View from Vesuvius: Italian Culture and the Southern Question. *v.3 p.197*

Views from the Other Shore: Essays on Herzen, Chekhov and Bakhtin. *v.2 p.798*

The Vigil: Poems. *v.2 p.159*

Viking Age Iceland. *v.3 p.234*

The Vikings in Britain. *v.3 p.63*

The Vikings. *v.3 p.235*

The VIkings. *v.3 p.236*

Vile Bodies. *v.2 p.388*

Vilimani: Labor Migration and Rural Change in Early Colonial Tanzania. *v.6 p.66*

Villa Decor: Distinctively French and Italian Style. . .*v.1 p.800*

Villa des Roses. *v.2 p.623*

Village and Family in Contemporary China. *v.4 p.734*

The Village and the Newspaper. *v.2 p.281*

Village Economies: The Design, Estimation, and Use of Villagewide Economic Models. *v.4 p.241, p.271*

Village Elders. *v.6 p.380*

Village England: A Social History of the Countryside. *v.4 p.772*

The Village in India. *v.4 p.772*

Village in the Vaucluse. *v.3 p.141*

Village Life and Labour. *v.3 p.115, p.124*

Village Life in China: A Study in Sociology. . .*v.6 p.187, p.206*

Village Life in Northern India. *v.4 p.704*

Village, Steppe, and State: The Social Origins of Modern Jordan. *v.6 p.620*

Village Voices: Forty Years of Rural Transformation in South India. *v.4 p.771*

The Ville: Cops and Kids in Urban America. *v.4 p.753*

Villette. *v.2 p.270*

The Vimalakirti Sutra. *v.1 p.564*

Vincenzo Bellini: Norma. *v.1 p.199, p.230, p.231, p.308, p.309*

A Vindication of Political Virtue: The Political Theory of Mary Wollstonecraft. *v.4 p.492, p.502,v.6 p.442*

A Vindication of the Rights of Men; A Vindication of the Rights of Woman; An Historical and Moral View of the French Revolution. *v.2 p.319*

A Vindication of the Rights of Woman: With Strictures on Political and Moral Subjects. *v.4 p.745*

A Vindication of the Rights of Woman. *v.6 p.432*

Vinnie Ream: An American Sculptor. *v.1 p.779*

The Vintage Book of Latin American Stories. *v.2 p.666*

The Vintage Book of Modern Indian Literature. . . .*v.2 p.763*

Vintage Didion. *v.2 p.143*

Vintage Lopez. *v.2 p.149*

Vintage Murakami. *v.6 p.232*

Vintage Years of the Theatre Guild, 1928-1939. . . . .*v.1 p.118, p.146, p.150, p.153*

The Viol: History of an Instrument. *v.1 p.391*

Violence Against Lesbians and Gay Men. *v.6 p.386*

Violence Against Women in Medieval Texts. *v.6 p.560*

Violence and Addiction Equation: Theoretical and Clinical Issues in Substance Abuse and Relationship Violence. *v.5 p.512, p.522*

Violence and Civil Disorder in Italian Cities, 1200-1500. . . . .*v.4 p.700*

Violence and Crime in Cross-National Perspective. . .*v.4 p.751*

Violence and Great Estates in the South of Italy: Apulia, 1900-1922. . . . .*v.3 p.202*

Violence and Nonviolence: Pathways to Understanding. .*v.4 p.750*

Violence, Conflict, and Politics in Colombia. *v.3 p.358*

Violence in Colombia: The Contemporary Crisis in Historical Perspective. *v.3 p.273, p.358*

Violence in Gay and Lesbian Domestic Partnerships. .*v.6 p.377*

Violence in Republican Rome. *v.3 p.26*

Violence: Reflections from a Christian Perspective. . .*v.1 p.643*

The Violence Within/The Violence Without: Wallace Stevens and the Emergence of a Revolutionary Poetics. . . .*v.2 p.123*

Violent Betrayal: Partner Abuse in Lesbian Relationships. *v.6 p.377*

The Violent Foam: New and Selected Poems. *v.2 p.677*

Violent Home. *v.4 p.742*

The Violet Hour: The Violet Quill and the Making of Gay Culture. *v.6 p.392*

Violet to Vita: The Letters of Violet Trefusis to Vita Sackville-West, 1910-1921. . . . .*v.2 p.380*

Violette Leduc. *v.2 p.521*

The Violin: A Research and Information Guide. .*v.1 p.167, p.390*

Viramma: Life of an Untouchable. *v.4 p.40*

Virgil: A Study in Civilized Poetry. *v.2 p.446*

Virgil: Aeneid I-VI. *v.2 p.447, p.448*

Virgil: Aeneid VII and VIII. *v.2 p.447*

Virgil: Aeneid VII-XII. *v.2 p.448*

Virgil: Aeneid. *v.2 p.447*

Virgil and the Augustan Reception. *v.2 p.447*

Virgil and the Moderns. *v.2 p.448*

Virgil: Eclogues and Georgics. *v.2 p.447*

Virgil: Eclogues. *v.2 p.447*

Virgil: Greece and Rome, New Surveys in the Classics, No. 28. . . . .*v.2 p.446*

Virgil: The Aeneid. *v.2 p.447*

Virgil Thomson Reader: Selected Writings, 1924-1984. . . . .*v.1 p.217, p.363,v.6 p.408*

Virgile, non. *v.2 p.534*

Virgil's Aeneid: A Critical Description. *v.2 p.446*

Virgil's Aeneid: Cosmos and Imperium. *v.2 p.447*

Virgil's Aeneid: Interpretation and Influence. *v.2 p.446*

Virgil's Epic Technique. *v.2 p.446*

Virgil. *v.2 p.446*

The Virgin and the Gypsy. v.2 p.362
Virgin Encyclopedia of Jazz. v.6 p.30
The Virgin Encyclopedia of Reggae. v.1 p.292
Virgin Land: The American West as Symbol and Myth. .v.3 p.519
The Virgin of the Andes: Art and Ritual In Colonial
  Cuzco. v.3 p.263
The Virgin, the King, and the Royal Slaves of el Cobre:
  Negotiating Freedom in Colonial Cuba, 1670-1780. .v.3 p.308
Virginia: A Commonwealth Comes of Age: An Illustrated
  History. v.3 p.499
Virginia: A Guide to the Old Dominion. v.3 p.501
Virginia: A History. v.3 p.500
The Virginia Adventure: Roanoke to James Towne: An
  Archaeological and Historical Odyssey. v.4 p.14
Virginia: Bourbonism to Byrd, 1870-1925. . . . . .v.3 p.500
The Virginia Company of London, 1606-1624. . . .v.3 p.499
The Virginia Conservatives, 1867-1879; a Study in
  Reconstruction Politics. v.3 p.500
Virginia: The New Dominion, a History from 1607 to the
  Present. v.3 p.499
Virginia Wolf's Rediscovered Essays: Sources and
  Allusions. v.2 p.393
Virginia Woolf: A Biography. v.2 p.392
Virginia Woolf: A Critical Reading. v.2 p.392
Virginia Woolf: A Feminist Slant. v.2 p.393
Virginia Woolf A to Z: A Comprehensive Reference for
  Students, Teachers, and Common Readers to Her Life, Work
  and Critical Reception. v.2 p.392
Virginia Woolf: A Writer's Life. v.2 p.392
Virginia Woolf: An Inner Life. v.2 p.392
Virginia Woolf and London: The Sexual Politics of the
  City. v.2 p.393, v.6 p.731
Virginia Woolf and the Essay. v.2 p.393
Virginia Woolf and the Fictions of Psychoanalysis. . .v.2 p.392
Virginia Woolf Icon. v.2 p.393
Virginia Woolf: Sources of Madness and Art. v.2 p.393
Virginia Woolf, the Intellectual, and the Public Sphere. .v.2 p.392
Virginia Woolf's London. v.2 p.392, v.6 p.730
Virginia Woolf's Reading Notebooks. v.2 p.393
Virginia Woolf's Women. v.2 p.392
Virginia Woolf. v.2 p.392, p.393
The Virginian: A Horseman of the Plains. . . .v.2 p.128, p.129
Virginians at Home: Family Life in the Eighteenth
  Century. v.3 p.500
Virginia's Native Son: The Election and Administration of
  Governor L. Douglas Wilder. v.3 p.499, p.500
Virgins and Viragos: A History of Women in Scotland from
  1080-1980. . . . . .v.3 p.92, p.124, p.132
Virgins of God: The Making of Asceticism in Late
  Antiquity. v.1 p.653
Virtual Art: From Illusion to Immersion. v.1 p.771
Virtual Decisions: Digital Simulations for Teaching Reasoning
  in the Social Sciences and Humanities. v.4 p.178
Virtual Equality: The Mainstreaming of Gay and Lesbian
  Liberation. .v.6 p.388
Virtual Herbarium. v.1 p.811

The Virtual High School: Teaching Generation V. . . .v.4 p.322
Virtual Jamestown. v.3 p.406
Virtual Justice: The Flawed Prosecution of Crime in
  America. v.4 p.471
The Virtual Library of Botany / Plant Biology
  (Biosciences). v.5 p.206
Virtual Library of Genetics. v.5 p.144
Virtual library: Science: Chemistry: History of
  Chemistry. v.5 p.262
Virtual Music: Computer Synthesis of Musical Style. .v.1 p.386
Virtual Music: How the Web Got Wired for Sound. . .v.1 p.386
Virtual Organization: Toward a Theory of Societal
  Transformation Stimulated by Information
  Technology. .v.4 p.718
Virtual Politics: Faking Democracy in the Post-Soviet
  World. v.4 p.599
Virtual Reality: The Revolutionary Technology of
  Computer-Generated Artificial Worlds - and How It Promises
  to Transform Society. v.5 p.408
Virtual Schools: Planning for Success. v.4 p.321
Virtual Sovereignty: Nationalism, Culture and the Canadian
  Question. v.3 p.535
Virtual Student: A Profile and Guide to Working with Online
  Learners. v.4 p.322
Virtual Tibet: Searching for Shangri-La from the Himalayans to
  Hollywood. v.6 p.241
Virtually Normal. v.6 p.387
Virtue, Commerce, and History: Essays on Political Thought and
  History, Chiefly in the Eighteenth Century. v.3 p.107
Virtue Is More Important Than Riches. v.2 p.814
The Virtue of Selfishness. v.1 p.504
Virtue, Vice, and Personality: The Complexity of
  Behavior. v.5 p.651
Virtues and Vices: And Other Essays in Moral
  Philosophy. .v.1 p.484
The Virtues. .v.1 p.651
Virtuoso Mariachi. v.1 p.293
The Virtuoso. .v.2 p.259
Virtuous Orphan: or The Life of Marianne. v.2 p.481
A Visa for a Dream: Dominicans in the United States. .v.6 p.530
Visible Differences: How Race Will Matter to Americans in the
  Twenty-First Century. v.4 p.730
The Visible Poor: Homelessness in the United States. .v.4 p.750
Visible Saints: The History of a Puritan Idea. . . .v.1 p.588
Visible Speech: The Diverse Oneness of Writing
  Systems. v.2 p.560
Visigothic Spain, 409-711. . . . . .v.3 p.237
Visigothic Spain: New Approaches. v.3 p.237
Vision and Art: The Biology of Seeing. v.1 p.703
Vision and Difference: Femininity, Feminism, and Histories of
  Art. v.6 p.473
Vision and Image in Early Christian England. .v.1 p.672, p.687
Vision and Mind: Selected Readings in the Philosophy of
  Perception. .v.5 p.607
Vision and Refuge: Essays on the Literature of the Great
  Plains. v.2 p.7

Vision and Time: Historical Perspective of an Africa-Centered Paradigm. *v.6 p.14*

A Vision Betrayed: The Jesuits in Japan and China 1542-1742. . . . .*v.1 p.647*

Vision of 2050 Agriculture in China: Dare to Dream. . .*v.5 p.29*

A Vision of Britain through Time. *v.6 p.735*

The Vision of Modern Dance: In the Words of Its Creators. *v.1 p.26, p.40*

The Vision of Rome in Late Renaissance France. . . .*v.3 p.146*

Vision of Self in Early Vedanta. *v.1 p.418, p.419*

Vision, Race, and Modernity: A Visual Economy of the Andean Image World. *v.3 p.331*

The Visionary Company; a Reading of English Romantic Poetry. *v.2 p.183*

Visionary Gardens: The Modern Landscapes of Ernst Cramer. *v.1 p.815*

The Visionary Package. *v.4 p.144*

Vision/Re-Vision: Adapting Contemporary American Fiction by Women to Film. *v.6 p.326*

Visions and Heat: The Making of the Indonesian Revolution. *v.6 p.176*

Visions and Voices: Native American Painting from the Philbrook Museum of Art. *v.1 p.734*

Visions d'Anna. *v.2 p.538*

Visions of Adventure: N. C. Wyeth and the Brandywine Artists. *v.1 p.716, p.717*

Visions of American Agriculture. *v.5 p.13*

Visions of Cody. *v.2 p.93*

Visions of Gerard: A Novel. *v.2 p.93*

Visions of Jewish Education. *v.4 p.308*

Visions of Modernity: American Business and the Modernization of Germany. *v.3 p.170*

Visions of Paradise: Primordial Titles and Mesoamerican History in Cuernavaca. *v.3 p.285*

Visions of Sound: Musical Instruments of First Nations Communities in Northeastern America. *v.1 p.295, p.296, p.389,v.6 p.699*

Visions of the City: Utopianism, Power, and Politics in Twentieth-Century Urbanism. *v.6 p.725*

Visions of the Cosmos. *v.5 p.65*

Visions of the East: Orientalism in Film. *v.6 p.329*

Visions of the End: Apocalyptic Traditions in the Middle Ages. *v.1 p.600, p.645*

Visions of the Land: Science, Literature and the American Environment from the Era of Exploration to the Age of Ecology. *v.6 p.287*

Visions of the Past: The Challenge of Film to Our Idea of History. *v.6 p.315*

Visions of the People: Industrial England and the Question of Class, C. 1848-1914. . . . .*v.6 p.742*

Visions of Wild America. *v.5 p.234*

Visit to a Small Planet. *v.2 p.127*

The Visitors and Fred and Madge. *v.2 p.374*

The Visit. *v.2 p.606*

Visual and Other Pleasures. *v.6 p.473*

The Visual Arts: A History. *v.1 p.668*

Visual Arts in the Twentieth Century. *v.1 p.680*

Visual Basic 2005 in a Nutshell. *v.5 p.347*

Visual Complex Analysis. *v.5 p.491*

Visual Culture: Images and Interpretations. *v.1 p.700*

A Visual Dictionary of Architecture. *v.1 p.783*

Visual Digital Culture. *v.1 p.771*

The Visual Display of Quantitative Information. *v.4 p.174, v.5 p.481, p.588*

Visual Effects Cinematography. *v.6 p.352*

Visual Effects for Film and Television. *v.6 p.352*

The Visual Index of Artists' Signatures and Monograms.*v.1 p.664*

Visual Intelligence: How We Create What We See. . .*v.5 p.607*

The Visual Mind II. *v.1 p.702*

Visual Music: Synaesthesia in Art and Music since 1900. . . . .*v.1 p.677*

Visual Pedagogy: Media Cultures in and Beyond the Classroom. *v.4 p.347*

Visual Perception: Essential Readings. *v.5 p.607*

Visual Persuasion: The Role of Images in Advertising.*v.1 p.715*

Visual Space Perception: A Primer. *v.5 p.606, p.607*

Visualization and Imaging in Transport Phenomena. . .*v.5 p.86*

Visualizing Labor in American Sculpture: Monuments, Manliness, and the Work Ethic, 1880-1935.*v.1 p.776, p.777*

Visualizing Your Business: Let Graphics Tell the Story. *v.4 p.173*

Vita d'un uomo : tutte le poesie. *v.2 p.723*

La Vita Nuova. *v.2 p.702, p.703*

Vita Sackville-West: Selected Writings. *v.2 p.381*

Vita Sexualis. *v.6 p.231*

Vita: The Life of V. Sackville-West. *v.2 p.380*

Vital Connections: Politics, Social Security and Inequality in Chile. *v.3 p.352*

Vital Contradictions: Characterization in the Plays of Ibsen, Strindberg, Chekhov, and O'Neill. . .*v.1 p.80, p.83, p.109*

Vital Forces: The Discovery of the Molecular Basis of Life. *v.5 p.79, p.127, p.154*

Vital Harmonies: Molecular Biology and Our Shared Humanity. *v.5 p.126, p.127*

The Vital Lie: Reality and Illusion in Modern Drama. *v.2 p.187, p.188*

Vital Signs 2006: the Trends That Are Shaping Our Future. *v.5 p.357, p.360, p.367*

The Vital South: How Presidents Are Elected.*v.4 p.550, p.556*

Vitamin C: Its Chemistry and Biochemistry. *v.5 p.329*

Vitamin D: New Perspectives in Drawing. *v.1 p.722*

A Vittorini Omnibus: The Twilight of the Elephant, in Sicily, La Garibaldina. *v.2 p.723*

Vittorio Alfieri. *v.2 p.710*

ViVa: A Bibliography of Women's History. *v.6 p.449*

Viva Baseball!: Latin Major Leaguers and Their Special Hunger. *v.4 p.809, p.834, p.851, p.852, p.897*

Viva Kennedy: Mexican Americans in Search of Camelot. *v.6 p.538*

Viva la Muerte (Baal Babylone). *v.2 p.507*

Viva Mexico! Viva la Independencia!: Celebrations of September 16. . . . .*v.3 p.290*

Vivaldi: The Four Seasons and Other Concertos, Op. 8. . . . .*v.1 p.184, p.239, p.364, p.365*

Vivaldi. *v.1 p.187, p.365*

Vivir para Contarla. *v.2 p.683*

The Vivisector. *v.2 p.750*

Vladimir Nabokov, 1941-1951: The Real Life of Sebastian Knight; Bend Sinister; Speak, Memory. *v.2 p.104*

Vladimir Nabokov, 1955-1962: Lolita; Pnin; Pale Fire; Lolita: A Screenplay. *v.2 p.104*

Vladimir Nabokov, 1969-1974: ADA, or Ardor; Transparent Things; Look at the Harlequins!. *v.2 p.104*

Vladimir Nabokov Lolita: A Reader's Guide to Essential Criticism. *v.2 p.104, p.105*

Vladimir Nabokov: The American Years. *v.2 p.104*

Vladimir Nabokov: The Russian Years. *v.2 p.104*

Vladimir Nabokov's Lolita: A Casebook. *v.2 p.105*

Vladimir Odoevsky and Romantic Poets. *v.2 p.802*

The Vocabulary of Organic Chemistry. *v.5 p.289*

The Vocation of a Teacher: Rhetorical Occasions, 1967-1988. . . . .*v.2 p.566, p.579*

The Vocation of Man. *v.1 p.460*

Vocational Development. *v.5 p.577, p.578*

☐ Vocational Information Center. *v.4 p.305*

Vocational Interests: Meaning, Measurement and Counseling Use. *v.5 p.578*

Vocationalisation of Secondary Education Revisited. . .*v.4 p.305*

Voces Femeninas de Hispanoamerica. *v.2 p.665*

Vodou Nation: Haitian Art Music and Cultural Nationalism. *v.4 p.26*

Vogel's Textbook of Practical Organic Chemistry. *v.5 p.292, p.293*

Vogel's Textbook of Quantitative Inorganic Analysis. .*v.5 p.309*

The Voice of Egypt: Umm Kulthum, Arabic Song, and Egyptian Society in the Twentieth Century. *v.1 p.286, p.363,v.6 p.637*

The Voice of Evidence in Reading Research. *v.4 p.364*

The Voice of Genius: Conversations with Nobel Scientists and Other Luminaries. *v.5 p.394*

The Voice of Reason: Essays in Objectivist Thought. *v.1 p.510*

Voice of the City: Vaudeville and Popular Culture in New York. *v.1 p.35*

The Voice of the Poor in the Middle Ages: An Anthology of Documents from the Cairo Geniza. *v.6 p.596, p.597*

☐ The Voice of the Shuttle. *v.2 p.549, p.727*

The Voice of the Turtle: An Anthology of Cuban Stories.*v.2 p.671*

Voice of Victorian Sex: Arthur H. Clough, 1819-1861.*v.2 p.278*

Voice That Is Great Within Us: American Poetry of the Twentieth Century. *v.2 p.22*

Voices Against the State: Nicaraguan Opposition to the FSLN. *v.3 p.301*

Voices from an Empire: A History of Afro-Portuguese Literature. *v.2 p.693, p.695, p.697*

Voices from Ancient Egypt: An Anthology of Middle Kingdom Writings. *v.6 p.644, p.645*

Voices from Chernobyl: The Oral History of a Nuclear Disaster. *v.3 p.228*

Voices from Four Directions: Contemporary Translations of the Native Literatures of North America. *v.6 p.699*

Voices from Iran: The Changing Lives of Iranian Women. *v.6 p.632*

Voices from Madagascar: An Anthropology of Contemporary Francophone Literature. *v.2 p.541*

Voices from Prison: An Ethnographic Study of Black Male Prisoners. *v.6 p.277*

Voices from S-21: Terror and History in Pol Pot's Secret Prison. *v.6 p.170*

Voices from Southeast Asia: The Refugee Experience in the United States. *v.6 p.95, p.120, p.138*

Voices from the Field: Readings in Criminal Justice Research Methods and Research Methods in Criminal Justice.*v.6 p.246*

☐ Voices from the Gaps: Women Artists and Writers of Color. *v.6 p.476*

Voices from the Harlem Renaissance. *v.2 p.19*

Voices from the Ming-Qing Cataclysm: China in Tigers' Jaws. *v.6 p.188*

Voices from the Rocks: Nature, Culture and History in the Matopos Hills of Zimbabwe. *v.6 p.77*

Voices from Within: Early Personal Narratives of Bengali Women. *v.6 p.154*

Voices in Bali: Energies and Perceptions in Vocal Music and Dance Theater. *v.6 p.174, p.176*

Voices in the Evening. *v.2 p.717*

Voices in the Mirror: An Autobiography. *v.6 p.18, p.27*

Voices in the Shadows. . .*v.2 p.818, v.3 p.248, v.6 p.478, p.479*

Voices of a New Chicana/o History. *v.6 p.532*

Voices of a People: The Story of Yiddish Folksong. . .*v.1 p.300*

Voices of a People's History of the United States. .*v.3 p.380, p.445*

Voices of Ancient Philosophy: An Introductory Reader.*v.1 p.419*

Voices of Decline: The Postwar Fate of U. S. Cities. .*v.6 p.710*

Voices of Hope in the Struggle to Save the Planet. . *v.5 p.740*

Voices of Multicultural America: Notable Speeches Delivered by African, Asian, Hispanic and Native Americans. . . .*v.2 p.28*

Voices of Protest: Huey Long, Father Coughlin and the Great Depression. *v.3 p.439, p.446, p.466*

Voices of Resistance: Oral Histories of Moroccan Women. *v.6 p.61, p.643*

Voices of Resurgent Islam. *v.1 p.554*

Voices of Revolution, 1917. . . . .*v.3 p.221*

Voices of Revolution: The Dissident Press in America.*v.4 p.404*

Voices of Russian Literature: Interviews with Ten Contemporary Writers. *v.2 p.799*

Voices of Successful African American Men. *v.6 p.40*

Voices of the American Past: Documents in United States History, Set. *v.3 p.372*

Voices of the American Past: Documents in United States History. *v.3 p.372*

Voices of the Country: Interviews with Classic Country Performers. *v.1 p.275*

Voices of the New Arab Public: Iraq, Al-Jazeera and Middle East Politics Today. *v.4 p.415, v.6 p.594*

Voices of the Self: A Study of Language Competence.*v.5 p.620*

A Void. *v.2 p.533*

Vol. 1, The South Atlantic. *v.5 p.433*

Vol. 2, The North Atlantic. *v.5 p.433*

Vol. 3, The Gulf of Mexico and The Caribbean. . . . *v.5 p.433*

Vol. 4A, The Eastern Mediterranean. *v.5 p.433*

Vol. 4B, The Western Mediterranean. *v.5 p.433*

Vol. 5, The Arctic Ocean. *v.5 p.433*

Volatile Bodies: Toward a Corporeal Feminism. . . . *v.6 p.436*

Volcanic Worlds: Exploring the Solar System's
Volcanoes. *v.5 p.434, p.437*

Volcanism. *v.5 p.437*

Volcanoes in Human History: The Far-Reaching Effects of
Major Eruptions. *v.5 p.437*

Volcanoes. *v.5 p.437*

The Volga Tatars: A Profile in National Resilience. . *v.3 p.213*

Volkswagen Blues. *v.2 p.541*

The Volleyball Coaching Bible. *v.4 p.869, p.905*

Voltaire: A Biography. *v.2 p.484*

Voltaire Almighty: A Life in Pursuit of
Freedom. *v.2 p.484, v.3 p.147*

Voltaire Revisited. *v.2 p.484*

Voltaire: Treatise on Tolerance. *v.1 p.454, p.455*

Volume the First. *v.2 p.266*

Volume the Second. *v.2 p.266*

Volume the Third. *v.2 p.266*

Volumetric Analysis, 1942-1957, 3 vols. *v.5 p.268*

La Voluntad. *v.2 p.656*

The Voluntary City: Choice, Community, and Civil
Society. *v.4 p.545, p.546,v.6 p.722*

The Von Balthasar Reader. *v.1 p.571*

Voraussetzungen Einer Erzahlung, Kassandra: Frankfurter
Poetik-Vorlesungen. *v.2 p.620*

Das Vorbild: Roman. *v.2 p.612*

Voss. *v.2 p.750*

The Vote: Bush, Gore, and the Supreme Court. . . . *v.4 p.462*

Voter Turnout and the Dynamics of Electoral Competition in
Established Democracies since 1945. . . . . . .*v.4 p.577*

Voters, Patrons, and Parties: The Unreformed Electorate of
Hanoverian England 1734-1832. *v.3 p.114, v.4 p.604, p.606*

Votes and Violence: Electoral Competition and Ethnic Riots in
India. *v.4 p.618*

Votes for Women: The Struggle for Suffrage
Revisited. *v.4 p.518, p.519,v.6 p.430, p.440*

The Votes That Counted: How the Court Decided the 2000
Presidential Election. *v.4 p.462*

Voting Radical Right in Western Europe. *v.4 p.601*

Vouchers Within Reason: A Child-Centered Approach to
Education Reform. *v.4 p.450*

Vowels and Consonants: An Introduction to the Sounds of
Languages. *v.2 p.562*

Vox Compact Spanish and English Dictionary. . . .*v.2 p.636*

Vox Diccionario de Uso del Español de America y
Españ. *v.2 p.637*

Vox Modern Spanish and English Dictionary:
English-Spanish/Spanish-English. *v.2 p.635*

Voyage Around My Room: Selected Works of Xavier de
Maistre. *v.2 p.498*

Voyage in the Dark. *v.2 p.769*

The Voyage of the Beagle: Charles Darwin's Journal of
Researches. *v.5 p.231*

The Voyage of the Beagle: Journal of Researches into the
Natural History and Geology of the Countries
Visited During the Voyage of H. M. S. Beagle Round the
World. *v.5 p.236*

Voyage Out. *v.2 p.394*

Voyage Through Time: Walks of Life to the Nobel
Prize. *v.5 p.262*

A Voyage to Pagany. *v.2 p.136*

Voyager's Grand Tour: To the Outer Planets and
Beyond. *v.5 p.719*

Voyages en France. *v.2 p.502*

Voyages en Italie. *v.2 p.502*

Voyages of Discovery: Three Centuries of Natural History
Exploration. *v.3 p.322, v.5 p.223, p.230*

Voyages of Samuel de Champlain, 1604-1618. . . . *v.3 p.538*

Le voyeur. *v.2 p.525*

The Voyeur. *v.2 p.525*

Vsevolod Meyerhold. *v.1 p.109, p.139, p.153*

A vuelo de Pajaro: Chi xik'anik Tz'ikin. *v.2 p.674*

Vulnerable and Invulnerable Children: Theory, Research, and
Intervention. *v.5 p.671*

Vulnerable but Invincible: A Longitudinal Study of Resilient
Children and Youth. *v.5 p.672*

Vyacheslav Ivanov: Poet, Critic and Philosopher. . .*v.2 p.805*

Vygotsky's Educational Theory in Cultural
Context. *v.4 p.357, v.5 p.571*

Vygotsky's Psychology: A Biography of Ideas. . . .*v.5 p.597*

W

W. A. Mozart: Così Fan Tutte. *v.1 p.188, p.228, p.343*

W. A. Mozart: Die Entführung aus dem
Serail. *v.1 p.188, p.228, p.343*

W. A. Mozart: Die Zauberflöte. *v.1 p.188, p.228, p.343*

W. A. Mozart: Idomeneo. *v.1 p.192, p.232, p.344*

W. B. Yeats: A Life: The Apprentice Mage, 1865-1914, Vol.
I. *v.2 p.326*

W. B. Yeats: A Life: The Arch-Poet, 1915-1939. . . .*v.2 p.326*

W. B. Yeats: Man and Poet. *v.2 p.326*

W. B. Yeats: The Critical Heritage. *v.2 p.326*

W. B. Yeats, the Tragic Phase; a Study of the Last
Poems. *v.2 p.326*

W. D. Howells: Selected Criticism. *v.2 p.42*

W. E. B. Du Bois: Biography of a Race, 1868-1919. . *v.6 p.26*

W. Eugene Smith and the Photographic Essay. *v.1 p.769*

W. H. Auden: A Commentary. *v.2 p.329*

W. H. Auden and Chester Kallman: Libretti and Other Dramatic
Writings by W. H. Auden, 1939-1973. . . . . . .*v.2 p.329*

W. H. Auden Collected Poems. *v.2 p.329*

W. H. Auden: The Critical Heritage. *v.2 p.329*

W. I. Thomas on Social Organization and Social
Personality. *v.4 p.684*

W, or the Memory of Childhood. *v.2 p.533*

W, ou, Le souvenir d'enfance. *v.2 p.533*

W. Somerset Maugham: A Study of the Short Fiction. *v.2 p.370*

The W. Somerset Maugham Reader: Novels, Stories, Travel
Writing. *v.2 p.371*

W. Somerset Maugham. *v.2 p.370*

☐ Wachowicz's Web World: Web Sites for Discerning Finance
    Students. *v.4 p.88*

Wacousta: The Prophecy. *v.2 p.733*

Wade Hampton and the Negro: The Road Not Taken. .*v.3 p.425*

The Wadsworth Anthology of Drama. *v.1 p.69, p.129*

Wage Dispersion: Why Are Similar Workers Paid
    Differently? *v.4 p.203, p.244, p.254, p.266*

Wage Labour and Capital. *v.4 p.236, p.238*

Wage-Earning Women: Industrial Work and Family Life in the
    United States, 1900-1930. . . . .*v.3 p.444*

The Wager. *v.2 p.692*

The Wages of Affluence: Labor and Management in Postwar
    Japan. *v.6 p.224*

The Wages of Sin: Sex and Disease, Past and Present. .*v.4 p.746*

Waging Nonviolent Struggle: 20th Century Practice and 21st
    Century Potential. *v.4 p.650*

Wagner and His Operas. *v.1 p.203, p.233, p.366*

The Wagner Companion. *v.1 p.195, p.365*

The Wagner Compendium: A Guide to Wagner's Life and
    Music. *v.1 p.200, p.365, p.366*

Wagner Handbook. *v.1 p.200, p.201, p.366*

Wagner on Conducting. *v.1 p.205, p.366, p.403*

Wagner's das Rheingold. *v.1 p.196, p.229, p.365*

Wagner's Ring: A Listener's Companion and
    Concordance. *v.1 p.198, p.230, p.365*

Wagner's 'Ring' and Its Symbols: The Music and the
    Myth. *v.1 p.196, p.197, p.229, p.365*

Wagner. *v.1 p.205, p.366*

Wahhabi Islam: From Revival and Reform to Global
    Jihad. *v.6 p.625, p.626*

The Wahhabi Mission and Saudi Arabia. *v.6 p.626*

Wahhabism: A Critical Essay. *v.6 p.625*

Waiting: A Novel. *v.2 p.147*

Waiting for Aphrodite: Journeys into the Time Before
    Bones. *v.5 p.156*

Waiting for Godot: A Tragicomedy in Two Acts. . . .*v.2 p.333*

Waiting for Godot. *v.2 p.332, p.509*

Waiting for God. *v.1 p.458, p.652*

Waiting for Lefty and Other Plays. *v.2 p.108*

Waiting for the Barbarians. *v.2 p.754*

Waiting for the Dark, Waiting for the Light: A Novel. .*v.3 p.189*

Waiting for the Dawn: A Plan for the Prince. .*v.4 p.619, v.6 p.186*

Waiting for the Dog to Sleep. *v.2 p.789, p.790*

Waiting for the Unicorn: Poems and Lyrics of China's Last
    Dynasty, 1644-1911. . . . .*v.6 p.210*

Waiting for the Wild Beasts to Vote. *v.2 p.545*

The Waiting List: An Iraqi Woman's Tales of
    Alienation. *v.6 p.655*

The Waiting Years. *v.6 p.229*

A Wake for the Living: Poems. *v.2 p.811*

A Wake in Ybor City. *v.6 p.509*

Wake the Town and Tell the People: Dancehall Culture in
    Jamaica. *v.1 p.294*

Wake up, America!: World War I and the American
    Poster. *v.1 p.718*

Wakefulness: Poems. *v.2 p.57*

ⓔ Waking Sleeping Beauty: Feminist Voices in Children's
    Novels. *v.6 p.480*

Waking the Dictator: Veracruz, the Struggle for Federalism and
    the Mexican Revolution, 1870-1927. . . . . . .*v.3 p.284*

Walden: A Fully Annotated Edition. *v.2 p.53*

Walden Two. *v.4 p.500*

Wales in British Politics: 1868-1922. . . . .*v.3 p.132*

Wales: The Shaping of a Nation. *v.3 p.132*

Walford's Guide to Reference Material, Vol. 1. . . .*v.5 p.405*

A Walk in the Sun. *v.2 p.58*

A Walk on the Wild Side. *v.2 p.56*

Walker and Ghost Dance: Plays. *v.2 p.770, p.771*

Walker Evans. *v.1 p.766*

Walking and Orienteering: How to Cross Hills, Back Country
    and Rough Terrain in Safety and Confidence: A
    Professional Manual for Hikers, Paddlers, Horse Trekkers
    and Extreme Cyclists. *v.4 p.788*

Walking Games and Activities. . *v.4 p.797, p.798, p.799, p.800*

Walking in the Shade: 1949 to 1962. . . . .*v.2 p.365*

Walking the Line. *v.1 p.780*

Walking the Victorian Streets: Women, Representation, and the
    City. *v.6 p.748*

Walking Zero: Discovering Cosmic Space and Time along the
    Prime Meridian. *v.5 p.405, p.406*

Wall Street and Government Fraud: How They Deceive
    Us. *v.4 p.86*

Wall Street: From Its Beginnings to the Fall of
    Enron. *v.4 p.100, p.146, p.155, p.162*

The Wall Street Journal Guide to the Top Business Schools
    2006. . . . .*v.4 p.176*

The Wall Street Journal Guide to Understanding Money and
    Investing: An Easy-to-Understand, Easy-to-Use
    Primer That Helps Take the Mystery Out of Money, Indexes,
    Treasury Bills, Stocks, Commodities, Options, Bonds,
    Tracking Performance, Risk/Return, Mutual Funds, Futures,
    and Inflation. *v.4 p.96*

The Wall Street Journal Guide to Understanding Personal
    Finance: Mortgages, Banking, Taxes, Investing,
    Financial Planning, Credit, Paying for Tuition. . . .*v.4 p.96*

Wall Street People: True Stories of the Great Barons of
    Finance. *v.4 p.89, p.146, p.147, p.155, p.162*

Wall Street People: True Stories of Today's Masters and
    Moguls. *v.4 p.88, p.89, p.147, p.155, p.162*

Wall Street Words: An A to Z Guide to Investment Terms for
    Today's Investor. *v.4 p.97*

Wallace Nutting and the Invention of Old America. .*v.1 p.802*

Wallace Stegner: A Biography. *v.2 p.121*

Wallace Stegner: A Study of the Short Fiction. . . .*v.2 p.121*

Wallace Stevens: A Literary Life. *v.2 p.124*

Wallbangin': Graffiti and Gangs in L. A. *v.4 p.714*

The Walleye War: The Struggle for Ojibwe Spearfishing and
    Treaty Rights. *v.6 p.689, p.694, p.696*

Wallington's World: A Puritan Artisan in Seventeenth-Century
    London. *v.3 p.92, p.122*

Walls and Mirrors: Mexican Americans, Mexican Immigrants,
    and the Politics of Ethnicity. . . .*v.4 p.764, v.6 p.529, p.538*

Walls Built on Sand: Migration, Exclusion and Society in
Kuwait. . . . .*.v.6 p.627*

The Walls Came Tumbling Down: The Collapse of Communism
in Eastern Europe. . . . .*.v.3 p.208*

Walls of Heritage, Walls of Pride: African American
Murals. . . . .*.v.1 p.704*

Wall. . . . .*.v.1 p.779*

The Wall. . . . .*.v.2 p.81*

The Walnut Trees of Altenburg. . . . .*.v.2 p.522*

Walt in Wonderland: The Silent Films of Walt Disney. *.v.6 p.308*

Walt Whitman: A Gay Life. . . . .*.v.6 p.403*

Walt Whitman: An Encyclopedia. . . . .*.v.2 p.54*

Walt Whitman and Modern Music: War, Desire and the Trials of
Nationhood. . . . .*.v.2 p.54*

Walt Whitman and the Visual Arts. . . . .*.v.2 p.54*

Walt Whitman of the New York Aurora, Editor at Twenty-Two:
A Collection of Recently Discovered Writings. *.v.2 p.54, p.55*

Walt Whitman: Selected Poems. . . . .*.v.2 p.54*

Walt Whitman: The Centennial Essays. . . . . . .*.v.2 p.53*

Walt Whitman: The Measure of His Song. . . . . .*.v.2 p.54*

Walt Whitman: The Poem as Private History. . . .*.v.2 p.53*

Walt Whitman's America: A Cultural Biography. . . .*.v.2 p.54*

Walt Whitman's Camden Conversations. . . . . . .*.v.2 p.54*

Walt Whitman's Native Representations. . . . . . .*.v.2 p.53*

Walt Whitman. . . . .*.v.2 p.54*

Walter Benjamin and Art. . . . .*.v.1 p.702, p.770*

Walter Benjamin and the Arcades Project. . . .*.v.6 p.710*

Walter Gordon and the Rise of Canadian Nationalism. *.v.3 p.540*

Walter Johnson: Baseball's Big Train. . . . .*.v.4 p.852, p.898*

Walter Lippmann and the American Century. . . . .*.v.4 p.409*

Walter Pater: Lover of Strange Souls. . . . .*.v.2 p.302*

Walter Pater: Three Major Texts. . . . .*.v.2 p.302, p.303*

Walter Reuther: The Most Dangerous Man in Detroit. *.v.4 p.127*

Walter Scott. . . . .*.v.2 p.306, p.307*

Walter Sickert: The Prints: A Catalogue Raisonné. . .*.v.1 p.755*

Walther Nernst and the Transition to Modern Physical
Science. . . . .*.v.5 p.260*

Walther von der Vogelweide: The Single-Stanza Lyrics. *.v.2 p.594*

Waltzing in the Dark: African American Vaudeville and Race
Politics in the Swing Era. . . . .*.v.1 p.18*

Wanda Gag: A Catalogue Raisonné of the Prints. . . .*.v.1 p.758*

The Wanderers. . . . .*.v.2 p.756*

The Wanderer. . . . .*.v.2 p.628*

Wandering in the Garden, Waking from a Dream: Tales of
Taipei Characters. . . . .*.v.6 p.213, p.214*

Wandering Peoples: Colonialism, Ethnic Spaces, and Ecological
Frontiers in Northwestern Mexico,
1700-1850. . . . .*.v.3 p.269, p.287*

The Wandering Scholars. . . . .*.v.2 p.450*

Wang Shiwei and "Wild Lilies": Rectification and Purges in the
Chinese Communist Party, 1942-1944. . . . . .*.v.4 p.620*

ⓔ The Waning of the Communist State: Economic Origins of
Political Decline in China and Hungary. . . . . .*.v.4 p.509*

The Waning of the Middle Ages. . . . .*.v.6 p.563*

The Waning of the Old South Civilization, 1860-1880's. *.v.3 p.495*

The Waning of the Renaissance, 1550-1640. .*.v.1 p.600, v.3 p.70*

Wanted Dead or Alive: The American West in Popular
Culture. . . . .*.v.6 p.323*

The Wanting Seed. . . . .*.v.2 p.336*

The Wapshot Chronicle. . . . .*.v.2 p.67*

The Wapshot Scandal. . . . .*.v.2 p.67*

War: A Cruel Necessity. . . . .*.v.5 p.584*

The War after the War. . . . .*.v.4 p.562, p.646, p.648*

The War Against Cliche: Essays and Reviews,
1971-2000. . . . .*.v.2 p.329*

The War Against Proslavery Religion: Abolitionism and the
Northern Churches, 1830-1865. . . . .*.v.3 p.420*

War against the Idols: The Reformation of Worship from
Erasmus to Calvin. . . . .*.v.1 p.601*

The War Against the Jews, 1933-1945. . . . .*.v.1 p.548*

War Against the Poor: The Underclass and Antipoverty
Policy. . . . .*.v.4 p.754*

War Against the Weak: Eugenics and America's Campaign to
Create a Master Race. . . . .*.v.4 p.775*

War and Children. . . . .*.v.4 p.735*

War and Cinema: The Logistics of Perception. . . . .*.v.6 p.323*

War and Destiny: How the Bush Revolution in Foreign and
Military Affairs Redefined American Power. *.v.4 p.560, p.564*

War and Economic Development. . . . .*.v.3 p.42*

War and Economy in the Third Reich. . . . .*.v.3 p.173*

War and Film in America: Historical and Critical
Essays. . . . .*.v.6 p.323*

War and Gender: How Gender Shapes the War System and Vice
Versa. . . . .*.v.6 p.441*

War and Genocide: A Concise History of the
Holocaust. . . . .*.v.3 p.82, v.4 p.651*

War and Genocide: Organized Killing in Modern
Society. . . . .*.v.4 p.653*

War and Government in the French Provinces: Picardy,
1470-1560. . . . .*.v.3 p.144*

War and Human Nature. . . . .*.v.5 p.584*

War and Imperialism in Republican Rome: 327-70 B. C. *.v.3 p.25*

War and Intervention: A Global Survey of Peace
Operations. . . . .*.v.4 p.670*

War and Law since 1945. . . . .*.v.4 p.478*

War and Nature: Fighting Humans and Insects with Chemicals
from World War I to Silent Spring. . . . .*.v.6 p.296*

War and Peace in Israeli Politics: Labor Party Positions on
National Security. . . . .*.v.4 p.615, v.6 p.614*

War and Peace in the Middle East: A Critique of American
Policy. . . . .*.v.6 p.595*

War and Peace. . . . .*.v.2 p.809*

War and Politics. . . . .*.v.3 p.35*

ⓔ War and Popular Culture: Resistance in Modern China,
1937-1945. . . . .*.v.6 p.193*

War and Popular Culture: Resistance in Modern China,
1937-1945. . . . .*.v.1 p.693*

War and Press Freedom: The Problem of Prerogative
Power. . . . .*.v.4 p.459*

War and Punishment: The Causes of War Termination and the
First World War. . . . .*.v.4 p.649*

War and Reason: Domestic and International
Imperatives. *v.4 p.646*

War and Secession: Pakistan, India, and the Creation of
Bangladesh. *v.6 p.148*

War and Society in Ancient Mesoamerica. *v.3 p.261*

War and Society in Renaissance Europe,
1450-1620. . . . .*v.3 p.35, p.36, p.70,v.4 p.766*

War and the American Presidency. *v.4 p.642, p.643*

War and the Media: Reportage and Propaganda,
1900-2003. . . . .*v.4 p.406*

War and the Red Cross: The Unspoken Mission. . .*v.4 p.670*

War and the Works of J. R. R. Tolkien. *v.2 p.386*

War and Trade in West Indies. *v.3 p.107*

War As I Knew It. *v.3 p.461*

War Betwixt Englishmen: Brazil Against Argentina on the River
Plate. *v.3 p.277*

War by Other Means: National Liberation and
Revolution. *v.4 p.622*

War Crimes and Realpolitik: International Justice from World
War I to the 21st Century. *v.4 p.653, v.6 p.257*

War Crimes: Brutality, Genocide, Terror, and the Struggle for
Justice. *v.4 p.653*

War Crimes: Confronting Atrocity in the Modern World. .*v.6 p.257*

War Cruel and Sharp: English Strategy under Edward III,
1327-1360. . . . .*v.3 p.91, p.144*

War, Diplomacy, and Informal Empire: Britain, France and Latin
America, 1836-1852. . . . .*v.3 p.345*

War, Economy and Society, Nineteen Thirty-Nine to Nineteen
Forty-Five. *v.3 p.81*

The War Film. *v.6 p.322*

The War for America, 1775-1783. . . . .*v.3 p.409*

The War for Independence: A Military History. . . .*v.3 p.413*

The War for Korea, 1945—1950: A House Burning. .*v.6 p.237*

The War for Lebanon: 1970-1985. . . . .*v.6 p.606*

The War for Palestine: Rewriting the History of 1948. .*v.6 p.611*

The War for the Public Mind: Political Censorship in
Nineteenth-Century Europe. *v.3 p.74*

War for the Union: 1861-1862. . . . .*v.3 p.431*

The War for the Union: The Organized War, 1863-1864, Vol.
7. . . . .*v.3 p.431*

The War for the Union: The Organized War to Victory,
1864-1865, Vol. 8. . . . .*v.3 p.431*

The War for the Union: War Becomes Revolution, 1862-1863,
Vol. 6. . . . .*v.3 p.431*

War from the Top: German and British Military Decision
Making During World War II. *v.3 p.82*

A War Imagined: The First World War and English
Culture. *v.3 p.79*

War in a Time of Peace: Bush, Clinton, and the
Generals. *v.3 p.472*

The War in Bosnia-Herzegovina: Ethnic Conflict and
International Intervention. . . .*v.3 p.246, p.247, p.248, p.249*

War in European History. *v.3 p.36*

The War in Heaven: Paradise Lost and the Tradition of Satan's
Rebellion. *v.2 p.255*

War in the Land of Egypt. *v.6 p.663*

War in the Middle Ages. *v.3 p.35, v.6 p.566*

War in the Modern World. *v.3 p.36*

War, Justice, and Public Order: England and France in the Later
Middle Ages. *v.3 p.69, p.96, p.143, p.144*

War Land on the Eastern Front: Culture, National Identity, and
German Occupation in World War I. *v.3 p.161*

War Law: Understanding International Law and Armed
Conflict. *v.4 p.646*

A War Like No Other: How the Athenians and Spartans Fought
the Peloponnesian War. *v.3 p.17, p.18*

War Movies: The Belle and Blade Guide to Classic War
Videos. *v.6 p.322*

War, Nationalism and Peasants: Java under the Japanese
Occupation, 1942-1945. . . . .*v.6 p.178*

The War of 1812. . . . .*v.3 p.416*

The War of American Independence: Military Attitudes, Policies
and Practice, 1763-1789. . . . .*v.3 p.413*

War of Another Kind: A Southern Community in the Great
Rebellion. *v.4 p.520*

The War of Atonement, October 1973. . . . .*v.6 p.614*

A War of Information: The Conflict Between Public and Private
U.S. Foreign Policy on El Salvador, 1979-1992. . .*v.3 p.390*

A War of Nerves: Soldiers and Psychiatrists in the Twentieth
Century. *v.5 p.585*

War of Shadows: The Struggle for Utopia in the Peruvian
Amazon. *v.3 p.329*

The War of the End of the World. *v.2 p.686*

The War of the Revolution. *v.3 p.410*

The War of the Saints. *v.2 p.689*

War of the Unstamped: A History of the Movement to Repeal
the British Newspaper Tax, 1830-1836. . . . . .*v.6 p.742*

The War of the Worlds. *v.2 p.320*

A War of Words: Language and Conflict in the Middle
East. *v.6 p.583*

War on Labor and the Left: Understanding America's Unique
Conservatism. *v.4 p.123*

The War on Our Freedoms: Civil Liberties in an Age of
Terrorism. *v.4 p.564, p.572, p.660*

The War on the Bill of Rights: And the Gathering
Resistance. *v.4 p.563, p.572*

War on the Land: Ecology and Politics in Central
America. *v.3 p.270*

War on the Mind. *v.5 p.585*

The War Poems of Siegfried Sassoon. *v.2 p.380*

The War Prose. *v.2 p.345*

War, Prosperity and Depression: The U. S. Economy,
1917-1945. . . . .*v.3 p.440, p.447*

War Stories and Poems. *v.2 p.297*

A War to Be Won: Fighting the Second World War,
1937-1945. . . . .*v.3 p.81*

The War to End All Wars: The American Military Experience in
World War I. *v.3 p.468*

War to the Knife: Bleeding Kansas, 1854-1861. . . .*v.3 p.397*

War Trash: A Novel. *v.2 p.147*

War under Heaven: Pontiac, the Indian Nations, and the British
Empire. *v.6 p.685*

War with Catiline, War with Jugurtha - Selections from the
Histories - Doubtful Works. *v.2 p.442*

War with Mexico. *v.3 p.418, p.419*

The War with Spain in 1898. . . . .*v.3 p.401, p.438*

War with the Newts. *v.2 p.782, p.783*

War Without Mercy: Race and Power in the Pacific War. *v.6 p.223*

A Warbler's Song in the Dusk: The Life and Writings of Otomo
  Yakamochi (718-785). *v.6 p.229*

The Warden. *v.2 p.318*

Ward's Automotive Yearbook. *v.4 p.153*

Ward's world motor vehicle data. *v.4 p.153*

The Warehouse Prison: Disposal of the New Dangerous
  Class. *v.6 p.275*

Warfare and Agriculture in Classical Greece. *v.3 p.18*

Warfare and Diplomacy in Pre-Colonial Nigeria: Essays in
  Honor of Robert Smith. *v.6 p.71*

Warfare and Diplomacy in Pre-Colonial West Africa. . *v.6 p.69*

Warfare and Society in Europe, 1792-1914. . . .*v.4 p.628, p.648*

Warfare and Welfare: Integrating Security Policy into
  Socio-Economic Policy. *v.4 p.262, p.267*

Warfare at Sea, 1500-1650: Maritime Conflicts and the
  Transformation of Europe. *v.3 p.35*

Warm Climates in Earth History. *v.5 p.445*

Warm the Children, O Sun. *v.2 p.813*

Warped Passages: Unraveling the Mysteries of the Universe's
  Hidden Dimensions. *v.5 p.541*

Warrant for Genocide: Key Elements of Turko-Armenian
  Conflict. *v.4 p.652*

Warranted Christian Belief. *v.1 p.523, p.595*

The Warrior and the Priest: Woodrow Wilson and Theodore
  Roosevelt. *v.3 p.440, p.468*

Warrior for Gringostroika: Essays, Performance Texts, and
  Poetry. *v.6 p.499*

Warrior in Two Camps: Ely S. Parker, Union General and
  Seneca Chief. *v.6 p.681*

Warrior Poet: A Biography of Audre Lorde. .*v.6 p.24, p.43, p.401*

Warriors at Work: How Guinea Was Really Set Free. . *v.6 p.73*

The Warrior's Camera: The Cinema of Akira Kurosawa. *v.6 p.336*

Wars, Internal Conflicts, and Political Order: A Jewish
  Democracy in the Middle East. *v.6 p.613*

The Wars of French Decolonization: Modern Wars in
  Perspective. *v.4 p.584*

The Wars of Napoleon. *v.3 p.152*

Wars of the Ancient Greeks. *v.3 p.12*

The Wars of the Roses: Peace and Conflict in Fifteenth-Century
  England. *v.3 p.99, p.100*

Wars on Terrorism and Iraq: Human Rights, Unilateralism, and
  U.S. Foreign Policy. *v.4 p.565*

Wars, Parties and Nationalism : Essays on the Politics and
  Society of Nineteenth-Century Latin America. . . .*v.3 p.345*

The Wars We Took to Vietnam: Cultural Conflict and
  Storytelling. *v.6 p.322*

The Warsaw Diary of Adam Czerniakow: Prelude to
  Doom. *v.3 p.83*

The Warsaw Uprising of 1944. . . . .*v.3 p.254*

Wartime. *v.3 p.247, p.248*

Warton's History of English Poetry, Set. *v.2 p.179*

War. *v.3 p.35*

Warwick Illustrated Encyclopedia of Nature. . . .*v.5 p.77, p.225*

Was the Red Flag Flying There?: Marxist Politics and the
  Arab-Israeli Conflict in Egypt and Israel,
  1948-1965. . . . .*v.6 p.616, p.639*

The Washing of the Spears: The Rise and Fall of the Zulu
  Nation. *v.6 p.79*

Washington: A Centennial History. *v.3 p.532*

Washington: A Guide to the Evergreen State. *v.3 p.532*

Washington and Rome: The History of Catholicism in American
  Culture. *v.1 p.575*

Washington Comes of Age: The State in the National
  Experience. *v.3 p.533*

Washington Community: Eighteen Hundred to Eighteeen
  Twenty-Eight. *v.3 p.415*

Washington D. C.: A City and Capital. *v.3 p.493*

Washington, D. C. *v.2 p.127*

Washington Irving: An American Study, 1802-1832. . *v.2 p.42*

Washington Irving: Three Western Narratives. *v.2 p.42*

Washington Journal: A Diary of the Events of
  1973-1974. . . . .*v.3 p.469, p.470*

Washington, Somoza and the Sandinistas: State and Regime in
  U. S. Policy Toward Nicaragua, 1969-1981. . . .*v.3 p.391*

Washington Through Two Centuries. *v.3 p.493*

Washington's Crossing. *v.3 p.409*

Washington's History: The People, Land, and Events of the Far
  Northwest. *v.3 p.532, p.533*

Washington's Partisan War, 1775-1783. . . . .*v.3 p.409*

Washington. *v.3 p.493*

Waste and Want: A Social History of Trash. *v.6 p.296*

Waste Disposal in Academic Institutions. *v.5 p.266*

Wastewater Engineering: Treatment and
  Reuse. *v.5 p.369, p.379, p.380, p.706*

The Watcher and Other Stories. *v.2 p.715*

The Watcher of Waipuna and Other Stories. *v.6 p.102*

The Watcher on the Cast-Iron Balcony. *v.2 p.748*

Watching, from the Edge of Extinction. *v.5 p.181*

Watching the Dance Go By. *v.1 p.39*

Watching the Traffic Go By: Transportation and Isolation in
  Urban America. *v.5 p.700*

The Watchman Fell Asleep: The Surprise of Yom Kippur and Its
  Sources. *v.6 p.613*

The Watchman. *v.2 p.280*

Water: A Matrix of Life. *v.5 p.313*

Water Aerobics for Fitness and Wellness. *v.4 p.792*

Water and Womanhood: Religious Meanings of Rivers in
  Maharashtra. *v.1 p.535*

The Water Babies: A Fairy Tale for a Land-Baby. . .*v.2 p.296*

Water Chemistry. *v.5 p.705*

The Water Encyclopedia. *v.5 p.313*

Water for People, Water for Life: The United Nations World
  Water Development Report. *v.4 p.667*

Water: Global Common and Global Problems. *v.5 p.702*

Water Law. *v.4 p.463*

Water Lillies: An Anthology of Spanish Women Writers from
  the Fifteenth Through the Nineteenth Century. . . .*v.2 p.644*

Water Music. *v.2 p.141*

The Water of the Wondrous Isles. *v.2 p.301, p.302*

Water Resources and Development. *v.5 p.703*

Water Resources Engineering. *v.5 p.368, p.380, p.703*

Water Resources: Health, Environment and
Development. *v.5 p.703*

Water Resources Management: Principles, Regulations, and
Cases. *v.5 p.368, p.380*

Water Resources Planning and Management. *v.5 p.703*

Water Resources Planning. *v.5 p.19*

Water Resources Sustainability. *v.5 p.703*

Water Supply and Pollution Control. *v.5 p.369, p.380*

Water Treatment: Principles and Design. *v.5 p.704*

Water Use, Management, and Planning in the United
States. *v.5 p.703*

Waterfront Workers: New Perspectives on Race and
Class. *v.4 p.130*

Watergate: Chronology of a Crisis. *v.3 p.468*

The Watergate Investigation Index: House Judiciary Committee
Hearings and Report on Impeachment. . .*v.3 p.441, v.4 p.436*

Waterland. *v.2 p.380*

Waterlings. *v.2 p.813*

☐ The Waterloo Directory of English Newspapers and
Periodicals, 1800-1900. . . . .*v.6 p.735*

Watermark: Vietnamese American Poetry and
Prose. *v.6 p.92, p.141*

Water-Resources Engineering. *v.5 p.702*

The Water's Edge and Beyond: Defining the Limits to Domestic
Influence on United States Middle East Policy. . . .*v.3 p.387*

Watership Down: A Novel. *v.2 p.328*

Watson and DNA: Making a Scientific Revolution. . .*v.5 p.122*

The Watsons. *v.2 p.266*

Watteau's Painted Conversations: Art, Literatura, and Talk in
Seventeenth- and Eighteenth-Century France. . . .*v.1 p.749*

Waugh Abroad: The Travel Writing of Evelyn Waugh. .*v.2 p.388*

☐ Wavelet Tutorial. *v.5 p.279*

Wavelets in Intelligent Transportation Systems. . . .*v.5 p.699*

Wavelets: Tools for Science and Technology. . .*v.5 p.494, p.501*

Waverley: Or 'Tis Sixty Years Since. *v.2 p.308*

The Waves at Genji's Door: Japan Through Its Cinema. .*v.6 p.336*

Waves, Photons, Atoms. *v.5 p.561*

Waves, Tides and Shallow-Water Processes. *v.5 p.430*

The Waves. *v.2 p.394*

Waving the Flag: Constructing a National Cinema in
Britain. *v.6 p.339*

The Way Forward?: Christian Voices on Homosexuality and the
Church. *v.1 p.595*

The Way I Was. *v.1 p.250, p.328*

A Way in the World. *v.2 p.769*

The Way It Was and Other Writings. *v.6 p.535, p.543*

The Way Nature Works. *v.5 p.220, p.222*

The Way of All Flesh. *v.2 p.273*

Way of Death: Merchant Capitalism and the Angolan Slave
Trade, 1730-1830. . . . .*v.6 p.75*

A Way of Hope: An Autobiography. *v.4 p.129*

The Way of Stretching: Flexibility for Body and
Mind. *v.4 p.791, p.874*

The Way of the Brush: Painting Techniques of China and
Japan. *v.1 p.751*

The Way of the Carpenter: Tools and Japanese
Architecture. *v.6 p.221*

The Way of the Cell: Molecules, Organisms, and the Order of
Life. *v.5 p.154*

The Way of the Pipa: Structure and Imagery in Chinese Lute
Music. *v.1 p.289*

Way of the World and Other Plays. *v.2 p.244*

Way Out There in the Blue: Reagan, Star Wars and the End of
the Cold War. *v.3 p.471*

The Way to Nicea: The Dialectical Development of Trinitarian
Theology. *v.1 p.639*

The Way to Rainy Mountain. *v.2 p.150, v.6 p.698*

The Way to Tin Pan Alley: American Popular Song,
1866-1920. . . . .*v.1 p.275*

Way up North in Dixie: A Black Family's Claim to the
Confederate Anthem. *v.1 p.282*

The Way We Live Now: American Plays and the AIDS
Crisis. *v.6 p.412*

Way We Live Now. *v.2 p.318*

Way We Think: Conceptual Blending and the Mind's Hidden
Complexities. *v.5 p.608*

The Way We Wore: Styles of the 1930s and '40s. . .*v.6 p.332*

Way West: Stories, Essays and Verse Accounts,
1963-1993. . . . .*v.2 p.144*

The Way West. *v.2 p.78, p.79*

Wayfarers. *v.2 p.628*

The Wayfarer. *v.6 p.233*

Wayne Morse: A Political Biography. *v.3 p.457*

Wayne Thiebaud. *v.1 p.748*

The Ways and Power of Love: Types, Factors, and Techniques
of Moral Transformation. *v.4 p.694, p.695*

Ways of Escape and a Sort of Life. *v.2 p.350*

The Ways of Paradox and Other Essays. *v.1 p.444*

The Ways of Rain: And Other Poems by Hugo Lindo. .*v.2 p.676*

Ways of Seeing: The Scope and Limits of Visual
Cognition. *v.5 p.607*

Ways of the Hand: A Rewritten
Account. *v.1 p.382, p.383, p.403, p.404*

The Ways of White Folks. *v.2 p.87*

Ways to the Center: An Introduction to World Religions. .*v.1 p.525*

Ways with Words: Language, Life and Work in Communities
and Classrooms. *v.4 p.357*

The Wayward and the Seeking: A Collection of Writings by Jean
Toomer. *v.2 p.126*

The Wayward Bus. *v.2 p.123*

We Alone Will Rule: Native Andean Politics in the Age of
Insurgency. *v.3 p.326*

We Always Lie to Strangers: Tall Tales from the Ozarks. .*v.2 p.21*

We Answer Only to God: Politics and the Military in Panama,
1903-1947. . . . .*v.3 p.305*

We Are Everywhere: A Historical Sourcebook of Gay and
Lesbian Politics. *v.6 p.358, p.363, p.386*

We Are the Stories We Tell: The Best Short Stories by North American Women since 1945. . . . .*v.2 p.26, p.583*

We Came All the Way from Cuba So You Could Dress Like This?: Stories. *v.6 p.508*

We Came Naked and Barefoot: The Journey of Cabeza de Vaca across North America. *v.6 p.534*

We Can Sleep Later: Alfred D. Hershey and the Origins of Molecular Biology. *v.5 p.81, p.129*

We Cannot Delay, July 1, 1939-December 6, 1941, Vol. 2. . . . .*v.3 p.460*

We Don't Exactly Get the Welcome Wagon: The Experiences of Gay and Lesbian Adolescents in Child Welfare Systems. *v.4 p.756, v.6 p.377*

We Eat the Mines and the Mines Eat Us: Dependency and Exploitation in Bolivian Tin Mines. *v.3 p.324, v.4 p.34*

We Have Always Lived in the Castle. *v.2 p.90*

We Have Eaten the Forest: The Story of a Montagnard Village in the Central Highlands of Vietnam. *v.6 p.166*

We Hold the Rock: The Indian Occupation of Alcatraz Island, 1969-1971. . . . .*v.6 p.689, p.694*

We Keep America on Top of the World: Television Journalism and the Public Sphere. *v.4 p.414*

We Must Have Certainty: Four Essays on the Detective Story. *v.2 p.580*

We Must Love One Another or Die: The Life and Legacies of Larry Kramer. *v.6 p.402, p.412*

We Should Never Meet: Stories. *v.6 p.102, p.141*

We Specialize in the Wholly Impossible: A Reader in Black Women's History. *v.6 p.5, p.6, p.44*

We the Dangerous: New and Selected Poems. *v.6 p.104*

We, the Jury: The Jury System and the Ideal of Democracy. *v.4 p.470, v.6 p.270*

We the People: An Introduction to American Politics. .*v.4 p.516*

We the People: Foundations, Vol. 1. . . . . . .*v.4 p.451, p.452*

We the People: Transformations. *v.4 p.452*

We the Students: Supreme Court Cases for and about Students. *v.4 p.450*

We, the Tikopia: A Sociological Study of Kinship in Primitive Polynesia. *v.4 p.42, p.43*

We Took the Streets: Fighting for Latino Rights with the Young Lords. *v.6 p.540*

We Wear the Mask: African Americans Write American Literature, 1760-1870. . . . .*v.2 p.9, p.10*

We Were All Slaves: African Miners, Culture and Resistance at the Enugu Government Colliery, Nigeria. *v.6 p.71*

We Were the Mulvaneys. *v.2 p.152*

We Will Not Dance on our Grandparents' Tombs: Indigenous Uprisings in Ecuador. *v.3 p.333*

We Wish to Inform You That Tomorrow We Will Be Killed with Our Families: Stories from Rwanda. . . .*v.4 p.715, v.6 p.65*

The Weak Body of a Useless Woman: Matsuo Taseko and the Meiji Restoration. *v.6 p.228*

Weak Interactions of Leptons and Quarks. *v.5 p.553*

The Weakness of Civil Society in Post-Communist Europe. *v.4 p.640*

Wealth and Democracy: A Political History of the American Rich. *v.4 p.726*

The Wealth and Poverty of Nations: Why Some Are So Rich and Some So Poor. *v.3 p.40, v.4 p.237, p.265*

Wealth and Power in Provincial Mexico: Michoacán from the Late Colony to the Revolution. *v.3 p.285*

Wealth of a Nation to Be: The American Colonies on the Eve of the Revolution. *v.3 p.409*

Wealth of Nations. *v.4 p.220*

Weapons and Hope: International Edition. *v.4 p.656*

The Weather and Climate of Australia and New Zealand. *v.4 p.385*

Weather Bird: Jazz at the Dawn of Its Second Century. .*v.1 p.259*

Weather, Climate and Climate Change: Human Perspectives. *v.5 p.426*

The Weather for Poetry: Essays, Reviews, and Notes on Poetry, 1977-1981. . . . .*v.2 p.82*

The Weather Makers: How Man Is Changing the Climate and What It Means for Life on Earth. *v.5 p.371*

Weathering: An Introduction to the Scientific Principles. .*v.5 p.439*

The Weaver-God, He Weaves: Melville and the Poetics of the Novel. *v.2 p.48, p.49*

The Weaver's Knot: The Contradictions of Class Struggle and Family Solidarity in Western France, 1750-1914. . .*v.3 p.149*

Weavers of Revolution: The Yarur Workers and Chile's Road to Socialism. *v.3 p.356*

Weavers of Song: Polynesian Music and Dance. *v.1 p.289*

Weaving Identities: Construction of Dress and Self in a Highland Guatemala Town. *v.3 p.267*

Weaving New Worlds: Southeastern Cherokee Women and Their Basketry. *v.1 p.806, v.6 p.472, p.473, p.678, p.705*

The Weaving of Mantra: Kûkai and the Construction of Esoteric Buddhist Discourse. *v.1 p.567*

Weaving Science Inquiry and Continuous Assessment: Using Formative Assessment to Improve Learning. *v.4 p.362*

Weaving the Visions: New Patterns in Feminist Spirituality. *v.1 p.528*

Weaving the Web: The Original Design and Ultimate Destiny of the World Wide Web by Its Inventor. *v.5 p.338, p.342*

Web Advertising: New Forms of Communication on the Internet. *v.4 p.428*

Web and Software Development: A Legal Guide. . . .*v.4 p.441*

The Web and the Rock. *v.2 p.138*

Web Bloopers: 60 Common Web Design Mistakes, and How to Avoid. *v.5 p.338*

☐ Web Gallery of Art. *v.1 p.711*

Web of Life: A New Understanding of Living Systems. .*v.6 p.288*

☐ Web of Science. *v.5 p.256*

Web-Based Career Counseling: A Guide to Internet Resources for Researching a Career and Choosing A Major. . .*v.4 p.167*

☐ WebElements Periodic Table. *v.5 p.280*

☐ WebElements. *v.5 p.407*

Weber and Islam: A Critical Study. *v.1 p.559*

☐ Palestinian Education: Teaching for Peace or War?: Hearing Before a Subcommittee of the Committee Appropriations, United States Senate, One Hundred Eighth Congress, First Session, Special Hearing, October 30, 2003, Washington, DC. *v.4 p.337*

The Wedding: A Novel. *v.2 p.95*

The Wedding of Zein and Other Stories. *v.6 p.663*

The Wedding. *v.2 p.792*

Wedgwood: The First Tycoon. *v.1 p.802*

Weed-Crop Competition: A Review. *v.5 p.11, p.24*

Weeds. *v.2 p.91, p.92*

A Week on the Concord and Merrimack Rivers; Walden, or, Life
    in the Woods; the Maine Woods; Cape Cod. *v.2 p.53*

A Week on the Concord and Merrimack Rivers. *v.3 p.489*

Weekend Warriors: Alcohol in a Micronesian
    Culture. *v.4 p.45, p.46*

▢ Weekly Compilation of Presidental Statements. . .*v.4 p.481*

Weg Zuruck. *v.2 p.618*

Weighing the Odds: A Course in Probability and
    Statistics. *v.4 p.179*

The Weight of the World. *v.2 p.617*

Weight Training: Steps to Success. *v.4 p.792*

The Weimar Culture: The Outsider as Insider. *v.3 p.170*

The Weimar Republic Sourcebook. *v.3 p.170*

The Weimar Republic. *v.3 p.170*

Weird English. *v.2 p.190*

Weird Ideas That Work: 11 1/2 Practices for Promoting,
    Managing and Sustaining Innovation. *v.4 p.74*

Weird Ideas That Work. *v.4 p.67*

Welcome to the Dreamhouse: Popular Media and Postwar
    Suburbs. *v.6 p.448*

Welcome to the Genome: A User's Guide to the Genetic Past,
    Present, and Future. *v.5 p.130*

Welcome to the Monkey House. *v.2 p.158*

Welcome to the Real World: You've Got an Education, Now Get
    a Life!. *v.4 p.95*

Welcoming the Undesirables: Brazil and the Jewish
    Question. *v.3 p.341*

Welding Handbook, (2002), Vol. 1. . . . . . .*v.5 p.736, p.737*

Welding Metallurgy and Weldability of Stainless Steels. .*v.5 p.737*

Welding Metallurgy. *v.5 p.737*

Welfare, Modernity, and the Weimar State. *v.3 p.170*

The Welfare of Children. *v.4 p.756*

Welfare Realities: From Rhetoric to Reform. *v.4 p.754*

Welfare's End. *v.4 p.755, v.6 p.441, p.470*

The Well at the World's End. *v.2 p.302*

The Well of Loneliness: A 1920s Classic of Lesbian
    Fiction. *v.2 p.351, v.6 p.397*

We'll Understand It Better by and By: Pioneering African
    American Gospel Composers. *v.6 p.30*

The Well Wrought Urn: Studies in the Structure of
    Poetry. *v.2 p.179, p.568*

The Well-Being of Children and Families: Research and Data
    Needs. *v.5 p.639*

Well-Being: Positive Development Across the Life
    Course. *v.5 p.651*

Well-Being: The Foundations of Hedonic Psychology. *v.5 p.670*

Wellesley Index to Victorian Periodicals
    1824-1900. . . . .*v.6 p.735, p.752*

Wellington. *v.3 p.91*

Wellness Centers: A Guide for the Design
    Professional. *v.4 p.786, p.790, p.881, p.884*

The Wellness Guide to Lifelong Fitness. *v.4 p.791*

The Well-Ordered Police State: Social and Institutional Change
    Through Law in the Germanies and Russia,
    1660-1800. . . . .*v.3 p.167*

A Well-Ordered Thing: Dmitrii Mendeleev and the Shadow of
    the Periodic Table. *v.3 p.44*

The Well-Tempered Announcer: A Pronunciation Guide to
    Classical Music. *v.1 p.159, p.160*

Well-Tempered Women: Nineteenth-Century Temperance
    Rhetoric. *v.6 p.431, p.448*

Welsh Nationalism in the Twentieth Century: The Ethnic Option
    and the Modern State. *v.4 p.607*

Wendell and Ann Phillips: The Community of Reform,
    1840-1880. . . . .*v.3 p.419*

A Werewolf Problem in Central Russia and Other
    Stories. *v.2 p.807*

The Werewolf. *v.2 p.628*

The Werkbund: Design Theory and Mass Culture before the
    First World War. *v.1 p.713*

Werke: Abetilung III: Die Gemeinsamen Werke, Vol.
    46. . . . .*v.2 p.593*

Werke: Gesamtausgabe in drei Bänden. *v.2 p.602*

Werke in einem Band. *v.2 p.595, p.596*

Werke in fünf Bänden. *v.2 p.596*

Werke in Sechs Banden. *v.2 p.597*

Werke, in vier Bänden. *v.2 p.602*

Werke in Zehn Banden. *v.2 p.599*

Werke in zwei Bänden. *v.2 p.600*

Werke, Schriften und Briefe. *v.2 p.596*

Werke, Set. *v.2 p.596*

Werke und Briefe: Historisch-Kritische
    Gesamtausgabe. *v.2 p.600, p.602*

Werke und Briefe in Zwolf Banden. *v.2 p.600*

Werke und Briefe. *v.2 p.600*

Werke. *v.2 p.596, p.599, p.600, p.601, p.609, p.610*

Wesley and the People Called Methodists. *v.1 p.586*

Wessex Poems. *v.2 p.291, p.292*

West Africa Partitioned: The Elephants and the Grass, Vol.
    2. . . . .*v.6 p.68*

West Africa Partitioned: The Loaded Pause, 1885-1889, Vol.
    1. . . . .*v.6 p.68*

West Africa: Quest for God and Gold, 1454-1578. . . .*v.6 p.68*

West African Challenge to Empire: Culture and History in the
    Volta-Bani Anti-Colonial War. *v.6 p.74*

West African Christianity: The Religious Impact. *v.6 p.69*

West African Kingdoms in the Nineteenth-Century. . . .*v.6 p.68*

West African Popular Theatre. *v.2 p.751*

West African Worlds, Paths Through Socio-Economic Change,
    Livelihoods and Development. *v.4 p.384*

The West: An Illustrated History. *v.3 p.519*

The West Bank Handbook: A Political Lexicon. *v.6 p.616*

West Bank/East Bank: The Palestinians in Jordan,
    1949-1967. . . . .*v.6 p.621*

The West Beyond the West: A History of British
    Columbia. *v.3 p.546*

The West European Party System. *v.4 p.602*

The West from the Fathers to the Reformation. . . . *.v.1 p.615*

The West from the Reformation to the Present Day. . *.v.1 p.615*

West German Industry and the Challenge of the Nazi Past, 1945-1955. . . . . *.v.3 p.177*

West Germany under Construction: Politics, Society, and Culture in the Adenauer Era. . . . . *.v.3 p.177*

The West Indian in Panama. . . . . *.v.3 p.305*

West of Everything: The Inner Life of Westerns. . . *.v.6 p.325*

West of the Border: The Multicultural Literature of the Western American Frontiers. . . . . *.v.2 p.15*

West of Wichita: Settling the High Plains of Kansas, 1865-1890. *.v.3 p.524*

The West: The history of a region in Confederation. . *.v.3 p.545*

West Virginia, a Guide to the Mountain State. . . . . *.v.3 p.501*

West Virginia: A History. . . . . *.v.3 p.501*

Westcott's Plant Disease Handbook. . . . . *.v.5 p.47*

Westering Women and the Frontier Experience, 1800-1915. *.v.6 p.455*

Western and Frontier Film and Television Credits: 1903-1995, Vol. 1. . . . . *.v.6 p.324*

Western Aristocracies and Imperial Court, A. D. 364-425. . . . . *.v.3 p.31, p.32*

Western Attitudes toward Death: From the Middle Ages to the Present. . . . . *.v.4 p.742*

The Western Church in the Later Middle Ages. . . . . *.v.1 p.600, v.6 p.572*

Western European Costume Thirteenth to Seventeenth Century. . . . . *.v.1 p.150*

Western European Party Systems: Continuity and Change. . . . . *.v.4 p.601*

Western European Party Systems: Trends and Prospects. *.v.4 p.602*

Western Fertilizer Handbook. . . . . *.v.5 p.48, p.49*

The Western Impact on World Music: Change, Adaptation, and Survival. . . . . *.v.1 p.283*

Western Lands and the American Revolution. . . . . *.v.3 p.407*

Western Movies: A TV and Video Guide to 4200 Genre Films. . . . . *.v.6 p.324*

Western Music and Its Others: Difference, Representation, and Appropriation in Music. . . . . *.v.1 p.378*

Western Mysticism: A Guide to the Basic Works. . . *.v.6 p.570*

Western Mysticism: Augustine, Gregory, and Bernard on Contemplation and the Contemplative Life. . . . *.v.1 p.652*

The Western: Parables of the Western Dream. . . . . *.v.6 p.325*

Western Philosophy: An Illustrated Guide. . . . . . *.v.1 p.417*

Western Plainchant: A Handbook. . . . . *.v.1 p.177*

The Western Response to State-Supported Terrorism. *.v.4 p.564*

Western Sahara: Roots of a Desert War. . . . . . . *.v.6 p.61*

Western Society and the Church in the Middle Ages. . *.v.3 p.58*

The Western Story: A Chronological Treasury. . . . . *.v.2 p.27*

Western Times and Water Wars: State, Culture, and Rebellion in California. . . . . *.v.4 p.697, p.759*

Western Views of Islam in the Middle Ages. . . . . *.v.1 p.559*

Western Warfare in the Age of the Crusades, 1000-1300. . . . . *.v.6 p.556, p.567*

The Western Way of War: Infantry Battle in Classical Greece. . . . . *.v.3 p.18*

The Westerners. . . . . *.v.3 p.518*

Westerns and American Culture, 1930-1955. . . . . *.v.6 p.324*

Westerns: Films through History. . . . . *.v.6 p.325*

Westerns in a Changing America, 1955-2000. . . . . *.v.6 p.324*

Westerns: Making the Man in Fiction and Film. . . . *.v.6 p.324*

The Westminster Dictionary of Christian Theology. . *.v.1 p.594*

The Westminster Guide to the Books of the Bible. . . *.v.1 p.615*

The Westminster Handbook to Patristic Theology. . . *.v.1 p.633*

The Westminster Handbook to Reformed Theology. . *.v.1 p.589*

West's Encyclopedia of American Law. . . . . *.v.4 p.437*

The West's Road to 9/11: Resisting, Appeasing, and Encouraging Terrorism since 1970. . . . . *.v.4 p.658*

Westward Expansion: A History of the American Frontier. . . . . *.v.3 p.380*

Westward Ha!. . . . . *.v.2 p.111*

Westward Ho, Vol. 1. . . . . *.v.2 p.296*

Westward Ho, Vol. 2. . . . . *.v.2 p.296*

Wet: On Painting, Feminism and Art Culture. . . . . *.v.6 p.473*

Wetland Plants: Biology and Ecology. . . . *.v.5 p.53, v.6 p.290*

Wetlands: An Approach to Improving Decision Making in Wetland Restoration and Creation. . . . . *.v.5 p.173, p.179, p.180, p.242*

Wetlands: An Overview of the Issues. . . . . *.v.5 p.242*

Wetlands Ecosystems in Asia: Function and Management. *.v.5 p.178*

Wetlands: Environmental Gradients, Boundaries, and Buffers. . . . . *.v.5 p.357*

Wetlands: Mitigating and Regulating Development Impacts. . . . . *.v.5 p.177*

Wetlands. . . . . *.v.4 p.393, v.5 p.53, p.357, p.380*

We. . . . . *.v.2 p.810*

Wexford: An Omnibus. . . . . *.v.2 p.379*

Weymouth Sands. . . . . *.v.2 p.373*

Wörterbuch Chemie Deutsch/Englisch: Dictionary of Chemistry German/English. . . . . *.v.5 p.258*

Wörterbuch der deutschen Umgangssprache. . . . . *.v.2 p.621*

The Whale Caller: A Novel. . . . . *.v.2 p.756*

A Whale Hunt: Two Years on the Olympic Peninsula with the Makah and Their Canoe. . . . . *.v.6 p.695*

The Whale Rider. . . . . *.v.2 p.746*

Wharton:Novellas and Other Writings: Madame de Treymes; Ethan Frome; Summer; Old New York; the Mother's Recompense; a Backward Glance. . . . . *.v.2 p.132*

What a Producer Does: The Art of Moviemaking (Not the Business). . . . . *.v.6 p.351*

What African American Parents Want Educators to Know. . . . . *.v.4 p.310*

What Am I?: Descartes and the Mind-Body Problem. *.v.1 p.453*

What America Owes the World: The Struggle for the Soul of Foreign Policy. . . . . *.v.3 p.385*

What an Art Director Does: An Introduction to Motion Picture Production Design. . . . . *.v.6 p.349*

What Are the Chances?: Voodoo Deaths, Office Gossip and Other Adventures in Probability. . . . . *.v.4 p.178*

What Are the Questions?: Other Essays. . . . . . . *.v.4 p.270*

What Becomes of the Broken Hearted. . . . . *.v.2 p.744*

What Becomes of the Brokenhearted: A Memoir. .*v.6 p.401, p.402*

What Can She Know?: Feminist Theory and the Construction of Knowledge. *v.6 p.460, p.461, p.462*

What Can You Do with a Law Degree?: A Lawyer's Guide to Career Alternatives. *v.4 p.440*

What Can You Do with a Major in Biology: Real People. Real Jobs. Real Rewards. *v.5 p.244*

What Can You Do with a Major in Business?: Real People. Real Jobs. Real Rewards. *v.4 p.168*

What CEOs Expect from Corporate Training: Building Workplace Learning and Performance Initiatives That Advance Organizational Goals. *v.4 p.79*

What Color Is Your Parachute? 2006. . . . . *v.4 p.166*

What Computers Still Can't Do: A Critique of Artificial Reason. *v.5 p.339, p.343*

What Did the Biblical Writers Know and When Did They Know It?: What Archaeology Can Tell Us about the Reality of Ancient Israel. *v.1 p.617, p.619*

What Did the Internment of Japanese Americans Mean? *v.6 p.134*

What Did They Say about Gays? *v.6 p.360*

What Difference Does a Husband Make?: Women and Marital Status in Nazi and Postwar Germany. *v.3 p.53, p.172*

What Do I Teach for 90 Minutes?: Creating a Successful Block-Scheduled English Classroom. *v.4 p.288*

What Do We Expect to Learn from Our History?: The First Symposium on History in Landscape Architecture. .*v.1 p.813*

What Do You Care What Other People Think?: Further Adventures of a Curious Character. *v.5 p.542*

What Does It Mean to Be Well-Educated?: And More Essays on Standards, Grading, and Other Follies. *v.4 p.327*

What Does the World Want from America?: International Perspectives on U. S. Foreign Policy. *v.3 p.483*

What Emotions Really Are: The Problem of Psychological Categories. *v.5 p.653*

What Engineers Know and How They Know It: Analytical Studies from Aeronautical History. *v.5 p.718*

What Every Chemist Should Know about Patents. .*v.5 p.264*

What Every Special Educator Must Know: The Ethics, Standards, and Guidelines for Special Educators. *v.4 p.278, p.315, p.316*

What Every Teacher Should Know about Classroom Management. *v.4 p.284*

What Every Teacher Should Know about Student Assessment. *v.4 p.287*

What Evolution Is. *v.5 p.194*

What Functions Explain: Functional Explanation and Self-Reproducing Systems. *v.5 p.170, p.194*

What Gardens Mean. *v.1 p.819*

What Genes Can't Do. *v.5 p.135, p.136*

What Good Are the Arts? *v.1 p.702*

What Happened to the Soviet Union?: How and Why American Sovietologists Were Caught by Surprise. *v.3 p.223*

What Happens in Hamlet. *v.2 p.233*

What Has Christianity Ever Done for Us?: How It Shaped the Modern World. *v.1 p.595*

What I Remember. *v.4 p.193, p.273*

What If China Doesn't Democratize?: Implications for War and Peace. *v.4 p.619*

What Is a Crime?: Defining Criminal Conduct in Contemporary Society. *v.6 p.250*

What Is a Law of Nature? *v.1 p.498*

What Is Art? *v.1 p.481, v.2 p.809*

What Is Calculus About? *v.5 p.485*

What Is Called Thinking? *v.1 p.470*

What Is Community Justice?: Case Studies of Restorative Justice and Community Supervision. *v.6 p.278*

What Is Cool?: Understanding Black Manhood in America. *v.4 p.745*

What Is Dance?: Readings in Theory and Criticism. . .*v.1 p.41*

What Is Enlightenment?: Eighteenth-Century Answers and Twentieth-Century Questions. *v.3 p.72*

What Is Form Criticism? *v.1 p.616*

What Is Gnosticism? *v.1 p.646*

What Is Historical Materialism?: A Reader. *v.1 p.509*

What Is Judaism?: An Interpretation for the Present Age. *v.1 p.551*

What Is Knowledge? *v.1 p.474*

What Is Literature? and Other Essays. *v.2 p.528, p.576*

What Is Mathematics?: An Elementary Approach to Ideas and Methods. *v.5 p.458*

What Is Packaging Design?: Essential Design Handbook. *v.1 p.717*

What Is Painting?: Representation and Modern Art. . .*v.1 p.726*

What Is Philosophy? *v.1 p.416, p.417*

What Is Product Design? *v.1 p.717*

What Is Redaction Criticism? *v.1 p.616*

What Is Remembered? *v.2 p.124*

What Is Romanticism? *v.2 p.461*

What Is Sarbanes-Oxley? *v.4 p.109, p.111, p.112*

What Is Symbolism? *v.2 p.461*

What Is This Thing Called Jazz? *v.1 p.262*

What Is This Thing Called Science?: An Assessment of the Nature and Status of Science and Its Methods. . . *v.5 p.401*

What Is to Be Done? *v.4 p.506, p.508*

What Is Transparency? *v.4 p.87*

What Is Typography? *v.1 p.719*

What Is World Literature? *v.2 p.568*

What It Means to Be 98% Chimpanzee: Apes, People, and Their Genes. *v.4 p.14, p.15*

What It Takes to Be #1: Vince Lombardi on Leadership. *v.4 p.697, p.698*

What Kind of Europe? *v.4 p.383*

What Kind of Nation: Thomas Jefferson, John Marshall, and the Epic Struggle to Create a United States. *v.4 p.452*

What Lesbians Do in Books: Lesbians as Writers, Readers and Characters in Literature. *v.6 p.393*

What Liberal Media?: The Truth about Bias and the News. *v.4 p.416*

What Lips My Lips Have Kissed: The Loves and Love Poems of Edna St. Vincent Millay. *v.2 p.97*

What Made Pistachio Nuts?: Early Sound Comedy and the Vaudeville Aesthetic. *v.6 p.312*

What Makes Biology Unique?: Considerations on the Autonomy of a Scientific Discipline. *v.5 p.80*

What Makes Sammy Run? . . . . *.v.2 p.115*

What Makes the Lion Yawn?: A Zoogoer's Guide to Animal
    Behavior. . . . . *.v.5 p.83, p.166*

What Makes Women Sick: Gender and the Political Economy of
    Health. . . . . *.v.6 p.443, p.456*

What Matters in College: Four Critical Years
    Revisited. . . . . *.v.4 p.289, p.330*

What Matters Most: How a Small Group of Pioneers Is
    Teaching Social Responsibility to Big Business, and Why Big
    Business Is Listening. . . . . *.v.4 p.52, p.54*

What Mystery Do I Read Next?: A Reader's Guide. . *.v.2 p.580*

What Our Families Need: Toward a Policy Agenda for Lesbian
    and Gay Families. . . . . *.v.6 p.376, p.387, p.388*

What Price the Moral High Ground?: Ethical Dilemmas in
    Competitive Environments. . . . . *.v.4 p.53*

What Remains. . . . . *.v.1 p.767*

What Research Has to Say about Reading Instruction. *.v.4 p.363*

What Schools Are For. . . . . *.v.4 p.339*

What Science Is and How It Works. . . . . *.v.5 p.399*

What Scientists Think. . . . . *.v.5 p.96, p.230, p.231*

What Shape Is a Snowflake?: Magical Numbers in
    Nature. . . . . *.v.5 p.90, p.229, p.502*

What Should Teachers Know about Technology: Perspectives
    and Practices. . . . . *.v.4 p.352*

What Social Class Is in America: The American Dream and
    Social Class. . . . . *.v.4 p.725*

What Social Classes Owe to Each Other. . . . . . *.v.4 p.770*

What Stalin Knew: The Enigma of Barbarossa. . . . *.v.3 p.227*

What Style Is It?: A Guide to American
    Architecture. . . . . *.v.1 p.788, p.789*

What Successful Teachers Do: 91 Research-Based Classroom
    Strategies for New and Veteran Teachers. . . . . *.v.4 p.347*

What Teachers Need to Know: The Knowledge, Skills and
    Values Essential to Good Teaching. . . . . . . *.v.4 p.347*

What the Best CEOs Know: 7 Exceptional Leaders and Their
    Lessons for Transforming Any Business. . . . . . *.v.4 p.71*

What the Best MBAs Know: How to Apply the Greatest Ideas
    Taught in the Best Business Schools. . . . . . *.v.4 p.177*

What the Bible Really Says about Homosexuality: Millennium
    Edition. . . . . *.v.6 p.373*

What the Buddha Taught. . . . . *.v.1 p.565*

What the Dormouse Said: How the Sixties Counterculture
    Shaped the Personal Computer Industry. . . *.v.4 p.772, p.773*

What the Twilight Says: Essays. . . . . *.v.2 p.576*

What They Heard: Music in America, 1852-1881, from the
    Pages of "Dwight's Journal of Music". . . . . . *.v.1 p.279*

What to Listen for in Music. . . . . *.v.1 p.247, p.318*

What to Listen for in Rock: A Stylistic Analysis. . *.v.1 p.275*

What Was Socialism, and What Comes Next?: Princeton Studies
    in Culture - Power - History. . . . . *.v.3 p.208*

What We Knew: Terror, Mass Murder, and Everyday Life in
    Nazi Germany. . . . . *.v.3 p.172*

What We Owe to Each Other. . . . . *.v.1 p.485*

What Were the Crusades? . . . . *.v.3 p.63*

What Will We Do?: Preparing a School Community to Cope
    with Crises. . . . . *.v.4 p.353*

What Workers Want. . . . . *.v.5 p.579*

What Works in Corrections: Reducing the Criminal Activities of
    Offenders and Delinquents. . . . . *.v.6 p.272*

What Works in Distance Learning: Guidelines. . . . *.v.4 p.322*

What Works in Policing. . . . . *.v.6 p.263*

What'd I Say?: The Atlantic Story, 50 Years of
    Music. . . . . *.v.1 p.268, p.383*

Whatever Happened to the Soul?: Scientific and Theological
    Portraits of Human Nature. . . . . *.v.1 p.526*

Whatever. . . . . *.v.2 p.530*

What's Black about It?: Insights to Increase Your Share of A
    Changing African-American Market. . . . . . . *.v.4 p.138*

What's Going On?: California and the Vietnam
    Era. . . . . *.v.4 p.711, v.6 p.113, p.114*

What's Happening in the Mathematical Sciences. . . *.v.5 p.457*

What's in the Air: Natural and Man-Made Air
    Pollution. . . . . *.v.5 p.312, p.313*

What's That Sound?: Intoduction to Rock and Its
    History. . . . . *.v.1 p.267*

What's the Big Idea?: Creating and Capitalizing on the Best
    Management Thinking. . . . . *.v.4 p.66, p.72*

What's the Good of Education?: The Economics of Education in
    the UK. . . . . *.v.4 p.297*

What's to Become of the Boy?: Or, Something to Do with
    Books. *.v.2 p.604*

What's Welsh for Zen: The Autobiography of John
    Cale. . . . . *.v.1 p.210, p.267, p.315*

What's Wrong with Postmodernism?: Critical Theory and the
    Ends of Philosophy. . . . . *.v.1 p.512*

What's Wrong with the Criminal Justice System: Ideology,
    Politics and the Media. . . . . *.v.6 p.248*

What's Wrong with the World. . . . . *.v.2 p.277*

What's Your Corporate IQ?: How the Smartest Companies
    Learn, Transform, Lead. . . . . *.v.4 p.79*

Wheat and Wheat Improvement. . . . . *.v.5 p.22, p.25*

Wheater's Functional Histology: A Text and Colour
    Atlas. *.v.5 p.159*

Wheat. . . . . *.v.5 p.19, p.20, p.24*

Wheel of Fire. . . . . *.v.2 p.235*

The Wheel of Life: The Autobiography of a Western
    Buddhist. . . . . *.v.1 p.561*

Wheelchair Basketball. . . . . *.v.4 p.842, p.854*

☐ Wheelchair Sports Worldwide. . . . . *.v.4 p.842, p.843*

Wheels for the World: Henry Ford, His Company, and a Century
    of Progress. . . . . *.v.4 p.153*

When a Flower Is Reborn: The Life and Times of a Mapuche
    Feminist. . . . . *.v.3 p.354, p.355*

When Abortion Was a Crime: Women, Medicine and Law in the
    United States, 1867-1973. . . . . *.v.6 p.455, p.471*

When All Else Fails: Government as the Ultimate Risk
    Manager. *.v.4 p.92*

When Allies Differ: Anglo-American Relations During the Suez
    and Falklands Crises. . . . . *.v.3 p.391*

When and Where I Enter: The Impact of Black Women on Race
    and Sex in America. . *.v.4 p.729, p.730, v.6 p.25, p.38, p.43*

When Baby Boom Women Retire. . . . . *.v.6 p.456*

When Baghdad Ruled the Muslim World. . . . . . . *.v.6 p.585*

When Bosses Ruled Philadelphia: The Emergence of the Republican Machine, 1867-1933. . . .*v.4 p.551, p.552, p.553*

When Brazil Was Modern: A Guide to Architecture, 1928-1960. . . . .*v.1 p.788*

When Cells Die II: A Comprehensive Evaluation of Apoptosis and Programmed Cell Death. *v.5 p.159*

When China Ruled the Seas: The Treasure Fleet of the Dragon Throne, 1405-1433. . . . .*v.6 p.204*

When Colombia Bled: A History of the Violencia in Tolima. *v.3 p.357*

When Corporations Leave Town: The Costs and Benefits of Metropolitan Job Sprawl. *v.4 p.543*

When Courts and Congress Collide: The Struggle for Control of America's Judicial System. *v.4 p.541*

When Cultures Clash: Strategies for Strengthened Police-Community Relations. *v.6 p.265*

When Cultures Collide: Leading Across Cultures. . . .*v.4 p.56*

When Drag Is Not a Car Race: An Irreverent Dictionary of over 400 Gay and Lesbian Words and Phrases. *v.6 p.358*

When Elephants Weep: The Emotional Lives of Animals. *v.5 p.615*

When Farmers Voted Red: The Gospel of Socialism in the Oklahoma Countryside, 1910-1924. . . . .*v.4 p.548*

When Federalism Works. *v.4 p.525*

When Generations Collide: Who They Are. Why They Clash. How to Solve the Generational Puzzle at Work. . .*v.4 p.132*

When Genius Failed: The Rise and Fall of Long-Term Capital Management. *v.4 p.96, p.98, p.100*

When God Is a Customer: Telugu Courtesan Songs by Ksetrayya and Others. *v.6 p.152*

When God Is Silent. *v.1 p.650*

When Good Companies Do Bad Things: Responsibility and Risk in an Age of Globalization. *v.4 p.145*

When Good People Behave Badly. *v.4 p.130*

When Heaven and Earth Changed Places: A Vietnamese Woman's Journey from War to Peace. *v.6 p.93, p.140*

ⓔ When Heroes Love: The Ambiguity of Eros in the Stories of Gilgamesh and David. *v.6 p.391, p.646, p.664*

When I Was Puerto Rican. *v.6 p.490, p.508, p.509*

When Jesus Came, the Corn Mothers Went Away: Marriage, Sexuality and Power in New Mexico, 1500-1846. .*v.6 p.534*

When Knowledge Is Power: Three Models of Change in International Organizations. *v.4 p.629*

When Luck Runs Out: Help for Compulsive Gamblers and Their Families. *v.4 p.777*

When Men Revolt and Why. *v.4 p.760*

When Nationalism Began to Hate: Imagining Modern Politics in Nineteenth-Century Poland. *v.3 p.253*

When Nature Goes Public: The Making and Unmaking of Bioprospecting in Mexico. *v.6 p.283*

When Oberlin was King of the Gridiron: The Heisman Years. *v.4 p.804, p.858, p.893*

When Old Technologies Were New: Thinking about Electric Communication in the Late Nineteenth Century. . .*v.4 p.416*

When Pride Still Mattered: A Life of Vince Lombardi. .*v.4 p.859*

When Prisoners Come Home: Parole and Prisoner Reentry. *v.4 p.753, v.6 p.278*

When Prophecy Fails. *v.4 p.720, v.5 p.645*

When Rain Clouds Gather. *v.2 p.756*

When Romeo Was a Woman: Charlotte Cushman and Her Circle of Female Spectators. *v.6 p.413, p.414*

When Russia Learned to Read: Literacy and Popular Literature, 1861-1917. . . . .*v.3 p.217*

When Self-Consciousness Breaks: Alien Voices and Inserted Thoughts. *v.4 p.693*

When Sparks Fly: Igniting Creativity in Groups. .*v.4 p.66, p.80*

When the Bough Breaks: Forever after the Death of a Son or Daughter. *v.5 p.651*

When the Eagle Screamed: The Romantic Horizon in American Expansionism, 1800-1860. . . . .*v.3 p.385*

When the Elephants Dance: A Novel. *v.6 p.179*

When the Emperor Was Divine: A Novel. *v.6 p.101*

When the Game Was Black and White: The Illustrated History of Baseball's Negro Leagues. *v.4 p.804, p.831, p.850, p.890, p.891, p.896*

When the Giants Were Giants: Bill Terry and the Golden Age of New York Baseball. *v.4 p.853*

When the King Took Flight. *v.3 p.151*

When the Marching Stopped: The Politics of Civil Rights Regulatory Agencies. *v.4 p.529*

When the Moon Waxes Red: Representation, Gender and Cultural Politics. *v.6 p.88, p.90, p.112*

When the Old Left Was Young: Student Radicals and America's First Mass Student Movement, 1929-1941. . . . .*v.4 p.331*

When the Spirits Dance Mambo: Growing up Nuyorican in el Barrio. *v.1 p.19, p.20, v.6 p.491, p.545*

When the Time Comes. *v.2 p.510*

When the War Was Over: The Failure of Self-Reconstruction in the South, 1865-1867. . . . .*v.3 p.435*

When the Yankees Came: Chaos and Conflict in the Occupied South, 1861-1865. . . . .*v.4 p.519*

When Their World Falls Apart: Helping Families and Children Manage the Effects of Disasters. *v.4 p.758*

When Things Go Wrong: Organizational Failures and Breakdowns. *v.4 p.85*

When Titans Clashed: How the Red Army Stopped Hitler. *v.3 p.175*

When Topology Meets Chemistry: A Topological Look at Molecular Chirality. *v.5 p.298, p.498, p.499, p.501*

When We Were Good: The Folk Revival. *v.1 p.295*

When We Were Orphans. *v.2 p.355*

When Women Come First: Gender and Class in Transnational Migration. *v.4 p.44*

When Work Disappears: The World of the New Urban Poor. *v.4 p.759, v.6 p.720*

Where Angels Fear to Tread. *v.2 p.346*

Where Are You Going, Where Have You Been?: Selected Early Stories. *v.2 p.152*

Where Cultures Meet: Frontiers in Latin American History. *v.3 p.260*

Where Did Our Love Go?: The Rise and Fall of the Motown Sound. *v.1 p.269*

Where I'm Calling From: Selected Stories. *v.2 p.142*

Where Land and Water Meet: A Western Landscape Transformed. *v.6 p.295*

Where Science and Politics Meet. .*v.5 p.394, p.404, p.405, p.412*

Where Shall I Wander: New Poems. *v.2 p.57*

Where She Danced . . .: American Dancing,
1880-1930. . . . .*v.1 p.9, p.26*

Where Texts and Children Meet. *v.2 p.582*

Where the Animals Are: A Guide to the Best Zoos, Aquariums
and Wildlife Attractions in North America. *v.5 p.84*

Where the Body Meets the Memory: An Odyssey of Race,
Sexuality and Identity. *v.6 p.113, p.132*

Where the Boys Are: Cuba, Cold War America, and the Making
of a New Left. *v.3 p.309*

Where the Girls Are: Growing up Female with the Mass
Media. *v.4 p.416, v.5 p.620, p.624,v.6 p.448*

Where the Jackals Howl and Other Stories. *v.6 p.651*

Where the Law Ends: The Social Control of Corporate
Behavior. *v.4 p.444*

Where the Pavement Ends: Five Native American
Plays. *v.1 p.124, v.6 p.699*

Where the Pavement Ends: One Woman's Bicycle Trip Through
Mongolia, China and Vietnam. *v.1 p.124*

Where the Sky Began: Land of the Tallgrass Prairie. . .*v.5 p.241*

Where the Winds Sleep : Man's Future on the Moon, a
Projected History. *v.5 p.720*

Where Three Roads Meet: Novellas. *v.2 p.142*

Where White Men Fear to Tread: The Autobiography of Russell
Means. *v.6 p.694*

Where Women Work: A Study of Yoruba Women in the Market
Place and in the Home. *v.4 p.39*

Which Mary?: The Marys of Early Christian Tradition. .*v.1 p.642*

Which MBA?: A Critical Guide to the World's Best
MBAs. *v.4 p.176*

Which People's War?: National Identity and Citizenship in
Wartime Britain 1939-1945. . . . .*v.3 p.81*

Which Rights Should Be Universal? *v.4 p.513, p.670*

Which Way Did the Bicycle Go?: And Other Intriguing
Mathematical Mysteries. *v.5 p.469*

A Whig Embattled. *v.3 p.417*

Whiggery and Reform, 1830-41: The Politics of
Government. *v.3 p.114*

Whigs and Hunters. *v.3 p.109, p.131, p.132*

The Whirligig of Politics: The Democracy of Cleveland and
Bryan. *v.3 p.437*

The Whirlpool. *v.2 p.289*

Whispered Silences: Japanese Americans and World War
II. *v.6 p.116, p.134*

The Whispering Pond: A Personal Guide to the Emerging Vision
of Science. *v.5 p.403*

Whispering to Fool the Wind: Poems. .*v.6 p.502, p.503, p.511*

Whispers on the Color Line: Rumor and Race in
America. *v.2 p.17*

Whispers: The Voices of Paranoia. *v.5 p.661*

[e] Whistleblower Law: A Guide to Legal Protections for
Corporate Employees. *v.4 p.131*

Whistleblower Law: A Guide to Legal Protections for Corporate
Employees. *v.4 p.109*

The White Album. *v.2 p.143, p.144*

White Apples and the Taste of Stone: Poems 1946-2006. .*v.2 p.82*

White Bears and Other Unwanted Thoughts: Suppression,
Obsession and the Psychology of Mental Control. .*v.5 p.609*

White by Law: The Legal Construction of Race. . . .*v.4 p.457*

The White Castle. *v.6 p.667*

White Collar: The American Middle Classes. *v.4 p.724*

White Crow: The Life and Times of the Grand Duke Nicholas
Mikhailovich Romanov, 1859-1919. . . . .*v.3 p.220*

The White Devil. *v.2 p.235, p.236*

White Diaspora: The Suburb and the Twentieth-Century
American Novel. *v.6 p.731*

White Eagle, Red Star: The Polish-Soviet War, 1919-20. .*v.3 p.253*

White Fire: The Influence of Emerson on Melville. .*v.2 p.38, p.49*

White Gold: The Extraordinary Story of Thomas Pellow and
Islam's One Million White Slaves. *v.6 p.60*

The White Guard. *v.2 p.801*

White House Daze: The Unmaking of Domestic Policy in the
Bush Years. *v.3 p.473*

The White House: Its Historic Furnishings and First
Families. *v.1 p.801*

The White House Looks South: Franklin D. Roosevelt, Harry S.
Truman, Lyndon B. Johnson. *v.3 p.474*

[▭] White House Office of Faith-Based and Community
Initiatives. *v.5 p.672*

The White House Remembered. *v.3 p.378*

The White House: The First Two Hundred Years. . . .*v.3 p.493*

The White House Years. *v.3 p.459, p.460*

The White Image in the Black Mind: A Study of African
American Literature. *v.4 p.416*

White Land, Black Labor: Caste and Class in Late
Nineteenth-Century Georgia. *v.3 p.503*

The White Logic: Alcoholism and Gender in American
Modernist Fiction. *v.2 p.3*

White Magic and Other Poems. *v.2 p.789*

White, Male and Middle Class: Explorations in Feminism and
History. *v.6 p.434*

White Man's Burden: Historical Origins of Racism in the
United States. *v.3 p.398*

The White Man's Indian: Images of the American Indian from
Columbus to the Present. *v.6 p.681, p.682, p.697*

White Men on Race: Power, Privilege, and the Shaping of
Cultural Consciousness. *v.4 p.729*

The White Minority in the Caribbean. *v.3 p.297*

White Mischief: A Cultural History of Cocaine. . . .*v.4 p.777*

White Money/Black Power: The Surprising History of African
American Studies and the Crisis of Race in Higher
Education. *v.6 p.14*

White Mule. *v.2 p.136*

White Niggers of America. *v.3 p.536*

The White Nile. *v.6 p.51*

White over Black: American Attitudes Toward the Negro,
1550-1812. . . . .*v.6 p.7*

The White Peacock. *v.2 p.362*

White Raven. *v.2 p.792*

White Skins/Black Masks: Representation, Colonialism and
Cultural Cross-Dressing. *v.2 p.176*

Title Index

White Supremacy and Black Resistance in Pre-Industrial South Africa: The Making of the Colonial Order in the Eastern Cape, 1770-1865. . . . .*v.6 p.78, p.79*

White Teacher. *v.4 p.310*

White Teeth. *v.2 p.380*

White Terror: The Ku Klux Klan Conspiracy and Southern Reconstruction. *v.3 p.402, p.438*

White Women's Rights: The Racial Origins of Feminism in the United States. *v.6 p.435*

Whitebark Pine Communities: Ecology and Restoration. *v.5 p.40, v.6 p.292*

White/Black Race Mixing: An Essay on the Stereotypes and Realities of Interracial Marriage. *v.4 p.737*

White-Collar Crime and Criminal Careers. . . .*v.6 p.253, p.255*

Whitehall and the Wilderness: The Middle West in British Colonial Policy 1760. . . . .*v.3 p.513*

Whiteness and Trauma: The Mother-Daughter Knot in the Fiction of Jean Rhys, Jamaica Kincaid and Toni Morrison. *v.2 p.769*

Whiteness in the Novels of Charles W. Chesnutt. *v.2 p.32*

Whiteness of a Different Color: European Immigrants and the Alchemy of Race. *v.4 p.571*

Whites: Stories. *v.2 p.154*

Whitewashed Adobe: The Rise of Los Angeles and the Remaking of Its Mexican Past. *v.3 p.531*

Whitman Between Impressionism and Expressionism: Language of the Body, Language of the Soul. *v.2 p.54*

A Whitman Chronology. *v.2 p.54*

Whitman in His Own Time: A Biographical Chronicle of His Life, Drawn from Recollections, Memoirs, Interviews by His Friends and Associates. *v.2 p.54*

Whitman: Poetry and Prose. *v.2 p.54*

Whitman, Slavery and the Emergence of Leaves of Grass. *v.2 p.54*

Whitman's and Dickinson's Contemporaries: An Anthology of Their Verse. *v.2 p.22*

Whitman's Manuscripts: Leaves of Grass, 1860. . . . .*v.2 p.53*

Whitman's Poetry of the Body: Sexuality, Politics, and the Text. *v.2 p.53, p.54*

Whitman's Presence: Body, Voice, and Writing in Leaves of Grass. *v.2 p.54*

Whitman's Wild Children. *v.2 p.53*

Whittaker Chambers: A Biography. *v.3 p.450, p.463*

Who Are the People of God?: Early Christian Models of Community. *v.1 p.655*

Who Cares?: Institutional Barriers to Health Care for Lesbian, Gay and Bisexual Persons. *v.6 p.377*

Who Commits Crimes?: A Survey of Prison Inmates. .*v.6 p.276*

Who Controls Teacher's Work?: Power and Accountability in America's Schools. *v.4 p.283*

Who Controls the Internet?: Illusions of a Borderless World. *v.4 p.115*

Who Gets the Good Jobs?: Combatting Race and Gender Disparities. *v.4 p.133*

Who Governs?: Democracy and Power in an American City. *v.6 p.722*

▢ Who is Leading Our Schools? An Overview of School Administrators and Their Careers. *v.4 p.281*

Who Is She? *v.2 p.749*

Who Is White?: Latinos, Asians, and the New Black/Nonblack Divide. *v.6 p.125*

Who Knows: From Quine to a Feminist Empiricism. *v.6 p.461, p.463*

Who Makes Public Policy?: The Struggle for Control Between Congress and the Executive. *v.4 p.526, p.527*

Who Moved My Cheese?: An Amazing Way to Deal with Change in Your Work and in Your Life. *v.4 p.79*

Who Owns Academic Work?: Battling for Control of Intellectual Property. *v.4 p.446*

Who Owns History?: Rethinking the Past in a Changing World. *v.3 p.374, p.376*

Who Owns Information?: From Privacy to Public Access. *v.4 p.445, p.446*

Who Owns Native Culture? *v.4 p.33*

Who Pays for Student Diversity?: Population Changes and Educational Policy. *v.4 p.281*

Who Remembers the Sea. *v.2 p.542*

Who Rules America? Power, Politics, and Social Change. *v.4 p.702*

Who Rules Iran? the Structure of Power in the Islamic Republic. *v.6 p.632*

Who Runs for the Legislature? *v.4 p.530*

Who Set You Flowin'?: The African-American Migration Narrative. *v.6 p.25*

Who Shall Lead Them?: The Future of Ministry in America. *v.1 p.650*

Who Supports the Family: Gender and Breadwinning in Dual-Earner Marriages. *v.4 p.732, v.6 p.467*

Who Walk in Darkness. *v.2 p.58*

Who Wants to Be a Scientist?: Choosing Science As a Career. *v.5 p.398*

ⓔ Who Was Saint Patrick? *v.3 p.58*

Who Was That Man?: A Present for Mr. Oscar Wilde. .*v.2 p.320*

Who Was Who in American Art: 400 Years of Artists Active in America, 1564-1975. . . . .*v.1 p.664*

Who Were the Fascists?: Social Roots of European Fascism. *v.4 p.768*

Who What and Where of America: Understanding the Census Results. *v.4 p.179*

Who Will Care for Us?: Aging and Long-Term Care in a Multicultural America. *v.4 p.751*

Who Would Have Thought It? *v.6 p.503*

Who Wrote That Song? *v.1 p.167, p.251, p.270*

Who Wrote the Book of Life?: A History of the Genetic Code. *v.5 p.122*

Whole Days in the Trees. *v.2 p.516*

The Whole Enchilada: Hispanic Marketing 101. . . . .*v.4 p.138, v.6 p.526*

The Whole Music of Passion: New Essays on Swinburne. *v.2 p.313*

A Whole New Ball Game: An Interpretation of American Sports. *v.4 p.806, p.816*

The Whole Truth: The Watergate Conspiracy by Sam Ervin. *v.3 p.470*

Wholeness and the Implicate Order. *v.5 p.541*

Who's Afraid of the WTO? *v.4 p.55, p.61, p.664*

Who's He When He's at Home: A James Joyce
Directory. *v.2 p.357*

Who's Not Working and Why: Employment, Cognitive Skills,
Wages, and the Changing U. S. Labor Market. . . *v.4 p.305*

Who's Running America?: The Bush Restoration. . . *v.4 p.724*

Who's Who in Age of Alexander the Great: Prosopography of
Alexander's Empire. *v.3 p.19, p.20*

Who's Who in Contemporary Gay and Lesbian History: From
World War II to the Present Day. *v.6 p.357*

Who's Who in Economics. *v.4 p.193*

Who's Who in Gay and Lesbian History: From Antiquity to
World War ll. *v.6 p.357*

Who's Who in Non-Classical Mythology. *v.1 p.527*

Who's Who in Science and Engineering
1998-1999. . . . . *v.5 p.397, p.398*

Who's Who of Indian Writers, 1999: End-Century Edition. Vol.
1, (A-M). *v.6 p.147*

Who's Who of Indian Writers, 1999: End-Century Edition. Vol.
2, (N-Z). *v.6 p.147*

Who's Who of Indian Writers, 1999. . . . . *v.6 p.147*

Who's Who of Indian Writers: Supplementary Volume,
1990. . . . . *v.6 p.148*

Who's Who of Pulitzer Prize Winners. *v.4 p.403*

Whose America?: Culture Wars in the Public Schools. *v.4 p.762*

Whose Bible Is It?: A History of the Scriptures Through the
Ages. *v.1 p.615*

Whose Body? *v.2 p.382*

Whose Broad Stripes and Bright Stars?: The Trivial Pursuit of
the Presidency, 1988. . . . . *v.3 p.447*

Whose Detroit?: Politics, Labor, and Race in a Modern
American City. *v.3 p.517*

Whose Justice? Which Rationality? *v.1 p.484, p.514*

Whose Master's Voice?: The Development of Popular Music in
Thirteen Cultures, 41. . . . . *v.1 p.268*

Whose Science? Whose Knowledge?: Thinking from Women's
Lives. *v.6 p.439, p.462*

Why America Stopped Voting: The Decline of Participatory
Democracy and the Emergence of Modern A. . . *v.4 p.549*

Why Americans Split Their Tickets: Campaigns, Competition,
and Divided Government. *v.4 p.550*

Why Americans Still Don't Vote: And Why Politicians Want It
That Way. *v.4 p.549*

Why Angels Fall: A Journey Through Orthodox Europe from
Byzantium to Kosovo. *v.3 p.245*

Why Are All the Black Kids Sitting Together in the Cafeteria?:
And Other Conversations about Race. *v.4 p.310*

Why Asia?: Contemporary Asian and Asian American
Art. *v.6 p.87*

Why Be Moral?: The Egoist Challenge. *v.1 p.504*

Why Be Moral? *v.1 p.504*

Why Buildings Fall Down: How Structures Fail. . . *v.5 p.697*

Why Christianity of all religions? *v.1 p.597*

Why Deliberative Democracy?. *v.4 p.504*

Why Did the Socialist System Collapse in Central and East
European Countries?: The Case of Poland, the
Former Czechoslovakia and Hungary. *v.3 p.208*

Why Did the Soviet Union Collapse?: Understanding Historical
Change. *v.3 p.229*

Why Did They Kill?: Cambodia in the Shadow of
Genocide. *v.6 p.170*

Why Do I Write?: An Exchange of Views Between Elizabeth
Bowen, Graham Greene and V. S.
Pritchett. *v.2 p.335, p.349, p.378*

Why Do Men Barbecue?: Recipes for Cultural
Psychology. *v.5 p.637, p.638*

Why Geography Matters: Three Challenges Facing America:
Climate Change, the Rise of China, and Global
Terrorism. *v.4 p.373*

Why Globalization Works. *v.4 p.56, p.58, p.666*

Why God Won't Go Away: Brain Science and the Biology of
Belief. *v.5 p.635*

Why Haven't You Written?: Selected Stories,
1950-1970. . . . . *v.2 p.755*

Why Hitler Came into Power. *v.3 p.171*

Why Horace?: A Collection of Interpretations. . . . *v.2 p.434*

Why I Am a Separatist. *v.3 p.536*

Why Is It So Hard to Get Good Schools? *v.4 p.325*

Why Lenin? Why Stalin? Why Gorbachev?: The Rise and Fall
of the Soviet System. *v.3 p.223*

Why Life Speeds up As You Get Older: How Memory Shapes
our Past. *v.5 p.610*

Why Marriage Matters: America, Equality, and Gay People's
Right to Marry. *v.6 p.389*

Why Men Won't Ask for Directions: The Seductions of
Sociobiology. *v.5 p.653, p.657*

Why Not the Best? *v.3 p.456, p.467, p.468*

Why Not Victory?: A Fresh Look at American Foreign
Policy. *v.3 p.452*

Why Nothing Works: The Anthropology of Daily Life. *v.4 p.22*

Why Orwell Matters. *v.2 p.374*

Why Parents Matter: Parental Investment and Child
Outcomes. *v.5 p.640*

Why Parties?: The Origin and Transformation of Political
Parties in America. *v.4 p.552, p.578*

Why People Buy Things They Don't Need. *v.4 p.138*

Why People Buy. *v.4 p.139*

Why Poor People Stay Poor: Urban Bias in World
Development. *v.4 p.265*

Why Read the Classics?. *v.2 p.714*

Why Smart People Can Be So Stupid. *v.5 p.609, p.656*

Why Societies Need Dissent. *v.4 p.497, p.695*

Why Some Like It Hot: Food, Genes, and Cultural
Diversity. *v.5 p.136*

Why Study the Past?: The Quest for the Historical
Church. *v.1 p.598*

Why Study the Past? *v.1 p.656*

Why Suya Sing: A Musical Anthropology of an Amazonian
People. *v.1 p.294*

Why Switzerland? *v.3 p.245*

Why Terrorism Works: Understanding the Threat, Responding to
the Challenge. *v.4 p.658*

Why the Allies Won. *v.3 p.81*

Why the Confederacy Lost. *v.4 p.519*

Why the Crimean War?: A Cautionary Tale. *v.3 p.219*

Why the Lyrical Ballads? *v.2 p.324*

Why the North Won the Civil War. *v.3 p.395, p.430*

Why the South Lost the Civil War. *v.4 p.519*

Why the Wealthy Give: The Culture of Elite
Philanthropy. *v.4 p.719*

Why Things Are the Way They Are. *v.5 p.540*

Why Vietnam Invaded Cambodia: Political Culture and the
Causes of War. *v.6 p.168*

Why We Fought: Forging American Obligations in World War
II. *v.3 p.481*

Why We Hate. *v.6 p.252*

Why We Lost the ERA. *v.6 p.470*

Why We Shop: Emotional Rewards and Retail
Strategies. *v.5 p.586*

Why Women Protest: Women's Movements in
Chile. *v.3 p.352, v.4 p.710*

Whylah Falls. *v.2 p.733, p.734*

Wickedness. *v.1 p.484*

Wickerby: An Urban Pastoral. *v.5 p.242*

Wide Sargasso Sea. *v.2 p.769*

Wide-Field Astrophotography: Exposing the Universe, Starting
with a Common Camera. *v.5 p.65*

The Widening Circle of Genocide. *v.4 p.652*

Widening Gap: Development in the 1970's. . .*v.4 p.260, p.271*

The Widening Gate: Bristol and the Atlantic Economy,
1450-1700. . . . .*v.3 p.91*

A Widening Sphere: Changing Roles of Victorian
Women. *v.6 p.749*

A Wider Range: Travel Writing by Women in Victorian
England. *v.6 p.478*

A Wider View of the Universe: Henry Thoreau's Study of
Nature. *v.2 p.52*

☐ WIDNET: Women In Development Network
Database. *v.6 p.425*

Widows in White: Migration and the Transformation of Rural
Italian Women, Sicily, 1880-1928. . . . .*v.3 p.202*

Widows: North America. *v.4 p.741*

Widows, Vol. I: The Middle East, Asia, and the Pacific. *v.4 p.741*

Widows. *v.2 p.680*

WIE Elementary Differential Equations and Boundary Value
Problems, Textbook and Student Solutions Manual. *v.4 p.206*

Wie Urban Geography International Edition. *v.4 p.395*

Wieland: Or, the Transformation. *v.2 p.31*

Wielki Slownik Angielsko-Polski - The Great English-Polish
Dictionary. *v.2 p.775*

Wielki Slownik Polsko-Angielski - The Great Polish-English
Dictionary. *v.2 p.775*

The Wife of Bath. *v.2 p.208*

Wife to Mr. Milton and the Isles of Unwisdom. . . .*v.2 p.348*

Wiiliam Wordsworth : A Critical Anthology. *v.2 p.324*

☐ Wiki Spectroscopy. *v.5 p.270*

Wilberforce. *v.3 p.109*

Wild Africa. *v.5 p.236*

The Wild and Scenic Rivers of America. *v.5 p.174*

The Wild and the Sown: Botany and Agriculture in Western
Europe, 1350-1850. . . . .*v.3 p.42*

The Wild Ass's Skin. *v.2 p.486*

Wild Beasts and Idle Humors: The Insanity Defense from
Antiquity to the Present. *v.5 p.598*

Wild Bill: The Legend and Life of William O. Douglas. *v.4 p.468*

Wild Britain: A Traveller's Guide. *v.5 p.237*

Wild Cat Falling. *v.2 p.747*

Wild Cats of the World. *v.6 p.292*

Wild France: A Traveller's Guide. *v.5 p.237*

The Wild Geese. *v.6 p.231, p.232*

The Wild God of the World: An Anthology of Robinson
Jeffers. *v.2 p.91*

Wild Grass: Three Stories of Change in Modern China. *v.4 p.620*

Wild Heart: A Life: Natalie Clifford Barney and the Decadence
of Literary Paris. *v.6 p.403*

The Wild Hunter in the Bush of the Ghosts: Standard
Edition. *v.2 p.757*

Wild Ireland: A Traveller's Guide. *v.5 p.237*

The Wild Iris. *v.2 p.146*

🄴 Wild Lily, Prairie Fire: China's Road to Democracy, Yan'an
to Tian'anmen, 1942-1989. . . . .*v.6 p.192*

The Wild Man from Sugar Creek: The Political Career of
Eugene Talmadge. *v.3 p.502, p.503*

Wild Minds: What Animals Really Think. *v.5 p.614*

Wild Oats. *v.2 p.252*

Wild Ocean: America's Parks under the Sea. *v.5 p.83*

A Wild Peculiar Joy: The Selected Poems. *v.2 p.736*

A Wild Sheep Chase. *v.6 p.232*

Wild Solutions: How Biodiversity Is Money in the
Bank. *v.6 p.298*

Wild Spain: A Traveller's Guide. *v.5 p.237*

Wild Swans: Three Daughters of China. *v.6 p.193, p.199, p.217*

Wild Tales. *v.2 p.780*

Wild Thoughts from Wild Places. *v.5 p.223*

Wild to the Heart. *v.5 p.169, p.220*

Wild Town. *v.2 p.125*

Wilderness and the American Mind. *v.3 p.369, v.6 p.289*

Wilderness Ethics: Preserving the Spirit of
Wildness. *v.5 p.224, p.250*

Wilderness Manhunt: The Spanish Search for la Salle. *v.3 p.506*

The Wilderness Movement and the National
Forests. *v.5 p.223, p.235*

Wilderness Preservation: A Cross-Cultural Comparison of
Canada and the United States. *v.5 p.175, p.179*

Wilderness Preservation: A Reference Handbook. . .*v.5 p.181*

Wilderness Tips. *v.2 p.734*

Wilderness Visionaries. *v.5 p.231*

☐ Wildfinder - Mapping the World's Species. *v.5 p.224, p.233*

Wildlife and Western Heroes: Alexander Phimister Proctor,
Sculptor. *v.1 p.781*

Wildlife Ecology and Management. *v.5 p.19, p.356*

Wildwoods Wisdom: Encounters with the Natural
World. *v.5 p.221*

The Wiles of Men and Other Stories. *v.6 p.658*

The Wiley Encyclopedia of Energy and the Environment, Set. *v.5 p.359*

The Wiley Engineer's Desk Reference: A Concise Guide for the Professional Engineer. *v.5 p.679*

Ⓔ Wiley Guide to Chemical Incompatibilities. *v.6 p.286*

▢ Wiley Interscience Reference Tables. *v.5 p.257*

Wiley Registry of Mass Spectral Data: With NIST 2005 Spectral Data. *v.5 p.271*

Wiley/NBS Registry of Mass Spectral Data. *v.5 p.271*

Wiley's English-Spanish Spanish-English Chemistry Dictionary, 1. . . . .*v.5 p.258*

Wilhelm Busch. *v.2 p.603*

Wilhelm Meister's Apprenticeship. *v.2 p.598*

Wilhelm Raabe: The Fiction of the Alternative Community. *v.2 p.601*

Wilhelm Raabe. *v.2 p.599*

Wilkes and Liberty. *v.3 p.95, p.109*

Wilkie Collins. *v.2 p.281*

Will and Vision: How Latecomers Grow to Dominate Markets. *v.4 p.135*

Will Genocide Ever End? *v.4 p.653*

Will in the World: How Shakespeare Became Shakespeare. *v.2 p.227*

Will It Fly? How to Know If Your New Business Idea Has Wings... Before You Take the Leap. *v.4 p.68*

Will Power: Essays on Shakespearean Authority. . . .*v.2 p.233*

Will the Real Jesus Please Stand Up?: A Debate Between William Lane Craig and John Dominic Crossan. . .*v.1 p.642*

Will to Believe and Other Essays in Popular Philosophy and Human Immortality. *v.1 p.439*

The Will to Change; Poems 1968-1970. . . . . . .*v.2 p.115*

The Will to Kill: Making Sense of Senseless Murder. .*v.6 p.252*

Will You Miss Me When I'm Gone?: The Carter Family and Their Legacy in American Music. *v.1 p.276, p.316*

Willa Cather: A Critical Biography. *v.2 p.66, p.67*

Willa Cather: A Memoir. *v.2 p.67*

Willa Cather and Others. *v.2 p.67*

Willa Cather: Double Lives. *v.2 p.67*

Willa Cather: The Writer and Her World. *v.2 p.67*

Willa Cather. *v.2 p.66*

Willard and Spackman's Occupational Therapy. . . .*v.5 p.535*

Willard W. Waller on the Family, Education, and War: Selected Papers. *v.4 p.732*

Willem Marinus Dudok, a Dutch Modernist: A Bio-Bibliography. *v.1 p.662, p.697*

Willful Liberalism: Voluntarism and Individuality in Political Theory and Practice. *v.4 p.515*

William Appleman Williams: The Tragedy of Empire. *v.3 p.373, p.374*

William Billings of Boston: Eighteenth-Century Composer. *v.1 p.279, p.311*

William Blake: A Literary Life. *v.2 p.238*

William Blake and the Daughters of Albion. *v.2 p.239*

William Blake: The Complete Illuminated Books. *v.1 p.716, v.2 p.239*

William Blake: The Painter at Work. *v.1 p.748*

William Blake: The Seer and His Visions. *v.2 p.240*

William Blake's Theory of Art. *v.2 p.239*

William Blake. *v.2 p.240*

William Burroughs and the Secret of Fascination. . .*v.2 p.64*

William Byrd: A Guide to Research. . .*v.1 p.165, p.181, p.315*

William Byrd: Gentleman of the Chapel Royal. *v.1 p.180, p.315*

William Carleton, Irish Peasant Novelist: A Preface to His Fiction. *v.2 p.275*

William Carlos Williams and Alterity: The Early Poetry. *v.2 p.135*

William Carlos Williams and the Diagnostics of Culture. *v.2 p.136*

William Carlos Williams: Autobiography. *v.2 p.136*

William Carlos Williams: Selected Poems. *v.2 p.136*

William Christenberry. *v.1 p.767*

William Cobbett: The Poor Man's Friend. . . .*v.3 p.109, p.131*

William Collins and Eighteenth-Century English Poetry. *v.2 p.243, p.244*

William Cowper of the Inner Temple, Esq: A Study of His Life and Works to the Year 1768. . . . .*v.2 p.244*

William Cowper: Selected Letters. *v.2 p.244*

William Cowper. *v.2 p.244*

William Dean Howells: A Writer's Life. *v.2 p.42*

William Dean Howells: An American Life. *v.2 p.42*

William Dunbar: Selected Poems. *v.2 p.214*

William E. Borah and American Foreign Policy. . . .*v.3 p.460*

William Ellery Channing: Selected Writings. *v.1 p.590*

William Everson: The Life of Brother Antoninus. . . .*v.2 p.70*

William Faulkner: A Critical Study. *v.2 p.74*

William Faulkner A to Z: The Essential Reference to His Life and Work. *v.2 p.73*

William Faulkner and Southern History. *v.2 p.75*

William Faulkner: His Life and Work. *v.2 p.74*

William Faulkner Novels 1930-35: As I Lay Dying, Sanctuary, Light in August, Pylon. *v.2 p.74*

Ⓔ William Faulkner: Self-Presentation and Performance. *v.2 p.75*

William Faulkner: Six Decades of Criticism. *v.2 p.75*

William Faulkner: The Abstract and the Actual. . . .*v.2 p.73*

William Faulkner: The Yoknapatawpha Country. . . .*v.2 p.73*

William Faulkner: Toward Yoknapatawpha and Beyond. *v.2 p.73*

William Faulkner's As I Lay Dying: A Critical Casebook. *v.2 p.73*

William Faulkner's Yoknapatawpha: "A Kind of Keystone in the Universe". *v.2 p.74*

William Faulkner. *v.2 p.74*

William Gibbs McAdoo: A Passion for Change, 1863-1917. . . . .*v.3 p.456*

William Grant Still: A Study in Contradictions. *v.1 p.224, p.282, p.358*

William Harvey's de Motu Cordis: A New Translation and Latin Edition. *v.5 p.510*

William Hazlitt, Critic of Power. *v.2 p.293*

William Hazlitt. *v.2 p.293*

William Hickling Prescott: Representative Selections with Introduction, Bibliography and Notes. *v.2 p.49*

William Howard Taft: Chief Justice. *v.4 p.468*

William Howard Taft, Confident Peacemaker: The Evolution Idea: World Ordered Diplomacy. *v.3 p.439*

William I. Myers and the Modernization of American Agriculture. *v.5 p.6*

William J. Spillman and the Birth of Agricultural Economics. *v.5 p.14*

William Jaffe's Essays on Walras. *v.4 p.213, p.217*

William James: Sister Carrie; Jennie Gerhardt; Twelve Men. *v.2 p.70*

William Jennings Bryan: Political Puritan, 1915-1925. .*v.3 p.433*

William Lawes (1602-1645): Essays on His Life, Times and Work. *v.1 p.182, p.335*

The William Lowell Putnam Mathematical Competition, 1985-2000: Problems, Solutions and Commentary. *v.5 p.458, p.459*

The William Lowell Putnam Mathematical Competition: Problems and Solutions, 1938-1964. . . . .*v.5 p.458*

The William Lowell Putnam Mathematical Competition: Problems and Solutions 1965-1984. . . . .*v.5 p.457*

William Lyon Mackenzie King. *v.3 p.539*

William Makepeace Thackeray: A Literary Life. *v.2 p.315*

William Marshal: Knight-Errant, Baron and Regent of England, Vol. 13. . . . .*v.3 p.98*

William Marshal: The Flower of Chivalry. *v.6 p.556*

William Maxwell: A Literary Life. *v.2 p.97*

William McKinley and His America. *v.3 p.437*

William Morris: A Life for Our Time. *v.2 p.301*

William Morris: Centenary Essays. *v.2 p.301*

William Morris: Romantic to Revolutionary. *v.2 p.302*

William Morris: The Construction of a Male Self, 1856-1872. . . . .*v.2 p.301*

William Morris. *v.1 p.720, p.802,v.2 p.301*

William Osler: A Life in Medicine. *v.5 p.509*

William Penn: An Historical Biography Founded on Family and State Papers. *v.3 p.491*

William Penn. *v.1 p.585, v.3 p.492*

William Randolph Hearst and the American Century. .*v.4 p.150*

William S. Burroughs at the Front: Critical Reception, 1959-1989. . . . .*v.2 p.64*

William S. Burroughs. *v.2 p.64*

William Saroyan: A Study of Short Fiction. *v.2 p.118*

The William Saroyan Reader. *v.2 p.118*

William Shakespeare: A Compact Documentary Life. .*v.2 p.227*

William Shakespeare: A Study of Facts and Problems, Vol. I. *v.2 p.226, p.227*

William Shakespeare: Records and Images. *v.2 p.227*

William Shakespeare: The Complete Works. *v.2 p.225*

William Shakespeare, Vol. II. *v.2 p.226*

William Shenstone: An Eighteenth-Century Portrait. . .*v.2 p.260*

William Sidney Porter (O. Henry): A Reference Guide. .*v.2 p.51*

☐ William Still Underground Railroad Foundation Website. *v.6 p.37*

William Thackeray. *v.2 p.316*

William the Conqueror: The Norman Impact upon England. *v.3 p.97, p.98*

William the Silent: William of Nassau, Prince of Orange, 1533-1584. . . . .*v.3 p.205*

William Trevor: The Collected Stories. *v.2 p.385*

William Wordsworth - the Major Works: Including The Prelude. *v.2 p.325*

William Wordsworth: A Life. *v.2 p.323*

William Wordsworth: The Borders of Vision. *v.2 p.324*

William Wordsworth. *v.2 p.324*

William Wycherley and the Comedy of Fear. *v.2 p.264*

William Wycherley. *v.2 p.264*

Williams Hematology. *v.5 p.521*

Williams Obstetrics. *v.5 p.524*

Willies Textbook of Endocrinology. *v.5 p.518*

Willie's Game: An Autobiography of Willie Mosconi. .*v.4 p.855*

Willing Migrants: Soninke Labor Diasporas, 1848-1960. . . . .*v.6 p.73, p.74*

Williwaw. *v.2 p.127, p.128*

Wilson the Diplomatist: A Look at His Major Foreign Policies. *v.3 p.474*

Wilsonian Statecraft: Theory and Practice of Liberal Internationalism During World War One. . .*v.3 p.464, p.465*

Wilsonianism: Woodrow Wilson and His Legacy in American Foreign Relations. *v.3 p.465*

Wilson's Ghost: Reducing the Risk of Conflict, Killing, and Catastrophe in the 21st Century. *v.4 p.562*

Wimbledon: The Official History. *v.4 p.847, p.864*

Win or Lose: A Social History of Gambling in America. .*v.4 p.777*

Wind and Solar Power Systems: Design, Analysis, and Operation. *v.5 p.709*

Wind Effects on Structures: Fundamentals and Applications to Design. *v.5 p.696*

Wind Energy Comes of Age. *v.5 p.363*

Wind Energy in the Built Environment. *v.5 p.696*

Wind Engineering: A Handbook for Structural Engineering. *v.5 p.697, p.698*

A Wind in the Door. *v.2 p.149*

The Wind in the Willows. *v.2 p.347*

🕮 Wind Loads on Structures. *v.5 p.686*

Wind Loads on Structures. *v.5 p.693*

The Wind of the Hundred Days: How Washington Mismanaged Globalization. *v.4 p.663, p.664*

Wind Power for Home and Business: Renewable Energy for the 1990's and Beyond. *v.5 p.708, p.709*

Wind Power in View: Energy Landscapes in a Crowded World. *v.5 p.709*

Wind Power: Renewable Energy for Home, Farm, and Business. *v.5 p.363, p.708*

Wind, Sand and Stars. *v.2 p.526, p.527*

The Wind Spirit: An Autobiography. *v.2 p.534*

The Wind That Swept Mexico: The History of the Mexican Revolution of 1910-1942. . . . .*v.3 p.293*

Wind Tunnel Modelling and Ventilation Design. . . .*v.5 p.695*

Wind Turbine Technology: Fundamental Concepts of Wind Turbine Engineering. *v.5 p.363*

☐ WINDandSEA: The Oceanoic and Atmospheric Siences Internet Locator. *v.5 p.428*

The Winding Passage: Essays and Sociological Journeys, 1960-1980. . . . .*v.4 p.679*

The Window: New and Selected Poems. *v.6 p.651*

Window on the Black Sea: Bulgarian Poetry in Translation. *v.2 p.779*

Windows and Mirrors: Interaction Design, Digital Art, and the Myth of Transparency. *v.1 p.770*

Windows for the Crown Prince: An American Woman's Four Years as Private Tutor to the Crown Prince of Japan. .*v.6 p.228*

Windows on the World Economy with Economic Applications. *v.4 p.196*

The Winds of Change: Climate, Weather, and the Destruction of Civilizations. *v.4 p.394, v.5 p.426*

Winds of Death: Iraq's Use of Poison Gas Against Its Kurdish Population. *v.6 p.599, p.604*

Windsor Report. *v.1 p.582*

Windswept: A Passionate View of the Prairie Grasslands. *v.5 p.241*

Windthorst: A Political Biography. *v.3 p.169*

The Windy City Wars: Labor, Leisure, and Sport in the Making of Chicago. *v.4 p.783, p.784, p.805, p.881*

Wine: An Introduction. *v.5 p.52*

The Wine Atlas of California. *v.5 p.53*

Wine Science: Principles, Practice, Perception. *v.5 p.52*

Wine, Women and Death: Medieval Hebrew Poems on the Good Life. *v.6 p.566, p.574*

Winemaking Basics. *v.5 p.52, p.53*

Winemaking: From Grape Growing to Marketplace. . .*v.5 p.52*

Wines in the Wilderness: Plays by African American Women from the Harlem Renaissance to the Present. . .*v.6 p.15, p.23*

Wines: Their Sensory Evaluation. *v.5 p.52*

Winesburg, Ohio. *v.2 p.57*

Winfield Scott and the Profession of Arms. *v.3 p.399*

Wing Theory. *v.5 p.718*

Wings of Gauze: Women of Color and the Experience of Health and Illness. *v.6 p.443*

Wings of Madness: Alberto Santos-Dumont and the Invention of Flight. *v.3 p.341*

The Wings of the Dove: Authoritative Text, the Author and the Novel, Criticism. *v.2 p.44*

The Winner Names the Age: A Collection of Writings. .*v.2 p.116*

Winnie the Pooh 80th Anniversary Edition. *v.2 p.368*

Winning Business: How to Use Financial Analysis and Benchmarks to Outscore Your Competition. . . .*v.4 p.178*

Winning Field Hockey for Girls. *v.4 p.799, p.800, p.840, p.857, p.858*

Winning Hearts and Minds: British Governments, the Media and Colonial Counter-Insurgency, 1944-1960. . . . . .*v.3 p.87*

Winning Lacrosse for Girls. *v.4 p.838, p.862, p.863*

Winning Modern Wars: Iraq, Terrorism, and the American Empire. *v.4 p.561, p.563*

Winning of the Midwest: Social and Political Conflict, 1888-1896. . . . .*v.3 p.506*

The Winning of the West: From the Alleghanies to the Mississippi, 1769-1776. . . . .*v.3 p.381*

The Winning of the West: From the Alleghanies to the Mississippi, 1777-1783. . . . .*v.3 p.381*

The Winning of the West: Louisiana and the Northwest, 1791-1807. . . . .*v.3 p.381*

The Winning of the West: The Founding of the Trans-Alleghany Commonwealths, 1784-1790. . . . .*v.3 p.381*

Winning Raquetball: Skills, Drills, and Strategies. . .*v.4 p.864*

Winning Sounds Like This: A Season with the Women's Basketball Team at Gallaudet, the World's Only University for the Deaf. *v.4 p.835, p.842, p.853*

Winning: The Design of Sport. *v.4 p.870*

Winning the Dust Bowl. *v.6 p.699*

Winning the Games Scientists Play. *v.5 p.409*

Winning the Loser's Game: Timeless Strategies for Successful Investing. *v.4 p.94*

Winning the Vote: The Triumph of the American Woman Suffrage Movement. *v.4 p.554, p.568*

Winning Volleyball for Girls. *v.4 p.840, p.869*

Winning Ways for Your Mathematical Plays, Vol. 1. . . . .*v.5 p.457, p.468*

Winning Ways for Your Mathematical Plays, Vol. 2. . . . .*v.5 p.457, p.468*

Winning Ways for Your Mathematical Plays, Vol. 3. . . . .*v.5 p.457, p.468*

Winning Ways for Your Mathematical Plays, Vol. 4. . . . .*v.5 p.457, p.468*

Winning Wrestling Moves. *v.4 p.870*

Winning. *v.4 p.82*

Winnipeg: A Social History of Urban Growth, 1874-1914. . . . .*v.4 p.700, v.6 p.710*

Winslow Homer and the Critics: Forging a National Art in the 1870s. *v.1 p.737*

Winslow Homer and the Illustrated Book. *v.1 p.720*

Winslow Homer. *v.1 p.737*

Winston S. Churchill: The Wilderness Years. *v.3 p.118*

Winter Count. *v.2 p.149*

Winter in Majorca. *v.2 p.500*

The Winter King: Frederick V of the Palatinate and the Coming of the Thirty Years' War. *v.3 p.188*

Winter Love: Ezra Pound and H. D. *v.2 p.89, p.111*

Winter Night: Selected Poems of Attila Jozsef. . . .*v.2 p.786*

Winter: Notes from Montana. *v.2 p.140*

Winter of Artifice. *v.2 p.105*

The Winter of Our Discontent. *v.2 p.123*

Winter Pollen: Occasional Prose. *v.2 p.353*

The Winter's Tale. *v.2 p.224*

Winthrop's Boston: Portrait of a Puritan Town, 1630-1649. . . . .*v.3 p.488*

Wiping the War Paint off the Lens: Native American Film and Video, Vol. 10. . . . .*v.6 p.700*

Wired for Sound: Engineering and Technologies in Sonic Cultures. *v.1 p.283, p.386, p.387*

Wired Women: Gender and New Realities in Cyberspace. *v.6 p.439*

Wireless Communications: Principles and Practice. . .*v.5 p.726*

Wirtschaftspsychologie: Behavioral Economics. Behavioral Finance. Arbeitswelt. *v.4 p.263, p.264*

Wisconsin: A Guide to the Badger State. *v.3 p.517*

Wisconsin: A History. *v.3 p.517*

Wisconsin's Past and Present: A Historical Atlas. .*v.3 p.517, p.518*

Wisdom, Intelligence, and Creativity
Synthesized. *v.5 p.572, p.613, p.656, p.657*

The Wisdom Literature. *v.1 p.621*

Wisdom of Ben Shira. *v.1 p.624*

The Wisdom of Catholicism. *v.1 p.572*

The Wisdom of Crowds: Why the Many Are Smarter Than the
Few and How Collective Wisdom Shapes Business,
Economies, Societies and Nations. *v.4 p.51, p.135,v.5 p.649*

The Wisdom of Crowds. *v.5 p.649*

The Wisdom of Practice: Essays on Teaching, Learning, and
Learning to Teach. *v.4 p.348*

The Wisdom of Solomon. *v.1 p.624*

The Wisdom of Teams: Creating the High-Performance
Organization. *v.4 p.80*

The Wisdom of the Body. *v.5 p.509*

The Wisdom of the Genes: New Pathways in Evolution. .*v.5 p.198*

Wise and Foolish Kings: The House of Valois. . . .*v.3 p.143*

The Wise Men: Architects of the American Century. . *v.3 p.455*

The Wise Men of Foreign Affairs: The History of the Council
on Foreign Relations. *v.3 p.454*

Wisecracker: The Life and Times of William Haines,
Hollywood's First Openly Gay Star. *v.6 p.418*

Wishbone. *v.6 p.104*

Wising up the Marks: The Amodern William Burroughs. .*v.2 p.64*

Wit: A Play. *v.2 p.144*

Wit and the Writing of History: The Rhetoric of Historiography
in Imperial Rome. *v.2 p.426*

The Wit in the Dungeon: The Remarkable Life of Leigh
Hunt--Poet, Revolutionary, and the Last of the
Romantics. *v.2 p.290*

Witch Craze: Terror and Fantasy in Baroque Germany. *v.3 p.52*

Witch Hunting, Magic and the New Philosophy: An Introduction
to Debates of the Scientific Revolution,
1450-1750. . . . .*v.5 p.410, p.411*

The Witch of Edmonton. *v.2 p.218*

The Witch of Exmoor. *v.2 p.344*

Witchcraft in Europe, 400-1700: A Documentary
History. *v.3 p.70, v.6 p.569*

Witchcraft in the Middle Ages. *v.6 p.569*

Witchcraft, Oracles and Magic among the
Azande. *v.4 p.36, v.6 p.59*

Witchcraft Persecutions in Bavaria: Popular Magic, Religious
Zealotry and Reason of State in Early Modern
Europe. *v.3 p.165*

The Witchcraft Sourcebook. *v.6 p.569*

The Witches of Eastwick. *v.2 p.157*

With a Crooked Stick: The Films of Oscar
Micheaux. *v.6 p.329, p.330, p.341*

With All and for the Good of All: The Emergence of Popular
Nationalism in the Cuban Communities of the United States,
1848-1898. . . . .*v.3 p.312*

With Amusement for All: A History of American Popular
Culture Since 1830. . . . .*v.4 p.712*

With an Air Debonair: Musical Theatre in America,
1785-1815. . . . .*v.1 p.253*

With Bleeding Footsteps: Mary Baker Eddy's Path to Religious
Leadership. *v.1 p.583, p.584*

With Broadax and Firebrand: The Destruction of the Brazilian
Atlantic Forest. *v.3 p.268, p.339*

With Eyes Toward Zion: Scholars Colloquium on America-Holy
Land Studies. *v.6 p.610*

With Eyes Toward Zion: Themes and Sources in the Archives of
the United States, Breat Britain, Turkey and Israel, 2. .*v.6 p.610*

With Her Machete in Her Hand: Reading Chicana
Lesbians. *v.6 p.392, p.498, p.512*

With His Pistol in His Hand: A Border Ballad and Its
Hero. *v.2 p.109*

With His Pistol in His Hand, a Border Ballad and Its
Hero. *v.6 p.523, p.524*

With Justice for Some: Protecting Victims in Criminal
Trials. *v.6 p.270*

With Liberty for Some: 500 Years of Imprisonment in
America. *v.4 p.752, v.6 p.273*

With Malice Aforethought: A Study of the Crime and
Punishment for Homicide. *v.6 p.252*

With Malice Toward All?: The Media and Public Confidence in
Democratic Institutions. *v.4 p.558*

With Malice Toward None: The Life of Abraham
Lincoln. *v.3 p.426*

With Malice Toward Some: How People Make Civil Liberties
Judgments. *v.5 p.643, p.644*

With Napoleon in Russia. *v.3 p.152*

With No Apologies: The Personal and Political Memoirs of
United States Senator Barry M. Goldwater. *v.3 p.458*

With or Against the World?: America's Role among the
Nations. *v.3 p.450*

With Reagan: The Inside Story. *v.3 p.475*

With Scarcely a Ripple: Anglo-Canadian Migration into the
United States and Western Canada, 1880-1920. . . *v.4 p.765*

With Speed and Violence: Why Scientists Fear Tipping Points in
Climate Change. *v.4 p.394*

With Stalin Against Tito: Cominformist Splits in Yugoslav
Communism. *v.3 p.246, p.247, p.248*

With the Boys: Little League Baseball and Preadolescent
Culture. *v.4 p.745*

With the Flow. *v.2 p.495*

With the Old Corps in Nicaragua. *v.3 p.301*

With the Precision of Bats. *v.2 p.780*

With the Stroke of a Pen: Executive Orders and Presidential
Power. *v.4 p.462*

With Voice and Pen: Coming to Know Medieval Song and How
it Was Made. *v.1 p.178*

Within Her Power: Propertied Women in Colonial
Virginia. *v.6 p.452*

Within the Plantation Household: Black and White Women of
the Old South. *v.6 p.452*

Without an Alphabet, Without a Face: Selected Poems. .*v.6 p.664*

Without Authority. *v.1 p.652*

Without God, Without Creed: The Origins of Unbelief in
America. *v.1 p.545*

Without Hatreds or Fears: Jorge Artel and the Struggle for Black
Literacy Expression in Colombia. *v.4 p.336*

Without Honor: Defeat in Vietnam and Cambodia. . *v.6 p.168*

Without Miracles: Universal Selection Theory and the Second Darwinian Revolution. *v.5 p.202*

Without: Poems. . . . . *.v.2 p.82*

Witi Ihimaera: A Changing Vision. . . . . *.v.2 p.741*

A Witkiewicz Reader: The Life and Work of Stanislaw Ignacy Witkiewicz. . . . . *.v.2 p.792*

The Witlings and the Woman Hater. . . . .*.v.2 p.242*

Witness Against the Beast: William Blake and the Moral Law. . . . . *.v.2 p.240*

Witness for Peace: A Story of Resistance. *v.3 p.302*

Witness for the Defense: The Accused, the Eyewitness and the Expert Who Puts Memory on Trial. . . .*v.5 p.592, v.6 p.271*

The Witness of Preaching. *v.1 p.649*

Witness to America: An Illustrated Documentary History of the United States from the Revolution to Today. .*v.3 p.365, p.371*

Witness to History, 1929-1969. . . . .*v.3 p.456*

Witness to Hope: The Biography of Pope John Paul II. .*v.1 p.580*

Witness to Power: The Nixon Years. *v.3 p.470*

The Witnesses: War Crimes and the Promise of Justice in the Hague. *v.4 p.654*

Witness. *v.3 p.446*

WITSEC: Inside the Federal Witness Protection Program. *v.6 p.271*

A Wittgenstein Dictionary. *v.1 p.471, p.472*

Wittgenstein on Rules and Private Language: An Elementary Exposition. *v.1 p.472*

Wittgenstein's Lectures: Cambridge, 1932-1935 from the Notes of Alice Ambrose and Margaret Macdonald. *v.1 p.472*

Wittgenstein's Philosophical Investigations: An Introduction. *v.1 p.472*

Wittgenstein's Place in Twentieth-Century Analytic Philosophy. *v.1 p.468, p.502*

Wittgenstein's Tractatus: An Introduction. *v.1 p.472*

Wittgenstein. *v.1 p.471, p.472*

Wives and Daughters. *v.2 p.288*

Wives and Midwives: Childbirth and Nutrition in Rural Malaysia. *v.4 p.46*

Wives and Property: Reform of the Married Women's Property Law in Nineteenth-Century England. *v.6 p.747*

Wives at War and Other Stories. *v.2 p.756*

Wives of the Leopard: Gender, Politics, and Culture in the Kingdom of Dahomey. *v.4 p.610, p.611,v.6 p.453*

Wizards and Scientists: Explorations in Afro-Cuban Modernity and Tradition. *v.3 p.312*

The Wiz. *v.1 p.254, p.409, p.410*

Wo Warst Adam. *v.2 p.604*

A Wobbly Life: IWW Organizer E. F. Doree. *v.4 p.128*

Wodehouse: A Life. *v.2 p.390*

Woldman's Engineering Alloys. *v.5 p.736*

Wole Soyinka: Politics, Poetics, and Postcolonialism. . . . .*.v.2 p.757, p.758*

Wole Soyinka. . . . .*.v.2 p.757, p.758*

Wolfe Tone: Prophet of Irish Independence. *v.3 p.137*

Wolfgang Amadeus Mozart: A Guide to Research. *v.1 p.164, p.189, p.343*

The Wolfpen Notebooks: A Record of Appalachian Life. .*v.2 p.117*

Wolfram's Parzival: Five Essays with an Introduction. .*v.2 p.595*

A Wollstonecraft Anthology. . . . .*.v.2 p.319*

Wolsey. . . . .*.v.3 p.100, p.121*

Woman and Society in the Spanish Drama of the Golden Age: A Study of the Mujer Varonil. *v.2 p.640*

Woman and the Demon: The Life of a Victorian Myth. .*v.2 p.174*

Woman at Point Zero. *v.6 p.657*

Woman Defamed and Woman Defended: An Anthology of Medieval Texts. . . . .*.v.2 p.196, v.6 p.559*

Woman Far Walking. . . . .*.v.2 p.746*

The Woman from Hamburg: And Other True Stories. .*v.2 p.790*

A Woman in Jerusalem. *v.6 p.652*

The Woman in the Body: A Cultural Analysis of Reproduction. *v.4 p.47, v.6 p.444*

Woman in the Crested Kimono: The Life of Shibue Io and Her Family Drawn from Mori Ogai's Shibue Chusai. . .*v.6 p.227*

The Woman in White. *v.2 p.280, p.281*

A Woman Killed with Kindness. . . . .*.v.2 p.219*

Woman, Native, Other: Writing Postcoloniality and Feminism. . . . .*.v.6 p.89, p.97, p.112, p.479*

Woman of the River. *v.2 p.674*

The Woman of the Wolf and Other Stories. . . . . .*.v.6 p.399*

The Woman Question: Society and Literature in Britain and America, 1837-1883: Defining Voices. . . .*v.6 p.747, p.761*

The Woman Question: Society and Literature in Britain and America, 1837-1883: Literary Issues. *v.6 p.747, p.761*

The Woman Question: Society and Literature in Britain and America, 1837-1883: Social Issues. *v.6 p.747, p.761*

The Woman Reader, 1837-1914. . . . .*v.6 p.738*

A Woman Soldier's Own Story: The Autobiography of Xie Bingying. . . . .*.v.6 p.202, p.217*

Woman Suffrage and the Origins of Liberal Feminism in the United States, 1820-1920. . . . .*v.6 p.431*

The Woman Suffrage Movement in Canada. . . . .*.v.4 p.590*

The woman Taken in Adultery and The Poggenpuhl Family. *v.2 p.596*

The Woman That Never Evolved: With a New Preface and Bibliographical Updates. *v.4 p.744*

The Woman Triathlete. . . . .*.v.4 p.836, p.863, p.866*

The Woman Warrior and China Men. . . . . . .*.v.6 p.94, p.100*

The Woman Who Walked into Doors. . . . .*.v.2 p.343*

The Woman Within. *v.2 p.79*

Womanguides: Readings Toward a Feminist Theology. .*v.1 p.528*

Woman's Body, Woman's Right: A Social History of Birth Control in America. . . . .*.v.4 p.569*

Woman's Body, Woman's Right: Birth Control in America. *v.4 p.775*

Woman's Body, Woman's Word: Gender and Discourse in Arabo-Islamic Writing. *v.6 p.662*

Woman's Fiction: A Guide to Novels by and about Women in America, 1820-70. . . . .*v.2 p.8*

A Woman's Guide to Menopause and Perimenopause. .*v.5 p.523*

The Woman's Guide to Peak Performance. . . .*v.4 p.801, p.880*

A Woman's Guide to Sexual Health. *v.5 p.523, p.524*

A Woman's Guide to the Language of Success. *v.4 p.173*

A Woman's Kingdom: Noblewomen and the Control of Property in Russia, 1700-1861. . . . .*v.3 p.216, v.6 p.452*

Woman's "True" Profession: Voices from the History of Teaching. *v.4 p.282, p.283*

The Woman's Part: Feminist Criticism of Shakespeare. .*v.2 p.230*

A Woman's Place: An Oral History of Working Class Women, 1890-1940. . . . .*v.3 p.92, p.115, p.131*

A Woman's Version of the Faust Legend: The Seven Strings of the Lyre. *v.2 p.500*

Woman's World - Woman's Empire: The Woman's Christian Temperance Union in International Perspective, 1880-1930. . . . .*v.4 p.776*

A Woman. *v.2 p.713*

Wombs and Alien Spirits: Women, Men and the Zar Cult in Northern Sudan. *v.4 p.30*

Women: A Feminist Perspective. *v.6 p.427*

Women Against Censorship. *v.4 p.747, v.6 p.456, p.468*

Women Against the Good War: Conscientious Objection and Gender on the American Home Front, 1941-1947. .*v.3 p.441*

Women and Aging: A Guide to the Literature. *v.6 p.445*

Women and American Foreign Policy: Lobbyists, Critics, and Insiders. *v.4 p.566, p.568*

Women and Borderline Personality Disorder: Symptoms and Stories. *v.5 p.661*

Women and Bullfighting: Gender, Sex and the Consumption of Tradition. *v.4 p.818, p.837, p.856*

Women and Cancer: A Gynecologic Oncology Nursing Perspective. *v.5 p.520, p.523, p.530*

Women and Ceramics: Gendered Vessels. *v.1 p.707*

Women and Change in the Caribbean. *v.4 p.31, v.6 p.457*

Women and Children Last: The Plight of Poor Women in Affluent America. *v.6 p.458*

Women and Christian Origins. *v.1 p.599*

Women and Class in Japanese History. *v.6 p.226*

Women and Community in Oman. *v.6 p.627*

Women and Confucian Cultures in Premodern China, Korea, and Japan. *v.6 p.181, p.217*

Women and Democracy: Latin America and Central and Eastern Europe. *v.6 p.441*

Women and Demons: Cultic Healing in Islamic Egypt. *v.6 p.635, p.638*

Women and Depression: A Lifespan Perspective. . .*v.5 p.659*

Women and Elective Office: Past, Present, and Future. .*v.6 p.443*

Women and Gender in Early Jewish and Palestinian Nationalism. *v.6 p.610*

Women and Gender in Early Modern Europe. *v.3 p.52, v.6 p.452, p.453*

Women and Gender in Islam: Historical Roots of a Modern Debate. *v.1 p.557, v.6 p.449, p.458*

☐ Women and Gender Studies in Latin America. . . .*v.6 p.463*

Women and Globalization in the Arab Middle East: Gender, Economy and Society. *v.6 p.582, p.583*

Women and Goddess Traditions: In Antiquity and Today. *v.1 p.528*

Women and Health in America: Historical Readings. .*v.5 p.523*

Women and Health: Power, Technology, Inequality and Conflict in a Gendered World. *v.5 p.524*

Women and Information Technology: Research on Under-Representation. *v.5 p.342*

Women and Kinship: Comparative Perspectives on Gender in South and South-East Asia. *v.6 p.153, p.154*

Women and Literature in Britain, 1150-1500. . .*v.6 p.560, p.565*

Women and Literature in Britain, 1500-1700. . . . .*v.6 p.480*

Women and Madness. *v.5 p.659*

Women and Male Violence: The Visions and Struggles of the Battered Women's Movement. *v.4 p.752*

Women and Mass Communications in the 1990s: An International, Annotated Bibliography. *v.6 p.448*

Women and Men in Management. *v.6 p.457, p.458*

Women and Men in Renaissance Venice: Twelve Essays on Patrician Society. *v.3 p.199*

Women and Men Police Officers: Status, Gender, and Personality. *v.6 p.260*

Women and Minorities in Science: Strategies for Increasing Participation. *v.5 p.398*

Women and Music: A History. *v.1 p.379, v.6 p.475*

Women and Music: A Selective Annotated Bibliography on Women and Gender Issues in Music, 1987-1992. . .*v.6 p.474*

Women and Music in America since 1900: An Encyclopedia. *v.6 p.474*

Women and Music in Cross-Cultural Perspective. . . .*v.6 p.474*

Women and Nature: Saving the "Wild" West. *v.6 p.292*

Women and Peace: Feminist Visions of Global Security. .*v.6 p.442*

Women and Philosophy: Toward a Theory of Liberation. .*v.6 p.461*

Women and Politics in Chile. *v.3 p.353*

Women and Politics in the Third World. *v.6 p.439, p.440*

Women and Politics in Uganda: The Challenge of Associational Autonomy. *v.6 p.443*

Women and Politics Worldwide. *v.6 p.441*

Women and Power in the Middle East. *v.6 p.593*

Women and Redemption: A Theological History. . . .*v.6 p.460*

Women and Religion in Early America, 1600-1850: The Puritan and Evangelical Traditions. *v.1 p.607*

Women and Religion: The Original Sourcebook of Women in Christian Thought. *v.1 p.642*

Women and Religion. *v.1 p.528*

Women and Revolution in Africa, Asia, and the New World. *v.3 p.284, v.6 p.442, p.443*

Women and Revolution in Iran. *v.6 p.632*

Women and Social Movements in Latin America: Power from Below. *v.3 p.283, v.6 p.432, p.458*

☐ Women and Social Movements in the United States, 1600-2000. . . . .*v.6 p.449*

Women and Society in Greek and Roman Egypt: A Sourcebook. *v.3 p.11*

Women and Spirituality. *v.1 p.651*

Women and Spirtual Equality in Christian Tradition. . .*v.1 p.656*

Women and Sport: Interdisciplinary Perspectives. *v.4 p.823, p.835,v.6 p.437*

Women and the American Economy: A Look to the 1980s. *v.4 p.272, p.273*

Women and the City: Gender, Space, and Power in Boston, 1870-1940. . . . .*v.6 p.711*

Women and the Conquest of California 1542-1840. . .*v.3 p.530*

Women and the Economic Miracle: Gender and Work in
Postwar Japan. *v.6 p.218*

Women and the English Renaissance: Literature and the Nature
of Womankind, 1540-1620. . . . .*v.2 p.170*

Women and the Family in the Middle East: New Voices of
Change. *v.6 p.592*

Women and the First World War. *v.3 p.53, p.78, p.208*

Women and the Israeli Occupation: The Politics of
Change. *v.6 p.618*

Women and the Italian Resistance,
1943-45. . . . .*v.3 p.54, p.203,v.6 p.455*

Women and the Law in the Roman Empire: A Sourcebook on
Marriage, Divorce and Widowhood. *v.3 p.23*

Women and the Limits of Citizenship in the French
Revolution. *v.3 p.53, p.150*

Women and the Nation's Narrative: Gender and Nationalism in
Twentieth Century Sri Lanka. *v.2 p.760*

Women and the Political Process in Twentieth-Century
Iran. *v.6 p.631*

Women and the Politics of Empowerment. *v.6 p.440*

Women and the War Story. *v.6 p.478, p.659*

Women and the Women's Movement in Britain
1914-1999. . . . .*v.4 p.604*

Women and Urban Change in San Juan, Puerto Rico,
1820-1868. . . . .*v.3 p.321*

Women and War in Lebanon. *v.6 p.606*

The Women and War Reader. *v.6 p.465*

Women and War. *v.6 p.464*

Women and Work in Developing Countries: An Annotated
Bibliopgraphy. *v.6 p.456*

Women and Writing in Russia and the U. S. S. R.: A
Bibliography of English-Language Sources. . . . *v.2 p.796*

Women Anthropologists: A Biographical Dictionary. *v.4 p.3, p.4*

Women, Art, and Power and Other
Essays. *v.1 p.706, p.707,v.6 p.473, p.475*

Women, Art, and Society. *v.1 p.706, v.6 p.472*

Women Artists: A Historical, Contemporary and Feminist
Bibliography. *v.6 p.473*

Women Artists: An Illustrated History. *v.6 p.472*

Women Artists in History: From Antiquity to the
Present. *v.1 p.707, v.6 p.473*

Women Artists in the U. S.: Guide on the Fine and Decorative
Arts, 1750-1986. . . . .*v.6 p.472*

Women Artists of Color: A Bio-Critical Sourcebook to 20th
Century Artists in the Americas. *v.1 p.706, v.6 p.472*

Women As Healers: Cross-Cultural Perspectives. . . .*v.4 p.47*

Women As Single Parents: Confronting Institutional Barriers in
the Courts, the Workplace, and the Housing
Market. *v.6 p.465, p.467*

Women As Widows: Support Systems. *v.4 p.741, v.6 p.465, p.467*

Women at Crossroads: A Prostitute Community's Response to
AIDS in Urban Senegal. *v.6 p.471*

Women at the Front: Hospital Workers in Civil War
America. *v.4 p.522*

Women at the Gates: Gender and Industry in Stalin's
Russia. *v.3 p.225*

Women, Autobiography, Theory: A Reader. *v.6 p.477*

Women, Biology and Public Policy. *v.6 p.442*

Women College Basketball Coaches. *v.4 p.838, p.854*

Women Composers: The Lost Tradition Found. . . .*v.1 p.379*

Women, Creole Identity, and Intellectual Life in Early
Twentieth-Century Puerto Rico. *v.3 p.321*

Women, Crime, and Custody in Victorian
England. *v.3 p.55, v.6 p.744, p.745, p.749*

Women Designers in the U.S.A., 1900-2000: Diversity and
Difference. *v.1 p.706, p.714*

Women, Development, and the UN: A Sixty-Year Quest for
Equality and Justice. *v.4 p.634*

Women During the Civil War: An Encyclopedia. . . *v.6 p.452*

Women, Feminism, and Aging: A New Look at Theory and
Practice. *v.6 p.444*

Women, Feminism and Social Change in Argentina, Chile, and
Uruguay, 1890-1940. . . . . *v.3 p.346, p.348, p.354*

Women Film Directors: An International Bio-Critical
Dictionary. *v.6 p.474*

Women Filmmakers in Mexico: The Country of Which We
Dream. *v.6 p.340*

Women Filmmakers of the African and Asian Diaspora:
Decolonizing the Gaze, Locating Subjectivity. . . .*v.6 p.333*

Women, Fire, and Dangerous Things. . . .*v.4 p.20, v.5 p.619*

The Women Founders: Sociology and Social Theory, 1830-1930,
A Text with Readings. *v.4 p.680*

The Women, Gender and Development Reader. . . . *v.6 p.458*

Women, Gender and Human Rights: A Global
Perspective. *v.6 p.430, p.432*

Women, Gender and Social
Psychology. *v.6 p.429, p.446, p.467, p.470*

Women Go Global. *v.4 p.662, v.6 p.432*

Women, Household and Change. *v.3 p.354*

Women Immigrants, 1945 to the Present. *v.6 p.470*

The Women Impressionists: A Sourcebook. *v.1 p.725*

Women in a Violent World: Feminist Analyses and Resistance
Across Europe. *v.6 p.469*

Women in Academe: Progress and Prospects. *v.4 p.289*

Women in Africa and the African Diaspora: A
Reader. *v.6 p.11, p.46, p.47*

Women in African Colonial Histories: An Introduction. *v.6 p.53*

Women in African Economies: From Burning Sun to
Boardroom. *v.6 p.458*

Women in Agriculture and Rural Development. *v.5 p.13*

Women in American Education, 1820-1955: The Female Force
and Educational Reform. *v.6 p.462*

Women in American Theatre. *v.1 p.120, p.121*

Women in Ancient Greece. *v.3 p.13*

Women in Ancient Persia, 559-331 B. C. *v.6 p.450*

Women in Ancient Persia, 559-331 BC. *v.3 p.11*

Women in Anglo-Saxon England. *v.6 p.559*

Women in Arab Society: Work Patterns and Gender Relations in
Egypt, Jordan and Sudan. *v.6 p.583*

Women in Baseball: The Forgotten
History. *v.4 p.803, p.834, p.849*

Women in Buddhism: Images of the Feminine in the Mahayana
Tradition. *v.1 p.566*

Women in Chemistry and Physics: A Biobibliographic Sourcebook. *v.5 p.261*

Women in Chemistry: Their Changing Roles from Alchemical Times to the Mid-20th Century. *v.5 p.261*

Women in Contemporary Mexican Politics. *v.6 p.442*

Women in Contemporary Spain. *v.3 p.242*

Women in Early Medieval Europe, 400-1100. .*v.3 p.51, v.6 p.559*

Women in Early Modern England 1550-1720. .*v.3 p.52, v.6 p.452*

Women in Emergent Morocco: Changes and Continuities. *v.6 p.643*

Women in England, 1870-1950: Sexual Divisons and Social Change. *v.3 p.113*

Women in Europe Since 1700. . . . .*v.3 p.51*

Women in European History. *v.3 p.50*

Women in Frankish Society: Marriage and the Cloister, 500-900. . . . .*v.6 p.561*

Women in German History: From Bourgeois Emancipation to Sexual Liberation. *v.3 p.159*

Women in Global Migration, 1945-2000: A Comprehensive Multidisciplinary Bibliography. *v.4 p.667*

Women in Hellenistic Egypt: From Alexander to Cleopatra. *v.6 p.451, p.635*

Women in Higher Education: Empowering Change. . .*v.6 p.462*

Women in Higher Education. *v.4 p.292, p.293*

Women in Igbo Life and Thought. *v.4 p.700*

Women in India and Pakistan: The Struggle for Independence from British Rule. *v.6 p.158*

Women in Indian Religions. *v.1 p.541*

Women in Industry. *v.4 p.253*

Women in Iran from 1800 to the Islamic Republic. . .*v.6 p.629*

Women in Iran from the Rise of Islam to 1800. . . . .*v.6 p.435, p.452, p.630*

Women in Israel: A State of Their Own. *v.6 p.614*

Women in Kuwait: The Politics of Gender. *v.6 p.627*

Women in Latin American History: Their Lives and Views. *v.3 p.283*

Women in Life Science Careers. *v.5 p.222*

Women in Love. *v.2 p.362, p.363*

Women in Management Worldwide: Facts, Figures and Analysis. *v.6 p.456*

Women in Mathematics: Scaling the Heights. . .*v.5 p.459, p.464*

Women in Mathematics: The Addition of Difference. *v.5 p.458, p.466, v.6 p.439*

Women in Mathematics. *v.5 p.467*

Women in Medieval English Society. *v.6 p.560*

Women in Medieval Europe: 1200 - 1500. . . . . . .*v.3 p.51*

Women in Medieval History and Historiography. . . .*v.6 p.561*

[e] Women in Medieval Society. *v.6 p.451*

Women in Medieval Society. *v.6 p.561*

Women in Middle Eastern History: Shifting Boundaries in Sex and Gender. *v.6 p.454, p.593*

Women in Music: An Anthology of Source Readings from the Middle Ages to the Present. *v.1 p.379*

Women in Music: An Encyclopedic Biobibliography. *v.1 p.160, p.379, v.6 p.474*

Women in Music Guide to Research. *v.1 p.169, p.379*

Women in Nineteenth Century Egypt. *v.6 p.638*

Women in Nineteenth-Century Europe. *v.3 p.53*

Women in Old Norse Society. *v.3 p.51, v.6 p.560*

Women in Public and Private Law Enforcement. . .*v.6 p.260*

Women in Racing: In Their Own Words. *v.4 p.837, p.848*

Women in Romanticism: Mary Wollstonecraft, Dorothy Wordsworth and Mary Shelley. *v.2 p.310, p.322*

Women in Russia, 1700-2000. . . . . .*v.3 p.53, p.211, v.6 p.454*

Women in Russian Literature after Glasnot: Female Alternatives. *v.2 p.797*

Women in Science: Antiquity Through Nineteenth Century - A Biographical Dictionary with Annotated Bibliography. *v.5 p.398*

Women in Science: Career Processes and Outcomes. *v.5 p.398, p.399, v.6 p.439*

Women in Scientific and Engineering Professions. . . .*v.5 p.398*

Women in Scripture: A Dictionary of Named and Unnamed Women in the Hebrew Bible, the Apocryphal/Deuterocanonical Books and New Testament. *v.1 p.616*

Women in Sport: Issues and Controversies. . . .*v.4 p.814, p.835*

Women in Sport: Olympic Encyclopaedia of Sports Medicine. *v.4 p.825, p.873*

Women in Sub-Saharan Africa. *v.6 p.52*

Women in the Biological Sciences: A Biobibliographic Sourcebook. *v.5 p.221*

Women in the Celtic Church: Ireland C. 450-1150. . .*v.1 p.609*

Women in the Early Church. *v.1 p.599*

Women in the Field: America's Pioneering Women Naturalists. *v.5 p.229, p.230*

Women in the Fine Arts: From the Seventh Century B. C. to the Twentieth Century A. D. *v.6 p.472*

Women in the Inquisition: Spain and the New World. .*v.3 p.239*

Women in the Kibbutz. *v.6 p.616*

Women in the Martial Arts. *v.4 p.838, p.863*

Women in the Metropolis: Gender and Modernity in Weimar Culture. *v.3 p.170*

Women in the Middle Ages: An Encyclopedia. . . .*v.6 p.561*

Women in the Middle Ages. *v.6 p.560*

Women in the Muslim World. *v.6 p.458, p.468*

[e] Women in the Qur'an, Traditions, and Interpretation. *v.6 p.460*

Women in the Third World: An Encyclopedia of Contemporary Issues. *v.6 p.425*

Women in Tibet: Past and Present. *v.6 p.241*

Women in Twentieth-Century Britain: Social, Cultural and Political Change. *v.3 p.55, v.6 p.455*

Women in Utopia: The Ideology of Gender in the American Owenite Communities. *v.4 p.499*

Women in Western Political Thought. . . .*v.4 p.488, p.490, p.493, p.517, v.6 p.441, p.442*

Women in World History: A Biographical Encyclopedia, Set. *v.6 p.425*

[▢] Women in World History. *v.3 p.50*

Women in World Religions. *v.1 p.529*

Women, Knowledge, and Reality: Explorations in Feminist Philosophy. *v.6 p.461*

Women, Labour and Politics in Trinidad and Tobago: A History. *v.6 p.442, p.458*

Women, Madness and Medicine. *v.5 p.660, v.6 p.446*

Women Making Constitutions: New Politics and Comparative Perspectives. *v.6 p.440*

Women Making Music: The Western Art Tradition, 1150-1950. . . . . *v.1 p.378, v.6 p.474*

Women, Marriage, and Politics, 1860-1914. . . . . *v.3 p.112, p.113,v.6 p.765*

Women, Media, and Consumption in Japan. *v.6 p.222*

Women, Media and Politics. *v.6 p.448*

Women, Media and Sport: Challenging Gender Values. *v.4 p.835, p.901, p.902*

Women, Medicine, Ethics and the Law. *v.5 p.524*

Women, Men and Gender: Ongoing Debates. . .*v.6 p.430, p.446*

Women, Men, and the International Division of Labor. .*v.4 p.28*

Women, Migration and Citizenship: Making Local, National and Transnational Connections. *v.4 p.668*

Women Musicians of Venice: Musical Foundations, 1525-1855. . . . . *v.1 p.378*

Women Novelists in Spain and Spanish America. . . *v.2 p.638*

Women of Algiers in Their Apartment. *v.2 p.545*

Women of America. *v.6 p.453*

The Women of Brewster Place. *v.2 p.151*

The Women of Colonial Latin America. *v.3 p.283*

Women of Color and Southern Women: A Bibliography of Social Science Research 1975-1988. Annual Supplement, 1989. . . . . *v.6 p.8, p.47*

Women of Color: Integrating Ethnic and Gender Identities in Psychotherapy. *v.6 p.111, p.122, p.141, p.445*

The Women of Country Music: A Reader. *v.1 p.265, p.377, p.378*

Women of Deh Koh: Lives in an Iranian Village. . . *v.6 p.629*

Women of Fire and Spirit: History, Faith, and Gender in Roho Religion in Western Kenya. *v.4 p.36*

Women of Iron and Velvet: French Women Writers After George Sand. *v.2 p.457*

Women of Jordan: Islam, Labor, and the Law. *v.6 p.620*

The Women of Mexico City, 1790-1857. . . . . *v.3 p.282, p.288,v.6 p.453*

Women of Phokeng: Consciousness, Life Strategy, and Migrancy in South Africa, 1900-1983. . . . . . . *v.6 p.78*

Women of Prague: Ethnic Diversity and Social Change from the 18th Century to the Present. *v.3 p.190*

The Women of Provincetown, 1915-1922. *v.1 p.79, p.81, p.120*

Women of Sand and Myrrh. *v.6 p.657*

The Women of Suye Mura. *v.6 p.222*

Women of the American South. *v.6 p.452*

Women of the Beat Generation: The Writers, Artists, and Muses at the Heart of a Revolution. *v.2 p.11*

Women of the Civil Rights Movement. *v.6 p.431*

Women of the Fertile Crescent: Modern Poetry by Arab Women. *v.6 p.658, p.659*

Women of the Harlem Renaissance. *v.6 p.28, p.47*

Women of the Mexican Countryside, 1850-1990: Creating Spaces, Shaping Transitions. *v.3 p.292, v.6 p.454*

Women of the Northern Plains: Gender and Settlement on the Homestead Frontier, 1870-1930. . . . . *v.3 p.523*

Women of the Place: Kastom, Colonialism and Gender in Vanuatu. *v.4 p.31*

Women of the Press in Nineteenth-Century Britain. *v.6 p.448, p.740, p.748, p.754*

Women of the Renaissance. *v.3 p.52*

Women of Value: Feminist Essays on the History of Women in Economics. *v.4 p.273*

Women of Wisdom. *v.1 p.566*

Women on High: Pioneers of Mountaineering. *v.4 p.789, p.835*

Women on Love: Eight Centuries of Feminine Writing. .*v.2 p.456*

Women on the Edge: Four Plays. *v.2 p.410*

Women on the Front Lines: Meeting the Challenge of an Aging America. *v.6 p.444*

Women on the Margins: Three Seventeenth-Century Lives. *v.3 p.51, p.52, p.322*

Women on the Verge: Japanese Women, Western Dreams. *v.6 p.448, p.454, p.479*

Women on the Verge: Seven Avant-Garde American Plays. *v.1 p.67, p.87, p.121*

The Women on the Wall. *v.2 p.121*

Women Philosophers of the Early Modern Period. *v.1 p.436, p.437*

Women Poets of Spain, 1860-1990: Toward a Gynocentric Vision. *v.6 p.480*

Women Police. *v.6 p.260*

Women, Prison, and Crime. *v.6 p.278*

Women Pulitzer Playwrights: Biographical Profiles and Analyses of the Plays. *v.1 p.58, p.121*

Women Reading Women Writing: Self-Invention in Paula Gunn Allen, Gloria Anzaldua, and Audre Lorde. *v.6 p.479*

Women, Religion, and Social Change in Brazil's Popular Church. *v.3 p.339*

A Women Remaking Politic South. *v.6 p.441*

Women, Science and Technology: A Reader in Feminist Science Studies. *v.5 p.398, v.6 p.439*

Women Scientists in America: Before Affirmative Action, 1940-1972. . . . . *v.5 p.398*

Women Scientists in America: Struggles and Strategies to 1940. . . . . *v.5 p.398*

Women Scientists in Fifties Science Fiction Films. . . *v.6 p.319*

Women, Sex and the Law. *v.4 p.472*

Women Singing in the Snow: A Cultural Analysis of Chicana Literature. *v.6 p.480, p.502, p.515*

Women, Sport, and Culture. *v.4 p.814, p.834,v.6 p.437*

Women Suffrage and the New Democracy. *v.4 p.519*

Women, the Family, and Freedom: The Debate in Documents, 1750-1880, Vol. I. *v.3 p.52*

Women, the Family, and Freedom: The Debate in Documents, 1880-1950, Vol. II. *v.3 p.52*

Women: The Last Colony. *v.6 p.457*

Women, the State, and Political Liberalization: Middle Eastern and North African Experiences. *v.6 p.591*

Women, the State and Revolution: Soviet Family Policy and Social Life, 1917-1936. . .*v.3 p.53, p.208, p.222,v.6 p.454, p.464, p.466*

Women, the State, and Welfare. *v.4 p.754*

Title Index

Women Travel Writers and the Language of Aesthetics, 1716-1818. . . . .*v.6 p.477*

Women Who Kill: With Previously Unpublished Material on the "Battered Women's Syndrome". *v.4 p.752*

Women Who Live Evil Lives: Gender, Religion, and the Politics of Power in Colonial Guatemala, 1650-1750. .*v.3 p.263, p.298*

Women Who Taught: Perspectives on the History of Women and Teaching. *v.4 p.283*

Women Who Write Plays: Interviews with Contemporary American Dramatists. *v.1 p.121*

Women with Mustaches and Men Without Beards: Gender and Sexual Anxieties of Iranian Modernity. *v.6 p.630*

Women Without Class: Girls, Race and Identity. . . .*v.4 p.723*

Women Without Men: A Novel of Modern Iran. *v.6 p.672*

Women, Work and Family. *v.6 p.458*

[e] Women, Work, and Wages: Equal Pay for Jobs of Equal Value. *v.4 p.255*

Women, Work, and Wages: Equal Pay for Jobs of Equal Value. *v.4 p.254*

[□] Women working, 1870-1930. . . . .*v.6 p.455*

Women Writers and Poetic Identity: Dorothy Wordsworth, Emily Bronte and Emily Dickinson. . . .*v.2 p.270, p.271, p.322*

Women Writers, from Page to Screen: A Guide to Literary Sources. *v.6 p.305, p.306, p.325, p.327*

Women Writers in France: Variations on a Theme. . .*v.2 p.455*

Women Writers in Russian Literature. *v.6 p.478*

Women Writers of Early Modern Spain: Sophia's Daughters. *v.2 p.644*

Women Writers of the Middle Ages: A Critical Study of Texts from Perpetua to Marguerite Porete. *v.6 p.559*

Women Writers of Traditional China: An Anthology of Poetry and Criticism. *v.6 p.207, p.478*

[□] Women Writers Project. *v.6 p.476*

Women, Writing, and the Industrial Revolution. *v.6 p.481, p.483, p.485*

Women Writing in India: 600 BC to the Present, Vol. I. *v.2 p.763, p.764, v.6 p.147, p.148*

Women Writing in India: The Twentieth Century. *v.2 p.763, v.6 p.148*

Women's America: Refocusing the Past. *v.6 p.450*

The Women's Atlas of the United States. *v.6 p.425*

Women's Autobiographies in Contemporary Iran. . .*v.6 p.632*

The Women's Awakening in Egypt: Culture, Society, and the Press. *v.6 p.636*

[e] Women's Education, Autonomy, and Reproductive Behaviour: Experience from Developing Countries. .*v.6 p.447*

Women's Education in the Third World: An Annotated Bibliography. *v.4 p.314*

Women's Education in the United States, 1780-1840. .*v.6 p.463*

Women's Experience of Modernity, 1875-1945. . . . .*v.2 p.6*

Women's Experiences with HIV/AIDS: An International Perspective. *v.6 p.443*

Women's Gymnastics a History: 1966 to 1974. .*v.4 p.838, p.862*

Women's Health: A Primary Care Clinical Guide. . . .*v.5 p.524*

Women's Health: Complexities and Differences. . . .*v.6 p.444*

Women's Health from Womb to Tomb. *v.6 p.443*

Women's Health: Readings on Social, Economic, and Political Issues. *v.5 p.524*

Women's History and Ancient History. *v.6 p.451*

Women's Identities at War: Gender, Motherhood and Politics in Britain and France During the First World War. . . .*v.3 p.53*

Women's Indian Captivity Narratives. *v.6 p.478*

Women's Issues in Thrombosis and Hemostasis. . . .*v.5 p.521*

Women's Legal Guide: A Comprehensive Guide to Legal Issues Affecting Every Woman. *v.4 p.442, v.6 p.469*

Women's Letters from Ancient Egypt, 300 BC - AD 800. .*v.3 p.10*

The Women's Liberation Movement in America. . . .*v.6 p.430*

Women's Life in Greece and Rome: A Source Book in Translation. *v.3 p.13, v.6 p.451*

Women's Lives in Colonial Quito: Gender, Law, and Economy in Spanish America. *v.3 p.332*

Women's Lives in Medieval Europe: A Sourcebook. . .*v.6 p.559*

Women's Lives, Men's Laws. *v.4 p.442*

The Women's Movement and the Transition to Democracy in Chile. *v.3 p.352*

Women's Movement and Women's Employment in Nineteenth Century Britain. *v.3 p.53, v.6 p.431, p.457*

Women's Movements and Public Policy in Europe, Latin America, and the Caribbean: The Triangle of Empowerment. *v.3 p.283, v.6 p.441*

Women's Movements in International Perspective: Latin America and Beyond. *v.6 p.431*

Women's Participation in Mexican Political Life. *v.3 p.295, v.6 p.442*

Women's Pictures: Feminism and Cinema. *v.6 p.474*

Women's Poetry in France, 1965-1995: A Bilingual Anthology. *v.2 p.464*

Women's Poetry, Late Romantic to Late Victorian: Gender and Genre, 1830-1900. . . . .*v.2 p.173, p.174, p.184*

Women's Religions in the Greco-Roman World: A Sourcebook. *v.1 p.531*

Women's Rights: A Global View. *v.6 p.432*

Women's Rights, Human Rights: International Feminist Perspectives. *v.6 p.442*

The Women's Rights Movement in Iran: Mutiny, Appeasement, and Repression from 1900 to Khomeini. *v.6 p.631*

Women's Soccer: Techniques, Tactics and Teamwork. *v.4 p.837, p.867*

Women's Sport and Spectacle: Gendered Television Coverage and the Olympic Games. *v.4 p.835, p.845, p.902*

[□] Women's Sport Foundation (US). *v.4 p.783, p.790, p.794, p.802, p.834*

Women's Sports: A History. *v.4 p.806, p.836, v.6 p.437*

Women's Studies: A Recommended Bibliography. . . .*v.6 p.426*

Women's Studies Encyclopedia. *v.4 p.678, v.6 p.426*

[□] Women's Studies International. *v.6 p.432*

[□] Women's Studies Programs, Departments, & Research Centers. *v.6 p.463*

Women's Suffrage in America: An Eyewitness History. *v.6 p.430, p.431*

The Women's Torah Commentary: New Insights from Women Rabbis on the 54 Weekly Torah Portions. *v.1 p.553*

The Women's Victory- and after: Personal Reminiscences, 1911-1918. . . . .*v.4 p.273*

Women's Voices Across Musical Worlds. *v.1 p.378, v.6 p.473, p.474*

Women's Voices from the Rainforest. *v.3 p.270*

Women's Voices, Women's Lives: Documents in Early American History. *v.6 p.451*

Women's Words: The Feminist Practice of Oral History. *v.6 p.449, p.476*

Women's Work and Wages: A Selection of Papers from the 15th Arne Ryde Symposium on Economics of Gender and Family in Honor of Anna Bugge and Knut Wicksell. .*v.4 p.240*

Women's Work: Development and the Division of Labor by Gender. *v.6 p.457*

Women's Work in the World Economy. *v.4 p.273*

e Women's Work, Men's Work: Sex Segregation on the Job. *v.4 p.254*

Women's Working Lives in East Asia. *v.6 p.218, p.219*

e Women's Works in Stalin's Time: On Lidiia Chukovskaia and Nadezhda Mandelstam. *v.2 p.798, p.804*

Women's Writing on the First World War. *v.6 p.478*

Women. *v.1 p.767, v.2 p.534*

▢ WomenWatch: UN Information and Resources on Gender Equality and the Empowerment of Women. *v.6 p.436*

The Wonder: A Woman Keeps a Secret. *v.2 p.243*

The Wonder of American Toys: 1920-1950. . . . . .*v.1 p.714*

The Wonderful Dog and Other Tales. *v.2 p.810*

Wonderful Town: New York Stories from the New Yorker. *v.2 p.584*

Wondrous Difference: Cinema, Anthropology, and Turn-of-the-Century Visual Culture. *v.6 p.310*

Wondrous Strange: The Life and Art of Glenn Gould. *v.1 p.209, p.327*

Wong's Clinical Manual of Pediatric Nursing. .*v.5 p.525, p.527*

Won't You Join the Dance?: A Dancer's Essay into the Treatment of Psychosis. *v.1 p.51*

Wood and Wood Products. *v.5 p.691*

Wood Beyond the World. *v.2 p.302*

Wood Engineering Handbook. *v.5 p.688*

Wood Handbook: Wood As an Engineering Material. .*v.5 p.691*

Wood in the Landscape: A Practical Guide to Specification and Design. *v.1 p.818*

Wood Structure and Identification. *v.5 p.41*

Wood: World of Woodwork and Carving. *v.1 p.810*

The Woodcut Art of J. J. Lankes. *v.1 p.758*

The Woodcut Artist's Handbook: Techniques and Tools for Relief Printmaking. *v.1 p.760*

Woodcuts of Women: Stories. *v.6 p.499*

Woodcutters and Witchcraft: Rationality and Interpretive Change in the Social Sciences. *v.4 p.688*

Woodrow Wilson: 1913-1921. . . . .*v.3 p.466*

Woodrow Wilson and a Revolutionary World, 1913-1921. . . . .*v.3 p.474*

Woodrow Wilson and the Balance of Power. *v.3 p.467*

Woodrow Wilson and the Politics of Morality. . . .*v.3 p.466*

Woodrow Wilson and World Politics: America's Response to War and Revolution. *v.3 p.474*

Woodrow Wilson and World War I, 1917-1921. . . . .*v.3 p.440, p.470, p.471*

Woodrow Wilson As I Know Him. *v.3 p.481*

Woodrow Wilson: Revolution, War and Peace. *v.3 p.442, p.443, p.474*

Woodrow Wilson. *v.3 p.465*

The Woods Stretched for Miles: An Anthology of Contemporary Nature Writing from the South. *v.5 p.79, p.234*

Woodstock Census. *v.4 p.736*

Woodstock: Oral History. *v.1 p.271*

Woodwind Instruments and Their History. . . .*v.1 p.388, p.389*

Woodwinds: Fundamental Performance Techniques. *v.1 p.398, p.399*

Woolf and Lessing: Breaking the Mold. *v.2 p.366*

Wooster Proposes, Jeeves Disposes. *v.2 p.390*

Word and Image in Japanese Cinema. *v.6 p.337*

Word and Object. *v.1 p.444, p.490*

The Word as Scalpel: A History of Medical Sociology. *v.4 p.774, v.5 p.511*

A Word Child. *v.2 p.372*

Word Crimes: Blasphemy, Culture, and Literature in Nineteenth-Century England. *v.6 p.744*

A Word for Nature: Four Pioneering Environmental Advocates, 1845-1913. . . . .*v.6 p.287*

The Word from Paris: Essays on Modern French Writers and Thinkers. *v.2 p.460*

Word, Image, and the New Negro: Representation and Identity in the Harlem Renaissance. *v.2 p.10*

The Word in the World: Evangelical Writing, Publishing, and Reading in America, 1789-1880. . . . .*v.4 p.720*

A Word Index to Plato. *v.1 p.423*

The Word Made Self: Russian Writings on Language, 1860-1930. . . . .*v.2 p.776, p.793*

The Word of God and the Languages of Man: Interpreting Nature in Early Modern Science and Medicine. .*v.5 p.388*

The Word of God and the Word of Man. *v.1 p.596*

Word on the Street: Debunking the Myth of a Pure Standard English. *v.2 p.552*

Word Play: What Happens When People Talk. . . .*v.5 p.623*

Word Virus: The William S. Burroughs Reader. . . .*v.2 p.64*

Word-by-Word Translations of Songs and Arias: German and French. *v.1 p.394, p.411*

Word-by-Word Translations of Songs and Arias: Italian. *v.1 p.396, p.412*

Word-Hoard: An Introduction to Old English Vocabulary. *v.2 p.205, p.550*

Words Alone: The Poet T. S. Eliot. *v.2 p.71*

Words and Deeds in Renaissance Rome: Trials Before the Papal Magistrates. *v.3 p.200*

Words and Images: Chinese Poetry, Calligraphy, and Painting. *v.6 p.208*

Words and Life. *v.1 p.442*

Words and Music in the Middle Ages: Song, Narrative, Dance and Drama, 1050-1350. . . . .*v.1 p.178*

Words and Objections: Essays on the Work of W. V. Quine. *v.1 p.441*

Words and Rules: The Ingredients of Language. *v.5 p.621, p.623*

Words and Spaces: An Anthology of Twentieth Century Musical Experiments in Language and Sonic Environments. *v.1 p.224*

Words and the Poet: Characteristic Techniques of Style in Vergil's Aeneid. *v.2 p.446*

Words Cannot Be Found: German Colonial Rule in Namibia: An Annotated Reprint of the 1918 Blue Book. *v.6 p.76*

Words from the Land. *v.5 p.235*

Words into Flesh. *v.6 p.648*

Words Matter: Conversations with Asian American Writers. *v.6 p.95*

The Words of Cesar Chávez. *v.4 p.124*

Words of Fire: An Anthology of African-American Feminist Thought. *v.6 p.427*

Words That Bind: Judicial Review and the Grounds of Modern Constitutional Theory. *v.4 p.454*

Words to Outlive Us: Eyewitness Accounts from the Warsaw Ghetto. *v.3 p.84*

Words to Say It. *v.2 p.528*

The Wordsmiths: Oscar Hammerstein II and Alan Jay Lerner. *v.1 p.249, p.328, p.335, p.336*

The Words. *v.2 p.528*

Wordsworth : Language as Counter-Spirit. *v.2 p.323*

Wordsworth: A Collection of Critical Essays. *v.2 p.322*

Wordsworth: A Critical Introduction. *v.2 p.323*

Wordsworth: A Life. *v.2 p.322*

Wordsworth and Coleridge: Lyrical Ballads. *v.2 p.323*

Wordsworth and Coleridge: The Making of the Major Lyrics, 1802-1804. . . . . *v.2 p.324*

Wordsworth and Coleridge: The Radical Years. . . . *v.2 p.324*

Wordsworth and "The Recluse". *v.2 p.323, p.324*

Wordsworth and the cultivation of women. *v.2 p.324*

Wordsworth and the Enlightenment: Nature, Man, and Society in the Experimental Poetry. *v.2 p.323*

Wordsworth and the Poetry of Encounter. *v.2 p.323*

Wordsworth and the Poetry of Human Suffering. . . *v.2 p.322*

Wordsworth and the Victorians. *v.6 p.738, p.755*

Wordsworth: The Sense of History. *v.2 p.324*

Wordsworth's Great Period Poems: Four Essays. . . *v.2 p.324*

Wordsworth's Historical Imagination : The Poetry of Displacement. *v.2 p.324*

Wordsworth's Poetry, 1787-1814. . . . . *v.2 p.323*

Wordsworth's Second Nature: A Study of the Poetry and Politics. *v.2 p.323*

Work, 1961-1973. . . . . *v.1 p.11*

Work: A Story of Experience. *v.2 p.31*

Work and Control in a Peasant Economy: A History of the Lower Tchiri Valley in Malawi, 1859-1960. . . . *v.6 p.297*

Work and Days: With Prolegomena and Commentary. *v.2 p.413*

Work and Family in the United States: A Critical Review and Agenda for Research and Policy. . . . *v.4 p.733, v.6 p.457*

Work and Leisure. *v.4 p.250*

Work and Life Integration: Organizational, Cultural, and Individual Perspectives. *v.5 p.580*

Work and Motivation. *v.5 p.579, p.580*

Work and Revolution in France: The Language of Labor from the Old Regime to 1848. . . . . *v.3 p.149*

Work Careers: A Developmental Perspective. *v.5 p.577*

The Work Ethic in Industrial America, 1850-1920. . . . . *v.3 p.444, p.449*

Work, Family, Health, and Well-Being. *v.5 p.638*

Work in a 24/7 Economy: Challenges for American Families. *v.5 p.581*

Work in America: An Encyclopedia of History, Policy, and Society. *v.4 p.123*

Work of Cities. *v.6 p.722*

The Work of Living Art: A Theory of the Theatre. . . *v.1 p.138*

The Work of William Morris. *v.2 p.302*

The Work of Words: The Writing of Susanna Strickland Moodie. *v.2 p.733*

Work, Society, and Politics: The Culture of the Factory in Later Victorian England. *v.3 p.113, v.6 p.743*

Work Your Way Around the World. *v.4 p.169*

Work, Youth, and Schooling: Historical Perspectives on Vocationalism in American Education. . . *v.4 p.305, p.353*

Worker Activism after Successful Union Organizing. *v.4 p.127*

Worker in the Cane: A Puerto Rican Life History. . . *v.4 p.41*

Workers Against Work: Labor in Paris and Barcelona During the Popular Fronts. *v.3 p.242*

Workers and Working Class in the Ottoman Empire and the Turkish Republic, 1839-1950. . . . . . . *v.6 p.591, p.622*

Workers' Control in Latin America. *v.4 p.124*

Workers' Culture in Imperial Germany. . . *v.3 p.169, v.4 p.803*

Workers' Culture in Weimar Germany: Between Tradition and Commitment. *v.3 p.170*

Workers in the Dawn. *v.2 p.289, p.290*

Workers, Neighbors and Citizens: The Revolution in Mexico City. *v.3 p.293*

Workers on the Nile: Nationalism, Communism, Islam, and the Egyptian Working Class, 1882-1954. . . . . . *v.6 p.636*

Workers on the Waterfront: Seamen, Longshoremen, and Unionism in the 1930s. *v.4 p.128*

Workers or Citizens: Democracy and Identity in Rosario, Argentina, 1912-1930. . . . . *v.3 p.348*

The Worker's Party and Democratization in Brazil. . *v.3 p.341*

Workers' Rights As Human Rights. *v.4 p.131*

Workers, Women, and Social Change in Poland, 1870-1939. . . . . *v.3 p.253, p.254*

Workforce Education for Latinos: Politics, Programs, and Practices. *v.4 p.304, p.305, v.6 p.527*

Workforce Scorecard. *v.4 p.120*

The Workhouse. *v.6 p.743, p.761, p.766*

Working Abroad: The Complete Guide to Overseas Employment. *v.4 p.171*

Working Across Cultures: A Professional's Guide to Cultural Understanding. *v.4 p.762*

Working but Poor: America's Contradiction. *v.4 p.253, p.254, p.265*

Working Daughters of Hong Kong: Female Piety or Power in the Family? *v.6 p.206*

Working for Change: Making a Career in International Public Service. *v.4 p.166, p.167*

Working Girls: Gender and Sexuality in Popular Cinema. *v.6 p.475*

Working in the World: Jimmy Carter and the Making of American Foreign Policy. *v.4 p.560, p.561*

Working Knowledge: How Organizations Manage What They Know. *v.4 p.78*

Working Memory. *v.5 p.609*

Working Out in Japan: Shaping the Female Body in Tokyo Fitness Clubs. *v.4 p.792, p.819*

▢ Working Paper Sites of Political Science. *v.4 p.482*

Working Papers on Canadian Politics. *v.4 p.587*

Working: People Talk about What They Do All Day and How They Feel about What They Do. *v.4 p.717*

The Working Poor: Invisible in America. . . . *v.4 p.726, p.727*

Working Safely in the Chemistry Laboratory. *v.5 p.266*

Working the Garden: American Writers and the Industrialization of Agriculture. *v.6 p.287*

Working to Learn: Transforming Learning in the Workplace. *v.4 p.304, p.305*

Working Toward Whiteness: How America's Immigrants Became White - The Strange Journey from Ellis Island to the Suburbs. *v.4 p.571*

Working Virtually: Challenges of Virtual Teams. . . . *v.4 p.80*

Working with Culture: Psychotherapeutic Interventions with Ethnic Minority Children and Adolescents. *v.6 p.122*

Working with Lesbian, Gay, Bisexual, and Transgender College Students: A Handbook for Faculty and Administrators. *v.6 p.386*

Working with Women Offenders in Correctional Institutions. *v.6 p.277, p.278*

Working Wives, Working Husbands. *v.4 p.734, v.6 p.465, p.467*

Working Women in Renaissance Germany. *v.6 p.451*

Working Women, Working Men: Sao Paulo and the Rise of Brazil's Industrial Working Class, 1900-1955. . . *v.3 p.343*

The Working-Class Majority: America's Best-Kept Secret. *v.4 p.727*

The Workings of Language: From Prescriptions to Perspectives. *v.2 p.553*

Workplace Dispute Resolution: Directions for the Twenty-First Century. *v.4 p.121*

Workplace Intervention: The Bottom Line on Helping Addicted Employees Become Productive Again. *v.4 p.130*

Workplace Justice Without Unions. *v.4 p.131*

Workplace Strategies and Facilities Management: Building in Value. *v.4 p.113*

Works: A Facsimile of the William Morris Kelmscott Chaucer, with the Original 87 Illus by Edward Burne: Jones, Together with an Introd. by John T. Winterich and a Glossary for the Modern Reader. *v.2 p.207*

Works: A Tale of a Tub, the Case Is Altered, Everyman Out of His Humour. *v.2 p.220*

Works: An Historical Survey of the Texts, the Stage History of the Plays, Commentary on the Plays. *v.2 p.220*

The Works and Correspondence of David Ricardo: Biographical Miscellany. *v.4 p.221*

The Works and Correspondence of David Ricardo: General Index. *v.4 p.221*

The Works and Correspondence of David Ricardo: Letters, 1810-1815. . . . . *v.4 p.220, p.221*

The Works and Correspondence of David Ricardo: Letters, 1816-1818. . . . . *v.4 p.221*

The Works and Correspondence of David Ricardo: Letters, 1819-June 1821. . . . . *v.4 p.221*

The Works and Correspondence of David Ricardo: Letters, July 1821-1823. . . . . *v.4 p.221*

The Works and Correspondence of David Ricardo: Notes on Malthus. *v.4 p.220*

The Works and Correspondence of David Ricardo: Pamphlets and Papers, 1809-1811. . . . . *v.4 p.221*

The Works and Correspondence of David Ricardo: Pamphlets and Papers, 1815-1823. . . . . *v.4 p.221*

The Works and Correspondence of David Ricardo: Principles of Political Economy and Taxation. *v.4 p.221*

The Works and Correspondence of David Ricardo: Principles of Political Economy, Vol. 1. . . . . *v.4 p.221*

The Works and Correspondence of David Ricardo: Speeches and Evidence. *v.4 p.221*

The Works and Correspondence of David Ricardo, Vol. 1-11. . . . . *v.4 p.220*

Works: Batholomew Fair; The Devil Is an Ass; The Staple of News; The New Inn; The Magnetic Lady. . . . *v.2 p.220*

Works: Cynthia's Revels, Poetaster, Sejanus His Fall, Eastward Ho. *v.2 p.220*

[Works. English & German. 1983] Goethe edition. . *v.2 p.597*

Works in Verse and Prose. *v.2 p.213*

The Works of Anne Bradstreet in Prose and Verse. . . *v.2 p.28*

The Works of Aphra Behn. *v.2 p.238*

The Works of Charles and Mary Lamb, Set. *v.2 p.298*

Works of Cyril Tourneur. *v.2 p.222*

The Works of D. H. Lawrence. *v.2 p.363*

The Works of David Ricardo, Esq., M. P.: With a Notice of the Life and Writings of the Author [1846]. *v.4 p.221*

The Works of George Berkeley, Vol. 1. . . . . . . *v.1 p.449*

The Works of George Berkeley, Vol. 2. . . . . . . *v.1 p.449*

Works of Hesiod and the Homeric Hymns. *v.2 p.413*

The Works of Irving Fisher, Set. *v.4 p.200, p.225*

The Works of John Ruskin. *v.2 p.306*

The Works of Jonathan Edwards. *v.1 p.584*

The Works of Joseph Addison; Including the Whole Contents of B.P. Hurd's Edition, with Letters and Other Pieces Not Found in Any Previous Collection; and Macaulay's Essay on His Life and Works, ed., with Critical and Explanatory Notes, by George Washington Greene. *v.2 p.236*

The Works of Philo. *v.1 p.546*

The Works of Ralph Vaughan Williams. . . . *v.1 p.217, p.363*

The Works of Robert Browning, Set. *v.2 p.271*

▢ The works of Saint Augustine [electronic resource] : a translation for the 21st century. *v.1 p.592*

The Works of Sir John Suckling. *v.2 p.260*

The Works of Sir Thomas Malory, Vol. II. *v.2 p.212*

The Works of Sir Thomas Malory, Vol. I. *v.2 p.212*

The Works of Sir Thomas Malory. *v.2 p.212*

The Works of Stefan George. *v.2 p.609*

The Works of Stephen Crane: Bowery Tales; Maggie and George's Mother. *v.2 p.36*

The Works of the Right Honourable Joseph Addison. *v.2 p.236*

The Works of Thomas Deloney. *v.2 p.213*

Works of Thomas Middleton. *v.2 p.221*

The Works of Thomas Otway; Plays, Poems, and Love-Letters. *v.2 p.252*

The Works of Thomas Traherne I: Inducements to Retiredness, a Sober View of Dr Twisses His Considerations, Seeds of Eternity or the Nature of the Soul, the Kingdom of God. *v.2 p.263*

The Works of William Collins. *v.2 p.243*

Works on Vision. *v.1 p.449*

Works: Preface, Daily Round, Divinity of Christ, Origin of Sin, Fight for Mansoul, Against Symmachus 1, Vol. 1. *v.2 p.442*

Works, Pts. I-IV. *v.2 p.215*

Works, Set. *v.2 p.241*

Works, Vol. 10. . . . . *v.2 p.220*

Works, Vol. 11. . . . . *v.2 p.219*

Works, Vol. 1. . . . . *v.2 p.219*

Works, Vol. 2. . . . . *v.2 p.219*

Works, Vol. 5. . . . . *v.2 p.220*

Works, Vol. 7. . . . . *v.2 p.219, p.220*

Works. *v.2 p.251, p.258*

The World According to Garp. *v.2 p.147*

The World According to Pimm: A Scientist Audits the Earth. *v.5 p.357, v.6 p.294*

World Agriculture and the Environment: A Commodity-by-Commodity Guide to Impacts and Practices. *v.5 p.14*

World Agriculture: Towards 2015/2030: An FAO Study. *v.5 p.12*

The World Almanac and Book of Facts 2005. . . . . *v.4 p.374*

The World and a Very Small Place in Africa: A History of Globalization in Niumi, the Gambia. *v.6 p.69*

World Architecture Index: A Guide to Illustrations, 12. *v.1 p.711*

The World as Power. *v.1 p.538*

The World As Will and Representation, Vol. 1. . . . *v.1 p.466*

The World As Will and Representation, Vol. 2. . . . *v.1 p.466*

A World at Arms: A Global History of World War II. *v.3 p.81, p.82*

World at Risk: A Global Issues Sourcebook. *v.4 p.662*

World Atlas: Featuring Maps from the Rand McNally Goode's World Atlas. *v.4 p.380*

World Atlas of Coral Reefs. *v.4 p.393*

World Atlas of Epidemic Diseases. *v.4 p.381*

The World Atlas of Language Structures. *v.4 p.18*

World Atlas of the Oceans. *v.5 p.429*

World Bank and Urban Development: From Projects to Policy. *v.4 p.260, p.268*

A World Challenged: Fighting Terrorism in the Twenty-First Century. *v.4 p.661*

World Changes in Divorce Patterns. *v.4 p.740*

World Christianities C.1914-C.2000. . . . . . *v.1 p.611, p.612*

World Conqueror and World Renouncer. *v.1 p.562*

World Consumer Lifestyles Databook: Key Trends. *v.4 p.139, v.5 p.585*

The World Crisis and American Responsibility. . . . *v.3 p.453*

The World Crisis in Education: A View from the Eighties. *v.4 p.325*

World Cultures and Geography: Western Hemisphere and Europe. *v.4 p.383*

World Development Report 1978-2006 with Selected World Development Indicators 2005: Indexed Omnibus. . *v.4 p.373*

World Development Report 2004: Making Services Work for Poor People. *v.4 p.260*

World Development Report 2005: Investment Climate, Growth and Poverty. *v.4 p.59, p.60, p.665*

World Development Report 2006: Equity and Development. *v.4 p.260*

World Drug Report 2005, Set. *v.4 p.655*

World Economic and Social Survey, 2004: International Migration. *v.4 p.667*

World Economic and Social Survey: 2004 Supplement: World Economic Situation and Prospects. *v.4 p.666*

World Economic and Social Survey 2004: Trends and Policies in the World Economy. *v.4 p.666*

World Economic and Social Survey 2005: Financing for Development. *v.4 p.666*

World Economic Situation and Prospects 2005. . . . *v.4 p.666*

The World Economy and National Economies in the Interwar Slump. *v.4 p.237*

A World Elsewhere: The Place of Style in American Literature. *v.2 p.6*

World Encyclopedia of Aircraft Manufacturers: From the Wright Brothers to the Present. *v.4 p.151*

World Encyclopedia of Contemporary Theatre, Set. . . *v.1 p.61*

The World Encyclopedia of Contemporary Theatre. *v.1 p.61*

The World Encyclopedia of Parliaments and Legislatures, Set. *v.4 p.575*

World Energy and Nuclear Directory. *v.5 p.739*

World Energy Assessment: Energy and the Challenge of Sustainability: Overview. *v.5 p.452*

World Enough and Time: The Life of Andrew Marvell. *v.2 p.252*

World Fire: The Culture of Fire on Earth. *v.5 p.31*

A World Fit for People: Thinkers from Many Countries Address the Political, Economic, and Social Problems of Our Time. *v.4 p.504*

The World Food Problem: Tackling the Causes of Undernutrition in the Third World. *v.5 p.34*

World Graphic Design: Contemporary Graphics from Africa, the Arab World, the Far East and Latin America. . . *v.1 p.712*

World Health Report 2006: Working Together for Health. *v.4 p.669*

World Health Report. *v.4 p.669*

World Heritage. *v.1 p.821*

World History Atlas. *v.4 p.380*

The World History of Beekeeping and Honey Hunting. *v.5 p.26, p.27, p.54*

A World History of Christianity. *v.1 p.598*

A World History of Photography. *v.1 p.763*

A World History of Physical Education: Cultural, Philosophical, Comparative. *v.4 p.797*

World History of the Dance. *v.1 p.5, p.49*

The World I Left Behind: Pieces of a Past. *v.3 p.228*

The World in Depression, 1929-1939. . . . .*v.4 p.244*

The World in the Evening. *v.2 p.356*

ⓔ The World in Your Head: A Gestalt View of the Mechanism
of Conscious Experience. *v.5 p.613*

The World Is a Ghetto: Race and Democracy since World War
II. *v.4 p.731, p.767, p.768*

The World Is a Wedding. *v.2 p.119*

The World Is Flat: A Brief History of the Twenty-First
Century. *v.3 p.483, v.4 p.89*

The World Is Not for Sale: Farmers Against Junkfood. .*v.6 p.297*

The World Is Our Home: Society and Culture in Contemporary
Southern Writing. *v.2 p.13*

World Labour Report 2000: Income Security and Social
Protection in a Changing World. *v.4 p.254*

▢ World Lecture Hall. *v.4 p.294*

World Light. *v.2 p.625*

▢ World LII. *v.4 p.436, p.475, p.476, p.477*

World Meetings: United States and Canada. *v.5 p.405*

World Migration, 2005: Costs and Benefits of International
Migration. *v.4 p.667*

World Monetary Units: An Historical Dictionary, Country by
Country. *v.4 p.188*

World Music: A Very Short Introduction. *v.1 p.283*

World Music: The Basics. *v.1 p.283*

The World Next Door: South Asian American Literature and the
Idea of America. *v.6 p.97, p.98, p.138*

World Nuclear Power: A Geographical Appraisal. . . .*v.5 p.740*

World of Anatomy and Physiology, Set. *v.5 p.95, p.156*

The World of Bede. *v.2 p.203*

The World of Black Singles: Changing Patterns of Male-Female
Relations. *v.4 p.738, v.6 p.466, p.467*

The World of Buddhism. *v.1 p.564*

The World of Catholic Renewal, 1540-1770. . . . .*v.1 p.612*

A World of Difference? *v.4 p.336*

The World of Earl Hines. *v.1 p.258, p.332*

The World of E-Government. *v.4 p.546, p.547*

The World of el Cid: Chronicles of the Spanish
Reconquest. *v.3 p.65, p.237*

The World of Goods. *v.4 p.28*

The World of Humanism, 1453-1517. . . . .*v.3 p.70*

A World of Its Own: Race, Labor, and Citrus in the Making of
Greater Los Angeles,
1900-1970. . . . . . .*v.3 p.531, v.6 p.535, p.549, p.712*

The World of Jean Anouilh. *v.2 p.506*

The World of Jimmy Carter: U. S. Foreign Policy,
1977-1981. . . . .*v.3 p.474, p.475*

World of Late Antiquity. *v.3 p.30*

The World of Lawrence Durrell. *v.2 p.344*

The World of Learning. *v.5 p.397*

A World of Love. *v.2 p.335*

The World of Mathematics, Set. *v.5 p.459*

A World of Nations: The International Order since 1945. .*v.4 p.628*

The World of Ngugi Wa Thiong'o. *v.2 p.758*

The World of Odysseus. *v.2 p.413, v.3 p.15*

A World of Our Own: Women as Artists since the
Renaissance. *v.1 p.705, v.6 p.472*

World of Plants: The Missouri Botanical Garden. . . .*v.5 p.83*

The World of Scripting Languages. *v.5 p.346*

World of Sorrow: The African Slave Trade to Brazil. .*v.3 p.336*

The World of Tennessee Williams. *v.2 p.134*

The World of the Ancient Greeks. *v.3 p.12*

The World of the Imagination: Sum and Substance. . .*v.1 p.481*

The World of the Untouchable: The Paraiyars of India. .*v.6 p.153*

The World of Theatre: 2000 Edition. *v.1 p.55, p.61, p.128*

The World of Theatre. *v.1 p.55, p.61, p.62, p.128*

The World of Tupac Amaru: Conflict, Community, and Idenity
in Colonial Peru. *v.3 p.326*

A World of Widows. *v.4 p.741*

World of Wilderness: Essays on the Power and Purpose of Wild
Country. *v.5 p.227*

The World of Yesterday. *v.2 p.616, v.3 p.184*

World on Fire: How Exporting Free Market Democracy Breeds
Ethnic Hatred and Global Instability. .*v.4 p.256, p.261, p.262*

World Out of Balance: Navigating Global Risks to Seize
Competitive Advantage. *v.4 p.69*

World Outside the Window: The Selected Essays of Kenneth
Rexroth. *v.2 p.114, p.115*

World Painting Index, 1973-1980, Set. *v.1 p.711*

World Painting Index, 1980-1989. . . . .*v.1 p.711*

World Painting Index, 1990-1999. . . . .*v.1 p.711*

World Philosophers and Their Works, 3 vols. .*v.1 p.416, v.5 p.405*

World Philosophy: A Contemporary Bibliography, No.
3. . . . .*v.1 p.416, v.5 p.405*

World Population Monitoring, 2003: Population, Education and
Development. *v.4 p.663*

World Population Policies 2003. . . . .*v.4 p.669*

World Population to 2300. . . . .*v.4 p.668*

World Public Sector Report 2003: E-Government at the
Crossroads. *v.4 p.547*

World Radio Television Handbook. *v.4 p.157*

World Records in Chemistry. *v.5 p.259*

World Regional Geography. *v.4 p.396*

World Resources, 1992-93: A Guide to the Global
Environment. *v.5 p.357, p.367, p.370, p.378*

World Resources: The Wealth of the Poor: Managing
Ecosystems to Fight Poverty. *v.6 p.299, p.301*

A World Restored: Europe after Napoleon. *v.3 p.76*

World Revolution and Family Patterns. *v.4 p.739*

World Rock Art. *v.1 p.668*

The World Rushed In: The California Gold Rush
Experience. *v.3 p.531*

A World Safe for Capitalism: Dollar Diplomacy and America's
Rise to Global Power. *v.3 p.318*

World Security and Equity. *v.4 p.262*

World Soils. *v.5 p.48*

The World Split Open: How the Modern Women's Movement
Changed America. *v.6 p.455*

The World Sport Psychology Sourcebook. *v.4 p.877*

World Sports Encyclopedia. *v.4 p.848*

The World That Trade Created: Society, Culture, and the World Economy 1400 to the Present. . . .*v.4 p.57, p.147,v.6 p.145*

The World Trade Organization: A Very Short Introduction. *v.4 p.61*

The World Trading System: Law and Policy of International Economic Relations. *v.4 p.435*

A World Transformed: The Collapse of the Soviet Empire, the Unification of Germany, Tiananmen Square, the Gulf War. *v.3 p.467*

World Trends in Environmental Education. *v.5 p.353*

The World Turned: Essays on Gay History, Politics, and Culture. *v.4 p.569, v.6 p.386*

A World Turned Upside Down: Radical Ideas During the English Revolution. *v.3 p.103, p.121, p.128*

The World Turned Upside Down. *v.3 p.103, p.121*

The World Upside Down: Cross-Cultural Contact and Conflict in Sixteenth-Century Peru. *v.3 p.326*

A World View of Criminal Justice: Hunger for Justice.*v.6 p.269*

The World War II Black Regiment That Built the Alaska Military Highway: A Photographic History. . . .*v.6 p.5, p.16*

The World War II Combat Film: Anatomy of a Genre. .*v.6 p.322*

The World War II Desk Reference: With the Eisenhower Center for American Studies. *v.3 p.382*

World War II, Film, and History. *v.6 p.322*

World Wars Through the Female Gaze. *v.6 p.476*

World Water Resources at the Beginning of the Twenty-First Century. *v.5 p.359, p.371, p.380*

The World We Have Lost: Further Explored. *v.3 p.92*

The World We Have Lost. *v.4 p.704*

World Who's Who in Science: From Antiquity to the Present. *v.5 p.394*

The World Wide Web and Contemporary Cultural Theory: Magic, Metaphor, Power. *v.4 p.761*

☐ The World Wide Web Virtual Library: Biotechnology Information Directory Section. *v.5 p.217*

World Wildlife Fund Guide to Extinct Species of Modern Times. *v.5 p.224*

World Within Walls: Japanese Literature of the Pre-Modern Era, 1600-1867. . . . .*v.6 p.230*

World Within World: The Autobiography of Stephen Spender. *v.2 p.384*

The World Without a Self: Virginia Woolf and the Novel. *v.2 p.393*

A World Without Walls: Freedom, Development, Free Trade and Global Governance. *v.4 p.665*

World Writers in English. *v.2 p.728*

World Youth Report 2003: The Global Situation of Young People. *v.4 p.662*

World Youth Report 2005: Young People Today, and in 2015. . . . .*v.4 p.663*

Worldly Goods: A New History of the Renaissance.*v.3 p.70, p.71*

The Worldly Philosophers: The Lives, Times, and Ideas of the Great Economic Thinkers. *v.3 p.40*

The Worldly Philosophers: The Lives, Times and Ideas of the Great Economic Thinkers. *v.4 p.209*

Worldmark Encyclopedia of the Nations. *v.4 p.374*

Worldmark Encyclopedia of the States. *v.3 p.484*

WorldMinds: Geographical Perspectives on 100 Problems. *v.4 p.374*

Worlds Apart: Globalization and the Environment. . .*v.4 p.667*

Worlds Apart: Measuring International and Global Inequality. *v.4 p.261, p.266*

Worlds Apart: Relationships between Families and Schools. *v.4 p.303*

The World's Banker: A Story of Failed States, Financial Crises, and the Wealth and Poverty of Nations. . .*v.4 p.244, p.265*

World's End. *v.2 p.141*

The World's Game: A History of Soccer. *v.4 p.844, p.867*

The World's Greatest Fix: A History of Nitrogen and Agriculture. *v.5 p.5*

Worlds in Collision: Terror and the Future of Global Order. *v.4 p.658*

Worlds in Consciousness: Mythopoetic Thought in the Novels of Virginia Woolf. *v.2 p.393*

Worlds in the Sky: Planetary Discovery from Earliest Times Through Voyager and Magellan. *v.5 p.68*

The World's Largest Wetlands: Ecology and Conservation. *v.4 p.392*

Worlds Made Flesh: Reading Medieval Manuscript Culture. *v.6 p.569*

The World's Master Paintings: Catalogue and Location Index, Set. *v.1 p.726*

Worlds of Art: Painters in Victorian Society. . .*v.3 p.111, p.128*

The Worlds of Christopher Columbus. . .*v.3 p.73, p.404, p.406*

Worlds of Knowing: Global Feminist Epistemologies.*v.6 p.462*

Worlds of Music: An Introduction to the Music of the World's Peoples. *v.1 p.284*

The Worlds of Nam June Paik. *v.1 p.773*

Worlds of Pain: Life in the Working-Class Family. .*v.4 p.706*

The Worlds of Petrarch. *v.2 p.706*

Worlds of Power: Religious Thought and Political Practice in Africa. *v.1 p.542*

The Worlds of Truman Capote. *v.2 p.66*

Worlds of Women: The Making of an International Women's Movement. *v.6 p.432*

Worlds of Wonder, Days of Judgment: Popular Religious Belief in Early New England. *v.3 p.405*

Worlds on Fire: Volcanoes on the Earth, the Moon, Mars, Venus and Io. *v.5 p.434*

The World's Water 2004-2005: The Biennial Report on Freshwater Resources. *v.5 p.19, v.6 p.293*

The World's Writing Systems. *v.2 p.560, v.4 p.18*

World-Systems Analysis: An Introduction. *v.4 p.759*

☐ Worldwatch Institute. *v.5 p.369, p.377*

Worldwide Government Directory: With International Organizations. *v.4 p.574*

The Worldwide History of Telecommunications. *v.4 p.420*

☐ Worldwide Internet Music Resources. *v.1 p.173*

Worldwide Political Science Abstracts. *v.4 p.481*

World-Wide Shakespeares. *v.1 p.76, p.101, p.135*

Worldwide Trends in Youth Sport. *v.4 p.840*

☐ The World-Wide Web Virtual Library: Neuroscience (Biosciences). *v.5 p.164, p.165*

The World-Wide Web Virtual Library: Physiology & Biophysics (Biosciences). *v.5 p.163*

The Worm in the Apple: How the Teacher Unions Are Destroying American Education. *v.4 p.282*

Wormholes: Essays and Occasional Writings. . . *v.2 p.346, p.347*

Wormwood Forest: A Natural History of Chernobyl. . .*v.5 p.364*

Worship as Theology: Foretaste of Glory Divine. . . .*v.1 p.654*

Worship in Medieval and Early Modern Europe: Change and Continuity in Religious Practice. *v.1 p.654*

The Worth Book of Softball: A Celebration of America's True National Pastime. *v.4 p.868*

Worthy Monuments: Art Museums and the Politics of Culture in Nineteenth-Century France. *v.1 p.828*

A Worthy Tradition: Freedom of Speech in America. *v.4 p.459*

Would You Convict?: 17 Cases That Challenged the Law. *v.4 p.471, v.6 p.268*

The Wound and the Bow: Seven Studies in Literature. *v.2 p.576*

The Wounded Heart: Writing on Cherríe Moraga. *v.6 p.504, p.516*

Wounded Knee 1973: A Personal Account. *v.6 p.694*

Wounding the West: Montana, Mining and the Environment. *v.5 p.706*

Wounds in the Rain: A Collection of Stories Relating to the Spanish-American War of 1898. . . . .*v.2 p.36*

Woven Stone. *v.2 p.151*

Wozzeck. *v.1 p.209, p.228, p.309, p.407*

The WPA Guide to 1930s Alabama. *v.3 p.505*

The WPA Guide to 1930s Kansas. *v.3 p.524*

The WPA Guide to 1930s Nevada. *v.3 p.529*

The WPA Guide to 1930s New Mexico. *v.3 p.528*

The WPA Guide to 1930s Oklahoma. *v.3 p.523*

The WPA Guide to Kentucky. *v.3 p.511, p.512*

The WPA Guide to New York City. *v.3 p.490*

Wrapped in Rainbows: The Life of Zora Neale Hurston. *v.2 p.80, v.6 p.16, p.23*

Wrestling and Hyper-Masculinity. . . . *v.4 p.818, p.863, p.870*

Wrestling with God and Men: Homosexuality in the Jewish Tradition. *v.6 p.374*

The Wretched of the Earth. *v.6 p.10, p.32, p.56, p.642*

Wright American Fiction: 1851-1875. . . . .*v.2 p.18*

Wright: Early Works: Lawd Today!; Uncle Tom's Children; Native Son. *v.2 p.138*

Wright: Later Works: Black Boy and the Outsider. . *v.2 p.138*

Wright Morris Revisited. *v.2 p.103*

A Wrinkle in Time. *v.2 p.149*

Write All These Down: Essays on Music. *v.1 p.247*

Write Screenplays That Sell - The Ackerman Way: Revelations of a Remarkable Teacher. *v.6 p.352*

Writer and Public in France: From the Middle Ages to the Present Day. *v.2 p.456*

The Writer and the World: Essays. *v.2 p.769*

The Writer As Naysayer: Miroslav Krleza and the Aesthetic of Interwar Central Europe. *v.2 p.818, p.819*

A Writer at War: Vasily Grossman with the Red Army, 1941-1945. . . . .*v.2 p.804, v.3 p.227*

The Writer of Modern Life: Essays on Charles Baudelaire. *v.2 p.488*

Writer Sollers. *v.2 p.532*

Writers and Readers in Medieval Italy: Studies in the History of Written Culture. *v.6 p.569*

Writers and Their Background: John Dryden. . *v.2 p.246, p.247*

A Writer's Diary. *v.2 p.394*

A Writer's Eye: Collected Book Reviews. *v.2 p.130*

A Writer's Notebook. *v.2 p.371*

Writers of the Indian Diaspora: A Bio-Bibliographical Critical Sourcebook. *v.2 p.762*

Writers of the Spanish Colonial Period. *v.2 p.664*

Writers on Writing: Collected Essays from the New York Times. *v.2 p.566, p.584*

Writers on Writing: The Art of the Short Story. *v.2 p.574*

A Writer's Reality. *v.2 p.686*

The Writer's Reference Guide to Spanish: The Authoritative Handbook for Writers, Editors, Student. . . *v.2 p.635, p.636*

The Writer's Sense of the Past: Essays on Southeast Asian and Australasian Literature. *v.2 p.761*

The Writer's Voice. *v.2 p.574*

Writin' Is Fightin': Thirty-Seven Years of Boxing on Paper. *v.6 p.27*

Writing a New World: Two Centuries of Australian Women Writers. *v.2 p.742*

Writing about Music: An Introductory Guide. *v.1 p.174*

Writing about Nature. *v.5 p.232*

Writing Across Cultures: Gender Politics and Difference in the Fiction of Buchi Emecheta. *v.2 p.754*

Writing: African Historiography, 1960-1980. . . . . .*v.6 p.53*

Writing African History. *v.6 p.51*

Writing AIDS: Gay Literature, Language, and Analysis. *v.6 p.393*

Writing American History: Essays on Modern Scholarship. *v.3 p.374*

Writing and Being. *v.2 p.755*

Writing and Designing Manuals: Operator Manuals, Service and Maintenance Manuals for International Markets. . *v.5 p.681*

Writing and Inscription in Golden Age Drama. *v.2 p.640*

Writing and Presenting Scientific Papers. *v.5 p.681*

Writing and Revising the Disciplines. *v.2 p.565*

Writing and Speaking in the Technology Professions: A Practical Guide. *v.5 p.680*

Writing Arabic: A Practical Introduction to Ruq'ah Script. *v.6 p.654*

Writing Cases. *v.4 p.177, p.178*

Writing Culture: The Poetics and Politics of Ethnography. *v.4 p.23*

Writing Dancing in the Age of Postmodernism. *v.1 p.25, p.26, p.38, p.40*

Writing Degree Zero. *v.2 p.575*

Writing Development: Magic in the Brain. *v.4 p.361*

Writing, Directing, and Producing Documentary Films and Videos. *v.4 p.413*

Writing Double: Women's Literary Partnerships. . . .*v.6 p.479*

Writing Feature Articles. *v.4 p.407*

Writing Fiction: A Guide to Narrative Craft. *v.2 p.579*

Writing for an Endangered World: Literature, Culture, and Environment in the U. S. and Beyond. *v.6 p.287*

Writing for the Pedal Harp: A Standardized Manual for Composers and Harpists. *v.1 p.393, p.398*

Writing Geographical Exploration: Thomas James and the Northwest Passage 1631-33. . . . .*v.4 p.378*

Writing Himself into History: Oscar Micheaux, His Silent Films and His Audiences. *v.6 p.329, p.340*

Writing Home: American Women Abroad, 1830-1920. .*v.6 p.480*

Writing in Motion. *v.1 p.28, p.30, p.42*

Writing in Sumer: The Invention of Cuneiform. *v.3 p.5*

Writing in the Dark, Dancing in the New Yorker: An Arlene Croce Reader. *v.1 p.39*

Writing in the Margins: The Ethics of Expatriation from Lawrence to Ondaatje. *v.2 p.760, p.761*

Writing in the Teaching and Learning of Mathematics. .*v.5 p.463*

Writing India, 1757-1990: The Literature of British India. *v.2 p.762*

The Writing Life of James D. Watson: Professor, Promoter, Provocateur. *v.5 p.78, p.79, p.127*

Writing Los Angeles: A Literary Anthology. *v.2 p.21, p.22, v.6 p.730*

Writing Natural History: Dialogues with Authors. . . .*v.5 p.232*

Writing Naturally: A Down-to-Earth Guide to Nature Writing. *v.5 p.232*

Writing New York: A Literary Anthology. *v.2 p.21*

The Writing of Canadian History: Aspects of English-Canadian Historical Writing 1900-1970. . . . .*v.3 p.535*

The Writing of History in Nineteenth Century Egypt: A Study in National Transformation. *v.6 p.58, p.637*

Writing on the Body: Female Embodiment and Feminist Theory. *v.6 p.436, p.478*

Writing Papers in the Biological Sciences. *v.5 p.245*

Writing Projects for Mathematics Courses: Crushed Clowns, Cars, and Coffee to Go. *v.5 p.462*

Writing Reaction Mechanisms in Organic Chemistry. .*v.5 p.296*

Writing Realism: Howells, James, and Norris in the Mass Market. *v.2 p.41, p.46, p.49*

Writing Reports to Get Results: Quick, Effective, Results Using the Pyramid Method. *v.4 p.172*

Writing Research: Transforming Data into Text. . . .*v.4 p.689*

Writing Self, Writing Nation. *v.6 p.96, p.112*

Writing Short Scripts. *v.6 p.353*

Writing South Africa: Literature, Apartheid, and Democracy, 1970-1995. . . . .*v.2 p.750*

Writing Systems: A Linguistic Introduction. *v.2 p.564*

Writing Systems: An Introduction to Their Linguistic Analysis. *v.4 p.22*

Writing the Broadway Musical. *v.1 p.404*

Writing the Character-Centered Screenplay. *v.6 p.352*

Writing the Nation in Reformation England, 1530-1580. .*v.2 p.170*

Writing the Oral Tradition: Oral Poetics and Literate Culture in Medieval England. *v.6 p.568*

Writing the Radical Center: William Carlos Williams, John Dewey, and American Cultural Politics. . . .*v.2 p.135, p.136*

Writing the Siege of Leningrad: Women's Diaries, Memoirs, and Documentary Prose. *v.3 p.227*

Writing under the Raj: Gender, Race, and Rape in the British Colonial Imagination, 1830-1947. . . . . .*v.6 p.157, p.158*

Writing up Qualitative Research. *v.4 p.687*

Writing War: Fiction, Gender, and Memory. *v.2 p.191*

Writing Was Everything. *v.2 p.575*

Writing Western History: Essays on Major Western Historians. *v.3 p.518*

Writing with Intent: Essays, Reviews, Personal Prose: 1983-2005. . . . .*v.2 p.734*

Writing Without Teachers. *v.2 p.565*

Writing Women in Korea: Translation and Feminism in the Colonial Period. *v.6 p.237, p.238*

Writing Women's Worlds: Bedouin Stories. *v.6 p.596*

Writings about John Cage. *v.1 p.217, p.315*

Writings in Indian History, 1985-1990. . . . .*v.6 p.682*

Writings of Charles S. Peirce: A Chronological Edition: Vol. 1, 1857-1866. . . . .*v.1 p.440*

Writings of Charles S. Peirce: A Chronological Edition: Vol. 2, 1867-1871. . . . .*v.1 p.440*

Writings of Charles S. Peirce: A Chronological Edition: Vol. 3, 1872-1878. . . . .*v.1 p.440*

Writings of Charles S. Peirce: A Chronological Edition, Vol. 4: 1879-1884. . . . .*v.1 p.440*

Writings of Charles S. Peirce: A Chronological Edition, Vol. 5, 1884-1886. . . . .*v.1 p.440, p.441*

The Writings of Christine de Pizan. *v.2 p.469*

The Writings of the New Testament: An Interpretation. .*v.1 p.624*

Writings of the Young Marx on Philosophy and Society. .*v.1 p.465*

The writings of Willaim Gilmore Simms. Centennial edition. *v.2 p.51*

The Writings of William Carlos Williams: Publicity for the Self. *v.2 p.136*

Writings on Ballet and Music. *v.1 p.24, p.45, p.46*

Writings on Cities. *v.6 p.710*

Writings on Economics. *v.4 p.217, p.218, p.231*

Writings on Glass: Essays, Interviews, Criticism. .*v.1 p.217, p.326*

Writings on International Economics. *v.4 p.255*

Writings on Music, 1965-2000. . . . .*v.1 p.222, p.350*

Writings on Music. *v.1 p.207, p.367*

The Writings. *v.2 p.48*

Written Arabic: An Approach to the Basic Structures. .*v.6 p.653*

Written in Blood: Newly Revised Edition. *v.3 p.315*

Written in Water: The Collected Prose Poems. *v.2 p.657*

Written on the Body. *v.2 p.387, v.6 p.400*

Written Text and the Rise of Literate Culture in Classical Greece. *v.2 p.401*

Wrongly Convicted: Perspectives on Failed Justice. . .*v.6 p.270*

Wrongs of Passage: Fraternities, Sororities, Hazing, and Binge Drinking. *v.4 p.288, p.289*

⬜ WSSLINKS: Women and Gender Studies Websites. .*v.6 p.433*

The WTO and Anti-Dumping. *v.4 p.257, p.262*

The WTO, Trade and the Environment. *v.4 p.257, p.258, p.268, v.5 p.29*

The Wu Liang Shrine: The Ideology of Early Chinese Pictorial Art. *v.1 p.778*

Wuthering Heights. *v.2 p.270*

⬜ WWW Sites of Interest to Musicologists. *v.1 p.172*

🖵 The WWW Virtual Library - Developmental
Biology. *v.5 p.161*

🖵 WWW Virtual Library: Forestry, Forest Genetics & Tree
Breeding. *v.5 p.145*

🖵 WWW Virtual Library: Forestry. *v.5 p.206*

🖵 WWW Virtual Library: Microscopy. *v.5 p.86*

🖵 The WWW Virtual Library: Model Organisms. . . .*v.5 p.204*

🖵 The WWW Virtual Library: Science Fairs. *v.5 p.244*

🖵 The WWW Virtual Library Whale Watching Web. *v.5 p.212*

WWW.Advertising: Advertising and Marketing on the World
Wide Web. *v.4 p.428*

🖵 www.eMedicine.com. *v.5 p.509*

Wyatt: The Critical Heritage. *v.2 p.216*

Wyndham Lewis: Collected Poems and Plays. *v.2 p.367*

Wyndham Lewis: Painter and Writer. *v.2 p.366, p.367*

Wyoming: A Guide to Its History, Highways, and
People. *v.3 p.526*

Wyoming: From Territory to Statehood. *v.3 p.526*

X

Xala. *v.2 p.545*

Xenakis: His Life in Music. *v.1 p.215, p.368*

Xenophon and the History of His Times. *v.2 p.422*

Xenophon's Anabasis, Bks. 1-4. . . . .*v.2 p.422, p.423*

Xenophon. *v.2 p.422*

XML 1. 1 Bible. *v.5 p.346*

XML and Java: Developing Web Applications. *v.5 p.338, p.349*

🖵 X-Ray Crystallography Research Guide (U.
Wisconsin-Madison). *v.5 p.284*

X-Ray Fluorescence Spectrometry. *v.5 p.273*

X-Raying the Pharaohs. *v.6 p.57*

Xuanzang: A Buddhist Pilgrim on the Silk
Road. *v.6 p.185, p.203, p.239*

Xuxa: The Mega Marketing of Gender, Race, and
Modernity. *v.3 p.342*

Y

Y No Se lo Trago la Tierra. *v.6 p.503*

Yacoubian Building. *v.6 p.657, p.658*

🖵 Yahoo! Finance. *v.4 p.93, p.101, p.103*

🖵 Yahoo! Search Directory: Material Science >
Metallurgy. *v.5 p.731*

🖵 Yahoo! Search Directory: Metallurgy >
Corrosion. *v.5 p.734*

🖵 Yahoo! Search Directory Science: Chemistry. . . .*v.5 p.260*

🖵 Yahoo! Search Directory. *v.5 p.255*

Yakuza: Japan's Criminal Underworld. *v.6 p.251*

The Yakuza Movie Book: A Guide to Japanese Gangster
Films. *v.6 p.306, p.317*

The Yale Anthology of Twentieth-Century French
Poetry. *v.2 p.464*

The Yale Companion to Chaucer. *v.2 p.209, p.210*

The Yale Dictionary of Art and Artists. *v.1 p.665*

The Yale Edition of the Works of Samuel Johnson. . .*v.2 p.250*

The Yale Gertrude Stein. *v.2 p.122*

🖵 Yale Global Online. *v.4 p.55*

The Yale Guide to Women's Reproductive Health: From
Menarche to Menopause. *v.5 p.523, v.6 p.444*

Yamamoto: The Man Who Planned Pearl Harbor. . . .*v.6 p.227*

Yang Tai Chi Chuan. *v.4 p.793*

Yangtze Valley and Beyond. *v.6 p.214*

Yankee City. *v.4 p.708*

Yankee from Olympus: Justice Holmes and His Family. *v.4 p.467*

Yankee from the West. *v.3 p.464*

Yankee Go Home?: Canadians and Anti-Americanism. *v.3 p.537*

A Yankee in Canada, with Anti-Slavery and Reform
Papers. *v.3 p.544*

Yankee No!: Anti-Americanism in U. S.- Latin American
Relations. *v.3 p.305*

Yankee Science in the Making. *v.5 p.389, p.394*

Yankee Theatre: The Image of America on the Stage,
1825-1850. . . . .*v.1 p.115*

Yanko the Musician and Other Stories. *v.2 p.791, p.792*

Yanks: The Epic Story of the American Army in World War
I. *v.3 p.470*

Yard, Street, Park: The Design of Suburban Open
Space. *v.1 p.797*

Yardbird Suite: A Compendium of the Music and Life of Charlie
Parker. *v.1 p.170, p.261, p.346*

Yawar Fiesta. *v.3 p.328*

Yaws' Handbook of Physical Properties for Hydrocarbons and
Chemicals: Physical Properties for More Than 41,000
Organic and Inorganic Chemical Compounds: Coverage for C1
to C100 Organics and Ac to Zr Inorganics. . . .*v.5 p.287*

Ybor City Chronicles: A Memoir. *v.6 p.490, p.536*

Year in Life of a Shinto Shrine. *v.1 p.541*

The Year of Decision. *v.3 p.519*

The Year of Liberty. *v.3 p.135, p.137, p.138*

The Year of Living Dangerously. *v.2 p.747, v.6 p.178*

The Year of Magical Thinking. *v.2 p.144*

The Year of Stalingrad: A Historical Record and a Study of
Russian Mentality, Methods and Policies. *v.3 p.228*

Year of the Elephant: A Moroccan Woman's Journey Toward
Independence. *v.6 p.655*

The Year of the Four Emperors. *v.3 p.29*

The Year of the Frog: A Novel. *v.2 p.812*

The Year of the Salamis, 480-479 B.C.: The Greco-Persian
Wars. *v.3 p.17*

A Year of the Stars: A Month-by-Month Journey of
Skywatching. *v.5 p.70*

The Yearbook of Education Law, 2001. . . . .*v.4 p.451*

Yearbook of the United Nations 2003, Vol. 57. *v.4 p.635, p.636*

Yearbook of the United Nations Collection on CD-ROM
1946-2002: Network Version. *v.4 p.632*

The Yearling. *v.2 p.113*

The Year-Round Messier Marathon Field Guide: With Complete
Maps, Charts and Tips to Guide You to Enjoying the
Most Famous List of Deep-Sky Objects. *v.5 p.63*

The Years As Catches. v.2 p.69

Years of Decision American Politics 1890. . . .v.3 p.438, p.439

Years of Discord: American Politics and Society,
1961-1974. . . . . .v.3 p.439, p.466

The Years of Hunger: Soviet Agriculture, 1931-1933. .v.3 p.225

The Years of Persecution, 1933-1939. . . . . . .v.3 p.83, p.84

Years of Poverty, Years of Plenty. v.4 p.722, p.737

Years of Renewal. v.3 p.460

Years of Upheaval. v.3 p.460

The Years with Ross. v.2 p.126

The Years. v.2 p.394

Yeast: A Problem. v.2 p.296

Yeats: A Collection of Critical Essays. v.2 p.327

Yeats and Anglo-Irish Literature: Critical Essays. . .v.2 p.327

Yeats at His Last. v.2 p.327

Yeats the Man and the Masks. v.2 p.326

Yeats: The Nineteenth Century Matrix. v.2 p.326

Yeats the Playwright: A Commentary on Character and Design
in the Major Plays. v.2 p.327

Yeat's Vision and the Later Plays. v.2 p.327

Yeats. v.2 p.326

Yehuda Amichai: A Life of Poetry, 1948-1994. . . .v.6 p.647

Yekl: A Tale of the New York. v.2 p.32

Yell-Oh Girls!: Emerging Voices Explore Culture, Identity, and
Growing up Asian American. v.6 p.94

A Yell-Oh Girls! Emerging Voices Explore Culture, Identity and
Growing up Asian. v.6 p.113, p.122

Yellow Back Radio Broke Down. v.2 p.154

The Yellow Cross: The Story of the Last Cathars. . .v.6 p.573

Yellow Dog. v.2 p.329

Yellow Fever, Black Goddess: The Coevolution of People and
Plagues. v.5 p.365, p.366

Yellow Journalism: Puncturing the Myths, Defining the
Legacies. v.4 p.403, p.404

Yellow Light: Poems. v.6 p.103

Yellow Light: The Flowering of Asian American Arts. .v.6 p.88

The Yellow Peril: Chinese Americans in American Fiction,
1850-1940. . . . . .v.6 p.98, p.128

Yellow: Race in America Beyond Black and
White. v.4 p.729, p.731,v.6 p.108, p.125

The Yellow Sofa. v.2 p.689

Yellow: Stories. v.6 p.101

The Yellow Wallpaper: A Dual-Text Critical Edition. . .v.2 p.39

The Yellow Wallpaper: A Sourcebook. v.2 p.39

The Yellow Wind. v.6 p.614

Yellowface: Creating the Chinese in American Popular Music
and Performance, 1850s-1920s. v.1 p.296

The Yellowstone Story: A History of Our First National
Park. v.3 p.525

Yellowstone: The Creation and Selling of an American
Landscape, 1870-1903. . . . . . .v.5 p.18, v.6 p.295

The Yemen Arab Republic: Development and Change in an
Ancient Land. v.6 p.628

Yemen: The Search for a Modern State. v.6 p.628

Yemenite Jewry: Origins, Culture, and Literature. . .v.6 p.596

Yerma. v.2 p.659

Yes Yoko Ono. v.1 p.773

Yesterday in Mexico: A Chronicle of the Revolution
1919. . . . . .v.3 p.292

Yesterday's Soldiers: European Military Professionalism in
South America, 1890-1940. . . . . .v.3 p.276

Les yeux d'Elsa. v.2 p.507

Yiddish Proletarian Theatre: The Art and Politics of the Artef,
1925-1940. . . . . .v.1 p.126

The Yiddish Theatre: New Approaches. v.1 p.126

Yin Yu Tang: The Architecture and Daily Life of a Chinese
House. v.1 p.788

YMCA Personal Training Manual. v.4 p.792

Yo!: A Novel. v.6 p.505

Yo Voy Sonando Caminos. v.2 p.661

Yobo: Korean American Writing in Hawai'i. . . .v.6 p.91, p.135

The Yoder Case: Religious Freedom, Education, and Parental
Rights. v.4 p.308

Yoga and Psychology: Language, Memory, and
Mysticism. v.5 p.633

Yoga in Modern India: The Body Between Science and
Philosophy. v.4 p.790, p.792, p.793, p.802, p.803

Yogaku: Japanese Music in the 20th Century. v.1 p.288

Yohannes IV of Ethiopia: A Political Biography. . . .v.6 p.64

Yokohama, California. v.6 p.101

Yoruba Dance: Semiotics, Movement and Yoruba Body Attitude
in Communication. v.1 p.14

The Yoruba Diaspora in the Atlantic World. v.3 p.303

Yoruba from Cuba: Selected Poems of Nicolás Guillén. .v.2 p.672

Yoruba: Nine Centuries of African Art and Thought. . .v.1 p.690

The Yoshida Memoirs: The Story of Japan in Crisis. . .v.6 p.229

You and Your Genes. v.5 p.134

You Are Not a Stranger Here. v.2 p.160

You Are Not Alone: Bjorn Melhus. v.1 p.773

You Are on Indian Land: Alcatraz Island,
1969-1971. . . . . .v.6 p.689, p.694

You Belong in a Zoo!: Tales from a Lifetime Spent with Cobras,
Crocs, and Other Creatures. v.5 p.250

You Better Work!: Underground Dance Music in New
York. v.1 p.268

You Call This an Election?: America's Peculiar
Democracy. v.4 p.549

You Can Do the Math: Overcome Your Math Phobia and
Make Better Financial Decisions. v.4 p.175

You Can't Catch Death: A Daughter's Memoir. v.2 p.58

You Can't Do Both. v.2 p.328

You Don't Love Yourself. v.2 p.527

You Must Remember This. v.2 p.152

You Need to Be a Little Crazy: The Truth about Starting and
Growing Your Business. v.4 p.68

You, the People: The United Nations, Transitional
Administration, and State-Building. v.4 p.585

Young Adolf. v.2 p.330

Young Adventure a Book of Poems by Stephen Vincent
Benet. v.2 p.61

Young America: The Daguerreotypes of Southworth & Hawes. . . . . *.v.1 p.764*

The Young and Evil. . . . . *.v.6 p.396*

Young and Innocent?: The Cinema in Britain, 1896-1930. . . . . *.v.6 p.339*

Young Bob La Follette: A Biography of Robert M. La Follette, Jr. 1895-1953. . . . . *.v.3 p.460*

Young Charles Lamb, 1775-1802. . . . . *.v.2 p.298*

Young Children's Thinking about Biological World. . *.v.5 p.245*

The Young Entrepreneur's Edge: Using Your Ambition, Independence, and Youth to Launch a Successful Business. . . . . *.v.4 p.167*

Young Frederick Douglas: The Maryland Years. . . . *.v.3 p.421*

The Young Hemingway. . . . . *.v.2 p.85*

Young Japan: Yokohama and Yedo, a Narrative of the Settlement and the City from the Signing of the Treaties in 1858, to the Close of the Year 1879. with a Glance at the Progress of Japan During a Period of Twenty-One Years, Vol. 2. *.v.6 p.223*

The Young Lloyd George. . . . . *.v.3 p.94, p.117*

Young Men and Fire. . . . . *.v.5 p.31*

Young Men in Spats. . . . . *.v.2 p.391*

The Young Naturalist. . . . . *.v.5 p.223*

Young Poets of a New Bulgaria: An Anthology. . . . *.v.2 p.780*

Young Poets of a New Romania. . . . . *.v.2 p.816*

Young Researchers: Informational Reading and Writing in the Early and Primary Years. . . . . *.v.4 p.364*

Young Sam Johnson. . . . . *.v.2 p.250*

Young Shakespeare. . . . . *.v.2 p.227*

The Young Towns of Lima: Aspects of Urbanization in Peru. . . . . *.v.3 p.330*

The Youngest Parents: Teenage Pregnancy As It Shapes Lives. . . . . *.v.4 p.736*

Your Call Is Important to Us: The Truth about Bullshit. *.v.4 p.141*

Your Face Tomorrow: Fever and Spear. . . . . . . *.v.2 p.661*

☐ Your Federal Income Tax for Individuals. . . . . *.v.4 p.464*

Your First Resume: For Students and Anyone Preparing to Enter Today's Tough Job Market. . . . . *.v.4 p.169*

Your Isadora: The Love Story of Isadora Duncan and Gordon Craig Told Through Letters and Diaries. . . . . *.v.1 p.13*

Your Money or Your Life: Economy and Religion in the Middle Ages. . . . . *.v.6 p.558, p.572*

ⓔ Your Move: A New Approach to the Study of Movement and Dance : Teacher's Guide. . . . . *.v.1 p.38*

Your Name Here: Poems. . . . . *.v.2 p.57*

Your Next Business Strategy: The Case for Dynamic Friction and Loose Specialization. . . . . *.v.4 p.73*

Your Practicum in Psychology: A Guide for Maximizing Knowledge and Competence. . . . . *.v.5 p.675, p.676*

☐ Your Right to Federal Records: Questions and Answers on the Freedom of Information Act and the Privacy Act. *.v.4 p.464*

Your Rights in the Workplace. . . . . *.v.4 p.131*

Your Supervised Practicum and Internship: Field Resources for Turning Theory into Action. . . . . *.v.5 p.676*

You're Not from Around Here, Are You?: A Lesbian in Small-Town America. . . . . *.v.6 p.401*

Yours, Plum: The Letters of P. G. Wodehouse. *.v.2 p.391, p.392*

Youth Aggression and Violence: A Psychological Approach. . . . . *.v.5 p.628, p.631, p.662*

The Youth and Adult Aquatic Program Manual. *.v.4 p.792, p.797*

Youth and History: Tradition and Change in European Age Relations, 1770 to Present. . . . . *.v.4 p.736*

Youth, Education, and Sexualities: An International Encyclopedia. . . . . *.v.6 p.386*

Youth, Identity, Power: The Chicano Movement. *.v.6 p.539, p.541*

Youth in Cities: A Cross-National Perspective. . . . *.v.4 p.753*

Youth in Revolutionary Russia: Enthusiasts, Bohemians, Delinquents. . . . . *.v.3 p.222*

Youth: Scenes from Provincial Life II. . . . . . . *.v.2 p.754*

Youth Sport and the Law: A Guide to Legal Issues. . . . . *.v.4 p.785, p.882, p.900*

Youth, University, and Canadian Society: Essays in the Social History of Higher Education. . . . . *.v.4 p.333*

Youth Without Youth and Other Novellas. . . . . . *.v.2 p.817*

You've Had Your Time: The Second Part of the Confessions. . . . . *.v.2 p.336*

Yuan Mei: Eighteenth Century Chinese Poet. . . . . *.v.6 p.188, p.203, p.212*

Yucatán's Maya Peasantry and the Origins of the Caste War. . . . . *.v.3 p.289*

The Yugoslav Auschwitz and the Vatican: The Croatian Massacre of the Serbs During World War II. . . . *.v.3 p.248*

The Yugoslav Experiment 1948-1974. . . . . . . *.v.3 p.247*

Yugoslavia and Its Historians: Understanding the Balkan Wars of the 1990s. . . . . *.v.3 p.247*

Yugoslavia as History: Twice There Was a Country. . *.v.3 p.247*

Yugoslavia As History: Twice There Was a Country. . *.v.3 p.248*

Yugoslavia at the Paris Peace Conference: A Study in Frontiermaking. . . . . *.v.3 p.247*

The Yugoslavs. . . . . *.v.3 p.247, p.248*

Yurugu: An Afrocentric Critique of European Cultural Thought and Behavior. . . . . *.v.6 p.3, p.19*

Yvain: The Knight of the Lion. . . . . *.v.2 p.466*

Yves Brunier: Landscape Architect. . . . . *.v.1 p.813*

Yvor Winters: Selected Poems. . . . . *.v.2 p.128*

Z

Zaat. . . . . *.v.6 p.660*

Zach Lamar Cobb: El Paso Customs and Intelligence During the Mexican Revolution, 1913-1918. . . . . *.v.3 p.291*

Zachary Taylor. . . . . *.v.3 p.420, p.436*

The Zahir: A Novel of Obsession. . . . . *.v.2 p.690*

Zaire Country Studies: Area Handbook. . . . . . . *.v.6 p.62*

Zalmoxis. . . . . *.v.2 p.816*

Zambia: Between Two Worlds. . . . . *.v.6 p.77*

Zami: A New Spelling of My Name: A Biomythography. . . . . *.v.6 p.402*

Zanzibar: Its Society and Its Politics. . . . . . . *.v.6 p.66*

The Zanzibar Revolution and Its Aftermath. . . . . *.v.6 p.66*

Zanzibar under Colonial Rule: Eastern African Studies. *.v.6 p.66*

La Zapatera Prodigiosa. . . . . *.v.2 p.658*

Zappa: A Biography. . . . . *.v.1 p.219, p.272, p.369*

Zarumilla-Marañón: The Ecuador-Peru Dispute. . . . *.v.3 p.278*

Zarzuela: Spanish Operetta, American Stage. . . . . *.v.1 p.233, p.246, p.247*

Der Zauberer: Das Leben des Deutschen Schriftstellers Thomas Mann. *v.2 p.613*

Zayde: A Spanish Romance. *v.2 p.474*

Zayni Barakat. *v.6 p.656*

The Zealous Intruders. *v.6 p.611*

Zeb Vance: North Carolina's Civil War Governor and Gilded Age Political Leader. *v.4 p.542*

Zebrafish Genome Resources. .*v.5 p.104, p.109, p.213, p.214*

Zebulon Pike's Arkansas Journal: In Search of the Southern Louisiana Purchase Boundary Line. *v.3 p.520*

Zechariah 9-14: A New Translation with Introduction and Commentary. *v.1 p.623*

Zeffirelli: An Autobiography. *v.6 p.419*

Zelda: A Biography. *v.2 p.77*

Zell: The Governor Who Gave Georgia Hope. *v.3 p.503*

Zen and Japanese Culture. *v.1 p.476, p.562*

Zen and Philosophy: An Intellectual Biography of Nishida Kitaro. *v.1 p.476*

Zen and Shinto: The Story of Japanese Philosophy. . .*v.1 p.476*

Zen and the Brain: Toward an Understanding of Meditation and Consciousness. *v.5 p.632*

Zen Enlightenment: Origins and Meaning. *v.1 p.567*

Zen in the Art of Archery. *v.4 p.802, p.847*

Zen Master Dogen: An Introduction with Selected Writings. *v.1 p.568*

Zenobia. *v.2 p.779*

Zeno's Conscience. *v.2 p.724*

Zephaniah: A New Translation with Introduction and Commentary. *v.1 p.622*

Zettel. *v.1 p.472*

Zeus and Hera: Archetypal Image of Father, Husband, and Wife. *v.1 p.532*

Zeus. *v.1 p.532*

Zibaldone: A Selection by Giacomo Leopardi. *v.2 p.711*

Zibaldone, vol. 1: 1. Autografo 1-2341. . . . . . .*v.2 p.711*

Zibaldone, vol. 2: Autografo 2342-4526. . . . . . .*v.2 p.711*

Zibaldone, vol. 3: Commento. Bibliografia. Indice analitico. Indici filologici. *v.2 p.711*

The Zigzag Kid. *v.6 p.648*

The Zimbabwe Culture: Origins, Growth, and Decline of Precolonial States in Southern Zambezia. *v.6 p.77*

Zion Before Zionism: Eighteen Thirty-Eight to Eighteen Eighty. *v.6 p.609, p.610*

The Zionist Idea: A Historical Analysis and Reader. . .*v.1 p.549*

Zitate und Aussprueche. *v.2 p.621*

Zohar: The Book of Enlightenment. *v.1 p.550*

Zola: A Life. *v.2 p.504*

Zola: Germinal. *v.2 p.504*

Zone. *v.2 p.540*

Zoo: A History of Zoological Gardens in the West. *v.1 p.818, v.5 p.82*

Zoo and Aquarium History: Ancient Animal Collections to Zoological Gardens. *v.5 p.84*

The Zoo Book: A Guide to America's Best. *v.5 p.84*

Zoo Book. *v.5 p.84*

Zoo: The Modern Ark. *v.5 p.84*

Zooarchaeology. *v.4 p.7*

Zoobabies. *v.5 p.84*

Zoology: Forty-Nine Science Fair Projects. *v.5 p.228, p.229, p.244*

Zoology: High-School Science Fair Experiments. *v.5 p.228, p.229, p.244, p.245*

Zoos and Animal Rights: The Ethics of Keeping Animals. .*v.5 p.83*

Zoos and Game Reserves. *v.5 p.82*

Zoos. *v.5 p.84*

Zoot Suit and Other Plays. *v.1 p.125, v.6 p.504, p.518*

The Zoot-Suit Riots: The Psychology of Symbolic Annihilation. *v.6 p.536, p.540*

ZooWeb. *v.5 p.82, p.227*

Zora Neale Hurston: A Life in Letters. . . .*v.6 p.16, p.18, p.44*

Zora Neale Hurston: A Literary Biography. *v.6 p.17*

Zora Neale Hurston and a History of Southern Life. . .*v.2 p.82*

Zora Neale Hurston and American Literary Culture. . .*v.2 p.82*

A Zora Neale Hurston Companion. *v.2 p.80, v.6 p.24*

Zoroastrianism: An Introduction to Ancient Faith. . . .*v.1 p.538*

Zoroastrians: Their Religious Beliefs and Practices. . .*v.1 p.538*

Zouk: World Music in the West Indies. *v.1 p.292*

Zoyka's Apartment: A Tragic Farce in Three Acts. . . .*v.2 p.802*

Zukofsky's A: An Introduction. *v.2 p.138, p.139*

Zulfi Bhutto of Pakistan: His Life and Times. . .*v.6 p.162, p.163*

The Zuni Man-Woman. *v.6 p.371*

The Zuni Man-Woman. *v.4 p.31*

Zwingli: An Introduction to His Thought. . . .*v.1 p.581, p.603*

Zwingli. *v.3 p.245*

Zydeco!. . . . .*v.1 p.15 Numeric Titles*

Numeric Titles

The 1. 5 Generation: Becoming Korean American in Hawai'i. *v.6 p.135*

10 Downing Street. *v.4 p.604, p.605, p.606*

The 100 Absolutely Unbreakable Laws of Business Success. *v.4 p.68*

100 Best Corporate Citizens. *v.4 p.54*

100 Distinguished European Chemists (18th, 19th, and 20th Centuries). *v.5 p.260*

100 Great Poems of the Twentieth Century. *v.2 p.583*

100 Key Documents in American Democracy. *v.3 p.372*

100 Masters of Mystery and Detective Fiction, 2 vols. .*v.2 p.580*

100% Money. *v.4 p.199, p.224*

100 Selected Poems. *v.2 p.68*

100 Suns: 1945-1962. . . . .*v.1 p.767*

100 Years of American Nursing: Celebrating a Century of Caring. *v.5 p.529*

1001 Chemicals in Everyday Products. *v.5 p.264*

1001 Natural Wonders: Places You Must See Before You Die. *v.5 p.224*

101 Best Resumes for Grads. *v.4 p.168*

101 Careers in Mathematics. *v.5 p.460*

101 Chambers: Congress, State Legislatures, and the Future of Legislative Studies. *v.4 p.550*

101 Stories of the Great Ballets: The Scene-by-Scene Stories of the Most Popular Ballets, Old and New. *v.1 p.3*

101 Turkish Idiomatic Expressions. *v.6 p.665*

11 September 2001: War, Terror and Judgement. . . .*v.3 p.483*

110 Experiences for Multicultural Learning. *v.5 p.676*

The 120 Days of Sodom and Other Writings. *v.2 p.483*

1200 Mexican Artists: An Identification Guide to Painters, Graphic Artist, Sculptors and Photographers. .*v.1 p.666, p.685*

125 Original Audition Monologues. *v.1 p.143*

The 13th Element: The Sordid Tale of Murder, Fire and Phosphorus. *v.5 p.308, p.309*

The 13th Valley: A Novel. *v.2 p.143*

14 - 18: Understanding the Great War. *v.3 p.78*

1476-1776. . . . .*v.2 p.554*

150 Years of Popular Musical Theatre. *v.1 p.92, p.93*

15,000 Spanish Verbs: Fully Conjugated in All the Tenses Using Pattern Verbs. *v.2 p.637*

15-Minute Cover Letter: Write an Effective Cover Letter Right Now. *v.4 p.169*

1660-1678. . . . .*v.2 p.200*

1676: The End of American Independence. *v.3 p.500*

1789: The Emblems of Reason. *v.2 p.459*

1791: Mozart's Last Year. *v.1 p.190, p.344*

1816: America Rising. *v.4 p.487*

1848: The British State and the Chartist Movement. . *v.4 p.604*

1848: The Revolution of the Intellectuals. *v.3 p.76*

1848: The Revolutionary Tide in Europe. *v.3 p.76*

1876: A Novel. *v.2 p.127*

1900-1919: All-American Ads. *v.4 p.141*

1912: Wilson, Roosevelt, Taft and Debs - The Election That Changed the Country. *v.3 p.468*

1922: The Birth of Irish Democracy. *v.3 p.134*

1922: the Birth of Irish Democracy. *v.3 p.134, p.138*

1933: Essays and "How We Think". *v.1 p.443*

1948 and After: Israel and the Palestinians. *v.6 p.611*

1949, the First Israelis. *v.6 p.615*

1956 and All That: The Making of Modern British Drama. *v.2 p.189*

The 1956 Hungarian Revolution: A History in Documents. *v.4 p.641*

1968: A Student Generation in Revolt. *v.4 p.326*

1999 Harvard Business School Core Collection: An Author, Title and Subject Guide. *v.4 p.180*

19th Century American Women Writers. *v.2 p.7, p.8*

19th Century Art. *v.1 p.680*

19th Century European Painting: David to Cezanne. . *v.1 p.727*

19th Century Schoolbooks. *v.4 p.324*

19th-Century Chamber Music. *v.1 p.198, p.239*

19th-Century Piano Music. *v.1 p.205, p.243*

1Agricultural Bioethics: Implications of Agricultural Biotechnology. *v.5 p.7*

2 Peter, Jude. *v.1 p.630*

20 Common Problems: End-of-Life Care. *v.5 p.532*

200 Best Jobs for College Graduates. *v.4 p.167*

The 2000 Presidential Campaign: A Communication Perspective. *v.4 p.558*

20,000 Leagues under the Sea. *v.2 p.504*

20,000+ Words: Spelled and Divided for Quick Reference. *v.2 p.556*

2001: A Space Odyssey. *v.2 p.337*

2001 Race Odyssey: African Americans and Sociology. .*v.4 p.730*

2002 Census of Agriculture. *v.4 p.151*

The 2003 World Almanac - US Government and Defense. *v.4 p.150*

2004 Green Book. *v.5 p.672*

2004 International Petroleum Encyclopedia. *v.4 p.160*

2004 Public Human Services Directory, Vol. 64. . . . .*v.5 p.672*

2005 Current Text, Vol. 12. . . . .*v.4 p.104, p.105*

2005 Original Pronouncements, Vol. 13. . . . .*v.4 p.104, p.105*

2006 Graduate Programs in Physics, Astronomy, and Related Fields. *v.5 p.544, p.545*

The 2006 Report on Footwear. *v.4 p.153*

The 2006-2011 World Outlook for Footwear. *v.4 p.153*

2007 Artists and Graphic Designers Market. . .*v.1 p.667, p.712*

201 Arabic Verbs. *v.6 p.654*

201 Hebrew Verbs. *v.6 p.646*

201 Turkish Verbs: Fully Conjugated in All the Tenses. .*v.6 p.665*

20/20: 20 New Sounds of the 20th Century. *v.1 p.212*

20th Century French Drama. *v.2 p.461*

20th-Century Ceramics. *v.1 p.775, p.807, p.808*

20th-Century Italian Poems. *v.2 p.700*

21st Century African American Social Issues: A Reader. .*v.6 p.40*

21st Century Leisure: Current Issues. *v.4 p.783*

A 22 and 23. . . . .*v.2 p.139*

22 and 50 Poems. *v.2 p.68*

25 Top Consulting Firms: Wetfeet Insider Guide. . . .*v.4 p.65*

25 Years of the Safe Drinking Water Act: History and Trends. *v.6 p.295, p.300*

2-D Proteome Analysis Protocols. *v.5 p.117*

3 Exemplary Novels. *v.2 p.662*

36 Children. *v.4 p.310*

36 Days: The Complete Chronicle of the 2000 Presidential Election Crisis. *v.3 p.466, p.467*

365 Answers about Human Resources for the Small Business Owner: What Every Manager Needs to Know about Work Place Law. *v.4 p.87*

3-D Seismic Interpretation. *v.5 p.444*

3D Toons: Creative 3D Design for Cartoonists and Animators. *v.6 p.348*

4000 Years of Women in Science. *v.6 p.438*

40th Publication Design Annual. *v.1 p.719*

44 Hungarian Short Stories. *v.2 p.785*

45 RPM: A Visual History of the Seven-Inch Record. .*v.1 p.717*

5 Giants of Advertising. *v.4 p.141*

50 Designers/50 Costumes: Concept to Character. . . .*v.6 p.349*

50 Key Concepts in Gender Studies. *v.6 p.426*

50 Years a Keynesian and Other Essays. *v.4 p.225*

50 Years of DNA. *v.5 p.121*

500 Best-Loved Song Lyrics. *v.1 p.411*

500 Nations: An Illustrated History of North American Indians. *v.6 p.682*

501 Hebrew Verbs. *v.6 p.645*

501 Portuguese Verbs. *v.2 p.638*

53 Days. *v.2 p.533*

The 60's Communes: Hippies and Beyond. *v.4 p.740*

65 Successful Harvard Business School Application Essays: With Analysis by the Staff of the Harbus, the Harvard Business School Newspaper. *v.4 p.176*

69 A.D.: The Year of Four Emperors. *v.3 p.29*

The 7 Lively Arts. *v.1 p.35, p.118*

722 Miles: The Building of the Subways and How They Transformed New York. *v.6 p.713*

75 Years of the Oscar: The Official History of the Academy Awards. *v.6 p.346*

75 Years of the Turkish Republic. *v.6 p.624*

777 Mathematical Conversation Starters. .*v.5 p.458, p.460, p.461*

87th Precinct. *v.2 p.97*

9 Contemporary Jewish Plays: From the New Play Commission of the National Foundation for Jewish Culture. .*v.1 p.68, p.126*

The 9-11 Commission Report: Final Report of the National Commission on Terrorist Attacks Upon the United States, Official Government Edition. *v.4 p.481*

The 9/11 Commission Report: Final Report of the National Commission on Terrorist Attacks upon the United States. *v.4 p.564, p.659*

99 Canadian Writers Before 1890. . . . .*v.2 p.730*

99 Percent Inspiration: Tips, Tales and Techniques for Liberating Your Business Creativity. *v.4 p.66*